## Eight Simple Guides for the Use of this Dictionary

This DICTIONARY has been designed to give you the word or the meaning you desire; and it has been designed to lead you directly to it. By following these eight simple guides you will arrive at the word or the meaning you desire with certainty, with speed, and with the utmost ease.

1. Look up idioms under the noun, whether the idiom consists of a preposition and a noun or a verb and a noun (See Explanatory Note 29, p. xiv).
2. Look up prepositions under the word (verb or noun) associated syntactically with them; also under the prepositions themselves (See Explanatory Note 37, p. xvi).
3. Look up the adjective meanings of a word at the beginning of the entry, the verb meanings at the end, and other meanings in between, according to the functional sequence established for the treatment of words on the basis of the parts of speech (See Explanatory Note 23, p. xiii). You will be greatly aided in finding changes in part of speech by the boldface perpendicular lines used in many entries (See Explanatory Note 38, p. xvi).
4. Look up abbreviations and proper nouns in the same alphabetical listing as common words (See Explanatory Note 19, p. xiii).
5. Look up all words spelled alike under one and the same entry, whether spelled with an initial capital or not (See Explanatory Notes 21 and 22, p. xiii).
6. Look up feminine nouns that have identical spelling with the feminine form of an adjective under the masculine form of the adjective (See Explanatory Note 24, p. xiii).
7. Look up verb phrases under the transitive or intransitive treatment of the verb according as the verb (not the verb phrase as a whole) is transitive or intransitive (See Explanatory Note 36, p. xvi).
8. Look up English solid, hyphenated, and spaced compounds as lexical units. For example, *soft-boiled egg* is found as a separate entry and not under *soft* or *boiled* or *egg* (See Explanatory Note 27, p. xiv).

## Ocho Sencillas Indicaciones para el Uso de este Diccionario

Este DICCIONARIO ha sido planeado para proporcionar al usuario la palabra o la acepción deseada; y para conducirle de un modo directo a dicha palabra o acepción. Siguiendo estas ocho sencillas indicaciones, encontrará el usuario la palabra o la acepción que desea con seguridad, con rapidez y con la mayor facilidad.

1. Búsquense los modismos bajo el nombre, sea un modismo que conste de una preposición y un nombre o uno que conste de un verbo y un nombre (Véase Nota Explicativa 29, pág. xiv).
2. Búsquense las preposiciones bajo la palabra (verbo o nombre) que va asociada con ellas sintácticamente; y también bajo las preposiciones mismas (Véase Nota Explicativa 37, pág. xvi).
3. Búsquense las acepciones adjetivales de las palabras al principio del artículo, las acepciones verbales al fin y las demás acepciones entre ambas, según el orden funcional establecido para el tratamiento de las palabras a base de las partes de la oración (Véase Nota Explicativa 23, pág. xiii). Las líneas perpendiculares impresas en negrillas, que se encuentran en muchos artículos, ayudarán muchísimo a hallar cambios de una parte de la oración a otra (Véase Nota Explicativa 38, pág. xvi).
4. Búsquense las abreviaturas y los nombres propios en la misma lista alfabética de las palabras comunes (Véase Nota Explicativa 19, pág. xiii).
5. Búsquense todas las palabras escritas de la misma manera bajo un mismo artículo, ya sea que vayan escritas con mayúscula inicial o no (Véanse Notas Explicativas 21 y 22, pág. xiii).
6. Búsquense los nombres femeninos que se escriben de la misma manera que la forma femenina de un adjetivo bajo la forma masculina del adjetivo (Véase Nota Explicativa 24, pág. xiii).
7. Búsquense las frases verbales bajo el tratamiento transitivo o intransitivo del verbo según que el verbo (y no la frase verbal en su conjunto) sea transitivo o intransitivo (Véase Nota Explicativa 36, pág. xvi).
8. Búsquense como unidades léxicas independientes los compuestos ingleses sólidos, los unidos con guión y los escritos como dos o más vocablos separados. Por ejemplo, *soft-boiled egg* se encuentra como artículo separado y no bajo *soft* ni bajo *boiled* ni bajo *egg* (Véase Nota Explicativa 27, pág. xiv).

# *The Williams*
# SPANISH & ENGLISH DICTIONARY

EXPANDED EDITION

# *The Williams*
# SPANISH & ENGLISH DICTIONARY

EXPANDED EDITION

***Edwin B. Williams***
*University of Pennsylvania*

SPANISH-ENGLISH ENGLISH-SPANISH

complete in one volume

Charles Scribner's Sons • New York

Printed in the United States of America

3 5 7 9 11 13 15 17 19 O/C 20 18 16 14 12 10 8 6 4 2

Library of Congress Catalog Card Number 72-11299

SBN 684-13284-2 (cloth)
684-13294-x (cloth, thumb indexed)

# Preface

A bilingual dictionary is a bridge between two cultures. If these two cultures are among the great cultures of the world, it is important that this bridge be a sturdy and trustworthy medium through which they may become better known to each other and through which they may collaborate to their mutual enhancement and the benefit of the world at large.

It was with the purpose of building this bridge between Anglo-Saxon and Hispanic culture on a sounder footing than had ever been done before that I embarked on the task of designing and compiling this dictionary over fifteen years ago.

At the outset it was necessary to establish principles for the treatment of words, criteria for their acceptance, and standards for the relative space to be accorded them. It was also necessary to survey the history and current status of English lexicography, Spanish lexicography, and English and Spanish bilingual lexicography, as I had been doing for many years prior to the initiation of this work and as I continued to do throughout its compilation, its revision, and its subsequent expansion.

This has involved considerations of frequency and range. Probably at no time in the history of the world has language change been more rapid than in the past fifteen or twenty years. The acceleration of events, the rise of new concepts of life and government, the spread of new interests, the invention of new devices, and the discovery of new relationships in matter, individuals, and societies have brought into English and Spanish thousands of new words and meanings. Obsolete Spanish and English words, many of them not indicated as such in other dictionaries, many of them of little relative value, and many of them carried over from dictionary to dictionary during the past century, had to be eliminated to make way for

# Prólogo

Un diccionario bilingüe es un puente entre dos culturas. Si estas dos culturas se hallan entre las culturas mayores del mundo, es importante que este puente sea de solidez y confianza tales que permita que a través de él se compenetren mejor la una con la otra y puedan colaborar hacia su mutua superación y para beneficio del mundo entero.

Fué con el propósito de construir este puente entre la cultura anglosajona y la hispánica sobre bases más firmes que jamás antes haya tenido, por lo que yo me empeñé en la tarea de planear y compilar este diccionario hace más de quince años.

Como punto de partida era necesario establecer principios para el modo de considerar las palabras, criterios para su aceptación y normas para el espacio relativo que se les debía fijar. También era necesario estudiar la historia y el estado actual de la lexicografía inglesa, la lexicografía española y la lexicografía bilingüe inglesa y española, cosa que había estado haciendo durante muchos años antes de iniciar esta obra y que continué haciendo durante su compilación, su revisión y su ampliación ulterior.

En esto han intervenido consideraciones de frecuencia y extensión. Probablemente jamás en la historia del mundo haya habido cambios en el idioma más rápidos que en los últimos quince o veinte años. La aceleración de los sucesos, el surgimiento de nuevos conceptos de vida y de gobierno, el acrecentamiento de nuevos intereses, la invención de nuevos dispositivos y el descubrimiento de nuevas relaciones en la materia, los individuos y las sociedades han injertado en el inglés y el español millares de nuevas palabras y de significados nuevos. Las palabras españolas e inglesas desusadas, muchas de ellas ni indicadas como tales en otros diccionarios, muchas de ellas relativamente de poco valor y muchas de ellas pasadas de diccionario en diccionario durante el último siglo tuvieron que eliminarse para hacer lugar a las palabras de importancia incuestionable de hoy día en

words of unquestioned importance today in all branches of human knowledge and human activity and interest, such as literature, music, art, archeology, philosophy, psychology, anthropology, religion, agriculture, engineering, chemistry, mathematics, physics, astronomy, business, commerce, industry, medicine, surgery, dentistry, veterinary medicine, international law, diplomacy, sports, and games. And special attention has been given to the neologisms of both English and Spanish connected with jet propulsion, nuclear physics, the wonder drugs, radio, television, aeronautics, aerospace technology, rocketry, astronautics, etc.

A bilingual and bidirectional dictionary should fulfill four purposes. For example, a Spanish and English bilingual dictionary should provide (1) Spanish words which an English-speaking person wishes to use in speech or writing (by means of the English-Spanish part), (2) English meanings of Spanish words which an English-speaking person encounters in speech or writing (by means of the Spanish-English part), (3) English words which a Spanish-speaking person wishes to use in speech or writing (by means of the Spanish-English part), and (4) Spanish meanings of English words which a Spanish-speaking person encounters in speech or writing (by means of the English-Spanish part). Thus two purposes serve the English-speaking person, two the Spanish-speaking person. And thus each of the two parts had to be designed to fulfill two purposes.

Much research in many fields of knowledge has been necessary to solve the problems of translation. Chemical, mineralogical, biochemical, and pharmaceutical glosses have been compiled on the basis of chemical formulae. Botanical, entomological, ichthyological, ornithological, zoölogical, and some bacteriological and virological glosses have been compiled on the basis of the Latin names of the

todos los ramos del conocimiento humano, y en las actividades e intereses humanos, como son la literatura, la música, el arte, la arqueología, la filosofía, la psicología, la antropología, la religión, la agricultura, la ingeniería, la química, las matemáticas, la física, la astronomía, el comercio, la industria, la medicina, la cirujía, la odontología, la medicina veterinaria, el derecho internacional, la diplomacia, los deportes y los juegos. Y se ha prestado atención especial a los neologismos tanto de inglés como de español, relacionados con la propulsión a chorro, la física nuclear, las drogas milagrosas, la radio, la televisión, la aeronáutica, la tecnología aero-espacial, la cohetería, la astronáutica, etc.

Un diccionario bilingüe y bidireccional debiera cumplir cuatro propósitos. Por ejemplo, un diccionario bilingüe español e inglés debiera proveer (1) palabras en español que una persona de habla inglesa desee emplear en la conversación o en la escritura—usando la parte de inglés-español, (2) los significados ingleses de palabras españolas que una persona de habla inglesa encuentre en el discurso o en la lectura—usando la parte de español-inglés, (3) palabras en inglés que una persona de habla hispana desee emplear en la conversación o en la escritura—usando la parte de español-inglés y (4) los significados españoles de palabras inglesas que una persona de habla hispana encuentre en el discurso o en la lectura —usando la parte de inglés-español. De esta manera dos propósitos sirven a la persona de habla inglesa, dos a la persona de habla hispana. Y fué por esto que se idearon las dos partes del diccionario para que cada una cumpliera plenamente sus dos propósitos.

Han sido necesarias muchas pesquisas en todos los terrenos del conocimiento para solventar los problemas de la traducción. Se han compilado las glosas químicas, mineralógicas, bioquímicas y farmacéuticas a base de fórmulas químicas. Se han compilado las glosas botánicas, entomológicas, ictiológicas, ornitológicas, zoológicas y algunas bacteriológicas y virológicas

genus and species. And although etymologies are not included, the study of the etymology and phonology of words has often contributed to the precise solution of many difficult translations.

The two parts have been compiled concurrently and thus have an intimate structural relationship seldom found in bilingual dictionaries. The Spanish is both peninsular and Spanish American, while the English is both American and British. The work contains over 130,000 separate entries about equally divided between the two parts. These entries are enriched by the inclusion of thousands of idioms, and the language of everyday life is presented in words and phrases in both parts.

Two grammars, an English grammar written in Spanish and a Spanish grammar written in English, present in full detail the pronunciation of both languages and the inflection of nouns, adjectives, and verbs. English pronunciation, with variants, is shown by a simplified adaptation of the International Phonetic Alphabet.

The work of revision and expansion was begun immediately after the appearance of the first edition early in 1955 and has been carried on without interruption since that time. In this period many mighty changes have taken place in the world and these changes have brought into existence many new words and meanings, and many new ideas about lexicography also. In 1956 the Spanish Academy published the eighteenth edition of its dictionary and while it sanctioned some new words in this edition and displayed a slight tendency toward permissiveness in matters of pronunciation and spelling in its *Nuevas normas* of 1959 it remains basically prescriptive in theory and practice. In 1961 the G. and C. Merriam Company published Webster's *Third New International Dictionary Unabridged.* This work is extremely permissive, partic-

a base de los nombres latinos de los géneros y las especies. Y aunque no se han incluído las etimologías, el estudio de la etimología y la fonología ha contribuído a menudo a dar con la solución precisa de muchas traducciones difíciles.

Las dos partes se han compilado concurrentemente, con lo que tienen una relación estructural íntima que rara vez se encuentra en los diccionarios bilingües. El español es tanto el peninsular como el de la América Hispana, al igual que el inglés es tanto el que se usa en los Estados Unidos de Norteamérica como el de las islas Británicas. La obra contiene más de 130.000 artículos distintos que están más o menos igualmente divididos en ambas partes. Estos artículos están enriquecidos con la inclusión de miles de modismos y el idioma de la vida cotidiana se presenta en palabras y frases en ambas partes.

Dos gramáticas, una de inglés escrita en español y otra de español escrita en inglés, presentan con todo detalle la pronunciación de ambos idiomas y la inflexión de los nombres, adjetivos y verbos. La pronunciación del inglés, con sus variantes, se enseña mediante una adaptación simplificada del alfabeto fonético internacional.

La tarea de revisión y ampliación se inició a raíz de la aparición de la primera edición a principios de 1955 y se ha llevado a cabo sin interrupción desde aquel entonces. Durante este lapso muchos y grandes cambios han ocurrido en el mundo, cambios que han dado origen a muchas palabras y acepciones nuevas, como también nuevas ideas en el campo de la lexicografía. En 1956 la Real Academia Española publicó la décimoctava edición de su diccionario y aunque sancionó algunas palabras nuevas y demostró una ligera tendencia hacia lo permisivo en cuanto a pronunciación y ortografía en sus *Nuevas normas* de 1959, permanece fundamentalmente prescriptiva tanto en la teoría como en la práctica. En 1961 la Compañía G. and C. Merriam publicó *Webster's Third New International Dictionary Unabridged.* Esta obra es sumamente

ularly in the matter of usage, and has awakened increased interest in problems of lexicography and language in academic circles and the press.

In this Expanded Edition I have chosen an eclectic course between the prescriptiveness of the Academy and the permissiveness of Webster's Third. I have emphasized the language of contemporary literature, the language of everyday speech, and the language of science and technology and thus have introduced thousands of new words and meanings of varied status, many of which have not appeared in any other monolingual or bilingual dictionary. At the same time, feeling that the status of a word is just as important as any other aspect of the word, especially for users of a foreign tongue, I have labeled all words that deviate from standard usage with the labels that have been customarily used for the purpose.

In addition to the large increase in the main body of the dictionary I have inserted in the Center Section the following new features: a Breve historia de la lengua inglesa, a Brief History of the Spanish Language, a table of Model Regular Verbs (so arranged as to show the parallelisms of the simple and compound tenses), tables of Spanish and English Cognates, an abstract of the *Nuevas normas de prosodia y ortografía* of the Spanish Academy, and Conversion Tables (for converting elements of the British and American system of weights and measures into the metric system and vice versa).

This dictionary was originally conceived with the hope that it would contribute to greater understanding between Spanish-speaking and English-speaking peoples and thus to universal peace among the nations of the world. It should be mentioned now that this same hope was ever-present in the work of revision and expansion.

permisiva, especialmente en cuestiones de uso, y ha despertado mucho mayor interés en los problemas de la lexicografía y el lenguaje en los círculos académicos y en la prensa.

En esta Edición Aumentada he seguido un camino ecléctico entre el prescriptivo de la Academia y el permisivo del nuevo Webster. He hecho hincapié en el lenguaje de la literatura contemporánea, el lenguaje de uso diario y el lenguaje científico y tecnológico, con lo que he introducido miles de palabras y acepciones nuevas de diferentes categorías, muchas de las cuales no figuran en ningún otro diccionario monolingüe ni bilingüe. Al mismo tiempo, convencido de que la categoría de una palabra es tan importante como cualquier otro aspecto de ella, especialmente para los usuarios de una lengua extranjera, he calificado todas las palabras que se apartan del uso ordinario con las designaciones que se emplean habitualmente para tal efecto.

Además del gran aumento en el texto del diccionario, he incluído en la Sección Central los siguientes elementos nuevos: una Breve historia de la lengua inglesa, una Brief History of the Spanish Language, un cuadro de Modelos de conjugación de los verbos regulares (dispuesto de modo que demuestra el paralelismo de los tiempos simples y compuestos), tablas de palabras cognadas españolas e inglesas, un resumen de las *Nuevas normas de prosodia y ortografía* de la Real Academia Española y Tablas de conversión (para convertir elementos del sistema británico y norteamericano de pesas y medidas en el sistema métrico y viceversa).

Este diccionario se concibió desde el principio con la esperanza de que contribuiría a un mayor entendimiento entre los pueblos hispanohablantes y anglohablantes y por tanto a la paz universal entre las naciones del mundo. Cabe ahora mencionar que esta misma esperanza ha estado siempre presente en la obra de revisión y ampliación.

*Philadelphia*—EDWIN B. WILLIAMS

# Table of Contents — Índice de Materias

## Explanatory Notes

1. Subject and usage labels are printed in roman and in parentheses and refer to the preceding entry or phrase (printed in boldface).

## Notas Explicativas

1. Las designaciones de tema y uso se han impreso en letra redonda y entre paréntesis y se refieren al vocablo o frase que anteceden (impresos en negrillas);

**arco** *m* (geom. & elec.) arc; (anat. & arch.) arch
**shy** [ʃaɪ] *adj* . . . ; **to be shy on** (slang) estar escaso de

However, when they come immediately, i.e., without any intervening punctuation mark, after a target word, they refer to that target word and the preceding words grouped with it if there are any.

Sin embargo, cuando siguen inmediatamente, es decir, sin signo de puntuación intermedia, a un vocablo de la lengua-traductora, se refieren a este vocablo y los vocablos precedentes agrupados con él si los hay.

**sidewalk** [ˈsaɪd,wɔk] *s* acera; banqueta, vereda (Am.)

2. Subject and usage labels are generally in the form of abbreviations but they are sometimes full English words.

2. Las designaciones de tema y uso se dan generalmente en forma de abreviaturas pero algunas veces se dan las palabras completas en inglés.

**entropy** [ˈentrəpɪ] *s* (*pl:* **-pies**) (thermodynamics) entropía

3. Subject and usage labels are designed to be readily understood by both English-speaking and Spanish-speaking persons. In case of uncertainty ready reference can be had to the single alphabetical list of them on the end papers at the end of this book.

4. The subject label (bot.) is used with names of plants but not with names of fruits.

3. Las designaciones de tema y uso se escriben de manera que sean de facilísima comprensión tanto para las personas de habla inglesa como para las de habla hispana. En caso de duda se puede hacer pronta consulta en la única lista alfabética de las mismas en las guardas al final de este libro.

4. La designación de tema (bot.) se usa con los nombres de las plantas pero no con los nombres de los frutos.

**toronjo** *m* (bot.) grapefruit
**toronja** *f* grapefruit (*fruit*)

5. In view of the fact that bilingual dictionaries are consulted more frequently and by a larger number of users in pursuit of the meaning of foreign words than of foreign words themselves, definitions, particularizing words and phrases, and synonyms used to particularize are provided in the target language. They are printed in italics and in parentheses, and refer to the preceding word or phrase (printed in ordinary roman).

5. En vista de que los diccionarios bilingües se consultan más frecuentemente y por un número mayor de usuarios en busca de las acepciones de palabras extranjeras que de las palabras extranjeras mismas, las definiciones, los vocablos y frases particularizantes y los sinónimos que se usan con fines particularizadores van suministrados en la lengua-traductora. Van impresos en itálicas y entre paréntesis y se refieren al vocablo o frase que anteceden (impresos en redondas corrientes).

| | |
|---|---|
| DEFINITION: | **oriente** *m* east; . . . ; orient (*luster of the pearl*) |
| PARTICULARIZING WORD: | **suicide** [ˈsuɪsaɪd] o [ˈsjuɪsaɪd] *s* suicidio (*acción*); suicida (*persona*) |
| PARTICULARIZING PHRASE: | **shutter** [ˈʃʌtər] *s* cerrador; . . . contraventana (*para el exterior de las vidrieras*) |
| SYNONYM: | **férvido -da** *adj* fervid (*hot, boiling; vehement*) |

6. The particularizing word or phrase may be (a) a noun (to particularize the meaning of an adjective), (b) a noun in apposition (to particularize the meaning of another noun), (c) a direct object (to particularize the meaning of a verb), (d) a subject (to particularize the meaning of a verb), (e) an adjectival expression (to particularize the meaning of a noun), or (f) an adverbial expression (to particularize the meaning of a verb).

6. El vocablo o frase particularizante puede ser (a) un substantivo (para particularizar el significado de un adjetivo), (b) un substantivo en aposición (para particularizar el significado de otro sustantivo), (c) un complemento directo (para particularizar el significado de un verbo), (d) un sujeto (para particularizar el significado de un verbo), (e) una expresión adjetival (para particularizar el significado de un sustantivo) o (f) una expresión adverbial (para particularizar el significado de un verbo).

(a) **desperate** [ˈdɛspərɪt] *adj* . . . ; heroico (*p.ej., remedio*)
(b) **homicidio** *m* homicide (*act*)
(c) **pack** [pæk] *s* . . . ; *va* . . . ; hacer (*el baúl, la maleta*)
(d) **sag** [sæg] *s* . . . ; *vn* bajar (*los precios*)
(e) **abismo** *m* abyss; trough (*of a wave*)
(f) **felpar** *va* . . . ; (poet.) to carpet (*with grass or flowers*)

7. The Latin names of genus and species are given when needed for purposes of particularization.

7. Los nombres en latín de los géneros y las especies se dan cuando se necesitan para particularizar.

**oso marino** (zool.) fur seal (*Callorhinus alascanus*)

8. Abbreviations of grammatical terms are printed in italics and not in parentheses and refer to the preceding entry (printed in boldface).

8. Las abreviaturas de términos gramaticales se han impreso en itálicas y no entre paréntesis y se refieren al artículo antecedente (en negrillas).

**danés -nesa** *adj* Danish; *mf* Dane; *m* Danish (*language*)

9. The abbreviations *(cap.)* and *(l.c.)* are printed in italics and in parentheses, refer to the preceding entry, and are placed before the abbreviation indicating the part of speech.

9. Las abreviaturas *(cap. = mayúscula)* y *(l.c. = minúscula)* se han impreso en itálicas y entre paréntesis, se refieren al artículo antecedente y se han colocado antes de la abreviatura que indica la parte de la oración.

**python** [ˈpaɪθɑn] o [ˈpaɪθən] *s* (zool.) pitón; (*cap.*) *s* (myth.) Pitón
**Henry** [ˈhɛnrɪ] *s* Enrique; (*l.c.*) *s* (*pl:* **-ries** o **-rys**) (elec.) henrio

10. Irregular plurals are printed in boldface and in parentheses and are placed after the abbreviation indicating the part of speech, except that irregular Spanish plurals that apply to both the noun and adjective use of a word are placed immediately after the entry, that is, before the abbreviation *adj.*

10. Los plurales irregulares se han impreso en negrillas y entre paréntesis y se han colocado después de la abreviatura que indica la parte de la oración, excepto los plurales irregulares en español que se aplican tanto al substantivo como al adjetivo que se han colocado inmediatamente después del artículo, es decir, antes de la abreviatura *adj.*

**tooth** [tuθ] *s* (*pl:* **teeth**) diente
**infeliz** (*pl:* **-lices**) *adj* unhappy; (coll.) simple and good-natured; *m* wretch, poor soul

11. Irregular English comparatives and superlatives are printed in boldface and in parentheses and are placed after the abbreviation indicating the part of speech.

11. Los comparativos y superlativos irregulares en inglés se han impreso en negrillas y entre paréntesis y se han colocado después de la abreviatura que indica la parte de la oración.

**hot** [hɑt] *adj* (*comp:* **hotter;** *super:* **hottest**) caliente

12. The irregular forms of English verbs are printed in boldface and in parentheses and are placed before the abbreviation indicating the part of speech.

12. Las formas irregulares de los verbos ingleses se han impreso en negrillas y entre paréntesis y se han colocado antes de la abreviatura que indica la parte de la oración.

**run** [rʌn] *s* carrera; . . . (*pret:* **ran;** *pp:* **run;** *ger:* **running**) *va* correr

13. Irregular plural endings are shown by giving that part of the word that is necessary to complete the form after dropping the last orthographic syllable of the singular.

13. Las terminaciones irregulares del plural se han indicado dando la parte de la palabra necesaria para completar la forma después de suprimir la última sílaba ortográfica del singular.

**cemetery** [ˈsɛmɪˌtɛrɪ] *s* (*pl:* **-ies**) cementerio

14. The same method is used to show the irregular endings of English comparatives, superlatives, preterits, past participles, and gerunds.

14. El mismo método se usa para enseñar las terminaciones irregulares de los comparativos, superlativos, pretéritos, participios y gerundios ingleses.

**happy** [ˈhæpɪ] *adj* (*comp:* **-pier;** *super:* **-piest**) feliz
**forget** [fɔrˈgɛt] (*pret:* **-got;** *pp:* **-gotten** o **-got;** *ger:* **-getting**) *va* olvidar

15. Key forms of English and Spanish verbs are listed as separate entries with cross reference to the infinitive.

15. Las formas principales de los verbos en inglés y español se han incluído como artículos separados, con referencia al infinitivo.

**forgiven** [fɔrˈgɪvən] *pp de* **forgive**
**tuve** *1st sg pret ind of* **tener**

16. Numbers referring to the model conjugations of irregular Spanish verbs are placed before the abbreviation indicating the part of speech. If the verb may also be conjugated regularly, this is indicated by the addition of '& regular'.

16. Los números que se refieren a las conjugaciones modelo de los verbos irregulares españoles se han colocado antes de la abreviatura que indica la parte de la oración. Si el verbo se conjuga también regularmente, se indica, añadiendo '& regular'.

**poner** **§69** *va* to put, place, lay, set
**vidriar** **§90** & **regular** *va* to glaze

Some model conjugations show a combination of two irregularities.

Algunas conjugaciones modelo muestran una combinación de dos irregularidades.

**torcer** **§87** *va* to twist; to bend; to turn

17. The regimen of English and Spanish verbs is shown with respect to a following noun, infinitive, or gerund.

17. El régimen de los verbos ingleses y españoles se ha dado respecto al nombre, infinitivo o gerundio que sigue.

**set** [sɛt] . . . *va* . . . ; **to set afire** poner fuego a, pegar fuego a
**keep** [kip] . . . *va* . . . ; **to keep** + *ger* hacer + *inf*, p.ej., **I am sorry to keep you waiting** siento hacerle esperar

18. Some verbs, traditionally considered to be intransitive but actually transitive, are designated as transitive for the first time herein.

18. Algunos verbos, tradicionalmente considerados intransitivos pero que realmente son transitivos, se designan como transitivos por primera vez.

**agradar** *va* to please

19. Abbreviations and proper nouns are all included in the alphabetical body of the dictionary.

19. Las abreviaturas y los nombres propios están todos incluídos en el cuerpo alfabético del diccionario.

**jeopardy** ['dʒɛpərdɪ] *s* riesgo, peligro
**Jephthah** ['dʒɛfθə] *s* (Bib.) Jefté
**Jer.** abr. de **Jeremiah**

20. Proper nouns include given names, place names, Biblical names, mythological names, classical names, gentile nouns, and the names of some of the great figures of history.

20. Los nombres propios incluyen los nombres de pila y de lugares, nombres bíblicos, mitológicos, clásicos, gentilicios y los de algunas de las grandes figuras de la historia.

21. Words with the same spelling are combined in a single entry regardless of variation in part of speech, meaning, etymology, or pronunciation.

21. Las palabras escritas con las mismas letras se combinan en un solo artículo a pesar de su diferencia como partes de la oración, y de su significado, etimología o pronunciación.

**wind** [wɪnd] *s* viento . . . ; [waɪnd] *s* vuelta, recodo; . . . *va* enrollar, envolver; [waɪnd] o [wɪnd] . . . *va* sonar (*un instrumento de viento*)

22. Accordingly, common nouns and proper nouns that are spelled alike except for the initial capital are combined in a single entry.

22. De acuerdo con lo anterior, los nombres comunes y los nombres propios escritos con las mismas letras, excepto la mayúscula inicial, se han combinado en un solo artículo.

**scotia** ['skoʃɪə] o ['skoʃə] *s* (arch.) escocia, nacela; (*cap.*) ['skoʃə] *s* (poet.) Escocia

23. All words are treated in a fixed functional sequence, as follows: adjective, adverb, preposition, conjunction, interjection, noun, transitive verb, intransitive verb, and reflexive verb.

23. Todas las palabras se han tratado en su función fija y consecutiva, como sigue: adjetivo, adverbio, preposición, conjunción, interjección, sustantivo, verbo transitivo, verbo intransitivo y verbo reflexivo.

**after** ['æftər] o ['ɑftər] *adj* siguiente; *adv* después; *prep* después de; según; *conj* después que o después de que
**acostar** §77 *va* to lay, to lay down; to put to bed; (naut.) to bring alongside, to bring inshore; *vn* to lean, list; *vr* to lie down, to go to bed; (Am.) to be confined (with child)

Occasional exceptions occur, particularly in English nouns whose adjective function is sometimes treated in second place.

Sin embargo, se dan excepciones, particularmente con sustantivos ingleses cuya función adjetival se ha tratado a veces en segundo lugar.

**university** [ˌjunɪ'vʌrsɪtɪ] *s* (*pl:* **-ties**) universidad; *adj* universitario

24. If a Spanish feminine noun is the same in form as the feminine form of an adjective, it is entered under the adjective.

24. Si un nombre femenino español está en la forma misma que la forma femenina de un adjetivo, se lo inserta bajo el adjetivo.

**alazán -zana** *adj* sorrel, reddish-brown; *mf* sorrel horse; *f* wine press; olive-oil press

If this removes it from its alphabetical position, it is entered also in its alphabetical position with a cross reference to the adjective.

Si esto saca el nombre de su lugar alfabético, se lo inserta también en el lugar que le corresponda alfabéticamente y con una referencia al adjetivo.

**fecha** *f* see **fecho**
**fechación** *f* dating
**fechador** *m* (Am.) canceling stamp
**fechar** *va* to date
**fecho -cha** *adj* issued, executed; *f* date

25. The gender of the first noun of a pair of Spanish nouns separated by 'or' is indicated only after the second noun if both nouns are masculine and the first one ends in o or if both nouns are feminine and the first one ends in a.

25. El género del primer nombre de un par de nombres españoles separados por 'or' se indica sólo después del segundo nombre si ambos nombres son masculinos y el primero termina con o, o si ambos nombres son femeninos y el primero termina con a.

**hartazgo** or **hartazón** *m* fill, bellyful
**Antígona** or **Antígone** *f* (myth.) Antigone

26. A masculine and a feminine noun differing only in ending are combined in one entry if they have at least one meaning in common.

26. Un nombre masculino y uno femenino que difieren sólo en su terminación se combinan en un solo artículo si tienen por lo menos un significado que les sea común.

**nieto -ta** *mf* grandchild; *m* grandson; *f* granddaughter

27. All compound English words, whether written with hyphens or as two or more separate words, are listed as separate entries. The pronunciation of the elements not joined by a hyphen is given only if the word does not exist elsewhere in the dictionary as a separate entry.

27. Todas las palabras inglesas compuestas, bien se escriban con guiones o bien como dos o más palabras separadas, están incluídas como artículos separados. La pronunciación de los elementos que no van unidos por un guión se ha dado solamente si la palabra no existe en otra parte del diccionario como artículo separado.

**acetic acid** *s* (chem.) ácido acético
**Saint Vitus's dance** ['vaɪtəsɪz] *s* (path.) baile de San Vito

28. Spanish expressions consisting of a noun and an adjective or a noun and an adjective phrase are listed under the noun.

28. Las expresiones españolas que constan de un nombre y un adjetivo o de un nombre y una frase adjetival se han insertado bajo el nombre.

**ácido -da** *adj* acid; . . . ; *m* (chem.) acid; **ácido acético** acetic acid
**avión** *m* airplane; (orn.) martin; . . . ; **avión de caza** (aer.) pursuit plane

29. Prepositional phrases and expressions containing a verb and a noun are listed under the noun.

29. Las frases preposicionales y las expresiones que contienen un verbo y un nombre se incluyen bajo el nombre.

**quiet** ['kwaɪət] *adj* quieto; . . . ; *s* quietud; **on the quiet** a las calladas, de callada
**pie** *m* foot; . . . **perder pie** to lose one's footing

30. All subentries are listed alphabetically, those in which the entry word is not the first word coming before those in which it is.

30. Todos los artículos secundarios están en lista alfabética, poniéndose en primer lugar aquéllos cuya primera palabra no es la del artículo principal y en segundo lugar aquéllos cuya primera palabra lo es.

**vino** *m* wine; **bautizar** or **cristianizar el vino** to water wine; **dormir el vino** to sleep off a drunk; **tener mal vino** to be a quarrelsome drunk; **vino cubierto** dark-red wine; **vino de cuerpo** strong-bodied wine; **vino de Jerez** sherry wine; . . . ; **vino generoso** generous rich wine

31. The pronunciation of all English words is shown by a simplified adaptation of the International Phonetic Alphabet. (See note 27 above.) And common variant pronunciations are also given.

31. La pronunciación de todas las palabras inglesas se indica por medio de una adaptación simplificada del alfabeto fonético internacional. (Véase la nota 27.) Y también se dan las variaciones de pronunciación comunes.

**laugh** [læf] o [lɑf] *s* risa
**long** [lɔŋ] o [lɑŋ] *adj* (*comp:* **longer** [ˈlɔŋgər] o [ˈlɑŋgər]; *super:* **longest** [ˈlɔŋgɪst] o [ˈlɑŋgɪst]) largo

32. The Spanish conjunction **o** is always changed to **u** before English orthographic **o** but is only changed to **u** before the phonetic symbols [ɔ] and [o].

32. La conjunción española **o** se cambia siempre en **u** antes de la **o** ortográfica inglesa, pero se cambia en **u** antes de los únicos símbolos fonéticos [ɔ] y [o].

**octet** u **octette** [ɑkˈtɛt] *s* (mus.) octeto; (pros.) octava; grupo de ocho
**orange** [ˈɑrɪndʒ] u [ˈɔrɪndʒ] *s* naranja (*fruto*)
**overt** [ˈovʌrt] u [oˈvʌrt] *adj* abierto, manifiesto; premeditado
**octavo** [ɑkˈtevo] o [ɑkˈtɑvo] *adj* en octavo; *s* (*pl:* **-vos**) libro en octavo

33. The two parts of the dictionary are the converse of each other. However, they are not symmetrical because of differences in lexicographical procedure particularly in the matter of the treatment of compounds. (See notes 27 and 28 above.)

33. Las dos partes del diccionario son recíprocas la una de la otra. Con todo, no son simétricas a causa de las diferencias de procedimiento lexicográfico en cuanto al tratamiento de los compuestos. (Véanse notas 27 y 28 arriba.)

34. Grammatical information (pronunciation of English words, part of speech, gender of Spanish nouns, feminine of Spanish adjectives, and irregular forms of inflected words) is given for the source language in each part of the dictionary.

34. Los informes gramaticales (pronunciación de las palabras inglesas, parte de la oración, género de los nombres españoles, forma femenina de los adjetivos españoles y formas irregulares de palabras sujetas a la flexión) se dan para la lengua-fuente en las dos partes del diccionario.

**hindú -dúa** *adj & mf* (*pl:* **-dúes -dúas**) Hindu or Hindoo
**get** [gɛt] (*pret:* **got;** *pp:* **got** o **gotten;** *ger:* **getting**) *va* obtener, recibir

However, in order to match the meanings of the two languages, syntactical and lexical construction is shown in both the source and the target languages. Thus a transitive verb or expression is glossed by a transitive verb or expression, an intransitive verb or expression by an intransitive verb or expression, a mass noun by a mass noun, and a countable by a countable or by a mass noun accompanied by an appropriate counter.

Sin embargo, para igualar las acepciones de los dos idiomas, la construcción sintáctica y léxica se muestra tanto en la lengua-fuente como en la lengua-traductora. Así, un verbo o giro transitivo va glosado por un verbo o giro transitivo, uno intransitivo por uno intransitivo, un nombre no contable por un nombre no contable y uno contable por uno contable o por uno no contable acompañado de una palabra que hace posible la enumeración.

**rival** [ˈraɪvəl] *s . . . ; va* rivalizar con
**mueble** *adj . . . ; m* piece of furniture; cabinet (*e.g., of a radio*); **muebles** *mpl* furniture

When the gender of a Spanish noun varies with its meaning, it is also shown in the English-Spanish part of the dictionary.

Cuando el género de un nombre español varía con su acepción, aquél se indica también en la parte de inglés-español del diccionario.

**order** [ˈɔrdər] *s* orden *m* (*sucesión metódica de la cosas; . . .*); orden *f* (*mandato; . . .*)

35. When the subject and/or object of a verb are necessary to the understanding of the translation of the verb, although not part of the translation, they are included in parentheses and printed in italics.

35. Cuando el sujeto o el objeto o ambos son necesarios para la comprensión de la traducción del verbo, aunque no forman parte de dicha traducción, se encierran entre paréntesis y se imprimen en itálicas.

**grabar** *va* . . . ; to record (*a sound, a song, a phonograph record, etc.*)
**frost** [frɔst] o [frɑst] *s* . . . ; *va* . . . ; escarchar (*p.ej., confituras*); quemar (*el hielo las plantas*); deslustrar (*el vidrio*)

As personal a is considered to be part of the object, it is included in parentheses with the object.

Ya que se considera a la preposición a antes del acusativo como parte inseparable de dicho acusativo, se encierra dentro del mismo paréntesis.

**trap** . . . *va* entrampar; atrapar (*a un ladrón*)
**pass** . . . *va* . . . aprobar (*un proyecto de ley; un examen; a un alumno*)

36. Verb phrases in which the verb is transitive are entered under the treatment of the transitive verb, those in which the verb is intransitive under the treatment of the intransive verb. Thus the same verb phrase often occurs twice in the same vocabulary entry.

36. Las frases verbales en las cuales el verbo es transitivo se presentan bajo el tratamiento del verbo transitivo y aquellas en las cuales el verbo es intransitivo bajo el tratamiento del verbo intransitivo. De suerte que la misma frase verbal se encuentra a menudo dos veces en el mismo artículo.

**take** [tek] *s* . . . ; . . . ; *va* . . . ; **to take off** quitarse (*p.ej., el sombrero*); descontar; (coll.) imitar, parodiar; . . . ; *vn* . . . ; **to take off** levantarse; salir; (aer.) despegar

Accordingly, although the verb phrase as a whole may be transitive, it is entered under the treatment of the intransitive verb when the verb itself of the verb phrase is intransitive.

Por consiguiente, aunque la frase verbal en su conjunto pueda ser transitiva, se encontrará bajo el tratamiento del verbo intransitivo cuando el verbo mismo de la frase verbal es intransitivo.

**taste** [test] *s* . . . ; *va* gustar; probar; *vn* saber; **to taste like** u **of** saber a

37. While prepositions are treated comprehensively in their alphabetical position in the dictionary, they are treated also and with more direct applicability and usefulness under the words (verbs and nouns) with which they are closely associated syntactically and idiomatically.

37. Al paso que las preposiciones van tratadas detalladamente en su puesto alfabético en el diccionario, van tratadas también y con aplicación y utilidad más directas bajo los vocablos (verbos y nombres) con los cuales están asociadas · sintáctica e idiomáticamente.

**jump** [dʒʌmp] *s* . . . ; *vn* . . . ; **to jump at** saltar sobre; apresurarse a aceptar (*una invitación*); apresurarse a aprovechar (*la oportunidad*)

38. In long or complicated vocabulary entries, change in part of speech, inflection, function of verbs (transitive, intransitive, etc.), gender of Spanish nouns, and pronunciation of English words is marked with a boldface perpendicular line in place of the usual semicolon.

38. En los artículos largos o complicados, los cambios en la parte de la oración, la flexión, la función de los verbos (transitiva, intransitiva, etc.), el género de los nombres españoles y la pronunciación de las palabras inglesas van señalados con una línea perpendicular impresa en negrilla en vez del punto y coma de costumbre.

**pick** [pɪk] *s* pico; . . . ; flor (*lo más excelente*) **|** *va* escoger; recoger (*p.ej., flores*)
**corte** *m* cut; . . . ; **corte de traje** suiting **|** *f* court; yard

**A, a** *f* first letter of the Spanish alphabet
**A.** abr. of **Alteza & aprobado**
**a** *prep* (to indicate place whither) to, e.g., **va a Buenos Aires** he is going to Buenos Aires; **bajan a la estación** they are going down to the station; **viaje a la luna** trip to the moon; (as indirect object) to, e.g., **escribo a Carlos** I am writing to Charles; **dieron algo al pobre** they gave something to the beggar; (to express addition) to, e.g., **añade agua al vino** he adds water to the wine; (with a following infinitive after certain verbs) to, e.g., **voy a hacerlo** I am going to do it; **aprendemos a bailar** we are learning to dance; **comienza a llover** it is beginning to rain; (with a following infinitive in certain expressions) to, e.g., **a decir verdad** to tell the truth; (with a following infinitive to express condition) if, unless, e.g., **a no ser por** if it were not for, but for; **a saberlo yo** if I had known it; **a no venir él** unless he comes; (to express limit of change or motion in time or place) to, e.g., **de la juventud a la vejez** from youth to old age; **de las tres a las cuatro de la tarde** from three to four in the afternoon; **de calle a calle** from street to street; (in idiomatic expressions) to, e.g., **cara a cara** face to face; **a mi gusto** to my taste; (to indicate location) at, e.g., **sentado a la mesa** seated at the table; **me esperaba a la puerta** he was waiting for me at the door; **a tres kilómetros de Madrid** at three kilometers from Madrid; **a lo lejos** at a distance; **a veinticinco grados sobre cero** at twenty-five degrees above zero; (in telling time) at, e.g., **a los ocho** at eight o'clock; **a medianoche** at midnight; (to express price, rate, etc.) at, e.g., **a cien pesetas la libra** at a hundred pesetas a pound; **a veinte nudos** at twenty knots; (in idiomatic expressions) at, e.g., **a la vista** at sight; **al fin** at last; **al principio** at the beginning; **al menos** at least; **a solicitud de** at the request of; **a veces** at times; **a la ventura** at random; after, e.g., **a los dos meses** after two months; by, e.g., **hecho a mano** made by hand; **a fuerza de** by dint of; **a la luz de la luna** by moonlight; **al año** by the year; **dos a dos** two by two; **poco a poco** little by little; from, e.g., **compré el cuadro a Carlos** I bought the picture from Charles; **gané la apuesta a Juan** I won the bet from John; **quité la navaja al gamberro** I took the knife from the hoodlum; **a lo que veo** from what I see; in, e.g.; **a guisa de** in the manner of; **al aire libre** in the open air; **a mi servicio** in my service; **a poco** in a little while; **a pesar de** in spite of; **a la francesa** in the French manner; **a lo rústico** in rustic style; on, e.g., **a causa de** on account of; **a bordo** on board; **al día siguiente** on the following day; **a caballo** on horseback; **a pie** on foot; **a la derecha** on the right; **a condición de que** on condition that; **al contrario** on the contrary; within, e.g., **al alcance de** within reach of; (to indicate the addition of another substance or ingredient), e.g., **acero al carbono** carbon steel; **bronce al aluminio** aluminum bronze; (to indicate a substance with which an object is treated or prepared), e.g., **cuadro al óleo** oil painting; (to indicate the direct object with substantives standing for definite persons and personified abstractions, in grammatical language after such verbs as **modificar** and **regir,** and sometimes with place names that are used without the definite article), e.g., **quieren al niño** they love the child; **encontré a Pedro** I met Peter; **no ví a nadie** I saw nobody; **llama a la Muerte** he summons Death; **el adjetivo modifica al nombre** the adjective modifies the noun; **visitó (a) Madrid el año pasado** he visited Madrid last year; (in certain miscellaneous phrases), e.g., **¡al ladrón!** stop thief!; **a lo que dice** according to what he says; **a lo que parece** as it seems; **a que no . . .** I'll bet . . . not, e.g., **a que no sabe Vd. mi nombre** I'll bet you don't know my name; **¡a ver!** let's see!; **al** + *inf* on + *ger*, e.g., **al llegar a la oficina** on arriving at the office
**Aarón** *m* (Bib.) Aaron
**ab.** abr. of **abad**
**aba** *f* aba (*woolen cloth and garment*)
**ababa** *f* or **ababol** *m* (bot.) poppy
**abacá** *m* (bot.) abacá (*plant and fiber*)
**abacería** *f* grocery, grocery store
**abacero -ra** *mf* grocer
**abacial** *adj* abbatial
**ábaco** *m* abacus; (arch.) abacus; (min.) wash-trough
**abacorar** *va* (Am.) to press closely, to attack boldly, to undertake with daring; (Am.) to monopolize; (Am.) to catch, to surprise; *vn* (Am.) to hold improperly (*in dancing*)
**abactor** *m* cattle thief
**abad** *m* abbot; (dial.) parish priest
**abadejo** *m* (ichth.) codfish; (ent.) Spanish fly, blister beetle; (orn.) wren, firecrest; **abadejo largo** (ichth.) ling
**abadengo -ga** *adj* abbatial; *m* abbacy (*estate and jurisdiction*)
**abadernar** *va* (naut.) to fasten with short ropes
**abadesa** *f* abbess; (Am.) proprietress of a bawdy house
**abadía** *f* abbey; abbacy
**abadiato** *m* abbacy
**abafo -fa** *adj* undyed
**abajadero** *m* slope, incline
**abajador** *m* stable boy; (min.) pit boy; (surg.) depressor
**abajeño -ña** *adj* (Am.) (pertaining to the) lowland; *mf* (Am.) lowlander
**abajero -ra** *adj* (Am.) lower, under; *f* (Am.) bellyband, belly strap; (Am.) saddlecloth
**abajino -na** *adj* (Chile) Northern; *mf* (Chile) Northerner
**abajo** *adv* down, below, underneath; downwards; downstairs; **más abajo de** lower than (*below*); **río abajo** downstream; **abajo de** down; *interj* down with . . . !
**abalanzar §76** *va* to balance, to weigh; to hurl; *vr* to hurl oneself, to rush; to venture; (Am.) to rear (*said of a horse*); **abalanzarse a** to spring at; to rush into; **abalanzarse sobre** to pounce upon
**abalaustrado -da** *adj* var. of **balaustrado**
**abaldonamiento** *m* debasement, affront
**abaldonar** *va* to debase, affront
**abaleador -dora** *mf* farmer who sweeps up after winnowing
**abalear** *va* (agr.) to sweep up (*grain*) after winnowing; (Am.) to shoot
**abaleo** *m* (agr.) sweeping up after winnowing; (Am.) shooting
**abalizar §76** *va* (naut.) to mark with buoys; *vr* (naut.) to take bearings
**abalone** *m* (zool.) abalone
**abalorio** *m* glass bead; beadwork; **no valer un abalorio** to be not worth a continental
**abaluartar** *va* to bulwark, to fortify with bastions
**aballestar** *va* (naut.) to haul, to pull
**abama** *f* (bot.) bog asphodel
**abanar** *va* to fan
**abandalizar §76** *va & vr* var. of **abanderizar**

**abanderado -da** *adj* standardbearing; (mil.) color; *m* standardbearer, flagman
**abanderar** *va* (naut.) to register (*a ship*)
**abanderizador -dora** *mf* agitator; revolutionist
**abanderizar §76** *va* to organize into bands; *vr* to band together
**abandonado -da** *adj* abandoned; slovenly
**abandonamiento** *m* abandon, abandoning
**abandonar** *va* to abandon; *vr* to abandon oneself, to yield, to give up
**abandonismo** *m* defeatism
**abandonista** *adj & mf* defeatist
**abandono** *m* abandon, abandonment; **darse al abandono** to go to the dogs
**abanicada** *f* fanning, fanning motion
**abanicar §86** *va* to fan
**abanicazo** *m* tap with a fan, blow with a fan; big fan; blast (*e.g., of hot air*)
**abanico** *m* fan; fan-shaped object; (coll.) sword; (arch.) fanlight, fan window; (naut.) derrick, crane; (Am.) semaphore; **en abanico** fan-shaped; **abanico de chimenea** fire screen
**abanillo** *m* frilled collar; fan
**abanino** *m* frill, ruff
**abaniquear** *va* to fan
**abaniqueo** *m* fanning; gesticulation; (aut.) shimmy (*of front wheels*)
**abaniquería** *f* fanmaker's shop; fan store
**abaniquero -ra** *mf* fanmaker; fan dealer
**abano** *m* fan; ceiling fan, flychaser
**abanto -ta** *adj* skittish, shy, timid; *m* (orn.) Egyptian vulture
**abañar** *va* to sift, to grade by sifting
**abaratamiento** *m* cheapening
**abaratar** *va* to cheapen, to make cheap; to lower (*prices*); *vn & vr* to get cheap
**abarca** *f* sandal; wooden shoe
**abarcado -da** *adj* sandaled
**abarcador -dora** *adj* inclusive
**abarcadura** *f* or **abarcamiento** *m* embrace; inclusion, inclusiveness, encompassment
**abarcar §86** *va* to embrace; to include, take in, encompass; to surround, enclose; (Am.) to corner, to monopolize; **quien mucho abarca poco aprieta** grasp all, lose all
**abarcón** *m* pole ring of carriage
**abarloar** *va* (naut.) to bring alongside
**abarquero -ra** *mf* sandal maker; sandal dealer
**abarquillamiento** *m* curling up
**abarquillar** *va & vr* to curl up
**abarracar §86** *vn* to set up barracks; *vr* to go into barracks
**abarrado -da** *adj* blemished with stripes
**abarraganamiento** *m* illicit cohabitation
**abarraganar** *vr* to cohabit illicitly
**abarrajar** *va* to overwhelm (*an enemy*); to throw hard; *vr* to stumble, slip, fall
**abarrancadero** *m* place full of pitfalls, hard road, difficult situation
**abarrancamiento** *m* fall into a ditch; obstruction; (naut.) running aground; predicament
**abarrancar §86** *va* to open cracks or fissures in; to throw into an opening; to stop up; *vn* (naut.) to run aground; *vr* to fall into an opening or ditch; to become stopped up; (naut.) to run aground; to get into a jam
**abarrar** *va* to throw hard
**abarredera** *f* broom; sweeper
**abarrotar** *va* to bar, fasten with bars; to bind, fasten; (naut.) to stow or pack (*cargo*); to overstock; to jam, to pack (*e.g., a theater*); *vn* (cards) to finesse; *vr* (Am.) to become a glut in the market
**abarrote** *m* (naut.) packing; **abarrotes** *mpl* (Am.) groceries
**abarrotería** *f* (Am.) grocery, grocery store
**abarrotero -ra** *mf* (Am.) grocer
**abasidas** *mpl* Abbassides
**abastardar** *va* to degrade; *vn* to degenerate
**abastecedor -dora** supplying; *mf* supplier, provider
**abastecer §34** *va* to supply, provide, provision
**abastecimiento** *m* supplying, provisioning
**abastero** *m* (Am.) wholesale cattle dealer
**abastionar** *va* to fortify with bastions
**abasto** *m* supply; provisioning; tavern; **dar abasto** to be sufficient; **dar abasto a** to satisfy; to supply
**abatanado -da** *adj* skilled
**abatanar** *va* to beat or full (*cloth*); to beat, to whip; to overcome, to conquer
**abatatar** *va* (Am.) to intimidate; *vr* (Am.) to get timid; (Am.) to become agitated
**abate** *m* abbé
**abatí** *m* (Am.) corn; (Am.) corn whiskey
**abatible** *adj* collapsible, folding
**abatido -da** *adj* downcast; abject, contemptible; depreciated; *f* (fort.) abatis
**abatimiento** *m* knocking down; lowering; shooting down; dismantling; depression, discouragement; (aer.) leeway, drift angle; (naut.) leeway
**abatir** *va* to knock down; to take down, to lower; to shoot down; to take apart; to humble; to depress, to discourage; to draw (*a line*); *vn* (aer.) to drift; (naut.) to have leeway; *vr* to be humbled; to become discouraged; to swoop down; to drop, to fall
**abayado -da** *adj* berry-like
**abazón** *m* cheek pouch (*of monkeys*)
**abdicación** *f* abdication; renouncing
**abdicar §86** *va* to abdicate; to renounce; *vn* to abdicate; **abdicar de** to renounce; **abdicar en** to abdicate in favor of
**abdomen** *m* (anat. & zool.) abdomen
**abdominal** *adj* abdominal
**abducción** *f* (physiol. & log.) abduction
**abducir §38** *va* (physiol.) to abduct
**abductor -tora** *adj* (physiol.) abducent; *m* (physiol.) abductor
**abecé** *m* A B C (*alphabet; elements of a subject*)
**abecedario** *m* A B C's; primer; **abecedario manual** manual alphabet
**abedul** *m* (bot.) birch
**abeja** *f* (ent.) bee; **abeja albañila** (ent.) mason bee; **abeja carpintera** (ent.) carpenter bee; **abeja de miel** or **doméstica** (ent.) honeybee; **abeja machiega, maesa** or **maestra** queen bee; **abeja neutra** or **obrera** worker (*bee*); **abeja reina** queen bee
**abejar** *m* apiary
**abejarrón** *m* (ent.) bumblebee
**abejaruco** *m* (orn.) bee eater
**abejear** *vn* to swarm; to buzz
**abejeo** *m* swarming; buzzing
**abejero -ra** *adj* (pertaining to the) bee; *mf* beekeeper; *m* (orn.) bee eater; *f* apiary; (bot.) balm (*Melissa officinalis*)
**abejón** *m* (ent.) bumblebee; (ent.) drone
**abejorreo** *m* buzz, buzzing
**abejorro** *m* (ent.) bumblebee; (ent.) cockchafer
**abejuno -na** *adj* (pertaining to the) bee
**Abelardo** *m* Abelard
**abelmosco** *m* (bot.) abelmosk
**abellacado -da** *adj* mean, villainous
**abellacar §86** *va* to make mean; *vr* to become mean
**abellotado -da** *adj* acorn-shaped
**abemoladamente** *adv* sweetly, softly
**abemolar** *va* to soften, ease (*the voice*); (mus.) to mark with a flat
**abencerraje** *adj* (coll.) coarse, ill-mannered; **abencerrajes** *mpl* Abencerrages (*Moorish family in Granada in fifteenth century*)
**abéndula** *f* vane (*of water wheel*)
**aberenjenado -da** *adj* eggplant-shaped, eggplant-colored
**aberración** f aberration; (astr. & opt.) aberration; **aberración cromática** (opt.) chromatic aberration
**aberrante** *adj* aberrant
**aberrar** *vn* to err, be mistaken
**aberrugado -da** *adj* warty
**abertal** *adj* easily split or cracked; badly fenced; *m* crack, opening
**abertura** *f* aperture; opening; crack, slit, crevice; wide valley; cove, inlet; openness, frankness; (phonet.) opening
**abesana** *f* var. of **besana**
**abesón** *m* (bot.) dill
**abestiado -da** *adj* beast-like, bestialized
**abéstola** *f* plowstaff
**abetal** *m* fir forest
**abete** *m* pair of hooks used to hold cloth on the cutting table; (bot.) fir
**abetinote** *m* fir rosin

**abeto** *m* (bot.) fir; **abeto blanco, abeto de hojas de tejo** or **abeto plateado** (bot.) silver fir; **abeto del Norte, abeto falso** or **abeto rojo** (bot.) spruce
**abetuna** *f* fir sprout
**abetunar** *va* var. of **embetunar**
**abey** *m* (bot.) jacaranda
**abiar** *m* (bot.) oxeye
**Abidos** *f* Abydos
**abierto -ta** *adj* open; frank; (Am.) generous; (Am.) conceited; **a cielo abierto** in the open air; **a pecho abierto** frankly; *pp of* **abrir;** *f* vent (*in coat*)
**abigarrado -da** *adj* variegated, motley; incoherent, confused
**abigarrar** *va* to paint in several colors; to daub in several colors, to streak
**abigeato** *m* cattle stealing
**abigeo** *m* cattle thief, rustler
**abigotado -da** *adj* mustachioed
**abijar** *va* (Am.) to incite, sic (*a dog*); (Am.) to scare away (*cattle*)
**abintestato** *m* (law) settlement of an intestate estate
**ab intestato** *adv* (Lat.) intestate; (coll.) neglected, unprotected
**abiogénesis** *f* abiogenesis
**abiosis** *f* abiosis
**abiótico -ca** *adj* abiotic
**abirritación** *f* abirritation
**abirritante** *adj* abirritant
**abirritar** *va* (med.) to abirritate
**abisagrar** *va* to put hinges on
**abisal** *adj* abyssal
**abiselar** *va* to bevel
**abisinio -nia** *adj & mf* Abyssinian; *m* Abyssinian (*language*); (*cap.*) *f.* Abyssinia
**abismal** *adj* abysmal; *m* shingle nail, slate nail; pin, peg
**abismar** *va* to cast into an abyss; to cast down; to humble; to spoil, ruin; *vr* to cave in; to sink; to be humbled; to give oneself up (*e.g., to sorrow, meditation*); to lose oneself (*e.g., in reading*); (Am.) to be surprised
**abismático -ca** *adj* abysmal
**abismo** *m* abyss; trough (*of a wave*)
**abita** *f* var. of **bita**
**abitaque** *m* joist, beam, rafter
**abitar** *va* (naut.) to bitt
**abitón** *m* (naut.) bitt, topsail bitt
**abizcochado -da** *adj* biscuit-like; bisque-like
**abjuración** *f* abjuration, abjurement
**abjurar** *va* to abjure; *vn* to perjure oneself; **abjurar de** to abjure
**ab.l** abr. de **abril**
**ablación** *f* (surg.) ablation
**ablactación** *f* ablactation, weaning
**ablactar** *va* to ablactate, to wean
**ablana** *f* (prov.) hazelnut
**ablandabrevas** *mf* (*pl:* **-vas**) (coll.) good-for-nothing
**ablandador -dora** *adj* soothing, mollifying
**ablandahigos** *mf* (*pl:* **-gos**) (coll.) good-for-nothing
**ablandamiento** *m* softening; soothing, mollification; softening up (*by bombardment*)
**ablandar** *va* to soften; to soothe, mollify; to loosen (*bowels*); to soften up (*by bombardment*); *vn* to moderate (*said of weather*); *vr* to soften; to relent; to moderate (*said of weather*)
**ablandativo -va** *adj* soothing, mollifying
**ablandecer §34** *va* to soften
**ablano** *m* (prov.) hazel
**ablaqueación** *f* hollow for water or air around plants and trees
**ablativo** *m* (gram.) ablative, ablative case; **ablativo absoluto** (gram.) ablative absolute
**ablefaria** *f* ablepharia
**ablegado** *m* (eccl.) ablegate
**ablegar §59** *va* to send away, to get rid of
**ablepsia** *f* ablepsia
**ablución** *f* ablution
**abluente** *adj & m* (med.) detergent
**abnegación** *f* abnegation
**abnegar §29** *va & vr* to abnegate
**abobado -da** *adj* stupid, stupid-looking
**abobamiento** *m* stupidity
**abobar** *va* to make stupid; *vr* to grow stupid
**abocadear** *va* to tear away or out by mouthfuls
**abocado -da** *adj* vulnerable; mild, smooth (*wine*); **abocado a** verging on
**abocamiento** *m* biting; approach; meeting, interview
**abocar §86** *va* to bite, seize with the mouth; to transfer by pouring; to bring up, bring nearer; *vn* (naut.) to enter a river, channel, etc.; **abocar en** (naut.) to enter into the mouth of (*a river, channel, etc.*); *vr* to approach; to have an interview
**abocardado -da** *adj* bell-mouthed
**abocardar** *va* to widen or spread the mouth of (*a tube or pipe*)
**abocardo** *m* var. of **alegra**
**abocetar** *va* to sketch; to paint hastily
**abocinamiento** *m* flare, flaring
**abocinar** *va* to shape like a trumpet; to flare; *vn* to fall on the face; *vr* to take the shape of a trumpet; to flare; to walk with head lowered (*said of a horse*)
**abochornado -da** *adj* overheated; flushed, ashamed
**abochornar** *va* to burn up, overheat; to make blush; *vr* to blush; to wilt, wither
**abofellar** *va & vn* to puff out, to swell
**abofeteador -dora** *adj* slapping; insulting; *mf* slapper; insulter
**abofetear** *va* to slap in the face
**abogacía** *f* law, legal profession
**abogada** *f* lawyeress (*woman lawyer; lawyer's wife*)
**abogadear** *vn* (coll.) to be a poor lawyer; (coll.) to be a shyster; (coll.) to talk in legal jargon
**abogaderas** *fpl* (Am.) specious arguments, quibbling
**abogadesco -ca** *adj* lawyerish, lawyerlike
**abogadil** *adj* lawyerish
**abogadismo** *m* legal interference
**abogado** *m* mediator; lawyer; **abogado del diablo** (eccl. & fig.) devil's advocate; **abogado de secano** quack lawyer, quack, charlatan; **abogado firmón** shyster who will sign anything; **abogado trampista** shyster
**abogalia** or **abogalla** *f* (bot.) nutgall
**abogar §59** *vn* to plead, intercede; **abogar por** to advocate, to back
**abohardillado -da** *adj* var. of **abuhardillado**
**abolengo** *m* ancestry, descent; inheritance
**abolición** *f* revocation, repeal; (hist.) abolition
**abolicionismo** *m* abolitionism
**abolicionista** *mf* abolitionist
**abolir §53** *va* to revoke, to repeal
**abolorio** *m* ancestry
**abolsado -da** *adj* full of pockets, puckered, baggy
**abolsar** *vr* to form pockets, to get baggy
**abollado -da** *adj* rough, uneven; fluted, frilled; *m* puffs, tufts (*in a dress*)
**abolladura** *f* dent; embossing; bump, bruise
**abollar** *va* to dent; to emboss; to bump, to bruise; to stun; *vr* to dent, be dented; to get bumped, to get bruised
**abollonadura** *f* embossing
**abollonar** *va* to emboss
**abomaso** *m* (anat.) abomasum
**abombar** *va* to make convex, to make bulge; to crown (*a road*); (coll.) to stun, confound; *vr* (Am.) to rot, decompose; (Am.) to get drunk
**abominable** *adj* abominable
**abominación** *f* abomination
**abominar** *va* to abominate; *vn* **abominar de** to abominate
**abonable** *adj* payable
**abonado -da** *adj* trustworthy; likely; *mf* subscriber; commuter
**abonador -dora** *mf* guarantor, surety; (agr.) manurer; *m* cooper's auger; *f* (agr.) fertilizer spreader (*implement*)
**abonamiento** *m* vouching, backing; bail, security
**abonanzar §76** *vn* to clear up (*said of weather or a complicated situation*); (naut.) to abate, become less rough (*said of wind or sea*)
**abonar** *va* to vouch for, to answer for; to certify; to improve; to fertilize; to take the subscription of; to pay; to credit; **abonar en cuenta a** to credit to the account of; *vn* to clear up (*said of the weather*); *vr* to subscribe
**abonaré** *m* promissory note

**abono** *m* manure, fertilizer; subscription; credit; instalment; voucher, guarantee; **ser de abono** to be to the good; **abono compuesto** (agr.) compost; **abono verde** (agr.) leaf mold
**aboquillado -da** *adj* tipped (*cigaret*)
**aboquillar** *va* to put a mouth or nozzle on; to widen, to widen the mouth of; to bevel
**abordable** *adj* approachable
**abordador** *m* (naut.) boarder
**abordaje** *m* (naut.) boarding; (naut.) collision, running afoul
**abordar** *va* to approach; to accost; to undertake, to plan; (naut.) to board (*said of one ship with respect to another*); (naut.) to run afoul of; (naut.) to dock; *vn* (naut.) to run afoul; (naut.) to put in, put into port
**abordo** *m* (naut.) var. of **abordaje**
**abordonado -da** *adj* (Am.) striped, ribbed
**aborigen** *adj & m* aboriginal; **aborígenes** *mpl* aborigines
**aborlonado -da** *adj* (Am.) ribbed
**aborrachado -da** *adj* bright red
**aborrascar §86** *vr* to get stormy
**aborrecedor -dora** *adj* abhorring, hating; *mf* abhorrer, hater
**aborrecer §34** *va* to abhor, hate, detest; to bore; to alienate, antagonize; to abandon or desert (*eggs or young*); (coll.) to waste, throw away; *vr* to be bored
**aborrecible** *adj* abhorrent, detestable
**aborrecimiento** *m* abhorrence, hate, detestation
**aborregado -da** *adj* fleecy (*clouds*); mackerel (*sky*)
**aborregar §59** *vr* to get covered with light fleecy clouds; to fall madly in love; (Am.) to get dull or stupid
**aborricar §86** *vr* var. of **emborricar**
**abortamiento** *m* abortion
**abortar** *va & vn* to abort
**abortista** *mf* abortionist
**abortivo -va** *adj* abortive; *m* abortive medicine
**aborto** *m* abortion; **aborto de la naturaleza** monster
**abortón** *m* abortion (*of an animal*); skin of aborted lamb
**aborujar** *va* to pack, make lumpy; *vr* to get lumpy; to be wrapped up
**abosar** *va* (Am.) to revive (*cock in cockfighting*)
**abotagado -da** *adj* bloated, swollen
**abotagamiento** *m* bloating, swelling
**abotagar §59** *vr* to get bloated, to swell up
**abotellar** *vr* to get full of bubbles (*said of glass*)
**abotijar** *vr* to become pot-bellied
**abotinado -da** *adj* boot-shaped; closed over instep (*said of trousers*); having feet of different color from rest of leg
**abotonador** *m* buttonhook
**abotonar** *va* to button; *vn* to bud; to form buttons (*said of an egg cracked while boiling*)
**abovedado -da** *adj* arched, vaulted; *m* vaulting
**abovedar** *va* to arch, to vault; to crown (*a road*)
**aboyado -da** *adj* with oxen (*said of a place that is so rented*)
**aboyar** *va* (naut.) to lay buoys in, to mark with buoys
**abozalar** *va* to muzzle
**abra** *f* bay, cove; vale, valley; crack, fissure; (Am.) clearing
**abracadabra** *m* abracadabra
**abracadabrante** *adj* (hum.) killing, amazing, breath-taking
**abracapalo** *m* (bot.) tropical American orchid (*Epidendrum nodosum*)
**abracijo** *m* (coll.) hug, embrace
**Abrahán** *m* Abraham
**abrahonar** *va* to seize by the clothing
**abrasador -dora** *adj* very hot, burning
**abrasamiento** *m* catching fire, burning; ardor, passion
**abrasar** *va* to set afire, to burn; to destroy by gunfire; to parch; to nip (*said of cold*); to squander (*money*); to shame; *vn* to burn; *vr* to burn; to be parched; to be nipped (*by cold*); (fig.) to be on fire (*i.e., to be very hot; to be agitated by violent passion*)
**abrasilado -da** *adj* Brazil-red
**abrasión** *f* abrasion; erosion; (med.) abrasion; intestinal irritation
**abrasivo -va** *adj & m* abrasive
**abrazadera** *f* band, clasp, clamp; tieback; (print.) bracket; (aut.) snap-on; **abrazadera para papeles** paper clip
**abrazador -dora** *adj* embracing
**abrazamiento** *m* embracing
**abrazar §76** *va* to embrace; to clasp, throw one's arms around; to include, take in, take up; to embrace (*e.g., Catholicism*); *vr* to embrace; **abrazarse a, con** or **de** to embrace; to clasp, throw one's arms around
**abrazo** *m* hug, embrace
**abrebocas** *m* (*pl:* **-cas**) (surg.) mouth prop, mouth gag
**abrebotellas** *m* (*pl:* **-llas**) bottle opener
**abrecarta** *m* (*pl:* **-tas**) knife (*for slitting envelopes*)
**abrecoches** *m* (*pl:* **-ches**) doorman
**ábrego** *m* southwest wind
**abrelatas** *m* (*pl:* **-tas**) can opener; tin opener (Brit.)
**abrenuncio** *interj* fie!; by no means!
**abreostras** *m* (*pl:* **-tras**) oyster knife
**abrevadero** *m* drinking trough, watering place
**abrevador -dora** *adj* watering; *mf* one who waters livestock; *m* drinking trough
**abrevar** *va* to water (*cattle*); to give a drink to; to irrigate; to wet, soak; to size (*before painting*); to wet down (*a wall—for stuccoing*); *vn* to water cattle; to drink, to quench the thirst; *vr* to drink, to quench the thirst; **abrevarse en** to be bathed in (*e.g., blood, tears*)
**abreviación** *f* abbreviation (*making shorter*); abridgment; lessening, shortening; hastening
**abreviadamente** *adv* in an abridged form, summarily
**abreviado -da** *adj* abridged, condensed, summary
**abreviador -dora** *adj* abbreviating; abridging; shortening; *mf* abbreviator; *m* (eccl.) abbreviator
**abreviaduría** *f* (eccl.) office of papal abbreviator
**abreviamiento** *m* var. of **abreviación**
**abreviar** *va* to abbreviate; to abridge; to lessen, shorten, lighten; to cut short; to hasten; *vn* to be quick; **¡abrevia!** hurry!; **abreviar con** to make short work of; **abreviar en** + *inf* to be brief in + *ger*, to not take long to + *inf*
**abreviatura** *f* abbreviation (*shortened form*); **en abreviatura** in abbreviation; (coll.) in a hurry
**abreviaturía** *f* var. of **abreviaduría**
**abribonar** *vr* to become a loafer; to become a rascal
**abridero -ra** *adj & m* freestone
**abridor -dora** *adj* opening; *m* opener (*person or thing*); freestone; grafting knife; child's gold eardrop; **abridor de botellas** bottle opener; **abridor de guantes** glove stretcher; **abridor de láminas** engraver; **abridor de latas** can opener; **abridor en hueco** diesinker
**abrigadero** *m* shelter, windbreak
**abrigado -da** *adj* (Am.) heavy, warm (*clothes*); *m & f* shelter, windbreak
**abrigador -dora** *adj* warm (*clothing*); (Am.) concealing; *mf* (Am.) concealer; *m* (Am.) jacket
**abrigaño** *m* shelter, windbreak
**abrigar §59** *va* to shelter; to help, protect; to nourish, cherish, foster (*hopes, plans, etc.*); *vr* to take shelter; to wrap oneself up
**abrigo** *m* shelter; aid, support; fostering; cover, wrap; overcoat; (naut.) harbor, shelter; **al abrigo de** protected from, sheltered from, under the protection of; **de mucho abrigo** heavy (*said of clothing*); **abrigo antiaéreo** air-raid shelter; **abrigo de entretiempo** topcoat, spring-and-fall coat
**ábrigo** *m* var. of **ábrego**
**abril** *m* April; springtime (*of life*); summer (*i.e., year*), e.g., **tener quince abriles** to have seen fifteen summers; **estar hecho un abril** to be all dressed up, to be dressed to kill; **los dieciséis abriles** sweet sixteen
**abrileño -ña** *adj* (pertaining to) April
**abrillantador** *m* cutter and polisher of precious stones

**abrillantamiento** *m* cutting into facets; shining, polishing, brightening
**abrillantar** *va* to cut into facets, to cut facets in; to shine, polish, brighten; to enhance
**abrimiento** *m* opening
**abrir** *m* opening; **en un abrir y cerrar de ojos** (coll.) in the twinkling of an eye; **§17,** 9 *va* to open; to unlock, unfasten; to engrave, carve; (Am.) to clear (*woodland*); to whet (*the appetite*); to dig (*the foundations*); *vn* to open; *vr* to open; **abrirse a** or **con** to open up to, to unbosom oneself to
**abrochador** *m* buttonhook
**abrochadura** *f* or **abrochamiento** *m* buttoning, hooking, fastening
**abrochar** *va* to button, to hook, to fasten
**abrogación** *f* abrogation
**abrogar §59** *va* abrogate
**abrojal** *m* thistly spot of ground
**abrojín** *m* (zool.) purple shell
**abrojo** *m* (bot. & mil.) caltrop; thistle, thorn; thorny tip of scourge; **abrojos** *mpl* (naut.) hidden rocks
**abroma** *m* (bot.) devil's-cotton
**abromado -da** *adj* darkened with heavy mist or clouds
**abromar** *vr* (naut.) to get covered with shipworms
**abroncar §86** *va* to embarrass, ridicule; (coll.) to bore, annoy
**abroquelado -da** *adj* shaped like a shield
**abroquelar** *va* (naut.) to boxhaul; *vr* to shield oneself
**abrótano** *m* (bot.) southernwood; **abrótano hembra** (bot.) lavender cotton
**abrotoñar** *vn* to bud, to sprout
**abrumador -dora** *adj* crushing, oppressing, wearisome; overwhelming
**abrumar** *va* to crush, oppress, weary; to overwhelm; to annoy; *vr* to get foggy
**abrupto -ta** *adj* abrupt, steep; rough, rugged
**abrutado -da** *adj* brutalized, brutish, bestial
**Absalón** *m* (Bib.) Absalom
**absceso** *m* (path.) abscess; **absceso de fijación** (med.) fixation abscess
**abscisa** *f* (geom.) abscissa
**abscisión** *f* abscission
**absenta** *f* absinthe (*drink*)
**absentismo** *m* absenteeism
**absentista** *mf* absentee; absentee landlord
**ábsida** *f* or **ábside** *m* (arch.) apse
**absidiolas** *fpl* (arch.) apse chapels
**absidiolo** *m* (arch.) apsidiole
**absintina** *f* (chem.) absinthin
**absintio** *m* (bot.) absinthe
**absintismo** *m* (path.) absinthism
**absolución** *f* absolution; **absolución de la demanda** (law) dismissal of complaint, finding for the defendant; **absolución de la instancia** (law) dismissal of the case; **absolución libre** (law) acquittal, verdict of not guilty
**absoluta** *f* see **absoluto**
**absolutismo** *m* absolutism
**absolutista** *mf* absolutist
**absoluto -ta** *adj* absolute; (coll.) arbitrary, despotic; *m* absolute; **en absoluto** absolutely; absolutely not; *f* dogmatic statement; (log.) universal proposition; (mil.) discharge
**absolvederas** *fpl;* **tener buenas absolvederas** (coll.) to be an indulgent confessor
**absolver §63** & **§17,** 9 *va* to absolve; (law) to acquit
**absorbencia** *f* absorbency
**absorbente** *adj* absorbent; absorbing; *m* absorbent; **absorbente higiénico** sanitary napkin
**absorber** *va* to absorb; to use up, wipe out; to attract, captivate
**absorbible** *adj* absorbable
**absorción** *f* absorption
**absortar** *va* to entrance; *vr* to be entranced
**absorto -ta** *adj* absorbed; entranced
**abstemio -mia** *adj* abstemious; *mf* abstemious person
**abstención** *f* abstention
**abstencionismo** *m* nonparticipation (*especially in political matters*)
**abstencionista** *adj* nonparticipating; *mf* nonparticipant
**abstendré** *1st sg fut ind of* **abstener**
**abstener §85** *vr* to abstain, to refrain; **abstenerse de** + *inf* to abstain or refrain from + *ger*
**abstengo** *1st sg pres ind of* **abstener**
**abstergente** *adj & m* abstergent
**absterger §49** *va* to cleanse (*a wound*)
**abstersión** *f* abstersion
**abstersivo -va** *adj* abstersive
**abstinencia** *f* abstinence
**abstinente** *adj* abstinent, abstemious; *mf* abstainer
**abstracción** *f* abstraction; withdrawal, retirement; **hacer abstracción de** to take away, leave out of account, disregard
**abstraccionismo** *m* (f.a.) abstractionism
**abstraccionista** *adj & mf* (f.a.) abstractionist
**abstractivamente** *adv* abstractly
**abstracto -ta** *adj* abstract; **en abstracto** in the abstract
**abstraer §88** *va* to abstract (*a quality*); *vn* **abstraer de** to do without, leave aside; *vr* to be abstracted or absorbed; **abstraerse de** to do without, leave aside
**abstraído -da** *adj* withdrawn, in seclusion; abstracted, absorbed
**abstraigo** *1st sg pres ind of* **abstraer**
**abstraje** *1st sg pret ind of* **abstraer**
**abstruso -sa** *adj* abstruse
**abstuve** *1st sg pret ind of* **abstener**
**absuelto -ta** *pp of* **absolver**
**absurdidad** *f* absurdity
**absurdo -da** *adj* absurd; *m* absurdity
**abubilla** *f* (orn.) hoopoe
**abuchear** *va & vn* to boo, to hoot
**abucheo** *m* booing, hooting
**abuela** *f* see **abuelo**
**abuelastra** *f* stepgrandmother
**abuelastro** *m* stepgrandfather
**abuelo -la** *mf* grandparent; *m* grandfather; **abuelos** *mpl* grandparents; grandfather and grandmother; ancestors; *f* grandmother; old woman; **cuénteselo a su abuela** (coll.) tell that to the marines
**abuenar** *va* to calm, pacify
**abufar** *vr* (Am.) to swell
**abuhardillado -da** *adj* (arch.) dormered
**abulense** *adj* (pertaining to) Ávila; *mf* native or inhabitant of Ávila
**abulia** *f* apathy; (psychopath.) abulia
**abúlico -ca** *adj* apathetic; *mf* apathetic person
**abultado -da** *adj* bulky, massive
**abultamiento** *m* enlarging; bulk
**abultar** *va* to enlarge; (fig.) to enlarge, exaggerate; *vn* to be bulky
**abundamiento** *m* abundance, plenty; **a mayor abundamiento** furthermore; with all the more reason
**abundancia** *f* abundance
**abundante** *adj* abundant
**abundar** *vn* to abound; **abundar de** to abound in or with; **abundar en** to abound in or with; to espouse (*an opinion*)
**abundo** or **abundosamente** *adv* abundantly
**abundoso -sa** *adj* abundant
**abuñolar §77** *va* to fry (*eggs*) fluffy and brown; to rumple, crumple
**abuñuelar** *va* var. of **abuñolar**
**abur** *interj* (coll.) bye-bye!, so long!
**aburar** *va* to burn up
**aburelado -da** *adj* reddish brown
**aburguesado -da** *adj* middle-class
**aburguesar** *vr* to become bourgeois, to become middle-class
**aburilar** *va* to engrave (with a burin)
**aburrición** *f* (coll.) boredom
**aburrido -da** *adj* bored; tiresome, boring
**aburrimiento** *m* boredom
**aburrir** *va* to bore, weary, tire; to abandon, desert; (coll.) to spend, put in, while away; (coll.) to venture; *vr* to get bored; **aburrirse con, de,** or **por** to get bored with
**aburujar** *va & vr* var. of **aborujar**
**abusar** *vn* to go too far, to take advantage; **abusar de** to abuse (*to make bad use of*); to take advantage of, to impose on or upon
**abusión** *f* abuse; superstition; omen, augury; (rhet.) catachresis
**abusionero -ra** *adj* superstitious

**abusivo -va** *adj* abusive (*wrongly used*)
**abuso** *m* abuse (*misuse; bad practice, injustice*); imposition
**abusón -sona** *adj* (coll.) presumptuous; *mf* (coll.) imposer
**abutilón** *m* (bot.) flowering maple
**abyección** *f* abjectness, abjection
**abyecto -ta** *adj* abject
**A.C.** abr. of **año de Cristo**
**acá** *adv* here, around here; **de ayer acá** since yesterday; **¿de cuándo acá?** since when?; **desde entonces acá** since then, since that time; **más acá** here closer; **muy acá** right here
**acabable** *adj* achievable, attainable; endable
**acabado -da** *adj* finished, complete, perfect; worn-out, exhausted; *m* finish
**acabador -dora** *adj* finishing; *mf* finisher
**acabalar** *va* to complete
**acaballadero** *m* stud farm; mating season
**acaballado -da** *adj* horselike, like a horse's
**acaballar** *va* to cover (*a mare*)
**acaballerado -da** *adj* gentlemanly
**acaballerar** *va* to treat as a gentleman; *vr* to behave like a gentleman
**acaballonar** *va* (agr.) to ridge, to work ridges in
**acabamiento** *m* completion, finishing; end; exhaustion; death
**acabar** *va* to end, terminate, finish, complete; (Am.) to flay, excoriate; *vn* to end, come to an end; to die; **no acabar de decidirse** to be unable to make up one's mind; **acabar con** to finish, put an end to, wipe out; to end in; **acabar de** + *inf* to finish + *ger;* to have just + *pp*, e.g., **acabo de llegar** I have just arrived; **acababa de llegar** I had just arrived; **acabar por** to end in; **acabar por** + *inf* to end or finish by + *ger*; *vr* to end, come to an end; to be exhausted; to be all over; to run out of, e.g., **se me acabó el pan** I have run out of bread
**acabestrar** *va* to accustom to the halter
**acabestrillar** *vn* to go hunting with an ox as a shield
**acabildar** *va* to organize into a group
**acabo** *m* completion
**acabóse** *m* (coll.) windup, pay-off, limit
**acacia** *f* (bot.) acacia; **acacia bastarda** (bot.) blackthorn; **acacia de tres espinas** (bot.) honey locust; **acacia falsa** (bot.) acacia, locust tree; **acacia rosa** (bot.) rose acacia
**acachetar** *va* (taur.) to finish off with the dagger
**acachetear** *va* to pat, to slap
**academia** *f* academy; (f.a.) academy figure; **Academia General del Aire** Air Force Academy (U.S.A.); Royal Air Force College (Brit.); **Academia General Militar** Military Academy (U.S.A.); Royal Military College (Brit.)
**académico -ca** *adj* academic (*pertaining to an academy or school; classical, literary; theoretical; mannered*); *mf* academician; member (*of an academy*)
**academizar §76** *va* to academize
**Academo** *m* (myth.) Academus
**Acadia** *f* Acadia
**acadiense** *adj & mf* Acadian
**acaecedero -ra** *adj* possible
**acaecer §34** *vn* to happen, occur
**acaecimiento** *m* happening, occurrence
**acafresna** *f* (bot.) service tree
**acajú** *m* (*pl:* **-júes**) (bot.) cashew tree
**acalabrotado -da** *adj* (naut.) cable-laid
**acalabrotar** *va* (naut.) to weave into a cable of three ropes of three strands each
**acalambrar** *vr* to contract with cramps (*said of muscles*)
**acalefo -fa** *adj & m* (zool.) acalephan
**acalenturar** *vr* to become feverish
**acalia** *f* (bot.) marsh mallow
**acalicino -na** *adj* (bot.) acalycine
**acalorado -da** *adj* fiery, excited; warm; heated
**acalorar** *va* to warm, to heat; to encourage, incite, inspire; to stir up, inflame; *vr* to warm up; to become heated
**acalote** *m* (Am.) stretch of river cleared of floating vegetation; (orn.) Mexican wood ibis
**acallantar** or **acallar** *va* to silence, to quiet, to pacify; to silence by bribery
**acaller** *m* (archaic) potter
**acamaleonado -da** *adj* chameleon-like
**acamar** *va* to blow over, to beat down (*said of wind or rain acting on plants*)
**acampador -dora** *mf* camper
**acampamento** *m* camping; camp, encampment
**acampanado -da** *adj* bell-shaped
**acampanar** *va* to shape like a bell; *vr* to become bell-shaped
**acampar** *va, vn & vr* to encamp
**acampo** *m* pasture, grassland
**ácana** *m & f* (bot.) mastic bully, mastic tree, wild olive (*Sideroxylon mastichodendron*); (bot.) acana (*Labourdonnaisia albescens*)
**acanalado -da** *adj* channeled; fluted, grooved
**acanalador** *m* grooving plane
**acanaladura** *f* fluting, groove, striation; corrugation
**acanalar** *va* to flute, to groove; to corrugate; to channel
**acanallado -da** *adj* vile, degraded
**acandilado -da** *adj* peaked, pointed; (coll.) erect
**acanelado -da** *adj* cinnamon-colored, cinnamon-flavored
**acanelonar** *va* to flog with cat-o'-nine-tails
**acanillado -da** *adj* striped, ribbed
**acanilladura** *f* flaw, uneven weaving
**acansinar** *vr* (coll.) to get tired, to become lazy
**acantáceo -a** *adj* (bot.) acanthaceous
**acantalear** *vn* (prov.) to hail hen's eggs; (prov.) to rain pitchforks
**acantarar** *va* to measure by pitcherfuls
**acantilado -da** *adj* full of rocks (*said of surface of sea*); steep, precipitous; *m* cliff, escarpment, palisade
**acantilar** *va* (naut.) to run (*a ship*) on the rocks; to dredge; *vr* (naut.) to run on the rocks
**acantio** *m* (bot.) cotton thistle, Scotch thistle
**acanto** *m* (bot. & arch.) acanthus
**acantocéfalo -la** *adj & m* (zool.) acanthocephalan
**acantonamiento** *m* (mil.) cantonment, quarters; (mil.) quartering
**acantonar** *va* (mil.) to canton, to quarter; *vr* (mil.) to be cantoned, to be quartered; **acantonarse en** to limit one's activities (*studies, interests, etc.*) to
**acantopterigio -gia** *adj & m* (ichth.) acanthopterygian
**acañaverear** *va* to wound with sharp-pointed reeds
**acañonear** *va* to cannonade
**acaparador -dora** *adj* monopolizing; absorbing, engrossing; *mf* monopolizer
**acaparamiento** *m* monopolizing, monopoly; hoarding
**acaparar** *va* to monopolize; to corner; to hoard; (fig.) to monopolize (*e.g., the conversation*); to seize, grasp
**acaparrar** *vr* to come to terms, to make a deal
**acaparrosado -da** *adj* blotchy (*said of, e.g., the complexion*)
**acapizar §76** *vr* (coll.) to grapple, to come to grips
**acaponado -da** *adj* effeminate, unmanly
**acaracolado -da** *adj* spiral, winding
**acarambanado -da** *adj* var. of **carambanado**
**acaramelado -da** *adj* carameled; caramel-colored; (coll.) overpolite, oversweet
**acaramelar** *va* to caramel, to caramelize; *vr* to caramel, to caramelize; (coll.) to be oversweet (*especially toward a woman*)
**acarar** *va* to bring face to face
**acardenalar** *va* to make black-and-blue; *vr* to get black-and-blue
**acareamiento** *m* facing, confronting
**acarear** *va* to bring face to face; to face, confront, brave
**acariciador -dora** *adj* caressing; *mf* caresser
**acariciar** *va* to caress; to cherish (*to treat with affection; to cling to, e.g., a hope*)
**acárido** *m* (zool.) acarid, mite
**acarnerado -da** *adj* sheeplike
**ácaro** *m* (zool.) acarus, mite; **ácaro de la sarna** (ent.) itch mite; **ácaro del queso** or **ácaro doméstico** (ent.) cheese mite
**acaroide** *f* acaroid gum or resin
**acarpo -pa** *adj* (bot.) acarpous

**acarraladura** *f* (Am.) run (*in stockings*)
**acarralar** *va* to drop (*a thread*); *vr* to be nipped by the frost (*said of grapes*)
**acarrar** *vr* to seek the shade (*said of sheep*)
**acarreadizo -za** *adj* transportable
**acarreador -dora** *adj* carrying, transporting; *mf* carrier; *m* carrier of grain to thrashing floor
**acarreamiento** *m* cartage, carrying, transportation
**acarrear** *va* to cart, to transport, to carry along; to cause, to entail, to occasion; *vr* to bring upon oneself, incur
**acarreo** *m* cartage, drayage
**acartonado -da** *adj* like cardboard; wizened
**acartonar** *vr* (coll.) to dry up like cardboard, to shrivel up, to become wizened
**acasamatado -da** *adj* casemated
**acaserado -da** *adj* (Am.) regular; (Am.) home-loving; *mf* (Am.) regular customer; (Am.) homebody, stay-at-home
**acaserar** *vr* (Am.) to be a regular customer; (Am.) to become attached; (Am.) to be a stay-at-home
**acaso** *m* chance, accident; **al acaso** at random; *adv* maybe, perhaps; **por si acaso** in case; for any eventuality
**acastañado -da** *adj* chestnut-colored
**acastorado -da** *adj* (like) beaver
**acatable** *adj* worthy of respect
**acatadamente** *adv* respectfully
**acataléctico -ca** or **acatalecto -ta** *adj & m* acatalectic
**acatalepsia** *f* (philos.) acatalepsy; (med.) acatalepsia
**acatamiento** *m* reverence, awe
**acatar** *va* to revere, to hold in awe; to observe
**acatarrar** *va* (Am.) to bother, molest; *vr* to catch cold; (Am.) to get tipsy
**Acates** *m* (myth.) Achates
**acatólico -ca** *adj* non-Catholic
**acaudalado -da** *adj* rich, well-to-do
**acaudalar** *va* to accumulate, acquire (*knowledge, money, etc.*)
**acaudillador -dora** *adj* leading, commanding; *mf* leader, commander
**acaudillamiento** *m* leading, command
**acaudillar** *va* to lead, command; to be the leader of; to direct; *vr* to choose a leader
**acaule** *adj* (bot.) acaulescent
**Acaya** *f* Achaea
**acceder** *vn* to accede; to agree; **acceder a** + *inf* to agree to + *inf*
**accesibilidad** *f* accessibility
**accesible** *adj* accessible; attainable; approachable
**accesión** *f* accession, acquiescence; accessory; access, entry; (med.) attack of intermittent fever
**accesional** *adj* intermittent
**accésit** *m* second prize, honorable mention
**acceso** *m* access, approach; attack, fit, spell, e.g., **acceso de tos** coughing spell, fit of coughing; access, outburst (*e.g., of anger*); **acceso del Sol** (astr.) apparent motion of the sun toward the equator; **acceso dirigido desde tierra** (aer.) ground-controlled approach; **acceso forzoso** (law) easement, right of way; **acceso prohibido** no admittance
**accesorio -ria** *adj* accessory; *m* accessory, fixture, attachment; **accesorios** *mpl* (theat.) properties; **accesorias** *fpl* annex (*building*)
**accidentado -da** *adj* agitated, troubled; stormy, restless; rough, uneven; *mf* victim, casualty
**accidental** *adj* accidental; acting, temporary, pro tem; *m* (mus.) accidental
**accidentalizar** §76 *va* (mus.) to mark with accidentals
**accidentar** *va* to injure, hurt; *vr* to faint
**accidente** *m* accident; roughness, unevenness (*in a surface*); fainting spell; (gram. & mus.) accident; **por accidente** by accident
**Accio** *m* Actium
**acción** *f* action; (com.) share (*of stock*); (com.) stock certificate; **en acción** in action; **acción de gracias** thanksgiving; **acción de guerra** battle; **acción directa** direct action; **acción eslabonada** (phys.) chain reaction; **acción liberada** (com.) stock dividend; (com.) paid-up stock
**accionado** *m* action (*mechanism*)
**accionar** *va* (mach.) to drive; *vn* to gesticulate
**accionista** *mf* shareholder, stockholder; **accionista que como tal figura en el libro-registro de la compañía** stockholder of record
**accípitre** *m* (orn.) goshawk; (surg.) accipiter
**acebadamiento** *m* var. of **encebadamiento**
**acebadar** *va & vr* var. of **encebadar**
**acebal** *m*, **acebeda** *f*, or **acebedo** *m* plantation of holly trees
**acebo** *m* (bot.) holly, ilex
**acebollado -da** *adj* having cup shake or ring shake (*said of timber*); like an onion
**acebolladura** *f* cup shake, ring shake
**acebrado -da** *adj* var. of **cebrado**
**acebuchal** *adj* (pertaining to the) wild olive; *m* grove of wild olives
**acebuche** *m* (bot.) wild olive (*tree*)
**acebucheno -na** *adj* (pertaining to the) wild olive
**acebuchina** *f* wild olive (*fruit*)
**acecido** *m* var. of **acezo**
**acecinar** *va* to dry-cure, to dry-salt; *vr* to get thin and wrinkled
**acechadera** *f* ambush
**acechador -dora** *adj* spying; *mf* spyer, person who spies
**acechamiento** *m* or **acechanza** *f* spying, watching
**acechar** *va* to spy on, to watch
**aceche** *m* copperas
**acecho** *m* spying; **al acecho** or **en acecho** spying, on the watch
**acechón -chona** *adj* (coll.) spying; **hacer la acechona** (coll.) to spy, to lie in ambush, to watch
**acedar** *va* to make sour; (fig.) to sour, to embitter; *vr* to turn sour; to wither
**acedera** *f* (bot.) sorrel (*Rumex acetosa*); **acedera menor** (bot.) oxalis, wood sorrel
**acederaque** *m* (bot.) China tree, bead tree, azederach
**acederilla** *f* (bot.) sheep sorrel; (bot.) oxalis, wood sorrel
**acedía** *f* sourness, acidity; crabbedness, unpleasantness; heartburn; (ichth.) plaice
**acedo -da** *adj* sour, tart, acid; crabbed, disagreeable
**acéfalo -la** *adj* acephalous
**aceguero** *m* woodsman who gathers dead timber
**aceitada** *f* spilt oil; cake made with oil
**aceitado** *m* oiling, lubricating
**aceitar** *va* to oil, apply oil to
**aceitazo** *m* thick dirty oil
**aceite** *m* oil; olive oil; (paint.) medium; **dejarle a uno freír en su aceite** (coll.) to let someone stew in his own juice; **aceite alcanforado** camphorated oil; **aceite combustible** fuel oil; **aceite de algodón** cottonseed oil; **aceite de ballena** whale oil; **aceite de ben** oil of ben, behen oil; **aceite de cacahuete** peanut oil; **aceite de coco** coconut oil; **aceite de colza** colza oil, rape oil; **aceite de comer** table oil; **aceite de creosota** creosote oil; **aceite de crotón** croton oil; **aceite de esperma** sperm oil; **aceite de fusel** fusel oil; **aceite de gaulteria** oil of wintergreen; **aceite de hígado de bacalao** cod-liver oil; **aceite de linaza** linseed oil; **aceite de Macasar** Macassar oil; **aceite de nerolí** (chem.) neroli oil; **aceite de oliva** olive oil; **aceite de palma** palm oil; **aceite de palo** copaiba balsam; **aceite de pescado** fish oil; **aceite de pie de buey** neat's-foot oil; **aceite de ricino** castor oil; **aceite de vitriolo** oil of vitriol; **aceite esencial** essential oil; **aceite esencial de rosas** attar of roses; **aceite mineral** mineral oil; **aceite secante** (paint.) drying oil; **aceite vegetal** vegetable oil; **aceite volátil** volatile oil
**aceitera** *f* see **aceitero**
**aceitería** *f* oil shop; oil business
**aceitero -ra** *adj* (pertaining to) oil; *mf* oil dealer; oiler; *f* oilcan; (mach.) oil cup; (ent.) oil beetle; **aceiteras** *fpl* cruet stand
**aceitillo** *m* thin oil; (Am.) oil perfume; (bot.) mountain damson (*Simarouba amara*); (bot.) snowberry (*Chiococca*)

**aceitón** *m* thick dirty oil; olive oil dregs
**aceitoso -sa** *adj* oily, greasy
**aceituna** *f* olive (*fruit*); **llegar a las aceitunas** (coll.) to arrive late; **aceituna corval** jumbo olive; **aceituna de la reina** or **aceituna gordal** queen olive; **aceituna manzanilla** little round olive, manzanilla; **aceituna negra** ripe olive; **aceituna rellena** stuffed olive; **aceituna zapatera** spoilt olive; **aceituna zorzaleña** crescent olive
**aceitunado -da** *adj* olive, olive-colored; *f* olive harvest; batch of olives
**aceitunero -ra** *mf* olive dealer; olive picker; *m* olive storehouse
**aceituní** *m* (*pl:* **-níes**) rich medieval oriental fabric; arabesque; olive-colored velvet
**aceitunil** *adj* olive, olive-colored
**aceitunillo** *m* (bot.) West Indian storax (*Agotoxylum punctatum*)
**aceituno** *m* (bot.) olive (*tree*)
**acelajado -da** *adj* cloud-colored
**acelajar** *vr* to get cloudy
**aceleración** *f* hastening; acceleration
**acelerada** *f* (aut.) speed-up (*of motor*)
**aceleradamente** *adv* hastily, hurriedly
**acelerador -dora** or **-triz** (*pl:* **-trices**) *adj* hastening; accelerating; *m* (aut.) accelerator
**aceleramiento** *m* var. of **aceleración**
**acelerar** *va* to hasten, hurry; to accelerate; to advance (*e.g., a date*); *vr* to hasten, hurry; to accelerate
**acelerómetro** *m* (aer.) accelerometer
**acelerón** *m* acceleration, speed-up
**acelga** *f* (bot.) Swiss chard; **acelga silvestre** (bot.) sea lavender
**acémila** *f* beast of burden, sumpter, mule; (coll.) drudge; (coll.) beast, brute
**acemilar** *adj* (pertaining to the) mule; (pertaining to the) stable
**acemilería** *f* mule stable
**acemilero -ra** *adj* (pertaining to the) stable; *m* muleteer
**acemita** *f* bran bread
**acemite** *m* bran and flour mixed; porridge
**acendrado -da** *adj* pure, refined; stainless, spotless
**acendrar** *va* to purify, refine; to make stainless
**acensuar** §33 *va* to tax (*a possession*)
**acento** *m* accent; **acento agudo** acute accent; **acento circunflejo** circumflex accent; **acento de altura** pitch accent; **acento grave** grave accent; **acento ortográfico** written accent; **acento primario** primary accent; **acento prosódico** stress accent; **acento secundario** secondary accent; **acento tónico** tonic accent
**acentuación** *f* accentuation; emphasis
**acentuadamente** *adv* with an accent; markedly
**acentual** *adj* accentual
**acentuar** §33 *va* to accent; to accentuate, emphasize; *vr* to be accentuated, to become marked, to be aggravated; to become heavy, become bulky
**aceña** *f* water-driven flour mill
**aceñero** *m* miller in a water-driven flour mill
**acepar** *vn* to take root
**acepción** *f* acception, acceptation, meaning; **acepción de personas** partiality, discrimination
**acepillado** *m* planing
**acepilladora** *f* planer, planing machine
**acepilladura** *f* planing; **acepilladuras** *fpl* shavings, turnings
**acepillar** *va* to plane; to brush; (coll.) to polish, to smooth
**aceptabilidad** *f* acceptability
**aceptable** *adj* acceptable
**aceptación** *f* acceptance; (com.) acceptance; **aceptación de personas** partiality, discrimination
**aceptador -dora** *adj* accepting; *mf* acceptor
**aceptante** *adj* accepting; *mf* acceptor; (com.) acceptor
**aceptar** *va* to accept; (com.) to accept; **aceptar a** + *inf* to agree to + *inf*
**acepto -ta** *adj* acceptable, welcome
**acequia** *f* drain, irrigation ditch
**acequiar** *va* to build drains or irrigation ditches in, to equip with drains or irrigation ditches; *vn* to build drains or irrigation ditches
**acequiero** *m* irrigation ditch tender
**acera** *f* sidewalk; row of houses; (arch.) facing (*of wall*)
**aceráceo -a** *adj* (bot.) aceraceous
**acerado -da** *adj* (pertaining to) steel; sharp, cutting, biting
**acerar** *va* to acierate; to lay sidewalks in or along; to make sharp or biting; to harden, to steel; to face (*a wall*); to stucco; *vr* to harden, to get hard, cruel, or pitiless; to steel oneself
**acerato -ta** *adj* (zool.) acerous (*without horns*)
**acerbidad** *f* acerbity
**acerbo -ba** *adj* sour, bitter; harsh, sharp, cruel
**acerca** *adv* **acerca de** about, concerning, with regard to
**acercamiento** *m* approach, bringing near, drawing near, rapprochement
**acercar** §86 *va* to bring near or nearer; *vr* to approach, come near or nearer; to be warm (*i.e., near what one is looking for*); **acercarse a** to approach; **acercarse a** + *inf* to come near (in order) to + *inf*
**ácere** *m* var. of **arce**
**acería** *f* steel mill
**acerico** *m* small cushion; pincushion
**acerilla** *f* stronghold or tower on a cliff
**acerillo** *m* var. of **acerico**
**acerina** *f* see **acerino**
**acerineo -a** *adj* (bot.) aceraceous
**acerino -na** *adj* (poet.) steel; *f* (ichth.) ruff
**acernadar** *va* var. of **encernadar**
**acero** *m* steel; sword, weapon; courage, spirit; **aceros** *mpl* temper; (coll.) appetite; **tener buenos aceros** (coll.) to have a lot of courage; (coll.) to be good and hungry; **acero adamascado** Damascus steel, damask steel; **acero al hogar abierto** open-hearth steel; **acero al manganeso** manganese steel; **acero al molibdeno** molybdenum steel; **acero al níquel** nickel steel; **acero al vanadio** vanadium steel; **acero Bessemer** Bessemer steel; **acero colado** cast steel; **acero damasquino** Damascus steel, damask steel; **acero de aleación** alloy steel; **acero de alta velocidad** or **de corte rápido** high-speed steel; **acero de crisol** crucible steel; **acero de herramientas** tool steel; **acero dulce** soft steel; **acero duro** hard steel; **acero fundido** cast steel; **acero inmanchable** or **inoxidable** stainless steel; **acero intermedio** or **mediano** medium steel; **acero rápido** high-speed steel; **acero suave** soft steel
**acerocromo** *m* chromium steel, chrome steel
**acerola** *f* azarole, Neapolitan medlar (*fruit*)
**acerolo** *m* (bot.) azarole, Neapolitan medlar (*shrub*)
**aceroníquel** *m* nickel steel
**aceroso -sa** *adj* (bot.) acerose or acerous
**acérrimo -ma** *adj super* very acrid; very strong, vigorous or tenacious; very bitter (*e.g., enemy*)
**acerrojar** *va* to bolt, to fasten or lock with a bolt
**acertado -da** *adj* right, fit; sure, skillful; sure, well-aimed
**acertador -dora** *adj* skillful; *mf* good guesser
**acertajo** *m* (coll.) var. of **acertijo**
**acertamiento** *m* var. of **acierto**
**acertante** *mf* winner
**acertar** §18 *va* to hit, to hit upon; to guess right, to figure out correctly; to find, to find easily; to do (*something*) right or skillfully; *vn* to be right, to succeed; to guess right; to grow, to thrive (*said of plants*); **acertar a** + *inf* to happen to + *inf;* to succeed in + *ger;* **acertar con** to find, to find easily; to come upon, to happen upon
**acertijo** *m* riddle, conundrum
**aceruelo** *m* small packsaddle; pincushion
**acervo** *m* heap; store, fund, hoard; joint property; **acervo común** undivided estate
**acérvula** *f* (anat.) acervulus cerebri, brain sand
**acetábulo** *m* (anat., bot. & zool.) acetabulum
**acetanilida** *f* (chem.) acetanilid
**acetato** *m* (chem.) acetate; **acetato de vinilo** (chem.) vinyl acetate
**acético -ca** *adj* (chem.) acetic

**acetificación** *f* acetification
**acetificar** §86 *va & vr* to acetify
**acetilénico -ca** *adj* acetylene; acetylenic
**acetileno** *m* (chem.) acetylene
**acetilo** *m* (chem.) acetyl
**acetímetro** *m* acetometer
**acetín** *m* (bot.) barberry
**acetona** *f* (chem.) acetone
**acetonemia** *f* (path.) acetonemia
**acetonuria** *f* (path.) acetonuria
**acetosa** *f* see **acetoso**
**acetosilla** *f* var. of **acederilla**
**acetoso -sa** *adj* acetous; *f* (bot.) sorrel
**acetre** *m* small bucket; holy-water vessel
**acezar** §76 *vn* to pant, to gasp
**acezo** *m* panting, gasping
**acezoso -sa** *adj* panting, gasping
**aciago -ga** *adj* unlucky, ill-fated, evil
**acial** *m* barnacles or twitch (*device to keep an animal still*); (her.) barnacles
**aciano** *m* (bot.) bluebottle, cornflower
**aciar** *m* var. of **acial**
**acíbar** *m* aloes; bitterness, sorrow
**acibarar** *va* to make bitter with aloes; to embitter
**aciberar** *va* to grind fine
**acicalado -da** *adj* dressy; dressed up, spruced up; shiny; *m* polish, burnish
**acicalador -dora** *adj* polishing, burnishing; *m* polishing tool, burnishing tool
**acicaladura** *f* or **acicalamiento** *m* polishing, burnishing; polish; dressiness
**acicalar** *va* to polish, burnish (*e.g., a sword*); to dress, to dress up; (mas.) to finish, to point (*a wall*); *vr* to get dressed up
**acicate** *m* long-pointed spur; incentive, inducement
**acíclico -ca** *adj* acyclic
**aciculado -da** *adj* (bot. & zool.) aciculate
**acicular** *adj* acicular
**aciche** *m* paver's hammer
**acidalio -lia** *adj* (myth.) Acidalian (*pertaining to Venus*)
**acidaque** *m* Mohammedan's dowry to his wife
**acidez** *f* acidity
**acidífero -ra** *adj* acidiferous
**acidificación** *f* acidification
**acidificar** §86 *va & vr* to acidify
**acidímetro** *m* acidimeter
**acidioso -sa** *adj* lazy, lax
**ácido -da** *adj* acid; (chem.) acid; (petrog.) acid, acidic; *m* (chem.) acid; **ácido acético** acetic acid; **ácido acrílico** acrylic acid; **ácido arábico** arabic acid; **ácido arsénico** arsenic acid; **ácido ascórbico** ascorbic acid; **ácido barbitúrico** barbituric acid; **ácido benzoico** benzoic acid; **ácido bórico** boric acid, boracic acid; **ácido bromhídrico** hydrobromic acid; **ácido butírico** butyric acid; **ácido carbólico** carbolic acid; **ácido carbónico** carbonic acid; **ácido cerótico** cerotic acid; **ácido cianhídrico** hydrocyanic acid; **ácido ciánico** cyanic acid; **ácido cítrico** citric acid; **ácido clorhídrico** hydrochloric acid; **ácido clórico** chloric acid; **ácido esteárico** stearic acid; **ácido férrico** ferric acid; **ácido fluorhídrico** hydrofluoric acid; **ácido fólico** folic acid; **ácido fórmico** formic acid; **ácido fosfórico** phosphoric acid; **ácido fosforoso** phosphorous acid; **ácido fulmínico** fulminic acid; **ácido gálico** gallic acid; **ácido glicérico** glyceric acid; **ácido graso** fatty acid; **ácido hipocloroso** hypochlorous acid; **ácido hipofosfórico** hypophosphoric acid; **ácido hipofosforoso** hypophosphorous acid; **ácido hiposulfuroso** hyposulfurous acid; **ácido láctico** lactic acid; **ácido levulínico** levulinic acid; **ácido málico** malic acid; **ácido mangánico** manganic acid; **ácido metacrílico** methacrylic acid; **ácido muriático** muriatic acid; **ácido nicotínico** nicotinic acid; **ácido nítrico** nitric acid; **ácido nucleico** or **nucleínico** nucleic acid; **ácido oleico** oleic acid; **ácido oxálico** oxalic acid; **ácido pantoténico** pantothenic acid; **ácido perclórico** perchloric acid; **ácido permangánico** permanganic acid; **ácido pícrico** picric acid; **ácido prúsico** prussic acid; **ácido salicílico** salicylic acid; **ácido sulfhídrico** sulfhydric or sulphydric acid (*hydrogen sulfide*); **ácido sulfúrico** sulfuric acid; **ácido sulfuroso** sulfurous acid; **ácido tánico** tannic acid; **ácido tantálico** tantalic acid; **ácido tártrico** tartaric acid; **ácido tiociánico** thiocyanic acid; **ácido tiónico** thionic acid; **ácido tiosulfúrico** thiosulfuric acid; **ácido úrico** uric acid; **ácido yodhídrico** hydriodic acid
**acidófilo -la** *adj & m* acidophil
**acidógeno -na** *adj* acid-forming (*said of food*)
**acidómetro** *m* hydrometer
**acidosis** *f* (path.) acidosis
**acidular** *va* to acidulate, to make sour; to saturate (*water*) with carbonic acid; *vr* to get sour
**acídulo -la** *adj* acidulous
**acierto** *m* lucky hit, good shot; good guess; tact, prudence; skill, ability; success; accuracy, precision; rightness
**ácigos** *m* (anat.) azygos
**aciguatado -da** *adj* suffering from fish poisoning; yellowish, jaundiced
**aciguatar** *vr* to be sick with fish poisoning
**acijado -da** *adj* greenish
**acije** *m* copperas
**acijoso -sa** *adj* containing copperas, like copperas
**acimboga** *f* citron (*fruit*)
**ácimo -ma** *adj* var. of **ázimo**
**acimut** *m* (*pl:* **-muts**) azimuth
**acimutal** *adj* azimuthal
**acintle** *m* (orn.) helldiver, pied-billed grebe
**ación** *f* stirrup strap
**acipado -da** *adj* close-woven
**acirate** *m* boundary ridge; ridge between two furrows; rectangular flower plot; walk between rows of trees
**acitara** *f* zither; wall, railing, parapet; chair cover, saddle cover
**acitrón** *m* candied citron
**acivilar** *vr* (Am.) to be married by civil ceremony
**aclamación** *f* acclaim, acclamation, applause; **por aclamación** by acclamation
**aclamador -dora** *adj* acclaiming, applauding; *mf* acclaimer, applauder
**aclamar** *va & vn* to acclaim, to applaud
**aclaración** *f* brightening; rinsing; clearing; explanation
**aclarador -dora** *adj* explanatory
**aclarar** *va* to brighten, to brighten up; to make clear, to thin; to rinse; to clear out (*e.g., a thicket*); to explain; *vn* to brighten, to get bright; to clear up; to dawn; *vr* to brighten, to get bright; to clear up
**aclaratorio -ria** *adj* explanatory
**aclástico -ca** *adj* (opt.) aclastic
**acleido -da** *adj & m* (anat.) acleidian
**aclimatación** *f* acclimation, acclimatization
**aclimatar** *va & vr* to acclimate, to acclimatize
**aclínico -ca** *adj* (phys.) aclinic; *m* opera glasses
**aclocar** §95 *vn* to brood; *vr* to brood; to sprawl; to squat
**aclorhidria** *f* (path.) achlorhydria
**acmé** *m* (med.) acme
**acne** *f* (path.) acne
**acobardamiento** *m* intimidation; cowardliness
**acobardar** *va* to cow, to intimidate; *vr* to become frightened
**acobijar** *va* (agr.) to hill
**acobijo** *m* (agr.) hill
**acobrado -da** *adj* coppery
**acoceador -dora** *adj* kicking
**acoceamiento** *m* kicking; (coll.) ill-treatment
**acocear** *va* to kick; (coll.) to ill-treat, to trample upon
**acocil** *m* (zool.) Mexican crayfish (*Cambarus montezumae*); **estar como un acocil** (Am.) to blush, to flush
**acocotar** *va* var. of **acogotar**
**acocote** *m* (Am.) long gourd used to suck out the juice of the maguey
**acochar** *vr* to crouch, to squat, to stoop over
**acochinar** *va* (coll.) to corner and slay; to humble, to scare; to corner (*in checkers*); *vr* to wallow; to get smeared up
**acodado -da** *adj* bent in an elbow
**acodadura** *f* bending; leaning; (hort.) layerage

**acodalamiento** *m* propping, shoring
**acodalar** *va* to prop up, to shore up
**acodar** *va* to lean (*e.g., the arm*); (hort.) to layer; to prop; to square (*timber*); *vr* to lean (on the elbows)
**acoderar** *va* (naut.) to tie up alongside the dock, to moor with a spring, to moor broadside
**acodiciar** *va* to covet; *vr* **acodiciarse a** or **de** to covet
**acodillar** *va* to bend into an elbow; *vr* to double up; to bow, to bend, to crumple
**acodo** *m* (hort.) layer
**acogedizo -za** *adj* easy to gather, gathered at random
**acogedor -dora** *adj* welcoming, kindly; *mf* welcomer
**acoger** §49 *va* to welcome, receive; to accept; *vr* to take refuge; **acogerse a** to take refuge in; to have recourse to
**acogeta** *f* shelter, cover, refuge
**acogible** *adj* welcome, acceptable
**acogido -da** *mf* inmate of poorhouse; *m* flock admitted to pasture for a price; *f* welcome, reception; meeting place, confluence; refuge; shelter; protection; (com.) acceptance; **dar acogida a** (com.) to honor (*e.g., a draft*); **tener buena acogida** to be well received
**acogimiento** *m* welcome, welcoming
**acogollar** *va* to cover up (*plants*); *vn & vr* to sprout, to bud
**acogombradura** *f* (agr.) hilling
**acogombrar** *va* (agr.) to hill (*plants*)
**acogotar** *va* to kill with a blow on the back of the neck; to knock down by grabbing by the back of the neck; to conquer, to subdue
**acohombrar** *va* var. of **acogombrar**
**acojinamiento** *m* (mach.) cushioning
**acojinar** *va* to quilt, to pad; to stuff; (mach.) to cushion (*a piston*)
**acolada** *f* accolade; (arch., mus. & paleog.) accolade
**acolar** *va* (her.) to unite (*two coats of arms*) under one crest; (her.) to add (*certain distinctive symbols*) to the escutcheon
**acolchado** *m* cushions (*of a carriage or auto*); riprap; revetment of straw and reeds
**acolchar** *va* to quilt, to pad; (naut.) to intertwine (*strands*)
**acolchonar** *va* (Am.) var. of **acolchar**
**acolitado** *m* (eccl.) order of acolyte
**acolitazgo** *m* (eccl.) acolythate; (eccl.) order of acolyte; acolytes (*of a church*)
**acólito** *m* acolyte; altar boy; (coll.) satellite, shadow
**acología** *f* acology
**acollador** *m* (naut.) lanyard
**acollar** §77 *va* to surround (*base of tree trunk*) with earth; to shear the neck of (*sheep*); (naut.) to haul on (*the lanyards*); (naut.) to calk
**acollarado -da** *adj* ring-necked (*said of animals*)
**acollarar** *va* to put a collar on; to hitch up; to leash; *vr* (coll.) to get married
**acollonar** *va* (coll.) to scare, to intimidate
**acombar** *va* var. of **combar**
**acomedido -da** *adj* (Am.) obliging
**acomedir** §94 *vr* (Am.) to be obliging
**acomejenar** *vr* (Am.) to become infested with termites
**acometedor -dora** *adj* aggresive; enterprising; *mf* aggressor; enterprising person
**acometer** *va* to attack; to overcome suddenly; to undertake; to widen into; *vn* to attack
**acometida** *f* attack, assault; house or service connection (*of wires or pipes*)
**acometimiento** *m* attack, assault; temptation; sewer connection
**acometividad** *f* aggressiveness
**acomodable** *adj* adaptable
**acomodación** *f* accommodation, arrangement; (physiol.) accommodation
**acomodadizo -za** *adj* accommodating, obliging
**acomodado -da** *adj* convenient, suitable; moderately priced; comfort-loving; well-to-do
**acomodador -dora** *adj* accommodating, obliging; *mf* usher (*in theaters*); *f* usherette
**acomodamiento** *m* convenience, suitability; transaction
**acomodar** *va* to accommodate, to arrange; to usher (*in theaters*); to reconcile; to suit; to supply, furnish; *vn* to be suitable, be fitting; *vr* to comply, adapt oneself; to come to terms; **acomodarse a** or **con** to comply with; **acomodarse a** + *inf* to settle down to + *inf;* **acomodarse de** to supply oneself with, to be supplied with; to hire out as
**acomodaticio -cia** *adj* accommodating, obliging; sycophantic; (iron.) elastic
**acomodo** *m* arrangement, adjustment; lodgings; job, position; (Am.) neatness, tidiness, spruceness
**acompañado -da** *adj* accompanied, attended; busy, frequented; (Am.) tipsy; *mf* consultant; *m* (Am.) sewer covering
**acompañador -dora** *adj* accompanying, attending; *mf* companion, attendant; accompanist
**acompañamiento** *m* accompaniment; retinue, escort; (mus.) accompaniment; (theat.) supernumeraries, extras; (Am.) food eaten with coffee, tea, or chocolate
**acompañanta** *f* female companion, attendant, or escort; (mus.) woman accompanist; (prov.) governess
**acompañante** *adj* accompanying; *m* companion, attendant, escort; (mus.) accompanist
**acompañar** *va* to accompany, go with; to enclose (*in a letter, etc.*); to share with, to sympathize with; (mus.) to accompany; (Am.) to point (*e. g., brickwork*); *vr* to consult
**acompasado -da** *adj* rhythmic, regular; slow; easy-going, steady; cautious
**acompasar** *va* to measure with a compass; to make rhythmical; to mark the rhythm or cadence of; to distribute evenly
**acomplexionado -da** *adj* var. of **complexionado**
**acomunar** *vr* to join forces, make common cause
**acón** *m* (Am.) flatboat
**aconcagüés -güesa** or **aconcagüino -na** *adj* (pertaining to) Aconcagua; *mf* native or inhabitant of Aconcagua
**aconchabar** *vr* (coll.) to confabulate, to conspire, to gang up
**aconchar** *va* to make shell-like; to push to safety; (naut.) to beach, to run aground; (Am.) to shame; *vr* to become shell-like; to take shelter; (naut.) to become beached, to run aground; (Am.) to be a sponger; to form a deposit
**acondicionado -da** *adj* conditioned; **bien acondicionado** well-disposed; in good condition; of good quality; **mal acondicionado** ill-disposed; in bad condition; of poor quality
**acondicionador -dora** *adj* conditioning; *mf* conditioner; **acondicionador de aire** air conditioner
**acondicionamiento** *m* conditioning; municipal testing bureau of silk and cotton fabrics; **acondicionamiento del aire** air conditioning
**acondicionar** *va* to condition, to arrange, make fit; to put in condition; to repair; to season; *vr* to qualify; to get placed, find a job
**acongojadamente** *adv* sorrowfully, with anguish
**acongojar** *va* to grieve, afflict, to distress; *vr* to grieve, be distressed; to faint
**aconitina** *f* (chem.) aconitine
**acónito** *m* (bot.) aconite, monkshood
**aconsejable** *adj* advisable
**aconsejador -dora** *adj* counseling, advising; *mf* counselor, adviser
**aconsejar** *va* to advise, to counsel, to warn; **aconsejar** + *inf* to advise to + *inf;* *vr* to seek advice, to get advice; **aconsejarse de** or **con** to advise with, to consult with, to seek or get advice from; **aconsejarse mejor** to think better of it
**aconsonantar** *va & vn* to rhyme
**acontecedero -ra** *adj* possible
**acontecer** §34 *vn* to happen
**acontecimiento** *m* happening, event
**acopar** *va* to make cuplike, to hollow out; *vn* to spread out
**acopetado -da** *adj* crested, tufted

**acopiador -dora** *adj* gathering; *mf* gatherer, collector, buyer; monopolist; (Am.) agricultural export buyer
**acopiamiento** *m* gathering, collecting; supply, store
**acopiar** *va* to gather together
**acopio** *m* gathering, collecting; assortment, stock; abundance
**acoplado** *m* (Am.) trailer; (Am.) tow (*of barges*)
**acoplador** *m* (mach. & rad.) coupler
**acopladura** *f* joining, fitting
**acoplamiento** *m* coupling, joining; connection, joint, splice; (elec.) connection, hookup; (Am.) clutch; (Am. rail.) coupling; **acoplamiento de cono** cone coupling; **acoplamiento de fricción** friction coupling; (Am.) friction clutch; **acoplamiento de manguito** sleeve coupling; **acoplamiento de rebajo** (carp.) rabbeted joint; **acoplamiento en serie** (elec.) series connection; **acoplamiento inductivo** (elec.) linkage, flux linkage; **acoplamiento universal** universal joint
**acoplar** *va* to join, couple, fit together; to hitch; to bring together for breeding; to unite, reconcile; (elec.) to connect, to hook up; (Am. rail.) to couple (*cars*); *vr* to be reconciled; to be intimate; to mate
**acoquinamiento** *m* intimidation
**acoquinar** *va* to intimidate
**acorar** *va* to oppress, afflict; (Am.) to intimidate, to quiet; *vr* to be grieved; to be stifled; to wilt, to die (*said of plants*)
**acorazado -da** *adj* armored, armor-plated; ironclad; (coll.) forbidding, contrary; *m* battleship; ironclad; **acorazado de bolsillo** pocket battleship
**acorazamiento** *m* armor, armor-plating
**acorazar §76** *va* to cover with armor, to armorplate; *vr* (coll.) to steel oneself
**acorazonado -da** *adj* heart-shaped
**acorchamiento** *m* withering, shriveling
**acorchar** *va* to turn into cork, to give an appearance of cork to; to line with cork; *vr* to become cork-like or spongy; to dry up, wither, shrivel; to become corky or pithy; to get sluggish, to get numb; to become morally benumbed
**acorchetar** *va* to bracket
**acordada** *f* decree, order; authorization; curved ruler
**acordadamente** *adv* by common consent; after due reflection
**acordancia** *f* harmony, agreement
**acordar §77** *va* to decide, to agree upon; to grant, to authorize; to reconcile, to harmonize; to arrange; to make smooth; to make level or flush; to remind, to remind of; to tune; *vn* to agree, be in agreement; to blend, to harmonize; **acordar** + *inf* to agree to + *inf; vr* to be agreed, reconciled, harmonized; to remember; **si mal no me acuerdo** (coll.) if I remember correctly; **acordarse de** to remember; **acordarse de** + *inf* to remember to + *inf*, e.g., **se acordó de hacerlo** he remembered to do it; **acordarse de** + *perf inf* to remember + *ger*, e.g., **se acordaba de haberlo hecho** he remembered doing it
**acorde** *adj* agreed, in accord; harmonious, in tune; *m* accord, harmony; (mus.) chord
**acordelar** *va* to align with a cord, to measure with a cord, to lay out with a chalk line
**acordemente** *adv* var. of **acordadamente**
**acordeón** *m* accordion; **en acordeón** accordion (*pleats*)
**acordeonado -da** *adj* accordion (*pleats*)
**acordeonista** *mf* accordionist
**acordonamiento** *m* cording, lacing; milling, knurling; drawing a cordon around a place; roping off
**acordonar** *va* to cord, to lace, to fasten with cords; to mill, bead, knurl (*coins, etc.*); to draw a cordon around, to surround; to rope off (*a street*); (Am.) to align, to lay out by line
**acores** *mpl* (path.) milk crust
**acornar §77** *va* to attack with the horns, to butt, to gore; to shape like a horn; to make horny; *vn* to become horn-shaped; to become horny; to grow horns
**acorneador -dora** *adj* butting; *mf* animal given to butting
**acornear** *va* to butt; (Am.) to drive away, put to flight
**ácoro** *m* (bot.) sweet flag; **ácoro bastardo, falso** or **palustre** (bot.) flagon
**acorralamiento** *m* corralling, cornering; intimidation
**acorralar** *va* to corral, to corner; to intimidate
**acorrucar §86** *vr* to crouch, to huddle; to curl up to keep warm
**acortamiento** *m* cutting down, shortening, slackening; shrinking, contraction; (astr.) curtation
**acortar** *va* to cut down, to shorten, to reduce; to check, stop; to pull up (*a horse*); to slacken (*speed*); (Am.) to tone down (*a statement*); **acortar la vela** (naut.) to shorten sail; *vr* to become shorter; to be timid; to hold back; to slow down; to shrink, to contract
**acorullar** *va* (naut.) to ship (*oars*)
**acorvar** *va* to curve, to bend
**acosamiento** *m* var. of **acoso**
**acosar** *va* to harass, to pursue relentlessly; (taur.) to corral and test the mettle of
**acosijar** *va* (Am.) var. of **acosar**
**acoso** *m* harassment, relentless pursuit; (taur.) corralling and testing the mettle of a bull
**acostado -da** *adj* lying down; leaning, bent over; in bed; closely related; friendly; favored; (naut.) on beam ends; *f* (Am.) childbirth; (Am.) (sexual) intercourse
**acostamiento** *m* laying down; lying down, reclining; support, favor, protection; (archaic) stipend, emolument
**acostar §77** *va* to lay, to lay down; to put to bed; (naut.) to bring alongside, to bring inshore; *vn* to lean, to list; *vr* to lie down, to go to bed; (Am.) to be confined (with child)
**acostillado -da** *adj* ribbed
**acostumbrado -da** *adj* accustomed; usual, customary
**acostumbrar** *va* to accustom; **acostumbrar a** + *inf* to accustom (*someone*) to + *inf; vn* to be accustomed; **acostumbrar** + *inf* or **acostumbrar a** + *inf* to be accustomed to + *inf; vr* to accustom oneself; to become accustomed; **acostumbrarse a** + *inf* to be or become accustomed to + *inf*
**acotación** *f* boundary mark, landmark; annotation, marginal note; elevation mark
**acotada** *f* tree nursery
**acotamiento** *m* boundary mark, landmark; annotation, marginal note; elevation mark; stage direction; (Am.) shoulder (*of road*)
**acotar** *va* to survey, to map, to mark off; to annotate; to fix, to set up; to admit, to accept; to check, to verify; to vouch for; to choose, to select; to pollard, to cut off top branches of; to mark elevations on (*maps, etc.*)
**acotiledón -dona** *adj* (bot.) acotyledonous; *m* (bot.) acotyledon
**acotiledóneo -a** *adj* (bot.) acotyledonous
**acotillo** *m* sledge hammer
**acoyotado -da** *adj* (Am.) coyote-colored
**acoyundar** *va* to yoke (*oxen*)
**acoyuntar** *va* to yoke (*two horses of different owners*)
**acoyuntero** *m* farmer who yokes his horse with that of another farmer
**acre** *adj* acrid; austere, severe; biting, mordant; quarrelsome; *m* acre
**acreaje** *m* (Am.) acreage
**acrecencia** *f* increase, growth; accrual
**acrecentamiento** *m* accretion; increase, growth; promotion
**acrecentar §18** *va* to increase; to promote, to foster, to make flourish; *vr* to increase, to grow; to bud, to blossom
**acrecer §34** *va* to increase, enlarge; *vn* (law) to devolve or to be added (*said of share of an estate given up by an heir voluntarily or by death*); *vr* to increase, to grow larger
**acreción** *f* (mineral. & path.) accretion
**acreditación** *f* accreditation; (educ.) accreditation
**acreditar** *va* to accredit; to credit, to give a reputation to; to credit to; to get the reputation for; to do credit to; (com.) to credit; (educ.) to

accredit; *vr* to get a reputation; **acreditarse de loco** to act crazy
**acreedor -dora** *adj* accrediting, crediting; deserving; **acreedor a** deserving of; *mf* creditor; **acreedor hipotecario** mortgagee
**acreencia** *f* (Am.) balance in favor of creditor
**acribador -dora** *adj* sifting; *mf* sifter
**acribadura** *f* sifting; (fig.) riddling
**acribar** *va* to sift; (fig.) to riddle
**acribillar** *va* to riddle; to riddle with wounds, bites, stings, etc.; (coll.) to harass, to plague, to pester; **acribillar a balazos** to riddle with bullets; **acribillar a preguntas** to riddle with questions
**acriflavina** *f* (pharm.) acriflavine
**acrílico -ca** *adj* (chem.) acrylic
**acriminación** *f* incrimination; exaggeration of guilt
**acriminador -dora** *adj* incriminating; *mf* accuser
**acriminar** *va* to incriminate, to accuse; to exaggerate the gravity of (*a defect, weakness, misdeed, etc.*)
**acrimonia** *f* acridness; acrimony
**acrimonioso -sa** *adj* acrid; acrimonious
**acriollar** *vr* (Am.) to take on Spanish American ways
**acrisolado -da** *adj* pure; tried, tested; honest, reliable
**acrisolar** *va* to purify; to bring out, to reveal (*the truth*)
**acristalado -da** *adj* glass-enclosed, glassed-in
**acristianar** *va* (coll.) to Christianize; (coll.) to christen, to baptize; to beautify; *vr* (coll.) to become Christian, to get religious
**acritud** *f* var. of **acrimonia**
**acrobacia** *f* acrobatics (*feats or performances*)
**acróbata** *mf* acrobat
**acrobático -ca** *adj* acrobatic
**acrobatismo** *m* acrobatics (*art or profession*)
**acrofobia** *f* (path.) acrophobia
**acrógena** *f* (bot.) acrogen
**acromático -ca** *adj* achromatous; (opt., biol. & mus.) achromatic
**acromatina** *f* (biol.) achromatin
**acromatismo** *m* achromatism
**acromatizar §76** *va* to achromatize
**acromatopsia** *f* (path.) achromatopsia, color blindness
**acromatosis** *f* (path.) achromatosis
**acromegalia** *f* (path.) acromegaly
**acrónimo** *m* acronym
**acrópolis** *f* (*pl:* **-lis**) acropolis; **la Acrópolis** the Acropolis
**acrósporo** *m* (bot.) acrospore
**acróstico -ca** *adj* acrostical; *m* acrostic
**acrostolio** *m* (naut.) rostrum, acroterium; (naut.) spur, beak, ram (*of classical war vessel*)
**acrotera** *f* (arch.) acroterium
**acta** *f* minutes; certificate of election; **actas** *fpl* lives (*of saints, martyrs, etc.*); transactions (*of a learned society*); **levantar acta** to draw up the minutes; **tomar acta de** (coll.) to take note of; **acta de matrimonio** marriage certificate; **acta de nacimiento** birth certificate; **acta de nacionalidad** (naut.) registry certificate; **acta notarial** affidavit; **Actas de los Apóstoles** (Bib.) Acts of the Apostles
**actea** *f* (bot.) danewort, dwarf elder
**actinia** *f* (zool.) actinia, sea anemone
**actínico -ca** *adj* actinic
**actinio** *m* (chem.) actinium
**actinismo** *m* actinism
**actinómetro** *m* actinometer
**actinomicina** *f* (pharm.) actinomycin
**actinomicosis** *f* (path.) actinomycosis
**actitud** *f* attitude; (fig.) attitude (*feeling, outlook*); **en actitud de** + *inf* showing an intention to + *inf*, getting ready to + *inf*
**activación** *f* activation, promotion
**activador -dora** *adj* activating, moving; *mf* activator, mover; *m* (chem.) activator
**activar** *va* to activate; to expedite, to hasten
**actividad** *f* activity; **en actividad** active, operating; **en plena actividad** in full swing
**activista** *mf* activist
**activo -va** *adj* active; *m* (com.) assets; (com.) credit side (*of an account*); **en activo** in active service
**acto** *m* act; event; public function; commencement (*of school*); (theat.) act; (educ.) thesis; sexual intercourse; **en el acto** at once; on the spot; **hacer acto de presencia** to honor with one's presence, to pay one's respects in person; **acto continuo** right afterwards; **acto de presencia** formal attendance; **acto inaugural** opening, opening ceremonies, dedication; **Actos de los Apóstoles** (Bib.) Acts of the Apostles; **acto seguido** right afterwards; **acto seguido de** right after
**actor** *m* actor, agent; (theat.) actor; (law) actor, plaintiff; **primer actor** (theat.) leading man; **actor de carácter** (theat.) character actor
**actora** *f* (law) actor, plaintiff (*woman*)
**actriz** *f* (*pl:* **-trices**) (theat.) actress; **primera actriz** (theat.) leading lady
**actuación** *f* action; activity; operation; performance; acting; behavior
**actuado -da** *adj* skilled, experienced
**actual** *adj* present, present-day; up-to-date
**actualidad** *f* present time; present condition; timeliness; question of the moment; **actualidades** *fpl* current events; newsreel; **en la actualidad** at the present time; **ser de gran actualidad** to be of great importance at the moment; **actualidad gráfica** news in pictures; **actualidad escénica** theater news
**actualizar §76** *va* to make up-to-date, to bring up to date
**actualmente** *adv* at present, at the present time
**actuar §33** *va* to actuate, to put into action; *vn* to act; to perform; to take action; **actuar de** to act as; **actuar sobre** to act on or upon
**actuarial** *adj* actuarial
**actuario -ria** *adj* actuarial; *mf* actuary; **actuario de seguros** actuary
**acuadrillar** *va* to band together; to command (*a band*); *vr* to band together
**acuafortista** *mf* etcher, aquafortist
**acuantiar §90** *va* to fix or set the amount of
**acuaplano** *m* aquaplane
**acuarela** *f* water color
**acuarelista** *mf* water-colorist, aquarellist
**acuario** *m* aquarium; (*cap.*) *s* (astr.) Aquarius
**acuartelado -da** *adj* (her.) quartered
**acuartelamiento** *m* quartering, billeting; quarters; (her.) quartering
**acuartelar** *va* to quarter, to billet; to divide (*land*) into lots; (naut.) to bear (*sail*) to windward; (her.) to quarter (*a shield*); *vr* to quarter, take up quarters; to withdraw, retire
**acuarteronado -da** *adj* & *mf* mulatto, quadroon
**acuartillar** *vn* to bend in the quarters under a heavy load or through weakness
**acuático -ca** or **acuátil** *adj* aquatic
**acuatinta** *f* aquatint
**acuatintista** *mf* aquatinter
**acuatizaje** *m* (aer.) alighting on water
**acuatizar §76** *vn* (aer.) to alight on water
**acubilar** *va* to round up (*cattle*) for the night
**acucia** *f* zeal, diligence, haste; keen desire; sharpness (*of pain*)
**acuciadamente** *adv* zealously, hastily; keenly, eagerly
**acuciador -dora** *adj* keen, excruciating
**acuciamiento** *m* goading, prodding, hastening
**acuciante** *adj* keen, burning (*desire*); acute (*problem*)
**acuciar** *va* to goad, to prod, to hasten; to harass; to desire keenly; *vr* to hasten
**acucioso -sa** *adj* zealous, hasty; keen, eager
**acuclillar** *vr* to squat, to crouch down
**acucharado -da** *adj* spoon-shaped
**acuchilladizo** *m* gladiator; fencer
**acuchillado -da** *adj* knife-shaped, knife-like; full of stabs; cautious through bitter experience; slashed (*said of a garment*)
**acuchillador -dora** *mf* stabber, fighter, bully
**acuchillar** *va* to stab; to stab to death; to slash (*a garment*); to smooth down (*a piece of wood*); to cleave (*the air*); *vr* to fight with knives or swords
**acudimiento** *m* aid, succor; approach

**acudir** *vn* to come up, to respond; to come to the rescue; to hang around; to apply, to resort; to produce, to yield; **acudir a** + *inf* to come to + *inf*
**acueducto** *m* aqueduct; (anat.) aqueduct
**ácueo -a** *adj* aqueous
**acuerdado -da** *adj* aligned with a cord or rope
**acuerdo** *m* accord; agreement; memory, remembrance; **de acuerdo** in accord; **de acuerdo con** in accord with; **de común acuerdo** with one accord; **estar en su acuerdo** to be in one's right mind; **estar, quedar,** or **ponerse de acuerdo** to be in agreement; **llegar a un acuerdo con** to come to an understanding with; **volver en su acuerdo** to come to; to change one's mind
**acuernar** *va* (taur.) to look at or butt toward one side, to have the habit or defect of attacking on only one side
**acuerpar** *va* (Am.) to back up, defend
**acuidad** *f* acuity; visual acuity
**acuitadamente** *adv* with grief, sorrowfully, grievously
**acuitar** *va* to afflict, to grieve; *vr* to grieve, to be grieved
**acular** *va* to back up; (coll.) to force into a corner; *vr* (naut.) to back up on a shoal
**acullá** *adv* yonder, over there
**acumen** *m* acumen, keenness
**acuminado -da** *adj* acuminate; (bot. & zool.) acuminate
**acumulación** *f* accumulation
**acumulador -dora** *adj* accumulating; *mf* accumulator; *m* (elec.) storage battery; **acumulador de ferro-níquel** (elec.) iron-nickel alkaline cell; **acumulador de plomo-ácido** (elec.) lead acid cell; **acumulador flotante** (elec.) floating battery; **acumulador hierro-níquel** (elec.) iron-nickel alkaline cell; **acumulador níquel-cadmio** (elec.) nickel-cadmium battery
**acumular** *va* to accumulate, to gather; to store up; to charge with; *vn* to accumulate; *vr* to accumulate, to gather
**acumulativo -va** *adj* cumulative
**acúmulo** *m* accumulation; (bact.) clump
**acunar** *va* to rock in a cradle, to cradle; (fig.) to cradle (*to nurture during infancy*)
**acuñación** *f* coining, minting; wedging
**acuñador** *m* coiner, minter; wedge; tamper; (print.) shooting stick
**acuñar** *va* to coin, to mint; to wedge; to key, to lock; to tamp (*ties*); (print.) to quoin
**acuosidad** *f* wateriness, aqueousness
**acuoso -sa** *adj* watery, aqueous; juicy
**acupuntura** *f* (surg.) acupuncture
**acurrucar §86** *va* to wrap up; *vr* to huddle; to squat
**acusable** *adj* accusable
**acusación** *f* accusation
**acusado -da** *adj* accused; marked; *mf* accused
**acusador -dora** *adj* accusing; *mf* accuser
**acusar** *va* to accuse; to show; to acknowledge (*receipt*); to announce (*winning cards*); **acusar de** + *inf* to accuse of + *ger*; *vr* to confess; **acusarse de** to confess (*a crime*); to confess being; **acusarse de haber** + *pp* to confess having + *pp*
**acusativo -va** *adj* accusative, accusing; (gram.) accusative; *m* (gram.) accusative
**acusatorio -ria** *adj* accusatory
**acuse** *m* acknowledgment (*of receipt*); announcement (*of winning cards*); winning card; **acuse de recibo** acknowledgment of receipt
**acusete** *m* talebearer, informer
**acusón -sona** *adj* (coll.) talebearing; *mf* (coll.) tattler, talebearer
**acústico -ca** *adj* acoustic; *m* hearing aid; *f* (phys.) acoustics; **acústica arquitectural** acoustics (*acoustic properties of a room or building*)
**acusticón** *m* acousticon
**acusuco** *m* (Am.) wild desire, great anxiety
**acutángulo -la** *adj* acute-angled
**acutí** *m* (*pl:* **-tíes**) (zool.) agouti
**achacar §86** *va* to impute, to attribute
**achacoso -sa** *adj* sickly, ailing; indisposed
**achaflanar** *va* to chamfer, to bevel
**achagrinado -da** *adj* shagreen, shagreened
**achampañado -da** *adj* sparkling, effervescent, like champagne
**achantar** *vr* (coll.) to hide away from danger; (coll.) to comply, to submit
**achaparrado -da** *adj* stubby; chubby; runty
**achaparrar** *vr* to grow stunted
**achaque** *m* sickliness, unhealthiness; indisposition; weakness, fault; (coll.) monthlies; (coll.) pregnancy; excuse, pretext; matter, subject; (law) fine
**achaquiento -ta** *adj* var. of **achacoso**
**acharolar** *va* var. of **charolar**
**achatamiento** *m* flattening
**achatar** *va* to flatten; *vr* to get flat
**achicado -da** *adj* childish, childlike; abashed; disconcerted, confused
**achicador** *m* scoop (*for bailing water*); bailer
**achicadura** *f* or **achicamiento** *m* reduction in size; bailing
**achicar §86** *va* to make smaller; to humble, to intimidate; to drain, to bail out; to make childish; (Am.) to kill
**achicoria** *f* (bot.) chicory
**achicharradero** *m* inferno (*any hot place*)
**achicharrar** *va* to scorch; to bother, to bedevil; *vr* to get scorched
**achichinque** *m* (min.) scooper, bailer (*workman*)
**achilenado -da** *adj* (Am.) like a Chilean; (Am.) pro-Chilean
**achinado -da** *adj* Chinese-looking; (Am.) half-breed; (Am.) degraded; (Am.) copper-colored; (Am.) Indian-looking (*in color or features*)
**achinar** *va* (coll.) to intimidate, scare
**achinelado -da** *adj* slipper-shaped
**achiotal** *m* plantation of annatto trees
**achiote** *m* (bot.) annatto tree
**achique** *m* bailing, scooping, draining
**achispado -da** *adj* tipsy
**achispar** *va* to make tipsy; *vr* to get tipsy
**-acho -cha** *suffix aug & pej* e.g., **hombracho** husky big fellow; **populacho** mob, rabble; **terminacho** vulgar term
**achocadura** *f* hurling or dashing against a wall; hitting, striking, stoning
**achocar §86** *va* to hurl or dash against a wall; to hit, to strike, to stone; (coll.) to hoard
**achocolatado -da** *adj* chocolate, chocolate-colored
**achochar** *vr* (coll.) to begin to dote, to go into one's dotage
**acholado -da** *adj* (Am.) part white, part Indian; (Am.) abashed, cowed
**acholar** *vr* (Am.) to be abashed, to be ashamed
**achote** *m* var. of **achiote**
**achubascar §86** *vr* to get cloudy and threatening (*said of the sky*)
**achucutar** or **achucuyar** *vr* (Am.) to become discouraged; (Am.) to wither, to spoil
**achuchar** *va* to incite, urge on; (coll.) to crumple, crush; to push around, jostle
**achuchón** *m* (coll.) crumpling, crushing; jostling
**achulado -da** *adj* (coll.) rough, tough
**achulapar** or **achular** *vr* to get rough and ill-mannered
**achunchar** *va* (Am.) to embarrass, to foil; (Am.) to cast the evil eye on
**achuñuscar §86** *va* to crumple, to crush
**achura** *f* (Am.) guts (*of an animal*)
**Ada** *f* Ada
**adafina** *f* Jewish stew
**adagio** *m* adage; (mus.) adagio
**adala** *f* (naut.) pump dale
**adalid** *m* chief, commander; guide, leader; champion (*of a cause, a movement, etc.*)
**adamado -da** *adj* womanish, soft; chic, stylish; gaudy (*said of a woman*)
**adamantino -na** *adj* adamantine
**adamar** *vr* to become thin, to become effeminate, to look like a woman
**adamas** *m* adamant, diamond
**adamascado -da** *adj* damask; damascene
**adamascar §86** *va* to damask (*to weave like damask*); to damascene
**adámico -ca** *adj* Adamic; left by the tide (*said of sand and other sediment*)
**Adán** *m* Adam; (*l.c.*) *m* (coll.) dirty, ragged fellow; (coll.) lazy, careless fellow

**adaptabilidad** *f* adaptability
**adaptable** *adj* adaptable
**adaptación** *f* adaptation
**adaptador** *m* adapter
**adaptante** *adj* adapting, adaptive
**adaptar** *va* to adapt, to fit
**adaraja** *f* (mas.) toothing
**adarce** *m* dried salt froth, incrustation of salt spray
**adarga** *f* oval or heart-shaped leather shield
**adargar §59** *va* to shield, protect
**adarme** *m* sixteenth part of ounce (*179 centigrams*); bit, driblet
**adarvar** *va* to stun, to bewilder; *vr* to be stunned, to be overwhelmed
**adarve** *m* (fort.) walk behind parapet on top of wall
**adatar** *va* to enter in a ledger; to credit
**adaza** *f* (bot.) sorghum
**A. de C.** abr. of **año de Cristo**
**adecenamiento** *m* grouping or dividing in tens
**adecenar** *va* to group or divide in tens
**adecentar** *va* to make decent or proper; to tidy up, to clean up; *vr* (coll.) to put on a clean shirt, to dress up
**adecuación** *f* fitting, adaptation
**adecuado -da** *adj* fitting, suitable
**adecuar** *va* to fit, adapt
**adefagía** *f* voracity
**adéfago -ga** *adj* voracious
**adefesio** *m* (coll.) nonsense, absurdity; (coll.) outlandish outfit; (coll.) ridiculous fellow, queer-looking guy; **decir** or **hablar adefesios** to talk nonsense
**adefina** *f* var. of **adafina**
**adehala** *f* gratuity, extra, perquisite
**adehesamiento** *m* converting into pasture
**adehesar** *va* to convert into pasture
**Adelaida** *f* Adelaide
**adelantadamente** *adv* beforehand, in advance
**adelantado -da** *adj* precocious; bold, rash; fast (*said of a watch or clock*); **por adelantado** in advance; *m* (archaic) governor of a province
**adelantamiento** *m* anticipation; advancement, progress, improvement, promotion
**adelantar** *va* to move forward, to move ahead; to get ahead of, to outstrip; to hasten (*e.g., one's step*); to advance, promote; to make (*e.g., payment*) in advance; to improve; *vn* to advance, get along, improve; to be fast (*said of a watch or clock*); *vr* to move forward, to move ahead; to gain, be fast (*said of a watch or clock*); **adelantarse a** or **de** to get ahead of, to outstrip
**adelante** *adv* ahead; forward; in the opposite direction, e.g., **un hombre que viene por el camino adelante** a man coming in the opposite direction; **de aquí en adelante** from now on, henceforth; **en adelante** in the future; **hacia adelante** forward; **más adelante** farther on; later; *interj* ahead!, go ahead!; come in!
**adelanto** *m* advance, progress; advancement; payment in advance
**adelfa** *f* (bot.) oleander, rosebay
**adelfal** *m* field of oleanders
**adelfilla** *f* (bot.) spurge laurel; **adelfilla pelosa** (bot.) willow herb (*Epilobium hirsutum*)
**adelgazamiento** *m* thinness, slenderness; hairsplitting
**adelgazar §76** *va* to make thin or slender; to taper; to purify, refine; to split hairs regarding; **adelgazar el entendimiento** to sharpen one's wits; **adelgazar la voz** to raise the pitch of one's voice; *vn* to get thin or slender; *vr* to get thin or slender; to taper; to split hairs
**Adelina** *f* Adeline
**adema** *f* var. of **ademe**
**ademador** *m* (min.) shorer
**ademán** *m* attitude; gesture; (paint. & sculp.) attitude; **ademanes** *mpl* manners; **en ademán de** + *inf* showing an intention to + *inf*, getting ready to + *inf*; **hacer ademán de** + *inf* to make a move to + *inf*
**ademar** *va* (min.) to shore, to shore up
**además** *adv* moreover, besides; **además de** in addition to, besides
**ademe** *m* (min.) shore, strut, prop; shoring
**Adén** *m* Aden
**adenia** *f* (path.) adenia
**adenitis** *f* (path.) adenitis
**adenoidectomía** *f* adenoidectomy
**adenoideo -a** *adj* adenoid, adenoidal
**adenoma** *m* (path.) adenoma
**adensar** *vr* to become thick or thicker
**adentellar** *va* to sink one's teeth into; to criticize bitingly; (mas.) to leave toothing in (*e.g., a wall*)
**adentrar** *vn* & *vr* to go in, to go into; **adentrarse en el mar** to go further out to sea
**adentro** *adv* inside, within; **mar adentro** out at sea; **ser muy de adentro** to be like a member of the family; **tierra adentro** inland; **adentros** *mpl* very inmost being, very inmost thoughts; **en** or **para sus adentros** to oneself, to himself, etc.
**adepto -ta** *adj* adept; *mf* follower; adept (*in alchemy, magic, etc.*)
**aderezamiento** *m* dressing; adornment, embellishment
**aderezar §76** *va* to dress, to prepare, to embellish; to cook, to season; to repair; to mix (*drinks*); to lead, show the way to; *vr* to dress, to get ready
**aderezo** *m* dressing; seasoning, condiment; adornment, finery; equipment; set of jewels
**aderra** *f* rope made of esparto; trappings; trimmings; stiffening
**adestrado -da** *adj* (her.) dexterwise
**adestrador -dora** *adj* & *mf* var. of **adiestrador**
**adestrar §18** *va* & *vr* var. of **adiestrar**
**adeudado -da** *adj* indebted, in debt
**adeudar** *va* to owe; to be liable or subject to (*duties, taxes, etc.*); to charge, to debit; *vn* to become related by marriage; *vr* to run into debt, to become indebted
**adeudo** *m* debt, indebtedness; custom duty; charge, debit
**adherencia** *f* adhesion (*sticking fast*); bond, relationship; (path. & phys.) adhesion; **tener adherencias** to have connections
**adherente** *adj* adherent; *m* adherent; requisite; accessory; dressing
**adherir §62** *vn* & *vr* to adhere, to stick; **adherir a** or **adherirse a** to be attached to; to espouse, to embrace
**adhesión** *f* adherence or adhesion (*steady attachment*); (phys.) adhesion
**adhesividad** *f* adhesiveness; addiction; sociability
**adhesivo -va** *adj* & *m* adhesive
**adiabático -ca** *adj* adiabatic
**adiafa** *f* (archaic) treat or gift to sailors at the end of a voyage
**adiaforesis** *f* (path.) adiaphoresis
**adiamantado -da** *adj* diamondlike
**adición** *f* addition; marginal note (*on bill or account*); (Am.) check (*in hotel or restaurant*); **adición de la herencia** (law) acceptance of an inheritance
**adicional** *adj* additional
**adicionar** *va* to add; to add to
**adicto -ta** *adj* devoted; belonging, supporting; adjunct; *mf* devotee; supporter, partisan
**adiestrable** *adj* trainable; docile
**adiestrador -dora** *adj* training; teaching; *mf* trainer; teacher; guide
**adiestramiento** *m* training; teaching; leading
**adiestrar** *va* to train; to teach; to lead, direct, guide; *vr* to train, to practice; **adiestrarse a** + *inf* to train oneself to + *inf*, to practice + *ger*
**adietar** *va* to put on a diet
**adifés** *adv* (Am.) on purpose
**adinamia** *f* (path.) adynamia
**adinámico -ca** *adj* adynamic
**adinerado -da** *adj* moneyed, wealthy
**adinerar** *va* (prov.) to turn into cash; *vr* (coll.) to get rich
**adintelado -da** *adj* straight, flat (*said of an arch or vault*)
**adiós** *m* (*pl:* **adioses**) adieu, good-by; *interj* adieu!, good-by!; hello!
**adiosito** *interj* bye-bye!
**adipocira** *f* adipocere
**adiposidad** *f* adiposity
**adiposis** *f* (path.) adiposis
**adiposo -sa** *adj* adipose

**adipsia** *f* (path.) adipsia
**adir** *va* (law) to accept (*an inheritance*)
**aditamento** *m* addition; attachment, accessory
**aditivo -va** *adj & m* additive
**adiva** *f* (zool.) jackal; **adivas** *fpl* (vet.) vives
**adive** *m* (zool.) jackal
**adivina** *f* see **adivino**
**adivinable** *adj* guessable
**adivinación** *f* prophecy; guessing, divination; solving; **adivinación del pensamiento** mind reading
**adivinador -dora** *adj* divinatory; *mf* prophesier; guesser, diviner; good guesser; **adivinador del pensamiento** mind reader
**adivinaja** *f* (coll.) riddle, puzzle
**adivinamiento** *m* var. of **adivinación**
**adivinanza** *f* riddle; divination, guess
**adivinar** *va* to prophesy; to guess, to divine; to solve (*a riddle or puzzle*); to read (*someone's mind or thoughts*); *vn* to divine
**adivinatorio -ria** *adj* divining, divinatory
**adivino -na** *mf* fortuneteller, soothsayer, prophet; guesser; *m* (ent.) praying mantis; *f* (prov.) riddle, puzzle
**adjetivación** *f* modification; adjective use
**adjetivadamente** *adv* adjectively
**adjetival** *adj* adjectival
**adjetivar** *va* to modify (*a noun*); to apply an epithet to; to use as an adjective; *vr* to become an adjective
**adjetivo -va** *adj* adjective, adjectival; *m* adjective; **adjetivo gentilicio** adjective of nationality
**adjudicación** *f* adjudging, awarding
**adjudicador -dora** *adj* adjudging; *mf* adjudger
**adjudicar** **§86** *va* to adjudge (*to award*); *vr* to appropriate
**adjudicatario -ria** *mf* awardee, grantee
**adjuntar** *va* to join, connect; to add; to enclose (*in a letter*)
**adjunto -ta** *adj* adjunct; added, attached; enclosed (*in a letter*); *mf* adjunct, associate; *m* (gram.) adjunct
**adjuración** *f* (archaic) conjuration (*invoking by a sacred name*)
**adlátere** *m* var. of **a látere**
**Admeto** *m* (myth.) Admetus
**adminicular** *va* (law) to strengthen, reinforce
**adminículo** *m* adminicle, aid, auxiliary; accessory, gadget; meddler; (law) adminicle (*corroborative proof*); **adminículos** *mpl* emergency equipment
**administración** *f* administration
**administrador -dora** *adj* administrating; *mf* administrator; **administrador de aduanas** collector of customs; **administrador de correos** postmaster; **administrador judicial** administrator (*of an estate*); **administradora judicial** administratrix (*of an estate*)
**administrar** *va* to administer
**administrativo -va** *adj* administrative
**admirabilísimo -ma** *adj super* very or most admirable
**admirable** *adj* admirable
**admiración** *f* admiration; wonder; exclamation point
**admirador -dora** *adj* admiring; (coll.) beauty-loving; *mf* admirer; (coll.) beauty-lover, devotee of the fair sex
**admirando -da** *adj* admirable
**admirar** *va* to admire; to surprise; *vr* to admire, to wonder; **admirarse de** to wonder at
**admirativo -va** *adj* admiring; admirable
**admisibilidad** *f* admissibility
**admisible** *adj* admissible; allowable
**admisión** *f* admission; (mach.) intake
**admitancia** *f* (elec.) admittance
**admitir** *va* to admit; to allow, to allow for; to accept, recognize; **admitir** + *inf* to agree to + *inf*
**admonición** *f* admonition
**adm.**[or] abr. of **administrador**
**adnato -ta** *adj* (bot. & zool.) adnate; *f* (anat.) conjunctiva
**-ado -da** *suffix adj* -ate, e.g., **separado** separate; **apasionado** passionate; -ed, e.g., **bienaventurado** blessed; -y, e.g., **ondulado** wavy; -shaped, e.g., **acorazonado** heart-shaped; -colored, e.g., **naranjado** orange-colored; (bot. & zool.) -ate, e.g., **cordado** chordate; **espatulado** spatulate; *suffix m* -acy, e.g., **papado** papacy; -ate, e.g., **prelado** prelate; **senado** senate; -ful, e.g., **brazado** armful; **puñado** handful; -ing, e.g., **pisonado** tamping; **planchado** ironing; *suffix f* -ad, e.g., **tríada** triad; **Ilíada** Iliad; -ade, e.g., **brigada** brigade; **limonada** lemonade; **mascarada** masquerade; -ful, e.g., **cucharada** spoonful; **palada** shovelful; blow, stroke, stab, e.g., **martillada** blow or stroke with a hammer; **plumada** stroke of pen; **puñalada** stab with a dagger; pack, drove, e.g., **perrada** pack of dogs; **vacada** drove of cattle
**adobado** *m* pickled meat
**adobador -dora** *mf* repairer, dresser; pickler; tanner
**adobajes** *mpl* pickled meat in barrels
**adobar** *va* to repair, restore; to prepare, to dress; to trim (*a lamp*); to cook, stew; to pickle (*meat, fish*); to tan (*hides*); to fertilize; to hammer and fit (*a horseshoe*)
**adobasillas** *m* (*pl:* **-llas**) chair mender
**adobe** *m* adobe
**adobeño -ña** *adj* adobe-like; (pertaining to the) adobe
**adobera** *f* adobe mould; adobe factory; (Am.) adobe-shaped cheese; (Am.) mould for adobe-shaped cheese
**adobería** *f* adobe factory; tannery
**adobino -na** *adj* (pertaining to the) adobe
**adobo** *m* repairing; dressing; trimming; cooking; pickling, pickle, pickled meat or fish; tanning, tanning mixture
**adocenado -da** *adj* commonplace, ordinary
**adocenar** *va* to arrange or divide in dozens; to confuse with the rabble, to put in a lower class
**adoctrinamiento** *m* indoctrination, teaching, instruction
**adoctrinar** *va* to indoctrinate, to teach, to instruct
**adolecer** **§34** *vn* to fall sick, become ill; **adolecer de** to suffer from; (fig.) to suffer from; *vr* to sympathize, be sorry
**adolescencia** *f* adolescence
**adolescente** *adj & mf* adolescent
**Adolfo** *m* Adolph
**adolorado -da** or **adolorido -da** *adj* sore, aching; grieving, sorrowful
**adomiciliar** *va & vr.* var. of **domiciliar**
**adonde** *conj* where, whither
**adónde** *adv* where?, whither?; where, whither, e.g., **dígame Vd. adónde va** tell me where you are going
**adondequiera** *adv* anywhere; **adondequiera que** wherever, whithersoever
**adónico -ca** *adj & m* Adonic
**adonis** *m* (*pl:* **-nis**) Adonis (*handsome young man*); (*cap.*) *s* (myth.) Adonis
**adonizar** **§76** *vn & vr* to be a dandy, to be dandified; to be puffed up, be conceited
**adopción** *f* adoption
**adopcionismo** *m* adoptionism
**adopcionista** *adj & m* adoptionist
**adoptable** *adj* adoptable
**adoptador -dora** or **adoptante** *adj* adopting; *mf* adopter
**adoptar** *va* to adopt
**adoptivo -va** *adj* adoptive; strange, artificial, sham
**adoquín** *m* paving stone, paving block; dolt
**adoquinado** *m* cobblestone paving
**adoquinar** *va* to pave, to pave with cobblestones
**-ador -dora** *suffix adj* -ing, e.g., **acusador** accusing; **trabajador** working, hard-working; *suffix mf* -er, e.g., **acusador** accuser; **trabajador** worker; *suffix m* -er, e.g., **mostrador** counter; *suffix f* -er, e.g., **apisonadora** road roller
**ador** *m* turn to irrigate
**adorable** *adj* adorable
**adoración** *f* adoration, worship; **Adoración de los Reyes** (eccl.) Epiphany
**adorador -dora** *adj* adoring, worshiping; *mf* adorer, worshiper; **adorador del fuego** fire worshiper; *m* suitor
**adorar** *va & vn* to adore, to worship

**adormecedor -dora** *adj* soporific, sleep-producing
**adormecer §34** *va* to put to sleep; to calm, lull, ease; to quiet; *vr* to go to sleep, to fall asleep; to get numb; **adormecerse en** to persist in (*vices, pleasures, etc.*)
**adormecido -da** *adj* sleepy, drowsy; numb; calm, inactive
**adormecimiento** *m* falling asleep; sleepiness; numbness
**adormidera** *f* (bot.) opium poppy; **adormidera espinosa** (bot.) prickly poppy
**adormilar** *vr* to doze
**adormir §45** *va* to put to sleep; *vr* to go to sleep
**adormitar** *vr* to doze
**adornado -da** *adj* adorned, ornate; gifted, endowed; *m* adornment
**adornar** *va* to adorn; to embroider (*a story*)
**adornista** *mf* decorator
**adorno** *m* adornment, decoration; **adornos** *mpl* finery; **de adorno** ornamental (*e.g., plants*); **adorno de escaparate** window dressing; (fig.) window dressing
**adosado -da** *adj* (her.) addorsed
**adosar** *va* to lean; to push close; **adosar a** to lean (*something*) against; to push close to; to place with the back against
**adquirente** *mf* acquirer, purchaser
**adquiridor -dora** *mf* acquirer
**adquirir §56** *va* to acquire
**adquisición** *f* acquisition, acquirement
**adquisidor -dora** *mf* acquirer
**adquisitivo -va** *adj* (law) acquisitive
**adquisividad** *f* acquisitiveness
**adra** *f* turn; section of people of a town
**adraganto** *m* (bot.) tragacanth
**adral** *m* sideboard (*of a wagon*)
**adrede** or **adredemente** *adv* on purpose, purposely
**adrenalina** *f* (physiol. & pharm.) adrenalin
**adresógrafo** *m* addressograph
**adrián** *m* bunion; nest of magpies
**Adriano** *m* Adrian; Hadrian
**Adriático -ca** *adj* & *m* Adriatic
**adrizar §76** *va* (naut.) to right, to straighten
**adscribir §17,** 9 *va* to attribute; to assign, appoint
**adscripción** *f* attribution; assignment, appointment
**adscripto -ta** or **adscrito -ta** *pp of* **adscribir**
**adsorbente** *adj* adsorptive
**adsorber** *va* to adsorb
**adsorción** *f* adsorption
**aduana** *f* customhouse; **aduana seca** inland customhouse
**aduanar** *va* to enter (*goods*) at the customhouse; to pay duty on
**aduanero -ra** *adj* (pertaining to the) customhouse; *m* customhouse officer
**aduanilla** *f* (prov.) general store
**aduar** *m* Arab settlement; gipsy camp; (Am.) Indian camp or ranch
**adúcar** *m* floss, coarse silk; coarse silk cloth
**aducción** *f* adduction; (physiol.) adduction
**aducir §38** *va* to adduce; (physiol.) to adduct
**aductor** *adj* (physiol.) adducent; *m* (physiol.) adductor
**aduendado -da** *adj* fairylike
**adueñar** *vr* to take possession
**adufa** *f* lock, sluice
**adufe** *m* tambourine; (coll.) rattle-brained person
**aduja** *f* (naut.) turn, coil, fake
**adujada** *f* (naut.) coil (*of rope or cable*)
**adujar** *va* (naut.) to coil (*a rope or cable*); *vr* (naut.) to curl up (*e.g., to sleep*)
**aduje** *1st sg pret ind of* **aducir**
**adula** *f* common pasture
**adulación** *f* adulation
**adulador -dora** *adj* adulating, fawning; *m* adulator; *f* adulatress
**adular** *va* to adulate, to flatter, to fawn on
**adularia** *f* (mineral.) adularia
**adulatorio -ria** *adj* adulatory
**adulón -lona** *adj* (coll.) fawning, groveling; *mf* (coll.) bootlicker
**adúltera** *f* see **adúltero**
**adulteración** *f* adulteration
**adulterante** *adj* & *m* adulterant
**adulterar** *va* to adulterate; to wangle (*an account*); *vn* to adulterize, to commit adultery; *vr* to become adulterated
**adulterino -na** *adj* adulterine, adulterous; bastard; false, fake
**adulterio** *m* adultery
**adúltero -ra** *adj* adulterous; *m* adulterer; *f* adulteress
**adultez** *f* (Am.) adulthood
**adulto -ta** *adj* & *mf* adult
**adulzar §76** *va* to sweeten; to make more ductile, to soften (*metals*)
**adumbración** *f* (paint.) shadow
**adumbrar** *va* to shade; to conceal
**adunación** *f* or **adunamiento** *m* uniting, gathering
**adunar** *va* & *vr* to unite, join, gather
**adunco -ca** *adj* arched, curved
**adunia** *adv* in abundance
**adustez** *f* grimness, sternness, sullenness, gloominess
**adustión** *f* (surg.) cauterization
**adusto -ta** *adj* scorching hot; grim, stern, sullen, gloomy
**aduzco** *1st sg pres ind of* **aducir**
**advendré** *1st sg fut ind of* **advenir**
**advenedizo -za** *adj* foreign; strange; immigrant; parvenu, upstart; (Am.) inexperienced; *mf* foreigner; stranger, newcomer, outsider; immigrant; parvenu, upstart; nouveau riche; (Am.) novice, beginner
**advengo** *1st sg pres ind of* **advenir**
**advenidero -ra** *adj* coming, future
**advenimiento** *m* advent, coming; accession (*of a pontiff or sovereign*); **esperar el santo advenimiento** (coll.) to wait in vain; **segundo advenimiento** Second Advent
**advenir §92** *vn* to come, to arrive; to happen
**adventicio -cia** *adj* adventitious; (anat., biol. & med.) adventitious; *f* (anat.) adventitia
**adventismo** *m* Adventism
**adventista** *mf* Adventist
**adverado -da** *adj* certified
**adverbial** *adj* adverbial
**adverbializar §76** *va* to adverbialize
**adverbio** *m* adverb
**adversario -ria** *mf* adversary; **adversarios** *mpl* adversaria (*notes*)
**adversativo -va** *adj* & *f* (gram.) adversative
**adversidad** *f* adversity (*misfortune*)
**adverso -sa** *adj* adverse
**advertencia** *f* observation; notice, remark; warning; foreword
**advertidamente** *adv* deliberately, on purpose; with open eyes
**advertido -da** *adj* capable, clever, wide-awake
**advertir §62** *va* to notice, observe; to point out; to notify, warn, advise; *vn* **advertir en** to notice, observe; to take into account; *vr* to notice, become aware
**Adviento** *m* (eccl.) Advent
**advine** *1st sg pret ind of* **advenir**
**advocación** *f* name given to a church, chapel, or altar in dedication to the Virgin or a saint
**adyacencia** *f* adjacency
**adyacente** *adj* adjacent
**adyuvante** *adj* & *m* adjuvant
**aechadero** *m* sifting floor
**aechador -dora** *adj* sifting; *mf* sifter
**aechaduras** *fpl* siftings, chaff
**aechar** *va* to sift (*grain*)
**aecho** *m* sifting (*of grain*)
**Aelfrico** *m* Aelfric
**aeración** *f* aeration; ventilation; air conditioning
**aerear** *va* to aerate
**aéreo -a** *adj* aerial, (pertaining to) air; overhead, elevated; light, airy, fanciful; (poet.) tall, lofty
**aerífero -ra** *adj* aeriferous
**aerificación** *f* aerification
**aerificar §86** *va* to aerify
**aeriforme** *adj* aeriform
**aéro-atómico -ca** *adj* air-atomic
**aeróbico -ca** *adj* (bact.) aerobic
**aerobio** *m* (bact.) aerobe
**aerobús** *m* passenger plane

**aerodinámico -ca** *adj* aerodynamic; streamlined; *f* aerodynamics
**aeródromo** *m* aerodrome, airdrome; **aeródromo de urgencia** (aer.) emergency landing field
**aeroembolismo** *m* (path.) aeroembolism
**aeroescala** *f* var. of **aeroscala**
**aerofagia** or **aerofagía** *f* (path.) aerophagia, air swallowing
**aerofaro** *m* aerial beacon
**aerofluyente** *adj* streamlined
**aerofobia** *f* (path.) aerophobia
**aeroforme** *adj* streamlined
**aeróforo -ra** *adj* aeriferous; *m* (med. & min.) aerophore
**aerofoto** *f* aerophotograph
**aerofotografía** *f* aerophotography (*art or process*); aerophotograph (*picture*)
**aerofotografiar §90** *va* to photograph from the air
**aerofumigación** *f* crop dusting
**aerógrafo** *m* atomizer, air brush
**aerograma** *m* aerogram (*message carried by aircraft; radiogram*)
**aerolínea** *f* air line
**aerolito** *m* aerolite
**aerología** *f* aerology
**aerólogo -ga** *mf* aerologist
**aeromancía** *f* aeromancy
**aeromántico -ca** *adj* aeromantic; *mf* aeromancer
**aeromapa** *m* air map
**aeromecánico -ca** *adj* aeromechanical; *f* aeromechanics
**aeromedicina** *f* aviation medicine
**aerómetro** *m* aerometer
**aeromodelismo** *m* model-airplane building
**aeromodelista** *mf* model-airplane builder
**aeromodelo** *m* model airplane
**aeromotor** *m* windmill; aeromotor, aircraft motor
**aeromoza** *f* (aer.) air hostess, stewardess
**aeronato -ta** *adj* born in an aircraft in flight
**aeronauta** *mf* aeronaut
**aeronáutico -ca** *adj* aeronautic, aeronautical; *m* aeronautical engineer; *f* aeronautics
**aeronave** *f* airship; **aeronave cohete** rocket ship
**aeropista** *f* (aer.) landing strip
**aeroplano** *m* aeroplane
**aeroplano-nodriza** *m* (aer.) tanker plane
**aeropostal** *adj* air-mail
**aeropropulsor** *m* (aer.) airplane engine; **aeropropulsor por reacción** (aer.) jet engine
**aeropuerto** *m* airport
**aeroscala** *f* (aer.) fuel stop, transit point
**aeroscopio** *m* aeroscope
**aerosol** *m* (physical chem.) aerosol
**aerostación** *f* aerostation
**aeróstata** *mf* aerostat (*person*)
**aerostático -ca** *adj* aerostatic, aerostatical; *f* aerostatics
**aeróstato** *m* aerostat (*craft*)
**aerostero -ra** *adj* (pertaining to) aviation; *m* flyer; airman (*enlisted man*)
**aeroterapia** *f* aerotherapeutics, aerotherapy
**aeroterrestre** *adj* air-ground
**aerotransportado -da** *adj* airborne
**aerovía** *f* airway
**afabilidad** *f* affability
**afabilísimo -ma** *adj super* very or most affable
**afable** *adj* affable
**afabulación** *f* putting into the form of a fable; moral of a fable
**afabular** *va* to put into the form of a fable
**áfaca** *f* (bot.) lathyrus
**afamado -da** *adj* famed, noted, famous
**afamar** *va* to make famous; *vr* to become famous
**afán** *m* hard work; physical labor; anxiety, worry; zeal, eagerness; task, duty
**afanadamente** *adv* laboriously, zealously
**afanador -dora** *adj* hard-working, laborious; *mf* hard-worker, toiler
**afanar** *va* to press, harass, hurry; *vn* to strive, toil, labor; *vr* to busy oneself; to strive, toil, labor; **afanarse** + *ger* to busy oneself + *ger;* **afanarse en** or **por** + *inf* to strive to + *inf*
**afaníptero -ra** *adj* (zool.) aphanipterous
**afanita** *f* var. of **anfibolita**
**afanoso -sa** *adj* hard, heavy, laborious; hard-working
**afarallonado -da** *adj* craggy, cliffy
**afarolar** *vr* (Am.) to get all excited, to make a fuss
**afasia** *f* (path.) aphasia
**afeamiento** *m* making ugly, defacement; blame, condemnation
**afear** *va* to make ugly, to deform, deface; to blame, condemn
**afeblecer §34** *vr* to grow thin, to grow feeble
**afección** *f* affection; change, effect; (med.) affection
**afectabilidad** *f* susceptibility
**afectable** *adj* susceptible
**afectación** *f* affectation
**afectado -da** *adj* affected
**afectar** *va* to affect (*to pretend to have or feel; to assume*); to desire eagerly; to earmark; to sadden, afflict; to mortgage, to encumber; *vr* to be moved or stirred
**afectivo -va** *adj* affective, emotional
**afecto -ta** *adj* fond; annexed, attached; inclined, subject; harmed; **afecto de** affected with (*a disease*); *m* emotion; affection; moral instinct; **afecto moral** or **afecto superior** sense of human dignity
**afectuosidad** *f* affection, fondness
**afectuoso -sa** *adj* affectionate
**afeitada** *f* (Am.) shave, shaving
**afeitadera** *f* safety razor
**afeitado** *m* shave, shaving
**afeitanar** *va* (mach.) to cut off, to shear off
**afeitar** *va* to shave; to adorn, embellish; to paint (*e.g., the face*); to trim (*horse's mane or tail; branches, leaves of plant*); (taur.) to shave (*the bull's horns*); *vr* to shave; to paint; to become bored
**afeite** *m* fixing, arranging, adornment; cosmetic, make-up; grease paint, rouge
**afelio** *m* (astr.) aphelion
**afelpar** *va* to make like velvet or plush
**afeminación** *f* effeminacy; effemination
**afeminado -da** *adj* effeminate
**afeminamiento** *m* effeminacy; effemination
**afeminar** *va & vr* to effeminate
**aferente** *adj* (physiol.) afferent
**aféresis** *f* (*pl:* **-sis**) (gram.) aphaeresis
**aferrado -da** *adj* stubborn, obstinate
**aferramiento** *m* seizing, grasping; (naut.) mooring, anchoring; (naut.) furling; insistence, persistence
**aferrar** *va* to seize, grasp; to catch; to hook; (naut.) to moor, anchor; (naut.) to furl; *vn* (naut.) to moor, anchor; to insist; **aferrar a, con** or **en** to stick to (*e.g., an opinion*); **aferrar de** or **en** to seize, grasp; *vr* to interlock, to hook together; to insist; to cling; **aferrarse a, con,** or **en** to stick to (*e.g., an opinion*)
**aferruzado -da** *adj* angry, irate
**afestonado -da** *adj* festooned
**Afganistán, el** Afghanistan
**afgano -no** *adj & mf* Afghan; *m* Afghan (*language*)
**afianzable** *adj* bailable
**afianzamiento** *m* guarantee, security, bail; support, prop; fastening; (fig.) backing, support
**afianzar §76** *va* to guarantee, to vouch for; to fasten; to support, to prop up; to grasp; (fig.) to support, to back, to strengthen; *vr* to hold fast, to steady oneself
**afición** *f* fondness, liking, taste; zeal, ardor; fans, public; **de afición** as an amateur; (sport) amateur; **tomar afición a** to take a liking to; **afición ciega razón** love is blind
**aficionado -da** *adj* fond; amateur; *mf* amateur; lover, follower, fan
**aficionar** *va* to cause to like; *vr* **aficionarse a** to become fond of; to become a lover or follower of; **aficionarse a** + *inf* to become fond of + *ger*
**afiche** *m* (Am.) poster
**afidávit** *m* affidavit
**afídidos** or **áfidos** *mpl* (ent.) aphides
**afiebrado -da** *adj* feverish
**afijación** *f* (gram.) affixation

**afijo** *adj masc* (gram.) conjunctive (*pronoun*); *m* (gram.) affix
**afiladera** *f* grindstone
**afilado -da** *adj* sharp; pointed; peaked
**afilador -dora** *adj* sharpening; *m* sharpener, grinder (*person*); steel, knife sharpener; razor strop
**afiladura** *f* grinding, sharpening
**afilalápices** *m* (*pl:* **-ces**) pencil sharpener
**afilamiento** *m* peakedness (*of nose, fingers, face, etc.*)
**afilar** *va* to whet, grind, sharpen; to put a point or edge on; to strop (*a razor*); *vr* to sharpen, get sharp; to get thin or pointed (*said of nose, fingers, face, etc.*)
**afiliación** *f* affiliation
**afiliar §90 & regular** *va & vr* to affiliate; **afiliarse a** to affiliate oneself with, to affiliate with
**afiligranado -da** *adj* filigreed; fine, delicate; thin, slender
**afiligranar** *va* to filigree; to adorn, embellish
**áfilo -la** *adj* (bot.) aphyllose
**afilón** *m* steel, knife sharpener; razor strop
**afilorar** *va* (Am.) to adorn, bedeck
**afilosofado -da** *adj* like a philosopher, having the pretentions of a philosopher
**afín** *adj* near, bordering; like, similar; related; *mf* relative by marriage
**afinación** *f* refining, completion; (mus.) tuning
**afinadamente** *adv* completely, perfectly; smoothly, delicately
**afinador** *m* (mus.) tuner (*person*); (mus.) tuning hammer, tuning key
**afinadura** *f* var. of **afinación**
**afinamiento** *m* refining, completion; (mus.) tuning; refinement
**afinar** *va* to purify, refine, polish, perfect; to trim (*edges of a book*); (mus.) to tune; (mus.) to sing or play in tune
**afincado -da** *adj* owning real estate
**afincamiento** *m* settlement, location
**afincar §86** *vn & vr* var. of **fincar**
**afinidad** *f* affinity; (biol. & chem.) affinity; **por afinidad** by marriage
**afino** *m* refinement (*of metals*)
**afirmación** *f* affirmation
**afirmadamente** *adv* firmly
**afirmador -dora** *adj* affirming; *mf* affirmer
**afirmar** *va* to strengthen, secure, fasten; to assert, to affirm; *vn* to affirm; *vr* to be fastened, to hold fast; to make oneself firm, to steady oneself
**afirmativo -va** *adj & f* affirmative
**afistular** *va* to make fistulous
**aflato** *m* wind, draft; (fig.) afflatus
**aflautado -da** *adj* high-pitched; fluty, flutelike
**aflechado -da** *adj* arrow-shaped; (bot.) sagittate
**aflicción** *f* affliction, sorrow, grief
**aflictivo -va** *adj* afflictive
**aflicto -ta** *adj* afflicted
**afligidamente** *adv* sorrowfully, with affliction
**afligimiento** *m* var. of **aflicción**
**afligir §42** *va* to afflict, to grieve; *vr* to grieve; **afligirse de** + *inf* to be grieved at + *ger;* **afligirse con, de,** or **por** to be grieved at
**aflijón -jona** *adj* (Am.) gloomy, weepy
**aflogístico -ca** *adj* aphlogistic
**aflojamiento** *m* slackening, relaxing; loosening; diminution, abatement
**aflojar** *va* to slacken, to relax, to let go; to loosen (*e.g., a screw, the bowels*); *vn* to slacken, to relax, to slow up; to lessen, to abate; *vr* to come loose; to slacken; (Am.) to break wind
**aflorado -da** *adj* fine, elegant, excellent; (pertaining to) flour
**afloramiento** *m* (min.) outcrop, outcropping
**aflorar** *va* to sift; *vn* to crop out, crop up; (min.) to crop out, to outcrop
**afluencia** *f* flowing; inflow, influx; flow; rush (*of people*); affluence, abundance; crowd, jam; fluency, eloquence
**afluente** *adj* flowing; affluent, abundant; fluent, eloquent; *m* affluent, tributary
**afluir §41** *vn* to flow, to inflow; to pour (*said of a crowd of people, of a river, etc.*)
**aflujo** *m* (med.) afflux
**afmo.** or **af.mo** abr. of **afectísimo**
**afofar** *va* to make fluffy, make spongy; *vr* to become fluffy, become spongy
**afogarar** *va & vr* to burn
**afollar §77** *va* to blow (with bellows); to fold in the shape of bellows
**afondar** *va, vn & vr* to sink
**afonía** *f* (path.) aphonia
**afónico -ca** *adj* (path. & phonet.) aphonic
**afonización** *f* (phonet.) unvoicing
**afonizar §76** *va & vr* to unvoice
**áfono -na** *adj* aphonous
**aforado -da** *adj* privileged; assessed
**aforador** *m* gauger; appraiser; stream gauge; (coll.) winebibber
**aforamiento** *m* gauging, measuring; appraisement
**aforar** *va* to gauge, to measure; to appraise; (hyd.) to gauge; (law) to grant by emphyteusis; **§77** *va* to privilege, to grant privileges to (*a town*)
**aforestalación** *f* afforestation
**aforismo** *m* aphorism
**aforístico -ca** *adj* aphoristic
**aforo** *m* gauging, measuring; appraisement; seating capacity
**aforrar** *va* to line; (naut.) to serve (*a cable*); *vr* to put on heavy underwear; (coll.) to gorge
**aforro** *m* lining; (naut.) serving
**afortunado -da** *adj* fortunate; happy; stormy, tempestuous; *mf* lucky person
**afortunar** *va* to make happy
**afosar** *vr* (mil.) to entrench, dig in
**afoscar §86** *vr* to become misty or hazy
**afrailar** *va* to cut back, to trim (*trees, branches of trees*)
**afrancesado -da** *adj* Frenchified; *adj & mf* Francophile (*especially as applied to Spaniards in the eighteenth and nineteenth centuries*)
**afrancesamiento** *m* Francophilism; Gallicization
**afrancesar** *va* to Frenchify; to Gallicize; *vr* to Frenchify; to Gallicize; to become a Francophile
**afrecho** *m* bran
**afrenillar** *va* (naut.) to bridle (*the oars*)
**afrenta** *f* affront
**afrentar** *va* to affront; *vr* to be ashamed
**afrentoso -sa** *adj* insulting, ignominious
**afretar** *va* (naut.) to scrub and clean (*the hull*)
**África** *f* Africa; **el África del Norte** North Africa; **el África del Sudoeste** South-West Africa; **el África Ecuatorial Francesa** French Equatorial Africa; **el África Occidental Francesa** French West Africa; **el África Occidental Portuguesa** Portuguese West Africa; **el África Oriental Portuguesa** Portuguese East Africa
**africado -da** *adj* (phonet.) affricative; *f* (phonet.) affricate
**africanista** *mf* Africanist
**africano -na** *adj & mf* African
**áfrico** *m* var. of **ábrego**
**afriza** *f* (orn.) surfbird
**afroamericano -na** *adj & mf* Afro-American
**afro-asiático -ca** *adj* Afro-Asian
**afrodisia** *f* (path.) aphrodisia
**afrodisíaco -ca** *adj & m* aphrodisiac
**Afrodita** *f* (myth.) Aphrodite; (zool.) Aphrodite (*marine annelid*)
**afronitro** *m* wall saltpeter
**afrontamiento** *m* confrontation; meeting face to face
**afrontar** *va* to confront, to bring face to face; to face, to defy, to meet face to face; *vr* **afrontarse con** to confront, to meet face to face
**afta** *f* (path.) aphtha
**af.to** abr. of **afecto**
**aftoso -sa** *adj* aphthous; *f* (Am.) foot-and-mouth disease
**afuera** *adv* outside; *interj* look out!, gangway!; **afueras** *fpl* outskirts
**afuetear** *va* (Am.) to whip, to flog
**afufa** *f* (coll.) flight
**afufar** *vn & vr* (coll.) to flee, run away
**afufón** *m* (coll.) flight
**afusión** *f* (med.) affusion
**afuste** *m* (mil.) gun carriage

**afutrar** *vr* (Am.) to doll up
**agachada** *f* trick, wile; trickiness
**agachadiza** *f* (orn.) snipe; **hacer la agachadiza** (coll.) to duck (*to avoid being seen or as if to avoid being seen*)
**agachar** *va* (coll.) to bow, to lower (*e.g., the head*); *vr* (coll.) to crouch, squat; (coll.) to cower; (coll.) to fade out of sight
**agalbanado -da** *adj* var. of **galbanoso**
**agalerar** *va* (naut.) to tip (*an awning*)
**agáloco** *m* (bot.) agalloch, eaglewood
**agalla** *f* (bot.) nutgall; gill (*of fish*); ear lobe (*of bird*); windgall (*of horse*); **agallas** *fpl* beaks (*of shuttle*); tonsils; tonsilitis; (coll.) courage, energy, guts
**agallado -da** *adj* galled; *m* decoction of gallnuts
**agallón** *m* (bot.) large gallnut; hollow silver bead; large wooden bead
**agalludo -da** *adj* (Am.) stingy; (Am.) cunning; (Am.) daring, bold
**Agamenón** *m* (myth.) Agamemnon
**agamí** *m* (*pl:* **-míes**) (orn.) trumpeter
**agamitar** *vn* to bleat like a small deer
**ágamo -ma** *adj* (biol.) agamic
**agamogénesis** *f* (biol.) agamogenesis
**agamuzado -da** *adj* var. of **gamuzado**
**agangrenar** *vr* to gangrene
**Aganipe** *f* (myth.) Aganippe
**ágape** *m* banquet; love feast
**agar-agar** *m* agar, agar-agar
**agarbado -da** *adj* var. of **garboso**
**agarbanzado -da** *adj* like a chickpea; of the color of chickpeas
**agarbanzar** §76 *vn* to bud, sprout
**agarbar** *vr* to crouch, stoop, cower
**agarbillar** *va* to tie or bind in sheaves
**agareno -na** *adj & mf* Mohammedan
**agárico** *m* (bot.) agaric; **agárico blanco** (pharm.) agaric
**agarrada** *f* see **agarrado**
**agarradero** *m* handle; hold, grip; (coll.) shelter, protection; (naut.) anchorage
**agarrado -da** *adj* stingy, close-fisted; *f* (coll.) scrap, fight, brawl
**agarrador -dora** *adj* grasping, seizing; *m* flatiron holder; bailiff
**agarrafar** *va* (coll.) to grab, to clutch, to clinch
**agarrar** *va* to grasp, grab; to catch, take hold of; to filch; (coll.) to get, obtain; *vn* to take hold; to take root; to stick (*said of paint*); **agarrar de** to take hold of; **agarrar para** (Am.) to strike out for; *vr* to grasp each other, to grapple; to have a good hold, be on a sound footing; to worry; (coll.) to take hold of (*said of a disease*), e.g., **se le agarró la calentura** (coll.) the fever took hold of him; **agarrarse a** or **de** to seize, take a firm hold of
**agarre** *m* var. of **agarradero**
**agarro** *m* grasp, hold
**agarrochador** *m* goader
**agarrochar** *va* to goad, to prick with a spear
**agarrón** *m* (Am.) grab; (Am.) jerk; (Am.) hard throw; (Am.) row, fight, brawl
**agarrotamiento** *m* binding, jamming; stiffness
**agarrotar** *va* to bind with ropes; to squeeze hard, to pinch; to garrote; *vr* to get stiff, to get numb; to stick, get stuck; to bind, to jam
**agasajador -dora** *adj* kind, considerate, attentive
**agasajar** *va* to treat affectionately, to entertain royally, to shower with attentions, to lionize
**agasajo** *m* kindness, attention, show of affection; lionization; gift, favor; treat, refreshment; party (*in honor of someone*)
**ágata** *f* (mineral.) agate; (*cap.*) *s* Agatha; **ágata musgosa** (mineral.) moss agate
**agavanza** *f* dog rose (*fruit*)
**agavanzo** *m* (bot.) dog rose (*plant and fruit*)
**agave** *f* (bot.) agave
**agavillador -dora** *mf* binder (*of sheaves*); *f* binder (*machine*)
**agavillar** *va* to tie or bind in sheaves; *vr* to band together, to gang up
**agazapar** *va* (coll.) to seize, to grab; *vr* (coll.) to hide; (coll.) to crouch, to squat
**agencia** *f* agency; (Am.) pawnshop; **agencia de noticias** news agency
**agenciar** *va* to promote, to manage to bring about; *vr* to get along; to manage; to be put into effect
**agencioso -sa** *adj* active, diligent
**agenda** *f* notebook; agenda
**agenesia** *f* (physiol.) agennesis
**agente** *m* agent; policeman; (gram.) agent; **agente consular** consular agent; **agente de policía** policeman; detective; **agente provocador** agent provocateur; **agente reductor** (chem.) reducing agent; **agente secreto** secret agent; **agente viajero** agent, traveling salesman
**Ageo** *m* (Bib.) Haggai
**agérato** *m* (bot.) ageratum; (bot.) sweet maudlin
**agermanar** *vr* to join a gang of thieves; (Am.) to become Germanized, to imitate the Germans
**agestado -da** *adj* featured; **bien agestado** well-featured; **mal agestado** ill-featured
**agestión** *f* accumulation
**ageusia** *f* (path.) ageusia
**agibílibus** *m* (*pl:* **-bus**) (coll.) smartness, ability to look out for oneself; (coll.) smart fellow, fellow who knows how to look out for himself
**agible** *adj* feasible, workable
**agigantado -da** *adj* gigantic; notable, extraordinary
**agigantar** *va* to make huge, enormous, or immense; *vr* to become huge, enormous, or immense
**ágil** *adj* agile; light, flexible
**agilidad** *f* agility; lightness
**agilitar** or **agilizar** §76 *va* to make agile, to limber; to enable; *vr* to limber up
**agio** *m* agio; speculation; usury
**agiotador** *m* speculator; usurer
**agiotaje** *m* var. of **agio**
**agiotar** *vn* to speculate; to practice usury
**agiotista** *m* var. of **agiotador**
**agitable** *adj* agitable
**agitación** *f* agitation
**agitado -da** *adj* agitated, excited; blustering; rough (*sea*); exalted
**agitador -dora** *adj* agitating; *mf* agitator; *m* agitator, stirrer, shaker
**agitanado -da** *adj* gypsylike, gypsy
**agitar** *va* to agitate, to shake, to wave; to stir; to excite; *vn* to agitate (*to stir up discussion*); *vr* to be agitated; to shake, to wave; to get excited; to get rough (*said of the sea*)
**Aglaya** *f* (myth.) Aglaia
**aglobar** *va* to make into a ball, to heap together; to include
**aglomeración** *f* agglomeration; built-up area; density (*of building*); crowd
**aglomerado -da** *adj* agglomerate; (bot.) agglomerate; *m* briquet, coal briquet; (geol.) agglomerate
**aglomerante** *m* agglomerant, binder
**aglomerar** *va & vr* to agglomerate
**aglutinación** *f* agglutination
**aglutinado -da** *adj* agglutinate
**aglutinante** *adj* agglutinative; *m* sticking plaster; cementing material; (elec.) binder
**aglutinar** *va* to agglutinate; to stick together; to bind; *vr* to agglutinate; to cake
**aglutinina** *f* (biochem.) agglutinin
**agnación** *f* agnation
**agnado -da** *adj & mf* agnate
**agnición** *f* (rhet.) recognition
**agnocasto** *m* (bot.) agnus castus, chaste tree
**agnosticismo** *m* agnosticism
**agnóstico -ca** *adj & mf* agnostic
**agnusdéi** *m* Agnus Dei
**agobiado -da** *adj* weighed down; bent over
**agobiador -dora** or **agobiante** *adj* exhausting, oppressive
**agobiar** *va* to bow, to weigh down, to overburden; to exhaust, oppress; *vr* to bow, to be bowed; **agobiarse con, de,** or **por** to be weighed down or overburdened with
**agobio** *m* bowing; burden, exhaustion, oppression
**agogía** *f* water outlet, drainage canal
**agolpamiento** *m* thronging, crowding, rush
**agolpar** *vr* to throng, crowd together, flock
**agonal** *adj* agonistic; **agonales** *fpl* agones

**agonía** *f* agony (*anguish; death struggle*); yearning; end; **agonías** *m* (coll.) whiner, gloomy person

**agónico -ca** *adj* (pertaining to) death or dying; agonic

**agonioso -sa** *adj* (coll.) petulant, insistent

**agonístico -ca** *adj* agonistic; *f* agonistics

**agonizante** *adj* dying; *mf* dying person; *m* monk of the order of St. Camillus who assists the dying; prompter at university examinations

**agonizar §76** *va* to assist or attend (*the dying*); (coll.) to harass, importune; *vn* to be in the throes of death; to be dying out (*said, e.g., of a fire*)

**ágono -na** *adj* (geom.) agonic

**ágora** *f* agora

**agorador -dora** *adj & mf* var. of **agorero**

**agorafobia** *f* (psychopath.) agoraphobia

**agorar §19** *va* to predict, foretell, have a presentiment of; to prophesy

**agorero -ra** *adj* fortunetelling; ill-omened; superstitious; *mf* fortuneteller; foreteller of doom

**agorgojar** *vr* to be infested with grubs, mites, etc. (*said of grain*)

**agostadero** *m* summer pasture; summer-pasture time

**agostamiento** *m* burning, parching, withering

**agostar** *va* to burn up, parch, wither; to plow to get rid of August weeds; to kill untimely; *vn* to burn up, parch, wither; to graze on stubbles in the dry season; to spend August; *vr* to fade away (*said of hope, happiness, etc.*)

**agosteño -ña** *adj* (pertaining to) August

**agostero -ra** *adj* (pertaining to) August; *m* harvest helper; religious mendicant begging grain at harvest time

**agostino -na** *adj* (pertaining to) August

**agostizo -za** *adj* sickly, scrawny; (pertaining to) August; born in August

**agosto** *m* August; harvest, crop; harvest time; **hacer su agosto** (coll.) to make hay while the sun shines

**agotable** *adj* exhaustible

**agotado -da** *adj* exhausted; sold out; out-of-print

**agotador -dora** *adj* exhausting

**agotamiento** *m* exhaustion; draining; consumption

**agotar** *va* to wear out, exhaust, use up; to drain, drain off; to run through (*money*); *vr* to become exhausted, to be used up; to give out; to go out of print, to go out of stock, to be selling out

**agovía** *f* var. of **alborga**

**agracejina** *f* barberry (*fruit*)

**agracejo** *m* stunted little grape; (bot.) barberry; (prov.) fallen olive (*before ripening*)

**agraceño -ña** *adj* tart, sour

**agracero -ra** *adj* yielding unripe grapes; *f* cruet for green-grape juice

**agraciado -da** *adj* graceful, charming; pretty, nice; *mf* winner

**agraciar** *va* to grace, make graceful; to favor, honor, reward; to award; to pardon

**agracillo** *m* (bot.) barberry

**agradabilidad** *f* agreeableness

**agradabilísimo -ma** *adj super* very or most agreeable

**agradable** *adj* agreeable

**agradar** *va* to please, to be pleasing to; **agradar** + *inf* to please (*someone*) to + *inf*, to like to + *inf; vn* to be pleasing; *vr* to be pleased; **agradarse de** to be pleased at

**agradecer §34** *va* to thank; to reward; to be thankful or grateful for; **agradecerle a uno (que)** + *subj* to thank someone to + *inf*, e.g., **le agradeceremos llene la adjunta tarjeta** we will thank you to fill out the enclosed card; **agradecerle a uno una cosa** to thank a person for something

**agradecido -da** *adj* thankful, grateful; rewarding

**agradecimiento** *m* thanks, thankfulness, gratefulness

**agrado** *m* affability; pleasure, liking; **ser del agrado de** to be to the liking of

**agramadera** *f* scutch, brake

**agramador -dora** *adj* hemp-braking, flax-braking; *m* scutcher (*person*); scutch (*instrument*)

**agramaduras** *fpl* hemp refuse

**agramar** *va* to scutch, to brake (*flax or hemp*)

**agramilar** *va* to trim (*bricks*); to paint to resemble bricks; to mark out, to mark with a marking gauge

**agramiza** *f* stalk of hemp; hemp refuse

**agrandamiento** *m* enlargement, aggrandizement

**agrandar** *va* to enlarge, aggrandize; *vr* to grow larger; to aggrandize oneself

**agranelar** *va* to grain, to pebble (*leather*)

**agranitado -da** *adj* granitelike, granite

**agranujado -da** *adj* grain-shaped, grainlike, grained; pimply; rascally

**agranujar** *va* to grain, give a granular finish to; *vr* to become grained; (coll.) to turn into a rascal, to get to be worthless

**agrarianismo** *m* agrarianism

**agrariense** *adj & mf* agrarian

**agrario -ria** *adj* agrarian

**agravación** *f* aggravation, exaggeration, worsening

**agravador -dora** *adj* aggravating, oppressing

**agravamiento** *m* var. of **agravación**

**agravante** *adj* aggravating

**agravar** *va* to weigh down, make heavier; to increase (*taxes*); to aggravate; to make worse; to exaggerate; to oppress; *vr* to become aggravated; to get worse

**agravatorio -ria** *adj* aggravating; (law) mandatory

**agraviamiento** *m* wrong, offensiveness

**agraviante** *adj* offending, offensive

**agraviar** *va* to wrong, to offend; *vr* to take offense; **agraviarse de** or **por** to be offended at

**agravio** *m* wrong, offense; burden, weight; **agravios de hecho** assault and battery

**agravioso -sa** *adj* offensive, insulting

**agraz** *m* (*pl:* **-graces**) sour grape, sour grapes; sour-grape juice; (bot.) red-berried mistletoe; (bot.) mountain currant; (coll.) bitterness, displeasure; **echar el agraz en el ojo a** to hurt, to injure the feelings of; **en agraz** prematurely

**agrazada** *f* verjuice, green-grape juice

**agrazar §76** *va* to annoy, embitter; *vn* to taste sour, have a sour taste

**agrazón** *m* wild grape; wild-gooseberry bush; (coll.) displeasure, annoyance

**agrecillo** *m* (bot.) barberry

**agredir §53** *va* to attack, assault; to insult

**agregación** *f* aggregation

**agregado -da** *mf* (Am.) tenant farmer; (Am.) household guest; *m* aggregate; concrete block; acting employee; attaché

**agregar §59** *va* to add; to annex; to attach, to detail; to admit; to appoint; *vr* to join; to intrude

**agremán** *m* braid, ribbon

**agremiación** *f* unionization

**agremiado** *m* union man, unionist

**agremiar** *va* to unionize; *vr* to become unionized

**agresión** *f* aggression

**agresividad** *f* aggressiveness, self-assertion

**agresivo -va** *adj* aggressive; offensive

**agresor -sora** *adj* aggressive; *mf* aggressor

**agreste** *adj* rustic, country; wild, rough; uncouth

**agrete** *adj* sourish

**agriar §90 & regular** *va* to make sour; to exasperate, to aggravate; *vr* to sour, turn sour; to become exasperated

**agriaz** *m* (*pl:* **-griaces**) (bot.) China tree

**agrícola** *adj* agricultural; (pertaining to the) farm; *mf* agriculturalist

**agricultor -tora** *mf* agriculturalist, agriculturist; farmer

**agricultura** *f* agriculture

**agridulce** *adj* bittersweet

**agriera** *f* (Am.) heartburn

**agrietamiento** *m* cracking; crack

**agrietar** *va & vr* to crack

**agrifolio** *m* (bot.) holly

**agrilla** *f* var. of **acedera**

**agrillar** *vr* var. of **grillar**

**agrimensor** *m* surveyor

**agrimensura** *f* surveying
**agrimonia** *f* (bot.) agrimony
**agringar** §59 *vr* (Am.) to act like a gringo
**agrio -gria** *adj* sour, acrid; citrus (*fruit*); uneven, rough; brittle, unmalleable; (fig.) sour, mordant; *m* sour juice; sour gravy; **agrios** *mpl* citrus fruit; citrus fruit trees; citrus juices
**agrión** *m* (bot.) China tree; (vet.) callus on horse's knee
**Agripa** *m* Agrippa
**agripalma** *f* (bot.) motherwort
**agrisado -da** *adj* grayish
**agrisetado -da** *adj* flowered-silk
**agro** *m* land, countryside
**agronometría** *f* soil science
**agronomía** *f* agronomy
**agronómico -ca** *adj* agronomic
**agrónomo** *m* agronomist
**agropecuario -ria** *adj* farm, farming (*pertaining to cattle and crop raising*)
**agróstide** *f* (bot.) redtop
**agrumar** *va & vr* to clot, to curd
**agrupación** *f* grouping, group, cluster, crowd
**agrupar** *va & vr* to group, to cluster
**agrura** *f* sourness, acerbity; citrus fruit trees; **agruras** *fpl* citrus fruit
**ag.to** abr. of **agosto**
**agua** *f* water; tide; slope (*of a roof*); (naut.) leak; (naut.) sea route; **aguas** *fpl* waters, mineral springs; water, urine; water, sparkle (*of precious stones*); watered effect (*e.g., of silk*); **bailarle a uno el agua** to dance attendance on a person; **cubrir aguas** to have under roof; to have the roof put on; **cubrir aguas en** to put the roof on (*a new building*); **entre aguas** floating under water; **entre dos aguas** (coll.) undecided, without taking sides; **hacer agua** (naut.) to make water (*to leak*); **hacer aguas** to make water (*to urinate*); **hacerle a uno la boca agua** to make one's mouth water; **hacerse** or **volverse agua de cerrajas** (coll.) to fizzle out, to flop; **hacerse agua en la boca** to melt in one's mouth; **¡hombre al agua!** man overboard!; **pescar en agua turbia** (coll.) to fish in troubled waters; **tan claro como el agua** as clear as crystal; **agua abajo** downstream; **agua amoniacal** (chem.) ammonia water; **agua arriba** upstream; **agua bendita** holy water; **agua blanda** soft water; **agua corriente** running water; **agua de alhucema** lavender water; **agua de azahar** orange-flower water; **agua de cepas** (coll.) wine; **agua de cerrajas** (coll.) trash, trifle; **agua de Colonia** eau de Cologne; **agua de cristalización** (chem.) water of crystallization; **agua delgada** soft water; **agua de bebida** drinking water; **agua de espliego** lavender water; **agua de Javel** Javel water; **agua de nafa** orange-flower water; **agua de pantoque** (naut.) bilge water; **agua de pie** running water; **agua de rosas** rose water; **agua de seltz** seltzer water; **agua de socorro** emergency baptism; **agua de Vichy** Vichy water; **agua dulce** fresh water; **agua fuerte** aqua fortis; etching; **agua gaseosa** carbonated water; **agua helada** ice water; **agua herrada** water in which a red-hot iron has been cooled; **agua lluvia** rain water; **agua manantial** spring water; **agua mineral** mineral water; **agua mineromedicinal** mineral water (*for medicinal use*); **agua nieve** sleet; **agua oxigenada** hydrogen peroxide; **agua pesada** (chem.) heavy water; **agua regia** aqua regia; **aguas de albañal** sewage; **aguas de creciente** rising tide; **aguas de menguante** ebb tide; **aguas madres** mother liquid; **aguas mayores** equinoctial tide; feces; **aguas menores** ordinary tide; urine, urination; **aguas muertas** neap tide; **aguas negras** sewage; **aguas vivas** spring tide; **agua viento** driving rain, driving rain and snow; **agua viva** running water, spring
**aguacatal** *m* avocado orchard
**aguacate** *m* (bot.) avocado (*tree and fruit*); pear-shaped emerald
**aguacero** *m* shower, heavy shower
**aguacibera** *f* water to start growth in new-sown ground
**aguacha** *f* foul, stagnant water
**aguachar** *m* pool, puddle; *va* to flood; (Am.) to tame, domesticate; *vr* (Am.) to get fat (*said of horses*)
**aguacharnar** *va* to flood
**aguachento -ta** *adj* (Am.) watery (*e.g., fruit*)
**aguachinar** *va* (dial.) var. of **aguacharnar**
**aguachirle** *m* cheap wine; slosh, slipslop; trifle
**aguada** *f* see **aguado**
**aguadero -ra** *adj* rain, e.g., **capa aguadera** rain cloak; *m* watering place; **aguaderas** *fpl* framework for water vessels on horseback or muleback; (orn.) upper wing coverts
**aguadija** *f* water in a pimple or sore
**aguado -da** *adj* watery, watered; soaked; abstemious; spoiled, interrupted; (Am.) weak, washed out; *f* source of water; mine flood; water coloring; water color; gouache (*method and picture*); (naut.) water supply; (rail.) watering station; **hacer aguada** (naut.) to take water
**aguador -dora** *mf* water carrier, water vendor; *m* paddle, bucket (*of waterwheel*); (orn.) black phoebe
**aguaducho** *m* stall for selling water, refreshment stand; flood, freshet
**aguadura** *f* (vet.) hoof abscess; (vet.) surfeit
**aguafiestas** *mf* (*pl:* **-tas**) kill-joy, wet blanket, crapehanger
**aguafortista** *mf* etcher, aquafortist
**aguafuerte** *f* aqua fortis; etching; **grabar al aguafuerte** to etch
**aguafuertista** *mf* etcher, aquafortist
**aguagoma** *f* gum water
**aguaitacamino** *m* (orn.) goatsucker
**aguaitada** *f* (Am.) var. of **aguaitamiento**
**aguaitamiento** *m* spying, watching
**aguaitar** *va* to spy upon, lie in wait for
**aguajaque** *m* fennel gum
**aguajas** *fpl* var. of **ajuagas**
**aguaje** *m* watering place; water supply; strong sea current; tidal wave; wake (*of ship*)
**agualluvia** *f* rain water
**aguamala** *f* (zool.) jellyfish
**aguamanil** *m* ewer, wash jug, wash pitcher; washstand
**aguamanos** *m* (*pl:* **-nos**) water for washing hands; washstand
**aguamar** *m* (zool.) jellyfish
**aguamarina** *f* aquamarine (*mineral and color*)
**aguamarincrisolita** *f* (mineral.) aquamarine chrysolite
**aguamasa** *f* (Am.) crushed corn washings
**aguamelado -da** *adj* soaked or bathed in honey and water
**aguamiel** *f* hydromel, honey and water; maguey juice
**aguanieve** *f* sleet
**aguanieves** *f* (*pl:* **-ves**) (orn.) wagtail
**aguanosidad** *f* wetness, wateriness; aqueous substance (*in the body*)
**aguanoso -sa** *adj* wet, watery, soaked
**aguantable** *adj* tolerable, bearable, endurable
**aguantaderas** *fpl* (coll.) long-suffering, forbearance
**aguantar** *va* to hold (*e.g., one's breath*); to hold back (*laughter*); to hold up, sustain; to bear, endure, tolerate, stand; *vn* to last, hold out; *vr* to restrain oneself; to hold on
**aguante** *m* patience, endurance; strength, vigor
**aguañón** *adj* see **maestro**
**aguapié** *m* small wine; slosh, slipslop; running water
**aguar** §23 *va* to water; to spoil, mar, throw cold water on; to lighten (*a burden*); *vr* to collapse from overwork or drinking when overheated (*said of beasts of burden*); to flood; to become thin or watery
**aguardada** *f* wait, waiting
**aguardadero** *m* var. of **aguardo**
**aguardador -dora** *adj* waiting; *mf* person who waits
**aguardar** *va* to await, to wait for; to give an extension of time to; *vn* to wait; **aguardar a** + *inf* to wait to + *inf;* **aguardar a que** + *subj* to wait until + *ind*
**aguardentado -da** *adj* brandied; tipsy, drunk
**aguardentería** *f* liquor store

**aguardentero -ra** *mf* brandy maker; brandy vendor; *f* liquor flask, brandy flask
**aguardentoso -sa** *adj* brandy; brandyish; whisky (*voice*)
**aguardiente** *m* brandy; rum, spirituous liquor (*any intoxicating liquor*); **aguardiente de cabeza** first running (*from still*); **aguardiente de caña** rum; **aguardiente de cerezas** cherry brandy; **aguardiente de manzana** applejack
**aguardillado -da** *adj* having a garret; like a garret
**aguardo** *m* hiding place, hunter's blind
**aguarrás** *m* (*pl:* **-rrases**) oil of turpentine
**aguasal** *f* brine; pickle
**aguasar** *vr* to become countrified
**aguasol** *m* chickpea mildew; (Am.) corn stubble
**aguate** *m* (Am.) prickle (*of cactus, etc.*)
**aguatero -ra** *mf* (Am.) water carrier, water vendor
**aguatinta** *f* var. of **acuatinta**
**aguatocha** *f* water pump
**aguatoso -sa** *adj* (Am.) spiny, prickly
**aguaturma** *f* (bot.) Jerusalem artichoke (*plant and tuber*)
**aguaverde** *f* (zool.) green jellyfish
**aguaviento** *m* driving rain, driving rain and snow
**aguavientos** *m* (*pl:* **-tos**) (bot.) Jerusalem sage
**aguavilla** *f* (bot.) bearberry
**aguaza** *f* aqueous humor; sap
**aguazal** *m* pool, puddle
**aguazar** **§76** *va* to make marshy; to flood; *vr* to become marshy
**aguazo** *m* (paint.) gouache (*picture*)
**aguazoso -sa** *adj* var. of **aguanoso**
**aguazul** *m* or **aguazur** *m* var. of **algazul**
**agudeza** *f* acuteness; acuity; sharpness; briskness; witticism
**agudización** *f* sharpening; aggravation
**agudizar** **§76** *va* to sharpen, make more acute; *vr* to become aggravated, to get worse
**agudo -da** *adj* acute; sharp; keen; brisk; witty; (gram.) oxytone
**Águeda** *f* Agatha
**agüera** *f* irrigation ditch
**agüero** *m* augury; forecast; omen, sign; **ser de buen agüero** to augur well; **ser de mal agüero** to augur ill
**aguerrido -da** *adj* inured to war, inured, hardened
**aguerrir** **§53** *va* to inure to war, to inure, to harden; *vr* to become inured to war, to become inured, to become hardened
**aguijada** *f* goad, spur; plowstaff
**aguijador -dora** *adj* goading, inciting; *mf* goader, inciter
**aguijadura** *f* goading, inciting
**aguijar** *va* to goad, incite, urge on, hasten; to hasten (*one's steps*); *vn* to hurry along, to move fast
**aguijón** *m* spur, goad; sting (*of insects*); prickle, thorn (*of plants*); stimulus, incitement; **cocear** or **dar coces contra el aguijón** (coll.) to kick against the pricks
**aguijonada** *f* prick, sting; prick with goad or spur
**aguijonar** *va* var. of **aguijonear**
**aguijonazo** *m* var. of **aguijonada**
**aguijonear** *va* to goad, spur, incite, urge on; to sting
**águila** *f* (orn.) eagle; (fig.) eagle (*emblem; U.S. coin*); (Am.) swindler, cheat; (*cap.*) *f* (astr.) Eagle; **águila barbuda** (orn.) bearded eagle, bearded vulture, lammergeier; **águila caudal** (orn.) golden eagle; **águila de cabeza blanca** (orn.) bald eagle, white-headed eagle; **águila gallinera** (orn.) Egyptian vulture; **águila imperial** (orn.) imperial eagle; **águila marina** (orn.) sea eagle, white-tailed eagle; **águila moneva** (orn.) harpy eagle (*Pithecophaga jefferyi*); **águila pescadora** (orn.) fish hawk; **águila ratonera** (orn.) buzzard; **águila real** (orn.) golden eagle; *m* lively person, keen person; (ichth.) eagle ray
**aguileño -ña** *adj* aquiline; sharp-featured; *f* (bot.) columbine
**aguilera** *f* eagle's nest, eyrie
**aguilón** *m* large eagle; boom, jib (*of crane or derrick*); gable (*of roof*); slate or tile cut obliquely; square terra-cotta pipe
**aguilucho** *m* (orn.) eaglet
**agüilla** *f* moisture, seepage
**aguinaldo** *m* Christmas gift, Epiphany gift; (bot.) bindweed; (Am.) Christmas carol
**agüista** *mf* resorter, frequenter of a spa
**aguja** *f* needle (*for sewing; of phonograph; obelisk*); bodkin; hatpin; steeple, spire; hand (*of watch, clock, etc.*); pointer (*of dial, etc.*); style (*of sundial*); (rail.) switch rail; (ichth.) sailfish; (ichth.) needlefish; (bot.) lady's-comb; needlework; **agujas** *fpl* ribs (*of animal*); (rail.) switch; **alabar sus agujas** to blow one's own horn; **buscar una aguja en un pajar** to look for a needle in a haystack; **cuartear la aguja** (naut.) to box the compass; **aguja capotera** darning needle; sail needle; **aguja colchonera** tufting needle; **aguja de coser** sewing needle; **aguja de gancho** crochet needle; **aguja de hacer media** knitting needle; **aguja de mar** (ichth.) garfish; (ichth.) sailfish; **aguja de marear** mariner's needle, ship's needle; **aguja descarriladora** derail switch; **aguja de zurcir** darning needle; **aguja hipodérmica** hypodermic needle; **aguja imanada** or **magnética** magnetic needle; **aguja para marcar** center punch; **aguja salmera** upholsterer's needle; **aguja saquera** pack needle, packing needle
**agujazo** *m* prick or jab with a needle
**agujerar** or **agujerear** *va* to pierce, perforate, make a hole or holes in
**agujería** *f* needle factory
**agujero** *m* hole; maker or vendor of needles; pincushion; **quien acecha por agujero, ve su duelo** curiosity killed a cat; **agujero de hombre** manhole
**agujeruelo** *m* little hole
**agujeta** *f* needle (*of a syringe*); shoestring; (archaic) lace, string, or shoestring with tips; (orn.) godwit; **agujetas** *fpl* stitches, twinges
**agujetería** *f* (archaic) shoestring shop
**agujetero -ra** *mf* (archaic) maker or vendor of shoestrings; switch tender; *m* (Am.) needle case, pincushion
**agujón** *m* hatpin; (ichth.) needlefish
**agujuela** *f* brad
**aguosidad** *f* wateriness; aqueous humor, lymph
**aguoso -sa** *adj* watery
**agur** *interj* (coll.) bye-bye!, so long!
**agusanamiento** *m* worminess
**agusanar** *vr* to get wormy
**Agustín** *m* Austin, Augustine; **San Agustín** Saint Augustine; St. Augustine (*Florida city*)
**agustinianismo** *m* Augustinianism
**agustiniano -na** or **agustino -na** *adj & mf* Augustinian
**agutí** *m* (*pl:* **-tíes**) var. of **acutí**
**aguzadero -ra** *adj* sharpening; *m* place where wild boars whet their tusks; *f* sharpener, whetstone
**aguzador -dora** *adj* sharpening; *mf* sharpener; *f* drill sharpener
**aguzadura** *f* sharpening; steel or iron for ploughshare
**aguzamiento** *m* sharpening
**aguzanieves** *f* (*pl:* **-ves**) (orn.) wagtail
**aguzar** **§76** *va* to sharpen, to point, to whet; to incite, stir up; to stare at; **aguzar las orejas** to prick up one's ears; **aguzar la vista** to look sharp; **aguzar los dientes** (coll.) to whet one's appetite
**aguzonazo** *m* lunge, thrust, stab
**ah** *interj* ah!; **¡ah del barco!** ship ahoy!
**ah-chis** *interj* kerchoo!
**ahebrado -da** *adj* fibrous, thready
**ahechadero** *m* var. of **aechadero**
**ahechador -dora** *adj & mf* var. of **aechador**
**ahechaduras** *fpl* var. of **aechaduras**
**ahechar** *va* var. of **aechar**
**ahecho** *m* var. of **aecho**
**ahelear** *va* to make bitter; *vn* to taste bitter
**ahelgado -da** *adj* jag-toothed, snaggle-toothed
**aherrojamiento** *m* fettering, shackling
**aherrojar** *va* to fetter, to shackle; to subjugate, oppress

**aherrumbrar** *va* to rust; to give the taste or color of iron to; *vr* to rust; to take on the taste or color of iron
**ahervorar** *vr* to generate heat (*said of stored grain*)
**ahí** *adv* there; **de ahí que** with the result that; **por ahí** that way; about, more or less
**ahidalgado -da** *adj* noble, high-born, chivalrous
**ahigadado -da** *adj* liver-colored; (archaic) fearless, intrepid
**ahijadero** *m* (prov.) sheep nursery
**ahijado -da** *mf* godchild; protégé
**ahijar** §99 *va* to adopt; to impute; *vn* to beget offspring; to sprout
**ahilar** §99 *va* to line up; *vn* to go in single file; *vr* to faint from hunger; to grow thin through illness; to grow poorly; to turn, to grow sour (*said, e.g., of wine*)
**ahílo** *m* faintness, weakness
**ahincadamente** *adv* hard, insistently, earnestly
**ahincar** §86 & §99 *va* to press, urge; to importune; *vr* to hasten
**ahínco** *m* earnestness, zeal, ardor
**ahitar** §99 *va* to surfeit, cloy, satiate, stuff; *vr* to get surfeited
**ahitera** *f* (coll.) acute indigestion, bellyache
**ahíto -ta** *adj* surfeited, gorged, stuffed; disgusted, fed up; having indigestion; *m* surfeit; indigestion
**ahobachonado -da** *adj* (coll.) lazy, shiftless
**ahobachonar** *vr* (coll.) to become lazy or shiftless
**ahocicar** §86 *va* to stick the nose of (*a dog or cat*) in the dirt it has made; (coll.) to get the best of (*a person*) in an argument; *vn* (naut.) to dip the bows under; (Am.) to give in (*in an argument*)
**ahocinado** *m* gorge, narrow passage (*in stream or river*)
**ahocinar** *vr* to pass through a narrow gorge (*said of streams, rivers, etc.*)
**ahogadero** *m* hangman's rope; crowded place; throatband, throatlatch
**ahogadizo -za** *adj* easily drowned or stifled; dry, pulpy, hard to swallow (*said of fruit*); sinkable, nonfloating (*said of wood*)
**ahogado -da** *adj* drowned, suffocated; close, unventilated; sunk, swamped, overwhelmed; **morir** or **perecer ahogado** to drown; *mf* drowned person, suffocated person
**ahogador -dora** *mf* choker; *m* choker, collar
**ahogamiento** *m* drowning; suffocation, choking
**ahogar** §59 *va* to drown; to suffocate, smother, quench, choke; to slake (*lime*); to soak (*plants*); to oppress; to kill (*e.g., a legislative bill*); to quench, extinguish; to stalemate; to drown (*e.g., one's sorrows*); *vr* to drown, suffocate, smother; to drown oneself
**ahogo** *m* oppression, constriction; shortness of breath; great sorrow or affliction; pinch, stringency
**ahoguijo** *m* (vet.) quinsy
**ahoguío** *m* oppression or constriction (of the chest)
**ahombrado -da** *adj* (coll.) mannish
**ahombrar** *vr* to become mannish
**ahondar** *va* to deepen; to make deeper, to dig deeper; to probe, to go deep into, to study thoroughly; *vn* to go deep; to go deeper; to sink, to dip; to become thoroughly versed; *vr* to go deep; to sink, to dip
**ahonde** *m* deepening; digging; probing
**ahora** *adv* now; in a little while; a little while ago; **de ahora en adelante** from now on; **por ahora** for the present; **ahora bien** now then, so then; **ahora mismo** right now; **ahora que** but
**ahorcado -da** *adj* hanging, hanging by the neck; ruined; grieved; anxious, worried; *mf* hangee, person who has been hanged or who has hanged himself; person condemned to be hanged
**ahorcadura** *f* hanging
**ahorcajar** *vr* to sit astride, to get astride; **ahorcajarse en** to sit astraddle on, to straddle
**ahorcaperro** *m* (naut.) slip knot; (naut.) running bowline
**ahorcar** §86 *va* to hang (*to execute*); *vr* to hang, be hanged; to hang oneself; (mach.) to jam, get caught
**ahorita** *adv* (coll.) right now, right away; (coll.) just now, a minute ago
**ahormar** *va* to put on a form or last; to shape, fit, adjust; to break in (*e.g., shoes*); to mold (*someone's character*)
**ahornagamiento** *m* parching
**ahornagar** §59 *vr* to become parched (*said of the earth and its crops*)
**ahornar** *va* to put into the oven or furnace; *vr* to burn on the outside before being baked inside (*said of bread*)
**ahorquillado -da** *adj* forked; (shaped like a) hairpin
**ahorquillar** *va* to prop up (*limbs of trees*) with forks; to shape like a fork or a hairpin
**ahorrable** *adj* easy to save or spare
**ahorradamente** *adv* freely, easily
**ahorrado -da** *adj* saving, thrifty; free, emancipated
**ahorrador -dora** *adj* saving; freeing; *mf* saver; emancipator
**ahorramiento** *m* saving, economy; emancipation
**ahorrar** *va* to save, to spare; to free (*e.g., a slave*); *vr* to save or spare oneself; **no ahorrarse con nadie** or **no ahorrárselas con nadie** to be afraid of nobody
**ahorrativa** *f* see **ahorrativo**
**ahorratividad** *f* frugality; (coll.) stinginess
**ahorrativo -va** *adj* saving, thrifty, stingy; *f* economy
**ahorrillos** *mpl* small savings
**ahorro** *m* economy; saving (*e.g., of time*); **ahorros** *mpl* savings
**ahoyadura** *f* digging holes; hole
**ahoyar** *va* to dig holes in
**ahuate** *m* (Am.) prickly down (*of certain plants*)
**ahuatoso -sa** *adj* (Am.) spiny, prickly
**ahuchador -dora** *adj* hoarding, miserly; *mf* hoarder, miser
**ahuchar** §99 *va* to hoard
**ahuchear** *va* to whistle at, to hiss
**ahucheo** *m* whistling, hissing
**ahuecado -da** *adj* hollow; (fig.) hollow (*sound, voice*)
**ahuecador** *m* crinoline; hoops (*of hoop skirt*); curved chisel
**ahuecamiento** *m* hollowing; hollow, hollowness; loosening, softening; swaggering
**ahuecar** §86 *va* to hollow, hollow out; to loosen, soften, fluff up (*earth, wool, etc.*); to make (*the voice*) deep and solemn; *vn* (coll.) to beat it; *vr* to swagger, to put on airs
**ahuehué** *m* or **ahuehuete** *m* (Am.) Montezuma cypress
**ahuesado -da** *adj* bonelike, bony
**ahuevar** *va* to make egg-shaped; to clarify (*wine*) with white of eggs
**ahumada** *f* see **ahumado**
**ahumadero** *m* smokehouse
**ahumado -da** *adj* smoked, smoky; (Am.) drunk; *m* smoking, curing; *f* smoke signal
**ahumamiento** *m* smoking, curing with smoke
**ahumar** §99 *va* to treat with smoke, to fill with smoke, to cure with smoke; *vn* to be smoky, to emit smoke; *vr* to get smoked up; to look smoky, to taste smoky; (coll.) to get tipsy, get drunk
**ahurragado -da** *adj* badly cultivated
**ahusado -da** *adj* tapering; spindle-shaped
**ahusamiento** *m* taper, tapering
**ahusar** *va & vr* §99 *va & vr* to taper
**ahuyentar** *va* to put to flight; to scare away; to drive away, to drive out, banish; *vr* to flee, run away
**aijada** *f* goad, spur
**ailanto** *m* (bot.) ailanthus
**aína** or **aínas** *adv* (archaic) soon; (archaic) easily; (archaic) almost
**aindiado -da** *adj* (Am.) Indian-looking
**airado -da** *adj* angry, irate; wild, violent; depraved
**airamiento** *m* anger, wrath

**airar** §75 *va* to anger; *vr* to get angry; **airarse con** or **contra** to get angry with (*a person*); **airarse de** or **por** to get angry at (*a thing*)
**aire** *m* air; pace (*way of stepping: walk, trot, gallop, etc.*); **al aire libre** in the open air; **darse aire** to fan oneself; **darse aires** to put on airs; **darse aires de** to claim to be, to boast of being; **estar en el aire** (coll.) to be in the wind (*to be impending*); **¿qué aires traen a Vd. acá?** (coll.) what brings you here?, what are you doing here?; **tomar el aire** to go out to get some fresh air, to go out for a walk; **volar por los aires** to fly through the air; **aire acondicionado** air conditioning; **aire colado** cold draft; **aire comprimido** compressed air; **aire detonante** firedamp; **aire líquido** liquid air
**aireación** *f* aeration
**airear** *va* to air, ventilate; to aerate; *vr* to get aired, to take the air; to catch a cold
**airón** *m* aigrette; panache; (elec.) aigrette; (orn.) heron, gray heron
**airosidad** *f* gracefulness, elegance, majesty
**airoso -sa** *adj* airy; drafty; breezy; graceful, light; grand, resplendent; successful; **quedar** or **salir airoso** to come off with flying colors
**aislación** *f* insulation; **aislación de sonido** soundproofing
**aislacionismo** *m* isolationism
**aislacionista** *adj & mf* isolationist
**aisladamente** *adv* singly, alone
**aislador -dora** *adj* isolating; insulating; *m* (elec.) insulator
**aislamiento** *m* isolation, detachment; insulation; insulating material
**aislar** §75 *va* to isolate; to detach, separate; to insulate; *vr* to be isolated, to live in seclusion
**ajá** *interj* (coll.) fine!, good!, aha!
**ajada** *f* garlic sauce
**ajadizo -za** *adj* easily mussed or crumpled
**ajadura** *f* withering; mussing; tampering; wear and tear
**ajaja** *f* (orn.) spoonbill
**ajamiento** *m* withering; mussing, rumpling; tampering; abuse, insult
**ajamonar** *vr* (coll.) to get fat and middle-aged (*said of a woman*); (Am.) to wither, to dry up
**ajaquecar** §86 *vr* to get a headache
**ajar** *m* garlic field; *va* to wither; to muss, rumple; to tamper with; to abuse; *vr* to wither, to wither away, to waste away; to get mussed
**ajaraca** *f* (arch.) arabesque
**ajarafe** *m* tableland; flat roof, terrace
**ajardinar** *va* to landscape
**aje** *m* complaint, indisposition, weakness
**ajedrea** *f* (bot.) savory; **ajedrea de jardín** (bot.) savory, summer savory
**ajedrecista** *mf* chess player
**ajedrez** *m* chess; chess set
**ajedrezado -da** *adj* checkered; *m* checkerwork
**ajedrista** *mf* chess player
**ajenabe** *m* or **ajenabo** *m* (bot.) mustard
**ajengibre** *m* var. of **jengibre**
**ajenjo** *m* (bot.) absinthe, wormwood; absinthe (*drink*)
**ajeno -na** *adj* another's; contrary, inappropriate; free; foreign; different; insane; **estar ajeno de** (coll.) to be uninformed about, be unaware of; **estar ajeno de sí** to be detached, distinterested; **ajeno a** unbecoming to; not connected with; unmindful of
**ajenuz** *m* (bot.) love-in-a-mist
**ajeo** *m* cry of hunted partridge
**ajerezado -da** *adj* sherry-type (*wine*)
**ajesuitado -da** *adj* (Am.) jesuitical (*crafty*)
**ajete** *m* young garlic; garlic sauce
**ajetrear** *va* to harass, to exhaust; *vr* to bustle about, to wear oneself out
**ajetreo** *m* bustle
**ají** *m* (*pl:* **ajíes**) (bot.) chili (*plant and fruit*); chili sauce; **ponerse como un ají** (Am.) to turn red as a tomato
**ajiaceite** *m* garlic and olive-oil sauce
**ajiaco** *m* (Am.) chili sauce; (Am.) Spanish stew seasoned with garlic; **estar como ajiaco** (Am.) to be in a bad humor
**ajicola** *f* (paint.) glue made of boiled animal skins and garlic
**ajilimoje** *m* or **ajilimójili** *m* (coll.) pepper-and-garlic sauce; **ajilimojes** *mpl* or **ajilimójilis** *mpl* (coll.) accessories
**ajillo** *m* (bot.) woody vine of trumpet-creeper family (*Cydista aequinoctialis*)
**ajimez** *m* (*pl:* **-meces**) (arch.) mullioned window
**ajipa** *f* (bot.) artichoke, Jerusalem artichoke
**ajipuerro** *m* (bot.) wild leek
**ajironar** *va* to trim with braid; to tear into shreds
**-ajo -ja** *suffix dim & pej* e.g., **colgajo** rag, tatter; **lagunajo** puddle; **migaja** crumb
**ajo** *m* (bot.) garlic; clove of garlic; garlic sauce; face paint; (coll.) shady business; (coll.) obscenity; **ajos** *mpl* garlic; **harto de ajos** ill-bred; **revolver el ajo** (coll.) to stir up a row; **tieso como un ajo** proud and haughty; **ajo blanco** (bot.) garlic; Andalusian garlic sauce; **ajo de chalote** (bot.) shallot; **ajo moruno** (bot.) chive; **ajo silvestre** (bot.) moly (*Allium moly*); *interj* goo!, dada! (*to make a baby talk*)
**ajobar** *va* (coll.) to carry on one's back, to struggle along with
**ajobilla** *f* (zool.) clam
**ajobo** *m* burdening, burden, heavy load, heavy task
**ajolote** *m* (zool.) axolotl, mud puppy
**ajomate** *m* (bot.) conferva
**ajonje** *m* birdlime
**ajonjear** *va* (*Am.*) to fondle, caress
**ajonjera** *f* or **ajonjero** *m* (bot.) carline thistle
**ajonjolí** *m* (*pl:* **-líes**) (bot.) sesame
**ajoqueso** *m* dish of garlic and cheese
**ajorca** *f* bracelet, anklet, bangle
**ajornalar** *va* to hire by the day; *vr* to hire out by the day
**ajote** *m* (bot.) water germander
**ajuagas** *fpl* (vet.) malanders
**ajuanetado -da** *adj* bunionlike; having bunions
**ajuar** *m* housefurnishings; bridal equipment, trousseau; **ajuar de cocina** kitchen utensils
**ajudiado -da** *adj* Jewish, Jewlike
**ajuiciado -da** *adj* wise, sensible, prudent
**ajuiciar** *va* to bring to one's senses; *vn & vr* to come to one's senses, to mend one's ways
**ajumar** *vr* (Am.) to get drunk
**ajustado -da** *adj* just, right; close-fitting, tight
**ajustador** *m* jacket, close-fitting jacket; corselet; finisher, fitter; (print.) pager
**ajustamiento** *m* var. of **ajuste**
**ajustar** *va* to fit, adapt, adjust; to engage, hire; to arrange, arrange for; to reconcile; to settle; to fasten (*e.g., one's safety belt*); (print.) to page; **ajustar cuentas con** to settle accounts with; *vn* to fit; *vr* to fit; to get adjusted; to engage oneself; to be engaged, be hired; to hire out; to come to an agreement; **ajustarse a** + *inf* to agree to + *inf*
**ajuste** *m* fit (*of clothes*); fitting, adjustment; hiring; arrangement; reconciliation; settlement; agreement; (print.) paging
**ajusticiado -da** *mf* executed criminal
**ajusticiar** *va* to punish with death, to execute
**al** contraction of **a** and **el; al** + *inf* on + *ger*, e.g., **al llegar** on arriving
**ala** *f* wing; brim (*of hat*); auricle (*of heart*); fin (*of fish, torpedo, etc.*); leaf (*of door, table, etc.*); flange; mudguard; (naut.) studdingsail; (theat.) wing; **alas** *fpl* boldness; courage; importance; **ahuecar el ala** (coll.) to beat it; **caérsele a uno las alas** to lose heart; **cortarle a uno las alas** to clip one's wings; **volar con sus propias alas** to stand on one's own feet; **ala en delta** (aer.) delta wing; **ala en flecha** (aer.) backswept wing; *m* (sport) wing; (football) end
**Alá** *m* Allah
**alabado** *m* hymn in praise of the sacrament
**alabador -dora** *adj* eulogistic; *mf* praiser
**alabamiento** *m* praise
**alabamio** *m* (chem.) alabamine
**alabancero -ra** *adj* (coll.) fawning, flattering
**alabancioso -sa** *adj* (coll.) boastful
**alabanza** *f* praise; **amontonar alabanzas sobre** to heap praises on
**alabar** *va* to praise; *vr* to be pleased or satisfied; to boast; **alabarse de** to boast of being
**alabarda** *f* halberd

**alabardado -da** *adj* halberd-shaped; (bot.) hastate
**alabardazo** *m* blow or wound with a halberd
**alabardero** *m* halberdier; (theat.) paid applauder, claqueur
**alabastrado -da** *adj* alabaster, like alabaster
**alabastrino -na** *adj* alabastrine; *f* translucent sheet of alabaster
**alabastro** *m* alabaster
**álabe** *m* drooping branch of tree; bucket, paddle (*of water wheel*); wooden cog (*in flour mill*); side mat (*in wagons*)
**alabear** *va & vr* to warp
**alábega** *f* (bot.) basil
**alabeo** *m* warping
**alacena** *f* closet set in wall, cupboard; (naut.) locker
**alacrán** *m* (ent.) scorpion; link (*on metal button*); bridle-curb (*of harness*); **alacrán cebollero** (ent.) mole cricket; **alacrán marino** (ichth.) angler
**alacranado -da** *adj* stung by a scorpion; vice-ridden, disease-ridden
**alacranera** *f* (bot.) scorpion grass
**alacridad** *f* alacrity
**alacha** *f* or **alache** *m* (ichth.) anchovy
**alada** *f* see **alado**
**aladares** *mpl* hair falling over the temples
**aladica** *f* winged ant
**aladierna** *f* (bot.) evergreen buckthorn, alatern
**Aladino** *m* Aladdin
**alado -da** *adj* alate; winged (*having wings; swift*); *f* fluttering of wings
**aladrero** *m* (min.) timberman; (prov.) plowmaker
**aladroque** *m* (ichth.) anchovy
**alafia** *f* (coll.) pardon
**álaga** *f* (bot.) spelt
**alagadizo -za** *adj* subject to flooding
**alagar** §59 *va* to flood, to make ponds or lakes in
**alagartado -da** *adj* motley, variegated
**alajú** *m* (*pl:* **-júes**) paste made of nuts, honey, and spices
**ALALC** *f* abr. of **Asociación Latinoamericana de Libre Comercio**
**alamar** *m* frog (*button and loop on garments*)
**alambicado -da** *adj* distilled; overrefined, precious, oversubtle; doled out sparingly
**alambicamiento** *m* distillation; overrefinement, affectation, pedantry
**alambicar** §86 *va* to distill; to scrutinize; to refine to excess, make oversubtle; to sell cheap with a large turnover
**alambique** *m* still, alembic; **por alambique** sparingly
**alambor** *m* beveling; (fort.) scarp
**alamborado -da** *adj* beveled, sloped
**alambrado -da** *adj* (pertaining to) wire; *m* wire mesh, chicken wire; (mil.) wire entanglement; *f* wire mesh, chicken wire; wire fence; (mil.) barbed wire, wire entanglement; (elec.) wiring
**alambraje** *m* (elec.) wiring
**alambrar** *va* to enclose with wire, to fence with wire, to string with wire; to wire (*for electricity*)
**alambre** *m* wire; **alambre cargado** live wire; **alambre de entrada** (rad.) lead-in wire; **alambre de espino** or **de púas** barbed wire; **alambre de tierra** (rad.) ground wire; **alambre gemelo** (telv.) twin lead; **alambre para artefactos** (elec.) fixture wire; **alambre para timbres eléctricos** annunciator wire; **alambre sin aislar** bare wire
**alambrecarril** *m* aerial railway, cable or funicular railway, cableway, rope railway
**alambrera** *f* see **alambrero**
**alambrería** *f* wire shop
**alambrero -ra** *mf* wireworker; *m* (coll.) telegraph maintenance man; *f* screen; bell-shaped screen to place over a fire or embers; screen cover for food
**alámbrico -ca** *adj* wire
**alambrista** *mf* tightrope walker
**alameda** *f* poplar grove; tree-lined walk or avenue, mall
**alamín** *m* inspector of weights and measures; irrigation superintendent
**álamo** *m* (bot.) poplar; **álamo blanco** (bot.) white poplar; **álamo de Italia** (bot.) Lombardy poplar; **álamo negro** (bot.) black poplar; **álamo temblón** (bot.) aspen
**alampar** *vr* to have a craving; **alamparse por** to crave
**alamud** *m* bolt for door or window
**alanceado -da** *adj* (bot.) lanceolate
**alanceador** *m* spearman
**alancear** *va* to spear, to lance
**alandrear** *vr* to become dry, stiff, and white (*said of silkworms*)
**alanés** *m* large Mexican deer
**alano** *m* mastiff, great Dane; (*cap.*) *m* Alan, Allen
**alantoideo -a** *adj* allantoid
**alantoides** *f* (anat.) allantois
**alanzar** §76 *va* to strike or wound with a lance, to spear
**alaqueca** *f* (mineral.) carnelian
**alar** *adj* wing; (bot.) alar; *m* overhanging roof; horsehair snare; *va* (naut.) to haul
**alárabe** or **alarbe** *adj* Arabic, Arabian; *mf* Arab, Arabian; rough, unmannerly person
**alarde** *m* (mil.) review; show, display, ostentation; **hacer alarde de** to make a show of, to boast of
**alardear** *vn* to boast, brag, show off; **alardear de** to boast of
**alardoso -sa** *adj* showy, ostentatious
**alargada** *f* extension, lengthening; **dar la alargada** (Am.) to let out more string (*for a kite*)
**alargadera** *f* (chem.) adapter; (mach.) extension
**alárgama** *f* (bot.) African rue
**alargamiento** *m* lengthening, extension, prolongation; increase
**alargar** §59 *va* to lengthen, extend, stretch, prolong; to increase; to hand, to reach; to let out, to pay out (*e.g., a rope*); *vr* to go away, withdraw, separate; to lengthen, be prolonged; to expatiate, be long-winded
**alarguez** *m* (bot.) rosewood
**alaria** *f* smoothing tool (*of potters*)
**Alarico** *m* Alaric
**alarida** *f* shouting, yelling, uproar
**alarido** *m* shout, yell, howl, whoop, squeal
**alarifazgo** *m* profession of architect
**alarife** *m* architect; builder; (Am.) clever fellow, sharper
**alario -ria** *adj* alary
**alarma** *f* alarm; (aer.) alert; **falsa alarma** false alarm; **alarma aérea** air-raid warning; **alarma de incendios** fire alarm; **alarma de ladrones** burglar alarm
**alarmante** *adj* alarming
**alarmar** *va* to alarm; to call to arms; *vr* to become alarmed
**alármega** *f* var. of **alárgama**
**alarmista** *mf* alarmist
**alaroz** *m* (*pl:* **-roces**) framework closing a doorway with opening for small door; mullion
**alastrar** *va* to throw back (*the ears*); (naut.) to ballast; *vr* to lie flat, to cower (*said of hunted animals*)
**a látere** *m* (coll.) side-kick
**alaterno** *m* var. of **aladierna**
**alatinadamente** *adv* according to Latin, like Latin
**alatinado -da** *adj* affected, puristic
**alatrón** *m* wall saltpeter
**alavanco** *m* wild duck
**alavense** or **alavés -vesa** *adj* (pertaining to) Álava; *mf* native or inhabitant of Álava
**alazán -zana** *adj* sorrel, reddish-brown; *mf* sorrel horse; *f* wine press; olive-oil press
**alazo** *m* blow or stroke with a wing
**alazor** *m* (bot.) safflower, bastard saffron
**alba** *f* see **albo**
**albacara** *f* (fort.) projecting tower
**albacea** *m* executor; **albacea dativo** executor appointed by the court; *f* executrix
**albaceazgo** *m* executorship
**albacora** *f* (ichth.) albacore; (ichth.) swordfish; early fig
**albada** *f* dawn; aubade, morning music; (bot.) soapwort
**albahaca** *f* (bot.) basil

**albahaquero** *m* flowerpot
**albaicín** *m* hilly quarter (*of a town*); (*cap.*) *m* gypsy cave-dwelling quarter of Granada, Spain
**albaida** *f* (bot.) anthyllis
**albalá** *m & f* (*pl:* **-laes**) (archaic) royal letter patent; (archaic) statement, proof; (archaic) customhouse receipt
**albanega** *f* hair net; net for catching small game
**albanés -nesa** or **albano -na** *adj & mf* Albanian; *m* Albanian (*language*)
**Albania** *f* Albania
**albañal** *m* sewer, drain; slop basin, slop can, slop jar
**albañalero** *m* slop man; sewer cleaner
**albañil** *m* mason, bricklayer
**albañila** *f* (ent.) mason bee
**albañilería** *f* masonry, brickwork, bricklaying
**albaquía** *f* balance due
**albar** *adj* white; *va* to whiten, to shine; to make (*iron*) red-hot
**albarán** *m* rent sign; duplicate list of purchases
**albarazado -da** *adj* whitish; leprous; streaked with black, yellow, and red; (Am.) of mixed white, Chinese, and Indian blood
**albarazo** *m* (path.) tetter, ringworm; (path.) alphos
**albarca** *f* sandal
**albarcoque** *m* apricot (*fruit*)
**albarcoquero** *m* (bot.) apricot tree
**albarda** *f* packsaddle
**albardado -da** *adj* saddleback (*with back of a different color*)
**albardar** *va* to put a packsaddle on; to lard (*fowls*)
**albardear** *va* (Am.) to vex, annoy
**albardela** *f* small saddle, training saddle
**albardería** *f* packsaddle shop
**albardero** *m* packsaddle maker or vendor
**albardilla** *f* small packsaddle; thick coat of wool; shoulder pad (*for carrying water*); iron holder, pot holder; cope, coping; raised earthen border (*of walk or garden*); larding (*for fowl*)
**albardín** *m* (bot.) matweed
**albardón** *m* large packsaddle; saddle pad
**albarejo** *m* white wheat, summer wheat
**albareque** *m* fishing net
**albarico** *m* white wheat, summer wheat
**albaricoque** *m* apricot (*fruit*)
**albaricoquero** *m* (bot.) apricot tree
**albarillo** *m* lively dance tune; white apricot
**albarizo -za** *adj* whitish; *f* saltwater pond or lake
**albarrada** *f* dry wall; earthen wall; entrenchment, defensive earthwork
**albarranilla** *f* (bot.) squill
**albarrano -na** *adj & mf* (dial.) gypsy; see **cebolla & torre**
**albarraz** *m* (bot.) stavesacre
**albatros** *m* (*pl:* **-tros**) (orn.) albatross
**albayaldar** *va* to coat or cover with white lead
**albayalde** *m* white lead
**albazano -na** *adj* dark-chestnut
**albear** *vn* to turn white; (Am.) to get up early
**albedrío** *m* free will; caprice, fancy, wilfulness; (law) precedent, unwritten law; **al albedrío de** according to the pleasure of; **libre albedrío** free will
**albéitar** *m* veterinarian
**albeitería** *f* veterinary medicine, veterinary surgery
**albellanino** *m* (bot.) cornel tree
**albellón** *m* sewer, drain
**albenda** *f* embroidered white linen hangings
**albendera** *f* (archaic) gadabout
**albengala** *f* turban gauze
**albéntola** *f* fine-meshed fishing net
**alberca** *f* pond, pool, tank, reservoir, cistern; (Am.) swimming pool; **en alberca** roofless
**albérchiga** *f* clingstone peach
**albérchigo** *m* (bot.) clingstone-peach tree; clingstone peach; (prov.) apricot
**alberchiguero** *m* (bot.) clingstone-peach tree
**albergada** *f* cover, shelter, protection
**albergar** §59 *va* to shelter, harbor; to lodge, give lodging to; to house; *vn & vr* to take shelter; to lodge, to take lodgings
**albergue** *m* shelter, refuge, lodging; lair, burrow, den; **albergue de carretera** wayside inn
**albericoque** *m* apricot (*fruit*)
**albero -ra** *adj* white; *m* white earth, pipe clay; dishcloth
**alberquero** *m* tender of tanks or pools
**Alberto** *m* Albert; **Alberto Magno** Albertus Magnus
**albica** *f* white clay
**albicante** *adj* whitening, bleaching
**albido -da** *adj* whitish
**albigense** *adj* Albigensian; **albigenses** *mpl* Albigenses
**albihar** *m* (bot.) oxeye
**albillo -lla** *adj* white (*grape or wine*)
**albín** *m* hematite; dark carmine
**albina** *f* see **albino**
**albinismo** *m* albinism
**albino -na** *adj* albinic; *mf* albino; *f* salt-water marsh, salt deposit
**Albión** *f* (poet.) Albion (*England*)
**albita** *f* (mineral.) albite
**albitana** *f* fence to protect plants; (naut.) apron
**albo -ba** *adj* (poet.) white, snow-white; *f* dawn; alb (*priest's white linen robe*)
**alboaire** *m* glazed tiling (*in archways and vaulted roofs*)
**albohol** *m* (bot.) lesser bindweed
**albollón** *m* sewer, drain
**albóndiga** *f* meat ball, fish ball
**albondigón** *m* hamburger, Hamburg steak
**alboque** *m* flageolet, pastoral pipe; small cymbal
**albor** *m* whiteness; dawn; **albor de la vida** childhood, youth; **albores** *mpl* dawn
**alborada** *f* dawn; aubade, morning music; dawn attack; reveille; morning watch
**albórbola** *f* shouting, cheering, joyful yelling
**alborear** *vn* to dawn
**alborga** *f* matweed sandal
**albornía** *f* large glazed earthenware vessel
**alborno** *m* alburnum, sapwood
**albornoz** *m* (*pl:* **-noces**) coarse woolen stuff, terry cloth; burnoose; beach robe, bathrobe (*of terry cloth*); cardigan
**alboronía** *f* stew of eggplant, tomatoes, squash, and peppers
**alboroque** *m* treat given at the close of a deal
**alborotadizo -za** *adj* excitable, jumpy
**alborotado -da** *adj* hasty, rash
**alborotador -dora** *adj* inciting to riot; *mf* agitator, rioter
**alborotapueblos** *mf* (*pl:* **-blos**) (coll.) rabble rouser; (coll.) gay noisy person
**alborotar** *va* to agitate, stir up, arouse, excite; *vn* to make a racket, to clatter; to rampage; *vr* to become agitated, get excited; to riot; to get rough (*said of the sea*)
**alboroto** *m* agitation, disturbance, excitement; riot, noise, uproar; **alborotos** *mpl* (Am.) honey-coated popcorn
**alborozador -dora** *adj* cheering, joy-bringing; *mf* bringer of joy and gladness
**alborozar** §76 *va* to cheer, gladden, overjoy
**alborozo** *m* joy, merriment
**albotín** *m* (bot.) terebinth
**albriciar** *va* (archaic) to bring good news to, to reward for good news, to congratulate
**albricias** *fpl* reward for good news; present asked for or given on the occasion of some happy event; **en albricias de** as a token of; *interj* good news!, congratulations!
**albudeca** *f* tasteless melon; watermelon
**albufera** *f* saltwater lagoon
**albugíneo -a** *adj* albugineous
**albugo** *m* (path.) albugo; white spot (*on nails*)
**albuhera** *f* lake, lagoon, reservoir
**álbum** *m* (*pl:* **álbumes**) album; **álbum de recortes** scrapbook
**albumen** *m* (bot.) albumen
**albúmina** *f* (biochem.) albumin
**albuminado -da** *adj* albuminous; covered with a coat of albumin
**albuminaje** *m* (phot.) emulsification
**albuminar** *va* (phot.) to emulsify
**albuminímetro** *m* albuminimeter
**albuminoide** *m* albuminoid

**albuminoideo -a** *adj* albuminoid
**albuminoso -sa** *adj* albuminous
**albuminuria** *f* (path.) albuminuria
**albur** *m* (ichth.) dace; first two cards drawn by banker at monte (*card game*); risk, chance, hazard
**albura** *f* pure whiteness; white of egg; alburnum
**alburno** *m* var. of **alborno**
**alca** *f* (orn.) auk
**alcabala** *f* (archaic) sales tax; **alcabala del viento** (archaic) sales tax paid by outside merchant
**alcabalero** *m* (archaic) sales-tax collector
**alcacel** *m* or **alcacer** *m* (bot.) green barley
**alcací** *m* (*pl:* **-cíes**) (bot.) wild artichoke
**alcachofa** *f* (bot.) artichoke (*plant and head*)
**alcachofado -da** *adj* artichoke-shaped; *m* artichoke stew
**alcachofal** *m* artichoke bed; field of wild artichokes
**alcachofero -ra** *adj* (yielding the) artichoke; *mf* artichoke seller; *f* (bot.) artichoke
**alcahaz** *m* (*pl:* **-haces**) large bird cage
**alcahazada** *f* cageful of birds
**alcahazar** **§76** *va* to put or keep (*birds*) in a cage
**alcahuete -ta** *mf* bawd, procurer, go-between; harborer, screen, fence (*for criminals or stolen goods*); (coll.) schemer; (coll.) gossip, talebearer; *m* (theat.) curtain dropped for short intermission
**alcahuetear** *va* to procure (*for prostitution*); to harbor (*criminals or stolen goods*); (coll.) to scheme for; *vn* to pander
**alcahuetería** *f* pandering, procuring; harboring (*of criminals or stolen goods*); (coll.) trick, deceit, scheming
**alcaicería** *f* raw-silk market or exchange, bazaar
**alcaide** *m* governor or warden of a castle, fortress, or prison
**alcaidesa** *f* governor's lady, warden's wife, jailer's wife
**alcaidía** *f* position of governor or warden of a castle, fortress, or prison; governor's house, warden's house
**alcalaíno -na** *adj* (pertaining to) Alcalá de Henares, Alcalá de los Gazules, or Alcalá la Real (*Spanish cities*); *mf* native or inhabitant of Alcalá de Henares, Alcalá de los Gazules, or Alcalá la Real
**alcalareño -ña** *adj* (pertaining to) Alcalá de Guadaira, Alcalá del Río, or Alcalá del Valle (*Spanish cities*); *mf* native or inhabitant of Alcalá de Guadaira, Alcalá del Río, or Alcalá del Valle
**alcaldada** *f* abuse of authority, petty tyranny
**alcalde** *m* mayor, chief burgess; **tener el padre alcalde** to have a friend at court; **alcalde de monterilla** small-town mayor; **alcalde ordinario** mayor and justice of the peace combined, in colonial times
**alcaldear** *vn* to lord it, to be bossy
**alcaldesa** *f* mayoress
**alcaldesco -ca** *adj* (coll.) mayoral, mayor's
**alcaldía** *f* mayoralty; town hall, city hall
**alcalescencia** *f* (chem.) alkalescence
**alcalescente** *adj* (chem.) alkalescent
**álcali** *m* (chem.) alkali; **álcalis térreos** (chem.) alkaline earths
**alcalímetro** *m* alkalimeter
**alcalinidad** *f* alkalinity
**alcalino -na** *adj* alkaline
**alcalinotérreo -rrea** *adj* (chem.) alkaline-earth
**alcalizar** **§76** *va* to alkalize
**alcaloide** *m* alkaloid
**alcalóidico -ca** *adj* alkaloidal
**alcalosis** *f* (physiol.) alkalosis
**alcaller** *m* potter; pottery
**alcallería** *f* pottery, collection of pottery
**alcamonías** *fpl* aromatic seeds for flavoring; *m* (coll.) pander, go-between
**alcana** *f* (bot.) henna; (bot.) alkanet
**alcance** *m* pursuit; special delivery (*of mail*); late news (*in newspapers*); reach, arm's length; range (*e.g., of a gun*); scope, purview; extent; capacity, comprehension, intelligence; import, significance; coverage; balance due; deficit; **al alcance de** within reach of, within range of; **al alcance de la mano** within reach; **andarle** or **irle a uno en los alcances** to spy on a person; **dar alcance a** to catch up with; **de cortos alcances** of limited intelligence; **de gran alcance** long-range; **seguir los alcances a** to pursue; **alcance agresivo** striking range; **alcance de la vista** eyesight, eyeshot; **alcance del oído** earshot
**alcancía** *f* child's bank; bin, hopper, chute; (mil.) grenade; (Am.) poor box
**alcándara** *f* (archaic) perch for falcons; (archaic) clothes rack
**alcandía** *f* (bot.) sorghum, Indian millet
**alcandial** *m* field of sorghum
**alcandora** *f* signal fire, beacon
**alcanfor** *m* camphor
**alcanforada** *f* (bot.) stinking ground pine (*Camphorosma monspeliacum*)
**alcanforar** *va* to camphorate; *vr* (Am.) to hide, to disappear
**alcanforero** *m* (bot.) camphor tree
**alcántara** *f* cover for velvet in the loom
**alcantarilla** *f* drain, conduit, sewer, culvert; small bridge
**alcantarillado** *m* sewering, sewage system
**alcantarillar** *va* to sewer, to lay sewers in
**alcanzable** *adj* attainable
**alcanzadizo -za** *adj* reachable, attainable
**alcanzado -da** *adj* needy, hard up
**alcanzadura** *f* (vet.) attaint
**alcanzar** **§76** *va* to catch up to, to overtake; to reach; to grasp; to perceive (*to see, hear, smell*); to live through; to obtain, to attain; to understand; **alcanzar de cuenta a** to find lacking; **alcanzar en** to find (*someone*) indebted for the amount of; *vn* to succeed; to carry (*said of firearm*); **alcanzar a** + *inf* to manage to + *inf;* **alcanzar a** or **hasta** to attain to, to reach, to reach up to; **alcanzar a oír** to manage to hear, to overhear; **alcanzar a ver** to catch sight of, to set sight on; **alcanzar para** to be sufficient for; *vr* to overreach (*said of a horse*)
**alcaparra** *f* (bot.) caper (*plant and berry*)
**alcaparrado -da** *adj* prepared with capers
**alcaparral** *m* caper field
**alcaparrera** *f* or **alcaparro** *m* (bot.) caper (*plant*)
**alcaparrón** *m* caper (*bud or berry*)
**alcaparrosa** *f* var. of **caparrosa**
**alcaraván** *m* (orn.) stone curlew, thick-knee
**alcaravea** *f* (bot.) caraway (*plant and seed*)
**alcarceña** *f* (bot.) tare
**alcarcil** *m* artichoke, wild artichoke
**alcarracero -ra** *mf* maker of unglazed porous jugs; *m* shelf or cupboard for unglazed porous jugs
**alcarraza** *f* unglazed porous jug (*for cooling water by evaporation*)
**alcarria** *f* barren plateau
**alcartaz** *m* (*pl:* **-taces**) paper cone
**alcatara** *f* (archaic) still
**alcatifa** *f* fine rug or carpet; filling of earth or cinders under tile or brick
**alcatraz** *m* (*pl:* **-traces**) (orn.) gannet, solan; (orn.) pelican; (bot.) arum; paper cone
**alcaucí** *m* (*pl:* **-cíes**) (bot.) wild artichoke
**alcauciar** *va* (Am.) to shoot to death
**alcaudón** *m* (orn.) shrike
**alcayata** *f* tenterhook; meat hook; spike
**alcazaba** *f* fortress (*within a walled town*)
**alcázar** *m* alcazar, fortress; castle, royal palace; (naut.) quarterdeck
**alcazuz** *m* (bot.) licorice
**alc.de** abr. of **alcalde**
**alce** *m* (zool.) elk, moose; cut (*in card playing*)
**alcedo** *m* maple grove
**alcélafo** *m* (zool.) bubal, hartebeest
**Alcestes** *f* (myth.) Alcestis
**Alcibíades** *m* Alcibiades
**alcino** *m* (bot.) wild basil
**alción** *m* (orn.) kingfisher, halcyon; (myth.) halcyon; (*cap.*) *m* (astr.) Alcyone
**alciónеos** *mpl* (meteor. & myth.) halcyon days
**alcista** *adj* bullish (*tending to rise in price*); rising, upward (*e.g., trend in cost of living*); *mf* bull (*in stock market*)

**Alcmena** *f* (myth.) Alcmene
**alcoba** *f* bedroom; **alcoba de respeto** guest room
**alcocarra** *f* grimace, face
**alcofa** *f* rush or wicker basket or hamper
**alcohol** *m* alcohol; kohl; (mineral.) galena; **alcohol absoluto** absolute alcohol; **alcohol de grano** grain alcohol; **alcohol de madera** wood alcohol; **alcohol desnaturalizado** denatured alcohol; **alcohol etílico** ethyl alcohol; **alcohol metílico** methyl alcohol, wood alcohol; **alcohol para fricciones** rubbing alcohol; **alcohol vinílico** vinyl alcohol
**alcoholado -da** *adj* having dark hair around the eyes (*said of an animal*); *m* (pharm.) alcoholate, spirit
**alcoholar** *va* to distill alcohol from; to blacken with kohl
**alcoholato** *m* (pharm.) alcoholate
**alcoholaturo** *m* (pharm.) alcoholature
**alcoholero -ra** *adj* (pertaining to) alcohol; *f* vessel for holding kohl (*cosmetic*); alcohol plant or factory
**alcohólico -ca** *adj* alcoholic; (med.) alcoholic; *mf* (med.) alcoholic
**alcoholímetro** *m* alcoholometer
**alcoholismo** *m* (path.) alcoholism
**alcoholización** *f* alcoholization
**alcoholizado -da** *adj & mf* (med.) alcoholic
**alcoholizar §76** *va* to alcoholize; to fortify (*wines*); *vr* to become alcoholic
**alcolla** *f* large glass pitcher, vial, or cruet
**alconcilla** *f* rouge
**alcor** *m* hill, eminence
**Alcorán** *m* Alcoran, Koran
**alcoránico -ca** *adj* Koranic
**alcoranista** *m* Koranist
**alcornocal** *m* woods or forest of cork oaks
**alcornoque** *m* (bot.) cork oak; (coll.) blockhead
**alcornoqueño -ña** *adj* cork-oak
**alcorque** *m* cork-soled shoe; trench around base of plant or tree to hold irrigation water
**alcorza** *f* frosting of sugar and starch; **ser una alcorza** (Am.) to be a crybaby
**alcorzar §76** *va* to frost with sugar and starch; to adorn
**alcotán** *m* (orn.) lanner
**alcotana** *f* mason's or bricklayer's pickaxe
**alcrebite** *m* sulfur
**alcribís** *m* tuyère
**alcubilla** *f* basin, reservoir
**alcucero -ra** *adj* (coll.) sweet-toothed; (coll.) greedy; *mf* maker or vendor of olive-oil cans
**Alcuino** *m* Alcuin
**alcurnia** *f* ancestry, lineage, family
**alcuza** *f* olive-oil can; (Am.) water jug; (Am.) earthen bottle; (Am.) caster
**alcuzada** *f* canful of olive oil
**alcuzcuz** *m* couscous
**aldaba** *f* knocker, door knocker; bolt, crossbar; latch; hitching ring; **tener buenas aldabas** to have pull, to have influence; **aldaba dormida** deadlatch
**aldabada** *f* knock with a door knocker; sudden fright or shock
**aldabazo** *m* sharp knock with a door knocker
**aldabear** *vn* to knock with a door knocker
**aldabeo** *m* knocking with a door knocker
**aldabía** *f* crossbeam (*of door or partition*)
**aldabilla** *f* hook or catch (*for door or window*)
**aldabón** *m* knocker, door knocker; trunk or chest handle
**aldabonazo** *m* knock with a door knocker; sharp knock with a door knocker
**aldea** *f* village
**aldeaniego -ga** *adj* village, rustic, peasant
**aldeano -na** *adj* village; country, rustic; *mf* villager
**Aldebarán** *m* (astr.) Aldebaran
**aldehido** *m* (chem.) aldehyde
**aldehuela** *f* little village, hamlet
**aldeorrio** or **aldeorro** *m* small backward village
**alderredor** *adv* around, about
**aldino -na** *adj* Aldine
**aldiza** *f* (bot.) bluebottle, cornflower
**aldora** *f* (bot.) sorghum
**aldrán** *m* country wine peddler
**aleación** *f* alloy
**alear** *va* to alloy; to ally; *vn* to beat the wings; to move the arms up and down (*like wings*); to convalesce
**aleatorio -ria** *adj* aleatory
**alebrar §18** *vr* to lie flat (*like a rabbit*); to cower
**alebrastar** or **alebrestar** *vr* to lie flat (*like a rabbit*); to cower; (Am.) to rear; (Am.) to dash along; (Am.) to fall in love; (Am.) to become frightened; (Am.) to brighten up, to cheer up; (Am.) to get tipsy
**alebronar** *va* to cow, to intimidate; to frighten; *vr* to lie flat (*like a rabbit*); to cower; to become frightened
**aleccionador -dora** *adj* instructive, enlightening
**aleccionamiento** *m* instruction; training, coaching
**aleccionar** *va* to teach, instruct; to train, coach
**alece** *m* (ichth.) anchovy; ragout of fish liver
**alecrín** *m* (ichth.) tiger shark (*Galeocerdo arcticus*); (bot.) South American hardwood (*Holocalyx balansae*)
**aleche** *m* (ichth.) anchovy
**alechugar §59** *va* to curl in the shape of a lettuce leaf; to curl, fold, pleat, frill
**alechuguinar** *va* to make foppish; *vr* to become foppish, become a dude
**aleda** *f* propolis
**aledaño -ña** *adj* bordering; attached; *m* border, boundary
**alefangina** *f* (archaic) purgative pill containing aloes, nutmeg, etc.
**alefriz** *m* (naut.) rabbet, mortise
**alegación** *f* allegation
**alegamar** *va* to fertilize with silt; *vr* to get full of silt
**alegar §59** *va* to allege; *vn* (law) to plead
**alegato** *m* allegation; (law) allegation; (law) summing up, brief
**alegoría** *f* allegory
**alegórico -ca** *adj* allegoric
**alegorizar §76** *va* to allegorize
**alegra** *f* (naut.) pump auger
**alegrador -dora** *adj* cheering; *m* spill (*twisted paper for lighting*); reamer; **alegradores** *mpl* (taur.) banderillas
**alegrar** *va* to cheer, make glad; to brighten, enliven; to stir up (*a fire*); (naut.) to widen (*a hole*); *vr* to be glad, to rejoice; (coll.) to get tipsy; **alegrarse de, con,** or **por** to be glad of or because of; **alegrarse de** + *inf* to be glad to + *inf*
**alegre** *adj* glad, joyful; bright, gay; cheerful, merry, light-hearted; careless, reckless; (coll.) off-color; (coll.) tipsy; **alegre de cascos** scatterbrained
**alegreto** *m* (mus.) allegretto
**alegría** *f* joy, cheer, gladness; brightness, gaiety; (bot.) sesame; nougat of honey and sesame seeds; **alegría secreta, candela muerta** all who joy would win must share it
**alegro** *m* (mus.) allegro
**alegrón** *m* sudden upsurge of joy; flare-up, sudden blaze; (Am.) flirt
**alejado -da** *adj* distant, remote
**alejamiento** *m* farness, distance; removal, withdrawal; estrangement
**Alejandría** *f* Alexandria
**alejandrino -na** *adj* Alexandrian; Alexandrine; *mf* Alexandrine (*native or inhabitant of Alexandria*); *m* Alexandrine (*verse of twelve syllables in English, fourteen in Spanish*)
**Alejandro** *m* Alexander; **Alejandro Magno** Alexander the Great
**alejar** *va & vr* to move aside, to move away, to keep at a distance
**alejijas** *fpl* barley porridge
**Alejo** *m* Alexis
**alejur** *m* var. of **alajú**
**alelado -da** *adj* stunned, dumbfounded
**alelamiento** *m* stupidity, imbecility
**alelar** *va* to make stupid, to stupefy; *vr* to grow stupid or dull
**alelí** *m* (*pl:* **-líes**) (bot.) gillyflower
**aleluya** *m & f* hallelujah; *m* Easter time; *f* prints distributed at church on Holy Saturday; (bot.) hallelujah, wood sorrel; doggerel; daub; bag of bones, skinny fellow; **aleluya navideña** Christmas card; *interj* hallelujah!

**alema** *f* allotment of irrigation water; **alemas** *fpl* (Am.) public baths
**alemán -mana** *adj & mf* German; *m* German (*language*); *f* allemande (*dance*)
**alemanda** *f* allemande (*dance*)
**alemanesco -ca** *adj* var. of **alemanisco**
**Alemania** *f* Germany; **la Alemania Occidental** West Germany; **la Alemania Oriental** East Germany
**alemánico -ca** *adj* Germanic
**alemanisco -ca** *adj* damask; Germanic; *m* damask table linen
**alentado -da** *adj* brave, spirited; haughty, gallant; (Am.) well, in good health; *f* long breath, deep breath; **de una alentada** without catching one's breath
**alentador -dora** *adj* encouraging
**alentar** §18 *va* to encourage, inspire, cheer; **alentar a** + *inf* to encourage to + *inf; vn* to breathe; *vr* to get well, to recover
**aleonado -da** *adj* tawny, fulvous
**aleonar** *va* (Am.) to stir up, agitate
**alepantado -da** *adj* (Am.) distracted, fascinated
**alepídoto -ta** *adj* (ichth.) alepidote
**alepín** *m* bombazine
**Alepo** *m* Aleppo
**alerce** *m* (bot.) larch; **alerce africano** (bot.) sandarac
**alergeno** *m* (immun.) allergen
**alergia** *f* (path.) allergy
**alérgico -ca** *adj* allergic
**alero** *m* eaves; mudguard, splashboard
**alerón** *m* (aer.) aileron
**alerta** *m, adv & interj* see **alerto**
**alertar** *va* to alert
**alerto -ta** *adj* alert, watchful, vigilant; **alerta** *m* (mil.) alert; (mil.) watchword; **alerta** *adv* on the alert, alertly, watchfully; **estar alerta** to be on the alert; **alerta** *interj* watch out!, look out!
**alesaje** *m* bore (*of cylinder of motor*)
**alesna** *f* awl
**alesnado -da** *adj* awl-shaped; pointed; (bot.) subulate
**aleta** *f* small wing; fin (*of fish, etc.*); leaf (*of hinge*); blade (*of propeller*); (naut.) fashion piece; (aut.) fender, mudguard; (coll.) fin (*hand, arm*)
**aletada** *f* beating of wings, fluttering
**aletargamiento** *m* numbness, lethargy
**aletargar** §59 *va* to benumb, to make lethargic; *vr* to get benumbed, to fall into a lethargy
**aletazo** *m* stroke or flap of wing or fin
**aletear** *vn* to flutter, to beat or flap the wings or fins
**aleteo** *m* fluttering, flapping, beating; palpitation (*of heart*)
**aleto** *m* (orn.) osprey
**aletría** *f* (prov.) noodles, spaghetti
**aleudar** *va* to leaven, to ferment with yeast; *vr* to rise, become fermented
**aleurona** *f* (biochem.) aleurone
**aleutiano -na** *adj* Aleutian; *mf* Aleut, Aleutian (*native or inhabitant*); *m* Aleut (*language*)
**aleve** *adj* treacherous, perfidious; *mf* traitor, rebel; *m* treachery, perfidy
**alevilla** *f* (ent.) moth
**alevosa** *f* see **alevoso**
**alevosía** *f* treachery, perfidy
**alevoso -sa** *adj* treacherous, perfidious; *f* (vet.) frogtongue
**alexia** *f* (psychopath.) alexia
**alexifármaco -ca** *adj & m* alexipharmic
**alexina** *f* (biochem.) alexin
**aleya** *f* verse of the Koran
**alezo** *m* drawsheet (*in hospitals*)
**alfa** *f* alpha; **alfa y omega** alpha and omega
**alfábega** *f* (bot.) basil
**alfabético -ca** *adj* alphabetic
**alfabetización** *f* alphabetization; (Am.) teaching illiterates to read and write
**alfabetizar** §76 *va* to alphabetize; (Am.) to teach (*a person*) to read and write
**alfabeto** *m* alphabet; **alfabeto Morse** (telg.) Morse code; **alfabeto para sordomudos** deaf-and-dumb alphabet
**alfaguara** *f* gushing spring
**alfaida** *f* tidewater (*in a river*)
**alfajía** *f* quartering for doorframe or window frame; (prov.) roof timber
**alfajor** *m* var. of **alajú**
**alfalfa** *f* (bot.) alfalfa
**alfalfal** *m* alfalfa field
**alfalfe** *m* var. of **alfalfa**
**alfana** *f* big, fiery horse
**alfaneque** *m* (orn.) buzzard; (archaic) campaign tent
**alfanjado -da** *adj* cutlass-shaped
**alfanjazo** *m* stroke or wound with a cutlass
**alfanje** *m* cutlass; (ichth.) swordfish
**alfaque** *m* bar, shoal
**alfaquí** *m* (*pl:* **-quíes**) alfaqui (*expounder of the Koran*)
**alfar** *adj* galloping with front feet and trotting with rear feet; *m* pottery; clay; *vn* to gallop with front feet and trot with rear feet; (naut.) to pitch
**alfaraz** *m* (*pl:* **-races**) Moorish light-cavalry horse
**alfarda** *f* tax levied on Jews and Moors; special tax; (arch.) light beam
**alfardilla** *f* binding, trimming, gold or silver braid
**alfardón** *m* ring, washer; tax
**alfarería** *f* pottery; pottery store or stand; potter's workshop
**alfarero** *m* potter
**alfargo** *m* press of olive-oil mill
**alfarje** *m* olive crusher; carved and paneled ceiling
**alfarjía** *f* quartering for doorframe or window frame
**alféizar** *m* splay of door or window; embrasure
**alfeñicar** §86 *vr* (coll.) to become extremely thin; (coll.) to be finical, to be too nice
**alfeñique** *m* almond-flavored sugar paste; (coll.) thin, delicate person; prudery, squeamishness
**Alfeo** *m* (myth.) Alpheus
**alferazgo** ensigncy; second lieutenancy
**alferecía** *f* epilepsy; ensigncy; second lieutenancy
**alférez** *m* (*pl:* **-reces**) (mil.) second lieutenant; (mil.) subaltern (Brit.); **alférez de fragata** (nav.) ensign; **alférez de navío** (nav.) lieutenant (j.g.)
**alficoz** *m* (*pl:* **-coces**) (bot.) cucumber (*plant and fruit*)
**alfil** *m* bishop (*in chess*)
**alfiler** *m* pin; (elec.) prong (*of a tube*); **alfileres** *mpl* pin money; **de veinticinco alfileres** or **con todos sus alfileres** (coll.) dressed to kill; **no estar con sus alfileres** (coll.) to be in a bad humor; **pedir para alfileres** (coll.) to ask for a tip; (coll.) to ask for pin money; **pegar** or **prender con alfileres** (coll.) to put together in a shaky way; (coll.) to learn superficially; **alfiler de corbata** stickpin, scarfpin; **alfiler de madera** clothespin; **alfiler de París** wire nail; **alfiler de seguridad** safety pin
**alfilerar** *va* to pin, pin up
**alfilerazo** *m* pinprick; (fig.) dig, jab, innuendo
**alfilerillo** *m* finishing nail
**alfiletero** *m* pincase, needlecase
**alfitete** *m* semolina
**alfolí** *m* (*pl:* **-líes**) granary; salt warehouse
**alfoliar** §90 *va* (archaic) to store (*grain or salt*)
**alfolla** *f* hook, clasp; purple brocade
**alfombra** *f* carpet, rug; (path.) German measles; **alfombra de baño** bath mat; **alfombra de rezo** prayer rug; **alfombra mágica** magic carpet
**alfombrado** *m* carpeting
**alfombrar** *va* to carpet
**alfombrero -ra** *mf* carpet maker
**alfombrilla** *f* rug, runner; door mat; (path.) German measles
**alfombrista** *mf* carpet dealer; carpet repairer
**alfóncigo** *m* (bot.) pistachio (*tree and seed*)
**alfonsí** *adj masc* (*pl:* **-síes** or **-sinos**) Alphonsine
**alfónsigo** *m* var. of **alfóncigo**
**alfonsino -na** *adj* Alphonsine
**Alfonso** *m* Alphonso; **Alfonso el Sabio** Alphonso the Wise
**alforfón** *m* (bot.) buckwheat

**alforjas** *fpl* saddlebags, knapsack; provisions for traveling
**alforjón** *m* (bot.) buckwheat
**alforza** *f* pleat, tuck; innermost heart; (coll.) scar
**alforzar §76** *va* to pleat, to tuck
**alfoz** *m* (*pl:* **-foces**) narrow mountain pass; district, dependence; outskirts
**Alfredo** *m* Alfred; **Alfredo el Grande** Alfred the Great
**alga** *f* (bot.) alga; (bot.) seaweed
**algaba** *f* woods, thicket
**algaida** *f* jungle, brush, thicket; sandbank, dune
**algalia** *f* civet; (surg.) catheter; *m* (zool.) civet cat
**algaliar** *va* to perfume with civet
**algara** *f* thin skin (*of egg, onion, etc.*); raiding cavalry; cavalry raid
**algarabía** *f* Arabic; (coll.) gibberish, jabber; (*coll.*) din, clamor, uproar, confusion; (bot.) broomweed; (zool.) fulvous tree duck
**algaracear** *vn* (Am.) to spit snow, to snow lightly
**algarada** *f* outcry; catapult (*of ancient Romans*)
**algarero -ra** *adj* chattering, talkative; *m* raiding cavalryman
**algarrada** *f* catapult (*of ancient Romans*); bull baiting; fight with young bulls; driving bulls into pen
**algarroba** *f* (bot.) vetch; carob bean, locust bean
**algarrobilla** *f* (bot.) vetch
**algarrobo** *m* (bot.) carob; **algarrobo loco** (bot.) Judas tree; **algarrobo negro** (bot.) mesquite, honey mesquite
**algazara** *f* Moorish battle cry; uproar, tumult, din
**algazul** *m.* (bot.) ice plant
**álgebra** *f* algebra
**algebraico -ca** or **algébrico -ca** *adj* algebraic
**algebrista** *mf* algebraist
**algecireño -ña** *adj* (pertaining to) Algeciras; *mf* native or inhabitant of Algeciras
**algidez** *f* abnormal coldness
**álgido -da** *adj* cold, chilly; (bot. & zoöl.) of the frigid zone; (coll.) most active, most intense, decisive
**algo** *pron indef* something; **¿algo más?** anything else?; **algo por el estilo** something of the sort; *adv* somewhat, rather, a little
**algodón** *m* cotton; cotton wadding (*for ears*); (bot.) cotton plant; **estar criado entre algodones** to be brought up in comfort; **algodón de altura** upland cotton; **algodón en hojas** cotton batting; **algodón en rama** raw cotton, cotton wool; **algodón hidrófilo** absorbent cotton; **algodón pólvora** guncotton
**algodonal** *m* cotton plantation, cotton field
**algodonar** *va* to fill or stuff with cotton
**algodoncillo** *m* piece of cotton (*for the ear*); (bot.) milkweed, swamp milkweed
**algodonería** *f* cotton factory; cotton manufacture; cotton plantation
**algodonero -ra** *adj* (pertaining to) cotton; *mf* cotton dealer, cotton broker; cotton grower; *m* Levant cotton
**algodonoso -sa** *adj* cottony
**algología** *f* algology
**algonquino -na** *adj* (philol.) Algonquian; (geol.) Algonkian; *m* Algonquin (*North American Indian and his language*); (philol.) Algonquian; *f* (geol.) Algonkian
**algor** *m* (path.) algor
**algorfa** *f* grain loft
**algorín** *m* olive bin
**algoritmia** *f* (math.) algorism
**algorítmico -ca** *adj* algorithmic
**algoritmo** *m* (math.) algorism
**algoso -sa** *adj* algous
**alguacil** *m* bailiff, alguazil; (taur.) mounted police officer who heads the processional entrance of the bullfighters; (ent.) jumping spider
**alguacilazgo** *m* bailiwick
**alguacilillo** *m* (taur.) mounted police officer who heads the processional entrance of the bullfighters; (ent.) jumping spider
**alguarín** *m* (prov.) storeroom; (prov.) flour trough (*in flour mill*); (prov.) olive trough
**alguaza** *f* (prov.) hinge
**Alguer** Alghero (*Catalan-speaking Sardinian city*)
**alguien** *pron indef* somebody, someone
**algún** *adj indef* apocopated form of **alguno,** used only before masculine singular nouns and adjectives; *adv* **algún tanto** somewhat, a little
**alguno -na** *adj indef* some, any; (after noun) not any; **alguno de ellos** some one or another of them; **alguno que otro** some or another, an occasional; **alguna vez** sometimes; ever, e.g., **¿Ha estado Vd. alguna vez en España?** Have you ever been in Spain?; *pron indef* someone, some one; **algunos** some; **algunos de entre** some of
**alhaja** *f* jewel, gem, ornament, fine piece of furniture; (fig.) gem (*thing*); (coll.) gem (*person*); **buena alhaja** a sly fellow, a bad egg
**alhajar** *va* to bejewel; to furnish, to appoint
**alhámega** *f* var. of **alárgama**
**alhamel** *m* (prov.) beast of burden; (prov.) messenger; (prov.) muleteer
**alhandal** *m* colocynth, bitter apple (*fruit*)
**alharaca** *f* fuss, outcry, ado, ballyhoo; **hacer alharacas** to make a fuss
**alharaquiento -ta** *adj* fussy, emotional, strident, clamorous
**alhárgama** or **alharma** *f* var. of **alárgama**
**alhelí** *m* (*pl:* **-líes**) (bot.) gillyflower
**alhelicillo** *m* (bot.) alyssum, sweet alyssum
**alheña** *f* (bot.) henna; powdered henna; blight, mildew; **hecho alheña** or **molido como una alheña** (coll.) all fagged out
**alheñar** *va* to henna; to mildew, to blight; *vr* to henna (*e.g., one's hair*); to become mildewed, to become blighted
**alhócigo** *m* var. of **alfóncigo**
**alhoja** *f* (orn.) lark
**alholva** *f* (bot.) fenugreek (*plant and seed*)
**alhóndiga** *f* grain exchange
**alhorma** *f* Moorish camp; Moorish sanctuary or place of refuge (*around the tomb of a holy man*)
**alhorre** *m* meconium; skin eruption of newborn child
**alhoz** *m* (*pl:* **-hoces**) (archaic) var. of **alfoz**
**alhucema** *f* (bot.) lavender (*plant and dried flowers and leaves*)
**alhumajo** *m* pine needles
**alhurreca** *f* var. of **adarce**
**aliabierto -ta** *adj* with wings spread
**aliacán** *m* (path.) jaundice
**aliacanado -da** *adj* jaundiced
**aliáceo -a** *adj* garlicky
**aliado -da** *adj* allied; *mf* ally
**aliadófilo -la** *adj & mf* pro-Ally
**aliaga** *f* (bot.) furze, gorse
**aliagar** *m* furze field
**alianza** *f* alliance; wedding ring; (Bib.) covenant; **Santa Alianza** Holy Alliance; **Triple Alianza** Triple Alliance; **Alianza para el progreso** Alliance for Progress
**aliar §90** *va* to ally; *vr* to become allied; to form an alliance
**aliara** *f* drinking horn
**aliaria** *f* (bot.) garlic mustard
**alias** *m & adv* alias
**aliblanca** *f* (orn.) white-winged dove
**alible** *adj* nourishing, nutritive
**álica** *f* porridge of corn, wheat, and pulse
**alicaído -da** *adj* with drooping wings; (coll.) drooping, crestfallen; (coll.) discouraged, downhearted; (coll.) discountenanced
**alicántara** *f* (zool.) viper
**alicante** *m* (zool.) viper; Alicante wine
**alicantino -na** *adj* (pertaining to) Alicante; *mf* native or inhabitant of Alicante; *f* (coll.) trick, ruse
**alicatado** *m* tiling with arabesque designs
**alicatar** *va* to tile
**alicates** *mpl* pliers
**Alicia** *f* Alice; **Alicia en el país de las maravillas** Alice in Wonderland
**aliciente** *m* attraction, inducement, incentive
**alicortar** *va* to cut the wings of, to wing (*to wound*)
**alicuanta** *adj fem* (math.) aliquant
**alícuota** *adj fem* (math.) aliquot
**alidada** *f* alidade
**alienable** *adj* alienable

**alienación** *f* alienation; rapture
**alienado -da** *adj* insane; enraptured; distracted; *mf* insane person
**alienar** *va* to alienate; to enrapture
**alienismo** *m* alienism (*profession of alienist*)
**alienista** *mf* alienist
**aliento** *m* breath, breathing; enterprise, courage, spirit; **cobrar aliento** to revive, to take heart; **contener el aliento** to hold one's breath; **dejar sin aliento** to leave breathless; **de mucho aliento** long, endless, arduous (*work*); **de un aliento** without catching one's breath; without stopping; **mal aliento** bad breath; **nuevo aliento** second wind; **sin aliento** out of breath; **tomar aliento** to catch one's breath
**alifafe** *m* (vet.) tumor on horse's hock; (coll.) complaint, indisposition
**alifar** *va* (prov.) to polish, to burnish
**alifara** *f* (prov.) light lunch
**alifático -ca** *adj* (chem.) aliphatic
**alífero -ra** *adj* winged
**aliforme** *adj* wing-shaped
**aligación** *f* or **aligamiento** *m* bond, tie, connection; alloy
**aligar §59** *vr* to band together
**aligeramiento** *m* lightening; easing, alleviation; shortening; hastening
**aligerar** *va* to lighten; to ease, alleviate; to shorten; to hasten
**alígero -ra** *adj* (poet.) winged
**aligonero** *m* var. of **almez**
**aligustre** *m* (bot.) privet; **aligustre del Japón** (bot.) wax privet
**aligustrón** *m* (bot.) wax privet
**alijado -da** *adj* (naut.) light, unloaded
**alijador** *m* lighter (*ship*); lighterman; cotton ginner (*person*); smuggler; sander, sandpaperer
**alijar** *m* wasteland; Moorish tile; **alijares** *mpl* outlying commons; *va* to unload, to lighten (*a ship*); to unload (*contraband*); to gin (*cotton*); to sandpaper
**alijarar** *va* to apportion (*wasteland*) for cultivation
**alijarero** *m* farmer of wasteland
**alijo** *m* lighterage; ginning; smuggling; smuggled goods; contraband; (Am.) locomotive tender
**alilaya** *f* (Am.) flimsy excuse
**alileno** *m* (chem.) allylene
**alilo** *m* (chem.) allyl
**alimaña** *f* animal, small predatory animal, varmint
**alimañero** *m* gamekeeper who watches for and destroys predatory animals
**alimentación** *f* alimentation, nourishment, feed, feeding; **alimentación forzada** (mach.) force feed; (med.) force-feeding
**alimentador -dora** *adj* nourishing; *mf* nourisher; *m* stoker (*machine*); (elec.) feeder
**alimentar** *va* to nourish, to feed; to sustain, to maintain; to foster, to cherish; *vn* to be nourishing; *vr* to feed; **alimentarse con** or **de** to feed on or upon
**alimentario -ria** *adj* alimentary (*providing support*); *mf* pensioner
**alimenticio -cia** *adj* alimentary, nourishing, nutritional, food
**alimentista** *mf* pensioner
**alimento** *m* food, nourishment, aliment; encouragement, support; **alimentos** *mpl* foodstuffs; alimony; allowance; **alimento combustible** or **energético** carbohydrate; **alimento plástico** or **reparador** protein; **alimento respiratorio** or **termógeno** carbohydrate
**alimentoso -sa** *adj* nutritious
**álimo** *m* (bot.) saltbush
**alimoche** *m* (orn.) Egyptian vulture, Pharaoh's chicken
**alimón; al alimón** (taur.) with the cape held by two toreros
**alimonado -da** *adj* lemon (*in form, appearance, or color*)
**alimonar** *vr* to turn yellow (*said of leaves*)
**alindado -da** *adj* vain, foppish, dandified, mincing
**alindamiento** *m* marking off, setting boundaries
**alindar** *va* to mark off; to prettify; *vn* to border, be contiguous
**alindongar §59** *vr* (dial.) to overdress
**alineación** *f* alignment; (eng.) alignment; **fuera de alineación** out of alignment
**alineador -dora** *adj* aligning; *mf* aligner
**alineamiento** *m* building line; (archeol.) alignment
**alinear** *va & vr* to align, to line up
**aliñar** *va* to season, to dress (*food*); (Am.) to set (*a broken bone*)
**aliño** *m* seasoning, dressing; preparation; **aliño francés** French dressing
**aliñoso -sa** *adj* seasoned; careful, attentive
**alioli** *m* garlic and olive-oil sauce
**alionar** *va* (Am.) to stir up, agitate
**alionín** *m* (orn.) bottle tit
**alipata** *m* (bot.) blind-your-eyes, poison tree
**alípede** *adj* (poet.) winged, nimble, swift
**alípedo -da** *adj & mf* aliped
**aliquebrado -da** *adj* (coll.) drooping, crestfallen
**aliquebrar §18** *va* to break the wings of
**alirado -da** *adj* lyrate, lyre-shaped
**alirrojo -ja** *adj* red-winged
**alisado** *m* (action of) smoothing
**alisador -dora** *adj* polishing; *mf* smoother, polisher, finisher; *m* smoothing iron, smoothing blade; *f* surfacing machine, road scraper
**alisadura** *f* smoothing, polishing; surfacing; **alisaduras** *fpl* turnings, cuttings, shavings
**alisar** *m* alder grove or plantation; *va* to smooth; to sleek; to iron lightly
**aliseda** *f* alder grove or plantation
**alisios** *mpl* trade winds
**alisma** *f* (bot.) water plantain
**aliso** *m* (bot.) alder
**alistador -dora** *mf* enlister, enroller, recruiter
**alistamiento** *m* enlistment, enrolment, recruitment
**alistar** *va* to list; to enlist, enroll; to prepare, arrange; to stripe; *vr* to enlist, enroll; to get ready
**aliteración** *f* alliteration; paronomasia
**aliterado -da** *adj* alliterative
**alitierno** *m* (bot.) mock privet
**aliviador -dora** *adj* alleviative
**alivianar** *va* (Am.) to make lighter (*in weight*)
**aliviar** *va* to lighten; to alleviate, mitigate, soothe; to hasten, speed up
**alivio** *m* alleviation, relief
**alizar** *m* tile dado; tile (*of a dado*)
**alizarina** *f* (chem.) alizarin
**aljaba** *f* quiver
**aljama** *f* Moorish gathering, Jewish gathering; mosque, synagogue; Moorish quarter, ghetto
**aljamía** *f* Spanish of Moors or Jews; Spanish written in Arabic characters
**aljamiado -da** *adj* aljamía-speaking; written in Arabic characters (*said of Spanish*)
**aljarafe** *m* tableland; flat roof, terrace
**aljarfa** *f* or **aljarfe** *m* thick central part of fishing net
**aljerife** *m* large fishing net
**aljévena** *f* (prov.) washbowl, basin
**aljez** *m* gypsum
**aljezar** *m* gypsum pit
**aljezón** *m* gypsum rubbish
**aljibe** *m* tank barge, water tender; oil tanker; cistern, reservoir
**aljibero** *m* tender of a cistern or reservoir
**aljofaina** *f* washbowl, basin
**aljófar** *m* imperfect pearl; pearl trimming; (fig.) dewdrop
**aljofarar** *va* to adorn with pearls; to bepearl
**aljofifa** *f* floor mop
**aljofifar** *va* to mop (*a tiled floor*)
**aljonje** *m* birdlime
**aljonjera** *f* or **aljonjero** *m* (bot.) carline thistle
**aljonjolí** *m* (*pl:* **-líes**) (bot.) sesame
**aljor** *m* gypsum
**aljorozar §76** *va* (Am.) to smooth, to make smooth with plaster
**aljuba** *f* jubbah
**alma** *f* see **almo**
**almacén** *m* warehouse; store, department store; (phot.) magazine; (fig.) storehouse; (Am.) grocery store; **gastar (mucho) almacén** (coll.) to dress gaudily, be gaudily

dressed; (coll.) to be long-winded; **grandes almacenes** department store; **almacén de placas** (phot.) plateholder
**almacenaje** *m* storage (*cost, charges*)
**almacenamiento** *m* storage, storing
**almacenar** *va* to store; to store up, hoard
**almacenero** *m* storekeeper; warehouseman
**almacenista** *mf* shop owner; store clerk; warehouseman; (Am.) wholesale grocer
**almacería** *f* covered seedbed
**almáciga** *f* seedbed (*for later transplantation*); mastic
**almacigar** §59 *va* to scent or treat with mastic
**almácigo** *m* (bot.) mastic tree; seedbed
**almaciguero -ra** *adj* (pertaining to a) seedbed
**almádana** or **almádena** *f* stone hammer, spalling hammer
**almadía** *f* Hindoo canoe; raft
**almadiar** *vr* to get sick, become nauseated
**almadiero** *m* paddler, canoeist; raftsman
**almádina** *f* var. of **almádana**
**almadraba** *f* tuna fishing; tuna fishery; tuna-fish net
**almadrabero -ra** *adj* tuna-fishing; *mf* tuna fisher
**almadraque** *m* cushion, pillow; mattress
**almadreña** *f* wooden shoe
**almaganeta** *f* var. of **almádana**
**almagesto** *m* almagest
**almagra** *f* red ocher, ruddle
**almagrado -da** *adj* red-ocher (*color*)
**almagradura** *f* coloring with red ocher
**almagral** *m* ocher deposit
**almagrar** *va* to color with red ocher; to make bloody; (slang) to make bleed, to draw blood on; to stigmatize, to defame
**almagre** *m* red ocher
**almagrero -ra** *adj* red-ocher-bearing; *f* ocher deposit; ocher can
**almaizal** *m* or **almaizar** *m* Moorish gauze veil; (eccl.) humeral veil
**almajal** *m* var. of **almarjal**
**almajaneque** *m* (mil.) battering ram
**almajar** *m* var. of **almarjal**
**almajara** *f* (hort.) hotbed, forcing bed
**almajo** *m* var. of **almarjo**
**almalafa** *f* Moorish robe
**almanaque** *m* almanac; calendar; **hacer almanaques** (coll.) to meditate, to muse; **ser un almanaque del año pasado** to be out of date
**almanaquero -ra** *mf* maker or vendor of almanacs
**almancebe** *m* Guadalquivir fishing net
**almandina** *f* deep-red garnet
**almánguena** *f* red ocher
**almanta** *f* space between rows of trees; ground between two large furrows
**almarada** *f* poniard with triangular blade; wooden-handled poker; rope-sandalmaker's needle
**almarbatar** *va* to join (*two pieces of wood*)
**almarcha** *f* town on marshy ground
**almarga** *f* marlpit
**almarjal** *m* glasswort field; marsh, fen
**almarjo** *m* (bot.) glasswort; (chem.) barilla
**almaro** *m* (bot.) germander
**almarrá** *m* (*pl:* **-rraes**) cotton gin
**almarraja** or **almarraza** *f* glass sprinkling vessel
**almártaga** *f* (archaic) headstall; litharge
**almártega** *f* litharge
**almártiga** *f* (archaic) headstall
**almartigón** *m* halter (*for tying horse to manger*)
**almaste** *m*, **almástec** *m*, or **almástiga** *f* mastic
**almatrero** *m* shad fisherman
**almatriche** *m* irrigation trench
**almatroque** *m* shad net
**almatroste** *m* (Am.) var. of **armatoste**
**almazara** *f* oil mill, oil press
**almazarero** *m* oil-mill operator
**almazarrón** *m* red ocher
**almea** *f* almeh (*Oriental singing and dancing girl*); liquid storax; storax bark
**almear** *m* shock, stack; loft
**almecina** *f* var. of **almeza**
**almeja** *f* (zool.) clam; **almeja de los estanques** (zool.) swan mussel; **almeja redonda** (zool.) quahog, hard-shelled clam
**almejar** *m* clam bed
**almejía** *f* Moorish cloak of rough cloth
**almena** *f* (fort.) merlon
**almenado -da** *adj* battlemented, crenelated; *m* battlement
**almenaje** *m* battlement, battlements
**almenar** *s* cresset; *va* (fort.) to crenelate, to line or top with merlons
**almenara** *f* beacon fire; chandelier; overflow ditch, return ditch
**almendra** *f* almond (*fruit and stone; almond-shaped glass, diamond, etc.*); kernel (*of drupaceous fruit*); **almendra amarga** bitter almond; **almendra de Málaga** Jordan almond; **almendra garapiñada** praline
**almendrado -da** *adj* almond-shaped; *m* macaroon; *f* drink of milk and almonds; compliment
**almendral** *m* almond grove
**almendrate** *m* almond stew
**almendrera** *f* (bot.) almond tree; **florecer la almendrera** (coll.) to turn gray prematurely
**almendrero** *m* (bot.) almond tree; dish for almonds
**almendrilla** *f* almond-shaped file; fine gravel; buckwheat coal
**almendro** *m* (bot.) almond tree; **almendro amargo** (bot.) bitter almond
**almendrón** *m* (bot.) Malabar almond (*tree and nut*); (bot.) Brazil-nut tree; (bot.) Jamaica bayberry
**almendruco** *m* green almond
**almenilla** *f* merlon-shaped trimming
**almeriense** *adj* (pertaining to) Almería; *mf* native or inhabitant of Almería
**almete** *m* armet; soldier wearing armet
**almez** *m* (*pl:* **-meces**) (bot.) hackberry, nettle tree
**almeza** *f* hackberry (*fruit*)
**almezo** *m* (bot.) hackberry, nettle tree
**almiar** *m* haystack, hayrick
**almíbar** *m* simple syrup; fruit juice; **estar hecho un almíbar** (coll.) to be as sweet as pie
**almibarado -da** *adj* syrupy; (coll.) sugary, honeyed, flattering
**almibarar** *va* to preserve in syrup; to honey (*one's words*)
**almicantarada** or **almicantarat** *f* (astr.) almucantar
**almidón** *m* starch; **almidón de maíz** cornstarch
**almidonado -da** *adj* starched; (coll.) spruce, dapper; *m* starching
**almidonar** *va* to starch
**almidonería** *f* starch factory
**almijar** *m* place for drying olives or grapes before pressing
**almilla** *f* bodice, close-fitting jacket; undervest; (carp.) tenon; breast of pork
**almimbar** *m* mimbar (*pulpit in a mosque*)
**alminar** *m* minaret
**almiranta** *f* admiral's wife; flagship
**almirantazgo** *m* admiralty
**almirante** *m* admiral; female headgear; cone shell; (prov.) swimming coach
**almirez** *m* (*pl:* **-reces**) metal mortar
**almizclar** *va* to perfume with musk
**almizcle** *m* musk
**almizcleño -ña** *adj* musky; *f* (bot.) grape hyacinth
**almizclero -ra** *adj* musky; *m* (zool.) musk deer; *f* (zool.) muskrat
**almo -ma** *adj* (poet.) nourishing; (poet.) sacred, venerable; *f* soul, heart, spirit; living soul (*person*); strength, vigor; crux, heart (*of the matter*); pith (*of plants*); darling, sweetheart; bore (*of gun*); web (*of rail, etc.*); (elec.) core (*of cable*); newel (*of staircase*); (mus.) sounding-post (*of violin, etc.*); **dar el alma, entregar el alma, rendir el alma** to give up the ghost; **estar con el alma en la boca** or **entre los dientes** (coll.) to have one's heart in one's boots or mouth
**almocadén** *m* (archaic) infantry officer; (archaic) cavalry officer in command of a platoon; petty officer (*in Morocco*)
**almocafre** *m* dibble, weeding hoe

**almocárabes** *mpl* or **almocarbes** *mpl* (arch.) intertwining spiral or scroll-like figures
**almocatracía** *f* (archaic) duty on woolen goods
**almocela** *f* farmer's straw mattress; (archaic) hood
**almocrate** *m* (chem.) sal ammoniac
**almocrí** *m* (*pl:* **-críes**) reader of Koran in a mosque
**almodí** *m* (*pl:* **-díes**) public grain exchange
**almodón** *m* flour made from dampened wheat
**almodrote** *m* sauce of oil, cheese, and garlic; (coll.) mixture, hodgepodge
**almófar** *m* (arm.) mail coif (*worn under helmet*)
**almofía** *f* brass washbasin
**almofrej** *m* or **almofrez** *m* traveling bag for bedding
**almogama** *f* (naut.) var. of **redel**
**almogárabe** *m* (mil.) raider, forager
**almogataz** *m* Christianized Moor in Spanish army in Africa
**almogávar** *m* (mil.) raider, forager
**almogavarear** *vn* to go raiding, to go foraging
**almogavaría** or **almogavería** *f* (mil.) raiding troops, raiding party
**almohada** *f* pillow; cushion; pillowcase; (naut.) pillow; **consultar con la almohada** to sleep a thing over; **dar almohada a** (hist.) to raise to the nobility (*by the queen's inviting a woman to sit at her side on a cushion*); **almohada de aire** air cushion
**almohade** *adj* Almohade; **almohades** *mpl* Almohades (*Islamitic sect which controlled the Mussulman territory of North Africa and Spain in the 12th and 13th centuries*)
**almohadilla** *f* small pillow or cushion; sewing cushion; pad; harness pad; callus (*from saddle or harness*); cushion (*pad for gold leaf*); (arch.) bossage (*of an ashlar*); (arch.) bolster; (baseball) bag; **almohadilla higiénica** sanitary napkin; **almohadilla caliente eléctrica** electric hot pad, electric heating pad
**almohadillado -da** *adj* padded, cushioned; ashlared; *m* bossage; ashlar; **almohadillado rústico** rusticated or quarry-faced ashlar
**almohadillar** *va* to pad, to cushion; to dress (*an ashlar*)
**almohadón** *m* large pillow or cushion, round cushion, hassock; (arch.) springer
**almohatre** *m* (chem.) sal ammoniac
**almohaza** *f* currycomb
**almohazador** *m* currier, groom
**almohazar** **§76** *va* to curry, to currycomb
**almojábana** *f* cheese cake; cruller
**almojarifazgo** *m* import duty, export duty; custom house
**almojarife** *m* royal tax collector, revenue officer, customhouse officer
**almojaya** *f* (carp.) putlog
**almona** *f* shad fishery; (archaic) public stores; (prov.) soap factory
**almóndiga** *f* meat ball, fish ball
**almoneda** *f* auction; clearance sale
**almonedar** or **almonedear** *va* to auction; to sell out
**almonedero** *m* auctioneer
**almoraduj** *m* or **almoradux** *m* (bot.) sweet marjoram
**almorávid** *adj* Almoravide; **almorávides** *mpl* Almoravides (*North African tribe which dominated Arabic Spain from 1093 to 1148*)
**almorejo** *m* (bot.) bottle grass (*Setaria glauca*)
**almorí** *m* (*pl:* **-ríes**) honey cake
**almoronía** *f* var. of **alboronía**
**almorranas** *fpl* (path.) piles, hemorrhoids
**almorraniento -ta** *adj* suffering from piles
**almorrefa** *f* triangular tile
**almorta** *f* (bot.) grass pea
**almorzada** *f* double handful
**almorzar** **§52** *va* to eat for lunch, to lunch on; *vn* to have lunch, to lunch
**almotacén** *m* inspector of weights and measures; inspector's office
**almotacenazgo** *m* office of inspector of weights and measures
**almotacenía** *f* inspector's fee; office of inspector of weights and measures
**almozala** *f* quilt, blanket
**almozárabe** *adj* Mozarabic; *mf* Mozarab
**almud** *m* almud (*dry measure: 2 to 21 qts.; liquid measure: 5 to 32 qts.*)
**almudada** *f* ground sown with one almud of seed
**almudero** *m* keeper of dry measures
**almudí** *m* (*pl:* **-díes**) public grain exchange
**almudín** *m* var. of **almudí**
**almuecín** *m* or **almuédano** *m* muezzin
**almuérdago** *m* var. of **muérdago**
**almuerza** *f* double handful
**almuerzo** *m* lunch; luncheon set (*of dishes*)
**almunia** *f* orchard, farm
**alnado -da** *mf* stepchild
**alnico** *m* alnico (*alloy*)
**aló** *interj* (Am.) hello!, hey!
**alobadado -da** *adj* bitten by a wolf; (vet.) having carbuncular tumors
**alobunado -da** *adj* wolflike, wolf-colored
**alocado -da** *adj* mad, wild, reckless, foolish; *mf* madcap
**alocar** **§86** *va* to drive mad or crazy
**alocución** *f* allocution, address, speech
**alodial** *adj* (law) alodial
**alodio** *m* (law) alodium
**áloe** or **aloe** *m* (bot.) aloe; (pharm.) aloes
**aloético -ca** *adj* aloetic
**alófana** *f* (chem.) allophane
**alogamia** *f* (bot.) allogamy
**aloína** *f* (chem. & pharm.) aloin
**aloja** *f* metheglin, mead
**alojado -da** *mf* (Am.) guest, lodger; *m* soldier billeted in a private house
**alojamiento** *m* lodging; housing; quartering, billeting; lodgings, quarters; (naut.) crew's quarters
**alojar** *va* to lodge; to quarter, billet (*troops*); *vn* & *vr* to lodge; to be quartered or billeted
**alojería** *f* metheglin shop, mead shop
**alojero -ra** *mf* metheglin mixer or vendor; (theat.) box near the pit
**alomado -da** *adj* high-backed
**alomar** *va* to plow in wide furrows; *vr* to become strong in back and loins (*said of a horse*)
**alón** *m* wing without feathers
**alondra** *f* (orn.) lark; **alondra azul** (orn.) blue grosbeak
**alongamiento** *m* lengthening, prolongation; extension; distance, separation
**alongar** **§79** *va* to lengthen, prolong; to stretch, extend; to remove, to put at a distance; *vr* to move away
**alópata** *mf* allopath
**alopatía** *f* allopathy
**alopático -ca** *adj* allopathic
**alopecia** *f* (path.) alopecia
**alopecuro** *m* (bot.) foxtail grass
**alopiado -da** *adj* opiate
**aloque** *adj* light-red (*said of wine*); *m* light-red wine; mixture of light-red and white wine
**aloquecer** **§34** *vr* to go crazy, to lose one's mind
**aloquín** *m* stone inclosure of a wax bleachery
**alosa** *f* (ichth.) shad
**alotar** *va* (naut.) to reef, to stow
**alotropía** *f* allotropy
**alotrópico -ca** *adj* allotropic
**alotropismo** *m* allotropism
**alotropo** *m* allotrope
**alpaca** *f* (zool.) alpaca; alpaca (*wool and cloth; glossy black cloth made of wool and cotton*); German silver
**alpañata** *f* chamois skin, soft leather (*for polishing pottery before baking*)
**alpargata** *f* hemp sandal; espadrille
**alpargatado -da** *adj* shaped like a hemp sandal
**alpargatar** *vn* to make hemp sandals
**alpargate** *m* var. of **alpargata**
**alpargatería** *f* hemp-sandal shop or factory
**alpargatero -ra** *mf* maker or seller of hemp sandals
**alpargatilla** *mf* crafty, sneaking person
**alpechín** *m* foul-smelling juice that oozes from a heap of olives
**alpechinera** *f* vat for catching juice oozing from a heap of olives
**alpende** *m* tool house, tool shed; lean-to, penthouse
**alpérsico** *m* (bot.) peach (*tree and fruit*)

**Alpes** *mpl* Alps; **Alpes dináricos** Dinaric Alps; **Alpes julianos** Julian Alps; **Alpes réticos** Rhaetian Alps
**alpestre** *adj* alpine; Alpine
**alpicoz** *m* (*pl:* **-coces**) (prov.) var. of **alficoz**
**alpinismo** *m* Alpinism, mountain climbing
**alpinista** *mf* Alpinist, mountain climber
**alpino -na** *adj* Alpine
**alpiste** *m* (bot.) canary grass; alpist, canary seed, birdseed; **dejar alpiste a uno** (coll.) to disappoint someone; **quedarse alpiste** (coll.) to be disappointed
**alpistela** *f* sesame-seed cake
**alpistero -ra** *adj* canary-grass; canary-seed; *f* sesame-seed cake
**alpujarreño -ña** *adj* pertaining to the Alpujarras; *mf* native or inhabitant of the Alpujarras
**alquequenje** *m* (bot.) winter cherry, alkekengi
**alquería** *f* farmhouse
**alquermes** *m* kermes-colored alcoholic drink
**alquerque** *m* place in olive-oil mill for shredding crushed residue from first pressing
**alquez** *m* (*pl:* **-queces**) wine measure of 193 liters
**alquibla** *f* kiblah (*direction to which Moslems turn in prayer*)
**alquicel** *m* or **alquicer** *m* Moorish cloak; fabric for covering furniture
**alquifol** *m* alquifou (*lead sulfide for glazing pottery*)
**alquila** *f* "for hire" sign on a cab
**alquilable** *adj* rentable, for rent
**alquiladizo -za** *adj* for rent, for hire; hireling; *mf* hireling
**alquilador -dora** *mf* renter, hirer; proprietor, tenant
**alquilamiento** *m* rent, renting, hire, hiring
**alquilar** *va* to rent, to let, to hire; *vr* to hire, hire out; to be for rent; **se alquila** for rent
**alquilate** *m* (dial.) sales tax
**alquiler** *m* rent, rental, hire; **de alquiler** for hire; **alquiler de coches** car-rental service; **alquiler sin chófer** drive-yourself service
**alquilón -lona** *adj* cheap to rent, easy to hire; hireling; *mf* hireling; *m* hired cab or coach; *f* charwoman, cleaning woman
**alquimia** *f* alchemy
**alquímico -ca** *adj* alchemical
**alquimila** *f* (bot.) lady's-mantle, lion's-foot
**alquimista** *m* alchemist
**alquinal** *m* woman's headdress or veil
**alquitara** *f* still, alembic
**alquitarar** *va* to distil
**alquitira** *f* (bot.) tragacanth
**alquitrán** *m* tar; pitch; **alquitrán de hulla** coal tar; **alquitrán vegetal** wood tar
**alquitranado -da** *adj* (pertaining to) tar, tarred; *m* tarred cloth, tarpaulin
**alquitranadora** *f* tar-spraying machine
**alquitranar** *va* to tar
**alrededor** *adv* around; **alrededor de** around, about; (coll.) about (*practically*); **alrededores** *mpl* environs, outskirts
**alrota** *f* coarse tow, waste tow
**Alsacia** *f* Alsace
**Alsacia-Lorena** *f* Alsace-Lorraine
**alsaciano -na** *adj* & *mf* Alsatian
**álsine** *m* (bot.) chickweed
**alta** *f* see **alto**
**altabaque** *m* wicker basket, sewing basket
**altabaquillo** *m* (bot.) lesser bindweed
**altaico -ca** *adj* Altaic
**altamente** *adv* exceedingly, extremely
**altamisa** *f* var. of **artemisa**
**altanería** *f* upper air; soaring; falconry; haughtiness, arrogance
**altanero -ra** *adj* soaring, towering; haughty, arrogant
**altanos** *mpl* (naut.) winds blowing alternately offshore and off the sea
**altar** *m* altar; (found.) altar, flue bridge; **conducir al altar** to lead to the altar; **altar mayor** high altar
**altaricón -cona** *adj* (coll.) strapping, big and husky
**altarreina** *f* (bot.) yarrow
**altavoz** *m* (*pl:* **-voces**) (rad.) loudspeaker
**altea** *f* (bot.) althea
**altear** *vr* to rise, stand out
**alterabilidad** *f* alterability
**alterable** *adj* alterable
**alteración** *f* alteration; disturbance; agitation, irritation; uneven pulse, fast pulse; disorder, uprising; quarrel, altercation
**alteradizo -za** *adj* changeable, fickle
**alterado -da** *adj* altered; disturbed, agitated, upset; angered
**alterante** *adj* & *m* (med.) alterative
**alterar** *va* to alter; to disturb, to upset; to corrupt, to falsify; to agitate, irritate; to lessen, to cool; *vr* to alter; to be disturbed; to become agitated, to get irritated; to flutter (*said of the pulse*); to lessen, to cool
**alterativo -va** *adj* alterative (*causing change*)
**altercación** *f* or **altercado** *m* altercation, bickering
**altercador -dora** *adj* wrangling, bickering; *mf* wrangler, bickerer
**altercar §86** *vn* to altercate, to wrangle, argue, bicker
**álter ego** (Lat.) alter ego
**alternación** *f* alternation
**alternadamente** *adv* alternately
**alternador** *m* (elec.) alternator
**alternancia** *f* (elec.) alternation; **alternancia de generaciones** (biol.) alternation of generations
**alternante** *adj* alternate, alternating
**alternar** *va* to alternate; to vary; *vn* to alternate; to take turns; **alternar con** to go around with, be friendly with
**alternativo -va** *adj* alternating; *f* alternative, option; alternation; (taur.) ceremony by which a senior matador authorizes a novice matador to kill the bull, thus making the novice a full-fledged matador; **alternativas** *fpl* ups and downs; **tomar la alternativa** (taur.) to be dubbed a matador; **alternativa de cosechas** rotation of crops
**alterno -na** *adj* alternating; (bot. & geom.) alternate
**alteroso -sa** *adj* (naut.) top-heavy
**alteza** *f* height, elevation, sublimity; (*cap.*) *s* Highness (*title*)
**altibajo** *m* velvet brocade; downward cut or thrust (*with a sword*); **altibajos** *mpl* bumps, uneven ground; ups and downs, vicissitudes
**altilocuencia** *f* grandiloquence
**altilocuente** or **altílocuo -cua** *adj* grandiloquent
**altillo** *m* hillock; balcony (*in a store or shop, used as an office*); (Am.) attic
**altimetría** *f* altimetry
**altímetro -tra** *adj* altimetrical; *m* altimeter
**altiplanicie** *f* high plateau; (Am.) highland plain
**altiplano** *m* (Am.) highland plain
**altísimo -ma** *adj super* most high, very high; **el Altísimo** the Most High (*God*)
**altisonancia** *f* high-flown language
**altisonante** or **altísono -na** *adj* high-flown; high-sounding
**altitonante** *adj* (poet.) thundering
**altitud** *f* altitude
**altivar** *vr* to put on airs, to act haughtily
**altivecer §34** *va* to make haughty; *vr* to act haughtily, to become haughty
**altivez** *f* or **altiveza** *f* pride, haughtiness, arrogance
**altivo -va** *adj* proud, haughty, arrogant
**alto -ta** *adj* high; upper; deep; tall; loud; top; late (*hours*); early, remote (*e.g., Middle Ages*); arduous; noble, eminent; enormous; **de alto bordo** (naut.) of several decks, sea-going; (fig.) of importance; (fig.) high-up; **alta mar** high seas; **altas clases** upper classes; **altas horas** late hours; **alta traición** high treason; **alto horno** blast furnace; **alto relieve** alto-relievo, high relief; **alto** *adv* high up; loud, aloud, loudly; **alto** *interj* halt!; **¡alto ahí!** halt!, stop there!; **¡alto al fuego!** (mil.) cease fire!; **¡alto de aquí!** (coll.) out of here!; *m* height, altitude; depth; story, floor; roadbed; stop, halt; (mus.) alto; (Am.) pile, heap; **de alto a bajo** from top to bottom; **de lo alto** from above; **en alto** up high, up above; upward; **en lo alto de** on top of; **hacer alto** to

stop, to halt; **pasar por alto** to overlook, disregard, forget; **pasársele a uno por alto** to overlook, e.g., **eso se nos pasó por alto** we overlooked that; **ponerse tan alto** to take offense, to become hoity-toity; **alto el fuego** (mil.) cease fire; *f* courtly dance of German origin; dancing exercise; fencing bout; certificate of discharge from hospital; (mil.) certificate of induction into active service; acceptance as member of society or profession; **dar de alta** to discharge (*a patient*) from the hospital; (mil.) to admit, to enroll; **darse de alta** to join, become a member, be admitted; (mil.) to report for duty
**altoalemán -mana** *adj* High-German; *m* High German; **antiguo altoalemán** Old High German; **medio altoalemán** Middle High German
**altocúmulo** *m* (meteor.) alto-cumulus
**altoestrato** *m* var. of **altostrato**
**altoparlante** *m* (rad.) loudspeaker; **altoparlante dinámico** (rad.) dynamic speaker; **altoparlante electromagnético** (rad.) electromagnetic speaker
**altostrato** *m* (meteor.) alto-stratus
**altozanero** *m* (Am.) errand boy
**altozano** *m* hillock, knoll; hilly part of town; (Am.) paved terrace
**altramuz** *m* (*pl:* **-muces**) (bot.) lupine (*plant and seed*); (eccl.) voting bean
**altruísmo** *m* altruism
**altruísta** *adj* altruistic; *mf* altruist
**altura** *f* height, altitude; high seas; loftiness; (mus.) pitch; (naut.) latitude; point, stage, juncture; **alturas** *fpl* Heaven; **a estas alturas** at this point, at this juncture; **a la altura de** (naut.) off; **estar a la altura de** to be up to, to be equal to (*a task, undertaking, etc.*); **estar a la altura de las circunstancias** (coll.) to rise to the occasion; **por estas alturas** (coll.) around here; **altura de la vegetación** timber line
**alúa** *f* (ent.) fire beetle
**alubia** *f* string bean
**aluciar** *va* to shine, polish; *vr* to get dressed up
**alucinación** *f* hallucination
**alucinadamente** *adv* deludedly, with delusion
**alucinador -dora** *adj* hallucinatory, delusive
**alucinamiento** *m* (act of) hallucinating
**alucinante** *adj* dazzling
**alucinar** *va* to hallucinate, to delude; *vr* to be deluded, be dazzled
**alucita** *f* (ent.) moth
**alucón** *m* (orn.) tawny owl
**alud** *m* avalanche; (fig.) avalanche
**aluda** *f* see **aludo**
**aludel** *m* (chem.) aludel
**aludido -da** *adj* above-mentioned; alluded to
**aludir** *va* to allude to; *vn* to allude
**aludo -da** *adj* large-winged; *f* (ent.) winged ant
**alula** *f* (orn. & ent.) alula
**alumbrado -da** *adj* lighted; enlightened; (coll.) tipsy; (chem.) aluminous; *m* lighting, lighting system; **alumbrado de arco** arc light, arc lighting; **alumbrado fluorescente** fluorescent lighting; **alumbrado reflejado** indirect lighting; **alumbrados** *mpl* Illuminati (*mystical Spanish sect of 16th century*)
**alumbrador -dora** *adj* lighting, illuminating; enlightening; *mf* lighter; enlightener
**alumbramiento** *m* lighting; childbirth, accouchement; discovery and elevation of subterranean water
**alumbrar** *va* to light, illuminate; to show the way with a light to; to give sight to (*the blind*); to enlighten; to find (*subterranean water*); to remove the earth from around (*a vine*); to treat with alum; *vn* to have a child, to give birth; *vr* (coll.) to get tipsy
**alumbre** *m* (chem.) alum; **alumbre de cromo** (chem.) chrome alum; **alumbre de rasuras** (chem.) potassium carbonate; **alumbre de roca** (mineral.) alum rock; **alumbre sacarino** or **zacarino** saccharine alum
**alumbrera** *f* alum mine
**alumbroso -sa** *adj* aluminous
**alúmina** *f* (mineral.) alumina
**aluminato** *m* (chem.) aluminate
**alumínico -ca** *adj* aluminic
**aluminio** *m* (chem.) aluminum
**aluminita** *f* (mineral.) aluminite
**aluminoso -sa** *adj* aluminous
**aluminotermia** *f* aluminothermy
**alumnado** *m* student body; boarding school
**alumno -na** *mf* foster child; ward; pupil, student; **alumno de las Musas** poet
**alunado -da** *adj* lunatic; long-tusked (*said of a wild boar*); spoiled (*said of bacon*); (vet.) suffering from spasms
**alunar** *vr* to spoil (*said of bacon*); to have a crazy streak, to be not all there
**alunita** *f* (mineral.) alunite
**alunizar** **§76** *vn* to land on the moon
**alusión** *f* allusion
**alusivo -va** *adj* allusive
**alustrar** *va* to polish, to put a shine on, to give luster to
**alútero** *m* (ichth.) filefish
**alutrado -da** *adj* otter-colored
**aluvial** *adj* alluvial
**aluvión** *m* alluvion; alluvium; (law) alluvion; (fig.) flood
**aluzar** **§76** *va* (dial. & Am.) to light, illuminate
**alveario** *m* (anat.) alveary
**álveo** *m* bed of a stream
**alveolar** *adj* (anat. & phonet.) alveolar
**alvéolo** *m* (anat., phonet. & zool.) alveolus; bucket (*of a water wheel*)
**alverja** or **alverjana** *f* var. of **arveja**
**alverjilla** *f* (Am.) sweet pea
**alverjón** *m* (bot.) grass pea
**alvino -na** *adj* (med.) alvine
**alza** *f* rise, advance (*e.g., in prices*); leather between last and shoe; (print.) overlay; rear sight (*of firearms*); **jugar al alza** to bull the market
**alzacuello** *m* stock (*kind of cravat*)
**alzada** *f* see **alzado**
**alzadamente** *adv* for a cash settlement, for a lump sum
**alzadizo -za** *adj* easy to lift, easy to raise
**alzado -da** *adj* raised, lifted; fixed, settled; *m* cash settlement, lump sum; (arch.) front elevation; (b.b.) quire, gathering; (naut.) height (*of a ship*); *f* height (*of horse at withers*); (law) appeal
**alzadura** *f* raising, lifting
**alzafuelles** *mf* (*pl:* **-lles**) (coll.) flatterer, fawner; (Am.) squealer
**alzamiento** *m* raising, lifting; rise (*in prices*); overbid; uprising, insurrection; fraudulent bankruptcy
**alzapaño** *m* curtain hook, curtain holder; tieback
**alzapié** *m* snare, trap
**alzaprima** *f* lever, crowbar; wedge; (mus.) bridge (*in string instruments*)
**alzaprimar** *va* to raise with a lever or wedge; to arouse, incite, stir up
**alzapuertas** *m* (*pl:* **-tas**) dumb player, actor of small parts, supernumerary
**alzar** **§76** *va* to raise, lift, elevate, heave, hoist; to pick up; to carry off; to hide, lock up; to cut (*cards*); to elevate (*the host*); (b.b.) to gather; *vr* to rise, get up; to revolt; to become fraudulently bankrupt; to leave with one's winnings; (Am.) to run away; **alzarse a mayores** to get stuck up; **alzarse con** to flee with (*e.g., money*)
**alzaválvulas** *m* (*pl:* **-las**) (mach.) tappet
**allá** *adv* there, yonder; back there, long ago; **el más allá** the beyond (*life after death*); **más allá** farther away, farther over there, farther on; **más allá de** beyond; **no estar muy allá** (coll.) to not be very well; **por allá** thereabouts; that way; **tan allá** so far away; **allá en** over in; back in
**allanador -dora** *adj* leveling, flattening; *mf* leveler; *m* book for keeping gold leaf
**allanamiento** *m* leveling, flattening; submission, acquiescence; **allanamiento a la demanda** (law) acceptance of defendant's claim; **allanamiento de morada** housebreaking
**allanar** *va* to level, smooth, flatten; to overcome, iron out, get around (*e.g., a difficulty*); to subdue; to admit into; to break into (*a house*); *vn* to level off; *vr* to tumble down; to yield, submit; to humble oneself

**allegadizo -za** *adj* gathered or piled up at random
**allegado -da** *adj* near, close; related; partisan; (Am.) foster; *mf* relative; partisan, follower
**allegador -dora** *mf* gatherer, reaper; *m* board on which thrashed wheat is gathered
**allegamiento** *m* collecting, gathering, reaping; relationship, union, close friendship
**allegar** §59 *va* to collect, gather, reap; to add; *vn* to approach, to arrive; *vr* to approach, to arrive; **allegarse a** to become attached to, to become a follower of, to agree with
**allende** *adv* beyond, elsewhere; **de allende y de aquende** from both sides; **allende de** besides, in addition to; *prep* beyond; **de allende los mares** from overseas
**allí** *adv* there; then; **de allí que** with the result that; **por allí** that way; **allí dentro** in there
**alloza** *f* green almond
**allozar** *m* almond plantation or grove
**allozo** *m* (bot.) almond tree; (bot.) wild almond tree
**alludel** *m* var. of **aludel**
**allulla** *f* (Am.) corn-meal bread
**ama** *f* mistress (*of a household*); housekeeper; housewife, lady of the house; owner, landlady, proprietress; landlord's wife; **ama de brazos** child's nurse; **ama de casa** housewife; **ama de cría** wet nurse; **ama de gobierno** housekeeper; **ama de leche** wet nurse; **ama de llaves** housekeeper; **ama seca** dry nurse
**amabilidad** *f* amiability
**amabilísimo -ma** *adj super* very or most amiable or kind
**amable** *adj* amiable, affable, kind, lovable
**amacayo** *m* (bot.) jacobean lily
**amaceno -na** *adj* Damascene; *m* (bot.) damson (*tree*); *f* damson (*fruit*)
**amacollar** *vn & vr* to put forth clusters or bunches (*of sprouts*)
**amachetear** *va* to strike with a machete, to hack at
**amachinar** *vr* (Am.) to cohabit, to get intimate
**amacho -cha** *adj* (Am.) strong, vigorous, outstanding
**amadís** *m* chivalrous man
**amado -da** *adj & mf* beloved
**amador -dora** *adj* loving, fond; *mf* lover
**amadrigar** §59 *va* to welcome, take, shelter, receive with open arms; *vr* to burrow, to hole up; to seclude oneself, to live in retirement
**amadrinar** *va* to couple, yoke together; to act as godmother to, to act as bridesmaid to; (naut.) to fasten together, to splice; to sponsor, to second, to sanction; to reinforce, to strengthen
**amaestramiento** *m* teaching, coaching; training
**amaestrar** *va* to teach, to coach; to train (*an animal*)
**amagamiento** *m* (Am.) fissure, cleft
**amagar** §59 *va* to threaten, to hint, to show signs of; to feint; (dial.) to hide; *vn* to threaten, to look threatening, to be impending; **amagar a** + *inf* to move to + *inf;* to threaten to + *inf; vr* (dial.) to hide
**amago** *m* threat, menace; sign, indication, symptom; feint
**ámago** *m* beebread; nausea, loathing, disgust
**amainar** *va* (naut.) to lower, to shorten (*a sail*); to lessen, relax; *vn* to subside, die down (*said, e.g., of the wind*); to lessen; to yield; *vr* to lessen; to yield
**amaine** *m* (naut.) lowering, shortening; lessening, slacking; subsiding; yielding
**amaitinar** *va* to watch, to spy upon
**amajadar** *va* to fertilize (*a field*) with sheep; *vn* to seek shelter in the fold
**amalayar** *va* (Am.) to yearn for
**amalecita** *m* (Bib.) Amalekite
**amalgama** *f* (chem., mineral. & fig.) amalgam
**amalgamación** *f* amalgamation; (min.) amalgamation process
**amalgamar** *va & vr* (chem. & fig.) to amalgamate
**Amalia** *f* Amelia
**amamantamiento** *m* nursing, suckling
**amamantar** *va* to nurse, to suckle
**amán** *m* amnesty; (*cap.*) *m* (Bib.) Haman
**amancebamiento** *m* concubinage, cohabitation
**amancebar** *vr* to live in concubinage, to cohabit
**amancillar** *va* to stain, spot; to sully, tarnish, defame
**amanecer** *m* dawn, daybreak; **al amanecer** at daybreak; §34 *va* (poet.) to light up, illuminate; *vn* to dawn, to begin to get light; to begin to appear; to start the day, to get awake; **amanecer en** to be at (*a certain place*) at daybreak or in the morning; to awaken in
**amanecida** *f* dawn, daybreak
**amanerado -da** *adj* mannered, affected
**amaneramiento** *m* mannerism, affectation
**amanerar** *vr* to indulge in mannerisms, to become affected, to act affectedly
**amanita** *f* (bot.) amanita
**amanojado -da** *adj* bunchy
**amanojar** *va* to gather by the handful, to gather in bunches
**amansador -dora** *adj* taming; soothing, appeasing; *mf* tamer; horse breaker; soother, appeaser
**amansamiento** *m* taming, subduing; soothing, appeasement; tameness
**amansar** *va* to tame (*an animal*); to break (*a horse*); to soothe, to appease
**amanse** *m* (Am.) var. of **amansamiento**
**amantar** *va* to cloak, to blanket
**amante** *adj* fond, loving; *mf* (Am.) lover, paramour; *m* lover; (naut.) lift; *f* lover, sweetheart
**amantillar** *va* (naut.) to hoist by hauling on the lifts
**amantillo** *m* (naut.) lift, topping lift
**amanuense** *mf* amanuensis
**amañado -da** *adj* skilful, clever; faked; stacked (*said of cards*)
**amañar** *va* to do skilfully or cleverly; to fake; *vr* to be handy, to acquire skill, to become expert; **amañarse a** + *inf* to settle down to + *inf*
**amaño** *m* skill, cleverness, aptitude; **amaños** *mpl* tools, implements; machinations, trickery
**amapola** *f* (bot.) poppy, corn poppy
**amar** *va* to love
**amaracino -na** *adj* (pertaining to) sweet marjoram
**amáraco** *m* (bot.) sweet marjoram
**amaraje** *m* (aer.) alighting on water
**amarantáceo -a** *adj* (bot.) amaranthaceous
**amarantino -na** *adj* amaranthine; *f* (bot.) globe amaranth
**amaranto** *m* (bot.) amaranth
**amarar** *vn* (aer.) to alight on water
**amarchantar** *vr* (Am.) to become a customer, to deal regularly
**amarescente** *adj* bitterish
**amargaleja** *f* sloe (*fruit*)
**amargar** §59 *va* to make bitter; to embitter; to spoil (*a party, an evening*); *vn & vr* to become bitter; to become embittered
**amargo -ga** *adj* bitter; grievous; grieved; *m* bitterness; bitter-almond candy; **amargos** *mpl* bitters
**amargón** *m* (bot.) dandelion
**amargor** *m* bitterness; sorrow, grief
**amargoso -sa** *adj* bitter
**amarguera** *f* (bot.) shrubby hare's-ear
**amarguillo -lla** *adj* bitterish
**amargura** *f* bitterness; sorrow, grief
**amaricado -da** *adj* (coll.) effeminate
**amarilis** *f* (bot.) amaryllis; (*cap.*) *s* Amaryllis (*shepherdess*)
**amarilla** *f* see **amarillo**
**amarillear** *vn* to show yellow, to be yellowish
**amarillecer** §34 *vn* to become yellow
**amarillejo -ja** or **amarillento -ta** *adj* yellowish
**amarilleo** *m* showing yellow, yellowishness
**amarillez** *f* yellowness
**amarillo -lla** *adj* yellow; *m* yellow; jaundice; drowsiness of silk worms in damp weather; **amarillo indio** Indian yellow; *f* (vet.) sheep jaundice
**amarilloso -sa** *adj* yellowish
**amarinar** *va* to salt (*fish*); to man (*a ship*)
**amariposado -da** *adj* butterfly-shaped
**amaro** *m* (bot.) clary

**amarra** *f* martingale; (naut.) mooring line or cable; **amarras** *fpl* protection, support; **falsa amarra** (naut.) guest rope
**amarradero** *m* hitching post, hitching ring; tying place, ring for tying something; (naut.) bollard, mooring post; (naut.) mooring berth
**amarradijo** *m* (Am.) granny knot, bad knot
**amarradura** *f* mooring, moorage
**amarraje** *m* moorage (*charge for mooring*)
**amarrar** *va* to moor, lash, tie up; to stack (*cards*)
**amarrazones** *mpl* (naut.) ground tackle
**amarre** *m* mooring, tying, fastening; tie, splice; mooring rope, line, or cable; stacking (*cards*)
**amarro** *m* mooring line or cable; (Am.) pack of cigarets
**amartelado -da** *adj* amorous, in love; **estar amartelado** (coll.) to be cuddly
**amartelamiento** *m* (coll.) lovemaking, infatuation
**amartelar** *va* to make love to, to court, to woo; to love with devotion; to make jealous, to infatuate; *vr* to fall in love; to get jealous, to become infatuated
**amartillar** *va* to hammer; to cock (*a gun*)
**amasada** *f* (Am.) batch of dough; (Am.) batch of mortar
**amasadera** *f* kneading trough, kneading board, kneading machine
**amasadero** *m* kneading room
**amasador -dora** *adj* kneading; *mf* kneader; baker; *m* kneading room
**amasadura** *f* kneading; batch of dough
**amasamiento** *m* kneading; massaging
**amasandería** *f* (Am.) small bakery, small baker's shop
**amasandero** *m* (Am.) small baker
**amasar** *va* to knead; to prepare, to arrange; to massage; to cook up (*e.g., an intrigue*); to amass (*money, a fortune*)
**amasijo** *m* kneading; batch of dough; batch of mortar; job, task; plot, intrigue; medley, hodgepodge
**Amata** *f* Amy
**amate** *m* (bot.) rubber plant (*Ficus elastica*); (bot.) benjamin tree (*Ficus benjamina*)
**amatista** *f* amethyst
**amativo -va** *adj* amative
**amatorio -ria** *adj* amatory
**amaurosis** *f* (path.) amaurosis
**amayorazgar** §59 *va* (law) to entail, to leave in entail
**amazacotado -da** *adj* heavy, thick; ponderous, stodgy, awkward, clumsy
**amazona** *f* amazon (*masculine woman*); equestrienne, horsewoman; riding habit (*of woman*); ostrich plume; (orn.) Amazon (*parrot*); (myth.) Amazon
**Amazonas** *m* Amazon (*river*)
**Amazonia** *f* see **amazonio**
**amazónico -ca** *adj* Amazonian
**amazonio -nia** *adj* Amazonian; (*cap.*) *f* basin of the Amazon and its tributaries
**amazonita** *f* (mineral.) amazonite
**ambages** *mpl* ambages, quibbling, ambiguity; **sin ambages** without beating about the bush
**ambagioso -sa** *adj* ambagious, roundabout, ambiguous
**ámbar** *m* amber; **ámbar gris** ambergris; **ámbar negro** black amber
**ambarino -na** *adj* (pertaining to) amber; *f* musk, civet
**Amberes** *f* Antwerp
**amberino -na** *adj* (pertaining to) Antwerp; *mf* native or inhabitant of Antwerp
**ambición** *f* ambition
**ambicionar** *va* to be ambitious for, to desire earnestly, to strive for; **ambicionar** + *inf* to be ambitious to + *inf*
**ambicioso -sa** *adj* ambitious; eager, greedy; climbing, clinging (*plant, vine*); **ambicioso de figurar** social climber
**ambidexteridad** *f* or **ambidextrismo** *m* ambidexterity
**ambidextro -tra** *adj* ambidextrous
**ambientación** *f* atmosphere
**ambiental** *adj* environmental
**ambientar** *va* to give atmosphere to; to acclimate
**ambiente** *adj* ambient; *m* atmosphere; (fig.) atmosphere
**ambigú** *m* (*pl:* **-gúes**) buffet supper; buffet, refreshment bar, refreshment counter
**ambigüedad** *f* ambiguity
**ambiguo -gua** *adj* ambiguous; (gram.) common (*gender*)
**ambir** *m* (Am.) tobacco juice (*in pipestem*); (Am.) tobacco stain (*on fingers*)
**ámbito** *m* ambit, contour; limit, boundary line; compass, scope
**ambivalencia** *f* (psychol.) ambivalence
**ambivalente** *adj* ambivalent
**amblador -dora** *adj* ambling; *mf* ambler
**ambladura** *f* amble
**amblar** *vn* to amble, to pace
**ambleo** *m* short, thick wax candle; candlestick
**ambligonio -nia** *adj* (geom.) obtuse-angled
**ambliopía** *f* (path.) amblyopia
**ambo** *m* two-number combination in a lottery; (Am.) two-piece suit
**ambón** *m* ambo
**ambos -bas** *adj & pron indef* both; **ambos a dos** both
**ambrosía** *f* (bot., myth. & fig.) ambrosia
**ambrosíaco -ca** *adj* ambrosial
**ambrosiano -na** *adj* Ambrosian
**Ambrosio** *m* Ambrose
**ambucia** *f* (Am.) gluttony, greediness
**ambuesta** *f* double handful
**ambulacral** *adj* (zool.) ambulacral
**ambulacro** *m* hall, passage; (zool.) ambulacrum
**ambulancia** *f* ambulance; (mil.) field hospital; **ambulancia de correos** railway post office, post office car; **ambulancia de vía férrea** (mil.) hospital train
**ambulanciero -ra** *mf* ambulance driver
**ambulante** *adj* ambulant, walking; *m* railway mail clerk
**ambular** *vn* to ambulate
**ambulativo -va** *adj* roving, wandering
**ambulatorio -ria** *adj* ambulatory
**ambustión** *f* burning, scalding; (surg.) cauterization
**ameba** *f* var. of **amiba**
**amebeo** *m* amoebaeum (*dialogue in verse*)
**amechar** *va* to put a wick in; to lard (*meat, etc.*)
**amedrentador -dora** *adj* frightening; *mf* frightener
**amedrentar** *va* to frighten, scare; *vr* to get scared
**amelanquier** *m* (bot.) chokeberry
**amelga** *f* ridge between plowed furrows; plot of ground marked for planting
**amelgado -da** *adj* unevenly sown, unevenly growing; *m* (prov.) boundary mound
**amelgar** §59 *va* to plow regularly; to mark off with mounds to show boundaries
**amelonado -da** *adj* melon-shaped; (coll.) lovesick
**amelonar** *vr* (coll.) to fall madly in love
**amén** *m & interj* amen; **decir a todo amén** (coll.) to agree with everything; **en un decir amén** (coll.) in a jiffy; **amén de** (coll.) aside from, except for; (coll.) in addition to, besides
**amenaza** *f* threat, menace
**amenazador -dora** *adj* threatening, menacing; *mf* threatener
**amenazante** *adj* threatening, menacing, impending
**amenazar** §76 *va & vn* to threaten; **amenazar** + *inf* or **amenazar con** + *inf* to threaten to + *inf*
**amenguamiento** *m* lessening, diminution; belittlement; defamation
**amenguar** §23 *va* to lessen, diminish; to belittle, depreciate; to defame
**amenidad** *f* amenity
**amenizar** §76 *va* to make pleasant, to make agreeable, to add charm to
**ameno -na** *adj* pleasant, agreeable, charming
**amenorrea** *f* (path.) amenorrhea
**amentáceo -a** *adj* (bot.) amentaceous
**amentar** §18 *va* to fasten with a strap; to lace (*footwear*)
**amento** *m* (bot.) ament, catkin, cattail; (archaic) leather strap; (obs.) shoelace
**ameos** *m* (*pl:* **-os**) (bot.) bishop's-weed

**amerar** *va* to mix, to mix with water; *vr* to soak in, to percolate
**amerengado -da** *adj* like meringue; sweet, sugary; (coll.) prudish, overnice, prissy
**América** *f* America; **la América Central** Central America; **la América del Norte** North America; **la América del Sur** South America; **la América Latina** Latin America; **la Pequeña América** Little America (*Antarctic base*)
**americana** *f* see **americano**
**americanismo** *m* Americanism; (Am.) U.S. interference in the affairs of other nations of the Western Hemisphere
**americanista** *mf* Americanist
**americanización** *f* Americanization
**americanizar** §76 *va* to Americanize; *vr* to Americanize, to become Americanized
**americano -na** *adj & mf* American; Spanish American; *f* sack coat; **americana sport** sport coat
**americio** *m* (chem.) americium
**americomanía** *f* Americomania
**amerindio -dia** *adj* Amerindian; *mf* Amerind, Amerindian
**amerizar** §76 *vn* var. of **amarar**
**amestizado -da** *adj* like a half-breed
**ametalado -da** *adj* metallic; (fig.) metallic (*said, e.g., of voice*)
**ametista** *f* var. of **amatista**
**ametrallador** *m* machine gunner
**ametralladora** *f* machine gun; **ametralladora antiaérea** anti-aircraft gun
**ametrallar** *va* to machine-gun
**ametropía** *f* (path.) ametropia
**amezquinar** *vr* to complain
**amezquindar** *vr* to become sad
**amia** *f* (ichth.) cub shark; (ichth.) bowfin
**amianto** *m* asbestos
**amiba** *f* (zool.) amoeba
**amibiano -na** *adj* amoebic
**amibo** *m* var. of **amiba**
**amiboideo -a** *adj* amoeboid
**amicísimo -ma** *adj super* very or most friendly
**amida** *f* (chem.) amide
**amidina** *f* (chem.) amidine
**amidógeno** *m* (chem.) amidogen
**amidol** *m* (chem.) amidol
**amiento** *m* (archaic) leather strap; (obs.) shoelace
**amiga** *f* see **amigo**
**amigabilidad** *f* amicability, friendliness
**amigable** *adj* amicable, friendly; harmonious, concordant
**amigacho** *m* (coll.) chum, crony, husband's side-kick; (coll.) sugar daddy
**amigar** §59 *va* to bring together, to make friendly; *vr* to become friendly; to cohabit
**amígdala** *f* (anat.) amygdala; (anat.) tonsil; **amígdala palatina** (anat.) tonsil
**amigdalina** *f* (chem.) amygdalin
**amigdalitis** *f* (path.) tonsillitis
**amigdaloide** *adj* (mineral.) amygdaloid, amygdaloidal
**amigdalotomía** *f* (surg.) tonsillectomy
**amigo -ga** *adj* friendly; fond; **hacerse amigo de** to make friends with; **ser amigo de** to be fond of, to have a liking for; *mf* friend; sweetheart; **amigo del alma** or **amigo del corazón** bosom friend; *m* male paramour; *f* mistress, concubine; schoolmistress; kindergarten, girls' school; **amiga de noche** (bot.) tuberose
**amigote** *m* (coll.) old friend, pal
**amiláceo -a** *adj* amylaceous, starchy
**amilanado -da** *adj* cowardly; lazy
**amilanamiento** *m* terror, intimidation
**amilanar** *va* to terrify, intimidate, cow; *vr* to be terrified, be intimidated, be cowed
**amilasa** *f* (biochem.) amylase
**Amílcar** *m* Hamilcar
**amileno** *m* (chem.) amylene
**amílico -ca** *adj* (chem.) amylic; *m* (slang) rotgut, poor wine
**amilo** *m* (chem.) amyl
**amiloideo -a** *adj* amyloid
**amiloidosis** *f* (path.) amyloidosis
**amilopsina** *f* (chem.) amylopsin
**amillaramiento** *m* tax assessment
**amillarar** *va* to assess (*property*) for taxes
**amillonado -da** *adj* extremely rich
**amimar** *va* to pet, fondle, indulge
**amina** *f* (chem.) amine
**amínico -ca** *adj* (chem.) aminic
**aminoácidos** *mpl* (chem.) amino acids
**aminoración** *f* lessening, diminution; weakening
**aminorar** *va* to lessen, diminish; to weaken
**amir** *m* amir
**amistad** *f* friendship; friendly connection, friend; kindness; cohabitation, concubinage; affinity; **hacer las amistades** (coll.) to make up; **romper las amistades** (coll.) to fall out, to become enemies; **trabar amistad** to strike up a friendship
**amistar** *va* to bring together, to make friendly; *vr* to become friends, to become reconciled
**amistoso -sa** *adj* friendly
**amitigar** §59 *va* var. of **mitigar**
**amito** *m* (eccl.) amice
**amitosis** *f* (biol.) amitosis
**amnesia** *f* (path.) amnesia
**amnésico -ca** *adj* amnesic
**amnícola** *adj* growing along rivers
**amnios** *m* (*pl:* **-nios**) (anat.) amnion
**amniota** *adj & m* (zool.) amniote
**amniótico -ca** *adj* (anat.) amniotic
**amnistía** *f* amnesty
**amnistiar** §90 *va* to amnesty, to grant amnesty to
**am.º** abr. of **amigo**
**amo** *m* master (*of a household*); head of family; owner, landlord, proprietor; foster father; boss, foreman, overseer; **amos** *mpl* master and mistress; landlord and his wife; **el amo grande** (coll.) God; **ser el amo del cotarro** (dial.) to rule the roost
**amoblar** §77 *va* to furnish
**amodita** *f* (zool.) horned serpent
**amodorrado -da** *adj* drowsy, numb, sleepy
**amodorramiento** *m* drowsiness, numbness, sleepiness
**amodorrante** *adj* soporific; numbing
**amodorrar** *vr* to get drowsy; to grow numb; to fall asleep
**amodorrecer** §34 *va* to make drowsy, to make numb
**amodorrido -da** *adj* drowsy, numb, sleepy
**amófilo** *m* (ent.) sand wasp
**amogotado -da** *adj* knoll-shaped, humped
**amohecer** §34 *va & vr* to mold, mildew, rust
**amohinar** §99 *va* to vex, annoy; *vr* to get vexed, be annoyed
**amojamar** *va* to dry and salt (*tuna fish*); *vr* to wither, dry up
**amojelar** *va* (naut.) to seize (*a cable*)
**amojonamiento** *m* marking with landmarks; landmarks
**amojonar** *va* to mark off with landmarks, to put landmarks on
**amoladera** *f* grindstone, whetstone
**amolador -dora** *adj* grinding, sharpening; (coll.) boring, annoying, tedious; *mf* grinder, sharpener; *f* grinder, grinding machine
**amoladura** *f* grinding, sharpening; **amoladuras** *fpl* grindings
**amolar** §77 *va* to grind, sharpen; (coll.) to bore, annoy
**amoldamiento** *m* molding, fitting, modeling
**amoldar** *va* to mold, pattern, adjust, adapt, fit, model; *vr* to mold oneself, pattern oneself
**amole** *m* soap root, soap bark
**amollar** *va* (naut.) to ease off, to pay out (*rope, cable, etc.*); *vn* to play low (*in card games*); to yield, give, give in
**amollentar** *va* to soften
**amolletado -da** *adj* roll-shaped, loaf-shaped
**amomo** *m* (bot.) amomum
**amonar** *vr* (coll.) to get drunk
**amondongado -da** *adj* (coll.) flabby
**amonedación** *f* coining, coinage
**amonedar** *va* to coin, to mint
**amonestación** *f* admonition; marriage banns; **correr las amonestaciones** to publish the banns
**amonestador -dora** *adj* admonishing; *mf* admonisher
**amonestamiento** *m* admonishment

**amonestar** *va* to admonish; to publish the banns of
**amoniacal** *adj* ammoniacal
**amoníaco -ca** *adj* ammoniac, ammoniacal; *m* (chem.) ammonia; ammoniac (*gum resin*); **amoníaco líquido** (chem.) liquid ammonia
**amónico -ca** *adj* ammonic, (pertaining to) ammonium
**amonio** *m* (chem.) ammonium
**amonita** *f* (pal.) ammonite; *mf* (Bib.) Ammonite
**amontar** *va* to put to flight; *vr* to take cover, to flee to the woods
**amontazgar** §59 *va* var. of **montazgar**
**amontillado** *m* pale dry sherry
**amontonador -dora** *adj* heaping, accumulating, hoarding; *mf* gatherer, accumulator, hoarder
**amontonamiento** *m* heaping, piling, accumulation; hoarding, hoard
**amontonar** *va* to heap, pile, accumulate, hoard; *vr* to pile up, to collect, to gather; to be crowded, to crowd; (coll.) to get angry; to cohabit
**amor** *m* love; beloved; (*cap.*) *m* Cupid, Amor; **amores** *mpl* amour, love affair; (bot.) hedgehog parsley; **al amor del agua** with the current; obligingly; **al amor de la lumbre** at the fireside, in the warmth of the fire; **a su amor** at ease, leisurely; **de mil amores** with the greatest pleasure; **amor al uso** (bot.) cotton rose; **amor cortés** courtly love; **amor de hortelano** (bot.) bedstraw; **amor platónico** Platonic love; **amor propio** amour-propre
**amoral** *adj* amoral, unmoral
**amoralidad** *f* amorality
**amoratado -da** *adj* black-and-blue
**amoratar** *va* to turn purple; to make black and blue; *vn* to turn purple; to get black and blue
**amorcillo** *m* flirtation, passing fancy; (f.a.) little Cupid
**amordazamiento** *m* muzzling; (fig.) muzzling, gag
**amordazar** §76 *va* to muzzle; to gag; (fig.) to muzzle, to gag
**amorecer** §34 *va* to cover or serve (*a female sheep*); *vr* to be in rut (*said of sheep*)
**amorfia** *f* amorphia; organic deformity
**amorfismo** *m* amorphism
**amorfo -fa** *adj* amorphous
**amorgar** §59 *va* to drug (*fish*) with olive pulp
**amoricones** *mpl* (coll.) love glances, flirtations
**amorío** *m* (coll.) love-making; (coll.) love affair, flirtation
**amoriscado -da** *adj* Moorish, Moorish-looking
**amormado -da** *adj* suffering from glanders
**amormío** *m* (bot.) sea daffodil
**amoroso -sa** *adj* amorous; loving, affectionate; soft, malleable; mild, pleasant
**amorrar** *va* (naut.) to make pitch at the bow; (naut.) to beach head-on; *vn* & *vr* to hang one's head; (coll.) to sulk, to brood; (naut.) to dip the bows under
**amorronar** *va* (naut.) to roll and knot (*a flag*) to make a waft for hoisting as a signal of distress
**amortajar** *va* to shroud, to cover with a shroud, to lay out; to mortise
**amortecer** §34 *va* to lessen, deaden, muffle, tone down; *vr* to die away, to become faint, to be muffled; to faint
**amortecimiento** *m* lessening, deadening, muffling; faint, fainting; faintness
**amortiguación** *f* deadening, muffling; lessening, softening; dimming, damping; cushioning, absorbing; **amortiguación de las crecidas** flood control
**amortiguador -dora** *adj* deadening, muffling; lessening, softening; dimming, damping; *mf* deadener; lessener; dimmer, damper; *m* shock absorber; door check; bumper (*of automobile*); **amortiguador de luz** (aut.) dimmer; **amortiguador de ruido** (mach.) muffler
**amortiguamiento** *m* var. of **amortiguación**
**amortiguar** §23 *va* to deaden, muffle; to lessen, soften, tone down; to dim, to damp; to cushion (*a blow or shock*); to absorb (*a shock*); (elec.) to damp (*electromagnetic waves*)
**amortizable** *adj* amortizable
**amortización** *f* amortization, amortizement
**amortizar** §76 *va* to amortize; to pay off; to refund; to eliminate (*a position, office, etc.*)
**Amós** *m* Amos
**amoscar** §86 *vr* to become annoyed, peeved, or miffed
**amostachado -da** *adj* mustachioed
**amostazar** §76 *va* (coll.) to anger, provoke; *vr* (coll.) to become angry, get provoked
**amotinado -da** *adj* mutinous, rebellious, riotous; *mf* mutineer, insurgent, rebel
**amotinador -dora** *adj* rabble-rousing; mutinous, riotous; *mf* rabble rouser, mutineer, insurgent
**amotinamiento** *m* mutiny, uprising, insurrection
**amotinar** *va* to stir up, to upset; to incite to riot or mutiny; *vr* to be stirred up, to be upset; to rise up, to rebel, to riot, to mutiny
**amover** §63 *va* to remove, discharge, dismiss
**amovibilidad** *f* removability
**amovible** *adj* removable; detachable
**ampalagua** *f* (zool.) large boa
**amparador -dora** *adj* protecting, sheltering; *mf* protector, helper
**amparar** *va* to protect, shelter; *vr* to seek shelter; to defend oneself, to protect oneself; **ampararse a** to have recourse to, to seek the protection of; **ampararse de** to seek the protection of; to avail oneself of
**amparito** *m* stall (*e.g., in a market*)
**amparo** *m* protection, shelter, refuge; stall (*e.g., in a market*); aid, favor; (*cap.*) *f* Amparo (*female name*)
**ampélido** *m* (orn.) waxwing
**ampelita** *f* (mineral.) ampelite
**ampelografía** *f* ampelography
**amper** *m* (elec.) ampere
**amperaje** *m* (elec.) amperage
**amperímetro** *m* (elec.) ammeter; **amperímetro de hilo caliente** (elec.) hot-wire ammeter
**amperio** *m* (elec.) ampere; **amperio hora** *m* (*pl:* **amperios hora**) (elec.) ampere-hour
**amperio-vuelta** *f* (*pl:* **amperios-vueltas**) (elec.) ampere turn
**amperómetro** *m* var. of **amperímetro**
**ampervuelta** *f* (*pl:* **-tas**) (elec.) ampere turn
**amplexicaulo -la** *adj* (bot.) amplexicaul, amplexicauline
**ampliación** *f* amplification, enlargement, extension; (phot.) enlarging, enlargement
**ampliador -dora** *adj* amplifying, enlarging; *mf* amplifier, enlarger; *f* (phot.) enlarger
**ampliar** §90 *va* to amplify, enlarge, extend, broaden; (phot.) to enlarge
**ampliativo -va** *adj* amplifying, enlarging, amplificatory
**amplificación** *f* amplification; (elec.) amplification; **amplificación en cascada** (elec.) cascade amplification
**amplificador -dora** *adj* amplifying; *mf* amplifier; *m* (elec.) amplifier; **amplificador de poder** or **de potencia** (rad.) power amplifier
**amplificar** §86 *va* to amplify; (elec.) to amplify
**amplificativo -va** *adj* amplificative
**amplio -plia** *adj* ample; full, roomy; prolix; bold
**amplitud** *f* amplitude; roominess; (astr., elec. & mech.) amplitude
**ampo** *m* dazzling white; snowflake; **como el ampo de la nieve** white as the driven snow
**ampolla** *f* blister; bubble; cruet; round-bellied bottle; (med.) ampoule; (anat., bot., eccl., hist. & zool.) ampulla; bulb (*of electric-light or vacuum tube*)
**ampollar** *adj* blisterlike; bubble-shaped; bottle-shaped; bulbous; *va* to blister; to make bulbous; to hollow, to distend; *vr* to blister; to get bulbous; to be hollowed out, to distend
**ampolleta** *f* small vial, small bottle, small cruet; sandglass, hourglass; time taken by sand to run from top of sandglass; bulb, light bulb
**ampulosidad** *f* pomposity, bombast
**ampuloso -sa** *adj* pompous, bombastic
**amputación** *f* amputation
**amputar** *va* amputate
**amuchachado -da** *adj* boyish, boylike
**amueblar** *va* to furnish
**amugamiento** *m* setting up landmarks
**amugronamiento** *m* (hort.) layering

**amugronar** *va* (hort.) to layer
**amujerado -da** *adj* womanish, womanlike, effeminate
**amujeramiento** *m* womanishness, effeminacy
**amulatado -da** *adj* mulattolike
**amuleto** *m* amulet
**amunicionar** *va* to ammunition, supply with ammunition
**amunucar** §86 *vr* to grow sulky, to pout, scowl
**amuñecado -da** *adj* doll-like, puppetlike
**amura** *f* (naut.) tack of a sail; (naut.) beam of ship at one-eighth its length, measured from bow; **cambiar de amura** (naut.) to go about, to come about
**amurada** *f* (naut.) ship's side (*from within*)
**amurallar** *va* to wall, to wall in
**amurar** *va* (naut.) to fasten (*corner of sail*) for tacking; (naut.) to haul on (*a sail*) by the tack; *vn* (naut.) to tack
**amurcar** §86 *va* to gore
**amurco** *m* goring
**amurillar** *va* (hort.) to pile up earth around (*a tree*)
**amurrar** *vr* (Am.) to become glum, to become downcast
**amurriar** *vr* (prov.) var. of **amurrar**
**amusco -ca** *adj* brown
**amusgar** §59 *va* to throw back (*the ears*); to squint (*the eyes*) to see better
**amustiar** *va* & *vr* to wither
**Ana** *f* Ann, Anna, Anne; **Ana Bolena** Anne Boleyn; **Ana de Austria** Anne of Austria; **Ana Estuardo** Queen Anne; (*l.c.*) *f* ell (*measure*)
**anabaptismo** *m* Anabaptism
**anabaptista** *adj* & *mf* Anabaptist
**anabas** *s* (*pl:* **-bas**) (ichth.) anabas, climbing fish
**anabiosis** *f* anabiosis
**anabólico -ca** *adj* anabolic
**anabolismo** *m* (biol.) anabolism
**anacarado -da** *adj* mother-of-pearl (*in appearance*)
**anacardiáceo -a** *adj* (bot.) anacardiaceous
**anacárdico -ca** *adj* (chem.) anacardic
**anacardo** *m* (bot.) cashew (*tree and nut*)
**anaco** *m* (Peru & Bolivia) slit skirt of Indian women; (Ecuador) hair worn in single braid
**anacoluto** *m* (gram.) anacoluthon
**anaconda** *f* (zool.) anaconda
**anacoreta** *m* anchorite; *f* anchoress
**anacorético -ca** *adj* anchoritic
**anacoretismo** *m* anchoritism
**Anacreonte** *m* Anacreon
**anacreóntico -ca** *adj* Anacreontic
**anacrónico -ca** *adj* anachronistic, anachronous
**anacronismo** *m* anachronism
**ánade** *mf* duck; goose; **ánade cuchraretero** (orn.) shoveler; **ánade negro** (orn.) black scoter; **ánade salvaje** (orn.) mallard; **ánade silbador** (orn.) European widgeon
**anadear** *vn* to waddle
**anadeja** *f* duckling
**anadeo** *m* waddle, waddling
**anadino -na** *mf* duckling
**anadón** *m* duckling; nonfloating log
**anadromo -ma** *adj* anadromous
**anaeróbico -ca** *adj* anaerobic
**anaerobio -bia** *adj* anaerobic; *m* anaerobe
**anafase** *f* (biol.) anaphase
**anafe** *m* portable brazier
**anafilaxis** *f* (path.) anaphylaxis
**anáfora** *f* (rhet. & astrol.) anaphora
**anafre** *m* portable brazier
**anafrodisia** *f* (med.) anaphrodisia
**anafrodisíaco -ca** *adj* & *m* (med.) anaphrodisiac
**anafrodita** *adj* anaphroditous; sexually abstinent
**anáglifo** *m* anaglyph
**anagnórisis** *f* (rhet.) anagnorisis
**anagoge** *m* or **anagogía** *f* anagogics; mystical rapture, divine rapture
**anagrama** *m* anagram; **anagramas** *mpl* anagrams (*game*)
**anagramático -ca** *adj* anagrammatic, anagrammatical
**anagramatismo** *m* anagrammatism
**anal** *adj* (anat.) anal
**analectas** *fpl* analecta, analects
**analéptico -ca** *adj* analeptic
**anales** *mpl* annals
**analfabético -ca** *adj* illiterate
**analfabetismo** *m* illiteracy
**analfabeto -ta** *adj* & *mf* illiterate
**analgeno** *m* (pharm.) analgen
**analgesia** *f* (physiol.) analgesia; (med.) general anesthesia
**analgésico -ca** *adj* & *m* analgesic
**analgesina** *f* (pharm.) antipyrene
**análisis** *m* & *f* (*pl:* **-sis**) analysis; **análisis cualitativo** (chem.) qualitative analysis; **análisis cuantitativo** (chem.) quantitative analysis; **análisis espectral** spectrum analysis; **análisis gramatical** parsing
**analista** *mf* annalist; analyst (*analyzer; psychoanalyst*)
**analítico -ca** *adj* analytic, analytical; *f* (philos.) analytics
**analizable** *adj* analyzable
**analizador -dora** *mf* analyzer; analyst; *m* (opt.) analyzer
**analizar** §76 *va* to analyze; **analizar gramaticalmente** to parse
**analogía** *f* analogy; (gram.) inflection
**analógico -ca** *adj* analogical
**análogo -ga** *adj* analogous; similar; *m* analogue; (biol.) analogue
**anamita** *adj* & *mf* Annamese
**anamniótico -ca** *adj* anamniotic
**anamorfosis** *f* (*pl:* **-sis**) anamorphosis; (biol. & bot.) anamorphosis
**ananá** *m* (*pl:* **-naes**) (bot.) pineapple (*plant and fruit*)
**ananás** *m* var. of **ananá**
**Ananías** *m* (Bib.) Ananias
**anapelo** *m* (bot.) wolfsbane
**anapéstico -ca** *adj* anapestic
**anapesto** *m* anapest
**anaplastia** *f* (surg.) anaplasty
**anaplástico -ca** *adj* anaplastic
**anaptixis** *f* (phonet.) anaptyxis
**anaquel** *m* shelf (*in wall, closet, store, etc.*)
**anaquelería** *f* shelving
**anaranjado -da** *adj* & *m* orange (*color*); **anaranjado de metilo** methyl orange
**anarquía** *f* anarchy
**anárquico -ca** *adj* anarchic, anarchical
**anarquismo** *m* anarchism
**anarquista** *adj* anarchistic; *mf* anarch, anarchist
**anarquizar** §76 *va* to spread anarchism in (*a country or people*)
**anasarca** *f* (path.) anasarca
**anascote** *m* serge-like woolen material
**anastasia** *f* (bot.) mugwort
**anastático -ca** *adj* anastatic
**anastigmático -ca** *adj* (opt.) anastigmatic
**anastomizar** §76 *vr* var. of **anastomosar**
**anastomosar** *vr* to anastomose
**anastomosis** *f* (*pl:* **-sis**) (anat. & biol.) anastomosis
**anastomótico -ca** *adj* anastomotic
**anástrofe** *f* (gram.) anastrophe
**anata** *f* yearly income
**anatema** *m* & *f* anathema
**anatematismo** *m* anathematism, anathematization
**anatematización** *f* anathematization
**anatematizar** §76 *va* anathematize
**anatifa** *f* (zool.) goose barnacle
**anatolio -lia** *adj* & *mf* Anatolian
**anatomía** *f* anatomy; **anatomía macroscópica** gross anatomy
**anatómico -ca** *adj* anatomic, anatomical; *mf* anatomist
**anatomista** *mf* anatomist
**anatomizar** §76 *va* to anatomize; (paint. & sculp.) to bring out or emphasize (*the bones and muscles*)
**anavajado -da** *adj* knife-scarred
**anavia** *f* (prov.) bilberry
**Anaxágoras** *m* Anaxagoras
**Anaximandro** *m* Anaximander
**anca** *f* croup, haunch; rump, buttock; **a ancas** or **a las ancas** mounted behind another person (*on horseback*); **no sufrir ancas** (coll.) to take no joking

**ancado -da** *adj* (vet.) stringhalted, stringtied; seated behind another person (*on same mount*); *m* (vet.) stringhalt
**ancestral** *adj* ancestral
**ancianidad** *f* old age
**anciano -na** *adj* old, aged; *m* old man; (eccl.) elder; **el anciano de los días** Ancient of Days (*God*); *f* old woman
**ancilar** *adj* ancillary
**ancla** *f* (naut.) anchor; **echar anclas** to cast anchor; **levar anclas** to weigh anchor; **ancla de la esperanza** (naut.) sheet anchor
**ancladero** *m* anchorage, anchoring place
**anclaje** *m* anchorage; (dent.) anchor
**anclar** *vn* to anchor, to drop anchor
**anclote** *m* small anchor, kedge anchor
**anclotillo** *m* kedge anchor
**ancolia** *f* (bot.) columbine
**ancón** *m* (anat. & arch.) ancon; cove, bay
**anconada** *f* cove, bay
**áncora** *f* (naut., horol. & fig.) anchor
**ancoraje** *m* anchorage; anchoring; anchors
**ancorar** *vn* to anchor, to drop anchor
**ancorca** *f* yellow ocher
**ancorel** *m* stone sinker for fishing nets
**ancorería** *f* anchor foundry
**ancorero** *m* anchor smith
**ancudo -da** *adj* big-rumped
**ancusa** *f* (bot.) alkanet; **ancusa de tintes** (bot.) alkanet (*Alkanna tinctoria*)
**ancusina** *f* (chem.) alkanet
**anchar** *va, vn & vr* to widen, extend, enlarge
**ancheta** *f* small lot (*of goods*); gain, profit
**anchicorto -ta** *adj* wider than long; wide and short
**ancho -cha** *adj* broad, wide; full, ample, lax, loose, loose-fitting; **a sus anchas** in comfort, at ease, as one pleases; **ancho de conciencia** indulgent; free, lax; self-indulgent; *m* width, breadth; **ancho de vía** (rail.) track gauge
**anchoa** *f* (ichth.) anchovy; **anchoa de banco** (ichth.) bluefish
**anchor** *m* var. of **anchura**
**anchova** *f* (ichth.) anchovy
**anchuelo -la** *adj* widish, rather wide
**anchura** *f* width, breadth; extension; fullness, ampleness; ease, comfort, freedom, looseness
**anchuroso -sa** *adj* broad, wide, spacious
**andada** *f* see **andado**
**andadero -ra** *adj* passable, fit to walk or pass through; wandering, gadding; **andaderas** *fpl* gocart, walker (*to support child learning to walk*)
**andado -da** *adj* trodden, frequented; ordinary, common; worn, used; *f* thin, hard-baked cake or cracker; **andadas** *fpl* tracks (*of wild animals*); **volver a las andadas** (coll.) to backslide, to return to one's old tricks
**andador -dora** *adj* walking, fast-walking, swift; wandering, gadding; *mf* walker, runner; fast mover; great traveler; gadabout; *m* court messenger; footpath; **andadores** *mpl* leading strings (*to support child learning to walk*)
**andadura** *f* gait; walking, running; pace, amble
**andahuertas** *f* (*pl:* **-tas**) (orn.) garden warbler, whitethroat
**Andalucía** *f* Andalusia
**andalucismo** *m* Andalusianism
**andalucita** *f* (mineral.) andalusite
**andaluz -luza** *adj & mf* Andalusian; *m* Andalusian (*dialect*)
**andaluzada** *f* (coll.) tall story, Andalusian boastfulness
**andamiada** *f* or **andamiaje** *m* scaffolding, staging
**andamio** *m* scaffold; platform; skeleton; **andamio suspendido** hanging scaffold
**andana** *f* row, line, tier; **llamarse andana** (coll.) to take back a promise
**andanada** *f* (naut.) broadside; (taur.) covered section at top of grandstand; (coll.) scolding; (fig.) fusillade (*e.g., of questions*); **soltar la** or **una andanada a** to rake over the coals
**andancia** *f* (Am. & prov.) slight epidemic
**andaniño** *m* gocart (*to support child learning to walk*)
**andante** *adj* walking; errant; *m* (mus.) andante
**andantesco -ca** *adj* chivalrous, quixotic, (pertaining to a) knight-errant
**andantino** *m* (mus.) andantino
**andanza** *f* fate, fortune; (archaic) act, happening
**andar** *m* walk, gait, pace; go; passing (*e.g., of time*); **a largo andar** in time; **a más andar** at full speed ‖ §20 *va* to go (*e.g., two miles*); to go down or up (*a road*) ‖ *vn* to go, to move, to walk, to run; to go about, to travel; to act, to behave; to go, to run, to work (*said, e.g., of a clock*); to be, to feel; to continue, to keep on; to amble, to pace; to sail; to go by, to pass, to elapse (*said of time*); **¡anda!** (coll.) come now!; (coll.) fine!; (coll.) cut it out!; **andar a caballo** to ride horseback; **andar a gatas** to go on all fours; **andar andando** (Am.) to chase around; **andar bien** to keep good time (*said of a clock*); **andar bien de** to be well supplied with; **andar con** to handle; **andar en** to be engaged in; to be going on (*so many years old*); (coll.) to poke into; **andar en cuestiones** to wrangle; **andar reñidos** to be on bad terms ‖ *vr* to go by, to pass, to elapse (*said of time*); to go off, to go away; **andarse en** to give way to, to indulge in; (coll.) to poke into; **andarse por las ramas** to beat about the bush; **andarse sin** + *inf* to go or to do without + *ger*
**andaraje** *m* bucket wheel of noria; frame of garden roller
**andariego -ga** *adj* wandering, roving, gadding; swift, fleet-footed
**andarín -rina** *adj* fast-moving; *mf* fast walker, fast runner; professional runner; *f* (orn.) swallow
**andarivel** *m* ferry cable; cable ferry; aerial tramway, cableway; (naut.) hand rope; gantline
**andarríos** *m* (*pl:* **-ríos**) (orn.) wagtail
**andas** *fpl* litter; stretcher; bier with shafts; portable platform; **en andas** in triumph
**andén** *m* railway platform; boat landing; footpath; side path; sidewalk (*especially on bridge*)
**andero** *m* litter bearer; stretcher-bearer; bier bearer
**Andes** *mpl* Andes
**andinismo** *m* mountain climbing in the Andes
**andinista** *mf* mountain climber in the Andes
**andino -na** *adj & mf* Andean
**ándito** *m* exterior balcony (*going around or almost around a building*)
**andolina** *f* (orn.) swallow
**andorga** *f* (coll.) belly; **llenar la andorga** (coll.) to stuff oneself, to gorge
**andorina** *f* (orn.) swallow
**andorra** *f* (coll.) gadder (*woman*)
**andorrano -na** *adj & mf* Andorran
**andorrear** *vn* to gad about, to walk the streets, to tramp
**andorrero -ra** *adj* gadding, gadding about; *mf* gadder, wanderer
**andosco -ca** *adj* two-year-old (*cattle*)
**andrajero -ra** *mf* ragpicker
**andrajo** *m* rag, tatter; ragamuffin, scalawag; **estar en andrajos** to be in rags
**andrajoso -sa** *adj* ragged, raggedy
**Andrés** *m* Andrew
**andrina** *f* var. of **endrina**
**andrino** *m* var. of **endrino**
**androceo** *m* (bot.) androecium
**Androcles** *m* Androcles
**androfobia** *f* androphobia
**andrógeno** *m* (biochem.) androgen
**andrógino -na** *adj* androgynous; (bot.) androgynous; *mf* androgyne; *m* (bot.) androgyne
**androide** *m* android (*manlike automaton*)
**Andrómaca** *f* (myth.) Andromache
**Andrómeda** *f* (myth. & astr.) Andromeda
**andrómina** *f* (coll.) fraud, deceit, trick, lie, fib
**androsemo** *m* (bot.) androseme
**androsfinge** *m & f* (archeol.) androsphinx
**androsterona** *f* (biochem.) androsterone
**andulario** *m* long, trailing gown
**andullo** *m* fender, shield; plug tobacco; rolled tobacco leaf, pigtail
**andurriales** *mpl* byways, lonely spot, out-of-the-way place
**anduve** *1st sg pret ind of* **andar**

**anea** *f* (bot.) cattail, bulrush, reed mace (*Typha angustifolia*); (bot.) cattail, bulrush (*Typha latifolia*)
**aneblar** §18 *va* to cloud, darken; to cast a cloud over; *vr* to become clouded, get dark
**anécdota** *f* anecdote
**anecdotario** *m* stock or fund of anecdotes, collection of anecdotes
**anecdótico -ca** *adj* anecdotal
**anecdotista** *mf* anecdotist
**anega** *f* (bot.) dill
**anegable** *adj* subject to flooding
**anegación** *f* flooding; drowning; annihilation
**anegadizo -za** *adj* subject to frequent flooding; heavier-than-water
**anegamiento** *m* var. of **anegación**
**anegar** §59 *va* to flood; to drown; to sink; to annihilate; (aut.) to flood (*carburetor*); *vr* to become flooded; to drown; to sink; to be annihilated; (aut.) to become flooded; **anegarse en llanto** to be bathed in tears
**anegociado -da** *adj* busy, full of business
**anejar** *va* var. of **anexar**
**anejín** *m* or **anejir** *m* rhymed proverb set to music
**anejo -ja** *adj* annexed, attached; accessory; dependent; *m* annex; dependency; dependent church or benefice; supplement (*to a periodical*)
**aneldo** *m* (bot.) dill
**aneléctrico -ca** *adj & m* (phys.) anelectric
**anélido -da** *adj & m* (zool.) annelid
**anemia** *f* (path.) anemia; **anemia de los mineros** or **de los túneles** (path.) hookworm disease, tunnel disease; **anemia perniciosa** (path.) pernicious anemia
**anémico -ca** *adj* anemic
**anemometría** *f* anemometry
**anemómetro** *m* anemometer
**anemona, anemone** *f* or **anémone** *f* (bot.) anemone; **anemona de mar** (zool.) sea anemone
**anemoscopio** *m* anemoscope
**anepigráfico -ca** *adj* anepigraphic
**anequín; a anequín** or **de anequín** on a piecework basis (*for shearing sheep*)
**aneroide** *adj* aneroid
**anestesia** *f* anesthesia; **anestesia cruzada** crossed anesthesia; **anestesia de bloque** block anesthesia; **anestesia de conducción** conduction anesthesia; **anestesia espinal** spinal anesthesia; **anestesia general** general anesthesia; **anestesia local** local anesthesia; **anestesia medular** spinal anesthesia; **anestesia regional** conduction anesthesia
**anestesiador** *m* anesthetist
**anestesiar** *va* anesthetize
**anestésico** *adj & m* anesthetic
**anestesiología** *f* anesthesiology
**anestesiólogo -ga** *mf* anesthesiologist
**anestesista** *mf* anesthetist
**anestético -ca** *adj* anesthetic
**aneurisma** *m & f* (path.) aneurysm
**aneurismático -ca** *adj* aneurysmatic
**anexar** *va* to annex; to attach, append; to enclose
**anexidades** *fpl* annexes, supplements, appurtenances
**anexión** *f* annexation
**anexionar** *va* var. of **anexar**
**anexionismo** *m* annexationism
**anexionista** *adj & mf* annexationist
**anexo -xa** *adj* annexed, attached; accessory; dependent; *m* annex; dependency; **anexos** *mpl* (anat.) adnexa
**anfesibena** *f* var. of **anfisbena**
**anfetamina** *f* (pharm.) amphetamine
**anfibio -bia** *adj* amphibian; amphibious; *m* (aer. & biol.) amphibian
**anfíbol** *m* (mineral.) amphibole
**anfibolita** *f* (geol.) amphibolite
**anfibología** *f* amphibology
**anfibológico -ca** *adj* amphibological
**anfíbraco** *m* amphibrach
**anfión** *m* opium; (*cap.*) *m* (myth.) Amphion
**anfípodo -da** *adj & m* (zool.) amphipod
**anfisbena** *f* (zool.) amphisbaena
**anfiscios** *mpl* amphiscians (*inhabitants of tropics*)
**anfiteatro** *m* amphitheater; dissecting room
**Anfitrión** *m* (myth.) Amphitryon; (*l.c.*) *m* (coll.) host, lavish host; (coll.) escort (*of a lady*)
**Anfitrite** *f* (myth. & zool.) Amphitrite
**anfiumo** *m* (zool.) congo snake
**ánfora** *f* amphora; (eccl.) cruet for consecrated oils; (Am.) voting urn
**anfractuosidad** *f* anfractuosity
**anfractuoso -sa** *adj* anfractuous, winding, sinuous, tortuous
**angalete** *m* (Am.) miter box
**angaria** *f* (law) angaria
**angarillas** *fpl* handbarrow; panniers; cruet stand
**angaripola** *f* coarse colored linen; **angaripolas** *fpl* (coll.) gaudy trimmings, garish adornments
**ángaro** *m* beacon fire
**angarrio** *m* (Am.) living skeleton
**angas** *fpl;* **por angas o por mangas** (Am.) one way or another, by hook or by crook
**angazo** *m* rake for gathering shellfish
**ángel** *m* angel; grace, charm; **ángel caído** fallen angel; **ángel custodio** or **de la guarda** guardian angel; **ángel de mar** (ichth.) angelfish; **ángel patudo** (coll.) wolf in sheep's clothing; **tener ángel** to have charm
**Ángela** *f* Angela; **¡Ángela María!** I get you!
**angélica** *f* see **angélico**
**angelical** *adj* angelic or angelical
**angelico** *m* little imp of an angel
**angélico -ca** *adj* angelic or angelical; *f* (bot.) angelica; **angélica carlina** (bot.) carline thistle
**angelín** *m* (bot.) angelin
**angelito** *m* little angel; (fig.) little angel (*winsome or well-behaved child*)
**angelón** *m* large angel; **angelón de retablo** (coll.) awkward fat and chubby person
**angelote** *m* large figure of an angel; chubby child; (ichth.) angelfish
**ángelus** *m* (*pl:* **-lus**) Angelus
**angevino -na** *adj & mf* Angevin
**angina** *f* (path.) angina; **angina de pecho** (path.) angina pectoris
**angiocolitis** *f* (path.) angiocholitis
**angiografía** *f* (anat.) angiography
**angiología** *f* angiology
**angiospermo -ma** *adj* (bot.) angiospermous; *f* (bot.) angiosperm
**angla** *f* see **anglo**
**anglesita** *f* (mineral.) anglesite
**Anglia** *f* Anglia
**anglicanismo** *m* Anglicanism
**anglicano -na** *adj & mf* Anglican
**anglicismo** *m* Anglicism
**anglicización** *f* Anglicization
**anglo -gla** *adj* Anglian; *mf* Anglian; **anglos** *mpl* Angles; *f* cape, promontory
**angloamericano -na** *adj & mf* Anglo-American
**anglocatolicismo** *m* Anglo-Catholicism
**anglocatólico -ca** *adj & mf* Anglo-Catholic
**angloespañol -ñola** *adj* English-Spanish
**anglófilo -la** *adj & mf* Anglophile
**anglofobia** *f* Anglophobia
**anglófobo -ba** *adj & mf* Anglophobe
**angloíndio -da** *adj & mf* Anglo-Indian
**angloiranio -nia** *adj & mf* Anglo-Iranian
**anglomanía** *f* Anglomania
**anglómano -na** *mf* Anglomaniac
**anglonormando -da** *adj & mf* Anglo-Norman; *m* Anglo-Norman (*dialect*)
**anglonorteamericano -na** *adj & mf* Anglo-American
**angloparlante** *adj* English-speaking; *mf* speaker of English
**anglosajón -jona** *adj & mf* Anglo-Saxon; *m* Anglo-Saxon (*language*)
**angora** *mf* Angora (*cat or goat*)
**angostar** *va* to narrow, tighten, contract
**angosto -ta** *adj* narrow
**angostura** *f* narrowness; narrow place or passage; narrows; angostura (*medicinal bark*)
**angosturina** *f* (pharm.) angostura bitters
**angra** *f* cove, inlet
**angrelado -da** *adj* (her.) engrailed
**angstrom** *m* (*pl:* **-troms**) (phys.) angstrom
**anguarina** *f* sleeveless smock frock

**anguila** *f* (ichth.) eel; lash, whip; wiry fellow; **anguilas** *fpl* ways (*for launching a ship*); **escurrirse como una anguila** to be as slippery as an eel; **anguila agachadiza** (ichth.) snipe eel; **anguila de barro** (ichth.) mud eel; **anguila de cabo** (archaic) whip (*for flogging galley slaves*); **anguila eléctrica** (ichth.) electric eel
**anguilazo** *m* (naut.) lash (*stroke with rope's end*)
**anguilero -ra** *adj* for eels; *f* eel garth; eel basket
**anguílula** *f* (zool.) eelworm; **anguílula del vinagre** (zool.) vinegar eel
**anguina** *f* (vet.) inguinal vein
**angula** *f* grig (*young eel*)
**angular** *adj* angular
**angularidad** *f* angularity
**angulemia** *f* coarse cloth of hemp or tow; (*cap.*) *f* Angoulême; **angulemas** *fpl* flattery, coaxing
**ángulo** *m* angle; corner; **de ángulo ancho** (phot.) wide-angle; **en ángulo** at an angle; **ángulo agudo** acute angle; **ángulo complementario** complementary angle; **ángulo de ataque** (aer.) angle of attack; **ángulo de deriva** (aer. & naut.) drift angle; **ángulo de incidencia** (phys.) angle of incidence; **ángulo facial** facial angle; **ángulo obtuso** obtuse angle; **ángulo recto** right angle; **ángulos adyacentes** adjacent angles; **ángulos alternos** alternate angles
**angulosidad** *f* angularity
**anguloso -sa** *adj* angular (*said, e.g., of features*)
**angurria** *f* (coll.) strangury; (Am.) raging hunger
**angustia** *f* anguish, distress, affliction
**angustiado -da** *adj* distressed, grieved; greedy, grasping, mean
**angustiar** *va* to distress, afflict
**angustioso -sa** *adj* distressed, afflicted; grievous, worrisome
**angustura** *f* angostura (*medicinal bark*)
**anhelación** *f* panting, gasping; yearning
**anhelante** *adj* panting, gasping; eager, yearning
**anhelar** *va* to desire eagerly, to crave, to covet; *vn* to gasp, to pant; **anhelar** + *inf* to long to, to yearn to + *inf;* **anhelar por** to long for, to yearn for
**anhélito** *m* shortness of breath, hard breathing
**anhelo** *m* yearning, longing; gasp
**anheloso -sa** *adj* panting, breathless; eager, yearning
**anhídrido** *m* (chem.) anhydrid; **anhídrido carbónico** (chem.) carbon dioxide
**anhidrita** *f* (mineral.) anhydrite
**anhidro -dra** *adj* (chem.) anhydrous
**anhima** *f* (orn.) screamer
**anhinga** *f* (orn.) snakebird
**aní** *m* (*pl:* **-níes**) (orn.) ani
**Aníbal** *m* Hannibal
**anidación** *f* nesting
**anidar** *va* to shelter, take in; *vn & vr* to nestle, make one's nest; to live, dwell
**anieblar** *va & vr* var. of **aneblar**
**aniego** *m* var. of **anegación**
**anilina** *f* (chem.) anilin
**anilla** *f* curtain ring; ring, hoop; ring (*for gymnastics*); bow or loop (*of key*)
**anillado -da** *adj* ringed, ring-shaped, annulated; *m* (zool.) annelid
**anillar** *va* to form into rings or hoops; to make rings in; to fasten with rings or hoops; to put a ring on
**anillejo** or **anillete** *m* little ring, ringlet
**anillo** *m* ring; cigar band; (anat., arch. & bot.) annulus; (her. & zool.) annulet; (naut.) grommet; **de anillo** honorary; **venir como anillo al dedo** (coll.) to fit the case perfectly, to come in the nick of time; **anillo de boda** wedding ring; **anillo de collera** terret; **anillo de compromiso** engagement ring; **anillo de émbolo** piston ring; **Anillo del Nibelungo** (myth.) Ring of the Nibelung; **anillo de pedida** engagement ring; **anillos de Saturno** (astr.) rings of Saturn; **anillo sigilar** seal ring, signet ring
**ánima** *f* soul; soul in purgatory; bore (*of firearm*); (elec.) core (*of cable*); (found.) core (*of a mold*); web (*of rail*); **ánimas** *fpl* (eccl.) ringing of bells at sunset for prayers for souls in purgatory
**animación** *f* animation; liveliness; bustle, movement
**animado -da** *adj* animate; lively, animated
**animador -dora** *adj* animating; enlivening; encouraging, inspiring; *mf* animator; enlivener; inspirer; (mov.) animator; *m* master of ceremonies (*in night club, radio, etc.*)
**animadversión** *f* animadversion; enmity, ill will
**animal** *adj & m* animal
**animalada** *f* (coll.) stupidity
**animálculo** *m* animalcule
**animalejo** *m* little animal
**animalia** *f* animals, animal kingdom
**animalidad** *f* animality
**animalismo** *m* animalism
**animalista** *adj* animalistic; *mf* animalist
**animalización** *f* animalization
**animalizar** §76 *va* to animalize; *vr* to become animalized
**animalote** *m* big animal
**animalucho** *m* ugly animal; (coll.) big ignoramus
**animar** *va* to animate; to enliven; to encourage; to strengthen; to drive, impel; **animar a** + *inf* to encourage to + *inf; vr* to become enlivened; to take heart, cheer up, feel encouraged
**anime** *m* (bot.) courbaril (*tree and resin*)
**animero** *m* beggar for souls in purgatory
**anímico -ca** *adj* psychic
**animismo** *m* animism
**animista** *adj* animistic; *mf* animist
**animita** *f* (Am.) firefly
**ánimo** *m* soul; spirit; will, intention; attention, mind, thought; courage, valor; encouragement; **dar ánimo** or **ánimos a** to give encouragement to; **esparcir el ánimo** to relax, take it easy; **tener ánimo de** + *inf* to intend to + *inf*
**animosidad** *f* animosity; bravery, courage
**animoso -sa** *adj* brave, courageous, spirited
**aniñado -da** *adj* childish, babyish; (pertaining to a) baby
**aniñar** *vr* to become childish, to act childishly
**anión** *m* (elec.) anion
**aniquilación** *f* annihilation
**aniquilador -dora** *adj* annihilating, destructive, exhausting; *mf* annihilator, destroyer
**aniquilamiento** *m* annihilation
**aniquilar** *va* to annihilate; to destroy, exhaust; *vr* to be annihilated, to be wiped out; to decline, decay, waste away; to be humbled
**anís** *m* (bot.) anise (*plant and seed*); anise-flavored brandy
**anisado -da** *adj* anisated, flavored with anise; *m* anise-flavored brandy
**anisar** *m* patch of anise; *va* to anisate, to flavor with anise
**anisete** *m* anisette
**anisillo** *m* appetizer, relish
**anisofilo -la** *adj* (bot.) anisophyllous
**anisómero -ra** *adj* (bot.) anisomerous
**anisométrico -ca** *adj* (mineral.) anisometric
**anivelar** *va* to level; to even
**aniversario -ria** *adj & m* anniversary
**anjeo** *m* coarse linen; burlap
**anmetro** *m* (elec.) ammeter
**ano** *m* (anat.) anus
**anoche** *adv* last night
**anochecedor -dora** *adj* nocturnal, staying up late; *mf* night owl, nighthawk
**anochecer** *m* dusk, twilight, nightfall; §34 *vn* to grow dark; to be, arrive, or happen at nightfall; to end the day, go to sleep; *vr* to get dark; to get cloudy; (coll.) to slip away, to hide
**anochecida** *f* nightfall
**anódico -ca** *adj* anode, anodic
**anodinia** *f* anodynia
**anodino -na** *adj* anodyne; insignificant; innocuous; *m* anodyne
**anodizar** §76 *va* (metal.) to anodize
**ánodo** *m* (elec.) anode

**anofeles** *m* (*pl:* **-les**) (ent.) anopheles
**anomalía** *f* anomaly
**anomalístico -ca** *adj* (astr.) anomalistic
**anómalo -la** *adj* anomalous
**anomuro -ra** *adj* & *m* (zool.) anomuran
**anón** *m* or **anona** *f* (bot.) soursop
**anonáceo -a** *adj* (bot.) annonaceous
**anonadación** *f* or **anonadamiento** *m* annihilation, destruction; humiliation; discouragement
**anonadar** *va* to annihilate, destroy; to crush, overwhelm; to humiliate; *vr* to be humiliated; to be discouraged, be crushed
**anonimato** *m* or **anonimia** *f* anonymity
**anónimo -ma** *adj* anonymous; *m* anonym; anonymous letter, unsigned letter; anonymity; **conservar** or **guardar el anónimo** to preserve one's anonymity
**anorexia** *f* (path.) anorexia
**anormal** *adj* abnormal
**anormalidad** *f* abnormality
**anorza** *f* (bot.) bryony (*Bryonia alba*)
**anosmia** *f* (path.) anosmia
**anotación** *f* annotation; note, record; comment; (Am.) score (*in games*)
**anotador -dora** *mf* annotation; *m* (Am.) score card
**anotar** *va* to annotate; to note, to jot down; to comment on; to point out; to score (*a point*)
**anovelado -da** *adj* novelistic
**anoxemia** *f* (path.) anoxemia
**anqueta** *f* small rump; **estar de media anqueta** (coll.) to be uncomfortably seated
**anquialmendrado -da** *adj* narrow-rumped (*said of a horse*)
**anquiboyuno -na** *adj* bony-rumped (*said of a horse*)
**anquiderribado -da** *adj* low-buttocked (*said of a horse*)
**anquilosar** *va* & *vr* to ankylose
**anquilosis** *f* (path.) ankylosis
**anquirredondo -da** *adj* round-rumped (*said of a horse*)
**anquiseco -ca** *adj* thin-rumped (*said of a horse*)
**Anquises** *m* (myth.) Anchises
**ansa** *f* hanse (*medieval guild*)
**ánsar** *m* (orn.) goose; wild goose; (orn.) tule goose; **ánsar blanco** (orn.) lesser snow goose
**ansarería** *f* goose farm
**ansarero -ra** *mf* gooseherd; *f* goosegirl
**ansarino -na** *adj* anserine; *m* gosling
**ansarón** *m* goose, large goose
**anseático -ca** *adj* Hanseatic
**Anselmo, San** Saint Anselm
**ansia** *f* anxiety; anguish; longing, yearning; **ansias** *fpl* nausea
**ansiadamente** *adv* anxiously, yearningly
**ansiar §90 & regular** *va* to long for, yearn for, covet; **ansiar** + *inf* to yearn to, to be eager to + *inf; vn* (coll.) to be madly in love; **ansiar por** (coll.) to be madly in love with
**ansiedad** *f* anxiety, worry; pain
**ansioso -sa** *adj* anxious; anguished; longing, yearning; covetous
**ant.** abr. of **anticuado**
**anta** *f* (zool.) elk; (archeol.) menhir; (arch.) anta
**antagalla** *f* (naut.) spritsail reef band
**antagónico -ca** *adj* antagonistic
**antagonismo** *m* antagonism
**antagonista** *mf* antagonist
**antañazo** *adv* (coll.) a long time ago
**antaño** *adv* last year; of yore, long ago
**antañón -ñona** *adj* ancient, very old
**Antarés** *m* (astr.) Antares
**antártico -ca** *adj* antarctic; (*cap.*) *m* Antarctic (*ocean*); **la Antártica** Antarctica (*continent*)
**Antártida, la** Antarctica (*continent*)
**-ante** *suffix adj* -ing, e.g., **amante** loving; **hispanohablante** Spanish-speaking
**ante** *m* (zool.) elk; elk skin, buff; first course (*of a meal*); *prep* before, in the presence of; in front of; at, with; **ante todo** first of all
**anteado -da** *adj* buff (*orange yellow*)
**antealtar** *m* (eccl.) chancel
**anteanoche** *adv* night before last
**anteanteanoche** *adv* three nights ago
**anteanteayer** *adv* three days ago
**anteantier** *adv* (coll.) three days ago
**anteayer** *adv* day before yesterday
**antebrazo** *m* forearm
**antecama** *f* bedside rug
**antecámara** *f* antechamber, anteroom; lobby, hall
**antecapilla** *f* (eccl.) antechapel
**antecedente** *adj* antecedent; *m* antecedent; (gram., log. & math.) antecedent; **antecedentes** *mpl* antecedents
**anteceder** *va* to precede, go before
**antecesor -sora** *adj* preceding; *mf* predecessor; ancestor
**anteclásico -ca** *adj* preclassical
**antecoger §49** *va* to drag or pull forward
**antecolumna** *f* (arch.) free column
**antecoro** *m* (arch.) antechoir
**antecos** *mpl* antiscians
**antedata** *f* antedate
**antedatar** *va* to antedate
**antedecir §37** *va* (archaic) to foretell, predict
**antedespacho** *m* front office
**antedía** *adv* the day before, a day or two before
**antedicho -cha** *adj* aforesaid, aforementioned; *pp of* **antedecir**
**antedigo** *1st sg pres ind of* **antedecir**
**antedije** *1st sg pret ind of* **antedecir**
**antediluviano -na** *adj* antediluvian
**antediré** *1st sg fut ind of* **antedecir**
**antefija** *f* (arch.) antefix; gable end
**antefirma** *f* formal close (*of a letter*); title above signature
**antefoso** *m* (fort.) outer moat
**antehistórico -ca** *adj* prehistoric
**anteiglesia** *f* church porch; parochial church; parish
**antelación** *f* previousness, anticipation, planning; **con antelación** in advance
**antelio** *m* (meteor.) anthelion
**antemano; de antemano** beforehand, in advance
**antemeridiano -na** *adj* antemeridian
**antemio** or **antemión** *m* (f.a.) anthemion
**antemural** *m* (fort.) rampart, outwork; (fig.) rampart, defense, protection
**antena** *f* (ent.) antenna; (rad.) aerial, antenna; (naut.) lateen yard; **en antena** (rad.) on the air; **llevar a las antenas** (rad.) to put on the air; **antena de cuadro** (rad.) loop aerial or antenna; **antena de interior** (rad.) indoor aerial or antenna; **antena de amarre** (aer.) mooring mast (*of a dirigible*); **antena de radar** radar screen; **antena de rastreo** tracking antenna; **antena dipolo** (rad.) dipole antenna; **antena direccional** (rad.) directional antenna; **antena interior incorporada** (rad.) built-in antenna
**antenacido -da** *adj* born prematurely
**antenado -da** *adj* (ent.) provided with antennae; *mf* stepchild
**antenatal** *adj* antenatal
**antenoche** *adv* night before last; before sunset
**antenombre** *m* title, honorific
**anténulas** *fpl* feelers; antenules
**antenupcial** *adj* antenuptial
**Anteo** *m* (myth.) Antaeus
**anteojera** *f* spectacle case; patch (*worn over eye*); blinder, blinker
**anteojero** *m* maker or vendor of spectacles or eyeglasses
**anteojo** *m* eyeglass; spyglass, telescope; **anteojos** *mpl* spectacles, eyeglasses; opera glasses; binoculars; blinkers (*for horses*); **anteojo de larga vista** long-range telescope; **anteojo prismático** prism binocular; **anteojos bifocales** bifocals; **anteojos de campaña** field glass; **anteojos de predicador** pulpit glasses
**antepagar §59** *va* to pay in advance
**antepalco** *m* (theat.) small antechamber to a box
**antepasado -da** *adj* before last, e.g., **la semana antepasada** the week before last; **antepasados** *mpl* ancestors
**antepecho** *m* railing, guardrail; sill; parapet, breastwork; breast collar (*of harness*); footboard (*of carriage*)
**antepenúltimo -ma** *adj* antepenultimate; *f* antepenult

**antepondré** *1st sg fut ind of* **anteponer**
**anteponer** **§69** *va* to place before, place in front; to prefer; *vr* to get ahead; **anteponerse a** to get ahead of, overcome
**antepongo** *1st sg pres ind of* **anteponer**
**anteportada** *f* (print.) bastard title, half title
**anteportal** *m* porch, vestibule, entry
**anteproyecto** *m* preliminary sketch or plan; first draft
**antepuerta** *f* portière; (fort.) counterport
**antepuerto** *m* entrance to a mountain pass; (naut.) outer port; (naut.) outer anchorage
**antepuesto -ta** *pp of* **anteponer**
**antepuse** *1st sg pret ind of* **anteponer**
**antera** *f* (bot.) anther
**anterea** *f* (ent.) tussah (*silkworm*)
**anteridio** *m* (bot.) antheridium
**anterior** *adj* anterior, front, previous, preceding; earlier; front (*tooth*); (phonet.) front; **anterior a** previous to, earlier than
**anterioridad** *f* anteriority, priority, precedence; **con anterioridad** previously; **con anterioridad a** previous to, prior to
**antero** *m* tanner, leather dresser
**anterozoide** *m* (bot.) antherozoid
**antes** *adv* before, formerly; previously; sooner, soonest; rather; **cuanto antes** or **lo más antes** as soon as possible; **antes bien** rather, on the contrary; **antes de** before (*in time*); **antes de** + *inf* before + *ger*; **antes que** rather than; **antes (de) que** before (*in time*)
**antesacristía** *f* anteroom to the sacristy
**antesala** *f* antechamber; waiting room (*e.g., of a doctor's office*); **hacer antesala** to dance attendance, to kick one's heels
**antesis** *f* (bot.) anthesis
**antestatura** *f* (fort.) makeshift barricade or entrenchment
**antetemplo** *m* (arch.) porch, portico
**antever** **§93** *va* to foresee
**anteversión** *f* (bot.) anteversion
**antevíspera** *f* two days before
**antevisto -ta** *pp of* **antever**
**anti-** *prefix* anti-, e.g., **antisemítico** anti-Semitic; **antitoxina** antitoxin; **antipapa** antipope; ant-, e.g., **antiácido** antacid; contra-, e.g., **anticonceptivo** contraceptive; in-, e.g., **antiartístico** inartistic; non-, eg., **antirresbaladizo** nonskid; -proof, e.g., **antisonoro** soundproof; **antitérmico** heatproof; un-, e.g., **anticientífico** unscientific; **antideportivo** unsportsmanlike; **antieconómico** uneconomic
**antiácido -da** *adj & m* antacid
**antiaéreo -a** *adj* anti-aircraft; *m* anti-aircraft gun
**antiafrodisíaco -ca** *adj & m* (med.) anaphrodisiac
**antialcohólico -ca** *adj* antialcoholic; antisaloon (*league, propaganda, etc.*)
**antialcoholismo** *m* antialcoholism
**antiar** *m* antiar (*poisonous gum*)
**antiarina** *f* (chem.) antiarin
**antiartístico -ca** *adj* inartistic
**antibactérico -ca** *adj* antibacterial
**antibiosis** *f* (biol.) antibiosis
**antibiótico -ca** *adj & m* antibiotic
**anticartel** *adj invar* antitrust
**anticatarral** *adj & m* anticatarrhal
**anticátodo** *m* anticathode
**anticatólico -ca** *adj & mf* anti-Catholic
**anticiclón** *m* (meteor.) anticyclone
**anticiclonal** *adj* anticyclonic
**anticientífico -ca** *adj* unscientific
**anticipación** *f* anticipation; advance; **con anticipación** in advance
**anticipada** *f* see **anticipado**
**anticipadamente** *adv* in advance, beforehand
**anticipado -da** *adj* advance (*e.g., payment*); *f* unexpected thrust, treacherous attack
**anticipar** *va* to anticipate, advance, accelerate, hasten; to move up, to move ahead (*a scheduled event*); to advance (*money*); to lend; *vr* to happen early, take place earlier; **anticiparse a** to anticipate, get ahead of; **anticiparse a** + *inf* to + *inf* ahead of time, e.g., **se anticipó a salir sin esperar a sus amigos** he left ahead of time without waiting for his friends
**anticipo** *m* anticipation; forehandedness; deposit, advance payment; retaining fee
**anticlerical** *adj* anticlerical
**anticlericalismo** *m* anticlericalism
**anticlímax** *m* (rhet.) anticlimax
**anticlinal** *adj* anticlinal; *m* (geol.) anticline
**anticlinorio** *m* (geol.) anticlinorium
**anticloro** *m* (chem.) antichlor
**anticomunista** *adj & mf* anticommunist
**anticoncepción** *f* contraconception
**anticonceptivo -va** *adj & m* contraconceptive
**anticongelante** *m* antifreeze
**anticonstitucional** *adj* unconstitutional
**anticresis** *f* (*pl:* **-sis**) (law) antichresis
**anticrético -ca** *adj* antichretic
**anticristiano -na** *adj & mf* anti-Christian
**Anticristo** *m* Antichrist
**anticuado -da** *adj* antiquated; obsolete; old-fashioned
**anticuar** *va* to antiquate, make out of date; *vr* to become antiquated
**anticuario -ria** *adj* antiquarian; *m* antiquarian or antiquary; antique dealer
**anticuerpo** *m* (bact.) antibody
**antidáctilo** *m* anapest
**antidemocrático -ca** *adj* antidemocratic
**antideportivo -va** *adj* unsportsmanlike
**antiderrapante** *adj* nonskid
**antideslizante** *adj* nonslipping; nonskid
**antideslumbrante** *adj* antiglare
**antidetonante** *adj & m* antiknock
**antídoto** *m* antidote; (fig.) antidote
**antieconómico -ca** *adj* uneconomic or uneconomical
**antiemético -ca** *adj & m* antiemetic
**antier** *adv* (coll.) day before yesterday
**antiesclavista** *adj* antislavery; *m* abolitionist
**antiescorbútico -ca** *adj & m* antiscorbutic
**antiespañol -la** *adj* anti-Spanish
**antiespasmódico -ca** *adj* antispasmodic
**antiestético -ca** *adj* unesthetic
**antifaz** *m* (*pl:* **-faces**) veil, mask
**antifederalista** *adj* antifederal; *m* antifederalist
**antiflogístico -ca** *adj* antiphlogistic
**antífona** *f* (eccl.) antiphon; anthem
**antifonal** or **antifonario -ria** *adj & m* antiphonal
**antifonero** *m* precentor
**antífrasis** *f* (rhet.) antiphrasis
**antifricción** *m* antifriction; antifriction metal
**antigás** *adj invar* protecting from poisonous gases, gas (*e.g., mask*)
**antigénico -ca** *adj* antigenic
**antígeno** *m* (bact.) antigen
**Antígona** or **Antígone** *f* (myth.) Antigone
**antigramatical** *adj* ungrammatical
**antigripal** *adj* antigrippe
**antigualla** *f* antique; old story; ancient custom; (coll.) relic, antique; (coll.) faded rose, has-been
**antiguar** **§23** *vn* to attain seniority; *vr* to attain seniority; to become antiquated
**antigüedad** *f* antiquity; seniority; **antigüedades** *fpl* antiquities
**antiguo -gua** *adj* old; ancient; antique; **a la antigua** or **a lo antiguo** in the ancient manner; in an old-fashioned way; **de antiguo** from days gone by, from time immemorial; **en lo antiguo** in ancient times; *mf* old member; veteran; senior; **los antiguos** the ancients
**antiherrumbroso -sa** *adj* rustless, rust-resisting
**antihistamina** *f* (pharm.) antihistamine
**antihistamínico -ca** *adj & m* (pharm.) antihistamine
**antiinflacionista** *adj* anti-inflationary
**antijudío -a** *adj* anti-Jewish
**antilogaritmo** *m* (math.) antilogarithm
**antílope** *m* (zool.) antelope
**antillano -na** *adj & mf* Antillean, West Indian
**Antillas** *fpl* Antilles; **Antillas Francesas** French West Indies; **Antillas Mayores** Greater Antilles; **Antillas Menores** Lesser Antilles
**antimacasar** *m* antimacassar
**antimateria** *f* (phys.) antimatter
**antimilitarismo** *m* antimilitarism
**antimilitarista** *adj & mf* antimilitarist
**antimonárquico -ca** *adj* antimonarchical
**antimonial** *adj* (chem.) antimonial

**antimonio** *m* (chem.) antimony
**antimonita** *f* (chem. & mineral.) antimonite
**antinatural** *adj* unnatural
**antinodo** *m* (phys.) antinode
**antinomia** *f* antinomy
**antinómico -ca** *adj* antinomic
**antiobrero -ra** *adj* antilabor
**Antíoco** *m* Antiochus
**antioqueno -na** *adj & mf* Antiochian
**antioqueño -ña** *adj* (pertaining to) Antioquia, S.A.; *mf* native or inhabitant of Antioquia
**Antioquía** *f* Antioch
**antipapa** *m* antipope
**antipara** *f* folding screen; gaiter
**antiparásito** *m* (rad.) static eliminator
**antiparras** *fpl* (coll.) spectacles, eyeglasses
**antipartido** *adj invar & m* antiparty
**antipatía** *f* dislike, antipathy
**antipático -ca** *adj* disagreeable; antipathetic
**antipatinador -dora** *adj* nonskid
**antipatizar** §76 *vn* (Am.) to feel antipathy, arouse antipathy, be repugnant
**antipatriótico -ca** *adj* unpatriotic
**antipendio** *m* (eccl.) antependium
**antipirético -ca** *adj & m* antipyretic
**antipirina** *f* (pharm.) antipyrine
**antípoda** *adj* antipodal; *m* antipode (*anything directly opposite*); **antípodas** *mpl* antipodes (*places and people*); **Antípodas** *fpl* Antipodes (*islands*)
**antipoliomielítico -ca** *adj* antipolio
**antiprotón** *m* (phys. & chem.) antiproton
**antiproyectil** *adj* antimissile
**antiquísimo -ma** *adj super* very old; very or most ancient
**antirrábico -ca** *adj* antirabic
**antirraquítico -ca** *adj & m* antirachitic
**antirreligioso -sa** *adj* antireligious
**antirresbaladizo -za** *adj* nonskid
**antirrino** *m* (bot.) snapdragon
**antiscios** *mpl* antiscians of the temperate zones
**antisemita** *mf* anti-Semite
**antisemítico -ca** *adj* anti-Semitic
**antisemitismo** *m* anti-Semitism
**antisepsia** or **antisepsis** *f* antisepsis
**antiséptico -ca** *adj & m* antiseptic
**antisísmico -ca** *adj* earthquake-proof
**antisocial** *adj* antisocial
**antisonoro -ra** *adj* soundproof
**antisoviético -ca** *adj* anti-Soviet
**Antístenes** *m* Antisthenes
**antistrofa** *f* antistrophe
**antisubmarino -na** *adj* antisubmarine
**antitanque** *adj* (*pl:* **-ques**) antitank
**antitérmico -ca** *adj* heatproof; antipyretic
**antítesis** *f* (*pl:* **-sis**) antithesis
**antitético -ca** *adj* antithetical
**antitóxico -ca** *adj* antitoxic
**antitoxina** *f* (bact.) antitoxin
**antitrago** *m* (anat.) antitragus
**antiveneno** *m* antivenin
**antiviral** or **antivirulento -ta** *adj* antiviral
**antiviviseccionista** *adj & mf* antivivisectionist
**antociana** or **antocianina** *f* (biochem.) anthocyanin
**antodio** *m* (bot.) anthodium
**antófilo -la** *adj* flower-loving; *mf* flower lover
**antofita** *f* (bot.) anthophyte
**antojadizo -za** *adj* fickle, capricious, whimsical
**antojado -da** *adj* desirous, eager
**antojar** *vr* to seem; *vr & impers* to fancy, take a sudden fancy to or for; to seem, seem likely, imagine, e.g., **se me antoja que va a llover** it seems to me that it is going to rain; **antojársele a uno** + *inf* to have or take a notion to + *inf*, e.g., **se me antoja ir a paseo** I have a notion to go for a walk
**antojera** *f* blinker, blinder (*for horses*)
**antojito** *m* (Am.) tidbit, delicacy
**antojo** *m* passing fancy, whim, caprice; hasty judgment; **antojos** *mpl* moles, spots, warts; **a su antojo** as one pleases
**antojuelo** *m* whim, vagary
**antología** *f* anthology
**antólogo -ga** *mf* anthologist
**Antón** *m* Antony, Anthony
**Antonieta** *f* Antoinette
**antónimo -ma** *adj* antonymous; *m* antonym
**Antonino** *m* Antoninus
**Antonio** *m* Anthony, Antonius
**antonomasia** *f* (rhet.) antonomasia
**Antoñito** *m* Tony
**antorcha** *f* torch; **antorcha a soplete** blowtorch
**antorchar** *va* var. of **entorchar**
**antorchero** *m* torch holder or socket; cresset
**antozoos** *mpl* (zool.) anthozoans
**antraceno** *m* (chem.) anthracene
**antracita** *f* anthracite
**antracitoso -sa** *adj* anthracite
**antracnosis** *f* (bot.) anthracnose
**ántrax** *m* (path.) anthrax
**antreno** *m* (ent.) museum beetle
**antro** *m* antrum, cavern; den (*e.g., of crooks*); (anat.) antrum; **antro de Highmoro** (anat.) antrum of Highmore; **antro timpánico** (anat.) tympanic antrum
**antropofagía** *f* anthropophagy
**antropófago -ga** *adj* anthropophagic; **antropófagos** *mpl* anthropophagi
**antropoide** *adj* anthropoid; *m* (orn.) demoiselle
**antropoideo -a** *adj* anthropoidal; *m* (zool.) anthropoid, anthropoid ape
**antropología** *f* anthropology
**antropológico -ca** *adj* anthropological
**antropólogo -ga** *mf* anthropologist
**antropometría** *f* anthropometry
**antropométrico -ca** *adj* anthropometric
**antropomórfico -ca** *adj* anthropomorphic
**antropomorfismo** *m* anthropomorphism
**antropomorfo -fa** *adj* anthropomorphous; **antropomorfos** *mpl* (zool.) anthropoids
**antropopiteco** *m* (pal.) Anthropopithecus
**antruejo** *m* carnival (*the three days before Lent*)
**antuviada** *f* (coll.) sudden blow or bump
**antuviar** *va* (coll.) to strike or bump suddenly or without warning, to be first to strike
**antuvión** *m* (coll.) sudden blow or attack; **de antuvión** (coll.) suddenly, unexpectedly
**anual** *adj* annual
**anualidad** *f* annuity; year's pay; annual occurrence; annual payment
**anuario** *m* yearbook; directory; bulletin, catalogue (*e.g., of a university*); **anuario telefónico** telephone directory
**anúbada** *f* call to arms; feudal service; tribute paid in lieu of service
**anubarrado -da** *adj* cloudy, overcast; with clouds painted in
**anublado -da** *adj* (slang) blind
**anublar** *va* to cloud; to dim, darken, to obscure; to wither, to dry up (*plants*); *vr* to become cloudy; to be withered; to fade away (*said, e.g., of one's hopes*)
**anublo** *m* var. of **añublo**
**anudar** *va* to knot, to tie, to fasten; to join, to unite; to take up again (*a story*); *vr* to get knotted; to unite, be united; to fade away, wither, wilt, fail; **se le anudó la garganta** he got a lump in his throat; **se le anudó la lengua** his tongue stuck in his throat
**anuencia** *f* consent
**anuente** *adj* consenting
**anulable** *adj* voidable
**anulación** *f* annulment; nullification, revocation; cancellation; removal, discharge
**anular** *adj* annular; *m* ring finger; *va* to annul; to nullify, revoke; to cancel; to remove, unseat, discharge; *vr* to be deprived of authority; to be passed over; to be humiliated
**anuloso -sa** *adj* annular; full of rings
**anunciación** *f* announcement, annunciation; (*cap.*) *f* Annunciation
**anunciador -dora** *adj* advertising; *mf* announcer; annunciator; advertiser
**anunciante** *adj* advertising; *mf* advertiser
**anunciar** *va* to announce, to annunciate; to forebode; to advertise
**anuncio** *m* announcement; harbinger; omen; advertisement; **anuncios clasificados (en secciones)** classified advertisements; **anuncios por palabras** classified advertisements at so much per word
**anuo -nua** *adj* annual
**anúteba** *f* var. of **anúbada**
**anverso** *m* obverse

**anzuelo** *m* fishhook; lure, attraction; **picar en el anzuelo** or **tragar el anzuelo** (fig.) to swallow the bait, swallow the hook
**añacal** *m* carrier of grain to the mill; board for carrying bread
**añacalero** *m* (prov.) hod carrier
**añada** *f* year, season (*speaking of weather or crops*); vintage wine; tract of cultivated land
**añadible** *adj* addible
**añadido -da** *adj* added, additional; *m* false hair, switch
**añadidura** *f* addition, increase; extra weight, extra measure; **de añadidura** extra, into the bargain; **por añadidura** besides, after all
**añadir** *va* to add; to add to
**añafea** *f* rag paper, brown paper
**añafil** *m* straight Moorish trumpet
**añagaza** *f* bird call; decoy, lure; trap, trick
**añal** *adj* annual; year-old; *mf* year-old calf, kid, or lamb; *m* memorial a year after death
**añalejo** *m* (eccl.) liturgical calendar, ordinal
**añascar** §86 *va* (coll.) to gather together bit by bit
**añejamiento** *m* aging; turning stale
**añejar** *va* to age; to make stale; *vr* to age, become aged; to improve with age; to grow stale
**añejo -ja** *adj* aged (*said, e.g., of wine*); old, stale; musty, rancid
**añicos** *mpl* pieces, bits, shreds; **hacer añicos** to tear to smithereens; **hacerse añicos** (coll.) to take great pains, to wear oneself out
**añil** *m* (bot.) anil (*plant, color, and dye*); bluing (*for laundering*); indigo (*of the solar spectrum*)
**añilar** *va* to dye with indigo; to blue (*clothes*)
**añilería** *f* anil or indigo plantation; anil mill, indigo works
**añinero** *m* dresser of lambskin; dealer in lambskin
**añinos** *mpl* unshorn lambskin; lamb's wool
**año** *m* year; **años** *mpl* birthday; **cumplir años** to have a birthday; **cumplir . . . años** to be . . . years old, to reach the age of; **¡Feliz Año Nuevo!** Happy New Year!; **por los años de . . .** about the year . . . ; **tener . . . años (de edad)** to be . . . years old; **año anomalístico** (astr.) anomalistic year; **año astronómico** astronomical year; **año bisiesto** leap year; **año civil** calendar year, civil year; **año de Cristo** anno Domini; **año de gracia** year of grace; **año de nuestra salud** year of our Lord; **año económico** fiscal year; **año escolar** or **año lectivo** school year; **año lunar** lunar year; **año luz** (*pl:* **años luz**) (astr.) light-year; **año nuevo** new year; **año solar** solar year; **año trópico** (astr.) tropical year
**añojal** *m* fallow land
**añojo -ja** *mf* year-old calf or lamb
**añoranza** *f* loneliness, longing, sorrow, grief
**añorar** *va* to long for, to miss, to sorrow for, to grieve over; *vn* to pine, to sorrow, to grieve
**añoso -sa** *adj* old, aged, heavy with years
**añublado -da** *adj* var. of **anublado**
**añublar** *va & vr* var. of **anublar**
**añublo** *m* blight, mildew
**añudar** *va & vr* var. of **anudar**
**añusgar** §59 *vn* to strangle, choke; to get angry
**aojada** *f* (Am.) skylight; (Am.) transom
**aojador -dora** *mf* hoodoo
**aojadura** *f* or **aojamiento** *m* spell, curse; evil eye, bad luck
**aojar** *va* to cast the evil eye upon, to hoodoo, to jinx
**aojo** *m* evil eye, bad luck
**aonio -nia** *adj* Aonian
**aoristo** *m* (gram.) aorist
**aorta** *f* (anat.) aorta
**aórtico -ca** *adj* aortic
**aovado -da** *adj* oval, egg-shaped
**aovar** *vn* to lay eggs
**aovillar** *vr* to form a ball, curl up, shrink
**ap.** abr. of **aparte** & **apóstol**
**apabilar** *va* to trim (*a wick*)
**apabullar** *va* (coll.) to mash, crush, flatten; (coll.) to squelch
**apabullo** *m* (coll.) mashing, crushing, flattening; (coll.) squelching
**apacentadero** *m* pasture, grazing ground
**apacentador -dora** *adj* pasturing, grazing; nourishing; encouraging, fostering; *mf* nourisher, fosterer; *m* shepherd, herdsman
**apacentamiento** *m* pasturage, grazing; feed, fodder; fuel
**apacentar** §18 *va* to pasture, to graze; (fig.) to feed; *vr* to pasture, to graze; to feed; **apacentarse con** or **de** to feed on
**apacibilidad** *f* peacefulness; mildness, gentleness
**apacible** *adj* peaceful; mild, gentle
**apaciguador -dora** *adj* pacifying, calming, appeasing; *mf* pacifier, calmer, appeaser
**apaciguamiento** *m* pacification, calming, appeasement
**apaciguar** §23 *va* to pacify, calm, appease; *vr* to become peaceful, to grow calm, to calm down
**apache** *m* apache (*bandit*); Apache (*Indian*)
**apacheta** *f* (Am.) devotional heap of stones at the top of a mountain road
**apachico** *m* (Am.) package, bundle
**apachurrar** *va* (Am.) to mash, to crush, to mangle
**apadrinador -dora** *adj* sponsoring; backing, protecting; *mf* sponsor, backer, supporter; protector; *m* patron; second (*in a duel*); *f* patroness
**apadrinamiento** *m* sponsorship, sponsoring, support
**apadrinar** *va* to sponsor; to act as godfather for; to be best man for; to second (*in a duel*); to back, to support; to take under one's wing; to ride alongside (*a rider on a partly broken horse*)
**apagable** *adj* extinguishable
**apagabroncas** *m* (*pl:* **-cas**) (coll.) bouncer
**apagachispas** *m* (*pl:* **-pas**) (elec.) spark arrester
**apagadizo -za** *adj* fire-resisting
**apagado -da** *adj* out (*said of fire or light*); dull, weak, dim; calm, listless, spiritless; timid; slaked (*lime*)
**apagador -dora** *adj* extinguishing; dimming; muffling; *mf* extinguisher (*person*); *m* extinguisher (*of a candle*); damper (*of piano*)
**apagafuego** *m* fire extinguisher
**apagaincendios** *m* (*pl:* **-dios**) fire extinguisher
**apagamiento** *m* extinguishing; dimming, dulling; muffling; subsiding
**apagapenoles** *mpl* (naut.) leech lines
**apagar** §59 *va* to put out, to extinguish; to turn off (*lights, electric current, radio, etc.*); to tone down (*light or color*); to damp, to muffle (*sound*); to slake (*lime*); to silence (*enemy fire*); to quench (*thirst*); to soothe, to calm, to deaden (*pain*); *vn* **¡apaga y vámonos!** (coll.) dry up!; *vr* to go out, to be extinguished; to subside, to calm down, to die away, to fade away
**apagavelas** *m* (*pl:* **-las**) candle extinguisher, snuffers
**apagón -gona** *adj* (Am.) fire-resisting; *m* blackout (*as military precaution*); darkness (*e.g., from failure of electricity*)
**apagoso -sa** *adj* (Am.) poorly burning
**apainelado -da** *adj* (arch.) basket-handle (*said of an arch*)
**apaisado -da** *adj* elongated, oblong
**apajarado -da** *adj* (Am.) scatterbrained, flighty
**apalabrar** *va* to bespeak, to engage; to discuss, to consider; *vr* to agree, to come to an agreement
**apalache** *adj* Appalachian; **Apalaches** *mpl* Appalachians (*mountains*)
**apalachina** *f* (bot.) yaupon
**apalancar** §86 *va* to move or raise with a lever, to move or raise with a crowbar
**apaleamiento** *m* shoveling; beating, thrashing; piling, heaping
**apalear** *va* to shovel; to beat, thrash, drub; to pile up, to heap up
**apaleo** *m* thrashing; piling, heaping
**apanalado -da** *adj* honeycombed
**apancle** *m* (Am.) irrigation ditch
**apancora** *f* (zool.) spiny crab; (zool.) sea hedgehog
**apandar** *va* (coll.) to steal, to swipe
**apandillar** *va* to form into bands, form into gangs; *vr* to band together

**apandorgar** §59 *vr* (coll.) to get fat, put on weight; (Am.) to get lazy
**apanojado -da** *adj* (bot.) panicled
**apantallar** *va* (elec.) to shield, to screen; (Am.) to dazzle, to amaze
**apantanar** *va* to make swampy or marshy; to stick in a swamp; *vr* to get swampy or marshy; to get stuck in a swamp, get stuck in the mud
**apantuflado -da** *adj* slipper-shaped
**apañado -da** *adj* clothlike, thick-textured; clever, handy; fit, suitable
**apañadura** *f* grasping; stealing; repairing, repair, patch; trimming, edging
**apañar** *va* to pick up, to grasp; to seize, to steal; to dress; to repair, to mend; (coll.) to wrap up; *vr* (coll.) to be handy
**apaño** *m* grasping; stealing; repairing, repair; skill, handiness
**apañuscar** §86 *va* (coll.) to rumple, crumple; (coll.) to steal, to swipe; (Am.) to jam, to crowd
**apapagayado -da** *adj* parrot-like; shaped like the beak of a parrot
**apar** *m* or **apara** *m* (zool.) three-banded armadillo
**aparador** *m* sideboard, dresser, buffet; serving table; showcase; workshop
**aparadura** *f* (naut.) garboard, garboard strake
**aparar** *va* to prepare, to arrange; to adorn, to dress; to block, to head off; to stretch out the hands, cloak, or skirt to catch; to dress, to cultivate (*plants*); to close (*uppers of shoes*); (carp.) to dub (*with adz*)
**aparasolado -da** *adj* parasol-shaped; (bot.) umbellate
**aparatar** *vr* to get ready; to get dressed up; (prov. & Am.) to get cloudy, to look threatening
**aparato** *m* preparation; apparatus, device; display, ostentation, show; exaggeration, embroidery; literary baggage; sign; radio set; television set; telephone; (coll.) airplane; (anat.) apparatus; (surg.) application, bandage; (theat.) scenery, properties; (med.) syndrome; **ponerse al aparato** to come or to go to the phone; **aparato auditivo** hearing aid; **aparato crítico** apparatus criticus; **aparato de relojería** clockwork; **aparato fotográfico** camera; **aparato pulverizador** sprayer, spray outfit; **aparatos sanitarios** bathroom fixtures; **aparato tomavistas** motion-picture camera
**aparatosidad** *f* ostentation, showiness, pomposity
**aparatoso -sa** *adj* ostentatious, showy, pompous
**aparcamiento** *m* parking
**aparcar** §86 *va & vn* (aut. & mil.) to park
**aparcería** *f* (com.) partnership
**aparcero -ra** *mf* (com.) partner; sharer, coheir; sharecropper; (Am.) customer
**apareamiento** *m* making even; pairing, mating, matching
**aparear** *va* to make even; to pair, to mate, to match; *vr* to match; to pair, to mate
**aparecer** §34 *vn & vr* to appear; to turn up, to show up
**aparecido** *m* ghost, specter
**aparecimiento** *m* appearance
**aparedar** *va* to wall up
**aparejado -da** *adj* ready, fit, suitable
**aparejador** *m* foreman, overseer, supervisor, builder; (naut.) rigger
**aparejar** *va* to prepare; to threaten; to harness; to dress, to process; to prime, to size; (naut.) to rig, to rig out; (Am.) to pair, to mate (*animals*); *vr* to prepare, to get ready; to get dressed up
**aparejería** *f* (Am.) harness shop
**aparejo** *m* preparation, arrangement; harness, riding gear; (mas.) bond, bonding; set, kit, equipment; (naut.) rigging, sails and rigging; (naut.) gear, tackle, block and tackle; priming, sizing, filler; **aparejos** *mpl* tools, instruments, implements, equipment, accessories; **aparejo de gata** (naut.) cat tackle; **aparejo flamenco** or **holandés** (mas.) Flemish bond; **aparejo inglés** (mas.) English bond
**aparentar** *va* to feign, pretend, affect; to look to be (*so many years old*); **aparentar** + *inf* to seem to + *inf*; to pretend to + *inf*
**aparente** *adj* apparent, seeming; visible, evident; right, proper, suitable
**aparición** *f* appearance; apparition
**apariencia** *f* appearance, aspect; probability, sign, indication; **juzgar por las apariencias** to judge by appearances; **las apariencias engañan** things are not what they seem; **salvar las apariencias** to keep up appearances, to save face
**aparqueamiento** *m* parking
**aparquear** *va* (mil. & aut.) to park
**aparqueo** *m* var. of **aparqueamiento**
**aparrado -da** *adj* viny, vinelike, shrubby; chunky, stubby; spreading
**aparragar** §59 *vr* (Am.) to squat, crouch, bend
**aparrar** *va* to espalier; *vr* to spread; (Am.) to squat, crouch; to be chunky
**aparroquiado -da** *adj* established in a parish; having many customers, patients, or clients
**aparroquiar** *va* to get customers, patients, or clients for; *vr* to get customers, patients, or clients
**apartadero** *m* siding, sidetrack; turnout; road fork; sorting room (*for driving bulls into individual pens before fight*)
**apartadijo** *m* small part; alcove, offset, recess; **hacer apartadijos de** to break up, break apart
**apartadizo -za** *adj* shy, diffident, retiring; *m* alcove, offset, recess
**apartado -da** *adj* separated; distant, remote; aloof; different; side or back (*e.g., road*); *m* side room; distribution; post-office box; section; vocabulary entry; penning of bulls; governing board of cattle dealers; **hacer el apartado de** to distribute, to separate
**apartador -dora** *mf* separator, divider, sorter; *m* (Am.) stick (*for driving cattle*)
**apartamento** *m* apartment, apartment house
**apartamiento** *m* separation; withdrawal, retirement; remoteness, remote spot; aloofness; coldness, indifference; apartment
**apartar** *va* to separate; to take aside; to turn aside; to move away, push away; (law) to set aside, to waive; (rail.) to shunt; to sort (*cattle*); to pen (*bulls*); *vr* to separate; to move away, keep away, turn aside, stand aside; to withdraw, retire; to get divorced; (law) to withdraw from a suit, to desist
**aparte** *adv* apart, aside; **esto aparte** aside from this; **aparte de** apart from; *adj* separate; *prep* apart from; *m* aside (*remark*); indented line, new paragraph
**apartidar** *va* to back, support; *vr* to take sides
**aparvar** *va* to arrange (*grain*) for thrashing; to heap, gather together
**apasionado -da** *adj* passionate; passionately fond, devoted; tender, sore (*said of a part of body*); tender, loving; **apasionado a** or **por** passionately fond of, devoted to; *m* lover
**apasionamiento** *m* passion, enthusiasm, intense emotion; violence, vehemence
**apasionante** *adj* stirring, thrilling
**apasionar** *va* to appeal deeply to, make enthusiastic, arouse passionately; to afflict; *vr* to become impassioned; to fall madly in love; to be stirred up; **apasionarse de** or **por** to fall madly in love with, be crazy about
**apasote** *m* (bot.) wormseed
**apaste** *m* (Am.) earthen bowl, earthen vat
**apatanado -da** *adj* coarse, farmerish
**apatía** *f* apathy
**apático -ca** *adj* apathetic
**apatita** *f* (mineral.) apatite
**apátrida** *adj* stateless, without a country; *mf* stateless person, expatriate; *m* man without a country
**apatuscar** §86 *va* (slang) to do in a hurry, to botch
**apatusco** *m* (coll.) ornament, finery, trimming
**apayasar** *va* to make clownish; *vr* to be clownish, act the clown
**apazote** *m* var. of **apasote**
**apdo.** abr. of **apartado**
**apea** *f* hobble (*for horses*)

**apeadero** *m* horse block, carriage block; (rail.) flag stop, wayside station; platform, landing; resting place; temporary lodging, place to stay
**apeador** *m* surveyor
**apealar** *va* (Am.) to hobble (*a horse*)
**apeamiento** *m* dismounting, alighting; propping; surveying
**apear** *va* to dismount, help dismount; to help down, help out; to bring down, to fell; to remove, discharge; to overcome (*a difficulty*); to prop, prop up; to wedge, to block (*a wheel*); (coll.) to dissuade; to hobble, to fetter (*animals*); to survey; *vr* to dismount, alight, get off, get out; (coll.) to be dissuaded, back down; to stay, to stop, to put up
**apechugar** §59 *va* (Am.) to grab, seize forcibly; *vn* to push with the chest; **apechugar con** (coll.) to make the best of, to put up with
**apedazar** §76 *va* to piece out, to mend, to patch; to cut in pieces; to tear to pieces
**apedernalado -da** *adj* flinty, hard as flint; stonyhearted
**apedreado -da** *adj* variegated; speckled; pockmarked
**apedreador -dora** *adj* stoning, stone-throwing; *mf* stone thrower
**apedreamiento** *m* stoning; lapidation; pitting; hail, hailstorm; damage from hail
**apedrear** *va* to stone, throw stones at; to cut with stones, hail, etc.; to lapidate; to stone to death; to pit; *vn* to hail; *vr* to be damaged by hail; to become pitted
**apedreo** *m* var. of **apedreamiento**
**apegadamente** *adv* affectionately, devotedly
**apegar** §59 *vr* to become attached, to grow fond; **apegarse a** to become attached to, to grow fond of
**apego** *m* attachment, fondness
**apelable** *adj* appealable
**apelación** *f* appeal; (law) appeal; (coll.) medical consultation; (coll.) help, remedy
**apelado -da** *mf* (law) appellee
**apelambrar** *va* to flesh, to remove hair from (*hides*)
**apelante** *adj & mf* (law) appellant
**apelar** *vn* to appeal, make an appeal; to have recourse; to refer; (law) to appeal; **apelar de** (law) to appeal from
**apelativo -va** *adj & m* (gram.) appellative
**apeldar** *vn* (coll.) to flee, run away; **apeldarlas** (coll.) to run away
**apelde** *m* (coll.) flight; dawn bell (*in Franciscan monasteries*)
**Apeles** *m* Apelles
**apelmazado -da** *adj* compressed, compact; heavy, clumsy (*writing*)
**apelmazamiento** *m* compactness
**apelmazar** §76 *va* to compress, squeeze together; *vr* to cake
**apelotonar** *va* to form into a ball, make a ball of; *vr* to form a ball or balls, to curl up
**apellar** *va* to dress, soften (*leather*)
**apellidamiento** *m* calling, naming, appellation
**apellidar** *va* to call, to name; to call by one's surname
**apellido** *m* name; surname, last name, family name; cognomen, epithet, nickname; **apellido de soltera** maiden name
**apenachado -da** *adj* plumed, crested
**apenar** *va* to cause sorrow to; *vr* to grieve
**apenas** *adv* scarcely, hardly; with difficulty; **apenas si** scarcely, hardly; *conj.* no sooner, as soon as
**apencar** §86 *vn* (coll.) to buck up, to face the music
**apendectomía** *f* (surg.) appendectomy
**apéndice** *m* appendix, appendage; (aer.) appendix; (biol.) appendage; **apéndice cecal, vermicular,** or **vermiforme** (anat.) vermiform appendix
**apendicectomía** *f* (surg.) appendectomy
**apendicitis** *f* (path.) appendicitis
**apendicitomía** *f* var. of **apendicectomía**
**apendicular** *adj* appendicular
**Apeninos** *mpl* Apennines
**apeñuscar** §86 *va* var. of **apañuscar**
**apeo** *m* dismounting, alighting; felling; propping; survey, surveying; surveyor's plan
**apeonar** *vn* to run (*said of birds*)
**apepsia** *f* (path.) apepsia
**aperador** *m* farmer; wheelwright; (min.) foreman
**aperar** *va* to make (*wagons, farm equipment, etc.*); to repair
**apercancar** §86 *vr* (Am.) to rust, to mold, get moldy
**apercepción** *f* (philos.) apperception
**aperceptivo -va** *adj* (philos.) apperceptive
**apercibimiento** *m* preparation, provision; warning, notice; (law) summons
**apercibir** *va* to prepare; to provide; to warn; to perceive; (law) to summon; (Am.) to collect; *vr* to get ready; to be provided; **apercibirse de** to provide oneself with; to notice, to observe
**apercollar** §77 *va* (coll.) to grab by the neck; (coll.) to grab, to snatch; (coll.) to club, to stun or to kill by a blow on the back of the neck
**aperchar** *va* (Am.) to pile, to heap, to stack up
**aperdigar** §59 *va* to brown, to broil slightly
**apergaminar** *vr* to get like parchment; (coll.) to dry up, to become yellow and wrinkled
**aperiódico -ca** *adj* aperiodic
**aperitivo -va** *adj* (med.) aperitive; *m* (med.) aperitive; apéritif, appetizer
**aperlado -da** *adj* pearly, pearl-colored
**apernar** *va* to bolt, to pin; §18 *va* to seize (*game*) by the leg (*said of hunting dogs*)
**apero** *m* tools, equipment, outfit, gear; sheepfold; (Am.) saddle, riding gear
**aperreador -dora** *adj* (coll.) worrisome, harassing, tiresome; *mf* (coll.) plague, bore
**aperrear** *va* to set the dogs on; (coll.) to worry, harass, plague, pester; *vr* (coll.) to be worried, harassed, plagued
**aperreo** *m* (coll.) worry, harassment, toil
**apersogar** §59 *va* to tether (*an animal*), to tie by the neck
**apersonado -da** *adj;* **bien apersonado** presentable; **mal apersonado** unpresentable
**apersonamiento** *m* personal appearance; (law) appearance
**apersonar** *vr* to appear in person; to have an interview; (law) to appear
**apertura** *f* opening, beginning; opening a will; (chess) opening
**apesadumbrar** *va* to grieve, distress; *vr* to grieve, be distressed; **apesadumbrarse con** or **de** to be grieved at, be distressed at
**apesaradamente** *adv* sadly, sorrowfully
**apesarar** *va & vr* var. of **apesadumbrar**
**apesgar** §59 *va* to overwhelm, overburden
**apestado -da** *adj* nauseated; pestilential
**apestar** *va* to infect with a plague; to corrupt, vitiate; (coll.) to sicken, nauseate, plague; to infest, fill; *vn* to stink; *vr* to be infected with a plague; to become vitiated
**apestoso -sa** *adj* pestilent, infected; sickening; annoying; stinking
**apétalo -la** *adj* (bot.) apetalous
**apetecedor -dora** *adj* hungering, thirsting, craving, longing
**apetecer** §34 *va* to hunger for, to thirst for, to crave, to long for
**apetecible** *adj* desirable; appetizing, tempting
**apetencia** *f* hunger, appetite, craving
**apetite** *m* sauce, appetizer; incentive, inducement
**apetitivo -va** *adj* appetitive; appetizing
**apetito** *m* appetite; **abrir el apetito** to whet the appetite
**apetitoso -sa** *adj* appetizing, tasty; gourmand
**ápex** *m* apex; (gram. & hist.) apex
**apezonado -da** *adj* nipple-shaped
**apezuñar** *vn* to dig the hoofs into the ground
**apiadar** *va* to move to pity; to take pity on; *vr* to have pity; **apiadarse de** to have pity on
**apiaradero** *m* shepherd's account of the heads of his flock
**apiario -ria** *adj* beelike; *m* apiary
**apical** *adj* apical; (phonet.) apical
**apicarar** *vr* to go to the bad, become depraved
**ápice** *m* apex; crux; bit, whit, iota; **estar en los ápices de** (coll.) to be up in, to know all about
**apícola** *adj* apicultural; *mf* apiculturist
**apículo** *m* apiculus

**apicultor -tora** *mf* apiculturist
**apicultura** *f* apiculture
**apilada** *f* dried chestnut
**apilamiento** *m* piling, heaping, pile
**apilar** *va & vr* to pile, pile up
**apilonar** *va* (Am.) to pile, to pile up
**apimpollar** *vr* to sprout, to put forth shoots
**apiñado -da** *adj* cone-shaped; packed, congested
**apiñadura** *f* or **apiñamiento** *m* squeezing; crowding, jamming; crowd, jam
**apiñar** *va* to bunch, to squeeze together, to crowd, to jam; *vr* to bunch, be squeezed together; to crowd, become crowded or jammed; to grow densely
**apio** *m* (bot.) celery; celery plant, celery stalk; **apio de ranas** (bot.) field buttercup, blister plant
**apiolar** *va* to gyve (*falcons*); to tie up (*the legs of a dead animal*); (coll.) to seize, arrest; (coll.) to kill
**apio-nabo** *m* (bot.) celeriac
**apipar** *vr* (coll.) to gorge with food and drink
**apirético -ca** *adj* apyretic
**apirexia** *f* (path.) apyrexia
**apiri** *m* (Am.) mine worker
**apisonado** *m* tamping, packing
**apisonador -dora** *adj* tamping; rolling; *mf* tamper (*person*); *m & f* road roller; roller; **apisonador de vapor** or **apisonadora movida a vapor** steam roller; *m* tamper (*tool*)
**apisonamiento** *m* tamping; rolling
**apisonar** *va* to tamp, to pack down; to roll
**apitonar** *va* to pierce, to break through; to peck at; *vn* to begin to show; to bud, to sprout; *vr* (coll.) to abuse each other, to exchange insults
**apizarrado -da** *adj* slate, slate-colored
**aplacable** *adj* placable, appeasable
**aplacador -dora** *adj* placating, appeasing; *mf* placator, appeaser
**aplacamiento** *m* placation, appeasement, calming
**aplacar** §86 *va* to placate, appease, pacify, calm, satisfy; to quench (*thirst*)
**aplacer** §34 *va* to please, satisfy; *vr* to be pleased, to take pleasure
**aplacerado -da** *adj* smooth and shallow (*said of bottom of sea*)
**aplacible** *adj* pleasant
**aplacimiento** *m* pleasure, enjoyment
**aplanadera** *f* road drag, leveler, roller, road roller; tamper
**aplanador -dora** *adj* smoothing, leveling; *m* roller
**aplanamiento** *m* smoothing, leveling; planishing
**aplanar** *va* to smooth, make even; to planish; (coll.) to astound; *vr* to collapse, fall over; to become discouraged
**aplanchado** *m* ironing
**aplanchador -dora** *mf* ironer
**aplanchar** *va* to iron (*clothing*)
**aplanético -ca** *adj* (opt.) aplanatic
**aplantillar** *va* to carve to measure
**aplastador -dora** *adj* var. of **aplastante**
**aplastamiento** *m* flattening, smashing; (coll.) dumbfounding
**aplastante** *adj* astounding, dumbfounding
**aplastapapeles** *m* (*pl:* **-les**) (Am.) paperweight
**aplastar** *va* to flatten, smash, crush; (coll.) to leave speechless; (Am.) to weary, to bore; *vr* to become flat; (coll.) to be left speechless
**aplaudidor -dora** *adj* applauding; *mf* applauder
**aplaudir** *va & vn* to applaud
**aplauso** *m* applause; **aplausos** *mpl* applause
**aplayar** *vn* to overflow, to flood (*said of a river*)
**aplazamiento** *m* convening; summons; postponement
**aplazar** §76 *va* to convene; to summon; to postpone; to set a time or date for
**aplebeyar** *va* to degrade; *vr* to be degraded, to lower oneself
**aplicabilidad** *f* applicability
**aplicable** *adj* applicable
**aplicación** *f* application; diligence; appliqué
**aplicado -da** *adj* studious, industrious; applied; appliqué
**aplicar** §86 *va* to apply; to assign; to attribute; (law) to adjudge; *vr* to apply (*be pertinent*); to apply oneself; to devote oneself
**aplomado -da** *adj* lead-colored; solemn, serious
**aplomar** *va* to plumb (*with plumb line*); to make straight or vertical; *vn* to plumb, be vertical; *vr* to collapse, fall to the ground
**aplomo** *m* seriousness, gravity; aplomb, self-possession
**apnea** *f* (path.) apnea
**apocado -da** *adj* irresolute, diffident, vacillating, of little courage; humble, lowly
**Apocalipsis** *m* (Bib.) Apocalypse
**apocalíptico -ca** *adj* apocalyptic; (fig.) apocalyptic
**apocamiento** *m* irresolution, diffidence, vacillation, lack of courage; depression, low spirits
**apocar** §86 *va* to cramp, contract, restrict; to make smaller, to narrow; to humble, belittle; *vr* to humble oneself
**apocárpico -ca** *adj* (bot.) apocarpous
**apócema** *f* or **apócima** *f* (pharm.) apozem, decoction
**apocináceo -a** *adj* (bot.) apocynaceous
**apocopar** *va* (gram.) to apocopate
**apócope** *f* (gram.) apocope
**apócrifo -fa** *adj* apocryphal; Apocryphal
**apodar** *va* to nickname; to make fun of; to curse, slander
**apoderado -da** *adj* empowered, authorized; *m* proxy; attorney; agent (*e.g., of a bullfighter*)
**apoderar** *va* to empower, to grant the power of attorney to; *vr* **apoderarse de** to take hold of, to seize, to grasp; to take possession of
**apodíctico -ca** *adj* (log.) apodictic
**apodo** *m* nickname, sobriquet
**ápodo -da** *adj* apodal
**apódosis** *f* (*pl:* **-sis**) (gram.) apodosis
**apófige** *f* (arch.) apophyge
**apófisis** *f* (*pl:* **-sis**) (anat. & zool.) process; (anat., bot., geol. & zool.) apophysis; (bot.) struma; **apófisis alveolar** (anat.) alveolar process; **apófisis coracoides** (anat.) coracoid process; **apófisis estiloides** (anat.) styloid process
**apofonía** *f* (phonet.) ablaut
**apogeo** *m* (astr. & fig.) apogee
**apógrafo** *m* apograph, copy
**apolillado -da** *adj* mothy, moth-eaten
**apolilladura** *f* moth hole
**apolillar** *va* to eat (*said of moths*); *vr* to become moth-eaten
**Apolo** *m* (myth.) Apollo
**apologético -ca** *adj* apologetic; *f* apologetics
**apología** *f* apology, apologia
**apologista** *mf* apologist
**apologizar** §76 *va* to praise, to defend; *vn* to apologize (*to offer a defense*)
**apólogo** *m* apologue
**apoltronado -da** *adj* loafing, idle, lazy
**apoltronar** *vr* to loaf around, to become lazier and lazier; to sprawl
**Apollión** *m* (Bib.) Apollyon
**apomazar** §76 *va* to smooth or polish with pumice stone
**apomorfina** *f* (pharm.) apomorphine
**aponeurosis** *f* (*pl:* **-sis**) (anat.) aponeurosis
**aponeurótico -ca** *adj* aponeurotic
**aponeurótomo** *m* (surg.) aponeurotome
**apontaje** *m* var. of **apontizaje**
**apontar** *vn* var. of **apontizar**
**apontizaje** *m* (aer.) deck-landing
**apontizar** §76 *vn* to deck-land
**apontocar** §86 *va* to prop up
**apoplejía** *f* (path.) apoplexy
**apoplético -ca** *adj & mf* apoplectic
**apoquinar** *vn* (slang) to come across, to cough up
**aporcado** *m* or **aporcadura** *f* (agr.) hilling
**aporcar** §86 *va* (agr.) to hill (*plants*)
**aporcelanado -da** *adj* procelainlike; porcelanic
**aporisma** *m* (path.) ecchymoma
**aporismar** *vr* to become an ecchymoma
**aporrar** *vn* (coll.) to be unable to say a word; *vr* (coll.) to be a bore, be a nuisance
**aporreado -da** *adj* poor, wretched; rascally; *m* (Am.) chopped beef stew
**aporreadura** *f* or **aporreamiento** *m* cudgeling, beating, clubbing

**aporrear** *va* to cudgel, beat, club; to annoy, bother; *vr* to get a beating; to drudge, slave
**aporreo** *m* var. of **aporreadura**
**aportación** *f* addition, contribution; (law) dowry, portion
**aportadera** *f* pannier or box (*to be carried on each side of a beast's back*); grape tub
**aportadero** *m* (naut.) port, harbor; stopping place, outlet
**aportar** *va* to bring, contribute; to lead; to provide; to bring as dowry; to bring (*one's proper share*); *vn* (naut.) to reach port; to come out at an unexpected place, to show up
**aporte** *m* (Am.) contribution
**aportillar** *va* to breach, break open, break down; *vr* to collapse, tumble down
**aposentador** *m* host; (mil.) billeter
**aposentamiento** *m* lodging; settling down, taking one's place
**aposentar** *va* to put up, to lodge; *vr* to take lodging; to take one's place
**aposento** *m* room; inn; lodging; box (*in ancient theaters*)
**aposesionar** *va* to give possession to; *vr* to take possession
**aposición** *f* (gram.) apposition
**apositivo -va** *adj & m* (gram.) appositive
**apósito** *m* (med.) external application
**aposta** or **apostadamente** *adv* (coll.) on purpose
**apostadero** *m* stand, station, post; (mil.) post; (naut.) naval station; (naut.) naval district
**apostador -dora** *mf* or **apostante** *mf* bettor
**apostal** *m* good spot for fishing
**apostar** *va* to post, to station; **§77** *va* to bet, to wager; *vn* to bet; to compete; **apostar a que** to bet that; **apostar a** or **por** to bet on (*e.g., a horse*); *vr* to compete; **apostárselas a** or **con** (coll.) to compete with
**apostasía** *f* apostasy
**apóstata** *mf* apostate
**apostatar** *vn* apostatize
**apostema** *f* (path.) abscess, aposteme
**apostemar** *va* to form an abscess in; *vr* to abscess, become abscessed
**apostematoso -sa** *adj* apostematous
**apostemero** *m* (surg.) lancet
**apostilla** *f* note, comment
**apostillar** *va* to annotate (*a text*); *vr* to break out in pimples
**apóstol** *m* apostle; **apóstol de las gentes** or **los gentiles** (Bib.) Apostle of the Gentiles
**apostolado** *m* apostolate
**apostólicamente** *adv* apostolically; (coll.) poorly, unostentatiously
**apostólico -ca** *adj* apostolic or apostolical
**apostrofar** *va* to apostrophize; to scold, insult; to write with an apostrophe
**apóstrofe** *m & f* apostrophe (*addressed to absent person*); scolding, insult
**apóstrofo** *m* (gram.) apostrophe
**apostura** *f* gracefulness, neatness, spruceness; bearing
**apotegma** *m* apothegm (*short, instructive saying*)
**apotema** *f* (geom.) apothem
**apoteósico -ca** *adj* deific, deifying; glorifying
**apoteosis** *f* (*pl:* **-sis**) apotheosis
**apotrerar** *va* (Am.) to take (*horses*) to pasture
**apoyabrazos** *m* (*pl:* **-zos**) armrest
**apoyador** *m* bracket, support
**apoyadura** *f* flow of milk to the udders
**apoyalibros** *m* (*pl:* **-bros**) book end
**apoyapié** *m* or **apoyapiés** *m* (*pl:* **-piés**) (aut.) footrest
**apoyar** *va* to lean, rest, support; to hold up, prop; to back, abet; to droop (*the head; said of horses*); *vn* to lean, rest, be supported; *vr* to lean, rest, be supported; to depend, be based; **apoyarse en** to lean on; to rely on; to stress
**apoyatura** *f* (mus.) appoggiatura, grace note
**apoyo** *m* prop, support; backing, approval, aid, protection
**apraxia** *f* (path.) apraxia
**apreciable** *adj* appreciable; estimable; (coll.) nice, fine (*person*)
**apreciación** *f* appreciation, appraisal; smallest reading (*of an instrument or gauge*)
**apreciadamente** *adv* appreciatively
**apreciador -dora** *mf* appraiser
**apreciar** *va* to appreciate; to appraise, to estimate; to esteem
**apreciativo -va** *adj* appreciable (*e.g., error*)
**aprecio** *m* appreciation, esteem
**aprehender** *va* to apprehend, catch; to conceive, think; to seize, attach (*property*)
**aprehensión** *f* apprehension (*capture; fear*); (law) seizure, attachment
**aprehensivo -va** *adj* apprehensive (*perceptive; afraid, worried*)
**aprehensor -sora** *mf* captor
**apremiadamente** *adv* with insistence, urgently
**apremiador -dora** *adj* pressing, compelling; *mf* compeller
**apremiante** *adj* insistent, urgent
**apremiar** *va* to press, urge; to compel, force; to hurry; to harass, oppress; **apremiar** + *inf* to be urgent to + *inf*
**apremio** *m* pressure, constraint; compulsion; oppression; (law) judicial writ (*to compel payment or fulfilment*)
**aprendedor -dora** *adj* learning; *mf* learner
**aprender** *va & vn* to learn; **aprender a** + *inf* to learn to + *inf*
**aprendiz -diza** *mf* apprentice, beginner; **aprendiz de imprenta** printer's devil
**aprendizaje** *m* learning; apprenticeship; **hacer su aprendizaje** to serve one's apprenticeship; **pagar el aprendizaje** (coll.) to pay for one's inexperience
**aprensador -dora** *adj* pressing; *mf* presser
**aprensar** *va* to press; to crush, oppress
**aprensión** *f* apprehension (*fear, worry*); notion, strange idea; (coll.) shame
**aprensivo -va** *adj* apprehensive (*afraid, worried*)
**apresador -dora** *adj* seizing; *mf* captor
**apresamiento** *m* seizing; clutch, hold; capture
**apresar** *va* to seize, grasp; to capture, take prisoner
**apreso -sa** *adj* rooted, well rooted
**aprestador** *m* primer (*for paint*)
**aprestar** *va* to prepare, make ready; to prime (*for painting*); to size; *vr* to prepare, get ready; **aprestarse a** + *inf* to prepare to + *inf*, to get ready + *inf*
**apresto** *m* preparation, readiness; outfit, equipment; priming; size, sizing
**apresuración** *f* haste, hastening
**apresuradamente** *adv* hastily
**apresuramiento** *m* haste, hastiness, hastening
**apresurar** *va & vr* to hasten, hurry; **apresurarse a** + *inf* to hasten to + *inf*, to hurry to + *inf*
**apretadamente** *adv* hard, tight; tightly, closely
**apretadera** *f* strap, rope (*for tying, e.g., a trunk*); **apretaderas** *fpl* (coll.) insistence, pressure
**apretadero** *m* truss
**apretadizo -za** *adj* easily compressed
**apretado -da** *adj* tight, compact; difficult, dangerous; (coll.) stingy; close, intimate; strict; dense, thick; (coll.) dangerously ill
**apretador** *m* tightener; corset; hair net
**apretadura** *f* tightening; squeezing; compression
**apretar** **§18** *va* to tighten; to squeeze; to contract; to fit tight, to pinch; to press (*e.g., a button*); to hold tight, to hug; to importune, to hurry; to pursue closely, to harass; to treat harshly; to beset, to distress, to afflict; to dun; to make more severe; to clench (*the fists, the teeth*); to shake (*hands*); *vn* to get worse; to pinch; to insist; **¡aprieta!** (coll.) get out!, nonsense!; **apretar a correr** (coll.) to strike out on a run; **apretar con** (coll.) to close in on, to attack; *vr* to narrow, be compressed; to grieve, be distressed; to skimp; (Am.) to gorge
**apretazón** *f* (Am.) var. of **apretadura**
**apretón** *m* sudden pressure; quick hug; struggle, conflict; dash, short run; **apretón de manos** handshake
**apretujar** *va* (coll.) to jam, to press hard, to keep on pressing or squeezing; *vr* (coll.) to jam, to be packed in
**apretujón** *m* (coll.) hard squeeze
**apretura** *f* jam, crush; fix; distress, tightness, constriction; difficulty, trouble; need, want

**aprietapapeles** *m* (*pl:* **-les**) paper finger (*of typewriter*)
**aprietarropa** *m* clothespin
**aprietatuercas** *m* (*pl:* **-cas**) wrench; spintight, nut-driver
**apriete** *m* tightening
**aprieto** *m* jam, crush; fix; **poner en aprieto** to put pressure on, to put on the spot; **sacar de un aprieto** to get (*someone*) out of a jam
**aprioridad** *f* (philos.) apriority
**apriorismo** *m* (philos.) apriorism
**apriorístico -ca** *adj* aprioristic
**aprisa** *adv* fast, quickly, hurriedly
**apriscar** **§86** *va* to gather (*sheep*) into the fold
**aprisco** *m* sheepfold; place of refuge
**aprisionar** *va* to imprison; to shackle; to tie, bind
**aproar** *vn* (naut.) to turn the prow
**aprobación** *f* approbation, approval; pass, passing grade
**aprobado -da** *adj* excellent, estimable; *m* pass (*mark of passing an examination*)
**aprobante** *adj* approving
**aprobar** **§77** *va* to approve; to pass (*a student; an examination; a course*); *vn* to approve; to pass
**aproches** *mpl* access, approach; neighborhood; (mil.) approaches
**aprontamiento** *m* quick preparation, ready delivery
**aprontar** *va* to prepare quickly, to hand over without delay, to have ready
**apropiable** *adj* appropriable
**apropiación** *f* giving, gift; fitting, adaptation; appropriation
**apropiado -da** *adj* appropriate, proper, fitting
**apropiar** *va* to give, to give possession of; to fit, adapt, apply; *vr* to appropriate; **apropiarse de una cosa** or **apropiarse una cosa** to appropriate something
**apropincuar** *vr* (hum.) to approach, come near
**apropósito** *m* (theat.) occasional play
**aprovechable** *adj* available, usable
**aprovechado -da** *adj* saving, thrifty; miserly, stingy; diligent, studious, industrious; well-spent (*said of time*); *m* opportunist
**aprovechamiento** *m* use; profit, advantage; progress; improvement; progress in school; harnessing (*e.g., of waterfalls*)
**aprovechar** *va* to make use of, benefit from, profit by, take advantage of; to harness (*e.g., a waterfall*); *vn* to be useful, to avail; to progress, to improve; *vr* **aprovecharse de** to avail oneself of, to take advantage of
**aprovisionador** *m* supplier
**aprovisionamiento** *m* supplying; supplies, supply
**aprovisionar** *va* to supply, furnish, provision
**aproximación** *f* nearness, closeness; approximation; approach; rapprochement; consolation prize (*in a lottery*); **aproximación controlada desde tierra** (aer.) ground-controlled approach
**aproximado -da** *adj* approximate
**aproximar** *va* to bring near or nearer; to approximate; *vr* to come near or nearer; to approximate
**aproximativo -va** *adj* approximate
**ápside** *m* (astr.) apsis
**apsiquia** *f* (path.) apsychia
**áptero -ra** *adj* apterous
**aptitud** *f* aptitude; suitability
**apto -ta** *adj* apt; suitable; **apto para** + *inf* quick to + *inf;* suitable for + *ger*
**apuesto -ta** *adj* elegant, bedecked, spruce; *f* bet, wager
**Apuleyo** *m* Apuleius
**apulgarar** *vn* to press the or one's thumb; *vr* (coll.) to spot with mildew (*said of clean wash*)
**apulso** *m* (astr.) appulse; (opt.) contact of heavenly body with vertical wire of reticle
**apunar** *vr* (Am.) to suffer from mountain sickness
**apuntación** *f* pointing, aiming; note, annotation; scoring; (mus.) notation; composition of music; **apuntaciones** *fpl* (mus.) transcription for voice
**apuntado -da** *adj* pointed, sharp; (her.) counterpointed; (Am.) tipsy
**apuntador** *m* (theat.) prompter
**apuntalamiento** *m* prop, propping, underpinning
**apuntalar** *va* to prop, prop up, underpin
**apuntamiento** *m* pointing, aiming; note; sketch, outline; judicial report
**apuntar** *va* to point at; to point out, to mark; to note, to take note of; to aim; to aim at; to sharpen; to stitch; to darn; to patch; to fasten up, to fasten temporarily; to prompt (*a student in an examination*); to correct, to set aright; to put up, to stake; to sketch, to outline; (theat.) to prompt; *vn* to begin to appear; to dawn; to hint; **apuntar y no dar** (coll.) to fail to come through; *vr* to begin to sour (*said of wine*); (coll.) to get tipsy; to register, to sign up
**apunte** *m* note; sketch; prompter; promptbook; stake; rascal
**apuntillar** *va* (taur.) to finish off with the dagger
**apuñadar** *va* (prov.) to punch with the fist
**apuñalado -da** *adj* dagger-shaped
**apuñalar** *va* to stab
**apuñar** *va* to seize with the fist; to punch with the fist; *vn* to tighten one's hand
**apuñear** or **apuñetear** *va* (coll.) to punch with the fist
**apuracabos** *m* (*pl:* **-bos**) save-all (*candlestick in which candle burns to very end*)
**apuración** *f* purification; verification; consumption; annoyance, worry; hurry
**apuradamente** *adv* (coll.) precisely, punctually; (coll.) carefully; (coll.) with difficulty
**apurado -da** *adj* needy, hard up; hard, dangerous; (coll.) hurried, rushed
**apurador -dora** *adj* purifying, refining; exhausting; *m* save-all (*candlestick in which candle burns to very end*)
**apuramiento** *m* draining; verification, check
**apuranieves** *m* (*pl:* **-ves**) (orn.) wagtail
**apurar** *va* to purify, refine; to verify, clarify, clear up; to carry out, finish; to exhaust, drain, use up; to annoy; to hurry, press; *vr* to grieve, worry, fret; (Am.) to hurry, hasten; **apurarse por** + *inf* to strive to + *inf*
**apure** *m* (min.) refining, refinement
**apurismado -da** *adj* (Am.) weak, sickly
**apuro** *m* need, want, fix; grief, sorrow, affliction; (Am.) haste, urgency; **estar en el mayor apuro** to be in a bad fix, to be up against it, to be in dire straits
**aquejar** *va* to grieve, afflict, weary; to harass; *vr* to hurry; to complain
**aquejoso -sa** *adj* sad, afflicted, grieved
**aquel, aquella** *adj dem* (*pl:* **aquellos, aquellas**) that, that . . . yonder
**aquél, aquélla** *pron dem* (*pl:* **aquéllos, aquéllas**) that one, that one yonder; the one; the former; the first (*of three*); *m* (coll.) charm, appeal
**aquelarre** *m* witches' Sabbath
**aquello** *pron dem neut* that; that thing, that matter
**aquende** *adv* on this side; *prep* on this side of; **de aquende** on this side of
**aquénico -ca** *adj* achenial
**aquenio** *m* (bot.) achene
**aqueo -a** *adj & mf* Achaean
**aquerenciar** *vr* to become fond; **aquerenciarse a** to become fond of, to become attached to
**Aqueronte** *m* (myth.) Acheron
**aquí** *adv* here; **de aquí** from here; hence; **de aquí a** in, within; **de aquí en adelante** from now on; **de aquí que** hence; **por aquí** hereabouts; this way; **aquí dentro** in here
**aquiescencia** *f* acquiescence
**aquiescente** *adj* acquiescent
**aquietar** *va* to quiet, calm, pacify; *vr* to quiet down, become calm
**aquilatamiento** *m* assay; weighing, estimation, checking
**aquilatar** *va* to assay; to weigh the merit of, to check, to appreciate
**aquilea** *f* (bot.) yarrow
**Aquiles** *m* (myth.) Achilles
**aquilino -na** *adj* (poet.) aquiline
**aquilón** *m* north wind; north
**aquilonal** *adj* north-wind; northern; (pertaining to) winter

**aquillado -da** *adj* keel-shaped, keellike; wide-keeled
**Aquisgrán** *m* Aachen, Aix-la-Chapelle
**aquistar** *va* to get, acquire, win
**Aquitania** *f* Aquitaine
**aquitánico -ca** *adj* Aquitanian
**aquitano -na** *adj & mf* Aquitanian
**aquivo -va** *adj & mf* var. of **aqueo**
**ara** *f* altar; altar slab; communion table; **en aras de** in honor of; *m* (orn.) macaw
**árabe** *adj* Arab, Arabic; (arch.) Moresque; *mf* Arab; *m* Arabic (*language*)
**arabesco -ca** *adj* Arabic; (f.a.) arabesque; *m* (f.a.) arabesque
**Arabia, la** Arabia; **la Arabia Saudita** Saudi Arabia
**arábico -ca** *adj* Arabic
**arábigo -ga** *adj* Arabian, Arabic; *m* Arabic (*language*); **estar en arábigo** (coll.) to be Greek (*i.e., hard to understand*); **hablar en arábigo** (coll.) to talk gibberish
**arabismo** *m* Arabism
**arabista** *mf* Arabist
**arabizar** §76 *va* to Arabize, to make Arabic
**arable** *adj* arable
**aracanga** *m* (orn.) macaw
**aráceo -a** *adj* (bot.) araceous
**Aracne** *f* (myth.) Arachne
**arácnido -da** *adj* (zool.) arachnid, arachnidan; *m* (zool.) arachnid
**aracnoides** *m* (*pl:* **-des**) (anat.) arachnoid
**arada** *f* plowed land; plowing; day's plowing by a yoke of oxen
**arado** *m* plow; plowshare
**arador** *m* plowman; (ent.) itch mite
**aradura** *f* plowing
**Aragón** *m* Aragon (*river, region, and former kingdom of Spain*)
**aragonés -nesa** *adj & mf* Aragonese; *m* Aragonese (*dialect*)
**aragonesismo** *m* Aragonese expression or idiom
**aragonita** *f* or **aragonito** *m* (mineral.) aragonite
**araguato** *m* (zool.) ursine howler
**aralia** *f* (bot. & pharm.) aralia; (bot.) spikenard
**araliáceo -a** *adj* (bot.) araliaceous
**aramaico -ca** *adj & m* Aramaic (*language*)
**arambel** *m* hangings; rag, shred
**arameo -a** *adj* Aramaean; Aramaic; *mf* Aramaean; *m* Aramaic (*language*)
**aramio** *m* fallow land, fallow field
**arana** *f* trick, cheat
**arancel** *m* tariff
**arancelario -ria** *adj* (pertaining to) tariff, customs
**arandanedo** *m* bilberry patch; cranberry bog
**arándano** *m* (bot.) bilberry, whortleberry; **arándano agrio** (bot.) cranberry; **arándano encarnado** (bot.) mountain cranberry, cowberry
**arandela** *f* (mach.) washer; bobèche, disk to catch drippings of candle; guard on handle of lance; candle stand; (naut.) half-port
**arandillo** *m* (orn.) marsh warbler
**aranero -ra** *adj* cheating, tricky, swindling; *mf* cheat, trickster, swindler
**araña** *f* (ent. & mach.) spider; crowfoot (*to suspend awnings, etc.*); (ichth.) stingbull, greater weever; (bot.) love-in-a-mist; chandelier; (coll.) thrifty, calculating person; whore; **araña de mar** (zool.) spider crab; **araña de sobremesa** candelabrum; **araña epeira** (ent.) cross spider
**arañada** *f* scratch
**arañador -dora** *adj* scratching; *mf* scratcher; burler; scraper (*penurious saver; poor fiddler*); *m* burling iron
**arañamiento** *m* scratching, scratch; scraping
**arañar** *m* scratch; **arañar de la aguja** needle scratch; *va* to scratch; to scrape; (coll.) to scrape together; *vr* to scratch
**arañazo** *m* scratch (*with fingernail, pin, etc.*)
**arañero -ra** *adj* wild, haggard (*said of birds*)
**araño** *m* scratching, scratch
**arañuela** *f* (bot.) love-in-a-mist
**arañuelo** *m* (ent.) red spider; (ent.) spider grub; bird net
**aráquida** *f* peanut

**arar** *m* (bot.) sandarac tree; *va* to plow
**arasá** *m* (Am.) guava (*tree and fruit*)
**araucanista** *mf* Araucanist (*authority on Araucanian language and customs*)
**araucano -na** *adj* Araucanian; *mf* Araucanian, Araucan; *m* Araucanian or Araucan (*language*)
**araucaria** *f* (bot.) araucaria, Norfolk Island pine
**arbalestrilla** *f* (math.) arbalest, cross-staff
**arbellón** *m* sewer, drain, gutter
**arbitrable** *adj* arbitrable
**arbitrador -dora** *adj* arbitrating; *m* arbitrator; *f* arbitress
**arbitraje** *m* arbitration, arbitrage; **arbitraje de cambio** arbitrage of exchange
**arbitral** *adj* arbitral
**arbitramento** or **arbitramiento** *m* arbitrament
**arbitrar** *va* to arbitrate; to referee; (sport) to umpire; to contrive, bring together, assemble; *vn* to arbitrate; to referee; (sport) to umpire; *vr* to manage well; (coll.) to manage to get along well
**arbitrariedad** *f* abuse, outrage, arbitrary act
**arbitrario -ria** *adj* arbitrary
**arbitrio** *m* free will; means, ways, expedient; adjudication; **arbitrios** *mpl* excise taxes
**arbitrista** *mf* cure-all politician, wild-eyed dreamer
**árbitro -tra** *adj* independent, autonomous; *m* arbiter; (sport) umpire; *f* arbitress
**árbol** *m* tree; newel (*of winding stairs*); body (*of shirt*); (mach.) shaft, arbor, axle, spindle; (naut.) mast; (print.) shank; **árbol de Judas** or **de Judea** (bot.) Judas tree; **árbol de la cera** (bot.) wax myrtle (*Myrica cerifera*); (bot.) wax tree (*Rhus verniciflus; Myrica cerifera*); (bot.) wax palm (*Ceroxylon andicolum*); **árbol de la ciencia del bien y del mal** (Bib.) tree of knowledge of good and evil; **árbol del alcanfor** (bot.) camphor tree; **árbol de la leche** (bot.) cow tree; **árbol del amor** (bot.) Judas tree; **árbol de las calabazas** (bot.) calabash tree; **árbol de la vida** (Bib. & bot.) tree of life; (anat.) arbor vitae; **árbol del caucho** (bot.) rubber plant; **árbol del cielo** (bot.) tree of heaven; **árbol del diablo** (bot.) sandbox tree; **árbol de levas** (mach.) camshaft; **árbol del pan** (bot.) breadfruit, breadfruit tree; **árbol del paraíso** (bot.) China tree; **árbol del tomate** (bot.) tomato tree; **árbol del viajero** (bot.) traveler's tree; **árbol de mando** (mach.) drive shaft; **árbol de María** (bot.) calaba; **árbol de Navidad** Christmas tree; **árbol de pie** seedling; **árbol de sombra** shade tree; **árbol de vaca** (bot.) cow tree; **árbol frutal** fruit tree; **árbol genealógico** genealogical tree, family tree; **árbol motor** (mach.) drive shaft
**arbolado -da** *adj* wooded; high (*seas*); *m* woodland
**arboladura** *f* (naut.) masts and spars
**arbolar** *va* to hoist; to raise, set up; (naut.) to mast (*a ship*); *vr* to rear on the hind feet
**arbolario -ria** *adj & mf* (coll.) scatterbrain
**arboleda** *f* grove
**arboledo** *m* woodland
**arbolejo** *m* little tree
**arbolete** *m* little tree; branch on which to fasten lime twigs (*to catch birds*)
**arbolillo** *m* little tree; side of a blast furnace
**arbolista** *mf* arborist
**arbollón** *m* sewer, drain
**arborecer** §34 *vn* to grow, develop (*said of trees*)
**arbóreo -a** *adj* arboreal
**arborescencia** *f* arborescence
**arborescente** *adj* arborescent
**arboricultor** *m* arboriculturist
**arboricultura** *f* arboriculture
**arboriforme** *adj* arboriform
**arborización** *f* (anat. & mineral.) arborization
**arborizado -da** *adj* treelike
**arbotante** *m* (arch.) flying buttress
**arbustivo -va** *adj* shrubby
**arbusto** *m* (bot.) shrub
**arca** *f* chest, coffer; tank, reservoir; ark; tempering oven; **arcas** *fpl* coffers (*e.g., of the State*); hollow below the ribs; **arca cerrada**

pure heart of a maiden; quiet person; unknown quantity (*person*); **arca de agua** water tower; **arca de la alianza** (Bib.) ark of the covenant; **arca de Noé** Noah's ark; (coll.) lumber room; (coll.) house in which all sorts and conditions of people live
**arcabucear** *va* to shoot with a harquebus, to kill with a harquebusade
**arcabucería** *f* troop of harquebusiers; harquebuses; harquebusade; harquebus factory
**arcabucero** *m* harquebusier; harquebus maker
**arcabuco** *m* craggy thicket
**arcabuz** *m* (*pl:* **-buces**) harquebus
**arcabuzazo** *m* harquebus shot or wound
**arcacil** *m* (bot.) artichoke
**arcada** *f* (arch.) arcade; archway; (mus.) stroke of bow; **arcadas** *fpl* retching
**árcade** *adj & mf* Arcadian
**Arcadia, la** Arcadia
**arcádico -ca** *adj* (fig.) Arcadian (*simple, rural*)
**arcadio -dia** *adj & mf* Arcadian
**arcaduz** *m* (*pl:* **-duces**) *m* pipe, conduit; bucket; means, way
**arcaico -ca** *adj* archaic; (geol.) Archeozoic
**arcaísmo** *m* archaism
**arcaísta** *mf* archaist
**arcaizante** *adj* obsolescent; using obsolescent forms
**arcaizar** §97 *va & vn* to archaize
**arcángel** *m* archangel
**arcangélico -ca** *adj* archangelic
**arcano -na** *adj* arcane, hidden, secret; *m* arcanum
**arcar** §86 *va* to arch; to beat (*wool*)
**arce** *m* (bot.) maple; **arce blanco** (bot.) sycamore; **arce del azúcar** (bot.) sugar maple
**arcedianato** *m* archdeaconry
**arcediano** *m* archdeacon
**arcedo** *m* maple grove
**arcén** *m* border, edge, brim; curbstone (*of well*)
**arcilla** *f* clay; **arcilla figulina** potter's clay, argil
**arcillar** *va* to clay; (agr.) to clay
**arcilloso -sa** *adj* clayey
**arciprestazgo** *m* archpriesthood
**arcipreste** *m* archpriest
**arco** *m* (geom. & elec.) arc; (anat. & arch.) arch; bow; hoop; (sport) goal post; **arco abocinado** splayed arch; **arco adintelado** horizontal or straight arch; **arco apainelado** basket-handle arch; **arco arábigo** Moorish arch; **arco botarete** (arch.) flying buttress; **arco carpanel** basket-handle arch; **arco cigomático** (anat.) zygomatic arch; **arco conopial** ogee arch; **arco de herradura** horseshoe arch; **arco de medio punto** semicircular arch; **arco de todo punto** Gothic arch; **arco de triunfo** triumphal arch; memorial arch; **arco elíptico** elliptical arch; **arco en rampa** rampant arch; **arco escarzano** segmental arch; **arco iris** rainbow; **arco ojival** pointed arch; **arco peraltado** stilted arch; **arco por tranquil** rampant arch; **arco trebolado** trefoil arch; **arco triunfal** triumphal arch; memorial arch
**arcón** *m* bin, bunker; large chest
**arcosa** *f* (geol.) arkose
**archi-** *prefix* (coll.) very, extremely, e.g., **archiconocido** extremely well-known; **archiridículo** very silly
**archi** *adj* (coll.) super (*excellent, superfine*)
**archicofradía** *f* privileged brotherhood
**archidiácono** *m* archdeacon
**archidiócesis** *f* (*pl:* **-sis**) var. of **arquidiócesis**
**archiducado** *m* archduchy
**archiducal** *adj* archducal
**archiduque** *m* archduke
**archiduquesa** *f* archduchess
**archienemigo** *m* archenemy (*chief enemy*)
**archilaúd** *m* (mus.) large lute
**archimillonario -ria** *adj & mf* multimillionaire
**archipámpano** *m* (hum.) self-styled or imaginary tycoon
**archipiélago** *m* archipelago; (coll.) labyrinth, entanglement; (*cap.*) *m* Aegean Sea, Archipelago; **archipiélago de Francisco José** Franz Josef Land; **archipiélago de Joló** or **de Sulú** Sulu Archipelago; **archipiélago Malayo** Malay Archipelago
**archivador -dora** *adj* filing; *mf* file clerk; *m* filing cabinet; letter file
**archivar** *va* to file; to file away; to deposit in the archives; (coll.) to hide away
**archivero** *m* archivist; city clerk
**archivista** *m* archivist
**archivo** *m* archives; file, files; filing; public records; (fig.) model (*e.g., of perfection*); (Am.) office
**archivolta** *f* (arch.) archivolt
**arda** *f* (zool.) squirrel
**ardalear** *vn* to fail to fill out (*said of bunches of grapes*)
**árdea** *f* var. of **alcaraván**
**ardeida** *f* (orn.) heron
**ardentía** *f* heartburn; (naut.) phosphorescence (*of water*)
**ardentísimo -ma** *adj super* very or most ardent; very or most passionate; bright red
**arder** *va* to burn; (Am.) to itch; *vn* to burn, to blaze; (poet.) to shine, flash; **estar que arde** to be coming to a head, to be near the breaking point; **arder de** or **en** to burn with (*e.g., love, hate*); **arder en** to be ablaze with (*e.g., war*); **arder por** + *inf* to be burning to + *inf;* **arder sin llamas** to smolder; *vr* to burn; to burn up (*said of grain in hot, dry weather*)
**ardero** *m* squirrel dog
**ardid** *m* trick, artifice, ruse
**ardido -da** *adj* spoiled, burnt-up (*said of grain, olives, etc.*); bold, intrepid; (Am.) angry
**ardiendo** *adj invar* burning, hot
**ardiente** *adj* ardent, burning; passionate, fiery; feverish; red
**ardilla** *f* (zool.) squirrel; **andar como una ardilla** to be always on the go, to flit about; **ardilla de tierra** (zool.) gopher; **ardilla gris** (zool.) gray squirrel; **ardilla ladradora** (zool.) prairie dog; **ardilla listada** (zool.) chipmunk; **ardilla voladora** (zool.) flying squirrel
**ardillón** *m* (zool.) gopher (*Spermophilus*)
**ardimiento** *m* burning; intrepidity, courage
**ardiondo -da** *adj* intrepid, courageous
**ardite** *m* old Spanish coin of little value; **no me importa un ardite** (coll.) I don't care a hang; **no valer un ardite** (coll.) to be not worth a continental
**ardor** *m* ardor, heat, excitement, vehemence; zeal, eagerness; intrepidity, courage, dash
**ardoroso -sa** *adj* burning, fiery, enthusiastic; restive, balky
**arduidad** *f* arduousness
**arduo -dua** *adj* arduous, hard
**área** *f* area; are (*surface measure*); **área de la libra esterlina** sterling block
**areca** *f* (bot.) areca (*palm and nut*)
**arefacción** *f* drying
**arel** *m* large sieve (*for grain*)
**arelar** *va* to sieve or sift (*grain*)
**arena** *f* sand; grit, grindings; arena; **arenas** *fpl* arena; (path.) stones (*in bladder*); **arena de estufa** or **arena seca** (found.) dry sand; **arena movediza** quicksand; **arena verde** (found.) green sand
**arenáceo -a** *adj* arenaceous
**arenación** *f* sanding; mixing sand and lime; (med.) arenation
**arenal** *m* sandy ground, sand pit; desert; quicksand
**arenalejo** *m* small sandy spot
**arenar** *va* to spread sand over; to sand, to rub or polish with sand; *vn* to become covered with sand; (naut.) to run aground on sand
**arenario -ria** *adj* (living in) sand; *f* (bot.) sandwort
**arencar** §86 *va* to cure (*sardines*) like herring
**arenero -ra** *adj* (for) sand; *mf* sand dealer; *m* (rail.) sandbox; (taur.) boy who spreads and smooths sand after each bullfight
**arenga** *f* harangue; (coll.) scolding
**arengador -dora** *mf* haranguer; (coll.) scold
**arengar** §59 *va & vn* to harangue; (coll.) to scold
**arenilla** *f* fine sand used to dry wet ink, pounce; **arenillas** *fpl* granulated saltpeter; (path.) stones (*in bladder*)

**arenillero** *m* var. of **salvadera**
**arenisco -ca** *adj* sandy, gritty; (pertaining to) sand; *f* (mineral.) sandstone; **arenisca verde** greensand
**arenoso -sa** *adj* sandy
**arenque** *m* (ichth.) herring; **arenque de ojos grandes** (ichth.) walleyed herring
**arenquero -ra** *mf* herring vendor; *f* herring net; (slang) coarse, shameless woman
**aréola** *f* (anat., bot., path. & zool.) areola
**areolar** *adj* areolar
**areometría** *f* hydrometry
**areométrico -ca** *adj* hydrometric
**areómetro** *m* areometer, hydrometer
**Areópago** *m* Areopagus
**areóstilo** *m* (arch.) areostyle
**arepa** *f* (Am.) corn griddle cake
**Ares** *m* (myth.) Ares
**arestín** *m* (vet.) thrush
**arete** *m* eardrop, earring
**Aretusa** *f* (myth.) Arethusa
**arfada** *f* (naut.) pitching
**arfar** *vn* (naut.) to pitch
**argadijo** or **argadillo** *m* reel, bobbin; (coll.) blustering fellow
**argado** *m* prank, trick
**argal** *m* wine stone
**argala** *f* (orn.) adjutant, adjutant bird
**argalí** *m* (*pl:* **-líes**) (zool.) argali
**argalia** *f* (surg.) catheter
**argallera** *f* croze, crozing saw
**argamandel** *m* rag, tatter
**argamandijo** *m* (coll.) set of small tools or utensils
**argamasa** *f* mortar; **argamasa hidráulica** hydraulic mortar
**argamasar** *va* to mix (*mortar*); to mortar, to plaster; *vn* to make mortar
**argamasilla** *f* fine mortar
**argamasón** *m* large dry piece of mortar
**argán** *m* (bot.) argan tree; argan (*fruit of argan tree*); (mus.) Arab organ
**árgana** *f* (mach.) crane; wicker basket for packsaddles
**arganeo** *m* (naut.) anchor ring
**argavieso** *m* thunderstorm
**argayar** *v impers* to be a landslide
**argayo** *m* landslide; **argayo de nieve** (prov.) avalanche
**argel** *adj* with right hind foot white (*said of a horse*); (coll.) wretched, unfortunate; (*cap.*) *f* Algiers
**Argelia** *f* Algeria
**argelino -na** *adj & mf* Algerian
**argemone** *f* (bot.) argemone, prickly poppy; **argemone mejicana** (bot.) Mexican poppy
**argén** *m* (her.) argent
**argentado -da** *adj* silver-plated; silvery; slashed (*said of shoes*)
**argentán** *m* German silver
**argentar** *va* to silver; to trim with silver; to give a silver finish to; (fig.) to silver; *vr* (fig.) to silver
**argentario** *m* silversmith; master of the mint
**argénteo -a** *adj* silvery; silver-plated
**argentería** *f* embroidery of silver or gold
**argentero** *m* silversmith
**argentífero -ra** *adj* argentiferous
**argentina** *f* & **Argentina, la** see **argentino**
**argentinismo** *m* Argentinism
**argentinizar §76** *va* to Argentinize; *vr* to become Argentinized
**argentino -na** *adj* argentine, silvery; Argentine; *mf* Argentine, Argentinean; *m* argentino (*coin*); *f* (mineral.) argentine; (bot.) silverweed; **la Argentina** Argentina, the Argentine
**argentista** *m* freesilverite
**argento** *m* (poet.) argent, silver; **argento vivo** quicksilver; **argento vivo sublimado** (chem.) corrosive sublimate
**argentoso -sa** *adj* mixed with silver
**argila** or **argilla** *f* var. of **arcilla**
**argiloso -sa** *adj* var. of **arcilloso**
**argirol** *m* argyrol
**argivo -va** *adj & mf* Argive
**argo** *m* (chem.) argon
**argólico -ca** *adj* Argolic
**Argólida** or **Argólide, la** Argolis
**argolla** *f* large iron ring; staple; croquet (*game*); ring (*put in the snout of an animal*)
**argolleta** *f* little iron ring
**argoma** *f* (bot.) furze, gorse
**argón** *m* (chem.) argon
**argonauta** *m* (myth.) Argonaut; (zool.) argonaut, paper nautilus
**argonáutico -ca** *adj* (myth.) Argonautic
**Argos** *f* Argos (*ancient Greek town*); (myth.) Argo (*ship*); (astr.) Argo; *m* (myth.) Argus (*monster*); (*l.c.*) *m* Argus (*watchful person*); **ser un argos, estar hecho un argos** to be Argus-eyed
**argucia** *f* subtlety, sophistry; trick, deceit
**argüe** *m* capstan
**arguellar** *vr* (dial.) to become emaciated, to lose weight
**arguello** *m* (dial.) emaciation, loss of weight
**árguenas** or **árgueñas** *fpl* handbarrow; saddlebags
**argüir §21** *va* to argue (*to indicate, to prove; to accuse*); *vn* to argue; **argüir contra** to argue against
**argumentación** *f* argumentation
**argumentador -dora** *adj* argumentative; *mf* arguer
**argumental** *adj* of the argument
**argumentar** *va & vn* to argue
**argumentativo -va** *adj* argumentative (*containing argument*)
**argumentista** *mf* arguer
**argumento** *m* argument; **argumento ontológico** (philos.) ontological argument
**aria** *f* see **ario**
**Ariadna** *f* (myth.) Ariadne
**aricado** *m* light plowing, cross harrowing
**aricar §86** *va* to plow lightly, to harrow crosswise
**aridecer §34** *va* to make dry or arid; *vn & vr* to become dry or arid
**aridez** *f* aridity, dryness
**árido -da** *adj* arid; (fig.) dry (*dull, boring*); **áridos** *mpl* dry commodities
**Aries** *m* (astr.) Aries
**arieta** *f* (mus.) arietta, short air
**ariete** *m* battering ram; **ariete hidráulico** hydraulic ram
**arietino -na** *adj* like a ram's head
**arijo -ja** *adj* easily tilled or cultivated
**arilado -da** *adj* (bot.) arillate, ariled
**arilo** *m* (bot.) aril
**arillo** *m* earring; frame for neck stock (*of clerics*)
**arimez** *m* projection (*in a building*)
**arincar §86** *vr* (Am.) to be or become constipated
**ario -ria** *adj & mf* Aryan; *f* (mus.) aria
**arísaro** *m* (bot.) wake-robin
**arisblanco -ca** *adj* white-bearded (*said of wheat*)
**arisco -ca** *adj* churlish, surly, shy; wicked, vicious
**arisema** *f* (bot.) Indian turnip, jack-in-the-pulpit
**arisnegro -gra** or **arisprieto -ta** *adj* black-bearded (*said of wheat*)
**arista** *f* (arch.) arris; (bot.) awn; (geom.) edge; **arista de encuentro** (arch.) groin
**aristado -da** *adj* (bot.) bearded, awned
**aristarco** *m* Aristarch, severe critic
**Arístides** *m* Aristides
**aristocracia** *f* aristocracy
**aristócrata** *mf* aristocrat
**aristocrático -ca** *adj* aristocratic
**aristocratizar §76** *va* to give aristocratic form to (*the government*); to infuse with aristocratic ideas; *vn* to act aristocratically; *vr* to become aristocratic; to become an aristocrat
**Aristófanes** *m* Aristophanes
**aristofánico -ca** *adj* Aristophanic; *m* (rhet.) Aristophanic
**aristoloquia** *f* (bot.) birthwort
**aristón** *m* (arch.) edge, corner; (arch.) groin rib; (mus.) hand organ
**aristoso -sa** *adj* bearded, many-bearded (*said of wheat*)
**Aristóteles** *m* Aristotle
**aristotélico -ca** *adj & mf* Aristotelian
**aristotelismo** *m* Aristotelianism

**aritmético -ca** *adj* arithmetical; *mf* arithmetician; *f* arithmetic
**aritmo -ma** *adj* arrhythmic
**aritmomanía** *f* arithmomania
**aritmómetro** *m* arithmometer
**arjorán** *m* (bot.) Judas tree
**arlequín** *m* harlequin; harlequin ice cream, Neapolitan ice cream; **arlequín de Cayena** (ent.) harlequin beetle; (*cap.*) *m* Harlequin
**arlequina** *f* harlequina; burlesque dance; music for such a dance
**arlequinada** *f* harlequinade
**arlequinesco -ca** *adj* harlequin, harlequinesque
**arlo** *m* (bot.) barberry; fruit hung up for keeping
**arlota** *f* var. of **alrota**
**arma** *f* arm, weapon; branch of the service (*army, navy, air force*); **¡a las armas!** to arms!; **alzarse en armas** to rise up, rebel; **jugar a las armas** to fence; **llevar las armas** to bear arms; **pasar por las armas** to execute by shooting; **presentar armas** to present arms; **rendir las armas** to lay down one's arms; **sobre las armas** under arms; **tocar al arma** or **tocar arma** to sound the call to arms; **tomar (las) armas** to take up arms; **arma al hombro** (mil.) right shoulder arms; **arma atómica** atomic weapon; **arma blanca** steel blade (*sword*); **arma corta** pistol; **arma de fuego** firearm; **arma negra** foil; **armas parlantes** (her.) canting arms, rebus
**armada** *f* see **armado**
**armadera** *f* (naut.) main timber
**armadía** *f* raft, float
**armadija** *f* or **armadijo** *m* trap, snare
**armadillo** *m* (zool.) armadillo; **armadillo de tres fajas** (zool.) three-banded armadillo
**armado -da** *adj* armed; reinforced (*concrete*); (her.) armed; *m* man in armor in processions of Holy Week; *f* fleet, armada; navy; **Armada Invencible** Invincible Armada
**armador -dora** *adj* shipbuilding; *m* shipowner, outfitter; privateer; jacket
**armadura** *f* armature, armor; frame, framework, support; skeleton; guard (*around a tree*); (elec.) armature (*of condenser, magnet, motor, etc.*); (mach.) assembly; (mus.) key signature; reinforcement (*of concrete*); **armadura de pendolón** king truss
**armaga** *f* (bot.) rue
**Armagedón** *m* (Bib.) Armageddon
**armajal** *m* marsh, moor, fen
**armajo** *m* (bot.) glasswort
**armamentario** *m* medical arsensal
**armamentismo** *m* military preparedness
**armamentista** *adj* (pertaining to) armament; militarist; *mf* advocate of military preparedness; arms dealer
**armamento** *m* armament
**armar** *va* to arm; to load (*a weapon*); to fix (*a bayonet*); to mount, assemble, put together, set, adjust; to build, establish; to equip; to suit, fit, become; to reinforce (*e.g., concrete*); (coll.) to cause, start, stir up, cook up; (coll.) to arrange, prepare; (naut.) to fit out, to commission; **armar caballero** to knight; **armarla** (coll.) to start a row; (coll.) to cheat; *vn* to suit, be becoming; *vr* to arm, to arm oneself; to get ready; to become erect; (coll.) to start, break out; (Am.) to balk, be balky; (Am.) to make a killing; **armarse con** (coll.) to hold on to unfairly, to refuse to give up
**armario** *m* closet, wardrobe; **armario de luna** wardrobe with mirror in door; **armario frigorífico** refrigerator
**armatoste** *m* hulk (*crude, heavy machine or piece of furniture; fat, clumsy person*)
**armazón** *f* frame, framework; assemblage; skeleton; (aer.) chassis; (Am.) shelving
**armella** *f* screw eye, eyebolt
**armelluela** *f* little screw eye
**armenio -nia** *adj* & *mf* Armenian; *m* Armenian (*language*); (*cap.*) *f* Armenia
**armería** *f* arms museum; armory (*manufactory; art of armorer*); arms shop; (her.) armory
**armero** *m* armorer, gunsmith; rack or stand for arms, armrack
**armífero -ra** *adj* warlike
**armígero -ra** *adj* (poet.) bearing arms; warlike; *m* armor-bearer
**armilar** *adj* armillary
**armilla** *f* (arch.) astragal (*molding*); (arch.) surbase
**arminianismo** *m* Arminianism
**arminiano -na** *adj* & *mf* Arminian
**Arminio** *m* Arminius
**armiñado -da** *adj* ermine; ermined
**armiño** *m* (zool. & her.) ermine; **armiño de cola larga** (zool.) long-tailed weasel
**armipotente** *adj* (poet.) mighty in war
**armisonante** *adj* (poet.) resounding with arms
**armisticio** *m* armistice
**armón** *m* (arti.) limber
**armonía** *f* harmony
**armónico -ca** *adj* & *m* (mus. & phys.) harmonic; *f* (mus.) harmonica; **armónica de boca** (mus.) mouth organ
**armonio** *m* (mus.) harmonium
**armonioso -sa** *adj* harmonious
**armonización** *f* harmonization
**armonizar** **§76** *va* & *vn* to harmonize
**armuelle** *m* (bot.) orach
**arna** *f* beehive
**arnacho** *m* (bot.) restharrow
**Arnaldo** *m* Arnold
**arnaúte** *adj* & *mf* (archaic) Albanian
**arnés** *m* armor, coat of mail; harness; **arneses** *mpl* harness, trappings; outfit, equipment; accessories
**árnica** *f* (bot. & pharm.) arnica
**aro** *m* hoop; rim; (croquet) hoop, wicket; (bot.) cuckoopint; **entrar por el aro** (coll.) to have to go ahead against one's will; **aro de émbolo** piston ring; **aro de Etiopía** (bot.) arum, arum lily, calla lily
**aroma** *f* aroma (*flower*); *m* aroma, fragrance; aromatic gum, herb, balm, or wood
**aromaticidad** *f* aromacity
**aromático -ca** *adj* aromatic; *m* (chem. & med.) aromatic; *f* (bot.) aromatic
**aromatización** *f* aromatization
**aromatizar** **§76** *va* to aromatize; to flavor
**aromo** *m* (bot.) aroma, huisache (*tree*)
**aromoso -sa** *adj* aromatic
**arón** *m* (bot.) cuckoopint; (*cap.*) *m* (Bib.) Aaron
**arpa** *f* (mus.) harp; **arpa eolia** aeolian harp
**arpado -da** *adj* toothed, jagged; (poet.) singing (*said of birds*)
**arpadura** *f* scratch
**arpar** *va* to tear, rend, claw, scratch
**arpegio** *m* (mus.) arpeggio
**arpella** *f* (orn.) marsh harrier
**arpeo** *m* (naut.) grappling iron
**arpía** *f* (coll.) ugly shrew, jade; (coll.) harpy (*rapacious person*); (myth.) Harpy
**arpillera** *f* burlap, bagging, sackcloth
**arpista** *mf* harpist
**arpón** *m* harpoon
**arponado -da** *adj* like a harpoon
**arponar** or **arponear** *va* to harpoon; *vn* to wield the harpoon with skill
**arponero** *m* harpoon maker; harpooner
**arqueada** *f* (mus.) bow (*stroke with bow*)
**arqueador** *m* ship gauger; wool beater
**arqueaje** *m* or **arqueamiento** *m* (naut.) gauging; (naut.) tonnage
**arquear** *va* to arch; to beat (*wool*); to gauge (*a ship*); to check; to audit (*cash and other assets in hand*); *vn* to retch, be nauseated; *vr* to arch
**arquegonio** *m* (bot.) archegonium
**arqueo** *m* arching; (naut.) gauging; (naut.) tonnage; check, checking; audit of cash in hand
**arqueología** *f* archeology
**arqueológico -ca** *adj* archeological
**arqueólogo -ga** *mf* archeologist
**arqueozoico -ca** *adj* (geol.) Archeozoic
**arquería** *f* arcade, series of arches
**arquero** *m* archer, bowman; bow maker; treasurer, cashier; (sport) goalkeeper
**arquetipo** *m* archetype
**arquibanco** *m* bench with drawers under seat
**arquidiócesis** *f* (*pl:* **-sis**) archdiocese
**arquiepiscopal** *adj* archiepiscopal
**Arquímedes** *m* Archimedes
**arquimédico -ca** *adj* Archimedean
**arquimesa** *f* writing desk

**arquisinagogo** *m* chief rabbi
**arquitecto** *m* architect; **arquitecto de jardines** landscape gardener; **arquitecto paisajista** landscape architect
**arquitectónico -ca** *adj* architectonic
**arquitectura** *f* architecture
**arquitectural** *adj* architectural
**arquitrabe** *m* (arch.) architrave
**arquivolta** *f* var. of **archivolta**
**arrabá** *m* (*pl:* **-baes**) (arch.) semirectangular frame around Moorish arch
**arrabal** *m* suburb; **arrabales** *mpl* outskirts, environs
**arrabalero -ra** *adj* suburban; (coll.) ill-bred; *mf* suburbanite
**arrabio** *m* pig iron
**arracacha** *f* (bot.) arracacha; (Am.) stupidity
**arracada** *f* earring, earring with pendant
**arracimado -da** *adj* clustered
**arracimar** *vr* to cluster, to bunch
**arraclán** *m* (bot.) alder buckthorn
**arráez** *m* Moorish chieftain; master of a Moorish ship
**arraigadamente** *adv* firmly, securely
**arraigado -da** *adj* rooted; deep-rooted; owning property; **arraigadas** *fpl* (naut.) futtock shrouds
**arraigamiento** *m* taking root; deep-seated habit
**arraigar §59** *va* to establish, strengthen; *vn* to take root, become deep-rooted; *vr* to take root; to get settled, become a property owner
**arraigo** *m* rootage, taking root; solidity, stability, settling; property, real estate
**arralar** *vn* to become thin or sparse; to yield thin bunches of grapes
**arramblar** *va* to cover with sand and gravel (*said of a stream or torrent*); to sweep away; *vn* to make off; *vr* to be covered with sand and gravel
**arrancacepas** *m* (*pl:* **-pas**) stump puller
**arrancaclavos** *m* (*pl:* **-vos**) nail claw, nail extractor
**arrancada** *f* see **arrancado**
**arrancadera** *f* leading bell (*for cattle*)
**arrancadero** *m* starting point (*in a race*)
**arrancado -da** *adj* (coll.) poor, penniless; *f* start; sudden start; (rail.) jerky start; (naut.) quick start, sudden pick-up; (taur.) sudden charge (*of bull*)
**arrancador -dora** *adj* extracting; *m* (aut.) starter; **arrancador automático** (aut.) self-starter; *f* extracting machine
**arrancadura** *f* or **arrancamiento** *m* pulling out, extraction; snatching
**arrancapinos** *m* (*pl:* **-nos**) (coll.) dwarf (*little fellow*); (coll.) giant (*big fellow*)
**arrancar §86** *va* to root up, to pull out, to pull up; to snatch, to snatch away, to tear away; to wrest, to wring; to draw forth (*e.g.,* ***tears***); to make (*a ship*) go faster; **arrancar a** to snatch from, snatch away from; *vn* to start; to start on a run; to set sail; (coll.) to leave, go away; (arch.) to spring (*said of an arch or vault*); (taur.) to rush forward; **arrancar de** to come from, originate in
**arrancarraíces** *m* (*pl:* **-rraíces**) root puller
**arrancasiega** *f* pulling up the short grain while mowing
**arrancasondas** *m* (*pl:* **-das**) drill extractor, grab
**arranciar** *vr* to get rancid
**arranchar** *va* to arrange, put in order; (naut.) to brace sharp up, to haul close aft; (naut.) to skirt, to sail close to; *vr* to gather together, to live in the same barracks, to mess together
**arranque** *m* pulling up; impulse, fit; sudden start, jerk; outburst, sally (*of wit, etc.*); (arch.) spring (*of an arch*); start, starting; (aut.) starter, starting gear, starting; **arranque a mano** (aut.) hand cranking; **arranque automático** (aut.) self-starter, self-starting
**arrapar** *va* (slang) to snatch away
**arrapiezo** *m* rag, tatter; (coll.) whippersnapper
**arrapo** *m* rag, tatter
**arras** *fpl* deposit, pledge, earnest money; dowry; thirteen coins given by bridegroom to bride at wedding
**arrasado -da** *adj* satin; satiny
**arrasadura** *f* leveling with a strickle
**arrasamiento** *m* razing, demolition
**arrasar** *va* to smooth, to level; to rase, wreck, flatten, demolish; to fill to the brim; to strike, to level with a strickle; *vn* to clear up, to get clear (*said of sky*); *vr* to clear up, to get clear (*said of sky*); **arrasarse de** or **en agua** or **lágrimas** to fill with tears (*said of the eyes*)
**arrastraculo** *m* (naut.) driver, water sail
**arrastradamente** *adv* (coll.) imperfectly; (coll.) laboriously, arduously; (coll.) penuriously; (coll.) unhappily
**arrastradera** *f* (naut.) lower studding sail; trail rope, guide rope (*of balloon*)
**arrastradero** *m* log path, dragging road; place where dead animals are dragged from bull ring
**arrastradizo -za** *adj* dangling; trailing; beaten, frequented; cringing
**arrastrado -da** *adj* poor, wretched, miserable; (coll.) knavish, rascally; *mf* (coll.) knave, rascal
**arrastramiento** *m* dragging; crawling
**arrastrar** *va* to drag; to drag along, drag on; to drag down; to impel; to compel, to necessitate; **traer arrastrado** or **arrastrando** to weary, to harass; **arrastrar a uno a** + *inf* to drag or draw someone into + *ger*; *vn* to crawl, creep; to drag, trail, touch the floor or the ground; *vr* to crawl, creep; to drag, trail, touch the floor or the ground; to trail (*said of a plant or vine*); to drag on; to cringe
**arrastre** *m* drag, dragging; haulage, hauling; washout; crawl, crawl stroke; influence, force; (Am.) drag (*political or social influence*); (min.) slope of an adit; (taur.) dragging dead bull from the arena; **arrastre de espalda** backstroke (*in swimming*)
**arratonado -da** *adj* eaten by mice, eaten by rats
**arrayán** *m* (bot.) myrtle; **arrayán brabántico** (bot.) wax myrtle, bayberry
**arrayanal** *m* myrtle field
**arrayanilla** *f* (bot.) Saint-Andrew's-cross
**arráyaz** *m* or **arraz** *m* var. of **arráez**
**arre** *m* (coll.) nag, old nag; *interj* gee!, get up!
**arreador** *m* foreman, overseer; muleteer; (Am.) whip
**arrear** *va* to drive (*horses, mules, etc.*); to prod; to harness; *vn* (coll.) to hurry along; **¡arrea!** (coll.) get moving!; (coll.) do tell!; *vr* to be ruined, lose all one's money
**arrebañaderas** *fpl* grapnel (*for pulling something out of a well*)
**arrebañador -dora** *mf* gatherer, collector, scraper
**arrebañadura** *f* (coll.) gathering-up; **arrebañaduras** *spl* leavings gathered together
**arrebañar** *va* to gather up; to eat up
**arrebatadamente** *adv* headlong, recklessly
**arrebatadizo -za** *adj* excitable, inflammable
**arrebatado -da** *adj* reckless, rash, impetuous; ruddy, flushed (*said of countenance*)
**arrebatador -dora** *adj* captivating; raging, furious; stirring, exciting
**arrebatamiento** *m* snatching away, carrying off; captivation; rage, fury; rapture, ecstasy
**arrebatar** *va* to snatch; to carry away, carry off; to attract, captivate; to move, stir; to parch (*grain*); **arrebatar a** to snatch from, snatch away from; *vn* to snatch, grab; *vr* to be parched (*said of grain*); to be burned (*by excessive cooking*); to be carried away (*by some passion or emotion*)
**arrebatiña** *f* grabbing, scramble, scuffle
**arrebato** *m* rage, fury; rapture, ecstasy
**arrebol** *m* red (*of sunrise or sunset*); rouge; rosiness (*of cheeks*); **arreboles** *mpl* red clouds; **arrebol alpestre** alpenglow
**arrebolada** *f* red clouds (*of sunrise or sunset*)
**arrebolar** *va* to redden, make red; to rouge; *vr* to redden, turn red; to rouge
**arrebolera** *f* rouge case; (bot.) four-o'clock, marvel-of-Peru
**arrebollar** *vr* (prov.) to fall or rush headlong
**arrebozar §76** *va* to muffle; *vr* to muffle or wrap up one's face; to cluster, to swarm
**arrebujadamente** *adv* in confusion; equivocally; vaguely

**arrebujar** *va* to jumble together; to wrap, to cover; *vr* to wrap oneself all up
**arreciar** *vn* to grow worse, become more severe or violent; to rage; *vr* to grow worse, become more severe or violent; to grow stronger, to take on weight
**arrecife** *m* stone-paved road; stone ditch, dike; (naut.) reef; **arrecife de coral** coral reef
**arrecir** §53 *vr* to grow stiff with cold
**arrechucho** *m* (coll.) fit, impulse, impulsive act; (coll.) slight indisposition
**arredilar** *va* to fold, to corral
**arredomado -da** *adj* sly, canny
**arredondear** *va* to round off; *vr* to get round, become rounded
**arredramiento** *m* driving back; backing out; fear
**arredrar** *va* to drive back; to frighten; *vr* to move away; to draw back, to shrink; to be frightened
**arregazado -da** *adj* tucked up; turned up
**arregazar** §76 *va* to tuck up
**arreglado -da** *adj* regular; moderate; reasonable; moderately fixed; neat, orderly
**arreglar** *va* to adjust, regulate, settle; to put in order, arrange; to fix, to repair; (coll.) to alter (*to castrate or to spay*); *vr* to adjust, settle; to arrange; to conform; **arreglarse con** to come to terms with, to reach an agreement with; **arreglárselas** (coll.) to manage all right, to shift
**arreglo** *m* adjustment; arrangement; settlement; rule, order; agreement; **con arreglo a** according to
**arregostar** *va* to lure, entice; *vr* (coll.) to take a liking
**arregosto** *m* (coll.) liking, taste
**arrejacar** §86 *va* to harrow, rake, or hoe crosswise (*i.e., across the furrows*)
**arrejaco** *m* (orn.) blackmartin, European swift
**arrejada** *f* plowstaff
**arrejaque** *m* three-pronged fishing fork; (orn.) blackmartin, European swift
**arrejerar** *va* (naut.) to anchor with two anchors fore and one aft
**arrellanar** *vr* to loll, to sprawl, to sprawl in one's seat; to enjoy one's work
**arremangado -da** *adj* turned up, tucked up, upturned
**arremangar** §59 *va* to turn up (*sleeves*); to tuck up (*dress*); *vr* to turn up one's sleeves; to tuck up one's dress; (coll.) to take a firm stand; to be turned up
**arremango** *m* turning up, tucking up; sleeve turned up, dress tucked up; boldness, dash; **arremangos** *mpl* threats
**arrematar** *va* to finish, terminate
**arremetedero** *m* (mil.) place to attack a fortress
**arremetedor -dora** *adj* attacking; *mf* attacker, aggressor
**arremeter** *va* to spur (*a horse*); to attack, to assail; *vn* to rush forth, to attack; to offend, be offensive (*to look at*); **arremeter con, contra,** or **para** to rush upon, to attack
**arremetida** *f* or **arremetimiento** *m* attack; sudden start (*of a horse*); short, wild run; push
**arremolinar** *vr* to crowd, to crush; to mill about; to whirl
**arrendable** *adj* rentable
**arrendación** *f* var. of **arrendamiento**
**arrendadero** *m* ring in manger to which horses are tied
**arrendado -da** *adj* obedient to the reins
**arrendador -dora** *mf* renter; tenant; *m* landlord; ring in manger to which horses are tied; *f* landlady
**arrendajo** *m* (orn.) jay; (coll.) mimic
**arrendamiento** *m* rent, rental, renting; lease
**arrendar** §18 *va* to rent (*to grant or take temporary possession of*); to tie (*a horse*); to bridle; to rein; to mimic; *vr* to rent, be rented
**arrendatario -ria** *mf* renter, tenant
**arreo** *m* adornment, dress; piece of harness; **arreos** *mpl* female headdress; appurtenances, accessories; harness, trappings; *adv* successively, without interruption
**arrepápalo** *m* fritter
**arrepentido -da** *adj* repentant; *mf* penitent; *f* penitent woman who has retired to a convent
**arrepentimiento** *m* repentance; curl on neck; repair to a painting
**arrepentir** §62 *vr* to repent, be repentant; to back down, back out; **arrepentirse de** to repent (*some deed, a sin, etc.*); **arrepentirse de haber** + *pp* to repent having + *pp*
**arrepistar** *va* to grind (*rags*) into pulp
**arrepisto** *m* grinding of rags
**arrepollado -da** *adj* cabbage-headed
**arrepticio -cia** *adj* possessed by the devil
**arrequesonar** *vr* to curdle
**arrequives** *mpl* finery; (coll.) attendant circumstances
**arrestado -da** *adj* bold, audacious
**arrestar** *va* to arrest, to take prisoner; *vr* to rush ahead boldly; **arrestarse a** to rush boldly into
**arresto** *m* arrest, imprisonment; boldness, daring; **bajo arresto** under arrest
**arretín** *m* moreen
**arrevesado -da** *adj* complex, intricate; wild, unmanageable
**arrezafe** *m* field full of brambles
**arrezagar** §59 *va* to tuck up; to raise (*e.g., the hand*)
**arria** *f* drove (*of horses*)
**arriada** *f* flood
**arrial** *m* var. of **arriaz**
**arrianismo** *m* Arianism
**arriano -na** *adj & mf* Arian
**arriar** §90 *va* to flood; (naut.) to lower, to strike; (naut.) to loosen, slacken, let loose; *vr* to become flooded
**arriata** *f* or **arriate** *m* border, edge (*in garden*); trellis; highway, road
**arriaz** *m* (*pl:* **arriaces**) quillon (*of sword*); hilt
**arriba** *adv* up, upward; above, on high; upwards; upstairs; uptown; on top; (naut.) aloft; upwards of, e.g., **tiene doce años arriba** he is upwards of twelve years old; **calle arriba** up the street; **de arriba** from above; **de arriba abajo** from top to bottom, from the top down, from head to foot, from beginning to end; superciliously; **más arriba de** higher than, above; **río arriba** upstream; **arriba de** up; *interj* up with . . . !
**arribada** *f* arrival (*by sea*); **de arribada** (naut.) emergency
**arribaje** *m* (naut.) arrival; (naut.) landing beach
**arribar** *vn* to put into port; to arrive; (naut.) to fall off to leeward; (coll.) to come back (*in health or fortune*); **arribar a** + *inf* to manage to + *inf*
**arribazón** *m* abundance of fish in port and along the coast; abundance
**arribeño -ña** *adj* (Am.) upland, highland; *mf* (Am.) uplander, highlander
**arribismo** *m* ruthless ambition
**arribista** *adj & mf* upstart, parvenu
**arribo** *m* arrival
**arricés** *m* buckle of stirrup strap
**arricete** *m* shoal, bar
**arridar** *va* (naut.) to haul taut
**arriendo** *m* var. of **arrendamiento**
**arrieraje** *m* (Am.) muleteers; (Am.) driving of pack animals
**arriería** *f* driving of pack animals
**arriero** *m* driver of pack animal, muleteer
**arriesgado -da** *adj* risky, dangerous; bold, daring
**arriesgar** §59 *va* to risk, to jeopardize; *vr* to take a risk, to expose oneself to danger; **arriesgarse a** + *inf* to risk + *ger;* **arriesgarse en** to venture on; **arriesgarse fuera** to venture abroad, to venture out; **quien no se arriesga no pasa la mar** nothing venture, nothing win
**arriesgón** *m* (coll.) risk, venture
**arrimadero** *m* support; wainscot, wainscoting
**arrimadillo** *m* mat, matting (*fastened to wall*); wainscot, wainscoting; pitching pennies (*boy's game*)
**arrimadizo -za** *adj* movable; parasitic; *mf* sycophant
**arrimador** *m* backlog in fireplace

**arrimadura** *f* moving near
**arrimar** *va* to move up, bring close; to give (*a blow, punch, kick, etc.*); to get rid of, remove; to abandon, neglect; to give up (*a position, profession, etc.*); (naut.) to stow; **arrimar el hombro** to put one's shoulder to the wheel; *vr* to move up, come close; to gather together; (taur.) to work close to the bull; **arrimarse a** to come close to; to draw up to (*e.g., the curb*); to lean against; to get to (*the point*); to depend on, to trust; to snuggle up to
**arrime** *m* spot near goal (*in bowling*)
**arrimo** *m* moving near; support; help, aid; favor, protection; fondness, attachment; party wall; idle wall
**arrimón** *m* loafer, idler; **estar de arrimón** to hang around watching; **hacer de arrimón** (coll.) to hold on to the wall (*for fear of falling from drunkenness*)
**arrinconado -da** *adj* distant, remote, out of the way; forgotten, neglected, shelved
**arrinconamiento** *m* retirement, seclusion
**arrinconar** *va* to corner; to put away in a corner, to lay aside; to get rid of, remove; to abandon, neglect, shelve; *vr* (coll.) to live in seclusion, to withdraw from the world
**arriñonado -da** *adj* kidney-shaped
**Arrio** *m* Arius
**arriostramiento** *m* brace, bracing
**arriostrar** *va* to brace, to stay
**arriscado -da** *adj* bold, enterprising; free, brisk, easy; craggy
**arriscamiento** *m* risk, risk taking
**arriscar §86** *va* to risk; *vr* to take a risk; to be vain; to plunge over a cliff (*said of cattle*)
**arrisco** *m* risk
**arritmia** *f* (path.) arrhythmia
**arrítmico -ca** *adj* arrhythmic
**arrivismo** *m* var. of **arribismo**
**arrivista** *adj & mf* var. of **arribista**
**arrizafa** *f* garden, park
**arrizar §76** *va* (naut.) to reef, stow, lash
**arrizo -za** *adj* (bot.) arrhizal or arrhizous
**arroaz** *m* (*pl:* **-aces**) (zool.) dolphin
**arroba** *f* arroba (*Spanish weight of about 25 lbs. and Spanish liquid measure of varying value*)
**arrobadizo -za** *adj* easily entranced, always entranced; feigning entrancement
**arrobador -dora** *adj* entrancing
**arrobamiento** *m* entrancement, ecstasy
**arrobar** *va* to entrance; *vr* to be entranced
**arrobero -ra** *adj* weighing an arroba; *mf* local baker
**arrobo** *m* ecstasy
**arrocabe** *m* top crossbeam; wooden frieze
**arrocero -ra** *adj* (pertaining to) rice; *mf* rice grower, rice dealer; *m* (orn.) redwing, redwinged blackbird
**arrocinado -da** *adj* nag-like, worn-out; bestial; (slang) ignorant, stupid
**arrocinar** *va* to bestialize; *vr* to become bestialized; to fall madly in love
**arrodajar** *vr* (Am.) to sit down with one's legs crossed
**arrodelar** *va* to protect with a buckler; *vr* to be protected or armed with a buckler
**arrodillado -da** *adj* kneeling, on bended knee
**arrodilladura** *f* or **arrodillamiento** *m* kneeling
**arrodillar** *va* to make (*someone*) kneel; *vn & vr* to kneel, to kneel down
**arrodrigar §59** *va* to prop (*vines*)
**arrodrigonar** *va* to prop (*vines*)
**arrogación** *f* adoption; arrogation
**arrogancia** *f* arrogance; gracefulness, elegance, majesty
**arrogante** *adj* arrogant; graceful, elegant, majestic
**arrogar §59** *va* to adopt; *vr* to arrogate, to arrogate to oneself
**arrojadizo -za** *adj* easily thrown; to be thrown, for throwing
**arrojado -da** *adj* bold, dashing, fearless, foolhardy
**arrojallamas** *m* (*pl:* **-mas**) (mil.) flame thrower
**arrojar** *va* to throw, hurl; to emit, shed; to bring forth (*shoots, sprouts*); to yield; *vr* to throw oneself; to rush; to rush recklessly
**arroje** *m* (theat.) man who drops as counterweight to raise the curtain; **arrojes** *mpl* (theat.) stand from which he drops; (theat.) stage to right of spectators
**arrojo** *m* boldness, dash, fearlessness
**arrollado** *m* (elec.) coil
**arrollador -dora** *adj* violent, sweeping, devastating; *m* windlass; *f* (ent.) sewer, leaf sewer
**arrollamiento** *m* rolling, winding; (elec.) winding; **arrollamiento del inducido** (elec.) armature winding; **arrollamiento inductor** (elec.) field winding
**arrollar** *va* to roll; to roll up; to wind, to coil; to sweep away; to rout (*enemy*); to dumbfound, leave speechless; to ride roughshod over; (coll.) to knock down, to run over
**arromadizar §76** *va* to give a cold to; *vr* to catch cold
**arromanzar §76** *va* (archaic) to put into the vernacular (*i.e., any Romance language*), to translate into Spanish
**arromar** *va* to blunt, to dull; *vr* to get dull
**arromper** *va* (coll.) to plow (*untilled ground*)
**arrompido** *m* newly broken ground
**arronzar §76** *va* (naut.) to move with levers; (naut.) to haul and shore (*the anchor*); *vn* (naut.) to drift to leeward
**arropamiento** *m* wrapping
**arropar** *va* to wrap, wrap up; to mix syrup with (*wine*); *vr* to wrap oneself up, to bundle up
**arrope** *m* grape syrup; honey syrup
**arropea** *f* irons, fetters, shackles
**arropera** *f* vessel for grape syrup
**arropía** *f* taffy
**arropiero -ra** *mf* maker or vendor of grape juice syrup
**arrostrado -da** *adj* featured; **bien arrostrado** well-featured; **mal arrostrado** ill-featured
**arrostrar** *va* to face; to overcome; to show a liking for, to show an inclination for; *vn* to face; **arrostrar con** or **por** to face, to resist; *vr* to rush into the fight; **arrostrarse con** to defy
**arroyada** *f* gully; channel; freshet, flood
**arroyadero** *m* gully; channel
**arroyar** *va* to make gullies in (*said of the rain*); *vn* to pour, to come down in torrents; *vr* to get full of gullies (*from the rain*); to blight, be blighted
**arroyo** *m* stream, rivulet, brook; gutter (*in street*); street; (fig.) stream (*of tears, blood, etc.*); **estar en el arroyo** (coll.) to be homeless; **plantar** or **poner en el arroyo** (coll.) to put out of the house
**arroyuela** *f* (bot.) loosestrife
**arroyuelo** *m* little stream, rill
**arroz** *m* (bot.) rice (*plant and grain or seeds*); **arroz de los pieles rojas** (bot.) Indian rice, wild rice
**arrozal** *m* rice field
**arruar §33** *vn* to grunt (*said of wild boar*)
**arrufadura** *f* (naut.) sheer
**arrufar** *va* to wrinkle (*one's brow*); to scold; (naut.) to form the sheer of; *vn* (naut.) to be curved upward
**arrufianar** *vr* to be foul, to be depraved; to pander, be a panderer
**arrufo** *m* var. of **arrufadura**
**arruga** *f* wrinkle; crease, rumple
**arrugación** *f* or **arrugamiento** *m* wrinkling; creasing, rumpling, crumpling
**arrugar §59** *va* to wrinkle; to crease, rumple, crumple; to knit (*the brow*); *vr* to wrinkle, become wrinkled; to crease, rumple, crumple; to shrink, to shrivel
**arrugia** *f* gold mine
**arruinador -dora** *adj* ruining, destructive; *mf* ruiner, destroyer
**arruinamiento** *m* ruin, ruination, destruction, demolition
**arruinar** *va* to ruin, destroy, demolish; *vr* to go to ruin, to be destroyed
**arrullar** *va* to coo to; to lull to sleep, to sing to sleep; (coll.) to court, to woo; *vn* to coo; *vr* to bill (*said of doves*); to coo
**arrullo** *m* cooing and billing; lullaby
**arruma** *f* (naut.) division or partition in hold (*for stowing cargo*)

**arrumaco** *m* caress; odd dress or adornment; flattery, pretense; **arrumacos** *mpl* show of affection
**arrumaje** *m* (naut.) good stowage; (naut.) ballast
**arrumar** *va* (naut.) to stow; *vr* (naut.) to become overcast
**arrumazón** *f* (naut.) stowing; (naut.) good stowage; (naut.) ballast; (naut.) overcast horizon
**arrumazonar** *vr* to become overcast (*said of sky or horizon*)
**arrumbadas** *fpl* (naut.) wales of a row galley
**arrumbamiento** *m* (naut.) bearing, direction
**arrumbar** *va* to cast aside; to neglect, pay no attention to; to sweep aside, to silence; to line up (*wine casks*) along the wall of a wine cellar; (naut.) to determine the lay of (*a coast*); *vn* (naut.) to take bearings; *vr* (naut.) to take bearings; to get seasick
**arrumbe** *m* (Am.) rust
**arrurruz** *m* arrowroot (*starch*)
**arsáfraga** *f* (bot.) water parsnip
**arsenal** *m* arsenal, armory; shipyard, navy yard, dockyard; (fig.) arsenal
**arseniato** *m* (chem.) arsenate
**arsenical** *adj* arsenical
**arsénico -ca** *adj* arsenical; (chem.) arsenic; *m* (chem. & mineral.) arsenic
**arsenioso -sa** *adj* (chem.) arsenious
**arsenito** *m* (chem.) arsenite
**arseniuro** *m* (chem.) arsenide
**arsfenamina** *f* (pharm.) arsphenamine
**arsolla** *f* var. of **arzolla**
**art.** abr. of **artículo**
**arta** *f* (bot.) plantain; **arta de agua** (bot.) fleawort
**Artajerjes** *m* Artaxerxes
**artanica** or **artanita** *f* (bot.) cyclamen, sowbread
**arte** *m & f* art; trick, cunning; knack; fishing gear; **bellas artes** fine arts; **el séptimo arte** moving pictures; **no tener arte ni parte en** to have nothing to do with; **arte cisoria** (cook.) art of carving; **arte manual** craft; **arte mayor** Spanish verse of ten to twelve syllables with the following rhyme scheme: abbaacca; **arte menor** Spanish verse of six to eight syllables, sometimes in the form of a quatrain; **arte plumaria** art of embroidering featherwork; **artes gráficas** graphic arts; **artes liberales** *fpl* liberal arts; **arte típico** native craft; **artes y oficios** arts and crafts
**artefacto** *m* device, contrivance, appliance, fixture, artifact; (biol.) artifact; **artefactos de alumbrado** lighting fixtures; **artefactos sanitarios** bathroom fixtures
**artejo** *m* knuckle (*of fingers*); (zool.) arthromere
**Artemis** *f* (myth.) Artemis
**artemisa** *f* (bot.) mugwort, sagebrush; (*cap.*) *f* (myth.) Artemis
**artemisia** *f* (bot.) mugwort, sagebrush
**artera** *f* see **artero**
**arteria** *f* (anat.) artery; (elec.) feeder; (fig.) artery (*main highway*)
**artería** *f* craftiness, cunning; (slang) rascality
**arterial** *adj* arterial
**arterialización** *f* arterialization
**arterializar** §76 *va* to arterialize
**arterioesclerosis** *f* var. of **arteriosclerosis**
**arteriola** *f* arteriole
**arteriosclerosis** *f* (path.) arteriosclerosis
**arterioso -sa** *adj* arterious
**arteritis** *f* (path.) arteritis
**artero -ra** *adj* sly, cunning, artful; *f* bread stamp (*iron for marking bread to be sent to common bakery*)
**arteroesclerosis** *f* var. of **arteriosclerosis**
**artesa** *f* trough, kneading trough; Indian canoe
**artesanado** *m* craftsmen, mechanics
**artesanía** *f* craftsmanship; craftsmen, mechanics
**artesano -na** *mf* artisan, craftsman; *f* craftswoman
**artesiano -na** *adj* Artesian; artesian (*well*)
**artesilla** *f* small trough; trough in bucket wheel
**artesón** *m* kitchen tub; (arch.) coffer, caisson
**artesonado -da** *adj* (arch.) caissoned; *m* (arch.) caissoned ceiling
**artesonar** *va* (arch.) to adorn (*a ceiling or vault*) with caissons
**artesuela** *f* small trough, small bowl
**artético -ca** *adj & mf* arthritic
**ártico -ca** *adj* arctic; (*cap.*) *m* Arctic (*ocean*)
**articulación** *f* articulation; (anat., bot. & zool.) articulation, joint; (phonet.) articulation; **articulación universal** (aut.) universal joint
**articulado -da** *adj* articulate; articulated; *m* series of articles; (law) series of proofs; (zool.) articulate
**articular** *adj* articular; *va & vr* to articulate; to article; to question
**articulista** *mf* writer of articles
**artículo** *m* article; item; joint (*part between two articulations*); entry (*each alphabetized word in a dictionary, etc.*); (anat. & bot.) articulation; **artículo de costumbres** (lit.) article on manners and customs; **artículo definido** or **determinado** (gram.) definite article; **artículo de fondo** leader, editorial; **artículo indefinido** or **indeterminado** (gram.) indefinite article; **artículos de consumo** consumers' goods; **artículos de cuero** leather goods; **artículos de deporte** sporting goods; **artículos del culto** church supplies; **artículos de primera necesidad** basic commodities; **artículos para caballeros** men's furnishings
**artífice** *mf* artificer; craftsman (*artist*)
**artificial** *adj* artificial
**artificiero** *m* fireworks manufacturer; (mil.) artificer
**artificio** *m* artifice; craft, workmanship; device, appliance; trick, ruse; cunning
**artificioso -sa** *adj* skillful, ingenious; wary, cunning, artful, scheming, tricky, fake, deceptive
**artiga** *f* (agr.) burning and breaking a field; field burned and broken
**artigar** §59 *va* (agr.) to burn clear and break (*a field, etc.*)
**artilugio** *m* (coll.) jigger, thingamajig; (coll.) scheme, trick
**artillado** *m* artillery
**artillar** *va* to arm or equip with artillery
**artillería** *f* artillery; **artillería de sitio** siege artillery
**artillero** *m* artilleryman; artillerist
**artimaña** *f* trap; (coll.) trick, cunning
**artimón** *m* (naut.) mizzenmast
**artina** *f* boxthorn berry
**artiodáctilo -la** *adj & m* (zool.) artiodactyl
**artista** *mf* artist
**artístico -ca** *adj* artistic
**art.º** abr. of **artículo**
**arto** *m* (bot.) boxthorn
**artolas** *fpl* mule chair, cacolet
**artralgia** *f* (path.) arthralgia, pain in the joints
**artrítico -ca** *adj & mf* arthritic
**artritis** *f* (path.) arthritis; **artritis reumatoidea** (path.) rheumatoid arthritis
**artrómera** *f* (zool.) arthromere
**artrópodo -da** *adj & m* (zool.) arthropod
**arturiano -na** or **artúrico -ca** *adj* Arthurian
**Arturo** *m* Arthur; (astr.) Arcturus; **el rey Arturo** King Arthur
**Artús** *m* Arthur (*king*)
**arugas** *fpl* (bot.) camomile
**árula** *f* small altar
**arundíneo -a** *adj* arundineous, reedy
**aruñar** *va* (coll.) to scratch
**aruñazo** *m* (coll.) scratch
**arúspice** *m* haruspex, diviner, soothsayer
**aruspicina** *f* haruspicy, divination
**arveja** *f* (bot.) vetch, spring vetch, tare; (bot.) vetchling; (bot.) pea
**arvejal** *m* vetch field
**arvejana** *f* var. of **arveja**
**arvejo** *m* (bot.) pea
**arvense** *adj* (growing in a) field
**arvícola** *f* (zool.) vole, water rat
**arz.** abr. of **arzobispo**
**arzbpo.** abr. of **arzobispo**
**arzobispado** *m* archbishopric

**arzobispal** *adj* archiepiscopal
**arzobispo** *m* archbishop
**arzolla** *f* (bot.) centaury; (bot.) milk thistle
**arzón** *m* saddletree; **arzón delantero** saddlebow; **arzón trasero** cantle
**as** *m* ace (*in cards, dice, tennis, aviation*); **as de fútbol** football star; **as de guía** (naut.) bowline, bowline knot; **as del volante** (aut.) speed king
**asa** *f* handle (*of jug, basket, etc.*); juice; opportunity, pretext; (bact.) loop; **asa dulce** (pharm.) gum benzoin; **asa fétida** asafetida
**asacar** §86 *va* to produce, invent; to feign; to impute, attribute
**asación** *f* roasting; (pharm.) decoction
**asadero -ra** *adj* for roasting; *m* oven (*hot place*); (Am.) fresh cheese
**asado -da** *adj* roasted; **bien asado** well-done, done brown; **poco asado** rare, underdone; *m* roasting; roast
**asador** *m* spit; roasting jack
**asadura** *f* entrails; liver; (fig.) sluggishness; **asadura de puerco** haslet
**asaetear** *va* to shoot with an arrow; to wound or kill with an arrow; to bother, harass
**asaetinado -da** *adj* sateen
**asafétida** *f* asafetida
**asainetado -da** *adj* farcical
**asalariado -da** *adj* wage-earning; *mf* wage earner
**asalariar** *va* to fix wages for; *vr* to work for wages
**asalmonado -da** *adj* salmon-like; salmon, salmon-colored
**asaltante** *mf* assailant
**asaltar** *va* to assault, assail, storm; to overtake, come suddenly upon (*a person*)
**asalto** *m* assault, attack; surprise party; (box.) round; **tomar por asalto** to take by storm
**asamblea** *f* assembly, assemblage; (mil.) assembly; **Asamblea General** General Assembly
**asambleísta** *mf* member of an assembly; *m* assemblyman
**asar** *va* to roast; to bother, annoy, pursue; *vr* to be burning up, be exceedingly hot
**asarabácara** *f* (bot.) asarabacca
**asarero** *m* (bot.) blackthorn
**asargado -da** *adj* twilled, serge
**ásaro** *m* (bot.) asarabacca
**asativo -va** *adj* (pharm.) boiled in its own juice
**asaz** *adj & adv* (poet.) enough, aplenty
**asbestino -na** *adj* (pertaining to) asbestos
**asbesto** *m* asbestos
**asca** *f* (bot.) ascus
**ascalonia** *f* (bot.) shallot
**áscar** *m* army (*in Morocco*)
**áscari** *m* soldier (*in Morocco*)
**ascáride** *f* (zool.) ascarid
**ascendencia** *f* ancestry, line
**ascendente** *adj* up, ascending, ascendant; *m* (astrol.) ascendant
**ascender** §66 *va* to promote; *vn* to ascend, go up; to be advanced, be promoted; **ascender a** to amount to
**ascendiente** *adj* up, ascending, ascendant; *mf* ancestor; *m* ascendancy
**ascensión** *f* ascension; exaltation; (*cap.*) *f* Ascension (*ascending of Jesus; church festival; island of Atlantic*); **ascensión recta** (astr.) right ascension
**ascensional** *adj* ascensional
**ascensionista** *mf* balloonist; mountain climber
**ascenso** *m* ascent, promotion
**ascensómetro** *m* (aer.) climb indicator
**ascensor** *m* elevator; freight elevator; **ascensor hidráulico** hydraulic elevator
**ascensorista** *mf* elevator operator
**asceta** *mf* ascetic
**ascético -ca** *adj* ascetic
**ascetismo** *m* asceticism
**ascidia** *f* (zool.) ascidian
**ascios** *mpl* ascians
**asciro** *m* (bot.) St.-Andrew's-cross
**ascitis** *f* (path.) ascites
**Asclepio** *m* (myth.) Asclepius
**asco** *m* loathing, nausea, disgust; disgusting thing; **dar asco** (coll.) to turn the stomach, to disgust; **estar hecho un asco** (coll.) to be filthy; **hacer ascos de** (coll.) to turn one's nose up at, to pretend to be contemptuous of; **tener asco a** to be disgusted with, to have enough of
**ascomiceto -ta** *adj* (bot.) ascomycetous; *m* (bot.) ascomycete
**ascón** *m* (zool.) ascon
**ascórbico -ca** *adj* ascorbic
**ascospora** *f* (bot.) ascospore
**ascua** *f* ember; **arrimar el ascua a su sardina** to know how to take care of oneself; **estar en** or **sobre ascuas** (coll.) to be worried to death; **sacar el ascua con la mano del gato** or **con mano ajena** (coll.) to get someone else to pull one's chestnuts out of the fire; **¡ascuas!** ouch!
**Asdrúbal** *m* Hasdrubal
**aseado -da** *adj* clean, neat, tidy
**asear** *va* to adorn, clean up, polish, embellish; *vr* to clean up, tidy up
**asechamiento** *m* or **asechanza** *f* trap, snare, waylaying
**asechar** *va* to waylay, ambush
**asecho** *m* var. of **asechamiento**
**asedado -da** *adj* silken
**asedar** *va* to make (*e.g., flax*) soft as silk
**asediador -dora** *adj* besieging; *mf* besieger
**asediar** *va* to besiege, to blockade; (fig.) to besiege, to harass; to make love to, to throw oneself at
**asedio** *m* siege, blockade
**aseglarar** *vr* to act like a layman, to look like a layman
**asegundar** *va* to repeat at once
**asegurable** *adj* insurable
**aseguración** *f* insurance; insurance policy
**asegurado -da** *adj* assured; insured; *mf* insured
**asegurador -dora** *adj* insuring, underwriting; *mf* insurer, underwriter; fastener, fastening
**aseguramiento** *m* assurance; insurance; pass, permit; fastening
**aseguranza** *f* (prov.) firmness, security; (Am.) insurance
**asegurar** *va* to secure, make secure, fasten; to assure, guarantee; to assert; to seize, imprison; to insure; *vr* to make oneself secure; to make onself sure; to take out insurance
**aseidad** *f* (theol.) aseity
**asemejar** *va* to make like; to compare; to resemble; *vn & vr* to be similar; **asemejar a** or **asemejarse a** to be like, to resemble
**asendereado -da** *adj* beaten, frequented; overwhelmed with work or trouble
**asenderear** *va* to cut or open a path through; to pursue through paths and by-paths
**asenso** *m* assent; credence
**asentada** *f* see **asentado**
**asentaderas** *fpl* (coll.) buttocks
**asentadillas; a asentadillas** sidesaddle, woman-fashion
**asentado -da** *adj* sedate, judicious; stable, permanent; *f* sitting; **de una asentada** at one sitting
**asentador** *m* stonemason; strap, razor strop; wholesale merchant; turning chisel; **asentador de vía** (rail.) road foreman, roadmaster
**asentamiento** *m* establishment; settlement, settling; plot, land; judgment, wisdom
**asentar** §18 *va* to seat; to place; to fix, establish, found; to tamp down, to smooth, to level; to hone, sharpen; to note, to enter (*e.g., in a ledger*); to impart (*a blow*); to impress (*on the mind*); to affirm; to guess, suppose; (law) to award; to settle (*food with a drink*); *vn* to be suitable, be becoming; *vr* to sit down; to establish oneself, to be established; to not be digested (*said of food*); to settle (*said of a liquid or a building*)
**asentimiento** *m* assent
**asentir** §62 *vn* to assent
**asentista** *m* army contractor; builder, contractor
**aseñorado -da** *adj* pompous, lordly
**aseo** *m* cleanliness, neatness, tidiness; toilet, powder room
**asepsia** *f* (med.) asepsis
**aséptico -ca** *adj* aseptic
**asequible** *adj* accessible, obtainable

**aserción** *f* assertion
**aserradero** *m* sawmill
**aserradizo -za** *adj* for sawing; sawed
**aserrado -da** *adj* serrate, dented
**aserrador -dora** *adj* saw, sawing; *m* sawer, sawyer; (coll.) scraper, fiddler; *f* power saw
**aserradura** *f* saw cut; **aserraduras** *fpl* sawings, sawdust
**aserraduría** *f* sawmill
**aserrar §18** *va* to saw
**aserrería** *f* sawmill
**aserrín** *m* sawdust
**aserruchar** *va* to saw (*with a handsaw*)
**asertivo -va** *adj* assertive
**aserto** *m* assertion
**asesar** *vn* to become wise, to get sense
**asesinar** *va* to assassinate, murder; to plague, harass
**asesinato** *m* assassination, murder; **asesinato ritual** ritual murder
**asesino -na** *adj* murderous; *mf* assassin, murderer; *m* traitor, betrayer; *f* murderess
**asesor -sora** *adj* advising, advisory; *mf* adviser
**asesoramiento** *m* advising, counseling
**asesorar** *va* to advise; *vr* to seek advice; to get advice
**asesoría** *f* advising; adviser's fee; adviser's office
**asestadura** *f* aiming; shooting, firing
**asestar** *va* to aim; to shoot, fire; to deal (*a blow*); to try to hurt
**aseveración** *f* asseveration
**aseveradamente** *adv* positively, affirmatively
**aseverar** *va* to asseverate
**aseverativo -va** *adj* asseverative; (gram.) declarative (*sentence*)
**asexual** *adj* asexual
**asfaltado -da** *adj* (pertaining to) asphalt; *m* asphalting; asphalt paving
**asfaltar** *va* to asphalt
**asfáltico -ca** *adj* asphaltic, asphalt
**asfalto** *m* asphalt; (mineral.) asphalt
**asfíctico -ca** *adj* asphyctic, asphyxial
**asfixia** *f* asphyxiation; (path.) asphyxia
**asfixiante** *adj* asphyxiating
**asfixiar** *va* to asphyxiate; *vr* to be asphyxiated
**asfíxico -ca** *adj* var. of **asfíctico**
**asfódelo** *m* (bot.) asphodel
**asgo** *1st sg pres ind of* **asir**
**así** *adv* so, thus; **y así sucesivamente** and so on; **así así** so so; **así . . . como** both . . . and; **así como** as soon as; as well as; **así no más** (Am.) so so; **así que** as soon as; so that, with the result that; **así y todo** even so, anyhow; **por decirlo así** so to speak; *adj* such, e.g., **un hombre así** such a man; *conj* although; would that . . . !
**Asia** *f* Asia; **el Asia Menor** Asia Minor; **el Asia sudoriental** Southeast Asia
**asiaticismo** *m* Asiaticism
**asiático -ca** *adj & mf* Asian, Asiatic
**asibilación** *f* (phonet.) assibilation
**asibilar** *va & vr* (phonet.) to assibilate
**asidera** *f* (Am.) saddle strap with ring at each end
**asidero** *m* handle; handhold; (fig.) handle (*occasion, pretext*)
**asiduidad** *f* assiduity; frequency, persistence
**asiduo -dua** *adj* assiduous; frequent, persistent
**asiento** *m* seat; site; settling (*of a building*); bottom (*e.g., of a bottle or chair*); sediment; list, roll; collar band; entry (*e.g., in ledger*); indigestion; trading contract; wisdom, judgment, maturity; **asientos** *mpl* buttocks; **hacer asiento** to settle (*said of a building*); **tome Vd. asiento** have a seat; **asiento de pastor** (bot.) blue genista; **asiento de rejilla** cane seat; **asiento de válvula** valve seat; **asiento lanzable** (aer.) ejection seat
**asignable** *adj* assignable
**asignación** *f* assignation; salary; allowance
**asignado** *m* assignat (*paper money in French Revolution*)
**asignar** *va* to assign
**asignatura** *f* course, subject (*in school*)
**asilado -da** *mf* inmate (*in an asylum or home*)
**asilar** *va* to shelter, give refuge to; to place in an asylum; (agr.) to silo, to ensile; *vr* to take refuge, to take refuge in an asylum; to be placed in an asylum; (archaic) to seek sanctuary
**asilo** *m* asylum; home (*for sick, poor, etc.*); refuge, shelter, protection; (ent.) robber fly, hawk fly; **asilo de huérfanos** orphan asylum; **asilo de locos** insane asylum; **asilo de pobres** poorhouse; **asilo nocturno** night shelter, flophouse
**asilla** *f* fastener; slight pretext; collarbone; **asillas** *fpl* shoulder pole (*for carrying equal weights on each side*)
**asimetría** *f* asymmetry
**asimétrico -ca** *adj* asymmetric or asymmetrical
**asimiento** *m* seizing, grasp; attachment, affection
**asimilable** *adj* assimilable
**asimilación** *f* assimilation; understanding (*of another person, of a role, of a character*)
**asimilar** *va* to assimilate; to compare; to take in; *vn* to assimilate; to be alike; *vr* to assimilate (*e.g., food, knowledge*); **asimilarse a** to resemble
**asimilativo -va** *adj* assimilative
**asimina** *f* (bot.) papaw
**asimismo** *adv* in like manner, likewise, also
**asimplado -da** *adj* simple, simple-looking
**asincrónico -ca** *adj* asynchronous
**asincronismo** *m* asynchronism
**asíndeton** *m* (rhet.) asyndeton
**asinino -na** *adj* var. of **asnino**
**asíntota** *f* (math.) asymptote
**asir §22** *va* to seize, grasp; **tener asido** to hold on to; **asidos del brazo** arm in arm; *vn* to take root; *vr* to take hold; to fight, grapple; **asirse a** or **de** to seize, grasp, take hold of; **asirse con** to grapple with
**Asiria** *f* see **asirio**
**asiriano -na** *adj & mf* (archaic) Assyrian
**asirio -ria** *adj & mf* Assyrian; *m* Assyrian (*language*); (*cap.*) *f* Assyria
**asiriología** *f* Assyriology
**asiriólogo -ga** *mf* Assyriologist
**Asís** *f* Assisi
**asistencia** *f* attendance; assistence; reward; social work; persons present, audience; (Am.) upstairs parlor; (Am.) boarding house; (Am.) board; **asistencias** *fpl* allowance, support
**asistencial** *adj* of assistance
**asistenta** *f* (female) attendant, handmaid; day maid, charwoman
**asistente** *adj* attendant; attending, present; *m* assistant; attendant; bystander, spectator, person present; (mil.) orderly
**asistido -da** *mf* (Am.) roomer, boarder; *m* (Am.) miner
**asistir** *va* to assist, aid, help; to attend, to accompany; to serve, wait on; to take care of; *vn* to be present; to follow suit; **asistir a** to be present at, to attend
**asistolia** *f* (path.) asystole
**asistólico -ca** *adj* asystolic
**asma** *f* (path.) asthma
**asmático -ca** *adj & mf* asthmatic
**Asmodeo** *m* Asmodeus
**asna** *f* she-ass, jenny ass; **asnas** *fpl* rafters
**asnacho** *m* (bot.) restharrow
**asnada** *f* (coll.) asininity
**asnado** *m* (min.) side-wall timber
**asnal** *adj* (pertaining to a) donkey; (coll.) bestial, brutish
**asnalmente** *adv* (coll.) riding on a donkey; (coll.) bestially, brutishly
**asnallo** *m* (bot.) restharrow
**asnaucho** *m* (bot.) Spanish paprika
**asnería** *f* asses; asininity
**asnilla** *f* prop; shoring; trestle, sawbuck
**asnino -na** *adj* (pertaining to a) donkey
**asno** *m* ass, donkey, jackass; (fig.) ass
**asobarcar §86** *va* to take under the arm; to lift high (*one's skirts*)
**asobinar** *vr* to be sprawled out helpless; to fall in a lump
**asocarronado -da** *adj* crafty, cunning
**asociación** *f* association; (sport) association football, soccer
**asociacionismo** *m* (psychol.) associationism
**asociado -da** *adj* associated; associate; *mf* associate, partner

**asociamiento** *m* association
**asociar** *va* to associate; to take as partner; *vr* to associate; to become a partner; to become partners
**asociativo -va** *adj* associative
**asolación** *f* destruction, razing
**asolador -dora** *adj* destructive; *mf* destroyer
**asolamiento** *m* destruction, razing
**asolanar** *va* to parch, dry up (*said of the east wind*); *vr* to be too early, to ripen too early
**asolapar** *va* to make (*e.g., a tile*) overlap
**asolar** *va* to parch, burn; *vr* to become parched; §77 *va* to knock down, to destroy, to raze; *vr* to settle (*said of a liquid*)
**asoldadar** *va* var. of **asoldar**
**asoldar §77** *va* to hire
**asolear** *va* to sun; *vr* to bask; to get sunburned
**asoleo** *m* sunning, basking
**asomado -da** *adj* leaning, leaning out; tipsy; *f* brief appearance; spot from which something is first seen
**asomar** *va* to show, to stick out (*e.g., one's head*); to let show; *vn* to begin to show or appear; to show; *vr* to show, to stick out; to lean out; (coll.) to begin to get tipsy, to get tipsy; **asomarse a mirar** to lean out to look; to come out to look around; **asomarse a ver** to take a look at, to look in at, to look out at
**asombradizo -za** *adj* timid, shy
**asombrador -dora** *adj* astonishing, amazing
**asombrar** *va* to shade; to darken (*a color*); to frighten; to astonish, amaze; *vr* to be frightened; to be astonished or amazed; **asombrarse con** or **de** to be amazed at; **asombrarse de** + *inf* to be amazed to + *inf*
**asombro** *m* fear, fright, scare; astonishment, amazement; wonder; **no volver de su asombro** to not be able to get over it
**asombroso -sa** *adj* astonishing, amazing
**asomo** *m* appearance; sign, indication; **ni por asomo** by no means, not by a long shot
**asonada** *f* mob; row
**asonancia** *f* assonance; correspondence
**asonantado -da** *adj* assonanced
**asonantar** *va* to make assonant; *vn* to assonate
**asonante** *adj* assonant; *m & f* assonance (*sound, syllable, or letter*)
**asonar §77** *vn* to assonate
**asordar** *va* to deafen
**asosegar §29** *va* to calm, quiet; *vn & vr* to become calm, quiet down
**asotanar** *va* to dig or excavate for a cellar
**aspa** *f* X-shaped figure, crosspiece, cross stud; reel; wheel (*of windmill*); vane (*of windmill*); propeller blade; **en aspa** crosswise
**aspadera** *f* reel
**aspado -da** *adj* cross-shaped; with the arms outstretched; (coll.) tight-laced
**aspador -dora** *mf* reeler; *m* reel
**aspálato** *m* (bot.) rosewood
**aspalto** *m* (paint.) dark glaze
**aspar** *va* to reel; to crucify; (coll.) to vex, annoy; *vr* to writhe; to strive, take great pains
**aspaventero -ra** *adj* fussy, excitable; *mf* fussy, excitable person
**aspaviento** *m* fuss, excitement
**aspear** *vr* to bruise one's feet, to become footsore
**aspecto** *m* aspect; (astr., astrol. & gram.) aspect; **al** or **a primer aspecto** at first sight
**asperarteria** *f* (anat.) windpipe, trachea
**asperear** *vn* to taste bitter
**asperete** *m* bitterness, sourness
**aspereza** *f* roughness; harshness; bitterness, sourness; rudeness, coarseness, gruffness; asperity; **limar asperezas** (fig.) to smooth away the rough edges
**asperiego -ga** *adj* cider (*apple or apple tree*)
**asperilla** *f* (bot.) woodruff
**asperillo** *m* bitterness, sourness
**asperjar** *va* to sprinkle; to sprinkle with holy water
**áspero -ra** *adj* rough; harsh; bitter, tart; sour; rude, coarse, gruff; (phonet.) rough (*breathing*)
**asperón** *m* sandstone, grit, gritstone; grindstone
**asperonar** *va* to grind with sandstone and water, to rub with sandstone
**aspérrimo -ma** *adj super* very or most rough
**aspersión** *f* aspersion (*sprinkling*); sprinkling; spraying
**aspersor** *m* sprinkler
**aspersorio** *m* sprinkler, water sprinkler
**áspid** *m* or **áspide** *m* (zool.) asp, aspic
**aspidistra** *f* (bot.) aspidistra
**aspillera** *f* (fort.) embrasure, loophole; (fort.) machicolation
**aspillerar** *va* to embrasure; to machicolate
**aspiración** *f* aspiration; inhalation; suction; draft; intake; (mus.) short pause
**aspirado -da** *adj & f* (phonet.) aspirate
**aspirador -dora** *adj* (pertaining to) suction; *mf* inhaler; *m* aspirator; **aspirador de gasolina** (aut.) vacuum tank; **aspirador** or **aspiradora de polvo** vacuum cleaner
**aspirante** *adj* (pertaining to) suction; *m* applicant, candidate; **aspirante a cabo** (mil.) private first class; **aspirante de marina** (naut.) midshipman
**aspirar** *va* to suck, draw in; to inhale; (phonet.) to aspirate; *vn* to aspire; to inhale; **aspirar a** to aspire after or to; **aspirar a** + *inf* to aspire to + *inf*
**aspirina** *f* (pharm.) aspirin
**asplenio** *m* (bot.) spleenwort
**asquear** *va* to loathe, be nauseated at; *vn* to be nauseated
**asquerosidad** *f* loathsomeness; nausea; squeamishness
**asqueroso -sa** *adj* loathsome, disgusting; nauseated; squeamish
**asta** *f* spear; shaft; mast, flagpole, staff; handle (*of brush*); horn; antler; **a media asta** at half-mast; **dejar en las astas del toro** (coll.) to leave high and dry
**ástaco** *m* (zool.) crawfish, crayfish
**astado -da** *adj* horny; horned; *m* bull
**astático -ca** *adj* astatic
**astatino** or **ástato** *m* (chem.) astatine
**astenia** *f* (path.) asthenia
**asténico -ca** *adj & mf* asthenic
**aster** or **áster** *m & f* (bot. & biol.) aster
**asteria** *f* (mineral.) asteriated opal; (zool.) starfish
**asterisco** *m* asterisk
**asterismo** *m* (astr. & phys.) asterism
**asteroide** *adj* asteroid (*starlike*); *m* (astr.) asteroid
**asteroideo -a** *adj & m* (zool.) asteroidean
**Astianacte** *m* (myth.) Astyanax
**astigmático -ca** *adj* astigmatic
**astigmatismo** *m* (med.) astigmatism
**astigmómetro** *m* astigmometer
**astil** *m* handle (*of an ax*); shaft (*of arrow, of feather*); beam (*of balance*)
**astilla** *f* chip, splinter
**astillar** *va* to chip, to splinter; *vr* to chip, to splinter; (coll.) to be bursting (*with too much food or drink*)
**astillazo** *m* blow from flying chip
**Astillejos** *mpl* (astr.) Castor and Pollux
**astillero** *m* rack for spears, lances, etc.; shipyard, dockyard
**astilloso -sa** *adj* splintery
**astorgano -na** *adj* (pertaining to) Astorga; *mf* native or inhabitant of Astorga
**astracán** *m* astrachan; (theat.) drama of puns
**astracanada** *f* (coll.) cheap farce
**astrágalo** *m* (anat., arch. & arti.) astragal; (bot.) milk vetch
**astral** *adj* astral
**astrancia** *f* (bot.) astrantia; **astrancia mayor** (bot.) black sanicle, masterwort
**astreñir §74** *va* var. of **astringir**
**astricción** *f* astriction
**astrictivo -va** *adj* astrictive
**astrífero -ra** *adj* (poet.) starry
**astringencia** *f* astringency
**astringente** *adj & m* astringent
**astringir §42** *va* to constrict, compress; to bind, compel
**astriñir §25** *va* var. of **astringir**
**astro** *m* star, heavenly body; (fig.) star, luminary, leading light; **el astro de la noche** the moon; **el astro del día** the sun
**astródomo** *m* (aer.) astrodome
**astrofísico -ca** *adj* astrophysical; *f* astrophysics

**astrofotografía** *f* astrophotography
**astrofotometría** *f* astrophotometry
**astrolabio** *m* (astr.) astrolabe
**astrologar** §59 *va & vn* to astrologize
**astrología** *f* astrology
**astrológico -ca** *adj* astrological
**astrólogo -ga** *adj* astrological; *mf* astrologer
**astronauta** *m* astronaut
**astronáutico -ca** *adj* astronautic or astronautical; *f* astronautics
**astronave** *f* spaceship; **astronave tripulada** manned spaceship
**astronavegación** *f* space travel; astronavigation
**astronomía** *f* astronomy
**astronómico -ca** *adj* astronomic or astronomical; (coll.) astronomic or astronomical (*exceedingly large*)
**astrónomo -ma** *mf* astronomer
**astroso -sa** *adj* unfortunate, ill-fated; vile, contemptible; (coll.) shabby, ragged
**astucia** *f* astuteness; cunning; trick, artifice
**astucioso -sa** *adj* astute, cunning
**astur** *adj & mf* var. of **asturiano**
**asturianismo** *m* Asturian word or expression
**asturiano -na** *adj & mf* Asturian; *m* Asturian (*dialect*)
**Asturias** *f* Asturias
**asturión** *m* (ichth.) sturgeon; pony
**astuto -ta** *adj* astute, cunning, sly; tricky
**asuardado -da** *adj* spotted, stained
**asuertado -da** *adj* (Am.) lucky, fortunate
**asueto** *m* day off, short time off, brief vacation; (coll.) leisure, diversion, amusement
**asumir** *va* to assume (*command, responsibilities, great proportions, etc.*); to raise, elevate (*to a dignity*); *vr* to assume
**asunción** *f* assumption; elevation (*to a dignity*); (*cap.*) *f* (eccl.) Assumption; Asunción (*city*)
**asuncionista** *mf* Assumptionist
**asunto** *m* subject, matter; business, affair; theme; **asuntos exteriores** foreign affairs
**asuramiento** *m* burning; parching; worriment
**asurar** *va* to burn (*food*); to parch (*said of hot sun*); to worry, harass; *vr* to be burned; to be parched; to be worried or annoyed; to be burning up, be roasting
**asurcano -na** *adj* neighboring (*said of fields and their farmers*)
**asurcar** §86 *va* to furrow, to plow
**asustadizo -za** *adj* shy, scary, skittish
**asustador -dora** *adj* frightening
**asustar** *va* to scare, frighten; *vr* to be scared, frightened; **asustarse de, con,** or **por** to be frightened at; **asustarse de** + *inf* to be frightened to, to be afraid to + *inf*
**atabacado -da** *adj* tobacco-colored
**atabal** *m* kettledrum; kettledrummer; timbrel
**atabalear** *vn* to stamp (*said of a horse*); to drum (*with the fingers*)
**atabalero** *m* kettledrummer
**atabanado -da** *adj* with white spots (*said of a horse*)
**atabardillado -da** *adj* like spotted fever
**atabe** *m* vent (*in a pipe*)
**atabernado -da** *adj* sold by the glass (*said of wine*)
**atabladera** *f* drag (*for smoothing or leveling*)
**atablar** *va* to drag (*e.g., a field for leveling*)
**atacable** *adj* attackable, assailable
**atacadera** *f* blaster's rammer, tamping stick
**atacado -da** *adj* undecided, irresolute; stingy, mean
**atacador -dora** *mf* aggressor; *m* ramrod, rammer
**atacadura** *f* attaching, fastening, buttoning; (min.) plugging (*of blasting-powder holes*)
**atacamita** *f* (mineral.) atacamite
**atacante** *adj* attacking; *mf* attacker
**atacar** §86 *va* to attach, fasten, button, buckle; to pack, to jam; to ram, tamp; to attack; to corner, to contradict
**atacir** *m* (astrol.) division of celestial sphere into twelve houses
**ataderas** *fpl* (coll.) garters
**atadero** *m* cord, rope; place for tying; **no tener atadero** (coll.) to be in disorder; (coll.) to be full of nonsense
**atadijo** *m* (coll.) loose package
**atado -da** *adj* timid, shy; weak, irresolute; insignificant; hampered, cramped; *m* pack, bundle, roll
**atador -dora** *adj* binding; *mf* binder; *f* binding machine; **atadores** *mpl* bonnet strings
**atadura** *f* tying, binding, fastening; string, rope; knot, connection; bond, union; obstacle, shackle
**atafagar** §59 *va* to suffocate (*especially with strong odors*); to bother, harass
**atafea** *f* surfeit
**atafetanado -da** *adj* like taffeta
**ataguía** *f* cofferdam
**ataharre** *m* breeching
**atahona** *f* var. of **tahona**
**atahorma** *f* (orn.) harrier eagle
**ataifor** *m* round Moorish table
**atairar** *va* to put molding in (*doors and windows*)
**ataire** *m* molding
**atajadero** *m* dike, levee (*for directing and controlling irrigation*)
**atajadizo** *m* partition, wall
**atajador** *m* interceptor; (mach.) arrester; (Am.) stable boy
**atajar** *va* to stop, arrest, intercept, interrupt; to partition off; to take a short cut to meet or to head off; to cross off; *vn* to take a short cut; *vr* to be abashed, be confused with fear or shame
**atajo** *m* short cut; cut (*e.g., in a play*); flock; (fig.) short cut; **echar por el atajo** to duck (*to get expeditiously out of an unpleasant situation*)
**atalajar** *va* to harness and hitch
**atalaje** *m* harness; (coll.) outfit, equipment
**atalantar** *va* to please, to suit; to stun, daze; *vr* to be stunned
**atalaya** *f* watchtower; height, elevation; *m* guard, lookout
**atalayador -dora** *mf* lookout; spy, prier
**atalayar** *va* to watch from a watchtower; to spy on
**atalayero** *m* (mil.) scout
**ataludar** *va* to slope, batter
**atalvina** *f* var. of **talvina**
**atamán** *m* var. of **hetmán**
**atamiento** *m* (coll.) pusillanimity, timidity
**atanasia** *f* athanasia (*immortality*); (bot.) costmary; (print.) English (*14 points*)
**atanasiano -na** *adj* Athanasian
**Atanasio, San** Saint Athanasius
**atanor** *m* water pipe; athanor
**atanquía** *f* (coll.) depilatory ointment; coarse silk, floss
**atañadero -ra** *adj* applicable; concerning, pertaining
**atañer** §84 *va* to concern
**atapar** *va* to cover, cover up, hide; to stop up, plug
**ataque** *m* attack; (mil.) offensive trenches; **ataque aéreo** air attack, air raid; **ataque cardíaco** or **ataque de corazón** heart attack; **ataque en picado** (aer.) diving attack; **ataque por sorpresa** surprise attack
**ataquiza** *f* (hort.) layering
**ataquizar** §76 *va* (hort.) to layer (*a vine*)
**atar** *va* to tie, fasten, lace; to paralyze; **no atar ni desatar** (coll.) to talk nonsense; (coll.) to get nowhere, to lead nowhere; *vr* to stick (*to, e.g., an opinion*); to get tied up (*e.g., in difficulties*)
**ataracea** *f* marquetry, inlaid work; inlaid floor
**ataracear** *va* to inlay, to adorn with marquetry
**atarantado -da** *adj* bitten by a tarantula; scared, bewildered; (coll.) restless, boisterous
**atarantamiento** *m* stunning, daze, bewilderment
**atarantar** *va* to stun, daze; *vr* to be stunned
**ataraxia** *f* ataraxia
**ataráxico -ca** *adj* ataractic
**atarazana** *f* shipyard; spinner's shed; (prov.) wine vault
**atarazar** §76 *va* to bite, to tear or lacerate with the teeth
**atardecer** *m* late afternoon; §34 *vn* to draw towards evening; to be, arrive, or happen in the late afternoon
**atareado -da** *adj* busy

**atarear** *va* to assign a task to, to give a job to; *vr* to toil, to overwork; **atarearse a** + *inf* to be busy + *ger;* **atarearse con** or **en** to busy oneself with
**atarjea** *f* culvert, drainpipe, sewer; sewer connection (*from house*); **atarjea de alimentación** (rail.) feed trough, track tank
**atarquinar** *va* to cover with mud; *vr* to get covered with mud, to silt up
**atarraga** *f* (bot.) elecampane
**atarragar** **§59** *va* to hammer and fit (*a horseshoe*)
**atarrajar** *va* to thread, to tap
**atarraya** *f* casting net
**atarugamiento** *m* (coll.) confusion, timidity, bashfulness
**atarugar** **§59** *va* to fasten with pegs, pins, or wedges; to plug, to plug up; to stuff, fill; (coll.) to silence, shut up; *vr* (coll.) to get confused (*in speech*)
**atasajar** *va* to jerk (*meat*); to slash, hack; (coll.) to stretch across a horse
**atascadero** *m* mudhole, bog; obstruction, interference
**atascamiento** *m* obstruction; (path.) compression, constriction
**atascar** **§86** *va* to stop, stop up, clog; *vr* to become stopped up, to clog; to get stuck (*in the mud*); to stuff, to stuff oneself; (coll.) to get stuck (*in speech*)
**atasco** *m* clogging, jamming, sticking; obstruction
**ataúd** *m* casket, coffin
**ataudado -da** *adj* coffin-shaped
**ataujía** *f* damascene, damascene work (*incrustation of gold or silver wire and enamel in steel or copper*); (Am.) conduit, drain
**ataujiado -da** *adj* damascene, damascened (*having gold or silver wire incrusted in steel or copper*)
**ataujiar** **§90** *va* to damascene (*to adorn with gold or silver wire or enamel incrusted in steel or copper*)
**ataurique** *m* (arch.) Moorish ornamental plasterwork; carved foliage
**ataviar** **§90** *va* to dress, dress up, adorn
**atávico -ca** *adj* atavistic
**atavío** *m* dress, adornment; **atavíos** *mpl* finery
**atavismo** *m* (biol.) atavism
**ataxia** *f* ataxia; (path.) ataxia; **ataxia locomotriz progresiva** (path.) locomotor ataxia
**atáxico -ca** *adj & mf* ataxic
**Até** *f* (myth.) Ate
**atediante** *adj* boring, tiresome
**atediar** *va* to bore, tire; *vr* to become bored, be bored
**ateísmo** *m* atheism
**ateísta** *adj & mf* atheist
**ateístico -ca** *adj* atheistic
**atejado -da** *adj* overlapping
**ateje** *m* (bot.) tropical tree of genus *Cordia*
**atejonar** *vr* (Am.) to squat, cower, duck, hide; (Am.) to become sly, cunning
**atelaje** *m* harness; team
**atemorizar** **§76** *va* to scare, frighten; *vr* to become scared, become frightened; **atemorizarse de** or **por** to become scared or frightened at
**atemperación** *f* tempering, moderation; adjusting; cooling
**atemperante** *adj* tempering, softening; cooling
**atemperar** *va* to temper, soften, moderate; to adjust, accommodate; to cool; to condition (*air*)
**atemporalado -da** *adj* stormy, tempestuous
**Atena** *f* (myth.) Athena
**atenacear** *va* to tear the flesh of (*a person*) with nippers; to tie down; to torture
**Atenas** *f* Athens
**atenazar** **§76** *va* var. of **atenacear**
**atención** *f* attention; **atenciones** *fpl* attentions (*acts of courtesy, etc.*); business, duties, responsibilities; **en atención a** in view of; *interj* attention!; (mil.) attention!
**atendedor -dora** *mf* (print.) copyholder (*reader who follows copy as proofreader reads aloud*)
**atendencia** *f* attention, attending
**atender** **§66** *va* to attend to, pay attention to; to take care of; *vn* to attend, pay attention; (print.) to follow copy as proofreader reads aloud; **atender por** to answer to the name of (*said of an animal*)
**atendible** *adj* worthy of attention
**atendré** *1st sg fut ind of* **atener**
**Atenea** *f* see **ateneo**
**atenebrar** *vr* to become dark
**ateneo -a** *adj & mf* (poet.) Athenian; *m* athenaeum; (*cap.*) *f* (myth.) Athena
**atener** **§85** *vr* to abide; to depend, to rely; **atenerse a** to abide by; to depend on, to rely on
**atengo** *1st sg pres ind of* **atener**
**ateniense** *adj & mf* Athenian
**atentación** *f* illegality
**atentadamente** *adv* illegally; cautiously
**atentado -da** *adj* prudent, moderate; cautious; *m* attempt, assault; crime
**atentar** *va* to do illegally; to attempt, to try to commit; *vn* to attempt a crime; **atentar a** or **contra** to attempt (*e.g., the life of a person*); **§18** *vr* to grope; to restrain oneself
**atentatorio -ria** *adj* offensive; **atentatorio a** violating
**atento -ta** *adj* attentive; kind; polite, courteous; *f* favor (*letter of which one acknowledges receipt*)
**atenuación** *f* attenuation; extenuation (*of guilt, offense, etc.*); (rhet.) litotes
**atenuar** **§33** *va* to attenuate; to extenuate (*to make seem less serious*); *vn* to attenuate
**ateo -a** *adj* atheist, atheistic; *mf* atheist
**atercianado -da** *adj* suffering from tertian fever; *mf* person suffering from tertian fever
**aterciopelado -da** *adj* velvety
**aterecer** **§34** *vr* to become stiff with cold
**aterimiento** *m* stiffness from cold
**aterir** **§53** *vr* to become stiff with cold
**atermancia** *f* (phys.) athermancy
**atérmano -na** *adj* athermanous
**aterosclerosis** *f* (path.) atherosclerosis
**aterrada** *f* (naut.) landfall (*making or sighting land*)
**aterrador -dora** *adj* frightful, dreadful
**aterrajar** *va* to thread, to tap
**aterraje** *m* landing (*of boat or aircraft*)
**aterramiento** *m* ruin, destruction; terror; discouragement; landing
**aterrar** *va* to terrify; *vr* to become terrified; **§18** *va* to demolish, destroy; to cover with earth, to earth up; (min.) to dump; *vn* to land; *vr* to keep or stand inshore; **navegar aterrado** (naut.) to sail inshore
**aterrizaje** *m* (aer.) landing; **aterrizaje a ciegas** (aer.) blind landing; **aterrizaje aplastado** or **en desplome** (aer.) pancake landing; **aterrizaje forzado** or **forzoso** (aer.) forced landing; **aterrizaje sobre tres puntos** (aer.) three-point landing
**aterrizar** **§76** *vn* (aer.) to land
**aterronado -da** *adj* lumpish, cloddy
**aterronar** *va* to make lumpy, to clod; *vr* to become lumpy, to cake
**aterrorizar** **§76** *va* to terrify
**atesar** **§18** *va* (naut.) to haul taut
**atesoramiento** *m* hoarding
**atesorar** *va* to treasure, hoard up; to possess (*virtues, charm, etc.*)
**atestación** *f* attestation
**atestado -da** *adj* stubborn; *m* (law) attestation; **atestados** *mpl* (law) testimonials
**atestadura** *f* packing, cramming, stuffing; must for filling up casks
**atestamiento** *m* packing, cramming, stuffing
**atestar** *va* (law) to attest; **§18 &** **regular** *va* to pack, to stuff, to cram; to fill up (*wine casks*); (coll.) to stuff (*with food*)
**atestiguación** *f* or **atestiguamiento** *m* attestation, testifying, deposition, corroboration
**atestiguar** **§23** *va* to attest, to testify, to depose
**atetado -da** *adj* mammiform
**atetar** *va* to suckle
**atetillar** *va* (agr.) to make a pit around (*trunk of tree*), leaving some earth close to trunk
**atezado -da** *adj* tan; black
**atezamiento** *m* tanning; blackening

**atezar** §76 *va* to tan; to blacken; *vr* to tan; to become tanned; to get black
**atibar** *va* (min.) to fill up with muck and rubbish
**atiborrar** *va* to stuff; (coll.) to stuff (*with food*); *vr* (coll.) to stuff, to stuff oneself (*with food*)
**Ática** *f* see **ático**
**aticismo** *m* Atticism
**aticista** *mf* Atticist
**ático -ca** *adj & mf* Attic; *m* (anat. & arch.) attic; **el Ática** Attica
**atierre** *m* (min.) cave-in, deads; (Am.) filling with earth
**atiesador** *m* stiffener, stiffening
**atiesamiento** *m* stiffening
**atiesar** *va* to stiffen; to tighten; *vr* to stiffen, become stiff; to tighten, become tight
**atifle** *m* potter's trivet
**atigrado -da** *adj* tigerish; tiger-marked
**atigrar** *va* to mark like a tiger; *vr* to become tigerish
**atijara** *f* goods, business; transportation (*cost*); reward
**Atila** *m* Attila
**atildado -da** *adj* neat, stylish
**atildadura** *f* or **atildamiento** *m* marking with tilde; faultfinding; neatness, adornment, elegance
**atildar** *va* to put a tilde, dash, or accent mark over; to note, point out, find fault with; to clean, fix up, trim, adorn
**atinado -da** *adj* wise, keen, careful
**atinar** *va* to find, to come upon; *vn* to guess, guess right; to apply, be right; **atinar a** to guess; to find, to come upon; to hit (*e.g., the target*); **atinar a** + *inf* to manage to + *inf*, to succeed in + *ger*; **atinar con** to guess; to find, to come upon, to hit upon; **atinar en** to guess, guess right, hit upon
**atíncar** *m* borax
**atinconar** *va* (min.) to prop up, to shore up
**atípico -ca** *adj* atypical
**atiplar** *va* (mus.) to raise the pitch of to treble; *vr* (mus.) to rise to treble
**atirantar** *va* to make taut; to brace with stays or ties
**atiriciar** *vr* to become jaundiced
**atisbadero** *m* peephole
**atisbador -dora** *adj* watching, spying; *mf* watcher, spy
**atisbadura** *f* watching, spying
**atisbar** *va* to watch, spy on, observe
**atisbo** *m* watching, spying, observation; sign, token, show
**atisuado -da** *adj* like tissue
**atizadero** *m* poker; coal mouth (*of furnace*)
**atizador -dora** *adj* inciting, stirring; *m* poker; feeder
**atizar** §76 *va* to stir, to poke; to snuff; to rouse, to stir up; (coll.) to give, to let go (*e.g., a kick*)
**atizonar** *va* to bond with headers; to embed in a wall; (agr.) to smut, to taint with smut; *vn* (agr.) to smut, to blight
**atlante** *m* strong man; **atlantes** *mpl* (arch.) atlantes; (*cap.*) *m* (myth.) Atlas
**atlántico -ca** *adj* Atlantic; Atlantean; (*cap.*) *m* Atlantic (*ocean*)
**Atlántida** *f* Atlantis; **Atlántidas** *fpl* (astr. & myth.) Atlantides
**atlas** *m* (*pl:* **-las**) atlas (*book of maps; size of paper*); (anat.) atlas; (*cap.*) *m* (myth.) Atlas; **el Atlas** the Atlas Mountains
**atleta** *mf* athlete; athletic person; intellectual giant; great figure (*e.g., of literature*); champion (*of a cause*)
**atlético -ca** *adj* athletic; *f* athletics (*art or skill*)
**atletismo** *m* athletics (*principles of athletic training; games, sports, etc.*)
**atmósfera** *f* atmosphere; (fig.) atmosphere
**atmosférico -ca** *adj* atmospheric
**atoar** *va* (naut.) to tow; (naut.) to warp
**atocinado -da** *adj* (coll.) fat, fleshy
**atocinar** *va* to cut up (*a pig*); to make into bacon; (coll.) to assassinate; *vr* (coll.) to become angry; (coll.) to fall madly in love
**atocha** *f* (bot.) esparto
**atochada** *f* dike of esparto grass and mud
**atochal** *m* esparto field
**atochar** *m* esparto field; *va* to stuff or fill with esparto; to stuff or fill; *vr* (naut.) to jam
**atochón** *m* (bot.) esparto; (bot.) esparto panicle
**atol** *m* or **atole** *m* (Am.) atole (*drink made of maize meal*)
**atolón** *m* atoll
**atolondrado -da** *adj* amazed, bewildered; scatterbrained, reckless
**atolondramiento** *m* amazement, bewilderment; thoughtlessness, recklessness
**atolondrar** *va* to amaze, bewilder; *vr* to become amazed, become bewildered
**atolladero** *m* mudhole; difficulty, obstruction, blind alley, dead end
**atollar** *vn* to get stuck in the mud or in a mudhole; *vr* to get stuck in the mud or in a mudhole; (coll.) to get stuck
**atomicidad** *f* (chem.) atomicity
**atómico -ca** *adj* atomic
**atomismo** *m* atomism
**atomista** *mf* atomist
**atomístico -ca** *adj* atomistic; *f* atomistics
**atomizador** *m* atomizer
**atomizar** §76 *va* to atomize
**átomo** *m* atom; (chem.) atom; **átomo cálido** (phys.) hot atom
**átomo-gramo** *m* (*pl:* **átomos-gramos**) (chem.) gram atom
**atonal** *adj* (mus.) atonal
**atonalidad** *f* (mus.) atonality
**atonalismo** *m* (mus.) atonalism
**atondar** *va* to spur (*a horse*)
**atonía** *f* (path. & phonet.) atony; (phonet.) lack of stress
**atonicidad** *f* (med.) atonicity
**atónico -ca** *adj* (gram. & med.) atonic
**atónito -ta** *adj* overwhelmed, aghast
**átono -na** *adj* (gram. & med.) atonic
**atontadamente** *adv* stupidly
**atontamiento** *m* stunning, stupefaction; confusion, bewilderment; stupidity, imbecility
**atontar** *va* to stun, stupefy; to confuse, bewilder; *vr* to become stunned, become stupefied; to become confused, become bewildered
**atoramiento** *m* sticking; choking; obstruction
**atorar** *va* to obstruct; *vn* to stick; *vr* to stick; to choke; §77 *va* to chop (*wood*)
**atormentador -dora** *adj* tormenting; *mf* tormentor; torturer
**atormentar** *va* to torment; to torture
**atornillar** *va & vr* to screw, to screw on
**atorozonar** *vr* (vet.) to suffer from colic
**atorrante** *adj & mf* (Am.) good-for-nothing
**atortolar** *va* to rattle, intimidate; *vr* to become rattled or intimidated
**atortorar** *va* (naut.) to frap (*a cable*)
**atortujar** *va* to squeeze, to flatten
**atosigador -dora** *mf* poisoner; urger
**atosigamiento** *m* poisoning; pressing, urging
**atosigar** §59 *va* to poison; to press, harass; *vr* to be hurried
**atrabajado -da** *adj* overworked; belabored
**atrabancar** §86 *va & vn* to get through in a hurry
**atrabanco** *m* hurry, precipitation
**atrabiliario -ria** *adj* atrabilious
**atrabilis** *f* (med.) black bile; (fig.) ill-humor
**atracadero** *m* (naut.) landing, wharf, berth
**atracado -da** *adj* (coll.) stuffed; *f* (naut.) bringing alongside, mooring
**atracador** *m* (slang) holdup man
**atracar** §86 *va* to bring up; (naut.) to bring alongside; to waylay, to hold up; (coll.) to stuff (*with food and drink*); *vn* (naut.) to come alongside; *vr* (coll.) to stuff (*to eat and drink too much*); (Am.) to fight, quarrel
**atracazón** *m* (Am.) jam, mob
**atracción** *f* attraction; amusement (*in vaudeville, a circus, etc.*); **atracción capilar** (phys.) capillary attraction
**atraco** *m* holdup
**atracón** *m* (coll.) stuffing, gluttony
**atractivo -va** *adj* attractive; *m* attraction; attractiveness
**atractriz** (*pl:* **-trices**) *adj fem* attracting; *f* (phys.) force of attraction
**atraer** §88 *va* to attract; to draw (*e.g., a crowd*); *vr* to be attracted; to draw (*applause*)
**atrafagar** §59 *vn* to toil, make a great effort

**atragantado -da** *adj* choking (*with strong emotion*)
**atragantamiento** *m* choking
**atragantar** *va* to choke down; *vr* to choke; (coll.) to get mixed up (*in one's speech*); **atragantarse con** to choke on
**atraíble** *adj* attractable
**atraicionar** *va* to betray
**atraidorado -da** *adj* treacherous, traitorous
**atraigo** *1st sg pres ind of* **atraer**
**atraillar §75** *va* to leash; to pursue (*game*) with a dog in leash
**atraimiento** *m* attracting, attraction
**atraje** *1st sg pret ind of* **atraer**
**atrampar** *vr* to be trapped, to fall in the trap; to stop up (*said, e.g., of a pipe*); to catch, to stick (*said of bolt of lock that cannot be opened*); (coll.) to get entangled, to get stuck
**atramuz** *m* (*pl:* **-muces**) var. of **altramuz**
**atrancar §86** *va* to bar; to obstruct; *vn* (coll.) to stride, take large strides; (coll.) to read hastily and skipping words; *vr* (Am.) to be insistent
**atranco** or **atranque** *m* mudhole; difficulty, obstruction
**atrapador** *m* (mach.) trap, collector
**atrapamoscas** (*pl:* **-cas**) *f* (bot.) Venus's-flytrap
**atrapar** *va* (coll.) to catch, to trap (*especially, person or animal that is fleeing*); (coll.) to get (*something good or advantageous*); (coll.) to trap, take in, deceive
**atraque** *m* (naut.) bringing alongside, mooring
**atrás** *adv* back, backward; behind; previously; **desde muy atrás** a long time ago; for a long time; **días atrás** days ago; **hacerse atrás** to back up, move back, fall back; **hacia atrás** backwards; (coll.) the wrong way; **ir para atrás** to look younger every day; **atrás de** back of, behind; *interj* back up!, back out!
**atrasado -da** *adj* slowed, late; slow (*said of a watch or clock*); hard up, needy; back; past; due; in arrears; retarded; (coll.) backward, slow to learn; **mentalmente atrasado** mentally retarded; **atrasado de medios** poor, impoverished; **atrasado de noticias** behind the times; **atrasado en pagos** in arrears
**atrasar** *va* to slow, slow down; to slow down, retard (*watch or clock*); to set back, to turn back (*hands of watch or clock*); to leave behind; to hold back, to delay; to postdate (*an event, document, etc.*); *vn* to go slow, to be slow (*said of a watch or clock*); *vr* to go slow, to be slow; to lose time; to stay back, stay behind; to lag; to be late; to be in debt
**atraso** *m* slowness, delay; backwardness; lag
**atravesado -da** *adj* squint-eyed; crossbred, mongrel; wicked, treacherous, vile
**atravesador -dora** *adj* crossing; monopolizing; *m* (elec.) bushing (*of a transformer*)
**atravesaño** *m* var. of **travesaño**
**atravesar §18** *va* to put or lay (*e.g., a piece of timber*) across; to cross, to go through, to go over, to go across; to pierce; to cast the evil eye upon; to put up, to stake, to wager; to buy (*goods*) wholesale in order to sell retail; **atravesar . . . en** to put or lay (*e.g., a piece of timber*) across (*e.g., a street*); *vr* to butt in; to wrangle, fight; to get stuck (*said e.g., of a bone in the throat*)
**atrayente** *adj* attractive
**atreguado -da** *adj* mad, deranged; under truce
**atreguar §23** *va* to give a truce to; to grant an extension; *vr* to agree to a truce
**atrenzo** *m* (Am.) conflict, difficulty
**Atreo** *m* (myth.) Atreus
**atresia** *f* (med.) atresia
**atresnalar** *va* (agr.) to arrange (*sheaves*) in shocks
**atrever** *vr* to dare, to make bold; **atreverse a** to venture, to dare to undertake; **atreverse a** + *inf* to dare to + *inf;* **atreverse con** or **contra** to be impudent toward
**atrevido -da** *adj* bold, daring; impudent, forward
**atrevimiento** *m* boldness, daring; impudence, effrontery
**atrezo** *m* stage equipment, properties
**atribución** *f* attribution; assignment, power, function
**atribuíble** *adj* attributable
**atribuir §41** *va* to attribute; to assign
**atribulación** *f* tribulation, grieving
**atribular** *va* to grieve, afflict; *vr* to grieve, be grieved, lose heart
**atributivo -va** *adj* attributive; (gram.) attributive
**atributo** *m* attribute; (gram.) attribute
**atrición** *f* (phys. & theol.) attrition; (path.) bruise
**atril** *m* lectern; music stand
**atrilera** *f* ornamental cover of lectern or choir desk
**atrincheramiento** *m* intrenchment
**atrincherar** *va* to intrench, to fortify with trenches; *vr* to intrench, to dig in
**atrio** *m* atrium; hall, vestibule; parvis; (anat.) atrium
**atrípedo -da** *adj* (zool.) black-footed
**atrirrostro -tra** *adj* black-beaked
**atrito -ta** *adj* contrite
**atrocidad** *f* atrocity; (coll.) enormity; (coll.) stupidity; **¡qué atrocidad!** (coll.) how terrific!
**atrochar** *vn* to go by cross paths, to take a short cut
**atrofia** *f* atrophy
**atrofiar** *va & vr* to atrophy
**atrojar** *va* to garner (*grain*); *vr* (Am.) to be befuddled, to not know which way to turn
**atrompetado -da** *adj* bell-mouthed, trumpet-shaped
**atronado -da** *adj* reckless, thoughtless
**atronador -dora** *adj* deafening
**atronadura** *f* fissure in trunk of tree; (vet.) crepance
**atronamiento** *m* deafening; stun, stunning; (vet.) crepance
**atronar §77** *va* to deafen; to stun; to stop the ears of (*a horse*); to kill (*a bull*) by blow on nape of neck; *vn* to thunder; *vr* to be frightened at thunder (*said of chickens and silkworms*)
**atronerar** *va* (fort.) to make embrasures in
**atropar** *va* to round up in a gang; to gather (*grain, hay, etc.*); *vr* to gang together
**atropellado -da** *adj* hasty; violent, brusk; tumultous; sickly, decrepit
**atropellador -dora** *mf* trampler; brash person
**atropellamiento** *m* trampling; upsetting; abuse, insult
**atropellaplatos** *f* (*pl:* **-tos**) (coll.) slap-bang maid
**atropellar** *va* to trample under foot; to run over; to knock down; to push one's way through; to ride roughshod over or through; to do hurriedly; to disregard, to violate; *vn* to act hastily or recklessly; **atropellar por** to push one's way through; to disregard, to violate; *vr* to act hastily or recklessly
**atropello** *m* trampling; upsetting; (act of) running down, running over; abuse, insult; outrage, excess
**atropina** *f* (chem. & pharm.) atropine
**Átropos** *f* (myth.) Atropos
**atroz** *adj* (*pl:* **-troces**) atrocious; (coll.) huge. enormous
**atruhanado -da** *adj* scurrilous
**atto.** or **att.º** abr. of **atento**
**atuendo** *m* pomp, show; dress, adornment
**atufamiento** *m* anger, vexation, annoyance
**atufar** *va* to anger, vex, irritate; *vr* to get angry; to turn sour (*said of wine*); to get smelly (*said of food*); **atufarse con, de** or **por** to get angry at
**atufo** *m* anger, vexation, irritation
**atumultuar §33** *va & vr* var. of **tumultuar**
**atún** *m* (ichth.) tuna, tunny
**atunara** *f* tuna fishery
**atunero -ra** *mf* tuna dealer; *m* tuna fisherman; *f* tuna fishhook
**aturar** *va* (coll.) to close up tight
**aturbonar** *vr* to become overcast with thunderclouds
**aturdido -da** *adj* thoughtless, scatterbrained, reckless
**aturdidor -dora** *adj* amazing, bewildering, perplexing, deafening

**aturdimiento** *m* stun, stunning; amazement, bewilderment, confusion
**aturdir** *va* to stun; to amaze, bewilder, perplex; *vr* to be stunned; to be amazed, to become bewildered, to become perplexed
**aturrullamiento** *m* (coll.) bewilderment, perplexity
**aturrullar** *va* (coll.) to bewilder, to perplex, to dumbfound; *vr* (coll.) to become bewildered, become perplexed, become dumbfounded
**atusar** *va* to trim (*the hair*); to smooth (*the hair with hand and comb*); to trim (*plants*); *vr* to dress too fancily
**atutía** *f* tutty
**atuve** *1st sg pret ind of* **atener**
**auca** *f* (orn.) goose; (Am.) derby hat
**audacia** *f* audacity
**audaz** *adj* (*pl:* **-daces**) audacious
**audibilidad** *f* audibility
**audible** *adj* audible
**audición** *f* hearing; audition; concert; (law) hearing; (rad.) listening
**audiencia** *f* audience; audience chamber; hearing, listening; (law) hearing; royal tribunal; high court of justice (*in Spanish colony*); provincial high court
**audífono** *m* audiphone; hearing aid; earphone; handset
**audímetro** *m* audiometer
**audiofrecuencia** *f* (rad.) audio frequency
**audiología** *f* audiology
**audiómetro** *m* audiometer
**audión** *m* (rad.) audion
**audio-visual** *adj* audio-visual
**auditivo -va** *adj* auditory; *m* earpiece (*of telephone*)
**auditor** *m* judge advocate; auditor (*in school*); listener (*to radio*); (com.) auditor; **auditor de guerra** judge advocate (*in army*); **auditor de marina** judge advocate (*in navy*)
**auditoría** *f* judge advocate's office; (com.) auditorship
**auditorio** *m* audience; auditorium; studio, radio studio
**auge** *m* height, acme, zenith; boom; vogue; (astr.) apogee; **cobrar nuevo auge** to take on new life; **estar en auge** to be booming; to be in vogue; **tomar auge** to have great vogue, to be all the rage
**augita** *f* (mineral.) augite
**augur** *m* augur
**auguración** *f* auguring
**augurado** *m* augurate
**augural** *adj* augural, ominous, portentous
**augurar** *va* to augur; (Am.) to wish; *vn* to augur
**augurio** *m* augury; (Am.) wish, good wish
**augustal** *adj* Augustan
**augusto -ta** *adj* august; (*cap.*) *m* Augustus
**aula** *f* classroom, lecture room; (anat.) aula; (poet.) palace; **aula magna** assembly hall
**aulaga** *f* (bot.) furze, gorse
**aulagar** *m* furze field, gorse field
**áulico -ca** *adj* aulic; *m* aulic; courtier
**aulladero** *m* place where animals gather and howl
**aullador -dora** *adj* howling; *mf* howler; *m* (zool.) howler, howling monkey
**aullar** **§75** *vn* to howl
**aullido** *m* howl; (rad.) howling, squealing
**aúllo** *m* howl
**aumentación** *f* (rhet.) climax; (her.) augmentation
**aumentado -da** *adj* (mus.) augmented
**aumentador -dora** *adj* increasing, amplifying; *m* booster
**aumentar** *va* to augment, increase, enlarge; to promote; (coll.) to exaggerate; *vn* to augment, increase; *vr* to augment, increase; to multiply
**aumentativo -va** *adj & m* (gram.) augmentative
**aumento** *m* augmentation, increase, enlargement; promotion; **ir en aumento** to be on the increase
**aun** *adv* still; even; also; **ni aun** not even; neither; **aun cuando** although
**aún** *adv* still, yet
**aunar** **§75** *va* to join, unite; to mix, combine; *vr* to join, unite; to combine
**aunque** *conj* although, even though
**aúpa** *interj* up, up!; **de aúpa** (coll.) swanky
**aupar** **§75** *va* (coll.) to help up; to extol, praise; *vr* (coll.) to arise, to rise up, to be extolled, be praised
**aura** *f* gentle breeze; breath; popularity; dawn; orange (*color*); (orn.) turkey buzzard; (med.) aura
**aural** *adj* aural
**Aureliano** *m* Aurelian
**Aurelio, Marco** Marcus Aurelius
**áureo -a** *adj* aureate
**aureola** or **auréola** *f* (meteor. & theol.) aureole; (f.a. & fig.) aureole, halo
**aureolar** *va* to aureole, to halo; (Am.) to glorify
**aureomicina** *f* (pharm.) aureomycin
**aurícula** *f* (anat.) auricle; (bot.) auricula
**auriculado -da** *adj* (bot. & zool.) auriculate
**auricular** *adj* auricular; (anat.) auricular; *m* earpiece, receiver (*of telephone*); little finger; **auricular de casco** headphone
**aurífero -ra** *adj* auriferous, gold-bearing
**auriga** *m* (poet.) coachman, charioteer; (*cap.*) *m* (astr.) Auriga
**aurista** *mf* aurist
**aurora** *f* aurora, dawn; roseate hue; pink cheeks; (bot.) flower of an hour; (fig.) dawn, harbinger; (*cap.*) *f* (myth.) Aurora; **aurora austral** (meteor.) aurora australis; **aurora boreal** (meteor.) aurora borealis; **aurora polar** (meteor.) aurora
**auroral** *adj* auroral
**aurorino -na** *adj* (poet.) auroral
**aurragado -da** *adj* badly cultivated
**aurúspice** *m* var. of **arúspice**
**auscultación** *f* auscultation
**auscultar** *va* to auscultate; to sound out; *vn* to auscultate
**ausencia** *f* absence
**ausentado -da** *adj* absent
**ausentar** *va* to send away; *vr* to absent oneself
**ausente** *adj* absent; absent-minded; *mf* absentee;; *m* (law) missing person
**ausentismo** *m* absenteeism
**auspiciar** *va* (Am.) to support, foster, back
**auspicio** *m* auspice; **bajo los auspicios de** under the auspices of
**auspicioso -sa** *adj* (Am.) auspicious
**austeridad** *f* austerity
**austero -ra** *adj* austere; harsh, astringent; penitent; honest, incorruptible
**austral** *adj* austral
**Australasia, la** Australasia
**australasiático -ca** *adj & mf* Australasian
**australasino -na** *adj* Australasian
**Australia** *f* Australia
**australiano -na** *adj & mf* Australian
**Austria** *f* Austria
**austríaco -ca** *adj & mf* Austrian
**Austria-Hungría** *f* Austria-Hungary
**austro** *m* south wind
**austrohúngaro -ra** *adj & mf* Austro-Hungarian
**autarcía** *f* autarky (*economic self-sufficiency*)
**autárcico -ca** *adj* autarkic or autarkical
**autarquía** *f* autarchy; autarky (*economic self-sufficiency*)
**autárquico -ca** *adj* autarchic or autarchical; autarkic or autarkical
**auténtica** *f* see **auténtico**
**autenticación** *f* authentication
**autenticar** **§86** *va* to authenticate
**autenticidad** *f* authenticity
**auténtico -ca** *adj* authentic; real; *f* certification; certificate; **auténticas** *fpl* Authentics (*Novels of Justinian*)
**autillo** *m* (orn.) tawny owl; particular decree of Inquisition
**auto** *m* edict, judicial decree; short Biblical play; miracle play; auto; **auto de fe** auto-da-fe; **auto de prisión** commitment, warrant for arrest; **auto sacramental** Biblical play following a procession in honor of the Sacrament
**autoanálisis** *m* self-analysis
**autobiografía** *f* autobiography
**autobiográfico -ca** *adj* autobiographical
**autobiógrafo -fa** *mf* autobiographer

**autoblasto** *m* (biol.) autoblast
**autobomba** *f* motor pumper; motor fire engine
**autobombo** *m* self-glorification
**autobote** *m* powerboat, motorboat
**autobús** *m* (*pl:* **-buses**) bus, autobus
**autocamión** *m* autotruck, motor truck
**autocar** *m* bus, interurban bus; sightseeing bus
**autocarril** *m* (rail.) motorcar
**autocasa** *f* trailer (*mobile house*)
**autocebante** *adj* self-priming
**autoclave** *f* autoclave
**autoconciencia** *f* self-consciousness
**autocracia** *f* autocracy
**autócrata** *mf* autocrat
**autocrático -ca** *adj* autocratic
**autocrítica** *f* self-examination; self-criticism; criticism of a work by its author
**autoctonía** *f* autochthony
**autóctono -na** *adj* autochthonous; native; *mf* autochthon; native
**autodefensa** *f* self-defense
**autodestrucción** *f* self-destruction
**autodeterminación** *f* or **autodeterminismo** *m* (pol.) self-determination
**autodidacto -ta** *adj* self-taught, self-educated
**autodidaxia** *f* self-instruction
**autodirigido -da** *adj* self-directed
**autodisciplina** *f* self-discipline
**autodominio** *m* self-control
**autódromo** *m* automobile race course
**autoencendido** *m* self-ignition, pre-ignition
**autoenfriamiento** *m* self-cooling
**autoengaño** *m* self-deception
**autoenseñanza** *f* self-instruction
**auto-escuela** *f* driving school
**autofecundación** *f* (bot.) close fertilization
**autofretage** *m* autofrettage
**autogénesis** *f* (biol.) autogenesis
**autógeno -na** *adj* autogenous; *f* welding
**autogiro** *m* autogiro
**autogobierno** *m* self-government
**autografía** *f* autography
**autografiar** §90 *va* to autograph
**autográfico -ca** *adj* autographic
**autógrafo -fa** *adj & m* autograph
**autohipnosis** *f* autohypnosis, self-hypnotism
**autoinducción** *f* (elec.) self-induction
**autoinducido -da** *adj* (elec.) self-induced
**autoinductancia** *f* (elec.) self-inductance
**autoinfección** *f* (path.) autoinfection
**autointoxicación** *f* (path.) autointoxication
**autolicuador** *m* juice extractor
**autolimpiador -dora** *adj* self-cleaning
**automacia** *f* automatism
**autómata** *m* automaton; (coll.) automaton (*person*)
**automático -ca** *adj* automatic
**automatismo** *m* automatism
**automatización** *f* automation
**automatizar** §76 *va* to automate; (coll.) to make an automaton of, to deprive of independence
**automotor -tora** *adj* automotive; self-propelling; self-moving; *m* railway motor coach
**automotriz** *f* (*pl:* **-trices**) rail car, self-propelled railroad car
**automóvil** *adj & m* automobile
**automovilismo** *m* motoring; automobile industry
**automovilista** *adj* (pertaining to the) automobile; *mf* automobilist, motorist
**automovilístico -ca** *adj* (pertaining to the) automobile
**autonomía** *f* autonomy; cruising radius (*of a boat, airplane, etc.*)
**autonómico -ca** *adj* autonomic
**autonomista** *mf* autonomist
**autónomo -ma** *adj* autonomous, independent
**autopiano** *m* (Am.) player piano
**autopista** *f* automobile road, turnpike
**autoplastia** *f* (surg.) autoplasty
**autoplástico -ca** *adj* autoplastic
**autopolinización** *f* (bot.) self-pollination
**autopolinizar** §76 *va* (bot.) to self-pollinate
**autopropulsado -da** *adj* self-propelled
**autopropulsión** *f* self-propulsion
**autopropulsor -sora** *adj* self-propelling
**autoprotección** *f* self-protection
**autopsia** *f* autopsy
**autopsiar** *va* to autopsy
**autópsido -da** *adj* (mineral.) having metallic luster
**autor -tora** *mf* author; perpetrator (*of crime*); (archaic) theatrical manager; *f* authoress
**autoría** *f* (archaic) management of a theater
**autoridad** *f* authority; pomp, show, display
**autoritario -ria** *adj* authoritarian; authoritative; *mf* authoritarian
**autoritarismo** *m* authoritarianism
**autorización** *f* authorization
**autorizado -da** *adj* authoritative
**autorizamiento** *m* var. of **autorización**
**autorizar** §76 *va* to authorize; to legalize; to exalt, to enhance; **autorizar a** or **para** + *inf* to authorize to + *inf*
**autorradio** *m* auto radio
**autorreactor** *m* (aer.) ram-jet engine
**autorregistrador -dora** *adj* self-recording
**autorregulador -dora** *adj* self-regulating
**autorretrato** *m* self-portrait
**autorriel** *m* railway motor coach
**autoservicio** *m* self-service
**auto-stop** *m* hitchhiking; **hacer auto-stop** to hitchhike
**autosuficiencia** *f* self-sufficiency
**autosuficiente** *adj* self-sufficient
**autosugestión** *f* autosuggestion
**autosuperar** *vr* to outdo oneself
**autotaponador -dora** *adj* self-sealing
**auto-teatro** *m* drive-in motion-picture theater
**autotécnica** *f* automotive engineering
**autotécnico** *m* automotive engineer
**autótrofo -fa** *adj* (bot.) autotrophic
**autotropismo** *m* (bot.) autotropism
**autovía** *f* automobile road, turnpike; *m* railway motor coach
**autunita** *f* (mineral.) autunite
**Auvernia** *f* Auvergne
**auxiliador -dora** *adj* helping, aiding; *mf* helper, aider
**auxiliante** *adj* helping, aiding
**auxiliar** *adj* auxiliary; (gram.) auxiliary; *mf* auxiliary; aid, assistant; substitute teacher, professor's assistant; *m* (gram.) auxiliary (*verb*); §90 & **regular** *va* to help, aid, assist; to attend (*a dying person*)
**auxiliaría** *f* substitute teaching position; assistantship
**auxilio** *m* help, aid, assistance, relief; **acudir en auxilio a** or **de** to come to the help of; **primeros auxilios** first aid; **auxilio en carretera** (aut.) road service; **auxilio social** social work
**auxocromo** *m* (chem.) auxochrome
**avacado -da** *adj* cowlike, slow, heavy
**avadar** *vn & vr* to become fordable
**avahar** *va* to steam; to warm with vapor or breath; *vn* to steam, give out vapor; *vr* to steam, give out vapor; to warm one's hands with one's breath
**aval** *m* indorsement, backing; countersignature
**avalancha** *f* avalanche; (fig.) avalanche
**avalar** *va* (com.) to guarantee with an indorsement; to answer for (*a person*) with an indorsement; to enhance; to sanction; *vn* to shake with an earthquake
**avalentado -da** *adj* of a boaster or braggart; swaggering, bullying (*manner*)
**avalentonado -da** *adj* arrogant, boastful
**avalo** *m* slight movement; earthquake
**avalorar** *va* to estimate; to encourage
**avaluación** *f* valuation, appraisal
**avaluar** §33 *va* to appraise, estimate
**avalúo** *m* var. of **avaluación**
**avallar** *va* to wall in, to fence in
**avambrazo** *m* armlet (*of armor*)
**avance** *m* advance; payment in advance; removable front (*of carriage body*); (com.) balance; (com.) estimate; (mil.) advance, attack; (elec. & mach.) lead; (mach.) feed; (mov.) preview; **avance del encendido** (mach.) spark lead
**avante** *adv* (naut.) fore; **tomar por avante** (naut.) to broach to
**avantrén** *m* (mil.) limber
**avanzado -da** *adj* advanced; **avanzado de años** or **de edad** advanced in years; *f* (mil.) outpost, advance guard; (fig.) vanguard

**avanzar** §76 *va* to propose; to advance, increase; *vn* to advance; (com.) to have a favorable balance; (Am.) to vomit; *vr* to advance
**avanzo** *m* (com.) balance; (com.) estimate
**avaricia** *f* avarice
**avaricioso -sa** *adj* avaricious
**avariento -ta** *adj* avaricious, miserly; *mf* miser
**avaro -ra** *adj* miserly; *mf* miser
**avasallamiento** *m* subjection, enslavement
**avasallar** *va* to subject, enslave; *vr* to become a subject or vassal; to submit
**avatar** *m* avatar
**ave** *f* bird; fowl; **ave canora** songbird; **ave de corral** barnyard fowl; **ave del paraíso** bird of paradise; **ave de mar** seafowl; **ave de paso** bird of passage; (fig.) bird of passage; **ave de rapiña** bird of prey; **ave fría** (orn.) lapwing; **ave lira** (orn.) lyrebird; **ave nocturna** night bird; (fig.) night owl; **aves de cetrería** hawking birds; **ave tonta** (orn.) yellowhammer; **ave toro** (orn.) bittern, European bittern; **ave viajera** migratory bird; **ave zancuda** (orn.) wading bird
**avecilla** *f* birdie; **avecilla de las nieves** (orn.) wagtail
**avecinar** *va* to bring near; to domicile; *vr* to approach; to take up residence
**avecindamiento** *m* domicile; domiciliation
**avecindar** *va* to domicile; *vr* to take up residence, become a resident
**avechucho** *m* ugly bird; (coll.) scalawag, bum
**avefría** *f* (orn.) lapwing
**avejentado -da** *adj* aged, old-looking
**avejentar** *va & vr* to age before one's time
**avejigar** §59 *va, vn & vr* to vesicate, to blister
**avellana** *f* hazelnut; **avellana de la India** or **avellana índica** myrobalan
**avellanado -da** *adj* hazel, nut-brown; shriveled
**avellanador** *m* countersink, countersinking bit
**avellanal** *m* hazel plantation
**avellanar** *m* hazel plantation; *va* to countersink; *vr* to shrivel, shrivel up
**avellaneda** *f* or **avellanedo** *m* hazel plantation
**avellanero -ra** *mf* vendor of hazelnuts; *f* (bot.) hazel, hazel tree
**avellano** *m* (bot.) hazel
**avemaría** *f* Ave Maria; **al avemaría** at sunset; **en un avemaría** (coll.) in a twinkle; **saber como el avemaría** (coll.) to have a ready knowledge of
**Ave María** *interj* gracious goodness!
**avena** *f* (bot.) oats (*plant or seed*); (poet.) oat (*reed instrument*)
**avenado -da** *adj* fickle; crazy
**avenal** *m* oat field
**avenamiento** *m* draining, drainage
**avenar** *va* to drain
**avenate** *m* oatmeal gruel; (prov.) fit of madness
**avendré** *1st sg fut ind of* **avenir**
**avenencia** *f* deal, bargain; agreement
**avengo** *1st sg pres ind of* **avenir**
**avenido -da** *adj;* **bien avenidos** in agreement; **mal avenidos** in disagreement; *f* avenue; allée; flood, freshet; assemblage, gathering
**avenidor -dora** *mf* reconciler, mediator
**avenimiento** *m* reconciliation; agreement
**avenir** §92 *va* to reconcile; *vr* to agree, be reconciled; **avenirse a** to correspond to; to harken to; **avenirse a** + *inf* to agree to + *inf;* **avenirse con** to get along with
**aventador -dora** *adj* winnowing; *mf* winnower; *m* winnowing rake; blower, fan; esparto fan (*for fanning fire*); *f* winnowing machine
**aventadura** *f* (vet.) windgall
**aventajado -da** *adj* superior, outstanding, excellent; advantageous
**aventajar** *va* to advance, to raise, to give an advantage to; to put ahead, to prefer; to excel; *vr* to advance, to win an advantage; to excel
**aventamiento** *m* fanning; blowing; winnowing
**aventar** §18 *va* to fan; to blow; to winnow; to scatter to the winds; (coll.) to expel, drive away; *vr* to swell, swell up; (coll.) to flee, run away
**aventón** *m* (Am.) push; (Am.) lift (*free ride*); **pedir aventón** (Am.) to hitchhike
**aventura** *f* adventure; risk, danger, peril
**aventurado -da** *adj* venturesome, hazardous
**aventurar** *va* to adventure; to adventure, to hazard (*an opinion*); *vr* to adventure, take a risk; **aventurarse a** + *inf* to venture to + *inf;* to risk + *ger;* **quien no se aventura no pasa el mar** nothing venture nothing win
**aventurero -ra** *adj* adventurous, adventuresome, venturesome; *m* adventurer, soldier of fortune; *f* adventuress
**avergonzar** §98 *va* to shame, to put to shame; to embarrass; *vr* to be ashamed; to be embarrassed; **avergonzarse de** + *inf* to be ashamed to + *inf*
**avería** *f* aviary; flock of birds; breakdown, failure, damage, defect; (com.) damage; (naut.) average; **localizar averías** to shoot trouble; **avería gruesa** (naut.) general or gross average
**averiable** *adj* damageable, perishable
**averiar** §90 *va* to damage; *vr* to suffer damage, be damaged; to break down
**averiguable** *adj* ascertainable
**averiguación** *f* ascertainment; inquiry
**averiguador -dora** *adj* investigating, inquiring; *mf* investigator, inquirer
**averiguamiento** *m* var. of **averiguación**
**averiguar** §23 *va* to ascertain, find out
**averío** *m* flock of birds
**Averno** *m* (myth.) Avernus; hell
**averroísmo** *m* Averroism
**averroísta** *mf* Averroist
**averrugado -da** *adj* full of warts, warty
**averrugar** §59 *vr* to become warty
**aversión** *f* aversion; **cobrar aversión a** to take a dislike for
**avestruz** *m* (*pl:* **-truces**) (orn.) ostrich; (coll.) blockhead; **avestruz de América** or **de la pampa** (orn.) American ostrich, rhea
**avetado -da** *adj* veined, streaked
**avetarda** *f* var. of **avutarda**
**avetoro** *m* (orn.) bittern, European bittern
**avezar** §76 *va* to accustom; *vr* to become accustomed; **avezarse a** + *inf* to accustom oneself to + *inf*, to become accustomed to + *inf*
**aviación** *f* aviation; aviation corps
**aviador -dora** *adj* preparing, equipping; flying; *mf* preparer, equipper; aviator, flyer; *m* aviator, airman; (mil.) airman; (naut.) caulker's auger; (Am.) mining moneylender; **aviador postal** air-mail pilot; *f* airwoman, aviatrix
**aviar** *adj* (pertaining to a) bird; §90 *va* to get ready, prepare; (coll.) to equip, provide; (Am.) to lend (*money or equipment*); **estar, encontrarse** or **quedar aviado** (coll.) to be in a mess, to be in a jam; **dejar aviado** (coll.) to leave in the lurch; *vn* (coll.) to hurry, make haste; (aer.) to take off
**aviatorio -ria** *adj* (pertaining to) aviation
**aviatriz** *f* (*pl:* **-trices**) aviatrix
**avícola** *adj* bird-raising
**avicultor** *m* bird fancier, bird keeper
**avicultura** *f* aviculture
**avidez** *f* avidity, greediness
**ávido -da** *adj* avid, greedy, thirsty
**aviejar** *va & vr* to age before one's time
**avienta** *f* winnowing
**aviento** *m* long-pronged rakelike winnowing fork; pitchfork
**avieso -sa** *adj* distorted, irregular; evil-minded, perverse
**avigorar** *va* to invigorate, revive
**avilantar** *vr* to be insolent
**avilantez** *f* or **avilanteza** *f* boldness, insolence; meanness
**avilés -lesa** *adj* (pertaining to) Ávila; *mf* native or inhabitant of Ávila
**avillanado -da** *adj* rustic, peasant
**avillanamiento** *m* boorishness, debasement
**avillanar** *va* to make boorish, to debase; *vr* to become boorish, to become debased
**avinagrado -da** *adj* (coll.) vinegarish, crabbed
**avinagrar** *va* to sour, to make sour; *vr* to sour, to turn sour; to turn into vinegar
**avine** *1st sg pret ind of* **avenir**
**aviniendo** *ger of* **avenir**
**Aviñón** *f* Avignon
**aviñonense** or **aviñonés -nesa** *adj* (pertaining to) Avignon; *mf* native or inhabitant of Avignon

**avío** *m* preparation, provision; (Am.) loan; **avíos** *mpl* tools, equipment, outfit; **¡al avío!** hurry up!

**avión** *m* airplane; (orn.) martin; **avión a turbohélice** (aer.) turbo-prop plane; **avión birreactor** (aer.) twin-jet plane; **avión cohete** (aer.) rocket plane; **avión convertible** (aer.) convertiplane; **avión de caza** (aer.) pursuit plane; **avión de combate** (aer.) fighter; **avión a chorro, de chorro, de propulsión a chorro** or **a reacción** (aer.) jet plane; **avión de transporte** (aer.) transport; **avión de travesía** (aer.) air liner; **avión interceptor** (aer.) interceptor; **avión militar** (aer.) warplane; **avión transporte** (aer.) transport

**avión-correo** *m* mailplane

**avioneta** *f* (aer.) small plane

**avión-nodriza** *m* var. of **aeroplano-nodriza**

**avisacoches** *m* (*pl:* **-ches**) car caller

**avisado -da** *adj* prudent, wise; **mal avisado** rash, thoughtless

**avisador -dora** *adj* warning; *mf* informer, announcer; adviser, admonisher; *m* electric bell; **avisador de incendio** fire alarm

**avisar** *va* to advise, inform; to warn, admonish; to report on; **avisar a una persona una cosa** to notify a person of or about something

**aviso** *m* advice, information, notice; warning, admonishment; prudence, attention, care; dispatch boat; **poner sobre aviso de** to keep (*someone*) on the lookout for; **sobre aviso** on the lookout, on the watch

**avispa** *f* (ent.) wasp; crafty person; **avispa cavadora** (ent.) digger wasp; **avispa de barro** (ent.) mason wasp

**avispado -da** *adj* (coll.) brisk, lively, clever, wide-awake

**avispar** *va* to spur (*a horse*); (coll.) to stir up, prod, enliven; *vr* (coll.) to become stirred up; to fret, to worry

**avispero** *m* wasp's nest; swarm of wasps; mass of boils; (coll.) mess, complicated affair

**avispón** *m* (ent.) hornet

**avistar** *va* to descry; *vr* to have an interview

**avitaminosis** *f* (path.) avitaminosis

**avitelado -da** *adj* (pertaining to or like) vellum

**avituallamiento** *m* victualing, provisioning

**avituallar** *va* to victual; to supply, to provision; *vr* to victual

**avivadamente** *adv* briskly, lively

**avivador -dora** *adj* reviving, enlivening; *m* (arch.) quirk; plane for making quirks

**avivamiento** *m* reviving, enlivening

**avivar** *va* to revive, enliven, brighten; *vn & vr* to revive, brighten

**avizor** *m* watcher; **avizores** *mpl* (slang) eyes

**avizorador -dora** *mf* watcher, spyer

**avizorar** *va* to watch; *vr* to hide and watch, to spy

**avocación** *f* or **avocamiento** *m* (law) removal to a superior court

**avocar** **§86** *va* (law) to remove to a superior court

**avoceta** *f* (orn.) avocet

**avolcanado -da** *adj* volcanic

**avora** *f* (bot.) oil palm

**avucasta** *f* var. of **avutarda**

**avugo** *m* small early pear

**avuguero** *m* (bot.) pear tree

**avulsión** *f* (law) avulsion; (surg.) extirpation, excision

**avuncular** *adj* avuncular

**avutarda** *f* (orn.) great bustard

**avutardado -da** *adj* like a great bustard

**ax** *interj* ow!, ouch!

**axial** or **axil** *adj* axial

**axila** *f* (anat. & zool.) axilla; (bot.) axil or axilla

**axilar** *adj* axile; axillar; axillary; *f* (ent.) axillar

**axinita** *f* (mineral) axinite

**axiología** *f* axiology

**axioma** *m* axiom

**axiomático -ca** *adj* axiomatic

**axión** *m* (anat.) axion

**axis** *m* (*pl:* **-xis**) (anat.) axis; (zool.) axis deer

**axo** *m* square woolen cloth, worn by Peruvian women

**axoideo -a** *adj* (anat.) axoid, axoidean

**axón** *m* (anat.) axon; (anat. & physiol.) axon or axone

**ay** *m* sigh; *interj* alas!; ouch!; **¡ay de . . . !** woe to . . . !; **¡ay de mí!** ay me!, woe is me!

**aya** *f* governess, instructress

**ayate** *m* (Am.) cloth of maguey fiber

**ayatito** *m* (bot.) sego, sego lily

**Áyax** *m* (myth.) Ajax; **Áyax el Pequeño** (myth.) Ajax the Less

**ayear** *vn* to sigh, to utter sighs

**ayeaye** *m* (zool.) aye-aye

**ayer** *adv & m* yesterday

**ayo** *m* tutor

**ayocote** *m* (bot.) scarlet runner, scarlet runner bean

**ayuda** *f* aid, help, assistance; enema; **ayuda de parroquia** chapel of ease; *m* page; **ayuda de cámara** valet de chambre

**ayudador -dora** *adj* helping; *mf* helper

**ayudanta** *f* aid, assistant; (Am.) substitute (*teacher*); **ayudanta de cocina** kitchenmaid

**ayudante** *m* aid, assistant; (mil.) adjutant; **ayudante de campo** (mil.) aide-de-camp; **ayudante de profesor** assistant professor; **ayudante general** (mil.) adjutant general; *adj* assistant, adjutant

**ayudantía** *f* assistantship; (mil.) adjutancy

**ayudar** *va* to aid, help, assist; **ayudar a** + *inf* to help to + *inf*, to help + *inf*

**ayuga** *f* (bot.) mock cypress

**ayunador -dora** *adj* fasting; *mf* faster

**ayunar** *vn* to fast; to deprive oneself; (coll.) to go hungry

**ayuno -na** *adj* fasting; deprived; uninformed; **en ayunas** or **en ayuno** fasting, before breakfast; **estar** or **quedarse en ayunas** or **en ayuno** to be uninformed; to not catch on, to miss the point; *m* fast, fasting; **ayuno natural** fasting from midnight on

**ayunque** *m* anvil

**ayuntamiento** *m* town or city council, municipal government; town or city hall; sexual intercourse

**ayustar** *va* (naut.) to splice; (naut.) to scarf

**ayuste** *m* (naut.) splicing, splice; (naut.) scarfing, scarf

**azabachado -da** *adj* jet, jet-black

**azabache** *m* (mineral.) jet; (orn.) coal titmouse; **azabaches** *mpl* jet trinkets

**azabachero** *m* jet worker; jet vendor

**azabara** *f* (bot.) aloe

**azacán -cana** *adj* menial, drudging; *mf* drudge; *m* water carrier

**azacanar** *vr* to toil, drudge

**azacaya** *f* (prov.) water pipe

**azache** *adj* inferior (*said of silk from outside of cocoon*)

**azada** *f* hoe; blow with hoe

**azadazo** *m* blow with hoe

**azadilla** *f* little hoe; dibble, weeding hoe

**azadón** *m* hoe; grub hoe; **azadón de peto** or **de pico** mattock

**azadonada** *f* blow with a hoe

**azadonar** *va* to hoe, hoe up, dig with a hoe

**azadonazo** *m* var. of **azadonada**

**azadonero** *m* hoer

**azafata** *f* lady of the queen's wardrobe; (aer.) air hostess, stewardess

**azafate** *m* low, flat basket, tray, waiter

**azafrán** *m* (bot.) saffron; saffron (*stigmas and color*); (naut.) rudder frame; **azafrán bastardo, romí,** or **romín** (bot.) bastard saffron

**azafranado -da** *adj* saffron, saffroned

**azafranal** *m* saffron plantation

**azafranar** *va* to saffron (*to color or flavor*)

**azafranero -ra** *mf* saffron grower; saffron dealer

**azagadero** or **azagador** *m* cattle path

**azagaya** *f* assagai, javelin

**azahar** *m* orange blossom, lemon blossom, citron blossom

**azainadamente** *adv* perfidiously

**azalá** *m* (*pl:* **-laes**) Mohammedan prayer

**azalea** *f* (bot.) azalea

**azamboa** *f* citron (*fruit*)

**azamboero** *m* or **azamboo** *m* (bot.) citron (*tree*)

**azanahoriate** *m* preserved carrot; (coll.) insincere flattery

**azanca** *f* underground spring
**azar** *m* chance, hazard; accident, misfortune; fate, lot, destiny; losing card; losing throw (*at dice*); Jonah (*that which brings bad luck*); cushion side (*of billiard pocket*); hazard (*in a game*); **al azar** at random
**azarandar** *va* var. of **zarandar**
**azarar** *vr* to go awry; to get rattled
**azarbe** *m* irrigation trench
**azarbeta** *f* little irrigation trench
**azarcón** *m* minium; earthen pot; bright orange (*color*)
**azarja** *f* reel for winding raw silk
**azarolla** *f* var. of **acerola**
**azarollo** *m* var. of **acerolo**
**azaroso -sa** *adj* risky, hazardous; unfortunate
**Azerbeiyán, el** Azerbaijan
**ázimo -ma** *adj* azymous, unleavened
**azimut** *m* (*pl:* **-muts**) var. of **acimut**
**azimutal** *adj* var. of **acimutal**
**aznacho** *m* (bot.) Scotch pine
**aznallo** *m* (bot.) Scotch pine; (bot.) restharrow
**-azo -za** *suffix aug* e.g., **bribonazo** big rascal; **bocaza** big mouth; *suffix m* blow, e.g., **escobazo** blow with a broom; **puñetazo** blow with the fist, punch; shot, e.g., **cañonazo** cannon shot; **fusilazo** gunshot; wound, e.g., **flechazo** arrow wound; **sablazo** saber wound
**azoado -da** *adj* nitrogenous
**azoar** *va* to fix nitrogen in
**azoato** *m* nitrate
**ázoe** *m* (chem.) azote, nitrogen
**azofaifa** *f* var. of **azufaifa**
**azofaifo** *m* var. of **azufaifo**
**azófar** *m* brass, latten
**azogado -da** *adj* (coll.) restless, fidgety, turbulent; *m* quicksilver foil (*of a mirror*); **temblar como un azogado** (coll.) to shake like a leaf
**azogamiento** *m* quicksilver coating, silvering; (coll.) shaking, agitation, confusion
**azogar §59** *va* to coat with quicksilver, to silver (*a mirror*); *vr* to have mercurialism or mercury poisoning; (coll.) to shake, to become agitated, to become confused
**azogue** *m* quicksilver, mercury; market place; (coll.) mirror; **ser un azogue** (coll.) to be restless
**azoguejo** *m* small market place
**azoguería** *f* amalgamation works
**azoguero** *m* amalgamator; dealer in quicksilver
**azoico -ca** *adj* (chem. & geol.) azoic
**azolar §77** *va* to adz, to dub
**azolvar** *vr* to silt up, become obstructed
**azor** *m* (orn.) goshawk
**azoramiento** *m* excitement, confusion
**azorar** *va* to abash, disturb; to excite, stir up; *vr* to be abashed, be disturbed; to get excited, become upset
**Azores** *fpl* Azores
**azorramiento** *m* drowsiness; heavy-headedness; headache
**azorrar** *va* (naut.) to overload (*a boat*); *vr* to get drowsy; (naut.) to become threatening (*said of the atmosphere*); (naut.) to pitch (*from being overloaded*); (slang) to get drunk
**azotable** *adj* deserving a beating
**azotacalles** *mf* (*pl:* **-lles**) (coll.) gadabout, loafer; *f* (coll.) piano teacher
**azotado -da** *adj* variegated; *m* criminal whipped in public; penitent
**azotador -dora** *adj* whipping; *mf* whipper, flogger
**azotaina** *f* (coll.) whipping, flogging, spanking
**azotalenguas** *f* (bot.) bedstraw
**azotar** *va* to whip, to horsewhip, to scourge; to beat with the tail or the wings; to flail; to beat upon, beat down upon
**azotazo** *m* lash, lashing; slap, spanking
**azote** *m* whip; lash, spanking; (fig.) scourge; **el azote de Dios** the Scourge of God (*Attila*); **azotes y galeras** (coll.) tiresome fare
**azotea** *f* flat roof
**azotina** *f* (coll.) var. of **azotaina**
**azteca** *adj & mf* Aztec; *m* Aztec (*language*)
**aztor** *m* var. of **azor**
**azúcar** *m & f* sugar; **azúcar blanco** refined sugar; **azúcar cande** or **candi** rock candy; **azúcar de arce** maple sugar; **azúcar de flor** refined sugar; **azúcar de fruta** (chem.) fruit sugar; **azúcar de leche** sugar of milk; **azúcar de malta** malt sugar; **azúcar de plomo** (chem.) sugar of lead; **azúcar de remolacha** beet sugar; **azúcar de uva** grape sugar; **azúcar en polvo** powdered sugar; **azúcar en terrón** lump sugar; **azúcar moreno** or **negro** brown sugar
**azucarado -da** *adj* sugared, sugary; (coll.) sugary
**azucarar** *va* to sugar, to coat or ice with sugar; (coll.) to sugar, sugar over
**azucarera** *f* see **azucarero**
**azucarería** *f* (Am.) sugar store
**azucarero -ra** *adj* (pertaining to) sugar; *m* sugar master, sugar expert; confectioner; sugar bowl; (orn.) honey creeper; *f* sugar bowl; sugar refinery
**azucarillo** *m* brittle sugar bar (*made of sugar, white of egg, and lemon juice and used to sweeten water*)
**azucena** *f* (bot.) Madonna lily; **azucena amarilla** (bot.) day lily; **azucena atigrada** (bot.) tiger lily
**azucenilla** *f* (bot.) night-blooming gladiolus (*Gladiolus tristis*)
**azuche** *m* pile shoe
**azud** *m* or **azuda** *f* irrigation water wheel; dam, diversion dam
**azuela** *f* adz, chip ax
**azufaifa** *f* jujube (*fruit*)
**azufaifo** *m* (bot.) jujube (*tree*)
**azufrado -da** *adj* (pertaining to or like) sulfur; *m* sulfuring
**azufrador -dora** *adj* sulfuring; *m* drying machine; sulfuring machine (*for grapevines*)
**azufral** *m* sulfur mine
**azuframiento** *m* sulfuring, sulfuration
**azufrar** *va* to sulfur, sulfurate, sulphurize
**azufre** *m* (chem.) sulfur; brimstone; **azufre cañón** or **en canuto** roll sulfur; **azufre vegetal** (bot.) club moss
**azufrera** *f* sulfur mine
**azufrón** *m* powdered pyrites
**azufroso -sa** *adj* sulphury, sulphureous
**azul** *adj & m* blue; **dar el azul a** (coll.) to put on probation; **azul celeste** sky blue; **azul de mar** navy blue; **azul de metileno** methylene blue; **azul de Prusia** Prussian blue; **azul de ultramar** ultramarine (*pigment and color*); **azul marino** navy blue; **azul turquesa** turquoise blue; **azul turquí** indigo (*color*)
**azulado -da** *adj* blue, bluish
**azulaque** *m* var. of **zulaque**
**azular** *va* to color blue, to dye blue; *vr* to turn blue
**azulear** *va* to turn blue; *vn* to have a bluish cast, to look bluish, to turn blue
**azulejar** *va* to tile, cover with tiles
**azulejería** *f* tilework; tilemaking
**azulejero** *m* tilemaker
**azulejo** *m* glazed colored tile; (bot.) bluebottle, bachelor's-button; (orn.) bee eater; (orn.) indigo bunting; **azulejo antisonoro** acoustical tile
**azulenco -ca** *adj* blue, bluish
**azulete** *m* bluish cast, bluish hue; bluing
**azulino -na** *adj* bluish
**azuloso -sa** *adj* (Am.) bluish
**azumar** *va* to dye and oil (*the hair*)
**azumbrado -da** *adj* measured in azumbres; (coll.) drunk
**azumbre** *m* azumbre (*liquid measure: about 2 liters*)
**azur** *m* (her.) azure
**azurita** *f* (mineral.) azurite
**azuzamiento** *m* sicking; (coll.) teasing
**azuzar §76** *va* to sic (*a dog*); (coll.) to tease, stir up, incite
**azuzón -zona** *mf* (slang) troublemaker

# B

**B, b** *f* second letter of the Spanish alphabet
**B.** abr. of **Beato** and **Bueno** (*en examen*)
**baba** *f* drivel, spittle, slobber; mucus (*viscid animal secretion*); **caérsele a uno la baba** (coll.) to be overwhelmed with joy
**babada** *f* (vet.) stifle
**babador** *m* bib; apron top
**babaza** *f* froth, slobber; slime; (zool.) slug
**babazorro** *m* (coll.) boor, ill-bred fellow
**babear** *vn* to slobber, to drivel; to foam, to froth; (coll.) to be fascinated (*by a person of the opposite sex*); (coll.) to be overattentive (*to a woman*)
**babel** *m & f* babel, bedlam, confusion; (*cap.*) *m & f* Babel
**babeo** *m* slobbering, driveling
**babera** *f* beaver (*of helmet*); bib
**babero** *m* bib
**baberol** *m* beaver (*of helmet*)
**Babia** *f* mountainous region of León; **estar en Babia** to be absent-minded, to be stargazing
**babicha** *mf* (Am.) Italian; *m* (Am.) Italian (*language*); (Am.) cigar stump; **babichas** *fpl* (Am.) leavings; (Am.) dregs of pulque
**babieca** *adj* (coll.) simple, ignorant; *mf* (coll.) simpleton, ignoramus
**Babilonia** *f* see **babilonio**
**babilónico -ca** *adj* Babylonian; (fig.) Babylonian (*magnificent*)
**babilonio -nia** *adj & mf* Babylonian; *f* babel; confusion; (*cap.*) *f* Babylonia (*ancient empire*); Babylon (*ancient city; any great, rich, and wicked city*)
**babilla** *f* (vet.) stifle
**babirusa** *m* (zool.) babirusa
**bable** *m* Asturian (*dialect*); patois
**babor** *m* (naut.) port, larboard; **a babor** (naut.) aport; **de babor a estribor** (naut.) athwartships
**babosa** *f* see **baboso**
**babosear** *va* to slobber over
**baboso -sa** *adj* slobbery; immature, unfit; filthy, unkempt; (coll.) mushy (*with women*); (Am.) idiotic; *mf* (Am.) fool; *m* (ichth.) butterfly fish; *f* (zool.) slug
**babucha** *f* slipper; mule, heelless slipper
**babuíno** *m* (zool.) baboon
**baca** *f* top of stagecoach (*for passengers or baggage*); rainproof cover for stagecoach
**bacalada** *f* cured codfish
**bacaladero -ra** *adj* (pertaining to) codfish
**bacalao** or **bacallao** *m* codfish; (coll.) shriveled person; (Am.) cold-blooded person
**bacallar** *m* peasant, country fellow
**bacán** *m* (Am.) sport, bawd, pimp
**bacanal** *adj* bacchanal; bacchanalian; *f* bacchanal, bacchanalia (*orgy*); **bacanales** *fpl* bacchanals, Bacchanalia
**bacante** *f* bacchante; drunken, riotous woman; **bacantes** *fpl* Bacchae
**bácara** *f* (bot.) clary
**bacará** *m* baccara
**bácaris** *f* var. of **bácara**
**bacelar** *m* grape arbor; new vineyard
**bacera** *f* (vet.) anthrax, splenic fever
**baceta** *f* widow (*in card playing*)
**bacía** *f* basin, vessel; shaving dish
**bacífero -ra** *adj* (bot.) bacciferous
**báciga** *f* three-card game
**bacilar** *adj* bacillary
**bacilo** *m* bacillus; (anat.) rod (*in retina*)
**bacillar** *m* grape arbor; new vineyard
**bacín** *m* big chamber pot; poor box; (coll.) cur
**bacinada** *f* contents thrown from chamber pot; (coll.) contemptible action
**bacinero -ra** *mf* person who passes the plate for the poor box
**bacineta** *f* little chamber pot; small poor box; pan (*of gunlock*)
**bacinete** *m* basinet; cuirassier; (anat.) pelvis
**bacinica** or **bacinilla** *f* little chamber pot; small poor box
**Baco** *m* (myth.) Bacchus; (fig.) wine
**baconiano -na** *adj* Baconian
**baconista** *mf* Baconian
**bacteria** *f* bacterium
**bacteriano -na** *adj* bacterial
**bactericida** *adj* bactericidal; *m* bactericide
**bacteriófago** *m* (bact.) bacteriophage
**bacteriólisis** *f* bacteriolysis
**bacteriología** *f* bacteriology
**bacteriológico -ca** *adj* bacteriological
**bacteriólogo -ga** *mf* bacteriologist
**bacteriostasis** *f* (bact.) bacteriostasis
**bacteriostático -ca** *adj* bacteriostatic
**bactriano -na** *adj & mf* Bactrian
**báculo** *m* stick, staff; aid, consolation; **báculo del obispo, báculo pastoral** crozier, bishop's crozier
**bache** *m* hole, rut, pothole; sweating room for sheep (*to prepare them for shearing*); (radar) blip; **bache aéreo** (aer.) air pocket
**bachear** *va* to fill the ruts and holes in (*a road*)
**bachiller -llera** *adj* garrulous, loquacious; *mf* garrulous person, babbler; **bachiller** *mf* bachelor (*holder of degree*)
**bachilleramiento** *m* conferring the bachelor's degree; receiving the bachelor's degree
**bachillerar** *va* to confer the bachelor's degree on; *vr* to receive the bachelor's degree
**bachillerato** *m* baccalaureate, bachelor's degree
**bachillerear** *vn* to babble, prattle
**bachillería** *f* (coll.) babble, prattle; (coll.) gossip, groundless rumor
**bachorno** *m* (Am.) drudgery
**bachornoso -sa** *adj* (Am.) toilsome, laborious
**bada** *f* (zool.) rhinoceros
**badajada** *f* stroke (*of a bell*); (coll.) idle talk, nonsense
**badajazo** *m* stroke (*of a bell*)
**badajear** *vn* (coll.) to talk nonsense
**badajo** *m* clapper (*of bell*); (coll.) prattler, blatherskite
**badajocense** or **badajoceño -ña** *adj* (pertaining to) Badajoz; *mf* native or inhabitant of Badajoz
**badal** *m* muzzle; twitch (*to twist a horse's lip*)
**badán** *m* trunk (*of animal body*)
**badana** *f* (dressed) sheepskin; **zurrarle a uno la badana** (coll.) to tan someone's hide; (coll.) to give one a raking over the coals
**badazas** *fpl* (naut.) bonnet lacing
**badea** *f* tasteless melon; (coll.) dullard; (coll.) triviality
**badén** *m* gully, gutter (*channel made by rain water*); thank-you-ma'am; paved trench for a stream across a road; dry bed of stream
**baderna** *f* (naut.) thrummed cable
**badián** *m* (bot.) Chinese anise
**badiana** *f* (bot.) Chinese anise; badian (*fruit*)
**badil** *m* fire shovel
**badila** *f* fire shovel; **dar con la badila en los nudillos a** to rap the knuckles of; **badila de mesa** crumb tray
**badilazo** *m* blow with a fire shovel
**badilejo** *m* mason's trowel
**badomía** *f* nonsense, absurdity
**badulaque** *m* (coll.) nincompoop; (obs.) paint, make-up; (obs.) chopped-lung stew; (Am.) hell-raiser
**Baedeker** *m* Baedeker (*guidebook*)
**baga** *f* head of flax; (prov.) rope used to tie packs on beasts of burden

**bagacera** *f* bagasse drier
**bagaje** *m* beast of burden; military baggage
**bagajero** *m* driver of army beasts
**bagar** §59 *vn* to go to seed (*said of flax*)
**bagarino** *m* volunteer oarsman, paid oarsman (*not a slave*)
**bagasa** *f* prostitute, harlot, loose woman
**bagatela** *f* trinket; bagatelle, triviality; pinball
**bagazo** *m* bagasse; pressed pulp; flax straw, flax husk
**bagre** *adj* (Am.) showy, gaudy; (Am.) coarse, ill-bred; *m* (ichth.) catfish
**bagual** *adj* (Am.) wild, untamed; (Am.) dull, doltish
**baguarí** *m* (*pl:* **-ríes**) (orn.) South American crane
**baguío** *m* baguio (*cyclone in the Philippine Islands*)
**bah** *interj* bah!
**baharí** *m* (*pl:* **-ríes**) (orn.) sparrow hawk
**bahía** *f* bay
**bahorrina** *f* (coll.) slop; (coll.) riffraff
**bahuno -na** *adj* var. of **bajuno**
**baila** *f* (ichth.) hogfish
**bailable** *adj* danceable; with dancing; *m* ballet
**bailadero** *m* public dance hall, dance floor
**bailador -dora** *mf* dancer
**bailar** *va* to dance (*e.g., a polka*); to spin (*a top*); *vn* to dance; (fig.) to dance; to spin (*said of a top*); to wobble
**bailarín -rina** *mf* dancer; *m* dancer (*professional*); **bailarín de cuerda** ropedancer; *f* ballerina; **bailarina ombliguista** (coll.) belly dancer
**baile** *m* dance, ball; ballet; bailiff; **baile de etiqueta** dress ball, formal dance; **baile de los globos** bubble dance; **baile de máscaras** masquerade ball; **baile de San Vito** (path.) Saint Vitus's dance; **baile de trajes** costume ball, fancy ball; **baile serio** dress ball, formal dance
**bailete** *m* short ballet
**bailía** *f* bailiwick
**bailiaje** *m* commandery in the order of Malta
**bailiazgo** *m* bailiwick
**bailío** *m* knight commander of Malta
**bailotear** *vn* (coll.) to dance a lot and without grace, to hop about
**bailoteo** *m* (coll.) awkward dancing, hopping around
**baivel** *m* bevel square
**baja** *f* see **bajo**
**bajá** *m* (*pl:* **-jaes**) pasha
**bajaca** *f* (Am.) hair ribbon
**bajada** *f* slope; descent; swoop; (rad.) lead-in wire; **bajada de aguas** spout, downspout; **bajada de antena** (rad.) lead-in wire
**bajadizo -za** *adj* sloping gently, easy to go down
**bajagua** *f* (Am.) poor tobacco
**bajamanero** *m* (slang) sneak thief
**bajamar** *f* (naut.) low tide
**bajar** *va* to lower, to let down; to bring down; to descend, to go down (*stairs*); to bend down; to humble; *vn* to go down, to come down; to get off; **bajar de** to get off (*e.g., a trolley car*); *vr* to bend down; to humble oneself
**bajel** *m* ship, vessel
**bajelero** *m* boatman, skipper, master
**bajero -ra** *adj* lower, under
**bajete** *m* (coll.) shorty; (mus.) baritone; (mus.) counterpoint exercise
**bajeza** *f* lowness; lowliness, meanness, vileness
**bajial** *m* (Am.) winter marshland
**bajío** *m* shoal, sand bank; (Am.) lowland
**bajista** *mf* bear (*in stock market*); (mus.) bass viol player
**bajo -ja** *adj* low, lower, under; short (*in stature*); common, mean, vile; shallow; downcast; poor (*wine*); (mus.) bass; **por lo bajo** on the sly, secretly; (coll.) under one's breath; **bajo de cuerpo** short; *m* shoal, sandbank; (mus.) bass (*voice, score, singer, instrument, etc.*); **bajo profundo** (mus.) basso profundo; *f* fall, drop (*in prices*); casualty (*in war*); canceled subscription; **dar baja, ir de baja** or **ir en baja** to go down, to decline (*said, e.g., of prices*); **dar de baja** to drop (*from a list, society, etc.*); (mil.) to mark absent; **darse de baja** to drop out; **jugar a la baja** to bear the market; **bajo** *adv* down; low, in a low voice; **bajo** *prep* under
**bajoalemán -mana** *adj* Low-German; *m* Low German
**bajoca** *f* (prov.) string bean; (prov.) dead silkworm
**bajón** *m* decline, drop (*in health, wealth, etc.*); (mus.) bassoon; bassoon player
**bajonista** *mf* bassoon player, bassoonist
**bajorrelieve** *m* bas-relief
**bajuno -na** *adj* low, mean, vile
**bajura** *f* lowness, low or deep place, depth; shortness (*of stature*)
**bakelita** *f* var. of **baquelita**
**Bakú** *f* Baku
**bala** *f* bullet; bale (*of paper, cotton, etc.*); **bala dumdum** dumdum bullet; **bala fría** spent bullet; **bala perdida** stray bullet; **balas enramadas** (mil.) chain shot
**Balaán** *m* (Bib.) Balaam
**balaca** *f* (Am.) boast, boasting, bravado
**balacera** *f* (Am.) firing, shooting, stray shooting
**balada** *f* ballad; (mus.) ballade
**baladí** *adj* (*pl:* **-díes**) frivolous, trivial, paltry
**balador -dora** *adj* bleating, baaing
**baladrar** *vn* to scream, screech, whoop
**baladre** *m* (bot.) oleander, rosebay
**baladrero -ra** *adj* screaming, screeching; loud-mouthed
**baladro** *m* scream, screech, whoop
**baladrón -drona** *adj* boastful; *mf* boaster, braggart
**baladronada** *f* boasting, bragging; boastful word or deed
**baladronear** *vn* to boast, brag; to speak or act boastfully
**bálago** *m* chaff (*of hay or rye*); heap of chaff; soapsuds
**balaguero** *m* heap of chaff
**balaj** *m* or **balaje** *m* balas (*ruby spinel*)
**balalaika** *f* (mus.) balalaika
**balance** *m* rocking, swinging; hesitation, uncertainty; (com.) balancing, balance, balance sheet; (aer. & naut.) rolling; (Am.) rocking chair
**balancear** *va* to balance; *vn* to rock, swing; *vr* to rock, swing; to hesitate, waver
**balanceo** *m* balancing; rocking, swinging; hesitation
**balancero** *m* var. of **balanzario**
**balancín** *m* balance beam; rocker arm; singletree; (naut.) outrigger (*e.g., of canoe*); ropewalker's balancing pole; seesaw; balancer, halter (*of insect*)
**balandra** *f* (naut.) sloop
**balandrán** *m* cassock
**balandro** *m* (naut.) small sloop, fishing smack
**bálano** or **balano** *m* (anat.) glans of penis; (zool.) acorn barnacle
**balante** *adj* bleating
**balanza** *f* balance, scales; comparison, judgment; **en balanza** in the balance; **balanza de comercio** balance of trade; **balanza de compensación** (horol.) compensation balance; **balanza de pagos** balance of payments; **balanza de precisión** precision balance; **balanza de torsión** (phys.) torsion balance; (*cap.*) *f* (astr.) Scales
**balanzario** *m* weighmaster (*in mint*)
**balanzón** *m* cleaning pan (*of silversmith*)
**balar** *vn* to bleat; **balar por** (coll.) to pine for, to cry for
**balarrasa** *f* (coll.) strong brandy
**balastar** *va* (rail.) to ballast
**balasto** *m* (rail.) ballast
**balata** *f* (bot.) balata, bully tree
**balate** *m* terrace; narrow slope; edge, border (*of a ditch*); (zool.) slug
**balausta** *f* balausta (*any fruit like pomegranate*)
**balaustra** *f* (bot.) pomegranate tree
**balaustrado -da** *adj* balustered; *m* balustrade, circle of balusters; *f* balustrade, banisters
**balaustrar** *va* to adorn or enclose with a balustrade
**balaustre** *m* or **balaústre** *m* baluster, banister
**balay** *m* (Am.) wicker basket

**balazo** *m* shot; bullet wound; **acribillar a balazos** to riddle with bullets
**balboa** *m* balboa (*monetary unit of Panama*)
**balbucear** *va* to stammer (*e.g., excuses*); *vn* to stammer, stutter; to babble, prattle
**balbucencia** *f* or **balbuceo** *m* stammering, stuttering; babbling, prattling
**balbucir** §53 *vn* var. of **balbucear**
**Balcanes, los** the Balkans
**balcánico -ca** *adj* Balkan
**balcanizar** §76 *va* to Balkanize
**balcarrotas** *fpl* (Am.) sideburns, side whiskers; (Am.) locks of hair falling over sides of face
**balcón** *m* balcony; railing; large window with balcony
**balconaje** *m* balconies, row of balconies
**balconcillo** *m* little balcony
**balda** *f* see **baldo**
**baldadura** *f* or **baldamiento** *m* incapacity, disability
**baldaquín** *m* or **baldaquino** *m* baldachin, canopy, dais; (arch.) baldachin, ciborium
**baldar** *va* to cripple; to incapacitate; to inconvenience; to ruff, to trump
**balde** *m* bucket, pail; **de balde** free, for nothing; over, in excess; idle; **en balde** in vain
**baldear** *va* to wash (*decks, floors, etc.*) with pails of water; to bail out (*a ditch*)
**baldeo** *m* deckswabbing
**baldés** *m* sheepskin for gloves
**baldío -a** *adj* untilled, uncultivated; idle, lazy; careless; vagabond; vain, useless; baseless, unfounded; *m* wasteland
**baldo -da** *adj* lacking, out of (*a suit of cards*); *m* lack (*of a suit*); *f* closet shelf
**baldón** *m* insult, affront; blot, stain, disgrace
**baldonar** *va* to insult, to affront; to stain, disgrace
**baldosa** *f* floor tile, paving tile; (Am.) gravestone
**baldosado** *m* tile flooring, tile paving
**baldosar** *va* to floor or pave with tile
**baldosilla** *f* or **baldosín** *m* small square paving tile
**baldosón** *m* large paving tile, flagstone
**baldragas** *m* (*pl:* **-gas**) (coll.) easy-going fellow
**Balduíno** *m* Baldwin
**balduque** *m* narrow red tape
**balear** *adj* Balearic; *mf* native or inhabitant of the Balearic Islands; **las Baleares** the Balearic Islands; *va* (Am.) to shoot at, to shoot, to shoot to death
**baleárico -ca** *adj* Balearic
**baleo** *m* round mat; esparto fan (*for fanning fire*)
**balería** *f* or **balerío** *m* stock of balls or bullets (*of an army or fort*)
**balero** *m* bullet mold
**baleta** *f* small bale, small bundle
**baliaga** *adj & mf* Balinese
**balido** *m* bleat, bleating
**balín** *m* small bullet; **balines** *mpl* shot, buckshot
**balinés -nesa** *adj & mf* Balinese
**balista** *f* ballista
**balístico -ca** *adj* ballistic; *f* ballistics
**balistocardiografía** *f* ballistocardiography
**balistocardiógrafo** *m* ballistocardiograph
**balistocardiograma** *m* ballistocardiogram
**balita** *f* small bullet; small bale; (Am.) marble
**balitadera** *f* deer call
**balitar** or **balitear** *vn* to bleat all the time
**baliza** *f* buoy, beacon; danger signal (*on highway undergoing repairs*)
**balizaje** *m* (naut.) system of buoys; (aer.) airway lighting
**balizamiento** *m* marking with buoys or beacons
**balizar** §76 *va* to mark with buoys or beacons; to show, to mark off
**balneario -ria** *adj* bathing, mineral, medicinal; *m* spa, watering place
**balneoterapia** *f* treatment with baths, balneotherapy
**balomano** *m* handball
**balompédico -ca** *adj* (pertaining to) football, soccer
**balompié** *m* football, soccer
**balón** *m* football; bale; balloon; **balón a mano** handball
**baloncestista** *mf* basketball player
**baloncestístico -ca** *adj* (pertaining to) basketball
**baloncesto** *m* basketball
**balota** *f* small ball (*used in voting*); ballot
**balotada** *f* ballotade (*leap of horse*)
**balotaje** *m* (Am.) balloting
**balotar** *vn* to ballot
**balsa** *f* raft, balsa; float; pool, puddle; (bot.) balsa, corkwood
**balsadera** *f* or **balsadero** *m* ferry
**balsamea** *f* (bot.) balm of Gilead
**balsamera** or **balsamerita** *f* flask for balsam
**balsámico -ca** *adj* balsamic, balmy; soothing, healing
**balsamina** *f* (bot.) balsam apple; (bot.) balsam (*Impatiens balsamina*); **balsamina de jardín** (bot.) garden balsam
**balsamita** *f* (bot.) hedge mustard; (bot.) feverfew; (bot.) wall rocket; **balsamita mayor** (bot.) costmary; **balsamita menor** (bot.) tansy
**bálsamo** *m* balsam, balm; (fig.) balm (*something soothing*); **bálsamo de Judea** or **de la Meca** balm of Gilead (*resin and ointment*); **bálsamo de Tolú** tolu or tolu balsam
**balsar** *m* (Am.) swamp covered with underbrush
**balsear** *va* to cross (*a stream*) by ferry or raft, to ferry across (*a stream*)
**balsero** *m* ferryman
**balso** *m* rope netting; (bot.) corkwood
**balsopeto** *m* (coll.) bosom; (coll.) pouch worn on bosom
**Baltasar** *m* Balthasar; (Bib.) Belshazzar
**bálteo** *m* (arch.) balteus, baluster (*of Ionic capital*); (archaic) balteus (*kind of baldric*)
**báltico -ca** *adj* Baltic; (*cap.*) *m* Baltic
**balto -ta** *mf* Balt
**baluarte** *m* (fort. & fig.) bulwark
**balumba** *f* great bulk
**balumbo** *m* bulk, bulky thing
**ballena** *f* whale; whalebone; corset steel, stay; **la Ballena** (astr.) Cetus, the Whale
**ballenato** *m* whale calf
**ballener** *m* whale-shaped vessel (*of Middle Ages*)
**ballenero -ra** *adj* (pertaining to) whaling; *m* whaler (*person and ship*); (naut.) whaleboat (*long rowboat with a bold sheer at both ends*)
**ballesta** *f* crossbow, arbalest; carriage spring; auto spring
**ballestada** *f* crossbow shot
**ballestazo** *m* hit or wound from crossbow shot
**ballestear** *va* to shoot or to shoot at with a crossbow
**ballestera** *f* loophole for crossbows
**ballestería** *f* archery; bowmen; bowmen's quarters; store of crossbows
**ballestero** *m* crossbowman; maker of crossbows; royal armorer
**ballestilla** *f* singletree; (vet.) fleam; (naut.) forestaff, cross-staff
**ballestrinque** *m* (naut.) clove hitch
**ballet** *m* (*pl:* **-llets**) ballet
**ballico** *m* (bot.) Italian rye grass; **ballico perenne** (bot.) cockle, rye grass
**ballueca** *f* (bot.) wild oats
**bamba** *f* fluke (*in billiards*)
**bambalear** *vn & vr* var. of **bambolear**
**bambalina** *f* (theat.) flies, borders
**bambalúa** *m* (Am.) clumsy fellow
**bambanear** *vn & vr* var. of **bambolear**
**bambarotear** *vn* to be loud and noisy, to make a racket
**bambarria** *f* fluke, scratch (*in billiards*); *mf* dolt, idiot
**bambarrión** *m* (coll.) big fluke; (coll.) big idiot
**bambochada** *f* (paint.) drinking scene, scene of revelry
**bamboche** *m* (coll.) plump, ruddy fellow
**bamboleante** *adj* swinging, swaying
**bambolear** *vn & vr* to swing, sway, reel, totter, wobble
**bamboleo** *m* swinging, swaying, reeling, tottering, wobbling

**bambolla** *f* (coll.) show, sham; pageantry
**bambollero -ra** *adj* (coll.) showy, flashy
**bambonear** *vn & vr* var. of **bambolear**
**bamboneo** *m* var. of **bamboleo**
**bambú** *m* (*pl:* **-búes**) (bot.) bamboo (*plant and hollow stems*)
**bambuche** *m* (Am.) ridiculous clay figure
**bamburé** *m* (Am.) large toad
**banana** *f* (bot.) banana (*tree and fruit*); (rad.) plug
**bananal** *m* banana plantation
**bananero -ra** *adj* (pertaining to the) banana; *m* (bot.) banana tree
**banano** *m* (bot.) banana tree
**banas** *fpl* (Am.) banns
**banasta** *f* large basket, hamper
**banastero -ra** *mf* basket maker
**banasto** *m* large round basket
**Banato, el** the Banat
**banca** *f* bench; stand, fruit stand; banking; bank (*especially in gambling*); **hacer saltar la banca** to break the bank (*in gambling*); **tener banca** (coll.) to be influential; **banca de hielo** iceberg, ice field
**bancada** *f* large stone bench; bedframe, solepiece; thwart; (min.) stope
**bancal** *m* oblong plot, oblong orchard; terrace; bench cover
**bancario -ria** *adj* banking, bank
**bancarrota** *f* bankruptcy; (fig.) bankruptcy (*utter ruin*); **hacer bancarrota** to go bankrupt
**bancarrotero -ra** *adj & mf* bankrupt
**bance** *m* rail (*used to close a road*)
**banco** *m* bench; bank; school (*of fish*); **banco de ahorros** savings bank; **banco de emisión** bank of issue; **banco de hielo** iceberg; **banco de liquidación** clearing house; **banco de nieblas** fog bank; **banco de pruebas** testing bench; **banco de sangre** blood bank
**banda** *f* band; ribbon, sash; faction, party; gang; flock; bank, shore; border, edge; side; cushion (*of billiard table*); (mus. & rad.) band; **allá de la otra banda** on the other side; **de la banda de allá de** on the other side of; **irse a la banda** (naut.) to list; **banda de rodamiento** (aut.) tread; **banda de tambores** drum corps; **Banda Oriental** East Bank or Side (*Uruguay*); **bandas laterales** (rad.) sidebands; **banda sonora** (mov.) sound track; **banda transportadora** belt conveyor
**bandada** *f* flock of birds; (coll.) flock (*of people*)
**bandaje** *m* tire
**bandarria** *f* (naut.) iron maul, sledge hammer
**bandazo** *m* swerving, zigzagging; (naut.) blow of wave on side of ship; (naut.) lurch, violent jolt to one side
**bandeado -da** *adj* banded, striped
**bandear** *va* (Am.) to cross, go through; (Am.) to swim across; (Am.) to pursue, make love to; *vr* (Am.) to manage, to get along
**bandeja** *f* tray; (Am.) dish
**bandera** *f* flag, banner; **a banderas desplegadas** in the open; **con banderas desplegadas** (mil.) with flying colors (*with flags unfurled and waving*); **bandera blanca** white flag; **bandera de parlamento** or **de paz** flag of truce; **bandera de proa** (naut.) jack; **bandera morrón** waft, weft; **bandera negra** black flag (*of pirates*)
**bandereta** *f* banneret
**bandería** *f* band, faction
**banderilla** *f* banderilla (*barbed dart with banderole*); (print.) paper with corrections pasted on proof; **clavar, plantar** or **poner una banderilla a** (coll.) to taunt, to be sarcastic to; (coll.) to hit for a loan; **banderillas de fuego** (taur.) banderillas with firecrackers attached
**banderillear** *va* to thrust banderillas into (*neck or shoulder of bull*)
**banderillero** *m* banderillero (*bullfighter who thrusts banderillas into neck or shoulders of bull*)
**banderín** *m* little flag, banneret; camp colors; recruiting post; (rail.) flag
**banderita** *f* banderole
**banderizar** §76 *va & vr* var. of **abanderizar**
**banderizo -za** *adj* factional; fiery, excitable; seditious; *mf* factionist, partisan
**banderola** *f* banderole; (surv.) fanion; (Am.) transom
**bandicut** *m* (zool.) bandicoot
**bandidaje** *m* banditry; gang of bandits
**bandido** *m* bandit, outlaw
**bandín** *m* (naut.) stern seat
**banditismo** *m* banditry
**bando** *m* edict, proclamation; faction, party; side (*e.g., in bridge*); **bando de destierro** ban
**bandola** *f* mandolin; (naut.) jury mast; (Am.) red flag (*of bullfighters*)
**bandolera** *f* bandoleer; female bandit, moll; **en bandolera** across the shoulders
**bandolerismo** *m* brigandage
**bandolero** *m* brigand, robber, highwayman
**bandolín** *m* var. of **bandola**
**bandolina** *f* (mus.) mandolin; pomade, hair grease
**bandolón** *m* (mus.) mandola
**bandujo** *m* sausage
**bandullo** *m* (coll.) belly, guts, bowels
**bandurria** *f* (mus.) bandurria (*instrument of lute family*)
**baniano** *m* banian; (bot.) banian
**banjo** *m* banjo
**banjoísta** *mf* banjoist
**bánova** *f* light bedcover; (prov.) bedquilt
**banquero** *m* banker
**banqueta** *f* stool, footstool; (eng. & fort.) banquette; (Am.) sidewalk
**banquete** *m* banquet
**banquetear** *va, vn & vr* to banquet
**banquillo** *m* bench; footstool; defendant's seat; (Am.) scaffold
**banquisa** *f* iceberg, floe, ice field
**bantu** (*pl:* **-tus**) *adj & mf* Bantu
**bantú** (*pl:* **-tús** *or* **-túes**) *adj & mf* var. of **bantu**
**banzo** *m* cheek (*of a frame*)
**baña** *f* water hole, bathing hole (*for animals*)
**bañadera** *f* (Am.) bathtub
**bañadero** *m* var. of **bañil**
**bañado** *m* chamber pot; (Am.) marshy land
**bañador -dora** *adj* bathing; *mf* bather; *m* bathing tub or trough; bathing suit
**bañar** *va* to bathe; to dip; to coat by dipping; (fig.) to cover (*e.g., with glory*); (fig.) to overspread (*e.g., with smiles*); **estar bañado en agua de rosas** to walk on air; *vr* to bathe
**bañero -ra** *mf* bathhouse proprietor; bath attendant; *m* dipping tub (*for candle makers*); *f* bathtub
**bañil** *m* water hole, wallow (*where wild animals bathe*)
**bañista** *mf* bather; resorter, frequenter of a spa or seaside resort
**baño** *m* bath; bathing; bathroom; bathtub; bagnio (*Moorish or Turkish prison*); cover, coating; **baño de asiento** sitz bath; **baño de ducha** or **de lluvia** shower bath; **baño de maría** or **baño maría** double boiler, water bath, bain-marie; **baño del sol** sun bath; **baño de vapor** steam bath; **baño para pájaros** bird bath; **baño turco** Turkish bath
**bañomaría** *m* double boiler, water bath, bain-marie
**bao** *m* (naut.) beam, cross timber; **bao mayor** (naut.) beam (*main horizontal support*)
**baobab** *m* (bot.) baobab
**baptista** *adj & mf* Baptist
**baptisterio** *m* baptistry
**baque** *m* thud, thump; bump, bruise
**baquelita** *f* bakelite
**baqueta** *f* ramrod; drumstick; **a baqueta** or **a la baqueta** harshly, scornfully; **correr baquetas** or **pasar por baquetas** (mil. & fig.) to run the gauntlet
**baquetazo** *m* blow with a ramrod
**baquetear** *va* to make run the gauntlet; to inure; to bother, to disturb
**baquetudo -da** *adj* (Am.) sluggish, slow, phlegmatic
**baquía** *f* familiarity with region (*roads, paths, rivers etc.*); (Am.) skill, manual dexterity
**baquiano -na** *adj* skilful, expert; *mf* guide, pathfinder
**baquiar** *va* (Am.) to train (*animals*)

**báquico -ca** *adj* Bacchic; bacchic (*drunken, riotous*)
**baquira** or **báquira** *mf* (zool.) peccary
**bar** *m* bar, barroom; cocktail bar
**barahúnda** *f* uproar, tumult
**baraja** *f* deck or pack (*of playing cards*); confusion, mix-up; gang, mob; **jugar con dos barajas** (coll.) to act with duplicity, to be a double-crosser; **peinar la baraja** to riffle the cards
**barajado** *m* shuffling
**barajadura** *f* shuffling; quarrel, dispute
**barajar** *va* to shuffle (*playing cards*); to mix; to bandy about; (Am.) to parry, ward off; (Am.) to catch; *vn* to fight, quarrel; *vr* to become jumbled; to get mixed up
**Barajas** international airport of Madrid
**barajones** *mpl* (prov.) skis
**baranda** *f* railing; cushion (*of billiard table*)
**barandaje** *m* or **barandajo** *m* railing, balustrade
**barandal** *m* upper or lower rail of balustrade; railing, balustrade
**barandilla** *f* railing, balustrade; (naut.) guardrail
**baranguay** *m* baranguay (*Philippine canoe or boat; Philippine village of 50 to 100 families*)
**barata** *f* see **barato**
**baratador -dora** *mf* barterer
**baratar** *vn* (archaic) to barter
**baratear** *va* to sell cheaply, to sell at a bargain
**baratería** *f* (law) barratry; **baratería de capitán** or **patrón** (naut. law) barratry
**baratero -ra** *adj* (Am.) cheap (*charging low prices*); *m* fellow who exacts money from winning gamblers; (Am.) haggler
**baratía** *f* (Am.) cheapness
**baratija** *f* trinket, trifle
**baratillero -ra** *mf* second-hand dealer
**baratillo** *m* second-hand goods; second-hand shop; bargain counter; bargain sale; **de baratillo** cheap, second-rate
**barato -ta** *adj* cheap; *m* bargain sale; **dar de barato** (coll.) to admit for the sake of argument; **de barato** gratis, free; **echar** or **meter a barato** (coll.) to heckle; (coll.) to sneer at; *f* barter; cheapness; (Am.) bargain sale; **barato** *adv* cheap
**báratro** *m* (poet.) hell, inferno
**baratura** *f* cheapness
**baraúnda** *f* uproar, tumult
**baraustar** **§75** *va* to aim; to ward off
**barba** *f* chin; beard, whiskers; deckle edge, rough edge; gill or wattle (*of fowl*); (bot.) beard; (mach.) burr; **echarle a las barbas a uno** to throw in one's teeth; **hacer la barba** to shave (oneself); **hacer la barba a** to shave; to bore, annoy; to fawn on; **mentir por la barba** (coll.) to tell fish stories; **por barba** apiece; **barba cabruna** (bot.) goatsbeard; **barba de capuchino** (bot.) clover dodder; **barba de Júpiter** (bot.) houseleek; **barba española** (bot.) Spanish moss, Florida moss; **barbas de viejo** (bot.) Spanish moss, Florida moss; *m* (theat.) old man; **Barba Azul** Bluebeard
**barbacana** *f* (fort.) barbican; churchyard wall
**barbacoa** *f* (Am.) barbecue
**barbada** *f* see **barbado; la Barbada** see **barbado**
**barbadejo** *m* (bot.) wayfaring tree
**barbadija** *f* (bot.) laurustine
**barbado -da** *adj* bearded; barbed; deckle-edged; *m* shoot, sucker, seedling for transplanting; **plantar de barbado** to transplant (*a seedling*); *f* lower jaw of horse; bridle curb; (ichth.) dab; **la Barbada** Barbados
**barbaja** *f* (bot.) cut-leaved viper's-grass; **barbajas** *fpl* (agr.) first roots
**barbaján** *m* (Am.) rustic, hayseed
**barbar** *vn* to grow a beard; to breed bees; to strike root
**barbárico -ca** *adj* barbaric
**barbaridad** *f* barbarism; outrage; nonsense; (coll.) huge amount; **¡qué barbaridad!** how awful!
**barbarie** *f* barbarism, barbarity
**barbarismo** *m* (gram.) barbarism; illiteracy; barbarity; outrage; barbarians
**barbarizar** **§76** *va* to make barbarous; to fill with barbarisms; *vn* to make atrocious remarks
**bárbaro -ra** *adj* barbaric; barbarous; *mf* barbarian
**barbarote -ta** *adj* (coll.) cruel; (coll.) coarse
**barbaza** *f* shaggy beard
**barbear** *va* to reach with the chin; to be as high as; (Am.) to shave; (Am.) to flatter; *vn* to reach the same height; **barbear con** to be as high as
**barbechada** *f* fallowing
**barbechar** *va* to plow for seeding; to fallow
**barbechera** *f* series of fallows; fallowing; fallowing season
**barbecho** *m* fallow
**barbera** *f* see **barbero**
**barbería** *f* barbershop; barbering
**barberil** *adj* (pertaining to a) barber
**barbero -ra** *adj* (Am.) fawning, flattering; *m* barber; *f* barber's wife
**barbeta** *f* (fort.) barbette; (naut.) racking; **a barbeta** in barbette
**barbián -biana** *adj* (coll.) dashing, bold, handsome
**barbibermejo -ja** *adj* red-bearded
**barbiblanco -ca** *adj* var. of **barbicano**
**barbicacho** *m* chin ribbon or strap, cap or hat string
**barbicano -na** *adj* gray-bearded, white-bearded
**barbiespeso -sa** *adj* heavy-bearded, thick-bearded
**barbihecho -cha** *adj* fresh-shaved
**barbilampiño -ña** *adj* smooth-faced, beardless
**barbilindo -da** *adj* dapper, dandified
**barbiluengo -ga** *adj* long-bearded
**barbilla** *f* tip of chin; (carp.) rabbet; barbel (*growth in mouth of fish*)
**barbillera** *f* tuft of tow; chin strap (*to hold mouth of corpse shut*)
**barbinegro -gra** *adj* black-bearded
**barbiponiente** *adj* (coll.) beginning to grow a beard; (coll.) beginning, apprenticed
**barbiquejo** *m* chin strap, hat guard; (naut.) bobstay
**barbirrubio -bia** *adj* blond-bearded
**barbirrucio -cia** *adj* gray-bearded, with a grizzled beard
**barbitaheño -ña** *adj* red-bearded
**barbitonto -ta** *adj* simple, simple-looking
**barbiturato** *m* (chem.) barbiturate
**barbitúrico -ca** *adj* (chem.) barbituric
**barbo** *m* (ichth.) barbel; **barbo de mar** (ichth.) red mullet
**barbón** *m* bearded man; billy goat; Carthusian lay brother; (coll.) graybeard, solemn old person
**barboquejo** *m* var. of **barbiquejo**
**barbotar** *va & vn* to mutter, to mumble
**barbote** *m* beaver (*of helmet*)
**barbotear** *vn* to mumble
**barboteo** *m* mumbling
**barbudo -da** *adj* bearded, long-bearded, heavy-bearded; *m* shoot, sucker, seedling for transplanting
**barbulla** *f* (coll.) uproar, clamor, hubbub, hullabaloo
**barbullar** *va* to daub; *vn* (coll.) to blabber, to make a hullabaloo
**barbullón -llona** *adj* loudmouthed; *mf* noisy talker
**barbuquejo** *m* var. of **barbiquejo**
**barca** *f* small boat; (naut.) bark, barque
**barcada** *f* boatload; boat trip
**barca-goleta** *f* (naut.) barkentine
**barcaje** *m* ferrying; boat fare
**barcal** *m* wooden bowl or trough; dog dish
**barcarola** *f* (mus.) barcarole; rowing song
**barcarrón** *m* (naut.) hooker, tub
**barcaza** *f* lighter, barge; lighterage
**barcelonés -nesa** *adj* (pertaining to) Barcelona; *mf* native or inhabitant of Barcelona
**barceno -na** *adj* ruddy, auburn
**barceo** *m* (bot.) matweed
**barcia** *f* chaff
**barcinar** *va* (prov.) to gather in (*grain*)
**barcino -na** *adj* reddish-brown and white; *mf* (Am.) turncoat (*in politics*); *f* load of hay or straw; straw-net bag

**barco** *m* boat, vessel; shallow ravine; **el Barco fantasma** the Flying Dutchman; **barco marinero** good sailer; **barco náufrago** shipwreck; **barco velero** fast sailer
**barcolongo** or **barcoluengo** *m* (hist.) roundbow sailing vessel; (hist.) long, narrow two-master
**barcón** *m* large boat
**barchilón -lona** *mf* (Am.) orderly, nurse
**barda** *f* bard, horse armor; thatch; hedge; (naut.) low black cloud
**bardaguera** *f* (bot.) osier
**bardal** *m* thatched fence or wall
**bardana** *f* (bot.) burdock; **bardana menor** (bot.) cocklebur (*Xanthium strumarium*); (bot.) hedgehog parsley
**bardar** *va* to thatch; to bard (*a horse*)
**bardiota** *m* (archaic) Byzantine imperial guard
**bardo** *m* bard
**bardoma** *f* (prov.) filth, dirt, dung
**baremo** *m* ready reckoner; arithmetic (*book*); scale (*of marks, salaries, etc.*); table of rates
**barés** *m* barège
**barga** *f* river barge
**bargueño** *m* fancy inlaid gilt secretary
**baribal** *m* (zool.) black bear
**bario** *m* (chem.) barium
**barisfera** *f* (geol.) barysphere
**barita** *f* (mineral.) baryta
**baritel** *m* hoist, windlass
**baritina** *f* (chem.) barite
**barítono** *m* (mus.) baritone
**barjuleta** *f* knapsack, haversack; tool bag
**barloar** *va* (naut.) to bring alongside; *vn & vr* (naut.) to come alongside
**barloas** *fpl* (naut.) relieving tackles
**barloventear** *vn* (naut.) to ply or turn to windward; to wander from place to place
**barlovento** *m* (naut.) windward
**barman** *m* (*pl:* **-mans**) bartender
**barnacla** *f* (zool.) barnacle; (orn.) sea goose
**barniz** *m* (*pl:* **-nices**) varnish; glaze (*on pottery*); face paint; gloss, polish; smattering; **dar de barniz** to varnish (*e.g., a piece of furniture*); **barniz del Japón** (bot.) tree of heaven; **barniz aislador** electric varnish
**barnizado** *m* varnish, varnishing, coat of varnish; (f.a.) varnishing day
**barnizador -dora** *adj* varnishing; glazing; *mf* varnisher; glazer
**barnizar** **§76** *va* to varnish; to glaze (*pottery*); to polish, to shine
**barógrafo** *m* barograph
**barograma** *m* barogram
**barométrico -ca** *adj* barometric
**barómetro** *m* barometer; (fig.) barometer; **barómetro aneroide** aneroid barometer
**barón** *m* baron
**baronaje** *m* or **baronato** *m* baronage
**baronesa** *f* baroness
**baronía** *f* barony, baronage
**baronial** *adj* baronial
**baroscopio** *m* baroscope
**barquear** *va* to cross (*e.g., a river*) in a boat; *vn* to cross or go across in a boat
**barqueo** *m* boating, crossing in a boat
**barquero** *m* boatman
**barquía** *f* fishing boat, fishing smack
**barquilla** *f* cone mold; (aer.) nacelle; (naut.) log; log chip; **barquilla transbordadora** transporter car
**barquillero -ra** *mf* maker or seller of cones; *m* cone mold; waffle iron; harbor boatman; **barquillero de los estanques** (ent.) back swimmer
**barquillo** *m* cone (*e.g., for ice cream*); waffle; wafer stick
**barquín** *m* bellows
**barquinazo** *m* (coll.) hard jolt, fall, or upset of a carriage
**barquinera** *f* bellows
**barquino** *m* wineskin
**barra** *f* bar (*of metal, etc.; of sand in river or ocean; military badge; counter of barroom*); stick (*of dynamite*); railing in courtroom; (her. & mus.) bar; (mach.) rod; gross-spun or colored thread (*in a fabric*); **barra colectora** (elec.) bus bar; **barra de balas** bar bell; **barra de labios** or **para los labios** lipstick; **barra imantada** bar magnet; **barras paralelas** (sport) parallel bars
**barrabás** *m* (fig.) devil; (*cap.*) *m* (Bib.) Barabbas
**barrabasada** *f* devilishness, fiendish act
**barraca** *f* cabin, hut; small country house; (Am.) storage shed
**barracón** *m* barracks; fair booth; (mil.) permanent quarters
**barracuda** *f* (ichth.) barracuda
**barragán** *m* barragan; barragan raincoat
**barragana** *f* concubine
**barraganería** *f* concubinage
**barraganete** *m* (naut.) top-timber
**barramunda** *f* (ichth.) Burnett salmon; (ichth.) arapaima
**barranca** *f* ravine, gorge, gully; (Am.) channel made by running water
**barrancal** *m* locality full of ravines, place full of gullies
**barranco** *m* ravine, gorge, gully; (Am.) cliff, precipice; great difficulty, obstruction
**barrancoso -sa** *adj* full of ravines, gorges, or gullies; broken, uneven; steep, precipitous
**barranquear** *va* to drag (*logs*) down a ravine
**barranquera** *f* ravine, gorge, gully
**barrar** *va* to daub, smear; to bar, barricade
**barreal** *m* (Am.) mudhole, quagmire
**barrear** *va* to barricade; to bar, fasten with a bar; (prov.) to strike out, cross off; *vn* to graze one's opponent's armor; *vr* (prov.) to wallow in the mud (*said of wild boar*)
**barreda** *f* barrier
**barredero -ra** *adj* sweeping; drag; *m* baker's mop; *f* street sweeper; **barredera de alfombras** carpet sweeper
**barredor -dora** *adj* sweeping; *mf* sweeper; **barredora de nieve** snowplow
**barredura** *f* sweeping; **barreduras** *fpl* sweepings, refuse
**barrejobo** *m* (Am.) clearing, clean sweep
**barreminas** *m* (*pl:* **-nas**) (nav.) mine sweeper
**barrena** *f* drill, auger, gimlet; bit (*of drill*); crowbar; (aer.) spin; **entrar en barrena** (aer.) to go into a spin
**barrenado -da** *adj* drilled; (coll.) mad, crazy
**barrenar** *va* to drill; to scuttle (*a ship*); to undo, upset; to violate
**barrendero -ra** *mf* sweeper (*person*)
**barrendo** *m* (Am.) wildcat
**barrenero** *m* drill maker, drill dealer; (min.) driller, blaster
**barrenillo** *m* (ent.) boring insect, borer
**barreno** *m* large drill; bored hole; blast hole; pride, haughtiness; (Am.) mania, pet idea; **dar barreno a** to scuttle (*a ship*)
**barreña** *f* or **barreño** *m* dishpan
**barrer** *va* to sweep, to sweep away, to sweep clean; to graze; *vn* to sweep; **barrer hacia dentro** to look out for oneself; *vr* (Am.) to shy (*said of a horse*)
**barrera** *f* barrier; (mil.) barricade; (mil.) barrage; clay pit; crockery cupboard; gate; tollgate; (rail.) crossing gate; (taur.) wooden barrier or fence around inside of bull ring; (taur.) first row of seats; **barrera aduanera** customs barrier; **barrera de arrecifes** barrier reef; **barrera de globos** balloon barrage; **barrera del idioma** language barrier; **barrera del sonido** or **barrera sónica** sonic barrier; **barrera de paso a nivel** (rail.) crossing gate; **barrera térmica** thermal barrier
**barrero** *m* potter; mudhole; (Am.) salt marsh
**barreta** *f* small bar; shoe lining
**barretear** *va* to bar, fasten with a bar; to line (*a shoe*)
**barretina** *f* Catalan beret
**barriada** *f* ward, quarter, district, precinct; houses on edge of town
**barrica** *f* cask, large cask
**barricada** *f* barricade
**barrido** *m* sweeping, sweepings
**barriga** *f* belly; (fig.) belly (*of a container*); bulge (*in a wall*)
**barrigón -gona** or **barrigudo -da** *adj* big-bellied
**barriguera** *f* bellyband, cinch, girth
**barril** *m* barrel; earthen water jug
**barrilamen** *m* stock of barrels or casks
**barrilejo** *m* rundlet, small barrel

**barrilería** *f* stock of barrels or casks; barrel factory, barrel shop
**barrilero** *m* cooper, barrel maker, barrel dealer
**barrilete** *m* dog, clamp; (naut.) mouse; (zool.) fiddler crab; keg
**barrilla** *f* (bot. & chem.) barilla
**barrillar** *m* barilla plantation; barilla pit
**barrillero -ra** *adj* barilla-yielding
**barrillo** *m* pimple
**barrio** *m* ward, quarter, precinct; suburb; **andar** or **estar vestido de barrio** (coll.) to be dressed plainly; **el otro barrio** (coll.) the other world; **barrio bajo** slums; **barrio comercial** shopping district, business district; **Barrio Latino** Latin Quarter; **barrios externos** suburbs
**barrisco; a barrisco** jumbled together, indiscriminately
**barrita** *f* little bar; **barrita de pan** roll
**barritar** *vn* to trumpet (*said of elephants*)
**barrizal** *m* mudhole, mire
**barro** *m* mud; clay; earthenware; pimple, whelk
**barroco -ca** *adj & m* baroque
**barrocho** *m* barouche
**barrón** *m* large bar; (bot.) beach grass
**barroquismo** *m* baroque style, baroque taste; extravagance, bad taste
**barroso -sa** *adj* muddy; pimply
**barrote** *m* bar, heavy bar; bolt; cross brace
**barrueco** *m* baroque pearl
**barrumbada** *f* boast; boastful extravagance
**barruntador -dora** *adj* conjecturing, guessing; *mf* guesser
**barruntamiento** *m* conjecturing, guessing
**barruntar** *va* to conjecture, guess; to sense
**barrunte** *m* or **barrunto** *m* conjecture, guess; sign, token, show
**bartola; a la bartola** carelessly, in a carefree manner
**bartolillo** *m* little meat pie; cream tart
**bartolina** *f* (Am.) cell, dungeon; (Am.) solitary confinement
**Bartolomé** *m* Bartholomew
**bártulos** *mpl* household tools; dealings, business; steps, means, way; **liar los bártulos** (coll.) to pack up, to gather one's belongings; **preparar los bártulos** (coll.) to get set, to lay one's plans
**Baruc** *m* (Bib.) Baruch
**baruca** *f* (coll.) snare, trap
**barullo** *m* tumult, uproar, confusion
**barzal** *m* bramblebush, thicket
**barzoi** *m* borzoi (*Russian wolfhound*)
**barzón** *m* loitering, wandering, saunter, stroll; ring or loop of a yoke
**barzonear** *vn* to loiter, to wander around, to saunter, to stroll
**basa** *f* (arch.) base; basis, foundation
**basada** *f* stocks (*for shipbuilding*)
**basal** *adj* basal, basic
**basáltico -ca** *adj* basaltic, basalt
**basalto** *m* basalt
**basamento** *m* (arch.) base and pedestal (*of a column*)
**basanita** *f* basalt; (petrog.) basanite
**basar** *va* to base; to support; *vr* **basarse en** to base one's judgment on, to rely on
**basáride** *f* (zool.) cacomistle
**basca** *f* nausea, squeamishness; (coll.) fit of temper, angry mood
**bascosidad** *f* filth, dirt
**bascoso -sa** *adj* nauseated, squeamish
**báscula** *f* platform scale
**bascular** *vn* to tip, tilt, rock
**base** *f* base; basis; **a base de** on the basis of; **primera base** *f* (baseball) first base (*station*); **primera base** *m* (baseball) first base, first baseman (*player*); **segunda base** *f* (baseball) second base (*station*); **segunda base** *m* (baseball) second base, second baseman (*player*); **tercera base** *f* (baseball) third base (*station*); **tercera base** *m* third base, third baseman (*player*); **base aérea** air base; **base aeronaval** naval air base; **base robada** (baseball) stolen base
**basebolista** *mf* baseball player
**basicidad** *f* (chem.) basicity
**básico -ca** *adj* basic; (chem.) basic
**basidio** *m* (bot.) basidium
**basidiomiceto** *m* (bot.) basidiomycete
**basilar** *adj* basilar
**Basilea** *f* Basle, Basel
**basílica** *f* basilica; (anat.) basilic vein
**basiliense** *adj* (pertaining to) Basle; *mf* native or inhabitant of Basle
**basilio -lia** *adj & m* Basilian
**basilisco** *m* (zool. & myth.) basilisk; **estar hecho un basilisco** to be in a rage
**basquear** *vn* to be nauseated
**basquetbol** *m* basketball
**basquetbolista** *mf* basketball player
**basquiña** *f* basquine; skirt
**basta** *f* see **basto**
**bastaje** *m* porter, errand boy
**bastante** *adj* enough, sufficient; *adv* enough; fairly, rather
**bastantear** *va* (law) to recognize as valid, to admit the legality of
**bastantemente** *adv* sufficiently
**bastanteo** *m* (law) recognition, admission, validation
**bastar** *vn* to suffice, be enough, be more than enough, to abound; **¡basta!** that'll do!, cut it out!; **bastar** + *inf* or **bastar con** + *inf* **to** be enough to + *inf*; **bastar a** or **para** + *inf* to suffice to + *inf*; *vr* to be self-sufficient; **bastarse a sí mismo** to be sufficient unto oneself
**bastarda** *f* see **bastardo**
**bastardear** *va* to debase; to adulterate, contaminate; *vn* to degenerate, deteriorate, decline
**bastardelo** *m* notary's notebook
**bastardía** *f* bastardy; meanness, wickedness, indignity
**bastardillo -lla** *adj* (print.) italic; *f* (print.) italics
**bastardo -da** *adj & mf* bastard; *m* (print.) bastard type; (naut.) parrel rope; *f* bastard file
**baste** *m* stitch; saddle pad
**bastear** *va* to baste, to tack; to tuft
**bastedad** *f* coarseness, rudeness, roughness
**bastero** *m* maker or seller of packsaddles; harness maker
**basteza** *f* var. of **bastedad**
**bastidor** *m* frame; stretcher (*for canvas*); wing (*of stage scenery*); (phot.) plate holder; **entre bastidores** (theat. & fig.) behind the scenes
**bastilla** *f* (sew.) hem; bastille (*small fortress*)
**bastillar** *va* (sew.) to hem
**bastimentar** *va* to supply, provision
**bastimento** *m* vessel; supplies, provisions
**bastión** *m* bastion
**bastionado -da** *adj* (fort.) bastioned
**basto -ta** *adj* coarse, rude, rough; *m* packsaddle; club (*playing card*); **bastos** *mpl* clubs (*suit of playing cards*); **el basto** the ace of clubs; *f* coarse stitch; basting; basting stitch
**bastón** *m* cane, staff, baton; **empuñar el bastón** to seize the reins; **meter el bastón** to intercede; **bastón de esquiar** ski pole or stick; **bastón de estoque** sword cane
**bastonada** *f* or **bastonazo** *m* bastinado
**bastoncillo** *m* small cane or stick; narrow trimming lace; (anat.) rod (*in retina*)
**bastoncito** *m* (bact.) rod
**bastonear** *va* to cane, to beat, to cudgel
**bastoneo** *m* caning, beating, cudgeling
**bastonera** *f* cane stand, umbrella stand
**bastonería** *f* cane making; cane shop
**bastonero** *m* cane maker, cane dealer; master of ceremonies at a ball; jailer's assistant
**basura** *f* sweepings; rubbish, refuse, trash; horse manure
**basural** *m* (Am.) dump, trash pile; (Am.) manure pile
**basurero** *m* rubbish collector, trash collector; trash can; rubbish dump
**basuriento -ta** *adj* (Am.) full of rubbish or trash, dirty
**bata** *f* smock; dressing gown, wrapper; **bata de baño** bathrobe
**Bataán, el** Bataan
**batacazo** *m* thud, bump
**bataclán** *m* (Am.) burlesque show
**bataclana** *f* (Am.) show girl, stripteaser; (Am.) pinup girl
**batahola** *f* (coll.) hubbub, uproar

**batalla** *f* battle, fight; joust, tournament; wheel base; seat (*of saddle*); worry, uneasiness; (paint.) battle piece; **en batalla** in battle array; **librar batalla** to do battle, to join battle; **batalla campal** pitched battle
**batallador -dora** *adj* battling; *mf* battler; fighter; fencer
**batallar** *vn* to battle, fight, struggle; to fence; to hesitate, waver
**batallola** *f* (naut.) rail
**batallón** *m* (mil. & fig.) battalion
**batán** *m* fulling mill
**batanar** *va* to beat or full (*cloth*); to beat, to whip; to overcome, conquer
**batanear** *va* to beat, to thrash
**batanero** *m* fuller
**batanga** *f* bamboo outrigger (*in Philippine Islands*)
**bataola** *f* var. of **batahola**
**batata** *f* (bot.) sweet potato (*plant and tuber*); (Am.) timidity, bashfulness
**batatal** *m* sweet-potato field or patch
**batatazo** *m* (Am.) fluke, stroke of luck; **dar batatazo** (Am.) to win against all odds (*in a horse race*)
**bátavo -va** *adj & mf* Batavian
**batayola** *f* (naut.) rail
**batazo** *m* (baseball) hit; **buen batazo** (baseball) fair ball; **mal batazo** (baseball) foul ball
**bate** *m* beating, shaking; tamping pick; baseball bat
**batea** *f* tray; painted wooden tray; flat-bottomed boat; tray (*e.g., of a trunk*); (rail.) flatcar; (min.) washing trough
**bateado** *m* (baseball) batting
**bateador -dora** *adj* (baseball) batting, at bat; *mf* (baseball) batter
**batear** *va & vn* (baseball) to bat
**batel** *m* small boat, skiff
**batelero** *m* boatman
**bateo** *m* (coll.) baptism; (baseball) batting
**batería** *f* battery; battering; (elec.) battery (*two or more cells connected together*); (baseball) battery; footlights; **batería de cocina** set of kitchen utensils
**batey** *m* (Am.) sugar refinery; (Am.) sugar-refining machinery
**batibio** *m* (zool.) bathybius
**batiborrillo** or **batiburrillo** *m* hodgepodge
**baticola** *f* crupper
**batida** *f* see **batido**
**batidera** *f* mortar hoe, concrete hoe; stirrer; device for cutting honeycombs
**batidero** *m* constant beating or striking; rough ground; (fig.) going and coming; **batideros** *mpl* (naut.) washboard; (naut.) patch (*to protect sails from rubbing*)
**batido -da** *adj* beaten (*path*); chatoyant (*silk*); *m* batter; milk shake; beating; beat; (rad.) beat; *f* battue; search, reconnoitering
**batidor** *m* beater (*person or device*); scout, ranger; haircomb; (mus.) finger board; **batidor de oro** goldbeater
**batidora** *f* beater, mixer (*device*)
**batiente** *m* jamb; door (*each of a pair of double doors*)· damper (*of a piano*)
**batihoja** *m* goldbeater; sheet-metal worker
**batimento** *m* (paint.) shade, shading, shadow
**batimiento** *m* beating; (phys.) beat
**batín** *m* smoking jacket
**batintín** *m* (mus.) Chinese gong
**bationdeo** *m* flapping (*of a curtain, flag, etc.*)
**batiportar** *va* (naut.) to house (*a gun*)
**batiporte** *m* (naut.) sill (*of gun ports*)
**batir** *va* to beat; to beat down; to clap (*the hands*); to coin; **batir las olas** to ply the seas; **batir los talones** to take to one's heels; **batir tiendas** (mil.) to strike camp; *vr* to fight
**batiscafo** *m* bathyscaphe
**batisfera** *f* bathysphere
**batista** *f* cambric; **batista de Escocia** batiste
**batitú** *m* (*pl:* **-túes**) (orn.) upland plover
**bato** *m* rustic, simpleton ; (orn.) wood ibis
**batojar** *va* to beat down (*fruit from a tree*)
**batolito** *m* (geol.) batholith
**batología** *f* battology
**batómetro** *m* bathometer
**batracio** *adj & m* (zool.) batrachian
**batucar** §86 *va* to shake, to shake up, to stir together
**batuda** *f* jumping (*on a springboard*)
**batueco -ca** *adj* stupid, foolish, simple
**batuque** *m* (Am.) uproar, rumpus; (Am.) jamboree; **armar un batuque** (Am.) to raise a row
**batuquear** *va* var. of **batucar**
**baturrillo** *m* hodgepodge
**baturro -rra** *adj* (dial.) countrified; *mf* (dial.) peasant
**batuta** *f* (mus.) baton; **llevar la batuta** (coll.) to be in charge, to boss the show
**Baucis** *f* (myth.) Baucis
**baúl** *m* trunk; (coll.) belly; **baúl mundo** Saratoga trunk; **baúl perchero** or **ropero** wardrobe trunk
**baulería** *f* trunk shop
**baulero** *m* trunk maker or dealer
**bauprés** *m* (naut.) bowsprit
**bausán -sana** *adj* (Am.) idle, loafing; *mf* fool, idiot; (Am.) loafer; *m & f* straw soldier (*figure stuffed with straw*)
**bautismal** *adj* baptismal
**bautismo** *m* baptism; (eccl.) baptism; **bautismo de aire** first flight in an airplane; **bautismo de fuego** baptism of fire
**bautista** *adj* Baptist; *mf* baptizer; Baptist; **el Bautista** (Bib.) John the Baptist
**bautisterio** *m* baptistery
**bautizar** §76 *va* to baptise (*a person, a ship; to give a name to*); to throw water on (*a person*); (coll.) to dilute, to water (*wine*)
**bautizo** *m* baptism; christening party
**bauxita** *f* (mineral.) bauxite
**bávaro -ra** *adj & mf* Bavarian; *m* Bavarian (*dialect*)
**Baviera** *f* Bavaria; (*l.c.*) *f* (Am.) Bavarian beer, Munich beer
**baya** *f* see **bayo**
**bayadera** *f* bayadere (*female dancer and singer of India*)
**bayal** *adj* berry-like; bay; *m* lever used for turning stones
**Bayardo, señor de** seigneur de Bayard
**bayeta** *f* baize; floor mop
**bayetón** *m* bearskin (*shaggy woolen cloth for overcoats*)
**bayo -ya** *adj* bay; *m* bay; silkworm used as bait; *f* berry; (coll.) fun, joke, trick
**Bayona** *f* Bayonne
**bayonense** or **bayonés -nesa** *adj* (pertaining to) Bayonne; *mf* native or inhabitant of Bayonne
**bayoneta** *f* bayonet; (bot.) Spanish bayonet, Spanish dagger; **bayonetas** *fpl* troops, army; **bayoneta espada** sword bayonet
**bayonetazo** *m* bayonet thrust, bayonet wound
**bayonetear** *va* (Am.) to bayonet
**bayuca** *f* (coll.) inn, tavern, drinking place
**baza** *f* see **bazo**
**bazar** *m* bazar
**bazo -za** *adj* yellowish-brown; *m* yellowish brown; (anat.) spleen; *f* trick (*cards in one round*); **hacer baza** (coll.) to get along, to succeed; **meter baza (en)** (coll.) to butt in; **no dejar meter baza** (coll.) to not let (*a person*) get a word in edgewise; **baza rápida** (cards) quick trick
**bazofia** *f* offal, refuse, garbage, hogwash
**bazuca** *f* (mil.) bazooka (*portable rocket launcher*)
**bazucar** §86 *va* to stir by shaking; to tamper with
**bazuquear** *va* var. of **bazucar**
**bazuqueo** *m* stirring, shaking; **bazuqueo gástrico** intestinal rumblings
**be** *m* baa
**beatería** *f* cant, hypocrisy, sanctimony
**beaterio** *m* house of lay sisters
**beatificación** *f* beatification
**beatificar** §86 *va* to beatify
**beatífico -ca** *adj* beatific
**beatilla** *f* betille, fine linen
**beatísimo -ma** *adj super* most holy; **Beatísima madre** Holy Mother; **Beatísimo padre** Holy Father
**beatitud** *f* beatitude; Beatitude (*Pope*)
**beato -ta** *adj* happy, blessed; beatified; devout; prudish, bigoted; *mf* beatified person; devout

person; prude, bigot; *m* man who wears clerical dress but is not in a religious community; (coll.) churchgoer; *f* charity worker (*woman*); lay sister
**beatón -tona** *adj* hypocritical, bigoted; *mf* hypocrite, bigot
**Beatriz** *f* Beatrice
**beatucho -cha** *mf* (coll.) scheming hypocrite
**bebé** *m* baby; doll
**bebeco -ca** *adj* (Am.) albino
**bebedero -ra** *adj* drinkable; *m* water trough; drinking dish or pan (*for animals*); spout (*of drinking vessel*); (found.) sprue
**bebedizo -za** *adj* drinkable; *m* potion (*medicinal or poisonous*); philter
**bebedor -dora** *adj* drinking; *mf* drinker; hard drinker, toper
**beber** *m* drink, drinking; *va* to drink; to drink in; **beber los vientos por** to sigh for, to long for; *vn* to drink; **beber a la salud de** to drink to the health of; **beber de** or **en** to drink out of; **beber por la salud de** to drink to the health of; *vr* to drink, to drink up; (fig.) to drink in (*e.g., a book*)
**beberrón -rrona** *adj* (coll.) hard-drinking, drunk; *mf* (coll.) hard drinker, drunk, drunkard
**bebestible** *adj* drinkable; *m* drink
**bebezón** *m* (Am.) drunk, spree, drinking party
**bebible** *adj* (coll.) pleasant, drinkable
**bebido -da** *adj* tipsy; *f* drink; (Am.) potion, medicine; (prov.) break for a bite and a drink
**bebirina** *f* (pharm.) bebeerine
**bebistrajo** *m* (coll.) unpalatable drink, dose
**beborrotear** *vn* (coll.) to sip, to tipple
**beca** *f* scholarship, fellowship; sash worn over academic gown
**becabunga** *f* (bot.) brooklime
**becacín** *m* (orn.) whole snipe
**becacina** *f* (orn.) great or double snipe
**becado -da** *mf* (Am.) var. of **becario;** *f* (orn.) woodcock; **becada de los pantanos** (orn.) jacksnipe
**becafigo** *m* (orn.) beccafico, figpecker
**becar §86** *va* (Am.) to grant a scholarship or fellowship to
**becardón** *m* (orn.) snipe
**becario -ria** *mf* scholar, fellow, holder of a scholarship or fellowship
**becerra** *f* see **becerro**
**becerrada** *f* (taur.) fight of yearling calves
**becerrero** *m* keeper of herds of yearling calves
**becerril** *adj* (pertaining to a) calf
**becerrillo** *m* calfskin
**becerro -rra** *mf* yearling calf; *m* calfskin; **becerro de oro** (Bib. & fig.) golden calf; **becerro marino** (zool.) sea calf; *f* (bot.) snapdragon
**becoquín** *m* cap with strap under the chin
**becoquino** *m* (bot.) honeywort
**becuadro** *m* (mus.) natural sign
**bechamela** *f* béchamel sauce
**Bechuanalandia, la** Bechuanaland
**bedano** *m* heavy chisel
**bedel** *m* beadle
**bedelía** *f* beadleship
**bedelio** *m* bdellium
**beduíno -na** *adj & mf* Bedouin; *m* barbarian
**befa** *f* see **befo**
**befar** *va* to jeer at, to scoff at; *vn* to move the lips (*said of a horse*)
**befo -fa** *adj* blobber (*lip*); blobber-lipped; knock-kneed; *m* lip (*of an animal*); monkey; *f* jeer, scoff
**begonia** *f* (bot.) begonia
**begoniáceo -a** *adj* (bot.) begoniaceous
**behaviorismo** *m* behaviorism
**behén** *m* var. of **ben**
**behetría** *f* confusion, disorder, pandemonium
**béisbol** *m* baseball
**beisbolero -ra** or **beisbolista** *mf* (Am.) baseball player
**bejín** *m* (bot.) puffball; (coll.) touchy person, cross child
**bejuco** *m* (bot.) liana; **bejuco de corona** (bot.) bull briar
**bejuquillo** *m* Chinese gold necklace; ipecac
**Belcebú** *m* (Bib.) Beelzebub
**belcho** *m* (bot.) joint fir
**beldad** *f* beauty (*quality of beautiful; beautiful woman*)
**beldar §18** *va* to winnow with a rakelike fork
**belemnita** *f* (pal.) belemnite
**belén** *m* crèche; (coll.) confusion, bedlam; (coll.) madhouse; risk, hazard; (slang) gossip, lie; (*cap.*) *m* Bethlehem
**beleño** *m* (bot.) henbane
**belérico** *m* (bot.) myrobalan
**Belerofonte** *m* (myth.) Bellerophon
**belesa** *f* (bot.) leadwort
**belez** *m* or **belezo** *m* jar, vessel; piece of furniture
**belfo -fa** *adj* blobber (*lip*); blobber-lipped; *m* lip (*of an animal*); blobber lip
**belga** *adj & mf* Belgian
**bélgico -ca** *adj* Belgian; (*cap.*) *f* Belgium
**Belgrado** *f* Belgrade
**Bélice** Belize
**belicismo** *m* war spirit, militarism
**belicista** *adj* war, militaristic
**bélico -ca** *adj* warlike
**belicosidad** *f* bellicosity
**belicoso -sa** *adj* bellicose
**beligerancia** *f* belligerence, belligerency
**beligerante** *adj & m* belligerent
**belígero -ra** *adj* (poet.) warlike
**belio** *m* (phys.) bel
**Belisario** *m* Belisarius
**belísono -na** *adj* with warlike sound
**belitre** *adj* (coll.) low, mean, vile; *m* rogue, scoundrel
**belorta** *f* clasp ring of plow
**Beltrán** *m* Bertram
**beltranear** *vn* (coll.) to be crude, to be uncouth
**Beluchistán, el** Baluchistan
**beluga** *f* (zool.) beluga
**belvedere** *m* belvedere
**bellacada** *f* var. of **bellaquería**
**bellaco -ca** *adj* sly, cunning; wicked, knavish; balky; *mf* scoundrel, knave
**belladona** *f* (bot.) belladonna, banewort; (pharm.) belladonna
**bellaquear** *vn* to deceive, to cheat, to be crooked; to rear; (Am.) to be stubborn
**bellaquería** *f* slyness, cunning; wickedness, knavery
**belleza** *f* beauty (*quality of beautiful; beautiful woman*)
**bello -lla** *adj* beautiful, fair; **bello ideal** beau ideal; **la Bella durmiente** Sleeping Beauty
**bellorio -ria** *adj* mouse-colored
**bellorita** *f* (bot.) English daisy
**bellota** *f* acorn; acorn-shaped perfume box; (zool.) acorn barnacle; carnation bud; (coll.) Adam's apple; **bellota de mar** or **marina** (zool.) sea urchin
**bellote** *m* round-headed spike
**bellotear** *vn* to feed on acorns (*said of pigs*)
**bellotero -ra** *mf* acorn gatherer or vendor; *f* acorn season; acorn crop
**bembo -ba** *adj* (Am.) thick-lipped; (Am.) snouty; *mf* (Am.) thicklips (*person*); (Am.) simpleton; *m* (Am.) thick lip
**bembón -bona** *adj* (Am.) thick-lipped; (Am.) snouty
**bemol** *adj* (mus.) flat; *m* (mus.) flat; **doble bemol** (mus.) double flat; **tener bemoles** or **tener tres bemoles** (coll.) to be full of difficulties, to be a tough job
**bemolado -da** *adj* (mus.) flat, lowered a semitone
**ben** *m* (bot.) horse-radish tree
**bencedrina** *f* (pharm.) benzedrine
**benceno** *m* (chem.) benzene
**bencidina** *f* (chem.) benzidine
**bencina** *f* benzine
**bendecidor -dora** *adj* blessing, giving blessings
**bendecir §24** *va* to bless; to consecrate; to extol
**bendición** *f* benediction, blessing; grace (*at table*); **bendiciones** *fpl* wedding ceremony; **de bendición** legitimate; **que es una bendición** abundantly, with the greatest ease; **echar la bendición a** (coll.) to have nothing to do with, to say good-bye to; **bendición de la mesa** grace; **bendiciones nupciales** wedding ceremony
**bendigo** *1st sg pres ind of* **bendecir**

**bendije** *1st sg pret ind of* **bendecir**
**bendito -ta** *adj* saintly, blessed; happy; simple, silly; holy (*water*); **como el pan bendito** (coll.) as easy as pie; **ser un bendito** (coll.) to be a simpleton, be a simple-minded soul
**benedícite** *m* (eccl.) Benedicite; (coll.) benedicite (*as at table*)
**benedictino -na** *adj & mf* Benedictine; *m* benedictine (*liqueur*)
**Benedicto** *m* Benedict (*pope*)
**benedictus** *m* (eccl.) Benedictus
**beneficencia** *f* beneficence, charity, welfare; public welfare
**beneficentísimo -ma** *adj super* very or most beneficent or charitable
**beneficiación** *f* benefit; cultivation; exploitation; reduction, processing (*of ores*)
**beneficiado -da** *mf* person receiving the proceeds of a benefit performance; *m* (eccl.) beneficiary
**beneficial** *adj* pertaining to ecclesiastical benefices
**beneficiar** *va* to benefit; to cultivate (*land*); to exploit, to work (*a mine*); to reduce, to process (*ores*); to season; to serve (*a certain region or part of country*); (com.) to discount; (Am.) to slaughter (*cattle*); *vn* to benefit; *vr* **beneficiarse de** to take advantage of
**beneficiario -ria** *mf* beneficiary
**beneficio** *m* beneficence, benefaction; yield, profit; benefit; (theat.) benefit, benefit performance; (eccl.) benefice; exploitation (*of a mine*); smelting, ore reduction; **a beneficio de** for the benefit of
**beneficioso -sa** *adj* beneficial, profitable
**benéfico -ca** *adj* beneficent, charitable, benevolent; beneficial
**benemérito -ta** *adj* worthy, meritorious; *mf* worthy, notable; **benemérito de la patria** national hero
**beneplácito** *m* approval, consent
**benevolencia** *f* benevolence
**benevolentísimo -ma** *adj super* very or most benevolent or kind
**benévolo -la** *adj* benevolent, kind
**Bengala** *f* Bengal; (*l.c.*) *f* Bengal hemp; Bengal light; (aer.) flare
**bengalí** (*pl:* **-líes**) *adj & mf* Bengalese, Bengali; *m* Bengali (*language*); (orn.) Bengali
**bengalina** *f* bengaline
**benignidad** *f* benignity, benignancy
**benigno -na** *adj* benign, benignant, mild, kind; (path.) benign, benignant
**benito -ta** *adj & mf* Benedictine; (*cap.*) *m* Benedict
**benjamín** *m* baby (*youngest child*); (*cap.*) *m* Benjamin
**benjuí** *m* benzoin (*fragrant resin*)
**bentos** *m* (biol.) benthos
**benzoato** *m* (chem.) benzoate
**benzoico -ca** *adj* (chem.) benzoic
**benzoin** *m* (bot.) benzoin
**benzoína** *f* (chem.) benzoin
**benzol** *m* (chem.) benzol; (chem.) benzene
**beocio -cia** *adj* Boeotian; (fig.) Boeotian (*dull, stupid*); *mf* Boeotian; **la Beocia** Boeotia
**beodez** *f* drunkenness
**beodo -da** *adj & mf* drunk
**beorí** *m* (*pl:* **-ríes**) (zool.) American tapir
**beque** *m* (naut.) head (*of ship*); (naut.) beakhead
**berberecho** *m* (zool.) cockle (*Cardium edule*)
**berberí** (*pl:* **-ríes**) *adj & mf* Berber; *m* Berber (*language*); mother-of-pearl
**Berbería** *f* Barbary
**berberís** *m* (*pl:* **-rises**) (bot.) barberry (*shrub and fruit*)
**berberisco -ca** *adj & mf* var. of **bereber**
**bérbero** *m* (bot.) barberry (*shrub and fruit*)
**berbiquí** *m* (*pl:* **-quíes**) brace, carpenter's brace; **berbiquí y barrena** brace and bit
**berceo** *m* (bot.) matweed
**bercial** *m* field of matweed
**bereber** *adj & mf* Berber; *m* Berber (*language*)
**berenjena** *f* (bot.) eggplant
**berenjenal** *m* bed of eggplants; (coll.) predicament, kettle of fish, e.g., **en buen berenjenal nos hemos metido** (coll.) this is a fine kettle of fish we've got into
**bergamota** *f* bergamot (*lime; pear; perfume; snuff*)
**bergamote** *m* or **bergamoto** *m* (bot.) bergamot (*lime tree; pear tree*)
**bergante** *m* scoundrel, rascal
**bergantín** *m* (naut.) brig; **bergantín goleta** (naut.) brigantine, hermaphrodite brig
**beriberi** *m* (path.) beriberi
**berilio** *m* (chem.) beryllium
**berilo** *m* (mineral.) beryl
**berkelio** *m* (chem.) berkelium
**Berlín** *m* Berlin
**berlina** *f* berlin (*carriage*); closed front compartment (*of stagecoach or railroad car*); **en berlina** in a ridiculous position
**berlinés -nesa** *adj* (pertaining to) Berlin; *mf* Berliner
**Berlín-Este, el** East Berlin
**berlinga** *f* clothes pole; poker
**berlingar** §59 *va* to stir (*molten mass*) with poker
**Berlín-Oeste, el** West Berlin
**berma** *f* (fort.) berm
**bermejear** *vn* to turn bright red; to look bright red
**bermejizo -za** *adj* reddish; *m* (zool.) fruit bat, flying fox
**bermejo -ja** *adj* vermilion, bright red
**bermejón -jona** *adj* red, reddish
**bermejuela** *f* (ichth.) bitterling
**bermejura** *f* bright redness
**bermellón** *m* vermilion
**Bermudas, las** Bermuda
**bermudeño -ña** *adj & mf* Bermudian
**Berna** *f* Bern
**Bernabé** *m* Barnaby
**bernardina** *f* (coll.) tall story, extravagant boastful lie
**bernardo -da** *adj* Bernardine; *m* Bernardine monk; *f* Bernardine nun; (*cap.*) *m* Bernard
**bernegal** *m* drinking cup with scalloped edge
**bernés -nesa** *adj & mf* Bernese
**bernia** *f* rug; rug cloak
**bernicla** *f* (orn.) barnacle goose
**berra** *f* tall water cress
**berraza** *f* (bot.) water parsnip; tall water cress
**berrear** *vn* to low, to bellow
**berrenchín** *m* strong breath of angry boar; (coll.) rage, tantrum
**berrendo -da** *adj* two-colored; spotted; *m* (zool.) pronghorn
**berrera** *f* (bot.) water parsnip
**berrido** *m* lowing, bellowing; screech
**berrín** *m* (coll.) touchy person, cross child; small water cress
**berrinche** *m* (coll.) rage, tantrum
**berrinchudo -da** *adj* (Am.) cross, irascible
**berrizal** *m* water-cressy place
**berro** *m* (bot.) water cress (*plant and leaves that are used for salad*); **berro de caballo** (bot.) brooklime
**berrocal** *m* rocky spot
**berroqueño -ña** *adj* hard, resistant; hardened, hard-hearted; see **piedra**
**berrueco** *m* granite rock; baroque pearl; (path.) iritis
**berta** *f* bertha (*collar*); (*cap.*) *f* Bertha; (coll.) Bertha (*German cannon*)
**bertillonaje** *m* Bertillon system, bertillonnage
**berza** *f* (bot.) cabbage; **berzas** *fpl* cabbage (*for eating*); **mezclar berzas con capachos** (coll.) to bring up something irrelevant
**berzal** *m* cabbage patch
**besador -dora** *adj* kissing, fond of kissing
**besalamano** *m* unsigned note, written in the third person and marked B.L.M. (*kisses your hand*)
**besamanos** *m* levee, visit at court; throwing kisses
**besamela** *f* var. of **bechamela**
**besana** *f* furrow; furrowing; first furrow
**besar** *va* to kiss; (coll.) to graze, to touch; **a besar** (naut.) chock-a-block; **besar la mano** or **los pies** to give regards, to pay respects; *vr* (coll.) to bump heads together
**Besarabia, la** Bessarabia
**besico** *m* little kiss; **besico de monja** (bot.) Canterbury bell; (bot.) balloon vine, Indian heart

**beso** *m* kiss; kissing crust (*of bread*); bump; **beso de Judas** Judas kiss; **beso sonado** buss
**bestezuela** *f* little beast
**bestia** *f* beast; **gran bestia** (zool.) tapir; **bestia de carga** beast of burden; *mf* dunce, boor; *adj* stupid, boorish
**bestiaje** *m* beasts of burden
**bestial** *adj* beastly, bestial; (coll.) terrific (*extraordinarily great, intense, fine, beautiful, etc.*)
**bestialidad** *f* beastliness, bestiality; (coll.) stupidity
**bestializar** **§76** *vr* to live like a beast, to become bestialized
**bestiario** *m* gladiator; bestiary
**bestiaza** *f* big beast; big fool
**bestión** *m* big beast; big brute (*person*); (arch.) grotesque animal figure, chimera
**béstola** *f* plowstaff
**besucador -dora** *adj* (coll.) kissing; *mf* (coll.) kisser
**besucar** **§86** *va* (coll.) var. of **besuquear**
**besucón -cona** *adj* (coll.) kissing; *mf* (coll.) kisser
**besugo** *m* (ichth.) sea bream; (ichth.) red porgy
**besuguero -ra** *mf* fishmonger who sells sea breams; *f* fishing boat, fishing boat for fishing sea breams; fish pan for cooking sea breams
**besuguete** *m* (ichth.) little sea bream
**besuquear** *va* (coll.) to kiss repeatedly, to keep on kissing
**besuqueo** *m* (coll.) kissing, repeated kissing
**beta** *f* string, line, tape; beta
**betabel** *m* (Am.) beet
**Betania** *f* (Bib.) Bethany
**betarraga** or **betarrata** *f* (bot.) beet
**betatrón** *m* (phys.) betatron
**betel** *m* (bot.) betel
**Betelgeuze** *f* (astr.) Betelgeuse
**bético -ca** *adj & mf* Andalusian
**betijo** *m* stick fastened in the mouth of young goats to keep them from suckling but not from grazing
**Betis** *m* ancient name of the Guadalquivir
**betlemita** *mf* Bethlehemite
**betónica** *f* (bot.) hedge nettle, betony
**Betsabé** *f* (Bib.) Bathsheba
**Betsaida** *f* (Bib.) Bethsaida
**betuláceo -a** *adj* (bot.) betulaceous
**betuminoso -sa** *adj* var. of **bituminoso**
**betún** *m* bitumen; shoe polish, shoe blacking; (mach.) packing; **betún de Judea** bitumen of Judea, Jew's pitch; **betún de saliva** (coll.) elbow grease
**betunería** *f* pitch shop
**betunero** *m* pitch dealer
**bezante** *m* bezant (*coin*); (f.a. & her.) bezant
**bezo** *m* blubber lip; proud flesh
**bezoar** *m* bezoar
**bezudo -da** *adj* thick-lipped
**biangular** *adj* biangular
**biatómico -ca** *adj* (chem.) biatomic
**biaxil** *adj* biaxial
**biaza** *f* saddlebag
**bibásico -ca** *adj* (chem.) dibasic
**biberón** *m* nursing bottle
**bibijagua** *f* (ent.) leaf-cutting ant; (Am.) hustler
**Biblia** *f* Bible
**biblicista** *mf* Biblicist
**bíblico -ca** *adj* Biblical
**bibliófilo -la** *mf* bibliophile
**bibliografía** *f* bibliography
**bibliográfico -ca** *adj* bibliographic or bibliographical
**bibliógrafo -fa** *mf* bibliographer
**bibliomanía** *f* bibliomania
**bibliómano -na** *adj & mf* bibliomaniac
**biblioteca** *f* library; **biblioteca de consulta** reference library; **biblioteca de préstamo** lending library; **biblioteca rodante** bookmobile
**bibliotecario -ria** *mf* librarian
**B.I.C.** abr. of **Brigada de Investigación Criminal**
**bical** *m* (ichth.) male salmon
**bicameral** *adj* bicameral
**bicarbonato** *m* (chem.) bicarbonate; **bicarbonato sódico** or **de sosa** (chem.) bicarbonate of soda
**bicéfalo -la** *adj* bicephalous
**bicentenario -ria** *adj & m* bicentenary or bicentennial
**bíceps** *m* (*pl:* **-ceps**) (anat.) biceps
**bicerra** *f* (zool.) wild goat, mountain goat
**bici** *f* (coll.) bike (*bicycle*)
**bicicleta** *f* bicycle
**biciclista** *mf* bicyclist
**biciclo** *m* velocipede
**bicilíndrico -ca** *adj* two-cylinder
**bicípite** *adj* bicipital
**bicoca** *f* trifle, bagatelle
**bicolor** *adj* bicolor, bicolored
**bicóncavo -va** *adj* biconcave
**biconvexo -xa** *adj* biconvex
**bicoquete** *m* or **bicoquín** *m* two-pointed skullcap
**bicorne** *adj* (poet.) two-horned, two-pointed
**bicornio** *m* two-cornered hat
**bicos** *mpl* gold studs (*for velvet caps*)
**bicromato** *m* (chem.) bichromate
**bicromía** *f* two-color print
**bicuento** *m* (archaic) trillion (U.S.A.) (*one million million*)
**bicuspidado -da** *adj* bicuspidate
**bicúspide** *adj* bicuspid; (anat.) bicuspid; *m* (anat.) bicuspid
**bicha** *f* (superstitious use) snake; (archeol.) grotesque animal figure, chimera
**bichero** *m* boat hook
**bicho** *m* bug, vermin; beast; fighting bull; fool, simpleton; (coll.) brat, imp; **de puro bicho** (Am.) out of spite, out of pure envy; **mal bicho** wicked fellow, evil schemer; ferocious bull; **tener bicho** (Am.) to have a wild thirst; **bicho viviente** (coll.) living soul
**bidé** *m* bidet (*tub for sitz bath*)
**bidente** *adj* bidentate; *m* weeding hoe
**bidón** *m* can, tin can; drum (*container*)
**biela** *f* (mach.) connecting rod; (aut.) tie rod (*of steering system*)
**bielda** *f* wooden rake; winnowing
**bieldar** *va* to winnow with a rakelike fork
**bieldo** or **bielgo** *m* rakelike winnowing fork
**bielorruso -sa** *adj & mf* Byelorussian
**bien** *adv* well; properly, all right, readily; about; very, fully; indeed; **ahora bien** now then; **de bien en mejor** better and better; **más bien** rather; somewhat; **o bien** or else; **por bien** willingly; **si bien** while, though; **tener a bien** to deem wise or proper; **tener a bien** + *inf* to see fit to + *inf*; **y bien** now then, well; **bien a bien** willingly; **bien así como** or **bien como** just as; **bien que** although ‖ *conj* **no bien** as soon as, just as; scarcely; **bien . . . bien** either . . . or ‖ *m* good, welfare; property, piece of property; dearest, darling; **en bien de** for the sake of, for the benefit of; **bienes** *mpl* wealth, riches, property, possessions; **bienes de consumo** consumers' goods; **bienes de fortuna** worldly possessions; **bienes de producción** producers' goods; **bienes dotales** dower; **bienes gananciales** property acquired during married life; **bienes inmuebles** real estate; **bienes mostrencos** unclaimed property; **bienes muebles** personal property; **bienes parafernales** (law) paraphernalia; **bienes raíces** real estate; **bienes relictos** estate (*left by a decedent*); **bienes semovientes** livestock
**bienal** *adj & f* biennial
**bienamado -da** *adj* dearly beloved
**bienandante** *adj* happy, prosperous
**bienandanza** *f* happiness, prosperity, welfare
**bienaventurado -da** blissful, happy; blessed; simple
**bienaventuranza** *f* bliss, blessedness; well-being; **las bienaventuranzas** (theol.) the Beatitudes
**bienestar** *m* well-being, welfare, abundance
**bienfortunado -da** *adj* fortunate, lucky
**biengranada** *f* (bot.) botryoid goosefoot
**bienhablado -da** *adj* well-spoken
**bienhadado -da** *adj* fortunate, lucky
**bienhechor -chora** *adj* beneficent; *m* benefactor; *f* benefactress
**bienhechuría** *f* (Am.) improvements (*to real estate*)
**bienintencionado -da** *adj* well-meaning

**bienio** *m* biennium
**bienllegada** *f* welcome
**bienmandado -da** *adj* obedient, submissive
**bienmesabe** *m* meringue batter
**bienoliente** *adj* fragrant
**bienparecer** *m* compromise to save face
**bienpareciente** *adj* good-looking
**bienquerencia** *f* affection, fondness, good will
**bienquerer** *m* affection, fondness, good will; **§70** *va* to like, to be fond of, to be well-disposed toward
**bienqueriente** *adj* affectionate, fond, well-disposed
**bienquerré** *1st sg fut ind of* **bienquerer**
**bienquise** *1st sg pret ind of* **bienquerer**
**bienquistar** *va* to bring together, to reconcile; *vr* to become reconciled
**bienquisto -ta** *adj* well-thought-of
**bienteveo** *m* elevated wigwam from which to watch the vineyard; (orn.) Derby flycatcher
**bienvenido -da** *adj* welcome; *f* safe arrival; welcome; **dar la bienvenida a** to welcome
**bienvivir** *vn* to live in comfort; to live right
**bies** *m* bias
**bifásico -ca** *adj* (elec.) two-phase, diphase
**bífero -ra** *adj* (bot.) biferous
**bífido -da** *adj* bifid
**bifilar** *adj* bifilar; (elec.) two-wire
**bifloro -ra** *adj* biflorous
**bifocal** *adj* bifocal
**biforme** *adj* biform
**bifronte** *adj* (poet.) double-faced
**biftec** *m* (*pl:* **-tecs**) beefsteak
**bifurcación** *f* bifurcation; branch; junction
**bifurcado -da** *adj* bifurcate, forked
**bifurcar §86** *vr* to bifurcate, to fork, to branch
**biga** *f* two-horse carriage; (poet.) team of two horses
**bigamia** *f* bigamy
**bígamo -ma** *adj* bigamous; *mf* bigamist
**bigardear** *vn* (coll.) to bum around
**bigardía** *f* licentiousness; perversity; fake, dissimulation
**bigardo -da** *adj* licentious; wanton, perverse
**bigardón -dona** *adj* licentious; wanton, perverse; (dial.) lank and overgrown
**bígaro** *m* (zool.) sea snail, periwinkle
**bigarrado -da** *adj* var. of **abigarrado**
**bigarro** *m* var. of **bígaro**
**bignonia** *f* (bot.) bignonia
**bigorneta** *f* small anvil, stake
**bigornia** *f* two-horned anvil
**bigote** *m* mustache; (print.) dash rule; (found.) slag tap; **no tener malos bigotes** (coll.) to be not bad-looking (*said of a girl or woman*); **tener bigotes** (coll.) to have a mind of one's own; **bigote de gato** (rad.) cat whisker
**bigotera** *f* chamois mustache protector (*to keep points of mustache straight*); smear on upper lip; folding carriage seat; bow compass
**bigotudo -da** *adj* mustachioed
**bija** *f* (bot.) annatto tree; annatto (*dyestuff*)
**bilabiado -da** *adj* (bot.) bilabiate
**bilabial** *adj* & *f* (phonet.) bilabial
**bilateral** *adj* bilateral
**bilbaíno -na** *adj* (pertaining to) Bilbao; *mf* native or inhabitant of Bilbao
**biliar** or **biliario -ria** *adj* biliary
**bilingüe** *adj* bilingual
**bilingüismo** *m* bilingualism
**bilioso -sa** *adj* bilious; (fig.) bilious
**bilirrubina** *f* (biochem.) bilirubin
**bilis** *f* (physiol. & fig.) bile; **descargar la bilis** to vent one's spleen
**bilítero -ra** *adj* biliteral
**biliverdina** *f* (biochem.) biliverdin
**bilobular** *adj* bilobular
**bilocación** *f* bilocation
**bilocar §86** *vr* to be in two places at the same time
**bilocular** *adj* bilocular
**biltrotear** *vn* (coll.) to gad, run around
**biltrotera** *f* (coll.) gadabout
**billa** *f* pocketing a ball after it has struck another
**billalda** *f* tipcat (*boys' game*)
**billar** *m* billiards; billiard table; billiard room, billiard hall; **billar romano** pinball
**billarda** *f* var. of **billalda**
**billarista** *mf* (coll.) billiardist, billiard player
**billetaje** *m* tickets
**billete** *m* ticket; note; bill; **medio billete** half fare; **billete de abono** season ticket; commutation ticket; **billete de banco** bank note; **billete de ida y vuelta** round-trip ticket; **billete de regalo** complimentary ticket; **billete kilométrico** mileage book
**billetero -ra** *mf* vendor of lottery tickets; *m* & *f* billfold
**billón** *m* British billion; trillion (*in U.S.A.*)
**billonario -ria** *adj* & *mf* billionaire
**billonésimo -ma** *adj* & *m* billionth
**bímano -na** *adj* bimanous, two-handed; **bímanos** *mpl* (zool.) Bimana
**bimanual** *adj* bimanual, two-handed
**bimba** *f* (coll.) high hat
**bimembre** *adj* having two members, two-part
**bimensual** *adj* semimonthly
**bimestral** *adj* bimonthly
**bimestre** *adj* bimonthly; *m* period of two months; bimonthly payment (*of salary, debt, etc.*)
**bimetal** *m* two-metal element (*e.g., of thermostat*)
**bimetálico -ca** *adj* bimetallic
**bimetalismo** *m* bimetallism
**bimetalista** *adj* bimetallist, bimetallistic; bimetallic; *mf* bimetallist
**bimotor** *adj* twin-motor; *m* twin-motor plane
**bina** *f* second plowing or digging
**binación** *f* (eccl.) bination
**binadera** *f* weeding fork
**binado -da** *adj* (bot.) binate
**binador -dora** *adj* weeding; *mf* weeder; *f* weeding fork
**binar** *va* to plow or dig the second time; *vn* (eccl.) to celebrate two masses on the same day
**binario -ria** *adj* binary
**binaural** or **binauricular** *adj* binaural
**binazón** *f* second plowing or digging
**binocular** *adj* binocular
**binóculo** *m* binocle, binocular; spectacles, lorgnette
**binomial** *adj* binomial
**binomio -mia** *adj* binomial; *m* pair of names; hyphenated name; (alg. & biol.) binomial; **binomio de Newton** (alg.) binomial theorem
**bínubo -ba** *adj* twice married
**binza** *f* pellicle (*of eggshell; of onion*)
**biodinámico -ca** *adj* biodynamic; *f* biodynamics
**biofísico -ca** *adj* biophysical; *f* biophysics
**biogénesis** *f* (biol.) biogenesis
**biografía** *f* biography
**biografiado -da** *mf* biographee
**biográfico -ca** *adj* biographic or biographical
**biógrafo -fa** *mf* biographer
**biología** *f* biology
**biológico -ca** *adj* biologic or biological
**biólogo -ga** *mf* biologist
**biombo** *m* screen, folding screen
**biomédico -ca** *adj* biomedical
**biometría** *f* biometry
**biométrico -ca** *adj* biometric or biometrical
**biopsia** *f* (med.) biopsy
**bioquímico -ca** *adj* biochemical; *mf* biochemist; *f* biochemistry
**biostático -ca** *adj* biostatic or biostatical; *f* biostatics
**biota** *f* biota
**biótico -ca** *adj* biotic or biotical
**biotipo** *m* (biol.) biotype
**biotita** *f* (mineral.) biotite
**bióxido** *m* (chem.) dioxide
**bíparo -ra** *adj* (bot. & zool.) biparous
**bipartición** *f* bipartition, fission, splitting
**bipartido -da** or **bipartito -ta** *adj* bipartite
**bípede** *adj* biped
**bípedo -da** *adj* & *m* biped
**bipersonal** *adj* for two people
**bipétalo -la** *adj* (bot.) bipetalous
**bipinado -da** *adj* (bot.) bipinnate
**biplano** *m* (aer.) biplane
**biplaza** *m* (aer.) two-seater
**bipolar** *adj* bipolar; (elec.) double-pole
**biribís** *m* roulette
**biricú** *m* (*pl:* **-cúes**) sword belt
**birimbao** *m* (mus.) jews'-harp

**birlar** *va* to throw (*ball*) second time from place where it stopped; (coll.) to knock down with one blow, to kill with one shot; (coll.) to filch, to swipe; (coll.) to outwit
**birlí** *m* (*pl:* **-líes**) (print.) blank lower part (*of printed page*)
**birlibirloque; por arte de birlibirloque** magically, by magic
**birlocha** *f* kite
**birlocho** *m* surrey
**birlón** *m* (prov.) head pin (*in bowling*)
**birlonga** *f* omber (*card game*); **a la birlonga** (coll.) carelessly, sloppily
**Birmania** *f* Burma
**birmano -na** *adj & mf* Burmese; *m* Burmese (*language*)
**birreactor** *adj masc* (aer.) twin-jet
**birrectángulo -la** *adj* (geom.) birectangular
**birrefringencia** *f* birefringence
**birreme** *adj & f* bireme
**birreta** *f* biretta; (coll.) cardinalate
**birrete** *m* biretta; academic cap, mortarboard
**birretina** *f* small biretta, small cap; hussar's cap, grenadier's cap
**birria** *f* wobble (*of a spinning top*); clown; mess, sight; (Am.) grudge; **de birria** (Am.) half-heartedly
**bis** *adv* (mus.) bis; *interj* (theat.) encore!; *m* (theat.) encore
**bisabuelo -la** *mf* great-grandparent; *m* great-grandfather; *f* great-grandmother
**bisagra** *f* hinge; shoemaker's polisher of boxwood
**bisanuo -nua** *adj* (bot.) biennial
**bisar** *va* to repeat (*a song, performance, recitation, etc.*)
**bisayo -ya** *adj & mf* Bisayan or Visayan
**bisbís** *m* roulette
**bisbisar** *va* (coll.) to mutter, to mumble
**bisbiseo** *m* (coll.) muttering, mumbling
**bisbita** *f* (orn.) pipit, titlark
**bisecar** §86 *va* (geom.) to bisect
**bisección** *f* (geom.) bisection
**bisector -triz** *adj* (*pl:* **-tores -trices**) (geom.) bisecting; *f* (*pl:* **-trices**) (geom.) bisector or bisectrix
**bisel** *m* bevel, bevel edge
**biselar** *va* to bevel
**bisemanal** *adj* semiweekly, biweekly
**bisexual** *adj & m* bisexual
**bisiesto -ta** *adj* bissextile, leap (*year*); *m* bissextile, leap year; **mudar bisiesto** or **de bisiesto** (coll.) to change one's tune, to change one's ways
**bisílabo -ba** *adj* bisyllabic
**bismutismo** *m* (path.) bismuth poisoning
**bismutita** *f* (mineral.) bismutite
**bismuto** *m* (chem.) bismuth
**bisnieto -ta** *mf* great-grandchild; *m* great-grandson; *f* great-granddaughter
**biso** *m* (hist. & zool.) byssus
**bisojo -ja** *adj* squint-eyed, cross-eyed; *mf* cross-eyed person
**bisonte** *m* (zool.) bison; (zool.) buffalo
**bisoñada** *f* (coll.) greenhorn stunt or remark
**bisoñé** *m* wig for front of head
**bisoñería** *f* (coll.) var. of **bisoñada**
**bisoño -ña** *adj* green, inexperienced; (mil.) raw; *mf* greenhorn, rookie
**bispón** *m* roll of oilcloth
**bisté** *m* or **bistec** *m* beefsteak
**bistorta** *f* (bot.) bistort
**bistre** *m* (paint.) bister
**bistrecha** *f* advance, advance payment
**bisturí** *m* (*pl:* **-ríes**) (surg.) bistoury, lancet
**bisulco -ca** *adj* cloven-footed
**bisulfato** *m* (chem.) bisulfate
**bisulfito** *m* (chem.) bisulfite
**bisulfuro** *m* (chem.) bisulfide
**bisunto -ta** *adj* dirty, greasy
**bisutería** *f* costume jewelry, imitation jewelry
**bita** *f* (naut.) bitt; **bita de linguete** (naut.) pawl bitt; **bita de remolque** (naut.) towing bitt
**bitácora** *f* (naut.) binnacle
**bitadura** *f* (naut.) cable bitt
**bitongo -ga** *adj* (coll.) overgrown (*child*)
**bitoque** *m* bung; plug (*for muzzle of gun*)
**bitor** *m* (orn.) corn crake
**bítter** *m* bitters
**bituminizar** §76 *vr* to become bituminized
**bituminoso -sa** *adj* bituminous
**bivalencia** *f* (chem.) bivalence
**bivalente** *adj* (chem.) bivalent
**bivalvo -va** *adj* bivalve
**bixáceo -a** *adj* (bot.) bixaceous
**biyugado -da** *adj* (bot.) bijugate
**biza** *f* (ichth.) striped tunny
**Bizancio** *m* Byzantium
**bizantino -na** *adj & mf* Byzantine
**bizarrear** *vn* to act gallantly, to be magnanimous
**bizarría** *f* gallantry; loftiness, magnanimity; (arch.) bizarrerie
**bizarro -rra** *adj* gallant; lofty, magnanimous
**bizaza** *f* leather saddlebag
**bizcar** §86 *va* to wink (*the eye*); *vn* to squint
**bizco -ca** *adj* squint-eyed, cross-eyed; **quedarse bizco** (coll.) to be dazzled, be dumfounded; *mf* cross-eyed person
**bizcochada** *f* biscuit soup; slit roll
**bizcochar** *va* to bake a second time
**bizcochero -ra** *adj* (pertaining to a) biscuit or cake; *mf* biscuit or cake maker or dealer
**bizcocho** *m* biscuit (*bread and pottery*); cake, sponge cake; hardtack; bisque (*unglazed ceramic ware*); **bizcocho borracho** tipsy cake
**bizcorneto -ta** *adj* (Am.) squint-eyed, cross-eyed
**bizcotela** *f* sponge cake with icing
**bizma** *f* poultice
**bizmar** *va* to poultice
**bizna** *f* membrane (*between kernels of a nut*)
**biznaga** *f* (bot.) bishop's-weed; toothpick (*made from this plant*); (Am.) fishhook cactus
**biznieto -ta** *mf* var. of **bisnieto**
**bizquear** *vn* to squint
**blanca** *f* see **blanco**
**blancazo -za** *adj* (coll.) whitish
**blanco -ca** *adj* white (*like snow; applies also to grapes, wine, etc.*); fair (*complexion*); blank; water (*power*); (coll.) yellow (*cowardly*); *mf* white (*person*); (coll.) coward; *m* white (*color*); white star, white spot (*on horse*); blank; blank space; white page; interval; target; aim, goal; sizing; (print.) blank form; (her.) argent; **calentar al blanco** to heat to a white heat; **dar en el blanco** or **hacer blanco** to hit the mark; **en blanco** blank; **hacer blanco en** to hit; **quedarse en blanco** to fail to grasp the point; to be disappointed; **blanco abatible** collapsible target; **blanco de ballena** spermaceti; **blanco de España** whiting; **blanco de huevo** eggshell cosmetic; white of egg; **blanco de la uña** half moon of fingernail; **blanco del ojo** white of the eye; **blanco de plomo** white lead; *f* old coin of varying values; (mus.) minim; (*cap.*) *f* Blanch; **estar sin blanca** or **no tener blanca** to be broke; **blanca morfea** (vet.) tetter, ringworm; **Blanca Nieves** Snow White
**blancor** *m* whiteness
**blancote -ta** *adj* very white; dirty-white; (coll.) cowardly; *mf* (coll.) coward
**blancura** *f* whiteness; **blancura del ojo** (vet.) white spot on cornea
**blancuzco -ca** *adj* whitish; dirty-white
**blandeador -dora** *adj* softening, convincing
**blandear** *va* to soften, to convince, to persuade; to brandish; *vn & vr* to soften, to yield, to give in; to brandish
**blandengue** *adj* soft, easy-going; colorless, without character; *m* Argentine lancer
**blandiente** *adj* swaying, brandishing
**blandir** §53 *va, vn & vr* to brandish
**blando -da** *adj* bland, soft; tender (*eyes*); soft (*soap*); flabby; sensual; exquisite; indulgent; (coll.) cowardly; (phys.) soft (*ray; vacuum tube*); (mus.) flat; **más blando que una breva** (coll.) sweet as pie; **blando** *adv* softly, gently
**blandón** *m* wax candle; candlestick
**blandujo -ja** *adj* (coll.) softish
**blandura** *f* blandness, softness, gentleness; flattery, flirtation; white cosmetic; application, emolient; flabbiness; sensuality; mild weather
**blandurilla** *f* lavender pomade
**blanduzco -ca** *adj* (coll.) softish

**blanqueación** *f* whitening, bleaching; whitewashing; blanching
**blanqueador -dora** *adj* whitening, bleaching; whitewashing; *mf* whitener, bleacher; whitewasher
**blanqueadura** *f* or **blanqueamiento** *m* whitening, bleaching; whitewashing; blanching
**blanquear** *va* to whiten, to bleach; to whitewash; to tin; to blanch (*metals*); (cook. & hort.) to blanch; to wax (*honeycomb*); *vn* to blanch, to turn white
**blanquecer §34** *va* to whiten, to bleach; to blanch (*metals*)
**blanquecimiento** *m* bleaching; blanching of metals
**blanquecino -na** *adj* whitish
**blanqueo** *m* whitening, bleaching; whitewashing; blanching
**blanquería** *f* bleachery
**blanquete** *m* white cosmetic
**blanquición** *f* blanching of metals
**blanquillo -lla** *adj* whitish; white (*wheat, bread*); *m* (Am.) egg; (Am.) white peach
**blanquimento** or **blanquimiento** *m* bleacher, bleaching solution
**blanquinoso -sa** *adj* whitish
**blanquizal** *m* or **blanquizar** *m* chalk pit
**blanquizco -ca** *adj* white, whitish
**blao** *m* (her.) azure
**blasfemador -dora** or **blasfemante** *adj* blaspheming, blasphemous; *mf* blasphemer
**blasfemar** *vn* to blaspheme; **blasfemar contra** to blaspheme, to blaspheme against; **blasfemar de** to blaspheme, to curse (*e.g., virtue*)
**blasfematorio -ria** *adj* blasphemous
**blasfemia** *f* blasphemy; vile insult
**blasfemo -ma** *adj* blasphemous; *mf* blasphemer
**blasón** *m* heraldry, blazon; armorial bearings; (her.) charge; honor, glory
**blasonador -dora** *adj* boasting, bragging
**blasonar** *va* to emblazon (*heraldic shield*); (fig.) to emblazon, to extol; *vn* to boast, to brag; **blasonar de** to boast of being
**blasonería** *f* boasting, bragging
**blastema** *m* (embryol.) blastema
**blastocele** *m* (embryol.) blastocoele
**blastocisto** *m* (embryol.) blastocyst
**blastodermo** *m* (embryol.) blastoderm
**blástula** *f* (embryol.) blastula
**bledo** *m* (bot.) blite, goosefoot; (bot.) prostrate pigweed; **no dársele a uno un bledo de** (coll.) to not matter to a person, e.g., **no se me da un bledo de ello** that does not matter to me, that is of no importance to me
**blefaritis** *f* (path.) blepharitis
**blenda** *f* (mineral.) blende, zinc sulfide
**blenia** *f* (ichth.) blenny
**blenorrea** *f* (path.) blennorrhea
**blinda** *f* (fort.) blind
**blindado -da** *adj* shielded, armored
**blindaje** *m* (fort.) blindage; (naut.) armor; (elec.) shield
**blindar** *va* to armor; to armor-plate; (elec.) to shield
**b.l.m.** or **B.L.M.** abr. of **besa la mano**
**bloc** *m* (*pl:* **bloques**) pad (*of note paper*); tear-off calendar
**blocao** *m* (fort.) blockhouse
**blof** *m* bluff
**blofeador -dora** *adj* bluffing; *mf* bluffer
**blofear** *vn* to bluff
**blonda** *f* see **blondo**
**blondina** *f* narrow blond lace
**blondo -da** *adj* blond, flaxen, light; (Am.) curly; *f* blond lace
**bloque** *m* block; (mach.) cylinder block; pad; (print.) block; (pol.) block, bloc; block, lot (*of merchandise*); **bloque de hormigón** concrete block
**bloqueador -dora** *adj* blockading; *mf* blockader
**bloquear** *va* (mil. & naut.) to blockade; to brake (*car, train, etc.*); to block; (com.) to freeze
**bloqueo** *m* (mil. & naut.) blockade; (com.) freezing; **burlar, forzar** or **violar el bloqueo** to run the blockade; **bloqueo en el papel** paper blockade; **bloqueo horizontal** (telv.) horizontal hold; **bloqueo vertical** (telv.) vertical hold
**b.l.p.** or **B.L.P.** abr. of **besa los pies**
**blufar** *vn* var. of **blofear**
**blusa** *f* blouse; shirtwaist
**B.mo P.e** abr. of **Beatísimo Padre**
**boa** *f* (zool.) boa, boa constrictor; *m* boa (*scarf*)
**Boadicea** *f* Boadicea
**boardilla** *f* var. of **buhardilla**
**boato** *m* show, pomp; pageantry
**bobada** *f* folly, foolishness
**bobalías** *mf* (coll.) dolt, dunce, ass
**bobalicón -cona** *adj* (coll.) stupid, silly; *mf* (coll.) nitwit
**bobatel** *m* (coll.) simpleton
**bobático -ca** *adj* (coll.) foolish, silly, stupid (*deed or remark*)
**bobear** *vn* to talk nonsense, to act like a fool; to dawdle, to fool around
**bobera** *f* (Am.) folly, foolishness
**bobería** *f* folly, foolishness; trifle
**bóbilis; de bóbilis bóbilis** (coll.) for nothing; (coll.) without effort
**bobillo** *m* round glazed pitcher; lace worn around open neck
**bobina** *f* bobbin; (elec.) coil; **bobina de cesto** (rad.) basket coil; **bobina de chispas** spark coil; **bobina de choque** (elec.) choke coil; **bobina de encendido** spark coil, ignition coil; **bobina de impedancia** (elec.) impedance coil; **bobina de panal** (rad.) honeycomb coil; **bobina de regeneración** (rad.) tickler coil; **bobina de sintonía** (rad.) tuning coil; **bobina móvil** (rad.) voice coil; (elec.) moving coil; **bobina térmica** (elec.) heating coil; **bobina tipo canasto** (rad.) basket-weave coil
**bobinado** *m* (elec.) winding
**bobinadora** *f* winding machine
**bobinar** *va* to wind
**bobiné** *m* (Am.) bobbinet
**bobo -ba** *adj* simple, stupid; **bobo con** crazy about, mad about; *mf* simpleton, dunce; clown, jester
**boca** *f* mouth; taste, flavor; speech; entrance, portal (*to tunnel, subway, etc.*); pit (*of stomach*); **a boca** by word of mouth; **a boca de cañón** at close range; **a boca de jarro** without moderation (*with reference to drinking*); at close range; **a pedir de boca** to one's heart's content; exactly right; **buscar a uno la boca** to draw someone out; **decir con la boca chica** or **chiquita** (coll.) to offer as a mere formality; **decir** (*uno*) **lo que se le viene a la boca** (coll.) to say whatever comes into one's mind; **hablar por boca de ganso** (coll.) to say what one is told to say; **hacer boca** (coll.) to have some hors d'oeuvres; **meterse en la boca del león** (coll.) to put one's head in the lion's mouth; **no decir esta boca es mía** (coll.) to not say a word, to not say boo; **venirse a la boca a** to taste bad to, to regurgitate for; **boca abajo** face downward; **boca a boca** by word of mouth; **boca arriba** face upward; **boca de agua** hydrant; **boca de dragón** (bot.) snapdragon, dragon's-mouth; **boca de escorpión** evil tongue (*person*); **boca de gachas** (coll.) driveler; (coll.) babbler, jabberer; **boca del estómago** pit of stomach; **boca de riego** faucet, hydrant
**bocabarra** *f* (naut.) bar hole, socket (*of capstan*)
**bocacalle** *f* street entrance, street intersection
**bocacaz** *m* (*pl:* **-caces**) spillway, overflow
**bocací** *m* bocasine, colored buckram
**bocacha** *f* big mouth; wide-mouthed blunderbuss
**bocadear** *va* to break up, to divide into small parts or bits
**bocadillo** *m* thin middling linen; narrow tape or ribbon; snack; sandwich; stuffed roll; farmhand's bite or snack at ten A.M.; guava paste
**bocadito** *m* little bit; (Am.) cigarette (*wrapped in tobacco leaf*); **a bocaditos** piecemeal
**bocado** *m* mouthful, bite, morsel; bit; bridle; **bocados** *mpl* dried preserves; **con el bocado en la boca** (coll.) right after eating; **no te-**

**ner para un bocado** (coll.) to not have a cent, to be penniless; **bocado de Adán** Adam's apple; **bocado de gallina** (bot.) chickweed
**bocadulce** *m* (ichth.) smooth dogfish
**bocal** *m* narrow-mouthed pitcher; flume; narrows (*into a harbor*)
**bocallave** *f* keyhole
**bocamanga** *f* cuff, wristband; opening of sleeve
**bocamina** *f* mine entrance
**bocanada** *f* swallow; puff (*of smoke*); (coll.) boasting, bragging; **bocanada de gente** (coll.) rush, crush (*of people*); **bocanada de viento** gust of wind
**bocarte** *m* (min.) stamp mill
**bocartear** *va* to stamp, to crush (*ore*)
**bocateja** *f* front tile
**bocatijera** *f* carriage-pole socket
**bocaza** *f* big mouth; *mf* (coll.) blatherskite
**bocazo** *m* fizzle (*in blasting*)
**bocear** *vn* var. of **bocezar**
**bocel** *m* (arch.) solid cylindrical molding; edge (*of tumbler, etc.*); (carp.) molding plane; **cuarto bocel** (arch.) quarter round; **medio bocel** (arch.) half round
**bocelar** *va* to cut a molding on
**bocelete** *m* small molding plane
**bocera** *f* smear, stickiness (*on lips after eating or drinking*)
**boceto** *m* sketch, outline, model
**bocezar** **§76** *vn* to move the lips from side to side (*said of animals*)
**bocín** *m* hubcap (*of carriage*); hubcap of bass mat (*of cart*); feed pipe of overshot wheel
**bocina** *f* horn, trumpet; sea shell used as horn; phonograph horn; auto horn; speaking trumpet, ear trumpet; (Am.) blowgun
**bocinar** *vn* to blow the horn; to speak through a speaking trumpet
**bocinero** *m* hornblower, trumpeter
**bocio** *m* (path.) goiter
**bock** *m* (*pl:* **bocks**) beer glass (*of a quarter liter*)
**bocón -cona** *adj* (coll.) bigmouthed; (coll.) boastful; *mf* (coll.) spread eagle, braggart
**bocoy** *m* large barrel
**bocudo -da** *adj* bigmouthed
**bocha** *f* bowling ball; **bochas** *fpl* bowling
**bochar** *va* (bowling) to hit and move (*another ball*)
**bochazo** *m* stroke of one ball against another
**boche** *m* small hole in ground (*for boys' games*); Boche (*German*); (Am.) slight; **dar boche a** (Am.) to slight, to rebuff
**bochinche** *m* uproar, tumult; (Am.) mess, row, riot
**bochinchero -ra** *mf* noisemaker; (Am.) disturber of the peace, rioter; (Am.) sporty-looking roughneck
**bochista** *mf* expert bowler
**bochornazo** *m* sultry weather, stuffy weather
**bochorno** *m* sultry weather; hot summer breeze; flush; embarrassment; slight
**bochornoso -sa** *adj* sultry; stuffy; embarrassing; shameful, infamous
**boda** *f* marriage, wedding; **boda de negros** (coll.) noisy party, orgy; **bodas de Camacho** banquet, lavish feast; **bodas de diamante** diamond wedding, diamond jubilee; **bodas de oro** golden wedding; **bodas de plata** silver wedding
**bode** *m* billy goat
**bodega** *f* wine cellar, wine vault; vintage; pantry; storage vault, warehouse; (coll.) cellar; (naut.) hold (*of ship*); (coll.) tank (*hard drinker*); (Am.) grocery store; (Am.) freight station
**bodegón** *m* cheap restaurant; taproom; (paint.) still life
**bodegoncillo** *m* cheap little eating house; **bodegoncillo de puntapié** hash house on wheels
**bodegonear** *vn* to hang around taprooms
**bodegonero -ra** *mf* chophouse keeper; *m* bartender; *f* barmaid
**bodeguero -ra** *mf* cellarer, owner or keeper of a wine cellar; (Am.) grocer
**bodigo** *m* offering in church of a roll of fine wheat; dullard
**bodijo** *m* (coll.) unequal match, misalliance; (coll.) quiet wedding, simple wedding
**bodocazo** *m* hit made with ball of clay shot from crossbow
**bodón** *m* pool or pond that dries up in summer
**bodoque** *m* ball of clay shot from crossbow; lump; (coll.) dolt, dullard
**bodoquera** *f* mold for clay balls; cradle of crossbow; blowgun, peashooter
**bodorrio** *m* (coll.) unequal match, misalliance; (Am.) wedding party
**bodrio** *m* soup made of leavings; poorly seasoned stew; mixture of hog's blood and onions
**bóer** (*pl:* **bóeres**) *adj & mf* Boer
**boezuelo** *m* small ox; stalking ox (*used in hunting partridges*)
**bofe** *m* (coll.) lung; **bofes** *mpl* lights (*of sheep, pigs, etc.*); **echar el bofe** or **los bofes** (coll.) to toil, to drudge, to strive; **echar el bofe** or **los bofes por** (coll.) to burn to get, to be crazy about
**bofena** *f* var. of **bofe**
**bófeta** *f* thin stiff cotton fabric
**bofetada** *f* slap in the face; **dar de bofetada a** to slap in the face
**bofetán** *m* var. of **bófeta**
**bofetón** *m* hard slap in the face; (theat.) revolving-door trick
**boga** *f* vogue; rowing; stroke; (ichth.) ox-eyed cackerel, boce; **en boga** in vogue; *mf* rower
**bogada** *f* stroke (of oars)
**bogador -dora** *mf* rower
**bogar** **§59** *vn* to row; to sail
**bogavante** *m* strokesman; (zool.) lobster (*Homarus*)
**bogie** *m* (rail.) truck, bogie
**bogotano -na** *adj* (pertaining to) Bogotá; *mf* native or inhabitant of Bogotá
**bohardilla** *f* var. of **buhardilla**
**bohemia** & **Bohemia** *f* see **bohemio**
**bohemiano -na** *adj & mf* Bohemian
**bohémico -ca** *adj* Bohemian
**bohemio -mia** *adj & mf* Bohemian; gypsy; (fig.) Bohemian; *m* Bohemian (*language*); *f* (fig.) Bohemia; (fig.) Bohemianism; (Am.) wild oats; (*cap.*) *f* Bohemia
**bohemo -ma** *adj & mf* Bohemian
**bohena** *f* lung; pork-lung sausage
**bohío** *m* (Am.) hut; (Am.) brothel
**bohordo** *m* dart, short spear; (bot.) reed; (bot.) scape; (bot.) cattail spike
**boicot** *m* (*pl:* **-cots**) boycott
**boicotear** *va* to boycott
**boicoteo** *m* boycott, boycotting
**boíl** *m* ox stall
**boina** *f* beret
**boira** *f* mist, fog
**boj** *m* (bot.) boxwood; **boj de China** (bot.) orange jessamine
**boja** *f* (bot.) southernwood; bushes (*for rearing silkworms*)
**bojar** *va* to scrape (*leather*) clean; (naut.) to measure the perimeter of (*island or cape*); *vn* to measure (*said of the perimeter of island or cape*)
**boje** *m* var. of **boj**
**bojear** *va* (naut.) to measure the perimeter of (*island or cape*); *vn* (naut.) to measure (*said of the perimeter of island or cape*)
**bojedal** *m* growth of boxwood
**bojeo** *m* (naut.) measure of perimeter of island or cape; (naut.) perimeter of island or cape
**bojiganga** *f* traveling comedians; outlandish dress or disguise
**bojo** *m* (naut.) measure of perimeter of island or cape
**bol** *m* bowl; punch bowl; ninepin; dragnet; **bol arménico** or **de Armenia** Armenian bole
**bola** *f* ball; globe; bowling; shine, shoeshine; (cards) slam, grand slam; resentment; trick, deceit, lie; (naut.) signal made of two black disks crossed at right angles; (Am.) uprising, revolution; **bolas** *fpl* (Am.) bolas (*South American cowboy weapon*); **a bola vista** evidently, openly; **¡dale bola!** (coll.) that'll do!; **dejar rodar la bola** to let things take their course; **bola de alcanfor** camphor ball, moth ball; **bola de billar** billiard ball; **bola de**

cristal crystal ball (*used to divine the future*); **bola de nieve** snowball; (bot.) snowball; **bola de tenis** tennis ball; **bola negra** black ball; **bola rompedora** wrecking ball
**bolada** *f* throw (*of a ball*); love affair; lucky deal; (coll.) cinch; (Am.) prize (*in a raffle*)
**bolado** *m* meringue
**bolanchera** *f* (Am.) Paul Jones (*dance*)
**bolandista** *m* Bollandist
**bolardo** *m* (naut.) bollard
**bolazo** *m* hit with a ball; (Am.) nonsense; **de bolazo** (coll.) carelessly, hurriedly
**bolchevique** *adj & mf* Bolshevik
**bolcheviquismo** *m* Bolshevism
**bolcheviquista** *adj* Bolshevist, Bolshevistic; *mf* Bolshevist
**bolchevismo** *m* var. of **bolcheviquismo**
**bolchevista** *adj & mf* var. of **bolcheviquista**
**bolchevización** *f* Bolshevization
**bolchevizar** §76 *va* to Bolshevize
**boldina** *f* (pharm.) boldine
**boldo** *m* (bot.) boldo
**bolea** *f* (sport) volley
**boleada** *f* (Am.) shoeshine
**boleador** *m* (Am.) bootblack
**boleadoras** *fpl* (Am.) bola or bolas (*South American cowboy weapon*)
**bolear** *va* (coll.) to throw; (coll.) to play a mean trick on; to blackball; (Am.) to flunk; (Am.) to lasso with bolas; (Am.) to shine, to polish (*shoes*); *vn* to play for fun (*said of billiards and other games*); to bowl; to boast; to lie; *vr* to stumble; (Am.) to stumble and fall in a ball; (Am.) to falter, to waver; (Am.) to rear and tumble
**boleo** *m* bowling; bowling green; jolt, blow
**bolero -ra** *adj* truant; (coll.) lying; *mf* bolero dancer; (Am.) bootblack; *m* bolero (*dance and music; short jacket*); *f* bowling alley; **bolera encespada** bowling green
**boleta** *f* pass, entrance ticket; authorization; (mil.) billet; small package of tobacco; (Am.) certificate; (Am.) ballot
**boletería** *f* (Am.) ticket office
**boletero** *m* (Am.) ticket agent, ticket seller; (Am.) ticket collector
**boletín** *m* bulletin; ticket; pay warrant; (mil.) billet; **boletín de inscripción** registration form; **boletín de renovación** renewal form (*e.g., for subscription to a newspaper*)
**boleto** *m* ticket of admission; lottery ticket; (bot.) boletus, cepe; (Am.) ticket; **boleto de empeño** (Am.) pawn ticket; **boleto de señal** animal license, dog license
**bolichada** *f* fish caught with dragnet; (coll.) lucky break; **de una bolichada** (coll.) at one stroke
**boliche** *m* bowling; jack (*small ball for bowling*); bowling alley; small dragnet; small fish caught with dragnet; cup and ball (*game*); lead-smelting furnace; (naut.) bowline of a small sail; (Am.) store, shop; (Am.) hash house; (Am.) gambling den
**bolichear** *vn* (Am.) to fiddle around
**bólido** *m* (astr.) bolide, fireball; racer, racing car; (Am.) hot rod (*supercharged flivver*)
**bolígrafo** *m* ball point pen
**bolillo** *m* bobbin for making lace; form for stiffening lace cuffs; (zool.) coffin bone; (Am.) drumstick; (Am.) white bread; (Am. offensive) light-skinned person; (Am.) roll (*bread*); **bolillos** *mpl* candy bars
**bolín** *m* jack (*small ball for bowling*); **de bolín** (coll.) carelessly, thoughtlessly
**bolina** *f* (naut.) bowline; (naut.) flogging; (naut.) sounding line; (coll.) racket, row, dispute; **de bolina** (naut.) on a bowline, close-hauled; **echar de bolina** (coll.) to boast, brag; (coll.) to exaggerate
**bolineador -dora** *adj* (naut.) sailing well when close-hauled
**bolinear** *va* (naut.) to haul (*the bowline*); *vn* (naut.) to haul the bowline, to sail close-hauled; (naut.) to sail to windward
**bolinero -ra** *adj* (naut.) sailing well when close-hauled; (Am.) riotous, quarrelsome
**bolisa** *f* embers, hot coals
**bolístico -ca** *adj* bowling
**bolívar** *m* bolivar (*monetary unit of Venezuela*)
**Bolivia** *f* Bolivia
**bolivianismo** *m* Bolivianism
**boliviano -na** *adj & mf* Bolivian; *m* boliviano (*Bolivian monetary unit*)
**bolo** *m* ninepin, tenpin; dunce, ignoramus; bolus, big pill; bolt (*of food*); traveling comedians; newel (*of winding stairs*); (cards) slam; bolo (*Philippine knife*); **bolos** *mpl* bowling, ninepins, tenpins; **jugar a los bolos** to bowl
**Bolonia** *f* Bologna
**bolonio** *adj masc* (coll.) stupid, ignorant; *m* (coll.) ignoramus
**boloñés -ñesa** *adj & mf* Bolognese
**bolsa** *f* purse, pocketbook; bag, pouch; bag (*e.g., in trousers*); pouch (*e.g., of kangaroo*); (anat. & path.) pocket; (anat.) bursa; stock exchange, stock market; (min.) richest vein of gold; wealth, money; grant, award (*to a student, artist, etc.*); (box.) prize money; (Am.) pocket; **bolsas** *fpl* (anat.) scrotum; **jugar a la bolsa** to play the market, to speculate in stocks; **la bolsa o la vida** your money or your life; **no abrir fácilmente la bolsa** to be tight-fisted; **bolsa de agua caliente** hot-water bottle; **bolsa de hielo** ice bag; **bolsa de la tinta** ink sac; **bolsa de pastor** (bot.) shepherd's-purse; **bolsa de trabajo** employment bureau; **bolsa de viaje** traveling fellowship
**bolsear** *va* (Am.) to jilt; (Am.) to pick the pocket of; (Am.) to sponge on; *vn* (Am.) to pucker
**bolsería** *f* manufacture of purses, pocketbooks, or bags; purse, pocketbook, or bag business or store
**bolsero -ra** *mf* maker or seller of purses or pocketbooks; (Am.) sponger
**bolsillero** *m* pickpocket
**bolsillo** *m* pocket; pocketbook; money; **rascarse el bolsillo** (coll.) to fork out, to come across; **tener en el bolsillo** to have in one's pocket (*i.e., in one's control*); **bolsillo de parche** patch pocket
**bolsín** *m* curb market
**bolsiquear** *va* (Am.) to frisk the pockets of
**bolsista** *m* broker, stockbroker
**bolso** *m* bag, purse, pocketbook; (naut.) pocket (*in a sail*); **bolso de mano** handbag
**bolsón** *m* large purse; plank floor of olive crusher; (geol.) bolson; (mil.) pocket
**bolsudo -da** *adj* (Am.) baggy; (Am.) slow, heavy, lazy
**bolla** *f* (archaic) tax on manufacture of playing cards
**bolladura** *f* dent; embossing; bump, bruise
**bollar** *va* to mark (*fabrics*) with lead seal; to emboss
**bollería** *f* bakery, pastry shop
**bollero -ra** *mf* baker
**bollo** *m* bun, muffin; puff (*in a dress*); tuft (*in upholstery*); bump, lump, bruise; dent; (Am.) loaf of bread; **bollos** *mpl* (Am.) troubles, difficulties; **bollos de relieve** embossing, raised work
**bollón** *m* brass-headed nail or tack; (bot.) bud; button earring
**bollonado -da** *adj* trimmed with brass-headed nails or tacks
**bomba** *f* see **bombo**
**bombacha** *f* or **bombachas** *fpl* (Am.) loose-fitting breeches fastened at the bottom
**bombacho** *adj masc* loose-fitting (*breeches or trousers*)
**bombar** *va* to pump
**bombarda** *f* (archaic) bombard (*piece of ordnance; bomb vessel*); (mus.) borbardon (*organ stop and ancient wind instrument*)
**bombardear** *va* to bombard; to bomb; (phys.) to bombard
**bombardeo** *m* bombardment; bombing; **bombardeo de precisión** (aer.) precision bombing; **bombardeo de saturación** (aer.) saturation bombing; **bombardeo en picado** (aer.) dive bombing
**bombardero -ra** *adj* bombing; *m* bomber (*crewman and airplane*)
**bombardino** *m* (mus.) saxhorn

**bombardón** *m* (mus.) bass saxhorn
**bomba-reloj** *f* time bomb
**bombasí** *m* fustian
**bombástico -ca** *adj* bombastic
**bombazo** *m* bomb explosion; bomb hit; bomb damage
**bombé** *m* light two-wheeled carriage for two people
**bombear** *va* to bomb; (Am.) to pump; (Am.) to reconnoiter; to laud, to ballyhoo; to cheat; (Am.) to fire, to dismiss; *vr* to arch, to camber, to bulge
**bombeo** *m* bombing; (Am.) pumping; curving, bulging; crown (*of a road*)
**bombero** *m* pumper, pumpman; fireman (*who puts out fires*)
**bombilla** *f* lamp chimney; light bulb; thief tube; **bombilla de destello** or **bombilla relámpago** (phot.) flash bulb
**bombillo** *m* lamp chimney; light bulb; thief tube; (naut.) portable pump; trap (*in a toilet*)
**bombín** *m* derby, bowler
**bombista** *m* lamp maker; bomb maker; (coll.) booster
**bombo -ba** *adj* (coll.) dumfounded, aghast ‖ *m* bass drum; bass-drum player; (naut.) barge, lighter; ballyhoo; (Am.) lie, falsehood; **anunciar a bombo y platillo** (coll.) to ballyhoo; **dar bombo a** (coll.) to ballyhoo ‖ *f* pump; fire engine; bomb; lamp globe; high hat; (Am.) firecracker, skyrocket; **a prueba de bombas** bombproof; **caer como una bomba** (coll.) to fall like a bombshell; (coll.) to burst in unexpectedly; **dar a la bomba** (naut.) to use the pump (*in order to bail out water*); **estar en bomba** (Am.) to be drunk; **bomba alimenticia** feed pump; **bomba al vacío** vacuum pump; **bomba aspirante** suction pump; **bomba atómica** atomic bomb; **bomba centrífuga** centrifugal pump; **bomba cohete** rocket bomb; **bomba de cadena** chain pump; **bomba de carena** (naut.) bilge pump; **bomba de demolición** demolition bomb; **bomba de émbolo buzo** plunger pump; **bomba de engrase** grease gun; **bomba de fragmentación** fragmentation bomb; **bomba de hidrógeno** hydrogen bomb; **bomba de incendios** fire engine; **bomba de mano** hand pump, stirrup pump; (mil.) hand bomb; **bomba demoledora** demolition bomb; **bomba de neutrones** neutron bomb; **bomba de plástico** plastic bomb; **bomba de profundidad** depth bomb; **bomba de sentina** (naut.) bilge pump; **bomba estomacal** stomach pump; **bomba fétida** stink bomb; **bomba impelente** force or pressure pump; **bomba incendiaria** (mil.) incendiary bomb; **bomba volante** buzz bomb; **¡bomba!** attention, please!
**bombón** *m* bonbon
**bombona** *f* carboy
**bombonaje** *m* (bot.) jipijapa (*plant and leaves*)
**bombonera** *f* candy box, bonbonnière
**bombonería** *f* candy store
**Bona** *f* Bône
**bonachón -chona** *adj* (coll.) good-natured, unsuspecting
**bonaerense** *adj* (pertaining to) Buenos Aires; *mf* native or inhabitant of Buenos Aires
**bonancible** *adj* calm, gentle, serene
**bonanza** *f* (naut.) fair weather, clear skies; (min.) bonanza; (fig.) bonanza (*source of wealth*); **estar en bonanza** to be booming; **ir en bonanza** (naut. & fig.) to have clear sailing; (fig.) to get along famously
**bonapartista** *mf* Bonapartist
**bonarense** *adj & mf* var. of **bonaerense**
**bonazo -za** *adj* (coll.) kind, good-natured
**bondad** *f* kindness, goodness, gentleness, favor; **tener la bondad de** + *inf* to be good enough to + *inf*, please + *inf*
**bondadoso -sa** *adj* kind, good
**bonderizar §76** *va* to bonderize
**boneta** *f* (naut.) bonnet
**bonetada** *f* raising one's hat (*in salutation*)
**bonete** *m* hat, cap; cap (*of academic dress*); secular cleric; glass candy bowl; (anat. & fort.) bonnet; **a tente bonete** (coll.) with persistence
**bonetería** *f* hat shop; hat business
**bonetero** *m* hat maker or dealer; (bot.) spindle tree
**bonga** *f* (bot.) areca
**bongó** *m* bongo (*Afro-Cuban drum*)
**bonhomía** *f* (Am.) bonhomie
**boniato** *m* var. of **buniato**
**bonico -ca** *adj* nice, pretty, neat
**Bonifacio** *m* Boniface
**bonificación** *f* rise, increase; increased output; allowance, discount; (bridge) bonus
**bonificar §86** *va* to allow, to discount
**bonina** *f* (bot.) ringflower
**bonísimo -ma** *adj super* very good
**bonítalo** *m* (ichth.) bonito
**bonitamente** *adv* gropingly, stealthily, craftily; slowly, gradually
**bonito -ta** *adj* pretty; neat, spruce; *m* (ichth.) bonito
**bonizal** *m* growth of wild corn
**bonizo** *m* wild corn
**bono** *m* (com.) bond; scrip, voucher
**bonote** *m* cocoanut fiber, coir
**bonzo** *m* bonze, Buddhist monk
**boñiga** *f* cow dung
**boñigo** *m* pancake (*of cow dung*)
**Bootes** *m* (astr.) Boötes
**boqueada** *f* gasp of death
**boquear** *va* to pronounce, to utter; *vn* to gape, to gasp; to be in the throes of death; (coll.) to be about to end
**boquera** *f* sluice (*of irrigation canal*); window in hayloft; (path.) sore at angle of lips; (vet.) sore mouth
**boquerel** *m* nozzle
**boquerón** *m* wide opening, large hole; (ichth.) anchovy
**boquete** *m* gap, narrow passage; breach, opening
**boquiabierto -ta** *adj* open-mouthed
**boquiancho -cha** *adj* wide-mouthed
**boquiangosto -ta** *adj* narrow-mouthed
**boquiblando -da** *adj* tender-mouthed (*said of a horse*)
**boquiconejuno -na** *adj* rabbit-mouthed (*said of a horse*)
**boquiduro -ra** *adj* hard-mouthed (*said of a horse*)
**boquifresco -ca** *adj* fresh-mouthed (*said of a horse*); (coll.) outspoken
**boquilla** *f* opening in leg of trousers (*through which foot passes*); opening in irrigation canal; mouthpiece (*of wind instrument*); stem (*of pipe*); nozzle; burner; cigar holder, cigarette holder; clasp (*of purse*); **boquilla filtrónica** filter tip
**boquimuelle** *adj* tender-mouthed (*said of a horse*); easily duped or imposed upon; garrulous
**boquín** *m* coarse baize
**boquinegro -gra** *adj* black-mouthed (*said of an animal*); *m* (zool.) land snail (*Helix vermiculata*)
**boquirrasgado -da** *adj* wide-mouthed
**boquirroto -ta** *adj* wide-mouthed; (coll.) garrulous
**boquirrubio -bia** *adj* rosy-mouthed (*said of a child*); outspoken; garrulous; simple, naive; *m* (coll.) pretty boy
**boquiseco -ca** *adj* dry-mouthed
**boquituerto -ta** *adj* wry-mouthed, crooked-mouthed
**boquiverde** *adj* smutty, obscene, ribald
**boracita** *f* (mineral.) boracite
**boratado -da** *adj* borated
**borato** *m* (chem.) borato
**bórax** *m* (chem.) borax
**borbollar** or **borbollear** *vn* to bubble, to boil up
**borbollón** *m* bubbling, boiling; **a borbollones** impetuously, tumultuously
**borbollonear** *vn* to bubble, to boil up
**Borbón** *m* Bourbon
**borbónico -ca** *adj* Bourbonian or Bourbonic
**borbonismo** *m* Bourbonism
**borbor** *m* bubbling (*of spring water or boiling water*)
**borborigmo** *m* rumbling of the bowels
**borboritar** *vn* (coll.) to bubble, to boil up

**borbotar** or **borbotear** *vn* to bubble out, to bubble up
**borboton** *m* bubbling, boiling; **a borbotones** impetuously, tumultuously; **hablar a borbotones** (coll.) to speak in torrents
**borceguí** *m* (*pl:* **-guíes**) high shoe
**borceguinería** *f* shoeshop, shoe store
**borceguinero -ra** *mf* shoemaker; shoe dealer
**borcellar** *m* brim, edge (*of a container*)
**borda** *f* (naut.) gunwale; (naut.) mainsail (*of galley*); hut; **fuera de borda** outboard; **arrojar, echar** or **tirar por la borda** to throw overboard; (fig.) to throw overboard
**bordada** *f* (naut.) board (*stretch on one tack*); (coll.) walking back and forth; **dar bordadas** (naut.) to tack back and forth; (coll.) to keep walking back and forth
**bordado** *m* embroidering; embroidery; **bordado de realce** raised embroidery
**bordador -dora** *mf* embroiderer
**bordadura** *f* embroidery; (her.) bordure
**bordaje** *m* (naut.) side planks
**bordar** *va* to embroider; (fig.) to embroider, to embroider on
**borde** *m* edge, border, fringe; ledge; (naut.) board; **borde de ataque** (aer.) leading edge; **borde del mar** seaside, seashore; **borde de salida** (aer.) trailing edge; *adj* wild, uncultivated; bastard
**bordeado -da** *adj* hairbreadth, close, narrow
**bordear** *va* to border, to trim with a border; to skirt; (fig.) to border on; *vn* to stay on the edge; (naut.) to sail to windward
**bordelés -lesa** *adj* Bordelais, (pertaining to) Bordeaux; *mf* native or inhabitant of Bordeaux
**bordillo** *m* curb, curbing
**bordo** *m* (naut.) board; (naut.) tack; (Am.) ridge, furrow; (Am.) dike, dam; **a bordo** (naut.) on board; **al bordo** (naut.) alongside; **de alto bordo** (naut.) of several decks, seagoing; (fig.) of importance; (fig.) high-up; **rendir el bordo en** (naut.) to arrive at
**bordón** *m* pilgrim's staff; staff, guide (*person*); (mus.) bass string; (mus.) bass stop (*of organ*); (mus.) drone (*of bagpipe*); burden (*of poem or song*); pet word, pet phrase; snare (*of drum*)
**bordoncillo** *m* pet word, pet phrase
**bordonear** *vn* to grope along with a stick or cane; to go around begging
**bordonería** *f* groping; life of a tramp; tramping as a pilgrim
**bordonero -ra** *mf* tramp, vagabond
**bordura** *f* (her.) bordure
**boreal** *adj* boreal, northern
**Bóreas** *m* (myth.) Boreas; (*l.c.*) *m* Boreas (*north wind*)
**borgoña** *m* Burgundy (*wine*); **la Borgoña** Burgundy
**borgoñés -ñesa** or **borgoñón -ñona** *adj & mf* Burgundian; *m* Burgundian (*dialect*)
**borgoñota** *f* burgonet
**bórico -ca** *adj* (chem.) boric
**boricua** *adj & mf* (Am.) Puerto Rican
**borinqueño -ña** *adj & mf* Puerto Rican
**borla** *f* tassel; tuft; powder puff; tassel of academic cap; doctor's degree; **borlas** *fpl* (bot.) amaranth; **tomar la borla** to take a higher degree, to take the doctor's degree
**borlar** *vr* (Am.) to take a higher degree, to take the doctor's degree
**borlilla** *f* (bot.) anther
**borlón** *m* large tassel; dimity; **borlones** *mpl* (bot.) amaranth
**borne** *m* tip (*of lance*); (elec.) binding post, terminal; (bot.) flatpod; *adj* hard and brittle (*said of wood*)
**borneadero** *m* (naut.) berth of a ship at anchor; (naut.) turning basin
**borneadizo -za** *adj* easy to bend, easily warped
**bornear** *va* to twist, to bend; to model and carve (*a column or pillar*); to hoist and put (*building stones*) in place; to size up (*e.g., a board*) with one eye closed, to see if it is in line; *vn* (naut.) to swing at anchor; *vr* to warp, to bulge
**borneo** *m* twisting, bending; sway (*in dancing*); (naut.) swinging at anchor
**borní** *m* (*pl:* **-níes**) (orn.) marsh harrier
**boro** *m* (chem.) boron
**borona** *f* (bot.) millet; corn bread
**boronía** *f* var. of **alboronía**
**borra** *f* yearling ewe; thick wool; goat's hair; fuzz, nap; floss, burl; sediment, lees; trash, waste; (chem.) borax; **borra de algodón** cotton waste
**borracha** *f* see **borracho**
**borrachear** *vn* to booze; to rant, talk nonsense
**borrachera** *f* drunkenness; spree, carousing; high exaltation; (coll.) great nonsense; **tomar una borrachera** to go on a spree, go on a binge
**borrachero** *m* (bot.) stramonium
**borrachez** *f* drunkenness; mental aberration
**borrachín** *m* (coll.) drunk, drunkard
**borracho -cha** *adj* drunk; drinking; violet-colored; (coll.) blind, wild (*e.g., with jealousy*); **borracho perdido** blotto; *mf* drunk, drunkard; *f* (coll.) leather wine bottle
**borrachuela** *f* (bot.) darnel, bearded darnel
**borrachuelo** *m* brandied fritter
**borrado** *m* erasure
**borrador** *m* rough draft; rough copy; sketch; blotter, waste book, day book; (Am.) rubber eraser; (Am.) blackboard eraser
**borradura** *f* erasure
**borraj** *m* (chem.) borax
**borraja** *f* (bot.) borage
**borrajear** *va & vn* to scribble; to doodle
**borrajo** *m* embers, hot ashes
**borrar** *va* to efface, to strike out, to cross out; to erase, to rub out, to blot out; to blot, to smear with ink; to cloud, to darken, to obscure
**borrasca** *f* storm, tempest; danger, hazard; setback; revolution; (coll.) spree, orgy; (naut.) storm; **borrasca magnética** (phys.) magnetic storm
**borrascoso -sa** *adj* stormy; (fig.) stormy
**borrasquero -ra** *adj* (coll.) riotous, fond of revelry
**borratintas** *m* (*pl:* **-tas**) ink eradicator
**borregada** *f* flock of lambs
**borrego -ga** *mf* lamb; (coll.) simpleton; **borregos** *mpl* (coll.) fleecy clouds
**borreguero -ra** *adj* good for pasturing lambs; *mf* shepherd who tends lambs
**borreguil** *adj* (pertaining to a) lamb
**borrén** *m* saddle pad
**borrica** *f* she-ass; (coll.) stupid woman
**borricada** *f* drove of asses; ride on an ass; asininity
**borrico** *m* ass, donkey; sawhorse; (fig.) ass
**borricón** *m* or **borricote** *m* (coll.) drudge, plodder
**borrilla** *f* down, fuzz (*on fruit*)
**borriquero** *m* ass driver or tender
**borriquete** *m* sawhorse
**borro** *m* lamb (*between one and two years old*)
**borrón** *m* blot, ink blot; blemish; rough draft; first sketch; (fig.) blot, stain
**borronear** *va* to scribble; to outline
**borroso -sa** *adj* blurred, blurry, fuzzy; muddy, thick; dull, inconspicuous
**borrumbada** *f* var. of **barrumbada**
**boruca** *f* noise, uproar, hubbub
**borujo** *m* pack, lump; bagasse of olive pits
**borujón** *m* bump, lump; roll, bundle (*of clothing*)
**borusca** *f* dry leaves, falling leaves
**boscaje** *m* boscage; (paint.) woodland scene
**boscoso -sa** *adj* woodsy, bosky
**Bósforo** *m* Bosporus; (*l.c.*) *m* strait
**bosníaco -ca** or **bosnio -nia** *adj & mf* Bosnian
**bosque** *m* forest, woods, woodland; **bosque maderable** timberland
**bosquecillo** *m* copse, bosk
**bosquejar** *va* to sketch, to outline
**bosquejo** *m* sketch, outline
**bosquete** *m* woods, forest; grove
**bosquimán** *m* or **bosquimano** *m* Bushman (*roving hunter of South Africa*)
**bosta** *f* dung, manure
**bostezador -dora** *adj* always yawning

**bostezar** §76 *vn* to yawn, to gape
**bostezo** *m* yawn, gape; **bostezos** yawning
**bostón** *m* boston (*card game and dance*)
**bostonar** or **bostonear** *vn* to dance the boston
**bostoniano -na** *adj & mf* Bostonian
**bóstrice** *m* (bot.) bostryx
**bota** *f* see **boto**
**botacuchar** *vn* to meddle, to butt in
**botado -da** *adj* (Am.) (pertaining to a) foundling; (Am.) brazen; (Am.) simple, silly; (Am.) fired, discharged; (Am.) wasteful, prodigal, spendthrift; (Am.) cheap; (Am.) overcome with sleep from too much drinking; *mf* (Am.) foundling; *f* launching; staves for barrels; (Am.) firing (*of an employee*)
**botador** *m* pole (*to push a boat*); punch, nailset; nail puller; (dent.) pelican
**botadura** *f* launching
**botafuego** *m* linstock, match staff; (coll.) firebrand, quick temper (*person*)
**botafumeiro** *m* incensory; (coll.) flattery
**botagueña** *f* pork-haslet sausage
**botalón** *m* (naut.) boom; **botalón de foque** (naut.) jib boom; **botalón de petifoque** (naut.) flying jib boom
**botamen** *m* pots and jars of a drug store; (naut.) water casks on board
**botana** *f* plug, stopper; scar; patch, plaster; (Am.) hors d'oeuvre
**botanga** *f* (naut.) outrigger
**botánico -ca** *adj* botanic or botanical; *mf* botanist; *f* botany
**botanista** *mf* botanist
**botanizar** §76 *vn* to botanize
**botar** *va* to hurl, to fling; to throw away; to launch (*a boat*); to turn, to shift (*the helm or rudder*); (Am.) to waste, to squander; (Am.) to fire, to dismiss; *vn* to bounce; to jump, to caper; *vr* to buck (*to throw rider*); (Am.) to lie down
**botaratada** *f* (coll.) blustering, wildness; (coll.) smartness; (coll.) bragging; (Am.) profligacy
**botarate** *m* (coll.) blusterer, madcap; (coll.) smart aleck; (coll.) braggart; (Am.) spendthrift
**botarel** *m* (arch.) abutment, buttress
**botarga** *f* galligaskins; clownish outfit; clown
**botasilla** *f* (mil.) boots and saddles
**botavante** *m* (naut.) boarding pike
**botavara** *f* (naut.) sprit, gaff, boom, pole
**bote** *m* thrust, blow; jump, prance (*of horse*); small boat, rowboat; bounce; can; pot, jar; (Am.) jug, jail; (Am.) liquor bottle, gin bottle; **de bote en bote** (coll.) jammed, packed; **de bote y boleo** (coll.) hastily, thoughtlessly; **bote automóvil** powerboat; **bote de carnero** bucking of a horse; **bote de paso** ferryboat; **bote de porcelana** apothecary's jar; **bote de remos** rowboat; **bote de salvamento** or **bote salvavidas** lifeboat; **bote vivandero** bumboat; **bote volador** flying boat
**botella** *f* bottle; **botella de Leiden** (elec.) Leyden jar
**botellazo** *m* blow or hit with a bottle
**botellería** *f* bottle factory; bottles
**botellero** *m* bottle maker or dealer; bottle rack
**botellón** *m* (Am.) large water bottle; (Am.) carafe; (Am.) demijohn
**botería** *f* manufacture or business of wine bags, bottles, or casks; (naut.) wine casks
**botero** *m* maker or seller of wine bags, bottles, or casks; boatman, ferryman; skipper
**botica** *f* drug store, apothecary's shop; medicine; **de todo como en botica** (coll.) everything under the sun
**boticario -ria** *mf* druggist; *f* druggist's wife
**botija** *f* earthen jug; (Am.) buried treasure; (Am.) belly; **estar hecho una botija** (coll.) to be puffy, be puffed up; **decir más que botija verde a** or **poner como botija verde** (Am.) to heap insults on
**botijero -ra** *mf* maker or seller of earthen jars and jugs
**botijo** *m* earthen jar or jug with spout and handle; (coll.) chunky fellow
**botilla** *f* shoe; (Am.) bottle
**botillería** *f* ice-cream parlor, soft-drink store; liquor store; bar, saloon
**botillero -ra** *mf* ice-cream and soft-drink dealer; liquor dealer
**botillo** *m* leather wine bag
**botín** *m* boot; spat (*short gaiter*); buskin; booty, spoils; (Am.) sock
**botina** *f* high shoe
**botinero -ra** *adj* black-foot (*cattle*); *m* boot maker; boot dealer; (mil.) handler of booty
**botiquín** *m* medicine kit, medicine chest, first-aid kit; first-aid station; (Am.) retail wine store; **botiquín de emergencia** first-aid kit
**botito** *m* high shoe
**botivoleo** *m* (sport) hitting the ball on the bounce
**boto -ta** *adj* dull, blunt; (fig.) dull, slow; *m* leather wine or oil bag; *f* boot, shoe; leather wine bag; butt, pipe; water cask; liquid measure (*516 liters or 125 gallons*); **morir con las botas puestas** to die with one's boots on; **ponerse las botas** (coll.) to hit the jack pot, strike it rich; **bota de agua** gum boot; **bota de montar** riding boot
**botón** *m* button; knob; stem (*of watch*); tip (*of foil*); (bot.) bud; (elec.) push button; (mach.) crankpin; **botones** *msg* bellboy, bellhop, buttons; **botón de contacto** (elec.) push button; **botón de oro** (bot.) creeping crowfoot; (bot.) buttercup (*Ranunculus acris*); **botón de puerta** doorknob; **botón de sintonización** (rad.) tuning knob
**botonadura** *f* set of buttons
**botonar** *vn* (Am.) to bud
**botonazo** *m* thrust with foil
**botoncillo** *m* (bot.) buttonwood (*Conocarpus*)
**botonería** *f* button maker's shop
**botonero -ra** *mf* button maker or dealer; *f* (bot.) santolina; (elec.) panel of push buttons
**bototo** *m* (Am.) gourd for carrying water
**botulismo** *m* (path.) botulism
**botuto** *m* long stem of papaya; sacred war trumpet of Orinoco Indians
**bou** *m* (*pl:* **bous**) fishing by casting a net between two boats
**bóveda** *f* (arch.) vault, dome; cave, cavern; crypt; (anat.) vault; (aut.) cowl; **bóveda celeste** firmament, canopy of heaven; **bóveda claustral** (arch.) cloister vault; **bóveda de casquete esférico** (arch.) spherical vault; **bóveda en cañón** (arch.) barrel vault; **bóveda esquifada** (arch.) cavetto vault; **bóveda ojival** (arch.) quadripartite vault; **bóveda palatina** (anat.) palatine vault; **bóveda por arista** (arch.) cross vault; **bóveda vaída** (arch.) Byzantine dome or vault
**bovedilla** (arch.) small vault or arch; (naut.) counter
**bóvido -da** *adj* bovine, bovid
**bovino -na** *adj & m* bovine
**boxeador** *m* (sport) boxer; (Am.) brass knuckles
**boxear** *vn* to box
**boxeo** *m* boxing
**bóxer** *m* (*pl:* **bóxers**) boxer (*dog*); brass knuckles; Boxer (*of China*)
**boxibalón** *m* (sport) punching bag
**boxístico -ca** *adj* boxing
**boya** *f* (naut.) buoy; float (*for fishing net*); **boya de campana** (naut.) bell buoy; **boya pantalón** (naut.) breeches buoy; **boya salvavidas** (naut.) life buoy
**boyada** *f* drove of oxen
**boyal** *adj* (pertaining to) cattle
**boyante** *adj* buoyant; prosperous, lucky; (naut.) light (*carrying a small cargo or none at all*); (taur.) easy, mild
**boyar** *vn* to float, be afloat again
**boyardo** *m* boyar or boyard
**boyazo** *m* large ox
**boyera** or **boyeriza** *f* ox stable
**boyerizo** or **boyero** *m* oxherd, ox driver
**boyezuelo** *m* small ox, young ox
**boyuno -na** *adj* bovine
**boza** *f* (naut.) stopper
**bozal** *adj* just brought in (*said of Negro from Africa*); pure, unmixed (*said of Negro*); simple, stupid; wild, untamed; stammering (*child*); (coll.) novice, inexperienced; (Am.) speaking broken Spanish; *m* muzzle; bells on harness (*over nose of horse*); (Am.) headstall

**bozo** *m* down on upper lip; mouth, lips; lower part of face; headstall
**B.p.** abr. of **Bendición papal**
**br.** or **Br.** abr. of **bachiller**
**Brabante** *m* Brabant; (*l.c.*) *m* brabant (*linen*)
**braceada** *f* swinging the arms
**braceador** *m* brewer
**braceaje** *m* coining, minting; brewing; (found.) tapping; (naut.) fathoming, fathomage; (naut.) bracing the yards
**bracear** *va* to brew; (found.) to tap (*a furnace*); (naut.) to measure in fathoms; *vn* to swing the arms; to swim raising the arms out of the water; to struggle, to wrestle; (naut.) to brace the yards
**braceo** *m* swinging the arms; struggling
**braceral** *m* (arm.) brassart
**bracero -ra** *adj* (pertaining to the) arm; manual; thrown with the hand (*said of a weapon*); *m* man offering his arm to a lady; laborer; day laborer; brewer; sure-armed fellow (*in throwing or shooting*); **de bracero** arm in arm
**bracete** *m* small arm; **de bracete** (coll.) arm in arm
**bracil** *m* (arm.) brassart; upper arm
**bracmán** *m* var. of **brahmán**
**braco -ca** *adj* pug-nosed; *mf* setter (*dog*)
**bráctea** *f* (bot.) bract; (bot.) bractlet
**bractéola** *f* (bot.) bractlet, bracteole
**bradicardia** *f* (path.) bradycardia
**bradipepsia** *f* (path.) bradypepsia
**brafonera** *f* (arm.) rerebrace
**braga** *f* hoisting rope, lashing rope; diaper, clout; panties, step-ins; **bragas** *fpl* breeches, knickers, pants; panties, step-ins
**bragado -da** *adj* with the flanks of a different color from rest of body; wicked, ill-disposed; firm, energetic; *f* flat of the thigh (*of animals*)
**bragadura** *f* crotch
**bragazas** (*pl:* **-zas**) *adj* (coll.) easy, henpecked; *m* (coll.) easy mark, henpecked fellow
**braguero** *m* truss (*for rupture*); breeching (*of a gun*)
**bragueta** *f* fly (*flap on clothing*)
**braguillas** *m* (*pl:* **-llas**) (coll.) brat; boy wearing first pair of pants
**Brahma** *m* (rel.) Brahma
**brahmán** *m* Brahman
**brahmanismo** *m* Brahmanism
**brahmín** *m* var. of **brahmán**
**brama** *f* rut (*state and season*)
**bramadera** *f* whistle (*toy made to spin on end of a string*); horn call
**bramadero** *m* rutting or mating place (*of deer and other wild animals*)
**bramador -dora** *adj* roaring, howling
**bramante** *adj* roaring, howling; *m* twine, packthread; brabant (*linen*)
**bramantesco -ca** *adj* (arch.) Bramantesque
**bramar** *vn* to roar, to bellow; to storm, to bluster; (coll.) to cry out, to shriek
**bramido** *m* roar, bellow, howl; (coll.) outcry, shriek
**branca** *f* (archaic) point of horn; (archaic) row of prisoners; (obs.) branch of tree; **brancas** *fpl* (obs.) lion's claws; **branca ursina** (bot.) acanthus; **branca ursina alemana** or **espuria** (bot.) cow parsnip (*Heracleum sphodylium*)
**brancada** *f* dragnet, sweep net
**brancal** *m* frame (*of wagon or gun carriage*)
**brandal** *m* (naut.) backstay
**Brandeburgo** *m* Brandenburg (*city, province, and military decoration*)
**brandís** *m* greatcoat
**branquia** *f* (ichth.) gill, branchia
**branquial** *adj* branchial
**branquífero -ra** *adj* branchiferous
**braña** *f* summer pasture
**braquial** *adj* brachial
**braquicéfalo -la** *adj* (anthrop.) brachycephalic
**braquigrafía** *f* study of abbreviations
**braquiópodo** *m* (zool.) brachiopod
**braquiuro -ra** *adj* & *m* (zool.) brachyuran
**brasa** *f* live coal, red-hot charcoal; **estar en brasas** (coll.) to be on pins and needles; **estar hecho unas brasas** to be flushed, be red in the face
**brasca** *f* (found.) brasque, steep
**brascar** §86 *va* (found.) to brasque, to fettle
**braserillo** *m* small brazier
**brasero** *m* brazier; brasero (*place where heretics were burned*)
**brasil** *m* (bot.) brasiletto; brazilwood; Brazil red; rouge; **el Brasil** Brazil
**brasilado -da** *adj* Brazil-red
**brasileño -ña** *adj* & *mf* Brazilian
**brasilete** *m* (bot.) brasiletto; brazilwood
**brasilina** *f* (chem.) brazilin
**brasmología** *f* treatise on the tides; treatise on fermentation
**bravamente** *adv* bravely; well, skilfully; cruelly; hard, abundantly
**bravata** *f* bravado; **echar bravatas** to talk big
**braveador -dora** *adj* blustering, bullying; *mf* blusterer, bully
**bravear** *vn* to bluster, to boast, to four-flush
**bravera** *f* vent, chimney
**braveza** *f* fierceness, ferocity; bravery, courage; fury (*of the elements*)
**bravío -vía** *adj* fierce, ferocious, savage; wild, uncultivated; coarse, unpolished; (coll.) stubborn; *m* fierceness, ferocity
**bravo -va** *adj* brave; fine, excellent, great; elegant, spruce; (coll.) sumptuous, magnificent; wild, fierce, savage; game; rough (*sea; coast line*); angry, annoyed; (coll.) boasting, blustering; (coll.) ill-humored; strong (*chili*); (Am.) querulous; *m* bravo (*murderer*); **¡bravo!** bravo!
**bravonel** *m* braggart
**bravucón -cona** *adj* (coll.) four-flushing; *mf* (coll.) four-flusher
**bravuconada** *f* (coll.) four-flushing
**bravura** *f* fierceness, ferocity; gameness; bravery (*courage; fine appearance*); bravado, boasting; bruskness, ill-humor; (mus.) bravura
**braza** *f* (naut.) fathom; (naut.) brace (*rope*)
**brazada** *f* stroke with arms; armful; **brazada de pecho** breast stroke
**brazado** *m* armful, armload
**brazaje** *m* coining, minting; (naut.) fathomage
**brazal** *m* brassart (*of armor*); arm band; irrigation ditch; (naut.) headrail; **brazal de arquero** bracer
**brazalete** *m* bracelet; (arm.) brassart
**brazo** *m* arm (*of body, chair, sea, law, etc.*); foreleg (*of quadruped*); energy, enterprise; **brazos** *mpl* laborers, hands; backers, protectors; **a brazo partido** hand to hand; **asidos del brazo** arm in arm; **con los brazos abiertos** with open arms; **de brazos caídos** with arms folded; **hecho un brazo de mar** (coll.) gorgeously outfitted; **no dar su brazo a torcer** (coll.) to be stubborn, be persistent; **tener brazo** (coll.) to be husky; **brazo a brazo** hand to hand; **brazo derecho** right-hand man
**brazofuerte** *m* (zool.) ant bear
**brazola** *f* (naut.) coaming
**brazolargo** *m* (zool.) spider monkey
**brazuelo** *m* small arm; shoulder (*of animal*)
**brea** *f* tar, pitch, petroleum asphalt; (naut.) calking material; **brea seca** rosin
**brear** *va* (coll.) to abuse, to mistreat; (coll.) to play a joke on, to make fun of
**brebaje** *m* potion, dose; poison; unpleasantness; (naut.) grog
**breca** *f* (ichth.) dace; (ichth.) bleak
**brecina** *f* (bot.) broom heath
**brécol** *m* or **brécoles** *mpl* (bot.) broccoli
**brecolera** *f* woman who sells broccoli; (bot.) broccoli
**brecha** *f* breach, breakthrough; opening; impression; (geol.) breccia; **batir en brecha** (mil.) to breach; to get the better of; to floor
**brega** *f* struggle; fight, scrap, row; trick, joke; **andar a la brega** to toil, to work hard; **dar brega a** to play a trick on
**bregar** §59 *va* to work (*dough*) with a rolling pin; *vn* to struggle; to fight, to start a row; to toil, to work hard; to try hard to win out
**brema** *f* (ichth.) bream; (*cap.*) *f* Bremen
**bremense** *adj* (pertaining to) Bremen; *mf* native or inhabitant of Bremen

**bren** *m* bran
**brenca** *f* sluice post
**Brenero** *m* Brenner
**breña** *f* rough and brambly ground
**breñal** *m* or **breñar** *m* rough and brambly region
**breñoso -sa** *adj* rough and brambly; rocky, craggy
**breque** *m* (ichth.) bleak
**bresca** *f* honeycomb
**brescar** §86 *va* to extract honeycombs from (*a hive*)
**Bretaña** *f* Brittany; **la Gran Bretaña** Britain, Great Britain; (*l.c.*) *f* Brittany, Brittany cloth; (bot.) hyacinth
**brete** *m* fetters, shackles; tight spot, tight squeeze
**bretón -tona** *adj & mf* Breton; **bretones** *mpl* (bot.) Brussels sprouts
**breva** *f* purple fig, early fig; snap, cinch; flat cigar
**breval** *m* fig tree yielding early figs
**breve** *adj* short, brief; (gram.) short; **en breve** soon, shortly; in short; *m* apostolic brief; *f* (mus.) breve
**brevedad** *f* brevity, briefness, conciseness; **a** or **con la mayor brevedad** as soon as possible
**brevete** *m* note, memorandum
**breviario** *m* breviary, brief treatise; (eccl.) breviary; (print.) brevier
**brevipenne** *adj* (zool.) brevipennate
**brezal** *m* heath, moor
**brezo** *m* (bot.) heath, heather; **brezo albarino, blanco** or **castellano** (bot.) tree heath, brier
**brezoso -sa** *adj* heathery
**briaga** *f* hoisting rope, lashing rope; bass-weed rope
**Briareo** *m* (myth.) Briareus
**briba** *f* bumming, loafing; **andar a la briba** to bum around, to loaf around
**bribón -bona** *adj* bumming, loafing; rascally; *mf* bum, loafer; rascal, scoundrel
**bribonada** *f* rascality, knavery
**bribonazo** *m* big rascal
**bribonear** *vn* to bum around, to loaf; to be a rascal
**bribonería** *f* life of loafing; rascality
**bricbarca** *f* (naut.) bark
**bricho** *m* gold or silver spangle (*used in embroidery*)
**brida** *f* bridle; horsemanship; curb, check, restraint; splice plate; fishplate; flange; clamp; **bridas** *fpl* (rail.) couplers; (surg.) filaments around the lips of a wound; **a toda brida** at top speed
**bridar** *va* to flange
**bridecú** *m* (*pl:* **-cúes**) sword belt
**bridón** *m* small bridle; bridoon; horseman riding a bur saddle; horse fitted with a bur saddle; (poet.) spirited steed
**brigada** *f* brigade; squad, gang, party; fleet (*e.g., of tractors*); (mil.) brigade; (mil.) train; *m* (mil.) staff sergeant
**brigadero** *m* man in charge of military pack animals
**brigadier** *m* (mil.) brigadier, brigadier general
**brigadiera** *f* (coll.) brigadier general's wife
**brigantino -na** *adj* (pertaining to) Corunna; *mf* native or inhabitant of Corunna; *f* (arm.) brigandine
**Brígida** *f* Bridget
**Briján** *m;* **saber más que Briján** to be wide-awake, to be keen-witted
**brillante** *adj* brilliant, bright, shining; (fig.) brilliant; *m* brilliant (*sparkling stone*); metallic lustre
**brillantez** *f* brilliance; (fig.) brilliance
**brillantina** *f* brilliantine (*hair dressing; glossy fabric*); metal polish
**brillar** *vn* to shine, to sparkle
**brillo** *m* brilliance, brightness, lustre; splendor
**brilloso -sa** *adj* shiny
**brin** *m* fine canvas; (Am.) canvas (*for painting*)
**brincar** §86 *va* to bounce (*a child*) in one's arms; (coll.) to skip (*a word or passage*); to pass over (*another person because of a promotion*); *vn* to leap, to jump; (coll.) to be very touchy, to flare up
**brinco** *m* leap, jump; hop, bounce; fancy hair ornament; **en dos brincos** or **en un brinco** in an instant
**brindador -dora** *mf* toaster, person who proposes a toast
**brindar** *va* to offer; to invite; **brindar a** + *inf* to invite to + *inf;* **brindar a uno con una cosa** to offer someone something; *vn* to invite; to drink a toast; **brindar a** or **por** to drink to; to toast; **brindar con** to offer; *vr* to offer; **brindarse a** + *inf* to offer to + *inf*
**brindis** *m* (*pl:* **-dis**) toast (*to someone's health*); offer; invitation, treat; (taur.) dedication (*by the matador of the first bull killed to the presiding officer*)
**brinquillo** or **brinquiño** *m* gewgaw, trinket; Portuguese candy or sweet; **hecho un brinquiño** (coll.) all spruced up
**brinza** *f* (bot.) sprig, shoot, blade
**briñón** *m* nectarine (*fruit*)
**brío** *m* spirit; determination, enterprise; elegance; **cortar los bríos a uno** to cut someone's wings
**briofita** *f* (bot.) bryophyte
**briol** *m* (naut.) buntline
**briología** *f* bryology
**brionia** *f* (bot.) bryony
**brios** euphemistic form of **dios,** used in mild oaths
**brioso -sa** *adj* spirited; determined, enterprising; elegant
**briqueta** *f* briquet or briquette (*of coal*)
**brisa** *f* breeze; bagasse of pressed grapes; (poet.) zephyr
**brisca** *f* bezique (*card game*); brisque (*ace*)
**briscado -da** *adj* interwoven with silk and gold thread or silk and silver thread
**briscar** §86 *va* to weave with silk and gold or silver thread; to embroider with silk and gold or silver thread
**Briseida** *f* (myth.) Briseis
**brisera** *f* or **brisero** *m* (Am.) glass lamp shade
**brisote** *m* stormy breeze; steady, fresh breeze
**brístol** *m* Bristol board
**británico -ca** *adj* Britannic
**britano -na** *adj* British; *mf* Briton; Britisher; **los britanos** the British
**briza** *f* (bot.) quaking grass
**brizar** §76 *va* to rock in a cradle
**brizna** *f* chip, splinter, fragment; filament, string; blade (*e.g., of straw*); (fig.) grain (*of hope, conscience, etc.*)
**briznoso -sa** *adj* splintery; stringy
**brizo** *m* cradle
**brl.** abr. of **barril**
**broa** *f* biscuit, cracker; corn bread; shallow cove
**broca** *f* reel, bobbin (*in a shuttle*); drill, drill bit; shoemaker's tack; **broca de avellanar** countersinking bit; **broca de centrar** center drill
**brocadillo** *m* light brocade
**brocado -da** *adj* brocaded; *m* brocade
**brocal** *m* curbstone (*of well*); steel rim (*of shield*); cigarette holder; mouthpiece of leather wine bag
**brocamantón** *m* diamond brooch
**brocatel** *m* brocatel (*brocade and marble*)
**brocino** *m* bump, lump (*on head*)
**bróculi** *m* (bot.) broccoli
**brocha** *f* brush, stubby brush (*for painting, shaving, etc.*); loaded dice; **de brocha gorda** house (*painter*); (coll.) crude, heavy-handed
**brochada** *f* brush, stroke with a brush
**brochal** *m* header beam
**brochar** *va* (mach.) to broach
**brochazo** *m* dab, stroke (*with brush*)
**broche** *m* clasp, fastener, clip; hook and eye; brooch; hasp (*for book covers*); (Am.) cuff button; **broche de oro** punch line
**brocheta** *f* (cook.) skewer
**brochón** *m* large brush; whitewash brush, plasterer's brush
**brodio** *m* var. of **bodrio**
**broma** *f* joke, jest; fun, merriment; (cook.) oatmeal; (mas.) riprap; (zool.) shipworm; (Am.) disappointment; **de broma** in fun, as a joke; **decir en broma** to say jokingly; **gastar una broma (a)** to play a joke (on)

**bromar** *va* to gnaw, to bore (*said of a shipworm*)
**bromato** *m* (chem.) bromate
**bromazo** *m* poor joke
**bromear** *vn* to joke, to jest; to enjoy oneself, have a good time; to carouse, go on a spree; *vr* to joke, to jest; to chat and joke
**bromeliáceo -a** *adj* (bot.) bromeliaceous
**bromhídrico -ca** *adj* (chem.) hydrobromic
**brómico -ca** *adj* (chem.) bromic
**bromista** *adj* joking; *mf* joker
**bromo** *m* (chem.) bromin or bromine; (bot.) brome grass
**bromurado -da** *adj* (containing) bromine
**bromuro** *m* (chem.) bromide; **bromuro de potasio** (chem.) potassium bromide
**bronca** *f* see **bronco**
**bronce** *m* bronze (*alloy; object; powder*); (poet.) cannon, bell, trumpet, clarion; **bronce de aluminio** aluminum bronze; **bronce de campanas** bell metal; **bronce de magnesio** magnesium bronze; **bronce fosforoso** phosphor bronze
**bronceado -da** *adj* bronze, bronze-colored; tanned, sunburnt: *m* bronzing; bronze finish; bronze (*color*); tan, sunburn
**broncear** *va, vn & vr* to bronze; to tan
**broncería** *f* collection of bronzes; bronze work, brasswork; bronze or brass shop
**broncíneo -a** *adj* bronzelike
**broncista** *m* bronzesmith
**bronco -ca** *adj* coarse, rough; gruff, uncouth; raspy, harsh; hoarse; brittle (*metal*); *f* (coll.) row, wrangle, dispute; (coll.) poor joke; **armar una bronca** (coll.) to start a row
**bronconeumonía** *f* (path.) bronchopneumonia
**broncorrea** *f* (path.) bronchorrhea
**broncoscopia** *f* bronchoscopy
**broncoscopio** *m* bronchoscope
**bronquedad** *f* coarseness, roughness; gruffness, uncouthness; harshness; hoarseness; brittleness
**bronquial** *adj* bronchial
**bronquina** *f* (coll.) scrap, quarrel
**bronquio** *m* (anat.) bronchus, bronchial tube
**bronquíolo** *m* (anat.) bronchiole, smaller bronchus
**bronquítico -ca** *adj* bronchitic
**bronquitis** *f* (path.) bronchitis
**brontosauro** *m* (pal.) brontosaurus
**broquel** *m* shield, buckler; (fig.) shield
**broquelar** *vr* to shield oneself
**broquelazo** *m* stroke with a shield or buckler
**broquelillo** *m* earring
**broqueta** *f* (cook.) skewer, brochette
**brota** *f* shoot, bud
**brotadura** *f* sprouting, budding; springing, gushing; eruption (*of the skin*)
**brótano** *m* var. of **abrótano**
**brotar** *va* to sprout, to shoot forth; to cause, to produce; *vn* to sprout, to shoot forth, to bud; to spring, to gush; to break out (*on the skin*)
**brote** *m* shoot, bud; rash, pimples; breaking out in a rash; outburst; outbreak (*of a disease*); (dial.) bit, crumb, fragment
**brótola** *f* (ichth.) codling
**broza** *f* brushwood; rubbish, trash; brush, underbrush; printer's brush; (fig.) rubbish
**brozar** **§76** *va* (print.) to brush, to clean with a brush
**brozoso -sa** *adj* rubbishy, full of rubbish
**brucelosis** *f* (path. & vet.) brucellosis
**brucero** *m* brush or broom maker or dealer
**bruces** *mpl* lips; **a** or **de bruces** face downward, on one's face, prone
**brucina** *f* (pharm.) brucine
**brucita** *f* (mineral.) brucite
**brugo** *m* (ent.) plant louse; (ent.) oak larva
**bruja** *f* (orn.) barn owl; witch, sorceress; (coll.) hag; (coll.) shrew; (Am.) spook (*person wrapped in sheet*)
**Brujas** *f* Bruges
**brujear** *vn* to practice witchcraft
**brujería** *f* witchcraft, sorcery, magic
**brujesco -ca** *adj* witch
**brujidor** *m* var. of **grujidor**
**brujir** *va* var. of **grujir**
**brujo** *m* sorcerer, magician, wizard; (fig.) wizard
**brújula** *f* magnetic needle; compass; sight (*hole for aiming*); (fig.) guide; (*cap.*) *f* (astr.) Compasses; **brújula de inducción terrestre** (aer.) earth induction compass; **perder la brújula** to lose one's touch
**brujulear** *va* to uncover (*one's cards*) gradually; (coll.) to guess, to suspect; *vn* to know one's way around
**brulote** *m* fire ship
**bruma** *f* fog, mist
**brumador -dora** *adj* var. of **abrumador**
**brumal** *adj* foggy, misty
**brumar** *va* to crush, to overwhelm; to annoy
**brumazón** *m* heavy fog, thick mist
**brumo** *m* pure coating wax
**brumoso -sa** *adj* foggy, misty
**Brunilda** *f* Brunhild
**bruno -na** *adj* dark brown, blackish; brown; *m* (bot.) black plum
**bruñido** *m* burnishing, polishing
**bruñidor -dora** *adj* burnishing, polishing; *mf* burnisher, polisher; *m* burnisher (*tool*)
**bruñidura** *f* or **bruñimiento** *m* burnishing, polishing
**bruñir** **§25** *va* to burnish, to polish; (coll.) to put rouge on, to put make-up on
**bruño** *m* (bot.) black plum
**bruñón** *m* nectarine
**brus** *m* (naut.) deck mop
**brusco -ca** *adj* brusque; sudden; rough, gruff; sharp (*curve*); *m* (bot.) butcher's-broom; *f* camber, roundup; (Am.) brushwood
**brusela** *f* (bot.) myrtle, lesser periwinkle; **bruselas** *fpl* tweezers
**Bruselas** *f* Brussels
**bruselense** *adj* (pertaining to) Brussels; *mf* native or inhabitant of Brussels
**brusquedad** *f* brusqueness; suddenness; roughness, gruffness; sharpness (*of a curve*)
**brutal** *adj* brutal; sudden, unexpected; (coll.) terrific (*e.g., speed*); (coll.) stunning; (coll.) huge, colossal; *m* brute, beast
**brutalidad** *f* brutality; stupidity; (coll.) flock, slew
**brutalizar** **§76** *va* to brutalize
**brutear** *vn* (Am.) to talk nonsense, to bungle
**brutesco -ca** *adj* grotesque
**bruteza** *f* brutality; roughness, lack of polish
**bruto -ta** *adj* brute, brutish; stupid, ignorant; rough; gross; crude; (coll.) big, huge; **en bruto** in the rough; *mf* brute (*person*); ignoramus; *m* brute (*animal*); (coll.) dolt; (*cap.*) *m* Brutus
**bruza** *f* horse brush; printer's brush
**bruzar** **§76** *va* to brush, to clean with a brush
**bu** *m* (*pl:* **búes**) (coll.) bogeyman, bugaboo; **hacer el bu a** (coll.) to scare, to frighten, to say boo to; *interj* boo!
**búa** *f* pimple; (path.) bubo
**buarro** *m* var. of **buharro**
**buba** *f* (path.) syphilis; **bubas** *fpl* (path.) bubo
**búbalo -la** *mf* (zool.) bubal
**bubón** *m* (path.) bubo
**bubónico -ca** *adj* bubonic
**buboso -sa** *adj* buboed
**bucal** *adj* buccal
**bucanero** *m* buccaneer
**bucare** *m* or **búcare** *m* (bot.) bucare, coral tree
**Bucarest** *f* Bucharest
**búcaro** *m* fragrant clay; flower vase
**buccino** *m* (zool.) whelk
**buceador -dora** *mf* diver
**buceamiento** *m* diving
**bucear** *vn* to dive; to be a diver; to delve
**Bucéfalo** *m* Bucephalus; (*l.c.*) *m* (coll.) blockhead, jackass
**buceo** *m* diving
**bucero -ra** *adj* black-nosed (*said of a hound*)
**bucinador** *m* (anat.) buccinator
**bucle** *m* curl, ringlet, lock; bend, loop
**buco** *m* opening, gap; (zool.) buck
**bucólico -ca** *adj* bucolic; *m* bucolic poet; *f* bucolic (*poem*); (coll.) food; (coll.) meal
**bucráneo** *m* (arch.) bucranium
**buchada** *f* mouthful
**buche** *m* craw, crop, maw; belly; mouthful; bag, pucker (*in clothes*); bosom (*for secrets*); suck-

ling ass; **hacer buche** to be baggy, to pucker; **sacar el buche a uno** (coll.) to make someone tell all he knows
**buchete** *m* puffed-up cheek
**buchón -chona** *adj* (coll.) baggy, bulging; pouting (*pigeon*); *f* (orn.) pouter
**buchú** *m & f* (pharm.) buchu
**Buda** *m* Buddha
**búdico -ca** *adj* Buddhic
**budín** *m* pudding
**budinera** *f* pudding mold
**budión** *m* (ichth.) butterfly fish
**budismo** *m* Buddhism
**budista** *adj & mf* Buddhist
**buega** *f* (prov.) boundary mark
**buen** *adj* apocopated form of **bueno,** used only before masculine singular nouns
**buenaboya** *m* volunteer oarsman
**buenamente** *adv* easily, with ease; freely, voluntarily
**buenandanza** *f* var. of **bienandanza**
**buenaventura** *f* good luck; fortune (*told by fortuneteller*); **decirle a uno la buenaventura** to tell one's fortune, to tell someone his fortune
**buenazo -za** *adj* (coll.) kind, good-natured
**buenísimo -ma** *adj super* (coll.) very good
**bueno -na** *adj* good; kind; well; fine, e.g., **buen tiempo** fine weather; (iron.) fine; **a buenas** willingly; **a la buena de Dios** at random; **de buenas a primeras** suddenly; afresh, anew, from the beginning; **¿de dónde bueno?** (coll.) where do you come from?, what's the good news?; **el bueno de Juan** good old John; **estar de buenas** to be in a good mood; **por las buenas** willingly; **¡buena es ésa** or **ésta!** (coll.) that's a fine how-do-you-do!, that's a fine state of affairs!; **¡buenas!** greetings!; **¡bueno!** well!, all right!; that'll do!
**Buenos Aires** *m & f* Buenos Aires; **el Gran Buenos Aires** Greater Buenos Aires
**buenpasar** *m* well-being
**buey** *m* ox, bullock, steer; **trabajar como un buey** to work like an ox; **buey almizclado** or **almizclero** (zool.) musk ox; **buey de cabestrillo** ox used as a shield by hunter; **buey del Tibet** (zool.) yak; **buey giboso** (zool.) zebu; **buey suelto** (coll.) free agent; (coll.) bachelor; **buey marino** (zool.) sea cow (*Halicore*)
**bueyuno -na** *adj* bovine
**buf** *interj* (coll.) ugh!
**bufa** *f* see **bufo**
**bufalino -na** *adj* (pertaining to the) buffalo
**búfalo -la** *mf* (zool.) buffalo; **búfalo cafre** (zool.) Cape buffalo
**bufanda** *f* scarf, muffler
**bufar** *vn* to snort; (coll.) to snort, to puff (*e.g., with anger*); *vr* to swell, to heave
**bufete** *m* writing desk; law office; clients (*of lawyer*); (Am.) snack, refreshment; **abrir bufete** to open a law office
**bufetillo** *m* small desk
**bufido** *m* snort; (coll.) snort, puff (*e.g., of anger*)
**bufo -fa** *adj* farcical; clownish; *mf* buffoon; *f* jest, buffoonery
**bufón -fona** *adj* funny, comical, clownish; *mf* buffoon, clown; *m* fool, jester; peddler, street vendor
**bufonada** *f* jest, buffoonery; raillery, sarcasm
**bufonear** *vn* to play the clown; *vr* to jest, to make fun
**bufonesco -ca** *adj* farcical, clownish; coarse, rude, burlesque
**bufonizar** §76 *vn & vr* to jest, to make fun
**bugalla** *f* oak gall
**buganvilla** *f* (bot.) bougainvillea
**bugle** *m* (mus.) bugle
**buglosa** *f* (bot.) bugloss
**buharda** *f* dormer; dormer window; garret; (fort.) balcony, battlement (*designed for dropping weapons on attackers at foot of wall*)
**buhardilla** *f* dormer; dormer window; garret; (Am.) skylight
**buharro** *m* (orn.) scops owl
**buhedera** *f* loophole, embrasure
**buhedo** *m* pool or pond that dries up in summer; marl
**búho** *m* (orn.) eagle owl; (coll.) unsociable person; (slang) squealer
**buhonería** *f* peddler's kit; peddler's stock or wares
**buhonero** *m* peddler, hawker
**buído -da** *adj* sharp, pointed; fluted, grooved; weak, skinny
**buitre** *m* (orn.) vulture
**buitrero -ra** *adj* vulturine; *m* vulture hunter; *f* vulture trap
**buitrón** *m* fish trap (*made of osier*); partridge net; silver-smelting furnace; ashpit (*of furnace*)
**Bujara** *f* Bokhara or Bukhara (*city*); **la Bujara** Bokhara or Bukhara (*state*)
**bujarasol** *m* reddish fig (*of Murcia*)
**buje** *m* axle box, bushing
**bujeda** *f*, **bujedal** *m* or **bujedo** *m* var. of **bojedal**
**bujería** *f* bauble, gewgaw, trinket
**bujeta** *f* box made of boxwood; box, case; perfume bottle; perfume box
**bujía** *f* candle; candlestick; candle power; spark plug; (surg.) bougie; **bujía internacional** (phys.) international candle; **bujía normal** or **patrón** (phys.) standard candle
**bujía-pie** *m* (*pl:* **bujías-pies**) foot-candle
**bujiería** *f* chandlery
**bula** *f* bull, bulla
**bulario** *m* collection of papal bulls, bullary
**bulbillo** *m* (bot.) bulbil
**bulbo** *m* (anat. & bot.) bulb
**bulboso -sa** *adj* bulbous
**bulerías** *fpl* Andalusian song and dance
**buleto** *m* apostolic brief
**bulevar** *m* boulevard
**Bulgaria** *f* Bulgaria
**búlgaro -ra** *adj & mf* Bulgar, Bulgarian; *m* Bulgar, Bulgarian (*language*)
**bulí** *m* var. of **burí**
**bulimia** *f* (path.) bulimia (*insatiable hunger*)
**bulímico -ca** *adj & mf* bulimic, bulimiac
**bulo** *m* (coll.) false rumor
**bulón** *m* bolt; **bulón de grillete** shackle bolt
**bulonar** *va* to bolt
**bulto** *m* bulk, volume; bust, statue; bundle, package; piece of baggage; bump, swelling; form, body, shadow; (slang) carcass (*of a person*); (Am.) briefcase; **a bulto** broadly, by guess; **buscar el bulto a** (coll.) to lay for; **coger el bulto a** (coll.) to have in one's clutches; **de bulto** evident; (Am.) important; **escurrir** or **esquivar el bulto** (coll.) to duck, to dodge
**bululú** *m* (*pl:* **-lúes**) (archaic) strolling impersonator; (Am.) excitement, disturbance
**bulla** *f* noise, uproar; bustle, crowd
**bullabesa** *f* bouillabaisse
**bullaje** *m* crush, mix-up
**bullanga** *f* disturbance, riot
**bullanguero -ra** *adj* turbulent, rioting; *mf* disturber of the peace, rioter
**bullebulle** *mf* (coll.) bustler, busybody
**bullente** *adj* boiling, bubbling; frothy (*beer*); teeming, swarming
**bullicio** *m* bustle, rumble; brawl, wrangle; disturbance, excitement
**bullicioso -sa** *adj* bustling, rumbling; turbulent, restless; riotous; *mf* rioter
**bullidor -dora** *adj* bustling, turbulent
**bullir** §26 *va* to move, to budge; *vn* to boil, to bubble up; to swarm, to teem; to abound; to occur frequently; to bustle, to hustle; to stir, to budge; (coll.) to itch, be restless; *vr* to stir, to budge
**bullón** *m* bubbling dye (*in boiler*); stud (*for adorning bookbindings*); puff (*in a dress*)
**bumerang** *m* boomerang
**buna** *m* (chem.) buna
**buniatal** *m* sweet-potato patch
**buniato** *m* (bot.) sweet potato (*plant and tuber*)
**bunio** *m* (bot.) hardened bulb; (path.) bunion
**buñolería** *f* doughnut bakery
**buñolero -ra** *mf* doughnut maker or dealer
**buñuelo** *m* doughnut, cruller; (coll.) botch
**bupresto** *m* (ent.) buprestid, buprestid beetle

**buque** *m* capacity; hull (*of ship*); ship, vessel; (mus.) resonance box (*e.g., of guitar*); **buque almirante** admiral (*flagship of admiral*); **buque a rotores** rotor ship; **buque cablero** cable ship; **buque carguero** freighter; **buque cisterna** tanker; **buque correo** mailboat; **buque de cruz** square-rigger; **buque de desembarco** (nav.) landing craft, landing ship (*LST*); **buque de doble hélice** twin-screw ship; **buque de guerra** warship; **buque de ruedas** paddle-wheel steamer; **buque de transporte** transport; **buque de vapor** steamer, steamship; **buque de vela** sailboat; **buque escucha** vedette; **buque escuela** school ship; (nav.) training ship; **buque fanal** or **faro** lightship; **buque gemelo** sister ship; **buque hospital** hospital ship; **buque madre** (nav.) mother ship; **buque mercante** merchantman, merchant vessel; **buque portaminas** mine layer; **buque tanque** tanker; **buque teatro** showboat; **buque trampa** tramp steamer; **buque transbordador** train ferry; **buque velero** sailing vessel

**buqué** *m* bouquet (*of wine*)

**buquetero** *m* (Am.) flower vase

**bura** *m* (zool.) blacktail

**burato** *m* Canton crepe; transparent cloak or veil

**burbuja** *f* bubble

**burbujear** *vn* to bubble, to burble

**burbujeo** *m* bubbling, burbling

**burchaca** *f* var. of **burjaca**

**burche** *f* tower (*for defense*)

**burda** *f* see **burdo**

**burdégano** *m* hinny

**burdel** *m* brothel; disorderly house; *adj* libidinous, vicious

**Burdeos** *f* Bordeaux; (*l.c.*) *m* (*pl:* **burdeos**) Bordeaux (*wine*)

**burdo -da** *adj* coarse; *f* (naut.) backstay

**burel** *m* fid (*for opening strands of rope*)

**bureo** *m* court for trial of persons of royal household; amusement, diversion

**bureta** *f* (chem.) burette

**burga** *f* hot springs

**burgado** *m* (zool.) small brown snail

**burgalés -lesa** *adj* (pertaining to) Burgos; *mf* native or inhabitant of Burgos

**burgo** *m* (archaic) town, village

**burgomaestre** *m* burgomaster

**burgrave** *m* burgrave

**burgraviato** *m* burgraviate

**burgués -guesa** *adj* bourgeois, middle-class; (pertaining to a) town; *mf* bourgeois, person of the middle class; townsman

**burguesía** *f* bourgeoisie, middle class, **alta burguesía** upper middle class

**burí** *m* (bot.) buri palm, talipo palm

**buriel** *adj* dark red; *m* coarse woolen cloth

**buril** *m* burin, graver; (fig.) burin (*style or manner of engraver*); (dent.) explorer

**burilada** *f* stroke or mark made with a burin or chisel; shaving or chip cut with a burin or chisel; slither of silver to be assayed

**buriladura** *f* engraving; chiseling

**burilar** *va* to engrave with a burin; to chisel (*marble*)

**burjaca** *f* leather bag of pilgrim or beggar

**burla** *f* ridicule; sneering, scoffing; joke, jest; trick, deception; **de burlas** in fun, for fun; **burla burlando** by joking; unawares; on the quiet; **burla pesada** rough joke; **burlas aparte** joking aside

**burladero** *m* safety island, safety zone; covert in a bull ring; safety niche or recess in a tunnel

**burlador -dora** *adj* ridiculing; joking, jesting; disappointing; seducing; *mf* wag, jester, practical joker; *m* seducer of women; drinking cup full of holes (*used as a trick for the unwary*); hidden jet of water (*to squirt the unwary*)

**burlar** *va* to ridicule; to trick, to deceive, to disappoint; to outwit, to frustrate, to elude; to seduce (*a woman*); *vn* to scoff; **burlar de** to make fun of, to scoff at; *vr* to joke, to jest; **burlarse de** to make fun of, to scoff at

**burlería** *f* trick, deception; illusion; fish story, fairy tale; scorn, derision

**burlesco -ca** *adj* (coll.) funny, comic, jocular

**burlete** *m* weather strip or stripping

**burlisto -ta** *mf* (Am.) joker, jester; **burlisto grande** (orn.) Couch's kingbird

**burlón -lona** *adj* joking, jesting; *mf* joker, jester; *m* (orn.) mocking bird

**burlonería** *f* slyness, cunning

**buró** *m* (*pl:* **-rós**) writing desk, bureau; (Am.) night table

**burocracia** *f* bureaucracy

**burócrata** *mf* bureaucrat; jobholder

**burocrático -ca** *adj* bureaucratic

**burra** *f* see **burro**

**burrada** *f* drove of asses; asininity

**burrajear** *va* to scribble; to doodle

**burrajo -ja** *adj* (Am.) coarse, stupid; *m* dry stable dung (*used for fuel*)

**burreño** *m* var. of **burdégano**

**burrero** *m* herdsman who sells ass's milk; (Am.) owner or driver of asses

**burrillo** *m* liturgical calendar

**burro -rra** *adj* stupid, asinine; *m* jackass, donkey, burro; sawbuck, sawhorse; windlass; (naut.) feed pump; (Am.) stepladder; (fig.) jackass; **burro cargado de letras** (coll.) learned jackass; **burro de carga** drudge, slave (*man*); *f* she-ass; (fig.) ass, stupid woman; drudge, slave (*woman*)

**burrumbada** *f* (coll.) var. of **barrumbada**

**bursátil** *adj* stock, stock-market

**bursitis** *f* (path.) bursitis

**burujo** *m* var. of **borujo**

**burujón** *m* var. of **borujón**

**busaca** *f* (Am.) pocket (*of pool table*); (Am.) bag

**busardo** *m* (orn.) buzzard; (orn.) marsh harrier

**busca** *f* search, hunt, pursuit; (hunt.) party of beaters; **buscas** *fpl* (Am.) perquisites

**buscada** *f* search, hunt, pursuit

**buscador -dora** *adj* searching; **buscador del blanco** (mil.) homing (*e.g., torpedo*); *mf* searcher, seeker; *m* (astr.) finder

**buscahuella** *m* (aut.) spotlight

**buscaniguas** *m* (*pl:* **-guas**) (Am.) snake (*kind of firecracker*)

**buscapié** *m* hint; key (*to interpret obscure passages*); **buscapiés** *msg* (*pl:* **-piés**) snake, serpent (*kind of firecracker*)

**buscapleitos** *mf* (*pl:* **-tos**) (Am.) troublemaker

**buscapolos** *m* (*pl:* **-los**) (elec.) pole finder

**buscar §86** *va* to look for, to hunt for, to seek, to seek out; (Am.) to provoke; **buscar tres pies al gato** to pick a quarrel; *vr* to be selfish, to look out for oneself; **buscársela** (coll.) to manage to get along; (coll.) to ask for it, to be looking for trouble

**buscareta** *f* (orn.) wren

**buscarruidos** *m* (*pl:* **-dos**) (coll.) troublemaker

**buscavidas** *mf* (*pl:* **-das**) (coll.) snoop, busybody; (coll.) hustler

**busco** *m* miter sill (*of canal-lock gate*)

**buscón -cona** *mf* seeker, investigator, checker; petty thief; *m* (min.) prospector; *f* (coll.) loose woman

**busilis** *m* (*pl:* **-lis**) (coll.) difficulty, trouble; (coll.) dough (*money*); secret, mystery; **ahí está el busilis** (coll.) that's the trouble; **dar en el busilis** (coll.) to put one's finger on the trouble

**búsqueda** *f* search, hunt, pursuit

**busto** *m* bust

**bustrófedon** *m* boustrophedon

**butaca** *f* armchair, easy chair; orchestra seat

**butacama** *f* (aer. & rail.) sleeper seat

**butacón** *m* large easy chair

**butadieno** *m* (chem.) butadiene

**butano** *m* (chem.) butane

**buteno** *m* (chem.) butene

**butifarra** *f* Catalonian sausage; loose sock or stocking; (Am.) ham sandwich

**butifarrero -ra** *mf* maker or seller of Catalonian sausages

**butileno** *m* (chem.) butylene

**butilo** *m* (chem.) butyl

**butiondo -da** *adj* lewd, lustful

**butírico -ca** *adj* (chem.) butyric

**butirina** *f* (chem.) butyrin

**butiro** *m* butter

**butirómetro** *m* butyrometer
**butiroso -sa** *adj* butyrous
**butomáceo -a** *adj* (bot.) butomaceous
**butrino** *m* fish trap (*made of osier*)
**butrón** *m* var. of **buitrón**
**butuco -ca** *adj* (Am.) thick, stumpy
**buxáceo -a** *adj* (bot.) buxaceous
**buyo** *m* buyo (*chewing paste*)
**buz** *m* (*pl:* **buces**) kiss of gratitude, kiss of reverence; lip; **hacer el buz** (coll.) to bow and scrape
**buzamiento** *m* (geol.) dip
**buzar** **§76** *vn* (geol.) to dip
**buzarda** *f* (naut.) breasthook
**buzo** *m* diver (*especially in diving suit*); (orn.) buzzard; **buzo de los pantanos** (orn.) marsh harrier
**buzón** *m* canal, conduit; lid, cover; sluice (*of water course of mill*); (found.) plug; mailbox, letter box; letter drop; **buzón de alcance** special-delivery box; mailbox for last-minute mail

# C

**C, c** *f* third letter of the Spanish alphabet
**c.** abr. of **capítulo, compañía, corriente** & **cuenta**
**c/** abr. of **caja, cargo, contra** & **corriente**
**c.ª** abr. of **compañía**
**c/a** abr. of **cuenta abierta**
**C.A.** abr. of **corriente alterna**
**ca** *interj* (coll.) oh no!
**Caaba** *f* Kaaba (*at Mecca*)
**caama** *m* (zool.) hartebeest
**cabal** *adj* exact; complete, perfect, finished; **no estar en sus cabales** to be not all there, to not be in one's right mind; *adv* exactly; completely; *interj* right!
**cábala** *f* cabal; cabala; divination; lucky number (*to try for the lottery*); **cábalas** *fpl* guess, supposition
**cabalgada** *f* raid by horseback; booty brought back from a raid by horseback
**cabalgador -dora** *adj* upper (*said of one of crossed knees*); *m* rider, horseman; *f* rider, horsewoman
**cabalgadura** *f* mount, riding horse, riding animal; beast of burden; (coll.) nag
**cabalgar §59** *va* to ride (*a horse*); to mount (*a gun*); to cover (*a mare*); *vn* to ride horseback, to go horseback riding; to gallop; **cabalgar sobre** to run over into (*the next line; said of the sense of a line of poetry*)
**cabalgata** *f* cavalcade
**cabalista** *mf* cabalist; schemer
**cabalístico -ca** *adj* cabalistic
**cabalizar §76** *vn* to practice cabala
**caballa** *f* (ichth.) mackerel
**caballada** *f* drove of horses
**caballaje** *m* stud service; stud price; (Am.) horsepower
**caballar** *adj* (pertaining to the) horse, equine
**caballazo** *m* large heavy horse; (Am.) jolt with a horse, trampling with a horse
**caballear** *vn* (coll.) to go horseback riding, to like to go horseback riding
**caballejo** *m* little horse; nag; horse (*instrument of torture*)
**caballerango** *m* (Am.) stableman, horse trainer
**caballerato** *m* pontifical benefice granted to married layman
**caballerear** *vn* to claim to be a knight, to act the knight; to pretend to be somebody
**caballeresco -ca** *adj* knightly, chivalric; gentlemanly; quixotic
**caballerete** *m* (coll.) dude
**caballería** *f* horse, mule; mount; (mil.) cavalry; knights; knighthood, chivalry; order of knights; knight's share of booty; land measure of varying size in Spain and Spanish America; **andarse en caballerías** (coll.) to be overobsequious, to outdo oneself in compliments; **caballería andante** errantry, knight-errantry; **caballería ligera** (mil.) light horse, light cavalry; **caballería mayor** saddle horse; **caballería menor** ass, jackass
**caballeriza** *f* stable; stable hands
**caballerizo** *m* groom, stableman; **caballerizo mayor del rey** royal master of the horse
**caballero -ra** *adj* mounted, riding; gentlemanly; obstinate, persistent; *m* knight, nobleman; mister; gentleman; cavalier, rider, horseman; (fort.) cavalier; (orn.) sandpiper; **armar caballero** to knight; **ir caballero en** to ride (*e.g., a horse, mule*); **caballero andante** knight errant; **caballero cubierto** grandee who did not have to uncover in presence of king; boorish fellow who stands with his hat on; **caballero de industria** knave, adventurer, sharper; **Caballero de la triste figura** Knight of the Rueful Countenance (*Don Quijote*); **caballero del cisne** (myth.) swan knight; **caballero del Temple** Templar, Knight Templar
**caballerosidad** *f* chivalry, gentlemanliness
**caballeroso -sa** *adj* chivalrous, gentlemanly
**caballeta** *f* (ent.) grasshopper
**caballete** *m* small horse; hip, ridge (*of roof*); ridge (*between furrows*); easel; trestle, horse, sawbuck; gantry, barrelstand; horse (*instrument of torture*); hemp brake; chimney cap; bridge (*of nose*); breastbone; (Am.) rest (*for knife and fork*); **Caballete del pintor** (astr.) Painter's Easel
**caballista** *m* horseman; horsebreaker; cowboy; (dial.) mounted highwayman; *f* horsewoman
**caballito** *m* little horse; hobbyhorse (*stick with horse's head*); **caballitos** *mpl* merry-go-round; mechanical horse race (*for gambling*); **caballito del diablo** (ent.) dragonfly, darning needle; **caballito de mar** (ichth.) sea horse
**caballo** *m* horse; knight (*in chess*); playing card (*figure on horseback*) equivalent to queen; **caballos** *mpl* (mil.) horse, cavalry; **a caballo** on horseback; **a caballo de** astride; **a mata caballo** at breakneck speed; **de a caballo** mounted; **ir a caballo** to go or to ride horseback; **montar a caballo** to ride horseback; **un sesenta caballos** a sixty-horsepower automobile; **caballo aguililla** (Am.) swift-pacing horse; **caballo blanco** angel (*financial backer*); **caballo de agua** (zool.) river horse; (ichth.) sea horse; **caballo de aldaba** horse kept for gala occasions; **caballo de batalla** battle horse, charger; forte, specialty; main point (*of an argument*); **caballo de carga** pack horse; **caballo de carrera** race horse; **caballo de frisa** (mil.) cheval-de-frise; **caballo de fuerza** (mech.) French or metric horsepower (*736 watts*); **caballo de guerra** charger; **caballo del diablo** (ent.) dragonfly, darning needle; **caballo de mar** (zool.) river horse; (ichth.) sea horse; **caballo de montar** or **de silla** saddle horse; **caballo de palo** (coll.) ship, vessel; (coll.) wooden horse (*used for punishment*); **caballo de posta** post horse; **caballo de regalo** horse kept for gala occasions; **caballo de tiro** draft horse; **caballo de Troya** Trojan horse; **caballo de vapor** (mech.) French horsepower or metric horsepower (*736 watts*); **caballo de vapor inglés** horsepower (*746 watts*); **caballo entero** stallion; **caballo hora** (*pl:* **caballos hora**) (mech.) horsepower-hour; **caballo marino** (zool.) river horse; (ichth. & zool.) sea horse; **caballo mecedor** rocking horse, hobbyhorse; **caballo padre** stallion; **caballo regalado** gift horse, e.g., **a caballo regalado no se le mira el diente** never look a gift horse in the mouth; **caballo semental** studhorse
**caballón** *m* big clumsy horse; ridge (*between furrows*); dike, levee
**caballuno -na** *adj* (pertaining to the) horse, horselike
**cabaña** *f* cabin, hut; hovel; rustic bower (*in a garden*); drove, flock; flock of sheep and ewes; livestock; drove of grain-carrying horses or mules; (hunt.) shelter; (paint.) pastoral scene; balk line (*in billiards*); cattle-breeding ranch
**cabañal** *adj* sheep-and-cattle (*path*); *m* village of cabins or huts
**cabañería** *f* shepherd's weekly ration
**cabañero -ra** *adj* sheep-and-cattle; grain-carrying; *m* shepherd; drover
**cabañil** *adj* shepherd's-cabin; *m* mule-driver

**cabañuelas** *fpl* weather forecasting in January and August; first summer rains (*in Argentina and Bolivia*); winter rain (*in Mexico*); (archaic) Feast of Tabernacles (*in Toledo*); **estar cogiendo cabañuelas** (Am.) to be out of work
**cabaret** *m* (*pl:* **-rets**) cabaret, night club
**cabe** *m* stroke of ball; **dar un cabe a** (coll.) to hurt, to harm; **cabe de pala** (coll.) lucky break; *prep* (archaic & poet.) near, at the side of
**cabeceada** *f* (Am. & dial.) nod
**cabeceado** *m* thick stroke (*of certain letters*)
**cabeceamiento** *m* var. of **cabeceo**
**cabecear** *va* to write (*letters*) with thick strokes; to bind (*e.g., a rug*); to put a headband on (*a book*); to head (*wine*); to put a new foot on (*a stocking*); *vn* to nod (*in sleep*); to bob the head; to shake one's head (*in negation*); to slip to one side, to hang over; to lurch; (naut.) to pitch
**cabeceo** *m* nod, bob, shake (*of the head*); lurching; (naut.) pitch, pitching
**cabecera** *f* head (*of bed, table, etc.*); bedside; headboard; headwall; headwaters; end (*of house, lot, or field*); heading (*e.g., of a chapter of a book*); (print.) headpiece; headline (*of newspaper*); (law) heading (*of a document*); capital, county seat; fortified point on a bridge; pillow, bolster; **asistir** or **estar a la cabecera de un enfermo** to be in constant attendance on a sick person; **cabecera de cartel** (theat.) top billing; **cabecera de puente** (mil.) bridgehead
**cabeciancho -cha** *adj* broad-headed
**cabeciduro -ra** *adj* (Am.) stubborn
**cabecilla** *mf* (coll.) scalawag; *m* rebel leader; gang leader; ringleader
**cabellar** *vn* to grow hair; to put on false hair; *vr* to put on false hair
**cabellera** *f* head of hair; switch of hair; (astr.) coma (*of comet*); (bot.) mistletoe (*Phoradendron*)
**cabello** *m* hair (*of head*); **cabellos** *mpl* hair (*of head*); corn silk; **asirse de un cabello** (coll.) to be out for the main chance; **cortar un cabello en el aire** to have keen insight; **en cabello** with one's hair down; **en cabellos** bareheaded; **estar pendiente de un cabello** to be hanging by a hair; **traer por los cabellos** to drag in irrelevantly; **cabello del rey** (bot.) Florida moss, Spanish moss; **cabello de Venus** (bot.) maidenhair; **cabello merino** thick curly hair; **cabellos de ángel** fine vermicelli
**cabelludo -da** *adj* hairy, shaggy; fibrous
**caber §27** *vn* to fit, to go; to have enough room; to be admitted; to be possible; to befall, to happen; **no cabe duda** there is no doubt; **no cabe más** that's the limit; **no caber de** to be bursting with (*e.g., joy*); **no caber en sí** to be beside oneself; to be puffed up with conceit; **todo cabe en** anything (*bad*) can be expected of; **caber** + *inf* to be possible to + *inf;* **caber a** to happen to, to befall; **caber por** to be able to get through (*e.g., a door*)
**cabero -ra** *adj* (Am.) end, last; *m* (prov. & Am.) handle maker (*for farm implements*)
**cabestraje** *m* halters; fee paid to cattle drover
**cabestrante** *m* var. of **cabrestante**
**cabestrar** *va* to halter, put a halter on; *vn* to hunt using an ox as shield
**cabestrear** *va* (Am.) to lead by the halter; *vn* to be lead easily by the halter
**cabestrería** *f* halter shop
**cabestrero -ra** *adj* (dial.) wild but yielding to the halter; *m* maker and seller of halters and hemp ware
**cabestrillo** *m* sling (*to support hurt arm*); little chain worn as necklace; (carp.) strap, diagonal tie
**cabestro** *m* halter; trained ox, leading ox; (coll.) pander, pimp; (surg.) sling for broken jaw; **llevar** or **traer del cabestro** (coll.) to lead by the halter; (fig.) to lead by the nose
**cabete** *m* metal tip (*of rope*)
**cabeza** *f* head (*top part of body of man or animal; brains, intelligence; judgment; top part of page, of nail or pin, of a hammer; top of mountain; origin, source, e.g., of a river; front of a procession, army, etc.; chief, leader; chief command, leadership; person; individual; point of an arrow; rounded top of cabbage or lettuce; recording or reproducing part of tape recorder*); capital (*e.g., of a country*); **alzar la cabeza** (coll.) to be on one's feet (*after poverty or misfortune*); (coll.) to be up and around (*after an illness*); **andársele a uno la cabeza** (coll.) to be in a whirl; (coll.) to be on the skids; **calentarse la cabeza** (coll.) to be mentally exhausted; **dar de cabeza** (coll.) to lose one's wealth or standing; **dar en la cabeza a** to frustrate, to thwart; **de cabeza** on end; head first; by heart; on one's own, of one's own invention; **flaco de cabeza** befuddled, confused; **hacer cabeza** to be the head (*e.g., of a business*); **henchir la cabeza de viento a** (coll.) to flatter, to puff up; **ir cabeza abajo** (coll.) to be going downhill, to be on the decline; **irse de la cabeza** to go out of one's mind; **levantar la cabeza** (coll.) to be on one's feet (*after poverty or misfortune*); (coll.) to be up and around (*after an illness*); **mala cabeza** headstrong person; **meterse de cabeza** (coll.) to plunge headlong (*into a deal or business*); **metérsele a uno en la cabeza una cosa** (coll.) to get something in one's head; (coll.) to be bullheaded about something; **no levantar cabeza** to be deep in work, to be busy reading and writing; **no tener dónde volver la cabeza** to not know where to look for help; **otorgar de cabeza** to nod assent; **pasarle a uno por la cabeza** (coll.) to come into one's head; **perder la cabeza** to become befuddled, to go out of one's mind; **por su cabeza** on one's own (*without seeking advice*); **quebrantar la cabeza a** to humble the pride of; to bore to death; **quebrarse la cabeza** (coll.) to seek with diligence; **quebrarse la cabeza con** (coll.) to bother one's head about; **quitar a uno de la cabeza alguna cosa** (coll.) to put something out of someone's head; **romperse la cabeza** (coll.) to rack one's brains; **sentar la cabeza** (coll.) to settle down; **subírsele a uno a la cabeza** to go to one's head (*said of wine, success, etc.*); **tocado de la cabeza** (coll.) touched in the head; **cabeza de ajo** or **ajos** bulb of garlic; **cabeza de borrado** erase head (*of tape recorder*); **cabeza de combate** war head; **cabeza de chorlito** (coll.) scatterbrains; (Am.) forgetful person; **cabeza de la biela** (mach.) big end; **cabeza de lectura** playback head; **cabeza de mina** mine entrance; **cabeza de motín** ringleader; **cabeza de olla** (zool.) blackfish; **cabeza de partido** county seat; **cabeza de perro** (bot.) pilewort; **cabeza de playa** (mil.) beachhead; **cabeza de puente** (mil.) bridgehead; **cabeza de registro** or **cabeza grabadora** recording head; **cabeza de turco** (naut.) Turk's-head; (coll.) scapegoat, butt; **cabeza dura** (coll.) thick head (*person*); **cabeza mayor** head of cattle; **cabeza menor** head of sheep, goats, etc.; **cabeza perdida** countersunk head; **cabeza redonda** (coll.) blockhead
**cabezada** *f* butt (*with the head*); blow on the head; nod; headstall (*of a bridle*); pitch, pitching (*of a ship*); instep (*of boot*); (b.b.) headband; **dar cabezadas** to nod
**cabezal** *m* small pillow; bolster; header, header brick; (print.) heading; straw mattress of peasants; (surg.) compress; (mach.) headstock (*of a lathe*)
**cabezalero -ra** *mf* (law) executor
**cabezazo** *m* butt (*with the head*)
**cabezo** *m* hillock; summit, top; reef
**cabezón -zona** *adj* big-headed; headstrong; *m* hole for the head (*in a garment*); collarband; **llevar** or **traer de los cabezones** (coll.) to lead by the nose; **cabezón de serreta** cavesson
**cabezonada** *f* (coll.) stubbornness
**cabezorro** *m* (coll.) big misshapen head
**cabezota** *adj* (coll.) stubborn; *mf* (coll.) stubborn person; (coll.) big-headed person
**cabezudo -da** *adj* big-headed; (coll.) headstrong; heady (*wine*); *m* big-headed dwarf (*in carnival processions*); (ichth.) striped mullet

**cabezuela** *f* little head; coarse flour, middling; (bot.) capitulum or head (*inflorescence*); rose bud for making rose water; (bot.) broom centaury, cornflower
**cabida** *f* space, room, capacity; expanse; **dar cabida a** to make room for; **tener cabida** or **gran cabida** to have pull, to be in favor; **tener cabida en** to have a place in, to be included in
**cabila** *f* tribe (*in Morocco*)
**cabildada** *f* (coll.) hasty and unwise action of a chapter or council
**cabildear** *vn* to lobby
**cabildeo** *m* lobbying
**cabildero** *m* lobbyist
**cabildo** *m* cathedral chapter; chapter meeting; municipal council; council room; town hall
**cabilla** *f* steel bar, dowel, driftbolt; (naut.) belaying pin
**cabillo** *m* stalk, stem; end (*of a rope*)
**cabillón** *m* rung of rope ladder
**cabimiento** *m* space, room, capacity
**cabina** *f* cabin; cab (*e.g., of a truck*); booth (*for telephoning; for listening to phonograph records*); (aer.) cabin; (sport) dressing room; **cabinas de audición independientes** private listening booths
**cabio** *m* joist, rafter; trimmer; lintel, crosspiece
**cabizbajo -ja** *adj* crestfallen
**cable** *m* cable, rope, hawser; cable's length; (telg.) cable; **cable coaxial** coaxial cable; **cable de alambre** stranded cable; **cable de remolque** towline, towrope; **cable de retén** guy, guy wire
**cableado** *m* (elec.) cable (*in auto, radio, etc.*)
**cablear** *va* to fashion into a cable
**cablecarril** *m* cableway
**cablegrafiar** §90 *va & vn* to cable
**cablegráfico -ca** *adj* cable
**cablegrama** *m* cablegram, cable
**cablero -ra** *adj* cable (*e.g., ship*); *m* cable ship
**cabo** *m* end; handle; cape; small bundle; filament, thread, string; end, bit, small piece; chief, boss, foreman; finish, perfection; (naut.) cord, rope, cable; (mil.) corporal; **cabos** *mpl* eyes, eyebrows and hair; paws, nose, and mane (*of horse*); duds, pieces of clothing; miscellanies; **al cabo** finally, after all, **al cabo de** after, at the end of; **atar cabos** (coll.) to put two and two together; **dar cabo a** to finish, to perfect; **dar cabo de** to put an end to, to destroy; **El Cabo** Cape Town; **estar al cabo de** (coll.) to be informed about; **llevar a cabo** to carry out, accomplish; **ponerse al cabo de** to catch on to, to get the point of; **por ningún cabo** by no means; **cabo de año** anniversary memorial service; **Cabo de Buena Esperanza** Cape of Good Hope; **cabo de desgarre** (aer.) rip cord; **cabo de escuadra** (mil.) corporal; **Cabo de Hornos** Cape Horn; **cabo de maestranza** (naut.) foreman (*of a brigade of workmen*); **cabo de mar** (naut.) petty officer; **cabo de plumas** (Am.) penholder; **Cabo Finisterre** Cape Finisterre (*headland in northwest Spain*); Land's End (*southwest tip of England*); **cabo negro** (bot.) fishtail palm; **cabo suelto** (coll.) loose end (*unfinished business*); **Cabo Verde** Cape Verde
**cabotaje** *m* coasting trade, coastal traffic
**cabra** *f* (zool.) goat; (hist.) catapult; (Am.) loaded die; **cabra bezoar** (zool.) ibex (*Capra aegagrus*); **cabra de almizcle** (zool.) musk deer; **cabra montés** (zool.) ibex, wild goat
**cabrahigadura** *f* caprification
**cabrahigal** *m* field of caprifigs or wild figs
**cabrahigar** *m* field of caprifigs or wild figs; §59 *va* to caprificate
**cabrahigo** *m* (bot.) caprifig, wild fig (*tree and fruit*)
**cabrajo** *m* (zool.) lobster (*Homarus vulgaris*)
**cabré** *1st sg fut ind of* **caber**
**cabrear** *va* (vulg.) to burn up, exasperate; *vr* (Am.) to jump around
**cabrera** *f* goatherd (*woman*)
**cabrería** *f* goat-milk dairy; goat stable
**cabrerizo -za** *adj* goatish; *m* goatherd; *f* goat stable; goatherds' hut
**cabrero** *m* goatherd
**cabrestante** *m* capstan; **guarnir el cabrestante** to rig the capstan; **cabrestante para remolcar** towing winch
**cabria** *f* three-legged derrick, crab
**cabrieta** *f* jack, lifting jack
**cabrilla** *f* sawbuck, sawhorse; leg of a three-legged derrick; (ichth.) grouper; (ichth.) serran; **cabrillas** *fpl* (naut.) whitecaps; leg burns or blisters; game of skipping stones on water; (*cap.*) *fpl* (astr.) Pleiades
**cabrillear** *vn* to caper, to prance, to frisk; to sparkle, to flash; (naut.) to form whitecaps; (med.) to beat irregularly (*said of heart*)
**cabrilleo** *m* (naut.) forming of whitecaps
**cabrio** *m* rafter; joist
**cabrío -a** *adj* goatish; of goats; *m* herd of goats
**cabriola** *f* caper; skip, gambol; somersault; **dar** or **hacer cabriolas** to cut capers
**cabriolar** *vn* to caper, to prance, to frisk
**cabriolé** *m* cabriolet (*carriage and automobile*)
**cabriolear** *vn* to caper, to prance, to frisk
**cabritero -ra** *mf* dealer in kids (*young goats*)
**cabritilla** *f* kid, kidskin
**cabrito** *m* kid; **cabritos** *mpl* (Am.) popcorn
**cabrón** *m* buck, billy goat; complaisant husband, cuckold
**cabronada** *f* (coll.) indignity, shamelessness; (coll.) necessary evil
**cabrón-emisario** *m* (Bib.) scapegoat
**cabruno -na** *adj* (pertaining to the) goat
**cabujón** *m* uncut ruby; nail with diamond-shaped head; convex polished but uncut precious stone; **cabujones** *mpl* (print.) headpiece
**cabuya** *f* (bot.) century plant; pita fiber, pita hemp; rope, pita rope; (naut.) small ropes; **ponerse en la cabuya** (Am.) to catch on, to become fully informed
**cabuyera** *f* hammock cords
**cabuyería** *f* (naut.) small ropes
**cacahuacintli** *m* (Am.) hominy
**cacahual** *m* cacao plantation
**cacahuate** *m*, **cacahuete** *m* or **cacahuey** *m* (bot.) peanut (*plant, pod, and seed*)
**cacahuetero -ra** *mf* peanut vendor
**cacalote** *m* (Am.) raven; (Am.) popcorn; (Am.) break, blunder
**cacao** *m* (bot.) cacao (*tree and seed*); (Am.) chocolate; **pedir cacao** (Am.) to beg for mercy
**cacaotal** *m* var. of **cacahual**
**cacaotero** *m* (bot.) cacao (*tree*)
**cacaraña** *f* pit, pock (*in face*)
**cacarañado -da** *adj* pitted, pocked, pockmarked
**cacarañar** *va* (Am.) to pit
**cacareador -dora** *adj* cackling; (coll.) boasting
**cacarear** *va* (coll.) to exaggerate, exaggerate the importance of (*one's doings*); *vn* to cackle; to crow
**cacareo** *m* cackling; crowing; crying, yelling; (coll.) crowing, boasting
**cacarizo -za** *adj* (Am.) pock-marked
**cacatúa** *f* (orn.) cockatoo
**cacaxtle** *m* (Am.) crate
**cacea** *f* trolling; **pescar a la cacea** to troll
**cacear** *va* to stir with a dipper or ladle; *vn* to troll
**caceo** *m* stirring with a ladle; trolling
**cacera** *f* irrigating ditch or canal
**cacería** *f* hunt; hunting party; bag (*game caught*); (paint.) hunting scene
**cacerina** *f* cartridge pouch
**cacerola** *f* casserole, saucepan; (chem.) casserole
**caceta** *f* apothecaries' brass straining dipper
**cacica** *f* female Indian chief; chief's wife
**cacicato** or **cacicazgo** *m* position or territory of Indian chief; (coll.) bossism (*in politics*)
**cacillo** *m* small ladle or dipper; pannikin
**cacimba** *f* hole dug in beach for drinking water; bucket; (Am.) tub for collecting rain water
**cacique** *m* Indian chief; bossy person; (coll.) boss (*in politics*); (orn.) cacique; **cacique veranero** (orn.) hangbird, Baltimore oriole
**caciquesco -ca** *adj* (coll.) (pertaining to a) boss
**caciquismo** *m* (coll.) bossism
**cacle** *m* (Am.) leather sandal; (Am.) footwear
**caco** *m* pickpocket; (coll.) coward

**cacodilato** *m* (chem.) cacodylate
**cacodílico -ca** *adj* (chem.) cacodylic
**cacofonía** *f* cacophony
**cacofónico -ca** *adj* cacophonous
**cacomite** *m* (bot.) tigerflower
**cacoquimia** *f* (path.) cacochymia
**cactáceo -a** *adj* (bot.) cactaceous
**cacto** *m* (bot.) cactus
**cacumen** *m* (coll.) acumen
**cacha** *f* see **cacho**
**cachaco -ca** *adj* (Am.) sporty; *m* (Am.) sport
**cachada** *f* (Am.) thrust or wound made with the horns
**cachalote** *m* (zool.) sperm whale, cachalot
**cachamarín** *m* (naut.) coasting lugger
**cachanilla** *f* (bot.) arrowweed, arrowwood
**cachano** *m* (coll.) the devil; **llamar a cachano** (coll.) to ask in vain
**cachapa** *f* (Am.) corn bread
**cachar** *va* to break to pieces; to split (*wood*); to plough up
**cacharpari** *m* (Am.) farewell party, send-off party
**cacharrería** *f* crockery shop
**cacharrero -ra** *mf* crockery dealer
**cacharro** *m* crock, coarse earthen pot; piece of crockery (*still useful*); piece of junk (*any old machine that does not work well*); (Am.) notion, trinket
**cachava** *f* shinny (*game and stick*); crook, staff
**cachavazo** *m* stroke with shinny stick
**cachaza** *f* (coll.) slowness, sloth, phlegm; rum; first froth on boiling cane juice
**cachazudo -da** *adj* slow, slothful, phlegmatic; *mf* sluggard; *m* (zool.) tobacco worm
**cache** *adj* (Am.) slovenly
**cachear** *va* to frisk (*for weapons*)
**cachemarín** *m* (naut.) coasting lugger
**cachemir** *m* var. of **casimir**
**cachemira** *f* var. of **casimir;** (*cap.*) Cashmere
**cacheo** *m* frisking
**cachera** *f* homespun
**cachería** *f* (Am.) slovenliness; (Am.) small shop
**cacheta** *f* ward (*of lock*)
**cachetada** *f* (Am. & Canary Islands) slap in the face
**cachete** *m* punch in the face; cheek, swollen cheek; dagger
**cachetero** *m* dagger, short poniard; dagger man, puntillero (*bullfighter who gives coup de grâce with dagger*)
**cachetina** *f* (coll.) fist fight, brawl
**cachetudo -da** *adj* round-cheeked
**cachicamo** *m* (zool.) armadillo
**cachicán** *m* foreman, overseer; (coll.) sly fellow
**cachicuerno -na** *adj* horn-handled (*said of a weapon*)
**cachidiablo** *m* (coll.) hobgoblin; (coll.) person disguised as the devil; *adj* (coll.) mischievous, impish; (coll.) wild, unruly
**cachifollar** *va* (coll.) to make fun of, to humiliate
**cachigordete -ta** *adj* (coll.) stubby
**cachigordo -da** *adj* (coll.) squat
**cachillada** *f* breed, litter
**cachimba** *f* (Am.) spring, well; (Am.) pipe (*for smoking tobacco*); (Am.) pistol, revolver; (Am.) empty cartridge
**cachimbo** *m* (Am.) pipe; (Am.) sugar mill; **chupar cachimbo** (Am.) to smoke a pipe; (Am.) to suck its finger (*said of a baby*)
**cachipolla** *f* (ent.) shad fly, dayfly
**cachiporra** *f* billy, bludgeon
**cachiporrazo** *m* blow with a billy or bludgeon
**cachirulo** *m* liquor container; (naut.) small three-master; (slang) beau, lover; (prov.) kite; (prov.) hat, cap; (Am.) cloth or chamois patch (*for trousers*)
**cachivache** *m* (coll.) faker; **cachivaches** *mpl* broken crockery; pots and pans, kitchenware; trash, junk
**cacho -cha** *adj* bent, crooked; *m* crumb, bit, slice; (ichth.) chub; (Am.) horn; *f* side of the handle of a folding knife or razor; buttock (*of rabbit*); **hasta las cachas** (coll.) over head and ears
**cacholas** *fpl* (naut.) cheeks of the masts
**cachón** *m* breaker (*wave*); splashing jet of water; rapids (*in a river*); **cachones** *mpl* surf
**cachondo -da** *adj* in rut; (coll.) passionate; (slang) sexy (*woman*)
**cachopín -pina** *mf* var. of **cachupín**
**cachorreñas** *fpl* garlic soup
**cachorrillo** *m* pocket pistol; pup, cub
**cachorro -rra** *mf* pup, whelp, cub; *m* pocket pistol
**cachú** *m* (*pl:* **-chúes**) catechu
**cachucha** *f* rowboat; cap; cachucha (*Andalusian dance*)
**cachuchero** *m* maker or seller of caps; maker or seller of pincases
**cachucho** *m* oil measure equal to a sixth of a pound; pincase; rowboat; (ichth.) red West Indian snapper
**cachuela** *f* pork fricassee; fricassee of rabbit livers, hearts, and kidneys; gizzard
**cachuelo** *m* (ichth.) dace; (Am.) tip
**cachumbo** *m* (Am.) fruit shell (*used to make cups and other vessels*); (Am.) curl, corkscrew curl
**cachunde** *m* (pharm.) aromatic troche or pastil; catechu
**cachupín -pina** *mf* Spanish settler in America; *f* (Am.) strait jacket (*used for torture of prisoners*)
**cachupinada** *f* (coll.) gaudy party, gaudy gathering
**cachurear** *vn* (Am.) to rummage through the rubbish or trash
**cachurrera menor** *f* (bot.) cocklebur (*Xanthium spinosum*)
**cada** *adj indef* each; every (*followed by a numeral*), e.g., **cada tres meses** every three months; **cada tercer día** every third day; **cada cual** each one; **cada cuánto** how often; **cada día** + *comp* more and more; **cada quisque** (coll.) each one; **cada uno** each one; **cada vez** + *comp* more and more; **cada y siempre que** as soon as; *m* (bot.) juniper
**cadahalso** *m* wooden shed or shack
**cadalecho** *m* bed of branches
**cadalso** *m* stand, platform; scaffold
**cadañego -ga** *adj* annual, yearly
**cadañero -ra** *adj* annual, yearly; of a year's duration; having offspring every year
**cadarzo** *m* floss, floss silk (*threads of outer part of cocoon*)
**cádava** *f* (prov.) burnt stump of furze
**cadáver** *m* corpse, cadaver
**cadavérico -ca** *adj* cadaverous
**cadejo** *m* entangled hair; small hank or skein; batch of thread for making tassels
**cadena** *f* chain; chain gang; tie, brace; (chem. & rad.) chain; **cadena antideslizante** or **antirresbaladiza** tire chain; **cadena de agrimensor** surveyor's chain; **cadena de distribución** (aut.) timing chain; **cadena lateral** (chem.) side chain; **cadena para neumático** tire chain; **cadena perpetua** life imprisonment; **cadena sin fin** endless chain
**cadencia** *f* cadence; (mus.) cadence; (mus.) cadenza; **cadencia del paso** (mil.) cadence; **cadencia perfecta** (mus.) perfect cadence
**cadencioso -sa** *adj* rhythmical, cadenced
**cadenear** *va* to measure with the chain
**cadenero** *m* chainman, lineman
**cadeneta** *f* chain stitch; (b.b.) headband
**cadenilla** *f* small chain; **cadenilla de tiro** (elec.) pull chain
**cadente** *adj* declining, on the decline; rhythmic
**cadera** *f* (anat.) hip; flank (*of animal*); (zool.) coxa (*of arthropod*); **caderas** *fpl* bustle
**caderillas** *fpl* bustle
**caderudo -da** *adj* big-hipped
**cadetada** *f* (coll.) thoughtlessness, inconsiderate act
**cadete** *m* cadet; (Am.) apprentice
**cadí** *m* (*pl:* **-díes**) cadi
**cadillar** *m* field of hedgehog parsley
**cadillo** *m* (bot.) hedgehog parsley; (bot.) burdock; bristle, burr; **cadillos** *mpl* fag end, thrums
**cadmeo -a** *adj* Cadmean
**cadmía** *f* oxide of zinc which collects in the chimney of zinc-subliming furnaces

**cadmio** *m* (chem.) cadmium
**Cadmo** *m* (myth.) Cadmus
**cadozo** *m* whirlpool (*in river*)
**caducar** §86 *vn* to dote, to be in one's dotage; to be worn out, to be out-of-date; (com. & law) to lapse, to expire
**caduceo** *m* caduceus
**caducidad** *f* caducity (*feebleness, decrepitude; transitoriness*); (law) caducity (*lapse, expiration*); **incurrir en caducidad** to lapse, expire
**caduco -ca** *adj* caducous (*feeble, decrepit; transitory*); (bot. & law) caducous
**caduquez** *f* caducity
**caedizo -za** *adj* ready to fall, falling; fragile; weak, timid; (bot.) deciduous; **hacer caedizo** to drop, to lose (*on purpose*); *m* (Am.) lean-to
**caedura** *f* loose threads that fall from loom
**caer** §28 *vn* to fall, to tumble, to fall off; to droop; to be located, to be found; to fall due; to become faint (*said of colors*); to decline (*said of sun, day, wind, etc.*); to fall (*to be killed, e.g., in battle*); **estar al caer** to be about to happen; **no caigo** (coll.) I don't get it; **caer a** to face, to overlook; **caer bien** to fit, to hang well; to become, be becoming; to ride well; (coll.) to make a hit; **caer del burro** (fig.) to come down off one's horse; **caer de pies** to land on one's feet; **caer de plano** to fall flat; **caer en** to be found on or in (*a certain page or chapter*); **caer en cama** to fall ill; **caer en gracia** to be in favor; **caer en la cuenta** to catch on, to get the point; **caer enfermo** to fall ill; **caer en que** to realize that; **caer mal** to fit badly; to be unbecoming; to ride badly; (coll.) to fall flat ‖ *vr* to fall, to fall down; to be located, to be found; **caerse de sí mismo, caerse de su peso** or **caerse de suyo** to be self-evident; **caerse muerto de** to be struck dumb with (*e.g., fear*); **caerse redondo** to fall unconscious
**Cafarnaúm** Capernaum
**café** *m* coffee; coffee house; café; (bot.) coffee tree; (Am.) displeasure, unpleasant time; **café cantante** night club; **café de maquinilla** drip coffee; **café solo** black coffee; *adj* (Am.) tan, brown
**café-concierto** *m* (*pl:* **café-conciertos**) cabaret
**cafeína** *f* (pharm.) caffein
**cafetal** *m* coffee plantation
**cafetán** *m* caftan
**cafetera** *f* see **cafetero**
**cafetería** *f* cafeteria; (Am.) retail coffee shop
**cafetero -ra** *adj* (pertaining to) coffee; *mf* coffeegrower, coffee planter; coffee-bean picker, coffee gatherer; coffee seller; *f* coffee pot; **cafetera eléctrica** electric percolator
**cafetín** *m* small coffee shop
**cafeto** *m* (bot.) coffee plant, coffee tree
**cáfila** *f* (coll.) flock (*of people, animals, or things*); caravan
**cafre** *adj* & *mf* Kaffir or Kafir; savage; rustic, peasant
**caftán** *m* caftan
**cagaaceite** *m* (orn.) missel thrush
**cagaestacas** *m* (*pl:* **-cas**) (orn.) chat
**cagafierro** *m* slag, scoria
**cagajón** *m* horse or mule dung
**cagalaolla** *m* (coll.) clown, masquerader
**cágalo** *m* (orn.) jaeger
**cagar** §59 *va* (coll.) to spot, to spoil; *vn* to defecate; *vr* to defecate; to become frightened
**cagarrache** *m* washer of olive pits (*in olive-oil mill*); (orn.) missel thrush
**cagarria** *f* (bot.) morel
**cagarruta** *f* cow or sheep dung
**cagatintas** *m* (*pl:* **-tas**) (scornful) clerk, office worker
**cagón -gona** *adj* (coll.) cowardly; *mf* (coll.) coward
**caguanete** *m* cotton wool
**cahiz** *m* (*pl:* **-hices**) cahiz (*18.9 bushels*)
**cahuama** *f* (Am.) sea turtle
**caico** *m* (naut.) reef, shoal
**caído -da** *adj* fallen; turndown (*collar*); weak, languid; crestfallen; drooping (*eyelid, shoulder, etc.*); **caído en desuso** obsolete; **caídos** *mpl* income due; (min.) fallen material; **los caídos** the fallen (*in battle*); *f* fall, tumble; drop; collapse, failure; slip, blunder, lapse; fold (*e.g., of a curtain*); hang (*e.g., of clothing, of a curtain*); flop (*of a play*); (geol.) dip; (hyd.) head; (min.) slip; (naut.) calm; (naut.) depth or drop (*of a sail*); **caídas** *fpl* falling ends; coarse wool; (coll.) witticism; **a la caída de la hoja** in autumn; **a la caída de la tarde** in the late afternoon; **a la caída del sol** at sunset; **La Caída** the Fall (*sin of Adam*); **caída de agua** waterfall; **caída pluvial** rainfall; **caída radiactiva** (phys.) fallout
**Caifás** *m* (Bib.) Caiaphas
**caigo** *1st sg pres ind of* **caer**
**caimán** *m* (zool.) alligator, caiman; (coll.) schemer, sharper
**caimiento** *m* fall; weakness, decline
**caimito** *m* (bot.) star apple (*tree and fruit*)
**Caín** *m* (Bib.) Cain; **pasar las de Caín** to have a terrible time
**caique** *m* (naut.) caïque
**cairel** *m* wig; fringe; (arch. & naut.) breastrail
**cairelar** *va* to fringe, to trim with fringe
**cairino -na** *adj* & *mf* var. of **cairota**
**Cairo, El** Cairo
**cairota** *adj* (pertaining to) Cairo; *mf* native or inhabitant of Cairo
**caja** *f* box, case, chest; safe, strongbox; cashbox; cash; cashier's office; desk (*where bills are paid in a hotel*); coffin; case (*of watch*); drum; set (*of false teeth*); (elec.) box (*for switches, outlets, etc.*); cabinet (*e.g., of a radio*); body (*of carriage or car*); stock (*of firearm*); hole, hollow; socket; (carp.) mortise, recess; (elec.) jack; (mach.) housing, casing; shaft, well (*of staircase, elevator, etc.*); drum case or frame, drum; (print.) case; (bot.) capsule; **a caja y espiga** (carp.) mortise-and-tenon; **de caja alta** (print.) upper-case; **de caja baja** (print.) lower-case; **despedir** or **echar con cajas destempladas** (coll.) to send packing, to give the gate; **en caja** (coll.) in good shape, in good health; **caja clara** snare drum; **caja de aceite** (mach.) oil cup; **caja de ahorros** savings bank; **caja de cambio de marchas** (aut.) transmission-gear box; **caja de caudales** safe; **caja de cigüeñal** (aut.) crankcase; **caja de colores** paintbox; **caja de conexiones** (elec.) joint box, junction box; **caja de contacto** (elec.) receptacle; **caja de cortar al sesgo** (carp.) miter box; **caja de distribución** (mach.) valve chest; (elec.) junction box; **caja de embalaje** packing box or case; **caja de enchufe** (elec.) outlet; **caja de engranajes** gear case; **caja de fuego** firebox; **caja de fusibles** (elec.) fuse box; **caja de herramientas** tool box, tool chest; **caja de grasa** journal box; **caja de humos** smokebox; **caja de ingletes** (carp.) miter box; **caja de jubilaciones** pension fund; **caja del diferencial** (aut.) differential housing; **caja del eje** (mach.) journal box; **caja de menores** petty cash; **caja de música** music box; **caja de Pandora** (myth.) Pandora's box; **caja de Petri** Petri dish; **caja de puente trasero** (aut.) rear-axle housing; **caja de reclutamiento** (mil.) recruiting service; **caja de registro** manhole (*in street*); **caja de reloj** watchcase; **caja de resonancia** (mus. & fig.) sounding board; **caja de salida** (elec.) outlet box; **caja de sebo** (mach.) grease cup; **caja de seguridad** bank vault, safe; safe-deposit box; **caja de sorpresa** jack-in-the-box; **caja de vapor** steam box or chest; **caja de velocidades** (aut.) transmission-gear box; **caja de volquete** dump body (*of truck*); **caja fuerte** safe, bank vault; **caja postal de ahorros** postal or post-office savings; **caja registradora** cash register; **caja sorpresa** jack-in-the-box; **caja y espiga** (carp.) mortise and tenon
**caja-dique** *m* cofferdam
**cajel** *adj* see **naranja**
**cajera** *f* see **cajero**
**cajería** *f* box business, box store
**cajero -ra** *mf* boxmaker; teller, cashier; *f* groove, channel, recess
**cajeta** *f* little box; cigar case; (naut.) sennit; (Am.) butterscotch; *m* dude, sport, city guy
**cajetilla** *f* pack (*of cigarettes*)

**cajetín** *m* stamp, rubber stamp; (print.) box (*of type-holding tray*); (elec.) molding
**cajiga** *f* (bot.) gall oak
**cajigal** *m* grove of gall oaks
**cajista** *mf* (print.) compositor, typesetter
**cajo** *m* flange (*on back of book for boards to fit in*)
**cajón** *m* big box or case; bin; drawer; locker; space between shelves; stall, booth; shed; bier, coffin; (mil.) caisson; (taur.) box for transporting bulls; (Am.) dry-goods store; **ser de cajón** (coll.) to be customary; **cajón de aire comprimido** (eng.) caisson; **cajón de sastre** (coll.) odds and ends; (coll.) muddlehead; **cajón de suspensión** (naut.) caisson; **cajón hidráulico** (eng.) caisson
**cajonada** *f* (naut.) lockers
**cajonera** *f* chest of drawers in vestry; (hort.) cold frame
**cajonería** *f* set of drawers
**cajuela** *f* small box or case; groove, recess; (Am.) auto trunk
**cal** *f* lime; **de cal y canto** (coll.) strong, robust; **cal apagada** or **muerta** slaked lime; **cal hidráulica** hydraulic lime; **cal sodada** soda lime; **cal viva** quicklime
**cala** *f* cove, inlet; fishing ground; plug (*cut to sample a melon*); test core, test boring; (med.) suppository; (naut.) hold; (bot.) calla (*Zantedeschia aethiopica and Calla palustris*); **cala de construcción** (naut.) slip
**calabacear** *va* (coll.) to flunk; (coll.) to jilt
**calabacero -ra** *mf* calabash or pumpkin seller; *m* (bot.) calabash tree; *f* (bot.) calabash, pumpkin, squash
**calabacilla** *f* gourd-shaped eardrop; (bot.) squirting cucumber
**calabacín** *m* (bot.) small cylindrical calabash; (coll.) dolt
**calabacinate** *m* fried calabash or pumpkin
**calabacino** *m* gourd (*used as bottle, bowl, etc.*)
**calabaza** *f* calabash, pumpkin, squash, gourd (*fruit*); calabash, gourd (*bottle or bowl*); (coll.) dolt; **dar calabazas a** (coll.) to give the cold shoulder to; (coll.) to flunk; (coll.) to jilt; **salir calabaza** (coll.) to be a flop, to be a fizzle
**calabazada** *f* butt (*with the head*); blow on the head; **darse de calabazadas por** + *inf* (coll.) to break one's back to, to rack one's brains to + *inf*
**calabazar** *m* calabash or pumpkin plot
**calabazate** *m* candied calabash or pumpkin
**calabazazo** *m* blow with a pumpkin; (coll.) bump on the head
**calabazo** *m* gourd; wine gourd; (Am.) calabash (*drum*)
**calabobos** *m* (*pl:* **-bos**) (coll.) drizzle
**calabocero** *m* jailer
**calabozaje** *m* prisoner's fee to jailer
**calabozo** *m* calaboose, dungeon; cell; prison cell; (agr.) pruning hook, mattock
**calabrés -bresa** *adj & mf* Calabrian
**calabriada** *f* mixture, hodgepodge
**calabriar** *va* to mix up
**calabrotar** *va* var. of **acalabrotar**
**calabrote** *m* (naut.) cable-laid rope
**calada** *f* soaking; lowering of fishing net; diving, plunging; swoop (*of bird of prey*); openwork watchcase; **dar una calada a** (coll.) to rake over the coals
**caladero** *m* place for lowering fishing nets
**caladio** *m* (bot.) caladium
**caladizo -za** *adj* runny
**calado** *m* openwork, fretwork; plug (*in melon*); depth (*of water*); (naut.) draught; (sew.) drawn work; **en iguales calados** (naut.) on even keel
**calador** *m* borer, maker of openwork; calking iron; (surg.) probe
**caladre** *f* (orn.) calander
**caladura** *f* plugging (*a melon*)
**calafate** *m* calker; shipwright
**calafateador** *m* calker
**calafatear** *va* to calk; (mas.) to point; to plug, plug up
**calafateo** *m* calking
**calafatería** *f* calking; union or guild of calkers
**calafatín** *m* calker's boy or mate
**calafraga** *f* (bot.) saxifrage
**calagozo** *m* (agr.) pruning hook, mattock
**calahorra** *f* public granary; agency providing bread for poor
**calaíta** *f* (mineral.) turquoise
**calaje** *m* (elec.) angular displacement
**calamaco** *m* calamanco
**calamar** *m* (zool.) squid (*Loligo*); **calamar volante** (zool.) squid (*Ommastrephes*)
**calamarera** *f* squid-jigger
**calambac** *m* calambac (*wood*)
**calambre** *m* cramp; **calambre de los escribientes** writer's cramp; **calambre de los telegrafistas** telegrapher's cramp
**calambuco -ca** *adj* (Am.) pious, devout; *m* (bot.) calaba; (Am.) can, pail
**calamento** *m* submerging the fishing net: (bot.) calamint
**calamidad** *f* calamity
**calamina** *f* (mineral.) calamine
**calaminta** *f* (bot.) calamint
**calamistro** *m* (zool.) calamistrum
**calamita** *f* loadstone; magnetic needle
**calamitoso -sa** *adj* calamitous
**cálamo** *m* reed, stalk; (bot.) calamus, sweet flag; (poet.) reed, flute; (poet.) pen; **cálamo aromático** (bot.) sweet flag; (pharm.) calamus
**calamocano -na** *adj* (coll.) tipsy; (coll.) doddering
**calamoco** *m* icicle
**calamocha** *f* dark yellow ocher; (coll.) head
**calamón** *m* (orn.) sultana; brass tack; stay of the beam of an olive-oil mill
**calamorra** *f* (coll.) head; *adj* woolly-faced (*sheep*)
**calamorrada** *f* (coll.) butt (*with the head*)
**calamorrazo** *m* (coll.) bump on the head
**calandraca** *f* (naut.) hardtack and soup
**calandrajo** *m* rag; rag hanging from clothing; (coll.) sap, fool
**calandrar** *va* to calender (*paper*)
**calandria** *f* calender (*for giving paper glossy finish*); (orn.) calander; (chem.) calandria; treadmill cage (*of a hoisting whim*); person feigning illness in order to get into a hospital; (Am.) victoria (*coach*)
**cálanis** *m* (pharm.) calamus
**calaña** *f* model, sample, pattern; kind, nature, character, caliber; fan; guardrail, parapet
**calañés** *m* Andalusian hat with turned-up brim and low cone-shaped crown
**cálao** *m* (orn.) hornbill; **cálao rinoceronte** (orn.) rhinoceros hornbill
**calapatillo** *m* (ent.) weevil
**calapé** *m* (Am.) turtle roasted in its shell
**calapuerta** *f* holdback (*device to hold door open*)
**calar** *adj* lime, limy; *m* limestone quarry; *va* to pierce, perforate, permeate; to wedge; to soak; to cut openwork in (*paper, metal, etc.*); to cut a plug in (*a melon*); to make a core boring in; to bend (*a weapon*) forward; to fix (*a bayonet*); to lower (*a fishing net*) in the water; to sink (*a caisson*); to lower (*a drawbridge*); to treat with lime; (naut. & weaving) to draw; (coll.) to size up (*a person*); (coll.) to see through (*a person*); to slip in; (slang) to pick (*a pocket*); (Am.) to stare at; *vn* to cut, to hurt; to penetrate; (naut.) to draw; *vr* to become soaked or drenched; to slip in; to squeeze in; to swoop down (*said of birds of prey*); (coll.) to pull (*one's hat*) down on one's head; to stick (*one's glasses*) on; to miss fire; **calarse en** to slip in or into; **calarse hasta los huesos** to get soaked to the skin
**calato -ta** *adj* (Am.) naked
**calatraveño -ña** *adj* (pertaining to) Calatrava; *mf* native or inhabitant of Calatrava
**calavera** *f* skull; death's-head; (Am.) tail light; *m* daredevil, reckless fellow; roué, libertine
**calaverada** *f* recklessness, reckless act, escapade
**calaverar** *vn* (coll.) to become bald
**calaverear** *va* to make ugly, make hideous; *vn* (coll.) to act recklessly; (Am.) to carouse, to lead a wild life
**calbote** *m* chestnut or acorn bread; (dial.) roasted chestnut; **calbotes** *mpl* (dial.) string beans
**calca** *f* tracing; copy; (dial.) granary
**calcado** *m* tracing

**calcador -dora** *mf* tracer (*person*); *m* tracer (*instrument*)
**calcadura** *f* tracing
**calcáneo** *m* (anat.) calcaneus
**calcañal** *m* or **calcañar** *m* heel
**calcar** §86 *va* to trace; to copy, to imitate; to trample or tread on; **calcar en** to model (*e.g., one's style*) on
**calcáreo -a** *adj* calcareous
**Calcas** *m* (myth.) Calchas
**calce** *m* wedge; iron tire; iron tip, iron trimming; (Am.) foot, bottom (*of a document*)
**calcedonia** *f* (mineral.) chalcedony; (*cap.*) *f* Chalcedon
**calceolaria** *f* (bot.) calceolaria
**calcés** *m* (naut.) masthead
**calceta** *f* stocking; shackle, fetter; **hacer calceta** to knit
**calcetería** *f* hosiery; hosiery shop
**calcetero -ra** *mf* stocking maker or mender; hosier
**calcetín** *m* sock
**calcetón** *m* knitted stocking
**calcicloro** *m* (chem.) calcium chloride
**cálcico -ca** *adj* (chem.) calcic
**calcífero -ra** *adj* calciferous
**calcificación** *f* calcification
**calcificar** §86 *va & vr* to calcify
**calcímetro** *m* calcimeter
**calcina** *f* concrete
**calcinación** *f* calcination
**calcinar** *va & vr* to calcine; to burn
**calcio** *m* (chem.) calcium
**calcita** *f* (mineral.) calcite
**calcitrapa** *f* (bot.) star thistle
**calco** *m* tracing; copy, imitation
**calcografía** *f* chalcography; chalcograph; chalcograph shop; collection of chalcographs
**calcográfico -ca** *adj* chalcographic or chalcographical
**calcógrafo** *m* chalcographer
**calcomanía** *f* decalcomania
**calcopirita** *f* (mineral.) chalcopyrite
**calculable** *adj* calculable
**calculadamente** *adv* in a calculating way; deliberately
**calculador -dora** *adj* calculating; *mf* computer, calculator; *f* computer, calculating machine
**calcular** *va & vn* to calculate; to reckon
**calculatorio -ria** *adj* calculative
**calculista** *adj* planning, scheming; *mf* planner, schemer; rapid calculator
**cálculo** *m* calculation; conjecture; reflection; (math. & path.) calculus; **cálculo biliario** gallstone; **cálculo diferencial** (math.) differential calculus; **cálculo infinitesimal** (math.) infinitesimal calculus; **cálculo integral** (math.) integral calculus; **cálculo renal** (path.) kidney stone
**calculosis** *f* (path.) gallstones
**calculoso -sa** *adj* (path.) calculous; *mf* sufferer from gallstones
**Calcuta** *f* Calcutta
**calchona** *f* (Am.) bogey, goblin; (Am.) witch, hag
**calda** *f* warming, heating; **caldas** *fpl* hot baths, hot springs
**caldaico -ca** *adj* Chaldaic
**Caldea** *f* see **caldeo**
**caldeamiento** *m* heating
**caldear** *va* to heat, heat up; to weld; *vr* to become heated; to get overheated; (Am.) to get drunk; (Am.) to become overwrought
**caldeo -a** *adj & mf* Chaldean; *m* Chaldean (*language*); warming, heating; welding; (*cap.*) *f* Chaldea
**caldera** *f* boiler; pot, kettle; case of kettledrum; (min.) sump; (Am.) coffee pot, teapot; **las calderas de Pero Botero** (coll.) hell; **caldera de jabón** soap factory; **caldera de vapor** steam boiler; **caldera tubular de agua** water-tube boiler; **caldera tubular de humo** fire-tube boiler
**calderada** *f* boiler, kettle (*amount kettle or boiler can hold*)
**calderería** *f* boilermaking; boiler shop
**calderero** *m* boilermaker
**caldereta** *f* holy-water pot; fish stew; lamb stew
**calderilla** *f* holy-water vessel; bottom of a well; gutter; (bot.) currant; (min.) blind shaft, winze; copper coin; small change
**caldero** *m* kettle, pot, copper; (Am.) coffee pot, teapot; **caldero de colada** (found.) ladle
**calderón** *m* caldron; (mus.) pause (*hold and its symbol*); (print.) paragraph (*mark*); (zool.) blackfish, black whale; **calderones** *mpl* (bot.) globeflower
**calderoniano -na** *adj* Calderonian
**calderuela** *f* small kettle; vessel containing the light that hunters use to dazzle and catch partridges
**caldillo** *m* light broth; sauce for fricassee
**caldo** *m* broth, bouillon; sauce, dressing, gravy; salad dressing; liquid; (Am.) simple syrup; (Am.) sugar-cane juice; **caldos** *mpl* wet goods (*wine, olive oil, cider, vinegar, brandy, etc.*); spirituous liquors; **hacer el caldo gordo a** (coll.) to play into the hands of; **caldo de Burdeos** (hort.) Bordeaux mixture; **caldo de carne** beef tea; **caldo de cultivo** (bact.) broth; **caldo de la reina** eggnog
**caldoso -sa** *adj* full of broth
**calducho** *m* hogwash, slop
**caldudo -da** *adj* fond of broth; *f* (Am.) pie made of eggs, olives, and raisins
**cale** *m* slap, smack
**calé** *m* (slang) gypsy
**calecer** §34 *vn* to become hot
**caledonio -nia** *adj & mf* Caledonian
**calefacción** *f* heat, heating; **calefacción a panel radiante** radiant-panel heat; **calefacción a** or **por vapor** steam heat; **calefacción a vapor de baja presión** vapor heat; **calefacción central** central heating (*of a single building or house*); **calefacción por agua caliente** hot-water heat; **calefacción por aire caliente** hot-air heat
**calefaccionar** *va* to heat
**calefaccionista** *m* heating contractor
**calefaciente** *adj* (med.) heating, calefacient
**calefactor** *m* heater; heater man (*man who makes, installs, or repairs heating equipment*); (rad.) heater, heater element
**calefactorio** *m* calefactory (*in convents*)
**calefón** *m* (Am.) hot-water heater
**caleidoscopio** *m* var. of **calidoscopio**
**calendar** *va* to date (*a document*)
**calendario** *m* calendar; **hacer calendarios** (coll.) to meditate, to muse; (coll.) to make hasty and unfounded prophecies; **calendario escolar** school calendar; **calendario exfoliador** tear-off calendar; **calendario juliano** Julian calendar; **calendario gregoriano** Gregorian calendar; **calendario hebreo** Hebrew calendar
**calendarista** *mf* calendar maker
**calendas** *fpl* calends or kalends; **calendas griegas** Greek calends (*time that will never come*)
**caléndula** *f* (bot.) calendula
**calentador -dora** *adj* heating; *m* heater; warming pan; (coll.) turnip (*watch*); **calentador a gas** gas heater; **calentador de agua** water heater; **calentador de cama** warming pan
**calentamiento** *m* heating; inflammation (*e.g., of a sore*)
**calentar** §18 *va* to heat, heat up; to warm up; to warm (*a chair*); to hold (*a ball*) a moment before throwing it; (coll.) to beat; (Am.) to annoy, bother; **calentar al blanco** to make white-hot; **calentar al rojo** to make red-hot; *vr* to warm oneself; to heat up, to run hot; to warm up; to become heated (*in an argument*); to be in heat (*said of animals*); (Am.) to become annoyed; **calentarse la cabeza** to rack one's brains
**calentón** *m* (coll.) warm-up; (Am.) heater; **darse un calentón** (coll.) to come in and warm up
**calentura** *f* (path.) calenture, fever
**calenturiento -ta** *adj* feverish; exalted; (Am.) tubercular
**calenturón** *m* high fever
**calenturoso -sa** *adj* feverish
**caleño -ña** *adj* (pertaining to) lime
**calepino** *m* Latin dictionary
**calera** *f* see **calero**

**calería** *f* lime pit (*where lime is made and sold*)
**calero -ra** *adj* (pertaining to) lime; *m* lime burner; lime dealer; *f* limekiln; limestone quarry
**calesa** *f* chaise (*two-wheeled carriage*)
**calesera** *f* Andalusian jacket, bolero jacket
**calesero** *m* driver of a chaise
**calesín** *m* light chaise, fly
**calesinero** *m* driver of a light chaise
**caleta** *f* small inlet, cove
**caletre** *m* (coll.) judgment, acumen, brains
**cali** *m* (chem.) alkali
**calibeado -da** *adj* chalybeate
**calíbeo -a** *adj* steel-blue, chalybeous
**calibración** *f* calibration
**calibrado** *m* calibrating, calibration
**calibrador** *m* calipers; gauge; **calibrador de alambre** wire gauge; **calibrador fijo** caliper gauge
**calibrar** *va* to calibrate; to gauge
**calibre** *m* caliber; gauge; bore; calipers; (rail.) track gauge; (coll.) caliber (*quality of a thing*)
**calicanto** *m* stone masonry
**calicata** *f* (min.) test pit
**calicó** *m* calico
**calicular** *adj* (bot.) calycular
**calículo** *m* (anat. & zool.) calicle or calyculus; (bot.) calycle or epicalyx
**caliche** *m* pebble in a brick; flake or crust of lime
**calidad** *f* quality; qualification; capacity; condition, term; importance; nobility; **calidades** *fpl* moral qualities; **a calidad de que** provided, provided that; **en calidad de** in the capacity of, in quality of
**calidez** *f* warmth; heat, fire
**cálido -da** *adj* warm, hot (*climate, country*); hot, burning; warm (*color; welcome*)
**calidoscópico -ca** *adj* kaleidoscopic; (fig.) kaleidoscopic
**calidoscopio** *m* kaleidoscope; (fig.) kaleidoscope
**calientacamas** *m* (*pl:* **-mas**) bed warmer
**calientapiés** *m* (*pl:* **-piés**) foot warmer
**calientaplatos** *m* (*pl:* **-tos**) plate warmer, hot plate
**caliente** *adj* hot; heated; fiery; hot or warm (*near what one is looking for*); hot (*in rut*); **en caliente** while hot; at once; **caliente de cascos** hot-headed
**califa** *m* caliph
**califato** *m* caliphate
**calificable** *adj* qualifiable
**calificación** *f* qualification; proof; judgment; grade, mark (*in an examination*); standing (*in school*)
**calificado -da** *adj* attested, proved, qualified, competent
**calificador -dora** *mf* qualifier; censor; (eccl.) qualificator
**calificar §86** *va* to qualify, to characterize; to ennoble; to attest, to certify; to mark (*an examination paper*); (Am.) to register (*as a voter*); *vr* to give legal proof of one's noble birth; (Am.) to register (*as a voter*)
**calificativo -va** *adj* qualifying; (gram.) qualifying; *m* grade, mark (*in school*); (gram.) qualifier
**California** *f* see **californio**
**californiano -na** *adj & mf* Californian
**califórnico -ca** *adj* Californian
**californio -nia** *adj & mf* Californian; *m* (chem.) californium; (*cap.*) *f* California; **Baja California** Lower California
**cáliga** *f* caliga (*of Roman soldier; of bishop*)
**calígine** *f* (poet.) mist, darkness
**caliginoso -sa** *adj* (poet.) misty, dark
**caligrafía** *f* calligraphy, penmanship
**calígrafo -fa** *mf* calligrapher, good penman
**caligráfico -ca** *adj* calligraphic
**calima** *f* haze; (naut.) buoy made of a string of corks
**calimaco** *m* calamanco
**calimbo** *m* quality, character, brand
**calimoso -sa** *adj* hazy
**calina** *f* haze
**calinoso -sa** *adj* hazy
**Calíope** *f* (myth.) Calliope
**calípedes** *m* (*pl:* **-des**) (zool.) sloth
**calipso** *m* calypso (*improvised song*); *f* (bot.) calypso; (*cap.*) *f* (myth.) Calypso
**calisaya** *f* (pharm.) calisaya bark
**calistenia** *f* calisthenics
**calisténico -ca** *adj* calisthenic
**Calisto** *f* (myth.) Callisto
**cáliz** *m* (*pl:* **-lices**) (anat. & bot.) calyx; (bot., eccl. & poet.) chalice; cup of bitterness or sorrow; block (*to shape a hat*)
**calizo -za** *adj* (pertaining to) limestone or lime; *f* limestone
**calma** *f* see **calmo**
**calmante** *adj* soothing; (med.) sedative; *m* (med.) sedative; **calmante del dolor** pain reliever
**calmar** *va* to calm, to quiet; *vn* to abate, be becalmed; *vr* to calm, calm down
**calmazo** *m* (naut.) dead calm
**calmear** *vn* to ease up, to lessen (*said, e.g., of anger*)
**calmo -ma** *adj* barren, treeless; calm, quiet; *f* calm, calm weather; quiet, tranquillity; slowness, laziness; suspension, letup; (naut.) calm; **en calma** in abeyance, in suspension; (com.) steady (*market*); (naut.) calm, smooth (*sea*); **calma chicha** or **muerta** dead calm
**calmoso -sa** *adj* calm; (coll.) slow, lazy, sluggish
**calmudo -da** *adj* calm; (naut.) calm, light (*wind*); (Am.) easy-going
**caló** *m* gipsy slang, underworld slang
**calobiótica** *f* right living; innate sense of order
**calofriar §90** *vr* to chill, become chilled
**calofrío** *m* chill
**calomel** *m* or **calomelanos** *mpl* (pharm.) calomel
**calón** *m* rod for spreading nets; rod for measuring depth of water
**calor** *m* heat; warmth; heat wave; (fig.) heat, heatedness; (fig.) warmth, enthusiasm; **hacer calor** to be warm, to be hot (*said of weather*); **tener calor** to be warm, to be hot (*said of a person*); **calor específico** specific heat
**caloría** *f* (phys. & physiol.) calorie; **caloría gramo** or **caloría pequeña** gram calorie or small calorie; **caloría kilogramo** or **caloría grande** kilogram calorie or large calorie
**caloricidad** *f* (physiol.) caloricity
**calórico -ca** *adj* caloric; *m* (old chem.) caloric
**calorífero -ra** *adj* heat-producing; *m* heating system; heater, furnace; foot warmer
**calorificación** *f* calorification
**calorífico -ca** *adj* calorific
**calorífugo -ga** *adj* heat-resisting; noncombustible
**calorimetría** *f* calorimetry
**calorimétrico -ca** *adj* calorimetric or calorimetrical
**calorímetro** *m* calorimeter
**caloroso -sa** *adj* warm, hot; (fig.) warm, enthusiastic
**calosfrío** *m* chill
**calostro** *m* colostrum
**calotear** *va* (Am.) to cheat, to gyp
**caloyo** *m* new-born lamb or kid; raw recruit
**calpense** *adj* (pertaining to) Gibraltar; *mf* native of Gibraltar
**calpul** *m* (Am.) gathering, assembly; (Am.) Indian mound
**calseco -ca** *adj* cured with lime
**calta** *f* (bot.) caltha, marsh marigold
**calumnia** *f* calumny, slander
**calumniador -dora** *adj* slanderous; *m* calumniator, slanderer
**calumniar** *va* to calumniate, to slander
**calumnioso -sa** *adj* calumnious, slanderous
**caluroso -sa** *adj* warm, hot; (fig.) warm, enthusiastic
**calva** *f* see **calvo**
**Calvario** *m* (Bib.) Calvary; (*l.c.*) *m* calvary (*representation of crucifixion*); (fig.) cross (*suffering*); (coll.) series of misfortunes or sorrows; (coll.) debts; (coll.) baldy, bald fellow; (anat.) calvaria
**calvatrueno** *m* (coll.) complete baldness; (coll.) madcap, crazy fellow
**calvero** *m* clearing; clay pit

**calvete** *adj* baldish, somewhat bald
**calvez** *f* or **calvicie** *f* baldness
**calvijar** *m* var. of **calvero**
**calvinismo** *m* Calvinism
**calvinista** *adj* Calvinist; Calvinistic; *mf* Calvinist
**Calvino** *m* Calvin
**calvo -va** *adj* bald; bare, barren; *f* bald spot; barren spot, clearing; **calva de almete** crest of helmet
**calza** *f* (coll.) stocking; wedge; ribbon (*tied to an animal to distinguish it from others*); (Am.) gold filling (*of tooth*); **calzas** *fpl* hose, tights; breeches; shackles; **echarle a uno una calza** (coll.) to have someone's number; **en calzas prietas** in a tight fix; **tomar calzas de Villadiego** (coll.) to beat it; **calzas atacadas** patched breeches
**calzacalzón** *m* galligaskins
**calzada** *f* see **calzado**
**calzadera** *f* hemp cord (*for tying sandals*); brake block
**calzado -da** *adj* calced (*said, e.g., of a friar*); having feet of a different color (*said of an animal*); having feathers on the legs and feet (*said of birds*); *m* footwear; *f* causeway, highway; sidewalk; **Calzada de los Gigantes** Giant's Causeway (*in Ireland*)
**calzador** *m* shoehorn
**calzadura** *f* putting on shoes; wooden tire
**calzar §76** *va* to shoe, put shoes on, provide shoes for; to wear (*a certain size of shoe or glove*); to take (*a certain caliber of bullet*); to fit (*a person; said of a shoe*); to wedge, to shim, to chock; to scotch (*a wheel*); to block up, to put a wedge under (*e.g., the leg of a table*); (naut.) to chock; to tip, to trim with iron; (print.) to raise, to underlay; (Am.) to fill (*a tooth*); (hort.) to hill (*plants*); *vn* (Am.) to get the place sought for; **calzar bien** to wear good footwear; **calzar mal** to wear poor footwear; **calzar poco** (coll.) to not be very bright; *vr* to get a good position, to make a fortune; to put on (*shoes or gloves*); to wear
**calzo** *m* wedge, shim; (mach.) shoe; (mech.) fulcrum; (naut.) skid, chock; (print.) underlay
**calzón** *m* ombre (*game of cards*); roofer's strap (*to keep from slipping*); **calzones** *mpl* breeches; shorts; (Am.) trousers; (Am.) drawers; **calzarse** or **ponerse los calzones** (coll.) to wear the trousers
**calzonarias** *fpl* (Am.) suspenders
**calzonazos** *m* (*pl:* **-zos**) (coll.) softy, easygoing fellow, jellyfish
**calzoncillos** *mpl* drawers, underdrawers; shorts
**calzoneras** *fpl* (Am.) trousers buttoned down the sides
**calzonudo -da** *adj* (Am.) stupid, inept
**calzorras** *m* (*pl:* **-rras**) (coll.) var. of **calzonazos**
**callado -da** *adj* silent, quiet; secret; vague, mysterious; unmentioned; **estarse callado** to keep quiet; *f* (naut.) drop, abatement; dish of tripe; **a las calladas** (coll.) on the quiet; **dar la callada por respuesta** (coll.) to answer with silence; **de callada** (coll.) on the quiet
**callamiento** *m* silencing, quieting
**callana** *f* (Am.) crude Indian baking bowl; (Am.) flowerpot; (Am.) big watch; (Am.) useful slag; (Am.) metal-testing crucible
**callandico** or **callandito** *adv* (coll.) secretly, stealthily, softly
**callao** *m* pebble
**callar** *va* to silence, to hush up; to not mention; to keep (*a secret*); to quiet, to calm; *vn* to be silent, to keep silent, to become silent; to keep quiet, to stop playing or singing; **quien calla otorga** silence gives consent; **¡calla!** or **¡calle!** how strange!, you don't mean it!; *vr* to be silent, to keep silent, to become silent; to keep quiet, to stop playing or singing; to keep (*something*) to oneself; **callarse la boca** to shut up
**calle** *f* street; excuse, pretext; **abrir calle** (coll.) to open a path, to clear the way; **alborotar la calle** (coll.) to stir up the neighborhood; **dejar en la calle** (coll.) to deprive of one's livelihood; **echar a la calle** (coll.) to put out of the house; **hacer calle** (coll.) to open a path, to clear the way; **llevar** (or **llevarse**) **la calle a** to overwhelm; to confound, to silence; **para la calle** to take out (*said of food bought in a restaurant*); **quedarse en la calle** (coll.) to be at the end of one's means; **calle de árboles** alley, avenue of trees; **calle de travesía** cross street; **calle mayor** main street
**callear** *va* to clear (*passages between rows of vines*) of straggling stems and branches
**calleja** *f* side street, alley, by-street; (coll.) evasion, subterfuge, pretext; **sépase, ahora se sabrá, ya se verá** or **ya verán quién es Calleja** (coll.) you'll find out who I am; (coll.) you'll find out who he is
**callejear** *vn* to walk the streets, to loaf around the streets
**callejeo** *m* walking the streets, loafing around
**callejero -ra** *adj* (pertaining to the) street; fond of walking the streets; gadabout; *m* list of streets, street guide; addresses of newspaper subscribers
**callejo** *m* pitfall, trap
**callejón** *m* lane, alley; (taur.) passageway between barrier and stands; **callejón sin salida** blind alley; (coll.) impasse, deadlock
**callejuela** *f* side street, by-street, alley; (coll.) evasion, subterfuge, pretext
**callialto -ta** *adj* high-calked (*horseshoe*)
**callicida** *m & f* corn cure, corn remover
**callista** *mf* corncutter, chiropodist
**callo** *m* callus; corn (*on foot*); calk (*of horseshoe*); **callos** *mpl* tripe; **criar, hacer** or **tener callos** (coll.) to become callous (*unfeeling*)
**callón** *m* sharpening stone (*especially for awls*)
**callonca** *adj* half-roasted (*said of a chestnut or acorn*)
**callosa** *f* see **calloso**
**callosidad** *f* callosity
**calloso -sa** *adj* callous; *f* (bot. & biochem.) callose
**cama** *f* bed; couch; straw bedding or litter (*for animals*); lair; floor (*of wagon or cart*); side of melon resting on the ground; sheath (*of plow*); **caer en cama** or **en la cama** to fall sick; **estar en cama** to be confined to bed; **guardar cama** or **la cama** or **hacer cama** to be sick in bed; **hacer cama redonda** (coll.) to all sleep in the same bed; **hacer la cama** to make the bed; **hacerle la cama a uno** to work to harm someone behind his back; **media cama** single bed; **tenderle la cama a uno** (coll.) to set a trap for someone; (Am.) to help someone in his love affairs; **cama camera** single bed; **cama de matrimonio** double bed; **cama imperial** four-poster; **cama sencilla** single bed; **camas gemelas** twin beds; **cama turca** day bed (*couch without head and foot pieces*)
**camachuelo** *m* (orn.) linnet
**camada** *f* brood, litter; gang, den (*of thieves*); layer, stratum
**camafeo** *m* cameo
**camal** *m* halter of hemp; pole from which dead pig is hung; (arm.) camail
**camaleón** *m* (zool.) chameleon; (coll.) chameleon (*changeable person*)
**cama-litera** *f* (*pl:* **camas-literas**) double-decker (*bed*)
**camamila** *f* (bot.) camomile
**camándula** *f* rosary of one or three decades; (coll.) trickery, hypocrisy; **tener muchas camándulas** (coll.) to be full of tricks, to be full of hypocrisy
**camandulear** *vn* to be a hypocrite, to be untrustworthy
**camandulería** *f* prudery, priggishness; flattery
**camandulero -ra** *adj* (coll.) hypocritical, fawning; *mf* (coll.) hypocrite, flatterer
**cámara** *f* hall, parlor; chamber; bedroom; board, council; royal chamber; chamber, breech (*of firearm*); mow, granary; icebox; (aut.) inner tube; (min.) stall, chamber; (naut.) cabin; (nav.) wardroom; (aer.) cockpit; (anat.) chamber, cavity; (opt. & phot.) camera; bowels; **cámaras** *fpl* loose bowels; **de cámara** royal, e.g., **médico de cámara** royal physician; **irse de cámaras** to have an accident, to dirty oneself;

**cámara agrícola** grange (*organization of farmers*); **Cámara alta** Upper House; **cámara a popa** (naut.) stern sheets; **cámara apostólica** camera, papal treasury; **cámara ardiente** funeral chamber; **Cámara baja** Lower House; **cámara cinematográfica** motion-picture camera; **cámara clara** (opt.) camera lucida; **cámara compensadora** (com.) clearing house; **cámara de aire** (aut.) inner tube; (aer.) gasbag; **cámara de aire comprimido** pneumatic caisson; **cámara de combustión** (mach.) combustion chamber; **cámara de comercio** chamber of commerce; **cámara de compensación** (com.) clearing house; (hyd.) surge tank, surge chamber; **cámara de descompresión** decompression chamber; **cámara de fuelle** folding camera; **cámara de gas** or **de gases** gas chamber; **cámara de ionización** (phys.) ionization chamber; **cámara de las máquinas** (naut.) engine room; **Cámara de los Comunes** (Brit.) House of Commons; **Cámara de los Lores** (Brit.) House of Lords; **cámara de niebla** (phys.) cloud chamber; **cámara de oxígeno** (med.) oxygen tent; **cámara de pleno** plenum chamber; **Cámara de Representantes** (U.S.A.) House of Representatives; **cámara estrellada** Star Chamber (*in England*); **cámara fotográfica** camera; **cámara frigorífica** cold-storage room; **cámara indiscreta** candid camera; **cámara mortuoria** funeral chamber; **cámara múltiple** multiple-lens camera; **cámara oscura** (opt.) camera obscura; **cámara plegadiza** folding camera; **cámara televisora** television camera; *m* (mov.) cameraman

**camarada** *m* comrade, companion

**camaradería** *f* comradeship, camaraderie

**camaraje** *m* granary rent

**camaranchón** *m* garret, storeroom; (fig.) recess

**camarera** *f* waitress; maid, chambermaid; head maid; stewardess (*on ship or plane*); lady in waiting

**camarero** *m* waiter; valet; chamberlain; steward (*on ship or plane*)

**camareta** *f* (naut.) small cabin, deck cabin, midshipman's cabin

**camariento -ta** *adj* suffering from diarrhea

**camarilla** *f* camarilla, palace coterie, clique, cabal

**camarín** *m* boudoir; side room; (theat.) dressing room; niche behind altar containing an image; elevator car, shaft cage

**camarista** *m* minister of the royal council; *f* lady in waiting

**camarlengo** *m* papal chamberlain; lord in waiting of the kings of Aragon

**cámaro** *m* var. of **camarón**

**camarógrafo** *m* cameraman

**camarón** *m* (zool.) shrimp; (zool.) prawn (*Palaemon*); (Am.) tip, fee

**camaronero -ra** *mf* shrimp or prawn seller; *f* shrimp net

**camarote** *m* (naut.) stateroom, cabin

**camasquince** *mf* (*pl:* **camasquince**) (coll.) meddlesome person, kibitzer

**camastro** *m* rickety old bed; inclined bunk in barracks or guardhouse

**camastrón -trona** *adj* (coll.) tricky; *mf* (coll.) tricky person; (coll.) loafer

**camastronería** *f* (coll.) trickiness

**cambalachar** *va & vn* to swap, to exchange, to barter, to dicker

**cambalache** *m* swap, exchange, barter

**cambalachear** *va & vn* var. of **cambalachar**

**cámbaro** *m* (zool.) green crab

**cambiable** *adj* changeable; exchangeable

**cambiacorrea** *m* belt shifter

**cambiadiscos** *m* (*pl:* **-cos**) record changer

**cambiadizo -za** *adj* fickle, inconsistent

**cambiador -dora** *adj* exchanging, bartering; *m* (Am.) switch; (Am.) switchman; **cambiador de discos** record changer; **cambiador de frecuencia** (elec.) frequency changer

**cambial** *adj* (com.) (pertaining to) exchange

**cambiamiento** *m* change

**cambiante** *adj* changing; fickle; *mf* money changer; **cambiantes** *mpl* iridescence

**cambiar** *va* to change; to exchange; **cambiar el saludo** to exchange salutes; to exchange greetings; *vn* to change; **cambiar de** to change (*e.g., hats, clothes, trains*); **cambiar de sombrero con alguien** to exchange hats with someone; **cambiar de marcha** to shift gears; *vr* to change

**cambiavía** *m* (Am.) switch, turnout; (Am.) switchman

**cambiazo** *m* (coll.) gyp, fake, fraudulent exchange

**cambija** *f* raised water tank

**cambín** *m* fishing basket made of reeds

**cambio** *m* change; exchange; rate of exchange; (bot.) cambium; (aut.) shift; (rail.) switch; **en cambio** on the other hand; **en cambio de** in exchange for; instead of; **libre cambio** free trade; **cambio de hoja** change of subject; **cambio de hora** change of time; **cambio de marchas** or **de velocidades** (aut.) gearshift; **cambio de vía** (Am.) switch; **cambio exterior** or **extranjero** foreign exchange; **cambio minuto** change, small change

**Cambises** *m* Cambyses

**cambista** *mf* moneychanger, money broker; banker; *m* (Am.) switchman

**cámbium** *m* (*pl:* **-ums**) (bot.) cambium

**cambocho -cha** *adj* (Am.) bowlegged

**Camboya** *f* Cambodia

**camboyano -na** *adj & mf* Cambodian; *m* Cambodian (*language*)

**cambray** *m* chambray

**cambrayón** *m* cambric

**cambriano -na** or **cámbrico -ca** *adj & mf* Cambrian; *adj & m* (geol.) Cambrian

**cambrina** *f* (bot.) phlox

**cambrón** *m* (bot.) buckthorn; (bot.) boxthorn; (bot.) bramble; **cambrones** *mpl* (bot.) Christ's-thorn

**cambronal** *m* thicket of buckthorn, boxthorn, or brambles

**cambronera** *f* (bot.) boxthorn

**cambuj** *m* mask; cap used to keep baby's head straight

**cambujo -ja** *adj* reddish black (*donkey*); (Am.) half-breed; *mf* (Am.) half-breed

**cambullón** *m* (Am.) collusion, scheming, trickery; (Am.) trade, barter

**cambur** *m* (bot.) banana tree

**camedrio** *m* (bot.) germander, wall germander; **camedrio acuático** (bot.) water germander; **camedrio de los bosques** (bot.) wood germander

**camelar** *va* (coll.) to flirt with; (coll.) to cajole, to deceive

**camelia** *f* (bot.) camellia

**camelina** *f* (bot.) gold-of-pleasure, madwort

**camelo** *m* (coll.) flirtation; (coll.) joke; **dar camelo a** (coll.) to make fun of

**camelote** *m* camlet

**camella** *f* she-camel; ridge (*between furrows*); bow (*of yoke*); feed trough

**camellería** *f* camel stable; job of camel driver; camels

**camellero** *m* camel driver

**camello** *m* (zool.) camel; (naut.) camel (*to lift vessels*); **camello bactriano** (zool.) Bactrian camel; **camello pardal** (zool.) camelopard (*giraffe*)

**camellón** *m* drinking trough; sawhorse; ridge (*between furrows*); flower bed; camlet (*cloth*); (Am.) parkway

**camena** *f* (poet.) muse

**camerino** *m* (theat.) dressing room (*especially of star*)

**camero -ra** *adj* (pertaining to a) bed; single (*bed*); *mf* bedmaker; maker of bedding, maker of bed accessories; renter of beds; *m* (Am.) highway; *f* single bed

**Camerón** *m* Cameroons; **el Camerón francés** Cameroun

**cámica** *f* (Am.) slope of roof

**camilla** *f* stretcher; couch; table with heater underneath

**camillero** *m* stretcher-bearer

**caminador -dora** *adj* walking

**caminante** *adj* traveling; *mf* walker; traveler; passer-by; *m* groom who walks in front of master's horse

**caminar** *va* to walk (*a certain distance*); *vn* to travel, to journey; to go, to walk, to move; (coll.) to act, to behave
**caminata** *f* (coll.) hike, long walk; (coll.) jaunt, outing
**caminero -ra** *adj* (pertaining to a) road, highway; traveling, walking; *m* road laborer, road worker
**camino** *m* road, way, course, path; journey; runner (*on table or floor*); **abrir camino** to open a path or way; to find a way; **allanar el camino** (coll.) to smooth the way; **a medio camino (entre)** halfway (*between*); **de camino** in passing, on the way; traveling (*clothes, bags, etc.*); **echar camino adelante** to strike out; **en camino** on one's way; **ir de camino** to journey, to travel; **ir fuera de camino** to be mistaken; to be slipshod; to be out of all reason; **llevar camino de** + *inf* to show signs of + *ger;* **partir el camino con** to meet halfway; **traer a buen camino** to set right, to put back on the right path; **camino carretero** or **carretil** wagon or carriage road; **camino cubierto** (fort.) covered way; **camino de** on the way to; **camino de cintura** or **circunvalación** belt line; **camino de herradura** bridle path; **camino de hierro** railway; **camino de rueda** wagon or carriage road; **Camino de Santiago** Way of or to St. James (*Milky Way*); **camino de sirga** towpath; **camino real** highroad, highway; (fig.) highroad; **camino trillado** beaten path; **camino vecinal** town or county road
**camión** *m* camion; truck, motor truck; (Am.) bus, jitney; **camión cisterna** tank truck; **camión volquete** dump truck
**camionaje** *m* trucking, truckage
**camionero -ra** *adj* truck, trucking; *m* trucker, teamster
**camioneta** *f* light truck; (Am.) station wagon
**camión-grúa** *m* tow truck
**camionista** *m* trucker, teamster
**camisa** *f* shirt; chemise; (mach.) jacket, casing; (mach.) lining; thin skin (*of fruit*); slough (*of serpent*); mantle (*of gaslight*); folder (*for papers*); jacket (*of a book*); **cambiarse la camisa** to become a turncoat; **en camisa** in shirt sleeves; without dowry; **meterse en camisa de once varas** (coll.) to attend to other people's business; **perder hasta la camisa** to lose one's shirt; **camisa de agua** water jacket; **camisa de dormir** nightshirt; **camisa de fuerza** strait jacket; **camisa negra** *m* black shirt (*Fascist*); **camisa refrigerante** cooling jacket; **camisa parda** *m* brown shirt (*Nazi*)
**camisería** *f* shirt factory; shirt store, haberdashery
**camisero -ra** *mf* shirt maker; shirt dealer, haberdasher
**camiseta** *f* undershirt; sport shirt; mantle (*of gaslight*)
**camisola** *f* stiff shirt; ruffled shirt
**camisolín** *m* dickey, shirt front
**camisón** *m* nightshirt; shirt; (Am.) chemise
**camisote** *m* hauberk, haubergeon
**camita** *mf* Hamite; *f* little bed
**camítico -ca** *adj* Hamitic
**camomila** *f* (bot. & pharm.) camomile
**camón** *m* large bed; portable throne; (arch.) oriel; (arch.) arched rafter; felloe, section of a felloe; **camón de vidrios** glass partition
**camorra** *f* (coll.) quarrel, row; (dial.) hot dog; (*cap.*) *f* Camorra; **armar camorra** (coll.) to raise a row; **buscar camorra** (coll.) to look for trouble
**camorrear** *vn* (Am.) to quarrel
**camorrero -ra** *adj & mf* (Am.) var. of **camorrista**
**camorrista** *adj* (coll.) quarrelsome; *mf* (coll.) quarrelsome person; *m* Camorrist
**camote** *m* (Am.) sweet potato (*plant and tuber*); (Am.) onion; (Am.) rascal; (Am.) simpleton; **tomar un camote** (Am.) to become infatuated; **tragar camote** (Am.) to stammer, to falter
**camotear** *va* (Am.) to snitch; *vn* (Am.) to wander around aimlessly
**campa** *adj* treeless (*land*)
**campal** *adj* in the open country; pitched (*battle*)
**campamento** *m* encampment; camp
**campamiento** *m* excelling; show, display
**campana** *f* bell; canopy (*of electrical fixture*); bell glass, bell jar; (arch.) bell; parish, parish church; (Am.) spy, lookout; **a campana herida** or **tañida** with bell ringing; **por campana de vacante** (Am.) very seldom; **campana de buzo** diving bell; **campana de chimenea** funnel of a chimney; **campana de freno** (aut.) brake drum; **campana de vidrio** bell glass, bell jar; **campana eléctrica** electric bell
**campanada** *f* stroke of a bell; ringing of a bell; scandal (*sensational happening*)
**campanario** *m* belfry, bell tower, campanile; carillon
**campanear** *va* to ring (*bells*); to bruit about; *vn* to ring the bells, to ring the bells frequently; *vr* (coll.) to sway, to strut
**campanela** *f* rotation on one foot (*in Spanish dance*)
**campaneo** *m* bell ringing, frequent bell ringing; (coll.) sway, strut
**campanero** *m* bell founder; bell ringer; (ent.) praying insect; (orn.) bellbird
**campaneta** *f* small bell
**campanil** *adj* bell (*metal*); *m* belfry, bell tower
**campanilla** *f* bell, hand bell, doorbell; bubble; tassel; (anat.) uvula; (bot.) bellbind; **de campanillas** or **de muchas campanillas** (coll.) of great importance, of distinction; **campanilla de invierno** (bot.) snowdrop; **campanilla de otoño** (bot.) autumn snowflake; **campanilla de primavera** (bot.) spring snowflake; **campanilla eléctrica** electric bell
**campanillazo** *m* loud ring
**campanillear** *vn* to ring, to keep on ringing
**campanilleo** *m* ringing the bell
**campanillero** *m* bellman
**campano** *m* cowbell
**campanología** *f* campanology
**campanólogo -ga** *mf* campanologist
**campante** *adj* (coll.) proud, satisfied; (coll.) cheerful, buoyant
**campanudo -da** *adj* bell-shaped; wide, spreading; pompous, high-sounding
**campánula** *f* (bot.) bellflower, bluebell, campanula
**campanuláceo -a** *adj* (bot.) campanulaceous
**campaña** *f* (mil. & fig.) campaign; (naut.) cruise; level countryside; shift, work shift
**campañol** *m* (zool.) vole, meadow mouse
**campar** *vn* to excel, stand out; to camp; **campar por su cuenta** or **por sus respetos** (coll.) to do as one pleases
**campeador** *adj & m* champion in battle (*applied to the Cid*)
**campear** *vn* to go to pasture; to come out of the ground, come out of their lairs (*said of rabbits, etc.*); to grow green (*said of fields*); to work in the fields; to show up, to appear; to stand out; (mil.) to campaign; (mil.) to reconnoiter; (Am.) to round up the cattle
**campecico, campecillo** or **campecito** *m* little field
**campechana** *f* see **campechano**
**campechanería** or **campechanía** *f* (coll.) frankness, heartiness, good humor
**campechano -na** *adj* (coll.) frank, hearty, good-humored; *f* (Am.) mixed drink; (Am.) hammock
**campeche** *m* (bot.) logwood (*tree and wood*)
**campeón** *m* champion; (fig.) champion
**campeona** *f* championess
**campeonato** *m* championship
**campeonil** *adj* (pertaining to a) championship
**campero -ra** *adj* in the open, unsheltered; sleeping in the open (*said of domestic animals*); (Am.) good at farming; *m* farming friar or monk
**campesino -na** *adj* country; peasant; *mf* peasant; farmer; *m* countryman; *f* countrywoman
**campestre** *adj* country
**campilán** *m* campilan (*straight-edged sword of the Moros*)
**campillo** *m* small field; commons
**campiña** *f* stretch of farm land, countryside

**campirano -na** *adj & mf* (Am.) peasant; *m* (Am.) cowboy, broncobuster
**campo** *m* field; country; countryside; camp; crop; (her., phys. & sport) field; (fig.) field (*of various activities*); campus; ground, background; side (*in a contest*); **a campo raso** in the open; **a campo traviesa** or **travieso** across the fields, across country; **dar campo a** to give free range to; **en campo ajeno** (sport) away from home; **en campo propio** (sport) at home; **levantar el campo** (mil.) to break camp; (fig.) to consider finished, to give up; **quedar en el campo** to fall in battle or in a duel; **campo de Agramonte** bedlam; **campo de batalla** battlefield, battleground; **campo de concentración** concentration camp; **campo de deportes** athletic field; **campo de ejercicios** drill ground; **campo de emergencia** (aer.) emergency landing field; **campo de internamiento** internment camp; **campo de juego** playground; **campo del honor** field of honor (*of battle or duel*); **campo de minas** (mil. & nav.) mine field; **campo de pastoreo** grassland; **campo de pruebas** testing grounds; **campo de tiro** range, shooting range; **campo de trabajo** labor camp; **campo magnético** magnetic field; **campo raso** open country; **campo santo** cemetery; **campos elíseos** or **elisios** (myth.) Elysian Fields; **Campos Elíseos** Champs Elysées (*avenue in Paris*)
**camposanto** *m* cemetery
**camuesa** *f* pippin, sweeting (*apple*)
**camueso** *m* (bot.) pippin (*tree*); (coll.) simpleton, ignoramus
**camuflaje** *m* camouflage
**camuflar** *va* to camouflage
**camuñas** *fpl* mixture of seeds (*except wheat, barley, and rye*); *m* (*pl:* **-ñas**) goblin, bugaboo
**can** *m* dog; trigger (*of gun*); shoulder; bracket, corbel; khan; **Can mayor** (astr.) Canis Major, Great Dog; **Can menor** (astr.) Canis Minor, Little Dog
**cana** *f* see **cano**
**Canaán, Tierra de** (Bib.) Canaan, Land of Canaan
**canabíneo -a** *adj* (bot.) cannabinaceous
**canáceo -a** *adj* (bot.) cannaceous
**Canadá, el** Canada
**canadiense** *adj & mf* Canadian
**canadillo** *m* (bot.) joint fir
**canal** *m* canal; channel; (anat.) canal, duct; (rad. & telv.) channel; **el canal Ambrosio** Ambrose Channel; **Gran Canal** Grand Canal (*of China*); **canal de la Florida** Florida Straits; **canal de la Mancha** English Channel; **canal de Panamá** Panama Canal; **canal de Suez** Suez Canal; **canal digestivo** (anat.) alimentary canal; **Canal Grande** Grand Canal (*of Venice*); **canal semicircular** (anat.) semicircular canal ‖ *f* channel; gutter (*of roof*); gutter tile; pipe; conduit; long, narrow valley; fore edge (*of book*); groove, flute; dressed animal; **abierto en canal** split wide open; **abrir en canal** to cut in the middle from top to bottom; **canal para alambres** (elec.) conduit
**canalado -da** *adj* fluted, grooved, corrugated
**canaladura** *f* fluting, flute
**canaleja** *f* mill spout; (bot.) death cup
**canaleta** *f* wooden trough
**canalete** *m* paddle (*for canoeing*)
**canalí** *m* (*pl:* **-líes**) (Am.) paddle (*for canoeing*)
**canalización** *f* canalization; channeling; main, mains; piping; duct; installation of ducts; (elec.) wiring; (rad.) channeling; **canalización de consumo** (elec.) house current
**canalizar** §76 *va* to canalize; to pipe; to channel; (elec.) to wire
**canalizo** *m* (naut.) narrow channel, fairway
**canalón** *m* spout (*on side of house*); shovel hat; icicle; **canalones** *mpl* ravioli; **canalón de acera** cast-iron drain under sidewalk
**canalla** *f* (coll.) canaille, riffraff; *m* (coll.) cur, roughneck
**canallada** *f* meanness, currishness
**canallesco -ca** *adj* mean, low, base
**canana** *f* cartridge belt
**cananeo -a** *adj & mf* (Bib.) Canaanite
**canapé** *m* sofa; canapé (*appetizer*); **canapé cama** day bed
**Canarias** *fpl* see **canario**
**canariense** *adj & mf* Canarian
**canariera** *f* large cage for raising canaries
**canario -ria** *adj & mf* Canarian; *m* (orn.) canary, canary bird; (Am.) canary (*color*); (Am.) generous tipper; **Canarias** *fpl* Canaries; **¡canario!** great Scott!
**canasta** *f* basket, washbasket; canasta (*card game*)
**canastada** *f* basketful
**canastería** *f* basket business; baskets
**canastero -ra** *mf* basketmaker, basket dealer
**canastilla** *f* basket; layette; trousseau; **canastilla de la costura** sewing basket
**canastillo** *m* wicker tray
**canasto** *m* hamper; **¡canastos!** confound it!
**canastro** *m* hamper
**cancagua** *f* (Am.) fine building sand
**cáncamo** *m* (naut.) eyebolt; **cáncamo de argolla** ringbolt
**cancamurria** *f* (coll.) gloominess, blues
**cancamusa** *f* (coll.) ruse, artifice, fraud
**cancán** *m* cancan
**cancanear** *vn* (coll.) to stroll, to loaf about; (Am.) to stutter
**cancaneo** *m* (Am.) stuttering
**cáncano** *m* (coll.) louse
**cancel** *m* storm door; (Am.) folding screen
**cancela** *f* iron grating, iron door or gate
**cancelación** or **canceladura** *f* annulment, cancellation
**cancelar** *va* to annul, to cancel; to dispel, wipe out; to liquidate, pay off (*a debt*)
**cancelaría** *f* papal chancery
**cancelariato** *m* (eccl.) chancellorship
**cancelario** *m* (eccl.) chancellor (*who grants degrees*)
**cáncer** *m* (path.) cancer; (*cap.*) *m* (astr.) Cancer, Crab
**cancerado -da** *adj* cancerous; suffering from cancer; evil, corrupt
**cancerar** *va* to consume, destroy; to scold, punish; *vr* to have cancer; to become cancerous; to become depraved
**Cancerbero** *m* (myth. & fig.) Cerberus
**cancerígeno -na** *adj* cancerigenic
**cancerología** *f* study of cancer
**cancerólogo -ga** *mf* cancer expert, cancer specialist
**canceroso -sa** *adj* cancerous
**cancilla** *f* lattice gate (*of garden, barnyard, etc.*)
**canciller** *m* chancellor; **Canciller de hierro** Iron Chancellor (*Bismarck*); **Canciller del echiquier** (Brit.) Chancellor of the Exchequer; **Canciller mayor de Castilla** (archaic) Archbishop of Toledo
**cancilleresco -ca** *adj* (pertaining to a) chancellor or chancellery; formal, ceremonious
**cancillería** *f* chancellery, chancery; chancellorship
**canción** *f* song; lyric poem; **volver a la misma canción** (coll.) to sing the same old song; **canción de cuna** cradlesong; **canción popular** popular song; folk song
**cancionero** *m* anthology, collection of verse
**canciometa** *f* canzonet
**cancionista** *mf* singer; song composer; *m* songster; *f* songstress
**cancón** *m* (coll.) bugaboo; **hacer un cancón a** (Am.) to threaten, to bluff
**cancro** *m* (path.) cancer; (bot.) canker
**cancroide** *m* (path.) cancroid tumor
**cancroideo -a** *adj* cancroid
**cancha** *f* (sport) field, ground; race track; golf links; cockpit; path, way; (Am.) roasted beans or corn; **estar en su cancha** (Am.) to be in one's element; **cancha de tenis** tennis court; *interj* (Am.) gangway!
**canchal** *m* rocky ground or region
**canchalagua** *f* (bot.) gentian
**cancho** *m* boulder, rock; rocky ground
**candado** *m* padlock; **candados** *mpl* lateral lacunae (*of horse's hoof*)
**candaliza** *f* (naut.) brail
**candar** *va* to lock; to shut, to close up
**candeda** *f* chestnut blossom

**candela** *f* candle, taper; flare, torch; fire, light; candlestick; candle power; chestnut bloom; **en candela** (naut.) vertical; **candela romana** Roman candle
**candelabro** *m* candelabrum
**candelada** *f* bonfire; candles
**candelaria** *f* Candlemas; (bot.) great mullein
**candelecho** *m* elevated wigwam from which to watch the vineyard
**candelerazo** *m* blow with a candlestick
**candelero** *m* candlestick; metal olive-oil lamp; fishing torch; stanchion; **en candelero** in a position of authority
**candeleta** *f* (naut.) brail
**candelilla** *f* (surg.) bougie, catheter; (bot.) catkin; (Am.) glowworm; (Am.) ignis fatuus; **hacerle a uno candelillas** (coll.) to sparkle, to flash (*said of the eyes of a tipsy person*)
**candelita** *f* (orn.) redstart, warbler
**candeliza** *f* (naut.) brail
**candelizo** *m* (coll.) icicle
**candencia** *f* candescence
**candente** *adj* candent, candescent; red-hot
**candidación** *f* candying of sugar
**candidato -ta** *mf* candidate
**candidatura** *f* slate, list of candidates; candidacy
**candidez** *f* candor; innocence, simple-mindedness, gullibility; silly remark
**cándido -da** *adj* candid; innocent, simple-minded, gullible; white, snowy
**candiel** *m* meringue
**candil** *m* olive-oil lamp; tine (*of antler*); (Am.) chandelier; **candiles** *mpl* (bot.) wake-robin; (Am.) icicles
**candilada** *f* oil spilt from a lamp
**candileja** *f* lampion; oil receptacle (*of lamp*); (bot.) corn cockle; **candilejas** *fpl* footlights
**candilejo** *m* small oil lamp; sunset glow; (bot.) corn cockle; **candilejos** *mpl* (bot.) wake-robin
**candilera** *f* (bot.) lampwick
**candiletear** *vn* (prov.) to snoop
**candiletero -ra** *mf* (prov.) snooper
**candiota** *f* wine barrel; large earthen wine jug
**candiotera** *f* wine cellar; storage for wine barrels or jugs
**candongo -ga** *adj* (coll.) fawning, scheming; (coll.) loafing; *mf* (coll.) fawner, schemer; (coll.) loafer, shirker; *f* (coll.) fawning, scheming; (coll.) teasing; (coll.) draft mule; **dar candonga a** (coll.) to kid, to tease
**candonguear** *va* (coll.) to kid, to tease, to jolly; *vn* (coll.) to scheme one's way out of work
**candonguero -ra** *adj* (coll.) kidding, teasing
**candor** *m* candor; pure whiteness
**candoroso -sa** *adj* candid, frank, simple
**caneca** *f* glazed earthen bottle
**canecillo** *m* (arch.) corbel, console; bracket, support
**canela** *f* see **canelo**
**canelado -da** *adj* cinnamon-colored, cinnamon-flavored
**canelero** *m* (bot.) cinnamon (*tree or shrub*)
**canelina** *f* canella alba
**canelo -la** *adj* cinnamon, cinnamon-colored; *m* cinnamon (*tree or shrub*); *f* cinnamon (*bark and spice*); (coll.) something peachy; **canela de la China** (pharm.) cassia; **canela de Magallanes** Winter's bark
**canelón** *m* spout; icicle (*hanging from spout*); (sew.) tubular trimming; cinnamon candy; heavy end of whip
**canequí** *m* cannequin (*cotton cloth*)
**canesú** *m* (*pl:* **-súes**) guimpe
**caney** *m* (Am.) cabin, hut; (Am.) abode of an Indian chief; (Am.) bend (*in a river*)
**canfín** *m* (Am.) petroleum
**canfinflero** or **canflinflero** *m* (Am.) bawd, pimp
**canga** *f* cangue
**cangilón** *m* large pitcher or jug (*of earthenware or metal*); bucket (*of a bucket wheel*); dipper, scoop (*of a dredge*); (Am.) rut, wagon rut
**cangreja** *f* (naut.) fore-and-aft sail; **cangreja de mesana** (naut.) jigger; **cangreja de popa** (naut.) spanker
**cangrejal** *m* (Am.) crab bed
**cangrejero -ra** *mf* crab seller or dealer; *f* crab nest, crab bed
**cangrejo** *m* (zool.) crab; (naut.) gaff, spanker gaff; **sacar cangrejos** (rowing) to catch a crab; **cangrejo bayoneta** (zool.) king crab, horseshoe crab; **cangrejo de mar** (zool.) green crab; **cangrejo de río** (zool.) crawfish; **cangrejo ermitaño** (zool.) hermit crab
**cangrejuelo** *m* little crab
**cangrenar** *vr* to gangrene, to become gangrenous
**canguelo** *m* (slang) fear
**canguro** *m* (zool.) kangaroo
**caníbal** *adj & mf* cannibal
**canibalino -na** *adj* cannibalistic
**canibalismo** *m* cannibalism
**canica** *f* marbles (*game*); marble
**canicie** *f* whiteness (*of hair*)
**canícula** *f* dog days; (*cap.*) *f* (astr.) Dog Star
**canicular** *adj* canicular; **caniculares** *mpl* canicular days, dog days
**canicularlo** *m* beadle who keeps dogs out of church
**cánido -da** *adj* canine; *m* (zool.) canid
**canijo -ja** *adj* (coll.) sickly, infirm; *mf* (coll.) sickly person, weakling
**canil** *m* dog bread, dog cake
**canilla** *f* armbone, shinbone; tap (*in cask or barrel*); reel, bobbin; stripe, rib (*in cloth*)
**canillado -da** *adj* striped, ribbed
**canillero -ra** *mf* reel or bobbin maker; *m* tap-hole (*in cask or barrel*); (bot.) European elder; *f* shin guard; greave, jambe, jambeau
**caninez** *f* mad hunger
**canino -na** *adj* canine; *m* (anat.) canine, canine tooth; *f* dog excrement
**caniquí** *m* cannequin (*cotton cloth*)
**canisté** *m* or **canistel** *m* (bot.) lucuma; canistel (*fruit*)
**canje** *m* exchange
**canjeable** *adj* exchangeable
**canjear** *va* to exchange
**cano -na** *adj* gray, gray-haired; hoary, old; (poet.) white; *f* gray hair; measure equal to about two yards; (bot.) American fan palm; (Am.) jail; **echar una cana al aire** (coll.) to go on a lark, to cut loose
**canoa** *f* canoe; launch; (Am.) trough; **canoa automóvil** launch, motorboat
**canoero -ra** *mf* canoeist
**canófilo -la** *mf* dog fancier
**canon** *m* canon; (Bib., eccl. & mus.) canon; (eccl.) Canon (*part of the Mass which begins with Te igitur*); norm of human beauty; rate; royalty; tax; **cánones** *mpl* canon law; **gran canon** (print.) canon
**canonesa** *f* canoness
**canonical** *adj* canonical
**canonicato** *m* canonicate, canonry
**canónico -ca** *adj* (Bib. & eccl.) canonical; *f* (eccl.) canonical life
**canóniga** *f* (coll.) nap before eating
**canónigo** *m* canon (*churchman*)
**canonista** *m* canonist, canon lawyer
**canonización** *f* canonization
**canonizar** §76 *va* to canonize; to applaud, to approve
**canonjía** *f* canonry; (coll.) sinecure
**canoro -ra** *adj* singing, musical; sweet-singing (*bird*)
**canoso -sa** *adj* gray-haired, hoary
**canotié** *m* straw hat (*with low, flat crown*)
**cansado -da** *adj* tired, weary; worn-out, exhausted; tiresome, wearisome
**cansancio** *m* tiredness, weariness, fatigue
**cansar** *va* to tire; to weary, to bore; to harass; to exhaust (*a soil*); *vn* to tire, be tiresome; *vr* to tire, get tired; **cansarse de** + *inf* to get tired of + *ger;* **cansarse en** + *inf* to get tired + *ger*
**cansera** *f* (coll.) boredom, harassment
**cansino -na** *adj* tired, exhausted (*said of an animal*)
**cantable** *adj* singable; tuneful; sung slowly; *m* lyric (*words of musical passage of zarzuela*); musical passage (*of zarzuela*); (mus.) cantabile (*melodious, flowing passage*)
**cantábrico -ca** *adj* Cantabrian
**cantada** *f* (mus.) cantata
**cantador -dora** *mf* singer (*of popular songs*)
**cantal** *m* stone block; stony ground

**cantalear** *vn* to coo
**cantaleta** *f* tin-pan serenade, charivari, callithump; (Am.) constant scolding; **dar cantaleta a** (Am.) to make fun of, to laugh at; **la misma cantaleta** (Am.) the same old song
**cantaletear** *va* (Am.) to keep repeating, to say over and over again; (Am.) to make fun of, to laugh at
**cantalinoso -sa** *adj* rocky, stony (*ground*)
**cantalupo** *m* cantaloupe
**cantamisano** *m* var. of **misacantano**
**cantante** *adj* singing; *mf* singer; **cantante de ópera** opera singer
**cantar** *m* song; singing; chant; **ése es otro cantar** (coll.) that's another story; **cantar de gesta** (lit.) geste, romance; **Cantar de los Cantares** (Bib.) Song of Songs; *va* to sing; to sing of; to chant; **cantarlas claras** (coll.) to speak out; *vn* to sing; to chant; (coll.) to peach, to squeal; (coll.) to creak, to squeak; (naut.) to sing chanteys; (naut.) to whistle an order; **cantar de plano** (coll.) to make a full confession
**cántara** *f* jug; liquid measure equal to 13.16 liters
**cantarada** *f* jugful
**cantarera** *f* shelf for jugs
**cantarería** *f* jug shop, pottery
**cantarero** *m* potter
**cantárida** *f* (ent.) cantharis, Spanish fly; (pharm.) cantharides; blister plaster of cantharides; blister raised by cantharides
**cantarilla** *f* earthen jar
**cantarillo** *m* small jug
**cantarín -rina** *adj* fond of singing, always singing; *mf* singer, professional singer
**cántaro** *m* jug; jugful; ballot box; **llover a cántaros** to rain pitchforks
**cantata** *f* (mus.) cantata
**cantatriz** *f* (*pl:* **-trices**) singer, songstress
**cantazo** *m* blow with a big stone
**cante** *m* singing; popular song; **cante hondo, jondo** or **flamenco** Andalusian gypsy song or singing
**canteado -da** *adj* on edge, laid on edge
**cantear** *va* to pitch (*a stone*); to lay on edge
**cantera** *f* quarry, stone pit; talent, genius
**cantería** *f* stonecutting, stonework; stoneyard; masonry
**canterios** *mpl* roof girders
**cantero** *m* stonecutter; crust (*e.g., of bread*)
**canticio** *m* (coll.) tiresome singing
**cántico** *m* canticle; song
**cantidad** *f* quantity; **cantidad de movimiento** (mech.) momentum
**cantiga** *f* poem (*of troubadours*)
**cantil** *m* shelf (*on coast or under sea*); cliff
**cantilena** *f* song, ballad; cantilena; **la misma cantilena** (coll.) the same old song
**cantillo** *m* corner; pebble, little stone; jackstone; **cantillos** *mpl* jackstones
**cantimplora** *f* siphon; carafe, decanter; water bottle, canteen; wine flask; (eng.) weep hole; (Am.) powder flask; (Am.) mumps
**cantina** *f* canteen; wine cellar; lunchroom, luncheonette; lunch box; (rail.) station restaurant; (Am.) barroom
**cantinela** *f* var. of **cantilena**
**cantinera** *f* female sutler, vivandière; barmaid
**cantinero** *m* barkeeper, bartender
**cantizal** *m* stony ground
**canto** *m* song; singing; chant; canto; song (*lyric or ballad*); edge; corner; fore edge (*of book*); back (*of knife*); stone, pebble; crust (*of bread*); thickness (*e.g., of a board*); **de canto** on edge; on end; **canto ambrosiano** Ambrosian chant; **canto de corte** cutting edge; **canto del cisne** swan song; **canto flamenco** flamenco (*Andalusian gypsy singing*); **canto gregoriano** Gregorian chant; **canto llano** plain chant, plain song; **canto pelado** or **rodado** round stone, boulder
**cantón** *m* canton; region; cantonment; corner; (her.) canton
**cantonado -da** *adj* (her.) cantoned; *f* (archaic) corner; **dar cantonada a** (coll.) to shake off
**cantonal** *adj* cantonal
**cantonalismo** *m* cantonalism
**cantonar** *va & vr* var. of **acantonar**
**cantonear** *vn* to loaf at street corners; *vr* (coll.) to strut
**cantonero -ra** *mf* corner loafer; *m* gilding iron (*of bookbinder*); *f* angle iron, corner band, reinforcement (*of corner or edge*); corner shelf, corner table; streetwalker
**cantonés -nesa** *adj & mf* Cantonese
**cantor -tora** *adj* singing; sweet-singing; *m* singer, songster; minstrel; choirmaster; bard, poet; *f* songstress
**cantoral** *m* book of devotions
**Cantórbery** Canterbury
**cantorral** *m* stony ground
**cantoso -sa** *adj* stony, rocky
**cantuariense** *adj & mf* Canterburian
**cantueso** *m* (bot.) French lavender, stechados
**canturía** *f* vocal music; singing exercise; monotonous singing; singing quality (*of a composition*)
**canturrear** *va* (coll.) to hum, to sing; *vn* (coll.) to hum, to sing in a low voice
**canturreo** *m* (coll.) humming, singing in a low voice, crooning
**canturriar** *va & vn* (coll.) var. of **canturrear**
**cánula** *f* (surg.) cannula
**canular** *adj* cannular
**canut** *m* (orn.) knot
**canutero** *m* pincase
**canutillo** *m* var. of **cañutillo**
**canuto** *m* var. of **cañuto**
**caña** *f* cane, reed; stem, stalk; pipe; (bot.) giant reed; long bone (*of leg or arm*); leg (*of boot or stocking*); marrow; tipstock (*of firearm*); shank (*of anchor, drill, column, etc.*); wineglass (*stemless*); small glass (*of beer*); mine gallery; (naut.) tiller; (Am.) rum; (Am.) bluff; (Am.) boasting; **caña brava asiática** (bot.) bamboo; **caña de azúcar** sugar cane; **caña de Bengala** (bot.) rattan palm (*Calamus rotang*); **caña de Indias** (bot.) Indian reed, canna; **caña del pulmón** windpipe; **caña de pescar** fishing rod; **caña dulce** or **melar** sugar cane
**cañacoro** *m* (bot.) canna, Indian shot, Indian reed
**cañada** *f* gully, gulch; cattle path; (Am.) brook
**cañadilla** *f* (zool.) purple shell
**cañafístola** or **cañafístula** *f* (bot.) drumstick tree; cañafistula (*pods*)
**cañaheja** or **cañaherla** *f* (bot.) giant fennel
**cañal** *m* growth of reeds; fishgarth made of reeds, fishing channel
**cañamar** *m* hemp field
**cañamazo** *m* canvas; burlap; canvas for colored embroidery; embroidered hemp
**cañamelar** *m* sugar-cane plantation
**cañameño -ña** *adj* hempen, made of hemp
**cañamiel** *f* sugar cane
**cañamiza** *f* hemp refuse, hemp bagasse
**cáñamo** *m* (bot.) hemp (*plant and fiber*); hempen cloth; **cáñamo de Bengala** (bot.) sunn hemp; **cáñamo de Manila** Manila hemp; **cáñamo sisal** sisal hemp
**cañamón** *m* hempseed; **cañamones** *mpl* birdseed
**cañamoncillo** *m* fine mixing sand
**cañamonero -ra** *mf* hempseed vendor
**cañar** *m* growth of reeds; fishgarth made of reeds
**cañareja** *f* var. of **cañaheja**
**cañariego -ga** *adj* of a sheep that has died on the sheep path (*said of skin or hide*); accompanying the flock migrating between the north and south of Spain (*said of men, horses, and dogs*)
**cañarroya** *f* (bot.) wallwort
**cañavera** *f* (bot.) ditch reed
**cañaveral** *m* canebrake; reed field; sugar-cane plantation
**cañaverear** *va* var. of **acañaverear**
**cañazo** *m* blow with a reed or cane
**cañedo** *m* var. of **cañaveral**
**cañería** *f* pipe, pipe line; (mus.) organ pipes; **cañería de arcilla vitrificada** sewer pipe, soil pipe; **cañería maestra** main, gas or water main
**cañero** *m* pipe fitter, plumber; (dial.) angler; (Am.) sugar-cane dealer
**cañeta** *f* (bot.) ditch reed

**cañete** *m* small tube or pipe

**cañilavado -da** *adj* small-limbed (*said of a horse*)

**cañista** *m* pipe fitter, plumber

**cañiza** *f* coarse linen

**cañizal** *m* var. of **cañaveral**

**cañizo** *m* hurdle of reeds (*for drying fruit, rearing silkworms, shearing hats, etc.*); web of reeds and rope (*used as lath for ceilings*); (naut.) flake

**caño** *m* tube, pipe; ditch; gutter, sewer; channel (*into harbor or bay*); (mus.) organ pipe; mine gallery; spurt, jet; spout; cellar or cave for cooling water; wine cellar; **llover a caño libre** (coll.) to rain buckets

**cañón** *m* tube, pipe; cannon; barrel (*of gun*); shaft (*of column, elevator, etc.*); well (*of staircase*); (min.) gallery; shank (*of key*); stem (*of pipe, of feather*); quill; pinfeather; canyon; **cañón antiaéreo** anti-aircraft gun; **cañón antitanque** antitank gun; **cañón cohete** (mil.) rocket gun; **cañón de campaña** fieldpiece; **cañón de chimenea** flue, chimney flue; **cañón lanzaarpones** harpoon gun; **cañón lanzacabos** or **lanzacables** life-saving gun; **cañón obús** howitzer; **cañón rayado** rifled gun barrel

**cañonazo** *m* cannon shot

**cañonear** *va* to cannonade

**cañoneo** *m* cannonade, cannonry

**cañonera** *f* see **cañonero**

**cañonería** *f* cannon, cannonry; (mus.) set of organ pipes

**cañonero -ra** *adj* armed (*boat*); *m* gunner, cannoneer; gunboat; *f* (fort.) embrasure; (mil.) canteen (*store*); (Am.) holster

**cañoto** *m* (bot.) ditch reed

**cañucela** *f* slender cane or reed

**cañuela** *f* (bot.) fescue grass; **cañuela de oveja** (bot.) sheep's fescue

**cañutazo** *m* (coll.) gossip

**cañutería** *f* gold or silver embroidery; (mus.) set of organ pipes

**cañutero** *m* pincase

**cañutillo** *m* glass tube; bugle (*tubular glass bead*); gold or silver twist for embroidery

**cañuto** *m* internode (*of reed*); (coll.) gossip; tube, tubular container

**caoba** *f* (bot.) mahogany (*tree and wood*)

**caobana** *f* (archaic) mahogany (*tree*)

**caobo** *m* (bot.) mahogany (*tree*)

**caolín** *m* kaolin or kaoline

**caos** *m* chaos

**caótico -ca** *adj* chaotic

**cap.** abr. of **capitán & capítulo**

**capa** *f* cape, cloak, mantle; layer, bed; scum; coat (*e.g., of paint*); (mas.) bed, course; cigar wrapper; (anat. & geol.) stratum; (eccl.) cope; (naut.) primage; (fig.) cloak, mask; **a capa y espiga** mortise and tenon; **aguantarse a la capa** (naut.) to lie to; **andar de capa caída** (coll.) to be in a bad way (*in business, health, etc.*); **de capa y espada** cloak-and-sword; **de capa y gorra** plainly, informally; **estarse a la capa** (naut.) to lie to; **hacer de su capa un sayo** (coll.) to tend to one's own business, to keep one's own counsel; **so capa de** under the guise of, under the pretense of; **capa anual** (bot.) annual ring; **capa de balasto** (rail.) roadbed; **capa de Heaviside** (rad.) Heaviside layer; **capa del cielo** canopy of heaven; **capa de paseo** (taur.) dress cape; **capa freática** (eng.) water table; **capa magna** (eccl.) bishop's cope; **capa pluvial** (eccl.) cope, pluvial; **capa rota** (coll.) decoy, blind

**capacete** *m* casque, helmet

**capacidad** *f* capacity; capability; (elec. & phys.) capacity; **capacidad distribuída** (rad.) distributed capacity

**capacitación** *f* qualification, (act of) qualifying

**capacitancia** *f* (elec.) capacitance

**capacitar** *va* to enable, to qualify; to empower, to commission; *vr* to become enabled, become qualified

**capacitor** *m* (elec.) capacitor

**capacha** *f* frail, hamper; basket lid

**capachero** *m* porter or carrier using a basket

**capacho** *m* frail, hamper; basket lid; hempen pressing bag (*used in olive-oil presses*); bricklayer's hod; (orn.) barn owl

**capada** *f* (coll.) capeful (*contents of cape held as if it were an apron*)

**capadocio -cia** *adj & mf* Cappadocian

**capador** *m* gelder, castrator; gelder's whistle

**capadura** *f* gelding, castration; scar left by castration; second cutting of tobacco used for filling or wrappers

**capar** *va* to geld, to castrate; to curtail, to cut down

**caparazón** *m* caparison; horse blanket; feed bag; shell (*of insects or crustaceans*); carcass of fowl

**caparidáceo -a** *adj* (bot.) capparidaceous

**caparra** *f* cattle tick, sheep tick; earnest money

**caparrón** *m* (bot.) blossom

**caparrosa** *f* (chem.) vitriol; **caparrosa azul** (chem.) blue vitriol; **caparrosa blanca** (chem.) white vitriol; **caparrosa verde** (chem.) copperas, green vitriol

**capataz** *m* (*pl:* **-taces**) overseer, foreman; warden, steward

**capaz** *adj* (*pl:* **-paces**) capable, competent; capacious, spacious; **capaz de** capable of; with a capacity of; **capaz para** capable in; competent for; with room for

**capazo** *m* two-handled rush basket; blow with cloak

**capciosidad** *f* craftiness, deception

**capcioso -sa** *adj* crafty, deceptive

**capea** *f* (taur.) waving of cape at bull; (taur.) amateur free-for-all bullfight

**capeador** *m* (taur.) capeador (*bullfighter who waves cape before bull*)

**capear** *va* to take the cloak or cape away from; (coll.) to duck, dodge (*something unpleasant*); (taur.) to wave or flourish the cape at (*the bull*); (naut.) to weather (*a storm*); (coll.) to beguile, to take in; *vn* (naut.) to lay to; (Am.) to play hooky, to cut class

**capeja** *f* shabby cloak or cape

**capelán** *m* (ichth.) capelin

**capelina** *f* (surg.) capeline

**capelo** *m* cardinal's hat; cardinalate; **capelo rojo** red hat (*cardinal's hat; cardinalate*)

**capellada** *f* tip, toe piece (*of shoe*); patch on the vamp

**capellán** *adj masc* (Am.) fortune-hunting; *m* chaplain; (Am.) fortune hunter; **capellán castrense** or **de ejército** army chaplain; **capellán de la armada** or **de navío** navy chaplain

**capellanía** *f* fund left for religious purposes; chaplaincy

**capellina** *f* (arm. & surg.) capeline; (archaic) peasant's hood

**capeo** *m* (taur.) capework, waving of cape before bull

**capeón** *m* (taur.) young bull excited by waving of cape

**capero** *m* priest who wears a cope; cloak rack

**caperucita** *f* small pointed hood; **Caperucita Encarnada** or **Roja** Red Ridinghood, Little Red Ridinghood

**caperuza** *f* pointed hood; chimney cap; pipe cap; mantle (*of gaslight*); (mach.) hood

**capeta** *f* short cape

**capetiano -na** or **capetino -na** *adj & mf* Capetian

**capialzado** *m* curve or bend of arch; flashing over door or window

**capialzar §76** *va* to bend the face of (*an arch or lintel*) into an outward slope

**capialzo** *m* (arch.) slope of intrados

**capibara** *f* (zool.) capybara (*South American rodent*)

**capicúa** *m* palindrome

**capiculado -da** *adj* (philately) tête-bêche

**capichola** *f* ribbed silk

**capigorra** *m*, **capigorrón** *m* or **capigorrista** *m* (coll.) idler, loafer; dull cleric

**capilar** *adj* capillary; of the hair; *m* (anat.) capillary

**capilaridad** *f* capillarity

**capilla** *f* hood, cowl; chapel; death house; (mach.) bonnet, hood, cowl; (print.) proof sheet, advance sheet; (coll.) friar; **estar en**

capilla or **en la capilla** to be in the death house; (coll.) to be on pins and needles; (coll.) to be jittery about taking an examination; **estar expuesto en capilla ardiente** to be on view, to lie in state; **capilla ardiente** funeral chapel; oratory set up for funeral in the home; pallbearers; **capilla de la muerte** death house; **capilla mayor** chapel behind the high altar; **Capilla sixtina** Sistine Chapel
**capillada** *f* hoodful; blow with a hood
**capillejo** *m* skein of sewing silk
**capiller** *m* or **capillero** *m* chapelman, warden of a chapel, churchwarden
**capilleta** *f* small chapel; chapel-shaped niche
**capillo** *m* baby cap; hood; hood (*of falcon*); baptismal cap; cap of distaff; toe lining (*of shoe*); filler (*for cigars*); rabbit net; bud (*especially of rose*); cocoon; (metal.) cupel; (anat.) prepuce
**capilludo -da** *adj* like a hood or cowl; wearing a hood or cowl
**capipardo** *m* workingman
**capirotada** *f* dressing of eggs, herbs, garlic, etc.
**capirotazo** *m* fillip
**capirote** *m* hood (*covering face*); doctor's hood; cardboard or paper cone (*worn on head*); hood (*of falcon*); folding top (*of carriage*); fillip; *adj* with head of different color from that of body (*said of cattle*)
**capirucho** *m* (coll.) hood
**capisayo** *m* mantelet; bishop's vesture
**capiscol** *m* precentor
**capitación** *f* capitation; poll tax
**capitado -da** *adj* (bot.) capitate
**capital** *adj* capital; paramount; main, principal; essential; mortal (*enemy*); **lo capital** the main thing, the essential point; *m* capital; husband's estate at marriage; **capital circulante** (econ.) circulating capital; **capital de inversión** investment capital; **capital fijo** fixed capital; **capital lucrativo** productive capital; **capital social** capital stock; *f* capital (*city*); (fort.) capital
**capitalidad** *f* status as capital (*city*)
**capitalino -na** *adj* (Am.) of the capital; *mf* (Am.) dweller in the capital, native or inhabitant of the capital
**capitalismo** *m* capitalism
**capitalista** *adj* capitalist, capitalistic; *mf* capitalist; investor, share holder; *m* (taur.) apprentice bullfighter; (taur.) spectator who jumps into the ring at the end of the last fight
**capitalización** *f* capitalization; compounding (*of interest*)
**capitalizar §76** *va* to capitalize; to compound (*interest*)
**capitalmente** *adv* mortally
**capitán** *m* leader; captain (*e.g., of a football team*); (mil., naut. & nav.) captain; **capitán de bandera** (nav.) flag captain; **capitán de corbeta** (nav.) lieutenant commander; **capitán de fragata** (nav.) commander; **capitán del puerto** harbor master; **capitán de navío** (nav.) captain; **capitán general** (mil.) general (*of highest rank*); captain general; **capitán general de ejército** (mil.) General of the Army; **capitán general de la armada** (nav.) Admiral of the Fleet; **capitán preboste** (mil.) provost marshal
**capitana** *f* (nav.) flagship; captain's wife; (coll.) female leader
**capitanear** *va* to captain; to lead, to command
**capitanía** *f* captaincy; captainship; (mil.) company; anchorage (*toll*); **capitanía general** captain-generalcy
**capitel** *m* (arch.) capital; (arch.) spire; (tech.) capital (*of a still*)
**capitolino -na** *adj* Capitoline
**capitolio** *m* capitol; (*cap.*) *m* Capitol
**capitón** *m* (ichth.) striped mullet
**capitoste** *m* (coll.) boss, head
**capítula** *f* chapter (*passage of Scripture*)
**capitulación** *f* agreement; capitulation; **capitulaciones** *fpl* marriage contract, articles of marriage
**capitular** *adj* capitular; *m* capitulary; **capitulares** *fpl* (hist.) capitularies; *va* to accuse, to impeach; to agree on (*terms*); *vn* to capitulate; **capitular con** to capitulate to (*an enemy*); to compound or compromise with (*e.g., one's conscience*)
**capitulario** *m* prayer book
**capitulear** *vn* (Am.) var. of **cabildear**
**capituleo** *m* (Am.) var. of **cabildeo**
**capítulo** *m* chapter; chapter house; commission, errand; reprimand, reproof; (coll.) subject, matter; **llamar** or **traer a capítulo** to take to task, to bring to book; **capítulos** *mpl* main points (*of a speech or writing*); characteristics; **capítulos matrimoniales** articles of marriage
**capizana** *f* (arm.) crinière
**cap.ⁿ** abr. of **capitán**
**capnomancia** *f* capnomancy
**cap.º** abr. of **capítulo**
**capó** *m* (*pl;* **-pós**) (aut.) hood
**capoc** *m* kapok
**capolar** *va* to chop, mince, hash; (dial.) to cut the throat of, to behead
**capón -pona** *adj* castrated; *m* eunuch; capon; fillip on the head; bundle of brushwood; (naut.) anchor stopper; *f* (mil. & nav.) shoulder strap
**caponar** *va* (agr.) to tie up (*a vine*)
**caponera** *f* cage or coop for fattening capons; (fort.) caponier; (coll.) hospitable house, place of welcome; (coll.) coop (*jail*)
**capoquero** *m* (bot.) kapok tree, silk-cotton tree
**caporal** *m* chief, leader; cattle boss
**capota** *f* head of the teasel; capote (*top of a vehicle; bonnet with strings*); (aer.) cowling; (aut.) top
**capotaje** *m* somersault, upset
**capotar** *vn* to turn somersault (*said of a car*); (aer.) to nose over
**capote** *m* capote (*cloak*); mass of heavy clouds; bullfighter's bright-colored cape; (coll.) frown; (Am.) thrashing, beating; **dar capote a** (coll.) to flabbergast; (coll.) to leave (*a late-comer*) without anything to eat; (coll.) to not let (*someone*) take a single trick; (Am.) to take in, to bamboozle; **decir para su capote** to say to oneself; **echar un capote** (coll.) to turn the conversation; **capote de monte** poncho
**capotear** *va* to duck (*a responsibility*); (coll.) to beguile, take in; (taur.) to wave or flourish the cape at (*the bull*); (theat.) to cut, to make cuts in (*a performance*)
**capoteo** *m* (taur.) waving of cape before bull
**capotillo** *m* cape, mantelet
**capotudo -da** *adj* frowning
**capp.ⁿ** abr. of **capellán**
**caprario -ria** *adj* capric
**Capricornio** *m* (astr.) Capricorn; (*l.c.*) *m* (ent.) capricorn beetle
**capricho** *m* caprice; whim, fancy; keen desire; (mus.) capriccio, caprice
**caprichoso -sa** *adj* capricious; whimsical, willful
**caprichudo -da** *adj* whimsical, willful
**caprifoliáceo -a** *adj* (bot.) caprifoliaceous
**caprino -na** *adj* (pertaining to the) goat
**capriotada** *f* (Am.) goat's-milk pudding
**caprípede** or **caprípedo -da** *adj* (poet.) goat-footed
**capsaicina** *f* (chem.) capsaicin
**cápsula** *f* cap (*of a bottle*); laboratory dish; cartridge; capsule (*of space rocket*); (anat., bot., pharm. & zool.) capsule; **cápsula de cristal** (elec.) crystal cartridge; **cápsula fulminante** percussion cap; **cápsula manométrica** manometric capsule
**capsular** *adj* capsular; *va* to cap (*a bottle*)
**captación** *f* attraction, attractiveness; capture; winning; harnessing (*of water*); catchment; (rad.) tuning, tuning in, picking up; uptake (*of radioactive tracer*)
**captalización** *f* (wine mfg.) chaptalization
**captalizar §76** *va* to chaptalize
**captar** *va* to catch; to attract, to win, to capture (*e.g., confidence or affection*); to impound (*water*); to harness (*a waterfall*); to tune in (*a radio station*); to get, to pick up (*a radio signal*); to grasp, to get (*what someone says*); *vr* to attract, to win
**captor** *m* captor
**captura** *f* capture; catch
**capturar** *va* to capture

**capuana** *f* (coll.) beating, whipping
**capucha** *f* cowl; circumflex accent
**capuchina** *f* Capuchin nun; (bot.) Indian cress, garden nasturtium; (orn.) capuchin (*pigeon*); confection of egg yolks; (Am.) latch (*of door or window*)
**capuchino** *m* Capuchin (*monk*); (zool.) capuchin (*monkey*)
**capucho** *m* cowl, hood, capuchin
**capuchón** *m* lady's cloak with hood; short domino; (aut.) valve cap
**capulí** *m* (*pl:* **-líes**) (bot.) capulin; (bot.) calabur tree
**capulín** *m* var. of **capulí**
**capullo** *m* cocoon; coarse spun silk; acorn cup; bud (*especially of rose*); (anat.) prepuce; **en capullo** (coll.) in embryo
**capuz** *m* (*pl:* **-puces**) cowl; hooded cloak; dive, duck
**capuza** *f* (Am.) branding iron
**capuzar** **§76** *va* to duck; (naut.) to load (*a boat*) so that it draws more at the bow
**caquéctico -ca** *adj* cachectic or cachectical
**caquexia** *f* (path.) cachexia
**caqui** *m* (bot.) kaki, Japanese persimmon; khaki; *adj* khaki
**caquinos** *mpl* (Am.) cachinnation, uproarious laughter
**cara** *f* see **caro**
**carabao** *m* (zool.) carabao
**cárabe** *m* amber
**carabela** *f* (naut.) caravel
**carabelón** *m* small caravel
**carabina** *f* carbine; (coll.) chaperon; **ser la carabina de Ambrosio** (coll.) to be worthless
**carabinazo** *m* shot with a carbine; carbine wound
**carabinero** *m* carabineer; revenue guard
**cárabo** *m* (orn.) tawny owl; (ent.) carabus
**caracal** *m* (zool.) caracal
**caracol** *m* (zool.) snail; snail shell; sea shell; curl (*in hair*); spit curl; caracole (*of horse*); winding or spiral stairs; (anat.) cochlea; (arch.) spiral; (horol.) fusee; **¡caracoles!** confound it!; good gracious!; **hacer caracoles** to zigzag; **caracol real** (bot.) snailflower, corkscrew flower
**caracola** *f* (zool.) triton (*marine snail*); conch, triton (*shell*); trumpet
**caracolada** *f* fricassee of snails
**caracolear** *vn* (equit.) to caracole
**caracolejo** *m* small snail; small shell
**caracolero -ra** *mf* snail gatherer, snail vendor; *f* (bot.) pellitory
**caracolillo** *m* (bot.) Australian pea; pea-bean coffee; veined mahogany; **caracolillos** *mpl* shell-work trimmings or fringes; **caracolillo de olor** (bot.) sweet pea
**caracolito** *m* (bot.) gromwell
**carácter** *m* (*pl:* **caracteres**) character; (bot., zool., print. & theol.) character; brand (*on cattle*); **carácter adquirido** (biol.) acquired character; **carácter de imprenta** (print.) type; **carácter de letra** hand, handwriting; **carácter hereditario** (biol.) inherited character; **carácter recesivo** (biol.) recessive character
**característico -ca** *adj* characteristic; *m* (theat.) old man; *f* characteristic; (math. & rad.) characteristic; (theat.) old woman
**caracterización** *f* characterization
**caracterizado -da** *adj* distinguished, outstanding
**caracterizar** **§76** *va* to characterize; to confer a distinction on; to play (*a rôle*) effectively; *vr* (theat.) to dress and paint for a rôle
**caracul** *m* caracul (*curly fur*)
**caracha** *m* or **carache** *m* (vet.) itch, mange (*on llamas*)
**caracho -cha** *adj* violet-colored
**carado -da** *adj:* **bien carado** good-faced, kind-faced; **mal carado** evil-faced
**caradura** *m* (coll.) scoundrel
**caragilate** *m* (bot.) black-eyed bean
**caramanchel** *m* (naut.) roof or cover of hatchway; (coll.) refreshment stand
**caramanchón** *m* var. of **camaranchón**
**caramba** *interj* confound it!; gracious me!
**carambanado -da** *adj* frozen, frozen into an icicle
**carámbano** *m* icicle
**carambillo** *m* (bot.) saltwort
**carambola** *f* carom; (bot.) carambola (*tree and fruit*); trick, cheat; chance; (fig.) double shot; **por carambola** deviously; by chance, by luck
**carambolear** *vn* to carom
**carambolero** *m* (bot.) carambola (*tree*); lucky fellow
**carambolista** *mf* good carom shot (*person*)
**carambolo** *m* (bot.) carambola (*tree*)
**caramel** *m* (ichth.) atherine, silversides
**caramelizar** **§76** *va & vr* to caramelize
**caramelo** *m* caramel; lozenge, drop (*candy*)
**caramilla** *f* (mineral.) calamine
**caramillar** *m* growth of saltwort
**caramillo** *m* (bot.) saltwort; (mus.) shawm; crooked or shaky heap; gossiping, scheming
**caramilloso -sa** *adj* (coll.) var. of **quisquilloso**
**carantamaula** *f* (coll.) ugly false face; (coll.) ugly mug (*person*)
**carantoña** *f* (coll.) ugly false face, ugly face; (coll.) ugly old woman all dressed up and painted; **carantoñas** *fpl* (coll.) fawning, wheedling
**carantoñero -ra** *mf* (coll.) fawner, wheedler
**caraña** *f* caranna, caranna gum
**carapacho** *m* carapace; **meterse en su carapacho** to retire into one's shell; **salir del carapacho** to come out of one's shell
**carapato** *m* castor oil
**carape** *interj* var. of **caramba**
**caraqueño -ña** *adj* (pertaining to) Caracas; *mf* native or inhabitant of Caracas
**carasol** *m* solarium, sun porch, sunroom
**carátula** *f* mask; wire mask (*of beekeeper*); (Am.) title page; (Am.) face (*of watch*); (fig.) stage, theater
**caratulero -ra** *mf* mask maker or dealer
**carava** *f* peasant holiday gathering
**caravana** *f* caravan; (coll.) caravan (*band of travelers*)
**caravanera** *f* caravansary
**caravanero** *m* caravanner, caravanist
**caravansera** *f*, **caravanserrallo** *m* or **caravasar** *m* caravansary
**caray** *m* (zool.) tortoise; tortoise shell; *interj* confound it!; gracious me!
**carbinol** *m* (chem.) carbinol
**carbodinamita** *f* carbodynamite
**carbohidrato** *m* (chem.) carbohydrate
**carbohielo** *m* dry ice
**carbol** *m* (chem.) phenol
**carbólico -ca** *adj* carbolic
**carbolíneo** *m* carbolineum
**carbolización** *f* creosoting
**carbolizar** **§76** *va* to creosote
**carbón** *m* coal; charcoal; black crayon, carbon pencil; (elec.) carbon (*of a battery or an arc lamp*); (agr.) smut; **carbón animal** boneblack; **carbón antracitoso** anthracite coal; **carbón bituminoso** bituminous coal; **carbón de bujía** cannel coal; **carbón de leña** charcoal; **carbón de llama corta** hard coal; **carbón de llama larga** soft coal; **carbón de piedra** coal; **carbón graso** soft coal; **carbón mate** cannel coal; **carbón mineral** coal; **carbón tal como sale** run-of-mine coal; **carbón vegetal** charcoal
**carbonada** *f* charge of coal (*for furnace*); broiled meat; pancake
**carbonado** *m* carbonado, carbon diamond
**carbonalla** *f* refractory mortar for hearth of reverberatory furnace
**carbonatar** *va* to carbonate
**carbonato** *m* (chem.) carbonate; **carbonato de calcio** (chem.) calcium carbonate; **carbonato de potasio** (chem.) potassium carbonate; **carbonato de sodio** (chem.) sodium carbonate
**carboncillo** *m* fine coal; charcoal (*pencil*); black sand; carbon (*in cylinder*)
**carbonear** *va* to make charcoal of, turn into charcoal
**carboneo** *m* charcoal burning
**carbonera** *f* see **carbonero**
**carbonería** *f* coalyard; charcoal store; coal shed

**carbonero -ra** *adj* (pertaining to) coal, charcoal; coaling; *mf* coaldealer; charcoal burner; *f* charcoal kiln; bunker, coal bunker; coalbin; (Am.) coal mine
**carbónico -ca** *adj* carbonic
**carbonífero -ra** *adj* carboniferous; (geol.) Carboniferous; *m* (geol.) Carboniferous
**carbonilo** *m* (chem.) carbonyl
**carbonilla** *f* fine coal, pulverized coal; cinders; (aut.) carbon (*in cylinders*)
**carbonización** *f* carbonization
**carbonizar** *va & vr* to carbonize, to char; to burn up
**carbono** *m* (chem.) carbon
**carbonoso -sa** *adj* carbonaceous
**carborundo** *m* carborundum
**carboxilo** *m* (chem.) carboxyl
**carbunclo** *m* carbuncle (*ruby or garnet*); (path. & vet.) carbuncle
**carbunco** *m* (path. & vet.) carbuncle
**carbúnculo** *m* carbuncle (*ruby or garnet*)
**carburación** *f* carburetion
**carburador** *m* carburetor
**carburante** *m* fuel (*gas or liquid*)
**carburar** *va* to carburet
**carburo** *m* (chem.) carbide (*especially calcium carbide*); **carburo de calcio** (chem.) calcium carbide
**carcacha** *f* (Am.) jalopy
**carcaj** *m* quiver; socket or bucket (*for holding standard surmounted by cross*); (Am.) rifle case
**carcajada** *f* outburst of laughter, burst of laughter
**carcamal** *adj* (coll.) infirm; *m* (coll.) infirm old person
**carcamán** *m* tub (*clumsy boat*)
**carcasa** *f* (mil.) carcass; (mach.) frame
**Carcasona** *f* Carcassonne
**cárcava** *f* gully; ditch, earthwork; grave
**carcavón** *m* gully, gorge
**carcavuezo** *m* deep pit
**carcax** *m* (*pl:* **-cajes**) var. of **carcaj**
**carcayú** *m* (*pl:* **-yúes**) (zool.) wolverine, glutton
**carcaza** *f* var. of **carcaj**
**cárcel** *f* jail, prison; groove in which sluice gate slides; (carp.) clamp (*for holding together boards to be glued*)
**carcelaje** *m* jailer's fee; imprisonment
**carcelario -ria** *adj* (pertaining to) jail
**carcelería** *f* imprisonment; bail
**carcelero -ra** *adj* (pertaining to) jail; *mf* jailer, warden
**carcinógeno** *m* (path.) carcinogen
**carcinoma** *m* (path.) carcinoma
**cárcola** *f* treadle of a loom
**carcoma** *f* (ent.) wood borer; dust made by wood borer; anxiety; spendthrift; bore, pest (*person*)
**carcomer** *va* to bore; to gnaw away, gnaw away at, to undermine; *vr* to become undermined; to become worm-eaten
**carda** *f* carding; teasel (*head of plant; device for raising nap*); card (*brush*); rebuke; **carda para limas** file brush or card
**cardada** *f* carding (*roll of wool from carding machine*)
**cardador -dora** *mf* carder (*of wool*); *m* (zool.) julid, millepede
**cardal** *m* var. of **cardizal**
**cardamina** *f* (bot.) pepper cress
**cardamomo** *m* (bot.) cardamom
**cardán** *m* (mach.) universal joint
**cardar** *va* to card; to rebuke
**cardelina** *f* (orn.) linnet
**cardenal** *m* (eccl.) cardinal; (orn.) cardinal, cardinal bird; black-and-blue mark; **cardenal de Virginia** (orn.) eastern cardinal
**cardenalato** *m* cardinalate
**cardenalicio -cia** *adj* (pertaining to a) cardinal
**cardencha** *f* (bot.) teasel; card (*brush*)
**cardenchal** *m* teasel field
**cardenillo** *m* verdigris
**cárdeno -na** *adj* purple, violet; gray (*bull*); opaline (*water*)
**cardería** *f* carding shop
**cardíaca** *f* see **cardíaco**
**cardiáceo -a** *adj* heart-shaped
**cardíaco -ca** *adj* cardiac; *mf* cardiac (*sufferer from heart disease*); *f* (bot.) motherwort
**cardias** *m* (*pl:* **-dias**) (anat.) cardia
**cardillar** *m* field of Spanish oyster plants
**cardillo** *m* (bot.) Spanish oyster plant, golden thistle
**cardinal** *adj* cardinal
**cardinas** *fpl* (arch.) thistle leaves
**cardiografía** *f* cardiography
**cardiógrafo** *m* cardiograph
**cardiograma** *m* cardiogram
**cardiología** *f* cardiology
**cardiovascular** *adj* cardiovascular
**carditis** *f* (path.) carditis
**cardizal** *m* field full of thistles or brambles
**Card.**[l] abr. of **Cardenal**
**cardo** *m* (bot., arch. & her.) thistle; file brush or card; **cardo ajonjero** (bot.) carline thistle; **cardo alcachofero** (bot.) artichoke; **cardo bendito** (bot.) blessed thistle; **cardo borriqueño** or **borriquero** (bot.) cotton thistle, Scotch thistle; **cardo corredor** (bot.) field eryngo; **cardo de cardadores** (bot.) fuller's teasel; **cardo de comer** (bot.) cardoon; **cardo estrellado** (bot.) star thistle; **cardo lechar, lechero** or **mariano** (bot.) milk thistle; **cardo negro** (bot.) Canada thistle; **cardo santo** (bot.) holy thistle; **cardo yesquero** (bot.) cotton thistle; (bot.) globe thistle
**cardón** *m* carding; (bot.) teasel, wild teasel
**cardoncillo** *m* (bot.) milk thistle
**carducha** *f* big iron carding brush
**cardume** *m* or **cardumen** *m* school (*of fish*)
**carduzal** *m* var. of **cardizal**
**carduzar §76** *va* to card (*wool*); (hum.) to scratch with the nails
**carear** *va* to bring face to face; to compare; to lead (*cattle*); *vn* to face; **carear a** to face, to overlook (*e.g., a garden, the street*); *vr* to come face to face, to meet face to face; **carearse con** to face (*especially firmly or hostilely*)
**carecer §34** *vn* to be in want; **carecer de** to lack, be in need of
**carecimiento** *m* lack, want, need
**carelio -lia** *adj & mf* Karelian; (*cap.*) *f* Karelia
**carena** *f* (naut.) careen, careening (*cleaning and caulking*); (naut.) bottom (*part under-water*); (coll.) chiding, jeering, mocking; (poet.) bottom, ship; **dar carena a** (naut.) to careen (*to clean and caulk*)
**carenadura** *f* (naut.) careenage
**carenar** *va* (naut.) to careen (*to clean and caulk*)
**carencia** *f* lack, want, need, deficiency
**carencial** *adj* deficiency
**carenero** *m* (naut.) careener
**carente** *adj* lacking, devoid; **carente de** lacking, devoid of, in need of
**careo** *m* meeting, confrontation; comparison
**carero -ra** *adj* (coll.) dear, expensive (*charging high prices*)
**carestía** *f* scarcity; want; high cost of living, high prices; **carestía de la vida** high cost of living
**careto -ta** *adj* marked with a blaze (*said of a horse or cow*); *f* mask; fencing mask; **quitar la careta a** to unmask; **careta antigás** gas mask
**carey** *m* (zool.) hawksbill turtle; tortoise shell
**carga** *f* loading; load; freight, cargo; burden; weight; anxiety, worry; charge (*of a cannon, furnace, etc.*); responsibility, charge, obligation; (mil. & elec.) charge; (hyd.) head; (elec.) load; **a cargas** (coll.) in abundance; **con plena carga** (elec. & mach.) at full load; **echar la carga a** to put the blame on; **volver a la carga** to not give up, to keep coming back; **carga de caballería** cavalry charge; **carga de camión** truckload; **carga de espacio** (elec.) space charge; **carga de familia** dependent; **carga de profundidad** depth charge; **carga prosódica** (gram.) stress, stress accent; **carga pública** public charge (*person who is a burden or responsibility to the state or local government*); **carga útil** pay load
**cargadero** *m* loading platform; freight station; hopper, mouth of furnace; (arch.) lintel

**cargadilla** *f* (coll.) debt and accrued interest
**cargado -da** *adj* loaded; overcast, cloudy; sultry; strong, thick; copious; big with young; charged, hot (*wire*); **cargado de años** up in years; **cargado de espaldas** stoop-shouldered
**cargador** *m* loader, stevedore; stoker; ramrod; rammer; carrier, porter; **cargador de acumulador** (elec.) battery charger
**cargamento** *m* load; cargo, shipment; dependents
**cargante** *adj* (coll.) boring, annoying, tiresome
**cargar** §59 *va* to load; to load up, to overload; to weigh down on, to burden; to increase (*taxes*); to load (*a gun, a furnace, dice, etc.*); to charge; (mil. & elec.) to charge; to play (*a higher card*); (coll.) to weary, to bore; (coll.) to annoy; (coll.) to flunk; (Am.) to carry; (Am.) to wear; (Am.) to punish; **cargar a una persona** to place (*e.g., a task*) on someone; to entrust (*e.g., a responsibility*) to someone; to impose (*e.g., a tax*) on someone; to charge someone with (*an offense or crime*); **cargar a una persona de** to charge someone with being ‖ *vn* to load; to turn (*said of wind*); to incline, to tip; (phonet.) to fall (*said of accent*); to crowd; (coll.) to overeat, to drink too much; **cargar con** to pick up, to carry; to walk away with, steal; to take upon oneself; to shoulder (*a gun*); **cargar sobre** to rest on; to devolve on; to pester, to importune ‖ *vr* to turn (*said of wind*); to become overcast; (coll.) to become bored; (coll.) to become annoyed; (coll.) to break; **cargarse de** to have in abundance, to be overloaded with; to be bathed in (*tears*); (coll.) to get rid of
**cargareme** *m* voucher, deposit voucher
**cargazón** *f* cargo; heaviness (*in stomach, head, etc.; in literary style*); mass of heavy clouds; share, portion
**cargo** *m* burden, weight; blame, charge; job, post, position, duty; management; care, charge, responsibility; (law) count; (com.) charge; pile of olive-oil bags; load of pressed grapes; (naut.) freighter; **a cargo de** in charge of (*a person*); **girar a cargo de** (com.) to draw on; **hacer cargo a uno de una cosa** to charge someone with something; **hacerse cargo de** to take charge of; to look into; to grasp, to realize; to understand; **hacerse cargo de** + *inf* to take it upon oneself to + *inf;* **librar a cargo de** (com.) to draw on; **ser en cargo a** to be indebted to; **tomar a su cargo** to take upon oneself; **vestir el cargo** to look the part; **cargo de conciencia** sense of guilt, burden on one's conscience
**cargoso -sa** *adj* burdensome, onerous; annoying, bothersome
**carguero -ra** *adj* of burden (*said of animals*); freight, freight-carrying; *m* (Am.) beast of burden
**carguío** *m* load; cargo, freight
**cari** *m* curry (*sauce, powder, or stew*)
**caria** *f* (arch.) shaft (*of column*)
**cariacedo -da** *adj* sour-faced, unpleasant
**cariacontecido -da** *adj* (coll.) woebegone, down in the mouth
**cariacuchillado -da** *adj* scar-faced
**cariado -da** *adj* carious
**cariadura** *f* (path.) caries
**cariaguileño -ña** *adj* (coll.) sharp-featured
**carialegre** *adj* (coll.) smiling
**cariampollado -da** or **cariampollar** *adj* (coll.) fat-cheeked, round-faced
**cariancho -cha** *adj* (coll.) broad-faced
**cariar** §90 *va* to decay, cause to decay; *vr* to decay, become decayed
**cariátide** *f* (arch.) caryatid
**caríbal** *adj* & *mf* (obs.) var. of **caníbal**
**Caribdis** *f* (geog. & myth.) Charybdis
**caribe** *adj* Caribbean; *mf* Carib; *m* brute, savage; (ichth.) caribe
**caribú** *m* (*pl:* **-búes**) (zool.) caribou
**caricato** *m* buffo, buffoon
**caricatura** *f* caricature; cartoon
**caricaturar** *va* to caricature
**caricaturesco -ca** *adj* in caricature
**caricaturista** *mf* caricaturist; cartoonist
**caricaturizar** §76 *va* to caricature
**caricia** *f* caress, petting; endearment
**caricioso -sa** *adj* caressing, affectionate
**caricuerdo -da** *adj* (coll.) wise-looking
**carichato -ta** *adj* flat-faced
**caridad** *f* charity
**caridelantero -ra** *adj* (coll.) forward, brazen
**caridoliente** *adj* sad-looking
**cariedón** *m* (ent.) weevil
**carientismo** *m* (rhet.) disguised irony
**caries** *f* (path.) caries, decay (*e.g., of teeth*); (agr.) blight
**carifruncido -da** *adj* (coll.) wrinkle-faced
**carigordo -da** *adj* (coll.) fat-faced
**cariharto -ta** *adj* (coll.) round-faced
**carilampiño -ña** *adj* (Am.) smooth-faced, beardless
**carilargo -ga** *adj* (coll.) long-faced
**carilucio -cia** *adj* (coll.) glossy-faced
**carilla** *f* mask (*of beekeeper*); page (*of book*)
**carilleno -na** *adj* (coll.) full-faced
**carillón** *m* (mus.) carillon
**carimbar** *va* (Am.) to brand
**carimbo** *m* (Am.) branding iron
**carinegro -gra** *adj* swarthy; blackface
**cariño** *m* love, affection; fondness, fond attention; (Am.) gift, present; **cariños** *mpl* words of love, show of affection
**cariñoso -sa** *adj* loving, affectionate, endearing
**cariocinesis** *f* (biol.) karyokinesis
**cariofiláceo -a** *adj* (bot.) caryophyllaceous
**cariofilata** *f* (bot.) avens; **cariofilata acuática** (bot.) purple or water avens
**cariomitoma** *m* (biol.) karyomitome
**carioplasma** *m* (biol.) karyoplasm
**cariópside** *f* (bot.) caryopsis
**carioquinesis** *f* var. of **cariocinesis**
**cariosoma** *m* (biol.) karyosome
**cariotina** *f* (biol.) karyotin
**cariparejo -ja** *adj* (coll.) impassive, stone-faced
**carirraído -da** *adj* (coll.) brazen-faced
**carirredondo -da** *adj* (coll.) round-faced
**carisea** *f* kersey
**cariseto** *m* coarse wool
**carisma** *m* (theol.) charism
**carita** *f* little face; (bot.) mesquite; **dar** or **hacer carita** (Am.) to smile back (*said of a woman flirting*); **carita blanca** (zool.) capuchin (*monkey*)
**caritativo -va** *adj* charitable; **caritativo con, para** or **para con** charitable to or toward
**cariz** *m* appearance (*of sky or weather*); (coll.) look, aspect
**carlanca** *f* dog collar with sharp points around it (*to protect the dog*); **tener muchas carlancas** (coll.) to be underhanded
**carlancón -cona** *adj* underhanded; *mf* underhanded person
**carlear** *vn* to pant
**carleta** *f* file; French slate
**carlina** *f* (bot.) carline thistle
**carlinga** *f* (aer.) cockpit; (naut.) mast step
**carlismo** *m* Carlism
**carlista** *adj* & *mf* Carlist
**carlita** *f* eyeglass, lens
**Carlitos** *m* Charlie
**Carlomagno** *m* Charlemagne
**Carlos** *m* Charles
**Carlota** *f* Charlotte; (*l.c*) *f* charlotte (*pudding*); **carlota rusa** charlotte russe
**carlovingio -gia** *adj* & *m* Carlovingian
**carmañola** *f* carmagnole (*jacket, song, and dance*)
**carme** *m* villa, country house and garden
**Carmela** *f* Carmela (*familiar form of Carmen*)
**carmelina** *f* second crop of vicuña wool
**carmelita** *adj* (Am.) brown; *adj* & *mf* Carmelite; *f* nasturtium bud (*used in salads*)
**carmelitano -na** *adj* Carmelite
**carmen** *m* carmen, song, poem; villa, country house and garden; (*cap.*) *f* Carmen; Order of Our Lady of Mount Carmel
**carmenador** *m* teasler (*man or machine*); haircomb
**carmenadura** *f* teasling
**carmenar** *va* to unravel, disentangle; to teasel; (coll.) to pull the hair of; (coll.) to fleece, to swindle; *vr* to come unraveled

**carmes** *m* var. of **quermes**
**carmesí** (*pl:* **-síes**) *adj* crimson; *m* crimson; kermes powder; red silk (*fabric*)
**carmín** *m* carmine (*dyestuff and color*); (bot.) wild rose; (bot.) pokeweed; **carmín de índigo** indigo extract
**carminar** *va* to carmine; *vr* to become carmine (*in color*)
**carminativo -va** *adj & m* (med.) carminative
**carmíneo -a** *adj* carmine
**carminita** *f* (mineral.) carminite
**carnada** *f* bait; (coll.) bait, lure, trap
**carnadura** *f* muscularity, flesh, strength
**carnaje** *m* salt beef, jerked beef
**carnal** *adj* carnal; full (*brother, cousin, etc.*); *m* non-Lenten period
**carnalidad** *f* carnality
**carnalita** *f* (mineral.) carnallite
**carnaval** *m* carnival
**carnavalada** *f* carnival stunt
**carnavalesco -ca** *adj* (pertaining to) carnival
**carnaza** *f* inner face of hide or skin; bait; (coll.) fleshiness (*of a person*)
**carne** *f* flesh; meat; preserves; **cobrar carnes** (coll.) to put on flesh; **criar carnes** to put on fat, put on weight; **echar carnes** (coll.) to put on flesh; **en carnes** naked; without dowry; **en carne viva** raw (*skin or sore*); **en vivas carnes** naked; **no ser carne ni pescado** to be neither fish nor fowl, to be nondescript, to be colorless; **perder carnes** to lose flesh; **poner toda la carne en el asador** (coll.) to stake all, to put all one's eggs in one basket; **ser de carne y hueso** (coll.) to be only human; **temblarle a uno las carnes** (coll.) to be in deathly fear; **tener carne de perro** (coll.) to have an iron constitution; **carne asada al horno** baked meat; **carne asada en parrillas** broiled meat; **carne cediza** tainted meat; **carne de cañón** cannon fodder; **carne de cerdo** pork; **carne de cordero** lamb; **carne de gallina** goose flesh, goose pimples; **carne de horca** gallows bird; **carne de membrillo** preserved quinces; **carne de pelo** rabbit meat; **carne de pluma** fowl (*as food*); **carne de puerco** pork; **carne de res** (Am.) beef; **carne de ternera** veal; **carne de vaca** beef; **carne de venado** venison; **carne fiambre** cold meat; **carne mollar** lean meat; **carne sin hueso** (coll.) cinch, snap; **carne y sangre** flesh and blood
**carneada** *f* (Am.) butchering
**carnear** *va* (Am.) to slaughter, to butcher; (Am.) to take in, to deceive
**carnecilla** *f* bump, lump (*on body*)
**carnerada** *f* flock of sheep
**carneraje** *m* sheep tax
**carnereamiento** *m* penalty for damage caused by sheep
**carnerear** *va* to kill (*sheep and cattle*) for damage they caused
**carnerero** *m* shepherd
**carneril** *adj* (pertaining to) sheep
**carnerismo** *m* (Am.) sheepishness
**carnero** *m* (zool.) sheep; mutton; battering ram; (dial.) sheepskin; (Am.) sheep (*person*); charnel; charnel house; family vault; **cantar para el carnero** (Am.) to die; **no hay tales carneros** there's no truth to it; **carnero ciclán** (vet.) cryptorchid; **carnero de la sierra** or **de la tierra** (Am.) alpaca, vicuña, llama; **carnero del Cabo** (orn.) albatross; **carnero de simiente** ram for breeding; **carnero marino** seal; **carnero llano** wether
**carneruno -na** *adj* (pertaining to) sheep; sheeplike, rammish
**carnestolendas** *fpl* Shrovetide, carnival
**carnet** *m* (*pl:* **-nets**) notebook; bankbook; dance card; **carnet de chófer** driver's license, operator's license; **carnet de identidad** identification card
**carnicería** *f* meat market, butcher shop; (fig.) carnage
**carnicero -ra** *adj* carnivorous; bloodthirsty; fattening (*said of pasture*); (coll.) meat-devouring; *mf* butcher; (fig.) butcher (*person guilty of cruel slaughter*); *m* (zool.) carnivore
**cárnico -ca** *adj* (pertaining to) meat
**carnicol** *m* half of cloven hoof
**carnificación** *f* (path.) carnification
**carnificar** §86 *vr* to carnify
**carniseco -ca** *adj* skinny
**carnívoro -ra** *adj* carnivorous; *m* (zool. & bot.) carnivore
**carniza** *f* (coll.) offal (*of butchered animal*); (coll.) decayed meat
**carnosidad** *f* fleshiness, corpulence; proud flesh; carnosity
**carnosina** *f* (chem.) carnosine
**carnoso -sa** *adj* fleshy; marrowy; meaty (*of meat; like meat*)
**carnotita** *f* (mineral.) carnotite
**carnudo -da** *adj* fleshy
**carnuza** *f* coarse cheap meat
**caro -ra** *adj* dear, expensive; dear, beloved ‖ **caro** *adv* dear ‖ *f* face; look; mien, countenance; front, façade; facing; flat surface; heads (*of coin*); face (*of coin or medal*); side (*of phonograph record*); **a cara descubierta** openly; **a cara o cruz** heads or tails; **a dos caras** two-facedly; **dar la cara** to be willing to take the consequences; **dar la cara por otro** (coll.) to answer for someone else; **darle en cara a uno** to cast or throw in one's teeth; **de cara** opposite, facing; in the face; **echar a cara o cruz** to flip up, to flip a coin; **echarle en cara a uno** to cast or throw in one's teeth; **hacer cara a** to face, to resist, to meet boldly; **lavar la cara a** (coll.) to fawn on; **no volver la cara atrás** to not flinch; **tener buena cara** to look well; to look good; **tener cara de** + *inf* to look as if + *cond*, e.g., **esta tela tiene cara de romperse pronto** this cloth looks as if it would tear soon; **tener mala cara** to look ill; to look bad; **cara a** facing; **cara a cara** face to face; **cara adelante** facing forward; **cara al público** with an audience; **cara atrás** facing backward; **cara de acelga** (coll.) sallow face; **cara de ajo** (coll.) vinegar face; **cara de aleluya** (coll.) cheerful face; **cara de corcho** (coll.) shamelessness; **cara de cuaresma** dismal countenance; **cara de cuchillo** (coll.) hatchet face; **cara de hereje** (coll.) baboon, fright; **cara de pascua** (coll.) smiling face; **cara de rallo** (coll.) pocked face; **cara de viernes** (coll.) wan face, sorry countenance; **cara de vinagre** (coll.) sour face, vinegar aspect; **cara dura** (coll.) cheeky
**caroca** *f* paintings hung in streets in public celebrations; clownish farce; (coll.) false affection, hypocrisy
**carocha** *f* eggs (*of insect*)
**carochar** *vn* to lay eggs (*said of an insect*)
**Carolina** *f* see **carolino**
**carolingio -gia** *adj & m* Carolingian
**carolino -na** *adj* Caroline; (*cap.*) *f* Caroline; **la Carolina del Norte** North Carolina; **la Carolina del Sur** South Carolina
**caromomia** *f* dry flesh of a mummy (*once used in medicine*)
**Carón** *m* (myth.) Charon
**carona** *f* saddle padding; saddlecloth; part of back where saddle rests
**Caronte** *m* (myth.) Charon
**caroñoso -sa** *adj* full of galls, full of sores (*said of an old horse*)
**caroquero -ra** *adj* fawning, flattering; *mf* fawner, flatterer
**carosis** *f* (path.) deep stupor
**caroteno** *m* (chem.) carotene
**carótida** *f* (anat.) carotid
**carotídeo -a** *adj* carotid
**carotina** *f* var. of **caroteno**
**carozo** *m* corncob; (dial.) core (*e.g., of an apple*)
**carpa** *f* (ichth.) carp; part of a bunch of grapes; (Am.) awning, tent, circus tent; **carpa dorada** goldfish
**carpanel** *adj* see **arco**
**carpanta** *f* (coll.) raging hunger
**Cárpatos** *mpl* Carpathians, Carpathian Mountains
**carpe** *m* (bot.) hornbeam, yoke elm
**carpedal** *m* woods or growth of hornbeams
**carpelar** *adj* carpellary, carpellate
**carpelo** *m* (bot.) carpel

**carpeta** *f* table cover; folder; portfolio; invoice; curtain over tavern door; coating; paving; (Am.) office desk; (Am.) bookkeeping department; (Am.) slab
**carpetazo** *m* blow with a table cover; **dar carpetazo a** to table, to shelve, to set aside, to pigeonhole
**carpetero** *m* filing cabinet
**carpiano -na** *adj* (anat.) carpal
**carpidor** *m* (Am.) weeder (*tool*)
**carpincho** *m* (zool.) capybara (*South American rodent*)
**carpintear** *vn* to carpenter
**carpintería** *f* carpentry, carpentering; carpenter shop; **carpintería de modelos** patternmaking; **carpintería de taller** millwork
**carpinteril** *adj* (pertaining to a) carpenter
**carpintero** *m* carpenter; (orn.) woodpecker; **carpintero de armar** framer; **carpintero de banco** shop carpenter; **carpintero de blanco** joiner; **carpintero de buque** ship carpenter, shipwright; **carpintero de carreta** wheelwright; **carpintero de fino** joiner; **carpintero de navío** ship carpenter, shipwright; **carpintero de obra de afuera** framer; **carpintero de prieto** wheelwright; **carpintero de ribera** ship carpenter, shipwright; **carpintero modelista** patternmaker; **carpintero naval** ship carpenter, shipwright
**carpir** *va* to stun, to knock out; (Am.) to weed
**carpo** *m* (anat.) carpus
**carpobálsamo** *m* (bot.) balm of Gilead (*tree and fruit*)
**carpología** *f* carpology
**carquerol** *m* treadle cord (*of loom*)
**carquesa** *f* carquaise (*glass-annealing furnace*)
**carraco -ca** *adj* (coll.) old, decrepit; *f* (naut.) carrack (*galleon*); piece of junk; tub, hulk (*clumsy old boat*); rattle; ratchet, ratchet brace; **la Carraca** Cádiz navy yard
**carrada** *f* cartful, cartload
**carragaen** *m* (bot.) carrageen
**carral** *m* wine barrel
**carraleja** *f* (ent.) oil beetle
**carralero** *m* cooper
**carranca** *f* var. of **carlanca**
**carranza** *f* iron point (*on dog collar*)
**carraón** *m* spelt
**carrasca** *f* (bot.) kermes oak
**carrascal** *m* growth of kermes oaks; (Am.) stony place
**carrasco** *m* var. of **carrasca**
**carrascoso -sa** *adj* full of kermes oaks
**carraspada** *f* negus (*drink*)
**carraspear** *vn* to be hoarse, to hawk
**carraspeño -ña** *adj* rough, harsh; hoarse
**carraspeo** *m* hoarseness, hawking
**carraspera** *f* (coll.) hoarseness
**carraspique** *m* (bot.) candytuft
**carrasposo -sa** *adj* chronically hoarse; (Am.) rough
**carrasqueño -ña** *adj* kermes-oak; (coll.) rough
**carrasquera** *f* var. of **carrascal**
**carrasquilla** *f* (bot.) germander
**carrejo** *m* hall
**carrera** *f* run; race; race track; stretch, course; career; road; avenue, boulevard; row, line; part (*in hair*); rafter, girder, joist; (mach.) stroke (*of piston*); run (*in stocking*); (mus.) run; (naut.) route, run; **carreras** *fpl* horse racing, turf; **a carrera abierta** at full speed; **a la carrera** running; **dar carrera a** to provide an education for; **de carrera** hastily; without thinking; career (*used as adj*); **no poder hacer carrera con** (coll.) to make no headway with, to be unable to bring to reason; **tomar carrera** to take a running start (*before a jump*); **carrera al trote** trotting race; **carrera a pie** foot race; **carrera armamentista** or **carrera de los armamentos** armament race; **carrera a reclamar** selling race; **carrera ascendente** upstroke; **carrera de admisión** or **aspiración** intake stroke; **carrera de baquetas** (mil. & fig.) gauntlet; **carrera de caballos** horse race; **carrera de compresión** compression stroke; **carrera de consolación** (sport) consolation race; **carrera de encendido** ignition stroke; **carrera de escape** exhaust stroke; **carrera de expansión** expansion stroke; **carrera de galgos** greyhound race; **carrera de Indias** trade with South America (*from Spain*); **carrera de ladrillos** course of brick; **carrera de campanario** (sport) steeplechase; **carrera de maratón** (sport) marathon race; **carrera de obstáculos** obstacle race; steeplechase; **carrera de relevos** (sport) relay race; **carrera de resistencia** (sport) endurance race; **carrera descendente** downstroke; **carrera de vallas** (sport) hurdles, hurdle race; **carrera de ventas** selling race; **carrera espacial** space race; **carrera motriz** power stroke
**carrerilla** *f* (mus.) run of an octave
**carrerista** *mf* race-track fan; bicycle racer; race-track bettor; auto racer; *m* outrider; *f* (slang) streetwalker; *adj* horsy
**carrero** *m* cartwright; driver, teamster; track; (naut.) wake; handcar driver
**carreta** *f* cart
**carretada** *f* cartful, cartload; (coll.) great amount, great number; **a carretadas** (coll.) in abundance, in flocks
**carretaje** *m* cartage, drayage
**carretal** *m* rough ashlar stone
**carrete** *m* spool, bobbin, reel; fishing reel; (elec.) coil; **carrete de encendido** (aut.) ignition coil; **carrete de inducción** (elec.) induction coil; **carrete de película** film spool; **carrete de resistencia** (elec.) resistance coil; **carrete primario** (elec.) primary coil; **carrete secundario** (elec.) secondary coil
**carretear** *va* to cart, to haul; to drive (*a cart*); (aer.) to taxi; *vn* (aer.) to taxi; *vr* to pull hard (*said of oxen or mules*)
**carretel** *m* (naut.) reel, spool; (naut.) log reel; marking line (*of ship carpenter*); (prov.) fishing reel
**carretela** *f* calash
**carretera** *f* see **carretero**
**carretería** *f* carts, wagons; cart or wagon shop; cartwright work, wagon work; carting business
**carreteril** *adj* driver's, teamster's
**carretero -ra** *adj* (pertaining to a) wagon or carriage; *m* cartwright, wheelwright; driver, carter, teamster; charioteer; **jurar como un carretero** (coll.) to swear like a trooper; *f* highway; **carretera biviaria** two-lane highway; **carretera de cuatro vías** four-lane highway; **carretera de peaje** turnpike; **carretera de vía libre** express highway; **carretera matriz** through highway
**carretil** *adj* (pertaining to a) cart
**carretilla** *f* wheelbarrow; truck, baggage truck; gocart (*for learning to walk*); snake, serpent (*kind of firecracker*); pastry tube; **de carretilla** by rote, by heart, mechanically; **carretilla de mano** handcart
**carretillada** *f* wheelbarrow load; baggage-truck load
**carretillero** *m* wheelbarrow man; baggageman (*who pushes a truck*)
**carretón** *m* cart; gocart; portable grindstone (*with treadle*); (rail.) truck; **carretón de lámpara** pulley for raising and lowering lamps in church; **carretón de remolque** trailer
**carretonada** *f* cartload
**carretonero** *m* cart driver, cart pusher; drayman
**carricera** *f* (bot.) plume grass
**carricoche** *m* covered cart; old hack; (dial.) dung cart
**carricuba** *f* street sprinkler
**carriego** *m* fish trap (*made of osier*); basket for bleaching flax
**carril** *m* track, rut; furrow; lane, narrow road; rail; **carril de cremallera** rack rail; **carril de toma** (elec.) third rail
**carrilada** *f* track, rut
**carrilera** *f* track, rut; (Am.) sidetrack
**carrilero** *m* (Am.) railroader; (Am.) thief, bandit
**carrillada** *f* fat in hog's jowls; **carrilladas** *fpl* quaking of jaws
**carrillar** *m* (naut.) hoisting tackle
**carrillera** *f* jaw; chin strap, chin stay; cheekpiece (*of armor*)

**carrillo** *m* cheek; pulley; cart, truck; **comer a dos carrillos** (coll.) to have two sources of income; (coll.) to play both sides, to keep in with both sides
**carrilludo -da** *adj* round-cheeked
**carriola** *f* cariole; trundle bed, truckle bed
**carrizada** *f* (naut.) string of barrels being towed
**carrizal** *m* growth of ditch reed
**carrizo** *m* (bot.) ditch reed; **carrizo de las pampas** (bot.) pampas grass
**carro** *m* cart, wagon; truck; car, auto; railway car; streetcar; chariot; (mach.) carriage (*e.g., of a typewriter*); cartload, wagonload; carload; **el Carro** (astr.) the Dipper; **pare Vd. el carro** (coll.) hold your horses (*restrain yourself*); **tirar del carro** (coll.) to do all the work; **untar el carro** (coll.) to bribe; **carro alegórico** float (*in a parade*); **carro blindado** (mil.) armored car; **carro completo** (rail.) carload lot; **carro correo** (rail.) mail car; **carro cuba** (rail.) tank car; **carro de asalto** (mil.) heavy tank; **carro de carga** (rail.) freight car; **carro de combate** (mil.) combat car, tank; **carro de equipajes** (rail.) baggage car; **carro de guerra** chariot; **carro de hacienda** (Am.) stock car, cattle car; **carro de mudanza** moving van; **carro de plataforma** (rail.) flatcar; **carro de remolque** trailer; **carro de riego** street sprinkler; **carro entero** (rail.) carload lot; **carro frigorífico** (rail.) refrigerator car; **carro fuerte** platform carriage; **carro fúnebre** hearse; **carro ganadero** stock car, cattle car; **Carro Mayor** (astr.) Big Dipper; **Carro Menor** (astr.) Little Dipper; **carro nevera** (rail.) refrigerator car; **carro plano** (rail.) flatcar; **carro romano** chariot; **carro salón** (rail.) chair car; **carro transbordador** (rail.) transfer table, traverser
**carró** *m* (*pl:* **carrós**) (Am.) diamond (*playing card*); **carrós** *mpl* (Am.) diamonds (*suit of playing cards*)
**carrocería** *f* carriage shop; body (*e.g., of automobile*)
**carrocero -ra** *adj* (pertaining to a) carriage; (pertaining to a) body; *m* carriage maker, wheelwright
**carrocín** *m* shay (*light carriage*)
**carrocha** *f* eggs (*of insect*)
**carrochar** *vn* to lay eggs (*said of an insect*)
**carromatero** *m* cart driver
**carromato** *m* covered cart (*drawn by one horse or by two or more in single file*)
**carrón** *m* hod of bricks
**carronada** *f* carronade
**carroña** *f* see **carroño**
**carroñar** *va* to infect (*sheep*) with the scab
**carroño -ña** *adj* carrion (*rotten*); *f* carrion
**carroñoso -sa** *adj* carrion-smelling
**carroza** *f* coach, stately carriage; (naut.) awning; (Am.) hearse; **carroza alegórica** float
**carruaje** *m* carriage, vehicle
**carruajero** *m* driver, carriage driver
**carruco** *m* cart with solid wooden wheels
**carrucha** *f* pulley; reel, spool
**carrujado -da** *adj & m* var. of **encarrujado**
**carrusel** *m* cavalcade; carousel, merry-go-round
**carsaya** *f* kersey
**carta** *f* letter; chart; charter; playing card; map; bill of fare; **a carta cabal** thorough, in every respect; **a cartas vistas** with one's cards on the table; (coll.) with inside information; **a la carta** à la carte; **echar las cartas** to tell or read one's fortune with cards; **jugar a cartas vistas** to put one's cards on the table; (coll.) to act on inside information; **no saber a qué carta quedarse** to be unable to make up one's mind; **no ver carta** (coll.) to have a bad run of cards; **poner las cartas boca arriba** to put one's cards on the table; **tomar cartas en** (coll.) to get into, to take part in; **carta aérea** air-mail letter; **carta blanca** carte blanche; **carta certificada** registered letter; **carta credencial** (dipl.) credentials; **carta de crédito** letter of credit; **carta de fletamento** (naut.) charter party; **carta de marca** letter of marques; **carta de marear** ocean chart; **carta de Mercátor** (geog.) Mercator's chart; **carta de naturaleza** naturalization papers; **carta de pedido** letter ordering merchandise; **carta de presentación** letter of introduction; **carta de vecindad** registration certificate; **carta de venta** bill of sale; **carta general** form letter; **Carta Magna** Magna Charta; **carta meteorológica** weather map; **carta orden de crédito** (com.) letter of credit; **carta partida** (naut.) charter party; **carta por avión** air-mail letter; **carta postal** (Am.) postal card
**cartabón** *m* triangle (*used in drafting*); size stick (*for measuring foot*); gunner's quadrant; gusset plate; angle made by two slopes of a roof
**cartagenero -ra** *adj* (pertaining to) Cartagena; *mf* native or inhabitant of Cartegena
**cartaginense** or **cartaginés -nesa** *adj & mf* Carthaginian
**Cartago** *f* Carthage
**cártama** *f* or **cártamo** *m* (bot.) safflower, bastard saffron
**cartapacio** *m* notebook, memorandum book; dossier; satchel (*for schoolboy's books*); writing book (*with ruled lines for beginners*)
**cartapel** *m* silly document
**cartazo** *m* (coll.) letter or note of censure
**cartear** *vn* to play low cards (*to feel one's way*); *vr* to write to each other, to correspond
**cartel** *m* poster, placard, show bill; lampoon; cartel (*written challenge*); (econ.) cartel, trust; (dipl. & pol.) cartel; (taur.) fame, reputation; (theat.) bill; **dar cartel a** (coll.) to lend prestige to; (coll.) to headline; **se prohíbe fijar carteles** post no bills; **tener cartel** (slang) to make a hit, be the rage (*said of an actor, bullfighter, etc.*); **cartel de teatro** bill
**cartela** *f* (arch.) cartouche (*tablet for ornament or inscription*); bracket, support; tag, label; (arch.) bracket, console, corbel
**cartelero -ra** *adj* striking, catching, appealing; *m* billposter; *f* billboard; amusement page (*of newspaper*)
**cartelista** *mf* cartelist; lampooner; poster designer; billboard painter, sign painter
**cartelón** *m* show bill, poster; chart
**carteo** *m* correspondence, exchange of letters; play, playing (*of cards*)
**cárter** *m* (mach.) housing, case; **cárter de engranajes** (mach.) gear case; **cárter del cigüeñal** or **del motor** (mach.) crankcase
**cartera** *f* portfolio (*portable case for papers; office of minister; list of securities*); letter file, desk pad; pocket flap; (b.b.) tuck; **cartera de bolsillo** billfold, wallet
**cartería** *f* job of letter carrier; sorting room (*in post office*)
**carterista** *m* pickpocket
**cartero** *m* postman, mailman, letter carrier
**cartesianismo** *m* Cartesianism
**cartesiano -na** *adj & mf* Cartesian
**carteta** *f* lansquenet (*card game*)
**cartilagíneo -a** *adj* (ichth.) cartilaginous
**cartilaginoso -sa** *adj* cartilaginous, gristly; (ichth.) cartilaginous
**cartílago** *m* (anat.) cartilage
**cartilla** *f* primer, speller; short treatise; deposit book; identity card (*e.g., of servants*); liturgical calendar; **leer la cartilla a** (coll.) to lecture, to call down; **no estar en la cartilla** (coll.) to be unusual or extraordinary; **no saber la cartilla** (coll.) to be completely ignorant of the subject; **cartilla de abastecimiento** or **racionamiento** ration book
**cartillero -ra** *adj* (coll.) hackneyed; (coll.) ham
**cartivana** *f* (b.b.) hinge
**cartografía** *f* cartography
**cartográfico -ca** *adj* cartographic
**cartógrafo -fa** *mf* cartographer
**cartolas** *fpl* var. of **artolas**
**cartomancía** *f* fortunetelling with cards, cartomancy
**cartómetro** *m* chartometer
**cartón** *m* cardboard, pasteboard; carton, cardboard box; cartoon (*model for fresco, tapestry, etc.*); **cartón alquitranado** tar paper; **cartón de asbesto** asbestus board; **cartón de paja** strawboard; **cartón de yeso** plaster-

board, wallboard; **cartón embetunado** tar paper; **cartón piedra** papier-mâché; **cartón tabla** wallboard
**cartonajes** *mpl* cardboard products, cardboard boxes
**cartoné; en cartoné** (b.b.) in boards, bound in boards
**cartonería** *f* cardboard factory or shop; cardboard business
**cartonero -ra** *adj* (pertaining to) cardboard; *mf* cardboard maker or dealer
**cartuchera** *f* cartridge box; cartridge belt
**cartucho** *m* cartridge; roll of coins; paper cone or bag; (arch.) cartouche (*tablet for ornament or inscription*); **cartucho en blanco** blank cartridge
**cartuja** & **Cartuja** *f* see **cartujo**
**cartujano -na** *adj & m* Carthusian
**cartujo -ja** *adj* Carthusian; *m* Carthusian, Carthusian monk; (coll.) silent fellow, recluse; *f* Carthusian monastery, charterhouse; (*cap.*) *f* Carthusian order
**cartulario** *m* chartulary; archivist
**cartulina** *f* light or fine cardboard
**cartusana** *f* fancy braid
**carúncula** *f* (anat., bot. & zool.) caruncle; **carúncula lagrimal** (anat.) lachrymal caruncle
**carunculado -da** *adj* carunculate
**caruncular** *adj* caruncular
**carvajal** *m* woods of oak trees
**carvajo** or **carvallo** *m* (bot.) oak tree
**carvi** *m* caraway, caraway seeds
**casa** *f* house; home; household; apartment; firm; square (*e.g., of checkerboard*); **¡convida la casa!** the drinks are on the house!; **echar la casa por la ventana** (coll.) to go to a lot of expense (*to entertain or in other ways*); **empezar la casa por el tejado** to put the cart before the horse; **en casa** home, at home; **en casa de** at the home, office, shop, etc. of; **guardar la casa** to be confined to the house; **hacer casa** to get rich; **ir a buscar casa** to go house hunting; **no tener casa ni hogar** to have neither house nor home; **poner casa** to set up housekeeping; **por casa** at the house; **Casa Blanca** White House; **casa capitular** chapter house; **casa central** home office; **casa consistorial** town hall, city hall; **casa cuna** foundling home; **casa de asistencia** (Am.) boarding house; **casa de azotea** penthouse; **casa de banca** banking house; **casa de baños** bathhouse; **casa de beneficencia** settlement, settlement house; **casa de bombas** pump house; **casa de camas** bawdyhouse; **casa de campo** country house; **casa de caridad** poorhouse; **casa de citas** house of assignation; **casa de comercio** business house; **casa de comida** eating house; **casa de corrección** reform school, house of correction; **casa de correos** post office; **casa de departamentos** (Am.) apartment house; **casa de Dios** God's house, house of God (*church*); **casa de empeños** pawnshop; **casa de expósitos** foundling home or hospital; **casa de fieras** menagerie; **casa de huéspedes** boarding house; **casa de juego** gambling house; **casa de locos** madhouse; (fig.) madhouse; **casa de maternidad** maternity hospital; **casa de medianería** house between two others (*in a row*); **casa de modas** dress shop; **casa de moneda** mint; **casa de montería** hunting lodge; **casa de moradores** tenement house; **casa de niñas** disorderly house; **casa de oración** house of prayer; **casa de orates** insane asylum; **casa de placer** country house; **casa de posada** boarding house; **casa de postas** posthouse; **casa de préstamos** pawnshop; **casa de pupilos** boarding house; **casa de salud** private hospital; **casa de sanidad** health office; **casa de socorro** first-aid station, emergency hospital; **casa de tía** (coll.) jail; (hum.) tavern; **casa de vacas** dairy; **casa de vecindad** or **de vecinos** apartment house, tenement house; **casa editorial** publishing house; **casa grande** mansion; (hum.) big house (*jail*); **casa matriz** main office; **casa medianera** house between two others (*in a row*); **casa mortuoria** house of mourning (*where a death has occurred*); **casa pública** brothel; **casa real** royal palace; royal family; **Casa Rosada** Pink House (*official residence of chief executive of Argentina*); **casas baratas** low-cost housing; **casa solar** or **solariega** manor house, ancestral mansion
**casabe** *m* cassava flour; cassava bread; (ichth.) amberfish
**casaca** *f* dress coat, musketeer's coat; (coll.) wedding, marriage; **cambiar de casaca** or **volver casaca** or **la casaca** (coll.) to become a turncoat
**casación** *f* (law) cassation, annulment
**casacón** *m* greatcoat
**casadero -ra** *adj* marriageable
**casado -da** *adj* married; *mf* married person, spouse; *m* (print.) imposition
**casal** *m* country place; (Am.) pair (*male and female*)
**casalicio** *m* house, building, edifice
**casamata** *f* (fort. & naut.) casemate
**casamentero -ra** *adj* matchmaking; *mf* matchmaker
**casamiento** *m* marriage; wedding
**Casandra** *f* (myth. & fig.) Cassandra
**casapuerta** *f* vestibule, entrance
**casaquilla** *f* jacket
**casar** *m* hamlet; *va* to marry; to marry off (*a daughter*); to match, to harmonize; (law) to abrogate, annul, break; *vn* to marry, get married; to match, to harmonize; **casar con** to get married to; *vr* to marry, get married; **casarse con** to get married to; **casarse en segundas nupcias** to marry the second time; **no casarse con nadie** (coll.) to get tied up with nobody
**casarón** *m* large tumble-down house
**casatienda** *f* store and home in same building
**casca** *f* tanning bark; grape skins; marchpane
**cascabel** *m* tinkle bell, sleigh bell; rattlebrain; cascabel (*of a cannon*); **de cascabel gordo** (coll.) cheap, melodramatic; **ponerle cascabel al gato** (coll.) to bell the cat
**cascabelada** *f* noisy village celebration; (mus.) chimes (*of organ*); (coll.) piece of nonsense, indiscretion
**cascabelear** *va* (coll.) to cajole, to beguile; *vn* to jingle; (coll.) to behave in an inconsiderate manner
**cascabeleo** *m* jingle, jingling
**cascabelero -ra** *adj* (coll.) thoughtless, featherbrained; *mf* featherbrain; *m* baby's rattle
**cascabelillo** *m* little sweet plum
**cascabelito** *m* (bot.) locoweed
**cascabillo** *m* tinkle bell; glume, chaff, husk; cup of acorn
**cascaciruelas** *mf* (*pl:* **-las**) (coll.) contemptible good-for-nothing; **hacer lo que cascaciruelas** (coll.) to make a lot of fuss for nothing
**cascado -da** *adj* broken, infirm; weak, hollow (*voice*); *f* cascade, waterfall
**cascadura** *f* breaking, splitting
**cascajal** *m* or **cascajar** *m* place full of gravel, gravel pit; dump for grape skins
**cascajera** *f* place full of gravel, gravel pit
**cascajero** *m* (Am.) gravel pit; (Am.) gold mine not completely exhausted
**cascajo** *m* gravel, crushed stone; (coll.) broken crockery, rubbish, junk; **estar hecho un cascajo** (coll.) to be old and worn-out, to be a wreck
**cascajoso -sa** *adj* gravelly
**cascamajar** *va* to crush, to break up
**cascamiento** *m* breaking, splitting
**cascanueces** *m* (*pl:* **-ces**) nutcracker; (orn.) nutcracker
**cascapiñones** *m* (*pl:* **-nes**) pine-nut sheller; nutcracker for pine nuts; (orn.) hawfinch
**cascar** §86 *va* to crack, to split; (coll.) to break (*someone's health*); (coll.) to beat, to hit; *vn* to chatter; *vr* to crack, to split; (coll.) to break (*said of health, of the voice, etc.*)
**cáscara** *f* rind, peel, hull, shell; bark, crust; **¡cáscaras!** *interj* (coll.) upon my word!; **dar cáscaras de novillo a** (Am.) to whip, to beat; **ser de la cáscara amarga** (coll.) to be wild or flighty; (Am.) to be determined or resolute; **cáscara amarga** (pharm.) cascara

amarga; **cáscara rueda** (Am.) ring-around-a-rosy; **cáscara sagrada** (bot.) cascara or cascara buckthorn; (pharm.) cascara or cascara sagrada
**cascarela** *f* lansquenet (*card game*)
**cascarilla** *f* (pharm.) Peruvian bark, cinchona bark; (pharm.) cascarilla, sweetwood bark; foil (*metal*); powdered eggshell (*cosmetic*)
**cascarillero -ra** *mf* gatherer of cinchona, dealer in cinchona; *m* (bot.) cinchona
**cascarillo** *m* (bot.) cinchona
**cascarón** *m* eggshell; broken eggshell (*from which chick has emerged*); (arch.) calotte (*half cupola*); (Am.) cascaron (*filled with confetti*); **cascarón de nuez** (coll.) cockleshell (*light boat*)
**cascarrabias** *mf* (*pl:* **-bias**) (coll.) grouch, crab
**cascarria** *f* dried splashes of mud on lower part of clothing; (Am.) sheep dung stuck to wool
**cascarrón -rrona** *adj* (coll.) rough, harsh, gruff
**cascarudo -da** *adj* thick-shelled
**cascaruleta** *f* (coll.) chattering of teeth caused by hitting oneself on the chin
**casco** *m* skull; hoof; potsherd, broken piece; quarter (*of a fruit*); coat, shell (*of an onion*); crown (*of hat*); hulk (*of old ship*); hull (*of ship*); head (*of cask or barrel*); cask, vat, barrel; casque, headpiece; helmet (*of armor; of soldier, fireman, diver, etc.*); headset, headpiece; shell, container; bottle, liquid container; (dial. & Am.) slice (*e.g., of orange*); (mach.) shell, casing; tree (*of saddle*); **romperse los cascos** (coll.) to rack one's brains; **tener los cascos vacíos** (coll.) to be empty-headed; **casco de población** or **casco urbano** city limits
**cascote** *m* piece of rubble; rubbish, debris
**cascudo -da** *adj* large-hoofed
**caseación** *f* curdling
**caseasa** *f* (biochem.) casease
**caseico -ca** *adj* caseic
**caseificación** *f* (path.) caseation
**caseificar** §86 *va* to change into casein; to separate casein from (*milk*)
**caseína** *f* (biochem.) casein
**caseinógeno** *m* (biochem.) caseinogen
**cáseo -a** *adj* caseous; *m* curd
**caseoso -sa** *adj* caseous
**casera** *f* see **casero**
**casería** *f* country place, country house with outbuildings; housekeeping; (Am.) customers
**caserío** *m* country house; group of houses, hamlet
**caserna** *f* (fort.) armored barracks
**casero -ra** *adj* homemade; house (*e.g., dress*); home (*e.g., gathering*); home-loving; (sport) partial to home team; *mf* caretaker, janitor; renter; (Am.) huckster; *m* landlord; *f* landlady; housekeeper
**caserón** *m* var. of **casarón**
**caseta** *f* small house; bathhouse; stall (*at a fair*); booth
**casetón** *m* (arch.) coffer, caisson
**casi** *adv* almost, nearly; **casi casi** or **casi que** very nearly
**casia** *f* (bot.) cassia, stinking weed, ringworm bush
**casicontrato** *m* (law) quasi contract
**casilla** *f* hut, shack; cabin, booth; cab (*of locomotive or truck*); column or square (*on sheet of paper*); pigeonhole; square (*of checkerboard*); point (*of backgammon board*); ticket office; (aer.) nacelle, cockpit; (Am.) water closet; (Am.) bird trap; (Am.) post-office box; (dial.) lockup, jail; **sacar de sus casillas** (coll.) to jolt (*a person*) out of his old habits; (coll.) to drive crazy; **salir de sus casillas** (coll.) to forget oneself, to fly off the handle, to go wild; **casilla de correos** (Am.) post-office box
**casillero -ra** *mf* (rail.) crossing guard; *m* set of pigeonholes, filing cabinet; (sport) scoreboard
**casimba** *f* (Am.) well, spring
**casimir** *m* cashmere; cassimere
**casino** *m* casino; club; political club; clubhouse; recreation hall
**Casio** *m* Cassius
**Casiopea** *f* (myth. & astr.) Cassiopeia
**casis** *f* (bot.) cassis (*plant and liquor*); (zool.) queen conch
**casiterita** *f* (chem.) cassiterite
**casitienda** *f* var. of **casatienda**
**casmodia** *f* (path.) excessive yawning
**caso** *m* case; chance; event, happening; (gram. & med.) case; **dado caso que** supposing that; **de caso pensado** deliberately, on purpose; **en caso de** in case of, in the event of; **en el caso de que** in case; **en tal caso** in such a case; **en todo caso** in any case, at all events; **hacer al caso** (coll.) to be to the purpose; to be the point at issue; **hacer caso a** to mind, to notice; **hacer caso de** (coll.) to pay attention to, to take into account; **hacer caso omiso de** to pass over in silence, to not mention; **no venir al caso** to be beside the point; **poner por caso** to take as an example; **vamos al caso** (coll.) let's get to the point; **venir al caso** to be opportune, to be just the thing; **verse en el caso de** + *inf* to find oneself obliged to + *inf;* **caso de conformidad** in case you agree; **caso fortuito** mischance; act of God; **caso que** in case
**casón** *m* large house
**casorio** *m* (coll.) hasty marriage, unwise marriage
**caspa** *f* dandruff; scurf
**caspera** *f* fine comb for dandruff
**caspiano -na** *adj & mf* Caspian
**caspicias** *fpl* (coll.) offal, leavings
**caspio -pia** *adj & mf* Caspian
**caspiroleta** *f* (Am.) eggnog
**cáspita** *interj* well, well!, upon my word!
**casposo -sa** *adj* full of dandruff
**casquería** *f* tripe shop
**casquero** *m* tripe dealer
**casquetazo** *m* blow with the head
**casquete** *m* skullcap, calotte; cap; helmet; wig; canopy (*of parachute*); **casquete esférico** (geom.) zone of one base; **casquete polar** polar cap (*of Mars*); polar region (*of earth*)
**casquiacopado -da** *adj* cup-hoofed
**casquiblando -da** *adj* soft-hoofed
**casquiderramado -da** *adj* wide-hoofed
**casquijo** *m* gravel, ballast
**casquilucio -cia** *adj* (coll.) scatterbrained
**casquilla** *f* queen cell
**casquillo** *m* tip, cap, butt; ferrule; socket; sleeve, bushing; metal arrowhead; (Am.) horseshoe; cartridge case; metal part of pasteboard cartridge; **casquillos** *mpl* metal trimmings
**casquimuleño -ña** *adj* narrow-hoofed (*like mules*)
**casquivano -na** *adj* (coll.) scatterbrained
**casta** *f* see **casto**
**Castálidas** *fpl* (myth.) Castalides
**castaña** *f* see **castaño**
**castañar** *m*, **castañal** *m* or **castañeda** *f* woods of chestnut trees, chestnut grove
**castañero -ra** *mf* chestnut vendor; *m* (orn.) grebe
**castañeta** *f* castanet; snapping of the fingers; click with the tongue
**castañetada** *f* or **castañetazo** *m* click of castanets; cracking of roasting chestnut; cracking of joints
**castañeteado** *m* clicking of castanets
**castañetear** *va* to snap or to click (*the fingers*); to click off (*e.g., a seguidilla*) with the castanets; *vn* to click; to chatter (*said of teeth*); to crack (*said of knee joints*)
**castañeteo** *m* clicking (*of fingers or castanets*); chattering (*of teeth*)
**castaño -ña** *adj* chestnut, chestnut-colored ‖ *m* (bot.) chestnut, Spanish chestnut (*tree and wood*); chestnut (*color*); **pasar de castaño obscuro** (coll.) to be too much, to be too much trouble; **castaño de Indias** (bot.) horse chestnut ‖ *f* chestnut; demijohn; knot of hair, chignon; **sacarle a uno las castañas del fuego** to pull someone's chestnuts out of the fire; **castaña de Indias** horse chestnut; **castaña de Pará** Brazil nut
**castañola** *f* (ichth.) pomfret
**castañuelo -la** *adj* chestnut, chestnut-colored; *f* castanet; lewis (*used to hoist stones*); (bot.) plant of the sedge family (*Bulbocastanum in-*

*crassatanum*); **estar como unas castañuelas** (coll.) to be bubbling over with joy
**castellán** *m* castellan
**castellana** *f* see **castellano**
**castellanismo** *m* Castilianism
**castellanización** *f* Hispanicization
**castellanizar** §76 *va* to make (*a foreign word*) Spanish, to Hispanicize
**castellano -na** *adj & mf* Castilian; *m* Castilian, Spanish (*language*); castellan; lord of the castle; *f* chatelaine; assonanced octosyllabic verse of four lines
**castellar** *m* (bot.) St.-John's-wort
**casticidad** *f* purity, correctness (*in language*)
**casticismo** *m* purism
**casticista** *mf* purist
**castidad** *f* chastity, purity
**castigable** *adj* punishable
**castigación** *f* var. of **castigo**
**castigadera** *f* strap to tie clapper of wether's bell
**castigador -dora** *mf* punisher, castigator; *m* (coll.) seducer, Don Juan
**castigar** §59 *va* to punish, chastise; to castigate; to mortify (*the flesh*); to correct (*style, writing*); to cut down (*expenses*); (slang) to captivate, to break the heart of
**castigo** *m* punishment, chastisement; castigation; correction
**Castilla** *f* Castile; **¡ancha Castilla!** free and easy!; **Castilla la Nueva** New Castile; **Castilla la Vieja** Old Castile
**castillaje** *m* castle toll (*for passing through territory of castle*)
**castillejo** *m* small castle; gocart; scaffolding, trestlework
**castillería** *f* castle toll; castle-repair tax
**castillete** *m* small castle; **castillete de mina** gallows, headframe
**castillo** *m* castle; howdah; queen cell; **castillo en el aire** castle in Spain, castle in the air; **castillo de naipes** house of cards; **castillo de proa** (naut.) forecastle
**castilluelo** *m* castlet
**castina** *f* (metal.) limestone flux
**castizo -za** *adj* pure-blooded; pure, correct, chaste (*language*); real, genuine; prolific
**casto -ta** *adj* chaste, pure; *f* caste; race, breed; kind, quality; high breeding
**castor** *m* (zool.) beaver; beaver (*woolen cloth*)
**Cástor** *m* (myth., astr. & naut.) Castor; **Cástor y Pólux** (myth., astr. & naut.) Castor and Pollux
**castorcillo** *m* beaver cloth
**castoreño** *m* beaver (*hat*)
**castóreo** *m* castor, castoreum (*oily substance*)
**castorina** *f* beaver cloth; (chem.) castorin
**castra** *f* pruning; pruning season
**castración** *f* castration; pruning; extraction of honeycombs
**castradera** *f* honey extractor
**castrador** *m* castrator, sow-gelder
**castradura** *f* castration; scar left from castration
**castrametación** *f* (mil.) castrametation
**castrapuercas** *m* (*pl:* **-cas**) gelder's whistle
**castrar** *va* to castrate; to prune, cut back (*a plant*); to extract combs from (*hive*); to weaken
**castrazón** *f* extraction of honeycombs; season for extracting honeycombs
**castrense** *adj* (pertaining to the) army, military
**castro** *m* hopscotch; extraction of honeycombs; (dial.) headland
**castrón** *m* castrated goat
**casual** *adj* accidental, chance, casual; (gram.) case; **casuales** *mpl* priest's fee (*for baptism, marriage, funeral, etc.*)
**casualidad** *f* chance, accident; **por casualidad** by chance
**casuarina** *f* (bot.) beefwood, she-oak, swamp oak
**casuario** *m* (orn.) cassowary
**casuca** *f*, **casucha** *f* or **casucho** *m* shack, shanty
**casuísta** *adj* casuistic; *mf* casuist
**casuístico -ca** *adj* casuistic or casuistical; *f* casuistry; (med.) clinical report
**casulla** *f* chasuble
**casullero** *m* church-vestment tailor
**cata** *f* tasting, sampling; taste, sample; test pit; test boring
**catabolismo** *m* (biol.) catabolism
**catacaldos** *m* (*pl:* **-dos**) (coll.) rolling stone; (coll.) meddler, intruder
**cataclísmico -ca** *adj* cataclysmic
**cataclismo** *m* cataclysm
**catacresis** *f* (*pl:* **-sis**) (rhet.) catachresis
**catacumba** *f* catacomb
**catadióptrico -ca** *adj* (phys.) catadioptric
**catador** *m* taster, sampler
**catadura** *f* tasting, sampling; face, countenance
**catafalco** *m* catafalque
**cataforesis** *f* (med. & chem.) cataphoresis
**catalán -lana** *adj* Catalan; Catalonian; *mf* Catalan; *m* Catalan (*language*)
**catalanidad** *f* Catalan spirit or nature
**catalanismo** *m* Catalonian autonomy movement or doctrine; Catalanism (*word or expression*)
**catalanista** *mf* partisan of Catalonian autonomy; Catalanist (*one versed in Catalan*)
**catalasa** *f* (chem.) catalase
**cataléctico -ca** or **catalecto -ta** *adj* catalectic
**catalejo** *m* spyglass
**catalepsia** *f* (path.) catalepsis or catalepsy
**cataléptico -ca** *adj & mf* cataleptic
**catalicón** *m* var. of **diacatolicón**
**Catalina** *f* Catherine
**catalineta** *f* (ichth.) catalufa
**catálisis** *f* (chem.) catalysis
**catalítico -ca** *adj* catalytic
**catalizador** *m* (chem.) catalyst, catalyzer, catalytic agent
**catalogación** *f* cataloguing
**catalogador -dora** *adj* cataloguing
**catalogar** §59 *va* to catalogue
**catálogo** *m* catalogue
**catalpa** *f* (bot.) catalpa
**catalufa** *f* variegated carpet material; double taffeta; (ichth.) catalufa
**Cataluña** *f* Catalonia
**catamarán** *m* (naut.) catamaran
**catán** *m* catan, oriental cutlass
**cataplasma** *f* poultice; **cataplasma de mostaza** mustard plaster; *mf* (coll.) nuisance, pest, bore; (coll.) physical wreck (*person*)
**cataplum** *interj* bang!, boom!
**catapulta** *f* catapult; (aer.) catapult
**catapultar** *va* to catapult
**catar** *va* to taste, to sample; to look at, to examine, to check; to pass on; to look out for; to respect, to esteem; to extract combs from (*hive*)
**cataraña** *f* (orn.) sheldrake
**catarata** *f* cataract, waterfall; (path.) cataract; **abrirse las cataratas del cielo** to pour, to rain hard; **tener cataratas** (coll.) to be blind (*e.g., with ignorance*)
**catarina** *f* (Am.) pulque cup; (bot.) Mexican fire plant
**catarral** *adj* catarrhal
**catarro** *m* (path.) catarrh; head cold
**catarroso -sa** *adj* catarrhal; rheumy
**catarsis** *f* (aesthetics, med. & psychoanal.) catharsis
**catártico -ca** *adj* cathartic
**catasalsas** *mf* (*pl:* **-sas**) (coll.) var. of **catacaldos**
**catastral** *adj* cadastral
**catastro** *m* cadastre
**catástrofe** *f* catastrophe; (theat. & geol.) catastrophe
**catastrófico -ca** *adj* catastrophic
**cataviento** *m* (naut.) dogvane
**catavino** *m* cup for tasting wine; winetaster (*pipette*)
**catavinos** *m* (*pl:* **-nos**) winetaster (*person*); (coll.) rounder (*from one tavern to another*)
**Catay** *m* Cathay
**cateador** *m* prospecting hammer; (Am.) prospector
**catear** *va* to search for; to sample; (coll.) to flunk; (Am.) to explore, prospect for; (Am.) to break into, to search (*a house*)

**catecismo** *m* catechism
**catecú** *m* (*pl:* **-cúes**) catechu
**catecumenado** *m* catechumenate
**catecúmeno -na** *mf* (eccl. & fig.) catechumen
**cátedra** *f* chair, professorship; seat of the professor; class; subject; (eccl.) cathedra; **explicar una cátedra de** to hold a professorship of; **poner** or **sentar cátedra** to hold forth; **cátedra del Espíritu Santo** pulpit; **cátedra de San Pedro** Chair of Saint Peter (*papal see; actual chair*)
**catedral** *adj & f* cathedral
**catedralicio -cia** *adj* (pertaining to a) cathedral
**catedralidad** *f* status of a cathedral
**catedrática** *f* woman professor; professor's wife
**catedrático** *m* university professor; (eccl.) cathedraticum
**categoría** *f* category; class, kind; quality, condition; status, standing; **de categoría** of importance, prominent
**categórico -ca** *adj* categorical
**catenario -ria** *adj* catenary; *f* (math.) catenary
**catenular** *adj* catenulate
**cateo** *m* (Am.) sampling; (Am.) prospecting
**catequesis** *f* or **catequismo** *m* religious instruction, catechizing; teaching by questions and answers
**catequista** *mf* catechist
**catequístico -ca** *adj* catechistic (*pertaining to a catechism*); catechetical (*presented in the form of questions and answers*)
**catequizador -dora** *mf* forceful arguer
**catequizante** *adj* catechizing
**catequizar §76** *va* to catechize; to bring around, win over
**caterva** *f* throng, crowd, mob
**catéter** *m* (surg.) catheter
**cateterismo** *m* or **cateterización** *f* (surg.) catheterization
**cateterizar §76** *va* (surg.) catheterize
**cateto -ta** *mf* rustic, villager; *m* (geom.) leg (*of a right-angled triangle*)
**catetómetro** *m* (phys.) cathetometer
**catilinaria** *f* oration of Cicero against Catiline; vehement denunciation
**catín** *m* (metal.) copper crucible for forming rosettes
**catión** *m* (elec.) cation
**catite** *m* loaf of the finest sugar; light slap
**cato** *m* catechu
**catódico -ca** *adj* cathode, cathodic
**cátodo** *m* (elec.) cathode
**catolicidad** *f* catholicity; Catholicity, Catholicism
**catolicísimo -ma** *adj super* Most Catholic
**catolicismo** *m* Catholicism; **catolicismo romano** Roman Catholicism
**católico -ca** *adj* catholic; Catholic; **no estar muy católico** (coll.) to be under the weather; *mf* Catholic; **católico romano** Roman Catholic
**catolizar §76** *va & vr* to catholicize
**Catón** *m* Cato; (*l.c.*) *m* reader (*for children*); severe critic
**catoniano -na** *adj* Catonian
**catóptrico -ca** *adj* catoptric; *f* (opt.) catoptrics
**catorce** *adj* fourteen; **las catorce** two P.M.; *m* fourteen; fourteenth (*in dates*)
**catorceavo -va** *adj & m* var. of **catorzavo**
**catorceno -na** *adj* fourteenth
**catorzavo -va** *adj & m* fourteenth
**catre** *m* cot; **catre de tijera** folding cot
**catrecillo** *m* campstool, folding seat
**catricofre** *m* folding bed
**catrín -trina** *adj* (Am.) swell, sporty
**Catulo** *m* Catullus
**caucáseo -a** or **caucasiano -na** *adj & mf* Caucasian (*of the Caucasus*)
**caucásico -ca** *adj & mf* Caucasian (*white*)
**Cáucaso** *m* Caucasus
**cauce** *m* river bed; channel, trench; channel, passage; **cauce de salida** tailrace
**caución** *f* caution, precaution; (law) pledge, security, bond, bail
**caucionar** *va* to prevent (*harm or damage*); (law) to give security or bail for
**cauchal** *m* rubber plantation
**cauchero -ra** *adj* rubber; *m* rubber gatherer; rubber worker; *f* (bot.) rubber plant
**caucho** *m* rubber; (bot.) rubber plant; rubber raincoat; **caucho duro** or **endurecido** hard rubber; **caucho esponjoso** foam rubber; **caucho regenerado** reclaimed rubber; **caucho sintético** synthetic rubber; **caucho vulcanizado** vulcanized rubber
**cauchotar** *va* to rubberize, to cover with rubber
**cauda** *f* tail or train of bishop's cope
**caudal** *adj* of great volume (*e.g., river*); (zool.) caudal; *m* volume (*of water*); abundance; wealth; **caudal relicto** (law) estate
**caudaloso -sa** *adj* of great volume (*said of body or source of water*); abundant, wealthy
**caudatario** *m* priest who holds the train of bishop's cope
**caudato -ta** *adj* caudate
**caudatrémula** *f* (orn.) wagtail
**caudillaje** *m* leadership; (Am.) bossism
**caudillo** *m* chief, leader; military leader, chieftain, caudillo, head of the state
**caudimano** *adj* (zool.) having a prehensile tail (*like a beaver*)
**caudón** *m* (orn.) shrike
**caulescente** *adj* (bot.) caulescent
**caulícolo** *m* var. of **caulículo**
**caulícula** *f* (bot.) caulicle
**caulículo** *m* (arch.) cauliculus
**cauri** *m* cowrie (*shell used as money in parts of Africa*)
**cauro** *m* northwest wind
**causa** *f* cause; (law) cause, suit; (law) trial; (Am.) light lunch; (Am.) potato salad; **a** or **por causa de** on account of, because of; **hacer causa común con** to make common cause with
**causador -dora** *adj* causing; *mf* cause (*person*)
**causahabiente** *m* (law) assign
**causal** *adj* causal
**causalidad** *f* causality
**causante** *mf* cause (*person*); (law) principal, constituent
**causar** *va* to cause; (law) to sue
**causativo -va** *adj* causative
**causear** *va* (Am.) to defeat, overcome; *vn* (Am.) to have a bite, have a snack
**causeo** *m* (Am.) bite, snack
**causídico -ca** *adj* (law) causidical; *m* (law) advocate
**causón** *m* (path.) short intense fever
**cáustica** *f* see **cáustico**
**causticar §86** *va* to make caustic
**causticidad** *f* causticity; (fig.) causticity
**cáustico -ca** *adj* (chem., math., opt. & fig.) caustic; *m* (chem.) caustic; **cáustico lunar** lunar caustic; *f* (math. & opt.) caustic
**cautela** *f* caution; craft, cunning
**cautelar** *va* to prevent; *vr* to be on one's guard; **cautelarse de** to guard against
**cauteloso -sa** *adj* cautious, heedful, wary; crafty, cunning
**cauterio** *m* cautery; eradication (*of an evil*)
**cauterización** *f* cauterization
**cauterizar §76** *va* to cauterize; to eradicate (*an evil*); to brand
**cautín** *m* soldering iron
**cautivar** *va* to take prisoner; to attract, to win over; to charm, to captivate
**cautiverio** *m* or **cautividad** *f* captivity
**cautivo -va** *adj & mf* captive
**cauto -ta** *adj* cautious
**cava** *f* digging, cultivation (*of vines*); royal wine cellar; (fort.) moat; (anat.) vena cava
**cavacote** *m* mound made with a hoe and used as a marker
**cavadizo -za** *adj* soft, loose (*earth, sand*)
**cavador** *m* digger
**cavadura** *f* digging
**cavalillo** *m* irrigating ditch between two properties
**cavar** *va* to dig (*with hoe, etc.*); *vn* to go deep (*said, e.g., of a wound*); to paw; **cavar en** to go into thoroughly, to study deeply
**cavatina** *f* (mus.) cavatina; (dent.) cavity varnish
**cavazón** *f* digging
**caverna** *f* cavern

**cavernícola** *adj* cave-dwelling (*man or animal*); (coll.) reactionary; *mf* cave dweller; (coll.) political reactionary
**cavernosidad** *f* cave, cavern; hollowness; hollow sound
**cavernoso -sa** *adj* cavernous
**caveto** *m* (arch.) cavetto
**cavia** *f* trench around base of plant or tree to hold irrigation water; *m* (zool.) cavy
**cavial** *m* or **caviar** *m* caviar
**cavicornio -nia** *adj* (zool.) cavicorn
**cavidad** *f* cavity
**cavilación** *f* cavil, caviling; suspicion, mistrust; worry
**cavilar** *va* to cavil, to cavil at; *vn* to cavil; to worry, to fret
**cavilosidad** *f* suspicion, mistrust
**caviloso -sa** *adj* suspicious, mistrustful
**cavitación** *f* (mach. & path.) cavitation
**cayada** *f* or **cayado** *m* sheephook, shepherd's hook; crozier (*of bishop*); walking staff
**Cayena** *f* Cayenne
**cayente** *adj* falling
**cayo** *m* cay, key; **Cayo Hueso** Key West; **Cayos de la Florida** Florida Keys
**cayote** *m* var. of **chayote**
**cayuco** *m* (Am.) dugout canoe
**caz** *m* (*pl:* **caces**) millrace, flume; **caz de descarga** tailrace; **caz de traída** headrace
**caza** *f* chase, hunt, hunting; game; (aer.) pursuit; **a caza de** (coll.) in search of, on the hunt for; **andar a caza de** (coll.) to go hunting for; **dar caza** to give chase; **dar caza a** to go hunting for; to try to ferret out; to be on the lookout for; **ir de caza** to go hunting; **levantar la caza** (coll.) to try to attract attention; **llevar de caza** to take (*someone*) hunting; **caza al hombre** manhunt; **caza de grillos** fool's errand, wild-goose chase; **caza de pelo** fur, ground game; **caza de pluma** winged game; **caza mayor** big game; **caza menor** small game; *m* (aer.) pursuit plane; **caza de escolta** (aer.) escort fighter; **caza de reacción** or **caza reactor** (aer.) jet fighter
**cazabe** *m* cassava flour; cassava bread
**cazabombardero** *m* (aer.) fighter bomber
**cazaclavos** *m* (*pl:* **-vos**) nail puller
**cazadero** *m* hunting ground
**cazador -dora** *adj* hunting; chasing; *m* hunter; chaser; (mil.) chasseur; **cazador de alforja** trapper; **cazador de autógrafos** autograph seeker; **cazador de cabezas** head-hunter; **cazador furtivo** poacher; *f* huntress; jacket, hunting jacket
**cazamoscas** *m* (*pl:* **-cas**) (orn.) flycatcher
**cazanoticias** *m* (*pl:* **-cias**) newshawk
**cazaperros** *m* (*pl:* **-rros**) dogcatcher
**cazar** §76 *va* to chase; to hunt; to catch; (coll.) to wangle (*to get by scheming*); (coll.) to catch up (*in a mistake*); (coll.) to catch (*a mistake*); to take in (*to win over by trickery*); (naut.) to haul (*the sheets*) taut; **cazar vivo** to catch alive; *vn* to hunt; **cazar largo** (coll.) to be on one's toes, be alert
**cazarratas** *m* (*pl:* **-tas**) ratcatcher
**cazarreactor** *m* (aer.) jet fighter
**cazasubmarinos** *m* (*pl:* **-nos**) subchaser, submarine chaser
**cazata** *f* var. of **cacería**
**cazatorpedero** *m* (nav.) torpedo-boat destroyer
**cazcalear** *vn* (coll.) to buzz about
**cazcarria** *f* dried splashes of mud on lower part of clothing
**cazcarriento -ta** *adj* (coll.) splashed with mud
**cazcorvo -va** *adj* knock-kneed (*said of horses*)
**cazo** *m* dipper, ladle; glue pot; back of knife
**cazolero** *adj masc & m* var. of **cominero**
**cazoleta** *f* pan (*of musket lock*); bowl (*of tobacco pipe*); hand guard (*of sword*); boss (*of shield*); (mach.) pan, housing
**cazoletero** *adj masc & m* var. of **cominero**
**cazolón** *m* large earthen casserole
**cazón** *m* (ichth.) dogfish, shark; hunting dog; brown sugar
**cazonal** *m* tackle for shark fishing; (coll.) mess, entanglement
**cazonete** *m* (naut.) toggle
**cazudo -da** *adj* thick-backed (*said of a knife*)
**cazuela** *f* earthen casserole; minced meat and vegetables cooked in a casserole; (Am.) chicken stew; (theat.) upper gallery; (theat.) gallery for women
**cazumbrar** *va* to join (*staves of a barrel*) with oakum
**cazumbre** *m* cooper's oakum
**cazumbrón** *m* cooper
**cazurrería** *f* (coll.) sulkiness, sullenness
**cazurro -rra** *adj* (coll.) sulky, sullen
**cazuz** *m* (bot.) ivy
**c.c.** abr. of **centímetro cúbico** or **centímetros cúbicos** (*often used as a measure of cylinder displacement*)
**C.C.** abr. of **corriente continua**
**C. de J.** abr. of **Compañía de Jesús**
**ce** *interj* hey!, pst!
**ceanoto** *m* (bot.) New Jersey tea
**cearina** *f* (pharm.) cearin
**ceba** *f* fattening; feeding a furnace
**cebada** *f* barley; grain of barley; **cebada perlada** pearl barley
**cebadal** *m* barley field
**cebadar** *va* to feed barley to
**cebadazo -za** *adj* (pertaining to) barley
**cebadera** *f* nose bag; barley bin; hopper (*of furnace*); (naut.) spritsail
**cebadero** *m* barley dealer; mule carrying feed; lead mule; feeder of hawks; feeding place; mouth for charging a furnace or oven
**cebadilla** *f* (bot.) white hellebore; (bot.) sabadilla; hellebore snuff; sabadilla seeds (*used to kill head lice*)
**cebador** *m* priming horn; priming powder; (elec.) starter (*of fluorescent light*); (mach.) primer, priming cup
**cebadura** *f* fattening; priming
**cebar** *va* to fatten; to feed (*e.g., a furnace*); to bait (*a fishhook*); to prime (*gun, pump, gas engine, induction electric machine*); to light (*fireworks*); to start growth in (*new-sown ground*); to nourish (*e.g., anger, passion, hope; e.g., a person with hope*); to lure; to make (*a nut or screw*) catch; *vn* to take hold, to catch (*said of a nut or nail*); *vr* to rage (*said of a disease or epidemic*); **cebarse en** to become absorbed in; to vent one's fury on
**cebo** *m* feed, fattening; bait; incentive, lure; primer, charge; priming; **dar cebo a** to give grounds for; **cebo de fango** (ichth.) sand launce
**cebolla** *f* (bot.) onion (*plant and bulb*); bulb; strainer (*for foot valve*); oil receptacle (*of lamp*); **cebolla albarrana** (bot.) squill; **cebolla escalonia** (bot.) shallot
**cebollada** *f* onion stew; (bot.) globe daisy
**cebollar** *m* onion patch
**cebollero -ra** *adj* (pertaining to the) onion; *mf* onion dealer
**cebolleta** *f* tender onion; (bot.) Welsh onion
**cebollino** *m* young onion for transplanting; onion seeds; (bot.) chive; (bot.) onion set; **cebollino inglés** (bot.) Welsh onion
**cebollón** *m* large onion
**cebolludo -da** *adj* bulbous
**cebón -bona** *adj* fattened; *m* fattened animal
**ceboncillo** *m* fatling
**ceborrincha** *f* (bot.) wild onion
**cebra** *f* (zool.) zebra
**cebrado -da** *adj* having stripes like the zebra
**cebratana** *f* var. of **cerbatana**
**cebruno -na** *adj* var. of **cervuno**
**cebú** *m* (*pl:* **-búes**) (zool.) zebu
**ceca** *f* (archaic) mint; **andar de ceca en Meca** (coll.) to go from place to place, to go hither and thither
**cecal** *adj* caecal
**cecear** *vn* to lisp; to pronounce Spanish s like c and z (*i.e.,* [θ])
**ceceo** *m* lisping; pronunciation of Spanish s like c and z (*i.e.,* [θ])
**ceceoso -sa** *adj* lisping
**cecial** *m* fish dried and cured
**cecidia** *f* (bot.) gall, cecidium
**Cecilia** *f* Cecilia
**Cecilio** *m* Cecil
**cecina** *f* dried beef
**cecinar** *va* to dry-cure, to dry-salt
**cecografía** *f* writing of the blind

**cecógrafo** *m* device for helping the blind to write
**cechero** *m* (hunt.) watcher
**ceda** *f* bristle
**cedacería** *f* sieve shop
**cedacero** *m* sieve maker or dealer
**cedacillo** *m* (bot.) quaking grass
**cedazo** *m* sieve, bolt
**cedazuelo** *m* small sieve
**ceder** *va* to yield, give up, hand over, cede; *vn* to yield, give way, surrender; to decline, go down; to slacken, relax; **ceder de** to give up (*e.g., a claim*)
**cedilla** *f* cedilla
**cedizo -za** *adj* tainted, spoiled
**cedoaria** *f* (pharm.) zedoary
**cedras** *fpl* skin saddlebags
**cedria** *f* cedrium
**cédride** *f* cedar cone
**cedrino -na** *adj* cedar
**cedro** *m* (bot.) cedar; **cedro de España** (bot.) Spanish cedar; **cedro de las Antillas** (bot.) mahogany; **cedro del Líbano** (bot.) cedar of Lebanon; (fig.) potentate, tycoon; **cedro deodara** or **cedro de las Indias** (bot.) deodar; **cedro de Virginia** (bot.) juniper, red cedar; **cedro macho** (bot.) Spanish cedar
**cédula** *f* slip of paper or parchment; blank; form; certificate; government order; I.O.U.; **cédula de subscripción** subscription blank; **cédula de vecindad** identification papers; **cédula en blanco** blank check; **cédula personal** identification papers
**cedular** *va* to post, post up (*on the wall*)
**cedulón** *m* public notice, proclamation; lampoon
**cefalalgia** *f* (path.) cephalalgia, headache
**cefalea** *f* (path.) headache
**cefálico -ca** *adj* cephalic
**cefalitis** *f* (path.) encephalitis
**céfalo** *m* (ichth.) mullet, common mullet
**cefalocordado -da** *adj* (zool.) cephalochordate
**cefalópodo -da** *adj & m* (zool.) cephalopod
**cefalotórax** *m* (zool.) cephalothorax
**cefeido -da** *adj & f* (astr.) Cepheid; **cefeida variable** (astr.) Cepheid variable
**Cefeo** *m* (myth. & astr.) Cepheus
**céfiro** *m* zephyr (*wind; fabric*)
**cegajo** *m* two-year-old he-goat
**cegajoso -sa** *adj* blear, weepy
**cegar §29** *va* to blind; to block, plug, stop up; to wall up (*door or window*); *vn* to go blind; to become blinded (*e.g., by passion*); *vr* to become blinded (*e.g., by passion*)
**cegarra** *adj* (coll.) near-sighted, dim-sighted
**cegarrita** *adj* (coll.) squinting (*to see better*)
**cegato -ta** *adj* (coll.) near-sighted, dim-sighted
**cegatoso -sa** *adj* blear, weepy
**cegesimal** *adj* (phys.) centimeter-gram-second
**ceguedad** *f* blindness
**ceguera** *f* blindness; disease causing blindness; **ceguera nocturna** night blindness
**ceiba** *f* (bot.) ceiba tree, God tree, silk-cotton tree; (bot.) sea moss
**ceibal** *m* growth of ceiba trees; growth of ceibos
**ceibo** *m* (bot.) ceibo
**Ceilán** *m* Ceylon
**ceilanés -nesa** *adj & mf* Ceylonese
**ceja** *f* brow; eyebrow; (fig.) brow (*of hill*); projection; edging; rim, edge; flange; path at edge of woods; (mus.) fret; (mus.) capotasto; (naut.) opening in clouds; (Am.) clearing for a road; **dar entre ceja y ceja a** (coll.) to say to one's face; **fruncir las cejas** to knit one's brow; **hasta las cejas** deep (*e.g., in work*); **quemarse las cejas** (coll.) to burn the midnight oil; **tener entre ceja y ceja** (coll.) to look on (*a person*) with disfavor; (coll.) to persist in (*an intention*)
**cejadero** *m* holdback (*on a carriage*)
**cejador -dora** *adj* (Am.) shy, balky (*horse*); *m* holdback (*on a carriage*)
**cejar** *vn* to back up; to turn back; to slacken, relax
**cejijunto -ta** *adj* (coll.) beetle-browed; (coll.) scowling, frowning
**cejilla** *f* (mus.) capotasto
**cejo** *m* morning mist over a river or stream; esparto cord
**cejudo -da** *adj* beetle-browed
**cejuela** *f* (mus.) capotasto
**celada** *f* ambush, trap; (arm.) sallet; **caer en la celada** to fall into the trap; **celada borgoñota** (arm.) burgonet
**celador -dora** *adj* watching, on guard; *mf* caretaker; *m* watchman; maintenance man; proctor
**celaje** *m* cloud effect; skylight, transom; harbinger; (naut.) clouds; (paint.) clouds, burst of light through clouds
**celajería** *f* (naut.) clouds, mass of clouds
**celandés -desa** *adj* (pertaining to) Zeeland; *mf* Zeelander
**celar** *va* to see to (*observance of laws*); to watch over, keep a check on (*e.g., employees*); to keep an eye on (*out of jealousy or other concern*); to hide, conceal; to carve; to engrave; *vn* **celar sobre** to see to (*observance of laws*); **celar por** to watch out for (*e.g., protection of someone or something*)
**celastro** *m* (bot.) staff tree
**celda** *f* cell (*of honeycomb; small room in convent, prison, etc.*); (aer.) cell; **celda de castigo** solitary confinement
**celdilla** *f* cell (*of honeycomb*); niche; cavity; (bot.) cell (*loculus*)
**celebérrimo -ma** *adj super* very or most celebrated
**celebración** *f* celebration; holding (*e.g., of a meeting*)
**celebrante** *adj* celebrating, officiating; *mf* celebrator; *m* celebrant (*priest*)
**celebrar** *va* to celebrate; to welcome (*to accept or look upon with pleasure or approval*); to hold (*e.g., an interview, meeting*); to perform (*e.g., a marriage*); to say (*Mass*); *vn* to celebrate (*to say Mass*); to be glad; **celebrar** + *inf* to be glad to + *inf; vr* to be celebrated; to take place
**célebre** *adj* celebrated, famous; (coll.) funny, witty; (Am.) pretty
**celebridad** *f* celebrity (*quality and person*); celebration, pageant
**celedón** *m* celadon green
**celemín** *m* celemin (*Spanish dry measure: about half peck*)
**celenterado -da** *adj & m* (zool.) coelenterate
**célere** *adj* rapid, swift, quick
**celeridad** *f* celerity
**celerímetro** *m* speed gauge
**celesta** *f* (mus.) celesta
**celeste** *adj* celestial; heavenly (*body*); sky-blue; (mus.) soft (*pedal*); *mf* Celestial (*Chinese*); *m* sky blue; (mus.) celesta (*organ stop*)
**celestial** *adj* celestial, heavenly; (fig.) celestial, heavenly; (coll.) stupid, silly
**celestina** *f* bawd, procuress, go-between; (mineral.) celestite, celestine
**celíaco -ca** *adj* (anat.) coeliac; *f* (path.) coeliac flux
**celibato** *m* celibacy; (coll.) bachelor
**célibe** *adj* celibate, single, unmarried; *mf* celibate, single person, unmarried person
**célico -ca** *adj* (poet.) celestial
**celidonia** *f* (bot.) celandine; **celidonia menor** (bot.) pilewort
**celinda** *f* (bot.) syringa, mock orange
**celindrate** *m* dish seasoned with coriander
**celo** *m* zeal; distrust, envy; heat, rut; **celos** *mpl* jealousy; **en celo** in rut, in heat; **tener celos** to be jealous
**celofán** *m* or **celofana** *f* cellophane
**celoidina** *f* (chem.) celloidin
**celoma** *m* (anat. & zool.) coelom
**celomado -da** *adj & m* (zool.) coelomate
**celosía** *f* jalousie, slatted shutter; lattice, latticework; jealousy; (her.) lattice
**celoso -sa** *adj* jealous; zealous; distrustful, suspicious; (naut.) unsteady
**celotipia** *f* jealousy
**celsitud** *f* elevation, grandeur
**celta** *adj* Celtic; *mf* Celt; *m* Celtic (*language*)
**Celtiberia** *f* Celtiberia
**celtibérico -ca, celtiberio -ria, celtibero -ra** or **celtíbero -ra** *adj & mf* Celtiberian
**céltico -ca** *adj* Celtic
**celtismo** *m* Celticism

**celtista** *mf* Celticist, Celtist
**celtohispánico -ca** or **celtohispano -na** *adj* Celto-Hispanic
**célula** *f* (biol., elec. & pol.) cell; (aer.) cell, plane cell, cellule; **célula cribosa** (bot.) sieve cell; **célula de selenio** selenium cell; **célula fotoeléctrica** photoelectric cell; **célula germen** (biol.) germ cell; **célula mitral** mitral cell; **célula nerviosa** nerve cell; **célula sanguínea** blood cell; **célula voltaica** voltaic cell
**celulado -da** *adj* celled
**celular** *adj* cellular; cell, e.g., **prisión celular** cell house
**celulario -ria** *adj* cellular
**celulitis** *f* (path.) cellulitis
**celuloide** *m* celluloid; (fig.) celluloid (*motion-picture film*); **llevar al celuloide** to put on the screen
**celuloso -sa** *adj* cellulous; *f* (chem.) cellulose
**cellenco -ca** *adj* (coll.) decrepit
**cellisca** *f* sleet, sleet storm
**cellisquear** *vn* to sleet
**cello** *m* hoop
**cementación** *f* (metal.) cementation, casehardening
**cementar** *va* (metal.) to cement, to caseharden
**cementerio** *m* cemetery
**cementista** *mf* cement worker
**cemento** *m* cement; concrete; (anat., dent. & geol.) cement; **cemento armado** reinforced concrete; **cemento de goma** rubber cement; **cemento de Pórtland** or **cemento pórtland** Portland cement
**cementoso -sa** *adj* cement-like, cementitious
**cena** *f* supper; (*cap.*) *f* Last Supper
**cenaaoscuras** *mf* (*pl:* **-ras**) (coll.) recluse; (coll.) skinflint
**cenáculo** *m* cénacle, literary group; (*cap.*) *m* Cenacle (*room of Last Supper*)
**cenacho** *m* market basket
**cenadero** *m* supper room; summerhouse
**cenador -dora** *mf* diner-out; *m* arbor, bower, summerhouse; gallery around patio (*in houses in Granada*)
**cenaduría** *f* (Am.) eating house
**cenagal** *m* quagmire; (fig.) quagmire
**cenagoso -sa** *adj* muddy, miry
**cenar** *va* to have (*e.g., chicken*) for supper; *vn* to sup, to have supper
**cenceño -ña** *adj* thin, slender, lean
**cencerra** *f* cowbell
**cencerrada** *f* (coll.) charivari (*to celebrate the nuptials of a widower*)
**cencerrear** *vn* to jingle cowbells continuously; to jangle, to rattle; (coll.) to play out of tune, to play on an instrument that is out of tune
**cencerreo** *m* jingling of cowbells; jangle, rattle
**cencerro** *m* cowbell; **a cencerros tapados** (coll.) cautiously, stealthily; **cencerro zumbón** bell worn by foremost or leading animal
**cencerrón** *m* bunch of grapes left on the vine
**cencido -da** *adj* untrodden
**cendal** *m* sendal; gauze; (eccl.) humeral veil; barbs of feather; illusion
**cendolilla** *f* flighty young girl
**cendra** *f* cupel paste
**cendrada** *f* cupel; cupel paste
**cendradilla** *f* cupellation furnace
**cendrazo** *m* cupellation residue
**cenefa** *f* border, trimming; orphrey (*of chasuble*); (arch.) border; (naut.) weather cloth; (naut.) top rim
**cenestesia** *f* (psychol.) coenesthesis
**cení** *m* fine brass or bronze
**cenia** *f* irrigation water wheel; bucket wheel; irrigated garden
**cenicero** *m* ashpan; ash tray; ashpit, ash dump
**ceniciento -ta** *adj* ashen, ash-gray; *f* person or thing unjustly despised or disregarded; **la Cenicienta** Cinderella
**cenicilla** *f* (bot.) oidium
**cenit** *m* (astr. & fig.) zenith
**cenital** *adj* zenith, zenithal
**ceniza** *f* see **cenizo**
**cenizal** *m* ashpit
**cenizo -za** *adj* ashen, ash-gray; *mf* (coll.) wet blanket; *m* (bot.) white goosefoot; (bot.) oidium; (coll.) Jonah, jinx, hoodoo; *f* ash; ashes;
**cenizas** *fpl* ashes; (fig.) ashes (*mortal remains*); **huir de las cenizas y caer en las brasas** to jump from the frying pan into the fire; **cenizas de perla** pearlash; **cenizas de sosa** soda ash
**cenizoso -sa** *adj* ashy; ashen, ash-gray
**cenobio** *m* cenoby; (biol. & bot.) coenobium
**cenobita** *mf* cenobite
**cenobitismo** *m* cenobitism
**cenojil** *m* garter
**cenotafio** *m* cenotaph
**cenote** *m* (Am.) deep underground water reservoir
**cenozoico -ca** *adj* (geol.) Cenozoic
**censal** *adj* (pertaining to the) census
**censatario -ria** *mf* (law) lienee
**censo** *m* census; tax; perpetual lien or encumbrance; mortgage; **levantar el censo** to take the census; **ser un censo** (coll.) to be a constant drain (*on one's money*); **censo de por vida** life lien
**censor** *m* censor; censorious person; accountant; (educ.) proctor; **censor jurado de cuentas** certified public accountant
**censorino -na** or **censorio -ria** *adj* censorial; (educ.) proctorial
**censual** *adj* (pertaining to) census; (pertaining to a) lien
**censualista** *mf* (law) lienor
**censuario** *m* (law) lienee
**censura** *f* censure; censorship; censoring; **censura de cuentas** (com.) auditing
**censurable** *adj* censurable, reprehensible
**censurador -dora** *adj* censuring; censoring; *mf* censurer; censor
**censurar** *va* to censure; to censor
**censurista** *adj* censorious; *mf* censorious person, faultfinder
**centaura** or **centaurea** *f* (bot.) centaury; **centaura de jardín** (bot.) golden coreopsis
**centauro** *m* (myth.) centaur
**centavo -va** *adj* hundredth; *m* hundredth; cent
**centella** *f* flash (*of lightning; from flint*); (fig.) spark (*of genius; of love, etc.*); **echar centellas** (coll.) to blow up, hit the ceiling
**centellador -dora** *adj* flashing, sparkling, glimmering; *m* (phys.) scintillation counter
**centellar** or **centellear** *vn* to flash, to sparkle, to glimmer
**centelleo** *m* flashing, sparkling, glimmering
**centellón** *m* large flash or spark
**centena** *f* see **centeno**
**centenada** *f* hundred; **a centenadas** by the hundred
**centenal** *m* rye field; hundred
**centenar** *m* hundred; centenary (*celebration*); rye field; **a centenares** by the hundred
**centenario -ria** *adj* centenary or centennial; centenarian; *mf* centenarian; *m* centenary or centennial
**centenaza** *f* rye straw
**centenero -ra** *adj* good for growing rye (*said of soil*)
**centeno -na** *adj* hundredth; *m* (bot.) rye; *f* hundred; **las centenas** the hundreds (*the numbers 100, 200, 300, etc.*)
**centesimal** *adj* centesimal
**centésimo -ma** *adj* hundredth; *m* hundredth; (Am.) centime
**centiárea** *f* centiare
**centígrado -da** *adj* centigrade
**centigramo** *m* centigram
**centilitro** *m* centiliter
**centiloquio** *m* work of a hundred parts
**centimano** or **centímano** *adj* (myth.) hundred-handed
**centímetro** *m* centimeter
**céntimo -ma** *adj* hundredth; *m* hundredth; centime
**centinela** *mf* (may be used as feminine in speaking of a man) sentinel, sentry; watch, guard (*person*); **estar de centinela** to stand sentinel; **hacer centinela** to stand sentinel; to keep watch; **centinela de avanzada** vedette; **centinela de vista** prisoner's guard; **centinela perdida** (mil.) forlorn hope
**centinodia** *f* (bot.) knotgrass
**centípedo** *m* (zool.) centipede
**centiplicado -da** *adj* hundredfold

**centipondio** *m* hundredweight
**centola** or **centolla** *f* (zool.) thornback, maian (*Maia squinado*)
**centón** *m* crazy quilt; (lit.) cento
**centraje** *m* centering
**central** *adj* central; *f* main office, headquarters; (elec.) powerhouse; (telp.) central; (Am.) community sugar mill; **central de correos** main post office; **central de teléfonos** telephone exchange; **central generadora** (elec.) generating station; **central térmica** (elec.) steam power plant
**centralilla** *f* (telp.) local exchange, private exchange
**centralismo** *m* centralism
**centralista** *adj & mf* centralist
**centralización** *f* centralization
**centralizar** §76 *va & vr* to centralize
**centrar** *va* to center; (hunt.) to hit in the center; (mil.) to center (*fire, attack, etc.*); *vr* to center, be centered
**céntrico -ca** *adj* downtown; centric
**centrifugadora** *f* centrifugal machine
**centrifugar** §59 *va* to centrifuge
**centrífugo -ga** *adj* centrifugal; *f* centrifuge, centrifugal machine
**centrípeto -ta** *adj* centripetal
**centrisco** *m* (ichth.) shrimpfish
**centrista** *adj* (pertaining to the) center; *mf* (pol.) centrist
**centro** *m* center; middle; heart; business district, downtown; club; goal, purpose; **estar en su centro** to be in one's element; **centro de atracción** (astr.) center of attraction; **centro de control** control center; **centro de gravedad** (mech.) center of gravity; **centro de gravitación** (astr.) center of attraction; **centro de mesa** centerpiece; **centro de recepción** (mil.) reception center; **centro de substitución** (mil.) replacement center; **centro docente** educational institution; **centro ferroviario** rail center; **centro nervioso** (anat.) nerve center
**Centro América** *f* Central America
**centroamericano -na** *adj & mf* Central American
**centrobárico -ca** *adj* centrobaric
**centroesfera** *f* (biol.) centrosphere
**centroeuropeo -a** *adj* Central European
**centrosoma** *m* (biol.) centrosome
**cénts.** abr. of **céntimos**
**centuplicar** §86 *va* to centuple
**céntuplo -pla** *adj* centuple, hundredfold; *m* hundredfold
**centuria** *f* century; (hist.) century
**centurión** *m* centurion
**cenzalino -na** *adj* (pertaining to the) mosquito
**cénzalo** *m* (ent.) mosquito
**cenzontle** *m* (Am.) mocking-bird
**ceñideras** *fpl* overalls
**ceñido -da** *adj* tight, close-fitting; close; narrow-waisted, svelte, lithe; thrifty, economical
**ceñidor** *m* belt, girdle, sash
**ceñidura** *f* (act of) girding; fastening; abridgment
**ceñiglo** *m* (bot.) white goosefoot; **ceñiglo de jardín** (bot.) broom goosefoot
**ceñir** §74 *va* to gird; to encircle (*e.g., the brow*); to fasten around the waist, to fit around the waist; to fasten, to tie; to fit tightly; to abridge, shorten; (mil.) to besiege; *vn* (naut.) to sail close to the wind; *vr* to tighten one's belt, cut expenses; to limit oneself (*e.g., in words*); to adapt oneself; **ceñirse a** to hug, keep close to
**ceño** *m* frown; threatening aspect (*of clouds, sea, etc.*); band, ring, hoop; (vet.) dry and contracted hoof; **arrugar el ceño** to knit the brow, to frown
**ceñoso -sa** or **ceñudo -da** *adj* frowning; stern, grim, gruff
**ceo** *m* (ichth.) dory
**cepa** *f* stump (*of tree or plant*); stub (*of tail*); vinestalk; (arch.) footing; strain (*of a family*); **de buena cepa** of well-known quality
**cepacaballo** *m* (bot.) carline thistle
**cepáceo -a** *adj* garlicky
**cepeda** *f* land overgrown with heath
**cepejón** *m* thick end of broken branch; heavy root branching from trunk
**cepellón** *m* (hort.) ball (*left around root for transplanting*)
**cepera** *f* var. of **cepeda**
**cepillado** *m* var. of **acepillado**
**cepilladura** *f* var. of **acepilladura**
**cepillar** *va* var. of **acepillar**
**cepillo** *m* brush; (carp.) plane; charity box, poor box; (Am.) flatterer; **cepillo bocel** reed plane; **cepillo de alambre** wire brush; **cepillo de cabeza** hairbrush; **cepillo de dientes** toothbrush; **cepillo de ropa** or **para la ropa** clothesbrush; **cepillo para las uñas** nailbrush; **cepillo para los dientes** toothbrush
**cepo** *m* branch, bough; stock (*of anvil*); clamp, vise; snare, trap; reel (*for winding silk*); poor box; (naut.) stock (*of anchor*); stocks, pillory; **¡cepos quedos!** (coll.) quiet!, cut it out!
**ceporro** *m* old stump pulled up for firewood; (coll.) rude or uncouth fellow
**cequia** *f* var. of **acequia**
**cera** *f* wax; beeswax; wax candles (*burning at a function*); (orn.) cere; **ceras** *fpl* honeycomb; **hacer cera y pabilo de** (coll.) to lead by the nose; **ser como una cera** to be wax in one's hands; **cera aleda** bee glue; **cera de los oídos** earwax; **cera de lustrar** polishing wax; **cera de palma** palm wax; **cera de** or **para pisos** floor wax; **cera montana** montan wax
**cerafolio** *m* (bot.) chervil
**cerámico -ca** *adj* ceramic; *f* ceramics (*art; objects*); (archeol.) study of ceramics
**ceramista** *mf* ceramist
**cerapez** *m* shoemaker's wax
**cerasta** *f* or **ceraste** *m* (zool.) cerastes
**ceratias** *m* (astr.) twin-tailed comet
**cerato** *m* (pharm.) cerate
**cerbatana** *f* blowgun, peashooter; ear trumpet; (coll.) mouthpiece, spokesman, go-between
**Cerbero** *m* var. of **Cancerbero**
**cerca** *f* fence, wall; **cerca viva** hedge; *m* (coll.) close-up; **cercas** *mpl* (paint.) objects in foreground; **tener buen cerca** (coll.) to look good when close (*said of a person or thing*); *adv* near; **de cerca** near, nearly; at close range; **cerca de** near; about (*a certain number*); to, at the court of; **cerca de** + *inf* near + *ger*
**cercado** *m* fenced-in or walled-in garden or field; fence, wall
**cercador -dora** *adj* encircling, surrounding; *m* repoussé tool
**cercanía** *f* nearness, proximity; **cercanías** *fpl* neighborhood, vicinity
**cercano -na** *adj* near, close; adjoining, neighboring; **cercano a** + *inf* near + *ger*
**cercar** §86 *va* to fence in, to wall in, to hedge in; to encircle, to surround; to crowd around; (mil.) to besiege, lay siege to
**cercén; a cercén** all around, close
**cercenador -dora** *mf* clipper, trimmer
**cercenadura** *f* or **cercenamiento** *m* clipping, trimming; curtailment, reduction
**cercenar** *va* to clip, to trim, to trim the edges of; to curtail, to reduce
**cerceta** *f* (orn.) garganey; **cercetas** *fpl* spikes (*of young deer*); **cerceta de verano** (orn.) greenwing
**cercillo** *m* tendril (*of a vine*)
**cerciorar** *va* to inform, to assure (*a person*); *vr* to find out; **cerciorarse de** to find out about, to ascertain
**cerco** *m* fence, wall, enclosure; hoop; ring; rim, edge; casing or frame (*of door or window*); group, circle; (mil.) siege; (aut.) rim; iron tire; halo (*around sun or moon*); **alzar el cerco** (mil.) to raise the siege; **poner cerco a** (mil.) to lay siege to
**cercopiteco** *m* (zool.) cercopithecus, long-tailed African monkey
**cercha** *f* segment (*of rim of wheel*); (arch.) rib (*of center of arch*); flexible wooden rule for measuring concave or convex surfaces; (rail.) clearance gage
**cerchar** *va* (hort.) to layer
**cerchón** *m* (arch.) center, centering
**cerda** *f* bristle, horsehair; new-mown grain; snare (*to catch birds*); (zool.) sow
**cerdada** *f* herd of swine; swinishness

**cerdamen** *m* bunch of bristles (*for making brushes*)
**cerdear** *vn* to falter in the forelegs; to rasp, to grate (*said of a string instrument*); (coll.) to hold back, to look for excuses
**Cerdeña** *f* Sardinia; **la Cerdeña catalana** Alghero (*seaport in Sardinia where Catalan is still spoken*)
**cerdo** *m* (zool.) hog; dirty, sloppy fellow; ill-bred fellow; **cerdo de cría** pig not old enough to be slaughtered; **cerdo de mata** or **de muerte** pig old enough to be slaughtered; **cerdo de vida** pig not old enough to be slaughtered; **cerdo hormiguero** (zool.) aardvark; **cerdo marino** (zool.) porpoise, harbor porpoise
**cerdoso -sa** *adj* bristly
**cerdudo -da** *adj* bristly; hairy-chested
**cereal** *adj & m* cereal
**cerealista** *adj* (pertaining to) cereal, grain; *mf* grain producer, grain dealer
**cerebelo** *m* (anat.) cerebellum
**cerebración** *f* cerebration
**cerebral** *adj* cerebral
**cerebro** *m* (anat.) cerebrum (*brain; forebrain*); (fig.) brain, brains; **cerebro electrónico** electronic brain
**cerebroespinal** *adj* cerebrospinal
**cereceda** *f* cherry orchard
**cerecilla** *f* red pepper
**ceremonia** *f* ceremony; **de ceremonia** with all due ceremony; formal; **hacer ceremonias** to stand on ceremony; **por ceremonia** as a matter of form
**ceremonial** *adj* ceremonial; *m* ceremonial; (eccl.) ceremonial (*book*)
**ceremoniático -ca** *adj* extremely ceremonious
**ceremoniero -ra** *adj* (coll.) full of compliments
**ceremonioso -sa** *adj* ceremonious, overpolite; formal
**céreo -a** *adj* waxen
**cerería** *f* chandlery; royal chandlery
**cerero** *m* wax chandler; wax dealer; (bot.) wax myrtle; **cerero mayor** royal chandler
**Ceres** *f* (myth.) Ceres
**ceresina** *f* ceresin
**cerevisina** *f* brewers' yeast
**cereza** *f* cherry (*fruit*); cherry red (*of incandescent metals*)
**cerezal** *m* cherry orchard
**cerezo** *m* (bot.) cherry tree; cherry wood; **cerezo silvestre** (bot.) dogwood
**céridos** *mpl* (chem.) cerium metals
**cerífero -ra** *adj* ceriferous
**ceriflor** *f* (bot.) honeywort
**cerilla** *f* wax taper; wax match, paper match; earwax
**cerillero -ra** *mf* match vendor; *m & f* matchbox
**cerillo** *m* wax taper; (*dial.*) wax match
**cerina** *f* (chem.) cerin
**cerio** *m* (chem.) cerium
**cerita** *f* (mineral.) cerite
**cermeña** *f* pear (*fruit*)
**cermeño** *m* (bot.) pear tree; ill-bred fellow
**cernada** *f* cinder; leached ashes; sizing; (vet.) poultice made of ashes
**cernadero** *m* coarse linen cloth used for leaching ashes
**cerne** *m* heart (*of tree*)
**cernedero** *m* flour-sifter's apron; place for sifting flour
**cernedor** *m* screen, sieve, sifter
**cerneja** *f* or **cernejas** *fpl* fetlock (*tuft of hair*)
**cernejudo -da** *adj* heavily fetlocked
**cerner** §66 *va* to sift, to bolt; (Am.) to strain; to scan (*e.g., the horizon*); *vn* to bud, to blossom; to drizzle; *vr* to waddle; to soar, to hover; to impend, be imminent (*said of some evil or misfortune*); to threaten, to gather (*said, e.g., of a storm*); **cernerse sobre** to hang over (*to threaten*)
**cernícalo** *m* (orn.) sparrow hawk, kestrel; (coll.) rude ignoramus; **coger** or **pillar un cernícalo** (coll.) to get drunk
**cernidillo** *m* drizzle; waddling, wobbling
**cernido** *m* sifting; sifted flour
**cernidura** *f* sifting; **cerniduras** *fpl* screenings
**cernir** §43 *va* to sift
**cero** *m* zero; **ser un cero** or **ser un cero a la izquierda** (coll.) to not count, to be of no account; **cero absoluto** (phys.) absolute zero; **cero volado** (print.) superior zero, superior letter o
**cerollo -lla** *adj* mown while green and flexible
**cerón** *m* dross of honeycombs
**ceroplástica** *f* ceroplastics
**ceroso -sa** *adj* waxy
**cerote** *m* shoemaker's wax; (coll.) fright, fear
**cerotear** *va* to wax (*thread*); *vn* (Am.) to drip (*said of a candle*)
**cerótico -ca** *adj* (chem.) cerotic
**cerquillo** *m* fringe of hair around tonsure; welt (*of shoe*); (Am.) bangs
**cerquita** *adv* quite near, close by
**cerrada** *f* see **cerrado**
**cerradero -ra** *adj* lock; locking (*device*); *m* lock; keeper, strike (*of a lock*); purse strings; clasp; *f* lock; **echar la cerradera** (coll.) to turn a deaf ear
**cerradizo -za** *adj* easily locked
**cerrado -da** *adj* close, closed; secretive; obscure, incomprehensible; cloudy, overcast; sharp (*curve*); thick (*beard*); typical, out-and-out; (phonet.) close; (coll.) quiet, reserved; (coll.) dense, stupid; (coll.) with a heavy local accent; **cerrado de mollera** (coll.) crude, ignorant; *f* hide over backbone (*of an animal*)
**cerrador -dora** *adj* shutting, locking; *m* shutter; lock
**cerradura** *f* closing, shutting, locking; lock; **cerradura de cilindro** cylinder lock; **cerradura de dos vueltas** double-turn lock; **cerradura de embutir** mortise lock; **cerradura de golpe** or **de muelle** spring lock; **cerradura de seguridad** safety lock; **cerradura dormida** deadlock; **cerradura guarnecida al revés** rim lock; **cerradura recercada** mortise lock
**cerraja** *f* lock; (bot.) sow thistle; (bot.) corn sow thistle
**cerrajear** *vn* to be a locksmith
**cerrajería** *f* locksmith trade or business; locksmith's shop; light ironwork; hardware shop; builder's hardware
**cerrajero** *m* locksmith; hardware man, ironworker
**cerrajón** *m* big, steep hill
**cerramiento** *m* closing, shutting, locking; enclosure; partition wall; (arch.) roof
**cerrar** §18 *va* to close, to shut, to lock; to bolt; to turn off (*e.g., a radio*); to enclose; to clench (*the fist*); **cerrar con llave** to lock; **cerrar el ojo** (coll.) to close one's eyes (*to die*); *vn* to close; to close in, to make an attack; **cerrar con** to close in on (*an enemy*); **cerrar en falso** to not catch (*said of a door, lock, latch*); *vr* to close, to shut, to lock; to close, to heal (*said of a sore*); **cerrarse en** + *inf* to persist in + *ger;* **cerrarse en falso** to not heal right
**cerrazón** *f* gathering storm clouds; close-mindedness; (phonet.) closing (*of vowel*); (Am.) spur (*of mountain range*)
**cerrejón** *m* hillock
**cerrero -ra** *adj* running wild; unbroken (*colt*); (Am.) rough, unpolished; (Am.) bitter; (Am.) stubborn
**cerreta** *f* (naut.) headrail
**cerril** *adj* rough, uneven; wild, untamed; (coll.) rough, boorish
**cerrilla** *f* milling machine (*to mill coins*)
**cerrillar** *va* to mill, to knurl (*coins*)
**cerrillo** *m* (bot.) couch grass, twitch; (bot.) beard grass; **cerrillos** *mpl* milling cutter
**cerrión** *m* icicle
**cerro** *m* hill; neck of an animal; backbone; bunch of combed flax or hemp; **en cerro** bareback; **por los cerros de Úbeda** (coll.) off the track; (coll.) out of place, **echar por los cerros de Úbeda** (coll.) to talk nonsense
**cerrojazo** *m* slamming the bolt; **dar cerrojazo** to slam the bolt; (archaic) to adjourn (*the Cortes*) suddenly
**cerrojillo** *m* (orn.) coal titmouse
**cerrojo** *m* bolt
**cerrón** *m* burlap
**cerruma** *f* pastern

**certamen** *m* literary contest; match, contest; (obs.) challenge, duel, fight
**certero -ra** *adj* sure, certain, accurate; good (*shot*); well-aimed; well-informed
**certeza** *f* certainty
**certidumbre** *f* certainty; **certidumbre moral** moral certainty
**certificable** *adj* certifiable
**certificación** *f* certification; certificate
**certificado -da** *adj* registered; *m* registered letter or package; certificate; **certificado de estudios** (educ.) transcript; **certificado de origen** (com.) certificate of origin
**certificar** §86 *va* to certify; to certificate; to register (*a letter*); to assure
**certificatorio -ria** *adj* certificatory
**certinidad** *f* certainty
**certísimo -ma** *adj super* very or most certain
**certitud** *f* certainty
**cerúleo -a** *adj* cerulean
**ceruma** *f* var. of **cerruma**
**cerumen** *m* (physiol.) cerumen, earwax
**cerusa** *f* (chem.) ceruse
**cerusita** *f* (mineral.) cerussite
**cerval** *adj* deer; deerlike; intense (*fear*)
**cervantesco -ca, cervántico -ca** or **cervantino -na** *adj* (pertaining to) Cervantes
**cervantismo** *m* influence of Cervantes; expression or idiom of Cervantes
**cervantista** *mf* Cervantist
**cervantófilo -la** *mf* admirer of Cervantes; collector of editions of Cervantes
**cervario -ria** *adj* cervine, deer
**cervatica** *f* (ent.) green grasshopper
**cervatillo** *m* new-born fawn; (zool.) musk deer; (zool.) muntjac
**cervato** *m* fawn
**cerveceo** *m* fermentation of beer
**cervecera** *f* see **cervecero**
**cervecería** *f* brewery; beer saloon; **cervecería al aire libre** beer garden
**cervecero -ra** *adj* brewing; (pertaining to) beer; *mf* brewer; *f* (ichth.) alewife
**cerveza** *f* beer; **cerveza a presión** draught beer; **cerveza clara** light beer; **cerveza parda** dark beer; **cerveza de marzo** bock beer
**cervicabra** *f* (zool.) antelope
**cervical** *adj* cervical
**cervicitis** *f* (path.) cervicitis
**cervicular** *adj* cervical
**cérvido -da** *adj* (zool.) cervid
**cervigón** *m* var. of **cerviguillo**
**cervigudo -da** *adj* thick-necked
**cerviguillo** *m* thick nape of the neck, thick neck
**cervillera** *f* helmet
**cervino -na** *adj* cervine; **el Cervino** or **el monte Cervino** the Matterhorn
**cerviola** *f* (ichth.) amberfish
**cerviz** *f* (*pl:* **-vices**) (anat.) cervix; neck, nape of neck; base of brain; **bajar** or **doblar la cerviz** to humble oneself; **levantar la cerviz** to grow proud; **ser de dura cerviz** to be headstrong, be ungovernable
**cervuno -na** *adj* cervine, deer; deerlike; deerskin; deer-colored
**cesación** *f* or **cesamiento** *m* cessation, suspension
**cesante** *adj* jobless; out of office; on strike; on part pay; *mf* unemployed person; dismissed public employee
**cesantía** *f* dismissal; dismissal from public employment; pension of dismissed public employee; unemployment; unemployment compensation
**cesar** *va* to stop; (Am.) to dismiss; *vn* to cease, to stop, to desist; to quit, to leave; **sin cesar** ceaselessly; **cesar de** + *inf* to cease + *ger*
**César** *m* Caesar
**Cesarea** *f* Caesarea
**cesáreo -a** *adj* Caesarean (*imperial*); (surg.) Caesarean
**cesariano -na** *adj* Caesarean (*pertaining to Caesar*)
**cesarismo** *m* Caesarism
**cese** *m* cease; stoppage of salary; **cese de alarma** all-clear; **cese de fuego** cease fire
**cesible** *adj* (law) transferable
**cesio** *m* (chem.) cesium
**cesión** *f* cession; **cesión de bienes** (law) cessio bonorum
**cesionario -ria** *mf* grantee, assignee
**cesionista** *mf* grantor, assigner
**cesonario -ria** *mf* var. of **cesionario**
**césped** *m* or **céspede** *m* sod, turf, sward, lawn; (hort.) cortex growing over cut after pruning; **césped de Olimpo** (bot.) sea pink, thrift; **césped inglés** (bot.) Italian rye grass
**cespedera** *f* field or meadow where sod is cut
**cespitar** *vn* to waver, to totter
**cespitoso -sa** *adj* cespitose
**cesta** *f* basket; (sport) cesta, wickerwork racket; **cesta de costura** sewing basket
**cestada** *f* basketful
**cestería** *f* basketmaking; basket shop; basketwork
**cestero -ra** *mf* basketmaker, basket dealer
**cesto** *m* basket; washbasket; (hist.) cestus (*hand covering*); **estar hecho un cesto** (coll.) to be overcome with sleep or drink; **estar metido en el cesto** (coll.) to be peevish or fretful (*said of a child*); **ser un cesto** (coll.) to be crude and ignorant; **cesto de la colada** clothesbasket, washbasket
**cestodo** *m* (zool.) cestode
**cestón** *m* large basket; (fort.) gabion
**cestonada** *f* (fort.) gabionade
**cesura** *f* (pros.) caesura
**cetáceo -a** *adj* (zool.) cetacean, cetaceous; *m* (zool.) cetacean
**cetano** *m* (chem.) cetane
**cetilo** *m* (chem.) cetyl
**cetina** *f* whale oil, sperm oil; (chem.) cetin
**cetoína** *f* (ent.) flower beetle; **cetoína dorada** (ent.) rose chafer
**cetona** *f* (chem.) ketone
**cetoria** *f* fish tank, fishpond
**cetrarina** *f* (chem.) cetrarin
**cetrería** *f* falconry, hawking
**cetrero** *m* falconer; (eccl.) verger
**cetrino -na** *adj* sallow; jaundiced, melancholy
**cetro** *m* scepter; perch, roost (*for birds*); (eccl.) verge; **empuñar el cetro** to ascend the throne; **cetro de bufón** bauble; **cetro de locura** bauble, fool's scepter
**ceugma** *f* var. of **zeugma**
**ceutí** (*pl:* **-tíes**) *adj* (pertaining to) Ceuta; *mf* native or inhabitant of Ceuta
**cf.** abr. of **confesor**
**cg.** abr. of **centigramo** or **centigramos**
**C.I.** abr. of **cociente intelectual**
**c.ía** or **cía.** abr. of **compañía**
**cía** *f* (*anat.*) hipbone; (naut.) sternway
**ciaboga** *f* (naut.) turn, turning (*with oars or with rudder and engine*); **hacer ciaboga** to turn around in order to flee
**cianamida** *f* (chem.) cyanamide; **cianamida de calcio** (chem.) calcium cyanamide
**cianato** *m* (chem.) cyanate
**cianea** *f* (mineral.) lazulite
**cianhídrico -ca** *adj* (chem.) hydrocyanic
**ciánico -ca** *adj* (chem.) cyanic
**cianita** *f* (mineral.) cyanite
**cianofíceo -a** *adj* & *f* (bot.) cyanophycean
**cianógeno** *m* (chem.) cyanogen
**cianosis** *f* (path.) cyanosis
**cianótico -ca** *adj* (path.) cyanotic; cyanic (*blue*)
**cianotipia** *f* cyanotype, blueprinting
**cianotipo** *m* cyanotype, blueprint
**cianuración** *f* (min.) cyanide process
**cianurar** *va* to treat (*gold ore*) with the cyanide process
**cianuro** *m* (chem.) cyanide; **cianuro de potasio** or **cianuro potásico** (chem.) potassium cyanide; **cianuro de sodio** or **cianuro sódico** (chem.) sodium cyanide
**ciar** §90 *vn* (naut. & fig.) to back water
**ciático -ca** *adj* sciatic; *f* (path.) sciatica
**cibal** *adj* (pertaining to) food
**cibeleo -a** *adj* (poet.) of Cybele
**Cibeles** *f* (myth.) Cybele
**cibera** *f* wheat thrown into hopper to prime the mill; squashed fruit
**cibernética** *f* cybernetics
**cibiaca** *f* var. of **parihuela**
**cíbolo -la** *mf* (zool.) American bison
**ciborio** *m* (arch.) ciborium

**cicatear** *vn* (coll.) to be miserly, be stingy
**cicatería** *f* miserliness, stinginess
**cicatero -ra** *adj* miserly, stingy; *mf* miser, skinflint; *m* (slang) pickpocket
**cicatrícula** *f* (bot. & embryol.) cicatricle
**cicatriz** *f* (*pl:* **-trices**) cicatrix, scar; (bot.) cicatrix; (fig.) scar
**cicatrización** *f* cicatrization
**cicatrizar** **§76** *va* to cicatrize, to heal; *vr* to cicatrize, to heal; to scar
**cicércula** or **cicercha** *f* (bot.) grass pea
**cícero** *m* (print.) pica
**Cicerón** *m* Cicero
**cicerone** *m* cicerone
**ciceroniano -na** *adj* Ciceronian
**cicindela** *f* (ent.) tiger beetle
**cíclada** *f* cyclas (*of Roman women*)
**Cícladas** *fpl* Cyclades
**ciclamen** *m* (bot.) cyclamen
**ciclamina** *f* (chem.) cyclamin
**ciclamino** *m* (bot.) cyclamen
**ciclamor** *m* (bot.) Judas tree
**ciclar** *va* to polish (*a precious stone*)
**ciclatón** *m* cyclas (*medieval tunic*); ciclatoun (*medieval fabric*)
**cíclico -ca** *adj* cyclic or cyclical
**ciclismo** *m* cycling, bicycling; bicycle racing
**ciclista** *mf* cyclist, bicyclist; bicycle racer
**ciclización** *f* (chem.) ring formation
**ciclo** *m* cycle; term (*in school*); **ciclo de Artús** (lit.) Arthurian Cycle; **ciclo de Carnot** (phys.) Carnot cycle; **ciclo de cuatro tiempos** (mach.) four-cycle; **ciclo de dos tiempos** (mach.) two-cycle; **ciclo del nitrógeno** nitrogen cycle; **ciclo de Metón** (astr.) Metonic cycle
**cicloidal** *adj* cycloid, cycloidal
**cicloide** *f* (geom.) cycloid
**cicloideo -a** *adj* var. of **cicloidal**
**ciclómetro** *m* cyclometer
**ciclón** *m* cyclone
**ciclonal** *adj* cyclonal
**ciclónico -ca** *adj* cyclonic
**Cíclope** *m* (myth.) Cyclops
**ciclopentano** *m* (chem.) cyclopentane
**ciclópeo -a** *adj* cyclopean; (myth.) Cyclopean
**ciclópico -ca** *adj* Cyclopic
**cicloplejía** *f* (path.) cycloplegia
**ciclopropano** *m* (chem.) cyclopropane
**ciclorama** *m* cyclorama
**ciclostilo** or **ciclóstilo** *m* mimeograph
**ciclóstoma** *m* (ichth.) cyclostome
**ciclotrón** *m* (phys.) cyclotron
**-cico -ca** *suffix dim* var. of **-ico** and attached to polysyllables ending in **d, e, n, r,** or an accented vowel, e.g., **duendecico** elfkin; **corazoncico** dear little heart; **mujercica** cute little woman
**cicuta** *f* (bot.) hemlock, poison hemlock; hemlock (*poison*); **cicuta acuática** (bot.) water hemlock; **cicuta mayor** (bot.) hemlock, poison hemlock; **cicuta menor** (bot.) fool's-parsley
**cicutina** *f* (chem.) coniine
**cid** *m* leader, hero; **el Cid Campeador** Spanish hero of the wars against the Moors in the eleventh century
**cidiano -na** *adj* of the Cid
**Cidno** *m* Cydnus
**cidra** *f* citron (*fruit of Citrus medica*); citrus (*fruit of any plant of the genus Citrus*)
**cidrada** *f* citron (*candied rind*)
**cidral** *m* citron grove; (bot.) citron (*tree*)
**cidrato** *m* citron (*fruit*)
**cidrera** *f* or **cidrero** *m* (bot.) citron tree
**cidria** *f* cedrium
**cidro** *m* (bot.) citron (*Citrus medica*); (bot.) citrus (*any plant of the genus Citrus*)
**cidronela** *f* (bot.) balm (*Melissa officinalis*)
**ciegayernos** *m* (*pl:* **-nos**) (coll.) fraud, sham, humbug
**ciego -ga** *adj* blind; stopped, blocked; dark, dense; blank; (arch.) blind (*window, door, etc.*); (fig.) blind, e.g., **ciego de ira** blind with anger; **ciego con celos** blind with jealousy; *mf* blind person; *m* blind man; blood pudding; *f* blind woman; **a ciegas** blindly; without watching, without looking; thoughtlessly
**cieguecico -ca, cieguecillo -lla, cieguecito -ta** or **cieguezuelo -la** *mf* little blind person
**cielito** *m* darling, dearie; (Am.) ring dance and song of the Gauchos
**cielo** *m* sky, heaven; skies, climate, weather; top, ceiling, roof; canopy (*of a bed*); Heaven; (paint.) sky; **a cielo abierto** in the open air, outdoors; **a cielo descubierto** openly; **a cielo raso** in the open air, outdoors; in the country; **bajado del cielo** (coll.) marvelous, perfect; **escupir al cielo** to have something boomerang; **llovido del cielo** (coll.) heaven-sent; **mover cielo y tierra** (coll.) to move heaven and earth; **poner en el cielo** or **en los cielos** (coll.) to praise to the skies; **séptimo cielo** seventh heaven; (fig.) seventh heaven (*perfect felicity*); **tomar el cielo con las manos** (coll.) to hit the ceiling; **¡vaya Vd. al cielo!** (coll.) tell that to the marines!; **venirse el cielo abajo** (coll.) to rain pitchforks; **ver el cielo abierto** or **los cielos abiertos** (coll.) to see the light, to see one's way out (*of a difficulty*); **cielo de la boca** roof of the mouth; **cielo del hogar** crown sheet (*of firebox*); **cielo máximo** (aer.) ceiling; **cielo raso** ceiling, flat ceiling
**cielorraso** *m* ceiling, flat ceiling
**ciempiés** *m* (*pl:* **-piés**) (zool.) centipede; (coll.) disconnected nonsense (*in writing*)
**cien** *adj* hundred, a hundred, one hundred; **los Cien Días** the Hundred Days; *m* (coll.) a hundred, one hundred; **cien por cien** or **por ciento** hundred-per-cent
**ciénaga** *f* marsh, moor; mudhole
**ciencia** *f* science; knowledge; learning; **a ciencia cierta** with certainty; **a ciencia y paciencia** on sufferance; **de ciencia cierta** with certainty; **gaya ciencia** gay science (*amatory poetry*); **ciencia cristiana** Christian Science; **ciencia exacta** exact science; **ciencia física** physical science; **ciencia infusa** afflatus, divine afflatus; **ciencia natural** natural science; **ciencia social** social science; **ciencias ocultas** occult sciences
**cieno** *m* mud, slime, silt
**cienoso -sa** *adj* muddy, slimy, silty
**cientificismo** *m* scientific method
**científico -ca** *adj* scientific; *mf* scientist
**cientismo** *m* scientism
**cientista** *mf* scientist
**ciento** *adj & m* hundred, a hundred, one hundred; **por ciento** per cent; **por cientos** by the hundred; **un ciento de** a hundred, one hundred
**cientopiés** *m* (*pl:* **-piés**) (zool.) centipede
**cierna** *f* (bot.) anther (*of flower of wheat, the vine, etc.*)
**cierne** *m* (bot.) budding, blossoming; **en cierne** in blossom; in its infancy
**cierrarrenglón** *m* marginal stop (*of typewriter*)
**cierre** *m* closing, shutting, locking; snap, clasp, fastener; latch, lock, window latch; choke (*of carburetor*); close (*e.g., of stock market*); shutdown; (com.) closing (*of an account*); **cierre de cañón** breechblock; **cierre de portada** metal shutter (*for store window or door*); **cierre de puertas** door check; **cierre hermético** weather stripping; **cierre hidráulico** water seal; **cierre metálico** sliding metal shutter (*for store window or door*); **cierre cremallera** or **relámpago** zipper
**cierro** *m* closing, shutting, locking; (Am.) wall, fence; (Am.) envelope; **cierro de cristales** glass-enclosed balcony or porch
**cierto -ta** *adj* certain; a certain; fixed; **estar en lo cierto** to be right; to be sure of oneself; **de cierto** or **por cierto** for certain; **no, por cierto** certainly not; **cierto** *adv* certainly, surely
**cierva** *f* (zool.) hind
**ciervo** *m* (zool.) deer, stag, hart; spit curl; **ciervo del Cabo** (zool.) hartebeest; **ciervo de Virginia** (zool.) white-tailed deer; **ciervo mulo** (zool.) mule deer; **ciervo volante** (ent.) stag beetle
**cierzas** *fpl* vine shoots
**cierzo** *m* cold north wind
**cifosis** *f* (path.) kyphosis

**cifra** *f* cipher, figure, number; character; abridgment, summary; device, monogram, cipher; sum, amount; **en cifra** in code; secretly, enigmatically; in brief; **cifra arábiga** Arabic figure
**cifrado -da** *adj* cipher
**cifrador** *m* cipher device
**cifrar** *va* to cipher, to code; to abridge, to summarize; to calculate; **cifrar la dicha en** to base one's happiness on; **cifrar la esperanza en** to place one's hope in
**cifrario** *m* (com.) code
**cigala** *f* (zool.) squilla; (zool.) Norway lobster
**cigarra** *f* (ent.) locust, harvest fly
**cigarral** *m* orchard and picnic grounds (*in or near Toledo*)
**cigarrera** *f* see **cigarrero**
**cigarrería** *f* cigar store
**cigarrero -ra** *mf* cigar maker; cigar seller, cigar dealer; *f* cigar cabinet, cigar case; pocket cigar case
**cigarrillo** *m* cigarette; **cigarrillo con filtro** filter cigarette
**cigarrista** *mf* chain smoker
**cigarro** *m* cigar; cigarette; **cigarro de hoja** (Am.) cigar; **cigarro de papel** cigarette; **cigarro puro** cigar
**cigarrón** *m* big cigar; (ent.) grasshopper
**cigofiláceo -a** *adj* (bot.) zygophyllaceous
**cigoma** *f* (anat.) zygoma
**cigomático -ca** *adj* (anat.) zygomatic
**cigoñal** *m* well sweep; (mach.) crankshaft
**cigoñino** *m* (orn.) young stork
**cigoñuela** *f* (orn.) stilt
**cigoto** *m* (biol.) zygote
**ciguatera** *f* fish poisoning
**ciguato -ta** *adj* sick with fish poisoning
**cigüeña** *f* (orn.) stork; (mach.) crank, winch; **recibir a la cigüeña** (fig.) to have a visit from the stork; **cigüeña negra** (orn.) black stork
**cigüeñal** *m* var. of **cigoñal**
**cigüeñuela** *f* small crank; (orn.) stilt
**cija** *f* sheepfold; hayloft
**cilanco** *m* pool left by receding stream
**cilantro** *m* (bot.) coriander
**ciliado -da** *adj* ciliate, ciliated; *m* (zool.) ciliate
**ciliar** *adj* (anat.) ciliary
**cilicio** *m* sackcloth, haircloth, hair shirt
**cilindrada** *f* piston displacement, cylinder capacity
**cilindrado** *m* rolling
**cilindradora** *f* road roller
**cilindrar** *va* to roll
**cilíndrico -ca** *adj* cylindric or cylindrical
**cilindro** *m* cylinder; roll, roller; (Am.) barrel organ; **un cuatro cilindros** a four-cylinder motor; **un dos cilindros** a two-cylinder motor; **un ocho cilindros en V** an eight-cylinder V motor; **cilindro de caminos** road roller
**cilindroeje** *m* (anat. & physiol.) axis cylinder
**cilindroide** *adj* cylindroid; *m* (geom. & med.) cylindroid
**cilio** *m* cilium, eyelash; (bot. & zool.) cilium
**cilla** *f* granary; tithe
**cilleriza** *f* nun in charge of housekeeping in a convent
**cillerizo** *m* tithe man
**cillero** *m* tithe man; tithe barn; wine cellar; storehouse
**-cillo -lla** *suffix dim* var. of **-illo** and attached to polysyllables ending in **d, e, n, r,** or an accented vowel, e.g., **nubecilla** little cloud; **jardincillo** small garden; **dolorcillo** little pain
**cima** *f* top (*of tree*); top, summit (*of mountain*); (bot.) cyme; (bot.) sprout; (fig.) top, height; **dar cima a** to carry out, to complete; **mirar por cima** to pay slight attention to; **por cima** (coll.) at the very top; **cima helicoidea** (bot.) helicoid cyme
**cimacio** *m* (arch.) cyma, ogee
**cimarrón -rrona** *adj* (Am.) shy, wild; (Am.) wild (*plant*); (Am.) black or bitter (*maté*); (Am.) fugitive (*slave*); (Am.) lazy (*sailor*); *mf* (Am.) fugitive slave; *m* (Am.) lazy sailor
**cimarronear** *vn* (Am.) to drink black maté; *vr* (Am.) to flee, run away (*said of a slave*)
**cimbalaria** *f* (bot.) Kenilworth ivy
**cimbalero** *m* (mus.) cymbalist
**cimbalillo** *m* small bell
**cimbalista** *m* (mus.) cymbalist
**címbalo** *m* (mus.) cymbal
**cimbanillo** *m* var. of **cimbalillo**
**címbara** *f* short, broad scythe or sickle
**cimbel** *m* stool pigeon, decoy pigeon; cord to which a decoy is attached
**cimboga** *f* citron (*fruit*)
**cimborio** or **cimborrio** *m* (arch.) dome; dome (*of steam boiler, tank car, etc.*)
**cimbra** *f* (arch.) centering; inside curvature of an arch or vault; (naut.) curvature of a board
**cimbrado** *m* bending body at the waist (*in a Spanish dance*)
**cimbrar** *va* to swing, to sway, to bend; (coll.) to beat with a stick, to thrash; (arch.) to build the centering for (*an arch or vault*); *vn* to swerve; *vr* to swing, to sway, to bend
**cimbre** *m* subterranean gallery
**cimbreante** *adj* flexible, pliant
**cimbrear** *va, vn & vr* var. of **cimbrar**
**cimbreño -ña** *adj* flexible, pliant; agile, willowy
**cimbreo** *m* swinging, swaying, bending
**cimbronazo** *m* blow with flat of sword; (Am.) earthquake
**cimeno** *m* (chem.) cymene
**cimentación** *f* foundation, laying a foundation
**cimentar §18** *va* to found; to lay the foundation for (*a wall, building, etc.; a science, religion, etc.*)
**cimenterio** *m* var. of **cementerio**
**cimento** *m* (geol.) cement
**cimera** *f* see **cimero**
**cimerio -ria** *adj & mf* Cimmerian
**cimero -ra** *adj* top, uppermost; *f* crest (*of helmet*); (her.) crest
**cimicaria** *f* (bot.) dwarf elder
**cimiento** *m* foundation, groundwork; basis, source; **abrir los cimientos** to dig the foundations, to break ground
**cimillo** *m* stool (*pole to which decoy is fastened*)
**cimitarra** *f* scimitar
**cimo** *m* (path.) zyme; **cimo excitador** (biol.) zymogen
**cimofana** *f* (mineral.) cymophane
**cimogénesis** *f* (biochem.) zymogenesis
**cimógeno -na** *adj* zymogenic; *m* (biochem. & biol.) zymogen
**cimología** *f* zymology
**cimosis** *f* (*pl:* **-sis**) zymosis
**cimoso -sa** *adj* (bot.) cymose
**cimotecnia** *f* var. of **cimurgia**
**cimótico -ca** *adj* zymotic
**címrico -ca** *adj & m* Cymric
**cimurgia** *f* zymurgy
**cinabrio** *m* cinnabar (*mineral and color*)
**cinacina** *f* (bot.) Jerusalem thorn
**cinámico -ca** *adj* (chem.) cinnamic
**cinamomo** *m* (bot.) bead tree; (bot.) oleaster, Russian olive
**cinanquia** *f* (path.) quinsy
**cinc** *m* (*pl:* **cinces**) (chem.) zinc
**cinca** *f* fault, error (*in bowling*)
**cincar §86** *va* to zinc
**cincel** *m* chisel, cutter, graver
**cincelador** *m* sculptor; engraver; stonecutter; chipping hammer
**cinceladura** *f* chiseling, carving, engraving
**cincelar** *va* to chisel, carve, engrave
**cinceta** *f* (orn.) pipit, titlark
**cincino** *m* (bot.) helicoid cyme
**cincita** *f* (mineral.) zincite
**cinco** *adj* five; **las cinco** five o'clock; *m* five; fifth (*in dates*); **decir a uno cuántas son cinco** (coll.) to tell someone what's what; **¡choque Vd. esos cinco!** or **¡vengan esos cinco!** (coll.) shake! (*i.e., shake hands!*)
**cincocentista** *adj* fifteenth-century; *m* (f.a.) cinquecentist
**cincoenrama** *f* (bot.) cinquefoil
**cincograbado** *m* zinc etching, zincograph
**cincografía** *f* zinc etching, zincography
**cincomesino -na** *adj* five-month-old
**cincoso -sa** *adj* zincous
**cincuenta** *adj & m* fifty
**cincuentavo -va** *adj & m* fiftieth

**cincuentenario -ria** *adj & m* semicentennial
**cincuenteno -na** *adj* fiftieth; *f* fifty
**cincuentón -tona** *adj & mf* quinquagenarian
**cincha** *f* cinch (*of saddle*); **a revienta cinchas** at breakneck speed; (Am.) unwillingly
**cinchadura** *f* cinching
**cinchar** *va* to cinch; to band, to hoop
**cinchera** *f* part of body where cinch is worn; (vet.) girth sore
**cincho** *m* sash, girdle; iron hoop; iron tire; (vet.) dry and contracted hoof
**cinchuela** *f* small cinch; narrow ribbon
**cine** *m* (coll.) movie, movies; **en cine** (coll.) in the movies; **cine en colores** (coll.) color movies; **cine en relieve** (coll.) three-dimensional movie; **cine hablado** (coll.) talkie; **cine mudo** (coll.) silent movie; **cine sonoro** (coll.) sound movie, talkie
**cineasta** *mf* motion-picture producer; movie fan; *m* movie actor; *f* movie actress
**cinedrama** *m* screenplay
**cinegético -ca** *adj* cynegetic; *f* cynegetics, hunting
**cineísta** *mf* var. of **cineasta**
**cinelandia** *f* (coll.) movieland
**cinema** *m* var. of **cine**
**cinemadrama** *m* photoplay
**cinemateca** *f* film library
**cinemático -ca** *adj* kinematic; *f* kinematics
**cinematografía** *f* cinematography
**cinematografiar** **§90** *va & vn* to cinematograph, to film
**cinematográfico -ca** *adj* cinematographic, motion-picture
**cinematografista** *mf* motion-picture director
**cinematógrafo** *m* cinematograph, motion-picture projector, motion-picture theater; motion pictures
**cineración** *f* incineration
**cinerario -ria** *adj* cinerary; *f* (bot.) cineraria
**cinéreo -a** *adj* cinereous, ash-gray
**cinericio -cia** *adj* ashen; ash-gray
**cinescopio** *m* kinescope
**cinestéreo** *m* (mov.) three-D
**cinestesia** *f* kinaesthesia or kinesthesia
**cinestésico -ca** *adj* kinesthetic
**cineteatro** *m* movie house, motion-picture theater
**cinético -ca** *adj* kinetic; *f* kinetics
**cingalés -lesa** *adj* Singhalese; *mf* Singhalese; *m* Singhalese (*language*)
**cíngaro -ra** *adj* gypsy; *mf* zingaro
**cinglado** *m* shingling (*of iron*)
**cinglador** *m* shingler (*machine*)
**cinglar** *va* to shingle (*iron*); to scull (*to propel from the stern with one oar*)
**cíngulo** *m* cingulum (*of a priest's alb*); (anat., bot. & zool.) cingulum
**cínico -ca** *adj* cynic or cynical; Cynic; brazen, impudent; slovenly, untidy; *mf* cynic; *m* Cynic
**cínife** *m* (ent.) mosquito; (ent.) gallfly
**cinismo** *m* cynicism; Cynicism; brazenness, impudence
**cinocéfalo -la** *adj* cynocephalous; *m* (zool.) baboon
**cinoglosa** *f* (bot.) hound's-tongue
**Cinosura** *f* (astr.) Cynosure
**cinquén** *m* old Spanish coin (*five maravedis*)
**cinquero** *m* zinc worker, tinsmith
**cinta** *f* ribbon; tape, band, strip; film; measuring tape; curb (*along sidewalk*); (arch.) fillet, scroll; (Am.) can; **en cinta** tied down, repressed; **cinta adhesiva** adhesive tape; **cinta aisladora** or **aislante** friction tape; **cinta cinematográfica** moving-picture film; **cinta de embrague** (aut.) clutch band; **cinta de freno** (aut.) brake lining; **cinta de medir** tape measure; **cinta de teleimpresor** ticker tape; **cinta de transporte** belt conveyor; **cinta grabada de televisión** video tape; **cinta magnética** magnetic tape; **cinta magnetofónica** recording tape; **cinta métrica** tape measure; **cinta para cubrir** masking tape; **cinta perforada** paper tape, punched tape; **cinta pescadora** (elec.) fish wire
**cintado -da** *adj* beribboned
**cintagorda** *f* coarse hempen fishing net
**cintarazo** *m* blow with the flat of a sword
**cintarear** *va* (coll.) to strike with the broad of a sword
**cinteado -da** *adj* beribboned
**cintería** *f* ribbons; ribbon business; ribbon shop
**cintero -ra** *mf* ribbon weaver, ribbon dealer; *m* belt, girdle; hoisting line; (surv.) tapeman
**Cintia** *f* (myth.) Cynthia
**cintilar** *vn* var. of **centellear**
**cintillo** *m* hatband; ring set with precious stones, diamond ring; (Am.) hair ribbon
**cinto** *m* belt, girdle
**cintra** *f* (arch.) arch (*of an arch or vault*); **plena cintra** (arch.) semicircular arch
**cintrado -da** *adj* arched
**cintradora** *f* cambering machine
**cintrar** *va* to arch, bend, curve; to camber (*timber*)
**cintrel** *m* (arch.) guide rule for determining the angle of the various courses of an arch
**cintura** *f* waist; waistline; girdle; throat (*of chimney*); **meter en cintura** (coll.) to hold in check, to bring to reason
**cinturón** *m* sword belt; belt, sash; (fig.) belt, circle; **cinturón de castidad** chastity belt; **cinturón de asiento** seat belt; **cinturón de seguridad** safety belt (*of a lineman*); **cinturón de Venus** (myth.) cestus; (zool.) Venus's-girdle; **cinturón ortopédico** orthopedic belt; **cinturón salvavidas** (naut.) safety belt
**cipariso** *m* (poet.) cypress
**cipayo** *m* sepoy
**ciperáceo -a** *adj* (bot.) cyperaceous
**cipo** *m* memorial pillar; boundary stone; milestone, kilometer stone
**cipote** *adj* (Am.) stupid; (Am.) chubby, fat; *mf* (Am.) urchin, brat
**ciprés** *m* (bot.) cypress
**cipresal** *m* cypress grove
**cipresino -na** *adj* (pertaining to the) cypress
**ciprino -na** or **ciprio -pria** *adj & mf* Cyprian
**cipripedio** *m* (bot.) cypripedium
**ciquiricata** *f* (coll.) show of flattery, obsequiousness
**circasiano -na** *adj & mf* Circassian
**Circe** *f* (myth.) Circe; (*l.c.*) *f* cunning and deceitful woman
**circense** *adj* Circensian; (pertaining to a) circus
**circinado -da** *adj* (bot.) circinate
**circo** *m* circus; amphitheater; (geol.) cirque; **circo máximo** Circus Maximus
**circón** *m* (mineral.) zircon
**circona** *f* (chem.) zirconia
**circonio** *m* (chem.) zirconium
**circuición** *f* circling, surrounding
**circuir** **§41** *va* to circle, to surround
**circuito** *m* circuit; race course; network (*of roads or railroads*); (elec.) circuit; **corto circuito** (elec.) short circuit; **circuito abierto** (elec.) open circuit; **circuito cerrado** (elec.) closed circuit; **circuito de filamento** (rad.) filament circuit; **circuito de placa** (rad.) plate circuit; **circuito de rejilla** (rad.) grid circuit; **circuito de retorno por tierra** (elec.) earth-return circuit; **circuito fantasma** (elec.) phantom circuit; **circuito impreso** (elec.) printed circuit
**circulación** *f* circulation; traffic; **circulación rodada** vehicular traffic
**circulante** *adj* circulating
**circular** *adj* circular; *f* circular, circular letter; *va* to circulate; *vn* to circulate; **circular por** to walk around (*e.g., a garden*)
**circularidad** *f* circularity
**circulatorio -ria** *adj* circulatory
**círculo** *m* circle; club; clubhouse; **cuadrar el círculo** to square the circle; **círculo horario** (astr.) hour circle; **círculo máximo** (astr. & geom.) great circle; **círculo menor** (astr. & geom.) small circle; **círculo parhélico** (meteor.) parheliacal ring, parhelic circle; **círculo polar antártico** antarctic circle; **círculo polar ártico** arctic circle; **círculo vicioso** vicious circle
**circumambiente** *adj* circumambient, surrounding
**circumpolar** *adj* circumpolar
**circuncidar** *va* to circumcise; to clip, diminish, curtail

**circuncisión** *f* circumcision
**circunciso -sa** *adj* circumcised
**circundar** *va* to surround, encompass, go around
**circunferencia** *f* circumference
**circunferencial** *adj* circumferential
**circunferente** *adj* surrounding
**circunflejo -ja** *adj* (anat. & gram.) circumflex; *m* (gram.) circumflex
**circunfluente** *adj* circumfluent
**circunfuso -sa** *adj* circumfused
**circunlocución** *f* or **circunloquio** *m* circumlocution
**circunnavegación** *f* circumnavigation
**circunnavegador -dora** *mf* circumnavigator
**circunnavegar** §59 *va* to circumnavigate
**circunscribir** §17, 9 *va* to circumscribe; (geom.) to circumscribe; *vr* to become circumscribed; to hold oneself down
**circunscripción** *f* circumscription; subdivision (*of an administrative, military, electoral, or ecclesiastical territory*)
**circunscrito -ta** *pp of* **circunscribir;** *adj* circumscript
**circunspección** *f* circumspection
**circunspecto -ta** *adj* circumspect
**circunstancia** *f* circumstance; **en las circunstancias presentes** under the circumstances; **circunstancias agravantes** aggravating circumstances; **circunstancias atenuantes** extenuating circumstances
**circunstanciado -da** *adj* circumstantial, detailed, minute
**circunstancial** *adj* circumstantial
**circunstante** *adj* present; surrounding; *mf* bystander, onlooker
**circunterrestre** *adj* around the earth
**circunvalación** *f* circumvallation; (fort.) circumvallation
**circunvalar** *va* to surround; (fort.) to circumvallate
**circunvecino -na** *adj* adjacent, neighboring, surrounding
**circunvolar** §77 *va* to fly around
**circunvolución** *f* circumvolution; convolution; (anat.) convolution; **circunvolución cerebral** (anat.) cerebral convolution; **circunvolución de Broca** (anat.) convolution of Broca
**circunyacente** *adj* circumjacent
**cirenaico -ca** *adj & mf* Cyrenaic; **la Cirenaica** Cyrenaica
**Cirene** *f* Cyrene (*city*)
**cirial** *m* (eccl.) processional candlestick
**cirigallo -lla** *mf* gadabout
**cirigaña** *f* (dial.) flattery; (dial.) triviality; (dial.) disappointment
**cirílico -ca** *adj* Cyrillic
**Cirilo** *m* Cyril
**cirineo** *m* (coll.) helper
**cirio** *m* (eccl.) wax candle; **cirio pascual** (eccl.) paschal candle
**Ciro** *m* Cyrus
**cirolero** *m* (bot.) plum tree
**cirrípedo -da** *adj & m* (zool.) cirriped
**cirro** *m* (bot., zool. & meteor.) cirrus; (path.) scirrhus
**cirrocúmulo** *m* (meteor.) cirro-cumulus
**cirroestrato** *m* var. of **cirrostrato**
**cirrópodo -da** *adj & m* (zool.) cirriped
**cirrosis** *f* (path.) cirrhosis
**cirroso -sa** *adj* cirrous; scirrhous
**cirrostrato** *m* (meteor.) cirro-stratus
**cirrótico -ca** *adj* cirrhotic
**ciruela** *f* plum (*fruit*); **ciruela claudia** greengage; **ciruela de América** coco plum; **ciruela de fraile** long green plum; **ciruela de yema** yellow plum; **ciruela pasa** prune; **ciruela verdal** greengage
**ciruelo** *m* (bot.) plum tree; (coll.) dolt
**cirugía** *f* surgery; **cirugía cosmética, decorativa** or **estética** face lifting; **cirugía mayor** major surgery; **cirugía menor** minor surgery; **cirugía nerviosa** neurosurgery; **cirugía ortopédica** orthopedic surgery; **cirugía plástica** plastic surgery
**cirujano -na** *mf* surgeon; *m* (ichth.) surgeonfish
**cirujano-dentista** *m* dental surgeon
**cisalpino -na** *adj* cisalpine
**cisandino -na** *adj* cisandine
**cisatlántico -ca** *adj* cisatlantic
**cisca** *f* (bot.) ditch reed; (bot.) cogon grass
**ciscar** §86 *va* (coll.) to dirty, to soil; *vr* to soil one's bed or one's clothes
**cisco** *m* slack, culm, coal dust; (coll.) uproar, row, wrangling; **meter cisco** (coll.) to stir up a row
**ciscón** *m* cinders
**cisión** *f* incision
**cisípedo -da** *adj* finger-footed
**cisma** *m* schism; discord
**cismático -ca** *adj* schismatic or schismatical; (Am.) fastidious; (Am.) gossipy; *mf* schismatic
**cismontano -na** *adj* cismontane, situated on this side of the mountains
**cismoso -sa** *adj* troublemaking; gossipy; *mf* troublemaker; gossip
**cisne** *m* (orn.) swan; (fig.) swan (*poet*); (*cap.*) *m* (astr.) Cygnus, Swan; **cisne de Mantua** Mantuan Swan (*Virgil*); **cisne dirceo** Dircaean Swan (*Pindar*)
**cisoide** *f* (geom.) cissoid
**cispadano -na** *adj* cispadane, situated on the Roman side of the river Po
**cisquera** *f* coal-dust shop
**cisquero** *m* coal-dust dealer; pounce bag
**cistáceo -a** *adj* (bot.) cistaceous
**cistercience** *adj & m* Cistercian
**cisterna** *f* cistern; (anat.) cistern; **cisterna de desagüe** catch basin
**cisticerco** *m* (zool.) cysticercus
**cisticercosis** *f* (path.) cysticercosis
**cístico -ca** *adj* (anat.) cystic; *m* (anat.) cystic duct
**cistitis** *f* (path.) cystitis
**cistoscopio** *m* cystoscope
**cistotomía** *f* (surg.) cystotomy
**cisura** *f* fissure; incision; (anat.) sulcus; **cisura de Rolando** (anat.) sulcus of Rolando
**cita** *f* date, engagement, appointment; citation; quotation; reference; **darse cita** to make a date, to have an appointment (*with each other*); **cita a ciegas** (coll.) blind date
**citable** *adj* quotable
**citación** *f* citation, quotation; (law) citation, summons
**citado -da** *adj* above-mentioned
**citano -na** *mf* (coll.) so-and-so
**citar** *va* to make an appointment with; to cite, to quote; (law) to cite, to summon; (taur.) to incite, to provoke; *vr* to have a date, to keep a date
**citara** *f* wall the thickness of a brick
**cítara** *f* (mus.) cithara; (mus.) cither; (mus.) zithern; (mus.) zither
**citarilla** *f* thin brick wall
**citarón** *m* masonry foundation
**citasa** *f* (biochem.) cytase
**cite** *m* (taur.) incitement, challenge
**citereo -a** *adj* (poet.) Cytherean; (*cap.*) *f* (myth.) Cytherea
**citerior** *adj* hither, nearer, situated on this side
**citisina** *f* (pharm.) cytisine
**cítiso** *m* (bot.) cytisus
**-cito -ta** *suffix dim* var. of **-ito** and attached to polysyllables ending in **d, e, n, r,** or an accented vowel, e.g., **ciudadcita** pretty little city; **madrecita** dear little mother; **Carmencita** little Carmen; **mujercita** nice little woman; **papacito** dear papa
**cítola** *f* millclapper
**citología** *f* cytology
**citólogo -ga** *mf* cytologist
**citoplasma** *m* (biol.) cytoplasm
**citoplásmico -ca** *adj* (biol.) cytoplasmic
**citoquímica** *f* cytochemistry
**citote** *m* (coll.) citation, summons
**citramontano -na** *adj* var. of **cismontano**
**citrato** *m* (chem.) citrate; **citrato de magnesia** (med.) citrate of magnesia
**cítrico -ca** *adj* (chem.) citric
**citrícola** *adj* citrus-growing
**citrina** *f* lemon oil; (biochem.) citrin
**citrón** *m* var. of **limón**
**ciudad** *f* city; city council; **ciudad Condal** Barcelona; **ciudad de David** City of David (*Jerusalem; Bethlehem*); **ciudad de Dios** City of God (*heaven*); **ciudad del amor fraternal**

City of Brotherly Love (*Philadelphia*); **ciudad del Apóstol** Santiago de Compostela; **ciudad de las siete colinas** City of the Seven Hills (*Rome*); **ciudad del Betis** Seville; **Ciudad del Cabo** Cape Town; **ciudad de los Califas** Cordova; **ciudad de los mástiles** City of Masts (*London*); **ciudad de los Reyes** Lima, Peru; **Ciudad del Vaticano** Vatican City; **ciudad de María Santísima** Seville; **Ciudad Eterna** Eternal City (*Rome*); **ciudad Imperial** or **Imperial ciudad** Toledo; **ciudad jardín** garden city; **ciudad libre** free city; **ciudad prohibida** Forbidden City (*Lhasa, capital of Tibet; walled section of Pekin*); **Ciudad Santa** Holy City (*Jerusalem, Rome, Mecca, etc.*); **Ciudad Vaticana** Vatican City; **Ciudad** City (*word written on an envelope to indicate that the letter is to go to the city in which it is mailed*)

**ciudadanía** *f* citizenship

**ciudadano -na** *adj* (pertaining to the) city; civic; citizen; *mf* citizen; urbanite; *f* citizeness

**ciudadela** *f* (fort.) citadel; (Am.) tenement house

**civeta** *f* (zool.) civet cat

**civeto** *m* civet

**cívico -ca** *adj* civic; public-spirited; domestic; *m* (coll.) policeman

**civil** *adj* civil; civilian; *mf* civilian; *m* policeman

**civilidad** *f* civility

**civilista** *mf* authority on civil law, professor of civil law; (Am.) antimilitarist

**civilización** *f* civilization

**civilizador -dora** *adj* civilizing

**civilizar** **§76** *va & vr* to civilize

**civismo** *m* civism, good citizenship

**cizalla** *f* shears, sheet-metal shears; shearing machine; paper cutter; (surg.) bone forceps; chip, clipping (*of metal*); chips, shavings; **cizallas** *fpl* shears; **cizalla de guillotina** guillotine shears

**cizallar** *va* to shear

**cizaña** *f* (bot.) darnel; contagious vice, contaminating influence; discord; (Bib.) tare; **sembrar cizaña** to sow discord; **cizaña vivaz** (bot.) rye grass

**cizañador -dora** *mf* sower of discord, troublemaker

**cizañamiento** *m* sowing of discord, troublemaking

**cizañar** *va* to sow discord among, to alienate; *vn* to sow discord

**cizañero -ra** *mf* (coll.) sower of discord, troublemaker

**cl.** abr. of **centilitro** or **centilitros**

**clac** *m* (*pl:* **claques**) opera hat (*collapsible hat*); cocked hat

**cladócero -ra** *adj & m* (zool.) cladoceran

**cladodio** *m* (bot.) cladode, cladophyll

**claitonia** *f* (bot.) claytonia

**clamar** *va* to clamor for, cry out for; *vn* to clamor, cry out; **clamar al cielo** to cry to heaven; **clamar contra** to cry out against; **clamar por** to clamor for, cry out for

**clámide** *f* chlamys

**clamor** *m* clamor, outcry; plaint, whine; knell, toll

**clamoreada** *f* clamor, outcry; plaint, whine

**clamorear** *va* to clamor; *vn* to clamor; to toll

**clamoreo** *m* clamor, clamoring; toll, tolling

**clamoroso -sa** *adj* clamorous; crying, shrieking; buzzing (*noise*)

**clan** *m* clan

**clandestinidad** *f* clandestinity, secrecy, underhandedness

**clandestinista** *mf* (Am.) bootlegger

**clandestino -na** *adj* clandestine

**clanga** *f* (orn.) gannet, solan

**clangor** *m* (poet.) blare, sound of trumpet

**claque** *f* claque, hired clappers

**clara & Clara** *f* see **claro**

**claraboya** *f* skylight; transom; (arch.) bull's-eye; (arch.) clerestory

**clarar** *va* var. of **aclarar**

**clarea** *f* mulse, mulled wine

**clarear** *va* to brighten, light up; (Am.) to pierce through and through; *vn* to dawn; to clear up; *vr* to show through, be transparent (*said of a fabric*); (coll.) to show one's hand, give oneself away

**clarecer** **§34** *vn* to dawn

**clarens** *m* (*pl:* **-rens**) clarence (*carriage*)

**clareo** *m* clearing (*of a thicket or woods*)

**clarete** *m* claret

**clareza** *f* clarity, clearness

**claridad** *f* clarity, clearness; brightness, brilliance, glory; blunt remark; **claridades** *fpl* plain language, simple truth

**claridoso -sa** *adj* (Am.) blunt, plain-talking

**clarificación** *f* clarification; brightening

**clarificador** *m* clarifier

**clarificadora** *f* (Am.) clarifier (*in sugar refining*)

**clarificar** **§86** *va* to clarify; to brighten, light up; to clear (*e.g., a thicket*)

**clarífico -ca** *adj* bright, resplendent

**clarimente** *m* (archaic) face lotion

**clarimento** *m* (paint.) bright color

**clarín** *m* (mus.) clarion (*kind of trumpet; organ stop*); clarion player; fine cambric; (orn.) tropical thrush (*Myadestes unicolor*); (Am.) sweet pea

**clarinada** *f* clarion call; (coll.) uncalled-for remark

**clarinazo** *m* clarion call

**clarinero** *m* clarion player, bugler

**clarinete** *m* (mus.) clarinet; clarinetist

**clarinetista** *mf* clarinetist

**clarión** *m* chalk

**clarioncillo** *m* crayon

**clarisa** *f* Clare (*nun*)

**clarividencia** *f* clairvoyance (*clear-sightedness; supposed power to see things that are out of sight*)

**clarividente** *adj* clairvoyant; clear-sighted; *mf* clairvoyant (*person who claims to see things that are out of sight*)

**claro -ra** *adj* clear; bright; light (*in color*); thin (*liquid*); thin, sparse (*hair*); weak (*tea*); smart; famous, illustrious; light (*beer*); **a las claras** openly, publicly; clearly ‖ **claro** *adv* clearly; **¡claro!** sure!; of course!; **¡claro está!** or **¡claro que sí!** sure!, of course ‖ *m* gap, break; space, interval; glade, clearing; light (*window or opening*); skylight; (naut.) break (*in clouds*); **de claro en claro** obviously; from one end to the other; **pasar la noche de claro en claro** to not sleep a wink all night; **poner** or **sacar en claro** to explain, clear up; to copy (*a rough draft*); **claro de luna** brief moonlight (*on a dark night*) ‖ *f* white of egg; bald spot; thinly woven piece of cloth; temporary let-up or break (*in rain*) ‖ (*cap.*) *f* Clara, Clare

**claror** *m* brightness, splendor; **claror de luna** moonlight

**claroscuro** *m* (paint.) chiaroscuro; combination of fine and heavy strokes in penmanship

**clarucho -cha** *adj* (coll.) watery, thin

**clase** *f* class; classroom; **clases** *fpl* noncommissioned officers, warrant officers; **altas clases** upper classes; **fumarse la clase** (coll.) to cut class; **primera clase** (naut. & rail.) first class; **segunda clase** (naut. & rail.) second class; **tercera clase** (naut. & rail.) third class; **clase alta** upper class; **clase baja** lower class; **clase de cámara** or **clase intermedia** (naut.) cabin class; **clase de tropa** (mil.) noncommissioned officers; **clase media** middle class; **clase obrera** working class; **clases pasivas** pensioners; **clase turista** (aer. & naut.) tourist class

**clasicismo** *m* classicism

**clasicista** *adj* classicistic; *mf* classicist

**clásico -ca** *adj* classic, classical; outstanding; regular, everyday; *m* classic (*author*); classicist

**clasificación** *f* classification

**clasificador -dora** *adj* classifying; filing; *m* filing cabinet; (min.) classifier

**clasificar** **§86** *va* to classify

**clasismo** *m* class discrimination

**clasista** *adj* (pertaining to) class; *mf* advocate of class discrimination

**claudicación** *f* limping, limp

**claudicar** **§86** *vn* to limp; to bungle; (coll.) to back down

**Claudio** *m* Claude, Claudius

**claustra** *f* cloister
**claustral** *adj* cloistral
**claustro** *m* cloister; (anat.) claustrum; faculty (*of a school*)
**claustrofobia** *f* (path.) claustrophobia
**cláusula** *f* clause (*in a contract or other document*); (gram.) sentence; **cláusula de evicción de saneamiento** (law) warranty clause
**clausulado -da** *adj* choppy (*style*); *m* clauses, series of clauses
**clausular** *va* to close, finish; to terminate (*a contract*)
**clausura** *f* confinement, monastic life; adjournment, close; closing
**clausurar** *va & vr* to adjourn; to close
**clava** *f* club; (naut.) scupper; (anat.) clava
**clavadista** *mf* (Am.) diver
**clavadizo -za** *adj* nail-studded
**clavado -da** *adj* studded with nails; exact, precise; just right; stopped (*said of a watch*); sharp, e.g., **a las cinco clavadas** at five o'clock sharp; *m* (Am.) dive; **echar un clavado** (Am.) to take a dive
**clavadura** *f* pricking a horse's foot (*with horseshoe nail*)
**clavar** *va* to nail; to drive (*a nail*); to stick (*a dagger, a punch, etc.*); to prick (*a horse in shoeing*); to set (*a precious stone*); to fix (*eyes, attention, etc.*); (coll.) to cheat; *vr* (coll.) to get cheated; (Am.) to dive; **clavárselas** (Am.) to get drunk
**clavaria** *f* nail mould; (bot.) goatsbeard
**clavazón** *f* nails, stock of nails
**clave** *f* key (*to a code, puzzle, etc.*); (mus.) clef; (arch.) keystone; **echar la clave** to close, to wind up (*a deal, speech, etc.*); **clave de fa** (mus.) bass clef; **clave de sol** (mus.) treble clef; **clave telegráfica** (telg.) code word; *m* (mus.) harpsichord; *adj* key
**clavel** *m* (bot.) pink, carnation; **clavel coronado** (bot.) garden pink, grass pink; **clavel de China** (bot.) China pink; **clavel de las Indias** (bot.) French marigold; **clavel de ramillete** or **clavel de San Isidro** (bot.) sweet william; **clavel reventón** carnation, double-flowered carnation
**clavelito** *m* (bot.) dogbane
**clavelón** *m* (bot.) marigold
**clavellina** *f* (bot.) pink; **clavellina de pluma** (bot.) garden pink, grass pink
**claveque** *m* rock crystal (*cut to imitate a diamond*)
**clavero -ra** *mf* keeper of the keys; treasurer; *m* (bot.) clove tree; *f* nail hole; nail mould, heading stamp; line of boundary stones or landmarks
**claveta** *f* peg, wooden peg
**clavete** *m* tack; (mus.) plectrum
**clavetear** *va* to stud, to trim with studs, gold or silver tacks, etc.; to tip, to put a tip on (*a cord, string, ribbon, etc.*); to wind up, to settle
**clavicordio** *m* (mus.) clavichord
**clavícula** *f* (anat.) clavicle
**claviculado -da** *adj* (zool.) claviculate
**clavicular** *adj* clavicular
**claviforme** *adj* (bot. & zool.) clavate
**clavija** *f* pin, peg, dowel; treenail; (mach.) pintle; (mus.) peg (*of string instrument*); (elec.) plug; **apretar las clavijas a** (coll.) to put the screws on; **clavija de piso** (elec.) floor plug; **clavija hendida** cotter pin
**clavijero** *m* peg, hook, hanger; (mus.) pegbox (*e.g., of a guitar*); (mus.) wrest plank (*of piano*); (telp.) plug
**clavillo** or **clavito** *m* brad, tack; pin, rivet (*e.g., to hold scissors together*); (cook.) clove
**clavo** *m* nail; spike; corn (*on foot*); sharp pain; keen sorrow; headache; scab; (vet.) pastern tumor; (cook.) clove; (min.) rich vein; (Am.) drug on the market; **dar en el clavo** (coll.) to hit the nail on the head; **de clavo pasado** self-evident; easy; **remachar el clavo** (coll.) to make a bad situation worse; (coll.) to argue for a statement already proved; **clavo de alambre** wire nail; **clavo de especia** clove (*flower*); **clavo de herrar** horse nail, horseshoe nail; **clavo romano** brass-headed nail
**claxon** *m* klaxon
**cleistógamo -ma** *adj* (bot.) cleistogamous
**clemátide** *f* (bot.) clematis, virgin's-bower
**clemencia** *f* clemency
**clemente** *adj* clement; (*cap.*) *m* Clement
**Cleón** *m* Cleon
**clepsidra** *f* water clock, clepsydra
**cleptomanía** *f* kleptomania
**cleptomaníaco -ca** or **cleptómano -na** *adj & mf* kleptomaniac
**clerecía** *f* clergy; priesthood
**clerical** *adj* clerical; *m* clerical, clericalist
**clericalismo** *m* clericalism
**clericato** *m* or **clericatura** *f* clergy, priesthood
**clerigalla** *f* (scornful) priesthood, priests
**clérigo** *m* cleric, clergyman; (hist.) clerk (*scholar*); **clérigo de misa** priest
**clerizón** *m* chorister, acolyte
**clerizonte** *m* fake cleric; shabby priest
**clero** *m* clergy
**clerofobia** *f* priest hatred
**clerófobo -ba** *adj* priest-hating; *mf* priest hater
**cleveíta** *f* (mineral.) cleveite
**cliché** *m* cliché (*timeworn phrase or idea*)
**cliente** *mf* client; customer; patient (*of a physician*); guest (*of a hotel*)
**clientela** *f* clientele; customers; patronage, protection
**clima** *m* climate; (geog.) zone, country, clime; **clima artificial** air conditioning
**climatérico -ca** *adj* climacteric; (coll.) ill-humored; *m* climacteric
**climaterio** *m* climacteric
**climático -ca** *adj* climatic
**climatización** *f* air conditioning
**climatizar** §76 to air-condition
**climatología** *f* climatology
**clímax** *m* (*pl:* **-max**) (rhet.) climax
**clin** *f* var. of **crin**
**clincha** *f* (box.) clinch
**clínico -ca** *adj* clinical; *mf* clinician; (archaic) person asking for deathbed baptism; *f* clinic; private hospital; **clínica de reposo** convalescent home, nursing home
**clinómetro** *m* clinometer
**clinopodio** *m* (bot.) calamint
**Clío** *f* (myth.) Clio
**clípeo** *m* (archeol., bot. & zool.) clypeus
**clíper** *m* (naut. & aer.) clipper
**cliqueteo** *m* click, clicking
**clisado** *m* (print.) plating
**clisar** *va* (print.) to plate
**clisé** *m* (print.) cliché, plate; (print.) electrotype; (phot.) plate (*positive or negative*)
**clistel** *m* or **clister** *m* (med.) clyster, enema
**clisterizar** §76 *va* to clyster, to give an enema to; *vr* to give oneself an enema
**clitelo** *m* (zool.) clitellum
**Clitemnestra** *f* (myth.) Clytemnestra
**clitómetro** *m* clinometer
**clítoris** *m* (anat.) clitoris
**clivoso -sa** *adj* (poet.) sloping
**clo** *m* cluck
**cloaca** *f* sewer; (zool.) cloaca
**clocar** §95 *vn* to cluck
**Clodoveo** *m* Clovis
**Cloe** *f* Chloe
**clónico -ca** *adj* clonic
**clono** *m* (path.) clonus
**clopemanía** *f* var. of **cleptomanía**
**cloque** *m* boat hook; harpoon to catch tuna fish
**cloquear** *va* to harpoon (*tuna fish*); *vn* to cluck
**cloqueo** *m* cluck, clucking
**cloquera** *f* broodiness (*of a hen*)
**cloquero** *m* tuna-fish harpooner
**cloral** *m* (chem.) chloral
**clorato** *m* (chem.) chlorate; **clorato de potasio** (chem.) potassium chlorate
**clorhidrato** *m* (chem.) hydrochlorate
**clorhídrico -ca** *adj* (chem.) hydrochloric
**clórico -ca** *adj* (chem.) chloric
**Cloris** *f* (myth.) Chloris
**clorita** *f* (mineral.) chlorite
**clorítico -ca** *adj* chloritic
**clorito** *m* (chem.) chlorite
**cloro** *m* (chem.) chlorine
**clorofila** *f* (bot. & biochem.) chlorophyll
**clorofílico -ca** *adj* chlorophyllous
**clorofilina** *f* (biochem.) chlorophyllin
**clorofórmico -ca** *adj* chloroformic

**cloroformización** *f* (med.) chloroformization, chloroforming
**cloroformizar §76** *va* (med.) to chloroform
**cloroformo** *m* (chem.) chloroform
**cloromicetina** *f* (pharm.) chloromycetin
**cloropicrina** *f* (chem.) chloropicrin
**cloroplasto** *m* (bot.) chloroplast
**cloropreno** *m* (chem.) chloroprene
**clorosis** *f* (bot. & path.) chlorosis; **clorosis de Egipto** (path.) hookworm disease
**cloroso -sa** *adj* (chem.) chlorous
**clorótico -ca** *adj* chlorotic
**clortetraciclina** *f* (pharm.) chlortetracycline
**clorurar** *va* to chloridize, to convert into a chloride
**cloruro** *m* (chem.) chloride; **cloruro amónico** (chem.) ammonium chloride; **cloruro de cal** (chem.) chloride of lime; **cloruro de calcio** (chem.) calcium chloride; **cloruro de etilo** (chem.) ethyl chloride; **cloruro mercúrico** (chem.) mercuric chloride
**Cloto** *f* (myth.) Clotho
**club** *m* (*pl:* **clubs**) club; **club náutico** yacht club
**clubista** *mf* club member
**clueco -ca** *adj* broody; (coll.) decrepit; *f* brooder (*hen*)
**cluniacense** *adj & m* Cluniac
**cllo.** abr. of **cuartillo**
**cm.** abr. of **centímetro** or **centímetros**
**C.M.B.** or **c.m.b.** abr. of **cuyas manos beso**
**Cnosos** *f* Knossos
**coa** *f* sharp stick used by Indians for tilling; (Am.) hoe; (Am.) jail slang
**coacción** *f* coercion, compulsion, coaction; enforcement
**coaccionar** *va* to force, to compel
**coacervación** *f* piling, heaping
**coacervar** *va* to pile, to heap up
**coacreedor -ra** *mf* cocreditor
**coactar** *va* to coerce, to force
**coactivo -va** *adj* coercive, compelling
**coacusado -da** *adj* jointly accused; *mf* codefendant
**coadjutor -tora** *mf* coadjutor; *f* coadjutrix
**coadjutoría** *f* coadjuvancy
**coadministrador** *m* coadministrator
**coadunación** *f* or **coadunamiento** *m* close union, coadunation
**coadunar** *va & vr* to join closely together
**coadyutor** *m* coadjutor
**coadyuvante** *m* state's attorney; (med.) adjuvant
**coadyuvar** *va* to help, aid; **coadyuvar a** + *inf* to help to + *inf; vn* to contribute
**coagente** *mf* coagent, associate
**coagulación** *f* coagulation; curdling
**coagulador -dora** *adj* coagulating, coagulative
**coagulante** *adj* coagulating, coagulative; *m* coagulant
**coagular** *va & vr* to coagulate; to curdle
**coagulina** *f* (biochem.) coagulin
**coágulo** *m* (physiol.) coagulum, clot
**coala** *m* (zool.) koala
**coalescencia** *f* coalescence
**coalescente** *adj* coalescent
**coalición** *f* coalition
**coalicionista** *mf* coalitionist
**coaligar §59** *vr* var. of **coligar**
**coalla** *f* (orn.) woodcock
**coana** *f* (anat.) choana
**coapóstol** *m* fellow apostle
**coaptación** *f* coaptation
**coartación** *f* limitation, restriction; (med.) coarctation; obligation to be ordained within a limited time in order to enjoy a benefice
**coartada** *f* alibi; **probar la coartada** to prove an alibi
**coartar** *va* to limit, restrict
**coate -ta** *adj & mf* (Am.) var. of **cuate**
**coatí** *m* (*pl:* **-tíes**) (zool.) coati
**coautor -tora** *mf* coauthor, fellow author
**coaxial** *adj* coaxial
**coba** *f* (coll.) trick; (coll.) cajolery; (coll.) chat
**cobaltar** *va* to plate with cobalt
**cobáltico -ca** *adj* (chem.) cobaltic
**cobaltina** *f* (mineral.) cobaltite or cobaltine
**cobalto** *m* (chem.) cobalt
**cobarde** *adj* cowardly; timid, faint-hearted; dim (*sight*); *mf* coward
**cobardear** *vn* to be cowardly; to be timid, faint-hearted
**cobardía** *f* cowardice; timidity, faint-heartedness
**cobaya** *m* or **cobayo** *m* (zool.) guinea pig
**cobeligerante** *m* cobelligerent
**cobertera** *f* lid, potlid; procuress
**cobertizo** *m* shed
**cobertor** *m* bedcover, bedspread
**cobertura** *f* cover; covering; ceremony of conferring title on grandee of Spain (*which consists of his putting his hat on in the presence of king*)
**cobija** *f* imbrex tile; short mantilla; blanket; (Am.) horse blanket; **cobijas** *fpl* (Am.) bedclothes; **cobija eléctrica** electric blanket
**cobijamiento** *m* covering, closing
**cobijar** *va* to cover, to close; to lodge; to shelter; **en todo lo que el sol cobija** under the sun
**cobijo** *m* covering, closing; lodging (*without meals*); shelter, protection
**cobista** *adj* (coll.) fawning, flattering; *mf* (coll.) fawner, flatterer
**Coblenza** *f* Coblenz
**cobo** *m* (zool.) purse crab; (Am.) blanket
**cobra** *f* (hunt.) retrieve, retrieval; rope for yoking oxen; mares hitched to tread grain; (zool.) cobra
**cobrable** or **cobradero -ra** *adj* collectable; recoverable
**cobrador** *m* collector; conductor, trolley conductor; retriever (*dog*)
**cobranza** *f* collection; cashing; retrieval (*of game*)
**cobrar** *va* to recover (*something lost*); to collect; to cash; to charge; to acquire, get, win; to pull in (*a rope*); (hunt.) to retrieve; (Am.) to dun; **cobrar afición, odio, etc. a** to take a liking, dislike, etc. for; **cobrar ánimo** to take courage; **cobrar carnes** to put on flesh; **cobrar fuerzas** to gain strength; *vn* to get hit, e.g., **vas a cobrar** you're going to get hit; *vr* to recover (*e.g., from fear*); to come to
**cobre** *m* copper; brasses (*kitchen utensils*); **cobres** (mus.) brasses; **batir el cobre** (coll.) to hustle, work with energy; **mostrar el cobre** (Am.) to show one's bad side; **cobre quemado** copper sulfate; **cobre verde** malachite
**cobreado -da** *adj* copperplated; *m* copperplating
**cobreño -ña** *adj* copper
**cobrería** *f* copper work; copperworks
**cobrero** *m* coppersmith
**cobrizo -za** *adj* copper-colored; cupreous
**cobro** *m* collection; cashing; **poner en cobro** to put in a safe place; **ponerse en cobro** to withdraw to a safe place
**Coburgo** Coburg
**coca** *f* (bot. & pharm.) coca; little, round berry; woman's hair on one side of part in the center; (coll.) head; (coll.) rap on the head with the knuckles; kink, knot (*in a rope*); (Am.) shell, rind; **de coca** (Am.) free; (Am.) in vain; **coca de Levante** (bot.) India berry tree
**cocada** *f* coconut candy, coconut bar
**cocaína** *f* cocaine
**cocainismo** *m* (path.) cocainism
**cocainización** *f* cocainization
**cocainizar §76** *va* to cocainize
**cocar §86** *va* (coll.) to make a face at, to make faces at; (coll.) to cajole; (coll.) to make eyes at, to flirt with
**coccíneo -a** *adj* purple
**cocción** *f* cooking, boiling; baking, burning (*of brick*)
**cóccix** *m* (*pl:* **-cix**) (anat.) coccyx
**coceador -dora** *adj* kicking (*animal*)
**coceadura** *f* or **coceamiento** *m* kicking
**cocear** *vn* to kick; (coll.) to balk, to resist
**cocedero -ra** *adj* easy to cook, boil, or bake; *m* cookery, boiling room
**cocedizo -za** *adj* easy to cook, boil, or bake
**cocedor** *m* workman in charge of boiling syrup (*for making wine*); cookery, boiling room
**cocedura** *f* var. of **cocción**
**cocer §30** *va* to cook; to boil; to bake (*bread, etc.*); to fire (*bricks*); to brew, to seethe; to di-

gest; to ret; *vn* to cook; to boil; to ferment; to seethe; *vr* to be in great sorrow; to be greatly inconvenienced; **no cocérsele a uno el pan** (coll.) to become intensely impatient
**cocido -da** *adj* (coll.) experienced, skilled; *m* olla, Spanish stew
**cociente** *m* (math.) quotient; **cociente intelectual** intelligence quotient
**cocimiento** *m* cooking, boiling; baking; decoction; bath for dyeing
**cocina** *f* kitchen; cuisine, cooking; stove; pottage of greens; **cocina de campaña** camp kitchen; **cocina de presión** pressure cooker; **cocina económica** kitchen range; **cocina sin fuego** fireless cooker
**cocinar** *va* to cook; (Am.) to bake; *vn* (coll.) to meddle
**cocinero -ra** *mf* cook
**cocinilla** *f* kitchenette; chafing dish; cooker; fireplace; **cocinilla sin fuego** fireless cooker; *m* (coll.) meddler
**Cocito** *m* (myth.) Cocytus
**cóclea** *f* endless screw; (anat.) cochlea
**coclear** *adj* cochlear
**coclearia** *f* (bot.) scurvy grass
**coco** *m* (bot.) coco, coconut palm or tree; coconut; coconut husk or shell; (bact.) coccus; percale; India berry; (ent.) scale insect; (orn.) white ibis; topknot, chignon; (coll.) bogeyman; (coll.) face, grimace; (Am.) derby hat; **hacer cocos** (coll.) to make a face, to make faces; (coll.) to cajole; (coll.) to make eyes, to flirt; **ser un coco** (coll.) to be ugly as the devil
**cocobacilo** *m* (bact.) coccobacillus
**cocobolo** *m* (bot.) sea grape; (bot.) cocobolo (*Dalbergia retusa*)
**cocodriliano -na** *adj & m* (zool.) crocodilian
**cocodrilo** *m* (zool.) crocodile
**cocolmeca** *f* (bot.) greenbrier
**cócora** *adj* (coll.) boresome, annoying; *mf* (coll.) bore
**cocoso -sa** *adj* gnawed by scale insects
**cocotal** *m* coconut grove
**cocote** *m* var. of **cogote**
**cocotero** *m* (bot.) coco, coconut palm or tree
**coctel** *m* or **cóctel** *m* cocktail; cocktail party
**coctelera** *f* cocktail shaker
**cocuma** *f* (Am.) roast corn on the cob
**cocuyo** *m* (bot.) ironwood; (ent.) fire beetle
**cochambre** *m* (coll.) filthy, stinking thing; (coll.) filthiness, dirtiness
**cochambrería** *f* (coll.) lot of filthy, stinking things
**cochambrero -ra** or **cochambroso -sa** *adj* (coll.) filthy and stinking
**cocharro** *m* wooden or stone cup, crock or bowl
**cochastro** *m* sucking wild boar
**coche** *m* carriage; coach; car; taxi; hog; **arrastrar coche** (coll.) to set up a coach, to live in style; **caminar en el coche de San Francisco** to go or to ride on shank's mare; **echar coche** to set up a coach; **coche automotor** rail car; **coche bar** (rail.) club car; **coche bomba** fire engine; **coche celular** Black Maria, prison van; **coche cuna** baby carriage; **coche de alquiler** cab, hack; **coche de carreras** (aut.) racing car; **coche de correos** (rail.) postal car, railroad mail car; **coche de deporte** (aut.) pleasure car; **coche de equipajes** (rail.) baggage car; **coche de mercancías** (rail.) freight car; **coche de muchos caballos** (aut.) high-powered car; **coche de paseo** (aut.) passenger car; **coche de plaza** or **de punto** hack; **coche de serie** (aut.) stock car; **coche de turismo** (aut.) touring car; **coche de viajeros** (rail.) passenger car; **coche fúnebre** or **mortuorio** hearse; **coche motor** motor coach; **coche usado** used car
**cochear** *vn* to drive a coach; to go driving
**coche-bar** *m* (*pl:* **coches-bares**) (rail.) club car
**coche-cama** *m* (*pl:* **coches-camas** or **coches-cama**) (rail.) sleeping car
**cochecillo** *m* little coach; wheel chair; **cochecillo para inválidos** wheel chair; **cochecillo para niño** baby carriage
**coche-comedor** *m* (*pl:* **coches-comedores**) (rail.) diner, dining car
**coche-correo** *m* (*pl:* **coches-correo**) (rail.) postal car, railroad mail car
**coche-fumador** *m* (*pl:* **coches-fumadores**) (rail.) smoker, smoking car
**coche-habitación** *m* (*pl:* **coches-habitación**) trailer
**cochera** *f* see **cochero**
**coche-restaurante** *m* (*pl:* **coches-restaurantes** or **coches-restaurante**) (rail.) diner, dining car
**cocheril** *adj* (coll.) (pertaining to a) coach; coachman's
**cochero -ra** *adj* easily boiled or cooked; *m* coachman; coach driver; **cochero de punto** hackman; *f* coachman's wife; coach house; livery stable; garage; carbarn
**cocherón** *m* large coach house; engine house, roundhouse
**coche-salón** *m* (*pl:* **coches-salones** or **coches-salón**) (rail.) parlor car, chair car
**cochevira** *f* lard
**cochevís** *m* (orn.) crested lark
**cochifrito** *m* fricassee of lamb or goat
**cochinada** *f* (coll.) piggishness, filthiness; (coll.) dirty trick
**cochinata** *f* (naut.) rider
**cochinchina** *f* Cochin (*fowl*); **la Cochinchina** Cochin China; **cochinchina enana** Cochin Bantam
**cochinería** *f* (coll.) piggishness, filthiness; (coll.) coarseness, baseness
**cochinero -ra** *adj* for hogs (*said of food*)
**cochinilla** *f* (ent.) cochineal insect; (zool.) wood louse; cochineal (*dyestuff*); **cochinilla de humedad** (zool.) sow bug; **cochinilla de la laca** (ent.) lac insect; **cochinilla de San José** (ent.) San Jose scale
**cochinillo** *m* sucking pig
**cochino -na** *adj* (coll.) piggish, dirty, filthy; (coll.) stingy; *mf* hog; (coll.) pig, dirty person; *m* (ichth.) oldwife; (metal.) pig; *f* sow; trollop (*slovenly woman*)
**cochiquera** *f* (coll.) var. of **cochitril**
**cochite hervite** *adv, adj & m* helter-skelter
**cochitril** *m* (coll.) pigsty; (coll.) den, filthy room, hovel
**cochizo** *m* (min.) rich vein
**cocho -cha** *mf* (dial.) hog
**cochura** *f* cooking, boiling, baking; batch of dough
**coda** *f* (carp.) corner block (*in form of triangular prism*); (mus.) coda
**codadura** *f* (hort.) layer
**codal** *adj* (pertaining to the) elbow; *m* elbowpiece (*of armor*); frame (*of saw*); strut, prop, shore, trench brace
**codaste** *m* (naut.) sternpost
**codazo** *m* nudge, poke with the elbow; **dar codazo a** (Am.) to tip, tip off
**codear** *vn* to elbow; (Am.) to sponge, sponge one's way; *vr* to hobnob; **codearse con** to hobnob with
**codeína** *f* (chem.) codein or codeine
**codelincuencia** *f* complicity
**codelincuente** *mf* accomplice
**codeo** *m* elbowing, nudging; (Am.) sponging
**codera** *f* elbow patch; itch on the elbow; (naut.) stern fast
**codesera** *f* growth of cytisus
**codeso** *m* (bot.) flatpod; (bot.) hairy cytisus
**codeudor -dora** *mf* codebtor
**códice** *m* codex
**codicia** *f* covetousness, cupidity, greed
**codiciable** *adj* covetable
**codiciador -dora** *adj* coveting; *mf* coveter
**codiciar** *va & vn* to covet
**codicilar** *adj* codicillary
**codicilo** *m* (law) codicil
**codicioso -sa** *adj* covetous, greedy, grasping; eager, anxious; **berserk** (*bull*); (coll.) hardworking, industrious
**codificación** *f* codification
**codificar** §86 *va* to codify
**código** *m* code; codex; Justinian code; **código civil** civil law; **código de honor** code of honor; **código de Justiniano** Justinian code; **código de señales** signal code; **código de señales marítimas** marine code; **código in-**

**ternacional** (telg.) international code; **código penal** penal code; **código telegráfico** telegraph code
**codillo** *m* knee (*of quadrupeds*); stirrup; (mach.) elbow; angle iron; bend; stump (*remaining on trunk after branch has been cut*); codille (*in game of omber*); **jugársela a uno de codillo** (coll.) to outwit someone; **tirar al codillo a** (coll.) to do everything possible to ruin (*someone*)
**codo** *m* elbow (*of arm or sleeve*); (mach.) elbow; cubit; **alzar** or **empinar el codo** (coll.) to drink, to crook the elbow; **dar de codo a** (coll.) to nudge; (coll.) to spurn; **hablar por los codos** (coll.) to talk too much; **hasta los codos** (coll.) up to the elbows; **mentir por los codos** (coll.) to lie like a trooper; **roerse los codos de hambre** (coll.) to be hard up, be in great want
**codón** *m* leather dock for horse's tail
**codoñate** *m* preserved quinces
**codorniz** *f* (*pl:* **-nices**) (orn.) quail
**coeducación** *f* coeducation
**coeducacional** *adj* coeducational
**coeficiencia** *f* common cause; cooperation, joint effort
**coeficiente** *m* (math. & phys.) coefficient; **coeficiente de dilatación** (phys.) coefficient of expansion; **coeficiente diferencial** (math.) differential coefficient; *adj* coefficient
**coercer** **§91** *va* to coerce, to restrain
**coerción** *f* coercion, restraint; (phys.) coercive force
**coercitivo -va** *adj* coercive, restraining
**coetáneo -a** *adj & mf* contemporary
**coeterno -na** *adj* coeternal
**coevo -va** *adj* coeval
**coexistencia** *f* coexistence
**coexistente** *adj* coexistent
**coexistir** *vn* to coexist
**coextender** **§66** *vr* to coextend
**coextensión** *f* coextension
**coextensivo -va** *adj* coextensive
**cofa** *f* (naut.) top
**cofia** *f* coif; hair net; (arm.) coif (*pad under helmet*)
**cofiador** *m* (law) joint bondsman or surety
**cofiezuela** *f* small coif; small hair net
**cofín** *m* basket, fruit basket
**cofosis** *f* (path.) cophosis, deafness
**cofrada** *f* sister, member
**cofrade** *mf* member, fellow member; *m* brother (*of a confraternity, etc.*); *f* sister (*of a confraternity, etc.*)
**cofradía** *f* confraternity, brotherhood, sisterhood; union, association
**cofre** *m* coffer, chest, trunk; (fort.) coffer; (ichth.) trunkfish; **cofre de equipajes** trunk (*of automobile*)
**cofrero -ra** *mf* trunk maker or dealer
**cofto -ta** *adj & mf* var. of **copto**
**cogedero -ra** *adj* ready to be picked; *m* handle; *f* rod for gathering esparto grass; box for catching bees; fruit picker (*pole with catch on end*)
**cogedizo -za** *adj* easy to pick
**cogedor -dora** *mf* picker, gatherer; *m* dustpan; coal shovel, ash shovel
**cogedura** *f* picking, gathering
**cogegotas** *m* (*pl:* **-tas**) drip pan
**coger** **§49** *va* to pick, gather, collect; to seize, take hold of; to catch; to get; to overtake; to find; to take up, absorb; to hold; to cover, occupy; *vn* to be, to be located; (coll.) to fit; *vr* to get caught; (Am.) to steal; **cogerse los dedos** to burn one's fingers
**cogetrapos** *m* (*pl:* **-pos**) ragpicker, rag dealer
**cogida** *f* (coll.) picking, gathering, harvest; (taur.) hook (*with the horns*)
**cogido** *m* fold, gather (*in cloth*)
**cogitabundo -da** *adj* pensive, meditative
**cogitativo -va** *adj* cogitative (*possessing power of thought*)
**cognación** *f* blood relationship via the female line; relationship
**cognado -da** *adj & mf* cognate
**cognaticio -cia** *adj* cognatic
**cognición** *f* cognition (*process of knowing*)
**cognomento** *m* epithet, appellation
**cognoscitivo -va** *adj* cognitive
**cogollo** *m* heart (*of lettuce*); head (*of cabbage*); shoot (*of a plant*); top (*of tree*); (ent.) harvest fly; (fig.) cream, pick
**cogombrillo** *m* var. of **cohombrillo**
**cogombro** *m* (archaic) var. of **cohombro**
**cogón** *m* (bot.) cogon grass
**cogorda** *f* (bot.) bottle gourd
**cogorza** *f* (coll.) drunk, drunkenness
**cogotazo** *m* blow on the back of the neck
**cogote** *m* back of the neck; crest at back of helmet; **ser tieso de cogote** (coll.) to be stiff, be haughty
**cogotera** *f* havelock; sun curtain (*for horse's neck*)
**cogotudo -da** *adj* thick-necked; (coll.) proud, stiff-necked; (coll.) very rich; *m* (Am.) nouveau riche
**cogucho** *m* coarse sugar
**cogujada** *f* (orn.) crested lark
**cogujón** *m* point, tip, corner (*of a pillow, bag, etc.*)
**cogujonero -ra** *adj* with points or corners (*like those of a pillow*)
**cogulla** *f* cowl (*monk's hood and garment together*); **cogulla de fraile** (bot.) monkshood
**cogullada** *f* pendulous fold of skin under neck of hog
**cohabitación** *f* living together; cohabitation
**cohabitar** *vn* to dwell or live together; to cohabit
**cohecha** *f* (agr.) plowing just before sowing
**cohechador -dora** *adj* bribing; *mf* briber
**cohechar** *va* to bribe (*e.g., a judge*); (agr.) to plow just before sowing; *vn* to take a bribe
**cohecho** *m* bribing; (agr.) plowing season
**cohen** *mf* soothsayer; procurer
**coheredera** *f* coheiress
**coheredero** *m* coheir
**coherencia** *f* coherence
**coherente** *adj* coherent; (bot.) coherent
**cohesión** *f* cohesion; (phys.) cohesion
**cohesivo -va** *adj* cohesive
**cohesor** *m* (rad.) coherer
**cohete** *m* skyrocket; rocket; blasting fuse; (coll.) wind (*in intestines or being expelled*); **cohete de salvamento** (naut.) lifesaving rocket; **cohete de señales** (aer.) flare; *adj* (Am.) drunk
**cohetear** *va* (Am.) to blast
**cohetería** *f* rocketry
**cohetero -ra** *mf* maker or seller of skyrockets and fireworks; rocketeer
**cohibición** *f* restraint, restriction
**cohibir** **§99** *va* to restrain, restrict, check
**cohobación** *f* cohobation, redistillation
**cohobar** *va* (chem.) to cohobate, redistil
**cohobo** *m* deerskin
**cohollo** *m* var. of **cogollo**
**cohombral** *m* cucumber patch
**cohombrillo** *m* (bot.) small cucumber; **cohombrillo amargo** (bot.) squirting cucumber
**cohombro** *m* (bot.) cucumber (*plant and fruit*); cucumber-shaped fritter; **cohombro de mar** (zool.) sea cucumber
**cohonestar** *va* to palliate, to gloss over, to rationalize
**cohorte** *f* cohort
**coigual** *adj & mf* coequal
**coima** *f* rake-off of operator of a gambling house; concubine; (Am.) bribe
**coime** *m* croupier; score keeper at billiards
**coimero** *m* croupier
**coincidencia** *f* coincidence; **en coincidencia con** in agreement with
**coincidente** *adj* coincident
**coincidir** *vn* to coincide; to come together; to agree
**coinquilino -na** *mf* joint tenant, cotenant
**coinquinar** *va* to stain, soil; *vr* to become sullied
**cointeresado -da** *adj* jointly interested; *mf* party having a joint interest
**coipo** or **coipu** *m* (zool.) coypu
**coirón** *m* (bot.) ichu
**coito** *m* coition, coitus
**coja** *f* see **cojo**
**cojear** *vn* to limp, to halt; to wobble (*said, e.g., of a table*); (coll.) to slip, to lapse (*into vice or error*); (fig.) to limp (*said of verse*); **saber**

**de qué pie cojea alguien** to know someone's weakness
**cojera** *f* limp, lameness
**cojijo** *m* bug; peeve
**cojijoso -sa** *adj* peevish, querulous
**cojín** *m* cushion
**cojincillo** *m* pad
**cojinete** *m* small cushion; sewing cushion; bearing; pillow block; (rail.) chair; **cojinete de balas** ball bearing; **cojinete de cono** cone bearing; **cojinete de rodillos** roller bearing
**cojinillo** *m* little cushion; holder (*to seize something hot*)
**cojitranco -ca** *adj* (scornful) mean and lame
**cojo -ja** *adj* lame, halt; crippled; wobbly (*table*); game (*leg*); shaky, unsound (*argument*); *mf* lame person; cripple; *f* (coll.) lewd woman
**cojón** *m* testicle
**cojudo -da** *adj* not castrated
**cojuelo -la** *adj* lame, crippled; *mf* cripple
**cok** *m* var. of **coque**
**col.** abr. of **colonia** & **columna**
**col** *f* (bot.) cabbage; **coles** *fpl* cabbage (*for eating*); **col de Bruselas** (bot.) Brussels sprouts; **col de Laponia** (bot.) Russian turnip; **col marina** (bot.) sea kale
**col.ª** abr. of **colonia** & **columna**
**cola** *f* tail; tail end; end seat; end, bottom (*e.g., of the class*); trail, train (*of a gown*); queue (*line of people*); glue; (fig.) tail (*e.g., of a comet, a coat*); **colas** *fpl* (min.) tailings; **a la cola** (coll.) behind; **hacer cola** (coll.) to stand in line, to queue; **tener** or **traer cola** (coll.) to have serious consequences; **cola de caballo** horsetail; (bot.) horsetail; **cola de gato** (meteor.) cat's-tail (*cirrus*); **cola del dragón** (astr.) dragon's tail; **cola del pan** bread line; **cola de milano** or **de pato** dovetail; **cola de perro** (bot.) crested dog's-tail; **cola de pescado** isinglass (*gelatin*); fish glue; **cola de rata** (bot.) bottle brush, field horsetail; **cola de retal** or **de retazo** (paint.) size, sizing; **cola de tijera** (orn.) frigate bird; **cola de zorra** (bot.) meadow foxtail; **cola de zorrillo** (bot.) hop tree; **cola negra** (zool.) black-tail, mule deer
**colaboración** *f* collaboration; contribution (*to a journal or symposium*)
**colaboracionista** *mf* collaborationist
**colaborador -dora** *adj* collaborating; *mf* collaborator; contributor
**colaborar** *vn* to collaborate; to contribute
**colación** *f* collation (*comparison; light lunch*); conferring (*e.g., of a degree*); parish land; **sacar a colación** (coll.) to bring up, make mention of; **traer a colación** (coll.) to bring in, to bring up; (coll.) to adduce as proof; (coll.) to lug in irrelevantly
**colacionador -dora** *mf* collator
**colacionar** *va* to collate
**colactánea** *f* foster sister
**colactáneo** *m* foster brother
**colada** *f* buck (*lye; bleached clothing*); bucking; cattle run; gulch; (metal.) tap; (coll.) good sword; **salir en la colada** (coll.) to come to light, be shown up, be exposed
**coladera** *f* strainer, colander
**coladero** *m* strainer, colander; narrow pass; (min.) winze, ore chute; (coll.) easy school, pipe course
**coladizo -za** *adj* runny
**colador** *m* strainer, colander
**coladora** *f* woman who bucks clothes
**coladura** *f* straining; (coll.) nonsense, lying
**colágeno** *m* (biochem.) collagen
**colagogo -ga** *adj* & *m* (med.) cholagogue
**colaina** *f* cup shake, ring shake
**colambre** *f* var. of **corambre**
**colanilla** *f* door or window bolt
**colaña** *f* low partition; solid or closed stair railing
**colapez** *f* or **colapiscis** *f* isinglass (*gelatin*)
**colapsible** *adj* collapsible
**colapso** *m* (path. & fig.) breakdown, collapse; **colapso nervioso** nervous breakdown
**colapsoterapia** *f* collapse therapy
**colar** *va* to confer (*a degree or an ecclesiastical benefit*); **§77** *va* to strain; to pour; to cast; to drive, bore; to sink (*a shaft*); to bleach (*washed clothes*) in hot lye, to buck; to pass off (*a bad coin*); **colar el hueso por** (coll.) to squeeze oneself through; *vn* to ooze, to run; to squeeze through; to come in (*said, e.g., of air through a narrow opening*); to slip in (*said of a remark*); (coll.) to drink wine; **no colar** (coll.) to not be believed; **colar a fondo** (naut.) to sink; *vr* to seep, percolate; to slip or sneak in; to slip through; to slip, make a slip; to talk nonsense, to lie; **colarse de gorra** (coll.) to crash the gate
**colateral** *adj* collateral; *mf* collateral (*relative*); *m* (com.) collateral
**colativo -va** *adj* collative; cleansing
**colcótar** *m* (chem.) colcothar
**colcrén** *m* cold cream
**colcha** *f* bedspread, counterpane, quilt
**colchado -da** *adj* quilted, padded; *m* quilting; lay (*in ropemaking*)
**colchadura** *f* quilting; (naut.) laying (*of ropes*)
**colchar** *va* to quilt; (naut.) to lay (*strands of rope*)
**colchero -ra** *mf* quilt maker
**colchón** *m* mattress; **colchón de aire** air mattress; **colchón de muelles** bedspring, spring mattress; **colchón de pluma** feather mattress; **colchón de tela metálica** wire bed, bedspring; **colchón de viento** air mattress
**colchonería** *f* wool shop; mattress, pillow, and cushion shop
**colchonero -ra** *mf* mattress maker
**colchoneta** *f* long cushion (*for a sofa or bench*)
**coleada** *f* wag of the tail; (Am.) throwing a bull by twisting its tail
**coleador -dora** *adj* tail-wagging
**coleadura** *f* wagging the tail; (taur.) twisting the bull's tail; (aer.) fishtail
**colear** *va* (taur.) to grab (*a bull*) by the tail; (Am.) to throw (*a bull*) by twisting its tail; (Am.) to nag, harass; (Am.) to trail after (*a person*); (Am.) to flunk (*a student*); (Am.) to be approaching (*a certain age*); *vn* to wag the tail; (aer.) to fishtail; (Am.) to sway (*said of a train*); **todavía colea** (coll.) it's still unsettled
**colección** *f* collection; (path.) abscess, gathering
**coleccionador -dora** *mf* collector (*e.g., of coins*)
**coleccionar** *va* to collect (*e.g., coins*)
**coleccionista** *mf* collector (*e.g., of coins*)
**colecistectomía** *f* (surg.) cholecystectomy
**colecisto** *m* (anat.) cholecyst
**colecistostomía** *f* (surg.) cholecystostomy
**colecta** *f* assessment; purse, money collected for charity; (eccl.) collect; (eccl.) collection
**colectación** *f* collection (*e.g., of taxes*)
**colectar** *va* to collect (*e.g., taxes*)
**colecticio -cia** *adj* new, green, untrained; omnibus (*volume*)
**colectividad** *f* collectivity; whole; group; community, whole community; collective ownership
**colectivismo** *m* collectivism
**colectivista** *adj* collectivistic; *mf* collectivist
**colectivización** *f* collectivization
**colectivizar** **§76** *va* to collectivize; *vr* to become collectivized
**colectivo -va** *adj* collective; group; (gram.) collective
**colectomía** *f* (surg.) colectomy
**colector** *m* collector (*e.g., of taxes*); trap, catch basin; sewer; (elec.) commutator; (elec.) collector; **colector de admisión** intake manifold; **colector de escape** exhaust manifold
**colecturía** *f* collectorship; collector's office; tax office
**colédoco** *m* (anat.) common bile duct
**colega** *mf* colleague
**colegatario -ria** *mf* (law) joint legatee, colegatary
**colegiación** *f* association, organization into an association
**colegiado -da** *adj* collegiate
**colegial** *adj* collegiate, college; *m* collegian
**colegiala** *f* collegian, co-ed
**colegiar** *vr* to form an association
**colegiata** *f* collegiate church
**colegiatura** *f* scholarship, fellowship

**colegio** *m* college; school, academy; student body; **Colegio de cardenales** College of Cardinals; **colegio electoral** electoral college; polls
**colegir §72** *va* to gather, collect; to infer, to conclude
**colegislador -dora** *adj* colegislative
**coleo** *m* var. of **coleadura**
**coleóptero -ra** *adj* (ent.) coleopterous; *m* (ent.) coleopteran
**coleorriza** *f* (bot.) coleorhiza
**colera** *f* tail ornament (*for a horse*)
**cólera** *f* (physiol.) bile; anger, rage, choler; gummed white cotton fabric; **montar en cólera** to blow up, to hit the ceiling; *m* (path.) cholera; **cólera asiático** (path.) Asiatic cholera; **cólera de las gallinas** (vet.) chicken cholera; **cólera de los cerdos** (vet.) hog cholera; **cólera esporádico** (path.) cholera nostras; **cólera infantil** (path.) cholera infantum; **cólera morbo** (path.) cholera morbus; **cólera nostras** (path.) cholera nostras
**colérico -ca** *adj* choleric (*irascible*); choleraic (*pertaining to cholera*); sick with cholera; *mf* choleric or irritable person; person suffering from cholera
**coleriforme** *adj* choleriform
**colerina** *f* (path.) cholerine
**colesterina** *f* (biochem.) cholesterin
**colesterol** *m* (biochem.) cholesterol
**coleta** *f* pigtail; queue, cue; (coll.) postscript; (Am.) burlap; **cortarse la coleta** to quit the ring, give up bullfighting; to quit; **traer** o **tener coleta** (coll.) to lead to results of some moment
**coletazo** *m* lash, blow with the tail
**coleteo** *m* flop, flopping
**coletero** *m* (orn.) wren
**coletillo** *m* sleeveless jacket
**coleto** *m* buff jacket; (coll.) body, one's body, oneself; **decir para su coleto** (coll.) to say to oneself; **echarse al coleto** (coll.) to eat up, to drink up; (coll.) to read from cover to cover
**coletudo -da** *adj* (Am.) brazen, insolent
**colgadero -ra** *adj* fit to be hung up, fit to be kept; *m* hanger, hook; clothes rack
**colgadizo -za** *adj* hanging; lean-to, penthouse; *m* lean-to, penthouse
**colgado -da** *adj* pending, unsettled; drooping; **dejar colgado** (coll.) to frustrate, to disappoint; **quedarse colgado** (coll.) to be frustrated, to be disappointed
**colgador** *m* (print.) peel; clothes hanger
**colgadura** *f* hangings, drapery, tapestry
**colgajo** *m* rag, tatter; fruit hung up for keeping; (surg.) torn tissue (*used to heal over a wound*)
**colgandero -ra** *adj* hanging, suspended
**colgante** *adj* hanging; suspension; *m* hanger; drop, pendant; festoon; king post
**colgar §79** *va* to hang; to drape, to adorn with hangings; to flunk; to give a birthday present to; to attribute, to blame; (coll.) to hang (*e.g., a criminal*); *vn* to hang; to dangle; to droop; to depend; (telp.) to hang up; **colgar de** to hang from; to hang on (*e.g., a nail*)
**colibacilo** *m* (bact.) coli
**colibacilosis** *f* (path.) colibacillosis
**coliblanco -ca** *adj* white-tailed
**colibrí** *m* (*pl:* **-bríes**) (orn.) humming bird
**colicano -na** *adj* white-tailed
**cólico -ca** *adj* (anat. & path.) colic; *m* (path.) colic; *f* (path.) upset stomach
**colicuación** *f* melting, fusion; (path.) colliquation
**colicuar** *va* to melt, dissolve
**colicuecer §34** *va* var. of **colicuar**
**coliche** *m* (coll.) open house
**coliflor** *f* (bot.) cauliflower; (path.) cauliflower excrescence
**coligación** *f* connection, union; alliance
**coligado -da** *adj* bound together; allied; *mf* ally, confederate
**coligadura** *f* or **coligamiento** *m* var. of **coligación**
**coligar §59** *vr* to join forces, make common cause
**colilla** *f* butt, stump (*of cigar*)
**colillero -ra** *mf* cigar-butt picker
**colimación** *f* (astr. & opt.) collimation
**colimador** *m* (opt.) collimator
**colimbo** *m* (orn.) grebe
**colín -lina** *adj* bobtailed (*horse or mare*); *m* (orn.) bobwhite; **colín de Virginia** (orn.) bobwhite
**colina** *f* hill, knoll; cabbage seed; cabbage nursery; (biochem.) choline
**colinabo** *m* (bot.) rutabaga
**colindante** *adj* adjacent, contiguous, neighboring
**colindar** *vn* to be adjacent, be contiguous
**colineta** *f* pretty dish of sweets; (Am.) macaroon
**colino** *m* cabbage seed; cabbage nursery
**colinoso -sa** *adj* hilly
**coliquecer §34** *va* var. of **colicuar**
**colirio** *m* collyrium, eyewash
**colirrábano** *m* (bot.) kohlrabi
**colirrojo** *m* (orn.) redstart
**colisa** *f* (arti.) revolving platform; (arti.) swivel gun
**coliseo** *m* coliseum; (*cap.*) *m* Coliseum, Colosseum
**colisión** *f* collision; chafing, abrasion; bruise, bump
**colista** *mf* (hum.) queuer, person standing in line
**colitigante** *mf* colitigant
**colitis** *f* (path.) colitis
**colmadamente** *adv* in abundance
**colmado -da** *adj* abundant, full, overflowing; *m* sea-food restaurant; food store
**colmar** *va* to fill to overflowing; to fill, to stock; to fill in, to fill up; to crowd; to fulfill (*e.g., one's hopes*); to overwhelm; **colmar de** to shower with, to overwhelm with; **colmar el ojo** to fill the eye
**colmena** *f* beehive
**colmenar** *m* apiary
**colmenero -ra** *mf* beekeeper
**colmenilla** *f* (bot.) morel
**colmillada** *f* var. of **colmillazo**
**colmillar** *adj* (pertaining to an) eyetooth, tusk
**colmillazo** *m* bite with an eyetooth; gash made with a tusk
**colmillejo** *m* small eyetooth; small tusk
**colmillo** *m* eyetooth, canine tooth; tusk (*e.g., of elephant*); **enseñar los colmillos** (coll.) to show one's teeth; (coll.) to stiffen, show spirit; **escupir por el colmillo** (coll.) to boast, brag, bully; **tener el colmillo retorcido** (coll.) to be keen, be wide-awake
**colmilludo -da** *adj* having big eyeteeth; big-tusked; (coll.) keen, sharp-witted
**colmo -ma** *adj* filled to overflowing; *m* overflow, overflowing; (coll.) height, limit; thatch, thatched roof; topping (*e.g., of a dish of ice cream*); **a colmo** in abundance; **eso es el colmo** (coll.) that's the limit; **llegar a colmo** (coll.) to attain perfection; **llenar con colmo** to fill to overflowing; **para colmo de** to top off, as a finishing touch to
**colobo** *m* (zool.) guereza (*African monkey*)
**colocación** *f* placing; location; placement; investment; position, employment, job
**colocar §86** *va* to place, to put; to locate; to invest; to find a place or position for; to set (*a trap*); to find an outlet for (*a product*); to lay (*a keel*); *vr* to get placed, find a job; to sell; (sport) to place (*said of a horse in a race*)
**colocasia** *f* (bot.) taro
**colocolo** *m* colocolo (*South American wildcat*); singing mouse of Chile; (Chile) imaginary fish-shaped or lizard-shaped monster hatched from a rotten egg
**colocutor -tora** *mf* collocutor, conferee; party (*to a conversation*)
**colodión** *m* (chem.) collodion
**colodra** *f* milk bucket; wine bucket; drinking horn; **ser una colodra** (coll.) to be a toper
**colodrillo** *m* back of neck
**colofón** *m* colophon; (fig.) finishing touch
**colofonia** *f* colophony, rosin
**coloidal** *adj* colloidal
**coloide** *adj* & *m* (chem.) colloid
**coloideo -a** *adj* colloid, colloidal
**Colombia** *f* Colombia; **la Colombia Británica** British Columbia

**colombianismo** *m* Colombianism
**colombiano -na** *adj & mf* Colombian
**colombino -na** *adj* Columbian (*pertaining to Columbus*); (*cap.*) *f* Columbine
**colombio** *m* (chem.) columbium
**colombo** *m* (pharm.) calumba
**colombófilo -la** *mf* pigeon fancier
**colon** *m* (anat.) colon; (gram.) main clause; (gram.) colon, semicolon; **colon imperfecto** (gram.) dependent clause; **colon perfecto** (gram.) independent clause, main clause
**Colón** *m* Columbus; (*l.c.*) *m* colon (*monetary unit of Costa Rica and El Salvador*)
**colonato** *m* colonialism
**colonia** *f* colony; cologne; silk ribbon (*about an inch and a half wide*); community, development; (Am.) sugar plantation; (*cap.*) *f* Cologne; **la Colonia del Cabo** Cape Colony; **colonia veraniega** summer colony
**coloniaje** *m* (Am.) colonial period; (Am.) colonial system; (Am.) slavery
**colonial** *adj* colonial; overseas; **coloniales** *mpl* imported foods
**colonialismo** *m* colonialism
**colonialista** *adj* colonial (*country*)
**colónico -ca** *adj* colonic
**colonización** *f* colonization; land settlement
**colonizador -dora** *adj* colonizing; *mf* colonizer, colonist
**colonizar** §76 *va & vn* to colonize, to settle
**colono** *m* colonist, settler; colonial; farmer; tenant farmer; (Am.) Indian peasant
**coloquial** *adj* colloquial
**coloquíntida** *f* (bot.) colocynth
**coloquio** *m* colloquy, talk, conference
**color** *m* color; coloring; paint; rouge; **colores** *mpl* colors (*flag*); **de color** colored (*not black or white; of some other race than the white*); tan (*e.g., shoes*); **en todo color** in full color; **mudar de color** to change color (*to turn pale; to blush*); **sacar los colores a** to make blush; **salirle a uno los colores** to blush; **so color de** under color of, under pretext of; **verlo todo de color de rosa** to see everything through rose-colored glasses; **color al óleo** (paint.) oil color; **colores complementarios** complementary colors; **colores de anilina** aniline dyes; **color local** (lit. & paint.) local color; **color muerto** o **quebrado** faded color, wan color
**coloración** *f* coloration, coloring
**colorado -da** *adj* colored; red, reddish; off-color (*joke*); colored, specious; **ponerse colorado** (coll.) to blush
**coloradote -ta** *adj* (coll.) ruddy, sanguine, blowzy
**colorante** *adj & m* coloring
**colorar** *va* to color; to dye; to stain
**colorativo -va** *adj* coloring
**coloratura** *f* (mus.) coloratura
**colorear** *va* to color; (fig.) to color, to palliate; *vn* to redden, turn red (*said, e.g., of ripening fruit*)
**colorete** *m* rouge; **ponerse colorete** to rouge, to make up
**colorido -da** *adj* colorful; *m* coloring; (fig.) coloring
**colorimetría** *f* colorimetry
**colorímetro** *m* colorimeter
**colorín** *m* (orn.) linnet; bright color
**colorir** §53 *va* to color; (fig.) to color; *vn* to take on color
**colorista** *mf* colorist
**colosal** *adj* colossal
**colosense** *adj & mf* Colossian
**coloso** *m* colossus; **coloso de Rodas** Colossus of Rhodes
**colostomía** *f* (surg.) colostomy
**colquicina** *f* (chem.) colchicine
**cólquico** *m* (bot.) colchicum, autumn crocus; (pharm.) colchicum
**Cólquida, la** Colchis
**coludir** *vn* to be in collusion
**columbario** *m* columbarium
**columbino -na** *adj* columbine, dovelike; simple, innocent
**columbio** *m* var. of **colombio**
**columbrar** *va* to glimpse, descry; to guess
**columbrete** *m* (naut.) reef
**columela** *f* (arch., anat., bot. & zool.) columella
**columelar** *adj* canine (*tooth*); *m* canine tooth
**columna** *f* column; **quinta columna** fifth column; **columna adosada** (arch.) engaged column; **columna cerrada** (mil.) close column; **columna de dirección** (aut.) steering column; **columna embebida** (arch.) engaged column; **columna entorchada** (arch.) wreathed column; **columna entregada** (arch.) engaged column; **columna mingitoria** public urinal; **columna rostral** rostral column; **columna salomónica** (arch.) twisted column; **columnas de Hércules** Pillars of Hercules; **columna vertebral** (anat.) vertebral column, spinal column; **columna volante** (mil.) flying column
**columnación** *f* (arch.) columniation
**columnador** *m* tabulator (*of typewriter*)
**columnario -ria** *adj* columnar
**columnata** *f* (arch.) colonnade; (arch.) columniation
**columnista** *mf* columnist
**columpiar** *va* to swing; *vr* to swing; to seesaw; (coll.) to swing, sway, swagger
**columpio** *m* swing; seesaw; (Am.) dip in the road
**coluro** *m* (astr.) colure
**colusión** *f* collusion
**colusorio -ria** *adj* collusive
**colutorio** *m* gargle
**coluvie** *f* (archaic) gang of thugs; sewer, mudhole
**colza** *f* (bot.) colza, rape
**colla** *f* collet (*of armor*); squally weather preceding monsoons; (naut.) last packing of oakum; row of fish traps
**collada** *f* pass (*through mountains*); (naut.) steady blow
**collado** *m* hill, height; pass (*through mountains*)
**collar** *m* necklace; cord or chain (*hung around neck to hold insignia*); dog collar, horse collar; collar, band (*placed on neck of a prisoner*); frill, ring (*of feathers of different colors around neck of bird*); (mach.) collar
**collarejo** *m* small necklace
**collarín** *m* stock (*worn by clergy*); collar (*of a coat*); frill (*around neck of bird or animal*); (arch.) gorgerin
**collarino** *m* (arch.) gorgerin
**collazo** *m* farmhand (*who has been given some land to work for himself*); bondsman, serf
**colleja** *f* (bot.) corn salad
**collera** *f* horse collar; collar (*breast harness*); chain gang; (Am.) pair of cuff links; **collera de yugo** oxbow
**collerón** *m* fancy horse collar
**collón -llona** *adj* (coll.) cowardly; *mf* (coll.) coward
**collonada** *f* (coll.) cowardice, cowardly act
**collonería** *f* (coll.) cowardice
**coma** *f* (gram.) comma (*used also for the decimal point in Spanish*); (arch.) miserere, misericord; **sin faltar una coma** (coll.) in minutest detail; *m* (path.) coma; **coma vigil** (path.) coma vigil
**comabacilo** *m* (bact.) comma bacillus
**comadre** *f* midwife; mother or godmother (*with respect to each other*); gossip; (coll.) woman friend (*of another woman*); (coll.) go-between
**comadrear** *vn* (coll.) to gossip, to go around gossiping; (Am.) to enjoy oneself
**comadreja** *f* (zool.) weasel
**comadreo** *m* (coll.) gossip, gossiping
**comadrería** *f* (coll.) gossiping, idle gossip
**comadrero -ra** *adj* (coll.) gossipy; *mf* (coll.) gossip (*person*)
**comadrón** *m* accoucheur, man midwife; gynecologist
**comadrona** *f* midwife
**comal** *m* (Am.) round earthenware griddle (*for corncakes*)
**comalia** or **comalía** *f* (vet.) dropsy
**comalido -da** *adj* sickly
**comandancia** *f* command (*position or function; territory; troops, ships, etc. under one who commands*); commander's office; (mil.) majority

**comandanta** *f* (coll.) wife of commander, commandant, or major; (nav.) flagship
**comandante** *m* (mil.) commander; (mil.) commandant; (mil.) major; **comandante en jefe** commander in chief
**comandar** *va* (mil. & nav.) to command
**comandita** *f* (com.) silent partnership
**comanditar** *va* (com.) to invest in (*an undertaking*) as a silent partner
**comanditario -ria** *adj* silent; silent-partnership; *mf* silent partner
**comando** *m* (mil.) command; (mil.) commando; control; **comando a distancia** remote control
**comarca** *f* region, territory, province
**comarcal** *adj* regional, provincial
**comarcano -na** *adj* regional; bordering, neighboring
**comarcar** §86 *va* to line up (*trees*) at equal distances in every direction; *vn* to border
**comatoso -sa** *adj* comatose
**comátula** *f* (zool.) feather star
**comba** *f* see **combo**
**combadura** *f* bending, curving, warping, bulging; bend, belly, sag; camber
**combar** *va* to bend, to curve; *vr* to bend, to curve, to warp, to bulge, to sag
**combate** *m* combat, fight; struggle; **fuera de combate** hors de combat; **triunfar por fuera de combate** (box.) to win by a knockout
**combatido -da** *adj* aggressive, militant
**combatiente** *adj* combatant; *m* combatant; (orn.) ruff
**combatir** *va* to combat, to fight; to beat, to beat upon; to harass; *vn* to combat; to struggle; *vr* to combat, to fight
**combatividad** *f* combativeness
**combativo -va** *adj* combative
**combés** *m* open space; (naut.) half deck
**combinación** *f* combination; combination (*underwear*); plan, scheme; **combinación de trenes** (rail.) connection
**combinador** *m* (elec.) controller
**combinar** *va* to combine, to bring together; to work out; (chem.) to combine; *vr* to combine; (chem.) to combine
**combinatorio -ria** *adj* combinatory; (math.) combinatorial
**combleza** *f* mistress (*of a married man*)
**combo -ba** *adj* bent, warped, crooked; *m* stand for casks; *f* bend, curve, warp, bulge; skipping rope; game of skipping rope; camber (*of road*); **hacer combas** (coll.) to sway, to swing; **saltar a la comba** to jump rope, to skip rope
**comboso -sa** *adj* bent, curved, arched, bulging
**comburente** *adj* supporting combustion; *m* supporter of combustion
**combustibilidad** *f* combustibility
**combustible** *adj* combustible; *m* combustible; fuel
**combustión** *f* combustion; **poner en combustión** to inflame, to stir up, to agitate; **combustión espontánea** spontaneous combustion
**combusto -ta** *adj* burnt
**comedero -ra** *adj* eatable; *m* manger, feed trough; dining room; (Am.) pasture; (Am.) hangout; **limpiarle a uno el comedero** (coll.) to deprive someone of his livelihood
**comedia** *f* comedy; play, drama; theater; comedia (*Spanish verse drama*); (fig.) farce; (fig.) drama; **hacer la comedia** (coll.) to pretend, make believe; **comedia cómica** comedy (*humorous play*); **comedia de capa y espada** cloak-and-sword play; **comedia de carácter** comedy of character; **comedia de costumbres** comedy of manners; **comedia de enredo** comedy of intrigue; **comedia de figurón** Spanish drama of the seventeenth century depicting a ridiculous or extravagant vice or character; **comedia devota** Spanish mystery play (*based on Eucharist*)
**comediante -ta** *mf* hypocrite; *m* actor; *f* actress, comedienne
**comediar** *va* to divide into equal parts, to divide in half
**comedido -da** *adj* courteous, polite; moderate, frugal; (Am.) meddlesome; (Am.) obliging
**comedimiento** *m* courtesy, politeness; moderation; (Am.) meddlesomeness
**comedio** *m* middle; interval
**comediógrafo -fa** *mf* playwright; comedian (*writer*)
**comedión** *m* dull, tiresome play
**comedir** §94 *vr* to be courteous; to be moderate, control oneself; (Am.) to meddle; (Am.) to be obliging; **comedirse a** + *inf* (Am.) to offer to, to volunteer to + *inf*
**comedón** *m* (path.) blackhead
**comedor -dora** *adj* heavy-eating, hungry; *m* dining room; eating place, restaurant; dining-room suite; **comedor de beneficencia** soup kitchen
**comedorcito** *m* dinette
**comegente** *m* (slang) man-eater
**comején** *m* (ent.) white ant, termite
**comejenera** *f* nest of white ants; (Am.) dive, den
**comendador** *m* knight commander; commander (*of a military order*); prelate of an order, Mercedarian prelate
**comendadora** *f* mother superior, Mercedarian mother superior
**comendatario** *m* (eccl.) commendatary, commendator
**comendaticio -cia** *adj* (eccl.) commendatory (*letter*)
**comendatorio -ria** *adj* commendatory (*letter or document*)
**comendero** *m* (hist.) commendator
**comensal** *mf* retainer, dependent, servant; table companion; fellow diner; (biol.) commensal
**comensalía** *f* house companionship, table companionship
**comentador -dora** *mf* commentator
**comentar** *va* to comment on, to expound; *vn* to comment; (coll.) to gossip
**comentario** *m* commentary; **comentarios** *mpl* (coll.) chit-chat, gossip
**comentarista** *mf* commentator
**comento** *m* comment; commentary; fiction, falsehood; deceit, cheat
**comenzante** *adj* beginning; *mf* beginner
**comenzar** §31 *va & vn* to begin, to start, to commence; **comenzar a** + *inf* to begin to + *inf;* **comenzar** + *ger* to begin + *ger;* **comenzar por** + *inf* to begin by + *ger*
**comer** *m* food; *va* to eat; to feed on; to gnaw, to gnaw away; to corrode; to consume; to fade; to enjoy (*an income*); (checkers & chess) to take; to itch; **sin comerlo ni beberlo** (coll.) without having anything to do with it; **tener qué comer** (coll.) to have enough to live on; **comer vivo** (coll.) to have it in for; *vn* to eat; to dine, have dinner; to itch; **comer de todo** to eat everything; *vr* to be eaten; to eat up; to bite (*one's nails*); (coll.) to consume (*money*); to skip, skip over; to nullify; **comerse unos a otros** (coll.) to be at loggerheads
**comerciable** *adj* marketable; sociable
**comercial** *adj* commercial
**comercialidad** *f* marketability
**comercialización** *f* commercialization
**comercializar** §76 *va* to commercialize
**comerciante** *adj* trading, of traders, of merchants; *mf* trader, merchant; **comerciante al por mayor** wholesaler; **comerciante al por menor** retailer; **comerciante comisionista** commission merchant; *m* tradesman
**comerciar** *vn* to deal, to trade; to have dealings
**comercio** *m* commerce, trade; business; business interests; business center; store, shop; firm; intercourse, illicit intercourse; **comercio de artículos de regalo** gift shop; **comercio exterior** foreign trade; **comercio interior** domestic commerce; **comercio sexual** sexual intercourse; **comercio social** social intercourse
**comestible** *adj* eatable, comestible; *m* food, foodstuff, comestible
**cometa** *m* (astr.) comet; *f* kite
**cometario -ria** *adj* (pertaining to a) comet
**cometer** *va* to entrust; to commit (*an undertaking to someone; a mistake, a sin, a crime*); to employ (*a figure of speech*)
**cometido** *m* assignment, commission, duty; commitment; purpose

**comezón** *f* itch; (fig.) itch
**comible** *adj* (coll.) fit to eat
**comicastro** *m* ham, ham actor
**comicial** *adj* comitial
**comicidad** *f* comedy, comicalness
**comicios** *mpl* comitia; election; voting; **acudir a los comicios** to go to the polls
**cómico -ca** *adj* comic or comical; dramatic; *mf* comedian; actor; **cómico de la legua** strolling actor, barnstormer; ham; *f* comedienne; actress
**comida** *f* see **comido**
**comidilla** *f* repast; (coll.) hobby; (coll.) talk, gossip; **comidilla de la ciudad, del pueblo** or **de la vecindad** (coll.) talk of the town
**comido -da** *adj* fed; finished eating; **estar comido** to have finished eating; **comido por servido** (coll.) unprofitable, not worth while; *f* eating; food; meal; dinner; **comida corrida** (Am.) table d'hôte; **comidas y camas** board and lodging
**comienzo** *m* beginning, start; **a comienzos de** around the beginning of (*e.g., the month*); **dar comienzo** to have its (or their) beginnings
**comilitón** *m* var. of **conmilitón**
**comilitona** *f* (coll.) spread, feast
**comilón -lona** *adj* (coll.) hearty, heavy-eating, voracious; *mf* (coll.) big eater; *f* (coll.) big meal, hearty meal, spread
**comillas** *fpl* quotation marks
**cominear** *vn* (coll.) to fuss around like a woman (*said of a man*)
**cominería** *f* (coll.) fussiness
**cominero** *adj masc* (coll.) fussy (*man*); *m* (coll.) fussy fellow, betty
**Cominform** *f* Cominform
**cominillo** *m* (bot.) cockle, darnel
**comino** *m* (bot.) cumin; cuminseed; **no valer un comino** (coll.) to be not worth a continental; **comino rústico** (bot.) laserwort
**Comintern** *f* Comintern
**comiquear** *vn* to put on amateur plays
**comiquería** *f* (coll.) group of ham actors; (coll.) educational farce
**comiquillo** *m* ham, ham actor
**comisar** *va* to attach, to seize; to confiscate
**comisaría** *f* commissariat; (Am.) police station
**comisariato** *m* commissariat
**comisario** *m* commissary; commissioner; commissar; (mil.) commissary; **alto comisario** high commissioner; **comisario de a bordo** (naut.) purser
**comiscar §86** *va* (coll.) var. of **comisquear**
**comisión** *f* commission; committee; errand
**comisionado -da** *adj* commissioned; *mf* commissioner; committeeman
**comisionar** *va* to commission
**comisionista** *mf* commission agent; commission merchant; *adj* commission, working on a commission
**comis.°** abr. of **comisario**
**comiso** *m* attachment, seizure; confiscation; confiscated goods
**comisquear** *va* (coll.) to nibble at, keep nibbling at
**comistión** *m* commixture
**comistrajo** *m* (coll.) hodgepodge, mess
**comisura** *f* (anat., bot. & zool.) commissure; corner (*of lips, eyelids, etc.*)
**comité** *m* committee
**comitente** *adj & mf* constituent
**comitiva** *f* retinue, suite
**cómitre** *m* (naut.) galley boatswain
**comiza** *f* (ichth.) barbel
**como** *adv* as; like; how; so to speak, as it were; about; *conj* as; when; if; as soon as; so that; as long as; inasmuch as; that; **así como** as soon as; **la manera como** the way that; **tan luego como** as soon as; **como no** unless; **como no sea** unless it be; **como no sea para** + *inf* except to + *inf*, unless it be to + *inf;* **como que** because, inasmuch as; **como quien dice** so to speak; **como quiera que** however; since, inasmuch as; (archaic) although
**cómo** *adv* how?; why?; what?; how!; how, e.g., **no sé cómo explicar lo que hizo** I don't know how to explain what he did; **¿a cómo es . . . ?** how much is . . . ?; **¿cómo así?** how so?; **¿cómo no?** why not?; **¡cómo no!** (Am.) of course!
**cómoda** *f* see **cómodo**
**comodable** *adj* (law) susceptible of being lent
**comodante** *mf* (law) lender by commodation
**comodatario -ria** *mf* borrower by commodation
**comodato** *m* (law) commodation; (law) commodatum
**comodidad** *f* convenience; comfort; interest, advantage
**comodidoso -sa** *adj* (Am.) self-seeking
**comodín** *m* wild card, joker; gadget, jigger; excuse, alibi
**comodista** *adj* self-centered; selfish; comfort-loving
**cómodo -da** *adj* convenient, handy; comfortable (*person or thing*); comfort-loving; *f* commode, bureau, chest of drawers
**comodón -dona** *adj* (coll.) comfort-loving
**comodoro** *m* commodore
**comoquiera** *adv* anyway; **comoquiera que** however
**comp.ª** abr. of **compañía**
**compacción** *f* compactness
**compacidad** or **compactibilidad** *f* compressibility, contractility
**compacto -ta** *adj* compact; close (*e.g., weave*)
**compadecer §34** *va* to pity, to feel sorry for; *vr* to harmonize; **compadecerse con** to harmonize with; **compadecerse de** to pity, to feel sorry for
**compadecido -da** *adj* sympathetic
**compadraje** *m* cabal, clique
**compadrar** *vn* to become a godfather; to become friendly; to be congenial
**compadrazgo** *m* compaternity; cabal, clique
**compadre** *m* father or godfather (*with respect to each other*); (coll.) friend, companion
**compadrear** *vn* (coll.) to be close friends; (Am.) to show off
**compadrería** *f* friendship, companionship
**compadrito** *m* (Am.) bully
**compaginación** *f* arrangement, ordering; (print.) paging
**compaginador** *m* (print.) pager
**compaginar** *va* to arrange, to put in order, to bring together; (print.) to page, page up, make up; *vr* to fit, agree, gee
**companage** *m* or **compango** *m* cold cuts, cold dish
**compaña** *f* (coll.) company; (archaic) family
**compañerismo** *m* good fellowship, comradeship, companionship
**compañero -ra** *mf* companion; mate; partner; **compañero de armas** companion-at-arms, comrade in arms; **compañero de cama** bedfellow; **compañero de cuarto** or **de habitación** roommate; **compañero de juego** playfellow, playmate; **compañero de trabajo** fellow worker; **compañero de viaje** fellow traveler (*communist sympathizer*); *f* helpmeet (*wife*)
**compañía** *f* company; society; (com., mil. & theat.) company; **hacerle compañía a una persona** to keep someone company; **compañía anónima** (com.) stock company; **compañía comanditaria** or **en comandita** (com.) commandite (*partnership with one or more silent partners*); **compañía de desembarco** (nav.) landing force; **Compañía de Jesús** Society of Jesus; **compañía del ahorcado** (coll.) unsteady or inconstant companion; **compañía de la legua** (theat.) strolling players; **compañía de seguros** insurance company; **compañía matriz** parent company
**comparable** *adj* comparable
**comparación** *f* comparison; (gram.) comparison
**comparado -da** *adj* comparative
**comparador** *m* (coll.) comparer; (phys.) comparator
**comparar** *va* to compare
**comparativo -va** *adj* comparative; (gram.) comparative; *m* (gram.) comparative; *f* (gram.) conjunction of comparison
**comparecer §34** *vn* (law) to appear
**compareciente** *mf* (law) party appearing, party hereto
**comparencia** *f* (law) appearance
**comparendo** *m* (law) summons

**comparición** *f* (law) appearance; (law) summons
**comparsa** *f* (theat.) supernumeraries, extras; masquerade; *mf* (theat.) supernumerary, extra; (coll.) quiet person
**comparte** *mf* (law) joint party
**compartidor -dora** *mf* sharer, participant
**compartimiento** *m* division, distribution; compartment; (rail.) compartment; **compartimiento estanco** (naut.) watertight compartment
**compartir** *va* to divide; to share (*e.g., an opinion*)
**compás** *m* compass (*for showing directions*); compass or compasses (*for drawing curves, etc.*); (mus.) time, measure; (mus.) beat; (mus.) bar, measure; rule, measure; jurisdiction of a monastery; **a compás** (mus.) in time; **al compás de** in step with; **fuera de compás** (mus.) out of time, off beat; **llevar el compás** (mus.) to keep time; **perder el compás** (mus.) to get out of time; **compás de calibres** caliper compass, calipers; **compás de división** dividers; **compás mayor** (mus.) duple measure; **compás menor** (mus.) compound duple or quadruple time
**compasado -da** *adj* measured, moderate, prudent
**compasar** *va* to measure with a compass; to fit, to cut to size, to adapt or adjust with precision; (mus.) to mark off (*a composition*) in measures or bars
**compasible** *adj* pitiful; compassionate
**compasillo** *m* (mus.) compound duple or quadruple time
**compasión** *f* compassion; **mover a compasión** to move to compassion; **¡por compasión!** for pity's sake
**compasionado -da** *adj* passionate
**compasivo -va** *adj* compassionate
**compaternidad** *f* compaternity
**compatibilidad** *f* compatibility
**compatible** *adj* compatible
**compatricio -cia** or **compatriota** *mf* compatriot, fellow countryman
**compatrón** *m* var. of **compatrono**
**compatrono -na** *mf* joint patron
**compeler** *va* to compel; **compeler a** + *inf* to compel to + *inf*
**compendiador -dora** *adj* summarizing; *mf* summarizer
**compendiar** *va* to summarize, condense
**compendiariamente** *adv* in brief, in a word
**compendio** *m* compendium; **en compendio** in brief, in a word
**compendioso -sa** *adj* compendious
**compendista** *mf* writer of a compendium or digest; summarizer
**compendizar** §76 *va* var. of **compendiar**
**compenetración** *f* interpenetration, compenetration; mutual understanding
**compenetrar** *vr* to interpenetrate, to compenetrate; to have the same thoughts and feelings; to understand thoroughly; (Am.) to be convinced; **compenetrarse de** to absorb, take in
**compensación** *f* compensation; (com.) clearing; (sport) handicap (*in boat races*)
**compensador -dora** *adj* compensating; *m* compensator; compensating pendulum
**compensar** *va* to compensate; to compensate for, make up for; *vn* to compensate; *vr* to be compensated for
**compensativo -va** *adj* compensative
**compensatorio -ria** *adj* compensatory
**competencia** *f* competence or competency; adequacy, sufficiency; dispute; competition; area, domain, field; (law) competence or competency; **a competencia** in emulation, vying with each other; **de la competencia de** in the domain or bailiwick of; **en competencia de** in competition with; **sin competencia** unmatched (*e.g., prices*)
**competente** *adj* competent; adequate, sufficient; reliable; (law) competent
**competer** *vn* to be incumbent, to belong
**competición** *f* competition
**competidor -dora** *adj* competing; *mf* competitor
**competir** §94 *vn* to compete
**compilación** *f* compilation
**compilador -dora** *mf* compiler
**compilar** *va* to compile
**compinche** *mf* (coll.) chum, crony, pal
**complacedero -ra** or **complacedor -dora** *adj* pleasing
**complacencia** *f* complaisance; pleasure, satisfaction, complacency
**complacer** §34 *va* to please, to humor; *vr* to be pleased; **complacerse con, de** or **en** to be pleased with, take pleasure in, delight in; **complacerse** + *inf* or **en** + *inf* to be pleased to + *inf*, to take pleasure in + *ger*
**complacido -da** *adj* complacent, satisfied
**complaciente** *adj* complaisant; pleasing, agreeable; nice; indulgent
**complacimiento** *m* var. of **complacencia**
**complejidad** *f* complexity
**complejo -ja** *adj* complex; *m* complex; (psychol.) complex; **complejo B** (biochem.) B complex; **complejo de Electra** (psychoanal.) Electra complex; **complejo de Edipo** (psychoanal.) Oedipus complex; **complejo de inferioridad** inferiority complex
**complementar** *va* to complement
**complementario -ria** *adj* complementary
**complemento** *m* complement, addition; accessory; perfection, completion; (gram., math. & mus.) complement; **complemento directo** (gram.) direct object; **complemento indirecto** (gram.) indirect object
**completamiento** *m* completion
**completar** *va* to complete; to perfect
**completas** *fpl* see **completo**
**completivo -va** *adj* complemental; finished, perfect
**completo -ta** *adj* complete; full (*e.g., trolley car*); **completas** *fpl* (eccl.) compline, completory
**complexidad** *f* complexity
**complexión** *f* constitution; complexion
**complexionado -da** *adj* constituted; **bien complexionado** strong, robust; **mal complexionado** weak, frail
**complexional** *adj* constitutional
**complexo -xa** *adj* complex
**complicación** *f* complication
**complicado -da** *adj* complicated, complex
**complicar** §86 *va* to complicate; to involve; *vr* to become complicated; to become entangled or involved
**cómplice** *mf* accomplice, accessory
**complicidad** *f* complicity
**complot** *m* (*pl:* **-plots**) complot, plot, intrigue
**complotar** *vn* to complot, plot, intrigue
**complutense** *adj* (pertaining to) Alcalá de Henares; *mf* native or inhabitant of Alcalá de Henares; (*cap.*) *f* Complutensian Polyglot (*Bible polyglot printed in 1513-1517 in Alcalá de Henares*)
**componado -da** *adj* (her.) componé
**compondré** *1st sg fut ind of* **componer**
**componedor -dora** *mf* composer; compositor, typesetter; mender, repairer; arbitrator; **amigable componedor** (law) arbitrator; *m* (print.) stick, composing stick
**componenda** *f* compromise, deal; settlement; reconciliation
**componente** *adj* component; *m* component; member (*person*); *f* (mech.) component
**componer** §69 *va* to compose; to compound; (mus., lit. & print.) to compose; to make, to constitute; to arrange, to put in order; to mend, to repair; to adorn, to trim, to deck out; to pacify, to reconcile; to settle; (coll.) to strengthen, restore; (coll.) to settle (*the stomach*); to scheme up; (Am.) to set (*a bone*); *vn* to compose; *vr* to compose oneself; to get dressed; to make up (*with paint, powder, etc.; to become friends again*); **componerse de** to be composed of; **componerse con** to settle with, come to terms with; **componérselas** (coll.) to manage, to make out, to come to terms
**componible** *adj* adjustable; reparable, mendable; conciliable
**comporta** *f* grape basket or bucket
**comportable** *adj* bearable, tolerable
**comportamentismo** *m* (psychol.) behaviorism

**comportamentista** *adj* behavioristic; *mf* behaviorist
**comportamiento** *m* comportment, behavior, deportment
**comportar** *va* to bear, tolerate; (Am.) to entail; *vr* to comport oneself, to behave
**comporte** *m* behavior; bearing, carriage
**comportería** *f* grape-basket or grape-bucket business or shop
**comportero -ra** *mf* grape-basket or grape-bucket maker or dealer
**composición** *f* composition; settlement, compromise; agreement; composure; **hacer una composición de lugar** to size up the situation; to lay one's plans; **composición de fuerzas** (mech.) composition of forces
**compositivo -va** *adj* compositive, constituent; (gram.) combining (*particle*)
**compositor -tora** *mf* (mus.) composer; (Am.) trainer (*of race horses or fighting cocks*)
**compostelano -na** *adj* (pertaining to) Santiago de Compostela; *mf* native or inhabitant of Santiago de Compostela
**compostura** *f* composition, form, structure; agreement, settlement, adjustment; composure; circumspection; neatness, sleekness; repair, repairing; adulteration
**compota** *f* compote, preserves, sauce (*of fruit*)
**compotera** *f* compote, compotier
**compound** *adj indecl* (elec. & mach.) compound
**compra** *f* purchase, buy; shopping; day's marketing; **hacer compras** or **ir de compras** to go shopping
**comprable, compradero -ra** or **compradizo -za** *adj* purchasable
**comprador -dora** *adj* buying; *mf* buyer, purchaser; shopper
**comprar** *va* to buy, to purchase; (fig.) to buy, buy off (*by bribing*); **comprar a** or **de** to buy from; *vn* to shop
**compraventa** *f* transaction, buying and selling; second-hand business; (law) bargain
**comprendedor -dora** *adj* understanding
**comprender** *va* to understand; to comprehend; to comprize
**comprensibilidad** *f* comprehensibility
**comprensible** *adj* comprehensible, understandable
**comprensión** *f* comprehension, understanding; inclusion
**comprensivo -va** *adj* understanding; comprehensive; **comprensivo de** inclusive of
**comprensor -sora** *adj* inclusive, embracing; (theol.) blessed
**compresa** *f* (med.) compress; **compresa fría** (med.) cold pack ; **compresa higiénica** sanitary napkin
**compresibilidad** *f* compressibility
**compresible** *adj* compressible
**compresión** *f* compression; (pros.) synaeresis
**compresivo -va** *adj* compressive
**compresor -sora** *adj* compressing; *m* compressor; (anat., mach. & surg.) compressor; *f* (mach.) compressor
**comprimario -ria** *mf* (theat.) singer playing second or supporting roles
**comprimido -da** *adj* compressed; flattened; *m* (pharm.) tablet
**comprimir** *va* to compress; to repress, to restrain; *vr* to become compressed, to flatten out; to control oneself
**comprobable** *adj* provable, verifiable
**comprobación** *f* checking, verification; proof; **comprobación de averías** trouble shooting
**comprobante** *adj* proving, verifying; *m* proof; certificate, voucher, warrant, claim check
**comprobar** **§77** *va* to check, verify; to prove
**comprofesor -sora** *mf* colleague
**comprometedor -dora** *adj* (coll.) compromising
**comprometer** *va* to compromise, to involve, to bind; to endanger; to force, to oblige; to agree to entrust (*a matter to a third party*); *vr* to become compromised; to compromise oneself· to commit oneself; to become engaged; **comprometerse a** + *inf* to promise to + *inf*, to obligate oneself to + *inf*
**comprometido -da** *adj* awkward, embarrassing
**comprometimiento** *m* adjustment; danger, predicament; pledge, promise
**compromisario -ria** *mf* arbitrator, umpire; *m* electoral delegate
**compromiso** *m* compromise (*e.g., of a lawsuit*); engagement, appointment; commitment; pledge; compromising situation; embarrassment; betrothal; (canon law) compromise; **estar en compromiso** to be questioned, be in doubt; **poner en compromiso** to bring into question, cast doubt on
**comprovincial** *adj* & *m* (eccl.) comprovincial
**comprovinciano -na** *mf* comprovincial
**comps.** abr. of **compañeros**
**compuerta** *f* floodgate, sluice, lock; hatch, half door; draw (*of a drawbridge*); scapulary, shoulder strap (*to which cross was hung*)
**compuestamente** *adv* neatly, trimly; in an orderly fashion
**compuesto -ta** *adj* compound; composite; (gram.) compound; bedecked; composed, calm, circumspect; (arch.) Composite; *pp of* **componer;** *m* compound; composite; (chem.) compound; *f* (bot.) composite
**compulsa** *f* collating; (law) authentic copy
**compulsación** *f* collating
**compulsar** *va* to collate; (law) to make an authentic copy of
**compulsión** *f* compulsion
**compulsivo -va** *adj* compulsive, compulsory
**compunción** *f* compunction; sorrow, pity
**compungido -da** *adj* grieved, sorrowful, remorseful
**compungir** **§42** *va* to make remorseful; *vr* to feel remorse, be remorseful
**compungivo -va** *adj* pricking, stinging
**compurgación** *f* (law) compurgation
**compurgar** **§59** *va* (law) to try by compurgation; (Am.) to finish serving (*one's time in jail*)
**compuse** *1st sg pret ind of* **componer**
**computación** *f* computation
**computar** *va* & *vn* to compute
**computista** *mf* computer
**cómputo** *m* computation
**comulgante** *mf* (eccl.) communicant
**comulgar** **§86** *va* to administer communion to; *vn* to take communion
**comulgatorio** *m* communion rail, altar rail; communion window (*in a nunnery*)
**común** *adj* common; (gram.) common; **común de dos** (gram.) common (*noun*); **común de tres** (gram.) common (*adjective or adjectival ending in Latin*); *m* community; commonalty; water closet; **el común de las gentes** the general run of people, the common run of people; **en común** in common; **por lo común** commonly
**comuna** *f* commune; (dial.) main irrigation channel; (*cap.*) *f* Commune
**comunal** *adj* common; communal, community; *m* commonalty, common people
**comunero -ra** *adj* popular (*well-liked*); *m* shareholder, joint owner; **comuneros** *mpl* commoners (*in pasture lands*)
**comunicable** *adj* communicable; sociable, communicative, companionable
**comunicación** *f* communication; report, paper; rhetorical question; **comunicaciones** *fpl* communications (*telephone, mail, etc.*)
**comunicado** *m* communiqué; letter to the editor; official notice
**comunicador -dora** *adj* communicating
**comunicante** *adj* communicant; communicating; *mf* communicant; writer (*person who writes to inform or request*)
**comunicar** **§86** *va, vn* & *vr* to communicate
**comunicativo -va** *adj* communicative
**comunidad** *f* community; **comunidades** *fpl* popular uprisings (*especially in Castile under Charles I*); **de comunidad** jointly; **Comunidad Británica de Naciones** British Commonwealth of Nations; **comunidad de bienes** joint ownership
**comunión** *f* communion; political party; (eccl.) Communion; **comunión de los santos** (eccl.) communion of saints
**comunismo** *m* communism
**comunista** *adj* communist, communistic; *mf* communist
**comunistizante** *adj* communistically inclined; *mf* fellow traveler

**comunistizar §76** *va* to communize; *vr* to become communistic
**comunistoide** *adj* fellow-traveling; *mf* fellow traveler
**comunizar §76** *va* to communize
**comuña** *f* maslin (*mixture of wheat and rye*)
**con** *prep* with; in spite of; to, e.g., **amable con ella** kind to her; of: **soñar con** to dream of; **con** + *inf* by + *ger;* in spite of + *ger;* **con que** whereupon; and so; **con tal (de) que** provided that; **con todo** however, nevertheless
**conación** *f* (psychol.) conation
**conato** *m* endeavor, effort, try; attempt; (law) attempt, assault
**concadenación** *f* concatenation
**concadenar** *va* to concatenate, to link together
**concambio** *m* exchange
**concanónigo** *m* fellow canon
**concatenación** *f* concatenation
**concatenar** *va* to concatenate, to link together
**concausa** *f* concause, joint cause
**concavidad** *f* concavity
**cóncavo -va** *adj* concave; *m & f* concave, concavity, cavity
**cóncavoconvexo -xa** *adj* concavo-convex
**concebible** *adj* conceivable
**concebir §94** *va & vn* to conceive
**concedente** *adj* conceding, concessive
**conceder** *va* to concede, admit; to grant
**concedidamente** *adv* admittedly, avowedly, concededly
**concejal** *m* alderman; councilman
**concejala** *f* alderman's wife; councilman's wife; councilwoman
**concejil** *adj* (pertaining to the) council; common, public
**concejo** *m* town council; town hall; council meeting; foundling
**concento** *m* harmonious singing
**concentrabilidad** *f* faculty of concentration
**concentración** *f* concentration
**concentrado -da** *adj* concentrated; uncommunicative
**concentrar** *va* to concentrate; to center; to restrain, conceal; *vr* to concentrate; to center
**concéntrico -ca** *adj* concentric or concentrical
**concentuoso -sa** *adj* harmonious
**concepción** *f* conception; Immaculate Conception; feast of the Immaculate Conception; **Inmaculada Concepción** Immaculate Conception
**conceptear** *vn* to be full of conceits, to be witty
**conceptible** *adj* conceivable
**conceptismo** *m* (lit.) conceptism
**conceptista** *adj & mf* (lit.) conceptist
**conceptivo -va** *adj* conceptive
**concepto** *m* concept; conceit, fancy, witticism; opinion, judgment; cause, reason; **¿bajo qué concepto?** from what point of view?, for what reason?; **en concepto de** under the head of; **tener buen concepto de** or **tener en buen concepto** to hold in high esteem, to have a high opinion of
**conceptual** *adj* conceptual
**conceptualismo** *m* (philos.) conceptualism
**conceptualista** *adj* (philos.) conceptualistic; *mf* (philos.) conceptualist
**conceptuar §33** *va* to deem, to judge; **conceptuar a uno de** or **por** to deem someone to be
**conceptuoso -sa** *adj* witty, sententious, epigrammatic
**concernencia** *f* respect, connection, concern
**concerniente** *adj* relative, applicable; **concerniente a** concerning
**concernir §43** *va* to concern
**concertadamente** *adv* in concert, in harmony
**concertante** *adj* contracting; (mus.) concertante; *m* (mus.) concertante; (mus.) finale (*of an act of an opera*)
**concertar §18** *va* to concert; to arrange (*e.g., a marriage, peace*); to reconcile; to harmonize; to bargain for; to conclude (*an agreement*); to rouse (*game*); to mend, to repair; to set (*a broken bone*); to make agree; (gram.) to make agree; *vn* to concert; to harmonize; to agree; (gram.) to agree; *vr* to become reconciled, to come to terms; to harmonize; to agree; (Am.) to hire out
**concertina** *f* (mus.) concertina
**concertino** *m* (mus.) concertmaster
**concertista** *mf* (mus.) performer, soloist; (mus.) manager
**concerto** *m* (mus.) concerto
**concesible** *adj* grantable, concessible
**concesión** *f* concession, admission; grant
**concesionario** *m* concessionaire; dealer
**concesivo -va** *adj* concessive; (gram.) concessive
**concia** *f* forbidden section of woodland
**conciencia** *f* conscience; consciousness; awareness; **a conciencia** conscientiously; **en conciencia** in all conscience; **conciencia doble** (psycopath.) double consciousness
**concienzudo -da** *adj* conscientious, thorough
**concierto** *m* concert, agreement, harmony; (mus.) concert; (mus.) concerto; **de concierto** in concert
**conciliable** *adj* conciliable, reconcilable
**conciliábulo** *m* conciliabule
**conciliación** *f* conciliation; likeness, congruity; favor, esteem, protection
**conciliador -dora** *adj* conciliatory; *mf* conciliator
**conciliar** *adj* (pertaining to a) council; *m* council member; *va* to conciliate, to reconcile; to win; *vr* to win (*e.g., friendship*)
**conciliativo -va** *adj* conciliative
**conciliatorio -ria** *adj* conciliatory
**concilio** *m* (eccl.) council; council decrees; **concilio de Nicea** Nicene Council; **concilio de Trento** Council of Trent; **concilio ecuménico** (eccl.) ecumenical council
**concisión** *f* concision, conciseness
**conciso -sa** *adj* concise
**concitación** *f* agitation, incitement
**concitador -dora** *adj* inciting, stirring; *mf* agitator, inciter
**concitar** *va* to stir up, agitate, incite
**concitativo -va** *adj* inciting
**conciudadano -na** *mf* fellow citizen
**conclave** *m* or **cónclave** *m* conclave; (eccl.) conclave
**conclavista** *m* conclavist
**concluir §41** *va* to conclude; to convince; to silence, to overwhelm; (fencing) to disarm (*an adversary*) by catching the hilt of his sword; *vn & vr* to conclude, to end; **concluir de** + *inf* to finish + *ger*
**conclusión** *f* conclusion; **en conclusión** in conclusion
**conclusivo -va** *adj* concluding, final
**concluso -sa** *adj* (law) closed, concluded (*said of a trial*)
**concluyente** *adj* conclusive, convincing
**concoide** *f* (geom.) conchoid
**concoideo -a** *adj* conchoidal; (mineral.) conchoidal
**concoloro -ra** *adj* concolorous
**concomer** *vr* (coll.) to shrug one's shoulders, to give a shrug, to fidget with an itch
**concomimiento** or **concomio** *m* (coll.) shrug, shrug of the shoulders, fidgets
**concomitancia** *f* concomitance
**concomitante** *adj & m* concomitant
**concomitar** *va* to accompany, work with, go with
**concón** *m* (orn.) tawny owl
**concordación** *f* harmonizing, combining, coördination
**concordador -dora** *adj* conciliating; *mf* conciliator
**concordancia** *f* concordance, agreement; (gram. & mus.) concord; **concordancias** *fpl* concordance (*list of words with references*)
**concordante** *adj* concordant
**concordar §77** *va* to harmonize; to reconcile; (gram.) to make agree; *vn* to agree; (gram.) to agree; **concordar con** to agree with; (gram.) to agree with
**concordata** *f* or **concordato** *m* concordat; (eccl.) concordat
**concorde** *adj* in agreement
**concordia** *f* concord, harmony; agreement, settlement; double finger ring; **de concordia** by common consent
**concreado -da** *adj* (theol.) innate
**concreción** *f* concretion; (geol. & path.) concretion

**concrecionar** *va & vr* to concrete, to form into a mass, to form into concretions
**concrescencia** *f* concrescence; (biol.) concrescence; (path.) concretion
**concretar** *va* to concrete, make concrete; to specify; to explain; to thicken; to boil down (*a statement*); *vr* to limit oneself, to confine oneself; **concretarse a** + *inf* to limit oneself or confine oneself to + *inf*
**concretera** *f* (Am.) concrete mixer
**concreto -ta** *adj* concrete; *m* concretion; concrete; **en concreto** finally, to sum up
**concubina** *f* concubine
**concubinario -ria** *adj & m* concubinary
**concubinato** *m* concubinage
**concúbito** *m* coitus, concubitus
**concuerda; por concuerda** O.K. (*said of a true copy*)
**conculcación** *f* treading, trampling; violation
**conculcar §86** *va* to tread upon, trample under foot; to break, violate
**concuñada** *f* sister-in-law (*wife of one's husband's or wife's brother*)
**concuñado** *m* brother-in-law (*husband of one's wife's or husband's sister*)
**concupiscencia** *f* concupiscence
**concupiscente** *adj* concupiscent
**concupiscible** *adj* concupiscible
**concurrencia** *f* concurrence; attendance; crowd, gathering; competition, contest
**concurrente** *adj* concurrent; competing; *mf* contender
**concurrido -da** *adj* crowded, full of people
**concurrir** *vn* to concur; to gather, come together; to coincide (*in time*); to contend, to compete; **concurrir con** to come in with, to contribute (*e.g., money*)
**concursado** *m* (law) insolvent debtor
**concursante** *mf* competitor
**concursar** *va* (law) to declare insolvent
**concurso** *m* concourse, crowd; concurrence, backing, coöperation; contest, competition; show, exhibition (*with prizes*); (law) insolvency proceedings; **fuera de concurso** not competing; **concurso de acreedores** (law) meeting of creditors; **concurso hípico** horse show
**concusión** f concussion; extortion, shakedown; (path.) concussion
**concusionario -ria** *mf* extortioner
**concha** *f* shell; tortoise shell; shellfish; oyster; lower millstone; horseshoe bay; concha (*cigar*); sheltered inlet (*on seacoast*); (theat.) prompter's box; (anat.) concha; (arch.) conch, concha; **meterse en su concha** to retire into one's shell; **salir de la concha** to come out of one's shell; **tener muchas conchas** (coll.) to be sly, to be cunning; **concha de peregrino** scallop shell; (zool.) scallop; **concha de perla** mother-of-pearl
**conchabanza** *f* comfort; (coll.) ganging up
**conchabar** *va* to join, to unite; to mix (*wools of different qualities*); (Am.) to hire; (Am.) to get (*a job*); *vr* (coll.) to gang up; (Am.) to hire out
**conchabero** *m* (Am.) pieceworker
**conchabo** *m* (Am.) hiring; (Am.) hiring out; (Am.) work
**conchado -da** *adj* (zool.) shelled, shelly
**conchesta** *f* (dial.) snowdrift
**conchil** *m* (zool.) murex
**conchudo -da** *adj* (zool.) shelled, shelly; (coll.) sly, cunning, crafty
**conchuela** *f* (ent.) Mexican bean beetle
**condado** *m* earldom, countship; county
**condal** *adj* of an earl or count
**conde** *m* earl, count; gypsy chief; (dial.) foreman; **condes** *mpl* earl and countess, count and countess
**condecoración** *f* decoration (*especially with medal, badge, or ribbon; medal, badge, or ribbon itself*)
**condecorar** *va* to decorate (*with honors, medals, etc.*)
**condena** *f* sentence; penalty; transcript of sentence; **condena judicial** (law) conviction
**condenación** *f* condemnation; (theol.) damnation
**condenado -da** *adj* condemned; damned; (Am.) shrewd, clever; *mf* condemned; damned
**condenador -dora** *adj* condemning, incriminating; *mf* condemner
**condenar** *va* to condemn; to damn; to convict; to block up or shut off (*e.g., a window*); to close up, to padlock; **condenar a** + *inf* to condemn to + *inf; vr* to condemn oneself, confess one's guilt; to be damned (*to hell*)
**condenatorio -ria** *adj* condemnatory
**condensación** *f* condensation
**condensador -dora** *adj* condensing; *m* condenser; **condensador de derivación** or **de paso** (elec.) by-pass condenser; **condensador de placa** (rad.) plate condenser; **condensador de rejilla** (rad.) grid condenser; **condensador de sintonía** (rad.) tuning condenser; **condensador electrolítico** (rad.) electrolytic condenser; **condensador fijo** (elec.) fixed condenser; **condensador sintonizador** (rad.) tuning condenser; **condensador variable** (elec.) variable condenser
**condensar** *va* to condense; *vr* to condense, become condensed
**condesa** *f* countess; **condesa viuda** dowager countess
**condescendencia** *f* acquiescence, consent
**condescender §66** *vn* to acquiesce; **condescender a** to accede to; **condescender con** to yield to; **condescender en** + *inf* to acquiesce in + *ger*, to agree to + *inf*
**condescendiente** *adj* acquiescent, obliging
**condestable** *m* constable (*commander of armed forces in Middle Ages*); (nav.) deck petty officer, gunner
**condestablesa** *f* constable's wife
**condestablía** *f* constableship, constablewick
**condición** *f* condition, state; status, station, position; standing; circumstance; nature, temperament, character; **condiciones** *fpl* condition, state; aptitude, disposition; **a condición (de) que** on condition that, provided that; **tener condición** to have a bad temper
**condicionado -da** *adj* conditioned; conditional
**condicional** *adj* conditional; (gram.) conditional
**condicionamiento** *m* conditioning; adjustment; agreement
**condicionar** *va* to condition; to adjust; to prepare; (textiles) to condition; *vn* to agree, to fit
**condigno -na** *adj* condign (*punishment, censure*); appropriate, worthy; **condigno de** in accord with
**cóndilo** *m* (anat.) condyle
**condimentación** *f* seasoning
**condimentar** *va* to season, to treat with a condiment
**condimento** *m* condiment
**condiscípulo** *m* condisciple, fellow student
**condolencia** *f* condolence
**condoler §63** *vr* to condole, to sympathize; **condolerse de** to sympathize with, feel sorry for
**condolido -da** *adj* sad, sorrowful, touched
**condominio** *m* (law) joint ownership or possession; dual control, condominium
**condómino** *mf* (law) joint owner
**condonación** *f* condonation, forgiveness
**condonante** *adj* condoning, forgiving
**condonar** *va* to condone, to forgive
**cóndor** *m* (orn.) condor; **cóndor de California** (orn.) California condor
**condotiero** *m* condottiere
**condrila** *f* (bot.) gum succory
**condrioma** *m* (biol.) chondriome
**condriosoma** *m* (biol.) chondriosome
**condrología** *f* chondrology
**conducción** *f* leading, guiding; direction; conduction; transportation; piping; transfer, conveyance; (aut.) driving; agreement (*on prices or wages*); (phys. & physiol.) conduction; **conducción a derecha** or **a la derecha** (aut.) right-hand drive; **conducción a izquierda** or **a la izquierda** (aut.) left-hand drive; **conducción de noche** night driving; **conducción interior** (aut.) closed car
**conducencia** *f* conduction; transfer, conveyance
**conducente** *adj* conducive; leading
**conducir §38** *va* to lead, guide; to conduct, manage, direct; to convey, transport; to drive

(*a carriage, auto, etc.*); to hire, employ; *vn* to lead; to conduce, be suitable; *vr* to conduct oneself, behave
**conducta** *f* conduct, direction, management; guidance; conduct, behavior; convoy, conveyance; commission to enlist and bring in recruits; agreement made by a town with a doctor to attend its sick; **mejorar de conducta** to mend one's ways
**conductancia** *f* (elec.) conductance; **conductancia mutua** (elec.) mutual conductance
**conductero** *m* conductor of a convoy
**conductibilidad** *f* conductibility
**conductible** *adj* conductible
**conductividad** *f* conductivity
**conductivo -va** *adj* conductive
**conducto** *m* conduit, pipe; (elec.) conduit; (anat.) duct, canal; mediation, agency; channel; intermediary; **por conducto de** through; **conducto alimenticio** (anat.) alimentary canal; **conducto auditivo** (anat.) auditory canal; **conducto biliar** (anat.) bile duct; **conducto cístico** (anat.) cystic duct; **conducto de desagüe** sewer; (naut.) drain; **conducto de humo** flue; **conducto eyaculador** (anat.) ejaculatory duct; **conducto radicular** (anat. & dent.) root canal; **conducto regular** (mil.) channel; **conducto torácico** (anat.) thoracic duct
**conductor -tora** *adj* conducting, leading, guiding; (phys.) conductive; *m* conductor, leader, guide, mentor; driver, motorist; (phys. & rail.) conductor; (rail.) engineman, engine driver; (Am.) driver, teamster; **conductor huésped** (mus.) guest conductor
**condueño** *mf* part owner, joint owner
**conduerma** *f* (Am.) deep sleep, stupor
**conduje** *1st sg pret ind of* **conducir**
**condumio** *m* (coll.) grub, victuals; (coll.) food to eat with bread
**conduplicado -da** *adj* (bot.) conduplicate
**conduplicación** *f* (rhet.) reduplication
**condutal** *m* gutter, rain gutter
**conduzco** *1st sg pres ind of* **conducir**
**conectador** *m* connector; (elec.) connector; (elec.) outlet
**conectar** *va* to connect
**conectivo -va** *adj* connective
**coneja** *f* female rabbit
**conejal** *m* or **conejar** *m* rabbit warren
**conejero -ra** *adj* rabbit, rabbit-hunting; *mf* rabbit breeder; *f* burrow; rabbit warren; large cave; (coll.) joint, dive
**conejillo** *m* little rabbit; **conejillo de Indias** (zool.) guinea pig, cavy; (fig.) guinea pig
**conejo** *m* (zool.) rabbit; **conejo de Noruega** (zool.) lemming
**conejuno -na** *adj* (pertaining to a) rabbit; *f* cony, rabbit fur
**conexidades** *fpl* adjuncts, appurtenances
**conexión** *f* connection; **conexión en cascada** (elec.) cascade connection; **conexión en delta** (elec.) delta connection; **conexión en estrella** (elec.) star connection
**conexionar** *va* to connect; to put in touch; to compare, relate; *vr* to connect; to get in touch
**conexivo -va** *adj* connective
**conexo -xa** *adj* connected
**conf.** abr. of **confesor**
**confabulación** *f* confabulation; connivance, plotting, scheming, leaguing
**confabulador -dora** *mf* confabulator; conniver, plotter, schemer
**confabular** *vn* to confabulate; *vr* to connive, to plot, to scheme, to league together
**confalón** *m* gonfalon
**confaloniero** *m* gonfalonier
**confección** *f* making, confection; concoction; tailoring, suit making; ready-made suit; **confeccíon a medida** made-to-order suit
**confeccionado -da** *adj* ready-made
**confeccionar** *va* to make (*e.g., a suit of clothes*); to make up (*a prescription*)
**confeccionista** *mf* ready-made clothier
**confederación** *f* confederation, confederacy, alliance, league
**confederado -da** *adj & mf* confederate
**confederar** *va & vr* to confederate
**confederativo -va** *adj* confederative
**conferencia** *f* conference; interview; lecture; **conferencia en la cumbre** summit conference
**conferenciante** *mf* lecturer; conferee
**conferenciar** *vn* to confer, hold an interview
**conferencista** *mf* (Am.) lecturer
**conferir** §62 *va* to confer, bestow, award; to compare; *vn* to confer; to lecture
**confesa** *f* see **confeso**
**confesado -da** *mf* (coll.) penitent
**confesante** *adj* confessing; *mf* confessor (*of guilt, fault, sin, etc.*)
**confesar** §18 *va* to confess; (eccl.) to confess (*sins; a sinner*); **confesar de plano** to confess openly; **confesar haber** + *pp* to confess having + *pp; vn & vr* to confess; (eccl.) to confess; **confesar** or **confesarse a** to confess to (*God*); **confesarse con** to confess to (*a priest*)
**confesión** *f* confession; faith, religion, denomination; **confesión de Augsburgo** Augsburg Confession
**confesional** *adj* confessional
**confesionario** *m* confessional; rule or code of confession
**confesionista** *mf* Confessionist, Lutheran
**confeso -sa** *adj* confessed; converted (*Jew*); *mf* converted Jew; *m* lay brother; *f* widow who has become a nun
**confesonario** *m* confessional
**confesor** *m* confessor (*believer; priest*)
**confeti** *m* confetti
**confiabilidad** *f* trustworthiness, reliability
**confiable** *adj* trustworthy, reliable
**confiadamente** *adv* trustingly, confidently
**confiado -da** *adj* confiding, unsuspecting; self-confident, haughty
**confiador** *m* var. of **cofiador**
**confianza** *f* confidence; self-confidence; familiarity, informality; **de confianza** reliable; **en confianza** trustingly; in confidence
**confianzudo -da** *adj* (coll.) overfriendly, overfamiliar, presumptuous; (Am.) meddlesome
**confiar** §90 *va* to entrust, confide; to give confidence to; **confiar algo a** or **en uno** to entrust something to someone; *vn & vr* to trust; **confiar** or **confiarse de** or **en** to trust in, rely on
**confidencia** *f* confidence; secret; **hacer confidencias a** to confide in
**confidencial** *adj* confidential
**confidente -ta** *adj* trustworthy, faithful; *mf* confident, confidant; informer, detective; spy, secret agent; *m* love seat; *f* confidante
**configuración** *f* configuration
**configurar** *va* to form, to shape
**confín** *adj* bordering; *m* confine, border, boundary; **los confines** the confines
**confinación** *f* var. of **confinamiento**
**confinado -da** *adj* confined (*kept in confines under surveillance*); *m* prisoner
**confinamiento** *m* confinement (*restraint under surveillance*)
**confinante** *adj* bordering
**confinar** *va* to confine (*to restrain within limits*); *vn* to border; **confinar con** to border on; *vr* to shut oneself up, to keep onself confined
**confinidad** *f* nearness, proximity
**confirmación** *f* confirmation
**confirmadamente** *adv* firmly, surely, approvingly
**confirmador -dora** or **confirmante** *adj* confirming, confirmatory; *mf* confirmer
**confirmar** *va* to confirm
**confirmativo -va** *adj* confirmative
**confirmatorio -ria** *adj* confirmatory
**confiscación** *f* confiscation
**confiscar** §86 *va* to confiscate
**confitado -da** *adj* hopeful, confident
**confitar** *va* to candy; to preserve; to sweeten
**confite** *m* candy, bonbon, confection; **confites** *mpl* candy; **morder en un confite** (coll.) to be very close, to be very intimate
**confitería** *f* confectionery; confectionery store
**confitero -ra** *mf* confectioner; *f* candy box; candy jar
**confitura** *f* confection, confiture, preserve
**conflación** *f* melting, smelting
**conflagración** *f* conflagration

**conflagrar** *va* to set fire to, to burn
**conflátil** *adj* fusible
**conflicto** *m* conflict; struggle, anguish; fix, jam
**confluencia** *f* confluence
**confluente** *adj* confluent; *m* confluence (*of rivers*)
**confluir** §41 *vn* to flow together, to come together, to crowd, to meet
**conformación** *f* conformation
**conformador** *m* hat block; shoe tree; grader, road shaper
**conformar** *va* to conform; to adjust, harmonize; to shape; to block (*a hat*); *vn* to conform, to agree; *vr* to conform, to comply, to yield; **conformarse a** or **con** to resign oneself to, to submit to
**conforme** *adj* according, in agreement; conformable; **conforme con** in agreement with; resigned to; *adv* depending on circumstances; O.K.; **conforme a** according to, in accordance with; *conj* as; in proportion as, in the way that; as soon as; *m* approval
**conformemente** *adv* conformably; in agreement
**conformidad** *f* conformity, conformance; shape; compliance; forbearance; **de conformidad con** in accordance with, in agreement with; **en conformidad con** in compliance with
**conformismo** *m* conventionality; conformism
**conformista** *mf* conformist
**confort** *m* comfort
**confortable** *adj* comforting; comfortable (*e.g., chair, bed, room*)
**confortación** *f* comfort, consolation; strength, invigoration
**confortador -dora** *adj* comforting, consoling; *mf* comforter, consoler
**confortamiento** *m* var. of **confortación**
**confortante** *adj* comforting; tonic; *mf* comforter; *m* tonic; mitt
**confortar** *va* to comfort, console; to strengthen, enliven, invigorate
**confortativo -va** *adj* comforting, consoling; *m* comfort, consolation
**conforte** *m* var. of **confortación**
**confr.** abr. of **confesor**
**confracción** *f* breaking, fracture
**confraternal** *adj* confraternal
**confraternar** *vn* to be brotherly
**confraternidad** *f* confraternity
**confraternizar** §76 *vn* to be brotherly; to fraternize
**confricación** *f* rubbing; (path.) chafing; masturbation; Lesbianism
**confricar** §86 *va* to rub
**confrontación** *f* confrontation; propinquity; natural affinity, innate sympathy
**confrontar** *va* to confront (*to bring face to face; to compare*); *vn* to border; to get along, to agree; **confrontar con** to border on; to get along with, to agree with; *vr* to get along, to agree; **confrontarse con** to confront, to face; to get along with, to agree with
**confucianismo** *m* Confucianism
**confucianista** *adj & mf* Confucianist
**confuciano -na** *adj & mf* Confucian
**Confucio** *m* Confucius
**confulgencia** *f* combined brilliance
**confundible** *adj* confusable
**confundimiento** *m* confusion, bewilderment
**confundir** *va* to confuse; to mix, mix together, mix up; to confound; *vr* to become confused; to mix, to fuse; to become lost, become mingled (*e.g., in a crowd*)
**confusión** *f* confusion; **confusión de lenguas** (Bib.) confusion of tongues
**confuso -sa** *adj* confused; **en confuso** confusedly, in confusion
**confutación** *f* confutation
**confutador -dora** *adj* confutative; *mf* confuter
**confutar** *va* to confute
**confutatorio -ria** *adj* confutative
**conga** *f* see **congo**
**congelación** *f* congealing; freezing
**congelador** *m* freezer
**congeladora** *f* deep-freeze
**congelamiento** *m* var. of **congelación**
**congelante** *adj* freezing, refrigerant
**congelar** *va* to congeal; to freeze; (com.) to freeze (*assets, credits, etc.*); *vr* to congeal; to freeze
**congelativo -va** *adj* refrigerant
**congénere** *adj* congeneric; *m & f* congener; fellow
**congenial** *adj* congenial
**congeniar** *vn* to be congenial, to get along
**congénito -ta** *adj* congenital
**congerie** *f* congeries
**congestión** *f* congestion; (path.) congestion
**congestionar** *va* to congest; (path.) to congest; *vr* to congest, become congested
**congestivo -va** *adj* congestive
**conglobación** *f* conglobation; (fig.) concentration, integration
**conglobar** *va & vr* to conglobate, to form in a round mass
**conglomeración** *f* conglomeration
**conglomerado -da** *adj & m* conglomerate
**conglomerar** *va & vr* to conglomerate
**conglutinación** *f* conglutination
**conglutinante** *adj* conglutinant
**conglutinar** *va & vr* to conglutinate
**conglutinativo -va** *adj* conglutinative
**congo -ga** *adj & mf* Congo; *m* (zool.) congo monkey; (*cap.*) *m* Congo; **el Congo Belga** Belgian Congo; **el Congo Francés** French Congo; *f* (ent.) large poisonous ant; (zool.) hutia conga; (zool.) hutia carabali
**congoja** *f* anguish, grief
**congojar** *va & vr* var. of **acongojar**
**congojoso -sa** *adj* distressing; in anguish
**congoleño -ña** or **congolés -lesa** *adj & mf* Congoese or Congolese
**congosto** *m* canyon, narrow pass
**congraciador -dora** *adj* ingratiating
**congraciamiento** *m* ingratiation
**congraciar** *va* to win, win over; *vr* to win; **congraciarse con** to ingratiate oneself with
**congratulación** *f* congratulation
**congratular** *va* to congratulate; **congratular de** or **por** to congratulate on; *vr* to congratulate oneself, to rejoice
**congratulatorio -ria** *adj* congratulatory
**congregación** *f* congregation
**congregacionalismo** *m* congregationalism; Congregationalism
**congregacionalista** *adj* Congregational, Congregationalist; *mf* Congregationalist
**congreganista** *adj* congregational
**congregar** §59 *va & vr* to congregate
**congresal** *mf* (Am.) var. of **congresista**
**congresional** *adj* congressional, Congressional
**congresista** *mf* delegate; member of congress; *m* congressman; *f* congresswoman
**congreso** *m* congress; meeting, convention; intercourse; **Congreso de los Diputados** Congress (*of Spanish or Spanish American Cortes*)
**congrí** *m* (Am.) rice and bean stew
**congrio** *m* (ichth.) conger, conger eel; (coll.) saphead, dope
**congrua** *f* see **congruo**
**congruencia** *f* congruence; congruity; (math.) congruence; (geom.) congruity
**congruente** *adj* congruent; appropriate; (geom.) congruent, congruous
**congruo -grua** *adj* congruous; *f* supplementary emolument; adequate income for one who is about to be ordained a priest
**conicidad** *f* conicity
**conicina** *f* (chem.) coniine
**cónico -ca** *adj* conic or conical; *f* (math.) conic section
**conidio** *m* (bot.) conidium
**conidióforo** *m* (bot.) conidiophore
**conífero -ra** *adj* (bot.) coniferous; *f* (bot.) conifer
**coniforme** *adj* coniform, cone-shaped
**conirrostro -tra** *adj* (orn.) conirostral
**conivalvo -va** *adj* (zool.) cone-shelled
**coniza** *f* (bot.) fleawort
**conjetura** *f* conjecture
**conjeturador -dora** *adj* guessing; *mf* guesser
**conjetural** *adj* conjectural
**conjeturar** *va & vn* to conjecture, to guess, to surmise
**conjuez** *m* (*pl:* **-jueces**) cojudge

**conjugación** *f* conjugation; (biol. & gram.) conjugation
**conjugado -da** *adj* (bot. & math.) conjugate; *f* (bot.) conjugate
**conjugar** §59 *va* to conjugate; (biol. & gram.) to conjugate; *vr* to conjugate, to be joined, be fused; (biol. & gram.) to conjugate
**conjunción** *f* conjunction; combination; (astr., astrol. & gram.) conjunction; **conjunción coordinante** (gram.) coördinating conjunction; **conjunción disyuntiva** (gram.) alternative conjunction; **conjunción dubitativa** (gram.) dubitative conjunction; **conjunción subordinante** (gram.) subordinating conjunction
**conjuntado -da** *adj* (theat.) well integrated
**conjuntamente** *adv* conjointly
**conjuntar** *va* to combine, to bring together
**conjuntiva** *f* see **conjuntivo**
**conjuntival** *adj* conjunctival
**conjuntivitis** *f* (path.) conjunctivitis
**conjuntivo -va** *adj* conjunctive; (gram.) conjunctive; *f* (anat.) conjunctiva
**conjunto -ta** *adj* conjoint, conjunct; joined, allied, related; joint; *m* whole, entirety, ensemble; group; unit; (mus.) ensemble (*whole effect of united performance*); (theat.) chorus; **de conjunto** general; united; **en conjunto** as a whole; **en su conjunto** in its entirety
**conjura** or **conjuración** *f* conspiracy, plot
**conjurado -da** *mf* conspirator
**conjurador** *m* conjurer (*one who entreats*)
**conjuramentar** *va* to swear in; *vr* to take an oath
**conjurante** *mf* conjurer (*one who entreats*)
**conjurar** *va* to swear in; to conjure (*to entreat*); to conjure away; *vn* to conspire, to plot; *vr* to conspire, to plot; to join in a conspiracy
**conjuro** *m* conjuration (*magic form of words*); conjuration of evil spirits; adjuration, entreaty
**conllevador -dora** *mf* co-worker; fellow sufferer
**conllevancia** *f* cooperation; mutual toleration
**conllevar** *va* to coöperate in bearing (*a task, burden, etc.*); to bear, tolerate (*a person*); to suffer (*adversity*)
**conmemorable** *adj* commemorable
**conmemoración** *f* commemoration; **en conmemoración de** in commemoration of
**conmemorar** *va* to commemorate
**conmemorativo -va** *adj* commemorative, memorial
**conmemoratorio -ria** *adj* commemoratory
**conmensurabilidad** *f* commensurability
**conmensurable** *adj* commensurable; commensurate
**conmensuración** *f* commensuration
**conmensurar** *va* to make commensurate, to commensurate
**conmigo** with me, with myself
**conmilitón** *m* companion-at-arms, fellow soldier
**conminación** *f* commination
**conminar** *va* to threaten; to threaten with punishment
**conmiseración** *f* commiseration
**conmistión** *f* commixture
**conmisto -ta** *adj* commingled
**conmixtión** *f* var. of **conmistión**
**conmixto -ta** *adj* var. of **conmisto**
**conmoción** *f* commotion, disturbance; shock; arousing, stirring; excitement
**conmocionado -da** *adj* jolted, shocked, stunned
**conmoración** *f* (rhet.) repetition, elaboration
**conmovedor -dora** *adj* stirring, moving, touching
**conmover** §63 *va* to stir, stir up; to move, to touch, to affect; to shake, to upset; *vr* to be moved, be touched, be affected
**conmutable** *adj* commutable
**conmutación** *f* commutation; (elec. & law) commutation
**conmutador** *m* (elec.) change-over switch, commutating switch; (elec.) commutator; **conmutador de cuatro terminales** (elec.) four-way switch; **conmutador de tres terminales** (elec.) three-way switch; **conmutador de doble caída** (elec.) double-throw switch
**conmutar** *va* to commute; (elec.) to commutate; (law) to commute
**conmutativo -va** *adj* commutative
**conmutatriz** *f* (*pl:* **-trices**) (elec.) converter
**connacional** *m* fellow countryman
**connatural** *adj* connatural, inborn, inherent
**connaturalización** *f* adaptation, acclimation
**connaturalizar** §76 *va* to make connatural; *vr* to become accustomed, become acclimated
**connivencia** *f* connivance
**connivente** *adj* conniving; (anat. & bot.) connivent
**connotación** *f* connotation; distant relationship
**connotado -da** *adj* (Am.) notable, outstanding; *m* distant relationship
**connotar** *va* to connote
**connotativo -va** *adj* connotative
**connovicio -cia** *mf* fellow novice, beginner, or apprentice
**connubio** *m* (poet.) marriage
**connumerar** *va* to mention; to connumerate
**cono** *m* (geom. & bot.) cone; **cono de poleas** cone pulley; **cono de proa** nose cone (*of a rocket*); **cono de sombra** (astr.) umbra; **cono de viento** (aer.) wind sock
**conocedor -dora** *adj* knowing, expert; *mf* connoisseur, judge
**conocencia** *f* (law) confession
**conocer** §32 *va* to know (*by reasoning or learning; by perception or the senses; to be acquainted with, to recognize*); to meet, to get to know; to tell, to distinguish; to know carnally; (law) to try (*a case*); *vn* to know; **conocer de** or **en** to know, to have a knowledge of; **conocer de** (law) to try (*a case*); *vr* to know oneself; to know each other; to meet, to meet each other, to get acquainted
**conocible** *adj* knowable
**conocido -da** *adj* familiar, well-known; illustrious, distinguished; *mf* acquaintance
**conocimiento** *m* knowledge; understanding; consciousness; acquaintance; (com.) bill of lading; **conocimientos** *mpl* knowledge; **hablar con pleno conocimiento de causa** to know what one is talking about; **obrar con conocimiento de causa** to know what one is doing, know what one is up to; **perder el conocimiento** to lose consciousness; **poner en conocimiento** to inform, to let know; **por su real conocimiento** (Am.) for real money; **recobrar el conocimiento** to regain consciousness; **venir en conocimiento de** to come to know, to find out, take cognizance of; **conocimiento de embarque** (com.) bill of lading
**conoidal** *adj* conoidal
**conoide** *adj* conoid; *m* (geom.) conoid
**conoideo -a** *adj* conoidal, cone-shaped
**conopeo** *m* canopy (*fixed over shrine or carried over exalted personage*)
**conopial** *adj* see **arco**
**conozco** *1st sg pres ind of* **conocer**
**conque** *adv* and so, so then, well; *m* (coll.) condition, terms, understanding
**conquense** *adj* (pertaining to) Cuenca; *mf* native or inhabitant of Cuenca, Spain
**conquífero -ra** *adj* conchiferous
**conquiforme** *adj* shell-shaped, conchiform
**conquiliología** *f* conchology
**conquiliólogo -ga** *mf* conchologist
**conquista** *f* conquest (*act; person or thing*); **conquista normanda** Norman Conquest
**conquistable** *adj* conquerable; easy to get, attainable
**conquistador -dora** *adj* conquering; *mf* conqueror; *m* lady-killer; conquistador (*Spanish conqueror in America in the sixteenth century*); **el Conquistador** the Conqueror (*William I of England, James I of Aragon, Alfonso I of Portugal*)
**conquistar** *va* to conquer (*by force of arms*); to win over; **conquistar algo a alguien** to win something from someone
**Conrado** *m* Conrad
**conrear** *va* to work over; to grease (*wool*); to plow a second time
**conreinado** *m* coreign
**conreinar** *vn* to reign jointly

**consabido -da** *adj* well-known, above-mentioned
**consagración** *f* consecration
**consagrado -da** *adj* consecrate, consecrated; hallowed (*ground*); sanctioned, established, time-honored; stock (*phrase*)
**consagrante** *adj* consecrating; *mf* consecrator
**consagrar** *va* to consecrate; to devote; to dedicate; to deify, to apotheosize; to authorize (*a new word or meaning*); *vr* to devote oneself (*e.g., to study*); to consecrate oneself; to make a name for oneself; **consagrarse a** + *inf* to devote oneself to + *inf*
**consanguíneo -a** *adj* consanguineous
**consanguinidad** *f* consanguinity
**consciente** *adj* conscious
**conscripción** *f* (mil.) conscription
**conscripto** *m* (mil.) draftee
**consectario -ria** *adj* next, adjoining; *m* corollary
**consecución** *f* obtaining, acquisition, attainment
**consecuencia** *f* consequence; consistency; **en consecuencia** accordingly; **guardar consecuencia** to remain consistent; **por consecuencia** consequently; **sacar en consecuencia** to prove, to show; **traer a consecuencia** to bring in, bring up
**consecuente** *adj* consecutive; consistent; *m* (log. & math.) consequent
**consecutivo -va** *adj* consecutive; (gram.) consecutive
**conseguimiento** *m* var. of **consecución**
**conseguir §82** *va* to get, obtain; to bring about; **conseguir** + *inf* to succeed in + *ger*
**conseja** *f* story, fairy tale; cabal, conciliabule
**consejero -ra** *adj* advisory; *m* counselor, adviser; councilor; *f* counselor's wife; female adviser
**consejo** *m* advice, counsel; council; town or city council; board; **consejos** *mpl* advice; **tomar consejo** to take counsel, **un consejo** a piece of advice; **consejo de estado** council of state; **consejo de familia** board of guardians; **consejo de guerra** council of war; court-martial; **consejo de ministros** council of ministers, cabinet; **Consejo de Seguridad** Security Council
**consenciente** *adj* blinking at evil
**consenso** *m* consensus
**consensual** *adj* (law) consensual
**consentido -da** *adj* complaisant, indulgent (*husband*); pampered, spoiled; (Am.) proud, haughty
**consentidor -dora** *adj* acquiescent, yielding; (coll.) pampering; *mf* acquiescent person; (coll.) pamperer; *m* cuckold
**consentimiento** *m* consent
**consentir §62** *va* to allow, permit, tolerate; to admit; to pamper, spoil; *vn* to consent; to believe; to weaken, become loose (*said, e.g., of a piece of furniture or its parts*); **consentir** + *inf* to believe, to think that + *ind*, e.g., **consentí morir helado** I thought that I was freezing to death; **consentir con** to be indulgent with; **consentir en** to consent to; **consentir en** + *inf* to consent to + *inf; vr* to begin to split or crack up; (Am.) to be proud
**conserje** *m* janitor, concierge, porter
**conserjería** *f* janitorship, janitor's quarters; porter's desk, conciergerie
**conserva** *f* conserve, preserves; preserved food; pickles; (naut.) convoy; **navegar en conserva** or **en la conserva** (naut.) to sail in a convoy; **conservas alimenticias** canned goods; **conserva trojezada** minced preserves
**conservación** *f* conservation; maintenance, upkeep; preservation; self-preservation; **conservación de la energía** (phys.) conservation of energy; **conservación de la masa** (phys.) conservation of mass; **conservación de la materia** (phys.) conservation of matter; **conservación de suelos** soil conservation
**conservador -dora** *adj* preservative; (pol.) conservative; *mf* (pol.) conservative; *m* conservator; curator
**conservadorismo** *m* var. of **conservadurismo**
**conservaduría** *f* curatorship
**conservadurismo** *m* conservatism; British Conservative Party
**conservar** *va* to conserve, keep, maintain; to preserve; **bien conservado** well-preserved; *vr* to keep; to take good care of oneself
**conservatismo** *m* (Am.) conservatism
**conservativo -va** *adj* preservative
**conservatorio -ria** *adj* conservatory; *m* conservatory, conservatoire; (Am.) conservatory (*greenhouse*)
**conservera** *f* see **conservero**
**conservería** *f* preserve making
**conservero -ra** *adj* preserve, canning (*business, industry, etc.*); *mf* preserver, preserve maker; canner; *f* cannery
**considerabilísimo -ma** *adj super* very great, quite considerable
**considerable** *adj* considerable; large, great
**consideración** *f* consideration; **cargar** or **fijar la consideración en** to consider carefully, to look into thoroughly; **en consideración** under consideration; **en consideración a** in consideration of; **ser de consideración** to be of importance, be of concern; **tomar en consideración** to take into consideration
**consideradamente** *adv* carefully, watchfully
**considerado -da** *adj* considered; considerate; respected, esteemed
**considerando** *m* whereas; **considerando que** whereas
**considerar** *va* to consider; to treat with respect
**consigna** *f* order; slogan; (mil.) watchword; (rail.) checkroom
**consignación** *f* consignment; (com.) consignment; **a consignación** (com.) on consignment
**consignador** *m* (com.) consignor
**consignar** *va* to consign; to assign; to tell, relate; to point out; to indicate, state; (com.) to consign
**consignatario** *m* consignatary; (com.) consignee
**consigo** with him, with her, with them, with you; with himself, with herself, with themselves, with yourself, with yourselves
**consiguiente** *adj* consequent; consequential; resultant; **ir** or **proceder consiguiente** to act consistently; *m* consequence, result; (log.) consequent; **por consiguiente** or **por el consiguiente** consequently, therefore
**consiliario -ria** *mf* counselor, adviser
**consistencia** *f* consistence or consistency
**consistente** *adj* consistent; consisting
**consistir** *vn* to consist; **consistir en** to consist in; to consist of; **consistir en** + *inf* to consist in + *ger*
**consistorial** *adj* consistorial; *m* member of a consistory; councilman
**consistorio** *m* consistory; town council; town hall; **Consistorio divino** Throne of God
**cons.º** abr. of **consejo**
**consocio -cia** *mf* copartner; companion, comrade, fellow member
**consola** *f* console, console table; bracket; (arch., mus. & rad.) console
**consolación** *f* consolation; (cards) consolation (*fine paid by loser*)
**consolador -dora** *adj* consoling; *mf* consoler
**consolar §77** *va* to console
**consolativo -va** or **consolatorio -ria** *adj* consolatory
**consólida** *f* (bot.) comfrey; **consólida real** (bot.) delphinium, field larkspur
**consolidación** *f* consolidation
**consolidado -da** *adj* bonded (*debt*); **consolidados** *mpl* consolidated annuities
**consolidar** *va* to consolidate; to fund, to refund; to put together, to repair; *vr* to consolidate
**consonancia** *f* consonance or consonancy; harmony; rhyme; **en consonancia con** in accordance with
**consonantado -da** *adj* rhymed
**consonante** *adj* consonant; consonantal; rhyming; *m* rhyme word; *f* (gram.) consonant
**consonántico -ca** *adj* consonantal
**consonar §77** *vn* to rhyme; (mus.) to be in harmony; to be harmonious

**cónsone** *adj* consonous, harmonious; *m* (mus.) chord
**cónsono -na** *adj* consonous, harmonious
**consorcio** *m* consortium; partnership; fellowship, harmony
**consorte** *mf* consort; companion, partner; **consortes** *mpl* (law) colitigants; (law) accomplices
**conspicuo -cua** *adj* distinguished, outstanding, conspicuous
**conspiración** *f* conspiracy
**conspirado** *m* conspirer, conspirator
**conspirador -dora** *mf* conspirer, conspirator
**conspirar** *vn* to conspire; **conspirar a** + *inf* to conspire to + *inf*
**conspuir §41** *va* to decry, run down
**Const.** abr. of **Constitución**
**constancia** *f* constancy, steadiness; certainty; proof; (Am.) written evidence, documentary proof; **dejar constancia de** to prove, to establish
**constante** *adj* constant; clear, certain; *f* (math. & phys.) constant
**constantemente** *adv* constantly; surely, with certainty; regularly
**Constantino** *m* Constantine
**Constantinopla** *f* Constantinople
**Constanza** *f* Constance (*feminine proper name*)
**constar** *vn* to be clear, be certain; to be shown, be on record; to have the right rhythm (*said of verse*); **hacer constar** to state, to reveal; **constar de** to consist of, be composed of
**constatación** *f* proof, establishment (*of a fact*)
**constatar** *va* to state, show, establish, prove
**constelación** *f* (astr. & astrol.) constellation; climate, atmosphere; epidemic
**constelar** *va* to fill, cover, sprinkle
**consternación** *f* consternation
**consternar** *va* to dismay, terrify, consternate
**constipación** *f* cold, cold in the head; **constipación de vientre** constipation
**constipado** *m* cold, cold in the head
**constipar** *va* to cause (*someone*) to catch cold, to give a cold to; to constipate; to close or constrict (*pores or tissues*); to stop up (*nasal passages*); *vr* to catch cold; to become constipated
**constitución** *f* constitution
**constitucional** *adj* constitutional; *mf* constitutionalist
**constitucionalidad** *f* constitutionality
**constituidor -dora** *adj* constitutive
**constituir §41** *va* to constitute; to set up, to establish; **constituir en** to force into; *vr* to constitute oneself; **constituirse en** or **por** to set oneself up as
**constitutivo -va** *adj* & *m* constituent
**constituyente** *adj* constituent; component; (pol.) constituent; *m* constituent; component; **constituyentes** *fpl* (pol.) constituent assembly
**const.l** abr. of **constitucional**
**constreñidamente** *adv* constrainedly
**constreñimiento** *m* constraint, compulsion
**constreñir §74** *va* to constrain, to force; to compress, to oppress; to bind, make costive, constipate
**constricción** *f* constriction; (med.) constriction
**constrictivo -va** *adj* constrictive; styptic
**constrictor -tora** *adj* constricting; (med.) styptic; *m* (anat.) constrictor; (med.) styptic
**constringente** *adj* constringent
**construcción** *f* construction; structure, building; (gram.) construction; **construcción de buques, construcción naval** shipbuilding
**constructivo -va** *adj* constructive
**constructor -tora** *adj* constructing, building; construction (*e.g., company*); *mf* constructor, builder; **constructor de buques** shipbuilder
**construir §41** *va* to construct; (geom. & gram.) to construct
**constuprar** *va* to defile, corrupt
**consubstanciación** *f* (theol.) consubstantiation
**consubstancial** *adj* consubstantial
**consubstancialidad** *f* consubstantiality
**consuegra** *f* mother-in-law of one's child
**consuegro** *m* father-in-law of one's child
**consuelda** *f* (bot.) comfrey; (bot.) prickly or rough comfrey; **consuelda mayor** (bot.) comfrey; **consuelda media** (bot.) bugle, bugleweed; **consuelda real** (bot.) field larkspur; **consuelda sarracena** (bot.) goldenrod (*Solidago virgaurea*)
**consuelo** *m* consolation; joy, comfort; **sin consuelo** inconsolably; (coll.) to excess, without limit; (*cap.*) *f* Consuelo (*woman's name*)
**consueta** *m* (theat.) prompter
**consuetudinario -ria** *adj* customary, consuetudinary; *mf* habitual sinner
**cónsul** *m* consul; **cónsul general** consul general
**cónsula** *f* consul's wife
**consulado** *m* consulate; consulship; **consulado general** consulate general
**consular** *adj* consular
**consulesa** *f* (coll.) consul's wife
**consulta** *f* consulting; consultation; opinion (*of lawyer, doctor, etc.*)
**consultación** *f* consultation
**consultante** *adj* consulting
**consultar** *va* to consult; to take up, to discuss; to advise; to hand down an opinion on; *vn* to consult
**consultivo -va** *adj* consultative
**consultor -tora** *adj* consulting; *mf* consultant
**consultorio** *m* information bureau; doctor's office, clinic
**consumación** *f* consummation; termination, extinction; **la consumación de los siglos** the end of the world
**consumado -da** *adj* consummate; fulfilled; *m* consommé
**consumar** *va* to consummate
**consumero** *m* (slang) tax collector (*at city gates*); (slang) guard stationed to prevent smuggling
**consumible** *adj* consumable
**consumición** *f* consumption; drink (*bought in a café or restaurant*)
**consumido -da** *adj* (coll.) weak, thin, emaciated, worn-out; (coll.) worrying, fretful
**consumidor -dora** *adj* consuming; *mf* consumer; customer (*of a café or restaurant*)
**consumimiento** *m* consumption, destruction
**consumir** *va* to consume; to take (*the Eucharist*); (coll.) to harass, vex, wear down; *vr* to consume, waste away, languish; to long, to yearn; (coll.) to become harassed or vexed
**consumo** *m* consumption (*e.g., of food*); consumers; **consumos** *spl* octroi, tax on provisions (*being brought into town*)
**consunción** *f* consumption, destruction; (path.) consumption
**consuno; de consuno** in accord, together
**consuntivo -va** *adj* consumptive, consuming
**consustanciación** *f* var. of **consubstanciación**
**consustancial** *adj* var. of **consubstancial**
**consustancialidad** *f* var. of **consubstancialidad**
**contabilidad** *f* calculability; accountancy, accounting, bookkeeping
**contabilista** *mf* accountant, bookkeeper
**contabilizar §76** *va* to enter (*in ledger, on score card, etc.*)
**contable** *adj* countable; *m* accountant, bookkeeper
**contactar** *vn* to contact, be in contact
**contacto** *m* contact; (elec.) contact; **poner en contacto con** to put in contact or touch with; **ponerse en contacto con** to reach, to get in touch with
**contactor** *m* (elec.) contactor
**contadero -ra** *adj* countable; *m* narrow passage (*through which only one person or animal can pass at a time*)
**contado -da** *adj* scarce, rare; **contados -das** *adj pl* a few; **al contado** cash, for cash; **de contado** immediately, right away; **por de contado** naturally, of course
**contador** *m* counter; accountant; cash register; (law) auditor, receiver; meter (*for gas, water, electricity*); **contador automático** slot meter; **contador de abonado** house meter; **contador de centelleo** (phys.) scintillation counter; **contador de Geiger** (phys.) Geiger counter; **contador kilométrico** (aut.) speed-

ometer, odometer; **contador público titulado** certified public accountant
**contaduría** *f* accountancy; accountant's office; auditorship; (theat.) box office
**contagiar** *va* to affect by contagion; (fig.) to infect; (fig.) to communicate (*e.g., an emotion*); *vr* to become affected by contagion; (fig.) to become infected; **contagiarse de** to catch (*a disease*) by contagion
**contagio** *m* contagion
**contagiosidad** *f* contagiousness
**contagioso -sa** *adj* contagious
**contal** *m* string of beads for counting
**contaminación** *f* contamination; (philol.) contamination; (fig.) stain, blot
**contaminador -dora** *adj* contaminating
**contaminar** *va* to contaminate; to corrupt (*a text*); to profane, to break (*the law of God*); *vr* to become contaminated
**contante** *adj* ready (*money*)
**contar §77** *va* to count; to rate, consider; to charge, to debit; to tell, to relate; **dejarse contar diez** (box.) to take the count; **tiene sus días contados** or **sus horas contadas** his days are numbered; **contar . . . años** to be . . . years old; **contar una cosa por hecha** to consider a thing as good as done; *vn* to count; **a contar desde** beginning with; **contar con** to count on, rely on; to reckon with; **contar con** + *inf* to count on + *ger*, to expect to + *inf;* **contar con** or **por los dedos** to count on one's fingers
**contario** *m* var. of **contero**
**contemperar** *va* var. of **atemperar**
**contemplación** *f* contemplation; leniency, condescension; **gastar contemplaciones con** (coll.) to humor
**contemplador -dora** *adj* contemplating, contemplative; *mf* contemplator
**contemplar** *va* to contemplate; to be lenient to, to be condescending towards; *vn* to contemplate
**contemplativo -va** *adj* contemplative; lenient
**contemporaneidad** *f* contemporaneousness
**contemporáneo -a** *adj* contemporaneous; contemporary; *mf* contemporary (*person or thing*)
**contemporización** *f* temporizing, temporization
**contemporizador -dora** *adj* temporizing; *mf* temporizer
**contemporizar §76** *vn* to temporize
**contén** *m* curb; *2nd sg impv of* **contener**
**contención** *f* containment; containing, checking; contention, strife, emulation; (law) suit, litigation
**contencioso -sa** *adj* contentious; (law) contentious
**contendedor** *m* contestant
**contender §66** *vn* to contend, to contest
**contendiente** *adj* contending; *mf* contestant, contender
**contendor** *m* var. of **contendedor**
**contendré** *1st sg fut ind of* **contener**
**contenencia** *f* suspension in flight of birds of prey; (dancing) side step with pause
**contener §85** *va* to contain; *vr* to contain oneself
**contengo** *1st sg pres ind of* **contener**
**contenido -da** *adj* moderate, restrained; *m* contents; content
**contenta** *f* see **contento**
**contentadizo -za** *adj* easy to please; **bien contentadizo** easy to please; **mal contentadizo** hard to please
**contentamiento** *m* contentment
**contentar** *va* to content; (com.) to indorse; **ser de buen contentar** (coll.) to be easy to please; **ser de mal contentar** (coll.) to be hard to please; *vr* to be contented; **contentarse con** or **de** + *inf* to be satisfied with + *ger* or to + *inf*
**contento -ta** *adj* contented, glad; **no caber de contento** (coll.) to be bursting with joy; *m* contentment; **a contento** to one's satisfaction; *f* gift or treat to please someone; (com.) indorsement; (mil.) certificate of good conduct; (law) release
**contera** *f* tip (*e.g., of umbrella*); refrain; **por contera** (coll.) finally, at the end
**contérmino -na** *adj* conterminous
**contero** *m* (arch.) beading, beadwork
**conterráneo -a** *adj* of the same country; *m* fellow countryman; *f* fellow country woman
**contertuliano -na** or **contertulio -lia** *mf* party-goer, fellow member (*of a social group*)
**contesta** *f* (Am.) chat, conversation; (Am.) answer
**contestable** *adj* answerable
**contestación** *f* answer, reply; dispute, altercation; **contestación a la demanda** (law) answer, plea; **mala contestación** back talk, sauce
**contestar** *va* to answer; to confirm (*a witness, the deposition of a witness*); **contestar el timbre, la puerta, el teléfono, una carta, una pregunta, a una persona** to answer the bell, the door, the telephone, a letter, a question, a person; *vn* to answer; to agree; **contestar a** to answer (*e.g., a letter*)
**conteste** *adj* (law) confirming another witness; **estar contestes** to be in agreement
**contexto** *m* interweaving; interweaving of words; context
**contextuar §33** *va* to back with quotations
**contextura** *f* contexture; contexture of human body
**conticinio** *m* dead of night
**contienda** *f* contest, fight, dispute
**contigo** with thee, with you
**contigüidad** *f* contiguity
**contiguo -gua** *adj* contiguous
**continencia** *f* continence
**continental** *adj* continental; *m* office for local messages; local message
**continente** *adj* continent; *m* container; mien, countenance; bearing; continent; **Continente antártico** Antarctic Continent; **Continente Negro** Dark Continent
**contingencia** *f* contingency
**contingente** *adj* contingent; *m* contingent; share; quota; (mil.) contingent
**contingible** *adj* possible
**continuación** *f* continuation; continuance; **a continuación** later on, below; **a continuación de** right after; right behind
**continuadamente** *adv* continuously
**continuador -dora** *adj* continuing; *mf* continuer, continuator
**continuar §33** *va* to continue; *vn* to continue; **continuar** + *ger* to continue to + *inf*, to continue + *ger*; **continuará** to be continued (*said e.g., of a serial*); **continuar con** to continue with; to adjoin; *vr* to continue; **continuarse con** to connect with
**continuativo -va** *adj & f* (gram.) continuative
**continuidad** *f* continuity
**continuo -nua** *adj* continual; continuous; persevering; (mach.) endless; **a la continua** continuously; **de continuo** continuously; **continuo** *adv* continuously; *m* continuum; yeoman of the guard; **continuo espacio-temporal** or **continuo espacio tiempo** (phys.) space-time continuum
**contómetro** *m* comptometer
**contonear** *vr* to strut, to swagger
**contoneo** *m* strut, swagger
**contorcer §87** *vr* to twist oneself, to writhe
**contorción** *f* twisting, writhing, contortion
**contornado -da** *adj* (her.) contourné
**contornar** or **contornear** *va* to go around; to trace the contour of, to outline
**contorneo** *m* encircling; outline, outlining
**contorno** *m* contour, outline; **contornos** *mpl* environs; **en contorno** around, round about
**contorsión** *f* contortion
**contorsionista** *mf* contortionist
**contra** *prep* against; facing; *m* con (*opposite opinion*); (mus.) organ pedal; **contras** *mpl* lowest bass of organ; *f* (coll.) trouble, inconvenience; (fencing) counter; (Am.) play-off; (Am.) gift, extra (*to a customer*); **en contra de** against; **ir en contra de** to run counter to; **llevar la contra a** (coll.) to oppose, to disagree with
**contraabertura** *f* (surg.) counteropening
**contraalmirante** *m* rear admiral
**contraamura** *f* (naut.) preventer
**contraantena** *f* (rad.) counterpoise
**contraaproches** *mpl* (fort.) counterapproach

**contraárbol** *m* (mach.) countershaft
**contraarmiños** *mpl* (her.) ermines, counter-ermine
**contraatacar** §86 *va & vn* to counterattack
**contraataguía** *f* secondary cofferdam
**contraataque** *m* counterattack; **contraataques** *mpl* (fort.) fortified line of defense
**contrabajo** *m* (mus.) contrabass, double bass; (mus.) contrabassist
**contrabajón** *m* (mus.) double bassoon
**contrabajonista** *mf* double-bassoon player
**contrabalancear** *va* to counterbalance
**contrabalanza** *f* counterbalance; contrast
**contrabandear** *vn* to smuggle
**contrabandista** *adj* (pertaining to) contraband, smuggling; *mf* contrabandist, smuggler
**contrabando** *m* contraband· smuggling; **pasar de contrabando** to smuggle, to smuggle in; **contrabando de guerra** contraband of war
**contrabarrera** *f* (taur.) inner barrier; (taur.) second row of seats
**contrabasa** *f* pedestal
**contrabatería** *f* (mil.) counterbattery
**contrabatir** *va* (mil.) to fire back at (*enemy's battery*)
**contrabolina** *f* (naut.) auxiliary bowline
**contrabóveda** *f* (arch.) inverted vault or arch
**contrabovedilla** *f* (naut.) upper counter
**contrabracear** *va* to counterbrace
**contrabranque** *m* (naut.) stemson
**contrabraza** *f* (naut.) auxiliary brace
**contrabrazo** *m* drag link (*of steering gear*)
**contrabrazola** *f* (naut.) headledge
**contracaja** *f* (print.) upper right-hand corner of case for little-used type
**contracalle** *f* parallel side street
**contracambio** *m* exchange; (com.) re-exchange
**contracanal** *m* branch channel
**contracarril** *m* (rail.) guardrail
**contracarta** *f* var. of **contraescritura**
**contracción** *f* contraction; (econ.) recession
**contracédula** *f* counter decree
**contracepción** *f* contraception
**contraceptivo -va** *adj & m* contraceptive
**contracifra** *f* key to a cipher
**contraclave** *f* (arch.) voussoir next to keystone
**contracodaste** *m* (naut.) inner sternpost
**contracorriente** *f* countercurrent, crosscurrent; (fig.) backwash; **a contracorriente** upstream
**contractable** *adj* contractible
**contráctil** *adj* contractile; contractible, shrinkable
**contractilidad** *f* contractility
**contractivo -va** *adj* contractive
**contracto -ta** *adj* (gram.) contract
**contractual** *adj* contractual
**contractura** *f* contraction; (arch. & path.) contracture
**contracuartelado -da** *adj* (her.) counterquartered
**contracurva** *f* reverse curve
**contrachapado** *m* plywood
**contradanza** *f* contradance
**contradecir** §37 *va* to contradict; *vr* to contradict oneself
**contradicción** *f* contradiction
**contradiciendo** *ger of* **contradecir**
**contradictor -tora** *adj* contradictory (*person*); *mf* contradicter
**contradictorio -ria** *adj* contradictory; *f* (log.) contradictory
**contradicho -cha** *pp of* **contradecir**
**contradigo** *1st sg pres ind of* **contradecir**
**contradije** *1st sg pret ind of* **contradecir**
**contradique** *m* counterdike
**contradiré** *1st sg fut ind of* **contradecir**
**contradriza** *f* (naut.) auxiliary halyard
**contradurmiente** *m* (naut.) clamp
**contraeje** *m* (mach.) countershaft
**contraelectromotriz** *adj fem* counter electromotive
**contraemboscada** *f* counterambush
**contraer** §88 *va* to contract; to condense (*an idea*); (gram.) to contract; *vr* to contract; to be restricted; (Am.) to work hard, to apply oneself
**contraescalón** *m* riser (*of stairs*)
**contraescarpa** *f* (fort.) counterscarp
**contraescota** *f* (naut.) auxiliary sheet
**contraescotín** *m* (naut.) auxiliary topsail sheet
**contraescritura** *f* (law) countermand; (law) deed of invalidation
**contraespía** *mf* counterspy
**contraespionaje** *m* counterespionage
**contraestimulante** *m* (med.) counterstimulant
**contrafagot** *m* (mus.) contrafagotto, double bassoon
**contrafajado -da** *adj* (her.) counterfessed
**contrafallar** *va & vn* to overtrump
**contrafallo** *m* overtrump
**contrafase** *f* (rad.) push-pull amplification; **en contrafase** (rad.) push-pull
**contrafigura** *f* counterpart; (theat.) counterpart
**contrafilo** *m* back edge near the tip (*of a weapon*)
**contraflorado -da** *adj* (her.) counterflory
**contrafoque** *m* (naut.) foretopmast staysail
**contrafoso** *m* (theat.) subcellar; (fort.) outer ditch
**contrafuerte** *m* girth strap (*for saddletree*); stiffener for shoe (*inner strip of leather*); spur (*of mountain range*); (arch.) abutment, buttress, counterfort; (fort.) outwork, outer fort
**contrafuga** *f* (mus.) counterfugue
**contragolpe** *m* counterstroke; (path.) contrecoup; (mach.) return stroke; kickback; (box.) counter
**contraguardia** *f* (fort.) counterguard
**contraguía** *f* front left-hand animal in a team of four
**contrahacedor -dora** *adj* counterfeiting, imitative, fake; *mf* counterfeiter, imitator, fake; impersonator
**contrahacer** §55 *va* to counterfeit, imitate, copy; to forge; to feign; to mimic, impersonate; to pirate (*a book*); *vr* to feign
**contrahago** *1st sg pres ind of* **contrahacer**
**contraharé** *1st sg fut ind of* **contrahacer**
**contrahaz** *f* (*pl:* **-haces**) wrong side (*of cloth*)
**contrahecho -cha** *adj* counterfeit, faked; hunchbacked, deformed; *mf* hunchback; *pp of* **contrahacer**
**contrahechura** *f* counterfeit, fake
**contrahice** *1st sg pret ind of* **contrahacer**
**contrahierba** *f* (bot.) contrayerva; precaution
**contrahilo; a contrahilo** across the grain
**contrahuella** *f* riser (*of stairs*)
**contraigo** *1st sg pres ind of* **contraer**
**contraindicación** *f* (med.) contraindication
**contraindicante** *adj* (med.) contraindicating; *m* (med.) contraindicant
**contraindicar** §86 *va* (med.) to contraindicate
**contrainteligencia** *f* counterintelligence
**contrairritación** *f* (med.) counterirritation
**contrairritante** *adj & m* (med.) counterirritant
**contraje** *1st sg pret ind of* **contraer**
**contralateral** *adj* contralateral
**contralecho; a contralecho** (mas.) laid vertically
**contralmirante** *m* var. of **contraalmirante**
**contralor** *m* comptroller
**contralto** *m* (mus.) contralto (*voice*); *mf* (mus.) contralto (*person*)
**contraluz** *f* view against the light; **a contraluz** against the light
**contramaestre** *m* foreman; (naut.) boatswain; (nav.) warrant officer, petty officer; (orn.) tropic bird; **segundo contramaestre** (naut.) boatswain's mate; **contramaestre mayor de cargo** (nav.) chief petty officer
**contramalla** or **contramalladura** *f* double fishing net
**contramandar** *va* to countermand
**contramandato** *m* countermand
**contramangas** *fpl* oversleeves
**contramanivela** *f* drag link
**contramano; a contramano** the wrong way, in the wrong direction
**contramarca** *f* countermark
**contramarcar** §86 *va* to countermark
**contramarco** *m* (carp.) sash
**contramarcha** *f* countermarch; turning back; reverse, reversal; (naut.) evolution, maneuver; (mach.) fast and loose pulleys

**contramarchar** *vn* to countermarch; to turn back; to go into reverse, run in reverse
**contramarea** *f* (naut.) opposing tide
**contramedida** *f* countermeasure
**contramesana** *f* (naut.) aftermast
**contramina** *f* (mil.) countermine
**contraminar** *va* (mil. & fig.) to countermine
**contramuralla** *f* (fort.) countermure
**contramuro** *m* (arch.) low secondary wall; (fort.) countermure
**contranatural** *adj* unnatural
**contraofensiva** *f* (mil.) counteroffensive
**contraorden** *f* countermand, cancellation
**contrapalado -da** *adj* (her.) counterpaly
**contrapalanquín** *m* (naut.) auxiliary clew garnet
**contrapar** *m* rafter; eaves board
**contraparte** *f* counterpart (*complement*)
**contrapartida** *f* (com.) correction in double-entry bookkeeping
**contrapás** *m* half step (*in contredanse*); contredanse (*of Catalonia*)
**contrapasamiento** *m* going over to the other side, joining the other side
**contrapasar** *vn* to go over to the other side; (her.) to be counterpassant
**contrapaso** *m* back step; (mus.) counter passage
**contrapeado** *m* plywood
**contrapear** *va* (carp.) to place (*boards*) together with grains at right angles
**contrapelo; a contrapelo** against the hair; against the grain; backwards, the wrong way; **a contrapelo de** counter to, against
**contrapesar** *va* to offset, equalize, compensate, counterpoise, counterbalance
**contrapeso** *m* counterpoise, counterbalance, counterweight; makeweight (*to complete weight of meat, fish, etc.*); (rail.) counterbalance (*of locomotive wheel*)
**contrapeste** *m* pest preventive, remedy for the pest
**contrapilastra** *f* (carp.) astragal; (arch.) counterpilaster
**contrapondré** *1st sg fut ind of* **contraponer**
**contraponer** §69 *va* to set in front; to compare; to oppose; **contraponer a** to set up against; *vr* to be opposed, be opposite
**contrapongo** *1st sg pres ind of* **contraponer**
**contraposición** *f* contraposition; **en contraposición de** as contrasted with
**contrapozo** *m* counterblast
**contrapresión** *f* back pressure
**contraproducente** *adj* unproductive, self-defeating
**contraproposición** *f* counterproposition
**contrapropuesta** *f* counterproposal
**contraprueba** *f* (engraving) counterproof; (print.) second proof
**contrapuerta** *f* storm door; vestibule door; (fort.) counterport
**contrapuesto -ta** *pp of* **contraponer**
**contrapunta** *f* false edge (*of sword*); (mach.) tailstock
**contrapuntante** *mf* (mus.) counterpoint singer
**contrapuntar** *vr* var. of **contrapuntear**
**contrapuntear** *va* (mus.) to sing in counterpoint; *vn* to be sarcastic; *vr* to be sarcastic, to use abusive language; to be sarcastic to each other
**contrapuntista** *mf* (mus.) contrapuntist
**contrapuntístico -ca** *adj* (mus.) contrapuntal
**contrapunto** *m* (mus.) counterpoint
**contrapunzar** §76 *va* to rivet with a punch
**contrapunzón** *m* counterpunch; punch; nailset
**contrapuse** *1st sg pret ind of* **contraponer**
**contraquilla** *f* (naut.) keelson
**contraria** *f* see **contrario**
**contrariar** §90 *va* to oppose; to counteract, thwart; to annoy, provoke
**contrariedad** *f* contrariness, contrariety; opposition; interference, obstacle; annoyance, bother; disagreement, clash
**contrario -ria** *adj* contrary; opposite, opposed; hostile; harmful; *mf* enemy; opponent; rival; *m* opposite, contrary; contradiction; obstacle; **al contrario de** unlike; **en contrario** to the contrary; **por el** or **lo contrario** on the contrary; *f* contrary (*opposite*); **llevar la contraria a** (coll.) to oppose, to disagree with
**contrarreclamación** *f* counterclaim
**contrarreconocimiento** *m* (mil.) counterreconnaissance
**contrarreferencia** *f* cross reference
**contrarreforma** *f* counterreformation; (*cap.*) *f* Counter Reformation
**contrarregistro** *m* control (*of an account; of a scientific experiment*)
**contrarreguera** *f* lateral drain, cross ditch
**contrarréplica** *f* rejoinder; (law) rejoinder
**contrarrestar** *va* to resist, offset, counteract; (sport) to return (*a ball*)
**contrarresto** *m* resistance, counteraction; (sport) player who returns the ball
**contrarretablo** *m* (eccl.) altar slab
**contrarrevolución** *f* counterrevolution
**contrarriel** *m* (rail.) guardrail
**contrarroda** *f* (naut.) stemson
**contrarronda** *f* (mil.) counterround
**contrarrotura** *f* (vet.) plaster, poultice
**contrasellar** *va* to counterseal
**contrasello** *m* (hist.) counterseal
**contrasentido** *m* countersense, misinterpretation, mistranslation; contradiction; nonsense, piece of nonsense
**contraseña** *f* countersign, countermark; baggage check; (mil.) countersign, watchword; **contraseña de salida** (theat.) check
**contrastar** *va* to resist; to assay; to check (*weights and measures*); *vn* to resist; to contrast; **contrastar a, con** or **contra** to face up to
**contraste** *m* resistance; assay; assayer; assayer's office; assayer's seal; contrast; (naut.) sudden shift in the wind
**contrata** *f* contract
**contratación** *f* trade, commerce; deal, transaction; contract (*document*)
**contratante** *adj* contracting; *mf* contractor; covenanter, contracting party
**contratar** *va* to contract for; to engage, hire, take on
**contratiempo** *m* misfortune, disappointment, contretemps; (mus.) contretemps; **a contratiempo** (mus.) off beat
**contratista** *mf* contractor
**contrato** *m* contract; **contrato de compraventa** deal, bargain, contract
**contratorpedero** *m* (nav.) torpedo-boat destroyer
**contratreta** *f* counterplot
**contratrinchera** *f* var. of **contraaproches**
**contratuerca** *f* lock nut, jam nut
**contravalación** *f* (fort.) contravallation
**contravalar** *va* (fort.) to build a contravallation around or in front of
**contravapor** *m* back-pressure steam; **dar contravapor a** to reverse (*a steam engine*)
**contravención** *f* contravention, infringement, infraction
**contravendré** *1st sg fut ind of* **contravenir**
**contraveneno** *m* counterpoison; antidote; (fig.) antidote
**contravengo** *1st sg pres ind of* **contravenir**
**contravenir** §92 *vn* to act contrary; **contravenir a** to contravene, to infringe
**contraventana** *f* window shutter (*inside or outside*)
**contraventar** *va* to brace, to guy
**contraventor -tora** *adj* contravening; *mf* contravener
**contravidriera** *f* storm sash
**contravine** *1st sg pret ind of* **contravenir**
**contraviniendo** *ger of* **contravenir**
**contrayente** *adj* marriage-contracting; *mf* contracting party (*to a marriage*)
**contrayerba** *f* var. of **contrahierba**
**contrecho -cha** *adj* crippled, maimed
**contribución** *f* contribution; tax; **contribución de sangre** military service; **contribución directa** direct tax; **contribución indirecta** indirect tax; **contribución industrial** excise tax; **contribución territorial** land tax
**contribuidor -dora** *adj* contributory; taxpaying; *mf* contributor; taxpayer

**contribuir** §41 *va & vn* to contribute; **contribuir a** + *inf* to contribute to + *ger*
**contribulado -da** *adj* afflicted, grieved
**contributario -ria** *mf* fellow taxpayer
**contributivo -va** *adj* contributive, tax
**contribuyente** *adj* contributing; taxpaying; *mf* contributor; taxpayer
**contrición** *f* contrition
**contrincante** *m* opponent, rival, competitor
**contristar** *va* to sadden
**contrito -ta** *adj* contrite
**control** *m* check, control; control experiment; **control a cascada** (elec.) cascade control; **control de fuego** (nav.) fire control; **control de la frecuencia** (rad.) frequency control; **control de la natalidad** or **de los nacimientos** birth control; **control de volumen** (rad.) volume control; **control remoto** remote control
**controlable** *adj* controllable
**controlar** *va* to check, audit, control
**controversia** *f* controversy
**controversista** *mf* controversialist
**controvertible** *adj* controvertible
**controvertir** §62 *va* to controvert, dispute
**contubernio** *m* cohabitation; concubinage; vicious alliance
**contumacia** *f* contumacy; (law) contempt
**contumaz** *adj* (*pl:* **-maces**) contumacious; germ-bearing, disease-carrying; (law) guilty of contempt
**contumelia** *f* contumely
**contumelioso -sa** *adj* contumelious
**contundencia** *f* forcefulness, impressiveness
**contundente** *adj* bruising; forceful, impressive
**contundir** *va* to contuse, to bruise
**conturbación** *f* disquiet, anxiety, worry
**conturbar** *va* to disquiet, to upset, to trouble
**contusión** *f* contusion
**contusionar** *va* var. of **contundir**
**contuso -sa** *adj* bruised
**contutor** *m* coguardian
**contuve** *1st sg pret ind of* **contener**
**convalecencia** *f* convalescence
**convalecer** §34 *vn* to convalesce; to recover, get out of danger
**convaleciente** *adj & mf* convalescent
**convalidación** *f* confirming, confirmation
**convalidar** *va* to confirm
**convección** *f* (phys.) convection
**convecino -na** *adj* neighboring; *mf* fellow neighbor
**conveler** *vr* to twitch
**convencedor -dora** *adj* convincing; *mf* convincer
**convencer** §91 *va* to convince
**convencible** *adj* convincible
**convencimiento** *m* conviction; (act of) convincing
**convención** *f* convention
**convencional** *adj* conventional; *m* member of a convention
**convencionalidad** *f* conventionality
**convencionalismo** *m* conventionalism
**convendré** *1st sg fut ind of* **convenir**
**convengo** *1st sg pres ind of* **convenir**
**convenible** *adj* docile, compliant; reasonable, fair
**conveniencia** *f* propriety; fitness, suitability; advantage; agreement, conformity; convenience; **conveniencias** *fpl* property, income; perquisites; proprieties
**convenienciero -ra** *adj* selfish, thinking only of one's own convenience; comfort-loving
**conveniente** *adj* proper; fit, suitable; advantageous, profitable; convenient
**convenio** *m* covenant, pact; (com.) bankruptcy settlement
**convenir** §92 *vn* to be suitable, be becoming, be necessary, be important; to agree; to convene; **convenir** + *inf* to be important to + *inf;* **convenir en** + *inf* to agree to + *inf;* **conviene a saber** namely, to wit; *vr* to agree, come to an agreement; **convenirse en** + *inf* to agree to + *inf*
**conventícula** *f* or **conventículo** *m* conventicle
**conventillo** *m* (Am.) tenement house
**convento** *m* convent; monastery
**conventual** *adj & m* conventual
**conventualidad** *f* life in a convent or monastery; assignment to a convent or monastery
**convergencia** *f* convergence; concurrence, concordance
**convergente** *adj* convergent
**converger** §49 *vn* var. of **convergir**
**convergir** §42 *vn* to converge; to concur, concord
**conversa** *f* see **converso**
**conversable** *adj* conversable
**conversación** *f* conversation
**conversacional** *adj* conversational
**conversador -dora** *adj* conversing; *mf* conversationalist
**conversar** *vn* to converse; to live, dwell; to deal, traffic; (mil.) to wheel about
**conversible** *adj* var. of **convertible**
**conversión** *f* conversion; (alchem. & elec.) transformation; (rhet.) epistrophe; (mil.) conversion (*wheeling*); **conversión de la deuda** refunding of public debt
**conversivo -va** *adj* conversive
**converso -sa** *adj* converted; *mf* convert; *m* lay brother; *f* lay sister; (coll.) conversation, chat
**conversor** *m* (rad.) converter
**convertibilidad** *f* convertibility
**convertible** *adj* convertible
**convertidor** *m* (elec. & metal.) converter; (elec.) transformer; **convertidor Bessemer** Bessemer converter; **convertidor de frecuencia** (elec.) frequency converter; **convertidor de par** (aut.) torque converter; **convertidor sincrónico** (elec.) synchronous converter
**convertiplano** *m* (aer.) convertiplane
**convertir** §62 *va* to convert; to turn; *vr* to convert; to become converted; **convertirse en** to turn into, to become
**convexidad** *f* convexity
**convexo -xa** *adj* convex
**convicción** *f* conviction
**convicto -ta** *adj* convinced; convicted, found guilty; *mf* convict
**convidado -da** *mf* guest; *f* (coll.) treat (*to a drink*)
**convidador -dora** *adj* inviting; *mf* host
**convidar** *va* to invite; to treat; **convidar a** + *inf* to invite to + *inf;* to move to, to incite to + *inf;* **convidar a uno con una cosa** to offer something to someone; *vr* to volunteer one's services
**convincente** *adj* convincing
**convine** *1st sg pret ind of* **convenir**
**conviniendo** *ger of* **convenir**
**convite** *m* invitation; party, banquet; treat; **convite a escote** Dutch treat
**convivencia** *f* (act of) living together, life together
**conviviente** *adj* living together; *mf* companion
**convivir** *vn* to live together; **convivir con** to exist side by side with
**convocación** *f* convocation
**convocador -dora** *adj* summoning, convoking; *mf* convoker, convocator
**convocar** §86 *va* to convoke; to call (*a meeting, strike, etc.*)
**convocatorio -ria** *adj* summoning, convoking; *f* call, notice of a meeting
**convolución** *f* convolution
**convolutado -da** *adj* (bot.) convolute
**convolvuláceo -a** *adj* (bot.) convolvulaceous
**convólvulo** *m* (bot.) convolvulus; (ent.) measuring worm
**convoy** *m* convoy; (coll.) retinue; cruet stand; train, railway train
**convoyar** *va* to convoy
**conv.**[te] abr. of **conveniente**
**convulsión** *f* convulsion; (path.) convulsion
**convulsionar** *va* to convulse
**convulsivo -va** *adj* convulsive
**convulso -sa** *adj* convulsed, convulsive
**convulsoterapia** *f* (med.) convulsive treatment, shock treatment
**conyugal** *adj* conjugal
**cónyuge** *mf* spouse, consort, mate; **cónyuges** *mpl* couple, husband and wife
**coñac** *m* (*pl:* **-ñacs**) cognac
**coolí** *m* (*pl:* **-líes**) coolie
**cooperación** *f* coöperation

**cooperador -dora** *adj* coöperative; *mf* coöperator, co-worker
**cooperar** *vn* to coöperate; **cooperar a** + *inf* to coöperate in + *ger*
**cooperario** *m* coöperator, co-worker
**cooperativo -va** *adj* coöperative; *f* coöperative, coöperative society
**coopositor -tora** *mf* fellow competitor (*e.g., for a professorship*)
**cooptación** *f* coöptation
**cooptar** *va* coöpt
**coordenado -da** *adj* (math.) coördinate; *f* (math.) coördinate; **coordenadas cartesianas** (math.) Cartesian coördinates
**coordinación** *f* coördination
**coordinado -da** *adj & f* var. of **coordenado**
**coordinador -dora** *adj* coördinating; *mf* coördinator
**coordinamiento** *m* var. of **coordinación**
**coordinante** *adj* coördinating
**coordinar** *va & vn* to coördinate
**coordinativo -va** *adj* coördinative
**copa** *f* goblet, wineglass, cup, bowl; vase; crown (*of hat*); treetop; brazier; copa (*liquid measure equal to about a gill*); drink; sundae; (arch.) vase (*kind of finial*); roof or vault (*of a furnace*); playing card (*representing a bowl*) equivalent to heart; (sport) cup; (fig.) cup (*of sorrow, misfortune, etc.*); (*cap.*) *f* (astr.) Cup; **copas** *fpl* bosses of bridle; card suit corresponding to hearts; **tomarse una copa** to take a drink; **copa de oro** (bot.) California poppy
**copado -da** *adj* copped, crested; high-topped, bushy; *f* (orn.) crested lark
**copaiba** *f* (bot.) copaifera (*tree*); (pharm.) copaiba, copaiba balsam
**copal** *m* copal
**copar** *va* to cover (*the whole bet*); to sweep (*all posts in an election*); (mil.) to cut off and capture
**coparticipación** *f* joint partnership, copartnership, fellowship
**copartícipe** *mf* joint partner, copartner
**copayero** *m* (bot.) copaifera (*tree*)
**cope** *m* close-woven part of fishing net
**copear** *vn* to sell wine and liquor by the glass; to have a drink, to drink
**copela** *f* cupel
**copelación** *f* cupellation
**copelar** *va* to cupel
**Copenhague** *f* Copenhagen
**copépodo -da** *adj & m* (zool.) copepod
**copera** *f* cupboard, closet for glassware
**copernicano -na** *adj & mf* Copernican
**Copérnico** *m* Copernicus
**copero** *m* cupbearer; cabinet for wineglasses
**copeta** *f* small glass, small cup
**copete** *m* pompadour; tuft; forelock (*of horse*); crest (*of feathers; of a mountain*); top (*finial on piece of furniture*); topping (*e.g., of a dish of ice cream*); (carp.) triangular side of a hip roof; snobbishness; **de alto copete** important, aristocratic; **tener mucho copete** to be haughty, to be high-hat
**copetudo -da** *adj* copped, tufted; high, lofty; (coll.) haughty, snobbish; *f* (orn.) lark; (bot.) marigold
**copey** *m* (bot.) star-of-night; Ecuadoran bitumen
**copia** *f* abundance, plenty; copy; **copia al carbón** carbon copy; **copia del expediente académico** (educ.) transcript; **copia fiel** true copy
**copiador -dora** *adj* copying; *mf* copier, copyist; *m* letter book, letter file; duplicator, copying machine; *f* (mach.) copying lathe
**copiante** *mf* copier, copyist
**copiar** *va* to copy; to copy down
**copihue** *m* (bot.) Chilean bellflower (*Lapageria rosea*)
**copiloto** *m* (aer.) copilot
**copilla** *f* var. of **chofeta**
**copiosidad** *f* copiousness, abundance
**copioso -sa** *adj* copious, abundant; hearty (*meal*)
**copista** *mf* copyist, copier
**copla** *f* couplet; stanza; ballad, popular song; **coplas** *fpl* (coll.) verse, poetry; **coplas de ciego** (coll.) doggerel
**coplear** *vn* to compose or sing ballads
**coplero -ra** or **coplista** *mf* ballad vendor; poetaster
**copo** *m* flake; cot; bundle of cotton, flax, hemp, etc. (*to be spun*); bottom of purse net; fishing with purse net; **copo de nieve** snowflake
**copón** *m* large goblet, large cup; (eccl.) ciborium, pyx
**coposesión** *f* joint ownership
**coposesor -sora** *mf* joint owner
**coposo -sa** *adj* bushy, high-topped; flaky, woolly
**copra** *f* copra
**copretérito** *m* (gram.) imperfect (*indicative*)
**coproducción** *f* coproduction
**coprolito** *m* (pal.) coprolite
**copropietario -ria** *mf* joint owner
**cóptico -ca** *adj* Coptic
**copto -ta** *adj* Coptic; *mf* Copt (*person*); *m* Coptic (*language*)
**copudo -da** *adj* bushy, thick-topped (*tree or shrub*)
**cópula** *f* copula; (anat., gram., law, log. & med.) copula; (arch.) cupola
**copulación** *f* copulation
**copular** *vr* to copulate
**copulativo -va** *adj* copulative; *f* (gram.) copulative conjunction
**coque** *m* coke
**coqueluche** *f* (path.) whooping cough
**coquera** *f* head of a top; cavity or hollow in a stone; coke bin
**coqueta** *adj* coquettish, flirtatious; *f* coquette, flirt; roll, small loaf; blow on the palm of the hand with a ruler; dressing table
**coquetear** *vn* to flirt, to coquet; to try to please everybody
**coqueteo** *m* coquetting, flirting
**coquetería** *f* flirtation, coquetry; affectation, artificiality
**coquetilla** *f* little coquette
**coquetismo** *m* coquetry
**coquetón -tona** *adj* (coll.) coquettish, kittenish; *m* (coll.) ladykiller
**coquificar** §86 *va* to coke
**coquina** *f* (zool.) coquina, wedge shell
**coquinero** *m* (orn.) scaup, scaup duck
**coquito** *m* grimace made to make a baby laugh; cocoanut candy; (bot.) coquito, coquito palm; (orn.) Inca dove
**coquizar** §76 *va & vn* to coke
**coráceo -a** *adj* var. of **coriáceo**
**coracero** *m* cuirassier; (coll.) strong cigar
**coracina** *f* small breastplate
**coracoideo -a** *adj* coracoidal
**coracoides** *adj* coracoid; *m* (*pl:* **-des**) (anat.) coracoid
**coracha** *f* leather bag
**corada** *f* entrails
**coraje** *m* anger; mettle, spirit
**corajina** *f* (coll.) fit of anger
**corajudo -da** *adj* (coll.) ill-tempered
**coral** *adj* (mus.) choral; *m* (mus.) choral, chorale; (zool.) coral (*polyp, calcareous secretion, color, etc.*); (bot.) coral-bead tree; (bot.) coral vine; **corales** *mpl* coral beads; *f* (zool.) coral snake
**coralero -ra** *mf* worker or dealer in corals
**coralífero -ra** *adj* coralliferous
**coralígeno -na** *adj* coralligenous
**coralilla** *f* (bot.) pimpernel; (zool.) king snake
**coralillo** *m* (zool.) coral snake
**coralino -na** *adj* coralline; *f* (bot. & zool.) coralline
**corambre** *f* hides, skins; wine skin
**corambrero** *m* dealer in hides and skins
**Corán** *m* Koran
**coránico -ca** *adj* Koranic
**coranvobis** *m* (*pl:* **-bis**) (coll.) fat solemn-looking person
**coraza** *f* armor (*protective covering*); (arm. & zool.) cuirass; armor plate; (sport) guard, protector
**coraznada** *f* pith or marrow of pine tree; stew of animal hearts
**corazón** *m* heart; core; courage; (fig.) heart; **de corazón** heartily, sincerely; **decirle a uno el corazón una cosa** to have a presentiment of something; **hacer de tripas corazón** to pluck up courage; **llevar el co-**

**razón en la mano** to wear one's heart upon one's sleeve; **no tener corazón para** + *inf* to not have the heart to + *inf;* **partir** or **quebrantar el corazón de** to break the heart of; **corazón atlético** (path.) athlete's heart; **corazón grasoso** (path.) fatty heart
**corazonada** *f* impulsiveness; presentiment, hunch; (coll.) entrails
**corazoncillo** *m* (bot.) St.-John's-wort
**corbachada** *f* lash with a pizzle
**corbacho** *m* pizzle (*used as a whip*)
**corbata** *f* necktie, cravat; scarf; flap (*of a tire*); bow and streamer (*of a banner*); **corbata a la inglesa** ascot, ascot tie; **corbata a la mariposa** or **corbata de lazo** bow tie; **corbata de nudo corredizo** four-in-hand tie
**corbatería** *f* necktie shop
**corbatero -ra** *mf* necktie maker or dealer
**corbatín** *m* bow tie
**corbato** *m* cooler, cooling bath (*of a still*)
**corbeta** *f* (naut.) corvette, barque
**corbona** *f* basket
**Córcega** *f* Corsica
**corcel** *m* steed, charger
**corcesca** *f* barbed spear
**corcino** *m* small deer, young deer
**corcova** *f* hump, hunch
**corcovado -da** *adj* humpbacked, hunchbacked; *mf* humpback, hunchback
**corcovar** *va* to bend, to crook
**corcovear** *vn* to buck (*said of a horse*)
**corcoveta** *f* small hump; *mf* (coll.) humpback
**corcovo** *m* buck (*of a horse*); (coll.) crookedness
**corcusido** *m* (coll.) rough darning, rough patch
**corcusir** *va* (coll.) to darn or mend roughly
**corcha** *f* cork bark; cork bucket (*for cooling wine*); (naut.) laying of a rope
**corchar** *va* (naut.) to lay (*strands of rope*)
**corche** *m* cork-soled shoe
**corchea** *f* (mus.) quaver, eighth note
**corchero -ra** *adj* cork; *f* cork bucket (*for cooling wine*)
**corcheta** *f* eye (*of hook and eye*); rabbet (*in doorframe*)
**corchete** *m* hook and eye; hook (*of hook and eye*); (carp.) bench hook; bracket; horizontal brace; (print.) overrun; constable
**corcho** *m* cork; cork wine cooler; cork, cork stopper; cork-soled clog; cork box (*for carrying food*); cork mat; (angling) cork (*float*); beehive; **corcho bornizo** virgin cork; **corcho segundero** cork of second barking; **corcho virgen** virgin cork
**corchoso -sa** *adj* corky
**corchotaponero -ra** *adj* cork, cork-making, stopper-making (*industry*)
**corda** *f* (dial.) mountain range; **estar a la corda** (naut.) to be close-hauled, to be lying to
**cordado -da** *adj & m* (zool.) chordate
**cordaje** *m* cordage; strings of guitar; (naut.) rigging
**cordal** *m* (mus.) tailpiece (*of stringed instrument*); *f* wisdom tooth
**cordato -ta** *adj* cordate; (archaic) prudent, judicious
**cordel** *m* cord, string; five steps; cattle run; **a cordel** in a straight line; **cordel de la corredera** (naut.) log line
**cordelado -da** *adj* corded (*ribbon*)
**cordelazo** *m* lash with a rope
**cordelejo** *m* string; bantering; **dar cordelejo** to make fun, to banter
**cordelería** *f* cordmaking; cordage; cord shop; (naut.) rigging
**cordelero -ra** *mf* cordmaker, cord dealer
**cordellate** *m* grogram
**cordera** *f* ewe lamb; (fig.) lamb (*meek woman*)
**cordería** *f* cordage
**corderilla** *f* little ewe lamb
**corderillo** *m* lambskin (*dressed with wool on it*)
**corderino -na** *adj* (pertaining to a) lamb; *f* lambskin
**cordero** *m* lamb; lambskin (*dressed with wool on it*); (fig.) lamb (*meek fellow*); (*cap.*) *m* Lamb (*Christ*); **Divino Cordero** or **Cordero de Dios** Lamb of God; **cordero lechal** yeanling; **cordero pascual** paschal lamb; **cordero recental** sucking lamb
**corderuela** *f* little ewe lamb
**corderuelo** *m* little lamb
**corderuna** *f* lambskin
**cordezuela** *f* small cord or rope
**cordíaco -ca** *adj* var. of **cardíaco**
**cordial** *adj* cordial; middle (*finger*); *m* cordial, tonic
**cordialidad** *f* cordiality
**cordiforme** *adj* heart-shaped
**cordila** *f* (ichth.) young of the tunny
**cordilla** *f* guts of sheep (*fed to cats*)
**cordillera** *f* mountain range, chain of mountains
**cordillerano -na** *adj* Cordilleran
**cordita** *f* cordite
**Córdoba** *f* Cordova; (*l.c.*) *m* cordoba (*monetary unit of Nicaragua*)
**cordobán** *m* cordovan (*leather*)
**cordobana; andar a la cordobana** (coll.) to go naked
**cordobanero** *m* cordovan tanner
**cordobés -besa** *adj & mf* Cordovan
**cordón** *m* cordon (*cord or ribbon worn as ornament*); lace, lacing; milled edge of coin; strand (*of rope or wire*); (anat. & elec.) cord; (arch.) cordon, stringcourse, belt course; (fort., her., hort. & mil.) cordon; **cordones** *mpl* (mil.) aiguillettes; **cordón bleu** first-rate cook; **cordón espermático** (anat.) spermatic cord; **cordón sanitario** sanitary cordon; **cordón umbilical** (anat.) umbilical cord
**cordonazo** *m* blow with a cord or rope; **cordonazo de San Francisco** (naut.) autumn equinoctial storm
**cordoncillo** *m* rib, ridge; braid, piping; milling (*of coins*)
**cordonería** *f* cordmaking, ropemaking; lacemaking; lacework
**cordonero -ra** *mf* cordmaker, ropemaker; lacemaker
**cordura** *f* prudence, wisdom
**corea** *f* (path.) chorea; dance with singing; (*cap.*) *f* Corea or Korea; **la Corea del Norte** North Korea; **la Corea del Sur** South Korea
**coreano -na** *adj & mf* Corean or Korean; *m* Corean or Korean (*language*)
**corear** *va* to compose (*music*) for chorus; to accompany with a chorus, to choir; to answer in chorus; to join in singing (*a song*); to fawningly agree with (*someone's opinion*); *vn* to choir
**corecico** or **corecillo** *m* sucking pig
**coreo** *m* (pros.) choreus; (mus.) harmony
**coreografía** *f* choreography
**coreográfico -ca** *adj* choreographic
**coreógrafo -fa** *mf* choreographer
**coreópsida** *f* (bot.) coreopsis, calliopsis
**corezuelo** *m* sucking pig; skin of roast piglet
**cori** *m* (bot.) St.-John's-wort
**coriáceo -a** *adj* coriaceous
**coriámbico -ca** *adj & m* choriambic
**coriambo** *m* choriamb
**coriandro** *m* (obs.) var. of **cilantro**
**coribante** *m* Corybant (*priest of Cybele*)
**corifeo** *m* coryphaeus; (fig.) leader
**coriláceo -a** *adj* (bot.) corylaceous
**corimbo** *m* (bot.) corymb
**corimboso -sa** *adj* corymbose or corymbous
**corindón** *m* (mineral.) corundum
**coríntico -ca** *adj* Corinthian
**corintio -tia** *adj & mf* Corinthian
**Corinto** *f* Corinth
**Coriolano** *m* Coriolanus
**corión** *m* (embryol. & zool.) chorion; (anat. & zool.) corium
**corista** *mf* chorist; *m* choir priest; (theat.) chorus man; *f* (theat.) chorus girl, chorine
**corito -ta** *adj* naked; bashful, timid; *m* workman who carries the wine from press to vats; grape-treader
**coriza** *f* (path.) coryza; (prov.) sandal
**corladura** *f* gold varnish
**corlar** or **corlear** *va* to coat with gold varnish
**corma** *f* stocks (*for punishment*); annoyance, bother
**cormo** *m* (bot.) corm
**cormofita** *f* (bot.) cormophyte
**cormorán** *m* (orn.) cormorant
**cornac** *m* (*pl:* **-nacs**) or **cornaca** *m* mahout

**cornáceo -a** *adj* (bot.) cornaceous
**cornada** *f* thrust with horns; (fencing) upward thrust
**cornadiza** *f* stanchion (*for cattle*)
**cornado** *m* old copper coin; **no valer un cornado** (coll.) to be not worth a continental
**cornadura** *f* horns
**cornal** *m* strap for yoking oxen
**cornalina** *f* (mineral.) carnelian
**cornalón** *adj masc* big-horned (*said of a bull*)
**cornamenta** *f* horns, antlers
**cornamusa** *f* (mus.) bagpipe; (mus.) horn shaped like a French horn; (naut.) chock
**cornatillo** *m* horn-shaped olive
**córnea** *f* see **córneo**
**corneador -dora** *adj* butting, horning
**corneal** *adj* corneal
**corneana** *f* (geol.) hornfels
**cornear** *va* to butt, to horn
**cornecico, cornecillo** or **cornecito** *m* little horn
**corneja** *f* (orn.) crow, daw; (orn.) carrion crow; (orn.) scops owl
**cornejo** *m* (bot.) dogwood, cornel tree; **cornejo florido** (bot.) flowering dogwood; **cornejo hembra** (bot.) red dogwood; **cornejo macho** (bot.) cornelian cherry
**Cornelia** *f* Cornelia
**cornelina** *f* var. of **cornalina**
**Cornelio** *m* Cornelius
**córneo -a** *adj* horny, corneous; *f* (anat.) cornea; **córnea cónica** (path.) keratoconus; **córnea opaca** (anat.) sclera
**cornerina** *f* var. of **cornalina**
**corneta** *f* (mus.) bugle; (mus.) cornet; swineherd's horn; troop of horse; pennant; (mil.) cornet (*cavalry officer who carried flag*); **corneta acústica** ear trumpet; **corneta de llaves** cornet-à-pistons; **corneta de monte** hunting horn; *m* bugler; cornetist
**cornete** *m* (anat.) turbinated bone
**cornetilla** *f* hot pepper
**cornetín** *m* (mus.) cornet; cornetist
**cornezuelo** *m* (bot. & pharm.) ergot; crescent-shaped olive
**corniabierto -ta** *adj* with wide-spread horns
**cornial** *adj* horn-shaped
**corniapretado -da** *adj* with close-set horns
**corniblanco -ca** *adj* white-horned
**cornicabra** *f* (bot.) terebinth tree; crescent-shaped olive; (bot.) wild fig
**córnico -ca** *adj* Cornish; *m* Cornish (*language*)
**cornicorto -ta** *adj* short-horned
**corniforme** *adj* horn-shaped
**cornigacho -cha** *adj* with horns turned downward
**cornígero -ra** *adj* (poet.) horned
**cornija** *f* var. of **cornisa**
**cornijal** *m* corner (*of a cushion, building, etc.*); (eccl.) altar napkin
**cornijón** *m* (arch.) entablature; outer corner (*of a building*)
**cornijuelo** *m* (bot.) shadbush
**cornil** *m* var. of **cornal**
**cornillo** *m* (bot.) shadbush
**corniola** *f* var. of **cornalina**
**cornisa** *f* cornice (*of snow on a ridge*); (arch.) cornice
**cornisamento** or **cornisamiento** *m* (arch.) entablature
**cornisón** *m* var. of **cornijón**
**corniveleto -ta** *adj* with high, straight horns
**corno** *m* (bot.) dogwood; (mus.) horn; **corno inglés** (mus.) English horn
**Cornualles** *m* Cornwall
**cornucopia** *f* cornucopia; sconce with mirror
**cornudilla** *f* (ichth.) hammerhead
**cornudo -da** *adj* horned, antlered; cuckold; *m* cuckold
**cornúpeta** *adj* cornupete; *m* (coll.) bull
**coro** *m* chorus; choir; choir loft; (mus., arch. & theol.) choir; **a coros** alternately, responsively; **de coro** by heart; **hacer coro a** to echo; **coro mixto** mixed chorus
**corocha** *f* (ent.) vine fretter
**corografía** *f* chorography
**corográfico -ca** *adj* chorographic or chorographical
**corógrafo -fa** *mf* chorographer
**coroideo -a** *adj* choroid
**coroides** *adj & f* (anat.) choroid
**corojo** *m* or **corojo de Guinea** (bot.) African oil palm
**corola** *f* (bot.) corolla
**corolario** *m* corollary
**corona** *f* crown; wreath, garland; coronet; halo; tonsure; (astr., elec. & meteor.) corona; (dent.) crown; (vet.) coronet (*of horse's pastern*); crown (*coin*); **ceñir** or **ceñirse la corona** to assume the crown; **Corona austral** (astr.) Corona Australis; **Corona boreal** (astr.) Corona Borealis; **corona de flores** wreath, floral wreath; **corona de laurel** wreath, laurel wreath; **corona mural** (hist.) mural crown; **corona nupcial** bridal wreath
**coronación** *f* coronation, crowning; termination, completion
**coronado** *m* tonsured cleric; (bot.) aster, China aster
**coronal** *adj* coronal
**coronamento** or **coronamiento** *m* termination, completion; (arch.) crest, coping, top, crown; (naut.) taffrail
**coronar** *va* to crown; to cap, to top; (checkers) to crown
**coronario -ria** *adj* coronary; fine (*gold*); *f* second-hand wheel (*of clock or watch*)
**corondel** *m* (print.) column rule
**coronel** *m* colonel; (arch.) top molding; (her.) crown
**coronela** *f* colonel's wife
**coronelato** *m* (Am.) colonelcy
**coronelía** *f* colonelcy
**coronilla** *f* crown (*of head*); **andar** or **bailar de coronilla** (coll.) to grind away, to be hard at it; **dar de coronilla** (coll.) to bump one's head on the ground; **estar hasta la coronilla** (coll.) to be fed up
**coronio** *m* (chem.) coronium
**coroza** *f* conical paper hat worn as a mark of infamy; farmer's straw cape
**corozo** *m* (bot.) African oil palm; (bot.) cohune; cohune nut
**corpa** *f* (min.) lump of crude ore
**corpachón** *m* or **corpanchón** *m* (coll.) big body, big carcass; carcass of fowl
**corpazo** *m* (coll.) big body, big carcass
**corpecico, corpecillo** or **corpecito** *m* bodice, waist
**corpiño** *m* little body; bodice, waist; (Am.) brassière
**corporación** *f* corporation; association
**corporal** *adj* corporal, bodily; *m* (eccl.) corporal (*cloth*)
**corporativo -va** *adj* corporate, corporative
**corpóreo -a** *adj* corporeal
**corpudo -da** *adj* corpulent
**corpulencia** *f* corpulence
**corpulento -ta** *adj* corpulent; thick, heavy
**Corpus** *m* (eccl.) Corpus Christi
**corpuscular** *adj* corpuscular
**corpúsculo** *m* (bot. & physiol.) corpuscle; (chem. & phys.) corpuscle, particle; **corpúsculo de Malpighi** (anat.) Malpighian corpuscle
**corral** *m* corral, stockyard; barnyard; fishpond; open-air theater; blank left by a student in taking notes; **hacer corrales** (coll.) to play truant; **corral de madera** lumberyard; **corral de vacas** (coll.) pigpen (*place that is filthy or littered up*)
**corralada** *f* large corral
**corralero -ra** *adj* (pertaining to a) corral, barnyard; *mf* manure seller; *f* Andalusian dance and song; (dial.) hussy
**corraliza** *f* yard, court, corral
**correa** *f* leather strap, thong; leatheriness; (aer.) belt; (carp.) purlin; (mach.) belt, belting; (bot.) correa, native fuchsia; **correas** *fpl* duster made of strips of leather; **besar la correa** (coll.) to eat humble pie; **tener correa** (coll.) to take a kidding goodnaturedly; (coll.) to be tough; **correa conductora** belt conveyor; **correa de seguridad** (aer. & aut.) safety belt; **correa de ventilador** (aut.) fan belt; **correa de zapatos** leather shoestring; **correa transmisora** drive belt; **correa transportadora** belt conveyor

**correaje** *m* belts, belting
**correal** *m* deerskin (*used in garments*)
**correar** *va* to draw out (*wool*)
**correazo** *m* lash with a leather strap
**correcalles** *m* (*pl:* **-lles**) (coll.) loafer
**correcamino** *m* (orn.) road runner
**corrección** *f* correction; correctness
**correccional** *adj* & *m* correctional
**correctivo -va** *adj* corrective; (gram.) adversative; (gram.) restrictive; *m* corrective
**correcto -ta** *adj* correct
**corrector -tora** *adj* correcting, corrective; *m* corrector, correcting device; (print.) corrector, proofreader; superior, abbot (*in monastery of St. Francis of Paula*)
**corredera** *f* track, slide, rail, tongue, guide; shutter (*in a peephole*); upper millstone; race track; street; (mach.) slide valve; (ent.) roach; (naut.) log (*chip and line*); (naut.) log line; (surv.) target; **de corredera** sliding (*e.g., door*)
**corredizo -za** *adj* slide; sliding; slip
**corredor -dora** *adj* running; (orn.) ratite; *mf* runner; (sport) runner; (sport) racer; *m* corridor; porch, gallery; (com.) broker; (mil.) scout; (mil.) raider; (fort.) covert way; **corredor de apuestas** bookmaker, professional betting man; **corredor de bodas** (coll.) matchmaker; **corredor de noticias** (coll.) gossip; **corredor de posta** postrider; **Corredor Polaco** Polish Corridor; *f* (orn.) ratite
**corredura** *f* overflow
**correduría** *f* (com.) brokerage
**correería** *f* strap making; strap shop
**correero -ra** *mf* strap maker or seller
**corregencia** *f* coregency
**corregente** *mf* coregent
**corregibilidad** *f* corrigibility
**corregible** *adj* corrigible
**corregidor -dora** *adj* correcting; *m* corregidor (*Spanish magistrate; chief magistrate of Spanish town*); *f* wife of a corregidor
**corregimiento** *m* office of corregidor; district governed by a corregidor
**corregir §72** *va* to correct; to temper, to lessen; *vr* to mend one's ways
**corregüela** or **correhuela** *f* (bot.) lesser bindweed; (bot.) knotgrass; **corregüela hembra** (bot.) mare's-tail
**correinado** *m* coreign
**correjel** *m* shoe leather, sole leather
**correlación** *f* correlation
**correlacionar** *va* & *vr* to correlate
**correlativo -va** *adj* & *m* correlative
**correligionario -ria** *mf* coreligionist, coreligionary; colleague, confederate
**correncia** *f* (coll.) looseness of the bowels; (coll.) bashfulness
**correndilla** *f* (coll.) short run, dash
**correntío -a** *adj* running; (coll.) free and easy, agile; *f* (coll.) looseness of the bowels
**correntón -tona** *adj* gadabout; jolly, full of fun
**correntoso -sa** *adj* (Am.) swift, rapid (*stream*)
**correo** *m* courier, postman; mail; post office; mail train; (law) accomplice; **correos** *mpl* postal service; **echar al correo** to mail, to post; **correo aéreo** air mail; **correo marítimo** packet boat; **correo urgente** special delivery
**correón** *m* large leather strap
**correoso -sa** *adj* leathery, tough
**correr** *va* to run, to race (*a horse*); to run (*a risk*); to traverse, travel over; to overrun; to chase, pursue; to slide; to turn (*a key*); to draw (*a curtain*); to embarrass; to confuse; to auction; to have (*e.g., the same fate or lot*); (slang) to cut (*class*); (naut.) to furl, unfurl (*a sail*); (naut.) to outride (*a storm*); to rob, get by robbery; (taur.) to fight (*a bull*); (Am.) to throw (*a person*) out; **correrla** (coll.) to carouse around at all hours of the night ‖ *vn* to run; to race; to flow; to blow; to pass, elapse; to pass, be accepted; to circulate, be common, be common talk; **a todo correr** at full speed; **a todo turbio correr** no matter how bad things are; **que corre** current (*e.g., month*); **correr a** to sell at or for; **correr a** + *inf* to run to + *inf;* **correr a cargo de** or **por cuenta de** to be under, be under the administration of; **correr con** to be in charge of, to be on good terms with; to defray (*an expense*); **correr por** to sell at or for; to be in the care or the hands of; *vr* to turn (*right or left*); to become embarrassed; to become confused; to be ashamed; to slide, to glide, to slip; to run (*said of a candle or a color*); to go too far
**correría** *f* excursion; raid, foray
**correspondencia** *f* correspondence; communication, contact (*between two places*); connection, interchange (*of road, subway, etc.*); agreement, harmony; **correspondencia urgente** special delivery
**corresponder** *vn* to correspond; to communicate (*said, e.g., of two rooms*); **corresponder a** to return, reciprocate (*affection, a favor, etc.*); to belong to, to concern; **corresponderle a uno** + *inf* to be up to someone to + *inf,* to be the turn of someone to + *inf; vr* to correspond (*to write to each other*); to be in agreement or harmony
**correspondiente** *adj* correspondent; corresponding; respective; *mf* correspondent
**corresponsal** *mf* correspondent
**corresponsalía** *f* post of newspaper correspondent
**corretaje** *m* brokerage
**corretear** *va* (coll.) to run up and down, to race around; *vn* (coll.) to hang around; (coll.) to romp, to race around
**correteo** *m* (coll.) hanging around; (coll.) romping
**corretora** *f* nun who directs the choir
**correvedile** *mf* or **correveidile** *mf* (*pl:* **-le**) (coll.) gossip, mischief-maker; (coll.) go-between, pimp
**correverás** *m* (*pl:* **-rás**) (coll.) mechanical toy
**corrido -da** *adj* in excess (*said of a weight or measure*); cursive; experienced; flowing, fluent; in sequence, continuous, unbroken; abashed, confused; (coll.) wise, sharp; (Am.) fixed-price (*meal*); **de corrido** fluently, unhaltingly; offhand; *m* shed along the wall of a corral; (Am.) ballad, street ballad; *f* race; bullfight; course, run, travel; **de corrida** fast, without stopping; **corrida de banco** (Am.) run on the bank; **corrida de toros** bullfight
**corriente** *adj* running (*water*); current; ordinary, common; regular, usual; well-known; permissible; fluent; good-natured; **corriente y moliente** (coll.) regular ‖ *adv* all right, O.K. ‖ *m* current month; **al corriente** on time, promptly; **estar al corriente (de)** to be posted (on), be informed (about), be aware (of); **poner al corriente (de)** to acquaint (with), to inform (about); **tener al corriente (de)** to keep (*someone*) posted (on), keep (*someone*) informed (about) ‖ *f* current, stream; (elec.) current; (fig.) current, stream; **dejarse llevar de la corriente, irse con** or **tras la corriente** (fig.) to follow the crowd; **llevarle a uno la corriente** (coll.) to kowtow to someone; **seguir la corriente** (fig.) to follow the crowd; to follow the line of least resistance; **ir** or **navegar contra la corriente** to go against the tide, to fight an uphill battle; **corriente alterna** or **alternativa** (elec.) alternating current; **corriente continua** (elec.) direct current; **corriente de aire** draft; **corriente de filamento** (rad.) filament current; **corriente de convección** (elec.) convection current; **corriente de Foucault** (elec.) eddy current, Foucault current; **Corriente del Golfo** Gulf Stream; **corriente del Japón** Japan current; **corriente de placa** (rad.) plate current; **corriente de rejilla** (rad.) grid current; **corriente de saturación** (phys.) saturation current; **corriente parásita** (elec.) eddy current; (rad.) static, interference; **corriente sanguínea** blood stream
**corrientemente** *adv* fluently; flatly, plainly
**corrigendo -da** *mf* inmate of a jail or reformatory
**corrillero -ra** *mf* loafer, lounger, idler
**corrillo** *m* huddle, clique
**corrimiento** *m* running, sliding, gliding; watery discharge, rheum; embarrassment, shyness; vine blight (*from frost, rain, etc.*); landslide; (elec.) creepage; **corrimiento de fase** (elec.) phase lag

**corrincho** *m* gathering of riffraff
**corrivación** *f* corrivation, construction that channels several streams together
**corro** *m* group or circle of people; ring (*space*); ring-around-a-rosy; **escupir en corro** to butt into the conversation; **hacer corro** to make room, to make an open space; **hacer corro aparte** to start a separate ring or faction; **corro de bruja** or **de brujas** fairy ring (*circle formed in grass by growth of certain fungi*)
**corroboración** *f* strengthening; corroboration
**corroborante** *adj & m* corroborant
**corroborar** *va* to strengthen; to corroborate
**corroborativo -va** *adj* corroborative
**corrobra** *f* var. of **alboroque**
**corroer** §78 *va* to corrode; (fig.) to corrode (*to prey upon, eat away at*); *vr* to corrode
**corrompedor -dora** *adj* corrupting; *mf* corrupter
**corromper** *va* to corrupt; to spoil; to rot; to bribe; to seduce; (coll.) to annoy, disturb, inconvenience; *vn* to smell bad; *vr* to become corrupted; to spoil, to become spoiled; to rot
**corrosal** *m* (bot.) soursop
**corrosible** *adj* corrodible, corrosible
**corrosión** *f* corrosion; (geol.) erosion
**corrosivo -va** *adj & m* corrosive
**corr.te** abr. of **corriente**
**corrugación** *f* contraction, shrinkage; wrinkling (*of skin*); corrugation
**corrugado -da** *adj* corrugated
**corrugar** §59 *va* to corrugate
**corrumpente** *adj* corrupting, corruptive; (coll.) annoying, bothersome
**corrupción** *f* corruption; corruptness; stink, stench
**corruptela** *f* corruption; abuse
**corruptibilidad** *f* corruptibility
**corruptible** *adj* corruptible
**corruptivo -va** *adj* corruptive
**corruptor -tora** *adj & mf* var. of **corrompedor**
**corrusco** *m* (coll.) piece of bread, crust of bread
**corsa** *f* see **corso**
**corsario -ria** *adj* (naut.) privateering; *mf* (croquet) rover (*player*); *m* (naut.) corsair (*pirate; pirate ship; privateer*); *f* (croquet) rover ball
**corsé** *m* corset
**corsear** *vn* (naut.) to privateer, to cruise as a privateer
**corsetería** *f* corset shop; corset business, corset manufacturing
**corsetero -ra** *mf* corset maker or dealer
**corso -sa** *adj & mf* Corsican; *m* Corsican (*dialect*); (naut.) privateering; (Am.) drive, promenade; **armar en corso** (naut.) to arm as a privateer; **ir a corso** (naut.) to cruise as a privateer; **llevar** or **traer a corso** to transport posthaste; *f* (naut.) day's voyage; (dial.) sled, drag
**corta** *f* see **corto**
**cortaalambres** *m* (*pl:* **-bres**) wire cutter; cold chisel
**cortabolsas** *m* (*pl:* **-sas**) (coll.) pickpocket
**cortacallos** *m* (*pl:* **-llos**) corncutter
**cortacésped** *m* lawn mower
**cortacigarros** *m* (*pl:* **-rros**) cigar cutter
**cortacircuitos** *m* (*pl:* **-tos**) (elec.) fuse
**cortacorriente** *m* (elec.) switch
**cortada** *f* see **cortado**
**cortadero -ra** *adj* easy to cut; *f* blacksmith's chisel; beekeeper's knife
**cortadillo** *m* drinking cup; **echar cortadillos** (coll.) to speak with affectation; (coll.) to drink wine
**cortado -da** *adj* proportioned; choppy (*style*); (Am.) hard up; *m* drinking cup; cup of coffee with a touch of milk; caper, cabriole (*in dancing*); *f* (Am.) cut; **cortada de pelo** (Am.) haircut
**cortador -dora** *adj* cutting; *m* cutter (*person who cuts out garments, etc.*); butcher; (anat.) cutter (*incisor*); *f* cutter, cutting machine; slicing machine; mower; cutting board
**cortadura** *f* cutting; cut; slit, slash; clipping, cutout; (fort.) parapet; (geog.) cut (*between mountains*); **cortaduras** *fpl* cuttings, trimmings, parings, shreds
**cortafrío** *m* cold chisel
**cortafuego** *m* (forestry) fireguard; fire wall
**cortahielos** *m* (*pl:* **-los**) icebreaker, iceboat
**cortalápices** *m* (*pl:* **-ces**) pencil sharpener
**cortamente** *adv* scantily, sparingly; curtly
**cortante** *adj* cutting, sharp; *m* butcher; butcher knife, cleaver
**cortapapeles** *m* (*pl:* **-les**) paper cutter, paper knife
**cortapicos** *m* (*pl:* **-cos**) (ent.) earwig; **cortapicos y callares** (coll.) little children should be seen and not heard
**cortapiés** *m* (*pl:* **-piés**) (coll.) cut or slash at the legs
**cortapisa** *f* trimming (*made of different material from dress*); charm, wit; terms, conditions (*of a gift*); difficulty, interference
**cortaplumas** *m* (*pl:* **-mas**) penknife, pocketknife
**cortapuros** *m* (*pl:* **-ros**) cigar cutter
**cortar** *va* to cut; to cut away, to trim; to clip; to cut down; to cut off; to cut out, omit; to cut short, to stop; to cut up; to carve; to engrave; to cleave, chop, hew, hack; to dock; to prune; (elec.) to cut off (*the current*); (aut.) to cut off (*the ignition*); (Am.) to pick, to harvest; **cortar bien** to pronounce (*a language*) well; to read (*verse*) well; **cortar mal** to pronounce (*a language*) poorly; to read (*verse*) poorly; **cortar por la mitad** to bisect ‖ *vn* to cut; to be cutting (*said of wind or cold*); **cortar de vestir** to cut cloth, cut a pattern; (coll.) to gossip, talk evil ‖ *vr* to become confused, become speechless; to chap, to crack (*said of skin*); to curdle, turn sour
**cortarrenglón** *m* marginal stop (*of typewriter*)
**cortatubos** *m* (*pl:* **-bos**) pipe cutter (*tool*)
**cortaúñas** *m* (*pl:* **-ñas**) nail clippers, nail cutters
**cortavidrios** *m* (*pl:* **-drios**) glass cutter
**cortaviento** *m* windshield
**corte** *m* cut; cutting; edge (*of knife, sword, book*); cross section; cut, fit (*of a garment*); piece of material (*for a suit, trousers, etc.*); cutting room (*of military tailor*); reconciliation; (elec.) break; **corte de pelo** haircut; **corte de pelo a cepillo** crew cut; **corte de traje** suiting ‖ *f* court; yard; stable, fold; (Am.) court (*of justice*); **Cortes** *fpl* Parliament; **darse corte** (Am.) to put on airs; **hacer la corte a** to pay court to (*a person in power, a woman*); **la Corte** the Capital (*Madrid*); **corte celestial** Heaven; **Corte Suprema** (Am.) Supreme Court
**cortedad** *f* shortness; smallness; scantiness; dullness; bashfulness, shyness; **cortedad de medios** or **recursos** lack of funds
**cortejador -dora** *adj* courting, wooing, courtly; *m* courter, wooer, courtier
**cortejar** *va* to escort, attend, court; to woo, to court (*a woman*)
**cortejo** *m* court, courting; courtship; homage; cortege; entourage; gift, treat; (coll.) beau, paramour
**cortero** *m* (Am.) day laborer
**cortés** *adj* courteous, gracious, polite
**cortesana** *f* see **cortesano**
**cortesanazo -za** *adj* overpolite, obsequious
**cortesanía** *f* courtliness, courtesy; fawning, flattery
**cortesano -na** *adj* of the court, courtlike; courtly, courteous; fawning, flattering; *m* courtier; fawner; flatterer; *f* courtesan
**cortesía** *f* courtesy, graciousness, politeness; expression of respect at end of a letter; title of honor; grace, favor; gift, present; (com.) days of grace; (print.) blank space at end or beginning of a chapter; bow; curtsy; **hacer una cortesía** to make a bow; to curtsy; **por cortesía** by courtesy
**corteza** *f* bark; peel, skin, rind; crust; coarseness, crudeness; (anat. & bot.) cortex; (orn.) sand grouse; **corteza del cascarillo** (pharm.) cinchona bark
**cortezón** *m* heavy bark or crust
**cortezudo -da** *adj* barky, corticated; crude, crusty, unpolished
**cortezuela** *f* thin bark; thin peel, skin, or rind
**corticado -da** *adj* corticate, corticated
**cortical** *adj* cortical

**corticotropina** *f* (physiol. & pharm.) corticotropin
**cortijada** *f* group of farmhouses
**cortijero -ra** *mf* farmer; *m* farm boss
**cortijo** *m* farmhouse, farm; **alborotar el cortijo** (coll.) to raise a row, cause a riot
**cortil** *m* barnyard
**cortina** *f* curtain; shade, screen; (fort.) curtain; **correr la cortina** to pull the curtain aside (*to reveal something hidden*); **cortina de bambú** (fig.) bamboo curtain; **cortina de hierro** (fig.) iron curtain; **cortina de humo** smoke screen; **cortina de muelle** sustaining wall (*of a dike*)
**cortinaje** *m* set of curtains, pair of curtains
**cortinal** *m* fenced-in and cultivated field near a farm or village
**cortinilla** *f* shade, window shade; carriage curtain
**cortinón** *m* big heavy curtain
**cortiña** *f* (prov.) garden patch
**cortisona** *f* or **cortisono** *m* (physiol. & pharm.) cortisone
**corto -ta** *adj* short; small; scant, wanting; slight; dull; bashful, shy; speechless; stingy; **a la corta o a la larga** sooner or later; **desde muy corta edad** from earliest childhood; **corto de alcances** limited, short-witted; **corto de manos** slow (*at work*); **corto de oído** hard of hearing; **corto de resuello** short of breath, short-winded; **corto de vista** shortsighted; *f* clearing, cutting, cutting or felling of trees; **corto** *adv* short
**cortocircuitar** *va* (elec.) to short-circuit
**cortocircuito** *m* (elec.) short circuit; **poner en cortocircuito** (elec.) to short-circuit; **ponerse en cortocircuito** (elec.) to short-circuit, be short-circuited
**cortometraje** *m* (mov.) short
**cortón** *m* (ent.) mole cricket
**coruja** *f* (orn.) barn owl
**corulla** *f* (naut.) cordage room (*in a galley*)
**corundo** *m* var. of **corindón**
**Coruña, La** Corunna
**coruñes -ñesa** *adj* (pertaining to) Corunna; *mf* native or inhabitant of Corunna
**coruscación** *f* flash of a meteor; (poet.) coruscation
**coruscante** *adj* flashing, sparkling
**coruscar** §86 *vn* (poet.) to coruscate
**corusco -ca** *adj* (poet.) coruscating
**corva** *f* see **corvo**
**corvadura** *f* bend; curvature; (arch.) bend of an arch or vault
**corvato** *m* young crow, young rook
**corvecito** *m* little crow, little rook
**corvejón** *m* gambrel, hock; spur (*of a cock*); (orn.) cormorant
**corvejos** *mpl* gambrel, hock
**corveta** *f* curvet
**corvetear** *vn* to curvet
**córvidos** *mpl* (orn.) Corvidae
**corvino -na** *adj* corvine; *f* (ichth.) corvina; **corvina blanca** (ichth.) croaker; **corvina negra** (ichth.) black drum, drumfish
**corvo -va** *adj* arched, curved, bent; *m* pothook; (ichth.) corvina; *f* ham, bend or back of knee; (vet.) curb
**corzo -za** *mf* (zool.) roe deer
**corzuelo** *m* wheat left in the husk
**cosa** *f* thing; **a cosa hecha** as good as done, sure-fire; **como si tal cosa** (coll.) as if nothing had happened; **en cosa de** in a matter of; **no . . . alguna cosa** or **no . . . cosa** nothing; **no . . . gran cosa** not much, not very much; **no haber tal cosa** to be not so; **no ser gran cosa** to be of no importance, to not amount to much; **otra cosa** something else; **¿qué cosa?** what's new?; **¿qué es cosa y cosa?** what's the answer to this?; **cosa corta** pittance, trifle; **cosa de** a matter of; **cosa de cajón** matter of course; **cosa de entidad** something worth while; **cosa del otro jueves** (coll.) something unheard-of; (coll.) something out of date; **cosa de mieles** (coll.) something exquisite; **cosa de nunca acabar** bore, something tiresome; **cosa de oír** something worth hearing; **cosa de reír** laughing matter; **cosa de risa** something to laugh at; **cosa de ver** something worth seeing; **cosa en sí** (philos.) Ding an sich, thing-in-itself; **cosa nunca vista** (coll.) something unheard-of; **cosa perdida** hopeless or incorrigible person; **cosa rara** strange thing; strange to say; **cosas de** doings of, tricks of; **cosas del mundo** ups and downs; **cosas de viento** (coll.) frivolities; **cosa seria** serious matter; the real thing, a worthwhile proposition; **cosa y cosa** puzzle, riddle
**cosaco -ca** *adj & mf* Cossack; *m* brute
**cosario -ria** *adj* traveled, frequented; *m* carrier, messenger, deliveryman; hunter
**coscar** §86 *vr* (coll.) to shrug one's shoulders, to give a shrug
**coscarana** *f* (dial.) cracknel
**coscoja** *f* (bot.) kermes, kermes oak; dry leaves of kermes oak
**coscojal** *m* or **coscojar** *m* field of kermes oak
**coscojita** *f* var. of **coxcojilla**
**coscojo** *m* kermes, kermes berry; **coscojos** *mpl* iron bosses of horse's bit
**coscón -cona** *adj* (coll.) sly, crafty
**coscoroba** *f* (orn.) coscoroba
**coscorrón** *m* bump on the head, contusion
**cosecante** *f* (trig.) cosecant
**cosecha** *f* harvest, crop; harvest time; (fig.) crop (*e.g., of lies*); **de su cosecha** (coll.) of one's own invention, out of one's own head; **cosecha de vino** vintage
**cosechadora** *f* harvester (*machine*)
**cosechar** *va* to harvest, reap, gather; (Am.) to grow; *vn* to harvest
**cosechero -ra** *mf* harvester, reaper; vintner
**coselete** *m* corselet (*armor*); pikeman; (zool.) corselet (*thorax of insect*)
**coseno** *m* (trig.) cosine; **coseno verso** (trig.) coversed sine
**cose-papeles** *m* (*pl:* **-les**) stapler
**coser** *va* to sew; to rivet together; to lace (*a belt*); to join, unite closely; to stab; **coser a preguntas** to riddle with questions; **coser a puñaladas** (coll.) to cut or slash to pieces; *vn* to sew; **ser coser y cantar** (coll.) to be a cinch; *vr* **coserse con** or **contra** (coll.) to become closely united or associated with
**cosetada** *f* quick step, run
**cosicosa** *f* var. of **quisicosa**
**cosido** *m* sewing; **cosido de cama** sheet, quilt, and blanket stitched together
**cosidura** *f* (naut.) lashing
**cosignatario -ria** *adj & mf* cosignatory
**cosmético -ca** *adj & m* cosmetic
**cosmogonía** *f* cosmogony
**cosmogónico -ca** *adj* cosmogonic or cosmogonical
**cosmografía** *f* cosmography
**cosmográfico -ca** *adj* cosmographic or cosmographical
**cosmógrafo -fa** *mf* cosmographer
**cosmología** *f* cosmology
**cosmológico -ca** *adj* cosmological
**cosmólogo -ga** *mf* cosmologist
**cosmonauta** *m* cosmonaut
**cosmopolita** *adj* cosmopolitan; *mf* cosmopolitan; cosmopolite
**cosmopolitismo** *m* cosmopolitanism
**cosmorama** *m* cosmorama
**cosmos** *m* cosmos (*universe*); (bot.) cosmos
**coso** *m* enclosure for bullfighting; main street; (ent.) wood borer
**cospe** *m* chop, hack
**cospel** *m* blank (*from which to stamp coin*)
**cosque** *m* (coll.) bump on the head, contusion
**cosquilladizo -za** *adj* peevish, touchy
**cosquillar** *va* (archaic) to tickle
**cosquillas** *fpl* ticklishness; **buscarle a uno las cosquillas** (coll.) to try to annoy someone; **hacerle a uno cosquillas** (coll.) to stir up someone's curiosity; (coll.) to worry or scare someone; **no sufrir cosquillas** or **tener malas cosquillas** (coll.) to be impatient, be touchy
**cosquillear** *va* to tickle; to tease; to arouse the curiosity of; to make apprehensive; *vr* to become curious; to become annoyed; to enjoy oneself, to have a good time
**cosquillejas** *fpl* ticklishness
**cosquilleo** *m* tickling, tickling sensation

**cosquilloso -sa** *adj* ticklish; (fig.) touchy, ticklish
**costa** *f* cost, price; board and wages; coast; shore, bank; edge iron (*of shoemaker*); **costas** *fpl* (law) costs; **a costa de** at the expense of; **a toda costa** at any price; **barajar la costa** to sail close to shore; **condenar en costas** (law) to sentence to pay the costs; **ir** or **navegar costa a costa** to sail along the coast; **Costa Brava** Mediterranean coast from Pals to Tordera in province of Gerona, Spain; **Costa del Atlántico** Atlantic Coast; **Costa de los Esclavos** Slave Coast; **Costa del Pacífico** Pacific Coast; **Costa de Marfil** Ivory Coast; **Costa de Oro** Gold Coast; Côte-d'Or (*in France*); **Costa Firme** Spanish Main; **costa marítima** seacoast
**costado** *m* side (*of human body, of a ship*); (mil.) flank; (Am.) station platform; (min.) side face (*of a gallery*); **costados** *mpl* stock, ancestors
**costal** *adj* (anat.) costal; *m* bag, sack; tamper, stamper; **estar hecho un costal de huesos** (coll.) to be nothing but skin and bones; **costal de los pecados** human body (*full of sin*)
**costalada** *f* or **costalazo** *m* blow on the back or side (*from a fall*)
**costalejo** *m* small sack
**costalero** *m* (prov.) public errand boy; bearer of image of saint in Easter procession in Seville
**costanero -ra** *adj* coastal; sloping; *f* slope; **costaneras** *fpl* rafters
**costanilla** *f* short steep street
**costar §77** *va & vn* to cost; **costar trabajo** + *inf* to be hard to + *inf;* **cueste lo que cueste** cost what it may
**costarricense** *adj* Costa Rican
**costarriqueño -ña** *adj & mf* Costa Rican
**coste** *m* cost, price; **a coste y costas** at cost
**costear** *va* to defray the cost of; to sail along the coast of; *vn* to sail along the coast; *vr* to pay for itself; to pay one's way
**costeño -ña** *adj* coastal; coasting; *mf* (Am.) coast dweller
**costero -ra** *adj* coastal; *m* slab (*outside piece cut from log*); side wall (*of blast furnace*); *f* side of a bale or package; fishing season; coast; slope
**costezuela** *f* slight slope
**costilla** *f* rib; (anat., bot. & naut.) rib; (carp.) fur; (coll.) wealth, property; (coll.) rib (*wife, better half*); stave; rung; **costillas** *fpl* back, shoulders; **calentar** or **medir las costillas a** (coll.) to thrash, beat, cudgel; **costilla cervical** (anat.) cervical rib; **costillas falsas** (anat.) false ribs; **costillas flotantes** (anat.) floating ribs; **costillas verdaderas** (anat.) true ribs
**costillaje** *m* or **costillar** *m* (anat.) ribs; ribbing, framework; (carp.) furring; lagging (*of a tunnel*)
**costilludo -da** *adj* (coll.) broad-shouldered, heavy-set
**costo** *m* cost; (bot.) sawwort; costusroot; **a costo y costas** at cost; **costo de la vida** cost of living; **costo hortense** (bot.) costmary; **costo, seguro y flete** (com.) cost, insurance, and freight
**costoso -sa** *adj* costly, expensive; grievous
**costra** *f* scab, crust, scale; snuff (*of candle wick*); scab (*on a cut or wound*); **costra láctea** (path.) infantile impetigo
**costrada** *f* crumb pie
**costroso -sa** *adj* scabby, crusty, scaly
**costumbre** *f* custom; **de costumbre** usually; usual; **tener por costumbre** + *inf* to be in the habit of + *ger*
**costumbrista** *adj* (*novel, writer, painting, painter*) depicting regional manners, customs, scenes, etc.; *mf* writer who depicts regional manners and customs
**costura** *f* sewing, needlework; tailoring; seam; (mach.) seam, joint; (naut.) splice; **alta costura** fashion designing, haute couture; high fashion, high style; **de costura francesa** full-fashioned (*hose*); **sentar las costuras** to press the seams; **sentarle a uno las costuras** (coll.) to take someone to task
**costurera** *f* seamstress, dressmaker
**costurero** *m* sewing table; sewing room; sewing case
**costurón** *m* large seam; coarse seam; big scar
**cota** *f* coat of arms; coat of mail; quota, share; elevation; (top.) bench mark; (top.) datum level; **cota de armas** coat of arms, tabard; **cota de malla** coat of mail
**cotana** *f* mortise; mortise chisel
**cotangente** *f* (trig.) cotangent
**cotanza** *f* coutances (*fine linen*)
**cotarra** *f* side of a ravine
**cotarrera** *f* (coll.) gossip, gossipy woman; (slang) prostitute
**cotarro** *m* night lodging for beggars and tramps; side of a ravine; **alborotar el cotarro** (coll.) to stir up a row; **andar de cotarro en cotarro** (coll.) to fool around from one place to another
**cotejar** *va* to compare, collate
**cotejo** *m* comparison, collation
**cotense** *m* (Am.) coarse hemp
**coterráneo -a** *adj & mf* var. of **conterráneo**
**cotí** *m* (*pl:* **-tíes**) bedtick, ticking
**cotidiano -na** *adj* daily, everyday, quotidian
**cótila** *f* (anat.) cotyla, acetabulum
**cotiledón** *m* (bot. & embryol.) cotyledon
**cotiledóneo -a** *adj* (bot.) cotyledonous
**cotiloideo -a** *adj* (anat.) cotyloid
**cotilla** *mf* (coll.) tattletale; *f* (archaic) corselet, corset
**cotillear** *vn* to gossip
**cotilleo** *m* gossip
**cotillo** *m* face (*of a hammer*)
**cotillón** *m* cotillion
**cotín** *m* (sport) backstroke (*in returning a ball*)
**cotiza** *f* dent (*for the warp*); (her.) cotise; (Am.) Indian sandal
**cotización** *f* quotation (*of a price*); current price, price list; quota; dues
**cotizante** *adj* dues-paying; *mf* dues payer
**cotizar §76** *va* to quote (*a price*); to prorate; to cry out (*prices*) in the stock exchange; *vn* to collect dues; to pay dues
**coto** *m* enclosed pasture; preserve; landmark; boundary; (ichth.) sculpin; (pharm.) coto, coto bark; (zool.) howling monkey; (slang) churchyard; (slang) hospital; (Am.) goiter; **poner coto a** to check, to put a stop to; **coto social** workers' benefit society
**cotón** *m* cotton (*fabric*)
**cotona** *f* (Am.) man's work shirt; (Am.) sleeveless shirt; (Am.) blouse; (Am.) chamois jacket
**cotonada** *f* calico, print
**cotoncillo** *m* (paint.) button of maulstick
**cotonía** *f* dimity
**cotorra** *f* (orn.) parrot; (orn.) parakeet; (orn.) magpie; (coll.) chatterbox; (Am.) overnight hangout
**cotorrear** *vn* (coll.) to chatter, to gossip, to gabble
**cotorreo** *m* (coll.) chattering, gossip, gabble
**cotorrera** *f* female parrot; (coll.) chatterbox
**cotorrón -rrona** *adj* trying to be young, affecting youth
**cototo** *m* (Am.) bump
**cotral** *m & f* var. of **cutral**
**cotudo -da** *adj* cottony, hairy; (Am.) goitrous
**cotufa** *f* Jerusalem artichoke (*tuber of the plant*); tidbit, delicacy; **hacer cotufas** (Am.) to be fastidious; **pedir cotufas en el golfo** (coll.) to ask for the moon
**coturnado -da** *adj* buskined
**coturno** *m* buskin; **calzar el coturno** to write in the sublime style; to write tragedies; **de alto coturno** lofty, elevated, sublime
**cotutor** *m* coguardian
**covacha** *f* small cave; (Am.) cubbyhole; (Am.) shanty
**covachuela** *f* small cave; (archaic) office of crown minister (*in vaulted basement corridors of Royal Palace in Madrid*)
**covachuelista** *m* or **covachuelo** *m* (coll.) clerk; (coll.) government clerk
**covanilla** *f* or **covanillo** *m* basket for gathering grapes
**covezuela** *f* small cave
**coxa** *f* (ent.) coxa

**coxal** *adj* coxal; *m* (anat.) coxa
**coxalgia** *f* (path.) coxalgia
**coxálgico -ca** *adj* coxalgic
**coxcojilla** or **coxcojita** *f* hopscotch; **a coxcojita** hippety-hoppety
**coxcox; a coxcox** hippety-hoppety
**coxis** *m* (*pl:* **-xis**) var. of **cóccix**
**coxofemoral** *adj* coxofemoral
**coy** *m* (naut.) hammock, cot
**coyote** *m* (zool.) coyote, prairie wolf
**coyunda** *f* strap for yoking oxen; marriage; tyranny; sandal string
**coyuntero** *m* var. of **acoyuntero**
**coyuntura** *f* conjuncture, juncture; turn, chance, opportunity; (anat.) joint, articulation; **en coyuntura** at the right time
**coz** *f* (*pl:* **coces**) kick; butt (*of gun*); kick, recoil (*of gun*); ebb, reflux; kickback; big end (*of pole or mast*); (coll.) insult, churlishness; **dar coces** to kick; **tirar coces** to kick; (coll.) to kick (*to resist, to complain*)
**C.P.B.** or **c.p.b.** abr. of **cuyos pies beso**
**cps.** abr. of **compañeros**
**crabrón** *m* (ent.) hornet
**crac** *m* crash; **hacer crac** to crash, to fail; **crac financiero** crash, failure in business
**Cracovia** *f* Cracow
**crampón** *m* crampon, calk, climbing iron
**cramponado -da** *adj* (her.) cramponee
**cran** *m* (print.) nick
**craneal** or **craneano -na** *adj* cranial
**cráneo** *m* (anat.) skull, cranium
**craneología** *f* craniology
**craneometría** *f* craniometry
**craneotomía** *f* (surg.) craniotomy
**crápula** *f* drunkenness; licentiousness
**crapuloso -sa** *adj* drunken; licentious
**crascitar** *vn* to crow, to croak
**crasia** *f* crasis, temperament, constitution
**crasiento -ta** *adj* greasy
**crasis** *f* (*pl:* **-sis**) crasis; (gram.) crasis
**crasitud** *f* fatness, corpulence
**craso -sa** *adj* thick, coarse; fat, greasy; gross, crass (*error, ignorance, etc.*); (*cap.*) *m* Crassus
**crasuláceo -a** *adj* (bot.) crassulaceous
**cráter** *m* crater; (elec. & mil.) crater; (*cap.*) *m* (astr.) Crater
**crátera** *f* crater (*vessel*)
**cratícula** *f* wicket through which nuns receive communion
**crea** *f* crea (*linen fabric*)
**creación** *f* creation; **la Creación** the Creation
**creacionismo** *m* (philos. & theol.) creationism
**creador -dora** *adj* creative; *mf* creator; **el Creador** the Creator
**crear** *va* to create; *vr* to build up (*e.g., a clientele*); to trump up (*an excuse*)
**creativo -va** *adj* creative
**crecedero -ra** *adj* growing; large enough to allow for growth (*said of child's clothes*)
**crecepelo** *m* hair restorer
**crecer** §34 *vn* to grow, increase; to rise, to swell (*said of a stream or flood*); **crecer como la mala hierba** to grow wild; *vr* to assume more authority or importance; to get bolder and more daring
**creces** *fpl* increase, extra, excess; **con creces** in abundance, in excess; **de creces** growing (*said of a child*)
**crecido -da** *adj* large, big, grown; swollen; **crecidos** *mpl* wide stitches (*in knitting*); *f* freshet, flood
**creciente** *adj* crescent; growing, increasing; (phonet.) rising (*diphthong*); *m* (her.) crescent; **creciente de la luna** (astr.) crescent (*increasing moon*); *f* freshet, flood; **creciente del mar** (naut.) high tide, flood tide
**crecimiento** *m* growth, increase; rise (*in value*)
**crec.te** abr. of **creciente**
**credencia** *f* credence, sideboard; (eccl.) credence
**credencial** *adj* & *f* credential; **credenciales** *fpl* credentials
**credibilidad** *f* credibility
**crediticio -cia** *adj* (pertaining to) credit
**crédito** *m* credit; (com. & educ.) credit; **abrir crédito a** (com.) to give credit to; **a crédito** (com.) on credit; **dar crédito a** to give credence or credit to; to credit, to do credit to
**credo** *m* creed; credo; (mus.) credo; **con el credo en la boca** (coll.) with one's heart in one's mouth; **en un credo** (coll.) in a trice; **que canta el credo** (coll.) with an air of importance
**credulidad** *f* credulity
**crédulo -la** *adj* credulous
**creedero -ra** *adj* believable; **creederas** *fpl* (coll.) credulity; **tener buenas creederas** (coll.) to be too gullible
**creedor -dora** *adj* credulous
**creencia** *f* belief; credence; creed, persuasion
**creer** §35 *va* & *vn* to believe, to think; **¡ya lo creo!** (coll.) I should say so!; **creer en** to believe in (*e.g., God*); *vr* to believe; to believe oneself to be; **¡que te crees tú eso!** (iron.) you think so!
**crehuela** *f* crea (*linen fabric*)
**creíble** *adj* credible, believable
**crema** *f* cream; cold cream; shoe polish; (gram.) diaeresis; (fig.) cream (*e.g., of society*); **crema de afeitar** shaving cream; **crema de menta** crème de menthe; **crema desvanecedora** vanishing cream
**cremación** *f* cremation
**cremallera** *f* (mach.) rack; rack rail; zipper; **cremallera y piñón** rack and pinion
**cremástico -ca** *adj* chremastic, economic; *f* chremastics, economics
**crematorio -ria** *adj* & *m* crematory
**cremera** *f* creamer
**cremería** *f* (Am.) creamery
**cremómetro** *m* creamometer, cremometer
**cremona** *f* espagnolette, casement bolt; *m* Cremona (*violin*)
**crémor** *m* cream of tartar; **crémor tártaro** cream of tartar
**cremoso -sa** *adj* creamy
**crena** *f* (anat. & bot.) crenation
**crenado -da** *adj* (bot.) crenate
**crencha** *f* part (*of hair*); hair on each side of part
**creosol** *m* (chem.) creosol
**creosota** *f* creosote
**creosotar** *va* to creosote
**crep** *m* o **crepé** *m* crepe
**crepitación** *f* crepitation, crackling; (med.) crepitation
**crepitante** *adj* crepitant, crackling
**crepitar** *vn* to crepitate, to crackle
**crepuscular** *adj* crepuscular
**crepusculino -na** *adj* crepusculine, twilight
**crepúsculo** *m* twilight
**cresa** *f* egg of queen bee; maggot; flybow
**crescendo** *m* (mus.) crescendo
**Creso** *m* (biog. & fig.) Croesus
**cresol** *m* (chem.) cresol
**crespilla** *f* (bot.) morel
**crespina** *f* hair net
**crespo -pa** *adj* curled, crispy; curly; angry, vexed; turgid (*style*)
**crespón** *m* crape; **crespón de la China** crepe de Chine; **crespón fúnebre** crape; mourning band
**cresta** *f* crest (*of bird, of wave, of mountain, of helmet*); (anat., arch., bot., mach. & zool.) crest; **alzar** or **levantar la cresta a** (coll.) to cut short, to mortify; **cresta de gallo** cockscomb; (bot.) cockscomb, yellow rattle
**crestado -da** *adj* crested
**crestería** *f* (fort.) battlement; (arch.) openwork cornice, cresting
**crestillo** *m* (bot.) clematis
**crestomatía** *f* chrestomathy
**crestón** *m* large crest; crest (*of helmet*); (min.) outcrop
**crestudo -da** *adj* heavy-crested; haughty
**creta** *f* chalk; (*cap.*) *f* Crete
**cretáceo -a** *adj* cretaceous; (geol.) Cretaceous; *m* (geol.) Cretaceous
**cretácico** *m* (geol.) Cretaceous
**cretense** *adj* & *mf* Cretan
**crético -ca** *adj* Cretan, Cretic; *m* cretic (*metrical foot*)
**cretinismo** *m* (path.) cretinism
**cretino -na** *adj* cretinic; *mf* cretin
**cretona** *f* cretonne
**creyente** *adj* believing; *mf* believer
**creyón** *m* crayon

**crezneja** *f* var. of **crizneja**
**cría** *f* raising, rearing; breeding; keeping (*of bees*); brood, litter; suckling; nursing; fledgling; **cría caballar** horse breeding
**criada** *f* see **criado**
**criadero -ra** *adj* fruitful, prolific; *m* nursery, tree nursery; breeding place; fish hatchery; (min.) seam, vein; **criadero de ostras** oyster bed
**criadilla** *f* testicle (*of animal*); potato, tuber; small roll (*of bread*); **criadilla almizclada** (bot.) red truffle; **criadilla de tierra** (bot.) truffle
**criado -da** *adj* bred; **bien criado** well-bred; **mal criado** ill-bred; *mf* servant; *f* female servant, maid; wash bat; **criada de servir** housemaid
**criador -dora** *adj* creative; fruitful, abounding; nurturing; *mf* breeder, raiser; keeper (*of bees*); creator; *f* wet nurse
**criaduelo -la** *mf* little servant
**criamiento** *m* care, upkeep, maintenance
**crianza** *f* raising, rearing; nursing; lactation; breeding, manners; **buena crianza** good breeding; **mala crianza** bad breeding
**criar** §90 *va* to raise, rear, bring up; to breed, to grow; to nurse, nourish; to foster; to fatten (*an animal*); to create; **criar carnes** to put on fat, put on weight
**criatura** *f* creature; little creature (*child, baby*); creature (*person owing his position to another*)
**criba** *f* screen, sieve; (min.) jig
**cribado** *m* screening, sieving
**cribador -dora** *adj* screening, sieving; *mf* screener, siever, screen tender
**cribar** *va* to screen, to sieve
**cribo** *m* screen, sieve
**criboso -sa** *adj* sievelike
**cric** *m* (*pl:* **crics**) jack, lifting jack; **cric de cremallera** ratchet jack
**cricoides** *adj* (anat.) cricoid; *m* (*pl:* **-coides**) (anat.) cricoid
**cricquet** *m* (sport) cricket
**Crimea** *f* Crimea
**crimen** *m* crime; **crimen de guerra** war crime; **crimen de lesa majestad** lese majesty
**criminación** *f* crimination
**criminal** *adj* criminal; *mf* criminal; **criminal de guerra** war criminal
**criminalidad** *f* criminality
**criminalista** *mf* criminal lawyer; penologist, criminalist
**criminar** *va* to criminate
**criminología** *f* criminology
**criminológico -ca** *adj* criminological
**criminólogo -ga** *mf* criminologist
**criminoso -sa** *adj* criminal; *mf* criminal; (Am.) slanderer
**crimno** *m* wheat or spelt meal
**crin** *f* mane; horsehair; **crin vegetal** vegetable horsehair
**crinado -da** *adj* (poet.) long-haired
**crinito -ta** *adj* crinite (*comet*)
**crinoideo -a** *adj* (zool.) crinoid; *m* (zool.) crinoid, sea lily
**crinolina** *f* crinoline (*cloth*); (Am.) crinoline (*skirt*)
**crío** *m* (coll.) nursing infant; (coll.) infant
**criogénico -ca** *adj* cryogenic; *f* cryogenics
**criógeno -na** *adj* cryogenic; *m* cryogen
**criohidrato** *m* (chem.) cryohydrate
**criolita** *f* (mineral.) cryolite
**criología** *f* cryology
**criollismo** *m* (Am.) native character; (Am.) advocacy of native manners and customs and things in general
**criollo -lla** *adj & mf* Creole; native (*in Latin America*); hundred-per-cent Argentine, Colombian, Venezuelan, etc.
**criómetro** *m* cryometer
**crioscopia** *f* cryoscopy
**crioscopio** *m* cryoscope
**crióstato** *m* cryostat
**crioterapia** *f* (med.) cryotherapy
**cripta** *f* crypt; (anat.) crypt
**criptogámico -ca** *adj* cryptogamic
**criptógamo -ma** *adj* cryptogamous; *f* (bot.) cryptogam
**criptografía** *f* cryptography
**criptográfico -ca** *adj* cryptographic
**criptógrafo -fa** *mf* cryptographer (*person*); *m* cryptograph (*device*)
**criptograma** *m* cryptogram
**criptón** *m* (chem.) krypton
**crique** *m* var. of **cric**
**cris** *m* (*pl:* **crises**) creese (*dagger*)
**crisálida** *f* (ent.) chrysalis
**crisantema** *f* or **crisantemo** *m* (bot.) chrysanthemum
**Criseida** *f* (myth.) Chryseis; (myth.) Cressida (*in medieval redaction*)
**crisis** *f* (*pl:* **-sis**) crisis; depression (*economic*); mature judgment; **crisis de llanto** outburst of tears, fit of weeping; **crisis de vivienda** housing shortage; **crisis ministerial** cabinet crisis; **crisis nerviosa** nervous breakdown
**crisma** *m & f* (eccl.) chrism; *f* (slang) bean, head
**crismal** *adj & m* (eccl.) chrismal
**crismera** *f* chrismatory
**crismón** *m* chrismon
**crisoberilo** *m* (mineral.) chrysoberyl
**crisol** *m* crucible; (fig.) crucible
**crisolada** *f* charge of a crucible
**crisólito** *m* (mineral.) chrysolite
**crisopacio** *m* var. of **crisoprasa**
**crisopeya** *f* chrysopoeia (*transmuting into gold*)
**crisoprasa** *f* (mineral.) chrysoprase
**Crisóstomo, San Juan** Saint John Chrysostom
**crisotilo** *m* (mineral.) chrysotile
**crispadura** *f* or **crispamiento** *m* twitching
**crispar** *va* to cause to twitch; *vr* to twitch
**crispatura** *f* twitching
**crispir** *va* to grain, to marble
**crista** *f* (her.) crest
**cristal** *m* crystal (*glass; glass ornament*); (chem., mineral. & rad.) crystal; pane of glass; mirror, looking glass; crystal glass, flint glass; (poet.) crystal (*water*); **cristal cilindrado** plate glass; **cristal de patente** (naut.) bull's-eye (*glass in ship's side, deck, etc.*); **cristal de reloj** crystal, watch crystal; **cristal de roca** crystal, rock crystal; **cristal hilado** spun glass, glass wool; **cristal líquido** liquid crystal; liquid glass; **cristal tallado** cut glass
**cristalera** *f* China closet; sideboard; glass door
**cristalería** *f* glasswork; glassworks; glass store; glassware; closet of glassware
**cristalino -na** *adj* crystalline; *m* (anat.) crystalline lens
**cristalito** *m* (mineral.) crystallite
**cristalización** *f* crystallization
**cristalizador** *m* crystallizer (*vessel*)
**cristalizar** §76 *va & vr* to crystallize
**cristalofísica** *f* physics of crystalline substances
**cristalografía** *f* crystallography
**cristalográfico -ca** *adj* crystallographic or crystallographical
**cristaloide** *m* crystalloid
**cristaloideo -a** *adj* crystalloid
**cristaloquímica** *f* chemistry of crystalline substances
**cristel** *m* var. of **clister**
**Cristián** *m* Christian (*man's name*)
**cristianamente** *adv* Christianly, in a Christian manner
**cristianar** *va* (coll.) to christen, baptize
**cristiandad** *f* Christendom; Christianity (*conformity to Christian religion*); missionary's flock
**cristianesco -ca** *adj* Christian, imitating the Christian (*said of something Moorish*)
**cristianísimo -ma** *adj* Most Christian (*sovereign*)
**cristianismo** *m* Christianity; christening, baptism
**cristianización** *f* Christianization
**cristianizar** §76 *va* to Christianize
**cristiano -na** *adj* Christian; *mf* Christian; *m* soul, person; Spanish (*language*); (coll.) watered wine
**cristino -na** *mf* Cristino (*partisan of Maria Christina*); (*cap.*) *f* Christine

**Cristo** *m* Christ; crucifix; **donde Cristo dió las tres voces** (coll.) in the middle of nowhere; **poner como un cristo** (coll.) to abuse, to beat up
**Cristóbal** *m* Christopher
**cristofué** *m* (orn.) Venezuelan greenfinch
**cristus** *m* (*pl:* **-tus**) christcross; **no saber el cristus** (coll.) to be very ignorant
**crisuela** *f* drip pan (*of lamp*)
**criterio** *m* criterion; judgment, discernment
**crítica** *f* see **crítico**
**criticador -dora** *adj* criticizing, faultfinding; *mf* criticizer, faultfinder
**criticar** §86 *va* to criticize
**criticastro** *m* criticaster
**criticismo** *m* (philos.) criticism
**crítico -ca** *adj* critical; (Am.) faultfinding; *m* critic; (coll.) pedant; *f* criticism; critique; gossip; **alta crítica** high criticism; **crítica textual** textual criticism
**criticón -cona** *adj* (coll.) censorious, faultfinding; *mf* (coll.) critic, faultfinder
**critiquizar** §76 *va* (coll.) to overcriticize
**crizneja** *f* braid of hair; rope of osiers or rushes
**Croacia** *f* Croatia
**croar** *vn* to croak (*said of frogs*)
**croata** *adj* & *mf* Croatian; *m* Croatian (*language*)
**crocante** *m* almond brittle, peanut brittle
**croceína** *f* (chem.) crocein
**crocino -na** *adj* (pertaining to) saffron; *f* (chem.) crocin
**crocitar** *vn* to crow, to croak
**croché** *m* crochet, crochet work
**crochet** *m* (box.) hook
**cromado -da** *adj* chrome, chromium-plated; *m* chromium plating
**cromañón** *m* (anthrop.) Cro-Magnon
**cromañonense** *adj* (anthrop.) Cro-Magnon
**cromar** *va* to chrome (*to plate with chromium*)
**cromático -ca** *adj* chromatic; (mus.) chromatic; *f* chromatics
**cromatina** *f* (biol.) chromatin
**cromatismo** *m* chromatism
**cromato** *m* (chem.) chromate
**cromatóforo** *m* (biol.) chromatophore
**crómico -ca** *adj* (chem.) chromic
**crominancia** *f* (phys.) crominance
**cromismo** *m* (bot.) chromatism
**cromita** *f* (mineral.) chromite
**cromito** *m* (chem.) chromite
**cromo** *m* (chem.) chromium, chrome; chromo (*picture*)
**cromóforo** *m* (chem.) chromophore
**cromógeno -na** *adj* chromogenic; *m* (chem.) chromogen
**cromolitografía** *f* chromolithography; chromolithograph (*picture*)
**cromolitografiar** §90 *va* to chromolithograph
**cromolitográfico -ca** *adj* chromolithographic
**cromolitógrafo -fa** *mf* chromolithographer
**cromoplasma** *m* (biol.) chromoplasm
**cromoplasto** *m* (bot.) chromoplast
**cromoscopio** *m* (telv.) chromoscope, color tube
**cromosfera** *f* (astr.) chromosphere
**cromoso -sa** *adj* (chem.) chromous
**cromosoma** *m* (biol.) chromosome; **cromosoma sexual** (biol.) sex chromosome
**cromotipia** *f* chromotypy or chromotypography
**cromotipografía** *f* chromotypography
**cromotipográfico -ca** *adj* chromotypographic
**crónica** *f* see **crónico**
**cronicidad** *f* chronicity, chronic nature
**crónico -ca** *adj* chronic; inveterate (*vices*); longstanding; *f* chronicle; news, news chronicle, feature story; **Crónicas** *fpl* (Bib.) Chronicles
**cronicón** *m* brief chronicle
**cronista** *mf* chronicler; reporter, feature writer; **cronista de radio** newscaster, radio newscaster
**cronístico -ca** *adj* (pertaining to a) chronicle; chronicler's
**cronógrafo -fa** *mf* chronographer; *m* chronograph
**cronología** *f* chronology
**cronológico -ca** *adj* chronologic or chronological
**cronologista** *mf* or **cronólogo -ga** *mf* chronologist
**cronometrador -dora** *mf* (sport) timekeeper
**cronometraje** *m* (sport) clocking, timing
**cronometrar** *va* (sport) to clock, to time
**cronometría** *f* chronometry
**cronómetro** *m* chronometer; stop watch
**Cronos** *m* (myth.) Cronus
**cronoscopio** *m* chronoscope
**croqueta** *f* croquette
**croquis** *m* (*pl:* **-quis**) sketch
**croscitar** *vn* to crow, to croak
**crosse** *f* (sport) lacrosse; **jugar a la crosse** to play lacrosse
**crótalo** *m* (zool.) rattlesnake; castanet
**crotón** *m* (bot.) croton
**crotorar** *vn* to rattle (*said of a stork or crane*)
**cruce** *m* cross, crossing; crossroads; intersection; exchange (*e.g., of letters*); (elec.) crossed wires (*short*); **cruce a nivel** (rail.) grade crossing; **cruce de palabras** (philol.) blending; **cruce en trébol** cloverleaf, cloverleaf intersection (*in a highway*)
**crucera** *f* withers (*of horse*)
**crucería** *f* (arch.) boss (*in Gothic vaulting*)
**crucero** *m* (eccl.) crucifer, cross-bearer; crossroads; railroad crossing; timber; crosspiece; (nav.) cruiser; (naut. & aer.) cruise, cruising; (arch.) transept; (arch.) crossing (*where transept crosses nave*); (*cap.*) *m* (astr.) Southern Cross; **crucero a nivel** (rail.) grade crossing
**cruceta** *f* crosspiece (*e.g., of trelliswork*); (mach.) crosshead (*of connecting rod*); (naut.) crosstree
**crucial** *adj* crucial; (surg.) crucial
**cruciata** *f* (bot.) crosswort
**cruciferario** *m* (eccl.) crucifer, cross-bearer
**crucífero -ra** *adj* (bot.) cruciferous; *f* (bot.) crucifer
**crucificado -da** *adj* crucified; **el Crucificado** the Crucified (*Christ*)
**crucificar** §86 *va* to crucify; (coll.) to crucify (*to torture, torment*)
**crucifijo** *m* crucifix
**crucifixión** *f* crucifixion; (*cap.*) *f* Crucifixion
**cruciforme** *adj* cruciform, cross-shaped
**crucigrama** *m* crossword puzzle
**crucigramista** *mf* crossworder
**crucillo** *m* pushpin
**cruda** *f* see **crudo**
**crudelísimo -ma** *adj super* very or most cruel
**crudeza** *f* rawness, crudeness; unripeness; hardness (*of water*); roughness, severity, harshness; (coll.) blustering; **crudezas** *fpl* undigested food, indigestible food
**crudo -da** *adj* raw, crude; unripe; unbleached (*linen*); hard (*water*); raw (*weather*); **estar crudo** (Am.) to have a hangover; **medio crudo** rare (*meat*); *m* burlap; *f* (Am.) hangover
**cruel** *adj* cruel; intense (*cold*); fierce, bitter, bloody (*struggle, battle*)
**crueldad** *f* cruelty
**cruento -ta** *adj* bloody
**crujía** *f* corridor, hall; block, row of houses; ward, hospital ward; bay (*space between two walls*); (naut.) midship gangway; **pasar** or **sufrir una crujía** (coll.) to have a hard time of it; **crujía de piezas** suite of rooms
**crujidero -ra** *adj* crackling; creaking; chattering, clattering; rustling
**crujido** *m* crackle; creak; chatter, clatter; rustle
**crujiente** *adj* var. of **crujidero**
**crujir** *vn* to crackle; to creak; to chatter, clatter; to rustle
**crúor** *m* (physiol.) cruor; (poet.) blood
**crup** *m* (path.) croup
**crupal** *adj* croupous
**cruposo -sa** *adj* croupy
**crural** *adj* (anat.) crural
**crustáceo -a** *adj* crustaceous; (zool.) crustaceous, crustacean; *m* (zool.) crustacean
**crústula** *f* var. of **cortezuela**
**cruz** *f* (*pl:* **cruces**) cross; tails (*of a coin*); withers (*of quadruped*); (math.) plus sign; (naut.) crown (*of anchor*); (print.) dagger; top of trunk (*where horizontal branches begin*); (fig.) cross (*suffering, burden*); **de la cruz a la fecha** from beginning to end; **en cruz** crosswise; cross-shaped; in quarters; (her.)

quarterly; **Cruz del Sur** (astr.) Southern Cross; **cruz de Malta** Maltese cross; (bot.) scarlet lychnis; **cruz de San Andrés** Saint Andrew's cross; **cruz gamada** gammadion, fylfot, swastika; **cruz latina** Latin cross; **cruz potenzada** (her.) potent cross; **cruz roja** red cross; **Cruz Roja** Red Cross; **cruz trebolada** (her.) tréflé cross, botony cross; **cruz y raya** (coll.) I have my fill, that's enough
**cruzado -da** *adj* crossed; cross (*breed*); twilled; double-breasted; **con los brazos cruzados** with arms crossed, idle; *m* crusader; knight; *f* crusade; crossroads, intersection
**cruzamiento** *m* crossing; cross-breeding; (elec.) cross; **cruzamiento retrógrado** backcross
**cruzar** §76 *va* to cross; to cut across; to honor with the cross, confer the cross on; to twill; to exchange (*correspondence*); (naut.) to cruise, cruise over; **cruzarle a uno la cara** to lash someone in the face; *vn* to cross; to fold over (*said of clothing when it is full*); to cruise; *vr* to cross in front; to cross each other; to cross one another's path; to take the cross (*to join a crusade*); **cruzarse con** to pass (*e.g., another automobile*); **cruzarse de brazos** to cross one's arms, remain idle, do nothing
**cs.** abr. of **céntimos** & **cuartos**
**csardas** *f* (mus.) czardas
**c.ta** abr. of **cuenta**
**cte.** abr. of **corriente**
**ctetología** *f* ctetology
**c.to** abr. of **cuarto**
**cts.** abr. of **céntimos** & **cuartos**
**c/u** abr. of **cada uno**
**cuaba** *f* (bot.) Jamaica rosewood; (Am.) gyp
**cuaco** *m* (Am.) yucca flour; (Am.) horse
**cuad.** abr. of **cuadrado**
**cuaderna** *f* (naut.) frame; **cuaderna de escuadra** (naut.) square frame; **cuaderna maestra** (naut.) midship frame; **cuaderna sesgada** (naut.) cant frame
**cuadernal** *m* double or triple block
**cuadernillo** *m* (eccl.) liturgical calendar; quinternion
**cuaderno** *m* notebook; folder; (print.) quarternion; **cuaderno de bitácora** (naut.) logbook; **cuaderno de hojas cambiables** or **sueltas** loose-leaf notebook
**cuadra** *f* see **cuadro**
**cuadrada** *f* see **cuadrado**
**cuadradamente** *adv* exactly, fully
**cuadradillo** *m* ruler; plotting paper; square iron bar; gusset (*of shirt*); lump (*of sugar*)
**cuadrado -da** *adj* square; quadrate; perfect, complete; square-shouldered; *m* (geom. & math.) square; quadrate; ruler; clock (*in stockings*); gusset (*of shirt*); die (*for making coins*); (print.) quadrat; **de cuadrado** perfectly; full-faced (*view*); **dejar de cuadrado** to sting to the quick; **cuadrado mágico** magic square; *f* (mus.) breve
**cuadragenario -ria** *adj* & *mf* quadragenarian
**cuadragesimal** *adj* Quadragesimal
**cuadragésimo -ma** *adj* & *m* fortieth; *f* (eccl.) Lent; (eccl.) Quadragesima
**cuadral** *m* (carp.) angle brace
**cuadrangular** *adj* quadrangular; *m* (baseball) home run
**cuadrángulo -la** *adj* quadrangular; *m* quadrangle
**cuadrantal** *m* quadrantal (*liquid measure*)
**cuadrante** *m* fourth part of an inheritance; dial, face (*of watch, clock, etc.*); (astr. & geom.) quadrant; (carp.) angle brace; **cuadrante de sintonía** (rad.) tuning dial; **cuadrante solar** sundial
**cuadranura** *f* radial crack in trees (*sign of rotting*)
**cuadrar** *va* to square; to form into a square; to please; (math.) to square; (math.) to determine the square of; (taur.) to line up, to square off (*the bull*); **cuadrar** + *inf* (Am.) to be pleasing to + *inf*; *vn* to square, to conform; *vr* to stand at attention, to square one's shoulders; (coll.) become solemn, to assume a serious air
**cuadratín** *m* (print.) quadrat
**cuadratura** *f* (astr., elec. & math.) quadrature; **cuadratura del círculo** (math.) quadrature of the circle; (coll.) impossibility
**cuadrete** *m* small square
**cuadricenal** *adj* done every forty years
**cuadríceps** *m* (anat.) quadriceps; *adj* quadricipital
**cuadrícula** *f* quadrille ruling
**cuadricular** *adj* squared, in squares; *va* to graticulate, to quadrille
**cuadrienal** *ajd* & *f* quadrennial
**cuadrienio** *m* quadrennium, period of four years
**cuadrífido -da** *adj* (bot.) quadrifid
**cuadrifilar** *adj* four-wire
**cuadrifoliado -da** *adj* four-leaf
**cuadrifolio -lia** *adj* four-leaf; *m* (arch.) quatrefoil
**cuadriforme** *adj* quadriform
**cuadriga** *f* (hist.) quadriga
**cuadrilátero -ra** *adj* quadrilateral; *m* quadrilateral; (box.) ring
**cuadriliteral** or **cuadrilítero -ra** *adj* quadriliteral, four-letter
**cuadrilongo -ga** *adj* oblong, rectangular; *m* oblong, rectangle; (mil.) rectangular formation
**cuadrilla** *f* group, party, crew, troup, gang, squad; quadrille; (taur.) cuadrilla, quadrille; **cuadrilla de demolición** demolition squad
**cuadrillar** *vn* (Am.) to quadrille
**cuadrillazo** *m* (Am.) surprise attack; **dar cuadrillazo a** (Am.) to gang up on
**cuadrillero** *m* chief, leader, foreman; (orn.) tanager
**cuadrillo** *m* bolt, quarrel (*arrow*)
**cuadrimestre** *adj* & *m* var. of **cuatrimestre**
**cuadrimotor** *m* (aer.) four-motor plane
**cuadringentésimo -ma** *adj* & *m* four-hundredth
**cuadrinomio** *m* (alg.) quadrinomial
**cuadripartido -da** *adj* quadripartite
**cuadriplaza** *m* (aer.) four-seater
**cuadriplicar** §86 *va* var. of **cuadruplicar**
**cuadrisílabo -ba** *adj* & *m* var. of **cuatrisílabo**
**cuadriviario -ria** *adj* four-lane
**cuadrivio** *m* crossroads (*of four roads*); quadrivium (*four upper subjects of medieval seven liberal arts*)
**cuadrivista** *m* scholar trained in the quadrivium
**cuadríyugo** *m* four-horse chariot
**cuadro -dra** *adj* square ‖ *m* square; picture, painting; frame (*of picture, door, bicycle, etc.*); flower bed, patch; table, outline; staff, personnel; (lit.) picture; (mil.) square; (mil.) cadre; (print.) platen; (sport) team; (theat.) scene; (coll.) sight, mess; **a cuadros** checked; **en cuadro** square, e.g., **ocho pulgadas en cuadro** eight inches square; **en cuadro** (coll.) topsy-turvy; **estar** or **quedarse en cuadro** to be all alone in the world; to be on one's uppers; (mil.) to be skeletonized; **cuadro al óleo** oil painting; **cuadro conmutador** (elec. & telp.) switchboard; **cuadro de contador** (elec.) meter panel; **cuadro de costumbres** (lit.) sketch of manners and customs; **cuadro de distribución** (elec. & telp.) switchboard; **cuadro de mandos** panelboard; **cuadro de vidrio** pane of glass; **cuadro indicador** score board; (elec.) annunciator; **cuadro vivo** tableau ‖ *f* hall, large room; dormitory, ward; stable; croup, rump; (naut.) quarter; (Am.) block of houses, square
**cuadrúmano -na** *adj* (zool.) quadrumanous; *m* (zool.) quadrumane
**cuadrupedal** *adj* quadrupedal
**cuadrúpedo -da** *adj* quadruped; (coll.) doltish; *m* quadruped; (coll.) dolt
**cuádruple** *adj* & *m* quadruple
**cuadrúplex** *m* (telg.) quadruplex system
**cuadruplicación** *f* quadruplication
**cuadruplicar** §86 *va* to quadruplicate, to quadruple; *vr* to quadruple
**cuádruplo -pla** *adj* & *m* var. of **cuádruple**
**cuaga** *f* (zool.) quagga
**cuajada** *f* see **cuajado**
**cuajadillo** *m* fancy work on silk
**cuajado -da** *adj* dumfounded; *m* mincemeat; *f* curd; cottage cheese
**cuajadura** *f* curdling, coagulation
**cuajaleche** *m* (bot.) bedstraw, cheese rennet

**cuajamiento** *m* var. of **cuajadura**
**cuajar** *m* (zool.) rennet bag; *va* to curd, to curdle, to coagulate; to thicken, to jelly; to overdeck; (coll.) to please, to suit; *vn* (coll.) to jell, take shape; (coll.) to take hold, catch on, succeed; (Am.) to prattle; *vr* to curd, to curdle, to coagulate; to thicken, to jelly; to sleep soundly; (coll.) to become crowded
**cuajarón** *m* clot, grume
**cuajilote** *m* (bot.) tropical American tree (*Parmentiera edulis*)
**cuajo** *m* rennet; curdle; rennet bag; thickening (*of cane juice*); idle chatting; recess (*in school*); **de cuajo** by the roots
**cuakerismo** *m* var. of **cuaquerismo**
**cuákero -ra** *adj & mf* var. of **cuáquero**
**cual** *adj & pron rel* as, such as; **el cual** which, who; **por lo cual** for which reason; **cual . . . tal** like . . . like, e.g., **cual el padre, tal el hijo** like father like son; just as . . . so, e.g., **cual es Pedro, tal es Juan** just as Peter is, so is John, John is like Peter; *adv* as; **cual si** as if; *prep* like
**cuál** *adj & pron interr* which, what, which one; how!; **cuál . . . cuál** some . . . some
**cualicho** *m* (Am.) evil spirit, demon
**cualidad** *f* quality; characteristic
**cualímetro** *m* qualimeter
**cualitativo -va** *adj* qualitative
**cualquier** *adj indef* (*pl:* **cualesquier**) apocopated form of **cualquiera,** used only before nouns and adjectives
**cualquiera** (*pl:* **cualesquiera**) *pron indef* anyone; *pron rel* whichever; whoever; *adj indef* any; *adj rel* whichever; *m* anybody, nobody (*person of no account*)
**cuan** *adv* as
**cuán** *adv* how, how much
**cuando** *conj* when; in case (that); although; since; **aún cuando** even though; **de cuando en cuando** from time to time; **cuando más** at most; **cuando menos** at least; **cuando mucho** at most; **cuando quiera** whenever; *prep* (coll.) at the time of
**cuándo** *adv* when?, e.g., **¿cuándo llegará?** when will he arrive?; when, e.g., **no sé cuándo llegará** I don't know when he will arrive; **¿de cuándo acá?** since when?; how come?; **cuándo . . . cuándo** sometimes . . . sometimes
**cuandoquiera** *adv* any time; **cuandoquiera que** whenever
**cuantía** *f* quantity; importance, distinction; **de mayor cuantía** first-rate; grave, serious; **de menor cuantía** second-rate; of minor seriousness
**cuantiar** §90 *va* to estimate, to appraise
**cuántico -ca** *adj* (phys.) quantum
**cuantidad** *f* quantity
**cuantificar** §86 *va* to quantify
**cuantimás** *adv* (coll.) at least
**cuantímetro** *m* quantimeter
**cuantioso -sa** *adj* numerous, large, substantial
**cuantitativo -va** *adj* quantitative
**cuanto -ta** *adj & pron rel* as much as, whatever; **unos cuantos** some few; **cuanto** as much as, all that (which); **cuantos** as many as, all those who, everybody who; **cuanto** *adv* as soon as; as long as; **en cuanto** as soon as; while; insofar as; **en cuanto a** as to, as for; **por cuanto** inasmuch as; **por cuanto . . . por tanto** inasmuch as . . . therefore; **cuanto antes** as soon as possible; **cuanto más . . . tanto más** the more . . . the more, e.g., **cuanto más tiene tanto más desea** the more he has the more he wants; **cuanto más** at least; **cuanto más que** all the more because; **cuanto y más** at least; **cuanto y más que** all the more because; *m* (*pl:* **-ta**) (phys.) quantum
**cuánto -ta** *adj & pron interr* how much; **cuántos** how many; **cuánto** *adv interr* how, how much; how long; how long ago; **cada cuánto** how often
**cuaquerismo** *m* Quakerism
**cuáquero -ra** *adj & mf* Quaker; *f* Quakeress
**cuarcífero -ra** *adj* quartziferous
**cuarcita** *f* (mineral.) quartzite
**cuarenta** *adj & m* forty; **acusarle a uno las cuarenta** (coll.) to give someone a piece of one's mind
**cuarentavo -va** *adj & m* fortieth
**cuarentena** *f* forty, two score; quarantine; Lent; forty days, months, years, etc.; suspension of approval
**cuarentón -tona** *adj* forty-year-old; *mf* person forty years old
**cuaresma** *f* Lent; Lenten sermons
**cuaresmal** *adj* Lenten
**cuaresmario** *m* Lenten sermons
**cuarta** *f* see **cuarto**
**cuartago** *m* nag, pony
**cuartal** *m* dry measure equal to 5.60 liters; dry measure equal to 17.50 liters; quarter loaf of bread
**cuartán** *m* dry measure equal to 18.08 liters; oil measure equal to 4.15 liters
**cuartana** *f* (path.) quartan
**cuartanal** *adj* quartan
**cuartanario -ria** *adj* suffering from quartan
**cuartazos** *m* (scornful) fat slob
**cuartear** *va* to quarter; to divide; to zigzag over (*a road*); to bid a fourth higher for; to take the fourth place in (*a game*); (Am.) to whip, to lash; (naut.) to box (*the compass*); *vn* (taur.) to step aside, to dodge; (Am.) to compromise; *vr* to crack, split; (taur.) to step aside, to dodge
**cuartel** *m* quarter; section, ward (*of a city*); lot (*of ground*); flower bed; (her.) quarter; (mil.) barracks; (mil.) quarter (*clemency to conquered enemy*); (naut.) hatch (*door over hatchway*); (coll.) house, home; **cuarteles** *mpl* (mil.) quarters; **no dar cuartel a** to give no quarter to; **cuartel de bomberos** engine house, firehouse; **cuartel de la salud** (coll.) refuge, haven; **cuartel general** (mil.) headquarters
**cuartelada** *f* mutiny, military uprising
**cuartelar** *va* (her.) to quarter
**cuartelero -ra** *adj* barrack, soldier; *m* soldier charged with policing the barracks
**cuartelesco -ca** *adj* barrack, soldier
**cuartelillo** *m* (mil.) barracks; police station
**cuarteo** *m* quartering; dividing; dodging; crack, split
**cuartera** *f* dry measure equal to about 70 liters; land measure equal to about 30 acres; log, piece of lumber
**cuarterada** *f* land measure equal to about 7 sq. mi.
**cuarterola** *f* quarter cask
**cuarterón -rona** *mf* quadroon; *m* quartern, fourth; quarter pound; panel (*of a door*); wicket (*small door in larger one*)
**cuarteta** *f* quatrain with the rhyme abba; quatrain with second and fourth lines rhymed
**cuartete** *m* or **cuarteto** *m* quatrain (*poem*); quartet (*group of four*); (mus.) quartet or quartette
**cuartilla** *f* pastern (*of horse*); quarter sheet of paper; sheet of paper; quarter arroba; dry measure equal to 13.87 liters; liquid measure equal to 4.033 liters
**cuartillo** *m* dry measure equal to 1.156 liters; liquid measure equal to 0.504 liters
**cuartilludo -da** *adj* long-pasterned (*horse*)
**cuartizo** *m* quartersawed timber
**cuarto -ta** *adj* fourth; quarter ‖ *m* fourth; quarter; quarter-hour; room, bedroom; **cuartos** *mpl* (coll.) money, cash; **de tres al cuarto** of little importance; **echar su cuarto a espadas** (coll.) to butt into the conversation; **en cuarto** quarto (*said of a volume*); **hacer cuartos a** to quarter; **no tener un cuarto** (coll.) to not have a cent; **por cuarto cuartos** (coll.) for a song, for practically nothing; **tener buenos cuartos** (coll.) to be strong and husky; **cuarto creciente** first quarter (*of moon*); **cuarto de aseo** lavatory; **cuarto de baño** bathroom; **cuarto de dormir** bedroom; **cuarto de estar** living room; **cuarto de huésped** spare room, guest room; **cuarto de juegos** playroom, nursery; **cuarto delantero** forequarter; **cuarto de luna** (astr.) quarter; **cuarto menguante** last quarter (*of*

*moon*); **cuarto obscuro** (phot.) darkroom; **cuarto trasero** (cook.) rump (*e.g., of a cow*) ‖ *f* fourth, fourth part, quarter; (mus.) fourth; (naut.) point, rhumb (*of compass card*); four of a kind (*in cards*); span (*of hand*); (Am.) horse whip
**cuartón** *m* quartersawed timber; square field
**cuartucho** *m* shack, hovel
**cuarzo** *m* (mineral.) quartz
**cuarzoso -sa** *adj* quartzose or quartzous
**cuascle** *m* (Am.) horse blanket
**cuasi** *adv* almost; quasi
**cuasia** *f* (bot. & pharm.) quassia; **cuasia de Jamaica** (bot. & pharm.) bitterwood, Jamaica quassia
**cuasicontrato** *m* (law) quasi contract
**cuasidelito** *m* (law) quasi delict
**cuasimodo** *m* (eccl.) Quasimodo
**cuate -ta** *adj* (Am.) twin; (Am.) chummy; *mf* (Am.) twin; (Am.) chum, pal
**cuaternario -ria** *adj* quaternary; (chem.) quaternary; (geol.) Quaternary; *m* (geol.) Quaternary
**cuaterno -na** *adj* quaternary
**cuatí** *m* (*pl:* **-tíes**) var. of **coatí**
**cuatralbo -ba** *adj* having four white feet
**cuatrero** *m* horse thief, cattle thief, rustler
**cuatricromía** *f* four-color reproduction, four-color process
**cuatriduano -na** *adj* four-day-long
**cuatrienio** *m* var. of **cuadrienio**
**cuatrifilar** *adj* four-wire
**cuatrillizo -za** *mf* quadruplet
**cuatrillo** *m* lansquenet (*card game*)
**cuatrillón** *m* British quadrillion; septillion (*in U.S.A.*)
**cuatrimestre** *adj* four-month; *m* four months
**cuatrimotor** *adj masc* four-motor
**cuatrinca** *f* foursome; four of a kind (*in cards*)
**cuatripartito -ta** *adj* var. of **cuadripartido**
**cuatrirreactor** *m* (aer.) four-engine jet plane
**cuatrisílabo -ba** *adj* quadrisyllabic; *m* quadrisyllable
**cuatro** *adj* four; **las cuatro** four o'clock; *m* four; fourth (*in dates*); (mus.) quartet (*of voices*); **más de cuatro** (coll.) quite a number (*of people*)
**cuatrocentista** *adj* fifteenth-century; *m* (f.a.) quattrocentist
**cuatrocientos -tas** *adj & m* four hundred
**cuatrodoblar** *va* to quadruplicate
**cuatropea** *f* sales tax on horses; quadruped; cattle market place
**Cuatro Vientos** Madrid airport
**cuba** *f* cask, barrel; tub, vat; stack (*of blast furnace*); bucket (*of turbine*); (coll.) tub (*fat person*); (coll.) toper; **estar hecho una cuba** (coll.) to be tanked up; **cuba del flotador** float chamber (*of carburetor*); **cuba de riego** street sprinkler
**cubaje** *m* (Am.) cubing
**cubanismo** *m* Cubanism
**cubanizar** **§76** *va* to Cubanize
**cubano -na** *adj & mf* Cuban
**cubeba** *f* (bot. & pharm.) cubeb
**cubera** *f* (ichth.) snapper
**cubería** *f* cooperage; cooper's shop
**cubero** *m* cooper
**cubertura** *f* var. of **cobertura**
**cubeta** *f* keg, small cask or barrel; pail, small bucket; toilet bowl; cup or cistern (*of barometer*); (chem. & phot.) tray (*of glass, hard rubber, etc.*); (phot.) cuvette; (mus.) pedestal (*of harp*); (Am.) high hat; **cubeta de aceite** (mach.) oil well; **cubeta de goteo** drip pan
**cubeto** *m* small pail or bucket, small tub
**cúbica** *f* see **cúbico**
**cubicación** *f* cubing; cubic measure
**cubicar** **§86** *va* to determine the volume of; (math.) to cube
**cúbico -ca** *adj* cubic, cubical; (cryst. & math.) cubic; (math.) cube (*root*); *f* cubica (*fabric*)
**cubículo** *m* cubicle
**cubierta** *f* see **cubierto**
**cubiertamente** *adv* secretly, under cover
**cubierto -ta** *pp of* **cubrir** ‖ *m* cover, roof, shelter; cover (*place for one person at table*); knife, fork, and spoon; tray with napkin for serving bread and cakes; meal (*at a fixed price*); table d'hôte; **a cubierto de** under cover of (*e.g., darkness*); protected from (*e.g., the rain*); **bajo cubierto** under cover, indoors ‖ *f* cover; envelope; casing; roof; paper cover (*of a book*); shoe (*of a tire*); hood (*of motor*); (naut.) deck; **bajo cubierta** under separate cover; **entre cubiertas** (naut.) between decks; **cubierta alta** (naut.) upper deck; **cubierta corrida** flush deck; **cubierta de aterrizaje** (nav.) flight deck; **cubierta de cama** bedcover; **cubierta de guindaste** (naut.) spar deck; **cubierta de mesa** table cover; **cubierta de paseo** (naut.) promenade deck; **cubierta de salón** (naut.) saloon deck; **cubierta de vuelo** (nav.) flight deck; **cubierta principal** (naut.) main deck
**cubija** *f* (Am.) blanket
**cubijar** *va* var. of **cobijar**
**cubil** *m* lair, den (*of wild animals*); bed (*of stream*)
**cubilar** *m* lair, den; sheepfold; *vn* to take shelter overnight (*said of sheep and shepherd*)
**cubilete** *m* (cook.) copper pan or mold; pannikin; juggler's goblet, dicebox; mince pie; (Am.) high hat; (bot.) yellow pond lily; intrigue, wirepulling
**cubiletear** *vn* to juggle; to scheme, to intrigue; (Am.) to dabble in politics
**cubileteo** *m* jugglery
**cubiletero** *m* juggler; copper pan or mold
**cubilote** *m* (found.) cupola
**cubilla** *f* (ent.) oil beetle
**cubillo** *m* (ent.) oil beetle; earthen water jug
**cubismo** *m* (f.a.) cubism
**cubista** *adj & mf* (f.a.) cubist
**cubital** *adj* cubital
**cúbito** *m* (anat.) cubitus
**cubo** *m* bucket; hub (*of wheel*); socket (*of a candelabrum; of a wrench*); bayonet socket; reserve water tank (*for mill*); cube; (arch.) dado; (mach.) barrel, drum; (math.) cube; (Am.) finger bowl
**cuboides** *adj* (anat.) cuboid; *m* (*pl:* **-boides**) (anat.) cuboid, cuboid bone
**cubreasiento** *m* (aut.) seat cover
**cubrebandeja** *f* tray cloth
**cubrecabeza** *f* helmet (*e.g., of aviator*)
**cubrecadena** *f* chain guard
**cubrecama** *f* counterpane, bedspread
**cubrecorsé** *m* corset cover, underbodice
**cubrefuego** *m* curfew
**cubrejunta** *f* (carp.) fish
**cubremantel** *m* fancy tablecloth
**cubreneumático** *m* (aut.) tire cover
**cubrenuca** *f* havelock; neckguard
**cubreobjeto** or **cubreobjetos** *m* (*pl:* **-tos**) cover glass, cover slip (*for microscopic preparations*)
**cubrepantalones** *mpl* overalls
**cubreplatos** *m* (*pl:* **-tos**) dish cover
**cubrerrueda** *f* mudguard
**cubresexo** *m* G string, cache-sexe
**cubretablero** *m* (aut.) cowl
**cubretetera** *f* cozy, tea cozy
**cubrimiento** *m* covering
**cubrir** **§17,** 9 *va* to cover, cover over, cover up; to cover (*a mare*); (mil.) to cover (*e.g., a retreat*); *vr* to cover oneself; to become covered; to put one's hat on; to cover (*to settle a debt*)
**cuca** *f* see **cuco**
**cucamonas** *fpl* (coll.) fawning, wheedling
**cucaña** *f* greased pole to be walked on or climbed (*as a game*); (coll.) cinch
**cucañero -ra** *mf* (coll.) parasite, hanger-on
**cucar** **§86** *va* to wink; to make fun of; to sight (*game*); (Am.) to excite, stir up; *vn* to go off on a run (*said of cattle when bitten by flies*)
**cucaracha** *f* (ent.) cockroach, roach; (zool.) wood louse, pill bug
**cucarachero -ra** *adj* (Am.) amorous, lecherous; *f* cockroach trap
**cucarda** *f* cockade
**cuclillas; ponerse en cuclillas** to squat, to crouch
**cuclillo** *m* (orn.) cuckoo; (orn.) yellow-billed cuckoo; cuckold; **cuclillo de las lluvias** (orn.) yellow-billed cuckoo
**cuco -ca** *adj* crafty, sly; (coll.) nice, cute; *mf* crafty, sly person; *m* India berry; bogeyman;

(ent.) caterpillar; (orn.) cuckoo; (coll.) gambler; *f* (bot.) chufa; (ent.) caterpillar; (coll.) gambling woman; **mala cuca** (coll.) vicious, evil person
**cucú** *m* (*pl:* **-cúes**) cuckoo (*call of cuckoo*)
**cuculado -da** or **cuculiforme** *adj* cowled, cowl-like, cucullate
**cuculí** *f* (*pl:* **-líes**) (Am.) wild pigeon (*Melopelia meloda*); **jugar la** or **hasta la cuculí** (Am.) to shoot the works
**cuculla** *f* cowl; hood
**cucúrbita** *f* (archaic) retort
**cucurbitáceo -a** *adj* (bot.) cucurbitaceous
**cucurucho** *m* paper cone, cornet; ice-cream cone
**cucuy** *m* or **cucuyo** *m* var. of **cocuyo**
**cuchara** *f* spoon; ladle; scoop; trowel; dipper (*of power shovel*); (Am.) pickpocket; **media cuchara** (coll.) mediocre person; **meter su cuchara** (coll.) to meddle, to butt in, to put in one's oar; **cuchara de café** teaspoon; **cuchara de sopa** tablespoon
**cucharada** *f* spoonful; ladleful; scooping; **meter su cucharada** (coll.) to meddle, to butt in; **cucharada de café** teaspoonful; **cucharada de sopa** tablespoonful
**cucharadita** *f* teaspoon; teaspoonful
**cucharal** *m* shepherd's goatskin spoon bag
**cucharear** *va* to spoon, to ladle out; (hort.) to sprinkle
**cucharero -ra** *mf* spoon maker or dealer; *m* spoon rack
**cuchareta** *f* small spoon; Andalusian wheat; (orn.) shoveler; (vet.) liver rot, sheep rot
**cucharetear** *vn* (coll.) to stir the pot; (coll.) to meddle
**cucharetero -ra** *mf* maker of wooden ladles; dealer in wooden ladles; *m* spoon rack; petticoat fringe
**cucharilla** *f* small spoon, teaspoon; ladle (*of tinsmith*); liver disease of hogs; (surg.) curette
**cucharón** *m* large spoon; soup ladle, dipper; scoop; (orn.) spoonbill; (mach.) bucket; **despacharse con el cucharón** (coll.) to take care of oneself, to look out for number one; **cucharón de quijadas** grab bucket, clamshell bucket
**cucharro** *m* (naut.) harpings, buttocks
**cuchichear** *va & vn* to whisper
**cuchicheo** *m* whispering
**cuchichero -ra** *mf* whisperer
**cuchichiar** *vn* to call or cry (*said of partridge*)
**cuchilla** *f* knife, cutting tool; large knife, cleaver; blade (*of razor, of sword*); hogback, mountain ridge, runner (*of skate, sled, sleigh*); (elec.) blade (*of switch*); (poet.) sword; (archaic) halberd; **cuchilla de carnicero** butcher knife
**cuchillada** *f* slash, hack, gash; **cuchilladas** *fpl* quarrel, fight; slashes (*ornamental slits in garment*); **dar cuchillada** (coll.) to be the hit of the town (*said of a show*)
**cuchillar** *adj* (pertaining to a) knife; knifelike
**cuchilleja** *f* small knife or blade
**cuchillería** *f* cutlery; cutler's shop
**cuchillero** *m* cutler; iron band or clasp
**cuchillo** *m* knife; knife edge; gore (*in garment*); lower tusk (*of wild boar*); (carp.) upright; (naut.) triangular sail; **pasar a cuchillo** to put to the sword, put to death; **cuchillo de armadura** (arch.) gable frame; **cuchillo de cocina** kitchen knife; **cuchillo de monte** hunting knife; **cuchillo de vidriero** putty knife; **cuchillo puñal** bowie knife
**cuchipanda** *f* (coll.) merry feast
**cuchitril** *m* hole, corner, den, hut
**cuchuchear** *vn* to whisper; (coll.) to gossip
**cuchufleta** *f* (coll.) joke, joking, fun
**cuchufletear** *vn* (coll.) to joke, make fun
**cuchufletero -ra** *adj* (coll.) joking, funmaking; *mf* (coll.) joker, funmaker
**cuchumbo** *m* (Am.) dicebox; (Am.) dice (*game*)
**cudú** *m* (*pl:* **-dúes**) (zool.) kudu
**cuelga** *f* bunch of fruit hung up for keeping; (coll.) birthday present
**cuelgacapas** *m* (*pl:* **-pas**) cloak hanger
**cuelmo** *m* candlewood
**cuellicorto -ta** *adj* short-necked
**cuellierguido -da** *adj* stiff, haughty
**cuellilargo -ga** *adj* long-necked
**cuello** *m* neck; collar; shirt collar; **levantar el cuello** (coll.) to be on one's feet again (*after poverty or misfortune*); **cuello blando** soft collar; **cuello de camisa** shirtband, neckband; **cuello de cisne** gooseneck; **cuello de pajarita** or **cuello doblado** wing collar; piccadilly; **cuello duro** stiff collar; **cuello postizo** detachable collar
**cuenca** *f* wooden bowl; socket (*of eye*); valley; basin, river basin, watershed; **cuenca de captación** catchment area or basin; **cuenca de polvo** dust bowl
**cuencano -na** *adj* (pertaining to) Cuenca; *mf* native or inhabitant of Cuenca, Ecuador
**cuenco** *m* earthen bowl; hollow
**cuenda** *f* end or tie of a skein
**cuenta** *f* count, calculation; account; bill; bead (*of rosary*); check (*in a restaurant*); **abonar en cuenta a** to credit to the account of; **a cuenta** or **a buena cuenta** on account; **adeudar en cuenta a** to charge with, to charge to the account of; **a fin de cuentas** after all, in the last analysis; **ajustar cuentas con** (coll.) to settle accounts with; **caer en la cuenta** (coll.) to see, get the point; to realize; **cargar en cuenta a** to charge with, charge to the account of; **correr por cuenta de** to be under, be under the administration of; **dar buena cuenta de sí** to give a good account of oneself; **dar cuenta de** to use up, destroy; **darle cuenta a uno de una cosa** to give an account of something to someone; **darse cuenta de** (coll.) to realize, become aware of; **de cuenta** of importance; **de cuenta y riesgo de** for the account and risk of; **echar la cuenta sin la huéspeda** (coll.) to reckon without one's host; **en cuenta con** in account with; **en resumidas cuentas** to sum up, in short; **hacer cuenta de** to count on; to esteem; **hacer cuenta que** (coll.) to suppose that, to assume that; **llevar cuentas** to keep accounts; **más de la cuenta** too long; too much; **no tener cuenta con** to have nothing to do with; **perder la cuenta de** to lose account of; **por la cuenta** apparently; **por mi cuenta** to my way of thinking; **tener en cuenta** to take into account, bear in mind; **tener cuenta** to be worth while; **tomar en cuenta** to take into account, give credit for; **tomar por su cuenta** to take upon oneself, assume responsibility for; **vamos a cuentas** (coll.) let's settle this; **cuenta corriente** current account; charge account; checking account; **cuenta de gastos** expense account; **cuenta de la vieja** (coll.) counting on one's fingers; **cuenta en participación** joint account; **cuentas a cobrar** accounts receivable; **cuentas del gran capitán** account overdrawn; **cuentas galanas** (coll.) illusions, idle dreams; **cuentas por pagar** accounts payable; *interj* careful!, look out!
**cuentacorrentista** *mf* depositor, person with a checking account
**cuentadante** *mf* trustee
**cuentagotas** *m* (*pl:* **-tas**) dropper, medicine dropper
**cuentahilos** *m* (*pl:* **-los**) cloth prover, yarn tester; (coll.) pedant, hairsplitter
**cuentakilómetros** *m* (*pl:* **-tros**) (aut.) speedometer, odometer
**cuentamilla** *f* (naut.) log (*chip and line*); speedometer, odometer
**cuentapasos** *m* (*pl:* **-sos**) pedometer, odometer
**cuentero -ra** *adj* (coll.) gossipy; *mf* (coll.) gossip
**cuentezuela** *f* small account
**cuentista** *adj* (coll.) gossipy; *mf* (coll.) gossip; storyteller; story writer, short-story writer
**cuento** *m* story, tale; short story; prop, support; tip, ferrule; count; (coll.) evil story, gossip; (coll.) trouble, disagreement; (archaic) million; **contar cuentos** to tell tales; **degollar el cuento a** (coll.) to cut into the story of; **dejarse de cuentos** (coll.) to come to the point; **despachurrar** or **destripar el cuento a** (coll.) to butt into and finish the

story of; (coll.) to thwart the plans of; **ése es el cuento** (coll.) that's the gist of the matter; **estar en el cuento** to be well-informed; **hablar en el cuento** to speak to the point; **¡puro cuento!** pure fiction!; **quitarse de cuentos** (coll.) to come to the point; **sin cuento** countless; **traer a cuento** to bring up (*a subject*); **venir a cuento** (coll.) to be opportune; **cuento de hadas** fairy tale; **cuento del tío** or **del tocomocho** (Am.) gyp, swindle; **cuento de nunca acabar** (coll.) endless story, endless affair; **cuento de penas** (coll.) hard-luck story; **cuento de viejas** (coll.) wild story, nonsense; old wives' tale; **cuento largo** (fig.) long story

**cuentón -tona** *adj* (coll.) gossipy; *mf* (coll.) gossip

**cuera** *f* (archaic) leather jacket

**cuercíneo -a** *adj* (bot.) quercine

**cuercitrón** *m* (bot.) black oak, quercitron

**cuerda** *f* see **cuerdo**

**cuerdezuela** *f* var. of **cordezuela**

**cuerdo -da** *adj* sane; wise, prudent; *f* cord, rope, string; watch spring; (act or effect of) winding a watch or clock; fishing line; string of galley slaves (*tied together*); hanging (*execution by hanging*); (anat.) cord, tendon; (aer., anat., eng. & geom.) chord; (mus.) string; (mus.) voice (*bass, tenor, contralto, soprano*); (path.) stricture (*of urethra*); **acabarse la cuerda** to run down, e.g., **se acabó la cuerda** the watch ran down; **aflojar la cuerda** to ease up; **apretar la cuerda** to tighten up, become more severe; **bajo cuerda** secretly; underhandedly; **dar cuerda a** to wind (*a watch or clock*); to give free rein to, to give rope to; **por debajo de cuerda** secretly; underhandedly; **sin cuerda** unwound, rundown; **cuerda de piano** piano wire; **cuerda de presos** chain gang; **cuerda de suspensión** shroud, shroud line (*of parachute*); **cuerda de tripa** (mus.) catgut; **cuerda de volatinero** acrobat's rope; **cuerda espinal** (anat.) spinal cord; **cuerda floja** slack rope; **cuerda freno** or **cuerda guía** (aer.) dragrope; **cuerdas vocales** (anat.) vocal cords; **cuerda tesa** tightrope

**cuerezuelo** *m* var. of **corezuelo**

**cuerna** *f* vessel made of a horn; trumpet made of a horn, huntinghorn; antler

**cuernecillo** *m* (bot.) bird's-foot trefoil, babies'-slippers

**cuerno** *m* horn (*curved and extended growth; material*); (anat.) cornu; (ent.) horn (*antenna*); (fig.) horn (*of moon*); (mil.) wing; (mus. & naut.) horn; (vet.) callosity; **en los cuernos del toro** (coll.) in great danger; **levantar hasta los cuernos de la luna** (coll.) to praise to the skies; **saber a cuerno quemado** (coll.) to be unpleasant, be distasteful; **cuerno de Amón** (anat. & pal.) cornu ammonis; **cuerno de caza** huntinghorn; **cuerno de ciervo** hartshorn; (pharm.) hartshorn; **cuerno de la abundancia** horn of plenty; **Cuerno de Oro** Golden Horn; **cuerno de yunque** horn of an anvil; **cuerno inglés** (mus.) English horn; *interj* upon my word!

**cuero** *m* pelt, rawhide; leather; wine bag, wineskin; (coll.) toper; (Am.) whip; **en cueros** or **en cueros vivos** stark naked; **cuero cabelludo** scalp; **cuero de suela** sole leather; **cuero en verde** rawhide

**cuerpear** *vn* (Am.) to duck, to dodge

**cuerpecillo** *m* small body; corselet

**cuerpo** *m* body; substance; bulk; volume (*book*); trunk; waist; build (*of a person*); corpus (*of writings, laws, etc.*); corps, staff; corpse; (mil.) corps; (print.) point; (racing) length; **a cuerpo descubierto** unprotected; manifestly; **dar con el cuerpo en tierra** (coll.) to fall flat on the ground; **de cuerpo entero** full-length (*picture*); **de medio cuerpo** half-length (*picture*); **descubrir el cuerpo** to drop one's guard; to stick one's neck out; **en cuerpo** or **en cuerpo de camisa** in shirt sleeves; **estar de cuerpo presente** to be on view, to lie in state; to be present in person; **falsear el cuerpo** to dodge, to duck; **hacer del cuerpo** (coll.) to have a movement of the bowels; **hurtar el cuerpo** to dodge, to duck; **sacar el cuerpo** (Am.) to dodge, to duck; **tomar cuerpo** to grow (*said, e.g., of a rumor*); **cuerpo a cuerpo** hand to hand; **cuerpo astral** (theosophy) astral body; **cuerpo calloso** (anat.) corpus callosum; **cuerpo celeste** heavenly body; **cuerpo compuesto** (chem.) compound; **cuerpo de administración militar** (mil.) quartermaster corps; **cuerpo de aviación** air corps; **cuerpo de baile** corps de ballet; **cuerpo de bomberos** fire brigade, fire company; **cuerpo de ejército** (mil.) army corps; **cuerpo de guardia** (mil.) guard; (mil.) post of the guard; **cuerpo de inclusión** (path.) inclusion body; **cuerpo del delito** (law) corpus delicti; **cuerpo de redacción** editorial staff; **cuerpo de sanidad** sanitary corps; **cuerpo diplomático** diplomatic corps; **cuerpo extraño** foreign matter (*in an organism*); **cuerpo lúteo** (embryol.) corpus luteum; **cuerpo simple** (chem.) simple substance, element; **cuerpo volante** (mil.) flying column

**cuerudo -da** *adj* (Am.) slow, sluggish; (Am.) heavy-skinned; (Am.) thick-skinned, long-suffering

**cuerva** *f* female rook

**cuervo** *m* (orn.) raven; (*cap.*) *m* (astr.) Raven; **cuervo marino** (orn.) cormorant; **cuervo merendero** (orn.) rook

**cuesco** *m* stone (*of fruit*); millstone (*of olive-oil mill*); (min.) dross, scoria; (coll.) noisy windiness; **cuesco de lobo** (bot.) puffball; **cuesco grande de lobo** (bot.) giant puffball

**cuesta** *f* hill, slope; charity solicitation, charity drive; **a cuestas** on one's back or shoulders; **hacérsele a uno cuesta arriba** to be repugnant to a person; **hacérsele a uno cuesta arriba** + *inf* to find it hard to + *inf;* **ir cuesta abajo** to go downhill, be on the decline; **cuesta abajo** downhill; **cuesta arriba** uphill

**cuestación** *f* charity solicitation, charity drive

**cuestezuela** *f* little hill or slope

**cuestión** *f* question; affair, matter; dispute, quarrel; **andar en cuestiones** to wrangle; **en cuestión de** in a matter of; **cuestión batallona** controversial question, moot question; **cuestión candente** burning question; **cuestión de tormento** torture; **cuestión palpitante** burning question

**cuestionable** *adj* questionable

**cuestionar** *va* to question, controvert, dispute

**cuestionario** *m* questionnaire

**cuesto** *m* hill

**cuestor** *m* quaestor; solicitor for charity

**cuestuario -ria** or **cuestuoso -sa** *adj* lucrative, profitable

**cuestura** *f* quaestorship

**cuetear** *vr* (Am.) to go off, to blow up; (Am.) to get drunk; (Am.) to croak, to kick the bucket

**cueto** *m* fortified eminence; peak, rocky peak

**cueva** *f* cave; cellar; den (*of thieves or wild animals*)

**cuévano** *m* hamper, pannier (*especially for grapes*)

**cueza** *f* or **cuezo** *m* mortar trough

**cufifo -fa** *adj* (Am.) tipsy, fuddled

**cugujada** *f* (orn.) crested lark

**cugulla** *f* cowl

**cuicacoche** *m* (orn.) long-billed thrasher

**cuico -ca** *adj* (Am.) outside, foreign, strange; *m* (Am.) cop

**cuida** *f* girl who takes care of a younger girl (*in school*)

**cuidado** *m* care; concern; worry; **correr al cuidado de** to be the concern of, to be the lookout of; **de cuidado** dangerously; **estar con cuidado** to be worried, to be afraid; **estar de cuidado** (coll.) to be dangerously ill; **pierda Vd. cuidado** don't worry, forget it; **salir de cuidado** to be delivered; **tener cuidado** to be careful; *interj* look out!, beware! **¡cuidado con . . . !** look out for . . . !, beware of . . . !; **¡cuidado me llamo!** (coll.) look out for me!, you'd better behave!

**cuidadora** *f* (Am.) chaperon, nurse, caretaker

**cuidadoso -sa** *adj* careful, watchful, anxious, concerned

**cuidar** *va* to care for, watch over, take care of, take good care of; *vn* **cuidar de** to take care of; **cuidar de** + *inf* to care to + *inf; vr* to take care of oneself (*i.e., one's health, comforts, etc.*); **cuidarse de** to care about (*e.g., what people say*); **cuidarse de** + *inf* to be careful to + *inf;* to be careful about + *ger*
**cuido** *m* care (*e.g., of the house, the garden*)
**cuino** *m* (Am.) short-legged pig
**cuita** *f* trouble, worry, sorrow
**cuitado -da** *adj* troubled, worried; timid, shy
**cuitamiento** *m* timidity, shyness
**cuja** *f* bedstead; lance bucket
**cují** *m* (bot.) huisache
**cujón** *m* var. of **cogujón**
**culantrillo** *m* (bot.) maidenhair; **culantrillo bastardo** or **menor** (bot.) maidenhair spleenwort; **culantrillo de pozo** (bot.) maidenhair, Venus's-hair
**culantro** *m* (bot.) coriander
**culata** *f* haunch, buttock; butt (*of gun*); breech (*of cannon*); (elec.) keeper, yoke (*of magnet*); (mach.) head (*of cylinder*)
**culatada** *f* kick, recoil (*of firearm*)
**culatazo** *m* kick, recoil (*of firearm*); blow with the butt of a gun
**culcusido** *m* rough darning, rough patch
**culebra** *f* (zool.) snake; coil (*of still*); (coll.) sudden disturbance; (coll.) joke, trick; **saber más que las culebras** (coll.) to be foxy; **culebra de anteojos** (zool.) cobra; **culebra de cascabel** (zool.) rattlesnake; **culebra de herradura** (zool.) horseshoe snake
**culebrazo** *m* joke, trick
**culebrear** *vn* to wiggle, to wriggle, to wriggle along; to wind, to meander; to zigzag
**culebreo** *m* wiggling, wriggling; winding, zigzagging
**culebrilla** *f* (path.) tetter; rocking staff (*of loom*); crack (*in barrel of gun*); (bot.) green dragon
**culebrino -na** *adj* snaky, snake-like; *f* (mil.) culverin
**culebrón** *m* large snake; (coll.) crafty fellow; (coll.) evil woman
**culeco -ca** *adj* (Am.) home-loving
**culén** *m* (bot.) basil
**culero -ra** *adj* lazy; *m* diaper; *f* dirt spot in child's underpants; patch on seat of pants or drawers
**culí** *m* (*pl:* **-líes**) coolie
**culiblanco** *m* (orn.) wheatear, stonechat
**culinario -ria** *adj* culinary
**culinegro -gra** *adj* (coll.) black-rumped
**culipandear** *vr* (Am.) to shrink, to draw back in fear
**culminación** *f* culmination; height; (astr.) culmination
**culminante** *adj* culminant, predominant, top
**culminar** *va* to finish; to round out; *vn* to culminate; (astr.) to culminate; **culminar con** to end with, to wind up with
**culo** *m* seat, behind; anus; buttocks (*of animal*); bottom (*e.g., of a jar*); **volver el culo** (coll.) to run away; **culo de mal asiento** (coll.) restless person, fidgety person; **culo de vaso** (coll.) imitation stone
**culombio** *m* (elec.) coulomb
**culón -lona** *adj* big-rumped; *m* (coll.) retired soldier
**culote** *m* base (*of a projectile*); base (*of vacuum tube or incandescent lamp*)
**culpa** *f* blame, guilt, fault; **echar la culpa a uno de una cosa** to put the blame on someone for something; **tener la culpa** to be wrong, to be to blame; **tener la culpa de** to be to blame for; **Vd. tiene la culpa** it's your fault
**culpabilidad** *f* culpability, guiltiness
**culpabilísimo -ma** *adj super* very or most culpable or guilty
**culpable** *adj* culpable, blamable, guilty; *mf* culprit
**culpación** *f* inculpation, blame
**culpado -da** *adj* guilty; *mf* culprit
**culpar** *va* to blame, censure, accuse; *vr* to take the blame
**cultalatiniparla** *f* (hum.) euphuistic speech, macaronic speech
**cultedad** *f* (hum.) affectation, fustian
**culteranismo** *m* euphuism, cultism
**culterano -na** *adj* euphuistic, Gongoristic; *mf* euphuist, cultist
**cultero -ra** *adj* (hum.) high-flown
**cultiparlar** *vn* to speak in a euphuistic manner
**cultiparlista** *adj* euphuistic in speech; *mf* euphuist in speech
**cultipicaño -ña** *adj* mock-euphuistic, burlesquely euphuistic
**cultismo** *m* cultism (*Gongorism*); learned word
**cultivable** *adj* cultivable
**cultivación** *f* cultivation, tilling
**cultivador -dora** *adj* cultivating, farming; *mf* cultivator, farmer; *f* cultivator (*implement*)
**cultivar** *va* to cultivate; (bact.) to culture
**cultivo** *m* cultivation; farming; (bact.) culture; **cultivo de secano** dry farming; **cultivo de tejidos** (bact.) tissue culture
**culto -ta** *adj* cultivated, cultured; euphuistic; (philol.) learned; *m* worship; cult; cultus; **culto a la personalidad** personality cult
**cultor -tora** *adj* worshipful; worshiping; *mf* worshiper
**cultura** *f* culture; cultivation; **cultura física** physical culture; **cultura taurina** training as a bullfighter
**cultural** *adj* cultural
**culturar** *va* to cultivate, to till
**cumarú** *m* (bot.) coumarou
**Cumas** *f* Cumae (*ancient city of Italy*)
**cumbre** *f* summit; (fig.) acme, pinnacle; (naut.) ridgepole; *adj* top, greatest, crowning
**cumbrera** *f* summit; ridgepole, ridgepiece; lintel, doorhead
**cúmel** *m* kümmel
**cumiche** *m* (Am.) baby (*youngest member of a family*)
**cumínico -ca** *adj* (chem.) cumic
**cuminol** *m* (chem.) cuminole, cumaldehyde
**cumís** *m* kumiss
**cúmplase** *m* approval; (Am.) decree
**cumpleaños** *m* (*pl:* **-ños**) birthday
**cumplefaltas** *m* (*pl:* **-tas**) substitute, replacement (*person*)
**cumplidamente** *adv* fully, completely
**cumplidero -ra** *adj* expiring (*by a certain date*); necessary
**cumplido -da** *adj* full, complete; full (*said of a garment*); courteous, correct; *m* attention, courtesy, correctness; compliment; present; **deshacerse en cumplidos** to be overobsequious
**cumplidor -dora** *adj* reliable, trustworthy
**cumplimentar** *va* to compliment, congratulate; to pay a complimentary visit to; to execute (*an order*); to fill out (*a form, a questionnaire*)
**cumplimentero -ra** *adj* (coll.) effusive, full of compliments
**cumplimiento** *m* fulfillment; perfection; compliment; courtesy, correctness; formality; **de** or **por cumplimiento** as a matter of pure formality
**cumplir** *va* to execute, perform, fulfill; to keep (*a promise*); **cumplir años** to have a birthday; **cumplir . . . años** to be . . . years old, to reach the age of . . .; **cumplir una condena** to serve a term; **cumplir a una persona** + *inf* to behoove someone to + *inf*, to be necessary or important for someone to + *inf; vn* to fall due; to expire; to finish one's military service; to keep one's promise, to fulfill one's obligation; **por cumplir** as a mere formality; **cumpla yo, y tiren ellos** do right and fear no man; **cumplir con** to fulfill (*an obligation*); to fulfill one's obligation to; **cumplir por** to act on behalf of; to pay the respects of, e.g., **cumpla Vd. por mí** pay my respects; *vr* to come true, be fulfilled; to fall due; **cúmplase** approved
**cumquibus** *m* (coll.) boodle, wherewithal
**cumucho** *m* (Am.) crowd, heap
**cumular** *va* to cumulate
**cumulativo -va** *adj* cumulative
**cúmulo** *m* heap, cumulus; lot, great many; (meteor.) cumulus, thunderhead
**cumulocirro** *m* (meteor.) cumulo-cirrus
**cumuloestrato** *m* (meteor.) cumulo-stratus
**cúmulonimbo** *m* (meteor.) cumulo-nimbus

**cuna** *f* cradle; foundling home or asylum; (naut. & constr.) cradle; (fig.) cradle (*place of birth or origin*); family, lineage, birth; **cunas** *fpl* cat's cradle
**cunar** *va* to cradle, rock in a cradle
**cundido** *m* provision of olive oil, vinegar, and salt given to shepherds; olive oil, cheese, and honey given to children to make them eat bread
**cundir** *vn* to spread; to swell, puff up; to increase, multiply
**cuneado -da** *adj* (bot.) cuneate
**cunear** *va* to cradle, rock in a cradle; *vr* (coll.) to rock, to swing, to sway
**cuneco -ca** *mf* (Am.) baby (*youngest member of a family*)
**cuneiforme** *adj* cuneiform; (anat.) cuneiform; *m* (anat.) cuneiform; (bot.) cuneate
**cuneo** *m* rocking, swinging; (naut.) rolling
**cúneo** *m* (hist.) cuneus; (mil.) wedge
**cunero -ra** *adj* (taur.) unknown, unpedigreed (*bull*); (pol.) outside (*candidate*); *mf* foundling; *f* cradle rocker (*in royal palace*)
**cuneta** *f* ditch, gutter; catch drain
**cunicultor -tora** *adj* rabbit-raising; *mf* rabbit raiser or breeder
**cunicultura** *f* rabbit raising, rabbit breeding
**cuña** *f* wedge; paving stone in the form of truncated pyramid; (anat.) cuneiform; (print.) quoin; (coll.) backing, support; (coll.) backer; **ser buena cuña** (coll.) to push one's way in, to take up a lot of room
**cuñada** *f* sister-in-law
**cuñadía** *f* affinity, relationship by marriage
**cuñado** *m* brother-in-law
**cuñete** *m* keg; firkin
**cuño** *m* die for stamping coins, medals, etc.; stamp (*made by die*); (mil.) wedge; (fig.) mark, stamp
**cuociente** *m* (archaic) var. of **cociente**
**cuodlibético -ca** *adj* quodlibetic or quodlibetical
**cuodlibeto** *m* quodlibet; (coll.) witticism, joke
**cuota** *f* quota; share; rate; fare; tuition, tuition fee; **cuota de inmigración** immigration quota
**cuotidiano -na** *adj* var. of **cotidiano**
**cupe** *1st sg pret ind of* **caber**
**cupé** *m* coupé (*automobile and carriage*); **cupé comercial** business coupé; **cupé deportivo** sport coupé
**cupido** *m* gallant lover; cupid (*winged baby, symbol of love*); (*cap.*) *m* (myth.) Cupid
**cupla** *f* coupling; (mech.) couple; **cupla motora** (mech.) torque
**cuplé** *m* popular song
**cupletista** *f* popular singer (*woman*)
**cupo** *m* quota, share; *3d sg pret ind of* **caber**
**cupón** *m* coupon
**cupón-respuesta** *m* reply coupon
**cupresáceo -a** or **cupresíneo -a** *adj* (bot.) cupressineous
**cupresino -na** *adj* (poet.) cypress
**cúprico -ca** *adj* coppery; (chem.) cupric
**cuprífero -ra** *adj* cupriferous
**cuprita** *f* (mineral.) cuprite
**cuproníquel** *m* cupronickel
**cuproso -sa** *adj* (chem.) cuprous
**cúpula** *f* (arch., anat. & nav.) cupola; (arch.) dome; (bot. & zool.) cupule; **cúpula de arena** (rail.) sand dome; **cúpula de toma de vapor** (rail.) steam dome
**cupulífero -ra** *adj* (bot.) cupuliferous
**cupulino** *m* (arch.) cupola (*lantern over dome*)
**cuquería** *f* craftiness, slyness; (coll.) niceness, cuteness
**cuquillo** *m* (orn.) cuckoo
**cura** *m* curate; parish priest; (coll.) priest; **este cura** (coll.) I; *f* cure; care, treatment (*of a wound*); **no tener cura** (coll.) to be hopeless, be incorrigible; **ponerse en cura** to undergo treatment; **primera cura** first aid; **tener cura** to be curable; **cura de aguas** water cure; **cura de almas** care of souls; **cura de reposo** rest cure; **cura de urgencia** first aid
**curabilidad** *f* curability
**curable** *adj* curable
**curaca** *m* (Am.) boss, chief
**curación** *f* treatment; healing; cure, curing
**curadillo** *m* (ichth.) codfish
**curado -da** *adj* dry, hardened
**curador -dora** *mf* caretaker, overseer; healer; curer; (law) guardian
**curaduría** *f* (law) guardianship
**cúralotodo** *m* (*pl:* **-do**) var. of **sánalotodo**
**curalle** *m* (falc.) casting
**curandería** *f* or **curanderismo** *m* quackery
**curandero -ra** *mf* quack, healer
**curar** *va* to treat (*a sick person*); to heal; to cure (*a disease, an evil, a sick person; meat, fish, hides, etc.*); to season (*wood*); to see (*someone*) through an illness; to dress (*a wound*); *vn* to cure; to recover; **curar de** to recover from; to take care of; to care about, to mind, to pay attention to; *vr* to take treatment; to cure oneself; to cure; to recover; to season; (Am.) to get drunk; **curarse de** to recover from, to get over; **curarse en salud** to be forewarned
**curare** *m* curare
**curarizar** §76 *va* to curarize
**curasao** *m* curaçao (*liqueur*)
**curatela** *f* var. of **curaduría**
**curativo -va** *adj & f* curative
**curato** *m* curacy; parish
**curazao** *m* curaçao (*liqueur*); (*cap.*) *f* Curaçao
**curbaril** *m* (bot.) courbaril
**cúrcuma** *f* turmeric, curcuma root; curcumin
**curcuncho -cha** *adj* (Am.) stooped, hunchbacked; (Am.) annoyed, upset
**curcusilla** *f* var. of **rabadilla**
**curda** *f* see **curdo**
**Curdistán, el** Kurdistan
**curdo -da** *adj* Kurdish; *mf* Kurd; *m* Kurdish (*language*); *f* (coll.) drunkenness
**cureña** *f* gun carriage; gunstock in the rough; stay of crossbow; **a cureña rasa** (fort.) without a parapet, without breastwork; (coll.) without shelter
**cureñaje** *m* gun carriages
**curesca** *f* waste left after combing cloth
**cureta** *f* (surg.) curette
**curetaje** *m* (surg.) curettage
**curia** *f* (hist.) curia; care, carefulness; (law) bar; **Curia romana** Roman Curia
**curial** *adj* curial; *m* attorney; court clerk
**curialesco -ca** *adj* legalistic, hairsplitting (*style, etc.*)
**curiana** *f* (ent.) cockroach
**curie** *m* (phys.) curie
**curiel** *m* (Am.) guinea pig
**curieterapia** *f* curietherapy
**Curiles** *fpl* Kurile Islands
**curio** *m* (chem.) curium
**curiosear** *va* (coll.) to pry into; *vn* (coll.) to snoop, to pry around; (coll.) to browse around
**curioseo** *m* (coll.) snooping, prying; (coll.) browsing
**curiosidad** *f* curiosity; curio; neatness, cleanness; care, diligence
**curioso -sa** *adj* curious; odd, rare, quaint; neat, clean, tidy; careful, diligent; (Am.) cute; *mf* busybody
**Curlandia** *f* Courland
**curricán** *m* (fishing) spinning tackle; (Am.) plug
**currinche** *m* cub reporter; (coll.) hit playwright
**curro -rra** *adj* (coll.) sporty, flashy
**curruca** *f* (orn.) whitethroat; **curruca de cabeza negra** (orn.) blackcap; **curruca de los pantanos** (orn.) marsh warbler
**currutaco -ca** *adj* (coll.) dudish, sporty; *m* (coll.) dude, sport
**cursado -da** *adj* skilled, versed; taken (*as a course in school*)
**cursante** *adj* attending; *mf* student
**cursar** *va* to haunt, to frequent; to devote oneself to; to take, to attend; to study; to facilitate; to send, to circulate; to forward
**cursería** *f* cheapness, flashiness, vulgarity; (coll.) group of cheap flashy people
**cursi** *adj* (coll.) cheap, vulgar, flashy
**cursilería** *f* var. of **cursería**
**cursillista** *mf* student taking a short course
**cursillo** *m* short course (*in school*); short series of lectures
**cursivo -va** *adj* cursive; *f* cursive; italics
**curso** *m* course; price, quotation, current rate;

circulation, currency; program, series; textbook; **cursos** *mpl* loose bowels; **dar curso a** to forward; to give course to (*e.g., tears*); **en curso de impresión** in press; **curso académico** academic year; **curso legal** legal tender
**cursor** *m* (elec.) sliding contact; (mach.) slide; indicator (*of slide rule*); **cursor de procesiones** marshal
**curtación** *f* (astr.) curtation
**curtido** *m* tanning; tanning bark; **curtidos** *mpl* tanned leather; (Am.) pickles
**curtidor** *m* tanner
**curtidura** *f* tanning
**curtiduría** *f* tannery
**curtiembre** *f* (Am.) tannery
**curtiente** *adj* tanning; *m* tanning material
**curtimiento** *m* tanning; tan
**curtir** *va* to tan (*hides*); to tan, to sunburn; to harden, to inure; to season or harden by exposure to the weather; **estar curtido en** to be skilled or expert in; *vr* to become tanned, become sunburned; to become hardened, become inured; to become weather-beaten
**curubu** *m* (bot.) passionflower (*of Colombia*)
**curuca** *f* (orn.) barn owl, screech owl
**curucú** *m* (orn.) quetzal; (Am.) snake-bite poisoning
**curucucú** *m* (Am.) snake-bite poisoning
**curuguá** *m* (bot.) cassabanana
**curuja** *f* var. of **curuca**
**curul** *adj* curule
**curupay** *m* (bot.) curupay
**cururú** *m* (*pl:* **-rúes**) (zool.) Surinam toad
**curva** *f* see **curvo**
**curvadura** *f* (arch.) curvature of an arch or vault; (med.) painful exhaustion
**curvatón** *m* slight curve; (naut.) gusset, gusset stay
**curvatubos** *m* (*pl:* **-bos**) pipe bender
**curvatura** or **curvidad** *f* curvature
**curvilíneo -a** *adj* curvilinear; (coll.) curvaceous (*woman*)
**curvímetro** *m* curvometer
**curvo -va** *adj* curve, curved, bent; *f* curve, bend; (rail.) crossover; **curva de frecuencias** (statistics) frequency curve; **curva de nivel** contour line; **curva isobárica** (meteor.) isobar
**cusca** *f* (Am.) jag, drunk; (Am.) slattern, slut
**cuscurro** *m* end crust, crouton
**cuscús** *m* var. of **alcuzcuz**
**cúscuta** *f* (bot.) dodder
**cusir** *va* (coll.) var. of **corcusir**
**cusita** *adj & mf* (Bib.) Cushite
**cusma** *f* var. of **cuzma**
**cúspide** *f* peak (*of a mountain*); cusp, tip, apex; (anat.) cusp (*of a tooth*); (anat.) cuspid (*tooth*); (geom.) vertex (*of cone or pyramid*); (fig.) apex, top, extreme
**cuspídeo -a** *adj* cuspidate
**custodia** *f* custody, care; guard (*in charge of a prisoner*); shrine; (eccl.) monstrance; **custodia preventiva** protective custody
**custodiar** *va* to guard, watch over
**custodio** *m* guard, custodian
**cusumbe** *m* or **cusumbo** *m* var. of **coatí**
**cususa** *f* (Am.) rum
**cutáneo -a** *adj* cutaneous
**cúter** *m* (naut.) cutter (*sailboat with one mast*)
**cutí** *m* (*pl:* **-tíes**) bedtick, ticking
**cuticolor** *adj* cuticolor
**cutícula** *f* (anat. & bot.) cuticle
**cuticular** *adj* cuticular
**cutina** *f* (biochem.) cutin
**cutinización** *f* (bot.) cutinization
**cutio** *m* work, labor
**cutir** *va* to knock, to strike
**cutirreacción** *f* (med. & vet.) cutireaction
**cutis** *m & f* skin (*of human body, especially the face*); **cutis anserina** goose flesh
**cutitis** *f* (path.) dermatitis
**cutización** *f* (physiol.) cutization
**cutral** *m* old worn-out ox; *f* old cow that no longer bears
**cutre** *adj* miserly, stingy; *mf* miser, skinflint
**cuy** *m* (Am.) cavy
**cuyo -ya** *adj rel* whose; *m* (coll.) beau, lover
**cuz** *interj* here, here! (*to call a dog*)
**cuzcuz** *m* var. of **alcuzcuz**
**cuzo** *m* (prov.) doggie
**cuzma** *f* (Am.) sleeveless shirt or tunic of palm, cork, or wool fiber (*worn by South American Indians*)
**cuzqueño -ña** *adj* (pertaining to) Cuzco; *mf* native or inhabitant of Cuzco
**CV** abr. of **caballo de vapor**
**c/v** or **c/vta.** abr. of **cuenta de venta**
**czar** *m* var. of **zar**
**czarevitz** *m* var. of **zarevitz**
**czariano -na** *adj* var. of **zariano**
**czarina** *f* var. of **zarina**

# Ch

**Ch, ch** *f* fourth letter of the Spanish alphabet
**cha** *m* (*pl:* **chaes**) (Am.) tea
**chabacanada** or **chabacanería** *f* crudeness, vulgarity
**chabacano -na** *adj* awkward, clumsy; crude, cheap; *m* (Am.) apricot
**chabola** *f* hut, shack, shanty
**chacal** *m* (zool.) jackal
**chacanear** *va* (Am.) to spur, to goad
**chacarero -ra** *mf* (Am.) farm laborer, field worker
**chacarrachaca** *f* (coll.) racket, wrangling, row, brawl
**chacate** *m* (bot.) chacate
**chacina** *f* dried beef; pork seasoned for sausages
**chacó** *m* (*pl:* **-cós**) shako
**chacolí** *m* (*pl:* **-líes**) chacolí (*sour wine of Vizcaya, Spain*)
**chacolotear** *vn* to clatter (*said of loose horseshoe*)
**chacoloteo** *m* clattering (*of loose horseshoe*)
**chacona** *f* (mus.) chaconne
**chaconada** *f* jaconet (*thin cotton fabric*)
**chaconero -ra** *mf* chaconne writer or dancer
**chacota** *f* fun, noisy laughter, racket; **echar a chacota** (coll.) to sneer at; **hacer chacota de** (coll.) to make fun of
**chacotear** *vn* to laugh and make a lot of noise
**chacoteo** *m* noisy laughter
**chacotero -ra** *adj* loud-laughing; *mf* loud or noisy laugher, noisemaker
**chacra** *f* (Am.) small farm; (Am.) field marked off for cultivation
**chacuaco -ca** *adj* (Am.) ugly, repugnant; (Am.) crude, boorish; *m* (Am.) silver-smelting furnace; (Am.) cigar butt
**chacha** *f* (coll.) lass; (coll.) nursemaid
**chachalaca** *f* (orn.) chachalaca; (Am.) chatterbox (*person*)
**chachalaquero -ra** *adj* (Am.) loquacious, talkative
**cháchara** *f* (coll.) chatter, idle talk; **cháchara****s** *fpl* junk
**chacharear** *vn* (coll.) to chatter, to prate
**chacharero -ra** *adj* (coll.) chattering; *mf* (coll.) chatterbox
**chacho** *m* (coll.) boy, lad
**chafaldete** *m* (naut.) clew line
**chafaldita** *f* (coll.) jest, banter
**chafalditero -ra** *adj* (coll.) jesting, bantering
**chafalmejas** *mf* (*pl:* **-jas**) (coll.) dauber (*poor painter*)
**chafalonía** *f* old plate
**chafallar** *va* (coll.) to botch
**chafallo** *m* (coll.) botch, poor patch
**chafallón -llona** *adj* (coll.) botching; *mf* botcher
**chafandín** *m* pompous empty head
**chafar** *va* to flatten; to wrinkle, to rumple, to muss; (coll.) to cut short
**chafariz** *m* (*pl:* **-rices**) top of monumental fountain from which water spouts
**chafarotazo** *m* blow or stroke with a cutlass
**chafarote** *m* cutlass; (coll.) sword
**chafarrinada** *f* blot, stain, spot; daub (*poor painting*)
**chafarrinar** *va* to blot, stain, spot
**chafarrinón** *m* blot, stain, spot; **echar un chafarrinón a** (coll.) to be rude to; (coll.) to throw mud at
**chaflán** *m* chamfer; (arch.) cant
**chaflanar** *va* to chamfer
**chagrén** *m* or **chagrín** *m* shagreen
**chah** *m* shah
**chaira** *f* steel (*for sharpening knives*); shoemaker's blade
**chajá** *m* (*pl:* **-jaes**) (orn.) screamer, crested screamer
**chal** *m* shawl
**chalado -da** *adj* (coll.) addlebrained; (coll.) madly in love
**chalán -lana** *adj* horse-dealing; *mf* horse dealer; trader; (Am.) broncobuster, horsebreaker; *f* scow, flatboat, barge
**chalanear** *va* to drive (*deals*) shrewdly; (Am.) to break (*horses*); *vn* to dicker, to horse-trade
**chalaneo** *m* shrewd dealing, horse trading
**chalanería** *f* shrewdness in dealing, horse trading
**chalanesco -ca** *adj* horse-trading, sharp-dealing
**chalar** *vr* (dial.) to lose one's head; **chalarse por** (dial.) to become mad or crazy about
**chalate** *m* (Am.) skinny old nag
**chalaza** *f* (bot. & embryol.) chalaza
**chaleco** *m* vest, waistcoat; **chaleco salvavidas** life preserver
**chalet** *m* (*pl:* **chaletes**) chalet; villa
**chalí** *m* challie or challis
**chalina** *f* bow tie with long ends, scarf
**chalón** *m* shalloon
**chalote** *m* (bot.) shallot, scallion
**chalupa** *f* (naut.) shallop, small two-master; lifeboat; (Am.) corncake
**chalupero** *m* boatman, skipper; rower
**chama** *f* (slang) swapping, trading
**chamaco -ca** *mf* (Am.) urchin, youngster, kid
**chamada** *f* brushwood; (dial.) streak of bad luck
**chamagoso -sa** *adj* dirty, filthy; common, tawdry; (Am.) botched
**chamal** *m* (Am.) chiripá; (bot.) edible Dioön
**chamán** *m* shaman
**chamar** *va* (slang) to swap
**chamara** or **chamarasca** *f* brushwood; brush fire
**chamarilear** *va* var. of **chamar**
**chamarilero -ra** *mf* junk dealer, old-clothes dealer
**chamarillero -ra** *mf* junk dealer, old-clothes dealer; *m* gambler
**chamarillón -llona** *mf* poor player (*at cards*)
**chamariz** *m* (*pl:* **-rices**) (orn.) greenfinch
**chamarón** *m* (orn.) bottle tit, long-tailed titmouse
**chamarra** *f* sheepskin jacket
**chamarreta** *f* loose jacket
**chamba** *f* (coll.) fluke, scratch (*e.g., in billiards*)
**chambelán** *m* chamberlain; (Am.) atomizer, spray
**chambergo -ga** *adj* Schomberg (*regiment, uniform, etc., which existed in Madrid at time of Charles II*); *m* broad-brimmed soft hat; (orn.) reedbird; *f* narrow silk ribbon
**chamberguilla** *f* (dial.) narrow silk ribbon
**chamberí** *adj* (*pl:* **-ríes**) (Am.) showy, flashy
**chamberinada** *f* (Am.) ostentation, flashiness
**chambilla** *f* stone wall surmounted by iron grating
**chambón -bona** *adj* (coll.) clumsy, awkward (*in games*); unskillful; lucky; *mf* (coll.) foozler, bungler
**chambonada** *f* (coll.) clumsiness; (coll.) foozle; fluke, stroke of luck
**chambonear** *vn* to play awkwardly, to foozle
**chamborote** *adj* (Am.) long-nosed
**chambra** *f* house blouse or tunic, negligee
**chambrana** *f* trim (*around a door, window, etc.*); (Am.) shouting, uproar
**chamburgo** *m* (Am.) pool, stagnant water
**chamburo** *m* (bot.) papaw tree
**chamicera** *f* strip of burned woodland
**chamico** *m* (bot.) jimson weed, thorn apple; **dar chamico a** (Am.) to bewitch, seduce

**chamiza** *f* (bot.) chamiso; brush used as firewood
**chamizo** *m* half-burned tree; half-burned log or stick; chamiso-thatched hut; (coll.) hangout, joint
**chamorra** *f* see **chamorro**
**chamorrar** *va* (coll.) to shear (*the head*)
**chamorro -rra** *adj* (coll.) with head shorn, with hair cut; *f* (coll.) shorn head
**champán** *m* sampan; champagne (*wine*)
**champaña** *m* champagne (*wine*); **la Champaña** Champagne
**champañizar** **§76** *va* to make sparkling, make effervescent, champagnize
**champar** *va* (coll.) to talk meanly to, to remind (*someone*) of a favor
**champiñón** *m* mushroom
**champú** *m* (*pl:* **-púes**) shampoo
**champurrar** *va* (coll.) to mix, mix in
**chamuscado -da** *adj* (coll.) touched, infected (*with a vice or passion*)
**chamuscar** **§86** *va* to singe, to scorch; (Am.) to undersell
**chamusco** *m* singe, singeing
**chamusquina** *f* singe, singeing; (coll.) quarrel, row; **oler a chamusquina** (coll.) to look like a fight; (coll.) to be heresy
**chanada** *f* (coll.) trick, deceit
**chanca** *f* var. of **chancla**
**chancar** **§86** *va* (Am.) to crush (*stones*)
**chancear** *vn & vr* to joke, to jest
**chancero -ra** *adj* joking, jesting, merry
**chanciller** *m* chancellor
**chancillería** *f* chancery (*court of equity*)
**chancla** *f* worn-out shoe, shoe worn down at the heel; slipper
**chancleta** *f* slipper; **en chancleta** in slippers, in shoes without heels; *mf* (coll.) good-for-nothing
**chancletazo** *m* blow with slipper
**chancletear** *vn* to go about in slippers, to go about clattering one's slippers
**chancleteo** *m* clatter of slippers
**chanclo** *m* clog (*shoe with wooden sole*); overshoe, rubber
**chanco** *m* stilt
**chancro** *m* (path.) chancre
**chancroso -sa** *adj* chancrous
**cháncharras máncharras** *fpl* (coll.) subterfuge; **andar en cháncharras máncharras** (coll.) to beat about the bush
**chanchería** *f* (Am.) pork butcher's shop
**chancho -cha** *adj* (Am.) dirty, piggish; *m* (Am.) pig
**chanchullero -ra** *adj* (coll.) crooked; *mf* (coll.) crooked person
**chanchullo** *m* (coll.) crookedness; **andar en chanchullos** (coll.) to be up to some crookedness
**chanfaina** *f* stew of chopped lungs
**chanflón -flona** *adj* misshapen, crude
**changador** *m* (Am.) public errand boy
**changarro** *m* (Am.) little shop
**chango -ga** *adj* (Am.) quick, skilful; (Am.) sporty; (Am.) dull, stupid; *mf* (Am.) house servant; (Am.) monkey
**changote** *m* (found.) bloom
**changüí** *m* (*pl:* **-güíes**) (coll.) trick, deception; (slang) idle talk; **dar changüí a** (coll.) to trick
**chantaje** *m* blackmail
**chantajista** *mf* blackmailer
**chantar** *va* to put on; to stick, push, or force on; (coll.) to tell (*someone something*) straight from the shoulder; *vr* to put on, to clap on (*e.g., one's hat*)
**chantillón** *m* pattern, templet
**chanto** *m* (prov.) flagstone
**chantre** *m* cantor, precentor
**chantría** *f* precentorship
**chanza** *f* joke, jest; **de chanza** jokingly, in fun
**chanzoneta** *f* chansonnette; (coll.) joke, jest
**chanzonetero** *m* chansonnier
**chao** *m* chow (*dog*)
**chapa** *f* sheet, plate; veneer; flush (*on cheek*); rouge; (coll.) judgment, good sense; (Am.) lock; **chapas** *fpl* (game of) tossing coins; **chapa de patente** or **chapa matrícula** (aut.) license plate
**chapado -da** *adj* lined or covered with sheets or sheeting (*of metal*); veneered; nice, fine; **chapado a la antigua** old-fashioned
**chapalear** *vn* to splash; to clatter (*said of loose horseshoe*)
**chapaleo** *m* splashing; clatter (*of loose horseshoe*)
**chapaleta** *f* (hyd.) clack valve
**chapaleteo** *m* splash, splashing (*of water on the shore*); patter (*of rain*)
**chapapote** *m* (Am.) tar; chapapote, Mexican asphalt
**chapar** *va* to cover or line with metal sheeting; to veneer; to let go, to smack down (*something disagreeable*); to plate (*with gold or silver*)
**chaparra** *f* (bot.) kermes oak; chaparral (*thicket*)
**chaparrada** *f* downpour
**chaparral** *m* chaparral
**chaparrear** *vn* to rain hard, to pour
**chaparreras** *fpl* (Am.) chaps (*cowboy trousers*)
**chaparro** *m* (bot.) chaparro; chaparral (*thicket*); short, chubby person
**chaparrón** *m* downpour; (Am.) shower (*e.g., of insults*)
**chapatal** *m* mudhole
**chapeado -da** *adj* lined or covered with sheets or sheeting (*of metal*); veneered; *m* veneer; plywood
**chapear** *va* to cover or line with metal sheeting; to veneer; *vn* to clatter (*said of a loose horseshoe*)
**chapecar** **§86** *va* (Am.) to braid, to plait; (Am.) to string (*garlic, onions, etc.*)
**chapeo** *m* (coll.) hat
**chapera** *f* (mas.) board with wooden cleats (*for climbing*)
**chapería** *f* sheet metal; sheet-metal work
**chaperón** *m* (archaic) chaperon (*hood*)
**chapeta** *f* red spot on the cheek
**chapetón -tona** *adj* (Am.) awkward, green; *mf* (obs.) newly arrived and green Spanish soldier (*in Latin America*); (archaic) Spanish or European new arrival (*in Latin America*); *m* (Am.) silver disk (*on riding harness*)
**chapetonada** *f* (Am.) greenhornism (*of a foreigner*); (obs.) illness of Spanish or European new arrivals in Latin America (*from change of climate*)
**chapín -pina** *adj* (Am.) clubfooted; *m* chopine (*clog worn especially by women*); sandal, slipper, dance slipper; (bot.) lady's-slipper; (ichth.) trunkfish
**chapinazo** *m* blow with a clog
**chápiro** *m* (Am.) silver disk (*on riding harness*); **¡por vida del chápiro!**, **¡por vida del chápiro verde!** or **¡voto al chápiro!** (coll.) good grief!
**chapista** *mf* tinsmith; (aut.) body and fender repairman; **chapista carrocero** (aut.) body and fender repairman
**chapistería** *f* tinsmithing, sheet-metal work; body and fender repair shop
**chapitel** *m* (arch.) spire; (arch.) capital; (naut.) agate socket (*of needle*)
**chapitón -tona** *adj* (Am.) new (*in a job*); *mf* (Am.) novice; (Am.) newly arrived European in South America
**chapitonada** *f* (Am.) inexperience
**chapó** *m* (*pl:* **-pós**) four-hand pool or billiards; four-hand match
**chapodar** *va* to trim, to clear of branches
**chapodo** *m* branch trimmed from a tree
**chapón** *m* large blot (*of ink*)
**chapona** *f* house blouse or tunic
**chapotear** *va* to moisten, to sponge; *vn* to splash
**chapoteo** *m* sponging; splashing
**chapucear** *va* to botch, bungle
**chapucería** *f* botch, bungle, patchwork
**chapucero -ra** *adj* rough, crude; bungling, clumsy; cheating; *mf* bungler; amateur, dabster; *m* blacksmith; junk dealer
**chapulín** *m* (Am.) grasshopper
**chapurrar** *va* to jabber (*a language*); to jumble (*in conversation*); (coll.) to mix, to mix in
**chapurrear** *va* to jabber (*a language*); *vn* to jabber
**chapurreo** *m* jabbering

**chapuz** *m* (*pl:* **-puces**) duck, ducking (*sudden dip under water*); botch; bungling
**chapuza** *f* botch, bungle
**chapuzar** **§76** *va, vn & vr* to duck
**chapuzón** *m* ducking (*sudden dip under water*)
**chaqué** *m* cutaway coat, morning coat
**chaquehue** *m* (Am.) corn grits
**chaqueta** *f* jacket
**chaquete** *m* backgammon
**chaquetudo** *m* (ent.) potato beetle
**chaquira** *f* (Am.) glass bead
**charabán** *m* char-à-banc
**charada** *f* charade
**charadrio** *m* var. of **alcaraván**
**charamusca** *f* (Am.) candy twist; **charamuscas** *fpl* (Am.) brushwood, firewood
**charanga** *f* (mus.) brass band
**charango** *m* (Am.) bandurria (*kind of lute*)
**charanguero -ra** *adj* rough, crude; bungling, clumsy; *mf* bungler; *m* (prov.) peddler; (prov.) small coast-trading boat
**charca** *f* pool
**charcal** *m* puddly spot
**charco** *m* puddle; **pasar el charco** (coll.) to cross the pond (*the ocean*)
**charla** *f* (coll.) chat, chatting; (coll.) talk, lecture; (coll.) chatter, prattle; (orn.) missel thrush; **charla de chimenea** fireside chat
**charlador -dora** *adj* (coll.) prattling, garrulous; (coll.) gossiping; *mf* (coll.) prattler, chatterbox; (coll.) gossip
**charladuría** *f* prattling, small talk; gossip
**charlar** *vn* (coll.) to chat; (coll.) to chatter, to prattle
**charlatán -tana** *adj* prattling, garrulous; gossiping; charlatan; *mf* prattler, chatterbox; gossip; charlatan
**charlatanear** *vn* (coll.) to chatter, to prattle; (coll.) to gossip
**charlatanería** *f* loquacity, garrulity
**charlatanismo** *m* loquacity, garrulity; charlatanism
**charlotear** *vn* (coll.) to chatter, to prattle; (coll.) to gossip
**charloteo** *m* (coll.) chatter, prattle; (coll.) gossip
**charneca** *f* (bot.) mastic tree
**charnecal** *m* growth of mastic trees
**charnela** *f* hinge; (mach.) knuckle; (zool.) hinge (*of bivalve shell*); **charnela de dirección** (aut.) steering knuckle
**charneta** *f* (coll.) var. of **charnela**
**charol** *m* varnish, polish; patent leather; (Am.) painted metal tray; **calzarse las de charol** (Am.) to hit the jack pot; **darse charol** (coll.) to brag, to blow one's own horn
**charola** *f* (Am.) painted metal tray; (Am.) large eye, ugly big eye
**charolado -da** *adj* shiny
**charolar** *va* to varnish, polish, enamel, japan
**charolista** *mf* varnisher, polisher, gilder
**charpa** *f* pistol belt; sling (*to support hurt arm*)
**charquear** *va* (Am.) to jerk (*beef*); (Am.) to slash, to cut to pieces; (Am.) to malign, vilify
**charquetal** *m* puddly spot
**charqui** *m* (Am.) jerked beef
**charrada** *f* boorishness; country dance; (coll.) overfancy work or adornment
**charrán** *m* rascal
**charranada** *f* piece of rascality
**charranear** *vn* to be a rascal
**charranería** *f* rascality
**charrasca** *f* (hum.) dangling or trailing sword; (coll.) folding knife
**charrascal** *m* var. of **carrascal**
**charrasco** *m* (hum.) dangling or trailing sword
**charreada** *f* (Am.) rodeo
**charrería** *f* overfancy work or adornment
**charretera** *f* epaulet; garter; buckle (*of garter*); (coll.) shoulder pad (*for carrying water*)
**charro -rra** *adj* coarse, ill-bred; of Salamanca; (coll.) showy, flashy, loud; (coll.) overfancy; **estar** or **ir bien charro** (coll.) to be flashily dressed; *mf* peasant, rustic; peasant of province of Salamanca; *m* (Am.) Mexican horseman in fancy riding costume
**charrúa** *f* (naut.) small tugboat
**chartreuse** *m* chartreuse
**chasca** *f* see **chasco**
**chascar** **§86** *va* to click (*the tongue*); to crunch (*food*); to swallow; *vn* to crack (*to break with a sharp noise*)
**chascarrillo** *m* (coll.) snappy story
**chascás** *m* (mil.) schapska
**chasco -ca** *adj* (Am.) crinkly; crinkly-haired; *m* trick, joke; disappointment; **dar un chasco a** to play a trick on; **llevarse chasco** to be disappointed; *f* small branches cleaned from a tree
**chascón -cona** *adj* (Am.) disheveled; (Am.) bushy-haired
**chasis** *m* (*pl:* **-sis**) (aut. & rad.) chassis; (phot.) plateholder
**chasponazo** *m* scratch or dent made by a grazing bullet
**chasquear** *va* to crack (*e.g., a whip*); to play a trick on; to disappoint; to fail to keep (*a promise*); *vn* to crack (*to break with a sharp noise*); (Am.) to chatter (*said of teeth*); *vr* to come to naught; to become disappointed
**chasqui** *m* (Am.) Indian courier
**chasquido** *m* swish, crack of a whip; crack, cracking sound (*of something breaking*)
**chata** *f* see **chato**
**chatarra** *f* slag containing some iron; junk, scrap iron; **chatarra de acero** scrap steel
**chatarraje** *m* junk, scrap iron
**chatarrería** *f* junk yard
**chatarrero -ra** *mf* junk dealer, scrap-iron dealer
**chatedad** *f* (coll.) flatness
**chato -ta** *adj* flat; flat-nosed; blunt; (Am.) commonplace, humdrum; *m* (coll.) wine cup, wineglass; *f* scow, barge; bedpan; flatcar
**chatón** *m* large stone (*in its setting*)
**chatre** *adj* (Am.) all dressed up; *m* (Am.) short skirt
**chau** *interj* (Am.) so long!
**chaucha** *f* (Am.) small change, chicken feed; (Am.) bean; (Am.) early potato; (Am.) poverty; *adj* (Am.) poor, miserable
**chauche** *m* red-lead floor paint
**chaul** *m* blue Chinese silk
**chauvinismo** *m* chauvinism
**chauvinista** *adj* chauvinistic; *mf* chauvinist
**chaval -vala** *adj* (coll.) young; *m* (coll.) lad; *f* (coll.) lass
**chavasca** *f* var. of **chasca**
**chaveta** *f* (mach.) cotter, cotter pin, forelock; (mach.) key; **perder la chaveta (por)** (coll.) to go out of one's head (for)
**chavetera** *f* (mach.) keyway, key seat
**chavo** *m* (Am.) cent; (Am.) 350 sq. meters
**chayote** *m* (bot.) chayote (*plant and fruit*)
**chayotera** *f* (bot.) chayote (*plant*)
**chaza** *f* (sport) stopping the ball; (sport) mark where ball was stopped; **hacer chazas** to walk on the hind feet (*said of a horse*)
**chazador** *m* (sport) stop (*player*); (sport) marker
**chazar** **§76** *va* (sport) to stop or interfere with (*the ball*); (sport) to mark (*the spot where ball was stopped*)
**che** *interj* (Am.) hey!, say!
**checo -ca** *adj & mf* Czech; *m* Czech (*language*); (*cap.*) *f* Checa (*Soviet secret police*)
**checoeslovaco -ca** *adj & mf* Czecho-Slovak or Czecho-Slovakian
**Checoeslovaquia** *f* Czecho-Slovakia
**checoslovaco -ca** *adj & mf* Czecho-Slovak or Czecho-Slovakian
**Checoslovaquia** *f* Czecho-Slovakia
**chechén** *m* (Am.) poison ivy
**chécheres** *mpl* (Am.) trinkets, junk
**Chefú** Chefoo
**cheira** *f* var. of **chaira**
**chelín** *m* shilling; schilling
**chepa** *f* (coll.) hunch, hump
**cheque** *m* check; **cheque certificado** certified check; **cheque de viajeros** traveler's check
**Cherburgo** *f* Cherbourg
**cherna** *f* or **cherno** *m* (ichth.) giant perch, dusky perch; (ichth.) grouper
**cherva** *f* (bot.) castor-oil plant
**cheurón** *m* (her.) chevron; (arch.) chevron molding
**cheuronado -da** *adj* (her.) chevrony

**chía** *f* (hist.) short mourning cloak; (hist.) cowl worn as a mark of nobility; (bot.) chia (*any of several species of Salvia of Mexico*); chia seed; chia (*beverage*)
**chibalete** *m* (print.) composing cabinet
**chibuquí** *m* (*pl:* **-quíes**) chibouk
**chicada** *f* herd of sickly and underdeveloped sheep; childishness, childish act
**chicalote** *m* (bot.) Mexican poppy
**chicana** *f* baffle plate; (Am.) chicanery; (Am.) quibbling
**chicaneada** *f* (Am.) piece of chicanery
**chicaneo** *m* (Am.) chicane, chicanery
**chicanería** *f* (Am.) chicanery
**chicanero -ra** *mf* (Am.) chicaner; (Am.) shyster lawyer
**chicle** *m* chicle (*gumlike substance*); chewing gum; **chicle de burbuja, chicle de globo,** or **chicle hinchable** bubble gum
**chiclear** *vn* to chew gum
**chicloso -sa** *adj* (Am.) gummy, sticky
**chico -ca** *adj* small, little; *mf* child, youngster; *m* lad, little fellow; (coll.) young fellow; (coll.) my boy, old man; *f* lass, little girl; (coll.) my dear
**chicoco -ca** *mf* (coll.) husky youngster; (Am.) dwarf
**chicolear** *vn* (coll.) to make compliments; *vr* (Am.) to enjoy oneself
**chicoleo** *m* (coll.) compliment (*to a woman*)
**chicoria** *f* (bot.) chicory
**chicorro** *m* (coll.) husky guy
**chicorrotico -ca, chicorrotillo -lla** or **chicorrotito -ta** *adj* (coll.) small, tiny
**chicorrotín -tina** *adj* (coll.) small, tiny; *mf* (coll.) tiny child, tot
**chicotazo** *m* (Am.) lash, blow with a whip
**chicote -ta** *mf* (coll.) husky youngster; *m* (coll.) cigar; (coll.) cigar stub; (Am.) whip; (naut.) piece of rope, end of rope
**chicotear** *va* (Am.) to lash, whip, flog; (Am.) to dispatch, to kill; (Am.) to splash stucco on (*a wall*)
**chicozapote** *m* (bot.) sapodilla
**chicuelo -la** *adj* small, little; *m* little boy; *f* little girl
**chicha** *f* chicha, corn liquor; (coll.) meat; **de chicha y nabo** (coll.) insignificant, worthless; **ni chicha ni limonada** (coll.) neither fish nor fowl
**chícharo** *m* pea; (Am.) poor cigar; (Am.) apprentice
**chicharra** *f* (ent.) locust, harvest fly; kazoo; (coll.) chatterbox; (Am.) buzzer, noisy tool; **cantar la chicharra** (coll.) to be hot and sultry
**chicharrar** *va* to scorch; to bother, to bedevil
**chicharrear** *vn* (Am.) to chirp (*said of a cicada*)
**chicharrero** *m* (coll.) hot place or region
**chicharro** *m* cracklings (*residue of hogs' fat*); (ichth.) caranx
**chicharrón** *m* cracklings (*residue of hogs' fat*); burned or scorched food; (coll.) person scorched by the sun
**chiche** *f* (Am.) infant's toy; (Am.) trinket; (Am.) breast; (Am.) wet nurse
**chichear** *va, vn & vr* to hiss
**chicheo** *m* hiss, hissing
**chichigua** *f* (Am.) wet nurse; (Am.) shade tree; (Am.) small change; (Am.) trifle
**chichisbeo** *m* ardent wooing; ardent suitor
**chichón -chona** *adj* (Am.) joking; (Am.) large-breasted; *m* bump or lump on the head
**chichonera** *f* (coll.) wadded hat (*to protect a child's head from bumps*)
**chifla** *f* hissing; whistling; whistle; paring knife; **estar de chifla** (Am.) to be in a bad humor
**chifladera** *f* whistle
**chiflado -da** *adj* (coll.) daffy; *mf* (coll.) nut; (coll.) crank
**chifladura** *f* hissing; whistling; (coll.) daffiness; (coll.) whim, craze, wild idea
**chiflar** *va* to hiss (*e.g., an actor*); to gulp down (*wine or liquor*); to pare (*leather*); *vn* to whistle; (Am.) to sing (*said of birds*); *vr* (coll.) to become unbalanced; **chiflarse con** (coll.) to be or get nutty about
**chiflato** *m* whistle
**chifle** *m* whistle; bird call (*instrument*); powder flask, powder horn; (Am.) horn used to carry water
**chiflete** *m* whistle
**chiflido** *m* whistle; whistling sound
**chiflo** *m* whistle
**chiflón** *m* (Am.) cold blast (*of air*); (Am.) rapids; (Am.) flume; (Am.) slide of loose stone (*in a mine*)
**chigre** *m* (naut.) winch; (dial.) cider shop
**chilaba** *f* jelab or jellaba
**chilaquiles** *mpl* (Am.) casserole of tortillas, tomatoes, and chili
**chilar** *m* field of chilies
**chile** *m* (bot.) chili (*plant and fruit*); **chile con carne** (Am.) chile con carne or chili con carne; (*cap.*) *m* Chile
**chilenismo** *m* Chileanism
**chileno -na** or **chileño -ña** *adj & mf* Chilean
**chilindrina** *f* (coll.) trifle; (coll.) joke, funny story; (coll.) jest, banter
**chilindrinero -ra** *adj* (coll.) joking, storytelling; *mf* (coll.) joker, storyteller
**chilindrón** *m* Pope Joan (*card game*)
**chilipuca** *f* Sieva bean (*seed or bean*)
**chiltipiquín** *m* (bot.) chili (*plant and fruit*)
**chilla** *f* (hunt.) fox call, hare call; clapboard; (Am.) small fox
**chillado** *m* clapboard roof
**chillador -dora** *adj* shrieking, squeaking, screaming, squealing; *mf* screamer, squealer
**chillar** *vn* to shriek; to screech; to creak, to squeak; to hiss, to sizzle; to scream (*said of colors*); (hunt.) to call (*with fox call, etc.*); (Am.) to squeal (*to turn informer*); **no chillar** (Am.) to not say a word; *vr* (Am.) to be piqued, be offended
**chillería** *f* shrieks, screams, outcries; screaming and scolding
**chillido** *m* shriek, scream
**chillo** *m* (hunt.) fox call, hare call
**chillón -llona** *adj* (coll.) shrieking, screaming; shrill, screechy; high-pitched; loud (*color*); *m* lath nail; **chillón real** large nail, spike
**chimachima** *m* (orn.) chimachima
**chimango** *m* (orn.) chimango
**chimenea** *f* chimney, smokestack; fireplace, hearth; stovepipe, stovepipe hat; vent (*of parachute*); (naut.) funnel; (min.) shaft; stove; **caer por la chimenea** (coll.) to come unexpectedly and without effort; **chimenea francesa** fireplace, fireplace and mantel
**chimpancé** *m* (zool.) chimpanzee
**chimuelo -la** *adj* (Am.) toothless; *mf* (Am.) toothless person
**china** *f*. see **chino**
**chinampa** *f* artificial garden reclaimed from a lake (*near Mexico city*)
**chinanta** *f* chinanta (*Philippine weight, equal to 13 pounds 12 ounces*)
**chinarro** *m* large pebble, stone
**chinazo** *m* blow with a stone
**chincapino** *m* (bot.) chinquapin
**chinchar** *va* (coll.) to bother, to annoy; (coll.) to kill
**chincharrazo** *m* blow with the flat of a sword
**chincharrero** *m* buggy place; fishing smack
**chinche** *m & f* (ent.) bedbug; (ent.) bug; thumbtack; (coll.) bore, tiresome person; (Am.) grouch; **caer** or **morir como chinches** (coll.) to die like flies
**chincheta** *f* thumbtack
**chinchilla** *f* (zool.) chinchilla (*animal and fur*)
**chinchín** *m* street music; ballyhoo; (bot.) bottle gourd; (Am.) drizzle
**chinchorrería** *f* (coll.) mischievous gossip, mischievous piece of gossip; (coll.) impertinence, bother; (coll.) hoax
**chinchorrero -ra** *adj* (coll.) mischievous, gossipy; (coll.) impertinent, importunate
**chinchorro** *m* sweep net; small rowboat; hammock; (Am.) flock, drove
**chinchoso -sa** *adj* (coll.) boring, tiresome
**chiné** *adj* Chiné (*fabric*)
**chinela** *f* slipper; clog
**chinelón** *m* big slipper, high slipper
**chinero** *m* china closet

**chinesco -ca** *adj* Chinese; **chinescos** *mpl* (mus.) bell tree
**chingar** §59 *va* (coll.) to tipple (*wine or liquor*); (Am.) to bother, harass; (Am.) to bob; *vn & vr* (coll.) to tipple; (Am.) to misfire; (Am.) to fail
**chinguirito** *m* (Am.) cheap rum; (Am.) swig (*of liquor*)
**chinito -ta** *mf* (Am.) dearie
**chino -na** *adj* Chinese; *mf* Chinese; (Am.) half-breed (*cross between non-white races*); *m* Chinaman; Chinese (*language*); (Am.) boy, newsboy; **me es chino** it's Greek to me; *f* Chinese woman; china, porcelain; China silk; pebble; game of guessing which hand holds a pebble; (bot.) chinaroot; (Am.) half-breed maidservant; (Am.) top, spinning top; **la China** China
**chinoamericano -na** *adj* Sino-American
**chinuco** *m* Chinook (*Indian; language*); chinook (*wind*)
**chiolita** *f* (mineral.) chiolite
**chipé** *f* truth, goodness; **de chipé** (coll.) first-class, excellent
**chipén** *m* activity, excitement; **de chipén** (coll.) first-class, excellent
**chipichipi** *m* (Am.) mist, drizzle
**chipirón** *m* (zool.) squid
**Chipre** *f* Cyprus
**chipriota** or **chipriote** *adj & mf* Cypriote or Cyprian
**chiqueadores** *mpl* (Am.) medicated paper disks stuck on the temples to cure headache; (Am.) paper or tortoise-shell spangles (*old female adornment in Mexico*)
**chiquero** *m* pigsty; bull pen; (theat.) dressing room
**chiquichaque** *m* sawyer; noise of chewing
**chiquiguao** *m* (zool.) snapper, snapping turtle
**chiquigüite** *m* or **chiquihuite** *m* (Am.) reed basket
**chiquilicuatro** *m* (coll.) meddler, schemer
**chiquilín -lina** *mf* (Am.) tot, little youngster
**chiquillada** *f* childish prank, mischievousness
**chiquillería** *f* (coll.) crowd of small fry, crowd of youngsters
**chiquillo -lla** *mf* child, youngster
**chiquirritico -ca, chiquirritillo -lla** or **chiquirritito -ta** *adj* (coll.) small, tiny
**chiquirritín -tina** or **chiquitín -tina** *adj* (coll.) tiny; *mf* (coll.) tiny child, tot
**chiquito -ta** *adj* small, tiny; **andarse en chiquitas** (coll.) to beat about the bush; *mf* little one
**chiribita** *f* spark; (bot.) daisy; **chiribitas** *fpl* (coll.) spots in front of the eyes; **echar chiribitas** (coll.) to blow up, hit the ceiling
**chiribitil** *m* garret; hovel; (coll.) crib, cubbyhole
**chirigota** *f* (coll.) joke, joking, fun
**chirigotero -ra** *adj* (coll.) joking, funmaking
**chirimbolo** *m* (coll.) utensil, tool, implement, vessel; **chirimbolos de cocina** (coll.) kitchenware
**chirimía** *f* (mus.) hornpipe; *mf* hornpipe player
**chirimoya** *f* cherimoya (*fruit*)
**chirimoyo** *m* (bot.) cherimoya; **chirimoyo del Senegal** (bot.) sweetsop
**chirinola** *f* boys' game of bowling; trifle; **estar de chirinola** (coll.) to be in good spirits
**chiripa** *f* fluke, scratch (*in billiards*); (coll.) lucky stroke, piece of luck, fluke
**chiripá** *m* (Am.) chiripá (*blanket wrapped around waist and hips and thighs*)
**chiripear** *va* to win (*points*) by a fluke
**chiripero** *m* winner by a fluke; (coll.) lucky fellow
**chirivía** *f* (bot.) parsnip (*plant and root*); (orn.) wagtail
**chirla** *f* (zool.) small clam
**chirlador -dora** *adj* ranting
**chirlar** *vn* (coll.) to rant
**chirlata** *f* (coll.) gambling joint (*where stakes are copper and small silver coins*)
**chirle** *adj* (coll.) tasteless, insipid; *m* sheep manure, goat manure
**chirlo** *m* slash in the face; long scar on the face
**chirlomirlo** *m* tidbit; (orn.) thrush
**chirlota** *f* (orn.) meadow lark, eastern meadow lark
**chirona** *f* (coll.) jug, jail
**chirriadero -ra** or **chirriador -dora** *adj* hissing; creaking, squeaking; shrieking (*bird*)
**chirriante** *adj* hissing; creaking, squeaky
**chirriar** §90 *vn* to hiss, sizzle; to creak, squeak; to shriek (*said of birds*); to chirp (*said of crickets*); (coll.) to sing out of tune; (coll.) to be out of tune, to play out of tune (*said of a musical instrument*); *vr* (Am.) to go on a spree; (Am.) to shiver
**chirrido** *m* hiss, sizzle; creak, squeak; shrieking (*of birds*); chirping (*of crickets*)
**chirrío** *m* (coll.) var. of **chirrido**
**chirrión** *m* squeaky tumbrel
**chirrionero** *m* tumbrel driver
**chirula** *f* (mus.) fipple flute or pipe
**chirumen** *m* (coll.) judgment, acumen, brains
**chis** *interj* sh-sh!, hush!; **¡chis, chis!** hey!, pst!
**chiscón** *m* (coll.) hut, hovel
**chischás** *m* clash of swords
**chisgarabís** *m* (coll.) meddler, schemer
**chisguete** *m* (coll.) drink or swallow of wine; (coll.) squirt; **echar un chisguete** (coll.) to take a swig
**chisma** *f* (archaic) gossip
**chismar** *vn* (archaic) var. of **chismear**
**chisme** *m* gossip, piece of gossip; (coll.) trinket, gadget, jigger; **chismes** *mpl* gossip; articles, equipment (*e.g., for writing, shaving, etc.*); **chisme de vecindad** (coll.) idle talker, chatterbox
**chismear** *vn* to gossip
**chismería** *f* gossip, gossiping; cattiness
**chismero -ra** *adj & mf* var. of **chismoso**
**chismografía** *f* (coll.) gossiping, fondness for gossip
**chismorrear** *vn* (coll.) to gossip
**chismorreo** *m* (coll.) gossip, gossiping
**chismoso -sa** *adj* gossipy; catty; *mf* gossip
**chispa** *f* see **chispo**
**chispazo** *m* flying spark; burn from a spark; straw (*token, indication*); (coll.) gossip, tale, piece of gossip
**chispeante** *adj* sparkling (*writing, imagination, person*); (Am.) drizzly
**chispear** *vn* to spark; to sparkle; to drizzle; (fig.) to sparkle
**chispero -ra** *adj* sparking, sparkling (*firecracker*); *m* blacksmith; junk dealer; (rail.) spark arrester; (coll.) denizen of the Madrid underworld
**chispo -pa** *adj* (coll.) tipsy; *m* (coll.) swallow, drink; *f* spark; sparkle (*tiny diamond*); drop (*small amount*); lightning; (fig.) sparkle, wit; (coll.) drunk, drunken spree; (Am.) false rumor (bot.) coreopsis; **chispas** *fpl* sprinkle (*of rain*), e.g., **caen chispas** it is sprinkling; **¡chispas!** blazes!; **coger una chispa** (coll.) to go on a drunk; **dar chispa** (Am.) to work, to click; **echar chispas** (coll.) to blow up, hit the ceiling; (Am.) to be all dressed up; **ser una chispa** (coll.) to be a little hustler; **chispa de entrehierro** (elec.) jump spark
**chispoleto -ta** *adj* lively, wide-awake
**chisporrotear** *vn* (coll.) to spark, to sputter
**chisporroteo** *m* (coll.) sparking, sputtering
**chisposo -sa** *adj* sparking, sputtering
**chisquero** *m* leather bag (*fastened to belt*); pocket lighter
**chistar** *vn* to speak, be about to speak; **no chistar** to not say a word; **sin chistar ni mistar** (coll.) without saying a word
**chiste** *m* witticism; joke, funny thing; **caer en el chiste** (coll.) to get wise, to get the point; **contar un chiste** to tell a joke; **dar en el chiste** (coll.) to guess right, to do the right thing
**chistera** *f* fish basket; top hat; (sport) cesta, wickerwork racket
**chistoso -sa** *adj* witty; funny; *mf* wit (*person*)
**chistu** *m* var. of **chirula**
**chita** *f* (anat.) anklebone; boys' quoits; **a la chita callando** (coll.) in silence; (coll.) stealthily, secretly; **dar en la chita** (coll.) to hit the nail on the head; **tirar a dos chitas** (coll.) to try to kill two birds with one stone

**chitar** *vn* var. of **chistar**
**chiticalla** *mf* (coll.) clam, tight-lipped person; *f* (coll.) secret
**chiticallando** *adv* (coll.) in silence; (coll.) stealthily, secretly; **a la chiticallando** (coll.) in silence; (coll.) stealthily, secretly
**chito** *m* piece of wood on which stakes or bets are placed; **irse a chitos** (coll.) to bum around; *interj* sh-sh!, hush!
**chitón** *m* (zool.) chiton; *interj* sh-sh!, hush!
**chivarras** *fpl* (Am.) shaggy kid breeches
**chivatazo** *m* (slang) squealing, peaching
**chivateado -da** *adj* (Am.) cash (*payment*)
**chivatear** *va* (Am.) to cheat, deceive; *vn* (Am.) to give the war cry; *vr* (Am.) to get scared
**chivato** *m* (zool.) kid; (slang) squealer; (Am.) helper, apprentice
**chivetero** or **chivital** *m* fold for kids
**chivo -va** *mf* (zool.) kid; *m* billy goat; tank for the lees of olive oil
**cho** *interj* whoa!
**chocador -dora** *adj* shocking; *mf* shocker
**chocante** *adj* shocking; scurrilous; (Am.) tiresome
**chocar** §86 *va* to shock; to aggravate, irritate; (slang) to please; **¡chóquela!** or **¡choque Vd. esos cinco!** (coll.) shake! (*i.e., shake hands!*); *vn* to shock; to collide; to clash, to fight; **chocar con** to collide with; to clash with
**chocarrear** *vn & vr* to tell coarse jokes
**chocarrería** *f* coarse joke; scurrility
**chocarrero -ra** *adj* coarse, scurrilous; *mf* coarse joker
**choclar** *vn* to drive the ball through the hoop (*in croquet*)
**choclo** *m* clog (*shoe with wooden sole*); (Am.) low shoe; (Am.) ear of corn
**choclón** *m* driving ball through the hoop (*in croquet*)
**choco** *m* small cuttlefish
**chocolate** *m* chocolate; **chocolate a la española** thick chocolate (*beverage*); **chocolate a la francesa** thin chocolate (*beverage*)
**chocolatera** *f* see **chocolatero**
**chocolatería** *f* chocolate factory; chocolate shop
**chocolatero -ra** *adj* fond of chocolate; *mf* chocolate maker; chocolate dealer; *f* chocolate pot; (orn.) spoonbill
**chocolatín** *m* cake of chocolate
**chocha** *f* see **chocho**
**chochaperdiz** *f* (*pl:* **-dices**) (orn.) woodcock
**chochear** *vn* to dote, become childish; (coll.) to dote, be infatuated
**chochera** *f* dotage; doting act or word; **ser la chochera de** (Am.) to be the choice of, be the foible of
**chochez** *f* (*pl:* **-checes**) dotage; doting act or word
**chochín** *m* young or baby woodcock; (orn.) wren
**chochita** *f* (orn.) wren
**chocho -cha** *adj* doddering; doting; *m* lupine (*seed*); cinnamon candy; **chochos** *mpl* candy to quiet a child; *f* (orn.) woodcock; **chocha de mar** (ichth.) shrimpfish
**chofe** *m* lung
**chófer** *m* chauffeur; driver
**chofeta** *f* fire pan (*for lighting cigars*)
**cholo -la** *adj* (Am.) Indian; (Am.) half-breed (*Indian and white*); (Am.) half-civilized (*Indian*); *mf* (Am.) Indian; (Am.) half-breed; (Am.) half-civilized Indian; (Am.) boor, rustic; (Am.) coward; (Am.) darling; *m* (Am.) black dog; *f* (coll.) noodle, head; (coll.) brains, ability
**cholla** *f* (coll.) noodle, head; (coll.) brains, ability; (bot.) cholla; (Am.) calm, apathy, dullness
**chomite** *m* (Am.) coarse wool; woolen skirt (*worn by Mexican Indian women*)
**chompa** *f* (Am.) sweater; (Am.) iron bar; (Am.) hand drill
**chonta** *f* (bot.) tucuma
**chopa** *f* (ichth.) chopa, rudder fish; (naut.) topgallant poop
**chopal** *m*, **chopalera** or **chopera** *f* grove of black poplars
**chopo** *m* (bot.) black poplar; (coll.) musket, gun; **chopo blanco** (bot.) white poplar; **chopo de Italia** (bot.) Lombardy poplar; **chopo de la Carolina** (bot.) Carolina poplar; **chopo del Canadá** o **de Virginia** (bot.) cottonwood; **chopo lombardo** (bot.) Lombardy poplar
**chopontil** *m* (zool.) snapper, snapping turtle
**choque** *m* shock; impact, collision; (elec., med. & fig.) shock; (elec.) choke, choke coil; (mil.) clash, skirmish; (naut.) chock; **choque de agua, choque de ariete** water hammer; **choque glótico** (phonet.) glottal stop
**choquezuela** *f* (anat.) kneepan
**chorcha** *f* (orn.) woodcock
**chordón** *m* var. of **churdón**
**choricería** *f* sausage shop
**choricero -ra** *mf* sausage maker or dealer; *f* (mach.) sausage filler
**chorizo** *m* smoked pork sausage; ropewalker's pole
**chorla** *f* (orn.) sand grouse
**chorlito** *m* (orn.) golden plover; (coll.) scatterbrains; **chorlito blanco** (orn.) sanderling; **chorlito de manchas acaneladas** (orn.) solitary sandpiper; **chorlito de mar** (orn.) red phalarope; **chorlito de mar apizarrado** (orn.) northern phalarope; **chorlito dorado** (orn.) American golden plover; **chorlito gris** (orn.) black-bellied plover; **chorlito gritón peleador** (orn.) killdeer; **chorlito palmeado de pico largo** (orn.) stilt sandpiper; **chorlito pardo mayor** or **patiamarilla** (orn.) lesser yellowlegs; **chorlito playero** (orn.) black-bellied plover; **chorlito playero manchado** (orn.) spotted sandpiper; **chorlito siberiano** (orn.) Pacific golden plover; **chorlito verde** (orn.) American golden plover
**chorlo** *m* (mineral.) schorl, tourmaline; (mineral.) aluminum silicate; (orn.) curlew; (orn.) spotted sandpiper; (Am.) great-great-great-grandchild; **chorlo blanco nadador** (orn.) Wilson's phalarope; **chorlo de las playas** (orn.) surfbird; **chorlo grande de patas amarillas** (orn.) greater yellowlegs; **chorlo gris pecho negro** (orn.) black-billed plover; **chorlo gris pico largo** (orn.) long-billed dowitcher; **chorlo manchado** (orn.) spotted sandpiper; **chorlo menor de patas amarillas** (orn.) lesser yellowlegs; **chorlo nadador de pies lobados** (orn.) red phalarope; **chorlo pampa** (orn.) American golden plover; **chorlo real** (orn.) greater yellowlegs; **chorlo rojizo** (orn.) knot (*Calidris canutus rufus*); **chorlo rojizo de mar** (orn.) red phalarope
**chorrada** *f* (coll.) extra dash (*of a liquid*)
**chorreado -da** *adj* with dark vertical stripes (*said of cattle*)
**chorreadura** *f* spurting, spouting, gushing; dripping; (coll.) trickling; stain from constant dripping
**chorreante** *adj* dripping
**chorrear** *vn* to spurt, to spout, to gush; to drip; (coll.) to trickle
**chorreo** *m* spurting, spouting, gushing; dripping; (coll.) trickling
**chorreón** *m* gushing; dripping; stain from dripping; trickle
**chorrera** *f* spout, channel; mark left by running water; cut, gulley; rapids (*in a stream*); jabot; knight's, magistrate's, or pilgrim's pendant; (Am.) string, stream (*of things*)
**chorretada** *f* (coll.) squirt, sudden gush; (coll.) extra dash (*of a liquid*); **hablar a chorretadas** (coll.) to pour forth words
**chorrillo** *m* (coll.) constant stream (*e.g., of money*); **irse por el chorrillo** (coll.) to follow the current (*to do what others do*); **sembrar a chorrillo** (agr.) to sow with a funnel; **tomar el chorrillo de** + *inf* (coll.) to get the habit of + *ger*
**chorro** *m* spurt, jet; stream, flow; **a chorros** in abundance; **chorro de arena** sandblast; **chorro de voz** fullness of voice
**chorroborro** *m* (coll.) flood
**chorrón** *m* dressed hemp
**chortal** *m* puddle from a surface spring
**chotacabras** *m* (*pl:* **-bras**) (orn.) goatsucker, nighthawk
**chotear** *va* (Am.) to make fun of

**chotis** *m* schottische (*dance and music*)
**choto -ta** *mf* sucking kid; lamb
**chotuno -na** *adj* sucking (*kid*); weak, sickly (*lamb*); **oler a chotuno** to smell like a goat
**chova** *f* (orn.) rook; (orn.) Cornish chough; **chova pinariega** (orn.) alpine chough
**chovinismo** *m* var. of **chauvinismo**
**chovinista** *adj & mf* var. of **chauvinista**
**choz** *f* blow, surprise; **dar** or **hacer choz a** to surprise
**choza** *f* hut, cabin, lodge
**chozno -na** *mf* great-great-great-grandchild
**chozo** *m* small hut, small cabin
**chozpar** *vn* to caper, to gambol (*said of small animals*)
**chozpo** *m* caper, gambol
**chozpón -pona** *adj* capering, gamboling, frisky
**chozuela** *f* small hut, small cabin, shanty
**christmas** *m* (*pl:* **-mas**) Christmas card
**chubasco** *m* squall, shower, storm; (naut.) threatening cloud; temporary upset (*in one's plans*); **aguantar el chubasco** to weather the storm; **chubasco de agua** (naut.) rainstorm; **chubasco de nieve** blizzard; **chubasco de viento** (naut.) windstorm
**chubascoso -sa** *adj* showery, squally
**chubasquería** *f* (naut.) mass of threatening clouds on the horizon
**chubasquero** *m* raincoat
**chucero** *m* (mil.) pikeman
**chucrut** *m* or **chucruta** *f* sauerkraut
**chucha** *f* (coll.) female dog, bitch; (coll.) drunk, spree; (coll.) idleness; (Am.) opossum
**chuchaqui** *m* (Am.) hangover
**chuchear** *va* to trap (*small game*); *vn* to whisper
**chuchería** *f* trinket, knickknack; tidbit, delicacy; (hunt.) trapping small game
**chuchero -ra** *adj* (hunt.) for trapping small game; *m* (Am.) switch tender
**chucho** *m* (coll.) dog; (*cap.*) *m* child Jesus; (*l.c.*) *interj* get out of here! (*said to a dog*); down! (*said to restrain a dog*)
**chuchumeco -ca** *adj* (Am.) stunted, dwarfish; *mf* (coll.) little runt
**chueco -ca** *adj* (Am.) crooked, bent; (Am.) bow-legged; *f* stump (*of tree*); head of bone; hockey; hockey ball; (coll.) joke, trick
**chueta** *mf* (Balearic Islands) Chueta (*descendant of Christianized Jews*)
**chufa** *f* (bot.) chufa (*plant and tuber*)
**chufar** *va* to scoff at; *vn & vr* to scoff
**chufería** *f* orgeat shop
**chufero -ra** *mf* orgeat vendor; chufa vendor
**chufeta** *f* fire pan (*for lighting cigars*); (coll.) joke, jest
**chufleta** *f* (coll.) joke, jest
**chufletear** *vn* (coll.) to joke, to jest
**chufletero -ra** *adj* (coll.) joking, jesting; *mf* (coll.) joker, jester
**chula** *f* see **chulo**
**chulada** *f* vulgarity; light-heartedness, light-hearted remark
**chulama** *f* (slang) girl
**chulamo** *m* (slang) boy
**chulapo -pa** or **chulapón -pona** *adj* (coll.) smart, pert; *mf* (coll.) sporty person (*in lower classes of Madrid*)
**chulear** *va* (Am.) to flirt with
**chulería** *f* ease, charm, sparkle; flashiness, snap; group of sporty people (*in lower classes of Madrid*)
**chulesco -ca** *adj* smart, pert, sporty
**chuleta** *f* chop, cutlet; (carp.) fill-in; (coll.) slap, smack; (coll.) crib, pony
**chulo -la** *adj* flashy, snappy; foxy; (Am.) pretty, good-looking; *m* sporty fellow (*in lower classes of Madrid*); pimp; (taur.) attendant on foot; butcher's helper; *f* flashy dame (*in lower classes of Madrid*)
**chumacera** *f* (mach.) pillow block, journal bearing; (naut.) strip of wood through which tholepins are driven and whose purpose is to protect the gunwale; (naut.) rowlock, oarlock
**chumbera** *f* (bot.) prickly pear
**chunga** *f* (coll.) jest, fun; **estar de chunga** (coll.) to be in a jesting mood
**chungar** §59 *vr* (coll.) to jest, to joke
**chunguear** *vr* (coll.) var. of **chungar**
**chunguero -ra** *adj* (coll.) joking, full of fun
**chupa** *f* (mil.) frock; **poner como chupa de dómine** (coll.) to upbraid, to abuse
**chupada** *f* see **chupado**
**chupadero -ra** *adj* sucking; *m* teething ring
**chupado -da** *adj* (coll.) lean, skinny; **chupado de cara** (coll.) lantern-jawed; *f* suck, sucking; pull (*on a cigar*)
**chupador -dora** *adj* sucking; absorbent; *mf* (Am.) smoker; (Am.) heavy drinker; *m* teething ring
**chupadura** *f* suck, sucking
**chupaflor** *m* (Am.) hummingbird
**chupaleta** *f* (Am.) lollipop
**chupamieles** *m* (bot.) bugloss
**chupamirto** *m* (orn.) hummingbird
**chupar** *va* to suck; to absorb; to milk, to sap (*someone's wealth*); (Am.) to smoke; (Am.) to guzzle, to drink; *vn* to suck; *vr* to lose strength, to decline; to smack (*one's lips*)
**chuparrosa** *m* (Am.) hummingbird
**chupatintas** *mf* (*pl:* **-tas**) (coll.) office drudge
**chupeta** *f* short frock; (naut.) roundhouse; **chupeta de escala** (naut.) companion
**chupete** *m* pacifier (*rubber nipple for a baby*); (Am.) lollipop; **de chupete** (coll.) splendid, fine
**chupetear** *va & vn* to keep sucking gently
**chupeteo** *m* gentle steady sucking
**chupetín** *m* jerkin, waistcoat
**chupetón** *m* hard suck
**chupín** *m* short suck
**chupón -pona** *adj* (coll.) sucking; (coll.) swindling; *mf* (coll.) swindler; *m* (bot.) sucker; (mach.) sucker (*piston*)
**chupóptero** *m* (hum.) parasite, sponger
**chuquisa** *f* (Am.) party girl
**churdón** *m* (bot.) raspberry (*plant and fruit*); raspberry jam
**chureca** *f* (bot.) sweet pea
**churla** *f* or **churlo** *m* seroon
**churra** *f* see **churro**
**churrasco** *m* (Am.) barbecue
**churrasquear** *va* (Am.) to barbecue
**churre** *m* (coll.) thick, dirty grease; (coll.) dirt, grease, filth
**churretada** *f* large dirty spot (*on hands or face*); mass of dirty spots (*on hands or face*)
**churrete** *m* dirty spot (*on hands or face*)
**churretoso -sa** *adj* full of dirty spots
**churriana** *f* (slang) prostitute
**churriburri** *m* (coll.) var. of **zurriburri**
**churriento -ta** *adj* greasy
**churrigueresco -ca** *adj* (arch.) churrigueresque; flashy, loud, tawdry
**churriguerismo** *m* (arch.) churriguerism (*excess of ornamentation*)
**churriguerista** *m* (arch.) churriguerist
**churro -rra** *adj* coarse (*wool*); coarse-wooled (*sheep*); *mf* coarse-wooled sheep; *m* cucumber-shaped fritter; (coll.) botch; *f* (orn.) sand grouse
**churrullero -ra** *adj* gossipy, loquacious; *mf* gossip, chatterbox
**churruscar** §86 *va* to burn (*food*); *vr* to burn, become burnt (*said of food*)
**churrusco** *m* burnt toast
**churumbel** *m* (coll.) child, youngster
**churumbela** *f* (mus.) flageolet; (Am.) maté cup
**churumo** *m* (coll.) juice, substance
**chus** *interj* here, here! (*to call a dog*); **no decir chus ni mus** to not say boo
**chuscada** *f* drollery, pleasantry
**chusco -ca** *adj* droll, funny; *m* (Am.) mongrel (*dog*)
**chusma** *f* galley slaves; mob, rabble
**chuspa** *f* (Am.) bag
**chusquel** *m* (slang) house dog
**chutar** or **chutear** *va* to kick (*a football*)
**chuva** *f* (zool.) spider monkey
**chuza** *f* (Am.) strike (*in bowling*)
**chuzar** §76 *va* (Am.) to prick, to wound
**chuzo** *m* pike; (Am.) whip; **echar chuzos** (coll.) to boast, to brag; (coll.) to storm, to rage; **llover chuzos** (coll.) to rain pitchforks
**chuzón -zona** *adj* sly, crafty; witty, clever, adroit (*in conversation*)
**chuzonada** *f* var. of **bufonada**
**chuzonería** *f* joke, trick

# D

**D, d** *f* fifth letter of the Spanish alphabet
**D.** abr. of **don**
**D.ª** abr. of **doña**
**dable** *adj* possible, feasible
**daca** give me, hand over to me; **andar al daca y toma** (coll.) to be at cross purposes
**dacio -cia** *adj & mf* Dacian; **la Dacia** Dacia
**dación** *f* (law) yielding, handing over
**dactilado -da** *adj* finger-shaped
**dactilar** *adj* var. of **digital**
**dactílico -ca** *adj* dactylic
**dactiliografía** *f* dactyliography
**dactiliología** *f* dactyliology
**dáctilo** *m* dactyl
**dactilográfico -ca** *adj* typewriting
**dactilógrafo -fa** *mf* typist, typewriter; *m* typewriter (*machine*)
**dactilograma** *m* dactylogram, fingerprint
**dactilología** *f* dactylology, sign language
**dactiloscopia** *f* dactyloscopy
**dactiloscópico -ca** *adj* dactyloscopic
**dadaísmo** *m* Dadaism
**dádiva** *f* gift, present
**dadivar** *va* to give a present to, make gifts to
**dadivosidad** *f* generosity, liberality
**dadivoso -sa** generous, liberal
**dado -da** *adj* given; **dado que** given that; provided that, as long as; *m* die; (arch.) dado; (mach.) block; **dados** *mpl* dice; **el dado está tirado** (coll.) the die is cast; **cargar los dados** to load the dice; **correr el dado** (coll.) to be in luck; **dados cargados** loaded dice
**dador -dora** *adj* giving; *mf* giver, donor; bearer (*of a letter*); drawer (*of a bill of exchange*)
**Dafne** *f* (myth.) Daphne
**daga** *f* dagger; line of bricks in a kiln; **llegar a las dagas** (coll.) to get to the real difficulty
**daguerrotipar** *va* to daguerreotype
**daguerrotipo** *m* daguerreotype
**dala** *f* (naut.) pump dale
**dalia** *f* (bot.) dahlia
**Dalila** or **Dálila** *f* (Bib.) Delilah
**Dalmacia** *f* Dalmatia
**dálmata** *adj & mf* Dalmatian
**dalmático -ca** *adj* Dalmatian; *f* dalmatic (*vestment*)
**daltonismo** *m* (path.) Daltonism
**dalla** *f* scythe
**dallador** *m* mower, grass mower (*with scythe*)
**dallar** *va* to cut (*grass*) with the scythe
**dalle** *m* scythe
**dama** *f* lady, dame; lady of honor; king (*in checkers*); queen (*in chess and cards*); mistress, concubine; (found.) dam; (theat.) leading lady; **damas** *fpl* checkers; **muy dama** ladylike; **señalar dama** to crown a man (*in checkers*); **soplar la dama a** (checkers) to huff the king of; (coll.) to cut out (*a rival*); to beat (*someone*) to it; **dama cortesana** courtesan; **dama de noche** (bot.) night jasmine; **dama joven** (theat.) young lead
**damado -da** *adj* checkered
**damajuana** *f* demijohn
**damascado -da** *adj* damask; damascene
**damasceno -na** *adj & mf* Damascene
**damasco** *m* damask (*fabric*); (bot.) damson (*tree and fruit*); **Damasco** *f* Damascus
**damasina** *f* light damask, damassin
**damasquillo** *m* light damask, damassin; (dial.) apricot
**damasquina** *f* see **damasquino**
**damasquinado -da** *adj* damascene; *m* damascene (*steel or iron with water marking; incrustation of gold or silver wire and enamel in steel or copper*)
**damasquinar** *va* to damascene
**damasquino -na** *adj* Damascene; damascene; *f* (bot.) French marigold
**damería** *f* nicety, prudery; caution, circumspection
**damero** *m* checkerboard
**damisela** *f* young lady, damsel; courtesan
**damnación** *f* damnation
**damnificar** §86 *va* to damage, hurt, injure
**Damocles** *m* or **Dámocles** *m* (myth.) Damocles
**Damón** *m* (myth.) Damon
**Dánae** *f* (myth.) Danae
**Danaides** *fpl* (myth.) Danaides
**Danao** *m* (myth.) Danaus
**danchado -da** *adj* (her.) dentelated
**dandismo** *m* dandyism
**danés -nesa** *adj* Danish; *mf* Dane; *m* Danish (*language*)
**dango** *m* (orn.) gannet
**dánico -ca** *adj* Danish
**Daniel** *m* Daniel
**danta** *f* (zool.) tapir
**dantelado -da** *adj* (her.) dentelated
**dantesco -ca** *adj* Dantesque
**danubiano -na** *adj* Danubian
**Danubio** *m* Danube
**danza** *f* dance; dancing; habanera; mess, row; **armar una danza** (coll.) to start a row; **meter en la danza** (coll.) to drag into a deal or scheme, to involve; **baja danza** allemande; **danza de cintas** Maypole dance; **danza de espadas** sword dance; (coll.) quarrel, row; **danza de la muerte** dance of death; **danza macabra** danse macabre
**danzador -dora** *adj* dancing; *mf* dancer
**danzante** *adj* dancing; *mf* public dancer; (coll.) hustler; (coll.) scatterbrain, meddler
**danzar** §76 *va* to dance; *vn* to dance; (fig.) to dance; (coll.) to butt in
**danzarín -rina** *adj* dancing; *mf* dancer, fine dancer; (coll.) scatterbrain, meddler
**danzón** *m* danzón (*Cuban dance*)
**dañable** *adj* harmful; reprehensible
**dañado -da** *adj* bad, wicked; spoiled, tainted; damned; *mf* person damned
**dañar** *va* to hurt; to damage, to harm; to spoil; *vr* to become damaged; to spoil
**dañino -na** *adj* harmful, destructive; evil, wicked
**daño** *m* hurt; damage, harm; (Am.) witchcraft, enchantment; **a daño de** at the risk of; **en daño de** to the harm or detriment of; **hacerse daño** to hurt oneself
**dañoso -sa** *adj* harmful, injurious
**dar** §36 *va* to give; to cause; to yield; to hit, to strike; to strike, e.g., **el reloj da las tres** the clock is striking three; to deal (*cards*); to overtake, to attack (*said of fever, pain, etc.*); to wish (*e.g., good morning*); to take (*a walk, ride*); to promulgate; **dar a conocer** to make known; **dar de** to paint with (*e.g., varnish*); to smear with (*e.g., butter*); **dar de beber** to give something to drink; **dar de bofetones** to beat with a stick; **dar de comer a** to give something to eat to, to feed; **dar de palos** to slap in the face; **darle a uno por** + *inf* to get the idea of + *ger*, e.g., **a todos los niños de la vecindad les dió por jugar a la pelota** all the children in the neighborhood got the idea of playing ball; **dar por** to consider as; **dar prestado** to lend; **dar que decir** to give rise to complaint or criticism; **dar que hablar** to cause a lot of talk; to give rise to complaint or criticism; **dar que hacer** to cause annoyance or trouble; **dar que pensar** to set (*a person thinking*); to give rise to suspicion; **dar que sentir** to cause sorrow, to

cause harm; **dar, que van dando** (coll.) to hand it back, to return blow for blow, to return insult for insult; **dar y tomar** to discuss ‖ *vn* to fall; to occur, to arise; to strike, e.g., **dan las tres** it is striking three o'clock; **el reloj acaba de dar** the clock has just struck; to tell, intimate, e.g., **me da el corazón que** my heart tells me that; **dar a** to overlook, to face, to open on; **dar con** to meet, encounter, run into; to hit upon, to come upon; **dar de espaldas** to fall on one's back; **dar de sí** to stretch, to give; **dar en** to hit; to overlook; to fall into; to run into; to catch on to (*a joke*); to be bent on; **dar en** + *inf* to begin to + *inf;* to be bent on + *ger;* **dar en qué pensar** to give rise to suspicion; **dar sobre** to overlook; **dar tras** to pursue hotly; **dar y tomar sobre** to discuss, argue about ‖ *vr* to give oneself up; to yield, to give in; to occur, be found; **darse a** to give oneself over to, to devote oneself to; **darse a conocer** to make a name for oneself, to make oneself known; to get to know each other; **darse contra** to run into; **dárselas de** to pose as; **darse por** to be considered as; to consider oneself (or itself) as; **darse por aludido** to take the hint; **darse por entendido** to understand, to show an understanding; to be appreciative, to show appreciation; to be responsive; **darse por vencido** to give in, to give up

**dardabasí** *m* (*pl:* **-síes**) (orn.) kite, hawk

**Dardanelos** *mpl* Dardanelles

**dardanio -nia** *adj* Dardan, Dardanian

**dárdano -na** *adj & mf* Dardan, Dardanian; (*cap.*) *m* (myth.) Dardanus

**dardo** *m* dart; small lance; cutting remark; (arch.) dart; (ichth.) dace

**dares y tomares** *mpl* (coll.) give and take; (coll.) disputes, quarrels; **andar en dares y tomares con** (coll.) to quarrel with

**Darío** *m* Darius

**dársena** *f* inner harbor, dock

**darviniano -na** *adj* Darwinian, Darwinist

**darvinismo** *m* Darwinism

**darvinista** *mf* Darwinian, Darwinist

**dasocracia** *f* forestry

**dasocrático -ca** *adj* forest, forestry

**dasonomía** *f* forestry

**dasonómico -ca** *adj* forest, forestry

**data** *f* date; (com.) item; outlet of reservoir; **de larga data** of long standing; **estar de mala data** (coll.) to be in a bad humor

**datación** *f* dating

**datar** *va* to date; *vn* to date; **datar de** to date from

**dataría** *f* datary (*office*)

**datario** *m* datary (*cardinal*)

**dátil** *m* date (*fruit*); (zool.) date shell

**datilado -da** *adj* datelike

**datilera** *f* (bot.) date palm

**datismo** *m* (rhet.) excess of synonyms

**dativo -va** *adj & m* (gram.) dative

**dato** *m* datum; basis, fact

**datura** *f* (bot.) datura

**daturina** *f* (pharm.) stramonium

**dauco** *m* (bot.) wild carrot; (bot.) bishop's-weed

**David** *m* David

**davídico -ca** *adj* Davidic, Davidical

**daza** *f* (bot.) sorghum

**D.D.T.** *m* symbol of **diclorodifeniltricloroetano**

**de** *prep* (to express possession) of, -'s, e.g., **el coche de Juan** the car of John, John's car; **este coche es de Vd.** this car is yours; (to indicate membership) of, e.g., **la gente de la aldea** the people of the village; **los miembros de la academia** the members of the academy; (to express association), e.g., **gente de teatro** theater people; **médico de hospital** hospital physician; (to denote occupation or office) as, e.g., **trabaja de ingeniero** he works as an engineer; **está de presidente** he is acting as chairman, he is chairman now; (to express material) of, e.g., **un anillo de acero** a ring of steel; **medias de seda** silk stockings; (to indicate price), e.g., **el precio del sombrero es de seis dólares** the price of the hat is six dollars; (to express source or origin), e.g., **sal de mar** sea salt; **café de moca** Mocha coffee; (to express quality, characteristic, nature, or kind), e.g., **el señor de traje negro** the gentleman in the black suit; **casa de dos pisos** two-story house; **motor de cuatro cilindros** four-cylinder motor; **dolor de muelas** toothache; **discurso de elección** election speech; (to express dimension or size), e.g., **un viaje de cien kilómetros** a one-hundred-kilometer trip; **un buque de mil toneladas** a one-thousand-ton ship; (to express manner), e.g., **de buena gana** willingly; **de golpe** suddenly; (to express contents, what is contained) of, e.g., **un vaso de cerveza** a glass of beer; (to indicate the point of departure) from, e.g., **de París a Madrid** from Paris to Madrid; **salió de Londres esta mañana** he left London this morning; (to indicate time of occurrence) in, e.g., **de día** in the daytime; **de noche** in the nighttime; (to indicate the driving force), e.g., **máquina de vapor** steam engine; **bomba de hidrógeno** hydrogen bomb; (to indicate the purpose of an object), e.g., **banco de ahorros** savings bank; **máquina de coser** sewing machine; (to express cause) with, of, e.g., **temblar de miedo** to tremble with fear; **morir de hambre** to die of hunger; (to indicate the agent with the passive voice) by, e.g., **querido de todos** loved by everybody; **acompañado de un guía** accompanied by a guide; (between words in apposition), e.g., **la ciudad de Méjico** the city of Mexico; **el año de 1963** the year of 1963; **el pobre de mi hermano** my poor brother; (between words in apposition in interjectional phrases), e.g., **¡desgraciados de nosotros!** unhappy we!; (after **un millón, millones, un billón, billones,** etc.), e.g., **dos millones de habitantes** two million inhabitants; (after **hablar, opinar, pensar,** etc.) about, e.g., **no hemos hablado de ella** we did not speak about her; (with a following infinitive after certain verbs) to, e.g., **se alegró de vernos** he was glad to see us; (with a following infinitive after certain adjectives) to, e.g., **el ruso es difícil de aprender** Russian is hard to learn; **esta agua no es buena de beber** this water is not good to drink; (with a following infinitive to express condition) if, unless, e.g., **de haberlo sabido yo** if I had known it; **de no venir él** unless he comes; (after a comparative and before a numeral) than, e.g., **más de doscientos** more than two hundred; (to indicate the position of part of the body) on, e.g., **estar de rodillas** to be on one's (his, her, etc.) knees; **caer de cara** to fall on one's (his, her, etc.) face; **acostarse de lado** to lie on one's (his, her, etc.) side; (to form prepositional phrases with certain adverbs), e.g., **antes de las seis** before six o'clock; **cerca de la iglesia** near the church; **de a** (to express rate, value, weight, etc.), e.g., **un billete de a cinco dólares** a five-dollar bill; **un jamón de a veinte-cinco kilos** a twenty-five-kilogram ham; **de entre** from between; through, out of (*e.g., one's hands*)

**dé** *1st sg pres subj of* **dar**

**dea** *f* (poet.) goddess

**deambular** *vn* to ambulate, to stroll

**deambulatorio** *m* (arch.) ambulatory

**deán** *m* (eccl.) dean

**deanato** or **deanazgo** *m* (eccl.) deanship

**debajo** *adv* below, underneath; **debajo de** under, below, underneath

**debate** *m* debate; altercation, fight

**debatir** *va* to debate; to battle, to fight; *vn* to debate; *vr* to struggle

**debe** *m* (com.) debit

**debelación** *f* conquering, conquest

**debelador -dora** *adj* conquering; *mf* conqueror

**debelar** *va* to conquer, subdue

**deber** *m* duty; debt; school work, homework; **últimos deberes** last rites; *va* to owe; *v aux* must; **deber** + *inf* must, have to, ought to, should + *inf* (*to express necessity or obligation*); **deber de** + *inf* must + *inf* (*to express conjecture*); *vr* to be dedicated, be committed; **deberse a** to be due to

**debidamente** *adv* duly

**debido -da** *adj* just, reasonable, due, proper; **debido a** due to
**débil** *adj* weak; (gram.) weak (*vowel; verb*)
**debilidad** *f* weakness, debility; **debilidad mental** mental deficiency
**debilitación** *f* or **debilitamiento** *m* debilitation
**debilitar** *va* to debilitate; *vr* to weaken, become weak
**debitar** *va* (com.) to debit
**débito** *m* debit; **débito conyugal** conjugal obligation (to have offspring)
**debó** *m* (*pl:* **-boes**) scraper (*for skins*)
**Débora** *f* Deborah
**debutante** *m* debutant (*man*); *f* debutante (*woman*)
**debutar** *vn* to make one's debut
**década** *f* decade
**decadencia** *f* decadence
**decadente** *adj* decadent; *mf* (lit.) decadent
**decadentismo** *m* (lit.) decadence
**decadentista** *adj* & *mf* (lit.) decadent
**decaedro** *m* (geom.) decahedron
**decaer** §28 *vn* to decay; to fail, weaken, sink; (naut.) to drift from the course
**decágono -na** *adj* & *m* (geom.) decagon
**decagramo** *m* decagram
**decaigo** *1st sg pres ind of* **decaer**
**decaimiento** *m* decay; decline, weakness
**decalaje** *m* unwedging, unkeying; unscotching (*of a wheel*); shift; (elec.) phase shift; (aer.) stagger; **decalaje de escobillas** (elec.) brush shift
**decalcomanía** *f* decalcomania
**decalescencia** *f* (metal.) decalescence
**decalitro** *m* decaliter
**decálogo** *m* decalog
**decalvante** *adj* (med.) decalvant
**decalvar** *va* to shave the head of (*as punishment*)
**decámetro** *m* decameter
**decampar** *vn* to decamp
**decanato** *m* deanship; deanery; (eccl.) deanship
**decano -na** *adj* senior; *m* dean (*of a school*); (fig.) dean
**decantación** *f* decantation
**decantar** *va* to decant; to exaggerate, puff up; to exalt, to extol; *vn* **decantar por** to back up, support
**decapar** *va* to oxidize and clean the surface of (*a metal*)
**decapitación** *f* decapitation
**decapitar** *va* to decapitate
**decápodo -da** *adj* & *m* (zool.) decapod
**decárea** *f* decare
**decasílabo -ba** *adj* decasyllable, decasyllabic; *m* decasyllable
**decastéreo** *m* decastere
**decatlo** or **decatlón** *m* (sport) decathlon
**deceleración** *f* deceleration
**decelerar** *va, vn* & *vr* to decelerate
**decembrino -na** *adj* (pertaining to) December
**decena** *f* see **deceno**
**decenal** *adj* decennial
**decenario -ria** *adj* (pertaining to) ten; *m* decade; ten-bead rosary
**decencia** *f* decency, propriety; dignity; cleanliness, tidiness
**decenio** *m* decade
**deceno -na** *adj* & *m* tenth; *f* ten, about ten; (period of) ten days; (mus.) tenth (*interval and organ stop*); **las decenas** the tens (*the numbers 10, 20, 30, etc.*)
**decentar** §18 *va* to cut the first slice of; to begin to lose (*e.g., health*); *vr* to get bedsores
**decente** *adj* decent, proper; dignified; clean, decent-looking; respectable
**decenvir** *m* decemvir
**decenviral** *adj* decemviral
**decenvirato** *m* decemvirate
**decenviro** *m* decemvir
**decepción** *f* disappointment; deception
**decepcionar** *va* to disappoint
**deceso** *m* (obs.) decease, death
**deciárea** *f* deciare
**decibel** *m*, **decibelio** or **decíbelo** *m* (phys.) decibel
**decible** *adj* utterable, to be told
**decidero -ra** *adj* mentionable; **decideras** *fpl* (coll.) fluency
**decidido -da** *adj* decided; determined
**decidir** *va* to decide; to persuade; to decide on; **decidir a** + *inf* to persuade to + *inf; vn* to decide; **decidir** + *inf* to decide to + *inf; vr* to decide; **decidirse a** + *inf* to decide to + *inf*
**decidor -dora** *adj* facile, fluent, witty; *mf* pleasant talker, wit
**deciduo -dua** *adj* (bot. & zool.) deciduous
**deciestéreo** *m* decistere
**decigramo** *m* decigram
**decilitro** *m* deciliter
**decillón** *m* British decillion
**décima** *f* see **décimo**
**decimación** *f* decimation
**décimacuarta** *adj* & *f* var. of **décimocuarta**
**decimal** *adj* & *m* decimal
**decimalizar** §76 *va* to decimalize
**décimanona** *adj* & *f* var. of **décimonona**
**décimanovena** *adj* & *f* var. of **décimonovena**
**décimaoctava** *adj* & *f* var. of **décimoctava**
**décimaquinta** *adj* & *f* var. of **décimoquinta**
**décimaséptima** *adj* & *f* var. of **décimoséptima**
**décimasexta** *adj* & *f* var. of **décimosexta**
**décimatercera** *adj* & *f* var. of **décimotercera**
**décimatercia** *adj* & *f* var. of **décimotercia**
**decímetro** *m* decimeter
**décimo -ma** *adj* tenth; *m* tenth; tenth part of a lottery ticket; *f* tenth; (mus.) tenth; Spanish ten-line stanza of octosyllables with the following rhyme scheme: abba - accddc
**décimoctavo -va** *adj* eighteenth; *f* (mus.) eighteenth
**décimocuarto -ta** *adj* fourteenth; *f* (mus.) fourteenth
**décimonono -na** *adj* nineteenth; *f* (mus.) nineteenth (*interval and organ stop*)
**décimonoveno -na** *adj* nineteenth; *f* (mus.) nineteenth (*interval and organ stop*)
**décimoquinto -ta** *adj* fifteenth; *f* (mus.) fifteenth
**décimoséptimo -ma** *adj* seventeenth; *f* (mus.) seventeenth
**décimosexto -ta** *adj* sixteenth; *f* (mus.) sixteenth
**décimotercero -ra** *adj* thirteenth; *f* (mus.) thirteenth
**décimotercio -cia** *adj* thirteenth; *f* (mus.) thirteenth
**decir** *m* saying; say-so; **al decir de** according to; **decir de las gentes** talk (*unfavorable*) ‖ §37 *va* to say, to tell; to talk (*e.g., nonsense*); to speak (*the truth*); to show, reveal; to call; to read, e.g., **el artículo cuatro dice así . . .** article four reads thus . . .; **como quien dice** or **como si dijéramos** so to speak; **como quien no dice nada** and this is important; **como dijo el otro** as the fellow said; **ello dirá** we shall see; **el qué dirán** what people say; **es decir** that is to say; **mejor dicho** rather; **no hay más que decir** there is nothing more to do about it; **no decir ni malo ni bueno** to make no answer; **no digamos** as one might say; **por decirlo así** so to speak; **por decir mejor** rather, in other words; **¿qué dice?** what is it, e.g., **¡María! — ¿Qué dice, mamá?** Mary! What is it, mama?; **querer decir** to mean; **que digamos** to speak of, e.g., **no llueve que digamos** it isn't raining to speak of; what we might call, e.g., **no estaba muy limpio que digamos** he was not what we might call very clean; **decir entre sí** to say to oneself; **decir** + *inf* to say that + *ind*, e.g., **decía tener muchos amigos en Madrid** he said he had many friends in Madrid; **decirle a uno cuántas son cinco** (coll.) to tell a person what's what, to speak one's mind to a person; **decirle a uno que** + *subj* to tell someone to + *inf;* **decir misa** to say mass; **decir para sí** to say to oneself; **decir por decir** to talk for talk's sake; **decir que sí** to say yes; **decírselo a uno deletreado** (coll.) to spell it out to a person; **¡diga!** hello! (*on answering telephone*); **¡digo, digo!** say!, listen! ‖ *vn* to suit, to fit; **¿porqué dice?** why do you ask?, e.g., **Yo soy de Madrid. ¿Porqué dice?** I'm from Madrid. Why

do you ask?; **Vd. dirá** say when; **decir bien a** to suit, go well on; **decir con** to harmonize with; **decir mal a** to not suit, to not go well on ‖ *vr* to be said, to be told; to be called; to call oneself; **se dice** it is said, they say
**decisión** *f* decision
**decisivo -va** *adj* decisive
**declamación** *f* declamation
**declamador -dora** *adj* declaiming; *mf* declaimer
**declamar** *va & vn* to declaim
**declamatorio -ria** *adj* declamatory
**declarable** *adj* declarable
**declaración** *f* declaration; (bridge) bid
**declaradamente** *adv* manifestly, clearly
**declarante** *mf* declarant; (bridge) bidder
**declarar** *va* to declare; *vn* to declare; (law) to testify, to make a statement; *vr* to declare oneself; to arise, occur, take place, break out
**declarativo -va** *adj* declarative
**declaratorio -ria** *adj* declaratory
**declinable** *adj* declinable
**declinación** *f* declination; fall, decline; (astr. & magnetism) declination; (gram.) declension
**declinar** *va* to decline, refuse; (gram.) to decline; *vn* to decline, to turn down or away; to abate, diminish; to degenerate; (gram.) to decline
**declinatoria** *f* (law) declinatory plea
**declinatorio** *m* declinatory compass
**declive** *m* descent, declivity; slope (*amount of sloping*); **en declive** (fig.) on the decline
**declividad** *f* declivity
**declivio** *m* var. of **declive**
**decocción** *f* decoction; (pharm.) decoction
**decoloración** *f* decolorization, loss of color
**decolorar** *va* to decolorize; *vr* to lose color
**decollaje** *m* (aer.) take-off
**decollar** *vn* (aer.) to take off
**decomisar** *va* to confiscate, seize
**decomiso** *m* confiscation, seizure
**decoración** *f* decoration; memorizing, memorization; (theat.) set, scenery; **decoraciones** *fpl* (theat.) scenery; **decoración interior** interior decoration
**decorado -da** *adj* decorated; *m* decoration; (theat.) décor, scenery; memorizing
**decorador -dora** *mf* decorator
**decorar** *va* to decorate; to memorize
**decorativo -va** *adj* decorative
**decoro** *m* decorum; honor, respect
**decoroso -sa** *adj* decorous, decent; honorable, respectful
**decrecer §34** *vn* to decrease, diminish
**decreciente** *adj* decreasing, diminishing; (phonet.) falling (*diphthong*)
**decrecimiento** *m* decrease, diminution
**decremento** *m* decrement, decrease; (rad.) decrement
**decrémetro** *m* (rad.) decremeter
**decrepitación** *f* crackling
**decrepitar** *vn* to crackle
**decrépito -ta** *adj* decrepit
**decrepitud** *f* decrepitude; decline; **en la decrepitud** on the decline
**decrescendo** *m* (mus.) decrescendo
**decretal** *adj* decretal; *f* decretal; **decretales** *fpl* decretals
**decretalista** *m* (theol.) decretalist
**decretar** *va* to decree
**decretero** *m* list of decrees
**decretista** *m* decretist
**decreto** *m* decree
**decreto-ley** *m* decree law
**decretorio -ria** *adj* (med.) critical
**decúbito** *m* (med.) decubitus; (path.) decubitus (*ulcer*)
**decumbente** *adj* decumbent; (bot.) decumbent
**decuplar** *va* to decuple
**decuplicar §86** *va* to decuple
**décuplo -pla** *adj & m* decuple, tenfold
**decuria** *f* decury
**decurrente** *adj* (bot.) decurrent
**decursas** *fpl* arrears
**decurso** *m* course (*of time*)
**decuso -sa** or **decusado -da** *adj* decussate; (bot.) decussate
**dechado** *m* example, sample, model, standard; sampler (*embroidered cloth*)
**dedada** *f* touch (*small quantity, e.g., of honey, picked up on finger*); flip of finger; **dar una dedada de miel a** (coll.) to feed the hopes of
**dedal** *m* thimble; thimbleful; fingerstall
**dedalera** *f* (bot.) foxglove
**Dédalo** *m* (myth.) Daedalus; (*l.c.*) *m* labyrinth
**dedeo** *m* (mus.) finger dexterity
**dedicación** *f* dedication; dedicatory inscription on a building
**dedicante** *mf* dedicator
**dedicar §86** *va* to dedicate (*e.g., a church, a monument, a book, one's life*); to autograph (*a book, a photograph*); to devote (*e.g., one's time*); *vr* to devote oneself
**dedicativo -va** *adj* dedicative
**dedicatorio -ria** *adj* dedicatory; *f* dedication (*e.g., of a book*); autograph, inscription (*in a book, on a photograph*)
**dedil** *m* fingerstall
**dedillo** *m* small finger; **jugar al dedillo** (coll.) to cheat in weighing; **saber al dedillo** (coll.) to have at one's finger tips
**dedo** *m* finger; toe; finger's breadth, finger; (coll.) bit; **alzar el dedo** (coll.) to raise one's hand (*in taking an oath, etc.*); **cogerse los dedos** to burn one's fingers; **el dedo de Dios** the hand of God; **estar a dos dedos de** + *inf* (coll.) to be within an ace of + *ger;* **irse de entre los dedos** (coll.) to slip between the fingers; **no tener dos dedos de frente** (coll.) to have no brains; **poner el dedo en la llaga** to put one's finger on the sore spot; **poner los cinco dedos en la cara a** (coll.) to slap in the face; **tener en la punta de los dedos** (coll.) to have at one's finger tips; **dedo anular** ring finger; **dedo auricular** little finger; **dedo cordial, de en medio,** or **del corazón** middle finger; **dedo gordo** thumb; big toe; **dedo índice** index finger, forefinger; **dedo mayor** middle finger; **dedo médico** ring finger; **dedo meñique** little finger; **dedo mostrador** index finger, forefinger; **dedo pulgar** thumb; big toe; **dedo saludador** index finger, forefinger
**dedolación** *f* (surg.) dedolation
**dedolar §77** *va* (surg.) to cut (*skin*) obliquely
**deducción** *f* deduction; derivation; (mus.) diatonic scale
**deducible** *adj* deducible; deductible
**deducir §38** *va* to deduce; to deduct; (law) to allege
**deductivo -va** *adj* deductive
**deduje** *1st sg pret ind of* **deducir**
**deduzco** *1st sg pres ind of* **deducir**
**defalcar §86** *va* var. of **desfalcar**
**defasar** *va* (elec.) to dephase
**defecación** *f* defecation
**defecar §86** *va* to defecate, purify, refine; *vn* to defecate
**defección** *f* defection; insurrection; mean quirk
**defeccionar** *vn & vr* (Am.) to defect, desert
**defectible** *adj* unsure; faulty, defective
**defectivo -va** *adj* defective; (gram.) defective
**defecto** *m* defect; shortage, lack, absence; **defectos** *mpl* (print.) sheets left over or sheets lacking (*after printing*); **en defecto de** for lack of, in default of; **defecto de masa** (phys.) mass defect
**defectuosamente** *adv* imperfectly
**defectuoso -sa** *adj* defective, faulty
**defeminación** *f* masculinization
**defendedero -ra** *adj* defensible
**defendedor -dora** *mf* defender
**defender §66** *va* to defend; to protect; to delay, interfere with; (law) to defend; (archaic) to forbid, prohibit; *vr* to defend oneself; to get along
**defendible** *adj* defensible
**defenestración** *f* defenestration; violent dismissal or discharge
**defensa** *f* defense; (law & sport) defense; (naut.) skid; fender, guard; horn (*of bull*); tusk (*of elephant*); (Am.) bumper (*of automobile*); **defensa en profundidad** (mil.) defense in depth; *m* (football) back
**defensión** *f* defense, protection
**defensivo -va** *adj* defensive; *m* defense, protection; *f* defensive; **estar a la defensiva** to be on the defensive

**defensor -sora** *adj* defending; *mf* defender; (law) counsel for the defense
**defensoría** *f* (law) defense (*as a practice or service*)
**defensorio** *m* written defense
**deferencia** *f* deference
**deferente** *adj* deferential; (anat.) deferent
**deferir §62** *va* (law) to refer, transfer, delegate; *vn* to defer; **deferir a** to defer to (*e.g., the wishes of someone*)
**deficiencia** *f* deficiency, defect
**deficiente** *adj* deficient, defective
**déficit** *m* (*pl:* **-cit**) deficit; lack, shortage
**deficitario -ria** *adj* (pertaining to a) deficit, deficiency; lacking
**definible** *adj* definable
**definición** *f* definition; outcome; decision, verdict; (opt.) definition
**definido -da** *adj* definite; defined, sharp
**definidor -dora** *adj* defining; *mf* definer; *m* (eccl.) definitor
**definir** *va* to define; to determine, to settle; (paint.) to finish, to complete; *vr* (Am.) to clarify one's political position
**definitivo -va** *adj* definitive; **en definitiva** definitively; in short
**deflación** *f* (econ.) deflation
**deflagración** *f* (chem.) deflagration
**deflagrar** *vn* (chem.) to deflagrate
**deflector** *m* deflector, baffle; (naut.) deflector
**deflegmar** *va* (chem.) to dephlegmate
**deflexión** *f* deflection
**defoliación** *f* defoliation
**deformación** *f* deformation; (mach.) strain; (rad.) distortion
**deformado -da** *adj* deformed; out of shape
**deformar** *va* to deform; *vr* to become deformed
**deforme** *adj* deformed
**deformidad** *f* deformity; crude error; great offense, enormity
**defraudación** *f* defrauding; robbing, cheating; defeat; interception (*e.g., of light*)
**defraudador -dora** *mf* defrauder
**defraudar** *va* to defraud, to cheat; to disappoint; to defeat (*e.g., one's hopes*); to cut off (*light*); **defraudar algo a uno** to cheat someone out of something
**defuera** *adv* outside; **por defuera** outside, on the outside
**defunción** *f* death, demise
**degaullista** *adj & mf* de Gaullist
**degeneración** *f* degeneration; degeneracy; **degeneración amiloidea** (path.) amyloid degeneration; **degeneración grasosa** (path.) fatty degeneration; **degeneración hialina** (path.) hyaline degeneration
**degenerado -da** *adj & mf* degenerate
**degenerar** *vn* to degenerate
**degenerativo -va** *adj* degenerative
**deglución** *f* swallowing, deglutition
**deglutir** *va & vn* to swallow
**degollación** *f* throat-cutting, massacre; décolletage; **degollación de los inocentes** slaughter of the innocents
**degolladero** *m* neck, throttle; slaughterhouse; scaffold (*for capital punishment*); décolletage
**degollado** *m* décolletage, low neck; (orn.) rose-breasted grosbeak
**degollador -dora** *adj* throat-cutting; *mf* executioner
**degolladura** *f* throat-cutting; décolletage; joint (*between bricks*)
**degollante** *mf* (coll.) bore, fool
**degollar §19** *va* to cut in the throat, to cut in the neck; to kill, massacre; to cut (*a dress*) low in the neck; to spoil, to murder (*a performance, drama, etc.*); to bore, become obnoxious to
**degollina** *f* (coll.) slaughter, butchery
**degradación** *f* degradation (*demotion; depravity*); (geol.) degradation
**degradante** *adj* degrading
**degradar** *va* to degrade (*to demote, to demean; to deprave, to debase*); (geol.) to degrade; (mil.) to break
**degüello** *m* throat-cutting, massacre, slaughter; slender part, neck
**degustación** *f* tasting
**degustar** *va* to taste (*e.g., wines*); to savor
**dehesa** *f* pasture land, meadow; (taur.) range
**dehesar** *va* to convert into pasture
**dehesero** *m* keeper of pasture land
**dehiscencia** *f* (biol. & bot.) dehiscence
**dehiscente** *adj* dehiscent
**deicida** *adj* deicidal; *mf* deicide (*person*)
**deicidio** *m* deicide (*act*)
**deidad** *f* deity; (coll.) beauty
**deificación** *f* deification
**deificar §86** *va* to deify; *vr* (theol.) to become deified (*by divine union*)
**deífico -ca** *adj* deific
**deiforme** *adj* (poet.) godlike
**Deípara** *adj* Deipara (*pertaining to the Virgin Mary*)
**deísmo** *m* deism
**deísta** *adj* deistic; *mf* deist
**deja** *f* jut, projection
**dejación** *f* abandonment, relinquishment; **hacer dejación de** to abandon
**dejadez** *f* laziness, negligence; untidiness, slovenliness; fatigue, low spirits
**dejado -da** *adj* lazy, negligent; untidy, slovenly; dejected, low-spirited, listless; **dejado de la mano de Dios** vile, infamous, beyond redemption; bungling; *f* (sport) easy short return (*of ball*)
**dejamiento** *m* abandonment, relinquishment; laziness; untidiness; dejection
**dejar** *va* to leave; to abandon; to yield, produce; to appoint; to lend; **dejar** + *inf* to let + *inf*, to permit + *inf;* to let be + *pp*, *e.g.*, **dejar oír la voz** to let one's voice be heard; **dejar caer** to drop, let fall; **dejar feo a** (coll.) to slight; **dejar fresco a** (coll.) to discomfit, leave in the lurch; **dejar por** to leave as, to consider as; **dejar por** or **que** + *inf* to leave to be + *pp*, e.g., **dejó mucho trabajo por hacer** he left a lot of work to be done; **dejar ver** to show, to make it plain ‖ *vn* to stop; **no dejar de** + *inf* to not fail to + *inf;* **dejar de** + *inf* to stop or cease + *ger;* to fail to + *inf* ‖ *vr* to be careless or slovenly; to grow (*a beard, a mustache*); **dejarse** + *inf* to allow oneself to + *inf;* to allow oneself to be + *pp;* **dejarse a** to give oneself over to, to be devoted to; to yield to; **dejarse de** to cut out (*talk, nonsense*); to stop asking (*questions*); to stop making (*compliments*); to put aside (*doubts*); **dejarse de** + *inf* to stop + *ger;* **dejarse decir** to let slip (*in conversation*); **dejarse ver** to show up; to be evident, be easily seen
**dejillo** *m* accent (*of a region*); aftertaste
**dejo** *m* abandonment; end, stop; accent (*of a region*); slovenliness, neglect; aftertaste; (fig.) touch, aftertaste; drop (*in voice*)
**del** contraction of **de** and **el**
**delación** *f* accusation, denunciation, information
**delantal** *m* apron; workman's apron
**delante** *adv* before, in front, ahead; **delante de** before, in front of, ahead of
**delantero -ra** *adj* front; head; first; *m* postilion; nosing (*of stair tread*); (sport) forward; *f* front, front part; fore skirt; front (*of garment*); front row; front edge (*of book*); lead, advantage; cowcatcher; (taur.) front row (*of tendido bajo, i.e., third row counting barrera and contrabarrera*); **coger la delantera a** or **tomar la delantera a** to get ahead of, to outstrip; to get a start on; **tomar la delantera** to take the lead; **delanteras** *fpl* overalls
**delatable** *adj* accusable
**delatar** *va* to accuse, denounce, inform on; to reveal, divulge
**delator -tora** *adj* accusing, informing; *mf* accuser, denouncer, informer
**dele** *m* (print.) dele
**deleble** *adj* eradicable
**delectación** *f* delectation
**delegación** *f* delegation; (com.) branch; (Am.) police station
**delegado -da** *mf* delegate; (com.) agent, representative
**delegar §59** *va* to delegate
**deleitabilísimo -ma** *adj super* very or most delectable
**deleitable** *adj* delectable

**deleitación** *f* or **deleitamiento** *m* delectation, delight
**deleitar** *va* to delight; *vr* to delight, to take delight; **deleitarse con** or **en** to delight in, to take delight in; **deleitarse en** + *inf* to delight in or to take delight in + *ger*
**deleite** *m* delight
**deleitoso -sa** *adj* delightful, delicious
**deletéreo -a** *adj* deleterious, noxious
**deletreador -dora** *adj* spelling; *mf* speller
**deletrear** *va* to spell; to decipher; to interpret; *vn* to spell; to decipher
**deletreo** *m* spelling
**deleznable** *adj* perishable, fragile; crumbly; slippery; frail, unstable
**deleznar** *vr* to slip, slide
**délfico -ca** *adj* Delphian or Delphic
**delfín** *m* dauphin; (zool.) dolphin; (*cap.*) *m* (astr.) Dolphin
**delfina** *f* dauphiness
**Delfos** *f* Delphi
**delga** *f* (elec.) commutator bar
**delgadez** *f* thinness, leanness, slenderness; delicateness, tenuity, lightness; acuity, ingenuity
**delgado -da** *adj* thin, lean, slender, slim, lank; delicate, tenuous, light; acute, ingenious; (agr.) poor, exhausted; *m* flank (*of an animal*); (naut.) dead rise
**delgaducho -cha** *adj* thinnish, lanky
**deliberación** *f* deliberation
**deliberadamente** *adv* deliberately
**deliberante** *adj* deliberative
**deliberar** *va* to deliberate; **deliberar** + *inf* to come to a decision to + *inf; vn* to deliberate
**deliberativo -va** *adj* deliberative; (coll.) opinionated
**delicadez** *f* delicateness; touchiness; laziness
**delicadeza** *f* delicacy, delicateness; acuity, ingenuity; scrupulousness
**delicado -da** *adj* delicate; acute, ingenious; touchy, hard to please; cautious, scrupulous
**delicia** *f* delight
**delicioso -sa** *adj* delicious, delightful
**delictivo -va** or **delictuoso -sa** *adj* criminal
**delicuescencia** *f* deliquescence
**delicuescente** *adj* deliquescent
**delimitación** *f* delimitation
**delimitar** *va* to delimit
**delincuencia** *f* guilt, criminality, delinquency
**delincuente** *adj* guilty, criminal, delinquent; *mf* guilty person, criminal, delinquent
**delineación** *f* delineation
**delineador -dora** *adj* delineating; *mf* delineator, designer
**delineamento** or **delineamiento** *m* delineation
**delineante** *adj* delineating, drafting; *mf* delineator, draftsman
**delinear** *va* to delineate, to outline
**delinquimiento** *m* transgression, guilt, delinquency
**delinquir** **§39** *vn* to transgress, be guilty, be delinquent
**delio -lia** *adj & mf* Delian
**deliquio** *m* swoon, faint
**delirante** *adj* delirious
**delirar** *vn* to be delirious, to rave, to rant; to talk nonsense
**delirio** *m* delirium; nonsense
**delírium tremens** *m* (path.) delirium tremens
**delito** *m* crime, transgression; **delito de incendio** arson; **delito de lesa majestad** lese majesty
**Delos** *f* Delos
**delta** *f* delta; *m & f* delta (*of a river*)
**deltoides** *adj* deltoid (*triangular*); (anat.) deltoid; *m* (anat.) deltoid, deltoid muscle
**deludir** *va* to delude
**delusor -sora** *adj* delusive; *mf* deluder
**delusorio -ria** *adj* delusive, delusory
**demacración** *f* emaciation
**demacrar** *va & vr* to waste away
**demagogia** *f* demagoguery or demagogy
**demagógico -ca** *adj* demagogic
**demagogo -ga** *mf* demagog
**demanda** *f* demand; petition; claim; complaint; undertaking; begging; charity box (*carried by beggars*); lawsuit; quest (*of the Holy Grail*); (elec.) load; **ir en demanda de** to go looking for; **tener demanda** to be in demand; **demanda máxima** (elec.) peak load
**demandadero -ra** *mf* messenger (*in convents and prisons*); outside errand boy or girl
**demandado -da** *mf* (law) defendant
**demandador -dora** *mf* claimant, solicitor; (law) complainant, plaintiff
**demandante** *mf* (law) plaintiff, complainant
**demandar** *va* to demand; (law) to sue, file a suit against
**demarcación** *f* demarcation
**demarcador -dora** *adj* demarcating; *mf* demarcator
**demarcar** **§86** *va* to demarcate
**demás** *adj indef* other, rest of the, e.g., **la demás gente** the rest of the people; **estar demás** to be useless; to be in the way, be unwanted; **lo demás** the rest; **por lo demás** furthermore, besides; *pron indef* others; **los** or **las demás** the others, the rest; *adv* besides; **por demás** in vain; too, too much; **demás de** besides, in addition to
**demasía** *f* excess, superabundance, surplus; boldness, audacity; insolence, outrage; evil, guilt, wrong; **en demasía** too, too much, excessively
**demasiadamente** *adv* too, too much, excessively
**demasiado -da** *adj & pron indef* too much; **demasiados -das** *adj & pron indef pl* too many; **demasiado** *adv* too; too much, too hard
**demasiar** *vr* (coll.) to go too far, to exceed the bounds of reason
**demediar** *va* to divide in half; to reach the middle of; to use up half of; *vn* to be divided in half
**demencia** *f* dementia, insanity; **demencia precoz** (path.) dementia praecox
**dementar** *va* to drive crazy; *vr* to go crazy
**demente** *adj* demented, insane; *mf* lunatic, crazy person; *m* madman
**demérito** *m* demerit, unworthiness
**demeritorio -ria** *adj* undeserving
**Deméter** *f* or **Demetria** *f* (myth.) Demeter
**demisión** *f* yielding, submission, humility
**demiurgo** *m* (philos.) Demiurge
**democracia** *f* democracy
**demócrata** *adj* democratic; *mf* democrat
**democrático -ca** *adj* democratic
**democratización** *f* democratization
**democratizar** **§76** *va & vr* to democratize
**Demócrito** *m* Democritus
**Demogorgón** *m* (myth.) Demogorgon
**demografía** *f* demography
**demográfico -ca** *adj* demographic or demographical
**demoledor -dora** *adj* demolishing, destructive; *mf* demolisher
**demoler** **§63** *va* to demolish
**demolición** *f* demolition
**demonche** *m* (coll.) devil
**demoníaco -ca** *adj* demoniac or demoniacal; demonic; *mf* demoniac
**demonio** *m* demon; devil; **estar hecho un demonio** (coll.) to be wild, be crazy as the devil; **estudiar con el demonio** (coll.) to be full of devilishness
**demonismo** *m* demonism
**demonolatría** *f* demonolatry
**demonología** *f* demonology
**demonomancia** *f* demonomancy
**demontre** *m* (coll.) devil; *interj* the deuce!, the devil!
**demora** *f* delay; (naut.) bearing
**demorar** *va* to delay; *vn* to delay, tarry, linger; to be delayed; (naut.) to bear
**Demóstenes** *m* Demosthenes
**demostrabilidad** *f* demonstrability
**demostrable** *adj* demonstrable
**demostración** *f* demonstration
**demostrador -dora** *adj* demonstrating; *mf* demonstrator; *m* hand (*of clock*); gnomon (*of sundial*)
**demostrar** **§77** *va* to demonstrate; **demostrar** + *inf* to demonstrate that + *ind*
**demostrativo -va** *adj* demonstrative; (gram.) demonstrative; *m* (gram.) demonstrative
**demótico -ca** *adj* demotic

**demudación** *f* change, alteration; change of countenance
**demudar** *va* to change, to alter; to cloak, to disguise; *vr* to change, be changed; to change countenance, to color suddenly
**demulcente** *adj & m* demulcent
**demulsibilidad** *f* (chem.) demulsibility
**demulsionar** *va* (chem.) demulsify
**denario -ria** *adj* denary; *m* denarius
**dendriforme** *adj* dendriform
**dendrita** *f* (anat., physiol. & mineral.) dendrite
**dendrítico -ca** *adj* dendritic or dendritical
**dendrografía** *f* dendrography
**dendroide** *adj* dendroid
**dendrómetro** *m* dendrometer
**denegación** *f* denial, refusal
**denegar §29** *va* to deny, to refuse; (law) to deny, to refuse
**denegrecer §34** *va* to blacken, to darken; *vr* to become black, to turn dark
**denegrido -da** *adj* blackish
**dengoso -sa** *adj* overnice, prudish, affected
**dengue** *m* overniceness, prudery; cape with long points; sardine boat; (path.) dengue
**denguero -ra** *adj* overnice, prudish
**denigración** *f* defamation, revilement; insult
**denigrante** *adj* defamatory; insulting; *mf* defamer; insulter
**denigrar** *va* to defame, revile, sully; to insult
**denigrativo -va** *adj* defamatory; insulting
**denodado -da** *adj* brave, daring, bold
**denominación** *f* denomination
**denominadamente** *adv* distinctly, markedly
**denominador -dora** *adj* denominating; *mf* denominator; *m* (math.) denominator
**denominar** *va* to name, to indicate, to denominate
**denominativo -va** *adj* denominative; (gram.) denominative; *m* (gram.) denominative
**denostadamente** *adv* insultingly, abusively
**denostador -dora** *adj* insulting; *mf* insulter, abuser
**denostar §77** *va* to insult, abuse
**denostoso -sa** *adj* insulting
**denotación** *f* denotation
**denotar** *va* to denote
**denotativo -va** *adj* denotative
**densidad** *f* density; darkness; confusion; (fig.) solidity, fullness, substance; **densidad de flujo** (phys.) flux density
**densimetría** *f* densimetry
**densímetro** *m* densimeter
**denso -sa** *adj* dense; dark; confused; thick, crowded; (fig.) solid, full, rich
**dentado -da** *adj* toothed, dentate; (philately) perforated; *m* gear; teeth; (philately) perforation; **dentado de peine** (philately) comb perforation
**dentadura** *f* denture, set of teeth; **ablandarle a uno la dentadura** (coll.) to punch someone in the teeth, to knock someone's teeth out; **dentadura artificial** denture, set of artificial teeth
**dental** *adj* dental; (phonet.) dental; *m* tooth of threshing machine; moldboard (*of plow*); *f* (phonet.) dental
**dentalización** *f* (phonet.) dentalization
**dentalizar §76** *va* (phonet.) to dentalize; *vr* (phonet.) to become dentalized
**dentar §18** *va* to tooth, furnish with teeth; (philately) to perforate; **sin dentar** (philately) imperforate; *vn* to teethe
**dentario -ria** *adj* dental; *f* (bot.) toothwort
**dentejón** *m* yoke for oxen
**dentelaria** *f* (bot.) leadwort
**dentellado -da** *adj* denticulate; serrulate; bitten with the teeth; (arch.) denticulate; (her.) dentelated; *f* biting; bite; tooth mark; **a dentelladas** with the teeth
**dentellar** *vn* to chatter (*said of teeth*)
**dentellear** *va* to nibble, nibble at
**dentellón** *m* cam, tooth (*of lock*); (arch.) tooth (*of toothing*); (arch.) dentil
**dentera** *f* tooth edge; envy; eagerness, great desire; **dar dentera** to set the teeth on edge; to make eager or impatient
**dentezuelo** *m* little tooth
**dentición** *f* dentition, teething
**denticulación** *f* denticulation
**denticulado -da** *adj* denticulate
**denticular** *adj* denticular
**dentículo** *m* little tooth; (arch.) dentil; (bot. & zool.) dentation
**dentífrico -ca** *adj* tooth (*paste, etc.*); *m* dentifrice
**dentilabial** *adj & f* (phonet.) dentilabial
**dentilingual** *adj & f* (phonet.) dentilingual
**dentina** *f* (anat.) dentine
**dentirrostro -tra** *adj* dentirostral or dentirostrate; *m* (orn.) dentiroster
**dentista** *mf* dentist
**dentistería** *f* dentistry
**dentística** *f* (Am.) dentistry
**dentivano -na** *adj* (vet.) having long, wide teeth
**dentón -tona** *adj* having large, uneven teeth; *m* (ichth.) dentex
**dentro** *adv* inside, within; **por dentro** on the inside; **dentro de** inside, within; **dentro de poco** shortly; **dentro en** on the inside of; **dentro o fuera** (coll.) yes or no
**dentudo -da** *adj* having large, uneven teeth
**denudación** *f* denudation
**denudar** *va* to denude, lay bare; *vn* to be denuded; to be stripped of bark
**denuedo** *m* bravery, daring
**denuesto** *m* insult, abuse
**denuncia** *f* proclamation, announcement; foretelling; denunciation
**denunciación** *f* denunciation
**denunciador -dora** *mf* denouncer, denunciator
**denunciante** *mf* denouncer
**denunciar** *va* to proclaim; to foretell; to denounce, to denunciate, to squeal on; (dipl. & min.) to denounce
**denunciatorio -ria** *adj* denunciatory
**denuncio** *m* (min.) denouncement, denunciation
**deontología** *f* deontology; **deontología médica** medical ethics
**deparar** *va* to provide, furnish; to present
**departamental** *adj* departmental
**departamento** *m* department; compartment; naval district (*in Spain*); (rail.) compartment; apartment
**departidor -dora** *adj* conversing; *mf* converser, conversationalist
**departir** *vn* to chat, to converse
**depauperación** *f* impoverishment; weakening, exhaustion, depletion
**depauperar** *va* to pauperize, to impoverish; to weaken, exhaust, deplete; *vr* to become weakened, become exhausted
**dependencia** *f* dependence, dependency; branch, branch office; affair, charge, agency; relationship; friendship; employees, clerks; **dependencias** *fpl* accessories
**depender** *vn* to depend; **depender de** to depend on or upon
**dependienta** *f* female employee, clerk, store clerk
**dependiente** *adj* dependent; (pertaining to a) branch; *mf* dependent; employee, clerk, store clerk
**depilación** *f* depilation
**depilar** *va* to depilate
**depilatorio -ria** *adj & m* depilatory
**deplorable** *adj* deplorable
**deplorar** *va* to deplore
**depondré** *1st sg fut ind of* **deponer**
**deponente** *adj* (gram.) deponent; *mf* (law) deponent; *m* (gram.) deponent verb
**deponer §69** *va* to set aside, to put aside, to remove, to take down; to remove from office, to depose; to lay down (*arms*); (law) to depose, to depone; *vn* to have a movement (*of bowels*); (law) to depose, to depone; (Am.) to vomit
**depongo** *1st sg pres ind of* **deponer**
**depopulador -dora** *adj* devastating; *mf* destroyer, plunderer
**deportación** *f* deportation
**deportado -da** *mf* deportee
**deportante** *mf* sport fan; sportsman
**deportar** *va* to deport
**deporte** *m* sport; outdoor recreation
**deportismo** *m* sport, sports; love of sport or sports; participation in sports

**deportista** *adj* (pertaining to) sport; sporting; *mf* sport fan; *m* sportsman; *f* sportswoman
**deportivo -va** *adj* (pertaining to) sport, sports
**deposición** *f* deposition, deposal; removal (*from office*); bowel movement; (law) deposition
**depositador -dora** *adj* depositing; *mf* depositor
**depositante** *mf* depositor
**depositar** *va* to deposit; to store; to entrust; to confide; to check (*baggage*); to bond (*merchandise*); to commit (*a person*); to place (*a corpse*) in a receiving vault; (law) to free (*a young person*) from parental restraint; *vr* to deposit, to settle
**depositaría** *f* depository; public treasury; trust
**depositario -ria** *adj* depository; (pertaining to a) deposit; *mf* depositary, repository; *m* public treasurer
**depósito** *m* depot, warehouse; deposit; stack (*of books in a library*); dump; reservoir; tank; well (*of a fountain pen*); (mil.) depot; **en depósito** on deposit; **depósito anatómico** morgue; **depósito comercial** bonded warehouse; **depósito de agua** reservoir; water tank; **depósito (judicial) de cadáveres** morgue; **depósito de cereales** grain elevator; **depósito de equipajes** (rail.) checkroom; **depósito de gasolina** (aut.) gas tank; **depósito de locomotoras** (rail.) roundhouse; **depósito de municiones** munition dump
**depravación** *f* depravation, depravity
**depravado -da** *adj* depraved
**depravador -dora** *adj* depraving; *mf* depraver
**depravar** *va* to deprave; *vr* to become depraved
**deprecación** *f* entreaty, prayer
**deprecante** *adj* entreating, imploring
**deprecar** §86 *va* to entreat, to implore
**deprecativo -va** *adj* deprecative; (gram.) imperative; *m* (gram.) imperative (*with supplication or entreaty*)
**deprecatorio -ria** *adj* deprecatory
**depreciación** *f* depreciation (*in value*)
**depreciar** *va & vn* to depreciate (*to diminish in value*)
**depredación** *f* depredation; embezzlement; (law) depredation
**depredador -dora** *adj* depredating; predatory; *mf* depredator; predator
**depredar** *va* to depredate; to embezzle
**depresión** *f* depression; drop, dip; (path.) depression; (meteor.) depression, low; recess, recession (*e.g., in a wall*)
**depresivo -va** *adj* depressive
**depresor -sora** *adj* depressing; *mf* depressor; *m* (anat., physiol. & surg.) depressor; **depresor de la lengua** (med.) tongue depressor
**deprimente** *adj* depressive; depressing; depressant; *m* (med.) depressant
**deprimido -da** *adj* depressed, flattened; weakened; receding (*e.g., forehead*)
**deprimir** *va* to depress, to compress; to push in; to belittle; to humiliate; to weaken; *vr* to be or become depressed or compressed; to be or become humiliated; to be weakened, to become weak; to recede
**depuesto -ta** *pp of* **deponer**
**depuración** *f* purification; purging
**depurar** *va* to purify, refine, cleanse; to purge; *vr* to be or become purified, to be cleansed
**depurativo -va** *adj & m* (med.) depurative
**depuse** *1st sg pret ind of* **deponer**
**derecera** *f* straight road, straight path
**derecha** *f* see **derecho**
**derechamente** *adv* directly, straight; wisely, justly; properly
**derechazo** *m* blow with the right (*hand*); (box.) right
**derechero -ra** *adj* right, just, sure; *m* tax collector; *f* straightaway, straight road
**derechismo** *m* rightism
**derechista** *adj & mf* rightist
**derecho -cha** *adj* right; right-hand; right-handed; straight; standing, upright; *m* law; right; grant, privilege, exemption; road, path; right side (*e.g., of cloth*); **derechos** *mpl* dues, duties, fees, taxes; **según derecho** by right, by rights; **derecho canónico** canon law; **derecho civil** civil law; **derecho consuetudinario** common law; **derecho de asilo** right of asylum; **derecho de gentes** international law; **derecho de reunión** right of assembly; **derecho de propiedad literaria** copyright; **derecho de subscripción** (com.) right; **derecho de visita** right of search; **derecho divino** divine right; **derecho internacional** international law; **derecho romano** Roman law; **derechos civiles** civil rights; **derechos consulares** consular fees; **derechos de aduana** customhouse duties; **derechos de almacenaje** storage (*costs*); **derechos de autor** royalty; **derechos del hombre** rights of man; **derechos naturales** natural rights; **derechos reservados** copyright; *f* right hand; right-hand side; (pol.) right; **a derechas** right, rightly; **a la derecha** right, on the right, to the right; **derecho** *adv* directly, straight; rightly, wisely; **todo derecho** straight ahead
**derechura** *f* rightness, rectitude; directness, straightness; servants' wages; **en derechura** directly, straight; right away, without delay; with determination, steadfastly
**deriva** *f* (aer. & naut.) drift; (gun.) drift compensation; **ir a la deriva** (naut.) to drift, to be adrift
**derivación** *f* derivation; (gram., math. & med.) derivation; (gun.) drift; (elec.) shunt, shunt connection; **en derivación** (elec.) shunt, shunted; **derivación regresiva** (philol.) back formation
**derivado -da** *adj* derived; derivative; (gram.) derivative; (elec.) shunt, derived; *m* derivative, by-product; **derivado regresivo** (philol.) back formation, *f* (math.) derivative
**derivador** *m* (elec.) graduator
**derivar** *va* to derive; to turn (*e.g., one's attention*); to guide, to lead; (elec.) to shunt; *vn & vr* to derive, to be derived; (aer. & naut.) to drift
**derivativo -va** *adj & m* (gram. & med.) derivative
**derivo** *m* derivation, origin
**derivómetro** *m* (aer. & naut.) drift meter
**dermalgia** *f* (path.) skin neuralgia
**dermatitis** *f* (path.) dermatitis
**dermatoesqueleto** *m* (zool.) exoskeleton
**dermatografía** *f* (path.) dermatographia; dermatography (*description of skin*)
**dermatología** *f* dermatology
**dermatológico -ca** *adj* dermatological
**dermatólogo -ga** *mf* dermatologist
**dermatosis** *f* (path.) dermatosis
**dermesto** *m* (ent.) larder beetle
**dérmico -ca** *adj* dermic, dermal
**dermis** *f* (anat.) dermis, cutis
**dermografía** *f* or **dermografismo** *m* (path.) dermographia or dermographism
**-dero -ra** *suffix adj* -able, e.g., **casadero** marriageable; **comedero** eatable; -ible, e.g., **hacedero** feasible; *suffix m* used to indicate the place where something is performed, e.g., **desembarcadero** landing place; **lavadero** washing place; **picadero** riding school
**derogación** *f* abolition, elimination; decrease, deterioration, derogation
**derogar** §59 *va* to destroy, abolish, modify, reform (*a law, custom, etc.*)
**derogatorio -ria** *adj* abolishing, modifying, repealing
**derrabadura** *f* cutting or pulling out the tail; wound left after cutting tail
**derrabar** *va* to cut or pull out the tail of, to dock
**derrama** *f* apportionment of a tax; special tax
**derramadero** *m* dumping ground, dumping place; weir, spillway
**derramado -da** *adj* extravagant, prodigal, lavish
**derramamiento** *m* pouring, spilling, shedding; spreading, scattering, publishing; lavishing, wasting; waterflow, dispersion
**derramar** *va* to pour out, to spill, to shed; to spread, scatter, publish; to lavish, to waste; to apportion (*e.g., taxes*); *vr* to run over, to overflow; to spread, spread out; to open, flow, empty (*said of a stream*)
**derramasolaces** *mf* (*pl:* **-ces**) wet blanket

**derrame** *m* pouring, spill, shed; spread, dispersion; lavishing, waste; overflow; leakage; (arch.) splay, chamfering; slope; outlet; (med.) discharge, effusion
**derramo** *m* (arch.) splay, chamfering, flare, flanging
**derrapar** *vn* to skid
**derredor** *m* circumference; **al** or **en derredor** around, round about; **al** or **en derredor de** around; **por todo el derredor** all around, in every direction
**derrelicción** *f* dereliction, abandonment
**derrelicto** *m* (naut.) derelict (*ship*)
**derrelinquir** **§39** *va* to forsake, to abandon
**derrenegar** **§29** *vn* (coll.) to be a hater; **derrenegar de** (coll.) to be a hater of, to hate, loathe, detest
**derrengado -da** *adj* twisted, bent, crooked; lame, crippled, out of shape
**derrengadura** *f* crookedness; lameness, sore back
**derrengar** **§29** or **§59** *va* to break the back of, to cripple; to bend, make crooked; (dial.) to knock (*fruit*) from tree with a stick
**derrengo** *m* (dial.) stick for knocking fruit from tree
**derreniego** *m* (coll.) curse, blasphemy
**derretido -da** *adj* madly in love; *m* concrete
**derretimiento** *m* melting, thawing; intense love, mad passion
**derretir** **§94** *va* to melt, to thaw; to squander; (coll.) to change (*money*); *vr* to melt, to thaw; to be or fall madly in love; to be very susceptible, to fall in love easily; (coll.) to be worried, uneasy, or impatient
**derribador -dora** *adj* overthrowing; *mf* overthrower; *m* feller (*in abattoir*)
**derribar** *va* to demolish, destroy, tear down, knock down; to wreck; to fell; to overthrow; to subdue (*an emotion or passion*); to bring down, shoot down; to bring down, humiliate; *vr* to fall down, tumble down; to throw oneself on the ground
**derribo** *m* demolition, wrecking, overthrow; felling; bringing down (*of an enemy plane*); **derribos** *mpl* debris, rubble
**derrocadero** *m* rocky precipice
**derrocamiento** *m* flinging, throwing down, overthrow; demolition; ousting
**derrocar** **§86** or **§95** *va* to throw from a rock or precipice; to demolish, tear down, knock down; to overthrow, bring down, humble, oust
**derrochador -dora** *adj* squandering; *mf* squanderer, wastrel
**derrochar** *va* to waste, squander
**derroche** *m* waste, squandering, extravagance, profusion
**derrota** *f* rout, defeat; route, road, way; (naut.) course
**derrotado -da** *adj* threadbare, shabby
**derrotar** *va* to rout, put to flight; to defeat; to wear, wear out; to squander, waste; to ruin; *vr* (naut.) to drift from the course
**derrote** *m* upward thrust with the horns
**derrotero** *m* (naut.) ship's course, navigation route; route, course
**derrotismo** *m* defeatism
**derrotista** *adj & mf* defeatist
**derrubiar** *va & vr* to wash away, to wear away
**derrubio** *m* washout; alluvium
**derruir** **§41** *va* to tear down, to raze, to destroy, to ruin
**derrumbadero** *m* precipice, crag; hazard, risky business
**derrumbamiento** *m* plunge, headlong plunge; collapse, cave-in; (eng.) wrecking; **derrumbamiento de tierra** landslide
**derrumbar** *va* to throw headlong; *vr* to plunge headlong; to crumble, collapse; to fall in, cave in
**derrumbe** *m* precipice; fall; landslide; cave-in; (eng.) wrecking
**derrumbo** *m* precipice
**derviche** *m* dervish
**des-** *prefix* de-, e.g., **descornar** dehorn; **destronar** dethrone; dis-, e.g., **desconfiar** distrust; **descubrir** discover; un-, e.g., **desgraciado** unfortunate; **desigual** unequal; **desabotonar** unbutton; **desenganchar** unhook; under-, e.g., **desnutrido** underfed
**desabarrancar** **§86** *va* to pull out of a ditch; to extricate
**desabastecer** **§34** *va* to deprive of supplies or provisions
**desabejar** *va* to remove the bees from
**desabillé** *m* deshabille
**desabollador** *m* dent remover (*tool*)
**desabollar** *va* to knock the dents out of, to straighten, to flatten; *vr* to flatten out
**desabollonar** *va* var. of **desabollar**
**desabonar** *vr* to drop one's subscription
**desabono** *m* cancellation of subscription, discontinuance of subscription; damage, harm (*through gossip*)
**desabor** *m* tastelessness, insipidity
**desabordar** *vr* (naut.) to get clear of a ship; (naut.) to get clear of each other (*said of two ships which have run afoul of each other*)
**desaborido -da** *adj* tasteless, insipid; flimsy, insignificant; (coll.) dull, witless; *mf* (coll.) dull, witless person
**desabotonar** *va* to unbutton; *vn* to blossom, to bloom
**desabrido -da** *adj* tasteless, insipid, unseasoned; rough, unpleasant, uneven; gruff, surly; unseasonable, inclement; kicking, hard-kicking (*said of a gun*)
**desabrigado -da** *adj* lightly dressed; unsheltered; uncovered, unprotected, defenseless
**desabrigar** **§59** *va* to uncover, bare, undress; to deprive of shelter or protection; *vr* to uncover oneself, to undress, to take off clothing; to be deprived of shelter or protection
**desabrigo** *m* uncovering; lack of covering or clothing; lack of protection; unprotected place; abandonment, desertion
**desabrillantar** *va* to deprive of luster; *vr* to lose luster
**desabrimiento** *m* lack of seasoning, insipidity, flatness; bitterness, despondency; harshness; recoil (*of firearms*)
**desabrir** *va* to give a bad taste to; to embitter; *vr* to become embittered
**desabrochar** *va* to unsnap, to unbutton, to unfasten, to unclasp; to reveal; *vr* to become unfastened; (coll.) to unbosom oneself; **desabrocharse con** (coll.) to unbosom oneself to, to open up one's heart to
**desacalorar** *vr* to cool off; (fig.) to cool off (*from anger*)
**desacatador -dora** *adj* disrespectful, irreverent; *mf* disrespectful or irreverent person
**desacatamiento** *m* disrespect, irreverence
**desacatar** *va* to treat disrespectfully, to be disrespectful toward, to be irreverent toward
**desacato** *m* disrespect, irreverence, contempt
**desacedar** *va* to remove the roughness from
**desaceitado -da** *adj* unoiled
**desaceitar** *va* to remove the oil from
**desaceleración** *f* deceleration
**desacelerar** *va & vr* to decelerate
**desacerar** *va* to remove or wear away the steel from; *vr* to lose its steel surface or edge (*said, e.g., of a tool*)
**desacertado -da** *adj* wrong, unwise; wide of the mark
**desacertar** **§18** *vn* to be wrong
**desacidificar** **§86** *va* to remove the acidity from; to neutralize (*an acid*)
**desacierto** *m* error, mistake, blunder
**desacobardar** *va* to free of fear, to stiffen
**desacomodado -da** *adj* inconvenient; troublesome; out of service, unemployed; not well-to-do
**desacomodamiento** *m* inconvenience
**desacomodar** *va* to inconvenience, disturb; to discharge, dismiss; *vr* to lose one's job
**desacomodo** *m* discharge, dismissal
**desacompañamiento** *m* abandonment, lack of company
**desacompañar** *va* to abandon, leave the company of
**desaconsejado -da** *adj* ill-advised
**desaconsejar** *va* to dissuade, try to dissuade
**desacoplar** *va* to disconnect, to uncouple
**desacordado -da** *adj* discordant; (mus.) out of tune, inharmonious; (paint.) inharmonious (*in color*), out of proportion

**desacordar §77** *va* to put out of tune; *vr* to get out of tune; to become forgetful
**desacorde** *adj* discordant, inharmonious, incongruous
**desacorralar** *va* to take out of a corral or inclosure; (taur.) to bring (*a bull*) out into the ring or into an open field; (coll.) to get (*someone*) out of a hole or jam
**desacostumbrado -da** *adj* unaccustomed, unusual
**desacostumbrar** *va* to break of a habit or custom, to wean away
**desacotar** *va* to lay open (*a pasture or field*); to refuse, reject; *vn* to withdraw from a conference or deal
**desacoto** *m* opening a pasture or field
**desacreditar** *va* to discredit, bring discredit on; *vn* to discredit, to bring discredit
**desacuerdo** *m* discord, disaccord, disagreement; error, mistake; forgetfulness, forgetting; derangement; unconsciousness
**desaderezar §76** *va* to disarrange, to ruffle, to upset; *vr* to become disarranged, be put in disorder
**desadeudar** *va* to free from debt; *vr* to get out of debt
**desadormecer §34** *va* to awaken; to free from numbness; *vr* to awaken, get awake; to get free of numbness
**desadornar** *va* to remove the ornaments or decorations from; *vr* to be unadorned
**desadorno** *m* lack of ornaments, lack of decoration
**desadvertido -da** *adj* inattentive; unnoticed
**desadvertimiento** *m* inadvertence
**desadvertir §62** *va* to fail to notice, to not notice, to be unaware of
**desafear** *va* to make less ugly, to remove the ugliness of; *vr* to become less ugly, to lose one's or its ugliness
**desafección** *f* disaffection, dislike
**desafectar** *va* to dislike
**desafecto -ta** *adj* disaffected; opposed; *m* disaffection, dislike
**desaferrar** *va* to loosen, let go, unfasten; to make (*a person*) change his mind; (naut.) to raise (*the anchors*)
**desafiadero** *m* secret dueling ground
**desafiador -dora** *adj* challenging, defiant; *mf* challenger; duelist; feudist
**desafiar §90** *va* to challenge, dare, defy; to oppose, to face, to rival, to compete with; **desafiar a** + *inf* to challenge to + *inf; vn* to feud; *vr* to challenge each other; to compete
**desafición** *f* disaffection, dislike
**desaficionar** *va* to cause to dislike; *vr* to become disliked; **desaficionarse de** to lose one's liking for
**desafilar** *va* to dull, make dull; *vr* to dull, become dull
**desafinación** *f* dissonance, being out of tune
**desafinadamente** *adv* out of tune
**desafinado -da** *adj* out of tune, flat
**desafinar** *va* to put out of tune; to play or sing out of tune; *vn* to get out of tune; to play or sing out of tune; (coll.) to speak indiscreetly; *vr* to get out of tune; to play or sing out of tune
**desafío** *m* challenge, dare; rivalry, competition
**desaforado -da** *adj* disorderly, outrageous, impudent; huge, colossal, enormous; *mf* rowdy
**desaforar §77** *va* to encroach upon the rights of; *vr* to forget oneself, to act in an outrageous manner
**desaforrar** *va* to take the lining out of
**desafortunadamente** *adv* unfortunately
**desafortunado -da** *adj* unfortunate, unlucky
**desafuero** *m* excess, outrage, lawlessness
**desagarrar** *va* (coll.) to let go of, to loosen one's hold on
**desagraciado -da** *adj* graceless, ungraceful
**desagraciar** *va* to make ungraceful, to deprive of charm
**desagradable** *adj* disagreeable
**desagradar** *va* to displease; **desagradar** + *inf* to displease (*someone*) to + *inf*, to not like to + *inf; vn* to displease; *vr* to be displeased; **desagradarse de** to be displeased at
**desagradecer §34** *va* to be ungrateful for, to be unappreciative of
**desagradecido -da** *adj* ungrateful; **desagradecido a** ungrateful for (*a kindness*); **desagradecido con** or **para con** ungrateful to (*a person*)
**desagradecimiento** *m* ungratefulness, ingratitude
**desagrado** *m* displeasure
**desagraviar** *va* to make amends to, to indemnify
**desagravio** *m* amends, compensation, indemnification
**desagregación** *f* disintegration; (geol.) disintegration
**desagregar §59** *va & vr* to disintegrate
**desaguadero** *m* drain, outlet; (fig.) drain (*source of expense*)
**desaguador** *m* drain, outlet; irrigation drain
**desaguar §23** *va* to drain, empty; to waste, squander; *vn* to flow, to empty; *vr* to drain, be drained; to vomit; to have a movement (*of bowels*)
**desaguazar §76** *va* to drain, to empty
**desagüe** *m* drainage, sewerage; drain, outlet
**desaguisado -da** *adj* illegal, unreasonable; *m* wrong, offense, outrage
**desaherrojar** *va* to unshackle
**desahijar** *va* to separate young cattle from (*the dams*); *vr* to swarm
**desahitar** *vr* to get rid of indigestion
**desahogado -da** *adj* forward, brazen, impudent; clear, free, roomy; comfortable, in comfortable circumstances; (naut.) free-running, free-sailing
**desahogar §59** *va* to relieve, give comfort to; to give rein to (*desires, passions, etc.*); *vr* to ease one's discomfort, to take it easy, to get comfortable; to get out of trouble or worry, to recover; to let oneself go; to unbosom oneself, to open up one's heart; **desahogarse de** to unbosom oneself of; **desahogarse en** to burst forth in (*e.g., insults*)
**desahogo** *m* brazenness, impudence; ample room; comfort; ease; comfortable circumstances; outlet, relief; recovery; unbosoming, unburdening
**desahuciado -da** *adj* hopeless
**desahuciar** *va* to deprive of hope, to give up hope for; to oust, evict, dispossess; *vr* to lose all hope
**desahucio** *m* ousting, eviction, dispossession
**desahumado -da** *adj* weak, vapid (*liquor*)
**desahumar** *va* to free of smoke
**desainadura** *f* (vet.) loss of fat from overwork
**desainar §75** *va* to remove the fat from; to lessen the thickness or substance of; *vr* to lose fat
**desairadamente** *adv* ungracefully; scornfully
**desairado -da** *adj* slighted, snubbed; unattractive; unsuccessful
**desairar** *va* to slight, disregard, overlook, snub
**desaire** *m* ungracefulness, unattractiveness, lack of charm; slight, rebuff, disregard, snub
**desaislar §75** *va* to join, connect; *vr* to be no longer separated or isolated; to come out of seclusion
**desajustar** *va* to put out of order; *vr* to get out of order; to disagree, to fail to agree
**desajuste** *m* being out of order, disorder; disagreement
**desalabanza** *f* belittling, disparagement
**desalabar** *va* to belittle, disparage
**desalabear** *va* to straighten (*a warped board*)
**desalabeo** *m* straightening
**desalado -da** *adj* hasty, anxious, eager
**desalar** *va* to desalt, remove the salt from; to clip the wings of; *vr* to hasten, to rush; **desalarse por** + *inf* to be eager to + *inf*, to yearn to + *inf*
**desalazón** *f* desalting, removal of salt
**desalbardar** *va* to remove the packsaddle from
**desalentadamente** *adv* with discouragement; faintly, feebly
**desalentar §18** *va* to put out of breath; to discourage; *vr* to become discouraged
**desalfombrar** *va* to remove the rugs or carpets from
**desalforjar** *va* to take out of the saddlebags; *vr* (coll.) to loosen one's clothes (*because of heat*)

**desalhajar** *va* to remove the furniture from, to remove the appointments from (*a room*)
**desaliento** *m* discouragement; faintness, weakness
**desalineación** *f* disalignment, lack of alignment
**desalinear** *va* to put out of line or alignment, to disalign
**desaliñado -da** *adj* slovenly, dirty; careless, neglectful
**desaliñar** *va* to disarrange, to make slovenly, to dirty; *vr* to become disarranged, to become slovenly, become dirty
**desaliño** *m* slovenliness, dirtiness; carelessness, neglect; **desaliños** *mpl* long earrings
**desalivar** *vn & vr* to salivate
**desalmado -da** *adj* cruel, inhuman, merciless, soulless
**desalmamiento** *m* cruelty, inhumanity, soullessness
**desalmar** *va* to weaken; to disturb, upset; *vr* to become disturbed, to get upset; **desalmarse por** to have a longing for, to crave
**desalmenado -da** *adj* without merlons, stripped of merlons
**desalmidonar** *va* to remove the starch from
**desalojamiento** *m* dislodging, eviction, ejection
**desalojar** *va* to dislodge, to evict, to eject, to oust; to empty, to clear (*of people*); *vn* to leave, move out or away
**desalojo** *m* var. of **desalojamiento**
**desalquilado -da** *adj* unrented, vacant
**desalquilar** *va* to stop renting, to vacate; *vr* to be unrented, be vacant
**desalterar** *va* to calm, to quiet; *vr* to become calm, become quiet; to quench one's thirst
**desalumbrado -da** *adj* dazzled, dazed; unsure
**desalumbramiento** *m* blindness; loss of knack, unsureness
**desamable** *adj* unlovable
**desamado -da** *adj* unloved
**desamador -dora** *adj* hating; *mf* hater
**desamar** *va* to cease loving, to dislike, to hate, to detest
**desamarrar** *va* to untie, unlash; (naut.) to unmoor; to unbend ( *a rope*); *vr* to part; to come loose, get loose
**desamasado -da** *adj* undone, detached
**desamigado -da** *adj* unfriendly, estranged
**desamistar** *vr* to fall out, to quarrel, to become estranged
**desamoblar** §77 *va* to remove the furniture from
**desamoldar** *va* to change the form of; to throw out of proportion
**desamontonar** *va* to take apart, take away (*things piled in a heap*); to squander
**desamor** *m* coldness, indifference; hatred
**desamorado -da** *adj* unloving, cold-hearted, loveless
**desamorar** *va* to alienate the affections of; *vr* to stop loving
**desamoroso -sa** *adj* loveless, cold, scornful
**desamorrar** *va* (coll.) to make (*a person*) talk, to cheer (*a person*) up
**desamortajar** *va* to unshroud
**desamortización** *f* freedom from mortmain
**desamortizar** §76 *va* to free from mortmain
**desamotinar** *vr* to withdraw from a mutiny
**desamparadamente** *adv* without protection, helplessly
**desamparador -dora** *adj* forsaking; *mf* forsaker, deserter
**desamparar** *va* to abandon, forsake, leave; (law) to give up, to release
**desamparo** *m* abandonment, helplessness, lack of protection
**desamueblado -da** *adj* unfurnished
**desamueblar** *va* to remove the furniture from
**desanalfabetizar** §76 *va* to teach (*a person*) to read and write
**desanclar** or **desancorar** *va* (naut.) to weigh the anchor of; *vn* (naut.) to weigh anchor
**desandar** §20 *va* to retrace, go back over (*the road traveled*)
**desandrajado -da** *adj* ragged, in tatters
**desanduve** *1st sg pret ind of* **desandar**
**desangramiento** *m* excessive bleeding; complete draining
**desangrar** *va* to bleed copiously; to drain, draw a large amount of water from; (fig.) to bleed, impoverish; *vr* to bleed copiously, lose a great amount of blood
**desangre** *m* bleeding; drain, draining
**desanidar** *va* to dislodge, to oust; *vn* to leave the nest
**desanimación** *f* discouragement, low spirits, downheartedness
**desanimadamente** *adv* with discouragement, downheartedly
**desanimar** *va* to discourage, dishearten; *vr* to become discouraged, become disheartened
**desánimo** *m* discouragement, low spirits
**desanublar** *va* to brighten; to clarify; *vr* to get bright, to clear up
**desanudar** *va* to untie; to disentangle, clear up
**desaojadera** *f* charmer, woman who cures the evil eye
**desaojar** *va* to dispel the evil eye for
**desapacibilidad** *f* unpleasantness, disagreeableness
**desapacible** *adj* unpleasant, disagreeable
**desapadrinar** *va* to disapprove, disavow
**desaparear** *va* to separate (*the two of a pair*)
**desaparecer** §34 *va* to cause to disappear; *vn & vr* to disappear
**desaparecido -da** *adj* missing; extinct; **desaparecidos** *mpl* missing persons
**desaparecimiento** *m* disappearance
**desaparejar** *va* to unharness, unhitch; (naut.) to unrig
**desaparición** *f* disappearance
**desaparroquiar** *va* to remove from a parish; to drive customers away from; *vr* to lose one's parish; to lose customers
**desapasionado -da** *adj* dispassionate
**desapasionar** *va* to free of passion, love, or fondness; *vr* to overcome one's passion; to become indifferent or unconcerned; **desapasionarse de** to overcome one's passion for
**desapegar** §59 *va* to unglue; to loosen, detach; *vr* to come loose; to become indifferent
**desapego** *m* coolness, indifference, dislike
**desapercibidamente** *adv* without notice, without warning
**desapercibido -da** *adj* unprovided, wanting; unnoticed
**desapercibimiento** *m* unpreparedness
**desapestar** *va* to disinfect (*a person contaminated with the plague*)
**desapiadado -da** *adj* merciless, pitiless
**desaplacible** *adj* disagreeable
**desaplicación** *f* lack of application; idleness, laziness
**desaplicado -da** *adj* lazy, idle
**desaplicar** §86 *va* to make lazy or idle; *vr* to become lazy or idle
**desaplomar** *va* to put out of plumb; *vr* to get out of plumb
**desapoderado -da** *adj* headlong, impetuous; wild, violent
**desapoderamiento** *m* dispossession; depriving of power or authority
**desapoderar** *va* to dispossess; to deprive of power or authority; *vr* to become dispossessed; **desapoderarse de** to lose possession of
**desapolillar** *va* to free of moths; *vr* (coll.) to go out in the cold, to go out after being long indoors
**desaporcar** §86 *va* to remove the piled-up earth from around (*a plant*)
**desaposentar** *va* to drive out of one's room or quarters; to cast aside; *vr* to give up one's room or quarters
**desaposesionar** *va* to dispossess
**desapoyar** *va* to deprive of support
**desapreciar** *va* to depreciate (*to lessen the value of; to belittle*)
**desaprecio** *m* depreciation (*drop in value; belittling*)
**desaprender** *va* to unlearn; *vn* to forget what one has learned
**desaprensar** *va* to remove the gloss from (*fabrics*); to ease, to free

**desaprensión** *f* freedom from worry or fear, unapprehensiveness; unscrupulousness
**desaprensivo -va** *adj* unapprehensive, unworried; unscrupulous
**desapretar** §18 *va* to loosen; to relieve; (print.) to unlock; *vr* to loosen one's clothing
**desaprisionar** *va* to free from jail, to free from shackles; *vr* to extricate oneself, to get free
**desaprobación** *f* disapproval, deprecation
**desaprobar** §77 *va* to disapprove, to deprecate; *vn* to disapprove
**desapropiación** *f* or **desapropiamiento** *m* divestment, surrender (*of property*)
**desapropiar** *va* to divest, deprive; **desapropiar a una persona de** to divest or deprive a person of; *vr* to divest oneself; **desapropiarse de** to divest oneself of, to surrender, to transfer (*property*)
**desapropio** *m* var. of **desapropiación**
**desaprovechado -da** *adj* unproductive; lazy, indifferent
**desaprovechamiento** *m* ill use, poor use; unimprovement
**desaprovechar** *va* to make no use of, to use to no advantage; *vn* to lose one's advantage, to slip back
**desapuntalar** *va* to remove the props, supports, or shoring from
**desapuntar** *va* to unstitch; to put (*a gun or cannon*) out of aim
**desaquellar** *vr* (coll.) to be or feel discouraged
**desarbolar** *va* (naut.) to unmast, to dismast; to clear of trees
**desarbolo** *m* (naut.) unmasting a ship
**desarenar** *va* to clear of sand
**desareno** *m* clearing of sand
**desarmable** *adj* demountable
**desarmador** *m* hammer (*of gun*); (Am.) screwdriver
**desarmadura** *f* or **desarmamiento** *m* disarmament
**desarmar** *va* to disarm; to dismount, take apart, undo; to calm, to temper, to dissipate; (naut.) to lay up, to decommission; *vn* to disarm
**desarme** *m* disarmament; dismounting, dismantling; (naut.) decommissioning
**desarraigar** §59 *va* to uproot, root out, dig up; to extirpate, exterminate; to evict, throw out; to make (*a person*) change his opinion
**desarraigo** *m* uprooting; extermination
**desarrancar** §86 *vr* to withdraw (*from a group or association*)
**desarrapado -da** *adj* var. of **desharrapado**
**desarrebozadamente** *adv* openly, frankly, without concealment
**desarrebozar** §76 *va* to unmuffle, to uncover, to reveal
**desarrebujar** *va* to disentangle; to clarify, elucidate; to unbundle (*a person*); *vr* to unbundle oneself
**desarreglado -da** *adj* intemperate; unruly, disorderly, slovenly; out of order
**desarreglar** *va* to disarrange, to put out of order; *vr* to become disarranged, to get out of order
**desarreglo** *m* disarrangement, disorder, confusion, bad order
**desarrendamiento** *m* discontinuance of rent; voiding of a lease
**desarrendar** §18 *va* to unbridle; to stop renting; *vr* to shake off the bridle; to be unrented
**desarrimar** *va* to separate, to remove; to dissuade
**desarrimo** *m* lack of support
**desarrollable** *adj* developable
**desarrollar** *va* to unroll, unfold, unwind, unfurl; to develop; (math. & phot.) to develop; *vn* to unroll, unfold, unwind; to develop; *vr* to unfold, to develop; to take place
**desarrollo** *m* unrolling, unfolding, unwinding; development; (math. & phot.) development
**desarropar** *va* to unclothe, undress; *vr* to take one's clothes off, to undress
**desarrugadura** *f* unwrinkling
**desarrugar** §59 *va & vr* to unwrinkle
**desarrumar** *va* (naut.) to break out, to unstow; (naut.) to unload (*in order to examine hull*)
**desarticulación** *f* disarticulation; (surg.) disarticulation
**desarticular** *va* to disarticulate; to take apart; to tear apart, to break up; (surg.) to disarticulate; *vr* to disarticulate
**desartillar** *va* to remove the gun from (*a boat or fort*)
**desarzonar** *va* to unsaddle, to unhorse
**desasado -da** *adj* without handles; with broken handles
**desaseado -da** *adj* dirty, unclean, untidy
**desasear** *va* to make dirty, to leave untidy
**desasegurar** *va* to make uncertain; to make unsteady, to remove the supports from; to cancel the insurance on
**desasentar** §18 *va* to remove, move away; *vn* to displease, be disliked; to be unbecoming; *vr* to stand up, get up from one's seat
**desaseo** *m* dirtiness, uncleanliness, untidiness
**desasgo** *1st sg pres ind of* **desasir**
**desasimiento** *m* loosening, releasing; detachment, disinterest
**desasimilación** *f* (physiol.) disassimilation
**desasimilar** *va* (physiol.) to disassimilate; *vr* to be disassimilated
**desasir** §22 *va* to let go; to loosen, unfasten; *vr* to let loose; to come loose; **desasirse de** to let go; to give up; to get rid of
**desasistir** *va* to abandon, forsake
**desasnar** *va* (coll.) to give good manners to, to polish; *vr* (coll.) to acquire good manners
**desasociable** *adj* unsociable
**desasociar** *va* to disassociate (*two or more persons*)
**desasosegadamente** *adv* uneasily, worriedly, anxiously
**desasosegar** §29 *va* to disquiet, worry, disturb; *vr* to become disquieted, to worry, to get upset
**desasosiego** *m* disquiet, worry, anxiety
**desastado -da** *adj* hornless
**desastar** *va* to dehorn
**desastrado -da** *adj* unfortunate, unlucky; shabby, ragged; *mf* shabby person, ragged person
**desastre** *m* disaster; **ir al desastre** to go to pieces, to fall apart (*said, e.g., of a business*)
**desastroso -sa** *adj* unfortunate, disastrous
**desatacar** §86 *va* to unfasten, undo, unbutton
**desatadamente** *adv* freely, without restraint
**desatado -da** *adj* loose; mad, wild; fierce, violent
**desatadura** *f* untying, unfastening, loosening; solving, resolving
**desatancar** §86 *va* to unclog, to open up; *vr* to get out of the mud, get out of a rut
**desatar** *va* to untie, undo, unfasten; to solve, unravel; *vr* to come untied; to break loose (*said, e.g., of a storm*); to lose all reserve or restraint; to go too far, to forget oneself; to talk without restraint; **desatarse en** to burst forth in (*e.g., insults*)
**desatascar** §86 *va* to pull out of the mud, to pull out of a rut; to unclog; to extricate, release from a tight spot or difficulty; *vr* to get out of the mud, get out of a rut
**desataviar** §90 *va* to strip of adornment or ornaments, to disarray
**desatavío** *m* slovenliness, uncleanliness, disarray
**desate** *m* unrestraint, unrestrained talk; flood (*e.g., of words*); **desate del vientre** loose bowels
**desatención** *f* inattention, disregard; disrespect, discourtesy
**desatender** §66 *va* to pay no attention to, take no notice of; to slight, disregard
**desatentado -da** *adj* injudicious, thoughtless, unwise; extreme, severe, out of proportion
**desatentar** §18 *va* to cause to lose the sense of touch; to confuse, to perplex; *vr* to lose one's sense of touch; to become confused or perplexed
**desatento -ta** *adj* inattentive, disregardful; impolite, unmannerly
**desaterrar** §18 *va* (min.) to clear of rubbish and debris; (Am.) to move away, to clear away (*earth or mud*)

**desatesorar** *va* to spend (*one's treasure or hoardings*)
**desatiento** *m* loss of sense of touch; confusion, perplexity, uneasiness, worry
**desatierre** *m* (min.) dumping ground; (Am.) removal of earth or mud
**desatinado -da** *adj* unwise, foolish; wild, crazy; unruly, in disorder, confused; *mf* fool, blunderer
**desatinar** *va* to confuse, bewilder; *vn* to act or talk foolishly; to lose one's bearings; *vr* to lose one's bearings
**desatino** *m* folly, foolishness, nonsense; tactlessness, awkwardness, irrelevancy
**desatolondrar** *va* to bring to; *vr* to come to
**desatollar** *va* to pull out of the mud, to pull out of a rut; *vr* to get out of the mud, get out of a rut
**desatontar** *vr* to recover from being stunned
**desatorar** *va* (naut.) to break out, to unstow; (min.) to clear of rubbish or debris
**desatornillar** *va* to unscrew
**desatracar** **§86** *va* (naut.) to move away (*one boat from alongside another*); *vn* (naut.) to keep away from the coast; *vr* (naut.) to move away, to push off
**desatraer** **§88** *va* to separate, detach
**desatraigo** *1st sg pres ind of* **desatraer**
**desatraillar** **§75** *va & vr* var. of **destraillar**
**desatraje** *1st sg pret ind of* **desatraer**
**desatrampar** *va* to unclog
**desatrancar** **§86** *va* to unbolt, unbar; to unclog
**desatufar** *vr* to get out of the close air (*e.g., of a crowded room*); (fig.) to cool off, to quiet down
**desaturdir** *va & vr* to rouse from a daze or stupor
**desautoridad** *f* want of authority
**desautorización** *f* withdrawal of authority
**desautorizado -da** *adj* unauthorized; discredited
**desautorizar** **§76** *va* to deprive of authority or credit
**desavahado -da** *adj* free of clouds, mist, or steam; free, easy, calm
**desavahamiento** *m* airing; uncovering, cooling
**desavahar** *va* to air, ventilate; to let cool off, let the steam out of; *vr* to unburden oneself, to brighten up
**desavecindado -da** *adj* unoccupied, deserted
**desavecindar** *vr* to move, to move to another place
**desavendré** *1st sg fut ind of* **desavenir**
**desavenencia** *f* discord, disagreement, hostility
**desavengo** *1st sg pres ind of* **desavenir**
**desavenido -da** *adj* contrary, disagreeable; incompatible
**desavenir** **§92** *va* to make hostile, bring disagreement among, sow discord among; *vr* to disagree; **desavenirse con** or **de** to disagree with
**desaventajado -da** *adj* disadvantageous
**desaventura** *f* misfortune
**desaviar** **§90** *va* to mislead, lead astray; to deprive of needs or equipment; *vr* to be misled, to go astray; to be without necessary equipment
**desavine** *1st sg pret ind of* **desavenir**
**desaviniendo** *ger of* **desavenir**
**desavío** *m* leading astray, going astray; inconvenience, want of equipment
**desavisado -da** *adj* unadvised, uninformed
**desavisar** *va* to give different advice to, give new advice to
**desayudar** *va* to keep help from, to keep (*a person*) from being helped
**desayunado -da** *adj* with breakfast over; **estar desayunado** to have had breakfast
**desayunar** *vn* to breakfast; *vr* to breakfast; to receive the first news; **desayunarse con** to have breakfast on; **desayunarse de** to receive the first news of
**desayuno** *m* breakfast, light breakfast; breakfasting
**desazogar** **§59** *va* to remove the quicksilver from
**desazón** *f* tastelessness, insipidity; displeasure, bitterness, annoyance; discomfort, indisposition; unfitness for cultivation
**desazonado -da** *adj* indisposed; displeased; unfit for cultivation
**desazonar** *va* to make tasteless; to displease, annoy, embitter; *vr* to be displeased, annoyed, or embittered; to be indisposed, to feel ill; to become tasteless
**desazufrar** *va* to desulfurize
**desbabar** *vn & vr* to drivel, to slobber
**desbagar** **§59** *va* to extract (*flaxseed*) from the capsules
**desbancar** **§86** *va* (naut.) to clear of benches; to win the bank from; to cut out, to supplant
**desbandada** *f* disbandment; **a la desbandada** helter-skelter, in confusion
**desbandar** *vr* to run away, to flee in disorder; to disband; (mil.) to desert the colors
**desbarahustar** *va* var. of **desbarajustar**
**desbarahuste** *m* var. of **desbarajuste**
**desbarajustar** *va* to throw into confusion or disorder; *vr* to get out of order, to break down
**desbarajuste** *m* confusion, disorder
**desbaratadamente** *adv* in confusion, in disorder
**desbaratado -da** *adj* (coll.) corrupt, debauched
**desbaratador -dora** *mf* destroyer
**desbaratamiento** *m* ruin, destruction, downfall, upset
**desbaratar** *va* to spoil, disrupt, ruin, destroy; to waste, squander; to debunk; (mil.) to rout, throw into confusion; *vn* to talk nonsense; *vr* to talk or act unreasonably, to be unbalanced
**desbarate** *m* disruption, ruin, destruction; debunking; loose bowels; **desbarate de vientre** loose bowels
**desbarato** *m* ruin, destruction
**desbarbado -da** *adj* beardless
**desbarbar** *va* to cut the roots, vanes, or filaments of, to trim; (coll.) to shave; *vr* (coll.) to shave, get shaved
**desbarbillar** *va* to cut off the rootlets of (*young vines*)
**desbardar** *va* to unthatch
**desbarnizar** **§76** *va* to remove the varnish from
**desbarrancadero** *m* (Am.) precipice
**desbarrancar** **§86** *va* to level (*uneven ground*); (Am.) to throw over a precipice; *vr* (Am.) to fall over a precipice
**desbarrar** *va* to unbar; (Am.) to clear of mud; *vn* (sport) to throw the bar with all one's might but without taking aim; to slip away; to steal away; to talk nonsense, to act foolishly
**desbarretar** *va* to unbar, unbolt; to remove the lining of (*shoes*)
**desbarrigado -da** *adj* small-bellied
**desbarrigar** **§59** *va* (coll.) to slash in the belly, to rip open the belly of
**desbarro** *m* slip, blunder; slipping away; nonsense, folly
**desbastador** *m* dressing chisel
**desbastadura** *f* roughdressed effect
**desbastar** *va* to work or shape roughly, to roughdress, to scabble; to consume, waste, weaken; to polish, take off the rough edges of, educate; *vr* to take on polish
**desbaste** *m* roughdressing; roughdressed state
**desbastecido -da** *adj* without provisions or supplies
**desbautizar** **§76** *va* to change the name of; *vr* (coll.) to lose one's temper, become very impatient or angry
**desbazadero** *m* wet, slippery place
**desbeber** *vn* (coll.) to urinate
**desbecerrar** *va* to wean calves from (*their mothers*)
**desbloquear** *va* to break the blockade of, to relieve the blockade of; (com.) to unfreeze
**desbloqueo** *m* relieving a blockade; (com.) unfreezing
**desbocado -da** *adj* wide-mouthed (*said of a gun*); nicked (*said of a tool*); neckless (*jug*); runaway (*horse*); loose, licentious; (coll.) foulmouthed; (coll.) loosemouthed; *mf* (coll.) foulmouthed person
**desbocamiento** *m* running away; licentiousness; (coll.) abusiveness, insulting language, obscenity

**desbocar** §86 *va* to break the mouth or spout of; *vn* to empty (*said of a river*); to run, to open, to end (*said of a street*); *vr* to break loose, to run away (*said of a horse*); to burst forth in insults, to swear, to curse; to become debauched, to lead a life of violence
**desbonetar** *vr* (coll.) to take one's cap off
**desboquillar** *va* to remove or break the mouth, stem, or nozzle of
**desbordamiento** *m* overflowing, inundation; violence (*of conduct*)
**desbordante** *adj* overflowing
**desbordar** *vn* to overflow; *vr* to overflow; to lose one's self-control, to yield to evil
**desborde** *m* overflowing, inundation
**desbornizar** §76 *va* to remove the cork from (*a tree*)
**desborrar** *va* to burl; (prov.) to strip of shoots
**desbozalar** *va* unmuzzle
**desbragado -da** *adj* (coll.) without pants; (scornful) ragged, shabby; *mf* (scornful) ragged person
**desbravar** *va* to break in, to tame; *vn & vr* to become less wild; to abate, to moderate; to cool off, calm down; to lose strength (*said of liquors*)
**desbravecer** §34 *vn & vr* to become less wild; to abate, to moderate; to cool off, calm down; to lose strength (*said of liquors*)
**desbrazar** §76 *vr* to wave the arms with violence
**desbrevar** *vr* to lose body and strength (*said of wine*)
**desbridamiento** *m* unbridling; (surg.) débridement, removal of lacerated or contaminated material
**desbridar** *va* to unbridle; (surg.) to débride
**desbriznar** *va* to cut or divide into small parts; to chop up, to mince (*meat*); to remove the strings from (*vegetables*); to pull the stamens from (*saffron*)
**desbroce** *m* var. of **desbrozo**
**desbrozar** §76 *va* to clear of brush or underbrush, to clear of rubbish, to clean up
**desbrozo** *m* clearing of brush or underbrush, clearing of rubbish
**desbrujar** *va* to wear away, to destroy
**desbuchar** *va* to disgorge (*said of birds*); to tell (*secrets*); to remove the maw from (*a bird*); to remove the fat from
**desbulla** *f* oyster shell
**desbullador -dora** *mf* oyster opener, oyster vendor; *m* oyster fork
**desbullar** *va* to open (*an oyster*)
**descabal** *adj* incomplete, imperfect
**descabalamiento** *m* removal of parts, loss of parts, damage
**descabalar** *va* to make incomplete, to take away or lose parts of, to damage
**descabalgadura** *f* dismounting, alighting from a horse
**descabalgar** §59 *va* to dismount (*a gun*); to knock (*a gun*) out by destroying the carriage; *vn* to dismount, to alight from a horse
**descabellado -da** *adj* disheveled; rash, preposterous, wild
**descabellar** *va* to dishevel, to muss, to rumple; (taur.) to kill (*the bull*) by piercing the base of its brain with the sword; *vr* to become disheveled, to become mussed
**descabello** *m* (taur.) killing the bull by piercing the base of its brair with the sword
**descabestrar** *va* to unhalter
**descabezado -da** *adj* rash, wild, crazy
**descabezamiento** *m* beheading; quandary
**descabezar** §76 *va* to behead; to top (*e.g., a tree*); (coll.) to be about to get the best of (*e.g., a task*); **descabezar el sueño** to nod, to doze; *vn* to adjoin, to border; *vr* to shed the grain (*said of cereals*); to rack one's brain
**descabritar** *va* to wean goats from (*the mother*)
**descabullir** §26 *vr* to slip away, to sneak away; to avoid facing a problem; to refuse to face realities; **descabullirse de** to wriggle out of (*e.g., a difficulty*)
**descachar** *va* (Am.) to dehorn
**descacharrado -da** *adj* (Am.) dirty, ragged
**descachazar** §76 *va* (Am.) to skim froth from (*cane juice*)
**descaderado -da** *adj* narrow-hipped
**descaderar** *va* to injure the hips of; *vr* to injure one's hips
**descadillar** *va* to cut off the loose threads of (*the warp*)
**descaecer** §34 *vn* to decline, fade away
**descaecimiento** *m* weakness, debility; despondency, dejection
**descafilar** *va* to clean and smooth (*old bricks and stones*)
**descalabazar** §76 *vr* (coll.) to rack one's brain
**descalabrado -da** *adj* wounded in the head; worsted; **salir descalabrado** to come out the loser, to lose out
**descalabradura** *f* bump in the head; scab on the head
**descalabrar** *va* to hit, to hurt, to hit in the head; to damage, to ruin; *vr* to hurt one's head
**descalabro** *m* misfortune, damage, loss
**descalandrajar** *va* to tear to shreds
**descalcador** *m* (naut.) ravehook
**descalcar** §86 *va* (naut.) to remove oakum from (*seams*)
**descalce** *m* undermining
**descalcez** *f* barefootedness
**descalificación** *f* disqualification; (sport) disqualification
**descalificar** §86 *va* to disqualify (*to deprive of a right, etc.*); (sport) to disqualify
**descalzar** §76 *va* to take off (*footwear*); to take the shoes or stockings off (*a person*); to remove wedges or chocks from; to dig under, to undermine; *vr* to take off one's shoes and stockings; to take off one's gloves; to take off (*shoes or gloves*); to lose a shoe (*said of a horse*); to become discalced (*said of a friar*); **descalzarse de risa** to split one's sides with laughter
**descalzo -za** *adj* barefoot, unshod; discalced (*said, e.g., of a friar*); seedy, down at the heel
**descamación** *f* desquamation
**descamar** *vr* to desquamate
**descambiar** *va* to exchange back again
**descaminadamente** *adv* off the road; mistakenly, wrongly
**descaminado -da** *adj* off the road; lost, misguided; ill-advised
**descaminar** *va* to lead astray, to mislead, to misguide; to declare contraband; to seize (*smuggled goods*); to punish for smuggling; (Am.) to waylay, to hold up; *vr* to go astray, to get lost; to run off the road
**descamino** *m* leading astray; going astray; running off the road; nonsense; lack of tact; seizure of smuggled goods; smuggled goods seized
**descamisado -da** *adj* shirtless, ragged; poor, wretched; *m* ragamuffin; poor person; wretch; **Descamisados** *mpl* Spanish liberals of 1820; (Am.) followers of General Perón around 1950
**descamisar** *va* to remove the shirt of, to strip; to hull, to husk; (found.) to remove the mold from; (Am.) to ruin
**descampado -da** *adj* free, open, clear; **en descampado** in the open country
**descampar** *va* to clear (*a piece of land*); *vn* to stop work; to stop raining
**descanar** *va* (Am.) to thin out the gray hairs from
**descansadamente** *adv* easily, without trouble; tranquilly, calmly, peacefully
**descansadero** *m* stage, stopping place, resting place
**descansadillo** *m* (aut.) footrest
**descansado -da** *adj* easy; rested, refreshed; tranquil, unworried
**descansapié** *m* or **descansapiés** *m* (*pl:* **-piés**) (aut.) footrest
**descansar** *va* to help, to give a hand to; to rest (*e.g., one's head*); to support, to hold up; *vn* to rest; to be quiet; to stop work; to lie down; to lie (*be buried*); to rest, to lean; to sleep; to not worry; to lie fallow; **descansar en** to trust in
**descansillo** *m* landing (*of stairs*)
**descanso** *m* rest, quiet, stillness, peace; ease, relief; aid, help; landing (*of stairs*); (mach.) seat, bench, support, bracket; (mil.) parade rest; (theat.) intermission; rest (*peace of*

*death*); (Am.) bridge; (Am.) water closet; **a discreción descanso** (mil.) at ease; **en su lugar descanso** (mil.) parade rest; **descanso dominical** Sunday observance
**descantar** *va* to clear of stones
**descantear** *va* to smooth the angles or corners of, to round off; to splay, to chamfer, to edge
**descanterar** *va* to remove the crust, corners, or ends of
**descantillar** *va* to break off, to pare off, to chip off; to deduct, to subtract; to speak ill of
**descantillón** *m* gauge, pattern, rule, templet; square
**descantonar** *va* to pare off, to chip off; to take off (*corners*); to subtract
**descañonar** *va* to pluck; to shave against the grain; (coll.) to fleece, to swindle; (coll.) to break, to win the pot from
**descaperuzar** **§76** *va* to unhood, to uncowl; *vr* to take off one's hood, cowl, or hunting cap
**descaperuzo** *m* taking off one's hood, cowl, or hunting cap
**descapillar** *va* to take off the hood of
**descapiruzar** **§76** *va* (Am.) to dishevel, to muss the hair of; (Am.) to rumple, to crumple; (Am.) to dull (*velvet*) by rubbing the wrong way
**descapitalizar** **§76** *va* to deprive (*a town or city*) of its status as capital
**descapotable** *adj & m* (aut.) convertible
**descapotar** *va* to lower the top of (*an automobile*)
**descapsulador** *m* bottle opener
**descarado -da** *adj* impudent, shameless; saucy
**descaramiento** *m* impudence, shamelessness; sauciness
**descarar** *vr* to speak or behave in an impudent manner; to be saucy; **descararse a pedir** to have the nerve to ask for; **descararse con** to speak insolently to, to behave insolently towards
**descarbonatar** *va* to decarbonate, remove carbonic acid from
**descarburación** *f* decarbonization
**descarburador -dora** *adj* decarbonizing
**descarburar** *va* to decarbonize
**descarga** *f* unloading; discharge, firing (*of a gun, etc.*); clearing (*of a ship*); unburdening; (com.) discount; (elec.) discharge; **descarga de aduana** clearance through customhouse; **descarga superficial** (elec.) surface leakage
**descargadero** *m* unloading place, wharf
**descargador** *m* unloader; (naut.) lighterman; (ord.) wormer
**descargadura** *f* bone that a butcher takes out of a piece of meat
**descargar** **§59** *va* to unload; to ease (*one's conscience*); to shoot, to fire, to discharge; to free; to dump; to take the flap and bones from (*loin*); to deal, to inflict (*e.g., blows*); to clear, to acquit; to free (*e.g., of a debt*); (com.) to take up (*a draft*); (elec.) to discharge; (naut.) to brace (*a lee*); (naut.) to clear (*the sails or yards*); **descargar un golpe en, contra,** or **sobre** to strike a blow at; *vn* to empty (*said of a river*); to open (*said of a hall, walk, street, etc.*); to burst (*said of a storm*); *vr* to unburden oneself; to resign; **descargarse de** to get rid of; to clear oneself of (*a charge*); to resign from; **descargarse con** or **en una persona de una cosa** to unload something on someone
**descargo** *m* unloading; discharge, acquittal; acquittance (*of a debt*); receipt, release; (law) deposition favorable to defendant
**descargue** *m* unloading
**descariñar** *vr* to become cool, become indifferent
**descariño** *m* coolness, indifference
**descarnadamente** *adv* plainly, frankly, to the point
**descarnado -da** *adj* lean, thin, spare; bare; bony, cadaverous; **la descarnada** Death
**descarnador** *m* (dent.) scraper
**descarnadura** *f* removal of flesh
**descarnar** *va* to remove the flesh from; to wear down, wear away; to chip; to detach from the things of this world; *vr* to lose flesh
**descaro** *m* effrontery, impudence
**descarriamiento** *m* var. of **descarrío**
**descarriar** **§90** *va* to misguide, lead astray; to separate (*cattle*); *vr* to go astray; to go wrong
**descarrilador -dora** *adj* derailing; *mf* derailer; **descarrilador de trenes** train wrecker
**descarriladura** *f* or **descarrilamiento** *m* derailment
**descarrilar** *vn* to derail, to jump the track; (coll.) to get off the track, wander from the point; *vr* to derail, to jump the track
**descarrío** *m* going astray; ruin, damnation
**descartar** *va* to reject, cast aside; to discard; *vr* to discard; to shirk, evade; **descartarse de** to shirk, evade (*e.g., a commitment*)
**descarte** *m* rejection, casting aside; discarding; discard (*cards discarded*); shirking, evasion
**descasado -da** *adj* jumbled, mixed up
**descasamiento** *m* annulment (*of marriage*); divorce
**descasar** *va* to annul the marriage of; to disturb, to disturb the arrangement of; (print.) to change the arrangement of (*pages of a folio*); *vr* to separate by an annulment of marriage; to become disarranged
**descascar** **§86** *va* to peel, to shell; *vr* to break to pieces; to chatter, to bluster
**descascarar** *va* to peel, to shell; *vr* to peel off, to shell off
**descascarillado** *m* hulling, shelling
**descascarillar** *va & vr* to hull, to shell
**descaspar** *va* to remove the dandruff from
**descasque** *m* decortication (*especially of cork tree*)
**descastado -da** *adj* ungrateful, ungrateful to one's own
**descastamiento** *m* ingratitude
**descastar** *va* to exterminate (*destructive animals and insects*); *vr* to become depraved, to turn ingrate
**descatolizar** **§76** *va* to cause to give up Catholicism; *vr* to give up Catholicism
**descaudalado -da** *adj* ruined, penniless
**descebar** *va* to unprime (*a firearm*)
**descendencia** *f* descent (*family tree; issue*)
**descendente** *adj* descending, descendent, down
**descender** **§66** *va* to lower, take down, bring down; to descend, go down (*e.g., stairs*); *vn* to descend, go down, get down; to run, to flow; to be derived; to decline; (mus.) to descend; **descender a** to descend to, to stoop to; **descender a** + *inf* to go or come down to + *inf;* **descender de** to descend from
**descendiente** *mf* descendant
**descendimiento** *m* descent, lowering
**descensión** *f* descent, descending
**descenso** *m* descent (*act of descending; downward course in station, value, etc.*); decline, falling off; drop (*in temperature*); (path.) hernia, rupture, prolapse (*of uterus*)
**descentrado -da** *adj* off center, out of plumb
**descentralización** *f* decentralization
**descentralizador -dora** *adj* decentralizing
**descentralizar** **§76** *va* to decentralize
**descentrar** *va* to put off center; *vr* to get off center, to get out of line
**desceñido -da** *adj* loose, loose-fitting
**desceñidura** *f* unbelting, ungirding; loosening or removal of a belt, etc.
**desceñir** **§74** *va* to unbelt, ungird; to take off (*a belt, etc.*)
**descepar** *va* to pull up by the roots; to exterminate; (naut.) to remove the stocks from (*an anchor*)
**descerar** *va* to cut away the dry combs from (*a beehive*)
**descercar** **§86** *va* to destroy or tear down the wall or fence of; to raise the siege of; to force the enemy to raise the siege of
**descerco** *m* raising a siege
**descerebrar** *va* to brain, to dash out the brains of
**descerezar** **§76** *va* to pulp (*coffee berry*)
**descerrajado -da** *adj* (coll.) wicked, evil, corrupt
**descerrajadura** *f* lock-breaking
**descerrajar** *va* to break or tear off the lock of; (coll.) to shoot, discharge (*a shot*)
**descerrar** **§18** *va* to open

**descerrumar** *vr* to wrench its joints (*said of a horse*)
**descervigar** §59 *va* to twist the neck of (*an animal*); *vr* to humble oneself
**descifrable** *adj* decipherable
**descifrador** *m* decipherer; decoder
**descifrar** *va* to decipher; to decode
**descifre** *m* deciphering; decoding
**descimbramiento** *m* (arch.) removal of centers
**descimbrar** *va* (arch.) to remove the center of (*e.g., an arch*)
**descimentar** *va* to demolish the foundations of
**descinchar** *va* to ungird
**descivilizar** §76 *va* to uncivilize, to make uncivilized; *vr* to become uncivilized
**desclasificación** *f* (sport) disqualification
**desclasificar** §86 *va* (sport) to disqualify
**desclavador** *m* nail puller
**desclavar** *va* to remove the nails from, to unnail; to take (*a precious stone*) out of its setting
**desclorurar** *va* to remove sodium chloride from; to remove salt from (*the diet*)
**descoagular** *va* to dissolve (*a clot*)
**descobajar** *va* to pull the stem from (*grapes*)
**descobijar** *va* to uncover, to open; to deprive of shelter
**descocado -da** *adj* forward, insolent
**descocar** §86 *va* to clear (*trees*) of insects; *vr* to clean itself of fleas, etc. (*said of birds and other animals*); (coll.) to be impudent; (coll.) to act or speak insolently
**descocer** §30 *va* to digest
**descoco** *m* (coll.) impudence, insolence
**descochollado -da** *adj* (Am.) ragged, in tatters
**descodar** *va* (dial.) to unstitch, to rip
**descoger** §49 *va* to extend, spread, unfold
**descogollar** *va* to strip (*a tree*) of shoots; to take the heart out of (*vegetables*)
**descogotado -da** *adj* (coll.) low-necked
**descogotar** *va* to break the neck of; to dehorn (*a stag*)
**descohesor** *m* (rad.) decoherer
**descolar** *va* to dock, crop, or cut the tail off (*an animal*); to cut off the fag end of (*cloth*); (Am.) to slight; (Am.) to dismiss (*an employee*)
**descolchar** *va* (naut.) to untwist (*a cable*)
**descolgar** §79 *va* to take down; to unhook; to take down the draperies, hangings, etc. in; *vr* to slip down; to come down; to come on suddenly, to show up unexpectedly; **descolgarse con** (coll.) to come out with suddenly, to blurt out; **descolgarse de** or **por** to slip down (*e.g., a wall*)
**descoligado -da** *adj* unattached, unfederated
**descolmar** *va* to strike (*with a strickle*); to level off; to diminish
**descolmillar** *va* to pull out the eyeteeth or the fangs of
**descolocado -da** *adj* out of place, in the wrong place
**descolón** *m* (coll.) slight
**descoloración** *f* decolorization, color removal
**descoloramiento** *m* discoloring, discoloration
**descolorar** *va* & *vr* to discolor
**descolorido -da** *adj* discolored, faded, off color
**descolorimiento** *m* discoloring, discoloration
**descolorir** *va* & *vr* to discolor
**descollado -da** *adj* haughty; outstanding
**descollamiento** *m* var. of **descuello**
**descollante** *adj* outstanding
**descollar** §77 *vn* to stand out, excel
**descombrar** *va* to disencumber, to clear of obstacles
**descombro** *m* disencumbrance, clearing of obstacles
**descomedido -da** *adj* immoderate, excessive; rude, disrespectful, impolite
**descomedimiento** *m* rudeness, disrespect, impoliteness
**descomedir** §94 *vr* to be rude, be disrespectful
**descomer** *vn* (coll.) to have a movement of the bowels
**descomodidad** *f* inconvenience
**descompadrar** *va* (coll.) to break up the friendship of; *vn* (coll.) to be no longer friends, to fall out
**descompaginar** *va* to disorganize, to upset
**descompás** *m* excess, immoderateness
**descompasado -da** *adj* extreme, immoderate, out of all reason
**descompasar** *vr* to be extreme, be immoderate
**descompletar** *va* to make incomplete, to break (*e.g., a set of dishes*)
**descompondré** *1st sg fut ind of* **descomponer**
**descomponer** §69 *va* to decompose; to disturb, upset, discompose, disorganize; to put out of order; to alienate, set at odds; *vr* to decompose; to become distorted (*said of the face*); to fall to pieces (*with regard to health*); to get out of order; to lose one's temper; **descomponerse con** to fall out with
**descompongo** *1st sg pres ind of* **descomponer**
**descomposición** *f* decomposition; disturbance, disorder, disorganization; discomposure; discord
**descompostura** *f* decomposition; disorder, disorganization; untidiness; impudence, brazenness
**descompresión** *f* decompression
**descompuesto -ta** *adj* impudent, brazen, impolite; angry, exasperated; out of order; *pp of* **descomponer**
**descompuse** *1st sg pret ind of* **descomponer**
**descomulgado -da** *adj* wicked, perverse, evil
**descomulgar** §59 *va* to excommunicate
**descomunal** *adj* extraordinary, enormous, monstrous
**desconceptuar** §33 *va* to discredit; *vr* to become discredited
**desconcertado -da** *adj* unrestrained, wicked; out of order; disconcerted
**desconcertador** *m* disturber, tinkerer
**desconcertar** §18 *va* to put out of order, to disturb; to dislocate; to surprise, to disconcert, to baffle; *vr* to get out of order; to become dislocated; to become disconcerted; to get upset; to become estranged
**desconcierto** *m* disrepair, disorder; disagreement; unrestraint, imprudence; mismanagement; looseness of bowels
**desconcordia** *f* discord, disunion, disagreement
**desconchabar** *vr* (Am.) to become dislocated, to get out of joint
**desconchado** *m* scaly wall; chip, chipped place (*e.g., in china*)
**desconchar** *va* & *vr* to scale off, to chip, to chip off
**desconectar** *va* to detach; (elec. & mach.) to disconnect; *vr* to become detached; (elec. & mach.) to become disconnected
**desconexión** *f* disconnection
**desconfiado -da** *adj* distrustful, suspicious
**desconfianza** *f* distrust
**desconfiar** §90 *vn* to have no confidence; **desconfiar de** to have no confidence in, to distrust
**desconformar** *vn* to dissent, disagree; *vr* to disagree, to not go well together
**desconforme** *adj* disagreeing
**desconformidad** *f* nonconformity, unconformity, disconformity; disagreement
**descongelación** *f* melting, defrosting
**descongelador** *m* defroster
**descongelar** *va*, *vn* & *vr* to melt, to defrost; (com.) to unfreeze
**descongestión** *f* removal or lessening of congestion
**descongestionar** *va* to remove or lessen the congestion of; *vr* to become less congested
**descongojar** *va* to relieve, to console
**desconocedor -dora** *adj* ignorant
**desconocer** §32 *va* to not know, be ignorant of; to not recognize; to disown, disavow, deny; to slight, overlook, pretend not to know, disregard, ignore; to have nothing to do with; to fail to see; *vr* to be or become unrecognizable, to be or become quite changed; to be unknown
**desconocidamente** *adv* unknowingly
**desconocido -da** *adj* unknown; unrecognizable; ungrateful; strange, unfamiliar; quite changed, quite different; *mf* unknown, unknown person

**desconocimiento** *m* ignorance; disregard; ingratitude
**desconozco** *1st sg pres ind of* **desconocer**
**desconsentir §62** *va* to not consent to, to not acquiesce in
**desconsideración** *f* inconsiderateness
**desconsiderado -da** *adj* ill-considered; inconsiderate
**desconsiderar** *va* to be inconsiderate of; to fail to consider
**desconsolación** *f* grief, disconsolateness
**desconsolado -da** *adj* disconsolate, grief-stricken; disordered; weak (*said of the stomach*)
**desconsolador -dora** *adj* distressing
**desconsolar §77** *va* to grieve, to distress; *vr* to grieve, be distressed
**desconsuelo** *m* grief, disconsolation, disconsolateness; neediness, helplessness; stomach disorder
**descontable** *adj* discountable
**descontaminación** *f* decontamination
**descontaminar** *va* to decontaminate
**descontar §77** *va* to discount; to deduct; to rebate; to take for granted
**descontentadizo -za** *adj* hard to please, easily displeased
**descontentamiento** *m* discontentment, displeasure; disagreement, unfriendliness
**descontentar** *va* to dissatisfy, to displease; *vr* to be dissatisfied, to be displeased
**descontento -ta** *adj* discontent, discontented, displeased; *m* discontent, displeasure
**descontinuación** *f* discontinuation
**descontinuar §33** *va* to discontinue
**descontinuo -nua** *adj* discontinuous
**desconvendré** *1st sg fut ind of* **desconvenir**
**desconvengo** *1st sg pres ind of* **desconvenir**
**desconvenible** *adj* incongruous, incompatible, discrepant
**desconveniencia** *f* unsuitableness; incongruity; inconvenience
**desconveniente** *adj* unsuitable; incongruous; inconvenient
**desconvenir §92** *vn* to disagree; to be incongruous; to not match; *vr* to disagree; to be incongruous
**desconversable** *adj* unsociable, retiring
**desconvidar** *va* to cancel an invitation to; to take back (*something promised*)
**desconvine** *1st sg pret ind of* **desconvenir**
**desconviniendo** *ger of* **desconvenir**
**descopar** *va* to top (*a tree*)
**descorazonamiento** *m* broken-heartedness; discouragement, dejection
**descorazonar** *va* to tear out the heart of; to dishearten, discourage; *vr* to become disheartened or discouraged
**descorchador** *m* decorticator (*person or machine*); corkscrew
**descorchar** *va* to remove the bark or cork from (*cork oak*); to uncork; to break open (*a beehive*) in order to extract honey; to break open, to break into
**descorche** *m* removal of bark or cork
**descordar §77** *va* to unstring (*e.g., a musical instrument*)
**descorderar** *va* to separate lambs from (*mother*) in order to form new flocks
**descornamiento** *m* dehorning
**descornar §77** *va* to dehorn; *vr* (coll.) to rack one's brains in vain
**descorrear** *va* to shed or rub the velvet off (*the antlers*); *vn & vr* to shed or rub the velvet off the antlers (*said, e.g., of a young deer*)
**descorrer** *va* to run back over; to draw (*e.g., a curtain*); *vn & vr* to flow, to run off
**descorrimiento** *m* flow, flowing away
**descortés** *adj* discourteous, impolite
**descortesía** *f* discourtesy, impoliteness
**descortezador** *m* decorticator
**descortezadura** *f* removal of bark; bark removed
**descortezamiento** *m* removal of bark
**descortezar §76** *va* to strip off the bark of; to take off the crust of; to hull, to shell; (coll.) to polish, to civilize; *vr* (coll.) to become polished
**descortezo** *m* removal of bark
**descortinar** *va* (mil.) to demolish (*a curtain*)
**descosedura** *f* rip, ripping
**descoser** *va* to unstitch, to rip; **descoser la boca** to reveal a secret; *vr* to loose one's tongue; (coll.) to break wind
**descosido -da** *adj* indiscreet, imprudent; unconnected, desultory; slovenly, disorderly, immoderate, wild; **como un descosido** (coll.) wildly; **reír como un descosido** to laugh like a wild man; *m* open seam, tear, rip
**descostar** *vr* to move away
**descostillar** *va* to beat in the ribs, to bruise the ribs of; *vr* to fall flat on one's back
**descostrar** *va* to remove the crust from
**descotar** *va* to cut low in the neck
**descote** *m* low neck, low cut (*around neck*)
**descoyuntamiento** *m* dislocation; great fatigue, exhaustion
**descoyuntar** *va* to dislocate; to annoy, to bore; *vr* to become dislocated, to get out of joint
**descrecencia** *f* decrease, decreasing
**descrecer §34** *vn* to decrease, diminish
**descrecimiento** *m* decrease, diminution
**descrédito** *m* discredit
**descreer §35** *va* to disbelieve, discredit; to deny due credit to; *vn* to disbelieve
**descreído -da** *adj* unbelieving; *mf* unbeliever, disbeliever
**descreimiento** *m* unbelief, disbelief
**descremadora** *f* cream separator
**descremar** *va* to skim (*milk*)
**descrestar** *va* to remove the crest or comb of
**descrianza** *f* incivility, coarseness, rudeness
**descriar §90** *vr* to spoil, deteriorate, waste away
**describir §17,** 9 *va* to describe
**descripción** *f* description
**descriptible** *adj* describable
**descriptivo -va** *adj* descriptive
**descriptor -tora** *adj* descriptive; *mf* describer
**descrismar** *va* to remove the chrism from; (coll.) to wallop in the head, to break the skull of; *vr* (coll.) to lose one's temper; (coll.) to rack one's brain; (coll.) to break one's skull
**descristianar** *va* to remove the chrism from; (coll.) to wallop in the head, to break the skull of; *vr* (coll.) to break one's skull
**descristianizar §76** *va* to dechristianize; *vr* to become dechristianized
**descrito -ta** *pp of* **describir**
**descruce** *m* uncrossing
**descruzar §76** *va* to uncross, remove from a crossed position
**descto.** abr. of **descuento**
**descuadernar** *va* to unbind, take the binding off (*a book*); to undo, upset, put out of order; *vr* to get loose, come unbound
**descuadrillado** *m* (vet.) sprain in the haunch
**descuadrillar** *vr* to have a sprain in the haunches (*said of a horse*)
**descuajar** *va* to liquefy, to dissolve (*something clotted, coagulated, etc.*); to uproot, pull up by the roots; to eradicate (*a vice*); (coll.) to dishearten, discourage; *vr* to liquefy, be dissolved
**descuajaringar §59** *vr* (coll.) to collapse, be broken down with fatigue; (Am.) to fall to pieces
**descuaje** *m* or **descuajo** *m* pulling up by the roots, grubbing, clearing away underbrush
**descuartizamiento** *m* quartering; dividing into pieces, carving; quartering (*punishment*)
**descuartizar §76** *va* to quarter; to divide into pieces, to carve; to quarter (*as punishment*)
**descubierta** *f* see **descubierto**
**descubiertamente** *adv* clearly, openly, manifestly
**descubierto -ta** *pp of* **descubrir;** *adj* uncovered, bareheaded; under fire, under accusation; bare (*said, e.g., of a field*); *m* exposition of the holy sacrament; deficit, shortage; **al descubierto** (com.) short; openly; in the open; **en descubierto** (com.) overdrawn; **vender al descubierto** (com.) to sell short; *f* open pie, pie without top crust; (mil.) reconnoitering; (naut.) scanning horizon at sunrise and sunset; (naut.) morning and evening inspection of rigging; **a la descubierta** in the open; openly; reconnoitering

**descubridero** *m* lookout, eminence commanding a vast expanse
**descubridor -dora** *adj* discovering; *mf* discoverer; *m* (mil.) scout
**descubrimiento** *m* discovery; unveiling
**descubrir §17,** 9 *va* to discover, find out; to uncover, expose to view, lay open, reveal; to invent; to unveil (*a statue*); *vr* to take off one's hat, cap, etc.; to be discovered; to be uncovered; **descubrirse a** or **con** to open one's heart to
**descuello** *m* distinction, excellence; excessive height; haughtiness, loftiness
**descuento** *m* discount; deduction, rebate
**descuerar** *va* (Am.) to flay, to skin; (Am.) to flay, to criticize
**descuernacabras** *m* strong cold north wind
**descuerno** *m* (coll.) affront, slight
**descuidado -da** *adj* careless, negligent; dirty, slovenly; unaware, off guard
**descuidar** *va* to neglect, overlook; to free of worry; to distract, divert; *vn* to not bother, to not worry; *vr* to be distracted, be diverted; to not bother, to not worry; to become careless; **descuidarse de** to not bother about; **descuidarse de** + *inf* to neglect to + *inf;* **descuidarse de sí mismo** to neglect oneself
**descuidero -ra** *mf* sneak thief
**descuido** *m* carelessness, neglect, negligence; oversight, mistake, slip; thoughtlessness, faux pas, slight; **al descuido** with studied carelessness; **con descuido** without thinking
**descuitado -da** *adj* carefree
**descular** *va* to break the bottom of (*e.g., a bottle*)
**descumbrado -da** *adj* smooth, without a crest or peak; clean, free
**deschavetar** *vr* (Am.) to get rattled, to lose one's head
**deschuponar** *va* to strip (*a tree*) of shoots and suckers
**desde** *prep* since, from; after; **desde aquí** from here; **desde entonces** since then, ever since; **desde entonces a esta parte** since that time; **desde hace** for, e.g., **está aquí desde hace tres meses** he has been here for three months; **desde . . . hasta** from . . . to; **desde luego** at once; doubtless, of course; **desde que** since
**desdecir §37** *vn* to degenerate, to slip back; to differ; to decline; *vr* to retract; **desdecirse de** to retract, take back (*something said*)
**desdén** *m* disdain, scorn, contempt; **al desdén** with studied carelessness, with studied neglect
**desdentado -da** *adj* toothless, edentate; *m* (zool.) edentate
**desdentar §18** *va* to pull the teeth of
**desdeñable** *adj* despicable, contemptible
**desdeñadamente** *adv* scornfully, disdainfully
**desdeñador -dora** *adj* scornful, disdainful; *mf* scorner, disdainer
**desdeñar** *va* to scorn, to disdain; *vr* to be disdainful; **desdeñarse de** to loathe; **desdeñarse de** + *inf* to not deign to + *inf*
**desdeñoso -sa** *adj* scornful, disdainful
**desdevanar** *va* to unwind
**desdibujado -da** *adj* poorly drawn, badly outlined (*said of a drawing or a character in a book*)
**desdibujar** *vr* to become blurred, become clouded
**desdicha** *f* see **desdicho**
**desdichado -da** *adj* unfortunate, unlucky; miserable, unhappy, wretched; (coll.) backward, timid; *mf* wretch
**desdicho -cha** *pp of* **desdecir;** *f* misfortune; indigence, misery
**desdigo** *1st sg pres ind of* **desdecir**
**desdije** *1st sg pret ind of* **desdecir**
**desdinerar** *va* to impoverish
**desdiré** *1st sg fut ind of* **desdecir**
**desdoblamiento** *m* unfolding; splitting; elucidation; **desdoblamiento de la personalidad** disintegration of the personality
**desdoblar** *va & vr* to unfold, spread open; to split; to divide, break down
**desdorar** *va* to remove the gold from, remove the gilding from; to damage, sully (*e.g., reputation*); *vr* to lose its gold or gilding; to become damaged or sullied (*said, e.g., of reputation*)
**desdoro** *m* blemish, blot, stigma
**desdoroso -sa** *adj* damaging (*to reputation, etc.*)
**deseabilidad** *f* desirability
**deseable** *adj* desirable
**deseador -dora** *mf* desirer, wisher
**desear** *va* to desire, wish; **desear** + *inf* to desire to, to wish to + *inf*
**desecación** *f* drying, desiccation
**desecador -dora** *adj* desiccating; *m* drying room; dryer, desiccator
**desecamiento** *m* var. of **desecación**
**desecante** *adj* desiccant; *m* desiccant, drier
**desecar §86** *va* to dry, drain, desiccate; *vr* to dry up, drain, desiccate
**desecativo -va** *adj* desiccative
**desechable** *adj* disposable
**desechadamente** *adv* contemptibly, despicably
**desechar** *va* to cast aside, throw out; to think little of, to underrate; to blame, to censure; to drop (*an employee*); to turn (*a key to open door*)
**desecho** *m* remainder, residue; débris, rubbish, offal; castoff; contempt, low opinion; **desecho de hierro** scrap iron
**desedificación** *f* bad example
**desedificar §86** *va* to set a bad example for, to give a bad example to
**desegregación** *f* desegregation
**desegregar §59** *va* to desegregate
**deselectrización** *f* (elec.) discharge, discharging
**deselectrizar §76** *va* (elec.) to discharge (*a body*)
**desellar** *va* to unseal
**desembalaje** *m* unpacking
**desembalar** *va* to unpack
**desembaldosar** *va* to remove the bricks or paving tiles from (*a floor, a room, etc.*)
**desembalse** *m* loss of water in a dam
**desembanastar** *va* to take out of a basket; (coll.) to draw (*e.g., a sword*); to talk indiscreetly about; *vr* to break out, to break loose (*said of an animal*); (coll.) to alight from a carriage
**desembarazado -da** *adj* free, open; easy, unrestrained
**desembarazar §76** *va* to disembarrass, to disengage; to clear (*a road*); to empty (*a room*); *vr* to free oneself; to be cleared; to be emptied; **desembarazarse de** to get rid of
**desembarazo** *m* freedom; ease, naturalness, lack of restraint; (Am.) delivery, accouchement; **con desembarazo** readily, comfortably; quickly
**desembarcadero** *m* wharf, pier, landing place
**desembarcar §86** *va* to debark, disembark, unload; *vn* to debark, disembark, land, go ashore; to leave ship; (coll.) to alight; to end (*said of a staircase at landing*); *vr* to debark, disembark, land, go ashore
**desembarco** *m* debarkation, disembarkation, landing; landing (*of stairs*)
**desembargar §59** *va* to free, to disengage; (law) to raise the attachment or seizure of
**desembargo** *m* (law) raising of an attachment or seizure
**desembarque** *m* debarkation, disembarkation, unloading
**desembarrancar §86** *va & vn* to float (*said of a ship that ran aground*)
**desembarrar** *va* to clear of mud
**desembaular §75** *va* to take out of a trunk; (coll.) to unburden oneself of
**desembebecer §34** *vr* to come to, to recover one's senses
**desembelesar** *vr* to recover from one's amazement or stupefaction
**desemblantado -da** *adj* with changed countenance, with changed expression
**desemblantar** *vr* to change countenance, to color suddenly
**desembocadero** *m* exit, opening, outlet; mouth (*e.g., of river*)
**desembocadura** *f* mouth (*e.g., of river*); opening, outlet (*e.g., of street*); (Am.) channel (*between islands*)

**desembocar** §86 *vn* to flow, to empty; to end; **desembocar en** to flow or empty into; to end at (*said of a street*)
**desembojar** *va* to remove (*cocoons*) from rearing bushes
**desembolsar** *va* to empty out of a purse; to disburse, to pay out
**desembolso** *m* payment, expenditure; outlay; disbursement
**desemboque** *m* var. of **desembocadero**
**desemborrachar** *va & vr* to sober up
**desemboscar** §86 *va* to drive out of the woods; to bring out of ambush; *vr* to come out of the woods; to come out of ambush
**desembotar** *va* to remove the dullness from, to sharpen, to make sharp; *vr* to lose its dullness, to sharpen, to become sharp
**desembozar** §76 *va* to unmuffle, unmask; *vr* to unmuffle, unmask; to show one's true colors
**desembozo** *m* unmuffling, unmasking
**desembragar** §59 *va* (mach.) to disengage, to unclutch; (mach.) to disconnect (*e.g., a shaft*); *vn* to throw the clutch out
**desembrague** *m* (mach.) disengaging, disengagement
**desembravecer** §34 *va* to tame, domesticate; to calm, pacify; *vr* to become tame, to become domesticated
**desembravecimiento** *m* taming, domestication; calming
**desembrazar** §76 *va* to take (*something*) off the arm; to hurl (*a weapon*)
**desembriagar** §59 *va & vr* to sober up
**desembridar** *va* to unbridle
**desembrollar** *va* (coll.) to unravel, untangle
**desembrozar** §76 *va* var. of **desbrozar**
**desembuchar** *va* to disgorge (*said of birds*); to tell (*secrets*)
**desemejante** *adj* dissimilar, unlike; **desemejante de** unlike
**desemejanza** *f* dissimilarity, unlikeness, disagreement
**desemejar** *va* to disfigure, make look bad, change; *vn* to be unlike, to not look alike
**desempacar** §86 *va* to unpack, unwrap (*merchandise*); *vr* to cool off, calm down
**desempachar** *va* to relieve of indigestion; to free of timidity or bashfulness; *vr* to be relieved of indigestion; to get rid of one's timidity or bashfulness
**desempacho** *m* ease, calmness, unconcern
**desempalagar** §59 *va* to rid of nausea; *vr* to get rid of nausea
**desempañar** *va* to remove the blur, steam, smear, etc. from (*glass*); to remove the swaddling clothes from
**desempapelar** *va* to unwrap; to remove the paper from (*a wall, room, etc.*)
**desempaque** *m* unpacking, unwrapping
**desempaquetar** *va* to unpack, to unwrap
**desemparejar** *va* to unmatch, make unlike, uneven or unequal
**desemparentado -da** *adj* without relatives
**desempastelar** *va* (print.) to distribute (*mixed type*)
**desempatar** *va* to break the tie between, to break (*a tie vote*)
**desempate** *m* breaking the tie
**desempedrar** §18 *va* to remove the paving stones from, to unpave; (coll.) to pound (*the pavement*); **ir desempedrando la calle** (fig.) to dash down the street
**desempegar** §59 *va* to remove the pitch from
**desempeñado -da** *adj* clear, out of debt
**desempeñar** *va* to redeem, to recover, to take out of pawn or hock; to free from debt, to free from a commitment; to get (*a person*) out of a jam; to fulfill, carry out, accomplish; to fill (*a function*); to play (*a rôle*); *vr* to get out of a jam; to get out of debt
**desempeño** *m* redeeming a pledge; taking out of hock; payment (*of a debt*); discharge, fulfilment; performance, acting of a part
**desempeorar** *vr* to recover, to recover one's strength
**desemperezar** §76 *vn & vr* to shake off one's laziness
**desempernar** *va* to unbolt
**desempleo** *m* unemployment
**desemplomar** *va* to remove the lead from; to remove the seals from; (dent.) to take the filling out of; *vr* to come out (*said of a filling*)
**desemplumar** *va* to pluck, to take the feathers out of
**desempolvadura** *f* dusting, removal of dust or powder
**desempolvar** *va* to dust, to dust off; to renew; to brush up on; *vr* to brush up
**desempolvoradura** *f* var. of **desempolvadura**
**desempolvorar** *va* to dust, to dust off
**desemponzoñar** *va* to free from the effects of poison; to free of poison
**desempotrar** *va* to remove, take out (*something fixed or plugged in a wall*)
**desempozar** §76 *va* to remove from a well
**desenalbardar** *va* to remove the packsaddle from; to unharness
**desenamorar** *va* to destroy the love or affection of; *vr* to become cold or indifferent
**desenastar** *va* to take the handle or shaft off (*a tool, weapon, etc.*)
**desencabalgar** §59 *va* to dismount (*a gun*)
**desencabestrar** *va* to disentangle the feet of (*an animal*) from the halter
**desencadenamiento** *m* unchaining, unleashing; outbreak
**desencadenar** *va* to unchain, unleash, let loose; *vr* to be unchained, to break loose, to break out, to break forth
**desencajamiento** *m* dislocation; disjointedness; ricketiness, run-down appearance
**desencajar** *va* to dislocate; to throw out of joint, to disconnect; *vr* to get out of joint, become dislocated; to become contorted (*said of face or part of face*)
**desencaje** *m* var. of **desencajamiento**
**desencajonamiento** *m* unboxing, unpacking; (taur.) removal of bulls from box
**desencajonar** *va* to take out of a box, to unpack; to take (*bulls*) out of a box
**desencalabrinar** *va* to free of dizziness
**desencalcar** §86 *va* to loosen (*what was caked or packed*)
**desencallar** *va* to set (*a stranded ship*) afloat
**desencaminar** *va* to mislead, to lead astray
**desencantamiento** *m* disenchantment; disillusionment
**desencantar** *va* to disenchant; to disillusion; *vr* to become disenchanted; to become disillusioned
**desencantaración** *f* drawing lots
**desencantarar** *va* to draw (*lots*) from an urn; to exclude (*a name or names*) from balloting
**desencanto** *m* var. of **desencantamiento**
**desencapillar** *va* (naut.) to take the rigging from, to unrig
**desencapotar** *va* to take the cloak off (*a person*); to make (*a horse*) keep his head up; (coll.) to reveal, to manifest; *vr* to take off one's cloak; to keep its head up (*said of a horse*); to clear up (*said of sky*); to cool off, calm down
**desencaprichar** *va* to make (*a person*) give in; *vr* to give in, to give up a pet idea
**desencarcelar** *va* to free from jail, to set at liberty
**desencarecer** §34 *va* to lower the price of; *vn & vr* to come down (*in price*)
**desencarnar** *va* to keep (*dogs*) from eating game; to lose one's liking for; to disembody; *vr* to cast off the body, to die
**desencastillar** *va* to drive out of a castle; to reveal, make appear, show; to cause (*a person*) to fall from power, favor, etc.
**desencerrar** §18 *va* to unclose; to free from confinement; to reveal, to disclose
**desencintar** *va* to remove the ribbons from; to remove the curb of (*a sidewalk*)
**desenclavar** *va* to remove the nails from, to unnail; to expel or drive out forcibly
**desenclavijar** *va* to pull the pegs or pins out of; to let go, to disconnect
**desencoger** §49 *va* to spread out, to unfold; *vr* to lose one's timidity or bashfulness
**desencogimiento** *m* ease, naturalness
**desencoladura** *f* ungluing
**desencolar** *va* to unglue; *vr* to come unglued

**desencolerizar** §76 *va & vr* to calm down, to cool off
**desenconar** *va* to allay (*an inflammation*); to calm (*a person; a person's rancor or ill will*); *vr* to abate; to calm down; to soften up, get soft
**desencono** *m* allayment; calming, mitigation
**desencordar** §77 *va* to unstring (*e.g., a musical instrument*)
**desencordelar** *va* to unstring
**desencorvar** *va* to straighten
**desencovar** §77 *va* to get (*especially an animal*) out of a cave; to free of a risk or danger
**desencrespar** *va & vr* to uncurl, to unfrizzle
**desencuadernado -da** *adj* back on one's feet (*after fatigue or a beating*)
**desencuadernar** *va* to unbind, take the binding off (*a book*); *vr* to get loose, come unbound
**desenchufar** *va* to unplug, to disconnect
**desendemoniar** *va* to drive evil spirits out of; *vr* to be free of evil spirits
**desendiablar** *va* to drive evil spirits out of
**desendiosar** *va* to humble the vanity of, to bring down to earth
**desenfadaderas** *fpl* (coll.) resources, resourcefulness; **tener buenas desenfadaderas** (coll.) to be resourceful; (coll.) to be easygoing
**desenfadado -da** *adj* free, clear; ample, spacious; carefree, casual
**desenfadar** *va* to free of anger or annoyance; *vr* to cool off, calm down
**desenfado** *m* ease, freedom, naturalness; casualness; cheek, effrontery
**desenfaldar** *va* to untuck
**desenfardar** or **desenfardelar** *va* to unpack, to open
**desenfilada** *f* (mil.) defilade
**desenfilar** *va & vr* (fort. & mil.) to defilade
**desenfocado -da** *adj* out of focus
**desenfoque** *m* putting out of focus, distortion
**desenfrailar** *va* (prov.) to top (*a tree*); *vn* to leave the monastic life, become secularized; (coll.) to take a vacation; (coll.) to be freed, be emancipated; *vr* to leave the monastic life, become secularized
**desenfrenado -da** *adj* unbridled, licentious, wanton
**desenfrenamiento** *m* var. of **desenfreno**
**desenfrenar** *va* to unbridle, remove the bit from; *vr* to yield to vice and evil; to fly into a passion; to break loose (*said, e.g., of a storm*)
**desenfreno** *m* unruliness, licentiousness, wantonness; **desenfreno de vientre** loose bowels, diarrhea
**desenfundar** *va* to unsheathe
**desenfurecer** §34 *va* to quiet the anger of; *vr* to calm down, cool off
**desenganchar** *va* to unhook, unpin, unfasten; to uncouple; to unhitch, to unharness; *vr* to come unhooked, to come unfastened
**desengañadamente** *adv* openly, sincerely; (coll.) badly, poorly, carelessly
**desengañador -dora** *adj* disillusioning, disappointing
**desengañar** *va* to undeceive, disabuse; to disillusion; *vr* to become disillusioned
**desengaño** *m* disabusal; disillusionment; disappointment; plain fact, plain truth
**desengarrafar** *va* to release one's grip on
**desengarzar** §76 *va* to take out of a setting; to loosen, to disconnect
**desengastar** *va* to take (*e.g., a precious stone*) out of its setting
**desengomar** *va* to ungum; to unsize (*silk*)
**desengoznar** *va* to unhinge; to disconnect, upset, throw out of gear; *vr* to contort the body (*as in certain dances*)
**desengranar** *va & vr* to unmesh, disengage
**desengrane** *m* unmeshing, disengaging
**desengrasar** *va* to take the grease out of; *vn* (coll.) to get thin; (coll.) to take away the greasy taste by eating olives, fruit, etc.
**desengrase** *m* removal of grease
**desengraso** *m* (Am.) dessert
**desengrosar** §77 *va* to make thin, lean, or fine; *vr* to become thin, lean, or fine
**desengrudar** *va* to scrape or rub the paste off
**desenhebrar** *va* to unthread; (fig.) to unravel
**desenhornar** *va* to take out of the oven
**desenjaezar** §76 *va* to unharness, to take the trappings off (*a horse*)
**desenjalmar** *va* to take the packsaddle off (*a horse, mule, etc.*)
**desenjaular** *va* to take out of the cage; to take out of jail or out of confinement
**desenlabonar** *va* var. of **deseslabonar**
**desenlace** *m* outcome; denouement (*of drama*)
**desenladrillar** *va* to take up the bricks or tiles from (*floor*)
**desenlazar** §76 *va* to untie; to solve; to unravel (*plot of play*); *vr* to untie, come untied; to unfold (*said of plot of play*)
**desenlodar** *va* to clear of mud
**desenlosar** *va* to take up the flagstones in (*a room, patio, etc.*)
**desenlutar** *va* to make (*a person*) give up mourning; *vr* to give up mourning
**desenmallar** *va* to take (*fish*) out of the net
**desenmarañar** *va* to disentangle; to unravel
**desenmascaradamente** *adv* barefacedly
**desenmascaramiento** *m* unmasking; exposure, exposé
**desenmascarar** *va* to unmask; to expose; *vr* to unmask, take one's mask off
**desenmohecer** §34 *va* to clear of rust; *vr* to become clear of rust
**desenmudecer** §34 *va* to free of a speech impediment; *vn* to get rid of a speech impediment; to break a long silence
**desenojar** *va* to free of anger, to allay the anger of; *vr* to cool off, calm down; to amuse oneself
**desenojo** *m* coolness, calmness, freedom from anger
**desenredar** *va* to disentangle, resolve; to clear up, straighten out; *vr* to extricate oneself
**desenredo** *m* disentanglement; denouement (*of plot*)
**desenrollar** *va & vr* to unroll, unwind, unreel, unfurl
**desenroscar** §86 *va & vr* to untwine; to unscrew
**desensamblar** *va & vr* to disjoint
**desensañar** *va* to calm, to pacify; *vr* to calm down, to cool off
**desensartar** *va* to unstring, to unthread
**desensebar** *va* to strip of fat; *vn* to change one's pursuits to break the monotony; (coll.) to take away the greasy taste by eating olives, fruit, etc.
**desenseñamiento** *m* ignorance
**desenseñar** *va* to unteach (*something learned wrongly*)
**desensibilización** *f* desensitization
**desensibilizar** §76 *va* to desensitize; *vr* to become desensitized
**desensillar** *va* to unsaddle (*a horse*)
**desensoberbecer** §34 *va* to humble, to lessen the pride of; *vr* to become humbled, to lose one's pride
**desensortijado -da** *adj* uncurled; dislocated
**desentablar** *va* to rip the boards or planks from; to disturb, upset, confuse; to break off (*a friendship, bargain, etc.*)
**desentalingar** §59 *va* (naut.) to unbend (*a cable*)
**desentarimar** *va* to take up the inlaid floor or parquetry in
**desentender** §66 *vr* to not participate; to affect ignorance; **desentenderse de** to take no part in, to renounce; to detach oneself from, free oneself from; to pay no attention to; to affect ignorance of
**desenterrador** *m* exhumer
**desenterramiento** *m* unearthing, disinterment; (fig.) unearthing; (fig.) recall, recalling
**desenterrar** §18 *va* to unearth, disinter; to dig up; (fig.) to unearth, to dig up; (fig.) to remember, recall
**desentierramuertos** *mf* (*pl:* **-tos**) (coll.) defamer of the dead
**desentoldar** *va* to take the awning from; to strip of adornment
**desentonación** *f* var. of **desentono**
**desentonadamente** *adv* out of tune
**desentonado -da** *adj* out of tune, flat; inharmonious
**desentonamiento** *m* var. of **desentono**

**desentonar** *va* to humble the pride of; *vn* to be out of tune; to clash, to be out of harmony; *vr* to talk loud and disrespectfully
**desentono** *m* false note, dissonance; rude tone of voice
**desentornillar** *va* to unscrew
**desentorpecer §34** *va* to free of numbness; to polish, give a polish to (*a person*); *vr* to get rid of numbness, be freed of numbness; to take on a polish
**desentrampar** *va* (coll.) to free of debts; *vr* (coll.) to get out of debt
**desentrañamiento** *m* disembowelment, evisceration; giving one's all for love
**desentrañar** *va* to disembowel, to eviscerate; to dig deeply into, to figure out; *vr* to give one's all to one's beloved
**desentrenado -da** *adj* (sport) out of training
**desentrenamiento** *m* (sport) lack of training
**desentrenar** *vr* (sport) to be out of training, to slip
**desentristecer §34** *va* to cheer, comfort, banish the sadness of
**desentronizar §76** *va* to dethrone; to deprive of power, favor, or standing
**desentumecer §34** *va* to take out the numbness of, to relieve of numbness; *vr* to shake off the numbness
**desentumecimiento** *m* freedom from numbness
**desentumir** *va & vr* var. of **desentumecer**
**desenvainar** *va* to unsheathe; to stretch out (*the claws*); (coll.) to show, expose
**desenvelejar** *va* (naut.) to strip of sails
**desenvendar** *va* to unbandage
**desenvergar §59** *va* (naut.) to unbend (*a sail*)
**desenviolar** *va* to bless or purify (*a holy place that was desecrated*)
**desenvoltura** *f* ease, free and easy manner; fluency; lewdness (*chiefly in women*)
**desenvolvedor -dora** *adj* scrutinizing, curious, prying; *mf* investigator, curious person
**desenvolver §63 & §17,** 9 *va* to unroll, unfold; to unwrap; to develop (*e.g., a theme, one's mind, an industry*); to disentangle, unravel, clear up; *vr* to be forward, be too bold; to extricate oneself; to unroll; to develop, to evolve; to be unraveled, be cleared up
**desenvolvimiento** *m* unfolding; elucidation; development
**desenvuelto -ta** *pp of* **desenvolver;** *adj* easy, free and easy; fluent; bold, daring; forward, brazen
**desenzarzar §76** *va* to pull out of the brambles; (coll.) to separate and reconcile (*quarrelers*); (Am.) to clear (*a field*) of brambles
**deseo** *m* desire, wish; **coger a deseo** to succeed in gratifying one's desire for; **venir en deseo de** to desire, to want
**deseoso -sa** *adj* desirous
**desequido -da** *adj* very dry, too dry
**desequilibrado -da** *adj* unbalanced; (fig.) unbalanced
**desequilibrar** *va* to unbalance; *vr* to become unbalanced
**desequilibrio** *m* disequilibrium, imbalance, unbalanced condition; unbalanced mental condition
**deserción** *f* desertion; (law) forfeiture (*of right of appeal*)
**deserrado -da** *adj* free of error
**desertar** *va* to desert; (law) to forfeit (*right of appeal*); *vn* to desert; **desertar a** to go over to; **desertar de** to desert
**desértico -ca** *adj* desert
**desertor** *m* (mil. & fig.) deserter
**deservicio** *m* disservice
**deservir §94** *va* to disserve, do an ill turn to
**desescarchador** *m* defroster
**deseslabonar** *va* to cut the links of, to unlink
**desespaldar** *va* to wrench the back of, break the back of; to take the back off or out of (*e.g., a chair*); *vr* to wrench one's back, to break one's back
**desespañolizar §76** *va* to free of Spanish influence; *vr* to become free of Spanish influence; to give up one's Spanish nationality
**desesperación** *f* despair, desperation; **ser una desesperación** (coll.) to be unbearable
**desesperado -da** *adj* desperate, despairing; hopeless (*e.g., condition*); *mf* desperate person
**desesperante** *adj* despairing; exasperating, maddening
**desesperanza** *f* hopelessness
**desesperanzado -da** *adj* hopeless
**desesperanzar §76** *va* to make hopeless, to deprive of hope; to discourage; *vr* to lose hope
**desesperar** *va* to make hopeless, to deprive of hope, to drive to despair; (coll.) to exasperate, to drive wild; *vn* to be hopeless, to lose hope, to be driven to despair, to despair; (coll.) to be exasperated, be driven wild
**desespero** *m* var. of **desesperación**
**desestalinización** *f* destalinization
**desestalinizar §76** *va & vn* to destalinize
**desestancar §86** *va* to open (*something stopped up*); (com.) to open the market to, to make free of duty, to raise the monopoly on
**desestanco** *m* opening, clearing
**desestañado** *m* untinning, detinning; unsoldering
**desestañar** *va* to untin, to detin; to unsolder; *vr* to detin; to come unsoldered
**desesterar** *va* to remove the mats from (*floor, stairs*)
**desesterilizar §76** *va* to desterilize (*gold*)
**desestero** *m* removal of mats; season for removing mats
**desestima** or **desestimación** *f* low regard, disesteem; refusal, rejection
**desestimar** *va* to hold in low regard, to disesteem; to refuse, to reject
**deséxito** *m* failure
**desexualizar §76** *va* to desexualize
**desfachatado -da** *adj* (coll.) impudent, brazen, shameless
**desfachatez** *f* (coll.) impudence, brazenness, shamelessness
**desfajar** *va* to ungird, to unbind
**desfalcador -dora** *mf* defaulter
**desfalcar §86** *va* to remove part of, to lop off; to embezzle; to bring down in standing or favor; *vn* to embezzle, to defalcate
**desfalco** *m* removal, lopping off; embezzlement, defalcation
**desfallecer §34** *va* to weaken, to debilitate; *vn* to fall away, grow weak; to faint, faint away; **desfallecer de ánimo** to lose courage
**desfallecido -da** *adj* faint, fainting, languid
**desfalleciente** *adj* languishing, failing
**desfallecimiento** *m* weakening, debilitation; languor; faint, fainting
**desfasaje** *m* (elec.) phase displacement
**desfasar** *vn* (elec.) to be out of phase; to be out of tune; to not fit
**desfavorable** *adj* unfavorable
**desfavorecer §34** *va* to disfavor; to disfigure
**desfibrar** *va* to remove the fibers from
**desfiguración** *f* or **desfiguramiento** *m* disfigurement; deformation; alteration; distortion
**desfigurar** *va* to disfigure; to cloud, to darken; to disguise (*voice*); to change, to alter; to distort, misrepresent; *vr* to change countenance
**desfijar** *va* to pull off, to detach
**desfiladero** *m* defile, pass
**desfilar** *vn* to defile, march in review, parade; (coll.) to file by or out
**desfile** *m* defiling, marching in review, parade
**desflecar §86** *va* to remove the flakes from (*wool*) or frettings of (*cloth*)
**desflemar** *va* (chem.) to dephlegmate; *vn* to expel phlegm
**desflocar §95** *va* var. of **desflecar**
**desfloración** *f* or **desfloramiento** *m* defloration, deflowering
**desflorar** *va* to deflower; to treat superficially
**desflorecer §34** *vn & vr* to lose flowers, to wither
**desflorecimiento** *m* loss of flowers, withering
**desfogar §59** *va* to vent, make an opening in (*e.g., a furnace*); to slake (*lime*); (fig.) to vent (*e.g., one's anger*); to give loose rein to (*a horse*); *vn* (naut.) to break into rain and wind (*said of threatening clouds*); *vr* to vent one's anger, to blow off steam
**desfogonar** *va* to burst the vent of (*a gun*); *vr* to burst (*said of vent of gun*)

**desfogue** *m* vent; (Am.) drain hole (*in large aqueduct*); venting of emotions, venting of anger
**desfollonar** *va* to trim (*a plant*)
**desfondamiento** *m* (sport) collapse
**desfondar** *va* to break or remove the bottom of; to stave in; (naut.) to bilge, to knock in the bottom of (*a ship*); (agr.) to dig up (*the soil*) to a great depth; *vr* (naut.) to bilge; (sport) to collapse
**desfonde** *m* (agr.) digging the soil to a great depth
**desforestación** *f* deforestation
**desforestar** *va* to deforest
**desformar** *va* to deform
**desforrar** *va* to remove the lining of; to strip
**desfortalecer §34** *va* to dismantle, to demolish (*a fort*); to deprive a fortress of (*its garrison*)
**desfrenar** *va* to unbridle; *vn* (aut.) to take the breaks off; *vr* to yield to one's emotions or passions; to break loose (*said, e.g., of a storm*)
**desfruncir §50** *va* to unfold, to spread out
**desgaire** *m* slovenliness; affected carelessness; scornful attitude; **al desgaire** carelessly, with affected carelessness; scornfully
**desgajadura** *f* tearing, breaking; splitting of a branch from a tree
**desgajar** *va* to tear off, to break off; to split off (*a branch*); *vr* to come off, to come loose, to break off, to break away; **desgajarse el cielo** to become stormy, to rain hard
**desgaje** *m* tearing, breaking, splitting
**desgalgadero** *m* rocky slope; cliff, precipice
**desgalgar §59** *va* to throw headlong; *vr* to fall headlong, to rush headlong
**desgalichado -da** *adj* (coll.) sloppy, ungainly
**desgana** *f* lack of appetite; indifference; boredom, disgust; unwillingness; **a desgana** unwillingly, reluctantly
**desganado -da** *adj* not hungry; indifferent
**desganar** *va* to make indifferent; *vr* to lose one's appetite; to become indifferent; to be bored
**desganchar** *va* to lop or tear the branches off (*a tree*)
**desgano** *m* var. of **desgana**
**desgañitar** *vr* (coll.) to struggle and scream; (coll.) to scream oneself hoarse
**desgarbado -da** *adj* graceless, ungainly, uncouth
**desgargantar** *vr* (coll.) to shout oneself hoarse
**desgargolar** *va* to ripple (*flax or hemp*); to remove (*a board*) from a groove or notch
**desgaritar** *vn* to lose the way, to go astray; *vr* to lose the way, to go astray; to get separated from the fold; to abandon an undertaking
**desgarrado -da** *adj* torn, ripped; tattered; shameless, barefaced, licentious
**desgarradura** *f* var. of **desgarrón**
**desgarramiento** *m* tearing, rending
**desgarrar** *va* to tear, to rend; to cough up; *vr* to withdraw, retire
**desgarre** *m* tear, rent
**desgarro** *m* tear, rent; outburst; boldness, barefacedness, effrontery; boasting, braggadocio
**desgarrón** *m* large tear or rip; shred, tatter
**desgasificar §86** *va* to degas, to degasify
**desgastar** *va* to abrade, consume, wear away; to weaken, spoil, vitiate; *vr* to wear away, lose one's strength, decline
**desgaste** *m* abrasion, attrition, wear, wearing down, fray, fraying
**desgausamiento** *m* degaussing
**desgausar** *va* to degauss
**desgaznatar** *vr* (coll.) to shout oneself hoarse
**desglazador** *m* defroster
**desglosar** *va* to obliterate a note in (*a writing*); to set aside (*a question*); to detach (*a page or pages*); to break down, to analyse
**desglose** *m* obliteration of a note or gloss; separation; detachment; breakdown, analysis
**desgobernado -da** *adj* ungovernable, uncontrollable
**desgobernar §18** *va* to upset the government of; to misgovern; to dislocate (*bones*); (naut.) to steer poorly; *vn* (naut.) to steer poorly; *vr* to go through contortions (*as in certain dances*)
**desgobierno** *m* mismanagement, maladministration, misgovernment; dislocation
**desgolletar** *va* to break the neck of (*e.g., a bottle*); to loosen or remove (*clothing around the neck*)
**desgomar** *va* to ungum; to unsize (*silk*)
**desgonzar §76** *va* to unhinge; to disconnect, upset, throw out of gear; *vr* to be disconnected, upset, or thrown out of gear
**desgoznar** *va & vr* var. of **desengoznar**
**desgracia** *f* misfortune, bad luck; disfavor, disgrace; lack of charm or grace; unpleasantness, gruffness; **caer en desgracia** (coll.) to be in disfavor, to lose favor; **correr con desgracia** to have no luck; **por desgracia** unfortunately
**desgraciado -da** *adj* unfortunate; unhappy; graceless, ungraceful; ungracious, unpleasant, disagreeable; *mf* wretch, unfortunate
**desgraciar** *va* to displease; to spoil; *vr* to spoil; to decline, to degenerate; to fall out; to fail, to fall through
**desgramar** *va* to pull up the grass in (*a field*)
**desgranador -dora** *adj* shelling, threshing; *mf* sheller, thresher; *f* threshing machine
**desgranar** *va* to remove the grain from, to remove or pick the grapes from (*a bunch of grapes*), to shell (*e.g., peas*); to thresh; to sift (*powder*); *vr* to fall from the ear, to drop from the bunch; to shell, to seed; to come loose (*said of beads*); to wear away (*said of vent of firearms*)
**desgrane** *m* shelling, picking; coming loose (*of grain, grapes, beads, etc.*); threshing
**desgranzar §76** *va* to separate the chaff from; (paint.) to give (*colors*) the first grinding
**desgrasar** *va* to remove the grease from (*e.g., wool*)
**desgrase** *m* removal of grease
**desgravación** *f* lowering of duties or taxes; removal of lien or mortgage
**desgravar** *va* to lower duties or taxes on; to remove a lien or mortgage on
**desgreñar** *va* to dishevel; *vr* to get disheveled; to pull each other's hair, to get into a fight
**desguace** *m* roughhewing, roughdressing; taking down, disassembling of a boat
**desguarnecer §34** *va* to remove the ornaments from, to strip of trimmings; to strip down, to remove the accessories from; to unharness; to unman (*a fortress*); to disarm (*an opponent*)
**desguarnecimiento** *m* stripping; disarming
**desguazar §76** *va* to roughhew or roughdress (*timber*); to take down, to break down (*a ship*)
**desguince** *m* knife for cutting rags in paper mills; dodge, dodging
**desguindar** *va* (naut.) to lower, bring down; *vr* to slide down
**desguinzar §76** *va* to cut (*rags, in paper mills*)
**deshabillé** *m* deshabille or dishabille
**deshabitado -da** *adj* uninhabited, unoccupied
**deshabitar** *va* to move out of; to abandon, to desert (*a town or region*)
**deshabituación** *f* disuse, disusage
**deshabituar §33** *va* to make unaccustomed, to disaccustom; *vr* to become unaccustomed, become disaccustomed
**deshacedor -dora** *adj* undoing; *mf* undoer; **deshacedor de agravios** righter of wrongs
**deshacer §55** *va* to undo; to take apart; to untie, to open; to consume, diminish, destroy; to carve, cut up; to wear away; to put to flight, to rout; to melt, dissolve; to violate (*a treaty*); to right (*wrongs*); *vr* to get out of order, to break, to break to pieces; to go to pieces, to melt (*in the mouth*); to strive hard; to grow weak; to disappear; to be grieved, to be impatient; to bump, to bruise; **deshacerse de** to get rid of; **deshacerse en** to burst into (*tears*); to lavish (*praise, flattery*); **deshacerse por** + *inf* to strive hard to + *inf*
**deshago** *1st sg pres ind of* **deshacer**
**deshaldo** *m* spring trimming of honeycombs
**deshambrido -da** *adj* famished, starving
**desharé** *1st sg fut ind of* **deshacer**
**desharrapado -da** *adj* ragged, shabby
**desharrapamiento** *m* raggedness, shabbiness, poverty, indigence

**deshebillar** *va* to unbuckle
**deshebrar** *va* to ravel, to unthread; to tear to shreds
**deshecha** *f* see **deshecho**
**deshechizar** §76 *va* to take the spell or curse off (*a person*); to disappoint
**deshechizo** *m* breaking a spell or curse; disappointment
**deshecho -cha** *pp of* **deshacer;** *adj* strong, violent, hard; great, good (*luck*); *f* feint, simulation, sham, pretense; polite farewell; way-out; l'envoi (*of a poem*); **a la deshecha** with dissimulation; **hacer la deshecha** to feign, to pretend; (Am.) to pretend to be uninterested
**deshelador** *m* (aer.) deicer
**deshelar** §18 *va & vr* to melt, to thaw; to defrost; (aer.) to deice
**desherbar** §18 *va* to pull, pull up (*weeds*); to weed (*e.g., a field*)
**desheredación** *f* disinheritance
**desheredado -da** *adj* disinherited; underprivileged
**desheredamiento** *m* var. of **desheredación**
**desheredar** *va* to disinherit; *vr* to disgrace one's family, be a disgrace to one's family
**deshermanar** *va* to make unlike, to unmatch; *vr* to fail as a brother
**desherrar** §18 *va* to unchain, unshackle; to unshoe (*a horse*)
**desherrumbrar** *va* to clean of rust, to take the rust off; *vr* to get free of rust
**deshice** *1st sg pret ind of* **deshacer**
**deshidratación** *f* dehydration
**deshidratar** *va & vr* to dehydrate
**deshielo** *m* thaw, thawing; defrosting
**deshierba** *f* weeding
**deshilachado** *m* removal of ravels or frayings
**deshilachar** *va* to pull ravels or frayings from (*a fabric*); *vr* to fray
**deshilado -da** *adj* in a file; **a la deshilada** in file, in single file; clandestinely; *m* drawn work, openwork, hemstitching
**deshiladura** *f* unweaving; reduction of rags to a pulp (*in paper manufacturing*); pulp (*for manufacturing paper*)
**deshilar** *va* to unweave leaving a fringe; to shred (*meat*); to distract (*a swarm of bees*) to a new hive; *vn* to get thin
**deshilo** *m* distracting bees to new hive
**deshilvanado -da** *adj* disconnected, loose, incoherent, desultory
**deshilvanar** *va* (sew.) to unbaste, untack
**deshincar** §86 *va* to pull out, to pull up (*something driven in*)
**deshinchar** *va* to deflate (*a balloon, news, etc.*); to give vent to (*anger, annoyance, etc.*); *vr* to go down (*said of a swelling, tumor, etc.*); (coll.) to become deflated (*in self-esteem*)
**deshinchazón** *m* abatement of swelling
**deshipnotizar** §76 *va* to dehypnotize
**deshipotecar** §86 *va* to cancel the mortgage on, to free of mortgage
**deshojador** *m* stripper of leaves, defoliator
**deshojadura** *f* defoliation
**deshojar** *va* to defoliate, to strip the leaves off (*a plant or tree*); to tear the leaves out of (*a book*); *vr* to defoliate
**deshoje** *m* fall of leaves
**deshollejar** *va* to peel, pare, skin (*e.g., grapes*); to shell (*e.g., beans*)
**deshollinadera** *f* long-handled brush or broom
**deshollinador -dora** *adj* chimney-sweeping; *mf* chimney sweep, chimney sweeper; (coll.) scrutinizer; *m* long-handled brush or broom
**deshollinar** *va* to clean, to sweep (*a chimney*); to clean (*walls and ceiling*) with long-handled brush; (coll.) to scrutinize
**deshonestar** *vr* to act unbecomingly or indecently
**deshonestidad** *f* immodesty, indecency
**deshonesto -ta** *adj* immodest, indecent
**deshonor** *m* dishonor
**deshonorar** *va* to dishonor; to deprive of office or occupation; to deface, disfigure; *vr* to be dishonored
**deshonra** *f* dishonor, disgrace; dishonorable act; **tener a deshonra** to consider dishonorable
**deshonrabuenos** *mf* (*pl:* **-nos**) (coll.) slanderer; (coll.) black sheep
**deshonradamente** *adv* dishonorably, disgracefully
**deshonrador -dora** *adj* dishonorable, disgraceful; *mf* dishonorer, disgracer; *m* seducer
**deshonrar** *va* to dishonor, to disgrace; to violate, to seduce (*a woman*); to insult, defame; to scorn, despise
**deshonrible** *adj* (coll.) shameless, contemptible; *mf* (coll.) shameless person, contemptible person
**deshonroso -sa** *adj* dishonorable, ignominious, indecent
**deshora** *f* inopportune time, inconvenient time; **a deshora** or **a deshoras** inopportunely, at an inconvenient time; without preparation
**deshornar** *va* var. of **desenhornar**
**deshospedamiento** *m* refusal of lodging, inhospitality
**deshospedar** *va* to deprive of lodging, to refuse lodging to
**deshuesadora** *f* pitter (*device*)
**deshuesar** *va* to bone; to stone, to take the pits out of (*fruit*)
**deshumanar** *vr* to become dehumanized
**deshumanización** *f* dehumanization
**deshumanizar** §76 *va* to dehumanize
**deshumedecedor -dora** *adj* dehumidifying; *m* dehumidifier
**deshumedecer** §34 *va* to dehumidify, to dry up; *vr* to become dehumidified, to dry up
**deshumidificar** §86 *va* to dehumidify
**desiderátum** *m* (*pl:* **-rata**) desideratum
**desidia** *f* laziness, indolence
**desidioso -sa** *adj* lazy, indolent; *mf* lazy person
**desierto -ta** *adj* desert; deserted; *m* desert; wilderness; **predicar en desierto** (coll.) to preach to deaf ears; **Desierto Arábigo** *or* **de Arabia** Arabian Desert; **Desierto de Libia** Libyan Desert; **Desierto de Sahara** Sahara Desert
**designación** *f* designation, selection
**designar** *va* to plan (*a piece of work*); to designate, to appoint, to select
**designio** *m* design, purpose, plan
**desigual** *adj* unequal; rough, uneven, irregular, jerky; arduous, difficult; changeable, inconstant
**desigualar** *va* to make unequal; *vr* to become unequal; to get ahead
**desigualdad** *f* inequality; roughness, unevenness
**desilusión** *f* disillusion, disillusionment; disappointment
**desilusionar** *va* to disillusion; to disappoint; *vr* to be disillusioned; to be disappointed
**desimanación** *f* demagnetization
**desimanar** *va* to demagnetize; *vr* to become demagnetized
**desimantación** *f* var. of **desimanación**
**desimantar** *va & vr* var. of **desimanar**
**desimpondré** *1st sg fut ind of* **desimponer**
**desimponer** §69 *va* (print.) to break up the imposition of (*a form*)
**desimpongo** *1st sg pres ind of* **desimponer**
**desimpresionar** *va* to undeceive; to remove the impression of; *vr* to be undeceived; **desimpresionarse de** to free one's mind of
**desimpuesto -ta** *pp of* **desimponer**
**desimpuse** *1st sg pret ind of* **desimponer**
**desinclinar** *va* to disincline; *vr* to disincline, be disinclined
**desincorporar** *va & vr* to separate, to break up
**desincrustante** *m* disincrustant
**desincrustar** *va* to disincrust
**desinencia** *f* (gram.) termination, ending, desinence; **desinencia casual** (gram.) case ending
**desinfección** *f* disinfection
**desinfectante** *adj & m* disinfectant
**desinfectar** *va* to disinfect; *vr* to become disinfected
**desinfestar** *va* to disinfest
**desinficionar** *va & vr* var. of **desinfectar**
**desinflación** *f* or **desinflado** *m* deflation
**desinflamación** *f* decrease of inflammation, loss of inflammation

**desinflamar** *va* to remove the inflammation from; *vr* to lose its inflammation (*said of a wound, part of body, etc.*)
**desinflar** *va* to deflate; (coll.) to deflate (*a person*); *vr* to become deflated; (coll.) to be or become deflated
**desinsacular** *va* to draw lots on (*certain names*)
**desinsectación** *f* fumigation, freeing of insects
**desinsectar** *va* to fumigate, to free of insects
**desintegración** *f* disintegration
**desintegrar** *va & vr* to disintegrate
**desinterés** *m* disinterestedness
**desinteresado -da** *adj* disinterested, impartial; uninterested
**desinteresar** *vr* to lose interest
**desintonizar §76** *va* (rad.) to put out of tune; (rad.) to tune out
**desinvernar §18** *va* (mil.) to take out of winter quarters; *vn & vr* (mil.) to go out of or to leave winter quarters
**desistencia** *f* or **desistimiento** *m* desistence; (law) waiving a right
**desistir** *vn* to desist; (law) to waive a right; **desistir de** to desist from, to give up; **desistir de** + *inf* to stop, leave off + *ger*
**desjarretadera** *f* hooked knife for hamstringing or hocking animals
**desjarretar** *va* to hamstring, to hock; (coll.) to weaken, to bleed to excess
**desjarrete** *m* hamstringing, hocking
**desjugar §59** *va* to draw the juice from
**desjuiciado -da** *adj* devoid of judgment, senseless
**desjuntar** *va & vr* to disjoin, to sever, to separate
**deslabonar** *va* to unlink; to disconnect; to destroy; *vr* to come unlinked; to be disconnected; to be destroyed; to retire, to withdraw
**desladrillar** *va* var. of **desenladrillar**
**deslamar** *va* to clear of mud, to remove silt from
**deslastrar** *va* (naut.) to unballast, to remove the ballast from
**deslatar** *va* to remove the laths from
**deslavado -da** *adj* barefaced; *mf* barefaced person
**deslavadura** *f* superficial washing; fading, weakening
**deslavar** *va* to wash superficially; to fade, weaken, take the life out of
**deslavazar §76** *va* var. of **deslavar**
**deslazar §76** *va & vr* var. of **desenlazar**
**desleal** *adj* disloyal
**deslealtad** *f* disloyalty
**deslechugar §59** *va* to prune (*e.g., vines*); to strip leaves from; to trim off (*shoots*)
**deslechuguillar** *va* var. of **deslechugar**
**desleidura** *f* or **desleimiento** *m* dilution, thinning; dissolving
**desleír §73** *va* to dilute, to diffuse; to dissolve; to thin (*paint*); to be diffuse or prolix in (*thought*); *vr* to become diluted; to dissolve
**deslendrar §18** *va* to clean the nits out of (*hair*)
**deslenguado -da** *adj* shameless, foul-mouthed, scurrilous
**deslenguamiento** *m* (coll.) shamelessness, impudence, indecency
**deslenguar §23** *va* to cut the tongue of, to cut out the tongue of; *vr* (coll.) to blab, talk too much; (coll.) to speak or act shamelessly or indecently
**desliar §90** *va* to untie, unpack; to separate the refuse from (*the juice, in making wine*); (fig.) to unravel; *vr* to come untied
**desligadura** *f* untying, unbinding, loosening; unraveling, disentangling
**desligar §59** *va* to untie, to unbind; to unravel, to disentangle; to excuse, to exempt; to absolve from ecclesiastical censure; (mus.) to play or sing (*something*) staccato; *vr* to come loose, to come untied; to become disentangled
**deslindador** *m* surveyor
**deslindamiento** *m* determination of boundaries, demarcation; explanation, defining
**deslindar** *va* to bound, to mark the boundaries of; to explain, to define
**deslinde** *m* var. of **deslindamiento**
**deslingar §59** *va* (naut.) to unsling
**desliñar** *va* to clean (*fulled cloth, before sending it to the press*)
**deslío** *m* decanting new wine
**desliz** *m* (*pl:* **-lices**) sliding, slipping; slide (*smooth surface*); backslide; peccadillo, slip
**deslizable** *adj* sliding; weak, fragile, brittle
**deslizadero -ra** *adj* slippery; *m* slide, slippery spot; launching way; *f* (mach.) slide, guide
**deslizadizo -za** *adj* slippery
**deslizador** *m* (aer.) glider
**deslizamiento** *m* sliding, slipping; skid, skidding; **deslizamiento de tierra** landslide
**deslizante** *adj* sliding, gliding; slipping; skidding
**deslizar §76** *va* to slide, make slide; to let slip (*a remark*); *vn* to slide, glide; to slip; *vr* to slide, glide; to slip; to skid; to slip out (*said of a remark*); to slip away, sneak away; to backslide, slide back (*e.g., into a vice*)
**deslomadura** *f* breaking the back; (vet.) aponeurositis of the loins
**deslomar** *va* to strain or break the back of; *vr* to strain or break one's back, to work oneself to death
**deslucido -da** *adj* quiet, unshowy; dull, undistinguished
**deslucimiento** *m* tarnishing, dulling; lack of brilliance, dullness; lack of charm, grace, distinction; ungracefulness, uncouthness, failure
**deslucir §60** *va* to tarnish, to dull the luster of, to deprive of charm, grace, distinction; to discredit
**deslumbrador -dora** *adj* dazzling; bewildering, baffling
**deslumbramiento** *m* glare, dazzling; bewilderment, bafflement
**deslumbrante** *adj* dazzling; bewildering, baffling
**deslumbrar** *va* to dazzle; to bewilder, to baffle; *vr* to be dazzled; to be bewildered, be baffled
**deslustrado -da** *adj* dull, flat; frosted, ground (*glass*)
**deslustrador -dora** *adj* tarnishing, dulling; *mf* tarnisher
**deslustrar** *va* to tarnish, to dull, to dim; to frost (*glass*); to discredit; *vr* to tarnish, dull, dim
**deslustre** *m* tarnishing, dulling; dullness, dimness; dinginess; discredit, stain, stigma
**deslustroso -sa** *adj* ugly, unbecoming; disgraceful
**desluzco** *1st sg pres ind of* **deslucir**
**desmadejamiento** *m* enervation, weakness
**desmadejar** *va* to enervate, weaken; *vr* to become enervated, become weakened
**desmadrado -da** *adj* abandoned by the mother, motherless (*said of animals*)
**desmadrar** *va* to wean (*young cattle*)
**desmagnetizar §76** *va* to demagnetize; *vr* to become demagnetized
**desmajolar §77** *va* to pull up (*new vines*) by the root; to untie, to loosen (*shoes*)
**desmalladura** *f* undoing or cutting meshes
**desmallar** *va* to undo or cut the meshes of (*a net*)
**desmamar** *va* to wean
**desmamonar** *va* to cut the young shoots off (*a tree or vine*)
**desmán** *m* excess, misbehavior; mishap, misfortune; (zool.) desman
**desmanar** *vr* to stray from the flock or herd
**desmanchar** *va* (Am.) to clean of spots, to remove spots from (*clothing*)
**desmandado -da** *adj* disobedient, intractable, out of hand
**desmandar** *va* to cancel, countermand, revoke; to revoke (*a legacy, bequest*); *vr* to be impudent and ill-mannered; to go away, to keep apart; to stray from the flock or herd; to get out of hand
**desmanear** *va* to unfetter, to unshackle
**desmangar §59** *va* to take off the handle of
**desmanotado -da** *adj* (coll.) shy, awkward, unhandy
**desmantecar §86** *va* to take the butter out of
**desmantelado -da** *adj* dilapidated
**desmantelamiento** *m* dismantling; dilapidation

**desmantelar** *va* to dismantle; to dilapidate; (naut.) to unmast; (naut.) to unrig; *vr* to dilapidate (*to fall into disrepair or partial ruin*)
**desmaña** *f* clumsiness, awkwardness, laziness, bungling
**desmañado -da** *adj* clumsy, awkward, lazy; bungled
**desmarrido -da** *adj* languid, exhausted
**desmarrir** §53 *vr* to become exhausted; to grow sad
**desmatar** *va* to grub, dig up
**desmayado -da** *adj* languid, colorless, apathetic; dull (*color*)
**desmayar** *va* to dishearten, to depress; *vn* to lose heart; to falter; *vr* to faint
**desmayo** *m* depression; faltering; faint, fainting fit; (bot.) weeping willow; **sin desmayo** unfaltering; unfalteringly
**desmazalado -da** *adj* weak, weakened; downcast, dispirited
**desmedido -da** *adj* excessive; limitless, boundless
**desmedir** §94 *vr* to be impudent, to forget oneself
**desmedrado -da** *adj* run-down
**desmedrar** *va* to impair; *vn* to decline; *vr* to deteriorate
**desmedro** *m* impairment, deterioration, decline
**desmejora** *f* or **desmejoramiento** *m* impairment, deterioration, decline
**desmejorar** *va* to impair, to spoil; *vn* to decline, lose one's health; *vr* to be impaired, be spoiled; to decline, lose one's health; lose one's charm and attractiveness; (coll.) to grow thin, weak, old
**desmelar** §18 *va* to remove the honey from (*hive*)
**desmelenar** *va* to dishevel, to muss; *vr* to become disheveled, become mussed
**desmembración** *f* or **desmembramiento** *m* dismemberment
**desmembrar** §18 *va* to dismember; *vr* to become dismembered, to break up
**desmemoria** *f* forgetfulness, poor memory
**desmemoriado -da** *adj* forgetful, having a weak memory, having no memory
**desmemoriar** *vr* to become forgetful, to lose one's memory
**desmenguar** §23 *va* to lessen, to diminish, to break off
**desmentida** *f* contradiction, denial; **dar una desmentida a** to give the lie to
**desmentido** *m* (coll.) contradiction, denial
**desmentir** §62 *va* to belie; to give the lie to; to conceal (*e.g., evidence*); *vn* to be out of line, to be off level; *vr* to make an about-face, to contradict oneself
**desmenudear** *va & vn* (Am.) to sell at retail
**desmenuzable** *adj* crumbly
**desmenuzamiento** *m* crumbing, crumbling, shredding
**desmenuzar** §76 *va* to crumb, to crumble, to shred; to examine closely, to criticize severely; *vr* to crumb, to crumble, to shred
**desmeollamiento** *m* removal of marrow or pith
**desmeollar** *va* to take the marrow or pith from
**desmerecedor -dora** *adj* unworthy, undeserving
**desmerecer** §34 *va* to be or become unworthy of (*praise, reward, etc.*); to detract from, to spoil; *vn* to lose worth, to decline in value; to compare unfavorably; **desmerecer de** to compare unfavorably with
**desmerecimiento** *m* unworthiness
**desmesura** *f* immoderation, lack of restraint, excess
**desmesurado -da** *adj* disproportionate, extreme, excessive; insolent, impudent; *mf* insolent person, impudent person
**desmesurar** *va* to disturb, to put out of order; *vr* to be impudent, to be insolent, to go too far
**desmigajar** *va* to crumble, to grind up; to crumb; *vr* to crumble, to break up; to crumb
**desmigar** §59 *va* to crumble, to crumb (*bread*); *vr* to crumble, to crumb
**desmilitarización** *f* demilitarization
**desmilitarizar** §76 *va* to demilitarize
**desmineralización** *f* (med.) demineralization
**desmirriado -da** *adj* (coll.) lean, exhausted, emaciated, run-down
**desmocha** or **desmochadura** *f* topping; dehorning; cutting, excision
**desmochar** *va* to top (*a tree*); to dehorn (*a bull*); to cut (*a literary work, musical composition, etc.*)
**desmoche** *m* var. of **desmocha**
**desmocho** *m* toppings (*e.g., of trees*)
**desmodular** *va* (rad.) to demodulate
**desmogar** §59 *vn* to cast the horns (*said, e.g., of deer*)
**desmogue** *m* casting of horns
**desmolado -da** *adj* toothless
**desmonetización** *f* demonetization
**desmonetizar** §76 *va* to demonetize
**desmontable** *adj* demountable, detachable; *m* (aut.) tire iron
**desmontadura** *f* clearing; leveling; demounting; dismounting
**desmontaje** *m* (mach.) demounting, disassembling, takedown
**desmontar** *va* to clear (*land, woods*); to level (*ground*); to level off (*piles of earth, etc.*); to tear down; to dismount, take apart; to uncock (*a firearm*); to knock out (*enemy's guns*); to unhorse, to throw (*a rider*); *vn & vr* to dismount, to alight
**desmonte** *m* clearing; leveling; felling of trees; felled trees; brush; cut (*for a canal, highway, or railroad*)
**desmoñar** *va* to undo the hairknot of (*a woman*); *vr* to come loose, to get loose (*said of a hairknot*)
**desmoralización** *f* demoralization
**desmoralizador -dora** *adj* demoralizing
**desmoralizar** §76 *va* to demoralize; *vr* to become demoralized (*said of an army*)
**desmorecer** §34 *vr* to feel deeply or intensely; to stifle, to choke
**desmoronadizo -za** *adj* crumbly
**desmoronamiento** *m* wearing away; crumbling, decline, decay
**desmoronar** *va* to wear down, to wear away; *vr* to wear down, to wear away; to crumble, decline, decay
**desmostar** *vr* to lose must (*said of grapes*)
**desmotadera** *f* burler (*woman*); **desmotadera de algodón** cotton gin
**desmotador -dora** *mf* burler; *f* burling machine; **desmotadora de algodón** cotton gin
**desmotar** *va* to burl (*wool*); to gin (*cotton*)
**desmovilización** *f* demobilization
**desmovilizar** §76 *va* to demobilize
**desmullir** §26 *va* to undo, to spoil (*something soft or fluffy*)
**desmurador** *m* mouser (*cat*)
**desnacionalización** *f* denationalization
**desnacionalizar** §76 *va* to denationalize
**desnarigado -da** *adj* noseless; small-nosed
**desnarigar** §59 *va* to cut off the nose of; to punch or bang in the nose; *vr* to bump one's nose
**desnatadora** *f* cream separator
**desnatar** *va* to skim, to separate cream from; to cream, to take the choicest part of; to remove scum from; (found.) to remove the slag from
**desnaturalización** *f* denaturalization; (chem.) denaturation
**desnaturalizado -da** *adj* denaturalized; (chem.) denatured; unnatural (*parent, child*)
**desnaturalizar** §76 *va* to denaturalize; to denature, to pervert; (chem.) to denature; *vr* to become denaturalized; to lose one's citizenship
**desnazificación** *f* denazification
**desnazificar** §86 *va* to denazify
**desnegar** §29 *vr* to take back what one said, to retract
**desnervar** *va* to enervate
**desnevado -da** *adj* clear of snow
**desnevar** §18 *vn* to melt, to thaw
**desnieve** *m* melting, thaw
**desnitrificación** *f* denitrification
**desnitrificar** §86 *va* to denitrify
**desnivel** *m* unevenness, difference of level, drop

**desnivelación** *f* unleveling; unevenness, difference of level
**desnivelar** *va* to make uneven; *vr* to become uneven
**desnortado -da** *adj* (Am.) aimless
**desnucar** §86 *va* to dislocate or to break the back of the neck of; to kill (*an animal*) by a blow on the back of the neck; *vr* to dislocate one's neck, to break one's neck
**desnudamente** *adv* nakedly; clearly, openly, without concealment
**desnudar** *va* to undress; to lay bare, to denude, to strip; to draw (*the sword*); (coll.) to fleece; **desnudar a un santo para vestir a otro** (coll.) to rob Peter to pay Paul; *vr* to undress, to get undressed; to become evident, be revealed; **desnudarse de** to free oneself of, to cast aside (*e.g., bad habits*); to get rid of; to shed (*leaves, flowers, etc.*)
**desnudez** *f* nakedness, bareness, nudity
**desnudismo** *m* nudism
**desnudista** *mf* nudist; *f* stripteaser
**desnudo -da** *adj* naked, bare, nude; penniless; clear, evident; *m* (f.a.) nude
**desnutrición** *f* underfeeding, undernourishment, malnutrition
**desnutrido -da** *adj* underfed, undernourished
**desnutrir** *vr* to become undernourished, to suffer from undernourishment
**desobedecer** §34 *va & vn* to disobey
**desobediencia** *f* disobedience; **desobediencia civil** civil disobedience
**desobediente** *adj* disobedient
**desobligar** §59 *va* to free of an obligation; to antagonize, to alienate, to offend, to disoblige
**desobstrucción** *f* removal of obstructions or obstacles
**desobstruir** §41 *va* to free, to clear of obstructions, to clear of obstacles, to move obstacles out of the way of; *vr* to become free of obstructions, to open up
**desobstruyente** *adj & m* (med.) deobstruent
**desocupación** *f* unemployment; leisure
**desocupado -da** *adj* free, vacant, empty; unemployed; idle; free, not busy; *mf* unemployed, unemployed person
**desocupar** *va* to clear, to empty, vacate (*a place or space*); to take out, remove; to leave unoccupied; *vn* (coll.) to be delivered (*said of a woman*); *vr* to become clear, empty, vacated; to become unoccupied, become idle
**desodorante** *adj & m* deodorant
**desodorar** *va* to deodorize
**desodorización** *f* deodorization
**desodorizar** §76 *va* to deodorize
**desoigo** *1st sg pres ind of* **desoír**
**desoír** §64 *va* to not hear, to not heed, to be deaf to
**desojar** *va* to break the eye of (*e.g., of a needle*); *vr* to look hard, to strain one's eyes
**desolación** *f* desolation
**desolado -da** *adj* desolate; disconsolate
**desolador -dora** *adj* desolating; *mf* desolater
**desolar** §77 *va* to desolate, lay waste; *vr* to be desolate, be disconsolate
**desoldar** §77 *va* to unsolder; *vr* to come unsoldered
**desolladero** *m* slaughterhouse; (coll.) gyp store, gyp hotel; (coll.) gambling joint
**desollado -da** *adj* (coll.) brazen, impudent, shameless
**desollador -dora** *adj* skinning, flaying; fleecing; *mf* skinner, flayer; fleecer; *m* (orn.) butcher bird
**desolladura** *f* skinning, flaying; damage, hurt; scratch, bruise; fleecing, extortion
**desollar** §77 *va* to flay, to skin; to do great harm to; (fig.) to fleece; **desollar vivo** (coll.) to skin alive; (coll.) to flay (*to criticize severely*)
**desollón** *m* (coll.) scratch, bruise
**desopilación** *f* freeing or curing of obstructions, deoppilation
**desopilante** *adj* screamingly funny
**desopilar** *va* to free or cure of obstructions; to make howl with laughter; *vr* to become freed or cured of obstructions; to roar with laughter
**desopilativo -va** *adj & m* (med.) deoppilative, deobstruent
**desopinado -da** *adj* discredited
**desopinar** *va* to discredit, to defame
**desopresión** *f* freedom from oppression
**desoprimir** *va* to free from oppression
**desorbitado -da** *adj* out of proportion; popeyed (*from fear, terror, etc.*); crazy
**desorden** *m* disorder
**desordenado -da** *adj* disordered, disorderly, wild, unruly
**desordenamiento** *m* disorder, confusion
**desordenar** *va* to disorder, to throw into disorder, to put out of order; *vr* to get out of order; to be unruly or unmanageable; to go too far, to exceed all reason
**desorejado -da** *adj* (coll.) abject, infamous; (Am.) off tune (*said of a singer*); (Am.) brazen, shameless
**desorejamiento** *m* cutting off ears
**desorejar** *va* to cut off the ears of
**desorganización** *f* disorganization
**desorganizadamente** *adv* in a disorganized fashion
**desorganizador -dora** *adj* disorganizing; *mf* disorganizer
**desorganizar** §76 *va* to disorganize; *vr* to be or become disorganized
**desorientación** *f* leading astray, going astray; confusion; (psychopath.) disorientation
**desorientar** *va* to cause (*a person*) to lose his bearings or his way; to lead astray; to confuse; *vr* to lose one's bearings, to lose one's way; to go astray; to become confused
**desorillar** *va* to cut the selvage off, cut the border off, cut the edge off
**desortijado -da** *adj* (vet.) sprained, dislocated
**desortijar** *va* (agr.) to hoe or weed for the first time
**desosar** §40 *va* var. of **deshuesar**
**desovar** *vn* to spawn (*said of fish*); to oviposit (*said of insects*)
**desove** *m* spawning; spawning season; oviposition
**desovillar** *va* to unravel, disentangle; (fig.) to unravel, disentangle; to give heart to, to encourage; *vr* to become unraveled or disentangled, to be cleared up or solved
**desoxidable** *adj* deoxidizable
**desoxidación** *f* deoxidization
**desoxidante** *adj* deoxidizing; *m* deoxidizer
**desoxidar** *va* to deoxidize; *vr* to become deoxidized
**desoxigenación** *f* deoxygenation
**desoxigenante** *m* deoxidizer
**desoxigenar** *va* to deoxygenate, to deoxidize; *vr* to become deoxygenated, to become deoxidized
**desozonizar** §76 *va* to deozonize
**despabiladeras** *fpl* snuffers
**despabilado -da** *adj* wide-awake; (fig.) wide-awake
**despabilador -dora** *mf* snuffer; *m* snuffers
**despabiladura** *f* snuffing, snuff (*of a wick*)
**despabilar** *va* to trim, to snuff (*candle*); to snitch; (coll.) to dispatch (*a meal*); to dissipate (*a fortune*); (coll.) to dispatch, to kill; to brighten up, make alert; *vr* to brighten up, to become alert; to wake up; (Am.) to leave, go away
**despacio** *adv* slowly; at leisure; (Am.) in a low voice; *interj* easy there!; *m* (Am.) delay
**despacioso -sa** *adj* slow, sluggish
**despacito** *adv* (coll.) slowly, gently; *interj* easy!
**despachaderas** *fpl* (coll.) surly reply; (coll.) resourcefulness; **tener buenas despachaderas** (coll.) to not beat about the bush
**despachado -da** *adj* (coll.) brazen, impudent; ready, quick, resourceful
**despachador -dora** *adj* dispatching, shipping; *mf* dispatcher
**despachante** *m* (Am.) clerk, employee; **despachante de aduana** (Am.) customhouse broker
**despachar** *va* to dispatch, to expedite; to send, to ship; to decide, to settle; to dismiss, to discharge; to hurry; to sell; to wait on (*customers*); to attend to (*correspondence*); (coll.) to dispatch, to kill; *vn* to hurry, be expeditious; to come to a decision; to work, be employed; *vr* to hurry; (coll.) to be delivered (*said of a*

*woman*); **despacharse a su gusto** to speak one's mind
**despacho** *m* dispatch, expedition; shipping; dismissal; office, study, store, shop; dispatch, message; (law) mandamus; **estar al despacho** to be under consideration, to be pending; **tener buen despacho** to be capable and energetic; **despacho de aduana** clearance; **despacho de billetes** ticket office; **despacho de localidades** box office
**despachurramiento** *m* (coll.) smashing, squashing, crushing; (coll.) mangling, butchering; (coll.) squelching
**despachurrar** *va* (coll.) to smash, squash, crush; (coll.) to mangle, butcher, murder (*e.g., a speech*); (coll.) to squelch
**despajadura** *f* winnowing
**despajar** *va* to winnow (*grain*); (min.) to sift
**despaldar** *va* & *vr* var. of **desespaldar**
**despaldilladura** *f* breaking the back or shoulder of an animal
**despaldillar** *va* to break the back or shoulder of (*an animal*)
**despaletillar** *va* to break the back or shoulder of; (coll.) to pound in the back
**despalillador -dora** *mf* stripper (*of tobacco, etc.*)
**despalilladura** *f* stripping (*of tobacco, etc.*)
**despalillar** *va* to strip (*tobacco*); to separate (*grapes or raisins*) from the stalk, to stem
**despalmador** *m* (naut.) careenage, careening place; hoof-paring knife
**despalmadura** *f* (naut.) careenage (*cleaning and calking*); chamfering, beveling; paring a horse's hoof; parings (*of hoofs*)
**despalmar** *va* (naut.) to careen, to clean and calk (*bottom of a ship*); to chamfer, to bevel; to pare (*horse's hoof*); to pull up (*grass*)
**despalme** *m* paring a horse's hoof; cut or slash (*in tree trunk to bring down tree*)
**despampanador -dora** *mf* pruner of vines
**despampanadura** *f* pruning vines
**despampanante** *adj* (coll.) dumfounding, upsetting, disturbing; (coll.) stunning, terrific
**despampanar** *va* to prune (*vines*); to trim the suckers and shoots off (*vines*); (coll.) to astound, dumfound; *vn* (coll.) to open one's heart, to talk freely; *vr* (coll.) to give oneself a hard bump, to fall and hurt oneself
**despampanillar** *va* to prune (*vines*)
**despamplonar** *va* to thin the stems and shoots of; *vr* to sprain one's hand
**despancación** *f* (Am.) husking
**despancar** §86 *va* (Am.) to husk (*corn*)
**despancijar** *va* (coll.) to disembowel, to rip open the belly of; *vr* (coll.) to be disemboweled
**despanzurrar** *va* (coll.) to disembowel, to rip open the belly of; to smash; to slay, to kill; *vr* (coll.) to be disemboweled
**despapar** *vn* to raise its head too high (*said of a horse*)
**desparecer** §34 *vn* to disappear
**desparedar** *va* to remove the walls or partitions from
**desparejar** *va* to break the pair of
**desparejo -ja** *adj* rough, uneven; inconstant, fickle
**desparpajar** *va* to take apart in a bungling way, to take apart sloppily; *vn* & *vr* (coll.) to talk nonsense, to rave
**desparpajo** *m* (coll.) pertness, flippancy; (coll.) impudence, effrontery; (Am.) disorder
**desparramado -da** *adj* broad, open
**desparramador -dora** *adj* & *mf* spendthrift
**desparramamiento** *m* spreading, scattering, spilling; squandering, extravagance
**desparramar** *va* to spread, to scatter, to spill; to squander; *vr* to spread, to scatter, to spill, to be spilled; to make merry, to have a wild time
**despartidor -dora** *adj* separating; *mf* separator, divider
**despartimiento** *m* separation, division; reconciliation
**despartir** *va* to part, separate, divide, dispart; to reconcile, to make peace between; *vr* to separate, dispart
**desparvar** *va* (agr.) to pile up (*threshed grain*) for winnowing
**despasar** *va* & *vr* (naut.) to unreeve
**despatarrada** *f* (coll.) split (*in dancing*); **hacer la despatarrada** (coll.) to stretch out, feigning illness or death
**despatarrar** *va* (coll.) to make (*a person*) open his legs wide; to dumfound; *vr* (coll.) to open one's legs wide; (coll.) to fall to the ground or floor with legs widespread; to lie motionless
**despatillado** *m* (carp.) cut to make a tenon
**despatillar** *va* (carp.) to tenon; (naut.) to break off the fluke of (*an anchor*); to shave off the side whiskers of; *vr* to shave off one's side whiskers
**despavesaderas** *fpl* (Am.) snuffers
**despavesadura** *f* snuffing
**despavesar** *va* to snuff (*candle*); to blow the ashes off (*embers*)
**despavonar** *va* to remove the bluing from (*iron or steel*)
**despavorido -da** *adj* terrified, frightened
**despavorir** §53 *vn* & *vr* to be terrified, be aghast
**despeado -da** *adj* footsore
**despeadura** *f* or **despeamiento** *m* footsoreness
**despear** *vr* to bruise one's feet, to get one's feet sore
**despectivo -va** *adj* depreciatory, disparaging, contemptuous; (gram.) pejorative
**despechadamente** *adv* spitefully
**despechar** *va* to spite; to drive to despair; (coll.) to wean; *vr* to be spited; to despair
**despecho** *m* spite; despair; (Am.) weaning; **a despecho** unwillingly; **a despecho de** in spite of, despite; **por despecho** out of spite
**despechugadura** *f* carving the breast of a fowl; (coll.) baring one's breast
**despechugar** §59 *va* to carve the breast of (*a fowl*); *vr* (coll.) to uncover one's breast, to go with bare breast
**despedazamiento** *m* breaking to pieces, tearing to pieces, falling to pieces; abuse, ruination, destruction
**despedazar** §76 *va* to break to pieces, to tear to pieces; to ruin (*a reputation*); to break (*one's heart, the law*); *vr* to break or fall to pieces; **despedazarse de risa** to split one's sides laughing
**despedida** *f* farewell, leave-taking; leave, parting; dismissal, discharge; conclusion (*of a letter*); envoi (*to a poem*)
**despedimiento** *m* farewell; parting; dismissal
**despedir** §94 *va* to throw, to hurl; to emit, send forth, send out; to dismiss, to discharge; to see off; (fig.) to banish (*suspicion*); **despedir en la puerta** to see to the door; *vr* to take leave, say good-by; to give up one's job; **despedirse a la francesa** to take French leave; **despedirse de** to take leave of, say good-by to
**despedregar** §59 *va* to clear of stones
**despegable** *adj* detachable
**despegado -da** *adj* (coll.) harsh, unpleasant, gruff, surly
**despegadura** *f* loosening, detaching; opening
**despegar** §59 *va* to loosen (*something glued or sealed*); to detach; to open; *vn* (aer.) to take off; *vr* to get loose; to become alienated; **despegarse con** to not suit, to not go well with
**despego** *m* coolness, indifference; (coll.) gruffness; ingratitude
**despegue** *m* (aer.) take-off
**despeinado -da** *adj* uncombed, unkempt
**despeinar** *va* to take down the hair of; to muss the hair of; *vr* to take down one's hair; to muss one's hair
**despejado -da** *adj* clear, cloudless; unobstructed; easy, unconstrained; bright, sprightly, vivacious
**despejar** *va* to free, to clear; to clear up, to clarify, to explain; (math.) to find (*an unknown quantity*); *vr* to be free and easy, to be sprightly; to be amused; to clear up (*said of the weather*); to come out of a fever
**despejo** *m* clearing; grace, ease, sprightliness; talent, ability, understanding
**despelotar** *va* to dishevel; *vr* to get plump
**despeluzar** §76 *va* to muss the hair of; to make the hair of (*a person*) stand on end;

(Am.) to take everything from, to clean out; *vr* to be mussed; to stand on end (*said of the hair*)
**despeluznante** *adj* frightful, horrifying
**despeluznar** *va & vr* var. of **despeluzar**
**despellejadura** *f* skinning, flaying; scratch, bruise; (fig.) maligning, roasting
**despellejar** *va* to skin, flay; (fig.) to malign, to gossip about, to roast
**despenar** *va* to console; (coll.) to kill; (Am.) to make hopeless
**despendedor -dora** *adj & mf* spendthrift, prodigal
**despender** *va* to spend; to waste, squander, misspend
**despensa** *f* pantry, larder; (naut.) storeroom; provisions; daily marketing; office of steward, butlership
**despensería** *f* office of steward, butlership
**despensero -ra** *mf* steward, butler, dispenser; (naut.) storekeeper
**despeñadamente** *adv* hastily; audaciously, boldly
**despeñadero -ra** *adj* steep, precipitous; *m* crag, cliff, precipice; risk, danger
**despeñadizo -za** *adj* steep, precipitous
**despeñamiento** *m* var. of **despeño**
**despeñar** *va* to hurl over a cliff, to fling down a precipice; *vr* to hurl oneself over a cliff; to fall headlong; to plunge down; to plunge downward (*into vice, evil, etc.*); **despeñarse de un vicio a otro** to plunge downward from one vice to another
**despeño** *m* hurling over a cliff; plunge, plunge over a cliff; headlong fall; ruin, damnation; failure, collapse (*e.g., of a business*)
**despepitado** *m* (Am.) pitted preserved fruit
**despepitadora** *f* (Am.) cotton gin
**despepitar** *va* to seed, to remove the seeds from; (Am.) to stone (*fruit*); (Am.) to core (*an apple*); *vr* to scream in anger, to rush about screaming; (coll.) to strive, to struggle; **despepitarse por** (coll.) to be mad about
**despercudir** *va* to clean, to wash; *vr* (Am.) to brighten up
**desperdiciado -da** or **desperdiciador -dora** *adj & mf* spendthrift, prodigal
**desperdiciar** *va* to waste, squander; to fail to take advantage of, to miss
**desperdicio** *m* waste, squandering; leftover, residue; **desperdicios** *mpl* waste products; by-products; rubbish; **no tener desperdicio** (coll.) to be useful, to be fine; (iron.) to be fine
**desperdigamiento** *m* separation, scattering
**desperdigar** §59 *va* to separate, scatter
**desperecer** §34 *vr* to be extremely eager, to be burning
**desperezar** §76 *va* to shake off (*sleep*) by stretching; *vr* to stretch, to stretch one's arms and legs
**desperezo** *m* stretching, stretching the arms and legs
**desperfeccionar** *va* to impair, to damage
**desperfecto** *m* flaw, blemish, imperfection; slight damage
**desperfilar** *va* (paint.) to soften the lines of; (mil.) to camouflage the outlines of (*trenches, defenses, etc.*)
**despernado -da** *adj* weary, tired of walking
**despernar** §18 *va* to cut or injure the legs of; *vr* to cut or injure one's legs
**despersonalización** *f* depersonalization
**despertador -dora** *mf* awakener; *m* alarm clock; admonition, warning
**despertamiento** *m* awakening
**despertar** §18 *va* to awaken, to wake up; to arouse, to stir up; *vn & vr* to awaken, to wake up
**despesar** *m* displeasure, sorrow, regret
**despestañar** *va* to pluck the eyelashes of; *vr* to look hard, to strain one's eyes; (Am.) to go without sleep
**despezar** §31 *va* to taper (*a pipe or tube*); (arch.) to divide (*a stone wall, arch, vault, etc.*) into constituent parts
**despezo** *m* taper, tapering; (mas.) face of stone joining another; (arch.) division of stone wall, arch, or vault
**despezonar** *va* to take the umbo or nipple off (*a lemon, lime, etc.*); to divide, separate; *vr* to come off (*said of an umbo, nipple, end of an axle or spindle, etc.*)
**despezuñar** *vr* to become useless (*said of a horse's foot*); (Am.) to run, to rush; **despezuñarse por** to be eager about or for
**despiadado -da** *adj* unmerciful, merciless, ruthless
**despicar** §86 *va* to satisfy (*a person who was offended*); *vr* to be satisfied, to be requited
**despichar** *va* to squeeze dry; *vn* (slang) to croak, to die
**despidiente** *m* stick holding a hanging scaffold away from wall; **despidiente de agua** flashing
**despido** *m* dismissal, discharge, layoff
**despierto -ta** *adj* wide-awake; **soñar despierto** to daydream
**despiezo** *m* (arch.) division of stone wall, arch, or vault
**despilaramiento** *m* (Am.) removal of shoring (*in a mine*)
**despilarar** *va* (Am.) to remove the shoring from (*a mine*)
**despilfarrado -da** *adj* shabby, ragged; wasteful, prodigal; *mf* wasteful person, prodigal
**despilfarrador -dora** *adj* spendthrift, wasteful; *mf* spendthrift
**despilfarrar** *va* to squander, to squander recklessly, to waste; *vr* (coll.) to go on a spending spree
**despilfarro** *m* squandering, lavishness; waste, wastefulness, extravagance; shabbiness, slovenliness
**despimpollar** *va* to trim the useless shoots off (*a vine*)
**despinces** *mpl* burling tweezers
**despinochar** *va* to husk (*corn*)
**despintar** *va* to take the paint off (*e.g., a wall*); to distort, upset, reverse, disfigure, spoil; (Am.) to turn (*one's glance, one's eyes*) away; *vn* to slip back, to decline; **despintar de** to discredit (*e.g., one's ancestors*); *vr* to wash off, to fade; **no despintársele a uno** (coll.) to not fade from one's memory
**despinte** *m* (Am.) inferior ore
**despinzadera** *f* burler (*woman*); burling iron
**despinzar** §76 *va* to burl
**despinzas** *fpl* burling tweezers
**despiojar** *va* to delouse; (coll.) to free of misery; *vr* to be deloused
**despioje** *m* or **despiojo** *m* delousing
**despique** *m* satisfaction, requital
**despistar** *va* to throw off the scent, to throw off the track; *vr* to run off the track, run off the road
**despiste** *m* throwing off the scent; running off the track; losing one's way
**despitonado -da** or **despitorrado -da** *adj* (taur.) with a cracked or broken horn
**despizcar** §86 *va* to crush, break up, grind up; *vr* to be crushed, be broken up, be ground up; to bend all one's efforts
**desplacer** *m* displeasure; §34 *va* to displease
**desplanchar** *va* to wrinkle, rumple, muss (*something that was ironed*); *vr* to wrinkle, rumple, muss
**desplantación** *f* uprooting, eradication
**desplantador** *m* trowel, garden trowel
**desplantar** *va* to uproot; to turn or move (*something*) from the vertical; *vr* to turn or move from the vertical; to lose one's upright posture (*in dancing or fencing*)
**desplante** *m* irregular posture (*in dancing and fencing*); (Am.) boldness, impudence, boasting
**desplatar** *va* to remove the silver from
**desplate** *m* separation or removal of silver
**desplayado** *m* (Am.) sandy beach
**desplayar** *vn* to recede, recede from the beach (*said of the sea*)
**desplazado -da** *adj* displaced (*person*); *mf* displaced person
**desplazamiento** *m* displacement (*of a volume of water*); motion, move; movement; shift
**desplazar** §76 *va* to displace (*a volume of water*); to take the place of; *vr* to move; to shift
**desplegadura** *f* spreading out, unfolding; explanation; unfurling

**desplegar §29** *va* to spread, lay out, unfold; to display; to elucidate, explain; to unfurl; (mil.) to deploy; *vr* to spread out, open, unfold; (mil.) to deploy
**despleguetear** *va* to clip the tendrils from (*vines and runners*)
**despliegue** *m* spreading out, unfolding; display; unfurling; (mil.) deployment
**desplomar** *va* to put or knock out of plumb; *vr* to get out of plumb, to lean over; to topple over, to collapse; to fall over in a faint; (fig.) to crumble (*said, e.g., of a throne*); (aer.) to pancake
**desplome** *m* leaning; toppling, collapse; falling in a faint; crumbling, downfall; (arch.) overhang; (aer.) pancaking; **en desplome** (arch.) overhanging
**desplomo** *m* leaning
**desplumadura** *f* plucking, deplumation
**desplumar** *va* to pluck, deplume; (coll.) to fleece (*by deception or in gambling*); *vr* to molt
**desplume** *m* plucking; (coll.) fleecing
**despoblación** *f* depopulation
**despoblado** *m* deserted spot, wilderness; holding up, waylaying; **en despoblado** at a deserted spot, in the wilds
**despoblar §77** *va* to depopulate, to dispeople; to despoil, lay waste; *vr* to become depopulated
**despoetizar §76** *va* to divest of poetry, deprive of poetic qualities
**despojador -dora** *adj* despoiling, plundering; *mf* despoiler, plunderer
**despojar** *va* to strip, divest, despoil; to dispossess; *vr* to undress; **despojarse de** to take off (*a piece of clothing*); to give up, to relinquish, to divest oneself of
**despojo** *m* despoilment, despoliation; dispossession; plunder, spoils, booty; prey, victim; head, pluck, and feet of slaughtered animals; giblets; parts of wings, legs, head, and neck of fowl; **despojos** *mpl* leavings, scraps; mortal remains; second-hand building materials; (geol.) debris
**despolarización** *f* (chem. & phys.) depolarization
**despolarizador -dora** *adj* depolarizing; *m* (chem. & phys.) depolarizer
**despolarizar §76** *va* (chem. & phys.) to depolarize
**despoletar** *va* to defuse (*a mine or bomb*)
**despolvar** *va* to dust, to remove the dust or powder from
**despolvorear** *va* to dust, dust off; to scatter, dissipate; (Am.) to dust, sprinkle
**despopularización** *f* loss of popularity
**despopularizar §76** *va* to make unpopular; *vr* to become unpopular
**desportilladura** *f* chipping; chip, nick
**desportillar** *va* to chip, to chip the edge of, to chip the mouth or neck of (*a pitcher, bottle, etc.*); *vr* to chip, chip off
**desposado -da** *adj* handcuffed, manacled; recently married; *mf* newlywed
**desposar** *va* to marry (*to join as husband and wife*); *vr* to be betrothed, to get engaged; to get married
**desposeer §35** *va* to dispossess, to divest; *vr* to give up one's property; **desposeerse de** to divest oneself of
**desposeimiento** *m* dispossession
**desposorios** *mpl* betrothal, engagement; nuptials, marriage
**despostador** *m* (Am.) carver (*of slaughtered animals*)
**despostar** *va* (Am.) to cut up, carve up (*slaughtered animals*)
**desposte** *m* (Am.) carving, quartering
**déspota** *m* despot
**despótico -ca** *adj* despotic
**despotismo** *m* despotism; **despotismo ilustrado** enlightened despotism
**despotizar §76** *va & vn* to tyrannize
**despotricar §86** *vn & vr* (coll.) to talk without restraint, to rant
**despotrique** *m* (coll.) wild talk, ranting
**despreciable** *adj* despicable, contemptible
**despreciador -dora** *adj* scornful, contemptuous
**despreciar** *va* to despise, to scorn; to rebuff, to slight; to forget, to forgive, to overlook; to cast aside, to reject; *vr* to not deign; **despreciarse de** + *inf* to not deign to + *inf*
**despreciativo -va** *adj* depreciative, contemptuous
**desprecio** *m* scorn, contempt; slight, rebuff
**desprender** *va* to loosen; to detach; to give off, send out, emit, release, liberate; *vr* to loosen, to come loose; to come forth, to issue; **desprenderse de** to give up; to be clear from, be deduced from
**desprendido -da** *adj* generous, disinterested
**desprendimiento** *m* loosening, coming loose, detachment; emission, release, liberation; landslide; generosity, disinterestedness
**despreocupación** *f* impartiality, lack of bias; relaxation, unconcernedness; unconventionality
**despreocupado -da** *adj* impartial, unbiased; relaxed, carefree, unconcerned, unworried; unconventional; (Am.) sloppy, slovenly
**despreocupante** *adj* relaxing
**despreocupar** *vr* to divert one's mind, to forget one's worries, to relax
**desprestigiar** *va* to run down, to disparage; *vr* to lose one's reputation or standing, to lose caste
**desprestigio** *m* disparagement; loss of reputation, unpopularity
**desprevención** *f* improvidence, unpreparedness
**desprevenido -da** *adj* unprepared, off one's guard; **coger a una persona desprevenida** to catch somebody unawares
**desproporción** *f* disproportion
**desproporcionado -da** *adj* disproportional or disproportionate
**desproporcionar** *va* to disproportion
**despropositado -da** *adj* nonsensical, absurd
**despropósito** *m* nonsense, absurdity
**desproveer §35 & §17**, 9 *va* to deprive of essentials, deprive of supplies
**desprovisto -ta** *pp of* **desproveer;** *adj* unprovided, deprived, devoid
**despueble** *m* or **despueblo** *m* depopulation
**después** *adv* after, afterwards; later; next; **después de** after; next to; **después de** + *inf* after + *ger;* **después (de) que** after
**despulgar §59** *va* to remove the fleas from
**despulido -da** *adj* ground (*e.g., glass*)
**despulir** *va* to remove the polish from
**despulpador** *m* pulper (*machine*)
**despulpar** *va* to pulp (*to deprive of pulp*)
**despulsar** *va* to take the breath of, to lay low; *vr* to be eager
**despumación** *f* skimming
**despumadera** *f* skimmer
**despumar** *va* to skim
**despuntado -da** *adj* dull, blunt
**despuntadura** *f* dulling, blunting
**despuntar** *va* to dull, to blunt; to nip, nibble (*grass*); to cut away the dry combs of (*a beehive*); (naut.) to double (*e.g., a cape*); *vn* to begin to sprout or bud; to come on, to dawn (*said of the day, the morning, etc.*); to stand out; **despuntar en** or **por** to show an aptitude in or for; *vr* to become dull, be blunted
**despunte** *m* var. of **despuntadura**
**desquejar** *va* (hort.) to slip (*to take cuttings from*)
**desqueje** *m* (hort.) slipping
**desquerer §70** *va* to stop caring for, to no longer want
**desquerré** *1st sg fut ind of* **desquerer**
**desquiciamiento** *m* unhinging; upsetting, unsettling
**desquiciar** *va* to unhinge; to upset, unsettle, turn upside down, perturb; (coll.) to undermine, overthrow, deprive of favor or standing; *vr* to come unhinged; to become upset, to collapse
**desquicio** *m* (Am.) confusion, disorder, anarchy, ruin, destruction
**desquijaramiento** *m* breaking the jaws
**desquijarar** *va* to break the jaws of; *vr* to break one's jaws; **desquijararse de risa** (coll.) to laugh uproariously
**desquijerar** *va* (carp.) to tenon

**desquilatar** *va* to reduce the fineness of (*a gold alloy*); to devaluate, lower the value of
**desquise** *1st sg pret ind of* **desquerer**
**desquitar** *va* to retrieve, to recoup; to avenge; *vr* to retrieve a loss, win back one's money; to take revenge, get even; **desquitarse con** to get back at
**desquite** *m* retrieving, recovery; avenging, revenge, retaliation; (sport) return game, return match
**desrabotar** *va* to cut off the tail of (*especially sheep*)
**desramar** *va* to strip of branches
**desranchar** *vr* to leave, to decamp; (mil.) to disperse, break up (*said of soldiers in the same barracks or mess*)
**desraspadora** *f* stemming machine (*in wine making*)
**desraspar** *va* to stem (*grapes*)
**desrastrojar** *va* to remove the stubble from
**desratización** *f* deratting
**desratizar** §76 *va* to derat
**desrazonable** *adj* (coll.) unreasonable
**desreglar** *va & vr* var. of **desarreglar**
**desrelingar** §59 *va* (naut.) to detach the boltropes from (*sails*)
**desreputación** *f* (coll.) dishonor, discredit
**desrielar** *vn* (Am.) to jump the track
**desriñonar** *va* to break the back of, to cripple
**desrizar** §76 *va* to uncurl; (naut.) to unfurl, to let out by means of the reef points; *vr* to uncurl
**desroblar** *va* to unclinch, to unrivet
**destacado -da** *adj* outstanding, distinguished
**destacamento** *m* (mil.) detachment
**destacar** §86 *va* to emphasize, to highlight, to point up; to make stand out (*in a painting*); (mil.) to detail; *vn* (fig.) to stand out, be distinguished; *vr* to stand out, to project; (fig.) to stand out, be distinguished
**destaconar** *va* to wear down the heels of (*shoes*)
**destajador** *m* forging hammer
**destajar** *va* to arrange for, to contract for; to cut (*cards*)
**destajero -ra** or **destajista** *mf* pieceworker, jobber
**destajo** *m* piecework; job, contract; **a destajo** by the piece, by the job, on contract; eagerly, diligently; **hablar a destajo** (coll.) to talk too much
**destalinización** *f* destalinization
**destalinizar** §76 *va & vn* to destalinize
**destalonar** *va* to remove the heels from, to wear down the heels of; to detach (*a coupon*); to detach the coupon from; to level (*the hoofs of a horse*)
**destallar** *va* to prune useless stems or shoots from
**destapacorona** *m* (Am.) bottle opener
**destapada** *f* open pie, pie without top crust
**destapadero** *m* (elec.) knockout
**destapador** *m* bottle opener
**destapadura** *f* uncovering; uncorking; revelation
**destapar** *va* to uncover, take the cover or lid off; to open; to unplug, uncork; to reveal; *vr* to get uncovered; to throw off one's covers (*in bed*); **destaparse con** to open one's heart to
**destapiado** *m* place where mud walls have been torn down
**destapiar** *va* to tear down the mud walls around
**destapizar** §76 *va* to remove the hangings or draperies from; to take up the carpet from; *vn* to remove the hangings or draperies; to take up the carpet
**destaponar** *va* to unstop, to uncork (*to remove the stopper or cork from; to open up*)
**destarar** *va* to deduct the tare on
**destartalado -da** *adj* shabby, disordered; poorly furnished, poorly equipped
**destartalo** *m* (coll.) shabbiness, disordered condition
**destazador** *m* carver (*of slaughtered animals*)
**destazar** §76 *va* to cut up, carve up (*slaughtered animals*)
**destechadura** *f* unroofing
**destechar** *va* to unroof
**destejar** *va* to remove the tiles from the roof of, to untile; to remove the tiles from the coping of (*a wall*)
**destejer** *va* to unweave, unknit, unbraid; to upset, undo, disturb
**destellar** *va* to flash (*light, sparks, etc.*); *vn* to sparkle, to flash, to beam, to twinkle
**destello** *m* sparkle, flash, beam; (fig.) flash (*e.g., of insight*)
**destemplado -da** *adj* irregular, agitated (*pulse*); disagreeable, unpleasant (*e.g., voice*); out of tune; (f.a.) inharmonious
**destemplanza** *f* intemperance; inclemency (*of weather*); irregularity, agitation (*of the pulse*); indisposition; lack of moderation, excess
**destemplar** *va* to disturb the order or harmony of; to untune, put (*a musical instrument*) out of tune; to untemper, deprive (*a metal*) of temper; to steep, to infuse; *vr* to get out of tune; to lose its temper (*said of metal*); to become irregular (*said of the pulse*); to get excited; (Am.) to be on edge (*said of teeth*)
**destemple** *m* dissonance; slight indisposition; upset, disturbance; untempering
**destentar** §18 *va* to remove temptation from, to lead away from temptation
**desteñir** §74 *va* to discolor; to fade (*a color*); *vn & vr* to fade
**desternillar** *vr* to break one's cartilage or gristle; **desternillarse de risa** to split one's sides with laughter
**desterradero** *m* wilderness, waste, desert
**desterrado -da** *adj* exiled, banished; *mf* exile
**desterrar** §18 *va* to exile; to banish (*e.g., sadness*); to remove earth from (*roots*); *vr* to go into exile; to withdraw from the world
**desterronador** *m* (agr.) roller harrow
**desterronar** *va* to crush, to crumble (*soil, earth*), to crush the lumps of earth of (*a field*), to harrow
**destetadera** *f* weaning device attached to teats of cows
**destetar** *va* to wean; to separate (*a child*) from the comforts of home; to deprive of affection; *vr* to be weaned; to be separated from the comforts of home; **destetarse con** to have been brought up on
**destete** *m* weaning
**desteto** *m* weaned cattle; stable of weaned mules
**destiempo; a destiempo** inopportunely, untimely, out of season
**destiento** *m* shock, surprise
**destierre** *m* removal of dirt from ore
**destierro** *m* exile; wilderness, waste
**destilable** *adj* distillable
**destilación** *f* distillation; (physiol.) flow of humors; **destilación fraccionada** (chem.) fractional distillation
**destiladera** *f* still, distiller; filter; scheme, stratagem; (Am.) water filter
**destilado** *m* distillate
**destilador -dora** *adj* distilling; to be distilled; *mf* distiller; *m* water filter; still, alembic
**destilar** *va* to distill; to filter; to exude; *vn* to distill; *vr* to filter; to exude
**destilatorio -ria** *adj* distilling; *m* distillery; still, alembic
**destilería** *f* distillery, distilling plant
**destinación** *f* destination (*act of destining; purpose*)
**destinar** *va* to destine; to assign; to designate; **destinar a** + *inf* to destine (*e.g., money*) to + *inf;* **destinar para** to destine for
**destinatario -ria** *mf* addressee; consignee; recipient (*e.g., of homage, applause*)
**destino** *m* destiny; destination (*place to which a person is going or a thing is being sent; setting apart for a purpose*); office, employment; place of employment; **con destino a** bound for; (*cap.*) *m* (myth.) Destiny
**destiño** *m* blackish empty part of honeycomb
**destiranizado -da** *adj* free from tyranny
**destitución** *f* destitution, depriving; dismissal
**destituíble** *adj* removable
**destituir** §41 *va* to deprive; to dismiss, dismiss from office
**destocar** §86 *va* to take the hat or cap off (*a person*); *vr* to take off one's hat or cap

**destorcedura** *f* untwisting
**destorcer §87** *va* to untwist; to straighten (*something bent*); *vr* to untwist, become untwisted; (naut.) to drift, get off the course
**destornillado -da** *adj* inconsiderate, rash, mad, out of one's head
**destornillador** *m* screwdriver; **destornillador de trinquete** ratchet screwdriver
**destornillamiento** *m* unscrewing
**destornillar** *va* to unscrew; *vr* to unscrew; (fig.) to lose one's head, to act or talk like a wild man
**destoser** *vr* to cough (*in getting ready to talk or to attract attention*)
**destostar §77** *vr* to turn white again (*after sunburn*)
**destrabar** *va* to detach, loosen, separate; to untie, unfetter
**destraillar §75** *va* to uncouple, to unleash (*hounds*); *vr* to be unleashed
**destral** *m* hatchet
**destraleja** *f* little hatchet
**destralero** *m* hatchet maker or vendor
**destramar** *va* to undo the warp of, to unweave
**destrejar** *vn* to proceed with skill or dexterity
**destrenzar §76** *va* to unbraid, to unplait
**destreza** *f* skill, dexterity
**destrincar §86** *va* (naut.) to unlash
**destripacuentos** *m* (*pl:* **-tos**) (coll.) interrupter, butter-in
**destripamiento** *m* disembowelment; crushing, mangling
**destripar** *va* to gut, disembowel; to take the insides out of (*e.g., a pillow*); to crush, to mangle; (coll.) to spoil (*a story, by interrupting and revealing its outcome*)
**destripaterrones** *m* (*pl:* **-nes**) (coll.) clodhopper
**destrísimo -ma** *adj super* very or most skilful
**destriunfar** *va* to force (*another player*) to play trumps
**destrizar §76** *va* to break to pieces, to tear to shreds; *vr* to get angry, to be greatly distressed
**destrocar §95** *va* to swap back again
**destrón** *m* blind man's guide
**destronamiento** *m* dethronement; overthrow
**destronar** *va* to dethrone; to overthrow
**destroncadora** *f* stump puller
**destroncamiento** *m* detruncation; chopping down; dislocation; ruination; exhaustion
**destroncar §86** *va* to detruncate; to chop off, to chop down; to lop off; to maim, dislocate; to ruin, to bring to ruin; to exhaust, wear out; to interrupt; *vr* to be exhausted, be worn out
**destrozar §76** *va* to break to pieces, to shatter, to destroy; to squander; to annihilate, wipe out (*e.g., an army*)
**destrozo** *m* destruction; havoc; annihilation, massacre
**destrozón -zona** *adj* hard on clothing
**destrucción** *f* destruction
**destructibilidad** *f* destructibility
**destructible** *adj* destructible
**destructividad** *f* destructiveness
**destructivo -va** *adj* destructive
**destructor -tora** *adj* destructive; *mf* destroyer; *m* (nav.) destroyer
**destrueco** or **destrueque** *m* return of an exchange; re-exchange
**destruíble** *adj* destructible
**destruidor -dora** *adj* destructive; *mf* destroyer
**destruir §41** *va* to destroy; *vr* (alg.) to cancel each other
**desubstanciar** *va* var. of **desustanciar**
**desucación** *f* extraction of juice
**desucar §86** *va* to extract the juice from
**desudación** *f* wiping off sweat
**desudar** *va* to wipe the sweat off
**desuellacaras** *m* (*pl:* **-ras**) (coll.) scraper (*unskilful barber*); (coll.) scamp, scalawag
**desuello** *m* skinning, flaying; fleecing; boldness, shamelessness; **ser un desuello** (coll.) to be highway robbery (*said of exorbitant prices*)
**desuetud** *f* desuetude
**desulfuración** *f* desulfurization
**desulfurar** *va* to desulfurize
**desuncir §50** *va & vr* to unyoke
**desunión** *f* disunion
**desunir** *va* to take apart; to separate; to disunite; *vr* to come apart; to separate; to disunite
**desuñar** *va* to tear out the nails, claws, or fangs of; to pull up the dead roots of (*a plant*); *vr* (coll.) to work one's fingers to the bone; (coll.) to work hard and skilfully with one's hands; (coll.) to plunge into vice, gambling, thievery, etc.
**desurcar §86** *va* to remove the furrows from, take out the furrows of
**desurdir** *va* to remove the warp from, to unweave; to frustrate, to nip (*a plot*) in the bud
**desusado -da** *adj* out of use, out of date, obsolete; uncommon; rusty (*out of practice*)
**desusar** *va* to disuse, to stop using; *vr* to be no longer used, to go out of date
**desuso** *m* disuse; desuetude; **caído en desuso** obsolete
**desustanciar** *va* to deprive of substance, deprive of strength, weaken
**desvahar** *va* (agr.) to clean out the dry and withered parts of (*a plant*)
**desvaído -da** *adj* gaunt, tall and lanky; dull (*said of colors*)
**desvainar** *va* to shell (*beans, peas, etc.*)
**desvalido -da** *adj* destitute, helpless
**desvalijador** *m* robber, highwayman
**desvalijamiento** *m* theft of contents of a valise, trunk, etc.; robbery, plunder
**desvalijar** *va* to steal the contents of (*a valise, trunk, etc.*); to rob, plunder
**desvalijo** *m* var. of **desvalijamiento**
**desvalimiento** *m* abandonment, helplessness, disfavor
**desvalorar** *va* to devalue
**desvalorización** *f* devaluation
**desvalorizar §76** *va* to devalue
**desván** *m* garret, loft; **desván gatero** cockloft
**desvanecedor** *m* (phot.) mask
**desvanecer §34** *va* to cause to disappear or vanish, to dispel, to dissipate (*e.g., smoke, doubt, suspicion*); to break up (*e.g., a conspiracy*); to banish, cast aside (*a thought, idea, recollection*); to mask (*part of a photographic print*); *vr* to disappear, vanish; to be dissipated, to evanesce; to evaporate; to faint, to swoon; (rad.) to fade
**desvanecido -da** *adj* faint; proud, haughty, vain
**desvanecimiento** *m* disappearance, evanescence, dissipation; pride, haughtiness, vanity; faintness, giddiness, dizziness; fainting spell; (rad.) fading, fade-out
**desvarar** *va* to slide, to slip; (naut.) to refloat, set afloat (*a grounded ship*)
**desvariado -da** *adj* raving, delirious, crazy; disordered, nonsensical; long and wild (*said of branches of trees*)
**desvariar §90** *vn* to rave, rant, be delirious
**desvarío** *m* delirium, craziness; nonsense, wild idea, extravagance; inconstancy; caprice, whim; monstrosity
**desvedar** *va* to permit, to allow, to remove the prohibition from
**desvelado -da** *adj* wakeful, awake, sleepless; watchful, vigilant; anxious, worried, fearful
**desvelamiento** *m* var. of **desvelo**
**desvelar** *va* to keep awake; to reveal; *vr* to keep or stay awake, to go without sleep, to pass a sleepless night; to be watchful or vigilant; **desvelarse por** to be anxious about, be greatly concerned about
**desvelo** *m* wakefulness, lack of sleep; watchfulness, vigilance; anxiety, concern
**desvenar** *va* to remove the vein or filaments from; to strip (*tobacco*); to extract (*the ore*) from the veins; to arch the cannon of (*a horse's bit*)
**desvencijado -da** *adj* rickety, falling apart
**desvencijar** *va* to break, loosen, take apart
**desvendar** *va* to unbandage; *vr* to come unbandaged
**desveno** *m* port, tongue groove (*of horse's bit*)
**desventaja** *f* disadvantage
**desventajoso -sa** *adj* disadvantageous

**desventar** §18 *va* to vent, let the air out of
**desventura** *f* misfortune
**desventurado -da** *adj* unfortunate; faint-hearted; stingy; *mf* faint-hearted person; miser
**desvergonzado -da** *adj* unabashed, impudent; shameless; *mf* shameless person
**desvergonzar** §98 *vr* to be impudent or insolent; **desvergonzarse con** to be impudent or insolent to
**desvergüenza** *f* impudence, insolence; shamelessness
**desvestir** §94 *va & vr* to undress
**desvezar** §76 *va* to make unaccustomed; *vr* to become unaccustomed
**desviación** *f* deflection, deviation; detour; (med.) extravasation; (rad. & telv.) drift
**desviacionismo** *m* deviationism
**desviacionista** *mf* deviationist (*communist who does not hew to the party line*)
**desviadero** *m* (rail.) siding, turnout
**desviado -da** *adj* astray; off the track; devious
**desviar** §90 *va* to turn aside, to turn away, to deviate, to deflect; to dissuade, to sway; (rail.) to switch; to parry, ward off (*in fencing*); *vr* to turn aside, be deflected, to deviate, to swerve, to branch off; to be dissuaded
**desvío** *m* deflection, deviation; coldness, indifference, dislike; detour, turnout; (rail.) siding, sidetrack; wall support (*for hanging scaffolding*)
**desvirar** *va* to pare off the edges of (*a sole*); to trim (*a book*); (naut.) to unwind (*a cable or rope, on a capstan*)
**desvirgar** §59 *va* to deflower, to ravish
**desvirtuar** §33 *va* to weaken, detract from, spoil; *vr* to decline; to spoil, to become spoiled
**desvitalización** *f* devitalization
**desvitalizar** §76 *va* to devitalize
**desvitrificar** §86 *va* to devitrify; *vr* to become devitrified
**desvivir** *vr* to be eager, be anxious; **desvivirse por** to long for, be crazy about; **desvivirse por** + *inf* to be eager to, be anxious to + *inf*
**desvolvedor** *m* wrench, screw key
**desvolver** §63 & §17, 9 *va* to change, change the form of; to turn up (*the soil*); to loosen, to unscrew (*a nut or screw*)
**desvuelto -ta** *pp of* **desvolver**
**desyemar** *va* to remove the buds from; to remove the yolk from
**desyerba** *f* weeding; weeding hoe
**desyerbar** *va* var. of **desherbar**
**desyugar** §59 *va* to unyoke
**deszocar** §86 *va* to put (*a foot*) out of commission; (arch.) to remove the socle from (*a column*); *vr* to put one's foot out of commission
**deszumar** *va* to squeeze the juice out of
**detall** *m* retail; **al detall** retail, at retail
**detalladamente** *adv* in detail
**detallar** *va* to detail, to particularize, to tell in detail; to retail, to sell at retail
**detalle** *m* detail, particular; detailed account; (f.a.) detail; (Am.) retail; **en detalle** in detail
**detallista** *mf* person fond of detail; painter or writer skilled in detail; retailer
**detasa** *f* (rail.) rebate
**detección** *f* detection; (elec. & rad.) detection
**detectar** *va* to detect; (elec. & rad.) to detect
**detective** *m* detective
**detectivesco -ca** *adj* detective
**detector -tora** *adj* detecting; *m* detector; (elec. & rad.) detector; **detector a** or **de cristal** (rad.) crystal detector; **detector a válvula** (rad. & telv.) vacuum-tube detector; **detector de galena** (rad.) galena detector; **detector de mentiras** lie detector; **detector de minas** mine detector; *f* (rad. & telv.) vacuum-tube detector
**detén** *2d sg impv of* **detener**
**detención** *f* detainment, detention; delay; care, thoroughness; **detención ilegal** (law) detainer
**detendré** *1st sg fut ind of* **detener**
**detenedor -dora** *adj* stopping; *mf* detainer, stopper; *m* (mach.) arrester, catch
**detener** §85 *va* to stop, to check, to hold, to hold back; to detain, to arrest; to dam, to dam up; to keep, retain, reserve; **detener el aliento** to hold one's breath; *vr* to stop; to delay, to tarry, to linger, to pause; **detenerse a** + *inf* to stop to + *inf*; **¡detente, bala!** stop, bullet! (*words on the breast patch of the Carlists*)
**detengo** *1st sg pres ind of* **detener**
**detenidamente** *adv* carefully, thoroughly
**detenido -da** *adj* lengthy; timid, hesitant; mean, stingy, niggardly; careful, thorough; slow, dilatory; *mf* prisoner
**detenimiento** *m* var. of **detención**
**detentación** *f* (law) deforcement
**detentador** *m* (law) deforciant
**detentar** *va* to hold (*a position, title, etc.*); (law) to deforce
**detergente** *adj & m* detergent
**deterger** §49 *va* to deterge
**deterioración** *f* var. of **deterioro**
**deteriorar** *va & vr* to deteriorate
**deterioro** *m* deterioration
**determinabilidad** *f* determinability
**determinable** *adj* determinable
**determinación** *f* determination
**determinado -da** *adj* determined, resolute; determinate; certain; (gram.) definite (*article*)
**determinante** *adj* determinant; *m* determinant; (biol., log. & math.) determinant
**determinar** *va* to determine; to cause, bring about; to lead; **determinar a (una persona) a** + *inf* to lead or induce (*a person*) to + *inf*; **determinar** + *inf* to decide to + *inf*; *vr* to determine, to decide; **determinarse a** + *inf* to decide to + *inf*
**determinativo -va** *adj* determinative; (gram.) determinative
**determinismo** *m* (philos.) determinism
**determinista** *adj & mf* (philos.) determinist
**detersión** *f* detersion
**detersivo -va** *adj & m* detersive
**detersorio -ria** *adj & m* var. of **detergente**
**detestable** *adj* detestable
**detestación** *f* cursing; detestation
**detestar** *va* to curse; to detest; **detestar** + *inf* to hate to + *inf*, e.g., **detesto salir con la lluvia** I hate to go out in the rain; *vn* to detest; **detestar de** to detest
**detienebuey** *m* (bot.) restharrow
**detiento** *m* start, shock, upset
**detonación** *f* detonation; knock (*of an internal-combustion engine*)
**detonador** *m* detonator
**detonante** *adj* detonating
**detonar** *vn* to detonate
**detorsión** *f* sprain, twisting of a ligament, muscle, limb, or joint
**detracción** *f* detraction
**detractar** *va* to defame, vilify
**detractor -tora** *adj* detractive, disparaging; *mf* detractor, disparager
**detraer** §88 *va* to detract, take away; to defame, vilify
**detraigo** *1st sg pres ind of* **detraer**
**detraje** *1st sg pret ind of* **detraer**
**detrás** *adv* behind; **por detrás de** behind the back of; **detrás de** behind, back of
**detricción** *f* detrition
**detrimento** *m* damage, harm, loss, detriment
**detrítico -ca** *adj* (geol.) detrital
**detrito** *m* detritus, debris, dirt; (geol.) detritus
**detritus** *m* (*pl:* **-tus**) var. of **detrito**
**detuve** *1st sg pret ind of* **detener**
**Deucalión** *m* (myth.) Deucalion
**deudo -da** *mf* relative; *m* relationship, kinship; duty, obligation; *f* debt; indebtedness; (Bib.) debt (*sin*); **llenarse de deudas** to get deeply in debt; **deuda activa** asset, credit; **deuda de honor** or **deuda de juego** debt of honor; **deuda flotante** floating debt; **deuda pasiva** liability, debit; **deuda pública** public debt
**deudor -dora** *adj* indebted; *mf* debtor; **deudor hipotecario** mortgagor; **deudor moroso** delinquent (*in payment*)
**deuterio** *m* (chem.) deuterium
**deuterión** *m* (chem.) deuteron
**Deuteronomio** *m* (Bib.) Deuteronomy
**deutón** *m* (chem.) deuton (*i.e., deuteron*)
**deutoplasma** *m* (biol.) deutoplasm
**devalar** *vn* (naut.) to drift, to drift from the course

**devaluación** *f* devaluation
**devaluar §33** *va* to devalue
**devanadera** *f* winding frame
**devanado** *m* winding; (elec.) winding
**devanador -dora** *adj* winding; *m* core (*of a ball of yarn*); (Am.) winding frame
**devanar** *va* to wind, to spool, to roll; *vr* (Am.) to double up with laughter; (Am.) to writhe with pain
**devanear** *vn* to rave, talk nonsense; to fritter away one's time, to loaf around
**devaneo** *m* raving, nonsense, madness; loafing; flirtation
**devastación** *f* devastation
**devastador -dora** *adj* devastating; *mf* devastator
**devastar** *va* to devastate
**develación** *f* revelation, discovery; unveiling (*of, e.g., a statue*)
**develar** *va* to reveal, uncover; to unveil (*e.g., a statue*)
**devendré** *1st sg fut ind of* **devenir**
**devengar §59** *va* to earn (*wages*); to draw (*interest*)
**devengo** *m* earning; amount earned, earnings; *1st sg pres ind of* **devenir**
**devenir §92** *vn* to happen; (philos.) to become
**deviación** *f* var. of **desviación**
**devine** *1st sg pret ind of* **devenir**
**devoción** *f* devotion
**devocionario** *m* prayer book
**devolución** *f* return, restitution; (eccl.) devolution
**devolutivo -va** or **devolutorio -ria** *adj* (law) returnable
**devolver §63 & §17, 9** *va* to return, give back, send back; to requite, to pay back; (coll.) to vomit; *vr* (Am.) to return, come back
**devoniano -na** *adj & mf* Devonian; (geol.) Devonian
**devónico -ca** *adj* (geol.) Devonic, Devonian
**devorador -dora** *adj* devouring; *mf* devourer
**devorante** *adj* devouring
**devorar** *va* to devour; (fig.) to devour
**devotería** *f* (coll.) sanctimony, sanctimoniousness
**devoto -ta** *adj* devout; devoted; devotional; *mf* devotee; *m* object of devotion or worship
**devuelto -ta** *pp of* **devolver**
**dexiocardia** *f* var. of **dextrocardia**
**dextrina** *f* (chem.) dextrin or dextrine
**dextrocardia** *f* (anat.) dextrocardia
**dextrógiro -ra** *adj* (phys.) dextrogyrous
**dextrorrotatorio -ria** *adj* (phys.) dextrorotatory
**dextrorso -sa** *adj* (bot.) dextrorse
**dextrosa** *f* (biochem.) dextrose
**deyección** *f* (physiol.) dejection; (geol.) ejecta, ejection
**dezmable** *adj* tithable
**dezmatorio** *m* tithing; place where tithes are collected
**dezmeño -ña** *adj* (pertaining to) tithe
**dezmería** *f* tithe land
**dezmero -ra** *adj* (pertaining to) tithe; *mf* tither
**D.F.** abr. of **Distrito Federal**
**d/f** abr. of **días fecha**
**dg.** abr. of **decigramo** or **decigramos**
**Dg.** abr. of **decagramo** or **decagramos**
**dho.** abr. of **dicho**
**di** *2d sg impv of* **decir**
**dí** *1st sg pret ind of* **dar**
**día** *m* day; daytime; daylight; **días** *mpl* birthday; **a días** once in a while; **al día** a day, per day; up to date; **alcanzar en días** (coll.) to survive (*another person*); **al otro día** on the following day; **buenos días** good morning; **¡cualquier día!** I should say not!; **dar los buenos días a** to pass the time of day with; **dar los días a** to wish (*someone*) many happy returns of the day; to congratulate (*someone*) on his saint's day; **de día** in the daytime, in the daylight; **el día menos pensado** (coll.) when least expected; **el mejor día** some fine day; **en cuatro días** in a few days; **en días de Dios, en días del mundo** or **en los días de la vida** never; **en el día** nowadays; the same day; **en pleno día** in broad daylight; **en su día** in due time; **entrado en días** advanced in years; **ocho días** a week; **poner al día** to bring up to date; **ponerse al día** to catch up (*in one's debts*); **quince días** two weeks, a fortnight; **tener sus días** to have one's day, to be up in years; **un día sí y otro no** every other day; **vivir al día** to live from hand to mouth; **día de acción de gracias** Thanksgiving, Thanksgiving Day (*in U.S.A.*); **día de años** birthday; **día de año nuevo** New Year or New Year's Day; **día de asueto** day off, time off; **día de ayuno** fast day; **día de carne** meat day; **día de ceniza** Ash Wednesday; **día de Colón** Columbus Day; **día de cutio** or **de hacienda** workday; **día de engañabobos** the 28th of December, celebrated like April Fools' Day; **día de gracias** Thanksgiving Day (*in U.S.A.*); **día de guardar** (eccl.) holyday, holyday of obligation; **día de hogar** or **de huelga** day off; **día de inauguración** (f.a.) private viewing; **día de joya** court day; **día del idioma** anniversary of death of Cervantes (*23d of April*); **día del juicio** Day of Judgment; **día de la raza** Columbus Day, Discovery Day; **día de los caídos** Memorial Day; **día de los (santos) inocentes** (eccl.) Holy Innocents' Day (*December 28, popularly celebrated like April Fools' Day*); **día de pescado** fish day; **día de precepto** (eccl.) holyday, holyday of obligation; **día de ramos** Palm Sunday; **día de Reyes** Twelfth-night; **día de San Martín** Martinmas; **día de todos los santos** All Saints' Day; **día de trabajo** workday, weekday; **día de vigilia** fast day; **día diado** fixed day; **día feriado** (law) court holiday; holiday, day off; **día festivo** holiday; **día hábil** working day, business day; (law) court day; **día laborable** workday, weekday; **día lectivo** school day; **día onomástico** saint's day, birthday; **día puente** day taken off because it falls between two holidays; **días de demora** or **de estadía** (naut.) lay days; **días de gracia** (coll.) days of grace; **día útil** workday
**diabasa** *f* (mineral.) diabase
**diabetes** *f* (path.) diabetes
**diabético -ca** *adj & mf* diabetic
**diabetómetro** *m* diabetometer
**diabla** *f* (coll.) she-devil; carding machine; **a la diabla** (coll.) carelessly, any old way
**diablear** *vn* (coll.) to play pranks
**diablesa** *f* (coll.) she-devil
**diablesco -ca** *adj* diabolical, devilish
**diablillo** *m* imp; person disguised as devil; (coll.) schemer; **diablillo de Descartes** Cartesian devil, diver, or imp
**diablo** *m* devil; (mach.) devil; (billiards & pool) bridge, rest, cue rest; **¡diablos!** the devil!; **ahí será el diablo** (coll.) there will be the devil to pay; **como el diablo** (coll.) like the devil; **darse al diablo** (coll.) to get angry, go wild; **del diablo, de los diablos, de mil diablos,** or **de todos los diablos** a hell of a; **llevarse el diablo** (coll.) to turn out badly; **pobre diablo** (coll.) poor devil; **diablo cojuelo** tricky devil; **diablo encarnado** devil incarnate; **diablo marino** (ichth.) scorpene; **diablo punzante** (zool.) moloch; **diablos azules** (Am.) blue devils (*delirium tremens*)
**diablura** *f* devilment, deviltry (*mischief; daring*)
**diabólico -ca** *adj* diabolic, diabolical, devilish; (coll.) devilish (*very bad; mischievous*)
**diabolín** *m* chocolate drop
**diabolismo** *m* diabolism (*doctrine*)
**diábolo** *m* yo-yo
**diacatolicón** *m* (pharm.) purgative electuary
**diacitrón** *m* candied citron, candied lemon peel
**diacodión** *m* (pharm.) diacodion
**diaconado** *m* deaconry, diaconate
**diaconal** *adj* deaconal, diaconal
**diaconato** *m* deaconry, diaconate
**diaconía** *f* diaconia; deacon's house
**diaconisa** *f* deaconess
**diácono** *m* deacon
**diacrítico -ca** *adj* (gram. & med.) diacritic or diacritical

**diacronía** *f* diachrony
**diacrónico -ca** *adj* diachronic
**diadelfo -fa** *adj* (bot.) diadelphous
**diadema** *f* diadem; tiara (*ornamental coronet worn by women*)
**diademado -da** *adj* (her.) diademed
**diado -da** *adj* fixed (*day*)
**diafanidad** *f* diaphanousness, translucency
**diafanizar** §76 *va* to make diaphanous
**diáfano -na** *adj* diaphanous
**diáfisis** *f* (anat. & bot.) diaphysis
**diaforesis** *f* (med.) diaphoresis
**diaforético -ca** *adj* diaphoretic or diaphoretical; *m* diaphoretic
**diafragma** *m* diaphragm; **diafragma iris** (opt.) iris diaphragm
**diafragmático -ca** *adj* diaphragmatic
**diagnosis** *f* (*pl:* **-sis**) (bot., zool. & med.) diagnosis
**diagnosticar** §86 *va* to diagnose
**diagnóstico -ca** *adj* diagnostic; *m* diagnostic; diagnosis
**diagonal** *adj* diagonal; *f* diagonal; diagonal cloth
**diágrafo** *m* diagraph
**diagrama** *m* diagram
**diagramático -ca** *adj* diagrammatic
**diálaga** *f* (mineral.) diallage
**dialectal** *adj* dialectal
**dialectalismo** *m* dialecticism
**dialéctico -ca** *adj* dialectic or dialectical; sophistical; *m* dialectic (*philosopher*); dialectician; *f* dialectic, dialectics; sophistry
**dialecto** *m* dialect
**dialectología** *f* dialectology
**dialicarpelar** *adj* (bot.) dialycarpous
**diálisis** *f* (*pl:* **-sis**) dialysis
**dialítico -ca** *adj* dialytic
**dializador** *m* (physical chem.) dialyzer
**dializar** §76 *va* to dialyze
**dialogal** *adj* dialogic
**dialogar** §59 *va* to write in the form of a dialogue; *vn* to talk, to converse
**dialogismo** *m* (rhet.) dialogism, Wellerism
**dialogístico -ca** *adj* interlocutory, dialogistic
**dialogizar** §76 *vn* to dialogue, to converse
**diálogo** *m* dialogue; friendly relations
**dialoguista** *mf* dialogist (*writer*)
**dialtea** *f* (pharm.) marsh-mallow ointment
**diamagnético -ca** *adj & m* diamagnetic
**diamagnetismo** *m* diamagnetism
**diamantado -da** *adj* diamondlike
**diamantar** *va* to make shine or sparkle like diamonds
**diamante** *m* diamond; **diamante en bruto** diamond in the rough; (fig.) diamond in the rough; **diamante negro** black diamond (*carbon diamond*); **diamante rosa** rose diamond
**diamantífero -ra** *adj* diamantiferous
**diamantino -na** *adj* (pertaining to or like a) diamond; (poet.) hard, unshakable
**diamantista** *mf* diamond cutter; diamond merchant
**diamela** *f* (bot.) Arabian jasmine
**diametral** *adj* diametric, diametrical, diametral
**diámetro** *m* diameter
**diana** *f* (mil.) reveille; bull's-eye; (*cap.*) *f* (myth.) Diana; **hacer diana** to hit the bull's-eye or to score a bull's-eye
**dianche** *m* (coll.) devil; *interj* (coll.) the deuce!, the devil!
**diandro -dra** *adj* (bot.) diandrous
**diantre** *m* (coll.) devil; *interj* (coll.) the dickens!, the deuce!
**diapalma** *f* (pharm.) diapalma
**diapasón** *m* (mus.) diapason; (mus.) tuning fork; (mus.) pitch pipe; (mus.) finger board (*e.g., of violin*); **bajar el diapasón** (coll.) to lower one's voice, to change one's tune; **subir el diapasón** (coll.) to raise one's voice; **diapasón normal** (mus.) diapason normal
**diapédesis** *f* (physiol.) diapedesis
**diapente** *m* (ancient mus. & ancient pharm.) diapente
**diapositiva** *f* (phot.) diapositive; slide, lantern slide
**diaprea** *f* small round plum
**diaquilón** *m* (pharm.) diachylon
**diario -ria** *adj* daily; (Am.) street (*clothes*); **a diario** daily, everyday; *m* daily (*paper*); diary; daily household expenses, daily ration; day book; **diario de navegación** (naut.) log book; **diario hablado** (rad.) newscast
**diarismo** *m* (Am.) journalism
**diarista** *mf* diarist; *m* newspaperman
**diarrea** *f* (path.) diarrhea
**diartrosis** *f* (*pl:* **-sis**) (anat.) diarthrosis
**diascordio** *m* (pharm.) diascordium
**diasén** *m* (pharm.) senna purgative
**diáspero** *m* (mineral.) jasper
**Diáspora** *f* (Bib. & fig.) Diaspora
**diásporo** *m* (mineral.) diaspore
**diaspro** *m* var. of **diáspero**
**diastasa** *f* (biochem.) diastase
**diastásico -ca** *adj* (biochem. & surg.) diastasic
**diastasis** *f* (surg.) diastasis
**diástilo** *m* (arch.) diastyle
**diástole** *f* (physiol. & gram.) diastole
**diastólico -ca** *adj* diastolic
**diastrofismo** *m* (geol.) diastrophism
**diatérmano -na** *adj* (phys.) diathermanous
**diatermia** *f* (med.) diathermy
**diatérmico -ca** *adj* (med. & phys.) diathermic
**diatesarón** *m* (ancient mus., ancient pharm. & rel.) diatessaron
**diatésico -ca** *adj* diathetic
**diátesis** *f* (med.) diathesis
**diatomáceo -a** *adj* diatomaceous
**diatomea** *f* (bot.) diatom
**diatónico -ca** *adj* (mus.) diatonic
**diatriba** *f* diatribe
**dibásico -ca** *adj* (chem.) dibasic
**dibujante** *mf* sketcher, illustrator; *m* draftsman; *f* draftswoman
**dibujar** *va* to draw, to design; to sketch; to depict, to outline; *vr* to be outlined; to come to the surface (*said, e.g., of something concealed or hidden*)
**dibujo** *m* drawing; sketch; depiction; design; **no meterse en dibujos** (coll.) to attend to one's own business; **dibujo animado** animated cartoon
**dicacidad** *f* wittiness, sharpness, sarcasm
**dicasio** *m* (bot.) dichasium
**dicaz** *adj* (*pl:* **-caces**) witty, sharp, sarcastic
**dicción** *f* word; diction
**diccionario** *m* dictionary; **Diccionario de Autoridades** dictionary of Spanish Academy, whose first edition appeared from 1726 to 1739
**diccionarista** *mf* lexicographer
**dic.**[e] abr. of **diciembre**
**dicentra** *f* (bot.) dicentra, bleeding heart
**diciembre** *m* December
**diciendo** *ger of* **decir**
**diclino -na** *adj* (bot.) diclinous
**diclorodifeniltricloroetano** *m* (chem.) dichlorodiphenyl-trichloroethane
**dicloruro** *m* (chem.) dichloride, bichloride
**dicotiledón** *adj* (bot.) dicotyledonous; *m* (bot.) dicotyledon
**dicotiledóneo -a** *adj* (bot.) dicotyledonous
**dicotomía** *f* dichotomy; (astr., biol., bot. & log.) dichotomy; split fees (*among doctors*)
**dicotómico -ca** *adj* dichotomic
**dicótomo -ma** *adj* dichotomous
**dicroico -ca** *adj* dichroic
**dicroísmo** *m* dichroism
**dicromático -ca** *adj* dichromatic
**dicromatismo** *m* dichromatism
**dicromato** *m* (chem.) dichromate, bichromate
**dictado** *m* dictation; title of dignity or honor; **dictados** *mpl* dictates; **escribir al dictado** to take dictation; to take down (*something dictated*)
**dictador** *m* dictator
**dictadora** *f* dictaphone, dictating machine
**dictadura** *f* dictatorship
**dictáfono** *m* dictaphone
**dictamen** *m* dictum, opinion, judgment
**dictaminar** *va* to pass judgment on; *vn* to pass judgment
**díctamo** *m* (bot.) dittany; **díctamo blanco** (bot.) fraxinella
**dictar** *va* to dictate; to promulgate (*a law*); to inspire, to suggest; (Am.) to give (*a course*); (Am.) to deliver (*a lecture*); *vn* to dictate
**dictatorial** *adj* dictatorial (*pertaining to a dictator; imperious, overbearing*)

**dictatorio -ria** *adj* dictatorial (*pertaining to a dictator*)
**dicterio** *m* taunt, insult
**dictógrafo** *m* dictograph
**dicha** *f* see **dicho**
**dicharachero -ra** *adj* (coll.) vulgar, obscene, foul-mouthed
**dicharacho** *m* (coll.) vulgarity, obscenity
**dichero -ra** *adj* (coll.) witty; *mf* (coll.) wit
**dicho -cha** *adj* said; **mejor dicho** rather; *pp of* **decir; tener una cosa por dicha** to consider a matter settled; **dicho y hecho** no sooner said than done; *m* saying; pledge, promise of marriage; witticism, bright remark; (coll.) insulting remark; **dicho de las gentes** talk (*unfavorable*); *f* happiness, luck; **a dicha** or **por dicha** by chance
**dichón -chona** *adj* (Am.) sharp, sarcastic
**dichoso -sa** *adj* happy; fortunate, lucky; (coll.) annoying, tiresome; (iron.) lucky
**didáctico -ca** *adj* didactic or didactical; *f* didactics
**didáctilo -la** *adj* didactylous
**didelfo -fa** *adj & m* (zool.) didelphian
**didimio** *m* (chem.) didymium
**dídimo -ma** *adj* (bot. & zool.) didymous; *m* didymus (*testicle*)
**Dido** *f* (myth.) Dido
**diecinueve** *adj* nineteen; **las diecinueve** seven P.M.; *m* nineteen; nineteenth (*in dates*)
**diecinueveavo -va** *adj & m* nineteenth
**dieciochavo -va** *adj & m* eighteenth
**dieciocheno -na** *adj* eighteenth
**dieciochesco -ca** *adj* eighteenth-century
**dieciochismo** *m* eighteenth-century style or character
**dieciochista** *adj* eighteenth-century
**dieciocho** *adj* eighteen; **las dieciocho** six P.M.; *m* eighteen; eighteenth (*in dates*)
**dieciséis** *adj* sixteen; **las dieciséis** four P.M.; *m* sixteen; sixteenth (*in dates*)
**dieciseisavo -va** *adj* sixteenth; *m* sixteenth; **en dieciseisavo** sextodecimo (*book*)
**dieciseiseno -na** *adj* sixteenth
**diecisiete** *adj* seventeen; **las diecisiete** five P.M.; *m* seventeen; seventeenth (*in dates*)
**diecisieteavo -va** *adj & m* seventeenth
**diedro** *adj masc* (geom.) dihedral
**Diego** *m* James
**dieléctrico -ca** *adj & m* dielectric
**diente** *m* (anat.) tooth; tooth (*of saw, comb, rake, etc.*); tusk, fang; cog; **aguzar los dientes** to whet one's appetite; **apretar los dientes** to set one's teeth (*to prepare to resist*); **a regaña dientes** loathingly, with repugnance; **armado hasta los dientes** (coll.) armed to the teeth; **dar diente con diente** (coll.) to shake all over (*from fear or cold*); **decir entre dientes** (coll.) to mutter, to mumble; **de dientes afuera** (coll.) in bad faith; **enseñar los dientes** (coll.) to show one's teeth; **estar a diente** (coll.) to be famished; **hablar entre dientes** to chew one's words (*so as to be unintelligible*); (coll.) to mutter, to mumble; **mostrar los dientes** (coll.) to show one's teeth; **tener buen diente** to be a hearty eater; **tomar** or **traer entre dientes** (coll.) to have a grudge against; to speak ill of; **diente artificial** false tooth; **diente canino** (anat.) canine tooth, eye tooth; **diente de ajo** clove of garlic; (coll.) large, misshapen tooth; **diente de leche** milk tooth; **diente de león** (bot.) dandelion; **diente de lobo** burnisher; **diente de muerto** (bot.) grass pea; **diente de perro** sculptor's dented chisel; (arch.) dogtooth; (bot.) dogtooth violet; (sew.) featherstitch; (coll.) crude sewing; **diente incisivo** (anat.) incisor; **diente mamón** baby tooth; **diente molar** (anat.) molar, back tooth; **dientes de leche** baby teeth
**dientimellado -da** *adj* nick-toothed
**dientudo -da** *adj* var. of **dentudo**
**diéresis** *f* (*pl:* **-sis**) diaeresis
**Diesel** *m* Diesel engine or motor
**dieseleléctrico -ca** *adj* Diesel-electric
**dieselización** *f* equipment with Diesel engines, Dieselization
**diesi** *f* (mus.) diesis; (mus.) sharp
**diestro -tra** *adj* right; skilful, dexterous, handy; dexter; sagacious, shrewd; sly, artful; favorable, propitious; (her.) dexter; **a diestro y siniestro** right-and-left, wildly; *m* skilful fencer; bullfighter on foot; matador; bridle; *f* right hand; **juntar diestra con diestra** to join forces
**dieta** *f* diet (*regular food and drink; assembly*); (law) day's trip of ten leagues; **dietas** *fpl* per diem (*allowance*); pay, compensation (*e.g., of a legislator*); **estar a dieta** to be on a diet; **poner a dieta** to put on a diet; **dieta láctea** milk diet
**dietar** *va* to diet, to put on a diet
**dietario** *m* family budget; chronicler's record book
**dietético -ca** *adj* dietetic, dietary; *f* dietetics
**dietista** *mf* dietician or dietitian
**diez** *adj* ten; **las diez** ten o'clock; *m* (*pl:* **dieces**) ten; tenth (*in dates*); decade (*of Ave Marias*)
**diezmal** *adj* decimal
**diezmar** *va* to decimate; to tithe
**diezmero -ra** *mf* tither, collector of tithes
**diezmesino -na** *adj* ten-month
**diezmilésimo -ma** *adj & m* ten thousandth
**diezmilímetro** *m* tenth of a millimeter
**diezmo** *m* tithe
**difamación** *f* defamation
**difamador -dora** *adj* defaming; *mf* defamer
**difamar** *va* to defame
**difamatorio -ria** *adj* defamatory
**difásico -ca** *adj* (elec.) diphase, two-phase
**diferencia** *f* difference; (log.) differentia; **a diferencia de** unlike; **partir la diferencia** to split the difference; **diferencia de potencial** (phys.) difference of potential
**diferenciación** *f* differentiation
**diferenciador -dora** *adj* differentiating
**diferencial** *adj* differential; *m* (mach.) differential; *f* (math.) differential
**diferenciar** *va* to differentiate; (math.) to differentiate; *vn* to differ, to dissent; *vr* to differ, be different; to differentiate, become differentiated; to distinguish oneself; (bot.) to differentiate
**diferendo** *m* difference, disagreement
**diferente** *adj* different
**diferir** §62 *va* to defer, postpone, delay, put off; *vn* to differ, be different
**difícil** *adj* difficult, hard; **difícil de contentar** hard to please
**dificílimo -ma** *adj super* very or most difficult
**difícilmente** *adv* with difficulty
**dificultad** *f* difficulty; objection
**dificultador -dora** *adj* objecting, pessimistic; *mf* objector, pessimist
**dificultar** *va* to put obstacles in the way of, to make difficult; to consider difficult; **dificultar que** + *subj* to consider it difficult or unlikely that; *vn* to raise difficulties or objections; *vr* to become difficult
**dificultosamente** *adv* with difficulty
**dificultoso -sa** *adj* troublesome, difficult; (coll.) ugly, homely; (coll.) objecting, pessimistic
**difidación** *f* diffidation, declaration of war
**difidencia** *f* distrust
**difidente** *adj* distrustful
**difilo -la** *adj* (bot.) diphyllous
**difluencia** *f* diffluence
**difluente** *adj* diffluent
**difluir** §41 *vn* to flow away, to dissolve
**difracción** *f* diffraction
**difractar** *va* to diffract; *vr* to be diffracted
**difractivo -va** *adj* diffractive
**difrangente** *adj* diffractive
**difteria** *f* (path.) diphtheria
**diftérico -ca** *adj* diphtherial or diphtheritic
**difteritis** *f* (path.) diphtheritis
**difteroide** *adj* diphtheroid
**difuminar** *va* var. of **esfuminar**
**difumino** *m* var. of **esfumino**
**difundido -da** *adj* widespread, widely known
**difundir** *va* to diffuse, to disseminate, to spread; to divulge, to publish; (rad.) to broadcast; *vr* to spread
**difuntear** *va* to kill, to slay; *vr* to get killed, to die

**difunto -ta** *adj & mf* deceased; **difunto de taberna** dead-drunk; *m* corpse
**difusibilidad** *f* diffusibility
**difusible** *adj* diffusible
**difusión** *f* diffusion, dissemination, spread; diffuseness; (anthrop., chem. & phys.) diffusion; (rad.) broadcasting; **difusión normal** standard broadcasting
**difusionismo** *m* (anthrop.) diffusionist theory
**difusivo -va** *adj* diffusive
**difuso -sa** *adj* diffuse; broad, extended; prolix, wordy
**difusor -sora** *adj* diffusing; radiating; *m* diffuser
**digerible** *adj* digestible
**digerir §62** *va* (physiol. & chem.) to digest; (fig.) to digest (*to think over, to try to understand; to bear, to put up with*); *vr* to digest
**digestibilidad** *f* digestibility
**digestible** *adj* digestible
**digestión** *f* digestion; **de mala digestión** indigestible
**digestivo -va** *adj & m* digestive
**digesto** *m* (law) digest
**digestor** *m* digester (*closed vessel*)
**digitación** *f* (mus.) fingering
**digitado -da** *adj* digitate; (bot.) digitate; (mus.) fingered
**digital** *adj* digital; *f* (bot. & pharm.) digitalis
**digitalina** *f* (chem. & pharm.) digitalin
**digitígrado -da** *adj & m* (zool.) digitigrade
**dígito** *m* (arith.) digit; (astr.) digit or point
**dignación** *f* condescension
**dignar** *vr* to deign, condescend; **dignarse** + *inf* to deign to + *inf*, to condescend to + *inf*
**dignatario** *m* dignitary, official
**dignidad** *f* dignity; dignitary
**dignificación** *f* dignification
**dignificar §86** *va* to dignify; *vr* to become dignified
**digno -na** *adj* worthy, deserving; dignified; suitable, fitting; **digno de** + *inf* worthy of + *ger*
**digo** *1st sg pres ind of* **decir**
**digrafía** *f* or **dígrafo** *m* digraph
**digrama** *m* digram
**digresión** *f* digression; (astr.) digression
**digresivo -va** *adj* digressive
**dije** *1st sg pret ind of* **decir**; *m* amulet, charm, trinket; (coll.) jewel (*person*); (coll.) person all dressed-up; (coll.) handy person; **dijes** *mpl* boasting, bragging
**dilaceración** *f* dilaceration
**dilacerar** *va* to dilacerate, to tear to pieces; to damage (*honor, pride, etc.*)
**dilación** *f* delay
**dilapidación** *f* dilapidation, squandering
**dilapidar** *va* to dilapidate, to squander
**dilatabilidad** *f* dilatability
**dilatable** *adj* dilatable
**dilatación** *f* dilation, dilatation, expansion, distention; diffuseness, prolixity; calm, serenity, tranquility in sorrow or grief
**dilatado -da** *adj* vast, extensive, extended, numerous; diffuse, prolix
**dilatador -dora** *adj* dilating; *m* (anat. & surg.) dilator
**dilatar** *va* to dilate, expand; to defer, postpone; to spread (*e.g., fame*); (Am.) to delay; *vn* (Am.) to delay; *vr* to dilate, expand; to be deferred, be postponed; to spread; to be diffuse or prolix; (Am.) to delay
**dilatativo -va** *adj* dilative
**dilatómetro** *m* (phys.) dilatometer
**dilatorio -ria** *adj* (law) dilatory; *f* delay
**dilección** *f* true love
**dilecto -ta** *adj* dearly beloved
**dilema** *m* dilemma; (log.) dilemma
**diletante** *adj & mf* dilettante
**diletantismo** *m* dilettanteism
**diligencia** *f* diligence; stagecoach; caution, dispatch, speed; (coll.) errand; **hacer una diligencia** (coll.) to do an errand; (coll.) to have a bowel movement
**diligenciar** *va* to take steps to accomplish; to hasten
**diligenciero** *m* agent, representative
**diligente** *adj* diligent; prompt, quick
**dilogía** *f* ambiguity, double meaning
**dilucidación** *f* elucidation
**dilucidador -dora** *adj* elucidating; *mf* elucidator
**dilucidar** *va* to elucidate
**dilucidario** *m* commentary, exposition
**dilución** *f* dilution
**diluente** *m* thinner; (med.) diluent
**diluído -da** *adj* dilute
**diluir §41** *va* to dilute; to thin; *vr* to dilute, become diluted
**diluvial** *adj* (geol.) Recent
**diluviano -na** *adj* diluvian, diluvial; (geol.) Recent
**diluviar** *vn* to rain hard, to pour
**diluvio** *m* deluge; (fig.) deluge; **el Diluvio** (Bib.) the Deluge, the Flood
**dimanación** *f* springing; origination
**dimanar** *vn* to spring, spring up; **dimanar de** to spring from, arise from, originate in
**dimensión** *f* dimension; **cuarta dimensión** (math.) fourth dimension
**dimensional** *adj* dimensional
**dimensionar** *va* to determine the proportions of, to determine the size of
**dimes** *mpl;* **andar en dimes y diretes con** (coll.) to bicker with
**dimetría** *f* (med.) dimetria
**dímetro** *m* (pros.) dimeter
**diminución** *f* diminution
**diminuir §41** *va, vn, & vr* to diminish, to decrease
**diminutamente** *adv* sparingly; minutely
**diminutivo -va** *adj* diminishing; (gram.) diminutive; *m* (gram.) diminutive
**diminuto -ta** *adj* diminutive, tiny; defective, imperfect; (mus.) diminished
**dimisión** *f* demission, resignation
**dimisionario -ria** *adj* resigning; *mf* person resigning
**dimisorias** *fpl* (eccl.) dimissory letters; **dar dimisorias a** (coll.) to kick out, to fire; **llevar dimisorias** (coll.) to get kicked out, to get fired
**dimitente** *adj* resigning, retiring; *mf* person resigning
**dimitir** *va* to demit, to resign, to resign from; *vn* to demit, to resign
**dimorfismo** *m* dimorphism
**dimorfo -fa** *adj* dimorphous
**din** *m* (coll.) dough, money
**dina** *f* (phys.) dyne; (*cap.*) *f* Dinah
**Dinamarca** *f* Denmark
**dinamarqués -quesa** *adj* Danish; *mf* Dane; *m* Danish (*language*)
**dinámico -ca** *adj* dynamic; (fig.) dynamic; *f* dynamics
**dinamismo** *m* (philos.) dynamism
**dinamista** *adj* dynamistic; *mf* dynamist
**dinamita** *f* dynamite
**dinamitar** *va* to dynamite
**dinamitazo** *m* dynamite explosion
**dinamitero -ra** *adj* dynamiting; *m* dynamiter
**dínamo** *f* dynamo
**dinamoeléctrico -ca** *adj* dynamoelectric
**dinamometría** *f* (mech.) dynamometry
**dinamométrico -ca** *adj* dynamometric
**dinamómetro** *m* dynamometer
**dinamotor** *s* (elec.) dynamotor
**dinasta** *m* dynast
**dinastía** *f* dynasty
**dinástico -ca** *adj* dynastic or dynastical
**dinastismo** *m* loyalty to a dynasty
**dinerada** *f* or **dineral** *m* large amount of money
**dinerario -ria** *adj* monetary
**dinerillo** *m* (coll.) small amount of money
**dinero** *m* money; currency; wealth; **dinero contante** cash; **dinero contante y sonante** ready cash, spot cash; **dinero de bolsillo** pocket money; **dinero trocado** change
**dineroso -sa** *adj* rich, moneyed
**dinga** *f* dingey, dinghy
**dingo** *m* dingo (*wild dog*)
**dinornis** *m* (pal.) dinornis
**dinosaurio** *m* (pal.) dinosaur
**dinoterio** *m* (pal.) dinothere
**dintel** *m* (arch.) lintel, doorhead; threshold
**dintelar** *va* to provide with a lintel; to build in the form of a lintel

**diocesano -na** *adj & m* diocesan
**diócesi** *f* or **diócesis** *f* (*pl:* **-sis**) diocese
**Diocleciano** *m* Diocletian
**diodo** *m* (electron.) diode
**Diógenes** *m* Diogenes
**dioico -ca** *adj* (biol. & bot.) diecious or dioecious
**Diomedes** *m* (myth.) Diomedes
**dionea** *f* (bot.) Venus's-flytrap
**dionisia** *f* bloodstone; **Dionisias** *fpl* Dionysia (*festivals*)
**dionisíaco -ca** *adj* Dionysiac; **dionisíacas** *fpl* Dionysia (*festivals*)
**Dionisio** *m* Dionysius; Denis; **San Dionisio** Saint Denis
**Dionisios** *m* or **Dionisos** *m* (myth.) Dionysos or Dionysus
**dioptra** *f* sight (*of an instrument*); diopter, alidade
**dioptria** *f* (opt.) diopter (*unit*)
**dióptrico -ca** *adj* dioptric or dioptrical; *f* dioptrics
**diorama** *m* diorama
**diorámico -ca** *adj* dioramic
**diorita** *f* (mineral.) diorite
**dios** *m* god; (*cap.*) *m* God; **a la buena de Dios** (coll.) without cunning or malice; **estar con Dios** to be in heaven; **llamar a Dios de tú** to be wonderful, to be first-class; to be too familiar with everybody, to call everybody by his first name; **pasar las de Dios es Cristo** to go through fire and water; **permita Dios** God grant; **¡por Dios!** goodness!, for heaven's sake!; **¡válgame Dios!** bless me!, so help me God!; **¡vaya con Dios!** off with you!, be gone!; good-bye!; God's will be done!; **¡vive Dios!** by Jove!; **dios de los rebaños** or **de los pastores** shepherd god (*Pan*); **Dios mediante** God willing
**diosa** *f* goddess; (fig.) goddess (*very beautiful woman*)
**dioscoreáceo -a** *adj* (bot.) dioscoreaceous
**Dioscuros** or **Dióscuros** *mpl* (myth.) Dioscuri
**diostedé** *m* (orn.) toucan
**dióxido** *m* (chem.) dioxide; **dióxido de azufre** (chem.) sulfur dioxide
**dipétalo -la** *adj* (bot.) dipetalous
**diplejía** *f* (path.) diplegia; **diplejía espástica** (path.) cerebral palsy
**diploclamídeo -a** *adj* (bot.) diplochlamydeous
**diplococo** *m* (bact.) diplococcus
**diplodoco** *m* (pal.) diplodocus
**diploma** *m* diploma
**diplomacia** *f* diplomacy; **diplomacia del dólar** dollar diplomacy
**diplomado -da** *adj* having a diploma, graduate; *mf* diplomate, graduate
**diplomático -ca** *adj* diplomatic; *mf* diplomat, diplomatist; **diplomático de carrera** career diplomat; *f* diplomatics (*branch of paleography; diplomacy*)
**diplopía** *f* (med.) diplopia
**dipolar** *adj* dipolar
**dipolo** *m* (chem. & phys.) dipole
**dipsomanía** *f* (path.) dipsomania
**dipsomaníaco -ca** *adj* dipsomaniacal; *mf* dipsomaniac
**dipsómano -na** *adj & mf* dipsomaniac
**díptero -ra** *adj* (zool.) dipterous, dipteran, dipteral; (arch.) dipteral; *m* (zool.) dipteran; (arch.) dipteros (*building*)
**díptica** *f* diptych (*tablet*)
**díptico** *m* diptych (*picture*)
**diptongación** *f* diphthongization
**diptongar §59** *va & vr* to diphthongize
**diptongo** *m* diphthong
**diputación** *f* deputation; congress
**diputado -da** *mf* deputy; **diputado** *f* deputy, congresswoman
**diputador -dora** *adj & mf* constituent
**diputar** *va* to delegate, commission, depute; to deputize; to designate
**dique** *m* dike, dam, mole, jetty; dry dock; (dent.) dam; (geol.) dike; (fig.) check, stop, bar; **dique de carena** dry dock; **dique de caucho** or **goma** (dent.) rubber dam
**Dirce** *f* (myth.) Dirce
**dirceo -a** *adj* Dircaean
**diré** *1st sg fut ind of* **decir**
**dirección** *f* direction; course, trend, tendency; management, administration; address; directorship; office, administration office; guidance; (aut.) steering; **perder la dirección** to lose control of the car; **dirección de tiro** (nav.) fire control; **dirección obligatoria** or **única** one way
**direccional** *adj* directional
**directivo -va** *adj* directive, managing; *mf* director, manager; *f* board of directors, management
**directo -ta** *adj* direct; straight; (gram.) direct
**director -tora** *adj* guiding, directing, leading; managing, governing; *mf* director, manager; editor (*of a paper*); principal (*of a school*); (mus.) conductor; **director de escena** stage manager; **director de funeraria** funeral director; **director espiritual** spiritual director; **director general** director-general; *f* directress
**directorial** *adj* directorial
**directorio -ria** *adj* directory, directive; directorial; *m* directory (*body of directors; book of names*); directorate, directorship, board of directors; directive; (*cap.*) *m* Directoire
**directriz** *f* (*pl:* **-trices**) directive; (geom.) directrix
**dirigente** *mf* leader, head, director, executive
**dirigible** *adj & m* dirigible
**dirigir §42** *va* to direct, to manage; to turn; to steer (*an automobile*); to dedicate (*a work*); to address (*a letter; one's words, a speech, etc.*); *vr* to go, to betake oneself; to turn; **dirigirse a** to address oneself to, to address (*a person*); to apply to
**dirigismo** *m* state planning, state control
**dirimente** *adj* annulling
**dirimible** *adj* annullable
**dirimir** *va* to dissolve, annul; to solve (*a difficulty*); to settle (*a controversy*)
**disanto** *m* holy day, religious feastday
**discantar** *va* (mus.) to descant; *vn* to descant, to comment at length; (mus.) to descant
**discante** *m* descant; (mus.) descant; (coll.) folly
**discar §86** *va & vn* (telp.) to dial
**disceptación** *f* disceptation, debate, discussion
**disceptar** *vn* to discept, debate, discuss
**discernible** *adj* discernible, perceptible
**discernidor -dora** *adj* discerning; *mf* discerner
**discerniente** *adj* discerning; discriminating
**discernimiento** *m* discernment; (law) commitment
**discernir §43** *va* to discern, distinguish; (law) to entrust, to commit; *vn* to discern, distinguish
**disciplina** *f* discipline; teaching, instruction; whip, scourge
**disciplinable** *adj* disciplinable; pliant, teachable
**disciplinado -da** *adj* disciplined; many-colored (*said of flowers*)
**disciplinal** *adj* disciplinal
**disciplinar** *va* to discipline; to teach, instruct; to whip, to scourge
**disciplinario -ria** *adj* disciplinary
**disciplinazo** *m* lash
**discipulado** *m* discipleship; teaching, instruction; disciples, pupils
**discipular** *adj* discipular
**discípulo -la** *mf* pupil, student; disciple
**disco** *m* disk; record (*of phonograph*); (sport) discus; (astr., bot. & zool.) disk; (coll.) same old record, same old song; **disco de cola** (rail.) tail light; **disco de goma** washer (*e.g., for a spigot*); **disco de identificación** (mil.) identification tag; **disco de larga duración** long-playing record; **disco de Petri** Petri dish; **disco de señales** (rail.) semaphore; **disco explorador** (telv.) scanning disk; **disco rayado** (Am.) fixed idea; **disco selector** (telp.) dial
**discóbolo** *m* discus thrower
**discófilo -la** *mf* discophile, record lover
**discoidal** *adj* discoidal, disk-shaped
**díscolo -la** *adj* wayward, ungovernable, intractable; mischievous
**discoloro -ra** *adj* (bot.) discolor
**discómano -na** *mf* (coll.) var. of **discófilo**
**disconforme** *adj* disagreeing

**disconformidad** *f* nonconformity, unconformity, disconformity; disagreement
**discontinuación** *f* discontinuation
**discontinuar** §33 *va* to discontinue
**discontinuidad** *f* discontinuity
**discontinuo -nua** *adj* discontinuous
**disconvendré** *1st sg fut ind of* **disconvenir**
**disconvengo** *1st sg pres ind of* **disconvenir**
**disconveniencia** *f* unsuitableness; incongruity; inconvenience
**disconveniente** *adj* unsuitable; incongruous; inconvenient
**disconvenir** §92 *vn* to disagree; to be incongruous; to not match; *vr* to disagree; to be incongruous
**disconvine** *1st sg pret ind of* **disconvenir**
**discordancia** *f* discordance; (geol.) discordance
**discordante** *adj* discordant; (geol.) discordant
**discordar** §77 *vn* to disaccord; to be out of tune; to discord, to disagree; **discordar de** to disagree with
**discorde** *adj* discordant, opposed, in disagreement; (mus.) discordant, dissonant, out of tune
**discordia** *f* discord, disagreement
**discoteca** *f* (phonograph) record cabinet; record library
**discrasia** *f* (path.) dyscrasia
**discreción** *f* discretion; wit, sagacity; witticism; **a discreción** at discretion; (mil.) unconditionally (*at the mercy of an opponent*)
**discrecional** *adj* discretionary
**discrepancia** *f* discrepancy; dissent, disagreement; (mus.) discord
**discrepante** *adj* discrepant; dissenting, disagreeing; (mus.) discordant
**discrepar** *vn* to differ, disagree
**discretear** *vn* to try to be clever
**discreteo** *m* attempt at cleverness, attempted cleverness
**discreto -ta** *adj* discreet (*circumspect, cautious*); witty, sagacious; discrete (*separate; composed of distinct parts; marked by discretion*); (math. & med.) discrete
**discretorio** *m* (eccl.) council of seniors; (eccl.) council chamber
**discrimen** *m* hazard, risk, peril; difference
**discriminación** *f* discrimination; **discriminación racial** racial discrimination
**discriminante** *adj* discriminant, discriminating; *f* (math.) discriminant
**discriminar** *va* to discriminate, to distinguish; (Am.) to discriminate against; *vn* to discriminate
**discriminativo -va** *adj* discriminative
**discromatopsia** *f* (path.) dyschromatopsia
**discromía** *f* (path.) dyschroa
**disculpa** *f* excuse, apology
**disculpable** *adj* excusable; pardonable
**disculpadamente** *adv* pardonably
**disculpar** *va* to excuse; to offer as an excuse; (coll.) to pardon, to overlook; *vr* to excuse oneself, to apologize; **disculparse con** to make excuses to, to apologize to; **disculparse de** to make excuses for, to apologize for
**discurrir** *va* to invent, contrive; to infer, conjecture; *vn* to ramble, roam; to flow; to occur, take place; to think, reason; to discourse
**discursear** *vn* (coll.) to make a speech, to harangue
**discursista** *mf* great talker, idle talker
**discursivo -va** *adj* meditative
**discurso** *m* discourse, speech; course (*of time*); (gram.) speech; **discurso de la corona** King's Speech, Queen's Speech; **discurso de sobremesa** after-dinner speech
**discusión** *f* discussion; argument; **discusión de mesa redonda** round-table discussion
**discutible** *adj* disputable, debatable
**discutidor -dora** *adj* argumentative; *mf* arguer
**discutir** *va* to discuss; to argue about or over; to contradict, oppose; *vn* to discuss; to argue; **discutir sobre** to argue about or over
**disecable** *adj* dissectible
**disecación** *f* var. of **disección**
**disecado -da** *adj* (bot.) dissected (*leaf*)
**disecador -dora** *mf* var. of **disector**
**disecar** §86 *va* to dissect; to stuff (*dead animal*); to mount (*dead plant*); (fig.) to dissect
**disección** *f* dissection; anatomy; stuffing (*of dead animals*); mounting (*of dead plants*); (fig.) dissection (*critical analysis*)
**disector -tora** *mf* dissector
**diseminación** *f* dissemination; scattering
**diseminador -dora** *adj* disseminating, spreading; *mf* disseminator, spreader
**diseminar** *va* to disseminate; to scatter; *vr* to scatter
**disensión** *f* dissension; dissent
**disenso** *m* dissent, disagreement
**disentería** *f* (path.) dysentery; **disentería amibiana** (path.) amoebic dysentery
**disentérico -ca** *adj* dysenteric
**disentimiento** *m* dissent, disagreement
**disentir** §62 *vn* to dissent
**diseñador -dora** *mf* designer, sketcher
**diseñar** *va* to draw, design, sketch, outline
**diseño** *m* drawing, design, sketch, outline
**disépalo -la** *adj* (bot.) disepalous
**disertación** *f* dissertation, disquisition
**disertador -dora** *adj* disquisitive
**disertante** *adj* disquisitive, inquisitive; *mf* disquisitor, investigator; speaker
**disertar** *vn* to discourse in detail; **disertar acerca de** or **sobre** to discourse in detail on
**diserto -ta** *adj* fluent, eloquent
**disestesia** *f* (path.) dysesthesia
**disfagia** or **disfagía** *f* (path.) dysphagia
**disfasia** *f* (med.) dysphasia
**disfavor** *m* disfavor
**disformar** *va & vr* var. of **deformar**
**disforme** *adj* deformed; huge, monstrous
**disformidad** *f* deformity; hugeness, monstrousness
**disforzar** §52 *vr* (Am.) to be affected, prudish, finical
**disfraz** *m* (*pl:* **-fraces**) disguise
**disfrazar** §76 *va* to disguise
**disfrutar** *va* to enjoy, to have the benefit of, to take advantage of, to use; *vn* **disfrutar de** to enjoy, to have the use of; **disfrutar con** to enjoy, take enjoyment in (*e.g., music*)
**disfrute** *m* enjoyment, benefit, use
**disfumar** *va* var. of **esfumar**
**disfumino** *m* var. of **esfumino**
**disfunción** *f* (med.) dysfunction
**disgregación** *f* disintegration
**disgregador -dora** *adj* disintegrating; *mf* disintegrator
**disgregar** §59 *va* to disintegrate; *vr* to disintegrate; to disperse, break up
**disgregativo -va** *adj* disintegrating, disintegrative
**disgustado -da** *adj* tasteless, insipid, disagreeable; sad, sorrowful; displeased
**disgustar** *va* to displease; **disgustar** + *inf* to displease (*someone*) to + *inf*, to not like to + *inf; vr* to be displeased; to fall out; **disgustarse con** to be displeased at or with; to fall out with; **disgustarse de** to be displeased at or with; to be bored with, to be tired of
**disgusto** *m* disgust; annoyance, bother; worry, sorrow, grief; unpleasantness, quarrel, difference; **a disgusto** against one's will
**disgustoso -sa** *adj* unpleasant, disagreeable; tasteless
**disidencia** *f* dissidence; opposition; (eccl.) dissent
**disidente** *adj* dissident, dissentient; *mf* dissenter, dissident, dissentient; opponent
**disidir** *vn* to dissent; (eccl.) to dissent
**disilábico -ca** *adj* dissyllabic
**disílabo -ba** *adj* dissyllabic; *m* dissyllable
**disimetría** *f* dissymmetry
**disimétrico -ca** *adj* dissymmetric, dissymmetrical, unsymmetrical
**disímil** *adj* dissimilar
**disimilación** *f* dissimilation
**disimilar** *adj* dissimilar; *va & vr* to dissimilate
**disimilitud** *f* dissimilitude, dissimilarity
**disimulación** *f* dissimulation, dissembling
**disimulado -da** *adj* furtive, underhand, hypocritical; **a lo disimulado** or **a la disimulada** underhandedly; **hacer la disimulada** (coll.) to feign ignorance

**disimular** *va* to dissimulate, to dissemble; to disguise; to pardon, excuse; *vn* to dissimulate, to dissemble
**disimulo** *m* dissimulation, dissembling; tolerance, indulgence
**disipación** *f* dissipation; (fig.) dissipation (*dissolute way of life*)
**disipado -da** *adj* dissipated; spendthrift, prodigal; *mf* dissipated person, debauchee; spendthrift
**disipador -dora** *adj & mf* spendthrift
**disipar** *va* to dissipate; *vr* to dissipate, be dissipated, evanesce, disappear; to dissipate one's energies
**dislalia** *f* (med.) dyslalia
**dislate** *m* nonsense, absurdity
**dislocación** *f* dislocation; (geol.) dislocation, slip
**dislocadura** *f* dislocation
**dislocar §86** *va* to dislocate; to displace; *vr* to dislocate
**disloque** *m* (coll.) top notch, tops
**dismenorrea** *f* (path.) dysmenorrhea
**disminución** *f* diminution
**disminuir §41** *va, vn, & vr* to diminish, to decrease
**disnea** *f* (path.) dyspnea
**disociación** *f* dissociation
**disociador -dora** *adj* dissociative
**disociar** *va & vr* to dissociate
**disolubilidad** *f* dissolubility
**disoluble** *adj* dissoluble
**disolución** *f* dissolution; (fig.) dissolution (*e.g., of a family, partnership, government, treaty, contract*); dissoluteness, dissipation
**disolutivo -va** *adj* dissolutive
**disoluto -ta** *adj* dissolute; *mf* debauchee
**disolvente** *adj* dissolvent; demoralizing; *m* dissolvent, solvent
**disolver §63 & §17,** 9 *va* to dissolve; (law) to dissolve; to ruin, destroy; *vn* to dissolve; *vr* to dissolve
**disón** *m* (mus.) dissonance, discord
**disonancia** *f* dissonance; **hacer disonancia** to be out of harmony
**disonante** *adj* dissonant; *m* dissonant tone
**disonar §77** *vn* to be discordant, to lack harmony, to disagree; to sound bad; to be objectionable, to cause surprise
**dísono -na** *adj* dissonant
**dispar** *adj* unlike, unequal, different, disparate; odd (*that does not match*)
**disparada** *f* (Am.) sudden flight; **a la disparada** (Am.) at full speed, like a shot; (Am.) in mad haste; **de una disparada** (Am.) at once, right away; **tomar la disparada** (Am.) to take to one's heels, to run away
**disparadamente** *adv* hastily; absurdly, nonsensically
**disparadero** *m* trigger; **poner en el disparadero** (coll.) to drive mad, to drive to distraction
**disparador** *m* shooter; trigger; escapement (*of watch*); release (*on a camera*); (naut.) anchor tripper; **poner en el disparador** (coll.) to drive mad, to drive to distraction; **disparador de bombas** (aer.) bomb release
**disparar** *va* to shoot; to throw, to hurl; *vn* to talk nonsense; *vr* to dash away, dash off, rush away; to go off (*said, e.g., of a gun*); to be beside oneself
**disparatado -da** *adj* absurd, nonsensical; frightful, awful
**disparatador -dora** *adj* idle, nonsensical; *mf* idle talker
**disparatar** *vn* to talk nonsense, to blunder
**disparate** *m* foolish remark; crazy idea; piece of foolishness; blunder, mistake; (coll.) outrage
**disparatorio** *m* lot of nonsense, lot of hot air
**disparejo -ja** *adj* uneven, unequal, different, disparate; rough, broken
**disparidad** *f* disparity
**disparo** *m* shot, discharge, firing; absurdity, nonsense; (mach.) release, trip, start; **cambiar disparos** to exchange shots
**dispendio** *m* waste, squandering
**dispendioso -sa** *adj* expensive
**dispensa** *f* dispensation
**dispensable** *adj* dispensable
**dispensación** *f* dispensation
**dispensador -dora** *adj* dispensing; *mf* dispenser
**dispensar** *va* to dispense; to dispense with; to exempt, excuse; to pardon, absolve; **dispensar de** + *inf* to excuse from + *ger;* **dispensar que** + *subj* to excuse for + *ger*, e.g., **dispénseme que le detenga** excuse me for keeping you
**dispensaría** *f* (Am.) dispensary
**dispensario** *m* dispensary; **dispensario de alimentos** soup kitchen
**dispensatorio** *m* dispensatory (*book on medicines; dispensary*)
**dispepsia** *f* (path.) dyspepsia; **dispepsia ácida** (path.) acid dyspepsia; **dispepsia atónica** (path.) atonic dyspepsia; **dispepsia catarral** (path.) catarrhal dyspepsia; **dispepsia fermentativa** (path.) fermentative dyspepsia; **dispepsia flatulenta** (path.) flatulent dyspepsia; **dispepsia nerviosa** (path.) nervous dyspepsia
**dispépsico -ca** or **dispéptico -ca** *adj & mf* dyspeptic
**dispermia** *f* (biol.) dispermy
**dispersar** *va & vr* to disperse
**dispersión** *f* dispersion, dispersal; (phys.) dispersion
**dispersivo -va** *adj* dispersive
**disperso -sa** *adj* dispersed, scattered, separated; preoccupied
**dispirema** *f* (biol.) dispireme
**displacer §34** *va* (obs.) to displease
**displicencia** *f* coolness, indifference; discouragement; ill humor; contemptuousness
**displicente** *adj* disagreeable; peevish, fretful, ill-humored
**dispnea** *f* var. of **disnea**
**dispondré** *1st sg fut ind of* **disponer**
**disponer §69** *va* to dispose, arrange, line up, prepare; to direct, order, decree; **disponer** + *inf* to arrange to + *inf*, to provide for + *ger;* *vn* to dispose; **disponer de** to dispose of, to assign for a use; to make use of, make use of the services of, have at one's disposal; *vr* to prepare oneself, get ready; to line up; to get ready to die, to make one's will; **disponerse a** or **para** + *inf* to get ready to + *inf*
**dispongo** *1st sg pres ind of* **disponer**
**disponibilidad** *f* availability; **disponibilidades** *fpl* quick assets, available assets
**disponible** *adj* available, disposable
**disposición** *f* disposition, arrangement; layout; disposal; inclination, aptitude; preparation; elegance; predisposition; state of health; **a la disposición de** at the disposal of, at the service of; **estar en disposición de** + *inf* to be ready to + *inf;* to be in the mood to + *inf;* **última disposición** last will and testament
**dispositivo -va** *adj* dispositive; *m* device, apparatus
**disprosio** *m* (chem.) dysprosium
**dispuesto -ta** *pp of* **disponer;** *adj* comely, graceful; skilful, sprightly; ready, prepared; **bien dispuesto** well, in good health; well-disposed, favorable; **mal dispuesto** ill, indisposed; ill-disposed, unfavorable
**dispuse** *1st sg pret ind of* **disponer**
**disputa** *f* dispute, disputation; fight, struggle; contest; **sin disputa** beyond dispute
**disputador -dora** *adj* disputant; disputatious; *mf* disputant, disputer
**disputable** *adj* disputable, debatable
**disputar** *va* to dispute, to question; to debate, to argue over; to fight for; *vn* to dispute; to debate, to argue; to fight, to struggle
**disquero -ra** *mf* phonograph record dealer
**disquiria** *f* (path.) dyschiria
**disquisición** *f* disquisition
**disruptivo -va** *adj* (elec.) disruptive
**distal** *adj* (anat.) distal
**distancia** *f* distance; (fig.) distance (*coldness, unfriendliness*); **a distancia** at a distance; **distancia focal** (opt.) focal distance, focal length
**distanciar** *va* to place at a distance, to put further apart; to distance, to outdistance
**distante** *adj* distant

**distar** *vn* to be far, be distant; to be different; **distar de** + *inf* to be far from + *ger*
**distender** §66 *va* to distend; *vr* to distend; to unwind, to run down; to relax
**distensibilidad** *f* distensibility
**distensible** *adj* distensible
**distensión** *f* distension; relaxation of tension
**dístico -ca** *adj* (bot.) distichous; *m* distich
**distinción** *f* distinction; distinctness; **a distinción de** in distinction from or to
**distingo** *m* distinction; qualification, reservation
**distinguible** *adj* distinguishable
**distinguido -da** *adj* distinguished; polished, refined, urbane
**distinguir** §44 *va* to distinguish
**distintivo -va** *adj* distinctive; *m* badge, insignia; distinctive mark; distinction
**distinto -ta** *adj* distinct; different
**distocia** *f* (med.) dystocia
**dístomo -ma** *adj* (zool.) distomatous
**distorsión** *f* distortion; (rad. & fig.) distortion
**distorsionar** *va* to distort, twist, turn
**distracción** *f* distraction; diversion, amusement; seduction; embezzlement, misappropriation
**distraer** §88 *va* to distract (*e.g., the attention*); to divert, amuse, entertain; to divert, to draw off; to lead astray, to seduce; to embezzle
**distraído -da** *adj* distracted, absent-minded; dissolute, licentious; (Am.) careless, slovenly
**distraigo** *1st sg pres ind of* **distraer**
**distraimiento** *m* var. of **distracción**
**distraje** *1st sg pret ind of* **distraer**
**distribución** *f* distribution; electric supply system; (mach.) timing gears; (mach.) valve gears; **distribución de frecuencias** (statistics) frequency distribution
**distribuidor -dora** *adj* distributing; *mf* distributor; *m* (aut.) distributor; (mach.) slide valve; (print.) ink roller; **distribuidor automático** vending machine, slot machine; *f* (agr.) spreader (*e.g., of fertilizer*)
**distribuir** §41 *va* to distribute
**distributivo -va** *adj & m* distributive
**distrito** *m* district; (rail.) section; **distrito federal** federal district; **distrito postal** postal zone
**distrofía** *f* (path.) dystrophy; **distrofía muscular progresiva** (path.) muscular dystrophy
**distrófico -ca** *adj* dystrophic
**disturbar** *va* to disturb
**disturbio** *m* disturbance
**disuadir** *va* to dissuade; **disuadir de** + *inf* to dissuade from + *ger*
**disuasión** *f* dissuasion
**disuasivo -va** *adj* dissuasive
**disuelto -ta** *pp of* **disolver**
**disulfato** *m* (chem.) disulfate
**disulfuro** *m* (chem.) disulfide
**disuria** *f* (path.) dysuria
**disvulnerabilidad** *f* disvulnerability
**disyunción** *f* disjunction; (log.) disjunction
**disyunta** *f* (mus.) disjunct motion
**disyuntivo -va** *adj* disjunctive; *f* dilemma, disjunctive
**disyuntor** *m* (elec.) circuit breaker
**dita** *f* surety, bondsman; security, bond
**ditá** *m* (bot.) dita (*tree and bark*)
**ditaína** *f* (chem.) ditamin or ditamine
**diteísmo** *m* ditheism
**diteísta** *adj* ditheistic; *mf* ditheist
**diterpeno** *m* (chem.) diterpene
**ditirámbico -ca** *adj* dithyrambic
**ditirambo** *m* dithyramb
**ditisco** *m* (ent.) water beetle
**dítono** *m* (mus.) ditone
**diuca** *f* (orn.) South American sparrow (*Fringilla diuca*); *m* (Am.) teacher's pet
**diuresis** *f* (path.) diuresis
**diurético -ca** *adj & m* (med.) diuretic
**diurno -na** *adj* day, diurnal; *m* (eccl.) diurnal; **diurnos** *mpl* (ent.) butterflies (*as distinct from moths*); **diurnas** *fpl* (orn.) diurnal birds of prey
**diuturnidad** *f* diuturnity, long duration
**diuturno -na** *adj* diuturnal, lasting
**diva** *f* see **divo**
**divagación** *f* rambling, wandering, digression, divagation
**divagador -dora** *adj* rambling, wandering; discursive; *mf* rambler, wanderer
**divagar** §59 *vn* to ramble, wander, digress, divagate
**diván** *m* divan (*Turkish council and room where it meets; low sofa; collection of poems*); **diván arca** box couch; **diván cama** day bed
**divaricación** *f* divarication
**divaricado -da** *adj* (bot.) divaricate
**divergencia** *f* divergence or divergency
**divergente** *adj* divergent
**divergir** §42 *vn* to diverge
**diversidad** *f* diversity; plenty, abundance
**diversificación** *f* diversification
**diversificar** §86 *va* to diversify; *vr* to diversify, produce diversity
**diversiforme** *adj* diversiform
**diversión** *f* diversion; (mil.) diversion
**diverso -sa** *adj* diverse, different; **diversos -sas** *adj pl* several, various, many
**diverticular** *adj* diverticular
**diverticulitis** *f* (path.) diverticulitis
**divertículo** *m* (anat. & path.) diverticulum
**diverticulosis** *f* (path.) diverticulosis
**divertido -da** *adj* amusing, funny; (Am.) tipsy
**divertimiento** *m* diversion; distraction; (mus.) divertissement
**divertir** §62 *va* to divert, to amuse; (mil.) to divert; *vr* to be amused, to have a good time, to enjoy oneself, to celebrate; **divertirse en** + *inf* to amuse oneself + *ger*, to enjoy + *ger*
**dividendo** *m* (math. & com.) dividend
**divididero -ra** *adj* divisible
**dividir** *va* to divide; *vr* to divide; to separate, part company
**divieso** *m* (path.) boil
**divinal** *adj* (poet.) divine
**divinatorio -ria** *adj* divining, divinatory
**divinidad** *f* divinity; beauty (*person*)
**divinizar** §76 *va* to divinize, deify; to sanctify; to extol, to exalt
**divino -na** *adj* divine; (fig.) divine; **a lo divino** written or revised in sacred form
**divisa** *f* emblem; badge; heraldic device; motto; hope, goal, ideal; monetary standard; divisional coin; currency, foreign exchange; (taur.) colored bow to distinguish bull of each owner
**divisar** *va* to descry, to espy; (her.) to vary
**divisibilidad** *f* divisibility
**divisible** *adj* divisible
**división** *f* division; (math. & mil.) division
**divisional** *adj* divisional
**divisionario -ria** *adj* divisional
**divisivo -va** *adj* divisive
**divisor -sora** *adj* dividing; *mf* divider; *m* (math.) divisor; **común divisor** (math.) common divisor; **máximo común divisor** (math.) greatest common divisor; **divisor de fase** (elec.) phase splitter; **divisor de voltaje** (rad.) voltage divider
**divisorio -ria** *adj* dividing; *m* (print.) copyholder; *f* dividing line; (geog.) divide; (mus.) bar, bar line; **divisoria continental** continental divide
**divo -va** *adj* (poet.) divine, godlike; *m* (poet.) god; (mus.) opera star; *f* (poet.) goddess; (mus.) diva
**divorciar** *va* to divorce (*a married couple*); (fig.) to divorce; *vr* to divorce, get divorced; **divorciarse de** to divorce, to get a divorce from
**divorcio** *m* divorce; divergency (*in opinions*)
**divulgable** *adj* revealable
**divulgación** *f* disclosure; divulgation, publicity; popularization
**divulgador -dora** *adj* divulging; *mf* divulger, revealer
**divulgar** §59 *va* to divulge, to disclose, to publish abroad
**diyambo** *m* diiamb
**dizque** (Am.) probably, probably not, e.g., **él dizque lo hizo** (Am.) he probably did it; *m* (coll.) gossip, piece of gossip
**dl.** abr. of **decilitro** or **decilitros**
**Dl.** abr. of **decalitro** or **decalitros**
**dm.** abr. of **decímetro** or **decímetros**
**Dm.** abr. of **decámetro** or **decámetros**

**D.**[n] abr. of **don**
**dna.** abr. of **docena**
**do** *adv & conj* (archaic) where
**dobla** *f* doubling; old Spanish gold coin
**dobladillar** *va* to hem, to border
**dobladillo** *m* hem, border; heavy knitting thread
**doblado -da** *adj* thickset, stocky; uneven, rough; double-dealing, deceitful; *m* (mov.) dubbing
**doblador** *m* (mach.) bender (*of a pipe, rail, etc.*)
**doblaje** *m* (mov.) dubbing
**doblamiento** *m* doubling, folding, creasing, bending
**doblar** *va* to double, to fold, to crease, to bend; (naut.) to double (*a cape*); to turn, to round (*a corner*); to cause (*a person*) to change his opinion or intentions; (mov.) to dub (*a film in another language*); (Am.) to shoot down; (bridge) to double; *vn* to turn (*e.g., to the right or left*); to toll; (theat. & mov.) to double, to stand in; (bridge) to double; *vr* to double, to fold, to crease, to bend; to bow, to stoop; to yield, give in; to become uneven or rough
**doble** *adj* double, two-fold; thick, heavy; thickset, stocky; two-faced, deceitful; *adv* double, doubly, e.g., **doble culpable** doubly guilty; *mf* (theat. & mov.) double, stand-in; *m* fold, crease; toll, knell; margin (*in stock market*); beer glass (*of a quarter liter*); **al doble** doubly
**doblegable** *adj* easily folded; pliant, pliable
**doblegadizo -za** *adj* easily folded, easily bent
**doblegar §59** *va* to fold, to bend; to brandish, flourish; to sway, dominate, force to yield; to force (*a person*) to change his plans; *vr* to fold, to bend; to yield, to give in
**doblemente** *adv* doubly; deceitfully
**doblero** *m* (prov.) pretzel
**doblete** *adj* medium; *m* doublet (*false stone*); (philol.) doublet; (bridge) doubleton; (baseball) two-bagger, two-base hit
**doblez** *m* (*pl:* **-bleces**) fold, crease; cuff (*of trousers*); *m & f* double-dealing, duplicity
**doblón** *m* doubloon; **escupir doblones** (coll.) to make a vain display of wealth; **doblón de a ocho** piece of eight; **doblón de vaca** tripe
**doblonada** *f* pile of money; **echar doblonadas** (coll.) to exaggerate one's wealth
**doboquera** *f* blowgun, blowpipe
**dócar** *m* dogcart (*two-wheeled vehicle with two transverse seats back to back*)
**doce** *adj* twelve; **las doce** twelve o'clock; *m* twelve; twelfth (*in dates*)
**doceañista** *m* maker or follower of the Spanish Constitution of 1812
**doceavo -va** *adj & m* var. of **dozavo**
**docena** *f* see **doceno**
**docenal** *adj* sold by the dozen
**docenario -ria** *adj* made of twelve
**docencia** *f* teaching; (Am.) teaching staff
**doceno -na** *adj* twelfth, dozenth; *f* dozen; **docena del fraile** baker's dozen (*thirteen*)
**docente** *adj* educational, instructional, teaching
**docetismo** *m* Docetism
**dócil** *adj* docile; ductile, soft
**docilidad** *f* docility; ductility
**docimasia** *f* docimasy
**docimástico -ca** *adj* docimastic; *f* docimastic art
**Doct.** abr. of **Doctor**
**docto -ta** *adj* learned; (philol.) learned; *mf* scholar
**doctor -tora** *mf* doctor; **doctor angélico** Angelic Doctor (*Thomas Aquinas*); *f* (coll.) woman doctor; (coll.) doctor's wife; (coll.) bluestocking
**doctorado** *m* doctorate; doctorship (*learning*); studies leading to the doctorate
**doctoral** *adj* doctoral
**doctoramiento** *m* conferring the doctor's degree; taking the doctor's degree
**doctorando -da** *mf* candidate for the doctor's degree
**doctorar** *va* to give the doctor's degree to; (taur.) to authorize (*a novice*) to kill the bull, making him a full-fledged matador; *vr* to get the doctor's degree, to graduate as a doctor; (taur.) to become a full-fledged matador
**doctrina** *f* doctrine; teaching, instruction; wisdom, learning; preaching the Gospel; catechism; **doctrina cristiana** Christian doctrine; Institute of the Brothers of the Christian Schools; **doctrina de Monroe** Monroe Doctrine
**doctrinador -dora** *adj* teaching; *mf* teacher
**doctrinal** *adj* doctrinal; *m* manual of rules and precepts
**doctrinar** *va* to indoctrinate, to teach, to instruct
**doctrinario -ria** *adj & mf* doctrinaire
**doctrinarismo** *m* doctrinairism
**doctrinero** *m* teacher of Christian doctrine; (Am.) curate, parish priest
**doctrino** *m* orphan (*being raised in an asylum*); **parecer un doctrino** (coll.) to have a scared look
**documentación** *f* documentation; **documentación del buque** ship's papers
**documentado -da** *adj* documented, well-documented; well-informed; vouched-for
**documental** *adj* documental or documentary; *m* (mov.) documentary (*film*)
**documentalista** *mf* producer of documentary films
**documentar** *va* to document
**documento** *m* document; **documento de prueba** (law) exhibit
**docum.**[to] abr. of **documento**
**dodecaédrico -ca** *adj* (geom.) dodecahedral
**dodecaedro** *m* (geom.) dodecahedron
**dodecágono -na** *adj* (geom.) dodecagonal; *m* (geom.) dodecagon
**Dodecaneso, el** the Dodecanese Islands
**dodecasílabo -ba** *adj* dodecasyllabic; *m* dodecasyllabic verse
**dodó** *m* (*pl:* **-does**) (orn.) dodo
**dogal** *m* halter, noose, hangman's rope; oppression, tyranny; **estar con el dogal a la garganta** or **al cuello** to be in a jam, to be in a tight spot
**dogaresa** *f* dogaressa, doge's wife
**dogma** *m* dogma
**dogmático -ca** *adj* dogmatic or dogmatical
**dogmatismo** *m* dogmatism
**dogmatista** *mf* propounder of heretical doctrines
**dogmatizador** *m* or **dogmatizante** *m* dogmatist
**dogmatizar §76** *va & vn* to dogmatize
**dogo -ga** *mf* bulldog
**dogre** *m* dogger (*fishing boat*)
**doladera** *f* chip ax, broad ax; cooper's adze
**dolador** *m* hewer; stonecutter
**doladura** *f* shavings; chips
**dolaje** *m* wine absorbed by the cask
**dolamas** *fpl* or **dolames** *mpl* (vet.) hidden defects (*of a horse*); (Am.) complaint, indisposition (*of a person*)
**dolar §77** *va* to hew (*wood or stone*)
**dólar** *m* dollar
**dolencia** *f* ailment, complaint, indisposition
**doler §63** *va* to ache, to hurt, to pain; to grieve, to distress; to concern, be of concern to; **dolerle a uno el dinero** (coll.) to hate to spend money; **dolerle a uno** + *inf* to pain or grieve a person to + *inf; vn* to ache, to hurt, to pain; *vr* to complain; **dolerse con** to complain or lament to; **dolerse de** to complain about or of; to feel sorry for; to repent (*e.g., one's sins*)
**dolicocéfalo -la** *adj* (anthrop.) dolichocephalic
**dolido -da** *adj* complaining; grieved, hurt
**doliente** *adj* suffering, aching; ill, sick; sorrowful, sad; *mf* sufferer, sick person; mourner
**dolmen** *m* dolmen
**dolménico -ca** *adj* dolmenic
**dolo** *m* guile, deceit, fraud
**dolobre** *m* stone hammer
**dolomía** or **dolomita** *f* (mineral.) dolomite
**dolomítico -ca** *adj* dolomitic
**dolor** *m* ache, pain; grief, sorrow; regret, repentance; **Nuestra Señora de los Dolores** Mary of the Sorrows; **Dolores** *f* Dolores (*woman's name*); **dolor de cabeza** headache; **dolor de costado** pneumonia; **dolor de muelas** toothache; **dolor de oído** earache; **dolor de viudo** o **viuda** passing sorrow; **dolores**

de **Nuestra Señora** (eccl.) Dolors of Mary, sorrows of the Virgin Mary; **dolores del parto** labor pains
**dolora** *f* short sentimental and philosophic ballad, invented by Campoamor about 1846
**dolorido -da** *adj* sore, aching, painful; heartsick, grieving, disconsolate; *m* (dial.) chief mourner
**doloroso -sa** *adj* painful; pitiful, dolorous; **Dolorosa** *f* (f.a.) Sorrowing Mary; (coll.) weeping woman
**doloso -sa** *adj* guileful, deceitful, fraudulent
**doma** *f* taming, breaking; check, restraint
**domable** *adj* tamable, controllable
**domador -dora** *adj* taming; *mf* tamer; horsebreaker
**domadura** *f* taming; mastering, subduing
**domar** *va* to tame, to break, to break in; to master, to conquer, to subdue
**dombo** *m* dome
**domeñable** *adj* tamable, controllable, governable
**domeñar** *va* to tame, domesticate; to master, to subdue
**domesticable** *adj* domesticable
**domesticación** *f* domestication
**domesticar** §86 *va & vr* to domesticate
**domesticidad** *f* domesticity
**doméstico -ca** *adj* domestic; household; *mf* domestic (*servant*)
**domestiquez** *f* tameness
**Domiciano** *m* Domitian
**domiciliar** *va & vr* to domicile; to domiciliate
**domiciliario -ria** *adj* domiciliary; *mf* resident
**domicilio** *m* domicile; dwelling; **adquirir** or **contraer domicilio** to take up one's abode; **domicilio social** (com.) home office, company office
**dominación** *f* domination, dominance; (mil.) eminence, high ground; (sport) chinning; **dominaciones** *fpl* dominations (*high order of angels*)
**dominador -dora** *adj* dominating, controlling; domineering; *mf* dominator, ruler
**dominancia** *f* (biol.) dominance
**dominante** *adj* dominant; domineering; (astrol., biol. & mus.) dominant; *f* (mus.) dominant
**dominar** *va* to dominate; to domineer; to check, refrain, subdue, control; to handle perfectly (*a language*); to have a thorough knowledge of; *vn* to dominate; to domineer; *vr* to control oneself
**dominativo -va** *adj* dominating
**dómine** *m* Latin teacher; pedant; dominie, pedagogue
**domingada** *f* Sunday celebration, Sunday festival
**domingo** *m* Sunday; **guardar el domingo** to keep the Sabbath; **Santo Domingo** Saint Dominic; Santo Domingo (*city*); **domingo de adviento** Advent Sunday; **domingo de carnaval** Shrove Sunday; **domingo de cuasimodo** Quasimodo, Low Sunday; **domingo de la santísima trinidad** Trinity Sunday; **domingo de lázaro** or **de pasión** Passion Sunday; **domingo de ramos** Palm Sunday; **domingo de resurrección** Easter Sunday
**dominguero -ra** *adj* (coll.) Sunday
**dominguillo** *m* tumbler (*toy figure*)
**dominguito** *m* (orn.) yellowbird
**dominica** *f* see **dominico**
**domínica** *f* Sunday, Sabbath
**dominical** *adj* (pertaining to) Sunday; (pertaining to the) Sabbath; feudal (*fees*)
**dominicano -na** *adj* Dominican (*pertaining to Saint Dominic and to the Dominican Republic*); *mf* Dominican
**dominico -ca** *adj* Dominican (*pertaining to Saint Dominic*); *mf* Dominican; *f* (bot.) red periwinkle; **la Dominica** Dominica (*one of Lesser Antilles*)
**dominio** *m* dominion; domain; mastery (*e.g., of a foreign language*); (law) fee (*ownership*); **dominio absoluto** (law) fee simple; **dominio del aire** air supremacy; **dominio directo** (law) dominium directum; **dominio eminente** (law) eminent domain; **dominio público** (law) public domain; **dominio útil** (law) dominium utile
**dominó** *m* (*pl:* **-nós**) domino (*cloak with mask*); dominoes (*game*); set of dominoes
**dómino** *m* dominoes (*game*); set of dominoes
**dom.º** abr. of **domingo**
**domo** *m* (arch.) dome
**dompedro** *m* (bot.) four-o'clock, marvel-of-Peru
**don** *m* gift, present; natural gift, talent, faculty; Don (*Spanish title used before masculine Christian names, formerly given only to noblemen, now more widely used*); **don de acierto** tact, knack for doing the right thing; **don de errar** knack for doing the wrong thing; **don de gentes** charm, magnetism, winning manners; **don de lenguas** linguistic facility; **don de mando** ability to command; **Don Juan** Don Juan (*legendary Spanish nobleman; seducer of women*)
**dona** *f* (Am.) gift, legacy; **donas** *fpl* wedding presents given to the bride by the bridegroom
**donación** *f* donation; foundation, endowment
**donada** *f* lay sister
**donado** *m* lay brother
**donador -dora** *mf* giver, donor; **donador de sangre** blood donor
**donaire** *m* cleverness; bon mot, witticism; nimbleness, gracefulness
**donairoso -sa** *adj* clever; witty; nimble, graceful
**Donaldo** *m* Donald
**donante** *mf* donor; **donante de sangre** blood donor
**donar** *va* to give, donate
**donatario** *m* donee, donatory
**donatismo** *m* Donatism
**donatista** *adj & m* Donatist
**donativo** *m* gift, donation
**doncel** *m* bachelor (*young knight*); virgin (*man*); *adj* mild, mellow (*said, e.g., of wine*)
**doncella** *f* maiden, virgin; maid of honor; housemaid; lady's maid; (bot.) sensitive plant; (Am.) felon, whitlow; **Doncella del Lago** Lady of the Lake (*of Arthurian legend*); **Doncella de Orleáns** Maid of Orleans
**doncellez** *f* maidenhood, virginity
**doncellona** or **doncellueca** *f* maiden lady, spinster
**donde** *conj* where; wherein, in which; wherever; **por donde** whereby; **por donde quiera** anywhere, everywhere; **donde no** otherwise, if you don't; *prep* (Am.) at or to the house, store, office of
**dónde** *adv* where?, e.g., **¿dónde vive?** where does he live?; where, e.g., **dígame dónde vive** tell me where he lives; **¿a dónde?** where?, whither? **a dónde** where, whither; **¿de dónde?** whence?, from where?; **de dónde** whence, from where; **¿por dónde?** for what cause?, for what reason?; which way?
**dondequiera** *adv* anywhere; **dondequiera que** wherever
**dondiego** *m* fop, dandy, sport; (bot.) four-o'clock, marvel-of-Peru; **dondiego de día** (bot.) morning-glory; **dondiego de noche** (bot.) four-o'clock, marvel-of-Peru
**donillero** *m* sharper, smooth cheat
**donjonado -da** *adj* (her.) turreted
**donjuán** *m* (bot.) four-o'clock, marvel-of-Peru
**donjuanesco -ca** *adj* like Don Juan, philandering
**donjuanismo** *m* Don Juanism
**donosidad** *f* grace, wit, witticism
**donoso -sa** *adj* graceful, witty; (iron.) fine
**donostiarra** *adj* (pertaining to) San Sebastián; *mf* native or inhabitant of San Sebastián
**donosura** *f* gracefulness, wittiness, elegance
**doña** *f* doña (*Spanish title used before Christian names of married women or widows*)
**doñear** *vn* (coll.) to chase skirts, hang around women
**dopa** *f* (biochem.) dopa; **dopa oxidasa** (biochem.) dopaoxidase
**doquier** or **doquiera** *conj* wherever; **por doquier** on all sides, everywhere
**dorada** *f* see **dorado**
**doradilla** *f* (bot.) scale fern
**doradillo** *m* fine brass wire; (orn.) wagtail; satinwood

**dorado -da** *adj* gilt; golden; *m* gilt, gilding; (ichth.) dorado; (*cap.*) *m* (astr.) Dorado; **dorados** *mpl* gold or gilt trimmings (*on furniture*); **dorado de altura** (ichth.) dolphin; *f* (ichth.) gilthead
**dorador** *m* gilder
**doradura** *f* gilding
**doral** *m* (orn.) flycatcher
**dorar** *va* to cover with gold, to gild; to goldplate; (cook.) to brown; (fig.) to sugar-coat; *vr* to become golden (*said, e.g., of horizon*); (cook) to turn brown
**Dorcas** *f* (Bib.) Dorcas
**Dordoña** *f* Dordogne
**dórico -ca** *adj* Doric; *m* Doric (*dialect*)
**Dóride, la** Doris
**dorio -ria** *adj & mf* Dorian
**dormán** *m* dolman (*of Turks, hussars, etc.*)
**dormida** *f* see **dormido**
**dormidero -ra** *adj* soporific; *m* sleeping place of cattle; *f* (bot.) opium poppy; **dormideras** *fpl* (coll.) sleepiness; **tener buenas dormideras** (coll.) to be a ready sleeper, to go to sleep easily
**dormido -da** *adj* asleep; dormant; slow, dull; **dormido sobre** relying on, confident in; *f* sleeping period (*of silkworm*); night's resting place (*of animals and birds*); night's sleep; (Am.) lodging for the night
**dormidor -dora** *adj* sleepy; *mf* sleeper
**dormilón -lona** *adj* (coll.) sleepy; *mf* (coll.) sleepyhead; *f* earring; armchair for napping; (bot.) mimosa, sensitive plant
**dormir §45** *va* to put to sleep; (coll.) to sleep off (*e.g., wine*); *vn* to sleep; to stay overnight; **dormir sobre** to sleep over; *vr* to sleep; to go to sleep, to fall asleep; to go to sleep (*to become numb*)
**dormirlas** *m* hide-and-seek
**dormitar** *vn* to doze, to nap
**dormitivo -va** *adj & m* (med.) dormitive
**dormitorio** *m* dormitory; bedroom suit
**dornajo** *m* small round trough
**dornillo** *m* small trough; wooden bowl; wooden spittoon
**Dorotea** *f* Dorothy
**dorsal** *adj* dorsal; *m* (sport) number (*worn on front or back of shirt*)
**dorsiflexión** *f* dorsiflexion
**dorso** *m* back, dorsum
**dorsolumbar** *adj* dorsolumbar
**dorsoventral** *adj* dorsoventral
**dos** *adj* two; **las dos** two o'clock; *m* two; second (*in dates*); **en un dos por tres** (coll.) in a flash, in a second; **para entre los dos** between the two of us; **dos de mayo** national holiday of Spain, in commemoration of May 2, 1808, when the War of Independence against Napoleon I was begun
**dosalbo -ba** *adj* with two white feet (*said of a horse*)
**dosañal** *adj* biennial, two-year
**doscientos -tas** *adj & m* two hundred
**dosel** *m* canopy, dais
**doselera** *f* valance, drapery (*of canopy*)
**doselete** *m* (arch.) canopy (*over statue, tomb, etc.*)
**dosificación** *f* dosing, dosage; proportioning
**dosificador** *m* proportioner, mixing apparatus
**dosificar §86** *va* to dose (*a medicine*); to proportion (*ingredients*)
**dosimetría** *f* dosimetry
**dosimétrico -ca** *adj* dosimetric
**dosímetro** *m* dosimeter
**dosis** *f* (*pl:* **-sis**) dose; **dosis de paciencia** dose of patience
**dotación** *f* dowry; endowment; (aer.) crew; (sport) crew (*of oarsmen*); (naut.) complement; staff, personnel; equipment
**dotal** *adj* dotal; (pertaining to) endowment
**dotar** *va* to dower, give a dowry to; to endow; to equip; to man (*e.g., a ship*); to staff (*e.g., an office*); to fix the wages of; (fig.) to endow
**dote** *m & f* dowry, marriage portion; *m* stock of counters (*for playing cards*); *f* endowment, talent, gift; **dotes de mando** leadership, ability to command
**dovela** *f* (arch.) voussoir
**dovelaje** *m* (arch.) voussoirs of an arch
**doxología** *f* doxology; **gran doxología** greater doxology; **pequeña doxología** lesser doxology
**doy** *1st sg pres ind of* **dar**
**dozavado -da** *adj* twelve-sided, twelvefold
**dozavo -va** *adj & m* twelfth; **en dozavo** duodecimo, twelvemo
**d/p** abr. of **días plazo**
**draba** *f* (bot.) whitlow grass
**dracma** *f* drachm, drachma; (pharm.) dram, drachm
**Dracón** *m* Draco
**draconiano -na** *adj* Draconian; (fig.) Draconian; draconian
**draga** *f* dredge, dredging machine; dredger (*boat*)
**dragado** *m* dredging
**dragadora** *f* dredge
**dragaje** *m* var. of **dragado**
**dragaminas** *m* (*pl:* **-nas**) (nav.) mine sweeper
**dragar §59** *va* to dredge
**drago** *m* (bot.) dragon tree
**dragomán** *m* dragoman, interpreter
**dragón** *m* dragon (*fabulous animal*); (bot.) snapdragon; (ichth.) greater weever; (mil.) dragoon; (her.) wivern; (zool.) dragon, flying dragon; (vet.) dragon (*in horse's eye*); feed hole in reverberatory furnace; **dragón marino** (ichth.) greater weever; **dragón verde** (bot.) green dragon; **dragón volador** (zool.) flying dragon
**dragona** *f* dragoness; (mil.) shoulder knot; sword tassel
**dragonado -da** *adj* (her.) dragonné; *f* dragonnade
**dragonal** *m* var. of **drago**
**dragoncillo** *m* (mil.) dragon (*musket*); (bot.) tarragon
**dragonear** *vn* (Am.) to boast; (Am.) to flirt; **dragonear de** (Am.) to pass oneself off as; (Am.) to boast of being
**dragontea** *f* (bot.) green dragon
**dragontino -na** *adj* (pertaining to a) dragon
**drama** *m* drama (*play; genre; event or events in real life*)
**dramamina** *f* (pharm.) dramamine
**dramático -ca** *adj* dramatic; *mf* dramatist; actor; *f* dramatic art; drama (*genre*)
**dramatismo** *m* drama, dramatic effect
**dramatizable** *adj* dramatizable
**dramatización** *f* dramatization
**dramatizar §76** *va* to dramatize
**dramaturgia** *f* dramaturgy
**dramaturgo** *m* dramaturgist
**drapear** *va* to drape
**drástico -ca** *adj* drastic; (med.) drastic
**dravidiano -na** *adj & mf* Dravidian; *m* Dravidian (*language*)
**dren** *m* drain (*ditch, pipe, etc.*); (surg.) drain; **dren en cigarrillo** (surg.) cigarette drain
**drenaje** *m* drainage; (surg.) drainage
**drenar** *va* to drain
**Dresde** *f* Dresden
**dríada** or **dríade** *f* (myth.) dryad
**driblar** *va & vn* (sport) to dribble
**dril** *m* drill, denim; (zool.) drill (*baboon*)
**drino** *m* (zool.) long-nosed tree snake
**driza** *f* (naut.) halyard
**drizar §76** *va* (naut.) to hoist (*the yards*)
**dro.** abr. of **derecho**
**droga** *f* drug, medicine; trick, deceit; bother, annoyance; (Am.) bad debt; (Am.) drug on the market; **drogas mágicas, milagrosas** or **prodigiosas** wonder drugs
**drogmán** *m* var. of **dragomán**
**droguería** *f* drysaltery; drug business; drug store
**droguero -ra** *mf* drysalter; druggist
**droguete** *m* drugget
**droguista** *mf* drysalter; druggist; cheat, impostor
**drolático -ca** *adj* spicy, ribald
**dromedario** *m* dromedary; heavy animal; (coll.) brute (*person*)
**dromógrafo** *m* dromograph
**dromomanía** *f* (psychopath.) dromomania
**dromotrópico -ca** *adj* (physiol.) dromotropic
**drope** *m* (coll.) cur (*contemptible fellow*)
**drosera** *f* (bot.) sundew; (pharm.) drosera

**droseráceo -a** *adj* (bot.) droseraceous
**drosófila** *f* (ent.) drosophila
**drosómetro** *m* drosometer
**druida** *m* druid
**druidesa** *f* druidess
**druídico -ca** *adj* druidic or druidical
**druidismo** *m* druidism
**drupa** *f* (bot.) drupe, stone fruit
**drupáceo -a** *adj* (bot.) drupaceous
**druso -sa** *adj* Drusean; *mf* Druse; *f* (bot. & mineral.) druse
**dúa** *f* (min.) gang of workmen
**dual** *adj* dual; (gram.) dual; *m* (gram.) dual
**dualidad** *f* duality
**dualismo** *m* dualism
**dualista** *adj* dualistic; *mf* dualist
**duba** *f* earthen wall or enclosure
**dubio** *m* (law) doubtful point, doubt
**dubitable** *adj* doubtful, dubious
**dubitación** *f* dubitation, doubt
**dubitativo -va** *adj* dubitative
**ducado** *m* duchy, dukedom; ducat; **gran ducado** grand duchy
**ducal** *adj* ducal
**ducentésimo -ma** *adj & m* two-hundredth
**dúctil** *adj* ductile; (fig.) ductile, manageable, easy to handle
**ductilidad** *f* ductility
**ductivo -va** *adj* conducive
**ducha** *f* see **ducho**
**duchar** *va* to douche; to give a shower bath to; *vr* to douche; to take a shower bath
**ducho -cha** *adj* skilful, expert, experienced; *f* douche; shower bath; stripe; (med.) irrigation; **ducha en alfileres** needle bath
**duda** *f* doubt; **sin duda** beyond doubt; no doubt; without doubt
**dudable** *adj* doubtable, doubtful
**dudar** *va & vn* to doubt; **dudar de** to doubt; **dudar en** + *inf* to hesitate in + *ger*, to hesitate to + *inf*; **dudar haber** + *pp* to doubt having + *pp*
**dudoso -sa** *adj* doubtful, dubious
**duela** *f* stave (*of barrel*); **duela del hígado** (zool.) fluke, liver fluke
**duelaje** *m* var. of **dolaje**
**duelista** *m* duelist
**duelo** *m* grief, sorrow, affliction; mourning, bereavement; mourners; effort, strain; duel; **sin duelo** with abundance; **duelo judiciario** (hist.) judicial duel, trial or ordeal by battle
**duende** *m* elf, goblin, ghost; gold and silver cloth
**duendo -da** *adj* tame, gentle
**dueñesco -ca** *adj* (coll.) duennalike
**dueño -ña** *mf* owner, proprietor; **¡mi adorado dueño!** my beloved mistress! (*addressed to the woman one loves*); **ser dueño de** to own, to be master of; **ser dueño de** + *inf* to be free to, be at liberty to + *inf*; **hacerse dueño de** to take possession of; to master; **dueño de sí mismo** self-controlled; *m* landlord, master; *f* landlady, housekeeper, mistress; duenna; matron; (Am.) sweetheart; **dueña de casa** housewife
**duermevela** *m* (coll.) doze, light sleep; (coll.) fitful sleep; **a duermevela** (coll.) dozing, half-asleep
**duerna** *f* trough
**duerno** *m* (print.) double sheet (*folded together*)
**duetista** *mf* (mus.) duettist
**dueto** *m* (mus.) short duet
**dugón** *m* or **dugongo** *m* (zool.) dugong
**dula** *f* land irrigated from common ditch; common pasture land
**dulcamara** *f* (bot.) bittersweet
**dulce** *adj* sweet; rich; fresh (*water*); soft, ductile (*metal*); mild, gentle, pleasant; *m* candy, piece of candy; preserves; **dulces** *mpl* candy; **dulce de almíbar** preserved fruit; **un dulce** a piece of candy
**dulcedumbre** *f* sweetness
**dulcémele** *m* (mus.) dulcimer
**dulcería** *f* candy store, confectionery shop
**dulcero -ra** *adj* (coll.) sweet-toothed; *mf* confectioner; *f* candy dish, preserve dish
**dulcificacion** *f* sweetening; dulcification, mollification
**dulcificante** *m* (cook.) sweetening, sweetener
**dulcificar** §86 *va* to sweeten; to dulcify, mollify, appease; *vr* to sweeten, turn sweet
**dulcinea** *f* (coll.) sweetheart; ideal; (*cap.*) *f* Dulcinea (*peasant girl, Don Quijote's ideal*)
**dulcísono -na** *adj* (poet.) sweet-toned
**dulía** *f* dulia, worship of angels and saints
**dulzaina** *f* see **dulzaino**
**dulzainero** *m* flageolet player
**dulzaino -na** *adj* (coll.) too sweet, too rich; *f* (mus.) flageolet; (coll.) mess of sweets, mess of sweet food
**dulzamara** *f* var. of **dulcamara**
**dulzarrón -rrona** or **dulzón -zona** *adj* (coll.) too sweet, sickening, cloying
**dulzor** *m* sweetness; sweetness, pleasantness, gentleness
**dulzura** *f* sweetness; mildness (*e.g., of the weather*); sweetness, pleasantness, gentleness
**duma** *f* duma; (bot.) doom palm, doum palm
**dumdum** *f* dumdum, dumdum bullet
**duna** *f* dune
**Dunquerque** *m & f* Dunkirk
**dúo** *m* pair; (mus.) duet
**duodecenal** *adj* duodecennial
**duodecimal** *adj & m* duodecimal
**duodécimo -ma** *adj & m* twelfth
**duodécuplo -pla** *adj* duodecuple
**duodenal** *adj* duodenal
**duodenectomía** *f* (surg.) duodenectomy
**duodeno -na** *adj* twelfth; *m* (anat.) duodenum
**duomesino -na** *adj* two-month
**dup.do** abr. of **duplicado**
**dúplex** *m* duplex telegraphy; (metal.) duplex process
**dúplica** *f* (law) defendant's answer
**duplicación** *f* duplication, doubling
**duplicadamente** *adv* doubly
**duplicado** *m* duplicate; **por duplicado** in duplicate
**duplicador -dora** *adj* duplicating; *m* duplicator
**duplicar** §86 *va* to duplicate; to double; to repeat; (law) to answer (*plaintiff's reply*); *vr* to double
**duplicata** *f* duplicate
**dúplice** *adj* (obs.) double, duplex
**duplicidad** *f* duplicity; doubleness
**duplo -pla** *adj & m* double
**duque** *m* duke; (coll.) fold in mantilla; **gran duque** grand duke; (orn.) eagle owl; **duque de alba** (naut.) cluster of piles
**duquesa** *f* duchess; **gran duquesa** grand duchess; **duquesa viuda** dowager duchess
**dura** *f* see **duro**
**durabilidad** *f* durability
**durable** *adj* durable, lasting
**duración** *f* duration; endurance
**duradero -ra** *adj* lasting, serviceable
**duraluminio** *m* duralumin
**duramadre** *f* or **duramáter** *f* (anat.) dura mater
**duramen** *m* (bot.) duramen
**durante** *prep* during
**duraplastia** *f* (surg.) duraplasty
**durar** *vn* to last; to continue, to remain; to wear (*said of clothes*)
**durativo -va** *adj* durative; (gram.) durative, progressive
**duraznero** *m* (bot.) peach tree
**duraznilla** *f* peach (*fruit*)
**duraznillo** *m* (bot.) persicary, lady's-thumb
**durazno** *m* (bot.) peach tree; peach (*fruit*)
**durbar** *m* durbar
**durdo** *m* (ichth.) ballan, ballan wrasse
**dureno** *m* (chem.) durene
**Durero, Alberto** Albrecht or Albert Dürer
**dureza** *f* hardness; roughness; harshness; dullness (*in understanding*); (phys.) hardness (*of vacuum tube*); (med.) callosity; **dureza de corazón** hardheartedness; **dureza de oído** tone deafness; loss of hearing; **dureza de vientre** costiveness
**durián** *m* durian or durion (*fruit of Durio zibethinus*)
**durillo** *m* (bot.) laurustine; (bot.) dogwood
**durina** *f* (vet.) dourine
**durmiente** *adj* sleeping; *mf* sleeper; **dormir más que los siete durmientes** (coll.) to sleep all the time, to be a sleepyhead; **la**

**Bella durmiente** Sleeping Beauty; *m* girder, stringer, sleeper; (Am.) tie, crosstie; (Am.) steel bar (*to fasten a door*)

**duro -ra** *adj* hard; hard-boiled (*egg*); harsh, rough; unbearable; indifferent, cruel; stubborn, obstinate; stingy; inclement, stormy; (phys.) hard (*ray; vacuum tube*); (Am.) drunk; **estar muy duro con** to be hard on; **ser duro de pelar** (coll.) to be hard to deal with; (coll.) to be hard to get, to be hard to put across; **duro de corazón** hard-hearted; **duro de oído** tone-deaf; hard of hearing; **duro de oreja** hard of hearing; **duro** *adv* hard; *m* dollar (*Spanish coin worth 5 pesetas*); *f* (coll.) durability; **de mucha dura** (coll.) strong, durable (*cloth, clothing, etc.*)

**durra** *f* (bot.) durra

**duruculi** *m* (zool.) night ape

**duunvir** *m* duumvir

**duunviral** *adj* duumviral

**duunvirato** *m* duumvirate

**duunviro** *m* duumvir

**dux** *m* (*pl:* **dux**) doge

**d/v** abr. of **días vista**

# E

**E, e** *f* sixth letter of the Spanish alphabet
**E.** abr. of **este** (*oriente*)
**e** *conj* (used for **y** before a word beginning with the vowel sound **i**) and
**ea** *interj* hey!
**ebanista** *m* cabinetmaker
**ebanistería** *f* cabinetwork, cabinetmaking; cabinetmaker's shop
**ébano** *m* (bot.) ebony (*tree and wood*)
**ebenáceo -a** *adj* (bot.) ebenaceous
**ebonita** *f* ebonite
**ebriedad** *f* inebriety
**ebrio -bria** *adj* drunk; (fig.) blind (*e.g., with anger*); *mf* drunk
**ebrioso -sa** *adj* drinking; tipsy; *mf* drinker
**ebulición** *f* or **ebullición** *f* boiling, ebullition; bubbling; **en ebulición** in ferment
**ebullómetro** *m* ebulliometer
**ebulloscopio** *m* ebullioscope
**eburnación** *f* (path.) eburnation
**ebúrneo -a** *adj* (pertaining to) ivory
**eccehomo** *m* eccehomo; wretch, wreck (*person*)
**ec.**[co] abr. of **eclesiástico**
**Ecequiel** *m* (Bib.) Ezekiel (*prophet and book*)
**-ecer** *suffix v* -ish, e.g., **empobrecer** impoverish; **establecer** establish; **perecer** perish; and many other verbs, e.g., **entristecer** sadden; **parecer** appear
**-ecillo -lla** *suffix dim* var. of **-illo** and attached to monosyllables ending in a consonant, e.g., **panecillo** roll; **pececillo** little fish; to dissyllables with radical **ie** or **ue** and ending in **o** or **a**, e.g., **muestrecilla** small sample; **piedrecilla** little rock; and to dissyllables ending in **ia, io,** and **ua,** e.g., **gloriecilla** touch of glory; **fragüecilla** little forge
**-ecito -ta** *suffix dim* var. of **-ito** and attached to monosyllables ending in a consonant (including **y**), e.g., **florecita** little flower; **bueyecito** little ox; to dissyllables with radical **ie** or **ue** and ending in **o** or **a**, e.g., **piedrecita** little rock; **cuerpecito** little body; and to dissyllables ending in **ia, io,** and **ua,** e.g., **biestecita** little beast; **lengüecita** little tongue
**eclampsia** *f* (path.) eclampsia
**eclecticismo** *m* eclecticism
**ecléctico -ca** *adj & mf* eclectic
**Eclesiastés, el** (Bib.) Ecclesiastes
**eclesiástico -ca** *adj* ecclesiastic or ecclesiastical; *m* ecclesiastic; **el Eclesiástico** (Bib.) Ecclesiasticus
**eclesiastizar §76** *va* to transfer to ecclesiastical use or possession
**eclímetro** *m* clinometer
**eclipsar** *va* (astr. & fig.) to eclipse; (fig.) to outshine; *vr* (astr. & fig.) to be eclipsed; (fig.) to disappear
**eclipse** *m* (astr. & fig.) eclipse; **eclipse de Luna** lunar eclipse; **eclipse de Sol** solar eclipse; **eclipse parcial** partial eclipse; **eclipse total** total eclipse
**eclipsis** *f* (*pl:* **-sis**) (gram.) ellipsis
**eclíptico -ca** *adj* ecliptic or ecliptical; *f* ecliptic
**eclisa** *f* (rail.) fishplate
**eclisar** *va* (rail.) to fish
**écloga** *f* var. of **égloga**
**eclosión** *f* opening, blossoming, birth
**eco** *m* echo; rumbling; (*cap.*) *f* (myth.) Echo; **hacer eco** to correspond, be proportional; to attract attention; **tener eco** to spread, catch on, get popular
**ecoico -ca** *adj* echoic
**ecolalia** *f* (psychol.) echolalia
**ecología** *f* ecology
**ecólogo** *m* ecologist
**economato** *m* stewardship, guardianship; commissary (*store*)
**economía** *f* economy; want, misery; **economías** *fpl* savings; **economía dirigida** or **planificada** planned economy; **economía doméstica** home economics; **economía política** political economy, economics
**económico -ca** *adj* economic or economical; thrifty, saving; miserly, niggardly
**economista** *mf* economist
**economizador** *m* (mach.) economizer
**economizar §76** *va & vn* to economize; to save
**ecónomo** *m* supply priest; ecclesiastical administrator; guardian; steward
**ecrán** *m* (mov.) screen; (phot.) filter
**ectasia** *f* (path.) ectasia
**éctasis** *f* (pros.) ectasis
**ectoblasto** *m* (embryol.) ectoblast
**ectodermo** *m* (embryol.) ectoderm
**ectoparásito** *m* (zool.) ectoparasite
**ectopia** *f* (path.) ectopia
**ectoplasma** *m* (biol. & spiritualism) ectoplasm
**ectropión** *m* (path.) ectropion
**ecuación** *f* (math., astr. & chem.) equation; **ecuación cuadrática** (alg.) quadratic equation; **ecuación de primer grado** (alg.) linear equation; **ecuación de segundo grado** (alg.) quadratic equation; **ecuación diferencial** (math.) differential equation; **ecuación personal** personal equation; **ecuación simultánea** (alg.) simultaneous equation
**ecuador** *m* equator; **el Ecuador** Ecuador
**ecuánime** *adj* calm, composed, equanimous; impartial
**ecuanimidad** *f* equanimity; impartiality
**ecuatorial** *adj* equatorial; *m* (astr.) equatorial (*instrument*)
**ecuatorianismo** *m* Ecuadorianism
**ecuatoriano -na** *adj & mf* Ecuadoran, Ecuadorian
**ecuestre** *adj* equestrian
**ecuménico -ca** *adj* ecumenic or ecumenical
**ecúmeno** *m* inhabited part of the earth
**ecuóreo -a** *adj* (poet.) of the sea, aequorial
**eczema** *m & f* (path.) eczema
**eczematoso -sa** *adj* eczematous
**echacantos** *m* (*pl:* **-tos**) (coll.) empty-headed fellow
**echacorvear** *vn* (coll.) to pimp, to procure
**echacorvería** *f* (coll.) pimpery, procuring
**echacuervos** *m* (*pl:* **-vos**) (coll.) pimp, procurer; (coll.) cheat, gyp
**echada** *f* see **echado**
**echadera** *f* wooden shovel (*for putting bread in oven*)
**echadero** *m* place to rest, place to stretch out
**echadillo -lla** *adj & mf* (coll.) foundling
**echadizo -za** *adj* waste, discarded; spread around secretly; sent to spy; *mf* foundling; spy
**echado -da** *adj* lying down; (Am.) lazy, indolent, idle; *m* (min.) dip in vein; *f* throw; man's length (*stretched out on ground*); (Am.) boast, falsehood
**echador -dora** *adj* throwing, hurling; (Am.) boastful, bragging; *mf* (Am.) braggart; *m* waiter who pours coffee
**echadura** *f* setting (*of hens*); **echadura de pollos** brood of chicks
**echalumbre** *m* (orn.) junco
**echamiento** *m* throwing, hurling, throwing away
**echapellas** *m* (*pl:* **-llas**) wool soaker
**echaperros** *m* (*pl:* **-rros**) beadle who keeps dogs out of church
**echar** *va* to throw, cast, fling, throw away, throw out; to discharge, dismiss; to pour; to give out, issue, send forth, emit, publish; to

swallow, to take; to smoke (*cigar, cigaret*); to attribute, ascribe; to turn (*key*); to deliver (*speech, sermon, etc.*); to utter (*curses*); to put on (*a play*); to put forth, to begin to have or grow (*hair, teeth, shoots, etc.*); to impose, levy (*tax*); to acquire (*a stomach, bad disposition, etc.*); to deal (*cards*); to tell (*a fortune*); to mate, to couple (*male and female animals*); to cast (*a glance*); to shed (*blood*); to lay (*blame*); **echar abajo** to overthrow, demolish, ruin, destroy; to break down; **echar a pasear** (coll.) to dismiss harshly, to dismiss without ceremony; **echar a perder** to spoil, to ruin; **echar de menos** to miss; **echarla de** (coll.) to claim to be, to boast of being; **echarlo todo a rodar** (coll.) to upset everything, to spoil everything; (coll.) to fly off the handle; **echar menos** to miss ‖ *vn* to sprout; **echar a** + *inf* to begin to + *inf;* to burst out + *ger;* **echar a perder** to spoil, to ruin; **echar de ver** to notice; **echar por** to take up, go into (*a profession*); to turn toward (*the right or left*); to go down (*a road*) ‖ *vr* to throw or hurl oneself; to lie down, stretch out; to fall (*said of the wind*); to set (*said of a hen*); to throw on (*a wrap*); **echarse a** + *inf* to begin to + *inf;* to burst out + *ger;* **echarse a morir** (coll.) to give up in despair; **echarse a perder** to spoil, to be ruined; **echarse atrás** to back out; **echarse de ver** to be noticeable, to be easy to see; **echárselas de** to claim to be, to boast of being; **echarse sobre** to rush at, to fall upon

**echarpe** *m* & *f* sash

**echazón** *f* throwing; (naut.) jettison

**echiquier** *m* Exchequer

**echona** *f* (Am.) sickle

**edad** *f* age; **corta edad** youth, youthfulness; **de edad** older, e.g., **una señora de edad** an older woman; **en edad de quintas** of draft age; **mayor edad** majority; **menor edad** minority; **¿qué edad le echa Vd.?** how old do you think he is?; **¿qué edad tiene Vd.?** how old are you?; **edad antigua** ancient times; **edad crítica** change of life (*in women*); **edad de bronce** (myth.) bronze age; **edad de discreción** age of discretion; **edad de la máquina** machine age; **edad del bronce** (archeol.) Bronze Age; **edad del hielo** (geol.) ice age; **edad del hierro** (archeol.) Iron Age; **edad de oro** (myth.) golden age; **edad de piedra** (archeol.) Stone Age; **edad de plata** (myth.) silver age; **edad escolar** school age; **Edad Media** Middle Ages; **edad mental** (psychol.) mental age; **edad viril** prime of life

**edafología** *f* edaphology, soil science

**edda** *f* (lit.) Edda

**edecán** *m* aide-de-camp

**edelweiss** *f* (bot.) edelweiss

**edema** *m* (path.) edema

**edematoso -sa** *adj* edematous

**edén** *m* (Bib. & fig.) Eden

**edénico -ca** *adj* Edenic

**edición** *f* publication; edition; **la segunda edición de** the spit and image of; **edición crítica** critical edition; **edición diamante** (print.) diamond edition; **edición diplomática** diplomatic edition; **edición príncipe** first edition, editio princeps

**edicional** *adj* publishing

**edicto** *m* edict

**edificación** *f* building, construction; buildings; edification

**edificador -dora** *adj* building; edifying; *mf* builder

**edificante** *adj* edifying

**edificar** §86 *va* to build, construct, erect; to edify

**edificativo -va** *adj* edifying

**edificatorio -ria** *adj* building, constructing

**edificio** *m* building, edifice

**edil** *m* aedile, edile; councilman

**Edimburgo** *f* Edinburgh

**Edipo** *m* (myth.) Oedipus

**Edita** *f* Edith

**editar** *va* to publish

**editor -tora** *adj* publishing; *mf* publisher; editor (*writer of editorials*)

**editorial** *adj* publishing; editorial; *m* editorial; *f* publishing house

**editorialista** *mf* editor, editorial writer

**editorializar** §76 *vn* (Am.) to editorialize

**Edmundo** *m* Edmund

**-edor -dora** *suffix adj* -ing, e.g., **aprendedor** learning; **bebedor** drinking; *suffix mf* -er, e.g., **aprendedor** learner; **bebedor** drinker

**edrar** *va* (agr.) to dig (*vineyards*) the second time

**edredón** *m* eider down; quilt; feather pillow

**eduardiano -na** *adj* Edwardian

**Eduardo** *m* Edward

**educable** *adj* educable

**educación** *f* education; breeding; good manners; **educación de adultos** adult education; **educación física** physical education

**educacional** *adj* educational

**educador -dora** *adj* educating, training; *mf* educator

**educando -da** *adj* & *mf* student, pupil

**educar** §86 *va* to educate, to train; to rear, bring up

**educativo -va** *adj* educative

**educción** *f* eduction; exhaust (*of steam engine*)

**educir** §38 *va* to educe, bring out

**eductor** *m* steam ejector

**eduje** *1st sg pret ind of* **educir**

**edulcoración** *f* (pharm.) sweetening; (Am.) softening of water

**edulcorar** *va* (pharm.) to sweeten; (Am.) to soften (*water*)

**eduzco** *1st sg pres ind of* **educir**

**Eetes** *m* (myth.) Aeëtes

**EE.UU.** abr. of **Estados Unidos**

**efectismo** *m* striving for effect, sensationalism

**efectista** *adj* sensational, theatrical; *mf* sensationalist

**efectivamente** *adv* really, actually; effectively; sure enough

**efectividad** *f* effectiveness; (mil.) permanent status

**efectivo -va** *adj* real, actual; regular, permanent (*employment*); effective; **hacer efectivo** to carry out; to cash (*a check*); *m* cash; **efectivos** *mpl* (mil.) effectives, troops; **en efectivo** in cash; **efectivo en caja** cash in hand

**efecto** *m* effect; end, purpose; commercial document; article; (billiards) English; **efectos** *mpl* effects, property, merchandise; assets; **a efectos de** for the purpose of; **a efectos de** + *inf* for the purpose of + *ger;* **a ese** or **tal efecto** for that purpose; **al efecto** for the purpose; **de doble efecto** (mach.) double-acting; **de simple efecto** (mach.) single-acting; **en efecto** sure enough; **llevar a efecto** or **poner en efecto** to carry out, to put into effect; **por efecto de** as a result of; **surtir efecto** to have the desired effect, to work; **efecto de Doppler** (phys.) Doppler effect; **efecto de empaquetamiento** (phys.) packing effect; **efectos a pagar** bills payable; **efectos a recibir** bills receivable; **efectos de consumo** consumers' goods; **efectos sanitarios** plumbing fixtures; **efectos sonoros** (mov. & rad.) sound effects; **efecto útil** (mech.) efficiency, output

**efectuación** *f* accomplishment

**efectuar** §33 *va* to effect, carry out; *vr* to be carried out, to take place

**efedrina** *f* (pharm.) ephedrine

**efélide** *f* freckle, ephelis

**efeméride** *f* anniversary; **efemérides** *fsg* event, date; **efemérides** *fpl* ephemerides; diary, journal, record; **efemérides astronómicas** ephemerides

**efemérido** *m* (ent.) ephemerid

**efémero** *m* (bot.) stinking iris

**efendi** *m* effendi

**eferente** *adj* (physiol.) efferent

**efervescencia** *f* effervescence

**efervescente** *adj* effervescent

**efesino -na** or **efesio -sia** *adj* & *mf* Ephesian

**Éfeso** *f* Ephesus

**eficacia** *f* effectiveness, efficacy

**eficaz** *adj* (*pl:* **-caces**) effective, effectual, efficacious

**eficiencia** *f* efficiency; (mech.) efficiency

**eficiente** *adj* efficient

**efigie** *f* effigy; **ahorcar en efigie** to hang in effigy; **quemar en efigie** to burn in effigy
**efímero -ra** *adj* ephemeral; *f* (ent.) May fly
**eflorecer §34** *vr* (chem.) to effloresce
**eflorescencia** *f* (bot. & chem.) efflorescence
**eflorescente** *adj* (bot. & chem.) efflorescent
**efluvio** *m* effluvium; **efluvio eléctrico** luminous discharge, brush discharge
**Efraín** *m* (Bib.) Ephraim
**efugio** *m* evasion, subterfuge
**efusión** *f* effusion; (fig.) warmth, effusion; **efusión de sangre** bloodshed
**efusivo -va** *adj* effusive; (geol. & fig.) effusive
**egida** or **égida** *f* (myth. & fig.) aegis
**egílope** *m* (bot.) egilops, wild grass; (bot.) European wild oat; (path.) egilops
**egipcíaco -ca** or **egipciano -na** *adj & mf* Egyptian
**egipcio -cia** *adj & mf* Egyptian; *m* Egyptian (*language*)
**egiptano -na** *adj & mf* Egyptian; (obs.) gypsy
**Egipto** *m* Egypt; (myth.) Aegyptus
**egiptología** *f* Egyptology
**egiptológico -ca** *adj* Egyptological
**egiptólogo -ga** *mf* Egyptologist
**égira** *f* var. of **hégira**
**Egisto** *m* (myth.) Aegisthus
**eglantina** *f* (bot.) eglantine, sweetbrier
**eglefino** *m* (ichth.) haddock
**égloga** *f* eclogue
**egocéntrico -ca** *adj & mf* egocentric
**egoísmo** *m* egoism
**egoísta** *adj* egoistic; *mf* egoist
**ególatra** *adj* self-worshiping
**egolatría** *f* self-worship
**Egospótamos** *m* (hist.) Aegospotami
**egotismo** *m* egotism
**egotista** *adj* egotistic or egotistical; *mf* egotist
**egregio -gia** *adj* distinguished, eminent
**egresar** *va* (Am.) to withdraw (*money*); *vn* (Am.) to leave, go away; (Am.) to graduate
**egreso** *m* debit; (Am.) departure; (Am.) graduation
**egrisar** *va* to polish (*diamonds*)
**eh** *interj* eh!
**eíder** *m* (orn.) eider, eider duck
**einsteinio** *m* (chem.) einsteinium
**eje** *m* axis; axle, shaft; axletree; (math.) axis; (fig.) core, crux, main point; (*cap.*) *m* Axis (*Fascist bloc*); **eje de apoyo** knife edge (*of scale beam*); **eje de balancín** (mach.) rocker, rockershaft; **eje de carretón** axletree; **eje delantero** front axle; **eje de levas** (mach.) camshaft; **eje flotante** (mach.) floating axle; **eje óptico** (opt. & cryst.) optical axis; **eje principal** major axis; main shaft; **eje Roma-Berlín** Rome-Berlin axis; **eje trasero** rear axle
**ejecución** *f* execution; carrying out; (law) attachment, distraint
**ejecutable** *adj* feasible, practicable; (law) suable for debt, distrainable
**ejecutante** *adj* executing; *mf* performer, executant; (law) distrainor
**ejecutar** *va* to execute; to perform; to carry out; (law) to distrain
**ejecutivamente** *adv* promptly, with dispatch
**ejecutivo -va** *adj* executive; insistent, imperative; *m* (Am.) executive
**ejecutor -tora** *adj* executive; *mf* executive; executor; distrainor; **ejecutor de la justicia** executioner; **ejecutor testamentario** executor (*of a will*); **ejecutora testamentaria** executrix
**ejecutoria** *f* see **ejecutorio**
**ejecutoría** *f* (law) office of distrainor
**ejecutoriar** *va* to confirm; (law) to obtain (*a judgment*) in one's favor
**ejecutorio -ria** *adj* (law) executory; *f* pedigree, letters patent of nobility; decree
**ejemplar** *adj* exemplary; *m* exemplar; pattern; model; sample; example; precedent; copy (*of a book or magazine*); example (*warning to others*); **sin ejemplar** without precedent; as a special case; **ejemplar de cortesía** complimentary copy; **ejemplar muestra** sample copy
**ejemplaridad** *f* exemplary behavior, exemplary quality or character
**ejemplarizar §76** *va* (Am.) to set an example to; (Am.) to illustrate with an example
**ejemplificación** *f* exemplification, illustration
**ejemplificar §86** *va* to exemplify, illustrate
**ejemplo** *m* example, instance; **dar ejemplo** to set an example; **por ejemplo** for example, for instance; **seguir el ejemplo de** to follow the example of; **sin ejemplo** unexampled
**ejercer §91** *va* to practice, exercise; to exert; *vn* to practice; to hold office; **ejercer de** to practice as (*e.g., a lawyer*), to work as (*e.g., a newspaperman*)
**ejercicio** *m* exercise, drill; exertion; practice; tenure (*of office*); fiscal year; balance sheet; **hacer ejercicio** to take exercise; (mil.) to drill; **ejercicio antiaéreo** air-raid drill; **ejercicio económico** budget period; **ejercicios espirituales** spiritual retreat
**ejercitación** *f* exercise, practice
**ejercitante** *adj* exercising; *mf* incumbent; exercitant (*in a spiritual retreat*)
**ejercitar** *va* to exercise; to practice; to drill, to train; *vr* to exercise; to practice
**ejército** *m* army; (fig.) army; arm (*of national defense*); **los tres ejércitos** the three arms of the service; **ejército del aire** air force; **ejército de Salvación** Salvation Army; **ejército permanente** standing army
**ejidatario -ra** *mf* (Am.) squatter, settler on public land
**ejido** *m* commons, public land, communal farm
**ejión** *m* (arch.) corbel piece, purlin
**-ejo -ja** *suffix dim & pej* e.g., **caballejo** little horse, nag; **librejo** cheap book, poor book; **medianejo** fair to middling
**ejote** *m* (Am.) tender bean pod
**el** *art def masc* (*pl:* **los**) the; *pron dem masc* the one, that, e.g., **el de mi hermano** that of my brother
**él** *pron pers masc* he, him, it
**elaboración** *f* elaboration; working; development
**elaborado -da** *adj* elaborate, high-wrought; finished (*product*)
**elaborar** *va* to elaborate; (physiol.) to elaborate; to work (*e.g., wood*)
**elación** *f* haughtiness; magnanimity, nobility; pomposity (*of style*)
**elasmobranquio** *m* (ichth.) elasmobranch
**elástica** *f* see **elástico**
**elasticidad** *f* elasticity
**elástico -ca** *adj* elastic; *m* elastic; *f* knit undershirt; **elásticas** *fpl* (Am.) suspenders
**elastificar §86** *va* to make elastic, to elasticize
**elastina** *f* (biochem.) elastin
**elaterina** *f* (chem.) elaterin
**elaterio** *m* (bot.) squirting cucumber
**elayómetro** *m* oleometer, elaeometer
**elche** *m* apostate, renegade
**Eldorado** *m* El Dorado
**eleagnáceo -a** *adj* (bot.) elaeagnaceous
**eleático -ca** *adj & mf* Eleatic
**eleborastro** *m* (bot.) helleboraster
**eléboro** *m* (bot. & pharm.) hellebore; **eléboro negro** (bot.) Christmas rose, winter rose
**elección** *f* election; choice, free election; (theol.) election
**eleccionario -ria** *adj* (Am.) (pertaining to an) election, electoral
**electivo -va** *adj* elective
**electo -ta** *adj & m* elect
**elector -tora** *adj* electing; *mf* elector; *m* elector (*German prince*)
**electorado** *m* electorate
**electoral** *adj* electoral
**electorero** *m* heeler, henchman
**Electra** *f* (myth.) Electra
**electricidad** *f* electricity; **electricidad estática** static electricity; **electricidad vítrea** vitreous electricity
**electricista** *mf* electrician
**eléctrico -ca** *adj* electric or electrical
**electrificación** *f* electrification
**electrificar §86** *va* to electrify
**electriz** *f* (*pl:* **-trices**) electress (*wife or widow of an elector of old German Empire*)
**electrizable** *adj* electrifiable
**electrización** *f* electrification
**electrizador -dora** *adj* electrifying

**electrizar** §76 *va* to electrify; (fig.) to electrify; *vr* to become electrified
**electro** *m* amber; electromagnet; electrum (*alloy*)
**electroafeitadora** *f* electric shaver
**electrobomba** *f* motor-driven pump
**electrocardiógrafo** *m* electrocardiograph
**electrocardiograma** *m* electrocardiogram
**electrocirugía** *f* electrosurgery
**electrocución** *f* electrocution
**electrocutar** *va* to electrocute
**electrochoque** *m* electroshock
**electrodinámico -ca** *adj* electrodynamic; *f* electrodynamics
**electrodo** or **eléctrodo** *m* electrode; **electrodo de calomel** (physical chem.) calomel electrode
**electrodoméstico -ca** *adj* household-electric
**electrofónico -ca** *adj* electrophonic
**electróforo** *m* (phys.) electrophorus
**electrógeno -na** *adj* generating electricity; *m* electric generator
**electroimán** *m* electromagnet
**electrólisis** *f* electrolysis
**electrolítico -ca** *adj* electrolytic
**electrólito** *m* electrolyte
**electrolización** *f* electrolyzation
**electrolizar** §76 *va* to electrolyze
**electrología** *f* science or study of electricity
**electromagnético -ca** *adj* electromagnetic
**electromagnetismo** *m* electromagnetism
**electrometalurgia** *f* electrometallurgy
**electrometría** *f* electrometry
**electrométrico -ca** *adj* electrometric
**electrómetro** *m* electrometer
**electromotor -tora** or **-triz** (*pl:* **-trices**) *adj* electromotive; *m* electromotor, electric motor
**electrón** *m* (phys. & chem.) electron; **electrón voltio** (*pl:* **electrones voltios**) (phys.) electron volt
**electronegativo -va** *adj* electronegative
**electroneumático -ca** *adj* (mus.) electropneumatic
**electrónico -ca** *adj* electronic; *f* electronics
**electrón-voltio** *m* (*pl:* **electrones-voltios** or **electrón-voltios**) (phys.) electron volt
**electropositivo -va** *adj* electropositive
**electroquímico -ca** *adj* electrochemical; *f* electrochemistry
**electroscopio** *m* (phys.) electroscope
**electroshockterapia** *f* (med.) electro-convulsive treatment
**electrostático -ca** *adj* electrostatic; *f* electrostatics
**electrotecnia** *f* electrical engineering, electrotechnics
**electrotécnico -ca** *adj* electrotechnical
**electroterapia** *f* electrotherapy
**electrotipar** *va* to electrotype
**electrotipia** *f* electrotypy
**electrotipo** *m* electrotype
**electrotrén** *m* electric train
**electuario** *m* electuary
**elefancía** *f* (path.) elephantiasis
**elefancíaco -ca** *adj* & *mf* elephantiac
**elefanta** *f* female elephant
**elefante** *m* elephant; (coll.) jumbo; **elefante blanco** (fig.) white elephant; **elefante de mar** (zool.) walrus; **elefante marino** (zool.) sea elephant, elephant seal
**elefantiasis** *f* or **elefantíasis** *f* (path.) elephantiasis
**elefantino -na** *adj* elephantine
**elegancia** *f* elegance; style
**elegante** *adj* elegant; stylish; *mf* fashion plate (*person*)
**elegantizar** §76 *va* to make elegant, to give style to
**elegía** *f* elegy
**elegíaco -ca** *adj* elegiac
**elegibilidad** *f* eligibility
**elegible** *adj* eligible
**elegido -da** *adj* & *mf* elect, chosen
**elegir** §72 *va* to elect; to choose, select; **elegir** + *inf* to choose to + *inf*
**élego -ga** *adj* elegiac
**elemental** *adj* elemental; elementary
**elemento** *m* element; member; (anat. & biol.) element; (chem.) element, simple substance; (elec.) cell (*of a battery*); **los cuatro elementos** the four elements (*fire, air, water, and earth*); **los elementos** the elements (*first principles; atmospheric forces*); means, resources; **estar en su elemento** to be in one's element; **elemento calentador** (elec.) heating element; **elemento de caldeo** (rad.) heating element; **elemento de compuestos** (gram.) combining form, word element; **elemento primario** (elec.) primary cell; **elemento secundario** (elec.) secondary cell; **elemento trazador** (phys.) tracer element
**elemí** *m* (*pl:* **-míes**) elemi
**Elena** *f* Helen, Elaine; **Santa Elena** Saint Helena (*British island and colony in South Atlantic*)
**elenco** *m* list, table, catalogue; personnel; (theat.) cast
**eleómetro** *m* oleometer, elaeometer
**eleusino -na** *adj* & *mf* Eleusinian
**elevación** *f* elevation; (arch. & astr.) elevation; (eccl.) Elevation; **elevación a potencias** (math.) involution
**elevacristales** *m* (*pl:* **-les**) (aut.) window regulator
**elevado -da** *adj* high, elevated; lofty, sublime
**elevador -dora** *adj* elevating; *m* elevator; **elevador de granos** grain elevator; **elevador de tensión** (elec.) booster
**elevaje** *m* raising, rearing
**elevamiento** *m* elevation, exaltation
**elevar** *va* to elevate; (math.) to raise (*to a power*); **elevar hasta las nubes** to praise to the skies; *vr* to rise, ascend; to be elevated or exalted; to become vain or conceited
**elfino -na** *adj* elfin
**elfo** *m* elf
**Elí** *m* (Bib.) Eli
**Elías** *m* (Bib.) Elijah; Ellis, Eliot, Elliot
**elidir** *va* to strike out, nullify; to elide (*a sound*)
**elijación** *f* (pharm.) seething
**elijar** *va* (pharm.) to seethe
**eliminación** *f* elimination; (physiol.) elimination
**eliminador -dora** *adj* eliminating; *mf* eliminator; **eliminador de baterías** (rad.) battery eliminator
**eliminar** *va* to eliminate; (math. & physiol.) to eliminate
**eliminatoria** *f* (sport) elimination match, race, etc.
**elipse** *f* (geom.) ellipse
**elipsis** *f* (*pl:* **-sis**) (gram.) ellipsis
**elipsógrafo** *m* ellipsograph
**elipsoide** *m* & *f* (geom.) ellipsoid
**elíptico -ca** *adj* (geom. & gram.) elliptic or elliptical
**elíseo -a** *adj* Elysian; (*cap.*) *m* (Bib.) Elisha; (myth. & fig.) Elysium
**elisio -sia** *adj* Elysian; *m* (myth. & fig.) Elysium
**elisión** *f* elision
**élitro** *m* elytrum, shard (*of beetle*)
**elixir** or **elíxir** *m* elixir; **elixir paregórico** (pharm.) paregoric
**elocución** *f* elocution; diction, style
**elocuencia** *f* eloquence
**elocuente** *adj* eloquent
**elogiable** *adj* praiseworthy
**elogiador -dora** *adj* eulogistic; *mf* eulogist
**elogiar** *va* to praise, laud, eulogize
**elogio** *m* praise, eulogy; **elogios** *mpl* praise
**elogioso -sa** *adj* eulogistic
**Eloísa** *f* Eloise, Héloïse
**elongación** *f* (astr.) elongation
**elote** *m* (Am.) ear of green corn, ear of roasting corn
**elucidación** *f* elucidation
**elucidar** *va* to elucidate
**eludible** *adj* avoidable, escapable
**eludir** *va* to elude, evade; **eludir** + *inf* to avoid + *ger*
**elzevir** *m* (bibliog. & print.) Elzevir
**elzeviriano -na** *adj* Elzevir, Elzevirian
**elzevirio** *m* var. of **elzevir**
**ella** *pron pers fem* she, her, it; (coll.) trouble, e.g., **aquí fué ella** here's where the trouble was; **mañana será ella** the trouble will come tomorrow

**ello** *pron pers neut* it; (coll.) trouble, e.g., **aquí fué ello** here's where the trouble was; **ello es que** the fact is that; *adv* really, indeed; **ello no** by no means, not at all; **ello sí** most certainly; *m* (psychoanal.) id
**ellos, ellas** *pron pers pl* they, them
**E.M.** abr. of **Estado Mayor**
**Em.ª** abr. of **Eminencia**
**Ema** *f* Emma
**emaciación** *f* emaciation
**emanación** *f* emanation; **emanación del radio** (chem.) radium emanation
**emanar** *vn* emanate
**emancipación** *f* emancipation
**emancipador -dora** *adj* emancipating; *mf* emancipator
**emancipar** *va* to emancipate; *vr* to become emancipated; (coll.) to take too much liberty, to go too far
**Emanuel** *m* (Bib.) Immanuel
**emasculación** *f* emasculation
**emascular** *va* to emasculate
**embabiamiento** *m* (coll.) fascination, amazement, stupefaction
**embabucar** §86 *va* var. of **embaucar**
**embachar** *va* to pen (*sheep for shearing*)
**embadurnador -dora** *adj* daubing; *mf* dauber
**embadurnamiento** *m* daub, daubing
**embadurnar** *va* to daub, to bedaub, to besmear; *vn* to daub
**embaidor -dora** *adj* tricky, deceptive; *mf* trickster, deceiver, cheat
**embaimiento** *m* trickery, deception
**embaír** §53 *va* to trick, to deceive
**embajada** *f* embassy; ambassadorship; diplomatic message; (coll.) errand, mission; **buena embajada** (iron.) fine proposition
**embajador** *m* ambassador; **embajadores** *mpl* ambassador and wife
**embajadora** *f* ambassadress; ambassador's wife
**embajatorio -ria** *adj* ambassadorial
**embalador** *m* packer
**embalaje** *m* packing; package; (sport) sprint
**embalamiento** *m* packing; (sport) sprint
**embalar** *va* to pack; *vn* to beat the sea with oars to scare fish into the nets; (sport) to sprint; (aut.) to step on the gas; *vr* to race (*said of a motor*)
**embaldosado** *m* tile paving
**embaldosar** *va* to pave with tile
**embalsadero** *m* swamp, marsh
**embalsamador -dora** *adj* embalming; *mf* embalmer
**embalsamamiento** *m* embalming, embalmment
**embalsamar** *va* to embalm (*a corpse; to perfume the air*); *vr* to be or become perfumed; (Am.) to get full of pus
**embalsar** *va* to dam, to dam up; to put on a raft; (naut.) to sling, to hoist; *vr* to dam up
**embalse** *m* dam; damming; water dammed up; (naut.) slinging
**embalumar** *va* to load down, to overload; *vr* to take on too much, to overload oneself with work
**emballenado** *m* whalebone framework
**emballenar** *va* to bone, to stiffen with whalebones or stays
**emballestado -da** *adj* (vet.) foundered; *m* (vet.) founder
**embanastar** *va* to put into a basket; to overcrowd; *vr* to be overcrowded
**embancar** §86 *vn* to sail over the shoals; *vr* (found.) to stick to the walls of the furnace; (Am.) to silt up, to become dammed up
**embanderar** *va* to bedeck with flags or banners
**embanquetar** *va* (Am.) to put sidewalks on (*streets*)
**embarazada** *adj fem* pregnant; *f* pregnant woman
**embarazadamente** *adv* with difficulty
**embarazador -dora** *adj* embarrassing, disturbing
**embarazar** §76 *va* to embarrass, interfere with, hold up; to make pregnant; *vr* to be obstructed; to become pregnant
**embarazo** *m* embarrassment, interference, obstruction; timidity, awkwardness; pregnancy; indigestion
**embarazoso -sa** *adj* embarrassing; inconvenient, harmful; complicated, hard to solve
**embarbar** *va* (taur.) to throw (*the bull*) by seizing both horns
**embarbascar** §86 *vr* to become entangled in roots (*said of a plow*); to become entangled or confused
**embarbecer** §34 *vn* to grow a beard
**embarbillado** *m* (carp.) rabbet, rabbeting
**embarbillar** *va* (carp.) to rabbet
**embarcación** *f* boat, ship, vessel; embarkation (*of people*); **embarcación de alijo** tender
**embarcadero** *m* pier, wharf; (rail.) platform
**embarcador** *m* shipper
**embarcar** §86 *va* to embark; to ship; (fig.) to embark, to launch (*in an enterprise*); **embarcar agua** to ship water; *vn* to entrain; *vr* to embark, to go aboard; (naut.) to sign up, to ship; (fig.) to embark, become entangled (*in an enterprise*)
**embarco** *m* embarkation (*of people*)
**embardar** *va* to thatch
**embargar** §59 *va* to embargo; to paralyze; (law) to seize, to attach
**embargo** *m* indigestion; embargo; (law) seizure, attachment; **sin embargo** nevertheless, however
**embarnecer** §34 *vn* to get fat
**embarnecimiento** *m* fattening
**embarnizadura** *f* varnish, varnishing
**embarnizar** §76 *va* to varnish
**embarque** *m* shipment (*of goods*)
**embarrada** *f* (Am.) blunder
**embarrador -dora** *adj* cheating, scheming; *mf* cheat, schemer
**embarradura** *f* mud splash; smear, stain; (dial.) plastering; (Am.) vilification
**embarrancar** §86 *va* to run aground; to run into a ditch; to tie up, entangle, compromise; *vn* to run aground; to run into a ditch; *vr* to run into a ditch; to get tied up, get stuck
**embarrar** *va* to splash with mud; to smear, stain, bedaub; to pry up, lift with a bar; (dial.) to plaster; (Am.) to vilify; (Am.) to involve; **embarrarla** (Am.) to spoil everything; *vr* to take refuge in the trees (*said of partridges*)
**embarrilador** *m* packer of barrels
**embarrilar** *va* to barrel, to put in barrels
**embarrotar** *va* to bar, to fasten with bars
**embarullador -dora** *adj* (coll.) muddling; *mf* (coll.) muddler
**embarullar** *va* (coll.) to mix up, make a mess of; (coll.) to do carelessly, to do in a disorderly way
**embasamiento** *m* (arch.) foundation
**embastar** *va* to baste, to stitch; to put (*cloth*) in embroidering frame
**embaste** *m* basting, stitching
**embastecer** §34 *vn* to become fat; *vr* to become coarse
**embate** *m* blow, sudden attack; surf, dashing (*of waves*); gust (*of wind*); fresh summer sea breeze; impact; **embates de la fortuna** sudden changes of fortune
**embaucador -dora** *adj* deceptive, tricky; *mf* deceiver, trickster, swindler
**embaucamiento** *m* deception, trickery
**embaucar** §86 *va* to deceive, to trick, to bamboozle
**embaulado -da** *adj* crowded, packed, jammed
**embaular** §75 *va* to put into a trunk; (coll.) to gulp down
**embausamiento** *m* amazement, stupefaction
**embayar** *vr* (Am.) to get wrought up over nothing
**embazadura** *f* brown dye; astonishment, wonder
**embazar** §76 *va* to dye brown; to embrown; to astound; to embarrass, hinder; *vn* to be dumfounded; *vr* to get bored; to become surfeited
**embebecer** §34 *va* to entertain, to amuse, to enchant; *vr* to be enchanted; to be astounded
**embebecimiento** *m* enchantment; astonishment
**embebedor -dora** *adj* absorbent
**embeber** *va* to absorb, to soak up; to saturate, to soak; to take up, shorten; to fit, fit in; to insert; to imbed; to include; to contain; *vn* to shrink, contract; *vr* to be enchanted; to be

astounded; to become absorbed or immersed; to become well versed
**embebido -da** *adj* contracted, elided (*vowel*); (arch.) engaged (*column*)
**embecadura** *f* (arch.) spandrel
**embelecador -dora** *adj* deceiving, cheating; *mf* imposter, cheat
**embelecar §86** *va* to deceive, cheat, bamboozle
**embeleco** *m* fraud, imposition; bore; **embelecos** *mpl* cuteness
**embeleñar** *va* to dope, to stupefy; to charm, to fascinate
**embelesador -dora** *adj* charming, fascinating, entrancing
**embelesamiento** *m* charm, fascination, rapture, enchantment
**embelesar** *va* to charm, fascinate, enrapture; *vr* to be charmed, be fascinated, be enraptured
**embeleso** *m* delight, charming thing; entrancement
**embellaquecer §34** *vr* to become sly, to get deceitful
**embellecedor -dora** *adj* embellishing, beautifying; *m* (aut.) hubcap
**embellecer §34** *va* to embellish, to beautify
**embellecimiento** *m* embellishment, beautification
**embermejar** or **embermejecer §34** *va* to dye red, make red; to make blush; *vn* to turn red or reddish; *vr* to blush
**emberrenchinar** or **emberrinchar** *vr* (coll.) to fly into a rage, to become raving mad
**embestida** *f* attack, assault; (coll.) touch (*for loan or handout*)
**embestidor -dora** *adj* attacking; *m* (coll.) beat, sponger
**embestidura** *f* attack, assault
**embestir §94** *va* to attack, to assail; to hit, to strike; (coll.) to touch, to accost for a loan or handout; (coll.) to charge; *vn* (coll.) to rush forth, to charge, to attack; **embestir con** or **contra** to rush upon; to crash into
**embetunar** *va* to black, blacken; to bituminize; to cover with tar
**embicar §86** *va* (naut.) to top (*a yard*); (Am.) to tilt, to turn over (*in order to empty*); (Am.) to fit, insert; *vn* (Am.) to run aground
**embijar** *va* to paint vermilion; (Am.) to dirty, to smear
**embisagrar** *va* to hinge
**embizcar §86** *vn & vr* to be or to become cross-eyed
**emblandecer §34** *va* to soften, placate, mollify; *vr* to soften, yield; to be moved to pity
**emblanquecer §34** *va* to bleach, to whiten; *vr* to turn white
**emblanquecimiento** *m* bleaching, whitening
**emblema** *m* emblem
**emblemático -ca** *adj* emblematic or emblematical
**embobamiento** *m* fascination, amazement
**embobar** *va* to fascinate, hold in suspense; *vr* to be fascinated, to stand gaping; **embobarse con, de** or **en** to be fascinated at, to gape at
**embobecer §34** *va* to make foolish, to make silly; *vr* to become foolish, to get silly
**embocadero** *m* mouth, outlet, narrow channel
**embocado -da** *adj* mild, smooth (*said of wine*)
**embocadura** *f* nozzle; mouthpiece (*of musical instrument*); skill in playing wind instrument; tip (*of cigarette*); bit (*of bridle*); taste (*of wine*); passage, narrows (*from sea into a river*); stage entrance; (arch.) proscenium arch
**embocar §86** *va* to put in the mouth; to put (*into or through a narrow passage*); to undertake, to take on; (coll.) to gulp down; (coll.) to try to put over (*something false*); **embocarle algo a uno** (coll.) to force something on someone; (coll.) to spring something on someone; *vn & vr* to go or enter (*into or through a narrow passage*)
**embocinado -da** *adj* trumpet-shaped
**embodegar §59** *va* to store, store away (*wine, olive oil, etc.*)
**embojar** *va* to place bushes in (*shelves for silkworm rearing*)
**embojo** *m* bush (*of southernwood, scrub oak, etc., for silk worms*)
**embolada** *f* stroke (*of piston*)
**embolado** *m* (theat.) minor rôle; bull with wooden balls on horns; (coll.) trick, deception
**embolador -dora** *mf* (Am.) shoeblack, shoeshine
**embolar** *va* to fit or equip (*bull's horns*) with wooden balls; to size (*for gilding*); to shine, polish (*shoes*)
**embolectomía** *f* (surg.) embolectomy
**embolia** *f* (path.) embolus, clot; (path.) embolism; **embolia aérea** (path.) air bends
**embolismal** *adj* embolismic
**embolismar** *va* (coll.) to gossip about, carry tales about; (Am.) to stir up, incite
**embolismático -ca** *adj* confused, muddled, incomprehensible
**embolísmico -ca** *adj* embolismic
**embolismo** *m* embolism (*to regularize calendar*); confusion, complication; mess, entanglement; (coll.) gossip, lie, fraud
**émbolo** *m* (mach.) piston; (path.) embolus, clot; **émbolo buzo** (mach.) plunger
**embolsar** *va* to pocket, to take in
**embolso** *m* pocketing
**embonada** *f* (naut.) sheathing
**embonar** *va* to improve; (naut.) to sheathe; (Am.) to fertilize
**embono** *m* (naut.) sheathing
**emboñigar §59** *va* to smear with cow dung
**emboque** *m* passage through a small opening; (coll.) cheat, deception, hoax; (coll.) fooling, trifling, idle talk
**emboquillar** *va* to put a tip on (*a cigarette*); to prepare (*a hole*) for blasting; to cut an entrance in (*a shaft or tunnel*); (Am.) to point or chink (*joints*)
**embornal** *m* (naut.) scupper
**emborrachador -dora** *adj* intoxicating
**emborrachamiento** *m* (coll.) drunkenness
**emborrachar** *va* to intoxicate; *vr* to become intoxicated, to get drunk; to be blinded (*by passion*); to run, to run together (*said of colors*); **emborracharse con** or **de** to get drunk on (*e.g., gin*)
**emborrar** *va* to stuff, to pad; to card a second time; (coll.) to gulp down
**emborrascar §86** *va* to stir up, to aggravate; *vr* to get stormy; to fail (*said of a business*); (Am.) to peter out (*said of a mine*)
**emborrazamiento** *m* larding a fowl
**emborrazar §76** *va* to lard (*a fowl*)
**emborricar §86** *vr* (coll.) to get all confused; (coll.) to fall madly in love
**emborrizar §76** *va* to give first combing to (*wool*); (prov.) to bread (*food for frying*); (prov.) to sugar-coat (*cake*)
**emborronador -dora** *adj* blotting, scribbling; *mf* scribbler
**emborronar** *va* to blot, to cover with blots, to scribble; *vr* to blot, to become blotted
**emborrullar** *vr* (coll.) to squabble or wrangle loudly
**emboscada** *f* ambush, ambuscade; **caer en una emboscada** to fall into an ambush; to fall into a trap
**emboscado** *m* draft dodger
**emboscadura** *f* var. of **emboscada**
**emboscar §86** *va* to ambush, put in hiding for surprise attack; *vr* to ambush, lie in ambush; to hide in the woods, go deep into the woods; to dodge work, to dodge responsibilities by taking an easy job
**embosquecer §34** *vn* to become wooded
**embostar** *va* to fertilize with manure; (Am.) to plaster (*walls*) with a mixture of earth and manure
**embotado -da** *adj* blunt, dull; (Am.) black-pawed
**embotadura** *f* bluntness, dullness
**embotamiento** *m* dulling; dullness
**embotar** *va* to blunt, to dull; (fig.) to dull, stupefy, enervate, weaken; to put (*tobacco*) in a jar; (Am.) to put leather sheathes on (*the spurs of a game cock*); *vr* to get dull; (coll.) to put on boots
**embotellado -da** *adj* prepared (*speech*); *m* bottling; bottleneck
**embotellador -dora** *adj* bottling; *mf* bottler; *f* bottling machine

**embotellamiento** *m* bottling; bottling up; traffic jam
**embotellar** *va* to bottle; to tie up; (nav.) to bottle up
**emboticar** §86 *vr* (Am.) to stuff oneself with medicine
**embotijar** *va* to put or keep in jugs; (mas.) to pave (*a surface*) with a layer of jugs to support a tile floor; *vr* (coll.) to swell, to puff up; (coll.) to get angry
**embovedar** *va* to arch, to vault; to enclose in a vault
**embozadamente** *adv* cautiously, equivocally
**embozado -da** *adj* wrapped up, disguised; obscure, puzzling, equivocal; *mf* person with muffled or concealed face
**embozalar** *va* to muzzle
**embozar** §76 *va* to cover (*the face*) with cloak or muffler; to muffle; to muzzle; to dissemble, to disguise; *vr* to muffle oneself up, to pull one's cloak over one's face
**embozo** *m* muffler, part of cloak held over the face; folded part of sheet touching the face; cunning, slyness, faked concern; **con embozo** with caution, with concealment; **de embozo** disguised; **quitarse el embozo** (coll.) to remove one's mask, to lay one's cards on the table; **sin embozo** openly, frankly
**embrace** *m* curtain clasp
**embracilado -da** *adj* constantly carried around in someone's arms (*said of a child*)
**embragar** §59 *va* to engage by means of the clutch; (mach.) to connect (*e.g., a shaft*); (naut.) to sling; *vn* to throw the clutch in
**embrague** *m* clutch; throwing in the clutch; **embrague de cono** cone clutch; **embrague de mordaza** dog clutch, jaw clutch
**embravecer** §34 *va* to enrage, infuriate; *vn* to get strong, gather strength (*said of plants*); *vr* to get angry; to swell, get rough (*said of sea*); **embravecerse con** o **contra** to get angry at or with
**embravecido -da** *adj* angry, furious; wild, rough
**embravecimiento** *m* anger, fury, rage
**embrazadura** *f* grasp, clasping; clasp of shield
**embrazar** §76 *va* to fasten (*shield*) to left arm; *vn* (mach.) to mesh, engage (*said of gears*)
**embreadura** *f* tarring; caulking with tar or pitch
**embrear** *va* to cover or soak with tar or pitch; to caulk with tar or pitch
**embregar** §59 *vr* to quarrel, to wrangle
**embreñar** *vr* to hide in the brambles
**embriagador -dora** *adj* intoxicating
**embriagar** §59 *va* to intoxicate; to transport, to enrapture; *vr* to get drunk
**embriaguez** *f* intoxication, drunkenness; rapture
**embridar** *va* to bridle; to govern, check, restrain
**embriogenia** *f* (biol.) embryogeny
**embriogénico -ca** *adj* embryogenic
**embriología** *f* embryology
**embriológico -ca** *adj* embryologic or embryological
**embriólogo -ga** *mf* embryologist
**embrión** *m* (biol., bot. & fig.) embryo; **en embrión** in embryo
**embrional** *adj* embryonal
**embrionario -ria** *adj* embryonic
**embroca** *f* poultice
**embrocación** *f* (med.) embrocation
**embrocar** §86 *va* to turn over to empty; to place upside down; to wind on a bobbin; to tack (*soles of shoes*) to the last; (taur.) to catch between the horns; *vr* (Am.) to put (*a garment*) on over the head; (Am.) to fall on one's face
**embrochalado** *m* header, header beam
**embrochalar** *va* to support with a crossbeam, to frame with a header beam
**embrolla** *f* (coll.) var. of **embrollo**
**embrollador -dora** *adj* embroiling, confusing; *mf* embroiler, troublemaker
**embrollar** *va* to embroil
**embrollo** *m* embroilment; imbroglio; lie, trick, deception; impasse, muddle, awkward situation
**embrollón -llona** *adj & mf* (coll.) var. of **embrollador**
**embrolloso -sa** *adj* (coll.) tangled, confusing
**embromado -da** *adj* annoyed; misty, hazy; (Am.) sick, ill; (Am.) in trouble
**embromador -dora** *mf* jokester; trickster; tease
**embromar** *va* to joke with, to make fun of; to tease; to cheat, deceive; to delay, hold up; *vr* (Am.) to dally, loiter; (Am.) to be bored
**embroquelar** *vr* to shield oneself, to defend oneself
**embroquetar** *va* to skewer the legs of (*fowl*)
**embrujado -da** *adj* bewitching
**embrujamiento** *m* bewitchment
**embrujar** *va* to bewitch
**embrujo** *m* spell, charm; charmer
**embrutecedor -dora** *adj* brutalizing, stupefying
**embrutecer** §34 *va* to brutalize, to stupefy
**embrutecimiento** *m* brutalization, stupefaction
**embuchacar** §86 *va* (Am.) to wound (*a fighting cock*) in the craw; (Am. slang) to make pregnant; (Am.) to keep (*a secret*)
**embuchado** *m* pork sausage; blind, subterfuge; fraudulent voting
**embuchar** *va* to stuff (*an animal*) with minced meat, to cram the maw of (*an animal*); (coll.) to gulp down
**embudador -dora** *mf* funneler
**embudar** *va* to put a funnel in; to trick; to snare, ensnare
**embudista** *adj* tricky, scheming; *mf* trickster, schemer
**embudo** *m* funnel; trick, fraud; (mil.) shell hole; **embudo de bomba** (mil.) bomb crater
**embullamiento** *m* (Am.) var. of **embullo**
**embullar** *va* to key up, excite; *vr* to become keyed up, become excited
**embullo** *m* (Am.) excitement, revelry
**emburriar** *va* (dial.) to push
**emburujar** *va* to make lumpy; to pile up, to jumble; *vr* to get lumpy; (Am.) to wrap oneself up, to be wrapped up
**embuste** *m* lie, trick, fraud; **embustes** *mpl* trinkets, baubles
**embustear** *vn* to be always lying, to be tricky all the time
**embustería** *f* (coll.) trick, imposture, deceit
**embustero -ra** *adj* lying; tricky; *mf* liar; trickster
**embutidera** *f* rivet set
**embutido -da** *adj* recessed, flush; *m* inlay, marquetry; sausage; (Am.) lace embroidery
**embutidor** *m* nail set; rivet set
**embutir** *va* to insert; to stuff, pack tight; to shrink, condense; to inlay; to set flush; to hammer, to fashion (*sheet metal*); to countersink; (naut.) to worm; (coll.) to gulp down, to cram; *vr* to squeeze in; (coll.) to stuff oneself
**emelga** *f* var. of **amelga**
**emenagogo -ga** *adj & m* (med.) emmenagogue
**emergencia** *f* emergence; emergency; happening, incident; (bot.) emergence
**emergente** *adj* emergent
**emerger** §49 *vn* to emerge; to surface (*said of a submarine*)
**emeritense** *adj* (pertaining to) Mérida; *mf* native or inhabitant of Mérida
**emérito -ta** *adj* emeritus, retired
**emersión** *f* emersion; surfacing (*of a submarine*); (astr.) emersion
**emético -ca** *adj* emetic; *m* emetic; tartar emetic
**emétrope** *mf* emmetrope
**emetropía** *f* emmetropia
**E.M.G.** abr. of **Estado Mayor General**
**emigración** *f* emigration; migration
**emigrado -da** *mf* émigré
**emigrante** *adj & mf* emigrant
**emigrar** *vn* to emigrate; to migrate
**emigratorio -ria** *adj* (pertaining to) emigration; migratory
**Emilia** *f* Emily
**eminencia** *f* eminence; (eccl.) Eminence
**eminente** *adj* eminent
**emir** *m* emeer, emir

**emisario -ria** *mf* emissary
**emisión** *f* emission; issuance; broadcast; (com.) issue; **emisión seriada** (rad.) serial
**emisionario -ria** *adj* (com.) issuing
**emisivo -va** *adj* emissive
**emisor -sora** *adj* emitting; broadcasting; *m* radio transmitter; wireless transmitter; *f* broadcasting station
**emitir** *va* to emit, send forth; to broadcast; to utter, express; to issue, give out; (com.) to issue
**Em.mo** abr. of **Eminentísimo**
**emoción** *f* emotion
**emocionadamente** *adv* with emotion, with feeling
**emocional** *adj* emotional
**emocionalismo** *m* emotionalism
**emocionante** *adj* moving, stirring, touching; thrilling
**emocionar** *va* to move, to stir, to touch, to stir the heart of; *vr* to be moved, be moved to pity
**emoliente** *adj & m* emollient
**emolumento** *m* emolument
**emotividad** *f* emotion, expression of emotion
**emotivo -va** *adj* emotive; emotional
**empacadizo -za** *adj* (Am.) touchy, easily angered
**empacado -da** *adj* (Am.) grim, gruff; (Am.) stubborn
**empacador -dora** *adj* packing, crating; (Am.) balky, stubborn; *f* packing machine, baling machine
**empacar §86** *va* to pack, to crate; (Am.) to anger; *vr* to balk, get balky; to be stubborn; to get rattled, become confused; (Am.) to get angry
**empacón -cona** *adj* (Am.) stubborn; (Am.) balky
**empachado -da** *adj* awkward, backward, fumbling; surfeited, upset; (naut.) cluttered (*said of deck*)
**empachar** *va* to hinder, impede; to disguise; to overload, surfeit, upset, give indigestion to; *vr* to be embarrassed, to blush; to be upset, have indigestion
**empacho** *m* hindrance, obstacle; surfeit, indigestion; embarrassment, bashfulness
**empachoso -sa** *adj* surfeiting, sickening; shameful
**empadrar** *vr* to be too attached to one's father or one's parents (*said of a child*)
**empadronador** *m* census taker
**empadronamiento** *m* census; taking of census; registration
**empadronar** *va* to register, take the census of (*inhabitants for police, taxes, voting, etc.*); *vr* to register, be counted in the census
**empajada** *f* straw and bran soaked together for horses
**empajar** *va* to fill or cover with straw; to pack with straw; to bottom (*a chair*) with straw or rush; (Am.) to roof with straw; *vr* (coll.) to feather one's nest; (Am.) to get more than enough
**empajolar §77** *va* to fumigate with a sulphur match (*the inside of jugs, casks, etc., that have been washed*)
**empalagamiento** *m* var. of **empalago**
**empalagar §59** *va* to surfeit, pall, cloy; to bore, weary, annoy
**empalago** *m* surfeit, cloying; bore, annoyance
**empalagoso -sa** *adj* sickening, sickeningly sweet; mawkish; fawning; *mf* fawning bore
**empalamiento** *m* impalement
**empalar** *va* to impale
**empaliada** *f* bunting
**empaliar** *va* to decorate with bunting
**empalizada** *f* stockade, fence, palisade
**empalizar §76** *va* to stockade, to fence, to fence in
**empalmadura** *f* var. of **empalme**
**empalmar** *va* to join, connect, couple, splice; to combine; to palm (*a card*); *vn* to connect, make connections; to bisect; **empalmar con** to follow, to succeed; *vr* to hold a knife hidden between one's palm and sleeve
**empalme** *m* joint, connection, coupling, splice; combination; palming; (elec.) joint; (rail.) junction, connection
**empalmillar** *va* to welt (*a shoe*)
**empalmo** *m* (arch.) lintel
**empalomado** *m* loose-stone dam, dam of dry masonry
**empalomar** *va* (naut.) to sew (*boltrope and sail*)
**empalletado** *m* (naut.) mattress barricade
**empampar** *vr* (Am.) to get lost on the pampas
**empanada** *f* see **empanado**
**empanadilla** *f* pie; folding carriage step
**empanado -da** *adj* without windows or openings, unlighted, unventilated; breaded; *f* pie, meat pie, vegetable pie; fraud, concealment
**empanar** *va* (cook.) to bread; to sow with wheat; *vr* (agr.) to be choked with too much seed
**empandar** *va* to bend, to make sag; *vr* to bend, to sag
**empandillar** *va* to slip (*two or more cards together*) in order to cheat; to dupe, to hoax
**empanizado** *m* (Am.) bread crumbs
**empanizar §76** *va* (Am.) to bread (*e.g., a cutlet*)
**empantanar** *va* to flood, to swamp; to hold up, obstruct; *vr* to become flooded, become swamped
**empañado -da** *adj* misty; flat (*said, e.g., of voice*)
**empañadura** *f* swaddling, swaddling clothes
**empañar** *va* to swaddle; to dim, dull, blur, fog; to tarnish, to sully; *vr* to dim, dull, blur, fog; to film, to mist; to become sad or gloomy
**empañetar** *va* (Am.) to plaster
**empañicar §86** *va* (naut.) to hand, to furl
**empapagayar** *vr* to act like a parrot; to curve one's nose like the beak of a parrot
**empapamiento** *m* soaking, saturation; ecstasy, trance
**empapar** *va* to soak, saturate; to soak up; to drench, soak in, penetrate; *vr* to soak; to be soaked; (coll.) to be surfeited; **empaparse en** to soak in, to soak up, to saturate; to be imbued with
**empapelado** *m* paper, papering, paper hanging; paper lining
**empapelador -dora** *mf* paper hanger
**empapelar** *va* to wrap up in paper; to paper; to line with paper; to wallpaper
**empapirotar** *va & vr* to dress up, to dress elaborately
**empapuciar** or **empapujar** *va* (coll.) to stuff, to feed too much
**empaque** *m* packing; (coll.) look, appearance, mien; solemnness, stiffness; (Am.) nerve, brazenness
**empaquetado -da** *adj* snappily dressed; *m* (mach.) packing
**empaquetador -dora** *mf* packer; *f* packing machine
**empaquetadura** *f* packing; gasket
**empaquetar** *va* to pack; to jam, stuff, pack; to dress up; (mach.) to pack
**emparamentar** *va* to adorn, bedeck
**emparchar** *va* to apply plaster to; (naut.) to stop up (*a leak*) with rope mat
**emparedado -da** *mf* recluse; *m* sandwich
**emparedamiento** *m* immurement, confinement; prison; cloister
**emparedar** *va* to wall in, to immure, to confine
**emparejadura** *f* equaling, evening, matching
**emparejamiento** *m* matching; smoothing, leveling; evening up
**emparejar** *va* to pair, to match; to even, make even; to smooth, to level off; to close (*a door*) flush; *vn* to come up, catch up, come abreast; **emparejar con** to catch up with; to be even with; *vr* to pair, to match
**emparentado -da** *adj* related by marriage; related
**emparentar §18** *vn* to become related by marriage; **emparentar con** to marry into (*e.g., a rich family*)
**emparrado** *m* arbor, bower
**emparrar** *va* to embower
**emparrillado** *m* grate, grating, grillage, grid
**emparrillar** *va* to grill; *vr* (Am.) to go to bed
**emparvar** *va* to heap (*grain*) for thrashing
**empastador -dora** *mf* (Am.) bookbinder; *m* paste brush

**empastadura** *f* filling (*of a tooth*); (Am.) binding (*of a book*)
**empastar** *va* to cover or fill with paste; to bind (*a book*) with stiff covers; to fill (*a tooth*); (f.a.) to impaste; *vr* (Am.) to be covered with underbrush
**empaste** *m* filling (*of a tooth*); binding in stiff boards; (paint.) harmony of colors
**empastelamiento** *m* (print.) pieing
**empastelar** *va* (coll.) to settle in a hurry without regard to right or wrong; (coll.) to botch (*a word or words in typing*); (print.) to pie
**empatar** *va, vn & vr* to tie (*in games and elections*); **empatársela a uno** to tie someone (*in games and elections*)
**empate** *m* tie, draw; (Am.) penholder
**empatía** *f* (psychol.) empathy
**empavar** *va* (Am.) to kid, to razz
**empavesada** *f* (naut.) armings, waistcloths
**empavesado** *m* soldier provided with a shield; dressing of a ship, bunting
**empavesar** *va* to bedeck with flags or bunting; to dress (*a ship*); to veil (*a monument for ceremony of unveiling*)
**empavón -vona** *adj* (Am.) easily kidded
**empavonar** *va* to blue (*iron or steel*); (Am.) to grease; *vr* (Am.) to dress up
**empecatado -da** *adj* incorrigible, evil-minded, devilish; ill-starred, unlucky
**empecer §34** *va* (archaic) to damage, hurt; *vn* to stand in the way
**empecimiento** *m* (archaic) damage; obstacle
**empecinado -da** *adj* stubborn; *m* pitch maker
**empecinamiento** *m* stubbornness
**empecinar** *va* to dip in pitch; to fill with mud; *vr* (Am.) to be stubborn, to persist
**empedernido -da** *adj* hardened, hard-hearted; inveterate
**empedernir §53** *va* to harden; *vr* to harden, get hard; to become hard-hearted
**Empédocles** *m* Empedocles
**empedrado -da** *adj* cloud-flecked; pock-marked; (Am.) black-spotted (*horse*); *m* paving; stone paving
**empedrador** *m* stone paver
**empedramiento** *m* stone paving; pile of stones at base of bridge pier
**empedrar §18** *va* to pave with stones; to sprinkle, to bespatter
**empega** *f* pitch; mark made with pitch on sheep
**empegado** *m* tarpaulin
**empegadura** *f* coat of pitch; coating with pitch
**empegar §59** *va* to cover or coat with pitch; to mark (*sheep*) with pitch
**empego** *m* marking sheep with pitch
**empeguntar** *va* to mark (*sheep*) with pitch
**empeine** *m* pubes; instep; vamp; (bot.) cotton flower; (bot.) liverwort; (path.) tetter
**empeinoso -sa** *adj* tetterous
**empelar** *vn* to grow hair; to have like coats (*said of two or more horses*)
**empelazgar §59** *vn* (coll.) to get into a quarrel
**empelechar** *va* to cover or line with marble; to lay (*slabs of marble*)
**empelotar** *vr* (coll.) to get all tangled up or confused; to get involved in a row; (Am.) to strip, to take all one's clothes off
**empeltre** *m* (hort.) side graft
**empella** *f* vamp, upper
**empellar** *va* to push, shove, jostle
**empellejar** *va* to cover with skins, to line with skins
**empeller §46** *va* var. of **empellar**
**empellón** *m* push, shove; **a empellones** roughly, violently
**empenachar** *va* to adorn with plumes, to plume
**empenaje** *m* (aer.) empennage
**empenta** *f* prop, stay, shoring
**empentar** *va* (min.) to wall, wall up; (dial.) to push, shove
**empeñado -da** *adj* bitter, heated (*dispute*); persistent, determined
**empeñar** *va* to pawn; to pledge; to involve; to force, engage, compel; to begin (*a battle, dispute, etc.*); *vr* to bind oneself; to insist; to go in debt; to start (*said of a battle, dispute, etc.*); (naut.) to risk running aground; **empeñarse en** to engage in (*e.g., a battle, dispute*); to persist in, to insist on; to go in debt to the amount of; **empeñarse en** + *inf* to insist on + *ger;* **empeñarse por** to intercede for or in behalf of
**empeñero -ra** *mf* (Am.) pawnbroker
**empeño** *m* pledge, obligation, engagement; pawn; pawnshop; persistence, insistence; perseverance; eagerness, determination; endeavor, effort; favor, protection; pledge, backer, patron; **con empeño** eagerly, with determination
**empeñoso -sa** *adj* (Am.) eager, determined; (Am.) diligent
**empeoramiento** *m* impairment, worsening
**empeorar** *va* to make worse, impair; *vn & vr* to get worse
**empequeñecer §34** *va* to dwarf, to make smaller, to diminish; to belittle
**empequeñecimiento** *m* diminution, lessening; belittling
**emperador** *m* emperor; **emperadores** *mpl* emperor and empress
**emperatriz** *f* (*pl:* **-trices**) empress
**emperchar** *va* to hang on a clothes rack; *vr* to be caught in a snare
**emperdigar §59** *va* to prepare; to brown (*meat*); to broil (*partridges*)
**emperejilar** *va & vr* (coll.) to dress up, to dress fancily
**emperezar §76** *va* to make lazy; to delay, to slow down; *vr* to be or become lazy
**empergaminar** *va* to bind with parchment
**empericar §86** *vr* (Am.) to get drunk
**emperifollar** *va & vr* to dress up gaudily, to spruce up
**empernar** *va* to bolt, to bolt together
**empero** *conj* but; however
**emperrada** *f* tresillo (*card game*)
**emperramiento** *m* obstinacy, stubbornness
**emperrar** *vr* (coll.) to be or get obstinate or stubborn; (Am.) to cry, to burst out crying
**empetro** *m* (bot.) samphire
**empezar §31** *va & vn* to begin; **empezar a** + *inf* to begin to + *inf*, to begin + *ger;* **empezar por** + *inf* to begin by + *ger*
**empicar §86** *vr* to become too fond, to become infatuated, to be taken in
**empicotadura** *f* pillorying
**empicotar** *va* to pillory
**empiece** *m* (coll.) beginning
**empiema** *m* (path.) empyema; (surg.) operation to drain empyema
**empilar** *va* to pile, pile up
**empilonar** *va* (Am.) to pile up (*dried tobacco leaves*)
**empinado -da** *adj* high, lofty; stiff, stuck-up; (her.) saltant, salient; *f* (aer.) zooming; **irse a la empinada** to rear (*said, e.g., of a horse*)
**empinadura** *f* or **empinamiento** *m* elevation, raising; rising, towering
**empinar** *va* to raise, lift; to raise and tip over; (coll.) to crook (*the elbow*); (aer.) to zoom; *vn* (coll.) to drink, be a toper; *vr* to stand on tiptoe; to rear (*said, e.g., of a horse*); to rise high, to tower; (aer.) to zoom; (Am.) to overeat
**empingorotado -da** *adj* of high and influential social standing; proud, haughty
**empingorotar** *va* (coll.) to put on top; *vr* (coll.) to get up, to climb up (*e.g., on a table or chair*); (coll.) to be proud, be haughty
**empino** *m* (arch.) vertex of a cross vault
**empiñonado** *m* candied pine-nut kernel
**empíreo -a** *adj* empyrean or empyreal; *m* empyrean
**empireuma** *m* (chem.) empyreuma
**empírico -ca** *adj* empiric or empirical; *mf* empiricist
**empirismo** *m* empiricism
**empirista** *mf* empiricist
**empitonar** *va* (taur.) to catch with the horns
**empizarrado** *m* slate roof
**empizarrar** *va* to slate, to roof with slate
**emplastadura** *f* or **emplastamiento** *m* application of plasters; application of make-up or paint; make-up
**emplastar** *va* to apply a plaster to; to put make-up on; to smear up; (coll.) to tie up (*a deal*); *vr* to put on make-up; to smear oneself up

**emplastecer** §34 *va* (paint.) to smooth with filler
**emplástico -ca** *adj* sticky
**emplasto** *m* plaster, poultice; unsatisfactory compromise or settlement; (coll.) splotch (*on clothing or body*); (coll.) weakling; (coll.) misfit (*person*); patch, tire patch
**emplástrico -ca** *adj* var. of **emplástico**
**emplazamiento** *m* summoning; (law) summons; emplacement, location, site
**emplazar** §76 *va* to summons; (law) to summon; to place, locate
**empleado -da** *mf* clerk; employee
**emplear** *va* to employ, to engage; to use, use up; **estarle a uno bien empleado** (coll.) to serve someone right; *vr* to be employed; to busy oneself; **empleársele bien a uno** (coll.) to serve someone right
**empleita** *f* plaited strand of esparto grass; (Am.) straw hat
**empleitero -ra** *mf* plaiter and vender of esparto grass
**emplenta** *f* section of mud wall made in one form; wall plastered on only one side; masonry with rubble between the facings
**empleo** *m* employ, employment; use; public office; (mil.) rank
**empleomanía** *f* (coll.) zeal or eagerness to hold public office; (Am.) excessive number of people eager to hold public office
**emplomado** *m* lead roof
**emplomador** *m* leadworker
**emplomadura** *f* leadwork, leading; lead covering, lead lining; (Am.) plumbing
**emplomar** *va* to lead; to cover or roof with lead; to line with lead; to place a lead seal on (*e.g., a bale*); (Am.) to fill (*a tooth*)
**emplumar** *va* to put a feather or feathers on; to tar and feather; to thrash; **emplumarlas** (Am.) to flee, beat it; *vn* to fledge, to get feathers
**emplumecer** §34 *vn* to fledge, to get feathers
**empobrecedor -dora** *adj* impoverishing
**empobrecer** §34 *va* to impoverish; to weaken; *vn & vr* to become poor or impoverished
**empobrecimiento** *m* impoverishment
**empodrecer** §34 *vn & vr* to rot
**empolvado -da** *adj* (Am.) rusty (*out of practice*)
**empolvar** *va* to cover with dust; to powder, to put powder on; *vr* to become covered with dust; to become covered with powder; (Am.) to get rusty (*in knowledge or skill*)
**empolvoramiento** *m* covering with dust; powdering
**empolvorar** *va* var. of **empolvar**
**empolvorizar** §76 *va* var. of **empolvar**
**empollado -da** *adj* (coll.) shut-in; **ir bien empollado** (coll.) to be primed for an examination
**empolladura** *f* brooding; brood; brood of bees
**empollar** *va* to brood, hatch (*eggs*); (coll.) to bone up on; *vn* to breed (*said of insects*); (coll.) to grind, to study hard; **empollar sobre** (coll.) to bone up on
**empollón -llona** *mf* (scornful) grind (*student*)
**emponchado -da** *adj* (Am.) poncho-wearing; (Am.) suspicious-looking
**emponzoñador -dora** *adj* poisoning; *mf* poisoner
**emponzoñamiento** *m* poisoning
**emponzoñar** *va* to poison; to corrupt
**empopar** *va* (naut.) to turn (*the stern*) toward the wind; *vn* (naut.) to be down by the stern; (naut.) to sail before the wind
**emporcar** §95 *va* to soil, to dirty; *vn* to get soiled, get dirty
**emporio** *m* emporium; center of culture
**empotrado -da** *adj* built-in; set-in, recessed
**empotramiento** *m* planting, embedding, fastening; interlocking; (carp.) abutment, abutting joint
**empotrar** *va* to plant, embed, recess, fix in a wall; to scarf, to splice; *vn & vr* to interlock
**empozar** §76 *va* to throw or put into a well; to soak (*flax*); *vn* to form into puddles; *vr* (coll.) to fail to be carried out
**empradizar** §76 *va* to convert into pasture land
**emprendedor -dora** *adj* enterprising
**emprender** *va* to undertake; **emprenderla con** (coll.) to pester, to squabble with, to have it out with; **emprenderla para** (coll.) to set out for
**empreñar** *va* to impregnate, make pregnant; *vr* to become pregnant
**empresa** *f* enterprise, undertaking; motto, device; concern, company, firm; **la empresa** management (*as distinguished from labor*); **empresa anunciadora** advertising agency; **empresa constructora** building concern; **empresa de tranvías** traction company
**empresario -ria** *mf* contractor; industrialist, business leader; manager; theatrical manager; impresario; **empresario de circo** showman; **empresario de pompas fúnebres** undertaker; **empresario de publicidad** advertising man
**emprestar** *va* to borrow; (slang) to lend
**empréstito** *m* loan, government loan
**emprima** *f* first fruits
**emprimado** *m* second combing of wool
**emprimar** *va* to give a second combing to (*wool*); (paint.) to prime; (coll.) to hoodwink, to dupe, to defraud
**empringar** §59 *va & vr* var. of **pringar**
**empuchar** *va* to buck (*skeins of thread*)
**empujador -dora** *adj* pushing; *m & f* pusher; **empujadora niveladora** bulldozer
**empujar** *va* to push, to shove; to dismiss; to replace; *vn* to push, to shove; **empujad** or **empujar** push (*word on public door*)
**empujatierra** *f* bulldozer
**empuje** *m* push; thrust; (fig.) push, energy, enterprise; (phys.) thrust
**empujón** *m* push, hard shove; rapid progress; **a empujones** (coll.) roughly, violently; (coll.) by fits and starts; **tratar a empujones** (coll.) to push around
**empulgadura** *f* bending the bow of a crossbow; tenseness of string of crossbow
**empulgar** §59 *va* to bend the bow of (*a crossbow*); to fill with fleas
**empulguera** *f* wing of crossbow; **empulgueras** *fpl* thumbscrew (*instrument of torture*)
**empuntar** *va* to put a point on; **empuntarlas** (Am.) to beat it, run away
**empuñadura** *f* hilt (*of sword*); first words of a story; (Am.) handle (*e.g., of an umbrella*)
**empuñar** *va* to clutch, to grasp; to obtain (*a job*); **empuñar el cetro** to start to reign, to ascend the throne
**empuñidura** *f* (naut.) earing
**empurpurar** *va* to empurple
**emú** *m* (*pl:* **emúes**) (orn.) emu
**emulación** *f* emulation
**emulador -dora** *adj* emulative, emulating; *mf* emulator
**emular** *va & vn* to emulate; **emular con** to emulate, vie with
**emulgente** *adj* emulgent
**émulo -la** *adj* emulous; *mf* rival, emulator
**emulsión** *f* emulsion
**emulsionamiento** *m* emulsification
**emulsionar** *va* to emulsify
**emulsivo -va** *adj* emulsive
**emulsor** *m* emulsor, emulsifier
**emunción** *f* excretion
**emuntorio -ria** *adj & m* emunctory
**en** *prep* at, e.g., **estuvo en el teatro anoche** he was at the theater last night; in, e.g., **está en Madrid ahora** he is now in Madrid; **escribió la carta en francés** he wrote the letter in French; into, e.g., **entró en el cuarto silenciosamente** he came quietly into the room; by, e.g., **le conocí en el andar** I knew him by his walk; of, e.g., **pensaba en mis dos hermanos** I was thinking of my two brothers; on, e.g., **puso el libro en la mesa** he put the book on the table
**enaceitar** *va* to oil, grease; to spot with oil; *vr* to become oily or rancid
**enacerar** *va* to steel, make steely, harden
**enagua** *f* petticoat, underskirt; **enaguas** *fpl* petticoat
**enaguachar** *va* to spill water over, to soak with water, to flood; to upset the stomach of; *vr* to become upset (*from excessive eating or drinking*)

**enaguar §23** *va* to spill water over, to flood
**enaguazar §76** *va* to flood; *vr* to flood, become flooded
**enagüillas** *fpl* short skirt, kilt
**enajenable** *adj* alienable
**enajenación** *f* alienation; rapture; distraction, absence of mind; **enajenación mental** mental derangement
**enajenamiento** *m* var. of **enajenación**
**enajenar** *va* to transport, enrapture; to alienate, dispose of (*property*); to alienate (*a friend*); *vr* to be transported, enraptured; **enajenarse de** to get rid of (*property*); to become alienated from (*a friend*)
**enálage** *f* (gram.) enallage
**enalbar** *va* to make white-hot in a forge
**enalbardar** *va* to saddle, to put a packsaddle on; to dip in a batter; to lard (*a fowl*)
**enalmagrado -da** *adj* vile, despicable
**enalmagrar** *va* to color with red ocher
**enaltecer §34** to exalt, extol; *vr* to be exalted, be extolled
**enaltecimiento** *m* exaltation, exalting, extolling
**enamarillecer §34** *vn & vr* to become or to turn yellow
**enamoradamente** *adv* lovingly
**enamoradizo -za** *adj* susceptible (*to love*)
**enamorado -da** *adj* in love, lovesick; susceptible (*to love*); *mf* sweetheart; *m* lover
**enamorador -dora** *adj* wooing, love-making; *mf* wooer, love-maker, suitor
**enamoramiento** *m* love, love-making; falling in love
**enamorar** *va* to enamor, to inspire love in; to make love to; *vr* to fall in love; **enamorarse de** to fall in love with
**enamoricar §86** *vr* (coll.) to trifle in love, to be slightly in love
**enamoriscar §86** *vr* (dial. & Am.) var. of **enamoricar**
**enanchar** *va* (coll.) to widen
**enangostar** *va & vr* to narrow
**enanismo** *m* dwarfism, nanism
**enano -na** *adj* dwarfish; *mf* dwarf
**enante** *f* (bot.) water fennel
**enarbolar** *va* to hoist, raise on high, hang out (*e.g., a flag*); to brandish (*e.g., a sword*); *vr* to get angry; to rear
**enarcar §86** *va* to arch; to hoop (*barrels*)
**enardecer §34** *va* to inflame, to fire, to excite; *vr* to get excited; to become inflamed (*said, e.g., of a sore*)
**enardecimiento** *m* inflaming; excitement; inflammation (*e.g., of a sore*)
**enarenación** *f* sanding; coat of plaster (*in final preparation for painting a wall*)
**enarenar** *va* to sand, throw sand on; (min.) to mix fine sand with (*silver ore*) to speed amalgamation; *vn* (naut.) to run aground
**enarmonar** *va* to stand up; *vr* to rear
**enarmónico -ca** *adj* (mus.) enharmonic
**enartrosis** *f* (anat.) enarthrosis
**enastado -da** *adj* horned; antlered
**enastar** *va* to put a handle on, to put a shaft on
**enastillar** *va* to put a handle on
**encabalgamiento** *m* gun carriage; (pros.) enjambement
**encabalgar §59** *va* to provide with horses; *vn* to rest, to lean
**encaballado** *m* (print.) pieing, jumbling (*of type and lines*)
**encaballar** *va* to overlap; (print.) to pi; *vn* to rest, to lean; *vr* to overlap; (print.) to be pied
**encabellecer §34** *vr* to grow hair
**encabestradura** *f* (vet.) halter sore (*on pastern*)
**encabestrar** *va* to put (*a halter*) on; to lead by a halter; to subdue, to win over; *vr* to get a front leg entangled in the halter
**encabezado** *m* process of fortifying wines
**encabezamiento** *m* census, tax list, tax rate; heading, headline, title; caption; opening words (*of a document*); **encabezamiento de factura** billhead
**encabezar §76** *va* to draw up (*a tax list*); to head, to lead; to put a heading or title to; to fortify (*wine*); (carp.) to scarf, to join; *vr* to compromise, to settle
**encabillar** *va* to dowel, to pin
**encabrahigar §59** *va* var. of **cabrahigar**
**encabriar** *va* to put in the rafters for (*the roof*)
**encabritar** *vr* to rear (*said of a horse*); (aer. & naut.) to shoot up, to nose up
**encachado** *m* stone or concrete lining of bed of stream or sewer, riprap
**encachar** *va* to line with stones or concrete (*the bed of a stream, trench, or sewer*), to riprap
**encadar** *vr* to get scared, become intimidated
**encadenación** *f* chaining; connecting, connection; concatenation
**encadenado** *m* (arch.) buttress
**encadenadura** *f* or **encadenamiento** *m* var. of **encadenación**
**encadenar** *va* to chain, to enchain, to put in chains; to brace, to buttress; (mas.) to bond; to connect, tie together, bind; to tie down, immobilize; *vr* to be linked together, to hang together
**encajador** *m* enchaser; enchasing tool
**encajadura** *f* inserting, insertion, fitting; recess, groove, socket
**encajar** *va* to put, to insert; to enchase; to fit, make fit; to put in (*a joke or remark*); to put in (*a joke or remark*) inopportunely; to tell (*a story*) at the wrong time; to put away (*money*); to give, let go (*e.g., a blow*); (coll.) to throw, to hurl; **encajar una cosa a uno** (coll.) to force something on someone, to palm off something on someone; (coll.) to force someone to listen to something; *vn* to fit, to close right (*said, e.g., of a door*); to be fitting or appropriate; **encajar con** or **en** to fit into, to fit, to match; *vr* (coll.) to put on (*a garment*); to squeeze, to squeeze one's way; (coll.) to intrude, butt in
**encaje** *m* insertion; fitting, matching; recess, groove, socket; lace; inlay, mosaic; fit, look, appearance; **encaje de bolillos** bobbin lace, bone lace, pillow lace; **encaje de Malinas** malines, Mechlin lace
**encajero -ra** *mf* lacemaker; lace dealer
**encajetillar** *va* to put (*cigarettes or tobacco*) in packages or packs
**encajonado** *m* cofferdam; (mas.) coffer
**encajonamiento** *m* boxing, crating; narrowing (*of a stream or river*)
**encajonar** *va* to box, to case, to crate; to squeeze in or through; to dovetail; to coffer; to buttress; *vr* to narrow, to run through a narrow channel or ravine; to squeeze in or through
**encalabozar §76** *va* (coll.) to throw into jail
**encalabrinar** *va* to make dizzy (*said, e.g., of an odor*); to rattle, to fluster; *vr* (coll.) to get stubborn, to get a fixed idea in one's mind
**encalada** *f* metal ornament on harness
**encalado** *m* var. of **encaladura**
**encalador -dora** *mf* whitewasher; *m* lime pit, lime vat
**encaladura** *f* whitewashing; (agr.) liming
**encalar** *va* to whitewash; to lime (*hides*); (agr.) to lime; to sprinkle with lime, to treat with lime
**encalmado -da** *adj* (naut.) becalmed; (com.) quiet (*market*)
**encalmadura** *f* (vet.) overheating
**encalmar** *vr* (vet.) to be overheated; (naut.) to be becalmed
**encalostrar** *vr* to be sick with colostration, to get sick from the first milk
**encalvecer §34** *vn* to become bald
**encalladero** *m* (naut.) shoal, sand bank
**encalladura** *f* running aground
**encallar** *vn* to run aground; to fail; to get entangled in a deal
**encallecer §34** *vn* to get corns, get calluses; *vr* to get corns, get calluses; to become callous, become hardened
**encallejonar** *va & vr* to run down an alley or narrow passage
**encamación** *f* (min.) shoring, support
**encamar** *va* to stretch out on the ground or the floor; *vr* (coll.) to take to bed; to lie down, to hide (*said of game*); to bend over, to droop (*said of grain*)

**encamarar** *va* to store (*grain or fruit*)
**encambijar** *va* to store and distribute (*water*)
**encambrar** *va* var. of **encamarar**
**encambronar** *va* to hedge with brambles; to reinforce with iron
**encaminadura** *f* or **encaminamiento** *m* directing, forwarding
**encaminar** *va* to set on the way, to show the way to; to forward; to direct (*e.g., one's energies, one's attention*); **encaminar a** + *inf* to guide or direct (*someone*) to + *inf; vr* to set out, to be on one's way
**encamisada** *f* (mil.) camisade, night attack; night masquerade
**encamisar** *va* to put a shirt on (*a person*); to put slip covers on; to hide, conceal, disguise; *vr* to put one's shirt on; (mil.) to make a camisade or night attack
**encamo** *m* hiding place (*of game*)
**encampanado -da** *adj* bell-shaped
**encanalar** *va* to pipe, to channel
**encanalizar §76** *va* var. of **encanalar**
**encanallamiento** *m* corruption, depravity
**encanallar** *va* to corrupt, to deprave; *vr* to become corrupt, to get depraved; to associate with low company, to keep bad company
**encanar** *vr* to stiffen with anger (*said of an infant*)
**encanastar** *va* to put in a basket
**encancerar** *vr* to have cancer; to become cancerous
**encandecer §34** *va* to make white-hot, to make incandescent
**encandelar** *vn* to blossom with catkin
**encandiladera** *f* (coll.) procuress, bawd
**encandilado -da** *adj* (coll.) stiff, erect; (coll.) cocked (*hat*)
**encandiladora** *f* (coll.) var. of **encandiladera**
**encandilamiento** *m* glare
**encandilante** *adj* sparkling; dazzling
**encandilar** *va* to dazzle; (fig.) to dazzle, bewilder; (coll.) to stir (*a fire*); *vr* to sparkle, to flash (*said of eyes*)
**encanecer §34** *va* (poet.) to turn white; *vn & vr* to become gray or gray-haired; to become old; to become moldy
**encanijamiento** *m* weakening, emaciation
**encanijar** *va* to make sick or weak; *vr* to get sickly, become emaciated
**encanillar** *va* to wind on a spool
**encantación** *f* var. of **encantamento**
**encantado -da** *adj* satisfied, delighted; (coll.) absent-minded, in a trance; (coll.) empty and spacious, rambling (*said of a house*); *mf* (coll.) person on whom a spell has been cast
**encantador -dora** *adj* enchanting, charming, delightful; *mf* charmer; **encantador de serpientes** snake charmer; *m* enchanter; *f* enchantress
**encantamento** or **encantamiento** *m* spell; enchantment, charm, delight
**encantar** *va* to cast a spell on, to bewitch; to enchant, charm, delight; **encantar a uno** + *inf* to enchant, charm, delight someone to + *inf*
**encantarar** *va* to put into a jar or ballot box
**encante** *m* auction, public sale; auction house
**encanto** *m* var. of **encantamento**
**encantorio** *m* (coll.) var. of **encantamento**
**encantusar** *va* (coll.) to wheedle, to coax
**encanutar** *va* to shape like a tube; to put in a tube; to put (*a cigarette*) in a holder
**encañada** *f* gorge, ravine
**encañado** *m* water pipe; trellis of reeds
**encañador -dora** *mf* silk winder
**encañar** *va* to pipe; to drain with pipes; to prop up (*plants*) with reeds; to wind on a spool; *vn & vr* to form stalks (*said of cereals*)
**encañizada** *f* reed fence; reed fence to catch fish, weir
**encañizar §76** *va* to set up frame for (*silkworms*); to line (*a vault*) with a web of reeds and rope
**encañonar** *va* to pipe; to wind on a spool; to plait, to fold; to tip in (*a sheet of paper in a book*); *vn* to fledge out
**encapachadura** *f* pile of bags full of olives for pressing
**encapachar** *va* to put (*e.g., olives*) in bags for pressing
**encapar** *va* to put a cloak on; *vr* to put on one's cloak
**encapazar §76** *va* var. of **encapachar**
**encaperuzar §76** *va* to put a hood on; *vr* to put on one's hood
**encapillar** *va* to put a hood or cowl on; to hood (*a falcon*); (naut.) to rig (*the yards*); (min.) to start a new gallery in; **lo encapillado** (coll.) what one has on; *vr* (coll.) to put on (*a garment, especially over the head*)
**encapirotar** *va* to put a hood on; *vr* to put on one's hood
**encapotado -da** *adj* overcast, overclouded
**encapotadura** *f* or **encapotamiento** *m* grim look, frown
**encapotar** *va* to cloak; *vr* to put on one's cloak; to look grim, to frown; to become overcast, become overclouded; to pull the mouth down too close to the chest (*said of a horse*)
**encaprichar** *vr* to persist in one's whims; **encapricharse con** or **en** to whimsically set one's mind upon; **encapricharse por** (coll.) to be or become infatuated with
**encapuchar** *va* to put a cowl or hood on; *vr* to put one's cowl or hood on
**encapuzar §76** *va* to put a cowl on; *vr* to put on one's cowl
**encaracolado** *m* spiral adornment
**encaracolar** *va* to give a spiral shape or form to
**encarado -da** *adj* faced, featured, favored; **bien encarado** well-featured, well-favored; **mal encarado** ill-featured, ill-favored
**encaramar** *va* to raise, lift up, elevate; to praise, extol; (coll.) to elevate, dignify, exalt; *vr* to climb; to get on top; to rise, rise up; (Am.) to blush
**encaramiento** *m* aiming, pointing; facing, encounter
**encarar** *va* to aim, to point; to face (*a problem, question, etc.*); *vn & vr* to come face to face; **encararse a** or **con** to face, confront, stand up to
**encaratular** *vr* to put on a mask, to mask oneself
**encarcavinar** *va* to put in a grave, to bury; to suffocate, asphyxiate; to choke with a foul odor
**encarcelación** *f* or **encarcelamiento** *m* incarceration, imprisonment
**encarcelar** *va* to jail, incarcerate, imprison; (carp.) to clamp (*glued parts*); to plaster in, to imbed in mortar; (naut.) to woold; *vr* to stay indoors
**encare** *m* aiming
**encarecer §34** *va* to raise the price of; to raise (*the price or cost*); to extol; to overrate; to urge; **encarecer que** + *subj* to urge to + *inf; vn & vr* to rise in price
**encarecidamente** *adv* insistently, eagerly
**encarecimiento** *m* increase; extolling, overrating; **con encarecimiento** insistently, eagerly
**encargado -da** *mf* representative, person in charge, agent; **encargado de negocios** chargé d'affaires; **encargado de vía** (rail.) roadmaster, supervisor
**encargamiento** *m* duty, obligation
**encargar §59** *va* to entrust; to urge, to warn; to order (*goods*); to summon; to ask for, to request; **encargar algo a uno** to entrust someone with something, to put someone in charge of something; **encargar que** + *subj* to entrust with + *ger;* to urge to + *inf; vr* to take charge; **encargarse de** to be in charge of, to take charge of, to undertake; **encargarse de** + *inf* to take charge of + *ger*, to undertake to + *inf*
**encargo** *m* charge, commission, job, assignment, responsibility; warning; order; request; employment, office; **ni de encargo** (coll.) as if made to order
**encariñamiento** *m* endearment
**encariñar** *va* to awaken love or affection in; *vr* to become fond; **encariñarse con** to become fond of, become attached to
**encarna** *f* feeding entrails to hunting dogs
**encarnación** *f* incarnation; (theol.) Incarnation; (f.a.) flesh color, incarnadine
**encarnadino -na** *adj* reddish, pink
**encarnado -da** *adj* incarnate; red; flesh-colored, incarnadine; *m* flesh color, incarnadine

**encarnadura** *f* (surg.) healing characteristics of flesh; slash, cut (*of weapon*); feeding on entrails of game
**encarnamiento** *m* (med.) incarnation
**encarnar** *va* to incarnate, to embody; to bait (*fishhook*); to flesh (*hunting dog*); to mix, incorporate; to represent, to play; (f.a.) to give color of flesh to (*a statue*); *vn* to become incarnate; to incarn, heal over; to leave a strong impression; to be thrust into the flesh; to eat the entrails of game (*said of hunting dogs*)
**encarne** *m* first entrails given to hunting dogs
**encarnecer** **§34** *vn* to grow fat, put on flesh
**encarnizadamente** *adv* cruelly; fiercely, bitterly
**encarnizado -da** *adj* bloody, blood-shot; fierce, bitter, hard-fought
**encarnizamiento** *m* anger, fury; cruelty; fierceness, bitterness (*e.g., of a combat*)
**encarnizar** **§76** *va* to flesh (*a hunting dog*); to anger, infuriate; *vr* to be greedy for flesh (*said of animals*); to get angry, be infuriated; to fight bitterly; **encarnizarse con** or **en** to be merciless to, to treat inhumanly
**encaro** *m* stare, staring; aim, aiming; blunderbuss; rest for cheek (*on gunstock*)
**encarpetar** *va* to put in a portfolio, to file away; to table, to pigeonhole
**encarrilar** or **encarrillar** *va* to put back on the rails; to put on the right track, to set right; to guide, direct; *vr* to get stuck and slip off the pulley
**encarroñar** *va & vr* to rot
**encarrujado -da** *adj* curled, kinky; fluted; *m* fluting, shirring, gathering
**encarrujar** *vr* to curl, coil, kink
**encartar** *va* to outlaw, proscribe; to enroll, register; to register for taxes; to insert, slip in (*a card*); (cards) to lead (*a suit that can or must be followed*); *vr* (cards) to be unable to discard
**encarte** *m* leading a suit that can or must be followed; order of cards at end of hand
**encartonador** *m* bookbinder
**encartonar** *va* to put cardboard on, to cover or protect with cardboard; to bind (*books*) in boards
**encasamento** or **encasamiento** *m* (arch.) fascia
**encasar** *va* to set (*broken bone*)
**encascabelar** *va* to adorn with bells
**encascotar** *va* to fill with rubble, to mix with rubble
**encasillado** *m* set of pigeonholes; pattern of squares; list of government candidates
**encasillar** *va* to pigeonhole; to classify, sort out; to assign (*a candidate*) to a voting district
**encasquetar** *va* to stick (*a hat, cap, etc.*) on the head; to put (*an idea*) in someone's mind; to put in (*a remark*); *vr* to stick (*a hat, cap, etc.*) on one's head; to get (*an idea*) deeply rooted in one's mind
**encasquillador** *m* (Am.) horseshoer
**encasquillar** *va* to put a tip on; (mach.) to bush; (Am.) to shoe (*a horse*); *vr* to stick, get stuck (*said of a gun or a bullet in a gun*)
**encastar** *va* to improve (*breed*) by crossing; *vn* to breed
**encastillado -da** *adj* castellated; haughty, proud
**encastillamiento** *m* fortification with castles; withdrawal to a castle; scaffolding; stubborn adherence to one's opinion
**encastillar** *va* to fortify with castles; to pile up; to assemble a scaffold in order to build (*a building or other structure*); to build queen cells in (*beehives*); *vn* to build queen cells; *vr* to stick, to get stuck; to shut oneself up in a castle; to take to the hills; to proudly ensconce oneself; to stick to one's opinion, to refuse to give in
**encastrar** *va* (mach.) to engage, to mesh
**encastre** *m* (mach.) engaging, meshing; socket; groove; insert
**encatusar** *va* var. of **engatusar**
**encauchado** *m* (Am.) rubber-lined fabric; (Am.) rubber-lined poncho
**encauchar** *va* to cover with rubber
**encausar** *va* to prosecute, to sue
**encauste** *m* var. of **encausto**
**encausticar** **§86** *va* to wax (*a floor*)
**encáustico -ca** *adj* (f.a.) encaustic; *m* furniture polish, floor polish
**encausto** *m* (f.a.) encaustic
**encauzamiento** *m* channeling; guiding, directing; direction
**encauzar** **§76** *va* to channel (*a stream*); to guide, direct
**encavar** *vr* to hide, to hide in a cave, burrow, etc. (*said of game*)
**encebadamiento** *m* surfeit (*of an animal*)
**encebadar** *va* to surfeit (*an animal*); *vr* to surfeit
**encebollado** *m* beef stew with onions
**encebollar** *va* to season heavily with onions
**encefálico -ca** *adj* encephalic
**encefalitis** *f* (path.) encephalitis
**encéfalo** *m* (anat.) encephalon
**encefalomielitis** *f* (path.) encephalomyelitis
**encefalopatía** *f* (path.) encephalopathy
**enceguecer** **§34** *va* (Am.) to blind; *vn & vr* (Am.) to go blind
**encelado -da** *adj* (Am.) madly in love
**encelajar** *vr* to be covered with bright-colored clouds
**encelamiento** *m* jealousy
**encelar** *va* to make jealous; *vr* to become jealous; to be in rut
**enceldar** *va* to put in a cell
**encella** *f* cheese mold; basket
**encellar** *va* to mold (*cheese*)
**encenagado -da** *adj* mixed with mud
**encenagamiento** *m* getting muddied; wallowing in vice
**encenagar** **§59** *vr* to get into the mud; to become muddied; to wallow in vice
**encencerrado -da** *adj* wearing a bell (*said of an animal*)
**encencerrar** *va* to bell, put a bell on (*cattle*)
**encendaja** *f* dried brush, kindling
**encendedor -dora** *adj* lighting, kindling; *m* lighter; sparker, igniter; (elec.) starter (*of fluorescent light*); **encendedor automático** cigarette lighter, cigar lighter
**encender** **§66** *va* to light, kindle, set fire to, ignite; to turn on (*lights, radio, etc.*); to burn (*e.g., the tongue*); to instigate, stir up, excite; *vr* to be kindled, catch fire, ignite; to burn; to be stirred up, become excited; to blush
**encendidamente** *adv* ardently, keenly, eagerly
**encendido -da** *adj* bright, high-colored, inflamed; red, flushed; keen, enthusiastic; *m* (aut.) ignition
**encendimiento** *m* lighting, kindling, ignition; burning; glow, incandescence; ardor, intensity
**encenizar** **§76** *va* to cover with ashes; *vr* to get covered with ashes
**encentador -dora** *adj* beginning
**encentadura** *f* or **encentamiento** *m* beginning, start
**encentar** **§18** *va* to begin; to cut the first slice of; *vr* to get bedsores
**encentrar** *va* to center
**encepador** *m* stocker (*of a gun*)
**encepadura** *f* stocking; (carp.) tie joint
**encepar** *va* to put in the stocks; to stock (*a gun*); (naut.) to stock (*the anchor*); (carp.) to fasten or join with ties; *vn* to take deep root; *vr* to take deep root; (naut.) to be fouled on the anchor (*said of a cable*)
**encepe** *m* taking deep root
**encerado -da** *adj* waxy, wax-colored; hard (*said of a boiled egg*); *m* oilcloth; tarpaulin; wax sticking plaster; blackboard; waxing (*of floors and furniture*)
**encerador -dora** *mf* floor waxer (*person*); *f* floor-waxing machine
**enceramiento** *m* waxing
**encerar** *va* to wax; to smear with wax; to stiffen with wax; to thicken (*lime*); *vn & vr* to turn yellow, to ripen (*said of grain*)
**encernadar** *va* to cover with ashes, to plaster with ashes
**encerotar** *va* to wax (*thread*)
**encerradero** *m* sheepfold; pen for bulls before fight

**encerradura** *f* or **encerramiento** *m* locking up, confinement; encirclement; jail, lockup; retreat, retirement
**encerrar** **§18** *va* to shut in, lock in, lock up, confine; to encircle; to contain, to include; to involve, imply; *vr* to stay in the house; to lock oneself in; to go into seclusion
**encerrona** *f* (coll.) voluntary confinement; (coll.) trap; **dar una encerrona a** (coll.) to gang up on (*in gambling*); **hacer la encerrona** (coll.) to go into brief voluntary confinement
**encespedar** *va* to sod, to cover with sod
**encestar** *va* to put in a basket; (basketball) to put (*the ball*) through the basket
**encía** *f* (anat.) gum
**encíclica** *f* encyclical
**enciclopedia** *f* encyclopedia; **enciclopedia ambulante** or **viviente** walking encyclopedia
**enciclopédico -ca** *adj* encyclopedic
**enciclopedismo** *m* encyclopedism
**enciclopedista** *mf* encyclopedist
**encierro** *m* locking up, confinement; encirclement; inclusion; inclosure; prison, lockup; solitary confinement; (taur.) pen for bulls before fight; (taur.) driving bulls into pen before fight; retreat, retirement
**encima** *adv* above, overhead, at the top; besides, in addition; at hand, upon us; with you, e.g., **¿Tiene Vd. encima diez pesetas?** Do you have ten pesetas with you?; **de encima** (Am.) in the bargain; **echarse encima** to take upon oneself; **pasar por encima** to push right through; to push one's way to the top; **por encima** hastily, superficially; **por encima de** above, over; in spite of, against the will of; **quitar de encima a uno** to free one from, to take off one's shoulders; **quitarse de encima a** to shake off, get rid of; **encima de** on, upon; above, over
**encimar** *va* to put on top, to raise high; (Am.) to throw in; *vr* to rise above
**encimero -ra** *adj* top; superficial
**encina** *f* (bot.) holm oak, evergreen oak
**encinal** *m* or **encinar** *m* woods of oak, oak grove
**encinilla** *f* (bot.) germander
**encino** *m* (Am.) var. of **encina**
**encinta** *adj* pregnant, enceinte
**encintado -da** *adj* beribboned; *m* curb, curbing
**encintar** *va* to ribbon, beribbon; to install curbs in (*a street*)
**encismar** *va* to sow discord among
**encizañador -dora** *mf* var. of **cizañador**
**encizañamiento** *m* var. of **cizañamiento**
**encizañar** *va* var. of **cizañar**
**enclaustrar** *va* to cloister; to hide away
**enclavación** *f* nailing
**enclavadura** *f* pricking a horse's foot; groove, mortise; nails, nailing
**enclavamiento** *m* lock, locking; (med.) enclavement; (rail.) interlocking system (*of signals*)
**enclavar** *va* to nail; to prick (*a horse's foot*); to pierce, transfix; to lock; to enclave; (coll.) to deceive, cheat
**enclave** *m* (geog.) enclave
**enclavijar** *va* to pin, to dowel; to peg (*a string instrument*)
**enclenque** *adj* weak, feeble, sickly; *mf* sickly person
**enclítico -ca** *adj* (gram. & obstet.) enclitic; *m* (gram.) enclitic
**enclocar** **§95** *vn & vr* to brood
**encloquecer** **§34** *vn* var. of **enclocar**
**encobar** *vn & vr* to brood
**encobertado -da** *adj* (coll.) covered with a bedspread
**encobijar** *va* var. of **cobijar**
**encobrado -da** *adj* coppery
**encobrar** *va* to coat with copper
**encoclar** **§77** *vn & vr* var. of **enclocar**
**encocorar** *va* (coll.) to annoy greatly; *vr* (coll.) to be greatly annoyed
**encochado -da** *adj* coach-riding
**encodillar** *vr* to hole up in a bend of the burrow (*said of a ferret or hare*)
**encofrado** *m* (min.) planking, timbering; (min.) planked gallery; form (*for concrete*)
**encofrar** *va* (min.) to plank, to timber; to build a form for (*concrete*)
**encoger** **§49** *va* to shrink, contract; to intimidate, discourage; to let (*one's shoulders*) droop; *vn* to shrink, shrivel; *vr* to shrink, contract; to be bashful or timid; to cringe; **encogerse de hombros** to shrug one's shoulders
**encogido -da** *adj* timid, bashful
**encogimiento** *m* shrinking, shrinkage; timidity, bashfulness; crouch, crouching; **encogimiento de hombros** shrug, shrug of the shoulders
**encogollar** *vr* to climb to the treetops (*said of game*); to be proud, be haughty
**encohetar** *va* to harass (*an animal*) with firecrackers; *vr* (Am.) to get raving mad; (Am.) to get drunk
**encojar** *va* to cripple, to lame; *vr* to become lame; (coll.) to fall ill, to feign illness
**encolado** *m*, **encoladura** *f* or **encolamiento** *m* gluing; sizing; clarification (*of wine*)
**encolar** *va* to glue; to size; to throw out of reach; to clarify (*wine*); *vr* to be thrown out of reach, to be out of reach
**encolerizar** **§76** *va* to anger, irritate; *vr* to become angry
**encomendado** *m* vassal of a knight commander
**encomendamiento** *m* charge, commission
**encomendar** **§18** *va* to entrust, commend, commit; to knight; *vn* to hold a knight commandery or encomienda; *vr* to commend oneself, to commit oneself; to send regards
**encomendero** *m* encomendero (*holder of an encomienda*)
**encomiable** *adj* praiseworthy
**encomiador -dora** *adj* praising; *mf* encomiast
**encomiar** *va* to praise, to eulogize
**encomiasta** *m* encomiast
**encomiástico -ca** *adj* encomiastic
**encomienda** *f* charge, commission; praise, commendation; protection, favor; (eccl.) commendam; encomienda (*a Spanish dignity and estate; land in America and inhabiting Indians granted to Spanish colonists*); knight's cross (*of military orders*); (Am.) parcel-post package; **encomiendas** *fpl* regards, compliments; **en encomienda** (eccl.) in commendam
**encomio** *m* encomium
**encompadrar** *vn* (coll.) to become related as godfather and father; (coll.) to become close friends
**enconado -da** *adj* bitter, unfriendly
**enconamiento** *m* soreness, sore spot; rancor, ill will
**enconar** *va* to make sore, inflame; to poison (*someone's mind*); to irritate, aggravate, provoke; to rankle; *vr* to get sore, become inflamed; to become irritated or provoked; to rankle; (Am.) to filch, to snitch; **enconarse con** to be provoked at or with
**enconchado -da** *adj* (Am.) inlaid with pearl or mother-of-pearl
**enconchar** *vr* (Am.) to draw back into one's shell, to keep aloof
**encongar** **§59** *vr* (Am.) to get furious
**encono** *m* rancor, ill will
**enconoso -sa** *adj* sore, sensitive; harmful; rancorous, malevolent
**encontradizo -za** *adj* bobbing up all the time; **hacerse el encontradizo** to try to be met (seemingly) by chance
**encontrado -da** *adj* opposite; opposing, contrary; hostile; **estar encontrado con** to be at odds with; **estar encontrados** to be at odds
**encontrar** **§77** *va* to meet, to encounter; to find; *vn* to collide; *vr* to meet, to meet each other; to find oneself, to be found, to be situated, to be; to conflict; **encontrarse con** to meet, run into, run across, encounter; **encontrarse con que** to find to one's surprise that
**encontrón** *m* or **encontronazo** *m* jolt, collision
**encopetado -da** *adj* conceited, boastful; of noble descent, aristocratic; (Am.) drunk
**encopetar** *va* to raise (*the hair*) high over the forehead; *vr* to rise high over the forehead; to be conceited, to boast
**encorachar** *va* to put in a leather bag
**encorajar** *va* to give courage to; *vr* to fly into a rage
**encorajinar** *vr* (coll.) to get angry, fly into a rage

**encorar §77** *va* to cover with leather, to wrap in leather; to grow new skin over (*a sore*); *vn & vr* to grow new skin, to heal
**encorazado -da** *adj* covered with a cuirass; covered with leather
**encorchar** *va* to hive (*bees*); to cork (*bottles*)
**encorchetar** *va* to put hooks or clasps on; to fasten with hooks or clasps; to clamp
**encordadura** *f* strings (*of a musical instrument*)
**encordaje** *m* stringing (*of musical instrument or tennis racket*)
**encordar §77** *va* to string (*musical instrument, tennis racket, etc.*); to bind, to wrap (*with ropes, etc.*)
**encordelar** *va* to string; to tie with strings or cords
**encordonar** *va* to cord, to tie with cords
**encorecer §34** *va* to grow new skin over (*a sore*); *vn* to grow new skin, to heal
**encoriación** *f* healing (*of a sore or wound*)
**encornado -da** *adj* horned; **bien encornado** with good horns; **mal encornado** with poor horns
**encornadura** *f* horns, set of horns
**encornudar** *va* to cuckold, to make a cuckold of; *vn* to grow horns
**encorozar §76** *va* (Am.) to smooth up (*a wall*)
**encorralar** *va* to corral (*cattle*)
**encorrear** *va* to strap, to tie with a strap or straps
**encorsetar** *va & vr* to put a corset on, to lace a corset on tight
**encortinar** *va* to put curtains on; to provide with curtains
**encorvada** *f* stoop, bending; buck, bucking; cancan (*dance*); (bot.) hatchet vetch; **hacer la encorvada** (coll.) to malinger
**encorvadura** *f* or **encorvamiento** *m* bending, curving, curvature
**encorvar** *va* to bend, to curve; *vr* to bend over, to stoop; to buck; to be biased, be partial
**encostalar** *va* to bag, put in bags
**encostillado** *m* lagging (*in a mine or tunnel*)
**encostradura** *f* crust; (arch.) incrustation (*e.g., of marble*); whitewashing
**encostrar** *va* to cover with crust, to put crust on; to incrust (*e.g., marble*); *vr* to crust; to form a scab
**encovadura** *f* placing in the cellar; locking away, hiding
**encovar §77** *va* to put in the cellar; to keep, to lock away, to hide away; *vr* to hole up, to hide away
**encrasar** *va* to thicken; to fertilize
**encrespado -da** *adj* curly; rough, choppy; *m* curling the hair
**encrespador** *m* curling iron; hair curler
**encrespadura** *f* curling the hair
**encrespamiento** *m* curling; standing on end (*of hair*); roughness (*of waves*)
**encrespar** *va* to curl; to set (*the hair*) on end; to ruffle (*feathers*); to stir up (*the waves*); to anger; *vr* to curl; to stand on end; to become rough (*said of waves*); to become entangled; to bristle, to get angry
**encrestado -da** *adj* haughty, arrogant
**encrestar** *vr* to stiffen the crest or comb; to be haughty
**encrucijada** *f* crossroads; street intersection; ambush; chance to do harm
**encrudecer §34** *va* to make raw or sore; to irritate, exasperate; *vr* to get raw
**encruelecer §34** *va* to excite to cruelty, make cruel; *vr* to become cruel; to get furious
**encuadernación** *f* (b.b.) binding; bookbinding; bindery; **encuadernación a la holandesa** half binding; **encuadernación en pasta** cardboard binding
**encuadernador -dora** *mf* bookbinder; *m* clip, pin
**encuadernar** *va* to bind (*a book*); **sin encuadernar** unbound
**encuadramiento** *m* framing; encompassment
**encuadrar** *va* to frame; to fit in, to insert; to include; to encompass; (Am.) to summarize; *vn* to fit
**encuadre** *m* film adaptation (*of play, novel, etc.*); (mov. & telv.) frame; (telv.) vertical hold
**encuarte** *m* extra draft horse
**encubar** *va* to cask, to vat (*wine, etc.*); (min.) to shore up (*a shaft*)
**encubertar §18** *va* to trap, to caparison; to trap in mourning; to trap for war
**encubierta** *f* see **encubierto**
**encubiertamente** *adv* secretly; slyly, deceitfully; cautiously
**encubierto -ta** *pp of* **encubrir;** *f* fraud, deceit
**encubridizo -za** *adj* easily hidden, easily concealed
**encubridor -dora** *mf* concealer; (law) accessory after the fact
**encubrimiento** *m* concealment; (law) complicity
**encubrir §17,** 9 *va* to hide, conceal; to keep under cover; to feign, pretend; to include, comprise, involve; (law) to harbor, screen, conceal; *vr* to hide; to conceal one's identity, to disguise oneself
**encuentro** *m* meeting, encounter; clash, collision; find; joint; game, match; (print.) space, blank (*for insertion of letter of different color*); (mil.) encounter; **llevarse de encuentro** (Am.) to knock down, run over; (Am.) to drag down to ruin; **mal encuentro** unlucky encounter, foul play; **salir al encuentro a** to go to meet; to oppose, take a stand against; to get ahead of; **encuentro fronterizo** border clash
**encuerar** *va* (Am.) to strip, to undress; (Am.) to fleece
**encuesta** *f* inquiry; poll; survey (*e.g., of public opinion*)
**encuevar** *va & vr* var. of **encovar**
**encuitar** *vr* to grieve
**enculatar** *va* to cover (*a beehive*)
**encumbrado -da** *adj* high, lofty; stately, sublime; mighty, influential
**encumbramiento** *m* elevation, height, eminence; exaltation
**encumbrar** *va* to raise, elevate; to exalt, to honor, to dignify; to extol; to climb to the top of; *vr* to rise; to be highly honored; to be proud, be haughty; to tower; to be magniloquent
**encunar** *va* to put in the cradle; to catch between the horns
**encureñar** *va* to put on the gun carriage
**encurtido** *m* pickle
**encurtir** *va* to pickle (*fruit and vegetables*)
**enchancletar** *va* to put slippers on; to drag (*one's shoes*) like slippers
**enchapado** *m* veneer, overlay, plating
**enchapar** *va* to veneer, to overlay, to plate
**encharcada** *f* pool, puddle
**encharcamiento** *m* pooling, puddling
**encharcar §86** *va* to turn into a pool or puddle; to upset (*the stomach*); *vr* to turn into a pool or puddle; to wallow in vice
**enchavetar** *va* (mach.) to key
**enchilada** *f* (tresillo) stake in the pot; (Am.) corn cake seasoned with chili
**enchilado** *m* (Am.) shellfish stew with chili sauce; (bot.) chanterelle; (orn.) western meadow lark
**enchilar** *va* (Am.) to season with chili; (Am.) to anger; (Am.) to disappoint
**enchinar** *va* to pave with pebbles; (Am.) to curl (*hair*); *vr* to be covered with goose flesh
**enchinarrar** *va* to pave with cobbles
**enchiquerar** *va* to shut in the bull pen; (coll.) to jail
**enchironar** *va* (coll.) to jail
**enchivar** *vr* (Am.) to fly into a rage
**enchufable** *adj* fitting; plug-in
**enchufamiento** *m* fitting; connecting; merging
**enchufar** *va* to fit (*a pipe*); to connect (*two pipes*) together; (elec.) to connect, to plug in; to fit together; to merge (*two businesses*); *vn* to fit (*said of a pipe*); *vr* to merge
**enchufe** *m* fitting; male end (*of pipe*); joint (*of two pipes*); (elec.) connector, plug and jack, plug and receptacle; (elec.) plug; (elec.) receptacle; (coll.) political sinecure; **tener enchufe** (coll.) to have a drag, to have pull; **tener un enchufe** (coll.) to have a sinecure

**enchufismo** *m* (coll.) political sinecurism, holding an extra job through political influence
**enchufista** *mf* (coll.) political sinecurist, holder of an extra job through political influence
**enchuletar** *va* (carp.) to fill in
**ende; por ende** therefore
**endeble** *adj* feeble, weak; worthless; fragile, flimsy
**endeblez** *f* feebleness, weakness; worthlessness; fragility, flimsiness
**endécada** *f* eleven years
**endecágono -na** *adj* (geom.) hendecagonal; *m* (geom.) hendecagon, undecagon
**endecasílabo -ba** *adj* hendecasyllabic; *m* hendecasyllable
**endecha** *f* dirge; assonanced seven-syllabled quatrain; **endecha real** assonanced seven-syllabled quatrain whose last line is hendecasyllabic
**endechadera** *f* weeper, professional mourner
**endechar** *va* to sing a dirge to; *vr* to grieve, to mourn
**endehesar** *va* to put to pasture
**endejas** *fpl* (mas.) toothing
**endemia** *f* endemic
**endémico -ca** *adj* endemic
**endemoniado -da** *adj* possessed of the devil; furious, violent, wild; (coll.) devilish, fiendish; *mf* person possessed
**endemoniar** *va* to possess with the devil; (coll.) to anger, irritate; *vr* (coll.) to be angered or irritated
**endentado -da** *adj* (her.) serrated, indented
**endentar §18** *va* to mesh, to engage; to tooth, furnish with teeth; to key; *vn* to mesh, to engage
**endentecer §34** *vn* to teethe
**enderezadamente** *adv* straight, honestly
**enderezado -da** *adj* favorable, fitting, opportune; straight; fair, right
**enderezador -dora** *mf* good manager, person who knows how to straighten things out; *m* straightener (*tool*)
**enderezamiento** *m* straightening; standing
**enderezar §76** *va* to straighten; to stand up; to cock; to put in order, to regulate; to fix, to punish; to direct; to dedicate; (aer.) to flatten out; *vn* to go straight; *vr* to straighten; to stand up, to straighten up; to get back on a sound footing; to go straight; to go, to make one's way, to head; (aer.) to flatten out; **enderezarse a** + *inf* to take steps to + *inf*
**enderrotar** *va & vn* (naut.) to head
**endeudar** *vr* to run into debt; to acknowledge indebtedness
**endevotado -da** *adj* pious, devout; fond, devoted
**endiablada** *f* see **endiablado**
**endiabladamente** *adv* horribly
**endiablado -da** *adj* devilish; ugly, deformed; annoying, pestiferous; (Am.) complicated, difficult; (Am.) dangerous, risky; *f* noisy masquerade
**endiablar** *va* to entangle, confuse; to bewitch; (coll.) to pervert, to corrupt; *vr* to be furious, be in a rage; (coll.) to be perverted or corrupted
**endíadis** *f* (rhet.) hendiadys
**endibia** *f* (bot.) endive
**endilgar §59** *va* (coll.) to direct, send; (coll.) to help, to guide; (coll.) to hasten, expedite; (coll.) to spring, let go, unload (*something unpleasant*); *vr* (coll.) to slip away, slip out
**Endimión** *m* (myth.) Endymion
**endino -na** *adj* (coll.) wicked, vile
**endiosamiento** *m* pride, conceit, vanity; absorption, abstraction
**endiosar** *va* to deify; *vr* to be stuck-up; to be absorbed (*e.g., in reading*)
**endocardio** *m* (anat.) endocardium
**endocarditis** *f* (path.) endocarditis
**endocarpio** *m* (bot.) endocarp
**endocrino -na** *adj & f* (physiol.) endocrine
**endocrinología** *f* endocrinology
**endodermo** *m* (bot.) endodermis
**endoesqueleto** *m* (zool.) endoskeleton
**endogamia** *f* endogamy, inbreeding; (biol.) endogamy
**endogénesis** *f* (biol.) endogeny
**endógeno -na** *adj* endogenous
**endolinfa** *f* (anat.) endolymph
**endomingado -da** *adj* (worn on) Sunday; dressed in one's Sunday clothes
**endomingar §59** *vr* to dress up in one's Sunday clothes
**endomisio** *m* (anat.) endomysium
**endoparásito** *m* (zool.) endoparasite
**endoplasma** *m* (biol.) endoplasm
**endorsar** *va* var. of **endosar**
**endorso** *m* var. of **endoso**
**endosante** *mf* indorser
**endosar** *va* to indorse; to unload (*a task or something unpleasant*)
**endosatario -ria** *mf* indorsee
**endoscopio** *m* (med.) endoscope
**endose** *m* (Am.) var. of **endoso**
**endoselar** *va* to hang with a canopy or dais
**endosmosis** *f* or **endósmosis** *f* (phys., chem. & physiol.) endosmosis
**endoso** *m* indorsement
**endospermo** *m* (bot.) endosperm
**endospora** *f* (bot. & bact.) endospore
**endotecio** *m* (bot.) endothecium
**endotelio** *m* (anat.) endothelium
**endotérmico -ca** *adj* (chem.) endothermic
**endriago** *m* fabulous monster
**endrino -na** *adj* sloe-colored; *m* (bot.) sloe, blackthorn; *f* sloe (*fruit*)
**endrogar §59** *vr* (Am.) to run into debt
**endulzadura** *f* sweetening; mitigation
**endulzar §76** *va* to sweeten; to soften, mitigate, make bearable
**endurador -dora** *adj* saving, stingy
**endurancia** *f* (sport) endurance
**endurar** *va* to harden; to suffer, endure; to delay, put off; to save; *vr* to harden, get hard
**endurecer §34** *va* to harden; to inure; *vr* to harden; to become inured; to become hardened or cruel
**endurecido -da** *adj* hard, strong; inured, experienced; hard-hearted; tenacious, obstinate; (phys.) hard (*ray*)
**endurecimiento** *m* hardening; hardness; hard-heartedness; tenacity, obstinacy; **endurecimiento arterial** (path.) hardening of the arteries
**enea** *f* var. of **anea**
**eneágono** *m* (geom.) nonagon
**Eneas** *m* (myth.) Aeneas
**enebral** *m* growth of juniper trees
**enebrina** *f* juniper berry
**enebro** *m* (bot.) juniper; **enebro de la miera** (bot.) cade
**enechado -da** *adj & mf* foundling
**Eneida** *f* Aeneid
**enejar** *va* to put an axle or axles on; to fasten to the axle
**eneldo** *m* (bot.) dill
**enema** *f* (med.) enema; **enema de bario** or **enema opaca** (med.) barium enema
**enemigo -ga** *adj* enemy; inimical, hostile; *mf* enemy, foe; **el enemigo malo** the Evil One; **el enemigo número uno** the enemy number one; **enemigo jurado** sworn enemy; **enemigo público** public enemy; *f* enmity, ill will, hatred
**enemistad** *f* enmity
**enemistar** *va* to estrange, to make enemies of; *vr* to become enemies; **enemistarse con** to become estranged from
**éneo -a** *adj* (poet.) bronze, aënean
**energético -ca** *adj* (phys.) (pertaining to) energy; (elec.) (pertaining to) power; *f* energetics
**energía** *f* energy; **energía actual** (phys.) kinetic energy; **energía atómica** (phys.) atomic energy; **energía blanca** water power; **energía cinética** (phys.) kinetic energy; **energía eléctrica** electric power; **energía hidráulica** water power; **energía libre** (phys.) free energy; **energía potencial** (phys.) potential energy; **energía radiante** (phys.) radiant energy; **energía térmica** steam-generated power; **energía viva** (phys.) kinetic energy
**enérgico -ca** *adj* energetic
**energúmeno -na** *mf* energumen; wild person, crazy person
**enero** *m* January

**enervación** *f* enervation; weakening; effemination, effeminacy
**enervador -dora** *adj* enervating
**enervamiento** *m* enervation
**enervar** *va* to enervate; to weaken; to effeminate
**enésimo -ma** *adj* (math.) nth
**enfadadizo -za** *adj* irritable, peevish
**enfadar** *va* to annoy, to anger, to bother; *vr* to be annoyed, get angry
**enfado** *m* annoyance; anger, irritation; trouble, bother
**enfadoso -sa** *adj* annoying, bothersome
**enfaldador** *m* large pin for tucking up or fastening skirt
**enfaldar** *va* to lop off the lower branches of; *vr* to tuck up one's skirt
**enfaldo** *m* tucked-up skirt; hollow made by holding up skirt to carry something
**enfangar** **§59** *va* to muddy, cover with mud; *vr* to sink in the mud; to get involved in dirty business; to be sunk in vice
**enfardar** *va* to bale, to pack
**enfardelador -dora** *mf* packer
**enfardeladura** *f* bundling; packing
**enfardelar** *va* to bundle; to bale, to pack
**énfasis** (*pl:* **-sis**) *m & f* emphasis; *m* bombast, affectation
**enfático -ca** *adj* emphatic
**enfermar** *va* to sicken, make sick; *vn* to sicken, get sick; **enfermar del corazón** to have heart trouble
**enfermedad** *f* sickness, illness, disease; **enfermedad bronceada** or **enfermedad de Addison** (path.) Addison's disease; **enfermedad carencial** deficiency disease; **enfermedad del mosaico** (plant path.) mosaic disease; **enfermedad del sueño** (path.) sleeping sickness; **enfermedad de Parkinson** (path.) Parkinson's disease; **enfermedad de pecho** (path.) tuberculosis, consumption; **enfermedad de radiación** (path.) radiation sickness; **enfermedad mental** mental disease; **enfermedad por carencia** (med.) deficiency disease; **enfermedad profesional** occupational disease; **enfermedad venérea** veneral disease
**enfermera** *f* see **enfermero**
**enfermería** *f* infirmary; sanitarium; (naut.) sick bay; patients, sufferers
**enfermero -ra** *mf* nurse; **enfermera ambulante** visiting nurse
**enfermizo -za** *adj* sickly; unhealthy (*e.g., climate*)
**enfermo -ma** *adj* sick, ill; sickly; **caer enfermo** to take sick; **enfermo de amor** lovesick; *mf* patient; **el enfermo de Europa** the Sick Man of Europe (*Turkey*)
**enfermoso -sa** *adj* (Am.) sickish, sickly
**enfermucho -cha** *adj* (coll.) sickish
**enfervorizador -dora** *adj* inspiring, encouraging
**enfervorizar** **§76** *va* to inspire, encourage
**enfeudación** *f* (law) enfeoffment (*act and instrument*)
**enfeudar** *va* (law) to enfeoff (*to give as a fief*)
**enfielar** *va* to balance (*scales*)
**enfiestar** *vr* (Am.) to have a good time, to be on a lark
**enfilado -da** *adj* (her.) enfiled; *f* (mil.) enfilade
**enfilamiento** *m* enfilade, alignment
**enfilar** *va* to enfilade, to line up; to string (*e.g., pearls*); to aim; to go down, go up (*e.g., the street*); (mil.) to enfilade
**enfisema** *m* (path.) emphysema
**enfistolar** *va & vr* to turn into a fistula
**enfiteusis** *m & f* (law) emphyteusis
**enfiteuta** *mf* emphyteuta
**enfitéutico -ca** *adj* emphyteutic
**enflacar** **§86** *vn* to get thin
**enflaquecer** **§34** *va* to make thin; to weaken; *vn* to get thin; to flag, grow spiritless; *vr* to get thin, lose weight
**enflaquecimiento** *m* loss of flesh, loss of weight; weakening
**enflautado -da** *adj* (coll.) inflated, pompous
**enflautador -dora** *mf* (coll.) procurer, bawd
**enflautar** *va* to blow up, inflate; (coll.) to cheat, deceive; (coll.) to procure
**enflechado -da** *adj* with the arrow ready to shoot (*said of a bow*)
**enfloración** *f* enfleurage
**enflorar** *va* to flower, adorn with flowers
**enfocamiento** *m* focusing
**enfocar** **§86** *va* to focus; (fig.) to size up; *vr* to focus; **enfocarse a** + *inf* to focus one's attention on + *ger*
**enfoque** *m* focus, focusing; approach (*to a problem*)
**enfosado** *m* var. of **encebadamiento**
**enfoscar** **§86** *va* (mas.) to patch or fill with mortar; to trim with mortar; *vr* to become grumpy; to become immersed in business; to get cloudy
**enfrailado -da** *adj* cloistered; monkish
**enfrailar** *va* to make a monk or friar of; *vn & vr* to become a monk or friar
**enfranque** *m* shank (*of the sole of a shoe*)
**enfranquecer** **§34** *va* to enfranchise, to set free
**enfrascamiento** *m* entanglement, involvement
**enfrascar** **§86** *va* to bottle; *vr* to become entangled, become involved; to be overloaded with work; to be having a lot of fun
**enfrenador -dora** *mf* bridler
**enfrenamiento** *m* bridling; checking, restraining; (mach.) braking
**enfrenar** *va* to bridle; to check with the bit or bridle; (mach.) to brake; to check, restrain
**enfrentamiento** *m* confrontation; opposition; alignment
**enfrentar** *va* to confront, to put face to face; to face; to meet (*opposition*); *vn* to be opposite each other, to be facing; **enfrentar con** to be opposite, to be across from; *vr* to meet face to face; **enfrentarse con** to confront; to face, to stand up to, to cope with
**enfrente** *adv* in front, opposite; against, opposed to; **enfrente de** in front of, opposite; against, opposed to
**enfriadera** *f* bottle cooler, wine cooler, ice pail
**enfriadero** *m* cooling place; cold storage
**enfriador -dora** *adj* cooling; *m* cooling place
**enfriamiento** *m* cooling, refrigeration; (path.) cold
**enfriar** **§90** *va* to cool, to make cold, to chill; to temper; (Am.) to kill; *vn* to cool off, to turn cold; *vr* to cool off, to turn cold; to be tempered
**enfroscar** **§86** *vr* to become entangled, become involved
**enfullar** *va* (coll.) to make (*a game*) crooked
**enfundadura** *f* casing, sheathing
**enfundar** *va* to sheathe, to put (*e.g., a pillow*) in its case; to stuff, to fill; to contain; to muffle (*a drum*)
**enfurción** *f* var. of **infurción**
**enfurecer** **§34** *va* to infuriate, enrage; *vr* to rage, become infuriated
**enfurecimiento** *m* infuriation
**enfurruñamiento** *m* sulk, sulkiness
**enfurruñar** *vr* (coll.) to sulk; (dial.) to get cloudy
**enfurtir** *va* to full (*cloth*); to felt
**engabanado -da** *adj* overcoated, wearing an overcoat
**engace** *m* union, connection
**engafar** *va* to bend (*crossbow*); to hook; to half-cock (*a gun*)
**engaitador -dora** *adj* (coll.) beguiling, deluding, cozening, humbugging
**engaitar** *va* (coll.) to beguile, delude, cozen, humbug
**engalanar** *va* to adorn, bedeck; (naut.) to dress
**engalgar** **§59** *va* to scotch (*a wheel*); (naut.) to back (*an anchor*)
**engallado -da** *adj* straight, erect; haughty
**engallador** *m* checkrein
**engalladura** *f* var. of **galladura**
**engallar** *va* to stand up straight and haughty; *vr* to stand up straight and haughty; to raise the head held close to the chest (*said of a horse*)
**enganchador** *m* (rail.) brakeman; recruiting officer
**enganchamiento** *m* hooking, coupling; inveigling; recruiting
**enganchar** *va* to hook; to couple; to hang or catch on a hook; to hitch; (coll.) to inveigle; to inveigle into enlisting, to recruit; *vn* to be

hooked; to get caught (*e.g., on a hook*); *vr* to be hooked; to get caught (*e.g., on a hook*); to enlist
**enganche** *m* hooking; hook; inveigling; enlisting; recruiting of labor; (rail.) coupler, coupling
**engañabobos** (*pl:* **-bos**) *mf* (coll.) bamboozler; *m* (coll.) bamboozle
**engañadizo -za** *adj* easily deceived, deceivable
**engañador -dora** *adj* deceptive; winsome; *mf* cheat
**engañapastores** *m* (*pl:* **-res**) (orn.) goatsucker
**engañar** *va* to deceive, fool, cheat; to while away (*time*); to ward off (*hunger, sleep*); to make appetizing; *vr* to deceive oneself; to be mistaken
**engañifa** *f* (coll.) trick, cheat; (coll.) catchpenny
**engaño** *m* deceit, fraud; falsehood; mistake, misunderstanding; **llamarse a engaño** (coll.) to claim deception, to back out because of misrepresentation
**engañoso -sa** *adj* deceitful; deceptive
**engarabatar** *va* to hook; to make crooked; *vr* to get crooked
**engarabitar** *vn* (coll.) to climb; *vr* (coll.) to climb; to get stiff or numb (*from cold*)
**engarbar** *vr* to perch high (*said of birds*)
**engarbullar** *va* (coll.) to mix up, entangle
**engarce** *m* linking; enchasing; setting
**engargantadura** *f* meshing (*of gears*)
**engargantar** *va* to put into the throat; *vn* to mesh, to engage; *vr* to mesh, to engage; to put one's foot in the stirrup up to the instep
**engargante** *m* meshing (*of gears*)
**engargolado** *m* groove for sliding door; tongue-and-groove joint
**engargolar** *va* to groove, to mortise; to fit (*pipes*)
**engaritar** *va* to equip with sentry boxes; (coll.) to trick
**engarnio** *m* (coll.) var. of **plepa**
**engarrafar** *va* (coll.) to grapple, to seize tightly
**engarrar** *va* to seize
**engarro** *m* seizing, seizure
**engarzadura** *f* var. of **engarce**
**engarzar** **§76** *va* to link, to wire (*jewels*); to enchase; to curl
**engastador -dora** *mf* enchaser, setter
**engastar** *va* to enchase, to set, to mount
**engaste** *m* enchasing; setting, mounting; flat pearl
**engatado -da** *adj* thievish
**engatar** *va* (coll.) to cheat, to take in
**engatillado -da** *adj* having a high, thick neck (*said of a horse or bull*); *m* (mach.) flat-lock seaming, grooved seaming
**engatillar** *va* to clamp, to cramp; to fit (*floor beams*); to joint (*sheets of metal*) with flat-lock seams
**engatusador -dora** *adj* (coll.) wheedling, coaxing; *mf* (coll.) wheedler, coaxer
**engatusamiento** *m* (coll.) wheedling, coaxing, blandishment
**engatusar** *va* (coll.) to wheedle, to coax, to blandish; **engatusar para que** + *subj* to inveigle into + *ger*
**engavetar** *va* (Am.) to pigeonhole
**engavillar** *va* var. of **agavillar**
**engazar** **§76** *va* to link, to wire (*jewels*); to enchase; to curl; to dye in the cloth; (naut.) to strap (*blocks*)
**engendrador -dora** *adj* engendering, begetting, generating; *mf* begetter, generator
**engendramiento** *m* engendering, generation, begetting
**engendrar** *va* to engender, beget; (geom.) to generate
**engendro** *m* foetus; stunt (*animal or plant*); botch, bungle; (coll.) runt; (coll.) clownish person; **mal engendro** (coll.) unruly youth, young tough
**engeridor** *m* (hort.) grafter; grafting knife
**engibar** *va* to make humpbacked
**englandado -da** or **englantado -da** *adj* (her.) acorned
**englobar** *va* to include, lump together
**engolado -da** *adj* (her.) engouled
**engolfar** *vn* to go far out on the ocean; *vr* to go far out on the ocean; to become deeply absorbed, to be lost in thought; to let oneself go
**engolillado -da** *adj* wearing a ruff; wearing a lawyer's collar; (coll.) proud of observing old styles
**engolondrinar** *va* (coll.) to make vain or conceited; *vr* (coll.) to be or get vain or conceited; (coll.) to have a trifling love affair
**engolosinador -dora** *adj* alluring, tempting
**engolosinar** *va* to allure, to tempt; *vr* to take a liking; **engolosinarse con** to take a liking for
**engollamiento** *m* presumption, vanity
**engolletar** *vr* (coll.) to be vain or conceited
**engomado -da** *adj* starchy; (Am.) spruce, all dressed up; *m* gumming (*of a postage stamp*); gummy paste
**engomadura** *f* gumming; first coat which bees give to their hives
**engomar** *va* to gum (*fabrics, papers, etc.*)
**engorar** **§19** *va* to addle
**engorda** *f* (Am.) fattening; (Am.) animals being fattened
**engordadero** *m* fattening sty; fattening time; fodder for fattening
**engordador -dora** *adj* fattening; *mf* fattener
**engordar** *va* to fatten; *vn* to get fat; (coll.) to fatten, get fat (*rich*)
**engorde** *m* fattening
**engorro** *m* obstacle, nuisance, bother
**engorroso -sa** *adj* annoying, bothersome
**engoznar** *va* to hinge, to fasten with hinges
**Engracia** *f* Grace
**engranaje** *m* gearing, gears, gear; (fig.) bond, connection; **engranaje de distribución** (aut.) timing gears; **engranaje de marcha atrás** (aut.) reverse gear; **engranaje de tornillo sin fin** worm gear; **engranaje diferencial** differential gear
**engranar** *va* to gear; to unite, to interlock; *vn* to gear
**engrandar** *va* var. of **agrandar**
**engrandecer** **§34** *va* to enlarge, amplify, magnify; to enhance; to extol; to elevate, to exalt; *vr* to be exalted
**engrandecimiento** *m* enlargement, amplification; enhancement; praise; exaltation
**engrane** *m* gear, gearing; mesh, meshing
**engranerar** *va* to store (*grain*)
**engranujar** *vr* to become pimply; (coll.) to go to the bad
**engrapador -dora** *m & f* stapler
**engrapar** *va* to clamp, to cramp
**engrasación** *f* greasing, lubrication
**engrasadera** *f* grease cup
**engrasado** *m* var. of **engrase**
**engrasador -dora** *adj* grease, greasing; *mf* greaser; *m* grease cup; oiler (*of wool*)
**engrasamiento** *m* var. of **engrasación**
**engrasar** *va* to grease, lubricate; to smear or stain with grease; to foul; to dress (*cloth*); to fertilize; *vr* to get smeared or stained with grease; to foul
**engrase** *m* greasing, lubrication; grease
**engravar** *va* to gravel, to spread gravel over
**engravecer** **§34** *va* to make heavy; *vr* to get heavy
**engredar** *va* to clay, to chalk
**engreído -da** *adj* vain, conceited
**engreimiento** *m* vanity, conceit
**engreír** **§73** *va* to make vain or conceited; *vr* to become vain or conceited
**engreñado -da** *adj* disheveled
**engrescar** **§86** *va* to goad into fighting; to stir to merriment; *vr* to pick a fight; to be stirred to merriment, to join the merriment
**engrifar** *va* to curl, to crisp, to crimp; to make (*hair*) stand on end; *vr* to curl up; to stand on end; to rear
**engrillar** *va* to shackle, to put in irons; *vr* to shoot, sprout (*said of potatoes*)
**engrilletar** *va* to shackle, to fetter; (naut.) to shackle (*two lengths of chain*)
**engringar** **§59** *vr* to imitate the ways of foreigners (*especially Americans and Englishmen*)
**engrosamiento** *m* broadening; increase, enlargement

**engrosar §77** *va* to thicken, broaden; to enlarge; *vn* to get fat; *vr* to thicken, broaden; to become enlarged, to swell
**engrudador -dora** *mf* paster; *m* pasting brush or tool
**engrudamiento** *m* pasting
**engrudar** *va* to paste
**engrudo** *m* paste; belt dressing
**engruesar** *vn* to get fat
**engrumecer §34** *vr* to clot, to curdle
**engualdrapar** *va* to caparison
**enguantar** *va & vr* to put gloves on
**enguatar** *va* to line or interline with raw cotton
**enguedejado -da** *adj* in long locks; wearing long locks; (coll.) proud of one's long locks
**enguijarrado** *m* cobblestone paving
**enguijarrar** *va* to pave with cobblestones
**enguillar** *va* (naut.) to wind (*a heavy rope*) with a thin rope
**enguillotar** *vr* to rush in eagerly, to get involved
**enguirnaldar** *va* to enwreathe, to garland; to trim, bedeck
**enguizgar §59** *va* to incite, stimulate
**engullidor -dora** *mf* gulper, gobbler
**engullir §26** *va* to gulp down; (fig.) to swallow (*nonsense*)
**engurrio** *m* sadness, melancholy
**enhacinar** *va* var. of **hacinar**
**enharinar** *va* to cover with flour, to smear with flour
**enhastiar §90** *va* to cloy; to annoy, to bore
**enhastillar** *va* to put arrows in (*a quiver*)
**enhatijar** *va* to close or shut (*a beehive*) with esparto netting
**enhebillar** *va* to put a buckle on (*a strap*)
**enhebrar** *va* to thread (*a needle*); to string (*e.g., pearls*); (coll.) to rattle off (*e.g., lies*)
**enhenar** *va* to cover with hay
**enherbolar** *va* to poison (*arrows, etc.*) with herbs
**enhestador** *m* raiser, hoister
**enhestadura** *f* or **enhestamiento** *m* erection, raising, hoisting
**enhestar §18** *va* to erect, stand straight; to hoist, raise high; *vr* to stand straight or upright; to rise high
**enhielar** *va* to mix with gall, to make bitter
**enhiesto -ta** *adj* erect, straight, upright, raised
**enhilar** *va* to thread; to arrange in order, to marshal (*ideas*); to line up; to direct; *vn* to move
**enhorabuena** *adv* safely, luckily; all right, O.K.; **enhorabuena que** + *subj* it is all right that . . . ; *f* congratulations; **dar la enhorabuena a** to congratulate
**enhoramala** *adv* in an evil hour, under an unlucky star, unluckily; **enviar** or **mandar enhoramala** to send to the devil; **nacer enhoramala** to be born to an unhappy fate; **vete enhoramala** go to the devil
**enhorcar §86** *va* to string (*onions or garlic*)
**enhornar** *va* to put into an oven
**enhuecar §86** *va* var. of **ahuecar**
**enhuerar** *va, vn, & vr* to addle; (fig.) to addle
**enigma** *m* enigma, puzzle, riddle
**enigmático -ca** *adj* enigmatic or enigmatical
**enigmatista** *mf* person who talks in enigmas or riddles
**enjablar** *va* to insert (*barrelhead*) in croze
**enjabonado** *m* or **enjabonadura** *f* soaping, washing
**enjabonar** *va* to soap; to lather; (coll.) to softsoap; (coll.) to abuse, upbraid
**enjaezar §76** *va* to trap, to put trappings on, to harness
**enjaguadura** *f* var. of **enjuagadura**
**enjaguar §23** *va* var. of **enjuagar**
**enjalbegado** *m* whitewashing
**enjalbegador -dora** *adj* whitewashing; *mf* whitewasher
**enjalbegadura** *f* whitewashing
**enjalbegar §59** *va* to whitewash; to paint (*the face*); *vr* to paint one's face
**enjalma** *f* light packsaddle
**enjalmar** *va* to put (*a packsaddle*) on; *vn* to make packsaddles
**enjalmero** *m* packsaddle maker or dealer
**enjambradera** *f* cell of queen bee; bee which hums as signal for swarming
**enjambradero** *m* swarmer (*place where bees swarm*)
**enjambrar** *va* to swarm (*bees*); to empty (*a hive*); *vn* to swarm (*in order to form new colony*); to increase greatly, to multiply abundantly
**enjambrazón** *f* swarming (*of bees*)
**enjambre** *m* swarm; (fig.) swarm
**enjaquimar** *va* to put the headstall on (*an animal*)
**enjarciar** *va* (naut.) to rig
**enjardinar** *va* to arrange (*trees or flowers*) as in a garden; to turn or convert into a garden; *vr* to spend the day in the garden
**enjaretado** *m* grating, lattice work
**enjaretar** *va* to run (*a string, cord, ribbon, etc.*) through a casing or hem; to coerce; (coll.) to put across, to spring (*something unpleasant*); (coll.) to rush headlong through; *vr* (coll.) to insinuate oneself
**enjarrar** *vr* (Am.) to stand akimbo
**enjaular** *va* to cage; to jail, imprison; (min.) to load in the cage
**enjebar** *va* to steep (*cloth*) in lye before dyeing; to whiten with a thin coat of plaster; (Am.) to soap
**enjebe** *m* alum; lye; plaster whitening
**enjergar §59** *va* (coll.) to launch, to manage to get (*something*) started, to start (*something*) on a shoestring; (coll.) to string along (*words*) without rhyme or reason
**enjertación** *f* var. of **injertación**
**enjertar** *va* var. of **injertar**
**enjerto** *m* grafted plant; mixture, conglomeration
**enjimelgar §59** *va* (naut.) to fish (*a mast, beam, etc.*)
**enjoyar** *va* to bejewel; to embellish; to set with precious stones
**enjoyelado -da** *adj* wrought into jewels; bejeweled
**enjoyelador** *m* setter, jeweler
**enjuagadientes** *m* (*pl:* **-tes**) mouthwash
**enjuagadura** *f* rinse, rinsing; wash
**enjuagar §59** *va* to rinse, rinse out (*mouth, kettle, etc.*)
**enjuagatorio** *m* rinse, rinsing; wash, rinsing water; washbowl; mouthwash
**enjuague** *m* rinse, rinsing; wash, rinsing water; washbowl; mouthwash; plot, scheme
**enjugador** *m* drier; clotheshorse
**enjugamanos** *m* (*pl:* **-nos**) towel
**enjugaparabrisas** *m* (*pl:* **-sas**) windshield wiper
**enjugar §59** *va* to dry; to wipe, to wipe off; (fig.) to wipe out (*e.g., a debt*); *vr* to get thin, lose weight
**enjuiciamiento** *m* examining, judging; (law) suit; (law) trial; (law) sentence
**enjuiciar** *va* to examine, take under advisement, pass judgment on; (law) to sue; (law) to try; (law) to sentence
**enjulio** or **enjullo** *m* cloth beam, warp rod (*of loom*)
**enjuncar §86** *va* to cover with rush; to tie with rush ropes
**enjundia** *f* axunge; substance; force, vigor
**enjundioso -sa** *adj* fatty, greasy; substantial; (dial.) annoying, boring
**enjunque** *m* (naut.) heavy ballast, pig-iron ballast, kentledge
**enjuta** *f* see **enjuto**
**enjutar** *va* to dry (*e.g., plaster*)
**enjutez** *f* dryness
**enjuto -ta** *adj* lean, skinny; dry (*eyes; weather*); reserved, quiet, stolid; **enjutos** *mpl* brushwood; crackers, tidbits (*to excite thirst*); *f* (arch.) spandrel; (arch.) pendentive
**enlabiador -dora** *mf* humbug, bamboozler
**enlabiar** *va* to humbug, to bamboozle, to take in; to bring one's lips to, to press one's lips against
**enlabio** *m* humbug, bamboozle
**enlace** *m* lacing, linking, connection; liaison; relationship; marriage; engagement, betrothal; (chem.) linkage; (rail.) connection; (rail.)

crossover; **enlace domiciliario** (Am.) house service
**enlaciar** *va, vn & vr* to wither; to rumple
**enladrillado** *m* brick paving, brick pavement; bricklaying; brickwork
**enladrillador** *m* brick paver, bricklayer
**enladrilladura** *f* var. of **enladrillado**
**enladrillar** *va* to pave with bricks; to brick
**enlagunar** *va & vr* to flood
**enlajado** *m* (Am.) flagstone
**enlajar** *va* (Am.) to pave with flagstones
**enlamar** *va* to cover with silt
**enlanado -da** *adj* woolly
**enlardar** *va* (cook.) to baste
**enlatado** *m* canning
**enlatar** *va* to can; (dial. & Am.) to put a tin roof on, to roof with tin
**enlazador -dora** *adj* linking, connecting; *mf* connecter
**enlazadura** *f* or **enlazamiento** *m* var. of **enlace**
**enlazar §76** *va* to lace, to enlace, to link, to connect; to lasso; *vn* to connect (*said, e.g., of two trains*); *vr* to be linked, be connected; to connect, to interlock; to get married; to become related by marriage
**enlechar** *va* to grout
**enlegajar** *va* to arrange (*papers*) in a file; to file (*papers*)
**enlegamar** *va* to cover with mud; *vr* to get covered with mud; to silt up
**enlejiar §90** *va* to put (*clothes*) in lye; (chem.) to dissolve (*an alkaline substance*) in water
**enlenzar §31** *va* to strengthen (*woodwork, especially, wood carvings*) with adhesive tape
**enlerdar** *va* to slow down, to dull
**enlevaje** *m* (rowing) spurt
**enligar §59** *va* to smear with birdlime; *vr* to be caught with birdlime
**enlistonado** *m* laths, lathing
**enlistonar** *va* to lath, to batten
**enlizar §76** *va* to add leashes to (*a loom*)
**enlobreguecer §34** *va* to make dark; *vr* to get dark
**enlodadura** *f* or **enlodamiento** *m* muddying; muddiness
**enlodar** *va* to muddy, soil with mud; to plaster with mud; (chem.) to lute (*a joint, porous surface, etc.*); to seal with mud; to vilify, defame; *vr* to get muddied, be soiled with mud
**enlodazar §76** *va* to muddy, bemire; *vr* to mire, mire up
**enloquecedor -dora** *adj* maddening
**enloquecer §34** *va* to drive crazy, to madden, to distract; *vn* to go crazy; to become barren (*said of trees*)
**enloquecimiento** *m* madness, insanity
**enlosado** *m* flagstone paving
**enlosador** *m* flagstone paver
**enlosar** *va* to pave with flagstone
**enlozado -da** *adj* (Am.) enameled; *m* (Am.) enameling; (Am.) enamelware
**enlozanar** *vr* to be fresh, be luxuriant
**enlozar §76** *va* (Am.) to enamel (*especially iron*)
**enlucido** *m* plaster, coat of plaster; plastering
**enlucidor** *m* plasterer
**enlucimiento** *m* plastering; polishing
**enlucir §60** *va* to plaster (*walls*); to polish (*metal*)
**enlustrecer §34** *va* to brighten, to shine
**enlutado -da** *mf* person dressed in mourning; *m* mourning (*especially drapery*)
**enlutar** *va* to put in mourning, to dress in mourning; to darken; to sadden; *vr* to be in mourning, to dress in mourning
**enllantar** *va* to put a rim or tire on (*a wheel*)
**enllentecer §34** *va & vr* to soften
**enllocar §95** *vn & vr* var. of **enclocar**
**enmaderación** *f* wood construction, timber work; shoring
**enmaderado** *m* wood construction, timber work; timber
**enmaderamiento** *m* wood construction, timber work
**enmaderar** *va* to cover with boards or timber
**enmadrar** *vr* to become excessively fond of one's mother
**enmagrecer §34** *va* to make thin or skinny; *vn & vr* to get thin or skinny
**enmalecer §34** *va* to harm, spoil, corrupt
**enmalezar §76** *vr* to become overgrown with brush
**enmallar** *vr* to get caught in the meshes of the net (*said of a fish*)
**enmangar §59** *va* to put a handle on
**enmantar** *va* to put a blanket on, to cover with a blanket; to cover up, to wrap up; *vr* to be melancholy
**enmantecado** *m* (orn.) cowbird
**enmarañador -dora** *adj* entangling
**enmarañamiento** *m* tangle; entanglement, confusion
**enmarañar** *va* to tangle; to entangle, confuse, mix up; *vr* to get tangled; to become entangled or confused; to fall out, become enemies; to turn dark, turn cloudy
**enmarar** *vr* (naut.) to reach the high sea, to get out of sight of land
**enmarcar §86** *va* to frame
**enmaridar** *vn & vr* to marry, to take a husband
**enmarillecer §34** *vr* to turn pale, to turn yellow
**enmaromar** *va* to tie with a rope
**enmasar** *va* to mass (*troops*)
**enmascarado** *m* mask, person wearing a mask
**enmascaramiento** *m* camouflage
**enmascarar** *va* to mask; (fig.) to mask, disguise; *vr* to put on a mask, to masquerade
**enmasillar** *va* to putty
**enmatar** *vr* to hide in the bushes (*said of game*)
**enmelar §18** *va* to add honey to, to smear with honey; to sweeten; *vn* to make honey
**enmendación** *f* emendation, correction
**enmendador -dora** *mf* corrector, emender
**enmendadura** *f* emendation, correction
**enmendar §18** *va* to emend, to correct; to amend; to make amends for; *vr* to amend, to reform, to go straight
**enmienda** *f* emendation, correction; amendment; amends; **enmiendas** *fpl* (agr.) amendment
**enmohecer §34** *va* to make moldy; to rust; to cast aside, neglect; to dull (*e.g., the memory*); *vr* to get moldy; to rust; to fade away, disappear
**enmohecimiento** *m* getting moldy, moldiness; rusting; disappearance
**enmollecer §34** *va & vr* to soften
**enmondar** *va* var. of **deslinar**
**enmontar** *vr* (Am.) to be overgrown with weeds and brush
**enmordazar §76** *va* var. of **amordazar**
**enmostar** *va* to stain with grape juice; *vn* to become stained with grape juice
**enmudecer §34** *va* to hush, to silence; *vr* to be silent, to keep silent; to lose the power of speech
**enmuescar §86** *va* to notch; to mortise
**enmugrecer §34** *va* to soil, to cover with dirt
**enmustiar** *va & vr* to wither
**enneciar** *vr* to become foolish, get stupid
**ennegrecer §34** *va* to dye black, to blacken; *vn* to turn black; *vr* to turn black; to be dark or black (*said, e.g., of the future*)
**ennegrecimiento** *m* blackening, turning black
**ennoblecedor -dora** *adj* ennobling
**ennoblecer §34** *va* to ennoble; to adorn, embellish; *vr* to become ennobled
**ennoblecimiento** *m* ennoblement; nobility; fame, glory
**ennudecer §34** *vn* to stop growing, to wither
**en.º** abr. of **enero**
**enodio** *m* fawn, young deer
**enojada** *f* (Am.) anger, fit of anger
**enojadizo -za** *adj* ill-tempered, irritable
**enojar** *va* to anger, make angry; to annoy, vex; *vr* to get angry; **enojarse con** or **contra** to become angry with (*a person*); **enojarse de** to become angry at (*a thing*)
**enojo** *m* anger; annoyance, bother; **enojos** *mpl* annoyance, bother
**enojón -jona** *adj* (Am.) irritable, touchy
**enojoso -sa** *adj* annoying, bothersome, vexatious
**enología** *f* oenology
**enológico -ca** *adj* oenological
**enómetro** *m* oenometer
**Enona** *f* (myth.) Oenone

**enorgullecer** §34 *va* to make proud, to fill with pride; *vr* to be proud, to swell with pride; **enorgullecerse de** to pride oneself on or upon; **enorgullecerse de** + *inf* to pride oneself on + *ger*, to boast of + *ger*
**enorgullecimiento** *m* pride
**enorme** *adj* enormous; (coll.) terrific
**enormidad** *f* enormity
**enotecnia** *f* wine making; oenology
**enotécnico -ca** *adj* wine-making
**enquiciar** *va* to hang (*a door or window*); to put in order; to fasten, make firm
**enquillotrar** *vr* (coll.) to fall in love
**enquiridión** *m* handbook, manual, enchiridion
**enquistamiento** *m* encystment
**enquistar** *va & vr* to encyst
**enrabiar** *va* to enrage; *vn* to get or have rabies; *vr* to become enraged
**enraizar** §97 *vn* to take root
**enramada** *f* arbor, bower; decoration made of branches; shelter made of branches
**enramado** *m* (min.) lining made of branches; (naut.) frames (*of a ship*)
**enramar** *va* to intertwine (*branches*); to adorn with branches; to spread branches, flowers over (*a room, street, etc.*); (naut.) to set up (*the frames of a ship under construction*); *vn* to sprout branches; *vr* to hide in the branches
**enramblar** *va* to tenter (*cloth*)
**enrame** *m* intertwining or adorning with branches; **de enrame** climbing
**enranciar** *va* to make rancid; *vr* to become rancid
**enrarecer** §34 *va* to rarefy, make less dense; to make scarce; *vn* to become scarce; *vr* to rarefy, become less dense; to become scarce
**enrarecimiento** *m* rarefaction; scarceness, scarcity
**enrasado -da** *adj* plain; flush
**enrasamiento** *m* leveling, grading
**enrasar** *va* to make even or flush; to level, to grade; *vn* to be even or flush
**enrase** *m* leveling, grading; (mas.) leveling course
**enratonar** *vr* (coll.) to get sick from eating mice (*said of cats*)
**enrayar** *va* to put spokes in (*a wheel*); to scotch (*a wheel*) with a spoke
**enredadera** *adj fem* (bot.) climbing; *f* (bot.) vine, climbing plant; (bot.) bindweed
**enredador -dora** *mf* (coll.) gossip, tattler; (coll.) meddler, busybody
**enredar** *va* to catch in a net; to set (*snares, nets, or traps*); to tangle up; to involve, entangle; to start (*e.g., a fight*); to interweave, intertwine; to compromise, endanger; to alienate; *vn* to be frisky, to romp around; *vr* to get tangled up; to get involved or entangled; (coll.) to have an affair
**enredijo** *m* (coll.) tangle
**enredista** *mf* (Am.) var. of **enredador**
**enredo** *m* tangle; entanglement, complication; mischievous lie; restlessness, friskiness; plot (*e.g., of a play*)
**enredón -dona** *adj* scheming; *mf* schemer
**enredoso -sa** *adj* tangled, entangled, full of difficulties
**enrejado** *m* grating, lattice, trellis; lacing; bamboo curtain; openwork embroidery; **enrejado de alambre** wire netting
**enrejalar** *va* to pile (*bricks, boards, etc.*) alternately crisscross
**enrejar** *va* to put grates or grating on (*e.g., a window*); to grate, to lattice; to fence or surround with a grating; to share, fasten the share on (*a plow*); to cut (*feet of oxen or horses*) with plowshare; to pile (*bricks, boards, etc.*) alternately crisscross
**enrevesado -da** *adj* var. of **revesado**
**enriado** *m* retting
**enriador -dora** *mf* retter
**enriamiento** *m* retting
**enriar** §90 *va* to ret
**enrieladura** *f* laying rails; rails, tracks
**enrielar** *va* to make into ingots; to pour into the ingot mold; (Am.) to lay rails on (*a road*); to put on the rails; (fig.) to put on the right track
**enripiar** *va* to fill with rubble, to riprap
**Enrique** *m* Henry
**enriquecedor -dora** *adj* enriching, fertilizing
**enriquecer** §34 *va* to enrich; to enhance; to adorn; *vn* to get rich, to prosper; *vr* to become enriched; to get rich, to prosper
**enriquecimiento** *m* enrichment
**enriqueño -ña** *adj* of or like Henry II of Castile
**Enriqueta** *f* Henrietta, Harriet
**Enriquito** *m* Harry
**enriscado -da** *adj* craggy, full of cliffs
**enriscar** §86 *va* to raise; *vr* to rise; to hide or take refuge among the rocks
**enristrar** *va* to couch (*the lance*); to string (*e.g., onions*); to go straight to; to straighten out (*a difficulty*); (Am.) to recruit
**enristre** *m* couching the lance
**enrizamiento** *m* curling
**enrizar** §76 *va & vr* to curl
**enrocamiento** *m* rock fill, riprap
**enrocar** §95 *va* to put (*flax, hemp, wool, etc.*) on the distaff; §86 *va & vn* (chess) to castle; (croquet) to roquet
**enroco** *m* (Am.) var. of **enroque**
**enrodar** §77 *va* to subject to torture by the wheel
**enrodelado -da** *adj* armed with a buckler or shield
**enrodrigar** §59 *va* to prop, prop up (*plants*)
**enrodrigonar** *va* to prop up, to tie up (*plants*)
**enrojar** *va* to redden, make red; to heat (*furnace or oven*); *vr* to redden, turn red
**enrojecer** §34 *va* to redden, make red; to make red-hot; to make blush; *vn* to blush; *vr* to redden, turn red; to get red-hot; to flush; to get sore
**enrojecido -da** *adj* reddened; flushed; sore
**enrolar** *va* to enroll
**enrollado** *m* volute; (elec.) winding
**enrollar** *va* to wind, coil, reel, roll up, enroll; to pave with cylindrical stones
**enromar** *va* to blunt, to dull; *vr* to become blunt, get dull
**enronquecer** §34 *va* to make hoarse; *vn & vr* to grow hoarse
**enronquecimiento** *m* hoarseness
**enroñar** *va* to cover with scabs; to touch with filth; to rust, make rusty; *vr* to rust, get rusty
**enroque** *m* (chess) castling
**enroscadamente** *adv* twisting, coiling
**enroscadura** *f* twisting, coiling; twist, coil, convolution
**enroscar** §86 *va* to twist, to coil; to twist in, to screw in; *vr* to twist, to coil, to curl
**enrubiador -dora** *adj* bleaching
**enrubiar** *va* to make blond, to bleach (*hair*); *vr* to turn blond, to bleach
**enrubio** *m* bleaching; bleaching lotion
**enrudecer** §34 *va* to make rough or crude; to make dull or stupid
**enruinecer** §34 *vn* to become debased, to get worse and worse
**enrular** *va* (Am.) to curl (*hair*)
**ensabanada** *f* var. of **encamisada**
**ensabanado** *m* first coat of plaster
**ensabanar** *va* to wrap up in a sheet; (mas.) to apply the first coat of plaster to
**ensacador -dora** *mf* bagger; *m* bagging machine
**ensacar** §86 *va* to bag, to put in a bag
**ensaimada** *f* twisted coffee cake
**ensalada** *f* salad; hodgepodge; **ensalada de frutas** fruit salad; **ensalada repelada** mixed salad
**ensaladera** *f* salad bowl
**ensaladilla** *f* assorted candy; setting of varicolored jewels; hodgepodge
**ensalmador -dora** *mf* bonesetter; powwow (*person*)
**ensalmar** *va* to set (*a bone*); to powwow, to heal by incantation
**ensalmista** *m* powwow (*person*)
**ensalmo** *m* powwow, incantation (*for curing*); **por ensalmo** as if by magic
**ensalobrar** *vr* to turn salty or briny
**ensalzamiento** *m* extolling; exaltation
**ensalzar** §76 *va* to extol; to exalt, elevate
**ensambenitar** *va* to put the sanbenito on (*a person*)

**ensamblador** *m* joiner, assembler
**ensambladora** *f* (carp.) jointer
**ensambladura** *f* joining, assembling; joint; **ensambladura a cola de milano** dovetail joint; **ensambladura a media madera** halved joint; **ensambladura de caja y espiga** mortise-and-tenon joint; **ensambladura de inglete** miter joint; **ensambladura de lengüeta y ranura** tongue-and-groove joint; **ensambladura de pasador** pin-connected joint; **ensambladura enrasada** flush joint; **ensambladura francesa** scarf, scarf joint
**ensamblaje** *m* joining, assembling; joint, union; stolen fragments of another author's works
**ensamblar** *va* to join, connect, assemble, fit together; (carp.) to joint; **ensamblar a caja y espiga** to mortise; **ensamblar a cola de milano** to dovetail
**ensamble** *m* var. of **ensambladura**
**ensanchador -dora** *adj* widening, expanding, stretching; *m* expander, stretcher; reamer; glove stretcher; **ensanchador de neumáticos** tire spreader
**ensanchamiento** *m* extension, expansion
**ensanchar** *va* to widen, enlarge, extend; to ease, let out (*close-fitting garment*); to unburden (*one's heart*); *vn* to be high and mighty; to get fat; *vr* to widen, to expand; to be high and mighty
**ensanche** *m* widening, extension; extent; fold in seam (*for subsequent enlargement of garment*); extension (*e.g., of a street*); suburban development; **ensanche de banda** (rad.) band spread
**ensandecer** §34 *vn* to get silly, to get simple, become feeble-minded
**ensangostar** *va* var. of **angostar**
**ensangrentado -da** *adj* bloody, blood-stained, gory
**ensangrentamiento** *m* staining with blood; bathing in blood
**ensangrentar** §18 *va* to stain with blood; to bathe in blood; *vr* to rage, get furious, go wild; to rise up in sanguinary factions; **ensangrentarse con** or **contra** to be cruel to, to try to hurt
**ensañado -da** *adj* angry, irritated; merciless, vengeful; cruel, ferocious
**ensañamiento** *m* extreme cruelty, barbarity, brutality; (law) aggravation
**ensañar** *va* to anger, enrage; *vr* to exult in cruelty; to rage (*said, e.g., of a disease*); **ensañarse en** to exult in hurting (*a defenseless person*)
**ensarnecer** §34 *vn* to get the itch
**ensartar** *va* to string (*e.g., beads*); to thread; (coll.) to pierce, to run through, e.g., **el toro le ensartó el cuerno** the bull ran its horn through him; to rattle off (*e.g., lies*); *vr* to squeeze in
**ensay** *m* (*pl:* **-sayes**) var. of **ensaye**
**ensayador** *m* assayer; rehearser
**ensayalar** *vr* to wear sackcloth
**ensayar** *va* to try, try on, try out; to test; to assay; to rehearse; **ensayar a** + *inf* to teach to + *inf*, to train to + *inf*; *vr* to practice; **ensayarse a** + *inf* to practice + *ger*, to rehearse + *ger*
**ensaye** *m* assay (*of metals*)
**ensayismo** *m* essay (*literary genre*)
**ensayista** *mf* essayist; (Am.) assayer
**ensayo** *m* trying, testing; trial, test; (lit.) essay; assay; practice, exercise; rehearsal; (chem.) analysis; **ensayo de coro** choir practice; **ensayo general** (theat.) dress rehearsal
**ensebar** *va* to tallow, to rub or smear with tallow; (coll.) to grease
**enseguida** *adv* at once, immediately
**enselvado -da** *adj* wooded
**enselvar** *va* to place in the woods; *vr* to hide in the woods; to become wooded
**ensenada** *f* inlet, cove
**ensenar** *va* to embosom; (naut.) to run (*a boat*) into an inlet or cove
**enseña** *f* standard, ensign, colors
**enseñable** *adj* teachable
**enseñado -da** *adj* trained, educated, informed; housebroken (*dog, cat*); trained (*hunting dog*)
**enseñamiento** *m* teaching; education, instruction; (archaic) teaching, precept
**enseñante** *adj* teaching
**enseñanza** *f* teaching; education, instruction; lesson (*instructive event or warning example*); **segunda enseñanza** or **enseñanza media** secondary education (*education in high school or liceo*); **enseñanza objetiva** object teaching; **enseñanza primaria** or **primera** primary education; **enseñanza secundaria** secondary education; **enseñanza superior** higher education
**enseñar** *va* to teach, to train; to show, to point out; **enseñar a** + *inf* to teach to + *inf*, to teach how to + *inf*; **enseñar algo a alguien** to teach someone something; *vn* to teach
**enseñoreamiento** *m* seizure, possession
**enseñorear** *va* to put in possession; *vr* to take possession; to control oneself; **enseñorearse de** to take possession of
**enserar** *va* to cover with matweed
**enseres** *mpl* household goods, implements, utensils, equipment
**enseriar** *vr* (Am.) to become serious
**ensiforme** *adj* sword-shaped; (anat., bot. & zool.) ensiform
**ensilaje** *m* ensilage, silage
**ensilar** *va* to ensilage
**ensillado -da** *adj* saddle-backed; *f* saddleback (*hill*)
**ensilladura** *f* saddling; back of horse where saddle fits; curve of the back
**ensillar** *va* to saddle
**ensimismamiento** *m* engrossment, self-absorption, deep thought
**ensimismar** *vr* to lose oneself, to become absorbed in thought; (Am.) to be proud, be boastful
**ensoberbecer** §34 *va* to make proud; *vr* to become proud; to become insolent; to swell, get rough (*said of the sea*)
**ensoberbecimiento** *m* pride, haughtiness
**ensogar** §59 *va* to fasten or bind with a rope; to wrap (*a bottle*) in ropework
**ensolerar** *va* to fix stools to (*beehives*)
**ensolver** §63 & §17, 9 *va* to include, contain; to shorten, contract; (med.) to resolve, clear up
**ensombrecer** §34 *va* to darken, cloud; *vr* to become sad and gloomy
**ensombrerado -da** *adj* (coll.) wearing a hat, with hat on
**ensopar** *va* to dip, to dunk; to steep, to soak
**ensordecedor -dora** *adj* deafening
**ensordecer** §34 *va* to deafen, make deaf; (phonet.) to unvoice; *vn* to become deaf; to play deaf, to not answer; *vr* (phonet.) to unvoice
**ensordecimiento** *m* (act of) deafening; deafness
**ensortijamiento** *m* curling; curls, ringlets, kinks
**ensortijar** *va* to curl, to kink; to clasp (*one's hands*); to ring (*e.g., a swine's snout*); *vr* to curl, to kink
**ensotar** *vr* to go into a thicket, to hide in the bush
**ensuciador -dora** *adj* staining, soiling; defiling
**ensuciamiento** *m* staining, soiling; defilement
**ensuciar** *va* to dirty, stain, soil, smear; to sully, defile; *vn* to soil; **ensuciar en** to soil (*one's bed or one's clothes*); *vr* to soil oneself; (coll.) to take bribes; **ensuciarse en** to soil (*one's bed or one's clothes*)
**ensuelto -ta** *pp of* **ensolver**
**ensueño** *m* dream; daydream
**ensullo** *m* var. of **enjulio**
**entablación** *f* boarding, planking; flooring; church register
**entablado** *m* wooden framework; flooring (*of boards*)
**entabladura** *f* boarding, planking
**entablamento** *m* board roof
**entablar** *va* to board, board up; (surg.) to splint; to start (*e.g., a conversation*); to bring (*e.g., a suit or action*); to set up (*the men on checkerboard or chessboard*); *vr* to settle (*said of wind*)

**entable** *m* boarding, planking; position of men (*on checkerboard or chessboard*); (Am.) business, undertaking; (Am.) circumstances, setting
**entablerar** *vr* (taur.) to hug the fence, to stick close to the barrier (*said of bull*)
**entablillar** *va* (surg.) to splint; (Am.) to cut (*chocolate*) into blocks or tablets
**entablón -blona** *adj* (Am.) blustering, browbeating; *mf* (Am.) bully
**entablonado** *m* planking
**entado -da** *adj* (her.) enté; **entado en punta** (her.) enté en point
**entalamadura** *f* arched cover (*of cart or wagon*)
**entalamar** *va* to cover (*a wagon*) with an arched canvas cover
**entalegar §59** *va* to bag, put in a bag; to hoard (*money*)
**entalingadura** *f* (naut.) clinch
**entalingar §59** *va* (naut.) to clinch (*cable*) to the anchor
**entallador** *m* sculptor, carver; engraver; fitter
**entalladura** *f* or **entallamiento** *m* sculpture, carving; engraving; slot, groove, mortise; gash, slash
**entallar** *va* to sculpture, to carve; to engrave; to notch, make a cut in; to slot, to groove, to mortise; to tailor, to fit (*a garment*); *vn* to fit (*said of clothing*); to take shape, to fill out; (coll.) to fit, go well, be appropriate
**entallecer §34** *vn & vr* to shoot, to sprout
**entallo** *m* intaglio
**entapizada** *f* rug, carpet; (fig.) carpet (*e.g., of daisies*)
**entapizar §76** *va* to tapestry; to hang (*e.g., with tapestry*); to cover (*walls, chairs, etc.*) with a fabric; to overgrow (*said of weeds, etc.*)
**entarascar §86** *va & vr* to dress up too fancily
**entarimando** *m* hardwood floor, inlaid floor
**entarimar** *va* to put a hardwood floor or inlaid floor on or over; *vr* (coll.) to put on airs
**entarquinamiento** *m* (agr.) reclamation by siltation
**entarquinar** *va* to fertilize with silt; to smear or soil with mud or slime; to reclaim (*a swamp*) with silt
**entarugado** *m* paving of wooden blocks
**entarugar §59** *va* to pave with wooden blocks
**entasia** *f* (path.) entasia
**éntasis** *f* (arch.) entasis
**ente** *m* being; (coll.) guy, queer duck
**entecado -da** or **enteco -ca** *adj* sickly, weakly
**entejar** *va* to tile, to cover with tile
**entelarañado -da** *adj* cobwebby, full of cobwebs
**entelequia** *f* (philos.) entelechy
**enteleridо -da** *adj* shaking with cold or fright; (Am.) frail, sickly
**entelo** *m* (zool.) entellus
**entena** *f* (naut.) lateen yard
**entenado -da** *mf* stepchild
**entenallas** *fpl* small vise, hand vise
**entendederas** *fpl* (coll.) brains; **tener malas entendederas** (coll.) to have no brains
**entendedor -dora** *adj* understanding, intelligent; *mf* understanding person; **al buen entendedor, pocas palabras** a word to the wise is enough
**entender** *m* opinion, understanding; **a mi entender** or **según mi entender** in my opinion, according to my understanding; **§66** *va* to understand; to intend, to mean; to believe; *vn* to understand; **entender de** to be experienced as (*e.g., a carpenter*); to have authority to pass on, to be a judge of; **entender de razones** to listen to reason; **entender en** to be familiar with; to deal with, take care of; to have authority to pass on; *vr* to be understood; to be meant; to understand each other; to have a secret understanding; to know what one is up to; **entenderse con** to get along with; to have an understanding with; to concern
**entendidamente** *adv* skilfully, knowingly
**entendido -da** *adj* expert, skilled, trained, learned; **los entendidos** well-informed persons, informed sources; **no darse por entendido** to pay no attention, to pretend not to understand
**entendimiento** *m* understanding; (philos.) understanding
**entenebrecer §34** *va* to darken, make dark; *vr* to get dark
**entente** *f* (dipl.) entente
**enterado -da** *adj* informed, fully informed; (Am.) conceited, haughty; *m* insider
**enteralgia** *f* (path.) enteralgia
**enterar** *va* to inform, acquaint; *vn* (Am.) to get better, recover; *vr* to understand; to find out; **enterarse de** to find out about, learn about, become aware of; to understand
**entercar §86** *vr* to get stubborn
**enterectomía** *f* (surg.) enterectomy
**entereza** *f* entirety, completeness; perfection; integrity, fairness; firmness, constancy, fortitude; strictness, rigor; **entereza virginal** virginity
**entérico -ca** *adj* enteric
**enterísimo -ma** *adj super* most complete; (bot.) entire
**enteritis** *f* (path.) enteritis
**enterizo -za** *adj* solid, in one piece
**enternecedor -dora** *adj* affecting, touching, moving
**enternecer §34** *va* to touch, to move to pity; *vr* to be touched, to be moved to pity
**enternecidamente** *adv* compassionately, tenderly
**enternecimiento** *m* pity, compassion
**entero -ra** *adj* whole, entire, complete; honest, upright; sound, vigorous; firm, energetic; (coll.) strong, heavy (*fabric*); not castrated; (arith.) whole, integral; (bot.) entire; *m* (arith.) integer; **por entero** wholly, entirely, completely
**enterohepatitis** *f* (path.) enterohepatitis; **enterohepatitis infecciosa** (vet.) blackhead, infectious enterohepatitis
**enterología** *f* enterology
**enterostomía** *f* (surg.) enterostomy
**enterotomía** *f* (surg.) enterotomy
**enterrador** *m* gravedigger; (ent.) burying beetle
**enterramiento** *m* interment, burial; grave; tomb
**enterrar §18** *va* to inter, bury; (fig.) to bury (*to conceal by covering; to abandon, to forget*); to outlive, to survive; *vr* (fig.) to be buried, to hide away
**enterronar** *va* to cover with clumps of earth
**entesamiento** *m* stretching, tightness, tautness
**entesar §18** *va* to stretch, tighten, make taut
**entestado -da** *adj* stubborn, obstinate
**entestecer §34** *va & vr* to stiffen
**entibación** *f* shoring, timbering
**entibador** *m* (min.) timberman
**entibar** *va* (min.) to prop up, shore up; *vn* to rest, lean
**entibiadero** *m* cooling room, cooling bath
**entibiar** *va* to make lukewarm; to temper, moderate; *vr* to become lukewarm; to cool down, cool off
**entibo** *m* (min.) timber, timbering; foundation, support; (arch.) abutment
**entidad** *f* entity; organization; consequence, importance, moment
**entierramuertos** *m* (*pl:* **-tos**) gravedigger
**entierro** *m* interment, burial; grave; tomb; funeral; buried treasure
**entiesar** *va* to stiffen
**entigrecer §34** *vr* to get mad, to fly into a rage
**entimema** *m* (log.) enthymeme
**entinar** *va* to put into a vat; to put (*wool*) in the degreasing bath
**entintado** *m* (print.) inking
**entintar** *va* to ink; to ink in; to stain with ink; to dye
**entinte** *m* (print.) inking
**entizar §76** *va* to chalk (*billiard cue*)
**entiznar** *va* to soil with soot; to stain, to spot; to defame
**entoldado** *m* covering with awnings; tent, group of tents (*on beach front*)
**entoldamiento** *m* covering with awnings
**entoldar** *va* to cover with an awning; to adorn with hangings; *vr* to become overcast, get cloudy; to be proud and haughty

**entomizar** §76 *va* to tie esparto cord on (*boards to be plastered*)
**entomología** *f* entomology
**entomológico -ca** *adj* entomologic or entomological
**entomólogo -ga** *mf* entomologist
**entonación** *f* intoning; intonation; blowing of bellows; (phonet.) intonation
**entonadera** *f* bellows lever (*of an organ*)
**entonado -da** *adj* haughty, arrogant; (mus.) harmonious, in tune; *m* (phonet.) toning
**entonador -dora** *mf* bellows blower (*person*)
**entonamiento** *m* var. of **entonación**
**entonar** *va* to intone; to intonate; to sing (*something*) in tune; to blow (*an organ*) with bellows; to harmonize (*colors*); (mus., paint. & phot.) to tone; to tone up (*the body*); *vn* to sing in tune; *vr* to put on airs, be puffed up with pride
**entonces** *adv* then; and so; **de entonces acá** since then, since that time; **en aquel entonces** at that time; **pues entonces** well then
**entonelar** *va* to put in casks, to put in barrels
**entongar** §59 *va* (Am.) to pile up (*boxes and packing cases*); (Am.) to pile up in rows
**entono** *m* intoning; haughtiness, arrogance
**entontecer** §34 *va* to make foolish or silly; *vn & vr* to become foolish or silly
**entontecimiento** *m* foolishness, silliness
**entorchado -da** *adj* (arch.) wreathed; *m* wreathed cord; bullion (*twisted fringe of uniform*); **ganar los entorchados** to win one's stripes
**entorchar** *va* to twist (*candles*) to make a torch; to wreathe or twine (*a string or cord*) with silk or wire
**entorilar** *va* to drive (*a bull*) into the pen
**entornado -da** *adj* half-closed, on the jar
**entornar** *va* to upset; to half-close (*door; eyes*); *vr* to upset, to be upset
**entornillar** *va* to twist, to twist into a spiral; to screw, to screw on, to screw up
**entorpecer** §34 *va* to stupefy; to dull, benumb; to obstruct, delay, slow up; to make (*e.g., a piece of machinery*) stick; *vr* to stick, get stuck
**entorpecimiento** *m* stupefaction; dulling, benumbing; obstruction, delay; sticking, jamming
**entortadura** *f* or **entortamiento** *m* bending; crookedness
**entortar** §77 *va* to bend, make crooked; to make blind in one eye; *vr* to bend, get crooked
**entosigar** §59 *va* to poison
**entozoario** *m* (zool.) entozoan
**entrado -da** *adj* (Am.) meddling, self-assertive; **entrado en años** advanced in years; *f* entry, entrance; accession; entree; admission; arrival; beginning; hand (*at cards*); receipts; income; entry, entrance hall; (com.) entry; (cook.) entree; admission ticket; (elec.) input; (theat.) house (*audience; size of audience*); gate (*number of people paying admission; amount they pay*); (coll.) short call; (Am.) onslaught, rain (*e.g., of blows*); (Am.) down payment; **dar entrada a** to admit; to give an opening or chance to; (naut.) to give right of entry to (*a ship*); **mucha entrada** good house, good turnout; **entrada de explotación** operating revenue; **entrada de pavana** (coll.) twaddle, bombast; **entrada de taquilla** gate (*number of people paying admission; amount they pay*); **entrada general** (theat.) top gallery; **entrada llena** full house
**entradón** *m* (sport) big gate (*large attendance*)
**entrador -dora** *adj* (Am.) energetic, lively, hustling; (Am.) intruding, self-assertive
**entramado -da** *adj* half-timbered; *m* timber framework
**entramar** *va* to build the framework for, to make half-timbered
**entrambos -bas** *adj & pron indef* both
**entrampar** *va* to trap; to trick; (coll.) to entangle; (coll.) to burden with debt; *vr* to get trapped; (coll.) to become entangled; (coll.) to run into debt
**entrante** *adj* entering; incoming, inbound; next, coming; (math. & mil.) re-entering; *mf* entrant; **entrantes y salientes** (coll.) hangers-on; *m* (naut.) flood tide
**entraña** *f* internal part; heart, center; **entrañas** *fpl* entrails; (fig.) entrails (*e.g., of the earth*); heart, feeling, will; (fig.) temper, disposition
**entrañable** *adj* close, intimate; deep-felt
**entrañar** *va* to bury deep, to enwomb; to contain, involve; *vr* to be buried deep, be enwombed; to become very close or intimate
**entrañoso -sa** *adj* intimate, inmost
**entrapada** *f* crimson cloth (*for hangings and upholstery*)
**entrapajar** *va* to wrap up with rags, to bandage with rags
**entrapar** *va* to powder (*the hair*) to remove grease and dirt; to puff up (*the hair*) with powder and grease; (agr.) to fertilize (*a root*) with old rags; *vr* to get full of dust and dirt; to be dulled by grit
**entrapazar** §76 *va* to cheat, swindle
**entrar** *va* to bring in, to show in; to attack; to invade, take by force; to influence, to impress; (naut.) to overtake; *vn* to enter, go in, come in; to attack; to empty (*said of a river*); to have entree; to begin; to begin to be felt; to rise (*said of wind, tide, etc.*); to be understandable; **entrar a** + *inf* to go in to + *inf;* to begin to + *inf;* **entrar a matar** (taur.) to go in for the kill; **entrar bien** to be suitable; **entrar en** to enter; to enter into; to fit in or into; to take up, adopt; **entrar en el número de** to be counted among; **entrar por** to follow (*e.g., a custom, fashion*)
**entre** *prep* between; among; in the course of; **entre manos** at hand, in hand; **entre mí** to myself; **entre que** while; **entre tanto** meanwhile, in the meantime; **entre tú y yo** between you and me
**entreabierto -ta** *adj* half-open, ajar; *pp of* **entreabrir**
**entreabrir** §17, 9 *va* to half-open (*door; eyes*)
**entreacto** *m* entr'acte; small cigar
**entreancho -cha** *adj* neither broad nor narrow
**entrecalle** *f* (arch.) space between moldings
**entrecanal** *f* (arch.) fillet (*between two flutings*)
**entrecano -na** *adj* graying (*hair; person*)
**entrecarril** *m* (Am.) gage (*of rails*)
**entrecasco** *m* var. of **entrecorteza**
**entrecavar** *va* to loosen the earth around (*e.g., root of vine*); (dial.) to clear of weeds, to weed
**entrecejo** *m* space between eyebrows; frown; **con entrecejo** with a frown; **arrugar el entrecejo, fruncir el entrecejo** or **ponerse de entrecejo** to knit or to wrinkle one's brow, to frown
**entrecierre** *m* interlock; (elec.) interlocking connector
**entrecinta** *f* (arch.) collar beam
**entreclaro -ra** *adj* lightish, clearish
**entrecogedura** *f* catching, seizing; squeezing, overcoming
**entrecoger** §49 *va* to catch, seize; to press hard, to put down, to silence
**entrecomar** *va* to set off between commas, to set off between quotation marks
**entrecoro** *m* (eccl.) chancel
**entrecortado -da** *adj* intermittent, broken
**entrecortadura** *f* partial cut; intermittent interruption
**entrecortar** *va* to cut here and there; to break into now and then, to cut off from time to time
**entrecorteza** *f* ingrown bark (*defect in timber resulting from growing together of two branches*)
**entrecruzar** §76 *va & vr* to intercross; to interlace, interweave; to interbreed
**entrecubierta** *f* or **entrecubiertas** *fpl* (naut.) between-decks
**entrecuesto** *m* loin, sirloin; backbone (*of an animal*)
**entrechocar** §86 *vr* to collide, to clash
**entrechoque** *m* collision, clash
**entredicho** *m* interdiction, prohibition; (law) injunction; **estar en entredicho** to be under suspicion; **poner en entredicho** to cast doubt on
**entredoble** *adj* of medium thickness or weight

**entredós** *m* (sew.) insertion; entre-deux, console placed between two windows; (print.) long primer
**entrefilete** *m* short feature, special item (*in a newspaper*)
**entrefino -na** *adj* medium, of medium quality
**entreforro** *m* (naut.) parceling
**entrega** *f* delivery; surrender; fascicle, instalment, issue, number (*of a magazine, etc.*); abandon; (mas.) tailing; **por entregas** in instalments
**entregamiento** *m* delivery
**entregar §59** *va* to deliver; to surrender, hand over; to betray; to fit, insert, embed; **entregarla** (coll.) to die; *vr* to give in, to surrender; to devote oneself; to abandon oneself, to yield; **entregarse de** to take charge of, take possession of
**entreguismo** *m* (Am.) political defeatism
**entrehierro** *m* (phys.) air gap; (phys.) pole gap (*of cyclotron*); (elec.) spark gap; **entrehierro de chispa amortiguada** (elec.) quenched gap
**entrelargo -ga** *adj* fairly long
**entrelazado da** *adj* (her.) interlaced, interfretted; *m* interlace, interlacery
**entrelazar §76** *va* to interlace, interweave, entwine
**entrelínea** *f* writing between the lines, interlineation; (print.) space, lead
**entrelinear** *va* to write between the lines
**entreliño** *m* space between rows of trees or vines
**entrelistado -da** *adj* with colored stripes
**entreluces** *mpl* twilight; dawn
**entrelucir §60** *vn* to show through; to shine dimly
**entreluzco** *1st sg pres ind of* **entrelucir**
**entremediar** *va* to put between or in the midst of
**entremedias** *adv* in between; in the meantime; **entremedias de** between; among, in the midst of
**entremés** *m* side dish, hors d'oeuvre; interlude; (theat.) interlude (*inserted in a mystery*); (theat.) short scene or farce (*inserted in an auto or between two acts of a comedia*)
**entremesear** *va* to enliven (*a conversation*); *vn* to play in an entremés
**entremesil** *adj* (pertaining to an) entremés
**entremesista** *mf* writer or actor of entremeses
**entremeter** *va* to put in, insert; to fold (*a diaper*); *vr* to butt in, intrude, meddle
**entremetido -da** *adj* meddlesome; *mf* meddler, intruder
**entremetimiento** *m* interposition, insertion; meddlesomeness, intrusion
**entremezcladura** *f* intermingling, intermixing, intermixture
**entremezclar** *va & vr* to intermingle, to intermix
**entremiche** *m* (naut.) carling
**entremiso** *m* cheese vat, cheese shelf
**entremorir §45** & **§17,** 9 *vn* to flicker, die out, burn out
**entrenador** *m* (sport) trainer, coach
**entrenamiento** *m* (sport) training, coaching
**entrenar** *va & vr* (sport) to train, to coach
**entrencar §86** *va* to put rods or crosstrees in (*beehive*)
**entreno** *m* (sport) training
**entrenudo** *m* (bot.) internode
**entrenzar §76** *va* to plait, braid (*hair*)
**entreoído -da** *pp of* **entreoír;** *adj* half-heard; **saber de** or **por entreoídas** (coll.) to know from having heard some talk about
**entreoigo** *1st sg pres ind of* **entreoír**
**entreoír §64** *va* to hear vaguely, to hear something said about
**entreordinario -ria** *adj* middling
**entrepalmadura** *f* (vet.) ulcerous sore (*on horse's hoof*)
**entrepanes** *mpl* unsown ground (*amidst sown areas*)
**entrepañado -da** *adj* paneled
**entrepaño** *m* panel (*e.g., of door*); shelf; (arch.) pier (*wall between two openings*)
**entreparecer §34** *vr* to show through; to have some resemblance
**entrepaso** *m* rack pace (*of horse*)
**entrepeines** *mpl* comb wool
**entrepelado -da** *adj* pied, parti-colored (*said of a horse*)
**entrepelar** *va* to pluck irregularly; *vn* to be pied or parti-colored (*said of horses*)
**entrepernar §18** *vn* to intertwine the legs
**entrepierna** *f* or **entrepiernas** *fpl* (anat.) side of thigh between the legs; crotch; patches in the crotch of trousers or drawers; (Am.) bathing trunks
**entrepiso** *m* mezzanine, entresol; (min.) intermediate gallery
**entreplanos** *m* (*pl:* **-nos**) (aer.) gap
**entreplanta** *f* mezzanine
**entrepuente** *m* or **entrepuentes** *mpl* (naut.) between-decks
**entrepunzadura** *f* dull shooting pains
**entrepunzar §76** *vn* to have dull shooting pains
**entrerraído -da** *adj* worn in spots, threadbare in spots
**entrerrenglón** *m* space between lines, interline; (print.) space, lead
**entrerrenglonadura** *f* writing between the lines, interlineation
**entrerrenglonar** *va* to write between the lines
**entrerriel** *m* gage (*of railroad*)
**entrerrosca** *f* (mach.) nipple
**entresaca** or **entresacadura** *f* picking out, selection; sifting; thinning, pruning
**entresacar §86** *va* to pick out, select; to sift, cull; to thin out (*e.g., trees*); to prune (*branches*)
**entresijo** *m* (anat. & zool.) mesentery; arcanum, secret; obstacle; **tener muchos entresijos** to be complicated, be hard to figure out; to be cautious, be mysterious
**entresuelo** *m* mezzanine, entresol; (theat.) first balcony
**entresurco** *m* space between furrows
**entretalla** or **entretalladura** *f* bas-relief
**entretallar** *va* to carve, engrave; to carve or cut in bas-relief; to make openwork in; to intercept, obstruct; *vr* to fit together
**entretanto** *adv* meanwhile; *m* meanwhile, meantime; **por entretanto** in the meantime
**entretecho** *m* (Am.) attic, garret
**entretejedor -dora** *adj* interweaving
**entretejedura** *f* interweaving
**entretejer** *va* to interweave
**entretejimiento** *m* var. of **entretejedura**
**entretela** *f* (sew.) interlining; **entretelas** *fpl* (coll.) heartstrings, inmost being
**entretelar** *va* (sew.) to interline
**entretelones** *mpl* events behind the scenes, persons behind the scenes
**entretén** *2d sg impv of* **entretener**
**entretención** *f* (Am.) entertainment, amusement
**entretendré** *1st sg fut ind of* **entretener**
**entretenedor -dora** *adj* entertaining; *mf* entertainer
**entretener §85** *va* to entertain, amuse; to keep amused; to delay, put off; to make bearable, to allay (*pain*); to while away (*the time*); to deceive; to maintain, to keep up; **entretener el hambre** (coll.) to take a bite in order to stave off hunger till mealtime; (coll.) to try to forget one's hunger; *vr* to be amused, to amuse oneself; **entretenerse con** or **en** + *inf* to amuse oneself + *ger*
**entretengo** *1st sg pres ind of* **entretener**
**entretenido -da** *adj* entertaining, amusing; (rad.) undamped, continuous (*waves*); *f* entertainment; kept woman; **dar la entretenida a** or **dar con la entretenida a** to keep talking in order to avoid granting a request
**entretenimiento** *m* entertainment, amusement; maintenance, upkeep
**entretiempo** *m* spring or autumn (*the season between the seasons, i.e., between summer and winter*); **de entretiempo** lightweight (*coat*)
**entretuve** *1st sg pret ind of* **entretener**
**entreuntar §75** *va* to oil on the surface, oil lightly
**entreveía** *1st sg imperf ind of* **entrever**
**entrevenar** *vr* to spread through the veins
**entreventana** *f* (arch.) pier (*wall between two windows*)

**entreveo** *1st sg pres ind of* **entrever**
**entrever** §93 *va* to glimpse, descry; to guess, divine, suspect
**entreverar** *va* to mix in, to intermingle; *vr* to be intermixed, to intermingle; (Am.) to get mixed together without order; (Am.) to clash in hand-to-hand combat (*said of two forces of cavalry*)
**entrevero** *m* (Am.) intermingling; (Am.) jumble, confusion; (Am.) hand-to-hand combat between two forces of cavalry
**entrevía** *f* (rail.) gage
**entrevista** *f* see **entrevisto**
**entrevistar** *vr* to have an interview; **entrevistarse con** to interview, to talk with
**entrevisto -ta** *pp of* **entrever;** *f* interview
**entripado -da** *adj* in the belly; not cleaned (*said of a dead animal*); *m* bellyache; (coll.) anger, veiled displeasure
**entristecedor -dora** *adj* saddening
**entristecer** §34 *va* to sadden; to make gloomy; *vr* to sadden, become sad
**entristecimiento** *m* sadness, gloominess
**entrojar** *va* to garner (*grain*)
**entrometer** *va & vr* var. of **entremeter**
**entrometido -da** *adj & mf* var. of **entremetido**
**entrometimiento** *m* var. of **entremetimiento**
**entronar** *va* to enthrone
**entroncamiento** *m* relationship, connection; connection, junction (*of rail lines*)
**entroncar** §86 *va* to show or prove the relationship between; *vn* to be related, be connected; to connect (*said of two or more rail lines*); **entroncar con** to be or become related to
**entronerar** *va* (billiards) to pocket (*a ball*); *vr* to be pocketed, to fall into a pocket
**entronización** *f* enthronement; exaltation; popularization
**entronizar** §76 *va* to enthrone; to exalt; to promote, popularize; *vr* to be enthroned; to seize power; to become the vogue; to be puffed up with pride
**entronque** *m* var. of **entroncamiento**
**entropía** *f* (thermodynamics) entropy
**entruchada** *f* or **entruchado** *m* (coll.) decoy, trick, intrigue
**entruchar** *va* (coll.) to decoy, to trick
**entruchón -chona** *mf* (coll.) decoy, trickster
**entrujar** *va* to store (*especially olives*); (coll.) to pocket
**entubar** *va* to pipe; to install new tubes in (*a boiler*); (min.) to case, to line (*a shaft*)
**entuerto** *m* wrong, injustice, insult; **entuertos** *mpl* afterpains
**entullecer** §34 *va* to stop, check; *vn & vr* to become crippled, become paralyzed
**entumecer** §34 *va* to benumb, make numb; *vr* to become numb, to go to sleep (*said of limbs*); to swell, to surge
**entumecimiento** *m* numbness, deadness, torpor; swell, swelling
**entumir** *vr* to become numb, to go to sleep (*said of a limb*)
**entunicar** §86 *va* (paint.) to plaster for frescoing
**entupir** *va* to block, clog, stop up; to compress; *vr* to become blocked, clogged, or stopped up
**enturbiamiento** *m* muddiness; confusion, disorder
**enturbiar** *va* to stir up, to muddy; to obscure, to confuse, to derange; *vr* to get muddy; to become deranged or disordered
**entusiasmar** *va* to enthuse, enrapture; *vr* to enthuse, be enthusiastic
**entusiasmo** *m* enthusiasm
**entusiasta** *adj* enthusiastic; *mf* enthusiast
**entusiástico -ca** *adj* enthusiastic
**enucleación** *f* (surg.) enucleation
**enuclear** *va* to enucleate
**énula campana** *f* (bot.) elecampane
**enumeración** *f* enumeration
**enumerador -dora** *mf* enumerator; **enumerador censal** census taker
**enumerar** *va* to enumerate
**enumerativo -va** *adj* enumerative
**enunciación** *f* enunciation
**enunciado** *m* enunciation, statement
**enunciar** *va* to enounce, enunciate
**enunciativo -va** *adj* enunciative; (gram.) declarative
**enuresis** *f* (path.) enuresis
**envainador -dora** *adj* sheathing
**envainar** *va* to sheathe
**envalentonamiento** *m* boldness, daring; encouragement
**envalentonar** *va* to embolden, to encourage; *vr* to pluck up
**envalijar** *va* to put or pack in a valise
**envanecer** §34 *va* to make vain; *vr* to become vain; **envanecerse con, de, en,** or **por** to swell with pride at
**envanecimiento** *m* vanity, conceit
**envaramiento** *m* numbness, stiffness
**envarar** *va* to benumb, stiffen
**envarbascar** §86 *va* to infect (*water*) with mullein to stun the fish
**envasado** *m* packing, bottling, canning
**envasador -dora** *adj* packing; *mf* packer, filler; *m* large funnel
**envasar** *va* to pack, to package, to bottle, to can; to sack (*grain*); to insert; to thrust, push, poke (*a sword*); to drink (*e.g., wine*) to excess; *vn* to drink to excess; *vr* to stab oneself; to stab each other
**envase** *m* packing, bottling, canning; package, container, bottle, jar, can; **envase de hojalata** tin can
**envedijar** *vr* to get tangled; (coll.) to get into a fist fight
**envejecer** §34 *va* to age, make old; *vn* to age, grow old; to go out-of-date; to last a long time; *vr* to age, grow old; to go out-of-date
**envejecido -da** *adj* old, aged; tried, experienced
**envejecimiento** *m* aging; age
**envenenador -dora** *adj* poisoning; *mf* poisoner
**envenenamiento** *m* poisoning; **envenenamiento plúmbico** lead poisoning
**envenenar** *va* to poison; (fig.) to put an evil interpretation on (*someone's words or deeds*); (fig.) to envenom, to embitter; *vr* to take poison
**enverar** *vn* to turn golden-red (*said of ripening fruit*)
**enverdecer** §34 *vn & vr* to turn green, be covered with verdure
**enverdecimiento** *m* turning green; verdure
**envergadura** *f* breadth (*of sails*); (aer.) span, wingspread; spread (*of wings of bird*); (fig.) spread, compass, reach
**envergar** §59 *va* (naut.) to bend (*the sails*)
**envergue** *m* (naut.) sail rope, roband
**enverjado** *m* lattice, trellis, grillwork, grating
**envero** *m* golden red (*of ripening fruit*); golden-red grape
**envés** *m* wrong side; (coll.) back, shoulders
**envesado -da** *adj* showing the back side; *m* fleshy side of hide or skin
**envestir** §94 *va* var. of **investir**
**enviada** *f* fishing scow
**enviadizo -za** *adj* sent, regularly sent
**enviado** *m* messenger; envoy; **enviado extraordinario** envoy extraordinary
**enviajado -da** *adj* sloping, oblique
**enviar** §90 *va* to send; to ship; **enviar a** + *inf* to send to + *inf*
**enviciamiento** *m* corruption, vitiation; addiction
**enviciar** *va* to corrupt, vitiate, spoil; *vn* to have abundant leaves and little fruit; *vr* to become addicted, to become overfond; **enviciarse con** or **en** to become addicted to, to become overfond of
**envidador -dora** *mf* bidder, bettor (*at cards*)
**envidar** *va* to bid against, to bet against; *vn* to bid, to bet
**envidia** *f* envy; desire
**envidiable** *adj* enviable
**envidiar** *va* to envy, to begrudge; to desire
**envidioso -sa** *adj* envious; covetous, greedy
**envigado** *m* beams, joists
**envigar** §59 *va* to install the beams in (*a building*); *vn* to install the beams
**envilecedor -dora** *adj* debasing, degrading
**envilecer** §34 *va* to vilify, debase; *vr* to be debased, to degrade oneself; to cringe, grovel
**envilecimiento** *m* vilification, debasement, degradation; cringing, groveling

**envinado -da** *adj* (Am.) wine-colored
**envinagrar** *va* to put vinegar in or on; *vr* to sour, to turn sour
**envinar** *va* to put wine in (*water*)
**envío** *m* sending, shipment, remittance; autograph, inscription (*in a book*)
**envión** *m* push, shove
**envirotado -da** *adj* stiff, stuck-up
**enviscamiento** *m* smearing with birdlime
**enviscar §86** *va* to incite, provoke, stir up; to smear (*branches*) with birdlime; *vr* to be caught or stuck with birdlime
**envite** *m* stake; side bet; offer, invitation; push, shove; (bridge) bid; **al primer envite** at the start, right off
**enviudar** *vn* to become widowed, to become a widow or widower
**envoltorio** *m* bundle; wrapping; knot (*in cloth from mixture of different kind of wool*)
**envoltura** *f* cover, wrapper, envelope; swaddling clothes; (aer. & bot.) envelope
**envolvedor -dora** *mf* wrapping clerk, wrapper; *m* wrapping, cover; bed, cot, or table used for swaddling children
**envolvente** *adj* (mil.) encircling; *f* cover, housing
**envolver §63 & §17,** 9 *va* to wrap, wrap up; to swaddle; to wind; to imply, mean; to involve; to floor (*an opponent*); to surround; (mil.) to encircle; *vr* to wrap up; to become involved; to have an affair
**envolvimiento** *m* wrapping, envelopment; involvement; winding; wallowing place (*for animals*); (mil.) encirclement
**envuelto -ta** *pp of* **envolver**
**enyerbar** *vr* (Am.) to be overgrown with grass, be covered with grass
**enyesado** *m* plastering; treatment of wine with gypsum; treatment of soil with gypsum
**enyesadura** *f* plastering
**enyesar** *va* to plaster; to mix plaster with; (surg.) to put in a plaster cast; to treat (*wine or soils*) with gypsum
**enyugar §59** *va* to yoke
**enzainar** *vr* (coll.) to look askance, to look sidewise; (coll.) to become untrustworthy, to turn traitor
**enzalamar** *va* (coll.) to provoke, to incite
**enzamarrado -da** *adj* wearing an undressed sheepskin jacket
**enzarzar §76** *va* to throw into the brambles, to cover with brambles; to involve, involve in a dispute; to set hurdles for (*silkworms*); *vr* to get entangled in brambles; to get involved, get involved in a dispute
**enzima** *f* (biochem.) enzyme
**enzímico -ca** *adj* enzymatic
**enzootia** *f* (vet.) enzoötic
**enzunchar** *va* to bind with hoops or iron bands
**enzurdecer §34** *vn* to become left-handed
**enzurizar §76** *va* to sow discord among
**enzurronar** *va* to bag; (coll.) to put inside
**eoceno -na** *adj & m* (geol.) Eocene
**eoliano -na** *adj* (geol.) aeolian
**eólico -ca** *adj* Aeolian; (geol.) aeolian; *m* Aeolic (*dialect*)
**Eólide, la** Aeolis
**eolio -lia** *adj & mf* Aeolian; *adj & m* Aeolic (*dialect*)
**eolítico -ca** *adj* (archeol.) eolithic
**Eolo** *m* (myth.) Aeolus
**eón** *m* aeon; (Gnosticism) aeon
**Eos** *f* (myth.) Eos
**eosina** *f* (chem.) eosin
**epacta** *f* epact
**epactilla** *f* liturgical calendar
**epazote** *m* (bot.) Mexican tea
**E.P.D.** abr. of **en paz descanse**
**epéndimo** *m* (anat.) ependyma
**epéntesis** *f* (*pl:* **-sis**) (gram.) epenthesis
**epentético -ca** *adj* epenthetic
**eperlano** *m* (ichth.) smelt
**épica** *f* see **épico**
**epicáliz** *m* (*pl:* **-lices**) (bot.) epicalyx
**epicarpio** *m* (bot.) epicarp
**epicedio** *m* epicedium
**epiceno -na** *adj* (gram.) epicene
**epicentro** *m* epicenter
**epicíclico -ca** *adj* epicyclic
**epiciclo** *m* (astr. & geom.) epicycle
**epicicloide** *f* (geom.) epicycloid
**épico -ca** *adj* epic or epical; (fig.) epic, heroic, sublime; *m* epic poet; *f* epic poetry
**epicotilo** *m* (bot.) epicotyl
**Epicteto** *m* Epictetus
**epicureísmo** *m* Epicureanism
**epicúreo -a** *adj* Epicurean; epicurean; *mf* Epicurean; epicurean, epicure
**Epicuro** *m* Epicurus
**epidemia** *f* epidemic
**epidemial** *adj* var. of **epidémico**
**epidemicidad** *f* epidemicity
**epidémico -ca** *adj* epidemic or epidemical
**epidemiología** *f* epidemiology
**epidemiólogo -ga** *mf* epidemiologist
**epidérmico -ca** *adj* epidermal
**epidermis** *f* (anat.) epidermis
**epidota** *f* (mineral.) epidote
**Epifanía** *f* (eccl.) Epiphany; (*l.c.*) *f* epiphany (*apparition*)
**epífisis** *f* (*pl:* **-sis**) (anat.) epiphysis
**epífito -ta** *adj* epiphytic; *f* (bot.) epiphyte
**epifonema** *f* (rhet.) epiphonema
**epifora** *f* (path.) epiphora
**epigástrico -ca** *adj* epigastric
**epigastrio** *m* (anat. & zool.) epigastrium
**epigea** *f* (bot.) epigaea; **epigea rastrera** (bot.) trailing arbutus
**epigénico -ca** *adj* (geol.) epigene
**epiglotis** *f* (anat.) epiglottis
**epígono** *m* follower, disciple
**epígrafe** *m* epigraph; inscription; motto, device; title; headline
**epigrafía** *f* epigraphy
**epigráfico -ca** *adj* epigraphic
**epigrafista** *mf* epigrapher
**epigrama** *m* epigram
**epigramatario -ria** *adj* epigrammatic; *mf* epigrammatist; *m* collection of epigrams
**epigramático -ca** *adj* epigrammatic
**epilepsia** *f* (path.) epilepsy
**epiléptico -ca** *adj & mf* epileptic
**epilogación** *f* epilogue
**epilogal** *adj* epilogic; compendious
**epilogar §59** *va* to recapitulate, sum up
**epilogismo** *m* (astr.) computation
**epílogo** *m* epilogue; (rhet.) peroration
**epinicio** *m* song of victory
**epiplón** *m* (anat. & zool.) epiploön, omentum
**Epiro, el** Epirus
**episcopado** *m* episcopacy, episcopate
**episcopal** *adj* episcopal; Episcopal
**episcopalismo** *m* (eccl.) episcopalism; Episcopalianism
**episcopalista** *adj & mf* Episcopalian
**episcopologio** *m* catalogue of bishops
**episódico -ca** *adj* episodic or episodical
**episodio** *m* episode
**epispástico -ca** *adj & m* (med.) epispastic
**epistaxis** *f* (path.) epistaxis
**epistemología** *f* epistemology
**epistemológico -ca** *adj* epistemological
**epistilo** *m* (arch.) epistyle
**epístola** *f* epistle; (eccl.) Epistle
**epistolar** *adj* epistolary
**epistolario** *m* volume of letters; (eccl.) epistolary
**epistolero** *m* (eccl.) epistler
**epitafio** *m* epitaph
**epitalamio** *m* epithalamium
**epitelial** *adj* epithelial
**epitelio** *m* (anat.) epithelium
**epitelioma** *m* (path.) epithelioma
**epítema** *m* (med.) epithem
**epíteto** *m* epithet
**epítimo** *m* (bot.) clover dodder
**epitomar** *va* to epitomize
**epítome** *m* epitome
**epizootia** *f* epizoötic
**epizoótico -ca** *adj* epizoötic
**E.P.M.** abr. of **en propia mano**
**época** *f* epoch, age, time; (astr. & geol.) epoch; **formar** or **hacer época** to be epoch-making; **época glacial** (geol.) ice age; **época victoriana** Victorian age
**epoda** *f* or **epodo** *m* epode
**epónimo -ma** *adj* eponymous
**epopeya** *f* epic, epic poem; (fig.) epic

**épsilon** *f* epsilon
**epsomita** *f* (mineral.) epsomite
**equiángulo -la** *adj* (geom.) equiangular
**equidad** *f* equity; (law) equity; equableness (*of disposition*); reasonableness (*in prices or other terms*)
**equidistancia** *f* equidistance
**equidistante** *adj* equidistant
**equidistar** *vn* to be equidistant
**equidna** *f* (zool.) echidna
**équido** *m* (zool.) equid
**equilátero -ra** *adj* equilateral
**equilibración** *f* equilibration
**equilibrado -da** *adj* sensible, prudent
**equilibrar** *va* to balance, equilibrate; to balance (*the budget*); *vr* to balance, equilibrate
**equilibrio** *m* equilibrium, balance, equipoise; balancing (*of the budget*); **equilibrio europeo** or **equilibrio político** (dipl.) balance of power
**equilibrista** *adj* equilibristic; *mf* equilibrist, balancer, ropedancer
**equimosis** *f* (*pl:* **-sis**) black-and-blue mark, ecchymosis
**equino -na** *adj* equine; *m* equine; (arch. & zool.) echinus
**equinoccial** *adj* equinoctial; *f* equinoctial (*line*)
**equinoccio** *m* (astr.) equinox; **equinoccio otoñal** or **de otoño** (astr.) autumnal equinox; **equinoccio vernal** or **de primavera** (astr.) vernal equinox
**equinococo** *m* (zool.) echinococcus
**equinodermo** *m* (zool.) echinoderm
**equipaje** *m* baggage; piece of baggage; equipment; (naut.) crew; (mil.) baggage train; **equipaje de mano** hand baggage
**equipar** *va* to equip, fit out; to equip and provision (*a ship*)
**equiparación** *f* comparison; equalization
**equiparar** *va* to compare; to equalize, make equal or like
**equipier** *m* (*pl:* **-piers**) teammate
**equipo** *m* equipment, outfit; set; unit; crew; (sport) team; **equipo de novia** trousseau; **equipo de radio** radio set; **equipo de urgencia** first-aid kit
**equiponderancia** *f* equality in weight
**equiponderar** *vn* to be equal in weight
**equipotencial** *adj* (phys.) equipotential
**equisetáceo -a** *adj* (bot.) equisetaceous
**equiseto** *m* (bot.) equisetum, horsetail; **equiseto menor** (bot.) bottle brush, field horsetail
**equitación** *f* equitation, horsemanship
**equitativo -va** *adj* equitable
**equivaldré** *1st sg fut ind of* **equivaler**
**equivalencia** *f* equivalence
**equivalente** *adj & m* equivalent
**equivaler §89** *va* to be equivalent to, to be equal to; *vn* to be equivalent, to be equal
**equivalgo** *1st sg pres ind of* **equivaler**
**equivocación** *f* mistakenness; mistake
**equivocadamente** *adv* mistakenly, by mistake
**equivocado -da** *adj* mistaken, wrong
**equivocar §86** *va* to mistake; to mix (*to confuse completely*); *vr* to be mistaken, to make a mistake; to miss one's calling; **equivocarse con** to be mistaken for; **equivocarse de** to be mistaken in; **me equivoqué de camino** I took the wrong road; **se equivocó de casa** he went to the wrong house
**equívoco -ca** *adj* equivocal; *m* equivocation, ambiguity; pun; mix-up
**equivoquista** *mf* punster; equivocator
**-era** *suffix f* see **-ero**
**era** *f* era, age, period; (geol.) era; threshing floor; vegetable patch, garden bed; mixing board; **era arqueozoica** (geol.) Archeozoic era; **era atómica** atomic age; **era común** Common Era; **era cristiana** or **era de Cristo** Christian Era; **era de hortalizas** vegetable garden; **era vulgar** Vulgar Era; *1st sg imperf ind of* **ser**
**eral** *m* two-year-old bull
**erar** *va* to lay out patches or beds in (*a garden*)
**erario** *m* state treasury
**erasmiano -na** *adj & mf* Erasmian
**Erasmo** *m* Erasmus
**Erato** *f* (myth.) Erato
**erbio** *m* (chem.) erbium
**Erebo** *m* (myth.) Erebus (*underworld*)
**erección** *f* erection; establishment; tension; (physiol.) erection
**eréctil** *adj* erectile
**erectilidad** *f* erectility
**erector -tora** *adj* erecting; *mf* erector, builder
**eremita** *m* eremite, hermit
**eremítico -ca** *adj* eremitic; solitary
**eremitorio** *m* location of a hermitage or hermitages
**erepsina** *f* (biochem.) erepsin
**eres** *2d sg pres ind of* **ser**
**eretismo** *m* (physiol.) erethism
**ergástula** *f* or **ergástulo** *m* (hist.) slave prison
**ergio** *m* (phys.) erg
**ergosterol** *m* (pharm.) ergosterol
**ergotina** *f* (pharm.) ergotin
**ergotismo** *m* ergotism (*sophistry*); (plant path.) ergot; (path.) ergotism
**ergotizar §76** *vn* to ergotize, argue sophistically
**erguen** *m* (bot.) argan tree
**erguimiento** *m* raising, straightening
**erguir §47** *va* to raise, lift up, straighten; *vr* to swell with pride
**-ería** *suffix f* -ery, e.g., **cervecería** brewery; **tontería** foolery; **mojigatería** priggery; -ry, e.g., **carpintería** carpentry; **joyería** jewelry; **pedantería** pedantry; -ing, e.g., **barbería** barbering; **ingeniería** engineering; -ness, e.g., **niñería** childishness; **tontería** foolishness; and many other words, without a corresponding suffix in English, indicating a place where something is made or sold, e.g., **librería** bookstore; **zapatería** shoemaker's shop; shoe store
**erial** or **eriazo -za** *adj* unplowed, uncultivated; *m* unplowed land, uncultivated land
**erica** *f* (bot.) heath, heather
**ericáceo -a** *adj* (bot.) ericaceous
**Erico** *m* Eric
**erigir §42** *va* to erect, build; to establish; to elevate; *vr* to be elevated; **erigirse en** to be elevated to; to set oneself up as, to pose as
**Erín** *f;* **la Verde Erín** (poet.) Erin
**erina** *f* (surg.) tenaculum
**eringe** *f* (bot.) field eryngo
**Erinia** *f* (myth.) Erinys
**erío -a** *adj & m* var. of **erial**
**erisipela** *f* (path.) erysipelas
**erisipeloide** *f* (path.) erysipeloid
**erístico -ca** *adj* eristic; *f* eristic (*art of disputation*)
**eritema** *m* (path.) erythema
**eritreo -a** *adj & mf* Eritrean; Erythraean; (*cap.*) *f* Eritrea
**eritrina** *f* (chem.) erythrin
**eritrita** *f* (mineral.) erythrite
**eritroblasto** *m* (anat.) erythroblast
**eritrocito** *m* (anat.) erythrocyte
**eritroxiláceo -a** *adj* (bot.) erythroxylaceous
**erizado -da** *adj* spiny, bristly, bristling; **erizado de** bristling with
**erizar §76** *va* to set on end, make bristle; **estar erizado de** to bristle with (*e.g., difficulties*); *vr* to stand on end, to bristle
**erizo** *m* (zool.) hedgehog; (bot.) thistle; bur (*prickly involucre, e.g., of chestnut*); (mach.) pinwheel; (mach.) urchin (*of weaving machine*); cheval-de-frise (*along top of wall*); (coll.) harsh, unruly person; **erizo de mar** or **erizo marino** (zool.) sea urchin
**erizón** *m* (bot.) blue genista; **erizones** *mpl* (bot.) spiny yellow genista (*Genista horrida*)
**ermit.** abr. of **ermitaño**
**ermita** *f* hermitage
**ermitaño -ña** *mf* hermit; *m* eremite; (zool.) hermit crab
**ermitorio** *m* var. of **eremitorio**
**Ernesto** *m* Ernest
**-ero -ra** *suffix adj* e.g., **aduanero** customhouse; **guerrero** warlike; *suffix mf* -er, e.g., **carcelero** jailer; **extranjero** foreigner; **molinero** miller; *suffix m* -eer, e.g., **bucanero** buccaneer; **cañonero** cannoneer; **ingeniero** engineer; -ier, e.g., **alabardero** halberdier; **bombardero** bombardier; **cajero** cashier; **gondolero** gondolier; -ary, e.g., **granero** granary; and in many other words, without a

corresponding suffix in English, indicating the place where something is kept, e.g., **azucarero** sugar bowl; **tintero** inkwell; *suffix f* -ary, e.g., **abejera** apiary; **pajarera** aviary; and in many other words, without a corresponding suffix in English indicating the place where something is kept, e.g., **ensaladera** salad bowl; **sombrerera** hat box
**erogación** *f* distribution (*of property or wealth*); (Am.) gift, charity
**erogar** §59 *va* to distribute (*property, wealth*); to cause, give rise to
**Eros** *m* (myth.) Eros
**erosión** *f* erosion; (geol.) erosion
**erosionar** *va & vr* to erode
**erosivo -va** *adj* erosive; *m* erosive substance or agent
**erotema** *f* (rhet.) rhetorical question
**erótico -ca** *adj* erotic; *f* erotic poetry
**erotismo** *m* erotism
**erotomanía** *f* (path.) erotomania
**erotómano -na** *adj & mf* erotic
**errabundo -da** *adj* wandering
**erradicable** *adj* eradicable
**erradicación** *f* eradication
**erradicar** §86 *va* to eradicate
**erradizo -za** *adj* wandering; stumbling, fumbling
**errado -da** *adj* mistaken; unwise, unbecoming
**erraj** *m* fine coal made of crushed olive stones
**errante** *adj* wandering, roving; nomadic
**errar** §48 *va* to miss (*a target, one's calling*); (archaic) to fail; *vn* to wander; to err, be wrong or mistaken; *vr* to err, be wrong or mistaken
**errata** *f* erratum; printer's error
**errático -ca** *adj* wandering; (geol.) erratic
**errátil** *adj* wavering, fallible
**erróneo -a** *adj* erroneous
**erronía** *f* grudge, dislike; (archaic) incredulity; (archaic) stubbornness
**error** *m* error, mistake; **salvo error u omisión** barring error or omission; **error craso** blunder, break
**erso -sa** *adj & m* Erse
**erubescencia** *f* modesty, blushing; erubescence
**erubescente** *adj* red, blushing; erubescent
**eructación** *f* var. of **eructo**
**eructar** *vn* to belch, eruct; (coll.) to brag
**eructo** *m* belch, belching, eructation
**erudición** *f* erudition, learning
**erudito -ta** *adj* erudite, learned, scholarly; *mf* scholar, savant; **erudito a la violeta** highbrow, intellectual fourflusher
**eruginoso -sa** *adj* rusty
**erumpir** *vn* to erupt (*said of volcano*)
**erupción** *f* eruption; bursting forth, outburst; (path. & dent.) eruption
**eruptivo -va** *adj* eruptive
**erutar** *vn* var. of **eructar**
**eruto** *m* var. of **eructo**
**ervato** *m* var. of **servato**
**ervilla** *f* var. of **arveja**
**es** *3d sg pres ind of* **ser**
**Esaú** *m* (Bib.) Esau
**esbatimentar** *va* (paint.) to draw or paint a shadow in; *vn* to cause a shadow
**esbatimento** *m* (paint.) shade or shadow
**esbeltez** *f* or **esbelteza** *f* gracefulness, slenderness, elegance, litheness
**esbelto -ta** *adj* graceful, slender, well-built, svelte
**esbirro** *m* bailiff, constable; myrmidon, minion of the law
**esbozar** §76 *va* to sketch, outline
**esbozo** *m* sketch, outline
**escabechado -da** *adj* (coll.) with dyed hair; (coll.) painted, with painted face
**escabechar** *va* to pickle; (coll.) to flunk; (coll.) to kill, to slay, to stab to death; to dye (*the hair*); *vr* to dye one's hair; **escabecharse las canas** to dye one's hair
**escabeche** *m* pickle; pickled fish; hair dye
**escabechina** *f* (coll.) ravage, destruction
**escabel** *m* stool; footstool; (fig.) stepping stone (*means of advancement*)
**escabiosa** *f* see **escabioso**
**escabiosis** *f* (path.) scabies
**escabioso -sa** *adj* scabious, mangy; *f* (bot.) scabious; **escabiosa de Indias** (bot.) sweet scabious; **escabiosa mordida** (bot.) blue scabious
**escabro** *m* (vet.) scabs (*on sheep*); (plant path.) scaly bark
**escabrosidad** *f* scabrousness; harshness, roughness
**escabroso -sa** *adj* scabrous, risqué; harsh, rough, bumpy
**escabuche** *f* weeding hoe
**escabullimiento** *m* slipping or sneaking away, escape
**escabullir** §26 *vr* to slip away, to clear out, to sneak away, to escape
**escacado -da** *adj* (her.) checky
**escachar** *va* to squash, crush
**escacharrar** *va* to break (*an earthen pot*); to spoil, damage, ruin
**escachifollar** *va* var. of **cachifollar**
**escafandra** *f* or **escafandro** *m* diving suit, diving outfit; **escafandra espacial** space helmet
**escafandrista** *mf* diver
**escafilar** *va* var. of **descafilar**
**escafoides** *m* (anat.) scaphoid
**Escafusa** *f* Schaffhausen
**escajo** *m* var. of **escalio**
**escala** *f* ladder, stepladder; scale (*graduated line*); call (*of a boat*); port of call; stop (*of airplane*); (mus.) scale; **en escala de** on a scale of (*e.g., an inch to a mile*); **en grande escala** on a large scale; **en pequeña escala** on a small scale; **hacer escala en** (naut.) to call at; **escala cromática** (mus.) chromatic scale; **escala de cuerda** rope ladder; **escala de Jacob** (Bib.) Jacob's ladder; (bot.) Jacob's-ladder; **escala de jarcia** (naut.) Jacob's ladder; **escala de los vientos** wind scale; **escala de travesaños** peg ladder; **escala de viento** (naut.) rope ladder; **escala diatónica** (mus.) diatonic scale; **escala mayor** (mus.) major scale; **escala menor** (mus.) minor scale; **escala móvil** (econ.) sliding scale (*e.g., of salaries*)
**escalabrar** *va & vr* var. of **descalabrar**
**escalada** *f* escalade, scaling; climbing
**escalador -dora** *adj* burglarious; *mf* scaler, climber; burglar, housebreaker
**escalafón** *m* roster, register (*showing position, seniority, merits, etc.*)
**escalamera** *f* (naut.) rowlock, oarlock
**escalamiento** *m* scaling (*ascent by or as by ladder; measurement by a scale*); burglary
**escálamo** *m* (naut.) thole, tholepin
**escalar** *va* to escalade, to scale (*a wall*); to enter by scaling; to break in, to break through (*e.g., a wall*); to burglarize; to climb; to open the gates of (*a sluice, trench, channel, etc.*); to slit and clean (*a fish or other animal*) for curing or salting; *vn* to climb; (fig.) to make one's way up by fair means or foul; (naut.) to call; *vr* to escalate
**escalatorres** *mf* (*pl:* **-rres**) steeplejack, human fly
**Escalda** *m* Scheldt (*river*)
**escaldado -da** *adj* (coll.) cautious, wary, scared; (coll.) loose, lewd (*woman*)
**escaldadura** *f* scald, scalding
**escaldar** *va* to scald; to make red-hot; *vr* to be scalded; to chafe
**escaldo** *m* skald (*ancient Scandinavian bard*)
**escaleno -na** *adj* (geom. & anat.) scalene; *m* (anat.) scalenus
**escalenoedro** *m* (cryst.) scalenohedron
**escalentamiento** *m* (vet.) sorefoot
**escalera** *f* stairs, stairway; ladder; (cards) sequence; (poker) straight; **de escalera abajo** of the servants, from below stairs; **por la escalera abajo** down the stairs; **escalera ascensora** (Am.) moving stairway, escalator; **escalera automática** escalator; **escalera de caracol** winding stairs; **escalera de escape** fire escape; **escalera de ganchos** hook ladder; **escalera de gato** cat ladder; **escalera de husillo** winding stairs; **escalera de incendio** fire ladder; **escalera de mano** ladder; **escalera de papagayo** peg ladder; **escalera de salvamento** fire escape; **escalera de**

**servicio** service stairs, back stairs; **escalera de tijera** or **escalera doble** stepladder; **escalera espiral** spiral staircase; **escalera excusada** or **falsa** private stairs (*to bedrooms and apartments*); **escalera extensible** extension ladder; **escalera hurtada** secret stairway; **escalera interior** back stairs; **escalera mecánica** escalator; **escalera movible** ladder; **escalera móvil** or **rodante** moving stairway, escalator
**escalerilla** *f* low step; car step; short ladder; sequence of three or five (*in cards*); rack (*for pinion*); (vet.) mouth prop, jaw lever (*for exploring horse's mouth*)
**escalerista** *m* (Am.) stairbuilder
**escalerón** *m* large stairway; peg ladder
**escaleta** *f* frame for lifting carriages
**escalfado -da** *adj* blistered (*said of plastered wall*); poached (*egg*)
**escalfador** *m* barber's metal pitcher (*for heating water*); chafing dish; painter's torch
**escalfar** *va* to poach (*eggs*); to burn, to bake (*bread*) brown
**escalfarote** *m* hair-lined or hay-lined shoe or boot
**escalfeta** *f* var. of **chofeta**
**escalinata** *f* stone step, front step
**escalio** *m* wasteland to be cultivated
**escalmo** *m* (naut.) thole; heavy wedge
**escalo** *m* burglary, breaking in; digging for escape, digging for forcible entry
**escalofriado -da** *adj* chilly, chilled
**escalofriante** *adj* chilling; frightening, hair-raising
**escalofriar** **§90** *va* to cause (*someone*) to shudder
**escalofrío** *m* chill
**escalón** *m* step, rung; tread (*of step*); (fig.) echelon, step, stage, grade; (fig.) stepping stone (*to fulfill an ambition*); (mil.) echelon; (rad.) stage; **en escalones** irregularly, unevenly (*made or cut*)
**escalona** *f* (bot.) scallion
**escalonar** *va* to place at intervals, to space out, to spread out; to stagger (*e.g., working hours*); to mark off (*at intervals*); (mil.) to echelon
**escalonia** or **escaloña** *f* var. of **escalona**
**escalpar** *va* to scalp
**escalpelo** *m* (surg.) scalpel
**escama** *f* (zool. & bot.) scale; resentment, grudge; fear, suspicion
**escamado -da** *adj* (coll.) fearful, distrustful; *m* scalework; *f* embroidery in scalework
**escamadura** *f* scaling
**escamar** *va* to scale; (coll.) to frighten, to shake the confidence of; *vr* to scale; (coll.) to be scared, to lose confidence
**escamel** *m* sword-maker's anvil
**escamocho** *m* leavings (*of food and drink*)
**escamón -mona** *adj* fearful, apprehensive
**escamonda** *f* pruning
**escamondadura** *f* pruned branches
**escamondar** *va* to prune (*a tree*); (fig.) to trim, to prune
**escamondo** *m* var. of **escamonda**
**escamonea** *f* (bot. & pharm.) scammony
**escamonear** *vr* (coll.) to lose confidence, become suspicious
**escamoso -sa** *adj* scaly, squamous
**escamotar** *va* to make disappear by sleight of hand; to palm (*a card*); to whisk out of sight, to cause to vanish; to snitch, to swipe; *vr* to disappear
**escamoteable** *adj* retractable
**escamoteador -dora** *mf* prestidigitator; thief, swindler
**escamotear** *va & vr* var. of **escamotar**
**escamoteo** *m* sleight of hand; palming; snitching, swiping
**escampado -da** *adj* free, open, clear; *f* break in rain, clear spell
**escampar** *va* to clear out; *vn* to stop raining; to ease up, to stop
**escampavía** *f* (naut.) scout; (naut.) revenue cutter, coast guard cutter
**escampo** *m* emptying, clearing out; end of rain
**escamudo -da** *adj* scaly
**escamujar** *va* to prune (*especially olive trees*); to clear out (*branches*)
**escamujo** *m* pruning, clearing out of branches
**escancia** *f* pouring, serving, or drinking wine
**escanciador -dora** *mf* one who passes the wines or other drinks
**escanciar** *va* to pour, to serve, to drink (*wine*); *vn* to drink wine
**escanda** *f* (bot.) spelt (*wheat*)
**escandalar** *m* (naut.) compass room (*in a galley*)
**escandalera** *f* (coll.) commotion, excitement
**escandalizador -dora** *adj* scandalizing; *mf* scandalizer
**escandalizar** **§76** *va* to scandalize; to outrage; *vr* to be scandalized; to be angered or irritated
**escandalizativo -va** *adj* scandalous
**escándalo** *m* scandal; shameful conduct, bad example; commotion, uproar; surprise, wonder; **causar escándalo** to make a scene
**escandaloso -sa** *adj* scandalous; turbulent, violent, restless; *f* (naut.) gafftopsail; **echar la escandalosa** (coll.) to use harsh words, to scold abusively
**escandallar** *va* (naut.) to sound; to sample (*a product*)
**escandallo** *m* (naut.) sounding lead; sampling (*of a product*); (com.) cost accounting; **echar el escandallo** (naut.) to take soundings
**escandelar** *m* var. of **escandalar**
**escandia** *f* (bot.) emmer
**Escandinavia** *f* Scandinavia
**escandinavo -va** *adj & mf* Scandinavian
**escandio** *m* (chem.) scandium
**escandir** *va* to scan (*verse*)
**escansión** *f* scansion
**escantillar** *va* to measure off, to lay off
**escantillón** *m* pattern, templet; rule, gage
**escaña** *f* var. of **escanda**
**escaño** *m* settle, bench with back for two or more people; seat (*in parliament*); (Am.) park bench
**escañuelo** *m* footstool
**escapada** *f* escape, flight; escapade; run, quick trip; **en una escapada** at full speed
**escapadita** *f* quick getaway; flying trip
**escapamiento** *m* var. of **escapada**
**escapar** *va* to save, preserve, to free; to drive (*a horse*) hard; *vn* to escape; to slip away, to flee, to run away; **escapar a** to escape (*e.g., death*); *vr* to escape; to slip away, to flee, to run away; to escape, to leak (*said of gas, water, etc.*); **escaparse a** to escape from (*a person*); to escape (*death*); **escaparse de** to escape from (*e.g., jail*); **escapársele a uno** to let slip, to say inadvertently; to miss, to not notice; to escape one's notice
**escaparate** *m* show window; cabinet (*for displaying curios or specimens*)
**escaparatista** *mf* window dresser
**escapatoria** *f* escape, getaway; (coll.) subterfuge, evasion; (fig.) escape (*from responsibilities, duties, etc.*)
**escape** *m* escape; flight; leak; exhaust; exhaust valve; escapement (*of a watch*); **a escape** at full speed, on the run; **escape de áncora** (horl.) anchor escapement; **escape de rejilla** (rad.) grid leak; **escape libre** (mach.) cutout
**escapismo** *m* escapism
**escapista** *adj & mf* escapist
**escapo** *m* (arch., bot. & zool.) scape
**escápula** *f* (anat.) scapula, shoulder blade
**escapular** *adj* scapular; *va* (naut.) to double or to round (*a cape*)
**escapulario** *m* scapular, scapulary
**escaque** *m* square (*of checkerboard or chessboard*); (her.) square; **escaques** *mpl* chess
**escaqueado -da** *adj* checkered
**escara** *f* see **escaro**
**escarabajear** *va* (coll.) to harass, to worry; *vn* to crawl around, to swarm; to scrawl, to scribble
**escarabajeo** *m* (coll.) harassment, worry
**escarabajo** *m* (ent.) scarab, black beetle; (f.a.) scarabaeus; flaw (*in fabric or casting*); (coll.) runt; **escarabajos** *mpl* (coll.) scribbling, scrawl; **escarabajo de agua** (ent.) water beetle; **escarabajo enterrador** (ent.) burying beetle; **escarabajo estercolero** (ent.) dor, dorbeetle; **escarabajo patatero** (ent.)

potato beetle or bug; **escarabajo pelotero** (ent.) tumblebug; **escarabajo sepulturero** (ent.) burying beetle
**escarabajuelo** *m* (ent.) vine beetle
**escaramucear** *vn* var. of **escaramuzar**
**escaramujo** *m* (bot.) dog rose (*plant and fruit*); (zool.) barnacle (*Pollicipes cornucopia*)
**escaramuza** *f* skirmish
**escaramuzador** *m* skirmisher
**escaramuzar** **§76** *vn* to skirmish
**escarapela** *f* cockade; quarrel ending in hair pulling or fisticuffs
**escarapelar** *vn & vr* to quarrel, to wrangle (*said of women*); **escarapelársele a uno el cuerpo** to have goose flesh
**escaravia** *f* (bot.) skirret
**escarbadientes** *m* (*pl:* **-tes**) toothpick
**escarbador** *m* scraper, scratcher; pryer; plugging chisel
**escarbadura** *f* scraping, scratching
**escarbaorejas** *m* (*pl:* **-jas**) earpick
**escarbar** *va* to scratch, to scratch up (*the ground*); to dig into; to poke (*the fire*); to pick (*teeth, ears, etc.*); to pry into
**escarbo** *m* scraping, scratching
**escarcela** *f* large pouch; game bag; cuisse or cuish (*of armor*)
**escarceo** *m* evasion, digression; (naut.) small bubbling waves (*due to currents*); **escarceos** *mpl* prancing
**escarcina** *f* cutlass
**escarcha** *f* frost, hoarfrost
**escarchado -da** *adj* frosted; *m* frost-like embroidery of gold or silver; *f* (bot.) ice plant
**escarchar** *va* to frost, to put frosting on (*e.g., a cake*); to dilute (*potter's clay*); to spangle; *vn* to be frost, e.g., **esta noche ha escarchado** last night there was frost
**escarche** *m* frost-like embroidery of gold and silver
**escarcho** *m* (ichth.) red surmullet
**escarda** *f* weeding; weeding time; weeding hoe
**escardadera** *f* weeder (*woman*); weeding hoe
**escardador -dora** *mf* weeder (*person*); *m* weeding hoe
**escardadura** *f* weeding
**escardar** or **escardillar** *va* to weed, to weed out
**escardillo** *m* dibble, weeding hoe; flicker in the dark
**escariador** *m* reamer
**escariar** *va* to ream
**escarificación** *f* (agr. & surg.) scarification
**escarificador** *m* (agr.) scarifier, cultivator, harrow; (surg.) scarifier, scarificator
**escarificar** **§86** *va* (agr. & surg.) to scarify; (surg.) to remove the dead skin from
**escarioso -sa** *adj* (bot.) scarious
**escarizar** **§76** *va* (surg.) to remove the dead skin from
**escarlador** *m* comb polisher
**escarlata** *adj* scarlet; *f* scarlet (*color and cloth*); (path.) scarlet fever
**escarlatina** *f* (path.) scarlatina, scarlet fever; crimson woolen fabric
**escarmenar** *va* to comb (*wool, silk, etc.*); to take away (*money or something else*) as punishment; to cheat a little at a time
**escarmentar** **§18** *va* to punish severely; *vn* to learn by experience, to learn one's lesson; **escarmentar en cabeza ajena** to learn by another person's mistakes; **escarmentar en cabeza propia** to learn by one's own mistakes
**escarmiento** *m* punishment, penalty; lesson, example, warning; caution, wisdom
**escarnecedor -dora** *adj* scoffing, ridiculing; *mf* scoffer
**escarnecer** **§34** *va* to scoff at, to make fun of, to ridicule
**escarnecidamente** *adv* scoffingly, mockingly
**escarnecimiento** or **escarnio** *m* scoffing, derision, gibe
**escaro -ra** *adj* duck-toed; *m* (ichth.) scarus, parrot fish; *f* (path.) slough
**escarola** *f* (bot.) endive; head of endive; (archaic) ruff, frill
**escarolado -da** *adj* ruffled, frilled, curled
**escarolar** *va* var. of **alechugar**
**escarótico -ca** *adj & m* (med.) escharotic
**escarpa** *f* scarp, escarpment; (fort.) scarp, escarpment
**escarpado -da** *adj* steep; rough, rugged, craggy
**escarpadura** *f* scarp, escarpment; cliff, bluff; solleret (*of armor*)
**escarpar** *va* to scarp, to escarp; to rasp (*sculpture*)
**escarpe** *m* var. of **escarpadura**
**escarpelo** *m* rasp; (surg.) scalpel
**escarpia** *f* tenterhook; meat hook; spike
**escarpiador** *m* clamp, staple (*to fasten a pipe to a wall*)
**escarpidor** *m* large-toothed comb
**escarpín** *m* pump (*slipperlike shoe*); sock (*worn over stocking or other sock*)
**escarpión; en escarpión** in the form of a tenterhook
**escartivana** *f* var. of **cartivana**
**escarza** *f* (vet.) sore hoof (*from nail*)
**escarzano** *adj masc* segmental (*arch*)
**escarzar** **§76** *va* to clear (*a hive*) of black combs; to bend (*a stick*) into an arc by means of cords
**escarzo** *m* black comb without honey; removal of honey from hive; floss silk; punk
**escasear** *va* to give sparingly; to save, to spare, to avoid; to bevel, to cut at an angle; *vn* to be scarce, to become scarce
**escasero -ra** *adj* (coll.) sparing; (coll.) saving, frugal; (coll.) stingy; *mf* (coll.) skinflint
**escasez** *f* scarcity, shortness; want, need; stinginess
**escaso -sa** *adj* scarce; little, slight; scanty; parsimonious, frugal; stingy; scant, e.g., **media hora escasa** a scant half-hour; **escaso de** scant of, short of
**escatimar** *va* to scrimp; **escatimar a uno la comida** to scrimp someone for food; *vn* to scrimp
**escatimoso -sa** *adj* sly, scrimpy, mean
**escatología** *f* scatology; (theol.) eschatology
**escatológico -ca** *adj* scatological; eschatological
**escavanar** *va* to loosen and weed (*the ground*)
**escayola** *f* scagliola; stucco
**escayolar** *va* to overlay with scagliola; to stucco; (surg.) to put in a plaster cast
**escena** *f* scene; stage; incident, episode; **poner en escena** to stage (*a play*)
**escenario** *m* stage; setting; background
**escénico -ca** *adj* scenic (*pertaining to a stage or to stage effects*)
**escenificación** *f* staging, portrayal; adaptation for the stage
**escenificar** **§86** *va* to stage, to portray; to adapt for the stage
**escenografía** *f* scenography
**escenográfico -ca** *adj* scenographic or scenographical
**escenógrafo -fa** *adj* scenographic; *mf* scenographer
**escepticismo** *m* scepticism
**escéptico -ca** *adj* sceptic or sceptical; *mf* sceptic
**esciente** *adj* knowing
**escila** *f* (bot.) squill; (*cap.*) *f* (geog. & myth.) Scylla; **estar entre Escila y Caribdis** to be between Scylla and Charybdis
**escinco** *m* (zool.) skink
**escindible** *adj* fissionable
**escindir** *va* to split
**Escipión** *m* Scipio
**escirro** *m* (path.) scirrhus
**escirroso -sa** *adj* scirrhous
**escisión** *f* scission, fission; splitting; schism; (biol.) fission; (surg.) excision
**escita** *adj & mf* Scythian
**Escitia, la** Scythia
**escítico -ca** *adj* Scythian
**esclarea** *f* (bot.) clary
**esclarecedor -dora** *adj* enlightening; ennobling
**esclarecer** **§34** *va* to brighten, to light up; to explain, to elucidate; to enlighten; to ennoble; *vn* to dawn
**esclarecidamente** *adv* illustriously, nobly; brilliantly
**esclarecido -da** *adj* illustrious, noble; manifest, obvious

**esclarecimiento** *m* illumination; explanation, elucidation; enlightenment; ennoblement
**esclavina** *f* pelerine; tippet; pilgrim's cloak
**esclavista** *adj* proslavery; *mf* advocate of slavery
**esclavitud** *f* slavery
**esclavización** *f* enslavement
**esclavizar** **§76** *va* to enslave
**esclavo -va** *adj* enslaved; **esclavo de su palabra** faithful to one's word; *mf* slave; (fig.) slave, drudge
**esclavón -vona** *adj & mf* var. of **eslavón**
**esclavonio -nia** *adj & mf* var. of **eslavonio;** (*cap.*) *f* var. of **Eslavonia**
**esclerénquima** *m* (bot.) sclerenchyma
**esclerocio** *m* (bot.) sclerotium
**esclerodermia** *f* (path.) scleroderma
**escleroma** *m* (path.) scleroma
**esclerómetro** *m* sclerometer
**esclerosis** *f* (*pl:* **-sis**) (path. & bot.) sclerosis; **esclerosis en placas** or **esclerosis múltiple** (path.) multiple sclerosis
**escleroso -sa** *adj* sclerous; (path.) sclerotic
**esclerótico -ca** *adj & f* (anat.) sclerotic
**esclerotitis** *f* (path.) sclerotitis
**esclerotomía** *f* (surg.) sclerotomy
**esclusa** *f* lock, floodgate, sluice; **esclusa de aire** (eng.) caisson
**esclusada** *f* lockful; flood of water released to swell a river
**esclusero** *m* lock tender
**esc.º** abr. of **escudo**
**escoa** *f* (naut.) point of greatest curvature (*of a ship's rib*)
**escoba** *f* broom; (bot.) broom
**escobada** *f* sweep; quick sweeping
**escobadera** *f* woman sweeper
**escobajo** *m* old broom; grape stem (*with grapes removed*)
**escobar** *m* field of broom; *va* to sweep with a broom
**escobazar** **§76** *va* to sprinkle with a wet broom
**escobazo** *m* blow with a broom; sweep
**escobén** *m* (naut.) hawsehole
**escobera** *f* see **escobero**
**escobería** *f* broom factory; broom store
**escobero -ra** *mf* broom maker or vendor; *f* (bot.) Spanish broom
**escobeta** *f* brush, small broom
**escobilla** *f* brush, whisk, small broom; sweepings of gold or silver (*e.g., in a mint*); (bot.) teasel (*plant and bur*); (elec.) brush; **escobilla de afeitar** or **de barba** shaving brush; **escobilla de carbón** (elec.) carbon brush
**escobillado** *m* (Am.) brush (*in dancing*)
**escobillar** *va* to brush
**escobillón** *m* push broom; boiler-flue cleaner; (gun.) swab
**escobina** *f* chips from drilling; filings
**escobo** *m* broom thicket, brushwood
**escobón** *m* long-handled broom; short-handled broom; scrubbing brush; (bot.) broom
**escocedura** *f* chafing, chafed skin
**escocer** **§30** *va* to chafe; to annoy, to displease; *vn* to smart, to sting; *vr* to feel sorry; to chafe, become chafed
**escocés -cesa** *adj* Scotch; *mf* Scot; *m* Scotchman; Scotch (*dialect; whiskey*); *f* (mus.) écossaise
**escocia** *f* (arch.) scotia; codfish; (*cap.*) *f* Scotland; **la Nueva Escocia** Nova Scotia
**escocimiento** *m* smarting or stinging sensation; chafed skin
**escoda** *f* bushhammer
**escodadero** *m* place where deer rub the velvet off their antlers
**escodar** *va* to bushhammer, to carve or trim (*stone*) with bushhammer; to shake or rub (*the antlers*) to free them of velvet; (prov.) to cut off the tail of
**escofieta** *f* hair net
**escofina** *f* rasp
**escofinar** *va* to rasp
**escofión** *m* net headpiece
**escogedor -dora** *adj* choosing, selecting; *mf* chooser, selector
**escoger** **§49** *va* to choose, to select
**escogidamente** *adv* cleverly, wisely; completely, in an excellent manner; carefully
**escogido -da** *adj* selected; choice, select; **los escogidos** (theol.) the elect
**escogimiento** *m* choosing, selecting
**escolanía** *f* choirboys' school or association (*in Catalonia*)
**escolano** *m* choirboy (*pupil*)
**escolapio -pia** *adj* pertaining to the Scuole Pie (*religious schools founded in Rome in the seventeenth century*); *m* Escolapio, Piarist
**escolar** *adj* (pertaining to) school, scholastic; *m* pupil, scholar; **§77** *vn & vr* to squeeze one's way
**escolástica** *f* see **escolástico**
**escolasticismo** *m* scholasticism; (philos.) scholasticism
**escolástico -ca** *adj & mf* scholastic; *f* scholasticism
**escólex** *m* (*pl:* **escólex**) (zool.) scolex
**escoliador** *m* scholiast
**escoliar** *va* to comment, to gloss (*a text*)
**escoliasta** *m* scholiast
**escolimado -da** *adj* (coll.) weak, sickly
**escolimoso -sa** *adj* (coll.) impatient, restless
**escolio** *m* scholium
**escoliosis** *f* (path.) scoliosis
**escolopendra** *f* (zool.) scolopendra, centipede; (bot.) hart's-tongue
**escolta** *f* escort; attendant; (aer. & nav.) escort
**escoltar** *va* to escort, to attend
**escollar** *vn* (Am.) to hit a reef, to run aground on a reef; (Am.) to fail
**escollera** *f* rock fill; jetty, breakwater; row of rocks jutting out of the sea
**escollo** *m* reef, rock; (fig.) pitfall; (fig.) stumbling block
**escolloso -sa** *adj* dangerous, risky; thorny (*problem*)
**escombra** *f* clearing, clearing out
**escombrar** *va* to clear, to clear out
**escombrera** *f* dump, spoil bank
**escombro** *m* rubbish, debris; (ichth.) mackerel; **escombros** *spl* rubbish, debris; (min.) deads
**escomer** *vr* to wear away
**esconce** *m* corner, angle
**escondedero** *m* hiding place
**esconder** *m* hide-and-seek; *va* to hide; to harbor, to contain; *vr* to hide; to lurk
**escondidamente** *adv* secretly, hiddenly
**escondido -da** *adj* hidden, out of the way; **a escondidas** secretly, on the sly; **a escondidas de** without the knowledge of; **en escondido** secretly, on the sly
**escondillas; a escondillas** hiddenly, on the sly
**escondimiento** *m* hiding, concealment
**escondite** *m* hiding place; hide-and-seek; **jugar al escondite** to play hide-and-seek
**escondrijo** *m* hiding place; nook
**esconzado -da** *adj* angular
**escopeta** *f* shotgun; **aquí te quiero, escopeta** (coll.) now or never; **escopeta blanca** gentleman hunter; **escopeta de aire comprimido** air rifle; **escopeta de dos cañones** double-barreled shotgun; **escopeta de viento** air rifle; **escopeta negra** professional hunter
**escopetar** *va* (min.) to clear the earth from (*a gold mine*)
**escopetazo** *m* gunshot; gunshot wound; sudden bad news; (Am.) sarcasm, insult
**escopetear** *va* to shoot at with a shotgun; *vr* to shoot at each other with shotguns; **escopetearse a** (coll.) to shower each other with, e.g., **se escopeteaban a lisonjas** they showered each other with flattery; **se escopeteaban a improperios** they showered each other with insults
**escopeteo** *m* firing a shotgun; gunfire
**escopetería** *f* soldiers armed with shotguns; gunfire
**escopetero** *m* soldier armed with a shotgun, musketeer; gunner; armed guard; gunsmith
**escopladura** *f* chisel cut, notch, mortise
**escopleadora** *f* mortising machine
**escopleadura** *f* var. of **escopladura**
**escoplear** *va* to chisel
**escoplo** *m* turning chisel, woodworking chisel
**escopolamina** *f* (chem.) scopolamine
**escora** *f* (naut.) level line; (naut.) shore; (naut.) list

**escorar** *va* (naut.) to shore; *vn* (naut.) to list; (naut.) to reach low tide
**escorbútico -ca** *adj & mf* scorbutic
**escorbuto** *m* (path.) scorbutus, scurvy
**escorchar** *va* to flay, to skin
**escordio** *m* (bot.) water germander
**escoria** *f* scoria, dross, slag; (fig.) trash, dregs; (petrog.) scoria
**escoriáceo -a** *adj* scoriaceous
**escorial** *m* slag dump; lava bed; abandoned mine; **El Escorial** El Escorial (*town in central Spain*); the Escorial or the Escurial (*monastery, palace, and royal mausoleum at El Escorial, built in sixteenth century*)
**escoriar** *va* var. of **excoriar**
**escorificar** §86 *va* to scorify
**escorpena** or **escorpina** *f* (ichth.) scorpene
**Escorpio** *m* (astr.) Scorpio
**escorpioide** *f* (bot.) scorpion grass
**escorpión** *m* (ent.) scorpion; scorpion (*scourge; ancient catapult*); (ichth.) scorpion fish; (*cap.*) *m* (astr.) Scorpio; **tener lengua de escorpión** to have a biting tongue
**escorrozo** *m* (coll.) pleasure, enjoyment
**escorzado** *m* var. of **escorzo**
**escorzar** §76 *va* (f.a.) to foreshorten
**escorzo** *m* (f.a) foreshortening
**escorzón** *m* (zool.) toad
**escorzonera** *f* (bot.) viper's-grass
**escoscar** §86 *va* to remove the dandruff from; to hull, to shell; *vr* to shrug one's shoulders
**escota** *f* (naut.) sheet; **escota mayor** (naut.) mainsheet
**escotado -da** *adj* sharp, pointed; low-necked; *m* low neck (*in a dress*); armhole (*in armor*); (theat.) large trap door; notch, recess
**escotadura** *f* low neck (*in dress*); armhole (*in armor*); (theat.) large trap door; notch, recess
**escotar** *va* to cut (*something*) to fit; to draw water from (*e.g., a river*) through a drain or trench; *vn* to club together, to go Dutch
**escote** *m* low neck; tucker; share, quota, scot; **ir a escote** or **pagar a escote** to go Dutch
**escotero -ra** *adj* traveling light (*i.e., without baggage*); *f* (naut.) sheet hole; (naut.) chock
**escotilla** *f* (naut.) hatchway
**escotillón** *m* hatchway, bulkhead, trap door (*e.g., to a cellar*); (theat.) trap door; (naut.) small hatchway
**escotín** *m* (naut.) topsail sheet
**escotismo** *m* Scotism
**escozor** *m* smarting or stinging sensation; sorrow, grief
**escriba** *m* scribe (*teacher of Jewish law*)
**escribanía** *f* court clerkship; court clerk's office; portable writing desk; writing materials
**escribano** *m* court clerk; lawyer's clerk; clerk; (archaic) scrivener; (archaic) notary; **escribano del agua** (ent.) whirligig beetle
**escribido -da** *pp of* **escribir,** used only in expression **leído y escribido** (coll.) posing as learned
**escribidor** *m* (coll.) poor writer
**escribiente** *mf* clerk, office clerk; writer; **escribiente a máquina** typist
**escribir** *m* writing; §17, 9 *va & vn* to write; *vr* to enroll, to enlist; to write to each other; **no escribirse** to be impossible to describe, to be impossible to say
**escriño** *m* straw hamper; jewel case; hiding place; (prov.) cup of acorn
**escrit.ª** abr. of **escritura**
**escrita** *f* see **escrito**
**escritilla** *f* lamb's fry
**escrito -ta** *pp of* **escribir;** *adj* streaked; *m* writing; document, manuscript; (law) writ, brief; **por escrito** in writing; *f* (ichth.) spotted skate
**escritor -tora** *mf* writer
**escritorcillo -lla** *mf* writer of no account
**escritorio** *m* writing desk, escritoire; (print.) desk with sloping top; office; **escritorio ministro** office desk; **escritorio norteamericano** roll-top desk
**escritura** *f* writing; handwriting, script; (law) indenture, instrument; (law) sworn statement; (law) deed; **escritura al tacto** touch typewriting; **escritura a máquina** typewriting; **escritura de riesgo** (naut.) marine-insurance policy; (*cap.*) *f* Scripture; **Sagrada Escritura** Holy Scripture
**escriturar** *va* (law) to establish by affidavit, to execute (*e.g., a sale*) by means of a deed; to book (*e.g., an actor for a play*)
**escriturario -ria** *adj* (law) notarial; *m* Scripturist
**escrnía.** abr. of **escribanía**
**escrno.** abr. de **escribano**
**escrófula** *f* (path.) scrofula
**escrofularia** *f* (bot.) figwort
**escrofuloso -sa** *adj* scrofulous
**escrotal** *adj* scrotal
**escroto** *m* (anat.) scrotum
**escrupulillo** *m* slight scruple; jinglet
**escrupulizar** §76 *vn* to scruple, have scruples; to be overcautious
**escrúpulo** *m* scruple; (pharm.) scruple
**escrupulosidad** *f* scrupulosity, scrupulousness
**escrupuloso -sa** *adj* scrupulous
**escrutación** *f* scrutiny, examination
**escrutador -dora** *adj* searching; *mf* examiner, inspector; teller of votes, inspector of election returns
**escrutar** *va* to scrutinize; to count (*votes*)
**escrutinio** *m* scrutiny; inspection of election returns, counting of votes
**escrutiñador -dora** *mf* examiner, inspector, censor
**escuadra** *f* (carp.) square; triangle (*of draftsman*); bracket; angle iron, angle brace, gusset; squad, gang; (mil.) squad; (nav.) squadron; **a escuadra** square, at right angles; **falsa escuadra** bevel square; **fuera de escuadra** out of square; **escuadra de agrimensor** cross-staff; **escuadra falsa** bevel square
**escuadración** *f* squaring
**escuadrar** *va* (carp.) to square
**escuadreo** *m* squaring, quadrature
**escuadría** *f* dimensions of cross section
**escuadrilla** *f* (nav. & aer.) escadrille
**escuadrón** *m* flock, swarm; (mil.) squadron (*of cavalry*)
**escuadronista** *m* (mil.) cavalry tactician
**escualidez** *f* squalor; paleness, emaciation
**escuálido -da** *adj* squalid; pale, emaciated, thin
**escualo** *m* (ichth.) spiny dogfish
**escualor** *m* squalor
**escucha** *f* listening; chaperon (*in convents*); (mil.) scout, vedette; **estar de escucha** (coll.) to eavesdrop; *mf* listener
**escuchador -dora** *adj* listening
**escuchar** *va* to listen to; to heed, to mind; *vn* to listen; *vr* to speak with pompous deliberation, to be pleased at the sound of one's own voice
**escuchimizado -da** *adj* feeble, exhausted
**escudar** *va* to shield
**escuderaje** *m* shield service
**escuderear** *va* to wait on, to attend
**escudero** *m* shield-bearer, esquire; nobleman; lady's page; shield maker
**escuderón** *m* (coll.) fourflusher
**escudete** *m* escutcheon; (sew.) gusset; (carp.) escutcheon, escutcheon plate (*around keyhole*); (bot.) white water lily
**escudilla** *f* bowl
**escudo** *m* shield, buckler; (bot., her. & fig.) shield; (zool.) shield, scute, scutum; coat of arms; escutcheon, escutcheon plate (*around keyhole*); (naut.) backboard; **escudo de armas** coat of arms; **escudo térmico** heat shield (*of space capsule*)
**escudriñador -dora** *adj* scrutinizing, prying; *mf* scrutinizer, prier
**escudriñamiento** *m* scrutinizing, scrutiny
**escudriñar** *va* to scrutinize, to pry into
**escuela** *f* school; **hacer escuela** to start or found a school; to set a fashion; **escuela comercial** business college; **escuela de artes y oficios** trade school; **escuela de graduados** graduate school; **escuela de ingenieros de montes** forestry school; **escuela del hogar y profesional de la mujer** school of home economics; **escuela de párvulos** kindergarten; **escuela de verano** summer school; **escuela dominical** Sunday school; **Escuela Naval Militar** Naval Academy

(U.S.A.); Royal Naval College (Brit.); **escuela normal** normal school; **escuela para enfermeras** school of nursing; **escuela parroquial** parochial school; **escuela preparatoria** preparatory school
**escuelante** *m* (Am.) schoolboy; *f* (Am.) schoolgirl; *mf* (Am.) teacher
**escuelero -ra** *mf* (Am.) pupil; (Am.) teacher
**escuerzo** *m* (zool.) toad; (coll.) sickly-looking person
**escueto -ta** *adj* free, unencumbered; plain, bare, unadorned
**escuintle** *m* (Am.) mutt; (Am.) brat
**Esculapio** *m* (myth.) Aesculapius; (fig.) Aesculapian (*any physician*)
**esculcar** §86 *va* (Am.) to search, to frisk
**esculpidor** *m* sculptor; engraver
**esculpir** *va* to sculpture, to carve; to engrave
**escultismo** *m* scoutcraft, outdoor activities
**escultista** *mf* scout, athlete; *m* outdoorsman
**escultor** *m* sculptor
**escultora** *f* sculptress
**escultórico -ca** *adj* sculptural
**escultura** *f* sculpture
**escultural** *adj* sculptural, sculpturesque, statuesque
**escuna** *f* (naut.) schooner
**escupetina** *f* var. of **escupitina**
**escupidera** *f* cuspidor, spittoon; (prov. & Am.) chamber pot
**escupidero** *m* spitting place, place full of spit; (fig.) seat of scorn, embarrassing position
**escupido -da** *adj* the spit and image of, e.g., **María es escupida la madre** Mary is the spit and image of her mother; *m* spit, spittle
**escupidor -dora** *adj* spitting all the time; *mf* great spitter; *m* (prov. & Am.) cuspidor, spittoon; (Am.) round mat
**escupidura** *f* spit, spittle; fever blister or sore
**escupir** *va* to spit; to cast aside with scorn; to throw off; (fig.) to spit, to spit forth; *vn* to spit; **escupir a** to scoff at
**escupitajo** *m* (coll.) spit, spittle
**escupitina** *f* (coll.) spit, spittle; (coll.) spitting, constant spitting
**escupitinajo** *m* (coll.) var. of **escupitajo**
**escupo** *m* spit, spittle
**escurar** *va* to scour (*cloth*) before fulling
**escurialense** *adj* pertaining to El Escorial (*town*) and to the Escorial (*building*)
**escurra** *m* scoundrel, rascal
**escurreplatos** *m* (*pl:* **-tos**) dish rack, draining rack
**escurribanda** *f* (coll.) subterfuge, evasion; (coll.) looseness of bowels; (coll.) running (*of a sore*); (coll.) scuffle
**escurridero** *m* drainpipe, drain hole, outlet; drainboard; slippery place; (phot.) rack for drying plates
**escurridizo -za** *adj* slippery
**escurrido -da** *adj* narrow-hipped; wearing tight-fitting skirts; (Am.) abashed, ashamed
**escurridor** *m* colander; dish rack, draining rack; (phot.) rack for drying plates
**escurriduras** or **escurrimbres** *fpl* lees, dregs
**escurrimiento** *m* draining; dripping; (elec.) creepage; (fig.) slip
**escurrir** *va* to drain (*a vessel; a liquid; dishes*); to wring, to wring out; to slip; *vn* to drip, to ooze, to trickle; to slip, to slide; to be slippery; *vr* to drip, to ooze, to trickle; to slip, to slide; to escape, to slip away; to slip out (*said of a remark*); **escurrirse de entre las manos** to slip out of or through one's hands
**escusalí** *m* (*pl:* **-líes**) little apron
**Escútari** *m* Scutari
**escutelado -da** *adj* (bot., zool. & orn.) scutellate
**escutelo** *m* (bot. & zool.) scutellum
**escutiforme** *adj* scutiform, scutate
**Esdras** *m* (Bib.) Esdras
**esdrujulear** *vn* to use proparoxytones all the time
**esdrujulizar** §76 *va* to give a proparoxytonic accent to
**esdrújulo -la** *adj* (gram.) proparoxytonic; (*verse*) whose last word is accented on antepenult; *m* (gram.) proparoxytone

**ese, esa** *adj dem* (*pl:* **esos, esas**) that; **ese** *f* s (*letter*); S-shaped link (*of chain*); sound hole (*in violins*); **hacer eses** to zigzag, to reel (*from too much drink*)
**ése, ésa** *pron dem* (*pl:* **ésos, ésas**) that one; *f* your city
**esecilla** *f* little link
**esencia** *f* essence; gasoline; (chem.) essence; **en esencia** in essence; **quinta esencia** quintessence; **esencia de pera** banana oil
**esencial** *adj* & *m* essential
**esfacelar** *vr* (path.) to sphacelate
**esfacelo** *m* (path.) sphacelus
**esfágnea** *f* (bot.) sphagnum
**esfena** *f* or **esfeno** *m* (mineral.) sphene
**esfenoidal** *adj* sphenoidal
**esfenoides** *m* (anat.) sphenoid, sphenoid bone
**esfera** *f* (geom.) sphere; (fig.) sphere (*range, surroundings*); (poet.) sphere (*sky, heavens*); dial (*e.g., of clock*); **esfera armilar** armillary sphere; **esfera celeste** sphere, celestial sphere; **esfera de actividad** sphere of action; **esfera de influencia** (dipl.) sphere of influence
**esferal** *adj* var. of **esférico**
**esfericidad** *f* sphericity
**esférico -ca** *adj* sperical; *m* (sport) ball
**esferilla** *f* little sphere, little ball
**esferoidal** *adj* spheroidal
**esferoide** *m* (geom.) spheroid
**esferómetro** *m* spherometer
**esférula** *f* spherule
**esfigmógrafo** *m* (physiol.) sphygmograph
**esfinge** *f* sphinx; (fig.) sphinx (*mysterious person*); (fig.) sly, vengeful woman; (ent.) hawk moth
**esfínter** *m* (anat.) sphincter
**esforrocinar** *va* to trim runners from (*trunk of vine*)
**esforrocino** *m* (bot.) sarmentum or runner growing from trunk of vine
**esforzado -da** *adj* vigorous, courageous, enterprising
**esforzador -dora** *adj* encouraging
**esforzar** §52 *va* to strengthen, to invigorate; to encourage; *vr* to exert oneself; **esforzarse a, en** or **por** + *inf* to strive to + *inf*
**esfragístico -ca** *adj* sphragistic; *f* sphragistics
**esfuerzo** *m* effort; vigor, spirit, courage; stress
**esfumado -da** *adj* (paint.) sfumato
**esfumar** *va* (f.a.) to stump; (paint.) to tone down, to soften; *vr* to disappear, to fade away
**esfuminar** *va* (f.a.) to stump
**esfumino** *m* (f.a.) stump
**esgarrar** *va* to try to cough up (*phlegm*); to tear, rend; *vn* to clear one's throat
**esgrafiado** *m* (f.a.) sgrafitto
**esgrafiar** *va* (f.a.) to decorate with sgraffito
**esgrima** *f* fencing (*art*)
**esgrimidor** *m* fencer
**esgrimidura** *f* fencing (*act*)
**esgrimir** *va* to wield; to brandish; to swing (*e.g., a new argument*); *vn* to fence
**esgrimista** *mf* (Am.) fencer; (Am.) gyp, panhandler
**esguazable** *adj* fordable
**esguazar** §76 *va* to ford
**esguazo** *m* fording; ford
**esgucio** *m* (arch.) cavetto
**esguín** *m* (ichth.) samlet, parr
**esguince** *m* dodge, duck; feint; frown, scornful look; sprain, twist (*of a joint*)
**esguízaro -ra** *adj* & *mf* Swiss; **pobre esguízaro** (coll.) wretch, ragamuffin
**eslabón** *m* link (*of chain*); (fig.) link; steel (*for striking fire from flint; for sharpening knives*); **eslabón perdido** missing link (*between man and monkey*)
**eslabonador -dora** *adj* linking, interlinking
**eslabonamiento** *m* linkage, linking; interlinking, stringing together, sequence
**eslabonar** *va* to link; to interlink, to string together; *vr* to link
**eslalom** *m* slalom
**eslavo -va** *adj* Slav; Slavic; *mf* Slav; *m* Slavic (*language*)
**eslavoeclesiástico** *m* Church Slavic or Slavonic (*language*)
**eslavón -vona** *adj* & *mf* Slav

**eslavonio -nia** *adj & mf* Slavonian; (*cap.*) *f* Slavonia
**eslinga** *f* (naut.) sling
**eslingar** §59 *va* (naut.) to sling
**eslizón** *m* (zool.) seps
**eslora** *f* (naut.) length; **esloras** *fpl* (naut.) binding strakes (*of deck*)
**eslovaco -ca** *adj & mf* Slovak or Slovakian; *m* Slovak (*language*)
**Eslovaquia** *f* Slovakia
**Eslovenia** *f* Slovenia
**esloveno -na** *adj & mf* Slovene or Slovenian; *m* Slovenian (*language*)
**esmaltado** *m* enameling
**esmaltador -dora** *mf* enameler
**esmaltadura** *f* var. of **esmaltado**
**esmaltar** *va* to enamel; to adorn with bright colors; to adorn, to embellish
**esmalte** *m* enamel; enamel work; (anat.) enamel; smalt (*pigment and color*); (her.) tincture; **esmalte alveolado** or **tabicado** cloisonné; **esmalte campeado** or **vaciado** champlevé; **esmalte de uñas** or **esmalte para las uñas** nail polish
**esmaltín** *m* smalt
**esmaltina** *f* (mineral.) smaltite
**esméctico -ca** *adj* smectic
**esmerado -da** *adj* careful, painstaking
**esmeralda** *f* emerald
**esmeraldino -na** *adj* emerald (*in color*)
**esmerar** *va* to polish, to brighten; *vr* to take pains, to use great care; to get results; **esmerarse en** or **por** + *inf* to strive to + *inf*, to take pains to + *inf*
**esmerejón** *m* (orn.) goshawk; (orn.) merlin; small-caliber gun
**esmeril** *m* emery; small-caliber gun
**esmerilador** *m* grinder (*workman*)
**esmeriladora** *f* emery wheel, grinder
**esmerilar** *va* to grind, to polish with emery
**esmerillón** *m* swivel
**esmero** *m* great care; cleanliness, neatness
**Esmirna** *f* Smyrna
**esmirriado -da** *adj* var. of **desmirriado**
**esmoladera** *f* grindstone
**esmoquin** *m* var. of **smoking**
**esnob** *adj* snobbish; *mf* (*pl:* **esnobs**) snob
**esnobismo** *m* snobbery, snobbishness
**esnordeste** *m* east-northeast
**eso** *pron dem neut* that; **a eso de** about (*e.g., six o'clock*); **por eso** therefore, for that reason; **eso es** that's it; that is
**esófago** *m* (anat.) esophagus
**esópico -ca** *adj* Aesopian or Aesopic
**Esopo** *m* Aesop
**esotérico -ca** *adj* esoteric
**esotro -tra** *adj & pron dem* (archaic) that other
**esotropia** *f* (path.) esotropia
**espabiladeras** *fpl* snuffers
**espabilar** *va* to trim, to snuff (*candle*)
**espaciado -da** *adj* scattered; *m* (print.) spacing
**espaciador** *m* space bar
**espacial** *adj* spatial; (pertaining to) space
**espaciamiento** *m* spacing; expatiation
**espaciar** §90 (Am.) & **regular** *va* to space; to scatter, to spread; (print.) to space; (print.) to lead; *vr* to enlarge, to expatiate; to relax, to amuse oneself
**espacio** *m* space; room; period, interval; (mus.) interval; (print.) space; delay, slowness; **por espacio de** in the space of (*e.g., a year*); **espacio de almacenaje** storage space; **espacio de chispa** (elec.) spark gap (*of spark plug*); **espacio de pelo** (print.) hair space; **espacio euclidiano** (geom.) Euclidean space; **espacio exterior** outer space; **espacio vital** Lebensraum
**espaciosidad** *f* spaciousness
**espacioso -sa** *adj* spacious, roomy; slow, deliberate
**espachurrar** *va* var. of **despachurrar**
**espada** *f* sword; playing card (*representing a sword*) equivalent to spade; (ichth.) swordfish; **espadas** *fpl* card suit corresponding to spades; **entre la espada y la pared** between the devil and the deep blue sea; **envainar la espada** to sheathe the sword; **medir las espadas** to measure swords; **espada de Damocles** sword of Damocles; **espada de dos filos** two-edged sword; *m* swordsman; (taur.) matador
**espadachín** *m* swordsman, skilled swordsman; bully
**espadador -dora** *mf* scutcher, hemp or flax beater
**espadaña** *f* (bot.) cattail, bulrush, reed mace (*Typha latifolia*); bell gable; **espadaña fina** (bot.) flagon
**espadañada** *f* spewing of blood; abundance, large number
**espadañal** *m* meadow full of cattail
**espadañar** *va* to spread out (*the tail feathers*)
**espadar** *va* to swingle, to scutch
**espadarte** *m* (ichth.) swordfish
**espadería** *f* sword cutlery, sword shop
**espadero** *m* swordmaker, swordsmith, sword dealer
**espádice** *m* (bot.) spadix
**espadilla** *f* scull (*oar*); swingle; ace of spades; bodkin (*for lady's hair*); red insignia of order of Santiago
**espadillar** *va* to swingle
**espadín** *m* rapier
**espadón** *m* (coll.) brass hat (*in army and elsewhere*); (coll.) braggart soldier; eunuch
**espadrapo** *m* var. of **esparadrapo**
**espagírico -ca** *adj* metallurgic; spagyric, iatrochemical; *f* metallurgy; spagyric, iatrochemistry
**espahí** *m* (*pl:* **-híes**) spahi
**espalar** *va* to shovel (*e.g., snow*)
**espalda** *f* back; **espaldas** *fpl* back, shoulders; (mil.) rearguard; **a espaldas** or **a espaldas vueltas** treacherously; **a espaldas de** behind, back of (*a building*); **cargado de espaldas** round-shouldered; **dar de espaldas** to fall on one's back; **echarse a las espaldas** to forget about (*a worry, duty, etc.*); **echarse sobre las espaldas** to take on, to assume as a responsibility; **hablar por las espaldas de** to talk behind the back of; **no sacarle espaldas al trabajo** to keep one's shoulder to the wheel; **tener buenas espaldas** (coll.) to have broad shoulders; **volver las espaldas a** to turn a cold shoulder to
**espaldar** *m* back; backplate (*of armor*); back (*of chair*); shell, shield (*of turtle*); espalier, trellis; **espaldares** *mpl* wall hangings
**espaldarazo** *m* accolade; slap on the back; **dar el espaldarazo a** to approve, to validate, to recognize
**espaldarcete** *m* épaulière (*of armor*)
**espaldarón** *m* backplate (*of armor*)
**espaldear** *va* (naut.) to dash against the stern of (*a ship*)
**espalder** *m* stern rower (*in galley*)
**espaldera** *f* espalier, trellis; trellised wall
**espaldilla** *f* (anat.) scapula, shoulder blade; back (*of jacket*)
**espalditendido -da** *adj* (coll.) stretched out on one's back
**espaldón** *m* (carp.) mortise; (fort.) intrenchment
**espaldonar** *vr* (mil.) to hide from enemy fire
**espaldudo -da** *adj* broad-shouldered, heavy-set
**espalera** *f* espalier, trellis
**espalmadura** *f* parings (*of hoofs*)
**espalmar** *va* var. of **despalmar**
**espalto** *m* (paint.) dark glaze
**espantable** *adj* frightful, terrible
**espantada** *f* stampede (*flight*); cold feet
**espantadizo -za** *adj* shy, scary
**espantador -dora** *adj* frightening
**espantajo** *m* scarecrow (*figure; person*); (fig.) scarecrow, bugaboo
**espantalobos** *m* (*pl:* **-bos**) (bot.) bladder senna
**espantamoscas** *m* (*pl:* **-cas**) fly chaser; flytrap; fly net
**espantapájaros** *m* (*pl:* **-ros**) scarecrow (*figure*)
**espantar** *va* to scare, to frighten; to frighten away, to chase away; *vr* to become scared, to become frightened; to marvel, to wonder
**espanto** *m* fright, terror, consternation; threat; (Am.) ghost, spook
**espantoso -sa** *adj* frightful; awful, fearful, astounding

**España** *f* Spain; **la Nueva España** New Spain (*Mexico in colonial period*); **las Españas** Spain and the countries of Spanish America
**español -ñola** *adj* Spanish; **a la española** in the Spanish fashion or manner; *mf* Spaniard; *m* Spanish (*language*); **los españoles** the Spanish (*people*); *f* Spanish woman; **La Española** Hispaniola (*Santo Domingo*)
**españolado -da** *adj* Spanish-looking; *f* Spanish sort of remark, Spanish mannerism; (scornful) Spanish take-off (*by foreigners*)
**españolar** *va & vr* (coll.) var. of **españolizar**
**españolería** *f* var. of **españolada**
**españoleta** *f* ancient Spanish dance; (Am.) espagnolette
**españolismo** *m* love of Spain, Spanish patriotism; Spanish nature or essence; Hispanicism
**españolización** *f* Hispaniolization
**españolizar** §76 *va* to make Spanish or like Spanish; to make (*a word*) Spanish; *vr* to become Spanish, to adopt Spanish customs
**esparadrapo** *m* court plaster, sticking plaster
**esparaván** *m* (vet.) spavin; (orn.) sparrow hawk
**esparavel** *m* mortarboard, hawk; casting net
**esparceta** *f* (bot.) sainfoin
**esparciata** *adj & mf* Spartan
**esparcidamente** *adv* separately; here and there; merrily, freely
**esparcido -da** *adj* merry, gay, open, candid
**esparcidor -dora** *adj* scattering, spreading; relaxing, diverting; *mf* scatterer, spreader
**esparcilla** *f* (bot.) spurry, corn spurry; (bot.) sainfoin
**esparcimiento** *m* scattering, spreading; spreading abroad, dissemination; relaxation, diversion; joviality, openness, frankness; **esparcimiento de banda** (rad.) band spread
**esparcir** §50 *va* to scatter, to spread; to spread abroad; to relax, to divert; *vr* to scatter, to spread; to spread abroad; to disperse; to relax, to take it easy
**esparragado** *m* dish of asparagus
**esparragador -dora** *mf* asparagus grower
**esparragar** §59 *vn* to grow asparagus
**espárrago** *m* (bot.) asparagus (*plant and its shoots*); tent or awning pole; peg ladder; stud bolt; **espárragos** *mpl* asparagus (*for eating*)
**esparragón** *m* double-thread silk cloth
**esparraguero -ra** *mf* asparagus grower or dealer; *f* (bot.) asparagus (*plant*); asparagus bed; asparagus dish
**esparrancado -da** *adj* with one's legs wide apart; too wide apart or open
**esparrancar** §86 *vr* (coll.) to spread one's legs wide apart
**Esparta** *f* Sparta
**Espártaco** *m* Spartacus
**espartal** *m* esparto field
**espartano -na** *adj & mf* Spartan; (fig.) Spartan
**esparteña** *f* matweed sandal
**espartería** *f* esparto wear (*cordage, shoes, baskets, mats*); esparto-wear shop or business
**espartero -ra** *mf* esparto-wear maker or dealer
**espartilla** *f* horsebrush of esparto grass
**espartizal** *m* esparto field
**esparto** *m* (bot.) esparto or esparto grass
**esparver** *m* (orn.) sparrow hawk
**espasmo** *m* (path.) spasm; **espasmo cínico** (path.) cynic spasm
**espasmódico -ca** *adj* spasmodic, convulsive
**espasticidad** *f* (path.) spasticity
**espástico -ca** *adj* spastic
**espata** *f* (bot.) spathe
**espatarrada** *f* (coll.) var. of **despatarrada**
**espático -ca** *adj* (mineral.) spathic
**espato** *m* (mineral.) spar; **espato calizo** (mineral.) calcspar; **espato de Islandia** (mineral.) Iceland spar; **espato flúor** (mineral.) fluor spar; **espato pesado** (mineral.) heavy spar, barite
**espátula** *f* spatula; palette knife; putty knife; (orn.) shoveler, spoonbill; (bot.) stinking iris, gladdon
**espatulado -da** *adj* spatulate
**espatulomancía** *f* spatulamancy
**espaviento** *m* fuss, excitement
**espavorido -da** *adj* terrified, frightened
**especia** *f* spice
**especiado -da** *adj* spicy
**especial** *adj* special, especial; **en especial** especially
**especialidad** *f* specialty, speciality
**especialista** *adj & mf* specialist
**especialización** *f* specialization
**especializar** §76 *va, vn & vr* to specialize
**especiar** *va* to spice
**especie** *f* species; kind, sort; matter; objection, pretext, show, appearance; news, rumor; **en especie** in kind (*in goods or produce*); **escapársele a uno una especie** to be indiscreet, to talk too much; **la especie** the species (*mankind*); **soltar una especie** to try to draw a person out; **especies sacramentales** (eccl.) species
**especiería** *f* spice store; spicery (*spices*); spice business; grocery store
**especiero -ra** *mf* spice dealer; *m* spice box
**especificación** *f* specification
**especificar** §86 *va* to specify; to itemize
**especificativo -va** *adj* specificative; (gram.) restrictive
**específico -ca** *adj* specific; *m* specific (*medicine*); patent medicine
**espécimen** *m* (*pl:* **especímenes**) specimen
**especiosidad** *f* neatness, beauty; speciosity, speciousness
**especioso -sa** *adj* neat, beautiful; specious
**especiota** *f* (coll.) crazy idea; (coll.) hoax, fake news
**espectacular** *adj* spectacular
**espectáculo** *m* spectacle; **dar un espectáculo** to create a scene, to make a scene
**espectador -dora** *adj* watching; *mf* spectator
**espectral** *adj* spectral, ghostly; (phys.) spectral, spectrum
**espectro** *m* specter, phantom, ghost; (phys.) spectrum; **espectro de radio** radio spectrum; **espectro magnético** magnetic curves
**espectrógrafo** *m* spectrograph; **espectrógrafo de masa** or **de masas** (phys.) mass spectrograph
**espectroscopia** *f* spectroscopy
**espectroscópico -ca** *adj* spectroscopic
**espectroscopio** *m* spectroscope
**especulación** *f* contemplation; speculation; (com.) speculation; report, account, statement
**especulador -dora** *adj* speculating; *mf* speculator
**especular** *adj* specular; *va* to view, inspect, contemplate; to speculate about or on; *vn* to speculate; (com.) to speculate; (coll.) to manage to improve one's lot
**especulativo -va** *adj* speculative; *f* (philos.) faculty of speculation or reason
**espéculo** *m* (med. & surg.) speculum
**espejado -da** *adj* mirrorlike, smooth or bright (*as a mirror*); mirrored
**espejar** *va* var. of **despejar**
**espejear** *vn* to shine, to sparkle
**espejeo** *m* var. of **espejismo**
**espejería** *f* mirror shop
**espejero** *m* mirror maker or dealer
**espejismo** *m* (opt. & fig.) mirage
**espejo** *m* mirror, looking glass; (fig.) mirror; model; **espejo de cuerpo entero** pier glass, full-length mirror; **espejo de falla** (geol.) slickenside; **espejo de los incas** (mineral.) obsidian; **espejo de retrovisión** (aut.) rear-view mirror; **espejo de Venus** (bot.) Venus's-looking-glass; **espejo de vestir** pier glass, full-length mirror; **espejo retrovisor** (aut.) rear-view mirror; **espejo ustorio** burning glass
**espejuelo** *m* small looking glass; (mineral.) selenite; candied citron or pumpkin; (arch.) rose window with openings filled with selenite; (vet.) chestnut; (fig.) mirage; **espejuelos** *mpl* spectacles; lenses of spectacles
**espeleología** *f* speleology
**espeleólogo -ga** *mf* speleologist
**espelta** *f* (bot.) spelt
**espélteo -a** *adj* (pertaining to) spelt
**espelunca** *f* cave, cavern
**espeluzar** §76 *va & vr* var. of **despeluzar**

**espeluznante** *adj* hair-raising
**espeluznar** *va & vr* var. of **despeluzar**
**espeluzno** *m* (coll.) chill, terror
**espeque** *m* prop, support; lever, handspike
**espera** *f* wait, waiting; restraint, composure; respite; delay; (law) stay; (carp.) notch; (hunt.) blind, hunter's blind; **en espera** waiting; **en espera de** waiting for, while waiting for; **no tener espera** to be of the greatest urgency, to be unpostponable
**esperador -dora** *adj* expectant
**esperantista** *adj & mf* Esperantist
**esperanto** *m* Esperanto
**esperanza** *f* hope; hopefulness; **tener puesta su esperanza en** to pin one's faith on; **esperanza de vida** life expectancy
**esperanzado -da** *adj* hopeful (*having hope*)
**esperanzador -dora** *adj* hopeful (*causing or giving hope*)
**esperanzar** §76 *va* to give hope to, to make hopeful
**esperanzoso -sa** *adj* hopeful (*having great hope*)
**esperar** *va* to hope for; to hope; to expect; to await, to wait for; **ir a esperar** to go to meet; *vn* to hope; to wait; **esperar** + *inf* to hope to + *inf;* **esperar a que** + *subj* to wait until + *ind;* **esperar desesperando** to hope against hope; **esperar en** to put one's hope or trust in; **esperar que** + *fut ind* or *pres subj* to hope that + *fut ind;* **esperar sentado** to have a good wait, to wait for nothing; *vr* to expect
**esperezar** §76 *vr* to stretch, to stretch one's arms and legs
**esperezo** *m* stretching, stretching the arms and legs
**esperinque** *m* (ichth.) smelt
**esperma** *f* sperm; **esperma de ballena** spermaceti
**espermaceti** *m* spermaceti
**espermático -ca** *adj* spermatic
**espermatofita** *f* (bot.) spermatophyte
**espermatorrea** *f* (path.) spermatorrhea
**espermatozoide** *m* or **espermatozoo** *m* (zool.) spermatozoön
**espermófita** *f* var. of **espermatofita**
**espermogonio** *m* (bot.) spermogonium
**espernada** *f* open link (*at end of chain*)
**esperón** *m* (naut.) spur (*ram of war vessel*); (Am.) long wait
**esperonte** *m* (fort.) spur
**esperpento** *m* (coll.) fright (*ugly person or thing*); nonsense, absurdity
**espesador** *m* thickener
**espesamiento** *m* thickening (*act*)
**espesante** *m* thickening (*substance*)
**espesar** *m* thickness, depth (*of woods*); *va* to thicken; to make closer, to weave tighter; *vr* to thicken, to become thick or thicker
**espesativo -va** *adj* thickening
**espeso -sa** *adj* thick; heavy (*liquid*); dirty, greasy, untidy
**espesor** *m* thickness; (coll.) thickness (*of a liquid or gas*)
**espesura** *f* thickness; shock of hair; thicket; dirtiness, greasiness, untidiness
**espetaperro; a espetaperro** or **a espetaperros** (coll.) at full speed
**espetar** *va* to spit, to skewer; to pierce, to pierce through, to transfix; **espetarle a uno una cosa** (coll.) to spring something on someone; *vr* to be stiff and solemn; (coll.) to steady oneself, to settle, to settle down
**espetera** *f* scullery, kitchen rack
**espetón** *m* poker; iron pin; large pin; spit; poke, jab; (ichth.) needlefish
**espía** *mf* spy; tattletale, squealer; *m* (coll.) cop (*policeman*); *f* (naut.) warping; (naut.) warp
**espiar** §90 *va* to spy on; *vn* to spy; (naut.) to warp a ship; *vr* (naut.) to warp a ship
**espibia** *f*, **espibio** *m* or **espibión** *m* (vet.) sprain in the neck (*of horse*)
**espicanardi** *f* or **espicanardo** *m* (bot.) spikenard
**espiciforme** *adj* (bot.) spiciform
**espícula** *f* (anat., bot. & zool.) spicule
**espicular** *adj* spicular or spiculate
**espichar** *va* to prick; *vn* (coll.) to die; *vr* (Am.) to get thin
**espiche** *m* prick (*pointed weapon or instrument*); (naut.) peg, spigot
**espichón** *m* prick, stab (*wound*)
**espiga** *f* (bot.) spike, ear; (archeol. & surg.) spica; (carp.) tenon, pin, peg; (mach.) tongue; brad; clapper (*of bell*); stem (*of a key*); shank (*e.g., of a rivet*); fuse (*of a bomb*); (naut.) masthead; **espiga de la Virgen** (astr.) Spica; **espigas comprobadoras** (elec.) testing prongs
**espigadera** *f* gleaner
**espigado -da** *adj* spiky; ripe, seeded; spindly; tall, grown-up; (bot.) spicate
**espigador -dora** *mf* gleaner
**espigadura** *f* gleaning
**espigar** §59 *va* to glean; (fig.) to glean; to tenon, to pin, to dowel; *vn* to ear, to form ears (*said of cereals*); *vr* to grow tall
**espigo** *m* stem, shank
**espigón** *m* sting; point of a sharp tool or nail; sharp ear or spike; ear of corn; peak; breakwater
**espigueo** *m* gleaning; gleaning time
**espiguilla** *f* (bot.) spikelet; tape, fringe; (bot.) meadow grass
**espina** *f* thorn, spine; fishbone; (anat., bot. & zool.) spine; (fig.) thorn; doubt, uncertainty; **dar mala espina a** (coll.) to worry, to make anxious; **estar en espinas** (coll.) to be on pins and needles; **sacarse la espina** (coll.) to get even, make up a loss; **espina blanca** (bot.) cotton thistle; **espina de pescado** herringbone (*in fabrics*); **espina de pez** fishbone; **espina dorsal** (anat.) spinal column; **espina santa** or **vera** (bot.) Christ's-thorn, Jerusalem thorn
**espinaca** *f* (bot.) spinach; **espinacas** *fpl* spinach (*for eating*)
**espinadura** *f* prick, pricking
**espinal** *adj* spinal
**espinapez** *m* herringbone (*in hardwood or tile floor*); thorny matter, difficulty
**espinar** *m* thorny spot; (fig.) thorny matter; *va* to prick (*said of thorns*); to protect (*trees*) with thorn bushes; (fig.) to sting, to provoke; *vn* to prick
**espinazo** *m* (anat.) backbone; (arch.) keystone
**espinel** *m* trawl, trawl line
**espinela** *f* (mineral.) spinel
**espíneo -a** *adj* made of thorns; thornlike
**espinera** *f* (bot.) hawthorn
**espineta** *f* (mus.) spinet
**espingarda** *f* small cannon; long Moorish shotgun; (coll.) tall ungainly woman
**espinilla** *f* (anat.) shinbone; (path.) blackhead
**espinillera** *f* (sport) shin guard; greave, jambe
**espinillo** *m* (bot.) Jerusalem thorn, horse bean; (bot.) huisache
**espino** *m* (bot.) hawthorn; **espino artificial** barbed wire; **espino albar** or **blanco** (bot.) hawthorn; **espino cerval** or **hediondo** (bot.) buckthorn; **espino negro** (bot.) blackthorn
**espinochar** *va* to husk (*e.g., corn*)
**espinosismo** *m* Spinozism
**espinosista** *adj* Spinozistic; *mf* Spinozist
**espinoso -sa** *adj* thorny; bony (*fish*); spinous, spinose; (fig.) thorny; *m* (ichth.) stickleback
**espínula** *f* spinule
**espiocha** *f* pickaxe
**espión** *m* spy
**espionaje** *m* spying, espial; espionage
**espira** *f* turn (*of helix or spiral*); (elec.) turn (*of a winding*); (geom. & zool.) spire; (arch.) surbase (*of a pedestal*)
**espiración** *f* breathing; exhalation, expiration
**espiráculo** *m* (zool.) spiracle
**espirador -dora** *adj* (physiol.) expiratory
**espiral** *adj* spiral; *f* spiral spring; (horol.) hairspring; (geom.) spiral
**espirante** *adj & f* (phonet.) spirant
**espirar** *va* to breathe, to breathe out (*an odor*); to encourage; *vn* to breathe; to exhale; (poet.) to blow gently
**espirea** *f* (bot.) spiraea
**espirilo** *m* (bact.) spirillum
**espiritado -da** *adj* (coll.) ghostlike (*extremely thin*)

**espiritar** *va* to possess with the devil; (coll.) to stir, to disturb, to upset; to waste away; *vr* to be possessed with the devil; (coll.) to be stirred, disturbed, or upset; to waste away
**espiritismo** *m* spiritualism, spiritism
**espiritista** *adj* spiritualistic, spiritistic; *mf* spiritualist, spiritist
**espiritoso -sa** *adj* spirited; spirituous
**espiritrompa** *f* (zool.) proboscis (*of insects*)
**espíritu** *m* spirit; mind; ghost; (gram.) breathing (*in ancient Greek*); **espíritus** *mpl* spirits, demons; **espíritu de cuerpo** esprit de corps; **espíritu de equipo** spirit of teamwork; **Espíritu Santo** Holy Ghost, Holy Spirit; **dar, despedir** or **exhalar el espíritu** to breathe one's last
**espiritual** *adj* spiritual; energetic, lively; keen, susceptible, soulful; *f* spiritual (*religious song*)
**espiritualidad** *f* spirituality; energy, liveliness; keenness, susceptibility, soulfulness
**espiritualismo** *m* spiritualism (*as opposed to materialism*)
**espiritualista** *adj* spiritualistic; *mf* spiritualist
**espiritualización** *f* spiritualization
**espiritualizar** §76 *va* to spiritualize
**espirituoso -sa** *adj* var. of **espiritoso**
**espirogira** *f* (bot.) spirogyra
**espirómetro** *m* spirometer
**espiroqueta** *f* (bact.) spirochete
**espita** *f* tap, cock (*for a cask*); (coll.) tippler
**espitar** *va* to tap (*a cask or barrel*)
**espito** *m* peel (*hanger used for drying paper*)
**esplácnico -ca** *adj* splanchnic
**esplendente** *adj* (poet.) splendent
**esplender** *vn* (poet.) to shine
**esplendidez** *f* splendor; abundance; magnificence, show, pomp; generosity, lavishness; resplendence
**espléndido -da** *adj* splendid; abundant; magnificent; generous, lavish; resplendent
**esplendor** *m* splendor
**esplendoroso -sa** *adj* resplendent, magnificent; (poet.) brilliant, shining
**esplenectomía** *f* (surg.) splenectomy
**esplénico -ca** *adj* (anat.) splenetic, splenic
**esplenio** *m* (anat.) splenium; (anat.) splenius; bandage, compress
**esplenitis** *f* (path.) splenitis
**espliego** *m* (bot.) lavender (*plant and dried flowers and leaves*)
**esplín** *m* melancholy, hypochondria
**esplique** *m* bird snare
**espodumeno** *m* (mineral.) spodumene
**espolada** *f* prick with spur; **espolada de vino** (coll.) shot of wine
**espolazo** *m* var. of **espolada**
**espoleadura** *f* spurgall
**espolear** *va* to spur; (fig.) to spur on
**espoleta** *f* fuse (*of a bomb*); wishbone; **espoleta de explosión retardada** delayed-action fuse; **espoleta de percusión** percussion fuse; **espoleta de proximidad** proximity fuse; **espoleta de tiempos** time fuse
**espolín** *m* spur (*fastened with pin instead of straps*); shuttle for brocading flowers on silk; flowered brocade; (bot.) feather grass
**espolinar** *va* to brocade with flowers
**espolio** *m* despoliation; (eccl.) spolium
**espolique** *m* or **espolista** *m* groom who walks in front of master's horse
**espolón** *m* spur (*on leg of cock; of range of mountains*); fetlock (*projection on back of horse's leg*); spur, beak (*ram of war vessel*); mole, dike; jetty; cutwater (*of ship or bridge*); (arch.) buttress; (arti.) trail spade; (carp.) spur; (naut.) stem (*of bow*); (coll.) chilblain
**espolonada** *f* violent onslaught of horsemen
**espolvorear** *va* to dust (*to remove dust from; to sprinkle dust on*); to sprinkle (*e.g., sugar*); *vr* to dust off, come off (*said of dust*)
**espolvorizar** §76 *va* to dust, sprinkle with dust
**espondaico -ca** *adj* spondaic
**espondeo** *m* spondee
**espóndil** *m* (anat.) spondyl
**espondilitis** *f* (path.) spondylitis
**espóndilo** *m* var. of **espóndil**
**espongina** *f* (biochem.) spongin
**esponja** *f* sponge; (coll.) sponge, sponger; **beber como una esponja** to drink like a fish; **tirar la esponja** (coll.) to throw up (or in) or to toss up (or in) the sponge (*to acknowledge defeat*); **esponja de baño** bath sponge
**esponjado -da** *adj* proud, puffed up; (coll.) fresh, healthy; *m* brittle sugar bar (*made of white of egg and sugar, used to sweeten water*)
**esponjadura** *f* puffing up, fluffiness; conceit; (found.) flaw in casting
**esponjar** *va* to puff up, to make fluffy; *vr* to puff up, to become fluffy; (fig.) to be puffed up, be conceited; (coll.) to look fresh, to glow with health
**esponjera** *f* sponge tray, sponge rack
**esponjosidad** *f* sponginess
**esponjoso -sa** *adj* spongy
**esponsales** *mpl* betrothal, engagement
**esponsalicio -cia** *adj* (pertaining to a) betrothal, engagement
**espontanear** *vr* to own up; to open one's heart
**espontaneidad** *f* spontaneity
**espontáneo -a** *adj* spontaneous; (bot. & biol.) spontaneous; *m* (taur.) spectator who jumps into the ring to fight the bull
**espontón** *m* spontoon
**espontonada** *f* salute with a spontoon, blow with a spontoon
**espora** *f* (biol.) spore
**esporádico -ca** *adj* sporadic
**esporangio** *m* (bot.) sporangium
**esporidio** *m* (bot.) sporidium
**esporo** *m* var. of **espora**
**esporocarpo** *m* (bot.) sporocarp
**esporofila** *f* (bot.) sporophyll
**esporofito** *m* (bot.) sporophyte
**esporozoo -a** *adj & m* (zool.) sporozoan
**esportada** *f* basketful
**esportilla** *f* small two-handled basket
**esportillero** *m* carrier (*workman*); errand boy, street porter
**esportillo** *m* basket made of esparto grass; **coger el esportillo a** (coll.) to catch the attention of
**espórula** *f* (bot.) sporule
**esporulación** *f* (biol.) sporulation
**esposa** *f* see **esposo**
**esposado -da** *adj & mf* var. of **desposado**
**esposar** *va* to handcuff
**esposo -sa** *mf* spouse; *m* husband; *f* wife; **esposas** *fpl* manacles, handcuffs
**esprue** *m & f* (path.) sprue
**espuela** *f* spur; (fig.) spur (*incitement, stimulus*); **calzar espuela** to be a knight; **calzar la espuela a** to knight; **echar la espuela** (coll.) to take a nightcap together; **espuela de caballero** (bot.) delphinium, rocket larkspur; **espuela de galán** (bot.) Indian cress, garden nasturtium
**espuerta** *f* two-handled basket (*for carrying earth, rubble, etc.*); **a espuertas** in abundance
**espulgabueyes** *m* (*pl:* **-yes**) (orn.) oxpecker, beefeater
**espulgadero** *m* place where beggars clean themselves of lice or fleas
**espulgar** §59 *va* to delouse, to clean of lice or fleas; to examine closely, to scrutinize
**espulgo** *m* removal of lice or fleas; close examination, scrutiny; choice, careful selection
**espuma** *f* foam, spume, froth; scum; (fig.) cream; **crecer como (la) espuma** (coll.) to grow like weeds; (coll.) to have a meteoric rise; **espuma de caucho** foam rubber; **espuma de jabón** lather; **espuma de mar** (mineral.) meerschaum; **espuma de nitro** wall saltpeter
**espumadera** *f* skimmer; spray nozzle
**espumador -dora** *mf* skimmer
**espumaje** *m* foaminess, frothiness; scumminess
**espumajear** *vn* to froth at the mouth
**espumajo** *m* var. of **espumarajo**
**espumajoso -sa** *adj* foamy, frothy
**espumante** *adj* foaming, frothing; sparkling (*wine*)
**espumar** *va* to skim; *vn* to foam, to froth; to sparkle (*said of wine*); to grow or increase rapidly
**espumarajear** *vn* var. of **espumajear**
**espumarajo** *m* froth, frothing at the mouth; **echar espumarajos por la boca** (coll.) to froth at the mouth

**espúmeo -a** *adj* var. of **espumoso**
**espumero** *m* salina (*deposit of crystallized salt*)
**espumilla** *f* voile; (Am.) meringue
**espumillón** *m* heavy silk fabric
**espumoso -sa** *adj* foamy, frothy; scummy; lathery; sparkling (*wine*)
**espundia** *f* (path.) leishmaniasis; (vet.) cancerous ulcer (*of horses*)
**espurio -ria** *adj* spurious
**espurrear** or **espurriar** *va* to sprinkle with water by squirting from the mouth
**esputar** *va & vn* to spit
**esputazo** *m* splotch of spit
**esputo** *m* spit, saliva; sputum
**esq.** abr. of **esquina**
**esquebrajar** *va & vr* var. of **resquebrajar**
**esqueje** *m* (hort.) cutting, slip
**esquela** *f* note; announcement; death note; death notice; **esquela de defunción** or **esquela mortuoria** death note; death notice
**esquelético -ca** *adj* skeletal; thin, wasted
**esqueleto** *m* skeleton; (fig.) skeleton (*thin person; sketch, outline*); (Am.) blank form; **en esqueleto** incomplete, unfinished
**esquema** *m* scheme, schema, diagram; (philos.) schema
**esquemático -ca** *adj* schematic
**esquematismo** *m* schematism
**esquematizar** §76 *va* to sketch, to outline, to diagram
**esquena** *f* backbone; spine (*of a fish*)
**esquenanto** *m* (bot.) camel grass
**esquero** *m* leather bag (*fastened to belt*)
**esquí** *m* (*pl:* **esquís**) ski; skiing; (aer.) skid; **esquí acuático** water ski; water skiing; **esquí remolcado** skijoring
**esquiador -dora** *adj* ski; *mf* skier
**esquiar** §90 *vn* to ski
**esquíbala** *f* (path.) scybalum
**esquiciar** *va* to sketch
**esquicio** *m* sketch
**esquifada** *f* skiffload, boatload
**esquifar** *va* (naut.) to fit out, to man
**esquifazón** *f* (naut.) outfit, boat's crew
**esquife** *m* skiff; small boat, jolly boat; (arch.) cylindrical vault, barrel arch
**esquiismo** *m* skiing
**esquila** *f* hand bell; sacring bell, squilla; cowbell; sheepshearing; (bot.) squill; (ent.) whirligig beetle; (zool.) squill, mantis crab
**esquilador -dora** *mf* sheepshearer (*person*); *f* sheepshearer (*machine*)
**esquilar** *va* to shear, to fleece
**esquileo** *m* shearing, sheepshearing
**esquilimoso -sa** *adj* (coll.) fastidious, squeamish
**esquilmar** *va* to harvest; to impoverish; to drain, to exhaust (*the soil*); to steal, carry away; (fig.) to drain (*a source of wealth*)
**esquilmo** *m* harvest, farm produce; (fig.) harvest
**Esquilo** *m* Aeschylus
**esquilón** *m* large hand bell
**esquimal** *adj* Eskimoan; *mf* Eskimo
**esquina** *f* corner; (Am.) country store; **a la vuelta de la esquina** around the corner; **hacer esquina** to be on a corner (*said of a building*)
**esquinado -da** *adj* having a corner or corners; sharp-cornered; unsociable, intractable; piqued; angry
**esquinal** *m* angle iron, knee brace, gusset
**esquinancia** *f* var. of **esquinencia**
**esquinante** *m* or **esquinanto** *m* var. of **esquenanto**
**esquinar** *va* to be on the corner of, to form a corner with; *vn* **esquinar con** to be on the corner of, to form a corner with; *vr* to quarrel, to fall out; **esquinarse con** to quarrel with, to fall out with
**esquinazo** *m* (coll.) corner; (Am.) serenade; **dar esquinazo a** (coll.) to shake off; (coll.) to leave in the lurch
**esquinco** *m* var. of **escinco**
**esquinela** *f* greave, jambe
**esquinencia** *f* (path.) quinsy
**esquinera** *f* corner piece (*of furniture*)
**Esquines** *m* Aeschines
**esquinudo -da** *adj* sharp-cornered
**esquinzar** §76 *va* var. of **desguinzar**
**esquirla** *f* splinter (*of stone, glass; of bone*)
**esquirol** *m* scab, strikebreaker; (dial.) squirrel
**esquisto** *m* (geol.) schist; **esquisto aluminoso** alum schist
**esquistoso -sa** *adj* schistose or schistous
**esquitar** *va* to remit, to cancel (*a debt*)
**esquite** *m* (Am.) popcorn
**esquivada** *f* evasion, dodge; **esquivada lateral** (box.) side step
**esquivar** *va* to avoid, to shun, to evade; to dodge, to side-step; *vr* to withdraw, to shy away; to dodge, to side-step
**esquivez** *f* aloofness, gruffness, scorn
**esquivo -va** *adj* aloof, gruff, scornful; fleeting, elusive
**esquizado -da** *adj* mottled (*marble*)
**esquizocarpio** *m* (bot.) schizocarp
**esquizofrenia** *f* (path.) schizophrenia
**esquizofrénico -ca** *adj & mf* schizophrenic
**esquizomiceto** *m* (bot.) schizomycete
**essudeste** or **essueste** *m* east-southeast
**estabilidad** *f* stability
**estabilísimo -ma** *adj super* very or most stable
**estabilización** *f* stabilization
**estabilizador -dora** *adj* stabilizing; *mf* stabilizer (*person*); *m* stabilizer (*device*)
**estabilizar** §76 *va* to stabilize; *vr* to become stabilized
**estable** *adj* stable; *mf* steady or permanent guest (*e.g., at a boarding house*)
**establear** *va* to accustom to the stable; *vr* to become accustomed to the stable
**establecedor -dora** *adj* founding; *mf* founder
**establecer** §34 *va* to establish; to institute; *vr* to become a resident, to take up residence; to set up in business
**establecimiento** *m* establishment; place of business; settlement; ordinance, decree, statute; **Establecimientos de los Estrechos** Straits Settlements (*in Malay Peninsula*)
**establero** *m* stableman, groom
**establo** *m* stable; **establos de Augías** (myth.) Augean Stables
**estabulación** *f* stabling
**estabular** *va* to stable, to raise in a stable
**estaca** *f* stake, pale, picket; (hort.) cutting, stem cutting; club, cudgel; spike; (min.) claim
**estacada** *f* stockade, palisade; lists (*tilting field*); dueling ground; (fig.) predicament; **dejar en la estacada** to leave in the lurch; **quedar** or **quedarse en la estacada** to succumb in a duel, on the field of battle, etc.; to lose out; to fail hopelessly
**estacar** §86 *va* to tie (*an animal*) to a stake; to stake off; *vr* to stand stiff as a pole
**estacazo** *m* blow with a stake or a club; reverse, setback
**estación** *f* station; season; stop; resort; (astr. & eccl.) station; **vestir con la estación** to dress according to the season; **estación balnearia** bathing resort; **estación central** (elec.) power plant; **estación de aparcamiento** (aut.) parking station, parking lot; **estación de bandera** (rail.) flag station; **estación de cabeza** (rail.) terminal station; **estación de carga** freight station; **estación de clasificación** (rail.) classification yard; **estación de empalme** or **enlace** (rail.) junction; **estación de fin de línea** (rail.) terminal; **estación de fuerza** (elec.) power plant; **estación de gasolina** gas station, filling station; **estación de la seca** dry season; **estación de las lluvias** rainy season; **estación de paso** (rail.) way station; **estación de radiodifusión** (rad.) broadcasting station; **estación de servicio** (aut.) service station; **estación difusora** or **emisora** (rad.) broadcasting station; **estación elevadora** pumping station; **estaciones de la cruz** (eccl.) stations of the cross; **estación extrema** (rail.) terminal station; **estación gasolinera** gas station, filling station; **estación telefónica** telephone exchange; **estación termoeléctrica** steam power plant
**estacional** *adj* seasonal; stationary
**estacionalidad** *f* seasonal characteristic, seasonal demand

**estacionamiento** *m* stationing; (aut.) parking
**estacionar** *va* to station; (aut.) to park; *vn* (aut.) to park; *vr* to station oneself; to be stationed; to remain stationary; (aut.) to park; **se prohibe estacionarse** (aut.) no parking
**estacionario -ria** *adj* stationary; *mf* (archaic) stationer (*bookseller*)
**estacionero -ra** *mf* visitor to shrines in search of indulgences
**estacte** *f* oil of myrrh
**estacha** *f* (naut.) hawser; towline, harpoon rope
**estada** *f* stop, stay
**estadal** *m* linear measure of about 3.3 meters; blessed ribbon worn about the neck; **estadal cuadrado** square measure of about 11.2 square meters
**estadia** *f* (surv.) stadia
**estadía** *f* sitting (*e.g., before a painter*); (com.) demurrage; (Am.) stay
**estadillo** *m* register, roll, roster; (mil.) muster roll
**estadio** *m* stadium; stage, phase; furlong
**estadista** *m* statesman; statistician
**estadístico -ca** *adj* statistical; *m* statistician; *f* statistics
**estadiunense** *adj & mf* var. of **estadounidense**
**estadizo -za** *adj* stagnant (*water*); heavy, stifling (*air*)
**estado** *m* state, condition, station; status; state, government, country; statement, report; staff; **en estado (interesante)** or **en estado de buena esperanza** in the family way, pregnant; **los tres estados** the three estates (*noblemen, clergymen, and common people*); **Estados Unidos** *msg* or **los Estados Unidos** *mpl* the United States *ssg;* **mudar de estado** or **tomar estado** to take a wife; to go into the church; **estado civil** marital status; **estado de ánimo** state of mind; **estado de cosas** state of affairs; **estado de cuenta** (com.) statement; **estado de guerra** martial law; **estado de sitio** state of siege; **estado honesto** spinsterhood; **estado libre asociado** commonwealth; **Estado Libre de Irlanda** Irish Free State; **Estado Libre del Congo** Congo Free State; **Estado Libre de Orange** Orange Free State; **estado llano** commons, common people; **estado mayor** (mil.) staff; **estado mayor conjunto** (mil.) joint chiefs of staff; **estado mayor general** (mil.) general staff; **estados bálticos** Baltic States; **Estados Berberiscos** Barbary States; **estados generales** (hist.) States-General (*in France*); **Estados Malayos** Malay States; **Estados Malayos Federados** Federated Malay States; **estado sólido** (phys.) solid state; **estado tapón** buffer state
**estado-policía** *m* (*pl:* **estados-policías**) police state
**estadounidense** or **estadunidense** *adj* American, United States; *mf* American (*native or inhabitant of the United States*)
**estafa** *f* trick, swindle; swindling; stirrup
**estafador -dora** *mf* cheat, swindler
**estafar** *va* to defraud, to swindle; to overcharge
**estafermo** *m* revolving figure of an armed man, used as target in a game; dumfounded person; (coll.) simpleton
**estafeta** *f* post, courier; post office; branch post office; diplomatic mail; messenger
**estafetero** *m* postmaster; post-office clerk
**estafetil** *adj* post, courier; post-office
**estafilococo** *m* (bact.) staphylococcus
**estafiloma** *m* (path.) staphyloma
**estafisagria** *f* (bot.) stavesacre
**estagnación** *f* var. of **estancamiento**
**estagnar** *va* var. of **estancar**
**estajanovismo** *m* var. of **stajanovismo**
**estala** *f* (naut.) call, stop
**estalación** *f* class, category
**estalactita** *f* stalactite
**estalagmita** *f* stalagmite
**estalladura** *f* blowout
**estallar** *vn* to burst, to explode; to break out (*said, e.g., of a fire, a revolution, a war*); to break forth (*said of anger*); to burst with anger
**estallido** *m* report, explosion; crack, crash; outbreak (*e.g., of war*); **dar un estallido** to crash, to explode
**estambrar** *va* to spin or weave (*wool*) into worsted
**estambre** *m* worsted, woolen yarn; (bot.) stamen; (fig.) thread, course (*of life*)
**Estambul** *f* Stambul, Istanbul
**estamento** *m* estate (*each of four represented in Cortes of Aragon*)
**estameña** *f* tammy cloth, estamene
**estameñete** *m* light tammy cloth
**estaminado -da** *adj* (bot.) staminate (*having stamens and no pistils*)
**estamíneo -a** *adj* worsted; (bot.) stamineous
**estaminífero -ra** *adj* (bot.) staminate, staminiferous
**estaminodio** or **estaminodo** *m* (bot.) staminode or staminodium
**estampa** *f* print, stamp, engraving; swage; press, printing; track, footstep; aspect; **la propia estampa de** the very image of; **parecer la estampa de la herejía** (coll.) to be a sight, to be a mess (*to be ugly, to be shabbily dressed*); **estampa de Navidad** Christmas card
**estampación** *f* printing, stamping, engraving; swaging; embossing; (b.b.) tooling; **estampación en seco** (b.b.) blind tooling
**estampado** *m* printing, stamping, engraving; swaging; print, cotton print
**estampador** *m* stamper, engraver
**estampar** *va* to print, to stamp, to engrave; to swage; to sink (*e.g., one's foot in the mud*); to fix, to engrave (*on the mind*); (b.b.) to tool; (coll.) to dash, to slam; **estampar en seco** (b.b.) to blind-tool
**estampería** *f* stamp or print shop or business
**estampero -ra** *mf* stamp or print maker or dealer
**estampía; de estampía** suddenly, unexpectedly
**estampida** *f* crash, explosion, report (*of a gun*); (Am.) stampede
**estampido** *m* crash, explosion, report (*of a gun*)
**estampilla** *f* stamp, seal; rubber stamp (*of signature*); (Am.) stamp (*postage or revenue*)
**estampillado** *m* stamping; rubber-stamping
**estampillar** *va* to stamp; to rubber-stamp
**estancación** *f* stagnation; deadlock; state monopoly
**estancamiento** *m* stagnation; (fig.) stagnation, deadlock
**estancar** §86 *va* to stanch, to stem, to check; to hold up, to stall, to suspend (*a deal*); to deadlock; to corner (*a product*); to monopolize (*said particularly of the state*); *vr* to stagnate; to be a state monopoly
**estancia** *f* stay; room; dwelling; day in hospital; cost of day in hospital; stanza; (Am.) country place; (Am.) cattle ranch; (Am.) truck farm
**estanciero** *m* (Am.) farmer, rancher
**estanco -ca** *adj* stanch, watertight; **estanco al aire** airtight; *m* monopoly, state monopoly; cigar store, government store (*for sale of stamps, tobacco, matches, etc.*); archives; (Am.) liquor store
**estándar** *m* (Am.) standard
**estandardización** *f* standardization
**estandardizar** §76 *va* to standardize
**estandarización** *f* var. of **estandardización**
**estandarizar** §76 *va* var. of **estandardizar**
**estandarte** *m* standard, banner
**estandartización** *f* var. of **estandardización**
**estandartizar** §76 *va* var. of **estandardizar**
**estangurria** *f* (path.) strangury; catheter
**estannato** *m* (chem.) stannate
**estánnico -ca** *adj* (chem.) stannic
**estannoso -sa** *adj* (chem.) stannous
**estanque** *m* reservoir, basin; pond, pool
**estanquero -ra** *mf* storekeeper (*in store of government monopolies*); tobacconist; *m* reservoir attendant
**estanquidad** *f* watertightness
**estanquillero -ra** *mf* storekeeper (*in store of government monopolies*); tobacconist

**estanquillo** *m* government store, cigar store; (Am.) small shop; (Am.) tavern
**estantal** *m* (mas.) abutment
**estantalar** *va* to brace, to prop, to support
**estante** *adj* being, residing; fixed, permanent; *m* shelf; shelving; open bookcase; post, upright
**estantería** *f* shelving; book stacks
**estantigua** *f* phantom, hobgoblin; (coll.) lank, dirty and ragged person, big scarecrow
**estantío -a** *adj* inactive, stationary; slow, dull, lukewarm
**estañado** *m* tinning
**estañador** *m* tinman, tinner; soldering iron
**estañadura** *f* tinning; tinwork
**estañar** *va* to tin; to tin-plate; to solder
**estañero** *m* tinsmith; tinman (*dealer*)
**estaño** *m* (chem.) tin
**estapedio** *m* (anat.) stapedius
**estaquero** *m* year-old buck or doe
**estaquilla** *f* peg, pin, dowel; brad; spike
**estaquillador** *m* pegging awl
**estaquillar** *va* to peg, to fasten with pegs
**estar** §51 *v aux* (used with gerund to form the progressive form) to be, e.g., **le estoy escribiendo una carta** I am writing him a letter ‖ *vn* to be; to be in; to be ready; **¿a cuántos estamos?** what day of the month is it today?; **¿dónde estamos?** what have we come to?, can you imagine it?; **¡está bien!** all right!; **estamos a** today is (*a certain day of the month*); **estar a** to cost (*a certain amount*); **estar a dos velas** (coll.) to be hard up; **estar al caer** (coll.) to be about to happen; (coll.) to be about to strike (*the hour*); **estar a la que salta** (coll.) to be always ready to make the most of things; **estar a matar** (coll.) to be bitter enemies; **estar a obscuras** (coll.) to be in the dark (*ignorant*); **estar bien** to be well; **estar bien con** to be on good terms with; **estar con** to have an interview with; to agree with; to have (*a disease*); **estar con ánimo de** + *inf* to have a mind to, to have a notion to + *inf;* **estar de** to be (*for the time being*); **estar de caza** to be hunting, to be on a hunting trip; **estar de más** (coll.) to be de trop, to be in the way; (coll.) to be unnecessary; (coll.) to be idle; **estar de prisa** to be in a hurry; **estar de viaje** to be on a trip, to be traveling; **estar en** to understand, to be on to; to cost (*a certain amount*); **estar en ánimo de** + *inf* to have a mind to, to have a notion to + *inf;* **estar en grande** to have one's way in everything; to live in luxury; **estar en que** to be sure that; **estar en todo** to have a finger in everything; **estar mal** to be ill; **estar mal con** to be on bad terms with; **estar para** + *inf* to be about to + *inf;* **estar por** to be for, to be in favor of; **estar por** + *inf* to be in favor of + *ger;* to remain to be + *pp*, e.g., **la carta está por escribir** the letter remains to be written; to be about to (*e.g., happen*); to have a mind to, to have a notion to + *inf;* **estar que** + *ind* to be fairly + *ger*, e.g., **estaba que brincaba** he was fairly leaping (*e.g., with enthusiasm*); **estar sobre sí** to be wary, to be cautious; **¿está Vd.?** do you understand? ‖ *vr* to stay (*e.g., home*); to keep (*quiet*); **estarse de charla** to linger to chat; **estarse de más** (coll.) to be idle
**estarcido** *m* stencil (*letters and designs*)
**estarcir** §50 *va* to stencil
**estarna** *f* (orn.) gray partridge
**estatal** *adj* (pertaining to the) state
**estática** *m* (bot.) thrift, sea pink
**estático -ca** *adj* static; dumfounded, speechless; *f* (mech.) statics
**estatidad** *f* statehood
**estatificación** *f* nationalization (*of property*)
**estatificar** §86 *va* to nationalize (*property*)
**estatismo** *m* static state; statism
**estatista** *adj & mf* statist
**estatización** *f* (Am.) nationalization (*of property*)
**estatizar** §76 *va* (Am.) to nationalize (*property*)
**estatocisto** *m* (zool.) statocyst
**estatolito** *m* (zool.) statolith
**estator** *m* (mach. & elec.) stator
**estatorreactor** *m* (aer.) ram-jet engine
**estatoscopio** or **estatóscopo** *m* (phys.) statoscope
**estatua** *f* statue; **ahorcar en estatua** to hang in effigy; **quedarse hecho una estatua** (coll.) to stand aghast, to be struck with amazement; **estatua de la Libertad** Statue of Liberty; **estatua orante** (sculp.) orant statue; **estatua yacente** (sculp.) jacent statue
**estatuar** §33 *va* to statue, to make a statue of; to adorn with statues
**estatuario -ria** *adj* statuary; *m* statuary (*person*); *f* statuary (*art*)
**estatúder** *m* stadholder
**estatuderato** *m* stadholderate or stadholdership
**estatuilla** *f* statuette
**estatuir** §41 *va* to establish, arrange, prove
**estatuita** *f* statuette
**estatura** *f* stature
**estatutario -ria** *adj* statutory
**estatuto** *m* statute
**estaurolita** *f* (mineral.) staurolite
**estay** *m* (naut.) stay; **estay mayor** (naut.) mainstay
**este, esta** *adj dem* (*pl:* **estos, estas**) this; *m* east; east wind
**éste, ésta** *pron dem* (*pl:* **éstos, éstas**) this one; *f* this city (*where I am*)
**esté** *1st sg pres subj of* **estar**
**esteapsina** *f* (biochem.) steapsin
**estearato** *m* (chem.) stearate
**esteárico -ca** *adj* (chem.) stearic
**estearina** *f* (chem.) stearin
**estearopteno** *m* (chem.) stearoptene
**esteatita** *f* (mineral.) steatite
**esteatitoso -sa** *adj* (mineral.) steatitic
**esteatopigia** *f* (anthrop.) steatopygia
**esteba** *f* (naut.) steeve (*used for stowing bales of wool*); (bot.) meadow spear grass
**Esteban** *m* Stephen
**estebar** *va* to pack (*cloth*) in the dye kettle
**estefanita** *f* (mineral.) stephanite
**estegomía** *f* (ent.) stegomyia
**estegosauro** *m* (pal.) stegosaurus
**estela** *f* wake (*of a ship*); trail (*of a heavenly body, rocket, etc.*); (arch. & bot.) stele; (bot.) lady's-mantle
**estelar** *adj* stellar, sidereal; star
**estelario -ria** *adj* stellar; *f* (bot.) lady's-mantle
**estelífero -ra** *adj* (poet.) starry
**estelión** *m* (zool.) tarente; toadstone
**estelón** *m* toadstone
**estema** *m* (zool.) stemma (*simple eye of insect*)
**estemple** *m* (min.) stemple
**esténico -ca** *adj* (med.) sthenic
**estenocardia** *f* (path.) stenocardia
**estenografía** *f* stenography
**estenográfico -ca** *adj* stenographic
**estenógrafo -fa** *mf* stenographer
**estenosis** *f* (path.) stenosis, stricture
**estenotipia** *f* stenotypy; stenotype (*letter or group of letters*)
**estenotipiadora** *f* stenotype (*machine*)
**Estentor** *m* (myth.) Stentor
**estentóreo -a** *adj* stentorian
**estepa** *f* steppe, barren plain; (bot.) rockrose
**estepar** *m* field of rockroses
**estepilla** *f* (bot.) white-leaved rockrose
**estequiología** *f* stoichiology
**estequiometría** *f* stoichiometry
**éster** *m* or **ester** *m* (chem.) ester
**Ester** *f* Esther
**estera** *f* mat, matting; (mach.) apron; **esteras** *fpl* caterpillar tread; **cargado de esteras** (coll.) out of patience
**esterar** *va* to cover with a mat or mats; *vn* (coll.) to dress for winter ahead of time
**estercoladura** *f* or **estercolamiento** *m* dunging, manuring
**estercolar** *m* dunghill; §77 *va & vn* to dung, to manure
**estercolero** *m* dung collector; dunghill
**estercolizo -za** *adj* dungy, mucky
**estercóreo -a** *adj* stercoraceous
**estercuelo** *m* manuring, fertilizing
**esterculiáceo -a** *adj* (bot.) sterculiaceous
**estéreo** *m* stere
**estereóbato** *m* (arch.) stereobate

**estereocinema** *m* (mov.) three-D
**estereocromía** *f* stereochromy
**estereofonía** *f* stereophony
**estereofónico -ca** *adj* stereophonic
**estereofotografía** *f* stereophotography
**estereografía** *f* stereography
**estereográfico -ca** *adj* stereographic or stereographical
**estereograma** *m* stereogram
**estereoisomería** *f* (chem.) stereoisomerism
**estereometría** *f* stereometry
**estereopsis** *f* stereopsis
**estereóptico** *m* stereopticon
**estereoquímico -ca** *adj* stereochemical; *f* stereochemistry
**estereoscopia** *f* stereoscopy
**estereoscópico -ca** *adj* stereoscopic
**estereoscopio** *m* stereoscope
**estereotipar** *va* to stereotype; (fig.) to stereotype
**estereotipia** *f* stereotype; stereotypy
**estereotipo** *m* stereotype
**estereotomía** *f* stereotomy, stonecutting
**estereotropismo** *m* (biol.) stereotropism
**estereovisión** *f* stereovision
**esterería** *f* mat shop; mat business
**esterero -ra** *mf* mat maker or dealer; mat repairer, mat layer
**estéril** *adj* sterile; futile
**esterilidad** *f* sterility; futility
**esterilización** *f* sterilization
**esterilizador -dora** *mf* sterilizer; *m* sterilizer (*apparatus*)
**esterilizar** §76 *va* to sterilize; *vr* to become sterile
**esterilla** *f* small mat; straw mat; gold or silver plait; canvas; **esterilla de alambre** wire mesh
**esterlín** *m* bocasine, colored buckram
**esterlina** *adj fem* sterling (*pound*)
**esternal** *adj* (anat.) sternal
**esternón** *m* (anat.) sternum, breastbone
**estero** *m* matting; time for laying matting; estuary; tideland; (Am.) stream; (Am.) swamp
**esterquero** or **esterquilinio** *m* dunghill
**estertor** *m* stertor, râle, rhonchus; death rattle; **estertor agónico** death rattle
**estertoroso -sa** *adj* stertorous
**estesiómetro** *m* esthesiometer
**esteta** *mf* aesthete
**estético -ca** *adj* aesthetic, aesthetical; *mf* aesthetician; *f* aesthetics
**estetoscopia** *f* (med.) stethoscopy; stethoscopic findings
**estetoscópico -ca** *adj* stethoscopic
**estetoscopio** *m* (med.) stethoscope
**esteva** *f* plow handle, stilt
**estevado -da** *adj* bowlegged
**estevón** *m* var. of **esteva**
**estezado** *m* var. of **correal**
**estiaje** *m* low water
**estiba** *f* rammer; place for packing wool in bags; (naut.) stowage
**estibador** *m* (naut.) stevedore, longshoreman
**estibar** *va* to pack, to stuff; (naut.) to stow
**estibia** *f* var. of **espibia**
**estibina** *f* (chem.) stibine
**estibio** *m* (chem.) stibium
**estibonio** *m* (chem.) stibonium
**estiércol** *m* dung, manure
**estigio -gia** *adj* Stygian; (*cap.*) *f* (myth.) Styx
**estigioso -sa** *adj* Stygian, gloomy, mysterious
**estigma** *m* (bot., hist., path., zool. & fig.) stigma; **estigmas** *mpl* stigmata (*marks resembling the wounds on the body of Christ*)
**estigmatismo** *m* (opt. & path.) stigmatism
**estigmatización** *f* stigmatization
**estigmatizado** *m* (eccl.) stigmatic (*person bearing marks suggesting the wounds of Christ*)
**estigmatizador -dora** *adj* stigmatizing; *mf* stigmatizer
**estigmatizar** §76 *va* to stigmatize
**estilar** *va* to draw up (*a document*); to affect, to be given to; *vn & vr* to be in style; **estilarse** + *inf* to be the style to + *inf*
**estilete** *m* stiletto; stylet; style (*of a recording instrument*); (surg.) stylet
**estilicidio** *m* stillicide, dripping; (med.) stillicidium
**estilismo** *m* (lit.) excessive attention to style
**estilista** *mf* stylist; designer
**estilístico -ca** *adj* stylistic; *f* stylistics
**estilita** *adj* (eccl. hist.) stylitic; *m* (eccl. hist.) stylite
**estilización** *f* stylization; designing
**estilizar** §76 *va* to stylize; to design
**estilo** *m* style; stylus; gnomon; (bot. & print.) style; **al estilo de** in the style of; **de estilo** period (*chair, furniture, etc.*); **por el estilo** like that, of the kind; **por el estilo de** like; **estilo antiguo** (chron.) Old Style; **estilo culto** (lit.) euphuistic style; **estilo directo** (gram.) direct discourse; **estilo imperio** (f.a.) Empire; **estilo indirecto** (gram.) indirect discourse; **estilo llano** (lit.) simple style; **estilo nuevo** (chron.) New Style
**estilográfico -ca** *adj* stylographic; fountain-pen (*e.g., ink*); *f* fountain pen
**estilógrafo** *m* stylograph
**estiloides** *adj* (anat.) styloid
**estima** *f* esteem; (naut.) dead reckoning
**estimabilidad** *f* estimableness
**estimabilísimo -ma** *adj super* very or most estimable
**estimable** *adj* estimable, highly esteemed; appreciable
**estimación** *f* estimation, esteem; estimate
**estimador -dora** *adj* appreciative; estimating
**estimar** *va* to esteem; to estimate; to think, to believe; (coll.) to like, to be fond of; **estimar en poco** to hold in low esteem; *vr* to have great esteem for oneself; to esteem each other
**estimativo -va** *adj* respectful; *f* judgment; moral perception; instinct
**estimulación** *f* stimulation
**estimulante** *adj* stimulating, stimulant; *m* stimulant
**estimular** *va & vn* to stimulate; **estimular a** + *inf* to stimulate to + *inf*
**estímulo** *m* stimulus
**estinco** *m* var. of **escinco**
**estío** *m* summer
**estipe** *m* (bot. & zool.) stipe
**estipendiar** *va* to stipend, to give a stipend to
**estipendiario -ria** *adj & mf* stipendiary
**estipendio** *m* stipend; salary, wages
**estípite** *m* (arch.) pedestal in form of inverted truncated rectangular pyramid; (bot.) stipe
**estipticar** §86 *va* (med.) to constrict
**estipticidad** *f* stypticity, astringency
**estíptico -ca** *adj* styptic; constipated; mean, stingy; *m* styptic
**estípula** *f* (bot.) stipule
**estipulación** *f* stipulation
**estipulado -da** *adj* (bot.) stipulate
**estipular** *adj* (bot.) stipular; *va* to stipulate
**estipulilla** *f* (bot.) stipel
**estira** *f* currier's knife
**estirable** *adj* stretchy, stretchable
**estiracáceo -a** *adj* (bot.) styracaceous
**estiradamente** *adv* scarcely, hardly; violently; tensely
**estirado -da** *adj* stuck-up; soberly dressed; prim; (coll.) closefisted, pennypinching; **estirado en frío** (metal.) hard-drawn
**estirador** *m* stretcher
**estirajar** *va* (coll.) var. of **estirar**
**estirajón** *m* (coll.) var. of **estirón**
**estiramiento** *m* stretching; drawing (*of metals*)
**estirar** *va* to stretch; to draw (*metal or wire*); to iron lightly; (fig.) to stretch (*money*); (fig.) to stretch out (*a speech, job, appointment, etc.*); *vr* to stretch; to put on airs
**estirazar** §76 *va* (coll.) var. of **estirar**
**estireno** *m* (chem.) styrene
**Estiria** *f* Styria
**estirón** *m* jerk, tug; **dar un estirón** (coll.) to grow up quickly
**estirpe** *f* stock, race, family; pedigree; strain (*of a family*)
**estítico -ca** *adj* var. of **estíptico**
**estivación** *f* (bot. & zool.) aestivation
**estivada** *f* brushland turned up and burned in preparation for cultivation
**estival** *adj* aestival, summer
**estivo -va** *adj* (poet.) var. of **estival**

**esto** *pron dem neut* this; **en esto** at this point
**estocada** *f* thrust, stab, lunge; stab wound; deathblow; (fig.) blow (*something which causes suffering*); **estocada caída** (taur.) stab on the side
**estocafís** *m* unsplit smoked codfish
**Estocolmo** *f* Stockholm
**estofa** *f* quilted material; quality, class
**estofado -da** *adj* ornamented; *m* stew
**estofador -dora** *mf* quilter
**estofar** *va* to quilt; to size (*wood carvings*) for gilding; to distemper (*burnished gold*); to stew
**estoicismo** *m* stoicism; Stoicism
**estoico -ca** *adj* stoic, stoical; Stoic, Stoical; *mf* stoic; Stoic
**estola** *f* stole
**estolidez** *f* stupidity, imbecility
**estólido -da** *adj* stupid, imbecile
**estolón** *m* (eccl.) deacon's stole; (bot. & zool.) stolon
**estoma** *m* (anat., bot. & zool.) stoma
**estomacal** *adj* stomachic; (pertaining to the) stomach; *m* (med.) stomachic
**estomagar** §59 *va* to upset, give indigestion; to pall, to cloy; (coll.) to annoy, to vex
**estómago** *m* stomach; **revolver el estómago** to turn the stomach; **tener buen estómago** or **mucho estómago** (coll.) to be thick-skinned; (coll.) to have an easy conscience; **estómago de avestruz** (coll.) cast-iron stomach, iron digestion
**estomatical** *adj* stomachic
**estomático -ca** *adj* stomatic (*pertaining to the mouth*)
**estomaticón** *m* stomach plaster
**estomatitis** *f* (path.) stomatitis
**estomatología** *f* stomatology
**estomatoplastia** *f* (surg.) stomatoplasty
**estonio -nia** *adj & mf* Estonian; *m* Estonian (*language*); (*cap.*) *f* Estonia
**estopa** *f* tow; burlap; (mach.) packing; (naut.) oakum; **estopa de acero** steel wool; **estopa de algodón** cotton waste
**estopada** *f* tow for spinning
**estopear** *va* (naut.) to calk with oakum
**estopeño -ña** *adj* (pertaining to or made of) tow
**estoperol** *m* tow wick; (naut.) clout nail; (Am.) brass-headed tack
**estopilla** *f* fine part of flax or hemp; lawn, cambric; cheesecloth
**estopín** *m* blasting cap, exploder
**estopón** *m* coarse tow
**estopor** *m* (naut.) stopper
**estoposo -sa** *adj* (pertaining to) tow; towlike
**estoque** *m* rapier; tip of a sword; (bot.) sword lily, corn flag, gladiolus
**estoqueador** *m* swordsman; matador
**estoquear** *va* to stab with sword or rapier
**estoqueo** *m* thrusting, stabbing
**estor** *m* blind, shade, window shade
**estoraque** *m* (bot.) storax (*tree and balsam*)
**estorbador -dora** *adj* hindering, obstructing; annoying
**estorbar** *va* to hinder, to obstruct; to annoy, to inconvenience; **estorbarle a uno lo negro** (coll.) to dislike reading, to be illiterate; *vn* (coll.) to be in the way; **estorbar** + *inf* to prevent one from + *ger*
**estorbo** *m* hindrance, obstruction; annoyance
**estorboso -sa** *adj* hindering, obstructing; annoying
**estornija** *f* washer (*under linchpin*)
**estornino** *m* (orn.) starling; **estornino de los pastores** (orn.) grackle, myna
**estornudar** *vn* to sneeze
**estornudo** *m* sneeze, sneezing
**estornutativo -va** or **estornutatorio -ria** *adj* sternutative
**estotro -tra** *adj & pron dem* (archaic) this other
**estovar** *va* var. of **rehogar**
**estoy** *1st sg pres ind of* **estar**
**estrábico -ca** *adj* strabismal or strabismic
**estrabismo** *m* (path.) strabismus; **estrabismo convergente** (path.) cross-eye
**Estrabón** *m* Strabo
**estrabotomía** *f* (surg.) strabotomy
**estracilla** *f* rag; brown paper
**estrada** *f* road, highway; **batir la estrada** (mil.) to reconnoiter; **estrada encubierta** (fort.) covert way
**Estradivario** *m* Stradivarius; (*l.c.*) *m* Stradivarius (*violin*)
**estrado** *m* dais; stage, lecture platform; podium (*of orchestra conductor*); drawing room; drawing-room furniture; baker's table; **estrados** *mpl* court rooms; **citar para estrados** (law) to subpoena
**estrafalario -ria** *adj* (coll.) slovenly, sloppy; (coll.) wild, extravagant, outlandish; *mf* (coll.) screwball
**estragado -da** *adj* corrupt, depraved
**estragador -dora** *adj* corrupting, depraving
**estragamiento** *m* corruption, depravation
**estragar** §59 *va* to corrupt, to deprave, to vitiate, to spoil
**estrago** *m* damage, ruin, havoc; destruction, devastation; corruption; **estragos** *mpl* damage, ruin, havoc
**estragón** *m* (bot.) tarragon
**estrambote** *m* couplet, triplet, etc. (*at end of poem, especially a sonnet*)
**estrambótico -ca** adj (coll.) odd, queer, freakish
**estramonio** *m* (bot.) stramonium
**estrangol** *m* (vet.) strangullion
**estrangul** *m* (mus.) mouthpiece, reed
**estrangulación** *f* strangulation; (path. & surg.) strangulation; (mach.) choke, choking
**estrangulador** *m* throttle; (aut.) choke
**estrangular** *va* to strangle; (path. & surg.) to strangulate; (mach.) to choke; (mach.) to throttle; *vr* to strangle
**estranguria** *f* (path.) strangury
**estrapalucio** *m* (coll.) breakage, crash; (coll.) rumpus, fracas
**estraperlear** *vn* to deal in the black market, to be a black-market dealer
**estraperlismo** *m* black-market dealing; black marketeers
**estraperlista** *adj* black-market; *mf* black marketeer
**estraperlo** *m* black market
**estrapontín** *m* folding seat, flap seat (*in automobile, train, theater, etc.*); (aut.) jump seat
**Estrasburgo** *f* Strasbourg
**estratagema** *f* stratagem; craftiness
**estratega** *m* strategist
**estrategia** *f* strategy, strategics; **alta estrategia** (mil.) grand strategy
**estratégico -ca** *adj* strategic or strategical; *m* strategist, militarist
**estratego** *m* var. of **estratega**
**estratificación** *f* stratification
**estratificar** §86 *va & vr* to stratify
**estratigrafía** *f* stratigraphy
**estratigráfico -ca** *adj* stratigraphic
**estrato** *m* layer; (meteor.) stratus; (anat. & geol.) stratum
**estratocúmulo** *m* (meteor.) strato-cumulus
**estratosfera** *f* stratosphere
**estratosférico -ca** *adj* stratospheric
**estratovisión** *f* stratovision
**estrave** *m* (naut.) stem knee
**estraza** *f* rag
**estrechamiento** *m* narrowing; tightening; closer relations; rapprochement
**estrechar** *va* to narrow; to tighten; to hem in; to press, to pursue; to bring closer together; to force, to compel; to hug, to embrace; **estrechar la mano a** to grasp the hand of, to shake hands with; *vr* to contract; to squeeze; to come closer together; to hug, to embrace; to retrench; **estrecharse con** to persuade by friendly entreaty; **estrecharse en** to squeeze into; **estrecharse en los gastos** to cut down expenses; **estrecharse la mano** to shake hands
**estrechez** *f* narrowness; tightness; closeness, intimacy; strictness, austerity; want, poverty; urgency; trouble, jam; **hallarse en gran estrechez** to be in a jam, to be in dire straits; **estrechez de miras** (fig.) narrowness, narrow outlook
**estrecho -cha** *adj* narrow; tight; close, intimate; stingy; strict, rigid, austere; exact, punctual, conscientious; poor, indigent; mean-

spirited; **estrecho de conciencia** strict, austere, strait-laced; **estrecho de medios** in straitened circumstances; *m* fix, predicament; strait; channel; **poner en estrecho de** + *inf* to force to + *inf;* **estrecho de Gibraltar** Strait of Gibraltar; **estrecho de la Florida** Florida Strait; **estrecho de la Sonda** Sunda Strait; **estrecho de Magallanes** Strait of Magellan

**estrechón** *m* flapping (*of sails*); (coll.) handclasp, handshake

**estrechura** *f* narrowness, narrow passage; closeness, intimacy; strictness, austerity; trouble, jam

**estregadera** *f* scrubbing brush; scraper, foot scraper

**estregadero** *m* place on which animals rub themselves (*as deer rub their antlers*); place for washing and scrubbing clothes

**estregadura** *f* or **estregamiento** *m* rubbing, scrubbing, scouring

**estregar §29** *va* to rub hard, to scrub, to scour

**estregón** *m* hard rub, rough rub

**estrella** *f* star; (elec.) star; (mov.) star (*man or woman*); (print.) star, asterisk; (fig.) star (*person who stands out; destiny, fortune; white spot on forehead of horse*); **con estrellas** after sunset, before sunrise; **nacer con estrella** to be favored by fortune; **poner sobre las estrellas** to praise to the skies; **tener estrella** to be favored by fortune; **tener buena estrella** to be lucky; **tener mala estrella** to be unlucky; **ver las estrellas** (coll.) to see stars; **estrella de Belén** Star of Bethlehem; (bot.) Star-of-Bethlehem; **estrella de los Alpes** (bot.) edelweiss; **estrella de mar** (zool.) starfish; (bot.) aster, China aster; **estrella de rabo** comet; **estrella doble** (astr.) double star; **estrella enana** (astr.) dwarf star; **estrella fija** (astr.) fixed star; **estrella filante** or **fugaz** shooting star; **estrella polar** (astr.) polestar; **estrella poligonal** (geom.) star polygon; **estrellas y listas** Stars and Stripes; **estrella vespertina** evening star

**estrelladera** *f* (cook.) slice, turnover

**estrelladero** *m* egg pan (*of pastry cooks*)

**estrellado -da** *adj* starred, star-spangled; star-shaped; fried (*said of eggs*); star-faced (*said of horses*)

**estrellamar** *f* (zool.) starfish

**estrellar** *adj* star, starry; *va* to star, to spangle with stars; to fry (*eggs*); (coll.) to shatter, to dash to pieces; *vr* to be spangled with stars; to crash; (fig.) to crash

**estrellato** *m* (theat.) stardom

**estrellero -ra** *adj* holding its head high (*said of a horse*)

**estrellizar §76** *va* to beautify with stars

**estrellón** *m* large star; star (*kind of fireworks*); (coll.) stroke of luck; (Am.) collision, shock

**estremecer §34** *va* to shake; to rend (*the air*); (fig.) to shake, to perturb; *vr* to shake, to shiver, to shudder

**estremecimiento** *m* shaking, shiver, shivering, shuddering

**estrena** *f* gift of appreciation; (archaic) first use; (archaic) wedding, marriage

**estrenar** *va* to use or wear for the first time; to perform (*a play*) for the first time; to show (*a movie*) for the first time; to try out (*something new*); *vr* to make one's start, to appear for the first time; to make the day's first transaction; to open (*said of a play or movie*)

**entrenista** *mf* (theat.) first-nighter

**estreno** *m* beginning, debut; first performance, première; **estreno de una casa** housewarming

**estrenque** *m* heavy esparto rope

**estrenuidad** *f* strenuousness, activity; vigor, enterprise

**estrenuo -nua** *adj* strenuous, active, vigorous

**estreñido -da** *adj* constipated; stingy

**estreñimiento** *m* constipation

**estreñir §74** to bind, to constipate; **estreñir el bolsillo** (coll.) to be tight, to be stingy; *vr* to become constipated

**estrepada** *f* pull, pull in unison (*on a rope; on the oars*)

**estrépito** *m* noise, racket, uproar, crash; show, ostentation, fuss

**estrepitoso -sa** *adj* noisy, boisterous, deafening; notorious; shocking

**estreptococia** *f* (path.) streptococcic infection

**estreptocóccico -ca** *adj* streptococcic

**estreptococo** *m* (bact.) streptococcus

**estreptomicina** *f* (pharm.) streptomycin

**estreptotricina** *f* (pharm.) streptotrichin

**estría** *f* stria, flute, groove; (arch. & med.) stria

**estriación** *f* striation

**estriado -da** *adj* striated, grooved, fluted

**estriadura** *f* fluting, striation

**estriar §90** *va* to striate, to flute, to groove; *vr* to become fluted or grooved

**estribación** *f* (geog.) spur, counterfort

**estribadero** *m* prop, support

**estribar** *va* to rest on, to press down on; to fasten; *vn* to rest, to lean; to be based; **estribar en** + *inf* to be based on + *inf*

**estribera** *f* stirrup

**estribería** *f* stirrup factory or shop

**estriberón** *m* stepping stone; (mil.) temporary road

**estribillo** *m* burden, refrain, chorus; initial theme (*of a poem*); pet word or phrase

**estribo** *m* stirrup; (arch.) abutment, buttress; footboard; (aut.) running board; (mach.) brace, stay, stirrup; (carp.) joist hanger, cross prop; (geog.) spur, counterfort; (anat.) stapes; (taur.) white stirrup board at base of fence (*used to help a man escape over the fence*); (fig.) support, foundation; **perder los estribos** to talk nonsense; to lose one's head, fly off the handle; **tenerse en los estribos** to keep a steady head

**estribor** *m* (naut.) starboard

**estricnina** *f* (chem.) strychnine

**estricote; al estricote** hither and thither, from pillar to post

**estricto -ta** *adj* strict, severe; narrow (*meaning of a word*)

**estrictura** *f* (path.) stricture

**estridencia** *f* stridence

**estridente** *adj* strident

**estridor** *m* stridence; (path.) stridor

**estridulación** *f* stridulation; (zool.) stridulation

**estridular** *vn* to stridulate

**estriduloso -sa** *adj* stridulant, stridulous; (path.) stridulous

**estrige** *f* (orn.) barn owl; (orn.) little owl

**estrinque** *m* var. of **estrenque**

**estro** *m* inspiration (*of poet or artist*); rut, heat; orgasm; (ent.) botfly

**estróbilo** *m* (bot.) strobile; (zool.) strobile, strobila

**estrobo** *m* (naut.) grommet, becket

**estroboscopio** *m* stroboscope

**estrobotrón** *m* (electron.) strobotron

**estrofa** *f* strophe

**estrófico -ca** *adj* strophic

**estrógeno** *m* (biochem.) estrogen

**estroma** *m* (anat., biol. & bot.) stroma

**Estrómboli** *m* Stromboli

**estrona** *f* (biochem.) estrone

**estronciana** *f* (chem.) strontia

**estroncianita** *f* (mineral.) strontianite

**estroncio** *m* (chem.) strontium

**estropada** *f* var. of **estrepada**

**estropajear** *va* (mas.) to rub down or to scour (*a plastered wall*) in order to remove loose particles or dust

**estropajeo** *m* (mas.) rubbing or scrubbing a plastered wall

**estropajo** *m* esparto scrubbing brush; rag for scrubbing, mop, dishcloth; (bot.) luffa, dishcloth gourd; **servir de estropajo** (coll.) to do the dirty work, to be treated with indifference

**estropajoso -sa** *adj* (coll.) ragged, slovenly; (coll.) tough, leathery (*said, e.g., of meat*); (coll.) stammering

**estropear** *va* to abuse, to mistreat; to spoil, to ruin; to cripple, to maim; (mas.) to stir (*mortar*) a second time; *vr* to spoil, go to ruin; to fail

**estropeo** *m* abuse, mistreatment; damage; crippling

**estropicio** *m* (coll.) breakage, crash; (coll.) havoc, ruin; (coll.) rumpus, fracas
**estructura** *f* structure
**estructuración** *f* construction, organization
**estructural** *adj* structural
**estructurar** *va* to construct, to organize
**estruendo** *m* crash; confusion, uproar; (coll.) pomp; (Am.) detonating rocket
**estrujador -dora** *adj* squeezing; *f* squeezer; wine press
**estrujadura** *f* or **estrujamiento** *m* squeezing, pressing, crushing; mashing, bruising; (metal.) extrusion
**estrujar** *va* to squeeze, to press, to crush; to mash, to rumple, to bruise; (coll.) to drain, to exhaust; (metal.) to extrude
**estrujón** *m* squeezing, pressing, crushing; last pressing of grapes; (coll.) crush, jam
**estruma** *f* (path.) struma (*scrofula; goiter*)
**estrumoso -sa** *adj* strumous
**estuación** *f* flow of tide, flood tide
**estuante** *adj* hot, burning
**Estuardo, María** Mary Stuart
**estuario** *m* estuary; tideland
**estucador** *m* stucco plasterer
**estucar** §86 *va* to stucco
**estuco** *m* stucco
**estuche** *m* box, case; casket, jewel case; slipcase; sheath (*for scissors*); (coll.) handy fellow; **estuche de afeites** vanity case, compact
**estudiado -da** *adj* affected, mannered, studied
**estudiador -dora** *adj* (coll.) very studious
**estudiantado** *m* student body
**estudiante** *mf* student
**estudiantil** *adj* (coll.) (pertaining to a) student, college
**estudiantino -na** *adj* (coll.) student; **a la estudiantina** (coll.) like a student, like students; *f* group of students; student serenade; carnival masquerade in student disguise
**estudiantón** *m* (scornful) dull grind
**estudiar** *va* to study; to hear (*someone's lesson; an actor recite his lines*); to design; (f.a.) to copy (*nature or a model*); *vn* to study; **estudiar para médico** to study to become a doctor
**estudio** *m* study; studio; (mov. & rad.) studio; designing, planning; survey; (mus.) étude; **altos estudios** advanced studies
**estudiosidad** *f* studiousness
**estudioso -sa** *adj* studious; *m* student, scholar
**estufa** *f* stove; heater; foot stove; steam cabinet, steam room; hothouse; dryer; **estufa de desinfección** sterilizer
**estufador** *m* stewing pan
**estufero** *m* var. of **estufista**
**estufilla** *f* hand muff; foot stove; chafing dish
**estufista** *m* stovemaker; stove or heater repairman or dealer
**estulticia** *f* silliness, foolishness
**estulto -ta** *adj* silly, foolish
**estuoso -sa** *adj* hot, burning
**estupefacción** *f* stupefaction (*daze*); (coll.) stupefaction (*great amazement*)
**estupefaciente** *adj* & *m* (med.) narcotic, stupefacient
**estupefactivo -va** *adj* stupefying
**estupefacto -ta** *adj* stupefied, dumfounded
**estupendo -da** *adj* stupendous, wonderful; (coll.) famous, distinguished
**estupidez** *f* (*pl:* **-deces**) stupidity
**estúpido -da** *adj* & *mf* stupid
**estupor** *m* stupor; amazement, surprise
**estuprador** *m* rapist, violator
**estuprar** *va* to rape, to violate
**estupro** *m* rape, violation
**estuque** *m* var. of **estuco**
**estuquería** *f* stuccoing; stucco work
**estuquista** *m* stucco plasterer, stuccoist
**esturar** *va* & *vr* to burn, to parch, to scorch
**esturgar** §59 *va* to smooth off and finish (*pottery*)
**esturión** *m* (ichth.) sturgeon; **esturión blanco** (ichth.) white sturgeon, beluga
**estuve** *1st sg pret ind of* **estar**
**ésula** *f* (bot.) spurge
**esvarar** *vn* & *vr* to slide, to slip
**esvarón** *m* slide, slip
**esvástica** *f* var. of **svástica**
**esviaje** *m* skew
**-eta** *suffix dim* e.g., **aleta** fin; **historieta** anecdote; **placeta** small public square
**etalaje** *m* bosh (*of blast furnace*)
**etamín** *m* or **etamine** *m* etamine (*fabric*)
**etano** *m* (chem.) ethane
**etapa** *f* stage; (mil.) campaign or marching ration; (mil.) stage (*of journey*); (rad.) stage; **a pequeñas etapas** by easy stages; **de etapa única** single-stage
**etcétera** *f* the character &, which means **y lo demás; hacer por etcéteras** (coll.) to dash off
**-ete** *suffix dim & pej* e.g., **caballerete** dude; **lugarete** hamlet; **vejete** little old fellow
**Etelredo** *m* Ethelred
**éter** *m* aether or ether (*heavens; upper regions*); (phys.) aether or ether (*hypothetical medium*); (chem.) ether ($R_2O$)
**etéreo -a** *adj* aethereal or ethereal; (phys.) aethereal or ethereal; (chem.) ethereal
**eterificación** *f* (chem.) etherification
**eterificar** §86 *va* (chem.) etherify
**eterización** *f* (med.) etherization
**eterizar** §76 *va* to etherize
**eternal** *adj* eternal
**eternidad** *f* eternity
**eternizable** *adj* worthy of being immortalized
**eternizar** §76 *va* to eternize; to make endless, to prolong endlessly; *vr* to be endless or interminable; to never finish
**eterno -na** *adj* eternal
**etesio -sia** *adj* & *m* etesian
**ético -ca** *adj* ethic or ethical; (path.) consumptive; *mf* (path.) consumptive; *m* ethicist, moralist; *f* ethics
**etileno** *m* (chem.) ethylene
**etílico -ca** *adj* ethylic
**etilo** *m* (chem.) ethyl
**étimo** *m* var. of **étimon**
**etimología** *f* etymology, **etimología popular** folk etymology, popular etymology
**etimológico -ca** *adj* etymological
**etimologista** *mf* etymologist
**etimologizar** §76 *va* to etymologize (*a word*); *vn* to etymologize; (coll.) to pose as an etymologist
**etimólogo -ga** *mf* etymologist
**étimon** *m* (philol.) etymon
**etiología** *f* aetiology
**etíope** *adj* & *mf* Ethiopian; *m* (old chem.) ethiops
**Etiopía** *f* Ethiopia
**etiópico -ca** *adj* Ethiopic, Ethiopian; *m* Ethiopic (*language*)
**etiopio -pia** *adj* & *mf* Ethiopian
**etiqueta** *f* etiquette; formality; tag, label; formal dress, formal clothes; **de etiqueta** full-dress, formal; **estar de etiqueta** to have become cool toward each other; **etiqueta menor** semiformal dress
**etiquetar** *va* to tag, to label
**etiquetero -ra** *adj* ceremonious, formal; full of compliments
**etiquez** *f* (path.) consumption
**etites** *f* (mineral.) eaglestone
**etmoides** *adj* & *m* (anat.) ethmoid
**Etna, el** Mount Etna
**étneo -nea** *adj* Etnean
**étnico -ca** *adj* ethnic or ethnical; (gram.) gentilic
**etnografía** *f* ethnography
**etnográfico -ca** *adj* ethnographic or ethnographical
**etnógrafo -fa** *mf* ethnographer
**etnología** *f* ethnology
**etnológico -ca** *adj* ethnologic or ethnological
**etnólogo -ga** *mf* ethnologist
**Etolia, la** Aetolia
**etopea** or **etopeya** *f* (rhet.) ethopoeia
**etrurio -ria** *adj* & *mf* Etrurian
**etrusco -ca** *adj* & *mf* Etruscan; *m* Etruscan (*language*)
**etusa** *f* (bot.) fool's-parsley
**E.U.** abr. of **Estados Unidos**
**E.U.A.** abr. of **Estados Unidos de América**
**Eubea** *f* Euboea
**eucaína** *f* (pharm.) eucaine
**eucalipto** *m* (bot.) eucalyptus

**eucaliptol** *m* eucalyptol
**Eucaristía** *f* (eccl.) Eucharist
**eucarístico -ca** *adj* Eucharistic
**Euclides** *m* Euclid
**euclidiano -na** *adj* Euclidean; **no euclidiano** non-Euclidean
**eucologio** *m* (eccl.) euchology
**eucrasia** *f* (med.) eucrasia
**eudemonismo** *m* eudaemonism
**eudiómetro** *m* eudiometer
**eufémico -ca** *adj* euphemistic
**eufemismo** *m* euphemism
**eufemístico -ca** *adj* euphemistic
**eufonía** *f* euphony
**eufónico -ca** *adj* euphonic
**eufono -na** *adj* euphonious
**euforbiáceo -a** *adj* (bot.) euphorbiaceous
**euforbio** *m* (bot.) euphorbia, spurge; (pharm.) euphorbia (*dried herb*); (pharm.) euphorbium (*gum resin*)
**euforia** *f* (psychol.) euphoria; moment of glory; endurance, fortitude
**eufórico -ca** *adj* euphoric
**eufrasia** *f* (bot.) eyebright, euphrasy
**Éufrates** *m* Euphrates
**Eufrosina** *f* (myth.) Euphrosyne
**eufuísmo** *m* euphuism
**eufuísta** *adj* euphuistic; *mf* euphuist
**eufuístico -ca** *adj* euphuistic
**eugenesia** *f* eugenics
**eugenésico -ca** *adj* eugenic
**Eugenia** *f* Eugenia
**Eugenio** *m* Eugene
**Euménides** *fpl* (myth.) Eumenides
**eunuco** *m* eunuch
**eupatorio** *m* (bot.) eupatorium, boneset
**eupepsia** *f* (med.) eupepsia
**eupéptico -ca** *adj* eupeptic
**Eurasia** *f* Eurasia
**eurasiano -na** *adj & mf* Eurasian
**eureka** *interj* eureka!
**Eurídice** *f* (myth.) Eurydice
**Eurípides** *m* Euripides
**euritmia** *f* (f.a.) eurhythmy; (med.) normal rhythm of pulse
**eurítmico -ca** *adj* (f.a.) eurhythmic; (med.) normal, regular
**euro** *m* east wind
**Europa** *f* Europe; (myth.) Europa
**europeidad** *f* or **europeísmo** *m* Europeanism
**europeizante** *adj* Europeanizing; *mf* (Am.) advocate of European manners and customs
**europeizar** §76 *va* to Europeanize; *vr* to become Europeanized
**europeo -a** *adj & mf* European
**europio** *m* (chem.) europium
**éuscaro -ra** or **eusquero -ra** *adj & m* Basque (*language*)
**Eustaquio** *m* Eustace
**éustilo** *m* (arch.) eustyle
**eutanasia** *f* euthanasia; (med.) euthanasia, mercy killing
**euténica** *f* euthenics
**Euterpe** *f* (myth.) Euterpe
**eutiquiano -na** *adj & mf* Eutychian
**eutrapelia** *f* moderation (*in one's diversions*); simple pastime; lightheartedness
**eutrapélico -ca** *adj* moderate, simple; lighthearted
**eutropelia** *f* var. of **eutrapelia**
**Eva** *f* Eve
**evacuación** *f* evacuation; **evacuación de basuras** garbage disposal
**evacuado -da** *mf* evacuee
**evacuante** *adj & m* (med.) evacuant
**evacuar** *va* to evacuate; (mil.) to evacuate; to transact (*a deal*), to do (*an errand*); to drain (*a sore or humor*); to make (*a visit*); to carry out, to execute; **evacuar el vientre** to have a movement of the bowels; *vn* (mil.) to evacuate; to have a movement of the bowels
**evacuativo -va** *adj & m* (med.) evacuant
**evacuatorio -ria** *adj* evacuant; *m* public urinal
**evadido -da** *adj* escaped; *mf* escapee
**evadir** *va* to avoid; to evade; *vr* to evade; to flee, to escape
**evagación** *f* distraction; digression
**evaluación** *f* evaluation
**evaluador -dora** *adj* evaluating
**evaluar** §33 *va* to evaluate
**evanescente** *adj* evanescent; (bot.) evanescent
**evangélico -ca** *adj* evangelic or evangelical
**Evangelio** *m* gospel; Gospel, Evangel; (*l.c.*) *m* (coll.) gospel, gospel truth; **evangelios** *mpl* Gospel booklet with relics, worn around the neck of children; **decir** or **hablar el evangelio** to speak the gospel truth
**evangelismo** *m* evangelism
**evangelista** *m* gospeler, singer of the Gospel; (Am.) penman, scrivener, public writer; (*cap.*) *m* Evangelist
**evangelistero** *m* singer of Gospel in High Masses
**evangelización** *f* evangelization
**evangelizador -dora** *adj* evangelizing; *mf* evangelizer, evangelist
**evangelizar** §76 *va & vn* to evangelize
**Evang.º** abr. of **Evangelio**
**Evang.ta** abr. of **Evangelista**
**evaporable** *adj* evaporable
**evaporación** *f* evaporation
**evaporado -da** *adj* scatterbrained
**evaporador -dora** *adj* evaporating; *m* evaporator (*apparatus*)
**evaporar** *va* to evaporate; *vr* to evaporate (*change into vapor; vanish, disappear*)
**evaporizar** §76 *va, vn & vr* to vaporize
**evasión** *f* escape; evasion
**evasivo -va** *adj* evasive; *f* evasion
**evección** *f* (astr.) evection
**evento** *m* chance event, happening; **a todo evento** for any eventuality
**eventual** *adj* eventual, contingent
**eventualidad** *f* eventuality, contingency
**eversión** *f* destruction, ruin, desolation; (med.) eversion
**evicción** *f* (law) eviction, dispossession in virtue of an antecedent right
**evidencia** *f* evidence; obviousness; **en evidencia** in evidence; (coll.) in the open
**evidenciar** *va* to evidence, to make evident
**evidente** *adj* evident
**evisceración** *f* (surg.) evisceration
**evitable** *adj* avoidable, preventable
**evitación** *f* avoidance
**evitar** *va* to avoid, to shun; to keep off (*e.g., dust*); to prevent; **evitar** + *inf* to avoid + *ger*
**eviterno -na** *adj* unending, imperishable
**evo** *m* (poet.) age, aeon; (theol.) eternity
**evocación** *f* evocation
**evocador -dora** *adj* evoking; evocative
**evocar** §86 *va* to evoke
**evolución** *f* evolution; (biol., philos., mil. & nav.) evolution; change (*in attitude, plans, conduct, etc.*)
**evolucionar** *vn* to evolve; (mil. & nav.) to perform evolutions or maneuvers; to change (*in attitude, plans, conduct, etc.*)
**evolucionismo** *m* (biol.) evolution, evolutionism
**evolucionista** *adj* evolutionist, evolutionistic, evolutionary; *mf* evolutionist
**evolutivo -va** *adj* evolutionary
**evónimo** *m* (bot.) spindle tree, wahoo
**ex** *adj* ex- (*former*), e.g., **ex ministro** ex-minister; **su ex mujer** his ex-wife
**ex abrupto** (Lat.) abruptly, brashly; *m* abruptness, brash remark
**exacción** *f* exaction, requirement, demand; levy
**exacerbación** *f* exacerbation
**exacerbar** *va* to exacerbate; *vr* to become exacerbated
**exactitud** *f* exactness; punctuality
**exacto -ta** *adj* exact; punctual, faithful; complete
**exactor** *m* taxgatherer
**exageración** *f* exaggeration
**exagerado -da** *adj* exaggerated; exaggerating
**exagerador -dora** *adj* exaggerating; *mf* exaggerator
**exagerar** *va* to exaggerate
**exaltación** *f* exaltation
**exaltado -da** *adj* exalted; hot-headed, extreme
**exaltar** *va* to exalt; *vr* to become excited or wrought-up
**examen** *m* examination; **sufrir un examen** to take an examination
**examinador -dora** *mf* examiner

**examinando -da** *mf* examinee
**examinar** *va* to examine; to inspect; *vr* to take an examination; **examinarse de** to take an examination in; **examinarse de ingreso** to take entrance examinations
**exangüe** *adj* bloodless, anemic; exhausted, worn-out; dead
**exanimación** *f* exanimation
**exánime** *adj* exanimate, lifeless, in a faint
**exantema** *m* (path.) exanthema
**exantemático -ca** *adj* exanthematic
**exasperación** *f* exasperation
**exasperar** *va* to exasperate
**Exc.**ª abr. of **Excelencia**
**excandecencia** *f* anger, exasperation
**excandecer** §34 *va* to enrage, to incense; *vr* to become enraged
**excarcelación** *f* release from custody
**excarcelar** *va* to release (*a prisoner*)
**excava** *f* (agr.) removal of soil around a plant
**excavación** *f* excavation
**excavador -dora** *adj* excavating; *mf* excavator (*person*); *m* (dent. & surg.) excavator; *f* excavator, power shovel
**excavar** *va* to excavate; (agr.) to remove soil from around (*a plant*)
**excave** *m* digging, excavation
**excedencia** *f* excess; leave; leave pay
**excedente** *adj* excessive; excess, in excess; on leave; *m* excess, surplus; government employee on leave; **excedentes** *mpl* surplus property
**exceder** *va & vn* to exceed, to excel; **exceder de** to exceed; *vr* to exceed; to go too far, to go to extremes; **excederse a sí mismo** (coll.) to outdo oneself
**excelencia** *f* excellence or excellency; **por excelencia** par excellence; (*cap.*) *f* Excellency (*title*)
**excelente** *adj* excellent
**excelsitud** *f* loftiness, sublimity
**excelso -sa** *adj* lofty, elevated, sublime; **el Excelso** the Most High
**excéntrica** *f* see **excéntrico**
**excentricidad** *f* eccentricity; (coll.) eccentricity (*oddity, peculiarity*)
**excéntrico -ca** *adj* eccentric; erratic; (coll.) eccentric (*odd, peculiar*); *mf* (coll.) eccentric; *f* (mach.) eccentric
**excepción** *f* exception; **a excepción de** with the exception of
**excepcional** *adj* exceptional
**excepcionar** *va* (law) to protest against, to deny the validity of
**excepto** *prep* except
**exceptuar** §33 *va* to except; to exempt
**excerpta** or **excerta** *f* excerpt
**excesivo -va** *adj* excessive
**exceso** *m* excess; (fig.) excess (*abuse; eating or drinking too much*); **en** or **por exceso** to excess (*too much*); **exceso de equipaje** excess baggage; **exceso de peso** excess weight; **exceso de velocidad** speeding
**excipiente** *m* (pharm.) excipient
**excisión** *f* (surg.) excision
**excitabilidad** *f* excitability
**excitable** *adj* excitable
**excitación** *f* excitation, excitement; (phys. & physiol.) excitation
**excitador -dora** *adj* exciting; *m* (elec.) exciter (*for producing jump sparks*)
**excitante** *adj* exciting; stimulating; *m* (physiol.) excitant; (med.) stimulant
**excitar** *va* to excite; (elec. & physiol.) to excite; *vr* to become excited
**excitativo -va** *adj* excitative
**excitatriz** *f* (*pl:* **-trices**) (elec.) exciter (*for producing a magnetic field*)
**exclamación** *f* exclamation
**exclamar** *va & vn* to exclaim
**exclamativo -va** or **exclamatorio -ria** *adj* exclamatory
**exclaustración** *f* secularization
**exclaustrado -da** *mf* secularized ecclesiastic
**exclaustrar** *va* to secularize (*a monk*)
**excluir** §41 *va* to exclude
**exclusión** *f* exclusion; **con exclusión de** to the exclusion of
**exclusiva** *f* see **exclusivo**
**exclusive** *adv* exclusively
**exclusividad** *f* exclusive feature; exclusiveness; **con exclusividad** exclusively
**exclusivismo** *m* exclusivism
**exclusivista** *adj* exclusive, clannish; *mf* exclusivist
**exclusivo -va** *adj* exclusive; *f* turndown, rejection; sole right, special privilege; exclusive news release
**Exc.**ᵐᵒ abr. of **Excelentísimo**
**excogitar** *va* to excogitate, to think out
**ex combatiente** *m* ex-serviceman, veteran
**excomulgado -da** *adj* excommunicated; (coll.) pert, saucy; *mf* excommunicant, excommunicated person
**excomulgador** *m* excommunicator
**excomulgar** §59 *va* to excommunicate; to anathematize; (coll.) to proscribe, to ostracize; (coll.) to flay, to treat harshly
**excomunión** *f* excommunication
**excoriación** *f* excoriation, skinning
**excoriar** *va* to excoriate, to skin; *vr* to be excoriated; to skin oneself (*e.g., on the arm*)
**excrecencia** *f* excrescence
**excrecente** *adj* excrescent
**excreción** *f* (physiol.) excretion; evacuation
**excremental** *adj* excremental
**excrementar** *vn* to have an evacuation
**excrementicio -cia** *adj* excremental; (physiol.) waste (*matter*)
**excremento** *m* excrement
**excrescencia** *f* var. of **excrecencia**
**excreta** *f* (physiol.) excreta
**excretar** *va* (physiol.) to excrete; *vn* to eject the excrements
**excretorio -ria** *adj* (physiol.) excretory; *m* toilet
**exculpación** *f* exculpation, exoneration
**exculpar** *va* to exculpate, to exonerate
**excursión** *f* incursion; excursion
**excursionismo** *m* excursioning; touring
**excursionista** *adj* (pertaining to an) excursion; *mf* excursionist
**excusa** *f* excuse; basket with lid; **buscar excusa** to look for an excuse; **excusa es decir** it is unnecessary to say
**excusabaraja** *f* basket with lid
**excusable** *adj* excusable; avoidable
**excusadamente** *adv* unnecessarily
**excusado -da** *adj* exempt; unnecessary; reserved, set apart; *m* water closet, toilet
**excusador -dora** *adj* excusing; *m* substitute, vicar
**excusalí** *m* (*pl:* **-líes**) little apron
**excusapecados** *mf* (*pl:* **-dos**) indulgent person
**excusar** *va* to excuse; to avoid, to shun, to prevent; to exempt; to make unnecessary, to replace; **excusarle a uno de algo** to excuse someone for something; **excusar** + *inf* to not have to + *inf; vr* to excuse oneself; to apologize; **excusarse de** + *inf* to decline to + *inf*
**excusión** *f* (civil law) discussion
**execrable** *adj* execrable
**execración** *f* anathematization; execration
**execrador -dora** *adj* execrating; *mf* execrator
**execrando -da** *adj* execrable
**execrar** *va* to anathematize; to execrate
**execratorio -ria** *adj* execratory
**exedra** *f* (arch.) exedra
**exégesis** *f* (*pl:* **-sis**) exegesis
**exegético -ca** *adj* exegetic or exegetical
**exención** *f* exemption
**exencionar** *va* to exempt
**exentamente** *adv* freely; frankly, simply
**exentar** *va* to exempt
**exento -ta** *adj* exempt; clear, open, unobstructed; free, disengaged; deprived
**exequátur** *m* (*pl:* **-tur**) exequatur
**exequias** *fpl* obsequies, exequies
**exequible** *adj* attainable, feasible
**exergo** *m* exergue
**éxeunt** (Lat.) exeunt (*they go out*)
**exfoliación** *f* exfoliation
**exfoliador -dora** *adj* tear-off
**exfoliar** *va & vr* to exfoliate
**exhalación** *f* exhalation; shooting star; flash of lightning; fume, vapor
**exhalar** *va* to exhale, to emit (*gases, odors*); to breathe forth (*sighs, complaints*); **exhalar el**

**último suspiro** to breathe one's last; *vr* to exhale; to breathe hard (*from overexertion*); to hurry; to have a craving
**exhaustivo -va** *adj* exhaustive
**exhaustizar** **§76** *vr* to become exhausted
**exhausto -ta** *adj* exhausted; (coll.) wasted away
**exheredación** *f* disinheritance
**exheredar** *va* to disinherit
**exhibición** *f* exhibition; exhibit
**exhibicionismo** *m* (psychol.) exhibitionism
**exhibicionista** *mf* exhibitionist
**exhibir** *va* to exhibit; (law) to exhibit (*a document*); *vr* (coll.) to show oneself, to like to be seen
**exhilarante** *adj* exhilarating; laughing (*gas*)
**exhortación** *f* exhortation
**exhortador -dora** *adj* exhorting; *mf* exhorter
**exhortar** *va* to exhort; **exhortar a** + *inf* to exhort to + *inf*
**exhortativo -va** *adj* exhortative
**exhortatorio -ria** *adj* exhortatory
**exhorto** *m* (law) letters rogatory
**exhumación** *f* exhumation
**exhumador -dora** *mf* exhumer
**exhumar** *va* to exhume
**exigencia** *f* exigency, requirement, demand
**exigente** *adj* exacting, exigent, demanding
**exigible** or **exigidero -ra** *adj* exigible, requirable; payable on demand
**exigir** **§42** *va* to exact, to require, to demand, to call for; **exigir** + *inf* to require (*something*) to be + *pp*
**exigüidad** *f* exiguity, exiguousness; meagreness, smallness, scantiness
**exiguo -gua** *adj* exiguous; meagre, small, scanty
**exilado -da** *adj* & *mf* exile
**exilar** *va* to exile
**exilio** *m* exile
**eximente** *adj* (law) exempting
**eximio -mia** *adj* select, choice, superior, distinguished
**eximir** *va* to exempt; **eximir de** + *inf* to exempt from + *ger*
**exina** *f* (bot.) extine (*of pollen*)
**exinanición** *f* inanition, exinanition
**exinánido -da** *adj* exhausted, debilitated
**existencia** *f* existence; **existencias** *fpl* (com.) stock; **en existencia** (com.) in stock
**existencial** *adj* existentialist
**existencialismo** *m* (philos.) existentialism
**existencialista** *adj* & *mf* existentialist
**existente** *adj* existing, existent, extant
**existimación** *f* judgment, opinion
**existimar** *va* to judge, to deem, to esteem
**existimativo -va** *adj* putative
**existir** *vn* to exist
**existista** *adj* (Am.) me-too; *mf* (Am.) me-tooer
**éxit** (Lat.) exit (*he or she goes out*)
**éxito** *m* outcome, result; success; hit (*successful stroke, performance, etc.*); **éxito de librería** best seller (*book*); **éxito de taquilla** box-office hit, good box office; **éxito de venta** best seller; **éxito rotundo** smash hit
**exitoso -sa** *adj* (Am.) successful
**ex libris** *m* (*pl:* **-bris**) ex libris, bookplate
**exobiología** *f* exobiology
**éxodo** *m* exodus; (*cap.*) *m* (Bib.) Exodus
**exodoncia** or **exodontología** *f* exodontia
**exoftalmía** *f* (path.) exophthalmos or exophthalmia
**exoftálmico -ca** *adj* exophthalmic
**exoftalmos** *m* var. of **exoftalmía**
**exogamia** *f* exogamy; (biol.) exogamy
**exógeno -na** *adj* exogenous
**exoneración** *f* exoneration; discharge, dismissal; defecation
**exonerar** *va* to exonerate (*to relieve of an obligation*); to discharge; *vn* to defecate
**exónfalo** *m* (path.) exomphalos
**exorable** *adj* exorable
**exorar** *va* to beg, to entreat
**exorbitancia** *f* exorbitance or exorbitancy
**exorbitante** *adj* exorbitant
**exorcismo** *m* exorcism
**exorcista** *mf* exorcist; *m* exorcist (*priest*)
**exorcistado** *m* (eccl.) third minor order
**exorcizar** **§76** *va* to exorcise
**exordio** *m* exordium
**exornación** *f* adornment, embellishment
**exornar** *va* to adorn, to embellish
**exorno** *m* adornment, embellishment
**exosfera** *f* exosphere
**exósmosis** *f* (physical chem. & physiol.) exosmosis
**exospora** *f* (bot.) exospore
**exosqueleto** *m* (zool.) exoskeleton
**exostoma** *m* (bot.) exostome
**exostósico -ca** *adj* exostotic
**exostosis** *f* (*pl:* **-sis**) (bot. & path.) exostosis
**exoteca** *f* (zool.) exotheca
**exotecio** *m* (bot.) exothecium
**exotérico -ca** *adj* exoteric
**exotérmico -ca** *adj* (chem.) exothermic
**exoticidad** *f* exoticity
**exótico -ca** *adj* exotic; striking, stunning
**exotiquez** *f* exoticalness, exoticism
**exotismo** *m* exoticism
**exotospora** *f* (biol.) exotospore
**exotoxina** *f* (biochem.) exotoxin
**exotropía** *f* (path.) exotropia
**expandir** *va* & *vr* to spread, extend, expand
**expansibilidad** *f* expansibility
**expansible** *adj* expansible
**expansión** *f* expansion; expansiveness; relief, recreation, rest
**expansionar** *va* to expand (*e.g., production*); *vr* to expand; to open one's heart; to enjoy oneself, to relax, to take it easy
**expansionismo** *m* expansionism
**expansionista** *adj* & *mf* expansionist
**expansivo -va** *adj* expansive; (fig.) expansive
**expatriación** *f* expatriation
**expatriado -da** *adj* expatriate; *mf* expatriate, displaced person
**expatriar** **§90** & **regular** *va* to expatriate; *vr* to expatriate, to leave one's country
**expectación** *f* expectancy; (med.) expectation; **expectación de vida** life expectancy
**expectante** *adj* expectant
**expectativa** *f* expectation, expectancy; **estar en la expectativa de** to be expecting, to be on the lookout for; **expectativa de vida** expectation of life
**expectoración** *f* expectoration
**expectorante** *adj* & *m* expectorant
**expectorar** *va* & *vn* to expectorate
**expedición** *f* expedition; shipment; issuance; (fig.) expedition
**expedicionario -ria** *adj* expeditionary; *mf* expeditionist, member of an expedition
**expedidor -dora** *mf* sender, shipper; *m* dispenser (*device*)
**expediente** *m* expedient; expedition; (law) action, proceedings; dossier; record; reason, motive; supply, provision; **formar** or **instruir expediente a** to impeach (*a public official*); **expediente académico** (educ.) record
**expedienteo** *m* red tape; (law) execution (*of papers, etc.*)
**expedir** **§94** *va* to send, to ship, to remit; to issue; to expedite
**expeditar** *va* (Am.) to expedite
**expeditivo -va** *adj* expeditious
**expedito -ta** *adj* free, easy, ready, expeditious; clear, open
**expeler** *va* to expel, to eject
**expendedor -dora** *adj* spending; dealing, trading; vending; *mf* dealer, agent, retailer; ticket agent; distributer of counterfeit money
**expendeduría** *f* cigar store, retail store (*for sale of state-monopolized articles*); **expendeduría de billetes** (Am.) ticket office
**expender** *va* to expend; to sell on a commission; to sell at retail; to circulate (*counterfeit money*)
**expendición** *f* commission selling; retailing
**expendio** *m* expense; (Am.) shop, store; (Am.) ticket office; (Am.) retailing
**expensar** *va* (Am.) to defray (*expenses*)
**expensas** *fpl* expenses; **a expensas de** at the expense of
**experiencia** *f* experience (*practical knowledge gained by doing or living through things; something experienced, event participated in*); experiment; **aprender con su propria experiencia** to learn by experience
**experimentación** *f* experimentation

**experimentado -da** *adj* experienced
**experimentador -dora** *adj* experimenting; *mf* experimenter
**experimental** *adj* experimental
**experimentalismo** *m* experimentalism
**experimentar** *va* to test, to try, to try out; to experience, undergo, feel; *vn* to experiment
**experimentativo -va** *adj* experimental
**experimento** *m* experience; experiment
**experto -ta** *adj & m* expert
**expiable** *adj* expiable
**expiación** *f* expiation, atonement; cleansing, purification
**expiar §90** *va* to expiate, to atone for; to cleanse, to purify
**expiativo -va** *adj* expiative, expiatory
**expiatorio -ria** *adj* expiatory
**expilar** *va* to rob, to despoil
**expillo** *m* (bot.) feverfew
**expiración** *f* expiration
**expirante** *adj* expiring
**expirar** *vn* to expire (*to emit the breath; to die; to come to an end*)
**explanación** *f* leveling, grading; explanation, elucidation
**explanada** *f* esplanade; (fort.) esplanade
**explanar** *va* to level, to grade; to explain, to elucidate
**explantación** *f* (biol.) explantation
**explayar** *va* to extend, to enlarge; *vr* to extend, to spread out; to discourse at large; **explayarse con** to unbosom oneself to
**expletivo -va** *adj* expletive
**explicable** *adj* explicable, explainable
**explicación** *f* explanation, explication; **pedir explicaciones** to demand an explanation
**explicaderas** *fpl* (coll.) way of explaining; **tener buenas explicaderas** (coll.) to have a way of explaining things
**explicador -dora** *mf* explainer, commentator
**explicar §86** *va* to explain; to expound; *vr* to explain oneself; to understand, e.g., **ahora me lo explico** now I understand it
**explicativo -va** *adj* explanatory, explicative
**explicatorio -ria** *adj* explanatory, explicatory
**explícito -ta** *adj* explicit
**exploración** *f* exploration; (mil.) scouting; (telv.) scanning
**explorador -dora** *adj* exploring; exploratory; (telv.) scanning; *mf* explorer; *m* (mil.) scout; boy scout; (med.) explorer (*instrument*); (telv.) scanning disk
**exploramiento** *m* exploration
**explorar** *va & vn* to explore; (telv.) to scan; (mil.) to scout
**explorativo -va** *adj* explorative
**exploratorio -ria** *adj* exploratory
**explosímetro** *m* explosimeter
**explosión** *f* explosion; combustion (*e.g., of gasoline in a motor*); (phonet.) explosion
**explosivo -va** *adj* explosive; (phonet.) explosive; *m* explosive; *f* (phonet.) explosive
**explosor** *m* exploder, blasting machine
**explotable** *adj* workable; exploitable
**explotación** *f* running, operation; working; exploitation
**explotador -dora** *adj* running, operating; exploiting; *mf* operator; exploiter
**explotar** *va* to run, to operate (*e.g., a railroad*); to work (*a mine*); to exploit; *vn* to explode
**expoliación** *f* spoliation; (rhet.) repetition, elaboration
**expoliador -dora** *adj* spoliating; *mf* spoliator
**expoliar** *va* to spoliate, to despoil
**expolio** *m* spoliation
**expondré** *1st sg fut ind of* **exponer**
**exponencial** *adj* (math.) exponential
**exponente** *adj* explaining, expounding; *m* exponent; (alg.) exponent
**exponer §69** *va* to expose; to abandon (*a child*); to expound; to show; to put (*a corpse*) on view; (eccl.) to expose (*the Host*); *vn* (eccl.) to expose the Host; *vr* to expose oneself (*e.g., to a danger*)
**expongo** *1st sg pres ind of* **exponer**
**exportación** *f* export, exportation; exports
**exportador -dora** *adj* exporting; *mf* exporter
**exportar** *va & vn* to export
**exposición** *f* exposition; exposure (*exposing or being exposed; position as to points of compass*); (rhet.) exposition; (phot.) exposure; show, fair, exposition; **exposición universal** world's fair
**exposímetro** *m* (phot.) exposure meter, light meter
**expositivo -va** *adj* expositive
**expósito -ta** *adj* exposed or abandoned (*child*); *mf* foundling
**expositor -tora** *adj* expository; *mf* exponent; expositor, expounder, commentator; exhibitor
**expremijo** *m* cheese vat, cheese shelf
**exprés** *adj* express (*train*); *m* express train; caffè espresso; (Am.) express company
**expresable** *adj* (Am.) expressible
**expresado -da** *adj* above-mentioned
**expresamente** *adv* expressly
**expresar** *va* to express; to specify; *vr* to express oneself
**expresión** *f* expression; squeezing; (math.) expression; **expresiones** *fpl* regards
**expresionismo** *m* (f.a.) expressionism
**expresionista** *adj & mf* expressionist
**expresividad** *f* expressiveness
**expresivo -va** *adj* expressive; kind, affectionate
**expreso -sa** *adj* expressed; express (*clear, definite; for a particular purpose; train, car, elevator, etc.*); *m* express (*train; fast shipment*); (Am.) express company
**exprimible** *adj* expressible
**exprimidamente** *adv* stiffly; primly, prudishly; with affectation; grudgingly
**exprimidera** *f* or **exprimidero** *m* squeezer; **exprimidera de naranjas** orange squeezer
**exprimido -da** *adj* lean, skinny; stiff, stuck-up; prim, prudish; affected, overprecise
**exprimidor** *m* wringer; squeezer
**exprimir** *va* to express, to squeeze, to press out; to wring, wring out; to express vividly; (Am.) to empty (*a firearm*)
**ex profeso** *adv* on purpose, expressly
**expropiación** *f* expropriation
**expropiador -dora** *mf* expropriator
**expropiar** *va* to expropriate
**expuesto -ta** *adj* dangerous, hazardous; *pp of* **exponer**
**expugnable** *adj* expugnable, pregnable
**expugnación** *f* taking by storm
**expugnar** *va* to take by storm
**expulsador -dora** *mf* ejector
**expulsanieves** *m* (*pl:* **-ves**) snowplow
**expulsar** *va* to expel, to expulse, to drive out
**expulsión** *f* expulsion
**expulsivo -va** *adj* expulsive
**expulsor** *m* ejector (*of firearm*)
**expurgación** *f* expurgation
**expurgar §59** *va* to expurgate
**expurgatorio -ria** *adj* expurgatory
**expurgo** *m* expurgation; expurgated parts (*of a book*); elimination of green and damaged grapes before pressing
**expuse** *1st sg pret ind of* **exponer**
**exquisitez** *f* exquisiteness; excellence; affectation
**exquisito -ta** *adj* exquisite; consummate, excellent; genteel; affected
**exsicación** *f* exsiccation
**exsomático -ca** *adj* exsomatic
**exstrofia** *f* (path.) exstrophy
**éxtasi** *m* var. of **éxtasis**
**extasiar §90 & regular** *va* to delight, to enrapture; *vr* to go into ecstasies, to become enraptured
**éxtasis** *m* (*pl:* **-sis**) ecstasy
**extático -ca** *adj* ecstatic
**extemporal** *adj* unseasonable
**extemporaneidad** *f* unseasonableness; untimeliness
**extemporáneo -a** *adj* unseasonable; untimely, inopportune; (pharm.) magistral
**extender §66** *va* to extend, to stretch out, to spread, to spread out; to draw up (*a document*); *vr* to extend, to stretch out, to spread, to spread out; to go on and on (*talking, explaining, etc.*); (coll.) to be puffed up; **extenderse a** or **hasta** to reach, to amount to
**extendidamente** *adv* in detail, at great length
**extensible** *adj* stretchy, extensible

**extensión** *f* extension, extent, extensity; expanse; range; (psychol.) extensity; (telp.) extension
**extensivo -va** *adj* extensive; (agr.) extensive; **hacer extensivos a** to extend (*congratulations, good wishes, etc.*) to; **hacerse extensivo a** to extend to
**extenso -sa** *adj* extended, vast, extensive; **por extenso** in detail, at great length
**extensor -sora** *adj* extending; extensile; *m* (anat.) extensor; chest or muscle exerciser; **extensor de cubiertas** (Am.) tire spreader
**extenuación** *f* extenuation, emaciation, weakening
**extenuante** *adj* weakening, debilitating
**extenuar** §33 *va* to extenuate, to emaciate, to weaken
**extenuativo -va** *adj* emaciating, weakening
**exterior** *adj* exterior, external, outer, outside, outward; foreign; *m* exterior, outside; appearance, bearing; **al exterior** or **a lo exterior** on the outside; outwardly; **del exterior** from abroad; **en el exterior** on the outside; abroad; **en exteriores** (mov.) on location
**exterioridad** *f* exteriority, externality; externals, outward appearance, outward show; **exterioridades** *fpl* show, pomp
**exteriorista** *adj* outgoing, outgiving (*e.g., nature, personality*); *mf* extrovert
**exteriorización** *f* revelation, manifestation; (surg.) temporary removal (*of an internal organ*); (psychol.) doubling of personality
**exteriorizar** §76 *va* to reveal, to make manifest; *vr* to unbosom one's heart
**exteriormente** *adv* on the outside; outwardly, seemingly
**exterminable** *adj* exterminable
**exterminador -dora** *adj* exterminating; *mf* exterminator (*person*); *m* exterminator (*apparatus*)
**exterminar** *va* to exterminate
**exterminio** *m* extermination
**externado** *m* day school
**externo -na** *adj* external, outside; (anat.) external; *mf* day scholar, day pupil; day-school pupil
**extima** *f* (anat.) extima
**extina** *f* (bot.) extine
**extinción** *f* extinction; elimination, obliteration
**extinguible** *adj* extinguishable
**extinguir** §44 *va* to extinguish, to quench, to put out, to wipe out; to carry out, to fulfil; to spend, to serve (*a period of time*); *vr* to go out, to be extinguished; to become extinct
**extintivo -va** *adj* extinctive; (law) extinctive
**extinto -ta** *adj* extinguished; extinct; (Am.) dead, deceased
**extintor -tora** *adj* extinguishing; *m* fire extinguisher; **extintor de espuma** foam extinguisher; **extintor de granada** fire grenade
**extirpación** *f* extirpation
**extirpador -dora** *adj* extirpating; *mf* extirpator; *m* (agr.) cultivator
**extirpar** *va* to extirpate
**extorno** *m* (ins.) premium adjustment (*based on modification of policy*)
**extorsión** *f* extortion; damage, harm
**extorsionar** *va* to extort; to damage, harm
**extra** *adj* extra; **extra de** (coll.) besides, in addition to; *mf* (theat.) extra; *m* extra (*of a newspaper*); (coll.) extra (*gratuity*)
**extrabronquial** *adj* extrabronchial
**extrabucal** *adj* extrabuccal
**extrabulbar** *adj* extrabulbar
**extracapsular** *adj* extracapsular
**extracardíaco -ca** *adj* extracardial
**extracción** *f* extraction; number drawing (*in lottery*); **extracción de raíces** (math.) extraction of roots, evolution
**extracelular** *adj* extracellular
**extracístico -ca** *adj* extracystic
**extracorriente** *f* (elec.) extra current
**extracorto -ta** *adj* (rad.) ultrashort
**extractador -dora** *mf* abstractor
**extractar** *va* to abstract (*a writing*)
**extractivo -va** *adj* extractive; extractable
**extracto** *m* abstract (*of a writing*); (pharm.) extract; **extracto de índigo** indigo extract; **extracto de malta** malt extract
**extractor -tora** *mf* extractor; *m* extractor (*apparatus*); **extractor de aire** ventilator; **extractor de rueda** (aut.) wheel puller
**extracurricular** *adj* extracurricular
**extradición** *f* extradition
**extraditable** *adj* extraditable
**extradós** *m* (arch.) extrados
**extraelevado -da** *adj* (rad.) ultrahigh
**extraembrionario -ria** *adj* extraembryonic
**extraente** *adj* extracting; *mf* extractor
**extraer** §88 *va* to extract; to pull; (math.) to extract (*a root*)
**extraeuropeo -a** *adj* outside of Europe, non-European
**extrafino -na** *adj* extrafine
**extrafuerte** *adj* heavy-duty
**extragenital** *adj* extragenital
**extrahepático -ca** *adj* extrahepatic
**extraigo** *1st sg pres ind of* **extraer**
**extraje** *1st sg pret ind of* **extraer**
**extrajudicial** *adj* extrajudicial
**extralegal** *adj* extralegal
**extralimitación** *f* overstepping, taking advantage
**extralimitar** *vr* to overstep, to go too far
**extramedular** *adj* extramedullary
**extrameridiano -na** *adj* extrameridional
**extramural** *adj* extramural
**extramuros** *adv* beyond the walls, outside the town or city
**extranjería** *f* alienism, alienship
**extranjerismo** *m* xenomania; borrowing, foreignism
**extranjerizar** §76 *va* to mix foreign customs with; *vr* to become mixed with foreign customs
**extranjero -ra** *adj* foreign; *mf* foreigner; **extranjero enemigo** enemy alien; *m* foreign land; **del extranjero** from abroad; **en el extranjero, por el extranjero** abroad
**extranjía** *f* (coll.) alienship; **de extranjía** (coll.) foreign; (coll.) strange, unexpected
**extranjis; de extranjis** (coll.) foreign; (coll.) strange, unexpected; (coll.) secretly
**extraña** *f* see **extraño**
**extrañación** *f* or **extrañamiento** *m* banishment, expatriation
**extrañar** *va* to banish, to expatriate; to surprise; to find strange, to be surprised at; (dial. & Am.) to miss; **extrañar** + *inf* to surprise to + *inf*, e.g., **me extrañó encontrar a Vd. aquí** it surprised me to find you here; *vn* to be strange; *vr* to be surprised; to wonder; to refuse; **extrañarse de** + *inf* to be surprised to + *inf*
**extrañez** *f* or **extrañeza** *f* strangeness, peculiarity; estrangement; wonder
**extraño -ña** *adj* foreign; strange; extraneous; **extraño a** unconnected with; *mf* foreigner; stranger; *f* (bot.) China aster
**extraoficial** *adj* unofficial
**extraordinario -ria** *adj* extraordinary; extra; *m* extra dish; extra number (*of a periodical*); special mail
**extrapélvico -ca** *adj* extrapelvic
**extrapiramidal** *adj* extrapyramidal
**extraplacentario -ria** *adj* extraplacental
**extraplano -na** *adj* extra-flat
**extrapolación** *f* (math.) extrapolation
**extrapolar** *adj* extrapolar; *va & vn* (math.) to extrapolate
**extrapulmonar** *adj* extrapulmonary
**extrarradio** *m* outer edge of town
**extrarrápido -da** *adj* (phot.) extra-fast
**extrasensorial** *adj* extrasensory
**extraseroso -sa** *adj* extraserous
**extrasístole** *f* (med.) extrasystole
**extraterreno -na** *adj* extramundane
**extraterrestre** *adj* extraterrestrial; (astr.) extraterrestrial
**extraterritorial** *adj* extraterritorial
**extraterritorialidad** *f* extraterritoriality
**extrauterino -na** *adj* extrauterine
**extravagancia** *f* extravagance, folly, wildness, nonsense
**extravagante** *adj* extravagant, foolish, wild, nonsensical; in transit (*said of mail in post office*); **extravagantes** *fpl* (canon law) Extravagants or Extravagantes
**extravagar** §59 *vn* to ramble, to talk nonsense

**extravaginal** *adj* (anat. & bot.) extravaginal
**extravasación** *f* extravasation
**extravasar** *va* to extravasate; *vr* (physiol.) to extravasate
**extravascular** *adj* extravascular
**extravenar** *va & vr* to exude through the veins
**extraventricular** *adj* extraventricular
**extraversión** *f* (psychol.) extroversion or extraversion
**extraviadamente** *adv* astray; beside oneself; at random, wandering
**extraviar** **§90** *va* to lead astray; to mislead; to mislay, to misplace; *vr* to go astray; to wander; to get lost; to be wrong; to get out of line or out of alignment
**extravío** *m* misleading; misplacement; going astray; loss; misconduct; error, wrong; (coll.) annoyance
**extrema** *f* see **extremo**
**extremadamente** *adv* extremely
**extremado -da** *adj* extreme, excessive; consummate
**extremar** *va* to carry far, carry to the limit; *vr* to exert oneself to the utmost; **extremarse en** + *inf* to strive hard to + *inf*
**extremaunción** *f* (eccl.) extreme unction
**extremeño -ña** *adj* frontier; Estremenian; *mf* frontier dweller; Estremenian
**extremidad** *f* extremity; end, tip; **la última extremidad** one's last moment (*death*); **extremidades** *fpl* extremities (*hands and feet*)
**extremismo** *m* extremism
**extremista** *mf* extremist
**extremo -ma** *adj* extreme; ultimate; utmost; critical, desperate; *m* end, extremity, tip; extreme; point (*of a conversation, letter, etc.*); great care; winter pasture, winter grazing; (football) end; **al extremo de** to the point of; **con, de, en** or **por extremo** extremely; **de extremo a extremo** from one end to the other; **hacer extremos** to gush, be demonstrative; **pasar de un extremo a otro** to go from one extreme to the other; **extremo muerto** dead end; *f* (coll.) extremity (*extreme need*); (coll.) end, final moment (*of life*); (coll.) extreme unction
**extremosidad** *f* effusiveness, gushiness
**extremoso -sa** *adj* extreme; demonstrative, effusive; forthright
**extrínseco -ca** *adj* extrinsic
**extrofia** *f* var. of **exstrofia**
**extrorso -sa** *adj* (bot.) extrorse
**extroversión** *f* (path.) extroversion
**extrovertido -da** *mf* extrovert
**extrusión** *f* (metal.) extrusion
**exuberancia** *f* exuberance
**exuberante** *adj* exuberant
**exuberar** *vn* to exuberate
**exudación** *f* exudation
**exudado** *m* exudate
**exudar** *va & vn* to exude
**exulceración** *f* chafing, slight ulceration
**exulcerar** *va & vn* to chafe, to ulcerate lightly
**exultación** *f* exultation
**exultar** *vn* to exult
**exutorio** *m* (med.) issue, artificial ulcer (*for discharge of pus*)
**exvoto** *m* ex-voto, votive offering
**eyaculación** *f* (physiol.) ejaculation
**eyaculador -dora** *adj* (physiol.) ejaculatory
**eyacular** *va & vn* (physiol.) to ejaculate
**eyector** *m* (mach.) ejector
**-ez** *suffix f* -hood, e.g., **niñez** childhood; **viudez** widowhood; -ness, e.g., **altivez** haughtiness; **madurez** ripeness; **pequeñez** smallness; -ty, e.g., **aridez** aridity; **fluidez** fluidity; **rapidez** rapidity
**-eza** *suffix f* -ness, e.g., **grandeza** bigness; greatness; **ligereza** lightness; **limpieza** cleanliness; -ty, e.g., **certeza** certainty; **pureza** purity
**Ezequías** *m* (Bib.) Hezekiah
**Ezequiel** *m* (Bib.) Ezekiel (*prophet and book*)

# F

**F, f** *f* seventh letter of the Spanish alphabet
**F.** abr. of **fulano**
**fab.** abr. of **fabricante**
**f.a.b.** abr. of **franco a bordo**
**fabada** *f* Asturian bean soup with pork and sausage
**Fabián** *m* Fabian
**fabiano -na** *adj & mf* Fabian
**fabla** *f* imitation of Old Spanish
**fabordón** *m* (mus.) faux-bourdon
**fábrica** *f* manufacture; factory, plant, mill; building; fabric; masonry; invention; church rate; church funds; vestry, church board; **de fábrica** (pertaining to or made of) masonry; **fábrica de la moneda** mint; **fábrica de montaje** assembly plant
**fabricación** *f* fabrication, manufacture; **fabricación en serie** mass production
**fabricador -dora** *mf* fabricator, inventor, schemer
**fabricante** *mf* manufacturer; *m* factory owner, plant owner, mill owner
**fabricar** §86 *va* to fabricate, to manufacture; to devise, invent, bring about, forge
**fabricoide** *m* fabricoid
**fabril** *adj* manufacturing
**fabriquero** *m* manufacturer, factory owner; charcoal burner (*person*); churchwarden
**fabuco** *m* beechnut, mast (*food for animals*)
**fábula** *f* fable; rumor, gossip; talk (*e.g., of the town*); story, lie; plot, story, tale; **la Fábula** mythology; **fábulas milesias** Milesian tales
**fabulador** *m* var. of **fabulista**
**fabulario** *m* collection of fables, book of fables
**fabulista** *mf* fabulist
**fabuloso -sa** *adj* fabulous
**faca** *f* cutlass, falchion
**facción** *f* faction; feature; factious group; battle; **facciones** *fpl* features (*face*); **estar de facción** (mil.) to be on duty
**faccionar** *va* to incite to rebellion; *vr* to rebel
**faccionario -ria** *adj* factional; *mf* partisan, factionalist
**faccioso -sa** *adj* factious; rebellious; *mf* partisan; rebel
**faceto -ta** *adj* (Am.) affected, smart; (Am.) finicky; *f* facet; (arch., zool. & fig.) facet
**facial** *adj* facial; face; intuitive
**facie** *f* (cryst.) face
**facies** *f* (med.) face (*indicating a certain disease*); (biol.) facies
**fácil** *adj* easy; facile; pliant, yielding, docile; probable, likely; loose, wanton; **poco fácil a** not given to
**facilidad** *f* ease, easiness, facility; **facilidades** *fpl* facilities (*conveniences, means*); **facilidades de pago** easy payments
**facílimo -ma** *adj super* very or most easy
**facilitación** *f* facilitation; furnishing, providing
**facilitar** *va* to facilitate, to expedite; to furnish, to provide; (coll.) to oversimplify
**facilitón -tona** *adj* (coll.) brash, bumbling; *mf* (coll.) bumbler
**facineroso -sa** *adj* wicked, villainous; *mf* villain, rascal; criminal
**facistol** *m* lectern, choir desk
**facón** *m* (Am.) dagger; **pelar el facón** (Am.) to pull a knife
**faconazo** *m* (Am.) stab
**facóquero** *m* (zool.) wart hog
**facsímil** *m* var. of **facsímile**
**facsimilar** *adj* facsimile; *va* to facsimile, to make a facsimile of
**facsímile** *m* facsimile; **a facsímile** in facsimile
**fact.ª** abr. of **factura**
**factaje** *m* carriage, conveyance, delivery
**factible** *adj* feasible, doable
**facticio -cia** *adj* factitious
**factitivo -va** *adj* (gram.) causative
**factor** *m* commission merchant; baggageman; freight agent; factor (*element that helps to bring about a result*); (biochem., biol., law, math. & physiol.) factor; **factor de potencia** (elec.) power factor; **factor Rh** (biochem.) Rh factor
**factoraje** *m* factorage (*business of commission merchant*)
**factoría** *f* factory (*trading post in a foreign country*); factorage (*business of commission merchant*); (Am.) factory; (Am.) foundry
**factorial** *f* (math.) factorial
**factótum** *m* (coll.) factotum; (coll.) busybody; (coll.) confidant
**factura** *f* form, execution, workmanship; manufacture; invoice, bill; **según factura** as per invoice; **factura consular** consular invoice; **factura simulada** pro forma invoice
**facturación** *f* invoicing, billing; checking (*of baggage*)
**facturar** *va* (com.) to invoice, to bill; to check (*baggage*)
**fácula** *f* (astr.) facula
**facultad** *f* faculty; power; permission; option; knowledge, skill; school (*of a university*); (med.) strength, resistance; **facultad de altos estudios** school of advanced studies, graduate school
**facultar** *va* to empower, to authorize
**facultativo -va** *adj* (pertaining to a) faculty; of a doctor; facultative, optional; (biol.) facultative; *m* doctor (*physician or surgeon*)
**facundia** *f* eloquence, fluency; gift of gab
**facundo -da** *adj* eloquent, fluent; talkative
**facha** *f* (coll.) appearance, look; **ponerse en facha** (coll.) to get ready, be prepared; (naut.) to lie to; **facha a facha** face to face; *m & f* (coll.) ridiculous figure
**fachado -da** *adj*; **bien fachado** (coll.) good-looking; **mal fachado** (coll.) bad-looking; *f* façade; frontage; title page; (coll.) front, presence; **hacer fachada con** to face, overlook
**fachear** *vn* (naut.) to lie to
**fachenda** *f* (coll.) boasting, ostentation; *m* (coll.) boaster, show-off
**fachendear** *vn* (coll.) to boast, to show off
**fachendista, fachendón -dona** or **fachendoso -sa** *adj* (coll.) boastful, ostentatious; *mf* (coll.) boaster, show-off
**fachinal** *m* (Am.) marsh, marshland
**fachoso -sa** or **fachudo -da** *adj* ill-favored, funny-looking; boastful, ostentatious
**fada** *f* fairy, witch
**faena** *f* task, job, chore; work, toil; stunt; (taur.) windup; (taur.) stunt, skill, trick (*of bullfighters on a cattle-raising farm*); (mil.) fatigue, fatigue duty; (Am.) extra work, overtime; (Am.) morning work in the field; (Am.) gang of laborers
**faenero** *m* (Am.) farm hand
**faenza** *f* faïence
**faetón** *m* phaeton; (*cap.*) *m* (myth.) Phaethon
**fagáceo -a** *adj* (bot.) fagaceous
**fagocito** *m* (physiol.) phagocyte
**fagocitosis** *f* phagocytosis
**fagot** *m* (*pl:* **-gotes**) (mus.) bassoon; bassoonist
**fagotista** *m* (mus.) bassoonist
**faisán** *m* (orn.) pheasant; **faisán de Mogolia** (orn.) Mongolian pheasant; **faisán dorado** (orn.) golden pheasant; **faisán plateado** (orn.) silver pheasant

**faisana** *f* hen pheasant
**faisanería** *f* pheasant preserve, pheasantry
**faisanero -ra** *mf* pheasant raiser
**faja** *f* sash, girdle, belt; bandage; strip, band; sheet; zone; newspaper wrapper; plaster border (*of door or window*); lane (*of highway*); strip (*of landing field*); (arch. & surg.) fascia; (her.) fesse; (naut.) reef band; (rad.) channel; **faja abdominal** abdominal supporter; **faja de desgarre** (aer.) rip panel; **faja divisora** parting strip (*of a road*); **faja medical** supporter
**fajado** *m* mine timber
**fajadura** *f* wrapping; bandaging; swaddling; (naut.) parceling
**fajamiento** *m* wrapping; bandaging; swaddling
**fajar** *va* to wrap; to bandage; to swaddle; to put a wrapper on (*a newspaper or magazine*); (Am.) to beat, to thrash; (Am.) to give (*a slap, a whipping*); (Am.) to attack, jump on; *vr* to put on a sash or belt
**fajardo** *m* meat pie, mince pie
**fajeado -da** *adj* striped, banded, fasciated
**fajero** *m* knitted swaddling band; dealer in sashes, belts, etc.; clerk who wraps newspapers for mailing
**fajín** *m* sash (*badge of distinction*)
**fajina** *f* fagot, fascine; shock, rick; toil, task, chore; (fort.) fascine; (mil.) call to mess; (archaic) call to quarters; **meter fajina** to blab, to jabber
**fajinada** *f* (fort.) fascine work
**fajo** *m* bundle; **fajos** *mpl* swaddling clothes
**fajol** *m* (bot.) buckwheat
**fajón** *m* large sash; large strip or band; plaster border (*of door or window*)
**fakir** *m* var. of **faquir**
**falacia** *f* deceit; perfidy; (log.) fallacy
**falange** *f* phalanx; (anat. & zool.) phalanx; (iron.) array (*of people*); (poet.) army; (*cap.*) *f* (pol.) Falange
**falangero** *m* (zool.) phalanger
**falangeta** *f* (anat.) phalangette
**falangia** *f* (ent.) daddy longlegs
**falangiano -na** *adj* phalangeal
**falangio** *m* var. of **falangia**
**falangista** *adj & mf* Falangist
**falansterio** *m* phalanstery
**falaris** *f* (orn.) coot
**falárope** *m* (orn.) phalarope
**falaz** *adj* (*pl:* **-laces**) deceitful; perfidious; fallacious, deceptive, misleading
**falbalá** *m* (*pl:* **-laes**) (archaic) square flap sewed in the rear slit of the skirt of a coat; ruffle, flounce
**falca** *f* warp (*in a board*); (naut.) washboard; (dial.) wedge; (Am.) small still
**falcado -da** *adj* falcate
**falce** *f* sickle; curved knife; (anat.) falx
**falciforme** *adj* falciform
**falcinelo** *m* (orn.) glossy ibis
**falcón** *m* (arti.) falcon
**falconete** *m* (arti.) falconet
**falda** *f* skirt, dress; flap, fold; lap; loin (*e.g., of beef*); brim (*of hat*); foothill, lower slope (*of a mountain*); (arm.) skirt; (coll.) skirt (*woman*); **cosido** or **pegado a las faldas de** tied to the apron strings of
**faldamenta** *f* or **faldamento** *m* skirt; ugly, long skirt
**faldar** *m* (arm.) skirt (*of tasses*)
**faldear** *va* to climb (*a hill*); (Am.) to wind one's way up (*a hill*)
**faldellín** *m* short skirt; underskirt
**faldero -ra** *adj* skirt; lap; lady-loving; *m* lap dog; *f* skirt maker
**faldeta** *f* small skirt; (theat.) stage screen
**faldicorto -ta** *adj* short-skirted
**faldilla** *f* flap of a saddle; **faldillas** *fpl* skirts, coattails; (Am.) petticoat
**faldistorio** *m* faldstool
**faldón** *m* coattail; shirttail; skirt, tail; flap; saddle flap; top millstone; triangular slope (*of a hip roof*)
**faldriquera** *f* var. of **faltriquera**
**faldulario** *m* or **faldumenta** *f* trailing clothing
**falena** *f* (ent.) geometrid
**falencia** *f* fallacy, mistake; falsehood; (Am.) failure, bankruptcy
**falencioso -sa** *adj* fallacious, erroneous; false
**falibilidad** *f* fallibility
**falible** *adj* fallible
**fálico -ca** *adj* phallic
**falina** *f* (biochem.) phallin
**falismo** *m* phallicism or phallism
**falo** *m* phallus
**falsabraga** *f* (fort.) low outer rampart
**falsada** *f* swoop (*of bird of prey*)
**falsario -ria** *adj* falsifying; lying; *mf* falsifier, crook; liar
**falsarregla** *f* bevel square; guide lines (*for writing*)
**falsarrienda** *f* checkrein
**falseamiento** *m* falsification; counterfeit; forgery
**falsear** *va* to falsify; to misrepresent, to fake; to counterfeit; to forge; to pick (*a lock*); to bevel; to pierce (*armor*); *vn* to sag, buckle; to give, give way; to flag; to be out of tune
**falsedad** *f* falsehood; falsity
**falseo** *m* bevel; beveling
**falsete** *m* plug, tap; small door; falsetto (*voice*)
**falsetista** *m* falsetto (*person*)
**falsía** *f* falsity, treachery, duplicity
**falsificación** *f* falsification; counterfeit; forgery; fake
**falsificador -dora** *mf* falsifier; counterfeiter; forger; faker
**falsificar** §86 *va & vn* to falsify; to counterfeit; to forge; to fake
**falsilla** *f* guide lines (*for writing*)
**falso -sa** *adj* false; counterfeit; vicious (*horse*); *m* patch, reinforcement; (philately) forgery (*forged stamp*); **coger en falso** to catch in a lie; **de falso** or **en falso** without proper support; **envidar de falso** or **en falso** to bluff (*in betting*); (fig.) to invite half-heartedly; **sobre falso** without proper support
**falta** *f* see **falto**
**faltante** *adj* wanting, missing
**faltar** *va* to offend, to insult; *vn* to be missing; to be lacking, be wanting; to be short, fall short; to run out; to fail; to be absent; to be unfaithful; to die; to be impudent; to slip; to lack, need, be in need of, e.g., **me falta dinero** I lack money, I need money; **¡no faltaba más!** the very idea!, that's the last straw!; **faltar a** to go back on (*e.g., a promise*); **faltar a la clase** to cut class, be absent from class; **faltar a la verdad** to fail to tell the truth; **faltar a una cita** to break an appointment; **faltar . . . para** to be . . . to, e.g., **faltan diez minutos para las dos** it is ten minutes to two; **falta un cuarto para la una** it is a quarter to one; **faltar poco para** + *inf* to be near + *ger*, e.g., **falta poco para terminarse el año** the year is near ending; **faltar poco para que** + *subj* to come near + *ger*, e.g., **poco faltó para que cayese en el estanque** he came near falling into the pool; **faltar por** + *inf* to remain to be + *pp*, e.g., **faltan por escribir tres cartas** three letters remain to be written
**falto -ta** *adj* short, lacking, wanting; mean, lowly; short (*weight or measure*); (Am.) dull, stupid; **falto de** short of, lacking ‖ *f* lack, want; shortage; fault, mistake; misdemeanor, misdeed; flaw, defect; absence, cut; (sport) fault; **a falta de** for want of; **echar en falta** to miss; **hacer buena falta** to be badly needed; **hacer falta** to be needed, be necessary; to be lacking, be missing; to fail, to miss; to need, e.g., **me hacían falta esos papeles** I needed those papers; to miss, e.g., **Vd. me ha hecho mucha falta** I have missed you very much; **hacer falta** + *inf* to be necessary to + *inf;* **sin falta** without fail; **falta de ortografía** misspelling; **falta de pie** (tennis) foot fault
**faltón -tona** *adj* (coll.) dilatory, remiss
**faltoso -sa** *adj* (coll.) non compos mentis; (Am.) quarrelsome
**faltriquera** *f* pocket; handbag; **rascar** or **rascarse la faltriquera** (coll.) to cough up
**falúa** *f* (naut.) harbor felucca, tender
**falucho** *m* (naut.) felucca
**falla** *f* see **fallo**
**fallada** *f* (cards) ruff

**fallar** *va* to ruff, to trump; (law) to judge, pass judgment on; *vn* to fail, to miss; to sag, weaken; to miss fire; to break down; (law) to judge, pass judgment
**falleba** *f* espagnolette, door bolt
**fallecer §34** *vn* to decease, die; to fail, expire, run out
**fallecido -da** *adj* deceased, late
**fallecimiento** *m* decease, death; failure, expiration
**fallero -ra** *adj & mf* absentee (*worker or employee*); *f* queen of the falla (*in Valencia, Spain*)
**fallido -da** *adj* unsuccessful, sterile; uncollectible; without standing; bankrupt
**fallo -lla** *adj* (dial.) weak, faint; (Am.) silly, simple; **estar fallo a** to be out of (*cards of a certain suit*); *m* decision; short suit; (law) judgment, verdict; **tener fallo a** or **de** to be out of (*cards of a certain suit*); *f* defect; failure, breakdown; (geol. & min.) fault; (archaic) faille (*woman's scarflike headdress*); spectacular bonfire in Valencia on the eve of Saint Joseph's Day (*March 19th*)
**fama** *f* fame; reputation; rumor; (Am.) bull's-eye (*center of target and shot which hits it*); **correr fama** to be rumored; **es fama** it is rumored, it is said
**famélico -ca** *adj* famished, hungry, starving
**familia** *f* family; **en familia** en famille, in the family circle
**familiar** *adj* familiar; (pertaining to the) family, e.g., **lazos familiares** family ties; colloquial; **ser familiar a** to be familiar to; *m* familiar; member of the family; member of the household; household servant; acquaintance; familiar spirit; (eccl.) familiar; **familiar dependiente** dependent
**familiaridad** *f* familiarity
**familiarización** *f* familiarization
**familiarizar §76** *va* to familiarize; *vr* to become familiar; to become too familiar; **familiarizarse con** to familiarize oneself with, to become familiar with
**famoso -sa** *adj* famous; (coll.) famous (*excellent, first-rate*); (coll.) some, e.g., **famoso tarambana** (coll.) some crackpot
**fámula** *f* (coll.) maidservant
**fámulo** *m* famulus; (coll.) servant
**fanal** *m* beacon, lighthouse; lantern; bell glass, bell jar, glass cover; lamp shade; (fig.) torch, guide
**fanático -ca** *adj* fanatic or fanatical; *mf* fanatic; (sport) fan
**fanatismo** *m* fanaticism; (sport) fans
**fanatizador -dora** *mf* spreader of fanaticism
**fanatizar §76** *va* to make fanatical
**fandango** *m* fandango; disorder, topsy-turvy; (coll.) dance; (Am.) carousal
**fandanguear** *vn* (coll.) to carouse around
**fandulario** *m* var. of **faldulario**
**faneca** *f* (ichth.) bib
**fanega** *f* fanega (*1.58 bu. in Spain*); **fanega de tierra** fanegada (*1.59 acres in Spain*)
**fanegada** *f* fanegada (*1.59 acres in Spain*); **a fanegadas** (*coll.*) in great abundance
**fanerógamo -ma** *adj* (bot.) phanerogamous; *f* (bot.) phanerogam
**fanfarrear** *vn* var. of **fanfarronear**
**fanfarria** *f* (coll.) bluster, bragging; fanfare (*loud show; flourish of trumpets or hunting horns*); (mus.) fanfare; *m* (coll.) blusterer, braggart
**fanfarrón -rrona** *adj* (coll.) blustering, bragging; (coll.) flashy, trashy; *mf* (coll.) blusterer, braggart, sword rattler
**fanfarronada** *f* bluster, bravado, fanfaronade
**fanfarronear** *vn* to bluster, to brag
**fanfarronería** *f* (coll.) blustering, bragging, fanfaronading, sword rattling
**fanfurriña** *f* (coll.) pet, fit of peevishness
**fangal** *m* or **fangar** *m* quagmire, mudhole
**fango** *m* mud, mire; (fig.) mud; **llenar de fango** (fig.) to sling mud at
**fangoso -sa** *adj* muddy, miry; soft and sticky
**fanón** *m* (eccl.) fanon
**fantaseador -dora** *adj* daydreaming; *mf* daydreamer, dreamer
**fantasear** *va* to dream of; *vn* to fancy, to daydream; **fantasear de** to boast of being
**fantasía** *f* fantasy; fancy; imagery; (coll.) vanity, conceit; (naut.) dead reckoning; (mus.) fantasy, fantasia; **fantasías** *fpl* pearls, string of pearls; **de fantasía** fancy, colored; fancy, imitation (*e.g., jewelry*); **tocar por fantasía** (Am.) to play by ear
**fantasioso -sa** *adj* (coll.) vain, conceited
**fantasma** *m* phantom; stuffed shirt; (telv.) ghost; **fantasma magnético** magnetic curves; *f* scarecrow, hobgoblin
**fantasmagoría** *f* phantasmagoria
**fantasmagórico -ca** *adj* phantasmagorial or phantasmagoric
**fantasmal** *adj* phantasmal
**fantasmón -mona** *adj* (coll.) conceited; *mf* (coll.) stuffed shirt; *m* scarecrow
**fantástico -ca** *adj* fantastic; fanciful; conceited
**fantoche** *m* marionette, puppet; (coll.) nincompoop; (coll.) whippersnapper; (fig.) puppet
**fañado -da** *adj* one-year-old (*animal*)
**faquín** *m* porter, errand boy
**faquir** *m* fakir
**farachar** *va* to swingle, to scutch
**farádico -ca** *adj* faradic
**faradímetro** *m* faradmeter
**faradio** *m* (elec.) farad
**faradismo** *m* faradism; (med.) faradism
**faradización** *f* (med.) faradization
**faradizar §76** *va* (med.) to faradize
**faralá** *m* (*pl:* **-laes**) ruffle, flounce; (coll.) frill
**farallón** *m* cliff, headland; (min.) outcrop
**faramalla** *f* (coll.) claptrap; (coll.) sham, fake; (Am.) trash, rubbish; *mf* (coll.) gossip, schemer, cheat
**faramallero -ra** or **faramallón -llona** *adj* (coll.) gossiping, scheming, cheating; *mf* (coll.) gossip, schemer, cheat
**farándola** *f* farandole (*dance*); (dial.) ruffle, flounce
**farándula** *f* farandole (*dance*); confusion, web of lies; (coll.) wicked gossip; (Am.) jam (*of people*), buzz (*of voices*); (archaic) acting; company of actors, company of barnstormers
**farandulear** *vn* (coll.) to boast, to brag, to show off
**farandulero -ra** *adj* (coll.) gossiping, scheming; cheating; (pertaining to the) theater; *mf* (coll.) gossip, schemer, cheat; comedian, player
**Faraón** *m* Pharaoh; (*l.c.*) *m* faro (*card game*)
**faraónico -ca** *adj* Pharaonic
**faraute** *m* herald, messenger; prologue (*actor*); (coll.) busybody
**farda** *f* tax levied on Jews and Moors (*in Spain*); bundle of clothing; notch, mortise
**fardacho** *m* (zool.) lizard
**fardaje** *m* var. of **fardería**
**fardar** *va* to supply with clothes
**fardel** *m* bag (*carried over shoulder*); bundle; (coll.) slob
**fardela** *f* (orn.) shearwater; **fardela del Atlántico** (orn.) Manx shearwater
**fardería** *f* pile of bundles
**fardo** *m* bundle
**farellón** *m* cliff, headland
**farfalá** *m* (*pl:* **-laes**) ruffle, flounce
**farfallear** *vn* (dial.) to stammer, stutter
**farfallón -llona** *adj* (coll.) jabbering, spluttering; (coll.) hasty, bungling
**farfalloso -sa** *adj* (dial.) stammering, stuttering
**fárfara** *f* (bot.) coltsfoot; pellicle (*of eggshell*); **en fárfara** immature; half done
**farfolla** *f* husk, cornhusk; (coll.) sham, fake
**farfulla** *f* (coll.) sputtering; *mf* (coll.) sputterer; *adj* (coll.) sputtering
**farfulladamente** *adv* (coll.) sputteringly
**farfullador -dora** *adj* (coll.) sputtering; *mf* (coll.) sputterer
**farfullamiento** *m* (coll.) sputtering, gibbering
**farfullar** *va* (coll.) to sputter through (*e.g., a lesson*); (coll.) to stumble through (*a task*); *vn* (coll.) to sputter, to gibber
**farfullero -ra** *adj & mf* (coll.) var. of **farfullador**
**fargallón -llona** *adj* (coll.) hasty, bungling; (coll.) slovenly, untidy; *mf* (coll.) botcher, bungler

**farillón** *m* var. of **farallón**
**farináceo -a** *adj* (bot.) farinaceous
**faringe** *f* (anat.) pharynx
**faríngeo -a** *adj* pharyngeal
**faringitis** *f* (path.) pharyngitis
**faringoscopia** *f* pharyngoscopy
**faringoscopio** *m* pharyngoscope
**farinoso -sa** *adj* var. of **harinoso**
**farisaico -ca** *adj* pharisaic or pharisaical; Pharisaic
**farisaísmo** *m* pharisaism; Pharisaism
**fariseo** *m* pharisee; Pharisee; (coll.) tall, lanky good-for-nothing
**farmacéutico -ca** *adj* pharmaceutic or pharmaceutical; *mf* pharmacist, druggist; *f* pharmaceutics
**farmacia** *f* pharmacy, drug store; **farmacia de guardia** drug store open overtime, drug store open all night
**fármaco** *m* drug, medicine
**farmacognosia** *f* pharmacognosy
**farmacología** *f* pharmacology
**farmacólogo -ga** *mf* pharmacologist
**farmacopea** *f* pharmacopoeia
**farmacopola** *m* pharmacist, pharmacopolist
**farmacopólico -ca** *adj* pharmaceutical
**faro** *m* lighthouse, beacon; floodlight; lantern; (aut.) headlight, headlamp; (fig.) beacon; **faro aéreo** air beacon; **faro piloto** (aut.) spotlight; **faros de carretera** (aut.) bright lights; **faros de cruce** (aut.) dimmers; **faros de población** or **de situación** (aut.) parking lights
**farol** *m* lantern; lamp, light; street lamp; (rail.) headlight; (taur.) farol (*pase in which bullfighter swirls cape over his shoulders*); (coll.) conceited fellow; **farol de tope** (naut.) headlight
**farola** *f* street light, lamppost; beacon, lighthouse
**farolazo** *m* blow with a lantern; (Am.) swig, drink
**farolear** *vn* (coll.) to boast, to brag
**faroleo** *m* (coll.) boasting, bragging
**farolería** *f* (coll.) boasting, bragging; lamp or lantern shop
**farolero -ra** *adj* (coll.) boasting, bragging; *mf* (coll.) boaster, braggart; *m* lamp or lantern maker or dealer; lamplighter
**farolillo** *m* (bot.) Canterbury bell; (bot.) balloon vine, heartseed
**farolito** *m* small lantern; (bot.) winter cherry; **farolito de enredadera** (bot.) balloon vine, heartseed
**farolón -lona** *adj* (coll.) boasting, bragging; (coll.) *mf* boaster, bragger; *m* (coll.) large lamp or lantern
**farota** *f* (coll.) minx, vixen
**farotón -tona** *adj* (coll.) cheeky, brazen; *mf* (coll.) cheeky person
**farpa** *f* point of a scallop
**farpado -da** *adj* scalloped
**farra** *f* (ichth.) salmon trout; (Am.) revelry, spree
**fárrago** *m* farrago, hodgepodge
**farragoso -sa** *adj* confused, disordered
**farraguista** *mf* muddlehead
**farro** *m* peeled barley; spelt wheat
**farruco -ca** *adj* (coll.) bold, fearless; *mf* (coll.) Galician abroad, Asturian abroad; *f* farruca (*Spanish gypsy dance*)
**farruto -ta** *adj* (Am.) sickly
**farsa** *f* (theat.) farce; company of players; crude play, grotesque play; (fig.) farce, absurdity; (fig.) humbug
**farsanta** *f* (archaic) farce actress
**farsante** *adj* & *mf* (coll.) fake, humbug; *m* (archaic) farce actor
**farseto** *m* quilted jacket (*worn under armor*)
**farsista** *mf* author of farces
**fas; por fas o por nefas** rightly or wrongly, in any event
**fasces** *fpl* fasces
**fascia** *f* (anat. & surg.) fascia
**fascial** *adj* fascial
**fasciculado -da** *adj* fascicled
**fascículo** *m* fascicle or fasciculus (*of printed book*); (anat.) fascicle or fasciculus; (bot.) fascicle
**fascinación** *f* fascination; bewitchment, spell
**fascinador -dora** *adj* fascinating; *mf* fascinator
**fascinante** *adj* fascinating
**fascinar** *va* to fascinate; to bewitch; to cast a spell on, by a look, to cast the evil eye on
**fascismo** *m* fascism; (*cap.*) *m* Fascism
**fascista** *adj* & *mf* fascist; (*cap.*) *adj* & *mf* Fascist
**fascólomo** *m* (zool.) wombat
**fase** *f* phase; (astr., biol., elec. & phys.) phase; **en fase** (elec.) in phase; **fuera de fase** (elec.) out of phase; **fase partida** (elec.) split phase
**faseolina** *f* (biochem.) phaseolin
**fásoles** *mpl* (bot.) beans, string beans
**fastidiar** *va* to cloy, to sicken; to annoy, to bore; to disappoint; *vr* to get bored; to make a fool of oneself
**fastidio** *m* squeamishness; annoyance, boredom; profound dislike
**fastidioso -sa** *adj* cloying, sickening; annoying, boring; annoyed, displeased
**fastigio** *m* apex, tip, summit; (anat.) fastigium; (arch.) pediment, fastigium
**fasto -ta** *adj* happy, fortunate; *m* pomp, magnificence, show; **fastos** *mpl* fasti
**fastoso -sa** or **fastuoso -sa** *adj* vain, pompous; magnificent
**fatal** *adj* fatal; unfortunate; inevitable; bad, evil
**fatalidad** *f* fatality; fate; misfortune
**fatalismo** *m* fatalism
**fatalista** *adj* fatalistic; *mf* fatalist
**fatalmente** *adv* fatally; inevitably; badly, poorly
**Fata Morgana** *f* (meteor.) Fata Morgana
**fatídico -ca** *adj* fatidic; fateful
**fatiga** *f* fatigue; hardship; hard breathing; (mech. & physiol.) fatigue; **fatigas** *fpl* nausea
**fatigador -dora** or **fatigante** *adj* var. of **fatigoso**
**fatigar** §59 *va* to fatigue, to tire, to weary; to annoy, to harass; to rack (*one's brains*); *vr* to tire, get tired, tire oneself out
**fatigoso -sa** *adj* fatiguing, tiring; (coll.) trying, tedious
**fatuidad** *f* fatuity; conceit
**fatuo -tua** *adj* fatuous; conceited
**faucal** *adj* faucal
**fauces** *fpl* (anat.) fauces
**fauna** *f* fauna; (*cap.*) *f* (myth.) Fauna
**fáunico -ca** *adj* faunal
**fauno** *m* (myth.) faun
**fáustico -ca** *adj* Faustian
**fausto -ta** *adj* happy, fortunate; *m* pomp, magnificence, show; (*cap.*) *m* Faust
**faustoso -sa** *adj* magnificent
**fautor -tora** *mf* abetter, accomplice, instigator
**favila** *f* (poet.) ember, spark
**favo** *m* (path.) favus
**favonio** *m* (poet.) zephyr
**favor** *m* favor; (fig.) favor (*gift, token, ribbon*); **favores** *mpl* favors (*of a woman*); **a favor de** under cover of; with the aid of, by means of; in favor of; in behalf of; **estar en favor** to be in favor; **hágame Vd. el favor de** + *inf* do me the favor of + *ger;* **por favor** please; **tener a su favor** to have under one's wing; **vender favores** to peddle influence
**favorable** *adj* favorable
**favorecedor -dora** *adj* favoring; *mf* favorer; customer
**favorecer** §34 *va* to favor
**favoritismo** *m* favoritism
**favorito -ta** *adj* & *mf* favorite
**favoso -sa** *adj* favose
**faya** *f* faille (*silk cloth*)
**fayanca** *f* unstable posture; **de fayanca** carelessly
**faz** *f* (*pl:* **faces**) face; aspect; obverse; **faz a faz** face to face
**F.C.** or **f.c.** abr. of **ferrocarril**
**fe** *f* faith; fidelity; certificate; testimony, witness; **¡a fe mía!** upon my faith!; **a la buena fe** with simplicity, guilelessly; **dar fe de** to attest, to certify; **de buena fe** in good faith; **de mala fe** in bad faith; **hacer fe** to be valid, have validity; **la fe del carbonero** simple faith; **¡por mi fe!** upon my faith!; **tener fe en** to have faith in; **fe de bautismo** certificate of baptism; **fe de erratas** errata, list

of errata; **fe de nacimiento** birth certificate; **fe de óbito** death certificate
**fealdad** *f* ugliness
**Febe** *f* (myth.) Phoebe; (poet.) Phoebe (*moon*)
**febeo -a** *adj* (poet.) Phoebean
**feble** *adj* weak, feeble; lacking in weight or fineness (*said of a coin or alloy*); *m* foible, weak point
**feb.º** abr. of **febrero**
**Febo** *m* (myth.) Phoebus; (poet.) Phoebus (*sun*)
**febrero** *m* February
**febricitante** *adj* feverish
**febrífugo -ga** *adj & m* febrifuge
**febrígeno -na** *adj* fever-producing
**febril** *adj* febrile, feverish
**fecal** *adj* fecal
**fecalito** *m* (path.) fecalith
**fécula** *f* starch; fecula; dregs; **fécula de maranta** arrowroot (*starch*)
**feculento -ta** *adj* feculent (*foul, fecal*); starchy
**feculoso -sa** *adj* starchy
**fecundación** *f* fecundation; (biol.) fecundation
**fecundador -dora** *adj* fecundating
**fecundar** *va* to fecundate; (biol.) to fecundate
**fecundativo -va** *adj* fecundative
**fecundidad** *f* fecundity
**fecundizar §76** *va* to fecundate, to fertilize
**fecundo -da** *adj* fecund
**fecha** *f* see **fecho**
**fechación** *f* dating
**fechador** *m* (Am.) canceling stamp
**fechar** *va* to date
**fecho -cha** *adj* issued, executed; *f* date; day; **con fecha de** under date of; **¿cuál es la fecha de hoy?** what is the date?; **de antigua fecha** or **de larga fecha** of long standing; **hasta la fecha** to date
**fechoría** *f* misdeed, villainy
**federación** *f* federation
**federal** *adj & mf* federal
**federalismo** *m* federalism
**federalista** *adj & mf* federalist
**federar** *va* to federate; to federalize
**federativo -va** *adj* federative
**Federica** *f* Frederica
**Federico** *m* Frederick
**Fedra** *f* (myth.) Phaedra
**feérico -ca** *adj* fairy, fairylike
**fehaciente** *adj* authentic
**felá** *m* (*pl:* **-laes**) fellah
**felandrio** *m* (bot.) water fennel
**feldespático -ca** *adj* feldspathic or feldspathose
**feldespato** *m* (mineral.) feldspar
**felice** *adj* (poet.) happy
**felicidad** *f* felicity, happiness; luck, good luck
**felicísimo -ma** *adj super* very or most happy
**felicitación** *f* felicitation, congratulation
**felicitar** *va* to felicitate, congratulate; to wish happiness to
**félido -da** *adj* feline; *m* (zool.) felid
**feligrés -gresa** *mf* parishioner, church member
**feligresía** *f* parish (*members of parish*); country parish
**felino -na** *adj* (zool. & fig.) feline; *m* (zool.) feline
**Felipe** *m* Philip
**feliz** *adj* (*pl:* **-lices**) happy; lucky; felicitous
**felodermo** *m* (bot.) phelloderm
**felógeno** *m* (bot.) phellogen
**felón -lona** *adj* perfidious, treacherous, felonious; *mf* wicked person, felon
**felonía** *f* perfidy, treachery; (feud.) felony
**felpa** *f* plush; (coll.) drubbing; (coll.) sharp reprimand
**felpado -da** *adj* plushy, velvety
**felpar** *va* to cover with plush; (poet.) to carpet (*e.g., with grass or flowers*)
**felpilla** *f* chenille
**felpón** *m* (prov.) coarse velvet; (prov.) hard beating
**felposo -sa** *adj* felted; plushy
**felpudo -da** *adj* plushy, velvety, downy; *m* mat, plush mat
**felsita** *f* (mineral.) felsite
**f.e.m.** abr. of **fuerza electromotriz**
**femenil** *adj* feminine, womanly
**femenino -na** *adj* feminine; (bot.) female; (gram.) feminine; *m* (gram.) feminine; **el eterno femenino** (lit.) the eternal feminine
**fementido -da** *adj* false, treacherous, unfaithful
**feminidad** *f* femininity
**feminismo** *m* feminism
**feminista** *adj* feminist, feministic; *mf* feminist
**femoral** *adj* femoral
**fémur** *m* (anat.) femur, thighbone; (ent.) femur
**fenacetina** *f* (pharm.) phenacetin
**fenaquistiscopio** *m* phenakistoscope
**fenda** *f* crack, split
**fenecer §34** *va* to finish, to close; *vn* to die; to come to an end
**fenecimiento** *m* finish, termination; death
**fenianismo** *m* Fenianism
**feniano -na** *adj & m* Fenian
**fenice** *adj & mf* Phoenician
**fenicio -cia** *adj & mf* Phoenician; (*cap.*) *f* Phoenicia
**fénico -ca** *adj* (chem.) carbolic, phenic
**fenileno** *m* (chem.) phenylene
**fenilo** *m* (chem.) phenyl
**fénix** *m* (*pl:* **-nix** or **-nices**) (myth. & fig.) phoenix; **el fénix de los ingenios** Lope de Vega
**fenobarbital** *m* (pharm.) phenobarbital
**fenocristal** *m* (geol.) phenocryst
**fenogreco** *m* (bot.) fenugreek
**fenol** *m* (chem.) phenol
**fenolftaleína** *f* (chem.) phenolphthalein
**fenología** *f* phenology
**fenomenal** *adj* phenomenal; (fig.) phenomenal
**fenomenalismo** *m* (philos.) phenomenalism
**fenómeno** *m* phenomenon; (philos.) phenomenon; (coll.) monster, freak
**fenomenología** *f* (philos.) phenomenology
**fenotiacina** *f* (chem.) phenothiazine
**fenotipo** *m* (biol.) phenotype
**feo -a** *adj* ugly; **feo** *adv* (Am.) bad, e.g., **oler feo** to smell bad; *m* (coll.) slight; **dejar feo a** or **hacer un feo a** (coll.) to slight
**feote -ta** *adj* very ugly, hideous
**feracidad** *f* fertility, feracity
**feral** *adj* cruel, bloody, feral
**feraz** *adj* (*pl:* **-races**) fertile, feracious
**féretro** *m* bier, coffin
**feria** *f* fair; market; market-day crowd; deal, agreement; weekday; rest, repose; day off, holiday; (Am.) change; (Am.) tip; **ferias** *fpl* holiday gift to servants or the poor; **revolver la feria** (coll.) to upset the applecart
**feriado -da** *adj* see **día**
**ferial** *adj* week (*day*); *m* market; market place
**feriante** *adj* fairgoing; *mf* fairgoer
**feriar** *va* to buy, to sell, to exchange; to buy at the fair; to make a gift to; *vn* to take off, take a few days off
**ferino -na** *adj* wild, savage, ferine
**fermata** *f* (mus.) pause
**fermentable** *adj* fermentable
**fermentación** *f* fermentation; (fig.) fermentation
**fermentador -dora** *adj* fermenting
**fermentante** *adj* fermentive
**fermentar** *va & vn* to ferment; (fig.) to ferment
**fermentativo -va** *adj* fermentative
**fermento** *m* ferment
**fermio** *m* (chem.) fermium
**fernandina** *f* (archaic) farandine (*fabric*)
**Fernando** *m* Ferdinand
**Fern.do** abr. of **Fernando**
**feroce** *adj* (poet.) var. of **feroz**
**ferocidad** *f* ferocity
**ferocísimo -ma** *adj super* very or most ferocious
**feróstico -ca** *adj* (coll.) irritable, unruly; (coll.) very ugly
**feroz** *adj* (*pl:* **-roces**) ferocious
**ferrar §18** *va* to trim with iron, to cover with iron; to stamp or punch
**ferrato** *m* (chem.) ferrate
**férreo -a** *adj* ferreous; iron; tough, strong
**ferrería** *f* ironworks, foundry
**ferrete** *m* sulfate of copper; iron stamp or punch

**ferretear** *va* to trim with iron, to cover with iron; to stamp or punch; to work with iron
**ferretería** *f* ironworks; hardware; hardware store
**ferretero -ra** *mf* hardware dealer
**férrico -ca** *adj* (chem.) ferric
**ferrificar** §86 *vr* to turn into iron
**ferrizo -za** *adj* iron
**ferro** *m* (naut.) anchor
**ferroaluminio** *m* ferroaluminum
**ferrocarril** *m* railroad, railway; **ferrocarril aéreo** elevated railway; **ferrocarril de circunvalación** belt line; **ferrocarril de cremallera** rack railway; **ferrocarril de sangre** animal-drawn railway; **ferrocarril de vapor** steam railroad; **ferrocarril de vía angosta** narrow-gauge railway; **ferrocarril de vía normal** standard-gauge railway; **ferrocarril elevado** elevated railway; **ferrocarril funicular** funicular railway; **ferrocarril subterráneo** subway; **ferrocarril urbano** street railway
**ferrocarrilero -ra** *adj & m* (Am.) var. of **ferroviario**
**ferrocerio** *m* ferrocerium
**ferrocianuro** *m* (chem.) ferrocyanide
**ferroconcreto** *m* ferroconcrete
**ferrocromo** *m* ferrochrome or ferrochromium
**ferrohormigón** *m* ferroconcrete
**ferromagnético -ca** *adj* (phys.) ferromagnetic
**ferromanganeso** *m* ferromanganese
**ferrón** *m* ironworker
**ferroníquel** *m* ferronickel
**ferroprusiato** *m* (chem.) ferroprussiate
**ferroso -sa** *adj* ferrous; (chem.) ferrous
**ferrotipia** *f* (phot.) ferrotype (*process*)
**ferrotipo** *m* (phot.) ferrotype, tintype
**ferrotungsteno** *m* ferrotungsten
**ferrovía** *f* railway
**ferrovial** *adj* (pertaining to the) railroad, railway
**ferroviario -ria** *adj* (pertaining to the) railroad, railway, rail; *m* railroader
**ferrugiento -ta** *adj* iron, irony
**ferruginoso -sa** *adj* ferruginous; iron (*water*)
**fértil** *adj* fertile; (fig.) fertile
**fertilidad** *f* fertility
**fertilizable** *adj* fertilizable
**fertilización** *f* fertilization; **fertilización cruzada** (bot. & biol.) cross-fertilization
**fertilizador -dora** *adj* fertilizing; *mf* fertilizer
**fertilizante** *adj* fertilizing; *mf* fertilizer; *m* fertilizer (*e.g., manure*)
**fertilizar** §76 *va* to fertilize; *vr* to become fertile, become fertile again
**férula** *f* ferule; authority, rule; (bot.) giant fennel; (surg.) splint; **estar bajo la férula de** to be under the thumb of
**feruláceo -a** *adj* (bot.) ferulaceous
**ferventísimo -ma** *adj super* very or most fervent
**férvido -da** *adj* fervid (*hot, boiling; vehement*); burning (*thirst, fever*)
**ferviente** *adj* fervent
**fervor** *m* fervor
**fervorín** *m* short prayer
**fervorizar** §76 *va* to incite, inflame, inspire
**fervoroso -sa** *adj* fervent, fervid
**festejar** *va* to fete, entertain, honor; to court, woo; to celebrate; (Am.) to beat, thrash; *vr* to enjoy oneself, have a good time
**festejo** *m* feast, entertainment; courting, wooing; ovation, celebration; (Am.) revelry; **festejos** *mpl* public festivities
**festín** *m* feast, banquet
**festinación** *f* (Am.) hurry, haste
**festinar** *va* (Am.) to hurry, hasten
**festival** *m* festival, music festival
**festividad** *f* witticism; festivity; holiday
**festivo -va** *adj* witty; humorous; festive; festal, festival; (lit.) burlesque
**festón** *m* festoon
**festonar** or **festonear** *va* to festoon
**fetal** *adj* fetal
**feticida** *adj* feticidal; *mf* killer of a fetus
**feticidio** *m* feticide (*act*)
**fetiche** *m* fetish
**fetichismo** *m* fetishism
**fetichista** *adj* fetishistic; *mf* fetishist
**fetidez** *f* fetidity, foulness
**fétido -da** *adj* fetid, foul
**fetiquismo** *m* var. of **fetichismo**
**feto** *m* (embryol.) fetus
**fetor** *m* var. of **hedor**
**feúco -ca** or **feúcho -cha** *adj* very ugly, repulsive
**feudado -da** *adj* feudatory (*held as a fief*)
**feudal** *adj* feudal; feudalistic
**feudalidad** *f* feudality; feudalism
**feudalismo** *m* feudalism
**feudatario -ria** *adj & m* feudatory
**feudista** *m* (law) feudist
**feudo** *m* (law) feud; (law) fief; **feudos** *mpl* (hum.) bailiwick; **feudo franco** (law) freehold
**fez** *m* fez
**fiable** *adj* trustworthy, reliable
**fiado -da** *adj* trusting; **al fiado** on credit, on trust; **en fiado** on bail
**fiador -dora** *mf* bail (*person*); bondsman; **salir fiador por** to go bail for; *m* fastener; trigger; catch, pawl, stop; tumbler (*of a lock*); (Am.) chin strap
**fiambrar** *va* to prepare (*food*) for serving cold
**fiambre** *adj* cold, cold-served (*food*); (coll.) old, stale, out-of-date (*e.g., news*); *m* cold lunch, cold food; (coll.) stale news; **fiambres** *mpl* cold cuts; **de fiambre** (coll.) on credit, borrowed
**fiambrera** *f* lunch basket; dinner pail, lunch pail; portable food warmer
**fiambrería** *f* (Am.) delicatessen store; (Am.) grillroom
**fianza** *f* guarantee, surety; bond; bail (*guarantee and person giving guarantee*); **fianza carcelera** bail (*guarantee*)
**fiar** §90 *va* to guarantee, go surety for; to give credit to; to entrust, confide; to sell on credit; *vn* to trust; **fiar en** to trust in, put one's trust in; *vr* to trust; **fiarse a** or **de** to trust in, rely on
**fiasco** *m* fiasco
**fíat** *m* fiat
**fibra** *f* fiber; grain (*of wood*); (bot.) fibril (*root hair*); (min.) vein; (fig.) fiber, strength, vigor; **fibras del corazón** heartstrings (*deepest feelings*); **fibras de vidrio** fiberglas
**fibravidrio** *m* fiberglas
**fibrilación** *f* (path.) fibrillation
**fibrilla** *f* (anat. & bot.) fibril
**fibrina** *f* (bot. & physiol.) fibrin
**fibrinógeno** *m* (physiol.) fibrinogen
**fibrinoso -sa** *adj* fibrinous
**fibrocartílago** *m* (anat.) fibrocartilage
**fibroide** *adj* fibroid; *m* (path.) fibroid
**fibroideo -a** *adj* fibroid
**fibroína** *f* (biochem.) fibroin
**fibroma** *m* (path.) fibroma
**fibroso -sa** *adj* fibrous
**fíbula** *f* (anat. & archeol.) fibula
**fibular** *adj* fibular
**ficción** *f* fiction; (law) fiction
**ficcionario -ria** *adj* fictional
**fice** *m* (ichth.) hake
**ficología** *f* phycology
**ficticio -cia** *adj* fictitious
**ficha** *f* chip; domino (*piece*); slug; counter; token; filing card; record; police record; (elec.) plug; (Am.) check; (Am.) bad actor; **llevar ficha** to have a police record; **ser una buena ficha** (Am.) to be a sly fox; **ficha antropométrica** anthropometric chart; **ficha catalográfica** card, index card (*of a library*)
**fichador -dora** *mf* file clerk
**fichar** *va* to play (*a domino*); to file (*e.g., cards*); to make the anthropometric chart of; (coll.) to black-list
**fichero** *m* card index, filing cabinet, file case
**fidecomiso** *m* var. of **fideicomiso**
**fidedigno -na** *adj* reliable, trustworthy
**fideero -ra** *mf* vermicelli maker or dealer, spaghetti maker or dealer
**fideicomisario -ria** *adj & mf* (law) fideicommissary
**fideicomiso** *m* (law) fideicommissum; trusteeship (*of the UN*)
**fideicomitente** *mf* (law) fideicommissioner

**fidelería** *f* (Am.) vermicelli factory, spaghetti factory
**fidelidad** *f* fidelity; punctiliousness; **alta fidelidad** (rad.) high fidelity
**fidelísimo -ma** *adj super* very or most faithful
**fideo** *m* (coll.) skinny person; **fideos** *mpl* vermicelli
**Fidias** *m* Phidias
**fiduciario -ria** *adj & mf* fiduciary
**fiebre** *f* (path. & fig.) fever; **fiebre aftosa** (vet.) aphthous fever; **fiebre amarilla** (path.) yellow fever; **fiebre cerebral** (path.) brain fever; **fiebre continua** (path.) continued fever; **fiebre de garrapatas** (path.) tick fever; **fiebre de las Montañas Rocosas** (path.) Rocky Mountain spotted fever; **fiebre del heno** (path.) hay fever; **fiebre de Tejas** (vet.) Texas fever; **fiebre entérica** (path.) enteric fever; **fiebre láctea** (path.) milk fever; **fiebre ondulante** (path.) undulant fever; **fiebre paratifoidea** (path.) paratyphoid fever; **fiebre puerperal** (path.) puerperal fever; **fiebre reumática** (path.) rheumatic fever; **fiebre sextana** (path.) sextan; **fiebre tifoidea** (path.) typhoid fever; **fiebre tifoidea ambulante** or **ambulatoria** (path.) walking typhoid fever
**fiel** *adj* faithful; honest, trustworthy; exact; punctilious; sincere; *m* public inspector, inspector of weights and measures; pointer (*of scales*); pin (*of scissors*); **en fiel** balanced, in balance; **los fieles** the faithful; **fiel de romana** inspector of weights in a slaughterhouse
**fielato** *m* inspector's office; octroi (*office*)
**fieltrar** *va* to felt
**fieltro** *m* felt; felt hat, felt coat, felt rug
**fiemo** *m* (prov.) dung, manure
**fiera** *f* see **fiero**
**fierabrás** *m* (coll.) bully, spitfire; (coll.) little terror, brat
**fierecilla** *f* shrew
**fiereza** *f* fierceness, ferocity; cruelty; ugliness, deformity
**fiero -ra** *adj* fierce; terrible; cruel; ugly; tremendous; proud, haughty; **fieros** *mpl* boasts, threats; **echar** or **hacer fieros** to bluster; *f* wild animal; (taur.) bull; fiend (*person*); **ser una fiera para** (coll.) to be a fiend for (*e.g., work*)
**fierro** *m* (Am.) var. of **hierro**
**fiesta** *f* feast, holy day; holiday; festivity, celebration, party; **fiestas** *fpl* holidays, vacation; **aguar la fiesta** (coll.) to be a kill-joy; **estar de fiesta** (coll.) to be in a good mood, to be in a holiday mood; **hacer fiesta** to take off (*from work*); **hacer fiestas (a)** to fawn (on); **la fiesta brava** the fierce sport (*bullfighting*); **no estar para fiestas** (coll.) to be in no mood for joking; **por fin de fiesta** to top it off; **se acabó la fiesta** (coll.) let's drop it, that'll do; **tengamos la fiesta en paz** (coll.) cut it out; **fiesta de guardar** holy day; **fiesta de la hispanidad** or **fiesta de la raza** Columbus Day, Discovery Day; **fiesta del árbol** Arbor Day; **fiesta de precepto** holy day; **fiesta de todos los santos** All Saints' Day; **fiesta fija** or **inmoble** (eccl.) immovable feast; **fiesta movible** (eccl.) movable feast; **fiesta nacional** national holiday; national sport (*bullfighting*); **fiesta onomástica** saint's day, birthday; **fiesta simple** (eccl.) simple; **fiestas navideñas** Christmas holidays; **fiestas nemeas** Nemean games; **fiestas órficas** Orphic mysteries
**fiestero -ra** *adj* gay, merry, jolly; *mf* jolly person, merrymaker; party-goer
**fígaro** *m* barber; short jacket; (coll.) meddler, schemer
**figle** *m* (mus.) ophicleide; ophicleidist
**figón** *m* cheap eating house
**figonero -ra** *mf* keeper of a cheap eating house
**figulino -na** *adj* figuline
**figura** *f* figure; face, countenance; face card; (arith., geom., log. & rhet.) figure; (mus.) note (*showing length of sound*); (theat.) character; **hacer figura** to cut a figure; *m* (coll.) pompous fellow; *mf* sorry figure
**figuración** *f* figuration; representation; (mus.) figuration; (theat.) supers, extras; (Am.) role in society, distinguished role in society
**figurado -da** *adj* figurative (*language, style, etc.*); imaginary, illusory
**figuranta** *f* (theat.) figurante
**figurante** *m* (theat.) figurant
**figurar** *va* to figure, depict, trace; to represent; to feign; *vn* to figure (*to participate, appear, be conspicuous*); to be in the limelight; *vr* to figure, to imagine
**figurativo -va** *adj* figurative
**figurería** *f* grimace, face
**figurero -ra** *adj* (coll.) grimacing, fond of grimacing; *mf* (coll.) grimacer; maker or seller of small figures or statuettes
**figurilla** or **figurita** *f* figurine; marionette; *mf* (coll.) silly little runt
**figurín** *m* dummy, model, lay figure; fashion plate (*design; person*)
**figurina** *f* figurine
**figurón** *m* (coll.) stuffed shirt, pretentious nobody; **figurón de proa** (naut.) figurehead
**fija** *f* see **fijo**
**fijacarteles** *m* (*pl:* **-les**) billposter
**fijación** *f* fixation; fixing, fastening; posting; (chem., phot., psychoanal. & psychol.) fixation; **fijación del complemento** (bact.) complement fixation; **fijación del nitrógeno** (chem.) nitrogen fixation; **fijación de precios** price fixing
**fijado** *m* (phot.) fixing
**fijador -dora** *adj* fixing; *m* carpenter who hangs doors and windows; (mas.) pointer; (phot.) fixing bath; sprayer; hair set, hair spray
**fijamárgenes** *m* (*pl:* **-nes**) marginal stop (*of typewriter*)
**fijapeinados** *m* (*pl:* **-dos**) hair set, hair spray
**fijar** *va* to fix; to fasten; to paste, to glue; to drive (*a stake*); to post (*bills*); to set (*a date; the hair*); to establish (*e.g., residence*); (phot.) to fix; *vr* to become fixed, to settle; to notice; **fijarse en** to notice, to pay attention to; to imagine; **fijarse en** + *inf* to be intent on + *ger*
**fijativo -va** *adj & m* fixative
**fijeza** *f* firmness, solidity; steadfastness; fixity; **mirar con fijeza** to stare at
**Fijí** *m* Fiji (*islands*)
**fijiano -na** *adj & mf* Fijian
**fijo -ja** *adj* fixed; agreed upon; firm, solid, secure; fast; permanent; stationary; sure; determined; **de fijo** surely, without doubt; *f* hinge; trowel; **a la fija** (Am.) surely, without doubt; **ésa es la fija** (coll.) it is a sure thing; **ésta es la fija** this is it (*i.e., what is feared or hoped for*)
**fil** *m* (archaic) inspector of weights in a slaughter house; **estar en fil** or **en un fil** to be equally balanced, be alike; **fil derecho** leapfrog
**fila** *f* row, line, tier; file; rank; (coll.) hatred, dislike; **cerrar las filas** (mil.) to close ranks; **en fila** in a row; in single file; **en filas** (mil.) in active service; **llamar a filas** (mil.) to call to the colors; **pasarse a las filas de** to go over to; **ponerse en fila** to line up; **romper filas** (mil.) to break ranks; **salirse de la fila** to get out of line; **fila india** single file, Indian file
**filacteria** *f* phylactery; (f.a.) phylactery
**Filadelfia** *f* Philadelphia
**filadelfiano -na** *adj & mf* Philadelphian
**filadiz** *m* floss silk
**filamento** *m* filament; (bot. & elec.) filament
**filamentoso -sa** *adj* filamentous
**filandria** *f* (zool.) filander
**filandro** *m* (zool.) philander
**filantropía** *f* philanthropy
**filantrópico -ca** *adj* philanthropic or philanthropical
**filántropo -pa** *mf* philanthropist
**filar** *va* (naut.) to ease out, pay out slowly (*a cable*)
**filaria** *f* (zool.) filaria
**filariasis** *f* or **filariosis** *f* (path.) filariasis
**filarmonía** *f* love of harmony or music
**filarmónico -ca** *adj & mf* philharmonic
**filástica** *f* (naut.) rope yarn

**filatelia** *f* philately
**filatélico -ca** *adj* philatelic; *mf* philatelist
**filatelista** *mf* philatelist
**filatería** *f* fast talking (*to deceive*); prolixity
**filatero -ra** *adj* fast-talking (*to deceive*); prolix; *mf* fast talker; great talker
**filatura** *f* spinning; spinning mill
**Filemón** *m* (myth. & Bib.) Philemon
**fileno -na** *adj* (coll.) delicate, tiny
**filete** *m* filet or fillet (*of meat or fish*); narrow hem; small spit; snaffle bit; welt (*of shoe*); edge, rim; thread (*of screw*); (arch. & b.b.) fillet; (print.) ornamental bar or line
**fileteado** *m* threads (*of a screw*); (b.b.) tooling
**filetear** *va* to fillet; (b.b.) to tool; to thread (*e.g., a screw*)
**fileteo** *m* threading
**filetón** *m* heavy bullion (*for embroidering*)
**filfa** *f* (coll.) hoax, fake
**filheleno -na** *adj & mf* philhellene
**filiación** *f* filiation; description, characteristics; (mil.) regimental register
**filial** *adj* filial; *f* (com.) affiliate, subsidiary
**filiar** *va* to register; *vr* to enroll; to enlist
**filibote** *m* (naut.) flyboat
**filibustear** *vn* to filibuster (*to act as a military freebooter or buccaneer*)
**filibusterismo** *m* filibusterism
**filibustero** *m* filibuster (*freebooter, buccaneer*)
**filicida** *adj* filicidal; *mf* filicide (*person*)
**filicidio** *m* filicide (*act*)
**filiforme** *adj* filiform
**filigrana** *f* filigree; watermark (*in paper*); delicacy; cutie (*attractive child or young girl*); (bot.) lantana; (fig.) fancy work
**filigranado -da** *adj* var. of **afiligranado**
**filili** *m* (*pl:* **-líes**) (coll.) peach, honey (*fine person or thing*)
**filio** *m* (ent.) phyllium
**filipéndula** *f* (bot.) spirea filipendula, dropwort
**filipense** *adj & mf* Philippian
**filípico -ca** *adj* (poet.) Philippic; *f* philippic; (*cap.*) *f* (hist.) Philippic (*of Demosthenes; of Cicero*)
**filipichín** *m* moreen
**filipino -na** *adj* Filipine, Filipino, or Philippine; *mf* Filipino; **Filipinas** *fpl* Philippines (*islands*)
**Filipo** *m* Philip (*e.g., of Macedonia*); (poet.) Philip
**Filipos** *f* Philippi
**Filis** *f* Phyllis; (*l.c.*) *f* (poet.) charm, grace, delicacy; trinket, charm
**filisteísmo** *m* Philistinism
**filisteo -a** *adj* (Bib. & fig.) Philistine; *m* (Bib. & fig.) Philistine; tall, heavy fellow
**filita** *f* (mineral.) phyllite
**film** *m* (*pl:* **films**) film, moving picture; **film de bulto** or **film en relieve** three-dimensional film
**filmación** *f* filming
**filmar** *va & vr* to film
**fílmico -ca** *adj* (mov.) (pertaining to) film
**filmoteca** *f* film library
**filo** *m* edge, cutting edge; dividing line; ridge; (biol.) phylum; **al filo de** at, about (*e.g., sunset, ten o'clock*); **dar filo a, dar un filo a** or **sacar el filo a** to sharpen; **pasar al filo de la espada** to put to the sword; **por filo** exactly; **filo del viento** (naut.) direction of the wind
**filobús** *m* trolley bus, trackless trolley
**filocladio** *m* var. of **cladodio**
**filocomunista** *adj & mf* procommunist
**filodio** *m* (bot.) phyllode
**filófago -ga** *adj* phyllophagous
**filogénesis** *f* (biol.) phylogenesis
**filogenia** *f* (biol.) phylogeny
**filogénico -ca** *adj* phylogenic, phylogenetic
**filología** *f* philology
**filológico -ca** *adj* philological; *f* philology
**filólogo -ga** *mf* philologian, philologist
**filolumenista** *mf* matchbox collector
**filomanía** *f* (bot.) phyllomania
**filomela** *f* (poet.) philomela, philomel, or Philomel (*nightingale*); (*cap.*) *f* (myth.) Philomela
**filomena** *f* (poet.) philomela, philomel, or Philomel (*nightingale*)
**filomeno** *m* (orn.) cedarbird
**filón** *m* vein, seam, lode; (fig.) gold mine; **filón ramal** (min.) feeder
**filópodo -da** *adj & m* (zool.) phyllopod
**filosa** *f* see **filoso**
**filoseda** *f* silk and woolen cloth, silk and cotton cloth; schappe
**filoso -sa** *adj* (Am.) sharp, sharp-edged; *f* (bot.) hypocist
**filosofador -dora** *adj* philosophizing; *mf* philosophizer
**filosofar** *vn* to philosophize
**filosofastro** *m* philosophaster
**filosofear** *vn* var. of **filosofar**
**filosofía** *f* philosophy; **filosofía moral** moral philosophy
**filosófico -ca** *adj* philosophic or philosophical
**filósofo -fa** *mf* philosopher
**filotaxia** *f* (bot.) phyllotaxis
**filote** *m* (Am.) corn silk
**filoxera** *f* (ent.) phylloxera
**filtrable** *adj* filterable
**filtración** *f* filtration; leak, leakage; (fig.) leak (*of funds*)
**filtrado** *m* filtering; filtrate
**filtrador -dora** *adj* filtering; *mf* filterer; *m* filter
**filtraje** *m* filtering
**filtrar** *va* to filter, to filtrate; *vn* to leak (*said, e.g., of water or of roof*); *vr* to filter, to filtrate; (fig.) to disappear, to leak away (*said of money*)
**filtro** *m* filter; seaside fresh-water spring; philter, love potion; (elec. & opt.) filter; **filtro de bandas** (elec.) band filter, band-pass filter; **filtro de paso alto** (elec.) high-pass filter; **filtro de paso bajo** (elec.) low-pass filter; **filtro de paso de banda** (elec.) band filter, band-pass filter; **filtro paso inferior** (elec.) low-pass filter; **filtro paso superior** (elec.) high-pass filter
**filtrónico -ca** *adj* (pertaining to a) filter
**filtro-prensa** *m* (*pl:* **filtros-prensas**) filter press
**filudo -da** *adj* (Am.) sharp
**fílum** *m* (biol.) phylum
**filván** *m* featheredge (*on sharpened tool*)
**fillós** *mpl* fritter
**fimbria** *f* border (*of a skirt*); fringe
**fimo** *m* dung, manure
**fimosis** *f* (path.) phimosis
**fin** *m* (& *f*) end; end, purpose; **a fin de** + *inf* in order to + *inf;* **a fin de cuentas** after all; **a fin de que** in order that, so that; **a fines de** at the end of, toward the end of, late in (*a period of time*); **al fin** finally; **al fin del mundo** far, far away; **al fin y a la postre** or **al fin y al cabo** after all, in the end; **dar fin a** to put an end to, to stop; **dar fin de** to put an end to, to destroy, to wipe out; **en fin** finally, in a word, in short; well; **poner fin a** to put an end to, to stop; **por fin** finally, in a word, in short; **sin fin** endless; endlessly; **un sin fin de** no end of; **fin de semana** weekend
**finado -da** *adj* deceased, late; *mf* deceased
**final** *adj* final; *m* end; (mus.) finale; **por final** finally; *f* (sport) finals; **final de partida** windup (*of a game*)
**finalidad** *f* end, purpose
**finalismo** *m* (philos.) finalism
**finalista** *mf* (philos. & sport) finalist
**finalizar §76** *va* to end, terminate; (law) to execute (*a deed, contract, etc.*); *vn* to end, terminate
**finamiento** *m* end, conclusion; decease
**financiación** *f* financing
**financiamiento** *m* (Am.) financing
**financiar** *va* to finance
**financiero -ra** *adj* financial; *mf* financier
**finanzas** *fpl* finances
**finar** *vn* to die; *vr* to long, to yearn
**finca** *f* property, piece of real estate; (Am.) farm, ranch; **buena finca** (coll.) sly fellow, bad egg; **finca cafetera** coffee plantation
**fincabilidad** *f* real estate
**fincar §86** *vn* to buy up real estate; (Am.) to reside, rest, be found; *vr* to buy up real estate
**finchado -da** *adj* (coll.) conceited, vain
**finchar** *vr* (coll.) to be conceited
**finear** *va* to pole (*a boat*)

**Fineas** *m* Phineas
**finés -nesa** *adj* Finnic; Finnish; *mf* Finn (*member of any Finnic-speaking people; native of Finland*); *m* Finnic language
**fineza** *f* fineness; favor, kindness; little gift; (bridge) finesse
**fingido -da** *adj* false, deceptive; fake, sham; affected
**fingidor -dora** *adj* false, fake; *mf* faker
**fingimiento** *m* feigning, faking, pretense
**fingir §42** *va* to feign, pretend, fake; *vn* to feign, pretend; **fingir** + *inf* to feign to, to pretend to + *inf; vr* to feign to be, to pretend to be
**finible** *adj* endable, terminable
**finiquitar** *va* to settle, to close (*an account*); (coll.) to finish, wind up
**finiquito** *m* settlement, closing (*of an account*); **dar finiquito a** to settle, close out; (coll.) to finish, wind up
**finir** *vn* (archaic & Am.) to end
**finisecular** *adj* fin-de-siècle
**finítimo -ma** *adj* bordering, neighboring
**finito -ta** *adj* finite
**Finlandia** *f* Finland
**finlandés -desa** *adj* Finnish; *mf* Finn, Finlander; *m* Finnish (*language*)
**fino -na** *adj* fine; sheer; thin, slender; thin (*cloth, paper, sole of shoe, etc.*); pure (*water*); courteous, polite; cunning, shrewd; fond, true
**finoúgrio -gria** *adj* Finno-Ugric
**finta** *f* feint (*fake threat*)
**fintar** *vn* to feint
**finura** *f* fineness, excellence; courtesy, politeness; (aer.) fineness ratio
**finústico -ca** *adj* (coll.) overpolite, obsequious
**finustiquería** *f* (coll.) overpoliteness, obsequiousness
**fiñana** *m* black-bearded wheat
**fiord** *m* or **fiordo** *m* fiord
**fioritura** *f* trimming, adornment
**firma** *f* signature; (act of) signing; firm; **con mi firma** under my hand; **firma en blanco** blank signature
**firmal** *m* brooch
**firmamento** *m* firmament
**firmán** *m* firman
**firmante** *adj* signatory; *mf* signer, signatory
**firmar** *va & vn* to sign
**firme** *adj* firm, steady; hard, solid; staunch, unswerving; (com.) steady (*market*); **¡firmes!** (mil.) attention!; *adv* firmly, steadily; *m* roadbed; **de firme** hard; steadily; **en firme** (com.) firm; **en lo firme** in the right
**firmeza** *f* firmness; steadiness, constancy
**firmón** *m* shyster who will sign anything
**firuletes** *mpl* (Am.) finery, frippery
**fiscal** *adj* fiscal, (pertaining to a) treasury; *m* treasurer; district attorney, public prosecutor; busybody, informer
**fiscalía** *f* office of treasurer; office of district attorney
**fiscalización** *f* control, inspection; prosecution; prying, informing
**fiscalizar §76** *va* to control, to inspect; to oversee, superintend; to prosecute; to pry into, to talk about (*somebody's conduct*)
**fisco** *m* state treasury, exchequer
**fisga** *f* fishgig, fish spear; snooping; banter, raillery; (dial.) grain of spelt; (dial.) spelt bread; **hacer fisga a** to make fun of
**fisgador -dora** *adj* mocking, scoffing; *mf* mocker, scoffer
**fisgar §59** *va* to fish with a spear, to harpoon; to pry into, to spy on; *vn* to snoop; to mock, to scoff; *vr* to mock, to scoff
**fisgón -gona** *mf* (coll.) jester; (coll.) busybody
**fisgonear** *va* (coll.) to keep prying into (*other people's business*)
**fisgoneo** *m* (coll.) constant prying, constant nosiness
**fisible** *adj* fissionable
**físico -ca** *adj* physical; (Am.) finicky, prudish; *mf* physicist; *m* physique, look, appearance; (archaic & dial.) physician; *f* physics; **física nuclear** nuclear physics
**físicoquímico -ca** *adj* physicochemical; *mf* physicochemist; *f* physicochemisty
**físil** *adj* fissile, fissionable
**fisiocracia** *f* physiocracy
**fisiócrata** *adj* physiocratic; *mf* physiocrat
**fisiocrático -ca** *adj* physiocratic
**fisiografía** *f* physiography
**fisiográfico -ca** *adj* physiographic
**fisiógrafo -fa** *mf* physiographer
**fisiología** *f* physiology; **fisiología vegetal** plant physiology
**fisiológico -ca** *adj* physiological
**fisiólogo -ga** *mf* physiologist
**fisión** *f* (phys.) fission
**fisionable** *adj* fissionable
**fisionar** *va & vr* to split
**fisionomía** *f* physiognomy
**fisioterapia** *f* physiotherapy
**fisíparo -ra** *adj* (biol.) fissiparous
**fisípedo -da** *adj & m* (zool.) fissiped
**fisirrostro -tra** *adj* (orn.) fissirostral
**fisonomía** *f* physiognomy
**fisonómico -ca** *adj* physiognomic or physiognomical
**fisonomista** *mf* physiognomist
**fisónomo -ma** *mf* physiognomist
**fisostigmina** *f* (chem.) physostigmine
**fistol** *m* sly fellow; (Am.) necktie pin
**fistra** *f* (bot.) bishop's-weed
**fístula** *f* fistula; (path.) fistula; (mus.) reed
**fistular** *adj* fistular; *va* to make fistulous
**fistuloso -sa** *adj* fistulous
**fisura** *f* (anat., path. & min.) fissure; **fisura del paladar** cleft palate
**fita** *f* sketch, drawing (*of animated cartoon*)
**fitina** *f* (chem.) phytin
**fitófago -ga** *adj* (zool.) phytophagous
**fitogeografía** *f* phytogeography
**fitografía** *f* phytography
**fitográfico -ca** *adj* phytographic or phytographical
**fitógrafo -fa** *mf* phytographer
**fitolacáceo -a** *adj* (bot.) phytolaccaceous
**fitología** *f* botany, phytology
**fitopatología** *f* (bot. & med.) phytopathology
**fitoplancton** *m* (*biol.*) phytoplankton
**fitotomía** *f* phytotomy
**flabelado -da** *adj* flabellate
**flabeliforme** *adj* flabelliform
**flabelo** *m* (eccl., bot., & zool.) flabellum
**flaccidez** *f* flaccidity; softness
**fláccido -da** *adj* flaccid; soft
**flaco -ca** *adj* thin, skinny; weak; **flaco de cabeza** befuddled, confused; *m* weak spot, foible
**flacucho -cha** *adj* (coll.) thinnish
**flacura** *f* thinness, skinniness; weakness
**flagelación** *f* flagellation
**flagelado -da** *adj* (bot. & biol.) flagellate; *m* (bot.) flagellate
**flagelador -dora** *adj* flagellant; *mf* flagellator
**flagelante** *adj & mf* flagellant; *m* Flagellant
**flagelar** *va* to scourge, to whip, to flagellate; to flay, criticize severely
**flagelo** *m* scourge, whip; (biol.) flagellum; (fig.) scourge, calamity
**flagrancia** *f* (poet.) blazing, flaming
**flagrante** *adj* (poet.) blazing, flaming; occurring; **en flagrante** in the act
**flagrar** *vn* (poet.) to blaze, flame
**flama** *f* flame; reverberation
**flamante** *adj* bright, flaming; brand-new, spick-and-span
**flamberga** *f* (archaic) rapier, flamberg
**flameante** *adj* flamboyant; (arch.) flamboyant
**flamear** *va* to flame (*to sterilize with flame*); *vn* to flame; to flame with anger; to wave, flutter
**flamen** *m* (*pl:* **flámines**) (hist.) flamen
**flamenco -ca** *adj* Flemish; buxom; Andalusian gypsy (*dance, song, etc.*); (coll.) gypsyish, flashy, snappy; *mf* Fleming; *m* Flemish (*language*); Andalusian gypsy dance, song, or music; (orn.) flamingo; **los flamencos** the Flemish (*people*)
**flamenquilla** *f* small platter; (bot.) marigold
**flámeo -a** *adj* flamelike
**flamero** *m* torch holder, torch stand
**flamígero -ra** *adj* (poet.) flaming, flamelike; (arch.) flamboyant
**flámula** *f* streamer; (bot.) banewort
**flan** *m* custard, soufflé; blank (*from which to stamp coin*)

**flanco** *m* flank, side; (fort., mach., mil. & nav.) flank; (aut.) sidewall (*of tire*); **coger por el flanco** (coll.) to catch off guard; **conocerle** or **saberle a uno el flanco** to know someone's weak side
**Flandes** *f* Flanders
**flanear** *vn* to loaf, loaf around
**flanqueador -dora** *adj* flanking; *mf* flanker; *m* (mil.) flanker
**flanqueamiento** *m* var. of **flanqueo**
**flanquear** *va* to flank
**flanqueo** *m* flanking
**flaquear** *vn* to weaken, to flag, to give way; to become faint; to lose heart
**flaqueza** *f* thinness, skinniness; weakness, lack of strength; weakness, failing
**flato** *m* flatus, gas; (Am.) gloominess, melancholy
**flatoso -sa** *adj* flatulent, windy; (Am.) gloomy, melancholy
**flatulencia** *f* flatulence
**flatulento -ta** *adj* flatulent
**flatuosidad** *f* flatulence, windiness
**flatuoso -sa** *adj* var. of **flatoso**
**flauta** *f* (mus.) flute; **flauta del dios Pan** or **flauta de Pan** (mus.) Panpipe, Pan's pipes; *m* flautist, flutist
**flautado -da** *adj* flutelike; *m* (mus.) flute (*organ stop*)
**flauteado -da** *adj* flutelike, sweet
**flautear** *vn* to flute, play a flute
**flautero -ra** *mf* flute maker
**flautillo** *m* (mus.) shawm
**flautín** *m* (mus.) piccolo
**flautista** *mf* flautist, flutist
**flavo -va** *adj* fallow
**flébil** *adj* (poet.) sad, tearful, plaintive
**flebitis** *f* (path.) phlebitis
**flebosclerosis** *f* (path.) phlebosclerosis
**flebotomía** *f* phlebotomy, bloodletting
**flebotomiano** *m* phlebotomist
**fleco** *m* fringe; ragged edge; bangs; **flecos** *mpl* gossamer
**flecha** *f* arrow; sag, dip (*of cable*); (aer.) sweepback; (fort.) flèche; (mach.) shaft; **la flecha del parto** Parthian shot; **flecha de mar** (zool.) squid
**flechador** *m* archer, bowman
**flechadura** *f* (naut.) ratlines
**flechar** *va* to draw or stretch (*the bow*); to wound with an arrow; to kill with an arrow; (coll.) to infatuate; *vn* to be bent or stretched (*said of a bow in position to shoot an arrow*)
**flechaste** *m* (naut.) ratline
**flechazo** *m* arrow shot; arrow wound; (coll.) sudden passion, love at first sight
**flechería** *f* stock of arrows; shower of arrows
**flechero -ra** *adj* lovable, winsome; (Am.) tenacious, persevering; *mf* archer; arrow maker; *m* bowman; quiver
**flegmonoso -sa** *adj* var. of **flemonoso**
**fleje** *m* iron hoop or strap
**flema** *f* (physiol. & fig.) phlegm; **gastar flema** to be phlegmatic; to be slow to anger
**flemático -ca** *adj* phlegmatic or phlegmatical
**fleme** *m* veterinarian's fleam
**flemón** *m* (path.) phlegmon; (path.) gumboil
**flemonoso -sa** *adj* phlegmonous
**flemoso -sa** *adj* phlegmy
**flemudo -da** *adj* phlegmatic, lazy
**fleo** *m* (bot.) timothy
**flequillo** *m* bangs
**Flesinga** *f* Flushing
**fletador** *m* (naut.) charterer
**fletamento** *m* (naut.) chartering; (naut.) charter party
**fletante** *mf* shipowner
**fletar** *va* (naut.) to charter (*a ship*); (naut.) to load (*e.g., cattle*); (Am.) to hire (*a horse, carriage, etc.*); *vr* (Am.) to beat it, get out
**fletcherismo** *m* Fletcherism
**flete** *m* (naut.) freight, cargo; (naut.) freightage; (Am.) freight (*carried on land*); **falso flete** (naut.) dead freight
**flexibilidad** *f* flexibility
**flexible** *adj* flexible; soft (*hat*); *m* (elec.) cord, flexible cord; soft hat
**flexión** *f* flection; (gram.) flection, inflection
**flexional** *adj* (gram.) flectional, inflectional
**flexo** *m* gooseneck (*of a lamp*)
**flexor -xora** *adj* bending, flexing; *m* (anat.) flexor
**flexuoso -sa** *adj* flexuous
**flictena** *f* (path.) phlyctena, bulla
**flinflanear** *vn* to tinkle
**flinflaneo** *m* tinkling
**flirt** *m* flirting
**flirtación** *f* flirtation
**flirteador -dora** *adj* flirtatious; *mf* flirt (*person*)
**flirtear** *vn* to flirt
**flirteo** *m* flirting, flirtation
**flocadura** *f* fringe trimming
**floculento -ta** *adj* (chem.) flocculent
**floema** *m* (bot.) phloem
**flogístico -ca** *adj* (path. & old chem.) phlogistic
**flogisto** *m* (old chem.) phlogiston
**flogopita** *f* (mineral.) phlogopite
**flojear** *vn* to slacken, ease up, idle; to weaken
**flojedad** *f* looseness, slackness; limpness; laxity, laziness; weakness
**flojel** *m* nap (*of cloth*); down, soft feathers
**flojera** *f* (coll.) var. of **flojedad**
**flojo -ja** *adj* loose, slack; limp; lax, lazy, dilatory, languid; weak; light (*wind*); sagging, unsupported (*prices*); thin, poor (*writing*); (Am.) fearful, timid; **flojo de muelles** (coll.) incontinent (*unable to restrain natural evacuation*)
**floqueado -da** *adj* trimmed with fringe
**flor** *f* flower; blossom; flowers of wine; grain (*of leather*); (chem.) flowers; (fig.) bouquet, compliment; (fig.) flower (*choicest part*); **a flor de** at or near the surface of; even with; **a flor de agua** at water level; **andarse a la flor del berro** (coll.) to lead a life of pleasure; **dar en la flor** to get the knack; **decir flores a** to say pretty things to, to flirt with; **de mi flor** (coll.) excellent, magnificent; **echar flores a** to say pretty things to, to flirt with; **en flor** in flower, in blossom; **la flor de la canela** (coll.) the tops; **la flor y nata de** the flower of, the cream of; **flor de amor** (bot.) amaranth; **flor de antimonio** (chem.) flowers of antimony; **flor de azufre** (chem.) flowers of sulphur; **flor de calentura** (bot.) milkweed; **flor de embudo** (bot.) calla; **flor de harina** flour; **flor de la cera** (bot.) wax plant (*Hoya carnosa*); **flor de la edad** flower of life, bloom of youth; **flor de la maravilla** (bot.) tigerflower; (coll.) delicate convalescent; **flor de la oreja** sacred ear or sacred earflower; **flor de la Pascua** (bot.) poinsettia; **flor de la Trinidad** (bot.) pansy; **flor de la vida** flower of life, prime of life; (bot.) cotton rose; **flor de lazo** (bot.) tiger lily; **flor del campo** wild flower; **flor de lis** fleur-de-lis (*royal coat of arms of France*); (her.) fleur-de-lis; (bot.) jacobean lily; **flor de lis florenzada** (f.a.) fleur-de-lis; **flor del sol** (bot.) sunflower; **flor de mano** paper flower, artificial flower; **flor de príncipe** (bot.) red periwinkle; **flor de un día** (bot.) tigerflower; **flor de una hora** (bot.) flower of an hour; **flores cordiales** sudorific flowers; **flores de cantueso** (coll.) triviality
**flora** *f* flora; (*cap.*) *f* (myth.) Flora
**floración** *f* flowering, florescence
**florado -da** *adj* flowered; *f* (dial.) blossom time (*for beekeepers*)
**floral** *adj* floral
**florar** *vn* to flower, blossom, bloom
**florcita** *f* (Am.) little flower; **andar de florcita** (Am.) to stroll around with a flower in one's buttonhole, to loaf around
**flordelisado -da** *adj* (her.) fleury
**floreado -da** *adj* flowered; floury
**florear** *va* to flower, to decorate with flowers; to embellish with florid language; to stack (*cards*); to bolt (*flour*); to sort out; *vn* to quiver (*said of the tip of a sword*); to twang away (*on a guitar*); (coll.) to throw bouquets, to pay compliments
**florecer** **§34** *vn* to flower, blossom, bloom; to flourish; *vr* to become moldy
**florecido -da** *adj* moldy; blooming
**floreciente** *adj* florescent, inflorescent, flowering; flourishing
**florecimiento** *m* flowering, blossoming, blooming; continued prosperity

**Florencia** *f* Florence (*Italian city; feminine given name*)
**florentino -na** *adj & mf* Florentine
**florentísimo -ma** *adj super* very or most flourishing
**floreo** *m* idle talk; bright remark; quivering (*of tip of sword*); steady twanging (*of a guitar*); (mus.) flourish; **andarse con floreos** (coll.) to beat about the bush
**florería** *f* (Am.) florist's shop
**florero -ra** *adj* flattering, jesting; *mf* flatterer, jester; florist; *m* vase; flowerpot; potted flower; flower stand, jardiniere; (f.a.) flower piece; *f* flower girl
**florescencia** *f* (bot.) florescence, inflorescence
**floresta** *f* woods, grove; rural scene, rural setting; anthology
**florestero** *m* forest guard or warden
**floreta** *f* border or reinforcement on the edge of a girth
**floretazo** *m* stroke with a foil
**florete** *adj* first-class, superfine; *m* foil, fencing foil; medium-grade cotton fabric
**floretear** *va* to flower, to decorate with flowers; *vn* to fence
**floretista** *m* fencer
**floricina** *f* (chem.) phlorizin
**floricultor -tora** *mf* floriculturist, florist
**floricultura** *f* floriculture
**Florida, la** see **florido**
**floridano -na** *adj & mf* Floridan or Floridian
**floridez** *f* wealth of flowers, abundance of flowers; floweriness (*e.g., of style*)
**florido -da** *adj* flowery, florid, full of flowers; choice, select; (lit.) flowery, florid; **la Florida** Florida
**florífero -ra** *adj* floriferous
**florilegio** *m* anthology
**florín** *m* florin (*coin*)
**floripondio** *m* (bot.) floripondio; splotchy floral adornment; (lit.) floweriness, flowery style or language
**florista** *mf* florist; maker or seller of artificial flowers
**floristería** *f* flower shop
**florón** *m* large flower; (arch. & f.a.) finial; (arch.) rosette; (print.) tailpiece, vignette
**floronado -da** *adj* (her.) fleury (*said of a cross*)
**flósculo** *m* (bot.) floscule, floret
**flosculoso -sa** *adj* flosculous
**flota** *f* (naut., nav. & aer.) fleet; (fig.) fleet (*of cars, trucks, etc.*); **flota de guerra** navy; **flota en naftalina** (naut.) moth-ball fleet
**flotabilidad** *f* floatability; buoyancy
**flotable** *adj* floatable; navigable for rafts and logs
**flotación** *f* flotation; buoyancy; (metal.) flotation
**flotador -dora** *adj* floating; *mf* floater; *m* float (*e.g., of fish line*); (aer., bot. & mach.) float
**flotadura** *f* floating, flotation
**flotaje** *m* log driving
**flotamiento** *m* floating, flotation; log driving
**flotante** *adj* floating; flowing (*e.g., beard*)
**flotar** *vn* to float; to wave (*said, e.g., of a flag*)
**flote** *m* floating; **a flote** afloat; (fig.) on one's feet; **poner a flote** to float; **ponerse a flote** to get out of a jam
**flotilla** *f* flotilla
**flox** *m* (bot.) phlox
**fluctuación** *f* fluctuation; wavering, hesitation; (biol. & med.) fluctuation
**fluctuante** *adj* fluctuant
**fluctuar §33** *vn* to fluctuate; to bob up and down; to wave; to waver; to be in danger
**fluctuoso -sa** *adj* fluctuating, wavering
**fluencia** *f* flowing, running; source, spring; fluency; (elec.) creepage
**fluente** *adj* fluid, flowing; bleeding (*hemorrhoids*)
**fluidez** *f* fluidity; fluency (*of language or style*)
**flúido -da** *adj* fluid; fluent (*language, style*); *m* fluid
**fluir §41** *vn* to flow
**flujo** *m* flow, discharge, flux; looseness (*of bowels*); (chem., metal., phys. & path.) flux; (naut.) flow, rising tide; **flujo blanco** (path.) whites; **flujo de reír** constant laughing; **flujo de risa** fit of noisy laughter; **flujo de vientre** loose bowels; **flujo magnético** magnetic flux; **flujo y reflujo** ebb and flow
**flujómetro** *m* (phys.) fluxmeter
**fluminense** *adj* (pertaining to) Rio de Janeiro; *mf* native or inhabitant of Rio de Janeiro
**flúor** *m* (chem.) fluorin or fluorine; (chem.) flux
**fluoresceína** *f* (chem.) fluorescein
**fluorescencia** *f* fluorescence
**fluorescente** *adj* fluorescent
**fluorhídrico -ca** *adj* (chem.) hydrofluoric
**fluórico -ca** *adj* fluoric
**fluorina** or **fluorita** *f* (mineral.) fluorite, fluor, fluor spar
**fluorización** *f* fluoridation (*of drinking water*); (geol.) fluoridation
**fluorizar §76** *va* to fluoridate
**fluoroscopia** *f* fluoroscopy
**fluoroscópico -ca** *adj* fluoroscopic
**fluoroscopio** *m* fluoroscope
**fluoruro** *m* (chem.) fluoride
**fluvial** *adj* fluvial
**flux** *m* flush (*e.g., in poker*); (Am.) suit of clothes; **estar a flux** (Am.) to be penniless; **hacer flux** (coll.) to blow in everything without settling accounts; **tener flux** (Am.) to be lucky; **flux real** royal flush
**fluxión** *f* (math. & path.) fluxion; (path.) congestion; (path.) cold in the head; **fluxión de muelas** (path.) swollen cheek, abscessed tooth; **fluxión de pecho** (path.) inflammation of the lungs, pneumonia
**fluyente** *adj* fluid, flowing; fleeting
**f.º** abr. of **folio**
**fo** *interj* pew!
**fobia** *f* phobia
**foca** *f* (zool.) seal; **foca de trompa** (zool.) sea elephant; **foca fraile** (zool.) monk seal
**focal** *adj* focal
**focalización** *f* focalization
**focense** *adj & mf* Phocian
**Fócida, la** Phocis
**focino** *m* goad used to drive an elephant
**foco** *m* (math., med., phys., opt., seismol. & fig.) focus; center (*e.g., of vice*); core (*of an abscess*); source of light; (coll.) electric light, electric-light bulb; **fuera de foco** out of focus
**fóculo** *m* small hearth
**focha** *f* (orn.) European coot
**fodolí** *adj* (*pl:* **-líes**) meddlesome
**foena** *f* fish spear
**fofo -fa** *adj* fluffy, soft, spongy
**fofoque** *m* (naut.) middle jib
**fogaje** *m* fumage, hearth money (*tax*); (Am.) blush, flush; (Am.) fire, blaze
**fogarada** *f* blaze, fire, bonfire; (dial.) rash, eruption
**fogaril** *m* cresset
**fogarizar §76** *va* to start fires or bonfires in
**fogata** *f* blaze, bonfire; (mil.) mine, fougasse
**fogón** *m* firebox; cooking stove; (arti.) vent; (naut.) cookhouse; (Am.) gathering of soldiers and civilians around a fire; **fogón eléctrico** electric burner
**fogonadura** *f* (naut.) mast hole
**fogonazo** *m* powder flash
**fogonero** or **fogonista** *m* fireman (*of furnace, boiler, locomotive, etc.*)
**fogosidad** *f* fire, dash, spirit
**fogoso -sa** *adj* fiery, impetuous, spirited, vehement
**foguear** *va* to scale (*a gun*); to accustom to the smell of gunpowder; to inure; (coll.) to look daggers at
**fogueo** *m* target practice
**foguezuelo** *m* little fire
**foja** *f* (orn.) European coot; (law) leaf, sheet
**fol.** abr. of **folio**
**folgo** *m* foot-warming bag
**folía** *f* light music, popular music
**foliáceo -a** *adj* foliaceous
**foliación** *f* foliation (*of the leaves of a book*); (bot. & geol.) foliation
**foliado -da** *adj* (bot.) foliate
**foliar** *adj* foliar; *va* to foliate, to folio (*the leaves of a book*)
**foliatura** *f* foliature; foliation
**folicular** *adj* follicular
**folicularío** *m* (coll.) pamphleteer, news writer
**foliculina** *f* (biochem.) folliculin

**folículo** *m* (anat. & bot.) follicle
**folio** *m* folio (*leaf of a book*); (bookkeeping) folio; (print.) running head; **al primer folio** right off the bat; **de a folio** (coll.) enormous, tremendous; **en folio** in folio; **folio atlántico** atlas folio
**folíolo** *m* (bot.) foliole
**folklore** *m* folklore
**folklórico -ca** *adj* folkloric, (pertaining to) folklore
**folklorista** *mf* folklorist
**folla** *f* mixture, hodgepodge; (theat.) medley
**follada** *f* puff-paste pie
**follaje** *m* foliage; gaudy ornament; fustian; (arch.) foliage
**follajería** *f* (arch. & f.a.) foliation
**follar** *va* to foliate (*to shape like a leaf*); **§77** *va* to blow with bellows; *vr* to break wind without making a noise
**follero** or **folletero** *m* bellows maker or dealer
**folletín** *m* newspaper serial (*usually printed at bottom of page*)
**folletinesco -ca** *adj* serial; serial-like; exciting, intriguing
**folletinista** *mf* serial writer
**folletista** *mf* pamphleteer
**folleto** *m* pamphlet, brochure, tract, booklet
**folletón** *m* var. of **folletín**
**follón -llona** *adj* lazy, careless, indolent; arrogant, blustering, cowardly, worthless; *mf* lazy loafer; good-for-nothing; *m* noiseless rocket
**fomentación** *f* (med.) fomentation
**fomentador -dora** *adj* fomenting; promoting; *mf* fomenter; promoter
**fomentar** *va* to foment (*e.g., hatred*); to promote, encourage, foster; to warm; to enliven; (med.) to foment
**fomento** *m* fomentation; promotion, encouragement, fostering; improvement, development; warmth; (med.) fomentation
**fon** *m* (phonet.) phone
**fonda** *f* inn, restaurant
**fondable** *adj* (naut.) fit for anchoring
**fondado -da** *adj* reinforced in the heads (*said of a barrel*); (Am.) heeled, well-heeled
**fondeadero** *m* (naut.) anchorage (*place*)
**fondeado -da** *adj* (Am.) heeled, well-heeled
**fondear** *va* (naut.) to sound; to search (*a ship*); to scrutinize, examine closely; *vn* (naut.) to cast anchor; *vr* (Am.) to save up for a rainy day
**fondeo** *m* (naut.) search; (naut.) anchorage, casting anchor
**fondero -ra** *mf* (Am.) innkeeper
**fondillón** *m* dregs of a refilled cask; old Alicante wine
**fondillos** *mpl* seat (*of trousers*)
**fondista** *mf* innkeeper, restaurant keeper
**fondo** *m* bottom; back, rear; background; ground (*of a piece of cloth*); head (*of a barrel, boiler, etc.*); depth (*e.g., of a house*); fund; (anat.) fundus; (sport) distance, endurance; (fig.) bottom (*essence*); (fig.) fund, reservoir (*great amount*); **fondos** *mpl* funds (*money*); **a fondo** thoroughly; **a fondo perdido** without expecting to get the money back; **bajos fondos sociales** scum of the earth; underworld; **colar a fondo** (naut.) to sink; **dar fondo** (naut.) to cast anchor; **doble fondo** (naut.) double bottom; **echar a fondo** (naut.) to sink; **en el fondo** at bottom; **entrar en el fondo de** to get to the bottom of; **estar en fondos** to have funds available; **irse a fondo** (naut.) to founder; to fail (*said of a business venture*); **tener buen fondo** to be good-natured; **tener mal fondo** to be ill-natured; **fondo de amortización** sinking fund; **fondo falso** false bottom; **fondo rotativo** revolving fund; **fondo vitalicio** life annuity
**fondón -dona** *adj* (coll.) flabby, pursy
**fonducho** *m* cheap eating house
**fonema** *m* (phonet.) phoneme
**fonémico -ca** *adj* phonemic; *f* phonemics
**fonético -ca** *adj* phonetic; *f* phonetics
**fonetista** *mf* phonetician
**fónico -ca** *adj* phonic; *f* phonics
**fonil** *m* (naut.) large wooden funnel
**fonje** *adj* soft, fluffy
**fono** *m* earphone; phone
**fonocaptor** *m* (elec.) pickup
**fonografía** *f* phonography
**fonográfico -ca** *adj* phonographic
**fonógrafo** *m* phonograph
**fonograma** *m* phonogram
**fonolita** *f* (mineral.) phonolite
**fonología** *f* phonology
**fonológico -ca** *adj* phonologic or phonological
**fonólogo -ga** *mf* phonologist
**fonoscopio** *m* phonoscope
**fontal** *adj* fontal
**fontana** *f* (dial. & poet.) fountain
**fontanal** *adj* fontal; *m* spring; place abounding in springs
**fontanar** *m* spring
**fontanela** *f* (anat.) fontanel
**fontanería** *f* pipelaying; plumbing; water supply system, water department
**fontanero -ra** *adj* (pertaining to a) fountain; *m* pipelayer; plumber and electrician
**fontículo** *m* (med.) var. of **exutorio**
**foque** *m* (naut.) jib; (coll.) piccadilly (*collar*)
**foquillo** *m* flashlight bulb
**foquito** *m* flashlight bulb; dial light
**forajido -da** *adj* fugitive; *mf* fugitive, outlaw; bandit, malefactor
**foral** *adj* statutory
**foramen** *m* foramen; hole in nether millstone; (anat. & bot.) foramen
**foraminíferos** *mpl* (zool.) foraminifera
**foráneo -a** *adj* strange, foreign; *mf* stranger, outsider
**forastero -ra** *adj* outside, strange; *mf* outsider, stranger
**forbante** *m* pirate, freebooter
**forcejar** or **forcejear** *vn* to struggle; to contend
**forcejeo** or **forcejo** *m* struggle, struggling; resistance, opposition
**forcejón** *m* violent effort, violent tug
**forcejudo -da** *adj* husky, robust
**fórceps** *m* (*pl:* **-ceps**) (obstet. & zool.) forceps
**forcipresión** *f* or **forcipresura** *f* (surg.) forcipressure
**forense** *adj* forensic, legal
**forero -ra** *adj* statutory; *m* leaseholder
**forestal** *adj* (pertaining to a) forest
**forestería** *f* (Am.) forestry
**forillo** *m* (theat.) small back cloth (*seen through opening in backdrop*)
**forja** *f* forge; forging; concocting; ironworks, foundry; silversmith's forge; mortar; **forja a la catalana** Catalan forge or furnace
**forjador -dora** *adj* forging; *mf* forger; maker; smith, blacksmith
**forjadura** *f* forging
**forjar** *va* to forge; to build (*with stone and mortar*); (fig.) to forge (*e.g., lies*); **forjar a martinete** to drop-forge; *vr* to think up, to dream up
**forma** *f* form; shape; way; format; **de esta forma** in this way, in this wise; **de forma** of distinction; **de forma que** so that, with the result that; **en debida forma** in due form; **en forma** in form; (sport) in form
**formación** *f* formation; training; bullion, twisted fringe; (elec., geol. & mil.) formation; **formación de palabras** word formation; **formación en masa** (mil.) mass formation
**formador -dora** or **-triz** (*pl:* **-trices**) *adj* forming; *mf* former
**formaje** *m* cheese mold or vat
**formal** *adj* formal; serious (*matter*); sedate, settled; reliable; express, definite
**formaldehido** *m* (chem.) formaldehyde
**formalidad** *f* formality; seriousness; reliability
**formalina** *f* (chem.) formalin
**formalismo** *m* formalism; red tape
**formalista** *adj* formalistic; *mf* formalist
**formalizar** **§76** *va* to formalize; to formulate; to put in final form; to legalize; *vr* to become serious; to take offense
**formar** *va* to form; to train, educate; (elec.) to form (*plates of storage battery*); *vn* to form; to form a line; to embroider with chenille; *vr* to form; to form a line, stand in line, fall in; to take form; to grow, develop
**formativo -va** *adj* formative
**formato** *m* format

**formatriz** *adj fem* see **formador**
**formejar** *va* (naut.) to tie up (*a ship*); (naut.) to clear the decks of (*a ship*)
**formero** *m* (arch.) formeret, wall rib
**formiato** *m* (chem.) formate
**fórmico -ca** *adj* formic
**formidable** *adj* formidable; terrific
**formidoloso -sa** *adj* timorous; frightful, horrible
**formillón** *m* hat block
**formol** *m* (chem.) formol
**formón** *m* chisel; punch
**fórmula** *f* formula; prescription; recipe; **por fórmula** as a matter of form
**formulación** *f* formulation
**formulador -dora** *mf* formulator
**formular** *adj* formulary; *va* to formulate
**formulario -ria** *adj* formulary; formal; *m* formulary; form; (pharm.) formulary; **formulario de pedido** order blank
**fornicación** *f* fornication
**fornicador -dora** *adj* fornicating; *mf* fornicator
**fornicar §86** *vn* to fornicate
**fornicario -ria** *adj* fornicating; *mf* fornicator
**fornicio** *m* fornication
**fornido -da** *adj* robust, husky
**fornitura** *f* (print.) type melted down to complete a font; **fornituras** *fpl* (mil.) cartridge belt
**foro** *m* (hist. & law) forum; (law) emphyteusis; bar (*legal profession*); back, rear (*of stage*); **por tal foro** on such condition
**forragatear** *va* (coll.) to scribble, to scribble all over
**forraje** *m* forage; (coll.) hodgepodge
**forrajeador -dora** *adj* foraging; *m* forager
**forrajear** *va & vn* to forage
**forrajero -ra** *adj* forage; *f* forage rope; aiglet, lanyard; shoulder braid
**forrar** *va* to line; to cover (*book, umbrella, etc.*); (paint.) to stretch (*a canvas*); *vr* (Am.) to stuff oneself
**forro** *m* lining; cover; (her.) fur; (naut.) planking, sheathing; **no conocer ni por el forro** (coll.) to not know in the slightest; **no haber visto ni por el forro** (coll.) to have seen neither hide nor hair of; **ni por el forro** (coll.) not by a long shot; **forro de freno** (aut.) brake lining
**forsitia** *f* (bot.) forsythia
**fortachón -chona** *adj* (coll.) burly, husky, tough
**fortalecedor -dora** *adj* fortifying, strengthening
**fortalecer §34** *va* to fortify, to strengthen
**fortalecimiento** *m* fortification, strengthening; fortifications; tonic, fortifier
**fortaleza** *f* fortitude; strength, vigor; firmness; fortress, stronghold; **fortaleza volante** (aer.) flying fortress
**forte** *interj* (naut.) avast!
**fortepiano** *m* (mus.) pianoforte
**fortificación** *f* fortification
**fortificador -dora** *adj* fortifying
**fortificante** *adj* fortifying; *m* fortifier, tonic
**fortificar §86** *va & vn* to fortify
**fortín** *m* small fort; bunker
**fortísimo -ma** *adj super* very or most strong
**fortuitez** *f* fortuity
**fortuito -ta** *adj* fortuitous
**fortuna** *f* fortune; storm, tempest; **de fortuna** makeshift; **por fortuna** fortunately
**fortunón** *m* (coll.) windfall, great piece of luck
**forúnculo** *m* var. of **furúnculo**
**forzado -da** *adj* forced; forcible (*e.g., entry*); (fig.) forced (*e.g., smile*); hard (*labor*); *m* galley slave, convict
**forzador** *m* forcer; ravisher, violator
**forzal** *m* back (*of a comb*)
**forzamiento** *m* forcing
**forzar §52** *va* to force; (agr.) to force; **forzar a** + *inf* or **forzar a que** + *subj* to force to + *inf*
**forzosamente** *adv* necessarily; violently, by force
**forzoso -sa** *adj* inescapable, unavoidable; strong, husky, robust; hard (*labor*); forced (*e.g., landing, march*); *f* (coll.) squeeze (*pressure to do something*); **hacer la forzosa a** (coll.) to put the squeeze on
**forzudo -da** *adj* strong, husky, robust
**fosa** *f* grave; (anat.) fossa; (aut.) pit; **fosa de los leones** (Bib.) lions' den; **fosa séptica** septic tank
**fosal** *m* cemetery; (prov.) grave
**fosar** *va* to dig a ditch around; to moat
**fosco -ca** *adj* cross, sullen; dark; (naut.) threatening; *f* haze; (dial.) thicket, jungle
**fosfatar** *va* to phosphatize
**fosfático -ca** *adj* phosphatic
**fosfato** *m* (chem. & agr.) phosphate; **fosfato cálcico** (chem.) calcium phosphate
**fosfaturia** *f* (path.) phosphaturia
**fosfeno** *m* (physiol.) phosfene
**fosfina** *f* (chem.) phosphine
**fosfito** *m* (chem.) phosphite
**fosfonio** *m* (chem.) phosphonium
**fosforar** *va* to phosphorate
**fosforecer §34** *vn* to phosphoresce
**fosforero -ra** *mf* match vendor; *m* matchbox holder; *f* matchbox
**fosforescencia** *f* phosphorescence
**fosforescente** *adj* phosphorescent
**fosfórico -ca** *adj* (chem.) phosphoric
**fosforita** *f* (mineral.) phosphorite
**fósforo** *m* (chem.) phosphorus; match; (coll.) brilliance, talent; (*cap.*) *m* (poet.) Phosphor (*morning star*); **fósforo de seguridad** safety match
**fosforoscopio** *m* phosphoroscope
**fosforoso -sa** *adj* (chem.) phosphorous
**fosfurado -da** *adj* (chem.) phosphureted
**fosfuro** *m* (chem.) phosphide
**fosgeno** *m* (chem.) phosgene
**fósil** *adj & m* fossil; (fig.) fossil
**fosilífero -ra** *adj* fossiliferous
**fosilización** *f* fossilization
**fosilizar §76** *vr* to fossilize
**foso** *m* fosse, pit, hole; (fort.) fosse, moat; (theat.) pit
**fótico -ca** *adj* photic
**fotingo** *m* (coll.) jalopy, low-price car
**fotio** *m* (phys.) phot
**foto** *f* photo
**fotoactínico -ca** *adj* photoactinic
**fotocalco** *m* photoprint
**fotocelda** or **fotocélula** *f* (elec.) photocell
**fotocincografía** *f* photozincography
**fotocinesis** *f* (physiol.) photokinesis
**fotocinético -ca** *adj* photokinetic
**fotoconductividad** *f* (elec.) photoconductivity
**fotocopia** *f* photocopy
**fotocromía** *f* photochromy, color photography
**fotocromo** *m* photochrome
**fotodesintegración** *f* (phys.) photodisintegration
**fotodinámico -ca** *adj* photodynamic; *f* photodynamics
**fotodrama** *m* photoplay
**fotoeléctrico -ca** *adj* photoelectric
**fotoelectrón** *m* (physical chem.) photoelectron
**fotoesfera** *f* var. of **fotosfera**
**fotofija** *m* (sport) photo-finish camera
**fotofobia** *f* (path.) photophobia
**fotogénico -ca** *adj* (biol. & phot.) photogenic
**fotógeno -na** *adj* (biol.) photogenic; *m* (chem.) photogen
**fotograbado** *m* photoengraving
**fotograbador -dora** *mf* photoengraver
**fotograbar** *va* to photoengrave
**fotografía** *f* photograph (*picture*); photography (*art or process*); photograph gallery; **fotografía al magnesio** flashlight photograph; **fotografía en colores** color photography; **fotografía en relieve** photorelief
**fotografiar §90** *va* to photograph; to depict in photographic detail; *vn* to photograph
**fotográfico -ca** *adj* photographic
**fotógrafo -fa** *mf* photographer
**fotogrametría** *f* photogrammetry
**fotogramétrico -ca** *adj* photogrammetric or photogrammetrical
**fotolaboratorio** *m* photographic laboratory
**fotólisis** *f* photolysis
**fotolitografía** *f* photolithography; photolithograph
**fotolitografiar §90** *va* to photolithograph

**fotomecánico -ca** *adj* photomechanical
**fotometría** *f* photometry
**fotómetro** *m* photometer; light meter
**fotomicrografía** *f* photomicrography
**fotomontaje** *m* photomontage
**fotón** *m* (phys.) photon
**fotoperiodismo** *m* photojournalism
**fotopila** *f* (elec.) photovoltaic cell
**fotoquímico -ca** *adj* photochemical; *f* photochemistry
**fotorreconocimiento** *m* photoreconnaissance
**fotorrelieve** *m* photorelief
**fotosensible** or **fotosensitivo -va** *adj* photosensitive
**fotosfera** *f* (astr.) photosphere
**fotosíntesis** *f* (bot. & chem.) photosynthesis
**fotospectroscopio** *m* photospectroscope
**fotostatar** *va & vn* to photostat
**fotostático -ca** *adj* photostatic
**fotóstato** *m* photostat
**fototactismo** *m* or **fototaxis** *f* (biol.) phototaxis
**fototelegrafía** *f* phototelegraphy
**fototelegrafiar** §90 *va & vn* to phototelegraph
**fototelégrafo** *m* phototelegraph
**fototerapia** *f* phototherapeutics or phototherapy
**fototipia** *f* phototypy
**fototipo** *m* phototype
**fototipografía** *f* phototypography
**fototropismo** *m* (biol.) phototropism
**fototubo** *m* (elec.) phototube
**fotovoltaico -ca** *adj* photovoltaic
**fóvea** *f* fovea; (bot.) fovea; **fóvea central** (anat.) fovea centralis, central depression (*of retina*)
**Fr.** abr. of **Fray**
**fra.** abr. of **factura**
**frac** *m* (*pl:* **fraques**) swallow-tailed coat, full-dress coat, tails
**fracasar** *vn* to fail; to break to pieces
**fracaso** *m* failure; collapse, crash
**fracción** *f* fraction; faction, party; (math.) fraction; **fracción compleja** (math.) complex fraction; **fracción compuesta** (math.) compound fraction; **fracción continua** (math.) continued fraction; **fracción decimal** (math.) decimal fraction; **fracción impropia** (math.) improper fraction; **fracción periódica** (math.) periodic fraction; **fracción propia** (math.) proper fraction
**fraccionado -da** *adj* fractional
**fraccionador -dora** *adj* fractionating
**fraccionamiento** *m* breaking up, dismemberment; fractionization; (chem.) fractionation
**fraccionar** *va* to break up; to fractionize; (chem.) to fractionate
**fraccionario -ria** *adj* fractionary; fractional; fractional (*currency*)
**fractura** *f* fracture; breaking in, housebreaking; (geol. & surg.) fracture; **fractura complicada** (surg.) compound fracture; **fractura conminuta** (surg.) comminution, comminuted fracture
**fracturar** *va & vr* to fracture; to break open
**fraga** *f* (bot.) raspberry; thicket of brambles
**fragancia** *f* fragrance; good name
**fragante** *adj* fragrant; occurring; **en fragante** in the act
**fragaria** *f* (bot.) strawberry (*plant and fruit*)
**fragata** *f* (naut.) frigate; (orn.) frigate bird; **fragata ligera** (naut.) corvette
**frágil** *adj* fragile; frail; loose (*morally*); (Am.) poor, in want
**fragilidad** *f* fragility; frailty; looseness; lapse, moral lapse
**fragmentación** *f* fragmentation; (biol.) fragmentation
**fragmentar** *va* to break into fragments; *vr* to fragment
**fragmentario -ria** *adj* fragmentary
**fragmento** *m* fragment
**fragor** *m* crash, din, uproar
**fragoroso -sa** *adj* noisy, thundering
**fragosidad** *f* roughness, unevenness; thickness, denseness (*of a forest*); rough road; brambly path
**fragoso -sa** *adj* rough, uneven; brambly; noisy, thundering
**fragua** *f* forge; (fig.) hotbed; (fig.) fuel (*that feeds a passion*)
**fraguado** *m* setting, hardening
**fraguador -dora** *adj* scheming; *mf* schemer
**fraguar** §23 *va* to forge; (fig.) to forge (*e.g., lies*); (fig.) to hatch, brew, scheme; *vn* to set (*said, e.g., of cement*)
**fragura** *f* var. of **fragosidad**
**fraile** *m* friar; tuck (*at bottom of robe or skirt*); (print.) friar; (Am.) priest, cleric; (Am.) bagasse; **fraile de misa y olla** (coll.) friarling; **fraile negro** Black Friar (*Dominican*); **fraile rezador** (ent.) mantis, praying mantis
**frailear** *va* (dial.) to trim close to the trunk
**frailecillo** *m* little friar; (orn.) puffin
**frailengo -ga** or **fraileño -ña** *adj* (coll.) friary, monkish; priestlike
**frailería** *f* (coll.) friars
**frailero -ra** *adj* of a friar; (coll.) fond of priests, pious
**frailesco -ca** *adj* (coll.) var. of **frailengo**
**frailía** *f* priesthood
**frailillos** *mpl* (bot.) wake-robin
**frailuco** *m* (coll.) wretched little friar
**frailuno -na** *adj* (coll.) friarish; (Am.) priest-loving, clerical-minded
**frambesia** *f* (path.) yaws, frambesia
**frambuesa** *f* raspberry (*fruit*)
**frambueso** *m* (bot.) raspberry, raspberry bush
**frámea** *f* dart, javelin
**francachela** *f* (coll.) feast, spread; (coll.) carousal, high time; (Am.) excessive familiarity
**francachón -chona** *adj* (Am.) overfamiliar
**francalete** *m* strap with buckle
**francés -cesa** *adj* French; **a la francesa** in the French fashion or manner; **despedirse, irse** or **marcharse a la francesa** (coll.) to take French leave; *m* Frenchman; French (*language*); **el francés antiguo** Old French; **los franceses** the French (*people*); *f* Frenchwoman
**francesada** *f* typical French remark; French invasion of Spain in 1808
**francesilla** *f* French roll; (bot.) turban buttercup
**Francfort del Main** Frankfurt am Main
**Francfort del Oder** Frankfurt an der Oder
**Francia** *f* France
**franciano** *m* French (*dialect of Île de France*)
**francio** *m* (chem.) francium
**Francisca** *f* see **francisco**
**franciscano -na** *adj & mf* Franciscan
**francisco -ca** *adj & mf* Franciscan; (*cap.*) *m* Francis; *f* Frances
**francmasón** *m* Freemason
**francmasonería** *f* Freemasonry
**francmasónico -ca** *adj* Freemasonic
**Fran.co** abr. of **Francisco**
**franco -ca** *adj* frank; liberal, generous; free, open (*road*); gratis; loamy, rich (*soil*); Frankish; **franco a bordo** free on board; **franco de porte** postpaid; *mf* Frank; *m* franc; Frankish (*language*); tax-free days (*in a fair*)
**francoalemán -mana** *adj* Franco-German
**francobordo** *m* (naut.) freeboard
**francocanadiense** *adj* French-Canadian; *mf* French Canadian
**Franco Condado, el** Franche-Comté
**francófilo -la** *adj & mf* Francophile
**francófobo -ba** *adj & mf* Francophobe
**francolín** *m* (orn.) black partridge, francolin
**francoprovenzal** *adj & m* Franco-Provençal
**francote -ta** *adj* (coll.) frank, open-hearted, wholehearted
**francotirador** *m* franc-tireur; sniper
**Francho** *m* Frank
**franchote -ta** or **franchute -ta** *mf* (coll.) Frenchy
**franela** *f* flannel; **franela de algodón** cotton flannel
**frangente** *m* accident, mishap
**frangible** *adj* frangible
**frangir** §42 *va* to break up, to break to pieces
**frangollar** *va* (coll.) to bungle, dash off
**frangollo** *m* porridge, stew, mash; (coll.) mess, botch
**frangollón -llona** *adj* (Am.) bungling; *mf* (Am.) bungler
**frángula** *f* (bot.) alder buckthorn

**franja** *f* fringe; strip, band
**franjar** or **franjear** *va* to fringe
**franqueamiento** *m* var. of **franqueo**
**franquear** *va* to exempt; to grant; to enfranchise; to open, to clear (*the way*); to cross, get over; to free (*a slave*); to frank (*a letter*); *vr* to yield; to unbosom oneself; **franquearse a** or **con** to open one's heart to
**franqueo** *m* freeing, liberation; postage; franking (*of a letter*); **franqueo concertado** postal permit
**franqueza** *f* frankness; liberality, generosity; freedom
**franquía** *f* (naut.) sea room; **estar en franquía** (naut. & coll.) to be in the open; **ponerse en franquía** (naut. & coll.) to get in the open
**franquicia** *f* franchise; exemption, tax exemption; **franquicia postal** franking privilege
**franquista** *mf* supporter of General Franco
**fraque** *m* var. of **frac**
**frasca** *f* twigs, brushwood; (Am.) rumpus, excitement
**frasco** *m* bottle, flask; jar (*e.g., of olives*)
**frase** *f* phrase; sentence; idiom; **gastar frases** (coll.) to talk all around the subject, to talk without coming to the point; **frase compleja** (gram.) complex sentence; **frase hecha** saying, proverb; fixed or set expression, cliché; **frase musical** (mus.) phrase
**frasear** *va* to phrase; (mus.) to phrase; (coll.) to adorn with phrases; *vn* (coll.) to talk without saying anything
**fraseo** *m* phrasing; (mus.) phrasing
**fraseología** *f* phraseology; verbosity
**frasquera** *f* bottle carrier, bottle frame, cellaret
**frasqueta** *f* (print.) frisket
**fratás** *m* plastering trowel
**fratasar** *va* to smooth with plastering trowel
**fraterna** *f* see **fraterno**
**fraternal** *adj* fraternal, brotherly
**fraternar** *va* to reprimand sharply
**fraternidad** *f* fraternity, brotherhood
**fraternización** *f* fraternization
**fraternizar §76** *vn* to fraternize
**fraterno -na** *adj* fraternal, brotherly; *f* sharp reprimand
**fratría** *f* phratry
**fratricida** *adj* fratricidal; *mf* fratricide (*person*)
**fratricidio** *m* fratricide (*act*)
**fraude** *m* fraud
**fraudulencia** *f* fraudulence or fraudulency
**fraudulento -ta** *adj* fraudulent
**fray** *m* Fra
**frazada** *f* blanket
**freático -ca** *adj* phreatic
**frecuencia** *f* frequency; **alta frecuencia** high frequency; **baja frecuencia** low frequency; **con frecuencia** frequently; **frecuencia intermedia** (rad.) intermediate frequency; **frecuencia modulada** (rad.) frequency modulation; **frecuencia muy alta** (rad. & telv.) very high frequency; **frecuencia ultraalta** or **ultraelevada** (*rad.*) ultrahigh frequency
**frecuencímetro** *m* (elec.) frequency meter
**frecuentación** *f* frequentation
**frecuentador -dora** *mf* frequenter
**frecuentar** *va* to repeat, do over and over again; to frequent
**frecuentativo -va** *adj & m* (gram.) frequentative
**frecuente** *adj* frequent; common
**fregadero** *m* sink, kitchen sink
**fregado -da** *adj* (Am.) annoying, bothersome; (Am.) bold, daring; (Am.) stubborn; *m* rubbing; scrubbing; mopping; (coll.) mess; (coll.) rumpus, row
**fregador -dora** *mf* dishwasher; *m* sink; dishcloth; mop
**fregadura** *f* or **fregamiento** *m* rubbing; scrubbing; scouring; mopping; dishwashing
**fregar §29** *va* to rub; to scrub; to scour; to mop; to wash (*dishes*); (Am.) to annoy, bother; *vr* (Am.) to be bad off, be in a bad way
**fregatriz** *f* (*pl:* **-trices**) var. of **fregona**
**fregazón** *f* var. of **fregadura**
**fregona** *f* kitchenmaid, dishwasher
**fregonil** *adj* (coll.) (pertaining to a) kitchenmaid, dishwasher
**freidura** *f* frying
**freiduría** *f* fried-fish store
**freila** *f* nun of a military order; (archaic) lay sister
**freile** *m* knight of a military order; priest of a military order
**freimiento** *m* var. of **freidura**
**freír §73 & §17,** 9 *va* to fry; (coll.) to bore to death; *vn* to fry; **al freír será el reír** he laughs best who laughs last; **dejarle a uno freír en su aceite** (coll.) to let someone stew in his own juice; *vr* to fry; (coll.) to be bored to death; **freírsela a uno** (coll.) to scheme to deceive someone
**fréjol** *m* var. of **frijol**
**frémito** *m* roar
**frenada** *f* or **frenado** *m* braking
**frenaje** *m* braking; **frenaje de regeneración** (elec.) regenerative braking
**frenar** *va* to check, hold back, restrain; to brake
**frenazo** *m* sudden braking
**frenería** *f* bridle making; harness shop
**frenero** *m* bridle maker or dealer; (rail.) brakeman
**frenesí** *m* (*pl:* **-síes**) frenzy
**frenético -ca** *adj* phrenetic; fanatic; mad, frantic
**frénico -ca** *adj* phrenic; (anat.) phrenic
**frenillar** *va* var. of **afrenillar**
**frenillo** *m* (anat.) frenum; muzzle; (naut.) tarred rope; (naut.) bobstay; **no tener frenillo** or **no tener frenillo en la lengua** (coll.) to not mince one's words, to be too outspoken
**frenitis** *f* (path.) phrenitis
**freno** *m* bit; bridle; brake; (fig.) brake, curb, check, restraint; **hablar sin freno** to rave, to talk like a wild man; **morder el freno** to champ the bit; **tascar el freno** to champ the bit; (fig.) to bear with impatience; **freno de aire** air brake; **freno de cinta** band brake; **freno de cono** cone brake; **freno de contrapedal** coaster brake; **freno de estacionamiento** (aut.) parking brake; **freno de mano** hand brake; **freno de pedal** or **freno de pie** foot brake; **freno de puerta** door check; **freno hidráulico** hydraulic brake; **freno neumático** air brake
**frenología** *f* phrenology
**frenológico -ca** *adj* phrenological
**frenologista** *mf* or **frenólogo -ga** *mf* phrenologist
**frenopatía** *f* (path.) phrenopathy
**frental** *adj* frontal
**frente** *m & f* front (*e.g., of a building*); *m* obverse; (fort., mil. & pol.) front; (mil.) front rank, front line; *f* brow, forehead, face, head, front; **a frente** straight ahead; **al frente** in front; (com.) carried forward (*to opposite page*); **al frente de** in charge of; **arrugar la frente** to knit the brow, to frown; **con la frente levantada** (coll.) calmly; (coll.) brazenly; **de frente** forward; straight ahead; abreast; **del frente** (com.) carried forward (*from opposite page*); **en frente** in front, opposite; **en frente de** in front of, opposite; against, opposed to; **hacer frente a** to face; **llevar de frente** to carry forward, go right ahead with; **frente a** in front of; **frente a frente** face to face; **frente caliente** (meteor.) warm front; **frente de ondas** (phys.) wave front; **frente frío** (meteor.) cold front; **frente por frente de** right opposite
**frentón -tona** *adj* var. of **frontudo**
**freo** *m* channel, strait
**freón** *m* freon
**fres** *m* fringe
**fresa** *f* (bot.) strawberry (*plant and fruit*); ruff, fraise; countersinking bit; cutter (*of milling machine*); reamer; (dent.) burr
**fresado** *m* countersinking; milling; reaming
**fresadora** *f* milling machine
**fresal** *m* strawberry patch
**fresar** *va* to adorn or trim with friezes; to countersink, to mill, to ream
**fresca** *f* see **fresco**
**frescachón -chona** *adj* bouncing, buxom; (naut.) brisk (*wind*), moderate (*gale*)

**frescal** *adj* slightly salted; **frescales** *mf* (coll.) forward sort of person
**frescamente** *adv* recently, of late; offhand; brazenly
**frescar** **§86** *vn* (naut.) to blow up (*said of the wind*)
**fresco -ca** *adj* fresh; cool; buxom, ruddy; calm, unruffled; light (*cloth or clothing*); wet (*paint*); (naut.) strong (*breeze*); (coll.) fresh, cheeky ‖ *m* coolness, fresh air; fresh fish; fresh bacon; (f.a.) fresco (*art; picture*); (Am.) cool drink; **al fresco** in the night air; in the open air; (f.a.) in fresco; **dejar fresco** (coll.) to leave in the lurch; **estar fresco** (coll.) to be in a fine pinch; **hacer fresco** to be cool (*said of the weather*); **pintar al fresco** (f.a.) to fresco; **quedar fresco** (coll.) to be in a fine pinch; **quedarse tan fresco** (coll.) to show no offense, to be unconcerned; **tomar el fresco** to get some fresh air ‖ *f* fresh air; cool time of the day (*early morning or evening*); (coll.) blunt remark, piece of one's mind; **tomar la fresca** to get some fresh air; **salir con la fresca** to go out in the cool of the morning
**frescor** *m* freshness; cool, coolness; (paint.) flesh color
**frescote -ta** *adj* (coll.) buxom, plump and rosy
**frescura** *f* freshness; cool, coolness; greenness (*of a spot or region*); calmness, coolness; unconcern, offhand manner; sharp reply; (coll.) cheek
**fresero -ra** *mf* strawberry seller; *f* (bot.) strawberry (*plant*)
**fresnal** *adj* ash, ashen
**fresneda** *f* growth of ash trees
**fresnillo** *m* (bot.) fraxinella
**fresno** *m* (bot.) ash, ash tree; ash (*wood*)
**fresón** *m* Chilean strawberry (*fruit*); large strawberry
**fresquedal** *m* cool, damp, green spot
**fresquera** *f* see **fresquero**
**fresquería** *f* (Am.) ice-cream parlor
**fresquero -ra** *mf* fresh-fish peddler; *f* food cabinet, meat closet; icebox
**fresquilla** *f* flat-shaped peach
**fresquísimo -ma** *adj super* very or most fresh
**fresquista** *mf* frescoer
**freteado -da** *adj* (her.) fretted
**freudiano -na** *adj & mf* Freudian
**freudismo** *m* Freudianism
**frey** *m* Fra
**frez** *f* dung
**freza** *f* dung; spawning; spawning season; spawn, roe; feeding season of silkworms; hole dug by an animal
**frezada** *f* blanket
**frezar** **§76** *vn* to dung; to spawn; to feed (*said of silkworms*); to root or scratch
**friabilidad** *f* friability
**friable** *adj* friable
**frialdad** *f* coldness, frigidity; nonsense, stupidity; carelessness, laxity; (path.) impotence; (path.) frigidity (*abnormal sexual indifference*); (fig.) coldness, frigidity; (fig.) coolness
**friático -ca** *adj* chilly; awkward, stupid
**fricación** *f* rubbing; (phonet.) fricative sound
**fricandó** *m* fricandeau
**fricar** **§86** *va* to rub
**fricasé** *m* fricassee; **guisar a la fricasé** to fricassee
**fricativo -va** *adj & f* (phonet.) fricative
**fricción** *f* rub, rubbing; massage; (mech.) friction; (pharm.) rubbing liniment; (fig.) friction
**friccional** *adj* frictional
**friccionar** *va* to rub; to massage
**friega** *f* rubbing, massage; (Am.) annoyance, bother; (Am.) beating, whipping
**friera** *f* chilblain on the heel
**frígano** *m* (ent.) caddis fly
**Frigia** *f* see **frigio**
**frigidez** *f* frigidity; (path.) frigidity (*abnormal sexual indifference*)
**frígido -da** *adj* (poet.) cold, frigid
**frigio -gia** *adj & mf* Phrygian; (*cap.*) *f* Phrygia
**frigorífero** *m* freezing chamber
**frigorífico -ca** *adj* refrigerating; cold-storage; *m* refrigerator; (Am.) packing house, cold-storage plant
**frigorizar** **§76** *va* to freeze
**frijol** *m* or **fríjol** *m* (bot.) kidney bean; **frijol caballero** or **de Antibo** (bot.) hyacinth bean; **frijol de media luna** (bot.) Lima bean; **frijol de ojos negros** (bot.) black-eyed bean; **frijol iztagapa** (bot.) civet bean, Sieva bean
**frijolear** *va* (Am.) to bother, annoy
**frijolizar** **§76** *va* (Am.) to bewitch
**fringilago** *m* (orn.) great titmouse
**fringílido -da** *adj* (orn.) fringilloid; *m* (orn.) fringillid
**frío -a** *adj* cold, frigid; colorless, dull, weak; (fig.) cold, frigid; (fig.) cool; (fig.) cold (*remote from what one is looking for*); *m* cold, coldness; **fríos** *mpl* chills and fever; **no darle a una persona frío ni calentura** (coll.) to leave a person indifferent; **hacer frío** to be cold (*said of the weather*); **tener frío** to be cold (*said of a person*); **tomar frío** to catch cold
**friolento -ta** *adj* chilly
**friolero -ra** *adj* chilly; *f* trifle, trinket; snack, bite
**frisa** *f* frieze (*woolen cloth*); (fort.) fraise
**frisador -dora** *mf* friezer (*of cloth*)
**frisadura** *f* friezing (*of cloth*)
**frisar** *va* to frieze, to frizz (*cloth*); to rub; to pack, to line; to fit, to fasten; (naut.) to calk; *vn* to get along, to agree; to approach; **frisar con** or **en** to border on
**frisio -sia** *adj & mf* Frisian; *m* Frisian (*language*); (*cap.*) *f* Friesland
**friso** *m* (arch.) frieze; wainscot, dado
**frísol** *m* var. of **frijol**
**frisón -sona** *adj & mf* Frisian; *m* Frisian (*language*)
**frisuelo** *m* fritter; (bot.) kidney bean
**frita** *f* see **frito**
**fritada** *f* fry
**fritado** *m* fritting (*of materials for glass*)
**fritanga** *f* fry
**fritar** *va* to frit (*materials for glass*)
**fritilaria** *f* (bot. & ent.) fritillary
**frito -ta** *pp of* **freír**; *adj* fried; (coll.) bored to death, worried to death; *m* fry; *f* frit
**fritura** *f* var. of **fritada**
**frivolidad** *f* frivolity
**frivolité** *f* (sew.) tatting; **hacer frivolité** (sew.) to tat
**frívolo -la** *adj* frivolous
**friz** *f* flower of beech tree
**fronda** *f* (bot.) frond; (surg.) sling-shaped bandage; **frondas** *fpl* frondage
**fronde** *m* (bot.) frond (*of a fern*)
**frondescencia** *f* (bot.) frondescence
**frondescente** *adj* frondescent
**frondosidad** *f* frondage
**frondoso -sa** *adj* leafy; woodsy; shady; luxuriant
**frontal** *adj* frontal; *m* frontal; (anat., arch. & eccl.) frontal
**frontalera** *f* front (*of a bridle*); yoke pad (*for oxen*)
**frontera** *f* see **frontero**
**fronterizo -za** *adj* frontier, border; bordering; opposite
**frontero -ra** *adj* front; frontier, border; facing, opposite; *m* child's frontlet or brow pad; frontier commander; *f* frontier, border; frontage; front wall; binder of frail basket
**frontil** *m* yoke pad (*for oxen*)
**frontín** *m* (Am.) front (*of bridle*); (Am.) fillip
**frontino -na** *adj* marked in the face (*said of an animal*)
**frontis** *m* (*pl:* **-tis**) façade, front
**frontispicio** *m* frontispiece (*of a book*); (arch.) frontispiece; (coll.) face
**frontón** *m* gable (*over door or window*); (arch.) pediment; (sport) wall used in pelota; (sport) frontón, pelota court or building
**frontudo -da** *adj* big-browed; broad-faced
**frotación** *f* rubbing
**frotador -dora** *adj* rubbing; *mf* rubber; *m* (elec.) brush
**frotadura** *f* rubbing
**frotamiento** *m* rubbing; (mech.) friction
**frotar** *va & vr* to rub
**frote** *m* var. of **frotadura**
**frotis** *m* (*pl:* **-tis**) (bact.) smear
**fructífero -ra** *adj* fructiferous; fruitful
**fructificación** *f* fructification

**fructificar** §86 *vn* to fructify
**fructosa** *f* (chem.) fructose
**fructuosidad** *f* fruitfulness
**fructuoso -sa** *adj* fruitful, fructuous
**frufrú** *m* frou-frou, swishing, rustling (*of silk*)
**frugal** *adj* temperate (*in eating and drinking*)
**frugalidad** *f* temperance, sobriety
**frugívoro -ra** *adj* frugivorous
**fruición** *f* enjoyment, gratification, fruition; wicked joy, evil satisfaction (*in another's sorrow or trouble*)
**fruir** §41 *vn* to enjoy oneself, be gratified
**fruitivo -va** *adj* enjoyable
**frunce** *m* pleat; (sew.) shirr, shirring, gathering
**fruncido -da** *adj* frowning; stern, grim, gruff; *m* pleat; (sew.) shirr, shirring, gathering
**fruncimiento** *m* wrinkling; deceit, cheating; (sew.) shirring, gathering
**fruncir** §50 *va* to wrinkle, contract, pucker, pleat; to knit (*eyebrows*); to curl, purse (*lips*); to conceal, disguise (*truth*); (sew.) to shirr, to gather; *vr* to be shocked, to affect modesty
**fruslera** *f* see **fruslero**
**fruslería** *f* trifle, trinket; (coll.) futility, triviality
**fruslero -ra** *adj* frivolous, futile, trifling; *f* brass or copper turnings or chips
**frustración** *f* frustration
**frustráneo -a** *adj* unprofitable, vain
**frustrar** *va* to frustrate, to thwart; *vr* to be frustrated
**frústula** *f* (bot.) frustule
**fruta** *f* fruit (*e.g., apple, pear, strawberry*); (coll.) fruit (*result*); **frutas** *fpl* fruit, e.g., **me gustan las frutas** I like fruit; **fruta de hueso** stone fruit; **fruta del tiempo** fruit in season; **fruta de sartén** fritter, pancake; **fruta nueva** novelty; **fruta prohibida** forbidden fruit
**frutaje** *m* (paint.) fruit piece
**frutal** *adj* fruit (*tree*); *m* fruit tree
**frutar** *vn* to bear fruit
**frutecer** §34 *vn* (poet.) to bear fruit
**frutera** *f* see **frutero**
**frutería** *f* fruit store
**frutero -ra** *adj* fruit (*boat, dish, etc.*); *mf* fruiterer, fruit vendor; *m* fruit dish; doily for covering fruit; tray of imitation fruit; fruit cabinet; tilt-top fruit table; (paint.) fruit piece; *f* fruitwoman
**frutescente** *adj* frutescent
**frútice** *m* (bot.) shrub, frutex
**fruticoso -sa** *adj* fruticose
**fruticultura** *f* fruitgrowing, cultivation of fruit trees
**frutilla** *f* India berry (*used as bead for rosaries*); Chilean strawberry; (Am.) trichinosis
**frutillar** *m* (Am.) strawberry patch
**frutillero** *m* (Am.) strawberry grower; (Am.) strawberry hawker
**fruto** *m* (bot.) fruit (*part containing seeds*); (fig.) fruit (*result; product*), e.g., **el fruto de mucho trabajo** the fruit of much effort; **los frutos de la tierra** the fruits of the earth; **frutos** *mpl* produce, commodities; **sacar fruto** to derive benefit; **sin fruto** (coll.) fruitlessly, in vain; **fruto de bendición** legitimate offspring; **fruto del pan** breadfruit
**ftaleína** *f* (chem.) phthalein
**ftálico -ca** *adj* (chem.) phthalic
**ftalina** *f* (chem.) phthalin
**ftiocol** *m* (biochem.) phthiocol
**fu** *interj* spit! (*of cat*); faugh!, fie!; **ni fu ni fa** (coll.) neither one thing nor the other
**FUA** abr. of **frecuencia ultraalta**
**fucáceo -a** *adj* (bot.) fucaceous
**fúcar** *m* nabob, tycoon
**fucilar** *vn* to flash with sheet lightning; to flash, to shine
**fucilazo** *m* heat lightning, sheet lightning
**fuco** *m* (bot.) rockweed
**fucsia** *f* (bot.) fuchsia
**fucsina** *f* (chem.) fuchsin
**fucha** *interj* (Am.) ugh!, pew!
**fué** *3d sg pret ind of* **ir** *and* **ser**
**fuego** *m* fire; light (*to light a cigar, cigaret, etc.*); firing; light, beacon, lighthouse; hearth, home; burning sensation; rash, skin eruption; cold sore, fever blister; **a fuego y hierro** or **a fuego y sangre** without mercy, without quarter; violently, sweeping straight ahead; **abrir fuego** to open fire; **apagar los fuegos** (mil.) to quiet the enemy's fire; (coll.) to upset or get the best of an opponent; **dar fuego a** to give a light to; (naut.) to bream (*a ship's bottom*); **echar fuego** (coll.) to blow up, hit the ceiling; **echar fuego por los ojos** to look daggers; **entre dos fuegos** between two fires; **estar hecho un fuego** to be all stirred up; to be burning with anger; **hacer fuego** to fire, to shoot; **jugar con fuego** to play with fire; **levantar fuego** to stir up a row; **marcar a fuego** to brand; **meter a fuego y sangre** to lay waste; **pegar fuego a** to set fire to, to set on fire; **poner a fuego y sangre** to lay waste; **prender fuego a** to set fire to, to set on fire; **prenderse fuego** to catch fire, to catch on fire; **romper el fuego** to open fire; to stir up a row; **fuego de contacto** (arti.) contact firing; **fuego de San Antón** or **fuego de San Marcial** (path.) Saint Anthony's fire; **fuego de Santelmo** St. Elmo's fire; **fuego fatuo** ignis fatuus; **fuego graneado** drumfire; **fuego griego** Greek fire; **fuego nutrido** drumfire; **fuegos artificiales** fireworks; **fuegos en los labios** cold sore, fever blister; *interj* (mil.) fire!; **¡fuego de Dios!** or **¡fuego de Cristo!** confound it!
**fueguino -na** *adj & mf* Fuegian
**fuelle** *m* bellows; pucker, wrinkle, fold; folding carriage top; clouds over mountaintop, wind clouds; (phot.) bellows (*of folding camera*); (rail.) flexible cover (*between two cars of a vestibule train*); (coll.) gossip, talebearer
**fuente** *f* fountain; spring; running water (*in the house*); public hydrant; font, baptismal font; platter, tray; (fig.) source; **beber en buenas fuentes** (coll.) to be well-informed, to be well supplied with information; **fuente de alimentación** (elec.) source of current; (rad.) power pack; **fuente de beber** drinking fountain; **fuente de gasolina** gasoline pump; **Fuente de la juventud** Fountain of Youth; **fuente de poder** (elec.) source of current; (rad.) power pack; **fuente de sodas** soda fountain; **fuente luminosa** or **mágica** illuminated fountain; **fuente pieria** Pierian spring; **fuentes bien informadas** well-informed sources; **fuentes fidedignas** reliable sources; **fuentes termales** hot springs; **fuente surtidora** (elec.) source of current; (rad.) power pack
**fuer**; **a fuer de** as a, on the score of, by way of
**fuera** *adv* out, outside; away, out of town; **de fuera** outside; **desde fuera** from the outside; **por fuera** on the outside; **fuera de** outside, outside of; away from, out of; aside from; in addition to; **fuera de que** aside from the fact that; **fuera de sí** beside oneself
**fuereño -ña** *mf* (Am.) stranger, hick, yokel
**fuero** *m* law, statute; power, jurisdiction; code of laws; exemption, privilege; **fueros** *mpl* (coll.) pride, arrogance; **fuero interior** or **interno** conscience, inmost heart
**fuerte** *adj* strong; bad, severe; intense; rough; harsh; loud; hard; heavy; (gram.) strong (*vowel; verb*); **hacerse fuerte** to stick to one's guns; (mil.) to hole up, to dig in; *adv* loud; hard; heavily; *m* fort; forte, strong point
**fuerza** *f* force; strength; power; main body (*e.g., of an army*); literal meaning; **fuerzas** *fpl* (mil. & nav.) forces; **a fuerza de** by dint of, by force of; **a fuerza de brazos** or **de puños** (coll.) by hard work; **a la fuerza** by force, forcibly; **a viva fuerza** by main strength; **cobrar fuerzas** to recover one's strength; **en fuerza de** because of, on account of; **hacer fuerza** to strain, struggle; to be strained; to convince, persuade; **hacer fuerza de remos** to pull hard on the oars; **hacer fuerza de vela** (naut.) to crowd on sail; **mandar fuerza** to have great influence; **por fuerza** perforce, necessarily; by force; **ser fuerza** + *inf* to be necessary to + *inf;* **fuerza aérea** air force; **fuerza animal** animal power; **fuerza centrífuga** centrifugal force; **fuerza centrípeta** centripetal force; **fuerza**

**coercitiva** (phys.) coercive force; **fuerza contraelectromotriz** (elec.) back electromotive force, counter electromotive force; **fuerza de agua** water power; **fuerza de las señales** (rad.) signal strength; **fuerza de sangre** animal power; **fuerza electromotriz** electromotive force; **fuerza hidráulica** water power; **fuerza mayor** (law) force majeure, act of God; **fuerza motriz** motive power; **fuerza pública** police; **fuerza vital** vital force, vital principle; **fuerza viva** (phys.) kinetic energy
**fuetazo** *m* (Am.) lash
**fuete** *m* (Am.) whip, horsewhip
**fufar** *vn* to spit (*said of a cat*)
**fuga** *f* flight; leak; ardor, vigor; (mus.) fugue; **apelar a la fuga** or **darse a la fuga** to take flight, to run away, to be on the run; **poner en fuga** to put to flight; **ponerse en fuga** to take to flight
**fugacidad** *f* fugacity, evanescence
**fugada** *f* gust of wind
**fugar** §59 *vr* to flee, run away, escape
**fugaz** *adj* (*pl:* **-gaces**) fleeting, transitory, fugacious; (bot.) fugacious
**fugitivo -va** *adj & mf* fugitive
**fuguillas** *m* (*pl:* **-llas**) (coll.) hustler
**fui** *1st sg pret ind of* **ir** *and* **ser**
**fuina** *f* (zool.) stone marten, beech marten
**ful** *adj* (slang) bogus, sham
**fulano -na** *mf* so-and-so; **fulano de tal** John Doe; **fulano, sutano y mengano** Tom, Dick, and Harry; **fulano y mengano** John Doe and Richard Roe
**fular** *m* foulard
**fulcro** *m* (bot., ent., ichth. & mach.) fulcrum
**fulero -ra** *adj* (coll.) useless, unsatisfactory
**fulgente** *adj* fulgent, resplendent
**fúlgido -da** *adj* bright, resplendent; *m* (chem.) fulgide
**fulgor** *m* splendor, brilliance
**fulgurante** *adj* shining, dazzling, fulgurant
**fulgurar** *vn* to flash, to fulgurate
**fulgurita** *f* fulgurite
**fulguroso -sa** *adj* fulgurous
**fúlica** *f* (orn.) coot; **fúlica negra** (orn.) European coot
**fuliginoso -sa** *adj* fuliginous
**fulmicotón** *m* guncotton
**fulminación** *f* fulmination
**fulminante** *adj* fulminant; sudden; (med.) fulminant
**fulminar** *va* to strike with lighting; to strike dead; to fulminate, to thunder (*censure, threats, etc.*); to hurl, hurl forth; to brandish; *vn* to fulminate
**fulminato** *m* (chem.) fulminate; **fulminato mercúrico** (chem.) mercury fulminate
**fulmíneo -a** *adj* fulminous
**fulmínico -ca** *adj* fulminic
**fulminoso -sa** *adj* fulminous
**fullear** *vn* (coll.) to cheat
**fulleresco -ca** *adj* of crooks
**fullería** *f* cheating; trick, trickery
**fullero -ra** *adj* cheating, crooked; tricky; *mf* cheat, crook; tricky person; **fullero de naipes** cardsharp
**fullona** *f* (coll.) row, quarrel, wrangle
**fumable** *adj* smokable; (Am.) acceptable
**fumada** *f* puff (*of smoke*); Am. smoking
**fumadero** *m* smoking room; **fumadero de opio** opium den
**fumador -dora** *adj* smoking; *mf* smoker; **fumador de opio** opium smoker
**fumagina** *f* (plant path.) fumagine
**fumar** *va* to smoke (*e.g., a cigar*); *vn* to smoke; **se prohibe fumar** no smoking; **fumar en pipa** to smoke a pipe; *vr* (coll.) to squander; (coll.) to cut (*class*)
**fumarada** *f* puff, blast (*of smoke*); pipeful (*of tobacco*)
**fumaria** *f* (bot.) fumitory
**fumariáceo -a** *adj* (bot.) fumariaceous
**fumarina** *f* (chem. & pharm.) fumarine
**fumarola** *f* fumarole
**fumífero -ra** *adj* (poet.) smoking, smoke-producing
**fumífugo -ga** *adj* smokeless, smoke-dispersing
**fumigación** *f* fumigation; **fumigación aérea** crop dusting
**fumigador -dora** *mf* fumigator (*person*); *m* fumigator (*apparatus*)
**fumigante** *m* fumigant (*substance used for fumigation*)
**fumigar** §59 *va* to fumigate
**fumígeno -na** *adj* smoke-producing; *m* smoke producer (*apparatus*)
**fumista** *m* stove or heater repairman or dealer
**fumistería** *f* stove or heater shop
**fumívoro -ra** *adj* smokeless, smoke-consuming
**fumorola** *f* var. of **fumarola**
**fumosidad** *f* smokiness
**fumoso -sa** *adj* smoky
**funambulesco -ca** *adj* funambulatory; fantastic, extravagant
**funambulía** *f* ropewalking, ropedancing
**funámbulo -la** *mf* ropewalker, ropedancer
**función** *f* function; operation; duty, office, position; show, performance; **entrar en funciones** (coll.) to take office, to take up one's duties; **estar en funciones** (coll.) to be in office; (coll.) to be in session; **función de aficionados** amateur theatricals; **función de títeres** puppet show; **función potencial** (math.) potential function; **función secundaria** side show; **función trigonométrica** trigonometric function
**funcional** *adj* functional
**funcionalismo** *m* functionalism
**funcionamiento** *m* functioning; working, running, performance
**funcionar** *vn* to function; to work, to run
**funcionario** *m* functionary, official, public official, civil servant
**funcionarismo** *m* bureaucracy; job seeking
**funcionero -ra** *adj* (coll.) officious, self-important; (coll.) fussy
**fund.** abr. of **fundador**
**funda** *f* case, sheath, envelope, cover, slip; slip cover; holdall; **funda de almohada** pillowcase; **funda de asientos** seat cover; **funda de gafas** spectacle case; **funda de neumático** tire cover; **funda de pistolas** pistol case, holster
**fundación** *f* foundation
**fundadamente** *adv* with good reason; on good authority
**fundador -dora** *adj* founding; *mf* founder
**fundamental** *adj* fundamental; foundation
**fundamentalismo** *m* (rel.) fundamentalism
**fundamentalista** *mf* (rel.) fundamentalist
**fundamentar** *va* to lay the foundations of or for; to found, establish
**fundamento** *m* foundation; basis; grounds, reason; seriousness, reliability, trustworthiness; weft, woof
**fundar** *va* to found; to base; **fundar en** or **sobre** to found on or upon; to base on or upon; *vr* to be founded; to be based; **fundarse en** to base one's opinion on
**fundente** *adj* fusing; melting, molten; *m* (chem. & metal.) flux; (med.) dissolvent
**fundería** *f* smelter; foundry
**fundible** *adj* fusible
**fundición** *f* founding; smelting; fusion; smelter; foundry; forge; cast iron; (print.) font; **fundición gris** gray iron
**fundidor** *m* founder, smelter, foundryman
**fundillo** *m* (Am.) behind; (Am.) knockout (*beautiful woman*); **fundillos** *mpl* (Am.) seat (*of trousers*)
**fundilludo -da** *adj* (Am.) big-seated (*trousers*); (Am.) big-rumped; *m* (Am.) man, male; (Am.) easy mark, simp
**fundir** *va* to found (*a metal; a statue*); to smelt; to fuse; to melt; to mix (*paint*); to burn out (*an electric filament*); (Am.) to ruin; *vr* to smelt; to fuse; to melt; (fig.) to fuse, merge, blend; (Am.) to ruin oneself; (Am.) to be or become ruined
**fundo** *m* (law) country property
**fundón** *m* (Am.) long case or sheath; (Am.) riding habit
**fúnebre** *adj* funeral; funereal, gloomy
**funeral** *adj* funeral; funereal; *m* funeral (*often without the corpse*); **funerales** *mpl* funeral; **funeral de corpore insepulto** funeral (*with corpse present*)

**funerala; a la funerala** (mil.) with arms inverted (*as a token of mourning*)
**funerario -ria** *adj* funerary; funeral; *m* funeral director, mortician; *f* undertaking establishment; funeral parlor
**funéreo -a** *adj* (poet.) funereal
**funestar** *va* to soil, tarnish, profane, violate
**funestidad** *f* (Am.) calamity
**funesto -ta** *adj* fatal, ill-fated; sad, sorrowful; baneful (*e.g., influence*)
**fungible** *adj* expendable, consumable; (law) fungible
**fungicida** *adj* fungicidal; *m* fungicide
**fungir §42** *vn* (Am.) to act, function; (Am.) to loiter, to loaf; (Am.) to pinch hit
**fungo** *m* (path.) fungus
**fungoideo -a** *adj* fungoid
**fungología** *f* fungology
**fungosidad** *f* fungosity; (path.) fungosity
**fungoso -sa** *adj* fungous
**funiculado -da** *adj* (bot.) funiculate
**funicular** *adj & m* funicular
**funículo** *m* (anat., bot. & zool.) funiculus; (arch.) cable molding
**fuñique** *adj* slow, shy; dull, heavy
**furente** *adj* wild, raging
**furcífero -ra** *adj* forked; (zool.) furciferous
**fúrfura** *f* (path.) furfur
**furfuráceo -a** *adj* furfuraceous; (bot.) furfuraceous
**furgón** *m* van, wagon; (rail.) baggage car, freight car, boxcar; (rail.) caboose
**furgoneta** *f* light truck, delivery truck
**furia** *f* fury (*anger; violence; haste; angry person*); (*cap.*) *f* Fury; **a toda furia** like fury; **estar dado a las furias** to be in a fury
**furibundo -da** *adj* furious, enraged, frenzied
**furiente** *adj* var. of **furente**
**furierismo** *m* Fourierism
**furioso -sa** *adj* furious; tremendous; (her.) charging, leaping
**furo -ra** *adj* shy, diffident; (dial.) wild, untamed; *m* orifice (*in sugar mold*)
**furor** *m* furor, rage; **entrar** or **montar en furor** to fly into a rage; **hacer furor** to be the rage; **furor uterino** (path.) nymphomania
**furriel** *m* or **furrier** *m* fourrier (*quartermaster*); manager of the royal stables
**furtivo -va** *adj* furtive; clandestine, sneaky
**furúnculo** *m* (path.) boil, furuncle
**furunculoso -sa** *adj* furunculous
**fusa** *f* (mus.) demisemiquaver, thirty-second note
**fusca** *f* see **fusco**
**fuscina** *f* (biochem.) fuscin
**fusco -ca** *adj* fuscous, dark brownish-gray; *f* (orn.) black scoter
**fusé** *m* (horol.) fusee
**fuselado -da** *adj* streamlined; *m* streamlining
**fuselaje** *m* (aer.) fuselage
**fuselar** *va* (aer.) to streamline
**fusente** *adj* receding (*tide*)
**fusibilidad** *f* fusibility
**fusible** *adj* fusible; *m* (elec.) fuse; **fusible de cartucho** (elec.) cartridge fuse
**fusiforme** *adj* fusiform, spindle-shaped
**fusil** *m* gun, rifle; **fusil ametrallador** automatic rifle; **fusil de aguja** needle gun (*of Dreyse*); **fusil de chispa** flintlock (*musket*)
**fúsil** *adj* fusible
**fusilamiento** *m* shooting, execution
**fusilar** *va* to shoot, to execute; (coll.) to plagiarize
**fusilazo** *m* gunshot, rifle shot; heat lightning, sheet lightning
**fusilería** *f* guns, rifles; body of fusileers; fusillade
**fusilero -ra** *adj* (pertaining to a) gun, rifle; *m* fusileer; **fusilero de montaña** (mil.) chasseur
**fusión** *f* fusion; melting; (fig.) fusion; **fusión de empresas** (com.) merger; **fusión de voces** (philol.) blending
**fusionar** *va & vr* to fuse, to merge
**fusionismo** *m* (pol.) fusionism
**fusionista** *adj & mf* fusionist
**fusique** *m* bottle-shaped snuffbox; (coll.) tight-fitting garment
**fuslina** *f* smelter
**fusor** *m* smelting ladle
**fusta** *f* brushwood, twigs; coachman's whip; riding whip; (naut.) lateen-rigged vedette
**fustal** *m*, **fustán** *m* or **fustaño** *m* fustian (*coarse cloth*)
**fustazo** *m* lash
**fuste** *m* wood, timber; stem, shaft; saddletree; shank (*of bolt or rivet*); importance, substance, character; **fuste delantero** saddlebow
**fustete** *m* (bot.) fustic (*Cotinus coggygria; Chlorophora tinctoria and its wood*); (bot.) smoke tree, Venetian sumac (*Cotinus coggygria*)
**fustigación** *f* lashing, whipping; severe censure
**fustigar §59** *va* to lash, to whip; to censure severely
**fustina** *f* smelter; (chem.) fustin
**fut.** abr. of **futuro**
**fútbol** *m* football; **fútbol asociación** association football, soccer
**futbolista** *m* football player; soccer player
**futbolístico -ca** *adj* (pertaining to) football
**futesa** *f* trifle, triviality
**fútil** *adj* futile (*unimportant*); trifling, inconsequential, frivolous
**futileza** *f* (Am.) futility
**futilidad** *f* futility (*unimportance*); frivolousness
**futre** *m* (Am.) dude, dandy
**futura** *f* see **futuro**
**futurismo** *m* futurism
**futurista** *adj* futuristic; *mf* futurist
**futuro -ra** *adj* future; *m* future; (gram.) future; (coll.) fiancé; **futuros** *mpl* (com.) futures; *f* (law) reversion (*right of succeeding to an estate*); (coll.) fiancée
**Fz.** abr. of **Fernández**

# G

**G, g** *f* eighth letter of the Spanish alphabet
**g.** abr. of **gramo** or **gramos**
**G.** abr. of **gracia**
**gabacho -cha** *adj & mf* Pyrenean; (coll.) Frenchy; (Am.) gringo; *m* (coll.) Frenchified Spanish
**gabán** *m* overcoat, greatcoat
**gabardina** *f* gabardine; raincoat (*generally with belt*)
**gabarra** *f* barge; lighter; fishing sloop
**gabarrero** *m* bargeman; lighterman
**gabarro** *m* flaw, defect (*in a fabric*); filling, badigeon; pip (*disease of fowl*); bother; mistake (*in calculating*); (geol.) nodule
**gabazo** *m* var. of **bagazo**
**gabela** *f* tax; burden
**gabinete** *m* office (*of doctor, dentist, lawyer*); studio, study; boudoir; laboratory; cabinet (*of government; collection, display; private room*); **de gabinete** parlor, theoretical (*person*); **gabinete de aseo** washroom, lavatory, toilet; **gabinete de lectura** reading room
**gabinetero** *m* laboratory caretaker
**gablete** *m* gable (*over door or window*)
**Gabriel** *m* Gabriel
**gacel** *m* male gazelle
**gacela** *f* (zool.) gazelle
**gaceta** *f* gazette; sagger (*fire-clay box*); (Am.) newspaper; **mentir más que la gaceta** (coll.) to lie like a trooper
**gacetero -ra** *mf* news vendor, seller of newspapers; *m* gazeteer; newspaper man
**gacetilla** *f* gossip column, town talk (*in a newspaper*); short news item; (coll.) gossip (*person*)
**gacetillero** *m* gossip columnist
**gacetín** *m* (Am.) box (*of type-holding tray*)
**gacetista** *mf* newspaper reader; newsmonger
**gacha** *f* see **gacho**
**gacheta** *f* spring catch (*of lock*); paste
**gacho -cha** *adj* turned down; drooping, flopping; slouch (*hat*); with horns curved downward; *f* watery mass or mush; (Am.) earthenware bowl; **gachas** *fpl* pap, mush, porridge; (coll.) mud; (prov.) caresses; **a gachas** on all fours; **hacerse unas gachas** (coll.) to be mushy; **gachas de avena** oatmeal
**gachón -chona** *adj* (coll.) nice, cute; (prov.) spoiled, pampered
**gachonada** *f* (coll.) cuteness, charm
**gachonear** *va* (coll.) to flirt with; *vn* (coll.) to be cute
**gachonería** *f* (coll.) var. of **gachonada**
**gachumbo** *m* (Am.) fruit shell (*used to make cups and other vessels*)
**gachupín -pina, gachupo -pa** or **gachuzo -za** *mf* Spanish settler in America
**gádido** *m* (ichth.) gadid
**gaditano -na** *adj* (pertaining to) Cádiz; *mf* native or inhabitant of Cádiz
**gadolinio** *m* (chem.) gadolinium
**gaélico -ca** *adj* Gaelic; *mf* Gael; *m* Gaelic (*language*)
**gafa** *f* see **gafo**
**gafar** *va* to hook, to snatch with a hook, the claws, etc.
**gafe** *m* (coll.) hoodoo, jinx
**gafedad** *f* (path.) claw hand; (path.) anesthetic leprosy
**gafete** *m* hook and eye
**gafo -fa** *adj* claw-handed; (Am.) footsore; *f* hook (*for bending crossbow*); clamp, cramp; temple (*sidepiece of a pair of spectacles*); **gafas** *fpl* can hooks; spectacles, glasses; **unas gafas** a pair of glasses; **gafas de sol, gafas para sol, gafas parasoles** sunglasses
**gago -ga** *adj* (Am.) stuttering
**gaguear** *vn* (Am.) to stutter
**gaguera** *f* (Am.) stuttering
**gaicano** *m* (ichth.) remora
**gaita** *f* hornpipe; bagpipe; silly answer; chore, hard task; (coll.) neck; **estar de gaita** (coll.) to be in a gay mood; **templar gaitas a** (coll.) to humor; **gaita gallega** bagpipe
**gaitería** *f* flashy dress, gaudy dress
**gaitero -ra** *adj* (coll.) flashy, gaudy, showy; (coll.) garrulous; *m* bagpipe player
**gaje** *m* (archaic) gage (*e.g., of battle*); **gajes** *mpl* wages, salary; **gajes del oficio** (hum.) cares of office, unpleasant part of a job
**gajo** *m* branch of tree (*especially when broken off*); small stem (*of bunch of grapes*); bunch; kernel; slice (*e.g., of orange*); prong, tine (*e.g., of pitchfork*); spur (*of hills*); (bot.) lobe (*of leaf*); **gajo de nuez** nutmeat
**gajoso -sa** *adj* branched, branchy; stemmed; pronged
**gala** *f* festive dress or array; charm, elegance; choice, favorite; (poet.) pomp, show, splendor; (Am.) fee, tip; **galas** *fpl* finery, regalia; wedding presents; gifts, talents; beauties (*of diction, style, etc.*); **de gala** gala; full-dress; **hacer gala de** or **tener a gala** to make a show of; to take pride in, to glory in
**Galaad** *m* (Bib.) Gilead; Galahad (*of Round Table*)
**galabardera** *f* (bot.) dog rose (*plant and fruit*)
**Galacia** *f* Galatia
**galactagogo -ga** *adj & m* (med. & vet.) galactagogue
**galáctico -ca** *adj* (astr.) galactic
**galactita** or **galactites** *f* (mineral.) galactite
**galactómetro** *m* galactometer
**galactosa** *f* (chem.) galactose
**galafate** *m* slick thief; slicker; laborer; constable
**galaico -ca** *adj* Galician
**galaicoportugués -guesa** *adj & m* Galician-Portuguese
**galán** *m* fine-looking fellow; gallant, lover, suitor, ladies' man; (theat.) principal character; **primer galán** (theat.) leading man; **segundo galán** (theat.) second lead; **galán de noche** (bot.) night jasmine; **galán joven** (theat.) juvenile
**galancete** *m* (theat.) juvenile
**galanga** *f* (bot.) taro; (bot.) galingale (*Alpinia officinarum and rhizome*)
**galano -na** *adj* spruce, smartly dressed; graceful, elegant; rich, tasteful; (Am.) mottled
**galante** *adj* gallant, attentive to women; coquettish (*woman*); loose (*woman*)
**galanteador -dora** *adj* love-making; *m* gallant, lover, love-maker, flirt
**galantear** *va* to court, woo, make love to, flirt with
**galanteo** *m* courting, wooing, flirting
**galantería** *f* gallantry; charm, elegance; liberality, generosity
**galantina** *f* (cook.) galantine
**galanura** *f* charm, elegance
**galapagar** *m* place full of tortoises; breeding place for tortoises
**galápago** *m* (zool.) tortoise (*of genera Clemmys and Emys*); moldboard (*of plow*); centering arch; ingot (*of copper, lead, or tin*); hatch batten; brick mold; light saddle; (mil.) testudo, galapago; (coll.) sly fellow; **las Galápagos** the Galápagos Islands
**galapaguera** *f* tortoise pond
**galapo** *m* top, laying top (*used in making rope*)
**galardón** *m* reward, prize
**galardonador -dora** *adj* rewarding; *mf* rewarder

**galardonar** *va* to reward
**gálata** *adj & mf* Galatian
**Galatea** *f* (myth.) Galatea
**galaxia** *f* (mineral.) galactite; (astr.) galaxy
**galayo** *m* peak, cliff
**galbana** *f* (coll.) laziness, shiftlessness
**galbanado -da** *adj* galbanum-colored, yellowish
**galbanero -ra** *adj* (coll.) var. of **galbanoso**
**gálbano** *m* galbanum; **dar gálbano a** (coll.) to lead on, to deceive
**galbanoso -sa** *adj* (coll.) lazy, shiftless, indolent
**gálbula** *f* (bot.) galbulus, cone of cypress
**galdrufa** *f* (dial.) top, spinning top
**galeato** *adj masc* defensive (*preface*)
**galeaza** *f* (naut.) galleass
**galega** *f* (bot.) goat's-rue
**galena** *f* see **galeno**
**galénico -ca** *adj* Galenic
**galenismo** *m* Galenism
**galeno -na** *adj* (naut.) gentle, soft (*breeze*); (*cap.*) *m* Galen; (coll.) Galen (*physician*); (*l.c.*) *f* (mineral.) galena
**gáleo** *m* (ichth.) dogfish; (ichth.) swordfish
**galeón** *m* (naut.) galleon
**galeota** *f* (naut.) galiot
**galeote** *m* galley slave
**galera** *f* covered wagon; ward (*of hospital*); women's jail; row of reverberatory furnaces; line (*dividing two parts of fraction*); (carp.) jack plane; (naut. & print.) galley; (zool.) squilla, mantis crab; **galeras** *fpl* rowing on a galley (*as punishment*)
**galerada** *f* wagonload; (print.) galley, full galley; (print.) galley proof
**galerero** *m* driver of a covered wagon
**galería** *f* gallery; back porch; bay window; (ent.) bee moth; (fort., min., naut. & theat.) gallery; **hablar para la galería** (coll.) to play to the gallery; **galería de pinturas** picture gallery; **galería de popa** (naut.) stern gallery; **galería de tiro** shooting gallery; **galería fotográfica** photographic gallery; **galería visitable** manhole
**galerín** *m* (print.) galley
**galerita** *f* (orn.) crested lark
**galerna** *f* or **galerno** *m* stormy blast from the northwest (*on northern coast of Spain*)
**Gales** *f* Wales; **el país de Gales** Wales; **la Nueva Gales del Sur** New South Wales
**galés -lesa** *adj* Welsh; *m* Welshman; Welsh (*language*); **los galeses** the Welsh (*people*); *f* Welsh woman
**galfarro** *m* bum, loafer
**galgo -ga** *adj* (Am.) sweet-toothed; *mf* (coll.) gadabout; *m* greyhound; (fig.) greyhound (*ocean liner*); **galgo ruso** Russian wolfhound; *f* greyhound bitch; rolling stone; rash, mange; ankle ribbon; stretcher on which the poor are carried to the cemetery; hub brake (*on a wagon*); millstone for grinding olives; (Am.) gage (*of wire, sheet metal, etc.*)
**galgueño -ña** or **galguesco -ca** *adj* (pertaining to a) greyhound
**gálgulo** *m* (orn.) blue magpie
**Galia, la** Gaul
**galibar** *va* to fashion (*part of ship*) according to a template
**gálibo** *m* pattern, template; (naut.) template; (rail.) gabarit; (fig.) elegance
**galicado -da** *adj* Gallic, full of Gallicisms
**galicanismo** *m* (eccl.) Gallicanism
**galicano -na** *adj* (eccl.) Gallican; Gallic
**Galicia** *f* Galicia (*of Poland and of Spain*)
**galiciano -na** *adj & mf* Galician (*of Poland and of Spain*)
**galicismo** *m* Gallicism
**galicista** *adj* French, gallicizing; *mf* gallicizer, user of gallicisms
**gálico -ca** *adj* Gallic; (chem.) gallic; *m* (path.) syphilis
**galicoso -sa** *adj & mf* syphilitic
**galileo -a** *adj & mf* Galilean; **el Galileo** the Galilean, the Man of Galilee; *f* galilee (*porch*); (*cap.*) *f* Galilee
**galillo** *m* (anat.) uvula
**galimatías** *m* rigmarole, gibberish
**galináceo -a** *adj* var. of **gallináceo**
**galio** *m* (chem.) gallium; (bot.) bedstraw

**galiparla** *f* Frenchified Spanish
**galiparlista** *m* var. of **galicista**
**galipodio** *m* galipot or gallipot (*oleoresin*)
**galo -la** *adj* Gallic; *mf* Gaul; *m* Gaulish (*language*)
**galocha** *f* clog, wooden shoe
**galomanía** *f* Gallomania
**galón** *m* gallon; galloon; braid, stripe; (mil.) chevron
**galoneadura** *f* galloons, trimming
**galonear** *va* to trim with galloons or braid
**galonero -ra** *mf* galloon or braid maker or dealer
**galonista** *m* (coll.) student of a military academy who is allowed to wear the chevrons of corporal or sergeant as a reward
**galop** *m* or **galopa** *f* galop (*dance*)
**galopante** *adj* galloping
**galopar** *va* (Am.) to gallop (*a horse*); *vn* to gallop; to galop
**galope** *m* gallop; **a galope** or **de galope** at a gallop; in great haste; **a galope tendido** at full speed, on the run
**galopeado -da** *adj* hasty, sketchy; *m* (coll.) buffeting, punching, beating
**galopear** *vn* to gallop
**galopillo** *m* kitchen boy, scullion
**galopín** *m* ragamuffin; scoundrel; scullion; wise guy; (naut.) cabin boy; (coll.) loafer
**galopo** *m* scoundrel
**galorromano -na** *adj* Gallo-Roman
**Galván** *m* Gawain (*of Round Table and the Amadis of Gaul*)
**galvánico -ca** *adj* galvanic
**galvanismo** *m* galvanism
**galvanización** *f* galvanization
**galvanizar** **§76** *va* to galvanize; (fig.) to galvanize
**galvano** *m* (print.) electroplate
**galvanocauterio** *m* (med.) galvanocautery
**galvanometría** *f* galvanometry
**galvanométrico -ca** *adj* galvanometric
**galvanómetro** *m* galvanometer
**galvanoplastia** *f* galvanoplasty; electroplating
**galvanoplástico -ca** *adj* galvanoplastic; *f* galvanoplastics
**galvanoscopio** *m* galvanoscope
**galvanotropismo** *m* (biol.) galvanotropism
**galladura** *f* tread (*of an egg*)
**gallarda** *f* see **gallardo**
**gallardear** *vn & vr* to be graceful, elegant, gallant
**gallardete** *m* pennant, streamer; **gallardete azul** (naut.) blue ribbon (*prize*)
**gallardetón** *m* broad pennant with two tails
**gallardía** *f* gracefulness, elegance, gallantry, bravery; generosity; nobility
**gallardo -da** *adj* graceful, elegant, gallant, brave; generous; noble; fierce (*storm*); *f* galliard (*dance*)
**gallareta** *f* (orn.) European coot; **gallareta de pico blanco** (orn.) North American coot
**gallarito** *m* (bot.) lousewort (*Pedicularis sylvatica*)
**gallarón** *m* (orn.) little bustard
**gallaruza** *f* (archaic) hooded cloak
**gallear** *va* to tread (*said of a cock*); *vn* to stand out, excel; (coll.) to yell and threaten
**gallegada** *f* Galicians; Galicianism; Galician dance
**gallego -ga** *adj & mf* Galician (*of Spain*); *m* Galician (*dialect*)
**gallegoportugués -guesa** *adj & m* var. of **galaicoportugués**
**galleguismo** *m* Galicianism (*of Galicia, Spain*)
**galleo** *m* rough spot in a casting (*from rapid cooling*)
**gallero -ra** *adj* (Am.) cockfighting; *m* breeder of gamecocks; *f* cockpit
**galleta** *f* hardtack, ship biscuit, ship bread; cracker; biscuit; little pitcher; briquet (*of anthracite*); (coll.) slap
**gallina** *f* hen; **acostarse con las gallinas** (coll.) to go to bed with the chickens; **estar como gallina en corral ajeno** (coll.) to be like a fish out of water; **gallina brahma** brahma (*chicken*); **gallina ciega** blindman's buff; **gallina de agua** (orn.) coot; **gallina de Guinea** guinea hen; **gallina de río** (orn.)

coot; **gallina Guinea** or **pintada** guinea hen; **gallina sorda** (orn.) woodcock; *mf* chicken-hearted person; *adj* chicken-hearted
**gallináceo -a** *adj* (orn.) gallinaceous
**gallinazo -za** *mf* (orn.) turkey buzzard; *f* hen dung
**gallinería** *f* flock of hens; chicken market; cowardice
**gallinero -ra** *mf* chicken dealer, poultry dealer; *m* hencoop, henhouse; paradise, top gallery; poultry basket; madhouse
**gallineta** *f* (orn.) European coot; (orn.) woodcock; (Am.) guinea hen
**gallipato** *m* (zool.) Spanish newt, European salamandrid (*Pleurodeles waltlii*)
**gallipava** *f* large hen
**gallipavo** *m* (orn.) turkey; (coll.) sour note
**gallipollo** *m* cockerel
**gallipuente** *m* bridge without railing
**gallístico -ca** *adj* (pertaining to a) cock
**gallito** *m* somebody (*person of importance*); **gallito del lugar** cock of the walk; **gallito del rey** (ichth.) peacock fish
**gallo** *m* cock, rooster; false note, sour note; (coll.) boss; (box.) bantam weight; (ichth.) dory; **tener mucho gallo** (coll.) to be cocky; **gallo de bosque** (orn.) wood grouse; **gallo del corral** cock of the walk; **gallo de pelea** or **de riña** fighting cock, gamecock; **gallo de roca** (orn.) cock of the rock; **gallo en la garganta** frog in the throat; **gallo silvestre** (orn.) capercaillie, wood grouse
**gallocresta** *f* (bot.) wild sage, vervain sage
**gallofa** *f* food for pilgrims; alms, charity; vegetables for salad or soup; French roll; liturgical calendar; talk, gossip
**gallofar** or **gallofear** *vn* to bum, beg, loaf around
**gallofero -ra** or **gallofo -fa** *adj* bumming, begging, loafing; *mf* bum, beggar, loafer
**gallón** *m* sod, turf; (arch.) echinus
**gallote -ta** *adj* (dial. & Am.) cocky
**gama** *f* gamma; doe, female fallow deer; (mus. & fig.) gamut
**gamado -da** *adj* formed with four capital gammas; see **cruz**
**gamarra** *f* martingale
**gamarza** *f* (bot.) African rue
**gamba** *f* (zool.) prawn (*Pandalus*)
**gámbaro** *m* var. of **cámaro**
**gambax** *m* (*pl:* **gambax**) acton
**gamberrada** *f* hooliganism
**gamberrismo** *m* hooliganism, rowdyism; hooligans, rowdies
**gamberro -rra** *adj & mf* libertine; *m* hooligan, rowdy, hoodlum, roughneck; *f* (dial.) prostitute
**gambesina** *f* or **gambesón** *m* acton
**gambeta** *f* crosscaper; caper, prance
**gambetear** *vn* to caper, to prance
**gambeto** *m* cloak, mantle; cap used to keep baby's head straight
**gambir** *m* (pharm.) gambier
**gambito** *m* gambit
**gamboa** *f* (bot.) quince
**gambota** *f* (naut.) counter timber
**gambusino -na** *mf* (Am.) prospector; (Am.) adventurer, fortune hunter
**gamella** *f* bow (*of yoke*); feed trough; camlet (*cloth*); (min.) pan
**gamellón** *m* trough for treading grapes; long ridge
**gametangio** *m* (bot.) gametangium
**gameto** *m* (biol.) gamete
**gametofita** *f* or **gametofito** *m* (bot.) gametophyte
**gametogénesis** *f* (biol.) gametogenesis
**gamo** *m* buck, male fallow deer
**gamofilo -la** *adj* (bot.) gamophyllous
**gamogénesis** *f* (biol.) gamogenesis
**gamón** *m* (bot.) asphodel
**gamonal** *m* field of asphodel; (Am) landlord; (Am.) powerful and abusive landlord; (Am.) political boss
**gamonalismo** *m* (Am.) bossism
**gamonito** *m* shoot, sucker
**gamopétalo -la** *adj* (bot.) gamopetalous
**gamosépalo -la** *adj* (bot.) gamosepalous
**gamuno -na** *adj* buck (*skin*)
**gamuza** *f* (zool.) chamois; chamois (*leather*); vici, vici kid (*leather*)
**gamuzado -da** *adj* chamois-colored
**gana** *f* desire; **darle a uno la (real) gana de** + *inf* (coll.) to feel like + *ger*, e.g., **me da la gana de comer** I feel like eating; **de buena gana** willingly; **de gana** in earnest; willingly; **de mala gana** unwillingly; **tener gana** or **ganas de** + *inf* to feel like + *ger*, to have a mind to + *inf;* **tener ganas a** (coll.) to pick a fight with; **venir en gana a** to come into the head of, e.g., **dice lo que le venga en gana** he says whatever comes into his head
**ganadería** *f* cattle; cattle ranch; cattle raising, animal husbandry; livestock; brand, stock; (taur.) breeding ranch
**ganadero -ra** *adj* (pertaining to) cattle, livestock; *mf* cattle dealer; cattle breeder; *m* cattleman
**ganado** *m* cattle, livestock; stock of bees; (coll.) flock or mob of people; **ganado caballar** horses; **ganado cabrío** goats; **ganado de cerda** swine; **ganado de cría** cattle for breeding; **ganado lanar** sheep; **ganado mayor** cows, bulls, horses, and mules; **ganado menor** sheep, goats, etc.; **ganado menudo** young cattle; **ganado merino** merino sheep; **ganado moreno** swine; **ganado ovejuno** sheep; **ganado porcino** swine; **ganado vacuno** cattle, bovine cattle
**ganador -dora** *adj* winning; hard-working; *mf* winner; earner
**ganancia** *f* gain, profit; (elec.) gain; (Am.) extra, bonus; **ganancias y pérdidas** (com.) profit and loss
**ganancial** *adj* (pertaining to) profit
**ganancioso -sa** *adj* gainful, profitable; winning; *mf* winner
**ganapán** *m* errand boy, messenger; drudge; penniless fellow; (coll.) coarse fellow
**ganapanería** *f* drudgery
**ganapierde** *m & f* giveaway (*game of checkers*); **jugar al** or **a la ganapierde** to play giveaway
**ganar** *va* to earn; to gain; to win; to reach; to cross; to beat, defeat; to outstrip, win out over; to take over, to win over; **ganar algo a alguien** to win something from someone; **ganar de comer** to earn a living; *vn* to earn; to improve; *vr* to earn (*e.g., a livelihood*); to win over; (Am.) to hide, take refuge; (Am.) to slip away, disappear
**ganchada** *f* (Am.) favor
**ganchero** *m* log driver; gentle mount; (Am.) odd-jobber
**ganchete** *m* small hook; **a medio ganchete** (coll.) half, half-done; **de medio ganchete** carelessly, sloppily
**ganchillo** *m* crochet, crochet work; crochet needle; **hacer ganchillo** to crochet
**gancho** *m* hook; fishhook; coaxer, enticer; pimp; (Am.) hairpin; (Am.) lady's saddle; **echar el gancho a** (coll.) to hook in, to land; **tener gancho** (coll.) to have a way with the men; **gancho de botalones** (naut.) gooseneck
**ganchoso -sa** or **ganchudo -da** *adj* hooked
**gándara** *f* low wasteland
**gandaya** *f* (coll.) bumming, loafing, idleness; netting; **andar a la gandaya, buscar** or **correr la gandaya** or **ir por la gandaya** (coll.) to bum one's way, to be a tramp
**gandinga** *f* (min.) concentrate, washed fine ore
**gandujado** *m* accordion pleating
**gandujar** *va* to pleat, shirr, fold
**gandul -dula** *adj* (coll.) loafing, idling; (coll.) sly, crafty; *mf* (coll.) loafer, idler
**gandulear** *vn* to loaf, to idle
**gandulería** *f* (coll.) loafing, idleness
**ganeta** *f* (zool.) genet
**ganforro -rra** *mf* (coll.) scoundrel
**ganga** *f* (min.) gangue; (orn.) pin-tailed sand grouse; (orn.) upland plover; bargain; cinch, snap
**ganglio** *m* (anat. & path.) ganglion; **ganglio linfático** (anat.) lymph gland or node
**ganglionar** *adj* ganglionic
**gangocho** *m* (Am.) burlap
**gangosidad** *f* snuffliness, nasality
**gangoso -sa** *adj* snuffling, nasal

**gangrena** *f* (path.) gangrene
**gangrenar** *va & vr* to gangrene
**gangrenoso -sa** *adj* gangrenous
**gangsterismo** *m* gangsterism
**ganguear** *vn* to snuffle, to talk through the nose
**gangueo** *m* snuffle, talking through the nose
**ganguero -ra** *adj & mf* var. of **ganguista**
**gánguil** *m* (naut.) dump scow; (naut.) fishing sailboat with sweep net; sweep net
**ganguista** *adj* (coll.) bargain-hunting; (coll.) self-seeking; *mf* (coll.) bargain hunter; (coll.) self-seeker; *m* (coll.) lucky fellow
**Ganimedes** *m* (myth.) Ganymede
**ganoideo -a** *adj & m* (ichth.) ganoid
**ganoso -sa** *adj* desirous; (Am.) spirited (*horse*)
**gansa** *f* see **ganso**
**gansada** *f* (coll.) stupidity
**gansarón** *m* (orn.) goose; tall, lanky fellow
**ganso -sa** *mf* slob, dope, dullard, rube; *m* (orn.) goose; gander; **ganso bravo** wild goose; **ganso de corbata** (orn.) Canada goose; **ganso monjita** (orn.) barnacle goose; **ganso monjita atlántico** (orn.) American brant (*Branta bernicla hrota*); *f* goose (*female*)
**Gante** *f* Ghent
**gantés -tesa** *adj* (pertaining to) Ghent; *mf* native or inhabitant of Ghent
**ganzúa** *f* picklock (*hook; thief*); (coll.) pumper (*of secrets*)
**ganzuar** §33 *va* to open with a picklock; (coll.) to pump (*secrets*)
**gañán** *m* farm hand; rough, husky fellow
**gañanía** *f* gang of farm hands; lodge for farm hands
**gañido** *m* yelp, yelping; croak, croaking
**gañiles** *mpl* (zool.) larynx (*of animal*); gills of tunny fish
**gañir** §25 *vn* to yelp; to croak; (coll.) to wheeze
**gañón** *m* or **gañote** *m* (coll.) throat, gullet; (dial.) fritter
**garabatada** *f* hooking; hookful
**garabatear** *va* to scribble; *vn* to hook; to beat about the bush; to scribble
**garabateo** *m* hooking; scribbling
**garabato** *m* hook; pothook (*hooked rod; scrawl*); dibble, weeding hoe; (coll.) charm, winsomeness; **garabatos** *mpl* awkward movements of hands and fingers; **garabato de carnicero** meathook
**garabatoso -sa** *adj* full of scribbling; winsome
**garabito** *m* stall in market place; hook
**garage** *m* or **garaje** *m* garage
**garajista** *m* garage man
**garambaina** *f* gaudy trimming; (coll.) trinket; **garambainas** *fpl* simpering, smirking; scribbling
**garante** *adj* responsible; *mf* guarantor
**garantía** *f* guarantee, guaranty
**garantir** §53 *va* to guarantee
**garantizar** §76 *va* to guarantee
**garañón** *m* stud jackass; stud camel; libertine; (Am.) stallion
**garapacho** *m* carapace; wooden or cork bowl
**garapiña** *f* sugar-coating, icing; embroidered braid or galloon; (Am.) iced pineapple juice
**garapiñar** *va* to candy; to sugar-coat, to ice (*e.g., a cake*)
**garapiñera** *f* ice-cream freezer; cooler (*for wine and other drinks*)
**garapita** *f* net to catch small fish
**garapito** *m* (ent.) water bug, back swimmer
**garapullo** *m* paper dart
**garatura** *f* scraper (*used in tanning*)
**garatusa** *f* (coll.) coaxing, wheedling
**garbancero -ra** *adj* (pertaining to the) chickpea; *mf* chickpea dealer
**garbanzal** *m* chickpea patch
**garbanzo** *m* (bot.) chickpea (*plant and seed*); **garbanzo negro** (fig.) black sheep
**garbanzuelo** *m* (vet.) spavin
**garbar** *va* to sheaf or sheave
**garbear** *va* (dial.) to sheaf or sheave; *vn* to put on airs, to be full of pretense
**garbera** *f* (agr.) shock
**garbías** *mpl* fried cake made of herbs, cheese, eggs, and flour
**garbillador -dora** *adj* sieving, screening, riddling; *mf* siever, screener, riddler
**garbillar** *va* to sieve, to screen, to riddle
**garbillo** *m* sieve, screen, riddle; screened ore, riddled ore
**garbino** *m* southwest wind
**garbo** *m* fine bearing, jaunty air; grace, elegance; gallantry, magnanimity
**garbón** *m* male partridge
**garboso -sa** *adj* spruce, natty, sprightly, jaunty; generous
**garbullo** *m* noise, confusion
**garcero** *m* (Am.) heronry
**garceta** *f* (orn.) lesser egret (*Egretta garzetta*); side lock (*of hair*)
**gardenia** *f* (bot.) gardenia
**garduño -ña** *mf* (coll.) sneak thief; *f* (zool.) stone marten, beech marten
**garete; al garete** (naut. & fig.) adrift
**garfa** *f* claw
**garfada** *f* clawing
**garfear** *vn* to hook
**garfio** *m* hook; gaff; **garfios de trepar** climbing irons
**gargajeada** *f* var. of **gargajeo**
**gargajear** *vn* to spit phlegm
**gargajeo** *m* spitting or ejection of phlegm
**gargajiento -ta** *adj & mf* var. of **gargajoso**
**gargajo** *m* phlegm
**gargajoso -sa** *adj* hawking; *mf* hawker (*of phlegm*)
**garganta** *f* throat; instep; neck, throat (*e.g., of a river, vase*); gorge, ravine; sheath (*of plow*); (arch.) shaft; (arch.) gorge; (bot.) throat; (mach.) groove (*of a sheave*); **tener buena garganta** to have a good voice, to sing well
**gargantada** *f* throatful (*e.g., of blood*); (coll.) throatful (*swallow*)
**gargantear** *va* (naut.) to strap; *vn* to warble
**garganteo** *m* warble, warbling
**gargantilla** *f* necklace
**gárgara** *f* gargling; **gárgaras** *fpl* (Am.) gargle (*liquid*); **hacer gárgaras** to gargle
**gargarear** *vn* (Am.) var. of **gargarizar**
**gargarismo** *m* gargling; gargle (*liquid*)
**gargarizar** §76 *vn* to gargle
**gárgol** *adj* addle (*egg*); *m* gain, croze (*groove*)
**gárgola** *f* head of flax; (arch.) gargoyle
**garguero** or **gargüero** *m* gullet; windpipe
**garifo -fa** *adj* natty, spruce, showy
**gariofilea** *f* (bot.) wild carnation
**garita** *f* watchtower; sentry box; porter's lodge; water closet, privy (*with one seat*); cab (*of truck, power shovel, etc.*); railroad-crossing box; hut, hovel; (Am.) octroi; (Am.) city gate; **garita de centinela** sentry box; **garita de señales** (rail.) signal tower
**gariteear** *vn* (coll.) to frequent gambling houses, to hang around gambling joints
**garitero** *m* owner of a gambling house; gambler
**garito** *m* gambling den; gambling profits
**garla** *f* (coll.) talk, chatter, prattle
**garlador -dora** *adj* (coll.) chattering, prattling; *mf* (coll.) chatterer, prattler
**garlar** *vn* (coll.) to talk, chatter, prattle
**garlito** *m* fish trap; (coll.) trap, snare; **caer en el garlito** (coll.) to fall into the trap; **coger en el garlito** (coll.) to catch in the act
**garlocha** *f* goad, goad stick
**garlopa** *f* (carp.) jointer plane, trying plane
**garlopar** *va* (carp.) to plane
**garlopín** *m* (carp.) jack plane, fore plane
**garma** *f* (dial.) steep slope
**garnacha** *f* gown, robe (*e.g., of a judge*); company of strolling players; grenache (*grape; wine*)
**garniel** *m* muleteer's leather bag; muleteer's girdle
**Garona** *m* Garonne
**garra** *f* claw, talon; catch, claw, hook; (fig.) claw (*hand*); **caer en las garras de** (coll.) to fall into the clutches of; **echar la garra a** (coll.) to get one's hands on, to arrest; **sacar de las garras de** (coll.) to free from
**garrafa** *f* carafe, decanter
**garrafal** *adj* awful, terrific
**garrafiñar** *va* (coll.) to snatch, snatch away
**garrafón** *m* carboy, demijohn
**garrama** *f* (coll.) filching, stealing
**garramar** *va* (coll.) to filch, to steal
**garrancha** *f* (bot.) spadix; (coll.) sword

**garranchada** *f* or **garranchazo** *m* slash, gash
**garrancho** *m* broken branch
**garranchuelo** *m* (bot.) crab grass
**garrapata** *f* (ent.) chigger, cattle tick, sheep tick; (mil.) disabled horse
**garrapatear** *vn* to scrawl, scribble
**garrapatero** *m* (orn.) cowbird, buffalo bird
**garrapato** *m* pothook, scrawl
**garrapiñar** *va* var. of **garapiñar**
**garrapiñera** *f* var. of **garapiñera**
**garrar** or **garrear** *vn* (naut.) to drag the anchor
**garrido -da** *adj* handsome, spruce, elegant
**garroba** *f* carob bean
**garrobal** *m* growth of carob trees
**garrobilla** *f* chips of carob wood used for staining
**garrocha** *f* goad, goad stick; (sport) pole (*used in pole vault*)
**garrochear** *va* var. of **agarrochar**
**garrochón** *m* (taur.) lance
**garrofa** *f* carob bean
**garrón** *m* spur, talon; paw
**garrotal** *m* plantation of slips or cuttings of olive trees
**garrotazo** *m* blow with a cudgel
**garrote** *m* club, cudgel; garrote (*method of execution; iron collar used for this*); (hort.) olive cutting; (Am.) brake; **dar garrote a** to garrote
**garrotero -ra** *adj* (Am.) stingy; *m* (Am.) brakeman
**garrotillo** *m* (path.) croup
**garrubia** *f* (bot.) black-eyed bean; carob bean
**garrucha** *f* pulley, sheave
**garrucho** *m* (naut.) cringle
**garrudo -da** *adj* big-clawed; (Am.) brawny, husky
**garrulador -dora** *adj* var. of **gárrulo**
**garrulería** *f* chatter, prattle
**garrulidad** *f* garrulity, garrulousness
**gárrulo -la** *adj* chirping; garrulous; noisy (*said of the wind*); *m* (orn.) jay
**garúa** *f* (Am.) drizzle
**garuar** §33 *vn* (Am.) to drizzle
**garujo** *m* concrete
**garulla** *f* loose grapes; (coll.) mob, rabble
**garullada** *f* (coll.) mob, rabble
**garzo -za** *adj* blue; *m* (bot.) agaric; *f* (orn.) heron; (orn.) crane, blue crane; **garza real** (orn.) heron, gray heron (*Ardea cinerea*)
**garzón** *m* boy; youth, stripling; (orn.) blue crane, great blue heron
**garzota** *f* (orn.) night heron; plumage, crest
**gas** *m* gas; **gas amoníaco** (chem.) ammonia gas; **gas carbónico** (chem.) carbonic-acid gas, carbon dioxide; **gas cloacal** sewer gas; **gas combustible natural** natural gas; **gas de aceite** oil gas; **gas de agua** water gas; **gas de alumbrado** illuminating gas; **gas de carbón** or **de hulla** coal gas; **gas de guerra** (mil.) poison gas; **gas de los pantanos** marsh gas; **gas exhilarante** or **hilarante** laughing gas; **gas inerte** (chem.) inert gas; **gas lacrimógeno** tear gas; **gas mostaza** mustard gas; **gas natural** natural gas; **gas pobre** producer gas; **gas raro** (chem.) rare gas; **gas tóxico** (mil.) poison gas; **gas vesicante** blister gas
**gasa** *f* gauze, chiffon; crepe (*token of mourning*); **gasa antiséptica** antiseptic gauze; **gasa de alambre** wire gauze
**gascón -cona** *adj* Gascon; boastful; *mf* Gascon
**gasconada** *f* gasconade
**gasconés -nesa** *adj & mf* Gascon
**gasconismo** *m* Gasconism
**Gascuña** *f* Gascony
**gaseamiento** *m* gassing
**gasear** *va* to gas (*to attack, poison, or asphyxiate with gas*); (chem.) to gas
**gaseiforme** *adj* gasiform
**gaseoso -sa** *adj* gaseous, gassy; *f* soda water, carbonated water
**gasificación** *f* gasification
**gasificar** §59 *va* to gasify; to elate, exalt; *vr* to gasify
**gasiforme** *adj* var. of **gaseiforme**
**gasista** *m* gas fitter; gasworker
**gasoducto** *m* gas pipe line
**gasógeno** *m* gas generator, gas producer; mixture of benzine and alcohol used for lighting and for removal of spots
**gas-oil** *m* diesel oil
**gasoleno** *m* or **gasolina** *f* gasolene or gasoline
**gasolinera** *f* powerboat, gasoline motor boat; gas station, filling station
**gasómetro** *m* gasometer; gasholder, gas tank
**Gaspar** *m* Jasper
**gastable** *adj* expendable
**gastadero** *m* (coll.) waster (*way of wasting time, money, patience, etc.*)
**gastado -da** *adj* used up; worn-out; spent; crummy (*joke*)
**gastador -dora** *adj & mf* spendthrift; *m* convict; (mil.) sapper, pioneer, axeman
**gastadura** *f* rub, wear, worn spot
**gastamiento** *m* waste; wear; consumption
**gastar** *va* to spend; to waste; to wear; to wear out; to be hard on (*e.g., shoes*); to use up; to lay waste; to always show; to wear (*e.g., a beard*); to keep (*e.g., a carriage*); to play (*a joke*); **gastarlas** (coll.) to act, to behave; *vn* to spend; **gastar de** to spend; *vr* to waste away; to wear; to wear out; to become used up
**gasterópodo -da** *adj & m* var. of **gastrópodo**
**gasto** *m* cost, expense; wear; flow, rate of flow; **cubrir gastos** to cover expenses; **hacer el gasto** (coll.) to do most of the talking; (coll.) to be the subject of conversation; **pagar los gastos** to foot the bill; **gastos de conservación** or **de entretenimiento** upkeep, maintenance; **gastos de explotación** operating expenses; **gastos de primer establecimiento** initial expenses, initial costs; **gastos de representación** incidental expenses, allowances; **gastos de sostenimiento** upkeep, maintenance; **gastos menudos** petty expenses
**gastoso -sa** *adj* spendthrift, extravagant
**gastralgia** *f* (path.) gastralgia
**gastrectomía** *f* (surg.) gastrectomy
**gástrico -ca** *adj* gastric
**gastritis** *f* (path.) gastritis
**gastroenteritis** *f* (path.) gastroenteritis
**gastroenterología** *f* gastroenterology
**gastrointestinal** *adj* gastrointestinal
**gastronomía** *f* gastronomy
**gastronómico -ca** *adj* gastronomic or gastronomical
**gastrónomo -ma** *mf* gastronome or gastronomer, gourmet
**gastrópodo -da** *adj & m* (zool.) gastropod
**gastrovascular** *adj* gastrovascular
**gástrula** *f* (embryol.) gastrula
**gata** *f* she-cat; low-hanging cloud on mountainside; (bot.) restharrow; (coll.) woman of Madrid; (Am.) working girl; **a gatas** on all fours; **gata parida** (coll.) skeleton (*skinny person*)
**gatada** *f* catlike act; cats; litter of cats; sudden turn of a hare when pursued; (coll.) sly trick
**gatallón -llona** *adj* (coll.) scoundrelly; *mf* (coll.) scoundrel
**gatatumba** *f* (coll.) fake respect, fake emotion, fake pain
**gatazo** *m* (coll.) gyp; **dar gatazo a** (coll.) to gyp
**gateado -da** *adj* catlike; cat-colored; grained; striped; *m* creeping, crawling, climbing; (coll.) scratching, clawing; gateado (*tropical American cabinet wood*)
**gateamiento** *m* creeping, crawling, climbing; (coll.) scratching, clawing
**gatear** *va* (coll.) to scratch, to claw; (coll.) to snitch; *vn* to creep, crawl, climb, go on all fours
**gatera** *f* see **gatero**
**gatería** *f* (coll.) cats; (coll.) gang of roughnecks; (coll.) hypocrisy, fake humility
**gatero -ra** *adj* full of cats; *mf* cat dealer; cat lover; *f* cathole; hiding place; (naut.) hawsehole
**gatesco -ca** *adj* (coll.) catlike, feline
**gatillazo** *m* click of trigger; **dar gatillazo** (coll.) to be disappointing, to be a flop
**gatillo** *m* trigger; hammer, cock (*of firearm*); dentist's forceps; clamp; nape (*of bull*); (coll.) little pickpocket

**gato** *m* (zool.) cat; tomcat; jack, lifting jack; hooking tongs; moneybag; clamp; sly fellow; sneak thief; (coll.) native of Madrid; (Am.) outdoor market; (Am.) hot-water bottle; **dar** or **vender gato por liebre** (coll.) to cheat, to gyp; **gato cazador** mouser; **gato de algalia** (zool.) civet cat; **gato de Angora** Angora cat; **gato de cremallera** rack-and-pinion jack, ratchet jack; **gato de nueve colas** cat-o'-nine-tails; **gato desmurador** mouser; **gato de tornillo** screw jack, jackscrew; **gato encerrado** something fishy (coll.); **gato hidráulico** hydraulic jack; **gato maltés** Maltese cat; **gato manés** Manx cat; **gato montés** (zool.) wildcat; **gato rodante** dolly; **gato volador** or **volante** (zool.) flying cat, flying lemur
**gatuno -na** *adj* cat, catlike; *f* (bot.) restharrow
**gatuña** *f* (bot.) restharrow
**gatuperio** *m* hodgepodge; (coll.) trick, scheme, intrigue
**gauchada** *f* (Am.) Gaucho stunt, sly trick; (Am.) kindness, favor
**gauchaje** *m* (Am.) gathering of Gauchos, gang of Gauchos
**gauchesco -ca** *adj* Gaucho
**gaucho -cha** *adj* warped, uneven; sly, crafty; coarse, rude; (Am.) Gaucho; *m* (Am.) Gaucho; (Am.) good horseman; *f* (Am.) mannish woman; (Am.) loose woman
**gaudeamus** *m* (*pl:* **-mus**) (coll.) feasting, celebrating, merrymaking
**gaulteria** *f* (bot.) gaultheria, wintergreen
**gausio** *m* (phys.) gauss
**gavaje** *m* gavage
**gavanza** *f* dog rose (*flower*)
**gavanzo** *m* (bot.) dog rose
**gaveta** *f* drawer, till; (aut.) glove compartment
**gavetero** *m* furniture maker
**gavia** *f* ditch, drain; (naut.) topsail; (naut.) maintopsail; (orn.) gull; (min.) gang of basket passers
**gavial** *m* (zool.) gavial
**gaviero** *m* (naut.) topman, mastman
**gavieta** *f* (naut.) mizzenmast crow's-nest, bowsprit crow's-nest
**gaviete** *m* (naut.) cathead
**gavilán** *m* (orn.) sparrow hawk; nib (*of pen*); quillon (*of cross guard of sword*); hair stroke (*in writing*); pappus; metal tip (*of a goad*); (Am.) ingrowing nail
**gavilla** *f* sheaf, bundle; gang of thugs
**gavillero** *m* row of sheaves
**gavina** *f* var. of **gaviota**
**gavión** *m* (fort. & hyd.) gabion; (coll.) big wide hat
**gaviota** *f* (orn.) gull, herring gull; **gaviota salteadora** (orn.) jaeger
**gaviotín** *m* (orn.) tern (*Sterna hirundo*)
**gavota** *f* gavotte (*dance and music*)
**gaya** *f* see **gayo**
**gayadura** *f* colored stripes, colored striping
**gayar** *va* to trim with colored stripes
**gayo -ya** *adj* gay, bright, showy; *m* (orn.) bluejay; *f* colored stripe; (orn.) magpie
**gayola** *f* cage; (coll.) jail; (prov.) raised lookout in a vineyard
**gayomba** *f* (bot.) Spanish broom; (bot.) yellow lupine
**gayuba** *f* (bot.) bearberry
**gayubal** *m* bearberry field
**gaza** *f* (naut.) loop, bend
**gazafatón** *m* (coll.) var. of **gazapatón**
**gazapa** *f* (coll.) lie
**gazapatón** *m* (coll.) bloomer (*in speech*)
**gazapera** *f* rabbit warren; (coll.) gang, gang of thugs; (coll.) brawl, row; (vet.) distemper (*of cats*)
**gazapina** *f* (coll.) gang, gang of thugs; (coll.) brawl, row
**gazapo** *m* young rabbit; sly fellow; slip, error; squatty person; (coll.) big lie
**gazmiar** *vn* to nibble all the time; *vr* (coll.) to complain
**gazmoñada** or **gazmoñería** *f* priggishness
**gazmoñero -ra** or **gazmoño -ña** *adj* priggish, strait-laced, demure; *mf* prig
**gaznápiro -ra** *mf* gawk, boob
**gaznar** *vn* var. of **graznar**
**gaznatada** *f* or **gaznatazo** *m* punch in the gullet
**gaznate** *m* gullet, throttle; fritter
**gaznatón** *m* punch in the gullet; fritter
**gazné** *m* (Am.) large colored kerchief
**gazpacho** *m* cold vegetable soup, gazpacho
**gazuza** *f* (coll.) hunger
**gea** *f* description of the minerals of a region; (*cap.*) *f* (myth.) Gaea
**geco** *m* (zool.) gecko, tarente
**Gedeón** *m* (Bib.) Gideon
**gedeonada** *f* (coll.) platitude, commonplace
**gehena** *m* (Bib.) Gehenna
**géiser** *m* geyser
**geisha** *f* geisha
**gel** *m* (chem. & phys.) gel
**gelación** *f* gelation
**gelatina** *f* gelatin
**gelatinificar** §86 *va* to gelatinize
**gelatinoso -sa** *adj* gelatinous
**gélido -da** *adj* gelid, frigid
**gelsemio** *m* (bot.) yellow jasmine; (pharm.) gelsemium
**gema** *f* gem, precious stone; (bot.) bud, gemma; wane (*of board or plank*)
**gemación** *f* (bot. & zool.) gemmation
**gemebundo -da** *adj* full of groans
**gemelo -la** *adj* & *mf* twin; *m* (anat.) gemellus; **gemelos** *mpl* twins; binoculars; cuff links, set of buttons; **Gemelos** *mpl* (astr.) Gemini (*constellation*); **gemelos de campo** field glasses; **gemelos de teatro** opera glasses; **gemelos fraternos** fraternal twins; **gemelos homólogos** or **idénticos** identical twins; **gemelos heterólogos** fraternal twins; *f* (bot.) Arabian jasmine
**gemido** *m* moan, groan; wail, whine; howl, roar, whistle; (poet.) sigh
**gemidor -dora** *adj* moaning, groaning; wailing, whining; howling, roaring, whistling
**gemífero -ra** *adj* gemmiferous, full of gems or precious stones; (bot.) gemmate; (bot. & zool.) gemmiferous
**gemificar** §86 *vn* (bot.) to gemmate
**geminación** *f* gemination; (phonet. & rhet.) gemination
**geminado -da** *adj* geminate
**geminar** *va* & *vr* to geminate
**Géminis** *m* (astr.) Gemini (*constellation and sign of zodiac*); (*l.c.*) *m* (pharm.) plaster (*of ceruse and wax*)
**gemíparo -ra** *adj* (biol.) gemmiparous
**gemiquear** *vn* (dial. & Am.) to whine
**gemiqueo** *m* (dial. & Am.) whining
**gemir** §94 *vn* to moan, groan; to wail, whine; to howl, roar, whistle; to pine away, to grieve
**gémula** *f* (bot., zool. & biol.) gemmule
**gen** *m* (biol.) gene
**genciana** *f* (bot.) gentian (*plant and root*); **genciana amarilla** (bot.) bitterwort
**gencianáceo -a** *adj* (bot.) gentianaceous
**gencianilla** *f* (bot.) bitterwort
**gendarme** *m* gendarme
**gendarmería** *f* gendarmerie
**genealogía** *f* genealogy
**genealógico -ca** *adj* genealogical
**genealogista** *mf* genealogist
**generación** *f* generation; **generación espontánea** (biol.) spontaneous generation
**generador -dora** *adj* generating; *mf* generator; *m* (elec.) generator (*dynamo*); (mach.) generator (*steam boiler, etc.*); **generador de barrido** (telv.) sweep generator
**general** *adj* general; vast, enormous; widely informed; *m* (mil.) general, general officer; (rel.) general; **en general** or **por lo general** in general; **general de brigada** (mil.) brigadier general; **general de división** (mil.) major general; **general en jefe** (mil.) general in chief; **generales** *fpl* personal data (*such as name, age, nationality*)
**generala** *f* general's wife; call to arms
**generalato** *m* generalship; generals of an army
**generalero** *m* (prov.) customhouse officer
**generalidad** *f* generality; bulk, majority; Catalan legislative assembly; (prov.) custom duties
**generalísimo** *m* generalissimo
**generalización** *f* generalization
**generalizador -dora** *adj* generalizing

**generalizar** §76 *va & vn* to generalize; *vr* to become generalized
**generar** *va* to generate; (elec.) to generate
**generativo -va** *adj* generative
**generatriz** *f* (*pl:* **-trices**) (elec. & geom.) generatrix
**genérico -ca** *adj* generic; (gram.) indefinite (*article*); (gram.) common (*noun*); (gram.) indicating gender (*said of an ending*)
**género** *m* kind, sort; manner, way; material (*textile fabric*); (biol. & log.) genus; (f.a. & lit.) genre; (gram.) gender; **géneros** *mpl* material, goods, merchandise; **de género** (f.a.) genre, e.g., **pintor de género** genre painter; **género chico** (theat.) one-act comedy; **género de punto** knit goods, knitwear; **género humano** humankind, human race; **género ínfimo** (theat.) light vaudeville; **género novelístico** fiction; **género picaresco** (theat.) burlesque; **género tipo** (biol.) type genus
**generosidad** *f* generosity
**generoso -sa** *adj* generous; highborn; brave; excellent, superb; warm (*heart*); generous, rich (*wine*)
**genésico -ca** *adj* genesic
**génesis** *f* (*pl:* **-sis**) genesis; **el Génesis** (Bib.) Genesis
**geneticista** *mf* geneticist
**genético -ca** *adj* genetic; *f* genetics
**genetista** *mf* geneticist
**geniado -da** *adj* tempered; **bien geniado** well-tempered, good-natured; **mal geniado** ill-tempered
**genial** *adj* inspired, brilliant, genius-like; cheerful, pleasant; temperamental
**genialidad** *f* peculiarity; genius
**geniano -na** *adj* (anat. & zool.) genial
**geniazo** *m* (coll.) strong temper
**genicida** *adj & mf* var. of **genocida**
**genicidio** *m* var. of **genocidio**
**geniculación** *f* geniculation
**geniculado -da** *adj* geniculate
**geniecillo** *m* (coll.) strong temper; (f.a.) cupid
**genio** *m* temper; disposition, temperament; genius; character, force; (myth.) genie, jinni; (coll.) fire, spirit
**genioso -sa** *adj* ill-natured
**genipa** *f* (bot.) genipap
**genista** *f* (bot.) Spanish broom; (bot.) genista
**genital** *adj* genital; **genitales** *mpl* (anat.) testicles; (anat.) genitals
**genitivo -va** *adj & m* (gram.) genitive
**génitourinario -ria** *adj* genitourinary
**genízaro -ra** *adj & m* var. of **jenízaro**
**Gen.**[1] abr. of **general**
**genocida** *adj* genocidal; *mf* genocide (*person*)
**genocidio** *m* genocide (*act*)
**genol** *m* (naut.) futtock
**genoma** *m* (biol.) genom
**genotipo** *m* (biol.) genotype
**Génova** *f* Genoa
**genovés -vesa** *adj & mf* Genoese
**Genoveva** *f* Genevieve, Winifred
**gente** *f* people; troops; (naut.) complement; (coll.) folks (*relatives*); **de gente en gente** from generation to generation; **hacer gente** to recruit; (coll.) to draw a crowd; **la gente chic** the smart set; **ser gente** (Am.) to be somebody; **gente baja** lower classes, rabble; **gente bien** (coll.) nice people; **gente de alpargata** simple folk; **gente de barrio** loafers; **gente de bien** decent people; **gente de blusa** working people; **gente be bronce** gypsies; **gente de capa negra** (coll.) decent citizens; **gente de capa parda** (coll.) countryfolk; **gente de carda** or **de la carda** (coll.) scoundrels, bullies; **gente de coleta** (coll.) bullfighters; **gente de color** colored people; **gente de escalera abajo** (coll.) underdogs; **gente de gallaruza** (coll.) countryfolk; **gente de gavilla** crooks, thugs; **gente de la cuchilla** (coll.) butchers; **gente de la garra** (coll.) thieves; **gente de la vida airada** bullies, libertines; **gente del bronce** (coll.) lively people; **gente del gordillo** common people, plebeians; **gente del polvillo** (coll.) masons; **gente de pardillo** or **del pardillo** country people, peasants; **gente del rey** convicts; **gente de mal vivir** thugs, underworld; **gente de mar** seafaring people; **gente de medio pelo** people of limited means; **gente de paz** friend (*in answer to "Who is there?"*); **gente de pelo** or **de pelusa** (coll.) well-to-do people; **gente de pluma** (coll.) clerks; **gente de poco más o menos** (coll.) nincompoop, nobody; **gente de razón** (Am.) white people; **gente de seguida** gangsters, bandits; **gente de su majestad** convicts; **gente de toda broza** (coll.) loafers, bums; **gente de trato** tradespeople; **gente de traza** responsible people; **gente forzada** convicts; **gente gorda** (coll.) people of standing; **gente menuda** (coll.) small fry; (coll.) common people; **gente perdida** bums; **gente principal** outstanding people
**gentecilla** *f* mob, rabble
**gentil** *adj* gentile, heathen; genteel, elegant; strange, wondrous; terrific; *mf* gentile, heathen
**gentileza** *f* gentility, elegance, politeness; gallantry; show, splendor; ease, smoothness; **gentilezas** *fpl* beauties, adornments (*of language, style, etc.*)
**gentilhombre** *m* (*pl:* **gentileshombres**) gentleman (*attendant to person of high rank*); messenger to the king; kind sir, my good man; **gentilhombre de cámara** gentleman in waiting
**gentilicio -cia** *adj* national; family; (gram.) gentile; *m* (gram.) gentile
**gentílico -ca** *adj* heathenish
**gentilidad** *f* or **gentilismo** *m* heathendom
**gentilizar** §76 *va* to heathenize; *vn* to observe heathen rites
**gentío** *m* crowd, throng, mob
**gentualla** or **gentuza** *f* rabble, scum of society
**genuflexión** *f* genuflection or genuflexion
**genuino -na** *adj* genuine
**geocéntrico -ca** *adj* geocentric or geocentrical
**geoda** *f* (geol.) geode
**geodesia** *f* geodesy
**geodésico -ca** *adj* geodesic, geodetic
**geodesta** *mf* geodesist
**geofagía** *f* geophagy
**geofísico -ca** *adj* geophysical; *mf* geophysicist; *f* geophysics
**geófita** *f* (bot.) geophyte
**Geofredo** *m* Geoffrey
**geognosia** *f* geognosy
**geografía** *f* geography; **geografía física** physical geography; **geografía lingüística** linguistic geography
**geográfico -ca** *adj* geographic or geographical
**geógrafo -fa** *mf* geographer
**geoide** *m* geoid
**geología** *f* geology
**geológico -ca** *adj* geologic or geological
**geólogo -ga** *mf* geologist
**geomagnético -ca** *adj* geomagnetic
**geomancía** *f* geomancy
**geomántico -ca** *adj* geomantic; *mf* geomancer
**geómetra** *mf* geometer, geometrician; *m* (zool.) geometer, inchworm, measuring worm
**geometral** *adj* var. of **geométrico**
**geometría** *f* geometry; **geometría analítica** analytic geometry; **geometría del** or **en el espacio** solid geometry; **geometría euclidiana** Euclidian geometry; **geometría no euclidiana** non-Euclidian geometry; **geometría plana** plane geometry; **geometría proyectiva** projective geometry
**geométrico -ca** *adj* geometric or geometrical
**geométrido** *m* (ent.) geometrid
**geometrizar** §76 *va* to geometrize; *vn* to geometrize; (coll.) to pretend to be a geometrician
**geomorfología** *f* geomorphology
**geopolítico -ca** *adj* geopolitical; *f* geopolitics
**geoponía** *f* geoponics
**geopónico -ca** *adj* geoponic; *f* geoponics
**geoquímica** *f* geochemistry
**georama** *m* georama
**georgiano -na** *adj & mf* Georgian
**geórgica** *f* georgic (*poem*)
**Georgina** *f* Georgiana, Georgina (*woman's name*)
**geosinclinal** *adj & m* (geol.) geosynclinal
**geotactismo** *m* or **geotaxia** *f* geotaxis
**geotectónico -ca** *adj* geotectonic; *f* geotectonics

**geotérmico -ca** *adj* geothermal
**geotrópico -ca** *adj* geotropic
**geotropismo** *m* (biol.) geotropism
**geraniáceo -a** *adj* (bot.) geraniaceous
**geranio** *m* (bot.) geranium; **geranio de rosa** (bot.) rose geranium; **geranio malva** (bot.) nutmeg geranium
**Gerardo** *m* Gerald, Gerard
**gerbo** *m* var. of **jerbo**
**gerencia** *f* management; managership, directorship; manager's office
**gerente** *m* manager, director; **gerente de publicidad** advertising manager; **gerente de ventas** sales manager
**geriatría** *f* geriatrics
**geriatra** *adj* geriatrical; *mf* geriatrician, geriatrist
**geriátrico -ca** *adj* geriatrical
**gerifalte** *m* (orn.) gerfalcon; (slang) thief; **como un gerifalte** superbly
**germandrina** *f* (bot.) germander, wall germander
**germanesco -ca** *adj* slang, gypsy
**Germania** *f* (hist. & fig.) Germania
**germanía** *f* slang or jargon of gypsies and thieves
**germánico -ca** *adj* Germanic; *m* Germanic (*group of languages*)
**germanio** *m* (chem.) germanium
**germanismo** *m* Germanism
**germanista** *mf* Germanist
**germanización** *f* Germanization
**germanizar** §76 *va & vr* to Germanize
**germano -na** *adj* Germanic, Teutonic; *mf* German, Teuton; *m* brother-german
**germanófilo -la** *adj & mf* Germanophile
**germanófobo -ba** *adj & mf* Germanophobe
**germen** *m* (bact., biol., embryol. & fig.) germ; **germen plasma** germ plasm
**germicida** *adj* germicidal; *m* germicide
**germinación** *f* germination
**germinador -dora** *adj* germinating; *m* germinator
**germinal** *adj* germinal; germ
**germinante** *adj* germinant
**germinar** *vn* to germinate
**germinativo -va** *adj* germinative
**germón** *m* (ichth.) albacore (*Germo alalunga*)
**gerontología** *f* gerontology
**Gertrudis** *f* Gertrude
**gerundense** *adj* (pertaining to) Gerona; *mf* native or inhabitant of Gerona
**gerundiada** *f* (coll.) bombastic expression
**gerundiano -na** *adj* (coll.) bombastic
**gerundino** *m* gerundive (*in Latin grammar*)
**gerundio** *m* gerund, present participle; (coll.) bombastic writer or speaker
**gesta** *f* (archaic) gest (*metrical romance; feat, exploit*)
**gestación** *f* gestation; (fig.) gestation
**gestaltismo** *m* Gestalt psychology
**gestapo** *f* Gestapo (*Nazi secret police*)
**gestatorio -ria** *adj* gestatory; gestatorial (*chair*)
**gestear** *vn* var. of **gesticular**
**gestería** *f* crudity, vulgarity
**gesticulación** *f* face; grimace
**gesticular** *vn* to make a face, to make faces; to gesture
**gestión** *f* step, measure; management
**gestionar** *va* to pursue, prosecute, strive for; to manage; to take steps to attain or to accomplish
**gesto** *m* face; grimace, wry face; look, appearance; gesture; **estar de buen gesto** to be in a good humor; **estar de mal gesto** to be in a bad humor; **hacer gestos** to make faces; to gesture; **hacer gestos a** to make faces at; to look askance at; **poner gesto** to look annoyed; **gesto de manos** gesture
**gestor -tora** *adj* managing; *m* manager
**gestoría** *f* management
**gestudo -da** *adj* (coll.) cross-looking
**Getsemaní** *m* (Bib.) Gethsemane
**ghetto** *m* ghetto
**giba** *f* hump; (coll.) annoyance, inconvenience
**gibado -da** *adj* humped, hunchbacked
**gibar** *va* to hump, to hunch; (coll.) to annoy, bother
**gibelino -na** *adj & m* Ghibelline
**gibón** *m* (zool.) gibbon
**gibosidad** *f* gibbosity
**giboso -sa** *adj* gibbous, humped
**Gibraltar** Gibraltar
**gibraltareño -ña** *adj* (pertaining to) Gibraltar; *mf* native or inhabitant of Gibraltar
**giga** *f* jig (*dance and music*)
**giganta** *f* giantess; (bot.) sunflower
**gigante** *adj* giant, gigantic; *m* giant; giant figure (*in a procession*); (slang) middle finger; **gigante en tierra de enanos** (coll.) little runt; (coll.) big fish in a little pond
**giganteo -a** *adj* gigantean; *f* (bot.) sunflower
**gigantesco -ca** *adj* gigantic
**gigantez** *f* giantism; gigantic size
**gigantilla** *f* little giantess; big-headed masked figure; little fat girl; little fat woman
**gigantismo** *m* (path.) giantism or gigantism
**gigantón -tona** *mf* huge giant; *m* giant figure (*in a procession*); **echar los gigantones a** (coll.) to rake over the coals
**gigote** *m* chopped-meat stew; **hacer gigote** (coll.) to chop into small pieces
**gijonense** or **gijonés -nesa** *adj* (pertaining to) Gijón; *mf* native or inhabitant of Gijón
**Gil** *m* Giles
**gilbertio** *m* (phys.) gilbert
**Gilberto** *m* Gilbert
**gilí** *adj* (*pl:* **-líes**) (coll.) foolish, stupid
**gilvo -va** *adj* honey-colored
**gimnasia** *f* gymnastics; **gimnasia sueca** calisthenics, light gymnastics, setting-up exercise
**gimnasio** *m* gymnasium
**gimnasta** *mf* gymnast
**gimnástico -ca** *adj* gymnastic; *f* gymnastics
**gímnico -ca** *adj* athletic, gymnastic
**gimnospermo -ma** *adj* gymnospermous; *f* (bot.) gymnosperm
**gimnoto** *m* (ichth.) electric eel
**gimotear** *vn* (coll.) to whine
**gimoteo** *m* (coll.) whining
**ginandro -dra** *adj* (bot.) gynandrous
**ginebra** *f* gin (*drink*); bedlam; din; (mus.) xylophone; (*cap.*) *f* Geneva; (myth.) Guinevere; **ginebra holandesa** Holland gin
**ginebrada** *f* puff-paste pie
**ginebrés -bresa** or **ginebrino -na** *adj & mf* Genevan or Genevese
**gineceo** *m* (bot.) gynoecium, gynaeceum; (hist.) gynaeceum (*women's apartments*)
**ginecología** *f* gynecology
**ginecológico -ca** *adj* gynecological
**ginecólogo -ga** *mf* gynecologist
**ginesta** *f* (bot.) Spanish broom
**gineta** *f* (zool.) genet
**gingidio** *m* (bot.) bishop's-weed
**gingival** *adj* gingival
**gingivitis** *f* (path.) gingivitis
**gínglimo** *m* (anat.) ginglymus, hinge joint
**gingo** *m* (bot.) gingko
**giniatría** *f* gyniatrics
**ginóforo** *m* (bot.) gynophore
**ginsén** *m* (bot.) ginseng (*plant and root*)
**gipsófila** *f* (bot.) gypsophila, babies'-breath
**gira** *f* var. of **jira**
**girado -da** *mf* (com.) drawee
**girador -dora** *mf* (com.) drawer
**giralda** *f* weathercock (*in form of person or animal*); **la Giralda** the Giralda (*square tower of cathedral of Seville, Spain, surmounted by bronze statue of Faith, which turns in the wind*)
**giraldete** *m* (eccl.) sleeveless rochet
**giraldilla** *f* small weathercock
**giramachos** *m* (*pl:* **-chos**) tap wrench
**girándula** *f* girandole
**girante** *adj* revolving
**girar** *va* to pay (*a visit*); (com.) to draw; *vn* to turn; to gyrate, to rotate; to revolve; to trade; (com.) to draw
**girasol** *m* (bot.) sunflower; sycophant
**giratorio -ria** *adj* revolving; gyratory; *f* revolving bookcase
**giravión** *m* gyroplane
**girino** *m* (ent.) whirligig; (obs.) tadpole
**giro -ra** *adj* (Am.) black-and-white (*cock*); yellow (*cock*); (Am.) cocky; *m* turn; gyration, rotation; revolution; turn, trend, course;

threat, boast; gash, slash; expression; turn (*of phrase*); line (*of business*); trade; (com.) draft; **giro a la vista** (com.) sight draft; **giro electrónico** (phys.) spin, electron spin; **giro postal** money order; *f* var. of **jira**
**giroaleta** *f* (naut.) gyrofin
**girocompás** *m* gyrocompass
**giroestabilizador** *m* (aer. & naut.) gyrostabilizer
**giroflé** *m* (bot.) clove
**girola** *f* (arch.) apse aisle
**girómetro** *m* gyrometer
**girón** *m* var. of **jirón**
**girondino -na** *adj & m* (hist.) Girondist
**giropiloto** *m* (aer.) gyropilot
**giroplano** *m* (aer.) gyroplane
**giroscópico -ca** *adj* gyroscopic
**giroscopio** or **giróscopo** *m* gyroscope
**girostático -ca** *adj* gyrostatic; *f* gyrostatics
**giróstato** *m* gyrostat
**gis** *m* (archaic) chalk; (Am.) slate pencil
**giste** *m* var. of **jiste**
**gitanada** *f* gypsylike trick; fawning, flattery
**gitanear** *vn* to lead the life of a gypsy; to fawn, to flatter
**gitanería** *f* fawning, flattery; band of gypsies; gypsy life; gypsyism
**gitanesco -ca** *adj* gypsy, gypsyish
**gitanismo** *m* gypsies; gypsy life, gypsy lore; gypsyism
**gitano -na** *adj* gypsy; sly, tricky; flattering, honey-mouthed; *mf* gypsy; *m* Gypsy (*language*)
**glabro -bra** *adj* (bot. & zool.) glabrous
**glaciación** *f* glaciation, freezing
**glacial** *adj* glacial; frigid (*zone*); (chem.) glacial; (fig.) cold, indifferent
**glaciar** *m* glacier
**glaciario -ria** *adj* glacial
**glacis** *m* (*pl:* **-cis**) glacis; (fort.) glacis
**gladiador** *m* or **gladiator** *m* gladiator
**gladiatorio -ria** *adj* gladiatorial
**gladio** *m* (bot.) cattail, reed mace; (zool.) gladius
**gladíolo** *m* (bot.) cattail, reed mace; (bot.) gladiolus; (anat.) gladiolus (*mesosternum*)
**glande** *m* (anat.) glans penis
**glándula** *f* (anat. & bot.) gland; **glándula carótida** (anat.) carotid gland; **glándula cerrada** (anat.) ductless gland; **glándula endocrina** (anat.) endocrine gland; **glándula lagrimal** (anat.) lachrymal gland; **glándula mamaria** (anat.) mammary gland; **glándula paratiroides** (anat.) parathyroid gland; **glándula pineal** (anat.) pineal gland; **glándula pituitaria** (anat.) pituitary gland; **glándula prostática** (anat.) prostate gland; **glándula salival** (anat.) salivary gland; **glándula sebácea** (anat.) sebaceous gland; **glándula submaxilar** (anat.) submaxillary gland; **glándula sudorípara** (anat.) sweat gland; **glándula suprarrenal** (anat.) adrenal gland, suprarenal gland; **glándula tiroides** (anat.) thyroid gland
**glandular** *adj* glandular
**glanduloso -sa** *adj* glandulous
**glasé** *m* glacé silk
**glaseado -da** *adj* glacé; glossy, shiny
**glasear** *va* to calender, to satin; to glacé (*fruit, leather, etc.*); (paint.) to glaze
**glasto** *m* (bot.) woad
**glauberita** *f* (chem.) glauberite
**glaucio** *m* (bot.) horn poppy
**glauco -ca** *adj* glaucous; (bot.) glaucous; *m* (zool.) glaucus, sea slug
**glaucoma** *m* (path.) glaucoma
**glaucomatoso -sa** *adj* glaucomatous; *mf* sufferer from glaucoma
**gleba** *f* clod or lump of earth turned over by plow; estate, landed property
**glena** *f* (anat.) glenoid cavity
**glenoideo -a** *adj* glenoid
**glera** *f* gravel pit
**glicérico** *adj* (chem.) glyceric
**glicérido** *m* (chem.) glyceride
**glicerilo** *m* (chem.) glyceryl
**glicerina** *f* glycerin
**glicerol** *m* (chem.) glycerol
**glicina** *f* (bot.) Chinese wistaria; (chem.) glycine
**glicogénico -ca** *adj* glycogenic
**glicógeno** *m* (biochem.) glycogen
**glicol** *m* (chem.) glycol
**glifo** *m* (arch.) glyph
**glioma** *m* (path.) glioma
**gliptografía** *f* glyptography
**global** *adj* total; global, world-wide
**globo** *m* globe; balloon; globe, lamp shade; cell (*of dirigible*); **en globo** as a whole; in broad outlines; in bulk; **globo aerostático** balloon; **globo barrera** (mil.) barrage balloon; **globo cautivo** captive balloon; **globo celeste** (astr.) celestial globe; **globo cometa** kite balloon; **globo de fuego** (astr.) bolide; **globo del ojo** (anat.) eyeball; **globo de observación** observation balloon; **globo libre** free balloon; **globo piloto** pilot balloon; **globo sonda** sounding balloon, trial balloon; (fig.) trial balloon (*statement made to test public opinion*); **globo terráqueo** or **terrestre** globe (*earth; map of earth in form of sphere*)
**globoso -sa** *adj* globose, globate
**globular** *adj* globular; *va* to make round, to shape like a globe
**globulina** *f* (biochem.) globulin; **globulina gama** (physiol.) gamma globulin
**glóbulo** *m* globule; (bot.) globule; (physiol.) corpuscle; **glóbulo blanco** (physiol.) white corpuscle; **glóbulo rojo** (physiol.) red corpuscle
**globuloso -sa** *adj* globulose
**glogló** *m* var. of **gluglú**
**glomérula** *f* (bot.) glomerule
**glomérulo** *m* (anat.) glomerulus
**gloria** *f* glory; gloria (*fabric; halo*); ladylock (*pastry*); **estar en sus glorias** (coll.) to be in one's glory; **ganar la gloria** to go to glory (*to die*); **oler a gloria** (coll.) to smell heavenly; **saber a gloria** (coll.) to taste heavenly; (*cap.*) *m* (eccl.) Gloria
**gloriar §90** *va* to glory, to glorify; *vr* to glory; **gloriarse de** to glory in (*e.g., one's achievements*); **gloriarse en** to glory in (*e.g., the Lord*)
**glorieta** *f* arbor, bower, summerhouse; square, public square; traffic circle
**glorificable** *adj* glorifiable
**glorificación** *f* glorification
**glorificar §86** *va* to glorify; *vr* to be covered with glory; to glory
**glorioso -sa** *adj* glorious; proud, boastful; *f* (bot.) glory lily; **echar de la gloriosa** to boast of one's exploits, to show off; **la Gloriosa** the Virgin
**glosa** *f* gloss; gloss (*form of poem*); (mus.) variation
**glosador -dora** *adj* glossing; glossatorial; *mf* glosser; *m* glossator
**glosar** *va* to gloss; (Am.) to scold; *vn* to gloss; to find fault
**glosario** *m* glossary
**glose** *m* glossing, commenting
**glosectomía** *f* (surg.) glossectomy
**glosis** *f* (zool.) glossa
**glositis** *f* (path.) glossitis
**glosopeda** *f* (vet.) foot-and-mouth disease
**glótico -ca** *adj* glottal
**glotis** *f* (*pl:* **-tis**) (anat.) glottis
**glotón -tona** *adj* gluttonous; *mf* glutton; *m* (zool.) glutton (*Gulo gulo*)
**glotonear** *vn* to be gluttonous, to gormandize
**glotonería** *f* gluttony
**gloxínea** *f* (bot.) gloxinia
**glucina** *f* (chem.) glucina
**glucinio** *m* (chem.) glucinium or glucinum
**glucoproteína** *f* (biochem.) glycoprotein
**glucosa** *f* (biochem.) glucose
**glucósido** *m* (chem.) glucoside
**glucosuria** *f* (path.) glycosuria
**gluglú** *m* gurgle, glug; gobble (*of turkey*); **hacer gluglú** to gurgle, to glug
**gluglutear** *vn* to gobble (*said of a turkey*)
**gluma** *f* (bot.) glume
**gluten** *m* gluten
**glutenoso -sa** *adj* glutenous
**glúteo -a** *adj* (anat.) gluteal
**glutinoso -sa** *adj* glutinous
**gnatión** *m* (anat.) gnathion
**gneis** *m* (geol.) gneiss

**gnéisico -ca** *adj* gneissic
**gnómico -ca** *adj* gnomic
**gnomo** *m* gnome; (myth.) gnome
**gnomon** *m* gnomon
**gnosticismo** *m* Gnosticism
**gnóstico -ca** *adj & mf* Gnostic
**gnu** *m* var. of **ñu**
**goa** *f* (metal.) pig, bloom
**gob.** abr. of **gobierno**
**gobelino** *m* goblin
**gobernable** *adj* governable
**gobernación** *f* governing; government; interior, department of the interior; (Am.) territory
**gobernador -dora** *adj* governing; *m* governor; *f* woman governor; governor's wife
**gobernalle** *m* rudder, helm
**gobernante** *adj* ruling; *mf* ruler; *m* (coll.) self-appointed head
**gobernar** §18 *va* to govern; to guide, direct; to control, rule; to steer; *vn* to govern; to steer, e.g., **este buque no gobierna bien** this boat does not steer well
**gobernoso -sa** *adj* (coll.) orderly
**gobierna** *f* weather vane
**gobierno** *m* government; governor's office, governor's residence; governership; management, control, rule; guidance; navigability (*of a ship*); **de buen gobierno** navigable (*ship*); **para su gobierno** for your guidance; **servir de gobierno** (coll.) to serve as guide; **gobierno de monigotes** puppet government; **gobierno doméstico** housekeeping; **gobierno exilado** government in exile; **gobierno local** local government; **gobierno títere** puppet government
**gobio** *m* (ichth.) gudgeon; (ichth.) goby
**gob.no** or **gob.o** abr. of **gobierno**
**gob.r** abr. of **gobernador**
**goce** *m* enjoyment
**gocete** *m* (archaic) collar of mail; (archaic) shield of mail for armpit
**gocho -cha** *mf* (coll.) hog
**godesco -ca** *adj* gay, merry
**godo -da** *adj* Gothic; *mf* Goth; Spanish noble; (Am. scornful) Spaniard
**Godofredo** *m* Godfrey
**goecia** *f* black magic
**gofo -fa** *adj* stupid, crude; (paint.) dwarf (*figure*)
**gol** *m* (football) goal
**gola** *f* gullet; (arm.) gorget; (fort.) gorge; (mil.) gorget (*military badge*); (arch.) cyma, ogee
**goldre** *m* quiver (*for arrows*)
**goleta** *f* (naut.) schooner
**golf** *m* (sport) golf
**golfán** *m* (bot.) white water lily
**golfear** *vn* (coll.) to live the life of a ragamuffin
**golfería** *f* mob of ragamuffins; knavery
**golfín** *m* (zool.) dolphin
**golfista** *mf* (sport) golfer
**golfo -fa** *mf* little scoundrel, ragamuffin (*of Madrid*); *m* gulf; open sea, main; faro (*game*); chaos, confusion; great number, multitude; (coll.) tramp, bum; **golfo Arábigo** Red Sea; **golfo de Adén** Gulf of Aden; **golfo de Bengala** Bay of Bengal; **golfo de Botnia** Gulf of Bothnia; **golfo de Corinto** Gulf of Corinth; **golfo de Gascuña** Bay of Biscay; **golfo de Méjico** Gulf of Mexico; **golfo de Panamá** Gulf of Panama; **golfo de San Lorenzo** Gulf of St. Lawrence; **golfo de Valencia** Gulf of Valencia; **golfo de Venecia** Gulf of Venice; **golfo de Vizcaya** Bay of Biscay; **golfo Pérsico** Persian Gulf
**Gólgota, el** (Bib.) Golgotha
**Goliat** *m* (Bib.) Goliath
**golilla** *f* gorget, ruff; magistrate's collar; sleeve, collar (*of terra-cotta pipe*); pipe flange; (Am.) necktie; (Am.) erectile bristles (*of fowl*); **ajustar** or **apretar la golilla a** (coll.) to bring to reason; (coll.) to hang, to garrote; *m* (archaic) magistrate; (archaic) civilian
**golondrina** *f* wanderer; (orn.) swallow; (ichth.) swallow fish; **golondrina cola tijera** (orn.) barn swallow (*Hirundo erythrogastra*); **golondrina de mar** (orn.) tern (*Hydrochelidon*); **golondrina purpúrea** (orn.) purple martin
**golondrinera** *f* (bot.) swallowwort, celandine
**golondrino** *m* male swallow; vagabond; deserter; (path.) tumor under armpit
**golondro** *m* desire, whim; (coll.) sponger; **andar de golondro** (coll.) to have a lot of wild ideas; **campar de golondro** (coll.) to be a sponger, live by one's wits
**golosear** *vn* var. of **golosinar**
**golosina** *f* sweet, delicacy, tidbit; eagerness, appetite, greediness; trifle; attraction
**golosinar** or **golosinear** *vn* to go around nibbling on sweets, to be always indulging in sweets
**golosmear** *vn* to sniff the cooking
**goloso -sa** *adj* sweet-toothed; gluttonous; greedy; *mf* gourmand
**golpazo** *m* bang, heavy blow, stroke, or knock; hard slap; pounding
**golpe** *m* blow, hit, beat, knock; stroke; bruise, bump; heartbeat; crowd, throng; flap (*of pocket*); trimming; mass, abundance; blow (*misfortune*); surprise, wonder; witticism; high spot; **a golpe seguro** with certainty; **caer de golpe** to collapse; **dar golpe** to make a hit, to be a sensation; **dar golpe a** to taste; **dar golpe en bola** to come off with flying colors; **de golpe** suddenly, all at once; **de golpe y porrazo** or **zumbido** (coll.) slambang; **de un golpe** at one stroke, at one time; **matar a golpes** to beat to death; **no dar golpe** to not do a stroke of work; **golpe de agua** water hammer; **golpe de arco** (mus.) bowing; **golpe de ariete** water hammer; **golpe de estado** coup d'état; **golpe de fortuna** lucky hit, stroke of luck; **golpe de gancho** (box.) hook; **golpe de gracia** coup de grâce, finishing stroke; **golpe de mano** (mil.) surprise attack; **golpe de mar** surge, heavy sea; **golpe de ojo** insight; glance; **golpe de pechos** beating one's bosom or breast; **golpe de teatro** dramatic turn of events; **golpe de tijera** scissors kick (*in swimming*); **golpe de tos** coughing spell, fit of coughing; **golpe de viento** (naut.) gust of wind; **golpe de vista** glance, look; **golpe en vago** miss; flop, failure; (baseball) strike; **golpe inverso** (box.) jab; **golpe lateral** (box.) swing; **golpe mortal** deathblow; **golpe teatral** dramatic turn of events
**golpeadero** *m* spot worn from beating; place struck by falling water; beating sound
**golpeador -dora** *adj* striking, beating, knocking; *mf* striker, beater, knocker; *m* (Am.) door knocker
**golpeadura** *f* striking, hitting, beating, knocking
**golpear** *va* to strike, hit, beat, knock; to bruise, bump; *vn* to beat, to knock; to tick; to knock (*said of an automobile motor*)
**golpeo** *m* var. of **golpeadura**
**golpete** *m* door catch, window catch (*to hold door or window open*); **jugar de golpete** (coll.) to cheat in weighing
**golpetear** *va & vn* to beat, knock, hammer, pound; to rattle
**golpeteo** *m* beating, knocking, hammering, pounding; rattling
**gollería** *f* dainty, delicacy; (coll.) favor, extra
**golletazo** *m* blow on the neck of a bottle (*to open it*); sudden termination of negotiations; (taur.) stab in the lungs
**gollete** *m* throat, neck; neck (*e.g., of bottle*); neckband (*of religious habit*); **estar hasta el gollete** (coll.) to have enough, to be out of patience; to be full (*of food*); to be stuck
**gollizno** or **gollizo** *m* gully, ravine
**golloría** *f* var. of **gollería**
**goma** *f* gum, rubber; eraser, rubber; elastic, rubber band; tire; mucilage; (path.) gumma; (plant path.) gumming disease; (Am.) hangover; **goma adragante** tragacanth; **goma arábiga** gum arabic; **goma de borrar** eraser, rubber; **goma de mascar** chewing gum; **goma elástica** gum elastic; **goma espumosa** foam rubber; **goma guta** gamboge; **goma laca** shellac; **goma para pegar** mucilage; **goma quino** kino gum

**gomaguta** *f* gamboge
**gomecillo** *m* (coll.) blind man's guide
**gomero -ra** *adj* (pertaining to) gum, rubber; *m* rubber man, rubber producer; rubber-plantation worker; (bot.) gum tree
**gomia** *f* dragon (*in Corpus Christi procession*); bugaboo, bugbear; (coll.) glutton; waster, destroyer (*agent, cause*)
**gomífero -ra** *adj* gummiferous, gum-bearing
**gomista** *mf* dealer in rubber goods
**Gomorra** *f* (Bib.) Gomorrah or Gomorrha
**gomorresina** *f* gum resin
**gomosería** *f* dudishness
**gomosidad** *f* gumminess; stickiness
**gomosis** *f* (plant path.) gummosis
**gomoso -sa** *adj* gummy; (pertaining to) gum; *m* dude, dandy
**gónada** *f* (anat.) gonad
**gonce** *m* var. of **gozne**
**góndola** *f* gondola; (rail.) gondola
**gondolero** *m* gondolier
**gonfalón** *m* var. of **confalón**
**gonfaloniero** *m* var. of **confaloniero**
**gongo** *m* gong
**gongorino -na** *adj* Gongoristic; *mf* Gongorist
**gongorismo** *m* Gongorism
**gongorizar** §76 *vn* to be Gongoristic, to use Gongorisms
**gonia** *f* (biol.) gonium
**gonidio** *m* (bot.) gonidium
**goniometría** *f* goniometry
**goniómetro** *m* goniometer; **goniómetro de aplicación** contact goniometer
**gonococo** *m* (bact.) gonococcus
**gonóforo** *m* (bot. & zool.) gonophore
**gonorrea** *f* (path.) gonorrhea
**gonorreico -ca** *adj* gonorrheal
**gorbión** *m* var. of **gurbión**
**gordal** *adj* big, large-size
**gordana** *f* animal fat
**gordiano -na** *adj* Gordian
**gordiflón -flona** or **gordinflón -flona** *adj* (coll.) chubby, pudgy
**gordo -da** *adj* fat, stout, corpulent, plump; fatty, greasy, oily; big, large; coarse; whopping big; hard (*water*); **hablar gordo** (coll.) to talk big; **se armó la gorda** (coll.) there was a big hullabaloo; *m* fat, suet; (coll.) first prize (*in lottery*)
**gordolobo** *m* (bot.) mullein, great mullein
**gordura** *f* fatness, stoutness, corpulence; fat, grease
**gorfe** *m* deep whirlpool
**gorga** *f* hawk's meal; whirlpool
**gorgojar** *vr* var. of **agorgojar**
**gorgojo** *m* (ent.) grub, weevil; (coll.) dwarf, tiny person
**gorgojoso -sa** *adj* grubby, weevily
**gorgón** *m* (Am.) concrete
**Gorgona** *f* (myth.) Gorgon
**gorgonear** *vn* to gobble (*said of a turkey*)
**gorgóneo -a** *adj* Gorgon, Gorgonian
**gorgonzola** *m* Gorgonzola (*cheese*)
**gorgorán** *m* grogram
**gorgorita** *f* little bubble; (coll.) trill
**gorgoritear** *vn* (coll.) to trill
**gorgorito** *m* (coll.) trill; **hacer gorgoritos** (coll.) to trill
**gorgorotada** *f* gulp
**gorgotear** *vn* to gurgle, burble
**gorgoteo** *m* gurgle, burble, burbling
**gorgotero** *m* peddler, hawker
**gorguera** *f* ruff; (arch.) gorgerin; (arm.) gorget
**gorguz** *m* (*pl:* **-guces**) javelin; pole used for removing pine cones
**gorigori** *m* (coll.) mournful singing at a funeral
**gorila** *m* (zool.) gorilla
**gorja** *f* gorge, throat; **estar de gorja** (coll.) to be full of joy
**gorjal** *m* (arm.) gorget; (eccl.) scarf
**gorjear** *vn* to warble, to trill; *vr* to gurgle (*said of a baby*)
**gorjeo** *m* warble, trill; warbling; gurgle (*of a baby*)
**gorjerete** *m* (surg.) gorget
**gorra** *f* cap; busby; sponging, bumming; **andar de gorra** to sponge; **colarse de gorra** (coll.) to crash the gate; **comer de gorra** to eat at the expense of other people; **hablarse de gorra** (coll.) to bow without speaking, to greet each other without speaking; **vivir de gorra** to live on other people; **gorra de pelo** (mil.) bearskin cap; **gorra de visera** cap
**gorrada** *f* tipping the hat
**gorrear** *vn* (Am.) to sponge
**gorrero -ra** *mf* maker of caps and headwear, dealer in caps and headware; (coll.) sponger
**gorretada** *f* tipping the hat
**gorrilla** *f* small cap; peasant's hat
**gorrín** *m* var. of **gorrino**
**gorrinada** *f* pigs, drove of pigs; (coll.) piggishness
**gorrinera** *f* pigpen, pigsty; (coll.) pigpen (*filthy place*)
**gorrinería** *f* dirt, filth; piggishness
**gorrino -na** *mf* sucking pig; hog; (fig.) pig
**gorrión** *m* (orn.) sparrow; **gorrión triguero** (orn.) bunting
**gorriona** *f* female sparrow
**gorrionera** *f* (coll.) den of thugs, den of vice
**gorrista** *adj* sponging; *mf* sponger
**gorro** *m* cap, bonnet; baby's bonnet; **aguantar el gorro** to give in; **apretarse el gorro** (coll.) to beat it, to duck out; **gorro de dormir** nightcap; **gorro frigio** liberty cap
**gorrón -rrona** *adj* sponging; *mf* sponger, dead beat; *m* pebble; lazy silkworm; tailings; pivot; (mach.) gudgeon, journal; *f* prostitute
**gorronal** *m* pebbly spot
**gorronear** *vn* to sponge
**gorullo** *m* ball, lump (*e.g., of wool*)
**gorupo** *m* granny knot
**gosipino -na** *adj* cotton, cottony
**gota** *f* drop; (path.) gout; **gotas** *fpl* drops (*medicine*); touch of rum or brandy dropped in coffee; **llover a gotas espaciadas** to sprinkle, to rain in scattered drops; **sudar la gota gorda** (coll.) to work one's head off; **gota a gota** drop by drop
**goteado -da** *adj* splattered, speckled
**gotear** *vn* to drip; to dribble; to sprinkle (*to rain in scattered drops*)
**goteo** *m* dripping; dribbling
**gotera** *f* leak; drip, dripping; mark left by dripping water; valance; (plant path.) tree disease caused by infiltration of water into trunk; **goteras** *fpl* (coll.) aches, pains; **estar lleno de goteras** (coll.) to be full of aches and pains
**goterón** *m* big raindrop; (arch.) throat
**gótica** *f* see **gótico**
**goticismo** *m* Gothicism
**gótico -ca** *adj* Gothic; (f.a.) Gothic; (print.) black-letter; noble, illustrious; *m* Gothic (*language*); (f.a.) Gothic; *f* (print.) black letter, Old English
**Gotinga** *f* Göttingen
**gotón -tona** *adj & mf* Goth
**gotoso -sa** *adj* gouty; *mf* gout sufferer
**goyesco -ca** *adj* (pertaining to) Goya; in the style of Goya
**gozar** §76 *va* to enjoy, possess; *vn* to enjoy oneself; **gozar de** to enjoy, possess; *vr* to enjoy oneself; to rejoice; **gozarse en** + *inf* to enjoy + *ger*
**gozne** *m* hinge
**gozo** *m* joy, rejoicing; blaze from dry chips of wood; **gozos** *mpl* couplets in praise of the Virgin; **brincar** or **saltar de gozo** (coll.) to leap with joy; **no caber en sí de gozo** (coll.) to be beside oneself with joy
**gozoso -sa** *adj* joyful; **gozoso con** or **de** joyful over
**gozque** *m* or **gozquejo** *m* little yapper (*dog*)
**gr.** abr. of **gramo**
**Graal** *m* var. of **Grial**
**grabación** *f* engraving; recording (*of phonograph record*); **grabación de alambre** wire recording; **grabación sobre cinta** tape recording
**grabado** *m* engraving (*act, art, plate, and picture*); picture, print, cut; recording (*of phonograph record*)
**grabador -dora** *adj* recording; *mf* engraver; *f* recorder; **grabadora de alambre** wire recorder; **grabadora de cinta** tape recorder
**grabadura** *f* engraving

**grabar** *va* to engrave; to record (*a sound, a song, a phonograph record, etc.*); (fig.) to engrave (*e.g., on the memory*); **grabar en** or **sobre cinta** to tape-record; *vr* to become engraved (*on the memory*)
**grabazón** *f* carved onlays
**gracejada** *f* (Am.) clownishness, cheap comedy
**gracejar** *vn* to be engaging, be fascinating (*in what one says*); to have a light touch, be witty
**gracejo** *m* charm, winsome manner; lightness, wit; (Am.) clown
**gracia** *f* grace (*gracefulness, charm; favor; pardon*); joke, witticism, witty remark; point (*of a joke*); (theol.) grace; (coll.) name, e.g., **¿cuál es su gracia de Vd.?** what is your name?; **gracias** *fpl* thanks; **caer de la gracia de** to get into the bad graces of; **caer en gracia a** to please, be pleasing to; **dar en la gracia de decir** (coll.) to harp on; **de gracia** gratis, gratuitously; **decir dos gracias a uno** (coll.) to tell someone a thing or two; **en gracia a** because of; **estar en gracia cerca de** to be in the good graces of; **hacer gracia** to please, be pleasing; **hacer gracia de algo a uno** to exempt or free someone from something; **hacerle a uno gracia** to strike someone as funny; **las Gracias** (myth.) the Graces; **¡linda gracia!** nonsense!; **no estar de gracia** or **para gracias** to be in no mood for joking; **no verle la gracia a uno** to not think that someone is funny; **pedir una gracia** to ask a favor; **tener gracia** to be funny, be astounding; **gracia de Dios** air and sunshine; daily bread; **gracia de niño** cuteness, brightness (*of a child*); **gracias a** thanks to (*because of; owing to*); **¡gracias!** thanks!; **¡gracias a Dios!** thank heavens!
**graciable** *adj* gracious, kindly; easy to grant
**grácil** *adj* gracile, thin, slender; tiny
**graciola** *f* (bot.) hedge hyssop
**graciosamente** *adv* gracefully; graciously; wittily; gratis
**graciosidad** *f* gracefulness; graciousness; wit, wittiness
**gracioso -sa** *adj* graceful; attractive; gracious; witty; free, gratis, gratuitous; strange; *mf* (theat.) comic, clown; *m* (theat.) gracioso (*gay, comic character in Spanish comedy*)
**Graco** *m* Gracchus
**grada** *f* step; row of seats, gradin; grandstand, tiers of seats; grille or wicket in the parlor of a convent; step in front of altar; (agr.) harrow; slip (*inclined plane on which ship is built*); (min.) stope; **gradas** *fpl* stone steps (*in front of building*); **grada de discos** (agr.) disk harrow
**gradación** *f* gradation; (gram.) comparison (*of adjective*)
**gradado -da** *adj* stepped
**gradar** *va* (agr.) to harrow
**gradeo** *m* (agr.) harrowing
**gradería** *f* rows of seats (*in an amphitheater or stadium*); bleachers; stone steps (*in front of building, in garden, etc.*); **gradería cubierta** grandstand
**gradiente** *m* (math. & meteor.) gradient; (Am.) gradient (*slope*)
**gradilla** *f* small stepladder; tile mold, brick mold; (chem.) tube rack; (eccl.) gradin
**gradina** *f* gradine
**gradinar** *va* to carve with a gradine
**gradíolo** *m* var. of **gladíolo**
**grado** *m* step; grade, degree; grade (*class in school*); (educ.) degree (*e.g., of bachelor*); (gram., math. & mus.) degree; (mil.) rank; **grados** *mpl* (eccl.) minor orders; **a mal de mi grado** against my wishes, unwillingly; **de buen grado** willingly, gladly; **de grado** willingly, gladly; **de grado en grado** by degrees; **de grado o por fuerza** willy-nilly; **de mal grado** unwillingly; **de su grado** willingly; **en alto grado** to a great extent; **en grado superlativo** or **en sumo grado** in the highest degree; **mal de mi grado** against my wishes, unwillingly; **¡grado a Dios!** thank heavens!
**graduable** *adj* adjustable
**graduación** *f* graduation; grading; standing; strength (*of spirituous liquor*); (mil.) rank
**graduador** *m* (elec.) graduator
**gradual** *adj* gradual; *m* (eccl.) gradual
**graduando -da** *adj* graduating; *mf* graduate, candidate for a degree
**graduar** §33 *va* to graduate; to grade; to regulate (*e.g., a spigot, valve, potentiometer*); to estimate, evaluate, appraise; to graduate (*a student*); **graduar de** to graduate (*a student*) as (*e.g., a bachelor*); (mil.) to give the rank of (*e.g., captain*) to; **graduar de** or **por** to grade as (*good, bad, etc.*); *vr* to graduate, be graduated; **graduarse de** to receive the degree of (*e.g., bachelor*)
**grafía** *f* spelling; (gram.) graph
**gráfico -ca** *adj* graphic or graphical; printing; illustrated; picture, camera; *m* diagram; *f* graph; picture
**grafila** or **gráfila** *f* knurl, milled edge of coin
**grafioles** *mpl* S-shaped cakes or biscuits
**grafito** *m* graphite; (archeol.) graffito
**grafología** *f* graphology
**grafomanía** *f* graphomania
**grafómetro** *m* graphometer
**grafospasmo** *m* writer's cramp
**gragea** *f* small colored candy; sugar-coated pill
**grajear** *vn* to caw; to chatter; to gurgle (*said of a baby*)
**grajero -ra** *adj* (pertaining to the) rook or crow; full of or haunted by rooks or crows
**grajiento -ta** *adj* (Am.) foul, noisome
**grajo -ja** *mf* (orn.) rook, crow; **grajo de pico amarillo** (orn.) chough, alpine chough
**gral.** abr. of **general**
**grama** *f* (bot.) Bermuda grass; **grama del norte** (bot.) couch grass, quitch; **grama de olor** or **de los prados** (bot.) vernal grass
**gramaje** *m* weight (*in grams of a sheet of paper one meter square*)
**gramal** *m* field of Bermuda grass, quitch field
**gramalote** *m* (bot.) guinea grass
**gramalla** *f* coat of mail
**gramática** *f* see **gramático**
**gramatical** *adj* grammatical
**gramático -ca** *adj* grammatical; *mf* grammarian; *f* grammar; **gramática parda** (coll.) shrewdness, craftiness
**gramatiquear** *vn* (coll.) to bore with questions of grammar, to be always correcting someone's grammar
**gramatiquería** *f* (coll.) grammatical hairsplitting
**gramil** *m* gauge, marking gauge, joiner's gauge
**gramilla** *f* scutching board; (bot.) joint grass
**gramíneo -a** *adj* gramineous
**graminívoro -ra** *adj* graminivorous
**gramión** *m* (chem.) gram ion
**gramo** *m* gram
**gramofónico -ca** *adj* phonograph
**gramófono** *m* gramophone
**gramola** *f* console phonograph; portable phonograph
**gramoso -sa** *adj* Bermuda-grass
**grampa** *f* clamp
**gran** *adj* apocopated form of **grande,** used before nouns of both genders in the singular
**grana** *f* seeding; seeding time; seed; (ent.) cochineal; kermes (*dyestuff*); red; fine scarlet cloth; **dar en grana** to go to seed; **grana del paraíso** (bot.) cardamon; **grana encarnada** (bot.) pokeberry
**granada** & **Granada** *f* see **granado**
**granadera** *f* grenadier's pouch
**granadero** *m* grenadier
**granadilla** *f* (bot.) passionflower (*plant and flower*); passion fruit
**granadino -na** *adj* (pertaining to) Granada; *mf* native or inhabitant of Granada; *m* pomegranate flower; *f* grenadine (*fabric; syrup*)
**granado -da** *adj* choice, select, distinguished; mature, expert; tall, lanky; *m* (bot.) pomegranate; **granado blanco** (bot.) rose of Sharon; *f* pomegranate (*fruit*); grenade; (*cap.*) *f* Granada; la **Nueva Granada** New Granada; **granada de mano** hand grenade; **granada de metralla** shrapnel; **granada extintora** fire grenade
**granalla** *f* granulated metal; filings; **granalla de carbón** carbon granules
**granangular** *adj* (opt.) wide-angle

**granar** *va* to grain (*powder*); *vn* to seed
**granate** *m* garnet (*stone and color*); **granate almandino** deep-red garnet; *adj invar* garnet
**granazón** *f* seeding; **no llegar a granazón** to fall by the wayside
**Gran Bretaña, la** Great Britain
**grande** *adj* big, large; great; *m* grandee; **en grande** as a whole; on a grand scale; in a big way; **grande de España** grandee, Spanish grandee
**grandevo -va** *adj* (poet.) aged, hoary
**grandeza** *f* bigness, largeness; greatness; grandeur; size; grandeeship; grandees
**grandilocuencia** *f* grandiloquence
**grandilocuente** or **grandílocuo -cua** *adj* grandiloquent
**grandillón -llona** *adj* (coll.) oversize, overgrown
**grandiosidad** *f* grandeur, magnificence
**grandioso -sa** *adj* grandiose, grand
**grandísono -na** *adj* (poet.) high-sounding, resounding
**grandor** *m* size
**grandote -ta** *adj* (coll.) pretty big, biggish
**grandullón -llona** *adj* (coll.) var. of **grandillón**
**graneado -da** *adj* ground; spattered; heavy and continuous (*firing*)
**graneador** *m* stipple graver
**granear** *va* to sow; to grain (*powder; a lithographic stone*); to stipple
**granel; a granel** at random; loose, in bulk; lavishly, in abundance
**granelar** *va* to grain (*leather*)
**graneo** *m* sowing; stippling
**granero -ra** *adj* (pertaining to) grain; *mf* grain dealer; *m* granary; (fig.) granary (*region*)
**granetazo** *m* blow with a punch; punch mark
**granete** *m* center punch
**granetear** *va* to punch, mark with a punch
**granetería** *f* grain business
**granetero -ra** *mf* grain dealer
**granévano** *m* (bot.) goat's-thorn, tragacanth
**granguardia** *f* (mil.) grand guard
**granífugo -ga** *adj* hail-dispersing
**granilla** *f* grape seed
**granillo** *m* fine grain; profit, gain
**granilloso -sa** *adj* granular
**granítico -ca** *adj* granite; granitic
**granito** *m* granite; **echar un granito de sal** (coll.) to add spice to what one says
**granívoro -ra** *adj* granivorous
**granizada** *f* hailstorm; (fig.) hailstorm; (Am.) ice drink
**granizado** *m* water ice
**granizal** *m* (Am.) hailstorm
**granizar** §76 *va* to hail; to sprinkle; *vn* to hail
**granizo** *m* hail; (fig.) hail (*abundance*)
**granja** *f* grange, farm; dairy; country place; **granja escuela** farm school
**granjeador -dora** *adj* (Am.) ingratiating; *mf* (Am.) ingratiating person
**granjear** *va* to gain, to earn; to win, win over; *vr* to win, win over; to draw (*applause*)
**granjeo** *m* gain, profit; winning
**granjería** *f* farming, husbandry; gain, profit
**granjero -ra** *mf* farmer; *m* husbandman
**grano** *m* grain; grape, berry; (path.) pimple; grain (*weight*); **granos** *mpl* grain; **con un grano de sal** with a grain of salt; **ir al grano** (coll.) to come to the point; **grano de belleza** beauty spot; **grano de café** coffee bean; **granos de amor** (bot.) gromwell
**granoso -sa** *adj* granular (*surface*)
**granuja** *f* loose grape; grapestone, grapeseed; *m* scoundrel; (coll.) waif, little waif
**granujada** *f* rascality, deviltry
**granujería** *f* gang of scalawags; rascality
**granujo** *m* (coll.) pimple, pustule
**granujoso -sa** *adj* pimpled, pimply, pustular
**granulación** *f* granulation
**granular** *adj* granular; pimply; *va* to granulate; *vr* to granulate; (path.) to granulate
**granulita** *f* or **granulito** *m* (geol.) granulite
**gránulo** *m* granule; (bot. & pharm.) granule
**granuloso -sa** *adj* granular; (path.) granular; *f* (chem.) granulose
**granza** *f* (bot.) madder; pea coal; **granzas** *fpl* chaff; screenings, siftings; dross
**granzón** *m* piece of ore that won't pass through sieve; **granzones** *mpl* knots of hay that won't pass through sieve and that are left uneaten by cattle
**grañón** *m* boiled wheat grains
**grao** *m* beach, shore
**grapa** *f* staple; clip, clamp
**grasa** *f* see **graso**
**grasera** *f* vessel for fat or grease; (cook.) dripping pan
**grasería** *f* tallow chandler's shop
**grasero** *m* slag dump
**graseza** *f* fattiness, greasiness
**grasiento -ta** *adj* greasy
**grasilla** *f* pounce (*fine powder*)
**graso -sa** *adj* fatty, greasy; (chem.) fatty; *m* fattiness, greasiness; *f* fat, grease; pounce (*fine powder*); (chem.) fat; (Am.) shoe polish, shoe shine; **grasas** *fpl* slag; **grasa de ballena** blubber
**grasones** *mpl* porridge, wheat porridge
**grasoso -sa** *adj* fatty, greasy
**grasura** *f* var. of **grosura**
**grata** *f* see **grato**
**gratar** *va* to clean or burnish with a wire brush
**gratificación** *f* gratification, reward, fee; bonus
**gratificador -dora** *adj* gratifying; rewarding; tipping; *mf* gratifier; rewarder; tipper
**gratificar** §86 *va* to gratify; to reward; to tip, to fee
**gratil** *m* or **grátil** *m* (naut.) leech; (naut.) slings (*middle part of yard*)
**gratín** *m;* **al gratín** (cook.) au gratin
**gratis** *adv* gratis
**gratisdato -ta** *adj* gratis, free
**gratitud** *f* gratitude
**grato -ta** *adj* pleasing; free; (Am.) grateful; *f* favor (*letter*); wire brush
**gratonada** *f* chicken stew
**gratuitamente** *adv* gratuitously; free, gratis
**gratuito -ta** *adj* gratuitous
**gratulación** *f* gratulation
**gratular** *va* to congratulate; *vr* to rejoice
**gratulatorio -ria** *adj* gratulatory, congratulatory
**grauvaca** *f* (geol.) graywacke
**grava** *f* gravel; crushed stone; **grava provechosa** (min.) pay dirt
**gravamen** *m* burden, obligation; encumbrance; assessment
**gravar** *va* to burden, to encumber; to assess (*property*)
**gravativo -va** *adj* burdensome, heavy; dragging, heavy (*pain*)
**grave** *adj* heavy (*having weight*); grave, serious, solemn; hard, difficult; annoying; ill, sick; grave, deep, low (*sound*); noble, majestic (*music*); (gram.) paroxytone; (gram.) grave (*accent*)
**gravear** *vn* to rest, press, weigh
**gravedad** *f* gravity; (phys. & mus.) gravity; **de gravedad** seriously; **gravedad nula** weightlessness
**gravedoso -sa** *adj* heavy, pompous
**gravela** *f* (path.) gravel
**grávida** *f* see **grávido**
**gravidez** *f* gravidity
**grávido -da** *adj* gravid; (poet.) full, loaded, abundant; *f* pregnant woman
**gravimetría** *f* gravimetry
**gravimétrico -ca** *adj* gravimetric or gravimetrical
**gravitación** *f* (phys.) gravitation
**gravitacional** *adj* gravitational
**gravitar** *vn* to gravitate; to rest, press; **gravitar sobre** to be a burden to; to encumber; to live on (*another person*)
**gravoso -sa** *adj* onerous, burdensome, costly; boring, tiresome
**graznador -dora** *adj* cawing, croaking; cackling
**graznar** *vn* to caw, to croak; to cackle; to not know what one is talking about; to cackle (*in singing*)
**graznido** *m* caw, croak; cackle; chatter, jabber; cackle, cackling (*of a singer*)
**greba** *f* greave
**greca** *f* see **greco**
**Grecia** *f* Greece

**greciano -na** or **grecisco -ca** *adj* Grecian
**grecismo** *m* Grecism
**grecizar** §76 *va & vn* to Grecize
**greco -ca** *adj & mf* Grecian, Greek; *f* Grecian fret
**grecolatino -na** *adj* Greco-Latin
**grecorromano -na** *adj* Greco-Roman
**greda** *f* clay, fuller's earth
**gredal** *adj* clayey; *m* clay pit
**gredoso -sa** *adj* clayey
**gregal** *adj* gregarious; *m* northeast wind (*in Mediterranean*)
**gregario -ria** *adj* gregarious; slavish
**gregoriano -na** *adj* Gregorian
**Gregorio** *m* Gregory
**greguería** *f* shouting, hubbub; **greguerías** *fpl* (lit.) impressionistic imagery in epigrammatic prose
**gregüescos** *mpl* pantaloons, wide breeches (*worn in sixteenth and seventeenth centuries*)
**greguisco -ca** *adj* Grecian
**greguizar** §76 *va* to Grecize
**gremial** *adj* (pertaining to a) union; *m* guildsman; union man, union member; (eccl.) gremial
**gremio** *m* guild, corporation; society, association; union, trade union; lap; **gremio solteril** single blessedness
**grenchudo -da** *adj* long-haired, long-maned
**greña** *f* shock, tangled mop (*of hair*); entanglement; (prov.) heap of grain to be thrashed; (prov.) first leaves of new shoot; **andar a la greña** (coll.) to pull each other's hair; (coll.) to get into a hot argument
**greñudo -da** *adj* shock-headed; dishevelled; *m* shy horse
**gres** *m* sandstone; siliceous clay; stoneware
**gresca** *f* clamor, uproar; quarrel, row
**grey** *f* flock; group, party; people, nation; congregation (*of faithful*)
**Grial** *m* Grail; **Santo Grial** Holy Grail
**griego -ga** *adj* Greek; *mf* Greek; (coll.) greek (*cheat, sharper*); *m* Greek (*language*); **hablar en griego** (coll.) to talk unintelligibly
**grieta** *f* crack, crevice, fissure; chap (*in skin*)
**grietado -da** *adj* crackled; *m* (f.a.) crackle (*cracked surface*); (f.a.) crackleware
**grietar** *vr* to crack, to split; to become chapped
**grietoso -sa** *adj* cracky, cracked
**grifa** *f* see **grifo**
**grifería** *f* faucets, spigots; spigot shop
**grifo -fa** *adj* curly, tangled; (Am.) bristly, bristling; (Am.) haughty, arrogant; (Am.) drunk; (Am.) colored; **ponerse grifo** (Am.) to stand on end (*said of hair*); *mf* (Am.) mulatto; (Am.) drug addict; *m* faucet, spigot, cock; (myth.) griffin; (Am.) gas station; *f* hashish, marijuana
**grifón** *m* large faucet or spigot
**grigallo** *m* (orn.) capercaillie
**grilla** *f* female cricket; (rad.) grid; (coll.) lie; **¡ésa es grilla!** (coll.) you expect me to believe that!
**grillar** *vr* to shoot, sprout
**grillera** *f* cricket hole; cricket cage
**grillero** *m* jailer (*who shackles prisoners*); cricket dealer
**grillete** *m* fetter, shackle
**grillo** *m* (ent.) cricket; shoot, sprout; drag, obstacle; gyve; **grillos** *mpl* fetters, shackles; **andar a grillos** (coll.) to trifle away one's time; **grillo cebollero** or **real** (ent.) mole cricket
**grillotalpa** *f* (ent.) mole cricket
**grima** *f* annoyance, horror; **dar grima a** to annoy, horrify, grate on the nerves of
**grimoso -sa** *adj* annoying, horrifying
**grímpola** *f* (naut.) pennant, streamer
**gringo -ga** *mf* (scornful) foreigner; (Am.) gringo (*Anglo-Saxon*); *m* (coll.) gibberish
**griñolera** *f* (bot.) rose box
**griñón** *m* wimple; nectarine
**gripal** *adj* of grippe, grippal
**gripe** *f* (path.) grippe
**gris** *adj* gray; dull, gloomy; *m* gray; (zool.) miniver, Siberian squirrel; (coll.) cold, cold wind; **hacer gris** (coll.) to be sharp, be brisk (*said of weather*)
**grisáceo -a** *adj* grayish
**grisalla** *f* (f.a.) grisaille
**grisar** *va* to polish (*diamonds*)
**griseta** *f* flowered silk; grisette; (plant path.) tree disease caused by infiltration of water into trunk
**grisiento -ta** *adj* (Am.) grayish
**grisú** *m* (*pl:* **-súes**) (min.) firedamp
**grita** *f* outcry, shout; tumult, hubbub; **dar grita a** (coll.) to hoot at
**gritador -dora** *adj* crying, shouting, screaming; *mf* crier, shouter, screamer
**gritar** *vn* to cry out, to shout
**gritería** *f* or **griterío** *m* outcry, shouting, uproar
**grito** *m* cry, shout; scream, shriek; **a grito herido** or **pelado** in a loud shriek; **alzar el grito** (coll.) to raise one's voice brazenly; **asparse a gritos** (coll.) to scream wildly (*said of a child*); (coll.) to shout at the top of one's voice; **estar en un grito** to moan in constant pain; **el último grito** (coll.) the latest thing, all the rage; **poner el grito en el cielo** (coll.) to raise the roof, to complain loudly; **poner el grito en el cielo contra** (coll.) to cry out against
**gritón -tona** *adj* (coll.) shouting, screaming; *mf* (coll.) shouter, screamer
**griva** *f* (orn.) missel thrush
**gro.** abr. of **género**
**gro** *m* grosgrain
**groar** *vn* to croak (*said of frogs*)
**Grocio** *m* Grotius
**groelandés -desa** *adj & mf* var. of **groenlandés**
**Groelandia** *f* var. of **Groenlandia**
**groenlandés -desa** *adj* Greenlandic; *mf* Greenlander
**Groenlandia** *f* Greenland
**groera** *f* (naut.) rope hole
**gromo** *m* bud
**grosella** *f* currant (*fruit*); **grosella silvestre** gooseberry (*fruit*)
**grosellero** *m* (bot.) currant (*plant*); **grosellero silvestre** (bot.) gooseberry (*plant*)
**grosería** *f* grossness, coarseness, crudeness; churlishness, rudeness; stupidity; vulgarity
**grosero -ra** *adj* gross, coarse, rough, crude; churlish, rude; stupid; vulgar; *mf* churl, boor, mucker
**grosísimo -ma** *adj super* very or most thick or bulky; very coarse; very stout
**grosor** *m* thickness, bulk
**grosulariáceo -a** *adj* (bot.) grossulariaceous
**grosura** *f* fat, suet, tallow; meat, meat diet; parts of animals (*head, legs, intestines, etc.*); coarseness; ordinariness, vulgarity; (obs.) Saturday
**grotesco -ca** *adj* grotesque (*ridiculous*); (f.a.) grotesque; *m* (f.a.) grotesque
**grúa** *f* crane, derrick; **grúa corredera** or **corrediza** traveling crane; **grúa de auxilio** wrecking crane; **grúa de caballete** gantry crane; **grúa de tijera** shears (*hoisting device*)
**grúa-remolque** *m* tow truck
**grueso -sa** *adj* thick, bulky, heavy, big, gross; coarse, ordinary; stout; rough, heavy (*seas*); heavy (*line; rug, carpet*); *m* thickness; bulk; heavy stroke (*in writing*); **en grueso** in gross or in the gross; *f* gross (*twelve dozen*)
**gruir** §41 *vn* to crunk (*said of a crane*)
**grujidor** *m* glazier's nippers; glass cutter
**grujir** *va* to trim (*glass*) with nippers
**grulla** *f* (orn.) crane; **grulla de Numidia** (orn.) Numidian crane, demoiselle crane
**grullada** *f* flock of cranes; (coll.) gang of loafers; (coll.) platitude
**grumete** *m* (naut.) cabin boy, ship's boy
**grumo** *m* clot; curd; bunch, cluster; bud; wing tip (*of bird*); (arch.) Gothic finial
**grumoso -sa** *adj* clotty; curdly; bunchy, clustered
**gruñente** *adj* grunting; growling; *m* (slang) grunter (*hog*)
**gruñido** *m* grunt; growl; grumble; creak; (coll.) scolding
**gruñidor -dora** *adj* grunting; growling; (coll.) grumbling, discontent; *mf* grunter; growler; (coll.) grumbler

**gruñimiento** *m* grunting; growling; grumbling
**gruñir §25** *vn* to grunt; to growl; to grumble; to creak (*said, e.g., of a door*)
**gruñón -ñona** *adj* (coll.) grumbly, grumpy
**grupa** *f* croup, rump (*of horse*)
**grupada** *f* squall
**grupera** *f* crupper; pillion, cushion back of saddle for baggage
**grupeto** *m* (mus.) turn, grupetto
**grupo** *m* group; (mach. & elec.) unit, set; granny knot; **grupo carboxilo** (chem.) carboxyl group; **grupo de carga** (elec.) battery-charging unit or set; **grupo de motor y generador** (elec.) motor generator set; **grupo electrógeno** (elec.) generator unit, generating unit; **grupo motopropulsor** (elec.) electric drive, motor drive; (aer.) power plant; **grupo motor** (aut.) power plant; **grupo sanguíneo** blood group, blood type
**gruta** *f* grotto; **gruta Coriciana** Corycian Cave
**grutesco -ca** *adj* & *m* (f.a.) grotesque
**gruyère** *m* Gruyère, Swiss cheese
**gte.** abr. of **gerente**
**guaca** *f* (Am.) Indian tomb; (Am.) hidden treasure; (Am.) Indian altar
**guacal** *m* (Am.) crate
**guacamayo -ya** *adj* (Am.) flashy, sporty; *m* (orn.) macaw
**guacamole** *m* (Am.) avocado salad
**guacia** *f* (bot.) acacia (*plant and gum*)
**guaco** *m* (bot.) guaco; (orn.) curassow
**guachapear** *va* (coll.) to splash with the feet; (coll.) to botch, bungle; *vn* to clatter, to clank
**guacharaca** *f* (orn.) chachalaca
**guácharo -ra** *adj* sickly, dropsical; *m* (orn.) oilbird
**guachinango -ga** *adj* (Am.) cunning, flattering; *mf* (offensive term used by Cubans) Mexican; *m* (ichth.) red snapper; *f* (Am.) wooden bar (*across a door or window*)
**guacho -cha** *adj* (Am.) homeless, motherless, orphan; (Am.) odd, unmatched (*e.g., shoe*)
**guadafiones** *mpl* fetterlock (*shackle*)
**guadal** *m* bog, swamp; (Am.) bamboo grass; (Am.) dune, sand hill
**Guadalupe** *f* Guadeloupe
**guadamací** *m* (*pl:* **-cíes**) embossed leather, stamped leather; **guadamací brocado** gold or silver embossed leather
**guadamacil** *m* var. of **guadamací**
**guadamacilería** *f* embossed-leather business; embossed-leather shop
**guadamacilero** *m* embossed-leather maker or dealer
**guadamecí** *m* (*pl:* **-cíes**) var. of **guadamací**
**guadamecil** *m* var. of **guadamací**
**guadaña** *f* scythe
**guadañador -dora** *adj* mowing; *f* mowing machine
**guadañar** *va* to scythe, to mow
**guadañero** *m* scytheman, mower
**guadañeta** *f* squid-jigger
**guadañil** *m* var. of **guadañero**
**guadaño** *m* harbor boat
**guadapero** *m* (bot.) wild pear (*tree*); boy who carries food out to the harvestmen
**guadarnés** *m* harness room; harness keeper
**guadijeño -ña** *adj* (pertaining to) Guadix; *mf* native or inhabitant of Guadix; *m* poniard
**guadua** *f* (bot.) guadua (*Guadua latifolia and stems*)
**guadual** *m* growth of guaduas
**guagua** *f* trifle, triviality; (Am.) bus; (Am.) paca (*rodent*); (Am.) orange scale (*insect*); **de guagua** (coll.) free, gratis; *mf* (Am.) baby
**guagüero -ra** *adj* (Am.) paca-hunting (*e.g., dog*); *mf* (Am.) sponger; (Am.) bus driver
**guaicán** *m* (ichth.) remora
**guaira** *f* (naut.) leg-of-mutton sail; (Am.) smelting furnace (*of Indians*)
**guairabo** *m* (orn.) night heron
**guairo** *m* small vessel with two leg-of-mutton sails
**guaita** *f* (archaic) night watch, night sentinel
**guajada** *f* (Am.) nonsense, folly
**guajalote** *m* (Am.) turkey (*fowl*)
**guájar** *m* & *f* or **guájaras** *fpl* craggy section of mountains
**guaje** *adj* (Am.) foolish, crazy; (Am.) knavish; *m* (Am.) calabash, gourd; (Am.) junk, trinket; (Am.) nobody, good-for-nothing; (Am.) fool; **hacer guaje** (Am.) to deceive
**guajear** *vn* (Am.) to play stupid
**guájete; guájete por guájete** (coll.) tit for tat
**guajiro -ra** *adj* (Am.) rustic, boorish; *mf* white peasant of Cuba; (Am.) peasant, stranger; *f* Cuban peasant song
**guajolote** *m* (Am.) turkey (*fowl*); (Am.) simpleton
**gualda** *f* see **gualdo**
**gualdado -da** *adj* yellow-dyed
**gualdera** *f* (carp.) bridgeboard, horse; (arti.) trail
**gualdo -da** *adj* yellow; *f* (bot.) weld, dyer's rocket
**gualdrapa** *f* housing, trappings; (coll.) dirty rag hanging from clothing
**gualdrapazo** *m* flap or flapping sound of sail (*against rigging*)
**gualdrapear** *va* to alternate, to line up in alternation; *vn* to flap (*said of sails*)
**gualdrapeo** *m* flapping of sails
**gualdrapero** *m* raggedy fellow
**Gualterio** *m* Walter
**guamá** *m* or **guamo** *m* (bot.) guamá
**guanábana** *f* soursop (*fruit*)
**guanábano** *m* (bot.) soursop (*tree*)
**guanaco** *m* (zool.) guanaco
**Guanahaní** *f* Watling
**guanajo -ja** *adj* (Am.) dull, stupid; *m* (Am.) turkey
**guanana** *f* (orn.) blue goose; **guanana blanca** (orn.) lesser snow goose; **guanana prieta** (orn.) tule goose
**guando** *m* (Am.) handbarrow
**guanero -ra** *adj* (pertaining to) guano; *m* guano ship; (coll.) guano tycoon; *f* guano deposit; **guaneras** *fpl* guano islands
**guango** *m* (Am.) pigtail (*of Indian women*)
**guanidina** *f* (chem.) guanidine
**guanín** *m* (Am.) base gold
**guanina** *f* (bot.) stinking weed; (chem.) guanine
**guano** *m* guano; (bot.) palm tree
**guantada** *f* or **guantazo** *m* slap
**guante** *m* glove; **guantes** *mpl* tip, fee; **adobar los guantes a** (coll.) to treat, to tip; **arrojar el guante** to throw down the gauntlet; **echar el guante a** (coll.) to grasp, seize; **echar un guante** to collect for charity; **recoger el guante** to take up the gauntlet; **salvo el guante** (coll.) excuse my glove (*in shaking hands*)
**guantelete** *m* gauntlet; (surg.) gauntlet
**guantera** *f* see **guantero**
**guantería** *f* glove business; glove shop
**guantero -ra** *mf* glover, glove maker or dealer; *m* & *f* glove compartment
**guañín** *m* var. of **guanín**
**guañir §25** *vn* (prov.) to squeal (*said of pigs*)
**guao** *m* (bot.) guao (*Comocladia*); (bot.) sumac; **ser como la sombra del guao** or **tener peor sombra que un guao** (Am.) to be a jinx
**guapamente** *adv* (coll.) showily; (coll.) boldly; (coll.) very well, fine
**guapear** *vn* (coll.) to bluster, to act tough; (coll.) to dress in a showy manner, to be sporty
**guapetón -tona** *adj* (coll.) big and handsome; (coll.) flashy, sporty; (coll.) fearless, dauntless; *m* (coll.) bully, toughy
**guapeza** *f* (coll.) good looks; (coll.) showiness, flashiness; (coll.) boldness, daring; (coll.) bravado
**guapo -pa** *adj* (coll.) handsome, good-looking; (coll.) showy, flashy; (Am.) bold, daring; *m* bully; gallant, lady's man; **guapos** *mpl* (dial.) trinkets; **echarla de guapo** (coll.) to bluster, to act tough
**guapote -ta** *adj* (coll.) kindly, good-natured; (coll.) pretty, nice
**guapura** *f* (coll.) good looks
**guaracha** *f* guaracha (*old Spanish dance and music*)
**guarache** *m* (Am.) sandal; (Am.) tire patch

**guaraní** (*pl:* **-níes**) *adj & mf* Guarani; *m* Guarani (*language*)
**guarapo** *m* juice of sugar cane; guarapo (*fermented juice of sugar cane*)
**guarda** *mf* guard, keeper, custodian; (Am.) trolley-car conductor; *m* guard; caretaker **guarda de la aduana** customhouse officer; **guarda forestal** forest ranger; *f* guard, custody; observance (*of a law*); guard (*e.g., of sword*); ward (*of lock or key*); (b.b.) flyleaf; **guardas** *fpl* (b.b.) end paper
**guardabarrera** *mf* (rail.) gatekeeper
**guardabarros** *m* (*pl:* **-rros**) splashboard; (aut.) fender, mudguard
**guardabosque** *m* forest keeper, gamekeeper; (Am.) shortstop
**guardabrazo** *m* (arm.) brassard
**guardabrisa** *m* (aut.) windshield; (naut.) glass lamp shade (*for candles*)
**guardacabo** *m* (naut.) thimble
**guardacabras** *mf* (*pl:* **-bras**) goatherd
**guardacadena** *m* chain guard
**guardacalor** *m* asbestos insulation (*e.g., of a boiler*)
**guardacantón** *m* spur stone, corner spur stone
**guardacarril** *m* var. of **contracarril**
**guardacartas** *m* (*pl:* **-tas**) letter file
**guardacartuchos** *m* (*pl:* **-chos**) cartridge box
**guardacenizas** *m* (*pl:* **-zas**) ashpan
**guardacoches** *m* (*pl:* **-ches**) car watcher
**guardacostas** *m* (*pl:* **-tas**) revenue cutter, coast guard cutter; **guardacostas** *mpl* coast guard (*service*)
**guardador -dora** *adj* guarding, protecting; keeping, preserving; observant, regardful, mindful; stingy; *m* guardian; keeper; observer (*e.g., of laws*); (archaic) guardian of the spoils of war
**guardaespaldas** *m* (*pl:* **-das**) bodyguard
**guardaesquinas** *m* (*pl:* **-nas**) (coll.) corner loafer
**guardafango** *m* (aut.) mudguard, fender
**guardafrenos** *m* (*pl:* **-nos**) (rail.) brakeman, flagman
**guardafuego** *m* fender, fireguard (*of fireplace*); (naut.) breaming board
**guardaguas** *m* (*pl:* **-guas**) (naut.) batten to keep water out of portholes
**guardagujas** *m* (*pl:* **-jas**) switchman
**guardainfante** *m* farthingale; (naut.) whelps (*of capstan*)
**guardajoyas** *m* (*pl:* **-yas**) jewel case
**guardalado** *m* rail, railing (*e.g., of a bridge*)
**guardalmacén** *mf* storekeeper; warehouseman; (Am.) station master
**guardalobo** *m* (bot.) poet's cassia
**guardalodos** *m* (*pl:* **-dos**) (Am.) mudguard
**guardamalleta** *f* lambrequin, valance; (arch.) bargeboard
**guardamancebo** *m* (naut.) manrope
**guardamano** *m* guard of a sword
**guardameta** *m* (sport) goalkeeper
**guardamonte** *m* trigger guard; forest keeper; poncho
**guardamozo** *m* var. of **guardamancebo**
**guardamuebles** *m* (*pl:* **-bles**) warehouse (*for furniture*); furniture storeroom; palace guard or keeper of furniture
**guardamujer** *f* (archaic) lady in waiting
**guardanieve** *m* snowshed
**guardapelo** *m* locket
**guardapesca** *m* (naut.) fish warden's boat
**guardapolvo** *m* cover, cloth (*to protect from dust*); duster (*lightweight coat*); inner lid (*of watch*); flashing, hood (*over door or window*)
**guardapuente** *m* bridge guard
**guardapuerta** *f* storm door; portière
**guardar** *va* to guard; to keep; to preserve, protect; to watch, watch over; to show (*consideration*); to save, e.g., **¡Dios guarde a la Reina!** God save the Queen!; *vn* to keep, to save; **¡guarda!** look out!, watch out!; *vr* to be on one's guard; to keep (*affection, hate, etc.*) for each other; **guardarse de** to guard against, watch out for, look out for; **guardarse de** + *inf* to guard against + *ger*, to take care not to + *inf;* **guardársele a uno** to store up vengeance against someone
**guardarraya** *f* (Am.) boundary line
**guardarriel** *m* var. of **contracarril**
**guardarrío** *m* (orn.) kingfisher
**guardarropa** *mf* wardrober, keeper of the wardrobe; *m* wardrobe (*room, closet, etc.*); checkroom, cloakroom; (bot.) lavender cotton; check boy; *f* check girl, hat girl
**guardarropía** *f* (theat.) wardrobe
**guardarruedas** *m* (*pl:* **-das**) spur stone, corner spur stone; (rail.) wheel guard
**guardasilla** *f* chair rail
**guardatimón** *m* (naut.) stern chaser
**guardaventana** *f* storm window
**guardavía** *m* (rail.) trackwalker, flagman, lineman
**guardavientos** *m* (*pl:* **-tos**) chimney pot; windbreak
**guardavivo** or **guardavivos** *m* (*pl:* **-vos**) bead, corner bead
**guardería** *f* guard, guardship; **guardería infantil** day nursery
**guardesa** *f* woman guard; guard's wife
**guardia** *f* care, protection; guard (*body of armed men; position in fencing*); (naut.) watch; **de guardia** on duty; on guard; **en guardia** on guard; (fencing) on guard; **montar la guardia** to mount guard; **guardia civil** rural police; **guardia de asalto** shock corps; **guardia de corps** bodyguard (*group of guards*); **guardia nacional** national guard; **guardia suiza** Swiss guards; *m* guard, guardsman; **guardia civil** rural policeman; **guardia de corps** bodyguard (*single guard*); **guardia marina** *m* midshipman; **guardia municipal** or **guardia urbano** policeman
**guardiacivil** *m* rural policeman
**guardián -diana** *mf* guardian; *m* (eccl.) guardian; (naut.) heavy hawser
**guardianía** *f* (eccl.) guardianship (*of Franciscans*)
**guardilla** *f* attic; attic room; end tooth (*of a comb*); (sew.) guard
**guardillón** *m* loft, attic; top attic
**guardín** *m* (naut.) tiller cable, tiller chain
**guardoso -sa** *adj* careful, tidy; thrifty; stingy
**guarecer** §34 *va* to take in, give shelter or protection to; to keep, preserve; to treat (*a sick person*); *vr* to take refuge, take shelter
**guariao** *m* (orn.) limpkin
**guarida** *f* den, lair (*of animals*); shelter; cover, hide-out; haunt, hangout; stamping grounds
**guarín** *m* sucking pig
**guarismo** *m* cipher, figure, number
**guarne** *m* (naut.) turn (*of a cable*)
**guarnecedor -dora** *adj* trimming; binding; plastering; *mf* trimmer; binder; plasterer
**guarnecer** §34 *va* to trim; to bind, to edge; to equip, to provide; to stucco, to plaster; to harness; to set (*jewels*); to garrison; to line (*brakes*); to bush (*a bearing*); (cook.) to garnish
**guarnecido** *m* stucco, plaster
**guarnés** *m* var. of **guadarnés**
**guarnición** *f* trimming; binding, edging; provision; stuccoing, plastering; setting (*of jewels*); flounce; garrison (*troops*); guard (*of sword*); lining (*of brakes, clutch, etc.*); packing (*of piston*); (cook.) garnish; **guarniciones** *fpl* harness; fittings, fixtures; **guarniciones de alumbrado eléctrico** electric-light fixtures; **guarniciones de gas** gas fixtures
**guarnicionar** *va* to garrison
**guarnicionería** *f* harness making; harness maker's shop
**guarnicionero -ra** *mf* harness maker or dealer
**guarniel** *m* muleteer's leather bag
**guarnigón** *m* young quail
**guarnir** §53 *va* to trim; (naut.) to reeve, to rig
**guaro** *m* small parrot; (Am.) rum
**guarro -rra** *mf* hog
**guarte** *interj* look out!
**guasa** *f* see **guaso**
**guasca** *f* (Am.) rawhide
**guasear** *vr* (coll.) to joke, jest, kid; **guasearse de** (coll.) to poke fun at
**guasería** *f* (Am.) dullness, heaviness, timidity; (Am.) coarseness, crudity
**guaso -sa** *adj* (Am.) coarse, crude, uncouth; *mf* (Am.) peasant; *f* (coll.) dullness, heaviness, churlishness; (coll.) joking, kidding; (ichth.) West Indian jewfish

**guasón -sona** *adj* (coll.) dull, heavy, churlish; (coll.) funny, comical, humorous; *mf* (coll.) dullard, dolt; (coll.) joker, kidder
**guasquear** *va* (Am.) to rawhide, to flog
**guata** *f* wad, padding, raw cotton; (Am.) padded cotton blanket; (Am.) belly, paunch; (Am.) warping, bulging; **echar guata** (Am.) to get fat; (Am.) to become prosperous
**guataca** *f* (Am.) spade; (Am.) big ear; *m* (Am.) big-eared fellow
**guatacudo -da** *adj* (Am.) big-eared
**Guatemala** *f* Guatemala
**guatemalteco -ca** *adj & mf* Guatemalan
**guatemaltequismo** *m* Guatemalanism
**guateque** *m* Cuban shindig; party; afternoon party
**guatil** *m* (bot.) genipap
**guau** *m* (bot.) woodbine, Virginia creeper; bowwow (*of dog*); *interj* bowwow!
**guay** *interj* (poet.) woe!; **tener muchos guayes** to be full of woes; to be full of aches and pains; **¡guay de . . . !** (poet.) woe to . . . !; **¡guay de mí!** (poet.) woe is me!
**guaya** *f* lament, complaint
**guayaba** *f* guava, guava apple (*fruit*); guava jelly; (Am.) lie, fake; **guayabas** *fpl* (Am.) bulging eyes
**guayabera** *f* man's short blouse
**guayabo** *m* (bot.) guava (*tree*)
**guayacán** *m* or **guayaco** *m* (bot.) guaiacum, lignum vitae
**guayacol** *m* (chem.) guaiacol
**Guayana** *f* Guiana; **la Guayana Francesa** French Guiana; **la Guayana Holandesa** Dutch Guiana; **la Guayana Inglesa** British Guiana
**guayanés -nesa** *adj & mf* Guianan or Guianese
**guayín** *m* (Am.) light covered carriage
**guayina** *f* (Am.) station wagon
**guayule** *m* (bot.) guayule (*shrub and rubber*)
**gubarte** *m* (zool.) humpback (*whale*)
**gubernamental** *adj* governmental; government; strong-government (*e.g., advocate*)
**gubernativo -va** *adj* governmental
**gubia** *f* (carp.) gouge
**guedeja** *f* long hair; lion's mane; **guedejas** *fpl* shaggy coat (*of animal*)
**guedejón -jona, guedejoso -sa** or **guedejudo -da** *adj* long-haired; heavy-maned
**güeldo** *m* bait consisting of shrimps and other crustaceans
**Güeldres** Gelderland
**güelfo -fa** *adj* Guelfic or Guelphic; *m* Guelf or Guelph
**güemul** *m* (zool.) guemal or guemul (*South American deer: Hippocamelus bisulcus*)
**Guepeu** *f* Ogpu (*Soviet secret police*)
**güero -ra** *adj & mf* (Am.) blond
**guerra** *f* war, warfare; conflict, struggle; billiards; **armar en guerra** (nav.) to commission; **dar guerra** (coll.) to annoy, harass, be troublesome; **entrar en guerra** to go to war; **Gran Guerra** Great War; **guerra a muerte** war to the death; **guerra atómica** atomic war; **guerra bacilar, bacteriana** or **bacteriológica** germ war, germ warfare; **guerra biológica** biological warfare; **guerra blanca** cold war; **guerra civil** civil war; **guerra de Crimea** Crimean War; **guerra de guerrillas** guerrilla warfare; **guerra de la Independencia** War of Independence; **guerra de las dos Rosas** War of the Roses; **guerra del opio** Opium War; **guerra de los Cien Años** Hundred Years' War; **guerra de los Siete Años** Seven Years' War; **guerra de los Treinta Años** Thirty Years' War; **guerra del Peloponeso** Peloponnesian War; **guerra del Transvaal** Boer War; **guerra de nervios** war of nerves; **guerra de ondas** radio jamming; **guerra de precios** price war; **guerra de Troya** (myth.) Trojan War; **guerra entre Norte y Sur** Civil War, War between the States (*in the United States*); **guerra Francoprusiana** Franco-Prussian War; **guerra fría** cold war; **guerra hispanoamericana** Spanish-American War; **Guerra Mundial** World War; **guerra psicológica** psychological warfare; **guerra química** chemical warfare; **guerra relámpago** blitzkrieg; **guerra santa** holy war; **guerra sin cuartel** war without quarter; **guerras púnicas** Punic Wars; **guerra total** total war
**guerreador -dora** *adj* warlike; warring; *mf* warrior, fighter
**guerrear** *vn* to war, wage war, fight; to resist, put up an argument
**guerrero -ra** *adj* (pertaining to) war; warlike; warring; mischievous; *mf* fighter; *m* warrior, fighting man, soldier; *f* tight-fitting military jacket
**guerrilla** *f* band of skirmishers; band of guerrillas; guerrilla warfare
**guerrillear** *vn* to skirmish; to fight guerrilla warfare
**guerrillero** *m* guerrilla; guerrilla leader
**guía** *mf* guide; leader; adviser, mentor; *m* (mil.) guide; *f* guide; guidance; guidebook, directory; leader (*horse*); road marker (*for snowstorms*); marker (*for river navigation*); handle bar; young shoot (*left on vine for training others*); shoot, sprout; fence (*of a saw*); turned-up end of mustache; customhouse permit; (mach.) guide; (min.) leader; (naut.) guy; (rail.) timetable; (Am.) tip (*of stock, branch, etc.*); **guías** *fpl* reins for driving leader horses; **a guías** driving four-in-hand; **echarse con las guías** or **con guías y todo** to ride roughshod; **guía oficial de España** Spanish government yearbook; **guía sonora** sound track (*of film*); **guía telefónica** telephone directory; **guía vocacional** vocational guidance
**guiadera** *f* (mach.) guide
**guiador -dora** *adj* guiding; *mf* guide, leader
**guiar** §90 *va* to guide, to lead; to steer, to drive; to pilot; to train (*a plant*); *vn* to shoot, to sprout; *vr* to be guided; **guiarse de** or **por** to be guided by, to go by
**Guido** *m* Guy
**guiguí** *m* (*pl:* **-guíes**) (zool.) flying squirrel
**guija** *f* pebble; (bot.) grass pea
**guijarral** *m* place full of large pebbles and cobbles
**guijarreño -ña** *adj* full of cobbles, cobbly; hard; flint-hearted; hefty, robust
**guijarro** *m* large pebble, cobble
**guijarroso -sa** *adj* full of cobbles, cobbly, rocky
**guijeño -ña** *adj* gravelly, pebbly; hard-hearted
**guijo** *m* gravel; (mach.) gudgeon
**guijón** *m* caries, tooth decay
**guijoso -sa** *adj* pebbly, gravelly
**guileña** *f* (bot.) columbine
**güilogis** *m* (f.a.) guilloche
**guilla** *f* rich harvest
**guillado -da** *adj* (coll.) daffy
**guilladura** *f* (coll.) daffiness, craziness
**guillame** *m* (carp.) rabbet plane
**guillar** *vr* to leave, to flee; to become unbalanced
**Guillermina** *f* Wilhelmina
**Guillermo** *m* William
**güillín** *m* var. of **huillín**
**Guill.º** abr. of **Guillermo**
**guillomo** *m* (bot.) Juneberry, shadberry, serviceberry
**guillote** *adj* lazy, idle; simple, credulous; *m* harvester; iron pin
**guillotina** *f* guillotine; paper cutter; (surg. & law) guillotine; **de guillotina** sash (*window*)
**guillotinar** *va* to guillotine
**guimbalete** *m* pump handle
**guimbarda** *f* (carp.) grooving plane
**guinchar** *va* to goad, prod, prick
**guincho** *m* goad, prod; (orn.) American osprey
**guinda** *f* sour cherry (*fruit*); (naut.) height of masts; **guinda garrafal** sweet cherry (*fruit*)
**guindal** *m* (bot.) sour cherry (*tree*); (naut.) hawser; (naut.) crane
**guindalera** *f* sour-cherry orchard
**guindaleta** *f* (naut.) rope, hempen rope
**guindaleza** *f* (naut.) hawser
**guindamaina** *f* (naut.) dipping the colors (*as a salute*)
**guindar** *va* to hoist, to hang up; (coll.) to win; (coll.) to hang, to string up
**guindaste** *m* (naut.) jib crane
**guindilla** *f* small sour cherry; Guinea pepper (*fruit*); *m* (coll.) cop, policeman

**guindillo** *m* small sour cherry tree; **guindillo de Indias** (bot.) Guinea pepper (*plant*)
**guindo** *m* (bot.) sour cherry (*tree*); **guindo griego** (bot.) sweet cherry (*tree*)
**guindola** *f* (naut.) boatswain's chair; (naut.) life buoy; (naut.) log chip
**guineo -a** *adj* Guinea; Guinean; *m* Guineaman; banana; *f* guinea (*coin*); (*cap.*) *f* Guinea; **la Guinea Española** Spanish Guinea; **la Guinea Francesa** French Guinea; **la Guinea Portuguesa** Portuguese Guinea; **la Nueva Guinea** New Guinea
**guinga** *f* gingham
**guinja** *f* jujube
**guinjo** *m* (bot.) jujube tree
**guínjol** *m* var. of **guinja**
**guinjolero** *m* var. of **guinjo**
**guiñada** *f* wink; (naut.) yaw
**guiñador -dora** *adj* winking; *mf* winker
**guiñadura** *f* var. of **guiñada**
**guiñapiento -ta** *adj* ragged, raggedy
**guiñapo** *m* rag, tatter; tatterdemalion; reprobate
**guiñaposo -sa** *adj* var. of **guiñapiento**
**guiñar** *va* to wink (*an eye*); *vn* to wink; (naut.) to yaw; *vr* to wink at each other
**guiño** *m* wink; face, grimace; **hacerse guiños** to make faces at each other
**guión** *m* cross (*carried before prelate in procession*); royal standard; leader (*in a dance; among animals*); hyphen; dash; (mil.) guidon; outline; (mov. & theat.) scenario; (mus.) repeat sign; (rad. & telv.) script; **guión de las codornices** (orn.) corn crake; **guión de montaje** (mov.) cutter's script; **guión de rodaje** (mov.) shooting script
**guionista** *mf* (mov.) scenarist; (mov.) person who writes titles for a movie in a foreign language; scriptwriter
**guipur** *m* guipure
**güira** *f* (bot.) calabash tree
**guirigay** *m* (coll.) gibberish; hubbub, confusion
**guirindola** *f* jabot, frill
**guirlache** *m* almond brittle, peanut brittle
**guirnalda** *f* garland, wreath; (bot.) globe amaranth
**güiro** *m* (bot.) bottle gourd; (Am.) musical instrument made of a gourd; (Am.) green corn stalk
**guiropa** *f* meat stew
**guisa** *f* manner, wise, way; **a guisa de** like, in the manner of; by way of
**guisado** *m* stew; meat stew
**guisador -dora** or **guisandero -ra** *mf* cook
**guisante** *m* (bot.) pea (*plant and seed*); **guisante de olor** (bot.) sweet pea
**guisar** *va* to stew, to cook; to arrange, put in order; *vn* to cook
**guiso** *m* dish; seasoning
**guisote** *m* hash, poor dish
**guita** *f* twine; (coll.) money
**guitarra** *f* (mus.) guitar
**guitarrazo** *m* blow with a guitar
**guitarrear** *vn* to play the guitar
**guitarreo** *m* strumming on the guitar
**guitarrería** *f* guitar shop, string-instrument shop
**guitarrero -ra** *mf* guitar maker or dealer; guitarist; guitar enthusiast
**guitarresco -ca** *adj* (coll.) (pertaining to the) guitar
**guitarrillo** *m* small four-string guitar
**guitarrista** *mf* guitarist
**guitarro** *m* small four-string guitar; (coll.) little runt
**guitarrón** *m* big guitar; (coll.) sly rascal
**guitero -ra** *mf* twine maker or dealer
**guitón -tona** *mf* tramp, bum; (coll.) little scamp, rascal
**guitonear** *vn* to loaf, to bum around
**guitonería** *f* loafing, bumming, vagabondage; gang of bums
**guizacillo** *m* (bot.) hedgehog grass
**guizgar** §59 *va* var. of **enguizgar**
**guizque** *m* pole with a hook for reaching things
**gula** *f* gorging, guzzling; gluttony
**gules** *mpl* (her.) gules
**gulosidad** *f* gluttony
**guloso -sa** *adj* gorging, guzzling; gluttonous
**gulusmear** *vn* to sniff the cooking
**gullería** *f* var. of **gollería**
**gulloría** *f* favor, extra; (orn.) calander
**gúmena** *f* (naut.) heavy cable
**gumía** *f* Moorish dagger or poniard
**gumífero -ra** *adj* var. of **gomífero**
**gura** *f* (orn.) crowned pigeon
**gurbio -bia** *adj* curved
**gurbión** *m* (pharm.) euphorbium; coarse twisted silk
**guripa** *m* (slang) soldier
**guro** *m* (slang) bailiff, alguazil
**gurriato** *m* young sparrow
**gurrufero** *m* (coll.) ugly old nag
**gurrumino -na** *adj* weak, run-down; *m* (coll.) doting husband, henpecked husband; *f* uxoriousness
**gurrupié** *m* croupier; gamester's assistant
**gurullada** *f* (coll.) gang of loafers
**gurullo** *m* lump, knot
**gurvio -via** *adj* var. of **gurbio**
**gusanear** *vn* to swarm, to teem
**gusanera** *f* nest of worms; worm pit (*compost heap for breeding worms as food for chickens*); (coll.) ruling passion
**gusaniento -ta** *adj* wormy, grubby, maggoty
**gusanillo** *m* small worm; twist of gold, silver, or silk; twist stitch; spur (*of gimlet or bit*); **matar el gusanillo** (coll.) to take a shot of liquor before breakfast
**gusano** *m* worm; maggot; (fig.) worm (*poor soul, contemptible person*); **matar el gusano** (coll.) to take a shot of liquor before breakfast; **gusano de la conciencia** worm of conscience (*remorse*); **gusano de la manzana** apple worm; **gusano del queso** cheese skipper, cheese hopper; **gusano de luz** glowworm; **gusano de San Antón** wood louse; **gusano de seda** or **de la seda** silkworm; **gusano de tierra** earthworm; **gusano plano** flatworm; **gusano rojo** gapeworm
**gusanoso -sa** *adj* wormy, grubby
**gusarapiento -ta** *adj* wormy; dirty, filthy
**gusarapo** *m* waterworm, vinegar worm
**gustable** *adj* worth being tasted
**gustación** *f* tasting; taste
**gustadura** *f* tasting, sampling
**gustar** *va* to taste; to try, test, sample; to please, be pleasing to; to like, e.g., **no le gustaron a Juan estas manzanas** John did not like these apples; **gustar** + *inf* to like to + *inf*, e.g., **me gusta viajar** I like to travel; *vn* to like, e.g., **como Vd. guste** as you like; **gustar de** to like, e.g., **gusto de la música** I like music; **gustar de** + *inf* to like to + *inf*, e.g., **gusto de leer** I like to read
**gustativo -va** *adj* gustative
**gustatorio -ria** *adj* gustatory
**Gustavo** *m* Gustavus; **Gustavo Adolfo** Gustavus Adolphus
**gustazo** *m* (coll.) great pleasure, fiendish pleasure
**gustillo** *m* slight taste, touch
**gusto** *m* taste; flavor; liking; pleasure; caprice, whim; **a gusto** at will; as you like it; in comfort; **a gusto de** to the taste of, to the liking of; **con mucho gusto** with pleasure, gladly; **dar gusto a** to please; **encontrarse a gusto** or **estar a gusto** to be comfortable; to like it (*e.g., in the country*); **ser del gusto de** to be to the liking of; **tanto gusto** I was so glad to see you; glad to meet you; **tener gusto en** + *inf* to be glad to + *inf;* **tomar (el) gusto a** to take a liking for
**gustoso -sa** *adj* tasty; pleasant, agreeable; ready, willing, glad
**gutagamba** *f* (bot.) garcinia (*Garcinia morella*); gamboge, Ceylon gamboge
**gutapercha** *f* gutta-percha
**gutífero -ra** *adj* (bot.) guttiferous
**gutural** *adj* guttural; (phonet.) guttural
**guzla** *f* (mus.) gusla (*kind of rebec*)

**H, h** *f* ninth letter of the Spanish alphabet
**ha** *3d sg pres ind of* **haber;** *interj* ha!
**haba** *f* (bot.) bean, broad bean; bean (*of coffee, cocoa, etc.*); kernel; voting ball; (vet.) tumor on horse's palate; **son habas contadas** it's a sure thing; **haba caballuna** (bot.) horse bean; **haba de Egipto** (bot.) taro; **haba de las Indias** (bot.) sweet pea; **haba de San Ignacio** St.-Ignatius's-bean; **haba panosa** (bot.) horse bean; **haba tonca** tonka bean
**Habacuc** *m* (Bib.) Habakkuk
**habado -da** *adj* having a tumor on the palate (*said of a horse*); dappled (*horse*); mottled (*fowl*)
**Habana, La** see **habano**
**habanero -ra** *adj & mf* Havanese; *f* habanera (*dance and music*)
**habano -na** *adj* Havana (*tobacco; brown*); *m* Havana cigar; **La Habana** Havana
**habar** *m* bean patch
**hábeas corpus** *m* (law) habeas corpus
**haber** *m* salary, wages; (com.) credit, credit side; **haberes** *mpl* property, wealth ‖ §54 *va* to get hold of, to lay hands on; (archaic) to have, to get; **habido -da** taking place, held, e.g., **una conferencia habida en París** a conference held in Paris ‖ *v impers* ago, e.g., **cinco años ha** five years ago; (*3d sg pres ind:* **hay**) there to be, e.g., **mañana habrá función** there will be a show tomorrow; **¿cuánta distancia hay de aquí a . . .?** or **¿cuánto hay de aquí a . . .?** how far is it to . . .?; **no haber que** + *inf* to be unnecessary to + *inf;* to be useless to + *inf;* one should not + *inf;* **no hay de qué** you're welcome, don't mention it; **haber que** + *inf* to be necessary to + *inf* ‖ *v aux* to have, e.g., **he leído la carta** I have read the letter; **haber de** + *inf* must, to be to + *inf*, e.g., **ha de llegar antes de las seis** he is to arrive before six o'clock ‖ *vr* to behave oneself, conduct oneself; **habérselas con** to deal with, to have it out with
**haberío** *m* beast of burden; cattle
**habichuela** *f* (bot.) kidney bean, string bean; **habichuela verde** string bean
**habiente** *adj* (law) having, possessing
**hábil** *adj* skilful; capable; work (*day*); (law) competent
**habilidad** *f* skill; ability, capability; feat; scheme, trick
**habilidoso -sa** *adj* skilful
**habilitación** *f* qualification; financing; equipment; paymastership; **habilitaciones** *fpl* fixtures (*e.g., of a store*); **habilitación de la bandera** permission (*to a foreign vessel*) to engage in coasting trade
**habilitado -da** *adj* entitled, qualified; (philately) authorized, legalized; *m* paymaster
**habilitador -dora** *mf* outfitter, equipper
**habilitar** *va* to enable, to entitle, to qualify; to pass (*in an examination*); to finance (*a person*); to provide; to equip, fit out; to set up
**habitabilidad** *f* inhabitability
**habitable** *adj* inhabitable, habitable
**habitación** *f* habitation; house, dwelling; room; (biol.) habitat; **habitación del forastero** spare room; **habitación doble** double room; **habitación individual** single room; **habitación para los niños** nursery; **habitación popular** low-cost housing; **habitación salón** suite (*in a hotel*)
**habitáculo** *m* house, dwelling; hovel
**habitador -dora** *adj* inhabiting; *mf* inhabitant
**habitante** *mf* inhabitant
**habitar** *va* to inhabit, live in; to occupy (*e.g., an apartment*); *vn* to live
**habitat** *m* (biol.) habitat
**hábito** *m* habit (*custom; disposition acquired by repetition; dress*); **ahorcar** or **colgar el hábito** (coll.) to leave the priesthood, to doff the cassock, **tener por hábito** + *inf* to be in the habit of + *ger;* **tomar el hábito** to enter religion
**habituación** *f* habituation
**habituado -da** *mf* habitué
**habitual** *adj* habitual; usual, regular
**habituar** §33 *va* to habituate, accustom; **habituar a** + *inf* to accustom to + *inf; vr* to become habituated, become accustomed; **habituarse a** + *inf* to become accustomed to + *inf*
**habitud** *f* connection, relation
**habla** *f* speech (*faculty of speaking; manner of speaking; language, dialect; talk or address to a group of people*); **al habla** speaking; in contact, in communication; (naut.) within hailing distance; **¡al habla!** speaking! (*in answer to call of one's name on telephone*); **de habla latina** Romance-language-speaking; **negar** or **quitar el habla a** to not speak to (*because of a quarrel*); **perder el habla** to lose one's speech
**hablado -da** *adj* spoken; **bien hablado** well-tongued; well-spoken; **mal hablado** ill-tongued
**hablador -dora** *adj* talkative; gossipy; *mf* talker, chatterbox; gossip
**habladuría** *f* idle rumor; cut, sarcasm; gossip, piece of gossip
**hablanchín -china** *adj & mf* (coll.) var. of **hablador**
**hablante** *adj* speaking; *mf* speaker
**hablantín -tina** *adj & mf* (coll.) var. of **hablador**
**hablar** *va* to speak, to talk (*a language*); to talk (*e.g., nonsense*); **hablarlo todo** to spill everything; *vn* to speak, to talk; **dar que hablar** to cause talk; **es hablar por demás** it's wasted talk; **estar hablando** to be almost alive (*said of painting or sculpture*); **no hablar con** to not speak to (*because of a quarrel*); **hablar alto** to speak up; **hablar claro** to talk straight from the shoulder; *vr* to talk to each other; **hablárselo todo** to let nobody get a word in edgewise; to contradict oneself all the time
**hablilla** *f* story, gossip, piece of gossip
**hablista** *mf* speaker, good speaker
**habón** *m* wheal
**habré** *1st sg fut ind of* **haber**
**hacanea** *f* sturdy little horse
**hacedero -ra** *adj* feasible, practicable
**hacedor** *m* steward, manager; (*cap.*) *m* Maker (*God*)
**hacendado -da** *adj* landed, property-owning; *mf* property-owner; (Am.) rancher, cattle rancher
**hacendar** §18 *va* to transfer; **hacendarle a uno con** to transfer (*property*) to someone; *vr* to acquire property
**hacendero -ra** *adj* sedulous, thrifty; *f* community project or undertaking
**hacendista** *m* economist; fiscal expert; man of private means
**hacendoso -sa** *adj* diligent, industrious; thrifty
**hacer** §55 *va* to make; to do; to pack (*a trunk*); to give (*an order*); to cause; to accustom; to play (*a part*); to play the part of; to act, perform (*a play*); to pretend to be; to imagine (*someone*) to be; to hold, to contain; to have made; to ask (*a question*); **desde hace** for, e.g., **estoy aquí desde hace diez días** I have been here (for) ten days; **estaba allí**

desde hacía dos meses I had been there (for) two months; **hace** ago, e.g., **hace dos semanas** two weeks ago; **hacer con** to provide with; **hacer mucho (tiempo) que** to be a long time since; **hacer . . . que** to be . . . since, e.g., **hace un mes que Juan estuvo aquí** it is a month since John was here; **hacía un mes que Juan había estado aquí** it was a month since John had been here; **mañana hará un mes que Juan estuvo aquí** it will be a month tomorrow since John was here; **hacer** + *inf* to have + *inf*, e.g., **le haré llamar a su puerta** I shall have him knock at your door; to make + *inf*, e.g., **me hizo estudiar** he made me study; to have + *pp*, e.g., **haremos construir una casa** we shall have a house built; for expressions like **hacer calor** to be warm, to be hot (*said of weather*), see the noun ‖ *vn* to act; to matter; **hacer a** to fit; **hacer como que** + *ind* to pretend to + *inf;* **hacer de** to act as, work as; **hacer por** + *inf* to try to + *inf;* **hacer que** + *ind* to pretend to + *inf;* **hacer que** + *subj* to see to it that; to cause to + *inf* ‖ *vr* to make oneself; to become, get to be; to grow; to turn into; to imagine; **hacerse a** + *inf* to become accustomed to + *inf;* **hacerse a una parte** or **a un lado** to step aside, to withdraw; **hacerse con** to seize, get hold of, to make off with; **hacerse chiquito** or **el chiquito** (coll.) to sing small; **hacérsele a uno** + *adj* to strike or impress one as + *adj*, e.g., **lo que Vd. dijo se me hizo difícil de creer** what you said struck me as hard to believe; **hacerse viejo** (coll.) to kill time

**hacera** *f* var. of **acera**

**hacia** *prep* toward; near, about; **hacia abajo** downwards; **hacia adelante** forwards; **hacia arriba** upwards; **hacia atrás** backwards; (coll.) the wrong way; **hacia dentro** inwards; **hacia fuera** outwards

**hacienda** *f* farm, farmstead, country property; property, fortune, possessions; treasury; (Am.) ranch; (Am.) cattle, livestock; **haciendas** *fpl* household chores; **hacienda pública** public finance

**hacina** *f* (agr.) shock, stack; pile, heap

**hacinador -dora** *mf* stacker

**hacinamiento** *m* piling, heaping, stacking

**hacinar** *va* to pile, heap, stack

**hacha** *f* heavy wax candle with four wicks, torch, firebrand; axe; battle-axe; thatch; (coll.) expert

**hachar** *va* to hew with an axe; (Am.) to get the better of (*in an argument*)

**hachazo** *m* blow or stroke with an axe

**hachear** *va* to hew with an axe; *vn* to hack with an axe

**hachero** *m* torch stand; torchbearer; woodcutter; (mil.) sapper

**hachich** *m* or **hachís** *m* hashish

**hacho** *m* bunch of resinous wood or of tow and pitch (*for a torch*); beacon (*hill overlooking sea*)

**hachón** *m* large torch; cresset

**hachote** *m* (naut.) short, thick candle

**hachuela** *f* small axe; (Am.) hatchet

**hada** *f* fairy; (fig.) charmer (*fascinating woman*); (obs.) fate, destiny; **Hadas** *fpl* (myth.) Fates; **hada madrina** fairy godmother

**hadado -da** *adj* fateful; magic, wonder-working; **bien hadado** lucky; **mal hadado** ill-fated

**hadar** *va* to foretell; to predestine; to charm, cast a spell on

**Hades** *m* (myth. & Bib.) Hades

**hado** *m* fate, destiny

**hafiz** *m* (*pl:* **-fices**) warden

**hafnio** *m* (chem.) hafnium

**hagiografía** *f* hagiography

**hagiográfico -ca** *adj* hagiographic or hagiographical

**hagiógrafo** *m* hagiographer

**hagiología** *f* hagiology

**hago** *1st sg pres ind of* **hacer**

**haiga** *m* (slang) sporty-looking car; (slang) sporty-looking person

**Haití** *m* Haiti

**haitiano -na** *adj & mf* Haitian

**hala** *interj* get going!; come, come!, here, here!

**halagador -dora** *adj* flattering

**halagar** §59 *va* to cajole, fawn on; to gratify, to attract; to flatter

**halago** *m* cajolery; gratification; flattery; **halagos** *mpl* flattery, flattering words

**halagüeño -ña** *adj* attractive, charming; bright, rosy, promising; flattering

**halar** *va* (naut.) to haul, pull; *vn* (naut.) to pull ahead

**halazona** *f* (pharm.) halazone

**halcón** *m* (orn.) falcon; **halcón montano** haggard hawk; **halcón niego** eyas; **halcón palumbario** (orn.) pigeon hawk, merlin; **halcón peregrino** (orn.) peregrine falcon; **halcón peregrino patero** (orn.) duck hawk

**halconear** *vn* to act and dress brazenly in order to attract men

**halconera** *f* mew, place for falcons

**halconería** *f* hawking, falconry

**halconero** *m* hawker, falconer

**halda** *f* skirt; packing burlap; **de haldas o de mangas** (coll.) one way or another, right or wrong; **poner haldas en cinta** (coll.) to pull up one's skirts to run; (coll.) to roll up one's sleeves (*for work*)

**haldada** *f* skirtful

**haldear** *vn* to dash along with skirts flying

**haldeta** *f* flap

**haldudo -da** *adj* full-skirted

**hale** *interj* get going!

**haleche** *m* (ichth.) anchovy

**Halicarnaso** *f* Halicarnassus

**halieto** *m* (orn.) osprey, fish hawk

**halita** *f* (mineral.) halite (*rock salt*); (mineral.) websterite (*aluminite*); (petrog.) websterite

**hálito** *m* halitus, breath, vapor; (poet.) gentle breeze

**halitosis** *f* halitosis

**halo** *m* (meteor, f.a. & fig.) halo

**halófilo -la** *adj* (bot.) halophilous

**halófito -ta** *adj* (bot.) halophytic; *f* (bot.) halophyte

**halogenación** *f* halogenation

**halógeno** *m* (chem.) halogen

**haloideo -a** *adj & m* (chem.) haloid

**halón** *m* (meteor.) halo

**halozono** *m* var. of **halazona**

**halterio** *m* dumbbell; halter (*of insect*)

**haluro** *m* (chem.) halide

**hallaca** *f* var. of **hayaca**

**hallado -da** *adj* found; **bien hallado** unconstrained; **mal hallado** uneasy, constrained; *f* finding, discovery

**hallador -dora** *mf* finder

**hallar** *va* to find; *vr* to find oneself; to be; **no hallarse** to not like it, be annoyed; **hallarse bien con** to be satisfied with; **hallarse en todo** to butt in everywhere; to have one's hand in everything, to be mixed up in everything; **hallárselo todo hecho** to never have to turn a hand

**hallazgo** *m* finding, discovery; find; reward (*for finding something*), e.g., **cinco dólares de hallazgo** five dollars reward

**hallulla** *f* or **hallullo** *m* bread baked on embers or hot stones; (Am.) fine bread

**hamaca** *f* hammock

**hamacar** §86 *va* (Am.) to swing, to rock

**hamadríada** *f* (myth.) hamadryad

**hámago** *m* beebread; nausea, loathing, disgust

**hamamelidáceo -a** *adj* (bot.) hamamelidaceous

**hamamelina** *f* (pharm.) witch hazel

**hamaquear** *va & vr* (Am.) to swing, to rock

**hamaquero** *m* hammock maker; hammock bearer; hammock hook

**hambre** *f* hunger; famine; starvation; **entretener el hambre** (coll.) to take a bite to stave off hunger till mealtime; (coll.) to try to forget one's hunger; **matar de hambre** to starve (*a person*) to death; **morir de hambre** to starve to death, to die of starvation; **pasar hambre** to go hungry; **tener hambre** to be hungry; **tener hambre de** to be hungry for, to hunger for

**hambreador** *m* (Am.) food profiteer

**hambrear** *va* to starve, to famish; *vn* to starve, to famish, to hunger

**hambriento -ta** *adj* hungry; **hambriento de** hungry for (*e.g., wealth*)

**hambrón -brona** *adj* (coll.) starving; *mf* (coll.) starveling
**hambruna** *f* (Am.) mad hunger
**Hamburgo** *f* Hamburg
**hamburgués -guesa** *adj* (pertaining to) Hamburg; *mf* native or inhabitant of Hamburg; *f* hamburger (*sandwich*)
**hamita** *mf* Hamite
**hamo** *m* fishhook
**hampa** *f* vagrancy, rowdyism; (coll.) rowdies
**hampesco -ca** *adj* vagabond, rowdyish
**hampón** *m* rowdy, bully, tough
**han** *3d pl pres ind of* **haber**
**hangar** *m* (aer.) hangar
**hanoveriano -na** *adj & mf* Hanoverian
**hansa** *f* var. of **ansa**
**hanseático -ca** *adj* var. of **anseático**
**hanumán** *m* (zool.) langur
**haploide** *adj & m* (biol.) haploid
**haplología** *f* (philol.) haplology
**haragán -gana** *adj* idling, loafing, lazy; *mf* idler, loafer, good-for-nothing
**haraganear** *vn* to idle, to loaf, to hang around
**haraganería** *f* idleness, loafing, laziness
**harakiri** *m* hari-kari
**harambel** *m* var. of **arambel**
**harapiento -ta** *adj* ragged
**harapo** *m* rag, tatter; **andar** or **estar hecho un harapo** (coll.) to be in rags
**haraposo -sa** *adj* ragged
**haré** *1st sg fut ind of* **hacer**
**harem** *m* or **harén** *m* harem
**harfango** *m* (orn.) snowy owl
**harija** *f* mill dust, stive
**harina** *f* flour; **donde no hay harina, todo es mohina** poverty parts good company; **estar metido en harina** (coll.) to be deeply absorbed; (coll.) to be fat, be heavy; **ser harina de otro costal** (coll.) to be a horse of another color; **harina de maíz** corn meal
**harinero -ra** *adj* (pertaining to) flour; *m* flour dealer; flour bin or chest
**harinoso -sa** *adj* floury, mealy; farinaceous
**harma** *f* var. of **alárgama**
**harmonía** *f* var. of **armonía**
**harnero** *m* sieve; **estar hecho un harnero** to be riddled with wounds
**Haroldo** *m* Harold
**harón -rona** *adj* lazy; balky; *mf* lazy loafer
**haronear** *vn* to be slow, be lazy, idle around, to dawdle
**haronero** *m* sieve, sifter
**haronía** *f* laziness
**harpa** *f* var. of **arpa**
**harpía** *f* (coll.) ugly shrew, jade; (coll.) harpy (*rapacious person*); (zool.) harpy bat (*Nyctimene*); (myth.) Harpy
**harpillera** *f* burlap, bagging, sackcloth
**harre** *m & interj* var. of **arre**
**hartar** *va* to stuff, satiate; to satisfy, gratify; to tire, bore; **hartar de** to overwhelm with, deluge with; *vn* to stuff, be satiated; *vr* to stuff, be satiated; to tire, be bored
**hartazgo** *m* or **hartazón** *m* fill, bellyful; **darse un hartazgo** (coll.) to eat one's fill; **darse un hartazgo de** (coll.) to have or to get one's fill of (*e.g., peanuts, reading, eating*)
**harto -ta** *adj* full, satiated, fed up; much, very much; **harto de** full of, sick of, fed up with; **harto** *adv* quite, very; enough
**hartura** *f* fill, satiety; abundance; full satisfaction; **con hartura** in abundance, on a large scale
**has** *2d sg pres ind of* **haber**
**hasta** *adv* even; *prep* until, till; to, as far as, up to, down to; as much as; **hasta aquí** so far; **hasta después** good-by, so long; **hasta después de** until after; **hasta la vista** or **hasta luego** good-by, so long; **hasta mañana** see you tomorrow; **hasta no más** to the utmost; **hasta que** until, till; **hasta tanto que** until, till
**hastial** *m* gable end; (min.) side wall; bumpkin
**hastiar** **§90** *va* to sicken, cloy, surfeit; to annoy, bore
**hastío** *m* nausea, disgust, surfeit; annoyance, boredom
**hastioso -sa** *adj* sickening; annoying, boresome
**hataca** *f* large wooden ladle; rolling pin
**hatajar** *va & vn* to divide into small herds or flocks; to separate from the herd or flock
**hatajo** *m* small herd, small flock; (coll.) lot, flock (*e.g., of nonsense*)
**hatear** *va* (coll.) to pack up; *vn* to get one's outfit together; to bring provisions to shepherds
**hatería** *f* provisions, supplies, or equipment for several days (*for shepherds, farm hands, miners, etc.*)
**hatero -ra** *adj* pack (*animal*); *mf* (Am.) rancher; *m* pack carrier
**hatijo** *m* straw for beehives
**hato** *m* herd (*of cattle*); flock (*of sheep*); shepherds' hut; provisions for shepherds; everyday outfit; pack, bundle (*of clothes*); ring, clique; gang (*of thugs*); lot, flock (*of nonsense*); (Am.) cattle ranch; **liar el hato** (coll.) to pack, pack up, pack one's baggage; **menear el hato a** (coll.) to beat up; **revolver el hato** (coll.) to stir up trouble
**hawaiano -na** *adj & mf* Hawaiian; *m* Hawaiian (*language*)
**haxix** *m* var. of **hachich**
**hay** *3d sg pres ind of* **haber**
**haya** *1st sg pres subj of* **haber;** *f* (bot.) beech, beech tree; **La Haya** The Hague
**hayaca** *f* (Am.) mince pie
**hayal** *m* or **hayedo** *m* beech forest
**hayo** *m* (bot.) coca; (Am.) coca leaves prepared for chewing
**hayuco** *m* beechnut, mast (*food for hogs*)
**haz** *m* (*pl:* **haces**) bunch, bundle, fagot; sheaf; pencil, beam (*of rays*); (arch.) clustered column; (bot.) fascicle; (mil.) file of soldiers; (mil.) troops drawn up in divisions; *f* (*pl:* **haces**) face; surface (*of the earth*); right side (*e.g., of cloth*); **a sobre haz** on the surface; **en haz y en paz** by common consent; **hacer haz** to be in line, be flush; **ser de dos haces** to be two-faced; *2d sg impv of* **hacer**
**haza** *f* field (*for crops*)
**hazaleja** *f* towel
**hazaña** *f* deed, feat, exploit
**hazañería** *f* fuss (*trivial perturbation*)
**hazañero -ra** *adj* fussy, fluttery
**hazañoso -sa** *adj* gallant, courageous, heroic
**hazmerreír** *m* (coll.) butt, laughingstock
**he** *adv* lo, lo and behold; **he aquí** here is, here are, e.g., **he aquí a su hermano** here is your brother; **he allí** there is, there are, e.g., **helos allí** there they are; *1st sg pres ind of* **haber**
**hé** *2d sg impv of* **haber**
**hebdómada** *f* week, hebdomad; seven years
**hebdomadario -ria** *adj* hebdomadal or hebdomadary
**Hebe** *f* (myth.) Hebe
**hebilla** *f* buckle; **no faltar hebilla a** (coll.) to be tiptop, to be perfect
**hebillaje** *m* buckles, set of buckles
**hebillero -ra** *mf* buckle maker or dealer
**hebra** *f* thread, fiber; vein; grain (*in wood*); (fig.) thread (*of conversation*); **hebras** *fpl* (poet.) hair; **de una hebra** (Am.) all at once; **estar** or **ser de buena hebra** (coll.) to be strong and husky; **pegar la hebra** (coll.) to strike up a conversation; (coll.) to talk on and on
**hebraico -ca** *adj* Hebraic
**hebraísmo** *m* Hebraism
**hebraísta** *mf* Hebraist (*scholar skilled in Hebrew language and literature*)
**hebraizante** *adj* Hebraizing; *mf* Hebraist
**hebraizar** **§97** *vn* to Hebraize
**hebreo -a** *adj & mf* Hebrew; *m* Hebrew (*language*); (coll.) usurer
**Hébridas, las** the Hebrides; **Nuevas Hébridas** New Hebrides
**hebroso -sa** *adj* fibrous, stringy
**Hécate** *f* (myth.) Hecate
**hecatombe** *f* hecatomb
**hect.** abr. of **hectárea**
**hectárea** *f* hectare
**héctico -ca** *adj & mf* var. of **hético**
**hectiquez** *f* var. of **hetiquez**
**hectocótilo** *m* (zool.) hectocotylus
**hectógrafo** *m* hectograph
**hectogramo** *m* hectogram
**hectólitro** *m* hectoliter
**hectómetro** *m* hectometer

**Héctor** *m* (myth.) Hector
**Hécuba** *f* (myth.) Hecuba
**hechiceresco -ca** *adj* magical
**hechicería** *f* sorcery, wizardry, witchcraft; (fig.) charm, fascination
**hechicero -ra** *adj* magic; bewitching, charming, enchanting; *mf* magician, sorcerer; charmer, enchanter; *m* wizard, sorcerer; *f* witch, sorceress
**hechizar** §76 *va* to bewitch, cast a spell on; (fig.) to bewitch, charm, enchant, delight; *vn* to be charming, to enchant; to practice sorcery
**hechizo -za** *adj* fake, deceptive; detachable; made, manufactured; fit, suitable; skilful (*work*); (Am.) local, home (*product*); *m* spell, charm; magic, sorcery; (fig.) magic, sorcery, glamour; (fig.) charmer; **hechizos** *mpl* charms (*of a woman*)
**hecho -cha** *pp of* **hacer;** *adj* accustomed, inured; finished, perfect; ready-made; full-grown; **a lo hecho pecho** make the best out of a bad situation; **estar hecho** to be turned into, to be, to look like; **hecho y derecho** finished, complete; *m* fact; deed, act; matter; event; **de hecho** in fact; (law) de facto; **en hecho de verdad** as a matter of fact; **estar en el hecho de** to catch on to, to get the point of; **hecho consumado** fait accompli; **hecho de armas** feat of arms; **Hechos de los Apóstoles** (Bib.) Acts of the Apostles; **¡hecho!** O.K.!, all right!
**hechura** *f* make, making; creation, creature; form, shape, cut, build; workmanship; (Am.) drink, treat; **hechuras** *fpl* cost of making; **no tener hechura** to be impracticable
**hedentina** *f* stench, stink
**heder** §66 *va* to bore, annoy; *vn* to stink
**hediondez** *f* stench, stink
**hediondo -da** *adj* stinking; smelly; annoying, boring; filthy, dirty, obscene; *m* (bot.) bean trefoil; (zool.) skunk
**hedonismo** *m* hedonism
**hedonista** *mf* hedonist
**hedor** *m* stench, stink
**Hefestos** *m* (myth.) Hephaestus
**hegelianismo** *m* Hegelianism
**hegeliano -na** *adj & mf* Hegelian
**hegemonía** *f* hegemony
**hégira** *f* var. of **héjira**
**heguemonía** *f* var. of **hegemonía**
**héjira** *f* hegira (*Mohammedan era*)
**helada** *f* see **helado**
**Hélade** *f* Hellas (*Greece*)
**heladería** *f* (Am.) ice-cream parlor
**heladero -ra** *mf* (Am.) ice-cream maker or dealer; *f* (Am.) freezer, refrigerator; (Am.) ice-cream tray
**heladizo -za** *adj* easily frozen
**helado -da** *adj* cold; icy; (fig.) frozen (*with fear, surprise, etc.*); (fig.) cold, chilly; *m* cold drink; water ice; ice cream; **helado al corte** brick ice cream; **helado de barquillo** ice-cream cone; *f* freeze, freezing; frost (*freezing condition*); **helada blanca** hoarfrost
**helador -dora** *adj* freezing; *f* ice-cream freezer
**heladura** *f* crack in trunk of tree caused by cold
**helamiento** *m* freeze, freezing
**helar** §18 *va* to freeze; to congeal, harden; to astonish, dumfound; to discourage; *vn* to freeze; *vr* to freeze; to congeal, harden, set; to become frostbitten
**helechal** *m* fernland, fernery
**helecho** *m* (bot.) fern; **helecho acuático** (bot.) water fern, osmunda; **helecho arbóreo** (bot.) tree fern; **helecho florido** (bot.) flowering fern; **helecho macho** (bot.) male fern; **helecho real** (bot.) royal fern
**helena** & **Helena** *f* see **heleno**
**helénico -ca** *adj* Hellenic
**helenio** *m* (bot.) elecampane
**helenismo** *m* Hellenism
**helenista** *mf* Hellenist
**helenístico -ca** *adj* Hellenistic
**helenización** *f* Hellenization
**helenizar** §76 *va & vr* to Hellenize
**heleno -na** *adj* Hellenic; *mf* Hellene; *f* jack-o'-lantern, St. Elmo's fire; (*cap.*) *f* Helen of Troy
**helero** *m* glacier
**Helesponto** *m* Hellespont
**helgado -da** *adj* jag-toothed, snaggle-toothed
**helgadura** *f* gaps in teeth, uneven teeth
**helíaco -ca** *adj* (astr.) heliacal
**heliantemo** *m* (bot.) helianthemum
**heliantina** *f* helianthin
**helianto** *m* (bot.) helianthus
**hélice** *f* helix (*spiral*); (anat., elec. & geom.) helix; screw propeller; screw or propeller (*of boat*); propeller (*of airplane*); (mach.) fly
**hélico -ca** *adj* helical
**helicoidal** *adj* helicoidal
**helicoide** *adj* helicoid; *m* (geom.) helicoid
**helicoideo -a** *adj* (bot. & zool.) helicoid
**Helicón** *m* (hist., myth. & fig.) Helicon; (*l.c.*) *m* (mus.) helicon
**Helicónides** *fpl* (myth.) Muses
**heliconio -nia** or **-na** *adj* Heliconian; Muses'
**helicóptero** *m* (aer.) helicopter
**helio** *m* (chem.) helium
**heliocéntrico -ca** *adj* heliocentric
**heliograbado** *m* helioengraving
**heliografía** *f* heliography
**heliógrafo** *m* heliograph
**Helios** *m* (myth.) Helios
**helioscopio** *m* helioscope
**helióstato** *m* heliostat
**helioterapia** *f* heliotherapy
**heliotipia** *f* heliotype, heliotypy
**heliotropio** *m* var. of **heliotropo**
**heliotropismo** *m* (biol.) heliotropism
**heliotropo** *m* (bot. & mineral.) heliotrope
**helipuerto** *m* heliport
**helmintiasis** *f* (path.) helminthiasis
**helminto** *m* (zool.) helminth
**helmintología** *f* helminthology
**helvecio -cia** *adj & mf* Helvetian; **la Helvecia** Helvetia
**helvético -ca** *adj* Helvetic; *mf* Helvetian
**hemático -ca** *adj* hematic
**hematíe** *m* (physiol.) red cell
**hematina** *f* (physiol.) hematin
**hematita** or **hematites** *f* (mineral.) hematite
**hematocele** *m* (path.) hematocele
**hematócrito** *m* hematocrit
**hematopoyesis** *f* (physiol.) hematopoiesis
**hematosis** *f* (physiol.) hematosis
**hematoxilina** *f* (chem.) hematoxylin
**hembra** *adj* female, e.g., **un pez hembra** a female fish; (bot. & mach.) female; weak, thin, delicate; *f* female (*human or animal*); eye (*of hook and eye*); nut; strike (*of a lock*); (bot.) female; **hembra de terraja** (mach.) die; **hembra del timón** (naut.) rudder gudgeon; **hembras de la familia** distaff side
**hembraje** *m* (Am.) female flock or herd
**hembrear** *vn* to be drawn to the female (*said of animals*); to produce only females, to produce more females than males
**hembrilla** *f* eyebolt; (mach.) female
**hemélitro -tra** *adj* hemelytral; *m* (ent.) hemelytron or hemelytrum
**hemeralopía** *f* (path.) hemeralopia
**hemeroteca** *f* newspaper and magazine library, periodical library
**hemicelulosa** *f* (chem.) hemicellulose
**hemiciclo** *m* hemicycle (*half circle; semicircular structure*); floor (*of legislative body*)
**hemicránea** *f* (path.) hemicrania
**hemiédrico -ca** or **hemiedro -dra** *adj* (cryst.) hemihedral
**hemiesfera** *f* var. of **hemisferio**
**hemina** *f* (biochem.) hemin; (hist.) hemina
**hemíono** *m* (zool.) hemionus, kiang
**hemiplejía** *f* (path.) hemiplegia
**hemíptero -ra** *adj* (ent.) hemipterous
**hemisférico -ca** *adj* hemispherical
**hemisferio** *m* hemisphere; **hemisferios de Magdeburgo** (phys.) Magdeburg hemispheres
**hemisferoide** *m* (geom.) hemispheroid
**hemistiquio** *m* hemistich
**hemiterpeno** *m* (chem.) hemiterpene
**hemocianina** *f* (biochem.) hemocyanin
**hemofilia** *f* (path.) hemophilia
**hemofílico -ca** *adj* hemophilic; *mf* hemophiliac
**hemoglobina** *f* (biochem.) hemoglobin
**hemoleucocito** *m* (anat.) hemoleucocyte
**hemolisina** *f* (immun.) hemolysin

**hemólisis** *f* (immun.) hemolysis
**hemoptisis** *f* (path.) hemoptysis
**hemorragia** *f* (path.) hemorrhage
**hemorrágico -ca** *adj* hemorrhagic
**hemorroidal** *adj* hemorrhoidal
**hemorroidectomía** *f* (surg.) hemorrhoidectomy
**hemorroides** *fpl* (path.) hemorrhoids
**hemorroo** *m* (zool.) cerastes, horned viper
**hemos** *1st pl pres ind of* **haber**
**hemostático -ca** *adj & m* (med.) hemostatic
**hemostato** or **hemóstato** *m* hemostat
**henaje** *m* tedding
**henal** *m* hayloft
**henar** *m* hayfield
**henchidor -dora** *adj* filling; *mf* filler
**henchidura** *f* filling, stuffing; heave, swell (*of waves*)
**henchimiento** *m* filling, stuffing; (naut.) piece of wood used to fill in
**henchir §94** *va* to fill; to stuff; to heap (*e.g., with favors, insults*); *vr* to be filled; to stuff, stuff oneself
**hendedor -dora** *adj* cleaving, cracking, splitting
**hendedura** *f* cleft, crack, split
**hender §66** *va* to cleave, crack, split; to cleave (*the air, the water, the clouds, etc.*); to force one's way through; *vr* to cleave, crack, split
**hendible** *adj* cleavable; fissionable
**hendidura** *f* var. of **hendedura**
**hendiente** *m* downstroke of a sword
**hendimiento** *m* cleaving, cracking, splitting; fission
**heneador -dora** *adj* tedding; *mf* tedder, haymaker; *m* tedder (*machine*)
**henear** *va* to ted, to hay
**henequén** *m* (bot.) henequen (*plant and fiber*)
**henificación** *f* tedding, haying
**henificar §86** *va* to ted, to hay
**henil** *m* hayloft, haymow
**henna** *f* henna (*dye*)
**heno** *m* hay; (bot.) crimson clover; **heno blanco** (bot.) velvet grass
**henojil** *m* garter
**henoteísmo** *m* henotheism
**henrio** *m* (elec.) henry
**heñir §74** *va* to knead; **hay mucho que heñir** (coll.) there's still a lot to do
**heparina** *f* (pharm.) heparin
**hepático -ca** *adj* hepatic; *f* (bot.) hepatica, liverwort; **hepática estrellada** (bot.) woodruff
**hepatitis** *f* (path.) hepatitis
**hepatización** *f* (path.) hepatization
**heptaedro** *m* (geom.) heptahedron
**heptagonal** *adj* heptagonal
**heptágono -na** *adj* heptagonal; *m* (geom.) heptagon
**heptámetro** *m* heptameter
**heptangular** *adj* heptangular
**heptano** *m* (chem.) heptane
**heptarquía** *f* heptarchy; **la Heptarquía anglosajona** the Heptarchy
**heptasilábico -ca** *adj* heptasyllabic
**heptasílabo -ba** *adj* heptasyllabic; *m* heptasyllable
**Heptateuco** *m* (Bib.) Heptateuch
**Hera** *f* (myth.) Hera or Here
**Heracles** *m* (myth.) Heracles
**Heráclito** *m* Heraclitus
**heraldía** *f* heraldry (*office or duty of herald*)
**heráldico -ca** *adj* heraldic; *mf* heraldist; *f* heraldry
**heraldo** *m* herald
**herbáceo -a** *adj* herbaceous
**herbajar** *va* to graze, put to graze; *vn* to graze
**herbaje** *m* herbage; grazing fee; coarse woolen cloth
**herbajear** *va & vn* var. of **herbajar**
**herbajero** *m* renter of pasture
**herbar §18** *va* to dress (*hides*) with herbs
**herbario -ria** *adj* herbal; *m* herbarium (*treatise; room or building*); herbalist, botanist; rumen (*of ruminant*)
**herbazal** *m* grassland
**herbecer §34** *vn* to sprout; to turn green (*with grass*)
**herbero** *m* gullet (*of ruminants*)
**herbicida** *m* weed killer
**herbífero -ra** *adj* herbiferous
**herbívoro -ra** *adj* herbivorous
**herbolario -ria** *adj & mf* (coll.) scatterbrain; *m* herbalist (*botanist; herbman*); herb store
**herboristería** *f* herb store
**herborizar §76** *vn* to gather herbs
**herboso -sa** *adj* herby, grassy
**herciano -na** *adj* (elec.) Hertzian
**Herculano** *f* Herculaneum
**hercúleo -a** *adj* Herculean (*pertaining to Hercules*); herculean (*strong, courageous*)
**Hércules** *m* (astr. & myth.) Hercules; (*l.c.*) *m* strong man
**heredable** *adj* inheritable, hereditable
**heredad** *f* country property, country estate
**heredamiento** *m* inheritance; landed estate; (law) endowment
**heredar** *va & vn* to inherit
**heredero -ra** *adj* inheritable, inheriting; *mf* heir, inheritor; landowner, owner of a country estate; **heredero forzoso** (law) heir apparent; **heredero presuntivo** (law) heir presumptive; *m* heir; *f* heiress
**hereditario -ria** *adj* hereditary
**hereje** *mf* heretic
**herejía** *f* heresy; insult, outrage; (coll.) outrageous price
**herén** *f* var. of **yero**
**herencia** *f* inheritance, heritage; estate; (biol.) heredity; **herencia ligada al sexo** (biol.) sex-linkage
**heresiarca** *m* heresiarch
**herético -ca** *adj* heretic or heretical
**herido -da** *adj* hurt (*injured; offended*); wounded; **mal herido** seriously injured, seriously wounded; *mf* injured person, wounded person; **los heridos** the injured, the wounded; *m* wounded soldier; *f* injury, wound; insult, outrage; **renovar la herida** to open an old sore; **tocar en la herida** to sting to the quick
**herir §62** *va* to hurt, injure; to wound; to strike; to beat down upon; to play (*a stringed instrument*); to pluck (*a string*); to touch, to move; to offend
**herma** *m* (hist.) herma
**hermafrodismo** *m* var. of **hermafroditismo**
**hermafrodita** *adj* hermaphrodite, hermaphroditic; *m* hermaphrodite
**hermafroditismo** *m* (biol.) hermaphroditism
**hermafrodito** *adj & m* var. of **hermafrodita**
**hermana** *f* see **hermano**
**hermanable** *adj* brotherly, fraternal; compatible
**hermanado -da** *adj* like, mated, matched
**hermanamiento** *m* matching, mating; harmonizing; brotherly union
**hermanar** *va* to match, to mate; to join, combine; to harmonize (*e.g., opinions*); *vr* to match; to become brothers (*in spirit*)
**hermanastra** *f* stepsister
**hermanastro** *m* stepbrother
**hermanazgo** *m* or **hermandad** *f* brotherhood; sisterhood; sorority; close friendship; conformity, close relationship
**hermanear** *va* to call (*someone*) brother
**hermano -na** *adj* sister (*e.g., language*); *mf* mate, twin, companion; *m* brother; **hermanos** *mpl* brother and sister; **medio hermano** half brother; **primo hermano** first cousin; **hermano carnal** blood brother; **hermano de leche** foster brother; **hermano de madre** half brother by the same mother; **hermano de padre** half brother by the same father; **hermano político** brother-in-law; **hermanos de la doctrina (cristiana)** Christian Brothers; **hermanos siameses** Siamese twins; *f* sister; **media hermana** half sister; **prima hermana** first cousin; **ser prima hermana de** (coll.) to be much like; **hermana carnal** blood sister; **hermana de la caridad** Sister of Charity, Sister of Mercy; **hermana de leche** foster sister; **hermana de madre** half sister by the same mother; **hermana de padre** half sister by the same father; **hermana política** sister-in-law
**hermenéutico -ca** *adj* hermeneutic; *f* hermeneutics
**Hermes** *m* (myth.) Hermes

**hermeticidad** *f* airtightness; impenetrability
**hermético -ca** *adj* hermetic, airtight; impenetrable (*person, secret, etc.*); tight-lipped, tight-mouthed
**hermetismo** *m* secretiveness, secrecy
**Hermíone** *f* (myth.) Hermione
**hermoseador -dora** *adj* beautifying; *mf* beautifier
**hermoseamiento** *m* beautification, embellishment
**hermosear** *va* to beautify, embellish
**hermosilla** *f* (bot.) throatwort
**hermoso -sa** *adj* beautiful; handsome
**hermosura** *f* beauty; belle, beauty (*beautiful woman*)
**hernia** *f* (path.) hernia; **hernia estrangulada** (path.) strangulated hernia
**herniado -da** *adj* suffering from hernia; *mf* person suffering from hernia
**herniar** *vr* to herniate; to protrude
**herniario -ria** *adj* hernial; *f* (bot.) burstwort
**hernioso -sa** *adj & mf* var. of **herniado**
**hernista** *m* hernia surgeon
**Hero** *f* (myth.) Hero
**Herodes** *m* (Bib.) Herod; **andar** or **ir de Herodes a Pilatos** (coll.) to go from pillar to post, to be driven from pillar to post
**herodiano -na** *adj* Herodian
**Herodías** *f* (Bib.) Herodias
**Heródoto** *m* Herodotus
**héroe** *m* hero
**heroicidad** *f* heroicity, heroism; heroic deed
**heroico -ca** *adj* heroic; (med.) heroic; **a la heroica** in the heroic manner
**heroicocómico -ca** *adj* heroicomic, mock-heroic
**heroína** *f* heroine; (pharm.) heroin
**heroísmo** *m* heroism
**herpe** *m & f* (path.) herpes
**herpético -ca** *adj* herpetic
**herpetología** *f* herpetology
**herpil** *m* esparto net (*for carrying straw, melons, etc.*)
**herrada** *f* bucket
**herradero** *m* branding of cattle; place for branding cattle; (taur.) topsy-turvy bullring
**herrador** *m* horseshoer, farrier
**herradora** *f* (coll.) horseshoer's wife
**herradura** *f* horseshoe; **mostrar las herraduras** to kick; (coll.) to show one's heels
**herraj** *m* var. of **erraj**
**herraje** *m* iron fittings, iron trimmings, ironwork, hardware; fine coal made of crushed olive stones
**herramental** *adj* tool; *m* tool bag, toolbox
**herramienta** *f* tool; tools, set of tools; (coll.) horns (*of bull*); (coll.) grinders (*teeth*); **herramienta motriz** power tool; **herramientas de dotación** (aut.) tools that come with the car
**herrar §18** *va* to shoe (*a horse*); to brand (*cattle*); to trim with ironwork; to hoop (*a barrel*)
**herrén** *m* mixed fodder (*oats, rye, barley, etc.*)
**herrenal** *m* or **herreñal** *m* field of mixed grain
**herrería** *f* blacksmith shop; blacksmithing; ironworks; disturbance, uproar
**herrerillo** *m* (orn.) blue titmouse; (orn.) great titmouse
**herrero** *m* blacksmith; iron forger; **herrero de grueso** ironworker; **herrero de obra** steelworker, structural ironworker
**herreruelo** *m* (orn.) coal titmouse
**herrete** *m* tip (*of metal*)
**herretear** *va* to tip, put a metal tip on
**herrezuelo** *m* small piece of iron
**herrín** *m* rust
**herrón** *m* quoit; washer; iron bar (*used in planting*); (Am.) tip (*of spinning top*)
**herronada** *f* blow with iron bar; hard peck (*with bird's beak*)
**herrumbrar** *va & vr* var. of **aherrumbrar**
**herrumbre** *f* rust; taste of iron; (bot.) rust, plant rot
**herrumbroso -sa** *adj* rusty; (bot.) rusty
**hertziano -na** *adj* (elec.) Hertzian
**herventar §18** *va* to boil
**hervidero** *m* boiling; boiling spring, bubbling spring; rattle (*e.g., in the chest*); swarm (*of worms, of people, etc.*)
**hervidor** *m* cooker, boiler
**herviente** *adj* var. of **hirviente**
**hervir §62** *vn* to boil; to boil, to seethe (*said of the sea; of an angry person*); to swarm, to teem
**hervor** *m* boil, boiling; force, vigor, determination; fire, restlessness (*of youth*); **alzar** or **levantar el hervor** to begin to boil; **hervor de la sangre** skin rash
**hervoroso -sa** *adj* ardent, fiery, impetuous
**hesiense** *adj & mf* Hessian
**Hesíodo** *m* Hesiod
**hesitación** *f* hesitation
**hesitar** *vn* to hesitate
**Hesperia** *f* see **hesperio**
**Hespérides** *fpl* (myth.) Hesperides (*four nymphs*)
**hesperidina** *f* (chem.) hesperidin
**hesperidio** *m* (bot.) hesperidium
**hespérido -da** *adj* Hesperian (*western*)
**hesperio -ria** *adj* Hesperian (*of Spain or Italy*); (*cap.*) *f* Hesperia (*Spain or Italy*)
**héspero -ra** *adj* var. of **hesperio;** (*cap.*) *m* Hesperus (*evening star*)
**heteo -a** *adj & mf* var. of **hitita**
**hetera** *f* (hist.) hetaera; courtesan, prostitute
**heterocerco -ca** *adj* (ichth.) heterocercal
**heterocíclico -ca** *adj* (chem.) heterocyclic
**heteroclamídeo -a** *adj* (bot.) heterochlamydeous
**heteróclito -ta** *adj* heteroclite
**heterodinaje** *m* (rad.) heterodyning
**heterodinar** *va & vn* (rad.) to heterodyne
**heterodino -na** *adj* (rad.) heterodyne; *f* (rad.) heterodyne (*auxiliary oscillator*)
**heterodoxia** *f* heterodoxy
**heterodoxo -xa** *adj* heterodox; *mf* heterodox person
**heteroecia** *f* (biol.) heteroecism
**heterofilia** *f* (bot.) heterophylly
**heterofilo -la** *adj* (bot.) heterophyllous
**heterogamia** *f* heterogamy
**heterógamo -ma** *adj* (bot.) heterogamous
**heterogeneidad** *f* heterogeneity
**heterogéneo -a** *adj* heterogeneous
**heterónimo -ma** *adj* heteronymous; *m* heteronym
**heteroplastia** *f* (surg.) heteroplasty
**heterótrofo -fa** *adj* (biol.) heterotrophic
**hético -ca** *adj & mf* hectic
**hetiquez** *f* (path.) consumption
**hetmán** *m* hetman (*cossack chief*)
**heurístico -ca** *adj* heuristic
**hexacordo** *m* (mus.) hexachord
**hexaédrico -ca** *adj* hexahedral
**hexaedro** *m* (geom.) hexahedron
**hexafluoruro** *m* (chem.) hexafluoride
**hexagonal** *adj* hexagonal
**hexágono -na** *adj* hexagonal; *m* (geom.) hexagon
**hexagrama** *m* hexagram
**hexametilenotetramina** *f* (chem.) hexamethylenetetramine
**hexámetro -tra** *adj & m* hexameter
**hexángulo -la** *adj* hexangular
**hexano** *m* (chem.) hexane
**hexapétalo -la** *adj* (bot.) hexapetalous
**hexápodo -da** *adj* hexapod; *m* (ent.) hexapod
**Hexateuco** *m* (Bib.) Hexateuch
**hexosa** *f* (chem.) hexose
**hez** *f* (*pl:* **heces**) (fig.) scum, dregs; **heces** *fpl* lee, sediment, dregs; feces, excrement; (fig.) dregs
**Hg.** abr. of **hectogramo**
**hi** *interj* var. of **ji**
**Híadas** or **Híades** *fpl* (astr. & myth.) Hyades or Hyads
**hialino -na** *adj* hyaline (*glassy*); *f* (biochem.) hyaline
**hialita** *f* (mineral.) hyalite
**hialitis** *f* (path.) hyalitis
**hialoideo -a** *adj* hyaloid
**hialoides** *f* (anat.) hyaloid
**hialoplasma** *m* (biol.) hyaloplasm
**hialotecnia** or **hialurgia** *f* glass work
**hiante** *adj* (pros.) having hiatus
**hiato** *m* hiatus (*in a text*); (anat., gram. & pros.) hiatus
**hibernación** *f* (biol.) hibernation
**hibernal** *adj* hibernal

**hibernar** *vn* (biol.) to hibernate
**hibernés -nesa** or **hiberniano -na** *adj & mf* Hibernian
**hibérnico -ca** *adj* Hibernian
**hibisco** *m* (bot.) hibiscus
**hibridación** *f* hybridization
**hibridar** *va & vn* to hybridize
**hibridismo** *m* hybridism
**híbrido -da** *adj & m* hybrid
**hicaco** *m* (bot.) coco plum (*tree and fruit*)
**hice** *1st sg pret ind of* **hacer**
**Hicsos** *mpl* (hist.) Hyksos
**hidalgo -ga** *adj* noble, illustrious, imperious; *m* nobleman; *f* noblewoman
**hidalguete -ta** *mf* (coll.) impecunious noble
**hidalguez** *f* or **hidalguía** *f* nobility
**hidalguito -ta** *mf* cute little noble
**hidantoína** *f* (chem.) hydantoin
**hidátide** *f* (path.) hydatid
**hidatídico -ca** *adj* hydatid
**hidno** *m* (bot.) hydnum
**hidra** *f* hydra (*persistent evil*); (zool.) hydra (*polyp*); (zool.) poisonous sea snake (*Hydrus bicolor*); (*cap.*) *f* (astr. & myth.) Hydra
**hidracida** *f* (chem.) hydrazide
**hidrácido** *m* (chem.) hydracid
**hidracina** *f* (chem.) hydrazine
**hidrangea** *f* (bot.) hydrangea
**hidrargirismo** *m* (path.) hydrargyriasis
**hidrargiro** *m* (chem.) hydrargyrum
**hidratación** *f* (chem.) hydration
**hidratado -da** *adj* hydrous
**hidratar** *va & vr* (chem.) to hydrate
**hidrato** *m* (chem.) hydrate; **hidrato amónico** (chem.) ammonium hydroxide; **hidrato de carbono** (chem.) carbohydrate; **hidrato de cloral** (chem.) chloral hydrate
**hidráulico -ca** *adj* hydraulic; *m* hydraulician, hydraulic engineer; *f* hydraulics
**hídrico -ca** *adj* (chem.) hydric
**hidro** *m* (aer.) hydroplane
**hidroavión** *m* (aer.) hydroplane
**hidrocarburo** *m* (chem.) hydrocarbon
**hidrocefalía** *f* (path.) hydrocephalus
**hidrocéfalo -la** *adj* hydrocephalous
**hidrocele** *m* (path.) hydrocele
**hidrodeslizador** *m* gliding boat
**hidrodinámico -ca** *adj* hydrodynamic; *f* hydrodynamics
**hidroelectricidad** *f* hydroelectricity
**hidroeléctrico -ca** *adj* hydroelectric
**hidrófana** *f* or **hidrófano** *m* (mineral.) hydrophane
**hidrófido** *m* (zool.) sea serpent, sea snake, hydrophid
**hidrófilo -la** *adj* (chem.) hydrophile or hydrophilic; absorbent; *m* (ent.) water beetle
**hidrófita** *f* (bot.) hydrophyte
**hidrofobia** *f* (path.) hydrophobia
**hidrofóbico -ca** *adj* hydrophobic
**hidrófobo -ba** *adj* hydrophobic (*suffering from hydrophobia*); *mf* hydrophobe
**hidrófono** *m* hydrophone
**hidrófugo -ga** *adj* waterproof
**hidrogel** *m* (chem.) hydrogel
**hidrogenación** *f* (chem.) hydrogenation
**hidrogenar** *va* (chem.) to hydrogenate
**hidrogenión** *m* (chem.) hydrogen ion
**hidrógeno** *m* (chem.) hydrogen; **hidrógeno pesado** (chem.) heavy hydrogen
**hidrografía** *f* hydrography
**hidrográfico -ca** *adj* hydrographic
**hidrógrafo -fa** *mf* hydrographer
**hidroide** *m* (zool.) hydroid
**hidrólisis** *f* (chem.) hydrolysis
**hidrolítico -ca** *adj* hydrolytic
**hidrolizar** §76 *va & vr* (chem.) to hydrolize
**hidrología** *f* hydrology
**hidrólogo -ga** *mf* hydrologist
**hidromancía** *f* hydromancy
**hidromántico -ca** *adj* hydromantic
**hidromecánico -ca** *adj* hydromechanical; *f* hydromechanics
**hidromedusa** *f* (zool.) hydromedusa
**hidromel** *m* hydromel
**hidrometeoro** *m* (meteor.) hydrometeor
**hidrometría** *f* mechanics of water flow
**hidrómetro** *m* current gauge, water meter
**hidromiel** *m* var. of **hidromel**
**hidrópata** *mf* hydropath or hydropathist
**hidropatía** *f* hydropathy
**hidropático -ca** *adj* hydropathic
**hidropesía** *f* (path.) dropsy; (path.) hydrops
**hidrópico -ca** *adj* dropsical, hydropic; very thirsty; insatiable
**hidroplano** *m* hydroplane (*boat*); (aer.) hydroplane
**hidroponía** *f* hydroponics
**hidropónico -ca** *adj* hydroponic
**hidroquinona** *f* (chem.) hydroquinone
**hidrosfera** *f* hydrosphere
**hidrosis** *f* (path.) hidrosis
**hidrosol** *m* (chem.) hydrosol
**hidrostático -ca** *adj* hydrostatic; *f* hydrostatics
**hidrostato** or **hidróstato** *m* hydrostat
**hidrosulfito** *m* (chem.) hydrosulfite; **hidrosulfito sódico** (chem.) hydrosulfite, sodium hydrosulfite (*reducing agent*)
**hidrosulfuro** *m* (chem.) hydrosulfide
**hidrotecnia** *f* hydrotechny
**hidroterapia** *f* hydrotherapeutics or hydrotherapy
**hidroterápico -ca** *adj* hydrotherapeutic
**hidrotérmico -ca** *adj* hydrothermal
**hidrotórax** *m* (path.) hydrothorax
**hidrotropismo** *m* hydrotropism
**hidróxido** *m* (chem.) hydroxide; **hidróxido de calcio** (chem.) calcium hydroxide; **hidróxido de potasio** (chem.) potassium hydroxide; **hidróxido de sodio** (chem.) sodium hydroxide
**hidroxilamina** *f* (chem.) hydroxylamine
**hidroxilo** *m* (chem.) hydroxyl
**hidrozoico -ca** *adj* hydrozoic, hydrozoan
**hidrozoo** *m* (zool.) hydrozoan
**hidruro** *m* (chem.) hydride; **hidruro de litio** (chem.) lithium hydride
**hiedra** *f* (bot.) ivy; **hiedra terrestre** (bot.) ground ivy; **hiedra venenosa** (bot.) poison ivy
**hiel** *f* gall, bile; (fig.) bitterness, sorrow; **echar la hiel** (coll.) to strain, to overwork; **hiel de la tierra** (bot.) lesser centaury
**hielo** *m* ice; frost, cold; astonishment; **romper el hielo** (fig.) to break the ice; **hielo carbónico** dry ice; **hielo flotante** ice pack; **hielo seco** dry ice
**hiemación** *f* wintering; (bot.) winter blooming
**hiemal** *adj* winter, hiemal
**hiena** *f* (zool.) hyena; **hiena manchada** (zool.) spotted hyena; **hiena parda** (zool.) brown hyena; **hiena rayada** (zool.) striped hyena
**hienda** *f* dung
**hierático -ca** *adj* hieratic or hieratical
**hierba** *f* grass; herb; **hierbas** *fpl* grass, pasture; herb poison; vegetable soup (*for monks*); years of age (*said of animals*); **mala hierba** weed; (coll.) wayward young man; **y otras hierbas** (hum.) and many other things; **hierba amargosa** (bot.) ragweed; **hierba amarilla** (bot.) oxeye, oxeye daisy (*Heliopsis*); **hierba artética** (bot.) ground pine; **hierba ballestera** (bot.) white hellebore; **hierba belida** (bot.) buttercup, blisterflower; **hierba buena** (bot.) mint; **hierba callera** (bot.) sedum, orpine; **hierba cana** (bot.) groundsel; **hierba carmín** (bot.) pokeberry, pokeweed; **hierba centella** (bot.) marsh marigold; **hierba de ballesteros** (bot.) white hellebore; **hierba de clavo** (bot.) primrose willow; **hierba de Guinea** (bot.) Guinea grass; **hierba de hechiceros** (bot.) nightshade, black nightshade; **hierba de la culebra** (bot.) green dragon; **hierba de la golondrina** (bot.) celandine; **hierba del ala** (bot.) elecampane; **hierba de la madre** (bot.) toothwort; **hierba de la moneda** (bot.) moneywort; **hierba de la paciencia** (bot.) herb patience, spinach dock; **hierba de la plata** (bot.) honesty; **hierba de la rabia** (bot.) madwort; **hierba de las calenturas** (bot.) hedge hyssop; **hierba de las coyunturas** (bot.) joint fir; **hierba de las cucharas** (bot.) scurvy grass; **hierba de la segur** (bot.) hatchet vetch; **hierba de las golondrinas** (bot.) celandine; **hierba de las heridas** (bot.) selfheal; **hierba del asno** (bot.) evening primrose; **hierba de las quemaduras** (bot.)

groundsel; **hierba de las serpientes** (bot.) star thistle; **hierba de la tos** (bot.) rosette ramonda; **hierba de la Trinidad** (bot.) liverwort; **hierba del burro** (bot.) fireweed (*a wild lettuce*); **hierba del cáncer** (bot.) leadwort; **hierba del hígado** (bot.) liverwort; **hierba del maná** (bot.) manna grass, gloating fescue; **hierba del moro** (bot.) elecampane; **hierba de los canarios** (bot.) chickweed; **hierba de los canónigos** (bot.) corn salad; **hierba de los gatos** (bot.) rosette ramonda; **hierba de los indios** (bot.) comfrey; **hierba de los tiñosos** (bot.) burdock; **hierba del papa** (bot.) cat thyme; **hierba del Paraguay** (bot.) Paraguay tea; **hierba del pobre** (bot.) hedge hyssop; **hierba del Sudán** (bot.) Sudan grass; **hierba del toro** (bot.) hyssop loosestrife; **hierba de París** (bot.) herb Paris, truelove; **hierba de pordioseros** (bot.) traveler's-joy; **hierba de San Benito** (bot.) herb bennet; **hierba de San Cristóbal** (bot.) baneberry; **hierba de San Gerardo** (bot.) goutweed; **hierba de San Juan** (bot.) Saint-John's-wort; **hierba de San Lorenzo** (bot.) wood sanicle; **hierba de San Pablo** (bot.) cowslip, primrose; **hierba de San Pablo mayor** (bot.) oxlip, polyanthus; **hierba de San Roberto** (bot.) red shanks, fox geranium; **hierba de Santa Catalina** (bot.) touch-me-not; **hierba de Santa María** (bot.) costmary; **hierba de Santiago** (bot.) tansy ragwort; **hierba doncella** (bot.) large periwinkle, cut-finger; **hierba elefante** (bot.) elephant grass; **hierba estañera** (bot.) scouring grass, Dutch grass; **hierba fina** (bot.) Rhode Island bent; **hierba fuerte** (bot.) cat thyme; **hierba gatera** (bot.) catmint, catnip; **hierba hedionda** (bot.) jimson weed, thorn apple; **hierba lombriguera** (bot.) tansy; **hierba mate** (bot.) maté, Brazilian holly; **hierba medicinal** herb, medicinal herb; **hierba moli** (myth.) moly; **hierba mora** (bot.) nightshade, black nightshade; **hierba pajarera** (bot.) chickweed; **hierba pastel** (bot.) woad; **hierba peluda** (bot.) rosette ramonda; (bot.) rice cut-grass; **hierba piojera** (bot.) stavesacre; **hierba pulguera** (bot.) fleawort; **hierba puntera** (bot.) houseleek; **hierba Rhodes** (bot.) Rhodes grass; **hierba romana** (bot.) costmary; **hierba sagrada** (bot.) vervain; **hierba santa** (bot.) mint; **hierba sarracena** (bot.) costmary; **hierbas finas** fines herbes (*garnish made of chopped mushrooms, shallots, parsley, etc.*); **hierba tosera** (bot.) rosette ramonda; **hierba turca** (bot.) burstwort; **hierba velluda** (bot.) bulbous buttercup, meadow crowfoot

**hierbabuena** *f* (bot.) mint

**hiero** *m* var. of **yero**

**hierofanta** *m* or **hierofante** *m* hierophant

**hieroglífico -ca** *adj & m* var. of **jeroglífico**

**hierosolimitano -na** *adj & mf* var. of **jerosolimitano**

**hierro** *m* iron; brand (*stamped with hot iron*); **hierros** *mpl* irons (*chains, fetters, etc.*); **a hierro y fuego** without mercy, without quarter; violently, sweeping straight ahead; **llevar hierro a Vizcaya** to carry coals to Newcastle; **machacar en hierro frío** (coll.) to waste one's time (*in trying to change a person's nature*); **marcar con hierro** to brand; **hierro acanalado** corrugated iron; **hierro colado** cast iron; **hierro colado en barras** pig iron; **hierro de desecho** scrap iron; **hierro de marcar** branding iron; **hierro dulce** wrought iron; **hierro especular** (mineral.) specular iron; **hierro fundido** cast iron; **hierro galvanizado** galvanized iron; **hierro ondulado** corrugated iron

**hifa** *f* (bot.) hypha

**higa** *f* baby's fist-shaped amulet; scorn, contempt; **dar higa** to miss fire (*said of a gun*); **no dar dos higas por** (coll.) to not care a rap for

**higadilla** *f* or **higadillo** *m* liver (*of birds, fish, and other small animals*)

**hígado** *m* (anat.) liver; **hígados** *mpl* (coll.) guts, courage; **echar los hígados** (coll.) to strain, to overwork; **hasta los hígados** (coll.) from the bottom of one's heart; **malos hígados** ill will, hatred; **moler los hígados a** (coll.) to pester; **querer comer los hígados a** (coll.) to have a deep grudge against; **hígado de bacalao** cod liver

**Higea** or **Higía** *f* (myth.) Hygeia

**higiene** *f* hygiene; **higiene mental** mental hygiene; **higiene sexual** sex hygiene; **higiene social** social hygiene

**higiénico -ca** *adj* hygienic

**higienista** *adj & mf* hygienist; *m* public health doctor

**higienización** *f* hygienization

**higienizar** §76 *va* to hygienize, make hygienic

**higo** *m* fig (*fruit*); (vet.) thrush; **de higos a brevas** (coll.) once in a while; **no dársele a uno un higo de, no dar un higo por, no estimar en un higo** to not care a rap for; **no valer un higo** (coll.) to be not worth a continental; **higo chumbo** or **higo de tuna** prickly pear (*fruit*); **higo zafarí** sweet fig

**higrometría** *f* hygrometry

**higrométrico -ca** *adj* hygrometric

**higrómetro** *m* hygrometer

**higroscópico -ca** *adj* hygroscopic

**higroscopio** *m* hygroscope

**higuana** *f* var. of **iguana**

**higuera** *f* (bot.) fig tree; **higuera chumba** (bot.) prickly pear; **higuera de Bengala** (bot.) banyan; **higuera de Egipto** (bot.) caprifig, wild fig; **higuera del diablo, del infierno** or **infernal** (bot.) castor-oil plant; **higuera de Indias, de pala** or **de tuna** (bot.) prickly pear; **higuera loca** (bot.) jimson weed

**higuereta** or **higuerilla** *f* (bot.) castor-oil plant

**hija** *f* see **hijo**

**hijadalgo** *f* (*pl:* **hijasdalgo**) var. of **hidalga**

**hijastro -tra** *mf* stepchild; *m* stepson; *f* stepdaughter

**hijo -ja** *mf* child; young (*of an animal*); (fig.) child, fruit, result; **cada hijo de vecino** (coll.) every man Jack, every mother's son; **hijo de bendición** legitimate child; good child; **hijo de la cuna** foundling; **hijo del amor** love child; **hijo de leche** foster child; *m* son; native son; **hijos** *mpl* children, descendants; **Hijo de Dios** Son of God; **hijo del agua** good sailor; good swimmer; **Hijo del Hombre** Son of Man (*Jesus*); **hijo de su padre** (coll.) chip off the old block; **hijo de sus propias obras** self-made man; **hijo natural** love child; **hijo político** son-in-law; **hijo pródigo** prodigal son; *f* daughter; native daughter; **hija de Eva** daughter of Eve; **hija política** daughter-in-law

**hijodalgo** *m* (*pl:* **hijosdalgo**) var. of **hidalgo**

**hijuela** *f* see **hijuelo**

**hijuelero** *m* rural postman

**hijuelo -la** *mf* offspring; *m* little son, little child; (bot.) shoot, sucker; *f* little daughter, little girl; accessory; extra strip (*used to widen a garment*); extra little mattress placed under mattress to fill a hollow; branch drain; branch sewer; side path, crosspath; rural mail service (*off the main highway*); estate (*of decedent*); palm seed; (eccl.) pall (*to cover chalice*)

**hila** *f* row, line; thin gut; spinning; **hilas** *fpl* lint (*for dressing wounds*); (Am.) cotton waste; **a la hila** in single file

**hilable** *adj* spinnable, spinning, fit for spinning

**hilacha** *f* shred, raveling, fraying; **hilachas** *fpl* lint; **mostrar la hilacha** (Am.) to show one's worst side; **hilacha de acero** steel wool; **hilacha de algodón** cotton waste; **hilacha de vidrio** spun glass

**hilacho** *m* var. of **hilacha; hilachos** *mpl* (Am.) rags, tatters

**hilachoso -sa** *adj* shreddy, frayed, raveled

**hilada** *f* row, line; (mas.) course; **hilada atizonada** or **de cabezal** (mas.) header course; **hilada de coronación** (mas.) coping; **hilada de faja** (mas.) stretcher course; **hilada voladiza** (mas.) corbel course

**hiladillo** *m* braid

**hiladizo -za** *adj* spinnable

**hilado** *m* spinning; yarn, thread
**hilador -dora** *mf* spinner; *f* spinning machine
**hilandería** *f* spinning (*art*); spinning frame; spinning mill
**hilandero -ra** *mf* spinner; *m* spinning shop, spinning mill
**hilar** *va* to spin (*wool, thread, a cocoon, etc.*); to infer, conjecture; *vn* to spin; **hilar delgado** or **fino** (coll.) to hew close to the line; **hilar largo** (coll.) to drag on
**hilaracha** *f* var. of **hilacha**
**hilarante** *adj* mirthful, sprightful; laughing (*gas*)
**hilaridad** *f* hilarity
**Hilario** *m* Hilary
**hilatura** *f* spinning
**hilaza** *f* yarn, thread; uneven thread; coarse thread; **descubrir la hilaza** to show one's true nature
**hilera** *f* row, line; fine thread, fine yarn; ridgepole; (mach.) drawplate; (mas.) course; (mil.) file; (zool.) spinneret
**hilero** *m* ripple (*caused by two opposing currents*); stream, current
**hilio** *m* (anat.) hilum
**hilo** *m* thread; yarn; filament; string (*e.g., of pearls*); linen, linen fabric; light or thin wire; thin stream (*e.g., of water*); beam (*of light*); edge (*of razor, sword, etc.*); (bot.) hilum; (elec.) wire; (opt.) cross hair, cross wire; (zool.) thread (*of spider*); (fig.) thread (*of a speech, of life, etc.*); **a hilo** uninterruptedly; in line, parallel; **al hilo** along the thread, with the thread; **estar colgado de un hilo** (coll.) to hang by a thread; **irse al hilo** or **tras el hilo de la gente** to follow the crowd (*to do what others do*); **manejar los hilos** to pull strings; **perder el hilo de** to lose the thread of; **tomar el hilo** to pick up the thread (*e.g., of the conversation*); **vivir al hilo del mundo** (coll.) to follow the crowd; **hilo bramante** twine; **hilo cruzado** (opt.) cross hair, cross wire; **hilo de la muerte** end of life; **hilo de masa** (aut.) ground wire; **hilo de medianoche** midnight sharp; **hilo de mediodía** twelve noon sharp; **hilo dental** dental floss; **hilo de retorno** (elec.) return, return wire; **hilo de salmar** twine; **hilo de tierra** (rad.) ground wire; **hilos taquimétricos** (surv.) stadia hairs
**hilozoísmo** *m* (philos.) hylozoism
**hilván** *m* (sew.) tacking, basting; basting stitch; (Am.) hem; (Am.) basting thread; **hablar de hilván** (coll.) to jabber along
**hilvanar** *va* (sew.) to tack, to baste; to outline, to sketch; (coll.) to hurry (*a job*); (Am.) to hem; *vn* (sew.) to tack, to baste
**himalayo -ya** *adj* Himalayan; **el Himalaya** The Himalaya, The Himalayas
**himen** *m* (anat.) hymen
**himeneo** *m* marriage; hymeneal (*wedding song*); (bot.) courbaril; (*cap.*) *m* (myth.) Hymen
**himenio** *m* (bot.) hymenium
**himenóptero -ra** *adj* (zool.) hymenopterous; *m* (zool.) hymenopter
**Himeto** *m* Hymettus
**himnario** *m* hymnal, hymn book
**himno** *m* hymn; **himno nacional** national anthem
**himnología** *f* hymnology
**himplar** *vn* to roar, to bellow
**hin** *m* neigh, whinny
**hincadura** *f* driving, thrusting, sinking
**hincapié** *m* firm footing; foot stamping; emphasis; **hacer hincapié** (coll.) to take a firm stand; **hacer hincapié en** (coll.) to lay great stress on
**hincar** §86 *va* to stick, to drive, to thrust, to sink; to go down on, to fall on (*one's knee or knees*); *vr* to kneel, kneel down
**hinco** *m* post, pole (*sunk in the ground*)
**hincón** *m* boat post (*for fastening a boat to the shore*)
**hincha** *f* (coll.) grudge, ill will; *mf* (sport) rooter, fan
**hinchable** *adj* bubble (*chewing gum*)
**hinchado -da** *adj* swollen; swollen with pride; pompous, high-flown (*style, language*); *m* inflation (*of a tire*); *f* (sport) rooters, fans
**hinchar** *va* to swell; to inflate; to pump up; to embroider, exaggerate; *vr* to swell; to swell up, become puffed up (*with pride*)
**hinchazón** *f* swelling; conceit, vanity; bombast
**hinchismo** *m* (sport) rooters, fans
**hindí** *m* Hindi
**hindú -dúa** *adj* & *mf* (*pl:* **-dúes -dúas**) Hindu or Hindoo
**hinduísmo** *m* Hinduism
**Hindustán, el** var. of **el Indostán**
**hindustaní** *m* var. of **indostaní**
**hiniesta** *f* (bot.) Spanish broom
**hinojal** *m* fennel bed, fennel field
**hinojo** *m* (bot.) fennel; **de hinojos** kneeling, on one's knees; **hinojo acuático** (bot.) water fennel; **hinojo hediondo** (bot.) dill; **hinojo marino** or **marítimo** (bot.) samphire
**hintero** *m* kneading table (*of baker*)
**hioideo -a** *adj* hyoid
**hioides** *adj* hyoid; *m* (anat.) hyoid or hyoides
**hiosciamina** *f* (chem.) hyoscyamine
**hioscina** *f* (chem.) hyoscine
**hipabisal** *adj* (geol.) hypabyssal
**hipálage** *f* (rhet.) hypallage
**hipar** *vn* to hiccough; to pant; to whine; to be worn out; **hipar por** to long for, to want badly
**Hiparco** *m* Hipparchus
**Hipatia** *f* Hypatia
**hiperacidez** *f* hyperacidity
**hiperacusia** or **hiperacusis** *f* (path.) hyperacusis
**hiperbático -ca** *adj* hyperbatic
**hipérbaton** *m* (gram.) hyperbaton
**hipérbola** *f* (geom.) hyperbola
**hipérbole** *f* (rhet.) hyperbole
**hiperbólico -ca** *adj* (geom. & rhet.) hyperbolic
**hiperbolismo** *m* (rhet.) hyperbolism
**hiperbolizar** §76 *vn* to hyperbolize
**hiperboloide** *m* (geom.) hyperboloid
**hiperbóreo -a** *adj* hyperborean; *mf* hyperborean; (myth.) Hyperborean
**hipercinesia** *f* (path.) hyperkinesia
**hiperclorhidria** *f* (path.) hyperchlorhydria
**hipercrisis** *f* (med.) extreme crisis
**hipercrítico -ca** *adj* hypercritical; *m* severe critic, captious censor; *f* severe criticism
**hiperdulía** *f* (theol.) hyperdulia
**hiperemia** *f* (path.) hyperemia
**hiperestesia** *f* (path.) hyperesthesia
**Hiperión** *m* (myth.) Hyperion
**hipermetropía** *f* (path.) hypermetropia
**Hipermnestra** *f* (myth.) Hypermnestra
**hiperopía** *f* (path.) hyperopia
**hiperópico -ca** *adj* hyperopic
**hiperpirexia** *f* (path.) hyperpyrexia
**hiperpituitarismo** *m* (path.) hyperpituitarism
**hiperpnea** *f* (path.) hyperpnea
**hipersensibilidad** *f* (path.) hypersensitivity
**hipersensible** *adj* (path.) hypersensitive
**hipertensión** *f* (path.) hypertension, high blood pressure
**hipertenso -sa** *mf* person with high blood pressure
**hipertiroidismo** *m* (path.) hyperthyroidism
**hipertónico -ca** *adj* (chem. & physiol.) hypertonic
**hipertrofia** *f* (biol. & path.) hypertrophy
**hipertrofiar** *vr* to hypertrophy
**hipertrófico -ca** *adj* hypertrophic
**hípico -ca** *adj* hippic, equine, horse
**hipido** *m* whining
**hipismo** *m* horse breeding; horse racing
**hipnal** *m* (chem.) hypnale; (obs.) hypnale (*adder*)
**Hipnos** *m* (myth.) Hypnos
**hipnosis** *f* hypnosis
**hipnótico -ca** *adj* & *mf* hypnotic; *m* (med.) hypnotic (*sedative*)
**hipnotismo** *m* hypnotism
**hipnotista** *mf* hypnotist
**hipnotización** *f* hypnotization
**hipnotizador -dora** *adj* hypnotizing; *mf* hypnotizer
**hipnotizar** §76 *va* to hypnotize
**hipo** *m* hiccough; longing, keen desire; grudge; (phot.) hypo (*sodium hyposulfite*); **tener hipo contra** to have a grudge against; **tener hipo por** to crave

**hipoblasto** *m* (embryol.) hypoblast; (bot.) cotyledon of a grass
**hipobosco** *m* (ent.) horse tick
**hipocampo** *m* (anat., ichth. & myth.) hippocampus
**hipocausto** *m* (archeol.) hypocaust
**hipocicloide** *f* (geom.) hypocycloid
**hipoclorito** *m* (chem.) hypochlorite
**hipocloroso -sa** *adj* (chem.) hypochlorous
**hipocondría** *f* (path.) hypochondria
**hipocondríaco -ca** *adj & mf* hypochondriac
**hipocondrio** *m* (anat.) hypochondrium
**hipocorístico -ca** *adj* hypocoristic
**hipocotíleo** *m* (bot.) hypocotyl
**hipocrás** *m* hippocras
**Hipócrates** *m* Hippocrates
**hipocrático -ca** *adj* Hippocratic
**Hipocrene** *f* (myth.) Hippocrene
**hipocresía** *f* hypocrisy
**hipócrita** *adj* hypocritical; *mf* hypocrite
**hipodérmico -ca** *adj* hypodermic
**hipodermo -ma** *adj* (bot.) hypodermal
**hipódromo** *m* hippodrome
**hipófisis** *f* (*pl:* **-sis**) (anat.) hypophysis
**hipofosfito** *m* (chem.) hypophosphite
**hipofosfórico -ca** *adj* (chem.) hypophosphoric
**hipofosforoso -sa** *adj* (chem.) hypophosphorous
**hipogástrico -ca** *adj* hypogastric
**hipogastrio** *m* (anat. & zool.) hypogastrium
**hipogénico -ca** *adj* (geol.) hypogene
**hipogeo -a** *adj* (bot. & zool.) hypogeous; *m* (arch.) hypogeum
**hipogloso -sa** *adj* (anat.) hypoglossal; *m* (anat.) hypoglossal; (ichth.) halibut (*Hippoglossus*)
**hipogrifo** *m* (myth.) hippogriff
**hipoide** *adj* (mach.) hypoid
**Hipólito** *m* (myth.) Hippolytus
**hipopótamo** *m* (zool.) hippopotamus
**hiposo -sa** *adj* having hiccoughs
**hipóstasis** *f* (*pl:* **-sis**) (philos. & theol.) hypostasis
**hipostático -ca** *adj* hypostatic
**hipóstilo -la** *adj & m* (arch.) hypostyle
**hiposulfito** *m* (chem.) hyposulfite (*thiosulfate; salt of hyposulfurous acid*); **hiposulfito de sodio** (chem.) sodium hyposulfite ($Na_2S_2O_4$); (chem. & phot.) sodium hyposulfite ($Na_2S_2O_3$)
**hiposulfuroso -sa** *adj* (chem.) hyposulfurous
**hipotálamo** *m* (anat.) hypothalamus
**hipoteca** *f* mortgage; (law) hypothec; **¡buena hipoteca!** or **¡vaya una hipoteca!** (iron.) you can believe it, if you want to!
**hipotecación** *f* hypothecation
**hipotecar** §86 *va* to hypothecate, to mortgage
**hipotenusa** *f* (geom.) hypotenuse
**hipotermia** *f* (med.) hypothermia
**hipótesis** *f* (*pl:* **-sis**) hypothesis; **hipótesis nebular** (astr.) nebular hypothesis
**hipotético -ca** *adj* hypothetic or hypothetical
**hipotiroidismo** *m* (path.) hypothyroidism
**hipotónico -ca** *adj* (chem. & physiol.) hypotonic
**hipoxantina** *f* (chem.) hypoxanthine
**hipsometría** *f* hypsometry
**hipsómetro** *m* hypsometer
**hircino -na** *adj* hircine
**hirco** *m* (zool.) wild goat
**hircocervo** *m* (myth.) hircocervus
**hiriente** *adj* stinging, cutting, offensive
**hirma** *f* list, selvage
**hirsuto -ta** *adj* hirsute, bristly; (fig.) harsh, brusque, gruff
**hirviendo** *adj invar* boiling
**hirviente** *adj* boiling, seething
**hisca** *f* birdlime
**hiscal** *m* three-strand esparto rope
**hisopada** *f* sprinkling with holy water
**hisopar** *va* var. of **hisopear**
**hisopazo** *m* blow with an aspergillum
**hisopear** *va* to sprinkle with an aspergillum, to asperse
**hisopillo** *m* mouth swab; (bot.) winter savory
**hisopo** *m* (bot.) hyssop; (eccl.) aspergillum, hyssop; (Am.) brush, paint brush, shaving brush; **hisopo húmedo** wool fat, wool grease
**hispalense** *adj & mf* Sevillian
**Hispania** *f* Hispania
**hispánico -ca** *adj* Hispanic
**hispanidad** *f* Spanish nature, essence or spirit; Spanish solidarity, Spanish union
**Hispaniola** *f* former name of Santo Domingo
**hispanismo** *m* Hispanicism; Spanish studies, interest in Spanish language and literature
**hispanista** *mf* Hispanist
**hispanizar** §76 *va* to Hispanicize
**hispano -na** *adj* Hispanic, Spanish; Spanish American; *mf* Spaniard; Spanish American
**hispanoamericanizar** §76 *va* to make Spanish American; *vr* to become Spanish American
**hispanoamericano -na** *adj* Spanish American (*of America where Spanish is spoken*); Spanish-American (*of Spain and America or of Spain and the United States*); *mf* Spanish American (*native or inhabitant of America where Spanish is spoken*)
**hispanoárabe** *adj* Spanish-Arab or Spanish-Arabic; Hispano-Moresque
**hispanófilo -la** *adj & mf* Hispanophile
**hispanófobo -ba** *adj & mf* Hispanophobe
**hispanohablante** or **hispanoparlante** *adj* Spanish-speaking; *mf* speaker of Spanish
**hispanomarroquí** *adj* (*pl:* **-quíes**) Spanish-Moroccan
**híspido -da** *adj* hispid, bristly, spiny
**hispir** *va* to puff up, make fluffy; *vn & vr* to puff up, become fluffy
**histamina** *f* (chem.) histamine
**histerectomía** *f* (surg.) hysterectomy
**histéresis** *f* (phys.) hysteresis
**histeria** *f* (path.) hysteria
**histérico -ca** *adj* (path.) hysteric or hysterical
**histerismo** *m* (path.) hysteria
**histerotomía** *f* (surg.) hysterotomy
**histidina** *f* (chem.) histidine
**histólisis** *f* (biol.) histolysis
**histología** *f* histology
**histólogo -ga** *mf* histologist
**histona** *f* (biochem.) histone
**historia** *f* history; story, tale; painting of a historical subject; **historias** *fpl* (coll.) gossip, meddling; **armar historias** (Am.) to make trouble; **de historia** notorious; **dejarse de historias** (coll.) to come to the point; **la historia antigua** ancient history; **la historia contemporánea** contemporary history; **la historia medieval** or **media** medieval history; **la historia moderna** modern history; **la historia natural** natural history; **pasar a la historia** to become a thing of the past; **picar en historia** to turn out to be serious; **historia de lagrimitas** (coll.) sob story
**historiado -da** *adj* (arch.) historiated; (f.a.) richly adorned; (f.a.) storied (*painting, tapestry*); (coll.) overadorned
**historiador -dora** *mf* historian
**historial** *adj* historical; *m* record, dossier
**historiar** §90 & **regular** *va* to tell the history of; to tell the story of; (f.a.) to depict (*a historical event*)
**historicidad** *f* historicity
**histórico -ca** *adj* historic, historical
**historieta** *f* anecdote, brief account; **historieta gráfica** comic strip
**historiografía** *f* historiography
**historiógrafo -fa** *mf* historiographer
**histrión** *m* actor, histrion; juggler, clown, buffoon; fake, humbug
**histriónico -ca** *adj* histrionic
**histrionisa** *f* (archaic) actress, ballet dancer
**histrionismo** *m* histrionics; actors
**hita** *f* see **hito**
**híter** *m* (biol.) hyther
**hitita** *adj & mf* Hittite; *m* Hittite (*language*)
**hitleriano -na** *mf* Hitlerite
**hitlerismo** *m* Hitlerism
**hito -ta** *adj* fixed, firm; adjoining (*house, street*); black (*horse*); *m* landmark, milestone; peg, hob; quoits; aim, goal; **dar en el hito** to hit the nail on the head; **mirar de hito en hito** to eye up and down, to stare at; **mudar de hito** to not be able to keep still; (coll.) to keep trying new ways or methods; *f* brad, small headless cut nail; landmark, milestone
**hitón** *m* large headless cut nail
**hizo** *3d sg pret ind of* **hacer**
**hizono** *m* (chem.) hyzone

**Hl.** abr. of **hectolitro**
**Hm.** abr. of **hectómetro**
**Hno.** abr. of **Hermano**
**Hnos.** abr. of **Hermanos**
**hoazín** *m* (orn.) hoatzin
**hobachón -chona** *adj* (coll.) lumpish (*fat and sluggish*)
**hobachonería** *f* (coll.) lumpishness
**hobo** *m* var. of **jobo**
**hocicada** *f* blow with the snout; blow in the snout
**hocicar** §86 *va* to nuzzle; (slang) to keep on kissing; *vn* to nuzzle, to grub; to run into a snag; (naut.) to dip (*said of the bow of a ship*)
**hocico** *m* snout; (coll.) snout (*of person*); (coll.) face, sour face; **caer de hocicos** (coll.) to fall on one's face; **meter el hocico en todo** (coll.) to poke or put one's nose in everything; **poner hocico** (coll.) to make a face
**hocicón -cona** or **hocicudo -da** *adj* snouty, big-snouted
**hocino** *m* sickle; dale, glen; gorge, narrows
**hociquear** *va & vn* var. of **hocicar**
**hodómetro** *m* var. of **odómetro**
**hogaño** *adv* (coll.) this year; (coll.) nowadays, at the present time
**hogar** *m* fireplace, hearth; furnace; bowl (*of tobacco pipe*); home; household; home life; bonfire; **hogar substituto** (Am.) foster home
**hogareño -ña** *adj* home-loving; *mf* homebody, stay-at-home
**hogaza** *f* large loaf of bread; cobloaf
**hoguera** *f* bonfire
**hoja** *f* leaf (*of plant, book, door, folding door, spring, table, etc.; petal*); pad (*of aquatic plant*); sheet; blank (*sheet of paper*); foil; blade (*of knife, saw, sword, etc.*); runner (*of skates*); pane (*of glass*); veneer; side (*of hog*); sword; slat (*e.g., of Venetian blind*); land cultivated every other year; **desdoblar la hoja** (coll.) to open the subject again; **doblar la hoja** to close the subject for the time being; to change the subject, to digress; **poner como hoja de perejil** (coll.) to give a tongue lashing to; **tener hoja** to be counterfeit; **hoja batiente** casement sash; **hoja clínica** clinical chart; **hoja de afeitar** razor blade; **hoja de embalaje** packing slip; **hoja de encuadernador** (b.b.) end paper; **hoja de estaño** tin foil; **hoja de estudios** (educ.) transcript; **hoja de guarda** (b.b.) flyleaf; **hoja del anunciante** tear sheet; **hoja de lata** tin, tin plate; **hoja de nenúfar** lily pad; **hoja de paga** pay roll; **hoja de parra** fig leaf (*on a statue*); **hoja de pedidos** (com.) order blank; **hoja de plata** silver foil, silver leaf; **hoja de rodaje** (mov.) shooting record or report; **hoja de ruta** waybill; **hoja de servicios** record of service; (mil.) service record; **hoja de trébol** cloverleaf (*intersection*); **hoja maestra** master blade (*of spring*); **hojas alternas** (bot.) alternate leaves; **hojas del autor** (print.) advance sheets; **hoja suelta** leaflet, handbill; (b.b.) flyleaf; **hoja volante** leaflet, handbill
**hoja-bloque** *f* (*pl:* **hojas-bloque**) (philately) souvenir sheet
**hojalata** *f* tin, tin plate
**hajalatería** *f* tinwork; tinsmith's shop; sheet-metal work
**hojalatero** *m* tinsmith; sheet-metal worker
**hojaldrado -da** *adj* flaky
**hojaldrar** *va* to make into puff paste
**hojaldre** *m & f* puff paste
**hojaldrero -ra** or **hojaldrista** *mf* puff-paste baker
**hojaranzo** *m* (bot.) hornbeam; (bot.) oleander, rosebay
**hojarasca** *f* fallen leaves, dead leaves; excess foliage; vain show, bluff; trash, rubbish; (arch.) foliage
**hojaseca** *f* (ent.) leaf insect
**hojear** *va* to leaf through (*a book, a batch of papers*); *vn* to scale off; to flutter (*said of leaves of trees*)
**hojilla** *f* (Am.) cigaret paper; **hojilla magnética** (phys.) magnetic tracing, magnetic curves
**hojoso -sa** or **hojudo -da** *adj* leafy
**hojuela** *f* leaflet; pancake; foil; gold or silver braid; pressed-olive skins; **hojuela de estaño** tin foil
**hol.** abr. of **holandés**
**hola** *interj* hey!, ho!; hello!
**Holanda** *f* Holland; (*l.c.*) *f* fine chambray
**holandés -desa** *adj* Dutch; **a la holandesa** or **en holandesa** (b.b.) half-bound; *mf* Hollander; *m* Dutchman; Dutch (*language*); **el Holandés errante** the Flying Dutchman; **los holandeses** the Dutch (*people*); *f* Dutch woman
**holandeta** or **holandilla** *f* linen lining
**holgachón -chona** *adj* (coll.) ease-loving, idling; *mf* idler, loafer
**holgadero** *m* hangout
**holgado -da** *adj* idle, unoccupied; loose, full, roomy; comfortable; free; fairly well-off
**holganza** *f* idleness; ease, leisure; pleasure, enjoyment
**holgar** §79 *vn* to idle, to not work; to ease up, rest up; to be of no use, to be unnecessary; to be too loose, to not fit; to be glad; **holgar** + *inf* to be needless to + *inf;* **holgar con** or **de** to be glad at; *vr* to be glad; to be amused; **holgarse con** or **de** to be glad at; **holgarse de** + *inf* to be glad to + *inf*
**holgazán -zana** *adj* loafing, lazy; *mf* loafer, bum
**holgazanear** *vn* to loaf, to bum around
**holgazanería** *f* loafing, bumming, laziness
**holgón -gona** *adj* pleasure-loving; *mf* lizard, lounge lizard
**holgorio** *m* (coll.) gaiety, merriment, hilariousness
**holgueta** *f* (coll.) enjoyment, merriment
**holgura** *f* enjoyment, merriment; ease, comfort; looseness, fullness; (mach.) play
**holmio** *m* (chem.) holmium
**holocaína** *f* (pharm.) holocaine
**holocausto** *m* holocaust (*burnt offering; complete destruction by fire; wholesale destruction*); sacrifice, offering
**holoceno -na** *adj* (geol.) Holocene, Recent
**holoédrico -ca** *adj* (cryst.) holohedral
**Holofernes** *m* (Bib.) Holofernes
**hológrafo -fa** *adj & m* var. of **ológrafo**
**holoturia** *f* (zool.) holothurian, sea cucumber
**holladero -ra** *adj* traveled, trodden (*part of road*)
**holladura** *f* treading, trampling
**hollar** §77 *va* to tread, tread upon; (fig.) to tread under foot, to trample upon
**hollejo** *m* skin, peel, hull
**hollín** *m* soot
**hollinar** *va* (Am.) to make sooty, to soil with soot
**holliniento -ta** *adj* sooty
**hombracho** *m* husky big fellow
**hombrada** *f* manly thing; piece of folly; bravado
**hombradía** *f* manliness; courage
**hombre** *m* man; omber (*card game*); (coll.) my boy, old chap; (slang) husband, man; **buen hombre** good-natured fellow; **ser mucho hombre** to be a well-versed man; **ser muy hombre** to be a he-man; **ser todo un hombre** to be a full-grown man; **¡hombre al agua!** or **¡hombre a la mar!** man overboard!; **hombre bueno** man of legal age in good standing; (law) referee, arbiter; **hombre de armas** man-at-arms (*heavily armed soldier on horseback*); **hombre de bien** honest man, honorable man; **hombre de cabeza** man of talent; **hombre de campo** or **del campo** countryman; **hombre de criazón** or **hombre de remensa** serf; **hombre de dinero** man of means; **hombre de distinción** man of distinction; **hombre de estado** statesman; **hombre de fama** man of repute; **hombre de fondo** man of brains, man of great ability; **hombre de fondos** man of property; **hombre de guerra** man-at-arms (*military man*); **hombre de iglesia** man of the church, man of God; **hombre de la calle** man in the street (*average citizen*); **hombre de la situación** (Am.) man of the hour; **hombre del destino** Man of Destiny (*Napoleon*); **hombre de letras** man of letters; **Hombre de los Dolores** Man of Sorrows (*Jesus*); **hombre de mundo**

man of the world; **hombre de paja** straw man (*nonentity*); cat's-paw; **hombre de palabra** man of his word; **hombre de pelo en pecho** brave man; **hombre de prendas** man of parts; **hombre de suposición** man of straw; **hombre de veras** matter-of-fact fellow; serious fellow; **hombre hecho** grown man; well-educated man; **hombre mono** missing link; **hombre rana** (*pl:* **hombres rana**) frogman; **hombre viejo** (theol.) old man; *interj* upon my word!, man alive!

**hombrear** *vn* to try to act full-grown (*said of a boy*); to try to be somebody; to shoulder, push with the shoulder; to be mannish (*said of a woman*); to be a bully; **hombrear con** to strive to equal; *vr* **hombrearse con** to strive to equal

**hombrecillo** *m* homunculus, little man; (bot.) hop

**hombrera** *f* shoulder (*of garment*); shoulder padding; (arm.) pauldron; epaulet

**hombría** *f* manliness; **hombría de bien** honesty, honorableness

**hombrillo** *m* yoke (*of a shirt*); shoulder piece

**hombrituerto -ta** *adj* with shoulder raised (*in attitude of boasting*)

**hombro** *m* shoulder; (print.) shoulder; **a hombros de** on the shoulders of; **arrimar el hombro** to lend a hand, to put one's shoulder to the wheel; **echar al hombro** to take upon oneself; **encoger los hombros** to droop one's shoulders, to let one's shoulders droop (*in patience or resignation*); **encogerse de hombros** to shrug one's shoulders; to droop one's shoulders, to let one's shoulders droop (*in patience or resignation*); to crouch, to shrink with fear; to not answer; **escurrir el hombro** to shirk; **mirar por encima del hombro** to look down upon; **salir en hombros** to be carried off on the shoulders of the crowd; **hombro a hombro** (coll.) shoulder to shoulder

**hombrón** *m* (coll.) man of parts; (coll.) husky fellow

**hombruno -na** *adj* (coll.) mannish

**homenaje** *m* homage (*respect*); testimonial; gift; (feud.) homage; **en homenaje a** in honor of; **rendir homenaje a** to swear allegiance to; **homenaje de boca** lip service

**homenajear** *va* to honor, to fete

**homeópata** *adj* homeopathic; *mf* homeopath or homeopathist

**homeopatía** *f* homeopathy

**homeopático -ca** *adj* homeopathic

**homérico -ca** *adj* Homeric

**Homero** *m* Homer

**homicida** *adj* homicidal; cruel, inhuman; **homicida de sí mismo** (coll.) suicidal (*destructive of one's own health*); *mf* homicide (*person*)

**homicidio** *m* homicide (*act*); **homicidio intencional** voluntary manslaughter

**homilética** *f* homiletics; study of sacred authors

**homilía** *f* homily

**homiliario** *m* homiliarium

**homilista** *m* homilist

**hominal** *adj* human

**hominicaco** *m* (coll.) poor sap, nincompoop

**homocerco -ca** *adj* (ichth.) homocercal

**homoclamídeo -a** *adj* (bot.) homochlamydeous

**homocromía** *f* (zool.) protective coloration

**homofonía** *f* (phonet. & mus.) homophony

**homófono -na** *adj* (phonet.) homophonous; (mus.) homophonic

**homogeneidad** *f* homogeneity

**homogeneización** *f* homogenization

**homogeneizar** §76 *va* to homogenize

**homogéneo -a** *adj* homogeneous

**homogenización** *f* var. of **homogeneización**

**homogenizar** §76 *va* var. of **homogeneizar**

**homógrafo -fa** *adj* homographic; *m* homograph

**homologación** *f* equalization; (law) homologation; (sport) validation

**homologar** §59 *va* to make equal; (law) to homologate; (sport) to validate (*a record*)

**homología** *f* homology

**homólogo -ga** *adj* homologous

**homonimia** *f* homonymy

**homónimo -ma** *adj* homonymous; of the same name; *mf* namesake; *m* homonym

**homóptero -ra** *adj* (ent.) homopterous

**homosexual** *adj & mf* homosexual

**homosexualidad** *f* homosexuality

**homúnculo** *m* (coll.) homunculus; (coll.) guy, fellow

**honda** *f* see **hondo**

**hondazo** *m* blow with a sling

**hondear** *va* (naut.) to sound; (naut.) to unload

**hondero** *m* (hist.) slinger (*soldier*)

**hondigo** *m* sling

**hondillos** *mpl* patches in the crotch of trousers

**hondo -da** *adj* deep; low; *m* depth; bottom; *f* sling (*for hurling missiles; rope used for hoisting*); slingshot; **hondo** *adv* deep

**hondón** *m* bottom (*e.g, of a tumbler*); eye (*of needle*); foot piece (*of stirrup*); lowland

**hondonada** *f* lowland, bottom land

**hondura** *f* depth, profundity; **meterse en honduras** (coll.) to go beyond one's depth

**Honduras** *f* Honduras; **la Honduras Británica** British Honduras

**hondureñismo** *m* Honduranism

**hondureño -ña** *adj & mf* Honduran

**honestar** *va* to honor; to palliate, to excuse

**honestidad** *f* decency, decorum; honesty, uprightness; purity, chastity; modesty; fairness

**honesto -ta** *adj* decent, proper; honest, upright; pure, chaste; modest; fair, reasonable (*price*)

**hongo** *m* (bot.) mushroom; derby, bowler

**honor** *m* honor; honesty; **honores** *mpl* honors; honorary status or position; **en honor a la verdad** to tell the truth; **en honor de** in honor of; **hacer honor a** (coll.) to do or show honor to; (coll.) to honor (*one's signature*); **hacer los honores** to do the honors; **honores de la guerra** honors of war

**honorable** *adj* honorable (*worthy of honor*); (*cap.*) *adj* Honorable (*title*)

**honorario -ria** *adj* honorary; *m* honorarium, fee

**honorífico -ca** *adj* honorific, honorable

**honra** *f* honor; dignity; **honras** *fpl* memorial service; **tener a mucha honra** to be proud of

**honradez** *f* honesty

**honrado -da** *adj* honest, honorable; **honrado a carta cabal** fair and square

**honrador -dora** *adj* honoring; *mf* honorer

**honramiento** *m* honoring

**honrar** *va* to honor; *vr* to be honored; **honrarse de** + *inf* to deem it an honor to + *inf*

**honrilla** *f* concern (*at what people will say*); **por la negra honrilla** out of concern for what people will say

**honroso -sa** *adj* honorable (*behavior, position, etc.*)

**hopa** *f* long cassock; sack in which an executed criminal is placed

**hopalanda** *f* houppelande

**hopear** *va* (coll.) to throw out, to kick out; *vn* to wag the tail; to romp, race around

**hoplita** *m* hoplite

**hopo** *m* tuft, shock (*of hair*); bushy tail; **seguir el hopo a** ((coll.) to keep right after; **sudar el hopo** (coll.) to work hard, to sweat; **volver el hopo** (coll.) to beat it; *interj* get out of here!

**hoque** *m* var. of **alboroque**

**hora** *f* hour; time, e.g., **hora de acostarse** time to go to bed; time (*to die*), e.g., **ya le llegó la hora** or **la última hora** his time has come; **Horas** *fpl* (myth.) Hours; **a buena hora** (coll.) in good time, opportunely; (iron.) too late; **a la hora** on time; **a la hora de ahora** or **a la hora de ésta** (coll.) right now; **a la hora horada** on the dot; **a las pocas horas** within a few hours; **a las pocas horas de** + *inf* a few hours after + *ger;* **dar hora** to fix a time; **dar la hora** to strike (*said of a clock*); to be just right; (coll.) to be a knockout (*said of a beautiful woman*); **de última hora** late (*news*); up-to-date; latest, most up-to-date; **en buen** or **buena hora** or **en hora buena** safely, luckily; all right, O.K.; **en mal** or **mala hora** or **en hora mala** in an evil hour, unluckily; **fuera de horas** after

hours; **hasta altas horas** until late into the night; **las cuarenta horas** (eccl.) forty hours' devotion; **no ver la hora de** (coll.) to be hardly able to wait for; **por horas** by the hour; **¿qué hora es?** what time is it?; **hora cero** (mil.) zero hour; **hora de aglomeración** rush hour; **hora de clase** (educ.) class hour; **hora de comer** mealtime; **hora deshorada** (coll.) fatal hour; **hora de verano** daylight-saving time; **hora de verdad** (taur.) kill; **hora legal** or **oficial** standard time; **horas canónicas** canonical hours; **horas de consulta** office hours (*of a doctor*); **horas de ocio** leisure hours; **hora semestral** semester hour; **horas extraordinarias de trabajo** overtime; **horas menores** (eccl.) little hours; *adv* now
**horaciano -na** *adj* Horatian
**Horacio** *m* Horace
**horadación** *f* drilling, boring, piercing
**horadador -dora** *adj* drilling, boring, piercing; *mf* driller, borer
**horadar** *va* to drill, bore, pierce
**horado** *m* hole; cave, cavern
**hora-hombre** *f* (*pl:* **horas-hombre**) man-hour
**horario -ria** *adj* (pertaining to the) hour; *m* hour hand; timetable; clock; face (*of clock or watch*); **horario escolar** roster
**horca** *f* pitchfork; gallows, gibbet; forked prop (*for plants and trees*); string (*of onions or garlic*); **tener horca y cuchillo** (hist.) to have life-and-death power; (coll.) to be absolute boss, to be a tyrant; **Horcas Caudinas** Caudine Forks
**horcado -da** *adj* forked, forklike
**horcadura** *f* upper part of tree trunk; fork (*made by two branches*)
**horcajadas; a horcajadas** astride, astraddle
**horcajadillas; a horcajadillas** var. of **a horcajadas**
**horcajadura** *f* crotch (*formed by two legs or by two branches*)
**horcajo** *m* fork (*made by two streams*); yoke (*for mules*)
**horcate** *m* hames (*of harness*)
**horco** *m* string (*of onions or garlic*)
**horcón** *m* pitchfork; forked prop
**horchata** *f* orgeat
**horchatería** *f* orgeat shop or store
**horchatero -ra** *mf* orgeat maker or dealer
**horda** *f* horde
**hordiate** *m* pearl barley; barley water
**horizontal** *adj* horizontal; *f* horizontal; **buscar** or **tomar la horizontal** (Am.) to lie down
**horizonte** *m* horizon; (fig.) horizon
**horma** *f* form, mold; shoe tree, shoe last; block, hat block; dry wall; **hallar la horma de su zapato** (coll.) to find just the thing; (coll.) to meet one's match; **horma de bota** shoe tree, boot tree
**hormaza** *f* dry wall
**hormazo** *m* blow with a block or last; pile of stones
**hormiga** *f* (ent.) ant; itch; **ser una hormiga** to be very thrifty; **hormiga blanca** (ent.) white ant; **hormiga león** (ent.) ant lion; **hormiga roja** or **silvestre** (ent.) red ant (*Formica rufa*)
**hormigo** *m* sifted ashes used in smelting quicksilver; **hormigos** *mpl* dessert made of bread crumbs, crushed almonds, and honey; coarse parts of ground wheat
**hormigón** *m* concrete; **hormigón armado** reinforced concrete; **hormigón hidráulico** hydraulic mortar
**hormigonera** *f* concrete mixer
**hormigoso -sa** *adj* (pertaining to the) ant; full of ants; ant-eaten; itchy
**hormigueamiento** *m* var. of **hormigueo**
**hormigueante** *adj* swarming; crawly, creepy; teeming
**hormiguear** *vn* to swarm; to crawl, to creep (*with a sensation of insects*); to teem, to abound
**hormigueo** *m* swarming; crawling sensation; (coll.) worry, unrest
**hormiguero** *m* anthill; swarm, mob (*of people*); place swarming with people; pile of burned compost; (orn.) wryneck
**hormiguesco -ca** *adj* (pertaining to the) ant
**hormiguilla** *f* itch
**hormiguillo** *m* line of workmen passing material from one to the other; (vet.) founder
**hormilla** *f* buttonmold
**hormillón** *m* hat block
**hormón** *m* or **hormona** *f* (physiol.) hormone
**hormonal** *adj* hormonal
**hornabeque** *m* (fort.) hornwork
**hornablenda** *f* (mineral.) hornblende
**hornacina** *f* (arch.) niche
**hornacho** *m* (min.) horizontal opening; furnace for casting statues
**hornachuela** *f* hut, cabin
**hornada** *f* batch, bake (*of bread, bricks, etc.*); (coll.) crop (*of appointments, promotions, etc.*)
**hornaguear** *va* to dig (*the earth*) for coal
**hornaguero -ra** *adj* coal; wide, spacious; *f* coal
**hornaza** *f* jeweler's furnace; (f.a.) glazing yellow
**hornazo** *m* Easter cake filled with hard-boiled eggs; Easter present to Lenten preacher
**hornear** *va* (Am.) to bake; *vn* to bake; to be a baker
**hornería** *f* baking (*trade*); bakery
**hornero -ra** *mf* baker; *m* (orn.) baker, ovenbird
**hornija** *f* brushwood
**hornijero** *m* carrier of brushwood
**hornilla** *f* kitchen charcoal grate; pigeonhole (*recess for pigeons to nest*)
**hornillo** *m* small furnace; kitchen stove; fire pot; hot plate; bowl (*of tobacco pipe*); (mil.) fougasse; (min.) blast hole; **hornillo de atenor** athenor (*self-feeding furnace of alchemists*)
**horno** *m* furnace; kiln; oven; **alto horno** blast furnace; **horno de cal** limekiln; **horno de coque** coke oven; **horno de coquizar** coking oven; **horno de cuba** shaft furnace; **horno de fundición** smelting furnace; **horno de hogar abierto** open-hearth furnace; **horno de ladrillos** brickkiln; **horno de mufla** muffle furnace; **horno de pudelar** puddling furnace; **horno de regeneración** regenerative furnace; **horno de reverbero** or **de tostadillo** reverberatory furnace; **horno Siemens-Martin** open-hearth furnace
**horología** *f* horology
**horologio** *m* (eccl.) horologe
**horón** *m* large round hamper or frail
**horondo -da** *adj* var. of **orondo**
**horópter** *m* (opt.) horopter
**horoptérico -ca** *adj* horopteric
**horóptero** *m* var. of **horópter**
**horoscopar** *vn* to make horoscopes
**horoscopia** *f* horoscopy
**horoscopizar** §76 *vn* var. of **horoscopar**
**horóscopo** *m* (astrol.) horoscope; **sacar un horóscopo** (astrol.) to cast a horoscope
**horqueta** *f* fork, pitchfork; fork (*made by two branches*); (Am.) fork (*in river, road, etc.*)
**horquilla** *f* fork, pitchfork; forked pole; hairpin; fork (*of bicycle*); cradle (*of French telephone*); step or tread (*of stilts*); (aut.) clutch lever; (mach.) yoke
**horrendo -da** *adj* horrendous
**hórreo** *m* granary; (prov.) granary or barn raised on pillars (*for protection from mice and dampness*)
**horrero** *m* granary keeper or tender
**horribilísimo -ma** *adj super* very or most horrible
**horrible** *adj* horrible
**horridez** *f* horribleness
**hórrido -da** or **horrífico -ca** *adj* horrible, horrendous
**horripilación** *f* bristling of the hair; (path.) horripilation
**horripilante** *adj* hair-raising, terrifying
**horripilar** *va* to make the hair of (*someone*) stand on end; to terrify; *vn* to terrify; *vr* to be or become terrified
**horrisonante** or **horrísono -na** *adj* horrisonant
**horro -rra** *adj* enfranchised; free, untrammeled
**horror** *m* horror; horrid thing; atrocity; **¡qué horror!** how terrible!; horrors!; **tener en horror** to abhor, hate, detest; **tener horror a** to have a horror of

**horrorizar §76** *va* to horrify; *vr* to be horrified
**horroroso -sa** *adj* horrid, horrible; (coll.) hideous, ugly
**horrura** *f* filth, dirt, dross
**hortaliza** *f* vegetable
**hortatorio -ria** *adj* hortatory
**hortelano -na** *adj* (pertaining to a) garden; *m* gardener; orchardman; (orn.) ortolan; *f* gardener's wife
**hortense** *adj* (pertaining to a) garden
**hortensia** *f* (bot.) hydrangea; (bot.) hortensia; (*cap.*) *f* Hortense
**hortera** *f* wooden bowl; *m* (coll.) store clerk
**hortícola** *adj* horticultural; *m* horticulturist
**horticultor -tora** *mf* horticulturist
**horticultura** *f* horticulture
**Hos.** abr. of **Hermanos**
**hosanna** *m & interj* hosanna
**hosco -ca** *adj* dark; sullen, gloomy; proud, arrogant
**hoscoso -sa** *adj* rough, bristly
**hospedador -dora** *mf* host, one who provides lodging
**hospedaje** *m* lodging; cost of lodging
**hospedamiento** *m* lodging
**hospedar** *va* to lodge; *vr* to lodge, stop, put up
**hospedería** *f* hospice (*maintained by a religious order*); lodging; inn, hostelry
**hospedero -ra** *mf* host, innkeeper
**hospiciano -na** *mf* inmate of a poorhouse
**hospicio** *m* hospice; orphan asylum; poorhouse
**hospital** *m* hospital; **estar hecho un hospital** (coll.) to be full of aches and pains; (coll.) to be turned into a hospital (*said of a house full of sick people*); **hospital ambulante** (mil.) field hospital; **hospital de aislamiento** isolation hospital; **hospital de campaña** (mil.) field hospital; **hospital de la sangre** poor relations; **hospital de primera sangre** or **de sangre** (mil.) field hospital; **hospital robado** (coll.) bare house (*without furniture or adornments*)
**hospitalario -ria** *adj* hospitable; *mf* (hist.) hospitaler; (hist.) Hospitaler
**hospitalero -ra** *mf* hospital manager; hospitaler; hospitable person
**hospitalidad** *f* hospitality; hospitalization (*stay in a hospital*)
**hospitalización** *f* hospitalization
**hospitalizar §76** *va* to hospitalize
**hosquedad** *f* darkness; sullenness, gloominess; arrogance
**hostal** *m* var. of **hostería**
**hostelería** *f* hotel business; association of hotel keepers
**hostelero -ra** *mf* innkeeper; hotel keeper
**hostería** *f* inn, hostelry
**hostia** *f* sacrificial victim; wafer; (eccl.) wafer, Host
**hostiario** *m* wafer box; wafer mold
**hostiero -ra** *mf* wafer maker; *m* wafer box
**hostigamiento** *m* lashing, scourging; harassment; pestering
**hostigar §59** *va* to lash, scourge; to drive, harass; to pester, plague; (Am.) to cloy
**hostigo** *m* lash; weather-beaten wall; beating of wind and rain
**hostigoso -sa** *adj* (Am.) cloying, sickening
**hostil** *adj* hostile
**hostilidad** *f* hostility; **hostilidades** *fpl* hostilities (*warfare*); **cesar en las hostilidades** to cease hostilities; **romper las hostilidades** to start hostilities
**hostilizar §76** *va* to harry, to harass (*an enemy*); to make it hot for, to antagonize
**hotel** *m* hotel; mansion, villa
**hotelero -ra** *adj* (pertaining to a) hotel; *mf* hotelkeeper
**hotentote -ta** *adj & mf* Hottentot
**hovero -ra** *adj* blossom-colored (*horse*); egg-colored
**hoy** *adv & m* today; **de hoy a mañana** any time now; **de hoy en adelante** or **de hoy más** from now on, henceforth; **por hoy** for the present; **hoy día** nowadays; **hoy por hoy** at the present time, as of today
**hoya** *f* hole, pit, ditch; grave; valley; whirlpool; seedbed; (Am.) basin (*of river*); **tener un pie en la hoya** to have one foot in the grave
**hoyada** *f* low spot, depression
**hoyanca** *f* (coll.) potter's field, common grave for the poor
**hoyo** *m* hole; pockmark; grave
**hoyoso -sa** *adj* holey, full of holes
**hoyuela** *f* fonticulus, hollow at front of neck
**hoyuelo** *m* dimple; pitching pennies (*boy's game*); fonticulus, hollow at front of neck
**hoz** *f* (*pl:* **hoces**) sickle; defile, ravine; narrow pass; (anat.) falx; **de hoz y de coz** (coll.) headlong, recklessly; **la hoz y el martillo** the hammer and sickle; **meter la hoz en mies ajena** to mind other people's business; **hoz del cerebelo** (anat.) falx cerebelli; **hoz del cerebro** (anat.) falx cerebri
**hozada** *f* stroke with a sickle; grass (or other grain) cut with one stroke of sickle
**hozadero** *m* place where hogs root up the earth
**hozadura** *f* hole made by a rooting hog
**hozar §76** *va & vn* to root, to nuzzle
**hta.** abr. of **hasta**
**huacal** *m* (Am.) var. of **guacal**
**huachinango** *m* (ichth.) red snapper
**huanca** *f* (Am.) Indian reed horn
**huando** *m* (Am.) var. of **guando**
**huango** *m* (Am.) var. of **guango**
**huarache** *m* (Am.) var. of **guarache**
**huauzontli** *m* (Am.) goosefoot
**hube** *1st sg pret ind of* **haber**
**hucha** *f* large sheet; chest (*that can be used as a seat*); money box, toy bank; savings, nest egg
**huchear** *vn* to cry, shout, yelp
**huebra** *f* day's plowing of a yoke of oxen; pair of mules and plowman hired for a day; fallow
**huebrero** *m* plowman hired with pair of mules; owner of pair of mules who rents them out by the day
**hueca** *f* see **hueco**
**huecadal** *m* var. of **oquedal**
**hueco -ca** *adj* hollow; soft, fluffy, spongy; vain, conceited; deep, resounding (*voice*); affected, pompous (*style, language*); *m* hollow; interval; opening (*in wall for window, in a row of parked cars, etc.*); socket (*of a bone*); (coll.) opening (*vacancy*); **hueco de la axila** armpit; **hueco de la mano** hollow of the hand; **hueco del ascensor** elevator shaft; **hueco de escalera** stair well; *f* hollow; spiral groove in spindle (*to keep thread from slipping*)
**huecograbado** *m* photogravure
**huélfago** *m* (vet.) heaves
**huelga** *f* rest, leisure, idleness; sport, merriment; pleasant spot; strike (*of workmen*); (mach.) play (*between two parts*); (agr.) fallow (*period of being fallow*); **ir a la huelga** or **ponerse en huelga** to go on strike; **huelga de brazos caídos** sit-down strike; slowdown (*strike*); **huelga de hambre** hunger strike; **huelga de ocupación** sit-down strike; **huelga patronal** lockout; **huelga sentada** sit-down strike
**huelgo** *m* breath; room, space; play, allowance
**huelguista** *mf* striker
**huelguístico -ca** *adj* (pertaining to a) strike
**huelveño -ña** *adj* (pertaining) to Huelva; *mf* native or inhabitant of Huelva
**huella** *f* tread, treading; track, footprint; trace, mark; rut; tread (*of stairs*); (aut.) tread (*of tire*); **seguir las huellas de** to follow in the footsteps of; **huella dactilar** or **digital** fingerprint; **huella de sonido** (mov.) sound track
**huello** *m* walking (*condition of road for walking*); tread, hoofbeat; bottom of hoof
**huemul** *m* var. of **güemul**
**huérfago** *m* var. of **huélfago**
**huerfanato** *m* orphanage
**huérfano -na** *adj* orphan, orphaned; alone, deserted; *mf* orphan
**huero -ra** *adj* addle; (fig.) addle; (Am.) blond; **salir huero** (coll.) to turn out bad, to flop; *mf* (Am.) blond
**huerta** *f* garden, vegetable garden; fruit garden; irrigated region
**huertano -na** *adj* (pertaining to a) garden; *mf* gardener
**huertero -ra** *adj* (Am.) (pertaining to a) garden; *mf* (Am.) gardener

**huerto** *m* orchard; garden, kitchen garden
**huesa** *f* grave; **tener un pie en la huesa** to have one foot in the grave
**huesillo** *m* (Am.) dried peach
**hueso** *m* bone; stone, pit (*of fruit*); (fig.) hard job, drudgery; (Am.) junk, piece of junk; (Am.) good-for-nothing; **huesos** *mpl* bones (*mortal remains*); (coll.) hand; **desenterrar los huesos de uno** to drag someone's skeleton out of the closet; **calarse hasta los huesos** to get soaked to the skin; **estar en los huesos** to be nothing but skin and bones; **la sin hueso** (coll.) the tongue; **no dejarle a uno un hueso sano** (coll.) to pick someone to pieces; (coll.) to beat someone up, to give someone a good thrashing; **no poder con sus huesos** (coll.) to be all in; **soltar la sin hueso** (coll.) to wag one's tongue, to talk too much; (coll.) to pour forth insults; **tener los huesos molidos** to be fagged out; **hueso de la alegría** crazy bone, funny bone; **hueso de la suerte** wishbone; **hueso duro de roer** (coll.) a hard nut to crack; **hueso occipital** (anat.) occipital bone; **hueso temporal** (anat.) temporal bone
**huesoso -sa** *adj* bony
**huésped -peda** *mf* guest; lodger; stranger; host; (bot. & zool.) host; (archaic) innkeeper; **echar la cuenta sin la huéspeda** or **no contar con la huéspeda** (coll.) to reckon without one's host; **huésped de honor** guest of honor; *f* hostess
**hueste** *f* host (*army*); followers
**huesudo -da** *adj* big-boned
**hueva** *f* roe (*fish eggs*)
**huevar** *vn* to begin to lay (*said of birds*)
**huevera** *f* see **huevero**
**huevería** *f* egg store
**huevero -ra** *mf* egg dealer; *m* egg dish; *f* egg-cup; oviduct (*of birds*)
**huevo** *m* egg; (biol.) ovum; **huevo a la plancha** fried egg; **huevo al plato** shirred egg; **huevo de Colón** or **de Juanelo** something that looks hard at first but turns out to be easy; **huevo del té** tea ball; **huevo de zurcir** darning egg or gourd; **huevo de faltriquera** candied egg; **huevo duro** hard-boiled egg; **huevo en agua** soft-boiled egg; **huevo en cáscara** soft-boiled egg; **huevo escalfado** poached egg; **huevo estrellado** or **frito** fried egg; **huevo pasado por agua** soft-boiled egg; **huevos pericos** (Am.) scrambled eggs; **huevos revueltos** scrambled eggs; **huevo tibio** (Am.) soft-boiled egg
**huf** *interj* var. of **uf**
**Hugo** *m* Hugh
**hugonote -ta** *adj* Huguenotic; *mf* Huguenot
**huída** *f* flight; escape; leak; putlog hole; splay, flare (*at opening of a hole*); shying (*of a horse*)
**huidero -ra** *adj* fugitive; *m* cover, shelter (*of animals*)
**huidizo -za** *adj* fugitive; evasive
**huilota** *f* (orn.) mourning dove
**huillín** *m* (zool.) Chilean otter
**huir §41** *va* to flee, avoid, shun; to duck; *vn* to flee; to fly (*said, e.g., of time*); to slip (*from the memory*); *vr* to flee
**huisache** *m* (bot.) sponge tree
**hujier** *m* var. of **ujier**
**hule** *m* oilcloth, oilskin; rubber; (taur.) blood, goring
**hulear** *vn* (Am.) to gather rubber
**hulero -ra** *adj* (Am.) (pertaining to) rubber; *mf* rubber gatherer, rubber worker
**hulla** *f* coal, soft coal; **hulla azul** tide power; wind power; **hulla blanca** white coal, water power; **hulla grasa** soft coal; **hulla magra** hard coal; **hulla negra** short-flame coal; **hulla seca** hard coal
**hullero -ra** *adj* (pertaining to) coal; *f* colliery, coal mine
**humada** *f* smoke signal
**humanal** *adj* human
**humanar** *va* to humanize; *vr* to become more human; to become man (*said of Jesus Christ*); **humanarse a** + *inf* (Am.) to condescend to + *inf*
**humanidad** *f* humanity; (coll.) fatness, corpulence; **las humanidades** the humanities
**humanismo** *m* humanism
**humanista** *adj & mf* humanist
**humanístico -ca** *adj* humanistic
**humanitario -ria** *adj & mf* humanitarian
**humanitarismo** *m* humanitarianism
**humanizar §76** *va & vr* to humanize; to soften, to cool off, to calm down
**humano -na** *adj* human (*pertaining to man*); humane (*kind, merciful; civilizing*); *m* human
**humarada** *f* var. of **humareda**
**humarazo** *m* var. of **humazo**
**humareda** *f* cloud of smoke
**humazo** *m* dense smoke; poison smoke (*to drive rats from a ship*); **dar humazo a** (coll.) to smoke out
**Humberto** *m* Humbert
**humeada** *f* (Am.) puff of smoke
**humeante** *adj* smoky, smoking; steamy, steaming; reeking
**humear** *va* (Am.) to smoke, to fumigate; *vn* to smoke, give off smoke; to steam; to reek; to last, to persist (*said of traces of a quarrel, disturbance, etc.*); to be conceited, to be puffed up; *vr* to smoke, give off smoke
**humectación** *f* humidification
**humectador** *m* humidifier; humidor (*in textile mills*); moistener (*e.g., of stamps*)
**humectar** *va & vr* var. of **humedecer**
**humectativo -va** *adj* moistening, humectant
**humedad** *f* humidity, moisture, dampness; **humedad relativa** (meteor.) relative humidity
**humedal** *m* moist ground
**humedecer §34** *va* to humidify, moisten, dampen; to wet; to soak; *vr* to become moist, become damp; to become wet
**húmedo -da** *adj* humid, moist, damp; wet
**humera** *f* (coll.) drunk, spree
**humeral** *adj* (anat.) humeral; *m* (eccl.) humeral veil
**humero** *m* smokestack, chimney; (dial.) smokehouse
**húmero** *m* (anat.) humerus
**húmico -ca** *adj* (chem.) humic
**humifuso -sa** *adj* (bot.) humifuse
**humildad** *f* humility; humbleness
**humilde** *adj* humble
**humillación** *f* humiliation; (act of) humbling
**humilladero** *m* boundary crucifix, calvary, road shrine; prie-dieu
**humillador -dora** *adj* humiliating; *mf* humiliator
**humillante** *adj* humiliating
**humillar** *va* to humiliate; to humble; to bow (*one's head*); to bend (*one's body, knees, etc.*); *vr* to be humble; to humble oneself; to cringe, grovel
**humillo** *m* (vet.) pig fever; **humillos** *mpl* airs, conceit
**humina** *f* (biochem.) humin
**humo** *m* smoke; fume, steam; gauze; **humos** *mpl* airs, conceit; hearths, homes; **a humo de pajas** (coll.) lightly, thoughtlessly; **bajar los humos a** (coll.) to take down a peg; **echar más humo que una chimenea** to smoke like a chimney; **hacer humo** (coll.) to cook; (coll.) to stick around; (coll.) to smoke (*said, e.g., of a fireplace*); **irse todo en humo** to go up in smoke; **parar el humo** (coll.) to split hairs; **subírsele a uno el humo a las narices** (coll.) to get angry, be annoyed; **tragar el humo** to inhale (*in smoking*); **vender humos** (coll.) to scheme by claiming to have the inside track, to peddle influence
**humor** *m* humor; **buen humor** good humor; **mal humor** bad humor; **seguirle el humor a una persona** to humor a person; **humor ácueo** or **acuoso** (anat.) aqueous humor; **humor vítreo** (anat.) vitreous humor
**humorado -da** *adj;* **bien humorado** good-humored; **mal humorado** bad-humored; *f* sally, bit of humor, pleasantry; whim
**humorismo** *m* humor, humorousness
**humorista** *adj* humorous; *mf* humorist (*writer*)
**humorístico -ca** *adj* humorous (*writer, cartoon*)
**humoroso -sa** *adj* full of humor, watery
**humoso -sa** *adj* smoky; smoking; steamy
**humus** *m* humus
**hundible** *adj* sinkable

**hundimiento** *m* sinking; collapse; settling, cave-in; undoing; destruction; crash; disappearance
**hundir** *va* to sink; to plunge; to overwhelm; to confound, confute; to undo; to destroy, ruin; to crash, shatter; *vr* to sink, collapse; to settle, cave in; to come to ruin, be wiped out; to be turned upside down; to sink (*below the horizon*); (coll.) to vanish, disappear; **aunque se hunda el mundo** (coll.) let the heavens fall, come what may
**Hunfredo** *m* Humphrey
**húngaro -ra** *adj & mf* Hungarian; *m* Hungarian (*language*)
**Hungría** *f* Hungary
**húnico -ca** *adj* Hunnic
**huno -na** *adj* Hunnic; *mf* Hun
**hupe** *f* punk
**hura** *f* hole, burrow; coarse brush; carbuncle; (bot.) sandbox tree; **hura ruidosa** (bot.) sandbox tree
**huracán** *m* hurricane; (naut.) hurricane
**huracanado -da** *adj* hurricane-like, tempestuous
**huracanar** *vr* to hurricane, to blow like a hurricane
**hurañía** *f* shyness, diffidence
**huraño -ña** *adj* shy, diffident, retiring
**hurgar** §59 *va* to poke; (fig.) to stir up, incite; **peor es hurgallo** (*i.e.*, **hurgarlo**) (coll.) better let it alone, the less said the better; *vn* to poke; **hurgar en** to poke into
**hurgón** *m* poker; (coll.) thrust, stab
**hurgonada** *f* poke, poking; (coll.) thrust, stab
**hurgonazo** *m* thrust with a poker; (coll.) jab, thrust, stab
**hurgonear** *va* to poke (*the fire*); (coll.) to jab, to stab at
**hurgonero** *m* poker (*metal rod for stirring fire*)
**hurí** *f* (*pl:* **-ríes**) houri (*of Mohammedan paradise*)
**hurón -rona** *adj* (coll.) shy, diffident; *mf* (coll.) prier, snooper; (coll.) shy or diffident person; *m* (zool.) ferret; **hurón menor** (zool.) grison; *f* female ferret
**huronear** *va & vn* to ferret, hunt with a ferret; (coll.) to ferret, to pry
**huronera** *f* ferret hole; (coll.) lair, hiding place
**huronero** *m* ferreter
**huroniense** *adj & m* (geol.) Huronian
**hurra** *interj* hurrah!
**hurraca** *f* var. of **urraca**
**hurtacuerpo** *m* (Am.) cold shoulder, slight
**hurtadillas; a hurtadillas** stealthily, on the sly; **a hurtadillas de** unbeknown to
**hurtadineros** *m* (*pl:* **-nos**) (prov.) bank, toy bank
**hurtador -dora** *adj* thieving; *mf* thief
**hurtar** *va* to steal, filch; to cheat (*in weights or measures*); to wear away (*the soil*); to plagiarize; to move away, withdraw; **hurtar a** to steal from; **hurtar el cuerpo** to dodge, to duck; *vr* to withdraw, to hide; **hurtarse a** to hide from, to avoid, to duck
**hurto** *m* thieving; theft; (min.) driftway; **a hurto** stealthily, on the sly; **coger con el hurto en las manos** to catch with the goods
**husada** *f* spindleful
**húsar** *m* (mil.) hussar
**husero** *m* brow antler (*of a yearling deer*)
**husillo** *m* screw, worm (*of a press*); spindle; drain, overflow
**husita** *adj & mf* Hussite
**husitismo** *m* Hussitism
**husma** *f* (coll.) snooping; **andar a la husma** (coll.) to go snooping around
**husmeador -dora** *adj* scenting; (coll.) prying; *mf* scenter; (coll.) prier
**husmear** *va* to scent, to smell out; (coll.) to pry into; *vn* to become gamy or high, to smell bad (*said of meat*)
**husmeo** *m* scenting; (coll.) prying
**husmo** *m* high odor, gaminess; **andarse al husmo** to be on the scent; **estar al husmo** (coll.) to wait for a chance
**huso** *m* spindle; bobbin; drum (*of windlass*); **ser más derecho que un huso** (coll.) to be as straight as a ramrod; **huso esférico** (geom.) lune; **huso horario** time zone (*between two meridians*)
**huta** *f* hunter's blind
**hutía** *f* (zool.) hutia
**huy** *interj* ouch!
**huyente** *adj* receding (*forehead*); shifty (*glance*)

# I

**I, i** *f* tenth letter of the Spanish alphabet
**-ía** *suffix f* see **-ío**
**ib.** abr. of **ibídem**
**iba** *1st sg imperf ind of* **ir**
**Iberia** *f* Iberia
**ibérico -ca** or **iberio -ria** *adj* Iberian
**iberismo** *m* Iberism
**ibero -ra** *adj & mf* Iberian
**Iberoamérica** *f* Ibero-America
**iberoamericano -na** *adj & mf* Ibero-American
**íbice** *m* (zool.) ibex
**ibicenco -ca** *adj* (pertaining to) Iviza; *mf* native or inhabitant of Iviza
**ibídem** *adv* (Lat.) ibidem (*in the same place*)
**ibis** *f* (*pl:* **ibis**) (orn.) ibis
**Ibiza** *f* Iviza (*Balearic island*)
**ibón** *m* lake on slopes of Pyrenees
**ibseniano -na** *adj & mf* Ibsenian
**icaco** or **icaquero** *m* (bot.) coco plum (*tree and fruit*)
**icáreo -a** *adj* Icarian
**icario -ria** *adj* Icarian; (*cap.*) *m* (myth.) Icarius
**Ícaro** *m* (myth.) Icarus
**icástico -ca** *adj* natural, plain
**iceberg** *m* (*pl:* **-bergs**) iceberg
**icneumón** *m* (zool.) ichneumon; (ent.) ichneumon, ichneumon fly
**icnografía** *f* (arch.) ichnography
**-ico -ca** *suffix adj* -ic, e.g., **metálico** metallic; **público** public; **volcánico** volcanic; -ical, e.g., **crítico** critical; **lógico** logical; **músico** musical; para la comparación de **-ic** e **-ical**, véase **-ic** en la parte de inglés-español; (chem.) -ic, e.g., **cúprico** cupric; **sulfúrico** sulfuric; *suffix mf* -ic, e.g., **doméstico** domestic; -ician, e.g., **lógico** logician; **músico** musician; -ist, e.g., **botánico** botanist; **químico** chemist; *suffix m* -ic, e.g., **crítico** critic; **mecánico** mechanic; *suffix f* -ic, e.g., **aritmética** arithmetic; **música** music; -ics, e.g., **física** physics; **política** politics; **-ico -ca** (accented on penult) *suffix adj & m* Aragonese equivalent of **-ito,** sometimes with a touch of sarcasm, e.g., **elegantica** nice and stylish; **inocentico** kind of innocent; **angelico** imp of an angel
**icón** *m* (eccl.) icon
**icono** *m* icon (*image, picture*)
**iconoclasia** *f* or **iconoclasmo** *m* iconoclasm
**iconoclasta** *adj* iconoclastic; *mf* iconoclast
**iconógeno** *m* (phot.) developer (*chemical bath or reagent*)
**iconografía** *f* iconography
**iconográfico -ca** *adj* iconographic or iconographical
**iconólatra** *adj* iconolatrous; *mf* iconolater
**iconolatría** *f* iconolatry
**iconología** *f* iconology
**iconomanía** *f* iconomania
**iconoscópico -ca** *adj* (pertaining to the) iconoscope
**iconoscopio** *m* (telv.) iconoscope
**iconostasio** *m* (eccl.) iconostasion
**icor** *m* (path.) ichor (*from ulcer*)
**icoroso -sa** *adj* ichorous
**icosaedro** *m* (geom.) icosahedron
**ictericia** *f* (path.) icterus, jaundice
**ictericiado -da** *adj* jaundiced; *mf* person with jaundice
**ictérico -ca** *adj* icteric; jaundiced; *mf* person with jaundice
**ictíneo -a** *adj* fish-shaped; *m* submarine boat
**ictiófago -ga** *adj* ichthyophagous; *mf* ichthyophagist
**ictiol** *m* (pharm.) ichthyol
**ictiología** *f* ichthyology
**ictiológico -ca** *adj* ichthyologic or ichthyological
**ictiólogo -ga** *mf* ichthyologist
**ictiosauro** *m* (pal.) ichthyosaur or ichthyosaurus
**ictiosis** *f* (path.) ichthyosis
**ictiosismo** *m* (vet.) ichthyosism
**ichal** *m* field of ichu
**icho** or **ichú** *m* (bot.) ichu
**íd.** abr. of **ídem**
**ida** *f* see **ido**
**idea** *f* idea; **mudar de idea** to change one's mind; **idea fija** fixed idea
**ideación** *f* ideation
**ideal** *adj & m* ideal
**idealidad** *f* ideality
**idealismo** *m* idealism
**idealista** *adj* idealist, idealistic; *mf* idealist
**idealístico -ca** *adj* (philos.) idealistic
**idealización** *f* idealization
**idealizar** §76 *va* to idealize
**idear** *va* to think up, plan, devise
**ideario** *m* body of ideas or concepts
**ídem** *adj & pron* (Lat.) idem
**idemista** *adj* yes-saying; *mf* yes sayer
**idéntico -ca** *adj* identic or identical; very similar
**identidad** *f* identity, sameness
**identificación** *f* identification
**identificar** §86 *va* to identify
**ideografía** *f* ideograph
**ideográfico -ca** *adj* ideographic or ideographical
**ideograma** *m* ideogram
**ideología** *f* ideology
**ideológico -ca** *adj* ideologic or ideological
**ideólogo -ga** *mf* ideologist
**idílico -ca** *adj* idyllic
**idilio** *m* idyl
**idioeléctrico -ca** *adj* idioelectric or idioelectrical
**idioma** *m* language; speech, jargon; **idioma hablado** spoken language
**idiomático -ca** *adj* idiomatic; linguistic
**idiosincrasia** *f* idiosyncrasy
**idiosincrásico -ca** *adj* idiosyncratic
**idiota** *adj* idiotic; *mf* idiot
**idiotez** *f* idiocy; **idiotez mogólica** Mongolian idiocy
**idiótico** *m* idioticon
**idiotismo** *m* ignorance; idiom; idiocy
**idiotizar** §76 *va* to drive crazy; *vr* to go crazy
**ido -da** *adj* wild, scatterbrained; **los idos** the dead; *pp of* **ir**; *f* going; departure; sally; rashness; trail; **de ida y vuelta** round-trip; **idas y venidas** comings and goings
**idólatra** *adj* idolatrous; *m* idolater; *f* idolatress
**idolatrar** *va & vn* to idolize; **idolatrar en** to idolize
**idolatría** *f* idolatry; idolization
**idolátrico -ca** *adj* idolatrous
**ídolo** *m* idol; (fig.) idol
**idolología** *f* science dealing with idols
**Idomeneo** *m* (myth.) Idomeneus
**idoneidad** *f* fitness; suitability
**idóneo -a** *adj* fit; suitable
**-idor -dora** *suffix adj* -ing, e.g., **seguidor** following; **vividor** living; *suffix mf* -er, e.g., **seguidor** follower; **vividor** liver
**idumeo -a** *adj & mf* Idumaean or Idumean; (*cap.*) *f* (Bib.) Idumaea
**idus** *mpl* ides
**i.e.** abr. of **id est** (Lat.) **esto es, es decir**
**-iento -ta** *suffix adj* -y, e.g., **hambriento** hungry; **polvoriento** dusty; powdery; **sediento** thirsty; **sudoriento** sweaty

**Ifigenia** *f* (myth.) Iphigenia
**igl.ª** abr. of **iglesia**
**iglesia** *f* church; **entrar en la iglesia** to go into the church (*clerical profession*); **ir a la iglesia** to go to church; **llevar a la iglesia** to lead (*a woman*) to the altar; **iglesia colegial** collegiate church; **Iglesia de Inglaterra** Church of England; **Iglesia griega ortodoxa** Greek Orthodox Church; **Iglesia latina** Latin Church; **iglesia militante** church militant; **Iglesia ortodoxa** Orthodox Church; **iglesia triunfante** church triumphant
**iglesiero -ra** *adj* (Am.) churchgoing; *mf* (Am.) churchgoer
**iglú** *m* (*pl:* **-glúes**) igloo
**ignaciano -na** *adj & m* Ignatian, Jesuit
**Ignacio** *m* Ignatius
**ignaro -ra** *adj* ignorant
**ignavia** *f* laziness
**ignavo -va** *adj* lazy
**ígneo -a** *adj* igneous
**ignición** *f* ignition
**ignícola** *adj* fire-worshiping; *mf* fire worshiper
**ignífero -ra** *adj* igniferous
**ignífugo -ga** *adj & m* ignifuge
**ignito -ta** *adj* ignited, inflamed
**ignívomo -ma** *adj* (poet.) ignivomous
**ignominia** *f* ignominy
**ignominioso -sa** *adj* ignominious
**ignorancia** *f* ignorance
**ignorante** *adj* ignorant; *mf* ignoramus
**ignorar** *va* not to know, to be ignorant of
**ignoto -ta** *adj* unknown
**igorrote** *adj* Igorot; *m* Igorot or Igorrote
**igual** *adj* equal; smooth, level, even, uniform; equable, firm, constant; unchanging; indifferent; **me es igual** it is all the same to me, it makes no difference to me; *m* equal; sign of equality; **al igual de** like, after the fashion of; **al igual que** as; like; while, whereas; **en igual de** instead of; **sin igual** matchless, unrivaled; **igual que** as well as
**iguala** *f* equalization; agreement; annual fee; level
**igualación** *f* equalization; agreement
**igualado -da** *adj* with even plumage
**igualador -dora** *adj* equalizing; leveling; *mf* equalizer; leveler; **igualador de caminos** road planer; **igualador de dientes** jointer (*of saws*)
**igualamiento** *m* equalization
**igualar** *va* to equalize; to smooth, to level, to even, to smooth off; to match; to deem equal; to adjust, to face, to fit; (math.) to equate; to joint (*saws*); to set (*a clock or watch*); *vn & vr* to be equal; **igualar a** or **con** or **igualarse a** or **con** to equal, to be equal to
**igualdad** *f* equality, sameness; smoothness, evenness; **igualdad de ánimo** equability, equanimity
**igualitario -ria** *adj & mf* equalitarian
**igualmente** *adv* equally; likewise; (coll.) the same to you
**iguana** *f* (zool.) iguana
**iguanodonte** *m* (pal.) iguanodont
**igüedo** *m* (zool.) buck
**ijada** *f* flank (*of animal*); loin; stitch (*pain in the side*); **tener su ijada** to have its weak point
**ijadear** *vn* to pant, to quiver (*from fatigue*)
**ijar** *m* flank (*of animal*); loin
**ilación** *f* illation; order, connection
**ilapso** *m* trance, ecstatic trance
**ilativo -va** *adj* inferential, illative; *f* illative
**Il.ᵉ** abr. of **Ilustre**
**ilegal** *adj* illegal
**ilegalidad** *f* illegality
**ilegibilidad** *f* illegibility
**ilegible** *adj* illegible
**ilegitimar** *va* to make or prove illegitimate, to illegitimate
**ilegitimidad** *f* illegitimacy
**ilegítimo -ma** *adj* illegitimate
**íleo** *m* (path.) ileus
**ileocecal** *adj* ileocaecal
**íleon** *m* (anat.) ileum; (anat.) ilium
**ileso -sa** *adj* unharmed, unscathed; whole, untouched
**iletrado -da** *adj* unlettered, uncultured
**ilíaco -ca** *adj* (anat. & path.) ileac; (anat.) iliac; (myth.) Iliac
**Ilíada** *f* Iliad
**iliberal** *adj* illiberal
**iliberalidad** *f* illiberality
**ilicáceo -a** *adj* (bot.) ilicaceous
**ilíceo -a** *adj* oak
**ilicíneo -a** *adj* (bot.) ilicaceous
**ilicitano -na** *adj* (pertaining to) Elche; *mf* native or inhabitant of Elche
**ilícito -ta** *adj* illicit; unlawful; unjust
**ilicitud** *f* illicitness; unlawfulness; unjustness
**iliense** *adj* Ilian
**ilimitable** *adj* illimitable
**ilimitado -da** *adj* limitless, unlimited
**ilinio** *m* (chem.) illinium
**ilion** *m* (anat.) ilium; (anat.) ileum
**Ilión** *m* (myth.) Ilium or Ilion
**ilíquido -da** *adj* unliquidated
**Iliria** *f* see **ilirio**
**ilírico -ca** *adj* Illyric
**ilirio -ria** *adj & mf* Illyrian; (*cap.*) *f* Illyria
**iliterato -ta** *adj* illiterate
**Il.ᵐᵒ** abr. of **Ilustrísimo**
**ilógico -ca** *adj* illogical
**ilota** *mf* Helot; (fig.) helot
**ilotismo** *m* helotism
**iludir** *va* to elude, evade
**iluminación** *f* illumination; (f.a.) illumination; (f.a.) painting in distemper; **iluminación indirecta** indirect lighting
**iluminado -da** *adj* illuminated; **iluminados** *mpl* Illuminated, Illuminati
**iluminador -dora** *adj* illuminating; *mf* illuminator
**iluminar** *va* to illuminate; (f.a.) to illuminate
**iluminativo -va** *adj* illuminative
**iluminismo** *m* Illuminism
**ilusión** *f* illusion; delusion; zeal, enthusiasm, fanaticism; dream; **forjarse** or **hacerse ilusiones** to indulge in wishful thinking, to kid oneself; **ilusión óptica** optical illusion
**ilusionar** *va* to delude, to beguile; *vr* to be deluded, to have illusions, to indulge in wishful thinking
**ilusionismo** *m* prestidigitation
**ilusionista** *mf* illusionist, prestidigitator
**ilusivo -va** *adj* illusive
**iluso -sa** *adj* deluded; misguided; visionary
**ilusorio -ria** *adj* illusory
**ilustración** *f* illustration; learning; enlightenment; elucidation; illustrated magazine
**ilustrado -da** *adj* informed, learned; illustrated; enlightened
**ilustrador -dora** *adj* illustrative; enlightening; explicatory; *mf* illustrator
**ilustrar** *va* to illustrate; to make famous or illustrious; to shed glory on, to cause to shine; to enlighten; to elucidate; (theol.) to inspire; *vr* to be enlightened; to become famous
**ilustrativo -va** *adj* illustrative
**ilustre** *adj* illustrious
**ilustrísimo -ma** *adj super* very or most illustrious; (eccl.) Most Reverend (*bishop*)
**illicitano -na** *adj & mf* var. of **ilicitano**
**Illmo.** abr. of **Ilustrísimo**
**-illo -lla** *suffix dim* has the force of little, somewhat, rather and often indicates an attitude of indifference or depreciation, e.g., **cigarrillo** cigaret; **coquetilla** little coquette; **cucharilla** small spoon, teaspoon; **chiquillo** youngster; **abatidillo** somewhat downcast
**imagen** *f* image; picture; **a su imagen** in his own image; **imagen de bulto** statue, image in high relief; **imagen fantasma** (telv.) ghost image; **imagen real** (phys.) real image; **imagen virtual** (phys.) virtual image
**imaginable** *adj* imaginable
**imaginación** *f* imagination
**imaginar** *va, vn & vr* to imagine; **imaginarse** + *inf* to imagine + *ger*
**imaginario -ria** *adj* imaginary; *mf* painter or sculptor of religious images; *f* (mil.) reserve guard
**imaginativo -va** *adj* imaginative; *f* imagination; understanding
**imaginería** *f* fancy colored embroidery; carving or painting of religious images

**imaginero** *m* painter or sculptor of religious images
**imago** *m* (zool.) imago
**imán** *m* (mineral., phys. & fig.) magnet; (fig.) magnetism; imam; **imán de herradura** horseshoe magnet; **imán inductor** (elec.) field magnet
**imanación** *f* magnetization
**imanar** *va* to magnetize; *vr* to become magnetized
**imantación** *f* var. of **imanación**
**imantar** *va & vr* var. of **imanar**
**imbatible** *adj* unbeatable
**imbatido -da** *adj* unbeaten
**imbécil** *adj & mf* imbecile
**imbecilidad** *f* imbecility
**imbele** *adj* weak, feeble; defenseless, unfit to fight
**imberbe** *adj* beardless
**imbibición** *f* imbibition
**imbornal** *m* scupper, drain hole; (naut.) scupper
**imborrable** *adj* ineffaceable, ineradicable
**imbricación** *f* imbrication
**imbricado -da** *adj* imbricate or imbricated
**imbuir** §41 *va* to imbue; **imbuir de** or **en** to imbue with
**imitable** *adj* imitable; worthy of imitation
**imitación** *f* imitation; **a imitación de** in imitation of; **de imitación** imitation, e.g., **joyas de imitación** imitation jewelry; *adj* imitation, e.g., **joyas imitación** imitation jewelry
**imitado -da** *adj* imitated, copied; like; mock, sham; imitation, e.g., **perlas imitadas** imitation pearls
**imitador -dora** *adj* imitating, imitative; *mf* imitator
**imitar** *va* to imitate
**imitativo -va** *adj* imitative
**imoscapo** *m* (arch.) apophyge
**impacción** *f* impact; (dent. & med.) impaction
**impaciencia** *f* impatience; act or show of impatience
**impacientar** *va* to make impatient; *vr* to grow impatient
**impaciente** *adj* impatient
**impactado -da** *adj* (dent.) impacted
**impacto** *m* impact; hit; blow; mark (*left by a projectile*); (fig.) impact; **impacto de bala** bullet mark; **impacto directo** direct hit
**impagable** *adj* unpayable; priceless
**impalpabilidad** *f* impalpability
**impalpable** *adj* impalpable
**impanación** *f* (theol.) impanation
**impar** *adj* unmatched; (math.) odd, uneven; *m* (math.) odd number
**imparcial** *adj* impartial; nonpartisan
**imparcialidad** *f* impartiality; **extremar la imparcialidad** to lean over backward
**imparidad** *f* oddness, unevenness
**imparidígito -ta** *adj* (zool.) imparidigitate
**imparipinado -da** *adj* (bot.) imparipinnate
**imparisílabo -ba** or **imparisilábico -ca** *adj* (gram.) imparisyllabic
**impartible** *adj* indivisible
**impartir** *va* to distribute, transmit; (law) to seek, solicit
**impás** *m* (bridge) finesse
**impasibilidad** *f* impassibility, impassivity
**impasible** *adj* impassible, impassive
**impavidez** *f* intrepidity, fearlessness
**impávido -da** *adj* intrepid, fearless, dauntless
**impecabilidad** *f* impeccability
**impecable** *adj* impeccable
**impedancia** *f* (elec.) impedance
**impedido -da** *adj* crippled, paralytic
**impedimenta** *f* (mil.) impedimenta
**impedimento** *m* impediment, obstacle, hindrance; (law) impediment, disability
**impedir** §94 *va* to prevent; **impedir algo a uno** to prevent someone from doing something; **impedir** + *inf* or **impedir que** + *subj* to prevent or keep from + *ger*
**impeditivo -va** *adj* preventive, hindering
**impeler** *va* to impel; **impeler a** + *inf* to impel to + *inf*
**impender** *va* to spend, to invest
**impenetrabilidad** *f* impenetrability
**impenetrable** *adj* impenetrable
**impenitencia** *f* impenitence
**impenitente** *adj* impenitent; hardened, inveterate; *mf* impenitent
**impensa** *f* (law) expense, upkeep expense
**impensable** *adj* unthinkable
**impensado -da** *adj* unexpected
**imperador -dora** *adj* ruling, commanding
**imperante** *adj* ruling; prevailing; (astrol.) dominant
**imperar** *vn* to rule, reign, hold sway, prevail
**imperativo -va** *adj* imperative; imperious, dictatorial; (gram.) imperative; *m* imperative; (gram.) imperative; **imperativo categórico** (philos.) categorical imperative; *f* tone of command, commanding manner
**imperatoria** *f* (bot.) masterwort
**imperceptibilidad** *f* imperceptibility
**imperceptible** *adj* imperceptible
**imperdible** *adj* unlosable; *m* safety pin
**imperdonable** *adj* unforgivable, unpardonable
**imperecedero -ra** *adj* imperishable, undying
**imperfección** *f* imperfection
**imperfectivo -va** *adj* (gram.) imperfective
**imperfecto -ta** *adj* imperfect; (gram.) imperfect; *m* (gram.) imperfect
**imperforable** *adj* imperforable; (aut.) puncture-proof
**imperforación** *f* imperforation
**imperforado -da** *adj* imperforate
**imperial** *adj* imperial; *f* imperial, upper deck (*of diligence, bus, or trolley car*)
**imperialismo** *m* imperialism
**imperialista** *adj* imperialist, imperialistic; *mf* imperialist
**impericia** *f* inexpertness, unskilfulness
**imperio** *m* empire; dominion, sway; imperium; **celeste imperio** or **imperio celeste** Celestial Empire (*China*); **estilo imperio** (f.a.) Empire; **Sacro Imperio Romano-Germánico** Holy Roman Empire; **Imperio del sol naciente** Empire of the Rising Sun (*Japan*); **Imperio romano** Roman Empire
**imperioso -sa** *adj* imperious; imperative
**imperito -ta** *adj* inexpert, unskilled
**impermanencia** *f* impermanence
**impermanente** *adj* impermanent
**impermeabilidad** *f* impermeability
**impermeabilización** *f* waterproofing (*action*)
**impermeabilizante** *m* waterproofing (*material*)
**impermeabilizar** §76 *va* to make waterproof, to waterproof
**impermeable** *adj* impermeable; waterproof; impervious; *m* raincoat
**impermutable** *adj* impermutable; unexchangeable
**imperscrutabilidad** *f* inscrutability
**imperscrutable** *adj* inscrutable
**impersonal** *adj* impersonal; (gram.) impersonal
**impersonalidad** *f* impersonality
**impersonalizar** §76 *va* (gram.) to use (*a verb*) impersonally
**impersuasible** *adj* unpersuadable
**impersuasión** *f* unpersuadableness
**impertérrito -ta** *adj* dauntless, intrepid
**impertinencia** *f* irrelevance; impertinence
**impertinente** *adj* irrelevant; impertinent; fussy; **impertinentes** *mpl* lorgnette
**imperturbabilidad** *f* imperturbability
**imperturbable** *adj* imperturbable, unperturbable, unshakable
**imperturbado -da** *adj* unperturbed, undisturbed
**impétigo** *m* (path.) impetigo
**impetra** *f* permission, allowance
**impetración** *f* begging, petition; obtaining by entreaty
**impetrador -dora** *mf* impetrator
**impetrar** *va* to beg for; to obtain by entreaty
**ímpetu** *m* impetus; haste, violence; impetuousness
**impetuosidad** *f* impetuosity
**impetuoso -sa** *adj* impetuous
**impiedad** *f* pitilessness; impiety
**impiedoso -sa** *adj* pitiless
**impío -a** *adj* pitiless, cruel; impious
**impla** *f* wimple; material for making wimples
**implacabilidad** *f* implacability
**implacable** *adj* implacable

**implantación** *f* implantation; introduction
**implantar** *va* to implant; to introduce
**implaticable** *adj* unmentionable, not for conversation
**implicación** *f* contradiction; implication, complicity
**implicar** §86 *va* to implicate; to imply; *vn* to stand in the way, to imply contradiction
**implícitamente** *adv* implicitly, impliedly
**implícito -ta** *adj* implicit, implied
**imploración** *f* imploration, supplication, entreaty
**implorar** *va* to implore
**implosión** *f* implosion; (phonet.) implosion
**implosivo -va** *adj & f* (phonet.) implosive
**implotar** *vn* to burst inwards
**implume** *adj* featherless, unfeathered; unfledged
**impluvio** *m* impluvium
**impolarizable** *adj* impolarizable
**impolítico -ca** *adj* impolite, discourteous; *f* **impoliteness**, discourtesy
**impoluto -ta** *adj* unpolluted
**imponderabilidad** *f* imponderability, imponderableness
**imponderable** *adj & m* imponderable
**impondré** *1st sg fut ind of* **imponer**
**imponente** *adj* imposing; *mf* depositor
**imponer** §69 *va* to impose (*one's will, taxes, silence, etc.*); (print.) to impose; (eccl.) to impose (*the hands*); to instruct; to invest; to deposit (*money*); to impute falsely; *vn* to dominate, command respect; *vr* to assume (*e.g., an obligation*); to become trained; to command attention, impel recognition; **imponerse a** to dominate, command respect from; to get the best of; **imponerse de** to learn, find out
**impongo** *1st sg pres ind of* **imponer**
**imponible** *adj* taxable
**impopular** *adj* unpopular
**impopularidad** *f* unpopularity
**impopularizar** §76 *va* to make unpopular; *vr* to become unpopular
**importación** *f* import, importation; imports
**importador -dora** *adj* importing; *mf* importer
**importancia** *f* importance; size; concern, seriousness; **ser de la importancia de** to concern
**importante** *adj* important; large, considerable
**importar** *va* to import; to be worth, be valued at, amount to; to involve, imply; to concern; *vn* to import; to be important; to matter, make a difference
**importe** *m* amount
**importunación** *f* importuning, pestering
**importunar** *va* to importune
**importunidad** *f* importunity, annoyance; inopportunity, untimeliness
**importuno -na** *adj* importunate; inopportune
**imposibilidad** *f* impossibility
**imposibilitar** *va* to make unable; to make impossible, to prevent; *vr* to become unable; to become impossible; to become paralyzed
**imposible** *adj* impossible
**imposición** *f* imposition (*e.g., of one's will*); investiture; deposit (*of money*); (print.) make-up, imposition; (eccl.) imposition, laying on of hands; **imposición de manos** (eccl.) laying on of hands
**impositivo -va** *adj* (pertaining to) tax
**imposta** *f* (arch.) impost; (arch.) fascia; sill
**impostor -tora** *adj* cheating; slandering; *m* impostor; slanderer; *f* impostress; slanderer
**impostura** *f* imposture; slander
**impotable** *adj* undrinkable
**impotencia** *f* impotence; (path.) impotence
**impotente** *adj* impotent; (path.) impotent
**impracticabilidad** *f* impracticability, impassability
**impracticable** *adj* impracticable, impassable; impractical
**impráctico -ca** *adj* unpractical, impractical
**imprecación** *f* imprecation
**imprecar** §86 *va* to imprecate
**imprecatorio -ria** *adj* imprecatory
**imprecisión** *f* imprecision
**impreciso -sa** *adj* imprecise; vague, indefinite; inexact, inaccurate
**impregnación** *f* (phys.) impregnation
**impregnar** *va* (phys.) to impregnate, saturate; *vr* (phys.) to become impregnated, become saturated
**impremeditación** *f* unpremeditation
**impremeditado -da** *adj* unpremeditated
**imprenta** *f* printing; printing shop, printing house; press; printed matter; letterpress; **en imprenta** in press
**imprentar** *va* (Am.) to press, iron; (Am.) to mark
**imprescindible** *adj* essential, indispensable
**imprescriptible** *adj* imprescriptible, inalienable
**impresentable** *adj* unpresentable
**impresión** *f* printing; print, edition, issue; presswork; stamp, stamping; impression, impress, footprint; (phot.) print; (fig.) impression; **impresión dactilar** or **digital** fingerprint
**impresionabilidad** *f* impressionability, impressibility, susceptibility
**impresionable** *adj* impressionable, impressible
**impresionante** *adj* impressive; sensational
**impresionar** *va* to impress; to record (*a phonograph wire, tape or disk*); (phot.) to expose; *vn* to make an impression; *vr* to be impressed
**impresionismo** *m* (paint., lit. & mus.) impressionism
**impresionista** *adj* impressionistic; *mf* impressionist
**impreso -sa** *pp of* **imprimir;** *m* printed paper or book; **impresos** *mpl* printed matter
**impresor -sora** *adj* printing; *mf* printer (*workman or owner*); *f* wife of printer
**imprestable** *adj* unlendable
**imprevisible** *adj* unforeseeable
**imprevisión** *f* improvidence; oversight
**imprevisor -sora** *adj* improvident
**imprevisto -ta** *adj* unforeseen, unexpected; **imprevistos** *mpl* unforeseen expenses, emergencies
**imprimación** *f* priming; priming material
**imprimadera** *f* priming tool
**imprimador** *m* primer
**imprimar** *va* to prime
**imprimátur** *m* (*pl:* **-tur**) imprimatur
**imprimible** *adj* printable
**imprimir** *va* to impart (*fear, respect, etc.; motion*); §17, 9 *va* to print; to stamp, imprint, impress; to press (*a phonograph record*); to leave (*footprints*); (print.) to print
**improbabilidad** *f* improbability, unlikelihood
**improbable** *adj* improbable, unlikely
**improbar** §77 *va* to disapprove
**improbidad** *f* dishonesty, improbity
**ímprobo -ba** *adj* dishonest; arduous
**improcedencia** *f* lack of rightness; unfitness, untimeliness
**improcedente** *adj* not right; unfit, untimely
**improductivo -va** *adj* unproductive; unemployed
**impronta** *f* stamp, impress, impression; (fig.) stamp, mark
**impronunciable** *adj* unpronounceable
**improperar** *va* to insult, to revile
**improperio** *m* insult, indignity
**impropicio -cia** *adj* unpropitious, inauspicious
**impropiedad** *f* impropriety (*especially in language*)
**impropio -pia** *adj* improper, unsuited; foreign; (math.) improper
**improporción** *f* disproportion
**improporcionado -da** *adj* disproportionate
**improrrogable** *adj* unextendible
**impróspero -ra** *adj* unsuccessful
**impróvido -da** *adj* unprepared, improvident
**improvisación** *f* improvisation, extemporization; meteoric rise, undeserved success; (mus.) impromptu
**improvisadamente** *adv* unexpectedly, suddenly; extempore
**improvisado -da** *adj* unexpected, sudden
**improvisador -dora** *adj* improvising; *mf* improviser
**improvisamente** *adv* var. of **improvisadamente**
**improvisar** *va* to improvise, to extemporize; to utter extemporaneously; *vn* to improvise, to extemporize

**improviso -sa** *adj* unexpected, unforeseen; **al improviso** or **de improviso** unexpectedly, suddenly
**improvisto -ta** *adj* unexpected, unforeseen; **a la improvista** unexpectedly, suddenly
**imprudencia** *f* imprudence; **imprudencia temeraria** criminal negligence
**imprudente** *adj* imprudent
**impúber -bera** or **impúbero -ra** *adj* impuberate
**impublicable** *adj* unpublishable
**impudencia** *f* impudence; shamelessness
**impudente** *adj* impudent; shameless
**impudicia** or **impudicicia** *f* immodesty, impudicity
**impúdico -ca** *adj* immodest
**impudor** *m* immodesty, shamelessness
**impuesto -ta** *pp of* **imponer; estar** or **quedar impuesto de** to be informed of or about; *m* tax, impost
**impugnable** *adj* assailable, vulnerable
**impugnación** *f* opposition, impugnation
**impugnar** *va* to oppose, impugn, contest
**impulsar** *va* to impel; to drive; **impulsar a** + *inf* to impel to + *inf*
**impulsión** *f* impulsion; impulse, drive
**impulsividad** *f* impulsiveness
**impulsivo -va** *adj* impulsive
**impulso** *m* impulse; (mech.) impulse
**impulsor -sora** *adj* impelling; *mf* impeller
**impune** *adj* unpunished
**impunemente** *adv* with impunity
**impunidad** *f* impunity
**impureza** *f* impurity
**impurificación** *f* defilement
**impurificar** §86 *va* to make impure, to defile
**impuro -ra** *adj* impure
**impuse** *1st sg pret ind of* **imponer**
**imputable** *adj* imputable
**imputación** *f* imputation; assignment
**imputador -dora** *mf* imputer
**imputar** *va* to impute; to assign; (com.) to credit on account
**in-** *prefix* in-, e.g., **inconstante** inconstant; **inacción** inaction; **invadir** invade; (*before* **m**) im-, e.g., **inmediato** immediate; un-, e.g., **infeliz** unhappy; **inaudito** unheard-of
**inabarcable** *adj* unembraceable; that cannot be taken in or encompassed
**inabordable** *adj* unapproachable
**inabrogable** *adj* indefeasible
**inacabable** *adj* interminable
**inaccesibilidad** *f* inaccessibility
**inaccesible** *adj* inaccessible
**inacción** *f* inaction
**inacentuado -da** *adj* unaccented
**inaceptable** *adj* unacceptable
**inactividad** *f* inactivity
**inactivo -va** *adj* inactive
**inadaptabilidad** *f* unadaptability, inadaptability
**inadaptable** *adj* unadaptable, inadaptable
**inadaptado -da** *adj* unsuited, unsuitable; maladjusted
**inadecuación** *f* unsuitability; inadequacy
**inadecuado -da** *adj* unsuited, ill-suited; inadequate
**inadmisibilidad** *f* inadmissibility
**inadmisible** *adj* inadmissible; unallowable
**inadoptable** *adj* unadoptable
**inadvertencia** *f* inadvertence, oversight
**inadvertidamente** *adv* inadvertently; carelessly
**inadvertido -da** *adj* inadvertent, unwitting, inattentive; thoughtless, careless; unseen, unnoticed, unobserved
**inafectado -da** *adj* unaffected
**inagotable** *adj* inexhaustible, exhaustless
**inaguantable** *adj* intolerable, unsufferable
**inajenable** *adj* inalienable
**inalámbrico -ca** *adj* (elec.) wireless
**inalcanzable** *adj* unattainable, unreachable
**inalienabilidad** *f* inalienability
**inalienable** *adj* inalienable
**inalterabilidad** *f* unalterability
**inalterable** *adj* unalterable
**inalterado -da** *adj* unaltered
**inameno -na** *adj* unpleasant, disagreeable
**inamisible** *adj* unlosable
**inamistoso -sa** *adj* unfriendly
**inamovible** *adj* undetachable; built-in; unremovable, irremovable
**inamovilidad** *f* irremovability; tenure, permanent tenure
**inanalizable** *adj* unanalyzable
**inane** *adj* inane
**inanición** *f* inanition
**inanidad** *f* inanity
**inanimado -da** *adj* inanimate
**inánime** *adj* weak, spiritless, lifeless
**inapagable** *adj* unextinguishable
**inapeable** *adj* incomprehensible, inconceivable; stubborn, obstinate
**inapelable** *adj* unappealable; inevitable, unavoidable
**inapercibido -da** *adj* unnoticed
**inapetencia** *f* lack or loss of appetite
**inapetente** *adj* having no appetite, inappetent
**inaplazable** *adj* undeferrable
**inaplicable** *adj* inapplicable
**inaplicación** *f* inapplication, lack of application; inapplicability
**inaplicado -da** *adj* lazy, indolent, careless
**inapolillable** *adj* moth-free, moth-resisting
**inapreciable** *adj* inestimable; imperceptible; inappreciable
**inapto -ta** *adj* inapt
**inarmónico -ca** *adj* unharmonious; unharmonic, inharmonic
**inarrugable** *adj* wrinkle-free (*fabric*)
**inarticulado -da** *adj* inarticulate
**inartístico -ca** *adj* inartistic
**inasequibilidad** *f* inaccessibility
**inasequible** *adj* unattainable, inaccessible
**inasimilable** *adj* unassimilable
**inasistencia** *f* absence
**inastillable** *adj* nonshatterable, unshatterable, shatterproof
**inatacable** *adj* unattackable; unchallengeable, unquestionable; **inatacable por** resistant to, resisting
**inatención** *f* inattention
**inatento -ta** *adj* inattentive
**inaudible** *adj* inaudible
**inaudito -ta** *adj* unheard-of; astounding, extraordinary; outrageous, monstrous
**inauguración** *f* inauguration; unveiling
**inaugural** *adj* inaugural
**inaugurar** *va* to inaugurate; to unveil (*e.g., a statue*)
**inavenible** *adj* uncompromising, disagreeable
**inaveriguable** *adj* unascertainable
**inaveriguado -da** *adj* not ascertained, not checked
**inca** *mf* Inca; *m* Inca (*ruler*)
**incaico -ca** *adj* Inca, Incan
**incalculable** *adj* incalculable
**incalificable** *adj* unqualifiable; unspeakable
**incalmable** *adj* unsubduable
**incambiable** *adj* unchangeable; unexchangeable
**incandescencia** *f* incandescence
**incandescente** *adj* incandescent
**incansable** *adj* indefatigable, untiring
**incantable** *adj* unsingable
**incapacidad** *f* incapacity, inability, incapability
**incapacitar** *va* to incapacitate; to declare incompetent
**incapaz** *adj* (*pl:* **-paces**) incapable, unable; incompetent; not large enough; simple, stupid; crude, ignorant; (coll.) impossible, unbearable, frightful
**incarceración** *f* (path.) incarceration
**incasable** *adj* unmarriageable; unmarriable; opposed to getting married
**incásico -ca** *adj* var. of **incaico**
**incasto -ta** *adj* unchaste
**incautación** *f* (law) seizure, attachment
**incautar** *vr;* **incautarse de** to hold (*until claimed*); (law) to seize, to attach
**incauto -ta** *adj* unwary, heedless, incautious
**incendaja** *f* kindling
**incendiar** *va* to set on fire; *vr* to catch fire
**incendiario -ria** *adj* incendiary; *mf* incendiary, firebug
**incendio** *m* fire (*conflagration*); consuming passion
**incensación** *f* (act of) incensing or burning incense
**incensada** *f* swing of incense burner; flattery

**incensar** §18 *va* to incense, perfume with incense; (fig.) to incense, to flatter
**incensario** *m* incensory, censer, incense burner
**incensurable** *adj* unblamable
**incentivo -va** *adj & m* incentive
**inceremonioso -sa** *adj* unceremonious
**incertidumbre** *f* uncertainty, incertitude
**incertísimo -ma** *adj super* very or most uncertain
**incesable** *adj* unceasing
**incesante** *adj* incessant
**incesto** *m* incest
**incestuoso -sa** *adj* incestuous; *mf* incestuous person
**incidencia** *f* incidence; incident; (geom. & phys.) incidence; **por incidencia** by chance
**incidental** *adj* incidental
**incidente** *adj* incident; incidental; *m* incident
**incidir** *va* to cut, make an incision in; *vn* to fall; to fall into error; **incidir en** or **sobre** to impinge on, to strike
**incienso** *m* incense; frankincense; (bot.) southernwood; (fig.) incense
**incierto -ta** *adj* uncertain
**incindir** *va* to cut, make an incision in
**incinerable** *adj* incinerable; to be withdrawn from circulation and burned (*said of bank notes*)
**incineración** *f* incineration; **incineración de cadáveres** cremation
**incinerador** *m* incinerator
**incinerar** *va* to incinerate, to cremate
**incipiente** *adj* incipient
**incircunciso -sa** *adj* uncircumcised
**incircunscripto -ta** *adj* uncircumscribed
**incisión** *f* incision; caesura; incisiveness, sarcasm
**incisivo -va** *adj* incisive; barbed, caustic; (anat.) incisive; *m* (anat.) incisor
**inciso -sa** *adj* choppy (*style of writing*); (bot.) incised; *m* sentence; clause; comma
**incisorio -ria** *adj* incisory
**incitación** *f* incitation
**incitamento** or **incitamiento** *m* incitement
**incitar** *va* to incite; **incitar a** + *inf* to incite to + *inf*
**incivil** *adj* uncivil
**incivilidad** *f* incivility
**incivilizado -da** *adj* uncivilized
**inclasificable** *adj* unclassifiable
**inclaustración** *f* entry into a convent or monastery
**inclemencia** *f* inclemency; **a la inclemencia** exposed, shelterless
**inclemente** *adj* inclement
**inclinación** *f* inclination; bent, leaning; bow
**inclinado -da** *adj* inclined; **bien inclinado** well-disposed, good-natured; **mal inclinado** ill-disposed, ill-natured
**inclinar** *va* to incline, to bend, to bow; to move, impel, turn; *vn* to incline, bend, bow; **inclinar a** to resemble; *vr* to incline, be inclined, tend; to bow; **inclinarse a** to resemble; to be inclined to; **inclinarse a** + *inf* to be inclined to + *inf*
**inclinómetro** *m* inclinometer
**ínclito -ta** *adj* illustrious, distinguished
**incluir** §41 *va* to include; to inclose
**inclusa** *f* see **incluso**
**inclusero -ra** *adj* (coll.) raised as a foundling; *mf* (coll.) foundling
**inclusión** *f* inclusion; friendship
**inclusive** *adv* inclusively; *prep* including
**inclusivo -va** *adj* inclusive, including
**incluso -sa** *adj* inclosed; *f* foundling home or asylum; **incluso** *adv* inclusively; even; *prep* including
**incoación** *f* (law) initiation
**incoagulable** *adj* uncoagulable
**incoar** *va* (law) to initiate
**incoativo -va** *adj* (gram.) inchoative
**incobrable** *adj* irrecoverable; uncollectible
**incoercible** *adj* incoercible
**incógnito -ta** *adj* unknown; incognito; *mf* incognito (*person*); *m* incognito (*state*); **de incógnito** incognito; *f* (math. & fig.) unknown quantity
**incognoscible** *adj* unknowable
**incoherencia** *f* incoherence
**incoherente** *adj* incoherent
**íncola** *m* inhabitant
**incoloro -ra** *adj* colorless
**incólume** *adj* unharmed, sound, safe, untouched
**incolumidad** *f* safeness, security; preservation
**incombustibilidad** *f* incombustibility
**incombustibilización** *f* fireproofing
**incombustible** *adj* incombustible; fireproof; (fig.) cold, indifferent
**incombusto -ta** *adj* unburned
**incomerciable** *adj* unsalable, unmarketable; unnegotiable (*that cannot be got past*)
**incomible** *adj* (coll.) uneatable, inedible
**incomodar** *va* to incommode, inconvenience; *vr* to become vexed, get annoyed; to inconvenience oneself, to be inconvenienced
**incomodidad** *f* inconvenience; discomfort, uncomfortableness; anger, annoyance
**incómodo -da** *adj* inconvenient; uncomfortable; *m* inconvenience; discomfort
**incomparable** or **incomparado -da** *adj* incomparable
**incomparencia** *f* failure to appear
**incompartible** *adj* indivisible; unsharable
**incompasivo -va** *adj* pitiless, unsympathetic
**incompatibilidad** *f* incompatibility
**incompatible** *adj* incompatible; conflicting
**incompetencia** *f* incompetence or incompetency
**incompetente** *adj* incompetent
**incompetible** *adj* unmatchable (*price*)
**incomplejo -ja** *adj* incomplex, simple
**incompleto -ta** *adj* incomplete
**incomplexo -xa** *adj* incomplex, simple
**incomponible** *adj* unmendable, unrepairable
**incomportable** *adj* unbearable, intolerable
**incomposibilidad** *f* unmendable condition; incompatibility
**incomposible** *adj* unmendable; incompatible
**incomprable** *adj* unpurchasable
**incomprehensibilidad** *f* incomprehensibility
**incomprehensible** *adj* incomprehensible
**incomprendido -da** *adj* misunderstood
**incomprensibilidad** *f* incomprehensibility
**incomprensible** *adj* incomprehensible
**incomprensivo -va** *adj* unintelligent, ignorant
**incompresibilidad** *f* incompressibility
**incompresible** *adj* incompressible
**incomunicabilidad** *f* incommunicability
**incomunicable** *adj* incommunicable
**incomunicación** *f* isolation, solitary confinement
**incomunicado -da** *adj* incommunicado
**incomunicar** §86 *va* to isolate, put in solitary confinement; to close, shut off; *vr* to isolate oneself, become isolated
**inconcebibilidad** *f* inconceivability
**inconcebible** *adj* inconceivable
**inconciliable** *adj* irreconcilable
**inconcino -na** *adj* disarranged, disordered
**inconcluso -sa** *adj* unfinished
**inconcluyente** *adj* inconclusive
**inconcuso -sa** *adj* undeniable, unquestionable
**incondicional** *adj* unconditional
**inconducente** *adj* unconducive
**inconel** *m* inconel
**inconexión** *f* disconnection; irrelevance
**inconexo -xa** *adj* unconnected, disconnected; irrelevant
**inconfeso -sa** *adj* unconfessed
**inconfidencia** *f* distrust
**inconfidente** *adj* distrustful
**inconforme** *adj* in disagreement, out of sympathy
**inconfundible** *adj* unmistakable
**incongelable** *adj* uncongealable
**incongelado -da** *adj* uncongealed, unfrozen
**incongruencia** *f* incongruity
**incongruente** *adj* incongruent, incongruous
**incongruo -grua** *adj* incongruous
**inconmensurabilidad** *f* incommensurability
**inconmensurable** *adj* incommensurable, incommensurate
**inconmovible** *adj* firm, lasting; unyielding, inexorable
**inconmutable** *adj* immutable; unexchangeable
**inconocible** *adj* unknowable
**inconquistable** *adj* unconquerable; unbending

**inconsciencia** *f* unconsciousness; unawareness, insensibility; inattention, inadvertence
**inconsciente** *adj* unconscious; unaware, insensible; oblivious; **lo inconsciente** the unconscious
**inconsecuencia** *f* inconsequence; inconsistency
**inconsecuente** *adj* inconsequent, inconsequential; inconsistent
**inconsideración** *f* inconsiderateness
**inconsiderado -da** *adj* inconsiderate
**inconsiguiente** *adj* inconsistent
**inconsistencia** *f* inconsistency
**inconsistente** *adj* inconsistent
**inconsolable** *adj* inconsolable
**inconsonante** *adj* inconsonant
**inconstancia** *f* inconstancy
**inconstante** *adj* inconstant
**inconstitucional** *adj* unconstitutional
**inconstitucionalidad** *f* unconstitutionality
**inconstruíble** *adj* unbuildable
**inconsútil** *adj* seamless
**incontable** *adj* uncountable, countless
**incontaminado -da** *adj* uncontaminated
**incontenible** *adj* irrepressible
**incontestable** *adj* incontestable, unanswerable, unquestionable
**incontestado -da** *adj* unquestioned
**incontinencia** *f* incontinence; (path.) incontinence
**incontinente** *adj* incontinent; *adv* at once, instantly
**incontinenti** *adv* at once, instantly
**incontrastable** *adj* invincible; inconvincible
**incontratable** *adj* unruly; unsociable; undeniable
**incontrolado -da** *adj* uncontrolled
**incontrovertibilidad** *f* incontrovertibility
**incontrovertible** *adj* incontrovertible
**inconvencible** *adj* inconvincible
**inconvenible** *adj* intractable, uncompromising
**inconveniencia** *f* inconvenience; unsuitability; impoliteness, impropriety; absurdity, nonsense
**inconveniente** *adj* inconvenient; unsuitable; impolite; *m* obstacle, difficulty; damage
**inconversable** *adj* unsociable, uncommunicative, surly
**inconvertibilidad** *f* inconvertibility
**inconvertible** *adj* inconvertible
**incoördinación** *f* incoördination
**incordio** *m* (path.) bubo; (slang) nuisance, boor
**incorporación** *f* incorporation, embodiment; association, participation
**incorporadero** *m* (metal.) patio
**incorporado -da** *adj* sitting up (*from reclining position*); built-in
**incorporal** *adj* incorporeal, intangible
**incorporar** *va* to incorporate, to embody; *vr* to incorporate; to sit up (*from reclining position*); to associate, participate; **incorporarse a** to join (*a society*)
**incorporeidad** *f* incorporealness, incorporeity
**incorpóreo -a** *adj* incorporeal, bodiless
**incorrección** *f* incorrectness
**incorrecto -ta** *adj* incorrect
**incorregibilidad** *f* incorrigibility
**incorregible** *adj* incorrigible
**incorrupción** *f* incorruptness, purity
**incorruptibilidad** *f* incorruptibility
**incorruptible** *adj* incorruptible
**incorrupto -ta** *adj* uncorrupted, incorrupt; pure, chaste
**increado -da** *adj* uncreated
**incredibilidad** *f* incredibility
**incredulidad** *f* incredulity; disbelief
**incrédulo -la** *adj* incredulous; unbelieving; *mf* unbeliever, disbeliever
**increíble** *adj* incredible
**incrementar** *va* to increase
**incremento** *m* increase, increment; (math.) increment
**increpación** *f* chiding, rebuke
**increpador -dora** *adj* chiding; *mf* chider, rebuker
**increpar** *va* to chide, rebuke
**incriminación** *f* incrimination; exaggeration of guilt
**incriminar** *va* to incriminate; to exaggerate the gravity of (*a defect, weakness, misdeed, etc.*)
**incristalizable** *adj* uncrystallizable
**incruento -ta** *adj* bloodless
**incrustación** *f* incrustation; inlay
**incrustante** *adj* incrustive
**incrustar** *va* to incrust; to inlay; *vr* to incrust; to become engraved (*in the memory*)
**incubación** *f* incubation
**incubadora** *f* incubator
**incubar** *va & vn* to incubate; *vr* to brew, be brewing
**íncubo** *m* incubus; (med.) incubus
**incuestionable** *adj* unquestionable
**inculcación** *f* inculcation; (print.) locking
**inculcar** **§86** *va* to inculcate; (print.) to lock up; *vr* to be obstinate
**inculpabilidad** *f* inculpability, blamelessness, guiltlessness
**inculpable** *adj* inculpable, blameless, guiltless
**inculpación** *f* inculpation
**inculpadamente** *adv* faultlessly
**inculpado -da** *adj* faultless, innocent; accused, charged with guilt
**inculpar** *va* to blame, accuse, inculpate
**incultivable** *adj* untillable
**inculto -ta** *adj* uncultivated; untilled; uncultured; uncivilized
**incultura** *f* lack of cultivation; lack of culture
**incumbencia** *f* incumbency; duty, obligation; **ser de la incumbencia de** to be within the province of
**incumbente** *adj* incumbent; (bot. & zool.) incumbent
**incumbir** *vn* to be incumbent; **incumbir a** to be incumbent on; **incumbir a uno** + *inf* to become incumbent on one to + *inf*
**incumplido -da** *adj* unfulfilled; unpunctual
**incumplimiento** *m* nonfulfillment, unfulfillment, breach
**incumplir** *va* to not fulfill, to fail to fulfill
**incunable** *adj* incunabular; *m* incunabulum
**incurabilidad** *f* incurability
**incurable** *adj & mf* incurable
**incuria** *f* carelessness, negligence
**incurioso -sa** *adj* careless, negligent
**incurrimiento** *m* incurring
**incurrir** *vn* to become liable; **incurrir en** to incur
**incursión** *f* incursion, inroad, attack, raid
**incusar** *va* to accuse
**incuso -sa** *adj* incuse
**indagación** *f* investigation
**indagador -dora** *adj* investigating; *mf* investigator
**indagar** **§59** *va* to investigate
**indagatorio -ria** *adj* (law) investigatory
**indebido -da** *adj* undue; illegal, unlawful; improper
**indecencia** *f* indecency
**indecentada** *f* shame, infamy
**indecente** *adj* indecent
**indecible** *adj* unspeakable, unutterable
**indecisión** *f* indecision
**indeciso -sa** *adj* undecided; indecisive
**indeclinable** *adj* undeclinable; undeniable; (gram.) undeclinable, indeclinable
**indecoro** *m* indecorum
**indecoroso -sa** *adj* indecorous, improper
**indefectible** *adj* unfailing, indefectible
**indefendible** or **indefensible** *adj* indefensible
**indefensión** *f* defenselessness
**indefenso -sa** *adj* undefended, unguarded, defenseless
**indefinible** *adj* indefinable or undefinable; unexpressible; incomprehensible
**indefinido -da** *adj* indefinite, vague; limitless
**indehiscencia** *f* (bot.) indehiscence
**indehiscente** *adj* (bot.) indehiscent
**indelebilidad** *f* indelibility
**indeleble** *adj* indelible
**indeliberación** *f* lack of deliberation, indeliberation
**indeliberado -da** *adj* unpremeditated, indeliberate
**indelicadeza** *f* indelicacy
**indelicado -da** *adj* indelicate
**indemne** *adj* undamaged
**indemnidad** *f* indemnity (*security against damage or loss*)

**indemnización** *f* indemnification; indemnity; **indemnización por despido** severance pay
**indemnizar §76** *va* to indemnify; to reimburse
**indemostrable** *adj* undemonstrable, indemonstrable
**independencia** *f* independence
**independiente** *adj* independent; **independiente de** independent of; **independientes entre sí** independent of each other; *mf* independent
**independista** *adj* (pertaining to) independence; *mf* advocate of independence
**independizar §76** *va* to free, emancipate; *vr* to make oneself independent, become independent
**indescifrable** *adj* indecipherable
**indescriptible** *adj* undescribable, indescribable
**indeseable** *adj* undesirable
**indeseado -da** *adj* unwanted
**indesignable** *adj* undeterminable
**indesmallable** *adj* run-proof, hole-proof (*mesh or net*)
**indestructibilidad** *f* indestructibility
**indestructible** *adj* indestructible
**indeterminabilidad** *f* indeterminability
**indeterminable** *adj* undeterminable, indeterminable
**indeterminación** *f* indetermination
**indeterminado -da** *adj* indeterminate
**indeterminismo** *m* indeterminism
**indeterminista** *adj* indeterminist, indeterministic; *mf* indeterminist
**indevoción** *f* indevotion, impiety
**indevoto -ta** *adj* undevout; not fond, not devoted
**indezuelo -la** *mf* little Indian
**india** *f* & **la India** see **indio**
**indiada** *f* (Am.) gang of Indians
**indiana** *f* see **indiano**
**indianismo** *m* Indianism
**indianista** *mf* Indianist
**indiano -na** *adj* Spanish American; East Indian; West Indian; *mf* Spanish American; East Indian; West Indian; person back from America with great wealth; **indiano de hilo negro** (coll.) skinflint; *f* printed calico
**indicación** *f* indication; **por indicación de** at the direction of
**indicado -da** *adj* set, appointed; obvious, appropriate; **muy indicado** just the thing
**indicador -dora** *adj* indicating; indicatory; *mf* indicator; *m* indicator; (chem.) indicator; **indicadores de dirección** (aut.) turn signals
**indicán** *m* (chem. & biochem.) indican
**indicante** *adj & m* indicant
**indicanuria** *f* (path.) indicanuria
**indicar §86** *va* to indicate
**indicativo -va** *adj* indicative; (gram.) indicative; *m* (gram.) indicative; **indicativo de llamada** (telg.) call letters
**indicción** *f* indiction
**índice** *m* index; (math.) index; **índice de compresión** (mach.) compression index; **índice de libros prohibidos** (eccl.) Index; **índice de materias** table of contents; **índice de octano** (chem.) octane number or rating; **índice de oro** (chem.) gold number; **índice de refracción** (phys.) index of refraction; **índice en el corte** thumb index; **índice expurgatorio** (eccl.) Index Expurgatorius; **índice onomástico** index of proper names
**indiciar** *va* to suspect, surmise; to betoken, indicate
**indicio** *m* sign, token, indication; **indicios** *mpl* (chem.) traces; (law) evidence; **indicios vehementes** (law) circumstantial evidence
**índico -ca** *adj* East Indian
**indiferencia** *f* indifference
**indiferente** *adj* indifferent
**indiferentismo** *m* indifferentism
**indígena** *adj* indigenous; *mf* native
**indigencia** *f* indigence
**indigente** *adj* indigent; **los indigentes** the indigent
**indigerible** *adj* indigestible
**indigestar** *va* to make (*food*) indigestible; *vr* to have indigestion; to cause indigestion, to be indigestible; to be disliked, be unbearable
**indigestibilidad** *f* indigestibility
**indigestible** *adj* indigestible
**indigestión** *f* indigestion
**indigesto -ta** *adj* undigested
**indignación** *f* indignation
**indignado -da** *adj* indignant
**indignar** *va* to anger, irritate, make indignant; *vr* to get indignant; **indignarse con** or **contra** to become indignant at (*a person*); **indignarse de** or **por** to become indignant at (*a mean act*); **indignarse de** + *inf* to be or become indignant at + *ger*
**indignidad** *f* unworthiness; indignity
**indigno -na** *adj* unworthy; low, contemptible
**índigo** *m* (bot. & chem.) indigo; indigo (*of the solar spectrum*)
**indiligencia** *f* negligence, laziness
**indino -na** *adj* (coll.) saucy, mischievous
**indio -dia** *adj* Indian; blue; *mf* Indian (*of America or Asia*); *m* (chem.) indium; *f* wealth, riches; **la India** India; **Indias Occidentales** West Indies; **Indias Occidentales Holandesas** Dutch West Indies; **Indias Orientales** East Indies; **Indias Orientales Holandesas** Dutch East Indies
**indirecto -ta** *adj* indirect; *f* hint, innuendo; **indirecta del padre Cobos** broad hint
**indiscernibilidad** *f* indiscernibility
**indiscernible** *adj* indiscernible
**indisciplina** *f* indiscipline, lack of discipline
**indisciplinable** *adj* indisciplinable
**indisciplinado -da** *adj* undisciplined; insubordinate
**indisciplinar** *va* to disturb the discipline of; *vr* to disregard discipline, become undisciplined
**indiscreción** *f* indiscretion
**indiscreto -ta** *adj* indiscreet
**indisculpable** *adj* inexcusable
**indiscutible** *adj* unquestionable, indisputable, undeniable
**indisolubilidad** *f* indissolubility
**indisoluble** *adj* indissoluble
**indispensabilidad** *f* indispensability
**indispensable** *adj* indispensable; unpardonable
**indispondré** *1st sg fut ind of* **indisponer**
**indisponer §69** *va* to upset (*e.g., a plan*); to indispose; **indisponer a una persona con** to prejudice or set a person against; *vr* to become indisposed; **indisponerse con** to fall out with
**indispongo** *1st sg pres ind of* **indisponer**
**indisposición** *f* unpreparedness; indisposition; disagreement, unpleasantness
**indispuesto -ta** *pp* of **indisponer;** *adj* indisposed (*slightly ill*)
**indispuse** *1st sg pret ind of* **indisponer**
**indisputabilidad** *f* indisputability
**indisputable** *adj* indisputable
**indistinción** *f* indistinctness; identity; lack of distinction
**indistinguible** *adj* indistinguishable
**indistinto -ta** *adj* indistinct
**individuación** *f* individuation
**individual** *adj* individual; single (*e.g., room*)
**individualidad** *f* individuality
**individualismo** *m* individualism
**individualista** *adj* individualistic; *mf* individualist
**individualizar §76** *va* to individualize
**individualmente** *adv* individually
**individuamente** *adv* indivisibly, inseparately
**individuo -dua** *adj* individual; indivisible, inseparable; *mf* (coll.) individual (*person*); *m* individual; member, fellow (*of a society, etc.*); (biol.) individual; **su individuo** one's own self
**indivisibilidad** *f* indivisibility
**indivisible** *adj* indivisible
**indivisión** *f* indivision, entirety, oneness
**indiviso -sa** *adj* undivided; joint (*property*)
**indo -da** *adj & mf* Hindu; (*cap.*) *m* Indus (*river*)
**indoblegable** *adj* inflexible, unyielding
**indócil** *adj* indocile, unteachable
**indocilidad** *f* indocility, unteachableness
**indocto -ta** *adj* unlearned, ignorant
**indocumentado -da** *adj* unidentified, without identifying documents; *mf* nobody (*person of no account*)
**indochino -na** *adj & mf* Indochinese; **la Indochina** Indochina; **la Indochina Francesa** French Indochina
**indoeuropeo -a** *adj & m* Indo-European
**indofenol** *m* (chem.) indophenol

**indogermánico -ca** *adj & m* Indo-Germanic
**indol** *m* (chem.) indole
**índole** *f* temper, disposition; class, kind
**indolencia** *f* indolence; absence of pain or suffering
**indolente** *adj* indolent; (med.) indolent
**indoloro -ra** *adj* painless
**indomable** *adj* indomitable; uncontrollable
**indomado -da** *adj* untamed
**indomalayo -ya** *adj* Indo-Malayan
**indomeñable** *adj* var. of **indomable**
**indomesticable** *adj* untamable
**indomesticado -da** *adj* undomesticated
**indoméstico -ca** *adj* untamed; wild, undomesticated
**indómito -ta** *adj* untamable, indomitable; unruly
**indonesio -sia** *adj & mf* Indonesian; **la Indonesia** Indonesia
**Indostán, el** Hindustan
**indostanés -nesa** *adj* Hindustani; *mf* native or inhabitant of Hindustan
**indostaní** *m* Hindustani (*language*)
**indostánico -ca** *adj* Hindustani
**indostano -na** *adj & mf* var. of **indostanés**
**indotación** *f* lack of dowry
**indotado -da** *adj* without a dowry
**indoxilo** *m* (chem.) indoxyl
**indubitable** *adj* indubitable, doubtless
**indubitado -da** *adj* undoubted, certain
**inducción** *f* (log. & elec.) induction; **inducción electromagnética** (elec.) electromagnetic induction; **inducción mutua** (elec.) mutual induction
**inducido** *m* (elec.) armature (*of motor or dynamo*); **inducido de tambor** (elec.) drum armature
**inducir** §38 *va* to induce; (log.) to induce, to infer; (elec.) to induce; **inducir a** + *inf* to induce to + *inf;* **inducir en error** to lead into error
**inductancia** *f* (elec.) inductance; **inductancia mutua** (elec.) mutual inductance
**inductividad** *f* inductivity
**inductivo -va** *adj* inductive
**inductor -tora** or **-triz** (*pl:* **-trices**) *adj* inducing; inductive; *m* instigator; (elec.) inductor, field
**indudable** *adj* indubitable, certain, doubtless
**induje** *1st sg pret ind of* **inducir**
**indulgencia** *f* indulgence; **indulgencia plenaria** (eccl.) plenary indulgence
**indulgenciar** *va* to indulge, grant an indulgence to
**indulgente** *adj* indulgent
**indultar** *va* to pardon; to free, to exempt
**indulto** *m* pardon; exemption
**indumentario -ria** *adj* (pertaining to) clothing; *f* historical study of clothing; garb, clothing, dress
**indumento** *m* clothing; (bot.) indumentum
**induración** *f* induration; (med.) induration
**indurar** *va* (med.) to indurate
**indusio** *m* (bot.) indusium
**industria** *f* industry; effort, ingenuity; profession; **de industria** on purpose
**industrial** *adj* industrial; *m* industrialist
**industrialismo** *m* industrialism
**industrialización** *f* industrialization
**industrializar** §76 *va* to industrialize; *vr* to become industrialized
**industriar** *va* to train, teach, instruct; *vr* to manage, to get along
**industrioso -sa** *adj* industrious; hard-working; clever, skilful
**induzco** *1st sg pres ind of* **inducir**
**inedia** *f* fasting; inanition
**inédito -ta** *adj* unpublished; new, unknown
**ineducable** *adj* uneducable
**ineducación** *f* lack of education; unmannerliness
**ineducado -da** *adj* uneducated; ill-bred
**inefabilidad** *f* ineffability
**inefable** *adj* ineffable
**ineficacia** *f* inefficacy
**ineficaz** *adj* (*pl:* **-caces**) ineffective, ineffectual
**ineficiencia** *f* inefficiency
**ineficiente** *adj* inefficient
**inelasticidad** *f* inelasticity
**inelástico -ca** *adj* inelastic
**inelegancia** *f* inelegance or inelegancy
**inelegante** *adj* inelegant
**inelegibilidad** *f* ineligibility
**inelegible** *adj* ineligible
**ineluctable** *adj* ineluctable
**ineludible** *adj* inescapable, inevitable
**inenarrable** *adj* inexpressible, untold
**inencogible** *adj* unshrinkable
**inencontrable** *adj* unfindable
**inepcia** *f* silliness; ineptitude
**ineptitud** *f* inaptitude, ineptitude; gaucherie
**inepto -ta** *adj* inapt, inept; gauche
**inequidad** *f* inequity
**inequívoco -ca** *adj* unequivocal, unmistakable, unambiguous
**inercia** *f* inertia; (mech.) inertia; **inercia de la matriz** (med.) inertia
**inercial** *adj* inertial
**inerme** *adj* unarmed; (biol.) unarmed
**inerte** *adj* inert; slow, sluggish; inactive
**inerudito -ta** *adj* unscholarly
**inervación** *f* innervation
**Inés** *f* Agnes
**inescrutabilidad** *f* inscrutability
**inescrutable** or **inescudriñable** *adj* inscrutable
**inesperable** *adj* not to be hoped for, not to be expected
**inesperado -da** *adj* unexpected, unforeseen
**inestabilidad** *f* instability
**inestable** *adj* unstable, instable
**inestimabilidad** *f* inestimability
**inestimable** *adj* inestimable
**inestimado -da** *adj* unestimated; underestimated
**inestorbado -da** *adj* unchecked; undisturbed
**inevitabilidad** *f* inevitability
**inevitable** *adj* inevitable, unavoidable
**inexactitud** *f* inexactness
**inexacto -ta** *adj* inexact
**inexcusable** *adj* inexcusable; indispensable; inescapable, indefeasible
**inexhausto -ta** *adj* unexhausted
**inexistencia** *f* inexistence, nonexistence
**inexistente** *adj* inexistent, nonexistent
**inexorabilidad** *f* inexorability
**inexorable** *adj* inexorable
**inexperiencia** *f* inexperience
**inexperto -ta** *adj* inexperienced, inexpert
**inexpiable** *adj* inexpiable
**inexplicable** *adj* inexplicable, unexplainable
**inexplicado -da** *adj* unexplained
**inexplorado -da** *adj* unexplored
**inexplosible** *adj* unexplosive
**inexplotado -da** *adj* unexploited
**inexpresable** *adj* inexpressible
**inexpresivo -va** *adj* inexpressive
**inexpuesto -ta** *adj* (phot.) unexposed
**inexpugnabilidad** *f* inexpugnability, impregnability
**inexpugnable** *adj* inexpugnable, impregnable; firm, unpersuadable
**inextensible** *adj* unextendible, unstretchable
**inextenso -sa** *adj* unextended
**inextinguible** *adj* inextinguishable, unextinguishable; lasting, perpetual
**inextinto -ta** *adj* unextinguished
**inextirpable** *adj* ineradicable
**inextricabilidad** *f* inextricability
**inextricable** *adj* inextricable
**infacundo -da** *adj* ineloquent, not fluent
**infalibilidad** *f* infallibility
**infalible** *adj* infallible
**infamación** *f* defamation
**infamador -dora** *adj* defaming, slanderous; *mf* defamer
**infamante** *adj* opprobrious; (law) infamous (*punishment*)
**infamar** *va* to defame, discredit
**infamativo -va** *adj* defaming, slanderous
**infamatorio -ria** *adj* defamatory, libelous
**infame** *adj* infamous; (coll.) frightful; *mf* scoundrel
**infamia** *f* infamy
**infancia** *f* infancy; (fig.) infancy
**infando -da** *adj* frightful, unmentionable
**infanta** *f* female infant; infanta
**infantado** *m* appanage

**infante** *m* infant; infante; (mil.) infantryman; **infante de coro** (eccl.) choirboy; **infante de marina** (mil.) marine
**infantería** *f* infantry; **infantería de marina** marines, marine corps
**infanticida** *adj* infanticidal; *mf* infanticide (*person*)
**infanticidio** *m* infanticide (*act*)
**infantil** *adj* infantile, infant; innocent; infantile, childlike; children's
**infantilismo** *m* childishness; infantilism
**infanzón** *m* nobleman of limited rights
**infanzona** *f* noblewoman of limited rights
**infartación** *f* (path.) infarction
**infartar** *va* (path.) to produce an infarct in
**infarto** *m* (path.) infarct
**infatigabilidad** *f* indefatigability
**infatigable** *adj* indefatigable
**infatuación** *f* vanity, conceit
**infatuar** **§33** *va* to make vain or conceited; *vr* to become vain or conceited
**infausto -ta** *adj* unlucky, fatal
**infebril** *adj* feverless
**infección** *f* infection; **infección focal** (path.) focal infection
**infeccionar** *va* to infect
**infeccioso -sa** *adj* infectious
**infectar** *va* to infect; *vr* to become infected
**infectividad** *f* infectivity
**infectivo -va** *adj* infective
**infecto -ta** *adj* infected; foul, corrupt
**infecundidad** *f* sterility, infecundity
**infecundo -da** *adj* sterile, infecund
**infelice** *adj* (poet.) var. of **infeliz**
**infelicidad** *f* infelicity; misfortune
**infeliz** (*pl:* **-lices**) *adj* unhappy; (coll.) simple, good-hearted; *m* wretch, poor soul
**inferencia** *f* inference
**inferior** *adj* inferior; lower; **inferior a** inferior to; lower than; less than, smaller than; *m* inferior
**inferioridad** *f* inferiority
**inferir** **§62** *va* to infer; to entail, lead to; to cause, inflict; to offer (*e.g., an insult*)
**infernáculo** *m* hopscotch
**infernal** *adj* infernal; (coll.) infernal (*very bad, detestable*)
**infernar** **§18** *va* to damn; to vex, irritate
**infernillo** *m* chafing dish
**inferno -na** *adj* (poet.) infernal
**ínfero -ra** *adj* (bot.) inferior, lower, under
**infestación** *f* infestation
**infestar** *va* to infest; *vr* to become infested
**infesto -ta** *adj* (poet.) harmful
**inficionamiento** *m* infection
**inficionar** *va* to infect; *vr* to become infected
**infidelidad** *f* infidelity; unbelievers
**infidelísimo -ma** *adj super* very or most unfaithful
**infidencia** *f* faithlessness; treason
**infidente** *adj* faithless, disloyal; treasonable
**ínfido -da** *adj* faithless, disloyal
**infiel** *adj* unfaithful; inaccurate, inexact; infidel; *mf* infidel
**infiernillo** *m* chafing dish
**infierno** *m* hell; inferno; hades; chafing dish; **en el quinto infierno** or **en los quintos infiernos** (coll.) far, far away
**infigurable** *adj* incorporeal; unimaginable
**infiltración** *f* infiltration
**infiltrar** *va & vr* to infiltrate
**ínfimo -ma** *adj* lowest; least; humblest, most abject; meanest, vilest
**infinible** *adj* interminable
**infinidad** *f* infinity
**infinitesimal** *adj* infinitesimal
**infinitésimo** *m* (math.) infinitesimal
**infinitivo -va** *adj & m* (gram.) infinitive
**infinito -ta** *adj* infinite; *m* infinite; (math.) infinity; **a lo infinito** or **hasta lo infinito** ad infinitum; **el infinito** the Infinite (*God*); **infinito** *adv* infinitely, extremely, immensely
**infinitud** *f* infinitude
**infirmar** *va* (law) to invalidate
**inflación** *f* inflation; vanity, conceit
**inflacionismo** *m* inflationism
**inflacionista** *adj* inflationary; *mf* inflationist
**inflado** *m* inflation (*e.g., of a tire*)
**inflamabilidad** *f* inflammability
**inflamable** *adj* inflammable, flamable
**inflamación** *f* inflammation, ignition; enthusiasm, ardor; (path.) inflammation; **inflamación espontánea** spontaneous combustion
**inflamado -da** *adj* sore, inflamed
**inflamar** *va* to inflame; to set on fire; *vr* to inflame, become inflamed; to catch fire
**inflamatorio -ria** *adj* inflammatory
**inflamiento** *m* var. of **inflación**
**inflar** *va* to inflate; to exaggerate; to puff up with pride; *vn* to inflate; to be puffed up with pride
**inflativo -va** *adj* inflating
**inflatorio -ria** *adj* inflationary
**inflexibilidad** *f* inflexibility
**inflexible** *adj* inflexible; unbending, unyielding
**inflexión** *f* inflection; (geom. & gram.) inflection
**infligir** **§42** *va* to inflict; **infligir a** to inflict on
**inflorescencia** *f* (bot.) inflorescence (*arrangement*)
**influencia** *f* influence; (theol.) divine grace
**influenciar** *va* to influence
**influenza** *f* (path.) influenza
**influir** **§41** *vn* to influence, to have influence; to have great weight; **influir sobre** or **en** to influence, to have an influence on
**influjo** *m* influence; (naut.) rising tide
**influyente** *adj* influential
**infolio** *m* folio (*book*)
**inforciado** *m* infortiate
**información** *f* information; testimonial; (law) brief; (law) investigation, judicial inquiry; **abrir una información** (law) to begin legal proceedings; **a título de información** unofficially
**informador -dora** *adj* informing; *mf* informer; reporter
**informal** *adj* informal; unreliable; *m* unreliable fellow
**informalidad** *f* informality; unreliability
**informante** *mf* informant
**informar** *va* to inform; to shape, fill, give form to; *vn* to inform; (law) to plead; **informar contra** to inform against; *vr* to inquire, find out; **informarse de** to inquire into, find out about, investigate
**informativo -va** *adj* informational, informative; (pertaining to) news
**informe** *adj* shapeless, formless; *m* information; item of information, piece of information; notice; report; **informes** *mpl* information
**informidad** *f* shapelessness, formlessness
**infortificable** *adj* unfortifiable
**infortuna** *f* (astrol.) adverse influence of stars
**infortunado -da** *adj* unfortunate, unlucky
**infortunio** *m* misfortune; mishap
**infosura** *f* (vet.) founder
**infracción** *f* infraction, infringement, violation
**infraconsumo** *m* underconsumption
**infracto -ta** *adj* firm, steady, unshakable
**infractor -tora** *adj* violating; *mf* violator, transgressor
**infraestructura** *f* var. of **infrastructura**
**infrahumano -na** *adj* subhuman
**inframundo** *m* underworld
**infrangible** *adj* infrangible, unbreakable
**infranqueable** *adj* impassable
**infrarrojo -ja** *adj & m* infrared
**infrascripto -ta** or **infrascrito -ta** *adj* undersigned; hereinafter mentioned
**infrastructura** *f* (rail.) roadbed
**infrecuencia** *f* infrequence or infrequency
**infrecuente** *adj* infrequent
**infringir** **§42** *va* to infringe
**infructífero -ra** *adj* unfruitful; unprofitable
**infructuosidad** *f* unfruitfulness
**infructuoso -sa** *adj* fruitless, unfruitful
**ínfula** *f* infula; **ínfulas** *spl* conceit, airs; **darse ínfulas** to put on airs
**infumable** *adj* unsmokable; (coll.) unbearable
**infundado -da** *adj* unfounded, ungrounded, baseless
**infundible** *adj* infusible
**infundio** *m* (coll.) story, lie, fib
**infundioso -sa** *adj* (coll.) lying
**infundir** *va* to infuse; to instil

**infurción** *f* ground lease or rent
**infurtir** *va* to full (*cloth*); to felt
**infusibilidad** *f* infusibility
**infusible** *adj* infusible
**infusión** *f* infusion; sprinkling (*to baptize*); **estar en infusión para** (coll.) to be all set for
**infuso -sa** *adj* inspired, given (*by God*)
**infusorio -ria** *adj & m* (zool.) infusorian
**ingenerable** *adj* ingenerable
**ingeniar** *va* to think up, conceive, contrive; *vr* to manage; **ingeniarse a** or **para** + *inf* to manage to + *inf;* **ingeniarse a vivir** or **para ir viviendo** to manage to get along
**ingeniatura** *f* (coll.) ingenuity, cleverness
**ingeniería** *f* engineering
**ingenieril** *adj* engineering
**ingeniero** *m* engineer; **ingeniero de caminos, canales y puertos** government civil engineer; **ingeniero civil** civil engineer; **ingeniero del ejército** army engineer; **ingeniero de minas** mining engineer; **ingeniero de montes** forestry engineer; **ingeniero electricista** electrical engineer; **ingeniero mécanico** mechanical engineer; **ingeniero militar** army engineer; **ingeniero paisajista** landscape engineer; **ingeniero químico** chemical engineer
**ingenio** *m* talent, creative faculty; skill, wit, cleverness; talented person; apparatus, engine, machine; paper cutter; engine of war; (Am.) sugar mill, sugar plantation; **afilar** or **aguzar el ingenio** to sharpen one's wits
**ingeniosidad** *f* ingeniousness, ingenuity; wittiness
**ingenioso -sa** *adj* ingenious; witty
**ingénito -ta** *adj* unbegotten; innate, inborn
**ingente** *adj* huge, enormous
**ingenuidad** *f* ingenuousness
**ingenuo -nua** *adj* ingenuous; (archaic) freeborn
**ingerencia** *f* var. of **injerencia**
**ingeridura** *f* var. of **injeridura**
**ingerir §62** *va & vr* var. of **injerir**
**ingestión** *f* ingestion
**Inglaterra** *f* England; **la Nueva Inglaterra** New England
**ingle** *f* (anat.) groin
**inglés -glesa** *adj* English; **a la inglesa** in the English fashion or manner; *m* Englishman; English (*language*); **el inglés antiguo** Old English; **el inglés básico** Basic English; **el inglés medio** Middle English; **los ingleses** the English (*people*); *f* Englishwoman
**inglesar** *va* to Anglicize
**inglesismo** *m* Anglicism
**inglete** *m* angle of 45°; miter
**inglosable** *adj* unglossable
**ingobernable** *adj* ungovernable, uncontrollable, unruly
**ingramatical** *adj* ungrammatical
**ingratitud** *f* ingratitude, ungratefulness
**ingrato -ta** *adj* thankless (*ungrateful; not appreciated; unrewarding*); harsh, unpleasant; hard, cruel; sterile, unproductive (*soil*); *mf* ingrate
**ingravidez** *f* lightness, tenuousness; weightlessness
**ingrávido -da** *adj* light, tenuous; weightless
**ingrediente** *m* ingredient
**ingresado -da** *mf* admittee, new student
**ingresar** *va* to enter (*e.g., a child in an orphanage*); to deposit, transfer (*money*); *vn* to enter, become a member; to come in (*said of profits, etc.*); *vr* (Am.) to enlist
**ingreso** *m* entrance; ingress; admission; entry, receipts; **ingresos** *mpl* income, revenue
**íngrimo -ma** *adj* (Am.) solitary, alone
**inguinal** or **inguinario -ria** *adj* inguinal
**ingurgitación** *f* ingurgitation
**ingurgitar** *va* to ingurgitate, swallow greedily
**ingustable** *adj* unpalatable, unsavory
**inhábil** *adj* unable; unskilful; unqualified, incompetent; unfit
**inhabilidad** *f* inability, disability; unskilfulness; unfitness
**inhabilitación** *f* disqualification, incapacitation
**inhabilitar** *va* to disqualify, to disable, to incapacitate
**inhabitable** *adj* uninhabitable
**inhabitado -da** *adj* uninhabited
**inhacedero -ra** *adj* unfeasible
**inhalación** *f* (med.) inhalation
**inhalador** *m* (med.) inhaler
**inhalar** *va* (med.) to inhale
**inherencia** *f* inherence
**inherente** *adj* inherent
**inhestar §18** *va & vr* var. of **enhestar**
**inhibición** *f* inhibition
**inhibir** *va* to inhibit; (law) to stay (*a judge from further proceedings*); *vr* to stay out, stay on the side lines
**inhibitivo -va** *adj* inhibitive
**inhibitorio -ria** *adj* inhibitory
**inhiesto -ta** *adj* raised, upright
**inhonestidad** *f* immodesty, indecency
**inhonesto -ta** *adj* immodest, indecent
**inhospedable, inhospitable, inhospital** or **inhospitalario -ria** *adj* inhospitable
**inhospitalidad** *f* inhospitality
**inhóspito -ta** *adj* inhospitable (*affording no shelter or protection*)
**inhumación** *f* inhumation
**inhumanidad** *f* inhumanity
**inhumanitario -ria** *adj* unphilanthropic
**inhumano -na** *adj* inhuman, inhumane; (Am.) dirty, filthy
**inhumar** *va* to inhume
**iniciación** *f* initiation
**iniciado -da** *adj & mf* initiate
**iniciador -dora** *adj* initiating; *mf* initiator
**inicial** *adj & f* initial
**iniciar** *va* to initiate; *vr* to be initiated; (eccl.) to receive first orders
**iniciativo -va** *adj* initiative, initiating; *f* initiative; **tomar la iniciativa** to take the initiative
**inicio** *m* start, beginning, initiation
**inicuo -cua** *adj* iniquitous
**inigualado -da** *adj* unequaled; (math.) uneven
**inimaginable** *adj* unimaginable, inconceivable
**inimicísimo -ma** *adj super* very or most inimical or hostile
**inimitable** *adj* inimitable
**ininflamable** *adj* uninflammable
**ininteligente** *adj* unintelligent
**ininteligible** *adj* unintelligible
**ininterrumpido -da** *adj* uninterrupted
**iniquidad** *f* iniquity
**iniquísimo -ma** *adj super* very or most iniquitous
**injerencia** *f* interference, meddling
**injeridura** *f* (agr.) graft, stock of graft
**injerir §62** *va* (hort.) to graft; to insert, introduce; to ingest; (Am.) to swallow, take in; *vr* to interfere, to meddle
**injertación** *f* (hort. & surg.) grafting
**injertador** *m* (hort.) grafter
**injertar** *va* (hort. & surg.) to engraft, ingraft, graft
**injertera** *f* orchard of transplanted seedlings
**injerto** *m* (hort. & surg.) graft; **injerto cutáneo** (surg.) skin grafting
**injuria** *f* offense, insult; wrong, abuse; harm, damage
**injuriador -dora** *adj* offensive, insulting; abusive; *mf* offender, insulter
**injuriante** *adj* offending, insulting
**injuriar** *va* to offend, insult; to wrong, abuse; to harm, damage, injure
**injurioso -sa** *adj* offensive, insulting; abusive; harmful; profane (*language*)
**injusticia** *f* injustice
**injustificable** *adj* unjustifiable, unwarrantable
**injustificado -da** *adj* unjustified
**injusto -ta** *adj* unjust
**inllevable** *adj* unbearable, insupportable
**inmaculado -da** *adj* immaculate; **Inmaculada Concepción** Immaculate Conception
**inmadurez** *f* immaturity; flightiness
**inmanejable** *adj* unmanageable, unruly; unwieldy
**inmanencia** *f* immanence
**inmanente** *adj* immanent
**inmarcesible** or **inmarchitable** *adj* unfading; unwithering
**inmaterial** *adj* immaterial
**inmaterialidad** *f* immateriality

**inmaterialismo** *m* immaterialism
**inmaturo -ra** *adj* unripe; immature
**inmediación** *f* immediacy, immediateness; proximity, nearness; contact; **inmediaciones** *fpl* environs, neighborhood
**inmediatamente** *adv* immediately
**inmediato -ta** *adj* immediate; adjoining, close, next; next below; next above; **llegar** or **venir a las inmediatas** (coll.) to get down to brass tacks; **inmediato a** right next to; immediately preceding; immediately following
**inmedicable** *adj* immedicable, incurable
**inmejorable** *adj* unimprovable, unsurpassable, superb
**inmemorable** or **inmemorial** *adj* immemorial
**inmensidad** *f* immensity
**inmenso -sa** *adj* immense
**inmensurable** *adj* immensurable; unmeasurable
**inmerecido -da** *adj* unmerited, undeserved, unearned
**inmergir §42** *va* to immerse; *vr* to be immersed; to immerge
**inmérito -ta** *adj* unmerited; unjust
**inmeritorio -ria** *adj* not meritorious, undeserving
**inmersión** *f* immersion; dip; (surg.) immersion
**inmerso -sa** *adj* immersed
**inmigración** *f* immigration
**inmigrado -da** or **inmigrante** *adj & mf* immigrant
**inmigrar** *vn* to immigrate
**inminencia** *f* imminence or imminency
**inminente** *adj* imminent; early
**inmiscible** *adj* immiscible
**inmiscuir §41 & regular** *va* to mix; *vr* to meddle, interfere
**inmobiliario -ria** *adj* real-estate
**inmoble** *adj* immovable, unmovable; motionless; firm, constant
**inmoderación** *f* immoderation
**inmoderado -da** *adj* immoderate
**inmodestia** *f* immodesty
**inmodesto -ta** *adj* immodest
**inmódico -ca** *adj* excessive
**inmolación** *f* immolation
**inmolador -dora** *adj* immolating; *mf* immolator
**inmolar** *va* to immolate
**inmoral** *adj* immoral
**inmoralidad** *f* immorality
**inmortal** *adj* immortal, deathless; *mf* immortal
**inmortalidad** *f* immortality
**inmortalizar §76** *va* to immortalize
**inmortificación** *f* immortification, unrestraint, license
**inmortificado -da** *adj* immortified, unrestrained
**inmotivado -da** *adj* unmotivated, ungrounded
**inmoto -ta** *adj* unmoved
**inmovible** or **inmóvil** *adj* var. of **inmoble**
**inmovilidad** *f* immovability; immobility
**inmovilización** *f* immobilization
**inmovilizar §76** *va* to immobilize; to bring to a standstill; to tie up (*capital*) in merchandise of slow turnover
**inmudable** *adj* immutable
**inmueble** *adj* (law) immovable; *m* property, piece of real estate; **inmuebles** *mpl* immovables, real estate
**inmundicia** *f* dirt, filth; impurity, indecency
**inmundo -da** *adj* dirty, filthy; impure, indecent
**inmune** *adj* free, exempt; immune; **inmune contra** immune to
**inmunidad** *f* immunity; **inmunidad pasiva** (immun.) passive immunity
**inmunización** *f* immunization
**inmunizar §76** *va* to immunize
**inmunología** *f* immunology
**inmunólogo -ga** *mf* immunologist
**inmutabilidad** *f* immutability
**inmutable** *adj* immutable
**inmutación** *f* change, alteration
**inmutar** *va* to change, to alter; to disturb, upset; *vr* to change, to alter; to change countenance, to be out of countenance; **sin inmutarse** without batting an eye
**innatismo** *m* innatism
**innato -ta** *adj* innate, born, inborn; natural
**innatural** *adj* unnatural
**innavegable** *adj* unnavigable; unseaworthy
**innecesario -ria** *adj* unnecessary
**innegable** *adj* undeniable
**innegociable** *adj* unnegotiable
**innoble** *adj* ignoble
**innocuo -cua** *adj* innocuous
**innominable** *adj* unnameable
**innominado -da** *adj* unnamed; anonymous; (anat.) innominate
**innovación** *f* innovation
**innovador -dora** *adj* innovating; *mf* innovator
**innovamiento** *m* innovation
**innovar** *va* to innovate
**innumerabilidad** *f* innumerability
**innumerable** *adj* innumerable
**innúmero -ra** *adj* numberless, countless
**inobediencia** *f* inobedience
**inobediente** *adj* inobedient
**inobservable** *adj* inobservable, unobservable
**inobservancia** *f* inobservance, nonobservance
**inobservante** *adj* unobservant
**inocencia** *f* innocence
**Inocencio** *m* Innocent
**inocentada** *f* (coll.) simple remark, simple thing; (coll.) good-natured blunder; (coll.) practical joke; (coll.) April Fools' joke
**inocente** *adj & mf* innocent; **coger por inocente** to make an April fool of
**inocentón -tona** *adj* (coll.) simple, credulous; *mf* (coll.) simple, credulous person, dupe
**inocuidad** *f* innocuousness
**inoculable** *adj* inoculable
**inoculación** *f* inoculation
**inoculante** *adj* inoculating
**inocular** *va* to inoculate; (fig.) to contaminate, pervert; *vn* to inoculate; *vr* to be or become inoculated; (fig.) to be contaminated or perverted
**inocuo -cua** *adj* innocuous
**inodoro -ra** *adj* inodorous, odorless; *m* deodorizer; water closet, toilet
**inofensivo -va** *adj* inoffensive
**inoficioso -sa** *adj* inofficious, inoperative; (law) inofficious
**inolvidable** *adj* unforgettable
**inope** *adj* impecunious
**inoperable** *adj* (surg.) inoperable
**inoperancia** *f* inactivity, disuse
**inoperante** *adj* inoperative, ineffectual
**inopia** *f* poverty
**inopinable** *adj* indisputable
**inopinado -da** *adj* unexpected
**inoportunidad** *f* untimeliness, inopportuneness
**inoportuno -na** *adj* untimely, inopportune
**inordenado -da** *adj* disordered, in disorder
**inorgánico -ca** *adj* inorganic
**inorganizado -da** *adj* unorganized
**inoxidable** *adj* inoxidable, inoxidizable; stainless (*steel*)
**inquebrantable** *adj* unbreakable; unyielding; irrevocable
**inquietador -dora** *adj* disquieting; *mf* disturber
**inquietante** *adj* disquieting, disturbing
**inquietar** *va* to disquiet, to disturb, to worry; to stir up, harass, excite; *vr* to become disquieted, to worry; **inquietarse con, de** or **por** to get upset about, to worry about
**inquieto -ta** *adj* anxious, worried, restless
**inquietud** *f* disquiet, disquietude, inquietude, uneasiness, restlessness; concern
**inquilinato** *m* rent, lease; (Am.) rooming house
**inquilino -na** *mf* tenant, renter, lessee
**inquina** *f* aversion, dislike, ill will
**inquinamiento** *m* contamination
**inquinar** *va* to contaminate
**inquiridor -dora** *adj* inquiring; *mf* inquirer
**inquirir §56** *va* to inquire, inquire into, investigate; *vn* to inquire
**inquisición** *f* inquisition; (*cap.*) *f* Inquisition
**inquisidor -dora** *adj* inquiring; *mf* inquirer, inquisitor; (*cap.*) *m* (eccl.) Inquisitor
**inquisitivo -va** *adj* investigative
**inquisitoriado -da** *adj* condemned by the Inquisition
**inquisitorial** *adj* inquisitorial

**inquisitorio -ria** *adj* var. of **inquisitivo**
**inri** *m* I.N.R.I. (*initials of Iesus Nazarenus, Rex Iudaeorum, i.e., Jesus of Nazareth, King of the Jews*); (fig.) brand, stigma, insult
**insabible** *adj* unknowable
**insaciable** *adj* insatiable
**insaculación** *f* balloting by drawing lots
**insacular** *va* to cast (*ballots*) by drawing lots
**insalivación** *f* (physiol.) insalivation
**insalivar** *va* (physiol.) to insalivate
**insalubre** *adj* unhealthful, insalubrious, unsanitary, insanitary
**insalubridad** *f* unhealthfulness, unsanitary condition
**insalvable** *adj* insurmountable
**insanable** *adj* incurable
**insania** *f* insanity
**insano -na** *adj* insane; mad, wild
**insatisfecho -cha** *adj* unsatisfied
**inscribir §17,** 9 *va* to inscribe; (geom. & fig.) to inscribe; (law) to record; *vr* to enroll, register
**inscripción** *f* inscription; enrolment, registration
**inscrito -ta** *adj* (geom.) inscribed; *pp of* **inscribir**
**insecable** *adj* indivisible; (coll.) undryable, undrying
**insecticida** *adj* insecticide, insecticidal; *m* insecticide
**insectil** *adj* insectile
**insectívoro -ra** *adj* insectivorous; *m* (zool.) insectivore; *f* (bot.) insectivore
**insecto** *m* insect
**inseguridad** *f* insecurity, unsafeness; uncertainty
**inseguro -ra** *adj* insecure, unsafe; uncertain
**inseminación** *f* insemination; **inseminación artificial** artificial insemination
**inseminar** *va* to inseminate
**insenescencia** *f* agelessness
**insensatez** *f* insensateness, folly, brainlessness
**insensato -ta** *adj* insensate (*foolish, blind*)
**insensibilidad** *f* insensibility; hardheartedness
**insensibilizador** *m* deadener (*of pain*)
**insensibilizar §76** *va* to make insensible; *vr* to become insensible
**insensible** *adj* insensible; insentient; imperceptible; insensitive; hardhearted
**inseparabilidad** *f* inseparability
**inseparable** *adj* inseparable; indetachable; *mf* inseparable; *m* (orn.) lovebird
**insepulto -ta** *adj* unburied
**inserción** *f* insertion; (bot. & zool.) insertion
**inserir §62** *va* to insert; to graft; to ingest
**insertar** *va* to insert; *vr* (bot. & zool.) to be inserted
**inserto -ta** *adj* inserted
**inservible** *adj* useless
**insidia** *f* ambush; plotting
**insidiador -dora** *adj* waylaying; plotting; *mf* waylayer; plotter
**insidiar** *va* to ambush, waylay; to plot against
**insidioso -sa** *adj* insidious
**insigne** *adj* famous, noted, renowned
**insignia** *f* decoration, badge, device; standard; (naut.) pennant; **insignias** *fpl* insignia
**insignificancia** *f* insignificance
**insignificante** *adj* insignificant
**insinceridad** *f* insincerity
**insincero -ra** *adj* insincere
**insinuación** *f* insinuation, intimation, hint
**insinuante** *adj* insinuating, slick, crafty, engaging
**insinuar §33** *va* to insinuate; to suggest, hint at; *vr* to insinuate oneself; to work one's way; to flow, to run; to slip in, to creep in; to ingratiate oneself
**insinuativo -va** *adj* insinuative
**insipidez** *f* insipidity
**insípido -da** *adj* insipid
**insipiencia** *f* ignorance; lack of wisdom
**insipiente** *adj* ignorant; unwise
**insistencia** *f* insistence
**insistente** *adj* insistent
**insistir** *vn* to insist; **insistir en** or **sobre** to insist on or upon; **insistir en** + *inf* to insist on + *ger;* **insistir en que** + *subj* to insist that

**ínsito -ta** *adj* inbred, innate, inherent
**insociabilidad** *f* unsociability
**insociable** or **insocial** *adj* unsociable
**insolación** *f* insolation; (meteor.) insolation; (path.) sunstroke, insolation
**insolar** *va* to insolate; to expose, to expose to the sun; *vr* to take a sun bath; to get sunstruck
**insoldable** *adj* incapable of being soldered; irremediable; unmendable
**insolencia** *f* insolence
**insolentar** *va* to make insolent; *vr* to become insolent
**insolente** *adj* insolent; *mf* insolent person
**insólito -ta** *adj* unusual, unaccustomed
**insolubilidad** *f* insolubility
**insoluble** *adj* insoluble; insolvable
**insoluto -ta** *adj* unpaid
**insolvencia** *f* insolvency
**insolvente** *adj* insolvent
**insomne** *adj* sleepless
**insomnio** *m* insomnia, sleeplessness
**insondable** *adj* unfathomable, inscrutable
**insonorizar §76** *va* to soundproof
**insonoro -ra** *adj* soundproof, soundless
**insoportable** *adj* insupportable, unbearable; extremely annoying
**insoslayable** *adj* unavoidable
**insospechado -da** *adj* unsuspected
**insostenible** *adj* untenable, indefensible; unsustainable
**inspección** *f* inspection; inspectorship; inspector's office
**inspeccionar** *va* to inspect
**inspector -tora** *adj* inspecting; *mf* inspector
**inspiración** *f* inhalation; inspiration
**inspiradamente** *adv* inspiredly, with inspiration
**inspirador -dora** *adj* inspiring; (anat.) inspiratory; *mf* inspirer
**inspirante** *adj* inspiring
**inspirar** *va & vn* to inhale, breathe in; to inspire; **inspirar a** + *inf* to inspire to + *inf; vr* to be inspired; **inspirarse en** to be inspired by
**inspirativo -va** *adj* inspirational
**inspiratorio -ria** *adj* (anat.) inspiratory
**instabilidad** *f* var. of **inestabilidad**
**instable** *adj* var. of **inestable**
**instalación** *f* installation, instalment; plant, factory; equipment, outfit; arrangements, appointments; fittings; **instalaciones hoteleras** hotel facilities, hotel accommodations; **instalación sanitaria** plumbing
**instalador -dora** *mf* installer; **instalador de cañería** plumber; **instalador de líneas** lineman; **instalador sanitario** plumber
**instalar** *va* to install; *vr* to become installed; to settle
**instancia** *f* instance, request, entreaty; memorial; (law) instance; **a instancia de** at the instance of
**instantáneo -a** *adj* instantaneous; instant; *f* snapshot
**instante** *m* instant, moment; **a cada instante** all the time, at every moment; **al instante** right away, immediately; **en un instante** quickly, soon; **por instantes** uninterruptedly; any time
**instantemente** *adv* insistently, urgently
**instar** *va* to press, urge; **instar a** + *inf* or **instar a que** + *subj* to urge to + *inf; vn* to insist; to be urgent; **instar para, por** or **sobre** to insist on
**instauración** *f* restoration; reëstablishment
**instaurar** *va* to restore; to reëstablish
**instaurativo -va** *adj* restorative
**instigación** *f* instigation; **a instigación de** at the instigation of
**instigador -dora** *adj* instigating; *mf* instigator
**instigar §59** *va* to instigate
**instilación** *f* instillation
**instilar** *va* to instill
**instintivo -va** *adj* instinctive
**instinto** *m* instinct; **instinto de rebaño** herd instinct
**institución** *f* institution; (law) institution; **instituciones** *fpl* constitution (*of a government*); principles (*of an art or science*)

**institucional** *adj* institutional
**instituidor -dora** *adj* founding; *mf* founder
**instituir** §41 *va* to institute, found, establish; to teach, instruct
**instituta** *f* (law) institutes
**instituto** *m* constitution, rule (*e.g., of a religious order*); institute; high school; **instituto de segunda enseñanza** or **de enseñanza media** high school
**institutor -tora** *adj* founding; *mf* founder; teacher, instructor
**institutriz** *f* (*pl:* **-trices**) governess
**instridente** *adj* var. of **estridente**
**instrucción** *f* instruction, education; **instrucción pública** education, educational system; **instrucciones** *fpl* instructions, directions
**instructivo -va** *adj* instructive
**instructor -tora** *adj* instructing; *mf* teacher, instructor; *f* instructress
**instruído -da** *adj* well-educated, well-posted
**instruir** §41 *va* to instruct; to draw up; **instruir de, en,** or **sobre** to instruct about or on
**instrumentación** *f* instrumentation
**instrumental** *adj* instrumental; *m* instruments (*of music, surgery, etc.*); kit of instruments
**instrumentar** *va* (mus.) to instrument
**instrumentista** *mf* instrumentalist; instrument maker or dealer
**instrumento** *m* instrument; (mus.) instrument; (fig.) tool, cat's-paw; **instrumento de boquilla** (mus.) brass wind, brass-wind instrument; **instrumento de cuerda** (mus.) stringed instrument; **instrumento de lengüeta** (mus.) reed, reed instrument; **instrumento de percusión** (mus.) percussion instrument; **instrumento de precisión** precision instrument; **instrumento de punteo** (mus.) plucked instrument (*e.g., harp*); **instrumento de viento** (mus.) wind instrument
**insuave** *adj* rough; unpleasant, disagreeable
**insuavidad** *f* roughness; unpleasantness
**insubordinación** *f* insubordination
**insubordinado -da** *adj* insubordinate
**insubordinar** *va* to make insubordinate, incite to insubordination; *vr* to become insubordinate, to rebel
**insubsanable** *adj* irreparable
**insubsistencia** *f* impermanence, instability; lack of subsistence; groundlessness
**insubsistente** *adj* impermanent, unstable; lacking in subsistence; groundless
**insubstancial** *adj* unsubstantial, insubstantial
**insubstancialidad** *f* insubstantiality
**insubstituíble** *adj* irreplaceable
**insudar** *vn* to toil, to drudge, strive hard
**insuficiencia** *f* insufficiency, inadequacy; **insuficiencia mitral** (path.) mitral insufficiency
**insuficiente** *adj* insufficient, inadequate
**insuflación** *f* insufflation; blowing
**insuflador** *m* (med.) syringe
**insuflar** *va* to insufflate; to blow, to blow air in (*e.g., an organ*)
**insufrible** *adj* insufferable
**ínsula** *f* island; unimportant place
**insulano -na** *adj* (archaic) insular; *mf* (archaic) islander
**insular** *adj* insular; *mf* islander
**insularidad** *f* insularity
**insulina** *f* (med.) insulin
**Insulindia, la** Indonesia
**insulínico -ca** *adj* (pertaining to) insulin
**insulismo** *m* (path.) insulin shock
**insulsez** *f* tastelessness; dullness, heaviness
**insulso -sa** *adj* tasteless; dull, heavy
**insultante** *adj* insulting
**insultar** *va* to insult; to attack unexpectedly and with violence; *vr* to faint
**insulto** *m* insult; sudden attack; fainting spell; **insulto a superiores** (mil.) insubordination
**insumable** *adj* exorbitant
**insume** *adj* expensive
**insumergible** *adj* unsinkable
**insumir** *va* (Am.) to consume, use up (*money*); *vn* (Am.) to ooze
**insumiso -sa** *adj* unsubmissive
**insuperable** *adj* insuperable
**insuperado -da** *adj* unbeaten
**insurgente** *adj & mf* insurgent
**insurrección** *f* insurrection; (coll.) lack of deference
**insurreccional** *adj* insurrectionary
**insurreccionar** *va* to incite to rebellion; *vr* to rise up, to rebel
**insurrecto -ta** *adj* rebellious; *mf* insurrectionist
**insusceptibilidad** *f* insusceptibility
**insusceptible** *adj* insusceptible
**insustancial** *adj* var. of **insubstancial**
**insustancialidad** *f* var. of **insubstancialidad**
**insustituíble** *adj* var. of **insubstituíble**
**intacto -ta** *adj* intact, undamaged, unbroken
**intachable** *adj* irreproachable
**intangibilidad** *f* intangibility, untouchableness
**intangible** *adj* intangible, untouchable
**integérrimo -ma** *adj super* very or most complete, honorable, or irreproachable
**integrable** *adj* (math.) integrable
**integración** *f* integration
**integrado -da** *adj* in one piece
**integrador** *m* integrator
**integral** *adj* integral; (math.) integral; *f* (math.) integral; (math.) integral sign, sign of integration
**integrante** *adj* integrant, integral; constituent; *mf* member
**integrar** *va* to integrate; to form, make up; to reimburse; (math.) to integrate
**integridad** *f* integrity; virginity
**íntegro -gra** *adj* integral, whole, complete; honest, upright
**integumento** *m* integument; mask, disguise
**intelección** *f* understanding
**intelectivo -va** *adj* intellective; *f* understanding (*faculty*)
**intelecto** *m* intellect
**intelectual** *adj & mf* intellectual
**intelectualidad** *f* intellectuality; intelligentsia
**intelectualismo** *m* intellectualism
**intelectualoide** *m* (coll.) egghead, highbrow
**inteligencia** *f* intelligence, understanding; collusion; **estar en inteligencia con** to be in collusion with
**inteligenciado -da** *adj* well-informed
**inteligente** *adj* intelligent; trained, skilled
**inteligibilidad** *f* intelligibility
**inteligible** *adj* intelligible
**intemperancia** *f* intemperance
**intemperante** *adj* intemperate
**intemperie** *f* inclemency (*of weather*); **a la intemperie** in the open air, unsheltered
**intemperizar** §76 *va* to weather
**intempestivo -va** *adj* unseasonable, untimely, ill-timed
**intemporal** *adj* timeless
**intención** *f* intention; viciousness (*of an animal*); caution; **intenciones** *fpl* intentions (*with respect to marrying*); **con intención** deliberately, knowingly; **de intención** on purpose; **primera intención** (coll.) openness, readiness; (surg.) first intention; **segunda intención** underhandedness; (surg.) second intention
**intencionadamente** *adv* intentionally
**intencionado -da** *adj* intentioned, disposed; intentional; picaresque; **bien intencionado** well-intentioned; **mal intencionado** ill-intentioned, ill-disposed
**intencional** *adj* intentional; inner
**intendencia** *f* intendance; intendancy; (Am.) mayoralty
**intendenta** *f* intendant's wife; (Am.) mayor's wife
**intendente** *m* intendant; **intendente municipal** (Am.) mayor
**intensar** *va & vr* to intensify
**intensidad** *f* intensity
**intensificación** *f* intensification
**intensificar** §86 *va & vr* to intensify
**intensión** *f* intensity, intenseness
**intensivo -va** *adj* intensive
**intenso -sa** *adj* intense
**intentar** *va* to try, to attempt; to try out; to intend; (law) to initiate (*e.g., a suit*); **intentar** + *inf* to try to + *inf*
**intento** *m* intent, purpose; **de intento** on purpose

**intentona** *f* (coll.) foolhardiness, rash attempt
**interacción** *f* interaction, interplay
**interaliado -da** *adj* interallied
**interamericanismo** *m* inter-Americanism
**interamericano -na** *adj* inter-American
**interandino -na** *adj* inter-Andean
**intercadencia** *f* unevenness, irregularity; harshness; (med.) intercadence
**intercalación** *f* intercalation
**intercalar** *adj* intercalary; *va* to intercalate
**intercambiable** *adj* interchangeable
**intercambiar** *va & vr* to interchange
**intercambio** *m* interchange
**interceder** *vn* intercede
**intercelular** *adj* intercellular
**intercepción** *f* or **interceptación** *f* interception
**interceptar** *va* to intercept
**interceptor -tora** *adj* intercepting; *mf* interceptor; *m* separator; trap; (aer.) interceptor
**intercesión** *f* intercession
**intercesor -sora** *adj* interceding; *mf* intercessor
**intercesorio -ria** *adj* intercessory
**interciso -sa** *adj* cut into pieces (*said of a martyr*); **día interciso** (archaic) half holiday (*in the morning*)
**intercolonial** *adj* intercolonial
**intercolumnio** *m* (arch.) intercolumniation
**intercomunicación** *f* intercommunication
**intercomunicador** *m* intercom
**intercomunicar** §86 *vr* to intercommunicate
**interconectar** *va* to interconnect
**interconexión** *f* interconnection
**interconfesional** *adj* interdenominational
**intercontinental** *adj* intercontinental
**intercostal** *adj* (anat.) intercostal
**intercurrente** *adj* (path.) intercurrent
**intercutáneo -a** *adj* intercutaneous
**interdecir** §37 *va* to interdict
**interdental** *adj & f* (phonet.) interdental
**interdepartamental** *adj* interdepartmental
**interdependencia** *f* interdependence
**interdependiente** *adj* interdependent
**interdicción** *f* interdiction
**interdicto** *m* interdict
**interdicho -cha** *pp of* **interdecir**
**interdigital** *adj* interdigital
**interdigo** *1st sg pres ind of* **interdecir**
**interdije** *1st sg pret ind of* **interdecir**
**interdiré** *1st sg fut ind of* **interdecir**
**intereje** *m* (aut.) wheel base
**interés** *m* interest; **poner a interés** to put out at interest; **interés compuesto** compound interest; **intereses creados** vested interests; **interés simple** simple interest
**interesable** *adj* selfish, mercenary
**interesado -da** *adj* interested; selfish; *mf* interested person, interested party
**interesante** *adj* interesting
**interesar** *va* to interest; to give an interest to; to involve; **interesarle a uno** + *inf* to interest someone to + *inf; vn* to be interesting; *vr* to be interested; **interesarse en** or **por** to be interested in, to take an interest in
**interescolar** *adj* intercollegiate, interscholastic
**interesencia** *f* attendance
**interesente** *adj* present
**interestadal** *adj* interstate
**interestelar** *adj* interstellar
**inter-etapa** *adj invar* (rad.) interstage
**interfecto -ta** *adj* (law) murdered; *mf* (law) murdered person, victim of murder
**interferencia** *f* interference; (phys. & rad.) interference; **no interferencia** noninterference
**interferencial** *adj* (phys.) interferential
**interferir** §62 *va* to interfere with; *vn* to interfere; (phys.) to interfere
**interferómetro** *m* (phys.) interferometer
**interfoliar** *va* to interfoliate, to interleave
**interfono** *m* intercom
**intergubernamental** *adj* intergovernmental
**ínterin** *m* (*pl:* **interines**) temporary incumbency; (eccl.) Interim; *adv* meanwhile; *conj* (coll.) while, until, as long as
**interinamente** *adv* in the meantime; temporarily
**interinar** *va* to fill (*a post*) temporarily, to fill in an acting capacity
**interinidad** *f* temporariness; temporary incumbency
**interino -na** *adj* temporary, acting, interim
**interior** *adj* interior; inner, inside; (pertaining to) home; domestic; *m* interior; mind, soul; **interiores** *mpl* entrails, insides; **Interior** City (*word written on an envelope to indicate that the letter is to go to the city in which it is mailed*)
**interioridad** *f* inwardness; inside; **interioridades** *fpl* family secrets, private matters, inside story
**interiorizar** §76 *va* to keep well informed, to give inside information to; *vr* to keep well informed; **interiorizarse de** to find out about
**interiormente** *adv* on the inside; inwardly
**interjección** *f* (gram.) interjection
**interjectivo -va** *adj* (gram.) interjectional
**interlínea** *f* interline; (print.) space, lead
**interlineación** *f* interlineation
**interlineal** *adj* interlinear
**interlinear** *va* to interline; (print.) to space, to lead
**interlocutor -tora** *mf* interlocutor; speaker, party
**interlocutorio -ria** *adj* (law) interlocutory
**intérlope** *adj* interloping (*said of commerce and ships*)
**interludio** *m* (mus.) interlude
**interlunar** *adj* interlunar
**interlunio** *m* (astr.) interlunation
**intermaxilar** *adj* intermaxillary
**intermediar** *vn* to stand in the middle; to intermediate
**intermediario -ria** *adj* intermediary; mediating; *mf* intermediary; mediator; *m* (com.) middleman
**intermedio -dia** *adj* intermediate, intervening; (phonet.) medial; *m* interval, interim; (theat.) entr'acte, interlude, intermission; (mus.) intermezzo; **por intermedio de** (Am.) by means of
**interminable** *adj* interminable
**intermisión** *f* intermission; (path.) intermission
**intermiso -sa** *adj* interrupted, suspended
**intermitencia** *f* intermittence or intermittency; (path.) intermission
**intermitente** *adj* intermittent
**intermitir** *va* to intermit
**internación** *f* commitment, internment; penetration, moving inland
**internacional** *adj* international; (*cap.*) *f* International (*association*); Internationale (*hymn*); **Internacional Comunista** Communist International
**internacionalidad** *f* internationality
**internacionalismo** *m* internationalism
**internacionalista** *mf* internationalist
**internacionalización** *f* internationalization
**internacionalizar** §76 *va* to internationalize
**internado -da** *mf* (mil.) internee; *m* student boarding; boarding students; boarding school
**internamiento** *m* sending inland; commitment, internment; bedding (*of sick people*)
**internar** *va* to send inland; to commit, to intern; *vn* to move inland; *vr* to move inland; to worm one's way into another's confidence; to study deeply; to take refuge, hide
**internista** *mf* (med.) internist
**interno -na** *adj* internal; inward; inside; boarding; *mf* boarding-school student; **interno de hospital** intern
**internodio** *m* internode
**internuncio** *m* internuncio
**interoceánico -ca** *adj* interoceanic
**interocular** *adj* interocular
**interóseo -a** *adj* interosseous
**interpaginar** *va* to interpage
**interparietal** *adj* (anat.) interparietal
**interparlamentario -ria** *adj* interparliamentary
**interpelación** *f* beseeching; interpellation
**interpelar** *va* to ask aid or protection of; to ask for explanations; to interpellate
**interpenetración** *f* interpenetration
**interplanetario -ria** *adj* interplanetary

**interpolación** *f* interpolation; brief stop (*e.g., in a speech*)
**interpolar** *adj* interpolar; *va* to interpolate; to stop or interrupt for a moment; (math.) to interpolate
**interpondré** *1st sg fut ind of* **interponer**
**interponer** **§69** *va* to interpose; to appoint as mediator; *vr* to interpose, stand between, intercede
**interpongo** *1st sg pres ind of* **interponer**
**interposición** *f* interposition
**interprender** *va* to take by surprise
**interpresa** *f* taking by surprise, surprise action, surprise attack
**interpretable** *adj* interpretable
**interpretación** *f* interpretation
**interpretador -dora** *adj* interpreting; *mf* interpreter
**interpretar** *va* to interpret
**interpretativo -va** *adj* interpretative or interpretive
**intérprete** *mf* interpreter
**interpuesto -ta** *pp of* **interponer**
**interpuse** *1st sg pret ind of* **interponer**
**interracial** *adj* interracial
**interregno** *m* interregnum
**interrogación** *f* interrogation; (gram.) question mark, interrogation mark
**interrogado -da** *adj* questioned; *mf* person questioned, party questioned
**interrogante** *adj* questioning; interrogative; question (*mark*); *mf* questioner, interrogator; *m* question mark
**interrogar** **§59** *va & vn* to question, to interrogate
**interrogativo -va** *adj* interrogative; *m* (gram.) interrogative
**interrogatorio** *m* interrogatory
**interrumpidamente** *adv* interruptedly
**interrumpir** *va* to interrupt
**interrupción** *f* interruption
**interruptor -tora** *adj* interrupting; *m* (elec.) switch; **interruptor a palanca** (elec.) toggle switch; **interruptor automático** (elec.) circuit breaker; **interruptor de cuchilla** (elec.) knife switch; **interruptor del encendido** (aut.) ignition switch; **interruptor de reloj** (elec.) time switch; **interruptor de rótula** (elec.) toggle switch; **interruptor de una caída** (elec.) single-throw switch; **interruptor de volquete** (elec.) tumbler switch
**intersecar** **§86** *va & vr* to intersect
**intersección** *f* (geom.) intersection
**intersideral** *adj* intersidereal
**intersticial** *adj* interstitial
**intersticio** *m* interstice; interval
**intertrigo** *m* (path.) intertrigo
**intertropical** *adj* intertropical
**interuniversitario -ria** *adj* interuniversity, intercollegiate
**interurbano -na** *adj* interurban
**intervalo** *m* interval; (mus.) interval; **claro intervalo** lucid interval
**intervención** *f* intervention; supervision, inspection; participation; auditing; (surg.) operation; **no intervención** (dipl.) nonintervention; **intervención de los precios** price control
**intervencionista** *adj & mf* interventionist
**intervendré** *1st sg fut ind of* **intervenir**
**intervengo** *1st sg pres ind of* **intervenir**
**intervenir** **§92** *va* to take up, to work on; to inspect, to supervise; to audit; to offer to pay (*a draft*); to tap (*a telephone line*); (surg.) to operate on; *vn* to intervene; to intercede; to happen; to participate; *vr* to be found (*as a result of inspection*); **intervenírsele a uno** to be found on someone, e.g., **se le intervino una carta secreta** a secret letter was found on him, they found a secret letter on him
**interventor** *m* election supervisor; (com.) auditor
**interviev** *m & f* (*pl:* **-vievs**) interview
**interviuvador -dora** *mf* interviewer
**intervievar** *va* to interview
**intervine** *1st sg pret ind of* **intervenir**
**interviniendo** *ger of* **intervenir**
**intervistar** *vr* var. of **entrevistar**
**interviú** *m & f* interview
**intervocálico -ca** *adj* intervocalic
**interyacente** *adj* interjacent
**interzonal** *adj* interzonal or interzone
**intestado -da** *adj & mf* intestate
**intestinal** *adj* intestinal
**intestino -na** *adj* intestine (*internal; domestic*); *m* (anat.) intestine, intestines; **intestino ciego** (anat.) caecum; **intestino delgado** (anat.) small intestine; **intestino grueso** (anat.) large intestine; **intestinos** *mpl* (anat.) intestines
**intimación** *f* announcement, declaration; intimation (*announcement*)
**íntimamente** *adv* intimately; deeply
**intimar** *va* to intimate, to notify, to order; *vn* to become intimate or well-acquainted; *vr* to soak in; to become intimate or well-acquainted
**intimidación** *f* intimidation
**intimidad** *f* intimacy; homeyness; privacy
**intimidar** *va* to intimidate; *vr* to become intimidated
**íntimo -ma** *adj* intimate; innermost; homey; private
**intina** *f* (bot.) intine
**intitular** *va* to entitle; to give a title to; *vr* to give oneself a title, use a title; to be called
**intocable** *mf* untouchable (*person of lowest caste in India*)
**intocado -da** *adj* intact, untouched
**intolerabilidad** *f* intolerability
**intolerable** *adj* intolerable
**intolerancia** *f* intolerance
**intolerante** *adj & mf* intolerant
**intonso -sa** *adj* unshorn; ignorant, rustic; uncut (*said of a book or magazine*); *mf* ignorant person, rustic
**intoxicación** *f* (med.) poisoning, intoxication
**intoxicar** **§86** *va* (med.) to poison, intoxicate
**intracruce** *m* or **intracruzamiento** *m* inbreeding
**intradós** *m* (arch.) intrados
**intraducible** *adj* untranslatable
**intramolecular** *adj* intramolecular
**intramural** *adj* (anat.) intramural
**intramuros** *adv* intra muros, within the walls
**intramuscular** *adj* intramuscular
**intranquilidad** *f* worry, uneasiness; unrest
**intranquilizar** **§76** *va* to disquiet, to worry; *vr* to become disquieted, to worry
**intranquilo -la** *adj* worried, uneasy; restless
**intransferible** *adj* untransferable
**intransigencia** *f* intransigence or intransigency
**intransigente** *adj & mf* intransigent, irreconcilable, die-hard
**intransitable** *adj* impassable
**intransitivo -va** *adj* (gram.) intransitive
**intransmisible** *adj* untransmissible
**intransmutable** *adj* intransmutable
**intratabilidad** *f* intractability; unsociability
**intratable** *adj* intractable; unsociable; impassable
**intravenoso -sa** *adj* intravenous
**intrepidez** *f* intrepidity
**intrépido -da** *adj* intrepid
**intriga** *f* intrigue
**intrigante** *adj* intriguing, scheming; *mf* intriguer
**intrigar** **§59** *va* to intrigue, to excite the curiosity of; *vn* to intrigue; *vr* to be intrigued
**intrincación** *f* intricacy
**intrincado -da** *adj* intricate
**intrincamiento** *m* intricacy
**intrincar** **§86** *va* to confuse, entangle, complicate
**intríngulis** *m* (*pl:* **-lis**) (coll.) ulterior motive; (coll.) enigma, conundrum, mystery
**intrínseco -ca** *adj* intrinsic or intrinsical
**introducción** *f* introduction; insertion
**introducir** **§38** *va* to introduce; to insert, put in; *vr* to gain access; to interfere, intrude, meddle
**introductivo -va** *adj* introductory
**introductor -tora** *adj* introductory; *mf* introducer
**introduje** *1st sg pret ind of* **introducir**
**introduzco** *1st sg pres ind of* **introducir**
**introito** *m* (theat.) prologue; (eccl.) Introit
**intromisión** *f* insertion; meddling

**introrso -sa** *adj* (bot.) introrse
**introspección** *f* introspection
**introspectivo -va** *adj* introspective
**introversión** *f* introversion
**introverso -sa** *adj* introvert
**introvertido -da** *mf* introvert
**intrusar** *vr* to seize unlawfully
**intrusión** *f* intrusion; charlatanry, quackery
**intrusismo** *m* intrusion; practice of a profession without authority
**intruso -sa** *adj* intrusive; *mf* intruder, interloper; dishonest practitioner
**intubación** *f* (med.) intubation
**intuición** *f* intuition
**intuicionismo** *m* intuitionism
**intuir §41** *va* to intuit; to divine, to guess, to sense
**intuitivo -va** *adj* intuitive, intuitional
**intuito** *m* view, glance, look; **por intuito de** in view of
**intumescencia** *f* swelling, intumescence
**intumescente** *adj* swelling, intumescent
**intususcepción** *f* (biol. & path.) intussusception
**inulasa** *f* (biochem.) inulase
**inulina** *f* (chem.) inulin
**inulto -ta** *adj* (poet.) unavenged
**inundación** *f* inundation, flood
**inundar** *va* to inundate, to flood
**inurbanidad** *f* incivility, discourtesy
**inurbano -na** *adj* uncivil, discourteous
**inusitado -da** *adj* unusual; out of use
**inusual** *adj* unusual
**inútil** *adj* useless
**inutilidad** *f* uselessness, inutility; incapacity
**inutilizado -da** *adj* unused, unemployed
**inutilizar §76** *va* to make useless; *vr* to become useless; to be disabled
**invadeable** *adj* unfordable
**invadir** *va* to invade
**invaginación** *f* invagination
**invaginar** *va & vr* to invaginate
**invalidación** *f* invalidation
**invalidar** *va* to invalidate; to weaken, make helpless
**invalidez** *f* invalidity
**inválido -da** *adj & mf* invalid
**invar** *m* invar (*alloy*)
**invariabilidad** *f* invariability
**invariable** *adj* invariable
**invariante** *adj & f* invariant
**invasión** *f* invasion
**invasor -sora** *adj* invading; *mf* invader
**invectiva** *f* invective
**invectivar** *va* to inveigh against
**invencibilidad** *f* invincibility
**invencible** *adj* invincible
**invención** *f* finding; invention; **Invención de la Santa Cruz** (eccl.) Invention of the Cross
**invencionero -ra** *adj* inventive; cheating; *mf* inventor; cheat
**invendible** *adj* unsalable
**invendido -da** *adj* unsold
**inventar** *va* to invent
**inventariar §90 & regular** *va* to inventory
**inventario** *m* inventory
**inventivo -va** *adj* inventive; *f* inventiveness
**invento** *m* invention
**inventor -tora** *adj* inventive; *mf* inventor
**inverecundia** *f* shamelessness, insolence
**inverecundo -da** *adj* shameless, insolent
**inverisímil** *adj* improbable, unlikely
**inverisimilitud** *f* improbability, inverisimilitude
**invernación** *f* wintering; hibernation
**invernáculo** *m* hothouse, conservatory
**invernada** *f* wintertime; wintering; (Am.) pasture, pasturing, pasture land
**invernadero** *m* hothouse, conservatory; winter resort; winter pasture
**invernal** *adj* (pertaining to) winter; *m* (Am.) large winter stable (*in the Andes*)
**invernante** *mf* winter vacationist
**invernar §18** *vn* to winter; to be winter
**invernazo** *m* rainy season (*in Tropics*)
**inverne** *m* (Am.) winter pasture (*time*); (Am.) winter fattening
**invernizo -za** *adj* (pertaining to) winter; wintery
**inverosímil** *adj* improbable, unlikely
**inverosimilitud** *f* improbability, inverisimilitude
**inversión** *f* inversion; investment; subversion, overthrow; (gram.) inverted order
**inversionista** *adj* (pertaining to) investment; *mf* investor
**inverso -sa** *adj* inverse, opposite; **a** or **por la inversa** on the contrary; *m* (box.) jab
**inversor -sora** *adj* inverting, reversing; *m* reversing mechanism; (elec.) reverser
**invertasa** *f* (biochem.) invertase
**invertebrado -da** *adj & m* invertebrate
**invertido -da** *adj* inverted; *mf* (psychiatry) invert
**invertina** *f* (biochem.) invertase
**invertir §62** *va* to invert; to reverse; to invest; to spend
**investidura** *f* investiture; station, position
**investigación** *f* investigation
**investigador -dora** *adj* investigating; *mf* investigator
**investigar §59** *va* to investigate
**investir §94** *va* to invest (*to vest, install*); **investir de** or **con** to invest with
**inveterado -da** *adj* inveterate, confirmed
**inveterar** *vr* to become old; to become chronic
**invicto -ta** *adj* unconquered
**invidente** *adj* blind; *mf* blind person
**invierno** *m* winter; (Am.) rainy season
**invigilar** *vn* to watch with concern
**inviolabilidad** *f* inviolability
**inviolable** *adj* inviolable
**inviolado -da** *adj* inviolate
**invisibilidad** *f* invisibility
**invisible** *adj* invisible; (coll.) hiding; *m* (Am.) hair net; (Am.) invisible hairpin; **en un invisible** in less than no time
**invitación** *f* invitation
**invitado -da** *mf* person invited, guest
**invitar** *va* to invite; **invitar a** + *inf* to invite to + *inf*
**invocación** *f* invocation
**invocador -dora** *adj* invoking; *mf* invoker
**invocar §86** *va* to invoke
**invocatorio -ria** *adj* invocatory
**involución** *f* involution; (biol. & med.) involution; (math.) involution (*assemblage of pairs of collinear conjugate points*)
**involucrado -da** (bot.) involucrate
**involucrar** *va* to jumble; to introduce irrelevantly; *vr* to get jumbled
**involucro** *m* (bot.) involucre
**involuntariedad** *f* involuntariness
**involuntario -ria** *adj* involuntary
**involuta** *f* (arch.) volute; (geom.) involute
**invulnerabilidad** *f* invulnerability
**invulnerable** *adj* invulnerable
**inyección** *f* injection; **inyección hipodérmica** hypodermic injection
**inyectable** *adj* injectable
**inyectado -da** *adj* congested, inflamed
**inyectar** *va* to inject; *vr* to become congested
**inyector** *m* (mach.) injector
**iñiguista** *adj* Jesuitic; *mf* Jesuit
**-ío -ía** *suffix adj* e.g., **bravío** fierce; **cabrío** goatish; *suffix m* indicates a group or collection, e.g., **caserío** group of houses; **gentío** crowd of people; *suffix f* -y, e.g., **filosofía** philosophy; **geología** geology
**Ío** *f* (myth.) Io
**ion** *m* (chem. & phys.) ion; **ion hidrógeno** (*pl:* **iones hidrógeno**) (chem.) hydrogen ion
**iónico -ca** *adj* (chem. & phys.) ionic
**ionio** *m* (chem.) ionium
**ionización** *f* ionization
**ionizar §76** *va & vr* to ionize
**ionosfera** *f* ionosphere
**iota** *f* iota (*Greek letter*)
**iotacismo** *m* iotacism
**ipecacuana** *f* (bot.) ipecac or ipecacuanha (*plant, root, and medicine*)
**ir §57** *vn* to go; to come, e.g., **ya voy** I'm coming; to move, to walk; to be becoming, to fit, to suit; to be; to be at stake; to involve; **lo que va de** so far (as), e.g., **lo que va de este mes** so far this month; **lo que va de rodaje** so far as the filming has gone; **¡qué va!** of course not!; **¡vaya!** the deuce!; what a . . . !,

e.g., **¡vaya un hombre!** what a man!; **ir a** + *inf* to go to + *inf;* to be going to + *inf* (*expressing futurity*); **ir a buscar** to call for, to go get; **ir a parar en** to end up in; **ir con cuidado** to be careful; **ir con miedo** to be afraid; **ir con tiento** to be watchful; **ir de caza** to go hunting; **ir de pesca** to go fishing; **ir por** to go for, to go after; to follow (*a career*); **ir** + *pp* to be + *pp; vr* to go away; to ooze, to leak; to slip; to wear away; to get old; to break to pieces; to break wind; to lose control of natural evacuations; **la de vámonos** (slang) death; **irse de** to discard; **irse haciendo** to make one's way
**ira** *f* ire, wrath; **¡ira de Dios!** Lord help us!
**iraca** *f* (bot.) jipijapa; (Am.) Panama hat
**iracundia** *f* anger, angriness, wrath
**iracundo -da** *adj* angry, wrathful, ireful
**Irak, el** Irak or Iraq
**Irán, el** Iran
**iranés -nesa** or **iranio -nia** *adj & mf* Iranian; *m* Iranian (*language*)
**iraqués -quesa** or **iraquiano -na** *adj & mf* Iraqi; *m* Iraqi (*dialect*)
**irascibilidad** *f* irascibility
**irascible** *adj* irascible
**Irene** *f* Irene
**iridáceo -a** *adj* (bot.) iridaceous
**íride** *f* (bot.) gladdon, stinking iris
**iridescencia** *f* var. of **iridiscencia**
**iridescente** *adj* var. of **iridiscente**
**iridio** *m* (chem.) iridium
**iridiscencia** *f* iridescence
**iridiscente** *adj* iridescent
**iris** *m* (*pl:* **iris**) iris, rainbow; (anat. & opt.) iris; (mineral.) noble opal; **iris amarillo** (bot.) sweet flag; **iris de paz** peacemaker; (*cap.*) *f* (myth.) Iris
**irisación** *f* iridescence
**irisado -da** *adj* rainbow, rainbow-hued
**irisar** *va* to iris; *vn* to iridesce
**iritis** *f* (path.) iritis
**irlanda** *f* cotton cloth, woolen cloth; Irish linen; (*cap.*) *f* Ireland; **la Irlanda del Norte** or la **Irlanda Septentrional** Northern Ireland
**irlandés -desa** *adj* Irish; *m* Irishman; Irish (*language*); **los irlandeses** the Irish (*people*); *f* Irishwoman
**ironía** *f* irony
**irónico -ca** *adj* ironic, ironical
**ironizar §76** *va* to ridicule
**iroqués -quesa** *adj* Iroquoian; *mf* Iroquoian or Iroquois
**irracional** *adj* irrational, unreasoning; (math.) irrational
**irracionalidad** *f* irrationality
**irradiación** *f* irradiation; influence; (med.) irradiation; (rad.) broadcast
**irradiar** *va* to radiate; to irradiate; (rad.) to broadcast; *vn* to radiate
**irrazonable** *adj* unreasonable
**irreal** *adj* unreal
**irrealidad** *f* unreality
**irrealizable** *adj* unrealizable, unattainable
**irrebatible** *adj* irrefutable
**irreconciliable** *adj* unreconcilable, irreconcilable
**irreconciliado -da** *adj* unreconciled
**irreconocible** *adj* unrecognizable
**irrecuperable** *adj* irrecoverable, irretrievable
**irrecusable** *adj* unimpeachable
**irredentista** *mf* Irredentist
**irredento -ta** *adj* unredeemed (*region*)
**irredimible** *adj* irredeemable
**irreducible** or **irreductible** *adj* irreducible
**irreembolsable** *adj* not refunded
**irreemplazable** *adj* unreplaceable, irreplaceable
**irreflexión** *f* irreflection, rashness
**irreflexivo -va** *adj* unreflecting, thoughtless
**irreformable** *adj* irreformable, incorrigible
**irrefragable** *adj* irrefragable
**irrefrenable** *adj* unbridled, uncontrollable, irrepressible
**irrefutable** *adj* irrefutable
**irregenerado -da** *adj* unregenerate
**irregular** *adj* irregular; (bot., geom., gram. & mil.) irregular; *m* (mil.) irregular
**irregularidad** *f* irregularity; (coll.) embezzlement, irregularity
**irreligión** *f* irreligion
**irreligiosidad** *f* irreligiousness
**irreligioso -sa** *adj* unreligious; irreligious
**irrellenable** *adj* nonrefillable
**irremediable** *adj* irremediable
**irremisible** *adj* irremissible, unpardonable
**irremovible** *adj* irremovable
**irremunerado -da** *adj* unremunerated
**irrenovable** *adj* unrenewable
**irrenunciable** *adj* unrenounceable
**irreparable** *adj* irreparable
**irreprensible** *adj* irreprehensible, unexceptionable
**irrepresentable** *adj* unplayable
**irreprimible** *adj* irrepressible
**irreprochable** *adj* irreproachable, faultless
**irrescindible** *adj* unrescindable
**irresistible** *adj* irresistible
**irresoluble** *adj* unsolvable, unworkable
**irresolución** *f* irresolution, indecision
**irresoluto -ta** *adj* irresolute
**irrespeto** *m* (Am.) disrespect
**irrespetuoso -sa** *adj* disrespectful
**irrespirable** *adj* unbreathable
**irresponsabilidad** *f* irresponsibility
**irresponsable** *adj* irresponsible
**irrestañable** *adj* unstaunchable
**irresuelto -ta** *adj* irresolute, wavering, hesitant
**irreverencia** *f* irreverence
**irreverenciar** *va* to treat irreverently, to profane
**irreverente** *adj* irreverent
**irreversible** *adj* irreversible
**irrevocabilidad** *f* irrevocability
**irrevocable** *adj* irrevocable
**irrevocado -da** *adj* unrevoked
**irrigable** *adj* irrigable
**irrigación** *f* irrigation; (med.) irrigation
**irrigador** *m* irrigator; sprinkler
**irrigar §59** *va* to irrigate; (med.) to irrigate
**irrisible** *adj* laughable, ridiculous
**irrisión** *f* derision, ridicule; (coll.) butt, laughingstock
**irrisorio -ria** *adj* ridiculous, derisory; insignificant, ridiculously small
**irritabilidad** *f* irritability
**irritable** *adj* irritable
**irritación** *f* irritation; nullification
**irritadamente** *adv* angrily, vexedly
**irritador -dora** *adj* irritating
**irritamiento** *m* anger, irritation
**irritante** *adj & m* irritant
**irritar** *va* to irritate; (law) to irritate, to render null and void; to stir up; *vr* to become irritated, to be exasperated
**írrito -ta** *adj* (law) null and void
**irrogar §59** *va* to cause (*harm or damage*)
**irrompible** *adj* unbreakable
**irruir §41** *va* to raid, to invade; to assault
**irrumpir** *vn* to burst in, to irrupt; to invade; **irrumpir en** to burst into (*e.g., a room*)
**irrupción** *f* irruption; invasion
**irruptor -tora** *adj* irruptive
**irunés -nesa** *adj* (pertaining to) Irún; *mf* native or inhabitant of Irún
**-isa** *suffix f* -ess, e.g., **poetisa** poetess; **sacerdotisa** priestess
**Isaac** *m* Isaac
**Isabel** *f* Isabella, Elizabeth; **Isabel la Católica** Isabella I, queen of Castile and León
**isabelino -na** *adj* Isabelline; Elizabethan; light-bay; *mf* Isabelline; Elizabethan; *m* light-bay horse
**isabelita** *f* (ichth.) isabelita
**isagoge** *f* isagoge, introduction
**Isaías** m (Bib.) Isaiah
**isalóbara** *f* (meteor.) isallobar
**iscariote** *adj* traitorous; bold, brazen
**isíaco -ca** *adj* Isiac
**isidoriano -na** *adj* Isidorian
**Isidoro** *m* Isidore
**isidro -dra** *mf* (coll.) hick, yokel, jake
**Isis** *f* (myth.) Isis
**isla** *f* island; block (*of houses*); (fig.) island (*hill, grove of trees*); **las Mil Islas** the Thousand Islands; **la Isla de la Reunión** Reunion; **la**

**Isla del cabo Bretón** Cape Breton Island; **la Isla del Diablo** Devil's Island; **la Isla del Norte** North Island; **la Isla del Príncipe Eduardo** Prince Edward Island; **la Isla del Sur** South Island; **Isla de Man** Isle of Man; **la Isla de Pascua** Easter Island; **Isla de Pinos** Isle of Pines; **isla de seguridad** safety island, safety zone; **islas Afortunadas** (myth.) Fortunate Islands; **islas Aleutas, Aleutianas** or **Aleutinas** Aleutian Islands; **islas Almirantes** Admiralty Islands; **islas Anglonormandas** Channel Islands; **islas Bahamas** Bahama Islands; **islas Baleares** Balearic Islands; **islas Bisayas** Visayan Islands; **Islas Británicas** British Isles; **islas Canarias** Canary Islands; **islas Curiles** Kurile Islands; **islas de Barlovento** Windward Islands; **islas Carolinas** Caroline Islands; **islas de Cabo Verde** Cape Verde Islands; **islas de las Especias** Spice Islands; **islas de la Sociedad** Society Islands; **islas de la Sonda** Sunda Islands; **islas del Canal** Channel Islands; **islas del Dodecaneso** Dodecanese Islands; **islas de los Amigos** Friendly Islands; **islas de (los) Galápagos** Galápagos Islands; **islas de Sotavento** Leeward Islands; **Islas Filipinas** Philippine Islands; **islas Jonias** Ionian Islands; **islas Malvinas** Falkland Islands; **islas Normandas** Channel Islands; **islas Salomón** Solomon Islands; **islas Vírgenes** Virgin Islands; **islas Visayas** Visayan Islands
**Islam, el** Islam
**islámico -ca** *adj* Islamic
**islamismo** *m* Islamism
**islamista** *adj* Islamistic; *m* Islamist, Islamite
**islamita** *adj & m* Islamite
**islamizar** §76 *va, vn & vr* to Islamize
**islandés -desa** *adj* Icelandic; *mf* Icelander; *m* Icelandic (*language*)
**Islandia** *f* Iceland
**islándico -ca** *adj* Icelandic
**islario** *m* description of islands; map of islands
**isleño -ña** *adj* (pertaining to an) island; *mf* islander; (in Cuba) Canarian
**isleo** *m* island; island of ground (*surrounded by other ground of different nature*)
**isleta** *f* isle, islet
**islilla** *f* (anat.) collar bone
**islote** *m* small barren island; large jutting rock (*in sea*)
**Ismael** *m* (Bib.) Ishmael
**ismaelita** *mf* Ishmaelite
**ismo** *m* ism; isthmus
**isobárico -ca** *adj* isobaric
**isobaro -ra** *adj* isobaric; *m* (chem.) isobar; *f* (meteor.) isobar
**isoclino -na** *adj* isoclinal; *f* isoclinal line
**Isócrates** *m* Isocrates
**isocromático -ca** *adj* isochromatic
**isócrono -na** *adj* isochronal, isochronous
**isodáctilo -la** *adj* isodactylous
**isodinámico -ca** *adj* isodynamic
**isoete** *m* (bot.) quillwort
**isogloso -sa** *adj* isoglossal; *f* isogloss
**isogónico -ca** *adj* isogonic
**isógono -na** *adj* isogonic; *f* isogonic line
**Isolda** *f* (myth.) Iseult
**isomería** *f* (chem.) isomerism
**isomérico -ca** *adj* (chem.) isomeric, isomerical
**isomerismo** *m* (chem.) isomerism
**isómero -ra** *adj* (chem.) isomeric, isomerical; *m* (chem.) isomer
**isométrico -ca** *adj* isometric or isometrical
**isomorfismo** *m* (biol., chem. & mineral.) isomorphism
**isomorfo -fa** *adj* (biol., chem. & mineral.) isomorphic
**isoniacida** *f* (pharm.) isoniazid
**isoperímetro -tra** *adj* isoperimetric or isoperimetrical
**isópodo -da** *adj & m* (zool.) isopod
**isopreno** *m* (chem.) isoprene
**isoquímeno -na** *adj* (meteor.) isocheimenal; *f* (meteor.) isocheim
**isósceles** *adj* (geom.) isosceles
**isotermo -ma** *adj* isothermal; *f* isotherm
**isótero -ra** *adj* isotheral; *f* isothere
**isotopía** *f* isotopy
**isotópico -ca** *adj* isotopic
**isótopo** *m* (chem.) isotope
**isotropía** *f* (biol. & phys.) isotropy
**isotrópico -ca** *adj* (biol. & phys.) isotropic
**isotropo -pa** *adj* (biol. & phys.) isotropic, isotropous
**isquiático -ca** *adj* (anat.) ischial
**isquión** *m* (anat.) ischium
**Israel** *m* Israel
**israelí** (*pl* **-líes**) *adj & mf* Israeli
**israelita** *adj & mf* Israelite
**israelítico -ca** *adj* Israelitish
**Istambul** *f* Istanbul
**istmeño -ña** *adj & mf* isthmian
**ístmico -ca** *adj* isthmian, isthmic
**istmo** *m* isthmus; (anat.) isthmus; **istmo de Corinto** Isthmus of Corinth; **istmo de Panamá** Isthmus of Panama; **istmo de Suez** Isthmus of Suez
**istriar** §90 *va & vr* var. of **estriar**
**-ita** *suffix* see **-ito**
**Itaca** *f* Ithaca (*island west of Greece*)
**Italia** *f* Italy
**italianismo** *m* Italianism
**italianizar** §76 *va* to Italianize; *vr* to become Italianized
**italiano -na** *adj & mf* Italian; **a la italiana** in the Italian fashion or manner; *m* Italian (*language*)
**itálico -ca** *adj* Italic; (print.) italic; *f* (print.) italic, italics
**ítalo -la** *adj & mf* (poet.) Italian
**itea** *f* (bot.) itea
**ítem** *m* item, article, section; addition
**iterable** *adj* repeatable
**iteración** *f* iteration
**iterar** *va* iterate
**iterativo -va** *adj* iterative
**iterbia** *f* (chem.) ytterbia
**itérbico -ca** *adj* ytterbic
**iterbio** *m* (chem.) ytterbium
**itinerario -ria** *adj & m* itinerary
**-ito -ta** *suffix dim* has the force of little, nice and . . . , cute, dear, humble, somewhat, rather, etc. and is sometimes equivalent to English -y or -ie, e.g., **un poquito** a little bit; **hijita** little daughter; **tempranito** nice and early; **subidito** rather high; **perrito** doggie; **Juanito** Johnny; **Anita** Annie; is often added to adverbs, interjections, etc., e.g., **ahorita** right now; **¡adiosito!** bye-bye!; *suffix adj* -ite, e.g., **bipartito** bipartite; **finito** finite; *suffix adj & mf* **favorito** favorite; *suffix m* (chem.) -ite, e.g., **sulfito** sulfite; *suffix f* (com., explosives, mineral. & pal.) -ite, e.g., **vulcanita** vulcanite; **cordita** cordite; **dolomita** dolomite; **amonita** ammonite; **-ita** *adj & mf* -ite, e.g., **israelita** Israelite; **moscovita** Muscovite
**itria** *f* (chem.) yttria
**ítrico -ca** *adj* yttric
**itrio** *m* (chem.) yttrium
**Ixión** *m* (myth.) Ixion
**ixtle** *m* istle (*fiber*)
**izado** *m* hoisting
**izaga** *f* land full of rushes or reeds
**izaje** *m* (Am.) hoisting
**izar** §76 *va* (naut.) to hoist, haul up; **¡iza!** yo-heave-ho!
**-izo -za** *suffix adj* expresses the idea of tendency or susceptibility, e.g., **bermejizo** reddish; **enfermizo** sickly; **heladizo** easily frozen; -y, e.g., **cobrizo** coppery; **pajizo** strawy; *suffix m* e.g., **vaquerizo** cattle tender; *suffix f* e.g., **caballeriza** stable
**izote** *m* (bot.) Adam's-needle, bear grass; (bot.) Spanish dagger
**izq.°** abr. of **izquierdo**
**izquierda** *f* see **izquierdo**
**izquierdear** *vn* to go awry, to go wild, to go astray
**izquierdismo** *m* leftism
**izquierdista** *adj & mf* leftist
**izquierdizante** *adj* leftish; *mf* leftish person
**izquierdo -da** *adj* left; left-hand; left-handed; crooked; **a la izquierda** left, on the left, to the left; **levantarse del izquierdo** to get out of bed on the wrong side; *f* left hand; left-hand side; (pol.) left

# J

**J, j** *f* eleventh letter of the Spanish alphabet
**ja** *interj* ha!
**jabalcón** *m* strut, brace
**jabalconar** *va* to support with struts, to brace
**jabalí** *m* (*pl:* **-líes**) (zool.) wild boar; **jabalí de Erimanto** (myth.) Erymanthian boar; **jabalí de verrugas** (zool.) wart hog
**jabalina** *f* (hist. & sport) javelin; wild sow
**jabardear** *vn* to swarm (*said of bees*)
**jabardillo** *m* noisy swarm (*of insects or birds*); (coll.) noisy swarm (*of people*)
**jabardo** *m* afterswarm; poor swarm, small swarm; (coll.) noisy swarm (*of people*)
**jabato** *m* young wild boar
**jábega** *f* sweep net; fishing smack
**jabegote** *m* sweep-net fisherman
**jabeguero -ra** *adj* sweep-net; *m* sweep-net fisherman
**jabeque** *m* (naut.) xebec; (coll.) gash in the face
**jabí** *m* (*pl:* **-bíes**) (bot.) brasiletto (*tree and wood*); small wild apple; small grape of Granada
**jabillo** *m* (bot.) sandbox tree
**jabladera** *f* croze, crozing saw
**jable** *m* croze (*groove*)
**jabón** *m* soap; cake of soap; **dar jabón a** (coll.) to softsoap; **dar un jabón a** (coll.) to upbraid, rake over the coals; **jabón blando** soft soap; **jabón de afeitar** shaving soap; **jabón de Castilla** Castile soap; **jabón de tocador** or **de olor** toilet soap; **jabón de piedra** hard soap; **jabón de sastre** French chalk, soapstone; **jabón duro** hard soap; **jabón en polvo** soap powder; **jabón graso** soft soap; **jabón para la barba** shaving soap
**jabonado** *m* soaping; wash (*clothes washed or to be washed*)
**jabonadura** *f* soaping; **jabonaduras** *fpl* soapy water; soapsuds; **dar una jabonadura a** (coll.) to upbraid, to rake over the coals, to lambaste
**jabonar** *va* to soap; (coll.) to upbraid, to rake over the coals
**jaboncillo** *m* cake of toilet soap; French chalk; (bot.) soapberry, soapberry tree; **jaboncillo de sastre** French chalk
**jabonera** *f* see **jabonero**
**jabonería** *f* soap factory; soap store
**jabonero -ra** *adj* (pertaining to) soap; yellowish, dirty-white (*bull*); *mf* soapmaker; soap dealer; **jabonero de las Antillas** (bot.) chinaberry, wild China tree; *f* soap dish; (bot.) soapwort
**jaboneta** *f* or **jabonete** *m* cake of toilet soap
**jabonoso -sa** *adj* soapy
**jaca** *f* cob, jennet; gamecock
**jacal** *m* (Am.) hut, shack; (zool.) jackal
**jacalero -ra** *adj* (Am.) hut-dwelling; *mf* (Am.) hut dweller; **andar de jacalero** (Am.) to go on a spree
**jácara** *f* see **jácaro**
**jacarandá** *m* (bot.) jacaranda
**jacarandoso -sa** *adj* (coll.) gay, carefree; (coll.) sporty
**jacarear** *vn* to sing merry ballads; (coll.) to go serenading, to go singing in the street; (coll.) to be disagreeable, be offensive
**jacarero -ra** *adj* serenading; (coll.) gay, merry, witty; *mf* serenader; (coll.) jester, wag, wit
**jácaro -ra** *adj* braggart; *m* braggart, bully; *f* merry ballad; merry dance or tune; serenaders, night revelers; (coll.) story, argument; (coll.) lie, fake; (coll.) annoyance
**jácena** *f* girder; header beam
**jacerina** *f* coat of mail
**jacilla** *f* mark on the ground (*left by a thing that has stood for a long time*)
**jacintino -na** *adj* hyacinthine, violet
**jacinto** *m* (bot.) hyacinth; (mineral.) hyacinth, jacinth; (*cap.*) *m* (myth.) Hyacinthus; **jacinto de penacho** (bot.) tassel hyacinth; **jacinto estrellado** (bot.) Cuban lily, hyacinth of Peru; **jacinto racimoso silvestre** (bot.) grape hyacinth
**jaco** *m* nag, jade; (orn.) gray parrot; (obs.) coat of mail; (obs.) goatskin jacket
**Jacob** *m* (Bib.) Jacob
**jacobeo -a** *adj* of St. James
**jacobínico -ca** *adj* Jacobinic or Jacobinical
**jacobinismo** *m* Jacobinism
**jacobinizar §76** *va* to Jacobinize; *vn* to boast of or make a show of Jacobinism
**jacobino -na** *adj & mf* Jacobin
**jacobita** *mf* pilgrim to Santiago de Compostela; *m* Jacobite
**Jacobo** *m* James; Jacob
**jactancia** *f* boasting, bragging; boastfulness
**jactancioso -sa** *adj* boastful, bragging
**jactar** *vr* to boast, to brag; **jactarse de** + *inf* to boast of + *ger*
**jaculatorio -ria** *adj* ejaculatory; *f* ejaculation (*short, sudden prayer*)
**jade** *m* (mineral.) jade
**jadeante** *adj* panting, out of breath
**jadear** *vn* to pant
**jadeo** *m* panting
**jaecero -ra** *mf* harness maker
**jaez** *m* (*pl:* **jaeces**) harness, piece of harness; kind, stripe, quality, character; **jaeces** *mpl* trappings
**jaezar §76** *va* var. of **enjaezar**
**jafético -ca** *adj* Japhetic
**jagua** *f* (bot.) genipap
**jaguar** *m* (zool.) jaguar
**jaguarzo** *m* (bot.) rockrose
**jagüey** *m* (Am.) reservoir; (Am.) tiny mosquito; (bot.) Indian fig
**jaharrar** *va* to plaster
**jaharro** *m* plaster, plastering
**Jahel** *f* (Bib.) Jael
**jai alai** *m* jai alai (*Spanish game like rackets*)
**jaibería** *f* (Am.) slyness, trickiness
**Jaime** *m* James
**jaique** *m* hooded cape
**jairar** *va* to bevel (*leather*)
**jaire** *m* bevel cut
**jalapa** *f* (bot.) jalap
**jalar** *va* (coll.) to pull, to haul; (Am.) to flirt with; *vr* (Am.) to get drunk; (Am.) to beat it, get out
**jalbegador -dora** *adj & mf* var. of **enjalbegador**
**jalbegar §59** *va & vr* var. of **enjalbegar**
**jalbegue** *m* whitewash; whitewashing; paint, make-up
**jaldado -da, jalde** or **jaldo -da** *adj* bright-yellow
**jalea** *f* jelly; **hacerse una jalea** (coll.) to be madly in love
**jaleador -dora** *adj* cheering; *mf* cheerer
**jalear** *va* to cheer (*hounds; dancers*); to flirt with; (Am.) to bother, tease; *vn* to dance the jaleo; *vr* to dance the jaleo; to have a noisy time; to dance and sway
**jaleo** *m* cheering; noisy time, jamboree; jaleo (*vivacious Spanish solo dance*)
**jaletina** *f* gelatine; calf's foot jelly
**jalifa** *m* Spanish Moroccan caliph
**jalifato** *m* Spanish Moroccan caliphate
**jalisco -ca** *adj* (Am.) drunk; *m* (Am.) straw hat
**jalma** *f* light packsaddle
**jalmería** *f* packsaddle work
**jalmero** *m* packsaddle maker or dealer

**jalón** *m* stage; (surv.) flagpole, range pole; (Am.) jerk, tug; (Am.) swig, drink; **jalón de mira** (surv.) leveling rod
**jalonamiento** *m* staking, marking, laying out
**jalonar** *va* to lay out, stake out, mark out
**jalonero** *m* (surv.) rodman
**jaloque** *m* southeast wind
**jallullo** *m* (prov.) bread baked on embers or hot stones
**jamaica** *m* Jamaica, Jamaica rum; *f* (bot.) roselle, Jamaica sorrel; (Am.) charity fair; (*cap.*) *f* Jamaica
**jamaicano -na** *adj & mf* Jamaican
**jamar** *va* (coll.) to eat
**jamás** *adv* never; **jamás por jamás** never more
**jamba** *f* (arch.) jamb; (slang) loose woman; sweetheart
**jambaje** *m* (arch.) doorframe, window frame
**jámbico -ca** *adj* var. of **yámbico**
**jamelgo** *m* (coll.) jade, nag
**jamerdana** *f* sewer of an abattoir
**jamerdar** *va* to clean the guts of (*a slaughtered animal*); (coll.) to wash with a lick and a promise
**jamete** *m* samite
**jámila** *f* var. of **alpechín**
**jamón** *m* ham
**jamona** *adj fem* fat and middle-aged (*woman*); *f* fat and middle-aged woman
**jámparo** *m* (Am.) canoe, rowboat
**jamuga** *f* or **jamugas** *fpl* sidesaddle (*in form of folding chair*); **ir en jamugas** to ride sidesaddle
**jamurar** *va* to scoop out, bail out
**jándalo -la** *adj & mf* (coll.) Andalusian
**jangada** *f* (coll.) piece of folly; (coll.) dirty trick; raft; life-saving raft or float
**Janículo** *m* Janiculum
**Jano** *m* (myth.) Janus
**Jansenio** *m* Jansen
**jansenismo** *m* Jansenism
**jansenista** *adj* Jansenist, Jansenistic; *mf* Jansenist
**Jantipa** or **Jantipe** *f* Xanthippe
**japón -pona** *adj & mf* var. of **japonés; el Japón** Japan
**japonense** *adj & mf* var. of **japonés**
**japonés -nesa** *adj & mf* Japanese; *m* Japanese (*language*)
**japuta** *f* (ichth.) pomfret
**jaque** *m* check (*in chess*); saddlebag; (coll.) bully; (obs.) smooth hairdo; **dar jaque a** to check (*in chess*); **dar jaque mate a** to checkmate (*in chess*); **en jaque** in check (*in chess*); **estar muy jaque** (coll.) to be full of pep; **tener en jaque** to hold a threat over the head of; **jaque mate** checkmate (*in chess*); *interj* check! (*in chess*); **¡jaque de aquí!** get out of here!
**jaquear** *va* to check (*in chess*); to harass (*an enemy*); *vn* (coll.) to be a bully
**jaqueca** *f* headache, sick headache; **dar jaqueca a** (coll.) to bore to death
**jaquecoso -sa** *adj* boring, tiresome
**jaquel** *adj* (Am.) blood (*orange*); *m* (her.) square
**jaquelado -da** *adj* (her.) checky; square-faceted
**jaquemar** *m* jack (*figure of man which strikes time in a clock*)
**jaqueta** *f* (archaic & prov.) blouse, jacket
**jaquetilla** *f* small short loose coat
**jaquetón** *m* (zool.) man-eater (*shark*); (coll.) bully
**jáquima** *f* rope headstall
**jaquimazo** *m* blow with a headstall; (coll.) great disappointment
**jara** *f* see **jaro**
**jarabe** *m* syrup; sweet drink; **jarabe de pico** (coll.) empty talk, idle promise, lip service
**jarabear** *va* to prescribe syrups or potions for; *vr* to take syrups or potions, to take laxatives
**jaraíz** *m* (*pl:* **-íces**) wine press
**jaral** *m* growth of rockrose; puzzle, complication
**jaramago** *m* (bot.) wall rocket
**jaramugo** *m* tiny fish (*used as bait*)
**jarana** *f* (coll.) fun, merrymaking; (coll.) rumpus; (coll.) trick, deceit; (Am.) jest, joke; (Am.) small guitar; **ir de jarana** (coll.) to go on a spree, to go merrymaking
**jaranear** *vn* (coll.) to go on a spree, to go merrymaking; (coll.) to raise a rumpus
**jaranero -ra** *adj* merrymaking; fun-loving, gay, merry; *m* reveler
**jaranista** *adj* (Am.) var. of **jaranero**
**jarano** *m* sombrero
**jarazo** *m* arrow shot, arrow wound
**jarcia** *f* bundle; fishing tackle; (coll.) mess, jumble; **jarcias** *fpl* tackle, rigging; **jarcia de firme** or **jarcia muerta** (naut.) standing rigging; **jarcia trozada** junk (*old cable*)
**jarciar** *va* var. of **enjarciar**
**jardín** *m* garden, flower garden; park; flaw in an emerald; (baseball) field, outfield; (naut.) privy, latrine; **jardín botánico** botanical garden; **jardín central** (baseball) center field; **jardín de la infancia** kindergarten; **jardín del Edén** (Bib.) Garden of Eden; **jardín derecho** (baseball) right field; **jardín izquierdo** (baseball) left field; **jardín zoológico** zoölogical garden
**jardinaje** *m* (Am.) gardening
**jardinera** *f* see **jardinero**
**jardinería** *f* gardening, landscape gardening
**jardinero -ra** *mf* gardener; **jardinero adornista** landscape gardener; *m* (baseball) fielder, outfielder; *f* jardiniere; basket carriage; summer trolley car, open trolley car
**jardinista** *mf* garden expert
**jarear** *vr* (Am.) to flee, run away; (Am.) to swing, to sway; (Am.) to die of starvation
**jareta** *f* (sew.) casing
**jaretón** *m* broad hem
**jarife** *m* var. of **jerife**
**jarifo -fa** *adj* natty, spruce, showy
**jaripeo** *m* (Am.) rodeo
**jaro -ra** *adj* carroty; red (*hog or boar*); *m* thicket; small oak; (bot.) arum; *f* sharp-pointed arrow; (bot.) rockrose (*Cistus ladaniferus*); **jara blanca** (bot.) white-leaved rockrose
**jarocho -cha** *adj* brusque, bluff; *mf* brusque, insulting person; (Am.) peasant of Veracruz
**jaropar** *va* (coll.) to overdose with syrups and drugs; (coll.) to fix up a dose for
**jarope** *m* syrup; (coll.) nasty potion
**jaropear** *va* (coll.) to overdose with syrups and drugs; *vr* (coll.) to overdose oneself, take too much medicine
**jaropeo** *m* (coll.) overdosing oneself, abuse of medicine
**jarra** *f* pitcher, water pitcher; jug; **en jarras** or **de jarras** with arms akimbo
**jarrazo** *m* blow with a jar, jug, or pitcher
**jarrear** *va* to plaster; *vn* (coll.) to draw water or wine with a jug or pitcher; (prov.) to pour, to rain hard
**jarrero** *m* maker or seller of jars, jugs, etc.
**jarrete** *m* hock; gambrel; ham
**jarretera** *f* garter; (*cap.*) *f* Garter (*order; badge of the order*)
**jarro** *m* pitcher; **echar un jarro de agua (fría) a** (coll.) to pour cold water on
**jarrón** *m* vase; (arch.) urn
**Jartum** *f* Khartoum or Khartum
**Jasón** *m* (myth.) Jason
**jaspe** *m* (mineral.) jasper
**jaspeado -da** *adj* marbled, speckled, jaspered; jaspery; *m* marbling, speckling
**jaspeadura** *f* marbling, speckling
**jaspear** *va* to marble, to speckle
**jaspeo** *m* var. of **jaspeadura**
**jastial** *m* (prov.) var. of **hastial**
**jateo -a** *adj* fox-hunting; *mf* foxhound
**jato -ta** *mf* calf
**Jauja** *f* Cockaigne, Shangrila; **¿estamos aquí o en Jauja?** (coll.) where do you think you are?; **vivir en Jauja** (coll.) to live in the lap of luxury
**jaula** *f* cage; crate; (elec., mach. & min.) cage; (Am.) open freight car; **jaula de locos** insane asylum; (fig.) madhouse (*place of confusion*)
**jauría** *f* pack (*of hounds*)
**javanés -nesa** *adj & mf* Javanese; *m* Javanese (*language*)
**Javier** *m* Xavier
**jayán -yana** *mf* big brute of a person
**jazarán** *m* coat of mail

**jazmín** *m* (bot.) jasmine; **jazmín de Arabia** (bot.) Arabian jasmine; **jazmín de la India** (bot.) gardenia; **jazmín del Cabo** (bot.) Cape jasmine; **jazmín silvestre** (bot.) yellow jasmine
**jazz** *m* (mus.) jazz
**jazz-band** *m* jazz band
**J.C.** abr. of **Jesucristo**
**je** *interj* var. of **ji**
**jebe** *m* rock alum; India rubber; (bot.) rubber plant (*Hevea brasiliensis*)
**jedive** *m* khedive
**jefa** *f* female head or leader; **jefa de ruta** hostess (*on a bus*)
**jefatura** *f* chieftaincy, chieftainship; leadership; headquarters
**jefe** *m* chief, leader, head; boss; (her.) chief; (mil.) field officer; **en jefe** in chief; **mandar en jefe** (mil.) to be commander in chief; **quedar jefe** (Am.) to gamble away everything; **jefe de cocina** chef; **jefe de coro** choirmaster; **jefe de día** (mil.) officer of the day; **jefe de equipajes** (rail.) baggage master; **jefe de estación** (rail.) station agent, stationmaster; **jefe del estado** or **jefe del ejecutivo** chief executive; **jefe de meseros** (Am.) headwaiter; **jefe de redacción** editor in chief; **jefe de ruta** guide; hostess (*on a bus*); **jefe de tren** (rail.) conductor; **jefe supremo** commander in chief
**Jefté** *m* (Bib.) Jephthah
**Jehová** *m* Jehovah
**jehovismo** *m* Jehovism
**Jehú** *m* (Bib.) Jehu
**jeito** *m* anchovy net, sardine net
**jeja** *f* white wheat
**jején** *m* (ent.) gnat, mosquito
**jemal** *adj* as long as the distance between tip of thumb and tip of forefinger
**jeme** *m* space between tip of thumb and tip of forefinger when extended; (coll.) face (*of a woman*)
**jenabe** *m* or **jenable** *m* mustard
**jengibre** *m* (bot.) ginger (*plant, root, and spice*)
**jeniquén** *m* (Am.) henequen
**jenízaro -ra** *adj* mixed, hybrid; *m* Janizary
**Jenofonte** *m* Xenophon
**jeque** *m* sheik
**jerapellina** *f* old raggedy and torn garment
**jerarca** *m* hierarch; ruler
**jerarquía** *f* hierarchy; **de jerarquía** of importance, prominent
**jerárquico -ca** *adj* hierarchic or hierarchical
**jerarquizar** §76 *va* to hierarchize
**jerbo** *m* (zool.) jerboa
**jeremíaco -ca** *adj* Jeremian or Jeremianic
**jeremiada** *f* (coll.) jeremiad
**Jeremías** *m* (Bib.) Jeremiah; (*l.c.*) *mf* (*pl:* **-as**) (coll.) constant complainer
**jerez** *m* sherry
**jerezano -na** *adj* (pertaining to) Jerez; *mf* native or inhabitant of Jerez
**jerga** *f* coarse cloth; straw mattress; corduroy; jargon (*of a trade or special group; gibberish*); **en jerga** (coll.) unfinished
**jergal** *adj* of a trade, of a profession (*said, e.g., of a word or idiom*)
**jergón** *m* straw mattress; (mineral.) jargon; (coll.) ill-fitting clothes; (coll.) lummox
**Jericó** *f* Jericho
**jerifalte** *m* var. of **gerifalte**
**jerife** *m* shereef
**jerifiano -na** *adj* sherifian
**jerigonza** *f* slang; jargon (*of a trade or special group*); (coll.) gibberish, jargon; (coll.) folly, piece of folly
**jeringa** *f* syringe; enema; gun (*for projecting grease, etc.*); (coll.) plague, annoyance; **jeringa de engrase** or **grasa** grease gun; **jeringa hipodérmica** hypodermic syringe
**jeringación** *f* syringing; injection; (coll.) plague, annoyance
**jeringador -dora** *adj* (coll.) plaguing, pestering; *mf* (coll.) plague, pest
**jeringar** §59 *va* to syringe; to inject; to give an enema to; (coll.) to annoy, bore, molest; *vr* to give oneself an enema; (coll.) to be annoyed
**jeringazo** *m* injection, shot
**jeringuear** *va* (Am.) to plague, pester
**jeringuilla** *f* syringe (*for injecting fluids into body*); (bot.) syringa, mock orange
**Jerjes** *m* Xerxes
**jerofante** *m* var. of **hierofanta**
**jeroglífico -ca** *adj* hieroglyphic or hieroglyphical; *m* hieroglyphic; rebus
**jerónimo -ma** *adj & m* Hieronymite; (*cap.*) *m* Jerome
**jerosolimitano -na** *adj* (pertaining to) Jerusalem; *mf* native or inhabitant of Jerusalem
**jerpa** *f* (hort.) sterile shoot (*of vine*)
**jersey** *m* jersey (*sweater*)
**Jerusalén** *f* Jerusalem
**Jesé** *m* (Bib.) Jesse
**Jesucristo** *m* Jesus Christ
**jesuíta** *adj & m* Jesuit; (coll.) Jesuit (*intriguer*)
**jesuítico -ca** *adj* Jesuitic or Jesuitical; (coll.) Jesuitic or Jesuitical (*crafty*)
**jesuitisa** *f* Jesuitess
**jesuitismo** *m* Jesuitism; (coll.) jesuitism (*casuistry*)
**Jesús** *m* Jesus; bambino (*image of baby Jesus*); **en un decir Jesús** or **en un Jesús** in an instant; **hasta verte, Jesús mío** to the last drop; **¡Jesús, María y José!** my gracious!
**jeta** *f* pig face; pouched mouth; hog's snout; (coll.) phiz, mug; **estar con tanta jeta** (coll.) to make a long face; **poner jeta** (coll.) to pouch one's lips
**jetón -tona** or **jetudo -da** *adj* snouted; grim, gruff
**Jetró** *m* (Bib.) Jethro
**Jezabel** *f* (Bib.) Jezebel
**Jhs.** abr. of **Jesús**
**ji** *interj* he!; **¡ji, ji!** te-hee!; **¡ji, ji, ji!** he, he, he!
**jíbaro -ra** *adj & mf* (Am.) peasant
**jibia** *f* (zool.) cuttlefish
**jibión** *m* cuttlebone
**Jibraltar** var. of **Gibraltar**
**jibraltareño -ña** *adj & mf* var. of **gibraltareño**
**jícara** *f* chocolate cup; (Am.) calabash (*used as cup*)
**jicarazo** *m* blow with a chocolate cup; poisoning
**jícaro** *m* (Am.) calabash tree
**jicotea** *f* (zool.) mud turtle
**jifa** *f* offal (*of slaughtered animal*)
**jiferada** *f* blow with a slaughtering knife
**jifería** *f* slaughtering
**jifero -ra** *adj* (pertaining to the) slaughterhouse; (coll.) dirty, filthy, vile; *m* slaughtering knife; slaughterer, butcher
**jifia** *f* (ichth.) swordfish
**jifosuro** *m* (zool.) xiphosuran
**jiga** *f* var. of **giga**
**jigote** *m* var. of **gigote**
**jiguilete** *m* var. of **jiquilete**
**jijallar** *m* thicket of saltwort
**jijallo** *m* (bot.) saltwort
**jilguero** *m* (orn.) goldfinch, linnet
**jimagua** *adj & mf* (Am.) twin
**jimelga** *f* (naut.) fish (*of a mast*)
**jimenzar** §31 *va* (prov.) to ripple (*flax*)
**jimio** *m* var. of **simio**
**jinestada** *f* sauce made of milk, rice flour, dates, spices, etc.
**jineta** *f* riding with stirrups high and legs bent; sergeant's shoulder knot; (zool.) genet; **tener los cascos a la jineta** (coll.) to be a scatterbrain, to be a harum-scarum
**jinete** *m* horseman, rider; cavalryman; purebred horse; *f* horsewoman
**jineteada** *f* (Am.) horsebreaking
**jinetear** *va* (Am.) to break in (*a horse*); *vn* to ride around on horseback, to show off one's horsemanship; *vr* (Am.) to be puffed up
**jinglar** *vn* to swing, to rock
**jingoísmo** *m* jingoism
**jingoísta** *adj* jingo, jingoist, jingoistic; *mf* jingo, jingoist
**jínjol** *m* var. of **azufaifa**
**jinjolero** *m* var. of **azufaifo**
**jipato -ta** *adj* (Am.) pale, wan; (Am.) insipid
**jipi** *m* (coll.) Panama hat
**jipijapa** *f* (bot.) jipijapa; strip of jipijapa straw; *m* jipijapa, Panama hat
**jiquilete** *m* (Am.) indigo plant

**jira** *f* slip, strip; picnic, outing; tour; trip; swing, political trip
**jirafa** *f* (zool.) giraffe
**jirel** *m* rich caparison
**jíride** *f* (bot.) gladdon, stinking iris
**jirón** *m* shred, tatter, tear; pennant; (sew.) facing (*of skirt*); (her.) gyron; (fig.) shred, drop, bit; **hacer jirones** to tear to shreds
**jironado -da** *adj* shredded, tattered, torn
**jiste** *m* barm, froth, foam (*of beer*)
**jitomate** *m* (Am.) tomato
**jo** *interj* whoa!
**Joaquín** *m* Joachim
**Job** *m* (Bib.) Job; (*l.c.*) *m* (*pl:* **jobs**) (fig.) Job (*very patient man*)
**jobo** *m* (bot.) hog plum, yellow mombin
**jocoserio -ria** *adj* seriocomic, jocoserious
**jocosidad** *f* jocosity; jocularity; joke, witticism
**jocoso -sa** *adj* jocose; jocular
**jocotal** *m* (bot.) Spanish plum (*tree*)
**jocote** *m* Spanish plum (*fruit*)
**jocoyote** *m* (Am.) var. of **socoyote**
**jocundidad** *f* jocundity
**jocundo -da** *adj* jocund
**jofaina** *f* washbowl, basin
**jolgorio** *m* (coll.) var. of **holgorio**
**jolito** *m* rest, calm; **en jolito** disappointed
**joloano -na** *adj* Suluan; *mf* Sulu, Suluan
**jollín** *m* (coll.) merriment, jollification, uproar
**Jonás** *m* (Bib.) Jonah
**Jonatás** *m* Jonathan
**Jonia** *f* see **jonio**
**jónico -ca** *adj* Ionian, Ionic; (arch.) Ionic; *mf* Ionian
**jonio -nia** *adj* Ionian, Ionic; *mf* Ionian; (*cap.*) *f* Ionia
**jonrón** *m* (baseball) home run
**Jordán** *m* Jordan (*river*); (fig.) fountain of youth; (fig.) rebirth, regeneration; **ir al Jordán** (coll.) to be rejuvenated, to be born again
**Jordania** *f* Jordan (*country*)
**jordano -na** *adj & mf* Jordanian
**jorfe** *m* sustaining wall; cliff, precipice
**Jorja** *f* Georgia (*woman's name*)
**Jorge** *m* George
**jorguín** *m* wizard, sorcerer
**jorguina** *f* witch, sorceress
**jorguinería** *f* witchcraft, sorcery
**jornada** *f* day's journey; journey, trip, stage; workday (*number of hours of work*); day; session; battle; lifetime, span of life; passing (*death*); summer residence (*of diplomat or diplomatic corps*); undertaking; occasion, circumstance, event; (mil.) expedition; (archaic) act (*of a play*); **a grandes** or **a largas jornadas** by forced marches; **al fin de la jornada** in the end, at the wind-up; **caminar por sus jornadas** to proceed with circumspection; **echar** or **hacer mala jornada** to get nowhere, to make little or no progress; **jornada ordinaria** full time
**jornal** *m* salary, wage; day's wages; day's work; **a jornal** by the day; **jornal mínimo** minimum wage
**jornalar** *va* to hire by the day
**jornalero** *m* day laborer
**joroba** *f* hump; (coll.) annoyance, bother
**jorobado -da** *adj* humpbacked, hunchbacked; (coll.) annoyed, bothered, in a jam; *mf* humpback, hunchback
**jorobadura** *f* (coll.) annoyance, bother
**jorobar** *va* (coll.) to annoy, bother
**jorongo** *m* (Am.) poncho; (Am.) woolen blanket
**jorrar** *va* (archaic) to tow; see **red**
**jorro** *adj masc* (Am.) poor (*tobacco*); see **red**
**jos** *mpl* josses (*Chinese household divinities*)
**josa** *f* unfenced orchard
**Josafat** *m* (Bib.) Jehoshaphat
**José** *m* Joseph; **José de Arimatea** (Bib.) Joseph of Arimathea
**Josefa** or **Josefina** *f* Josephine
**Josefo** *m* Josephus
**Josías** *m* (Bib.) Josiah
**jostrado -da** *adj* banded and round-headed (*shaft*)
**Josué** *m* (Bib.) Joshua
**jota** *f* j (*letter*); jota (*Spanish dance*); jot, iota, tittle; vegetable soup; **no entender** or **no saber jota** or **una jota** (coll.) to be completely ignorant, to not know what is going on; **sin faltar una jota** (coll.) in minutest detail
**jotacismo** *m* use of **j** instead of **g** before **e** and **i**
**jovada** *f* (prov.) daywork (*of a pair of mules*)
**Jove** *m* (myth.) Jove
**joven** *adj* young; **ser joven de esperanzas** (coll.) to have a bright future; *mf* youth, young person; **de joven** as a youth, as a young man (or woman)
**jovencísimo -ma** *adj super* very young
**jovial** *adj* jovial; Jovian, Jovelike
**jovialidad** *f* joviality
**joviano -na** or **jovio -via** *adj* Jovian
**joya** *f* jewel, piece of jewelry; diamond brooch; gift, present; (arch. & arti.) astragal; (fig.) jewel (*person or thing*); **joyas** *fpl* trousseau; **joya de familia** heirloom; **joyas de fantasía** costume jewelry
**joyante** *adj* glossy (*silk*)
**joyel** *m* small jewel
**joyelero** *m* jewel case, casket
**joyería** *f* jewelry; jewelry shop; jewelry business
**joyero -ra** *mf* jeweler; *m* jewel case, casket; *f* (archaic) embroideress
**joyo** *m* (bot.) cockle
**joyón** *m* big, ugly jewel
**joyuyo** *m* (orn.) wood duck
**juaguarzo** *m* var. of **jaguarzo**
**Juan** *m* John; **Buen Juan** (coll.) sap, easy mark; **Juan de Gante** John of Gaunt; **Juan de las viñas** (fig.) puppet; **Juan Español** the Spanish people; the typical Spaniard; **Juan Lanas** (coll.) simpleton, poor devil; **Juan Palomo** (coll.) good-for-nothing
**Juana** *f* Jane, Jean, Joan; **juanas** *fpl* glove stretcher; **Juana de Arco** Joan of Arc, Jeanne d'Arc; **Juana la papisa** Pope Joan
**juanete** *m* bunion; high cheekbone; (naut.) topgallant; (naut.) topgallant sail; **juanete de proa** (naut.) foretopgallant sail; **juanete de sobremesana** (naut.) mizzen-topgallant sail; **juanete mayor** (naut.) main-topgallant sail
**juanetero** *m* (naut.) topman (*in charge of topgallants*)
**juanetudo -da** *adj* full of bunions
**Juanillo** *m* Jack, Johnny
**Juanita** *f* Jenny, Jeannette
**Juanito** *m* var. of **Juanillo**
**juarda** *f* stain, spot
**juardoso -sa** *adj* stained, spotted
**jube** *m* (arch.) jube, rood screen
**jubete** *m* mail-covered doublet
**jubilación** *f* retirement; pension
**jubilado -da** *adj* retired; *mf* pensioner
**jubilamiento** *m* var. of **jubilación**
**jubilar** *adj* jubilee (*e.g., indulgence*); *va* to retire; to pension; (coll.) to throw out, cast off; *vn* to rejoice; to retire; to be pensioned; *vr* to rejoice; to retire; to be pensioned; (Am.) to decline, go to pieces; (Am.) to play truant; (Am.) to be a past master (*in a game, vice, etc.*)
**jubilate** *m* Jubilate (*third Sunday after Easter*)
**jubileo** *m* (hist. & eccl.) jubilee; (coll.) great doings, much going and coming; **por jubileo** (coll.) once in a long while
**júbilo** *m* jubilation
**jubiloso -sa** *adj* jubilant
**jubón** *m* jerkin, tight-fitting jacket; **jubón de azotes** (coll.) public whipping
**júcaro** *m* tropical hardwood tree and its wood (*genus: Terminalia*)
**Judá** *m* (Bib.) Judah (*son of Jacob; kingdom; tribe*)
**judaico -ca** *adj* Judaic, Jewish; *f* spine of fossil sea urchin
**judaísmo** *m* Judaism
**judaíta** *mf* Judahite; Israelite
**judaizante** *adj* Judaizing; *mf* Judaizer, Judaist
**judaizar** **§97** *vn* to Judaize; to boast of being a Jew (*said of a person born a Christian*)
**Judas** *m* (*pl:* **-das**) (Bib. & fig.) Judas; effigy of Judas burned during Holy Week; **estar hecho** or **parecer un Judas** (coll.) to be sloppy, to go around in rags; **Judas Iscariote** (Bib.) Judas Iscariot
**Judea** *f* Judea

**judeo-español -ñola** *adj* Judaeo-Spanish; *mf* Judaeo-Spaniard; *m* Judaeo-Spanish (*dialect*)
**judería** *f* Jewry (*ghetto; race, people*)
**judía** *f* see **judío**
**judiada** *f* Jewish act; (coll.) cruelty; (coll.) usury
**judiar** *m* bean patch
**judicatura** *f* judicature; judgeship
**judicial** *adj* judicial (*pertaining to courts, judges, etc.*)
**judiciario -ria** *adj* astrological; *m* astrologer
**judío -a** *adj* Jewish; Judean; usurious; *mf* Jew; Judean; usurer; **judío de señal** (hist.) converted Jew wearing distinguishing badge on shoulder; *m* (orn.) common ani; **Judío errante** Wandering Jew; *f* Jewess; (bot.) kidney bean, string bean, haricot; **judía de careta** (bot.) black-eyed bean; **judía de España** or **judía escarlata** (bot.) scarlet runner, kidney bean; **judía de la peladilla** (bot.) Lima bean
**Judit** *f* Judith
**judo** *m* judo
**juego** *m* play, playing; game; gambling; cards (*game*); set; suit, suite; movement, works; motion; play (*of water, light, colors, etc.*); hand (*quota of cards of one player*); (mach.) play; (sport) field, court, alley, etc. (*according to sport*); (sport) game (*certain number of points won*); (fig.) game (*e.g., diplomacy*); **a juego** to match, e.g., **un pañuelo a juego** a handkerchief to match; **conocerle a uno el juego** to be on to someone; **descubrir su juego** (cards & fig.) to show one's hand; **en juego** at stake; **hacer el juego a** to play into the hands of; **hacer juego** to match; **hacer juego con** to match, to go with; **hacer su juego** to have one's way; **no ser cosa de juego** to be no laughing matter; **por juego** in fun, for fun; **verle a uno el juego** to be on to someone; **juego carteado** card game not played for money; **juego de ajedrez** chess, game of chess; **juego de alcoba** bedroom suit; **juego de azar** game of chance; **juego de bolas** (mach.) ball bearing; **juego de bolos** bowling; **juego de comedor** dining-room suit; **juego de compadres** (coll.) collusion; **juego de damas** checkers, game of checkers; **juego de envite** game played for money, gambling game; **juego de escritorio** desk set; **juego de la cuna** cat's cradle; **juego de la pulga** tiddlywinks; **juego del salto** leapfrog; **juego del tres en raya** game similar to tick-tack-toe, which is played with movable pebbles or counters instead of written ciphers and crosses; **juego de manos** juggling, legerdemain, sleight of hand; **juego de naipes** cards, card game; **juego de niños** child's play (*something easy*); **juego de palabras** pun, play on words; **juego de pelota** ball (*game*); pelota; **juego de piernas** footwork (*in sports and dancing*); **juego de por ver** (Am.) game played for fun (*not for money*); **juego de prendas** forfeits, game of forfeits; **juego de suerte** game of chance; **juego de tejo** shuffleboard; **juego de timbres** (mus.) glockenspiel; **juego de vocablos** or **voces** pun, play on words; **juego limpio** fair play; **juego público** gambling house; **juegos de sociedad** parlor games; **juegos ístmicos** Isthmian games; **juegos malabares** juggling, jugglery; flimflam; **juegos olímpicos** (hist.) Olympian games, Olympic games; Olympic games (*of modern times*); **juegos pitios** Pythian games; **juego sucio** (sport) foul play
**juerga** *f* (coll.) carousal, spree; **ir de juerga** (coll.) to go on a spree; **juerga de borrachera** (coll.) drinking bout, binge
**juerguista** *adj* (coll.) carousing, roistering; *mf* (coll.) carouser, roisterer
**juev.** abr. of **jueves**
**jueves** *m* (*pl:* **-ves**) Thursday; **Jueves gordo** or **lardero** Thursday before Shrove Tuesday; **Jueves santo** Maundy Thursday, Holy Thursday
**juez** *m* (*pl:* **jueces**) judge; **juez arbitrador** or **árbitro** (law) umpire; **juez de guardia** coroner; **juez de instrucción** examining magistrate; **juez de línea** (football) field judge; **juez de llegada** (sport) goal judge; **juez de palo** (coll.) ignorant judge; **juez de paz** justice of the peace; **juez de salida** (sport) starter; **juez de tiempo** (sport) timekeeper
**jugada** *f* play; throw, stroke; **mala jugada** mean trick, dirty trick
**jugador -dora** *mf* player; gambler; **jugador de manos** juggler
**jugar** §58 *va* to play (*e.g., a card, a knight, a game of chess*); to gamble; to stake, to risk; to gamble away; to wield (*a sword*); to work; to move (*e.g., hands, toes*); to match for, e.g., **jugar a uno las bebidas** to match someone for the drinks; *vn* to play; to gamble; to work; to match; to figure; to come into action (*said of weapons and firearms*); **jugar a** to play (*cards, tennis, etc.*); **jugar con** to toy with (*a person, a person's affections*); to match; **jugar en** to have a hand in; **jugar fuerte** or **grueso** to gamble heavily; *vr* to gamble, to risk (*one's salary, one's life*); to be at stake; **jugarse el todo por el todo** to stake all, to shoot the works
**jugarreta** *f* (coll.) bad play, poor play; (coll.) mean trick, dirty trick
**juglandáceo -a** or **juglándeo -a** *adj* (bot.) juglandaceous
**juglar** *m* (archaic) minstrel, jongleur; (archaic) juggler (*jester, buffoon*)
**juglaresco -ca** *adj* of minstrels, of jongleurs
**jugo** *m* juice; gravy; sauce; (fig.) gist, essence, substance; **en su jugo** (cook.) au jus; **sacar el jugo a** (fig.) to get the substance out of; **jugo de muñeca** (coll.) elbow grease; **jugo gástrico** (physiol.) gastric juice; **jugo pancreático** (physiol.) pancreatic juice
**jugosidad** *f* juiciness; substance, importance
**jugoso -sa** *adj* juicy; substantial, important
**juguete** *m* toy, plaything; joke, jest; gay song; (theat.) skit; (fig.) plaything, sport (*e.g., of fortune, passion, wind*); **de juguete** toy, e.g., **soldado de juguete** toy soldier; **por juguete** for fun, in fun; **juguete de movimiento** mechanical toy
**juguetear** *vn* to play, frolic, romp; (poet.) to blow lightly
**jugueteo** *m* playing, frolicking, romping
**juguetería** *f* toy business; toyshop; toys
**juguetero -ra** *adj* toy (*e.g., industry*); *mf* toy dealer; *m* whatnot, étagère
**juguete-sorpresa** *m* (*pl:* **juguetes-sorpresa**) jack-in-the-box
**juguetón -tona** *adj* playful, frisky
**juicio** *m* judgment; (law) trial; (log. & theol.) judgment; **asentar el juicio** to settle down, to come to one's senses; **el juicio final** or **universal** the Judgment or the Last Judgment; **estar en su cabal juicio** to be in one's right mind; **estar fuera de juicio** to be out of one's mind; **pedir en juicio** (law) to sue; **perder el juicio** to lose one's mind; **juicio de Dios** (hist.) ordeal (*to test guilt or innocence*)
**juicioso -sa** *adj* judicious, wise
**Jul.** abr. of **julio**
**julán** *m* (zool.) piddock
**julepe** *m* julep; mint julep; (coll.) scolding; (Am.) scare
**Julián** *m* Julian
**juliano -na** *adj* Julian; (*cap.*) *m* Julian; **Juliano el Apóstata** Julian the Apostate; *f* Juliana; (*l.c.*) *f* (bot.) damewort
**Julieta** *f* Juliet
**julio** *m* July; (phys.) joule; (*cap.*) *m* Julius
**julo** *m* lead cow, lead mule
**juma** *f* (Am.) drunk, spree
**jumento -ta** *mf* ass, donkey; *m* (coll.) ass, fool
**jumera** *f* (coll.) drunk, spree
**Jun.** abr. of **junio**
**juncáceo -a** *adj* (bot.) juncaceous
**juncada** *f* cylindrical fritter
**juncal** *adj* willowy, rushy; willowy (*form, body*); (prov.) handsome, elegant; *m* growth of rushes
**juncar** *m* clump of rushes, growth of rushes
**júnceo -a** *adj* rushy, rushlike
**juncia** *f* (bot.) sedge; **vender juncia** (coll.) to boast, to brag
**juncial** *m* growth of sedge
**junciana** *f* (coll.) vain show, bluff

**juncino -na** *adj* rushy
**junco** *m* junk (*Chinese ship*); rattan (*cane*); (bot.) rush, bulrush (*Juncus effusus*); **junco de esteras** (bot.) rush, bulrush (*Juncus effusus*); **junco de Indias** (bot.) rattan; **junco de laguna** (bot.) bulrush, tule; **junco florido** (bot.) flowering rush; **junco marinero, marino** or **marítimo** (bot.) bulrush, tule; **junco oloroso** (bot.) camel grass
**juncoso -sa** *adj* rushy
**jungla** *f* jungle
**junio** *m* June
**júnior** *m* (sport) novice
**junípero** *m* var. of **enebro**
**Juno** *f* (myth.) Juno
**junquera** *f* (bot.) rush, bulrush (*Juncus effusus*)
**junqueral** *m* growth of rushes
**junquillo** *m* (bot.) jonquil; (bot.) rattan palm; (arch.) bead; (carp.) strip of wood, reglet (*to fill or cover joints*); **junquillo amarillo** (bot.) jonquil; **junquillo de noche** (bot.) gladiolus (*Gladiolus tristis*); **junquillo oloroso** (bot.) jonquil
**junquito** *m* (orn.) junco
**junta** *f* see **junto**
**juntamente** *adv* together; at the same time
**juntar** *va* to join, unite; to gather, to gather together; to half-close; *vr* to gather, to gather together; to associate closely; to copulate
**juntera** *f* (carp.) jointer
**junterilla** *f* (carp.) rabbet plane
**junto -ta** *adj* joined, united; **juntos -tas** *adj pl* together; *f* meeting, conference; board, council; session; union, junction; seam; joint; washer, gasket; (arch.) joint; (Am.) junction (*of two rivers*); **junta a inglete** (carp.) miter, miter joint; **junta de cardán** (aut.) universal joint; **junta de comercio** board of trade; **junta de sanidad** board of health; **junta universal** (aut.) universal joint; **junto** *adv* together, at the same time; **en** or **por junto** all together, all told; **todo junto** at the same time, all at once; **junto a** near, close to; **junto con** along with, together with
**juntura** *f* joint, junction, seam; coupling; (anat.) joint
**Júpiter** *m* (astr. & myth.) Jupiter; **Júpiter tonante** or **tronante** (myth.) the Thunderer, Jupiter Tonans
**jura** *f* oath; pledge of allegiance
**jurado -da** *adj* sworn; **tenérsela jurada a** (coll.) to have it in for; *m* jury; juror, juryman
**jurador -dora** *mf* swearer
**juramentar** *va* to swear in; *vr* to take an oath, to be sworn in
**juramento** *m* oath; curse, swearword; **prestar juramento** to take oath; **prestar juramento a** to administer an oath to; **juramento de Hipócrates** Hippocratic oath
**jurar** *va* to swear; to swear allegiance to; to swear in; *vn* to swear (*to take an oath; to curse*); **jurar** + *inf* to swear to + *inf*, e.g., **juró decir la verdad** he swore to tell the truth; *vr* to swear; **jurársela a uno** or **jurárselas a uno** (coll.) to have it in for someone, to swear to get even with someone
**jurásico -ca** *adj* & *m* (geol.) Jurassic
**jurel** *m* (ichth.) caranx, saurel, yellow jack; (Am.) fear, terror; (Am.) drunk, drunkenness
**jurero** *m* (Am.) false witness
**jurídico -ca** *adj* juridical
**jurisconsulto** *m* jurisconsult
**jurisdicción** *f* jurisdiction
**jurisdiccional** *adj* jurisdictional
**jurisperito** *m* legal expert
**jurisprudencia** *f* jurisprudence
**jurista** *mf* jurist
**juro** *m* right of perpetual ownership; **de juro** with certainty, inevitably
**jusbarba** *f* (bot.) butcher's-broom
**justa** *f* see **justo**
**justador** *m* jouster, tilter
**justamente** *adv* justly; tightly; just; just at that time
**justar** *vn* to joust, to tilt
**justicia** *f* justice; rightness; (coll.) execution (*putting to death*); **de justicia** justly, deservedly; **hacer justicia a** to do justice to; **ir por justicia** to go to court, to bring suit; *m* judge, justice; (archaic) bailiff
**justiciable** *adj* actionable; justiciable
**justiciazgo** *m* judgeship, justiceship
**justiciero -ra** *adj* just, fair; stern, righteous
**justificable** *adj* justifiable
**justificación** *f* justification; (print.) justification
**justificado -da** *adj* just, right (*act*); just, upright (*person*)
**justificante** *m* written proof
**justificar** §86 *va* to justify; (print.) to justify
**justificativo -va** *adj* justificatory
**justillo** *m* waist, underwaist
**Justiniano** *m* Justinian
**justipreciar** *va* to estimate with precision
**justiprecio** *m* precise estimation
**justo -ta** *adj* just; exact, correct; tight; *mf* righteous person; **los justos** the just; *f* joust; contest; **justo** *adv* just; tight; right, in tune; in straitened circumstances
**Jutlandia** *f* Jutland
**juto -ta** *mf* Jute
**Juvenal** *m* Juvenal
**juvenil** *adj* juvenile, youthful
**juventud** *f* youth (*early period of life; early period; young people*)
**juvia** *f* (bot.) Brazil-nut tree
**juzgado** *m* court, tribunal
**juzgamundos** *m* (*pl:* **-dos**) (coll.) faultfinder
**juzgar** §59 *va* & *vn* to judge; **a juzgar por** judging by or from; **juzgar de** to judge, pass judgment on

# K

**K, k** *f* twelfth letter of the Spanish alphabet
**kan** *m* khan (*title; caravansary*)
**kanato** *m* khanate
**kantiano -na** *adj & mf* Kantian
**kantismo** *m* Kantianism
**kantista** *adj & mf* var. of **kantiano**
**kc.** abr. of **kilociclo**
**kepis** *m* (*pl:* **-pis**) var. of **quepis**
**keratina** *f* var. of **queratina**
**kermes** *m* (*pl:* **-mes**) var. of **quermes**
**kermesse** *f* var. of **quermese**
**keroseno** *m* kerosene, coal oil
**kg.** abr. of **kilogramo**
**kgm.** abr. of **kilográmetro**
**kilate** *m* var. of **quilate**
**kiliárea** *f* kiliare
**kilo** *m* kilo (*kilogram*)
**kiloamperio** *m* kiloampere
**kilocaloría** *f* (phys.) kilogram calorie, kilocalorie
**kilociclo** *m* kilocycle
**kilográmetro** *m* kilogrammeter
**kilogramo** *m* kilogram or kilogramme
**kilolitro** *m* kiloliter
**kilometraje** *m* kilometrage, distance in kilometers
**kilométrico -ca** *adj* kilometric
**kilómetro** *m* kilometer
**kilotonelada** *f* kiloton
**kilovatio** *m* kilowatt
**kilovatio-hora** *m* (*pl:* **kilovatios-hora**) kilowatt-hour
**kilovoltio** *m* kilovolt
**kimógrafo** *m* var. of **quimógrafo**
**kimono** *m* var. of **quimono**
**kindergarten** *m* kindergarten
**kinescopio** *m* (telv.) kinescope
**kino** *m* var. of **quino**
**kiosko** *m* var. of **quiosco**
**kirguís** *m* Kirghiz
**Kirie** *m* (eccl.) Kyrie
**kiwi** *m* (orn.) kiwi
**kl.** abr. of **kilolitro**
**klistrón** *m* (phys.) klystron
**km.** abr. of **kilómetro**
**kodak** *m & f* kodak
**kph.** abr. of **kilómetros por hora**
**krach** *m* var. of **crac**
**Kremlín** *m* Kremlin
**kulak** *m* kulak (*well-to-do Russian peasant*)
**kurdo -da** *adj & mf* var. of **curdo**
**kv.** abr. of **kilovatio**

# L

**L, l** *f* thirteenth letter of the Spanish alphabet
**la** *art def fem* the; *pron pers fem* her, it; you; *pron dem fem* the one, that, e.g., **la de mi hermano** that of my brother
**Labán** *m* (Bib.) Laban
**lábaro** *m* labarum; (hist.) labarum
**labela** *f* (ent.) labellum
**labelo** *m* (bot.) labellum
**laberíntico -ca** *adj* labyrinthine, mazy
**laberinto** *m* labyrinth, maze; (anat. & mach.) labyrinth; **el laberinto de Creta** (myth.) the Labyrinth
**labia** *f* (coll.) fluency, smoothness (*in speech*)
**labiado -da** *adj* (anat., zool. & bot.) labiate; *f* (bot.) labiate
**labial** *adj & f* labial
**labializar §76** *va* (phonet.) to labialize
**labiérnago** *m* (bot.) phillyrea, mock privet
**labihendido -da** *adj* harelipped
**lábil** *adj* liable to slip; unstable; (chem.) labile
**labilidad** *f* lability
**labio** *m* lip; lip, brim (*of glass or tumbler*); (anat., bot. & zool.) labium; (mach.) lip; (surg.) lip (*of wound*); (fig.) lips (*words, speech*); **labios** *mpl* (fig.) lips (*words, speech*); **chuparse los labios** to smack one's lips; **lamerse los labios** to lick one's lips; **leer en los labios** to lip-read; **morderse los labios** (coll.) to bite one's tongue; **no morderse los labios** (coll.) to speak out, to be outspoken; **labio inferior** lower lip; **labio leporino** harelip; **labio superior** upper lip
**labiodental** *adj & f* (phonet.) labiodental
**labiolectura** *f* lip reading
**labioso -sa** *adj* (Am.) fluent, smooth
**labor** *f* labor, work; farm work, farming, tilling; needlework, embroidery, fancywork; sewing school for little girls; thousand tiles, thousand bricks; **labores** *fpl* (min.) workings; **labor blanca** linen work, linen embroidery; **labor de ganchillo** crocheting
**laborable** *adj* workable; arable, tillable; work (*day*)
**laboral** *adj* (pertaining to) labor
**laborante** *adj* working; *m* political henchman
**laborar** *va* to work; *vn* to work; to scheme
**laboratorio** *m* laboratory
**laborear** *va* to work; (min.) to work (*a mine*); *vn* (naut.) to reeve
**laboreo** *m* working; tilling; (min.) working, exploitation; (naut.) reeving
**laboriosidad** *f* laboriousness
**laborioso -sa** *adj* laborious
**laborismo** *m* British Labour Party
**laborista** *adj* Labor (*party*); *mf* Laborite
**labra** *f* working, carving
**labrada** *f* see **labrado**
**labradero -ra** *adj* workable; arable, tillable
**labradío -a** *adj* arable, tillable; *m* tillable soil
**labrado -da** *adj* worked, wrought, fashioned; carved; figured, embroidered; *m* working, carving; cultivated field; **labrado de madera** wood carving; *f* fallow ground (*to be sown the following year*)
**labrador -dora** *adj* work; farm; *mf* farmer; peasant; *m* plowman; **el Labrador** Labrador (*in Newfoundland*); *f* (slang) hand
**labradoresco -ca** *adj* farm, peasant
**labradorita** *f* (mineral.) labradorite
**labrantín** *m* small farmer, poor farmer
**labrantío -a** *adj & m* var. of **labradío**
**labranza** *f* farming; farm, farm land; work
**labrar** *va* to work, to fashion; to carve; to till; to plow; to build; to cause, bring about; **sin labrar** crude, unfinished; *vn* to make a lasting impression; *vr* to carve out (*e.g., a future, a fortune*)
**labriego -ga** *mf* peasant
**labro** *m* (ichth.) wrasse; (zool.) labrum
**labrusca** *f* wild grapevine; (bot.) fox grape; (bot.) ivy vine (*Ampelopsis cordata*)
**laca** *f* lac (*resinous substance; color*); lacquer (*varnish and object coated with lacquer*); **laca de uñas** nail polish; **laca en grano** grained lac, seed-lac; **laco en palo** or **en rama** stick-lac
**lacayo** *m* lackey, footman, groom; knot of ribbons
**lacayuno -na** *adj* lackey, servile
**lacear** *va* to trim or bedeck with bows; to tie with a bow; to drive (*game*) within shot; to trap or snare (*small game*)
**lacedemón** *adj masc & m* Lacedaemonian
**Lacedemonia, la** see **lacedemonio**
**lacedemónico -ca** *adj* Lacedaemonian
**lacedemonio -nia** *adj & mf* Lacedaemonian; **la Lacedemonia** Lacedaemon
**laceración** *f* laceration
**lacerar** *va* to lacerate; (fig.) to damage (*honor, reputation, etc.*); *vn* to have lots of trouble, to be in want
**laceria** *f* trouble, bother, worry; poverty, want
**lacería** *f* bows, ornamental bows; (arch.) interlacery
**lacerioso -sa** *adj* troubled, worried; poor, needy
**lacero** *m* lassoer, roper; dogcatcher; poacher
**lacinia** *f* (bot.) lacinia
**laciniado -da** *adj* (bot.) laciniate
**lacio -cia** *adj* withered, faded; flaccid, languid; straight, lank (*hair*); **el Lacio** Latium
**lacón** *m* picnic (*shoulder of pork*)
**Laconia** *f* see **laconio**
**lacónico -ca** *adj* laconic
**laconio -nia** *adj & mf* Laconian; (*cap.*) *f* Laconia
**laconismo** *m* laconism
**lacra** *f* mark (*left by illness*); fault, defect; (Am.) sore, ulcer; (Am.) scab
**lacrar** *va* to lay low, to strike down; to damage, hurt; to seal (*with sealing wax*); *vr* to be stricken
**lacre** *m* sealing wax
**lácrima** *f* (archaic) tear; **lácrima cristi** Lachryma Christi (*wine*)
**lacrimal** *adj* lachrymal, tearful
**lacrimatorio -ria** *adj & m* lachrymatory
**lacrimógeno -na** *adj* tear, tear-producing
**lacrimoso -sa** *adj* lachrymose, tearful
**lactación** *f* var. of **lactancia**
**lactama** *f* (biochem.) lactam
**lactancia** *f* lactation
**lactar** *va & vn* to suckle
**lactasa** *f* (biochem.) lactase
**lactato** *m* (chem.) lactate
**lácteo -a** *adj* lacteous, milky
**lactescencia** *f* lactescence
**lactescente** *adj* lactescent; (bot.) lactescent
**lacticinio** *m* milk, milk food
**lacticinoso -sa** *adj* milky
**láctico -ca** *adj* lactic
**lactífero -ra** *adj* lactiferous
**lactobacilina** *f* acidophilus milk
**lactoflavina** *f* lactoflavin
**lactómetro** *m* lactometer
**lactona** *f* (chem.) lactone
**lactosa** *f* (chem.) lactose
**lactumen** *m* (path.) milk crust
**lacunario** *m* var. of **lagunar**
**lacustre** *adj* lacustrine; (geol.) lacustrine
**lacha** *f* (ichth.) anchovy; (ichth.) herring; (slang) shame; (dial.) ugly look; **ser de poca lacha** (coll.) to not amount to much
**lada** *f* (bot.) rockrose
**ládano** *m* labdanum

**ladear** *va* to tip, to tilt; to bend, to lean; *vn* to tip, to tilt; to bend, to lean; to go down; to turn away, to turn off; to deviate (*said of compass needle*); *vr* to tip, to tilt; to bend, to lean; to be even, be equal; (fig.) to lean (*to an opinion, party, etc.*); (Am.) to fall in love; **ladearse con** (coll.) to go at or to the side of; (coll.) to fall out with
**ladeo** *m* tipping, tilting; bending, leaning; bent, inclination
**ladera** *f* see **ladero**
**ladería** *f* (archaic) small plain on mountainside
**ladero -ra** *adj* side, lateral; *f* slope, hillside
**ladierno** *m* var. of **aladierna**
**ladilla** *f* (ent.) crab louse; **pegarse como ladilla** (coll.) to stick like a leech
**ladillo** *m* (print.) sidenote
**ladino -na** *adj* sly, cunning, crafty; fluent; foreign-language-speaking; (Am.) Ladino; *m* Ladin (*Romansh*); Ladino (*mixed Spanish and Hebrew*); (Am.) Ladino
**lado** *m* side; direction; room, space; mat (*used as side of cart*); favor, protection; (geom.) side; **lados** *mpl* advisers, backers; **al lado de** by the side of; **dejar a un lado** to skip, to leave aside; **de lado** tilted; square, e.g., **ocho pulgadas de lado** eight inches square; **de otro lado** on the other hand; **de un lado** on the one hand; **echar a un lado** to cast aside, to neglect; to wind up, bring to an end; **hacer lado** to make room; **hacerse a un lado** to step aside; **mirar de lado** or **de medio lado** to look askance at; to sneak a look at; **ponerse al lado de** to take sides with; **por el lado de** in the direction of; **por todos lados** on all sides; **tener lado izquierdo** (coll.) to have a lot of courage; **tirar por su lado** to pull for oneself; **lado débil** weak side, weak point; **lado de la epístola** (eccl.) Epistle side; **lado del evangelio** (eccl.) Gospel side
**ladón** *m* var. of **lada**
**ladra** *f* barking
**ladrador -dora** *adj* barking; (coll.) scowling
**ladrar** *va* to bark (*insults, orders, etc.*); *vn* to bark; (coll.) to bark (*to threaten idly*)
**ladrear** *vn* to keep on barking
**ladrería** *f* (path.) leprosy; (vet.) swine cysticercosis
**ladrido** *m* bark, barking; (coll.) blame, slander
**ladrillado** *m* brick floor, tile floor
**ladrillal** *m* brickyard
**ladrillar** *m* brickyard; *va* to pave with bricks; to brick
**ladrillazo** *m* blow with a brick
**ladrillero -ra** *mf* brickmaker; brick dealer; *f* brick mold
**ladrillo** *m* brick; tile; cake (*e.g., of chocolate*); **ladrillo de fuego** or **ladrillo refractario** firebrick
**ladrilloso -sa** *adj* brick; brick-red
**ladrón -drona** *adj* thieving, thievish; *mf* thief; *m* sluice gate; run (*on side of candle*); **ladrón de corazones** lady-killer
**ladronear** *vn* to go about thieving
**ladronera** *f* den of thieves; theft, robbery; bank, child's bank; sluice gate; (fort.) machicolation
**ladronería** *f* thievery; den of thieves; gang of thieves
**ladronerío** *m* (Am.) gang of thieves; (Am.) wave of thievery
**ladronesco -ca** *adj* (coll.) thieves'; *f* (coll.) gang of thieves
**ladronicio** *m* var. of **latrocinio**
**ladronzuelo -la** *mf* petty thief
**lagaña** *f* var. of **legaña**
**lagar** *m* wine press, olive press, apple press; winery; olive farm
**lagarada** *f* pressing of wine
**lagarejo** *m* trough for pressing wine; **hacer lagarejos a** (coll.) to squirt grape juice in the face of; **hacerse lagarejo** (coll.) to become bruised or crushed (*said of grapes*); (coll.) to roughhouse
**lagarero** *m* wine presser, olive presser
**lagareta** *f* trough for pressing wine; pool, puddle
**lagarta** *f* female lizard; (ent.) gypsy moth; (coll.) sly woman
**lagartado -da** *adj* var. of **alagartado**
**lagartero -ra** *adj* lizard-hunting; *f* lizard hole
**lagartija** *f* (zool.) green lizard; (zool.) wall lizard
**lagartijero -ra** *adj* lizard-hunting
**lagarto** *m* (zool.) lizard; (coll.) sly fellow; **lagarto cornudo** (zool.) horned toad; **lagarto de Indias** (zool.) alligator
**lagena** *f* (zool.) lagena
**lago** *m* lake; **el lago de Constanza** Lake of Constance; **Grandes Lagos** Great Lakes; **Gran Lago Salado** Great Salt Lake; **lago de amor** (her.) wake knot; **lago de Aral** Lake Aral; **lago de leones** (archaic) cave or den of lions; **lago de Tiberíades** Sea of Tiberias, Sea of Galilee
**lagotear** *va & vn* (coll.) to flatter
**lagotería** *f* (coll.) flattery
**lagotero -ra** *adj* (coll.) flattering; *mf* (coll.) flatterer
**lágrima** *f* tear; drop; tear (*of sap or juice*); juice exuded by ripe grapes; **beberse las lágrimas** (coll.) to hold back one's tears; **deshacerse en lágrimas** to weep bitterly; **llorar a lágrima viva** to shed bitter tears; **mover a lágrimas** to move to tears; **lágrima de Salomón** (bot.) lily of the valley; **lágrimas de cocodrilo** crocodile tears; **lágrimas de David** or **de Job** (bot.) Job's-tears
**lagrimable** *adj* tearful, deplorable
**lagrimal** *adj* lachrymal; (anat.) lachrymal; *m* (anat.) lachrymal caruncle
**lagrimar** *vn* to weep
**lagrimear** *vn* to weep easily, to be tearful; to run (*said of the eyes*)
**lagrimeo** *m* weeping; flow of tears (*from an illness*)
**lagrimón** *m* (iron.) tear, big tear
**lagrimoso -sa** *adj* tearful; watery (*eyes*)
**laguna** *f* lagoon; lacuna, gap; (anat., bot. & zool.) lacuna
**lagunajo** *m* puddle, pool
**lagunar** *m* (arch.) lacunar
**lagunero -ra** *adj* (pertaining to a) lagoon
**lagunoso -sa** *adj* full of lagoons
**laical** *adj* lay, laic
**laicismo** *m* secularism
**laicista** *adj & mf* secularist
**laicización** *f* laicization
**laicizar §76** *va* to laicize
**laico -ca** *adj*, lay, laic; *mf* lay person, laic
**laísmo** *m* use of **la** and **las** as indirect objects
**laísta** *mf* user of **la** and **las** as indirect objects
**laja** *f* slab, flagstone; (naut.) stone flat
**lakistas** *mpl* Lake poets (*Wordsworth, Coleridge, and Southey*)
**lama** *m* lama (*Buddhist priest in Tibet*); *f* mud, slime, ooze; surface film; lamé (*fabric*); (bot.) sea lettuce
**lamaísmo** *m* Lamaism
**lamaísta** *adj & mf* Lamaist
**lamarquismo** *m* Lamarckianism or Lamarckism
**lamarquista** *adj & mf* Lamarckian
**lamasería** *f* lamasery
**lambel** *m* (her.) label, lambel
**Lamberto** *m* Lambert
**lambrequín** *m* lambrequin; (her.) lambrequin
**lambrija** *f* worm; (coll.) skinny person
**lameculos** *mf* (*pl:* **-los**) (coll.) bootlicker
**lamedal** *m* mudhole
**lamedero** *m* salt lick
**lamedor -dora** *adj* licking; *mf* licker; *m* syrup; ruse, chicanery; **dar lamedor** (coll.) to lose at the beginning in order to take in one's opponent
**lamedura** *f* (act of) licking
**lamelar** *adj* lamellar
**lamelibranquio -quia** *adj & m* (zool.) lamellibranch
**lamentable** *adj* lamentable
**lamentación** *f* lamentation; **Lamentaciones de Jeremías** (Bib.) Lamentations
**lamentador -dora** *adj* lamenting, mourning; *mf* lamenter, mourner
**lamentar** *va, vn & vr* to lament, to mourn; **lamentar** + *inf* to be sorry to + *inf;* **lamentarse de** or **por** to lament, to mourn
**lamento** *m* lament

**lamentoso -sa** *adj* lamentable; plaintive, lamenting
**lameplatos** *mf* (*pl:* **-tos**) (coll.) glutton; (coll.) eater of scraps and leavings
**lamer** *va* to lick; to lap, lap against; to lick (*said of flames*); *vr* to lick (*e.g., one's lips*)
**lamerón -rona** *adj* (coll.) sweet-toothed
**lametada** *f* lick, lap
**lametón** *m* greedy lick
**lamia** *f* (ichth. & myth.) lamia
**lamiáceo -a** *adj* (bot.) lamiaceous
**lamido -da** *adj* scrawny, wan; prim; worn, frayed; smooth, sleek, glossy; (f.a.) fine; *f* (Am.) lick, licking
**lamiente** *adj* licking; lambent
**lamiero** *m* (bot.) dead nettle
**lámina** *f* lamina, sheet, plate, strip; engraving; copper plate; cut, picture; (anat., bot., geol. & zool.) lamina
**laminación** *f* lamination
**laminadero** *m* rolling mill (*factory*)
**laminado -da** *adj* laminate; laminated; *m* lamination; (metal.) rolling
**laminador -dora** *adj* laminating; rolling; *m* rolling-mill worker; rolling mill
**laminar** *adj* laminar; *va* to laminate; to roll (*iron or steel*); (dial.) to guzzle (*sweets*)
**laminilla** *f* lamella; (bot.) lamella
**laminoso -sa** *adj* laminose
**lamiscar** §86 *va* (coll.) to lick greedily
**lamoso -sa** *adj* muddy, slimy
**lampacear** *va* (naut.) to swab, to mop
**lampadario** *m* (eccl.) lampadary (*priest; lamppost*); floor lamp
**lampante** *adj* lamp (*oil*)
**lampar** *vr* var. of **alampar**
**lámpara** *f* lamp, light; grease spot, oil spot (*on clothing*); bough placed at door as love token; (rad.) vacuum tube; **atizar las lámparas** (coll.) to fill up the glasses again; **lámpara astral** astral lamp; **lámpara de Aladino** Aladdin's lamp; **lámpara de alcohol** spirit lamp; **lámpara de alto** stop light; **lámpara de arco** arc lamp, arc light; **lámpara de bolsillo** flashlight; **lámpara de carretera** (aut.) bright light; **lámpara de cruce** (aut.) dimmer; **lámpara de parada** stop light; **lámpara de pie** floor lamp; **lámpara de seguridad** safety lamp; **lámpara de sobremesa** table lamp; **lámpara de soldar** blowtorch; **lámpara de techo** ceiling light; (aut.) dome light; **lámpara de vapor de mercurio** (elec.) mercury-vapor lamp; **lámpara indicadora** pilot light; **lámpara inundante** floodlight; **lámpara piloto** or **lámpara testigo** pilot light
**lamparería** *f* lamp shop; lampistry
**lamparero -ra** *mf* lampmaker, lamp dealer; lampist, lamplighter
**lamparilla** *f* small lamp; rush candle; night light; (bot.) aspen; (coll.) glass of brandy
**lamparín** *m* lamp bracket (*used in churches*)
**lamparista** *mf* var. of **lamparero**
**lamparón** *m* big lamp; big grease spot; **lamparones** *mpl* (path.) king's evil; (vet.) streptothricosis
**lampatán** *m* (bot.) chinaroot
**lampazo** *m* (bot.) burdock; (bot.) toad lily, white water lily; (naut.) swab, mop; **lampazos** *mpl* (path.) rash
**lampiño -ña** *adj* hairless; beardless
**lampista** *mf* lampist, lamplighter; *m* plumber, tinsmith, electrician, glazier
**lampistería** *f* lampistry; shop of plumber, tinsmith, electrician, glazier, etc.
**lampo** *m* (poet.) flash of light
**lamprea** *f* (ichth.) lamprey; **lamprea glutinosa** (ichth.) hagfish
**lamprear** *va* to season with wine, honey, and sour gravy
**lampreazo** *m* (coll.) lashing, whipping
**lamprehuela** or **lampreílla** *f* (ichth.) sand pride, mud lamprey
**lámpsana** *f* (bot.) nipplewort
**lana** *f* wool; **lana de acero** steel wool; **lana de ceiba** kapok; **lana de escorias** mineral wool, rock wool; **lana de vidrio** glass wool; **lana mineral** mineral wool, rock wool
**lanado -da** *adj* lanate; *f* (arti.) sponge
**lanaje** *m* wool (*material and cloth made from it*)
**lanar** *adj* (pertaining to) wool; wool-bearing
**lanaria** *f* (bot.) soapwort
**lancasteriano -na** *adj & mf* Lancastrian
**lance** *m* cast, throw; catch, haul (*in a net*); play, move, turn, stroke; pass, chance, juncture; incident, event, episode; affair; row, quarrel; (taur.) move with cape; **de lance** cheap, at a bargain; second-hand; **echar buen lance** (coll.) to have a break; **tener pocos lances** (coll.) to be dull and uninteresting; **lance apretado** tight pinch, tight corner; **lance de fortuna** chance, accident; **lance de honor** affair of honor, challenge, duel
**lanceado -da** *adj* var. of **alanceado**
**lancear** *va* var. of **alancear**
**lancéola** *f* (bot.) ribwort
**lanceolado -da** *adj* (bot.) lanceolate
**lancera** *f* rack for lances
**lancería** *f* lances; troop of lancers
**lancero** *m* lancer, pikeman, spearman; **lanceros** *mpl* lancers (*dance and music*)
**lanceta** *f* (surg.) lancet
**lancetada** *f* or **lancetazo** *m* (surg.) lancing
**lancetero** *m* lancet case
**lancinante** *adj* piercing (*pain*)
**lancinar** *va* to lancinate, lacerate, pierce
**lancurdia** *f* small trout
**lancha** *f* barge, lighter; cutter; (naut.) longboat; (nav.) launch; snare for partridges; slab, flagstone; (Am.) mist, fog; (Am.) frost; **lancha automóvil** launch, motor launch; **lancha bombardera** or **cañonera** (nav.) gunboat; **lancha de auxilio** lifeboat (*stationed on shore*); **lancha de carreras** speedboat, race boat; **lancha de desembarco** (nav.) landing craft (*LCP*); **lancha de pesca** fishing smack; **lancha obusera** (nav.) gunboat; **lancha salvavidas** lifeboat (*on shipboard*); **lancha torpedera** (nav.) torpedo boat
**lanchada** *f* boatload
**lanchaje** *m* lighterage
**lanchar** *m* flagstone quarry; *vn* (Am.) to freeze
**lanchazo** *m* blow with a flat stone
**lanchero** *m* boatman, bargeman, lighterman
**lanchón** *m* lighter, flatboat
**landa** *f* swampland, moor
**landgrave** *m* landgrave
**landgraviato** *m* landgraviate
**landó** *m* (*pl:* **-dós**) landau
**landre** *f* small tumor (*in glands of neck, armpit, groin, etc.*); hidden pocket
**landrilla** *f* (vet.) tongue worm
**lanería** *f* wool shop; **lanerías** *fpl* woolens, woolen goods
**lanero -ra** *adj* (pertaining to) wool; *m* wool stapler; wool warehouse; (orn.) lanner
**langarucho -cha** *adj* (Am.) var. of **larguirucho**
**langaruto -ta** *adj* (coll.) var. of **larguirucho**
**langosta** *f* (ent.) locust; (zool.) spiny lobster; (coll.) scourge; (coll.) wastrel; **langosta a la Termidor** (cook.) lobster thermidor
**langostera** *f* lobster pot
**langostín** *m* or **langostino** *m* (zool.) prawn (*Peneus*)
**langostón** *m* (ent.) green grasshopper
**langrave** *m* var. of **landgrave**
**languedociano -na** *adj & mf* Languedocian
**languescente** *adj* languishing
**languidecer** §34 *vn* to languish
**languidez** *f* languor
**lánguido -da** *adj* languid, languorous
**lanífero -ra** *adj* (poet.) woolly; (bot.) downy
**lanificación** *f* or **lanificio** *m* woolwork
**lanilla** *f* nap; swanskin, canton flannel
**lanolina** *f* lanolin
**lanosidad** *f* (bot.) pubescence
**lanoso -sa** *adj* woolly
**lansquenete** *m* lansquenet (*foot soldier; card game*)
**lantano** *m* (chem.) lanthanum
**lanudo -da** *adj* woolly, fleecy
**lanuginoso -sa** *adj* lanuginous, downy
**lanza** *f* lance, pike; lancer, pikeman; wagon pole; nozzle; **medir lanzas** to cross swords; **romper lanzas** to intercede; to clear the way
**lanzabombas** *m* (*pl:* **-bas**) (aer.) bomb release; (mil.) trench mortar

**lanzacabos** *adj invar* line-throwing, life-saving
**lanzacohetes** *m* (*pl:* **-tes**) (mil.) rocket launcher
**lanzada** *f* see **lanzado**
**lanzadera** *f* shuttle; **parecer una lanzadera** (coll.) to buzz around, to hustle back and forth
**lanzadero** *m* log path, dragging road
**lanzadiscos** *m* (*pl:* **-cos**) var. of **lanzaplatos**
**lanzado -da** *adj* (sport) running (*start*); (naut.) raking, sloping (*mast*); *f* thrust or stroke with a lance
**lanzador -dora** *mf* thrower, hurler, slinger; **lanzador de lodo** (fig.) mudslinger; *m* (aer.) jettison gear; (baseball) pitcher
**lanzaespumas** *m* foam extinguisher
**lanzafuego** *m* linstock, match staff
**lanzahélices** *m* (*pl:* **-ces**) var. of **lanzaplatos**
**lanzahidroplanos** *m* (*pl:* **-nos**) (aer.) catapult
**lanzallamas** *m* (*pl:* **-mas**) (mil.) flame thrower
**lanzamiento** *m* launch, hurl, throw, fling; launching (*of a boat*); launching, shot (*of a rocket into space*); (law) dispossession; (naut.) steeve; (aer.) jump; (aer.) airdrop; (aer.) release
**lanzaminas** *m* (*pl:* **-nas**) (mil.) mine thrower; (nav.) mine layer
**lanzaplatos** *m* (*pl:* **-tos**) (sport) trap (*for throwing clay pigeons into the air*)
**lanzar** **§76** *va* to launch (*an arrow, curses, an offensive, a new product, a boat*); to hurl, to throw, to fling; to cast (*a glance*); to throw up, vomit; to put forth (*flowers, leaves*); to throw (*e.g., the javelin*); to toss, to toss out (*e.g., a remark*); (aer.) to airdrop; (aer.) to release (*a bomb*); (law) to dispossess; *vr* to launch; to hurl oneself, to throw oneself, to rush, to dash; to jump; (sport) to sprint; (aer.) to jump
**Lanzarote** *m* Lancelot (*of Round Table*)
**lanzatorpedos** *adj invar* (mil. & nav.) torpedo-launching; *m* (*pl:* **-dos**) (nav.) torpedo tube
**lanzazo** *m* thrust or stroke with a lance
**lanzón** *m* short and thick dagger
**laña** *f* clamp; rivet; green coconut
**lañador** *m* clamper; riveter (*of chinaware*)
**lañar** *va* to clamp; to rivet (*chinaware*); (prov.) to split (*a fish*) for salting
**laocio -cia** *adj & mf* Laotian
**Laocoonte** *m* (myth.) Laocoön
**laosiano -na** *adj & mf* var. of **laocio**
**lapa** *f* vegetable film (*produced by ferns, moss, etc.*); (bot.) burdock; (zool.) limpet
**lapachar** *m* swamp, marsh
**lápade** *f* (zool.) limpet
**lapicero** *m* pencil holder; mechanical pencil
**lápida** *f* tablet (*slab of stone for an inscription*); **lápida sepulcral** gravestone
**lapidación** *f* stoning to death, lapidation
**lapidar** *va* to stone to death, to lapidate
**lapidario -ria** *adj & m* lapidary
**lapídeo -a** *adj* stony, lapideous
**lapidificación** *f* lapidification
**lapidificar** **§86** *va & vr* to lapidify
**lapilla** *f* (bot.) hound's-tongue
**lapislázuli** *m* (mineral.) lapis lazuli
**lápiz** *m* (*pl:* **-pices**) black lead; pencil, lead pencil; **lápiz de labios** lipstick; **lápiz de pizarra** slate pencil; **lápiz de plomo** graphite; **lápiz encarnado** red ocher; **lápiz estíptico** styptic pencil; **lápiz labial** lipstick; **lápiz plomo** graphite; **lápiz rojo** red ocher; **lápiz tinta** indelible lead pencil
**lapizar** *m* black-lead mine, graphite mine; **§76** *va* to pencil
**lapo** *m* (coll.) blow with the flat of a sword, blow with a cane or stick; (Am.) drink, swig
**lapón -pona** *adj* Lappish; *mf* Lapp, Laplander (*native or inhabitant*); *m* Lappish (*language*)
**Laponia** *f* Lapland
**lapso** *m* lapse (*passing of time; slipping into guilt or error*)
**laqueado -da** *adj* lacquered; *m* lacquering
**laquear** *va* to lacquer
**Laquesis** *f* (myth.) Lachesis
**lardar** or **lardear** *va* (cook.) to baste; (cook.) to lard
**lardo** *m* back fat, lard fat
**lardón** *m* (print.) bite (*white spot*); marginal addition
**lardoso -sa** *adj* fatty, greasy
**lares** *mpl* home; **lares y penates** lares and penates (*household gods of Romans*)
**larga** *f* see **largo**
**largada** *f* (Am.) start, starting signal (*in a race*)
**largamente** *adv* at length, at large; at ease, in comfort; generously; long, for a long time
**largar** **§59** *va* to release, let go; to ease, slack, let up on; (coll.) to utter, let out; (naut.) to unfurl; (Am.) to throw; (Am.) to give, strike (*a hard blow*); *vr* to move away; (coll.) to beat it, sneak away; (naut.) to take to sea; (naut.) to come loose (*said of anchor*)
**largo -ga** *adj* long; generous, liberal; abundant; quick, ready; (coll.) shrewd, cunning; (phonet.) long; (naut.) loose, slack; **largos -gas** *adj pl* long, many (*e.g., years*); **a la larga** lengthwise; in the long run; in the end; at great length; **a lo más largo** at the most; **a lo largo** lengthwise; at great length; far away; **a lo largo de** along; along with; throughout; in the course of; far out in (*e.g., the sea*); **de largo** in a gown, in long robes; **hacerse a lo largo** (naut.) to get in the open sea; **ir para largo** to take a long time; **pasar de largo** to pass along, pass by, pass without stopping; to take a quick look, to be indifferent; to miss; **ponerse de largo** to come out, to make one's debut; **vestir de largo** to wear long clothes; **largo de lengua** loose-tongued; **largo de manos** ready-fisted; **largo de uñas** (coll.) light-fingered; **largo** *adv* abundantly; *m* length; (mus.) largo; **¡largo de aquí!** get out of here!; *f* long billiard cue; **dar largas a** to postpone, put off
**largor** *m* length
**larguero** *m* stringer; bolster; (aer.) longeron
**largueza** *f* length; largess, generosity
**larguirucho -cha** *adj* (coll.) gangling, lanky
**larguísimo -ma** *adj super* very long
**largura** *f* length
**largurucho -cha** *adj* (coll.) var. of **larguirucho**
**lárice** *m* (bot.) larch tree
**laricino -na** *adj* (pertaining to the) larch
**laricio** *m* var. of **lárice**
**laringe** *f* (anat.) larynx
**laríngeo -a** *adj* laryngeal
**laringitis** *f* (path.) laryngitis
**laringología** *f* laryngology
**laringólogo -ga** *mf* laryngologist
**laringoscopia** *f* laryngoscopy
**laringoscópico -ca** *adj* laryngoscopic
**laringoscopio** *m* laryngoscope
**larva** *f* (ent.) larva; mask; hobgoblin
**larvado -da** *adj* (path.) larval
**larval** *adj* larval
**las** *art def fem pl & pron pers & dem fem pl* see **los**
**lasca** *f* chip of stone; (dial.) slice
**lascar** *m* lascar (*East Indian sailor*); **§86** *va* to slacken, to pay out; (Am.) to bruise, to fray; *vr* (Am.) to bruise, to fray
**lascivia** *f* lasciviousness
**lascivo -va** *adj* lascivious; merry, playful, frisky
**laserpicio** *m* (bot.) laserwort
**lasitud** *f* lassitude
**laso -sa** *adj* tired, weary, exhausted; weak, wan, languid; untwisted (*silk thread*)
**lastar** *va* to pay up (*money*) for someone else; to suffer (*a punishment*) for someone else
**lástima** *f* pity; complaint; **dar, hacer** or **poner lástima** to be pitiful; **estar hecho una lástima** to be a sorry sight; **es lástima (que)** it is a pity (that); **¡qué lástima!** what a shame!, what a pity!; **¡qué lástima de saliva!** (coll.) what a waste of breath!
**lastimador -dora** *adj* hurtful, injurious
**lastimadura** *f* hurt, injury; bruise
**lastimar** *va* to hurt, injure; to bruise; to offend, to hurt; to pity; to move to pity; *vr* to hurt oneself; to bruise oneself; **lastimarse de** to complain about; to feel sorry for
**lastimero -ra** *adj* hurtful, injurious; pitiful, doleful
**lastimoso -sa** *adj* pitiful
**lastón** *m* (bot.) fescue grass
**lastra** *f* slab, flagstone
**lastrado** or **lastraje** *m* ballasting

**lastrar** *va* (naut. & aer.) to ballast
**lastre** *m* rock face; (naut. & aer.) ballast; (fig.) ballast (*steadiness*); (coll.) snack (*before drinking wine*); **lastre de agua** (naut. & aer.) water ballast
**lasún** *m* var. of **locha**
**lat.** abr. of **latín** & **latitud**
**lata** *f* see **lato**
**latamente** *adv* at great length; broadly
**latastro** *m* (arch.) plinth
**lataz** *m* (*pl:* **-taces**) (zool.) sea otter
**latebra** *f* den, hiding place
**latebroso -sa** *adj* furtive, secretive
**latencia** *f* (path.) latent period
**latente** *adj* latent
**lateral** *adj* lateral
**lateranense** *adj* Lateran
**látex** *m* (*pl:* **-tex**) (bot.) latex
**latido** *m* bark, yelp; beat, throb
**latiente** *adj* beating, throbbing
**latifundio** *m* large, run-down landed estate
**latifundista** *mf* large landowner
**latigazo** *m* lash; whipping (*of a cable*); lashing (*severe scolding*); crack of whip; (coll.) drink, swallow
**látigo** *m* whip, horsewhip; cinch strap; rope used in weighing with a steelyard; long plume around a hat; (coll.) bean pole (*person*)
**latigudo -da** *adj* (Am.) leathery
**latiguear** *va* (Am.) to lash; *vn* to crack a whip
**latigueo** *m* cracking a whip
**latiguera** *f* cinch strap
**latiguillo** *m* small whip; (bot.) stolon; (coll.) claptrap (*of an actor*); **de latiguillo** (coll.) claptrap
**latín** *m* Latin (*language*); (coll.) Latin word or phrase; **bajo latín** Low Latin; **decir** or **echar los latines a** (coll.) to marry, to officiate at the marriage of; (coll.) to bless; **saber latín** or **mucho latín** (coll.) to be very shrewd; **latín clásico** Classical Latin; **latín de cocina** dog Latin, hog Latin; **latín rústico** or **vulgar** Vulgar Latin
**latinajo** *m* (coll.) dog Latin; (coll.) Latin word or phrase
**latinamente** *adv* in Latin; in the Latin manner
**latinar** *vn* to speak or write Latin
**latinear** *vn* to speak or write Latin; (coll.) to use Latin words and phrases
**latinidad** *f* Latinity; Latin (*language*); **alta latinidad** period of Classical Latin; **baja** or **ínfima latinidad** Low Latin
**latiniparla** *f* excessive use of Latin words and phrases
**latinismo** *m* Latinism
**latinista** *mf* Latinist
**latinización** *f* Latinization
**latinizar** **§76** *va* to Latinize; *vn* (coll.) to use Latin words or phrases; *vr* to Latinize
**latino -na** *adj* Latin; (naut.) lateen; *mf* Latin (*person*)
**Latinoamérica** *f* Latin America
**latinoamericano -na** *adj* Latin-American; *mf* Latin American
**latir** *va* (Am.) to annoy, bore; *vn* to bark, yelp; to beat, throb
**latitud** *f* latitude; (fig.) latitude (*freedom, scope; climate, region*)
**latitudinal** *adj* latitudinal
**latitudinario -ria** *adj* & *mf* latitudinarian
**latitudinarismo** *m* latitudinarianism
**lato -ta** *adj* broad; (fig.) broad (*meaning of a word*); *f* log; batten, lath; tin plate; tin, tin can; (coll.) annoyance, bore; **estar en la lata** (Am.) to be penniless
**latón** *m* brass; (dial.) hackberry (*fruit*); **latón en hojas** or **planchas** latten; **latón rojo** red brass
**latonería** *f* brasswork; brassworks; brassware
**latonero** *m* brassworker, brazier; (dial.) hackberry, nettle tree
**latoso -sa** *adj* (coll.) annoying, boring
**latría** *f* (theol.) latria
**latrocinio** *m* thievery; thievishness
**latvio -via** *adj* & *mf* Latvian; (*cap.*) *f* Latvia
**laucha** *f* (Am.) mouse
**laúd** *m* (mus.) lute; (naut.) catboat; (zool.) leatherback
**laudabilidad** *f* laudability
**laudable** *adj* laudable
**láudano** *m* (pharm.) laudanum
**laudar** *va* (law) to render (*a decision*), to make (*an award*)
**laudatorio -ria** *adj* laudatory; *f* eulogy
**laude** *f* (archeol.) tombstone; **laudes** *fpl* (eccl.) lauds; **tocar a laudes** (coll.) to sing one's own praises
**laudo** *m* (law) decision, award, finding
**launa** *f* sheet of metal; slate clay; splint (*of ancient armor*)
**lauráceo -a** *adj* (bot.) lauraceous
**láurea** *f* see **láureo**
**laureado -da** *adj* laureate; laureled; *mf* laureate; (*cap.*) *f* military cross of Saint Ferdinand
**laureando** *m* graduate, candidate for a degree
**laurear** *va* to crown with laurel; to trim or adorn with laurel; to reward, honor, decorate
**lauredal** *m* growth of laurels
**laurel** *m* (bot.) laurel; (fig.) laurels (*of fame or victory*); **dormirse sobre sus laureles** to rest or sleep on one's laurels; **laurel cerezo** or **real** (bot.) cherry laurel; **laurel rosa** (bot.) oleander, rosebay
**laurentino -na** *adj* Laurentian; (geol.) Laurentian; *m* (geol.) Laurentian
**láureo -a** *adj* (pertaining to) laurel; *f* laurel wreath
**lauréola** *f* crown of laurel, laurel wreath; halo; (bot.) spurge laurel, daphne; **lauréola hembra** (bot.) mezereon
**lauro** *m* (bot.) laurel; (fig.) laurels (*fame*)
**lauroceraso** *m* (bot.) cherry laurel
**lauto -ta** *adj* rich, sumptuous
**lava** *f* lava; (min.) washing
**lavable** *adj* washable
**lavabo** *m* washstand (*bowl with faucets*); washroom, lavatory; (eccl. & hist.) lavabo; (eccl.) Lavabo (*towel*)
**lavacaras** *mf* (*pl:* **-ras**) (coll.) fawner, flatterer
**lavación** *f* wash
**lavacoches** *m* (*pl:* **-ches**) car washer
**lavadedos** *m* (*pl:* **-dos**) finger bowl
**lavadero** *m* laundry; washing place (*by a stream*); washboard; washtub; (min.) buddle; (Am.) placer
**lavado -da** *adj* (coll.) brazen, impudent; *m* wash, washing; laundry; (med.) lavage; (paint.) wash; **lavado a seco** or **lavado químico** dry cleaning; **lavado cerebral** or **de cerebro** brain washing
**lavador -dora** *adj* washing; *m* (phot.) washer; *f* washing machine; **lavadora de platos** or **de vajilla** dishwasher; **lavadora mecánica** automatic washer, automatic washing machine
**lavadura** *f* washing; washings (*dirty water; abraded material*); glove-leather dressing
**lavafrutas** *m* (*pl:* **-tas**) finger bowl
**lavaje** *m* wool washing; (surg.) swabbing
**lavajo** *m* water hole
**lavamanos** *m* (*pl:* **-nos**) washstand (*stand with basin and pitcher; bowl with faucets*); washbowl
**lavamiento** *m* wash, washing; enema
**lavanco** *m* wild duck; (orn.) widgeon (*Anas americana*)
**lavanda** *f* (bot.) lavender; lavender water
**lavandera** *f* laundress, laundrywoman, washwoman; (orn.) wagtail; (orn.) sandpiper (*Tringoides hypoleucus*)
**lavandería** *f* laundry
**lavandero** *m* launderer, laundryman
**lavándula** *f* (bot.) lavender
**lavaojos** *m* (*pl:* **-jos**) eyecup
**lavaparabrisas** *m* (*pl:* **-sas**) windshield washer
**lavaplatos** *mf* (*pl:* **-tos**) (coll.) dishwasher in a restaurant; *m* dishwasher (*machine*)
**lavar** *va* to wash; (mas., min., paint. & fig.) to wash; *vr* to wash
**lavativa** *f* enema (*liquid and apparatus*); (coll.) bore, bother, annoyance
**lavatorio** *m* wash; lavatory, washroom; (med.) wash, lotion; (eccl.) Maundy; (eccl.) lavatory
**lavazas** *fpl* dirty water, wash water
**lave** *m* (min.) washing
**lavotear** *va* & *vr* (coll.) to wash in a hurry
**lavoteo** *m* (coll.) quick wash

**laxación** *f* laxation, slackening, easing
**laxamiento** *m* laxation, slackening; laxness
**laxante** *adj & m* (med.) laxative
**laxar** *va* to slack, to ease; to loosen (*the bowels*); *vr* to slack, to ease
**laxativo -va** *adj & m* var. of **laxante**
**laxidad** or **laxitud** *f* slackness, laxity
**laxo -xa** *adj* lax (*slack; loose in morals*)
**lay** *m* lay (*poem*)
**laya** *f* spade; kind, quality
**layador** *m* spader, spademan
**layar** *va* to spade, dig with a spade
**Layo** *m* (myth.) Laius
**lazada** *f* bowknot
**lazar** §76 *va* to lasso
**lazareto** *m* lazaretto
**lazarillo** *m* blind man's guide
**lazarino -na** *adj* leprous; *mf* leper
**lázaro** *m* raggedy beggar; (*cap.*) *m* Lazarus; **estar hecho un lázaro** to be full of sores
**lazaroso -sa** *adj & mf* var. of **lazarino**
**lazo** *m* bow, knot, tie; bow tie; loop; bowknot; lasso, lariat; snare, trap; bond, tie; angle iron, tie bar; topiary design; **armar lazo a** (coll.) to set a trap for; **caer en el lazo** (coll.) to fall into the trap; **tender un lazo a** to lead into a trap; **lazo corredizo** running knot; **lazo de amor** truelove knot; **lazo de unión** (fig.) bond
**lazulita** *f* (mineral.) lazulite; (mineral.) lapis lazuli
**lb.** abr. of **libra**
**Ldo.** abr. of **Licenciado**
**le** *pron pers* to him, to her, to it; to you; him; you
**leal** *adj* loyal, faithful; devoted; reliable, trustworthy; *m* loyalist
**lealtad** *f* loyalty, fidelity; devotion; reliability, trustworthiness
**Leandro** *m* (myth.) Leander
**lebeche** *m* (naut.) southwest wind
**leberquisa** *f* (mineral.) magnetic pyrites
**lebrada** *f* rabbit fricassee
**lebrato** or **lebratón** *m* young hare, leveret
**lebrel -brela** *mf* whippet
**lebrero -ra** *adj* hare-hunting
**lebrillo** *m* tub, washtub
**lebrón** *m* large hare; (coll.) coward; (Am.) wise guy
**lebroncillo** *m* var. of **lebrato**
**lebruno -na** *adj* leporine, harelike
**lección** *f* lesson; reading (*interpretation of a passage*); (eccl.) lection; **dar una lección a** to give or teach a lesson to (*to reprove*); **dar la lección** to recite one's lesson; **echar lección** to assign the lesson; **tomar una lección a** to hear the lesson of
**leccionario** *m* (eccl.) lectionary
**leccionista** *mf* private tutor, coach
**lecitina** *f* (biochem.) lecithin
**lectivo -va** *adj* school (*day, year, etc.*)
**lector -tora** *adj* reading; *mf* reader; *m* lector; foreign-language instructor; meter reader; **lector mental** mind reader
**lectorado** *m* (eccl.) lectorate (*order*); modern-language instruction; professorship
**lectoría** *f* (eccl.) lectorate (*office*)
**lectura** *f* reading; public lecture; subject; culture; reading (*interpretation of a passage*); (elec.) playback; **ir con lectura** to know what one is about, to be purposive; **lectura chica** (print.) small pica; **lectura de la mente** mind reading; **lectura gorda** (print.) pica
**lecha** *f* (ichth.) milt (*secretion and gland*)
**lechada** *f* grout; slurry; pulp (*for making paper*); whitewash; **lechada de cal** milk of lime
**lechal** *adj* sucking; milky (*plant*); *m* milk (*of plant*)
**lechar** *adj* sucking; milky (*plant*); milk (*cow, plant, etc.*); *va* (Am.) to milk; (Am.) to whitewash
**lechaza** *f* var. of **lecha**
**lechazo** *m* suckling (*animal*); weaned lamb
**leche** *f* milk; **como una leche** (coll.) tender (*e.g., meat*); **dar a leche** to farm out (*sheep*); **estar con la leche en los labios** to lack experience; **estar en leche** to be still green or undeveloped (*said of plants and fruit*); (naut.) to be calm; **mamar en la leche** (coll.) to soak up as a child, to learn in childhood; **pedir leche a las cabrillas** to ask for the impossible; **leche condensada** condensed milk; **leche de coco** coconut milk; **leche de gallina** (bot.) star-of-Bethlehem; **leche de magnesia** (pharm.) milk of magnesia; **leche de manteca** buttermilk; **leche desnatada** skim milk; **leche en polvo** milk powder, powdered milk; **leche evaporada** evaporated milk; **leche homogeneizada** homogenized milk; **leche pasterizada** pasteurized milk
**lechecillas** *fpl* sweatbread; entrails
**lechera** *f* see **lechero**
**lechería** *f* dairy, creamery
**lechero -ra** *adj* milk; milch; (coll.) stingy, grasping; *m* milkman, dairyman; *f* milkmaid, dairymaid; milk can; milk pitcher; **lechera amarga** (bot.) milkwort
**lecheruela** or **lechetrezna** *f* (bot.) sun spurge
**lechigada** *f* brood, litter; (coll.) crew, gang, lot
**lechillo** *m* (bot.) hornbeam, American hornbeam
**lechín** *m* Andalusian olive (*tree and fruit*); (vet.) watery boil
**lechino** *m* (surg.) tent; (vet.) watery boil
**lecho** *m* bed; couch; (mas.) bed; (min.) floor; bed (*of river, road, etc.; base; layer, stratum*); **abandonar el lecho** to get up (*from illness*); **lecho de plumas** (fig.) feather bed (*comfortable situation*); **lecho de roca** bedrock
**lecho-litera** *m* (*pl:* **lechos-literas**) double-decker (*bed*)
**lechón -chona** *adj* (coll.) filthy, sloppy; *mf* sucking pig; (coll.) pig (*dirty person*); *m* pig; *f* sow
**lechoso -sa** *adj* milky; *m* (bot.) papaya (*tree*); *f* papaya (*fruit*)
**lechuga** *f* (bot.) lettuce; head of lettuce; frill; **lechugas** *fpl* lettuce (*leaves used in salad*); **lechuga romana** (bot.) romaine, romaine lettuce
**lechugado -da** *adj* lettuce-shaped
**lechuguero -ra** *mf* lettuce dealer
**lechuguilla** *f* wild lettuce; frill, ruff; (bot.) corn sow thistle; (bot.) lechuguilla
**lechuguino -na** *adj* fashionable, stylish; *mf* fashion plate; *m* small lettuce (*before transplanting*); (coll.) young flirt
**lechuzo -za** *adj* sucking (*mule*); owlish; *m* bill collector; summons server; (coll.) owl-faced fellow; *f* (orn.) barn owl, screech owl; (coll.) owl-faced woman; **lechuza blanca** (orn.) snowy owl
**ledo -da** *adj* (poet.) gay, merry, cheerful; (*cap.*) *f* (myth.) Leda
**leer** §35 *va* to read; *vn* to read; to lecture; **leer en** to read (*someone's thoughts*); **leer entre líneas** to read between the lines; *vr* to read, e.g., **este libro se lee con facilidad** this book reads easily
**leg.** abr. of **legal & legislatura**
**lega** *f* see **lego**
**legacía** *f* legateship; commission, message (*entrusted to a legate*)
**legación** *f* legation
**legado** *m* legacy; legate
**legajar** *va* (Am.) var. of **enlegajar**
**legajo** *m* file, dossier, docket, bundle of papers
**legal** *adj* legal; right, correct
**legalidad** *f* legality; rightness, correctness
**legalista** *adj* legalistic
**legalización** *f* legalization; authentication
**legalizar** §76 *va* to legalize; to authenticate (*a document, signature, etc.*)
**legamente** *adv* as a layman
**légamo** *m* slime, ooze
**legamoso -sa** *adj* slimy, oozy
**leganal** *m* pool of mud, mudhole
**légano** *m* var. of **légamo**
**legaña** *f* (path.) bleareye, rheum
**legañoso -sa** *adj* blear-eyed
**legar** §59 *va* to send as a legate or deputy; (law & fig.) to bequeath
**legatario -ria** *mf* (law) legatee, devisee
**legenda** *f* legend (*saint's life*)
**legendario -ria** *adj* legendary
**legibilidad** *f* legibility

**legible** *adj* legible
**legión** *f* legion; **constituir legión** to be legion; **legión de Honor** Legion of Honor; **legión extranjera** (mil.) foreign legion
**legionario -ria** *adj* legionary; *m* legionary; legionnaire
**legislación** *f* legislation
**legislador -dora** *adj* legislating, legislative; *mf* legislator
**legislar** *vn* to legislate
**legislativo -va** *adj* legislative
**legislatura** *f* session, term of a legislature; (Am.) legislature
**legisperito** *m* legalist, legal expert
**legista** *m* legalist, legal expert; law professor
**legítima** *f* see **legítimo**
**legitimación** *f* legitimation
**legitimar** *va* to legitimate; to establish or prove legally
**legitimidad** *f* legitimacy; rightness, justice
**legitimismo** *m* legitimism
**legitimista** *adj & mf* legitimist
**legítimo -ma** *adj* legitimate; fair, equitable; genuine; *f* (law) legitim
**lego -ga** *adj* lay; of a layman, uninformed; *m* layman; lay brother; *f* lay sister
**legón** *m* (agr.) hoe
**legra** *f* (surg.) bone scraper, periosteotome
**legración** *f* (surg.) periosteotomy
**legrado** *m* scraping of hides
**legradura** *f* var. of **legración**
**legrar** *va* to scrape (*hides*); (surg.) to scrape (*a bone*)
**legrón** *m* (surg.) large bone scraper or periosteotome (*of veterinarian*)
**legua** *f* league (*measure*); **a la legua, a legua, a leguas, de cien leguas, de mil leguas, de muchas leguas** or **de media legua** far, far away
**leguleyo** *m* pettifogger
**legumbre** *f* (bot.) legume; (bot.) vegetable
**legumina** *f* (biochem.) legumin
**leguminoso -sa** *adj* leguminous
**leíble** *adj* legible
**leído -da** *adj* well-read; **leído y escribido** (coll.) posing as learned; *f* reading
**leila** *f* Moorish dance
**leishmaniosis** *f* (path.) leishmaniasis or leishmaniosis
**leísmo** *m* use of **le** to the exclusion of **lo** and **la**
**leísta** *mf* user of **le** to the exclusion of **lo** and **la**
**leitmotiv** *m* (*pl:* **-tivs**) (mus.) leitmotiv; (Am.) fixed idea
**lejanía** *f* distance, remoteness; distant place
**lejano -na** *adj* distant, remote
**lejas** *adj fem pl* distant; **de lejas tierras** from distant lands
**lejía** *f* lye; (coll.) dressing-down, rebuke
**lejiadora** *f* washing machine
**lejío** *m* dyers' lye
**lejísimo** or **lejísimos** *adv* very far away
**lejitos** *adv* pretty far, rather far
**lejos** *adv* far; **a lo lejos** at a distance, in the distance; **de lejos, de muy lejos** or **desde lejos** from a distance; **estar lejos de** + *inf* to be far from + *ger;* **ir lejos** to go far; **lejos de** far from (*e.g., the city, one's mind*); *m* appearance at a distance; glimpse; distant point or spot (*in a painting*); **tener buen lejos** to look good at a distance
**lejuelos** *adv* var. of **lejitos**
**lelilí** *m* (*pl:* **-líes**) Moorish war cry
**lelo -la** *adj* stupid, dull; *mf* simpleton, dolt
**lema** *m* motto, slogan; theme, lemma
**lemnáceo -a** *adj* (bot.) lemnaceous
**lemniscata** *f* (geom.) lemniscate
**lemnisco** *m* lemniscus; ribbon, fillet; (anat.) lemniscus
**lempira** *m* lempira (*monetary unit of Honduras*)
**lémur** *m* (zool.) lemur; **lémures** *mpl* ghosts, apparitions; (myth.) lemures
**len** *adj* soft, untwisted (*silk or thread*)
**lena** *f* spirit, vigor
**lencería** *f* linen goods, dry goods; linen room, linen closet; linen shop, drygoods store; drygoods section (*of a city*)
**lencero -ra** *mf* linen dealer, drygoods dealer
**lendel** *m* gin race, gin ring
**lendrera** *f* fine comb, comb for removing nits or lice; (coll.) head full of lice
**lendrero** *m* place full of nits or lice
**lendroso -sa** *adj* nitty, lousy
**lene** *adj* soft; light; kind, agreeable
**lengua** *f* (anat.) tongue; (fig.) tongue (*language; bell clapper; animal's tongue used as food*); (fig.) tongue (*of land, of fire, of a shoe*); **andar en lenguas** (coll.) to be gossiped about; **buscar la lengua a** (coll.) to pick a fight with; **con la lengua de un palmo** (coll.) with great eagerness; **dar la lengua** (coll.) to chew the rag; **de lengua en lengua** from mouth to mouth; **echar la lengua por** or **echar la lengua de un palmo por** (coll.) to be eager for, to crave; (coll.) to strive for; **hacerse lenguas de** (coll.) to rave about; **irse** or **írsele a uno la lengua** (coll.) to blab; **mala lengua** (coll.) gossip, evil tongue; **malas lenguas** (coll.) gossips; (coll.) people; **morderse la lengua** to hold one's tongue; **sacar la lengua a** (coll.) to stick one's tongue out at; **soltar la lengua** to blow off steam; **tener en la lengua** (coll.) to have on the tip of one's tongue; **tener la lengua gorda** (coll.) to talk thick; (coll.) to be drunk; **tirar de la lengua a** (coll.) to draw out (*to persuade to talk*); **tomar en lenguas a** (coll.) to gossip about; **tomar lengua** or **lenguas** to pick up news; **trabársele** or **trastrabársele la lengua a uno** to become tongue-tied; **lengua canina** (bot.) hound's-tongue; **lengua cerval** or **cervina** (bot.) hart's-tongue; **lengua de buey** (bot.) ox-tongue; **lengua de ciervo** (bot.) hart's-tongue; **lengua de cordero** (bot.) plantain; **lengua de estropajo** (coll.) jabberer; **lengua de oc** langue d'oc; **lengua de oíl** langue d'oïl; **lengua de perro** (bot.) hound's-tongue; **lengua de trapo** (coll.) jabberer; **lengua franca** lingua franca; **lengua madre** or **matriz** mother tongue (*language from which another language is derived*); **lengua materna** mother tongue (*language naturally acquired by reason of nationality*); **lengua muerta** dead language; **lenguas aglutinantes** agglutinative languages; **lengua santa** Hebrew language; **lenguas modernas** modern languages; **lenguas vivas** living languages, modern languages; **lengua universal** universal language; **lengua vulgar** vernacular
**lenguadeta** *f* (ichth.) small sole
**lenguado** *m* (ichth.) sole; (ichth.) flounder (*Paralichthys brasiliensis*)
**lenguadoque** *m* langue d'oc
**lenguaje** *m* language; **lenguaje de los signos** sign language
**lenguarada** *f* var. of **lengüetada**
**lenguaraz** (*pl:* **-races**) *adj* foul-mouthed, scurrilous; garrulous, loquacious; accomplished in languages; *mf* linguist; (Am.) interpreter
**lenguaz** *adj* (*pl:* **-guaces**) garrulous
**lenguaza** *f* (bot.) bugloss
**lengüeta** *f* large bit; pointer (*of scales*); tongue (*of shoe*); ladyfinger; (anat.) epiglottis; (arch.) buttress; (carp. & mus.) tongue; (mus.) reed (*of reed instrument*); (mach.) feather, wedge; (Am.) paper cutter; (Am.) petticoat fringe; **a lengüeta y ranura** tongue-and-groove
**lengüetada** *f* licking, lapping
**lengüetear** *vn* to stick one's tongue out; to flicker, to flutter; (Am.) to jabber
**lengüetería** *f* (mus.) reedwork, reed stops (*of an organ*)
**lengüicorto -ta** *adj* (coll.) timid, reserved
**lengüilargo -ga** *adj* (coll.) foul-mouthed, scurrilous
**lengüita** *f* (ichth.) tongue-fish
**lenidad** *f* lenity, lenience
**lenificar** §86 *va* to soften; to soothe
**lenificativo -va** *adj* soothing
**Leningrado** *f* Leningrad
**leninismo** *m* Leninism
**leninista** *adj & mf* Leninist or Leninite
**lenitivo -va** *adj & m* lenitive
**lenocinio** *m* pandering, procuring
**lente** *m & f* (opt. & geol.) lens; magnifying glass; **lentes** *mpl* nose glasses; **lente de aumento** magnifying glass; **lente de contacto** or **len-**

te invisible contact lens; **lentes de náriz** or **de pinzas** pince-nez; **lentes polarizantes** polaroid lenses; **lente telefotográfico** telephoto lens; **lente tórica** or **toral** toric lens
**lentecer** §34 *vn & vr* to soften
**lenteja** *f* (bot.) lentil (*plant and seed*); pendulum bob, disk; **lenteja acuática** or **de agua** (bot.) lesser duckweed
**lentejar** *m* field of lentils
**lentejuela** *f* spangle, sequin; (bot.) lenticel
**lenticular** *adj* lenticular
**lentiscal** *m* thicket of mastic trees
**lentisco** *m* (bot.) mastic tree
**lentitud** *f* slowness; (fig.) slowness, sluggishness
**lento -ta** *adj* slow; sticky; low (*fire*)
**lenzuelo** *m* (agr.) sheet for carrying straw
**leña** *f* firewood, kindling wood; (coll.) beating, drubbing; **cargar de leña** (coll.) to beat, give a drubbing to; **echar leña al fuego** to make things worse, to stir up trouble; **llevar leña al monte** to carry coals to Newcastle
**leñador -dora** *mf* dealer in kindling wood; woodcutter; *m* woodman, woodsman
**leñame** *m* wood; stock or provision of firewood
**leñatero** *m* woodman, woodsman
**leñazo** *m* (coll.) blow with a cudgel
**leñera** *f* woodshed
**leñero** *m* wood dealer; wood purchaser; woodshed
**leño** *m* log; wood; (coll.) sap, dullard; (poet.) ship, vessel; **dormir como un leño** to sleep like a log; **leño hediondo** (bot.) bean trefoil
**leñoso -sa** *adj* woody, ligneous
**Leo** *m* (astr.) Leo
**león** *m* (zool.) lion; (ent.) ant lion; (fig.) lion (*very brave or strong man*); (*cap.*) *m* Leo (*man's name*); (astr.) Leo; **león de América** (zool.) mountain lion; **león de Nemea** (myth.) Nemean lion; **león marino** (zool.) sea lion
**leona** *f* lioness; brave, haughty woman
**leonado -da** *adj* tawny, fulvous
**Leonardo** *m* Leonard
**leonera** *f* cage or den of lions; (coll.) dive, gambling joint; attic, lumber room, junk room
**leonería** *f* boldness, fierceness
**leonero** *m* keeper of lions; (coll.) keeper of a gambling house
**leonés -nesa** *adj & mf* Leonese; *m* Leonese (*dialect*)
**leónica** *f* (anat.) ranine vein
**leónida** *f* (astr.) Leonid
**Leónidas** *m* Leonidas
**leonino -na** *adj* leonine; (law) one-sided (*contract*); *f* (path.) leontiasis
**Leonor** *f* Eleanor, Leonora, Leonore
**leontíasis** *f* (path.) leontiasis
**leontina** *f* watch chain
**leopardo** *m* (zool.) leopard
**leopoldina** *f* fob (*short chain*); (mil.) Spanish shako
**Leopoldo** *m* Leopold
**lepe** *m* (Am.) flip in the ear; **¡por vida de Lepe!** upon my soul!; **saber más que Lepe** to be very keen and wide-awake
**leperada** *f* (Am.) foulness, coarseness, vulgarity
**lépero -ra** *mf* (Am.) coarse person; (Am.) hoodlum
**lepidio** *m* (bot.) pepper cress
**Lépido** *m* Lepidus
**lepidolita** *f* (mineral.) lepidolite
**lepidóptero -ra** *adj* (ent.) lepidopterous; *m* (ent.) lepidopteron
**lepidosirena** *f* (ichth.) lepidosiren
**lepisma** *f* (ent.) bristletail, silverfish
**leporino -na** *adj* leporine, harelike
**lepra** *f* (path.) leprosy
**leprosería** *f* leprosarium
**leproso -sa** *adj* leprous; *mf* leper
**leptofilo -la** *adj* (bot.) leptophyllous
**leptorrino -na** *adj* (anthrop.) leptorrhine
**lercha** *f* reed on which fish and birds are strung and carried
**lerdo -da** *adj* slow, sluggish, dull, heavy; coarse, crude; *f* (vet.) tumor in pastern
**lerdón** *m* (vet.) tumor in pastern
**les** *pron pers* to them, to you; them, you
**lesbianismo** *m* Lesbianism
**lesbiano -na** or **lesbio -bia** *adj & mf* Lesbian; *f* Lesbian (*homosexual woman*)
**lésbico -ca** *adj* Lesbian
**lesión** *f* lesion; harm, injury; (path. & law) lesion
**lesionar** *va* to hurt, injure
**lesivo -va** *adj* harmful, injurious
**lesna** *f* awl
**lesnordeste** *m* east-northeast; east-northeast wind
**leso -sa** *adj* hurt, damaged, wounded; harmed, injured, offended; perverted; (Am.) simple, foolish
**lessueste** *m* east-southeast; east-southeast wind
**leste** *m* (naut.) east
**lesueste** *m* var. of **lessueste**
**letal** *adj* lethal
**letame** *m* manure
**letanía** *f* litany; (coll.) litany (*repeated series*)
**letárgico -ca** *adj* lethargic
**letargo** *m* lethargy
**letargoso -sa** *adj* lethargic (*producing lethargy*)
**Lete** *m* (myth.) Lethe (*river*)
**leteo -a** *adj* Lethean; (*cap.*) *m* (myth.) Lethe (*river*)
**lético -ca** *adj* Lettish
**letificar** §86 *va* to cheer, to enliven
**letón -tona** *adj* Lettish; *mf* Lett; *m* Lettish or Lett (*language*)
**Letonia** *f* Latvia
**letra** *f* letter (*of alphabet*); handwriting (*manner of writing*); words (*of a song*); (com.) draft; (print.) type (*character used in printing; such pieces collectively*); (fig.) letter (*literal meaning*); **letras** *fpl* letters (*literature*); (coll.) word, a line (*news, note*); **aceptar una letra** (com.) to accept a bill of exchange; **a la letra** to the letter (*literally*); **a letra vista** (com.) at sight; **bellas letras** belles lettres; **cuatro letras** or **dos letras** (coll.) a line (*short letter or note*); **en letras de molde** in print; **escribir en letra de molde** to print (*to write in letters resembling printed letters*); **las letras y las armas** the pen and the sword; **primeras letras** elementary education, three R's; **tener mucha letra** (coll.) to know one's way around; **letra a la vista** (com.) sight draft; **letra alemana** German script; **letra canina** dog's letter (*trilled r, i.e., rr*); **letra capital** capital letter; **letra de cambio** (com.) bill of exchange, draft; **letra de curia** court hand; **letra de imprenta** (print.) type; **letra de mano** handwriting; **letra de molde** printed letter; **letra futura** (print.) futura, Gothic; **letra gótica** (print.) black letter, Old English; **letra mayúscula** capital letter; **letra menuda** fine print; smartness, cunning; **letra minúscula** small letter; **letra muerta** dead letter (*unenforced law*); **letra negrilla** (print.) boldface; **letra redonda** (print.) roman
**letrado -da** *adj* lettered (*learned*); (coll.) pedantic; *m* lawyer; *f* (coll.) lawyer's wife
**Letrán, San Juan de** St. John Lateran (*church*)
**letrero** *m* label; sign, placard, poster
**letrilla** *f* short-line verse with a refrain at end of each strophe; (mus.) rondelet
**letrina** *f* latrine, privy, toilet; (fig.) cesspool (*filthy place*)
**letrista** *mf* writer of lyrics (*i.e., words of a song*); engrosser, calligrapher
**leucemia** *f* (path.) leukemia
**leucina** *f* (biochem.) leucine
**leucisco** *m* (ichth.) dace, roach
**leucita** *f* (mineral.) leucite
**leucobase** *f* (chem.) leuco base
**leucocitemia** *f* (path.) leucocythemia
**leucocito** *m* (physiol.) leucocyte
**leucocitosis** *f* (path.) leucocytosis
**leucoma** *m* (path.) leucoma
**leucomaína** *f* (biochem.) leucomaine
**leucón** *m* (zool.) leucon
**leucopenia** *f* (path.) leucopenia
**leucoplasto** *m* (bot.) leucoplast
**leucorrea** *f* (path.) leucorrhea
**leudar** *va* to leaven, to ferment with yeast; *vr* to rise, become fermented
**leudo -da** *adj* leavened, fermented

**leva** *f* weighing anchor; (mil.) levy; (naut.) swell; vane (*of water wheel*); (mach.) cam
**levada** *f* portion of silkworms moved from one place to another; flourish (*of sword, foil, etc.*); stroke (*of piston*); rise (*of sun, moon, stars*)
**levadero -ra** *adj* collectible, leviable
**levadizo -za** *adj* lift (*bridge*)
**levador** *m* piler (*in paper mill*); tricky thief; (mach.) cam
**levadura** *f* leaven; leavening; yeast; board; **levadura comprimida** yeast cake; **levadura de cerveza** brewer's yeast, beer yeast; **levadura química** baking soda
**levantacarril** *m* (rail.) track jack
**levantacoches** *m* (*pl:* **-ches**) auto jack
**levantado -da** *adj* elevated, lofty, sublime; proud, haughty; *f* getting up (*from bed*)
**levantador -dora** *adj* lifting, elevating; *mf* lifter, elevator; insurrectionist, rebel; (coll.) slanderer
**levantamiento** *m* rise, lift, elevation; insurrection, uprising, revolt; elevation, sublimity; survey; (geol.) upheaval; (mach.) exhaust port; (prov.) settlement (*of an account*); **levantamiento del cadáver** inquest; **levantamiento del censo** or **de los censos** census taking; **levantamiento de planos** or **levantamiento topográfico** surveying
**levantar** *va* to raise; to lift; to elevate; to straighten; to stir up, rouse, agitate; to adjourn; to clear (*the table*); to break (*camp*); to break up (*housekeeping*); to make (*a survey*); to start (*game*); to bear (*false witness*); to raise (*troops; a siege*); to weigh (*anchor*); *vr* to rise; to get up; to stand up; to straighten up; to rebel, rise up
**levantaválvulas** *m* (*pl:* **-las**) valve lifter
**levantaventana** *m* sash lift
**levante** *m* levanter (*wind*); East, Orient; (*cap.*) *m* Levant; northeastern Mediterranean shores of Spain; region around Valencia, Alicante, and Murcia; **de levante** ready to leave
**levantino -na** *adj* Levantine; of the northeastern Mediterranean shores of Spain; *mf* Levantine; native or inhabitant of the northeastern Mediterranean shores of Spain
**levantisco -ca** *adj* (archaic) Levantine; turbulent, restless; *mf* (archaic) Levantine
**levar** *va* (naut.) to weigh (*anchor*); *vr* (naut.) to set sail
**leve** *adj* light; slight, trivial, trifling
**levedad** *f* lightness; trivialness, levity
**Leví** *m* (Bib.) Levi
**leviatán** *m* (Bib. & fig.) leviathan
**levigación** *f* levigation
**levigar §59** *va* to levigate (*to mix with water so as to separate finer particles*)
**levirato** *m* (hist.) levirate
**levita** *m* (Bib.) Levite; deacon; *f* frock coat
**levitación** *f* levitation
**levítico -ca** *adj* Levitical; (*cap.*) *m* (Bib.) Leviticus
**levitón** *m* heavy frock coat
**levógiro -ra** *adj* (chem. & opt.) levorotatory
**levoglucosa** *f* (chem.) levoglucose
**levulina** *f* (chem.) levuline
**levulínico -ca** *adj* levulinic
**levulosa** *f* (chem.) levulose
**lewisita** *f* (mil.) lewisite
**léxico -ca** *adj* lexical; m lexicon; wordstock; vocabulary (*e.g., of an author*)
**lexicografía** *f* lexicography
**lexicográfico -ca** *adj* lexicographic
**lexicógrafo -fa** *mf* lexicographer
**lexicología** *f* lexicology
**lexicológico -ca** *adj* lexicologic or lexicological
**lexicólogo -ga** *mf* lexicologist
**lexicón** *m* lexicon
**ley** *f* law; loyalty, devotion; norm, standard; fineness (*of a metal*); **a ley de caballero** on the word of a gentleman; **a toda ley** according to principle; with the utmost sincerity; **dar la ley** to set an example; to set the pace, to impose one's will; **de buena ley** sterling, genuine; **tener** or **tomar ley a** to be or become devoted to; **venir contra una ley** to break a law; **ley antigua** Mosaic law; **ley de la selva** law of the jungle; **ley de las fases** (physical chem.) phase rule; **ley del embudo** (coll.) one-sided law; **ley del menor esfuerzo** line of least resistance; **ley de Moisés** law of Moses; **ley del talión** law of retaliation; **leyes suntuarias** sumptuary laws; **ley marcial** martial law; **ley mosaica** Mosaic law; **ley natural** natural law; **ley no escrita** unwritten law; **ley periódica** (chem.) periodic law; **ley sálica** Salic law; **ley seca** dry law
**leyenda** *f* legend; reading
**leyendario -ria** *adj* legendary
**leyente** *adj* reading; *mf* reader
**lezna** *f* awl
**Lía** *f* (Bib.) Leah; (*l.c.*) *f* plaited esparto rope; **lías** *fpl* lee, dregs; **estar hecho una lía** (coll.) to be drunk
**liana** *f* (bot.) liana or liane
**lianza** *f* (Am.) account, credit (*in a store*)
**liar §90** *va* to tie, bind; to tie up, wrap up; to roll (*a cigaret*); (coll.) to embroil, involve; **liarlas** (coll.) to beat it, to duck out; (coll.) to kick the bucket; *vr* to join together, be associated; to have a liaison; (coll.) to become embroiled, become involved; **liárselos** to roll one's own (*i.e., cigarets*)
**liara** *f* var. of **aliara**
**liásico -ca** *adj & m* (geol.) Liassic
**liatón** *m* esparto rope
**libación** *f* libation; (hum.) libation (*alcoholic drink*)
**libanés -nesa** *adj & mf* Lebanese
**Líbano, el** Lebanon (*republic at east end of Mediterranean*); the Lebanon Mountains
**libar** *va* to suck; to taste; *vn* to pour out a libation; to imbibe
**libelista** *m* libeler, lampoonist
**libelo** *m* libel, lampoon; (law) petition
**libélula** *f* (ent.) dragonfly
**líber** *m* (bot.) bast, liber
**liberación** *f* liberation; quittance; redemption (*e.g., of a mortgage*)
**liberador -dora** *adj* liberating; *mf* liberator
**liberal** *adj* liberal; quick, ready; (pol.) liberal; (Am.) liberal (*broad-minded*); *mf* (pol.) liberal
**liberalidad** *f* liberality
**liberalismo** *m* liberalism
**liberalización** *f* liberalization
**liberalizar §76** *va & vr* to liberalize
**liberar** *va* to free
**liberiano -na** *adj & mf* Liberian
**libérrimo -ma** *adj super* very or most free
**liberta** *f* freedwoman
**libertad** *f* liberty, freedom; **en libertad** at liberty, at large; **tomarse la libertad de** + *inf* to take the liberty to + *inf;* **tomarse libertades** to take liberties (*to be too familiar*); **libertad de comercio** free trade; **libertad de cultos** freedom of worship; **libertad de empresa** free enterprise; **libertad de enseñanza** academic freedom; **libertad de imprenta** freedom of the press; **libertad de los mares** freedom of the seas; **libertad de palabra** freedom of speech, free speech; **libertad de prensa** freedom of the press; **libertad de reunión** freedom of assembly
**libertadamente** *adv* brashly, wantonly, impudently
**libertado -da** *adj* free; bold, daring
**libertador -dora** *adj* liberating; *mf* liberator
**libertar** *va* to liberate, to set free; to free; to save, preserve (*from death, jail, etc.*)
**libertario -ria** *adj* anarchistic; *mf* anarchist
**liberticida** *adj* liberticidal; *mf* liberticide, destroyer of liberty
**libertinaje** *m* libertinism
**libertino -na** *adj & mf* libertine
**liberto** *m* freedman; probationer (*convicted delinquent on probation*)
**Libia** *f* see **libio**
**líbico -ca** *adj* Libyan
**libídine** *f* (psychol.) libido; lust, lewdness
**libidinoso -sa** *adj* libidinous
**libido** *f* (psychol.) libido
**libio -bia** *adj & mf* Libyan; **la Libia** Libya
**libón** *m* bubbling spring; pool
**libra** *f* pound (*weight, coin*); (*cap.*) *f* (astr.) Libra; **libra esterlina** pound sterling
**libración** *f* libration; (astr.) libration

**libraco** or **libracho** *m* cheap book, poor book
**librado -da** *adj* finished, ruined; **bien librado** successful; **mal librado** unsuccessful; *mf* (com.) drawee
**librador -dora** *mf* deliverer; *m* grocer's scoop; (com.) drawer
**libramiento** *m* deliverance, exemption; warrant (*for payment of money*)
**librancista** *m* (com.) holder of a draft
**libranza** *f* (com.) draft, bill of exchange; **libranza postal** money order
**librapié** *m* (mech.) foot-pound
**librar** *va* to free; to save, spare, deliver; to place (*e.g., one's hope*); to pass (*sentence*); to give, to join (*battle*); to decide; (com.) to draw; *vn* to be delivered, to give birth; to expel the placenta; to receive a visitor in the locutory (*said of a nun*); (com.) to draw; **a bien** or **a buen librar** as well as could be expected; **librar bien** to come off well, to succeed; **librar mal** to come off badly, to fail; *vr* to free oneself; to escape; **librarse de buena** (coll.) to get out of a jam, to have a close shave
**libratorio** *m* locutory
**librazo** *m* big book; blow with a book
**libre** *adj* free; single, unmarried; free, outspoken, brash; free, loose, licentious; guiltless, innocent; **libre de porte** postage prepaid, freight prepaid
**librea** *f* livery (*uniform*); coat (*of deer and other animals*); (coll.) servants; (fig.) livery (*outward appearance*); **llevar librea** to be a servant
**librear** *va* to sell by the pound
**librecambio** *m* free trade
**librecambista** *adj* free-trading; *mf* freetrader
**librejo** *m* var. of **libraco**
**librepensador -dora** *adj* freethinking; *mf* freethinker
**librepensamiento** *m* free thought, freethinking
**librería** *f* bookstore, bookshop; book business; bookshelf; library; **librería de viejo** second-hand bookshop
**libreril** *adj* book (*e.g., trade*)
**librero** *m* bookseller; (Am.) bookshelf, bookcase
**libresco -ca** *adj* book, bookish
**libreta** *f* loaf of bread; notebook; **libreta de banco** bankbook
**librete** *m* foot stove, foot brasier; booklet
**libretín** *m* booklet
**libretista** *mf* librettist
**libreto** *m* (mus.) libretto
**librillo** *m* tub, washtub; book (*of postage stamps, gold leaf, cigaret paper, etc.*); omasum (*of ruminant*); **librillo de cera** folded wax taper
**libro** *m* book; omasum (*of ruminant*); **ahorcar los libros** (coll.) to give up studying, to leave school; **a libro abierto** at sight; **el libro de Mormón** the book of Mormon; **hacer libro nuevo** (coll.) to turn over a new leaf; **libro a la rústica** paperbound book; **libro de actas** minute book; **libro de caballerías** romance of chivalry; **libro de caja** cashbook; **libro de cocina** cookbook; **libro de cheques** checkbook; **libro de chistes** joke book; **libro de lance** second-hand book; **libro de mayor venta** best seller; **libro de memoria** memo book; **libro de oro** Golden Book (*of Venetian nobility*); **libro de recuerdos** scrapbook; **libro de teléfonos** telephone book; **libro de texto** textbook; **libro diario** day book; **libro en folio** folio (*book*); **libro en rústica** paperbound book; **libro mayor** ledger; **libro procesional** or **procesionario** processional; **Libros sibilinos** Sibylline Books; **libro talonario** checkbook, stub book
**libro-registro** *m* (com.) book (*of a company*)
**licantropía** *f* lycanthropy
**licántropo** *m* lycanthrope
**licencia** *f* license (*permission; document showing such permission; abuse of liberty; licentiousness*); licentiate; master's degree; (mil.) furlough; **licencia absoluta** (mil.) discharge; **licencia de matrimonio** marriage license; **licencia poética** poetic license
**licenciado -da** *adj* licensed; free; pedantic; *mf* licenciate (*person who has a permit to practice a profession; holder of a licentiate or master's degree*); lawyer; (coll.) university student; (mil.) discharged soldier; **licenciado de presidio** freed prisoner; **Licenciado Vidriera** (coll.) namby-pamby
**licenciamiento** *m* graduation with a licentiate or master's degree; discharge of soldiers
**licenciar** *va* to license; to confer the degree of master on; (mil.) to discharge; *vr* to receive the master's degree; to be lewd; (mil.) to be discharged
**licenciatura** *f* licentiate, master's degree; graduation with a licentiate or master's degree; work leading to a licentiate or master's degree
**licencioso -sa** *adj* licentious
**liceo** *m* lyceum; lycée
**licio -cia** *adj* & *mf* Lycian; (*cap.*) *f* Lycia
**licitación** *f* bidding
**licitador -dora** *mf* bidder
**licitar** *va* to bid on; (Am.) to buy at auction, to sell at auction; *vn* to bid
**lícito -ta** *adj* licit; just, right; as prescribed
**licitud** *f* lawfulness; rightness
**lícnide** *f* or **licnis** *m* (bot.) lychnis
**licopodio** *m* (bot.) ground pine, lycopodium
**licor** *m* liquor (*spirituous beverage; any liquid*); liqueur (*spirituous liquor sweetened and flavored with aromatic substances*); (pharm.) liquor; **licores espiritosos** or **espirituosos** ardent spirits, spirituous liquors
**licorero -ra** *mf* (Am.) distiller; (Am.) liquor dealer; *f* cellaret
**licorista** *mf* distiller; liquor dealer
**licoroso -sa** *adj* spirituous, alcoholic; generous, rich (*wine*)
**lictor** *m* (hist.) lictor
**licuable** *adj* liquefiable
**licuación** *f* liquefaction; melting; (metal.) liquation
**licuador** *m* mechanical juice squeezer
**licuar** *va* to liquefy; to melt; (metal.) to liquate; *vr* to melt
**licuefacción** *f* liquefaction
**licuefacer** §55 *va* & *vr* to liquefy
**licuefactible** *adj* liquefiable
**licuefacto -ta** *adj* liquefied
**licuescencia** *f* liquescence
**licuescente** *adj* liquescent
**licurgo -ga** *adj* smart, keen; *m* lawmaker; (*cap.*) *m* Lycurgus
**lichera** *f* bedcover
**lid** *f* fight, combat; dispute, argument; **en buena lid** fairly, by fair means
**líder** *m* leader
**lidia** *f* & **Lidia** *f* see **lidio**
**lidiadero -ra** *adj* fighting, fit for fighting; *f* (Am.) quarreling, bickering
**lidiador -dora** *mf* fighter; *m* bullfighter
**lidiar** *va* to fight (*bulls*); *vn* to fight, to battle; to face up, to resist; **lidiar con** to contend with, to have to put up with
**lidio -dia** *adj* Lydian; (mus.) Lydian; *mf* Lydian; *f* fight; bullfight; (*cap.*) *f* Lydia
**lidita** *f* lyddite (*explosive*); (mineral.) Lydian stone
**liebratón** *m* var. of **lebrato**
**liebre** *f* (zool.) hare; coward; **coger una liebre** (coll.) to fall without hurting oneself; **levantar la liebre** (coll.) to do something to attract attention; **liebre de mar** or **liebre marina** (zool.) sea hare; (zool.) porcelain crab
**liebrecilla** *f* (bot.) bluebottle
**Lieja** *f* Liége
**liendre** *f* nit; **cascar** or **machacar las liendres a** (coll.) to beat up, to thrash; (coll.) to rake over the coals
**lientera** or **lientería** *f* (path.) lientery
**lientérico -ca** *adj* lienteric
**liento -ta** *adj* damp, dank
**lienza** *f* strip of cloth
**lienzo** *m* linen, linen cloth; linen handkerchief; face or front (*of a wall or building*); (fort.) curtain; (paint.) canvas; **lienzo de la Verónica** veronica (*representing Christ's face*)
**liga** *f* garter; league; alloy; birdlime; band, rubber band; bond, union; (bot.) mistletoe; **Liga anseática** Hanseatic League; **liga de goma** rubber band
**ligación** *f* ligation, binding, bond

**ligada** *f* ligature, tie, bond; (naut.) seizing, lashing
**ligado** *m* (mus. & print.) ligature
**ligador** *m* (surg.) ligator
**ligadura** *f* ligature, tie, bond; (mus. & surg.) ligature; (naut.) seizing, lashing
**ligamaza** *f* birdlime
**ligamen** *m* spell said to cause impotency
**ligamento** *m* ligament; (anat. & zool.) ligament
**ligamentoso -sa** *adj* ligamentous
**ligamiento** *m* tie, bond; union, harmony
**ligapierna** *f* garter
**ligar** §59 *va* to tie, bind; to alloy; to join, combine; (surg.) to ligate; (fig.) to bind, commit; *vn* (coll.) to flirt, to have an affair; *vr* to league together; (fig.) to become bound or committed
**ligazón** *f* bond, union; (naut.) futtock
**ligereza** *f* lightness; speed, rapidity, swiftness; fickleness, flightiness; indiscretion, tactlessness; **ligereza de mano** light touch, skill
**ligero -ra** *adj* light (*in weight; in arms or equipment; slight, delicate; agile, nimble; unimportant; superficial; flippant; fickle, flighty; cheerful; said also of food, wine, sleep*); weak (*e.g., tea*); **a la ligera** lightly; quickly; simply, unceremoniously; **de ligero** thoughtlessly; rashly; **ligero de cascos** scatterbrained, light-headed; **ligero de lengua** loose-tongued; **ligero de pies** light-footed; **ligero de ropa** scantily clad; **ligero** *adv* (Am.) fast, quickly, rapidly
**lignario -ria** *adj* ligneous
**lignificar** §86 *vr* to lignify
**lignina** *f* (bot.) lignin
**lignito** *m* (mineral.) lignite
**lignocelulosa** *f* lignocellulose
**ligón** *m* hoe
**ligroína** *f* (chem.) ligroin
**lígula** *f* (anat.) ligula; (bot. & zool.) ligula or ligule
**ligulado -da** *adj* ligulate
**ligur** or **ligurino -na** *adj & mf* Ligurian
**ligustre** *m* flower of privet
**ligustrino -na** *adj* (pertaining to) privet
**ligustro** *m* (bot.) privet
**lija** *f* (ichth.) dogfish; dogfish skin; sandpaper
**lijado** *m* sanding, sandpapering
**lijar** *va* to sand, to sandpaper
**lila** *f* (bot.) lilac (*shrub and flower*); *m* lilac (*color*); (*cap.*) *f* Lille
**lilac** *f* (*pl:* **lilaques**) (bot.) lilac (*shrub and flower*)
**lilaila** *f* (coll.) trickiness, cunning; Moorish war cry; (archaic) Berber fabric of silk and wool
**lilao** *m* (coll.) vain show
**liliáceo -a** *adj* (bot.) liliaceous
**liliputiense** *adj & mf* Lilliputian
**lima** *f* file (*tool*); sweet lime; (arch.) hip; (arch.) hip rafter; (bot.) sweet-lime tree; **lima de cola de rata** rattail file; **lima de doble picadura** double-cut file, cross-cut file; **lima delgada** slim file; **lima de mediacaña** half-round file; **lima de picadura sencilla** single-cut file; **lima de uñas** nail file; **lima hoya** (arch.) valley (*of a roof*); **lima muza** smooth file; **lima sorda** dead-smooth file; **lima tesa** (arch.) hip; **lima triangular** three-square file
**limador -dora** *mf* filer; *f* (mach.) shaper; power-file
**limadura** *f* filing; **limaduras** *fpl* filings
**limalla** *f* filings
**limar** *va* to file; to file down; to polish, touch up; to curtail, cut down; to smooth, smooth over
**limatón** *m* coarse round file
**limaza** *f* (zool.) slug
**limazo** *m* sliminess
**limbo** *m* edge; (astr., bot. & surv.) limb; (theol.) limbo; (coll.) distraction, diversion; **estar en el limbo** (coll.) to be distraught
**Limburgo** Limburg
**limen** *m* threshold; (psychol., physiol. & fig.) threshold
**limenso** *m* (Am.) honeydew melon
**limeño -ña** *adj & mf* Limean
**limero -ra** *mf* lime dealer; *m* (bot.) sweet-lime tree; *f* (naut.) rudderhole
**limeta** *f* long-necked bottle or flask
**liminal** *adj* (psychol.) liminal
**limitación** *f* limitation
**limitacorrientes** *m* (*pl:* **-tes**) (elec.) var. of **limitador de corriente**
**limitado -da** *adj* limited; dull-witted
**limitador** *m* limiter; **limitador de corriente** (elec.) clock meter; (elec.) slot meter, coin-operated meter; (elec.) current limiter
**limitáneo -a** *adj* limitary
**limitar** *va* to limit; to bound; to cut down, to reduce; **limitar a** + *inf* to limit to + *ger*; *vn* to be contiguous; **limitar con** to border on
**limitativo -va** *adj* limitative
**límite** *m* limit; **no tener límites** to know no limit
**limítrofe** *adj* bordering
**limnología** *f* limnology
**limo** *m* slime, mud
**limón** *m* shaft (*of wagon*); lemon; (arch.) string; (bot.) lemon, lemon tree; (Am.) lime (*fruit of Citrus aurantifolia*); **limón silvestre** May apple (*fruit*)
**limonado -da** *adj* lemon, lemon-colored; *f* lemonade
**limonar** *m* lemon grove
**limoncillo** *m* (bot.) citronella
**limoncito** *m* (bot.) limeberry, bergamot lime, orangeberry
**limoneno** *m* (chem.) limonene
**limonero -ra** *adj* shaft (*horse*); *mf* shaft horse; lemon seller or vendor; *m* (bot.) lemon, lemon tree; (Am.) lime tree (*Citrus aurantifolia*); *f* shaft (*of wagon*); shafts
**limonita** *f* (mineral.) limonite
**limosidad** *f* sliminess, muddiness
**limosina** *f* (aut.) limousine
**limosna** *f* alms
**limosnear** *vn* to beg
**limosnero -ra** *adj* almsgiving, charitable; *m* almsgiver, almoner; alms box; (Am.) beggar; *f* nun who collects alms; alms bag
**limoso -sa** *adj* slimy, muddy
**limpia** *f* see **limpio**
**limpiabarros** *m* (*pl:* **-rros**) scraper, foot scraper
**limpiabotas** *m* (*pl:* **-tas**) bootblack
**limpiacristales** *m* (*pl:* **-les**) windshield washer
**limpiachimeneas** *m* (*pl:* **-as**) chimney sweep
**limpiadera** *f* brush; plowstaff
**limpiadientes** *m* (*pl:* **-tes**) toothpick
**limpiador -dora** *adj* cleaning; *mf* cleaner
**limpiadura** *f* cleaning; **limpiaduras** *fpl* cleanings
**limpiaduría** *f* (Am.) dry-cleaning establishment
**limpialimas** *m* (*pl:* **-mas**) file card (*brush*)
**limpiamente** *adv* cleanly, in a clean manner; neatly; skillfully, with ease; simply, sincerely; honestly, unselfishly
**limpiametales** *m* (*pl:* **-les**) metal polish
**limpiamiento** *m* cleaning
**limpianieve** *m* snowplow
**limpiaoídos** *m* (*pl:* **-dos**) earpick
**limpiaparabrisas** *m* (*pl:* **-sas**) windshield wiper
**limpiaparrilla** *m* slice bar
**limpiapiés** *m* (*pl:* **-piés**) (Am.) door mat
**limpiapipas** *m* (*pl:* **-pas**) pipe cleaner
**limpiaplumas** *m* (*pl:* **-mas**) penwiper
**limpiapozos** *mf* (*pl:* **-zos**) cesspool cleaner
**limpiar** *va* to clean; to cleanse; to exonerate; to clean out, to prune (*a tree*); to shine (*shoes*); (coll.) to snitch; (coll.) to clean out (*someone in gambling*); (coll.) to clean up (*money in gambling*); (mil.) to mop up; **limpiarle a uno cierta cantidad** (coll.) to clean someone out of a certain amount of money; *vr* to clean, to clean oneself
**limpiatubos** *m* (*pl:* **-bos**) tube cleaner, flue scraper; swab, bailer
**limpiaúñas** *m* (*pl:* **-ñas**) orange stick, nail cleaner
**limpiavía** *f* (rail.) pilot, cowcatcher; **limpiavías** *m* (*pl:* **-as**) track cleaner
**limpiavidrio** *m* windshield wiper
**limpidez** *f* (poet.) limpidity
**límpido -da** *adj* (poet.) limpid

**limpieza** *f* cleaning; cleanness; cleanliness; neatness; ease, skill; chastity; honesty, disinterestedness; fair play; (fig.) house cleaning; **limpieza de bolsa** (coll.) lack of funds; **limpieza en seco** dry cleaning
**limpio -pia** *adj* clean; cleanly; neat, tidy; pure; chaste; clear, free; **dejar limpio** (coll.) to clean out (*of money*); **en limpio** net; **poner en limpio** to recopy clearly, to make a clear copy of; **quedar limpio** (coll.) to be cleaned out (*of money*); **sacar en limpio** to deduce, understand; to recopy clearly, to make a clear copy of; **limpio de polvo y paja** (coll.) free, for nothing; (coll.) net, after deducting expenses; *f* cleaning; **limpio** *adv* cleanly, in a clean manner; fair; **jugar limpio** to play fair
**limpión** *m* lick, quick cleaning; (coll.) cleaner; (Am.) dishcloth
**lín.** abr. of **línea**
**lina** *f* (Am.) coarse wool
**linaje** *m* lineage; class, description; **linajes** *mpl* people of high lineage; **linaje humano** humankind; **linaje puro** (biol.) pure line
**linajista** *m* genealogist
**linajudo -da** *adj* of high lineage, highborn; *mf* person of high lineage
**lináloe** *m* (bot.) aloe
**linalol** *m* (chem.) linaloöl
**linar** *m* flax field
**linaria** *f* (bot.) toadflax, snapdragon
**linaza** *f* flaxseed, linseed
**lince** *m* (zool.) lynx; keen, shrewd, or discerning person; (*cap.*) *m* (astr.) Lynx; **lince de las estepas** (zool.) caracal; *adj* keen (*sight, eyes*); keen, shrewd, discerning
**lincear** *va* (coll.) to see into, to see through
**linceo -a** *adj* lyncean; (poet.) keen (*sight, eyes*)
**linchamiento** *m* lynching
**linchar** *va* to lynch
**lindante** *adj* adjoining, bordering
**lindar** *vn* to be contiguous; **lindar con** to border on
**lindazo** *m* boundary
**linde** *m & f* limit, boundary
**lindero -ra** *adj* adjoining, bordering; *m* limit, edge; *f* limit, boundary
**lindeza** *f* prettiness, niceness; harmony, proportion, elegance; funny remark, witticism; (coll.) flirting; **lindezas** *fpl* (coll.) insults
**lindo -da** *adj* pretty, nice; fine, wonderful; **de lo lindo** a great deal; wonderfully; *m* (coll.) dude, sissy
**lindura** *f* prettiness, niceness; beauty (*beautiful woman*)
**línea** *f* line; lines (*outline of a figure, dress, etc.*); figure, waistline; **conservar la línea** to keep one's figure; **en toda la línea** all along the line; **la línea** (geog.) the line (*the equator*); **leer entre líneas** to read between the lines; **línea aclínica** (phys.) aclinic line; **línea agónica** (phys.) agonic line; **línea alámbrica** (elec.) line, wire; **línea de agua** water line; **línea de base** base line; **línea de batalla** line of battle; **línea de circunvalación** (rail.) belt line; (fort.) line of circumvallation; **línea de colimación** line of collimation; **línea de combate** line of battle; **línea de demarcación** (hist.) Line of Demarcation; **línea de empalme** (rail.) branch line; **línea de flotación** water line; **línea de fondo** (tennis) base line; (tennis) service line; **línea de fuego** (mil.) firing line; **línea de fuerza** (phys.) line of force; (elec.) power line; **línea de incidencia** line of incidence; **línea del lado** (tennis) side line; **línea del fuerte** (naut.) level line; **línea del partido** party line (*especially of Communist party*); **línea de media red** or **de mitad** (tennis) center service line; **línea de mira** (arti. & surv.) line of sight; **línea de montaje** assembly line; **línea de puntos** dotted line; **línea de respeto** limit of the marine belt; **línea de saque** or **de servicio** (tennis) service line; **línea de tierra** ground line; **línea de tiro** (mil.) line of fire; **línea férrea** railway; **línea geodésica** (math.) geodesic line; **línea internacional de cambio de fecha** international date line; **línea principal** (telp.) trunk line; **línea punteada** dotted line; **línea suplementaria** (mus.) ledger line, added line; **línea transversal** (geom.) transversal; **línea troncal** (rail.) trunk line
**lineal** *adj* lineal, linear
**lineamento** *m* lineament; **lineamentos** *mpl* lineaments (*especially of the face*)
**lineamiento** *m* lineament; **lineamientos** *mpl* (Am.) general outline, broad outline
**linear** *adj* linear (*leaf*); *va* to line; to sketch, outline; to delimit; to mark off, mark out
**linearidad** *f* linearity
**linfa** *f* (anat. & physiol.) lymph; (poet.) water
**linfadenitis** *f* (path.) lymphadenitis
**linfangitis** *f* (path.) lymphangitis
**linfático -ca** *adj* lymphatic; (fig.) lymphatic
**linfocito** *m* (anat.) lymphocyte
**lingote** *m* ingot; slug; (print.) slug; **lingote de hierro** pig iron
**linguado -da** *adj* (her.) langued
**lingual** *adj* lingual; (phonet.) lingual; *f* (phonet.) lingual
**linguete** *m* pawl, dog, ratchet
**lingüista** *mf* linguist (*person who studies linguistic phenomena*)
**lingüístico -ca** *adj* linguistic; *f* linguistics
**linimento** *m* liniment
**linina** *f* (biol. & chem.) linin
**linneano -na** *adj* Linnaean or Linnean
**lino** *m* (bot.) flax; flax fiber; linen; canvas; (poet.) sail
**linóleo** *m* linoleum
**linón** *m* lawn (*fabric*)
**linotipia** *f* linotype
**linotipista** *mf* linotyper or linotypist
**lintel** *m* var. of **dintel**
**linterna** *f* lantern; (arch. & mach.) lantern; (naut.) lantern (*of lighthouse*); **linterna de Aristóteles** (zool.) Aristotle's lantern; **linterna china** Japanese lantern; **linterna eléctrica** flashlight; **linterna mágica** magic lantern; **linterna sorda** dark lantern; **linterna veneciana** Japanese lantern
**linternazo** *m* blow with a lantern; (coll.) blow, smack
**linternero -ra** *mf* lantern maker or dealer
**linternón** *m* big lantern; (naut.) poop lantern
**liño** *m* row of trees, shrubs, or other plants
**liñuelo** *m* strand (*of a rope or cable*)
**lío** *m* bundle, package; batch (*of papers*); (coll.) muddle, mess; (coll.) liaison; **armar un lío** (coll.) to raise a row, stir up trouble; **hacerse un lío** (coll.) to get in a jam; **traer un lío con** (coll.) to have an affair with
**lionés -nesa** *adj & mf* Lyonese; **a la lionesa** (cook.) lyonnaise (*potatoes*)
**liorna** *f* (coll.) uproar, hubbub, confusion; (*cap.*) *f* Leghorn (*city*)
**lioso -sa** *adj* (coll.) scheming, trouble-making; (coll.) knotty, troublesome
**lipasa** *f* (biochem.) lipase
**lipoma** *m* (path.) lipoma
**liq.$^{n}$** abr. of **liquidación**
**líq.$^{o}$** abr. of **líquido**
**liquefacción** *f* liquefaction
**liquefacer** §55 *va & vr* to liquefy
**liquefactible** *adj* liquefiable
**liquefacto -ta** *adj* liquefied
**liquen** *m* (bot. & path.) lichen
**liquenina** *f* (chem.) lichenin
**liquenología** *f* lichenology
**liquenoso -sa** *adj* lichenous
**liquidable** *adj* liquefiable
**liquidación** *f* liquefaction; liquidation
**liquidador -dora** *adj* liquidating; *mf* liquidator; **liquidador de averías** insurance adjuster
**liquidámbar** *m* (bot.) liquidambar (*tree and liquid*)
**liquidar** *va & vr* to liquefy; to liquidate
**liquidez** *f* liquidity
**líquido -da** *adj* liquid; (com.) net; (phonet.) liquid; *m* liquid; (com.) net; **líquido amoniacal** ammoniacal liquor, ammonia liquor; **líquido imponible** taxable net; *f* (phonet.) liquid
**lira** *f* (mus.) lyre; inspiration, poetry (*of a given poet*); (*cap.*) *f* (astr.) Lyre or Lyra
**lirado -da** *adj* lyre-shaped; (bot.) lyrate

**liria** *f* birdlime
**lírico -ca** *adj* lyric, lyrical; (theat.) lyric (*musical, operatic*); (Am.) fantastic, utopian; *m* lyric poet; (Am.) visionary, utopian; *f* lyric poetry
**lirio** *m* (bot.) iris; **lirio amarillo** (bot.) yellow flag; **lirio blanco** (bot.) lily; **lirio de agua** (bot.) calla, calla lily; **lirio de Florencia** (bot.) fleur-de-lis, orris, Florentine iris; **lirio de los valles** (bot.) lily of the valley; **lirio de mar** (zool.) sea lily (*crinoid*); **lirio hediondo** (bot.) stinking iris, gladdon; **lirio tricolor** (bot.) red jasmine
**liriodendro** *m* (bot.) tulip tree, yellow pine
**lirismo** *m* lyricism
**lirón** *m* (zool.) dormouse; (bot.) water plantain; (fig.) sleepyhead
**lis** *f* (bot.) iris; (bot.) lily
**lisa** *f* see **liso**
**Lisandro** *m* Lysander
**Lisboa** *f* Lisbon
**lisboeta, lisbonense** or **lisbonés -nesa** *adj* (pertaining to) Lisbon; *mf* native or inhabitant of Lisbon
**lisencoísmo** *m* Lysenkoism
**lisera** *f* (fort.) berm
**lisiado -da** *adj* hurt, abused; crippled; eager, wild (*about something*); *mf* cripple
**lisiar** *va* to hurt, abuse; to cripple; *vr* to become crippled
**lisimaquia** *f* (bot.) loosestrife; **lisimaquia roja** (bot.) purple loosestrife, willow herb
**lisina** *f* (biochem.) lysin or lysine
**Lisipo** *m* Lysippus
**liso -sa** *adj* smooth, even; plain, unadorned (*clothes*); simple, plain-dealing; **liso y llano** simple, easy; *m* (min.) smooth face (*of a rock*); *f* (ichth.) spiny loach; (ichth.) gray mullet; (ichth.) striped mullet
**lisofobia** *f* (psycopath.) lyssophobia
**lisol** *m* lysol
**lisonja** *f* flattery; (her.) lozenge
**lisonjeador -dora** *adj* flattering; pleasing; *mf* flatterer
**lisonjear** *va & vn* to flatter; to please, delight; *vr* to flatter oneself
**lisonjero -ra** *adj* flattering; pleasing; *mf* flatterer
**lista** *f* see **listo**
**listado -da** *adj* striped
**listar** *va* to list
**listeado -da** *adj* var. of **listado**
**listel** *m* (arch.) listel, fillet; milled edge of coin
**listerina** *f* listerine
**listero** *m* timekeeper; roll taker, roll keeper
**listeza** *f* (coll.) readiness, quickness, alertness, craftiness
**listo -ta** *adj* ready, prepared; ready, quick, prompt; alert, wide-awake; **estar listo** to be finished (*with a task*); **pasarse de listo** (coll.) to bubble over, to go out on a limb; **más listo que Cardona** (coll.) as quick as lightning; **listo de manos** (coll.) light-fingered ‖ *f* list; roll; strip; colored stripe (*in a fabric*); roll call; **pasar lista** to call the roll; **lista de bajas** casualty list; **lista de comidas** bill of fare; **lista de correos** general delivery; **lista de espera** waiting list; **lista de frecuencia** frequency list (*of words*); **lista de pagos** pay roll; **lista de revista** (mil.) roll call; **lista negra** black list, black book
**listón -tona** *adj* white-striped, light-striped (*bull*); *m* tape, ribbon; strip (*of wood*); lath; (arch.) listel, fillet
**listonado** *m* lath, lathing
**listonar** *va* to build or construct with strips of wood
**listoncillo** *m* (carp.) bead
**lisura** *f* smoothness, evenness; candor, simplicity; (Am.) piece of impudence; (Am.) obscenity
**lit.** abr. of **literalmente**
**lita** *f* (vet.) tongue worm (*especially in a dog*)
**litargirio** *m* (chem.) litharge
**lite** *f* lawsuit
**litera** *f* litter; berth (*in boat or train*); **litera alta** upper berth; **litera baja** lower berth
**literal** *adj* literal
**literalidad** *f* literalness, literality
**literalismo** *m* literalism
**literalista** *adj* literalist, literalistic; *mf* literalist
**literario -ria** *adj* literary
**literato -ta** *adj* literary (*person*); *mf* literary person, writer
**literatura** *f* literature; **literatura de escape** escape literature
**litiasis** *f* (path.) lithiasis
**lítico -ca** *adj* lithic; (chem.) lithic
**litigación** *f* litigation
**litigante** *adj & mf* litigant
**litigar** §59 *va & vn* litigate
**litigio** *m* lawsuit, litigation; dispute, argument
**litigioso -sa** *adj* litigious
**litina** *f* (chem.) lithia
**litio** *m* (chem.) lithium
**litis** *f* (*pl:* **-tis**) lawsuit
**litisconsorte** *mf* (law) joint litigant
**litiscontestación** *f* (law) answer to an allegation; (law) litiscontestation
**litisexpensas** *fpl* (law) costs of a suit
**litispendencia** *f* (law) pending litigation
**litoclasa** *f* (geol.) lithoclase
**litófago -ga** *adj* (zool.) lithophagous
**litofotografía** *f* lithophotography
**litografía** *f* lithograph; lithography
**litografiar** §90 *va* to lithograph
**litográfico -ca** *adj* lithographic
**litógrafo -fa** *mf* lithographer
**litoideo -a** *adj* lithoid
**litología** *f* (geol. & med.) lithology
**litológico -ca** *adj* lithologic or lithological
**litomarga** *f* (mineral.) lithomarge
**litopón** *m* lithopone
**litoral** *adj* littoral, coastal; *m* littoral, coast, shore
**litorina** *f* (zool.) periwinkle
**litosfera** *f* lithosphere
**lítote** *f* (rhet.) litotes
**litotomía** *f* (surg.) lithotomy
**litotricia** *f* (surg.) lithotrity
**litotritor** *m* (surg.) lithotrite
**litráceo -a** *adj* (bot.) lythraceous
**litre** *m* (bot.) lithi
**litro** *m* liter
**Lituania** *f* Lithuania
**lituano -na** *adj & mf* Lithuanian; *m* Lithuanian (*language*)
**lituo** *m* (hist.) lituus (*augur's staff; trumpet*)
**liturgia** *f* liturgy
**litúrgico -ca** *adj* liturgic or liturgical
**liturgista** *m* liturgist
**liviandad** *f* lightness; fickleness; triviality; lewdness
**liviano -na** *adj* light; fickle; trivial; lewd; *m* leading donkey; **livianos** *mpl* lights, lungs
**lividez** *f* lividity
**lívido -da** *adj* livid
**Livio** *m* Livy
**livor** *m* lividness; evil, envy, hate; disorder
**lixiviador** *m* leach (*vessel*)
**lixiviar** *va & vr* to leach
**liza** *f* lists (*place of combat*); combat, contest; (ichth.) mullet; **entrar en liza** to enter the lists
**lizarol** *m* harness shaft (*of loom*)
**lizo** *m* warp; heddle, leash
**Lm.** abr. of **lumen**
**lo** *art def neut* (followed by masc form of adj) the, e.g., **lo hermoso** the beautiful; (the adj can often be translated by corresponding noun ending in -ness), e.g., **lo rápido de sus movimientos** the rapidness of his movements; (followed by adv or inflected adj) how, e.g., **me sorprende ver lo bien que habla Vd. el español** I am surprised to see how well you speak Spanish; **perdieron cuanto tenían a pesar de lo tacaños que eran** they lost all they had in spite of how stingy they were; **lo más** as . . . as, e.g., **lo más temprano posible** as early as possible; *pron pers* him, it; you; (with verb **estar, ser, parecer,** etc., it represents an adj or noun understood and is either not translated or is translated by 'so'), e.g., **estoy cansado pero ella no lo está** I am tired but she is not; **aunque no es rico, quiere parecerlo** although he is not rich, he wants to appear so; *pron dem* that; **de lo que** + *verb* more than + *verb*, e.g., **escri-**

**be mejor de lo que habla** he writes better than he speaks; **todo lo que** all that, e.g., **he perdido todo lo que tenía** I lost all I had; **lo de** the question of, the matter of, e.g., **lo de la guerra fría** the question of the cold war; **lo de que** the fact that, the statement that; **lo de siempre** the same old story; **lo que** what, e.g., **lo que Vd. necesita es ejercicio** what you need is exercise
**loa** *f* praise; prologue (*of medieval play*); short dramatic poem
**loable** *adj* laudable, praiseworthy
**loador -dora** *adj* eulogistic; *mf* eulogizer, eulogist
**loar** *va* to praise
**loba** *f* see **lobo**
**lobado -da** *adj* lobate
**lobagante** *m* (zool.) lobster (*Homarus*)
**lobanillo** *m* wen, cyst; gall
**lobato** *m* wolf cub
**lobelia** *f* (bot.) lobelia
**lobeliáceo -a** *adj* (bot.) lobeliaceous
**lobero -ra** *adj* (pertaining to the) wolf; *m* wolf hunter; *f* thicket infested with wolves
**lobezno** *m* wolf cub; wolfkin, little wolf
**lobina** *f* (ichth.) bass, sea bass
**lobo -ba** *adj* & *mf* (Am.) half-breed; *m* (zool.) wolf; (ichth.) loach; lobe; (coll.) drunk; **coger** or **pillar un lobo** (coll.) to get a jag on; **desollar** or **dormir un lobo** (coll.) to sleep off a drunk; **lobo cerval** or **cervario** (zool.) lynx; **lobo de mar** (ichth.) sea wolf, wolf fish; (coll.) old salt, sea dog (*experienced sailor*); **lobo marino** (zool.) seal; **lobo marsupial** (zool.) thylacine, Tasmanian wolf; **lobo solitario** (fig.) lone wolf; *f* she-wolf; ridge between furrows; soutane, cassock
**loboso -sa** *adj* full of wolves, infested with wolves
**lobotomía** *f* (surg.) lobotomy
**lóbrego -ga** *adj* gloomy (*dark; sad, melancholy*)
**lobreguecer §34** *va* to make dark, make gloomy; *vn* to grow dark
**lobreguez** *f* darkness; gloominess
**lobulado -da** *adj* lobate, lobed; lobulate; (arch.) foliated
**lobular** *adj* lobular; lobar
**lobulillo** *m* lobule
**lóbulo** *m* lobe; (arch.) foil
**lobuno -na** *adj* (pertaining to the) wolf, wolfish
**locación** *f* lease
**local** *adj* local; (med.) local; *m* rooms, quarters, premises: **local de negocios** place of business; **local prohibido** disorderly house
**localidad** *f* locality; accommodations (*e.g., on a train*); (theat.) seat
**localismo** *m* localism
**localización** *f* localization; location; **localización de averías** trouble shooting
**localizar §76** *va* to localize; to locate; to shoot (*trouble*); to limit, to limit the spread of; *vr* to be or become localized; to be located; (coll.) to become acclimated
**locatario -ria** *mf* renter, tenant
**locativo -va** *adj* (pertaining to a) lease; (gram.) locative; *m* (gram.) locative
**locería** *f* (Am.) chinaware; (Am.) set of china dishes; (Am.) pottery
**locero -ra** *mf* (coll.) var. of **ollero**
**loción** *f* wash, ablution; (pharm.) lotion
**loco -ca** *adj* crazy, mad, insane; wild, harum-scarum; awry; wonderful (*luck*); huge (*crop*); loose (*pulley*); (naut.) wild; **estar loco por** (coll.) to be crazy or mad about; **volver loco** to drive crazy; **loco de amor** madly in love; **loco de atar** (coll.) crazy as a bedbug, raving mad; **loco de contento** (coll.) mad with joy; **loco perenne** permanently mad; (coll.) full of fun; **loco rematado** (coll.) crazy as a bedbug, raving mad; *mf* insane person, lunatic, maniac; *m* fool (*jester*)
**locoísmo** *m* (vet.) loco disease
**locomoción** *f* locomotion
**locomotivo -va** *adj* locomotive
**locomotor -tora** or **-triz** (*pl:* **-trices**) *adj* locomotor; locomotive; **locomotora** *f* (rail.) engine, locomotive; **locomotora de empuje** (rail.) pusher engine; **locomotora de maniobras** (rail.) shifting engine; **locomotora de mercancías** (rail.) freight engine; **locomotora de viajeros** (rail.) passenger engine
**locomotora-ténder** *f* (*pl:* **locomotoras-ténder**) (rail.) tank engine, tank locomotive
**locomóvil** *adj* locomobile; *f* locomobile, tractor
**locro** *m* (Am.) meat and vegetable stew
**locuacidad** *f* loquacity
**locuaz** *adj* (*pl:* **-cuaces**) loquacious
**locución** *f* locution, expression; idiomatic phrase
**locuelo -la** *adj* (coll.) wild, frisky (*youngster*); *f* speech, way of speaking (*of an individual*)
**loculado -da** *adj* (bot.) loculate
**locular** *adj* locular
**loculicida** *adj* loculicidal
**lóculo** *m* (bot. & hist.) loculus
**locura** *f* madness, insanity; madness, folly; **locura de doble forma** (psychopath.) manic-depressive insanity
**locutor -tora** *mf* (rad.) announcer, commentator
**locutorio** *m* parlor, locutory (*in a nunnery*); telephone booth
**locha** *f* or **loche** *m* (ichth.) loach
**lodachar** *m*, **lodazal** *m* or **lodazar** *m* mudhole
**lodo** *m* mud; (chem.) lute (*substance used to close or seal a joint, porous surface, etc.*)
**lodoñero** *m* (bot.) guaiacum, lignum vitae
**lodoso -sa** *adj* muddy
**lofobranquio -quia** *adj* & *m* (ichth.) lophobranch
**loganiáceo -a** *adj* (bot.) loganiaceous
**logarítmico -ca** *adj* logarithmic or logarithmical
**logaritmo** *m* (math.) logarithm; **logaritmo vulgar** (math.) common logarithm
**logia** *f* lodge (*e.g., of Masons*); (arch.) loggia
**lógico -ca** *adj* logical; *mf* logician; *f* logic
**logístico -ca** *adj* (mil.) logistic or logistical; *f* (mil.) logistics
**logogrifo** *m* logogriph
**logomaquia** *f* logomachy
**logotipo** *m* (print.) logotype
**logrado -da** *adj* successful
**lograr** *va* to get, obtain; to attain; to produce, manage to produce; **lograr** + *inf* to succeed in + *ger*; *vr* to succeed, turn out well
**logrear** *vn* to be a moneylender; to profiteer
**logrería** *f* moneylending, usury; profiteering
**logrerismo** *m* (Am.) peculation
**logrero -ra** *adj* moneylending, usurious; profiteering; grasping; *mf* moneylender, usurer; profiteer; (Am.) sponger
**logro** *m* attainment; gain, profit; success; usury; **dar** or **prestar a logro** to lend at usurious rates
**loica** *f* (orn.) tanager
**Loira** *m* Loire
**loísmo** *m* use of **lo** for the accusative, instead of **le**
**loísta** *mf* user of **lo** for the accusative, instead of **le**
**lolardo** *m* Lollard
**loma** *f* long, low hill; **la loma de San Juan** San Juan Hill
**lombarda** *f* see **lombardo**
**Lombardía** *f* Lombardy
**lombardo -da** *adj* & *mf* Lombard; *f* (bot.) drumhead cabbage
**lombriguera** *f* hole in the ground made by a worm; wormy place; (bot.) tansy
**lombriz** *f* (*pl:* **-brices**) (zool.) worm, earthworm; (coll.) beanpole (*tall, skinny person*); **lombrices** *fpl* (path.) worms; **lombriz de los niños** (zool.) pinworm, threadworm; **lombriz de tierra** (zool.) earthworm; **lombriz intestinal** (zool.) intestinal worm; **lombriz solitaria** (zool.) tapeworm
**lombrosiano -na** *adj* Lombrosian
**lomear** *vn* to arch the back (*said of a horse*)
**lomentáceo -a** *adj* (bot.) lomentaceous
**lomento** *m* (bot.) loment
**lomera** *f* backstrap (*of harness*); ridgepole; (b.b.) backing
**lometa** *f* hill
**lomienhiesto -ta** *adj* var. of **lominhiesto**
**lomillería** *f* (Am.) harness maker's shop
**lomillo** *m* (sew.) cross-stitch; **lomillos** *spl* pads of packsaddle

**lominhiesto -ta** *adj* high-backed, high-cropped; (coll.) vain, conceited
**lomo** *m* back (*of animal, of book, of knife*); ridge between furrows; crease; loin; **lomos** *mpl* ribs; **lomo de asno** (rail.) hump
**lomudo -da** *adj* broad-backed
**lona** *f* canvas; (naut.) sailcloth; (poet.) sail; (Am.) burlap
**loncha** *f* slab, flagstone; slice, strip
**londinense** or **londonense** *adj* (pertaining to) London; *mf* Londoner
**Londres** *m* London; **el Gran Londres** Greater London
**long.** abr. of **longitud**
**longanimidad** *f* long-suffering, forbearance, magnanimity
**longánimo -ma** *adj* long-suffering, magnanimous
**longaniza** *f* pork sausage; (coll.) beanpole (*tall, skinny person*)
**longevidad** *f* longevity
**longevo -va** *adj* longevous, aged, very old
**longílocuo -cua** *adj* long-tongued, talkative
**longiloquio** *m* long, tiresome conversation
**longincuidad** *f* remoteness, distance; length (*of time*); length, extension
**longincuo -cua** *adj* remote, distant
**Longino** *m* Longinus
**longirrostro -tra** *adj* longirostral; (pal.) longirostrine
**longísimo -ma** *adj super* very long
**longitud** *f* longitude; length; **longitud de onda** (phys.) wave length
**longitudinal** *adj* longitudinal
**longividente** *adj* far-seeing, far-sighted
**longobardo -da** *adj & mf* Longobard
**longorón** *m* (zool.) piddock
**longuera** *f* long strip of land
**longuetas** *fpl* (surg.) bandages
**longuísimo -ma** *adj super* very long
**lonja** *f* exchange, market; grocery store; wool warehouse; slice; strap; stone step (*in front of church*); gallery, passageway
**lonjear** *va* (Am.) to cut (*hide*) into strips
**lonjeta** *f* bower, summerhouse
**lonjista** *mf* grocer
**lontananza** *f* far horizon; (paint.) background; **en lontananza** far away
**loor** *m* praise
**lopiano -na** *adj* (pertaining to) Lope de Vega
**lopista** *mf* authority on Lope de Vega
**loquear** *vn* to talk nonsense, to act like a fool; to have a high time, to carry on
**loquera** *f* see **loquero**
**loquería** *f* (Am.) madhouse, insane asylum
**loquero -ra** *mf* guard in an insane asylum; *m* (Am.) confusion, pandemonium; (Am.) madhouse (*place of confusion*); *f* insane asylum; (Am.) madness, insanity
**loquesco -ca** *adj* funny, jolly
**loquial** *adj* lochial
**loquios** *mpl* (obstet.) lochia
**lorán** *m* (naut.) loran
**lorantáceo -a** *adj* (bot.) loranthaceous
**loranto** *m* (bot.) mistletoe (*Loranthus*)
**lord** *m* (*pl:* **lores**) lord; Lord (*title*)
**lordosis** *f* (path.) lordosis
**loredo** *m* var. of **lauredal**
**Lorena, la** Lorraine
**lorenés -nesa** *adj* Lorrainese; *mf* Lorrainer
**Lorenzo** *m* Laurence or Lawrence
**loriga** *f* (arm. & zool.) lorica
**loriguillo** *m* (bot.) mezereon
**loris** *m* (*pl:* **-ris**) (zool.) loris; **loris cenceño** (zool.) slow loris
**loro -ra** *adj* dark-brown; blond; *m* (orn.) parrot; (bot.) cherry laurel; (ichth.) scarus; glass bedpan; (Am.) spy; **loro de mar** (ichth.) peacock fish
**lorza** *f* pleat, tuck
**Lor.zo** abr. of **Lorenzo**
**los, las** *art def pl* the; *pron pers pl* you, them; *pron dem* those, e.g., **los de mi hermano** those of my brother
**losa** *f* slab, flagstone; grave; **echar** or **poner una losa encima** to shut tight (*so that no news will leak out*)
**losado** *m* var. of **enlosado**
**Losana** *f* Lausanne
**losange** *m* lozenge, diamond; (geom. & her.) lozenge; (baseball) diamond
**losangeado -da** *adj* lozenged, lozenge-shaped; (her.) lozengy
**losanjado -da** *adj* (her.) lozengy
**losar** *va* var. of **enlosar**
**loseta** *f* small flagstone; **coger en la loseta** (coll.) to trick
**lota** *f* (ichth.) burbot
**lote** *m* lot, share, portion; lottery prize; (Am.) lot (*of ground*); (Am.) remnant; (Am.) swallow, swig; (Am.) dunce
**lotear** *va* (Am.) to divide into lots
**lotería** *f* lottery; lottery office; lotto (*game*); (fig.) gamble (*risk, chance*); **echar a la lotería** to put up (*money*) on the lottery
**lotero -ra** *mf* dealer in lottery tickets
**lotificar** §86 *va* (Am.) to divide into lots
**lotiforme** *adj* lotiform
**lotización** *f* (Am.) division into lots, development of new lots
**lotizar** §76 *va* (Am.) to divide into lots
**loto** *m* (bot., arch. & myth.) lotus; (bot.) lotus tree; **loto azul** (bot.) blue lotus, Egyptian lotus
**lotófago -ga** *adj* lotus-eating; *mf* lotus-eater
**Lovaina** *f* Louvain
**lovaniense** *adj* (pertaining to) Louvain; *mf* native or inhabitant of Louvain
**loxocosmo** *m* loxocosm
**loxodromia** *f* (naut.) loxodrome, rhumb line
**loxodrómico -ca** *adj* (naut.) loxodromic or loxodromical
**loxodromismo** *m* loxodromism
**loxoftalmía** *f* (path.) loxophthalmus
**loxótico -ca** *adj* loxotic
**loxotomía** *f* (surg.) loxotomy
**loyo** *m* (bot.) boletus
**loza** *f* crockery, earthenware; **loza fina** china, chinaware
**lozanear** *vn* to be luxuriant; to be full of life; to grow wild; *vr* to be luxuriant; to be full of life; to luxuriate, to take great delight
**lozanía** *f* verdure, luxuriance; vigor, exuberance; pride, haughtiness
**lozano -na** *adj* verdant, luxuriant; vigorous, exuberant; proud, haughty
**L.S.** abr. of **Locus Sigilli** (Lat.) **lugar del sello**
**lúa** *f* currying mitt; (prov.) saffron bag
**lubigante** *m* (zool.) lobster (*Homarus*)
**lubina** *f* var. of **lobina**
**lubricación** *f* lubrication
**lubricador -dora** *adj* lubricating; *mf* lubricator; *m* lubricator (*device*)
**lubricán** *m* dawn
**lubricante** *adj & m* lubricant
**lubricar** §86 *va* to lubricate
**lubricidad** *f* lubricity
**lúbrico -ca** *adj* lubricous (*slippery; lewd*)
**lubrificar** §86 *va* to lubricate
**Lucano** *m* Lucan
**Lucas** *m* Luke
**lucentísimo -ma** *adj super* very or most bright or shining
**lucera** *f* skylight, transom
**lucerna** *f* chandelier; loophole; (ichth.) flying gurnard; (*cap.*) *f* Lucerne
**lucérnula** *f* (bot.) corn cockle
**lucero** *m* Venus (*as morning or evening star*); bright star; light (*in a wall*); star (*in forehead of animal*); brilliance, splendor; **luceros** *mpl* (poet.) eyes; **lucero del alba** or **de la mañana** morning star (*Venus*); **lucero de la tarde** evening star (*Venus*)
**Lucía** *f* Lucy, Lucia
**Luciano** *m* Lucian
**lucidez** *f* lucidity; keenness; (psychol.) lucidity
**lucido -da** *adj* gracious, generous, magnificent; brilliant, successful; sumptuous, gorgeous
**lúcido -da** *adj* lucid (*clear, easy to understand*); (med.) lucid
**lucidor -dora** *adj* shining
**lucidura** *f* whitewash
**luciente** *adj* bright, shining, lucent
**luciérnaga** *f* (ent.) glowworm, firefly
**Lucifer** *m* Lucifer (*chief rebel angel; Venus as the morning star*); (*l.c.*) *m* overbearing fellow
**luciferasa** *f* (biochem.) luciferase

**luciferino -na** *adj* Luciferian; *f* (biochem.) luciferin
**lucífero -ra** *adj* (poet.) shining, dazzling; (*cap.*) *m* Lucifer (*Venus as the morning star*)
**lucífugo -ga** *adj* (biol.) lucifugous
**lucillo** *m* tomb, sepulcher
**lucimiento** *m* brilliancy, luster; show, display, dash; success; **quedar** or **salir con lucimiento** to come off with great success, to come off with flying colors
**lucio -cia** *adj* bright, shiny; *m* salt pool; (ichth.) pike, luce
**lución** *m* (zool.) blindworm, slowworm
**lucir §60** *va* to illuminate, light up; to show, to display, to put on; to help, benefit; to plaster; to sport (*e.g., a new suit*); *vn* to shine; (fig.) to shine (*to be brilliant, to excel*); *vr* to dress up; to come off well; (fig.) to shine (*to be brilliant, to excel*); (iron.) to flop
**lucrar** *va* to get, obtain; *vn & vr* to profit; **lucrar de** to profit from, make money on
**lucrativo -va** *adj* lucrative
**Lucrecia** *f* Lucrece or Lucretia
**Lucrecio** *m* Lucretius
**lucro** *m* gain, profit; **lucros y daños** profit and loss
**lucroso -sa** *adj* lucrative, profitable
**luctuoso -sa** *adj* sad, gloomy
**lucubración** *f* lucubration
**lucubrar** *va & vn* lucubrate
**Lúculo** *m* Lucullus
**lúcuma** *f* canistel (*fruit*)
**lucha** *f* fight; struggle; wrestling; wrestling match; quarrel; **lucha de clases** class struggle; **lucha de la cuerda** (sport) tug of war; **lucha por la vida** struggle for existence
**luchador -dora** *mf* fighter; struggler; wrestler
**luchar** *vn* to fight; to struggle; to wrestle; to quarrel; **luchar por** + *inf* to struggle to + *inf*
**lucharniego -ga** *adj* night-hunting (*dog*)
**ludibrio** *m* mockery, scorn, derision
**ludimiento** *m* rubbing
**ludión** *m* (phys.) Cartesian devil
**ludir** *va, vn & vr* to rub, rub together
**lúe** *f* var. of **lúes**
**luego** *adv* soon; at once; then; therefore, then; **con tres luegos** (coll.) in a hurry; **desde luego** right away; of course; **hasta luego** good-bye, so long; **luego como** as soon as; **luego de** after, right after; **luego de** + *inf* after + *ger;* **luego que** as soon as
**luengo -ga** *adj* long
**lúes** *f* (path.) pestilence; (path.) lues (*syphilis*); **lúes canina** (vet.) distemper
**luético -ca** *adj* luetic
**lugano** *m* (orn.) linnet (*Acanthis spinus*)
**lugar** *m* place, position; site, spot; seat; room, space; village, hamlet; (geom.) locus; **dar lugar** to make room; **dar lugar a** to give rise to; **dar lugar a que** + *subj* to give reason for + *ger;* to give rise to + *ger;* **en lugar de** instead of, in place of; **en primer lugar** in the first place; **hacer lugar** to make room; **hacerse lugar** to make a place for oneself; **no ha lugar** (law) petition refused; **tener lugar** to fit; to take place; **tener lugar de** to take the place of, to serve as; **lugar ciego** (rad.) blind spot; **lugar común** toilet, water closet; commonplace; **lugar de cita** tryst; **lugares estrechos** close quarters; **lugar geométrico** (geom.) locus; **lugar seguro** safe place
**lugarejo** *m* hamlet
**lugareño -na** *adj* (pertaining to a) village; *mf* villager
**lugarete** *m* hamlet
**lugarón** *m* dull country town
**lugartenencia** *f* lieutenancy
**lugarteniente** *m* lieutenant
**luge** *m* sled
**lugre** *m* (naut.) lugger
**lúgubre** *adj* dismal, gloomy, lugubrious
**luir §41** *va* (Am.) to rumple, to muss; (Am.) to polish (*pottery*); (naut.) to gall, to wear; *vr* (Am.) to rub, to wear away
**Luis** *m* Louis; Lewis; **Luis Felipe** Louis Philippe; **Luis Napoleón** Louis Napoleon
**luisa** *f* (bot.) lemon verbena; (*cap.*) *f* Louisa or Louise
**Luisiana, La** Louisiana
**luisianense** *adj & mf* Louisianan
**lujación** *f* var. of **luxación**
**lujar** *va* (Am.) to shine, to polish; (Am.) to rub; (Am.) to shine (*shoes*); *vr* to be dislocated
**lujo** *m* luxury; **de lujo** de luxe; **gastar mucho lujo** to live in high style; **lujo de** excess of, too much, too many
**lujoso -sa** *adj* luxurious; ostentatious; magnificent
**lujuria** *f* lust, lechery, luxury
**lujuriante** *adj* lustful; luxuriant
**lujuriar** *vn* to lust, to be lustful or lecherous; to couple, to pair (*said of animals*)
**lujurioso -sa** *adj* lustful, lecherous, lewd; *mf* lecher
**lula** *f* see **lulo**
**luliano -na** *adj* Lullian; *mf* Lullianist or Lullist
**lulismo** *m* philosophy of Raymond Lully
**lulista** *adj* Lullian; *mf* Lullianist or Lullist
**lulo -la** *adj* (Am.) lank, slender; *m* (Am.) bundle; *f* (prov.) squid
**lulú** *m* (*pl:* **-lúes**) spitz dog, Pomeranian
**lumaquela** *f* (petrog.) lumachel or lumachella
**lumbago** *m* (path.) lumbago
**lumbán** *m* (bot.) lumbang
**lumbar** *adj* lumbar
**lumbarización** *f* (path.) lumbarization
**lumbodinia** *f* (path.) lumbodynia
**lumbosacro -cra** *adj* lumbosacral
**lumbrada** *f* large fire, blaze
**lumbral** *m* var. of **umbral**
**lumbrarada** *f* var. of **lumbrada**
**lumbre** *f* fire, light; opening, light (*in a wall*); light (*to light a cigar or cigaret*); brightness, brilliance; knowledge, learning; (fig.) light (*of a countenance*); **lumbres** *fpl* tinder box; **a lumbre de pajas** (coll.) in a flash, like a flash; **a lumbre mansa** with slow flame; **echar lumbre** (coll.) to blow one's top; **ni por lumbre** (coll.) not for love or money; **ser la lumbre de los ojos de** to be the apple of the eye of; **lumbre del agua** surface of the water
**lumbrera** *f* light, source of light; louver (*opening to let in air and light*); skylight; dormer window; (carp.) slit (*in face of plane*); (mach.) port; (min.) ventilating shaft; (naut.) air duct; (fig.) light (*example, shining figure*); **lumbreras** *fpl* eyes; **lumbrera de admisión** (mach.) intake port; **lumbrera de escape** (mach.) exhaust port
**lumbrerada** *f* var. of **lumbrada**
**lumbrical** *adj* (anat.) lumbrical
**lumbricosis** *f* (path.) lumbricosis
**lumen** *m* (anat., bot. & phys.) lumen; **lumen hora** (*pl:* **lúmenes hora**) (phys.) lumen-hour
**luminal** *m* (pharm.) luminal
**luminar** *m* luminary; (fig.) luminary (*person*)
**luminaria** *f* (eccl.) altar lights; **luminarias** *fpl* lights, illumination (*for decoration*)
**lumínico -ca** *adj* photic; (pertaining to) light; lighting (*e.g., fixture*)
**luminífero -ra** *adj* luminiferous
**luminiscencia** *f* luminescence
**luminiscente** *adj* luminescent
**luminosidad** *f* luminosity
**luminoso -sa** *adj* luminous; (fig.) bright (*e.g., idea*)
**luminotecnia** *f* lighting engineering
**luminotécnico -ca** *adj* lighting; *m* lighting engineer
**lun.** abr. of **lunes**
**luna** *f* moon; moonlight; plate glass; mirror; lens, glass (*of spectacles*); (coll.) caprice, whim, wild idea; (ichth.) sunfish, moonfish; **dejar a la luna de Valencia** (coll.) to disappoint; **estar de buena luna** to be in a good humor; **estar de mala luna** to be in a bad humor; **ladrar a la luna** (coll.) to bark at the moon; **media luna** half moon; crescent (*shape of moon in first or last quarter; Mohammedanism; Turkish Empire*); **quedarse a la luna de Valencia** (coll.) to be disappointed; **luna creciente** crescent moon; **luna de agua** (bot.) white water lily; **luna de miel** honeymoon; **luna llena** full moon; **luna menguante** waning moon; **luna nueva** new moon
**lunación** *f* (astr.) lunation
**lunado -da** *adj* lunate; *f* (Am.) moonlight party

**lunanco -ca** *adj* with one quarter higher than the other (*said, e.g., of a horse*)
**lunar** *adj* lunar; *m* mole; polka dot; (fig.) stain, blot; (fig.) stigma; **lunar postizo** beauty spot
**lunaria** *f* (bot.) lunary; **lunaria menor** (bot.) moonwort
**lunático -ca** *adj* lunatic; temporarily unbalanced; *mf* lunatic; person temporarily unbalanced; moonstruck person
**lunecilla** *f* crescent-shaped jewel
**lunes** *m* (*pl:* **-nes**) Monday; **hacer san lunes** (Am.) to knock off on Monday; (Am.) to knock off on Monday because of a hangover; **lunes de carnaval** Shrove Monday
**luneta** *f* lens, glass (*of spectacles*); orchestra seat; front tile; lunette (*crescent-shaped ornament*); (arch. & fort.) lunette; (mach.) rest (*of a lathe*); (aut.) rear window
**lunetario** *m* (Am.) orchestra, parquet
**luneto** *m* (arch.) lunette
**lunfardo** *m* (Am.) thief; (Am.) underworld slang, thieves' Latin
**lunisolar** *adj* (astr.) lunisolar
**lúnula** *f* (anat. & zool.) lunule; (astr.) moon (*of other planets than the earth*); (geom.) lune; (opt.) meniscus
**lupa** *f* magnifying glass
**lupanar** *m* bawdyhouse, brothel
**lupanario -ria** *adj* (pertaining to a) bawdyhouse
**lupercales** *fpl* (hist.) Lupercalia
**lupia** *f* wen, cyst; (metal.) bloom; (Am.) bit, trifle; (Am.) witch doctor, quack; **lupias** *fpl* (Am.) small change
**lupino -na** *adj* lupine; *m* (bot.) lupine
**lupulina** *f* (bot.) black medic
**lúpulo** *m* (bot.) hop, hop vine; hops (*dried flowers of hop vine*)
**lupus** *m* (path.) lupus
**luquete** *m* slice of orange or lemon used to flavor wine; spot, hole (*in clothing*); bald spot; sulfur match or fuse; (arch.) dome (*of a Byzantine vault*); (Am.) unplowed patch in a fallow
**Lurdes** *f* Lourdes
**lúrida** *f* (orn.) golden oriole
**lurio -ria** *adj* (Am.) mad, crazy; (Am.) madly in love
**lurte** *m* (prov.) avalanche
**lusitanismo** *m* Lusitanism
**lusitano -na** *adj & mf* Lusitanian; Portuguese
**lustrabotas** *m* (*pl:* **-tas**) (Am.) bootblack
**lustración** *f* lustration
**lustral** *adj* lustral
**lustrar** *va* to shine, polish; to lustrate; *vn* to wander, roam
**lustre** *m* luster, gloss, shine, polish; shoe polish; (fig.) luster (*fame, glory*)
**lustrina** *f* lustrine; lustring; (Am.) shoe polish
**lustro** *m* lustrum (*five years*); chandelier; (hist.) lustrum
**lustroso -sa** *adj* shining, bright, lustrous
**lútea** *f* see **lúteo**
**lutecio** *m* (chem.) lutecium
**luteína** *f* (biochem. & physiol.) lutein
**lúteo -a** *adj* luteous; muddy, miry; mean, low, vile; *f* (orn.) golden oriole
**luteolina** *f* (chem.) luteolin
**luteoma** *m* (path.) luteoma
**luteranismo** *m* Lutheranism
**luterano -na** *adj & mf* Lutheran
**Lutero** *m* Luther
**lutidina** *f* (chem.) lutidine
**luto** *m* mourning; sorrow, bereavement; **lutos** *mpl* crape, mourning draperies; **aliviar el luto** to go out of deep mourning; **estar de luto** to be in mourning; **medio luto** half mourning; **luto riguroso** deep mourning
**lutocaro** *m* (Am.) trash cart
**lutria** *f* (zool.) otter
**Luvre** *m* Louvre (*museum*)
**lux** *m* (*pl:* **lux**) (phys.) lux
**luxación** *f* luxation, dislocation
**luxar** *va* to luxate, dislocate
**Luxemburgo** *m* Luxemburg
**luxemburgués -guesa** *adj* Luxemburgian; *mf* Luxemburger
**luz** *f* (*pl:* **luces**) light; window, opening, light; guiding light; (coll.) money; **luces** *fpl* enlightenment, culture; **a la luz de** in the light of; **a primera luz** at dawn; **a toda luz** or **a todas luces** everywhere; by all means; **dar a luz** to have a child; to give birth to; to bring out, publish; **echar luz** (coll.) to recover, get stronger; **echar luz sobre** to cast, shed, or throw light on; **entre dos luces** at twilight; (coll.) half-seas over, half drunk; **sacar a luz** to bring to light; **salir a luz** to come to light; to come out, be published; to take place; **ver la luz** to see the light, see the light of day; **luces de Bengala** (aer.) flares; **luces de carretera** (aut.) bright lights; **luces de cruce** (aut.) dimmers; **luz de balizaje** (aer.) marker light; **luz de Bengala** Bengal light; **luz de calcio** calcium light; **luz de frenado** brake light; **luz de magnesio** magnesium light; (phot.) flash bulb, flashlight; **luz de matrícula** license-plate light; **luz del mundo** (theol.) light of the World; **luz de parada** or **paro** stop light; **luz fría** cold light; **luz indicadora** pilot light; **luz negra** (phys.) black light; **luz trasera** tail light
**Luzbel** *m* Lucifer (*chief rebel angel, Satan*)
**luzco** *1st sg pres ind of* **lucir**
**Lx.** abr. of **lux**

# Ll

**Ll, ll** *f* fourteenth letter of the Spanish alphabet
**llaga** *f* ulcer; sore; torment, cause of pain or sorrow; (mas.) seam
**llagar §59** *va* to make sore; to hurt, to wound
**llagua** *f* var. of **yagua**
**llama** *f* flame, blaze; marsh, swamp; fiery passion; (zool.) llama; **salir de las llamas y caer en las brasas** to jump out of the frying pan into the fire; **llama manométrica** (phys.) manometric flame; **llama oxidante** (chem.) oxidizing flame; **llama reductora** (chem.) reducing flame
**llamada** *f* see **llamado**
**llamadera** *f* goad
**llamado -da** *adj* so-called; *m* call; *f* call; sign, signal (*to call someone*); knock, ring; reference, reference mark; (mil.) call, call to arms; **tocar** or **batir llamada** (mil.) to sound the call to arms; **llamada a filas** (mil.) call to the colors; **llamada a quintas** draft call
**llamador -dora** *mf* caller; *m* messenger; knocker; push button
**llamamiento** *m* call; divine inspiration
**llamar** *va* to call; to name; to summon; to call upon, to invoke; to attract; **estar llamado a** to have a natural aptitude for; *vn* to knock, to ring; *vr* to be called; (naut.) to veer; **¿cómo se llama Vd.?** what is your name?
**llamarada** *f* flare-up; flush; (fig.) flare-up, outburst
**llamargo** *m* marsh, swamp
**llamarón** *m* (Am.) var. of **llamarada**
**llamativo -va** *adj* thirst-raising; showy, flashy, gaudy
**llamazar** *m* marsh, swamp
**llambria** *f* steep rocky surface, steep face of a rock
**llame** *m* (Am.) bird net, bird trap
**llameante** *adj* flaming, blazing, flashing
**llamear** *vn* to flame, blaze, flash
**llampo** *m* (Am.) ore; (Am.) stone quarry
**llana** *f* see **llano**
**llanada** *f* plain, level ground
**llanero** *m* plainsman
**llaneza** *f* plainness, simplicity
**llano -na** *adj* smooth, even, level; plane; plain, simple; clear, evident; (phonet.) paroxytone; *m* plain; llano (*broad treeless plain*); landing (*of stairs*); side of a sheet of paper; *f* trowel; plain; **a la llana** simply; in the open; **de llano** plainly, openly
**llanque** *m* (Am.) rawhide sandal
**llanta** *f* felloe; rim (*of wheel*); tire; (bot.) kale; **llanta de goma** rubber tire; **llanta de oruga** track (*band of caterpillar tractor*)
**llantén** *m* (bot.) plantain; **llantén menor** (bot.) ribwort
**llantera** *f* (coll.) blubber, yammer
**llantería** *f* or **llanterío** *m* (Am.) weeping, wailing
**llantina** *f* (coll.) var. of **llantera**
**llanto** *m* weeping, crying; **en llanto** in tears
**llanura** *f* smoothness, evenness, level; plain; **llanura aluvial** flood plain
**llapa** *f* var. of **yapa**
**llapango -ga** *adj* (Am.) barefooted (*Indian*)
**llares** *fpl* pothanger
**llatar** *m* (prov.) rail fence
**llaupangue** *m* (bot.) pink francoa
**llauquear** *vr* (Am.) to fall to pieces, to come to ruin
**llave** *f* key; wrench, key; faucet, spigot; (elec.) switch; (print.) bracket; (mus.) key; (fig.) key (*means of solving a problem, secret, etc.; place controlling entrance to a sea, country, etc.*); **debajo de llave** under lock and key; **echar la llave a** to lock; **llave de afinar** (mus.) tuning key or hammer; **llave de cadena** chain tongs or wrench; **llave de caja** socket wrench; **llave de cambio** shift key; **llave de caño** pipe wrench; **llave de cubo** socket wrench; **llave de estufa** damper (*to control draft*); **llave de la mano** span of the hand; **llave del pie** distance from heel to instep; **llave de mandíbulas** or **llave dentada** alligator wrench; **llave de paso** stopcock; passkey; **llave de percusión** or **de pistón** percussion lock; **llave de purga** drain cock; **llave de salto** margin release, margin release key; **llave de tiempo atrasado** (elec.) delayed-time switch; **llave de trinquete** ratchet wrench; **llave espacial** space bar or key; **llave falsa** false key, picklock; **llave inglesa** monkey wrench; **llave maestra** master key, skeleton key; **llave para embutir** (elec.) flush switch, flushmounted switch; **llave para tubos** pipe wrench; **llaves de la iglesia** (eccl.) power of the keys; *adj* key
**llavero -ra** *mf* keeper of the keys; turnkey; *m* key ring
**llavín** *m* latchkey
**lleco -ca** *adj* virgin (*soil*)
**llegada** *f* arrival
**llegar §59** *va* to push, bring up; *vn* to arrive; to happen; to reach; to amount; to be equal; **llegar a** to arrive at; **llegar a** + *inf* to come to, to get to + *inf;* to succeed in + *ger;* **llegar a ser** to become; *vr* to move close, come near; to get, to go
**llena** *f* see **lleno**
**llenado** *m* filling
**llenador -dora** *adj* (Am.) filling (*food*)
**llenar** *va* to fill; to fill out; to fulfill; to satisfy; to overwhelm; to annoy, bother; *vn* to be full (*said of moon*); *vr* to fill, fill up, become full; (coll.) to stuff oneself; (coll.) to become annoyed; **llenarse a rebosar** to be filled to overflowing; **llenarse de** to get covered with; to be overwhelmed with; to be deeply in (*e.g., debt*)
**llenero -ra** *adj* full, entire, complete
**lleno -na** *adj* full; solid; **lleno a rebosar** full to overflowing; *m* fill, plenty; fulness, full enjoyment; perfection, completeness; full moon; full house (*e.g., in a theater*); **de lleno** fully, entirely; squarely; **lleno de la luna** full of the moon; *f* flood
**llenura** *f* fulness, abundance
**llera** *f* gravel pit
**lleta** *f* (bot.) sprout
**lleudar** *va & vr* var. of **leudar**
**lleuque** *m* (bot.) plum fir
**lleva** or **llevada** *f* carrying, conveying; ride; **lleva gratuita** free ride
**llevadero -ra** *adj* bearable, tolerable
**llevar** *va* to carry, to take, to lead; to carry away, take away; to yield; to keep (*accounts, books, etc.*); to carry on, to conduct (*correspondence*); to put (*a play on the screen, a program on the air*); to be in charge of, to manage; to lead (*a certain kind of life*); to bear (*arms*); to bear, to stand for; to suffer (*punishment*); to charge (*a certain price*); to take off, sever; to get, obtain; to win; to wear (*clothes*); to have been, e.g., **llevo mucho tiempo aquí** I have been here a long time; **lleva cinco días ausente** he has been absent five days; **llevo dos años de estudiar el español** I have been studying Spanish for two years; (arith.) to carry; **a todo llevar** for all kinds of wear (*said of clothing*); **llevar a** to exceed; to be ahead of (*by a certain distance*), e.g., **este vapor lleva cinco millas al otro** this

steamer is five miles ahead of the other one; to be heavier than (*by a certain weight*), e.g., **este muchacho lleva tres kilogramos a aquél** this boy is three kilograms heavier than that one; to be older than (*by a certain number of days, months, years, etc.*), e.g., **mi hijo lleva al suyo un año** my son is a year older than yours; **llevar a alguien a** + *inf* to take someone to + *inf;* to lead someone to + *inf;* **llevarla hecha** (coll.) to have it all figured out; **llevar las de perder** (coll.) to be in a bad way; **llevar puesto** to wear, to have on (*a garment*); **llevar** + *pp* to have + *pp*, e.g.,**lleva conseguidas muchas victorias** he has won many victories; **no llevarlas todas consigo** (coll.) to be scared ‖ *vn* to lead; to charge; **llevar y traer** (coll.) to go around gossiping ‖ *vr* to carry away; to take, take away; to seize; to carry off; to win, carry off; to get along; **llevarse algo a alguien** to take something away from someone, to steal something from someone; **llevarse bien** to get along together; **llevarse bien con** to get along with, to fit in with; **llevarse mal con** to be on bad terms with

**lloradera** *f* (coll.) blubbering, yammering

**llorador -dora** *adj* weeping; *mf* weeper

**lloraduelos** *mf* (*pl:* **-los**) (coll.) sobber, sniveler, crybaby

**lloralástimas** *mf* (*pl:* **-mas**) (coll.) sniveling skinflint, poverty-crying penny pincher

**lloramico** *m* weeping; **lloramicos** *mf* (*pl:* **-cos**) (coll.) crybaby

**lloranduelos** *m* (*pl:* **-los**) (coll.) var. of **lloraduelos**

**llorante** *adj* weeping

**llorar** *va* to weep; to weep over; to mourn; *vn* to weep, to cry; to drip; to water, to run (*said of the eyes*); (plant path.) to weep

**lloredo** *m* growth of laurels

**llorera** *f* (coll.) blubber, yammer

**llorica** *mf* whiner, crybaby

**lloriquear** *vn* to whimper, to whine

**lloriqueo** *m* whimper, whimpering, whining

**llorisquear** *vn* (Am.) var. of **lloriquear**

**llorisqueo** *m* (Am.) var. of **lloriqueo**

**lloro** *m* weeping, crying; tears

**llorón -rona** *adj* weeping, whining; (bot.) weeping; *mf* weeper, whiner; crybaby; *m* (bot.) weeping willow; pendulous plume; *f* weeper, hired mourner

**lloroso -sa** *adj* weeping, weepy; tearful, sad

**llovedero** *m* (coll.) rainy spell

**llovedizo -za** *adj* leaky (*roof*); rain (*water*)

**llover** §63 *va* to rain (*to send like rain*); *vn* to rain; **como llovido** unexpectedly; **como llovido del cielo** like manna from heaven; **llueva o no** rain or shine; **llueve** it is raining; *vr* to leak (*said of a roof*)

**llovido -da** *mf* stowaway

**llovioso -sa** *adj* var. of **lluvioso**

**llovizna** *f* drizzle

**lloviznar** *vn* to drizzle

**lloviznoso -sa** *adj* drizzled, wet from drizzle; (Am.) drizzly

**llueca** *f* brooding hen

**lluvia** *f* rain; rain water; (fig.) rain; (fig.) heap, mass, flock; **lluvia de estrellas** star shower; **lluvia de oro** heap of gold, great wealth; (bot.) golden chain, laburnum; (bot.) goldenrod; **lluvia radiactiva** fallout, radioactive fallout

**lluviosidad** *f* raininess

**lluvioso -sa** *adj* rainy

# M

**M, m** *f* fifteenth letter of the Spanish alphabet
**m.** abr. of **mañana, masculino, meridiano, metro** or **metros, milla, minuto** or **minutos** & **muerto**
**M.** abr. of **Madre (religiosa), Maestro, Majestad, mediano** & **Merced**
**m/** abr. of **mi** & **mes**
**m²** abr. of **metro cuadrado** & **metros cuadrados**
**M.ª** abr. of **María**
**maca** *f* flaw, blemish; spot, stain; bruise (*on fruit*); fraud, deceit
**Macabeo** *m* (Bib.) Maccabaeus; **macabeos** *mpl* (Bib.) Maccabees
**macábrico -ca** or **macabro -bra** *adj* macabre
**macaco -ca** *adj* (Am.) ugly, misshapen; *mf* (zool.) macaque; **macaco de la India** (zool.) rhesus; *f* (Am.) drunk, jag
**macadam** *m* macadam
**macadamizar §76** *va* to macadamize
**macadán** *m* var. of **macadam**
**macana** *f* (Am.) macana (*wooden sword or club*); trick, lie; drug on the market; (Am.) nonsense; (Am.) botch
**macanazo** *m* (Am.) blow with a macana; (Am.) great nonsense
**macanear** *vn* (Am.) to exaggerate, boast, joke
**macanudo -da** *adj* (coll.) stunning, terrific; (Am.) strong, husky; (Am.) swell, grand; (Am.) nonsensical
**macar §86** *vr* to rot from bruises (*said of fruit*)
**macareo** *m* tide rip in a river
**macarrón** *m* macaroon; (naut.) bulwark; **macarrones** *mpl* macaroni; (naut.) stanchions
**macarronea** *f* macaronic (*poem*)
**macarrónico -ca** *adj* macaronic
**macasar** *m* antimacassar
**macear** *va* to mace, to hammer, to pound; *vn* to be insistent, to bore
**macedón -dona** *adj* & *mf* Macedonian
**macedonia** *f* & **Macedonia** *f* see **macedonio**
**macedónico -ca** *adj* Macedonian
**macedonio -nia** *adj* & *mf* Macedonian; *f* macédoine (*salad; medley*); (*cap.*) *f* Macedonia; **macedonia de frutas** fruit salad
**macelo** *m* slaughterhouse
**maceo** *m* macing, hammering
**maceración** *f* maceration
**macerador -dora** *adj* macerating; *mf* macerater
**maceramiento** *m* var. of **maceración**
**macerar** *va* & *vr* to macerate
**macerina** *f* (Am.) saucer with device to hold chocolate cup
**macero** *m* macer, macebearer
**maceta** *f* tool handle; stone hammer, mason's hammer; flowerpot; vase for artificial flowers; (bot.) corymb; **maceta de aforrar** (naut.) serving mallet; **maceta de hojalatero** tinner's hammer
**macetero** *m* flowerpot stand
**macfarlán** *m* or **macferlán** *m* inverness, inverness cape
**macia** *f* var. of **macis**
**macicez** *f* solidity; massiveness
**macilento -ta** *adj* wan
**macillo** *m* hammer (*of piano*)
**macis** *f* mace (*spice*)
**macito** *m* tapper (*of a bell, decoherer, etc.*)
**macizar §76** *va* to fill in, make solid
**macizo -za** *adj* solid; massive; (fig.) solid, sound; *m* solid; flower bed; wall space; clump, mass; mountain mass, massif; (aut.) solid tire
**macla** *f* wooden flail; (mineral.) macle
**macle** *m* (her.) mascle
**maclura** *f* (bot.) Osage orange (*plant and fruit*)
**macolla** *f* cluster, bunch
**macollar** *vn* & *vr* var. of **amacollar**
**macón** *m* dry, brown honeycomb
**macramé** *m* macramé
**macrobiótico -ca** *adj* macrobiotic; *f* macrobiotics
**macrocito** *m* (path.) macrocyte
**macrocosmo** *m* macrocosm
**macrofísica** *f* macrophysics
**macrogameto** *m* (biol.) macrogamete
**macromolécula** *f* macromolecule
**macrosmático -ca** *adj* (zool.) macrosmatic
**macruro -ra** *adj* & *m* (zool.) macruran
**macsura** *f* area reserved in a mosque for caliph and imam
**macuache** *m* (Am.) ignorant Mexican Indian
**macuba** *f* maccaboy (*perfumed snuff*); (ent.) musk beetle
**macuco -ca** *adj* (Am.) strong, husky; (Am.) sly, cunning; (Am.) notable, important; *m* (Am.) overgrown boy
**mácula** *f* spot; stain, blemish; (anat., astr. & path.) macula; (coll.) deception, trick; **mácula solar** sunspot
**macular** *va* to spot; (print.) to mackle; *vr* (print.) to mackle
**maculatura** *f* (print.) mackle; (print.) mackled sheet of paper
**macuquero** *m* bootleg miner
**macuto** *m* (Am.) alms basket; (mil.) knapsack
**macha** *f* (zool.) tellina; (Am.) drunk, drunkenness; (Am.) joke, jest; (Am.) mannish woman
**machaca** *f* crusher; *mf* (coll.) bore; **¡dale, machaca!** (coll.) cut it out!
**machacadera** *f* crusher
**machacador -dora** *adj* crushing; *mf* crusher; *f* crusher (*machine*); **machacadora de martillos** hammer mill
**machacamiento** *m* crushing, pounding
**machacante** *m* (mil.) sergeant's aid
**machacar §86** *va* to crush, to mash, to pound; *vn* to be insistent, to bore
**machacón -cona** *adj* boring, tiresome; *mf* bore
**machaconería** *f* boresomeness, tiresomeness
**machada** *f* flock of billy goats; (coll.) stupidity
**machado** *m* hatchet
**machamartillo; a machamartillo** (coll.) firmly, tightly; blindly, with blind faith
**machaqueo** *m* crushing, pounding
**machaquería** *f* tiresomeness, dullness
**machaquero -ra** *adj* (coll.) boring; *mf* (coll.) bore
**machar** *va* to crush, grind; *vr* (Am.) to get drunk
**mache** *m* (phys.) Mache unit
**macheta** *f* cleaver
**machetazo** *m* blow or hack with a machete
**machete** *m* machete; cane knife
**machetear** *va* var. of **amachetear**
**machetero** *m* man who clears ground with a machete; cane cutter; (Am.) revolutionary; (Am.) grind (*student*); **machetero de salón** (Am.) parlor revolutionary
**machi** *m* or **machí** *m* (Am.) medicine man
**machihembradora** *f* (carp.) machine for cutting tongue and groove; (carp.) mortiser (*machine*)
**machihembrar** *va* (carp.) to feather; (carp.) to mortise
**machina** *f* derrick, crane; pile driver
**macho** *adj* male, e.g., **la comadreja macho** the male weasel; **la flor macho** the male flower; strong, tough; stupid; (bot. & mach.) male; *m* sledge hammer; square anvil; anvil block; abutment, pillar; male (*animal*); hemule; hook (*of hook and eye*); stupid fellow;

foreigner, Anglo-Saxon; (coll.) blond; pin, peg; (coll.) he-man; (mach.) male piece or part; **macho cabrío** he-goat, billy goat; **macho de aterrajar** (mach.) tap, screw tap; **macho de cabrío** he-goat, billy goat; **macho de terraja** (mach.) tap, screw tap
**machón** *m* pillar, buttress
**machona** *adj fem* mannish (*woman*)
**machorro -rra** *adj* barren, sterile; *f* barren female
**machota** *f* hammer, mallet; (coll.) mannish woman; **a la machota** (Am.) carelessly, any old way
**machote** *m* hammer, mallet; rough draft
**machucadura** *f* or **machucamiento** *m* crushing, pounding; bruise, contusion
**machucar §86** *va* to crush, to pound, to bruise
**machucón** *m* (Am.) crushing; (Am.) bruise
**machucho -cha** *adj* thoughtful, judicious; elderly
**machuelo** *m* small he-mule; germ; clove (*of garlic*); (Am.) tap
**madama** *f* madame; (coll.) missus; (bot.) garden balsam
**madamisela** *f* young lady, damsel; mademoiselle
**madamita** *m* (coll.) sissy
**madapolán** *m* madapollam
**madeja** *f* skein, hank; mass of hair; (coll.) listless fellow; **hacer madeja** to rope, become ropy; **madeja sin cuenda** (coll.) hopeless tangle; (coll.) muddlehead; (coll.) sloppy fellow
**madera** *f* wood; piece of wood; lumber, timber; horny part (*of hoof*); (coll.) knack, flair, makings, qualities; **no holgar la madera** (coll.) to work all the time; **saber a la madera** (coll.) to be a chip off the old block; **ser de mala madera** or **tener mala madera** (coll.) to be a lazy loafer; **madera alburente** sapwood; **madera aserradiza** lumber (*cut for use*); **madera contrachapada** plywood; **madera de corazón** heartwood; **madera de raja** split timber; **madera de sierra** lumber (*cut for use*); **madera fósil** lignite; **madera laminada** plywood; **madera plástica** plastic wood; **madera serradiza** lumber (*cut for use*); **maderas preciosas** fancy woods; *m* Madeira, Madeira wine
**maderable** *adj* timber-yielding
**maderada** *f* raft, float
**maderaje** *m* or **maderamen** *m* lumber, woodwork
**maderar** *va* var. of **enmaderar**
**maderería** *f* lumberyard
**maderero -ra** *adj* (pertaining to) lumber; *m* lumberman; carpenter
**maderista** *m* (Am.) lumberman
**madero** *m* log, beam; (coll.) dolt; ship, vessel
**madianita** *mf* (Bib.) Midianite
**Madona** *f* Madonna; (f.a.) Madonna
**mador** *m* moisture, slight sweat
**madoroso -sa** *adj* moist
**madrás** *m* madras
**madrastra** *f* stepmother; callous mother; nuisance; (bot.) apple mint
**madraza** *f* (coll.) doting mother
**madre** *f* mother; matron; womb; bed (*of river*); main sewer; main irrigation ditch; mother (*of vinegar*); sediment, dregs; (fig.) mother; **futura madre** expectant mother; **sacar de madre a** (coll.) to upset, disturb; **ser la madre del cordero** to be the real cause; **madre adoptiva** foster mother; **madre de Dios** (eccl.) Mother of God; **madre del clavo** clove; **madre de leche** wet nurse; **madre de perlas** (zool.) pearl oyster; **madre patria** mother country, old country; **madre política** mother-in-law; stepmother; **madre tierra** mother earth; *adj* mother, e.g., **lengua madre** mother tongue; **leona madre** mother lioness
**madrear** *vn* to look like one's mother; (coll.) to keep saying ma (*said of a child*); *vr* to turn, grow sour
**madrecilla** *f* ovary (*of a bird*)
**madreclavo** *m* clove of two-year growth
**madreña** *f* wooden shoe
**madreperla** *f* (zool.) pearl oyster; mother-of-pearl
**madrépora** *f* (zool.) madrepore
**madrepórico -ca** *adj* madreporic
**madrero -ra** *adj* mother-loving
**madreselva** *f* (bot.) honeysuckle, trumpet honeysuckle; **madreselva de jardín** (bot.) yellow honeysuckle
**madrigado -da** *adj* that has sired (*said of a bull*); twice-married (*said of a woman*); (coll.) experienced
**madrigal** *m* madrigal; (mus.) madrigal
**madrigalesco -ca** *adj* madrigalian; elegant, overnice
**madriguera** *f* burrow, den, lair; (fig.) den (*e.g., of thieves*)
**madrileño -ña** *adj* Madrid, Madrilenian; *mf* Madrilenian
**madrina** *f* godmother; patroness; protectress; prop, stanchion; shore, brace; strap for yoking two horses; (Am.) leading mare; (Am.) tame herd used to gather and lead untamed cattle; **madrina de bodas** bridesmaid; **madrina de guerra** war mother (*soldier's correspondent*)
**madrinazgo** *m* godmothership; sponsorship
**madrona** *f* main sewer; (bot.) toothwort; (coll.) doting mother
**madroncillo** *m* strawberry (*fruit*)
**madroñal** *m* growth of arbutus or strawberry trees
**madroñera** *f* (bot.) arbutus, strawberry tree; growth of arbutus or strawberry trees
**madroño** *m* (bot.) arbutus, strawberry tree; (bot.) madroño; madroño apple; fruit of strawberry tree; berry-shaped tassel
**madrugada** *f* dawn; early morning (*before sunrise*); early rising; **de madrugada** early, at the break of day
**madrugador -dora** *adj* early-rising; *mf* early riser
**madrugar §59** *vn* to get up early; to be ahead, to be out in front
**madrugón -gona** *adj* early-rising; *m* (coll.) very early rising, getting up very early; **dar madrugón** (coll.) to get up very early
**maduración** *f* ripening; maturation
**maduradero** *m* place for ripening fruit
**madurar** *va* to ripen; to mature; to maturate; to think out; *vn* to ripen; to mature; to maturate
**madurez** *f* ripeness; maturity
**maduro -ra** *adj* ripe; mature
**maese** *m* (obs.) messer, master; (obs.) journeyman; **maese coral** prestidigitation, sleight of hand
**maestra** *f* see **maestro**
**maestral** *m* northwest wind; queen cell
**maestralizar §76** *vn* (naut.) to decline to the northwest (*said of compass*)
**maestramente** *adv* masterly, in a masterly fashion, skilfully
**maestrante** *m* member of riding club
**maestranza** *f* riding club of noblemen; arsenal, armory; navy yard; (Am.) machine shop
**maestrazgo** *m* mastership (*of a military order*)
**maestre** *m* master (*of a military order*); (naut.) master; **gran maestre** grand master
**maestrear** *va* to direct, manage, take over; to cut back slightly (*a grapevine*); (mas.) to screed; *vn* to domineer, to be domineering
**maestresala** *m* (archaic) chief waiter, taster (*for a nobleman*)
**maestría** *f* mastery; mastership; trick, deceit; cure; master's degree
**maestril** *m* queen cell
**maestro -tra** *adj* masterful, masterly; main, principal; trained, e.g., **perro maestro** trained dog; master, e.g., **llave maestra** master key; **maestro mecánico** master mechanic; **maestros cantores** mastersingers; *m* master; teacher; maestro (*in music, painting, etc.*); (educ.) master; (naut.) mainmast; **gran maestro** grand master (*of Masons*); **maestro aguañón** master builder of water works; **maestro de armas** fencing master; **maestro de capilla** choirmaster; **maestro de ceremonias** master of ceremonies; **maestro de cocina** chef; **maestro de equitación** riding master; **maestro de escuela** elementary schoolteacher; **maestro de esgrima** fencing master; **maestro de obra prima** shoemaker

(*who makes shoes*); **maestro de obras** builder, master builder; **maestro de ribera** ship carpenter, shipwright; **maestro de taller** (Am.) master mechanic; *f* teacher; schoolmistress; teacher's wife; elementary school; (mas.) screed, guide line; (fig.) teacher (*such as adversity*); **maestra de escuela** schoolmistress
**Magallanes** *m* Magellan
**magallánico -ca** *adj* Magellanic
**magancear** *vn* (Am.) to bum, to loaf around
**magancería** *f* cheat, deceit
**magancés** *adj* evil, treacherous
**maganel** *m* (archaic) battering ram
**maganto -ta** *adj* wan, languid, spiritless
**maganza** *f* (Am.) bumming, loafing
**magaña** *f* trick, deceit; flaw (*in bore of a gun*)
**magarza** *f* (bot.) feverfew
**magarzuela** *f* (bot.) mayweed, stinking camomile
**Magdalena** *f* Magdalen, Madeleine; (*l.c.*) *f* (fig.) magdalene (*repentant prostitute*); oval-shaped biscuit; **estar hecha una magdalena** (coll.) to be inconsolable; **Santa María Magdalena** (Bib.) Mary Magdalene
**magdaleniense** *adj* (geol.) Magdalenian
**magdaleón** *m* (pharm.) cylindrical plaster or poultice
**magenta** *m* magenta
**magia** *f* magic; **magia blanca** white magic; **magia negra** black magic
**magiar** *adj & mf* Magyar; *m* Magyar (*language*)
**mágico -ca** *adj* magic or magical; *mf* magician; *f* magic
**magín** *m* (coll.) fancy, imagination; (coll.) keenness, ability
**magisterial** *adj* teaching
**magisterio** *m* teaching; teachers; teaching profession; guidance, leadership; solemnity, pomposity
**magistrado** *m* magistrate
**magistral** *adj* magistral, magisterial; master; masterly; (fort. & pharm.) magistral; *m* (metal.) magistral
**magistratura** *f* magistracy
**magma** *m* magma; (geol. & pharm.) magma
**magnanimidad** *f* magnanimity
**magnánimo -ma** *adj* magnanimous
**magnate** *m* magnate
**magnesia** *f* (chem.) magnesia
**magnesiano -na** *adj* magnesian
**magnésico -ca** *adj* magnesic
**magnesio** *m* (chem.) magnesium; (phot.) flashlight (*light; photograph*)
**magnesita** *f* (mineral.) magnesite
**magnético -ca** *adj* magnetic
**magnetismo** *m* magnetism; **magnetismo animal** animal magnetism; **magnetismo permanente** (phys.) permanent magnetism; **magnetismo remanente** (phys.) remanent magnetism; **magnetismo terrestre** terrestrial magnetism
**magnetita** *f* (mineral.) magnetite
**magnetización** *f* magnetization
**magnetizador -dora** *adj* magnetizing; *mf* magnetizer
**magnetizar** §76 *va* to magnetize
**magneto** *m & f* magneto
**magnetoeléctrico -ca** *adj* magnetoelectric
**magnetofón** *m* var. of **magnetófono**
**magnetofónico -ca** *adj* recording (*tape or wire*)
**magnetófono** *m* (phys.) magnetophone; wire recorder, tape recorder
**magnetómetro** *m* magnetometer
**magnetón** *m* (phys.) magneton
**magnetosfera** *f* magnetosphere
**magnetrón** *m* (rad.) magnetron
**magnicidio** *m* assassination of a great man
**magnificación** *f* (opt.) magnification; exaltation
**magnificador -dora** *adj* magnifying; extolling, exalting
**magnificar** §86 *va* (opt.) to magnify; to extol, to exalt
**magníficat** *m* Magnificat
**magnificencia** *f* magnificence
**magnificente** *adj* magnificent
**magnificentísimo -ma** *adj super* very or most magnificent
**magnífico -ca** *adj* magnificent; liberal, lavish
**magnitud** *f* magnitude; (astr. & math.) magnitude
**magno -na** *adj* great, e.g., **Alejandro Magno** Alexander the Great
**magnolia** *f* (bot.) magnolia
**mago -ga** *adj* magian, magical; Magian; *mf* magian, magician; *m* wizard; Magus, Magian; (zool.) tarsier; **magos de Oriente** Magi, Wise Men of the East
**magostar** *va* to roast (*chestnuts*) at a picnic
**magosto** *m* chestnut roast; roast chestnuts; picnic fire for roasting chestnuts
**magra** *f* see **magro**
**magrez** *f* thinness, leanness, meagerness
**magro -gra** *adj* thin, lean, meager; mean, paltry; *m* (coll.) loin of pork; *f* slice of ham; **¡magras!** *interj* (coll.) absolutely no!
**magrura** *f* var. of **magrez**
**maguar** *vr* (Am.) to be disappointed
**maguer** *conj* (obs.) although
**magüeta** *f* heifer
**magüeto** *m* young bull
**maguey** *m* (bot.) maguey
**maguillo** *m* (bot.) crab apple
**magujo** *m* (naut.) ravehook
**magulladura** *f* or **magullamiento** *m* bruise, bruising
**magullar** *va & vr* to bruise
**Maguncia** *f* Mainz
**magyar** *adj & mf* var. of **magiar**
**maharajá** *m* (*pl:* **-jaes**) maharaja
**mahatma** *m* mahatma; (theosophy) mahatma
**Mahoma** *m* Mohammed
**mahometano -na** *adj & mf* Mohammedan
**mahometismo** *m* Mohammedanism
**mahometista** *adj* Mohammedan; *mf* Mohammedan; Christianized Mohammedan who returns to Mohammedanism
**mahometizar** §76 *va* to Mohammedanize; *vn* to profess Mohammedanism
**mahón** *m* nankeen
**mahona** *f* mahone (*Turkish vessel*)
**mahonesa** *f* mayonnaise; (bot.) Mahon stock, Virginia stock
**maicena** *f* fine corn flour
**maicillo** *m* (bot.) gama grass; (Am.) gravel
**maído** *m* meow
**maillechort** *m* var. of **melchor**
**maimón** *m* monkey; **maimones** *mpl* Andalusian soup made with olive oil
**Maimónides** *m* Maimonides
**mainel** *m* railing, handrail
**maitinada** *f* dawn
**maitines** *mpl* (eccl.) matins
**maíz** *m* (bot.) maize, Indian corn; **maíz de Guinea** or **maíz morocho** (bot.) Guinea corn, durra; **maíz en la mazorca** corn on the cob
**maizal** *m* cornfield
**majada** *f* sheepfold; dung, manure
**majadal** *m* richly manured land
**majadear** *vn* to take shelter for the night (*said of sheep*); to manure
**majaderear** *va* (Am.) to pester, annoy
**majadería** *f* (coll.) folly, annoyance
**majaderillo** *m* bobbin for making lace
**majadero -ra** *adj* stupid, annoying; *mf* dolt, bore; *m* pestle, pounder; bobbin for making lace
**majador -dora** *adj* crushing, pounding, grinding; *mf* crusher, pounder, grinder
**majadura** *f* crushing, pounding, grinding
**majagranzas** *m* (*pl:* **-zas**) (coll.) stupid bore; (coll.) churl, peasant
**majagua** *f* (bot.) majagua, corkwood
**majal** *m* school of fish
**majamiento** *m* var. of **majadura**
**majano** *m* heap of loose stones (*in a field or at crossroads*)
**majar** *va* to crush, pound, mash, grind; (coll.) to annoy, harass
**majear** *va* (Am.) to cheat, deceive; *vn* to be a bully
**majenza** *f* (coll.) var. of **majeza**
**majestad** *f* majesty; (*cap.*) *f* Majesty (*title*)
**majestoso -sa** *adj* majestic
**majestuosidad** *f* majesty
**majestuoso -sa** *adj* majestic

**majeza** *f* (coll.) sportiness, gaudiness; insolence
**majo -ja** *adj* sporty, gaudy; pretty, nice; insolent; (coll.) all dressed up; *mf* sport (*flashy person*); *m* (coll.) bully
**majolar** *m* field of English hawthorn
**majoleta** *f* var. of **marjoleta**
**majoleto** *m* var. of **marjoleto**
**majorca** *f* var. of **mazorca**
**majuela** *f* haw or berry (*of Crataegus monogyna*); shoestring
**majuelo** *m* (bot.) English hawthorn (*Crataegus monogyna*); young fruit-yielding grapevine
**mal** *adj* apocopated form of **malo,** used only before masculine singular nouns; *adv* badly, poorly; wrong, wrongly; hardly, scarcely; with difficulty; **mal de fondos** short of money; **mal que bien** any old way; **mal que le pese** in spite of him; *m* evil; harm, damage; wrong; misfortune; disease, sickness; **de mal en peor** from bad to worse; **echar a mal** to scorn, have a poor opinion of; **estar mal** to be ill; **estar mal con** to be on the outs with; **parar en mal** to come to an evil end; **por mal de mis pecados** to my sorrow, unfortunately for me; **tener a mal** to be displeased with, to object to; **mal ardiente** (path.) St. Anthony's fire; **mal caduco** or **mal comicial** (path.) falling sickness; **mal de corazón** (path.) epilepsy; (path.) nausea; **mal de la puna** mountain sickness; **mal de las montañas** mountain sickness; **mal de la tierra** homesickness; **mal de los ardientes** (path.) St. Anthony's fire; **mal de mar** seasickness; **mal de ojo** evil eye; **mal de piedra** (path.) stone, urinary calculi; **mal de rayos** radiation sickness; **mal de vuelo** airsickness; **¡mal haya . . . !** curses on . . . !
**mala** *f* see **malo**
**malabar** *adj & mf* Malabarese; see **juego**
**malabárico -ca** *adj* Malabarese
**malabarismo** *m* juggling
**malabarista** *mf* juggler
**malacate** *m* (min.) whim (*hoisting machine*); (Am.) bobbin, spindle
**malacia** *f* (path.) depraved appetite
**malacitano -na** *adj & mf* var. of **malagueño**
**malacología** *f* malacology
**malacondicionado -da** *adj* evil, gruff, surly
**malaconsejado -da** *adj* ill-advised
**malacopterigio -gia** *adj & m* (zool.) malacopterygian
**malacostráceo -a** *adj & m* (zool.) malacostracan
**malacostumbrado -da** *adj* of bad habits; spoiled, pampered
**malacuenda** *f* burlap; oakum, tow
**málaga** *m* Malaga wine
**malagradecido -da** *adj* (Am.) ungrateful
**malagueño -ña** *adj* (pertaining to) Malaga; *mf* native or inhabitant of Malaga; *f* malaguena (*song and dance*)
**malagueta** *f* grains of paradise, melegueta pepper; (bot.) bayberry (*Pimenta acris*)
**malamente** *adv* badly, poorly; wrong, wrongly
**malandante** *adj* unfortunate, unlucky
**malandanza** *f* misfortune, bad luck
**malandar** *m* home-fed hog
**malandrín -drina** *adj* evil, wicked; *mf* scoundrel
**malanga** *f* (bot.) caladium
**Malaquías** *m* (Bib.) Malachi
**malaquita** *f* (mineral.) malachite
**malar** *adj & m* (anat.) malar
**malaria** *f* (path.) malaria
**malasio -sia** *adj & mf* Malaysian; **la Malasia** Malaysia
**malavenido -da** *adj* in disagreement
**malaventura** *f* misfortune
**malaventurado -da** *adj* unfortunate
**malaventuranza** *f* misfortune
**malayo -ya** *adj & mf* Malay, Malayan; *m* Malay (*language*); (*cap.*) *f* Malaya
**malbaratador -dora** *adj* underselling; squandering; *mf* underseller; squanderer
**malbaratamiento** *m* var. of **malbarato**
**malbaratar** *va* to undersell (*an article*); to squander
**malbaratillo** *m* second-hand shop
**malbarato** *m* underselling; squandering
**malcarado -da** *adj* evil-faced
**malcasado -da** *adj* mismated; undutiful (*spouse*)
**malcasar** *va* to mismate; *vn & vr* to be mismated
**malcaso** *m* treachery, perfidy
**malcocinado** *m* entrails; butcher shop (*where entrails are sold*)
**malcomer** *va & vn* to eat poorly, to eat lightly
**malcomido -da** *adj* underfed
**malcontento -ta** *adj* discontent; malcontent; *mf* malcontent
**malcoraje** *m* (bot.) herb mercury
**malcorte** *m* illegal cutting of timber
**malcriado -da** *adj* ill-bred
**malcriar §90** *va* (coll.) to spoil, pamper
**maldad** *f* badness, evil, wickedness
**maldecidor -dora** *adj* slanderous; *mf* detractor, slanderer
**maldecir §24** *va* to curse; *vn* to damn, to curse; to detract; **maldecir de** to slander, speak ill of, vilify
**maldiciente** *adj* cursing; slanderous; *mf* detractor, slanderer
**maldición** *f* malediction, curse; (coll.) curse, oath
**maldigo** *1st sg pres ind of* **maldecir**
**maldije** *1st sg pret ind of* **maldecir**
**maldispuesto -ta** *adj* indisposed; ill-disposed, unwilling
**maldito -ta** *adj* wicked; damned, accursed; **no saber maldita la cosa de** (coll.) to not know a single thing about; **maldito lo que me importa** (coll.) I don't give a damn about it; *m* Evil One (*Devil*); **los malditos** the damned; *f* (coll.) tongue; **soltar la maldita** (coll.) to talk without restraint, to talk freely; to pour forth a flood of curses
**maleabilidad** *f* malleability
**maleabilizar §76** *va* to make malleable
**maleable** *adj* malleable; (coll.) easily spoiled; (coll.) easily led astray
**maleante** *adj* corrupting; evil, wicked; (coll.) scoffing, malicious; *mf* hoodlum, rowdy; (coll.) scoffer
**malear** *va* to damage, spoil; to corrupt; *vr* to spoil; to become spoiled; to become corrupt; to sour, turn sour (*said of soil*)
**malecón** *m* levee, dike; sea wall
**maledicencia** *f* slander, scandal, evil talk
**maleficencia** *f* maleficence
**maleficiar** *va* to damage, harm; to curse, cast a spell on
**maleficio** *m* curse, spell; witchcraft, black magic
**maléfico -ca** *adj* maleficent; malevolent; spellcasting; *m* sorcerer
**malencarado -da** *adj* ill-featured, ill-favored, ugly
**malentendido** *m* misunderstanding
**maleolar** *adj* hammer-shaped; (anat.) malleolar
**maléolo** *m* (anat.) malleolus
**malestar** *m* malaise, indisposition
**maleta** *f* valise; **hacer la maleta** to pack up, to get ready for a trip; *m* (coll.) bungler, ham bullfighter
**maletero** *m* valise maker or dealer; porter, station porter
**maletín** *m* small bag, satchel; **maletín de grupa** (mil.) saddlebag
**malevolencia** *f* malevolence
**malévolo -la** *adj & mf* malevolent
**maleza** *f* weeds; thicket, underbrush
**malformación** *f* malformation
**malfuncionamiento** *m* malfunction
**malgastado -da** *adj* ill-spent
**malgastador -dora** *mf* wastrel, squanderer, spendthrift
**malgastar** *va* to waste, squander
**malhablado -da** *adj* foul-mouthed, foul-spoken
**malhadado -da** *adj* ill-starred, unfortunate
**malhecho -cha** *adj* malformed, deformed; *m* evil deed, misdeed
**malhechor -chora** *adj* malefactory; *mf* malefactor; *f* malefactress
**malherir §62** *va* to injure badly, to wound badly
**malhojo** *m* vegetable refuse
**malhumorado -da** *adj* ill-humored
**malicia** *f* evil; malice; slyness, trickiness; insidiousness; (coll.) suspicion

**maliciar** *va* to suspect; to spoil; *vr* to suspect; to become spoiled
**malicioso -sa** *adj* evil; malicious; sly, tricky; insidious; suspicious
**málico -ca** *adj* malic
**malignar** *va* to vitiate, corrupt; to spoil; *vr* to become vitiated; to spoil
**malignidad** *f* malignity, malignance
**maligno -na** *adj* malign, malignant, evil, unkind; (path.) malign, malignant
**malilla** *f* manilla (*second-best trump*)
**Malinas** *f* Mechlin or Malines
**malintencionado -da** *adj* ill-disposed, evil-disposed
**malmandado -da** *adj* unwilling, disobedient
**malmaridada** *adj fem* faithless (*wife*); *f* faithless wife
**malmeter** *va* to waste, squander; to alienate; to lead astray, to misguide
**malmirado -da** *adj* inconsiderate; disliked
**malo -la** *adj* bad; poor; evil; naughty, mischievous; sick; in bad shape; wrong; **a malas** on bad terms; **estar de malas** to be out of luck; **lo malo es que** the trouble is that; **por malas o por buenas** willingly or unwillingly; **ser malo de engañar** (coll.) to be hard to trick; **venir de malas** to have bad intentions; **malo con** or **para con** mean to; **malo de** +*inf* hard to+*inf*; *m* wicked person; **el Malo** the Evil One (*the Devil*); *f* mailbag; mail
**malogrado -da** *adj* late, ill-fated
**malogramiento** *m* var. of **malogro**
**malograr** *va* to miss, to waste; to spoil; *vr* to fail; to turn out badly; to come to an untimely end
**malogro** *m* failure; loss, waste (*e.g., of time*); disappointment; untimely death
**maloliente** *adj* malodorous, ill-smelling
**malón** *m* mean trick; (Am.) surprise attack; (Am.) Indian raid; (Am.) surprise party
**malparado -da** *adj* hurt, damaged; **salir malparado de** to come out worsted in
**malparar** *va* to mistreat, put in a bad way
**malparir** *vn* to miscarry
**malparto** *m* miscarriage
**malpigiáceo -a** *adj* (bot.) malpighiaceous
**malpraxis** *f* malpractice
**malquerencia** *f* dislike
**malquerer §70** *va* to dislike
**malquerré** *1st sg fut ind of* **malquerer**
**malquise** *1st sg pret ind of* **malquerer**
**malquistar** *va* to alienate; *vr* to become alienated
**malquisto -ta** *adj* estranged; disliked, unpopular
**malrotar** *va* to squander
**malsano -na** *adj* unhealthy
**malsín** *m* evil gossip; troublemaker
**malsonante** *adj* offensive, obnoxious
**malsufrido -da** *adj* impatient, unforbearing
**malta** *m* malt; *f* pitch, tar; (Am.) quality beer; (Am.) jug
**maltasa** *f* (biochem.) maltase
**maltés -tesa** *adj & mf* Maltese; *m* Maltese (*language*)
**maltosa** *f* (chem.) maltose
**maltrabaja** *mf* (coll.) lazy loafer
**maltrapillo** *m* (coll.) ragamuffin
**maltratamiento** *m* maltreatment, ill treatment, abuse
**maltratar** *va* to maltreat, ill-treat, abuse; to damage, harm, spoil
**maltrato** *m* var. of **maltratamiento**
**maltrecho -cha** *adj* battered, damaged, abused
**maltusianismo** *m* Malthusianism
**maltusiano -na** *adj & mf* Malthusian
**maluco -ca** or **malucho -cha** *adj* (coll.) slightly ill, sickish
**malva** *f* (bot.) mallow; **haber nacido con** or **en las malvas** (coll.) to be of humble birth; **ser una malva** or **como una malva** (coll.) to be meek and mild, to be as gentle as a lamb; **malva arbórea** (bot.) rose mallow, hollyhock; **malva común** (bot.) cheeseflower; **malva de hoja redonda** (bot.) dwarf mallow; **malva de olor** (bot.) nutmeg geranium; **malva loca, real** or **rósea** (bot.) rose mallow, hollyhock
**malváceo -a** *adj* (bot.) malvaceous
**malvado -da** *adj* evil, wicked; *mf* evildoer
**malvar** *m* growth of mallows; *va* to corrupt, to deprave
**malvarrosa** *f* (bot.) rose mallow, hollyhock
**malvasía** *f* malmsey (*wine*); malvasia grape
**malvavisco** *m* (bot.) marsh mallow
**malvender** *va* to sell at a loss, to undersell
**malversación** *f* malversation, graft, embezzlement
**malversador -dora** *mf* grafter, embezzler
**malversar** *va & vn* to graft, to embezzle
**malvezar §76** *va* to give bad habits to; *vr* to get bad habits
**malvís** *m* (orn.) song thrush, redwing
**malviz** *m* (*pl:* **-vices**) var. of **malvís**
**malla** *f* mesh; meshwork, network; mail (*of armor*); meshed or netted fabric; tights; bathing suit; (rad.) grid; **malla de alambre** wire mesh, wire netting
**mallar** *vn* to make meshing or network; to get caught in the meshes of a net (*said of a fish*)
**mallero** *m* mesh maker
**malletazo** *m* (sport) blow or stroke with a mallet
**mallete** *m* mallet; (naut.) partner; (sport) mallet (*in croquet and polo*)
**malleto** *m* beating maul (*used in paper mills*)
**mallo** *m* mallet; pall-mall (*game and alley*)
**Mallorca** *f* Majorca
**mallorquín -quina** *adj & mf* Majorcan; *m* Majorcan (*dialect*)
**mama** *f* (anat.) mamma; (coll.) mama or mamma (*mother*)
**mamá** *f* (*pl:* **-más**) (coll.) mama or mamma (*mother*)
**mamacallos** *m* (*pl:* **-llos**) simpleton, fool
**mamada** *f* sucking; sucking time; suck; (Am.) cinch
**mamadera** *f* breast pump; (Am.) nipple; (Am.) nursing bottle
**mamador -dora** *adj* sucking; *mf* sucker; (Am.) souse, drunk
**mamalón -lona** *adj* (Am.) loafing, sponging
**mamama** or **mamamama** *f* (Am.) granny, grandmother
**mamandurria** *f* (Am.) sinecure
**mamantón -tona** *adj* sucking (*animal*)
**mamar** *va* to suck; to take in or absorb as a child; (coll.) to swallow; (coll.) to wangle; **mamóla** (coll.) he was taken in; *vn* to suck; *vr* to get drunk; to have (*a scare*); (coll.) to swallow; (coll.) to wangle; **mamarse a uno** (coll.) to get the best of someone; (coll.) to take someone in; (coll.) to do away with someone; **mamarse el dedo** (coll.) to be taken in
**mamario -ria** *adj* mammary
**mamarrachada** *f* (coll.) collection of junk; (coll.) piece of folly; (coll.) daub
**mamarrachero -ra** or **mamarrachista** *mf* (coll.) botcher, dauber
**mamarracho** *m* (coll.) botch, mess, piece of junk, daub, scarecrow; (coll.) fellow, guy, milksop
**mambla** *f* mound, knoll
**mambrú** *m* (*pl:* **-brúes**) (naut.) kitchen funnel or stack
**mamelón** *m* mound, knoll, hillock; (anat. & bot.) mammilla
**mameluco -ca** *mf* mameluco, mestizo (*in Brazil*); *m* mameluke (*slave*); Mameluke (*soldier*); dolt, boob; *f* (Am.) prostitute
**mamella** *f* mammilla (*in neck of a goat*)
**mamey** *m* (bot.) mammee
**mamífero -ra** *adj* (zool.) mammalian; *m* (zool.) mammal, mammalian
**mamila** *f* breast; teat (*of a man*)
**mamilar** *adj* mammillary
**mammón** *m* (Bib.) Mammon
**mamola** *f* chuck (*under the chin*); **hacer la mamola a** to chuck under the chin; (coll.) to make a fool of
**mamón -mona** *adj* sucking; fond of sucking; *mf* suckling; *m* (bot.) shoot, sucker; (bot.) genip; *f* chuck (*under the chin*)
**mamoso -sa** *adj* sucking
**mamotreto** *m* notebook, memo book; (coll.) bulky book, bulky batch of papers; (coll.) piece of junk
**mampara** *f* screen; folding screen; small door

**mamparo** *m* (naut.) bulkhead
**mamperlán** *m* temporary railing
**mamporro** *m* bump, contusion
**mampostear** *va* to make or build of rubble
**mampostería** *f* rubblework
**mampostero** *m* rubble mason
**mampuesto -ta** *adj* rubble; *m* rough stone; parapet; (Am.) support for a gun in taking aim; **de mampuesto** spare; emergency; under cover, from a parapet; *f* (mas.) course
**mamujar** *va & vn* to suck intermittently
**mamullar** *va* to chew as if sucking; (coll.) to mumble, to mutter
**mamut** *m* (*pl:* **-muts**) (pal.) mammoth
**maná** *m* (Bib.) manna; (bot.) manna (*exudate of Fraxinus ornus and other plants*); godsend, salvation (*in form of cheap and abundant food*)
**manada** *f* flock, herd, pack, drove; handful; (coll.) crowd, mob
**manadero -ra** *adj* flowing, running; *m* source, spring; shepherd, herdsman
**manantial** *adj* flowing, running; *m* source, spring; (fig.) source, origin; **manantial de energía** (elec.) source of current
**manantío -a** *adj* flowing, running
**manar** *va* to pour forth, to run with; *vn* to pour forth, to run; (fig.) to abound, to run
**Manasés** *m* (Bib.) Manasseh
**manatí** *m* (*pl:* **-tíes**) (zool.) manatee, sea cow
**manato** *m* var. of **manatí**
**manaza** *f* big hand
**mancamiento** *m* maiming; lack, want
**mancar §86** *va* to maim (*especially in the hand*); *vn* (naut.) to abate, to slack (*said of wind*)
**manceba** *f* concubine
**mancebía** *f* brothel; wild oats; licentious living
**mancebo** *m* youth, young man; bachelor; clerk; helper (*e.g., in drug store or barbershop*)
**mancera** *f* plow handle
**mancerina** *f* var. of **macerina**
**mancilla** *f* spot, blemish
**mancillar** *va* to spot, blemish; (fig.) to spot, blemish
**mancipación** *f* enslavement; (law) conveyance, transfer
**mancipar** *va* to enslave; (law) to convey, transfer
**manco -ca** *adj* one-handed; one-armed; maimed; defective, faulty; *mf* one-handed person, one-armed person; **el manco de Lepanto** Cervantes; *m* (Am.) old nag
**mancome** *m* (bot.) sassy or sassywood
**mancomún; de mancomún** jointly, in agreement
**mancomunadamente** *adv* jointly, in agreement
**mancomunar** *va* to unite, combine; to pool; (law) to require joint payment or execution of; *vr* to unite, combine
**mancomunidad** *f* union, association; commonwealth
**mancornar §77** *va* to down (*a young bull*) and hold his horns on the ground; to tie a horn and a front leg of (*a steer*) with a rope; to tie (*two beasts*) together by the horns; (coll.) to join, bring together
**mancuerda** *f* rack (*torture*)
**mancuerna** *f* pair tied together; yoke fastened by the horns; **mancuernas** *fpl* (Am.) cuff links
**mancha** *f* spot, stain; speckle; patch; sketch; (fig.) stain, blot; (Am.) flock, school; **mancha amarilla** (anat.) yellow spot; **mancha ocular** (zool.) eyespot; **mancha solar** sun spot
**manchadizo -za** *adj* easily spotted or stained
**manchar** *va* to spot, stain; to speckle; (fig.) to stain, blot; **¡mancha!** wet paint!
**manchego -ga** *adj* (pertaining to) La Mancha; *mf* native or inhabitant of La Mancha
**manchón** *m* big spot; patch of heavy growth (*in a field*)
**manchoso -sa** *adj* (prov.) var. of **manchadizo**
**manchú -chúa** (*pl:* **-chúes** or **-chús** & **-chúas**) *adj & mf* Manchu; *m* Manchu (*language*)
**manchuriano -na** *adj & mf* Manchurian
**manda** *f* offer, gift; bequest, legacy
**mandadero -ra** *mf* messenger; *m* errand boy; office boy; *f* errand girl
**mandado** *m* order, command; errand; **hacer un mandado** to run an errand
**mandamás** *m* (slang) head man, big boss
**mandamiento** *m* order, command; (Bib.) commandment; (law) writ; **los cinco mandamientos** (coll.) the five fingers of the hand; **los diez mandamientos** (Bib.) the Ten Commandments; **mandamiento de arresto** or **prisión** (law) warrant of arrest
**mandante** *m* (law) mandator
**mandar** *va* to order; to command; to send; to bequeath; (Am.) to overlook, to dominate (*e.g., the countryside*); **mandar** + *inf* to order to + *inf*, to have + *inf*, e.g., **me mandó entrar** he had me come in; to order or have + *pp*, e.g., **mandó componer el reloj** he had the watch repaired; **mandar llamar** to send for; *vn* to command, be in command; to be the boss; **mandar decir que** to send word that; **mandar por** to send for; **mande Vd.** I beg your pardon; *vr* to get around (*said of a convalescent*); to be communicating (*said of rooms*); **mandarse con** to communicate with (*another room*); **mandarse por** to use (*e.g., a door, stairway*)
**mandarín -rina** *adj* mandarin; *m* mandarin; (coll.) official held in low esteem; *f* mandarin or tangerine (*fruit*); Mandarin (*language*)
**mandarino** *m* (bot.) mandarin (*tree*)
**mandarria** *f* (naut.) iron maul, sledge hammer
**mandatario** *m* agent; (law & dipl.) mandatary, mandatory; (Am.) chief executive; **primer mandatario** (Am.) chief executive (*of the country*)
**mandato** *m* mandate; (law & dipl.) mandate; (eccl.) maundy; (Am.) term (*of office*)
**mandíbula** *f* jaw; (anat. & zool.) mandible; **reír a mandíbula batiente** to roar with laughter
**mandibular** *adj* mandibular
**mandil** *m* apron; leather apron; cleaning rag; apron (*of Freemasons*)
**mandilar** *va* to wipe or clean (*a horse*) with a rag
**mandilete** *m* (fort.) cover of a loophole
**mandilón** *m* (coll.) coward
**mandinga** *m* (Am.) imp, little rogue
**mandioca** *f* (bot.) manioc (*plant and starch*)
**mando** *m* command; drive, control; **mandos** *mpl* controls; **alto mando** high command; **estar al mando** to be in command; **tener el mando y el palo** (coll.) to rule the roost, to be the boss; **tomar el mando** to take command; **mando a distancia** remote control; **mando a mano** hand control; **mando a punta de dedo** finger-tip control; **mando de las válvulas** (mach.) timing gears; **mando doble** (aut.) dual drive; **mando por botón** push-button control; **mando único** (rad.) single control
**mandoble** *m* two-handed slash or blow (*e.g., with a sword*); sharp reproof
**mandolina** *f* (mus.) mandolin
**mandón -dona** *adj* bossy; *mf* bossy person; *m* (Am.) boss, foreman (*in a mine*); (Am.) starter (*in horse race*)
**mandrachero** *m* keeper of a gambling house
**mandracho** *m* gambling house
**mandrágora** *f* (bot.) mandragora or mandrake
**mandrágula** *f* (coll.) mandragora or mandrake; (coll.) phantom, ghost
**mandria** *adj* cowardly; trifling, worthless
**mandril** *m* (mach.) mandrel or mandril; chuck; reamer; punch; (zool.) mandrill; **mandril de ensanchar** (mach.) driftpin
**mandrilado** *m* boring; reaming; (mach.) drifting
**mandrilar** *va* to bore (*a cylinder*); to ream; (mach.) to drift (*a hole*)
**mandrín** *m* (mach.) driftpin
**mandrinar** *va* var. of **mandrilar**
**mandrón** *m* stone or wood ball (*used as a missile*); mangonel (*catapult*)
**manducación** *f* (coll.) eating
**manducar §86** *va & vn* (coll.) to eat
**manducatoria** *f* (coll.) food, sustenance
**manea** *f* hopple (*rope or chain*)
**manear** *va* to hobble or hopple (*an animal*); to handle, to wield; (Am.) to trip with a rope

**manecilla** *f* small hand; hand (*of clock or watch*); clasp, book clasp; (print.) index, fist; (bot.) tendril
**manejabilidad** *f* manageability
**manejable** *adj* manageable
**manejado -da** *adj* managed, handled; **bien manejado** (paint.) loose; **mal manejado** (paint.) tight
**manejar** *va* to manage; to handle, to wield; (equit.) to manage (*a horse*); to drive (*an automobile*); *vr* to manage; to behave; to get around, move about
**manejo** *m* handling; management; scheming, intrigue; (equit.) manège; (Am.) driving; **manejo a distancia** remote control; **manejo doméstico** housekeeping; **manejos de corte** court intrigues
**maneota** *f* var. of **manea**
**manera** *f* see **manero**
**manerismo** *m* var. of **manierismo**
**manero -ra** *adj* tame (*falcon*); *f* manner; way; flap; slit (*in skirt*); (f.a. & lit.) manner (*e.g., of Raphael*); **maneras** *fpl* manners; **a la manera de** in the manner of; like; **de manera que** so that; **de ninguna manera** by no manner of means; **en gran manera** to a great degree; extremely; **sobre manera** exceedingly, beyond measure
**manes** *mpl* manes
**manés -nesa** *adj* Manx; *m* Manxman; Manx (*language*); **maneses** *mpl* Manx
**manezuela** *f* small hand; clasp; handle
**manga** *f* sleeve; hose; portmanteau (*laced together at the ends*); conical cloth strainer; scoop net; air shaft; wind scoop; waterspout; band of armed men; (bridge) game; (eccl.) manga; (naut.) beam (*widest part*); (Am.) crowd, mob; (Am.) cattle chute; (Am.) manga (*poncho*); **mangas** *fpl* profits, extras; **andar manga con hombro** (coll.) to be upside down, to be topsy-turvy; **en mangas de camisa** in shirt sleeves; **estar de manga** (coll.) to be in cahoots; **estar mangas por hombro** (coll.) to be topsy-turvy; **hacer mangas y capirotes** (coll.) to rush ahead without bothering about details; **hacerse** or **ir de manga** (coll.) to be in cahoots; **ser de manga ancha** or **tener manga ancha** to be indulgent, be easy-going; **manga de agua** waterspout, cloudburst; **manga de ángel** angel sleeve; **manga de camisa** shirt sleeve; **manga de jamón** leg-of-mutton sleeve; **manga de riego** watering hose; **manga de viento** whirlwind; **manga marina** waterspout; **manga perdida** sleeve with slit through which the arm projects
**mangajarro** *m* long, dirty sleeve
**mangaje** *m* length of hose
**mangana** *f* lasso
**manganear** *va* to lasso; (Am.) to vex, annoy
**manganeo** *m* lassoing
**manganesa** or **manganesia** *f* (mineral.) manganese dioxide, pyrolusite
**manganeso** *m* (chem.) manganese
**mangánico -ca** *adj* manganic
**manganilla** *f* trick, scheme, deceit
**manganita** *f* (chem.) manganite
**mangano** *m* (archaic) mangonel
**manganoso -sa** *adj* manganous
**mangante** *m* (coll.) cheat, loafer, good-for-nothing
**manglar** *m* mangrove swamp
**mangle** *m* (bot.) mangrove; *f* (mach.) mangle
**mango** *m* handle; (bot.) mango; **mango de cuchillo** (zool.) razor clam; **mango de escoba** broomstick; (aer.) stick, control stick
**mangón** *m* retailer; (Am.) corral
**mangonada** *f* blow or shove with the arm
**mangonear** *vn* (coll.) to loiter, to loaf around; (coll.) to meddle; (coll.) to dabble; **mangonear en** (coll.) to meddle in; (coll.) to dabble in
**mangoneo** *m* (coll.) meddling; (coll.) dabbling
**mangonero -ra** *adj* (coll.) meddlesome
**mangorrero -ra** *adj* rough, crude (*knife*); (coll.) handled; (coll.) worthless, useless; (coll.) idle, unemployed
**mangorrillo** *m* plow handle
**mangosta** *f* (zool.) mongoose
**mangostán** *m* (bot.) mangosteen (*tree*)
**mangosto** *m* mangosteen (*fruit*)
**mangote** *m* (coll.) long, wide sleeve; sleeve protector, cuffette
**mangual** *m* (mil.) flail, morning star
**manguardia** *f* wing wall, buttress (*of bridge*)
**manguera** *f* hose; waterspout; (naut.) funnel, air duct; (naut.) wind sail; **manguera contra incendios** fire hose
**manguero** *m* hoseman
**mangueta** *f* fountain syringe; door jamb; lever; neck (*of water-flushed toilet*); (aut.) stub axle
**manguita** *f* small sleeve; case, sheath
**manguitería** *f* furriery; fur shop
**manguitero** *m* furrier
**manguito** *m* muff; lace half sleeve; sleeve guard or protector; mantle (*of gaslight*); coffee cake; (mach.) sleeve; (mach.) coupling; **manguito para la muñeca** wristlet
**maní** *m* (*pl:* **-níes** or **-nises**) (bot.) peanut
**manía** *f* mania; (psychopath.) mania; **manía de grandezas** folie de grandeur, megalomania
**maniabierto -ta** *adj* open-handed, lavish
**maníaco -ca** *adj* maniac or maniacal; (psychopath.) manic; *mf* maniac
**manialbo -ba** *adj* white-footed (*horse*)
**manía-melancolía** *f* (psychopath.) manic-depressive insanity
**maniatar** *va* to tie the hands of, to manacle
**maniático -ca** *adj* maniacal; stubborn; queer; crazy (*enthusiastic*); *mf* maniac
**manicomio** *m* insane asylum, madhouse
**manicordio** *m* (mus.) manichord
**manicorto -ta** *adj* short-handed; (coll.) close-fisted, stingy; *mf* (coll.) skinflint
**manicuro -ra** *mf* manicure, manicurist; *f* manicure; manicuring
**manido -da** *adj* worn, stale; hackneyed; hidden, concealed; (Am.) full, swarming; (cook.) high; *f* haunt, hangout, den
**manierismo** *m* (f.a. & lit.) mannerism
**manifacero -ra** *adj* (coll.) scheming, meddlesome; *mf* (coll.) schemer, meddler
**manifactura** *f* manufacture; form, shape
**manifestación** *f* manifestation; demonstration (*public gathering to exhibit sympathy or opinion*)
**manifestante** *mf* manifestant; demonstrator
**manifestar** §18 *va* to manifest, make manifest; (eccl.) to expose (*the Host*); *vn* to demonstrate; *vr* to be or become manifest
**manifiesto -ta** *adj* manifest; *m* manifesto; (naut.) manifest; (eccl.) exhibition of the Host; **estar de manifiesto** to be manifest; **poner de manifiesto** to make manifest
**manigero** *m* boss of a gang of farmhands
**manigua** *f* Cuban jungle or thicket; **coger manigua** (Am.) to blush; **irse a la manigua** (Am.) to revolt
**manija** *f* handle; crank; clamp, collar; (rail.) coupling
**manilargo -ga** *adj* long-handed; ready-fisted; generous
**manilense** or **manileño -ña** *adj* Manila; *mf* native or inhabitant of Manila
**maniluvio** *m* (med.) hand bath
**manilla** *f* bracelet; handcuff, manacle; hand (*e.g., of watch*)
**manillar** *m* handle bar
**maniobra** *f* handling, operation; maneuver; (fig.) maneuver; (naut.) gear, tackle; **maniobras** *fpl* (rail.) shifting
**maniobrabilidad** *f* maneuverability
**maniobrable** *adj* maneuverable
**maniobrar** *vn* to work with the hands; to maneuver; (rail.) to shift; (fig.) to maneuver
**maniobrero -ra** *adj* (mil.) maneuvering; (mil.) skilled in maneuvering
**maniobrista** *adj* (naut.) skilled in maneuvering; *m* (naut.) skilful maneuverer
**maniota** *f* var. of **manea**
**manipodio** *m* (coll.) var. of **monipodio**
**manipulación** *f* manipulation
**manipulador -dora** *adj* manipulating; *mf* manipulator; *m* (telg.) key, telegraph key
**manipular** *va* to manipulate; (coll.) to manipulate (*to one's own purpose or advantage*)
**manipuleo** *m* (coll.) manipulation, maneuvering
**manípulo** *m* (hist. & eccl.) maniple

**maniqueísmo** *m* Manicheanism or Manicheism
**maniqueo -a** *adj & mf* Manichean
**maniquete** *m* black lace mitten
**maniquí** (*pl:* **-quíes**) *m* manikin, mannequin; dress form; (fig.) puppet; *f* mannequin, model
**manir** §53 *va* to keep (*game*) until it is high
**manirroto -ta** *adj* lavish, prodigal, spendthrift
**manita** *f* (chem.) mannitol, manna sugar
**manivacío -a** *adj* (coll.) empty-handed
**manivela** *f* crank; **manivela de arranque** starting crank
**manjar** *m* food, dish; tidbit, delicacy; pastime that gives a lift; **manjar blanco** blancmange; creamed chicken
**manjorrada** *f* (coll.) mess of food
**Man.l** abr. of **Manuel**
**mano** *f* hand; forefoot; coat (*e.g. of paint*); hand, round (*of a game*); hand (*of clock or watch*); turn; pestle, masher; trunk (*of elephant*); quire (*of paper*); mano, cylindrical grindstone (*for cocoa*); reprimand; **manos** *fpl* labor (*as distinguished from materials*); **abrir la mano** to accept gifts; to be generous; to be more lenient; **a la mano** at hand, on hand; within reach; easy to understand; **a mano** by hand; at hand; artificially; **a mano abierta** open-handedly; **a mano airada** violently; **a mano armada** armed (*e.g., attack*); insistently; **a manos llenas** generously; abundantly; **asentar la mano a** to give a beating; to reprimand; **asidos de la mano** hand in hand; **bajar la mano** to come down (*in price*); **bajo mano** underhandedly; **buenas manos** skill, dexterity; **caer en manos de** to fall into the hands of; **cerrar la mano** to be stingy; **¡dame esa mano!** (coll.) put it here!; **dar de manos** to fall flat on one's face; **dar la mano** to lend a hand; **darse las manos** to join hands; to shake hands (with each other); **de la mano** by hand, by the hand; **de las manos** hand in hand; **de manos a boca** suddenly, unexpectedly; **de primera mano** at first hand; first-hand; **de segunda mano** second-hand; **echar mano a** to seize; **echar mano a la bolsa** to take money out of one's purse; **echar mano de** to resort to; **echar una mano** to lend a hand; to play a game; **en buena mano está** (coll.) after you, you drink first; **escribir a la mano** to take dictation; **escribir a manos de** to write in care of; **estrecharse la mano** to shake hands; **ganarle a uno por la mano** to steal a march on someone; **imponer las manos** (eccl.) to lay hands on; **lavarse las manos de** to wash one's hands of; **llegar a las manos** to come to blows; **malas manos** awkwardness, lack of skill; **mudar de manos** to change hands; **probar la mano** to try one's hand; **salir a mano** (Am.) to come out even; **tener mano con** to have a pull with; **tener mano izquierda** (coll.) to have one's wits about one; **tomar la mano** to begin, to start in; to start the discussion; **untar la mano a** (coll.) to grease the palm of; **venir a las manos** to come to blows; **vivir de la mano a la boca** to live from hand to mouth; **mano a mano** face to face; on an equal footing; **mano de gato** cat's-paw; master hand, master touch (*of a person who has polished or edited the work of another person*); (coll.) make-up; **mano de obra** labor; **mano derecha** right-hand man; **mano de santo** (coll.) sure cure; **mano negra** Black Hand; **manos aguadas** butterfingers; **¡manos a la obra!** to work!, let's get to work!; **manos libres** outside earnings; **manos limpias** (coll.) clean hands; extras, perquisites; **manos muertas** (law) dead hand, mortmain; **mano sobre mano** idly; **manos puercas** (coll.) graft; *m* first to play, e.g., **soy mano** I'm first, I lead
**manobre** *m* (prov.) hod carrier
**manobrero** *m* keeper of irrigating ditches
**manojo** *m* handful, bunch, bundle; (Am.) hand (*of tobacco*); **a manojos** in abundance
**manojuelo** *m* small bunch or bundle
**manolesco -ca** *adj* loud, flashy, coarse
**manolo -la** *mf* Madrid sport; fast liver; (*cap.*) *m* Mannie
**manométrico -ca** *adj* manometric
**manómetro** *m* manometer
**manopla** *f* gauntlet; postilion's whip; (coll.) big hand; (Am.) brass knuckles
**manosa** *f* (chem.) mannose
**manosear** *va* to handle, finger; to fiddle with; to muss, rumple; (Am.) to pet, to fondle
**manoseo** *m* handling, fingering; fiddling; mussing, rumpling; (Am.) petting, fondling
**manota** *f* big hand
**manotada** *f* or **manotazo** *m* slap
**manoteado** *m* var. of **manoteo**
**manotear** *va* to slap, to smack; *vn* to gesticulate
**manoteo** *m* slapping; gesticulation
**manotón** *m* slap
**manquear** *vn* to be handless; to be one-handed; to be crippled; to pretend to be handless; to act crippled
**manquedad** *f* or **manquera** *f* lack of one or both hands or arms; crippled condition; defect
**mansalva; a mansalva** without danger, without running any risk; **a mansalva de** safe from
**mansarda** *f* mansard, mansard roof
**mansedumbre** *f* gentleness, mildness, meekness; tameness
**mansejón -jona** *adj* very gentle or tame
**mansera** *f* (Am.) vat for cane juice
**mansión** *f* stay; dwelling, abode; **hacer mansión** to stop, stay, put up; **mansión celestial** heavenly home
**mansito** *adv* (coll.) softly, quietly
**manso -sa** *adj* gentle, mild, meek; tame; *m* bellwether; farmhouse; (eccl.) manse
**mansurrón -rrona** *adj* extremely gentle, extremely meek; extremely tame
**manta** *f* blanket; large shawl; muffler; (mil.) mantelet; (coll.) beating; (Am.) coarse cotton cloth; (Am.) poncho; **a manta de Dios** copiously; **dar una manta a** (coll.) to toss in a blanket; **tirar de la manta** (coll.) to let the cat out of the bag; **manta de coche** lap robe; **manta de viaje** robe, rug, steamer rug
**mantaterilla** *f* coarse hempen blanketing
**manteador -dora** *adj* tossing; *mf* tosser
**manteamiento** *m* tossing in a blanket
**mantear** *va* to toss in a blanket; (Am.) to abuse, mistreat; *vn* (prov.) to gad (*said of a woman*)
**manteca** *f* lard; pomade; butter; (slang) dough (*money*); **como manteca** smooth as butter; **manteca de cacahuete** peanut butter; **manteca de cacao** cocoa butter; **manteca de cerdo** lard; **manteca de coco** coconut butter; **manteca de codo** (coll.) elbow grease; **manteca de puerco** lard; **manteca de vaca** butter
**mantecada** *f* slice of buttered bread; butter bun
**mantecado** *m* biscuit; custard ice cream, French ice cream
**mantecón** *m* (coll.) pampered fellow, mollycoddle
**mantecoso -sa** *adj* buttery
**manteísta** *m* student; day student
**mantel** *m* tablecloth; altar cloth; **levantar el mantel** or **los manteles** to clear the table
**mantelería** *f* table linen
**manteleta** *f* mantelet, lady's cape
**mantelete** *m* (mil.) mantelet; (eccl.) mantelletta; (her.) mantling
**mantelillo** *m* centerpiece (*of embroidery*)
**mantelito** *m* lunch cloth
**mantelo** *m* wide apron
**mantellina** *f* mantilla (*head scarf*)
**mantención** *f* (coll.) maintenance
**mantendré** *1st sg fut ind of* **mantener**
**mantenedor** *m* presiding officer of a contest
**mantener** §85 *va* to maintain, to keep; to keep up; *vr* to maintain oneself; to keep, to stay; to remain firm
**mantengo** *1st sg pres ind of* **mantener**
**mantenida** *f* (Am.) kept woman
**mantenido** *m* (Am.) gigolo (*man supported by a woman*)
**manteniente; a manteniente** with all one's might; with both hands
**mantenimiento** *m* maintenance; sustenance, food; living
**manteo** *m* tossing in a blanket; mantle, cloak

**mantequera** *f* see **mantequero**
**mantequería** *f* creamery
**mantequero -ra** *adj* (pertaining to) butter; *mf* butter maker or dealer; *f* churn, butter churn; butter dish
**mantequilla** *f* butter; butterfat; hard sauce; **mantequilla azucarada** hard sauce; **mantequilla derretida** drawn butter
**mantequillera** *f* (Am.) butter dish
**mantequillero** *m* (Am.) butter maker or dealer
**mantero -ra** *mf* blanket maker or dealer
**mantés -tesa** *adj* (coll.) scoundrely; *mf* (coll.) scoundrel
**mantilla** *f* mantilla (*head scarf*); horsecloth; (print.) blanket; **mantillas** *fpl* swaddling clothes; **estar en mantillas** (coll.) to be in its infancy (*said of an undertaking*)
**mantillo** *m* humus, vegetable mold; manure
**mantis** *f* (ent.) mantis; **mantis religiosa** (ent.) mantis, praying mantis
**mantisa** *f* (math.) mantissa
**manto** *m* mantle, cloak; large plain mantilla; mantel (*of fireplace*); robe, gown (*of priest, professor, etc.*); (geol.) stratum; (zool.) mantle; (fig.) cloak
**mantón -tona** *adj* with drooping wings; *m* shawl; **mantón de Manila** (coll.) embroidered silk shawl
**mantuano -na** *adj & mf* Mantuan
**mantudo -da** *adj* with drooping wings
**mantuve** *1st sg pret ind of* **mantener**
**manuable** *adj* handy, easy to handle, workable
**manual** *adj* manual, hand; handy; home; easy; easy-going; *m* manual, handbook; notebook
**manubrio** *m* handle; crank; (anat., bot. & zool.) manubrium
**manucodiata** *f* (orn.) bird of paradise
**manuela** *f* open hack (*used in Madrid*)
**manuella** *f* (naut.) capstan bar
**manufactura** *f* manufactory; manufacture
**manufacturar** *va* to manufacture
**manufacturero -ra** *adj* manufacturing
**manumisión** *f* (law) manumission
**manumiso -sa** *adj* free, emancipated
**manumisor** *m* manumitter
**manumitir** *va* (law) manumit
**manuscribir §17,** 9 *va & vn* to write by hand
**manuscrito -ta** *adj* manuscript, written by hand; *m* manuscript; *pp of* **manuscribir**
**manutención** *f* maintenance; board; protection, shelter
**manutendré** *1st sg fut ind of* **manutener**
**manutener §85** *va* (law) to maintain, support
**manutengo** *1st sg pres ind of* **manutener**
**manutisa** *f* var. of **minutisa**
**manutuve** *1st sg pret ind of* **manutener**
**manvacío -a** *adj* (coll.) var. of **manivacío**
**manzana** *f* apple (*fruit*); city block, block of houses; knob of a sword; knob (*on furniture*); **manzana asperiega** or **esperiega** cider apple; **manzana de Adán** Adam's apple; **manzana de la discordia** apple of discord, bone of contention; **manzana espinosa** (bot.) thorn apple
**manzanal** *m* apple tree; apple orchard
**manzanar** *m* apple orchard
**manzanera** *f* var. of **maguillo**
**manzanil** *adj* (pertaining to the) apple
**manzanilla** *f* (bot. & pharm.) camomile; manzanilla (*small round olive; pale dry sherry*); knob (*on furniture*); tip of chin; pad, cushion (*of foot of clawed animal*); **manzanilla de Indias** manchineel apple (*fruit*); **manzanilla fétida** or **hedionda** (bot.) stinking camomile; **manzanilla loca** (bot.) ringflower, oxeye; (bot.) Spanish or yellow camomile
**manzanillo** *m* (bot.) manchineel
**manzanita** *f* little apple; (bot.) manzanita; **manzanita de dama** Neapolitan medlar (*fruit*)
**manzano** *m* (bot.) apple, apple tree; **manzano enano de San Juan** or **del paraíso** (hort.) paradise, paradise apple
**maña** *f* see **maño**
**mañana** *f* morning; **de mañana** early in the morning; **en la mañana** in the morning; **muy de mañana** very early in the morning; **por la mañana** in the morning; **tomar la mañana** to get up early; (coll.) to take a shot of liquor before breakfast; *m* tomorrow; morrow (*future time*); *adv* tomorrow; **¡hasta mañana!** so long until tomorrow!; **pasado mañana** the day after tomorrow
**mañanero -ra** *adj* morning; early-rising
**mañanica** or **mañanita** *f* break of day, early morning; woman's knitted bed jacket
**mañear** *va & vn* to manage craftily
**mañerear** *vn* (Am.) to dawdle, to dillydally
**mañería** *f* sterility; feudal right of inheritance from one who dies without legitimate heirs
**mañero -ra** *adj* clever, shrewd; easy; (Am.) balky, mulish; (Am.) shy, scary
**maño -ña** *adj* (coll.) Aragonese; (dial. & Am.) dear, darling; *m* (dial. & Am.) brother; *f* skill, dexterity, cleverness; craftiness, cunning; vice, bad habit; bunch (*of flax, hemp, etc.*); (dial.) sauciness; (dial. & Am.) sister; **darse maña** to take care of oneself, to manage; **darse maña para** + *inf* to manage to, to contrive to + *inf*
**mañoco** *m* tapioca; (Am.) Indian corn meal
**mañoso -sa** *adj* skilful, clever; crafty, tricky; vicious
**mañuela** *f* craftiness, trickiness, meanness; **mañuelas** *mf* (*pl:* **-las**) (coll.) tricky person
**maorí** (*pl:* **-rís** or **-ríes**) *adj & mf* Maori
**mapa** *m* map; **mapa itinerario** road map; **mapa mundi** world map, map of the world; *f* (coll.) top (*finest of its lot or kind*); **llevarse la mapa** (coll.) to take the prize
**mapache** *m* (zool.) coon, raccoon
**mapamundi** *m* world map, map of the world
**mapanare** *f* (zool.) fer-de-lance; (zool.) bushmaster
**mapurite** *m* or **mapurito** *m* (zool.) skunk
**maque** *m* lacquer; (bot.) tree of heaven
**maquear** *va* to lacquer; (Am.) to varnish
**maqueta** *f* maquette; mock-up; (print.) dummy (*of a book*)
**maquí** *m* (*pl:* **-quíes**) (zool.) macaco; (bot.) maqui
**maquiavélico -ca** *adj* Machiavellian (*pertaining to Machiavelli; crafty, astute*)
**maquiavelismo** *m* Machiavellianism
**maquiavelista** *adj & mf* Machiavellian
**maquiavelizar §76** *vn* to be Machiavellian
**Maquiavelo** *m* Machiavelli
**maquila** *f* multure, miller's toll
**maquilar** *va* to exact toll for (*a grinding*)
**maquilero -ra** *mf* collector of miller's toll
**maquillador** *m* make-up man
**maquillaje** *m* (theat.) make-up
**maquillar** *va & vr* to make up
**máquina** *f* machine; engine; locomotive; edifice, mansion; plan, project; clippers; (lit. & theat.) machine; (fig.) machinery; (coll.) pile, heap, lot; (coll.) bike; **escribir a** or **con máquina** to typewrite; **máquina apisonadora** road roller; **máquina calculadora** computer; **máquina de afeitar** safety razor; **máquina de apostar** betting machine, gambling machine; **máquina de componer** (print.) typesetter; **máquina de coser** sewing machine; **máquina de dictar** dictating machine; **máquina de escribir** typewriter; **máquina de lavar** washing machine; **máquina de sumar** adding machine; **máquina de vapor** steam engine; **máquina de volar** flying machine; **máquina Diesel** Diesel engine; **máquina electrostática** (elec.) static machine; **máquina estenotipiadora** stenotype; **máquina fotográfica** camera; **máquina hiladora** spinning machine; **máquina infernal** infernal machine; **máquina parlante** talking machine; **máquina piloto** (rail.) pilot engine; **máquina sacaperras, tragamonedas** or **tragaperras** slot machine
**maquinación** *f* machination, scheming, plotting
**maquinador -dora** *adj* machinating, scheming, plotting; *mf* machinator, schemer, plotter
**máquina-herramienta** *f* (*pl:* **máquinas-herramientas**) machine tool
**maquinal** *adj* mechanical; (fig.) mechanical
**maquinar** *va & vn* to machinate, scheme, plot
**maquinaria** *f* machinery; applied mechanics; (fig.) machinery

**maquinilla** *f* winch; clippers; **maquinilla cortapelos** hair clippers; **maquinilla de afeitar** safety razor; **maquinilla de rizar** curling iron

**maquinismo** *m* (econ.) mechanization

**maquinista** *mf* machinist; engineer (*who runs an engine*); **primer maquinista** (naut.) engineer officer; **segundo maquinista** (naut.) machinist

**mar** *m & f* sea; tide, flood; (fig.) sea, e.g., **mar de lágrimas** sea of tears; (fig.) oceans, e.g., **la mar de trabajo** oceans of work; **alta mar** high seas; **a mares** copiously; **arrojarse a la mar** to plunge, take great risks; **baja mar** low tide; **correr los mares** to follow the sea; **de mar a mar** from one end to the other; (coll.) all dressed-up; **echar a la mar** (naut.) to launch; **hablar de la mar** (coll.) to talk wildly; to take up an endless subject; **hacerse a la mar** to put to sea; **la mar de** a lot of, lots of; **meter la mar en un pozo** to attempt the impossible; **meterse mar adentro** to go beyond one's depth; **mar alta** rough sea; **mar Amarillo** Yellow Sea; **mar ancha** high seas; **mar Arábigo** Arabian Sea; **mar Aral** Aral Sea; **mar Báltico** Baltic Sea; **mar Blanco** White Sea; **mar bonanza** calm sea; **mar Cantábrico** Bay of Biscay; **mar Caribe** Caribbean Sea; **mar Caspio** Caspian Sea; **mar de costado** beam sea; **mar de fondo** ground swell; **mar de Galilea** Sea of Galilee; **mar de Irlanda** Irish Sea; **mar de la China** China Sea; **mar de la China Meridional** South China Sea; **mar de la China Oriental** East China Sea; **mar de las Antillas** Caribbean Sea; **mar de las Indias** Indian Ocean; **mar del Coral** Coral Sea; **mar de leva** ground swell; **mar del Japón** Inland Sea, Sea of Japan; **mar del Norte** North Sea; **mar de los Sargazos** Sargasso Sea; **mar del sur** South Seas (*south of the equator*); **mar de Mármara** Sea of Marmara or Marmora; **mar de nubes** cloud bank; **mar de Omán** Gulf of Oman; **mar de Sargazos** Sargasso Sea; **mar Egeo** Aegean Sea (*of ancient times*); **mar Jonio** Ionian Sea; **mar larga** high sea; **mar Latino** Mediterranean Sea; **mar llena** high tide; **mar Mediterráneo** Mediterranean Sea; **mar Muerto** Dead Sea; **mar Negro** Black Sea; **mar Rojo** Red Sea; **mar tendida** swell (*of sea*); **mar Tirreno** Tyrrhenian Sea

**marabú** *m* (*pl:* **-búes**) (orn.) marabou (*bird and trimming*); (bot.) Cuban weed (*Diegrostachys nutans*)

**marabuto** *m* Mohammedan hermitage

**maraca** *f* (Am.) maraca (*dried gourd filled with seeds or pebbles and used for marking rhythm*); (Am.) game played with three dice marked with sun, gold coin (diamond), bowl (heart), star, moon, and anchor; (Am.) harlot

**maracá** *m* (Am.) maraca (*dried gourd used for marking rhythm*)

**maragato -ta** *adj* Maragato; *mf* Maragato (*descendant of Celtiberian inhabitants in León, Spain*)

**maraña** *f* thicket, jungle; silk waste; poor silk cloth; tangle (*of thread, hair, etc.*); complexity, puzzle; trick, scheme; (bot.) kermes oak

**marañal** *m* field of kermes oak

**marañar** *va* to tangle; to entangle; *vr* to get tangled; to become entangled

**marañero -ra** or **marañoso -sa** *adj* intriguing, scheming; *mf* intriguer, schemer; cheat

**marañón** *m* (bot.) cashew

**maraquiana** *f* (bot.) marijuana (*Nicotiana glauca*)

**marasmo** *m* (path.) marasmus; (fig.) depression, stagnation

**Maratón** *m* Marathon; (l.c.) *m* (sport) marathon

**maravedí** *m* (*pl:* **-dís, -dises** or **-díes**) maravedi

**maravilla** *f* wonder, marvel; (bot.) marigold, calendula; (bot.) four-o'clock, marvel-of-Peru; (bot.) ivy-leaved morning-glory; **a las maravillas** or **a las mil maravillas** magnificently; **a maravilla** wonderfully well; **hacer maravillas con** to do wonders with; **por maravilla** rarely, seldom, on occasion

**maravillar** *va* to astonish, amaze; *vr* to wonder, to marvel; **maravillarse con** or **de** to wonder at, to marvel at

**maravilloso -sa** *adj* wonderful, marvelous; **lo maravilloso** (lit.) the marvelous, the supernatural

**marbete** *m* stamp, label; baggage check; edge, border; rope, binding; **marbete engomado** sticker

**marca** *f* mark; stamp; sign; make; brand; score; height-measuring bar; march (*frontier; territory*); shipping mark; record (*e.g., of endurance*); (naut.) seamark, landmark; **de marca** outstanding; **de marca mayor** or **de más de marca** most outstanding; **marca de agua** watermark (*in paper*); **marca de fábrica** trademark; **marca de máximo calado** (naut.) Plimsoll line; **marca depositada** trademark; **marca de reconocimiento** (naut.) seamark, landmark; **marca de taquilla** box-office record; **marca privativa** trademark; **marca registrada** registered trademark

**marcación** *f* (naut.) relative bearing; (naut.) taking a ship's bearing

**marcado -da** *adj* marked, pronounced; *m* (print.) feeding

**marcador -dora** *adj* marking; branding; *mf* marker; brander; *m* marker; sampler (*embroidered cloth*); (sport) marker (*device for marking, e.g., a tennis court*); (sport) marker, scoreboard; (print.) feeder; (print.) feedboard

**marcaje** *m* (telp.) dialing; (sport) scoring

**marcapaso** *m* (med.) pacemaker (*to regulate heartbeat*)

**marcar §86** *va* to mark; to stamp; to brand; to embroider; to initial (*e.g., a handkerchief*); to designate; to lay out (*a task*); to point out, to stress; to show (*the hour*); to make (*a score*); to score (*a point*); to dial (*a telephone number*); *vr* to take its bearings (*said of a ship*)

**marcasita** *f* (mineral.) marcasite

**marceador -dora** *adj* shearing; *mf* shearer

**marcear** *va* to shear (*e.g., sheep*); *vn* to be Marchlike, to be rough as March (*said of weather*)

**Marcela** *f* Marcella

**Marcelo** *m* Marcellus

**marceño -ña** *adj* (pertaining to) March

**marceo** *m* springtime cleaning of honeycombs

**marcero -ra** *adj* shearing

**marcescencia** *f* (bot.) marcescence

**marcescente** *adj* (bot.) marcescent

**marcial** *adj* martial; plain, simple; (*cap.*) *m* Martial

**marcialidad** *f* martiality, martialness

**marciano -na** *adj & mf* Martian

**marco** *m* frame; standard (*of weights and measures*); framework; size stick (*for measuring foot*); mark (*coin; weight*); (*cap.*) *m* Mark, Marcus; **marco de imprimir** (phot.) printing frame

**márcola** *f* pruning hook

**marconigrama** *m* marconigram

**Marcos** *m* Mark

**marcha** *f* march; running, functioning; operation; rate of speed; course, path (*e.g., of rays of light*); departure; (mil. & mus.) march; (aut.) speed (*in relation to gears*); (fig.) march, course, progress; (dial.) bonfire; **a toda marcha** at full speed; **batir la marcha** or **batir marcha** (mus.) to strike up a march; **cambiar de marcha** to shift gears; **en marcha** under way; on the march; in motion; **poner en marcha** to start, to launch (*a project*); **ponerse en marcha** to start, to strike out; **primera marcha** (mach.) low gear; **segunda marcha** second (gear); **sobre la marcha** at once, right away; **marcha a rueda libre** (mach.) freewheeling; **marcha atrás** (mach.) reverse; **marcha de ensayo** trial run; **marcha del hambre** hunger march; **marcha directa** (mach.) high gear; **marcha en ralentí** or **en vacío** idling; **marcha forzada** (mil.) forced march; **marcha fúnebre** (mus.) dead march, funeral march; **marcha nupcial** (mus.) wedding march

**marchamar** *va* to mark at the customhouse

**marchamero** *m* customhouse marker

**marchamo** *m* customhouse mark; lead seal
**marchante** *adj* commercial; *m* dealer, merchant; (Am.) customer
**marchapié** *m* (naut.) footrope; running board (*of a carriage*)
**marchar** *vn* to march; to run; to work; to go; to go away, leave; to proceed, come along, progress; (mil.) to march; **marchar en ralentí** or **en vacío** to idle; *vr* to go away, leave
**marchitable** *adj* easily withered, perishable
**marchitamiento** *m* withering; languishing
**marchitar** *va* to wilt, to wither; *vr* to wilt, to wither; (fig.) to wilt, to languish
**marchitez** *f* withered state; languor
**marchito -ta** *adj* withered; languid
**marchoso -sa** *adj* (slang) breezy, jaunty; (prov.) sporty; (prov.) roisterous
**Mardoqueo** *m* (Bib.) Mordecai
**marea** *f* (naut.) tide; gentle sea breeze; dew, drizzle; street dirt washed away; **marea alta** high tide; **marea baja** low tide; **marea creciente** or **entrante** flood tide; **marea menguante, saliente** or **vaciante** ebb tide; **marea muerta** neap tide; **marea viva** spring tide
**mareado -da** *adj* nauseated, seasick, lightheaded
**mareaje** *m* navigation, seamanship; course (*of a ship*)
**mareamiento** *m* var. of **mareo**
**mareamotor -triz** (*pl:* **-trices**) *adj* tide-driven
**marear** *va* to navigate, sail; to hoist (*sails*); (coll.) to annoy; *vn* (coll.) to be annoying; *vr* to become nauseated, to become seasick; to get giddy; to become damaged at sea (*said of merchandise*)
**mareca** *f* (orn.) baldpate
**marecanita** *f* (mineral.) marekanite
**marejada** *f* ground swell; stirring, undercurrent (*of unrest*); **marejada de fondo** ground swell
**maremagno** or **mare mágnum** *m* (coll.) mess, confusion; (coll.) omnium-gatherum
**maremoto** *m* earthquake at sea; bore, tidal bore
**mare nóstrum** *m* mare nostrum (*our sea, i.e., the Mediterranean*)
**mareo** *m* nausea; seasickness; plane sickness; (coll.) annoyance
**mareógrafo** *m* marigraph
**marero** *adj masc* sea (*breeze or wind*)
**mareta** *f* surge; rumbling (*of a mob*); agitation, disturbance
**maretazo** *m* billow
**márfaga** *f* ticking
**marfil** *m* ivory; **marfil vegetal** ivory nut
**marfileño -ña** *adj* (pertaining to) ivory
**marfilino -na** *adj* (pertaining to) ivory; *f* imitation ivory
**marfuz -fuza** *adj* (*pl:* **-fuces** & **-fuzas**) rejected, cast aside; false, deceptive
**marga** *f* marl; ticking
**margal** *m* marlpit, marly ground
**margallón** *m* (bot.) dwarf fan palm
**margar** §59 *va* to marl
**margarita** *f* pearl; (bot.) daisy, marguerite; (mineral.) margarite; (naut.) sheepshank (*knot*); (zool.) periwinkle; (*cap.*) *f* Margaret, Marguerite; **echar margaritas a los cerdos** or **a los puercos** to cast pearls before swine; **margarita de los prados** (bot.) English daisy, bachelor's-button; **margarita mayor** (bot.) oxeye daisy
**margen** *m & f* margin; border, edge; note, marginal note; occasion; **al margen de** aside from; aloof from; outside of; independent of; **andarse por los márgenes** to beat about the bush; **dar margen para** to give occasion for; **dejar al margen** to leave out; **quedar al margen de** to be left on the outside of; **margen de seguridad** margin of safety
**marginado -da** *adj* (bot.) marginal
**marginador** *m* marginal stop (*of typewriter*)
**marginal** *adj* marginal
**marginar** *va* to write marginal notes in (*a text*); to leave a margin on (*a printed or written sheet*); (Am.) to line (*e.g., the bank of a river*)
**marginoso -sa** *adj* wide-margined
**margoso -sa** *adj* marly
**margrave** *m* margrave
**margraviato** *m* margraviate
**margravina** *f* margravine
**Marg.ta** abr. of **Margarita**
**marguera** *f* marlpit
**marhojo** *m* var. of **malhojo**
**maría** *f* (coll.) white wax taper; (*cap.*) *f* Mary
**mariache** *m* or **mariachi** *m* rousing type of Mexican popular music; musician who plays this music
**mariano -na** *adj* Marian; *m* Marion (*man's name*); *f* Marion, Marian, or Marianne
**marica** *f* (orn.) magpie; jack of diamonds; *m* (coll.) sissy, milksop
**maricangalla** *f* (naut.) ringtail
**Maricastaña; en tiempo** or **en tiempos de Maricastaña** in times of yore
**maricón** *m* (coll.) sissy; sodomite
**maridable** *adj* conjugal, matrimonial
**maridaje** *m* married life; (fig.) marriage, union
**maridar** *va* to combine, join, unite; *vn* to get married; to live as man and wife
**maridazo** *m* (coll.) doting husband, henpecked husband
**maridillo** *m* ridiculous little husband; foot stove
**marido** *m* husband
**mariguana** *f* (bot.) marijuana (*Cannabis sativa*); **mariguana falsa** (bot.) marijuana (*Nicotiana glauca*)
**mariguano** *m* (Am.) marihuana addict
**mariguanza** *f* (Am.) hocus-pocus; (Am.) pirouette; **mariguanzas** *fpl* (Am.) quackery, powwowing; (Am.) clowning
**marihuana** *f* var. of **mariguana**
**marimacho** *m* (coll.) mannish woman
**marimandona** *f* (prov.) bossy woman
**marimanta** *f* (coll.) hobgoblin, bugaboo
**marimarica** *m* (coll.) sissy, milksop
**marimba** *f* (mus.) marimba; (Am.) beating, flogging
**marimbero -ra** *mf* marimba player
**marimoña** *f* (bot.) turban buttercup
**marimorena** *f* (coll.) fight, row
**marina** *f* see **marino**
**marinaje** *m* var. of **marinería**
**marinar** *va* to salt, to marinate (*fish*); to man, to put a new crew on (*a ship*); *vn* to be a sailor
**marinear** *vn* to be a sailor; to get one's sea legs
**marinera** *f* see **marinero**
**marinería** *f* seamanship, sailoring; sailors, ship's crew
**marinero -ra** *adj* seaworthy, navigable; marine, sea; *m* mariner, seaman, sailor; (zool.) paper nautilus; **a la marinera** or **a lo marinero** sailor-fashion; **marinero de agua dulce** landlubber; **marinero matalote** lubber, landlubber; *f* sailor blouse; middy, middy blouse
**marinesco -ca** *adj* (pertaining to the) sailor; sailorly; **a la marinesca** sailor-fashion
**marinista** *mf* seascapist
**marino -na** *adj* marine, sea; *m* mariner, seaman, sailor; *f* navy (*personnel*); seascape, marine; seaside, shore; fleet; sailing, navigation; **marina de guerra** navy; **marina mercante** merchant marine
**Mario** *m* Marius
**marión** *m* (ichth.) sturgeon
**marioneta** *f* marionette
**maripérez** *f* hook to fasten frying pan to trivet
**mariposa** f (ent. & fig.) butterfly; (ichth.) butterfly fish; wing nut; butterfly valve; rushlight; prostitute; (Am.) blindman's buff; **mariposa nocturna** (ent.) moth
**mariposear** *vn* to be capricious, to be fickle; to flutter around
**mariposón** *m* (coll.) fickle flirt
**mariquita** *m* (coll.) sissy, milksop; *f* (ent.) ladybird; (*cap.*) *f* Molly, Polly
**marisabidilla** *f* (coll.) bluestocking, know-it-all
**mariscador -dora** *mf* gatherer of shellfish
**mariscal** *m* (mil.) marshal; veterinarian; blacksmith; **mariscal de campo** (mil.) field marshal; (archaic) major general
**mariscala** *f* marshaless
**mariscalato** *m* or **mariscalía** *f* marshalate

**mariscar** §86 *vn* to gather shellfish
**marisco** *m* shellfish; **mariscos** *mpl* seafood
**marisma** *f* marsh, swamp; salt marsh
**marismeño -ña** *adj* marsh, swamp; marshy, swampy
**marismo** *m* (bot.) orach
**marisqueo** *m* shellfishery
**marisquería** *f* seafood store
**marisquero -ra** *adj* shellfish; seafood; *mf* catcher of shellfish; shellfish dealer; seafood dealer
**marista** *adj & mf* (eccl.) Marist
**marital** *adj* marital
**marítimo -ma** *adj* maritime; marine, sea
**maritornes** *f* (*pl:* **-nes**) (coll.) ugly, mannish maidservant, wench
**marizápalos** *m* (*pl:* **-los**) (coll.) fight, row
**marjal** *m* marsh, moor, fen
**marjoleta** *f* haw or berry (*of Crataegus monogyna and C. oxyacantha*)
**marjoleto** *m* (bot.) English hawthorn (*Crataegus monogyna and C. oxyacantha*)
**marlota** *f* close-fitting Moorish gown
**marlotar** *va* to tie, pinch, squeeze; to cut, tear away; (archaic) to squander
**marmella** *f* var. of **mamella**
**marmita** *f* pot, boiler; **marmita de gigante** (geol.) pothole
**marmitón** *m* scullion, kitchen scullion
**mármol** *m* marble; marver (*for rolling hot glass*)
**marmolejo** *m* small marble column
**marmoleño -ña** *adj* (pertaining to) marble
**marmolería** *f* marble work; marble works
**marmolillo** *m* spur stone; dolt
**marmolista** *m* marble worker; marble dealer
**marmolización** *f* marbling
**marmolizar** §76 *va & vr* to marble
**marmoración** *f* stucco
**marmóreo -a** *adj* marmoreal
**marmoroso -sa** *adj* marble, marmoreal
**marmosete** *m* vignette
**marmota** *f* (zool.) marmot; worsted cap; sleepyhead; sleepy-headed woman; ugly wench; **marmota de Alemania** (zool.) hamster; **marmota de América** (zool.) ground hog, woodchuck
**maro** *m* (bot.) cat thyme; (bot.) clary
**marojal** *m* growth of red-berried mistletoes; growth of pubescent oak trees
**marojo** *m* (bot.) red-berried mistletoe (*Viscum cruciatum*); (bot.) pubescent oak, durmast
**maroma** *f* rope of hemp or esparto; (Am.) acrobatics
**maromear** *vn* (Am.) to walk a tightrope, to stunt; (Am.) to sway (*toward one party or the other*)
**maromero -ra** *mf* (Am.) tightrope walker
**marón** *m* (ichth.) sturgeon; ram, male sheep
**marquear** *va* to sow or plant in straight lines
**marqueo** *m* layout for planting trees
**marqués** *m* marquis; (coll.) one-eyed fellow; **marqueses** *mpl* marquis and marchioness
**marquesa** *f* marquise, marchioness; marquee (*over an entrance*); (coll.) one-eyed woman
**marquesado** *m* marquisate
**marquesina** *f* marquee (*over an entrance*); locomotive cab
**marquesita** *f* var. of **marcasita**
**marquesota** *f* (archaic) high stiff collar
**marqueta** *f* cake of crude wax
**marqueteador** *m* worker in marquetry
**marquetería** *f* marquetry (*inlaid work*); cabinetwork, woodwork
**marquiana** *f* var. of **maraquiana**
**marra** *f* gap (*in a row, e.g., of trees*); stone hammer, spalling hammer
**márraga** *f* ticking
**marrajo -ja** *adj* malicious, wicked (*bull*); sly, tricky; *m* (ichth.) shark
**marramao** or **marramáu** *m* caterwaul
**marramizar** §76 *vn* to caterwaul
**marrana** *f* see **marrano**
**marranada** *f* (coll.) piggishness, filthiness
**marranalla** *f* (coll.) rabble, riffraff
**marranchón -chona** *mf* pig
**marranería** *f* (coll.) var. of **marranada**
**marranillo** *m* little pig; sucking pig
**marrano -na** *adj* (coll.) dirty, sloppy; base, vile; *mf* hog; *m* male hog, boar; drum (*of water wheel*); timber (*of shaft or well*); (fig.) hog; axle (*of bucket wheel*); (fig.) cur; *f* sow; (coll.) slut
**marrar** *vn* to miss, fail; to go astray
**marras** *adv* (coll.) long ago, a long time ago; **de marras** (coll.) of a long time ago; (coll.) well-known; **hacer marras de** (Am.) to be a long time since
**marrasquino** *m* maraschino
**marrazo** *m* mattock
**marrear** *va* to strike with a stone hammer
**marrillo** *m* short, thick stick
**marro** *m* quoits (*played with a stone*); dodge, duck; slip, miss; tag (*game*); cat (*used in tipcat*)
**marrón** *adj invar* maroon (*very dark red*); tan (*shoes*); **marrón -rrona** *adj* (Am.) fugitive, runaway (*slave*); *m* maroon (*very dark red*); stone (*used as sort of quoit*); (Am.) maroon (*fugitive slave, descendant of fugitive Negro slaves in West Indies and Dutch Guiana; explosive*); **marrones** *mpl* marrons (*chestnuts preserved in syrup*)
**marronaje** *m* (Am.) fugitive slaves
**marroquí** (*pl:* **-quíes**) *adj & mf* Moroccan; *m* morocco, morocco leather
**marroquín -quina** *adj, mf & m* var. of **marroquí**
**marroquinería** *f* morocco-leather dressing; morocco-leather shop
**marrubial** *m* field of horehound
**marrubio** *m* (bot.) horehound; **marrubio acuático** (bot.) water horehound; **marrubio blanco** (bot.) white horehound
**marrueco -ca** *adj & mf* Moroccan; **Marruecos** *m* Morocco; **el Marruecos Español** Spanish Morocco; **el Marruecos Francés** French Morocco
**marrullería** *f* cajolery, wheedling
**marrullero -ra** *adj* cajoling, wheedling; *mf* cajoler, wheedler
**Marsella** *f* Marseilles
**marsellés -llesa** *adj* (pertaining to) Marseilles; *mf* native or inhabitant of Marseilles; *m* coarse jacket; (*cap.*) *f* Marseillaise (*French national song*)
**Marsias** *m* (myth.) Marsyas
**marsopa** or **marsopla** *f* (zool.) porpoise, harbor porpoise, sea hog
**marsupial** *adj & m* (zool.) marsupial
**mart.** abr. of **martes**
**marta** *f* (zool.) pine marten; (*cap.*) *f* Martha; **marta cebellina** (zool.) sable, Siberian sable; sable (*fur*); **marta del Canadá** (zool.) fisher
**martagón -gona** *mf* (coll.) crafty person; *m* (bot.) Turk's-cap lily
**Marte** *m* (astr. & myth.) Mars
**martellina** *f* marteline
**martes** *m* (*pl:* **-tes**) Tuesday; **martes de carnaval** Shrove Tuesday
**martillada** *f* blow or stroke with a hammer
**martillado** *m* (action of) hammering
**martillador -dora** *adj* hammering; *mf* hammerer
**martillar** *va* to hammer; to worry, torment
**martillazo** *m* hard blow with a hammer; (box.) chop
**martillear** *va* var. of **martillar**
**martilleo** *m* hammering; (fig.) hammering
**martillero** *m* (Am.) auctioneer
**martillete** *m* tinner's hammer
**martillo** *m* hammer; (anat.) hammer, malleus; (mus.) tuning hammer; auction house; scourge (*person*); **a macha martillo** strongly but crudely (*constructed*); **a martillo** by hammering, with a hammer; **de martillo** wrought, hammered (*metal*); **martillo de agua** (phys.) water hammer (*glass tube*); **martillo de caída** or **martillo pilón** drop hammer; **martillo percusor** or **percutor** (med.) percussion hammer; **martillo perforador** jackhammer; **martillo picador** (*pl:* **martillos picadores**) hammer drill, jackhammer; **martillo sacaclavos** claw hammer
**Martín** *m* Martin; **llegarle** or **venirle a uno su San Martín** (coll.) to pay for one's wild oats; **San Martín** (coll.) season for killing hogs; **martín cazador** (*pl:* **martín caza-**

**dores**) (orn.) laughing jackass; **martín del río** (orn.) night heron; **martín pescador** (*pl:* **martín pescadores**) (orn.) kingfisher
**martina** *f* (ichth.) sand cusk, cusk eel
**martinete** *m* drop hammer; pile driver; hammer (*of piano*); (orn.) night heron; **martinete de báscula** tilt hammer
**martingala** *f* trick, cunning; **martingalas** *fpl* breeches worn under armor
**Martinica, la** Martinique
**martinico** *m* (coll.) goblin, ghost
**mártir** *mf* martyr
**martirio** *m* martyrdom
**martirizar §76** *va* to martyrize, to martyr
**martirologio** *m* martyrology
**márts.** abr. of **mártires**
**martucha** *f* (zool.) kinkajou
**Maruja** *f* (coll.) Mary
**marullo** *m* surge, swell
**marxismo** *m* Marxism
**marxista** *adj & mf* Marxian or Marxist
**marzal** *adj* (pertaining to) March
**marzo** *m* March
**marzoleta** *f* var. of **marjoleta**
**marzoleto** *m* var. of **marjoleto**
**mas** *conj* but
**más** *adv* more; most; longer; faster; rather; **a lo más** at most, at the most; **a más** besides, in addition; **a más de** besides, in addition to; **a más y mejor** hard, copiously; to one's heart's content; **como el que más** as the next one (*i.e., as any or anybody*); **cuando más** at the most; **de más** extra; too much, too many; **en más de** at more than + *numeral;* **en más que** more highly than; for more than; **estar de más** to be unnecessary, be superfluous; to be in the way; **los más de** most of, the majority of; **ni más ni menos** neither more nor less; **no . . . más** no longer; **no . . . más nada** nothing more; **no . . . más que** only; **poco más o menos** little more or less, practically; **por más que** however much, no matter how much; **más bien** rather; **más de** more than + *numeral;* **más que** more than; better than; although; **más y más** more and more, harder and harder; **sin más ni más** (coll.) suddenly, in a rush, just like that, without more ado; *prep* plus; *m* more; plus (*sign*); **tener sus más y sus menos** (coll.) to have one's (or its) good points and bad points
**masa** *f* mass; dough; mash; nature, disposition; (phys.) mass; (elec.) ground (*e.g., of an automobile*); (Am.) flesh (*e.g., of fruit*); **en masa** in the mass; en masse; mass, e.g., **la inoculación en masa** mass inoculation; **las masas** the masses; **masa crítica** (phys.) critical mass
**masacre** *m* massacre
**masada** *f* farmhouse
**masadero** *m* farmer
**masaje** *m* massage
**masajear** *va* to massage
**masajista** *m* masseur; *f* masseuse
**masar** *va* to knead; to massage
**mascabado -da** *adj & m* muscovado
**mascada** *f* chew; chewing; (Am.) silk handkerchief
**mascador -dora** *adj* chewing; *mf* chewer, masticator
**mascadura** *f* chewing; chew; (naut.) fretting, galling (*of a cable*)
**mascar §86** *va* to chew; (coll.) to mumble, to mutter; *vr* (naut.) to fret, to gall
**máscara** *f* mask; masquerade (*costume*); (fig.) mask; **máscaras** *fpl* masque, masquerade; **arrancar** or **quitar la máscara a** (fig.) to unmask; **quitarse la máscara** (fig.) to take off one's mask; **máscara antigás, máscara contra gases** or **máscara de gases** gas mask; **máscara de cabeza** head shield (*of welder*); **máscara de seguridad** safety mask; **máscara respiratoria** respirator; *mf* (coll.) mask, masquerader, mummer
**mascarada** *f* masquerade; party of masqueraders
**mascarero -ra** *mf* costumer
**mascareta** *f* little mask
**mascarilla** *f* little mask; half mask; false face (*funny*); death mask; **mascarilla contra gases asfixiantes** gas mask
**mascarón** *m* large mask; false face; fright (*ugly person*); (arch.) mask; **mascarón de proa** (naut.) figurehead
**mascota** *f* mascot
**mascujada** *f* (coll.) mumbling
**mascujar** *va & vn* (coll.) to chew poorly or hurriedly; (coll.) to mumble, to mutter
**masculinidad** *f* masculinity
**masculinizar §76** *va* (gram.) to make masculine
**masculino -na** *adj* masculine; (bot.) male; (gram.) masculine; *m* (gram.) masculine
**mascullar** *va & vn* (coll.) to mumble, to mutter; (coll.) to chew hurriedly
**masecoral** *m* or **masejicomar** *m* sleight of hand
**masera** *f* kneading trough; cover for kneading trough
**masería** *f* var. of **masada**
**masetero** *m* (anat.) masseter
**masía** *f* (prov.) farmhouse; (prov.) farm
**másico -ca** *adj* (phys.) (pertaining to) mass
**masicoral** *m* var. of **masecoral**
**masicote** *m* massicot
**masiliense** *adj* (pertaining to) Marseilles; *mf* native or inhabitant of Marseilles
**masilla** *f* putty
**masita** *f* (mil.) pittance withheld for shoes and clothes; (Am.) cake
**maslo** *m* root (*of the tail of a quadruped*); stem
**masón** *m* mess of dough for fowls; Mason
**masonería** *f* Masonry
**masónico -ca** *adj* Masonic
**masonita** *f* (mineral.) masonite; masonite (*fiberboard*)
**masoquismo** *m* (path.) masochism
**masoquista** *adj* masochistic; *mf* masochist
**mastelerillo** *m* (naut.) topgallant mast; **mastelerillo de juanete** (naut.) foretopgallant mast; **mastelerillo de mayor** (naut.) maintopgallant mast
**mastelero** *m* (naut.) topmast; **mastelero de mayor** (naut.) maintopmast; **mastelero de proa** or **de velacho** (naut.) foretopmast
**masticación** *f* mastication; (tech.) mastication
**masticador** *m* masticator (*machine*); salivant bit
**masticar §86** *va* to masticate; to meditate upon; to mumble; to cover with mastic; (tech.) to masticate (*e.g., rubber*)
**masticatorio -ria** *adj & m* masticatory
**mástico** *m* var. of **mástique**
**mastigador** *m* salivant bit
**mástil** *m* (naut.) mast; (mus.) neck (*of violin*); upright; stalk; stanchion; stem, shaft (*of feather*)
**mastín -tina** *mf* mastiff; (coll.) dolt, ignoramus; **mastín danés** Great Dane
**mástique** *m* mastic
**mastitis** *f* (path.) mastitis
**masto** *m* (prov.) stock (*on which a graft is made*); male animal, cock
**mastodonte** *m* (pal.) mastodon
**mastoidectomía** *f* (surg.) mastoidectomy
**mastoideo -a** *adj* (anat.) mastoid
**mastoides** *adj & f* (anat.) mastoid
**mastoiditis** *f* (path.) mastoiditis
**mastranto** or **mastranzo** *m* (bot.) horse mint, apple mint
**mastuerzo** *m* (bot.) cress, peppercress, peppergrass; simpleton, dolt
**masturbación** *f* masturbation
**masturbar** *vr* to masturbate
**masurio** *m* (chem.) masurium
**masvale** *m* var. of **malvasía**
**mat.** abr. of **matemática**
**mata** *f* bush, shrub; blade, sprig; head of hair, crop of hair; brush, underbrush; (bot.) mastic tree; (metal.) matte; **saltar de la mata** (coll.) to come out of hiding; **mata parda** (bot.) chaparro (*oak*); **mata rubia** (bot.) kermes, kermes oak
**matabuey** *m* (bot.) shrubby hare's-ear
**matacabras** *m* (*pl:* **-bras**) cold blast from the north
**matacán** *m* dog poison; nux vomica; cobblestone; (fort.) machicolation
**matacandelas** *m* (*pl:* **-las**) candle extinguisher

**matacandil** *m* (bot.) London rocket; (prov.) spiny lobster
**matacandiles** *m* (*pl:* **-les**) (bot.) star-of-Bethlehem
**matachín** *m* merry-andrew; dance of merry-andrews; slaughterman; (coll.) bully
**matachinada** *f* merry-andrewism, clowning; (coll.) concern
**matadero** *m* abattoir, slaughter house; danger spot; (coll.) drudgery
**matador -dora** *mf* killer; *m* (taur. & cards) matador; **matador de mujeres** lady-killer
**matadura** *f* sore, gall
**matafuego** *m* fire extinguisher; fireman
**matagallos** *m* (*pl:* **-llos**) (bot.) Jerusalem sage
**matajudío** *m* (ichth.) striped mullet
**matalahuga** or **matalahuva** *f* var. of **anís**
**mátalas callando** *mf* (coll.) schemer
**matalobos** *m* (*pl:* **-bos**) (bot.) wolf's-bane
**matalón -lona** *adj* skinny and full of sores (*said of a horse*); *mf* skinny old nag
**matalotaje** *m* (naut.) ship stores; (coll.) mess, jumble
**matalote** *adj & mf* var. of **matalón;** *m* (naut.) next ship (*forward or astern, in a column of ships*)
**matamalezas** *m* (*pl:* **-zas**) weed killer
**matamoros** *m* (*pl:* **-ros**) (coll.) bully, braggart
**matamoscas** *m* (*pl:* **-cas**) fly swatter; fly-paper, piece of flypaper
**matanza** *f* slaughter, slaughtering, butchering; massacre; slaughtering season; pork products; (coll.) concern
**mataperrada** *f* (coll.) prank of a street urchin
**mataperros** *m* (*pl:* **-rros**) (coll.) street urchin; (Am.) harum-scarum
**matapiojos** *m* (*pl:* **-jos**) (ent.) dragonfly
**matapolvo** *m* light rain, sprinkling
**matapulgas** *f* (*pl:* **-gas**) (bot.) horse mint, apple mint
**matar** *va* to kill; to butcher (*animals for food*); to put out (*a fire, a light*); to slack (*lime*); to lay (*dust*); to dull; to mat (*metal*); to tone down (*a color*); to round off (*e.g., rough edges*); to gall (*a horse*); to spot (*a card*); to play a card higher than; to ruin, to wreck; to slay, to bore to death; (fig.) to kill (*time, hunger, etc.*); *vn* to kill; **estar a matar con** to be very much annoyed at; to be on the outs with; *vr* to kill oneself; to be killed; to drudge, overwork; to be grieved, be disappointed; **matarse con** to quarrel with; **matarse por** to struggle for; **matarse por** + *inf* to struggle to + *inf*
**matarife** *m* butcher, slaughterman
**matarratas** *m* rat poison; (coll.) rotgut
**matarrubia** *f* (bot.) kermes, kermes oak
**matasanos** *m* (*pl:* **-nos**) (coll.) quack doctor
**matasellar** *va* to cancel (*stamps*); to postmark
**matasellos** *m* (*pl:* **-llos**) canceler (*of postage stamps*); postmark
**matasiete** *m* (*pl:* **-te**) (coll.) bully, braggart
**matatías** *m* (*pl:* **-as**) (coll.) moneylender, pawnbroker
**matazarzas** *m* (*pl:* **-zas**) weed killer
**mate** *adj* dull, flat; *m* checkmate; (bot.) maté (*plant, leaves, and tea*); maté gourd; **dar mate ahogado a** (chess) to stalemate; **mate ahogado** (chess) stalemate; **mate amargo** or **cimarrón** black or bitter maté; **dar mate a** to checkmate; to make fun of, laugh at
**matear** *va* to plant at regular intervals; to make dull; (Am.) to checkmate; *vr* to sprout (*said of wheat*); to hunt through the bushes (*said of a hunting dog*); (Am.) to drink maté
**matemático -ca** *adj* mathematical; (coll.) obvious, unquestionable, *mf* mathematician; *f* mathematics; **matemáticas** *fpl* mathematics
**Mateo** *m* Matthew
**materia** *f* matter; stuff, material; subject; (path.) matter (*pus*); **en materia de** in the matter of, as regards; **entrar en materia** to go into the matter; **primera materia** raw material; **materia colorante** dyestuff; **materia médica** materia medica (*remedial substances; branch of medicine*); **materia prima** raw material
**material** *adj* material; physical (*effort*); crude; *m* material; equipment, matériel; (mil.) matériel; (print.) matter, copy; **ser material** (coll.) to be immaterial; **material fijo** (rail.) permanent way; **material móvil** or **rodante** (rail.) rolling stock
**materialidad** *f* materiality, corporeity; outward appearance; literal meaning; crudeness, coarseness; literalness
**materialismo** *m* materialism
**materialista** *adj* materialistic; *mf* materialist; *m* dealer in building material
**materialización** *f* materialization (*e.g., of thought*)
**materializar** **§76** *va* to materialize (*e.g., thought*); to realize (*profit*); *vr* to become materialistic
**maternal** *adj* maternal, mother (*e.g., love*)
**maternidad** *f* maternity; motherhood; maternity (*maternity hospital*)
**materno -na** *adj* maternal, mother (*e.g., tongue*)
**Matías** *m* Matthias
**matidez** *f* dullness, flatness
**matihuelo** *m* tumbler (*toy figure*)
**Matilde** *f* Matilda
**matinal** *adj* matinal, morning
**matinée** *m & f* matinée (*afternoon performance*); dressing gown, wrapper
**matitez** *f* flatness (*of a sound*)
**matiz** *m* (*pl:* **-tices**) hue, shade, nuance; (fig.) shade
**matizar** **§76** *va* to blend; to match (*in color*); to shade (*colors, sounds, etc.*); to adorn, bedeck (*e.g., a speech*)
**mato** *m* var. of **matorral**
**matojo** *m* (bot.) salsolaceous shrub (*Haloxylon articulatum*)
**matón** *m* (coll.) bully, browbeater; **matón sopista** (coll.) poverty-stricken bully
**matonismo** *m* (coll.) bullying, browbeating
**matorral** *m* thicket, underbrush
**matoso -sa** *adj* dense, thick, brushy
**matraca** *f* noisemaker (*wooden rattle*); pestering, harassment; pest, bore; **dar matraca a** (coll.) to jeer at, to taunt
**matracalada** *f* mob
**matracar** **§86** *vn* (Am.) to pester, be a pest
**matraquear** *vn* (coll.) to make a racket; (coll.) to jeer, to taunt
**matraqueo** *m* (coll.) racket; (coll.) jeering, taunting
**matraquista** *mf* (coll.) jeerer, taunter
**matraz** *m* (*pl:* **-traces**) flask, matrass; **matraz de lavado** (chem.) wash bottle
**matrería** *f* cunning, shrewdness
**matrero -ra** *adj* cunning, shrewd
**matriarca** *f* matriarch
**matriarcado** *m* matriarchy
**matriarcal** *adj* matriarchal
**matricaria** *f* (bot.) feverfew
**matricida** *adj* matricidal; *mf* matricide (*person*)
**matricidio** *m* matricide (*act*)
**matrícula** *f* register, roll, roster; license; registry; matriculation, registration
**matriculado -da** *adj & mf* matriculate
**matricular** *va & vr* to register, enroll; to matriculate
**matrimonesco -ca** *adj* (hum.) matrimonial
**matrimonial** *adj* matrimonial
**matrimonialmente** *adv* as husband and wife
**matrimoniar** *vn* to marry, get married
**matrimonio** *m* matrimony; marriage; married couple; **matrimonio de compañerismo** companionate marriage; **matrimonio de la mano izquierda** left-handed marriage; **matrimonio civil** civil marriage; **matrimonio consensual** common-law marriage; **matrimonio morganático** morganatic marriage; **matrimonio putativo** (canon law) putative marriage; **matrimonio rato** unconsummated marriage
**matritense** *adj & mf* var. of **madrileño**
**matriz** (*pl:* **-trices**) *adj* main, mother, first; *f* matrix (*womb; mold; impression of phonograph record*); screw nut; original draft; stub (*e.g., of checkbook*); (anat., biol., geol. & math.) matrix
**matrona** *f* matron; midwife; (coll.) matronly lady; matron (*in jail, custom house, etc.*)
**matronal** *adj* matronal, matronly
**matronaza** *f* matron

**maturrango -ga** *adj* (Am.) clumsy, rough; *mf* poor rider; *f* cajolery, trickery; (coll.) prostitute
**Matusalén** *m* (Bib. & fig.) Methuselah; **vivir más años que Matusalén** to be as old as Methuselah
**matute** *m* smuggling; smuggled goods; gambling den
**matutear** *vn* to smuggle
**matutero -ra** *mf* smuggler
**matutinal** or **matutino -na** *adj* matutinal, morning
**maula** *f* junk, trash; remnant; trick, trickery; *mf* (coll.) tricky person, poor pay, lazy loafer
**maulería** *f* remnant shop; trickery, trickiness
**maulero -ra** *mf* remnant dealer; trickster, cheat
**maullador -dora** *adj* meowing
**maullar** §75 *vn* to meow
**maullido** or **maúllo** *m* meow
**Mauricio** *m* Maurice or Morris; **la isla Mauricio** or **la isla de Mauricio** Mauritius
**máuser** *m* Mauser
**mausoleo** *m* mausoleum
**maxila** *f* (anat. & zool.) maxilla
**maxilar** *adj* & *m* (anat.) maxillary
**máxima** *f* see **máximo**
**máxime** *adv* chiefly, principally, especially
**Maximiliano** *m* Maximilian
**máximo -ma** *adj* maximum; top; superlative, superb; *m* maximum; *f* maxim; principle
**máximum** *m* maximum
**maxvelio** *m* (elec.) maxwell
**may.** abr. of **mayúscula**
**maya** *adj* & *mf* Maya or Mayan; *f* May queen; clown; (bot.) English daisy; (bot.) pinguin
**mayador -dora** *adj* meowing
**mayal** *m* flail; horse-drawn shaft of conical stone (*of olive-oil mill*)
**mayar** *vn* var. of **maullar**
**mayear** *vn* to be like May (*said of weather*)
**mayestático -ca** *adj* of majesty, royal
**mayido** *m* meow
**may.$^{mo}$** abr. of **mayordomo**
**mayo** *m* May; Maypole; **mayos** *mpl* serenading on the eve of May day
**mayólica** *f* majolica
**mayonesa** *f* mayonnaise
**mayor** *adj* greater; larger; older, elder; greatest; largest; oldest, eldest; elderly; major; main (*e.g., street*); high (*altar, mass*); (log. & mus.) major; **ser mayor de edad** to be of age; *m* superior, chief, head; **mayores** *mpl* elders; ancestors, forefathers; (eccl.) major orders; **al por mayor** wholesale; **por mayor** wholesale; summarily; **mayor de edad** major (*person of legal age*); **mayor general** staff officer; *f* (log.) major premise
**mayoral** *m* foreman, boss; head shepherd; stagecoach driver; (Am.) trolley-car conductor
**mayoralía** *f* flock, herd; shepherd's wages
**mayorana** *f* var. of **mejorana**
**mayorazga** *f* female owner of an entailed estate; heiress to an entailed estate
**mayorazgo** *m* primogeniture; right of primogeniture; entailed estate descending by primogeniture; heir to an entailed estate; first-born son
**mayordoma** *f* stewardess, housekeeper; wife of major-domo or steward
**mayordomear** *va* to manage, administer (*a household or estate*)
**mayordomía** *f* major-domoship, stewardship
**mayordomo** *m* major-domo, steward, butler
**mayoría** *f* superiority; majority (*being of full age; larger number or part*); **alcanzar su mayoría de edad** to come of age; **mayoría de edad** majority
**mayoridad** *f* superiority; majority (*full age*)
**mayorista** *adj* wholesale; *m* wholesaler
**mayoritario -ria** *adj* (pertaining to the) majority
**mayormente** *adv* chiefly, mainly
**mayúsculo -la** *adj* capital (*letter*); large; (coll.) tremendous, awful; *f* capital letter
**maza** *f* mace (*weapon; staff*); maul; hemp brake; drop hammer; pile driver; tup (*of drop hammer or pile driver*); heavy drumstick; hub; thick end of billiard cue; rag tied as a joke on a person's clothes; stick tied to a dog's tail; astounding pronouncement; (coll.) bore; (coll.) oracle; **la maza y la mona** constant companions; **maza de fraga** drop hammer; **maza de gimnasia** Indian club; **maza sorda** (bot.) reed mace
**mazacote** *m* barilla, kali; concrete; crude piece of work; (coll.) tough, doughy food; (coll.) bore
**mazada** *f* blow with a mace or club; **dar mazada a** (coll.) to hurt, injure
**mazado** *m* churning
**mazagatos** *m* (coll.) rumpus, row, wrangle
**mazagrán** *m* cold coffee and rum
**mazamorra** *f* crumbs; thick corn soup; (naut.) mess of broken hardtack
**mazapán** *m* marchpane or marzipan
**mazar** §76 *va* to churn (*milk*)
**mazarí** *m* (*pl:* **-ríes**) floor brick or tile
**mazarota** *f* (found.) deadhead
**mazazo** *m* var. of **mazada**
**mazdeísmo** *m* Mazdaism
**mazdeísta** *adj* Mazdean; *mf* Mazdaist
**mazmorra** *f* dungeon, underground dungeon
**maznar** *va* to knead; to beat (*hot iron*)
**mazo** *m* mallet, maul; bunch; clapper (*of bell*); stack (*e.g., of cards*); bore
**mazonado -da** *adj* (her.) masoned
**mazonería** *f* stone masonry; relief
**mazonero** *m* stone mason
**mazorca** *f* spindleful; ear of corn; cocoa bean; (carp.) spindle (*in a baluster*); **comer maíz en** or **de la mazorca** to eat corn on the cob
**mazorquera** *f* (bot.) selfheal
**mazorral** *adj* coarse, crude, rough
**mazurca** *f* (mus.) mazourka or mazurka
**m/c** abr. of **mi cargo, mi cuenta & moneda corriente**
**m/cta** abr. of **mi cuenta**
**m/cte** abr. of **moneda corriente**
**M.$^{e}$** abr. of **Madre**
**me** *pron pers & reflex* (used as object of verb) me, to me; myself, to myself
**meada** *f* urination, water; spot made by urine
**meadero** *m* urinal
**meados** *mpl* urine
**meaja** *f* crumb; **meaja de huevo** tread (*of an egg*)
**meajuela** *f* slavering chain (*of bit*)
**meándrico -ca** *adj* meandrous, meandering
**meandro** *m* meander; (f.a.) meander; wandering speech or writing
**mear** *va* to urinate on; *vn* & *vr* to urinate
**meato** *m* (anat.) meatus
**meauca** *f* (orn.) shearwater
**Meca** *f* mecca or Mecca (*place sought by many people*); **La Meca** Mecca (*city*); **la Meca del cine** movieland
**mecachis** *interj* var. of **caramba**
**mecánica** *f* see **mecánico**
**mecanicismo** *m* (biol. & philos.) mechanism
**mecanicista** *adj* (biol. & philos.) mechanistic; *mf* (biol. & philos.) mechanist
**mecánico -ca** *adj* mechanical; (coll.) low, mean; *m* mechanic; machinist; workman, repairman; driver, chauffeur; *f* mechanics; machinery, works; (coll.) meanness; (coll.) contemptible thing; **mecánicas** *fpl* (coll.) chores, household chores; **mecánica celeste** (astr.) celestial mechanics; **mecánica cuántica** (phys.) quantum mechanics
**mecanismo** *m* mechanism; **mecanismo de disparo** or **mecanismo gatillo** trigger mechanism
**mecanización** *f* mechanization
**mecanizar** §76 *va* to mechanize
**mecano -na** *adj* & *mf* Meccan; *m* Erector set
**mecanografía** *f* typewriting; **mecanografía al tacto** touch typewriting
**mecanografiar** §90 *va* & *vn* to type, to typewrite
**mecanográfico -ca** *adj* typewriting
**mecanógrafo -fa** *mf* typist, typewriter
**mecanoterapia** *f* mechanotherapy
**mecapal** *m* (Am.) strap of fiber, bark, or leather
**mecapalero -ra** *mf* (Am.) porter, messenger
**mecate** *m* (Am.) packthread; (Am.) boor
**mecedero** *m* stirrer, shaker
**mecedor -dora** *adj* swinging, rocking; *m* stirrer, shaker; swing; *f* rocker, rocking chair

**mecedura** *f* swinging, rocking
**Mecenas** *m* Maecenas; (*l.c.*) *m* (*pl:* **-nas**) (fig.) Maecenas
**mecenazgo** *m* Maecenasship, patronage
**mecer** §61 *va* to stir, to shake; to swing, to rock; *vr* to swing, to rock
**meconio** *m* meconium; poppy juice
**mecha** *f* wick; fuse, match; tinder; lock of hair; interlarding of bacon; bundle (*of threads*)
**mechar** *va* (cook.) to lard, to interlard
**mechazo** *m* (min.) fizzle (*of a blast fuse*); **dar mechazo** to fizzle
**mechera** *f* shoplifter (*woman*); larding pin
**mechero** *m* burner; socket (*of candlestick*); pocket lighter; jet; **mechero de gas** gas burner; **mechero de mariposa** fantail (*burner*); **mechero encendedor** pilot, pilot light (*e.g., of a gas stove*)
**mechinal** *m* putlog hole; (coll.) hovel
**mechón** *m* shock of hair; tuft, mop, shock
**mechoso -sa** *adj* thready, towy; shockheaded
**medalla** *f* medal; medallion
**medallero** *m* medal cabinet
**medallista** *mf* medalist (*engraver of medals*)
**medallón** *m* medallion; locket
**médano** *m* sandbank, dune
**medanoso -sa** *adj* sandy, duny
**medaño** *m* var. of **médano**
**media** *f* see **medio**
**mediacaña** *f* trochilus, scotia; gouge; half-round file; curling tongs (*for hair*); (print.) double rule
**mediación** *f* mediation; (astr., dipl. & mus.) mediation
**mediado -da** *adj* half-full; half over, e.g., **iba mediada la tarde** the afternoon was half over; **a mediados de** about the middle of
**mediador -dora** *adj* mediating, mediatorial; *mf* mediator; **mediador de cambio** medium of exchange
**medial** *adj* (bot. & zool.) median; (phonet.) medial
**mediana** *f* see **mediano**
**medianejo -ja** *adj* (coll.) fair to middling
**medianería** *f* party wall; party-line fence or hedge
**medianero -ra** *adj* middle, dividing; mediating; *mf* mediator; *m* owner of an adjoining house
**medianía** *f* halfway; moderate circumstances; mediocrity (*person*); (Am.) partition wall
**medianidad** *f* var. of **medianía**
**medianil** *m* sloping land or field; party wall
**mediano -na** *adj* middling, medium; average, fair, fairly good; (bot. & zool.) median; (coll.) mediocre; *m* (anat.) median; *f* long billiard cue; (geom.) median
**medianoche** *f* midnight; (*pl:* **mediasnoches**) *f* meat pie
**mediante** *adj* intervening; **Dios mediante** God willing; *prep* by means of, through
**mediar** *va* to make half-full; *vn* to be or get halfway; to be half over; to be in the middle; to mediate, to intervene; to elapse; to take place
**mediastino** *m* (anat.) mediastinum
**mediatamente** *adv* mediately, indirectly
**mediatinta** *f* (paint. & phot.) half-tone
**mediatizar** §76 *va* to control, get control of; to make a puppet of (*a government*)
**mediato -ta** *adj* mediate
**mediator** *m* ombre (*card game*)
**medible** *adj* measurable
**médica** *f* see **médico**
**medicable** *adj* medicable
**medicación** *f* medication
**medical** *adj* medical
**medicamento** *m* medicament, medicine; **medicamentos sulfas** (pharm.) sulfa drugs
**medicamentoso -sa** *adj* medicinal
**medicar** §86 *va* (archaic) to treat, to medicate (*a patient*); *vr* (archaic) to treat oneself, to doctor oneself
**medicastro** *m* (coll.) medicaster, quack
**medicina** *f* medicine (*science and art; remedy*); **medicina del espacio** space medicine; **medicina doméstica** home remedies; **medicina interna** internal medicine; **medicina preventiva** or **profiláctica** preventive medicine; **medicina social** socialized medicine; **medicina veterinaria** veterinary medicine
**medicinal** *adj* medicinal
**medicinamiento** *m* treatment, medication
**medicinante** *m* quack, healer; medical student who treats patients
**medicinar** *va* to treat (*a sick person*)
**medición** *f* measuring, measurement; metering
**médico -ca** *adj* medical; *m* doctor, physician; **médico de cabecera** family physician; **médico de plaza** bullring physician; **médico general** general practitioner; **médico partero** obstetrician; *f* woman doctor; doctor's wife
**médicolegal** *adj* medicolegal
**médicoquirúrgico -ca** *adj* medicochirurgical
**medicucho** *m* (coll.) var. of **medicastro**
**medida** *f* measurement; measure; step; moderation; (pros.) measure; **a medida de** in proportion to; according to; **a medida que** in proportion as; **en la medida que** to the extent that; **hecho a la medida** custom-made; **llenarse la medida** to drain the cup of sorrow; **tomarle a uno las medidas** to take one's measure; **tomar sus medidas** to size up a situation; **medida para áridos** dry measure; **medida para líquidos** liquid measure
**medidamente** *adv* with moderation
**medidor -dora** *adj* measuring; *mf* measurer; *m* gauge; (Am.) meter
**mediero -ra** *mf* hosier, stocking maker or dealer; stocking knitter; partner (*in farming or stock raising*); (Am.) partner (*in business*)
**medieval** *adj* medieval
**medievalidad** *f* medievalism (*medieval quality or nature*)
**medievalismo** *m* medievalism
**medievalista** *mf* medievalist
**medievo** *m* Middle Ages
**medina** *f* (Arab.) large city, metropolis
**medio -dia** *adj* half, half a, e.g., **media manzana** half an apple; a half, e.g., **media libra** a half pound; middle, intermediate; medium; medieval (*times*); mean, average; mid, e.g., **a media tarde** in mid afternoon; in the middle of, e.g., **a media comida** in the middle of the meal; **a medias** half-and-half, e.g., **dinero adquirido a medias por dos personas** money acquired half-and-half by two persons; half, e.g., **dueño a medias** half owner; **dormido a medias** half asleep; **ir a medias** to go halves, to go fifty-fifty ‖ **medio** *adv* half, e.g., **medio muerto** half dead; **medio . . . medio** half . . . half ‖ *m* (arith.) half; middle; medium, environment; step, measure; means; medium, spiritualistic medium; (bot. & bact.) medium; (baseball) shortstop; **medios** *mpl* means; (taur.) center (*of ring*); **a medio** half, e.g., **a medio vestir** half dressed; **de medio a medio** half-and-half; smack, plump; completely; **de por medio** half; in between, halfway; **desde en medio de** from the middle of; **echar por en medio** (coll.) to take the bull by the horns; **en medio** in the middle; in the meantime; **en medio de** in the middle of; in the midst of; in spite of; **entrar de por medio** to intercede; **estar de por medio** to mediate; **justo medio** happy medium, golden mean; **meterse de por medio** to intercede; **por medio de** by means of, through; **quitar de en medio** (coll.) to do away with, to get out of the way, to put out of the way; **quitarse de en medio** (coll.) to get out, get out of the way, duck; **tomar los medios** to take measures ‖ *f* stocking; half past, e.g., **las tres y media** half past three; (math.) mean; **dar la media** to strike half past; **media diferencial** (math.) arithmetical mean; **media media** or **media corta** (Am.) sock; **media proporcional** (math.) mean proportional, geometric mean; **medias de cristal** nylons, nylon stockings
**mediocre** *adj* mediocre, medium
**mediocridad** *f* mediocrity; mediocre circumstances
**mediodía** *m* noon, midday; south; (naut.) south wind; **en pleno mediodía** at broad noon; **hacer mediodía** to stop for the noon meal; **mediodía medio** (astr.) mean noon
**medioeval** *adj* var. of **medieval**

**medioevo** *m* Middle Ages
**mediooeste** *m* Middle West (*of the U.S.A.*)
**medio-oriental** *adj* Middle Eastern
**mediopaño** *m* light wool cloth
**mediquillo** *m* (coll.) medicaster, quack; Philippine Indian quack
**medir** **§94** *va* to measure; to scan (*verse*); *vn* to measure; *vr* to be moderate, act with moderation
**meditabundo -da** *adj* meditative
**meditación** *f* meditation
**meditador -dora** *adj* meditating, meditative
**meditar** *va* to meditate; to contemplate, to plan (*e.g., an escape*); *vn* to meditate
**meditativo -va** *adj* meditative
**Mediterráneo -a** *adj & m* Mediterranean
**médium** *mf* (*pl:* **-dium** or **-diums**) medium, spiritualistic medium
**mediúmnico -ca** *adj* mediumistic
**mediumnismo** *m* spiritualism
**medo -da** *adj* Median; *mf* Mede, Median
**medra** *f* growth, thriving, prosperity
**medrador -dora** *mf* schemer, person who is on the make
**medrana** *f* (coll.) fear
**medrar** *vn* to grow, thrive, prosper; **¡medrados estamos!** now look what's happened!
**medregal** *m* (ichth.) amberfish, pilot fish
**medriñaque** *m* medrinaque (*cloth used as padding for women's garments*); short peasant skirt
**medro** *m* growth, thriving; **medros** *mpl* progress, improvement
**medroso -sa** *adj* fearful, timid; dreadful, terrible
**medula** or **médula** *f* (anat.) medulla, marrow; (bot.) medulla, pith; (fig.) marrow, essence, gist; **medula espinal** (anat.) spinal cord; **medula oblonga** or **oblongada** (anat.) medulla oblongata
**medular** *adj* medullary; (fig.) pithy, marrowy
**meduloso -sa** *adj* marrowy; (bot.) pithy
**medusa** *f* (zool.) medusa, jellyfish; (*cap.*) *f* (myth.) Medusa
**medusar** *va* to frighten, scare
**Mefistófeles** *m* Mephistopheles
**mefistofélico -ca** *adj* Mephistophelian
**mefítico -ca** *adj* mephitic
**mefitis** *f* mephitis
**megaciclo** *m* (rad.) megacycle
**megáfono** *m* megaphone
**megalítico -ca** *adj* megalithic
**megalito** *m* (archeol.) megalith
**megalocéfalo -la** *adj* megalocephalous
**megalomanía** *f* (psychopath.) megalomania
**megalómano -na** *adj* megalomaniacal; *mf* megalomaniac
**megalosaurio** *m* (pal.) megalosaur
**mégano** *m* var. of **médano**
**megaterio** *m* (pal.) megathere
**megatón** *m* or **megatonelada** *f* megaton
**mego -ga** *adj* meek, gentle
**megohmio** *m* (elec.) megohm
**mehara** *m* or **mehari** *m* var. of **meharí**
**meharí** *m* (*pl:* **-ríes**) mehari (*swift African dromedary*)
**mehedí** *m* (*pl:* **-díes**) Mahdi
**Mej.** abr. of **Méjico**
**mejana** *f* islet (*in a river*)
**mejicanismo** *m* Mexicanism
**mejicano -na** *adj & mf* Mexican
**Méjico** *m* Mexico; **Nuevo Méjico** New Mexico; *f* Mexico City
**mejido -da** *adj* beaten with sugar and milk (*said of eggs*)
**mejilla** *f* cheek
**mejillón** *m* (zool.) mussel
**mejor** *adj* better; best; highest (*bidder*); *adv* better; best; rather; **a lo mejor** (coll.) like as not; (coll.) worse luck; **mejor dicho** rather; **mejor que** rather than; **mejor que mejor** all the better; **tanto mejor** so much the better
**mejora** *f* growth, improvement; alteration, renovation; higher bid; additional bequests
**mejorable** *adj* ameliorable, improvable
**mejoramiento** *m* amelioration, improvement
**mejorana** *f* (bot.) sweet marjoram
**mejorante** *m* ameliorant, improver
**mejorar** *va* to make better, to improve; to mend; to raise (*a bid*); to leave an additional bequest to; *vn & vr* to get better, to recover; to mend; to clear up (*said of weather*); to get along, to progress
**mejoría** *f* improvement (*in success, health, etc.*)
**mejunje** *m* mess, mixture, brew
**melado -da** *adj* honey-colored; *m* (Am.) thick cane syrup; honey cake sprinkled with seeds; *f* toast dipped in honey; dried marmalade
**meladora** *f* (Am.) last sugar-boiling pan
**meladucha** *f* coarse, mealy apple
**meladura** *f* concentrated cane syrup
**meláfido** or **meláfiro** *m* (geol.) melaphyre
**melámpiro** *m* (bot.) cowwheat
**melampo** *m* (theat.) prompter's candle or light
**melancolía** *f* melancholy; (path.) melancholia
**melancólico -ca** *adj* melancholy, melancholic; (path.) melancholic
**melancolizar** **§76** *va* to sadden, to give a melancholy aspect to; *vr* to become sad, become melancholy
**melanesio -sia** *adj & mf* Melanesian; **la Melanesia** Melanesia
**melanita** *f* (mineral.) melanite
**melanoma** *m* (path.) melanoma
**melanosis** *f* (path.) melanosis
**melapia** *f* pippin, pearmain
**melar** *adj* honey-sweet; **§18** *va* to fill (*combs*) with honey; *vn* to become filled with honey; to boil sugar-cane juice clear
**melaza** *f* molasses
**Melburna** *f* Melbourne
**melca** *f* (bot.) sorghum
**melcocha** *f* taffy, molasses candy
**melcochero -ra** *mf* maker or seller of molasses candy
**melchor** *m* German silver, nickel silver; (*cap.*) *m* Melchior
**melducha** *f* coarse mealy apple
**meleagrina** *f* (zool.) pearl oyster
**Meleagro** *m* (myth.) Meleager
**melena** *f* long lock of hair (*falling over face or eyes*); long hair (*falling over shoulders*); loose hair (*unbound*); mane (*of lion*); forelock (*of horse*); (path.) melena; **andar a la melena** (coll.) to pull each other's hair; (coll.) to get into a hot argument; **estar en melena** (coll.) to have one's hair down; **hacer venir** or **traer a la melena** (coll.) to put the screws on; **venir a la melena** (coll.) to yield, to give in
**melenera** *f* forehead of an ox; yoke pad
**meleno** *m* (coll.) peasant, rustic
**melenudo -da** *adj* shockheaded, bushy-headed
**melero -ra** *adj* honeyed; *mf* dealer in honey; *m* storage place for honey; *f* damage or rot of melons from rain or hail; (bot.) oxtongue
**melgacho** *m* (ichth.) spotted dogfish
**melgar** *m* field of medic or lucerne
**melgo -ga** *adj* twin
**meliáceo -a** *adj* meliaceous
**mélico -ca** *adj* melic
**melificado -da** *adj* var. of **melifluo**
**melificar** **§86** *va* to make or draw honey from (*flowers*); *vn* to make honey
**melifluencia** *f* mellifluence
**melifluidad** *f* mellifluence, mellifluousness
**melifluo -flua** *adj* mellifluent or mellifluous
**meliloto -ta** *adj* simple, stupid; *mf* simpleton, dolt; *m* (bot.) melilot, sweet clover
**melindre** *m* honey fritter; ladyfinger; tape, narrow ribbon; **melindres** *mpl* finickiness, prudery
**melindrear** *vn* to be finicky, be prudish
**melindrería** *f* finickiness, prudery
**melindrero -ra** *adj* var. of **melindroso**
**melindrizar** **§76** *vn* var. of **melindrear**
**melindroso -sa** *adj* finicky, prudish
**melinita** *f* melinite
**melisa** *f* (bot.) lemon balm, garden balm
**melito** *m* (pharm.) hydromel
**melocotón** *m* (bot.) peach, peach tree; peach (*fruit*); **melocotón en almíbar** canned peaches
**melocotonar** *m* peach orchard
**melocotonero** *m* (bot.) peach tree
**melodía** *f* melody

**melódico -ca** *adj* melodic
**melodión** *m* (mus.) melodeon
**melodioso -sa** *adj* melodious
**melodista** *mf* melodist
**melodrama** *m* melodrama
**melodramático -ca** *adj* melodramatic
**meloe** *m* (ent.) oil beetle
**melografía** *f* art of writing music
**meloja** *f* honey water
**melojar** *m* growth of pubescent oak trees
**melojo** *m* (bot.) pubescent oak, durmast
**melolonta** *m* (ent.) cockchafer
**melomanía** *f* melomania, love of music
**melómano -na** *mf* melomane, melomaniac, music lover
**melón** *m* (bot.) muskmelon; melon (*fruit*); dolt, ignoramus; (coll.) bald head; (zool.) ichneumon; **catar el melón** (coll.) to sound a person out; (coll.) to see what something is like; **decentar el melón** (coll.) to take a big risk; **melón de agua** watermelon; **melón de costa** (bot.) Turk's-head
**melonar** *m* melon patch
**meloncillo** *m* (zool.) ichneumon
**melonero -ra** *mf* melon raiser or dealer
**melonzapote** *m* (bot.) papaya, papaw
**melopeya** *f* (mus.) melopoeia
**melosa** *f* see **meloso**
**melosidad** *f* mildness, sweetness, mellowness
**melosilla** *f* oak blight
**meloso -sa** *adj* honeyed; mild, sweet, mellow; *f* (bot.) Chilean tarweed
**Melpómene** *f* (myth.) Melpomene
**melsa** *f* sloth, phlegm
**meltón** *m* melton
**mella** *f* nick, dent, notch; gap, hollow; harm, injury; **hacer mella a** to have an effect on; **hacer mella en** to harm, injure (*e.g., a reputation*)
**mellado -da** *adj* snaggle-toothed
**mellar** *va* to nick, dent, notch; to harm, injure (*honor, credit, etc.*); *vr* to nick, dent; to be harmed, be injured
**mellizo -za** *adj & mf* twin; *f* honey sausage
**mellón** *m* straw torch
**memada** *f* (coll.) piece of folly
**membrado -da** *adj* (her.) membered
**membrana** *f* (bot. & zool.) membrane; (telp. & rad.) diaphragm; **membrana fónica** (telp.) diaphragm; **membrana mucosa** (anat.) mucous membrane; **membrana pituitaria** (anat.) pituitary membrane; **membrana serosa** (anat.) serous membrane; **membrana timpánica** (anat.) tympanic membrane
**membranáceo -a** *adj* membranaceous
**membranoso -sa** *adj* membranous
**membrete** *m* letterhead; heading; address; invitation; note, memo
**membrillar** *m* quince-tree orchard; (bot.) quince tree
**membrillate** *m* quince preserves
**membrillero** *m* (bot.) quince tree
**membrillo** *m* (bot.) quince (*tree and fruit*)
**membrudo -da** *adj* burly, husky
**memeches; a memeches** (Am.) astride, on horseback
**memela** *f* (Am.) corn-meal pancake
**memento** *m* (eccl.) Memento
**memez** *f* (dial.) folly, nonsense
**memiso** *m* (bot.) calabur tree
**Memnón** *m* (myth.) Memnon
**memo -ma** *adj* simple, foolish; *mf* simpleton, fool
**memorable** *adj* memorable
**memoráculo** *m* memorial (*e.g., a monument*)
**memorando -da** *adj* var. of **memorable**
**memorándum** *m* (*pl:* **-dum**) memorandum; letterhead (*paper with letterhead*); professional services (*section of newspaper advertisements*); (Am.) certificate of deposit
**memorar** *va & vr* to remember
**memoratísimo -ma** *adj super* eternally remembered
**memoria** *f* memory; memoir; account, record; **memorias** *fpl* memoirs; regards; **de memoria** by heart; (prov.) with one's mouth wide-open; **encomendar a la memoria** to commit to memory; **en memoria de** in memory of; **hablar de memoria** (coll.) to say the first thing that comes to one's mind; **hacer memoria de** to bring up
**memorial** *m* memorandum book; memorial (*written statement making a petition*); (law) brief; **haber perdido los memoriales** (coll.) to have forgotten, to have lost the thread
**memorialista** *m* amanuensis
**memorión** *m* (coll.) terrific memory
**memorioso -sa** *adj* retentive, of retentive memory
**memorístico -ca** *adj* (pertaining to) memory
**memorizar §76** *va* to memorize
**mena** *f* (ichth.) picarel; (min.) ore; (naut.) size or thickness of cordage
**ménade** *f* (hist. & fig.) maenad
**menaje** *m* household furniture; school supplies
**Mencio** *m* Mencius
**mención** *f* mention; **en mención** in question, under discussion; **hacer mención de** to make mention of; **mención honorífica** honorable mention
**mencionar** *va* to mention
**menchevique** *m* Menshevik
**mendacidad** *f* mendacity
**mendaz** (*pl:* **-daces**) *adj* mendacious; *mf* liar
**mendelevio** *m* (chem.) mendelevium
**mendeliano -na** *adj* Mendelian
**mendelismo** *m* Mendelism, Mendelianism
**mendicación** *f* begging
**mendicante** *adj & mf* mendicant
**mendicidad** *f* mendicancy, mendicity
**mendiganta** *f* woman beggar
**mendigante** *adj* begging, mendicant; *mf* beggar, mendicant
**mendigar §59** *va* to beg, to beg for; *vn* to beg
**mendigo -ga** *mf* beggar
**mendiguez** *f* begging, beggary
**mendoso -sa** *adj* false, lying; mistaken, wrong
**mendrugo** *m* crust, crumb (*especially that given to beggars*)
**menear** *va* to stir; to shake; to wag; to wiggle; to manage; **peor es meneallo** (*i.e.,* **menearlo**) (coll.) better let it alone, the less said the better; *vr* to shake; to wag; to wiggle; (coll.) to hustle, bestir oneself
**menegilda** *f* (coll.) servant, housemaid
**Menelao** *m* (myth.) Menelaus
**meneo** *m* stirring; shaking; wagging; wiggling; hustling; (coll.) drubbing, flogging
**menester** *m* want, lack; need; job, occupation; **menesteres** *mpl* bodily needs; property; (coll.) tools, implements; **haber menester** to need; **ser menester** to be necessary; **ser menester** + *inf* to be necessary to + *inf*
**menesteroso -sa** *adj* needy; *mf* needy person
**menestra** *f* vegetable soup, vegetable stew; (coll.) hodgepodge; **menestras** *fpl* dried vegetables
**menestral -trala** *mf* artisan, mechanic
**menestralería** *f* artisanship
**menestralía** *f* artisans, mechanics (*as a group or class*)
**menestrete** *m* (naut.) nail puller
**Menfis** *f* Memphis
**meng.** abr. of **menguante**
**mengano -na** *mf* (coll.) so-and-so
**mengua** *f* diminution; decline, decay; want, lack; poverty; discredit; **en mengua de** to the discredit of; to the detriment of
**menguado -da** *adj* timid, cowardly; silly, foolish; mean, stingy; fatal; *m* drop stitch
**menguamiento** *m* var. of **mengua**
**menguante** *adj* diminishing; declining; waning; *f* decay, decline; low water; ebb tide; **menguante de la luna** waning of the moon
**menguar §23** *va* to lessen, diminish; to defame; *vn* to lessen, diminish; to decline, decay; to drop-stitch; to wane (*said of the moon*); to fall (*said of the tide*)
**mengue** *m* (coll.) devil
**menhir** *m* (archeol.) menhir
**menina** *f* young lady in waiting, maid of honor
**meníngeo -a** *adj* meningeal
**meninges** *fpl* (anat.) meninges
**meningitis** *f* (path.) meningitis; **meningitis cerebroespinal** (path.) cerebrospinal meningitis
**meningococo** *m* (bact.) meningococcus
**menino** *m* noble page of the royal family

**menique** *adj & m* (archaic) var. of **meñique**
**menisco** *m* (anat., opt. & phys.) meniscus
**menispermáceo -a** *adj* (bot.) menispermaceous
**menjuí** *m* var. of **benjuí**
**menjunje** *m* or **menjurje** *m* var. of **mejunje**
**menonita** *adj & mf* Mennonite
**menopausia** *f* (physiol.) menopause
**menor** *adj* less, lesser; smaller; younger; least; smallest; youngest; minor; (log. & mus.) minor; **menor de edad** minor; *m* minor; (eccl.) Minorite; **al por menor** retail; **por menor** retail; in detail, minutely; **menor de edad** minor; *f* (log.) minor premise
**Menorca** *f* Minorca
**menorete; al menorete** or **por el menorete** (coll.) at least
**menoría** *f* inferiority, subordination; minority (*time of being under age*)
**menorista** *mf* (Am.) retailer, retail dealer
**menorquín -quina** *adj & mf* Minorcan; *m* Minorcan (*dialect*)
**menorragia** *f* (path.) menorrhagia
**menos** *adv* less; fewer; lower; least; fewest; lowest; rather not; **al menos** at least; **a menos que** unless; **a lo menos** at least; **de menos** less, e.g., **un dólar de menos** a dollar less; **echar de menos** or **echar menos** to miss; **en menos que** at less than; **ir a menos** to be scarce; **lo menos** at least; **los** (or **las**) **menos** the fewest; **no poder menos de** + *inf* to not be able to help + *ger;* **no ser para menos** to be good cause, to be good reason, to not be surprising; **por lo menos** at least; **tener a menos** or **en menos** + *inf* to deem it beneath one to + *inf;* **tener en menos** to think little of; **venir a menos** to decay, to decline; **menos de** less than + *numeral;* **¡menos mal!** lucky you!, lucky break!, it might be worse!; **menos mal que** it's a good thing that; **menos que** less than ‖ *prep* less, minus; except; of or to (*in telling time*), e.g., **las dos menos cuarto** a quarter of two ‖ *m* minus (*sign*)
**menoscabar** *va* to lessen, reduce; to damage, spoil; to discredit
**menoscabo** *m* lessening, reduction; damage, loss; detriment, discredit
**menoscuenta** *f* part payment (*of a debt*)
**menospreciable** *adj* despicable, contemptible
**menospreciador -dora** *adj* scornful, contemptuous; *mf* scorner, despiser
**menospreciar** *va* to underestimate, undervalue; to scorn, despise
**menospreciativo -va** *adj* scornful, contemptuous
**menosprecio** *m* underestimation, undervaluation; scorn, contempt
**mensaje** *m* message; errand; **mensaje cifrado** cipher message
**mensajería** *f* stagecoach, public conveyance; **mensajerías** *fpl* transportation company; express service; express; shipping line; shipping office; **mensajerías** *msg* freight train
**mensajero -ra** *mf* messenger; *m* harbinger; freight train
**menso -sa** *adj* (Am.) silly, disagreeable
**menstruación** *f* menstruation
**menstrual** *adj* (physiol.) menstrual
**menstruar** §33 *vn* to menstruate
**menstruo -trua** *adj* menstruous; *m* menstruation; menses; (chem.) menstruum
**menstruoso -sa** *adj* menstruous
**mensual** *adj* menstrual, monthly; *f* monthly, monthly periodical
**mensualidad** *f* monthly pay, monthly allowance, monthly instalment
**ménsula** *f* brace, bracket; elbow rest; (arch.) corbel
**mensurabilidad** *f* mensurability
**mensurable** *adj* mensurable
**mensuración** *f* mensuration
**mensural** *adj* mensural
**mensurar** *va* to measure
**menta** *f* (bot.) mint; **menta romana** or **verde** (bot.) spearmint
**mentado -da** *adj* famed, renowned
**mental** *adj* mental
**mentalidad** *f* mentality, psychology
**mentalismo** *m* mind reading, clairvoyance
**mentalista** *mf* mind reader, clairvoyant
**mentar** §18 *va* to name, to mention
**mentastro** *m* (bot.) horse mint, apple mint
**mente** *f* mind; **leer mentes** to read minds; **tener en la mente** to have in mind
**mentecatería** or **mentecatez** *f* simpleness, folly
**mentecato -ta** *adj* simple, foolish; *mf* simpleton, fool
**mentidero** *m* (coll.) gathering place to talk and loaf
**mentido -da** *adj* false, deceptive
**mentidor -dora** *adj* false, lying; *mf* liar
**mentir** §62 *va* to disappoint, to fail to keep (*a promise*); *vn* to lie; to be false, be deceptive; to clash (*said of a color*); **¡miento!** my mistake!, my error!
**mentira** *f* lie; story, fiction; illusion, vanity; mistake, error; (coll.) white spot (*on fingernails*); (Am.) cracking of knuckles; **coger en una mentira** to catch in a lie; **de mentiras** in jest; **parece mentira** it's hard to believe; **mentira inocente** or **oficiosa** white lie
**mentirijillas; de mentirijillas** in fun, in jest; for fun (*not for money*)
**mentirilla** *f* fib, white lie; **de mentirillas** in fun, in jest; for fun (*not for money*)
**mentirón** *m* whopper, big lie
**mentiroso -sa** *adj* lying; full of mistakes; *mf* liar
**mentís** *m* (*pl:* **-tís**) insult; lie, flat denial; **dar un mentís a** to give the lie to
**mentol** *m* (chem.) menthol
**mentolado -da** *adj* mentholated
**mentón** *m* chin
**mentor** *m* mentor; (*cap.*) *m* (myth.) Mentor
**menú** *m* (*pl:* **-nús**) menu
**menuceles** *mpl* tithe of minor fruits
**menudamente** *adv* minutely, in detail; at retail
**menudear** *va* to do frequently, to repeat frequently; to tell in detail; (Am.) to sell at retail; *vn* to be frequent, to happen frequently; to rain, come down in abundance; to go into detail
**menudencia** *f* smallness; minuteness; meticulousness; trifle; **menudencias** *fpl* pork products; (Am.) giblets
**menudeo** *m* constant repetition; detailed account; retail; **al menudeo** at retail
**menudero -ra** *mf* retailer
**menudillo** *m* fetlock joint; **menudillos** *mpl* giblets
**menudo -da** *adj* small, slight; minute; common, vulgar; petty; futile, worthless; meticulous; *m* small change; rice coal; blood and entrails of beef; edible portions of fowl; tithe of minor fruits; **menudos** *mpl* small change; **a menudo** often; **por menudo** in detail; at retail
**menuzo** *m* bit, fragment, small piece
**meñique** *adj* little (*finger*); (coll.) little, tiny; *m* little finger
**meollar** *m* (naut.) spun yarn
**meollo** *m* (anat.) marrow; (bot.) pith; brain; brains, intelligence; marrow, gist, essence
**meolludo -da** *adj* marrowy; brainy, intelligent
**meón -ona** *adj* urinating, constantly urinating; dripping (*e.g., fog*); *f* newborn female infant
**meque** *m* slap, rap (*with the knuckles*)
**mequetrefe** *m* (coll.) whippersnapper, jackanapes
**merar** *va* to mix, to blend
**merca** *f* (coll.) purchase
**mercachifle** *m* peddler; small dealer
**mercachiflear** *vn* (coll.) to deal on a shoestring
**mercadear** *vn* to deal, to trade
**mercader -dera** *mf* merchant, dealer; **mercader de grueso** wholesale merchant; *f* tradeswoman; merchant's wife
**mercadería** *f* commodity; **mercaderías** *fpl* goods, merchandise; ledger
**mercado** *m* market; market place; **lanzar al mercado** to put on the market; **mercado bursátil** or **de valores** stock market; **Mercado Común Europeo** European Common Market; **mercado negro** black market
**mercadotecnia** *f* marketing
**mercaduría** *f* commodity
**mercal** *m* (Am.) tequila (*liquor*)

**mercancía** *f* trade, dealing; merchandise; piece of merchandise; **mercancías** *fpl* goods, merchandise; **mercancías** *msg* freight train
**mercante** *adj* merchant; *m* merchant; (naut.) merchantman
**mercantil** *adj* mercantile; mercenary
**mercantilismo** *m* mercantilism
**mercantilista** *adj & mf* mercantilist
**mercar** §86 *va* to buy, purchase
**merced** *f* favor, grace; mercy (*power, discretion*); **a merced** or **a mercedes** without pay, voluntarily; **estar a la merced de** to be at the mercy of; **muchas mercedes** many thanks; **vuestra merced** your grace, your honor, your worship; **merced a** thanks to; **merced de agua** free distribution of irrigating water
**mercedario -ria** *adj* of the Mercedarians; *mf* Mercedarian
**Mercedes** *f* Mercedes (*feminine name*)
**mercenario -ria** *adj* (mil. & fig.) mercenary; *mf* Mercedarian; *m* (mil.) mercenary; day laborer; salaried employee
**mercería** *f* haberdashery (*notions; notions store*); (Am.) dry-goods store; (Am.) hardware store
**mercerizar** §76 *va* to mercerize
**mercero** *m* haberdasher, notions dealer or clerk; (Am.) dry-goods merchant; (Am.) hardware merchant
**merciano -na** *adj & mf* Mercian
**mercología** *f* marketing (*transaction of business; study of the phenomena of the transaction of business*)
**mercológico -ca** *adj* (pertaining to) marketing
**merc.**[s] abr. of **mercaderías**
**mercurial** *adj* mercurial; (astr. & myth.) Mercurial; *m* (pharm.) mercurial; *f* (bot.) herb mercury
**mercurialismo** *m* (path.) mercurialism
**mercúrico -ca** *adj* (chem.) mercuric
**mercurio** *m* (chem.) mercury; (*cap.*) *m* (astr. & myth.) Mercury
**mercurioso -sa** *adj* (chem.) mercurous
**mercurocromo** *m* mercurochrome
**merdellón -llona** *mf* (coll.) sloppy servant
**merdoso -sa** *adj* (coll.) dirty, filthy
**merecedor -dora** *adj* deserving
**merecer** §34 *va* to deserve, to merit; to be worth; to win (*praise*); to attain (*one's goal*); **merecer** + *inf* to deserve to + *inf;* **merecer la pena** to be worth while; *vn* to deserve, be deserving; **merecer bien de** to deserve the gratitude of; *vr* to be fertile (*said of sheep*)
**merecido -da** *adj* deserved; *m* just deserts; **llevar su merecido** to get what's coming to one
**mereciente** *adj* deserving
**merecimiento** *m* desert, merit
**merendar** §18 *va* to lunch on, to have for lunch; to keep an eye on, to peep at; *vn* to lunch, to have lunch; *vr* to manage to get
**merendero** *m* lunchroom; summerhouse; picnic grounds
**merendilla** *f* light lunch
**merendona** *f* fine layout, fine spread
**merengar** §59 *va* to whip (*cream*)
**merengue** *m* meringue
**meretriz** *f* (*pl:* **-trices**) prostitute, harlot
**merey** *m* (bot.) cashew
**mergánsar** *m* or **mergo** *m* (orn.) cormorant
**mericarpo** *m* (bot.) mericarp
**meridiano -na** *adj* meridian; bright, dazzling; *m* meridian; **primer meridiano** prime meridian; *f* couch; afternoon nap; meridian, meridian line; **a la meridiana** at noon
**meridional** *adj* meridional, southern; *mf* meridional, southerner
**merienda** *f* lunch, light meal, afternoon snack; (coll.) hunchback; **merienda de negros** (coll.) bedlam; **juntar meriendas** (coll.) to join forces; (coll.) to make up
**merindad** *f* (archaic) royal judgeship of sheepwalks
**merino -na** *adj* merino; thick and curly (*hair*); *mf* merino (*sheep*); *m* shepherd of merinos; merino (*wool; fabric*); (archaic) royal judge of sheepwalks
**meristemo** *m* (bot.) meristem
**mérito** *m* merit, desert; worth, value; **méritos** *mpl* (law) merit; **hacer mérito de** to make mention of; **hacer méritos** to put one's best foot forward
**meritorio -ria** *adj* meritorious; *m* volunteer worker; learner (*without pay*)
**merla** *f* (orn.) blackbird
**merleta** *f* (her.) martlet
**merlín** *m* (naut.) marline; (*cap.*) *m* Merlin; **saber más que Merlín** to be very smart, to be a wizard
**merlo** *m* (ichth.) black wrasse; (Am.) simpleton, boob
**merlón** *m* (fort.) merlon
**merluza** *f* (ichth.) hake; (coll.) drunk, spree, jag
**merma** *f* decrease, reduction; (com.) leakage
**mermar** *va* to decrease, lessen, reduce; *vn* to decrease, diminish, shrink, dwindle
**mermelada** *f* marmalade
**mero -ra** *adj* mere; *m* (ichth.) hind, grouper, jewfish; (ichth.) giant perch
**merodeador -dora** *adj* marauding; *mf* marauder
**merodear** *vn* to maraud
**merodeo** *m* marauding
**merodista** *mf* marauder
**merovingio -gia** *adj & m* Merovingian
**merquén** *m* (Am.) mixed salt and chili
**mer.**[s] abr. of **mercancías**
**meruéndano** *m* (prov.) bilberry
**mes** *m* month; menses; monthly pay; **caer en el mes del obispo** (coll.) to come at the right time; **mes anomalístico** (astr.) anomalistic month; **meses mayores** months preceding harvest; last months of pregnancy; **mes lunar** lunar month
**mesa** *f* table; desk; counter; food, fare; tableland; landing (*of staircase*); facet; flat side (*of blade or tool*); game (*e.g., of billiards*); court, playing surface; board (*group of officers*); desk (*section of office*); mesa (*flat-topped hill*); **¡a la mesa!** let's eat!; **alzar la mesa** (coll.) to clear the table; **a mesa puesta** with no cost or worry; **estar a mesa y mantel de** to live on, live at the expense of; **hacer mesa gallega** or **limpia** to clean up (*in gambling*); **levantar la mesa** to clear the table; **media mesa** low-price table (*in a restaurant*); **poner la mesa** to set or lay the table; **quitar la mesa** (Am.) to clear the table; **tener a mesa y mantel** to feed, to support; **tener mesa** to keep open house; **mesa de altar** altar; **mesa de batalla** sorting table (*in post office*); **mesa de billar** billiard table; **mesa de cambios** commercial bank; **mesa de consola** console table; **mesa de extensión** extension table; **mesa de guarnición** (naut.) channel; **mesa de juego** gambling table, gaming table; **mesa de milanos** (coll.) scanty fare; **mesa de trucos** pool table; **mesa de té** coffee table, tea table; **mesa franca** open table; **mesa operatoria** (surg.) operating table; **mesa parlante** planchette; **mesa perezosa** drop table; **mesa redonda** common table; table d'hôte, ordinary; **Mesa Redonda** (myth.) Round Table (*at which King Arthur and knights sat*)
**mesada** *f* monthly pay, monthly allowance
**mesadura** *f* tearing the hair, pulling hair
**mesalina** *f* dissolute woman
**mesana** *f* (naut.) mizzen (*sail; mast*)
**mesar** *va* to tear, to pull out (*hair*); *vr* to pull each other's hair
**mescal** *m* (bot.) mescal (*plant and liquor*)
**mescolanza** *f* (coll.) var. of **mezcolanza**
**meseguería** *f* harvest watch; assessment to pay for harvest watch
**meseguero -ra** *adj* (pertaining to the) harvest; *m* harvest watchman; (prov.) vineyard watchman
**mesencéfalo** *m* (anat.) mesencephalon, midbrain
**mesénquima** *m* (embryol.) mesenchyme
**mesentérico -ca** *adj* mesenteric
**mesenterio** *m* (anat.) mesentery
**mesenteritis** *f* (path.) mesenteritis
**mesera** *f* (Am.) waitress
**meseraico -ca** *adj* var. of **mesentérico**

**mesero** *m* journeyman on monthly wages; (Am.) waiter
**meseta** *f* landing (*of staircase*); plateau; **meseta de guarnición** (naut.) channel
**mesiado** *m* var. of **mesiazgo**
**mesiánico -ca** *adj* Messianic
**mesianismo** *m* Messianism
**Mesías** *m* (Bib. & fig.) Messiah
**mesiazgo** *m* Messiahship
**mesilla** *f* landing (*of staircase*); sideboard; window sill; mantel, mantelpiece; night table; half-joking scolding
**mesillo** *m* first menses after childbirth
**mesita** *f* small table; **mesita portateléfono** telephone table
**mesitileno** *m* (chem.) mesitylene
**mesmedad** *f*; **por su misma mesmedad** (coll.) without outside help, all by oneself, all by itself
**mesmeriano -na** *adj* mesmerian; mesmeric; *mf* mesmerian
**mesmerismo** *m* mesmerism
**mesmerista** *mf* mesmerist
**mesnada** *f* armed retinue; company, band
**mesnadero** *m* member of an armed retinue
**mesoblasto** *m* (embryol.) mesoblast
**mesocarpio** *m* (bot.) mesocarp
**mesocéfalo -la** *adj* (anthrop.) mesocephalic
**mesodermo** *m* (bot.) mesoderm
**mesofilo** *m* (bot.) mesophyll
**mesófita** *f* (bot.) mesophyte
**mesogastrio** *m* (anat. & zool.) mesogastrium
**mesón** *m* inn, tavern; (phys.) meson; (Am.) showcase
**mesonaje** *m* street or quarter full of taverns
**mesonero -ra** *adj* (pertaining to an) inn, tavern; *mf* innkeeper, tavern keeper
**mesonista** *adj* (pertaining to an) inn, tavern
**mesorrino -na** *adj* (anthrop.) mesorrhine
**mesosfera** *f* mesosphere
**mesotórax** *m* (*pl:* **-rax**) (zool.) mesothorax
**mesotorio** *m* (chem.) mesothorium
**mesotrón** *m* (phys.) mesotron
**mesozoico -ca** *adj & m* (geol.) Mesozoic
**mesquite** *m* var. of **mezquite**
**mesta** *f* (archaic) association of cattle raisers; **mestas** *fpl* confluence (*of two streams*)
**mestal** *m* growth of shrubs
**mesteño -ña** *adj* stray; (Am.) wild, untamed (*animal*)
**mester** *m* (archaic) trade, craft, mystery; (archaic) genre, literary genre; **mester de clerecía** (archaic) clerical verse (*of Spanish literature of thirteenth and fourteenth centuries*); **mester de juglaría** (archaic) minstrelsy, verse of jongleurs (*of Spanish literature beginning with tenth century*)
**mesticia** *f* sadness
**mestizaje** *m* crossbreeding
**mestizar** §76 *va* to crossbreed
**mestizo -za** *adj* mixed, mongrel; half-blooded; hybrid; *mf* half-breed, half-blood; mestizo; mongrel; hybrid; *m & f* (Am.) bran bread
**mesto** *m* (bot.) false cork oak, bastard cork tree; (bot.) Turkey oak; (bot.) mock privet
**mestura** *f* maslin
**mesura** *f* gravity, dignity; politeness, reverence; calm, circumspection, restraint
**mesurado -da** *adj* grave, dignified; polite, respectful; calm, circumspect, restrained; moderate, temperate
**mesurar** *va* to moderate, to temper; *vr* to restrain oneself, act with restraint
**meta** *f* (sport & fig.) goal
**metabólico -ca** *adj* (physiol. & zool.) metabolic
**metabolismo** *m* (physiol.) metabolism; **metabolismo basal** (physiol.) basal metabolism
**metacarpiano -na** *adj & m* (anat.) metacarpal
**metacarpo** *m* (anat.) metacarpus
**metacentro** *m* metacenter
**metacrilato** *m* (chem.) methacrylate
**metacrílico -ca** *adj* methacrylic
**metacromatismo** *m* (physical chem.) metachromatism
**metacronismo** *m* metachronism
**metafase** *f* (biol.) metaphase
**metafísico -ca** *adj* metaphysical; *m* metaphysician; *f* metaphysics
**metafonía** *f* (phonet.) metaphony, umlaut
**metáfora** *f* metaphor; **mezclar las metáforas** to mix metaphors
**metafórico -ca** *adj* metaphorical
**metaforizar** §76 *va* to express metaphorically; *vn* to use metaphors
**metafrasis** *f* (*pl:* **-sis**) metaphrase
**metagénesis** *f* (biol.) metagenesis
**metal** *m* metal; brass, latten; quality, condition; timbre (*of voice*); money; (her.) metal; (mus.) brass; **el vil metal** (coll.) filthy lucre; **metal antifricción** antifriction metal; **metal blanco** nickel silver; **metal britannia** Britannia metal; **metal bruto** base metal; **metal campanil** bell metal; **metal común** base metal; **metal de babbitt** Babbitt metal; **metal de campana** bell metal; **metal de imprenta** type metal; **metal desplegado** expanded metal; **metal dúctil** soft metal; **metales alcalinotérreos** (chem.) alkaline-earth metals; **metal inglés** Britannia metal; **metal monel** Monel metal; **metal noble** noble metal
**metalado -da** *adj* alloyed, impure
**metalario** *m* metalist, metalworker
**metalepsis** *f* (*pl:* **-sis**) (rhet.) metalepsis
**metalero -ra** *adj* (Am.) (pertaining to) metal; *m* (Am.) metalworker
**metálico -ca** *adj* metallic; *m* metalist, metalworker; hard cash, coin; *f* metallurgy
**metalífero -ra** *adj* metal-bearing, metalliferous
**metalina** *f* metaline (*alloy*)
**metalista** *m* metalist, metalworker
**metalistería** *f* metalwork
**metalización** *f* metalization
**metalizado -da** *adj* (coll.) moneyed, rich; (coll.) money-mad
**metalizar** §76 *va* to metalize; *vr* to become metalized; to become mercenary; to become rich and hard-hearted
**metalografía** *f* metallography
**metalográfico -ca** *adj* metallographic
**metaloide** *m* nonmetal
**metaloideo -a** *adj* nonmetallic
**metaloterapia** *f* metallotherapy
**metalurgia** *f* metallurgy
**metalúrgico -ca** *adj* metallurgic; *m* metallurgist; metalworker
**metalurgista** *m* metallurgist; metalworker
**metalla** *f* scraps of gold leaf for mending
**metámero -ra** *adj* (chem. & zool.) metameric; *m* (zool.) metamere
**metamórfico -ca** *adj* metamorphic
**metamorfismo** *m* metamorphism
**metamorfosear** *va & vr* to metamorphose
**metamorfosis** *f* (*pl:* **-sis**) metamorphosis
**metano** *m* (chem.) methane
**metanol** *m* (chem.) methanol
**metaplasma** *m* (biol.) metaplasm
**metaplasmo** *m* (gram.) metaplasm
**metaproteína** *f* (biochem.) metaprotein
**metasomatismo** *m* (geol.) metasomatism
**metástasis** *f* (*pl:* **-sis**) (path.) metastasis
**metatarsiano -na** *adj & m* (anat.) metatarsal
**metatarso** *m* (anat. & zool.) metatarsus
**metate** *m* (Am.) stone on which corn and chocolate are ground
**metátesis** *f* (*pl:* **-sis**) (philol.) metathesis
**metatórax** *m* (*pl:* **-rax**) (zool.) metathorax
**metazoo** *m* (zool.) metazoan
**meteco -ca** *adj* strange; *mf* stranger, outsider
**metedor -dora** *mf* smuggler; *m* diaper
**metedurría** *f* smuggling
**metempsicosis** *f* or **metempsícosis** *f* (*pl:* **-sis**) metempsychosis
**metemuertos** *m* (*pl:* **-tos**) stagehand; busybody
**metencéfalo** *m* (anat.) metencephalon, hindbrain
**meteo** *m* weather broadcast
**meteórico -ca** *adj* meteoric; (fig.) meteoric
**meteorismo** *m* (path.) meteorism, tympanites
**meteorito** *m* meteorite
**meteorizar** §76 *va* (path.) to meteorize; *vr* to be affected by the weather (*said of the soil*); (path.) to become meteorized
**meteoro** or **metéoro** *m* meteor (*atmospheric phenomenon*); weather, kind of weather (*rain, snow, hail, etc.*)

**meteorología** *f* meteorology
**meteorológico -ca** *adj* meteorologic or meteorological
**meteorologista** *mf* or **meteorólogo -ga** *mf* meteorologist
**meter** *va* to put, to place, to insert; to take in (*a seam*); to smuggle; to make (*noise, trouble*); to cause (*fear*); to start (*a rumor, a row*); to tell (*lies*); to stake (*money*); to pocket (*a pool ball*); to hole (*a golf ball*); (Am.) to strike (*a blow*); *vr* to project, to extend; to butt in, to meddle; to become (*e.g., a soldier*); **meterse a** to set oneself up as; **meterse a** + *inf* to take it upon oneself to + *inf;* **meterse con** to pick a quarrel or fight with; **meterse en** to get into; to plunge into; to empty into (*said of a river*); **meterse en sí mismo** to keep one's own counsel
**metesillas** *m* (*pl:* **-llas**) stagehand
**meticulosidad** *f* shyness, fear; meticulousness
**meticuloso -sa** *adj* shy, fearful; meticulous, scrupulous
**metida** *f* see **metido**
**metidillo** *m* diaper
**metido -da** *adj* full, rich; close, tight; **estar muy metido con** to be on very close terms with; **estar muy metido en** to be deeply involved in; *m* punch, push; strong lye; diaper; loose leaf; (sew.) seam (*edges left after making a seam*); (coll.) harsh dressing-down; *f* pocketing a pool ball; holing a golf ball; (naut.) setting (*of sun, star, etc.*)
**metilamina** *f* (chem.) methylamine
**metilato** *m* (chem.) methylate
**metileno** *m* (chem.) methylene
**metílico -ca** *adj* (chem.) methylic
**metilo** *m* (chem.) methyl
**metimiento** *m* insertion; influence, upper hand
**metionina** *f* (biochem.) methionine
**metódico -ca** *adj* methodic or methodical
**metodismo** *m* Methodism
**metodista** *adj* & *mf* Methodist
**metodizar §76** *va* to methodize
**método** *m* method
**metodología** *f* methodology
**metol** *m* (chem.) metol
**métomentodo** *mf* (coll.) meddler, intruder
**metonimia** *f* (rhet.) metonymy
**metonímico -ca** *adj* metonymic or metonymical
**métopa** *f* (arch.) metope
**metraje** *m* distance in meters; meterage, measuring; (mov.) length of film in meters (*en inglés se usa* footage, *es decir, longitud de película en pies*); **de corto metraje** short (*movie*); **de largo metraje** full-length (*movie*)
**metralla** *f* grapeshot; shrapnel balls; shrapnel; scrap iron
**metrallar** *va* var. of **ametrallar**
**metrallazo** *m* discharge of grapeshot; discharge of shrapnel
**metralleta** *f* machine gun
**metrar** *va* to meter, to measure
**métrico -ca** *adj* metric, metrical; *f* metrics, art of metrical composition
**metrificación** *f* versification
**metrificador -dora** *mf* versifier
**metrificar §86** *va* to put into verse; *vn* to versify
**metrista** *mf* metrist, versifier
**metritis** *f* (path.) metritis
**metro** *m* meter (*unit; verse*); ruler; tape measure; subway; **metro patrón** standard meter; **metro plegadizo** folding rule
**metrología** *f* metrology
**metronómico -ca** *adj* metronomic
**metrónomo** *m* (mus.) metronome
**metrópoli** *f* metropolis; mother country; (eccl.) metropolis
**metropolitano -na** *adj* metropolitan; *m* subway; (eccl.) metropolitan
**metrorragia** *f* (path.) metrorrhagia
**Méx.** abr. of **México**
**mexicanidad** *f* Mexicanism, Mexican spirit
**mexicano -na** *adj* & *mf* (Am.) Mexican
**México** *m* (Am.) Mexico; **Nuevo México** New Mexico; *f* Mexico City
**meya** *f* (zool.) spider crab
**mezcal** *m* var. of **mescal**
**mezcla** *f* mixture; mortar; tweed; **mezcla pobre** (aut.) lean mixture; **mezcla rica** (aut.) rich mixture
**mezclable** *adj* mixable
**mezcladizo** *m* maslin
**mezclador -dora** *mf* mixer; **mezclador automático** combination faucet; *f* concrete mixer
**mezcladura** *f* or **mezclamiento** *m* mixture
**mezclar** *va* to mix; to blend; *vr* to mix; to mingle; to take part; to meddle; to intermarry
**mezclilla** *f* light tweed; (orn.) black-and-white warbler
**mezcolanza** *f* (coll.) mixture, hodgepodge, medley, jumble
**mezquinar** *va* (Am.) to be stingy with; *vn* (Am.) to be stingy
**mezquindad** *f* meanness, stinginess; poverty, need; smallness, tininess; wretchedness
**mezquino -na** *adj* mean, stingy; poor, needy; small, tiny; wretched, unlucky
**mezquita** *f* mosque
**mezquite** *m* (bot.) mesquite
**mezzo-soprano** *m* mezzo-soprano (*voice*); *f* mezzo-soprano (*woman*)
**mg.** abr. of **miligramo** or **miligramos**
**mho** *m* (elec.) mho
**mi** *adj poss* my; *m* (mus.) mi
**mí** (used as object of prepositions) *pron pers* me; *pron reflex* me, myself
**miaja** *f* crumb
**mialgia** *f* (path.) myalgia
**mialmas; como unas mialmas** (coll.) with the greatest pleasure
**miar §90** *vn* to meow
**miasma** *m* miasma
**miasmático -ca** *adj* miasmal or miasmatic
**miastenia** *f* (path.) myasthenia
**miau** *m* meow
**mica** *f* (mineral.) mica
**micáceo -a** *adj* micaceous
**micacita** *f* (mineral.) mica schist
**micado** *m* mikado
**micasquisto** *m* (mineral.) mica schist
**micción** *f* micturition
**micela** *f* (biol. & chem.) micelle
**micelar** *adj* micellar
**micelio** *m* (bot.) mycelium
**Micenas** *f* Mycenae
**micénico -ca** *adj* Mycenaean
**mico** *m* long-tailed monkey; (coll.) skinny fellow; (coll.) hoodlum; **dar** or **hacer mico** (coll.) to miss a date, to not keep a date; **dejar hecho un mico** (coll.) to abash, ruffle, upset; **quedarse hecho un mico** (coll.) to be abashed, ruffled, upset
**micología** *f* mycology
**micológico -ca** *adj* mycologic or mycological
**micólogo -ga** *mf* mycologist
**micosis** *f* (path.) mycosis
**micra** *f* micron
**microanálisis** *m* (chem.) microanalysis
**microbarógrafo** *m* microbarograph
**microbiano -na** *adj* microbial
**micróbico -ca** *adj* microbic
**microbio** *m* microbe
**microbiología** *f* microbiology
**microbiológico -ca** *adj* microbiological
**microbiólogo -ga** *mf* microbiologist
**microcéfalo -la** *adj* (anthrop. & path.) microcephalic
**microcito** *m* (path.) microcyte
**microclina** *f* (mineral.) microcline
**micrococo** *m* (bact.) micrococcus
**microcopia** *f* microcopy
**microcosmo** *m* microcosm
**microdisección** *f* microdissection
**microdonte** *adj* & *m* microdont
**microfaradio** *m* (elec.) microfarad
**microficha** *f* microcard
**microfilm** *m* microfilm
**microfilmación** *f* or **microfilmaje** *m* microfilming
**microfilmar** *va* to microfilm
**microfísica** *f* microphysics
**micrófito** *m* (bot.) microphyte
**microfónico -ca** *adj* microphonic
**micrófono** *m* microphone
**microfoto** *f* microphotograph

**microfotografía** *f* microphotography; microphotograph
**microgameto** *m* (biol.) microgamete
**micrografía** *f* micrography
**microgramo** *m* microgram
**micrometría** *f* micrometry
**micrométrico -ca** *adj* micrometric or micrometrical
**micrómetro** *m* micrometer
**micromilímetro** *m* micromillimeter
**micromovimiento** *m* micromotion
**micrón** *m* micron
**micronesio -sia** *adj & mf* Micronesian; **la Micronesia** Micronesia
**microonda** *f* (phys.) microwave
**microorganismo** *m* (bact.) microörganism
**micropelícula** *f* microfilm
**micrópilo** *m* (bot. & zool.) micropyle
**microquímica** *f* microchemistry
**microscopia** *f* microscopy
**microscópico -ca** *adj* microscopic or microscopical
**microscopio** *m* microscope; **microscopio electrónico** electron microscope
**microscopista** *mf* microscopist
**microsismo** *m* microseism
**microsoma** *m* (biol.) microsome
**microsporangio** *m* (bot.) microsporangium
**microsporo -ra** *adj* microsporous; *f* (bot.) microspore
**microsurco** *m* microgroove; *adj invar* microgroove
**microteléfono** *m* (telp.) handset (*telephone with receiver and mouthpiece on same handle*)
**micrótomo** *m* microtome
**micturición** *f* micturition
**Michigán** *m* Michigan
**michito** *m* (coll.) pussy, pussy cat
**micho -cha** *mf* (coll.) cat, puss
**mida** *f* (ent.) plant louse
**Midas** *m* (myth.) Midas
**midriasis** *f* (path.) mydriasis
**midriático -ca** *adj & m* mydriatic
**miedo** *m* fear; dread; **dar miedo a** to frighten; **de miedo** terrifically; **tener miedo (a)** to be afraid (of); **miedo cerval** intense fear
**miedoso -sa** *adj* (coll.) afraid, scared
**miel** *f* honey; molasses; (Am.) syrup; **dejar a media miel** or **con la miel en los labios** (coll.) to spoil the fun for; **hacerse de miel** to be peaches and cream; **miel rosada** (pharm.) honey of rose
**mielencéfalo** *m* (anat.) myelencephalon
**mielgo -ga** *adj & mf* twin; *f* plot of ground marked for planting; winnowing fork; (bot.) medic, lucerne; (ichth.) fox shark
**mielina** *f* (anat.) myelin
**mielitis** *f* (path.) myelitis
**miembro** *m* member; limb; **miembro de honor** honorary member; **miembro viril** (anat.) virile member; **miembro** *f* member, female member
**mientes** *fpl* mind, thought; **caer en mientes** or **en las mientes** to come to mind; **parar** or **poner mientes en** to consider, to reflect on; **traer a las mientes** to bring or to call to mind; **venírsele a uno a las mientes** to come to one's mind, to occur to one
**mientras** *conj* while; whereas; **mientras más (or menos) . . . más** (or **menos**) the more (or the less) . . . the more (or the less), e.g., **mientras más tiene más desea** the more he has the more he wants; **mientras que** while; whereas; **mientras tanto** meanwhile, in the meantime
**miera** *f* juniper oil; pine turpentine
**miérc.** abr. of **miércoles**
**miércoles** *m* (*pl:* **-les**) Wednesday; **miércoles corvillo** (coll.) Ash Wednesday; **miércoles de ceniza** Ash Wednesday
**mierra** *f* sled, stone drag
**mies** *f* grain, cereal; harvest time; (fig.) harvest (*of converts to Christianity*); **mieses** *fpl* grain fields
**miga** *f* bit; crumb (*soft part of bread*); substance; **migas** *fpl* fried crumbs; **hacer buenas migas (con)** to get along well (with); **hacer malas migas (con)** to get along badly (with); **hacerse migas** to be smashed to bits; **tener miga** (coll.) to have a point, to have something to it
**migaja** *f* crumb; bit; smattering; **migajas** *fpl* crumbs, leavings, offals; **reparar en migajas** (coll.) to bother about trifles
**migajón** *m* crumb; (coll.) substance
**migala** *f* (ent.) bird spider
**migar** §59 *va* to crumb (*bread*); to put crumbs in (*a liquid*)
**Mig.**[l] abr. of **Miguel**
**migración** *f* migration
**migraña** *f* (path.) migraine
**migrador -dora** or **migratorio -ria** *adj* migratory
**Miguel** *m* Michael; **Miguel Angel** Michelangelo
**miguelear** *va* (Am.) to make love to, to court
**migueleño -ña** *adj* (Am.) impolite, discourteous
**miguelete** *m* var. of **miquelete**
**Miguelito** *m* Mike, Micky
**mihrab** *m* (*pl:* **mihrabs**) mihrab
**mijar** *m* field of millet
**mijo** *m* (bot.) broomcorn millet; **mijo de sol agreste** (bot.) corn gromwell; **mijo gris** (bot.) gromwell
**mil** *adj & m* thousand, a thousand, one thousand; **a las mil y quinientas** (coll.) at an unearthly hour; **las mil y quinientas** (coll.) a mess of lentils; **las Mil y una noches** the Thousand and One Nights; **mil en grano** (bot.) burstwort
**miladi** *f* milady
**milagrear** *vn* to perform miracles
**milagrería** *f* tale of miracles
**milagrero -ra** *adj* superstitious; miracle-faking; miracle-working
**milagro** *m* miracle, wonder; votive offering; (theat.) miracle, miracle play; **colgar el milagro a** to put the blame on; **hacer milagros** to do wonders; **por milagro** for a wonder; **vivir de milagro** to have a hard time getting along; to have had a narrow escape
**milagrón** *m* (coll.) fuss, excitement
**milagroso -sa** *adj* miraculous; marvelous, wonderful
**milamores** *f* (bot.) red valerian
**Milán** *f* Milan
**milanés -nesa** *adj & mf* Milanese
**milano** *m* burr or down of thistle; (orn.) kite; (ichth.) flying gurnard
**Milcíades** *m* Miltiades
**mildeu** *m* or **mildiú** *m* (agr.) mildew; **mildeu de la patata** potato mildew or mold
**milefolio** *m* (bot.) milfoil
**milenario -ria** *adj* millenial; millenarian; *mf* millenarian; *m* millenium
**milenio** *m* millenium
**milenrama** *f* (bot.) yarrow
**milenta** *adj & m* (coll.) thousand, a thousand
**milépora** *f* (zool.) millepore
**milésimo -ma** *adj & m* thousandth, millesimal; *f* mill (*thousandth of monetary unit*)
**milesio -sia** *adj & mf* Milesian
**milés.**[s] abr. of **milésimas**
**Mileto** *f* Miletus
**milgranar** *m* field of burstwort
**milgranos** *m* (*pl:* **-nos**) (bot.) burstwort
**milhojas** *m* (*pl:* **-jas**) var. of **milenrama**
**mili** *f* (coll.) militia, army
**miliamperímetro** *m* (elec.) milliammeter
**miliamperio** *m* (elec.) milliampere
**miliar** *adj* miliary; (pertaining to a) mile; (path.) miliary
**miliario -ria** *adj* milliary; (pertaining to a) mile
**milibar** *m* millibar
**milicia** *f* militia; soldiery; art of warfare; military service; **milicia nacional** national guard
**miliciano -na** *adj* military; *m* militiaman
**miligramo** *m* milligram
**mililitro** *m* milliliter
**milímetro** *m* millimeter
**milimicrón** *m* millimicron
**milípedo** *m* (zool.) millepede
**milipulgada** *f* mil (*0.001 inch*)
**militante** *adj & mf* militant

**militar** *adj* military; (pertaining to the) army; *m* military man, soldier; *vn* to serve in the army; to go to war, to fight; to struggle; to militate (*for or against*)
**militara** *f* wife, daughter, or widow of a soldier
**militarismo** *m* militarism
**militarista** *adj & mf* militarist
**militarización** *f* militarization
**militarizar** §76 *va* militarize
**militarón** *m* (coll.) old campaigner; (coll.) militarist
**militarote** *m* (coll.) swashbuckler
**mílite** *m* soldier
**milivoltio** *m* (elec.) millivolt
**milmillonésimo -ma** *adj & m* billionth
**miloca** *f* (orn.) Tengmalm's owl
**milocha** *f* kite
**milor** *m* or **milord** *m* (*pl:* **-lores**) milord
**milpa** *f* (Am.) cornfield
**milpiés** *m* (*pl:* **-piés**) (ent.) centipede; (zool.) wood louse
**miltoniano -na** *adj* Miltonian or Miltonic
**milla** *f* mile; **milla marina** (naut.) nautical mile, geographical mile
**millar** *m* thousand; **a millares** by the thousand
**millarada** *f* thousand, about a thousand; **a millaradas** by the thousand, thousandfold; **echar millaradas** to boast of great wealth
**millo** *m* (bot.) millet; **millo de escoba** (bot.) broom millet, broomcorn millet
**millón** *m* million
**millonada** *f* million, about a million
**millonario -ria** *adj* millionaire; of a million or more inhabitants; *mf* millionaire
**millonésimo -ma** *adj & m* millionth
**mimar** *va* to pet, fondle; to pamper, indulge
**mimbar** *m* mimbar, Moslem pulpit
**mimbral** *m* osiery
**mimbrar** *va* to humble, to overwhelm
**mimbre** *m & f* osier, wicker, withe; (bot.) osier
**mimbrear** *vn & vr* to sway
**mimbreño -ña** *adj* willowy, withy
**mimbrera** *f* (bot.) osier, osier willow
**mimbreral** *m* osiery
**mimbrón** *m* var. of **mimbrera**
**mimbroso -sa** *adj* wicker
**mimeografiar** §90 *va* to mimeograph
**mimeógrafo** *m* mimeograph
**mímesis** *f* (rhet., biol. & path.) mimesis
**mimético -ca** *adj* (biol. & mineral.) mimetic
**mimetismo** *m* (biol.) protective coloration, mimetism
**mímico -ca** *adj* of mimes; mimic; *m* author of mimes; *f* mimicry; gesticulations; sign language
**mimicria** *f* (biol.) mimicry
**mimo** *m* mime; pampering, indulgence; finickiness, fussiness
**mimosa** *f* see **mimoso**
**mimosáceo -a** *adj* (bot.) mimosaceous
**mimoso -sa** *adj* pampered, spoiled; finicky, fussy; *f* (bot.) mimosa; **mimosa púdica** or **vergonzosa** (bot.) mimosa, sensitive plant
**mina** *f* mine; (min.) seam, vein, lode; lead (*of pencil*); (mil. & nav.) mine; (fig.) mine, storehouse, gold mine; (fig.) sinecure; (Am.) moll; **beneficiar una mina** to work a mine; **encontrar una mina** (fig.) to strike a gold mine; **volar la mina** to break one's silence; **voló la mina** the truth is out; **mina de carbón** coal mine; **mina de oro** gold mine; **mina hullera** coal mine
**minado** *m* mine working; (nav.) mining (*e.g., of a harbor*)
**minador -dora** *adj* mining; (nav.) mine-laying; *m* mining engineer; (mil.) miner; (nav.) mine layer
**minal** *adj* (pertaining to a) mine
**minar** *va* to mine; to undermine; to consume; to plug away at; (mil. & nav.) to mine; *vn* to mine
**minarete** *m* minaret
**mineraje** *m* mining; **mineraje a tajo abierto** strip mining
**mineral** *adj* mineral; *m* mineral; ore; fountainhead; mine; source, origin
**mineralización** *f* mineralization
**mineralizar** §76 *va* to mineralize; *vr* to become mineralized
**mineralogía** *f* mineralogy
**mineralógico -ca** *adj* mineralogical
**mineralogista** *mf* mineralogist
**minería** *f* mining; mines; miners; mine operators
**minero -ra** *adj* mining; *m* miner; mine operator; (fig.) source, origin
**mineromedicinal** *adj* mineral (*water*)
**Minerva** *f* (myth.) Minerva; (*l.c.*) *f* (eccl.) procession; (print.) small press; **de propia minerva** out of one's own head
**mingitorio** *m* upright urinal
**mingo** *m* object ball; **poner el mingo** (coll.) to stand out, excel, distinguish oneself; **tomar el mingo a** (coll.) to tease, to taunt
**mingón -gona** *adj* (Am.) spoiled (*child*)
**miniar** *va* to miniate, to illuminate (*a manuscript*); to paint in miniature
**miniatura** *f* miniature; **en miniatura** in miniature; *adj invar* miniature; toy (*e.g., dog*)
**miniaturesco -ca** *adj* miniature
**miniaturista** *mf* miniaturist
**miniaturización** *f* miniaturization
**miniaturizar** §76 *va* to miniaturize
**minifundio** *m* small farm
**minim** *m* (pharm.) minim
**mínima** *f* see **mínimo**
**minimización** *f* diminution, reduction; minimization; minimizing
**minimizar** §76 *va* to diminish, reduce; to minimize
**mínimo -ma** *adj* minimum; minimal; tiny, minute; least, smallest; *m* minimum; *f* tiny bit; minim; (mus.) minim
**mínimum** *m* minimum
**minino -na** *mf* (coll.) cat, kitty
**minio** *m* (chem.) minium
**ministerial** *adj* ministerial; *m* minister
**ministerio** *m* ministry; cabinet; government; **formar ministerio** to form a government; **ministerio de asuntos exteriores** foreign office; **ministerio de Asuntos Exteriores** Department of State (U.S.A.); Foreign Office (Brit.); **ministerio de Defensa Nacional** Department of Defense (U.S.A.); **ministerio de Hacienda** Treasury Department (U.S.A.); Treasury (Brit.); **ministerio de Justicia** Department of Justice (U.S.A.); Department of the Lord Chancellor (Brit.); **ministerio de la Gobernación** Department of the Interior (U.S.A.); Home Office (Brit.); **ministerio del Aire** Department of the Air Force (U.S.A.); Air Ministry (Brit.); **ministerio del Ejército** Department of the Army (U.S.A.); War Office (Brit.); **ministerio de Marina** Department of the Navy (U.S.A.); Board of Admiralty (Brit.)
**ministra** *f* woman minister; minister's wife
**ministrador -dora** *adj & mf* ministrant
**ministrante** *adj* ministrant; *mf* ministrant; trained nurse
**ministrar** *va* to administer; to supply; to minister; *vn* to minister
**ministril** *m* tipstaff; musician; wind instrument; minstrel (*retainer who sang and played for his lord*)
**ministro** *m* minister; bailiff, constable; (pol., dipl. & eccl.) minister; **primer ministro** prime minister, premier; **ministro de asuntos exteriores** foreign minister; **ministro de Asuntos Exteriores** Secretary of State (U.S.A.); Minister of Foreign Affairs (Brit.); **ministro de Gobernación** Home Secretary (Brit.); **ministro de Hacienda** Chancellor of the Exchequer (Brit.); **ministro de Justicia** Attorney General (U.S.A.); **ministro plenipotenciario** minister plenipotentiary; **ministro sin cartera** minister without portfolio; **ministro** *f* minister (*woman*)
**min.º** abr. of **ministro**
**mino** *interj* here, pussy!
**minoico -ca** *adj* Minoan
**minoración** *f* lessening, diminution; weakening
**minorar** *va* to lessen, diminish; to weaken
**minorativo -va** *adj* lessening, diminishing; laxative; *m* laxative

**minoría** *f* minority (*condition and time of being under age; smaller number or part*)
**minoridad** *f* minority (*being under age*)
**minorista** *adj* retail; *m* retailer; cleric holding minor orders
**minoritario -ria** *adj* (pertaining to the) minority
**Minos** *m* (myth.) Minos
**Minotauro** *m* (myth.) Minotaur
**minucia** *f* trifle; **minucias** *fpl* minutiae; (archaic) minor tithes
**minuciosidad** *f* minuteness; meticulousness; fussiness
**minucioso -sa** *adj* minute; meticulous; fussy
**minué** *m* minuet (*dance and music*)
**minuendo** *m* (math.) minuend
**minuete** *m* var. of **minué**
**minúsculo -la** *adj* small (*letter*); small, tiny; *f* small letter
**minuta** *f* see **minuto**
**minutar** *va* to make a draft of, to minute
**minutario** *m* notary's ledger
**minutería** *f* minute marks (*on face of clock or watch*); (elec.) automatic time switch (*used in hotel hallways*)
**minutero** *m* minute hand
**minutisa** *f* (bot.) sweet william
**minuto -ta** *adj* minute; *m* minute (*of an hour; of a degree*); *f* first draft, rough draft; memorandum; lawyer's bill; roll, list; bill of fare
**miñón** *m* border guard, forest guard; (prov.) slag; (prov.) iron ore
**miñona** *f* (print.) minion
**miñoneta** *f* (bot.) mignonette
**miñosa** *f* (zool.) earthworm
**mio** *interj* pussy, pussy!
**mío -a** *adj poss* mine, of mine; *pron poss* mine; **de mío** on my own accord; by myself
**miocardio** *m* (anat.) myocardium
**miocarditis** *f* (path.) myocarditis
**mioceno -na** *adj & m* (geol.) Miocene
**mioglobina** *f* (biochem.) myoglobin
**miógrafo** *m* myograph
**miología** *f* myology
**mioma** *m* (path.) myoma
**miope** *adj* myopic, near-sighted; (fig.) myopic; *mf* myope
**miopía** *f* (path.) myopia, near-sightedness
**miosis** *f* (path.) myosis
**miosota** *f* (bot.) German madwort
**miosotis** *m* (bot.) myosotis, forget-me-not; (bot.) German madwort
**Miqueas** *m* (Bib.) Micah
**miquelete** *m* miquelet
**mira** *f* sight; target; object, aim, purpose; level rod; **estar a la mira** to be on the lookout; **estar a la mira de que** to be on the lookout to see that; **poner la mira en** or **tener miras sobre** to have designs on; **mira esférica** globe sight
**mirabel** *m* (bot.) mock cypress; (bot.) sunflower
**mirabolano** or **mirabolanos** *m* (bot.) var. of **mirobálano**
**mirada** *f* see **mirado**
**miradero** *m* cynosure; concern, thing most watched; lookout, observatory
**mirado -da** *adj* thoughtful, cautious, circumspect; **bien mirado** well-thought-of; **mal mirado** little liked, looked on with disfavor; *f* glance, look; **apuñalar con la mirada** to look daggers at; **echar una mirada a** to take a look at
**mirador -dora** *adj* looking, overlooking; *m* watchtower; mirador; bay window, closed porch
**miradura** *f* glance, look
**miraguano** *m* (bot.) fan palm, thatch palm; (Am.) kapok
**miraje** *m* mirage
**miramelindos** *m* (*pl:* **-dos**) (bot.) balsam
**miramiento** *m* look; considerateness, regard; care, caution, circumspection; misgiving; **miramientos** *mpl* fuss, bother, worry
**miranda** *f* belvedere; eminence, vantage point
**mirar** *va* to look at; to watch; to contemplate, consider; to consider carefully, to be careful about; to esteem, have regard for; **mirar bien** to look with favor on, to like; **mirar mal** to look with disfavor on, to dislike; **mirar por encima** to glance at ‖ *vn* to look; to glance; **¡mira!** look!; look out!; **mirar a** to look at; to glance at; to aim at; to face, overlook; to concern; **mirar a** + *inf* to aim to + *inf;* **mirar por** to look after, to look out for ‖ *vr* to look at oneself; to look at each other; **mirar a sí** to know one's place; **mirarse en ello** to watch one's step; **mirarse en una persona** to be all wrapped up in a person; **mirarse unos a otros** to stand dumbfounded looking at each other
**mirasol** *m* (bot.) sunflower
**miríada** *f* myriad (*ten thousand; very great number*)
**miriámetro** *m* ten thousand meters
**miriápodo -da** *adj & m* var. of **miriópodo**
**miricáceo -a** *adj* (bot.) myricaceous
**mirificar** §86 *va* to exalt, extol
**mirífico -ca** *adj* marvelous, wonderful
**mirilla** *f* peephole; (surv.) target; (phot.) finder
**miriñaque** *m* crinoline; hoop skirt; bauble, trinket; (Am.) cowcatcher
**miriópodo -da** *adj & m* (zool.) myriapod
**mirística** *f* (bot.) nutmeg (*tree*)
**miristicáceo -a** *adj* (bot.) myristicaceous
**mirla** *f* (orn.) blackbird
**mirlamiento** *m* self-importance, airs
**mirlar** *vr* (coll.) to act important, to put on airs
**mirlo** *m* (orn.) blackbird; (coll.) affected expression of solemnity; **aguantar el mirlo** (coll.) to keep quiet, refuse to answer; **soltar el mirlo** (coll.) to jabber, to scold; **mirlo blanco** (coll.) rare bird; **mirlo de agua** (orn.) water ouzel
**mirmecófago -ga** *adj* myrmecophagous
**mirmecófilo -la** *adj* myrmecophilous; *m* (ent.) myrmecophile
**mirmecología** *f* myrmecology
**mirmecólogo -ga** *mf* myrmecologist
**Mirmidón** *m* (myth.) Myrmidon; (*l.c.*) *m* dwarf, tiny fellow
**mirobálano** *m* (bot.) myrobalan (*tree and fruit*)
**mirón -rona** *adj* onlooking; nosy, inquisitive; *mf* onlooker; kibitzer; busybody
**mirra** *f* myrrh
**mirrado -da** *adj* myrrhed
**mirrino -na** *adj* myrrhic
**mirtáceo -a** *adj* (bot.) myrtaceous
**mirtino -na** *adj* myrtiform
**mirto** *m* (bot.) myrtle; **mirto de Brabante** (bot.) gale, sweet gale
**misa** *f* (eccl. & mus.) mass; **cantar misa** to say mass; **como en misa** in dead silence; **decir misa** to say mass; **no saber de la misa la media** (coll.) to not know what it's all about; **oír misa** to hear mass; **misa cantada** High Mass; **misa de campaña** (mil.) mass in the field; outdoor mass; **misa del gallo** Christmas-eve mass; **misa de prima** early mass; **misa de réquiem** requiem mass; **misa mayor** High Mass; **misa rezada** Low Mass
**misacantano** *m* officiant at Mass, priest who says Mass for the first time
**misal** *m* (eccl.) missal, Mass book
**misantropía** *f* misanthropy
**misantrópico -ca** *adj* misanthropic
**misantropismo** *m* var. of **misantropía**
**misántropo** *m* misanthrope
**misar** *vn* (coll.) to say mass; (coll.) to hear mass
**misario** *m* (eccl.) acolyte
**miscegenación** *f* miscegenation
**misceláneo -a** *adj* miscellaneous; *f* miscellany; miscellanies
**miscible** *adj* miscible
**miserabilísimo -ma** *adj super* very or most miserable; very or most stingy
**miserable** *adj* miserable, wretched; mean, stingy; vile, wicked, despicable; *mf* wretch; cur, cad
**miseración** *f* pity, mercy
**miserando -da** *adj* pitiful
**miserear** *va* (coll.) to scrimp, to begrudge; *vn* (coll.) to be stingy
**miserere** *m* (eccl. & mus.) Miserere; (path.) ileus
**miseria** *f* misery, wretchedness; poverty; stinginess; (coll.) trifle, pittance; (slang) lice; **comerse de miseria** (coll.) to live in great poverty

**misericordia** *f* mercy, compassion; misericord (*dagger*); (arch.) miserere, misericord; (eccl.) misericord (*hall; dispensation*)
**misericordioso -sa** *adj* merciful
**misero -ra** *adj* (coll.) mass-loving, church-going
**mísero -ra** *adj* miserable, wretched; miserly, stingy
**misérrimo -ma** *adj super* very or most miserable or wretched; very or most miserly
**misión** *f* mission; food for harvesters; **misiones** *fpl* (eccl.) foreign missions; **ir a misiones** to go away as a missionary
**misional** *adj* missionary
**misionar** *va* to spread (*e.g., faith*); to spread the faith to; *vn* to conduct a mission, do missionary work
**misionario** *m* envoy, missionary; (eccl.) missionary
**misionero -ra** *adj* missionary; *m* (eccl.) missionary
**Misisipí** *m* Mississippi (*river and state*)
**misivo -va** *adj & f* missive
**mismamente** *adv* (coll.) exactly
**mismísimo -ma** *adj super* selfsame, very same
**mismo -ma** *adj & pron indef* same; own, very; self, e.g., **ella misma** herself; myself, yourself, himself, itself, e.g., **yo mismo** I myself; **su padre mismo** his father himself; **en España misma** in Spain itself; **así mismo** in like manner, likewise, also; **casi lo mismo** much the same; **lo mismo** the same thing; just the same; **lo mismo me da** (coll.) it's all the same to me; **por lo mismo** for the same reason, for that very reason; **mismo . . . que** same . . . as; **mismo** *adv* right, e.g., **ahora mismo** right now; **aquí mismo** right here; **en España mismo** right in Spain; **desde Sevilla mismo** right from Seville
**misogamia** *f* misogamy
**misógamo -ma** *adj* misogamic; *mf* misogamist
**misoginia** *f* misogyny
**misógino -na** *adj* misogynous; *mf* misogynist
**misoneísmo** *m* misoneism
**misoneísta** *mf* misoneist
**mispíquel** *m* (mineral.) mispickel
**mistagogo** *m* (hist.) mystagogue
**mistar** *vn* to mumble
**mistela** *f* flavored brandy; sweet wine
**misterio** *m* mystery; (theat.) mystery, mystery play; **misterios de Eleusis** Eleusinian mysteries
**misterioso -sa** *adj* mysterious
**mística** *f* see **místico**
**misticismo** *m* mysticism
**místico -ca** *adj* mystic, mystical; *mf* mystic; *m* (naut.) mistic; *f* mystical theology; literary mysticism
**misticón -cona** *adj* pietistic; *mf* pietist
**mistificación** *f* var. of **mixtificación**
**mistificar** §86 *va* var. of **mixtificar**
**mistifori** *m* (coll.) var. of **mixtifori**
**mistilíneo -a** *adj* var. of **mixtilíneo**
**mistral** *m* mistral (*wind*)
**mistura** *f* var. of **mixtura**
**Misurí** *m* Missouri (*river and state*)
**mita** *f* (zool.) mite, cheese mite; (Am.) Indian slave labor
**mitad** *f* half; middle; **a (la) mitad de** halfway through; **cara mitad** (coll.) better half (*husband and especially wife*); **en la mitad de** in the middle of; **la mitad de** half the, e.g., **la mitad del dinero** half the money; **mentir por la mitad de la barba** (coll.) to tell fish stories; **por la mitad** in the middle, in half; **mitad y mitad** half-and-half
**mítico -ca** *adj* mythic or mythical
**mitigación** *f* mitigation
**mitigador -dora** *adj* mitigating; *mf* mitigator
**mitigar** §59 *va* to mitigate, allay, appease; *vr* to mitigate
**mitigativo -va** *adj* mitigative
**Mitilene** *f* Mytilene
**mitin** *m* (*pl:* **mitins** or **mítines**) meeting, rally
**mito** *m* myth
**mitología** *f* mythology; **mitología nórdica** Norse mythology
**mitológico -ca** *adj* mythological; *mf* mythologist
**mitologista** *mf* or **mitólogo -ga** *mf* mythologist
**mitón** *m* mitt (*glove which leaves the fingers uncovered*)
**mitósico -ca** *adj* mitotic
**mitosis** *f* (biol.) mitosis
**mitra** *f* miter (*e.g., of a bishop; episcopal office or dignity*); chimney pot; (*cap.*) *m* (myth.) Mithras
**mitrado -da** *adj* mitered; *m* bishop, archbishop; (bot.) miter mushroom
**mitral** *adj* mitral; (anat.) mitral
**mitrar** *vn* (coll.) to be mitered, to become a bishop
**Mitrídates** *m* Mithridates
**mítulo** *m* (zool.) mussel
**mixedema** *f* (path.) myxedema
**mixomatosis** *f* (vet.) myxomatosis
**mixomiceto** *m* (bot.) myxomycete
**mixtela** *f* var. of **mistela**
**mixtificación** *f* hoax, mystification
**mixtificar** §86 *va* to hoax, to mystify
**mixtifori** *m* (coll.) hodgepodge
**mixtilíneo -a** *adj* mixtilineal
**mixtión** *f* mixture
**mixto -ta** *adj* mixed; *m* compound; match; explosive compound
**mixtura** *f* mixture; maslin
**mixturar** *va* to mix
**mixturero -ra** *adj* mixing; *mf* mixer; *f* (Am.) flower girl
**miz** *interj* pussy, pussy!
**mízcalo** *m* (bot.) edible milk mushroom (*Lactarius deliciosus*)
**mizo -za** *mf* (coll.) cat
**m/l** abr. of **mi letra**
**mm.** abr. of **milímetro** or **milímetros**
**m/m** abr. of **más o menos**
**Mm.** abr. of **miriámetro** or **miriámetros**
**m/n** abr. of **moneda nacional**
**mnemónico -ca** *adj* mnemonic; *f* mnemonics
**Mnemosina** or **Mnemósine** *f* (myth.) Mnemosyne
**mnemotecnia** *f* mnemotechny
**mnemotécnico -ca** *adj* mnemotechnic or mnemotechnical; *f* mnemotechnics
**moabita** *adj & mf* Moabite
**moaré** *m* var. of **muaré**
**mobiliario -ria** *adj* personal (*property*); *m* suit of furniture
**moblaje** *m* furniture, suit of furniture
**moblar** §77 *va* to furnish
**moca** *f* (Am.) mudhole; (Am.) wineglass; *m* Mocha coffee
**mocador** *m* handkerchief
**mocar** §86 *va* to blow the nose of; *vr* to blow one's nose
**mocarro** *m* (coll.) snot
**mocasín** *m* moccasin; (zool.) moccasin, cottonmouth; **mocasín de agua** (zool.) water moccasin
**mocasina** *f* moccasin
**mocear** *vn* to act young; to run around, to sow one's wild oats; to grow up; to run around after women
**mocedad** *f* youth; wild oats; licentious living
**mocejón** *m* (zool.) mussel
**moceril** *adj* youthful
**mocerío** *m* young people, crowd of young people
**mocero** *adj masc* woman-crazy; fast-living
**mocetón** *m* strapping young fellow
**mocetona** *f* buxom young woman
**mocil** *adj* youthful
**moción** *f* motion, movement; inclination, leaning; divine inspiration; motion (*in a deliberative assembly*); **hacer** or **presentar una moción** to make a motion
**mocionante** *mf* (Am.) mover (*of a proposition*)
**mocionar** *va* (Am.) to move (*to propose in a deliberative assembly*); *vn* (Am.) to move, make a motion
**mocito -ta** *adj* quite young; *mf* youngster
**moco** *m* mucus; snot; candle drippings; snuff (*of candlewick*); slag; **a moco de candil** by candle light; **llorar a moco tendido** (coll.) to cry like a baby; **quitar los mocos a** (coll.) to slap in the face; **moco del bauprés** (naut.)

dolphin striker, martingale; **moco de pavo** crest of a turkey; (bot.) cockscomb; (coll.) trifle
**mocoso -sa** *adj* snively, snotty; ill-bred, rude; saucy, flip; mean, good-for-nothing; *mf* brat
**mocosuelo -la** *mf* (coll.) brat; (coll.) meddler, schemer; (coll.) greenhorn
**mocosuena; traducir mocosuena** (coll.) to translate with cognates, to translate word for word
**mochada** *f* butt (*with the head*)
**mochales; estar mochales** (coll.) to be madly in love
**mochar** *va* to butt; (Am.) to dehorn
**mochazo** *m* blow with the butt of a gun
**mocheta** *f* thick or flat edge (*of a tool*); frame (*of door or window*); reëntering angle; (carp.) rabbet
**mochete** *m* (orn.) sparrow hawk
**mochil** *m* errand boy for farmers in the field
**mochila** *f* (mil.) knapsack; haversack; (mil.) ration (*for soldier or his horse*); tool bag; **de mochila** knapsack (*spray, pump, etc.*)
**mochín** *m* executioner
**mocho -cha** *adj* blunt, flat; stub-pointed; stub-horned; topped (*tree*); (coll.) cropped, shorn; *m* butt end
**mochuelo** *m* (orn.) little owl (*Athene noctua*); (print.) omission; **echarle a uno el mochuelo** (coll.) to give someone the worst of a deal; **cargar con el mochuelo** or **tocarle a uno el mochuelo** (coll.) to get the worst of a deal; **mochuelo de los bosques** (orn.) tawny owl
**moda** *f* fashion, mode, style; **a la moda** fashionable; **a la moda de** after the fashion of, in the style of; **de moda** in fashion, fashionable, popular; **fuera de moda** out of fashion; **pasar de moda** to go out of fashion
**modado -da** *adj;* **bien modado** (Am.) well-mannered; **mal modado** (Am.) ill-mannered
**modal** *adj* modal; **modales** *mpl* manners
**modalidad** *f* modality, way, manner, method; nature; kind
**modelación** *f* or **modelado** *m* modeling; molding
**modelaje** *m* modeling; molding; patternmaking
**modelar** *va* to model; to form, shape; to mold; *vr* to model; **modelarse sobre** to pattern oneself after
**modélico -ca** *adj* model
**modelismo** *m* patternmaking; molding
**modelista** *mf* patternmaker; molder
**modelo** *m* model; pattern; equal, peer; form, blank; style, e.g., **último modelo** latest style; **modelo vivo** live model; *mf* model, fashion model, mannequin; *adj invar* model, e.g., **una ciudad modelo** a model city
**moderación** *f* moderation
**moderador -dora** *adj* moderating; *mf* moderator; *m* (mach., phys. & chem.) moderator
**moderante** *m* (educ.) moderator
**moderantismo** *m* moderation; (pol.) conservatism
**moderar** *va* to moderate; to control, restrain; *vr* to moderate; to control onself, restrain oneself
**modernidad** *f* modernity
**modernismo** *m* modernism; neologism
**modernista** *adj* modernist, modernistic; *mf* modernist
**modernización** *f* modernization
**modernizar §76** *va & vr* to modernize
**moderno -na** *adj & m* modern
**modestia** *f* modesty
**modesto -ta** *adj* modest
**modicidad** *f* moderateness, reasonableness
**módico -ca** *adj* moderate, reasonable
**modificable** *adj* modifiable
**modificación** *f* modification
**modificador -dora** *adj* modifying; *mf* modifier
**modificante** *adj* modifying; *m* (gram.) modifier
**modificar §86** *va & vr* to modify
**modillón** *m* (arch.) modillion
**modismo** *m* idiom
**modista** *mf* dressmaker, modiste; **modista de sombreros** milliner
**modistería** *f* dressmaking; (Am.) ladies' dress shop
**modistilla** *f* (coll.) poor or unskilled dressmaker; seamstress, dressmaker's helper
**modisto** *m* ladies' tailor
**modo** *m* mode, manner, way, method; (gram.) mood or mode; (mus.) mode; **al modo** or **a modo de** like, in the manner of, on the order of; **al modo español** in the Spanish manner; **a mi modo** in my own way; **de buen modo** politely; **de ese modo** at that rate; **del mismo modo que** in the same way as; **de mal modo** impolitely, rudely; **de modo que** so that; so, and so; **de ningún modo** by no means; **de todos modos** at any rate, anyhow; **de un modo u otro** in one way or another, somehow; **en cierto modo** after or in a fashion; **por modo de** as, by way of; **sobre modo** extremely; **uno a modo de** a sort of, a kind of; **modo conjuntivo** (gram.) compound conjunction; **modo de ser** nature, disposition; **modo imperativo** (gram.) imperative mood; **modo indicativo** (gram.) indicative mood; **modo potencial** (gram.) potential mood; **modo subjuntivo** (gram.) subjunctive mood
**modorra** *f* see **modorro**
**modorrar** *va* to make drowsy, make heavy; *vr* to get drowsy, fall asleep; to become flabby (*said of fruit*)
**modorrilla** *f* (coll.) third night watch
**modorro -rra** *adj* drowsy, heavy; dull, stupid; flabby (*fruit*); poisoned by mercury (*in a mine*); (vet.) giddy; *f* drowsiness, heaviness; (vet.) gid, staggers
**modoso -sa** *adj* quiet, well-behaved
**modrego** *m* (coll.) awkward fellow, clumsy fellow
**modulación** *f* modulation; **modulación de altura** or **de amplitud** (rad.) amplitude modulation; **modulación de fase** (rad.) phase modulation; **modulación de frecuencia** (rad.) frequency modulation
**modulado -da** *adj* well-modulated; sweet, harmonious
**modulador -dora** *adj* modulating; *mf* modulator; *m* (rad.) modulator
**modular** *adj* modular; *va & vn* to modulate
**módulo** *m* modulus (*standard, norm*); module (*of a coin or medal*); (arch., hyd. & mach.) module; (phys.) modulus; (mus.) modulation
**moduloso -sa** *adj* harmonious
**moer** *m* moire; mohair
**mofa** *f* scoffing, jeering, mocking; **hacer mofa de** to scoff at, jeer at, make fun of
**mofador -dora** *adj* scoffing, jeering, mocking; *mf* scoffer, jeerer, mocker
**mofadura** *f* var. of **mofa**
**mofar** *vn & vr* to scoff, jeer, mock; **mofarse de** to scoff at, jeer at, make fun of
**mofeta** *f* (min.) blackdamp; mofette (*from a mine or from past volcanic activity*); (zool.) skunk, polecat
**moflete** *m* (coll.) jowl
**mofletudo -da** *adj* big-jowled, chubby-cheeked
**mogate** *m* glaze; **a** or **de medio mogate** carelessly
**mogato -ta** *adj & mf* var. of **mojigato**
**mogol -gola** *adj & mf* Mongol, Mongolian; **el gran Mogol** the Great Mogul; *m* Mongolian (*language*)
**Mogolia, la** Mongolia; **la Mogolia Exterior** Outer Mongolia; **la Mogolia Interior** Inner Mongolia
**mogólico -ca** *adj* Mongolian
**mogolismo** *m* Mongolism
**mogoloide** *adj & mf* Mongoloid
**mogollón** *m* sponging; **comer de mogollón** (coll.) to sponge
**mogón -gona** *adj* one-horned, single-horned; broken-horned
**mogote** *m* hummock, knoll; pile of faggots, stack of sheaves; budding antler
**mogrollo** *m* sponger; (coll.) roughneck
**moharra** *f* tip (*of lance, mast, etc.*); (Am.) spear (*for bullfighting*)
**moharrache** *m* or **moharracho** *m* clown
**mohatra** *f* fake sale; cheat
**mohecer §34** *va & vr* var. of **enmohecer**
**moheda** *f* or **mohedal** *m* bramblewood, jungle
**mohicano -na** *adj & mf* Mohican

**mohiento -ta** *adj* moldy, musty, mildewed
**mohín** *m* face, grimace, pouting
**mohíno -na** *adj* sad, gloomy; annoyed, peeved; black, black-nosed (*horse, cow, etc.*); *mf* hinny; *m* lone player (*against whom the rest gang up*); (orn.) blue magpie; *f* annoyance, displeasure
**moho** *m* (bot.) mold; rust, verdigris; laziness, sloth; **no criar moho** (coll.) to get no chance to grow stale; **moho del pan** bread mold
**mohoso -sa** *adj* moldy, musty, mildewed; rusty; stale (*joke*)
**Moisés** *m* Moses; (*l.c.*) *m* basket used as cradle
**mojado -da** *adj* wet; drenched, soaked; moist; (phonet.) liquid, mouillé; *m* (Am.) wetback; *f* wetting; drenching, soaking; stab
**mojador -dora** *adj* wetting; moistening; *mf* wetter; moistener; *m* moistener (*for fingers, stamps, etc.*)
**mojadura** *f* wetting; drenching, soaking; moistening
**mojama** *f* dry, salted tuna
**mojar** *va* to wet; to drench, soak; to dampen, moisten; (coll.) to stab; *vn* to dunk; **mojar en** (coll.) to get mixed up in; *vr* to get wet; to get drenched or soaked
**mojarra** *f* (ichth.) mojarra; (Am.) broad dagger
**mojarrilla** *mf* (coll.) jolly person
**moje** *m* gravy, sauce
**mojel** *m* (naut.) braided cord or cable
**mojera** *f* (bot.) whitebeam
**mojí** *m* (*pl:* **-jíes**) var. of **mojicón**
**mojicón** *m* muffin, bun; (coll.) punch in the face
**mojiganga** *f* mummery, masquerade, morris dance; clowning; (coll.) hypocrisy
**mojigatería** or **mojigatez** *f* hypocrisy; prudishness, sanctimoniousness
**mojigato -ta** *adj* hypocritical; prudish, sanctimonious; *mf* hypocrite; prude
**mojinete** *m* coping; ridge (*of roof*); caress, tap on the cheek; (Am.) gable
**mojo** *m* var. of **moje**
**mojón** *m* boundary stone, landmark, monument; pile, heap; turd; winetaster; quoits
**mojona** or **mojonación** *f* var. of **amojonamiento**
**mojonar** *va* var. of **amojonar**
**mojonera** *f* boundary, marked boundary; line of boundary stones or landmarks
**mojonero** *m* gauger
**mol** *m* (chem.) mol
**mola** *f* (path.) mole; (hist.) mole (*sacrificial cake*)
**molada** *f* batch of ground pigment
**molal** *adj* (chem.) molal
**molar** *adj* (anat., phys. & path.) molar; *m* (anat.) molar (*tooth*)
**molcajete** *m* stone mortar standing on a tripod
**moldar** *va* to mold; to put molding on
**moldavo -va** *adj & mf* Moldavian
**molde** *m* mold; matrix, cast, stamp; form, frame; pattern; model, ideal; (print.) form; **de molde** printed; fitting, to the purpose; **venir de molde** to be just right
**moldeado** *m* molding, casting
**moldeador -dora** *adj* molding; *m* molder; (carp.) molding machine; *f* (found.) molding machine
**moldear** *va* to mold; to cast; to put molding on
**moldeo** *m* molding; casting
**moldería** *f* molding (*preparation of molds*)
**moldura** *f* molding (*shaped strip of wood*)
**moldurar** *va* to put molding on
**moldurista** *m* molding maker
**mole** *adj* soft; *m* Mexican dish of meat or turkey cooked with chili and sesame sauce; *f* mass, bulk, heap
**molécula** *f* (chem. & phys.) molecule
**molécula-gramo** *f* (*pl:* **moléculas-gramos**) (chem.) gram molecule
**molecular** *adj* molecular
**molecular-gramo** *adj* gram-molecular
**moledero -ra** *adj* for grinding, to be ground; *f* grindstone; (coll.) bother, annoyance
**moledor -dora** *adj* grinding; (coll.) boring; *mf* grinder; (coll.) bore; *m* grinder, mill, crusher; roller (*of sugar mill*); *f* grinder, crusher
**moledura** *f* grinding, milling; fatigue, weariness
**molejón** *m* grindstone
**molendero -ra** *mf* miller, grinder; *m* chocolate grinder (*person*)
**moleño -ña** *adj* millstone (*rock*); *f* flint
**moler §63** *va* to grind, to mill; to annoy, harass; to tire out, to weary; to wear out, to spoil; (coll.) to chew; **a todo moler** wholeheartedly; **moler a palos** to beat up; *vr* to wear oneself out
**molero** *m* millstone maker or dealer
**molesquina** *f* moleskin
**molestador -dora** *adj* disturbing, annoying; *mf* disturber, annoyer
**molestar** *va* to molest, disturb; to annoy, bother; to tire, weary; *vr* to be annoyed; to bother; **molestarse con** to bother about or with; **molestarse en** + *inf* to bother to + *inf*, to take the trouble to + *inf*
**molestia** *f* molestation, annoyance, bother; discomfort, disturbance; unpleasantness, quarrel
**molesto -ta** *adj* annoying, bothersome; annoyed, bothered; uncomfortable
**molestoso -sa** *adj* (dial. & Am.) annoying, troublesome
**moleta** *f* muller; glass polisher; stamp, punch; roller; (print.) ink grinder
**moleteado** *m* knurl
**moletear** *va* to knurl
**moletón** *m* outing flannel, flannelet
**molibdato** *m* (chem.) molybdate
**molibdenita** *f* (mineral.) molybdenite
**molibdeno** *m* (chem.) molybdenum
**molibdenoso -sa** *adj* (chem.) molybdenous
**molíbdico -ca** *adj* (chem.) molybdic
**molicie** *f* softness; flabbiness; fondness for luxury, effeminacy; sensual pleasures
**molido -da** *adj* worn out, exhausted; see **oro**
**molienda** *f* grinding, milling; grist; mill; grinding season (*for sugar cane and olives*); (coll.) fatigue, weariness; (coll.) annoyance, bore, bother
**molificación** *f* softening
**molificar §86** *va & vr* to soften
**molimiento** *m* grinding; fatigue, weariness; discouragement
**molinar** *m* row of windmills
**molinería** *f* milling; milling industry; group of mills
**molinero -ra** *adj* (pertaining to a) mill; for grinding, to be ground; *mf* miller; *f* miller's wife
**molinete** *m* little mill; ventilating fan; windmill (*paper toy*); turnstile; twirl (*of cane*); brandish, flourish (*of sword*); (hyd.) current meter; (naut.) winch; drum (*of winch*)
**molinillo** *m* hand mill; chocolate beater; **molinillo de café** coffee grinder
**molino** *m* mill; grinder; restless person; **luchar con los molinos de viento** to tilt at windmills; **molino harinero** gristmill, flour mill; **molino de sangre** animal-driven mill; hand mill; **molino de viento** windmill (*machine; paper toy*); **molinos de viento** (fig.) windmills (*imaginary enemy*)
**Moloc** *m* (Bib.) Moloch; (*l.c.*) *m* (zool.) moloch
**móloc** *m* (Am.) mashed potatoes
**molondro** or **molondrón** *m* (coll.) lazy lummox
**moltura** *f* grinding
**molusco** *m* (zool.) mollusk
**molla** *f* lean meat; (prov.) soft part of bread
**mollar** *adj* soft, tender; easily shelled; mushy, pulpy; right, ripe; lean (*meat*); productive, easy; (coll.) gullible, easily taken in
**mollear** *vn* to give, to yield; to bend
**molledo** *m* fleshy part (*of leg, arm, etc.*); soft part of bread
**molleja** *f* gizzard; sweetbread; **criar molleja** (coll.) to grow lazy
**mollejón** *m* grindstone; (coll.) big fat loafer; (coll.) good-natured fellow
**mollera** *f* crown (*of head*); brains, sense; head, mind; **tener buena mollera** (coll.) to have a good head on one's shoulders; **cerrado de mollera** stupid; **duro de mollera** (coll.) stubborn, dull
**mollero** *m* (coll.) lean meat

**molleta** *f* biscuit; brown bread; **molletas** *fpl* snuffers
**mollete** *m* muffin, French roll; chubby cheek; fleshy part (*of arm*)
**molletudo -da** *adj* var. of **mofletudo**
**mollificar** §86 *va* var. of **molificar**
**mollino -na** *adj* drizzly; *f* drizzle
**mollizna** *f* drizzle
**molliznar** or **molliznear** *vn* to drizzle
**momentáneo -a** *adj* momentary
**momento** *m* moment; (mech.) moment; **a cada momento** at every moment, all the time; **al momento** at once; **de momento** present; suddenly; for the present; **de un momento a otro** at any moment; **en un momento** in a moment; **por momentos** continuously; any moment, presently; **momento angular** (mech.) angular momentum; **momento de inercia** (mech.) moment of inertia; **momento magnético** (phys.) magnetic moment; **momento psicológico** psychological moment
**momería** *f* clowning
**momero -ra** *adj* clowning; *mf* clown
**momia** *f* see **momio**
**momificación** *f* mummification
**momificar** §86 *va & vr* to mummify
**momio -mia** *adj* lean, skinny; *m* extra; bargain; **de momio** free, gratis; *f* mummy
**momista** *mf* bargain hunter
**Momo** *m* (myth.) Momus; (*l.c.*) *m* face, grimace, clowning; (coll.) caress, fondling; **hacer momos a** (coll.) to make eyes at (*a woman*)
**momórdiga** *f* (bot.) balsam apple
**mona** *f* see **mono**
**monacal** *adj* monachal
**monacato** *m* monkhood, monasticism
**monacillo** *m* altar boy, acolyte
**monacita** *f* (mineral.) monazite
**monacordio** *m* (mus.) manichord
**monada** *f* monkeyshine; monkey face, grimace; darling, cute little thing; cuteness; flattery; piece of foolishness; triviality, childishness
**mónada** *f* (biol., chem., philos. & zool.) monad
**monadélfico -ca** *adj* (bot.) monadelphous
**monadismo** *m* (philos.) monadism
**monago** *m* (coll.) altar boy, acolyte; **llenar el monago** (coll.) to eat
**monaguillo** *m* var. of **monacillo**
**monandria** *f* monandry; (bot.) monandry
**monándrico -ca** *adj* monandrous
**monandro -dra** *adj* (bot.) monandrous
**monaquismo** *m* monachism, monasticism
**monarca** *m* monarch; **los Monarcas de Oriente** the Wise Men of the East
**monarquía** *f* monarchy; **monarquía absoluta** absolute monarchy; **monarquía constitucional** constitutional monarchy
**monárquico -ca** *adj* monarchic or monarchical; *mf* monarchist
**monarquismo** *m* monarchism
**monarquista** *adj* monarchist, monarchistic; *mf* monarchist
**monasterial** *adj* monasterial
**monasterio** *m* monastery
**monasticismo** *m* var. of **monacato**
**monástico -ca** *adj* monastic or monastical
**monast.º** abr. of **monasterio**
**Moncenisio** *m* Mont Cenis
**monda** *f* see **mondo**
**mondadientes** *m* (*pl:* **-tes**) toothpick
**mondador -dora** *adj* cleaning; peeling, paring; *mf* cleaner; peeler, parer; *f* peeler, peeling machine
**mondadura** *f* pruning, trimming; **mondaduras** *fpl* peelings, parings
**mondaoídos** *m* (*pl:* **-dos**) earpick
**mondaorejas** *m* (*pl:* **-jas**) var. of **mondaoídos**
**mondar** *va* to clean; to prune, to trim; to peel, to pare, to hull, to husk; to cut the hair of; (coll.) to fleece; *vr* to lose one's hair (*e.g., after an illness*); to pick (*one's teeth*)
**mondarajas** *fpl* (coll.) peelings
**mondejo** *m* stuffed tripe
**mondo -da** *adj* clean, clear, pure; **mondo y lirondo** (coll.) pure, unadulterated; *f* pruning, trimming; parings, peelings; pruning season; clearing of a cemetery for further burials
**mondón** *m* stripped tree trunk
**mondonga** *f* (coll.) kitchen wench
**mondongo** *m* tripe; (coll.) guts
**mondonguería** *f* tripe shop
**mondonguero -ra** *mf* tripe dealer
**mondonguil** *adj* (coll.) (pertaining to) tripe
**monear** *vn* (coll.) to be a monkey, to make faces; (Am.) to boast
**moneda** *f* money; coin; mint; **la Moneda** Santiago, the government of Chile; **pagar en la misma moneda** to pay back in one's own coin; **moneda corriente** currency; (coll.) everyday matter, common knowledge; **moneda falsa** counterfeit; **moneda imaginaria** money of account; **moneda menuda** change; **moneda metálica** or **sonante** metal money, specie; **moneda suelta** change
**monedaje** *m* coining, minting; seigniorage
**monedar** or **monedear** *va* to coin, to mint
**monedero** *m* moneyer; moneybag; change purse; **monedero falso** counterfeiter
**monegasco -ca** *adj & mf* Monegasque
**monería** *f* monkeyshine; cuteness; triviality, childishness
**monesco -ca** *adj* (coll.) apish
**monetario -ria** *adj* monetary
**monetización** *f* monetization
**monetizar** §76 *va* to monetize
**monfí** *m* (*pl:* **-fíes**) (hist.) Moorish highwayman (*in Andalusia*)
**mongol -gola** *adj & mf* var. of **mogol**
**mongólico -ca** *adj* var. of **mogólico**
**mongolismo** *m* var. of **mogolismo**
**moniato** *m* var. of **buniato**
**monicaco** *m* (coll.) whippersnapper
**monición** *f* monition; remonstrance
**monigote** *m* lay brother; rag figure, stuffed form; botched painting, botched statue; (coll.) boob, sap; (fig.) puppet
**moniliforme** *adj* moniliform; (bot. & zool.) moniliform
**monillo** *m* waist, bodice
**monipodio** *m* (coll.) illegal deal, collusion, cabal
**monís** *f* trinket; **monises** *mpl* (coll.) money, dough
**monismo** *m* (philos.) monism
**monista** *adj* monist, monistic; *mf* monist
**mónita** *f* (coll.) smoothness, slickness
**monitor** *m* monitor; (hyd., naut. & rad.) monitor; (zool.) monitor, monitor lizard
**monitorio -ria** *adj* monitorial; monitory; *m* monitory; threat of excommunication; *f* monitory
**monja** *f* nun; **monjas** *fpl* lingering sparks in a burned piece of paper
**monje** *m* monk; recluse, anchorite; (orn.) great titmouse; **monje negro** Black Monk (*Benedictine*)
**monjía** *f* monkhood
**monjil** *adj* nunnish, nun's; *m* nun's dress; (archaic) mourning dress; angel sleeve
**monjío** *m* nunhood; taking the veil
**mono -na** *adj* (coll.) cute, cute little, nice; (Am.) red (*hair*); *m* (zool.) monkey, ape; mimic; (fig.) monkey (*in gestures*); squirt, whippersnapper; coveralls; (taur.) attendant on foot; (Am.) pile of fruit or vegetables (*in a store or market*); **estar de monos** (coll.) to be on the outs; **meter los monos a** (Am.) to scare the life out of; **mono araña** (zool.) spider monkey; **mono aullador, mono chillón** (zool.) howling monkey; **mono de Gibraltar** (zool.) Barbary ape; *f* (zool.) Barbary ape; female monkey; (coll.) copycat, ape; (taur.) guard for right leg; (coll.) drunk (*person*); (coll.) drunkenness; (coll.) hangover; **dormir la mona** (coll.) to sleep it off, to sleep off a drunk; **pillar una mona** (coll.) to go on a jag; **pintar la mona** (coll.) to act important; **quedarse como** or **quedarse hecho una mona** (coll.) to be disconcerted, to lose countenance
**monoatómico -ca** *adj* monoatomic
**monobásico -ca** *adj* (chem.) monobasic
**monocarpelar** *adj* monocarpellary
**monocarril** *m* var. of **monorriel**
**monócero -ra** *adj* monocerous; (*cap.*) *m* (astr.) Monoceros
**monoceronte** *m* or **monocerote** *m* (myth.) unicorn

**monocilíndrico -ca** *adj* single-cylinder
**monoclínico -ca** *adj* (cryst.) monoclinic
**monocordio** *m* (mus.) monochord
**monocotiledón** *m* (bot.) monocotyledon
**monocroico -ca** *adj* monochroic
**monocromático -ca** *adj* monochromatic
**monocromía** *f* monochromy
**monocromo -ma** *adj & m* monochrome
**monocular** *adj* monocular
**monóculo -la** *adj* monocular (*having only one eye*); *m* monocle; (surg.) monoculus
**monocultura** *f* (agr.) monoculture, cultivation of a single crop
**monodia** *f* (mus.) monody
**monódico -ca** *adj* monodic
**monofásico -ca** *adj* (elec.) monophase, single-phase
**monofilo -la** *adj* (bot.) monophyllous
**monofisita** *mf* (rel.) Monophysite
**monofónico -ca** *adj* monophonic
**monogamia** *f* monogamy; (zool.) monogamy
**monogámico -ca** *adj* monogamic
**monogamista** *adj* monogamist, monogamistic; *mf* monogamist
**monógamo -ma** *adj* monogamous; monogamistic; *mf* monogamist
**monogenismo** *m* (anthrop.) monogenism
**monogenista** *mf* monogenist
**monógino -na** *adj* (bot.) monogynous
**monografía** *f* monograph
**monográfico -ca** *adj* monographic; special (*course, theme, subject*)
**monografista** *mf* monographer
**monograma** *m* monogram
**monoico -ca** *adj* (bot.) monoecious
**monolítico -ca** *adj* monolithic
**monolito** *m* monolith
**monologar** §59 *vn* to engage in a monologue, to soliloquize
**monólogo** *m* monologue
**monologuista** *mf* monologuist
**monomanía** *f* monomania; **monomanía de grandezas** folie des grandeurs, megalomania
**monomaníaco -ca** or **monómano -na** *adj* monomaniacal; *mf* monomaniac
**monometálico -ca** *adj* (chem.) monometallic
**monometalismo** *m* monometallism
**monometalista** *adj & mf* monometallist
**monomio** *m* (alg.) monomial
**monono -na** *adj* (coll.) sweet, darling, cute
**monopastos** *m* (*pl:* **-tos**) sheave
**monopatín** *m* scooter (*child's vehicle*)
**monopétalo -la** *adj* (bot.) monopetalous
**monoplano** *m* (aer.) monoplane
**monoplaza** *m* (aer.) single-seater
**monoplejía** *f* (path.) monoplegia
**monopolio** *m* monopoly
**monopolista** *mf* monopolist
**monopolización** *f* monopolization
**monopolizador -dora** *adj* monopolizing; monopolistic; *mf* monopolizer
**monopolizar** §76 *va* to monopolize
**monóptero -ra** *adj* (arch.) monopteral
**monorriel** *m* monorail
**monorrimo -ma** *adj* monorhymed
**monosabio** *m* (taur.) costumed ring servant of picador
**monosacárido** *m* (chem.) monosaccharide
**monosépalo -la** *adj* (bot.) monosepalous
**monosilábico -ca** *adj* monosyllabic
**monosílabo -ba** *adj* monosyllabic; *m* monosyllable
**monospastos** *m* (*pl:* **-tos**) var. of **monopastos**
**monospermo -ma** *adj* (bot.) monospermous
**monóstrofe** *f* monostrophe
**monote** *m* (coll.) person transfixed (*with amazement, terror, etc.*); (coll.) pedant; (prov.) disturbance, riot
**monoteico -ca** *adj* monotheistic
**monoteísmo** *m* monotheism
**monoteísta** *adj* monotheist, monotheistic; *mf* monotheist
**monotipia** *f* (print.) monotype (*machine; method*)
**monotipista** *mf* monotyper
**monotipo** *m* (print.) monotype (*machine*)
**monotonía** *f* monotony
**monótono -na** *adj* monotonous
**monotrema** *adj & m* (zool.) monotreme
**monovalente** *adj* (chem. & bact.) monovalent
**monóxido** *m* (chem.) monoxide
**monroísmo** *m* Monroeism, Monroe Doctrine
**Mons.** abr. of **Monseñor**
**monseñor** *m* monseigneur; (eccl.) monsignor
**monserga** *f* (coll.) gibberish
**monstruo** *m* monster; **el monstruo de la naturaleza** Lope de Vega; **monstruo de Gila** (zool.) Gila monster
**monstruosidad** *f* monstrosity
**monstruoso -sa** *adj* monstrous
**monta** *f* mounting; sum, total; stud farm; account, e.g., **de poca monta** of little account, of little importance; (mil.) call to horse
**montacargas** *m* (*pl:* **-gas**) freight elevator, hoist
**montacarros** *m* (*pl:* **-rros**) automobile dealer
**montada** *f* see **montado**
**montadero** *m* horse block
**montado -da** *adj* mounted (*on horseback; in position for use; in a setting*); *m* horseman, trooper; *f* port, tongue groove (*of horse's bit*)
**montador** *m* mounter; horse block; fitter, erector, installer; (mov.) cutter
**montadura** *f* mounting; harness (*of a riding horse*); setting (*of a precious stone*)
**montaje** *m* montage; setting up; (mach.) mounting, assembly; (rad.) hookup; **montajes** *mpl* (arti.) mount
**montanear** *vn* to eat acorns and mast (*said of hogs*)
**montanera** *f* oak forest, acorn pasture for hogs; feeding of hogs on acorns; acorn-feeding season
**montanero** *m* forest ranger
**montano -na** *adj* (pertaining to a) mountain; montane
**montantada** *f* boasting; crowd, multitude
**montante** *m* post, upright; strut; transom; broadsword; amount; (arch.) mullion; *f* flood tide
**montantear** *vn* to wield the broadsword; to boast, to meddle
**montantero** *m* (archaic) fighter with a broadsword
**montaña** *f* mountain; forested region; **la Montaña** the province of Santander, Spain; **montaña de hielo** iceberg; **montaña rusa** roller coaster, switchback; **Montañas Rocosas** or **Roqueñas** Rocky Mountains, Rockies
**montañero -ra** *adj* mountaineering; *mf* mountain climber
**montañés -ñesa** *adj* (pertaining to a) mountain, highland; mountain-dwelling; (pertaining to) la Montaña; *mf* mountaineer, highlander; native or inhabitant of la Montaña; *m* dialect of la Montaña
**montañesismo** *m* fondness for mountains
**montañeta** *f* hill, small mountain
**montañismo** *m* mountaineering, mountain climbing
**montañoso -sa** *adj* mountainous
**montañuela** *f* var. of **montañeta**
**montaplatos** *m* (*pl:* **-tos**) dumbwaiter
**montar** *va* to mount; to get on; to ride (*a horse, a bicycle, a person's shoulders, etc.*); to set up, establish (*a service*); to amount to; to cock (*a gun*); to set (*a precious stone*); to cover (*a mare*); to wind (*a clock*); to fine (*for trespassing of cattle, etc.*); (mach.) to mount, to assemble; (elec.) to hook up; (mil.) to mount (*guard*); (naut.) to mount (*a certain number of cannon*); (naut.) to command (*a ship*); (naut.) to round (*a cape*); *vn* to mount; to get on top; to ride; to weigh, be important; **tanto monta** it's all the same; **¡montas!** (coll.) come now!; *vr* to mount; to get on top
**montaraz** (*pl:* **-races**) *adj* backwoods; wild, untamed; *m* warden, forester
**montazgar** §59 *va* to collect cattle toll from
**montazgo** *m* toll for passage of cattle
**monte** *m* mount, mountain; woods, woodland; obstruction, interference; backwoods, brush, wild country; bank, kitty; monte (*card game*); widow (*in card playing*); (coll.) dirty mop of hair; **andar a monte** (coll.) to take to the woods; (coll.) to be out of circulation; **el monte Ábila** Jebel Musa (*opposite Gibraltar*); **el**

monte Blanco Mont Blanc; **el monte Carmelo** Mount Carmel; **el monte de los Olivos** Mount Olive; **el monte Etna** Mount Aetna; **el monte Olivete** Mount Olivet; **el monte Palatino** the Palatine Hill; **el monte Parnaso** Mount Parnassus; **el monte Pelado** Mount Pelée; **el monte Sinaí** Mount Sinai; **monte alto** forest; **monte bajo** thicket, brushwood; **monte de piedad** pawnshop; **monte de Venus** (anat.) mons Veneris; **monte pío** pension fund (*for widows and orphans*); mutual benefit society; **montes Apalaches** Appalachian Mountains; **montes Balcanes** Balkan Mountains; **montes Grampianos** Grampian Hills; **montes Himalaya** Himalaya Mountains; **montes Laurentinos** Laurentian Mountains; **montes Urales** Ural Mountains

**montea** *f* hunting, beating the wood (*to rouse game*); stonecutting; (arch.) rise (*of an arch*); working drawing

**montear** *va* to hunt, to track down; to make a working drawing of; to arch, to vault

**montecillo** *m* mount, hillock

**montenegrino -na** *adj & mf* Montenegrin

**montepío** *m* pension fund (*for widows and orphans*); mutual benefit society

**montera** *f* cloth cap; skylight; head (*of boiler of a still*); huntress, huntswoman; bullfighter's hat; (naut.) moonsail

**monterería** *f* cap shop

**monterero -ra** *mf* cap maker or dealer

**montería** *f* hunt; hunting; big-game hunting; hunting party; (paint.) hunting scene; **andar de montería** to go hunting

**monterilla** *f* (naut.) moonsail

**montero** *m* hunter, huntsman

**montés** or **montesino -na** *adj* wild (*cat, goat, etc.*)

**montículo** *m* var. of **montecillo**

**montilla** *m* montilla (*a pale dry sherry*)

**monto** *m* sum, total

**montón** *m* pile, heap; crowd; (coll.) lot, great deal, great many; **a montones** (coll.) in abundance; **a, de** or **en montón** (coll.) together, taken together; **ser del montón** (coll.) to be quite ordinary; **montón de robo** widow (*at cards*); **montón de tierra** (coll.) feeble old person

**montonera** *f* (Am.) squad of mounted insurgents

**montuno -na** *adj* wooded; (Am.) rustic; (Am.) wild, untamed

**montuoso -sa** *adj* woody, wooded; rugged; hilly

**montura** *f* mount (*riding horse*); seat, saddle; harness (*of a riding horse*); mounting (*of precious stone, gun, telescope, etc*); frame (*of spectacles*); (mach.) mounting, assembly

**monumental** *adj* monumental

**monumento** *m* monument

**monzón** *m & f* monsoon

**monzónico -ca** *adj* monsoonal

**moña** *f* doll; mannequin (*lay figure*); ribbon, hair ribbon; bow of ribbons; (coll.) drunk

**moño** *m* topknot (*of hair, of ribbons; of feathers of certain birds*); top, crest; (Am.) forelock (*of horse*); (Am.) whim, caprice; **moños** *mpl* frippery; **ponerse moños** (coll.) to put on airs

**moñón -ñona** or **moñudo -da** *adj* topped, crested

**moquear** *vn* to snivel, to have a runny nose

**moqueo** *m* sniveling, runny nose

**moquero** *m* pocket handkerchief

**moqueta** *f* moquette

**moquete** *m* punch in the face, punch in the nose

**moquetear** *va* to punch in the nose; *vn* (coll.) to snivel all the time

**moquillo** *m* watery discharge (*from nose in cold weather*); (vet.) distemper; (vet.) pip

**moquita** *f* watery nose

**mor** *m* love; **por mor de** for love of; because of

**mora** *f* see **moro**

**morabito** *m* Mohammedan hermit; Mohammedan hermitage

**moráceo -a** *adj* (bot.) moraceous

**moracho -cha** *adj & m* light mulberry (*color*)

**morado -da** *adj & m* mulberry (*color*); *f* abode, house, dwelling; stay, sojourn

**morador -dora** *adj* dwelling, living; *mf* dweller, resident

**moradux** *m* var. of **almoraduj**

**moraga** *f* sheaf, bundle; fish fry

**moral** *adj* moral; *m* (bot.) black mulberry (*tree*); *f* morals (*ethics; conduct*); morale (*e.g., of soldiers*); (coll.) moral (*e.g., of a fable*)

**moraleja** *f* moral (*e.g., of a fable*)

**moralidad** *f* morality; moral (*e.g., of a fable*); morality play

**moralista** *m* moralist (*teacher or writer*)

**moralizador -dora** *adj* moralizing; *mf* moralizer

**moralizar §76** *va & vn* to moralize

**morapio** *m* (coll.) red wine

**morar** *vn* to live, dwell

**moratorio -ria** *adj* moratory; *f* moratorium

**moravo -va** *adj & mf* Moravian

**morbidez** *f* (paint.) morbidezza

**morbididad** *f* morbidity (*sick rate*)

**mórbido -da** *adj* (paint.) soft, delicate, mellow; morbid

**morbífico -ca** *adj* morbific or morbifical

**morbilidad** *f* var. of **morbididad**

**morbo** *m* disease, illness; **morbo comicial** (path.) epilepsy; **morbo gálico** (path.) syphilis; **morbo regio** (path.) jaundice

**morbosidad** *f* morbidity

**morboso -sa** *adj* morbid, diseased

**morcajo** *m* maslin, mixture of wheat and rye

**morcella** *f* spark from a candle

**morciguillo** *m* var. of **murciélago**

**morcilla** *f* see **morcillo**

**morcillero -ra** *mf* maker or seller of blood puddings; (coll.) gagging actor, adlibber

**morcillo -lla** *adj* reddish-black (*horse*); *m* fleshy part of arm; *f* black pudding, blood pudding; (coll.) gag (*interpolation by an actor*)

**morcón** *m* large blood pudding; (coll.) short stocky person; (coll.) sloppy person

**mordacidad** *f* mordacity; mordancy

**mordaga** *f* (coll.) drunk, drunkenness

**mordaz** *adj* (*pl:* **-daces**) mordacious; burning, corrosive; mordant; (fig.) mordacious, mordant, sarcastic

**mordaza** *f* gag; clamp, jaw; pincers, tongs; pipe vise; (fig.) gag; **poner la mordaza a** to gag (*to silence*); **mordaza dental** (surg.) gag

**mordedor -dora** *adj* biting; (fig.) biting, sarcastic; *mf* biter

**mordedura** *f* bite

**mordelón** *m* (Am.) bribe-taking officer, crooked cop

**mordente** *m* mordant; (mus.) mordent

**morder §63** *va* to bite; to nibble; to snatch; to wear away, wear down; to eat away; to gossip about, to ridicule; (Am.) to graft; *vn* to bite; to take hold; (Am.) to graft

**mordicación** *f* biting, stinging

**mordicante** *adj* burning, corrosive; mordant, sarcastic

**mordicar §86** *va & vn* to bite, to sting

**mordicativo -va** *adj* biting, corrosive

**mordido -da** *adj* wasted, worn; *m* (coll.) nibble, bite; *f* (Am.) bite; (Am.) petty graft, racket

**mordiente** *m* mordant

**mordihuí** *m* (*pl:* **-huíes**) (ent.) grub, weevil

**mordimiento** *m* var. of **mordedura**

**mordiscar §86** *va* to nibble at, to gnaw at; to champ; *vn* to nibble, to gnaw away; to champ

**mordisco** *m* nibble, bite

**mordisquear** *va & vn* var. of **mordiscar**

**moreda** *f* (bot.) black mulberry tree; growth of white mulberries

**morena** *f* see **moreno**

**morenez** *f* brownness, darkness

**morenillo** *m* paste of powdered charcoal and vinegar used by sheepshearer to treat cuts

**moreno -na** *adj* brown, dark brown; dark, dark-complexioned; (coll.) colored; (Am.) mulatto; *mf* (coll.) colored person; (Am.) mulatto; *m* brunet; *f* brunette; brown bread; rick (*of new-mown hay*); (geol.) moraine; (ichth.) moray; (path.) piles

**morenote -ta** *adj* very dark

**morera** *f* (bot.) white mulberry (*tree*)

**moreral** *m* growth of white mulberry trees
**morería** *f* Moorish quarter; Moorish land
**moretón** *m* (coll.) bruise, black-and-blue mark
**morfa** *f* (plant path.) citrus scab
**morfea** *f* (path.) morphea
**Morfeo** *m* (myth.) Morpheus
**morfema** *m* (gram.) morpheme
**morfina** *f* (chem.) morphine
**morfinismo** *m* (path.) morphinism
**morfinomanía** *f* drug habit
**morfinómano -na** *adj* addicted to drugs; *mf* drug addict
**morfogénesis** *f* morphogenesis
**morfógeno -na** *adj* (embryol.) morphogenic
**morfología** *f* (biol. & gram.) morphology
**morfológico -ca** *adj* morphologic or morphological
**morga** *f* foul-smelling juice that oozes from a heap of olives; (bot.) India berry tree
**Morgana** *f* (myth.) Fata Morgana, Morgan le Fay
**morganático -ca** *adj* morganatic
**moribundo -da** *adj* moribund, dying; *mf* moribund, dying person
**moriche** *m* (bot.) mirity palm
**moridero** *m* (Am.) unhealthy spot
**moriego -ga** *adj* Moorish
**morigeración** *f* moderation, temperance
**morigerado -da** *adj* moderate, temperate
**morigerar** *va* to moderate, restrain
**morilla** *f* (bot.) morel
**morillero** *m* var. of **mochil**
**morillo** *m* firedog, andiron
**morina** *f* (chem.) morin
**morir §45 & §17,** 9 *va* to die (*e.g., a painful death*); *vn* to die; to die away; **morir ahogado** to drown, to die by drowning; **morir de risa** to die laughing; **morir de viejo** to die of old age; **morir helado** to freeze to death; **morir por** to be crazy about, to pine for; **morir quemado** to burn to death; **morir vestido** (coll.) to die a violent death; *vr* to die; to be dying; to die out; to go to sleep (*said of a leg or arm*); **morirse por** to be crazy about, to pine for; **morirse por** + *inf* to be dying to + *inf*
**morisco -ca** *adj* Morisco, Moorish; *mf* Moor converted to Christianity (*after the Reconquest*); (Am.) Morisco (*offspring of mulatto and Spaniard*)
**morisma** *f* Mohammedanism; Moors, crowd of Moors
**morisqueta** *f* Moorish trick; mean trick; unsalted boiled rice
**morito** *m* (orn.) glossy ibis
**morlaco -ca** *adj* acting silly or ignorant; *m* (taur.) bull, big bull; **morlacos** *mpl* (Am.) dough, cash
**morlón -lona** *adj* acting silly or ignorant
**mormón -mona** *mf* Mormon; *m* (zool.) mormon, mandrill
**mormónico -ca** *adj* Mormon
**mormonismo** *m* Mormonism
**moro -ra** *adj* Moorish; Moslem; unbaptized; (coll.) unwatered (*wine*); dappled, spotted (*horse*); *mf* Moor; Moslem; Moro (*Mohammedan Malay of Philippine Islands*); **moro de paz** peaceful person; **moros en la costa** (coll.) trouble in the offing; *f* black mulberry (*fruit*); white mulberry (*fruit*); blackberry, brambleberry (*fruit*); (law) delay
**morocada** *f* butt of a ram
**morocho -cha** *adj* (Am.) strong, robust; (Am.) dark
**morojo** *m* fruit of strawberry tree
**morón** *m* mound, knoll; moron
**moroncho -cha** *adj* var. of **morondo**
**morondanga** *f* (coll.) hodgepodge
**morondo -da** *adj* stripped, bare (*of hair, leaves, etc.*)
**morónico -ca** *adj* moronic
**moronismo** *m* moronism
**morosidad** *f* slowness, tardiness; delinquency
**moroso -sa** *adj* slow, tardy, dilatory; delinquent
**morquera** *f* (bot.) winter savory
**morra** *f* top, crown (*of head*); mora (*game*); purr (*of cat*); **andar a la morra** (coll.) to come to blows; *interj* here pussy!
**morrada** *f* butt, butting; punch, slap
**morral** *m* nose bag; knapsack; game bag; wallet (*bag for traveling*); (coll.) boor, rustic
**morralla** *f* small fish; rabble, trash
**morrillo** *m* boulder; fat of neck (*of an animal*); (coll.) thick neck
**morriña** *f* (vet.) dropsy; (coll.) blues, melancholy, loneliness; **morriña de la tierra** (coll.) homesickness; **morriña negra** (vet.) blackleg
**morriñoso -sa** *adj* rachitic, sickly; (coll.) blue, melancholy, lonely
**morrión** *m* morion; helmet
**morrionera** *f* (bot.) wayfaring tree
**morro** *m* knob; knoll; pebble; snout; bulwark; ward (*of a lock*); **estar de morro** or **morros** (coll.) to be on the outs; **poner morro** to pucker one's lips, make a snout
**morrocotudo -da** *adj* (coll.) strong, heavy, thick; (coll.) weighty (*matter, business*); (Am.) rich; (Am.) big, enormous; (Am.) monotonous (*writing or work of art*)
**morrón** *adj* knotted (*flag*); *m* (coll.) crash, collision
**morroncho -cha** *adj* (prov.) mild, gentle
**morrongo -ga** or **morroño -ña** *mf* (coll.) cat
**morrudo -da** *adj* snouted; thick-lipped
**morsa** *f* (zool.) walrus; (Am.) vise
**morsana** *f* (bot.) bean caper
**mortadela** *f* Bologna sausage
**mortaja** *f* shroud, winding sheet; (carp.) mortise; (Am.) cigarette paper
**mortal** *adj* mortal; hard, killing, deadly; sure, definitive, conclusive; deathly pale; mortally ill, at death's door; *m* mortal
**mortalidad** *f* mortality (*mortal nature; death rate*)
**mortandad** *f* mortality, massacre, butchery
**mortecino -na** *adj* dead; dying; weak, failing; **hacer la mortecina** (coll.) to play dead, play possum
**morterada** *f* bowlful, batch (*mixed at one time in a mortar*); discharge of a mortar
**morterete** *m* small mortar (*used for salvos and public festivities*); floating candle
**mortero** *m* mortar (*bowl; mixture of lime, etc.*); (arti.) mortar; **mortero de trinchera** (arti.) trench gun or mortar
**morteruelo** *m* noise-making hemisphere (*toy*); fricassee of hog's liver
**mortífero -ra** *adj* deadly
**mortificación** *f* mortification
**mortificador -dora** or **mortificante** *adj* mortifying
**mortificar §86** *va & vr* to mortify
**mortuorio -ria** *adj* mortuary; funeral; *m* funeral
**morucho** *m* (taur.) young bull with wooden balls on horns
**morueco** *m* tup, ram
**mórula** *f* (embryol.) morula
**moruno -na** *adj* Moorish
**morusa** *f* (coll.) cash, money
**Mosa** *m* Meuse
**mosaico -ca** *adj* Mosaic (*of Moses*); (f.a.) mosaic; *m* tile; paving tile; (aer., f.a., & telv.) mosaic; **mosaico del tabaco** (plant path.) tobacco mosaic; **mosaico de madera** (f.a.) marquetry
**mosaísmo** *m* Mosaism
**mosca** *f* (ent.) fly; fly (*used in fishing*); imperial (*beard*); (coll.) cash, dough; (coll.) bore, nuisance; (coll.) disappointment; (Am.) sponger, parasite; **moscas** *fpl* sparks; **aflojar la mosca** (coll.) to shell out, to fork out; **papar moscas** (coll.) to gape, to gawk; **soltar la mosca** (coll.) to shell out, to fork out; **mosca abeja** (ent.) bee fly; **mosca borriquera** (ent.) horse tick; **mosca de burro** or **de caballo** (ent.) horsefly; **mosca de España** (ent.) Spanish fly; **mosca de la aceituna** (ent.) olive fly; **mosca de la carne** (ent.) flesh fly, meat fly; **mosca de las cerezas** (ent.) cherry fruit fly; **mosca de las frutas** (ent.) fruit fly; **mosca del olivo** (ent.) olive fly; **mosca del queso** (ent.) cheese fly; **mosca del vinagre** (ent.) vinegar fly, fruit fly; **mosca de mayo** (ent.) May fly; **mosca de sierra** (ent.) sawfly; **mosca de un día** (ent.) May fly; **mosca mediterránea** (ent.) fruit fly; **mosca muer-**

ta (coll.) hypocrite; **mosca picadora de los establos** (ent.) stable fly; **moscas blancas** snowflakes; **moscas volantes** muscae volitantes, spots before the eyes; *m* (box.) flyweight
**moscabado -da** *adj & m* var. of **mascabado**
**moscarda** *f* (ent.) flesh fly; (ent.) blowfly, bluebottle; egg of queen bee
**moscardear** *vn* to lay eggs (*said of queen bee*)
**moscardino** *m* (zool.) dormouse
**moscardón** *m* (ent.) botfly; (ent.) flesh fly; (ent.) hornet; (coll.) bore, annoyance (*person*)
**moscareta** *f* (orn.) flycatcher
**moscarrón** *m* var. of **moscardón**
**moscatel** *m* muscatel (*grape or wine*); (coll.) bore, nuisance
**moscella** *f* var. of **morcella**
**mosco** *m* (ent.) mosquito
**moscón** *m* large fly; (ent.) bluebottle; (ent.) flesh fly; (bot.) maple; (coll.) sly fellow
**moscona** *f* brazen woman, hussy
**mosconear** *va* to bore, bother, annoy; *vn* to make a nuisance of oneself
**Moscovia** *f* Muscovy
**moscovita** *adj & mf* Muscovite; *f* (mineral.) muscovite
**moscovítico -ca** *adj* Muscovitic
**Moscú** *f* Moscow
**Mosela** *m* Moselle
**mosén** *m* (prov.) father (*priest*); (obs.) sir (*title given to member of lesser nobility in Aragon*)
**mosqueador** *m* flyflap; (coll.) tail (*of horse or other animal*)
**mosquear** *va* to shoo (*flies*); to answer sharply; to beat, to whip; *vr* to shake off annoyances; to take offense
**mosqueo** *m* chasing flies; resentment
**mosquero** *m* flyflap, flytrap; fly swatter; flypaper
**mosquerola** or **mosqueruela** *f* (hort.) muscadine (*pear*)
**mosqueta** *f* (bot.) Japan globeflower; **mosqueta silvestre** (bot.) dog rose
**mosquetazo** *m* musket shot, musket wound
**mosquete** *m* musket
**mosquetería** *f* musketry (*troops; shooting*)
**mosquetero** *m* musketeer; (theat.) spectator with standing room in pit
**mosquetón** *m* snap hook, spring hook
**mosquil** or **mosquino -na** *adj* (pertaining to a) fly
**mosquitera** *f* or **mosquitero** *m* mosquito net or netting; fly net
**mosquito** *m* (ent.) mosquito; gnat; (coll.) tippler
**mostacera** *f* or **mostacero** *m* mustard pot
**mostacilla** *f* mustard-seed shot; tiny bead
**mostacho** *m* mustache; (coll.) spot on the face; (naut.) shroud (*of bowsprit*)
**mostachón** *m* macaroon
**mostachoso -sa** *adj* mustachioed
**mostagán** *m* (coll.) wine
**mostajo** *m* (bot.) whitebeam
**mostaza** *f* (bot.) mustard; mustard seed (*seed; dust shot*); mustard (*powder or paste*); **hacer la mostaza** (coll.) to give a bloody nose to each other (*said of boys*); **subírsele la mostaza a las narices** (coll.) to fly into a rage; **mostaza blanca** (bot.) white mustard; **mostaza de los alemanes** horseradish; **mostaza silvestre** (bot.) charlock
**mostazal** *m* mustard patch
**mostazo** *m* (bot.) mustard; strong, sticky must
**mostear** *vn* to yield must; to put must into vats; to mix must with old wine
**mostela** *f* (agr.) sheaf
**mostelera** *f* place where sheaves are stacked
**mostellar** *m* (bot.) whitebeam
**mostillo** *m* mustard sauce (*made of must and mustard*)
**mosto** *m* must (*unfermented juice*); **mosto de cerveza** wort
**mostrado -da** *adj* accustomed, inured
**mostrador -dora** *adj* showing, pointing; *mf* shower, pointer; *m* counter (*in a store*); bar; dial (*of clock*)
**mostrar** §77 *va* to show; *vr* to show; to show oneself to be
**mostrear** *va* to spot, to splash
**mostrenco -ca** *adj* unclaimed, ownerless; (coll.) homeless; (coll.) stray (*animal*); (coll.) slow, dull; (coll.) fat, heavy; *mf* (coll.) dolt, dullard
**mota** *f* speck, mote; burl, knot; hill, rise; fault; (Am.) powder puff
**motacila** *f* (orn.) wagtail
**mote** *m* riddle, enigma; device, emblem; nickname; (Am.) stewed corn
**motear** *va* to speck, speckle; to dapple, mottle
**motejador -dora** *adj* name-calling; scoffing; *mf* name-caller; scoffer
**motejar** *va* to call (*someone*) names; to scoff at, to ridicule; **motejar de** to brand as
**motejo** *m* name-calling; scoffing
**motel** *m* motel (*roadside hotel for motorists*)
**motete** *m* (mus.) motet
**motil** *m* var. of **mochil**
**motilar** *va* to shear (*the head*)
**motilidad** *f* (biol.) motility
**motilón -lona** *adj* hairless; short-haired; *m* (coll.) lay brother
**motín** *m* mutiny, uprising
**motivación** *f* motivation; rationalization
**motivar** *va* to motivate; to explain, to rationalize
**motivo -va** *adj* motive; *m* motive, reason; (f.a. & mus.) motif, motive; **con motivo de** because of; on the occasion of; **de su motivo** on his own accord; **motivo conductor** (mus.) leitmotif
**moto** *m* guidepost, landmark; *f* (coll.) motorcycle
**motobomba** *f* power pump; fire engine, fire truck
**motocamión** *m* motor truck
**motocicleta** *f* motorcycle
**motociclismo** *m* motorcycling
**motociclista** *mf* motorcyclist
**motociclo** *m* motorcycle
**motocultivo** *m* mechanical farming
**motocultor** *m* power cultivator
**motocultura** *f* var. of **motocultivo**
**motódromo** *m* motordrome
**motogrúa** *f* truck crane
**motolito -ta** *adj* simple, stupid; **vivir de motolito** to live on others, be a sponger; *f* (orn.) wagtail
**motón** *m* (naut.) block, pulley; **a rechina motón** stretched to the breaking point (*said of a cable*)
**motonáutico -ca** *adj* (pertaining to the) motorboat; *f* (art and science of) motorboating
**motonautismo** *m* (sport) motorboating
**motonave** *f* motor ship
**motonería** *f* (naut.) tackle, set of blocks or pulleys
**motoneta** *f* scooter, motor scooter; light three-wheel truck
**motoniveladora** *f* motor grader
**motopropulsor -sora** *adj* (elec.) motor-driven; (aer.) motor-and-propeller (*e.g., unit*)
**motor -tora** or **-triz** (*pl:* **-trices**) *adj* motor, motive; (anat.) motor; *m* motor; engine; **primer motor** (philos.) prime mover; **motor a chorro** or **a retropropulsión** (aer.) jet engine; **motor cohete** rocket motor; **motor de arranque** (aut.) starter, starting motor; **motor de combustión** combustion engine; **motor de combustión interna** or **motor de explosión** internal-combustion engine; **motor de cuatro tiempos** four-cycle engine; **motor de dos tiempos** two-cycle engine; **motor de gas** gas engine; **motor de inducción** (elec.) induction motor; **motor de jaula de ardilla** (elec.) squirrel-cage motor; **motor Diesel** Diesel engine or motor; **motor fuera de borda** outboard motor; **motor sincrónico** (elec.) synchronous motor; **motor térmico** heat engine; **motora** *f* small motorboat
**motor-convertidor** *m* (*pl:* **motores-convertidores**) (elec.) motor converter
**motor-generador** *m* (*pl:* **motores-generadores**) (elec.) motor generator
**motorismo** *m* motoring; motorcycling; motorcycle racing
**motorista** *mf* motorist; motorcyclist; motorcycle racer; *m* highway motorcycle policeman; (Am.) motorman, trolley motorman

**motorización** *f* motorization
**motorizar §76** *va* to motorize
**motosegadora** *f* power mower
**motosierra** *f* power saw
**motovelero** *m* (naut.) motor sailer
**motril** *m* errand boy
**mousse** *f* (cook.) mousse
**movedizo -za** *adj* moving; shaky, unsteady; quick, shifting; fickle, inconstant
**movedor -dora** *adj* moving; *mf* mover
**mover §63** *va* to move; to stir; to wag (*tail*); to stir up; to use (*influence, pull*); to abort; **mover a alguien a** + *inf* to move someone to + *inf*, to prompt someone to + *inf; vn* to abort, miscarry; to bud, sprout; (arch.) to spring (*said of an arch or vault*); *vr* to move; to be moved
**movible** *adj* movable; changeable, fickle; (astr.) movable
**móvil** *adj* movable; mobile; moving; changeable, fickle; *m* moving body; cause, motive, incentive
**movilidad** *f* mobility; fickleness; susceptibility; transportation
**movilización** *f* mobilization
**movilizar §76** *va, vn & vr* to mobilize
**movimiento** *m* movement; motion; moving; (f.a. & lit.) movement; (mus.) movement (*tempo*); **en movimiento** in motion; **movimiento browniano** (phys.) brownian movement; **movimiento continuo** perpetual motion; **movimiento de resistencia** resistance movement; **movimiento de vaivén** alternating motion; **movimiento ondulatorio** (phys.) wave motion; **movimiento paralelo** (mus.) parallel motion; **movimiento perdido** lost motion; **movimiento periódico** (phys.) periodic motion; **movimiento perpetuo** perpetual motion
**moyana** *f* bran biscuit for sheep dogs; (coll.) lie
**moyuelo** *m* fine bran
**moza** *f* see **mozo**
**mozalbete** *m* lad, young fellow
**mozallón** *m* strapping young workman
**mozancón** *m* strapping young fellow
**mozancona** *f* tall buxom lass
**mozárabe** *adj* Mozarabic; *mf* Mozarab (*Christian in Moslem Spain*)
**moznado -da** *adj* (her.) disarmed
**mozo -za** *adj* young, youthful; single, unmarried; *m* youth, lad; servant, waiter; porter; cloak hanger; **buen mozo** or **real mozo** good-looking, good-looking fellow; **mozo de caballerías** o **caballos** stable boy, hostler; **mozo de café** waiter; **mozo de cámara** (naut.) cabin boy; **mozo de campo y plaza** farm-and-house boy; **mozo de ciego** blind man's guide; **mozo de cocina** kitchen hand; **mozo de cordel** public errand boy; **mozo de cuadra** stable boy; **mozo de cuerda** public errand boy; **mozo de espada** bullfighter's servant; **mozo de espuelas** groom who walks in front of master's horse; **mozo de esquina** public errand boy; **mozo de estación** station porter; **mozo de estoques** (taur.) sword handler (*of matador*); **mozo de hotel** bellboy, bellhop; **mozo de paja y cebada** hostler at an inn; **mozo de restaurante** waiter; *f* girl, lass; wench, kitchen wench; mistress; wash bat; last hand, last game; **buena moza** or **real moza** good-looking, good-looking girl or woman; **moza de taberna** barmaid
**mozo-faquín** *m* (*pl:* **mozos-faquines**) porter
**mozuelo -la** *mf* youngster; *m* young fellow; *f* young girl
**m/p** abr. of **mi pagaré**
**M.P.S.** abr. of **Muy Poderoso Señor**
**mr.** abr. of **mártir**
**m/r** abr. of **mi remesa**
**mrd.** abr. of **merced**
**Mro.** abr. of **Maestro**
**mrs.** abr. of **maravedises & mártires**
**M.S.** abr. of **manuscrito**
**m.ˢ a.ˢ** abr. of **muchos años**
**M.SS.** abr. of **manuscritos**
**mtd.** abr. of **mitad**
**mu** *m* moo (*of cow*); *f* bye-bye (*sleep*); **ir a la mu** to go bye-bye

**muaré** *m* moire or moiré; *adj invar* moiré
**mucamo -ma** *mf* (Am.) servant, house servant
**múcara** *f* (naut.) shoal; (naut.) foul waters
**muceta** *f* hood (*e.g., of one holding a doctor's degree*); (eccl.) mozzetta
**mucilaginoso -sa** *adj* mucilaginous
**mucilago** or **mucílago** *m* mucilage
**mucina** *f* (biochem.) mucin
**mucoide** *m* (biochem.) mucoid
**mucosa** *f* see **mucoso**
**mucosidad** *f* mucosity; mucus
**mucoso -sa** *adj* mucous; *f* (anat.) mucosa
**mucronato -ta** *adj* mucronate
**múcura** *f* (Am.) water pitcher; (Am.) dolt, thickhead; (Am.) opossum
**mucus** *m* mucus
**muchacha** *f* see **muchacho**
**muchachada** *f* boyish prank, girlish prank; group of boys, group of girls; noisy crowd of youngsters
**muchachear** *vn* to act like a boy, act like a girl
**muchachería** *f* boyish prank, girlish prank; noisy crowd of youngsters
**muchachez** *f* boyishness, girlishness
**muchachil** *adj* boyish, girlish
**muchacho -cha** *adj* (coll.) boyish, girlish, youthful; *mf* (coll.) youth, young person; servant; *m* boy; *f* girl; maid; **muchacha de servir** servant girl
**muchachón** *m* overgrown boy
**muchedumbre** *f* crowd, multitude; flock (*of persons or things*); mob, rabble
**mucho -cha** *adj & pron* (*comp & super:* **más**) much, a lot of, a great deal of; a long (*time*); **muchos -chas** *adj & pron pl* (*comp & super:* **más**) many; **mucho** *adv* (*comp & super:* **más**) much, a lot, a great deal; hard; often; a long time; (coll.) yes, indeed; **con mucho** by far; **ni con mucho** or **ni mucho menos** not by a long shot, not by any means; **por mucho que** however much, no matter how much; **sentir mucho** to be very sorry; **ser mucho que no** + *subj* to be unlikely that...not, e.g., **mucho será que no llueva esta mañana** it is unlikely that it will not rain this morning; **mucho más** much more; **mucho que sí** (coll.) yes, indeed, *m* much; **tener en mucho** to hold in high esteem, to make much of; **tener mucho de** to take after
**muda** *f* see **mudo**
**mudable** *adj* changeable; fickle, inconstant
**mudada** *f* (Am.) change of clothes
**mudadizo -za** *adj* var. of **mudable**
**mudanza** *f* change; moving; inconstancy, fickleness; figure (*in a dance*); **estar de mudanza** to be moving (*from one house to another*); **hacer mudanza** or **mudanzas** to be changeable; to be fickle (*especially in love*)
**mudar** *m* (bot.) giant calotropis; *va* to change; to move; to shed, to molt; to change (*one's voice; said of a boy*); *vn* to change; **mudar de** to change (*clothing, location, one's mind, opinion*); *vr* to change; to change clothing or underclothing; to move; to move away; to have a movement of the bowels; **mudarse de** to change (*clothing, location, one's mind, one's opinion, etc.*)
**mudéjar** *adj* Mudejar; (arch.) Mudejar; *mf* Mudejar (*Mohammedan living under Spanish Christian king*)
**mudez** *f* dumbness, muteness; prolonged silence
**mudo -da** *adj* dumb, silent, mute; (gram.) mute (*letter*); (phonet.) voiceless, surd; *mf* mute (*person*); *f* change; change of voice; change of clothes; molt, molting; molting season; cosmetic; nest of birds of prey; **estar de muda** to be changing one's voice (*said of a boy*); **estar en muda** (coll.) to keep mum
**mueblaje** *m* var. of **moblaje**
**mueble** *adj* movable; *m* piece of furniture; cabinet (*e.g., of a radio*); **muebles** *mpl* furniture; **muebles de estilo** period furniture
**mueblería** *f* furniture factory, furniture store
**mueblero -ra** *adj* (pertaining to) furniture
**mueblista** *adj* (pertaining to) furniture; *mf* furniture maker, furniture dealer
**mueca** *f* face, grimace; **hacer muecas** to make faces

**muecín** *m* var. of **almuecín**
**muela** *f* millstone; grindstone; water for running a mill; mound, knoll; (anat.) back tooth, grinder; (bot.) grass pea; **haberle salido a uno la muela del juicio** to have cut one's wisdom teeth (*to be shrewd*); **muela cordal** wisdom tooth; **muela de esmeril** emery grinder, emery wheel; **muela del juicio** wisdom tooth; **muela de molino** millstone
**muelo** *m* stack of grain
**muellaje** *m* wharfage
**muelle** *adj* soft; easy, luxurious; *m* spring; pier, wharf, dock; chatelaine (*clasp worn at woman's waist*); (rail.) freight platform; **muelle de válvula** valve spring; **muelle real** (horol.) mainspring
**muérdago** *m* (bot.) mistletoe (*Viscum album*)
**muerdo** *m* (coll.) bite; (coll.) bit
**muergo** *m* (zool.) razon clam; wheat smut
**muermo** *m* (vet.) glanders; (bot.) muermo (*tree and wood*)
**muermoso -sa** *adj* glanderous
**muerte** *f* death; murder; Death (*skeleton with scythe*); **a muerte** to death, to the death; **dar la muerte a** to put to death; **de mala muerte** crummy, not much of a; **de muerte** implacably; hopelessly (*e.g., ill*); **estar a la muerte** to be at death's door; **tomarse la muerte por su mano** to take one's life in one's hands; **muerte civil** civil death, loss of rights; **muerte chiquita** (coll.) nervous shudder
**muerto -ta** *pp of* **morir** and **matar;** *adj* dead; flat, dull; slaked (*lime*); (elec.) dead; (rad.) dead-end; **estar muerto por** (coll.) to be crazy about; **muerto de** dying of (*e.g., hunger*); *mf* dead person, corpse; *m* dummy (*at cards*); **muertos** *mpl* (coll.) piles (*driven in ground*); **cargar con el muerto** (coll.) to be left holding the bag; **echar el muerto a** to put the blame on; **hacer** or **hacerse el muerto** to play possum; (coll.) to play deaf, to affect ignorance; **levantar un muerto** to vote using the name of a dead person; **tocar a muerto** to toll
**muesca** *f* notch, nick; (carp.) mortise
**muestra** *f* sample; sign (*in front of shop, hotel, etc.*); model, specimen; face, dial (*of watch or clock*); sampler; bearing; fag end of cloth (*with name of manufacturer*); set (*of dog in presence of game*); show, sign, indication; (mil.) review; (philately) specimen; **dar muestras de** to show signs of; **estar de muestra** to set (*said of a hunting dog*); **pasar muestra** to check carefully; (mil.) to review
**muestrario** *m* sample book, collection of samples
**muestreo** *m* (statistics) sampling
**muévedo** *m* abortion (*aborted fetus*)
**muezín** *m* var. of **almuecín**
**mufla** *f* muffle (*of a furnace*)
**muftí** *m* (*pl:* **-tíes**) mufti (*Mohammedan legal expounder*)
**muga** *f* landmark, boundary; spawning; fecundation of roe
**mugido** *m* moo, low; bellow; roar
**mugidor -dora** *adj* mooing, lowing; bellowing; roaring
**múgil** *m* var. of **mójol**
**mugir §42** *vn* to moo, to low; to bellow; to roar
**mugre** *f* dirt, filth
**mugriento -ta** *adj* dirty, filthy
**mugrón** *m* (hort.) layer (*of vine*); shoot, sprig, sucker
**mugronar** *va* (hort.) var. of **amugronar**
**mugroso -sa** *adj* var. of **mugriento**
**muguete** *m* (bot.) lily of the valley
**muharra** *f* var. of **moharra**
**mujer** *f* woman; wife; **ser mujer** to be a grown woman; **tomar mujer** to take a wife; **mujer de digo y hago** husky woman; **mujer de gobierno** housekeeper; **mujer del arte** or **de mal vivir** prostitute; **mujer de su casa** good manager (*of household*); **mujer fatal** vamp, vampire; **mujer mundana, perdida** or **pública** prostitute; **mujer policía** (*pl:* **mujeres policías**) policewoman
**mujercilla** *f* woman of no account; sissy
**mujeriego -ga** *adj* womanly; womanish; fond of women; **ir** or **montar a la mujeriega** or **a mujeriegas** to ride sidesaddle; *m* skirts, flock of women
**mujeril** *adj* womanly; womanish
**mujerío** *m* skirts, flock of women
**mujerona** *f* big strapping woman; matron
**mujerzuela** *f* woman of no account
**mújol** *m* (ichth.) mullet, striped mullet
**mula** *f* mule, she-mule; trash, junk; (Am.) ingrate, traitor; **en mula de San Francisco** on shank's mare; **hacer la mula** (coll.) to shirk, to back down, to back out
**mulada** *f* drove of mules
**muladar** *m* dungheap; trash heap; filth, corruption
**muladí** *m* (*pl:* **-díes**) Spaniard who embraced Mohammedanism
**mular** *adj* (pertaining to the) mule
**mulata** *f* see **mulato**
**mulatero** *m* mule hirer; muleteer
**mulato -ta** *adj & mf* mulatto; *f* (zool.) grapsoid
**mulero** *m* mule boy
**muleta** *f* crutch; prop, support; light lunch; (taur.) muleta (*staff with red flag*); (zool.) unio; **tener muletas** (coll.) to be as old as the hills
**muletada** *f* drove of mules
**muletero** *m* var. of **mulatero**
**muletilla** *f* cross-handle cane; braid frog; pet word, pet phrase; (taur.) muleta (*staff with red flag*)
**muletillero -ra** *mf* person always using pet words or phrases
**muleto** *m* young mule
**muletón** *m* swan's-down
**mulilla** *f* small mule; (zool.) eleven-banded armadillo; **mulillas de arrastre** (taur.) team of mules that drags dead bull from the arena
**mulo** *m* mule or hinny; **mulo castellano** mule (*offspring of male ass and mare*)
**mulso -sa** *adj* honeyed
**multa** *f* fine
**multar** *va* to fine
**multicelular** *adj* multicellular
**multicolor** *adj* many-colored, multicolored
**multicopista** *adj* duplicating, copying; *m* duplicator, copying machine
**multidentado -da** *adj* multidentate
**multiempleo** *m* (coll.) moonlighting
**multifacético -ca** *adj* many-sided
**multifásico -ca** *adj* var. of **polifásico**
**multifilar** *adj* multiple-wire
**multifloro -ra** *adj* (bot.) multiflorous, many-flowered
**multiforme** *adj* multiform
**multigrafiar §90** to multigraph
**multígrafo** *m* multigraph
**multigrávida** *adj fem* multiparous
**multilateral** *adj* multilateral (*participated in by more than two nations*)
**multilátero -ra** *adj* multilateral (*many-sided*)
**multimillonario -ria** *mf* multimillionaire
**multípara** *adj fem* multiparous; *f* multipara
**múltiple** *adj* multiple, manifold; *m* (mach.) manifold; **múltiple de admisión** intake manifold; **múltiple de escape** exhaust manifold
**multiplete** *m* (phys.) multiplet
**múltiplex** *adj* (rad. & telg.) multiplex
**multiplicable** *adj* multipliable
**multiplicación** *f* multiplication
**multiplicador -dora** *adj* multiplying; *mf* multiplier; *m* (math.) multiplier
**multiplicando** *m* (math.) multiplicand
**multiplicar §86** *va, vn & vr* to multiply
**multíplice** *adj* multiple, manifold
**multiplicidad** *f* multiplicity
**múltiplo -pla** *adj* multiple, manifold; (elec. & math.) multiple; *m* (elec. & math.) multiple; **mínimo común múltiplo** (math.) least common multiple; **en múltiplo** (elec.) in multiple
**multipolar** *adj* (anat. & elec.) multipolar or multipole
**multiseccional** *adj* multisectional, multistage
**multitud** *f* multitude
**multivalvo -va** *adj* multivalve
**mullido -da** *adj* fluffy, soft; ready, all set; *m* soft filling or stuffing (*for cushions, etc.*)

**mullir** §26 *va* to fluff, to soften; to beat up, to shake up (*a bed*); to ready, to get into shape; (agr.) to loosen (*the earth*) around a stalk; *vr* to become fluffy; to be beaten up or shaken up; **mullírselas a una persona** (coll.) to punish a person; (coll.) to be wise to a person
**mullo** *m* (ichth.) red mullet; (Am.) glass bead
**mundanal** *adj* var. of **mundano**
**mundanalidad** *f* worldliness
**mundanear** *vn* to be worldly-minded
**mundanería** *f* worldliness, sophistication; worldly behavior
**mundanesco -ca** *adj* worldly; *f* worldliness; worldly people
**mundanidad** *f* worldliness
**mundanismo** *m* worldliness; cosmopolitanism
**mundanista** *adj* worldly; cosmopolitan; *mf* worldly person; cosmopolitan
**mundano -na** *adj* mundane, worldly; loose (*woman*)
**mundial** *adj* world-wide, world
**mundialmente** *adv* throughout the world
**mundicia** *f* cleanness, cleanliness
**mundificación** *f* cleansing, purification
**mundificar** §86 *va* to cleanse, purify
**mundificativo -va** *adj* (med.) cleansing
**mundillo** *m* arched clotheshorse; cushion for making lace; warming pan; (bot.) cranberry tree, guelder-rose, snowball; world (*e.g., of politics, scholars, etc.* )
**mundinovi** *m* var. of **mundonuevo**
**mundo** *m* world; Saratoga trunk; savoir-vivre; (coll.) flock; (bot.) guelder-rose, snowball; **así va el mundo** so it goes; **correr mundo** to travel, go traveling; **desde que el mundo es mundo** (coll.) since the world began; **echar al mundo** to bring into the world; to bring forth, to create; **echarse al mundo** to debauch oneself; to become a prostitute; **el otro mundo** the other world (*future life*); **gran mundo** high society; **medio mundo** (coll.) half the world (*a lot of people*); **morir para el mundo** to give up the world, to go into seclusion; **Nuevo Mundo** New World; **tener mundo** or **mucho mundo** (coll.) to be experienced, be sophisticated; **todo el mundo** everybody; **ver mundo** to travel, to see the world; **mundo elegante** society, high society; **Mundo novísimo** Oceania
**mundología** *f* worldly experience, worldliness
**mundonuevo** *m* peep show, portable cosmorama
**munición** *f* munition, ammunition; supplies; load, charge (*of a gun*); buckshot; **de munición** (mil.) G.I., government issue; (coll.) done hurriedly; **municiones de boca** (mil.) food, provisions; **municiones de guerra** (mil.) war supplies; **munición menuda** bird shot
**municionamiento** *m* military supplies, ordnance stores
**municionar** *va* to munition, to supply with ammunition
**municionero -ra** *mf* supplier; *f* pouch for shot
**municipal** *adj* municipal; *m* policeman
**municipalidad** *f* municipality
**municipalización** *f* municipalization
**municipalizar** §76 *va* to municipalize
**munícipe** *m* citizen; councilman
**municipio** *m* municipality; council, town council
**munidad** *f* susceptibility (*to infection*)
**munificencia** *f* munificence
**munificente** or **munífico -ca** *adj* munificent
**muniquense** or **muniqués -quesa** *adj* (pertaining to) Munich; *mf* native or inhabitant of Munich
**munitoria** *f* art of fortification
**muñeca** *f* (anat.) wrist; doll; (coll.) doll (*tiny woman; pretty but silly girl*); manikin, dress form; stone marker; pounce bag; tea bag; (mach.) puppet; **menear las muñecas** (coll.) to hustle at a job; **muñeca de trapo** rag baby, rag doll; **muñeca parlante** talking doll
**muñeco** *m* doll (*toy puppet representing a male child or small animal*); puppet, manikin, dummy; effeminate fellow; (coll.) lad, little fellow; (fig.) puppet; **tener muñecos en la cabeza** to have an exaggerated opinion of oneself, to build castles in Spain
**muñequear** *vn* to fence from the wrist
**muñequera** *f* bracelet or strap (*for wrist watch*)
**muñequería** *f* (coll.) overdressing, exaggerated finery; (coll.) flock of youngsters
**muñequilla** *f* rubbing or polishing rag or bag; (mach.) pin; (mach.) chuck; (Am.) young ear of corn
**muñidor** *m* beadle; heeler, henchman; author, maker
**muñir** §25 *va* to summon; (pol.) to fix, to rig
**muñón** *m* stump (*of amputated limb*); (arti.) trunnion; (carp.) dowel; (mach.) gudgeon, journal; **muñón de dirección** (aut.) steering knuckle
**muñonera** *f* (arti.) trunnion plate; journal box, bearing
**muradal** *m* var. of **muladar**
**murajes** *mpl* (bot.) pimpernel
**mural** *adj* mural
**muralla** *f* wall, rampart; **Gran muralla** or **muralla de la China** Chinese Wall
**murallón** *m* large wall, heavy wall
**murar** *va* to wall, surround with a wall
**murceguillo** or **murciégalo** *m* var. of **murciélago**
**murciélago** *m* (zool.) bat; (ichth.) gurnard
**murecillo** *m* (anat.) muscle
**murena** *f* (ichth.) moray
**murga** *f* foul-smelling juice coming from a heap of olives; (coll.) band of street musicians; (coll.) tin-pan band; **dar murga a** (coll.) to bother, annoy
**murgón** *m* (ichth.) samlet, parr
**múrgula** *f* (bot.) morel
**muriático -ca** *adj* muriatic
**muriato** *m* (chem.) muriate
**múrice** *m* (zool.) murex; (poet.) murex, purple
**muriente** *adj* dying; faint (*e.g., light*)
**murino -na** *adj & m* (zool.) murine
**murmujear** *va & vn* (coll.) to murmur
**murmullar** *vn* to murmur
**murmullo** *m* murmur; whisper; ripple; rustle; (med.) murmur (*e.g., of heart*)
**murmuración** *f* gossip, gossiping
**murmurador -dora** *adj* murmuring; gossiping; *mf* murmurer; gossip
**murmurante** *adj* murmuring, rippling
**murmurar** *va* to murmur, to mutter; to murmur at; *vn* to murmur, to mutter; to whisper; to purl, to ripple; to rustle; (coll.) to gossip
**murmureo** *m* murmuring sound
**murmurio** *m* murmur; ripple; rustle
**muro** *m* wall; rampart; **muro de contención** dam; **muro de los lamentos** Wailing Wall; **muro supersónico** sonic barrier
**murria** *f* see **murrio**
**múrrino -na** *adj* murrhine
**murrio -rria** *adj* sad, dejected, sullen, morose; *f* (coll.) sadness, dejection, sullenness
**murta** *f* (bot.) myrtle; myrtle berry
**murtal** *m* or **murtela** *f* growth of myrtles
**murtón** *m* myrtle berry
**murucuyá** *f* (*pl:* **-yaes**) (bot.) passionflower
**murueco** *m* var. of **morueco**
**musa** *f* muse; (*cap.*) *f* (myth.) Muse; **soplarle a uno la musa** (coll.) to be inspired to write verse; (coll.) to be lucky at gambling
**musáceo -a** *adj* (bot.) musaceous
**musaraña** *f* (zool.) shrew, shrewmouse; bug, worm; floating speck in the eye; (coll.) misshapen figure; **mirar a las musarañas** (coll.) to stare vacantly; **pensar en las musarañas** (coll.) to be absent-minded; **musaraña de agua** (zool.) water shrew
**muscardina** *f* (zool.) muscardine
**muscaria** *f* (orn.) flycatcher
**muscarina** *f* (chem.) muscarine
**muscícapa** *f* var. of **muscaria**
**muscínea** *f* (bot.) bryophyte
**musco -ca** *adj* dark-brown; *m* (bot.) moss
**muscular** *adj* muscular
**musculatura** *f* musculature; muscularity
**músculo** *m* (anat.) muscle; (zool.) finback, razorback
**musculoso -sa** *adj* muscular
**muselina** *f* muslin
**museo** *m* museum; **museo de cera** waxworks
**muserola** *f* noseband
**musgaño** *m* (zool.) white-toothed shrew

**musgo -ga** *adj* dark-brown; *m* (bot.) moss; **musgo de Irlanda** (bot.) Irish moss; **musgo de Islandia** (bot.) Iceland moss; **musgo de roble** (bot.) oak moss; **musgo marino** (bot.) coralline; **musgo terrestre** (bot.) club moss
**musgoso -sa** *adj* mossy; moss-covered
**música** *f* see **músico**
**musical** *adj* musical
**musicalidad** *f* musicianship
**music-hall** *m* cabaret, burlesque show
**músico -ca** *adj* musical; *mf* musician; **músico mayor** bandmaster; *f* music; band; (coll.) noise, racket; **con buena música se viene** (coll.) that's a fine how-de-do; **con la música a otra parte** (coll.) get out, don't bother me; **música celestial** (coll.) nonsense, moonshine, piffle; **música clásica** classical music; **música coreada** choral music; **música de baile** dance music; **música de cámara** chamber music; **música de campanas** chimes; **música de danza** dance music; **música de fondo** background music; **música de iglesia** church music; **música de programa** program music; **música de salón** chamber music; **música instrumental** instrumental music; **música mundana** music of the spheres; **música negra** jazz music; **música popular** popular music; **música rítmica** music of stringed instruments; **música sacra** or **sagrada** sacred music; **música vocal** vocal music
**musicógrafo -fa** *mf* musicographer
**musicología** *f* musicology
**musicológico -ca** *adj* musicological
**musicólogo -ga** *mf* musicologist
**musiquero** *m* music cabinet
**musitar** *va & vn* to mumble, whisper
**musivo** *adj masc* mosaic (*gold*)
**muslera** *f* (arm.) cuisse or cuish
**muslim** or **muslime** *adj & mf* Moslem, Muslem or Muslim
**muslímico -ca** *adj* Moslemic, Mussulmanic
**muslo** *m* (anat.) thigh; drumstick (*of cooked chicken, turkey, etc.*)
**musmón** *m* (zool.) mouflon
**musola** *f* (ichth.) smooth hound
**musquerola** *f* var. of **mosquerola**
**mustaco** *m* cake made with must
**mustango** *m* (Am.) mustang
**mustela** *f* (ichth.) dog shark (*Mustelus vulgaris*); (zool.) weasel
**mustio -tia** *adj.* sad, gloomy; withered; (Am.) hypocritical
**musulmán -mana** *adj & mf* Mussulman
**muta** *f* pack of hounds
**mutabilidad** *f* mutability
**mutación** *f* mutation; change of weather, unsettled weather; (theat.) change of scene; (biol. & phonet.) mutation
**mutacional** *adj* mutational
**mutante** *m* (biol.) mutant
**mutarrotación** *f* (chem.) mutarotation
**mutilación** *f* mutilation
**mutilado -da** *adj* crippled; *mf* cripple; **mutilado de guerra** war cripple
**mutilador -dora** *adj* mutilating; *mf* mutilator
**mutilar** *va* to mutilate; to cripple
**mútilo -la** *adj* mutilated, armless; incomplete
**mutis** *m* (theat.) exit; **hacer mutis** (theat.) to exit; to say nothing, to keep quiet
**mutismo** *m* mutism; silence
**mutual** *adj* mutual
**mutualidad** *f* mutuality; mutual aid; mutual benefit society
**mutualismo** *m* mutualism
**mutualista** *adj* mutualistic; mutual-benefit-society; *mf* mutualist; member of a mutual benefit society
**mutuante** *mf* lender
**mutuario -ria** or **mutuatario -ria** *mf* borrower
**mútulo** *m* (arch.) mutule
**mutuo -tua** *adj* mutual; *m* (law) mutuum
**muy** *adv* very; very much, frequently; too, e.g., **está muy ocupado para poder dedicarse a los deportes** he is too busy to be able to devote himself to sports; very much of a, e.g., **muy mujer** very much of a woman; **muy de noche** late at night; **muy señor mío** Dear Sir
**muz** *m* (*pl:* **muces**) (naut.) upper extremity of cutwater
**muza** *f* see **muzo**
**muzárabe** *adj & mf* var. of **mozárabe**
**muzo -za** *adj* dead-smooth; *f* dead-smooth file

# N

**N, n** *f* sixteenth letter of the Spanish alphabet; (*l.c.*) *f* (alg.) n (*indefinite number*)
**n.** abr. of **nacido** & **noche**
**n/** abr. of **nuestro**
**N.** abr. of **Norte**
**naba** *f* (bot.) rape, cole
**nabab** *m* or **nababo** *m* nabob
**nabal** or **nabar** *adj* (pertaining to the) turnip; *m* turnip field
**nabería** *f* heap of turnips; turnip soup; turnip stand (*e.g., in a market*)
**nabí** *m* (*pl:* **-bíes**) Moorish prophet
**nabicol** *m* (bot.) turnip
**nabina** *f* rapeseed, turnip seed
**nabiza** *f* rape rootlets; rape oil; **nabizas** *fpl* turnip greens, turnip leaves
**nabo** *m* (bot.) turnip (*plant and root*); newel (*of winding stairs*); (naut.) mast; root of tail (*of quadrupeds*); **tener la cabeza más pelada que un nabo** to be as bald as a billiard ball; **nabo del diablo** (bot.) water fennel, water dropwort; **nabo de Suecia** (bot.) Swedish turnip; **nabo gallego, gordo** or **redondo** (bot.) rape, cole
**Nabot** *m* (Bib.) Naboth
**Nabucodonosor** *m* (Bib.) Nebuchadnezzar
**nácar** *m* mother-of-pearl, nacre
**nácara** *f* (Am.) kettle-drum
**nacarado -da** *adj* mother-of-pearl (*in material or appearance*)
**nacáreo -a** or **nacarino -na** *adj* mother-of-pearl (*in nature or appearance*)
**nacatamal** *m* (Am.) meat-filled tamale
**nacela** *f* (aer.) nacelle; (arch.) scotia; (anat.) fossa navicularis
**nacencia** *f* growth, tumor
**nacer §34** *vn* to be born; to bud, to begin to grow; to arise, take rise, originate, spring up, appear; to dawn; *vr* to bud, to shoot; to split (*said of seams*)
**nacido -da** *adj* natural, innate; apt, proper, fit; **bien nacido** of noble birth; **mal nacido** lowborn; **nacida** *adj fem* née or nee; *m* human being, offspring; growth, boil
**naciente** *adj* nascent; incipient, recent; resurgent; rising (*sun*); (chem.) nascent; *m* east; **nacientes** *fpl* source, headwaters
**nacimiento** *m* birth; origin, growth, beginning; lineage, descent; crèche (*Nativity scene*); spring (*of water*); **de nacimiento** from birth
**nación** *f* nation; **de nación** by birth; from birth; **la nación más favorecida** (dipl.) most favored nation; **naciones del Eje** Axis nations; **Naciones Unidas** United Nations; **nación miembro** (*pl:* **naciones miembros**) member nation
**nacional** *adj* national; domestic (*product*); *mf* national; *m* militiaman
**nacionalidad** *f* nationality
**nacionalismo** *m* nationalism
**nacionalista** *adj* nationalist, nationalistic; *mf* nationalist
**nacionalización** *f* nationalization
**nacionalizar §76** *va* to nationalize; to naturalize
**nacionalsocialismo** *m* National Socialism
**nacionalsocialista** *adj & mf* National Socialist
**nacista** *adj & mf* Nazi
**naco** *m* (Am.) rolled leaf of tobacco
**nacrita** *f* (mineral.) kaolinite
**nacho -cha** *adj* snub-nosed
**nada** *f* nothingness; *pron indef* nothing, not anything; very little; **de nada** don't mention it, you're welcome; **en nada** almost; *adv* not at all; well then; **nada más** only; **nada menos que** not less than
**nadada** *f* (Am.) swim
**nadaderas** *fpl* water bladder, water wings
**nadadero** *m* swimming place
**nadador -dora** *adj* swimming, floating; *mf* swimmer; *m* (Am.) float (*to hold up fishing nets*)
**nadar** *vn* to swim; to float; to fit loosely or too loosely; **nadar en** to revel in; **nadar en riqueza** to be rolling in wealth; **nadar en suspiros** to be full of sighs; **nadar entre dos aguas** to swim under water, to float under the surface; to carry water on both shoulders
**nadear** *va* to destroy, wipe out
**nadería** *f* trifle
**nadie** *m* nobody (*person of no importance*); **ser un don nadie** (coll.) to be a nonentity; *pron indef* nobody, not anybody, no one
**nadir** *m* (astr. & fig.) nadir
**nado; a nado** swimming, floating; **pasar a nado** to swim across
**nafa** *f* orange flower
**nafta** *f* naphtha; (Am.) gasoline
**Naftalí** *m* (Bib.) Naphtali
**naftaleno** *m* or **naftalina** *f* (chem.) naphthalene or naphthaline
**naftol** *m* (chem.) naphthol
**nagual** *m* (Am.) sorcerer, wizard; (Am.) inseparable companion (*said of an animal*)
**naguas** *fpl* petticoat
**Nahúm** *m* (Bib.) Nahum
**naife** *m* diamond of the first water
**naipe** *m* playing card; deck of cards; **naipes** *mpl* cards (*game*); **cortar el naipe** to cut the cards; **darle a uno el naipe** (coll.) to have good luck, to be a lucky player; **darle a uno el naipe por** (coll.) to have a knack for, e.g., **no le da el naipe por el tenis** he does not have a knack for tennis; **jugar a los naipes** to play cards; **pandillar el naipe** (slang) to stack the cards; **tener buen naipe** to be lucky (*in gambling*); **tener mal naipe** to be unlucky (*in gambling*); **naipe de figura** face card
**naipesco -ca** *adj* card, pertaining to cards
**naire** *m* mahout, elephant keeper
**naja** *f* (zool.) naja; **salir de naja** (slang) to scram, to beat it
**nalga** *f* buttock, rump
**nalgada** *f* shoulder, ham; blow on the buttocks, blow with the buttocks
**nalgar** *adj* gluteal, pertaining to the buttocks
**nalgatorio** *m* (coll.) posterior, buttocks
**nalgudo -da** *adj* with a big posterior
**nana** *f* (coll.) grandma; (Am.) child's nurse; lullaby, cradlesong
**nanear** *vn* to waddle
**nanquín** *m* nankeen or nankin
**nansa** *f* bow net, bag net; fish pond
**nansú** *m* nainsook
**nao** *f* ship, vessel
**naonato -ta** *adj* born on shipboard
**napa** *f* (Am.) sheet of underground water
**napea** *f* (myth.) wood nymph
**napelo** *m* (bot.) monkshood, wolf's-bane
**Napoleón** *m* Napoleon; (*l.c.*) *m* napoleon (*coin*)
**napoleónico -ca** *adj* Napoleonic
**Nápoles** *f* Naples
**napolitano -na** *adj* Neapolitan; *mf* Neapolitan (*person*); *m* Neapolitan (*dialect*)
**naque** *m* pair of strolling comedians
**naranja** *f* orange; **media naranja** (arch.) cupola; (coll.) sidekick; (coll.) better half; **naranja cajel** Seville or sour orange; **naranja de ombligo** navel orange; **naranja mandarina** mandarin orange; **naranja roja** or **sanguínea** blood orange; **naranja tangerina** tangerine

**naranjado -da** *adj* orange, orange-colored; *f* orangeade; orange juice; orange marmalade; coarse act or remark, vulgarity
**naranjal** *m* orange grove
**naranjero -ra** *adj* orange; orange-sized; *mf* orange vender; *m* (prov.) orange tree
**naranjilla** *f* green orange for preserving
**naranjo** *m* (bot.) orange tree; (coll.) boob
**Narbona** *f* Narbonne
**narbonense** or **narbonés -nesa** *adj* (pertaining to) Narbonne; *mf* native or inhabitant of Narbonne
**narceína** *f* (chem.) narceine
**narcisismo** *m* (psychoanal.) narcissism
**narciso** *m* (bot.) narcissus; fop, dandy; (*cap.*) *m* (myth.) Narcissus; **narciso trompón** (bot.) daffodil
**narcosis** *f* narcosis
**narcótico -ca** *adj* & *m* narcotic
**narcotina** *f* (chem.) narcotine
**narcotismo** *m* narcotism
**narcotizar** §76 *va* to narcotize, to dope
**nardo** *m* (bot. & pharm.) nard; (bot.) tuberose; spikenard (*of the ancients*); **nardo marítimo** (bot.) sea daffodil
**narguile** *m* hookah, narghile
**narigada** *f* (Am.) pinch of snuff
**narigón -gona** *adj* big-nosed; *mf* big-nosed person; *m* big nose
**narigudo -da** *adj* big-nosed; nose-shaped; *mf* big-nosed person
**nariguera** *f* nose ring
**nariz** *f* (*pl:* **-rices**) nose; nostril; sense of smell; bouquet (*of wine*); **hablar por las narices** to talk through the nose; **sonarse las narices** to blow one's nose; **tabicarse las narices** to hold one's nose; **tener agarrado por las narices** to lead by the nose; **nariz aguileña** aquiline nose; **nariz helénica** Grecian nose
**narizón -zona** *adj* (coll.) big-nosed
**narizota** *f* big ugly nose
**narrable** *adj* narratable
**narración** *f* narration
**narrador -dora** *adj* narrating; *mf* narrator
**narrar** *va* to narrate
**narrativo -va** *adj* narrative; *f* narrative (*story; skill in storytelling*)
**narria** *f* sled, sledge; drag (*sledge for conveying heavy bodies*); (coll.) big heavy woman
**narval** *m* (zool.) narwhal
**N.ª S.ª** abr. of **Nuestra Señora**
**nasa** *f* bow net, bag net; fish basket; bread basket; flour box
**nasal** *adj* & *f* nasal
**nasalidad** *f* nasality
**nasalización** *f* nasalization
**nasalizar** §76 *va* to nasalize
**nasardo** *m* (mus.) nasard
**nasica** *f* (zool.) proboscis monkey
**naso** *m* (coll.) big nose
**nástico -ca** *adj* (plant physiol.) nastic
**nata** *f* see **nato**
**natación** *f* swimming
**natal** *adj* natal; native; *m* birth; birthday
**natalicio -cia** *adj* natal; *m* birthday; birth
**natalidad** *f* natality, birth rate; **natalidad dirigida** planned parenthood
**Natán** *m* (Bib.) Nathan
**Natanael** *m* (Bib.) Nathanael
**natátil** *adj* natant; (bot.) natant, aquatic
**natatorio -ria** *adj* natatorial
**naterón** *m* cottage cheese
**natillas** *fpl* custard
**natío -a** *adj* natural, native; *m* birth; nature; **de su natío** naturally
**natividad** *f* birth, nativity; Christmas; Nativity (*festival commemorating birth of Christ, the Virgin Mary, or John the Baptist*)
**nativo -va** *adj* native; natural; natural-born; innate
**nato -ta** *adj* born, e.g., **criminal nato** born criminal; *f* cream; élite, best part; skim, scum; **natas** *fpl* whipped cream with sugar; **nata y flor** cream (*e.g., of society*)
**natrolita** *f* (mineral.) natrolite
**natrón** *m* (mineral.) natron
**natura** *f* genital organs; (archaic) nature
**natural** *adj* natural; native; (mus.) natural; *mf* native; *m* temper, disposition, nature; **al natural** au naturel; rough, unfinished; live (*e.g., program*); **del natural** (f.a.) from life, from nature
**naturaleza** *f* nature; nationality; genitals, female genitals; temperament, disposition; **segunda naturaleza** second nature; **naturaleza muerta** (f.a.) still life
**naturalidad** *f* naturalness; nationality
**naturalismo** *m* naturalism
**naturalista** *adj* naturalist, naturalistic; *mf* naturalist
**naturalización** *f* naturalization
**naturalizar** §76 *va* to naturalize; *vr* to become naturalized; to naturalize (*to live like the natives in a foreign country*)
**naturalmente** *adv* naturally; of course
**naturopatía** *f* naturopathy
**naufragar** §59 *vn* to be wrecked, to sink, to be shipwrecked; to fail
**naufragio** *m* shipwreck; failure, ruin
**náufrago -ga** *adj* shipwrecked; *mf* shipwrecked person; *m* (ichth.) shark
**náusea** *f* nausea, sickness, disgust; **dar náuseas a** to sicken, to disgust; **tener náuseas** to be nauseated, to be sick at one's stomach
**nauseabundo -da** *adj* nauseous, nauseating, loathsome, sickening
**nauseado -da** *adj* nauseated, sick
**nausear** *vn* to nauseate, to sicken, to become disgusted
**nauseativo -va** or **nauseoso -sa** *adj* var. of **nauseabundo**
**Nausica** or **Nausícaa** *f* (myth.) Nausicaä
**nauta** *m* mariner, sailor
**náutico -ca** *adj* nautical; *f* nautics
**nautilo** *m* (zool.) nautilus
**nava** *f* hollow plain between mountains
**navacero -ra** *mf* gardener in sandy marshland
**navaja** *f* folding knife; razor; tusk of wild boar; pocketknife, penknife; (zool.) razor clam; (coll.) evil tongue; **navaja de afeitar** razor; **navaja de injertar** grafter, grafting knife, grafting instrument; **navaja de seguridad** safety razor
**navajada** *f* or **navajazo** *m* slash, gash (*made with folding knife or razor*)
**navajero** *m* razor case; cloth for cleaning razor; cup for cleaning razor; knife wielder; razor wielder
**navajo** *m* pool of rain water
**naval** *adj* nautical; naval; **naval militar** naval
**navarro -rra** *adj* & *mf* Navarrese; *m* Navarrese (*dialect*); (*cap.*) *f* Navarre
**navazo** *m* pool of rain water; garden in sandy marshland
**nave** *f* ship, vessel; aisle (*of a shop, factory, store, etc.*); commercial ground floor; hall, shed, bay, building; **quemar las naves** to burn one's boats; **nave central** (arch.) nave; **nave del desierto** ship of the desert (*camel*); **Nave de San Pedro** Roman Catholic Church; **nave lateral** (arch.) aisle (*of nave*); **nave principal** (arch.) nave
**navecilla** *f* small ship; (eccl.) navicula (*censer*)
**navegabilidad** *f* navigability
**navegable** *adj* navigable (*said of a river, canal, etc.*)
**navegación** *f* navigation; sea voyage; **navegación a vela** sailing
**navegador -dora** or **navegante** *adj* navigating; *mf* navigator
**navegar** §59 *va* to navigate, to sail; *vn* to navigate, to sail; to move about
**navegatorio -ria** *adj* navigational
**navel** *f* (*pl:* **-vels**) navel orange
**naveta** *f* small ship; (eccl.) navicula (*censer*); small drawer
**navícula** *f* small ship; (bot.) navicula
**navicular** *adj* navicular, boat-shaped; *m* (anat.) navicular
**Navidad** *f* Christmas; Christmas time; **contar** or **tener muchas Navidades** to be pretty old; **¡Felices Navidades!** Merry Christmas!
**navidal** *m* Christmas card
**navideño -ña** *adj* Christmas, of Christmas
**naviero -ra** *adj* ship, shipping; *m* shipowner; outfitter

**navío** *m* ship, vessel; **Navío Argo** (astr.) Argo Navis; **navío de alto bordo** ship of the line; **navío de guerra** warship, ship of war; **navío de línea** ship of the line
**náyade** *f* (myth.) naiad
**nazareno -na** *adj* Nazarene; *mf* Nazarene; *m* penitent in Passion Week processions; **el Nazareno** or **el Divino Nazareno** the Nazarene
**nazareo -a** *adj & mf* Nazarene
**Nazaret** Nazareth
**nazi** *adj & mf* Nazi
**nazificar** §86 *va* to Nazify
**nazismo** *m* Nazism or Naziism
**názula** *f* cottage cheese
**N.B.** abr. of **nota bene**
**nébeda** *f* (bot.) catnip, catmint
**nebí** *m* (*pl:* **-bíes**) var. of **neblí**
**nebladura** *f* (agr.) damage from fog; (vet.) gid
**neblí** *m* (*pl:* **-blíes**) (orn.) stone falcon, merlin (*Falco aesalon*)
**neblina** *f* fog, mist
**neblinoso -sa** *adj* foggy, misty
**nebreda** *f* juniper plantation
**nebrina** *f* juniper berry
**nebrisense** *adj* pertaining to Lebrija; *mf* native or inhabitant of Lebrija
**nebular** *adj* (astr.) nebular
**nebulización** *f* nebulization
**nebulizar** §76 *va & vn* to nebulize
**nebulón** *m* scheming hypocrite
**nebulosa** *f* see **nebuloso**
**nebulosidad** *f* nebulosity, nebulousness; cloudiness; cloud, shadow; gloominess, sullenness
**nebuloso -sa** *adj* nebulous, cloudy, misty, hazy, vague; gloomy, sullen; (astr.) nebulous, nebular; *f* (astr.) nebula; **nebulosa espiral** (astr.) spiral nebula
**necear** *vn* to talk nonsense; to foolishly persist
**necedad** *f* foolishness, stupidity, folly
**necesario -ria** *adj* necessary: *f* water closet, privy
**neceser** *m* toilet case; sewing kit; **neceser de belleza** vanity, vanity case; **neceser de costura** workbasket
**necesidad** *f* necessity; need, want, starvation; urination, defecation; **de** or **por necesidad** of necessity
**necesitado -da** *adj* necessitous, poor, needy; **estar necesitado de** to be in need of; *mf* poor or needy person
**necesitar** *va* to require, necessitate; to need; **necesitar** + *inf* to have to, to need to + *inf; vn* to be in need; **necesitar de** to need, be in need of; *vr* to be needed, be necessary
**necio -cia** *adj* foolish, stupid, crazy; unwise, rash; stubborn, bullheaded; (Am.) touchy; *mf* fool; bullheaded person
**necrocomio** *m* morgue
**necrología** *f* necrology
**necromancia** or **necromancía** *f* necromancy
**necromántico -ca** necromantic; *m* necromancer
**necrópolis** *f* (*pl:* **-lis**) necropolis
**necropsia** or **necroscopia** *f* var. of **autopsia**
**necrosis** *f* (*pl:* **-sis**) (path. & bot.) necrosis
**néctar** *m* (myth., bot. & fig.) nectar
**nectáreo -a** *adj* nectareous
**nectarino -na** *adj* nectarine; *f* (orn.) honey creeper
**nectario** *m* (bot.) nectary
**necturo** *m* (zool.) mud puppy
**neerlandés -desa** *adj* Netherlandish, Dutch; *mf* Netherlander; *m* Dutchman; Netherlandish or Dutch (*language*); *f* Dutchwoman
**nefando -da** *adj* infamous, abominable
**nefario -ria** *adj* nefarious, heinous
**nefasto -ta** *adj* ominous, fatal, tragic
**nefoscopio** *m* nephoscope
**nefralgia** *f* (path.) nephralgia
**nefrectomía** *f* (surg.) nephrectomy
**nefridio** *m* (embryol.) nephridium
**nefrita** *f* (mineral.) nephrite
**nefrítico -ca** *adj* nephritic
**nefritis** *f* (path.) nephritis
**nefrolito** *m* (path.) nephrolith
**nefrotomía** *f* (surg.) nephrotomy
**negable** *adj* deniable
**negación** *f* negation; denial; refusal
**negado -da** *adj* unfit, incompetent; dull, indifferent
**negador -dora** *adj* denying; refusing; *mf* denier; refuser
**negar** §29 *va* to deny; to refuse; to prohibit; to disown, disclaim; to conceal; **negar haber** + *pp* to deny having + *pp; vn* to deny; (Am.) to misfire (*said of firearms*); *vr* to avoid; to refuse; to deny oneself to callers; **negarse a** to refuse (*something*); **negarse a** + *inf* to refuse to + *inf;* **negarse a sí mismo** to deny oneself, to practice self-denial
**negativa** *f* see **negativo**
**negativismo** *m* negativism
**negativo -va** *adj* negative; *m* (phot.) negative; *f* negative; denial; refusal; (phot.) negative
**negatrón** *m* (chem.) negatron
**negligencia** *f* negligence
**negligente** *adj* negligent
**negociabilidad** *f* negotiability
**negociable** *adj* negotiable
**negociación** *f* negotiation; matter, subject
**negociado** *m* department, bureau; business, affair
**negociador -dora** *adj* negotiating; *mf* negotiator
**negociante** *m* dealer, trader, businessman
**negociar** *va* to negotiate; to dicker for; *vn* to negotiate, to trade, to deal
**negocio** *m* business; affair, transaction, deal; job, work; profit; (Am.) store; (Am.) kitchen; **evacuar un negocio** to conclude a deal; **hacer su negocio** to look out for oneself
**negocioso -sa** *adj* businesslike
**negondo** *m* (bot.) box elder
**negra** *f* see **negro**
**negral** *adj* blackish
**negrear** *vn* to turn black, to be blackish
**negrecer** §34 *vn* to become black
**negrería** *f* Negroes, group of Negroes
**negrero -ra** *adj* slave-trading; (fig.) slave-driving; *mf* slave trader, slave driver; (fig.) slave driver; (Am.) friend of Negroes; *m* slave-trading vessel
**negreta** *f* (orn.) black scoter; (print.) boldface
**negrilla** *f* (zool.) black conger eel; (print.) boldface; (plant path.) fumagine
**negrillera** *f* plantation of elms, elm grove
**negrillo** *m* (bot.) elm tree; (prov.) blight; (Am.) black silver ore; (Am.) linnet
**negrito -ta** *mf* Negrito (*member of certain dwarfish Negroid peoples*); *f* (print.) blackface
**negro -gra** *adj* black; dark; gloomy, dismal; unhappy, fatal, evil, wicked; Negro; (coll.) broke, without means; **pasar las negras** (coll.) to be having a terrible time; *mf* (Am.) dear, darling; *m* black (*color, person*); **negro animal** boneblack; **negro de humo** lampblack; **negro de marfil** ivory black; **negro de platino** platinum black; *f* black (*woman or girl*): (mus.) quarter note; (Am.) honey, sweetheart
**negroide** or **negroideo -a** *adj* Negroid
**negror** *m* or **negrura** *f* blackness
**negruzco -ca** *adj* blackish, dark
**neguijón** *m* caries, tooth decay
**neguilla** *f* (bot.) corn cockle; corn cockle seed; (bot.) love-in-a-mist; age mark (*in horse's mouth*); cunning, rascality
**neguillón** *m* (bot.) corn cockle
**negundo** *m* (bot.) box elder
**Negus** *m* (*pl:* **-gus**) Negus (*emperor of Ethiopia*)
**Nehemías** *m* (Bib.) Nehemiah
**neis** *m* (geol.) gneiss
**nelumbio** *m* (bot.) nelumbo
**nema** *f* seal (*of a letter*)
**nematelminto** *m* (zool.) nemathelminth
**nematocisto** *m* (bot.) nematocyst
**nematoda** *m* (zool.) nematode
**neme** *m* (Am.) asphalt
**nemeo -a** *adj* Nemean
**Némesis** *f* (myth.) Nemesis
**nemoroso -sa** *adj* woody; sylvan; leafy
**Nemrod** *m* (Bib. & fig.) Nimrod
**nena** *f* (coll.) baby (*girl*)
**nene** *m* (coll.) baby (*boy*); villain
**neneque** *mf* (Am.) wretch, weakling
**nenúfar** *m* (bot.) white water lily; **nenúfar amarillo** (bot.) spatterdock, yellow water lily

**neo** *m* (chem.) neon
**neocatolicismo** *m* Neo-Catholicism
**neocatólico -ca** *adj & mf* Neo-Catholic
**neocelandés -desa** *adj* New Zealand; *mf* New Zealander
**neoclasicismo** *m* neoclassicism
**neoclásico -ca** *adj* neoclassic; *mf* neoclassicist
**neodimio** *m* (chem.) neodymium
**neoescocés -cesa** *adj & mf* Nova Scotian
**neoescolasticismo** *m* Neo-Scholasticism
**neófito -ta** *mf* neophyte
**neofobia** *f* aversion to the new
**neogranadino -na** *adj* pertaining to New Granada (*formerly Colombia and Panama*); *mf* native or inhabitant of New Granada
**neoguineano -na** *adj & mf* New Guinean
**neoiterbio** *m* (chem.) neoytterbium
**neolatino -na** *adj* Neo-Latin
**neolítico -ca** *adj* neolithic
**neología** *f* neology
**neologismo** *m* neologism
**neologista** or **neólogo -ga** *mf* neologist
**neomejicano -na** *adj & mf* New Mexican
**neomenia** *f* new moon; first day of the new moon
**neomicina** *f* (pharm.) neomycin
**neón** *m* (chem.) neon
**neoplasia** *f* or **neoplasma** *m* (path.) neoplasm
**neoplatonicismo** *m* Neo-Platonism
**neopreno** *m* neoprene
**neosalvarsán** *m* neosalvarsan
**neotenia** *f* (biol.) neoteny
**neotomismo** *m* Neo-Thomism
**neoyorquino -na** *adj* New York; *mf* New Yorker
**neozoico -ca** *adj* Neozoic
**Nepal, el** Nepal
**nepalés -lesa** *adj & mf* Nepalese; *m* Nepali (*language*)
**nepalí** *m* Nepali (*language*)
**nepente** *m* or **nepenta** *f* nepenthe (*magic potion*); (bot.) nepenthe
**neperiano -na** *adj* Napierian
**nepote** *m* relative and favorite of the Pope; (*cap.*) *m* Nepos
**nepotismo** *m* nepotism
**neptúneo -a** *adj* (poet.) Neptunian
**neptúnico -ca** *adj* (geol.) Neptunian
**neptunio** *m* (chem.) neptunium
**Neptuno** *m* (myth. & astr.) Neptune
**nequicia** *f* iniquity, perversity
**nereida** *f* (myth.) Nereid
**Nereo** *m* (myth.) Nereus
**nerol** *m* (chem.) nerol
**Nerón** *m* Nero
**nervadura** *f* nervation, ribbing; (bot. & ent.) nervure
**nerval** *adj* nerval
**nérveo -a** *adj* nerve, nerval
**nerviación** *f* nervation, nervure
**nervino -na** *adj & m* nervine
**nervio** *m* (anat. & bot.) nerve; rib (*of insect's wing*); (fig.) nerve (*physical and mental vigor*); string (*of musical instrument*); (arch.) rib in intrados of a vault; fillet (*rib in back of binding of a book*); (naut.) stay, span rope; **tener nervio** to be steadfast; **nervio auditivo** (anat.) auditory nerve; **nervio ciático** (anat.) sciatic nerve; **nervio medial** (bot.) midrib; **nervio olfativo** (anat.) olfactory nerve; **nervio óptico** (anat.) optic nerve
**nerviosidad** *f* nervosity; nervousness
**nerviosismo** *m* nervousness
**nervioso -sa** *adj* nervous; vigorous, energetic, sinewy; nerve (*tonic; tissue; disease*)
**nervosidad** *f* nervosity; flexibility, ductility; (bot.) nervation; potency (*of an argument*)
**nervoso -sa** *adj* var. of **nervioso**
**nervudo -da** *adj* strong-nerved, vigorous, energetic, sinewy
**nervura** *f* ribbing, backbone (*of book*); (bot.) nervation
**nesciencia** *f* nescience
**nesga** *f* (sew.) gore
**nesgar** §59 *va* to gore, to cut (*cloth*) on the bias
**Neso** *m* (myth.) Nessus
**néspera** *f* (bot.) medlar tree
**Néstor** *m* (myth.) Nestor
**nestoriano -na** *adj & mf* Nestorian
**neto -ta** *adj* pure, clean, neat; (com.) net; *m* (arch.) dado
**neuma** *m* (mus.) neume; *m & f* (rhet.) expression by nods, signs, or interjections
**neumático -ca** *adj* pneumatic; *m* tire, pneumatic tire; **neumático acordonado** cord tire; **neumático balón** balloon tire; **neumático de cordones** or **de cuerdas** cord tire; **neumático de recambio** or **de repuesto** spare tire; *f* pneumatics
**neumococo** *m* (bact.) pneumococcus
**neumonía** *f* (path.) pneumonia; **neumonía doble** (path.) double pneumonia
**neumónico -ca** *adj* pneumonic
**neumotórax** *m* (path. & med.) pneumothorax
**neuralgia** *f* (path.) neuralgia
**neurastenia** *f* (path.) neurasthenia
**neurasténico -ca** *adj & mf* neurasthenic
**neurectomía** *f* (surg.) neurectomy
**neuritis** *f* (path.) neuritis
**neurocirugía** *f* neurosurgery
**neuroglia** *f* (anat.) neuroglia
**neurología** *f* neurology
**neurológico -ca** *adj* neurological
**neurólogo -ga** *mf* neurologist
**neurona** *f* (anat.) neuron or neurone
**neurópata** *mf* neuropath
**neuropatía** *f* neuropathy
**neuropático -ca** *adj* neuropathic
**neuropsiquiatría** *f* neuropsychiatry
**neuroquirúrgico -ca** *adj* neurosurgical
**neurosis** *f* (*pl:* **-sis**) (path.) neurosis; **neurosis de ansiedad** (psychoanal.) anxiety neurosis; **neurosis de guerra** (path.) shell shock
**neurótico -ca** *adj & mf* neurotic
**neutoniano -na** or **neutónico -ca** *adj* Newtonian
**neutral** *adj & mf* neutral
**neutralidad** *f* neutrality
**neutralismo** *m* neutralism
**neutralista** *adj & mf* neutralist
**neutralización** *f* neutralization
**neutralizar** §76 *va* neutralize
**neutrino** *m* (phys.) neutrino
**neutro -tra** *adj* neuter; neutral (*e.g., in color*); (bot., chem., elec., phonet. & zool.) neutral; (gram.) neuter; (gram.) intransitive
**neutrón** *m* (phys.) neutron
**nevada** *f* see **nevado**
**nevadilla** *f* (bot.) whitlowwort
**nevado -da** *adj* snow-covered; snow-white; *f* snow, snowfall
**nevar** §18 *va* to make snow-white; *vn* to snow
**nevasca** *f* snowfall; snowstorm, blizzard
**nevatilla** *f* (orn.) wagtail
**nevazo** *m* snowfall
**nevazón** *f* (Am.) snowfall
**nevera** *f* see **nevero**
**nevería** *f* ice-cream parlor
**nevero -ra** *mf* ice dealer; ice-cream storekeeper; *m* place of perpetual snow; perpetual snow; *f* icebox, refrigerator; icehouse; **nevera eléctrica** electric refrigerator
**nevisca** *f* light snowfall, flurry; sleet
**neviscar** §86 *vn* to snow lightly; to sleet
**nevoso -sa** *adj* snowy
**nexo** *m* nexus; *adv* (slang) nix (*no*)
**ni** *conj* neither, nor; **ni . . . ni** neither . . . nor; **ni . . . siquiera** not even
**niacina** *f* (chem.) niacin
**niara** *f* straw rick
**nibelungo** *m* (myth.) Nibelung
**Nicaragua** *f* Nicaragua; (*l.c.*) *f* (bot.) balsam apple
**nicaragüense** or **nicaragüeño -ña** *adj & mf* Nicaraguan
**Nicea** *f* Nicaea
**niceno -na** *adj & mf* Nicene
**Nicolás** *m* Nicholas; **San Nicolás** Saint Nicholas; Santa Claus
**nicotina** *f* nicotine
**nicotínico -ca** *adj* nicotinic
**nicromo** *m* nichrome
**nictalopía** *f* nyctalopia
**nicho** *m* niche
**nidada** *f* nest (*of eggs*); brood, hatch
**nidal** *m* nest (*where hen lays eggs*); nest egg; haunt; source, basis, foundation
**nidificar** §86 *vn* to nest, to build a nest or nests

**nido** *m* nest; haunt; home; source; (fig.) nest (*of thieves, machine guns, etc.*); **caerse de un nido** (coll.) to be an easy mark; **de nido de abeja** honeycomb (*coil, radiator, etc.*)
**niebla** *f* fog, mist, haze; mildew; (fig.) fog, confusion; **hay niebla** it is foggy; **niebla artificial** smoke screen; **niebla meona** dripping fog
**niel** *m* niello
**nielado** *m* nielloing
**nielar** *va* to niello
**nieto -ta** *mf* grandchild; *m* grandson; **nietos** *mpl* grandchildren; *f* granddaughter
**nietzscheano -na** *adj & mf* Nietzschean
**nietzschismo** *m* Nietzscheism or Nietzscheanism
**nieve** *f* snow; (telv.) snow (*snowlike pattern*); (poet.) snow (*pure whiteness*); (slang) snow (*cocaine, heroin*); (Am.) water ice; **nieve carbónica** (chem.) carbon dioxide snow
**Níger** *m* Niger
**Nigeria** *f* Nigeria
**nigola** *f* (naut.) ratlin
**nigromancia** or **nigromancía** *f* necromancy
**nigromante** *m* necromancer
**nigromántico -ca** *adj* necromantic; *mf* necromancer
**nigua** *f* (ent.) chigoe, sand flea
**nihilismo** *m* nihilism
**nihilista** *adj* nihilistic; *mf* nihilist
**Nilo** *m* Nile; **Nilo Azul** Blue Nile
**nilón** *m* nylon
**nimbar** *va* to encircle with a halo
**nimbo** *m* nimbus, halo; (meteor.) nimbus
**nimboso -sa** *adj* cloudy, stormy, rainy
**nimiamente** *adv* excessively
**nimiedad** *f* excess, superfluity; fussiness, fastidiousness; trifle; (coll.) timidity
**nimio -mia** *adj* excessive; fussy, fastidious; stingy; small, negligible, worthless; (coll.) timid
**ninfa** *f* (myth., ent. & fig.) nymph; **ninfa marina** mermaid (*expert woman swimmer*)
**ninfea** *f* (bot.) white water lily
**ninfo** *m* (coll.) fop, dandy
**ninfomanía** *f* (path.) nymphomania
**ningún** *adj indef* apocopated form of **ninguno,** used only before masculine singular nouns and adjectives
**ninguno -na** *adj indef* no, not any; **de ninguna manera** by no means; *pron indef masc & fem* none, not any; neither, e.g., **ninguna de estas dos formas** neither of these forms; **ninguno** *pron indef* nobody, no one
**Nínive** *f* Nineveh
**ninivita** *adj* Ninevitical or Ninevitish; *mf* Ninevite
**niña** *f* see **niño**
**niñada** *f* childishness
**niñato** *m* unborn calf (*of butchered cow*)
**niñear** *vn* to act like a child
**niñera** *f* see **niñero**
**niñería** *f* childishness; trifle
**niñero -ra** *adj* child-loving, fond of children; *mf* dandler; *f* nursemaid, dry nurse
**niñeta** *f* pupil (*of the eye*)
**niñez** *f* childhood; childishness; (fig.) infancy; **segunda niñez** second childhood
**niño -ña** *adj* young, inexperienced; childlike, childish; *mf* child; **desde niño** from childhood; **niño azul** blue baby; **niño de la piedra** foundling; **niño expósito** foundling; **niño prodigio** infant prodigy; **niño travieso** imp; *m* child, boy; **niño bonito** fop, dandy, playboy; **niño de coro** (eccl.) choirboy; **niño de la bola** child Jesus, bambino; (coll.) lucky fellow; **niño de teta** suckling, babe in arms; **niño explorador** boy scout; **niño Jesús** child Jesus; bambino (*image of baby Jesus*); **niño gótico** fop, dandy, playboy; **niño zangolotino** (coll.) grown boy who passes as a child; *f* child, girl; (anat.) pupil (*of the eye*); **niña exploradora** girl scout; **niña del ojo** (coll.) apple of one's eye
**Níobe** *f* (myth.) Niobe
**niobio** *m* (chem.) niobium
**nipa** *f* (bot.) nipa palm
**nipón -pona** *adj & mf* Nipponese
**níquel** *m* (chem.) nickel
**niquelado** *m* or **niqueladura** *f* nickel plate
**niquelar** *va* to nickel-plate
**niquelina** *f* (mineral.) niccolite
**niquiscocio** *m* (coll.) trifle
**nirvana, el** nirvana or Nirvana
**níscalo** *m* (bot.) var. of **mízcalo**
**níspero** *m* (bot.) medlar (*tree and fruit*); (bot.) sapodilla; **níspero del Canadá** (bot.) shadberry, shadbush; **níspero del Japón** (bot.) loquat
**níspola** *f* medlar (*fruit*)
**nistagmo** *m* (path.) nystagmus
**nitidez** *f* brightness, clearness; sharpness
**nítido -da** *adj* bright, clear; sharp (*said of a photograph*)
**nitón** *m* (chem.) niton
**nitración** *f* (chem.) nitration
**nitral** *m* niter or saltpeter bed
**nitrar** *va* to nitrate, to nitrify
**nitrato** *m* (chem.) nitrate; **nitrato amónico** (chem.) ammonium nitrate; **nitrato de Chile** Chile saltpeter; **nitrato de plata** (chem.) silver nitrate; **nitrato de potasio** (chem.) potassium nitrate
**nitrería** *f* saltpeter works
**nítrico -ca** *adj* (chem.) nitric
**nitrificación** *f* nitrification
**nitrificar** §86 *va* to nitrify
**nitrilo** *m* (chem.) nitrile
**nitrito** *m* (chem.) nitrite
**nitro** *m* saltpeter, niter (*potassium nitrate*); **nitro de Chile** saltpeter, niter, Chile saltpeter (*sodium nitrate*)
**nitrobacterias** *fpl* (agr.) nitrobacteria
**nitrobenceno** *m* or **nitrobencina** *f* (chem.) nitrobenzene
**nitrocal** *f* nitrolime
**nitrocelulosa** *f* nitrocellulose
**nitrogenado -da** *adj* nitrogenous
**nitrógeno** *m* (chem.) nitrogen
**nitroglicerina** *f* nitroglycerine
**nitrólico -ca** *adj* (chem.) nitrolic
**nitrómetro** *m* nitrometer
**nitrosilo** *m* (chem.) nitrosyl
**nitroso -sa** *adj* (chem.) nitrous
**nitruro** *m* (chem.) nitride
**nivel** *m* level; **a nivel** at grade; **estar a un nivel** to be on the same footing; **nivel de aire** or **de burbuja** spirit level; **nivel del mar** sea level; **nivel de vida** standard of living
**nivelación** *f* leveling
**nivelada** *f* (surv.) sight
**nivelador -dora** *adj* leveling; *mf* leveler; *f* grader, road scraper
**nivelar** *va* to level; to even, to make even; to grade; to take the level of, to survey; to balance (*the budget*); *vr* to become level
**níveo -a** *adj* (poet.) snowy
**nivoso -sa** *adj* snowy
**nixtamal** *m* (Am.) corn steeped in lime water to make tortillas
**Niza** *f* Nice
**nizardo -da** *adj* (pertaining to) Nice; *mf* native or inhabitant of Nice
**N.º** abr. of **número**
**no** *adv* not; no; **¿no?** is it not so?; **¿cómo no?** why not?; of course, certainly; **creer que no** to think not, to believe not; **ya no** no longer; **no bien** no sooner; **no más que** not more than; only; **no sea que** lest; **no . . . sino** only; **no . . . ya** no longer
**nobabia** *f* (aer.) dope
**nobelio** *m* (chem.) nobelium
**nobiliario -ria** *adj* nobiliary; *m* peerage book, peerage list
**nobilísimamente** *adv super* very or most nobly
**nobilísimo -ma** *adj super* very or most noble
**noble** *adj* noble; *m* noble, nobleman; noble (*Spanish and English coin*)
**nobleza** *f* nobility
**noblote -ta** *adj* noble, generous
**noca** *f* (zool.) spider crab
**nocaut** *m* (box.) knockout
**nocedal** *m* var. of **nogueral**
**nocente** *adj* harmful; guilty
**noción** *f* notion, rudiment
**nocivo -va** *adj* noxious, harmful
**noctambulación** *f* noctambulation
**noctambulismo** *m* noctambulism

**noctámbulo -la** *adj* nighttime; night-wandering; *mf* nighthawk, night owl; nightwalker
**nocturno -na** *adj* night, nocturnal; lonely, sad, melancholy; *m* (mus.) nocturne
**nocharniego -ga** *adj* night-hunting (*dog*)
**noche** *f* night, nighttime; darkness; **a buenas noches** (coll.) in the dark; **a prima noche** or **a primera noche** shortly after dark; **buenas noches** good evening; good night; **de noche** at night, in the nighttime; **de la noche a la mañana** overnight; unexpectedly, suddenly; **esta noche** tonight; **hacer noche en** to spend the night in; **hacerse de noche** to grow dark; **muy de noche** late at night; **por la noche** at night, in the nighttime; **noche buena** Christmas Eve; **noche de bodas** wedding night; **noche de estreno** (theat.) first night; **noche de uvas** New Year's Eve; **noche intempestiva** (poet.) far into the night; **noche toledana** sleepless night; **noche vieja** New Year's Eve; watch night
**nochebuena** *f* Christmas Eve; (bot.) poinsettia
**nochebueno** *m* Christmas cake; Yule log
**nocherniego -ga** *adj* night-wandering
**nochizo** *m* (bot.) wild hazel
**nodal** *adj* nodal
**nodo** *m* (astr., med. & phys.) node
**No-Do** *m* (mov.) abr. of **Noticiario y Documentales** newsreel; newsreel theater
**nodriza** *f* wet nurse; (aut.) vacuum tank; (naut.) tender
**nodular** *adj* nodular
**nódulo** *m* nodule; (anat., geol. & min.) nodule
**Noé** *m* (Bib.) Noah
**Noemí** *f* Naomi
**nogada** *f* sauce of ground walnuts and spice for fish
**nogal** *m* (bot.) English walnut; walnut (*wood*); **nogal ceniciento** or **nogal de Cuba** (bot.) butternut; **nogal de la brujería** (bot.) witch hazel; **nogal negro** (bot.) black walnut
**nogalina** *f* walnut stain
**noguera** *f* (bot.) English walnut
**noguerado -da** *adj* walnut-colored
**nogueral** *m* walnut grove
**nogueruela** *f* (bot.) spurge
**nómada** or **nómade** *adj* nomad, nomadic; *mf* nomad
**nomadismo** *m* nomadism
**nombradamente** *adv* expressly
**nombradía** *f* fame, renown, reputation
**nombrado -da** *adj* famous, well-known
**nombramiento** *m* naming; appointment; (mil.) commission
**nombrar** *va* to name; to appoint; (mil.) to commission
**nombre** *m* name; fame, reputation; nickname; watchword; (gram.) noun; **dar el nombre** to give the watchword; **del mismo nombre** (elec.) like (*poles of a magnet*); **de nombres contrarios** (elec.) unlike (*poles of a magnet*); **en nombre de** in the name of; **hacerse un nombre** to make a name for oneself; **mal nombre** nickname; **no tener nombre** to be unspeakable; **poner nombre a** to give a name to; to set a price on; **por nombre de** by the name of; **nombre apelativo** or **común** (gram.) common noun; **nombre colectivo** (gram.) collective noun; **nombre comercial** firm name; **nombre de lugar** place name; **nombre de pila** first name, Christian name; **nombre de soltera** maiden name; **nombre postizo** alias; **nombre propio** (gram.) proper noun; **nombre substantivo** (gram.) noun; **nombre supuesto** alias; **nombre y apellido** full name
**nomenclador** *m* or **nomenclátor** *m* catalogue of names; technical glossary; nomenclator
**nomenclatura** *f* nomenclature
**nomeolvides** *f* (*pl:* **-des**) (bot.) forget-me-not; (bot.) German madwort
**nómina** *f* list, roll; pay roll; **nómina de sueldos** pay roll
**nominación** *f* naming, nomination; appointment
**nominador -dora** *adj* nominating; *mf* nominator
**nominal** *adj* nominal; noun, substantive
**nominalismo** *m* nominalism
**nominalista** *mf* nominalist
**nominar** *va* to name; to appoint
**nominativo -va** *adj* nominative (*having person's name*); (gram.) nominative; *m* (gram.) nominative
**nominilla** *f* voucher
**nómino** *m* nominee
**nomparell** *m* (print.) nonpareil
**non** *adj* (math.) odd, uneven; *m* (math.) odd number; **andar de nones** (coll.) to be idle; **estar de non** (coll.) to be unmatched; to be useless; **quedar de non** (coll.) to be alone, to be without a companion
**nona** *f* see **nono**
**nonada** *f* trifle, nothing
**nonagenario -ria** *adj & mf* nonagenarian
**nonagésimo -ma** *adj & m* ninetieth
**nonágono** *m* (geom.) nonagon
**nonato -ta** *adj* unborn, still nonexistent; ill-born; born by Caesarean operation
**noningentésimo -ma** *adj & m* nine hundredth
**nonio** *m* vernier; slide rule
**nono -na** *adj & m* ninth; *f* (eccl.) nones; **nonas** *fpl* (hist.) nones
**non séquitur** *m* non sequitur (*unfounded conclusion*)
**nopal** *m* (bot.) prickly pear; **nopal castellano** (bot.) Indian fig; **nopal de la cochinilla** (bot.) cochineal fig
**noque** *m* tanning vat
**noquear** *va* (box.) to knock out
**noquero** *m* tanner, leather dresser
**norabuena** *f* congratulation; *adv* fortunately
**Noráfrica** *f* North Africa
**noramala** *adv* var. of **enhoramala**
**noray** *m* (naut.) bollard, mooring
**norcoreano -na** *adj & mf* North Korean
**nordestada** *f* northeaster
**nordestal** *adj* northeast; northeastern; northeasterly
**nordeste** *m* northeast; northeaster; *adj* northeast; northeastern
**nordestear** *vn* (naut.) to turn from north toward east (*said of compass*)
**nórdico -ca** *adj* Nordic; Norse (*e.g., mythology*); *mf* Nordic; *m* Norse (*old Scandinavian language*)
**nordista** *m* Northerner (*in U.S. Civil War*)
**nordoccidental** *adj* northwestern
**noria** *f* chain pump, Persian wheel; Ferris wheel; (coll.) treadmill (*futile drudgery*)
**norma** *f* norm, standard; rule, regulation, method; (carp. & mas.) square
**normal** *adj* normal, standard; perpendicular, *f* normal school; perpendicular
**normalidad** *f* normality, normalcy
**normalista** *mf* normal-school student
**normalización** *f* normalization, standardization; regulation
**normalizar** **§76** *va* to normalize, standardize; to regulate
**normalmente** *adv* normally; perpendicularly
**Normandía** *f* Normandy
**normando -da** *adj* Norman; (arch.) Normanesque; *mf* Norman; *m* Norman French (*dialect*); Norseman, Northman
**normánico** *m* Norman French (*dialect*)
**normano -na** *adj & mf* var. of **normando**
**Norna** *f* (myth.) Norn
**nornordeste** *m* or **nornoreste** *m* north-northeast
**nornoroeste** *m* or **nornorueste** *m* north-northwest
**noroccidental** *adj* northwestern
**noroeste** *m* northwest; northwester; *adj* northwest; northwestern
**noroestear** *vn* (naut.) to turn from north toward west (*said of compass*)
**nortada** *f* norther, north wind
**norte** *m* north; north wind; North Pole; North Star; (fig.) lodestar, polestar (*guide*)
**norteafricano -na** *adj & mf* North African
**Norteamérica** *f* North America
**norteamericano -na** *adj & mf* North American; American (*i.e., of the U.S.A.*)
**nortear** *vn* (naut.) to steer to the north; (naut.) to turn northerly (*said of the wind*)
**norteño -ña** *adj* northern
**nórtico -ca** *adj* northern

**noruego -ga** *adj & mf* Norwegian; *m* Norwegian (*language*); (*cap.*) *f* Norway
**norueste** *m & adj* var. of **noroeste**
**noruestar** *vn* var. of **noroestear**
**nos** *pron pers & reflex* (used as object of verb) us, to us; ourselves, to ourselves; each other, to each other; *pron pers* (used as object of preposition in Biblical language) us; (fictitious plural, used as subject of verb or object of preposition, by high dignitaries of church and court) we; us
**nosocomial** *adj* (Am.) (pertaining to a) hospital
**nosocomio** *m* (Am.) hospital, public-health center
**nosotros -tras** *pron pers* (used as subject of verb and object of preposition; plural of modesty sometimes used by writers) we; us
**nostalgia** *f* nostalgia, homesickness
**nostálgico -ca** *adj* nostalgic, homesick
**nota** *f* see **noto**
**notabilidad** *f* notability (*quality; person*)
**notabilísimo -ma** *adj super* very or most notable
**notable** *adj* notable, noteworthy; *mf* notable, worthy
**notación** *f* notation
**notar** *va* to note, to notice, to annotate; to dictate; to criticize; to discredit
**notaría** *f* profession of notary; notary's office
**notariado -da** *adj* notarized; *m* profession of notary
**notarial** *adj* notarial
**notariato** *m* title of notary; practice of a notary
**notario** *m* notary, notary public
**noticia** *f* news; notice, information; knowledge; notion, rudiment; **una noticia** a news item; **noticia remota** vague notion, vague recollection; **noticias de actualidad** news of the day; **noticias de última hora** late news
**noticiar** *va* to notify, give notice to; to give notice of
**noticiario -ria** *adj* (pertaining to) news; *m* up-to-the-minute news; newsreel; (rad.) newscast; **noticiario cinematográfico** newsreel; **noticiario deportivo** sports news; **noticiario gráfico** picture page (*in a newspaper*); **noticiario teatral** theater news, theater page
**noticiero -ra** *adj* (pertaining to) news; *m* newsman; late news
**notición** *m* (coll.) big news, wild or fantastic story
**noticioso -sa** *adj* informed; learned, widely informed; (Am.) (pertaining to) news; (Am.) newsy; *m* (Am.) news item; (Am.) news report
**notificación** *f* notification
**notificar §86** *va* to notify (*to give notice of or to*); to report on; **notificar a una persona una cosa** to notify a person of something
**noto -ta** *adj* well-known; illegitimate; *m* south wind; *f* note; mark, grade (*in school*); check (*e.g., in a restaurant*); (mus.) note; **caer en nota** to get talked about, to cause a scandal; **tomar nota de** to take note of; **nota de adorno** (mus.) grace note; **nota marginal** marginal note; **nota tónica** (mus.) keynote
**notocordio** *m* (biol.) notochord
**notoriedad** *f* notoriety (*being well known or famous*)
**notorio -ria** *adj* notorious (*well-known*); evident, manifest
**nóumeno** *m* (philos.) noumenon
**nov.** abr. of **noviembre**
**nova** *f* (astr.) nova
**novación** *f* (law) novation
**novador -dora** *adj* innovating; *mf* innovator
**noval** *adj* newly broken (*said of land*)
**novar** *va* (law) to novate
**novatada** *f* hazing; beginner's blunder
**novato -ta** *adj* beginning; *mf* beginner; freshman
**novator -tora** *mf* innovator
**novecientos -tas** *adj & m* nine hundred
**novedad** *f* newness, novelty; surprise; happening; news; change; inconstancy; failing health; **novedades** *fpl* fashions; **hacer novedad** to unexpectedly cause great surprise; to make drastic changes; **sin novedad** as usual; without anything happening; safe; well
**novedoso -sa** *adj* novel; innovating; (Am.) fictional
**novel** *adj* new, inexperienced, beginning; *m* beginner
**novela** *f* novel, romance; story, lie; **novela caballista** cowboy story, novel of western life; **novela de clave** roman à clef; **novela policíaca** or **policial** detective story; **novela por entregas** serial
**novelador -dora** *mf* novelist
**novelar** *va* to novelize; *vn* to write novels; to tell stories
**novelería** *f* curiosity; fondness for fiction; worthless fiction
**novelero -ra** *adj* curious, fond of novelty; fond of fiction; gossipy; inconstant, fickle
**novelesco -ca** *adj* novelistic; fictional; like a novel, romantic, fantastic
**novelista** *mf* novelist
**novelístico -ca** *adj* fictional, (pertaining to the) novel; *f* fiction, novel; treatise on the novel
**novelizar §76** *va* to novelize, to fictionalize
**novembrino -na** *adj* (pertaining to) November
**noveno -na** *adj & m* ninth; *f* (eccl.) novena
**noventa** *adj & m* ninety
**noventavo -va** *adj & m* ninetieth
**noventón -tona** *adj & mf* nonagenarian
**novia** *f* fiancée; bride; **novia de guerra** war bride
**noviazgo** *m* engagement, courtship
**noviciado** *m* novitiate, apprenticeship; (eccl.) novitiate
**novicio -cia** *adj* inexperienced, beginning; *mf* novice, beginner, apprentice; (eccl.) novice
**noviembre** *m* November
**novilunio** *m* new moon
**novilla** *f* heifer
**novillada** *f* drove of young cattle; fight with young bulls
**novillero** *m* herdsman who cares for young cattle; stable for young cattle; pasture ground for young cattle; (taur.) aspiring fighter, untrained fighter; (coll.) truant
**novillo** *m* young bull; (coll.) cuckold; **novillos** fight with young bulls; **hacer novillos** to play truant
**novio** *m* suitor; fiancé; bridegroom; **novios** *mpl* engaged couple; bride and groom
**novísimo -ma** *adj super* newest, latest, most recent; *m* each of the last stages of man: death, judgment, hell, and heaven; **Novísima** *f* revised code of Spanish law (*1805*)
**novocaína** *f* novocaine
**noyó** *m* (*pl:* **-yoes**) noyau (*a cordial*)
**nro.** abr. of **nuestro**
**N.S.** abr. of **Nuestro Señor**
**N.S.J.C.** abr. of **Nuestro Señor Jesucristo**
**ntro.** abr. of **nuestro**
**nubado -da** *adj* clouded; cloud-shaped; *f* local shower; abundance, plenty
**nubarrada** *f* var. of **nubada**
**nubarrón** *m* large black cloud, storm cloud
**nube** *f* cloud (*fog suspended in air; crowd, multitude, flock; shadow in precious stones; sorrow, gloom*); light lace head scarf; white spot on cornea; **andar** or **estar por las nubes** to be sky-high (*in price*); **poner a uno por las nubes, subir a uno a las nubes** or **hasta las nubes** to praise someone to the skies; **subir a las nubes** to go sky-high (*in price*); **nube correo** scud; **nube de lluvia** rain cloud; **nube de polvo** dust cloud; **nube de verano** summer shower; (fig.) passing annoyance
**nubiense** *adj & mf* Nubian
**núbil** *adj* nubile, marriageable
**nubilidad** *f* nubility, marriageability
**nublado -da** *adj* cloudy; **está nublado** it is cloudy; *m* storm cloud; impending danger; multitude; abundance; **aguantar el nublado** to suffer resignedly, to take a disappointment resignedly; **descargar el nublado** to rain, snow, or hail hard; to unburden one's anger in explosive words
**nublar** *va & vr* var. of **anublar**
**nublo -bla** *adj* cloudy; *m* storm cloud; bunt, wheat smut
**nubloso -sa** *adj* cloudy; adverse, unfortunate

**nubosidad** *f* cloudiness; (meteor.) percentage of cloudiness (*at a given time*); (meteor.) cloud rate (*in a given period*)
**nuboso -sa** *adj* var. of **nubloso**
**nuca** *f* nape
**nucífraga** or **nucífraga** *f* (orn.) nutcracker
**nucleado -da** *adj* (bot.) nucleate
**nuclear** *adj* (phys.) nuclear
**nucleario -ria** *adj* nuclear, nucleate
**nucleasa** *f* (biochem.) nuclease
**nucleico -ca** *adj* nucleic
**nucleína** *f* (biochem.) nuclein
**nucleínico -ca** *adj* nucleic
**núcleo** *m* core, nucleus; kernel (*of nut*); stone (*of fruit*); (chem.) ring, nucleus; (elec.) core (*of an electromagnet*); (anat., biol. & phys.) nucleus; **núcleo bencénico** (chem.) benzene ring or nucleus
**nucléolo** *m* (biol.) nucleolus
**nucleón** *m* (phys.) nucleon
**nucleónico -ca** *adj* nucleonic; *f* nucleonics
**nudillo** *m* knuckle; knot in stockings; dowel, plug (*e.g., in a wall*); **dar con la badila en los nudillos a** to rap the knuckles of
**nudismo** *m* nudism
**nudista** *mf* nudist
**nudo -da** *adj* nude, naked; *m* knot; tie, union, bond; crux; node, plot, tangle; difficulty; crisis (*in drama*); juncture, center, point of crossing; (bot.) node; (naut.) knot; **cortar el nudo gordiano** (myth. & fig.) to cut the Gordian knot; **hacérsele a uno un nudo en la garganta** to get a knot in one's throat; **nudo corredizo** slip knot
**nudosidad** *f* knottiness; knot
**nudoso -sa** *adj* knotted, knotty
**nuecero -ra** *mf* walnut vender, nut vender
**nuégado** *m* nougat
**nuera** *f* daughter-in-law
**nuestrama** *f* mistress
**nuestramo** *m* master
**nuestro -tra** *adj poss* our; *pron poss* ours; **los nuestros** our friends, our men, our side
**nueva** *f* see **nuevo**
**Nueva Delhi** *f* New Delhi
**nuevamente** *adv* newly, recently; **again**
**Nueva Orleáns** *f* New Orleans
**Nueva York** *m & f* New York; **el Gran Nueva York** Greater New York
**Nueva Zelanda** *f* New Zealand
**nueve** *adj* nine; **las nueve** nine o'clock; *m* nine; ninth (*in dates*)
**nuevo -va** *adj* new; **de nuevo** again, anew; **¿qué hay de nuevo?** what's new?; **nuevo flamante** brand-new; *mf* novice; freshman; *f* news, fresh news
**nuevomejicano -na** *adj & mf* New Mexican
**Nuevo Méjico** *m* New Mexico
**nuez** *f* (*pl:* **nueces**) walnut; nut; Adam's apple; nut or frog (*of violin bow*); **apretar a uno la nuez** (coll.) to choke someone to death; **nuez de agallas** oak gall; **nuez de betel** betel nut; **nuez de cola** kola nut; (pharm.) kola; **nuez de especia** (bot.) nutmeg; **nuez de la garganta** Adam's apple; **nuez de marfil** ivory nut; **nuez dura** (bot.) hickory; hickory nut; **nuez encarcelada** (bot.) pecan (*tree and fruit*); **nuez moscada** (bot.) nutmeg; **nuez vómica** (bot.) nux vomica (*tree and seed*)
**nueza** *f* (bot.) bryony
**nulamente** *adv* with no effect
**nulidad** *f* nullity; incapacity; (coll.) nobody, person of no importance
**nulo -la** *adj* null, void, worthless
**núm.** abr. of **número**
**Numancia** *f* Numantia
**numantino -na** *adj & mf* Numantine or Numantian
**numen** *m* deity; inspiration
**numerable** *adj* numerable
**numeración** *f* numeration
**numerador -dora** *adj* numbering; *m* numerator; numbering; (math.) numerator; *f* numbering machine
**numeral** *adj* numeral
**numerar** *va* to numerate; to number; to calculate
**numerario -ria** *adj* numerary; *m* cash, coin, specie
**numérico -ca** *adj* numerical
**número** *m* number; lottery ticket; size (*e.g., of shoes*); (gram.) number; **números** *mpl* (poet. & mus.) numbers; **los Números** (Bib.) Numbers; **de número** regular (*said of members of an association*); **el mayor número** most, the majority; **los números centenares** the hundreds (*100, 200, 300, etc.*); **mirar por el número uno** to look out for number one (*oneself*); **sin número** without number, countless; **número arábigo** Arabic numeral; **número atómico** (chem.) atomic number; **número atrasado** back number (*of a newspaper, magazine*); **número cardinal** cardinal number; **número concreto** concrete number; **número de cetano** (chem.) cetane number; **número de guarismo** Arabic numeral; **número de masa** (phys.) mass number **número entero** whole number; **número equivocado** (telp.) wrong number; **número fraccionario** fractional number; **número impar** or **número non** odd number; **número másico** (phys.) mass number; **número mixto** mixed number; **número ordinal** ordinal number; **número par** even number; **número quebrado** fractional number; **número redondo** round number; **número romano** Roman numeral
**numeroso -sa** *adj* numerous
**númida** *adj & mf* Numidian
**numídico -ca** *adj* Numidian
**numisma** *m* coin, money
**numismático -ca** *adj* numismatic; *mf* numismatist; *f* numismatics
**numulario** *m* money broker
**nunca** *adv* never; **nunca jamás** never more
**nunciatura** *f* nunciature
**nuncio** *m* messenger; forerunner, harbinger; nuncio; **nuncio apostólico** nuncio, papal nuncio
**nupcial** *adj* nuptial
**nupcialidad** *f* marriage rate, nuptiality
**nupcias** *fpl* nuptials, marriage; **casarse en segundas nupcias** to marry the second time
**nutación** *f* (astr. & bot.) nutation
**nutra** or **nutria** *f* (zool.) otter
**nutricio -cia** *adj* nutritious, nutritive
**nutrición** *f* nutrition; (biol.) nutrition
**nutrido -da** *adj* great, intense, robust, vigorous, steady; full, abounding, rich, heavy
**nutrimento** or **nutrimiento** *m* nutriment, nourishment
**nutrir** *va* to nourish, to feed; to fill to overflowing; to supply, to stock; *vr* to be enriched
**nutritivo -va** *adj* nutritive, nutritious
**nutriz** *f* (*pl:* **-trices**) wet nurse

**Ñ, ñ** *f* seventeenth letter of the Spanish alphabet
**ñagaza** *f* var. of **añagaza**
**ñajú** *m* (bot.) okra or gumbo
**ñámbar** *m* (bot.) Jamaica rosewood
**ñame** *m* (bot.) yam (*vine and root*)
**ñandú** *m* (*pl:* **-dúes**) (orn.) nandu, American ostrich
**ñandutí** *m* (Am.) fine Paraguayan linenware
**ñangotar** *vr* (Am.) to squat, to squat down
**ñaño -ña** *adj* (Am.) close, intimate; (Am.) spoiled, overindulged; *m* (Am.) elder brother; *f* (Am.) elder sister; (Am.) nursemaid; (Am.) dear
**ñapa** *f* (Am.) lagniappe, something thrown in; **de ñapa** (Am.) in the bargain
**ñaque** *m* junk, pile of junk
**ñaruso -sa** *adj* (Am.) pock-marked
**ñeque** *adj* (Am.) drooping (*eyes*); (Am.) strong, vigorous; *m* (Am.) energy, pep; (Am.) slap, blow; **tener mucho ñeque** (Am.) to be full of pep
**ñilhue** *m* (Am.) sow thistle
**ñiquiñaque** *m* (coll.) trash (*person or thing*)
**ñisca** or **ñizca** *f* (Am.) bit, fragment
**ñoclo** *m* macaroon
**ñolombre** *m* (Am.) old peasant; **¡viene ñolombre!** (Am.) here comes the bogeyman!
**ñongo -ga** *adj* (Am.) slow, lazy, timid; (Am.) shapeless
**ñoñería** *f* timid act, whiny remark
**ñoñez** *f* timid act, whiny remark; timidity, whininess
**ñoño -ña** *adj* (coll.) timid and whiny; *mf* timid and whiny person
**ñorbo** *m* (Am.) passionflower
**ñu** *m* (zool.) brindled gnu, blue wildebeest
**ñudillo** *m* var. of **nudillo**
**ñudo** *m* knot
**ñudoso -sa** *adj* var. of **nudoso**
**ñufla** *mf* (Am.) good-for-nothing; *m* (Am.) worthless object
**ñuñu** *m* (bot.) blue-eyed grass
**ñuto -ta** *adj* (Am.) ground to dust or powder

**O, o** *f* eighteenth letter of the Spanish alphabet
**o** *conj* or; **o . . . o** either . . . or
**oasis** *m* (*pl:* **-sis**) oasis
**ob.** abr. of **obispo**
**obcecación** *f* obfuscation
**obcecar §86** *va* to obfuscate, blind
**obduración** *f* obduracy
**obedecedor -dora** *adj* obeying, obedient; *mf* obeyer
**obedecer §34** *va & vn* to obey; **obedecer a** to yield to, be due to, be in keeping with, arise from
**obediencia** *f* obedience; **a la obediencia** your obedient servant; **dar la obediencia a** to be submissive to
**obediente** *adj* obedient
**obelisco** *m* obelisk; (print.) dagger
**obencadura** *f* (naut.) shrouds
**obenque** *m* guy; **obenques** *mpl* (naut.) shrouds
**obertura** *f* (mus.) overture
**obesidad** *f* obesity
**obeso -sa** *adj* obese
**óbice** *m* hindrance, obstacle
**obispado** *m* bishopric
**obispal** *adj* episcopal
**obispalía** *f* palace of a bishop; bishopric
**obispar** *vn* to become a bishop, to be appointed bishop; to get married (*said of a woman*); *vr* to be disappointed; (coll.) to die
**obispillo** *m* boy bishop (*boy dressed as a bishop*); rump, croup (*of a fowl*); large pork sausage
**obispo** *m* bishop; **obispo sufragáneo** suffragan bishop; **obispo universal** Universal Bishop
**óbito** *m* decease, demise
**obituario** *m* obituary; (eccl.) obituary
**objeción** *f* objection
**objetante** *adj* objecting; *mf* objector; **objetante de conciencia** conscientious objector
**objetar** *va* to object; to raise (*difficulties, objections, etc.*); to set up, offer, present (*an opposing argument*); **no tener nada que objetar** to have no objections to make
**objetividad** *f* objectivity
**objetivo -va** *adj* objective; (gram.) objective; *m* objective (*end, aim*); (opt.) objective
**objeto** *m* object; subject matter; (gram.) object; **al objeto de** with the object of; **objetos de cotillón** favors (*small gifts such as streamers, noisemakers, hats, toy balloons*)
**oblación** *f* oblation
**oblada** *f* offering of bread on the occasion of a requiem
**oblato -ta** *adj & mf* (eccl.) oblate; *f* (eccl.) oblation
**oblea** *f* wafer; pill, tablet; **estar hecho una oblea** (coll.) to be nothing but skin and bones
**obleera** *f* wafer holder or box
**oblicuángulo -la** *adj* oblique-angled
**oblicuar** *va* to cant, to slant; *vn* to oblique; (mil.) to oblique
**oblicuidad** *f* obliquity; **oblicuidad de la eclíptica** (astr.) obliquity of the ecliptic
**oblicuo -cua** *adj* oblique
**obligación** *f* obligation; bond; debenture; **obligaciones** *fpl* family responsibilities; **correr obligación a** to be under obligation to
**obligacionista** *mf* bondholder
**obligado -da** *adj* obliged, grateful; submissive; (mus.) obbligato; *m* city or town contractor or supplier; (mus.) obbligato
**obligar §59** *va* to obligate; to oblige; to force; **obligar a** + *inf* to obligate to + *inf;* to oblige to + *inf*; to force to + *inf;* **obligar a que** or **para que** + *subj* to oblige to + *inf;* to force to + *inf; vr* to obligate oneself, to bind oneself; **obligarse a** + *inf* to obligate oneself to + *inf*
**obligatorio -ria** *adj* obligatory
**obliteración** *f* lack of memory; cancellation (*of postage stamps*); (med.) obliteration
**obliterar** *va* to cancel, to obliterate (*a postage stamp*); (med.) to obliterate
**oblongo -ga** *adj* oblong
**ob.º** abr. of **obispo**
**oboe** *m* (mus.) oboe; (mus.) oboist
**oboísta** *mf* (mus.) oboist
**óbolo** *m* mite (*small contribution*)
**obpo.** abr. of **obispo**
**obra** *f* work; building, construction; repair work; hearth (*of blast furnace*); **obras** *fpl* construction; repairs, alterations; **buena obra** charity, good works; **meter en obra** or **poner por obra** to undertake, to set to work on; **obra de** a matter of (*e.g., ten minutes*); **obra de consulta** reference work; **obra de El Escorial** (coll.) endless undertaking; **obra de manos** handwork; **obra de romanos** herculean task, Trojan task; immense, lasting piece of work; **obra maestra** masterpiece; **obra muerta** (naut.) rail, freeboard, upper works; **obra pía** charity; religious foundation; (coll.) profit, useful effort; **obra prima** shoemaking; **obras de campo** (fort.) fieldwork; **obra segunda** shoe repairing; **obras públicas** public works; **obra viva** (naut.) quickwork (*submerged part of ship when loaded*)
**obrada** *f* day's labor, day's plowing; land measure (*varying between 39 and 54 ares*)
**obrador -dora** *adj* working; *mf* worker; *m* workman; shop, workshop; *f* working woman
**obradura** *f* charge or pressing of an olive-oil mill
**obraje** *m* manufacture; mill, woolen mill
**obrajero** *m* foreman, superintendent
**obrar** *va* to build; to work, perform; to work (*e.g., wood*); *vn* to work; to act, operate, proceed; to be; to have a movement of the bowels; **obra en mi poder** I have at hand, I have in my possession; **obrar en contra de** to work against
**obrepción** *f* (law) concealment of the truth
**obrepticio -cia** *adj* obreptitious
**obrera** *f* see **obrero**
**obrería** *f* status of workman; money for church repairs; churchwarden's office or warehouse
**obrerismo** *m* laborism; labor; labor movement
**obrerista** *adj* (pertaining to) labor; *mf* laborist, laborite
**obrero -ra** *adj* working; (pertaining to) labor; *m* workman; worker; churchwarden; **los obreros** labor (*as distinguished from management*); *f* working woman; (ent.) worker
**obrero-patronal** *adj* labor-management
**obrizo -za** *adj* pure, refined (*gold*)
**obscenidad** *f* obscenity
**obsceno -na** *adj* obscene
**obscuración** *f* darkness, obscurity
**obscurantismo** *m* obscurantism
**obscurantista** *adj & mf* obscurantist
**obscurecer §34** *va* to darken; to dim, becloud; to discredit, to dim; to cloud, confuse; (paint.) to shade; *vn* to grow dark; *vr* to grow cloudy, to cloud over; to become dimmed; (coll.) to fade away, fade out
**obscurecimiento** *m* darkening, obscuration; clouding; fading; (paint.) shading
**obscuridad** *f* obscurity; darkness; gloominess
**obscuro -ra** *adj* obscure; dark; gloomy; uncertain, dangerous; (paint.) dark, shaded; **a obscuras** in the dark; (fig.) in the dark; *m* dark; (paint.) dark, shading; **hacer obscuro** to be dark (*because of night or clouds*)
**obsecración** *f* obsecration
**obsecuencia** *f* obedience, submissiveness

**obsecuente** *adj* obedient, submissive
**obseder** *va* to obsess
**obsequiado -da** *mf* recipient; guest of honor
**obsequiador -dora** *adj* fawning; *mf* fawner, flatterer
**obsequiante** *adj* fawning; *mf* fawner, flatterer; *m* suitor
**obsequiar** *va* to fawn over, flatter, pay attentions to; to present; to give; to court, to woo
**obsequio** *m* fawning, flattery, obsequiousness; gift; attention, courtesy; **en obsequio de** in honor of; out of consideration for
**obsequiosidad** *f* obsequiousness; kindness, courtesy
**obsequioso -sa** *adj* obsequious; obliging, courteous
**observable** *adj* observable
**observación** *f* observation
**observador -dora** *adj* observant; *mf* observer
**observancia** *f* observance; deference, respectfulness (*toward elders or superiors*); **poner en observancia** to enforce in a most conscientious fashion
**observante** *adj* observant
**observar** *va* to observe
**observatorio** *m* observatory
**obsesión** *f* obsession
**obsesionante** *adj* obsessing, haunting, harassing
**obsesionar** *va* to obsess
**obsesivo -va** *adj* obsessive
**obseso -sa** *adj* obsessed, possessed
**obsidiana** *f* (mineral.) obsidian
**obsidional** *adj* (pertaining to a) siege; obsidional (*coins; crown*)
**obstaculizar** §76 *va* to prevent; to obstruct
**obstáculo** *m* obstacle
**obstante** *adj* standing in the way; **no obstante** however, nevertheless; in spite of; **no obstante** + *inf* in spite of + *ger*
**obstar** *vn* to stand in the way; **obstar a** or **para** to hinder, check, oppose
**obstetricia** *f* obstetrics
**obstétrico -ca** *adj* obstetrical; *m* obstetrician; *f* obstetrics
**obstinación** *f* obstinacy
**obstinado -da** *adj* obstinate
**obstinar** *vr* to be obstinate; **obstinarse en** + *inf* to be obstinate in + *ger*, to persist in + *ger*
**obstrucción** *f* obstruction; (path.) stoppage
**obstruccionismo** *m* obstructionism
**obstruccionista** *adj & mf* obstructionist
**obstructivo -va** *adj* obstructive
**obstructor -tora** *adj* obstructing, obstructive
**obstruir** §41 *va* to obstruct, to interfere with; to block (*e.g., a doorway*); to stop up (*e.g., a pipe*)
**obtemperar** *va* to obey, yield to
**obtención** *f* (act of) obtaining, obtainment, obtention
**obtendré** *1st sg fut ind of* **obtener**
**obtener** §85 *va* to obtain; to keep, preserve
**obtengo** *1st sg pres ind of* **obtener**
**obtenible** *adj* obtainable
**obturación** *f* obturation, stopping, plugging
**obturador -triz** (*pl:* **-dores -trices**) *adj* stopping, plugging; *m* stopper, plug; (aut.) choke; (aut.) throttle; (phot.) shutter, obturator; (surg.) obturator; **obturador de guillotina** (phot.) drop shutter
**obturar** *va* to obturate, to plug, to stop up; (aut.) to throttle
**obtusángulo -la** *adj* obtuse-angled
**obtuso -sa** *adj* obtuse; (fig.) obtuse
**obtuve** *1st sg pret ind of* **obtener**
**obué** *m* var. of **oboe**
**obús** *m* howitzer; shell; plunger (*of tire valve*)
**obvención** *f* extra, bonus
**obvencional** *adj* incidental
**obverso -sa** *adj* obverse
**obviar** §90 & **regular** *va* to obviate; to remove (*e.g., doubts*); *vn* to stand in the way
**obvio -via** *adj* obvious; unnecessary
**obyecto** *m* objection
**obyurgación** *f* objurgation
**oca** *f* (orn.) goose; (bot.) oca; royal goose (*game*)
**ocarina** *f* (mus.) ocarina
**ocasión** *f* occasion, opportunity, chance; bargain; **aprovechar la ocasión** to improve the occasion; **asir, coger** or **tomar la ocasión por el copete, por la melena** or **por los cabellos** (coll.) to take time by the forelock; **con ocasión de** on the occasion of; **de ocasión** second-hand; **en varias ocasiones** on several occasions
**ocasionado -da** *adj* dangerous; exposed, subject, liable; annoying, provocative
**ocasional** *adj* occasional; causal; causing; responsible (*cause*); accidental, incidental
**ocasionar** *va* to cause, to occasion; to stir up; to endanger
**ocaso** *m* west; setting (*of a heavenly body*); sunset; decline; end, death
**occidental** *adj* occidental; western; Occidental; *mf* Occidental
**occidentalización** *f* westernization
**occidentalizar** §76 *va* to westernize; to Occidentalize
**occidente** *m* occident; (*cap.*) *m* Occident
**occipital** *adj* occipital; *m* (anat.) occipital, occipital bone
**occipucio** *m* (anat.) occiput
**occisión** *f* violent death
**occiso -sa** *adj* killed; *mf* person killed, victim
**Oceanía, la** Oceania
**oceánico -ca** *adj* oceanic; *mf* South Sea Islander
**Oceánidas** *fpl* (myth.) Oceanids
**océano** or **oceano** *m* ocean; (fig.) ocean (*vast expanse of anything*); (*cap.*) *m* (myth.) Oceanus; **gran Océano** Pacific Ocean; **océano Antártico** Antarctic Ocean; **océano Ártico** Arctic Ocean; **océano Atlántico** Atlantic Ocean; **océano Austral** Antarctic Ocean; **océano Glacial del Norte** Arctic Ocean; **océano Glacial del Sur** Antarctic Ocean; **océano Índico** Indian Ocean; **océano Pacífico** Pacific Ocean
**oceanografía** *f* oceanography
**oceanográfico -ca** *adj* oceanographic or oceanographical
**oceanógrafo -fa** *mf* oceanographer
**ocelado -da** *adj* ocellate
**ocelo** *m* (zool.) ocellus (*simple eye of some invertebrates; eyelike spot on wings of certain birds*)
**ocelote** *m* (zool.) ocelot
**ocena** *f* (path.) ozena
**ociar** *vn & vr* to idle, to loiter
**ocio** *m* idleness, leisure; distraction, pastime
**ociosidad** *f* idleness
**ocioso -sa** *adj* idle; useless; *mf* idler
**oclocracia** *f* mob rule, ochlocracy
**ocluir** §41 *va* (chem. & dent.) to occlude; *vr* (dent.) to occlude
**oclusal** *adj* (anat. & dent.) occlusal
**oclusión** *f* (chem., dent., med. & phonet.) occlusion
**oclusivo -va** *adj* occlusive; *f* (phonet.) occlusive
**ocotal** *m* (Am.) pine grove
**ocote** *m* (Am.) ocote pine, torch pine; (Am.) ocote torch
**ocozol** *m* (bot.) sweet gum
**ocre** *m* (mineral.) ocher; **ocre amarillo** yellow ocher; **ocre rojo** red ocher
**ocroso -sa** *adj* ocherous
**octaédrico -ca** *adj* octahedral
**octaedro** *m* (geom.) octahedron
**octagonal** *adj* octagonal
**octágono -na** *adj* octagonal; *m* octagon
**octanaje** *m* (chem.) octane number; **de alto octanaje** high-octane
**octano** *m* (chem.) octane
**octava** *f* see **octavo**
**Octaviano** *m* Octavian
**octavilla** *f* handbill; eight-syllable verse
**octavín** *m* (mus.) piccolo
**Octavio** *m* Octavius
**octavo -va** *adj* eighth; *mf* octoroon; *m* eighth; **en octavo** octavo (*said of a volume*); *f* (mus., pros. & eccl.) octave; (pros.) hendecasyllabic octave, rhymed abababcc
**oct.**^e abr. of **octubre**
**octeto** *m* (mus.) octet or octette
**octillón** *m* British octillion
**octingentésimo -ma** *adj & m* eight hundredth
**octobrino -na** *adj* (pertaining to) October

**octogenario -ria** *adj & mf* octogenarian
**octogésimo -ma** *adj & m* eightieth
**octogonal** *adj* var. of **octagonal**
**octógono -na** *adj & m* var. of **octágono**
**octosilábico -ca** *adj* octosyllabic
**octosílabo -ba** *adj* octosyllabic; *m* octosyllable (*verse*)
**octóstilo -la** *adj* (arch.) octastyle
**octubre** *m* October
**óctuple** *adj & m* octuple
**octuplicar §86** *va & vr* to octuple
**óctuplo -pla** *adj & m* var. of **óctuple**
**oculado -da** *adj* big-eyed
**ocular** *adj* ocular; *m* (opt.) eyeglass, eyepiece, ocular
**oculista** *mf* oculist
**oculística** *f* ophthalmology
**óculo** *m* (arch.) oculus, œil-de-bœuf
**ocultación** *f* occultation; hiding, concealment; (astr.) occultation
**ocultante** *adj* blinding (*e.g., smoke*)
**ocultar** *va* to hide, conceal; **ocultar una cosa a** or **de una persona** to hide a thing from a person; *vr* to hide; **ocultársele a uno** to be hidden from one
**ocultismo** *m* occultism
**ocultista** *mf* occultist
**oculto -ta** *adj* hidden, concealed; occult; **de oculto** incognito; stealthily; **en oculto** secretly
**ocupación** *f* occupation; occupancy; employment
**ocupacional** *adj* occupational
**ocupado -da** *adj* busy; occupied; pregnant
**ocupador -dora** *adj* occupying; *mf* occupier
**ocupante** *adj* occupying; *mf* occupant; **ocupantes** *mpl* occupying forces
**ocupar** *va* to occupy; to busy, keep busy; to employ; to bother, annoy; to attract the attention of; *vr* to become occupied; to be busy; to become preoccupied; **ocuparse con, de** or **en** to be busy with, be engaged in; to pay attention to; **ocuparse de** + *inf* to bother to + *inf*, to take the trouble to + *inf*
**ocurrencia** *f* occurrence; witticism; bright idea; **ocurrencia de acreedores** (law) meeting of creditors
**ocurrente** *adj* witty
**ocurrir** *vn* to occur, to happen; to come; to occur (*to come to mind*); **ocurrir a** to have recourse to; **ocurrírsele a uno** + *inf* to occur to one to + *inf*
**ochavado -da** *adj* eight-sided
**ochavar** *va* to make eight-sided, to make octagonal
**ochavear** *vn* (coll.) to be stingy
**ochavo** *m* octagon, octagonal building
**ochavón -vona** *mf* (Am.) octoroon
**ochenta** *adj & m* eighty
**ochentavo -va** *adj & m* eightieth
**ochenteno -na** *adj* eightieth; *f* eighty
**ochentón -tona** *adj & mf* (coll.) octogenarian
**ocho** *adj* eight; **las ocho** eight o'clock; *m* eight; eighth (*in dates*)
**ochocientos -tas** *adj & m* eight hundred; **el Ochocientos** the Nineteenth Century
**ochotona** *f* (zool.) pika
**oda** *f* ode
**odalisca** *f* odalisque
**odeón** *m* odeum
**Odesa** *f* Odessa
**odiable** *adj* hateful
**odiar** *va* to hate
**Odín** *m* (myth.) Odin
**odio** *m* hatred; **tener odio a** to hate
**odiosidad** *f* odiousness, hatefulness; hatred
**odioso -sa** *adj* odious, hateful
**Odisea** *f* (myth.) Odyssey; (*l.c.*) *f* (fig.) odyssey
**Odiseo** *m* (myth.) Odysseus
**Odoacro** *m* Odoacer
**odómetro** *m* odometer, taximeter; pedometer
**odontalgia** *f* (path.) odontalgia, toothache
**odontálgico -ca** *adj* odontalgic
**odontoblasto** *m* (anat.) odontoblast
**odontoceto -ta** *adj & m* (zool.) odontocete
**odontología** *f* odontology
**odontológico -ca** *adj* odontological
**odontólogo -ga** *mf* odontologist
**odorante** *adj* odorous, fragrant
**odorífero -ra** *adj* odoriferous
**odre** *m* goatskin wine bag; (coll.) drunk, drunkard
**odrería** *f* wineskin shop
**odrero** *m* wineskin maker or dealer
**odrezuelo** *m* small wineskin
**odrina** *f* oxskin wine bag
**OEA** *f* OAS (*Organization of American States*)
**oerstedio** *m* (elec.) oersted
**oesnoroeste** *m* or **oesnorueste** *m* west-northwest
**oessudoeste** *m* or **oessudueste** *m* west-southwest
**oeste** *m* west; west wind
**Ofelia** *f* Ophelia
**ofendedor -dora** *adj* offending; *mf* offender
**ofender** *va & vn* to offend; to harm; *vr* to take offense
**ofensa** *f* offense
**ofensivo -va** *adj* offensive; *f* offensive; **en la ofensiva** on the offensive; **tomar la ofensiva** to take the offensive; **ofensiva de paz** peace offensive
**ofensor -sora** *adj* offending; *mf* offender
**oferente** *adj* offering; *mf* offerer
**oferta** *f* offer; gift, present; **oferta y demanda** supply and demand
**ofertorio** *m* (eccl.) offertory
**oficial** *adj* official; *m* official, officer; skilled workman; clerk, office worker; journeyman; (mil. & nav.) commissioned officer; **oficial de complemento** (mil.) reserve officer; **oficial general** (mil.) general officer
**oficiala** *f* craftswoman, skilled working woman
**oficialía** *f* clerkship; status of journeyman
**oficialidad** *f* officers, body of officers; official nature
**oficiante** *m* (eccl.) officiant
**oficiar** *va* to announce officially in writing; to celebrate (*mass*); to officiate at; *vn* (eccl.) to officiate; **oficiar de** (coll.) to act as, behave as
**oficina** *f* office; pharmacist's laboratory; shop; (fig.) factory (*e.g., of lies*); **oficinas** *fpl* offices (*parts of house devoted to household work*); **oficina de objetos perdidos** lost-and-found department; **oficina matriz** home office
**oficinal** *adj* (pharm.) officinal
**oficinesco -ca** *adj* office, clerical; bureaucratic
**oficinista** *mf* clerk, office worker
**oficio** *m* office, occupation; rôle, function; craft, trade; memo, official note; (eccl.) office; **buenos oficios** (dipl.) good offices; **de oficio** officially; professional; (sport) professional; **desempeñar el oficio de** to play the rôle of; **Santo Oficio** Holy Office, Inquisition; **tomar por oficio** (coll.) to take to, to keep at; **oficio de difuntos** (eccl.) office of the dead; **oficio público** public office; **oficio servil** common labor
**oficiosidad** *f* diligence; complaisance, obligingness; officiousness
**oficioso -sa** *adj* diligent; obliging; officious, meddlesome; profitable; unofficial; (dipl.) officious
**ofidio -dia** *adj & m* (zool.) ophidian
**Ofir** *m* (Bib.) Ophir
**ofita** *f* (mineral.) ophite
**Ofiuco** *m* (astr.) Ophiucus
**ofrecedor -dora** *mf* offerer
**ofrecer §34** *va* to offer; *vn* to offer; **ofrecer** + *inf* to offer to + *inf; vr* to offer; to offer oneself; to happen; **ofrecerse a** + *inf* to offer to + *inf*
**ofreciente** *adj & mf* var. of **oferente**
**ofrecimiento** *m* offer, offering; **ofrecimiento de presentación** introductory offer
**ofrenda** *f* offering; gift
**ofrendar** *va* to make offerings of; to contribute, make a contribution of
**oftalmía** *f* (path.) ophthalmia
**oftálmico -ca** *adj* ophthalmic
**oftalmología** *f* ophthalmology
**oftalmológico -ca** *adj* ophthalmological
**oftalmólogo -ga** *mf* ophthalmologist
**oftalmoscopia** *f* ophthalmoscopy
**oftalmoscopio** *m* ophthalmoscope
**ofuscación** *f* or **ofuscamiento** *m* obfuscation, blindness, bewilderment, confusion
**ofuscar §86** *va* to obfuscate, dazzle, confuse

**ogaño** *adv* var. of **hogaño**
**ogro** *m* ogre; (coll.) ogre (*person*)
**Oh** *interj* O!, Oh!
**óhmetro** *m* var. of **ohmímetro**
**óhmico -ca** *adj* ohmic
**ohmímetro** *m* (elec.) ohmmeter
**ohmio** *m* (elec.) ohm
**oíble** *adj* audible
**oída** *f* hearing; **de** or **por oídas** by hearsay
**oídio** *m* (bot. & plant path.) oïdium, powdery mildew
**oído** *m* hearing (*sense*); (anat.) ear; (arti.) vent, priming hole; **abrir los oídos** to lend an ear; **abrir tanto oído** or **tanto el oído** to be all ears; **aguzar los oídos** to prick up one's ears; **al oído** by listening; confidentially; **dar oídos** to lend an ear, to listen favorably; **decir al oído** to whisper; **de oído** by ear; **entrar por un oído y salir por el otro** to go in one ear and out the other; **hacer oídos de mercader** to turn a deaf ear; **pegarse al oído** to stick in one's ears (*said, e.g., of a song*); **prestar el oído** or **los oídos** (coll.) to lend an ear; **prestar oído a** (coll.) to give ear to; **regalar el oído a** (coll.) to tickle the ear of, to flatter; **ser todo oídos** (coll.) to be all ears; **tener oído** or **buen oído** to have a good ear (*for music*); **tener oído para la música** to have an ear for music; **oído medio** (anat.) middle ear
**oidor -dora** *mf* hearer; *m* (archaic) judge
**oidoría** *f* (archaic) judgeship
**oigo** *1st sg pres ind of* **oír**
**oír** §64 *va* to hear; to listen to; to attend (*lectures*); **¡ahora lo oigo!** the first I've heard about it!; **oír** + *inf* to hear + *inf*, e.g., **oí entrar a mi hermano** I heard my brother come in; to hear + *ger*, e.g., **oí cantar a la muchacha** I heard the girl singing; to hear + *pp*, e.g., **oí tocar la campana** I heard the bell rung; **oír decir que** to hear that, to hear it said that; **oír hablar de** to hear about, to hear tell of; *vn* to hear; to listen; **¡oiga!** the idea!, the very idea!; *vr* to like to hear oneself talk
**oíslo** *mf* (coll.) darling; *f* (coll.) beloved wife
**ojada** *f* (Am.) skylight; (Am.) putlog hole
**ojal** *m* buttonhole; eyelet; grommet
**ojalá** *interj* God grant!, would to God!
**ojaladera** *f* buttonhole maker
**ojalador -dora** *mf* buttonhole maker
**ojaladura** *f* set of buttonholes
**ojalar** *va* to sew buttonholes in
**ojalatero** *m* (coll.) armchair partisan, stay-at-home well-wisher (*in a civil war*)
**ojaranzo** *m* (bot.) hornbeam
**ojeada** *f* glance; **echar una ojeada a** to cast a glance at; **buena ojeada** eyeful
**ojeador** *m* (hunt.) beater of game
**ojear** *va* to eye, stare at; to hoodoo, cast the evil eye upon; to start, to rouse (*game*); to frighten, to startle
**ojén** *m* anisette
**ojeo** *m* (hunt.) beating for game
**ojera** *f* eyecup, eyeglass; **ojeras** *fpl* rings under the eyes
**ojeriza** *f* grudge, ill will
**ojeroso -sa** *adj* with rings under the eyes
**ojerudo -da** *adj* with heavy rings or dark circles under the eyes
**ojete** *m* eyelet, eyehole; (coll.) behind
**ojetear** *va* to make eyelets in
**ojetera** *f* strip of eyelets (*for lacing, e.g., a corset*); stamp or punch to make metal eyelets
**ojialegre** *adj* (coll.) bright-eyed
**ojienjuto -ta** *adj* (coll.) dry-eyed, tearless
**ojigallo** *m* (Am.) wine spiked with brandy
**ojigarzo -za** *adj* (coll.) var. of **ojizarco**
**ojillo** *m* eyelet, grommet
**ojimel** *m* or **ojimiel** *m* (pharm.) oxymel
**ojimoreno -na** *adj* (coll.) brown-eyed
**ojinegro -gra** or **ojiprieto -ta** *adj* (coll.) black-eyed
**ojirrisueño -ña** *adj* (coll.) bright-eyed
**ojituerto -ta** *adj* cross-eyed
**ojiva** *f* (arch.) ogive; **ojiva de lanceta** (arch.) lancet, lancet arch
**ojival** *adj* ogival; (arch.) ogival
**ojizaino -na** *adj* (coll.) squint-eyed, squinty
**ojizarco -ca** *adj* (coll.) blue-eyed
**ojo** *m* (anat.) eye; (fig.) eye (*e.g., of needle, cheese, tools; center of flower; round window; glance, look; watchful look; way of thinking, appreciation*); bow (*of key*); opening, well (*of stairs*); span, bay (*of bridge*); spring (*of water*); speck of grease (*in soup*); size (*of type*); face (*of type*); scrubbing (*with soap*); **abrir el ojo** to keep one's eyes open; **abrirle los ojos a uno** to open someone's eyes (*to disabuse someone*); **abrir los ojos** to open one's eyes (*to become disillusioned*); to have an eye to the main chance; **a cierra ojos** half-asleep; recklessly, rashly; **a los ojos de** in the eyes of; **a ojo** by sight, by guess; **a ojos vistas** visibly, openly; **con buenos ojos** favorably; **costar un ojo de la cara** to cost a mint, to cost a gold mine; **dar en los ojos** to be self-evident; **delante de los ojos de uno** before one's eyes; **de ojos almendrados** almond-eyed; **echar el ojo a** (coll.) to have an eye on (*to regard with desire*); **hacer del ojo** to wink at each other (*to indicate a secret understanding*); **hacerse ojos** to look sharply; **hasta los ojos** up to one's ears (*e.g., in love, in work*); **más ven cuatro ojos que dos** two heads are better than one; **mirar con ojos de carnero degollado** to make sheep's eyes (at); **no pegar el ojo** (coll.) to not sleep a wink all night; **no quitar los ojos de** to not take one's eyes off; **poner los ojos en blanco** to roll one's eyes; **saltar a los ojos** to be self-evident; **tener los ojos en** to have an eye on, to keep an eye on; **valer un ojo de la cara** to be worth a mint; **ojo avizor** eagle eye; **ojo clínico** or **médico** medical aptitude, ability to diagnose; **ojo de buey** (arch.) bull's-eye; (bot.) oxeye; **ojo de gato** tiger-eye (*gem*); (mineral.) cat's-eye; **ojo de la cerradura** keyhole; **Ojo del Toro** (astr.) Bull's-eye; **ojo de pavo real** (ent.) peacock butterfly (*Vanessa io*); **ojo de poeta** or **de Venus** (bot.) black-eyed Susan (*Thunbergia alata*); **ojo eléctrico** electric eye; **ojo mágico** (rad.) magic eye; **ojo por ojo** an eye for an eye; **ojos saltones** or **reventones** bulging eyes; *interj* beware!; look out!; attention!; **¡mucho ojo!** be careful!, watch out!; **¡ojo con . . . !** beware of . . . !; look out for . . . !; **¡ojo, mancha!** fresh paint!
**ojoso -sa** *adj* eyey, full of eyes, full of holes
**ojuelos** *mpl* sparkling eyes; spectacles
**ola** *f* wave, billow; surge, swell (*e.g., of a crowd of people*); **ola de calor** heat wave; **ola de frío** cold wave; **ola de marea** tidal wave
**olaje** *m* var. of **oleaje**
**ole** *m* or **olé** *m* bravo; *interj* bravo!
**oleáceo -a** *adj* (bot.) oleaceous
**oleada** *f* big wave; beating of the waves; surge, swell (*of a crowd of people*); wave (*e.g., of strikes*); big crop of olive oil
**oleaginosidad** *f* oiliness
**oleaginoso -sa** *adj* oily, oleaginous
**oleaje** *m* surge, rush of waves; rough sea
**olear** *va* to administer extreme unction to; *vn* to surge, to swell (*said of the sea*); *vr* to grease oneself (*for wrestling*)
**oleario -ria** *adj* oily
**oleastro** *m* (bot.) wild olive
**oleato** *m* (chem.) oleate
**oleaza** *f* watery dregs in olive-oil mill
**olécranon** *m* (anat.) olecranon
**oledero -ra** *adj* odorous
**oledor -dora** *adj* smelling; (Am.) fawning
**oleico -ca** *adj* (chem.) oleic
**oleícola** *adj* olive-growing, olive-oil-producing
**oleicultor -tora** *mf* olive grower, olive-oil producer
**oleicultura** *f* olive growing, production of olive oil
**oleífero -ra** *adj* (bot.) oleiferous
**oleína** *f* (chem.) olein
**óleo** *m* oil; holy oil; oil, oil painting
**oleoducto** *m* pipe line
**oleografía** *f* oleograph
**oleomargarina** *f* oleomargarin or oleomargarine
**oleómetro** *m* oleometer
**oleorresina** *f* oleoresin
**oleosidad** *f* oiliness
**oleoso -sa** *adj* oily

**oler** **§65** *va* to smell; to look into, pry into; to sniff, sniff out (*e.g., a secret*); *vn* to smell, to be fragrant, to smell bad; **no oler bien** (coll.) to look suspicious; **oler a** to smell of, smell like; to reek with; to smack of; **oler donde guisan** (coll.) to know one's way around, to have an eye on the main chance
**olfacción** *f* olfaction
**olfatear** *va* to smell, scent, sniff; (coll.) to scent (*trouble, a good deal, etc.*)
**olfateo** *m* smell, smelling, scent
**olfativo -va** *adj* olfactory
**olfato** *m* smell, sense of smell; scent (*smell left in passing*); keenness, keen insight
**olfatorio -ria** *adj* olfactory
**olíbano** *m* frankincense
**oliente** *adj* smelling, odorous
**oliera** *f* (eccl.) chrismal (*vessel*)
**oligarca** *m* oligarch
**oligarquía** *f* oligarchy
**oligárquico -ca** *adj* oligarchic or oligarchical
**oligisto** *m* (mineral.) oligist
**oligoceno -na** *adj* & *m* (geol.) Oligocene
**Olimpia** *f* (geog.) Olympia
**Olimpíada** *f* Olympiad
**olímpicamente** *adv* haughtily, boastfully
**olímpico -ca** *adj* Olympian; Olympic; haughty, boastful
**olimpiónico** *m* winner in the Olympian games
**Olimpo, el** (geog., myth. & fig.) Mount Olympus
**Olinto** *f* Olynthus
**oliscar** **§86** *va* to smell, scent, sniff; to investigate; *vn* to smell bad (*said of spoiled meat*)
**olisquear** *va* (coll.) to smell, scent, sniff; (coll.) to investigate
**oliva** *f* (bot.) olive (*tree and fruit*); olive (*color*); (anat.) olive; (orn.) barn owl; (fig.) olive branch, peace
**oliváceo -a** *adj* olivaceous
**olivar** *adj* olive; *m* olive grove; *va* to trim off the lower branches of; *vr* to bubble in baking (*said of bread*)
**olivarda** *f* (orn.) green goshawk; (bot.) elecampane
**olivarero -ra** *adj* olive (*growing, industry, etc.*); *mf* olive grower
**olivastro** *m* (bot.) wild olive; **olivastro de Rodas** (bot.) aloe
**olivera** *f* (bot.) olive tree
**Oliverio** *m* Oliver
**olivero** *m* olive storage
**olivífero -ra** *adj* (poet.) grown with olive trees
**olivillo** *m* (bot.) phillyrea, mock privet
**olivino** *m* (mineral.) olivine
**olivo** *m* (bot.) olive (*tree*); **tomar el olivo** (taur.) to duck behind the barrier; (slang) to beat it; **olivo silvestre** (bot.) wild olive
**olmeda** *f* or **olmedo** *m* elm grove
**olmo** *m* (bot.) elm
**ológrafo -fa** *adj* & *m* holograph
**olomina** *f* (ichth.) minnow
**olor** *m* odor; promise, hope; **estar al olor** (coll.) to be on the scent; **tener en mal olor** to hold in bad odor; **olor de santidad** odor of sanctity
**olorizar** **§76** *va* to perfume
**oloroso -sa** *adj* odorous, fragrant
**olote** *m* (Am.) cob, corncob
**olvidadizo -za** *adj* forgetful; ungrateful; **hacerse olvidadizo** or **el olvidadizo** to pretend to be forgetful
**olvidado -da** *adj* forgetful; ungrateful; **estar olvidado** (coll.) to be ancient history
**olvidar** *va* & *vn* to forget; **olvidar** + *inf* to forget to + *inf; vr* to forget oneself; **olvidarse de** to forget; **olvidarse de** + *inf* to forget to + *inf;* **olvidársele a uno** to forget, e.g., **se me olvidó mi pasaporte** I forgot my passport; **olvidársele a uno** + *inf* to forget to + *inf*, e.g., **se me olvidó cerrar la ventana** I forgot to close the window
**olvido** *m* forgetfulness; oblivion; **enterrar en el olvido** to cast into oblivion
**olla** *f* pot, kettle; stew; eddy, whirlpool; (coll.) stomach; **recordar las ollas de Egipto** to remember happier days; **olla carnicera** large kettle, boiler; **olla de fuego** (mil.) incendiary grenade; **olla de grillos** (coll.) pandemonium; **olla de** or **a presión** pressure cooker; **olla podrida** Spanish stew (*made of meat, fowl, sausage, vegetables, etc.*)
**ollao** *m* (naut.) eyelet hole (*of sail*)
**ollar** *adj* soft (*stone*); *m* horse's nostril
**ollería** *f* pottery; earthenware shop
**ollero -ra** *mf* potter; dealer in earthenware
**olluco** *m* var. of **ulluco**
**olluela** *f* small pot or kettle
**omaso** *m* (zool.) omasum
**omatidio** *m* (zool.) ommatidium
**ombligo** *m* navel, umbilicus; umbilical cord; (fig.) center, heart; **ombligo de Venus** (bot.) Venus's-navelwort
**ombliguero** *m* navel bandage for infants
**ombliguismo** *m* belly dancing
**ombría** *f* shade, shady place
**ombú** *m* (*pl:* **-búes**) (bot.) umbra tree
**omega** *f* omega
**omental** *adj* omental
**omento** *m* (anat.) omentum
**ómicron** *f* (*pl:* **omícrones**) omicron
**ominar** *va* to omen, to presage
**ominoso -sa** *adj* ominous
**omisión** *f* omission; neglect
**omiso -sa** *adj* neglectful, remiss, careless
**omitir** *va* to omit; to overlook, neglect; **no omitir esfuerzos** to spare no efforts; **omitir** + *inf* to omit + *ger*
**ómnibus** *m* (*pl:* **-bus**) bus, omnibus; **ómnibus de dos pisos** double-decker; *adj* accommodation (*train*)
**omnímodo -da** *adj* all-embracing, all-inclusive
**omnipotencia** *f* omnipotence
**omnipotente** *adj* omnipotent
**omnipresencia** *f* omnipresence
**omnipresente** *adj* omnipresent
**omnisapiente** *adj* omniscient
**omnisciencia** *f* omniscience
**omnisciente** or **omniscio -cia** *adj* omniscient
**omnívoro -ra** *adj* omnivorous; *m* omnivore
**omóplato** *m* (anat.) shoulder blade
**-ón -ona** *suffix aug* & *pej* e.g., **cortinón** big heavy curtain; **hombrón** husky fellow; **mujerona** strapping big woman; **solterona** old maid; *suffix pej* e.g., **mandón** bossy; **respondón** saucy; **tragón** gluttonous; *suffix m* used to form nouns which denote result of action expressed by verb, e.g., **empujón** push; **resbalón** slide, slip; **salpicón** splash; *suffix dim* e.g., **callejón** lane, alley; **plumón** down; **ratón** mouse; **volantón** fledgling
**onagra** *f* (bot.) evening primrose
**onagro** *m* (zool.) onager
**Onán** *m* (Bib.) Onan
**onanismo** *m* onanism
**once** *adj* eleven; **las once** eleven o'clock; **estar a las once** (coll.) to be crooked (*said, e.g., of a part of clothing*); **hacer** or **tomar las once** (coll.) to take a bite or snack in the forenoon; *m* eleven; eleventh (*in dates*); (football) eleven (*team*)
**oncear** *va* to weigh out by ounces
**onceavo -va** *adj* & *m* var. of **onzavo**
**oncejera** *f* snare to catch birds
**oncejo** *m* (orn.) black martin, European swift
**onceno -na** *adj* & *m* eleventh
**oncijera** *f* var. of **oncejera**
**oncología** *f* oncology
**onda** *f* wave; flicker; curl, wave (*in hair*); (phys.) wave; (sew.) scallop; **de toda onda** (rad.) all-wave; **onda amortiguada** (elec.) damped wave; **onda corta** (rad.) short wave; **onda de choque** (aer.) shock wave; blast wave (*of a nuclear explosion*); **onda electromagnética** (phys.) electromagnetic wave; **onda herciana** or **hertziana** (elec.) Hertzian wave; **onda larga** (rad.) long wave; **onda luminosa** (phys.) light wave; **onda media** or **normal** (rad.) standard broadcast wave; **onda portadora** or **portante** (rad.) carrier wave; **ondas cerebrales** (med.) brain waves; **ondas continuas** or **ondas entretenidas** (rad.) continuous waves; **ondas encefálicas** (med.) brain waves; **onda sonora** (phys.) sound wave
**ondatra** *m* (zool.) muskrat
**ondeado -da** *adj* wavy; *m* waving, waviness
**ondeante** *adj* waving, undulating; flowing

**ondear** *va* to wave (*e.g., the hair*); *vn* to wave; to ripple; to flow; to flicker; to be wavy; *vr* to wave, to sway, to swing

**ondeo** *m* waving, rippling; flickering; swaying

**ondina** *f* (myth.) undine

**ondisonante** *adj* (poet.) babbling, rippling

**ondógrafo** *m* ondograph

**ondoso -sa** *adj* wavy

**ondulación** *f* undulation; wave; wave motion; **ondulación al agua** water wave; **ondulación permanente** permanent wave

**ondulado -da** *adj* undulate, rippled, wavy; rolling (*e.g., country*); corrugated; *m* wave (*in hair*); **ondulado al agua** finger wave

**ondulante** *adj* undulant; waving

**ondular** *va* to wave (*the hair*); *vn* to undulate; to wriggle

**ondulatorio -ria** *adj* undulatory

**oneroso -sa** *adj* onerous; (law) onerous

**Onfala** *f* (myth.) Omphale

**ónice** *m* or **ónique** *m* (mineral.) onyx

**oniromancia** or **oniromancía** *f* oneiromancy

**ónix** *m* (mineral.) onyx

**onomancia** or **onomancía** *f* onomancy

**onomástico -ca** *adj* onomastic; of proper names; *m* saint's day, birthday; *f* onomasticon, list of proper names; study of proper names

**onomatología** *f* onomatology

**onomatopeya** *f* onomatopoeia

**onomatopéyico -ca** *adj* onomatopeic or onomatopoetic

**onomatopeyismo** *m* (Am.) onomatopoeia

**onoquiles** *f* (bot.) alkanet, dyer's alkanet

**ontina** *f* (bot.) white sage

**ontogenia** *f* ontogeny

**ontología** *f* ontology

**ontológico -ca** *adj* ontological

**ontologismo** *m* (theol.) ontologism

**ONU** *f* UN (*United Nations*)

**onubense** *adj* (pertaining to) Huelva; *mf* native or inhabitant of Huelva

**onz.** abr. of **onza**

**onza** *f* ounce; (zool.) ounce; **onza de oro** Spanish doubloon

**onzavo -va** *adj & m* eleventh

**oocito** *m* (biol.) oöcyte

**ooforectomía** *f* (surg.) oöphorectomy

**ooforitis** *f* (path.) oöphoritis

**oogonio** *m* (bot.) oögonium

**oolítico -ca** *adj* oölitic

**oolito** *m* (mineral.) oölite

**oología** *f* oölogy

**oosfera** *f* (bot.) oösphere

**oósporo -ra** *adj* (bot.) oösporous; *m* (bot.) oöspore

**opacar** §86 *va* (Am.) to cloud, darken; *vr* (Am.) to become cloudy, to become obscure

**opacidad** *f* opacity; sadness, gloominess

**opaco -ca** *adj* opaque; sad, gloomy

**opado -da** *adj* swollen, puffed

**opalescencia** *f* opalescence

**opalescente** *adj* opalescent

**opalino -na** *adj* opaline

**ópalo** *m* (mineral.) opal

**opción** *f* option; (com.) option

**ópera** *f* (mus.) opera; **ópera bufa** (mus.) opera buffa; (mus.) opéra bouffe, comic opera; **ópera cómica** (mus.) comic opera; **ópera espiritual** (mus.) oratorio; **ópera semiseria** (mus.) light opera; **ópera seria** (mus.) grand opera

**operable** *adj* operable; practical, feasible; (surg.) operable

**operación** *f* operation; **operación cesárea** (surg.) Caesarean operation

**operacional** *adj* operational

**operado -da** *mf* patient operated on

**operador -dora** *adj* operating, operative; *mf* operator; (surg.) operator, operative surgeon; (telg. & telp.) operator

**operante** *adj* operating, active

**operar** *va* (surg.) to operate on (*a person or a part of body*); **operar a uno de una cosa** (surg.) to operate on someone for something; *vn* to work; to operate (*said, e.g., of a drug or medicine*); (com., mil., nav. & surg.) to operate; *vr* (surg.) to be operated on

**operario -ria** *mf* operative (*worker; laborer*); *m* workman; *f* working woman

**operativo -va** *adj* operative

**operatorio -ria** *adj* operating, working; (surg.) operating, operative

**opérculo** *m* (bot. & zool.) operculum

**opereta** *f* (mus.) operetta

**operista** *mf* opera singer; (Am.) composer of operas

**operístico -ca** *adj* operatic

**operoso -sa** *adj* laborious

**opiáceo -a** *adj* opiate (*containing opium; bringing sleep; quieting*)

**opiado -da** *adj & m* opiate

**opiático -ca** *adj* var. of **opiáceo**

**opiato -ta** *adj, m & f* opiate

**opilación** *f* (path.) obstruction; (path.) amenorrhea; (path.) dropsy

**opilar** *va* to obstruct; *vr* to have amenorrhea

**opilativo -va** *adj* obstructive, constipating

**opimo -ma** *adj* rich, fruitful, abundant

**opinable** *adj* moot

**opinar** *vn* to opine; to judge, pass judgment

**opinión** *f* opinion, view, judgment; reputation, public image; **cambiar** or **mudar de opinión** to change one's mind; **casarse con su opinión** (coll.) to stick to one's opinion; **ser de opinión que** to be of the opinion that; **opinión pública** public opinion

**opio** *m* (pharm.) opium

**opíparo -ra** *adj* sumptuous, magnificent (*banquet*)

**oploteca** *f* museum of ancient weapons, museum of arms

**opobálsamo** *m* balm of Gilead (*resin*)

**opondré** *1st sg fut ind of* **oponer**

**oponente** *adj* (anat.) opponent

**oponer** §69 *va* to put up, to offer (*e.g., resistance*); to juxtapose; **oponer una cosa a otra** to oppose something to something else, to set up something against something else; *vr* to oppose each other; to face each other, be juxtaposed; **oponerse a** to oppose, be opposed to; to be against, to resist; to compete for (*e.g., a professorship*)

**opongo** *1st sg pres ind of* **oponer**

**oponible** *adj* opposable

**opopónace** *f* (bot.) Hercules' allheal

**opopónaco** *m* (pharm.) opopanax

**oporto** *m* port (*wine*)

**oportunidad** *f* opportuneness; opportunity; occasion; **oportunidades** *fpl* opportune remarks, witticisms; **aprovechar la oportunidad** to seize the opportunity; **con toda oportunidad** in due time, in ample time

**oportunismo** *m* opportunism

**oportunista** *adj* opportunistic; *mf* opportunist

**oportuno -na** *adj* opportune; witty

**oposición** *f* opposition; competitive examinations

**oposicionista** *adj & mf* (pol.) oppositionist

**opositor -tora** *adj* rivaling, competing; *mf* opponent; competitor (*for a position*)

**opoterapia** *f* organotherapy

**opresión** *f* oppression; pressure

**opresivo -va** *adj* oppressive

**opresor -sora** *adj* oppressive; *mf* oppressor

**oprimir** *va* to oppress; to squeeze, to press

**oprobiar** *va* to defame, to revile

**oprobio** *m* opprobrium

**oprobioso -sa** *adj* opprobrious

**opsonina** *f* (bact.) opsonin

**optar** *va* to assume (*an office*); *vn* to opt; **optar a** or **por** to opt or decide in favor of, to choose; **optar a** or **por** + *inf* to decide to + *inf*, to choose to + *inf*

**optativo -va** *adj* optative, optional; (gram.) optative; *m* (gram.) optative (*mood*)

**óptico -ca** *adj* optic, optical; *mf* optician; *f* optics; optician's office; optical store; stereoscope

**óptimamente** *adv* to perfection

**optimates** *mpl* worthies, grandees

**optimismo** *m* optimism

**optimista** *adj* optimistic; *mf* optimist

**óptimo -ma** *adj super* very good, best, optimum

**optometría** *f* optometry

**optometrista** *mf* optometrist

**optómetro** *m* optometer

**opuesto -ta** *pp of* **oponer;** *adj* opposite, contrary; (bot.) opposite

**opugnación** *f* attack, assault; refutation

**opugnador -dora** *adj* attacking, assaulting; *mf* attacker
**opugnar** *va* to attack, to lay siege to; to oppugn
**opulencia** *f* opulence
**opulento -ta** *adj* opulent
**opúsculo** *m* short work, opuscule
**opuse** *1st sg pret ind of* **oponer**
**oque; de oque** (coll.) gratis
**oquedad** *f* hollow; (fig.) hollowness
**oquedal** *m* growth of tall trees without underbrush
**oqueruela** *f* kink in thread
**ora;** *conj* **ora . . . ora** now . . . then, now . . . now
**oración** *f* oration; speech; prayer; hour of prayer; (gram.) sentence; (gram.) clause; **oraciones** *fpl* prayers, call to prayer; **hacer oración** to pray; **oración compuesta** (gram.) compound sentence; **oración dependiente** (gram.) clause; (gram.) dependent clause; **oración dominical** Lord's prayer; **oración fúnebre** funeral oration; **oración principal** (gram.) main sentence; **oración simple** (gram.) simple sentence; **oración subordinada** (gram.) dependent clause, subordinate clause
**oracional** *adj* (gram.) sentential, (pertaining to the) sentence; *m* prayer book
**oráculo** *m* oracle; (fig.) oracle (*wise person; wise answer*); **oráculo délfico** Delphic oracle
**orador -dora** *mf* orator, speaker; petitioner; **orador de plazuela** soapbox orator; **orador de sobremesa** after-dinner speaker; *m* preacher
**oraje** *m* rough weather
**oral** *adj* oral
**orangista** *m* Orangeman
**orangután** *m* (zool.) orang-outang
**orante** *adj* (f.a.) orant, in the posture of prayer
**orar** *vn* to pray; to speak, make a speech; **orar por** to pray for
**orate** *mf* lunatic; (coll.) crazy person, wild person
**oratorio -ria** *adj* oratorical; *m* oratory (*small chapel*); (mus.) oratorio; *f* oratory
**orbe** *m* orb; world; (ichth.) globefish
**orbicular** *adj* orbicular
**órbita** *f* (anat., astr., phys. & fig.) orbit; **fuera de sus órbitas** (coll.) out of one's head
**orbital** *adj* orbital
**orca** *f* (zool.) killer whale
**Órcadas** *fpl* Orkney Islands
**orcaneta** *f* (bot.) alkanet, dyer's alkanet; **orcaneta roja** (bot.) alkanet, dyer's alkanet
**orco** *m* (zool.) killer whale; (poet.) Hades, the lower world; (*cap.*) *m* (myth.) Orcus
**orchilla** *f* (bot. & chem.) archil
**órdago; de órdago** (coll.) swell, real, e.g., **un discurso de órdago** a swell speech; **una bofetada de órdago** a real smack on the face
**ordalías** *fpl* (hist.) ordeal (*trial by fire, water, etc.*)
**orden** *m* order (*way one thing follows another; formal or methodical arrangement; peace, quiet; class, category*); (arch., biol., gram. & math.) order; (eccl.) order (*sixth sacrament*); (mil.) order (*formation*); **en orden** in order; **en orden a** with regard to; **llamar al orden** to call to order; **poner en orden** to put in order; **por su orden** in order (*of succession*); **orden de batalla** (mil.) order of battle, battle array; **orden de colocación** (gram.) word order; **orden de la misa, orden del culto** (eccl.) ordinal; **orden del día** order of the day (*in a legislative body*); **orden de marcha** working order; **Orden Nuevo** (pol.) New Order ‖ *f* order (*command; honor society; fraternal organization*); (eccl.) order (*monastic brotherhood; grade or rank of Christian ministry*); (mil.) order (*command*); (theol.) order (*any of nine grades of angels*); **a la orden de** (com.) to the order of; **estar a la orden del día** to be the order of the day (*i.e., the prevailing custom*); **estar a las órdenes de** to be at the service of; **sagradas órdenes** (eccl.) holy orders; **por orden de** by order of; **orden de allanamiento** (law) search warrant; **orden de caballería** order of knighthood; **orden de la Jarretera** (Brit.) Order of the Garter; **orden del Cister** Cistercian Order; **orden del día** (mil.) order of the day; **orden de San Agustín** Augustinian Order; **órdenes mayores** (eccl.) major orders; **órdenes menores** (eccl.) minor orders; **órdenes sagradas** (eccl.) holy orders
**ordenación** *f* order; ordering; auditor's office; (arch. & paint.) ordinance, balance; (eccl.) ordination; **ordenación de montes** forestry; **ordenación urbana** city planning
**ordenado -da** *adj* orderly; *f* (geom.) ordinate
**ordenador** *m* chief auditor; computer
**ordenamiento** *m* ordering, arrangement; law, decree; set of laws
**ordenancista** *adj* strict, rigid; *mf* martinet
**ordenando** or **ordenante** *m* (eccl.) ordinand
**ordenanza** *f* ordinance (*law, decree*); order, system; command; (arch. & paint.) ordinance; **ser de ordenanza** (coll.) to be the rule; *m* errand boy; (mil.) orderly
**ordenar** *va* to arrange; to order; (eccl.) to ordain; **ordenar** + *inf* to order to + *inf; vr* (eccl.) to become ordained, to take orders; **ordenarse de sacerdote** to become ordained as priest
**ordeña** *f* (Am.) milking
**ordeñadero** *m* milk pail
**ordeñador -dora** *adj* milking; *mf* milker; *f* milk maid; milking machine
**ordeñar** *va* to milk; to strip (*e.g., olives*) from a branch by a milking motion
**ordeño** *m* milking; **a ordeño** with milking motion; stripping olives from the branch
**ordiate** *m* barley water
**ordinal** *adj* orderly; ordinal; *m* ordinal
**ordinariez** *f* (coll.) coarseness, crudeness
**ordinario -ria** *adj* ordinary; daily (*expenses*); *m* ordinary (*judge; bishop*); daily household expenses; delivery man; **de ordinario** ordinarily; **ordinario de la misa** (eccl.) ordinary, Ordinary of the Mass
**ordo** *m* (eccl.) ordinal
**ordoviciense** *adj & m* (geol.) Ordovician
**oréada** or **oréade** *f* (myth.) Oread
**orear** *va* to air; *vr* to become aired, to dry in the air; to take an airing
**oreas** *m* (*pl:* **-as**) (zool.) eland
**orégano** *m* (bot.) wild marjoram
**oreja** *f* (anat.) ear, outer ear; flap (*of shoe*); flatterer; gossip; (mach.) lug, flange, ear; **aguzar las orejas** to prick up one's ears; **apearse por las orejas** (coll.) to take a tumble (*from a horse*); (coll.) to give a stupid answer; **bajar las orejas** (coll.) to come down from one's perch; **calentar a uno las orejas** (coll.) to dress someone down; **con las orejas caídas** or **gachas** (coll.) crestfallen; **con las orejas tan largas** all ears; **descubrir** or **enseñar las orejas** (coll.) to show the cloven hoof, to give oneself away; **mojar la oreja** to be looking for a fight; **tirar la oreja** or **las orejas, tirar de la oreja a Jorge** (coll.) to play cards for money; **ver las orejas al lobo** to be in great danger; **oreja de fraile** (bot.) asarabacca; **oreja de mercader** deaf ears; **oreja de monje** (bot.) Venus's-navelwort; **oreja de oso** (bot.) auricula, bear's-ear; **oreja de ratón** (bot.) snowberry; **oreja marina** (zool.) abalone
**orejano -na** *adj* unbranded (*cattle*)
**orejeado -da** *adj* (coll.) listening, ready to answer
**orejear** *vn* to shake or wiggle the ears; to act reluctantly; to whisper
**orejera** *f* earflap, earcap, earlap; earmuff; earthboard (*of plow*)
**orejeta** *f* lug
**orejón** *m* strip of dried peach; pull on the ear; dog's-ear (*of page of book*); (fort.) orillion
**orejudo -da** *adj* long-eared, big-eared
**orejuela** *f* little ear; handle (*of tray*)
**orenga** *f* (naut.) floor timber; (naut.) frame
**oreo** *m* breeze, fresh air; airing
**oreoselino** *m* (bot.) mountain parsley
**Orestes** *m* (myth.) Orestes
**orfanato** *m* orphanage
**orfanatorio** *m* (Am.) orphanage

**orfandad** *f* orphanage, orphanhood; abandonment, neglect
**orfebre** *m* goldsmith, silversmith
**orfebrería** *f* gold or silver work
**orfelinato** *m* (Am.) orphanage
**Orfeo** *m* (myth.) Orpheus
**orfeón** *m* glee club, choral society
**orfeonista** *mf* member of a glee club or choral society
**órfico -ca** *adj* Orphean, Orphic; **órficas** *fpl* Orphic mysteries
**orfo** *m* (ichth.) sea bream
**organdí** *m* (*pl:* **-díes**) organdy
**organero** *m* organ maker, organ builder
**organicismo** *m* (biol., med. & philos.) organicism
**organicista** *adj* & *mf* organicist
**orgánico -ca** *adj* organic
**organillero -ra** *mf* organ-grinder
**organillo** *m* barrel organ, hand organ, hurdy-gurdy
**organismo** *m* organism; agency, organization; (biol.) organism; **organismo cimógeno** (biol.) zymogenic organism; **organismo patógeno** (biol.) pathogenic organism
**organista** *mf* (mus.) organist
**organización** *f* organization; **organización científica del trabajo** scientific management
**organizador -dora** *adj* organizing; *mf* organizer
**organizar** §76 *va* & *vr* to organize
**órgano** *m* (mus. & physiol.) organ; part (*of a machine*); (bot.) organ-pipe cactus; organ (*means, instrument; medium*); **órgano de campanas** (mus.) carillon, glockenspiel; **órgano de cilindro** (mus.) barrel organ; **órgano de la voz** (anat.) vocal organ; **órgano de lengüetas** (mus.) reed organ; **órgano de los sentidos** (physiol.) sense organ; **órgano de manubrio** hand organ, street organ; **órgano móvil** (mach.) moving part; **órgano sensorio** (physiol.) sense organ; **órganos genitales** (anat.) genital organs
**organografía** *f* organography
**organología** *f* organology
**organoterapia** *f* organotherapy
**orgánulo** *m* (biol.) tiny organism
**orgasmo** *m* (physiol.) orgasm
**orgástico -ca** *adj* orgasmic or orgastic
**orgia** or **orgía** *f* orgy; **orgias** or **orgías** *fpl* orgies (*of ancient Greece*)
**orgiástico -ca** *adj* orgiastic
**orgullo** *m* haughtiness; pride
**orgulloso -sa** *adj* haughty, conceited; proud
**oribe** *m* goldsmith
**orientable** *adj* adjustable
**orientación** *f* orientation; prospect, exposure; bearings; (naut.) trimming the sails
**orientador -dora** *adj* leading; *mf* leader
**oriental** *adj* oriental; eastern; Oriental; *mf* Oriental
**orientalismo** *m* Orientalism
**orientalista** *mf* Orientalist
**orientalizar** §76 *va* to Orientalize
**orientar** *va* to orient, to orientate; to guide, direct; (naut.) to trim (*a sail*); *vr* to orient oneself, to find one's bearings
**oriente** *m* east; source, origin; youth; east wind; orient (*luster of the pearl*); (*cap.*) *m* Orient; **Cercano Oriente** Near East; **Extremo Oriente** or **Lejano Oriente** Far East; **gran oriente** grand lodge (*of Masons*); **Próximo Oriente** Near East; **Oriente Medio** Middle East
**orificación** *f* (dent.) gold filling
**orificador** *m* (dent.) plugger
**orificar** §86 *va* (dent.) to fill with gold
**orífice** *m* goldsmith
**orificio** *m* orifice, hole
**oriflama** *f* oriflamme
**orifrés** *m* orphrey
**origen** *m* origin; extraction, descent; **en el origen** at the beginning
**Orígenes** *m* Origen
**original** *adj* original; queer, odd, quaint; *m* original; character, queer duck; **de buen original** on good authority; **original de imprenta** (print.) copy
**originalidad** *f* originality; queerness, oddness, quaintness
**originar** *va* & *vr* to originate, to start
**originario -ria** *adj* originating, native; original
**orilla** *f* border, edge; margin; bank, shore; sidewalk; fresh breeze; shoulder (*of road*); **orillas** *fpl* (Am.) outskirts; **a la orilla** near, on the brink; **salir a la orilla** to manage to get through
**orillar** *va* to put a border or edge on; to trim; to settle, to arrange; *vn* & *vr* to skirt the edge, come up to the shore
**orillo** *m* list, selvage
**orín** *m* rust; **orines** *mpl* urine; **tomarse de orín** to get rusty
**orina** *f* urine
**orinal** *m* chamber pot, urinal; **orinal del cielo** (coll.) rainy place, rainy region
**orinar** *va* to pass, to urinate (*e.g., blood*); *vn* & *vr* to urinate
**oriniento -ta** *adj* rusty
**orinque** *m* (naut.) buoy rope
**oriol** *m* (orn.) oriole
**Orión** *m* (astr.) Orion
**oriundez** *f* origin
**oriundo -da** *adj* & *mf* native; **ser oriundo de** to come from, to hail from
**orla** *f* border, edge, margin; fringe, trimming; (her.) orle
**orlador -dora** *mf* borderer, edger
**orladura** *f* border, edge, trimming
**orlar** *va* to border, to put an edge on; to trim, trim with a fringe
**Orleanista** *adj* & *mf* Orleanist
**orlo** *m* Alpine horn; (arch.) plinth; (mus.) horn stop (*of an organ*)
**ormesí** *m* (*pl:* **-siés**) watered silk fabric
**ormino** *m* (bot.) wild sage
**orn.** abr. of **orden**
**ornado -da** *adj* ornate
**ornamentación** *f* ornamentation
**ornamental** *adj* ornamental
**ornamentar** *va* to ornament, adorn, decorate
**ornamento** *m* ornament; adornment; **ornamentos** *mpl* (eccl.) ornaments
**ornato** *m* adornment, show
**ornitodelfo -fa** *adj* & *m* (*zool.*) monotreme, ornithodelphian
**ornitología** *f* ornithology
**ornitológico -ca** *adj* ornithological
**ornitólogo -ga** *mf* ornithologist
**ornitomancia** or **ornitomancía** *f* ornithomancy
**ornitorrinco** *m* (zool.) duckbill, ornithorhyncus
**orno** *m* (bot.) manna ash
**oro** *m* gold; playing card (*representing a gold coin*) equivalent to diamond; **oros** *mpl* card suit corresponding to diamonds; **de oro y azul** (coll.) all dressed up; **poner de oro y azul** (coll.) to rake over the coals; **ponerle colores al oro** to gild the lily; **oro batido** gold foil, gold leaf; **oro coronario** fine gold; **oro de ley** standard gold; **oro en barras** bullion; **oro en libritos** gold leaf; **oro molido** ormolu; **oro mosaico** or **musivo** mosaic gold
**orobanca** *f* (bot.) broomrape
**orobancáceo -a** *adj* (bot.) orobanchaceous
**orobias** *m* fine incense
**orogenia** *f* orogeny
**orogénico -ca** *adj* orogenic
**orografía** *f* orography
**orográfico -ca** *adj* orographic or orographical
**orología** *f* orology
**orómetro** *m* orometer
**orondo -da** *adj* big-bellied (*bottle*); hollow, puffed up; (coll.) pompous; (Am.) calm, unflustered
**oropel** *m* tinsel; brass foil; accomplishment (*in some social art or grace*); flowery speech; (fig.) tinsel; **gastar mucho oropel** (coll.) to put on a front
**oropelar** *va* to tinsel, to trim with tinsel; to fake
**oropelero -ra** *mf* tinsel maker or dealer; flamboyant orator
**oropelesco -ca** *adj* tinselly, tawdry
**oropéndola** *f* (orn.) golden oriole
**oropimente** *m* (mineral.) orpiment

**oroya** *f* basket of rope railway
**orozuz** *m* (bot.) licorice
**orquesta** *f* (mus.) orchestra; (theat.) orchestra (*space occupied by musicians*); **orquesta de cámara** chamber orchestra; **orquesta de cuerda** string orchestra; **orquesta típica** regional orchestra (*which plays music typical of its place of origin*)
**orquestación** *f* orchestration
**orquestal** *adj* orchestral
**orquestar** *va* to orchestrate
**orquestina** *f* small orchestra
**orquidáceo -a** *adj* (bot.) orchidaceous
**órquide** *f* (bot.) orchis
**orquídea** *f* (bot.) orchid
**orquitis** *f* (path.) orchitis
**orre; en orre** loose, in bulk
**ortega** *f* (orn.) sand grouse
**orticón** *m* (telv.) orthicon
**ortiga** *f* (bot.) nettle; **ser como unas ortigas** (coll.) to be a grouch; **ortiga de mar** (zool.) sea nettle, jellyfish; **ortiga hedionda** (bot.) hedge nettle
**ortigal** *m* nettle field
**ortivo -va** *adj* (astr.) ortive
**orto** *m* rise (*of sun or star*)
**ortoclasa** *f* var. of **ortosa**
**ortocromático -ca** *adj* (phot.) orthochromatic
**ortodoncia** *f* orthodontia
**ortodoxia** *f* orthodoxy
**ortodoxo -xa** *adj* orthodox
**ortoepia** *f* orthoëpy
**ortoépico -ca** *adj* orthoëpic
**ortofonía** *f* orthophony
**ortogénesis** *f* (biol.) orthogenesis
**ortognato -ta** *adj* orthognathous
**ortogonal** *adj* orthogonal
**ortografía** *f* (gram. & geom.) orthography
**ortografiar** **§90** *va & vn* to spell
**ortográfico -ca** *adj* orthographic or orthographical
**ortógrafo -fa** *mf* orthographer
**ortología** *f* orthoëpy
**ortológico -ca** *adj* orthoëpic
**ortólogo -ga** *mf* orthoëpist
**ortopedia** *f* orthopedics
**ortopédico -ca** *adj* orthopedic; *mf* orthopedist
**ortopedista** *mf* orthopedist
**ortóptero -ra** *adj* (ent.) orthopterous; *m* (ent.) orthopteran
**ortorrómbico -ca** *adj* (cryst.) orthorhombic
**ortosa** *f* (mineral.) orthoclase
**ortotropismo** *m* (bot.) orthotropism
**ortótropo -pa** *adj* (bot.) orthotropous
**oruga** *f* (bot.) rocket; rocket sauce; (ent.) caterpillar; (mach.) caterpillar (*device moving on endless belts*)
**orujo** *m* bagasse of grapes or olives
**orvallar** *vn* (dial.) to drizzle
**orvalle** *m* (bot.) wild sage
**orvallo** *m* (dial.) drizzle, dew
**orza** *f* gallipot, crock; (naut.) luffing; (naut.) luff; **orza central de deriva** (naut.) centerboard
**orzaga** *f* (bot.) orach
**orzar** **§76** *vn* (naut.) to luff, to round to
**orzaya** *f* nursemaid
**orzuelo** *m* (path.) sty; snare (*to catch birds*); trap (*to catch wild animals*)
**orzura** *f* (chem.) minium
**os** *pron pers & reflex* (used as object of verb and corresponds to **vos** and **vosotros**); you, to you; yourself, to yourself; yourselves, to yourselves; each other, to each other; *interj* shoo!
**osa** *f* (zool.) she-bear; **Osa mayor** (astr.) Great Bear, Ursa Major; **Osa menor** (astr.) Little Bear, Ursa Minor; **el Osa** Ossa, Mount Ossa
**osadía** *f* boldness, daring
**osado -da** *adj* bold, daring
**osambre** *m* or **osamenta** *f* skeleton; bones
**osar** *m* ossuary, charnel house; *vn* to dare; **osar** + *inf* to dare + *inf*, to dare to + *inf*
**osario** *m* ossuary, charnel house
**oscense** *adj* (pertaining to) Huesca; *mf* native or inhabitant of Huesca
**oscilación** *f* oscillation; fluctuation; wavering, hesitation
**oscilador -dora** *adj* oscillating; *m* oscillator; (rad.) oscillator; **oscilador de relajación** (elec.) relaxation oscillator
**oscilante** *adj* oscillating, oscillatory
**oscilar** *vn* to oscillate; to waver, hesitate; (phys.) to oscillate
**oscilatorio -ria** *adj* oscillatory
**oscilógrafo** *m* (phys.) oscillograph
**oscilograma** *m* (phys.) oscillogram
**osciloscopio** *m* (phys.) oscilloscope
**oscino -na** *adj & f* (orn.) oscine
**oscitación** *f* gaping, yawning, oscitancy
**oscitancia** *f* careless oversight
**osco -ca** *adj & mf* Oscan; *m* Oscan (*language*)
**osculación** *f* (geom.) osculation
**osculador -dora** *adj* (geom.) osculatory
**osculatorio -ria** *adj* osculatory
**osculatriz** *f* (*pl:* **-trices**) (geom.) osculatrix
**ósculo** *m* osculation, kiss; (zool.) osculum (*of a sponge*)
**oscurantismo** *m* var. of **obscurantismo**
**oscurantista** *adj & mf* var. of **obscurantista**
**oscurecer** **§34** *va, vn & vr* var. of **obscurecer**
**oscurecimiento** *m* var. of **obscurecimiento**
**oscuridad** *f* var. of **obscuridad**
**oscuro -ra** *adj & m* var. of **obscuro**
**osear** *va* var. of **oxear**
**Oseas** *m* (Bib.) Hosea
**osecico, osecillo** or **osecito** *m* little bone
**óseo -a** *adj* osseous, bony
**osera** *f* bear's den
**osero** *m* ossuary
**osezno** *m* cub or whelp of a bear
**osezuelo** *m* little bone
**Osián** *m* Ossian
**osiánico -ca** *adj* Ossianic
**osianismo** *m* Ossianism
**osículo** *m* (anat.) ossicle
**osificación** *f* ossification
**osificar** **§86** *va & vr* to ossify
**osífraga** *f* or **osífrago** *m* (orn.) ossifrage
**Osiris** *m* (myth.) Osiris
**osmanlí** (*pl:* **-líes**) *adj & m* Osmanli
**osmio** *m* (chem.) osmium
**ósmosis** *f* (chem. & physiol.) osmosis
**osmótico -ca** *adj* osmotic
**-oso -sa** *suffix adj* -ous, e.g., **famoso** famous; **maravilloso** marvelous; -ful, e.g., **doloroso** painful; **espantoso** frightful; -y e.g., **jugoso** juicy; **rocoso** rocky; (chem.) -ous, e.g., **nitroso** nitrous; **sulfuroso** sulfurous
**oso** *m* (zool.) bear; **hacer el oso** (coll.) to make a fool of oneself; (coll.) to be overdemonstrative (*in love*); **oso bezudo** (zool.) sloth bear; **oso blanco** (zool.) polar bear; **oso colmenero** (zool.) honey badger; **oso del Tibet** (zool.) black bear; **oso gris** (zool.) grizzly bear; **oso hormiguero** (zool.) ant bear, anteater; **oso lavador** (zool.) coon, raccoon; **oso marino** (zool.) fur seal (*Callorhinus alascanus*); **oso marítimo** (zool.) polar bear; **oso negro** (zool.) black bear; **oso pardo** (zool.) brown bear
**ososo -sa** *adj* bony, osseous
**osta** *f* (naut.) guy, vang
**ostaga** *f* (naut.) tie
**oste** *interj* var. of **oxte**
**osteítis** *f* (path.) osteitis
**ostensible** *adj* visible, manifest
**ostensión** *f* show, manifestation; (eccl.) ostension
**ostensivo -va** *adj* ostensive; clear, obvious
**ostensorio** *m* (eccl.) monstrance
**ostentación** *f* showing; ostentation
**ostentador -dora** *adj* ostentatious; *mf* ostentatious person
**ostentar** *va* to show; to display, make a show of; *vr* to show off; to boast
**ostentativo -va** *adj* ostentatious
**ostento** *m* portent, prodigy
**ostentoso -sa** *adj* ostentatious
**osteoblasto** *m* (anat.) osteoblast
**osteolita** *f* (mineral.) osteolite
**osteología** *f* osteology
**osteológico -ca** *adj* osteological
**osteólogo -ga** *mf* osteologist
**osteoma** *m* (path.) osteoma
**osteomalacia** *f* (path.) osteomalacia
**osteomielitis** *f* (path.) osteomyelitis

**osteópata** *mf* osteopath, osteopathist
**osteopatía** *f* osteopathy
**osteopático -ca** *adj* osteopathic
**osteotomía** *f* (surg.) osteotomy
**ostial** *m* mouth of a harbor; pearl-growing shell; pearl fishery
**ostiario** *m* (eccl.) ostiary
**ostión** *m* large oyster
**ostra** *f* (zool.) oyster; **ostra perlera** (zool.) pearl oyster
**ostráceo -a** *adj* oyster; (zool.) ostraceous
**ostracismo** *m* ostracism
**ostral** *m* oyster bed, oyster farm
**ostrera** *f* see **ostrero**
**ostrería** *f* oysterhouse
**ostrero -ra** *adj* (pertaining to the) oyster; *m* oysterman; oyster bed, oyster farm; (orn.) oyster bird; *f* oysterwoman; (dial.) oyster bed
**ostrícola** *adj* oyster-raising, oyster-growing
**ostricultura** *f* oyster culture
**ostro** *m* large oyster; south; south wind; (zool.) purple (*mollusk and purple dye*)
**ostrogodo -da** *adj & mf* Ostrogoth
**ostugo** *m* corner; bit, whit
**osudo -da** *adj* bony
**osuno -na** *adj* bearish, bearlike
**otacústico -ca** *adj* otacoustic
**otalgia** *f* (path.) otalgia
**otálgico -ca** *adj* otalgic
**O.T.A.N., la** Nato (*North Atlantic Treaty Organization*)
**otáñez** *m* (coll.) old nobleman or esquire who served and accompanied a lady
**O.T.A.S.E., la** Seato (*Southeast Asia Treaty Organization*)
**-ote -ta** *suffix aug* e.g., **animalote** big animal; **grandote** biggish; **terminote** big word; **manota** big hand; *suffix dim* e.g., **camarote** stateroom, cabin; **islote** small barren island
**oteador -dora** *adj* watchful, spying; *mf* watcher, spy, lookout
**otear** *va* to survey, look down upon or over; to watch, keep an eye on
**Otelo** *m* Othello
**otero** *m* hillock, knoll
**oteruelo** *m* mound, hummock
**otitis** *f* (path.) otitis
**oto** *m* (orn.) tawny owl
**otocisto** *m* (zool.) otocyst
**otoesclerosis** *f* var. of **otosclerosis**
**otolaringología** *f* otolaryngology
**otología** *f* otology
**otólogo -ga** *mf* otologist
**otomán** *m* ottoman (*corded silk fabric*)
**otomano -na** *adj & mf* Ottoman; *f* ottoman (*sofa*)
**Otón** *m* Otto
**otoñada** *f* autumn time; autumn pasturage
**otoñal** *adj* autumnal, autumn, fall
**otoñar** *vn* to spend the autumn; to grow in autumn; *vr* (agr.) to soften up from autumn rains (*said of the ground*)
**otoñizo -za** *adj* autumnal
**otoño** *m* autumn, fall; fall crop of hay
**otorgadero -ra** *adj* grantable
**otorgador -dora** *adj* granting; *mf* grantor
**otorgamiento** *m* consent; grant; granting, conferring; approval; (law) execution of a document
**otorgante** *mf* grantor; (law) maker (*of a deed*)
**otorgar** §59 *va* to agree to; to grant, to confer; (law) to execute (*e.g., a deed*)
**otorrea** *f* (path.) catarrh of the ear
**otorrinolaringología** *f* otorhinolaryngology
**otorrinolaringólogo -ga** *mf* otorhinolaryngologist
**otosclerosis** *f* (path.) otosclerosis
**otoscopia** *f* otoscopy
**otoscopio** *m* otoscope
**otramente** *adv* otherwise; in a different way
**otro -tra** *adj indef* other, another; *pron indef* other one, another one; **algún otro** someone else, somebody else; **al otro día** on the next day; **al otro día de** + *inf* on the day after + *ger;* **como dijo el otro** as someone said; **el otro día** the other day; the next day; **¡ésa es otra!** (coll.) that's a fine thing!; **ser muy otro** (coll.) to be quite changed; **¡otra!** (theat.) encore; **otro tanto** as much, the same thing
**otrora** *adv* formerly, of yore
**otrosí** *adv* furthermore
**ova** *f* (bot.) sea lettuce; (arch.) egg (*in egg-and-dart ornaments*); **ovas** *fpl* roe
**ovación** *f* ovation
**ovacionar** *va* to give an ovation to
**ovado -da** *adj* ovate; oval; impregnated (*fowl*)
**oval** or **ovalado -da** *adj* oval
**ovalar** *va* to make oval
**oválico -ca** *adj* oval, oval-shaped
**óvalo** *m* oval; (arch.) egg (*in egg-and-dart ornaments*)
**ovante** *adj* victorious, triumphant
**ovar** *vn* to lay eggs
**ovárico -ca** *adj* ovarian
**ovario** *m* (anat. & bot.) ovary; (arch.) egg-ornamented molding
**ovariotomía** *f* (surg.) ovariotomy
**ovaritis** *f* (path.) ovaritis
**ovecico, ovecillo** or **ovecito** *m* small egg
**oveja** *f* ewe, female sheep; **oveja negra** (fig.) black sheep; **oveja perdida** (fig.) lost sheep
**ovejero -ra** *adj* (pertaining to) sheep; *mf* sheep raiser; *m* shepherd; *f* shepherdess
**ovejuela** *f* young ewe
**ovejuno -na** *adj* (pertaining to) sheep
**overo -ra** *adj* blossom-colored (*horse*); egg-colored; *f* ovary of a bird
**ovetense** *adj* (pertaining to) Oviedo; *mf* native or inhabitant of Oviedo
**ovezuelo** *m* small egg
**ovículo** *m* (arch.) oviculum
**Ovidio** *m* Ovid
**óvido -da** *adj & m* ovine; **óvidos** *mpl* (zool.) Ovidae
**oviducto** *m* (anat.) oviduct
**oviforme** *adj* oviform
**ovil** *m* sheepcote
**ovillar** *va* to wind up (*e.g., wool*); to sum up; *vn* to form into a ball; *vr* to curl up into a ball
**ovillo** *m* ball of yarn; ball, heap; tangled ball; **hacerse un ovillo** (coll.) to cower, to recoil; (coll.) to get all tangled up (*in speech*)
**ovino -na** *adj & m* ovine
**ovio -via** *adj* var. of **obvio**
**ovíparo -ra** *adj* oviparous
**oviscapto** *m* (zool.) ovipositor
**ovoide** or **ovoideo -a** *adj* ovoid
**óvolo** *m* (arch.) ovolo
**ovoso -sa** *adj* full of roe
**ovovivíparo -ra** *adj* ovoviviparous
**ovulación** *f* (biol.) ovulation
**ovular** *adj* ovular
**óvulo** *m* (biol. & bot.) ovule
**ox** *interj* shoo! (*to scare away fowl*)
**oxalato** *m* (chem.) oxalate
**oxalidáceo -a** *adj* (bot.) oxalidaceous
**oxálico -ca** *adj* oxalic
**oxalme** *m* brine mixed with vinegar
**oxe** *interj* var. of **ox**
**oxear** *va & vn* to shoo
**oxfordiano -na** *adj & mf* Oxfordian
**oxfordiense** *adj & m* (geol.) Oxfordian
**oxhídrico -ca** *adj* (chem.) oxyhydrogen
**oxhidrilo** *m* (chem.) hydroxyl
**oxiacanto -ta** *adj* thorny; *f* (bot.) hawthorn, whitethorn
**oxiacetilénico -ca** *adj* oxyacetylene
**oxidable** *adj* oxidizable
**oxidación** *f* oxidation
**oxidante** *adj* oxidizing; *m* (chem.) oxidizer
**oxidar** *va* to oxidize; *vr* to oxidize; to get rusty; (fig.) to get rusty (*said of one's knowledge of a subject*)
**óxido** *m* (chem.) oxide; **óxido amarillo** yellow oxide; **óxido de aluminio** (chem.) aluminum oxide; **óxido de carbono** (chem.) carbon monoxide; **óxido de cinc** (chem.) zinc oxide; **óxido de hierro** (chem.) iron oxide; **óxido de mercurio** (chem.) mercuric oxide; **óxido nitroso** (chem.) nitrous oxide
**oxigenación** *f* oxygenation
**oxigenar** *va* oxygenate; *vr* (chem.) to become oxygenated; to take the air, to go out for fresh air
**oxígeno** *m* (chem.) oxygen
**oxigonio -nia** *adj* (geom.) acute-angled
**oxihemoglobina** *f* (biochem.) oxyhemoglobin

**oximel** *m* or **oximiel** *m* (pharm.) oxymel
**oxirrino -na** *adj* (zool.) oxyrhine
**oxítono -na** *adj* & *m* (phonet.) oxytone
**oxizacre** *m* bittersweet drink
**oxoniense** *adj* & *mf* Oxonian
**oxozono** *m* (chem.) oxozone
**oxte** *interj* get out!, beat it!; **sin decir oxte ni moxte** (coll.) without opening one's mouth
**oye** *3d sg pres ind & 2d sg impv of* **oír**
**oyente** *mf* hearer; listener (*to radio*); auditor (*in school*)
**oyes** *2d sg pres ind of* **oír**
**ozona** *f* var. of **ozono**
**ozonizar** **§76** *va* & *vr* to ozonize
**ozono** *m* (chem.) ozone
**ozonosfera** *f* ozonosphere, ozone layer
**ozonuro** *m* (chem.) ozonide
**ozostomía** *f* (path.) ozostomia

# P

**P, p** *f* nineteenth letter of the Spanish alphabet
**P.** abr. of **Padre, Papa & Pregunta**
**p.ª** abr. of **para**
**P.A.** abr. of **Por ausencia & Por autorización**
**pabellón** *m* pavilion; bell tent; flag, banner; stack (*of guns*); building (*e.g., of an exposition*); canopy (*over bed, throne, altar*); summerhouse; (anat. & arch.) pavilion; (mus.) bell (*of wind instrument*); (naut.) flag, colors; protection; **pabellón de conveniencia** (naut.) flag of convenience; **pabellón nacional** national flag
**pabilo** or **pábilo** *m* wick; snuff (*of candle*)
**pabilón** *m* flax or wool hanging from distaff
**pablar** *vn* (hum.) to jabber
**Pablo** *m* Paul; **¡guarda, Pablo!** (coll.) careful there!
**pábulo** *m* pabulum; (fig.) support, encouragement, fuel
**paca** *f* (zool.) spotted cavy; bale
**pacana** *f* (bot.) pecan (*tree and fruit*)
**pacanero** *m* (bot.) pecan (*tree*)
**pacatería** or **pacatez** *f* mildness, gentleness
**pacato -ta** *adj* mild, gentle
**pacay** *m* (*pl:* **-cayes** or **-caes**) (bot.) pacay (*tree and fruit*)
**pacedero -ra** *adj* pasturable
**pacedura** *f* pasture
**pacense** *adj* (pertaining to) Badajoz; *mf* native or inhabitant of Badajoz
**paceño -ña** *adj* (pertaining to) La Paz (*Bolivia*); *mf* native or inhabitant of La Paz
**pacer §34** *va* to pasture, graze; to gnaw, eat away; *vn* to pasture, graze
**paciencia** *f* patience; almond cooky
**paciente** *adj & mf* patient; *m* (gram.) patient, recipient of an action
**pacienzudo -da** *adj* patient, long-suffering
**pacificación** *f* pacification; peace, calm, quiet
**pacificador -dora** *adj* pacifying; *mf* pacifier, peace-maker
**pacificar §86** *va* to pacify; *vn* to sue for peace; *vr* to calm down
**pacífico -ca** *adj* pacific; (*cap.*) *adj & m* Pacific (*ocean*)
**pacifismo** *m* pacifism
**pacifista** *adj* pacifist, pacifistic; *mf* pacifist
**paco** *m* (zool.) paco, alpaca; (mineral.) paco; Moorish sniper; sniper; (*cap.*) *m* Frank
**pacón** *m* (bot.) soap tree
**pacotilla** *f* goods carried by seamen or officers free of freight; merchandise; bother, annoyance; deal, venture; trash, junk; **hacer la pacotilla** (coll.) to pack up; **hacer su pacotilla** (coll.) to make a cleanup; **ser de pacotilla** to be shoddy, to be poorly made
**pacotillero -ra** *mf* (Am.) peddler
**pactar** *va* to agree to, to agree upon; *vn* to come to an agreement; to temporize
**pacto** *m* pact, covenant
**pachá** *m* (*pl:* **-chaes**) var. of **bajá**
**pachón -chona** *adj* (Am.) woolly, shaggy; *m* pointer (*dog*); phlegmatic fellow, sluggard
**pachorra** *f* (coll.) sluggishness, indolence
**pachorrudo -da** *adj* (coll.) sluggish, indolent
**pachucho -cha** *adj* overripe; weak, drooping
**pachulí** *m* (*pl:* **-líes**) (bot.) patchouli
**padecer §34** *va* to suffer; to endure; to be victim of (*a mistake, illusion, etc.*); *vn* to suffer; **padecer con** or **de** to suffer from
**padecimiento** *m* suffering
**padilla** *f* small frying pan; bread oven
**padrastro** *m* stepfather; bad father; obstacle; hangnail; (mil.) eminence, high ground
**padrazo** *m* (coll.) indulgent father
**padre** *m* father; stallion, sire; (eccl.) father; **padres** *mpl* parents; ancestors; **de padre y muy señor mío** (coll.) hard, terrific (*e.g., beating*); **santos padres** fathers of the church; **padre de la patria** Father of his Country; (hum.) Solon (*legislator*); **padre de pila** godfather; **padre político** father-in-law; step-father; **Padre Santo** Holy Father; **Padres apostólicos** Apostolic Fathers; **padres conscriptos** conscript father; **padres de la iglesia** fathers of the church; *adj* (Am.) swell, grand
**padrear** *vn* to resemble one's father; to breed (*said of a male animal*)
**padrenuestro** *m* (*pl:* **padrenuestros**) Lord's Prayer; paternoster (*prayer and bead*)
**padrillo** *m* (Am.) stallion
**padrina** *f* godmother
**padrinazgo** *m* godfathership; sponsorship, patronage
**padrino** *m* godfather; sponsor; second (*in a duel*); **padrinos** *mpl* godfather and godmother; **padrino de boda** best man, groomsman
**padrón** *m* poll, census; pattern, model; memorial column; note of infamy; (coll.) indulgent father; (Am.) stallion
**padrote** *m* (Am.) pimp, procurer; (Am.) gigolo
**paella** *f* saffron-flavored stew of chicken, seafood, and rice with vegetables
**paf** *interj* bang!
**paflón** *m* (arch.) soffit
**pág.** abr. of **página**
**paga** *f* pay, payment; wages, salary; fine; requital; **buena paga** good pay (*person*); **mala paga** poor pay (*person*)
**pagable** *adj* payable
**pagadero -ra** *adj* payable; *m* time of payment, term, grace
**pagado -da** *adj* pleased, cheerful; **estamos pagados** we're quits; **pagado de sí mismo** self-satisfied, conceited
**pagador -dora** *adj* paying; *mf* payer; paymaster; paying teller
**pagaduría** *f* disbursement office, paymaster's office
**pagamento** or **pagamiento** *m* payment
**paganismo** *m* paganism
**paganizar** *va & vn* to paganize
**pagano -na** *adj & mf* pagan; *m* (coll.) easy mark, scapegoat
**pagar §59** *va* to pay; to pay for; to return (*e.g., a kindness, a visit*); **pagarla** or **pagarlas** (coll.) to pay for it; *vn* to pay; **a luego pagar** cash, for cash; *vr* to become fond, become enamored; to yield to flattery; to boast, make a show; to be satisfied
**pagaré** *m* promissory note, I.O.U.
**pagd.º** abr. of **pagado**
**pagel** *m* (ichth.) red surmullet
**página** *f* page; (fig.) page (*of history*)
**paginación** *f* pagination
**paginar** *va* to page
**pago** *adj* (coll.) paid; *m* payment; district, region (*especially of vineyards or olive groves*); **en pago de** in payment of or for; **pago a la entrega** cash on delivery; **pago a plazos** installment payment, installment plan
**pagoda** *f* pagoda
**pagote** *m* (coll.) easy mark, scapegoat
**pagro** *m* (ichth.) porgy
**paguro** *m* (zool.) hermit crab
**paila** *f* large pan
**pailebote** *m* (naut.) small sleek schooner
**painel** *m* panel
**pairar** *vn* (naut.) to lie to
**pairo** *m* (naut.) lying to

**país** *m* country, land; back of fan; (f.a.) landscape; **el país de Gales** Wales; **el País Vasco** the Basque Country; **los Países Bajos** the Low Countries (*Belgium, The Netherlands, and Luxemburg*); The Netherlands (*Holland*); **país satélite** satellite country
**paisaje** *m* landscape; (f.a.) landscape
**paisajista** *mf* landscape painter, landscapist
**paisajístico -ca** *adj* (pertaining to) landscape
**paisana** *f* see **paisano**
**paisanaje** *m* peasantry; civilians; fellow citizenship
**paisano -na** *adj* of the same country; (Am.) rustic, boorish; *mf* peasant; *m* countryman; civilian; (orn.) road runner; **de paisano** in civies; *f* countrywoman
**paisista** *mf* landscape painter
**paja** *f* straw; chaff (*husk of wheat, oats, rye, etc.*); trash, rubbish, chaff, deadwood; **en un quítame allá esas pajas** (coll.) in a jiffy; **no dormirse en las pajas** (coll.) to not let the grass grow under one's feet; **no importar una paja** to be of no utter use or importance; **no levantar paja del suelo** to not lift a hand, to not do a stroke of work; **paja centenaza** rye straw; **paja de madera** excelsior; **paja pelaza** beaten barley straw; **¡pajas!** no less so!
**pajado -da** *adj* straw-colored; *f* chaff (*to be used as fodder*)
**pajar** *m* haystack, hayrick, straw loft
**pájara** *f* paper kite; paper rooster; bird; crafty female; **pájara pinta** game of forfeits
**pajarear** *vn* to go out to catch birds; to loaf around; (Am.) to shy (*said of a horse*)
**pajarel** *m* (orn.) redpoll
**pajarera** *f* see **pajarero**
**pajarería** *f* flock of birds, large number of birds; bird store; pet shop
**pajarero -ra** *adj* (coll.) bright, cheerful; (coll.) bright-colored, gaudy; *m* bird dealer, bird fancier; *f* aviary; large bird cage
**pajarilla** *f* (bot.) columbine; paper kite; paper rooster; milt, spleen (*of hog*)
**pajarita** *f* paper kite; paper rooster; bow tie; wing collar, piccadilly; (bot.) toadflax, snapdragon; **pajarita de las nieves** (orn.) wagtail
**pájaro** *m* bird; crafty fellow; expert; **matar dos pájaros de una pedrada** to kill two birds with one stone; **pájaro bobo** (orn.) penguin; **pájaro carpintero** (orn.) woodpecker; **pájaro de cuenta** (coll.) big shot; **pájaro gato** (orn.) catbird; **pájaro gordo** (coll.) big shot; **pájaro mosca** (*pl:* **pájaros moscas**) (orn.) hummingbird; **pájaro polilla** (orn.) kingfisher; **pájaro sastre** (orn.) tailorbird; **pájaro trompeta** (orn.) trumpeter; **pájaro verdugo** (orn.) butcherbird
**pajarota** or **pajarotada** *f* hoax, canard
**pajarote** *m* large bird
**pajarraco** or **pajaruco** *m* ugly big bird; (coll.) sly fellow, sneaky fellow
**pajaza** *f* fodder refuse
**pajazo** *m* (vet.) spot or scar on cornea of horse
**paje** *m* page; valet; dressing table; (naut.) cabin boy; **paje de hacha** linkboy
**pajear** *vn* to feed well on straw; (coll.) to act, behave
**pajecillo** *m* washstand
**pajel** *m* var. of **pagel**
**pajera** *f* see **pajero**
**pajería** *f* straw store; (coll.) bore, annoyance
**pajero -ra** *mf* straw dealer; *f* straw loft
**pajil** *adj* (pertaining to a) page (*boy*)
**pajilla** *f* cigarette; cigarette rolled in corn husk; lock spring
**pajita** *f* straw, drinking straw
**pajizo -za** *adj* straw, strawy; straw-colored
**pajolero -ra** *adj* annoying, pestiferous; voluble, convivial
**pajón** *m* coarse straw
**pajoso -sa** *adj* strawy, full of straw
**pajote** *m* straw mat for covering plants
**pajuela** *f* short straw; sulphur match or fuse; (Am.) match; (Am.) gold or silver toothpick
**pajuncio** *m* (scornful) page (*boy*)
**pajuno -na** *adj* var. of **pajil**
**pajuz** *m* or **pajuzo** *m* rotted straw used for manure
**Pakistán, el** Pakistan
**pakistanés -nesa** *adj* Pakistani
**pakistaní** (*pl:* **-níes**) *adj & mf* var. of **pakistano**
**pakistano -na** *adj & mf* Pakistani
**pal** *m* (her.) pale
**pala** *f* shovel; blade (*of hoe, spade, oar, etc.*); scoop; racket; upper (*of shoe*); scraper; setting (*of precious stones*); flat surface (*of tooth*); leaf (*of hinge*); paddle; peel (*of baker*); cake turner; (mil. & nav.) shoulder strap; (coll.) cunning, craftiness; bucket (*of power shovel*); **meter la pala** (coll.) to be slick, to be crooked; **pala de doble concha** clamshell bucket, grab bucket; **pala mecánica** power shovel
**palabra** *f* word; speech; words (*of a song*); (*cap.*) *f* (theol.) Word (*second person of Trinity*); **bajo su palabra** on one's word; **cruzar palabras con** to exchange words with; to have words with; **cuatro palabras** a word, a few words; **dar la palabra a** to give the floor to; **dar palabra y mano** to give one's word; to give one's word in marriage; **dar su palabra** to give one's word; **decir a medias palabras** to hint at; **de palabra** by word of mouth; **dirigir la palabra a** to address; to direct one's words to; **dos palabras** a word, a few words; **en una palabra** in a word; **pedir la palabra** to ask for the floor; **remojar la palabra** (coll.) to wet one's whistle; **sobre su palabra** on one's word; **tener la palabra** to have the floor; **tener palabras** to have words, to have words with each other; **tomar la palabra** to take the floor; **tomarle a una persona la palabra** to take a person at his word; **trabarse de palabras** to have words, get into an argument; **última palabra** last word; (fig.) last word (*most up-to-date style; thing that cannot be improved*); **usar de la palabra** to speak, make a speech; **venir contra su palabra** to go against one's word; **palabra clave** key word; **palabra de Dios** Word of God; **palabra de enchufamiento** portmanteau word; **palabra de matrimonio** promise of marriage; **palabra esdrújula** (phonet.) proparoxytone; **palabra llana** (phonet.) paroxytone; **palabras al aire** (coll.) hot air; **palabras cruzadas** word square; crossword puzzle; **palabras mayores** words (*angry words, quarrel*); *interj* hey!, say!; word of honor!
**palabrada** *f* wordiness, flow of words; vulgarity (*word*)
**palabreja** *f* minor word, incidental word
**palabreo** *m* (coll.) chatter
**palabrería** *f* (coll.) wordiness; (coll.) empty promises
**palabrerío** *m* (Am.) wordiness, windiness, hot air
**palabrero -ra** *adj* wordy, windy; *mf* windbag
**palabrimujer** *adj masc* (coll.) female-voiced; *m* (coll.) fellow with a female voice
**palabrista** *adj & mf* var. of **palabrero**
**palabrita** *f* pointed word; **palabritas mansas** *mf* honey-tongued schemer
**palabrón -brona** *adj* wordy, windy
**palabrota** *f* vulgarity (*word*)
**palaciano -na** *adj* (pertaining to the) palace, court
**palaciego -ga** *adj* (pertaining to the) palace, court; *m* courtier
**palacio** *m* palace; mansion; building; **Palacio de la Alborada** official residence of the chief executive of Brazil, in Brasilia; **Palacio de la Moneda** official residence of the chief executive of Chile, in Santiago; **palacio municipal** city hall
**palacra** or **palacrana** *f* gold nugget
**palada** *f* shovelful; stroke (*of an oar*)
**paladar** *m* (anat.) palate; (fig.) palate (*taste; gourmet*); **paladar blando** (anat.) soft palate; **paladar duro** (anat.) hard palate
**paladear** *va* to taste, to relish; to clean the mouth or palate of (*an animal*); to rub the palate of (*a baby*) with something sweet; to take a liking for; *vn* to show a desire for suck-

ing (*said of a baby*); *vr* to taste; **paladearse con** to taste, to relish
**paladeo** *m* tasting, relishing
**paladial** *adj & f* (phonet.) palatal
**paladín** *m* paladin
**paladino -na** *adj* public, open; *m* paladin
**paladio** *m* (chem.) palladium
**paladión** *m* palladium (*protection*); (*cap.*) *m* (myth.) Palladium
**palado -da** *adj* (her.) paly
**palafito** *m* (archeol.) palafitte, lake dwelling
**palafrén** *m* palfrey; groom's horse
**palafrenero** *m* groom, stableboy; equerry
**palahierro** *m* shaft socket of a millstone
**palamallo** *m* pall-mall (*game*)
**palamedea** *f* (orn.) screamer
**palamenta** *f* (naut.) oarage, set of oars
**palanca** *f* (mach. & mech.) lever; pole (*for carrying a weight*); crowbar; (fort.) outwork made of stakes and earth; (fig.) soul, prime mover; (Am.) friend with pull; **palanca de cambio** (aut.) gearshift lever; **palanca de gancho** cant hook; **palanca de mando** (aer.) control stick; **palanca de mayúsculas** shift key (*of typewriter*); **palanca portatipos** type bar (*of typewriter*)
**palancada** *f* move made with a lever, leverage
**palancana** or **palangana** *f* washbowl
**palanganero** *m* washstand (*stand with basin and pitcher*)
**palangre** *m* boulter, trawl, trotline
**palangrero** *m* boulterer, trawler
**palanquera** *f* stockade; (fort.) log rampart
**palanquero** *m* leverman; (archaic) blower of bellows; (Am.) brakeman; (Am.) timberman
**palanqueta** *f* jimmy; dumbbell; lever; (nav.) bar shot; (Am.) honeyed popcorn
**palanquilla** *f* billet (*square iron rod*)
**palanquín** *m* errand boy, porter; palankeen or palanquin; (naut.) double tackle
**Palas** *f* (myth.) Pallas; **Palas Atenea** (myth.) Pallas Athene
**palasán** *m* (bot.) rattan, rotang
**palastro** *m* sheet iron, plate steel; plate of lock
**palatal** *adj* palatal; (phonet.) palatal; *f* (phonet.) palatal
**palatalización** *f* palatalization
**palatalizar** **§76** *va & vr* to palatalize
**palatina** *f* see **palatino**
**palatinado** *m* palatinate; (*cap.*) *m* Palatinate
**palatino -na** *adj* (anat.) palatal; palatine; Palatine; *m* Palatine; **el Palatino** the Palatine; *f* tippet (*scarf*)
**palatizar** **§76** *va* to palatalize
**palatosquisis** *f* cleft palate
**palay** *m* paddy (*rice in husk*)
**palazo** *m* blow with a shovel
**palazón** *m* woodwork, timber
**palco** *m* (theat.) box; (theat.) bench, row of seats; **palco de platea** (theat.) parquet box; **palco escénico** (theat.) stage
**paleador** *m* shoveler; stoker
**palear** *va* to beat, to pound; to shovel
**palenque** *m* paling, palisade; arena; (fig.) arena; **tener la vida en un palenque** (coll.) to be in great danger
**palentino -na** *adj* (pertaining to) Palencia; *mf* native or inhabitant of Palencia
**paleobotánica** *f* paleobotany
**paleografía** *f* paleography
**paleográfico -ca** *adj* paleographic
**paleógrafo -fa** *mf* paleographer
**paleolítico -ca** *adj* paleolithic
**paleontología** *f* paleontology
**paleontólogo -ga** *mf* paleontologist
**paleoterio** *m* (pal.) palaeothere
**paleozoico -ca** *adj & m* Paleozoic
**palería** *f* draining, drainage
**palero** *m* shovel maker or dealer; drainer; shoveler; (mil.) pioneer, sapper
**palestino -na** *adj & mf* Palestinian; (*cap.*) *f* Palestine
**palestra** *f* palaestra; wrestling; struggle, dispute
**paléstrico -ca** *adj* palaestric
**palestrita** *m* wrestler
**paleta** *f* small shovel; fire shovel; trowel; paddle; blade, bucket, vane; (anat.) shoulder blade; (paint.) palette, pallet; (Am.) lollipop; **de paleta** ready, at hand; **en dos paletas** (coll.) in a jiffy
**paletada** *f* trowelful; blow with a shovel; **en dos paletadas** (coll.) in a jiffy
**paletazo** *m* blow with a shovel or trowel; side thrust with the horn
**paletear** *va* to beat (*hides*); *vn* to row without advancing; to go around without advancing (*said of paddle wheel*)
**paletero** *m* two-year-old fallow deer
**paletilla** *f* (anat.) shoulder blade; sternum cartilage; **poner la paletilla en su lugar a** (coll.) to rake over the coals
**paleto** *m* fallow deer; rustic, yokel
**paletó** *m* (*pl:* **-toes**) (archaic) overcoat, paletot
**paletón** *m* bit or web (*of key*)
**paletoque** *m* man's doublet or jacket
**pali** *adj & m* Pali
**palia** *f* (eccl.) altar cloth; (eccl.) pall, pallium
**paliacate** *m* (Am.) bandanna
**paliación** *f* palliation
**paliadamente** *adv* secretly, hiddenly
**paliar** **§90** & **regular** *va* to palliate
**paliativo -va** *adj & m* palliative
**paliatorio -ria** *adj* concealing, veiling
**palidecer** **§34** *vn* to pale, turn pale
**palidez** *f* paleness, pallor
**pálido -da** *adj* pale, pallid
**paliducho -cha** *adj* palish
**palillero -ra** *mf* toothpick maker or dealer; *m* toothpick holder
**palillo** *m* knitting-needle holder; toothpick; drumstick; tobacco stem; bobbin (*for making lace*); **palillos** *mpl* pins (*sometimes used in billiards*); chopsticks; castanets; (coll.) rudiments; (coll.) trifles
**palimpsesto** *m* palimpsest
**palíndromo -ma** *adj* palindromic; *m* palindrome
**palingenesia** *f* palingenesis
**palingenésico -ca** *adj* palingenetic
**palinodia** *f* backdown, recantation, palinode; **cantar la palinodia** to eat crow
**palio** *m* (anat., eccl. & hist.) pallium; cloak, mantle; baldachin, dais, canopy; (hist.) prize (*silk cloth*) for winning a horse race
**palique** *m* (coll.) chit-chat, small talk
**paliquear** *vn* (coll.) to chat, gossip
**palisandro** *m* (bot.) palisander, Brazilian rosewood
**palitroque** *m* stick
**paliza** *f* beating
**palizada** *f* fenced-in enclosure; stockade; embankment
**palma** *f* palm (*of hand*); (bot.) palm (*tree and leaf*); sole (*of hoof*); (fig.) palm; **palmas** *fpl* clapping, applause; **andar en palmas** to be highly esteemed; **batir palmas** to clap, applaud; **llevarse la palma** to bear the palm, to carry off the palm; **palma brava** (bot.) fan palm (*Corypha minor*); **palma de cera** (bot.) wax palm; **palma indiana** (bot.) coconut palm; **palma loca** (bot.) yucca; **palma real** (bot.) royal palm
**palmáceo -a** *adj* (bot.) palmaceous
**palmacristi** *f* (bot.) palma Christi
**palmado -da** *adj* palmate; (bot. & zool.) palmate; (slang) broke; *f* slap; hand, applause, clapping; **dar palmadas** to clap hands
**palmar** *adj* (anat.) palmar; clear, evident; *m* palm grove; fuller's thistle; *vn* (coll.) to die
**palmario -ria** *adj* clear, evident
**palmatoria** *f* ferule; candlestick
**palmeado -da** *adj* palmate; (bot. & zool.) palmate
**palmear** *va* (print.) to level (*a form*); (Am.) to pat, to slap; *vn* to clap; *vr* (naut.) to go aloft hand over hand
**palmense** *adj* (pertaining to) Las Palmas; *mf* native or inhabitant of Las Palmas, Canary Islands
**palmeo** *m* measuring by spans or palms
**pálmer** *m* micrometer caliper
**palmera** *f* elephant's ear (*cake*); (bot.) date palm; **palmera de betel** (bot.) betel palm; **palmera de las Antillas** (bot.) royal palm; **palmera de sombrilla** (bot.) talipot; **palmera enana** or **de abanico** (bot.) dwarf fan palm

**palmeral** *m* grove of date palms
**palmero** *m* palmer (*pilgrim from Holy Land*); caretaker of palm trees
**palmesano -na** *adj* (pertaining to) Palma; *mf* native or inhabitant of Palma, Majorca
**palmeta** *f* ferule; blow with a ferule
**palmetazo** *m* blow with a ferule; severe scolding
**palmiche** *m* (bot.) royal palm; nut of royal palm; (Am.) Palm Beach (*fabric*)
**palmífero -ra** *adj* (poet.) palmiferous
**palmilla** *f* blue woolen cloth; inner sole
**palmípedo -da** *adj & f* (zool.) palmiped
**palmitato** *m* (chem.) palmitate
**palmitieso -sa** *adj* flat-hoofed (*horse*)
**palmito** *m* (bot.) palmetto, dwarf fan palm; sprout (*of palm*); (coll.) face (*of a woman*); (coll.) slender figure (*of a woman*)
**palmo** *m* span, palm; **crecer a palmos** (coll.) to grow by leaps and bounds; **dejar con un palmo de narices** (coll.) to disappoint; **tener medido a palmos** to know every inch of
**palmotear** *vn* to clap
**palmoteo** *m* clapping; striking with a ferule
**palo** *m* stick; whack, blow with a stick; staff; handle; (naut.) mast; wood; execution on gallows; suit (*at cards*); (print.) hook or stroke (*of an ascender or descender*); (her.) pale; **dar palos de ciego** to lay about, to swing wildly; **de tal palo tal astilla** like father like son; **servir del palo** to follow suit; **palo áloe** aloes, aloes wood; **palo brasil** brazilwood; **palo campeche** logwood; **palo de áloe** aloes, aloes wood; **palo de barranco** (bot.) American hornbeam; **palo de Campeche** logwood; **palo de Cuba** (bot.) fustic; **palo de escoba** broomstick; **palo de hierro** (bot.) ironwood; **palo de jabón** soapbark, quillai bark; **palo de hule** (bot.) rubber tree; **palo de lanza** (bot.) lancewood; **palo de las Indias** lignum vitae (*wood*); **palo del Brasil** brazilwood; **palo de mesana** (naut.) mizzenmast; **palo de planchar** ironing board; **palo de rosa** (bot.) tulipwood (*tree and wood*); **palo de trinquete** (naut.) foremast; **palo dulce** licorice root; **palo en alto** big stick (*military or political coercive power*); **palo mayor** (naut.) mainmast; **palo santo** lignum vitae (*wood*)
**paloma** *f* (orn.) pigeon, dove; (fig.) dove, meek person, easy-going person; prostitute; (naut.) sling of yard; (slang) high collar; (slang) brandy and soda; **palomas** *fpl* whitecaps; **paloma brava** (orn.) stock dove; **paloma buchona** pouter (*pigeon*); **paloma capuchina** (orn.) capuchin (*pigeon*); **paloma colipava** (orn.) fantail; **paloma de pitahaya** (orn.) white-winged dove; **paloma emigrante** (orn.) passenger pigeon; **paloma mensajera** homing pigeon; **paloma silvestre** (orn.) stock dove; **paloma torcaz** (orn.) ringdove, wood pigeon; **paloma triste** (orn.) mourning dove; **paloma volcanera** (orn.) wood pigeon (*Columba fasciata*); **paloma zorita, zura, zurana** or **zurita** (orn.) rock dove
**palomadura** *f* (naut.) boltrope tie
**palomar** *adj* hard-twisted (*twine*); *m* pigeon house, dovecot
**palomariego -ga** *adj* domestic (*pigeon*)
**palomear** *vn* to hunt pigeons, to shoot pigeons; to breed pigeons
**palomera** *f* see **palomero**
**palomería** *f* pigeon shooting
**palomero -ra** *mf* pigeon breeder or fancier, pigeon seller; *f* small pigeon house; bleak spot
**palometa** *f* (mach.) pillow block; (ichth.) pomfret; (ichth.) weever; (ichth.) palometa (*Parona signata*)
**palomilla** *f* doveling; small butterfly; white horse; back (*of horse*); wall bracket; (bot.) alkanet (*Alkanna tinctoria*); (bot.) fumitory; (ent.) grain moth; (mach.) pillow block, journal bearing; (print.) galley rack; **palomillas** *fpl* whitecaps
**palomina** *f* pigeon droppings; (bot.) fumitory
**palomino** *m* young stock dove; palomino (*horse*); (coll.) dirty spot on shirttail
**palomita** *f* doveling; (Am.) piece of popcorn; (Am.) darling; **palomitas** *fpl* (Am.) popcorn
**palomo** *m* cock pigeon; (orn.) ringdove
**palor** *m* pallor
**palotada** *f* stroke with a drumstick; **no dar palotada** (coll.) to not do or say the right thing; (coll.) to be dilatory
**palote** *m* stick, drumstick; scribbled downstroke
**paloteado** *m* stick dance; (coll.) noisy scuffle
**palotear** *vn* to knock sticks together; to wrangle
**paloteo** *m* noise of sticks knocking together; (coll.) noisy scuffle
**palpabilidad** *f* palpability
**palpable** *adj* palpable
**palpación** *f* touching, feeling; groping; (med.) palpation
**palpadura** *f* or **palpamiento** *m* touching, feeling; groping
**palpar** *va* to touch, to feel; to grope through; to find self-evident; (med.) to palpate; *vn* to grope
**pálpebra** *f* eyelid
**palpebral** *adj* palpebral
**palpitación** *f* palpitation
**palpitante** *adj* palpitating; throbbing; thrilling; burning, of the moment (*said of an event, issue, etc.*)
**palpitar** *vn* to palpitate, to throb; to flash, to break forth (*said of an emotion*)
**pálpito** *m* thrill, excitement; (Am.) presentiment
**palpo** *m* palpus, feeler
**palta** *f* (Am.) avocado (*fruit*)
**palto** *m* (Am.) avocado tree
**palúdico -ca** *adj* marshy; marsh, malarial
**paludismo** *m* (path.) malaria
**palurdo -da** *adj* rustic, boorish; *mf* rustic, boor
**palustre** *adj* marshy, boggy; *m* trowel
**pallador** *m* (Am.) wandering minstrel
**pallaquear** *va* (Am.) var. of **pallar**
**pallar** *va* to extract (*metal*) from ore
**pallete** *m* (naut.) fender mat, cargo mat
**pallón** *m* assay button (*of gold or silver*)
**pamela** *f* woman's wide-brimmed straw hat; picture hat; (*cap.*) *f* Pamela (*woman's name*)
**pamema** *f* (coll.) trifle, bagatelle; (coll.) bunkum, humbug; (coll.) flattery
**pampa** *f* pampa; **La Pampa** the Pampas
**pámpana** *f* vine leaf; **tocar** or **zurrar la pámpana a** (coll.) to drub, to thrash
**pampanada** *f* juice of vine shoots
**pampanaje** *m* large growth of tendrils or shoots; froth, bluff; show, tinsel
**pampanilla** *f* loincloth; kilt worn by Indians
**pampanito** *m* (ichth.) pompano
**pámpano** *m* tendril; vine leaf; (ichth.) gilthead
**pampanoso -sa** *adj* full of tendrils
**pampelmusa** *f* var. of **pamplemusa**
**pampero -ra** *adj & mf* (Am.) pampean; *m* (Am.) pampero (*southwest wind from the Andes over the pampas*)
**pampirolada** *f* garlic sauce; (coll.) nonsense, simpleness
**pamplemusa** *f* (bot.) shaddock (*tree and fruit*); (bot.) grapefruit (*tree and fruit*)
**pamplina** *f* (bot.) chickweed; (bot.) large-flowered hypecoum; (coll.) nonsense, trifle, silly remark; **pamplina de agua** (bot.) brookweed; **pamplina de canarios** (bot.) chickweed
**pamplinada** *f* (coll.) nonsense, trifle
**pamplinero -ra** or **pamplinoso -sa** *adj* simple, silly
**pamporcino** *m* (bot.) cyclamen, sowbread
**pamposado -da** *adj* (coll.) idle, lazy
**pampringada** *f* toast dipped in gravy; (coll.) nonsense, triviality
**pan** *m* bread; loaf, loaf of bread; wheat; food; pie dough; cake (*e.g., of soap, wax*); gold foil or leaf, silver foil or leaf; (*cap.*) *m* (myth.) Pan; **panes** *mpl* grain, breadstuff; **a pan y agua** on bread and water; **buscar pan de trastrigo** (coll.) to be looking for trouble; **como el pan bendito** (coll.) as easy as pie; **de pan llevar** arable, tillable (*land*); **ganarse el pan** to earn one's livelihood; **llamar al pan pan y al vino vino** to call a spade a spade; **venderse como pan bendito** (coll.) to sell like hot cakes; **pan ázimo** unleavened bread; **pan bazo** brown bread; **pan candeal** white bread; **pan casero** homemade bread;

**pan de azúcar** sugar loaf (*mass of sugar; hat; hill*); **pan de cuco** (bot.) stonecrop; **pan de gluten** gluten bread; **pan del día** fresh bread; **pan de munición** army bread; prison bread; **pan de oro** gold leaf, gold foil; **panes de la proposición** (Bib.) shewbread; **pan porcino** (bot.) sowbread; **pan negro** black bread; **pan rallado** bread crumbs; **pan tierno** fresh bread; **pan y quesillo** (bot.) shepherd's-purse
**pana** *f* plush, velveteen, corduroy; (naut.) flooring board; (aut.) breakdown; **pana abordonada** or **acanillada** corduroy
**pánace** *f* (bot.) Hercules' allheal
**panacea** *f* panacea
**panadear** *va* to make (*flour*) into bread; *vn* to make bread, to be in the bread business
**panadeo** *m* making bread
**panadería** *f* bakery; baking business
**panadero -ra** *mf* baker; **panaderos** *mpl* clog dance
**panadizo** *m* (path.) felon, whitlow; (coll.) sickly person
**panado -da** *adj* breaded, bread-crumbed; flavored with toast
**panal** *m* honeycomb; hornet comb; lemon-flavored meringue
**panamá** *m* (*pl:* **-maes**) panama, panama hat; (*cap.*) *m* Panama (*country*); *f* Panama, Panama City
**panameño -ña** *adj & mf* Panamanian
**panamericanismo** *m* Pan-Americanism
**panamericanista** *mf* Pan-Americanist
**panamericano -na** *adj* Pan-American
**panarábico -ca** *adj* Pan-Arabian
**panario -ria** *adj* (pertaining to) bread
**panarizo** *m* var. of **panadizo**
**panarra** *m* (coll.) lazy simpleton
**panatela** *f* long thin spongecake
**Panateneas** *fpl* (hist.) Panathenaea
**panática** *f* (naut.) store of bread
**panatier** *m* var. of **panetero**
**panca** *f* (Am.) cornhusk
**pancada** *f* contract for lump sale
**pancarpia** *f* garland of flowers
**pancarta** *f* placard, poster
**pancellar** *m* or **pancera** *f* (arm.) belly plate
**pancista** *adj* weaseling, non-committal; *mf* weaseler
**pancrático -ca** *adj* var. of **pancreático**
**páncreas** *m* (*pl:* **-creas**) (anat.) pancreas
**pancreático -ca** *adj* pancreatic
**pancreatina** *f* (biochem.) pancreatin
**pancromático -ca** *adj* panchromatic
**pancho** *m* (ichth.) spawn of sea bream; (coll.) paunch, belly; (*cap.*) *m* (Am.) Frank
**panda** *m* see **pando**; *f* see **pando**
**pandanáceo -a** *adj* (bot.) pandanaceous
**pandear** *vn & vr* to warp, to bulge, to buckle, to sag, to bend
**pandectas** *fpl* (com.) index book; (*cap.*) *fpl* Pandects
**pandemia** *f* pandemic
**pandémico -ca** *adj* pandemic
**pandemonio** o **pandemónium** *m* pandemonium (*place*)
**pandeo** *m* warping, bulging, buckling, sagging, bending
**pandera** *f* (mus.) tambourine
**panderada** *f* tambourines; tambourine players; (coll.) nonsense
**panderazo** *m* blow with a tambourine
**pandereta** *f* (mus.) tambourine
**panderete** *m* (mus.) tambourine; brick wall in which bricks are laid on edge
**pandereteear** *vn* to celebrate playing the tambourine, to sing and dance and play the tambourine
**pandereteo** *m* celebrating and playing the tambourine, singing and dancing and playing the tambourine
**panderetero -ra** *mf* tambourine player; tambourine maker or dealer
**pandero** *m* (mus.) tambourine; paper kite; (coll.) jabberer, silly chatterbox
**pandiculación** *f* stretching, pandiculation
**pandilla** *f* party, faction; gang, band; picnic, excursion; stacking cards
**pandillaje** *m* banding together; leaguing, intriguing
**pandillar** *va* to form into bands or gangs; **pandillar el naipe** (slang) to stack the cards
**pandillero** or **pandillista** *m* gang leader
**pando -da** *adj* bulging; slow-moving; slow, deliberate; *m* plain between two mountains; *f* gallery of a cloister; **panda** *m* (zool.) panda; **panda gigante** (zool.) giant panda
**pandorada** *f* evil, misfortune
**pandorga** *f* kite; (coll.) fat, lazy woman
**panecillo** *m* roll, manchet, crescent; crescent (*crescent-shaped object*)
**panegírico -ca** *adj* panegyrical; *m* panegyric
**panegirista** *mf* panegyrist
**panegirizar** §76 *va* to panegyrize, to eulogize
**panel** *m* panel; (elec.) panel; (naut.) removable floor board
**panela** *f* prism-shaped cake; corncake; (her.) poplar leaf (*on a shield*)
**panenteísmo** *m* (theol.) panentheism
**panera** *f* granary; bread basket; (dial.) bread tray
**panero** *m* baker's basket; round mat
**paneslavismo** *m* Pan-Slavism
**paneslavista** *adj* Pan-Slav or Pan-Slavic; *mf* Pan-Slavist
**panetela** *f* (cook.) panada; panetella (*cigar*)
**panetería** *f* pantry of royal palace
**panetero -ra** *mf* pantler
**Panfilia** *f* Pamphylia
**panfilismo** *m* extreme gentleness, great mildness
**pánfilo -la** *adj* slow, sluggish; discouraged; *mf* sluggard
**panfletista** *mf* pamphleteer
**panfleto** *m* pamphlet
**pangelín** *m* (bot.) angelin
**pangénesis** *f* (biol.) pangenesis
**pangermanismo** *m* Pan-Germanism
**pangermanista** *adj* Pan-German, Pan-Germanic; *mf* Pan-German
**pangolín** *m* (zool.) pangolin
**panhelénico -ca** *adj* Panhellenic
**panhelenismo** *m* Panhellenism
**paniaguado** *m* (archaic) servant, minion; (coll.) protégé, favorite
**pánico -ca** *adj* panic, panicky; *m* panic
**panícula** *f* (bot.) panicle
**paniculado -da** *adj* (bot.) paniculate
**panicular** *adj* pannicular
**panículo** *m* (anat.) panniculus; **panículo adiposo** (anat.) panniculus adiposus
**paniego -ga** *adj* bread-eating; wheat-bearing; *m* (dial.) charcoal bag
**panificación** *f* panification, making bread
**panificar** §86 *va* to make (*flour*) into bread; to convert (*pasture land*) into wheat fields
**panique** *m* (zool.) flying fox
**panislamismo** *m* Pan-Islamism
**panislamista** *adj* Pan-Islamic; *mf* Pan-Islamist
**panizal** *m* field of foxtail millet; (dial.) foam on cider
**panizo** *m* (bot.) Italian millet, foxtail millet; (Am.) gangue; **panizo de las Indias** (bot.) Indian corn; **panizo negro** (bot.) sorghum
**panjí** *m* (*pl:* **-jíes**) (bot.) China tree
**panocha** *f* ear of grain; ear of corn; (bot.) panicle; bunch of small fish fried with tails sticking together; bunch of fruit hung up for keeping; (Am.) panocha (*brown sugar; candy made from it*)
**panoja** *f* ear of grain; ear of corn; (bot.) panicle; bunch of small fish fried with tails sticking together; bunch of fruit hung up for keeping
**panol** *m* var. of **pañol**
**panoli** *m* (slang) simpleton
**panoplia** *f* panoply; wall trophy; study of ancient weapons
**panorama** *m* panorama
**panorámico -ca** *adj* panoramic
**panoso -sa** *adj* mealy
**panqué** *m* or **panqueque** *m* pancake
**pantagruélico -ca** *adj* Pantagruelian or Pantagruelic
**pantalón** *m* trousers; **pantalones** *mpl* trousers, pants, pantaloons; **calzarse** or **ponerse los pantalones** (coll.) to wear the pants, to

wear the trousers (*said of a wife*); **pantalón de agua** (aer.) emergency water ballast bag (*built in two sections and resembling a pair of trousers suspended at the waist, each leg being full of water and the valve being at the lower end of each leg*); **pantalón de salvamento** (naut.) breeches buoy; **pantalones de equitación** riding breeches; **pantalones de golf** golf trousers, knickerbockers; **pantálon rana** coveralls

**pantalla** *f* lamp shade; fire screen; motion-picture screen; television screen; person standing in front of another, person standing in the way; blind (*person concealing another's actions*); (phys.) screen; (fig.) screen (*moving pictures*); (Am.) fan; **llevar a la pantalla** to put (*a play*) on the screen; **servir de pantalla a** to be a blind for (*someone*); **pantalla acústica** (rad.) baffle; **pantalla de chimenea** fire screen; **pantalla fluorescente** (phys.) fluorescent screen; **pantalla plateada** silver screen (*movies*); **pantalla televisora** television screen

**pantanal** *m* swampland

**pantanizar** §76 *vr* to become marshy or swampy; to dam up

**pantano** *m* bog, marsh, swamp; dam, reservoir; trouble, obstacle, morass; **Pantanos Pontinos** Pontine Marshes

**pantanoso -sa** *adj* marshy, swampy; muddy; knotty, difficult

**pantasana** *f* seine

**panteísmo** *m* pantheism

**panteísta** *adj* pantheistic; *mf* pantheist

**panteístico -ca** *adj* pantheistic

**panteón** *m* pantheon; mausoleum; cemetery

**pantera** *f* (zool.) panther (*Panthera pardus*)

**pantógrafo** *m* pantograph; (elec.) pantograph

**pantómetra** *f* pantometer

**pantomima** *f* pantomime

**pantomímico -ca** *adj* pantomimic

**pantomimo** *m* pantomimist

**pantoque** *m* (naut.) bilge

**pantorrilla** *f* calf (*of leg*)

**pantorrillera** *f* padded stocking

**pantorrilludo -da** *adj* thick-calved

**pantoténico -ca** *adj* pantothenic

**pantufla** *f* slipper, house slipper

**pantuflazo** *m* blow with a slipper, slippering

**pantuflo** *m* var. of **pantufla**

**panza** *f* paunch; belly (*e.g., of a vase*); (zool.) paunch, rumen (*of ruminant*); **panza de burra** (coll.) dark overcast (*sky*)

**panzada** *f* push with the belly; (coll.) bellyful

**panzón -zona** *adj* big-bellied; *m* big belly

**panzudo -da** *adj* big-bellied, paunchy

**pañal** *m* diaper; shirttail; **pañales** *mpl* swaddling clothes; infancy; early stages

**pañalón** *m* (coll.) sloppy-looking person

**pañería** *f* dry goods; cloths; dry-goods store, dry-goods department (*of a store*); cloth store, cloth department

**pañero -ra** *adj* dry-goods, cloth; *mf* dry-goods dealer, clothier

**pañete** *m* light, thin cloth; **pañetes** *mpl* trunks (*worn by fishermen*); breechcloth (*of crucifix*)

**pañito** *m* small cloth; **pañito de adorno** doily

**pañizuelo** *m* var. of **pañuelo**

**paño** *m* cloth; paper (*e.g., of needles*); breadth (*of cloth*); spot (*on face*); growth over eye; blur (*in mirror, precious stone, etc.*); hanging, drapery; (naut.) sailcloth, canvas; (Am.) shawl, kerchief; **al paño** (theat.) off-stage; **conocer el paño** (coll.) to know one's business, to know what one is up to; **poner el paño al púlpito** (coll.) to hold forth, to speak ex cathedra; **paño de adorno** antimacassar; **paño de altar** altar cloth; **paño de arrás** arras; **paño de cáliz** (eccl.) chalice veil; **paño de cocina** washrag, dishcloth; **paño de lágrimas** recourse, stand-by, helping hand; **paño de limpiar** cleaning rag; **paño de manos** towel; **paño de mesa** tablecloth; **paño de tumba** crape; **paño mortuorio** pall, hearsecloth; **paño pardillo** sacking, cheap coarse cloth; **paños calientes** (coll.) half measures; **paños menores** underclothing

**pañol** *m* (naut.) storeroom

**pañolería** *f* handkerchief shop; handkerchief business

**pañolero -ra** *mf* handkerchief maker or seller; *m* (naut.) storekeeper, yeoman

**pañoleta** *f* fichu; triangular plot of ground

**pañolón** *m* large shawl, scarf

**pañoso -sa** *adj* ragged, in rags; *f* (coll.) cloak, cloth cape

**pañuelo** *m* handkerchief; shawl; **pañuelo de bolsillo** or **de la mano** pocket handkerchief; **pañuelo de hierbas** bandana; **pañuelo para el cuello** scarf

**papa** *f* potato; (coll.) fake, hoax; (coll.) food, grub; (Am.) snap, cinch; **papas** (coll.) pap; **echar papas** (Am.) to fib, to lie; **no saber ni papa** (Am.) to not know a thing; **papa de caña** (bot.) Jerusalem artichoke; *m* pope; (coll.) papa; **papa negro** black pope

**papá** *m* (*pl:* **-pás**) (coll.) papa; **papás** *mpl* papa and mama

**papable** *adj* papable; eligible

**papacito** *m* (Am.) papa, daddy

**papada** *f* double chin; dewlap

**papadilla** *f* flesh under the chin

**papado** *m* papacy

**papafigo** *m* (orn.) figpecker; (orn.) golden oriole

**papagaya** *f* female parrot

**papagayo** *m* (orn.) parrot; (bot.) Joseph's-coat; (bot.) caladium; (ichth.) wrasse, peacock fish; (ichth.) roosterfish, papagallo; chatterbox; **papagayo de noche** (orn.) oilbird

**papahigo** *m* winter cap (*covering head, ears, and neck*)

**papahuevos** *m* (*pl:* **-vos**) (coll.) simpleton; (Am.) big-headed dwarf (*in a procession*)

**papaína** *f* (biochem.) papain

**papal** *adj* papal; *m* (Am.) potato field

**papalino -na** *adj* papal; *f* sunbonnet; (coll.) drunk (*spell of drinking*)

**papamoscas** *m* (*pl:* **-cas**) (orn.) flycatcher; (coll.) simpleton

**papanatas** *m* (*pl:* **-tas**) (coll.) simpleton, gawk

**papandujo -ja** *adj* (coll.) too soft, overripe

**papar** *va* to eat without chewing; (coll.) to eat; (coll.) to pay little attention to, to pass over hurriedly

**páparo** *m* gawk, gump

**paparote -ta** *mf* simpleton, boob

**paparrabias** *mf* (*pl:* **-bias**) (coll.) grouch, crab

**paparrasolla** *f* hobgoblin

**paparrucha** *f* (coll.) hoax; (coll.) trifle, inconsequentiality

**paparruchada** *f* (Am.) triviality, bagatelle

**papasal** *m* trifle, pastime

**papatoste** *m* var. of **papanatas**

**papaveráceo -a** *adj* (bot.) papaveraceous

**papavientos** *m* (*pl:* **-tos**) (orn.) goatsucker

**papaya** *f* papaya (*fruit*)

**papayo** *m* (bot.) papaya (*tree*)

**pápaz** *m* (used by African Moors) Christian priest

**papazgo** *m* papacy

**papel** *m* paper; piece of paper; rôle, part; character, figure; **desempeñar** or **hacer un papel** to play a rôle; **hacer papel** to cut a figure, to be somebody; **hacer buen papel** to make a good showing, to come out all right; **hacer el papel de** to play the rôle of; **hacer gran papel** to splurge, to cut a wide swath; **hacer mal papel** to come out badly, to fail; **tener buenos papeles** to have good backing; to be in the right; **traer los papeles mojados** (coll.) to bear false news; **papel alquitranado** tar paper; **papel biblia** Bible paper; **papel buscapolos** (elec.) pole-determining paper; **papel carbón** carbon paper; **papel cebolla** onionskin; **papel continuo** paper in rolls; **papel corrugado** corrugated paper; **papel cuché** art paper; **papel de barba** (theat.) rôle of an old man; **papel de barbas** untrimmed paper; **papel de calcar** tracing paper; **papel de cartas** letter paper; **papel de China** India paper; **papel de cúrcuma** (chem.) curcuma paper, turmeric paper; **papel de empapelar** or **de entapizar** wallpaper; **papel de escribir** writing paper; **papel de esmeril** emery paper; **papel de estaño** tin foil; **papel de estraza** brown wrapping paper; **papel de excusado** toilet paper;

**papel de filtro** filter paper; **papel de fumar** cigarette paper; **papel de lija** sandpaper; **papel de luto** mourning paper; **papel de marquilla** drawing paper; **papel de música** music paper; **papel de oficio** foolscap; **papel de ozono** (chem.) ozone paper; **papel de periódico** newsprint; **papel de seda** onionskin; tissue paper; **papel de segundón** second fiddle; **papel de tornasol** litmus paper; **papel higiénico** toilet paper; **papel mojado** scrap of paper; (coll.) trifle, triviality; **papel moneda** paper money; **papel pergamino** parchment paper; **papel pintado** wallpaper; **papel rayado** ruled paper; **papel satinado** glazed paper; **papel secante** blotting paper; **papel sepia** (phot.) sepia paper; **papel viejo** waste paper; **papel vitela** vellum paper; **papel volante** printed leaflet, handbill

**papelear** *vn* to look through papers; (coll.) to cut a figure, make a show

**papelejo** *m* scrap of paper

**papeleo** *m* looking through papers; red tape

**papelera** *f* see **papelero**

**papelería** *f* stationery store; scattered paper, mess of papers

**papelerío** *m* lot of paper; scattered paper, mess of papers

**papelero -ra** *adj* boastful, showy; (pertaining to) paper; *mf* paper manufacturer, paper dealer, stationer; *m* (bot.) paper mulberry; (Am.) paper boy; *f* paper case; writing desk; lot of papers; wastebasket

**papeleta** *f* slip of paper; card, file card; pawn ticket; examination paper; ballot; (coll.) tough problem; **no saberse la papeleta** to not know one's business; **papeleta de empeño** or **del monte** pawn ticket; **papeleta de fichero** filing card

**papeletizar** **§76** *va* to abstract on slips of paper or cards

**papelillo** *m* cigarette; paper (*of powdered medicine*)

**papelina** *f* tall drinking glass; poplin

**papelista** *m* papermaker, paper manufacturer; paper dealer, stationer; paper hanger; archivist

**papelón -lona** *adj* (coll.) bluffing, four-flushing; *mf* (coll.) bluffer, fourflusher; *m* worthless piece of paper; thin cardboard; (Am.) crystallized cane syrup

**papelonear** *vn* (coll.) to bluff, to four-flush

**papelorio** *m* mess of paper or papers

**papelote** *m* worthless paper, worthless piece of paper; (Am.) kite, child's kite

**papel-prensa** *m* newsprint

**papelucho** *m* var. of **papelote**

**papera** *f* goiter; mumps; **paperas** *fpl* scrofula

**papero** *m* pap pot; pap

**papialbillo** *m* (zool.) genet

**papiamento** *m* Curaçao Creole (*language of Curaçao and other Netherlands colonies of South America*)

**papila** *f* (anat. & bot.) papilla; **papila del gusto** (anat.) taste bud

**papilar** *adj* papillary

**papilionáceo -a** *adj* (bot.) papilionaceous

**papiloma** *m* (path.) papilloma

**papilla** *f* pap; guile, deceit

**papillote** *m* hair twisted in curlpaper; *f* (cook.) papillote, paper wrapper

**papín** *m* homemade sweet cake

**papión** *m* (zool.) papion

**papiráceo -a** *adj* papyraceous

**papiro** *m* (bot.) papyrus; papyrus (*strip of pith of this plant; record written on papyrus*)

**papirolada** *f* var. of **pampirolada**

**papirotada** *f* fillip; (coll.) folly, piece of stupidity

**papirotazo** *m* fillip

**papirote** *m* fillip; (coll.) nincompoop

**papisa** *f* popess; **Juana la papisa, la papisa Juana** Pope Joan

**papismo** *m* papistry, popery

**papista** *adj & mf* papist

**papístico -ca** *adj* papistic or papistical

**papo** *m* craw, maw; dewlap; puff (*in a dress*); (bot.) pappus; **papo de viento** (naut.) pocket in partly opened sail

**papón** *m* bogeyman

**paporrear** *va* to whip, to flog

**papú -púa** (*pl:* **-púes** & **-púas**) *adj & mf* Papuan

**Papuasia, la** Papua

**papudo -da** *adj* big-crawed; goitery

**papujado -da** *adj* full-gorged; swollen, puffed up

**pápula** *f* (path.) papule

**papuloso -sa** *adj* papulose

**paq.** abr. of **paquete**

**paquear** *va* to snipe at; *vn* to snipe

**paquebote** *m* packet boat

**paqueo** *m* sniping

**paquete -ta** *adj* (coll.) chic, dolled up; (Am.) insincere, self-important; *m* package, parcel, bundle, bale; packet boat; (coll.) sport, dandy; **en paquete aparte** under separate cover, in a separate package; **paquete de planchas fotográficas** film pack; **paquete regalo** (*pl:* **paquetes regalos**) gift package; **paquetes postales** parcel post (*service*)

**paquetería** *f* smallwares, notions

**paquetero -ra** *adj* packing, wrapping; *mf* parcel maker, wrapper; general distributor of bundles of newspapers; *m* (dial.) smuggler

**paquidermo -ma** *adj* (zool.) pachydermous; *m* (zool.) pachyderm

**paquisandra** *f* (bot.) pachysandra

**Paquistán, el** Pakistan

**Paquita** *f* Fanny

**par** *adj* like, similar, equal; (math.) even ‖ *m* pair, couple; principal rafter; peer (*equal; nobleman*); (elec. & mech.) couple; (math.) even number; **a pares** in twos; **al par** equally; jointly; at the same time; **de par en par** wide-open; completely; overtly; **en par de** on par with, equal to; **sin par** peerless, matchless, unequaled; **par de fuerzas** (mech.) couple; **¿pares o nones?** odd or even? (*guessing game*); **par motor** (mech.) torque; **par térmico** (elec.) thermocouple; **par termoeléctrico** (elec.) thermoelectric couple ‖ *f* par; **a la par** equally; jointly; at the same time; (com.) at par; **a la par con** abreast with; **a la par que** as well as; while, at the same time that; **bajo la par** (com.) below par or under par; **sobre la par** (com.) above par

**para** *prep* to, for; towards; compared to; by (*a certain time*); **para** + *inf* in order to + *inf;* about to + *inf;* **para con** towards; **para mí** for me; to myself; **para que** in order that, so that; **¿para qué?** for what reason?

**pára** *3d sg pres ind of* **parar**

**parabién** *m* congratulation; **dar el parabién a** to congratulate

**parábola** *f* parable; (geom.) parabola

**parabólico -ca** *adj* parabolic; (geom.) parabolic

**paraboloide** *m* (geom.) paraboloid

**parabrisa** *m* or **parabrisas** *m* (*pl:* **-sas**) windshield; **parabrisas panorámico** (aut.) wraparound windshield

**paracaídas** *m* (*pl:* **-das**) parachute; **salvarse en paracaídas** to parachute to safety; **paracaídas piloto** pilot chute

**paracaidismo** *m* parachute jumping

**paracaidista** *mf* parachutist; *m* (mil.) paratrooper

**Paracelso** *m* Paracelsus

**paracentesis** *f* paracentesis

**paracleto** or **paráclito** *m* Paraclete

**paracronismo** *m* parachronism

**parachispas** *m* (*pl:* **-pas**) spark arrester; (elec.) spark arrester

**parachoques** *m* (*pl:* **-ques**) (rail.) bumper, bumping post; (aut.) bumper

**parada** *f* see **parado**

**paradera** *f* sluice gate, floodgate; fishing seine

**paradero** *m* end; whereabouts; stopping place; (Am.) railroad station

**paradiclorobenceno** *m* (chem.) paradichlorobenzene

**paradigma** *m* (gram. & fig.) paradigm

**paradina** *f* scrub pasture with sheep pens

**paradisíaco -ca** *adj* paradisiacal

**paradislero** *m* hunter on the watch; newsmonger

**parado -da** *adj* slow, spiritless, witless; idle, out of work, unemployed; stopped; closed; (Am.) straight, standing; (Am.) proud, stiff; **salir mejor parado** to come off better | *f* stop; end; stay, suspension; shutdown; stake (*in gambling*); dam; stall (*for cattle*); stud farm; parry (*in fencing*); relay (*of horses*); post (*for keeping horses for relays*); (mil.) parade, dress parade, review; (mus.) pause; **doblar la parada** to double the stakes; to double one's bid; **salir a la parada a** to go to meet; **parada de taxi** taxi stand; **parada en cuarta** (fencing) parry of or in carte or quarte; **parada en primera** (fencing) parry of or in prime; **parada en segunda** (fencing) parry of or in seconde; **parada en tercera** (fencing) parry of or in tierce
**paradoja** *f* see **paradojo**
**paradójico -ca** *adj* paradoxical
**paradojo -ja** *adj* paradoxical; *f* paradox
**parador -dora** *adj* stopping; heavy-betting; *mf* heavy bettor; *m* inn, wayside inn, hostelry; **parador de turismo** motel
**paraestatal** *adj* government-coöperating, government-affiliated (*e.g., agency*)
**parafina** *f* paraffin
**parafraseador -dora** *adj* paraphrasing; *mf* paraphraser
**parafrasear** *va* to paraphrase
**paráfrasis** *f* (*pl:* **-sis**) paraphrase
**parafraste** *m* paraphrast
**parafrástico -ca** *adj* paraphrastic
**paragoge** *f* (gram.) paragoge
**paragógico -ca** *adj* paragogic
**paragolpes** *m* (*pl:* **-pes**) (rail.) buffer, bumper
**paragrafía** *f* (path.) paragraphia
**parágrafo** *m* paragraph
**paragranizo** *m* canvas cover to protect crops from hail
**paraguas** *m* (*pl:* **-guas**) umbrella
**paraguatán** *m* (bot.) Central American madder (*Sickingia tinctoria*)
**Paraguay, el** Paraguay
**paraguaya** *f* see **paraguayo**
**paraguayano -na** *adj & mf* Paraguayan
**paraguayo -ya** *adj & mf* Paraguayan; *f* flat-shaped peach
**paragüería** *f* umbrella store
**paragüero -ra** *mf* umbrella maker; umbrella vendor; *m* umbrella stand
**parahuso** *m* pump drill
**paraíso** *m* paradise; paradise (*top gallery of theater*); **paraíso de los bobos** (coll.) air castles; **paraíso terrenal** paradise, garden of Eden
**paraje** *m* place, spot; state, condition
**parajismero -ra** *adj* grimacing
**parajismo** *m* face, grimace
**paral** *m* putlog; (naut.) ground ways
**paraláctico -ca** *adj* parallactic
**paralaje** *f* parallax
**paralar** *va* to putlog
**paralasis** *f* (*pl:* **-sis**) var. of **paralaje**
**paralaxi** *f* var. of **paralaje**
**paraldehido** *m* (chem.) paraldehyde
**paralela** *f* see **paralelo**
**paralelar** *va* to parallel, to compare
**paralelepípedo** *m* (geom.) parallelepiped or parallelepipedon
**paralelismo** *m* parallelism
**paralelizar** §76 *va* to parallel, to compare
**paralelo -la** *adj* parallel; *m* (geog. & fig.) parallel; **en paralelo** (elec.) in parallel; *f* (geom. & fort.) parallel; **paralelas** *fpl* (sport) parallel bars
**paralelogramo** *m* (geom.) parallelogram
**paralipómenos** *mpl* (Bib.) Paralipomena
**paralipsis** *f* (*pl:* **-sis**) (rhet.) paralipsis
**parálisis** *f* (*pl:* **-sis**) paralysis; **parálisis agitante** (path.) paralysis agitans; **parálisis cerebral infantil** (path.) cerebral palsy; **parálisis infantil** (path.) infantile paralysis
**paraliticar** §86 *vr* to become paralyzed
**paralítico -ca** *adj & mf* paralytic
**paralización** *f* paralization
**paralizador -dora** *adj* paralyzing
**paralizar** §76 *va* to paralyze; (fig.) to paralyze; *vr* to become paralyzed

**paralogismo** *m* (log.) paralogism
**paralogizar** §76 *va* to try to convince with specious arguments; *vr* to paralogize
**paramagnético -ca** *adj* paramagnetic
**paramagnetismo** *m* paramagnetism
**paramecio** *m* (zool.) paramecium
**paramentar** *va* to adorn, bedeck; to caparison; to face, to surface
**paramento** *m* adornment, ornament; hangings; caparison; face, surface; **paramentos sacerdotales** (eccl.) liturgical vestments
**paramera** *f* bleak, barren country
**parámetro** *m* (math.) parameter
**páramo** *m* high barren plain; bleak windy spot; (Am.) cold drizzle
**parancero** *m* birdcatcher
**parangón** *m* comparison
**parangona** *f* (print.) paragon
**parangonar** *va* to compare
**paranieves** *m* (*pl:* **-ves**) snow fence
**paraninfo** *m* assembly hall, auditorium; speaker at opening exercises (*of a university*); bringer of joy; (poet.) best man, groomsman
**paranoia** *f* (path.) paranoia
**paranoico -ca** *adj & mf* paranoiac
**paranoya** *f* var. of **paranoia**
**paranza** *f* hunter's hut or blind
**parapetar** *va* to fortify with parapets; *vr* to fortify oneself with parapets; to protect oneself
**parapeto** *m* parapet; (fort.) parapet
**paraplejía** *f* (path.) paraplegia
**parapléjico -ca** *adj & mf* paraplegic
**parapoco** *mf* (*pl:* **parapoco**) (coll.) numskull
**parapsicología** *f* parapsychology
**parar** *m* lansquenet (*card game*); *va* to stop; to check; to change; to prepare; to put up, to stake; to parry; to order; to get, acquire; to fix (*attention*); (hunt.) to point (*game*); (print.) to set; (Am.) to prick up (*ears*); *vn* to stop; to put up (*e.g., in a hotel*); **sin parar** right away; **parar en** to become; to run to (*said of a train or rail line*); **parar a las manos de** or **en poder de** to come into the hands of; *vr* to stop; to stop work; to turn, to become; to be ready for danger; to stand up on end (*said, e.g., of hair*); (Am.) to stand up; **pararse a** + *inf* to stop to + *inf*, to pause to + *inf;* **pararse en** to pay attention to
**pararrayo** or **pararrayos** *m* (*pl:* **-yos**) lightning rod; lightning arrester; **pararrayo de cuernos** horn lightning arrester
**parasanga** *f* parasang
**parasceve** *m* parasceve
**paraselene** *f* (meteor.) paraselene
**parasicología** *f* var. of **parapsicología**
**parasimpático -ca** *adj & m* (anat. & physiol.) parasympathetic
**parasíntesis** *f* (gram.) parasynthesis
**parasismo** *m* var. of **paroxismo**
**parasitario -ria** *adj* parasitic
**parasiticida** *adj & m* parasiticide
**parasítico -ca** *adj* parasitic
**parasitismo** *m* parasitism
**parásito -ta** *adj* parasitic; (elec.) stray; *m* (biol. & fig.) parasite; **parásitos atmosféricos** (rad.) atmospherics, static
**parasito -ta** *adj & m* var. of **parásito**
**parasitología** *f* parasitology
**parasitológico -ca** *adj* parasitological
**parasitólogo -ga** *mf* parasitologist
**parasol** *m* parasol; (bot.) umbel
**parata** *f* step terrace
**paratífico -ca** or **paratifoide** *adj* paratyphoid
**paratifoidea** *f* (path.) paratyphoid fever
**paratiroideo -a** *adj* parathyroid
**paratiroides** *adj & m* parathyroid
**paratopes** *m* (*pl:* **-pes**) (rail.) bumper, bumping post
**paraulata** *f* (orn.) Venezuelan thrush
**paraván** *m* screen
**paraviento** *m* screen; bicycle windshield (*of celluloid*)
**parca** *f* & **Parcas** *fpl* see **parco**
**parce** *m* reward card (*in school*)
**parcela** *f* plot, piece of ground; particle
**parcelación** *f* or **parcelamiento** *m* parceling (*of land*)
**parcelar** *va* to parcel, to divide into lots
**parcial** *adj* partial; partisan; *mf* partisan

**parcialidad** *f* partiality; faction, party; clique; partisanship; sociability, friendliness
**parcidad** *f* var. of **parquedad**
**parcimonia** *f* var. of **parsimonia**
**parcionero -ra** *adj* participant; *mf* participant; accomplice
**parcísimo -ma** *adj super* very or most frugal; very or most moderate
**parco -ca** *adj* frugal, sparing; moderate; *f* (poet.) death; **Parcas** *fpl* (myth.) Parcae, Fates
**parcha** *f* (bot.) passionflower
**parchar** *va* (Am.) to mend, to patch
**parchazo** *m* large plaster; (naut.) bang of a sail against mast or yard; (coll.) gyp, swindle; **pegar un parchazo a** (coll.) to gyp, to swindle
**parche** *m* plaster, sticking plaster; patch; drum; drumhead; daub, botch, splotch; **pegar un parche a** (coll.) to gyp, to swindle; **parche poroso** porous plaster
**parchesí** *m* parcheesi
**parchista** *m* (coll.) sponger
**pardal** *adj* rustic; *m* (orn.) linnet; (orn.) swallow; (zool.) leopard; (zool.) camelopard; (bot.) wolfsbane; (coll.) sly fellow
**pardear** *vn* to be drabbish, to appear drab
**pardejón -jona** *adj* (Am.) drabbish
**pardela** *f* (orn.) small sea gull
**pardiez** *interj* (coll.) by Jove!
**pardillo -lla** *adj* drab; *m* (orn.) redpoll, linnet; (coll.) sly fellow
**pardisco -ca** *adj* var. of **pardusco**
**pardo -da** *adj* brown; drab; dark; cloudy; dull, flat (*voice*); dark (*beer*); (Am.) mulatto; *mf* (Am.) mulatto; *m* brown; drab; (zool.) leopard
**pardusco -ca** *adj* drabbish, grayish
**pareado -da** *adj* in the form of a couplet, rhymed; *m* couplet
**parear** *va* to pair; to match; (taur.) to thrust banderillas in; *vr* to pair off
**parecencia** *f* resemblance, likeness
**parecer** *m* opinion; look, mien, countenance; **a mi parecer** to my mind, in my opinion; **por el bien parecer** for appearance, to save appearances; §34 *vn* to appear; to show up; to look, to seem; **a lo que parece** or **al parecer** apparently; **cambiar** or **mudar de parecer** to change one's mind; **me parece que sí** I guess so, so it seems to me; **¿qué le parece?** what do you think?, what is your opinion?; **según parece** apparently; **parecer** + *inf* to seem to + *inf*; *vr* to look alike, to resemble each other; **parecerse a** to look like
**parecido -da** *adj* like, similar; **parecidos -das** *adj pl* alike, e.g., **estas casas son parecidas** these houses are alike; **bien parecido** good-looking; **mal parecido** ill-favored, hard-looking; **parecido a** like, e.g., **esta casa es parecida a la otra** this house is like the other one; *m* similarity, resemblance, likeness
**pared** *f* wall; **dejar pegado a la pared** (coll.) to nonplus; **entre cuatro paredes** shut in, withdrawn; **hasta la pared de enfrente** (coll.) to the limit, with all one's might; **pared maestra** main wall; **pared medianera** partition wall, party wall; **pared por medio** partition wall; next door; **pared supersónica** sonic barrier
**paredaño -ña** *adj* adjoining, separated by a wall
**paredón** *m* wall standing amid ruins; thick wall
**paregórico -ca** *adj* & *m* paregoric
**pareja** *f* see **parejo**
**parejero -ra** *adj* even, equal; (Am.) servile, cringing; *m* (Am.) steed, race horse
**parejo -ja** *adj* equal, like; even, smooth; **por parejo** or **por un parejo** alike, on a par; *f* pair, couple; dancing partner (*male or female*); **parejas** *fpl* pair (*of cards*); **correr parejas** or **a las parejas** to be abreast, arrive together; to go together, match, be equal; **correr parejas con** to keep up with, to keep abreast of
**parejura** *f* equality, similarity; evenness, smoothness
**paremia** *f* paroemia, proverb
**paremiología** *f* paroemiology
**paremiólogo -ga** *mf* paroemiologist
**parénesis** *f* (*pl:* **-sis**) admonition, exhortation
**parenético -ca** *adj* admonitory
**parénquima** *m* (anat. & bot.) parenchyma
**parenquimatoso -sa** *adj* parenchymatous
**parental** *adj* parental
**parentela** *f* kinsfolk, relations
**parenteral** *adj* parenteral
**parentesco** *m* relationship; bond, tie
**paréntesis** *m* (*pl:* **-sis**) (gram.) parenthesis; (fig.) parenthesis, break, interval; **dentro de un paréntesis** or **entre paréntesis** in parentheses; **entre paréntesis** or **por paréntesis** parenthetically; by the way
**parentético -ca** *adj* parenthetic or parenthetical
**pareo** *m* pairing; matching
**paresa** *f* peeress
**paresia** or **paresis** *f* (path.) paresis
**parético -ca** *adj* & *mf* paretic
**pargo** *m* (ichth.) porgy; **pargo colorado** (ichth.) dog snapper; **pargo criollo** or **guachinango** (ichth.) red snapper, muttonfish, mutton snapper
**parhelia** *f* var. of **parhelio**
**parhélico -ca** *adj* parheliacal or parhelic
**parhelio** *m* (meteor.) parhelion
**parhilera** *f* ridgepole
**paria** *mf* & **parias** *fpl* see **pario**
**paría** *f* peerage
**parián** *m* (Am.) market
**parición** *f* parturition time of cattle
**parida** *adj fem* recently delivered; *f* woman recently delivered
**paridad** *f* parity; comparison
**paridera** *adj* prolific (*female*); *f* parturition; parturition time; parturition place
**paridora** *adj* prolific (*female*)
**pariente -ta** *adj* related; *mf* relative; (coll.) spouse
**parietal** *adj* parietal; (anat., bot. & zool.) parietal; *m* (anat.) parietal
**parificación** *f* exemplification
**parificar** §86 *va* to exemplify, to show by comparison
**parigual** *adj* & *m* like, equal
**parihuela** *f* or **parihuelas** *fpl* handbarrow; stretcher
**pario -ria** *adj* & *mf* Parian; **paria** *mf* pariah (*of low caste of India and Burma*); outcast, pariah; **parias** *fpl* tribute, homage; (anat.) placenta
**paripé** *m* (slang) arrogance, haughtiness; **dar el paripé a** (slang) to cajole, deceive; **hacer el paripé** (slang) to put on airs
**paripinado -da** *adj* (bot.) paripinnate
**parir** *va* to bear, to give birth to, to bring forth; *vn* to give birth; to lay eggs; to come forth, to come to light; to express oneself, to talk well
**Paris** *m* (myth.) Paris
**París** *m* Paris
**parisiense** *adj* & *mf* Parisian
**parisilábico -ca** or **parisílabo -ba** *adj* parisyllabic
**parisino -na** *adj* (coll.) Parisian
**paritario -ria** *adj* labor-management (*board*)
**parla** *f* ease, facility in speaking; chatter, gossip
**parlador -dora** *adj* chattering, gossiping; *mf* chatterbox, gossip
**parladuría** *f* chatter, gossip, talk
**parlaembalde** *mf* (*pl:* **parlaembalde**) (coll.) chatterbox
**parlamentar** *vn* to talk, chat; to parley
**parlamentario -ria** *adj* parliamentary; *mf* parliamentarian
**parlamentarismo** *m* parliamentarism
**parlamento** *m* parliament; parley; speech; (theat.) speech; **Parlamento Largo** (hist.) Long Parliament
**parlanchín -china** *adj* (coll.) chattering, jabbering; *mf* (coll.) chatterer, jabberer; *m* (orn.) garden warbler
**parlante** *adj* talking
**parlar** *vn* to speak with facility; to chatter, to gossip, to talk too much; to talk (*said, e.g., of a parrot*)
**parlatorio** *m* talk, chat; parlor
**parlería** *f* loquacity, garrulity; gossip; (poet.) song of birds; (poet.) babbling of brooks

**parlero -ra** *adj* loquacious, garrulous; gossipy; singing, song (*bird*); expressive (*eyes*); babbling (*brook or spring*)
**parleta** *f* (coll.) chat, idle talk, gabble
**parlón -lona** *adj* (coll.) talkative; *mf* (coll.) talker
**parlotear** *vn* (coll.) to prattle, jabber
**parloteo** *m* (coll.) prattle, jabber
**Parménides** *m* Parmenides
**parmesano -na** *adj & mf* Parmesan; *m* Parmesan (*cheese*)
**parnasiano -na** *adj* Parnassian
**parnaso** *m* Parnassus (*collection of poems*); **el Parnaso** Mount Parnassus
**parné** *m* (slang) dough, cash
**paro** *m* shutdown, work stoppage; lockout; (orn.) titmouse; (Am.) throw (*of dice*); **paro carbonero** (orn.) great titmouse; **paro forzoso** layoff, unemployment
**parodia** *f* parody, travesty
**parodiar** *va* to parody, to travesty
**paródico -ca** *adj* parodical
**parodista** *mf* parodist
**parola** *f* (coll.) fluency, volubility; (coll.) chat, idle talk
**parolero -ra** *adj* (coll.) chattering, jabbering
**pároli** *m* paroli, leaving one's stake and winnings in the pot
**parolina** *f* (coll.) var. of **parola**
**paronimia** *f* paronymy
**parónimo -ma** *adj* paronymous; *m* paronym
**paronomasia** *f* paronomasia
**parótida** *f* (anat.) parotid; **parótidas** *fpl* (path.) mumps
**parotideo -a** *adj* (anat.) parotid, parotidean; (path.) parotitic
**paroxismal** *adj* paroxysmal
**paroxismo** *m* paroxysm; (path.) paroxysm
**paroxítono -na** *adj & m* (phonet.) paroxytone
**parpadear** *vn* to blink, to wink; to flicker
**parpadeo** *m* blinking, winking; flicker
**párpado** *m* eyelid
**parpar** *vn* to quack
**parque** *m* park; parking; parking space; parking lot; park, garden (*for wild animals*); equipment, outfit; (mil.) park; **parque de atracciones** amusement park; **parque de incendios** fire station; **parque de recreo** pleasure ground; amusement park; **parque para caballos** paddock; **parque zoológico** zoölogical garden
**parquear** *va* var. of **aparquear**
**parquedad** *f* frugality; moderation
**parqueo** *m* (Am.) parking
**parquet** *m* market, stock market
**parra** *f* (bot.) grapevine; earthen jar; **subirse a la parra** (coll.) to blow up, to hit the ceiling
**parrado -da** *adj* spreading
**parrafada** *f* (coll.) confidential interview
**parrafeada** *f* (Am.) confidential chat
**parrafear** *vn* to chat confidentially
**parrafeo** *m* confidential chat
**párrafo** *m* paragraph; (coll.) chat; **echar párrafos** (coll.) to gossip away; **echar un párrafo** (coll.) to chat, have a chat; **párrafo aparte** (coll.) changing the subject
**parragón** *m* assayer's standard silver bar
**parral** *m* vine arbor, grape arbor; place full of vine arbors; wild, untrimmed vineyard; large earthen jar for honey
**parranda** *f* (coll.) spree, party; **andar de parranda** (coll.) to go out on a spree, to go out to celebrate
**parrandear** *vn* (coll.) to go out on a spree, to go out to celebrate
**parrandero -ra** *adj* (coll.) reveling; *mf* (coll.) reveler
**parrandista** *mf* (coll.) reveler, carouser
**parrar** *vn* to spread out (*said of trees and plants*)
**parricida** *adj* patricidal; parricidal; *mf* patricide (*person*); parricide (*person*)
**parricidio** *m* patricide (*act*); parricide (*act*)
**parrilla** *f* grill, gridiron, broiler; grate, grating; earthen jug; grille (*e.g., of auto*); grill, grillroom; **asar a la parrilla** to broil
**parriza** *f* wild grapevine
**parro** *m* (orn.) duck
**párroco** *m* parson, parish priest
**parrocha** *f* (ichth.) small sardine; canned sardine
**parrón** *m* wild grapevine
**parroquia** *f* parish; parochial church; clientele, customers
**parroquial** *adj* parochial
**parroquialidad** *f* parochialism
**parroquiano -na** *adj* parochial, parish; *mf* parishioner; customer
**parsi** *adj* Parsic; *mf* Parsee or Parsi; *m* Parsee or Parsi (*dialect*)
**parsimonia** *f* parsimony; moderation
**parsimonioso -sa** *adj* parsimonious; moderate
**parsismo** *m* Parseeism
**parte** *f* part; share; party; side; direction; (theat. & mus.) part; (law) party; **partes** *fpl* parts, gifts, talent; faction; parts, genitals; **a parte de** apart from; **de buena parte** on good authority; **de la parte de** on the part of; **de un mes a esta parte** for about a month (*past*); **de parte a parte** from one end to the other, through and through; from one to the other; **de parte de** on the side of; on behalf of; **echar a mala parte** to look upon with disapproval; to use (*a word or phrase*) improperly; **en buena parte** in good part (*without taking offense*); **en ninguna parte** nowhere; **en parte** in part; **hacer las partes de** to act on behalf of; **la mayor parte** most, the majority; **por la mayor parte** for the most part; **por mi (su) parte** for or on my (his) part; **por otra parte** in another direction; elsewhere; on the other hand; **por todas partes** everywhere; **salva sea la parte** (coll.) excuse me for not mentioning where (*i.e., in what part of the body*); **tener parte con una mujer** to have intercourse with a woman; **tomar a mala parte** to look upon with disapproval; to use (*a word or phrase*) improperly; **tomar parte en** to take part in; **parte actora** (law) prosecution; plaintiff; **parte alicuanta** (math.) aliquant part; **parte alícuota** (math.) aliquot part; **parte de la oración** or **parte del discurso** (gram.) part of speech; **parte del león** lion's share; **parte de por medio** small-part actor; **partes contratantes** (dipl.) contracting parties; **parte por parte** in full; **partes naturales, pudendas** or **vergonzosas** privates, private parts; *m* dispatch, communiqué; **dar parte a** to inform; *adv* part, partly
**parteaguas** *m* (*pl:* **-guas**) divide, ridge; **parteaguas continental** continental divide
**partear** *va* to assist (*a woman*) in childbirth
**parteluz** *m* (*pl:* **-luces**) (arch.) mullion, sash bar
**partencia** *f* departure
**partenogénesis** *f* (biol.) parthenogenesis
**partenogenético -ca** *adj* parthenogenetic
**Partenón** *m* Parthenon
**partenueces** *m* (*pl:* **-ces**) nutcracker
**partera** *f* midwife
**partería** *f* midwifery
**partero** *m* accoucheur, man midwife
**parterre** *m* flower bed
**partesana** *f* (archaic) halberd
**Partia** *f* Parthia
**partible** *adj* divisible, separable
**partición** *f* partition, division
**particionero -ra** *adj & mf* participant
**participación** *f* communication, notification; participation; share (*in a lottery ticket*)
**participante** *adj* notifying; participant; *mf* notifier; participant; accomplice
**participar** *va* to communicate; to inform; **participar una cosa a una persona** to notify or inform a person of something; *vn* to participate; **participar de** to partake of; **participar en** to partake in, to participate in
**partícipe** *adj & mf* participant
**participial** *adj* participial
**participio** *m* (gram.) participle; **participio activo** or **de presente** (gram.) present participle; **participio pasivo** or **de pretérito** (gram.) past participle, perfect participle
**pártico -ca** *adj* Parthian
**partícula** *f* particle; (eccl., gram. & phys.) particle; **partícula nobiliaria** nobiliary particle; **partícula prepositiva** (gram.) prefix

**particular** *adj* particular; peculiar; private, personal; *m* particular (*item, point*); matter, subject; individual; private individual; **en particular** in particular; in private
**particularidad** *f* particularity; intimacy
**particularización** *f* particularization; specialization
**particularizar** §76 *va & vn* to particularize; *vr* to be distinguished, to stand out; **particularizarse en** + *inf* to specialize in + *ger*
**partida** *f* see **partido**
**partidamente** *adv* separately
**partidario -ria** *adj* partisan; *mf* partisan, supporter
**partidismo** *m* partisanship
**partidista** *adj & mf* partisan
**partido -da** *adj* generous, open-handed; (her.) party ‖ *m* (pol.) party; decision; profit, advantage; step, measure; deal, agreement; protection, support; match (*prospective partner in marriage*); district, county; area or circuit under care of a physician or surgeon; (sport) team; (sport) game, match; (sport) handicap, odds; (dial.) room; (Am.) part (*in hair*); **sacar partido de** to derive profit from; **tomar partido** to make up one's mind, take a stand, take sides; **partido conservador** (pol.) conservative party; **partido de desempate** (sport) play-off ‖ *f* departure; entry, item; certificate; party, group, band, gang; band of guerrillas; game; hand (*of cards*); set (*of tennis*); lot, shipment; (fig.) departure (*death*); (coll.) behavior; (Am.) part (*in hair*); **buena partida** (coll.) good turn; **echar una partida** to play a game (*e.g., of cards*); **mala partida** (coll.) mean trick; **partida de bautismo** certificate of baptism; **partida de campo** picnic; **partida de caza** hunting party; **partida de defunción** death certificate; **partida de matrimonio** marriage certificate; **partida de nacimiento** birth certificate; **partida de pesca** fishing party; **partida doble** (com.) double entry; **partida serrana** (coll.) dirty trick, double cross; **partida sencilla** or **simple** (com.) single entry
**partidor** *m* divider, separator, cleaver, splitter; (math.) divisor; **partidor de tensión** (rad.) voltage divider
**partidura** *f* part (*in hair*)
**partija** *f* small part; partition
**partil** *adj* (astrol.) partile
**partimento** or **partimiento** *m* partition, division
**partiquino -na** *mf* (mus.) singer of small parts
**partir** *va* to divide; to distribute; to share; to split, split open; to break, crack; to gash; (math.) to divide; (coll.) to upset, disconcert; *vn* to start, depart, leave, set out; to make up one's mind; **a partir de** beginning with; **partir a** + *inf* to start out to, to depart to + *inf;* **partir de** to reckon from; *vr* to become divided or split; to crack, to split
**partisano -na** *mf* (mil.) partisan
**partitivo -va** *adj* partitive; (gram.) partitive
**partitura** *f* (mus.) score
**parto -ta** *adj & mf* Parthian; *m* childbirth, delivery, labor; newborn child; product, offspring; prospect; brain child; **el parto de los montes** a great cry, but little wool; **estar de parto** to be in labor; **parto del ingenio** brain child
**parturición** *f* parturition
**parturienta** or **-te** *adj* parturient (*woman*); *f* woman in confinement
**párulis** *m* (*pl:* **-lis**) (path.) gumboil; (path.) phlegmon
**parva** *f* see **parvo**
**parvada** *f* heaps of unthreshed grain; flock, covey
**parvedad** *f* smallness, minuteness; light breakfast (*on fast days*)
**parvero** *m* long pile of grain for winnowing
**parvidad** *f* var. of **parvedad**
**parvificar** §86 *va* to make small; to diminish, lessen
**parvo -va** *adj* small, little; *f* light breakfast (*on fast days*); heap of unthreshed grain; heap, pile
**parvulez** *f* smallness; simpleness, innocence
**parvulista** *mf* kindergartner, kindergarten teacher
**párvulo -la** *adj* small, tiny; simple, innocent; humble, timid; *mf* child, tot; kindergartner (*child*)
**pasa** *f* see **paso**
**pasable** *adj* passable, fair
**pasacalle** *m* quickstep; (mus.) lively march; (mus.) passacaglia
**pasacaminos** *m* (*pl:* **-nos**) runner (*of carpet*)
**pasacólica** *f* (path.) upset stomach
**pasada** *f* see **pasado**
**pasadero -ra** *adj* passable; fair, good enough; *f* stepping stone; colander; walkway, catwalk; (naut.) spun yarn
**pasadía** *f* subsistence, fair subsistence; (Am.) picnic in the country
**pasadillo** *m* two-face embroidery
**pasadizo** *m* passage, corridor, hallway, alley; catwalk
**pasado -da** *adj* past; gone by; overripe, spoiled; stale; overdone; burned out; out-of-date, antiquated; (gram.) past; **lo pasado, pasado** let bygones be bygones; **pasado de maduro** overripe; *m* past; (mil.) deserter; (gram.) past; **pasados** *mpl* ancestors; **pasado próximo** recent past; *f* passage, passing; weft thread; **de pasada** in passing, hastily; **mala pasada** (coll.) mean trick
**pasador -dora** *adj* smuggling; *mf* smuggler; *m* door bolt; bolt, pin (*e.g., of hinge*); hatpin; brooch; stickpin; safety pin; strainer; colander; (naut.) marlinspike; **pasador de enganche** (rail.) coupling pin; **pasador de horquilla** cotter pin
**pasadura** *f* passage, transit; convulsive sobbing (*of a child*)
**pasagonzalo** *m* (coll.) tap, slight tap, flick
**pasaje** *m* passage; fare; fares; passengers; (mus.) passage; (naut.) strait; **cobrar el pasaje** to collect fares; **de pasaje** passenger
**pasajero -ra** *adj* passing, fleeting; common, frequented (*road, street, etc.*); migratory (*bird*); *mf* passenger; **pasajero no presentado** no-show (*passenger who fails to notify the company that he is not going to use his reservation*)
**pasajuego** *m* (sport) return of a serve
**pasamanar** *va* to passement, to trim with lace
**pasamanería** *f* passementerie, lace; passementerie or lace shop; lacemaking
**pasamanero -ra** *mf* passementerie maker or dealer
**pasamano** *m* passement, lace; handrail; (naut.) gangway
**pasamiento** *m* passage, transit
**pasamontaña** *m* or **pasamontañas** *m* (*pl:* **-ñas**) balaclava helmet, cap comforter, ski mask
**pasante** *adj* (her.) passant; *m* tutor; docent; assistant (*of a teacher, lawyer, or doctor*); **pasante de pluma** barrister's clerk
**pasantía** *f* tutorage, tutorship; docentship; assistantship
**pasapán** *m* (coll.) gullet
**pasapasa** *m* legerdemain
**pasaportar** *va* to issue a passport to
**pasaporte** *m* passport; (mil.) transportation (*for a soldier*); (fig.) passport
**pasar** *m* livelihood; **un buen pasar** enough to get along on ‖ *va* to pass; to cross, go through or over; to take across; to send, transfer, transmit; to slip in (*contraband*); to spend; to swallow; to excel; to stand, stand for, overlook; to undergo, to suffer; to go through (*a book*); to dry in the sun; to tutor, give private lessons in; to study with and assist (*a doctor or lawyer*); **pasar en blanco, en claro** or **por alto** to disregard; to omit, leave out, skip; **pasarlo** to be (*said of health*); to get along; to live; **pasarlo bien** to enjoy oneself, to have a good time ‖ *vn* to pass; to go; to pass away; to pass over (*said, e.g., of a fit of anger*); to happen; to last, to do; to spread; to get along; to yield; to come in, e.g., **pase Vd.** come in; **ir pasando** to manage to get along; **pasar a** + *inf* to go on to + *inf;* to stop by to + *inf;* **pasar a ser** to become; **pasar de** to go beyond, to exceed; to go above; to get beyond being;

**pasar de** + *inf* to go beyond + *ger;* **pasar de ... años** to be more than ... years old; **pasar por** to pass by, down, through, over, etc.; to pass as, to pass for; to stop or call at; **pasar por encima** to push right through; to push one's way to the top; **pasar sin** to do without; **pasar y traspasar** to pass back and forth ‖ *vr* to pass; to go; to excel; to pass over (*said, e.g., of a fit of anger*); to get along; to pass away; to take an examination; to leak; to be porous; to go too far; to become overripe, become overcooked, become tainted; to rot; to melt; to burn out; to not fit, to be loose (*said of a key, of a screw, etc.*); **pasarse al enemigo** to go over to the enemy; **pasarse de** + *adj* to be too + *adj;* **pasarse de** + *noun* to become + *noun;* **pasársele a uno** to forget, e.g., **se me pasó lo que me dijo Vd.** I forgot what you told me; **pasársele a uno** + *inf* to forget to + *inf*, e.g., **se me pasó abrir la ventana** I forgot to open the window; **pasarse por** to stop or call at; **pasarse sin** to to do without

**pasarela** *f* footbridge; catwalk; gangplank

**pasarríos** *m* (*pl:* **-rríos**) (zool.) basilisk, lizard

**pasatapas** *m* (*pl:* **-pas**) (elec.) bushing (*of a transformer*)

**pasatiempo** *m* pastime

**pasavante** *m* (nav.) safe-conduct

**pasavolante** *m* hasty act, thoughtlessness

**pascua** *f* Passover; Easter; Twelfth-night; Pentecost; Christmas; **pascuas** *fpl* Christmas holiday (*from Christmas to Twelfth-night*); **dar las pascuas** to wish a Happy New Year; **estar como una pascua** or **unas pascuas** (coll.) to be bubbling over with joy; **¡Felices Pascuas!** Merry Christmas!; **santas pascuas** (coll.) there's no choice, I give up; **Pascua de flores** Easter; **Pascua del Espíritu Santo** Pentecost; **Pascua de Navidad** Christmas; **Pascua de Resurrección** or **Pascua florida** Easter; **Pascuas navideñas** Christmas holiday (*from Christmas to Twelfth-night*)

**pascual** *adj* paschal

**pascueta** *f* (bot.) fireweed (*a wild lettuce*)

**pascuilla** *f* first Sunday after Easter

**pase** *m* pass (*permit; manipulation of mesmerist; free ticket*); exequatur; feint (*in fencing*); (taur.) pass (*move in which bullfighter, after inciting bull with muleta, allows him to pass by*); **pase de cortesía** complimentary ticket

**paseante** *adj* strolling; *mf* stroller; **paseante en corte** (coll.) loafer

**pasear** *va* to walk (*a child, a horse*); to promenade, show off; to cast (*a glance*); *vn* to take a walk; to go for a ride; **enviar** or **mandar a uno a pasear** (coll.) to send someone on his way, to dismiss a person without ceremony; *vr* to take a walk; to go for a ride; to wander, ramble; to take it easy; **pasearse a caballo** to go horseback riding; **pasearse en automóvil** to take an automobile ride; **pasearse en bicicleta** to go bicycling; **pasearse en canoa** to go boating; **pasearse en coche** to go for a ride

**paseata** *f* (coll.) walk, ride

**paseíllo** *m* processional entrance of the bullfighters

**paseo** *m* walk, stroll, promenade; ride; drive; avenue; **dar un paseo** to take a walk; to take a ride; **echar, enviar** or **mandar a uno a paseo** (coll.) to send someone on his way, to dismiss a person without ceremony; **ir de paseo** to go walking, to go out for a walk; to go for a ride; **sacar a paseo** to take out for a walk; to take out for a ride; **paseo de caballos** bridle path; **paseo de la cuadrilla** (taur.) processional entrance of the bullfighters

**pasero -ra** *adj* pacing, walking (*horse*); *mf* raisin seller; *f* drying of fruit; drying hurdle, drying room

**pasibilidad** *f* passibility, sensibility

**pasible** *adj* passible, sensible; deserving

**pasicorto -ta** *adj* making short steps

**pasiega** *f* nurse

**pasiflora** *f* (bot.) passionflower

**pasifloráceo -a** *adj* (bot.) passifloraceous

**pasilargo -ga** *adj* making long steps

**pasillo** *m* short step; passage, corridor; (sew.) basting stitch; (theat.) short piece, sketch

**pasión** *f* passion; (*cap.*) *f* (rel. & f.a.) Passion; **tener pasión por** to have a passion for

**pasional** *adj* passional

**pasionaria** *f* (bot.) passionflower (*plant and flower*)

**pasionario** *m* (eccl.) Passion songbook

**pasioncilla** *f* passing emotion; ugly grudge

**pasionero** *m* (eccl.) Passion singer; priest assigned to a hospital

**pasionista** *m* (eccl.) Passion singer

**pasitamente** *adv* gently, softly

**pasito** *m* short step; *adv* gently, softly

**pasitrote** *m* short trot

**pasividad** *f* passivity, passiveness

**pasivo -va** *adj* passive; retirement (*pension*); (gram.) passive; *m* (com.) liabilities; (com.) debit side (*of an account*)

**pasmar** *va* to chill; to frostbite; to stun, benumb; to dumfound, astound; *vr* to chill; to become frostbitten; to be astounded; to get lockjaw; to become dull or flat (*said, e.g., of colors*)

**pasmarota** or **pasmarotada** *f* (coll.) feigned spasm; (coll.) exaggerated show of surprise

**pasmarote** *m* (coll.) flabbergasted person

**pasmo** *m* (path.) cold; (path.) lockjaw, tetanus; astonishment; wonder, prodigy; **de pasmo** astonishingly

**pasmón -mona** *adj* open-mouthed, gawky; *mf* gawk

**pasmoso -sa** *adj* astounding; awesome

**paso -sa** *adj* dried (*fruit*) ‖ *m* step, pace; step (*of stairs*); gait, walk; go (*in traffic*); passing; passage; step, measure, démarche; permit, pass; strait; footstep, footprint; incident, happening; basting stitch; exequatur; pitch (*of propeller, nut, screw*); (elec.) pitch; (rad.) stage; (theat.) short piece, sketch, skit; **abrir paso** to open a path or way; to clear the way; **abrirse paso** to make one's way; **a buen paso** at a good pace or rate, hurriedly; **a cada paso** at every step, at every turn; **a dos pasos de** a short distance from; **a ese paso** at that rate; **aflojar el paso** (coll.) to slow down; **alargar el paso** (coll.) to hasten one's steps; **al paso** in passing, on the way; (chess) en passant; **al paso que** while, whereas; **al paso que vamos** at the rate we are going; **a paso de caracol** at a snail's pace; **a paso de carga** with leaps and bounds; **a paso de tortuga** at a snail's pace; **apretar** or **avivar el paso** (coll.) to hasten one's steps; **avanzar a grandes pasos** to make great or rapid strides; **buen paso** high living; **caminar a paso fino** to single, to single-foot; **ceder el paso** to step aside, to make way, to stay back, to keep clear, to let pass; **dar paso a** to give rise to; **dar pasos** to take steps; **dar un paso** to take a step; **de paso** in passing; at the same time; **de paso para** on the way to; **estar de paso** to be passing through; **llevar el paso** to keep step; **marcar el paso** (mil.) to mark time; (Am.) to obey humbly; **por sus pasos contados** in the usual way; **romper paso** to break step; **salir al paso a** to run into, to waylay; to buck, oppose; to confront; **salir del paso** (coll.) to get out of a jam, get out of a difficulty; **seguir los pasos a** to keep an eye on, to check; **seguir los pasos de** (fig.) to follow the footsteps of; **volver sobre sus pasos** to retrace one's steps; **paso a nivel** (rail.) grade crossing; **paso a paso** step by step; **paso de ambladura** or **andadura** amble; **paso de ganado** cattle crossing; **paso de ganso** (mil.) goose step; **pasa doble** (mil.) military march, quickstep; **paso en falso** slip, false step; **paso fino** single-foot (*of a horse*); **paso ligero** pitapat; (mil.) double time, double-quick; **paso polar** (elec.) pole pitch; **pasos de gigante** (sport) giant's stride; **paso único** (aut.) one line, single line ‖ *f* raisin; kink (*of Negro's hair*); (naut.) channel; **estar hecho una pasa** (coll.) to be all dried up, to be full of wrinkles; **pasa de Corinto** currant ‖ **paso** *adv* gently, softly; **¡paso!** easy there!

**pasodoble** *m* (mil.) military march, quickstep

**pasoso -sa** *adj* (Am.) porous; (Am.) sweaty

**pasote** *m* var. of **pazote**

**paspa** *f* (Am.) crack in the lips (*from cold and wind*)
**paspié** *m* (mus.) passepied (*music and dance*)
**pasquín** *m* pasquinade, lampoon; billboard
**pasquinada** *f* squib, lampoon
**pasquinar** *va* to pasquinade, to lampoon
**pasta** *f* paste, dough, pie crust, soup paste; mash; pulp (*for making paper*); cardboard; (b.b.) board binding; filling (*of a tooth*); (mineral. & ceramics) paste; (coll.) dough (*money*); cookie; **pastas** *fpl* noodles, macaroni, spaghetti, etc.; **de buena pasta** kindly, well-disposed; **media pasta** (b.b.) half binding; **pasta de hígado de ganso** pâté de foie gras; **pasta dentífrica** tooth paste; **pasta española** (b.b.) marbled leather binding, tree calf; **pasta seca** cookie
**pastadero** *m* pasture land
**pastaflora** *f* sponge cake
**pastar** *va* to lead to the pasture; *vn* to graze
**pasteca** *f* (naut.) snatch block
**pastel** *m* pie; pastry roll; meat pie; pastel (*drawing; crayon*); pastil or pastille (*pastel for crayons; crayon*); settlement, pacification; cheat, trick (*in shuffling cards*); (coll.) plot, deal; (bot.) woad; (print.) pi; (print.) smear
**pastelear** *vn* to temporize, to weasel
**pastelejo** *m* small pie
**pastelería** *f* pastry; pastry shop; pastry cooking
**pastelero -ra** *mf* pastry cook; (coll.) easy-going person, weaseler
**pastelillo** *m* tart, cake; pat (*e.g., of butter*); **pastelillo de hígado de ganso** pâté de foie gras
**pastelista** *mf* pastelist
**pastelito** *m* patty
**pastelón** *m* meat pie
**pastenco -ca** *adj* newly weaned (*cattle*)
**pasterización** *f* pasteurization
**pasterizar §76** *va* to pasteurize
**pastero** *m* workman who throws crushed olives into pressing bags
**pasteurizar §76** *va* var. of **pasterizar**
**pastilla** *f* tablet, lozenge, drop; dab (*soft mass*); cake (*of soap, chocolate, etc.*)
**pastinaca** *f* (bot.) parsnip; (ichth.) sting ray
**pastizal** *m* pasture for horses
**pasto** *m* pasture; grass; food, nourishment; (fig.) food (*e.g., for thought, gossip*); **a pasto** to excess; in abundance; **a todo pasto** freely, without restriction; **de pasto** ordinary, everyday
**pastor** *m* shepherd; **el Buen Pastor** (Bib.) the Good Shepherd; **pastor protestante** pastor, protestant minister
**pastora** *f* shepherdess; (bot.) poinsettia
**pastoral** *adj* pastoral; *f* (eccl. & lit.) pastoral; (mus.) pastoral or pastorale
**pastorear** *va* to shepherd (*flocks or souls*)
**pastorela** *f* shepherd's song; pastoral (*lyric poem*); (lit.) pastourelle
**pastoreo** *m* shepherding, pasturing
**pastoría** *f* shepherding; shepherds
**pastoricio -cia** or **pastoril** *adj* pastoral
**pastosidad** *f* pastiness, doughiness; mellowness
**pastoso -sa** *adj* pasty, doughy; mellow (*voice*); (paint.) pastose
**pastura** *f* pasture; fodder
**pasturaje** *m* pasturage, pasture land; pasturing fee
**pata** *f* paw, foot, leg; pocket flap; leg (*of furniture*); (hum.) leg (*of human being*); (orn.) duck (*female of drake*); **a cuatro patas** (coll.) on all fours; **a la pata llana** plainly, frankly; **enseñar la pata** (coll.) to show the cloven hoof, to give oneself away; **estirar la pata** (coll.) to kick the bucket; **meter la pata** (coll.) to butt in, to upset everything, to put one's foot in it; **sacar la pata** (coll.) to show the cloven hoof, to give oneself away; **salir** or **ser pata** or **patas** to be a tie; to be tied; **saltar a la pata coja** to hop; **tener mala pata** to be unlucky; **pata de araña** (mach.) oil groove; **pata de cabra** crowbar; **pata de gallina** radial crack in trees (*sign of rot*); **pata de gallo** crow's-foot (*at corner of eye*); (coll.) bull, blunder; (coll.) absurdity, piece of nonsense; **pata de palo** peg leg (*leg and person*); **pata es la traviesa** tit for tat; **pata galana** (coll.) game leg; (coll.) lame person; **pata hendida** cloven hoof; **patas arriba** (coll.) on one's back, upside down; (coll.) topsy-turvy; **patas** *m* (*pl:* **-tas**) (coll.) devil
**pataco -ca** *adj* churlish; *mf* churl; *f* (bot.) Jerusalem artichoke
**patada** *f* kick; stamp, stamping (*of foot*); (coll.) step; (coll.) footstep, track; **a patadas** (coll.) on all sides; **dar la patada a** to kick out
**patagio** *m* (zool.) patagium
**patagón -gona** *adj* Patagonian; (coll.) big-footed; *mf* Patagonian
**patagónico -ca** *adj* Patagonian
**patagorrilla** *f* or **patagorrillo** *m* haslet (*dish*)
**patalear** *vn* to kick; to stamp the feet
**pataleo** *m* kicking; stamping
**pataleta** *f* (coll.) feigned fit or convulsion
**patán** *adj masc* (coll.) churlish, boorish, loutish; *m* (coll.) churl, boor, lout; (coll.) villager, peasant
**patanería** *f* (coll.) churlishness, boorishness, loutishness
**pataplún** *interj* ker-plunk!
**patarata** *f* foolishness, simpleness; affectation; overpoliteness
**pataratero -ra** *adj* simple; affected; overpolite
**patarráez** *m* (*pl:* **-rraíces**) (naut.) preventer shroud
**patata** *f* (bot.) potato; **patata de caña** (bot.) Jerusalem artichoke; **patatas fritas** fried potatoes; **patatas majadas** mashed potatoes
**patatal** *m* or **patatar** *m* potato patch
**patatear** *vr* to flunk
**patatero -ra** *adj* (pertaining to the) potato; potato-eating; (coll.) up from the ranks; *mf* potato seller
**patatús** *m* (coll.) fainting fit
**pateadura** *f* or **pateamiento** *m* kicking, stamping; noisy protest; (coll.) severe dressing down
**patear** *va* (coll.) to kick; (coll.) to trample on, tread on; (coll.) to treat roughly; *vn* (coll.) to stamp one's foot (*in anger*); (coll.) to bustle around, to make a fuss; (Am.) to kick (*said of a gun*)
**patela** *f* (anat., archeol. & zool.) patela; (zool.) limpet
**patelar** *adj* (anat.) patellar
**patélula** *f* (bot.) patella
**patena** *f* large medal worn around the neck by peasant women; (eccl.) paten
**patentar** *va* to patent
**patente** *adj* patent, clear, evident; *f* grant, privilege, warrant; **de patente** (Am.) excellent, first-class; **patente de circulación** (aut.) owner's license; **patente de corso** (naut.) letters of marque; **patente de invención** patent; **patente de sanidad** (naut.) bill of health
**patentizar §76** *va* to make evident, to reveal
**pateo** *m* (coll.) kicking, stamping
**páter** *m* (mil.) padre; **páter familias** (Roman law) paterfamilias
**paternal** *adj* paternal; fatherly; paternalistic
**paternalismo** *m* paternalism
**paternidad** *f* paternity; fatherhood; **paternidad literaria** authorship
**paterno -na** *adj* paternal
**paternóster** *m* (*pl:* **paternóster**) paternoster; big tight knot
**pateta** *m* (coll.) devil; (coll.) cripple (*in feet or legs*)
**patético -ca** *adj* pathetic
**patetismo** *m* pathos
**patiabierto -ta** *adj* (coll.) bowlegged
**patialbillo** *m* (zool.) genet
**patialbo -ba** or **patiblanco -ca** *adj* white-footed
**patibulario -ria** *adj* of the scaffold; horrifying, hair-raising
**patíbulo** *m* scaffold (*for executions*)
**paticojo -ja** *adj* (coll.) lame, crippled
**patidifuso -sa** *adj* (hum.) silly, stunned, agape, flabbergasted
**patiecillo** *m* small patio
**patiestevado -da** *adj* bandy-legged, bowlegged
**patihendido -da** *adj* cloven-footed, cloven-hoofed

**patilla** *f* small paw or foot; chape (*of buckle*); pocket flap; (naut.) compass; (elec.) connecting lead (*of a vacuum tube*); (Am.) watermelon; **patillas** *fpl* sideburns, side whiskers; **patillas** *m* (coll.) the devil
**patilludo -da** *adj* bewhiskered
**patín** *m* small patio; (orn.) petrel; skate; skid, slide, runner; (aer.) skid; (elec.) contact shoe; (rail.) base (*of rail*); (naut.) skiff; **patín de cola** (aer.) tail skid; **patín de cuchilla** or **de hielo** ice skate; **patín de ruedas** roller skate
**pátina** *f* patina
**patinadero** *m* skating rink
**patinador -dora** *mf* skater; **patinador de fantasía** fancy skater; **patinador de figura** figure skater
**patinaje** *m* skidding; skating; **patinaje artístico** figure skating; **patinaje de fantasía** fancy skating; **patinaje de figura** figure skating
**patinar** *va* to patinate, give an artificial patina to; *vn* to skate; to skid; to slip, to spin
**patinazo** *m* skid, sudden skid; slipping, spinning
**patinejo** *m* small patio
**patinete** *m* scooter (*child's vehicle*)
**patinillo** *m* small patio
**patio** *m* patio, court, yard; campus; (metal.) patio; (rail.) yard, switchyard; (theat.) orchestra; **patio de carga** (rail.) freight yard; **patio de maniobras** (rail.) switchyard; **patio de recreo** playground
**patipollo** *m* duckling
**patiquebrar §18** *va* to break the leg of (*an animal*); *vr* to break a leg
**patita** *f* small paw or foot; **poner de patitas en la calle** (coll.) to throw out, to bounce
**patitieso -sa** *adj* (coll.) paralyzed (*in feet or legs*); (coll.) dumfounded; stiff, haughty; lifeless, dead
**patito** *m* duckling, young duck; **el Patito Feo** the Ugly Duckling
**patituerto -ta** *adj* crooked-legged; (coll.) crooked, lopsided, misshapen
**patizambo -ba** *adj* knock-kneed
**pato** *m* (orn.) duck, drake; **el pato Donaldo** Donald Duck; **pagar el pato** (coll.) to be the goat; **pato almizclado** (orn.) Muscovy duck; **pato bobo** (orn.) booby; **pato canelo** (orn.) sheldrake; **pato cuchareta** (orn.) shoveler (*Spatula clypeata*); **pato chiquito** (orn.) teal, blue-winged teal; **pato de flojel** (orn.) eider, eider duck; **pato mandarín** (orn.) mandarin duck; **pato marrueco** (orn.) widgeon; **pato negro** (orn.) black scoter; **pato pelucón** (orn.) canvasback; **pato picazo** (orn.) widgeon; **pato real** (orn.) mallard; **pato sierra** (orn.) goosander, merganser; **pato silbador** (orn.) widgeon; **pato silvestre** (orn.) mallard; **pato zarcel** (orn.) blue-winged teal
**patochada** *f* (coll.) blunder, stupidity
**patogénesis** *f* or **patogenia** *f* pathogenesis or pathogeny
**patogénico -ca** *adj* pathogenic
**patógeno -na** *adj* pathogenic (*producing disease*)
**patojo -ja** *adj* crooked-legged, waddling (*like a duck*); *mf* (Am.) young person
**patología** *f* pathology; **patología vegetal** plant pathology
**patológico -ca** *adj* pathologic or pathological
**patólogo -ga** *mf* pathologist
**patón -tona** *adj* (coll.) big-footed, big-pawed
**patoso -sa** *adj* smart-alecky
**patota** *f* (Am.) gang of young thugs
**Patr.** abr. of **Patriarca**
**patraña** *f* (coll.) fake, humbug, hoax
**patrañero -ra** *mf* (coll.) fake, humbug (*person*)
**patrañoso -sa** *adj* (coll.) fake
**patria** *f* see **patrio**
**patriarca** *m* patriarch
**patriarcado** *m* patriarchate; patriarchy
**patriarcal** *adj* patriarchal; *f* patriarch's church; patriarchate (*territory*)
**patriciado** *m* patriciate
**patricio -cia** *adj* patrician; (Am.) American-born; *m* patrician
**patrimonial** *adj* patrimonial
**patrimonialidad** *f* (eccl.) birthright
**patrimonio** *m* patrimony
**patrio -tria** *adj* native, home; paternal; *f* country (*land where one is a citizen*); mother country, fatherland, native land; birthplace; (fig.) home (*e.g., of the arts*); **patria celestial** heavenly home; **patria chica** native heath
**patriota** *mf* patriot
**patriotería** *f* (coll.) spread-eagleism, exaggerated patriotism
**patriotero -ra** *adj* (coll.) spread-eagle, exaggeratedly patriotic; *mf* (coll.) spread-eagleist
**patriótico -ca** *adj* patriotic
**patriotismo** *m* patriotism
**patrístico -ca** *adj* patristic; *f* patristics
**patrocinador -dora** *adj* sponsoring; *mf* sponsor, patron; (rad. & telv.) sponsor
**patrocinar** *va* to favor, sponsor, patronize; (rad. & telv.) to sponsor
**patrocinio** *m* favor, sponsorship, patronage; (rad. & telv.) sponsorship
**Patroclo** *m* (myth.) Patroclus
**patrología** *f* patrology
**patrón -trona** *mf* sponsor, protector; patron saint; *m* patron; landlord; owner, master; boss, foreman; host; skipper (*of a boat*); pattern; standard (*of measure, of money*); stock (*on which a graft is made*); **patrón oro** gold standard; **patrón picado** stencil (*sheet to make letters and designs*); *f* patroness; landlady; owner, mistress; hostess; (naut.) galleon ranking next to flagship
**patronal** *adj* patronal; employers'
**patronar** *va* var. of **patronear**
**patronato** *m* employers' association; foundation; board of trustees; patronage; **patronato de turismo** organization to encourage touring
**patronazgo** *m* var. of **patronato**
**patronear** *va* to skipper
**patronía** *f* skippership
**patronímico -ca** *adj & m* patronymic
**patrono -na** *mf* sponsor, protector; employer; *m* patron; landlord; boss, foreman; lord of the manor; **los patronos** management; *f* patroness; landlady
**patrulla** *f* (aer., mil. & nav.) patrol; gang, band
**patrullaje** *m* (aer., mil. & nav.) patrolling
**patrullar** *va & vn* (aer., mil. & nav.) to patrol
**patrullero -ra** *adj* (pertaining to) patrol; *m* (naut.) patrol ship
**patuá** *m* (*pl:* **-tuaes**) patois
**patudo -da** *adj* (coll.) big-footed, big-pawed
**patués** *m* patois
**patulea** *f* (coll.) disorderly soldiers; (coll.) mob, gang of roughnecks; (coll.) group of noisy brats
**patullar** *vn* to stamp around; (coll.) to make a fuss, to hustle around; (coll.) to chat
**paují** *m* (*pl:* **-jíes**) (orn.) cashew bird
**paujil** *m* var. of **paují**
**paúl** *m* bog, marsh
**paular** *m* bog, marsh; *vn* (coll.) to talk, chat; **ni paula ni maula** doesn't even open his mouth; **sin paular ni maular** without saying boo
**paulatino -na** *adj* slow, gradual
**paulilla** *f* (ent.) grain moth
**paulina** *f* & **Paulina** *f* see **paulino**
**paulinista** *adj & mf* Paulinist
**paulino -na** *adj* Pauline; *f* decree of excommunication; (coll.) censure, reproof; (coll.) poison-pen letter; (*cap.*) *f* Pauline
**paulonia** *f* (bot.) paulownia
**pauperismo** *m* pauperism
**paupérrimo -ma** *adj super* very or most poor
**pausa** *f* pause; slowness, delay; (gram.) pause; (mus.) rest
**pausado -da** *adj* slow, calm, deliberate; **pausado** *adv* slowly, calmly, deliberately
**pausar** *va & vn* to slow down
**pauta** *f* ruler; guide lines (*for writing*); guideline, rule, guide, standard, model; (mus.) ruled staff; **marcar la pauta a** to set the pace for
**pautada** *f* (mus.) musical staff
**pautador** *m* paper ruler (*person*)
**pautar** *va* to rule (*paper*); to give directions for

**pava** *f* (orn.) turkey hen; furnace bellows; Paul Jones (*dance*); (coll.) dull, colorless woman; **pelar la pava** (coll.) to make love at a window; **pava real** (orn.) peahen
**pavada** *f* flock of turkeys; (coll.) dullness, inanity
**pavana** *f* pavan (*dance and music*)
**pavear** *vn* (Am.) to talk nonsense; (Am.) to make love at a window
**pavero -ra** *mf* turkey raiser and dealer; *m* Andalusian broad-brimmed hat
**pavés** *m* pavis, large shield; **alzar** or **levantar sobre el pavés** to elevate to leadership, to glorify
**pavesa** *f* ember, spark; **estar hecho una pavesa** (coll.) to be weak and exhausted; **ser una pavesa** (coll.) to be meek and mild
**pavesada** *f* var. of **empavesada**
**pavezno** *m* young turkey
**pavía** *f* (bot.) pavy, clingstone peach (*tree and fruit*)
**pávido -da** *adj* (poet.) timid, fearful
**pavimentación** *f* paving
**pavimentar** *va* to pave
**pavimento** *m* paving, pavement
**paviota** *f* (orn.) sea gull
**pavipollo** *m* young turkey
**pavisoso -sa** *adj* dull, graceless
**pavita** *f* (orn.) sunbird, sun bittern
**pavitonto -ta** *adj* stupid, foolish
**pavo** *m* (orn.) turkey; turkey cock; (coll.) dull, colorless fellow; **comer pavo** (coll.) to be a wallflower; **ponerse hecho un pavo** (slang) to blush; **pavo de matorral** (orn.) brush turkey; **pavo real** (orn.) peacock
**pavón** *m* bluing, browning, bronzing (*of iron or steel*); (orn.) peacock; (ent.) peacock butterfly; (*cap.*) *m* (astr.) Peacock
**pavonado -da** *adj* dark-blue; gun-metal; *m* bluing, browning, bronzing (*of iron or steel*); *f* (coll.) stroll, short walk; (coll.) show, vain display
**pavonar** *va* to blue, to brown, to bronze (*iron or steel*)
**pavonear** *vn & vr* to strut, swagger, show off
**pavoneo** *m* strutting, swaggering
**pavor** *m* fear, terror
**pavorde** *m* (eccl.) provost
**pavordear** *vn* to swarm (*said of bees*)
**pavordía** *f* (eccl.) provostship
**pavoroso -sa** *adj* frightful, terrible
**pavura** *f* var. of **pavor**
**paya** *f* (Am.) improvised song, accompanied on the guitar
**payasada** *f* clownishness, clownish stunt, clownish remark
**payasear** *vn* (Am.) to be clownish
**payasería** *f* (Am.) clownishness; (Am.) clown's life
**payaso** *m* clown; laughingstock
**payés -yesa** *mf* Catalan peasant
**payo -ya** *adj* rustic, peasant; *m* churl, gump
**payuelas** *fpl* (path.) chicken pox
**paz** *f* (*pl:* **paces**) peace; peacefulness; (eccl.) pax (*ceremony and tablet*); **¡a la paz de Dios!** (coll.) God be with you!; **dejar en paz** to leave alone; **descansar en paz** to rest in peace; **estar en paz** to be even; to be quits; **hacer las paces con** to make peace with, to come to terms with; **no dar paz a** to give no rest to; **poner en paz** or **poner paz entre** to reconcile; **salir en paz** (coll.) to break even (*in gambling*); *interj* peace!, quiet!
**pazguatería** *f* simpleness, doltishness
**pazguato -ta** *adj* simple, doltish; *mf* simpleton, dolt
**pazote** *m* (bot.) wormseed, Mexican tea
**pazpuerca** *adj fem* (coll.) sluttish; *f* (coll.) slut
**pbro.** abr. of **presbítero**
**pche** or **pchs** *interj* pshaw!
**P.D.** abr. of **posdata**
**P.[e]** abr. of **Padre**
**pea** *f* drunkenness, drunken spree
**peaje** *m* toll
**peajero** *m* toll collector, tollkeeper
**peal** *m* foot (*of stocking*); knitted legging; (coll.) good-for-nothing
**peán** *m* (hist.) paean
**peana** or **peaña** *f* base, pedestal, stand; hat block; window sill; altar step
**peatón** *m* walker, pedestrian; rural postman
**pebete** *m* punk, joss stick; fuse; (coll.) stinker (*thing*)
**pebetero** *m* perfume censer
**pebrada** *f* sauce of pepper, garlic, parsley, and vinegar
**pebre** *m & f* sauce of pepper, garlic, parsley, and vinegar; pepper; (Am.) mashed potatoes
**peca** *f* freckle
**pecable** *adj* peccable
**pecado** *m* sin; (coll.) devil; **de mis pecados** of mine; **por mal de mis pecados** to my sorrow, unfortunately for me; **siete pecados capitales** seven deadly sins; **pecado capital** capital sin; **pecado mortal** mortal sin; **pecado original** (theol.) original sin; **pecado venial** venial sin
**pecador -dora** *adj* sinning, sinful; *mf* sinner; *f* (coll.) prostitute
**pecaminoso -sa** *adj* sinful
**pecante** *adj* sinning; excessive
**pecar** **§86** *vn* to sin; to go astray; **pecar de** + *adj* to be too + *adj*
**pecarí** *m* (*pl:* **-ríes**) (zool.) peccary
**pécari** *m* var. of **pecarí**
**pecblenda** *f* var. of **pechblenda**
**pece** *m* ridge between furrows; *f* mud or mortar for walls or other building
**pececico, pececillo** or **pececito** *m* little fish
**peceño -ña** *adj* pitchy
**pecera** *f* fish globe, fish bowl
**pecezuela** *f* small piece
**pecezuelo** *m* little foot; little fish
**peciento -ta** *adj* pitchy (*in color*)
**peciluengo -ga** *adj* long-stalked
**pecina** *f* fishpool; slime
**pecinal** *m* slime hole, swamp
**pecinoso -sa** *adj* slimy
**pecio** *m* (naut.) flotsam
**peciolado -da** *adj* petiolate
**pecíolo** *m* (bot. & zool.) petiole
**pécora** *f* head of sheep; **buena pécora** or **mala pécora** (coll.) schemer (*generally a woman*)
**pecorea** *f* cattle stealing; marauding, looting; hanging around, staying out
**pecorear** *va* to steal (*cattle*); *vn* to maraud, to loot
**pecoso -sa** *adj* freckly, freckle-faced
**pecten** *m* (zool.) pecten
**pectina** *f* (chem.) pectin
**pectinado -da** *adj* pectinate
**pectíneo -a** *adj* pectinate; (anat.) pectineal; *m* (anat.) pectineus
**pectinibranquio -quia** *adj* (zool.) pectinibranchian
**pectoral** *adj* pectoral; *m* pectoral; breastplate (*of Jewish high priest*); (pharm.) pectoral; (eccl.) pectoral cross
**pecuario -ria** *adj* (pertaining to) cattle
**peculado** *m* peculation
**peculiar** *adj* peculiar
**peculiaridad** *f* peculiarity
**peculio** *m* (law) peculium; small fund, small savings
**pecunia** *f* (coll.) cash, dough
**pecuniario -ria** *adj* pecuniary
**pechar** *va* to pay as a tax; to fulfill; to take on (*a disagreeable burden or responsibility*); (Am.) to bump or push with the chest; (Am.) to drive one's horse against; (Am.) to strike for a loan; *vn* **pechar con** to take on (*a disagreeable burden or responsibility*)
**pechblenda** *f* (mineral.) pitchblende
**peche** *m* pilgrim's scallop; *adj* (Am.) thin, sickly
**pechera** *f* see **pechero**
**pechería** *f* taxes; tax roll
**pechero -ra** *adj* taxable; *mf* taxpayer; commoner, plebeian; *m* bib; *f* shirt front, shirt bosom; vestee; chest protector; bib (*of apron*); breast strap (*of harness*); (coll.) bosom
**pechiblanco -ca** *adj* white-breasted
**pechicolorado** *m* (orn.) redpoll, linnet
**pechina** *f* pilgrim's scallop; (arch.) pendentive
**pechirrojo** *m* (orn.) redpoll
**pechisacado -da** *adj* (coll.) vain, arrogant
**pecho** *m* (anat.) chest; breast, bosom; teat; heart, courage; slope, hill; voice, strength of

voice; tax, tribute; **abrir el pecho** to unbosom oneself; **a pecho abierto** frankly; **a pecho descubierto** unprotected, unarmed; openly, frankly; **dar el pecho** to nurse, to suckle; (coll.) to face it out; **de dos pechos** double-breasted; **descubrir el pecho** to unbosom oneself; **de un solo pecho** single-breasted; **echar el pecho al agua** (coll.) to put one's shoulder to the wheel; (coll.) to speak out; **en pechos de camisa** (Am.) in shirt sleeves; **entre pecho y espalda** deep, in the heart; **tomar a pecho** to take to heart; **tomarse a pechos** (Am.) to take seriously, to make an issue of; (Am.) to take offense at; **¡pecho al agua!** take heart!, put your shoulder to the wheel!; **pecho amarillo** (orn.) yellowthroat, Maryland yellowthroat; **pecho de pichón** (path.) pigeon breast
**pechuelo** *m* small breast
**pechuga** *f* breast (*of fowl*); (coll.) breast, bosom; (coll.) slope, hill; (Am.) brass, cheek; (Am.) treachery, perfidy
**pechugón -gona** *adj* (coll.) big-chested; (Am.) brazen, forward; *mf* (Am.) sponger; *m* slap or blow on the chest; fall on the chest; hard push, strong effort
**pechuguera** *f* deep cough
**pedagogía** *f* pedagogy
**pedagógico -ca** *adj* pedagogic or pedagogical
**pedagogo -ga** *mf* pedagogue; mentor
**pedaje** *m* toll
**pedal** *m* pedal, treadle; (mus.) pedal; **pedal de freno** (aut.) brake pedal; **pedal suave** or **celeste** (mus.) soft pedal
**pedalear** *vn* to pedal
**pedalero** *m* (mus.) pedal board, pedal keyboard
**pedáneo -a** *adj* (law) petty, puisne
**pedanía** *f* district
**pedante** *adj* pedantic; *mf* pedant; *m* (archaic) home tutor
**pedantear** *vn* to be pedantic
**pedantería** *f* pedantry
**pedantesco -ca** *adj* pedantic
**pedantismo** *m* pedantry
**pedato -ta** *adj* (bot.) pedate
**pedazo** *m* piece; **a pedazos** in pieces; **caerse a pedazos** to fall apart; (coll.) to be broken-down, to let oneself go to pieces; (coll.) to be kindly, be unsuspecting; (coll.) to be fagged out; (coll.) to be stumbly, to be awkward; **hacer pedazos** (coll.) to break to pieces; **hacerse pedazos** (coll.) to fall to pieces; (coll.) to strain, wear oneself out, overexercise; **morirse por sus pedazos** (coll.) to be madly in love; **ser un pedazo de pan** (coll.) to be kindly, be the quintessence of kindness; **pedazo de alcornoque, de animal** or **de bruto** (coll.) dolt, imbecile, good-for-nothing; **pedazo del alma, de las entrañas** or **del corazón** (coll.) darling, apple of one's eye (*child*); **pedazo de pan** crumb (*small amount*); song (*small price*)
**pedazuelo** *m* small piece, bit
**pederasta** *m* pederast
**pederastia** *f* pederasty
**pedernal** *m* flint (*variety of quartz; piece used for striking fire*); flintiness; flint-hearted person
**pedernalino -na** *adj* flinty; (fig.) flinty
**pedestal** *m* pedestal
**pedestre** *adj* pedestrian; (fig.) pedestrian
**pedestremente** *adv* on foot; (fig.) in a pedestrian manner
**pedestrismo** *m* pedestrianism; walking; foot racing; cross-country racing
**pedestrista** *mf* walker; foot racer; cross-country racer
**pediatra** *mf* pediatrician
**pediatría** *f* pediatrics
**pediátrico -ca** *adj* pediatric
**pedicelo** *m* (bot. & zool.) pedicel
**pedicoj** *m* jump, hop (*on one foot*)
**pedicular** *adj* pedicular
**pedículo** *m* (bot.) pedicle
**pedicuro -ra** *mf* pedicure (*person*)
**pedido** *m* request; (com.) order; **a pedido** on request; **pedido de ensayo** (com.) trial order
**pedidor -dora** *adj* insistent, importunate
**pedidura** *f* asking, begging
**pedigón -gona** *adj* (coll.) insistent, importunate
**pedigüeño -ña** *adj* insistent, demanding, bothersome
**pediluvio** *m* foot bath
**pedimento** *m* petition; (law) claim, bill
**pedio -dia** *adj* (anat.) (pertaining to the) foot
**pedipalpo** *m* (zool.) pedipalpus
**pedir §94** *va* to ask, to ask for; to request; to demand, require; to need; to ask for the hand of, to ask for in marriage; to order (*merchandise*); (gram.) to govern; **pedir algo a alguien** to ask someone for something; **pedir prestado a** to borrow from; *vn* to ask; to beg; (law) to bring claim, bring suit; **a pedir de boca** opportunely; as desired; **venir a pedir de boca** to be just the thing; to come at the right time
**pedo** *m* wind, flatulence; **andar pedo** (Am.) to be drunk
**pedorrero -ra** *adj* flatulent; *f* flatulence; **pedorreras** *fpl* tights
**pedorreta** *f* sound made to imitate the breaking of wind
**pedorro -rra** *adj* flatulent
**pedrada** *f* stoning; hit or blow with a stone; mark or bruise made by a stone; rosette, bow (*for hair or hat*); (coll.) hint, taunt; **como pedrada en ojo de boticario** (coll.) apropos, just in time; **matar a pedradas** to stone to death
**pedral** *m* (naut.) stone used to hold a net or cable in place
**pedrea** *f* stoning; fight with stones; hailing
**pedregal** *m* stony ground
**pedregoso -sa** *adj* stony, rocky; suffering from gallstones; *mf* sufferer from gallstones
**pedrejón** *m* boulder
**pedreñal** *m* flintlock, firelock
**pedrera** *f* quarry, stone quarry
**pedreral** *m* packsaddle for carrying stones
**pedrería** *f* precious stones, jewelry
**pedrero** *m* stonecutter; slinger
**pedreta** or **pedrezuela** *f* small stone
**pedrisca** *f* var. of **pedrisco**
**pedriscal** *m* stony ground
**pedrisco** *m* shower of stones, stoning; heap of loose stones; hailstones; hailstorm
**pedrisquero** *m* hailstorm
**pedriza** *f* stony spot; stone fence
**Pedro** *m* Peter; **Pedro el Ermitaño** Peter the Hermit; **Pedro el Grande** Peter the Great
**pedroche** *m* stony ground
**pedrusco** *m* rough stone, boulder
**pedunculado -da** *adj* pedunculate
**peduncular** *adj* peduncular
**pedúnculo** *m* (anat., bot. & zool.) peduncle, stalk
**peer §35** *vn & vr* to break wind
**pega** *f* sticking; pitch varnish; drubbing; catch question (*in an examination*); (coll.) trick, joke; (ichth.) remora; (min.) firing a blast; (orn.) magpie; **de pega** (slang) fake; **pega reborda** (orn.) shrike
**pegadillo** *m* little patch, little plaster; (Am.) lace; **pegadillo de mal de madre** (coll.) bore, nuisance
**pegadizo -za** *adj* sticky; contagious; sponging, parasitic; false, imitation
**pegado** *m* patch, sticking plaster
**pegador** *m* paper hanger; billposter; (min.) blaster
**pegadura** *f* sticking
**pegajosa** *f* see **pegajoso**
**pegajosidad** *f* stickiness
**pegajoso -sa** *adj* sticky; catching, contagious; alluring, tempting; (coll.) soft, gentle, mellow; (coll.) mushy; *f* (bot.) marvel-of-Peru
**pegamento** or **pegamiento** *m* sticking, joining; glue, cement
**pegamoscas** *m* (*pl:* **-cas**) (bot.) catchfly
**pegapega** *f* (bot.) bedstraw
**pegar §59** *va* to stick, to paste; to fasten, attach, tie; to post (*bills*); to set (*fire*); to transmit, communicate (*a disease*); to beat; to let go (*a blow, slap, etc.*); to let out (*a cry*); to take (*a jump, a run*); to sew on (*a button*); **no pegar el ojo** (coll.) to not sleep a wink all night; **pegar un tiro a** to shoot; *vn* to stick, to catch;

to take root, take hold; to cling; to join, be contiguous; to make an impression; to fit, to match; to be fitting; to pass, be accepted; to beat; to knock; to stumble; *vr* to stick, to catch; to take root, take hold; to burn to the bottom of the pan; to hang on, stick around; to be catching (*said of a disease*); **pegársela a uno** (coll.) to make a fool of someone
**pegarropa** *m* (bot.) beggar's-lice
**pegásides** *fpl* (myth.) Muses
**Pegaso** *m* (myth. & astr.) Pegasus
**pegata** *f* (coll.) cheat, swindle, fraud
**pegmatita** *f* (petrog.) pegmatite
**pego** *m* cheating by sticking two cards together; **dar** o **tirar el pego** to make two cards stick together; (coll.) to dazzle, to cheat
**pegote** *m* pitch plaster; sticking plaster; (coll.) sticky mess; (coll.) hanger-on, sponger; (coll.) crude addition (*to a writing or a work of art*)
**pegotear** *vn* (coll.) to hang around, to sponge
**pegotería** *f* (coll.) hanging around, sponging
**pegual** *m* (Am.) saddle strap with ring at each end
**peguera** *f* pitch pit (*in which pine wood is burned to yield pitch*); place for heating pitch for marking sheep
**peguero** *m* pitch maker or dealer
**pegujal** *m* small fund; small holdings; fund of knowledge
**pegujalejo** *m* tiny holdings
**pegujalero** *m* small farmer
**pegujar** *m* var. of **pegujal**
**pegujarero** *m* var. of **pegujalero**
**pegujón** *m* or **pegullón** *m* lump or ball of wool or hair
**pegunta** *f* pitch mark on sheep
**peguntar** *va* to mark (*sheep*) with pitch
**pehuén** *m* (bot.) monkey puzzle
**peina** *f* var. of **peineta**
**peinado -da** *adj* combed; groomed; effeminate; (lit.) overnice; *m* hairdo, coiffure; **peinado al agua** finger wave; *f* combing
**peinador -dora** *mf* hairdresser; *m* wrapper, dressing gown, peignoir; *f* combing machine
**peinadura** *f* combing; combings
**peinar** *va* to comb; to riffle (*cards*); *vr* to comb one's hair
**peinazo** *m* (carp.) rail (*e.g., of a door*)
**peine** *m* comb; instep; reed (*of a loom*); (coll.) sly fellow, tricky fellow; (zool.) pecten; **a sobre peine** lightly, slightly; **peine de balas** cartridge clip; **peine de pastor** or **de Venus** (bot.) lady's-comb
**peinera** *f* see **peinero**
**peinería** *f* comb factory or shop
**peinero -ra** *mf* comb maker or dealer; *f* comb case
**peineta** *f* ornamental comb, back comb
**peinetero -ra** *mf* comb maker or dealer
**Peipín** *m* Peiping
**p.ej.** abr. of **por ejemplo**
**peje** *m* fish; (coll.) slicker, slick guy; **peje ángel** (ichth.) angelfish; **peje araña** (ichth.) scorpion fish; **peje diablo** (ichth.) scorpene
**pejebuey** *m* (zool.) manatee
**pejegallo** *m* (ichth.) roosterfish
**pejemuller** *m* (zool.) manatee
**pejepalo** *m* unsplit smoked codfish
**pejerrey** *m* (ichth.) atherine
**pejesapo** *m* (ichth.) angler
**pejiguera** *f* (coll.) bother, nuisance
**p.ejm.** abr. of **por ejemplo**
**pekinés -nesa** *adj & mf* var. of **pequinés**
**pela** *f* barking (*e.g., of a cork oak*)
**pelada** *f* see **pelado**
**peladero** *m* place for scalding slaughtered hogs or fowl; (coll.) den of cardsharps; (Am.) wasteland
**peladilla** *f* sugar almond; pebble
**peladillo** *m* (bot.) clingstone peach (*tree and fruit*); **peladillos** *mpl* wool stripped from the pelt
**pelado -da** *adj* bare; bald; barren; peeled; poor, penniless; even (*ten, twenty, hundred, etc.*); (Am.) ill-bred; *f* pelt, sheepskin (*stripped of wool*)
**pelador -dora** *adj* peeling; *mf* peeler
**peladura** *f* peeling, barking
**pelafustán -tana** *mf* (coll.) good-for-nothing
**pelagallos** *m* (*pl:* **-llos**) (coll.) tramp, bum
**pelagatos** *m* (*pl:* **-tos**) (coll.) wretch, outcast, ragamuffin
**pelágico -ca** *adj* pelagic
**pelagra** *f* (path.) pellagra
**pelagroso -sa** *adj* pellagrous
**pelaire** *m* wool carder
**pelairía** *f* wool carding
**pelaje** *m* coat, fur, pelage; (coll.) stripe (*sort, type*)
**pelambrar** *va* var. of **apelambrar**
**pelambre** *m* batch of hides to be fleshed; steeping liquid; hair; hair scraped from skins; lack of hair, bare spots
**pelambrera** *f* fleshing room; bushiness, hairiness; (path.) alopecia
**pelambrero** *m* flesher, steeper
**pelamen** *m* (coll.) var. of **pelambre**
**pelamesa** *f* scuffle, hair-pulling scuffle; bunch of hair
**pelandusca** *f* (coll.) prostitute, whore
**pelantrín** *m* small farmer; (Am.) pauper
**pelar** *va* to cut (*hair*); to pluck, pull out (*hair, feathers*); to peel, skin, husk, hull, shell, bark; to show (*the teeth*); (coll.) to clean out (*in gambling*); (Am.) to beat, to thrash; (Am.) to slander; *vr* to peel off; to lose one's hair; to get a haircut; (Am.) to clear out, make a getaway; **pelárselas** (coll.) to be efficient, expeditious, enthusiastic; (coll.) to kick the bucket (*to die*); **pelárselas por** (coll.) to crave; **pelárselas por** + *inf* to crave to + *inf*
**pelarela** *f* (path.) alopecia
**pelarruecas** *f* (*pl:* **-cas**) (coll.) woman who makes a living spinning
**pelasgo -ga** *adj & mf* Pelasgian
**pelaza** or **pelazga** *f* (coll.) quarrel, row
**peldaño** *m* step (*of stairs*)
**pelea** *f* fight; quarrel; struggle; **pelea de gallos** cockfight
**peleador -dora** *adj* fighting; quarrelsome; *mf* fighter
**pelear** *vn* to fight; to quarrel; to struggle; *vr* to fight, fight each other; to part company
**pelechar** *va* (coll.) to keep in food and clothing; *vn* to shed (*said of animals*); to get new hair; to fledge; (coll.) to be better off, to take a turn for the better
**pelele** *m* stuffed figure (*of straw and rags*); baby's knitted sleeping suit; (coll.) simpleton, laughingstock, lightweight
**Peleo** *m* (myth.) Peleus
**peleón -ona** *adj* (coll.) pugnacious, quarrelsome; (coll.) cheap, ordinary (*wine*); *m* (coll.) cheap wine; *f* (coll.) row, scuffle, altercation, fracas
**pelerina** *f* pelerine
**pelete** *m* punter (*in gambling*); (coll.) poor fellow, nobody; **en pelete** naked
**peletería** *f* furriery; fur shop; (Am.) shoe store
**peletero -ra** *mf* furrier; (Am.) shoe dealer, shoe merchant; *m* (Am.) shoe salesman
**pelgar** *m* (coll.) var. of **pelagallos**
**peliagudo -da** *adj* furry, long-haired; (coll.) arduous, ticklish; (coll.) tricky
**peliblanco -ca** *adj* white-haired
**peliblando -da** *adj* soft-haired
**pelicano -na** *adj* gray-haired
**pelícano** *m* (orn.) pelican
**pelicorto -ta** *adj* short-haired
**película** *f* pellicle; film; (phot. & mov.) film; motion picture; (Am.) blunder, break; **película de dibujo** (mov.) animated cartoon; **película de largo metraje** (mov.) full-length film; **película de seguridad** (phot.) safety film; **película en carretes** (phot.) roll film; **película en colores** (phot. & mov.) color film; **película en paquetes** (phot.) film pack; **película hablada** (mov.) talking film; **película sonora** (mov.) sound film
**pelicular** *adj* pellicular, filmy
**peliculero -ra** *adj* moving-picture; *mf* scenario writer; *m* movie actor; *f* movie actress
**peligrar** *vn* to be in danger
**peligro** *m* danger, peril, risk; **correr peligro** to be in danger; **fuera de peligro** out of danger; **ponerse en peligro de paz** to be alerted for war; **peligro amarillo** yellow peril

**peligrosidad** *f* dangerousness
**peligroso -sa** *adj* dangerous, perilous
**pelilargo -ga** *adj* long-haired
**pelillo** *m* (coll.) trifle, trifling difference; **echar pelillos a la mar** (coll.) to bury the hatchet; **no pararse en pelillos** (coll.) to not bother about trifles, to pay no attention to small matters; **no tener pelillos en la lengua** (coll.) to speak right out
**pelilloso -sa** *adj* (coll.) touchy
**pelinegro -gra** *adj* black-haired
**Pelión, el** Pelion; **levantar el Pelión sobre el Osa** to heap Pelion upon Ossa
**pelirrojo -ja** *adj* red-haired, redheaded; *mf* redhead
**pelirrubio -bia** *adj* fair-haired, blond; *m* blond; *f* blonde
**pelitieso -sa** *adj* straight-haired, stiff-haired
**pelitre** *m* (bot.) bertram, pellitory of Spain
**pelitrique** *m* (coll.) trifle, trinket
**pelma** *m* (coll.) flat mass; undigested food; *mf* (coll.) lump, poke, sluggard; (slang) easy mark
**pelmacería** *f* slowness, heaviness, pokiness
**pelmazo** *m* flat mass; undigested food; (coll.) lump, poke, sluggard
**pelo** *m* hair; down (*on skin, fruit, etc.*); nap (*of cloth*); grain (*in wood*); fiber, filament; coat (*of animal*); flaw (*in precious stones*); raw silk; color (*of horse*); kiss (*in billiards*); split (*in hoof*); hair or thread (*caught on tip of a pen*); cross hair (*of optical instrument*); hair trigger; hairspring (*of watch*); trifle; **al pelo** with the hair, with the nap; (coll.) perfectly, to the point; **a medios pelos** (coll.) tipsy; **a pelo** with the hair, with the nap; (coll.) timely, in good time; **con todos sus pelos y señales** chapter and verse; **contra pelo** backwards; against the hair or nap; (coll.) inopportunely; **cortar un pelo en el aire** to be sharp, be keen; **de medio pelo** (coll.) four-flushing; (coll.) trifling; **echar pelos a la mar** (coll.) to bury the hatchet; **en pelo** bareback; **escapar por un pelo** to escape by a hairbreadth, to have a narrow escape; **estar hasta por encima de los pelos** (coll.) to have one's fill, to be fed up; **hacer el pelo a** to do the hair of; to fix the hair of; **hacerse el pelo** to do one's hair; to fix one's hair; to have one's hair cut; **no tener pelo de tonto** (coll.) to be wide-awake; **no tener pelos en la lengua** (coll.) to be outspoken, to not mince words; **ponerle a uno los pelos de punta** to make one's hair stand on end; **relucirle a uno el pelo** (coll.) to be sleek, be well fed; **tomar el pelo a** (coll.) to make fun of, to make a fool of; **venir a pelo** to come in handy; **venir al pelo a** to suit perfectly; **pelo a la garçonne** shingle; **pelo arriba** against the hair; **pelo de camello** camel's hair; **pelo de cofre** or **de Judas** red hair; redhead (*person*); **pelos absorbentes** (bot.) root hair; **pelos de la estadia** (surv.) stadia hairs; **pelos y señales** (coll.) minutest details
**pelón -lona** *adj* bald, hairless; (coll.) dull, stupid; (coll.) poor, penniless; *m* (Am.) dried peach; *f* (path.) alopecia; (Am.) prostitute; (Am.) death
**pelonería** *f* (coll.) want, poverty
**pelonía** *f* (path.) alopecia
**Pélope** *m* (myth.) Pelops
**peloponense** *adj* & *mf* Peloponnesian
**peloponesíaco -ca** *adj* Peloponnesian
**Peloponeso** *m* Peloponnesus
**pelosilla** *f* (bot.) mouse-ear
**peloso -sa** *adj* hairy
**pelota** *f* ball; ball game; handball; (Am.) boat made of cowhide; **dejar en pelota** (coll.) to strip; (coll.) to clean out, leave penniless; **en pelota** stripped, naked; **estar la pelota en el tejado** (coll.) to be up in the air, to be of uncertain outcome; **no tocar pelota** (coll.) to not get to the root of the difficulty; **pelota acuática** (sport) water polo; **pelota de viento** football, basketball (*inflated with air*); **pelota medicinal** medicine ball; **pelota rodada** (baseball) grounder; **pelota vasca** (sport) pelota
**pelota-base** *f* baseball
**pelotari** *mf* pelota player
**pelotazo** *m* blow or hit with a ball
**pelote** *m* goat's hair
**pelotear** *va* to audit (*an account*); *vn* to knock a ball around (*without playing a game*); to wrangle, to argue; **pelotear con** to play ball with (*e.g., a pillow*)
**pelotera** *f* (coll.) brawl, row
**pelotería** *f* heap of balls; pile of goat's hair
**pelotero** *m* ball maker; ballplayer; (coll.) brawl, row
**pelotilla** *f* pellet; ball of wax and broken glass attached to end of scourge; **hacer la pelotilla a** (coll.) to soft-soap
**pelotillero -ra** *adj* fawning, cringing
**pelotón** *m* large ball; ball of hair; gang, crowd; (mil.) platoon; **pelotón de fusilamiento** firing squad; **pelotón de los torpes** (mil.) awkward squad
**peltraba** *f* (slang) game bag
**peltre** *m* spelter, pewter
**peltrería** *f* pewter factory; pewter business
**peltrero** *m* pewterer, pewter worker or dealer
**peluca** *f* wig; (coll.) wig (*one who wears a wig; severe reprimand*)
**pelucón -cona** *adj* wig-wearing; bewigged; (Am.) conservative; *m* big bushy wig; *f* gold doubloon
**peluche** *m* plush
**peludo -da** *adj* hairy, shaggy, furry; *m* bast mat
**peluquería** *f* hairdresser's (shop), barbershop
**peluquero -ra** *mf* hairdresser, barber; wigmaker
**peluquín** *m* scratchwig; peruke
**pelusa** *f* down; fuzz, nap; (coll.) jealousy, envy (*of a child*)
**pelusilla** *f* fuzz; (bot.) mouse-ear
**pelviano -na** *adj* pelvic
**pelvímetro** *m* pelvimeter
**pelvis** *f* (*pl:* **-vis**) (anat.) pelvis
**pella** *f* pellet; puff (*of pastry*); rough casting; tender head of cauliflower; raw lard; (orn.) gray heron; (coll.) sum of money, debt, theft; **hacer pella** (slang) to play hooky
**pellada** *f* pellet; batch of mortar or plaster
**pelleja** *f* hide; skin; undressed sheepskin; (coll.) prostitute
**pellejería** *f* leather dressing; skinnery; skins, hides; (Am.) jam, trouble
**pellejero -ra** *mf* leather dresser; skinner
**pellejina** *f* small skin
**pellejo** *m* skin; pelt, rawhide; peel, rind; wineskin; (fig.) hide, skin (*life*); (coll.) sot, drunkard; **dar, dejar** or **perder el pellejo** (coll.) to die; **estar** or **hallarse en el pellejo de otro** to be in somebody else's shoes; **no tener más que el pellejo** (coll.) to be nothing but skin and bones; **salvar el pellejo** (coll.) to save one's skin
**pellejudo -da** *adj* flabby, baggy
**pelleta** *f* var. of **pelleja**
**pelletería** *f* var. of **pellejería**
**pelletero** *m* var. of **pellejero**
**pellica** *f* robe or coverlet of fine furs; small dressed skin; jacket of fine skins
**pellico** *m* shepherd's jacket (*made of skins*)
**pellijero** *m* var. of **pellejero**
**pellín** *m* (bot.) antarctic or mountain beach
**pelliquero** *m* maker of shepherd's jackets
**pelliza** *f* pelisse; (mil.) dolman
**pellizcar** §86 *va* to pinch; to nip; to take a pinch of; *vr* (coll.) to long, to pine
**pellizco** *m* pinch; nip; bit, pinch; **pellizco de monja** cookie
**pello** *m* fine fur jacket
**pellón** *m* or **pellote** *m* fur cloak or robe
**pelluzgón** *m* bunch or tuft of hair
**pena** *f* see **peno**
**penable** *adj* penal, punishable
**penachera** *f* crest; plume, panache
**penacho** *m* crest; plume, panache; arrogance, haughtiness; (bot.) tassel
**penachudo -da** *adj* crested, plumed
**penachuelo** *m* small crest; small plume
**penadamente** *adv* painfully, with great effort
**penadilla** *f* narrow-mouthed drinking vessel
**penado -da** *adj* afflicted, grieved; arduous, difficult; narrow-mouthed (*vessel*); *mf* convict
**penal** *adj* penal; *m* penitentiary

**penalidad** *f* trouble, hardship; punishability; (law) penalty
**penalista** *mf* penologist
**penante** *adj* suffering, afflicted; *m* (coll.) suitor
**penar** *va* to penalize; to punish; *vn* to suffer; to linger (*although suffering or dying*); to suffer, to be tormented (*in Hell*); **penar por** to pine for, to long for; *vr* to grieve, to sorrow
**penates** *mpl* penates
**penca** *f* pulpy leaf (*e.g., of cactus*); pulpy part (*of leaf*); cowhide (*used for flogging*); **coger una penca** (Am.) to get drunk; **hacerse de pencas** (coll.) to let oneself be coaxed
**pencazo** *m* lash with a cowhide
**penco** *m* (bot.) Indian fig; (coll.) jade, hack, nag; (Am.) boor
**pencudo -da** *adj* having pulpy leaves
**pendanga** *f* jack of diamonds; (coll.) prostitute
**pendejo** *m* pubes (*hair*); (coll.) coward; (Am.) fool
**pendencia** *f* dispute, quarrel, fight; (law) pending litigation
**pendenciar** *vn* to dispute, quarrel, fight, wrangle
**pendenciero -ra** *adj* quarrelsome; *mf* wrangler
**pendenzuela** *f* little dispute or quarrel
**pender** *vn* to hang, dangle; to depend; to be pending
**pendiente** *adj* pendent, hanging, dangling; pending; under way; awaiting, expecting; **estar pendiente de** to depend on; to hang on (*e.g., someone's words*); to be in process of; *m* earring, pendant; watch chain; *f* slope, grade; dip, pitch; curve (*of a graph*)
**pendil** *m* woman's mantle; **tomar el pendil** (coll.) to leave, go away
**péndol** *m* (naut.) boot-topping
**péndola** *f* pendulum (*of clock*); clock (*with pendulum*); queen post; bridging brace; feather; pen, quill
**pendolaje** *m* (naut.) right of seizure
**pendolario** *m* penman
**pendolear** *vn & vr* to dangle, to swing
**pendolero -ra** *adj* (coll.) loose, dangling, sloppy
**pendolista** *mf* copyist, calligrapher; *m* penman
**pendolón** *m* large pendulum; king post
**pendón** *m* banner, standard, pennon; (bot.) shoot, tiller; (coll.) slattern
**pendonear** *vn* (coll.) var. of **pindonguear**
**pendular** *adj* of a pendulum
**péndulo -la** *adj* pendent, hanging; *m* pendulum; clock; **péndulo compensado** or **de compensación** compensation pendulum; **péndulo de segundos** seconds pendulum; **péndulo de torsión** torsion pendulum; **péndulo matemático** mathematical pendulum
**pene** *m* (anat.) penis
**peneca** *mf* (Am.) first-grade pupil; *f* (Am.) first grade (*in school*)
**penela** *f* flatboat, canal boat
**Penélope** *f* (myth.) Penelope
**peneque** *adj* (coll.) drunk
**penetrabilidad** *f* penetrability
**penetrable** *adj* penetrable
**penetración** *f* penetration; (fig.) penetration, insight; **penetración pacífica** (pol.) peaceful penetration
**penetrador -dora** *adj* keen, penetrating
**penetrante** *adj* penetrating; (fig.) penetrating
**penetrar** *va* to penetrate; to pierce; to grasp, fathom; to see through (*someone's intentions*); *vn* to penetrate; **penetrar en, entre** or **por entre** to penetrate into; *vr* to grasp, fathom; to realize; to become convinced; **penetrarse de** to become impregnated with; to become imbued with
**penetrativo -va** *adj* penetrative
**pénfigo** *m* (path.) pemphigus
**penicilina** *f* (pharm.) penicillin
**penígero -ra** *adj* (poet.) winged, feathered
**penillanura** *f* (geol.) peneplain
**península** *f* peninsula; **Península Balcánica** or **de los Balcanes** Balkan Peninsula; **península del Labrador** Labrador; **Península Ibérica** Iberian Peninsula; **península Malaya** or **de Malaca** Malay Peninsula
**peninsular** *adj & mf* peninsular
**penique** *m* penny
**penisla** *f* var. of **península**

**penit.** abr. of **penitente**
**penitencia** *f* penitence; penance; **hacer penitencia** to do penance; to eat sparingly; to take potluck
**penitenciado -da** *adj* punished by the Inquisition; punished; *mf* (Am.) convict
**penitencial** *adj* penitential; *m* (eccl.) penitential, penitential book
**penitenciar** *va* to impose penance on; to punish
**penitenciaría** *f* penitentiary; (eccl.) penitentiary
**penitenciario -ria** *adj* penitentiary; *m* (eccl.) penitentiary (*officer*)
**penitenta** *f* penitent woman; female confessant
**penitente** *adj & mf* penitent
**pennado -da** *adj* pennate
**penninervio -via** *adj* (bot.) penninervate
**peno -na** *adj & mf* Carthaginian ‖ *f* punishment; penalty; pain; hardship, toil; sorrow, grief; effort, trouble; choker (*jeweled collar*); (orn.) penna; **penas** *fpl* (Am.) ghosts; **a penas** hardly; **a duras penas** with great difficuty; **merecer la pena** to be worth while; **¡qué pena!** what a pity!; **so pena de** under penalty of; **última pena de la vida** death; **valer la pena** to be worth while; **valer la pena** + *inf* to be worth while to + *inf*, e.g., **no vale la pena ir al teatro esta noche** it isn't worth while to go to the theater this evening; **valer la pena de** + *inf* to be worth + *ger*, e.g., **aquella ciudad no vale la pena de visitarse** that city is not worth visiting; **pena capital** capital punishment; **pena infamante** loss of civil rights, banishment; **pena de muerte** death penalty, capital punishment; **pena de la vida** capital punishment
**penol** *m* (naut.) yardarm, peak
**penología** *f* penology
**penológico -ca** *adj* penological
**penologista** *mf* **penólogo -ga** *mf* penologist
**penoso -sa** *adj* arduous, difficult; suffering, afflicted; (coll.) conceited; (Am.) shy, timid
**pensado -da** *adj* deliberate, thought-out; **bien pensado** advised, wise; **de pensado** on purpose; **mal pensado** evil-minded; foolish, unwise
**pensador -dora** *adj* thinking; *m* thinker
**pensamiento** *m* thought; suspicion; (bot.) pansy; **en un pensamiento** in a twinkling, in a jiffy; **ni por pensamiento** not even in thought
**pensar** §18 *va* to think; to think over; to think of (*a card, a number, etc.*); to feed (*animals*); **pensar** + *inf* to intend to + *inf;* to almost + *inf;* **pensar de** to think of (*to have a certain opinion of*); *vn* to think; **sin pensar** unexpectedly; **pensar en** to think of (*to direct one's thoughts to*); **pensar en** + *inf* to think of + *ger*; *vr* to think; **pensárselo mejor** to think better of it, to change one's mind
**pensativo -va** *adj* pensive, thoughtful
**pensel** *m* (bot.) turnsole
**penseque** *m* (coll.) oversight, inadvertence
**pensil** *adj* pensile; *m* enchanted garden
**Pensilvania** *f* Pennsylvania
**pensilvano -na** *adj & mf* Pennsylvanian
**pensión** *f* pension, annuity; allowance; boarding house; board; fellowship (*for study*); grant-in-aid; bother, disadvantage; burden; **pensión completa** room and board
**pensionado -da** *mf* pensioner; fellow; *m* dormitory; boarding school
**pensionar** *va* to pension; to burden
**pensionario** *m* pensionary, magistrate
**pensionista** *mf* pensioner; boarder; pupil of a boarding school; **medio pensionista** day boarder (*in a school*)
**pentaclo** *m* pentacle
**pentadáctilo -la** *adj* pentadactyl
**pentaedro** *m* (geom.) pentahedron
**pentagonal** *adj* pentagonal
**pentágono -na** *adj* pentagonal; *m* (geom.) pentagon; **el Pentágono** the Pentagon (*building of U.S. Department of Defense in Washington*)
**pentágrama** or **pentagrama** *m* (mus.) staff, musical staff
**pentámero -ra** *adj* (bot. & zool.) pentamerous
**pentámetro -tra** *adj & m* pentameter
**pentano** *m* (chem.) pentane

**pentarquía** *f* pentarchy
**pentasílabo -ba** *adj* pentasyllabic; *m* pentasyllable
**Pentateuco** *m* (Bib.) Pentateuch
**pentatlo** *m* (sport) pentathlon
**pentatónico -ca** *adj* pentatonic
**pentavalente** *adj* (chem.) pentavalent
**Pentecostés** *f* Pentecost
**pentodo** or **péntodo** *m* (elec.) pentode
**pentosa** *f* (chem.) pentose
**pentosana** *f* (chem.) pentosan
**penúltimo -ma** *adj* penultimate; next to last; *f* (phonet.) penult
**penumbra** *f* penumbra; semidarkness, half-light
**penuria** *f* penury (*dearth*)
**Penyab** *m* Punjab
**peña** *f* rock, boulder; cliff; peen (*of hammer*); club, group, circle; **durar por peñas** to last a long time
**peñascal** *m* spiry terrain, rocky country
**peñasco** *m* spire of rock, pinnacle, crag; strong silk; (zool.) murex; (anat.) petrous portion (*of temporal bone*)
**peñascoso -sa** *adj* rocky, craggy
**peño** *m* (dial.) foundling
**peñol** *m* var. of **peñón**
**péñola** *f* pen, quill
**peñón** *m* rock, spire; **peñón de Gibraltar** Rock of Gibraltar
**peón** *m* pedestrian; foot soldier; laborer; pawn (*in chess*); man (*in checkers*); top, peg top; spindle, axle; hive; (taur.) attendant, assistant; (Am.) farm hand; **peón caminero** road laborer; **peón de albañil** or **de mano** hod carrier; **peón ferrocarrilero** (rail.) section hand
**peonada** *f* day's work of a laborer; gang of laborers
**peonaje** *m* gang of laborers; squad of foot soldiers
**peonería** *f* day's plowing
**peonía** *f* (bot.) peony; (bot.) rosary pea; (obs.) land in conquered territory given to an infantryman to settle on
**peonza** *f* whip top, whipping top; (coll.) noisy little squirt; **a peonza** (coll.) on foot
**peor** *adj & adv* worse; worst; **peor que peor** worse and worse
**peoría** *f* worseness; worsening
**pepa** *f* (Am.) seed (*e.g., of apple*); (Am.) marble; (*cap.*) *f* Jo, Jozy
**Pepe** *m* Joe
**pepián** *m* var. of **pipián**
**Pepillo** or **Pepín** *m* Joe
**pepinar** *m* cucumber patch
**pepinillo** *m* (bot.) gherkin (*Cucumis anguria and fruit; small cucumber used for pickles*); **pepinillo del diablo** (bot.) squirting cucumber
**pepino** *m* (bot.) cucumber; **no dársele a uno un pepino de** or **por** (coll.) to not care about, to not give a fig for
**pepita** *f* pip (*small seed*); melon seed; nugget; (vet.) pip; **no tener pepita en la lengua** (coll.) to speak freely, to speak without restraint; (*cap.*) *f* Jozy
**Pepito** *m* Joe
**pepitoria** *f* giblet fricassee with egg sauce; medley, hodgepodge
**pepitoso -sa** *adj* pippy (*full of pips*); suffering from pip
**peplo** *m* (hist.) peplum
**pepón** *m* (bot.) watermelon
**pepona** *f* large paper doll
**pepónide** *f* (bot.) pepo
**pepsina** *f* (biochem.) pepsin
**péptico -ca** *adj* peptic
**péptido** *m* (biochem.) peptide
**peptizar** §76 *va* (chem.) to peptize
**peptona** *f* (biochem.) peptone
**pequén** *m* (orn.) burrowing owl (*of Chile*)
**pequeñez** *f* (*pl:* **-ñeces**) smallness; infancy; trifle; (fig.) smallness
**pequeñín** *m* little one, baby, child
**pequeño -ña** *adj* little, small; young; low, humble; **en pequeño** briefly, in a word; on a small scale
**pequeñuelo -la** *adj* very small, tiny; very young; *mf* baby, tot
**pequín** *m* pekin; (*cap.*) *m* Pekin
**pequinés -nesa** *adj* Pekinese; *mf* Pekinese (*native of Pekin; dog*)
**pera** *f* pear (*fruit*); goatee, imperial; cinch, sinecure; pear-shaped bulb (*of camera shutter, auto horn, etc.*); (elec.) pear-shaped switch; **partir peras con** (coll.) to be on intimate terms with; **ponerle a uno las peras a cuatro** or **a ocho** (coll.) to put the squeeze on someone
**perada** *f* pear jam; pear brandy
**peral** *m* (bot.) pear, pear tree
**peraleda** *f* orchard of pear trees
**peraltar** *va* (arch.) to stilt; (rail.) to bank, to superelevate
**peralte** *m* (arch.) stilt; (arch.) height, rise; (rail.) superelevation
**peralto** *m* (geom.) height
**perantón** *m* (bot.) mock cypress; large fan; (coll.) tall person
**perborato** *m* (chem.) perborate
**perca** *f* (ichth.) perch; **perca de mar** (ichth.) sea bass
**percal** *m* percale
**percalina** *f* percaline
**percance** *m* mischance, misfortune; **percances** *mpl* perquisites
**percatar** *vr* to be on one's guard; **percatarse de** to notice, to become aware of, to suspect; to beware of, to guard against
**percebe** *m* (zool.) barnacle (*Pollicipes cornucopia*); (coll.) fool, ignoramus
**percebimiento** *m* var. of **apercibimiento**
**percentil** *m* percentile
**percepción** *f* perception; percept; collection
**perceptibilidad** *f* perceptibility; collectability
**perceptible** *adj* perceptible; collectable
**perceptivo -va** *adj* perceptive (*having the faculty of perceiving*); perceptual (*pertaining to perception*)
**perceptor -tora** *adj* percipient; *mf* percipient; collector (*e.g., of taxes*)
**Perceval** *m* Percival
**percibidero -ra** *adj* perceptible
**percibir** *va* to perceive; to collect
**percibo** *m* collecting, collection
**perclorato** *m* (chem.) perchlorate
**percloruro** *m* (chem.) perchloride
**percocería** *f* small piece of hammered silverware
**percuciente** *adj* percutient, percussive
**percudir** *va* to tarnish, to dull; to spread through; *vr* to spot with mildew (*said of clean wash*)
**percusión** *f* percussion; (med.) percussion
**percusor** *m* (med.) percussor (*person who strikes; percussion hammer*); firing pin
**percutir** *va* to percuss
**percutor** *m* firing pin
**percha** *f* perch, pole, roost; clothes tree; coat hanger; coat hook; barber pole; napping (*of cloth*); snare (*to catch birds*); perch for a falcon; (naut.) spar, rough log; (ichth.) perch; **estar en percha** to be in the bag
**perchar** *va* to nap (*cloth*)
**perchero** *m* rack, clothes rack
**percherón -rona** *adj & mf* Percheron
**perchón** *m* poorly pruned shoot (*of vine*)
**perchonar** *vn* to leave poorly pruned shoots on the vine; to lay snares for game
**perdedero** *m* cause of loss; gambling den; den of vice; rabbit's burrow
**perdedor -dora** *adj* losing; *mf* loser
**perder** §66 *va* to lose; to waste, squander; to miss (*e.g., a train, an opportunity*); to flunk (*a course*); to ruin; to spoil; *vn* to lose; to fade; *vr* to lose one's way, get lost, go astray; to miscarry; to sink, go to the bottom; to become ruined; to spoil, get spoiled; to fall into disuse; to lose one's virtue (*said of a woman*); **perderse en** to fall all over oneself in (*e.g., excuses*); **perderse por** to be madly in love with
**perdición** *f* perdition; loss; unbridled passion; outrage; ruination
**pérdida** *f* loss; waste; damage, ruination; **estar** or **ir a pérdidas y ganancias** to share profit and loss; **no tener pérdida** (coll.) to be easy to find; **pérdidas blancas** (path.) whites
**perdidamente** *adv* madly, wildly; uselessly

**perdidizo -za** *adj* supposed to be lost; **hacer perdidizo** (coll.) to hide; (coll.) to drop, to lose (*on purpose*); **hacerse perdidizo** (coll.) to lose on purpose (*in a game*); **hacerse el perdidizo** (coll.) to make oneself scarce
**perdido -da** *adj* stray, wild (*bullet*); wide, loose (*sleeve*); countersunk; fruitless, unsuccessful; dissolute; off, spare, idle (*hours*); absent, distracted; confirmed, inveterate; **perdido por** mad about; *m* profligate, rake; (print.) extra printing (*to make up for spoiled sheets*); **al perdido** carelessly, sloppily
**perdidoso -sa** *adj* losing, unlucky; easily lost
**perdigar §59** *va* to brown, to broil slightly; (coll.) to make ready, prepare
**perdigón** *m* young partridge; decoy partridge; shot; (coll.) profligate; (coll.) heavy loser (*in gambling*); (coll.) failure (*student who failed*); **perdigón zorrero** buckshot
**perdigonada** *f* shot with bird shot; wound caused by bird shot
**perdigonera** *f* pouch for shot
**perdiguero -ra** *adj* partridge-hunting; *m* pointer, setter; game dealer
**perdimiento** *m* loss, waste, ruin
**perdis** *m* (*pl:* **-dis**) (coll.) rake, good-for-nothing
**perditancia** *f* (elec.) leakage conductance, leakance
**perdiz** *f* (*pl:* **-dices**) (orn.) partridge; **perdiz blanca** (orn.) rock ptarmigan; **perdiz, o no comerla** (coll.) whole hog or none; **perdiz pardilla** (orn.) gray partridge; **perdiz real** or **roja** (orn.) red-legged partridge
**perdón** *m* pardon, forgiveness; (coll.) burning drop of oil, wax, etc.; **con perdón** by your leave
**perdonable** *adj* pardonable
**perdonador -dora** *adj* forgiving; *mf* pardoner; *m* (eccl.) pardoner
**perdonar** *va* to pardon, forgive, excuse; **no perdonar** to not miss, to not omit
**perdonavidas** *m* (*pl:* **-das**) (coll.) bully
**perdulario -ria** *adj* careless, sloppy; vicious, incorrigible
**perdurable** *adj* lasting, long-lasting; everlasting; *f* durance, everlasting (*a material*)
**perdurar** *vn* to last, last a long time, survive
**perecear** *va* (coll.) to put off, delay (*out of laziness, indifference, etc.*)
**perecedero -ra** *adj* perishable; mortal; *m* (coll.) misery, extreme want; danger spot
**perecer §34** *vn* to perish; to suffer, become exhausted; to be in great want; **perecer ahogado** to drown; *vr* to pine; **perecerse de risa** to be dying of laughter; **perecerse por** to pine for, to be dying for; to be mad about (*e.g., a woman*)
**perecimiento** *m* perishing, end, death
**pereda** *f* orchard of pear trees
**peregrinación** *f* or **peregrinaje** *m* peregrination; pilgrimage
**peregrinar** *vn* to peregrinate; to go as a pilgrim; to journey through life
**peregrinidad** *f* rareness, strangeness
**peregrino -na** *adj* wandering, traveling; peregrine, foreign; rare, strange; singular; beautiful, excellent; mortal; migratory (*bird*); *mf* pilgrim
**perejil** *m* (bot.) parsley; (coll.) frippery, tawdry dress or ornaments; **perejiles** *mpl* (naut.) pennants and banners hoisted to bedeck a ship; (coll.) handles (*titles, etc.*); (coll.) frippery; **perejil de mar** (bot.) samphire; **perejil de monte** (bot.) mountain parsley; **perejil de perro** (bot.) fool's-parsley; **perejil marino** (bot.) samphire
**perenal** *adj* var. of **perenne**
**perencejo** *m* var. of **perengano**
**perendeca** *f* (coll.) prostitute
**perendengue** *m* earring; trinket, cheap ornament
**perene** *adj* var. of **perenne**
**perengano -na** *mf* so-and-so
**perenne** *adj* perennial; (bot.) perennial
**perennidad** *f* perenniality
**perentoriedad** *f* peremptoriness; urgency
**perentorio -ria** *adj* peremptory; urgent
**perero** *m* fruit parer
**pereza** *f* laziness; slowness
**perezoso -sa** *adj* lazy; slow, dull, heavy; *mf* lazybones; sleepyhead; *m* (zool.) sloth
**perfección** *f* perfection; **a la perfección** to perfection
**perfeccionamiento** *m* perfection, improvement
**perfeccionar** *va* to perfect, improve
**perfeccionista** *mf* perfectionist
**perfectibilidad** *f* perfectibility
**perfectible** *adj* perfectible
**perfectivo -va** *adj* perfective
**perfecto -ta** *adj* perfect; (gram.) perfect; *m* (gram.) perfect
**perfidia** *f* perfidy
**pérfido -da** *adj* perfidious
**perfil** *m* profile; side view; cross section; thin stroke (*in writing*); trimming; outline, sketch; skyline; (iron mfg.) shape; **perfiles** *mpl* finishing touches; courtesies; **perfil aerodinámico** (aer.) streamlining
**perfilado -da** *adj* long and thin (*face*); well-formed (*nose*); delicate (*features*); streamlined
**perfiladura** *f* profiling, outlining; outline
**perfilar** *va* to profile, to outline; to perfect, to polish, to finish; *vr* to be outlined; to show one's profile, to stand sideways; (coll.) to dress up
**perfoliado -da** *adj* (bot.) perfoliate; *f* (bot.) hare's-ear
**perfoliata** *f* (bot.) hare's-ear
**perfolla** *f* cornhusk
**perforación** *f* perforation; drilling, boring; puncture; punch
**perforador -dora** *adj* perforating; drilling; *mf* perforator; *m* (telg.) perforator; *f* pneumatic drill, compressed-air drill, rock drill; (mach.) perforator
**perforante** *adj* perforating; armor-piercing
**perforar** *va* to perforate; to drill, to bore; to puncture; to punch (*e.g., card*)
**perforista** *mf* keypuncher
**performance** *f* (sport) performance
**perfumadero** *m* perfuming pan
**perfumador -dora** *mf* perfumer; *m* perfuming pan; perfume atomizer
**perfumar** *va* to perfume
**perfume** *m* perfume
**perfumear** *va* var. of **perfumar**
**perfumería** *f* perfumery
**perfumero -ra** or **perfumista** *mf* perfumer
**perfunctorio -ria** *adj* perfunctory
**perg.** abr. of **pergamino**
**pergal** *m* leather paring for sandal thongs
**pergaminero** *m* parchment-maker, parchment seller
**pergamino** *m* parchment
**Pérgamo** *f* Pergamum
**pergeniar** *va* to comprehend, to know thoroughly
**pergenio** *m* (coll.) appearance, looks
**pergeñar** *va* to execute; to perform with skill; to grasp thoroughly
**pergeño** *m* (coll.) appearance, looks
**pérgola** *f* pergola; roof garden
**peri** *f* (myth.) peri
**periantio** *m* (bot.) perianth
**pericardíaco -ca** *adj* pericardiac
**pericardio** *m* (anat.) pericardium
**pericarditis** *f* (path.) pericarditis
**pericarpio** *m* (bot.) pericarp, seedcase, seed vessel
**pericia** *f* skill, expertness
**pericial** *adj* expert; *m* expert; customhouse officer
**Pericles** *m* Pericles
**periclitar** *vn* to be in jeopardy, to be unsound or shaky
**perico** *m* periwig; large asparagus; large fan; queen of clubs; (naut.) mizzen-topgallant sail; (orn.) parakeet; (slang) chamber pot; (*cap.*) *m* Pete; **perico de los palotes** anybody, so-and-so; **perico entre ellas** (coll.) lady's man; **perico ligero** (zool.) sloth
**pericón -cona** *adj* fit for all uses (*said of a horse or mule*); *m* large fan; queen of clubs
**pericráneo** *m* (anat.) pericranium
**peridoto** *m* (mineral.) chrysolite, peridot
**perieco -ca** *adj* perioecic; **periecos** *mpl* perioeci

**periferia** *f* periphery; surroundings
**periférico -ca** *adj* peripheral
**perifollo** *m* (bot.) chervil; **perifollos** *mpl* (coll.) finery, frippery; **perifollo oloroso** (bot.) sweet cicely, sweet fern
**perifonear** *va* to broadcast
**perifonía** *f* broadcasting
**perífono** *m* broadcasting apparatus
**perifrasear** *vn* to periphrase
**perífrasi** *f* or **perífrasis** *f* (*pl:* **-sis**) periphrase or periphrasis
**perifrástico -ca** *adj* periphrastic
**perigallo** *m* loose skin under the chin; bright-colored hair ribbon; sling made of twine; (coll.) tall, lanky person; (naut.) topping lift
**perigeo** *m* (astr.) perigee
**periginia** *f* perigyny
**perihelio** *m* (astr.) perihelion
**perilustre** *adj* very illustrious
**perilla** *f* pear-shaped figure or ornament; goatee, imperial; pommel (*of saddlebow*); knob; lobe (*of ear*); **de perilla** or **de perillas** (coll.) apropos, to the point
**perillán -llana** *adj* rascally, crafty; *m* rascal, crafty fellow
**perillo** *m* scalloped cookie
**perímetro** *m* perimeter
**perimisio** *m* (anat.) perimysium
**perínclito -ta** *adj* illustrious, heroic
**perineal** *adj* perineal
**perineo** *m* (anat.) perineum
**perineurio** *m* (anat.) perineurium
**perinola** *f* teetotum; pear-shaped figure or ornament; (coll.) pert little woman
**perioca** *f* argument, summary
**periodicidad** *f* periodicity; regularity
**periódico -ca** *adj* periodic; periodical; *m* periodical; newspaper
**periodismo** *m* newspaper work, journalism
**periodista** *mf* journalist; *m* newspaperman; *f* newspaperwoman
**periodístico -ca** *adj* (pertaining to the) newspaper, journalistic
**periodización** *f* division into periods
**período** *m* period; (gram.) compound sentence; (phys.) cycle; **período de incubación** (path.) incubation period; **período glacial** (geol.) glacial period; **período lectivo** term (*in school*); **período medio** (phys.) half life (*of radioactive substance*)
**periodontal** *adj* periodontal
**periostio** *m* (anat.) periosteum
**periostitis** *f* (path.) periostitis
**peripatético -ca** *adj* Peripatetic; (coll.) ridiculous, wild (*in one's opinions*); *m* Peripatetic
**peripato** *m* Peripateticism; Peripatetics
**peripecia** *f* peripeteia, vicissitude
**periplo** *m* periplus (*voyage around coast or island; account of such voyage*); trip, journey
**períptero -ra** *adj* (arch.) peripteral
**peripuesto -ta** *adj* (coll.) dudish, all spruced up, sporty
**periquear** *vn* to be too free, take too much liberty (*said of a woman*)
**periquete** *m* (coll.) jiffy; **en un periquete** (coll.) in a jiffy
**periquillo** *m* sugarplum
**periquito** *m* (orn.) parakeet; (naut.) skysail; **periquito de Australia** (orn.) budgerigar, zebra parakeet
**periscio -cia** *adj* periscian; **periscios** *mpl* periscii
**periscópico -ca** *adj* periscopic
**periscopio** *m* periscope
**perisodáctilo -la** *adj & m* (zool.) perissodactyl
**perisología** *f* pleonasm, verbiage
**peristalsis** *f* (*pl:* **-sis**) (physiol.) peristalsis
**peristáltico -ca** *adj* peristaltic
**peristaltismo** *m* var. of **peristalsis**
**peristilo** *m* (arch.) peristyle
**perístole** *f* (physiol.) peristole, peristalsis
**perístoma** *m* (bot.) peristome
**peritación** *f* work of an expert
**peritaje** *m* work of an expert; expert's fee; training course for experts
**perito -ta** *adj* skilled, skilful; expert; *m* expert
**peritoneal** *adj* peritoneal
**peritoneo** *m* (anat.) peritoneum
**peritonitis** *f* (path.) peritonitis
**perjudicador -dora** *adj* harmful, injurious; *mf* harmer, injurer
**perjudicar** **§86** *va* to harm, damage, impair, prejudice
**perjudicial** *adj* harmful, injurious, prejudicial
**perjuicio** *m* harm, injury, damage, prejudice; **en perjuicio de** to the detriment of; **sin perjuicio de** without affecting
**perjurador -dora** *adj* perjured; *mf* perjurer
**perjurar** *vn* to commit perjury; to swear, be profane; *vr* to commit perjury; to perjure oneself
**perjurio** *m* perjury
**perjuro -ra** *adj* perjured; *mf* perjurer; *m* perjury
**perla** *f* pearl; (fig.) pearl, jewel (*person or thing*); (pharm.) pearl, capsule; (f.a.) pearl; **de perlas** perfectly; **perla de ampolla** blister pearl
**perlado -da** *adj* pearled; pearly
**perlático -ca** *adj* palsied, paralyzed; *mf* paralytic
**perlería** *f* collection of pearls
**perlero -ra** *adj* (pertaining to the) pearl
**perlesía** *f* (path.) palsy, paralysis
**perlífero -ra** *adj* pearl-bearing
**perlino -na** *adj* pearl, pearl-colored
**perlita** *f* (metal. & petrog.) perlite; (mineral.) phonolite
**perlongar** **§59** *va* to sail along; *vn* to sail along the coast; (naut.) to pay out a cable
**permaloy** *m* permalloy
**permanecer** **§34** *vn* to stay, remain
**permaneciente** *adj* staying; permanent
**permanencia** *f* permanence; stay, sojourn; **permanencias** *fpl* (educ.) study hours
**permanente** *adj* permanent; *f* permanent (*wave*); **permanente en frío** cold wave (*in hair*)
**permanganato** *m* (chem.) permanganate; **permanganato de potasio** (chem.) potassium permanganate
**permangánico -ca** *adj* permanganic
**permansión** *f* var. of **permanencia**
**permeabilidad** *f* permeability
**permeable** *adj* permeable
**permeancia** *f* (elec.) permeance
**pérmico -ca** *adj & m* (geol.) Permian
**permisible** *adj* permissible
**permisión** *f* permission
**permisivo -va** *adj* permissive
**permiso** *m* permission; permit; time off; tolerance (*in coinage*); leave; **con permiso** on leave; excuse me; **de permiso** on leave; **permiso de circulación** (aut.) owner's license; **permiso de conducir** (aut.) driver's license
**permisor -sora** *adj* var. of **permitidor**
**permistión** *f* mixture, concoction
**permitidero -ra** *adj* permissible
**permitidor -dora** *adj* permitting
**permitir** *va* to permit, to allow; **permitir** + *inf* to permit or allow to + *inf;* to enable to + *inf;* **permitir que** + *subj* to permit or allow to + *inf; vr* to be permitted; to allow oneself (*e.g., a criticism*); **no se permite fumar** no smoking; **permitirse** + *inf* to take the liberty to + *inf*
**permuta** *f* barter, exchange
**permutable** *adj* exchangeable; permutable
**permutación** *f* interchange, exchange; permutation; (math.) permutation
**permutar** *va* to interchange; to barter; to permute
**pernada** *f* kick; leg (*of some object*)
**pernaza** *f* big leg, thick leg
**perneador -dora** *adj* strong-legged
**pernear** *vn* to kick, shake the legs; (coll.) to fuss, to hustle, to fret
**perneo** *m* (dial.) hog market
**pernera** *f* leg (*of trousers*)
**pernería** *f* (naut.) stock of bolts
**perneta** *f* small leg; **en pernetas** barelegged
**pernete** *m* small bolt, pin, peg
**perniabierto -ta** *adj* bowlegged
**pernicioso -sa** *adj* pernicious
**pernil** *m* thigh (*of animal*); leg (*of trousers*)
**pernio** *m* hinge
**perniquebrar** **§18** *va* to break the leg or legs of; *vr* to break one's leg or legs

**pernituerto -ta** *adj* crooked-legged
**perno** *m* bolt; eye (*of hook-and-eye hinge*); **perno de expansión** expansion bolt; **perno roscado** screw bolt
**pernoctar** *vn* to spend the night, to spend the night away from home
**pernotar** *va* to note, observe
**pero** *conj* but, yet; *m* (bot.) permain; (coll.) but, objection; (coll.) fault, defect; **poner pero a** (coll.) to find fault with
**perogrullada** *f* (coll.) platitude, inanity
**perol** *m* kettle (*in form of hemisphere*)
**perón** *m* (Am.) pear-shaped apple
**peroné** *m* (anat.) fibula
**peroneo -a** *adj* fibular
**peroración** *f* peroration; (coll.) harangue
**perorar** *vn* to perorate; (coll.) to orate
**perorata** *f* harangue, declamation, tiresome speech
**peroxiácido** *m* (chem.) peroxyacid
**peróxido** *m* (chem.) peroxide; **peróxido de hidrógeno** (chem.) hydrogen peroxide; **peróxido de plomo** (chem.) lead dioxide ($O_2Pb$)
**perpendicular** *adj & f* perpendicular
**perpendicularidad** *f* perpendicularity
**perpendículo** *m* plumb bob; pendulum; (geom.) altitude of a triangle
**perpetración** *f* perpetration
**perpetrador -dora** *mf* perpetrator
**perpetrar** *va* to perpetrate
**perpetua** *f* see **perpetuo**
**perpetuación** *f* perpetuation
**perpetuar** §33 *va* to perpetuate; *vr* to be perpetuated
**perpetuidad** *f* perpetuity
**perpetuo -tua** *adj* perpetual; life; *f* (bot.) globe amaranth; **perpetua amarilla** (bot.) everlasting flower; **perpetua encarnada** (bot.) globe amaranth
**perpiaño** *m* (mas.) bondstone, perpend
**Perpiñán** *f* Perpignan
**perplejidad** *f* perplexity; worry, anxiety
**perplejo -ja** *adj* perplexed; worried, anxious; baffling, perplexing
**perpunte** *m* pourpoint (*quilted doublet*)
**perquirir** §56 *va* to seek out, investigate
**perra** *f* see **perro**
**perrada** *f* pack of dogs; drudgery; (coll.) dirty trick, meanness, treachery
**perrengue** *m* (coll.) irascible fellow, grouch; (coll.) Negro
**perrera** *f* doghouse, kennel; tantrum; drudgery; (coll.) poor pay (*person*)
**perrería** *f* pack of dogs; gang of thieves; angry word; (coll.) dirty trick, meanness, treachery
**perrero** *m* beadle who keeps dogs out of church; master of the hounds; dog fancier; dogcatcher
**perrezno** *m* puppy
**perrillo -lla** *mf* puppy; *m* trigger
**perrito** *m* doggie
**perro -rra** *adj* (coll.) wicked, mean; (coll.) hard, bitter, troublesome; (Am.) rash, stubborn; (Am.) selfish, stingy; *m* dog; (mach.) dog, pawl; **a otro perro con ese hueso** tell that to the marines; **el perro del hortelano** dog in the manger; **perro ardero** squirrel dog; **perro caliente** (slang) hot dog; **perro cobrador** retriever; **perro chico** (coll.) copper coin (*five centimes*); **perro dalmático** coach dog; **perro de aguas** spaniel; **perro de ajeo** bird dog, retriever; **perro de lanas** poodle; **perro de muestra** pointer, setter; **perro de pastor** sheep dog, shepherd dog; **perro de San Bernardo** Saint Bernard; **perro faldero** lap dog; **perro hiena** (zool.) Cape hunting dog; **perro jabalinero** boarhound; **perro lebrel** whippet; **perro lebrero** rabbit dog; **perro lobero** wolf dog; **perro lulú** spitz dog; **perro maestro** trained dog; **perro marino** (ichth.) dogfish, shark; **perro ovejero** sheep dog, shepherd dog; **perro pastor alemán** German shepherd dog; **perro policía** police dog; **perro pomerano** Pomeranian (*dog*); **perro raposero** foxhound; **perro rastrero** trackhound; **perro viejo** (coll.) wise old owl; *f* bitch; tantrum; (coll.) drunk, drunkenness
**perro-lazarillo** *m* (*pl:* **perros-lazarillo**) Seeing Eye dog
**perroquete** *m* (naut.) topgallant mast
**perruno -na** *adj* canine, dog; *f* dog bread, dog cake
**persa** *adj & mf* Persian; *m* Persian (*language*)
**persecución** *f* pursuit; persecution; annoyance, harassment
**persecutorio -ria** *adj* (pertaining to) persecution; persecutional
**Perséfone** *f* (myth.) Persephone
**perseguidor -dora** *mf* pursuer; persecutor; *f* (Am.) hangover
**perseguimiento** *m* var. of **persecución**
**perseguir** §82 *va* to pursue; to persecute; to annoy, harass
**Perseida** *f* (astr.) Perseid
**Perseo** *m* (myth. & astr.) Perseus
**persevante** *m* pursuivant, pursuivant of arms
**perseverancia** *f* perseverance
**perseverante** *adj* persevering
**perseverar** *vn* to persevere; **perseverar en** + *inf* to persevere in + *ger*
**persiano -na** *adj & mf* Persian; *f* flowered silk; slatted shutter; (aut.) louver; **persiana de tiro** or **persiana interior americana** Venetian blind
**persicaria** *f* (bot.) persicary, lady's-thumb; (bot.) prince's-feather
**pérsico -ca** *adj* Persian; *m* (bot.) peach (*tree and fruit*)
**persignar** *vr* to cross oneself, make the sign of the cross; to make the first sale of the day; (coll.) to cross oneself in surprise
**pérsigo** *m* (bot.) peach (*tree and fruit*)
**persistencia** *f* persistence or persistency
**persistente** *adj* persistent
**persistir** *vn* to persist; **persistir en** + *inf* to persist in + *ger*
**persona** *f* person; personage; (gram. & theol.) person; **personas** *fpl* people; **conjunta persona** spouse (*man or wife*); **de persona a persona** tête à tête, man to man; **en persona** in person; **en la persona de** in the person of; **hacer de su persona** (coll.) to have a bowel movement; **por persona** per capita; **por su persona** in person; **primera persona** (gram.) first person; **segunda persona** (gram.) second person; **tercera persona** (gram.) third person; **persona agente** (gram.) agent; **persona desplazada** displaced person; **persona grata** persona grata; **persona jurídica** (law) juristic person; **persona paciente** (gram.) recipient of the action
**personada** *adj* (bot.) personate (*corolla*)
**personado** *m* (eccl.) benefice without jurisdiction; (eccl.) incumbent of a benefice without jurisdiction
**personaje** *m* personage; (theat.) personage, character; somebody (*person of importance*)
**personal** *adj* personal; *m* personnel, staff, force; staff expenses (*of an office*)
**personalidad** *f* personality; (law) personality; **personalidad desdoblada** split personality
**personalismo** *m* selfishness; personality
**personalista** *adj* selfish, self-seeking
**personalización** *f* personalization
**personalizar** §76 *va* to personalize; to make personal remarks about; (gram.) to make (*an impersonal verb*) personal; *vr* to become personal
**personar** *vr* var. of **apersonar**
**personería** *f* solicitorship; (law) personality
**personero** *m* solicitor; delegate
**personificación** *f* personification
**personificar** §86 *va* to personify
**personilla** *f* (coll.) queer little person
**personudo -da** *adj* husky
**perspectivo -va** *adj* perspective; *m* expert in perspective; *f* perspective; outlook, prospect; appearance; deceptive appearance; **perspectiva lineal** linear perspective
**perspicacia** or **perspicacidad** *f* perspicacity, discernment; keen sight
**perspicaz** *adj* (*pl:* **-caces**) perspicacious, discerning; keen-sighted
**perspicuidad** *f* perspicuity
**perspicuo -cua** *adj* perspicuous
**perspiración** *f* perspiration
**perspirar** *vn* to perspire
**persuadidor -dora** *mf* persuader

**persuadir** *va* to persuade; **persuadir a** + *inf* to persuade to + *inf;* **persuadir a que** + *subj* to persuade to + *inf; vr* to become persuaded or convinced
**persuasible** *adj* credible, plausible
**persuasión** *f* persuasion
**persuasivo -va** *adj* persuasive; *f* persuasion, persuasiveness
**persuasor -sora** *mf* persuader
**pertenecer §34** *vn* to belong; to pertain, to concern; *vr* to be independent
**pertenecido** *m* property
**perteneciente** *adj* pertaining
**pertenencia** *f* property; ownership; appurtenance, accessory; province, domain; **ser de la pertenencia de** to be under the ownership of; to be in the bailiwick or province of
**pértiga** *f* pole, rod, staff; (sport) pole (*used in pole vault*)
**pertigal** *m* pole, rod, staff
**pértigo** *m* tongue (*of wagon*)
**pertiguería** *f* office of verger
**pertiguero** *m* verger
**pertinacia** *f* pertinacity; persistence (*e.g., of a disease*)
**pertinaz** *adj* (*pl:* **-naces**) pertinacious; persistent (*e.g., headache*)
**pertinencia** *f* pertinence, relevance
**pertinente** *adj* pertinent, relevant
**pertrechar** *va* to supply, provide, equip; to prepare, to implement
**pertrechos** *mpl* supplies, provisions, equipment; tools; **pertrechos de guerra** ordnance
**perturbación** *f* perturbation; disturbance; upset
**perturbadamente** *adv* in confusion
**perturbado -da** *adj* insane; *mf* insane person
**perturbador -dora** *adj* perturbing; disturbing; *mf* perturber; disturber
**perturbar** *va* to perturb; to disturb; to upset, disconcert; to confuse, interrupt
**Perú, el** Peru
**peruanismo** *m* Peruvianism
**peruano -na** *adj & mf* Peruvian
**peruétano** *m* (bot.) wild pear; end, tip, projection
**perulero -ra** *adj & mf* Peruvian; *mf* person who has returned wealthy from Peru; *m* round earthen jug with small mouth
**Perusa** *f* Perugia
**peruviano -na** *adj & mf* Peruvian
**perversidad** *f* perversity
**perversión** *f* perversion; (psycopath.) perversion
**perverso -sa** *adj* perverse; profligate, depraved; *mf* profligate
**pervertido -da** *adj* (psychopath.) perverse; *mf* (psychopath.) pervert
**pervertidor -dora** *adj* perverting, depraving; *mf* perverter
**pervertimiento** *m* perversion, corruption
**pervertir §62** *va* to pervert; *vr* to become perverted
**pervigilio** *m* sleeplessness, wakefulness
**pervinca** *f* (bot.) periwinkle
**pervivencia** *f* persistence, survival
**pervulgar §59** *va* to divulge, proclaim
**peryódico -ca** *adj* (chem.) periodic
**peryoduro** *m* (chem.) periodide
**pesa** *f* weight (*of scales, clock, gymnasium, etc.*); **tirar la pesa** (sport) to put the shot; **pesas y medidas** weights and measures
**pesacartas** *m* (*pl:* **-tas**) letter scales
**pesada** *f* see **pesado**
**pesadez** *f* heaviness; clumsiness, slowness; annoyance; tiresomeness, dullness; harshness; (phys.) gravity
**pesadilla** *f* nightmare; (fig.) nightmare
**pesado -da** *adj* heavy; clumsy, sluggish, slow; tiresome, dull; harsh; *f* quantity weighed at one time
**pesador -dora** *mf* weigher
**pesadumbre** *f* sorrow, grief; trouble; weight, heaviness
**pesaje** *m* weighing; paddock
**pesalicores** *m* (*pl:* **-res**) hydrometer
**pésame** *m* condolence; **dar el pésame por** to present one's condolences for, to extend one's sympathy for or on
**pesante** *adj* having weight
**pesantez** *f* (phys.) gravity
**pesar** *m* sorrow, regret; **a pesar de** in spite of; *va* to weigh; to grieve, to make sorry; (fig.) to weigh; **mal que me (le, etc.) pese** whether I (you, etc.) like it or not; **pesar** + *inf* or **pesar de** + *inf* to be sorry that + *ind*, e.g., **me pesa haber firmado esa protesta** I am sorry that I signed that protest; **pesar sus palabras** to weigh one's words; **pese a** in spite of; **pese a que** in spite of the fact that; **pese a quien pese** regardless, whether they like it or not; *vn* to weigh; to have weight; to be heavy; to cause sorrow, cause regret; (fig.) to weigh (*to have influence, be important*)
**pesario** *m* (med.) pessary
**pesaroso -sa** *adj* sorrowful, regretful
**pesca** *f* fishing; catch (*of fish*); **ir de pesca** to go fishing; **llevar de pesca** to take (*someone*) fishing; **pesca de bajura** offshore fishing; **pesca de gran altura** deep-sea fishing
**pescada** *f* (ichth.) hake; dried and cured fish
**pescadería** *f* fish market; fish store; fish stand
**pescadero -ra** *mf* fish dealer; fishmonger; *f* fishwoman
**pescadilla** *f* (ichth.) codling; (ichth.) weakfish; **pescadilla de red** or **pescadilla real** (ichth.) pescadilla (*Sagenichthys ancylodon*)
**pescado** *m* fish (*that has been caught*); salted codfish
**pescador -dora** *adj* fishing; *mf* fisher; *m* fisherman; (ichth.) angler; *f* fisherwoman
**pescante** *m* coach box; (aut.) front seat; jib (*of derrick*); (naut.) davit; (theat.) trap door
**pescar §86** *va* to fish; to catch (*fish*); to fish for; to fish out; (elec.) to fish; (coll.) to manage to get; (coll.) to catch, catch up (*e.g., in a lie*); *vn* to fish
**pescozada** *f* or **pescozón** *m* slap in the neck, slap on the head
**pescozudo -da** *adj* thick-necked
**pescuezo** *m* neck; haughtiness
**pescuño** *m* colter wedge (*of plow*)
**pese** see **pesar**
**pesebre** *m* crib, rack; manger; (Am.) crèche
**pesebrera** *f* row of mangers; mangers
**pesebrón** *m* boot (*of a coach*)
**peseta** *f* peseta (*Spanish monetary unit*); **cambiar la peseta** (coll.) to get sick and vomit
**pésete** *m* curse
**pesetero -ra** *adj* greedy, grasping; (costing a) peseta
**pesia** *interj* confound it!
**pesiar** *vn* to curse
**pesillo** *m* small scales (*for weighing coins*)
**pesimismo** *m* pessimism
**pesimista** *adj* pessimistic; *mf* pessimist
**pésimo -ma** *adj super* very bad, abominable, miserable
**peso** *m* weight; scale, balance; burden, load; judgment, good sense; (fig.) weight (*importance; burden*); peso (*Spanish American monetary unit*); **a peso de dinero, oro** or **plata** at a very high price; **caerse de su peso** to be self-evident; **de peso** of due weight; of sound judgment, serious, important; **en peso** in the air; entirely; on the fence; **llevar el peso de la batalla** to bear the brunt of the battle; **reducir peso** to reduce (*to lose weight, e.g., by exercising*); **peso atómico** (phys.) atomic weight; **peso en vivo** live weight; **peso específico** (phys.) specific gravity; **peso fuerte** (box.) heavyweight; **peso gallo** (box.) bantamweight; **peso ligero** or **liviano** (box.) lightweight; **peso mediano** or **medio** (box.) middleweight; **peso mediano fuerte** or **peso medio fuerte** (box.) light heavyweight; **peso mediano ligero** or **peso medio ligero** (box.) welterweight; **peso molecular** (phys.) molecular weight; **peso mosca** (box.) flyweight; **peso muerto** dead weight; (aer.) dead load; **peso pesado** (box.) heavyweight; **peso pesado ligero** (box.) light heavyweight; **peso pluma** (box.) featherweight
**pésol** *m* pea
**pesón** *m* balance, scales
**pesor** *m* (prov. & Am.) weight, gravity
**pespuntador -dora** *mf* backstitcher

**pespuntar** *va & vn* to backstitch
**pespunte** *m* backstitch, backstitching
**pespuntear** *va & vn* var. of **pespuntar**
**pesquera** *f* see **pesquero**
**pesquería** *f* fishery (*business; place*); fishing
**pesquero -ra** *adj* fishing (*boat, industry, etc.*); *m* fishing boat; *f* fishery; fishing ground; weir, garth
**pesquis** *m* acumen, keenness
**pesquisa** *f* inquiry, investigation; *m* (Am.) cop, policeman
**pesquisador -dora** *mf* investigator
**pesquisante** *adj* investigating, investigative
**pesquisar** *va* to inquire into, to investigate
**pestalociano -na** *adj* (educ.) Pestalozzian
**pestaña** *f* eyelash; flange; fluke (*of anchor*); edging (*lace*); index tab; (aut.) tire rim; **pestañas** *fpl* (bot.) cilia; **no mover pestaña** to not bat an eye; **no pegar pestaña** (coll.) to not sleep a wink; **pestañas vibrátiles** (biol.) cilia
**pestañear** *vn* to wink, to blink; **no pestañear ante un peligro** to not flinch in the face of a danger; **sin pestañear** without batting an eye
**pestañeo** *m* winking, blinking
**pestañoso -sa** *adj* with long eyelashes; (biol.) ciliate
**peste** *f* pest, plague; epidemic; stink, stench; corruption, depravity; evil; (coll.) wealth, abundance; (Am.) head cold; (Am.) smallpox; **decir** or **hablar pestes de** (coll.) to talk against, to criticize; **echar pestes (contra)** (coll.) to fume (at); **peste blanca** white plague (*tuberculosis*); **peste bubónica** (path.) bubonic plague
**pestífero -ra** *adj* pestiferous; stinking, noxious
**pestilencia** *f* pestilence
**pestilencial** *adj* pestilential, pestiferous
**pestilencioso -sa** *adj* pestilential (*having to do with pestilence*)
**pestilente** *adj* pestilent, pestiferous
**pestillo** *m* bolt (*of a lock*); door latch; **pestillo de golpe** night bolt, spring bolt
**pestiño** *m* honey fritter
**pestorejazo** *m* var. of **pestorejón**
**pestorejo** *m* var. of **cerviguillo**
**pestorejón** *m* blow on the back of the neck
**pesuña** *f* hoof; dry dirt stuck on a person's feet
**pesuño** *m* toe, digit (*half of cloven hoof*); **pesuño falso** dewclaw
**petaca** *f* cigar case; tobacco pouch; leather-covered chest; leather-covered hamper; (Am.) trunk; **petacas** *fpl* (Am.) big hips (*of a woman*)
**pétalo** *m* (bot.) petal
**petanque** *m* silver ore
**petar** *va* (coll.) to please
**petardear** *va* to blow open with petards; to swindle, to take in; *vn* (aut.) to backfire
**petardeo** *m* swindling; (aut.) backfire
**petardero** *m* petardeer; swindler
**petardista** *mf* swindler, cheat
**petardo** *m* petard; bomb; swindle, cheat; **pedir un petardo a** (coll.) to swindle
**petate** *m* sleeping mat; bedding (*of service man or prisoner*); (coll.) luggage; (coll.) cheat; (coll.) poor soul; **liar el petate** (coll.) to pack up and get out; (coll.) to kick the bucket
**petenera** *f* Andalusian popular song
**petequia** *f* (path.) petechia
**petera** *f* (coll.) brawl, row; stubbornness, temper
**peteretes** *mpl* (coll.) sweets, tidbits
**peterrear** *vn* (coll.) to crackle
**peticano** or **peticanon** *m* (print.) double pica
**petición** *f* petition; plea; request; (law) claim, bill; **petición de mano** formal betrothal; **petición de principio** (log.) petitio principii
**peticionar** *va* (Am.) to petition
**peticionario -ria** *mf* petitioner
**petifoque** *m* (naut.) flying jib
**petigrís** *m* squirrel (*fur*)
**petillo** *m* stomacher
**petimetra** *f* showy or gaudy woman
**petimetre** *m* dude, sport, dandy
**petirrojo** *m* (orn.) redbreast
**petitorio -ria** *adj* petitionary; *m* (coll.) tiresome and repeated demand; drug catalogue; *f* (coll.) petition
**peto** *m* breastplate; plastron; peen; (zool.) plastron; (taur.) mattress covering (*to protect horses*); (ichth.) wahoo
**petral** *m* breastband, breast collar
**Petrarca** *m* Petrarch
**petraria** *f* petrary, ballista
**petrarquesco -ca** *adj* Petrarchan, Petrarchian
**petrarquismo** *m* Petrarchism
**petrel** *m* (orn.) petrel; **petrel de la tempestad** (orn.) stormy petrel; **petrel gigante** (orn.) giant fulmar
**pétreo -a** *adj* stony; rocky
**petrificación** *f* petrifaction or petrification
**petrificar** §86 *va & vr* to petrify
**petrífico -ca** *adj* petrifactive, petrifying
**Petrogrado** *f* Petrograd
**petrografía** *f* petrography
**petrolato** *m* (pharm.) petrolatum
**petróleo** *m* petroleum; **petróleo combustible** fuel oil; **petróleo crudo** crude oil; **petróleo de alumbrado** kerosene; **petróleo de hogar** or **de horno** furnace oil; **petróleo lampante** kerosene
**petrolero -ra** *adj* (pertaining to) oil, petroleum; incendiary; radical; *mf* oil dealer, kerosene dealer; incendiary; radical; *m* oil man; (naut.) oil tanker; pétroleur; *f* pétroleuse
**petrolífero -ra** *adj* petroliferous
**petrología** *f* petrology
**petroquímico -ca** *adj* petrochemical
**petroso -sa** *adj* petrous; (anat.) petrous
**petulancia** *f* flippancy, pertness, insolence
**petulante** *adj* flippant, pert, insolent
**petunia** *f* (bot.) petunia
**peucédano** *m* (bot.) hog's-fennel
**peyorativo -va** *adj* depreciatory; (gram.) pejorative
**pez** *m* (*pl:* **peces**) fish; long heap (*e.g., of wheat*); (coll.) reward, just desert; (rel.) fish (*symbol*); (fig.) fish (*good swimmer*); **como un pez en el agua** (coll.) snug as a bug in a rug; **salga pez o salga rana** (coll.) blindly, hit or miss; **pez aguja** (ichth.) garfish; **pez ballesta** (ichth.) triggerfish; **pez caimán** (ichth.) garfish, alligator gar; **pez cofre** (ichth.) cowfish; **pez de color** goldfish; **pez de plata** (ent.) silverfish; **pez de rey** (ichth.) atherine; **pez de San Pedro** (ichth.) dory; **pez eléctrico** (ichth.) electric ray; **pez elefante** (ichth.) elephant fish, **pez espada** (ichth.) swordfish; **pez gallo** (ichth.) elephant fish; **pez gordo** (coll.) big shot, tycoon; **pez hoja** (ichth.) paddle fish; **pez limón** (ichth.) amber jack (*Seriola lalandi*); **pez luna** (ichth.) sunfish, moonfish; **pez martillo** (ichth.) hammerhead; **pez mujer** (zool.) manatee; **pez palo** dried codfish; **pez saltador** (ichth.) skipjack; **pez sierra** (ichth.) sawfish; **pez vela** (ichth.) sailfish; **pez víbora** (ichth.) stingbull; **pez volador** flying fish; (ichth.) flying gurnard; **pez zorro** (ichth.) tiger shark ‖ *f* pitch, tar; meconium; **pez griega** or **rubia** rosin
**pezolada** *f* fag end
**pezón** *m* stem; nipple, teat; pivot; pin (*of key*); point (*of land*); umbo (*of lemon, lime, etc.*)
**pezonera** *f* nipple shield; linchpin
**pezpalo** *m* var. of **pejepalo**
**pez-papagayo** *m* (*pl:* **peces-papagayos**) (ichth.) parrot fish
**pezpita** *f* or **pezpítalo** *m* (orn.) wagtail
**pezuelo** *m* fringe at end of cloth
**pezuña** *f* hoof
**P.G.M.** abr. of **Primera Guerra Mundial**
**pi** *f* (math.) pi
**piache; tarde piache** (coll.) too late
**piada** *f* peeping, chirping; (coll.) mimic phrase or expression
**piador -dora** *adj* peeping, chirping; (coll.) begging
**piadoso -sa** *adj* merciful; pitiful; pious, devout
**piafar** *vn* to paw, to stamp (*said of a horse*)
**piale** *m* (Am.) throwing a lasso
**piamadre** *f* or **piamáter** *f* (anat.) pia mater
**Piamonte, el** Piedmont
**piamontés -tesa** *adj & mf* Piedmontese

**pian** *m* (path.) pian
**pianino** *m* upright piano
**pianista** *mf* pianist; piano manufacturer; piano dealer
**pianístico -ca** *adj* pianistic; (pertaining to the) piano
**piano** *m* piano; **gran piano** grand piano; **piano cuadrado** square piano; **piano de cola** grand piano; **piano de manubrio** piano organ, street piano; **piano de media cola** baby grand; **piano de mesa** square piano; **piano recto** or **vertical** upright piano
**pianoforte** *m* (mus.) pianoforte
**pianola** *f* pianola
**piar** §90 *vn* to peep, to chirp; (coll.) to cry, whine
**piara** *f* herd (*of swine*); drove (*of mules, etc.*)
**piariego -ga** *adj* herd-owning
**piastra** *f* piaster
**pica** *f* pike; pikeman; (taur.) goad; stonecutter's hammer; (path. & vet.) pica, vitiated appetite; (Am.) pique, resentment
**picabueyes** *m* (*pl:* **-yes**) (orn.) oxpecker, beefeater
**picacero -ra** *adj* magpie-chasing (*said of a hawk*)
**picacho** *m* sharp peak
**picada** *f* see **picado**
**picadero** *m* riding school; (taur.) training field (*for picadors*); boat skid, boat block
**picadillo** *m* hash; minced pork (*for sausages*)
**picado -da** *adj* perforated; traced in perforations; pitted; cut (*tobacco*); cracked (*ice*); piqued; choppy (*sea*); *m* mincemeat; (aer.) dive; *f* peck; bite (*of insect or fish*); (surv.) line of stakes; staking out; (Am.) path, trail; (Am.) narrow ford; (Am.) dive; (Am.) knock (*at door*); **echar una picada a** (Am.) to hit for a loan
**picador** *m* horsebreaker; picador (*mounted bullfighter who thrusts a goad into bull*); worker with a pick; operator of pneumatic tool; chopping block; (slang) picklock (*thief*); **picador de limas** (mach.) file cutter
**picadora** *f* tobacco-shredding machine; **picadora de carne** meat chopper
**picadura** *f* bite, prick, sting; nick, cut; puncture; cut tobacco; (dent.) slight cavity
**picafigo** *m* (orn.) figpecker
**picaflor** *m* or **picaflores** *m* (*pl:* **-flores**) (orn.) hummingbird
**picagallina** *f* (bot.) chickweed
**picagrega** *f* (orn.) shrike
**picahielos** *m* (*pl:* **-los**) ice pick
**picajón -jona** or **picajoso -sa** *adj* (coll.) touchy, peevish
**pical** *m* crossroads
**picamaderos** *m* (*pl:* **-ros**) (orn.) green woodpecker
**picana** *f* (Am.) goad
**picanear** *va* (Am.) to goad; (Am.) to stir up, goad on
**picante** *adj* biting, pricking, stinging; piquant; racy; (Am.) highly seasoned; *m* acrimony, mordancy; piquancy; (Am.) highly seasoned sauce
**picaño -ña** *adj* lazy, shameless, ragged; *m* patch (*on shoe*)
**picapedrero** *m* stonecutter, quarrier
**picapica** *f* itch-producing vegetable powder, leaves, etc.
**picapinos** *m* (*pl:* **-nos**) (orn.) great spotted woodpecker
**picapleitos** *m* (*pl:* **-tos**) (coll.) quarrelsome fellow; (coll.) pettifogger, shyster
**picaporte** *m* latch; latchkey; knocker, door knocker
**picaposte** *m* (orn.) woodpecker
**picapuerco** *m* (orn.) spotted woodpecker (*Dryobates medius*)
**picar** §86 *va* to prick, pierce, puncture; to punch (*a ticket*); to sting; to bite; to burn; to peck; to nibble, pick at; to pit, to pock; to mince, chop up, cut up; to stick, to poke; to spur; to goad; (sew.) to pink; to perforate; to harass, pursue; to itch; to tame; to stipple; to roughen; to pique, annoy; (taur.) to goad ‖ *vn* to itch; to burn (*said of sun*); to nibble; to have a smattering; to put on the finishing touches; to catch, be catching; to pick up (*said of business*); (coll.) to bite (*to be caught, as by a trick*); (coll.) to move along; (aer.) to dive; **picar en** to nibble at; to be somewhat of a; to dabble in; **picar muy alto** (coll.) to aim high, to expect too much ‖ *vr* to become moth-eaten; to prick, to begin to turn sour; to begin to rot; to become decayed (*said of a tooth*); to become ripply (*said of surface of sea*); to swoop down; to become piqued, to take offense; **picarse de** to boast of being
**picaraza** *f* (orn.) magpie
**picardear** *va* to train in knavishness; *vn* to be a knave or rascal; to play tricks; to be mischievous; *vr* to go bad, to acquire bad habits
**picardía** *f* knavery, crookedness; scheming, trickiness; mischief; vileness, lewdness; gang of crooks; **la Picardía** Picardy; **picardías** *fpl* insults
**picardihuela** *f* prank, mischievousness
**picardo -da** *adj & mf* Picard; *m* Picard (*dialect*)
**picaresco -ca** *adj* roguish, rascally; picaresque; rough, coarse, crude; (coll.) witty, humorous, gay; *f* gang of rogues; rascality
**picaril** *adj* roguish, rascally
**pícaro -ra** *adj* roguish, crooked; scheming, tricky; low, vile; mischievous; *mf* rogue, crook; schemer; *m* (lit.) picaro; **pícaro de cocina** scullion, kitchen boy
**picarón -rona** *adj* (coll.) roguish, mischievous; *mf* rogue, picaroon; *m* (Am.) cruller
**picarrelincho** *m* (orn.) green woodpecker
**picatoste** *m* buttered toast; fried bread
**picazo -za** *adj* piebald; *m* piebald (*horse*); jab, jab with a pike or spear; (coll.) peck; (orn.) young magpie; *f* (orn.) magpie; **picaza chillona** or **manchada** (orn.) shrike; **picaza marina** (orn.) flamingo
**picazón** *f* itch; itching; (coll.) annoyance, displeasure
**píceo -a** *adj* piceous, pitchy; *f* (bot.) spruce, spruce tree
**Picio** *m;* **más feo que Picio** ugly as the devil
**pick-up** *m* pickup; phonograph
**picnóstilo** *m* (arch.) pycnostyle
**pico** *m* beak, bill; spout (*of pitcher*); beak (*of anvil*); corner (*e.g., of handkerchief*); nib, tip, sharp point; peak; pick, pickax; talkativeness; pile, lot (*of money*); (coll.) mouth; (elec.) peak; (naut.) bill (*of anchor*); (naut.) peak (*of a sail*); (naut.) bow, prow; (orn.) woodpecker; **andar a picos pardos** (coll.) to loaf around; **callar el pico** (coll.) to shut up, to keep one's mouth shut; **darse el pico** to bill (*said, e.g., of doves*); **hincar el pico** (coll.) to kick the bucket; **perder por el pico** (coll.) to talk too much for one's good; **tener mucho pico** (coll.) to talk too much, to tell all one knows; **y pico** odd, e.g., **doscientos y pico** two hundred odd; a little after, e.g., **a las dos y pico** a little after two o'clock; **pico barreno** or **carpintero** (orn.) woodpecker; **pico cangrejo** or **pico de cangreja** (naut.) gaff, spanker gaff; **pico de cigüeña** (bot.) stork's bill, heron's-bill; **pico de marfil** (orn.) ivorybill; **pico de oro** (fig.) silver-tongue; **pico duro** (orn.) grosbeak, pine grosbeak; **pico gordo** (orn.) hawfinch, grosbeak; **pico tijera** (orn.) skimmer, shearwater; **pico verde** (orn.) green woodpecker
**picocarpintero** *m* (orn.) woodpecker
**picón -cona** *adj* with upper teeth projecting (*said of a horse*); (Am.) touchy, sensitive; *m* kidding, teasing; charcoal for brasiers; broken rice
**picor** *m* smarting of the palate (*from something eaten*); itch, itching
**picoso -sa** *adj* pock-marked
**picota** *f* pillar or column on which heads of executed criminals were displayed; pillory; peak, point, spire; (naut.) cheek (*of pump*); **poner en picota** to hold up to public scorn
**picotada** *f* or **picotazo** *m* peck; sting
**picote** *m* goat's-hair cloth; glossy silk
**picotear** *va* to peck; *vn* to toss the head (*said of a horse*); (coll.) to chatter, jabber, gab; *vr* (coll.) to wrangle (*said of women*)
**picotella** *f* (orn.) nuthatch
**picotería** *f* (coll.) chattering, jabbering
**picotero -ra** *adj* (coll.) chattering, jabbering; *mf* chatterer, jabberer; *m* (orn.) waxwing

**picotijera** *m* (orn.) skimmer, shearwater
**picotillo** *m* rough goat's-hair cloth
**picozapato** *m* (orn.) shoebill
**picrato** *m* (chem.) picrate
**pícrico -ca** *adj* picric
**picto -ta** *adj* Pictish; *mf* Pict
**pictografía** *f* pictograph, picture writing
**pictográfico -ca** *adj* pictographic
**pictórico -ca** *adj* pictorial
**picuda** *f* see **picudo**
**picudilla** *f* crescent olive; (orn.) rail; (ichth.) picudilla
**picudo -da** *adj* beaked; pointed; long-snouted; (coll.) jabbering; *m* poker, rapier; (ent.) boll weevil; *f* (ichth.) barracuda
**pichana** *f* (Am.) broom
**pichel** *m* pewter tankard
**pichihuén** *m* (ichth.) walking fish
**pichincha** *f* (Am.) bargain, lucky break
**pichón -chona** *mf* (coll.) darling; *m* young pigeon; **pichón de paso** (Am.) passenger pigeon
**pidientero** *m* beggar
**pidón -dona** *adj* (coll.) var. of **pedigüeño**
**pie** *m* foot; footing; foothold; base, stand; stem (*of goblet*); foot (*unit of length; measure of verse*); footboard; trunk; young tree; sediment; foundation; origin; cause, reason; last player; foot, bottom (*of page*); caption; (theat.) cue; **a cuatro pies** on all fours; **al pie de** near; about, almost; **al pie de fábrica** (com.) at the factory; **al pie de la letra** literally; **al pie de la obra** (com.) delivered; **andar, caminar** or **ir con pie** or **pies de plomo** (coll.) to move with caution; **a pie** on foot, walking; **a pie enjuto** dryshod; without risk; without effort; **a pie juntillas, a pie juntillo,** or **a pies juntillos** with feet together; firmly, steadfastly; **buscar cinco** (or **tres**) **pies al gato** (coll.) to be looking for trouble; **dar pie a** to give cause for; **de a pie** foot (*soldier*); **del pie a la mano** at any moment; **de pie** or **de pies** standing; up and about; firm, steady; firmly, steadily; permanently; **de pies a cabeza** from head to foot; **en pie** standing; up and about; firm, steady; firmly, steadily; permanently; on the hoof; **en pie de guerra** on a war footing; **hacer pie** to have a good footing; **ir a pie** to go on foot, to walk; **írsele a uno los pies** to slip (*e.g., on the ice*); (fig.) to slip, to blunder; **irse por pies** or **por sus pies** to get away (*from another person*); **morir al pie del cañón** to die in the harness, to die with one's boots on; **nacer de pie** or **de pies** to be born with a silver spoon in one's mouth; **no dar pie con bola** (coll.) to keep on making mistakes, to make one mistake after another; **perder pie** to lose one's footing; **poner pies con cabeza** (coll.) to turn upside down; **ponerse de pie** or **en pie** to rise, to stand up; **tenerse en pie** to stay on one's feet, to remain standing; **volver pies atrás** to retrace one's steps; **pie calcáneo** (path.) clubfoot; **pie contrahecho** (path.) splayfoot; **pie de amigo** prop, support; **pie de atleta** (path.) athlete's foot; **pie de banco** silly remark; **pie de cabra** crowbar; (zool.) barnacle (*Pollicipes cornucopia*); **pie de carnero** (naut.) Samson post; **pie de guerra** war footing, war-time footing; **pie de imprenta** (print.) imprint, printer's mark; **pie de león** (bot.) lion's-foot; (bot.) edelweiss; **pie derecho** upright, stanchion; **pie de rey** caliper square, slide caliper; **pie de tabla** board foot; **pie de trinchera** (path.) trench foot; **pie marino** sea legs; **pie plano** (path.) flatfoot; **pie quebrado** (poet.) short line; **pie talo** (path.) clubfoot; **pie zambo** (path.) splayfoot
**pie-bujía** *f* (*pl:* **pies-bujías**) foot-candle
**piececillo** or **piececito** *m* little foot
**piecezuela** *f* little piece
**piecezuelo** *m* little foot
**piedad** *f* piety; pity, mercy
**piedra** *f* stone; rock; block; footstone; flint; heavy hailstone; (path.) stone; **a piedra y lodo** tight-shut; **de piedra en seco** dry-stone; **lanzar la primera piedra** to cast the first stone; **no dejar piedra por mover** to leave no stone unturned; **no dejar piedra sobre piedra** to raze to the ground, to wipe out; **poner la primera piedra** to lay the corner stone; **piedra angular** cornerstone; (fig.) cornerstone, keystone; **piedra arenisca** sandstone; **piedra azul** (chem.) bluestone; **piedra berroqueña** milestone; **piedra calaminar** (mineral.) calamine; **piedra caliza** limestone; **piedra de afilar** grindstone; **piedra de albardilla** copestone; **piedra de alumbre** (mineral.) alum rock, alum stone; **piedra de amolar** grindstone; **piedra de chispa** flint; **piedra de escándalo** bone of contention, object of indignation; **piedra de granizo** hailstone; **piedra de la luna** (mineral.) moonstone; **piedra de molino** millstone; **piedra de pipas** (mineral.) meerschaum; **piedra de toque** (mineral. & fig.) touchstone; **piedra filosofal** philosopher's stone; **piedra fina** precious stone; **piedra franca** freestone; **piedra fundamental** foundation stone; **piedra imán** loadstone; **piedra infernal** lunar caustic (*silver nitrate*); **piedra lipis** copper sulfate; **piedra melodreña** whetstone; **piedra meteórica** meteoric stone; **piedra miliar** or **miliaria** milestone; (fig.) milestone; **piedra pómez** pumice, pumice stone; **piedra preciosa** precious stone; **piedra viva** solid rock; **piedra voladora** millstone for grinding olives
**piedrezuela** *f* little stone
**piel** *f* skin; hide, pelt; fur; leather; peel, skin (*of fruit*); leather (*e.g., used to bind books*); **dar** or **soltar la piel** (coll.) to die; **ser de la piel del diablo** (coll.) to be a limb of the devil or of Satan, to be a harum-scarum; **piel de cabra** goatskin; **piel de foca** sealskin; **piel de gallina** goose flesh; **piel roja** *m* (*pl:* **pieles rojas**) redskin (*American Indian*)
**piélago** *m* sea; high sea; countless number
**pie-libra** *f* (*pl:* **pies-libras**) (mech.) foot-pound
**piemia** *f* var. of **pioemia**
**pienso** *m* feed, feeding (*in the stable*); **ni por pienso** by no means, don't think of it
**pie-poundal** *m* (mech.) foot-poundal
**piérides** *fpl* (myth.) Muses
**pierio -ria** *adj* Pierian
**pierna** *f* leg; post, upright; branch or leg (*of a compass*); downstroke (*of a letter*); (mach.) fork, shank; **a pierna suelta** or **tendida** (coll.) at ease, carefree; **dormir a pierna suelta** or **tendida** (coll.) to sleep soundly; **en piernas** barelegged; **estirar la pierna** (coll.) to lie down on the job; (coll.) to kick the bucket; **estirar** or **extender las piernas** to stretch one's legs, to go for a walk; **ser una buena pierna** (Am.) to be good-natured, be a good fellow
**piernitendido -da** *adj* with legs extended
**piesgo** *m* var. of **piezgo**
**pietismo** *m* Pietism
**pietista** *mf* Pietist
**pieza** *f* piece (*part, e.g., of a machine; single musical composition; play, drama; gun, cannon; man in checkers, chess, etc.; coin*); piece or article (*of clothing, of furniture*); space (*in time or place*); room; disappointment; **buena pieza** hussy; sly fox; **de una pieza** in one piece, solid; (Am.) honest, upright; **quedarse en una pieza** or **hecho una pieza** (coll.) to stand motionless, to be dumfounded; **pieza de recambio** spare part, extra; **pieza de recibo** reception room; **pieza de repuesto** spare part, extra; **pieza de respeto** special room, spare room; **pieza de tesis** thesis play; **pieza polar** (elec.) pole piece
**piezgo** *m* foot of a hide (*used to carry a liquid*); wineskin
**piezoelectricidad** *f* piezoelectricity
**piezoeléctrico -ca** *adj* piezoelectric
**piezómetro** *m* piezometer
**pífano** *m* fife; fifer
**pifia** *f* (billiards) miscue; (coll.) miscue, slip; **hacer pifia** to wheeze (*said of a voice or wind instrument*)
**pifiar** *va* (billiards) to make a miscue of (*a stroke*); *vn* (billiards) to miscue; to wheeze in playing the flute
**pigargo** *m* (orn.) fish hawk
**Pigmalión** *m* (myth.) Pygmalion
**pigmentación** *f* (biol.) pigmentation

**pigmentar** *va* to pigment; *vr* to pigment, become pigmented
**pigmentario -ria** *adj* pigmentary
**pigmento** *m* pigment
**pigmeo -a** *adj & mf* pygmy
**pignoración** *f* pledge, pledging; pawning; security
**pignorar** *va* to pledge; to pawn; to put up as security
**pigre** *adj* slothful, lazy
**pigricia** *f* sloth, laziness
**pigro -gra** *adj* var. of **pigre**
**pihua** *f* sandal
**pihuela** *f* jess (*on hawk's leg*); obstacle, hindrance; **pihuelas** *fpl* shackles, fetters
**pijama** *m* pajamas
**pijota** *f* var. of **pescadilla**
**pila** *f* basin; trough; sink; font, holy-water font; pile, heap; (elec., her. & phys.) pile; (elec.) battery, cell; **sacar de pila a** to stand godfather for; **pila atómica** (phys.) atomic pile; **pila de bicromato** (elec.) bichromate cell; **pila de gravedad** (elec.) gravity cell; **pila de linterna** flashlight battery; **pila húmeda** or **líquida** (elec.) wet cell, wet battery; **pila seca** (elec.) dry cell, dry battery; **pila voltaica** (elec.) voltaic battery, voltaic pile
**pilada** *f* batch of mortar; cloth fulled at one time; pile, heap
**pilar** *m* basin, bowl (*of fountain*); pillar; stone post, milestone; (fig.) pillar (*person*); *va* to pound, crush (*grain*)
**pilastra** *f* (arch.) pilaster
**pilatero** *m* fuller (*of cloth*)
**Pilatos** *m* Pilate
**píldora** *f* pill; (coll.) bad news; **dorar la píldora** (coll.) to gild the pill
**pildorero** *m* pill roller (*device*)
**píleo** *m* cardinal's biretta
**pilero** *m* workman who kneads potter's clay with his feet
**pileta** *f* basin, bowl (*of sink*); sink; small font or stoup; **pileta de natación** swimming pool
**pilocarpina** *f* (chem.) pilocarpine
**pilón** *m* pylon; water basin, drinking trough; loaf of sugar; mortar, pestle; counterpoise (*in olive press*); drop hammer; drop or ball (*of steelyard*); **pilón abrevadero** watering trough
**piloncillo** *m* (Am.) brown sugar
**pilonero -ra** *adj* (coll.) newsmongering; *mf* (coll.) newsmonger
**pilongo -ga** *adj* thin, lean; peeled and dried (*chestnut*)
**pílori** *m* pillory, stocks
**pilórico -ca** *adj* pyloric
**píloro** *m* (anat.) pylorus
**pilosidad** *f* pilosity
**piloso -sa** *adj* pilose, hairy, of hair
**pilotaje** *m* piling, pilework; (naut. & aer.) pilotage
**pilotar** *va* to pilot
**pilote** *m* pile (*for building*)
**pilotear** *va* to pilot; (Am.) to back, support
**piloto** *m* (aer., naut. & fig.) pilot; (naut.) mate, first mate; (ichth.) pilot fish; (Am.) hail fellow well met; **piloto de prueba** (aer.) test pilot; **piloto de puerto** harbor pilot
**piltraca** or **piltrafa** *f* skinny flesh; loot; **piltracas** or **piltrafas** *fpl* scraps, scraps of food; (Am.) rags, old clothes
**pillada** *f* (coll.) rascality
**pillador -dora** *adj* pillaging, plundering; thieving; *mf* pillager, plunderer; thief
**pillaje** *m* pillage, plunder
**pillar** *va* to pillage, plunder; to catch; (coll.) to catch (*e.g., in a lie*)
**pillastre** *m* or **pillastrón** *m* (coll.) rogue, rascal, big rascal
**pillear** *vn* (coll.) to be a rascal, act like a rascal
**pillería** *f* (coll.) rascality; (coll.) gang of scalawags
**pillete** *m* (coll.) little scamp
**pillín** *m* (coll.) little scamp; **pillín de aúpa** (coll.) sporty little devil
**pillo -lla** *adj* (coll.) roguish, rascally; (coll.) sly, crafty; (coll.) licentious; *m* (coll.) rogue, rascal, scalawag; (coll.) crafty fellow; (orn.) ibis
**pilluelo** *m* (coll.) scamp, little scamp
**pimental** *m* pepper patch
**pimentero -ra** *mf* pepper seller; *m* (bot.) pepper, black pepper; pepperbox; **pimentero falso** (bot.) pepper tree or shrub
**pimentón** *m* large pepper; cayenne pepper, red pepper; paprika
**pimienta** *f* pepper, black pepper; allspice, pimento; (bot.) allspice tree; **comer pimienta** (coll.) to get angry; **ser como una pimienta** (coll.) to be alert, be wide-awake; **tener mucha pimienta** (coll.) to be away up (*in price*); **pimienta de agua** (bot.) smartweed; **pimienta de Chiapas** or **de Tabasco** grains of paradise; **pimienta inglesa** allspice, pimento; **pimienta loca** or **silvestre** (bot.) chaste tree; **pimienta negra** black pepper
**pimiento** *m* (bot.) pepper, black pepper; (bot.) Guinea pepper; **pimiento de cornetilla** (bot.) chili; hot pepper, chili
**pimpante** *adj* smart, spruce
**pimpido** *m* (ichth.) dogfish
**pimpín** *m* boys' pinching game
**pimpina** *f* (Am.) earthen water jug with long spout
**pimpinela** *f* (bot.) salad burnet
**pimplar** *va* (coll.) to drink (*wine*)
**pimpleo -a** *adj* of the Muses
**pimpollada** *f* or **pimpollar** *m* grove or planting of young trees
**pimpollear** *vn* to sprout, to bud
**pimpollecer §34** *vn* var. of **pimpollear**
**pimpollejo** *m* small sucker, shoot, or sprout
**pimpollo** *m* sucker, shoot, sprout; rosebud; young tree; (coll.) handsome child; (coll.) handsome young person
**pimpolludo -da** *adj* full of suckers, shoots, or buds
**pina** *f* see **pino**
**pinabete** *m* (bot.) fir tree
**pinacoide** *m* (cryst.) pinacoid
**pinacoteca** *f* picture gallery
**pináculo** *m* pinnacle; (arch. & fig.) pinnacle
**pinado -da** *adj* (bot.) pinnate
**pinar** *m* pine grove, pinery
**pinarejo** *m* small pine grove
**pinariego -ga** *adj* (pertaining to the) pine
**pinastro** *m* (bot.) pinaster, cluster pine
**pinatar** *m* growth of young pines
**pinatífido -da** *adj* (bot.) pinnatifid
**pinatisecto -ta** *adj* (bot.) pinnatisected
**pinaza** *f* (naut.) pinnace
**pincarrasca** *f* (bot.) Aleppo pine
**pincarrascal** *m* grove of Aleppo pines
**pincarrasco** *m* var. of **pincarrasca**
**pincel** *m* brush; (fig.) brush (*painter; style of painting*); painting; pencil, beam (*of light, etc.*); **pincel aéreo** air brush; **pincel de pelo de camello** camel's-hair brush
**pincelación** *f* (med.) penciling
**pincelada** *f* stroke (*with a brush*); touch, finish, flourish
**pincelar** *va* to paint; to paint a portrait of; to picture; (med.) to pencil
**pincelero -ra** *mf* maker of brushes, dealer in brushes, seller of brushes; *m* brush case
**pincelote** *m* coarse brush
**pincerna** *mf* cupbearer, server of drinks
**pinciano -na** *adj* (pertaining to) Valladolid; *mf* native or inhabitant of Valladolid
**pincha** *f* kitchenmaid
**pinchadura** *f* or **pinchamiento** *m* prick, puncture
**pinchar** *va* to prick, jab, pierce, puncture; to stir up, provoke; **no pinchar ni cortar** to have no influence, be of no account
**pinchaúvas** *m* (*pl:* **-vas**) (coll.) grape thief (*at market*); (coll.) cur, contemptible fellow; (slang) necktie pin, stickpin
**pinchazo** *m* prick, jab; puncture; prodding, provocation; **a prueba de pinchazos** (aut.) puncture-proof
**pinche** *m* scullion, kitchen boy; helper, apprentice
**pincho** *m* thorn, prick; prod (*pointed object*)
**pinchón** *m* (orn.) chaffinch
**pinchudo -da** *adj* thorny, prickly
**pindárico -ca** *adj* Pindaric
**Píndaro** *m* Pindar

**Pindo** *m* Pindus
**pindonga** *f* (coll.) gadabout (*woman*)
**pindonguear** *vn* (coll.) to gad about (*said of a woman*)
**pineal** *adj* pineal
**pineda** *f* pine grove; braid for garters
**pingajo** *m* (coll.) rag, tatter
**pingajoso -sa** *adj* ragged, tattered
**pinganello** *m* icicle
**pinganitos; en pinganitos** (coll.) in prosperity, in a high place
**pingar** §59 *vn* to drip; to jump
**pingo** *m* (coll.) rag, tatter; (coll.) ragamuffin; (coll.) horse; (Am.) nag; **pingos** *mpl* (coll.) cheap duds (*of female*); **andar, estar** or **ir de pingo** (coll.) to gad about (*said of a woman*)
**pingorota** *f* summit, pinnacle
**pingorote** *m* (coll.) end, tip, projection
**pingorotudo -da** *adj* (coll.) high, lofty, elevated
**pingotear** *vn* (Am.) to frolic, gambol
**pingue** *m* (naut.) turret steamer, pinkie
**pingüe** *adj* oily, greasy, fat; rich, abundant, fertile, profitable
**pingüedinoso -sa** *adj* fatty; juicy, greasy
**pingüica** *f* (bot.) manzanita (*Arctostaphylus pungens*)
**pingüino** *m* (orn.) penguin
**pinguosidad** *f* fat, fattiness, greasiness
**pinífero -ra** *adj* (poet.) full of pines, pine-bearing
**pinillo** *m* (bot.) ground pine; (bot.) mock cypress; **pinillo oloroso** (bot.) ground pine
**pinino** *m* (Am.) var. of **pinito**
**pinito** *m* first step; **hacer pinitos** to begin to walk; (fig.) to take the first steps
**pinjante** *m* pendant (*jewel*); (arch.) pendant
**pinnado -da** *adj* var. of **pinado**
**pinnípedo -da** *adj* & *m* (zool.) pinniped
**pino -na** *adj* steep; *m* (bot.) pine, pine tree; first step; **en pino** standing; **hacer pinos** to begin to walk; (fig.) to take the first steps; **pino albar** (bot.) Scotch pine; **pino araucano** (bot.) monkey puzzle; **pino carrasco** or **carrasqueño** (bot.) Aleppo pine; **pino cembro** (bot.) Swiss pine; **pino doncel** (bot.) Italian stone pine; **pino marítimo** (bot.) cluster pine, pinaster; **pino negral** (bot.) larch, Corsican pine; **pino negro** (bot.) Swiss mountain pine; **pino piñón** (bot.) piñon; **pino piñonero** (bot.) stone pine (*Pinus pinea*); **pino pudio** (bot.) larch; **pino rodeno** (bot.) cluster pine, pinaster; **pino salgareño** (bot.) larch, Corsican pine; **pino tea** (bot.) pitch pine ‖ *f* felloe (*section of rim of wheel*); pointed or conical mound
**pinocha** *f* pine needle
**Pinocho** *m* Pinocchio
**pinole** *m* pinole (*powder used in making chocolate*)
**pinoso -sa** *adj* piny
**pinsapal** *m* grove of Spanish firs
**pinsapo** *m* (bot.) Spanish fir
**pinta** *m* see **pinto;** *f* see **pinto**
**pintacilgo** *m* var. of **jilguero**
**pintada** *f* see **pintado**
**pintadera** *f* pastry tube
**pintadillo** *m* var. of **jilguero**
**pintado -da** *adj* spotted, mottled; tipsy; accented (*with a written accent*); (dial.) pockmarked; **estar** or **venir pintado** or **como pintado** to be just the thing; **el más pintado** (coll.) the aptest one, the shrewdest one; (coll.) the best one; *m* painting (*act*); *f* (orn.) guinea hen; (ichth.) sierra
**pintamonas** *mf* (*pl:* **-nas**) (coll.) dauber (*poor painter*)
**pintar** *va* to paint; to draw (*a letter, an accent mark, etc.*); to picture, depict; to exaggerate; to amount to; to put a written accent on; to spread icing or a design on (*a cake*) with pastry tube; **pintarla** (coll.) to put it on, to put on airs; *vn* to paint; to begin to turn red, begin to ripen; (coll.) to show, to turn out; **pintar como querer** to indulge in wishful thinking; *vr* to paint, to paint oneself, put on make-up; to begin to turn red, begin to ripen; to imagine; **pintarse solo para** (coll.) to show great aptitude for
**pintarrajar** or **pintarrajear** *va* (coll.) to daub; *vr* (coll.) to be daubed
**pintarrajo** *m* (coll.) daub (*badly painted picture*)
**pintarroja** *f* (ichth.) dogfish
**pintear** *vn* to drizzle
**pintiparado -da** *adj* similar; **pintiparado a** similar to, like, just like; **pintiparado para** just the thing for
**pintiparar** *va* to liken, make like; (coll.) to compare
**pinto -ta** *adj* (Am.) pinto; *m* (Am.) pinto (*bean*); **estar entre Pinto y Valdemoro** (coll.) to be half-seas over; *f* spot, mark, sign; dot; pint; lines near edge of Spanish playing card showing suit; **pinta** *m* (coll.) scoundrel
**pintojo -ja** *adj* spotted, mottled
**pintón -tona** *adj* ripening (*said of grapes*); medium-baked (*brick*); *m* (ent.) corn borer
**pintor -tora** *mf* painter (*artist; artisan*); **pintor de brocha gorda** painter, house painter; (coll.) dauber; **pintor de mala muerte** (coll.) dauber; **pintor paisajista** landscape painter
**pintoresco -ca** *adj* picturesque
**pintoresquismo** *m* picturesqueness
**pintorrear** *va* (coll.) to daub; *vr* (coll.) to be daubed
**pintura** *f* painting; paint; **hacer pinturas** (coll.) to prance; **no poder ver ni en pintura** to not be able to stand the sight of; **pintura a la aguada** (f.a.) water color; **pintura al agua** cold-water paint; **pintura al encausto** (f.a.) encaustic painting; **pintura al fresco** (f.a.) fresco; **pintura al óleo** (f.a.) oil painting; **pintura al pastel** (f.a.) pastel (*drawing*); **pintura al temple** (f.a.) tempera; **pintura alumínica** aluminum paint; **pintura bronceada** bronze paint; **pintura de aceite** oil paint; **pintura de aluminio** aluminum paint
**pinturero -ra** *adj* (coll.) showy, conceited; *mf* (coll.) show-off
**pínula** *f* (opt.) sight
**pinza** *f* clothespin; spring clamp; **pinzas** *fpl* pincers (*tool; claws of crab, etc.*); tweezers; (dent. & surg.) forceps; **pinza hemostática** hemostat
**pinzón** *m* (orn.) finch; (orn.) chaffinch; pump handle; **pinzón real** (orn.) bullfinch
**pinzote** *m* (naut.) whipstaff; (naut.) pintle
**piña** *f* fir cone, pine cone; knob; plug; cluster, knot; (bot.) pineapple; (metal.) pina or piña (*residuary cone of silver*); (naut.) wall knot; **piña de ratón** (bot.) pinguin
**piñal** *m* (Am.) pineapple plantation, pinery
**piñata** *f* pot; hanging pot of candy which is broken by blindfolded children with a stick at a masked ball the first Sunday of Lent
**piñón** *m* (mach. & orn.) pinion; piñon (*seed*); (bot.) physic nut; **piñón de Indias** (bot.) physic nut; **piñón de linterna** (mach.) lantern pinion; **piñón diferencial** (aut.) pinion gear
**piñonata** *f* shredded-almond preserves
**piñonate** *m* pine-kernel candy
**piñoncillo** *m* (orn.) pinion (*of wing*)
**piñonear** *vn* to click (*said of a gun being cocked*); (coll.) to become a young man, to reach the age of puberty; (coll.) to become an old fool, to become flirtatious (*said of a mature man*)
**piñoneo** *m* click (*of a gun being cocked*)
**piñonero** *m* (orn.) bullfinch
**piñuela** *f* figured silk; cypress nut; (bot.) pinguin
**piñuelo** *m* var. of **erraj**
**pío -a** *adj* pious; merciful, compassionate; pied, dappled (*horse*); *m* peeping, chirping (*of chickens*); (coll.) intense desire; (*cap.*) *m* Pius; **no decir ni pío** to not breathe a word, to say absolutely nothing
**piocha** *f* jeweled head adornment; artificial flower made of feathers; pick, pickax
**pioemia** *f* (path.) pyaemia
**piogenia** *f* (path.) formation of pus
**piogénico -ca** or **piógeno -na** *adj* pyogenic
**piojento -ta** *adj* lousy
**piojería** *f* lousiness; lousy place; (coll.) misery, poverty

**piojillo** *m* bird louse, plant louse; **matar el piojillo** (coll.) to carry on an underhanded business
**piojo** *m* (ent.) louse; bird louse; **como piojos en costura** (coll.) packed in like sardines; **piojo de mar** (zool.) whale louse; **piojo pegadizo** (ent.) crab louse; (coll.) hanger-on, pest, parasite; **piojo resucitado** (coll.) upstart, parvenu
**piojoso -sa** *adj* lousy; mean, stingy
**piojuelo** *m* little louse; green fly, plant louse
**piola** *f* (naut.) houseline
**pión, piona** *adj* peeping, chirping
**pionero -ra** *adj* pioneering; *mf* pioneer
**pionía** *f* seed of coral tree, bucare beans
**piornal** *m* or **piorneda** *f* growth of Spanish broom
**piorno** *m* (bot.) Spanish broom; (bot.) cytisus
**piorrea** *f* (path.) pyorrhea
**pipa** *f* pipe (*for smoking tobacco*); wine cask, hogshead; butt (*liquid measure*); pip (*of orange, melon, etc.*); (arti.) fusee; (mus.) pipe, reed; **fumar en pipa** to smoke a pipe; **pipa de espuma de mar** meerschaum pipe; **pipa de paz** pipe of peace; **pipa de riego** watering cart; **pipa de tierra** clay pipe
**pipar** *vn* to smoke a pipe
**piperáceo -a** *adj* (bot.) piperaceous
**pipería** *f* casks, hogsheads; (naut.) water barrels, supply barrels
**piperina** *f* (chem.) piperine
**pipeta** *f* pipette
**pipí** *m* (*pl:* **-píes**) (orn.) honey creeper, pitpit
**pipián** *m* ragout of chicken and mutton with bacon and crushed almonds
**pipiar** §90 *vn* to peep, to chirp
**pipiolo** *m* (coll.) novice, greenhorn; (coll.) brat, urchin
**pipirigallo** *m* (bot.) sainfoin
**pipirijaina** *f* (coll.) company of strolling players
**pipiripao** *m* (coll.) sumptuous party
**pipiritaña** or **pipitaña** *f* boy's flute made of green cane
**pipistrela** *f* (zool.) bat
**pipo** *m* (orn.) lesser spotted woodpecker
**piporro** *m* (coll.) bassoon
**pipote** *m* keg
**pique** *m* pique, resentment; zeal, eagerness; (ent.) chigger; (naut.) crotch; spade (*playing card*); (Am.) shaft (*of mine*); **piques** *mpl* spades (*suit of playing cards*); **a pique** steep, jagged; (naut.) apeak; **a pique de** + *inf* in danger of + *ger;* on the verge of + *ger;* **echar a pique** (naut.) to sink (*a ship*); (fig.) to ruin, destroy; **irse a pique** (naut.) to sink; (fig.) to become ruined or destroyed; **tener un pique con** to be piqued at
**piqué** *m* piqué (*fabric*)
**piquera** *f* bung, bunghole; taphole; outlet or iron runner (*of blast furnace*); burner
**piquería** *f* troop of pikemen
**piquero** *m* pikeman; (orn.) booby
**piqueta** *f* pick, pickax; mason's hammer
**piquetaje** *m* staking out
**piquete** *m* sharp jab; small hole; survey pole; stake, picket; (mil.) picket; (Am.) pen, yard (*for animals*); (Am.) edge (*of scissors*); **piquete de ejecución** firing squad; **piquete de huelguistas** picket; **piquete de salvas** firing squad
**piquetero** *m* (min.) tool boy
**piquetilla** *f* gad, wedge; mason's pickaxe
**piquillo** *m* small beak or bill; picot
**piquituerto** *m* (orn.) crossbill
**pira** *f* pyre
**piragón** *m* var. of **pirausta**
**piragua** *f* pirogue; (sport) shell, single shell; (Am.) tailflower; (Am.) aroid
**piragüero -ra** *mf* person who steers a pirogue
**piragüista** *m* (sport) oarsman
**piral** *m* fabulous butterfly which lived in fire; (ent.) moth; **piral de la vid** (ent.) vine moth
**piramidal** *adj* pyramidal
**pirámide** *f* pyramid; **la gran Pirámide** the Great Pyramid; **las Pirámides** the Pyramids
**Píramo** *m* (myth.) Pyramus
**piranga** *f* (orn.) redbird, scarlet tanager
**pirano** *m* (chem.) pyran
**pirata** *m* pirate; hard-hearted wretch; *adj* piratical
**piratear** *vn* to pirate, to practice piracy
**piratería** *f* piracy; robbery; cruelty
**pirático -ca** *adj* piratical
**pirausta** *f* fabulous butterfly which lived in fire
**pirca** *f* (Am.) dry-stone wall
**pirco** *m* (Am.) succotash
**pirenaico -ca** *adj* Pyrenean
**Pireo, el** Peiraeus, Piraeus
**pirético -ca** *adj* pyretic
**piretología** *f* pyretology
**pirexia** *f* (path.) pyrexia
**piribenzamina** *f* (pharm.) pyribenzamine
**pírico -ca** *adj* (pertaining to) fire or fireworks
**piridina** *f* (chem.) pyridine
**piriforme** *adj* pyriform, pear-shaped
**pirinaico -ca** *adj* var. of **pirenaico**
**pirineo -a** *adj* Pyrenean; **Pirineos** *mpl* Pyrenees
**pirita** *f* (mineral.) pyrites; **pirita de cobre** (mineral.) copper pyrites; **pirita de hierro** or **pirita marcial** (mineral.) iron pyrites
**piritoso -sa** *adj* pyritic, pyritous
**pirlitero** *m* (bot.) English hawthorn (*Crataegus monogyna*)
**pirobolista** *m* (mil.) mine builder
**piroelectricidad** *f* pyroelectricity
**pirófago -ga** *adj* fire-eating; *mf* fire-eater
**piróforo** *m* (chem.) pyrophorus
**pirogálico -ca** *adj* pyrogallic
**pirogalol** *m* (chem.) pyrogallol
**pirograbado** *m* pyrography, pyrogravure
**pirolusita** *f* (mineral.) pyrolusite
**piromancia** or **piromancía** *f* pyromancy
**piromanía** *f* pyromania
**pirómetro** *m* pyrometer
**piropear** *va* (coll.) to flatter, to compliment, to flirt with
**piropeo** *m* (coll.) flattery, flirtation
**piropo** *m* garnet, carbuncle; (coll.) flattery, compliment, flirtatious remark
**piróscafo** *m* steamship
**piroscopio** *m* (phys.) pyroscope
**pirosfera** *f* pyrosphere
**pirosis** *f* (path.) pyrosis
**pirotecnia** *f* pyrotechnics
**pirotécnico -ca** *adj* pyrotechnic or pyrotechnical; *m* pyrotechnist, powder maker, fireworks manufacturer
**piroxena** *f* or **piroxeno** *m* (mineral.) pyroxene
**piroxilina** *f* pyroxylin
**Pirra** *f* (myth.) Pyrrha
**pirrar** *vr* (coll.) to long, to be eager; **pirrarse por** (coll.) to long for, to be eager for
**pírrico -ca** *adj* pyrrhic; Pyrrhic
**Pirro** *m* Pyrrhus
**pirrol** *m* (chem.) pyrrole
**pirrónico -ca** *adj* Pyrrhonistic; *mf* Pyrrhonist
**pirronismo** *m* Pyrrhonism
**pirueta** *f* pirouette
**piruétano** *m* (bot.) wild pear
**piruetear** *vn* to pirouette
**piruja** *f* flip young woman
**pirul** *m* (Am.) pepper tree
**pirulí** *m* (*pl:* **-líes**) candy on a stick, lollipop
**pisa** *f* tread, trampling, stamping; pressing of olives or grapes; volley of kicks
**pisada** *f* tread; footstep (*sound or mark*); footprint; trampling; **seguir las pisadas de** to walk in the steps of, to follow in the footsteps of
**pisadera** *f* (Am.) tread (*of stairs*)
**pisador -dora** *adj* high-stepping, prancing; *m* grape-treader
**pisadura** *f* treading; footstep
**pisapapeles** *m* (*pl:* **-les**) paperweight
**pisar** *va* to trample, tread on, step on, stamp on; to tamp, pack down; to tread, to press with the feet; to lie on or over, to cover part of; to ram; to infringe on; to cover (*a female bird*); (fig.) to tread all over, to abuse; (mus.) to pluck (*strings*); to strike (*keys*); *vn* to be right above (*said of one floor with respect to another*); **pisar firme** (Am.) to step high, be out on top; *vr* (Am.) to fail, to be disappointed
**pisasfalto** *m* pissasphalt, mineral tar
**pisaúvas** *m* (*pl:* **-vas**) grape-treader

**pisaverde** *m* (coll.) fop, coxcomb, dandy
**piscator** *m* almanac
**piscatorio -ria** *adj* piscatorial
**piscicultor -tora** *mf* pisciculturist, fish breeder
**piscicultura** *f* pisciculture, fish culture, fish breeding
**piscifactoría** *f* fish hatchery
**pisciforme** *adj* pisciform, fish-shaped
**piscina** *f* fishpool, fishpond; swimming pool; (eccl.) piscina; **revolver la piscina** (Am.) to stir up trouble
**Piscis** *m* (astr.) Pisces
**piscívoro -ra** *adj* piscivorous, fish-eating
**pisco** *m* Peruvian brandy; (Am.) brandy jug; (Am.) turkey
**piscolabis** *m* (*pl:* **-bis**) (coll.) snack, bite, treat
**pisicorre** *f* (Am.) station wagon
**pisiforme** *adj* pisiform, pea-shaped; (anat.) pisiform
**Pisístrato** *m* Pisistratus
**piso** *m* tread, treading; floor, flooring; floor, story; surface (*e.g., of a road*); apartment, flat; rent; (aut.) tread (*of tire*); (geol.) stage; (min.) level; **buscar piso** to look for a place to live; **piso alto** upper floor, top floor; **piso bajo** ground floor, first floor; **piso principal** main floor, second floor
**pisón** *m* tamper, rammer
**pisonear** *va* var. of **apisonar**
**pisotear** *va* to trample, to tramp on, to tread under foot; (fig.) to tread all over, to abuse
**pisoteo** *m* trampling; abuse
**pisotón** *m* heavy tread on someone's foot
**pista** *f* track; trace, trail; clew; race track; alley (*of bowling alley*); (aer.) runway; **estar sobre una pista** to be on the scent; **seguir la pista a** (coll.) to be on the trail of; **pista de aterrizaje** (aer.) landing field; **pista de despegue** (aer.) takeoff field; **pista de patinar** skating rink; **pista sonora** sound track
**pistachero** *m* (bot.) pistachio (*tree*)
**pistacho** *m* pistachio (*nut*)
**pistadero** *m* pestle, crusher, squeezer
**pistar** *va* to crush, to squeeze
**pistero** *m* drinking cup (*for invalids*)
**pistilado -da** *adj* (bot.) pistillate
**pistilo** *m* (bot.) pistil
**pisto** *m* chicken broth (*for the sick*); vegetable cutlet; jumbled speech or writing; mess (*unpleasant state of affairs*); **a pistos** (coll.) sparingly, scantily; **darse pisto** (coll.) to put on airs
**pistola** *f* pistol; sprayer, gun, nozzle; rock drill; pistole (*coin*); **pistola ametralladora** submachine gun; **pistola de arzón** horse pistol; **pistola engrasadora** grease gun
**pistolera** *f* holster
**pistolerismo** *m* gangsterism
**pistolero** *m* pistol-shooting gangster; operator of a rock drill
**pistoletazo** *m* pistol shot
**pistolete** *m* pistolet, pocket pistol
**pistón** *m* (mach. & mus.) piston; percussion cap
**pistonear** *vn* to knock (*said of an internal-combustion engine*)
**pistoneo** *m* knock, knocking (*of an internal-combustion engine*)
**pistonudo -da** *adj* (coll.) stunning, grand
**pistoresa** *f* poniard, short dagger
**pistraje** *m* or **pistraque** *m* slops
**pistura** *f* crushing, squeezing
**pita** *f* (bot.) American aloe, century plant; pita, pita fiber, pita thread; hiss, hissing; glass marble; hen
**pitaco** *m* stem of century plant
**pitada** *f* whistle, sound of a whistle; impropriety; whistling, hissing; (Am.) puff (*on a cigar, etc.*)
**Pitágoras** *m* Pythagoras
**pitagórico -ca** *adj & mf* Pythagorean
**pitahaya** *f* (bot.) cereus, night-blooming cereus
**pitancería** *f* distribution of doles or rations; place of distribution of doles or rations
**pitancero** *m* distributor of doles or rations; choir superintendent; (eccl.) steward
**pitanga** *f* (bot.) Surinam cherry (*Eugenia uniflora*)
**pitanza** *f* dole, ration; price; (coll.) daily bread
**pitaña** *f* var. of **legaña**
**pitañoso -sa** *adj* var. of **legañoso**
**pitar** *va* to distribute the dole to; to pay, pay off; to whistle disapproval of (*a bullfighter*); *vn* to blow a whistle, to whistle; to blow the horn, to honk; (coll.) to talk nonsense; **no pitar** (coll.) to not be in vogue, to not be popular
**pitarra** *f* var. of **legaña**
**pitarroso -sa** *adj* var. of **legañoso**
**pitazo** *m* whistle, whistling; honk (*of horn*)
**pitecántropo** *m* (anthrop.) pithecanthropus
**pitezna** *f* trigger (*of a trap*)
**Pitias** *m* (myth.) Pythias
**pitido** *m* whistle, whistling
**pitillera** *f* cigarette maker (*woman*); cigarette case
**pitillo** *m* cigarette
**pítima** *f* saffron poultice; (coll.) drunk, drunkenness
**pitio -tia** *adj* Pythian
**pitío** *m* var. of **pitido**
**pitipié** *m* scale (*with graduated spaces*)
**pitiriasis** *f* (path.) pityriasis
**pitirre** *m* (orn.) kingbird
**pito** *m* whistle; horn, auto horn; fife; fifer; cigarette; jackstone; (ent.) tick; (orn.) woodpecker; earthen vessel containing water which produces a whistling sound when air is blown into spout; **hacer un pito catalán a** (Am.) to thumb one's nose at; **no dársele a uno un pito de** (coll.) to not care or to not give a damn for, e.g., **no se me da un pito de lo que dice** I don't care a damn for what he says; **no tocar pito en** (coll.) to have no hand in; **no valer un pito** (coll.) to be not worth a damn; **pito real** (orn.) green woodpecker; **pitos flautos** (coll.) foolery, folly
**pitoflero -ra** *mf* (coll.) punk musician; (coll.) gossip, busybody
**pitómetro** *m* (hyd.) pitometer
**pitón** *m* lump, protuberance; sprig, young shoot; tenderling, budding horn; tip (*of horn*); nozzle, spout; (zool.) python; (*cap.*) *m* (myth.) Python
**pitonisa** *f* pythoness; witch, siren
**pitorra** *f* (orn.) woodcock
**pitorrear** *vr* (coll.) to jeer, scoff
**pitorreo** *m* (coll.) jeering, scoffing
**pitorro** *m* nozzle, spout
**pitpit** *m* (orn.) pitpit
**pitreo** *m* var. of **pitaco**
**Pitsburgo** *f* Pittsburgh
**pituco -ca** *adj* (Am.) thin, weak, feeble; (Am.) dandyish; *m* (Am.) dandy, dude
**pituita** *f* pituite, mucus, phlegm
**pituitario -ria** *adj* pituitary
**pituitoso -sa** *adj* pituitous
**pituso -sa** *adj* tiny, cute; *mf* tot
**piular** *vn* to peep, chirp
**piulido** *m* peeping, chirping
**piune** *m* (bot.) Chilean medicinal tree (*Lomatia ferruginea*)
**piuquén** *m* (orn.) Chilean wild brant
**piuria** *f* (path.) pyuria
**pivotar** *vn* to pivot
**pivote** *m* pivot
**píxide** *f* (eccl.) pyx
**pixidio** *m* (bot.) pyxidium
**piyama** *m* var. of **pijama**
**pizarra** *f* shale, slate; slate (*for roofs; for writing on*); blackboard (*of any material*)
**pizarral** *m* shale bed
**pizarreño -ña** *adj* slaty, slate-colored; shaly
**pizarrería** *f* slate quarry, shale quarry
**pizarrero** *m* slater
**pizarrín** *m* slate pencil
**pizarrón** *m* large slate; **pizarrón anotador** score board
**pizarroso -sa** *adj* slate-colored; full of slate
**pizate** *m* var. of **pazote**
**pizca** *f* (coll.) mite, whit, jot; **ni pizca** (coll.) not a bit
**pizcar** §86 *va* (coll.) to pinch
**pizco** *m* (coll.) pinch, pinching
**pizmiento -ta** *adj* pitch-colored
**pizpereta** or **pizpireta** *adj* brisk, lively, smart (*woman*)
**pizpirigaña** *f* boys' pinching game

**pizpita** *f* or **pizpitillo** *m* (orn.) wagtail
**placa** *f* plaque (*badge of an order*); plaque, tablet; plate, slab, sheet; (anat., elec., phot., rad. & zool.) plate; (Am.) spot, scab; **placa acribillada** (bot.) sieve plate; **placa de cuarzo** (elec.) quartz plate; **placa de matrícula** (aut.) license plate; **placa giratoria** turntable (*for locomotives, etc.; of phonograph*)
**placabilidad** *f* placability
**placable** *adj* placable
**placaminero** *m* (bot.) persimmon
**placativo -va** *adj* placatory
**placear** *va* to retail (*foodstuffs*); to reveal, make known
**placebo** *m* (eccl. & med.) placebo
**placel** *m* (naut.) sandbank, reef; pearl-fishery
**pláceme** *m* congratulation; **dar el pláceme a** to congratulate; **estar de plácemes** to be in luck
**placenta** *f* (anat., bot. & zool.) placenta
**placentario -ria** *adj* placental; *m* (zool.) placental
**placentero -ra** *adj* pleasant, agreeable
**placer** *m* (min.) placer; (naut.) sandbank, reef; pearl-fishery; pleasure; **a placer** at one's convenience; §67 *va* to please; **que me place** willingly, with pleasure
**placero -ra** *adj* public, market-place; *mf* market vendor; loafer, town gossip
**placeta** or **placetuela** *f* small public square
**placibilidad** *f* agreeableness
**placible** *adj* agreeable
**placidez** *f* placidity
**plácido -da** *adj* placid
**placiente** *adj* pleasing, agreeable
**plácito** *m* opinion, judgment
**plafón** *m* (arch.) soffit
**plaga** *f* plague; pest; scourge, calamity; abundance; sore, ulcer; clime, region; point (*of compass*)
**plagado -da** *adj* plagued, infested; smitten
**plagar** §59 *va* to plague, infest; **plagar de minas** to sow with mines; *vr* to become plagued or infested
**plagiar** *va* to plagiarize; (Am.) to abduct, kidnap
**plagiario -ria** *adj* plagiaristic; *mf* plagiarist
**plagio** *m* plagiarism; (Am.) abduction, kidnaping
**plagioclasa** *f* (mineral.) plagioclase
**plagiostomo -ma** *adj* & *m* (ichth.) plagiostome
**plagiotropismo** *m* (bot.) plagiotropism
**plagiotropo -pa** *adj* (bot.) plagiotropic
**plaid** *m* plaid
**plan** *m* plan; level, height; (med.) régime; (min.) mine floor; (naut.) floor timber; **plan de estudios** or **plan escolar** curriculum; **plan quinquenal** five-year plan
**plana** *f* see **plano**
**planada** *f* plain, level ground
**planador** *m* planisher
**planco** *m* (orn.) gannet, solan
**plancton** *m* (biol.) plankton
**plancha** *f* plate, sheet (*of metal*); gangplank; iron, flatiron; ironing; horizontal suspension (*in gymnastics*); (print.) plate; (coll.) blunder, break; (Am.) flatcar; (Am.) dental plate; **a la plancha** grilled; **tirarse una plancha** to make a break, to put one's foot in it; **plancha de blindaje** armor plate; **plancha de caldera** boiler plate; **plancha de sastre** tailor's goose; **plancha portainstrumentos** (aut.) instrument panel
**planchada** *f* gangplank; (arti.) apron
**planchado** *m* ironing, pressing
**planchador -dora** *mf* ironer; *f* ironer (*machine*)
**planchar** *va* to iron, to press (*clothing*); *vn* (Am.) to be a wallflower
**planchear** *va* to plate, to cover with metal plates or sheets
**plancheta** *f* (surv.) plane table
**planchón** *m* large or heavy plate (*of metal*); (Am.) glacier
**planeación** *f* planning; planing
**planeador** *m* (aer.) glider
**planear** *va* to plan, to outline; to plane (*a board*); *vn* (aer.) to volplane, to glide
**planeo** *m* planning; (aer.) volplane, gliding
**planera** *f* (bot.) planer tree
**planeta** *m* (astr. & astrol.) planet
**planetario -ria** *adj* planetary; (mach.) planetary; *m* planetarium
**planetesimal** *adj* & *m* planetesimal
**planetícola** *mf* dweller on another planet
**planetista** *m* astrologer
**planetoide** *m* (astr.) planetoid
**planga** *f* (orn.) gannet, solan
**planicidad** *f* flatness
**planicie** *f* level ground, plain
**planificar** §86 *va* to plan
**planilla** *f* (Am.) list, roll, schedule; (Am.) panel (*of candidates for office*); (Am.) ballot; (Am.) commutation ticket (*for trolleys and busses*)
**planimetría** *f* planimetry
**planimétrico -ca** *adj* planimetric or planimetrical
**planímetro** *m* planimeter
**planisferio** *m* planisphere
**plankton** *m* var. of **plancton**
**plano -na** *adj* plane; level; smooth, even; flat ‖ *m* plan; map; plane; (aer.) plane, wing; (b.b.) board; **caer de plano** to fall flat; **cantar de plano** (coll.) to make a clean breast of it; **de plano** clearly, plainly, flatly; flat; **levantar un plano** (surv.) to make a survey; **primer plano** foreground; **plano acotado** contour map; **plano de cola** (aer.) tail plane; **plano de deriva** (aer.) tail fin; **plano de dirección** (aer.) vertical stabilizer; **plano de incidencia** (opt.) plane of incidence; **plano de nivel** datum plane, datum level; **plano de profundidad** (aer.) horizontal stabilizer; **plano de prueba** (phys.) proof plane; **plano focal** (opt.) focal plane; **plano inclinado** (mech.) inclined plane; cable railway ‖ *f* flat country, plain; trowel; cooper's plane; handwriting (*of a beginner*); (print.) page; **a plana renglón** or **a plana y renglón** line for line; just right; **corregir** or **enmendar la plana a** to find fault with; to excel; **primera plana** first page; **plana curvada** drawknife; **plana mayor** (mil.) staff
**planocóncavo -va** *adj* plano-concave
**planoconvexo -xa** *adj* plano-convex
**planta** *f* (bot.) plant; sole (*of foot*); foot; planting; plan; project; floor; floor plan, ground plan; roster (*of an office staff*); stance (*in fencing and dancing*); plant, factory; **de planta** from the ground up; **echar plantas** to swagger, to bully; **tener buena planta** (coll.) to make a fine appearance; **planta baja** ground floor; **planta del sortilegio** (bot.) witch hazel; **planta de maceta** or **de tiesto** potted plant; **planta noble** ground floor; **plantas de adorno** (hort.) ornamental plants; **planta siempre verde** (bot.) evergreen
**plantación** *f* planting; plantation
**plantador -dora** *mf* planter; (Am.) planter (*colonist*); *m* dibble; *f* planter (*machine*)
**plantagináceo -a** *adj* (bot.) plantaginaceous
**plantaina** *f* var. of **llantén**
**plantaje** *m* plants, planting
**plantar** *adj* (anat.) plantar; *va* to plant; to establish, to found; (coll.) to plant (*a blow*); (coll.) to jilt; (coll.) to throw (*into the street, into prison*); to leave dumfounded; *vr* to stand, take a stand; (coll.) to balk (*said of an animal*); (coll.) to land, to get, to arrive; to gang together
**plantario** *m* seedbed
**plante** *m* ganging together
**planteamiento** *m* planning; establishment, execution; statement, exposition; framing (*of a question*)
**plantear** *va* to plan, to outline (*e.g., a deal*); to establish, to execute, to carry out; to state, to set up, to expound, to pose; to raise (*a question*); *vn* (archaic) to weep, sob, whine
**plantel** *m* nursery, nursery garden; establishment, plant (*educational institution*); group, gathering
**planțificación** *f* planning; (coll.) planting a blow; throwing, hurling (*e.g., into the street, jail, etc.*)

**plantificar** §86 *va* to plan, to outline; (coll.) to plant (*a blow*); (coll.) to throw (*into the street, into prison*); *vr* (coll.) to get, to arrive
**plantígrado -da** *adj & m* (zool.) plantigrade
**plantilla** *f* plantlet, young plant; insole; reinforced sole (*of stocking or sock*); model, pattern, template; staff (*e.g., of employees*); roster (*of office force*); plan, design; ladyfinger (*cake*); **echar plantillas al calzado** to half-sole shoes; **ser de plantilla** to be on the regular staff
**plantillar** *va* to put insoles in (*shoes*); to reinforce the sole of (*a stocking or sock*)
**plantillero -ra** *adj* swaggering; *mf* swaggerer, bully
**plantío -a** *adj* planted; ready to be planted; *m* planting, growth, patch
**plantista** *m* landscape gardener; (coll.) swaggerer, bully
**plantón** *m* shoot (*to be transplanted*); graft, cion; guard, watchman; soldier punished with extra guard duty; waiting, standing around; **dar un plantón** to be long in coming, to keep someone waiting; **estar de** or **en plantón** (coll.) to stand around (*for a long time*); **llevarse un plantón** (coll.) to be kept standing
**planudo -da** *adj* flat-bottomed
**plañidero -ra** *adj* weeping, mournful; *f* weeper, professional mourner, hired mourner
**plañido** or **plañimiento** *m* lamentation, wailing, weeping
**plañir** §25 *va* to lament, grieve over; *vn* to lament, grieve, bewail
**plaqué** *m* plate, plating (*of gold or silver*)
**plaquear** *va* to plate, to silver-plate
**plaqueta** *f* (anat.) plaquette, blood platelet
**plaquín** *m* hauberk, coat of mail
**plasma** *m* (anat., phys. & physiol.) plasma; **plasma sanguíneo** blood plasma; *f* (mineral.) plasm
**plasmación** *f* molding, shaping
**plasmador -dora** *adj* creative; *mf* molder, creator; (*cap.*) *m* Creator
**plasmar** *va* to mold, shape
**plasmático -ca** *adj* plasmatic
**plasmodio** *m* (biol.) plasmodium
**plasmólisis** *f* (physiol.) plasmolysis
**plasmoquina** *f* (pharm.) plasmochin
**plasmosoma** *m* (pharm.) plasmosome
**plasta** *f* paste, soft mass; flattened object, flattened mass; (coll.) poor job, bungle
**plaste** *m* sizing, filler
**plastecer** §34 *va* to size, to fill
**plastecido** *m* sizing, filling
**plástica** *f* see **plástico**
**plasticidad** *f* plasticity
**plástico -ca** *adj* plastic; *m* plastic (*substance*); *f* plastic (*art of modeling*); plastic arts
**plastificar** §86 *va & vr* to plasticize
**plastilina** *f* plasticine
**plastrón** *m* (fencing) plastron
**plata** *f* (chem.) silver; silver (*coin or coins*); wealth; money; **como una plata** (coll.) clean, shining; **en plata** (coll.) briefly, to the point; (coll.) plainly; (coll.) in sum; **quedarse sin plata** to be broke; **plata agria** (mineral.) stephanite; **plata alemana** German silver; **plata córnea** (mineral.) horn silver; **plata de piña** spongy silver; **plata dorada** silver gilt; **plata labrada** silverware; **plata roja** ruby silver
**platabanda** *f* border, edge; flower bed; (arch.) flat molding; splice plate, fishplate
**plataforma** *f* platform; (rail.) platform car, flatcar; (rail.) roadbed; (rail.) turntable; (geog.) platform; (mach.) index plate; (fig.) platform (*statement of policy of political party*); **plataforma giratoria** (rail.) turntable
**platal** *m* (coll.) lot of money
**platalea** *f* (orn.) pelican
**platanáceo -a** *adj* (bot.) platanaceous
**platanal** *m* or **platanar** *m* plantation of plantains
**platanero -ra** *adj* (pertaining to the) banana; *m* (bot.) plantain, banana
**plátano** *m* (bot.) plantain, banana (*Musa paradisiaca and fruit*); (bot.) plane tree; **plátano de occidente** (bot.) American plane tree; **plátano de oriente** (bot.) plane tree; **plátano falso** (bot.) sycamore maple; **plátano guineo** (bot.) banana
**platea** *f* (theat.) orchestra, parquet
**plateado -da** *adj* silver-plated; silver (*in color*); *m* silver plating; silver (*color*)
**plateador** *m* silver plater
**plateadura** *f* silver plating; silver (*used in plating*)
**platear** *va* to coat or plate with silver
**platel** *m* platter, tray
**platelminto** *m* (zool.) platyhelminth
**platén** *m* platen (*of typewriter*)
**plateresco -ca** *adj* (arch.) plateresque
**platería** *f* silversmith's shop; trade of silversmith
**platero** *m* silversmith; jeweller; **platero de oro** goldsmith
**plática** *f* talk, chat; talk, informal lecture; sermon; **libre plática** (naut.) pratique
**platicar** §86 *va* to talk over (*a matter*); to discuss; to preach; *vn* to talk, to chat; to discuss; to preach
**platija** *f* (ichth.) plaice
**platilla** *f* thin middling linen
**platillo** *m* plate; saucer; pan (*of scales*); stew; extra dish (*in a monastery*); subject of gossip; (mus.) cymbal; **platillo volador** or **volante** flying saucer
**platina** *f* platen; stage (*for microscope*); (chem.) platinum; (print.) imposing table
**platinar** *va* to platinize
**platiniridio** *m* platiniridium
**platino** *m* (chem.) platinum
**platinocianuro** *m* (chem.) platinocyanide
**platinoide** *m* platinoid
**platinotipia** *f* (phot.) platinotype
**platirrino -na** *adj & m* (zool.) platyrrhine
**plato** *m* dish; plate; course (*at meals*); daily fare; pan (*of scales*); subject of gossip; (arch.) ornamented metope; (mach.) plate, disk; (mach.) chuck; (poker) pot; **comer en un mismo plato** (coll.) to be close friends; **entre dos platos** with much bowing and bending; **hacer plato** to pass the food; **nada entre dos platos** (coll.) much ado about nothing; **ser plato de segunda mano** (coll.) to feel neglected, to be left out in the cold; **plato de segunda mano** (coll.) discard, castoff; **plato frutero** fruit dish; **plato fuerte** main course; **plato giratorio** turntable (*of phonograph*); **plato sopero** soup dish; **plato trinchero** trencher (*wooden platter*); dish
**plató** *m* (*pl:* **-tós**) (mov.) set
**platón** *m* large plate; (Am.) washbowl, basin; (Am.) platter; (*cap.*) *m* Plato
**platónico -ca** *adj* Platonic
**platonismo** *m* Platonism
**platonista** *mf* Platonist
**platudo -da** *adj* (Am.) rich, well-to-do
**platuja** *f* var. of **platija**
**plausibilidad** *f* praiseworthiness; acceptability, agreeableness
**plausible** *adj* praiseworthy; acceptable, agreeable, pleasing
**plausivo -va** *adj* applauding
**plauso** *m* var. of **aplauso**
**plaustro** *m* (poet.) cart, wagon
**plautino -na** *adj* Plautine
**Plauto** *m* Plautus
**playa** *f* beach, shore, strand; **playa de baños** bathing beach; **playa infantil** sand pile (*for children to play in*)
**playado -da** *adj* beach-lined
**playazo** *m* long, wide beach
**playero -ra** (pertaining to the) beach; *mf* fishmonger; **playero turco** (orn.) ruddy turnstone; *f* fishwoman; Andalusian song; beach shoe
**playón** *m* large beach
**playuela** *f* small beach
**plaza** *f* plaza, square; market, market place; town, city; fortified town or city; space, room; yard; office, employment; character, reputation; place, seat; **sacar a plaza** (coll.) to bring out into the open; **sentar plaza** (mil.) to enlist; **un cuatro plazas** a four-seater; **plaza de armas** (mil.) parade ground; (Am.)

public square; **plaza de gallos** cockpit (*for cockfights*); **plaza de toros** bull ring; **plaza fuerte** (fort.) stronghold, fortress, garrison; **plaza mayor** main square; **plaza montada** mounted soldier
**plazco** or **plazgo** *1st sg pres ind of* **placer**
**plazo** *m* term, time, extension; time limit; date of payment; instalment; **a largo plazo** long-range; (com.) long-term; **a plazo** on credit, on time; in instalments; **en breve plazo** within a short time; **vender a plazo** to sell on credit; to sell short
**plazoleta** *f* small square; small square or plaza in a public walk or garden
**plazuela** *f* small square
**ple** *m* handball
**pleamar** *f* (naut.) high tide, high water
**plébano** *m* parish priest
**plebe** *f* plebs, common people; (hist.) plebs
**plebeísmo** *m* plebeianism
**plebeyez** *f* (coll.) plebeianism
**plebeyo -ya** *adj & mf* plebeian
**plebiscitario -ria** *adj* (pertaining to a) plebiscite, plebiscitary
**plebiscito** *m* plebiscite
**pleca** *f* (print.) thin line or rule
**plectognato -ta** *adj & m* (zool.) plectognath
**plectro** *m* (mus.) plectrum; (poet.) inspiration
**plegable** *adj* folding; pliable
**plegadamente** *adv* in folds; confusedly; wholesale
**plegadera** *f* paper folder, paper knife
**plegadizo -za** *adj* folding; pliable
**plegado** *m* var. of **plegadura**
**plegador -dora** *adj* folding; *mf* folder; *m* folder, folding machine
**plegadura** *f* fold; plait, pleat, crease
**plegamiento** *m* fold; plait, pleat, crease; (geol.) fold
**plegar §29** *va* to fold; to plait, to pleat, to crease; to fold over; *vr* to yield, give in
**plegaria** *f* prayer; noon call to prayer
**pleguería** *f* folds, plaits
**pleguete** *m* (bot.) tendril
**pleistoceno -na** *adj & m* (geol.) Pleistocene
**pleita** *f* plaited strand of esparto grass
**pleiteador -dora** *mf* pleader, litigant
**pleitear** *va & vn* (law) to plead, to litigate
**pleitista** *adj* litigious; *mf* litigious person
**pleito** *m* litigation, lawsuit; dispute, quarrel; fight, battle; **pleito de acreedores** bankruptcy proceedings; **pleito homenaje** (feud.) homage
**plenamar** *f* var. of **pleamar**
**plenario -ria** *adj* plenary
**plenilunio** *m* full moon
**plenipotencia** *f* full powers
**plenipotenciario -ria** *adj & mf* plenipotentiary
**plenitud** *f* plenitude, fullness; **plenitud de los tiempos** fullness of time
**pleno -na** *adj* full; joint (*session*); **en plena bahía** out in the bay, in the open bay; **en plena calle** in the middle of the street, right in the street; **en plena cara** right in the face, smack in the face; **en plena carrera** in the middle of the race; in full career; **en plena ciudad** in the heart of the city; **en plena cosecha** in the middle of the harvest; **en plena faena** in the midst of his (her, your, etc.) task; **en plena guerra** in the midst of war; **en plena intriga** in the midst of plotting; **en plena juventud** in the flower of youth; **en plena marcha** in full swing; **en plena noche** in the depth of night; **en plena retirada** in full retreat; **en plena temporada** at the height of the season; **en plena urbe** in the heart of the city; **en plena vista** in plain sight, in full view; **en pleno bloqueo** at the height of the blockade; **en pleno campo** in the open country; **en pleno día** in broad daylight; **en pleno invierno** in the deep (or depth) of winter, in midwinter; **en pleno mar** in the open sea; **en pleno mediodía** at broad noon, at high noon; **en pleno río** in midstream; **en pleno trabajo** in the thick of work; **en pleno verano** at the height of summer, in midsummer; **en pleno viento** in the full force of the wind; exposed to the wind on all sides; **en pleno vigor** in full vigor; in full swing; *m* plenum; full meeting (or session); (bowling) strike
**pleocroísmo** *m* (cryst.) pleochroism
**pleonasmo** *m* pleonasm
**pleonástico -ca** *adj* pleonastic
**pleópodo** *m* (zool.) swimmeret, pleopod
**plepa** *f* (coll.) mess (*person or thing full of defects*)
**plesiosauro** *m* (pal.) plesiosaur
**pletina** *f* iron plate, flange, shim
**pletismógrafo** *m* (physiol.) plethysmograph
**plétora** *f* plethora; superabundance; (path.) plethora
**pletórico -ca** *adj* plethoric; **pletórico de** overflowing with
**pleura** *f* (anat. & zool.) pleura
**pleural** *adj* pleural
**pleuresía** *f* (path.) pleurisy
**pleurítico -ca** *adj* pleuritic
**pleuritis** *f* (path.) pleuritis
**pleurodinia** *f* (path.) pain in the side
**pleurodonto -ta** *adj* (zool.) pleurodont
**pleuronecto -ta** *adj & m* (ichth.) pleuronectid
**pleuroneumonía** *f* (path.) pleuropneumonia
**plexiglás** *m* plexiglass
**plexo** *m* (anat. & zool.) plexus; **plexo solar** (anat.) solar plexus
**Pléyade** *f* Pleiad; **Pléyades** *fpl* (myth & astr.) Pleiades
**plica** *f* (law) escrow; (mus. & path.) plica
**pliego** *m* sheet (*of paper*); folder; cover, envelope; sealed letter or document; bid, specifications; **pliego cerrado** (naut.) sealed orders; **pliego de comprobar** (print.) proof; **pliego de condiciones** bid, specifications; **pliego de prensa** (print.) page proof; **pliego de principios** (print.) proof of front matter
**pliegue** *m* fold, pleat, crease; (geol.) fold; **pliegue acordeonado** or **en acordeón** (sew.) accordion pleat; **pliegue de tabla** (sew.) box pleat
**plieguecillo** *m* small sheet; small fold; small folder
**Plinio** *m* Pliny; **Plinio el Antiguo** Pliny the Elder; **Plinio el Joven** Pliny the Younger
**plinto** *m* (arch.) plinth; baseboard
**pliocénico -ca** or **plioceno -na** *adj & m* (geol.) Pliocene
**plisado** *m* pleat; pleating
**plisar** *va* to pleat
**plomada** *f* carpenter's lead pencil; plummet; plumb bob; sinker or sinkers (*of a fishing net*); scourge tipped with lead balls; (naut.) sounding lead
**plomar** *va* to seal with lead
**plomazo** *m* shot, gunshot
**plomazón** *f* cushion (*of goldsmith or silversmith*)
**plombagina** *f* plumbago, graphite
**plomería** *f* lead roofing; leadwork; plumbing
**plomero** *m* lead worker; plumber
**plomífero -ra** *adj* plumbiferous; *mf* (coll.) bore, nuisance
**plomizo -za** *adj* leaden; lead-colored
**plomo** *m* (chem.) lead; lead (*piece of lead; plumb bob, plummet; bullet*); sinker; (elec.) fuse; (coll.) bore; **a plomo** plumb, perpendicularly; (coll.) just right; **caer a plomo** to fall flat; **plomo azul** blue lead (*pigment*)
**plomoso -sa** *adj* var. of **plomizo**
**Plotino** *m* Plotinus
**plugo** *3d sg pret ind of* **placer**
**pluma** *f* feather; feathers; quill; plume; pen; penmanship; writer; (fig.) pen; (Am.) faucet; **dejar correr la pluma** to write away, to write for dear life; **escribir a vuela pluma** to write freely, to let onself go (*in writing*); **vivir de la pluma** to live by one's pen; **pluma esferográfica** (Am.) ball point pen; **pluma estilográfica** or **pluma fuente** (*pl:* **plumas fuente**) fountain pen; **pluma secundaria** (orn.) secondary feather
**plumado -da** *adj* feathered; *f* flourish, stroke (*of pen*); penful
**plumafuente** *f* fountain pen
**plumaje** *m* plumage; plumes, crest
**plumajería** *f* abundance of plumes
**plumajero** *m* plumist, feather dresser

**plumazo** *m* feather pillow, feather mattress; stroke (*of pen*); **de un plumazo** (coll.) with one fell stroke
**plumazón** *m* plumage, abundance of plumes; crest
**plumbado -da** *adj* sealed with a lead seal
**plumbagina** *f* var. of **plombagina**
**plumbagináceo -a** *adj* (bot.) plumbaginaceous
**plúmbeo -a** *adj* lead; heavy as lead
**plúmbico -ca** *adj* lead; (chem.) plumbic
**plumeado** *m* (f.a.) hatching
**plumear** *va* (f.a.) to hatch
**plumeo** *m* (f.a.) hatching
**plúmeo -a** *adj* feathery
**plumería** *f* or **plumerío** *m* feathers, wealth of feathers
**plumerillo** *m* (bot.) milkweed
**plumero** *m* penholder (*rack*); duster, feather duster; school companion (*box for pens and pencils*); **plumeros** *mpl* (bot.) goldenrod
**plumífero -ra** *adj* (poet.) feathered
**plumilla** *f* small feather, plumelet; point (*of fountain pen*); (bot.) plumule; **plumilla inglesa** (print.) script
**plumión** *m* (orn.) plumule
**plumista** *m* scrivener, clerk; feather or plume maker or dealer
**plumón** *m* (orn.) plumule; down; feather bed
**plumoso -sa** *adj* downy, feathery, plumose
**plúmula** *f* (bot.) plumule
**plural** *adj* (gram.) plural; manifold; *m* (gram.) plural; **plural de modestia** (gram.) editorial plural; **plural mayestático** (gram.) royal plural
**pluralidad** *f* plurality; **a pluralidad de votos** by a majority of votes
**pluralizar** §76 *va* to pluralize
**plus** *m* extra, bonus; **plus marca** *f* (sport) record
**pluscuamperfecto -ta** *adj & m* (gram.) pluperfect
**plusmarca** *f* (sport) record
**plusmarquista** *adj* (sport) record-breaking; *mf* (sport) record breaker
**plusvalía** *f* increased value, appreciation
**Plutarco** *m* Plutarch
**plúteo** *m* shelf, bookshelf; (hist.) pluteus
**Pluto** *m* (myth.) Plutus
**plutocracia** *f* plutocracy
**plutócrata** *mf* plutocrat
**plutocrático -ca** *adj* plutocratic
**Plutón** *m* (myth. & astr.) Pluto
**plutoniano -na** *adj* Plutonian
**plutónico -ca** *adj* (geol.) plutonic; (myth. & geol.) Plutonic
**plutonio** *m* (chem.) plutonium
**Plutos** *m* (myth.) Pluto
**pluvial** *adj* pluvial; rain
**pluviómetro** *m* pluviometer, rain gauge
**pluviosidad** *f* rainfall; raininess
**pluvioso -sa** *adj* pluvious, rainy
**pneumático -ca** *adj* var. of **neumático**
**pno.** abr. of **pergamino**
**p.º** abr. of **pero**
**P.º** abr. of **Pedro**
**poa** *f* (naut.) bridle
**pobeda** *f* white-poplar grove
**población** *f* population; village, town, city
**poblacho** *m* shabby old town or village
**poblado -da** *adj* populated; thick, bushy; *m* community
**poblador -dora** *adj* founding, settling; *mf* founder, settler
**poblano -na** *mf* (Am.) townsman, villager
**poblar** §77 *va* to people, populate; to found, settle, colonize; to stock (*a farm, a fishpond, a beehive*); to plant (*e.g., with trees*); *vn* to settle, colonize; to multiply, be prolific; *vr* to become full, covered, or crowded
**poblazo** *m* var. of **poblacho**
**poblezuelo** *m* small village
**pobo** *m* (bot.) white poplar
**pobre** *adj* poor; **más pobre que las ratas** or **una rata** (coll.) poor as a church mouse; **pobre de espíritu** poor in spirit; **¡pobre de mí!** poor me!; **pobre de solemnidad** poor as a church mouse; *mf* beggar, pauper; *m* poor man; poor devil
**pobrería** *f* var. of **pobretería**
**pobrero** *m* distributor of alms
**pobrete -ta** *adj* poor; wretched; (coll.) sorry-looking; *mf* wretch, unfortunate; *f* (coll.) prostitute
**pobretear** *vn* (coll.) to play poor, to act poor
**pobretería** *f* poor, poor people; beggars; poverty, wretchedness
**pobreto** *m* wretch, unfortunate
**pobretón -tona** *adj* poor, needy; *m* poor man
**pobreza** *f* poverty, want; poorness; vow of poverty
**pobrezuelo -la** *adj* poorish
**pobrismo** *m* poor, poor people; beggars
**pócar** *m* poker
**pocero** *m* well digger, well driller; cesspool cleaner
**poceta** *f* (Am.) basin, bowl
**pocilga** *f* pigpen; (fig.) pigpen
**pocillo** *m* sump, catch basin; chocolate cup
**pócima** *f* potion, concoction
**poción** *f* potion, dose
**poco -ca** *adj* little; few, e.g., **hay poca gente aquí** there are few people here; **pocos -cas** *adj pl* few; **poco** *adv* little; **poco** + *adj* un-, e.g., **poco inteligente** unintelligent; **a poco** shortly, shortly afterwards; **a poco de** + *inf* shortly after + *ger;* **dentro de poco** shortly; **en poco** almost; **estar en poco que** + *subj* to come near + *ger;* **otro poco** a little more; **por poco** almost, nearly; **tener en poco** to hold in low esteem, be scornful of; **un poco** a little; **un poco de** a little; **unos pocos** a few; **poco a poco** little by little; **¡poco a poco!** easy there!
**póculo** *m* drinking cup or glass
**pocha** *f* see **pocho**
**pochi** *adj* (Am.) short, too short
**pocho -cha** *adj* faded, discolored; overripe; rotten; (Am.) chubby; *mf* (Am.) U.S.-born Mexican; *f* (Am.) lie, trick, cheat
**poda** *f* pruning; pruning season
**podadera** *f* pruning knife or hook, billhook
**podador -dora** *adj* pruning; *mf* pruner
**podagra** *f* (path.) gout, podagra
**podar** *va* to prune
**podazón** *f* pruning season
**podenco** *m* hound
**podenquero** *m* keeper of the hounds
**poder** *m* power; hands; (law) power of attorney, proxy; **a poder de** by dint of; **caer en poder de** (mil.) to fall to; **de poder a poder** hand to hand; **el cuarto poder** the fourth estate (*the press, journalism*); **en poder de** in the power of; in the hands of; **obra en mi poder** I have at hand, I have in my possession; **plenos poderes** full powers; **por poderes** by proxy; **poder adquisitivo** or **poder de adquisición** purchasing power; **poder aéreo** air power; **poder aéreo atómico** atomic air power ‖ §68 *vn* to be possible; to be able, to have power or strength; **a más no poder** as hard as possible; **hasta más no poder** to the utmost; **no poder con** to not be able to stand, to not be able to manage; **no poder más** to be exhausted, to be all in; **no poder menos de** + *inf* to not be able to help + *ger;* **poder mucho** to have power or influence; **poder poco** to have little power or influence ‖ *v aux* **poder** + *inf* to be able to + *inf,* may, can, might, could + *inf;* **no poder ver** to not be able to stand
**poderdante** *mf* (law) constituent
**poderhabiente** *mf* (law) attorney, proxy
**poderío** *m* power, might; wealth, riches; sway, jurisdiction
**poderoso -sa** *adj* powerful, mighty; wealthy, rich
**podíatra** *mf* podiatrist
**podiatría** *f* podiatry
**podio** *m* (arch.) podium
**podódromo** *m* race track (*for foot races*)
**podofilino** *m* (pharm.) podophyllin
**podofilo** *m* podophyllum
**podofilotoxina** *f* (chem.) podophyllotoxin
**podómetro** *m* pedometer
**podón** *m* large pruning hook, large billhook
**podre** *m & f* pus, corruption
**podré** *1st sg fut ind of* **poder**
**podrecer** §34 *va, vn & vr* to rot
**podrecimiento** *m* var. of **podredura**

**podredumbre** *f* corruption, putrefaction; pus; gnawing sorrow
**podredura** or **podrición** *f* corruption, putrefaction
**podridero** *m* var. of **pudridero**
**podrido -da** *adj* rotten, putrid
**podrigorio** *m* (coll.) person full of aches and pains
**podrimiento** *m* var. of **pudrimiento**
**podrir** *va, vn & vr* var. of **pudrir** and used only in the *inf & pp*
**poema** *m* poem; **poema en prosa** prose poem; **poema sinfónico** (mus.) symphonic poem
**poemático -ca** *adj* poetic
**poesía** *f* poetry; poem; **bella poesía** (fig.) fairy tale (*untrue story*); **poesías órficas** Orphic hymns
**poeta** *m* poet
**poetastro** *m* poetaster
**poético -ca** *adj* poetic or poetical; *f* poetics
**poetisa** *f* poetess
**poetizar** §76 *va & vn* to poetize
**poíno** *m* gantry, barrelstand
**poiquilotermo -ma** *adj* (zool.) poikilothermal
**polaco -ca** *adj* Polish; *mf* Pole; **los polacos** the Polish; *m* Polish (*language*); *f* Polish dance
**polacra** *f* (naut.) polacre
**polaina** *f* legging
**polar** *adj* pole; polar; *f* polestar
**polaridad** *f* polarity
**polarímetro** *m* polarimeter
**polariscopio** *m* polariscope
**polarización** *f* polarization; **polarización de rejilla** (rad.) grid bias
**polarizador -dora** *adj* polarizing; *m* (opt.) polarizer
**polarizar** §76 *va* to polarize; *vr* to become polarized; to concentrate
**polaroide** *m* polaroid
**polca** *f* (mus.) polka
**polcar** §86 *vn* to polka, dance the polka
**polea** *f* pulley; (naut.) tackle
**poleadas** *fpl* porridge
**poleame** *m* (naut.) set of pulleys, tackle
**polémico -ca** *adj* polemic or polemical; *f* polemic (*controversy*); polemics (*art*)
**polemista** *mf* polemist
**polemizar** §76 *vn* to start a polemic
**polemoniáceo -a** *adj* (bot.) polemoniaceous
**polemonio** *m* (bot.) Greek valerian, Jacob's-ladder
**polen** *m* (bot.) pollen
**polenta** *f* polenta
**poleo** *m* cold wind, cold blast; (bot.) pennyroyal; (coll.) bombast, strutting
**poleví** *m* (*pl:* **-víes**) var. of **ponleví**
**poliandria** *f* polyandry; (bot.) polyandry
**poliándrico -ca** *adj* polyandrous
**poliandro -dra** *adj* (bot.) polyandrous
**poliarquía** *f* polyarchy
**polibásico -ca** *adj* (chem.) polybasic
**polibasita** *f* (mineral.) polybasite
**policárpico -ca** *adj* (bot.) polycarpic or polycarpous
**pólice** *m* thumb
**policía** *f* police; policing; politeness; cleanliness, neatness; body of ordinances regarding public order; **policía militar** military police; **policía secreta** secret police; **policía urbana** street cleaning; *m* policeman
**policíaco -ca** *adj* (pertaining to the) police; detective (*story*)
**policial** *adj* (pertaining to the) police; detective (*story*); *m* policeman
**Policiano** *m* Politian
**policitación** *f* unaccepted promise or offer
**policlínica** *f* polyclinic
**policopia** *f* multigraph
**policromar** *va* to polychrome
**policromía** *f* polichromy
**policromo -ma** *adj* polychrome
**polichinela** *m* punchinello; (*cap.*) *m* Punch
**polidipsia** *f* (path.) excessive thirst
**Polidoro** *m* (myth.) Polydorus
**polidrupa** *f* (bot.) berry (*of strawberry, blackberry, etc.*)
**poliédrico -ca** *adj* polyhedral
**poliedro** *m* (geom.) polyhedron
**polietileno** *m* (chem.) polyethylene
**polifacético -ca** *adj* (fig.) many-sided
**polifagia** or **polifagía** *f* (path.) polyphagia
**polifásico -ca** *adj* (elec.) polyphase, multiphase
**Polifemo** *m* (myth.) Polyphemus
**polifilético -ca** *adj* polyphyletic
**polifonía** *f* (mus. & phonet.) polyphony
**polifónico -ca** or **polífono -na** *adj* polyphonic
**polígala** *f* (bot.) milkwort; **polígala de Virginia** (bot.) snakeroot
**poligamia** *f* polygamy
**poligámico -ca** *adj* polygamic
**polígamo -ma** *adj* polygamous; *mf* polygamist
**poligenismo** *m* polygenism
**poliglota** *f* see **poligloto**
**poliglotía** *f* knowledge of many languages
**poligloto -ta** *adj & mf* polyglot; *f* polyglot Bible
**poligonal** *adj* polygonal
**polígono -na** *adj* polygonal; *m* (geom.) polygon
**poligrafía** *f* polygraphy
**polígrafo** *m* polygraph (*prolific writer; copying machine*); ball point pen; (med.) polygraph
**polilla** *f* (ent.) moth, clothes moth; (ent.) carpet moth; moths; (fig.) ravager, destroyer; **polilla de los museos de historia natural** (ent.) museum beetle; **polilla de los paños** (ent.) carpet moth; **polilla de los tapices** (ent.) carpet beetle
**polillera** *f* (bot.) moth mullein
**polimatía** *f* wide learning
**polimería** *f* polymerism
**polimerización** *f* polymerization
**polimerizar** §76 *va & vr* to polymerize
**polímero -ra** *adj* polymeric; *m* (chem.) polymer
**Polimnia** *f* (myth.) Polyhymnia
**polimorfismo** *m* polymorphism
**polimorfo -fa** *adj* polymorphous
**polín** *m* roller; skid
**polinesio -sia** *adj & mf* Polynesian; **la Polinesia** Polynesia
**polineuritis** *f* (path.) polyneuritis
**polínico -ca** *adj* pollinic or pollinical
**polinífero -ra** *adj* polliniferous
**polinio** *m* (bot.) pollinium
**polinización** *f* (bot.) pollination; **polinización cruzada** (bot.) cross-pollination
**polinizar** §76 *va* to pollinate
**polinómico -ca** *adj* polynomial
**polinomio** *m* (alg.) polynomial
**polinosis** *f* (path.) pollinosis, hay fever
**polinuclear** *adj* polynuclear
**polio** *m* (bot.) poly; *f* (path.) polio
**poliomielitis** *f* (path.) poliomyelitis
**polipasto** *m* tackle
**polipero** *m* (zool.) polypary
**polipétalo -la** *adj* (bot.) polypetalous
**pólipo** *m* (zool.) polyp; (path.) polyp or polypus
**polipodio** *m* (bot.) polypody, sweet fern
**polisarcia** *f* (path.) polysarcia, obesity
**polisemia** *f* polysemy
**polisémico -ca** or **polisemo -ma** *adj* polysemous
**polisilábico -ca** *adj* polysyllabic
**polisílabo -ba** *adj* polysyllabic; *m* polysyllable
**polisíndeton** *m* (rhet.) polysyndeton
**polisintético -ca** *adj* polysynthetic
**polisón** *m* bustle (*of woman's dress*)
**polispasto** *m* var. of **polipasto**
**polista** *adj* polo-playing; *mf* poloist, polo player
**polistilo -la** *adj* (arch.) polystyle; (bot.) polystylous; *m* (arch.) polystyle
**polistireno** *m* (chem.) polystyrene
**Politburó** *m* Politburo
**politécnico -ca** *adj* polytechnic
**politeísmo** *m* polytheism
**politeísta** *adj* polytheistic; *mf* polytheist
**política** *f* see **político**
**politicastro** *m* petty politician, corrupt politician
**político -ca** *adj* political; tactful; polite, courteous; -in-law, e.g., **padre político** father-in-law; *mf* politician; *f* politics; policy; manners, politeness, courtesy; **política de acorralamiento** policy of encirclement; **política de café** parlor politics; **política de campanario** (coll.) petty politics; **política de cerco** policy of encirclement; **política de la**

**buena vecindad** Good Neighbor Policy; **política del palo en alto** policy of the big stick; **política de partido** party politics; **política de poder** power politics; **política exterior** foreign policy
**politicón -cona** *adj* overpolite, obsequious; fond of politics
**politiquear** *vn* (coll.) to dabble in politics, to play politics; (coll.) to chatter politics
**politiqueo** *m* (coll.) dabbling in politics; (coll.) political chatter
**politiquería** *f* political chicanery
**politiquero -ra** *mf* political schemer
**politiquilla** *f* parlor politics
**politiquillo** *m* parlor politician
**politonal** *adj* polytonal
**politonalidad** *f* (mus.) polytonality
**poliuria** *f* (path.) polyuria
**polivalencia** *f* (bact. & chem.) polyvalence, multivalence
**polivalente** *adj* (bact. & chem.) polyvalent, multivalent
**póliza** *f* check, draft; contract, policy; tax stamp; custom-house permit; admission ticket; lampoon; **póliza de seguro** insurance policy; **póliza dotal** endowment policy
**polizón** *m* bum, tramp; stowaway
**polizonte** *m* (coll.) cop, policeman
**polo** *m* support, foundation; water ice on a stick, popsicle; polo (*Andalusian dance*); (hist.) polo (*corvée exacted from Philippine natives by Spanish*); (astr., geog., biol., elec. & math.) pole; (sport) polo; **polo acuático** or **de agua** (sport) water polo; **polo norte magnético** North Magnetic Pole; **polo sur magnético** South Magnetic Pole
**polonés -nesa** *adj* Polish; *mf* Pole; *m* Polish (*language*); *f* polonaise (*overdress*); (mus.) polonaise
**Polonia** *f* Poland
**polonio** *m* (chem.) polonium
**poltrón -trona** *adj* idle, lazy, comfort-loving; *f* easy chair; (fig.) sinecure
**poltronería** *f* idleness, laziness
**poltronizar** **§76** *vr* to idle, loaf, get lazy
**polución** *f* (path.) pollution; **polución voluntaria** self-polution
**poluto -ta** *adj* dirty, filthy
**Pólux** *m* (myth. & astr.) Pollux
**polvareda** *f* cloud of dust; rumpus
**polvera** *f* compact, powder case
**polvificar** **§86** *va* to pulverize
**polvillo** *m* fine dust
**polvo** *m* dust; powder; pinch (*e.g., of snuff*); **polvos** *mpl* dust; powder; **en polvo** powdered; **hacer polvo a** (coll.) to overcome, destroy, wipe out; **morder el polvo** to bite or lick the dust; **sacudir el polvo a** (coll.) to give a beating to, to beat up; (coll.) to show up, refute; **tomar el polvo** (Am.) to beat it, disappear; **tomar un polvo** to take a pinch of snuff; **polvo de cantárida** (pharm.) cantharides; **polvo dentífrico** tooth powder; **polvos blancos faciales** face powder; **polvos calmantes** sleeping powder; **polvos de arroz** rice powder; **polvos de baño** bath powder; **polvos de estaño** putty powder; **polvos de gas** bleaching powder; **polvos de la madre Celestina** (coll.) hocus-pocus; prestidigitation; **polvos de Seidlitz** Seidlitz powder; **polvos de talco** talcum powder
**pólvora** *f* powder, gunpowder; fireworks; bad humor; briskness, liveliness; **correr como pólvora en reguero** to spread like wildfire; **gastar la pólvora en salvas** to fuss around for nothing; **ser una pólvora** (coll.) to be a live wire; **pólvora de algodón** guncotton; **pólvora gigante** giant powder; **pólvora sin humo** smokeless powder; **pólvora sorda** noiseless powder; (fig.) sneak, underhanded fellow
**polvoreamiento** *m* dusting, sprinkling
**polvorear** *va* to dust, sprinkle with dust or powder
**polvoriento -ta** *adj* dusty; powdery
**polvorín** *m* fine powder; powder magazine; powder flask; (Am.) spitfire; (Am.) tick
**polvorista** *m* powder maker; fireworks manufacturer
**polvorizable** *adj* var. of **pulverizable**
**polvorización** *f* pulverization
**polvorizar** **§76** *va* to dust, sprinkle with dust or powder; to pulverize
**polvoroso -sa** *adj* dusty; **poner pies en polvorosa** (coll.) to take to one's heels, to beat it
**polla** *f* pullet; (orn.) coot; (orn.) water hen, moor hen, gallinule; (coll.) lassie; stake, kitty; **polla de agua** (orn.) corn crake
**pollada** *f* hatch, covey; broadside
**pollancón -cona** *mf* large chicken; *m* (coll.) overgrown boy
**pollastre** *m* (coll.) sly fellow
**pollastro -tra** *mf* grown chicken; *m* (coll.) sly fellow
**pollazón** *f* hatch, brood
**pollera** *f* see **pollero**
**pollería** *f* poultry shop, poultry market; poultry business; poultry; young people, younger set
**pollero -ra** *mf* poulterer; *m* poultry yard; *f* poultry yard; chicken coop; gocart; (Am.) skirt
**pollino -na** *mf* ass, donkey; (fig.) jackass
**pollito -ta** *mf* chick; (coll.) chick, chicken (*young person*); **pollito unicolor** (orn.) Baird's sandpiper
**pollo** *m* chicken; young bee; (fig.) chicken (*young person*); sly fellow
**polluelo -la** *mf* chick; *m* (bot.) saltwort
**poma** *f* apple; smelling bottle; pomander
**pomáceo -a** *adj* (bot.) pomaceous
**pomada** *f* pomade
**pomar** *m* orchard, apple orchard
**pomarada** *f* apple orchard
**pomarrosa** *f* (bot.) rose apple
**pomelo** *m* (bot.) pomelo, shaddock; (bot.) grapefruit (*tree and fruit*)
**pomeranio -nia** or **pomerano -na** *adj & mf* Pomeranian
**pómez** *f* pumice stone
**pomífero -ra** *adj* (poet.) pomiferous
**pomo** *m* (bot.) pome; pommel (*of hilt of sword*); flacon; pomander; (dial.) bouquet; **pomo de puerta** doorknob
**pomología** *f* pomology
**pompa** *f* see **pompo**
**pompático -ca** *adj* pompous
**pompear** *vn* to make a show, be pompous; *vr* (coll.) to strut; (coll.) to move with pomp and ceremony
**Pompeya** *f* Pompeii
**pompeyano -na** *adj & mf* Pompeian
**Pompeyo** *m* Pompey
**pompo -pa** *adj* (Am.) dull; *f* pomp; soap bubble; swell, bulge; billowing or ballooning (*of clothes*); spread (*of peacock's tail*); (naut.) pump; **pompa de jabón** soap bubble; **pompa fúnebre** funeral; **pompas térmicas** (aer.) rising air currents
**pompón** *m* pompon
**pomponear** *vr* (coll.) to strut; (coll.) to move with pomp and ceremony
**pomposidad** *f* pomposity
**pomposo -sa** *adj* pompous; high-flown, highfalutin
**pómulo** *m* (anat.) cheekbone
**pon** *2d sg impv of* **poner**
**poncí** *m* (*pl:* **-cíes**) var. of **poncidre**
**poncidre** *m* or **poncil** *m* (bot.) citron (*tree and fruit*)
**Poncio** *m* Pontius
**ponchada** *f* bowlful of punch; (Am.) contents of a poncho (*held together by its four corners*); (Am.) portion, batch
**ponchadura** *f* (Am.) blowout; (Am.) strike-out
**ponchar** *va & vr* (Am.) to puncture, to blow out; (Am.) to strike out (*in baseball*)
**ponche** *m* punch (*drink*); **ponche de huevo** eggnog
**ponchera** *f* punch bowl
**poncho -cha** *adj* lazy, careless, easy-going; (Am.) chubby; *m* poncho; greatcoat
**ponderable** *adj* ponderable; (fig.) ponderable
**ponderación** *f* weighing; pondering; circumspection; balance, equilibrium; exaggeration; **sin ponderación** without the slightest exaggeration
**ponderado -da** *adj* tactful, prudent

**ponderador -dora** *adj* pondering; balancing; exaggerating
**ponderal** *adj* in weight, ponderal
**ponderar** *va* to weigh; to ponder, ponder over; to balance; to exaggerate; to praise to the skies; to weight (*statistically*)
**ponderativo -va** *adj* exaggerating
**ponderosidad** *f* ponderosity; gravity, seriousness, circumspection
**ponderoso -sa** *adj* ponderous, heavy; grave, serious, circumspect
**pondré** *1st sg fut ind of* **poner**
**ponedero -ra** *adj* placeable; egg-laying; *m* nest; nest egg
**ponedor -dora** *adj* egg-laying; trained to rear on hind legs (*said of a horse*); *m* bidder
**ponencia** *f* paper, report; (law) report; (law) post of reporter
**ponente** *m* (law) reporter, referee
**ponentino -na** or **ponentisco -ca** *adj* occidental, western; *mf* occidental, westerner
**poner** §69 *va* to put, place, lay, set; to arrange, dispose; to put in (*a remark*); to put on (*a play*); to set (*a table*); to assume, suppose; to impose (*a law, tax, etc.*); to wager, to stake; to lay (*eggs*); to set down, put down (*in writing*); to take (*time*); to cause (*e.g., fear*); to make, to turn; (aut.) to go in (*e.g., high gear*); **poner a** + *inf* to set (*someone*) to + *inf;* **poner a uno de** to treat someone as a; to set someone up as a; **poner en claro** to clear up, explain; **poner en limpio** to make a clean copy of, to recopy; **poner por encima** to prefer, to put ahead ‖ *vr* to put oneself; to become, to get, to turn; to set (*said of sun, stars, etc.*); to dress, dress up; to get spotted; to get, reach, arrive; to put on (*hat, coat, etc.*); **ponerse a** + *inf* to set out to, to begin to + *inf;* **ponerse al tanto de** to catch on to; **ponerse bien** to get along, become successful; **ponerse bien con** to get in with, get on the good side of; **ponerse tan alto** to take offense, to become hoity-toity
**pongo** *m* (zool.) orang-outang; (Am.) Indian servant; (Am.) gully, ravine; *1st sg pres ind of* **poner**
**ponientada** *f* steady west wind
**poniente** *m* west; west wind
**ponimiento** *m* placing, laying, setting
**ponleví** *m* (*pl:* **-víes**) shoe with high wooden heel
**ponqué** *m* (Am.) poundcake
**pontaje** *m* bridge toll, pontage
**pontana** *f* slab or flagstone on the bed of a stream
**pontazgo** *m* bridge toll
**pontear** *va* to build a bridge over; *vn* to build bridges
**pontederiáceo -a** *adj* (bot.) pontederiaceous
**pontezuela** *f* or **pontezuelo** *m* small bridge
**póntico -ca** *adj* Pontic
**pontificado** *m* pontificate; papacy
**pontifical** *adj* pontifical; **de pontifical** (coll.) in full dress; *m* pontifical (*book*); **pontificales** *mpl* pontificals
**pontificar** §86 *vn* (coll.) to pontificate
**pontífice** *m* (hist. & eccl.) pontiff, pontifex; **el Sumo Pontífice** or **el Pontífice Romano** (eccl.) the Sovereign Pontiff, the Supreme Pontiff (*the Pope*)
**pontificio -cia** *adj* pontifical
**pontil** *m* punty
**pontín** *m* pontin (*Philippine coasting vessel*)
**pontino -na** *adj* between two holidays
**ponto** *m* (poet.) sea; (*cap.*) *m* (myth.) Pontus; **el Ponto** Pontus (*country*); **Ponto Euxino** Euxine Sea, Pontus Euxinus (*ancient name of Black Sea*)
**pontocón** *m* kick
**pontón** *m* pontoon; pontoon bridge; log bridge; old ship tied up at a wharf and used as warehouse, hospital, or prison; hulk (*old ship used as prison*); **pontón flotante** pontoon bridge, floating bridge
**pontonero** *m* (mil.) pontonier
**ponzoña** *f* poison; (fig.) poison
**ponzoñoso -sa** *adj* poisonous
**popa** *f* (naut.) poop, stern; **a popa, en popa** (naut.) abaft
**popamiento** *m* scorn; fondling, caressing
**popar** *va* to scorn, despise; to fondle, caress
**pope** *m* pope (*of Greek Orthodox Church*)
**popel** *adj* (naut.) sternmost
**popelina** *f* poplin
**poplíteo -a** *adj* (anat.) popliteal
**popote** *m* (Am.) straw for brooms; (Am.) straw or tube (*for drinking*)
**populachería** *f* cheap popularity, appeal to the mob; rabble rousing
**populachero -ra** *adj* of the people, people's, popular; cheap, vulgar; rabble-rousing; *mf* rabble rouser
**populacho** *m* populace, mob, rabble
**popular** *adj* popular
**popularidad** *f* popularity
**popularización** *f* popularization
**popularizar** §76 *va* to popularize; *vr* to become popular
**populazo** *m* var. of **populacho**
**populeón** *m* poplar ointment
**populismo** *m* Populism
**populista** *m* Populist
**populoso -sa** *adj* populous
**popurrí** *m* (*pl:* **-rríes**) (mus.) potpourri, medley
**poquedad** *f* paucity, slightness, scantiness; scarcity; timidity; trifle
**póquer** *m* poker
**poquísimo -ma** *adj super* very little; **poquísimos -mas** *adj super pl* few, very few
**poquito -ta** *adj* very little; timid, shy; diminutive, slight; **a poquito** little by little; **a poquitos** in small quantities; **de poquito** (coll.) timid, inept; **un poquito (de)** a little bit (of)
**por** *prep* by; through, over; by way of, via; in (*e.g., the morning; Spain*); for; for the sake of, on account of; in exchange for, in place of; as; about (*e.g., Christmastime*); out of (*e.g., ignorance*); times, e.g., **tres por cuatro** four times three; **estar por** + *inf* to be on the point of + *ger*, be ready to + *inf;* to be still to be + *pp*, e.g., **la carta está por escribir** the letter is still to be written; **ir por** to go for, to go after; to follow (*a career*); **por ciento** per cent; **por entre** among, between; **por que** because; in order that; **por qué** why; **por** + *adj* + **que** however + *adj*, e.g., **por rico que sea** however rich he may be; **por** + *inf* in order to + *inf;* because of + *ger*
**porcachón -chona** or **porcallón -llona** *adj* (coll.) dirty, hoggish; *mf* (coll.) big hog; (coll.) fat slob
**porcelana** *f* porcelain; **porcelana mandarina** mandarin porcelain; **porcelana paria** Parian, Parian porcelain
**porcentaje** *m* percentage
**porcentual** *adj* percentage
**Porcia** *f* Portia
**porcino -na** *adj* porcine; *m* little pig; bruise, bump
**porción** *f* portion
**porcionero -ra** *adj & mf* participant
**porcionista** *mf* shareholder, participant; boarding-school pupil
**porcipelo** *m* (coll.) bristle
**porciúncula** *f* Franciscan jubilee (*celebrated August second*)
**porcuno -na** *adj* porcine; hoggish
**porche** *m* porch, portico
**pordiosear** *vn* to beg, to go begging
**pordioseo** *m* begging
**pordiosería** *f* begging, beggary
**pordiosero -ra** *adj* begging, mendicant; *mf* beggar
**porfía** *f* persistence, stubbornness, obstinacy; **a porfía** in emulation, in competition
**porfiado -da** *adj* persistent, stubborn, obstinate; opinionated
**porfiador -dora** *adj* persistent; *mf* persistent person, fighter
**porfiar** §90 *vn* to persist; to argue stubbornly; **porfiar en** + *inf* to persist in + *ger*
**porfídico -ca** *adj* porphyritic
**pórfido** *m* porphyry
**porfioso -sa** *adj* var. of **porfiado**
**porfolio** *m* picture folder
**poricida** *adj* (bot.) poricidal
**pormenor** *m* detail, particular
**pormenorizar** §76 *va* to detail, tell in detail; to itemize

**pornografía** *f* pornography
**pornográfico -ca** *adj* pornographic
**pornógrafo -fa** *mf* pornographer
**poro** *m* pore
**pororó** *m* (Am.) popcorn
**pororoca** *f* (Am.) tide rip (*in Río de la Plata*)
**porosidad** *f* porosity
**poroso -sa** *adj* porous
**poroto** *m* (Am.) bean, string bean; (Am.) runt, little runt; **tomar los porotos** (Am.) to eat, have something to eat
**porque** *conj* because; in order that
**porqué** *m* (coll.) why, reason, motive; (coll.) quantity, amount, share; (coll.) dough, money, wherewithal
**porquecilla** *f* small sow
**porquera** *f* wild boar's lair
**porquería** *f* (coll.) dirt, filth; (coll.) crudity; (coll.) trifle; (coll.) botch; (coll.) junk (*poor or harmful food*)
**porqueriza** *f* pigsty, pigpen
**porquerizo** or **porquero** *m* swineherd
**porquerón** *m* (coll.) catchpole
**porqueta** *f* (zool.) wood louse
**porquezuelo -la** *mf* piglet, little pig
**porra** *f* see **porro**
**porráceo -a** *adj* porraceous, leek-green
**porrada** *f* blow, bump; thwack, slap; (coll.) stupidity; pile, heap
**porrazo** *m* clubbing; blow; bump
**porrear** *vn* (coll.) to be importunate, make a nuisance of oneself
**porrería** *f* (coll.) folly, stupidity; (coll.) dullness, slowness
**porreta** *f* green leaves of leeks, garlic, or onions; **en porreta** (coll.) naked
**porretada** *f* pile, heap
**porrilla** *f* forge hammer; (vet.) osseous tumor in the joints
**porrillo** *m* mason's hammer; **a porrillo** (coll.) in abundance
**porrina** *f* small, green crop; green leaves of leeks
**porrino** *m* leek seed; leek ready for transplanting
**porro -rra** *adj* (coll.) dull, stupid; *m* (bot.) leek; *f* club, bludgeon; maul; (coll.) bore, nuisance; (coll.) boasting; (Am.) knot, entanglement (*of hair*); (Am.) rooters, backers; **mandar a la porra** (coll.) to send (*someone*) on his way, to dismiss without ceremony
**porrón -rrona** *adj* (coll.) slow, heavy, sluggish; *m* earthen jug; wine bottle with a long side spout
**porta-** *combining form* bearer, e.g., **portaestandarte** color bearer; handle, e.g., **portalimas** file handle; hanger, e.g., **portacaño** pipe hanger; -holder or holder, e.g., **portaplacas** plateholder; **portapapeles** paper holder; rack, e.g., **portabotellas** bottle rack; socket, e.g., **portalámparas** lamp socket; -stand or stand, e.g., **portatintero** inkstand; **portarretorta** retort stand
**porta** *f* (naut.) porthole; (fort.) cover of a loophole; (football) goal
**portaalmizcle** *m* (zool.) musk deer
**portaaviones** *m* (*pl:* **-nes**) aircraft carrier, airplane carrier, flattop
**portabandera** *f* (mil.) socket for flagpole
**portabombas** *m* (*pl:* **-bas**) (aer.) bomb carrier
**portabotellas** *m* (*pl:* **-llas**) bottle rack, bottle carrier
**portabrocas** *m* (*pl:* **-cas**) drill chuck, drill holder
**portacaja** *f* drum strap
**portacandado** *m* hasp
**portacaño** *m* pipe hanger
**portacartas** *m* (*pl:* **-tas**) pouch, mailbag
**portacojinete** *m* diestock
**portachuelo** *m* mountain pass
**portada** *f* see **portado**
**portadilla** *f* (print.) bastard title, half title
**portadiscos** *m* (*pl:* **-cos**) turntable
**portado -da** *adj;* **bien portado** well-dressed; well-behaved; **mal portado** poorly dressed; badly behaved; *f* front, façade; portal; title page; cover (*of magazine*); **falsa portada** (print.) half title
**portador -dora** *adj* (rad.) carrier (*wave*); *mf* carrier, bearer; (com.) bearer; **portador de gérmenes** (med.) carrier; *m* waiter's tray; *f* pannier or box (*carried on each side of beast's back*)
**portaequipaje** *m* (aut.) trunk
**portaequipajes** *m* (*pl:* **-jes**) baggage rack
**portaescobillas** *m* (*pl:* **-llas**) (elec.) brush holder
**portaestandarte** *m* (coll.) color bearer
**portaféretro** *m* pallbearer
**portafusible** *m* (elec.) cutout, cutout base
**portafusil** *m* sling (*of a rifle*)
**portaguantes** *m* (*pl:* **-tes**) (aut.) glove compartment
**portaguión** *m* (mil.) guidon
**portahachón** *m* torchbearer
**portaherramienta** *m* (mach.) chuck
**portaherramientas** *m* (*pl:* **-tas**) toolholder
**portainstrumentos** *adj* see **plancha**
**portaje** *m* var. of **portazgo**
**portal** *m* vestibule, entrance hall; porch, portico; arcade; town or city gate; portal (*of a tunnel*); (Am.) crèche
**portalada** *f* portal; large gate
**portalámparas** *m* (*pl:* **-ras**) (elec.) socket, lamp holder; **portalámparas de bayoneta** bayonet socket; **portalámparas de cadena** pull socket, chain-pull socket; **portalámparas de llave giratoria** key socket; **portalámparas de rosca** screw socket
**portalápiz** *m* (*pl:* **-pices**) pencil holder
**portaleña** *f* door board; (naut.) porthole
**portalero** *m* tax collector (*at city gates*)
**portalibros** *m* (*pl:* **-bros**) book straps (*for schoolbooks*)
**portalón** *m* gate; (naut.) gangway (*opening in side of ship*)
**portamantas** *m* (*pl:* **-tas**) blanket straps, blanket holder
**portamanteo** *m* portmanteau
**portaminas** *m* (*pl:* **-nas**) mechanical pencil
**portamira** *m* (surv.) rodman
**portamonedas** *m* (*pl:* **-das**) pocketbook, purse
**portaneumático** *m* (aut.) tire rack
**portante** *adj* (rad.) carrier (*wave*); *m* pace (*in which feet on same side are lifted and put down together*); **tomar el portante** (coll.) to leave, get out
**portantillo** *m* easy pace
**portanuevas** *mf* (*pl:* **-vas**) newsmonger
**portañola** *f* (naut.) porthole
**portañuela** *f* fly (*of trousers*); (Am.) carriage door
**portaobjetivo** *m* nosepiece (*of microscope*)
**portaobjeto** *m* slide (*for microscope*); stage (*of microscope*)
**portaollas** *m* (*pl:* **-llas**) potholder
**portapapeles** *m* (*pl:* **-les**) brief case; paper holder, paper stand
**portapaz** *m & f* (eccl.) pax
**portapechos** *m* (*pl:* **-chos**) (Am.) brassière
**portaplacas** *m* (*pl:* **-cas**) (phot.) plateholder
**portapliegos** *m* (*pl:* **-gos**) brief case
**portaplumas** *m* (*pl:* **-mas**) penholder (*handle*)
**portar** *va* (Am.) to carry, to bear; (hunt.) to retrieve; *vn* (naut.) to fill (*said of a sail*); *vr* to behave, to conduct oneself
**portarremos** *m* (*pl:* **-mos**) oarlock, rowlock; **portarremos exterior** outrigger (*of a racing shell*)
**portarretorta** *f* retort stand
**portarriendas** *m* (*pl:* **-das**) terret
**portasenos** *m* (*pl:* **-nos**) brassière
**portateléfono** *adj* see **mesita**
**portátil** *adj* portable
**portatintero** *m* inkstand
**portatipos** *adj* see **palanca**
**portatostadas** *m* (*pl:* **-das**) toast rack
**portaútil** *m* toolholder
**portaválvula** *m* (rad.) socket
**portavasos** *m* (*pl:* **-sos**) glass stand, glass rack
**portaventanero** *m* door and window maker
**portaviandas** *m* (*pl:* **-das**) dinner pail
**portaviento** *m* bustle pipe
**portaviones** *m* (*pl:* **-nes**) var. of **portaaviones**
**portavoz** *m* (*pl:* **-voces**) megaphone; (fig.) mouthpiece (*person, newspaper, etc.*)

**portazgar** §59 *va* to collect toll from
**portazgo** *m* toll, road toll
**portazguero** *m* tollkeeper
**portazo** *m* bang or slam (*of door*)
**porte** *m* carrying, portage; carrying charge, freight; postage; behavior, conduct; dress, bearing; nobility; size, capacity; (Am.) birthday present; **porte concertado** mailing permit; **porte pagado** postage prepaid, freight prepaid
**porteador** *m* carrier
**portear** *va* to carry, to transport (*for a price*); *vn* to slam; *vr* to migrate (*said especially of birds*)
**portento** *m* prodigy, wonder
**portentoso -sa** *adj* portentous, extraordinary
**porteño -ña** *adj* (pertaining to) Buenos Aires; (pertaining to) Valparaíso; pertaining to any large South American city with a port; *mf* native or inhabitant of Buenos Aires, Valparaíso, or any large South American city with a port
**porteo** *m* carrying, portage
**portera** *f* see **portero**
**portería** *f* porter's lodge; job of porter; main door (*of a convent*); (naut.) portholes
**portero -ra** *mf* doorkeeper; gatekeeper; (sport) goalkeeper; *m* porter, janitor; doorman; *f* portress, janitress
**portezuela** *f* little door; door (*of carriage, automobile, etc.*); pocket flap
**pórtico** *m* portico, porch; little gate; (arch.) portico, piazza
**portier** *m* (*pl:* **-tiers**) portiere, door curtain
**portilla** *f* (naut.) porthole; private cart road, private cattle pass; fly (*of trousers*)
**portillera** *f* private cart road, private cattle pass
**portillo** *m* gap, breach, opening; notch, nick; wicket (*of larger door or gate*); gate (*in fence or wall; of bird cage*); narrow pass (*between hills*); private or side entrance; (fort.) postern
**portón** *m* large door or gate; vestibule door, inner door
**portorriqueño -ña** *adj & mf* var. of **puertorriqueño**
**portuario -ria** *adj* (pertaining to a) port, harbor, dock; *m* dock hand, dock worker
**Portugal** *m* Portugal
**portugués -guesa** *adj & mf* Portuguese; **los portugueses** the Portuguese (*people*); *m* Portugese (*language*)
**portuguesada** *f* (coll.) exaggeration
**portuguesismo** *m* Lusitanism
**portulano** *m* collection of harbor charts
**porvenir** *m* future; (fig.) promise
**porvida** *interj* by the living God! (*to express threat or anger*)
**pos; en pos de** after, behind; in pursuit of
**posa** *f* knell, toll; pause during burial for singing responsory; **posas** *fpl* buttocks
**posada** *f* home, dwelling; inn, wayside inn; lodging; boarding house; camp; traveling case containing knife, fork, and spoon
**posadero -ra** *mf* innkeeper; *m* reed or esparto-grass mat (*used as a seat*); **posaderas** *fpl* buttocks
**posante** *adj* smooth-sailing (*boat*)
**posar** *va* to put down (*a load or burden*) in order to rest or catch one's breath; *vn* to put up, to lodge; to alight, to perch; to pose (*for a photograph; as a model*); *vr* to alight, to perch; to settle (*said of sediment, dust, etc.*); to rest
**posaverga** *f* (naut.) yard prop
**posbélico -ca** *adj* postwar
**poscafé** *m* after-dinner cordial
**poscombustión** *f* (aer.) afterburning
**poscomunión** *f* Postcommunion
**posdata** *f* postscript
**posdatar** *va* (coll.) to add a postscript to (*a letter*)
**pose** *f* pose (*position of body; affectation*); (phot.) exposure, time exposure
**poseedor -dora** *mf* owner, possessor; holder (*e.g., of a record*)
**poseer** §35 *va* to own, to possess, to hold; to have a mastery of (*e.g., a foreign language*); *vr* to control oneself
**poseído -da** *adj* possessed; *mf* person possessed; *m* private farm land
**Poseidón** *m* (myth.) Poseidon
**posesión** *f* possession; **tomar posesión de** to take up (*a post, an assignment*)
**posesionar** *va* to give possession to; *vr* to take possession
**posesionero** *m* pasture-owning cattleman
**posesivo -va** *adj* possessive; (gram.) possessive; *m* (gram.) possessive
**poseso -sa** *adj* possessed; *mf* person possessed
**posesor -sora** *mf* owner, possessor
**posesorio -ria** *adj* possessory
**posfecha** *f* postdate
**posfechar** *va* to postdate
**posfijo** *m* (gram.) postfix
**posgraduado -da** *adj & mf* var. of **postgraduado**
**posguerra** *f* postwar period
**posibilidad** *f* possibility; means, property; aptitude, ability
**posibilitar** *va* to make possible
**posible** *adj* possible; **hacer todo lo posible** to do one's best; **posibles** *mpl* means, income, property
**posición** *f* position; standing; (law) deposition; (mil.) fortified position
**positiva** *f* see **positivo**
**positivar** *va* (phot.) to make a positive of
**positivismo** *m* positivism
**positivista** *adj* positivistic; *mf* positivist
**positivo -va** *adj* positive; **de positivo** positively, beyond a doubt; *m* (gram.) positive; *f* (phot.) positive
**pósito** *m* public granary; cooperative; **pósito pío** public granary run for charity
**positrón** *m* (phys.) positron
**positura** *f* position, state, disposition
**posliminio** *m* var. of **postliminio**
**posma** *f* (coll.) dullness, sloth; *mf* (coll.) snail (*person*); *adj* (coll.) dull, slothful, sluggish
**posmeridiano -na** *adj* var. of **postmeridiano**
**poso** *m* sediment, dregs; grounds; rest, quiet, calm
**posología** *f* posology
**posón** *m* reed or esparto-grass mat (*used as a seat*)
**pospalatal** *adj & f* var. of **postpalatal**
**pospelo; a pospelo** against the lay of the hair, against the nap; (coll.) violently, forcibly
**pospierna** *f* thigh (*of an animal*)
**pospondré** *1st sg fut ind of* **posponer**
**posponer** §69 *va* to subordinate; to think less of, to hold in less esteem
**pospongo** *1st sg pres ind of* **posponer**
**posposición** *f* subordination
**pospuesto -ta** *pp of* **posponer**
**pospuse** *1st sg pret ind of* **posponer**
**posquemador** *m* (aer.) afterburner
**posta** *f* relay (*of post horses*); posthouse; stage; stake, wager (*at cards*); slice (*of meat or fish*); commemorative poster; (arch.) Vitruvian scroll; (archaic) post, military post; **a posta** (coll.) on purpose; **correr la posta** to ride post; **por la posta** riding post; (coll.) posthaste; *m* postrider, courier
**postal** *adj* postal; *f* postal, postal card
**postcomunión** *f* var. of **poscomunión**
**postdata** *f* var. of **posdata**
**postdiluviano -na** *adj* postdiluvian
**poste** *m* post, pole, pillar; punishment in school consisting in standing for a time on a given spot; (sport) starting or finishing marker (*of a race*); **dar poste a** (coll.) to keep (*someone*) waiting; **llevar poste** (coll.) to be kept waiting; (coll.) to stand for hours in front of one's sweetheart's house; **oler el poste** (coll.) to smell a rat; **ser un poste** (coll.) to be lumpish; (coll.) to be very deaf; **poste de alumbrado** lamppost; **poste de amarre** (aer.) mooring mast; **poste de llegada** (sport) winning post; **poste de partida** (sport) starting post; **poste de teléfonos** telephone post; **poste de telégrafo** telegraph pole; (fig.) beanpole (*tall, thin person*); **poste distribuidor de gasolina** gasoline pump; **poste indicador** road sign; **poste telegráfico** telegraph pole
**postelero** *m* (naut.) skid, fender

**postema** *f* abscess; bore, tiresome person; (coll.) grudge
**postemero** *m* (surg.) lancet
**postergación** *f* delay, postponement; holding back, passing over
**postergar** §59 *va* to delay, postpone; to hold back, to pass over
**postería** *f* or **posterío** *m* (Am.) posts, poles, row of posts
**posteridad** *f* posterity; posthumous fame
**posterior** *adj* posterior, back, rear; back (*tooth*); later, subsequent; (phonet.) back; **posterior a** later than
**posterioridad** *f* posteriority; **con posterioridad** subsequently, later on; **con posterioridad a** subsequent to, later than
**posteta** *f* sheets of paper used for packing books; (b.b.) signature, section
**postgraduado -da** *adj & mf* postgraduate
**postguerra** *f* postwar period
**posthipnótico -ca** *adj* posthypnotic
**postigo** *m* wicket (*small door in larger one*); shutter; postern (*small or back door or gate*)
**postila** *f* note, comment
**postilar** *va* to annotate (*a text*)
**postilla** *f* scab
**postillón** *m* postilion, postboy
**postilloso -sa** *adj* scabby, full of scabs
**postimagen** *f* (psychol.) afterimage
**postimpresionismo** *m* postimpressionism
**postimpresionista** *mf* postimpressionist
**postín** *m* (coll.) show, vanity, arrogance; **darse postín** (coll.) to put on airs
**postizo -za** *adj* false, artificial; detachable (*collar*); *m* switch, false hair; *f* castanet
**postliminio** *m* (law) postliminy
**postludio** *m* (mus.) postlude
**postmeridiano -na** *adj* postmeridian
**postnatal** *adj* postnatal
**postónico -ca** *adj* (phonet.) posttonic
**postoperatorio -ria** *adj* postoperative
**postor** *m* bidder (*at an auction*); **mayor** or **mejor postor** highest bidder
**postorbital** *adj* postorbital
**postpalatal** *adj & f* (phonet.) postpalatal
**postprandial** *adj* postprandial
**postración** *f* prostration; **postración nerviosa** nervous prostration
**postrador -dora** *adj* prostrative; *m* kneeling stool
**postrar** *va* to prostrate; to weaken, exhaust; *vr* to prostrate oneself; to be prostrated
**postre** *adj* last, final; **a la postre** or **al postre** at last, finally; **a la postre de** after; *m* dessert; last to play; **postres** *mpl* dessert; **llegar a los postres** to arrive late or too late
**postremero -ra** or **postremo -ma** *adj* last
**postrer** *adj* apocopated form of **postrero,** used only before masculine singular nouns and adjectives
**postrero -ra** *adj* last; *mf* last, last one
**postrimer** *adj* apocopated form of **postrimero,** used only before masculine singular nouns and adjectives
**postrimerías** *fpl* latter part; last stages of man: death, judgment, hell, and heaven
**postrimero -ra** *adj* last
**póstula** or **postulación** *f* postulation, petition; nomination; (eccl.) postulation
**postulado** *m* postulate; **postulado de las paralelas** (math.) parallel postulate
**postulador** *m* (eccl.) postulator
**postulanta** *f* (rel.) postulant
**postulante** *mf* petitioner; *m* (rel.) postulant
**postular** *va* to postulate, seek, demand, claim; to nominate; (eccl.) to postulate
**póstumo -ma** *adj* posthumous
**postura** *f* posture; stand, attitude; stake, wager; bid; pact, agreement; egg; eggs; egg-laying; transplanting; transplanted plant; **postura del sol** sunset
**potabilidad** *f* potability, potableness
**potabilizar** §76 *va* (Am.) to make potable or drinkable
**potable** *adj* potable, drinkable
**potación** *f* potation
**potaje** *m* pottage; mixture (*drink*); mixture, jumble; jumbled speech; **potajes** *mpl* vegetables
**potajería** *f* garden vegetables; storeroom for garden vegetables
**potala** *f* anchor stone; tub (*clumsy boat*)
**potar** *va* to correct and mark (*weights and measures*); to drink
**potasa** *f* (chem.) potash; **potasa cáustica** (chem.) caustic potash
**potásico -ca** *adj* potassic, potassium
**potasio** *m* (chem.) potassium
**pote** *m* pot; jug; flowerpot; **a pote** in abundance; **pote de la cola** glue pot
**potencia** *f* potency; power; (math., mech., opt. & phys.) power; (arti.) reach; (min.) thickness of a vein; **lo último de potencia** to the best of one's power; **potencia de choque** striking power; **potencia de fuego** (mil.) fire power; **potencia de salida sin distorsión** (elec.) undistorted output; **potencias A B C** A.B.C. powers (*Argentina, Brazil, and Chile*); **Potencias centrales** or **centroeuropeas** Central Powers; **potencia motora** or **motriz** motive power; **potencia mundial** world power
**potenciación** *f* (math.) involution
**potencial** *adj* potential; (gram.) potential; *m* potential; (elec., gram., math. & phys.) potential; **potencial humano** man power
**potencialidad** *f* potentiality
**potenciar** *va* to harness (*water power; a person's energy, interest, enthusiasm*); (math.) to raise (*to a power*)
**potenciómetro** *m* (elec.) potentiometer
**potentado** *m* potentate
**potente** *adj* potent, powerful; (coll.) big, huge
**potentila** *f* (bot.) potentilla
**potenza** *f* (her.) tau cross
**potera** *f* pulldevil
**poterna** *f* (fort.) postern
**potestad** *f* power; potentate; (math.) power; **potestades** *fpl* Powers (*sixth order of angels*); **patria potestad** (law) patria potestas
**potestativo -va** *adj* (law) facultative, optional
**potingue** *m* (hum.) dose, concoction
**potísimo -ma** *adj* very powerful
**potista** *mf* (coll.) toper, hard drinker, soak
**potosí** *m* pile of money; gold mine (*source of great wealth*)
**potra** *f* filly; (path.) scrotal hernia; (coll.) rupture; **tener potra** (coll.) to be lucky
**potrada** *f* herd of colts
**potranca** *f* young mare
**potrear** *va* (coll.) to bother, harass
**potrero -ra** *adj* of or for a colt or colts; *m* colt tender; pasture for colts; (coll.) rupture specialist; (Am.) cattle ranch
**potril** *m* pasture for colts
**potrilla** *f* filly; *m* (coll.) chipper old fellow
**potrillo** *m* (Am.) colt
**potro** *m* colt; wooden horse (*punishment*); obstetrical chair; stocks (*to sling a horse for shoeing*); pit for dividing a beehive; pest, great annoyance; **potro de madera** horse, vaulting horse
**potroso -sa** *adj* ruptured; (coll.) fortunate, lucky
**poundal** *m* (phys.) poundal
**poya** *f* fee for baking in public oven; hemp bagasse
**poyar** *vn* to pay the baking fee
**poyata** *f* shelf, bracket; cupboard, closet
**poyo** *m* stone bench built against the wall at the front door; judge's fee
**poza** *f* puddle; pool for breaking hemp
**pozal** *m* pail, bucket; coping or curbstone of a well; sump, catch basin
**pozanco** *m* puddle or pool along a river after a flood
**pozar** §76 *vn* to dig, to grub
**pozo** *m* well; pit; eddy, whirlpool; fish tank (*on a boat*); (min.) shaft; (naut.) hold; (Am.) pool, puddle; (Am.) spring, fountain; **pozo abisinio** driven well, drivewell; **pozo airón** bottomless pit; **pozo artesiano** artesian well; **pozo de aire** (aer.) air pocket; **pozo de ciencia** fountain of knowledge (*person*); **pozo de lanzamiento** launching silo; **pozo de lobo** (mil.) foxhole; **pozo negro** cesspool; **pozo séptico** septic tank
**pozuela** *f* small puddle

**pozuelo** *m* small well; sump, catch basin
**PP.** abr. of **Padres**
**P.P.** abr. of **porte pagado** & **por poder**
**p.p.do** abr. of **próximo pasado**
**prácrito** or **pracrito** *m* Prakrit
**práctica** *f* see **práctico**
**practicable** *adj* practicable
**practicaje** *m* pilotage
**practicanta** *f* prescription clerk; nurse
**practicante** *mf* prescription clerk; hospital nurse, hospital intern; *m* intern; surgeon (*for minor surgery*)
**practicar** **§86** *va* to practice; to bring about; to make, to cut (*a hole*); *vn & vr* to practice
**práctico -ca** *adj* practical; skilful, practiced; practicing (*e.g., churchman*); *m* practitioner, medical practitioner; (naut.) pilot; **práctico de puerto** harbor pilot; *f* practice; skill; **prácticas** *fpl* studies, apprenticeship, training
**practicón -cona** *mf* (coll.) old hand, practician
**pradal** *m* meadow, pasture
**pradejón** *m* small meadow
**pradeño -ña** *adj* (pertaining to a) meadow
**pradera** *f* meadowland; large meadow; prairie
**pradería** *f* meadowland
**praderoso -sa** *adj* (pertaining to a) meadow
**prado** *m* meadow, pasture; mall, walk, promenade; **a prado** grazing in the field; **prado de guadaña** meadow mowed annually
**Praga** *f* Prague
**pragmático -ca** *adj* pragmatic or pragmatical; *f* pragmatic sanction
**pragmatismo** *m* (philos.) pragmatism
**pragmatista** *adj & mf* (philos.) pragmatist
**pral.** abr. of **principal**
**pralte.** abr. of **principalmente**
**prandial** *adj* prandial
**prao** *m* proa (*Malay sailing boat*)
**praseodimio** *m* (chem.) praseodymium
**prasio** *m* (mineral.) prase
**prasma** *m* prasine, dark green agate
**pratense** *adj* pratal, living or growing in meadows
**pravedad** *f* depravity, wickedness
**pravo -va** *adj* depraved, wicked
**Praxiteles** *m* Praxiteles
**pre** *m* (mil.) daily pay
**preadamita** *m* preadamite
**preadamítico -ca** *adj* preadamic
**preadaptación** *f* (biol.) preadaptation
**preámbulo** *m* preamble; evasion; **no andarse** or **no detenerse en preámbulos** (coll.) to come to the point
**preamplificador** *m* (rad.) preamplifier
**prebélico -ca** *adj* prewar
**prebenda** *f* prebend; (coll.) sinecure; **prebendas** *fpl* patronage, political patronage
**prebendado** *m* prebend, prebendary
**prebendar** *va* to confer a prebend on
**prebostal** *adj* provostal, provost's
**prebostazgo** *m* provostship
**preboste** *m* provost
**precalentar** **§18** *va* to preheat
**precámbrico -ca** *adj & m* (geol.) Pre-Cambrian
**precariedad** *f* precariousness
**precario -ria** *adj* precarious
**precaución** *f* precaution; **precauciones contra accidentes** accident prevention
**precaucionado -da** *adj* precautionary
**precaucionar** *vr* to be cautious, take precautions
**precautelar** *va* to guard against, take precautions against
**precaver** *va* to try to prevent; to protect, to save; *vn & vr* to be on one's guard; **precaverse contra** or **de** to provide against, to guard against
**precavido -da** *adj* cautious, precautious
**precedencia** *f* precedence or precedency
**precedente** *adj* preceding, precedent; *m* precedent
**preceder** *va & vn* to precede
**precelente** *adj* most excellent
**preceptista** *adj* preceptive; *mf* preceptist
**preceptivo -va** *adj* preceptive, mandatory; *f* rules, principles; **preceptiva literaria** rules of composition, principles of writing
**precepto** *m* precept; order, injunction
**preceptor -tora** *mf* teacher, Latin teacher; *m* preceptor; *f* preceptress
**preceptoral** *adj* preceptorial
**preceptoril** *adj* (scornful) preceptorial
**preceptuar** **§33** *va* to lay down as a precept, to prescribe
**preces** *fpl* prayers, supplications
**precesión** *f* (mech.) precession; (rhet.) reticence; **precesión de los equinoccios** (astr.) precession of the equinoxes
**preciado -da** *adj* valued, esteemed; precious, valuable; proud, boastful
**preciador -dora** *mf* appraiser
**preciar** *va* to appraise, estimate; *vr* to boast; **preciarse de** to boast of being; **preciarse de** + *inf* to boast of + *ger*
**precinta** *f* strap, band; seal; corner patch or reinforcement; (naut.) parceling
**precintar** *va* to strap, bind; to seal
**precinto** *m* strapping, binding; seal; sealing strap; strap, band
**precio** *m* price; value, worth; esteem, credit; **al precio de** at the cost of; **a precio de coste** at cost; **a precios regalados** dirt-cheap; **no tener precio** to be priceless; **poner a precio** to offer a reward for; **poner precio a** to fix a price for; **precio de factura** invoice price; **precio de mercado** market price; **precio de situación** (Am.) cut price; **precio mínimo fijado** upset price; **precio tope** ceiling price
**preciosidad** *f* preciousness; beauty, charming thing
**preciosismo** *m* (lit.) preciosity
**precioso -sa** *adj* precious; valuable; witty, keen; (coll.) pretty
**preciosura** *f* (Am.) beauty, charming thing
**precipicio** *m* precipice; violent fall; ruin, destruction
**precipitación** *f* precipitation; (chem. & meteor.) precipitation; (fig.) precipitation, precipitance; **precipitación acuosa** rainfall
**precipitadamente** *adv* hastily, headlong
**precipitadero** *m* precipice, cliff
**precipitado -da** *adj* precipitant, precipitous; *m* (chem.) precipitate
**precipitante** *adj* precipitating; *m* (chem.) precipitant
**precipitar** *va* to precipitate; to rush, throw headlong, hurl; to hasten; (chem.) to precipitate; *vr* to rush, throw oneself headlong; (chem.) to precipitate
**precípite** *adj* teetering, about to fall
**precipitina** *f* (immun.) precipitin
**precipitoso -sa** *adj* risky, dangerous; precipitous, rash, reckless
**precipitrón** *m* (elec.) precipitron
**precipuo -pua** *adj* chief, principal
**precisar** *va* to state precisely, to specify; to fix, determine with precision; to need; **precisar a** + *inf* to force or oblige to + *inf*; *vn* to be necessary, be important; to be urgent; **precisar de** to need
**precisión** *f* necessity, obligation; precision; **precisiones** *fpl* data
**preciso -sa** *adj* necessary; precise
**precitado -da** *adj* aforesaid, above-mentioned
**precito -ta** *adj & mf* damned
**preclaro -ra** *adj* illustrious, famous
**precocidad** *f* precocity, precociousness
**precognición** *f* precognition
**precolombino -na** *adj* pre-Columbian
**preconcebir** **§94** *va* to preconceive
**preconcepción** *f* preconception
**preconfeccionado -da** *adj* ready-made
**preconización** *f* preconization; (eccl.) preconization
**preconizar** **§76** *va* to preconize, to commend publicly, to proclaim; (eccl.) to preconize
**preconocer** **§32** *va* to know in advance, to foreknow
**preconozco** *1st sg pres ind of* **preconocer**
**precordial** *adj* (anat.) precordial
**precoz** *adj* (*pl:* **-coces**) precocious; untimely
**precursor -sora** *adj* precursory, preceding, preliminary; *mf* precursor, forerunner; **el precursor de Cristo** the Forerunner (*John the Baptist*)

**predador -dora** or **predator -tora** *adj* predacious, predatory
**predecesor -sora** *mf* predecessor
**predecir** §37 *va* to predict, foretell
**predefinición** *f* (theol.) predetermination
**predefinir** *va* (theol.) to predetermine
**predestinaciano -na** *adj & mf* predestinarian
**predestinación** *f* predestination; (theol.) predestination
**predestinado -da** *adj* predestined; *mf* (theol.) predestinate
**predestinador -dora** *adj & mf* predestinarian
**predestinar** *va* to predestine, to predestinate
**predeterminación** *f* predetermination
**predeterminar** *va* to predetermine
**predial** *adj* predial, real, landed; attached to the land
**prédica** *f* sermon, protestant sermon; harangue
**predicable** *adj* preachable; predicable; *m* (log.) predicable
**predicación** *f* preaching, preachment
**predicaderas** *fpl* (coll.) gift of preaching
**predicado** *m* predicate
**predicador -dora** *adj* preaching; *mf* preacher; *m* pulpit orator; (ent.) praying mantis; (coll.) sermonizer
**predicamento** *m* (log.) predicament, category; esteem, reputation
**predicante** *adj & mf* predicant
**predicar** §86 *va* to preach; to praise to the skies; to scold, to preach to; to predicate; *vn* to preach; to predicate
**predicativo -va** *adj* predicative
**predicción** *f* prediction; **predicción del tiempo** weather forecasting
**predictor** *m* predictor; (aer.) predictor
**predicho -cha** *pp de* **predecir**
**predifunto -ta** *adj* predeceased
**predigerir** §62 *va* to predigest
**predigestión** *f* predigestion
**predigo** *1st sg pres ind of* **predecir**
**predije** *1st sg pret ind of* **predecir**
**predilección** *f* predilection
**predilecto -ta** *adj* favorite, preferred
**predio** *m* property, estate; **predio rústico** farmstead; **predio urbano** town property; country dwelling
**prediré** *1st sg fut ind of* **predecir**
**predispondré** *1st sg fut ind of* **predisponer**
**predisponer** §69 *va* to predispose
**predispongo** *1st sg pres ind of* **predisponer**
**predisposición** *f* predisposition
**predispuesto -ta** *adj* predisposed, biased, prejudiced; *pp of* **predisponer**
**predispuse** *1st sg pret ind of* **predisponer**
**predominación** *f* predomination
**predominancia** *f* predominance
**predominante** *adj* predominant
**predominar** *va* to predominate; *vn* to predominate; to stand out; **predominar a** or **sobre** to tower over
**predominio** *m* predominance, superiority
**preelección** *f* preëlection
**preelectoral** *adj* preëlectoral; preëlection
**preelegir** §72 *va* to elect beforehand; (theol.) to predestine
**preemción** *f* var. of **preempción**
**preeminencia** *f* preëminence
**preeminente** *adj* preëminent
**preempción** *f* preëmption
**preenfriar** §90 *va* to precool
**preescolar** *adj* preschool
**preestablecer** §34 *va* to preestablish
**preestreno** *m* (mov.) preview
**preexcelso -sa** *adj* most high, most sublime
**preexistencia** *f* preëxistence
**preexistente** *adj* preëxistent
**preexistir** *vn* to preëxist
**prefabricar** §86 *va* to prefabricate
**prefacio** *m* preface
**prefación** *f* prologue, introduction
**prefecto** *m* prefect; mayor; governor
**prefectura** *f* prefecture
**preferencia** *f* preference; **de preferencia** preferably
**preferencial** *adj* (econ.) preferential
**preferente** *adj* preferential; preferable, preferred
**preferentemente** *adv* chiefly; preferably
**preferible** *adj* preferable
**preferir** §62 *va* to prefer; **preferir** + *inf* to prefer to + *inf*
**prefiguración** *f* prefiguration, foreshadowing
**prefigurar** *va* to prefigure, to foreshadow
**prefijación** *f* prefixing
**prefijar** *va* to prefix, to prearrange, to predetermine; (gram.) to prefix
**prefijo -ja** *adj* (gram.) prefixed; *m* (gram.) prefix
**prefinición** *f* setting a time limit
**prefinir** *va* to set a time limit for
**prefloración** *f* (bot.) praefloration
**prefoliación** *f* (bot.) praefoliation
**preformación** *f* preformation
**prefulgente** *adj* brilliant, resplendent
**pregón** *m* proclamation, public announcement
**pregonar** *va* to proclaim, to announce publicly; to hawk (*merchandise; news; a secret*); to praise openly; to outlaw, proscribe
**pregonería** *f* office of common crier or town crier
**pregonero -ra** *adj* proclaiming, divulging; *mf* divulger; auctioneer; *m* common crier, town crier
**preguerra** *f* prewar period
**pregunta** *f* question; **andar, estar** or **quedar a la cuarta pregunta** (coll.) to be penniless; **coser a preguntas** to riddle with questions; **dejarse de preguntas** to stop asking questions; **hacer una pregunta** to ask a question
**preguntador -dora** *adj* questioning; inquisitive; *mf* questioner
**preguntar** *va* to ask, to question; *vn* to ask, to inquire; **preguntar por** to ask after or for; *vr* to ask oneself; to wonder
**preguntón -tona** *adj* (coll.) inquisitive; *mf* (coll.) inquisitive person
**pregustador** *m* taster, king's taster
**pregustar** *va* to taste (*food and drink before it is served to a king*)
**prehistoria** *f* prehistory
**prehistórico -ca** *adj* prehistoric or prehistorical
**preignición** *f* preignition
**preinsertar** *va* to preinsert
**prejudicio** or **prejuicio** *m* prejudgment; prejudice
**prejuzgar** §59 *va* to prejudge
**prelacía** *f* prelacy
**prelación** *f* preference
**prelada** *f* prelatess
**prelado** *m* prelate
**prelaticio -cia** *adj* prelatic, prelatish
**prelatura** *f* prelature
**preliminar** *adj & m* preliminary; **preliminares** *mpl* front matter (*of a book*)
**prelucir** §60 *vn* to shine ahead, to shine forth
**preludiar** *va* to prelude; (mus.) to try out (*an instrument or the voice*); *vn* to prelude; (mus.) to prelude; (mus.) to run over the scales
**preludio** *m* prelude; (mus.) prelude
**prelusión** *f* introduction, prelusion
**preluzco** *1st sg pres ind of* **prelucir**
**premarital** *adj* premarital
**prematuro -ra** *adj* premature; (law) impubic
**premédico -ca** *adj* premedical
**premeditación** *f* premeditation
**premeditado -da** *adj* premeditated
**premeditar** *va* to premeditate
**premiador -dora** *adj* rewarding; *mf* rewarder
**premiar** *va* to reward; to give an award to
**premidera** *f* treadle of a loom
**premio** *m* reward; prize; premium; **a premio** at a premium, with interest; **premio gordo** (coll.) first prize (*especially in Christmas lottery*); **premio Nóbel** Nobel prize; Nobel prize winner
**premiosidad** *f* tightness, closeness; bothersomeness; strictness; slowness, heaviness
**premioso -sa** *adj* tight, close; troublesome, bothersome; strict, rigid; slow, heavy, dull
**premiso -sa** *adj* presupposed, anticipated; sent in advance; (law) preceding; *f* (law & log.) premise; mark, token, clue; **premisa mayor** (log.) major premise; **premisa menor** (log.) minor premise
**premolar** *adj & m* (anat.) premolar
**premonitorio -ria** *adj* premonitory

**premonstratense** *adj & m* (eccl.) Premonstratensian
**premoriencia** *f* (law) predecease
**premoriente** *adj & mf* (law) predeceased
**premorir §45 & §17,** 9 *vn* (law) to die first, to predecease
**premostratense** *adj & m* var. of **premonstratense**
**premuerto -ta** *pp of* **premorir;** *adj* predeceased
**premura** *f* pressure, haste, urgency
**premuroso -sa** *adj* pressing, urgent
**prenatal** *adj* prenatal
**prenda** *f* pledge; security; pawn; jewel, household article (*especially if offered for sale*); garment, article of clothing; gift, talent; darling, loved one; **prendas** *fpl* forfeits (*game*); **dar en prenda** to pawn; **en prenda** in pawn; **en prenda de** as a pledge of, as proof of; **prenda de vestir** garment, article of clothing
**prendador -dora** *adj* pawning, pledging; *mf* pawner, pledger
**prendamiento** *m* pawning, pledging; fancy
**prendar** *va* to pawn, to pledge; to charm, to captivate; *vr* to take a liking, fall in love; **prendarse de** to take a liking to or for, to fall in love with; **prendarse de amor** to fall in love
**prendedero** *m* fillet, brooch, bandeau; stickpin
**prendedor** *m* catcher; fillet, brooch, bandeau; stickpin
**prendedura** *f* tread (*of an egg*)
**prender** *va* to seize, grasp; to catch, imprison; to catch (*e.g., on a hook*); to dress up; to pin, pin together; to fasten; *vn* to catch; to take root; to catch fire; to turn out well; **prender en** to catch on (*e.g., a hook*); *vr* to dress up; to be fastened; **prenderse en** to catch hold of
**prendería** *f* second-hand shop
**prendero -ra** *mf* second-hand dealer
**prendido -da** *adj* dressed up; (Am.) constipated; (Am.) drunk; **bien prendido** well dressed, well gotten up; **ir prendido en** (Am.) to be involved in; **mal prendido** poorly dressed; *m* adornment, woman's headdress; pattern pricked on parchment for bobbin lace; piece of bobbin lace; **prendido de flores** bouquet
**prendimiento** *m* seizure, capture; catching; rooting, taking root
**prenombre** *m* praenomen
**prenotar** *va* to note in advance
**prensa** *f* press; printing press; vise; (fig.) press, newspapers; (phot.) printing frame; **dar a la prensa** to publish; **entrar en prensa** to go tc press; **meter en prensa a uno** to put the squeeze on someone; **tener buena** (or **mala**) **prensa** to have a good (or bad) press; **prensa de filtrar** filter press; **prensa de imprenta** printing press; **prensa de vino** wine press; **prensa estopa** (mach.) stuffing box; **prensa hidráulica** hydraulic press; **prensa rotativa** (print.) rotary press; **prensa taladradora** drill press
**prensado** *m* pressing; luster, gloss (*from pressing*)
**prensador -dora** *adj* pressing; *mf* presser, press operator
**prensadura** *f* pressing, pressure
**prensaestopas** *m* (*pl:* **-pas**) (mach.) stuffing box
**prensalimones** *m* (*pl:* **-nes**) lemon squeezer
**prensar** *va* to press
**prensil** *adj* prehensile
**prensión** *f* prehension
**prensista** *m* (print.) pressman
**prensor -sora** *adj & f* (orn.) psittacine
**prenunciar** *va* to announce in advance, to presage
**prenuncio** *m* advance announcement, presage
**preñado -da** *adj* pregnant; sagging, bulging (*wall*); (fig.) pregnant; *m* pregnancy; fetus
**preñar** *va* (Am.) to make pregnant, to impregnate
**preñez** *f* pregnancy; fullness; threat, impending danger; inherent confusion
**preocupación** *f* preoccupation; preoccupancy; prejudice
**preocupadamente** *adv* with preoccupation; with prejudice
**preocupante** *adj* worrisome
**preocupar** *va* to preoccupy; *vr* to become preoccupied; to be prejudiced; **preocuparse con** or **por** to become preoccupied with; **preocuparse de** + *inf* to be concerned with + *ger*
**preopinante** *mf* previous speaker, first speaker
**preopinar** *vn* to give one's opinion earlier, to give one's opinion first
**preordinación** *f* preordination
**preordinar** *va* to preordain
**prep.** abr. of **preposición**
**prepalatal** *adj & f* (phonet.) prepalatal
**preparación** *f* preparation
**preparado** *m* (pharm.) preparation
**preparador -dora** *mf* preparer; preparator
**preparamento** or **preparamiento** *m* preparation
**preparar** *va* to prepare; **preparar a** or **para** + *inf* to prepare (*someone*) to + *inf; vr* to prepare, to get ready; **prepararse a** or **para** + *inf* to prepare to + *inf*, to get ready to + *inf*
**preparativo -va** *adj* preparative; *m* preparative, preparation
**preparatorio -ria** *adj* preparatory
**preponderancia** *f* preponderance
**preponderante** *adj* preponderant
**preponderar** *vn* to preponderate; to prevail
**prepondré** *1st sg fut ind of* **preponer**
**preponer §69** *va* to put before, to prefer
**prepongo** *1st sg pres ind of* **preponer**
**preposición** *f* preposition
**preposicional** *adj* prepositional
**prepositivo -va** *adj* prepositive
**prepósito** *m* chairman, president; (eccl.) provost
**prepositura** *f* chairmanship, presidency; (eccl.) provostship
**preposteración** *f* reversal, upset
**preposterar** *va* to reverse, upset
**prepóstero -ra** *adj* reversed, upset, out of order, inopportune
**prepotencia** *f* prepotency; haughtiness, pride
**prepotente** *adj* prepotent; haughty, overbearing
**prepucio** *m* (anat.) prepuce, foreskin
**prepuesto -ta** *pp de* **preponer**
**prepuse** *1st sg pret ind of* **preponer**
**prerrafaelismo** *m* Pre-Raphaelitism
**prerrafaelista** *adj & m* Pre-Raphaelite
**prerrogativa** *f* prerogative
**prerromanticismo** *m* preromanticism
**presa** *f* see **preso**
**presado -da** *adj* pale-green; *f* reservoir
**presagiar** *va* to presage, forebode, betoken
**presagio** *m* presage, omen, token
**presagioso -sa, presago -ga** or **présago -ga** *adj* foreboding, betokening
**presb.** abr. of **presbítero**
**presbicia** *f* (path.) presbytia, far-sightedness
**presbiope** *adj* presbyopic; *mf* presbyope
**presbiopía** *f* (path.) presbyopia
**présbita** or **présbite** *adj* presbytic, far-sighted; *mf* presbyte
**presbiterado** *m* priesthood
**presbiteral** *adj* sacerdotal, priestly
**presbiterato** *m* var. of **presbiterado**
**presbiterianismo** *m* Presbyterianism
**presbiteriano -na** *adj & mf* Presbyterian
**presbiterio** *m* presbytery
**presbítero** *m* presbyter; priest
**presciencia** *f* prescience, foreknowledge; **presciencia divina** (theol.) foreknowledge
**presciente** *adj* prescient
**prescindible** *adj* dispensable
**prescindir** *vn;* **prescindir de** to leave aside, leave out, disregard; to do without, dispense with; **prescindir de** + *inf* to avoid + *ger;* to do without + *ger*
**prescribir §17,** 9 *va* to prescribe; (law) to acquire by uninterrupted possession; *vn* to prescribe; to become invalid by default
**prescripción** *f* prescription; (law & med.) prescription; **prescripción adquisitiva** (law) acquisitive prescription
**prescriptible** *adj* prescriptible
**prescripto -ta** or **prescrito -ta** *pp of* **prescribir**
**presea** *f* gem, jewel
**preselector** *m* (telp.) preselector

**presencia** *f* presence; show, display; **en presencia de** in the presence of; **presencia de ánimo** presence of mind
**presencial** *adj* actual, in person
**presenciar** *va* to witness, be present at
**presentable** *adj* presentable
**presentación** *f* presentation; introduction; appearance (*e.g., of a new automobile, book*); **a presentación** (com.) on presentation
**presentado -da** *mf* presentee; *m* (eccl.) presentee
**presentador -dora** *mf* presenter; bearer
**presentalla** *f* votive offering
**presentáneo -a** *adj* quick-acting
**presentar** *va* to present; to introduce (*one person to another*); **presentar armas** (mil.) to present arms; *vr* to present oneself; to appear; to introduce oneself
**presente** *adj* present; **al presente** or **de presente** at present; **hacer presente** to notify of, to remind of; **la presente** this letter; **mejorando lo presente** present company excepted; **por el, la** or **lo presente** for the present; **tener presente** to bear or keep in mind; *m* present, gift; person present; (gram.) present; *interj* here!, present! (*in answering roll call*)
**presentemente** *adv* at present, now
**presentero** *m* (eccl.) sponsor
**presentimiento** *m* presentiment
**presentir** **§62** *va* to have a presentiment of
**presepio** *m* manger; stable
**presera** *f* (bot.) bedstraw
**presero** *m* keeper or tender of an irrigation ditch
**preservación** *f* preservation
**preservador -dora** *adj* preserving; *mf* preserver
**preservar** *va* to preserve, protect
**preservativo -va** *adj & m* preservative; preventive
**presidario** *m* var. of **presidiario**
**presidencia** *f* presidency; chairmanship; president's residence; president's office
**presidencial** *adj* presidential
**presidencialista** *adj* presidential
**presidenta** *f* president's wife; president (*woman*); chairwoman
**presidente** *m* president; chairman; **presidente electo** president-elect
**presidiar** *va* to garrison
**presidiario** *m* convict
**presidio** *m* garrison; penitentiary; citadel, fortress; prisoners, convicts; imprisonment; hard labor; aid, help; presidium
**presidir** *va* to preside over; to dominate; *vn* to preside
**presilla** *f* loop, fastener; clip; buttonhole stitching; shoulder strap (*of lady's garment*)
**presión** *f* pressure; **a presión** on draught (*beer*); **presión arterial** blood pressure; **presión atmosférica** atmospheric pressure, air pressure; **presión de inflado** tire pressure; **presión osmótica** osmotic pressure; **presión sanguínea** blood pressure
**presionar** *va* to press (*a button*); to put pressure on (*a person*)
**preso -sa** *adj* imprisoned; *mf* prisoner; convict; **coger preso a** or **poner preso a** to take prisoner; *f* seizure, capture; catch, prey; booty, spoils; dam; trench, ditch, flume; bit, morsel; talon, fang, tusk, claw; fishweir; (sport) hold, grip, grapple; **hacer presa** to seize, to hold tight; to take hold; to seize (*a chance, advantage, etc.*); **ser presa de** to be a victim of; to be a prey to; **presa de caldo** chicken broth
**prest** *m* var. of **pre**
**prestación** *f* lending; loan; service; (feudal law) service
**prestadizo -za** *adj* lendable
**prestado -da** *adj* lent, loaned; **dar prestado** to lend; **pedir** or **tomar prestado** to borrow
**prestador -dora** *adj* lending; *mf* lender
**prestamera** *f* (eccl.) benefice, church living
**prestamero** *m* (eccl.) incumbent of a benefice or church living
**prestamista** *mf* moneylender, pawnbroker
**préstamo** *m* lending; borrowing; loan; borrow, borrow pit; **dar a préstamo** to loan; **recibir en préstamo** or **tomar a préstamo** to borrow; **préstamo lingüístico** loan word, borrowing
**prestancia** *f* excellence, elegance, noble bearing
**prestante** *adj* excellent, elegant, noble
**prestar** *va* to lend, to loan; to give (*ear; help; news*); to pay (*attention*); to do (*a favor*); to render (*a service*); to take (*oath*); to keep (*silence*); to show (*patience*); *vn* to be useful; to give (*said, e.g., of a piece of cloth*); *vr* to lend oneself, to lend itself
**prestatario -ria** *adj* borrowing; *mf* borrower
**preste** *m* celebrant of high mass; (obs.) priest; **el Preste Juan** or **el Preste Juan de las Indias** Prester John
**presteza** *f* celerity, quickness
**prestidigitación** *f* prestidigitation
**prestidigitador -dora** *mf* prestidigitator
**prestigiador -dora** *adj* fascinating, captivating; *mf* faker, impostor
**prestigiar** *va* to accredit, sanction, glorify, lend luster to
**prestigio** *m* prestige; good standing; spell, fascination; illusion (*of sleight of hand*)
**prestigioso -sa** *adj* captivating, spellbinding; deceptive, illusory; famous, renowned
**prestimonio** *m* loan
**prestiño** *m* var. of **pestiño**
**presto -ta** *adj* quick, prompt, ready; nimble; **presto** *adv* right away
**presumible** *adj* presumable
**presumido -da** *adj* assuming, conceited, vain; *mf* vain pretender, would-be
**presumir** *va* to presume; *vn* to be conceited, to boast; **presumir de** + *adj* to boast of being + *adj*
**presunción** *f* presumption; conceit, vanity; (law) presumption
**presuntivo -va** *adj* presumptive
**presunto -ta** *adj* supposed, presumptive
**presuntuosidad** *f* conceit, vanity, priggery
**presuntuoso -sa** *adj* conceited, vain, priggish; *mf* conceited person, prig
**presupondré** *1st sg fut ind of* **presuponer**
**presuponer** **§69** *va* to presuppose; to budget
**presupongo** *1st sg pres ind of* **presuponer**
**presuposición** *f* presupposition
**presupuestal** *adj* budgetary
**presupuestar** *va* to budget
**presupuestario -ria** *adj* budgetary
**presupuesto -ta** *adj* presupposed, estimated; *pp of* **presuponer;** *m* reason, motive; supposition; budget; estimate
**presupuse** *1st sg pret ind of* **presuponer**
**presura** *f* anxiety, worry; speed, quickness; zeal, ardor, persistence
**presurizar** **§76** *va* (aer.) to pressurize
**presuroso -sa** *adj* speedy, quick, hasty; zealous, persistent
**pretal** *m* breastband, breast collar
**pretencioso -sa** *adj* conceited, vain; pretentious, showy
**pretender** *va* to pretend to, to claim; to try to do, to try for; **pretender** + *inf* to try to + *inf;* to claim to + *inf*
**pretendido -da** *adj* pretended
**pretendienta** *f* pretender, claimant (*woman*)
**pretendiente** *mf* pretender, claimant; office seeker; *m* suitor
**pretensión** *f* pretension; presumption; pursuit, effort
**pretensioso -sa** *adj* var. of **pretencioso**
**pretenso -sa** *adj* var. of **pretendido**
**pretensor -sora** *mf* pretender, claimant
**preterición** *f* preterition; (law & rhet.) preterition; **con preterición de** omitting, passing over
**preterir** **§62** *va* to overlook, disregard; (law) to not mention (*an heir in a will*)
**pretérito -ta** *adj* past; (gram.) past, preterit; *m* past; (gram.) past, preterit; **pretérito imperfecto** (gram.) imperfect; **pretérito indefinido** (gram.) preterit, past absolute; **pretérito perfecto** (gram.) present perfect; **pretérito anterior** (gram.) past anterior, second pluperfect
**pretermisión** *f* pretermission
**pretermitir** *va* to pretermit
**preternatural** *adj* preternatural

**pretextar** *va* to pretext, to use as a pretext
**pretexto** *m* pretext
**pretil** *m* parapet, railing (*of stone, brick, metal*); walk or road along a parapet; (Am.) ledge
**pretina** *f* girdle, belt; waistband
**pretinazo** *m* blow with a girdle
**pretinero -ra** *mf* maker of girdles, belts, or waistbands
**pretónico -ca** *adj* (gram.) pretonic
**pretor** *m* praetor; black water in places where tunnies are found
**pretorial** *adj* praetorian
**pretorianismo** *m* praetorianism, military interference in politics
**pretoriano -na** *adj & m* praetorian
**pretorio -ria** *adj* praetorian; *m* (hist.) praetorium; (Am.) front steps
**preuniversitario -ria** *adj* preuniversity
**prevaldré** *1st sg fut ind of* **prevaler**
**prevalecer §34** *vn* to prevail; to take root; to thrive; **prevalecer sobre** to prevail against or over
**prevaleciente** *adj* prevailing
**prevaler §89** *vn* (archaic) to prevail; *vr* **prevalerse de** to avail oneself of, to take advantage of
**prevalezco** *1st sg pres ind of* **prevalecer**
**prevalgo** *1st sg pres ind of* **prevaler**
**prevaricación** *f* collusion, connivance; transgression; (law) prevarication
**prevaricador -dora** *mf* transgressor; (law) prevaricator
**prevaricar §86** *vn* to collude, connive; to play false; to transgress; (law) to prevaricate; (coll.) to rave, to be delirious
**prevaricato** *m* corrupt practice; (law) prevarication
**prevención** *f* preparation; prevention; foresight; warning; prejudice; stock, supply; jail, lockup; (mil.) guardhouse; **a prevención** in case of emergency; **a prevención de que** ready in case that; **a** or **de prevención** spare; emergency
**prevendré** *1st sg fut ind of* **prevenir**
**prevengo** *1st sg pres ind of* **prevenir**
**prevenidamente** *adv* in advance, beforehand
**prevenido -da** *adj* prepared, ready; foresighted, forewarned; stocked, full
**prevenir §92** *va* to prepare, make ready; to forestall, prevent, anticipate; to overcome; to warn; to prejudice, predispose; *vn* to come up (*said, e.g., of a storm*); *vr* to get prepared, get ready; to come to mind; **prevenirse a** or **contra** to prepare against or for (*e.g., danger*); **prevenirse con** or **de** to provide oneself with; **prevenírsele a uno** to come to someone's mind
**preventivo -va** *adj* preventive; warning
**prever §93** *va* to foresee
**previne** *1st sg pret ind of* **prevenir**
**previniendo** *ger of* **prevenir**
**previo -via** *adj* previous, foregoing, preceding; preliminary; after, with previous, subject to, e.g., **previo acuerdo** subject to agreement
**previsible** *adj* foreseeable
**previsión** *f* prevision, foresight; foresightedness; forecast; **previsión del tiempo** weather forecasting; **previsión social** social security
**previsor -sora** *adj* far-seeing, foresighted, previsional
**previsto -ta** *pp of* **prever**
**prez** *m & f* honor, glory, worth
**Príamo** *m* (myth.) Priam
**priapismo** *m* (path.) priapism
**Príapo** *m* (myth.) Priapus
**priesa** *f* (archaic) var. of **prisa**
**prieto -ta** *adj* darking, black; stingy, mean; tight; compact; (Am.) dark-complexioned
**prima** *f* see **primo**
**primacía** *f* primacy; primateship; **detener la primacía** to hold the top place
**primacial** *adj* primatial; superior, supreme
**primado -da** *adj* primatial; *m* (eccl.) primate; primacy; *f* (coll.) gypping, rooking
**primal -mala** *adj & mf* yearling; *m* silk cord or braid
**primario -ria** *adj* primary; *m* (elec.) primary (*coil or winding*)
**primate** *m* worthy; (zool.) primate
**primavera** *f* spring, springtime; flowered silk; (bot.) cowslip, primrose; (orn.) robin (*Turdus migratorius*); (fig.) prime; **primavera de la China** (bot.) primrose, Chinese primrose
**primaveral** *adj* (pertaining to) spring
**primazgo** *m* cousinship; primacy
**primear** *vr* (coll.) to call each other cousin (*said of kings and noblemen*)
**primer** *adj* apocopated form of **primero**, used only before masculine singular nouns and adjectives
**primerísimo -ma** *adj super* very first
**primerizo -za** *adj* beginning; *mf* beginner, novice; *f* primipara
**primero -ra** *adj* first; former; early; primary; prime; raw (*material*); (arith.) prime; **de primero** at the outset; **primero** *adv* first (*in the first place; rather*); *m* first; **a primeros de** around the beginning of (*e.g., the month*)
**primevo -va** *adj* oldest
**primicerio -ria** *adj* first, top (*in rank or order*); *m* cantor, precentor
**primicia** *f* first fruits; **primicias** *fpl* (fig.) first fruits, beginnings
**primicial** *adj* primitial
**primichón** *m* silk skein
**primigenio -nia** *adj* original, primitive
**primilla** *f* pardon for the first offense
**primípara** *f* (obstet.) primipara
**primista** *m* small trader (*in stock market*)
**primitivo -va** *adj* primitive; *m* (f.a.) primitive
**primo -ma** *adj* first; prime (*excellent*); skillful; raw (*material*); (arith.) prime; **primo** *adv* in the first place; *mf* cousin; (coll.) booby, sucker, dupe; **primo carnal** or **primo hermano** first cousin, cousin-german; *f* early morning; bonus, bounty, subsidy; (eccl.) prime; (eccl.) first tonsure; (ins.) premium; (mil.) first quarter of the night; (mus.) treble (*string*)
**primogénito -ta** *adj & mf* first-born
**primogenitura** *f* primogeniture; birthright
**primor** *m* care, skill, elegance; beauty
**primordial** *adj* primordial
**primorear** *vn* to do a beautiful job, to perform with elegance
**primoroso -sa** *adj* careful, skillful, elegant; fine, exquisite
**primuláceo -a** *adj* (bot.) primulaceous
**princesa** *f* princess; princess royal; princesse dress; **princesa viuda** dowager princess
**principada** *f* (coll.) abuse of authority, petty tyranny
**principado** *m* princedom; principality; **principados** *mpl* (rel.) principalities
**principal** *adj* principal, main, chief; first, foremost; essential, important; famous, illustrious; (mus.) first; *m* principal, head, chief; main floor, second floor; (com. & law) principal; (mil.) main guard; (theat.) second balcony
**principalidad** *f* primacy, superiority, supremacy
**principalmente** *adv* above all else: principally
**príncipe** *m* prince; prince royal; **príncipes** *mpl* prince and princess; **portarse como un príncipe** to live like a prince; **príncipe consorte** prince consort; **príncipe de Asturias** heir apparent of the King of Spain; **príncipe de Gales** Prince of Wales; **príncipe de la Iglesia** Prince of the Church (*cardinal*); **príncipe de la paz** Prince of Peace (*Manuel de Godoy*); **príncipe de la sangre** prince of the blood; **príncipe de las tinieblas** Prince of Darkness; **príncipe de los ingenios** Cervantes; **príncipe negro** Black Prince; *adj* princeps, first (*edition*)
**principela** *f* (archaic) fine woolen fabric
**principesco -ca** *adj* princely
**principiador -dora** *adj* beginning; *mf* beginner
**principianta** *f* apprentice (*woman*)
**principiante** *adj* beginning; *mf* beginner, apprentice; novice, greenhorn
**principiar** *va, vn & vr* to begin; **principiar a** + *inf* to begin to + *inf*
**principio** *m* start, beginning; principle; source, origin; (chem.) principle; (cook.) entree; **principios** *mpl* front matter (*of a book*); **a principios de** around the beginning of (*e.g., the month*); **al principio** or **a los principios** in

the beginning, at first; **en principio** in principle; **en un principio** at the beginning; **por principio** on principle; **tener, tomar** or **traer principio de** to come or arise from; **principio de admiración** (gram.) inverted exclamation point; **principio de interrogación** (gram.) inverted question mark
**principote** *m* (coll.) upstart, parvenu
**pringada** *f* slice of bread dipped in gravy; grease spot
**pringamoza** *f* (bot.) nettle
**pringar §59** *va* to dip or soak in grease; to dip in boiling fat (*as punishment*); to spot or stain with grease; (coll.) to wound, make bleed; (coll.) to slander, run down; (Am.) to splash, spatter; *vn* (coll.) to participate, meddle; (Am.) to drizzle; *vr* to peculate
**pringón -gona** *adj* (coll.) greasy; *m* (coll.) smearing oneself with grease; (coll.) grease spot
**pringoso -sa** *adj* greasy
**pringote** *m* hodgepodge
**pringue** *m & f* grease, fat; grease spot
**pringuera** *f* dripping pan
**priodonte** *m* or **prionodonte** *m* (zool.) giant armadillo
**prior** *m* prior; curate
**priora** *f* prioress
**prioral** *adj* of a prior or prioress
**priorato** or **priorazgo** *m* priorate; priory
**prioridad** *f* priority
**prioste** *m* steward (*of a brotherhood*)
**prisa** *f* hurry, haste; urgency; fight; crush, crowd; **a prisa** or **de prisa** quickly, hurriedly; **a toda prisa** with the greatest speed; **correr** or **dar prisa** to be urgent; **correrle prisa a uno** + *inf* to be in a hurry to + *inf*, e.g., **no le corre prisa cumplir su cometido** he is not in a hurry to do his job; **dar prisa a** to rush, to hurry; **darse prisa** to hurry, make haste; **estar de prisa** or **tener prisa** to be in a hurry; **tener prisa en** or **por** + *inf* to be in a hurry to + *inf*
**priscal** *m* night shelter for cattle
**prisión** *f* seizure, capture; arrest; imprisonment; prison; bond, union; **prisiones** *fpl* chains, shackles, fetters; **reducir a prisión** to incarcerate
**prisionero -ra** *mf* (mil.) prisoner (*soldier or civilian*); (fig.) captive (*of love or passion*); **prisionero de guerra** prisoner of war; *m* setscrew; stud bolt
**prisma** *m* (geom., opt. & cryst.) prism; (fig.) mirage; **prisma de Nicol** (opt.) Nicol prism
**prismático -ca** *adj* prismatic; **prismáticos** *mpl* prism binocular
**priste** *m* (ichth.) sawfish
**prístino -na** *adj* pristine; primeval; pure, clear, transparent
**prisuelo** *m* muzzle for ferrets
**priv.** abr. of **privilegio**
**privación** *f* privation
**privada** *f* see **privado**
**privadamente** *adv* privily, privately
**privadero** *m* cesspool cleaner
**privado -da** *adj* private; *m* favorite (*at court*); *f* privy, cesspool; pile of dirt
**privanza** *f* favor at court
**privar** *va* to deprive; to forbid, prohibit; *vn* to be in vogue; to prevail; to be in favor (*especially at court*); *vr* to deprive oneself; **privarse de** to give up; **privarse de** + *inf* to give up + *ger*
**privativo -va** *adj* privative; private, personal, peculiar; (gram.) privative; **privativo de** peculiar to
**privilegiadamente** *adv* in a privileged way, with special consideration
**privilegiar** *va* to privilege, to grant a privilege to
**privilegio** *m* privilege; **privilegio de invención** patent
**pro** *m & f* profit, advantage; **¡buena pro!** good appetite!; **de pro** of note, of worth; **el pro y el contra** the pros and the cons; **en pro de** pro, in behalf of
**proa** *f* (naut.) prow; (aer.) nose
**proal** *adj* forward, (pertaining to the) prow
**pro-alemán -mana** *adj & mf* pro-German
**probabilidad** *f* probability, likelihood
**probabilismo** *m* (philos.) probabilism
**probable** *adj* probable, likely
**probación** *f* probation
**probado -da** *adj* tried, tested; sorely tried; proved
**probador -dora** *mf* tester; taster; sampler; fitter; *m* tester (*device*); **probador de baterías** (elec.) battery tester; **probador de válvulas** (rad.) tube tester
**probadura** *f* sampling, tasting
**probanza** *f* (law) inquiry; (law) proof, evidence
**probar §77** *va* to prove; to test; to try; to try on; to try out; to taste; to sample (*e.g., wine*) to fit; to suit, to agree with; **no probar** to not touch, to keep away from (*liquor*); *vn* **probar a** + *inf* to try to + *inf*; **probar de** to taste, take a taste of; *vr* to try on (*a suit of clothes*)
**probatorio -ria** *adj* probatory, probative; probational; *f* (law) time allowed for producing evidence
**probatura** *f* (coll.) trial, test
**probeta** *f* test tube; pressure gauge; beaker; powder prover
**probidad** *f* probity
**problema** *m* problem
**problemático -ca** *adj* problematic or problematical
**probo -ba** *adj* honest; fair, just
**probóscide** *f* (zool. & ent.) proboscis
**proboscidio -dia** *adj & m* (zool.) proboscidian
**proc.** abr. of **procesión**
**procacidad** *f* impudence, boldness
**procaz** *adj* (*pl:* **-caces**) impudent, bold
**procedencia** *f* origin, source; point of origin, point of departure; propriety
**procedente** *adj* coming, originating; proper
**proceder** *m* conduct, behavior; *vn* to proceed; to originate; to behave; to be proper; **proceder** + *inf* to be proper to + *inf*; **proceder a** + *inf* to proceed to + *inf*; **proceder contra** to proceed against, take action against; **proceder de** to proceed from, come from
**procedimiento** *m* procedure; proceeding; process; (law) proceedings; **procedimiento tricromo** three-color process
**procela** *f* (poet.) storm, tempest
**proceloso -sa** *adj* stormy, tempestuous
**prócer** *adj* high, lofty; *m* hero, leader, dignitary
**procerato** *m* heroic rôle, leadership
**proceridad** *f* height, loftiness; vigor, growth
**prócero -ra** or **procero -ra** *adj* high, lofty
**proceroso -sa** *adj* imposing, solemn, big and impressive-looking
**procesable** *adj* actionable, indictable
**procesado -da** *adj* legal; accused; *mf* accused, defendant
**procesal** *adj* legal
**procesamiento** *m* (law) prosecution; (law) indictment
**procesar** *va* (law) to sue, to prosecute; (law) to indict
**procesión** *f* procession; parade
**procesional** *adj & m* processional
**procesionaria** *f* (ent.) processional or processionary moth
**procesionario** *m* processional
**procesionista** *adj* (coll.) parade-loving; *mf* (coll.) parade lover, parade fan
**proceso** *m* process (*of time*); progress; (anat. & biol.) process; (law) suit, lawsuit; (law) trial; (med.) course, development (*of a disease*); **proceso verbal** (Am.) minutes, proceedings
**procio** *m* (chem.) protium
**Proción** *m* (astr.) Procyon
**proclama** *f* proclamation, manifesto; marriage banns
**proclamación** *f* proclamation; acclamation
**proclamar** *va* to proclaim; to acclaim
**proclítico -ca** *adj & m* (gram.) proclitic
**proclive** *adj* inclined, disposed, evil-disposed
**proclividad** *f* proclivity, evil proclivity
**Procne** *f* var. of **Progne**
**procomún** *m* or **procomunal** *m* public welfare, social welfare
**procónsul** *m* proconsul
**proconsulado** *m* proconsulate
**proconsular** *adj* proconsular
**procrastinar** *va* to procrastinate

**procreación** *f* procreation
**procreador -dora** *adj* procreative; *mf* procreator
**procreante** *adj* procreative
**procrear** *va* to procreate
**proctología** *f* proctology
**proctoscopio** *m* proctoscope
**procumbente** *adj* (bot.) procumbent
**procura** *f* power of attorney; attorneyship; business acumen
**procuración** *f* careful management; power of attorney; proxy; law office; attorneyship, solicitorship
**procurador** *m* solicitor, attorney; proxy; procurator (*for a monastery*)
**procuradora** *f* procuratrix (*especially for a nunnery*)
**procuraduría** *f* law office; proctorship; attorneyship, solicitorship
**procurar** *va* to strive for; to manage (*e.g., real estate*) as attorney; to yield, to produce; **procurar** + *inf* to try to, strive to + *inf*
**procurrente** *m* large peninsula
**Procustes** *m* or **Procusto** *m* (myth.) Procrustes
**prodición** *f* treachery
**prodigalidad** *f* prodigality
**prodigar §59** *va* to lavish; to squander, to waste; to spread widely; *vr* to be a show-off
**prodigio** *m* prodigy
**prodigiosidad** *f* prodigiousness; excellence
**prodigioso -sa** *adj* prodigious, marvelous; fine, excellent
**pródigo -ga** *adj* lavish; prodigal; *mf* prodigal; (law) prodigal
**prodrómico -ca** *adj* prodromal
**pródromo** *m* (path.) prodrome
**producción** *f* production; crop, yield, produce; **producción en masa** or **en serie** mass production
**producente** *adj* productive; producing
**producir §38** *va* to produce; to yield, to bear; to cause, bring about; *vr* to explain oneself; (Am.) to take place, happen
**productividad** *f* productivity
**productivo -va** *adj* productive
**producto** *m* product; proceeds; (chem. & math.) product; **producto alimenticio** foodstuff
**productor -tora** *adj* producing; *mf* producer
**produje** *1st sg pret ind of* **producir**
**produzco** *1st sg pres ind of* **producir**
**proejar** *vn* to resist with all one's might; to row against the current or the wind
**proel** *adj* (naut.) (pertaining to the) bow; *m* (naut.) bow oar, bowman
**proemial** *adj* proemial, prefatory, introductory
**proemio** *m* proem, preface, introduction
**proeza** *f* prowess; feat, stunt
**prof.** abr. of **profeta**
**profanación** *f* profanation
**profanador -dora** *adj* profanatory; *mf* profaner
**profanamiento** *m* var. of **profanación**
**profanar** *va* to profane
**profanidad** *f* profanity; indecency, immodesty
**profano -na** *adj* profane; worldly; indecent, immodest; lay; *mf* profane; worldly person; layman
**profecía** *f* prophecy; **las Profecías** (Bib.) the Prophets
**proferir §62** *va* to utter
**profesar** *va & vn* to profess
**profesión** *f* profession
**profesional** *adj* professional; *mf* professional; practitioner
**profesionalismo** *m* professionalism
**profeso -sa** *adj & mf* (rel.) professed
**profesor -sora** *mf* teacher; professor; **profesor adjunto** associate professor; **profesor agregado** assistant professor; **profesor de intercambio** exchange professor; **profesor honorario** emeritus professor; **profesor numerario** or **titular** full professor; **profesor visitante** visiting professor
**profesorado** *m* professorship; professorate; faculty; teaching staff; teaching profession
**profesoral** *adj* professorial
**profeta** *m* prophet; **el Profeta** the Prophet (*Mohammed*)
**profetal** or **profético -ca** *adj* prophetic
**profetisa** *f* prophetess
**profetizador -dora** *adj* prophesying; *mf* prophesier
**profetizar §76** *va & vn* to prophesy
**proficiente** *adj* progressing
**proficuo -cua** *adj* profitable, useful
**profiláctico -ca** *adj & m* prophylactic; preventive; *f* hygiene
**profilaxis** *f* prophylaxis
**prófugo -ga** *adj & mf* fugitive; *m* (mil.) slacker, draft dodger
**profundidad** *f* depth; profundity; (geom.) altitude, height
**profundizar §76** *va* to deepen, make deeper; to fathom, go deep into, get to the bottom of; *vn* to go deep into things; *vr* to deepen, become deep
**profundo -da** *adj* profound; deep; *m* profundity; (poet.) sea, deep; hell, underworld
**profusión** *f* profusion
**profuso -sa** *adj* profuse
**progenerado -da** *adj* illustrious, distinguished; ahead of the times
**progenie** *f* lineage, descent, parentage
**progenitor** *m* progenitor
**progenitura** *f* lineage, descent; primogeniture; right of primogeniture
**progesterona** *f* (biochem.) progesterone
**progimnasma** *m* (rhet.) preparatory exercise
**proglótide** *f* or **proglotis** *f* (zool.) proglottid
**prognatismo** *m* prognathism
**prognato -ta** *adj* prognathous
**Progne** *f* (myth.) Procne; (*l.c.*) *f* (poet.) swallow
**prognosis** *f* (*pl:* **-sis**) forecast (*especially of weather*); prognosis
**programa** *m* program; **programa continuo** (mov.) continuous showing; **programa de estudios** curriculum; **programa doble** (mov.) double feature; **programa vivo** (rad.) live program
**programación** *f* programing
**programar** *va* to program
**programático -ca** *adj* (pertaining to a) program
**progresar** *vn* to progress
**progresión** *f* progression; (math.) progression; **progresión aritmética** arithmetical progression; **progresión geométrica** geometric progression
**progresista** *adj & mf* (pol.) progressive
**progresivo -va** *adj* progressive
**progreso** *m* progress; **progresos** *mpl* progress (*of a disease, of a pupil, etc.*); **hacer progresos** to make progress
**prohibición** *f* prohibition; **prohibición de virar a la derecha** (aut.) no right-hand turn
**prohibicionista** *adj & mf* prohibitionist
**prohibir §99** *va* to prohibit, to forbid; **se prohíbe escupir** no spitting; **se prohíbe fijar carteles** post no bills; **se prohíbe fumar** no smoking; **se prohíbe el paso** no thoroughfare; **se prohíbe la entrada** keep out; **prohibir** + *inf* to forbid to + *inf*
**prohibitivo -va** *adj* prohibitive
**prohibitorio -ria** *adj* prohibitory
**prohijación** *f* adoption
**prohijador -dora** *mf* adopter
**prohijamiento** *m* var. of **prohijación**
**prohijar §99** *va* to adopt
**prohombre** *m* master (*of a guild*); leader; top man (*of a group*); (coll.) big shot
**prois** *m* (naut.) stone or post (*for fastening a boat*); (naut.) cable (*for tying up a boat*)
**prójima** *f* (coll.) slut, jade
**prójimo** *m* fellow man, fellow creature, neighbor; (coll.) fellow
**pról.** abr. of **prólogo**
**prolán** *m* (biochem.) prolan
**prolapso** *m* (path.) prolapse
**prole** *f* offspring, progeny
**prolegómeno** *m* prolegomenon
**prolepsis** *f* (*pl:* **-sis**) (rhet.) prolepsis
**proletariado** *m* proletariat
**proletario -ria** *adj & m* proletarian
**proletarizar §76** *va* to proletarianize; *vr* to become proletarianized
**proliferación** *f* proliferation
**prolífero -ra** *adj* (bot.) proliferous

**prolificación** *f* prolificacy
**proliferante** *adj* proliferating
**proliferar** *vn* (biol.) to proliferate; to proliferate
**prolífico -ca** *adj* prolific
**prolijidad** *f* tediousness; fussiness, fastidiousness; dullness, tiresomeness, rudeness
**prolijo -ja** *adj* too long, tedious; overcareful, fussy, fastidious; dull, tiresome, rude
**prolina** *f* (biochem.) proline
**prologar** §59 *va* to write a preface to or for; *vn* to prologuize
**prólogo** *m* prologue; preface
**prologuista** *mf* writer of prologues
**prolonga** *f* (arti.) prolonge
**prolongación** *f* prolongation, extension
**prolongadamente** *adv* at great length
**prolongado -da** *adj* prolonged; long
**prolongamiento** *m* var. of **prolongación**
**prolongar** §59 *va* to prolong, to extend; (geom.) to produce; *vr* to extend
**proloquio** *m* maxim, aphorism
**prolusión** *f* var. of **prelusión**
**promanar** *vn* to arise, originate
**promecio** *m* var. of **prometio**
**promediar** *va* to divide into two equal parts; to average; *vn* to mediate; to be half over
**promedio** *m* average, mean; middle
**promesa** *f* promise; pious offering; (fig.) promise (*something giving hope of success*)
**prometedor -dora** *adj* promising; *mf* promiser
**Prometeo** *m* (myth.) Prometheus
**prometer** *va* to promise; **prometer** + *inf* to promise to + *inf*; *vn* to promise; to give promise; *vr* to expect; to become engaged; **prometérselas felices** or **muy buenas** (coll.) to be too hopeful, to be overconfident
**prometido -da** *adj* engaged, betrothed; *m* fiancé; promise; *f* fiancée
**prometiente** *adj* promising
**prometimiento** *m* promise
**prometio** *m* (chem.) promethium
**prominencia** *f* prominence
**prominente** *adj* prominent, outstanding
**promiscuar** *vn* to eat meat and fish in the same meal during Lent and other fast days; to act inconsistently
**promiscuidad** *f* promiscuity; promiscuous intercourse; ambiguity
**promiscuo -cua** *adj* promiscuous; ambiguous
**promisión** *f* promise
**promisorio -ria** *adj* promissory
**promoción** *f* promotion; advancement; class, year, crop (*of persons promoted*)
**promontorio** *m* height, elevation; promontory, headland; bulky, unwieldly thing; (anat.) promontory
**promotor -tora** or **promovedor -dora** *adj* promotive; *mf* promoter
**promover** §63 *va* to promote; to further, to advance
**promulgación** *f* promulgation; publication, open declaration
**promulgador -dora** *adj* promulgating; *mf* promulgator; announcer
**promulgar** §59 *va* to promulgate; to proclaim, to publish abroad
**pronación** *f* (physiol.) pronation
**pronador** *m* (anat.) pronator
**pronefros** *m* (embryol.) pronephros
**proneidad** *f* proneness
**prono -na** *adj* prone
**pronombre** *m* pronoun; **pronombre complementario** object pronoun; **pronombre demostrativo** demonstrative pronoun; **pronombre indefinido** or **indeterminado** indefinite pronoun; **pronombre interrogativo** interrogative pronoun; **pronombre personal** personal pronoun; **pronombre posesivo** possessive pronoun; **pronombre relativo** relative pronoun; **pronombre sujeto** subject pronoun
**pronominado -da** *adj* (gram.) reflexive (*verb*)
**pronominal** *adj* (gram.) pronominal; (gram.) reflexive (*verb*)
**pronosticable** *adj* foretellable, predictable
**pronosticación** *f* prognostication
**pronosticador -dora** *adj* prognostic, prognosticating; *mf* prognosticator
**pronosticar** §86 *va* to prognosticate, to foretell
**pronóstico** *m* prognostic; almanac; (med.) prognosis; **de pronóstico gravísimo** in a serious condition; **de pronóstico reservado** in a critical condition
**prontitud** *f* promptness, promptitude; keenness, wittiness
**pronto -ta** *adj* quick, speedy; prompt; ready; **pronto** *adv* right away, soon; promptly; early; **lo más pronto posible** as soon as possible; **tan pronto como** as soon as; *m* jerk; (coll.) impulse, sudden impulse, fit of anger; **al pronto** right off; **de pronto** suddenly; hastily, without thinking; down (*payment*); **por de pronto** or **por lo pronto** for the present, provisionally
**prontuario** *m* notebook; compendium, handbook
**prónuba** *f* (poet.) bridesmaid
**pronunciable** *adj* pronounceable
**pronunciación** *f* pronunciation
**pronunciado -da** *adj* marked, pronounced; sharp (*curve*); steep (*hill*); bulky; *mf* rebel, insurgent
**pronunciador -dora** *adj* pronouncing; *mf* pronouncer
**pronunciamiento** *m* insurrection, uprising; (law) decree
**pronunciar** *va* to pronounce; to utter; to deliver, make (*a speech*); to decide on; *vr* to rebel; to declare oneself
**propagación** *f* propagation
**propagador -dora** *adj* propagating; *mf* propagator
**propaganda** *f* propaganda; advertising
**propagandismo** *m* propagandism
**propagandista** *adj* & *mf* propagandist
**propagandístico -ca** *adj* (pertaining to) propaganda
**propagar** §59 *va* to propagate; to spread, to extend; to broadcast; *vr* to propagate; to spread, to extend
**propagativo -va** *adj* propagative
**propalación** *f* spreading (*e.g., of rumors*)
**propalador -dora** *mf* divulger
**propalar** *va* to divulge, to spread
**propano** *m* (chem.) propane
**propao** *m* (naut.) breastwork
**proparoxítono -na** *adj* & *m* (phonet.) proparoxytone
**propasar** *vr* to go too far, to take undue liberty
**propender** *vn* to incline, tend, be inclined; **propender a** + *inf* to tend to + *inf*, to be inclined to + *inf*
**propensión** *f* propensity, liking; predisposition, susceptibility
**propenso -sa** *adj* inclined, prone, disposed
**propi** *f* (slang) tip
**propiciación** *f* propitiation
**propiciador -dora** *adj* propitiating; *mf* propitiator
**propiciar** *va* to propitiate; (Am.) to support, favor, sponsor
**propiciatorio -ria** *adj* propitiatory; *m* mercy seat; prie-dieu
**propicio -cia** *adj* propitious
**propiedad** *f* property; ownership; proprietorship; (f.a.) naturalness, likeness; **es propiedad** copyrighted; **propiedad horizontal** one-floor ownership in an apartment house; **propiedad literaria** copyright
**propienda** *f* listing attached to cheeks of an embroidery frame
**propietario -ria** *adj* proprietary; *m* proprietor; *f* proprietress
**propilo** *m* (chem.) propyl
**propina** *f* tip, fee; **de propina** (coll.) in the bargain
**propinación** *f* treat, invitation to drink; prescription or administration of medicine
**propinar** *va* to offer (*a drink*); to prescribe or administer (*medicine*); (coll.) to give (*e.g., a beating, a hard time*); *vr* to treat oneself to (*a drink*)
**propincuidad** *f* propinquity
**propincuo -cua** *adj* near, contiguous
**propio -pia** *adj* proper, suitable; peculiar, characteristic; natural; same; himself, herself, etc., e.g., **el propio capitán** the captain himself;

own, e.g., **mi propio hermano** my own brother; **el suyo propio** his very own; proper, e.g., **China propia** China proper; *m* messenger; native; **propios** *mpl* public lands, public property
**propóleos** *m* propolis, bee glue
**propón** *2d sg impv of* **proponer**
**propondré** *1st sg fut ind of* **proponer**
**proponedor -dora** *adj* proposing, propounding; *mf* proponent, propounder
**proponente** *adj* proposing, propounding
**proponer** §69 *va* to propose; to propound; to name, to present (*a candidate*); *vr* to plan; **proponerse** + *inf* to propose to + *inf*
**propongo** *1st sg pres ind of* **proponer**
**proporción** *f* proportion; opportunity; (math.) proportion; **proporciones** *fpl* proportions (*size; dimensions*)
**proporcionable** *adj* proportionable
**proporcionado -da** *adj* proportionate; proportioned; fit, suitable
**proporcional** *adj* proportional
**proporcionalidad** *f* proportionality
**proporcionar** *va* to proportion; to furnish, provide, supply, give; to adapt, adjust
**proposición** *f* proposition; **proposición dominante** (gram.) main clause, principal clause
**propósito** *m* aim, purpose, intention; subject matter; **a propósito** by the way; apropos, fitting; in place; **a propósito de** apropos of; **de propósito** on purpose; **fuera de propósito** irrelevant, beside the point, out of place
**propuesto -ta** *pp of* **proponer;** *adj* proposed; *f* proposal, proposition
**propugnáculo** *m* fortress; (fig.) bulwark
**propugnar** *va* to defend; to protect; to advocate
**propulsa** *f* repulse
**propulsante** *m* propellant
**propulsar** *va* to repulse; to propel, to drive; to promote
**propulsión** *f* repulse; propulsion; **propulsión a chorro** or **de chorro, propulsión a escape** or **de escape, propulsión por reacción** jet propulsion; **propulsión a cohete** rocket propulsion
**propulsor -sora** *adj* propellent, propulsive; *m* propellent; (rail. & fig.) booster; propeller
**propuse** *1st sg pret ind of* **proponer**
**pror.** abr. of **procurador**
**prora** *f* (poet.) prow
**prorrata** *f* prorate, quota; **a prorrata** pro rata
**prorratear** *va* to prorate, to apportion
**prorrateo** *m* apportionment; **a prorrateo** pro rata
**prórroga** or **prorrogación** *f* prorogation
**prorrogar** §59 *va* to prorogue; to defer, postpone
**prorrumpir** *vn* to spurt, shoot forth; to break forth, burst out
**prosa** *f* prose; (coll.) chatter, idle talk
**prosado -da** *adj* prose, in prose
**prosador -dora** *mf* prose writer; (coll.) chatterbox
**prosaico -ca** *adj* prose, prosaic; (fig.) prosaic, prosy
**prosaísmo** *m* prosaism, prosiness
**prosapia** *f* ancestry, lineage
**proscenio** *m* proscenium
**proscribir** §17, 9 *va* to proscribe, to outlaw
**proscripción** *f* proscription, exile, outlawry
**proscripto -ta** *pp of* **proscribir;** *mf* exile, outlaw
**proscriptor -tora** *adj* proscriptive; *mf* proscriber
**proscrito -ta** *pp & mf* var. of **proscripto**
**prosector** *m* prosector
**prosecución** *f* continuation, prosecution; pursuit
**proseguir** §82 *va* to continue, carry on; *vn* to continue
**proselitismo** *m* proselytism
**prosélito** *m* proselyte
**prosénquima** *f* (bot.) prosenchyma
**Proserpina** *f* (myth.) Proserpina or Proserpine
**prosificación** *f* prosification
**prosificar** §86 *va* to prosify, put into prose
**prosimiano -na** *adj & m* (zool.) prosimian
**prosista** *mf* prose writer; (coll.) chatterbox
**prosístico -ca** *adj* (pertaining to) prose
**prosita** *f* short piece of prose
**prosodia** *f* orthoëpy; prosody (*study of quantity in Greek and Latin verse*)
**prosódico -ca** *adj* orthoëpic; prosodic; stress (*accent*)
**prosodista** *mf* orthoëpist, phonologist
**prosopopeya** *f* (rhet.) prosopopoeia; (coll.) airs, pomposity, solemnity
**prospección** *f* prospecting (*for gold, oil, etc.*)
**prospectar** *va & vn* to prospect
**prospecto** *m* prospectus
**prospector -tora** *mf* prospector
**prosperado -da** *adj* prosperous (*rich*)
**prosperar** *va* to prosper, make prosper; *vn* to prosper, to thrive
**prosperidad** *f* prosperity
**próspero -ra** *adj* prosperous, thriving
**próstata** *f* (anat.) prostate
**prostatectomía** *f* (surg.) prostatectomy
**prostático -ca** *adj* prostatic, (pertaining to the) prostate; *m* prostate sufferer
**prosternar** *vr* to prostrate oneself
**próstesis** *f* (gram.) prosthesis
**prostético -ca** *adj* (gram.) prosthetic
**prostíbulo** *m* brothel
**próstilo** *m* (arch.) prostyle
**prostitución** *f* prostitution
**prostituir** §41 *va* to prostitute; *vr* to prostitute oneself; to become a prostitute
**prostituta** *f* prostitute
**prosudo -da** *adj* (Am.) pompous, solemn, formal; (Am.) domineering
**protactinio** *m* var. of **protoactinio**
**protagonista** *mf* protagonist
**protagonizar** §76 *va* to play the leading role of
**Protágoras** *m* Protagoras
**protalo** or **prótalo** *m* (bot.) prothallium
**prótasis** *f* (*pl:* **-sis**) (gram.) protasis
**protección** *f* protection; **protección aduanera** protective tariff; **protección civil** civil defense
**proteccionismo** *m* protectionism; protection of animals and plants
**proteccionista** *adj & mf* protectionist
**protector -tora** or **-triz** (*pl:* **-trices**) *adj* protective; *m* protector; *f* protectress
**protectorado** *m* protectorate
**protectoría** *f* protectorship, protectorate
**protectorio -ria** *adj* protective
**proteger** §49 *va* to protect
**protegida** *f* protégée
**protegido** *m* protégé
**proteico -ca** *adj* (biochem.) proteid, protein; (fig.) protean; (myth.) Protean
**proteido** *m* (biochem.) proteid
**proteína** *f* (biochem.) protein
**Proteo** *m* (myth. & fig.) Proteus
**proterozoico -ca** *adj & m* Proterozoic
**protervia** or **protervidad** *f* perversity
**protervo -va** *adj* perverse
**prótesis** *f* (gram. & surg.) prothesis or prosthesis
**protesta** *f* protest; protestation; promise, pledge; (law) protest
**protestación** *f* protestation; profession (*e.g., of faith*)
**protestante** *adj & mf* protestant; Protestant
**protestantismo** *m* Protestantism
**protestar** *va* to protest, asseverate; to profess (*one's faith*); (com.) to protest; *vn* to protest; **protestar de, contra** or **por** to protest (*to object to*)
**protesto** *m* (com.) protest
**protético -ca** *adj* (gram. & surg.) prothetic or prosthetic
**protio** *m* var. of **procio**
**protoactinio** *m* (chem.) protoactinium
**protocolar** *adj* protocolary; *va* to protocol
**protocolizar** §76 *va* to protocol
**protocolo** *m* protocol
**protógina** *f* (geol.) protogine
**protomártir** *m* protomartyr
**protón** *m* (phys. & chem.) proton
**protonema** *m* (bot.) protonema
**protonotario** *m* (eccl.) prothonotary
**protoplasma** *m* (biol.) protoplasm
**protoplásmico -ca** *adj* protoplasmic
**protórax** *m* (*pl:* **-rax**) (ent.) prothorax

**prototipo** *m* prototype
**protozoario -ria** or **protozoo -a** *adj* protozoan; *m* (zool.) protozoan, protozoön
**protozoología** *f* protozoölogy
**protráctil** *adj* protractile
**protuberancia** *f* protuberance; **protuberancias solares** (astr.) solar protuberances
**protuberante** *adj* protuberant
**protutor** *m* (law) guardian
**prov.ª** abr. of **provincia**
**provecto -ta** *adj* old, ripe
**provecho** *m* advantage, benefit; profit, gain; advance, progress; **¡buen provecho!** good luck!; good appetite!; **de provecho** useful, just right; decent
**provechoso -sa** *adj* advantageous, beneficial; profitable; useful
**proveedor -dora** *mf* supplier, provider, purveyor; steward
**proveeduría** *f* stewardship; storehouse
**proveer §35 & §17,** 9 *va* to provide, furnish; to supply; to resolve, settle; to confer, bestow; (law) to decree; *vn* to provide; **proveer a** to provide for; *vr* to have a movement of the bowels; **proveerse de** to provide oneself with
**proveído** *m* (law) interlocutory decree
**proveimiento** *m* provisioning
**provena** *f* (hort.) layer (*of vine*)
**provendré** *1st sg fut ind of* **provenir**
**provengo** *1st sg pres ind of* **provenir**
**proveniente** *adj* coming, originating, arising
**provenir §92** *vn* to come, originate, arise
**provento** *m* product, yield
**Provenza, la** Provence
**provenzal** *adj & mf* Provençal; *m* Provençal (*language*)
**proverbiador** *m* book of proverbs
**proverbial** *adj* proverbial
**proverbiar** *vn* (coll.) to use proverbs
**proverbio** *m* proverb; **Proverbios** *mpl* (Bib.) Proverbs
**proverbista** *mf* (coll.) proverbialist
**provicero** *m* prophet, diviner
**providencia** *f* providence, foresight; (*cap.*) *f* Providence
**providencial** *adj* providential
**providenciar** *va* to make provision for; to settle, arrange
**providente** *adj* provident; prudent
**próvido -da** *adj* provident, watchful; favorable, propitious
**provincia** *f* province; **en provincias** in the provinces (*not in Madrid*); **las Provincias Vascongadas** the Basque Provinces; **Provincias Marítimas** Maritime Provinces (*of Canada*)
**provincial** *adj* provincial; *m* (eccl.) provincial
**provincialismo** *m* provincialism
**provincianismo** *m* provinciality
**provinciano -na** *adj & mf* provincial
**provine** *1st sg pret ind of* **provenir**
**proviniendo** *ger of* **provenir**
**provisión** *f* provision; **provisiones** *fpl* provisions
**provisional** *adj* provisional
**proviso; al proviso** right away, at once
**provisor** *m* provider; (eccl.) vicar general
**provisora** *f* stewardess (*in a convent*)
**provisorato** *m* stewardship
**provisoría** *f* stewardship; storeroom, pantry (*in a convent*)
**provisorio -ria** *adj* provisory, provisional
**provisto -ta** *pp of* **proveer**
**provitamina** *f* (biochem.) provitamin
**provocación** *f* provocation
**provocador -dora** *adj* provoking; provocative; *mf* provoker
**provocante** *adj* provocative
**provocar §86** *va* to provoke; to forward, promote; to move, to incite, to tempt; **provocar a** + *inf* to provoke to + *inf;* to move to + *inf,* to tempt to + *inf;* *vn* to provoke; (coll.) to vomit
**provocativo -va** *adj* provocative
**proxeneta** *mf* go-between
**proximal** *adj* (anat.) proximal
**próximamente** *adv* soon, in the near future; proximately; approximately
**proximidad** *f* proximity; **proximidades** *fpl* neighborhood
**próximo -ma** *adj* next; near, neighboring; proximate, close; early; **próximo pasado** last (*month*)
**proyección** *f* projection; influence, distinction; **proyección cónica** conic projection; **proyección de Mercátor** (geog.) Mercator's projection
**proyectar** *va* to project (*a bullet; a film; a scheme*); to plan; to design (*e.g., a building*); (geom.) to project; **proyectar** + *inf* to plan to + *inf;* *vr* to project, stick out; to be projected, to fall (*said of a shadow*)
**proyectil** *m* projectile, missile; **proyectil buscador del blanco** homing missile; **proyectil dirigido** or **teleguiado** guided missile
**proyectista** *mf* projector, designer, planner; project administrator
**proyectivo -va** *adj* projective
**proyecto** *m* project; **proyecto de ley** bill (*in a legislative body*)
**proyector** *m* projector, searchlight; (mov.) projection machine
**proyectura** *f* (arch.) projection
**prudencia** *f* prudence
**prudencial** *adj* prudential
**prudenciar** *vr* (Am.) to be restrained, to hold oneself in
**prudente** *adj* prudent
**prueba** *f* proof; trial, test; examination; fitting (*e.g., of a suit of clothes*); sample (*of food or drink*); (math., phot. & print.) proof; (law) evidence, proof; (Am.) acrobatic stunt; (Am.) sleight of hand; **a prueba** on approval, on trial; perfect; **a prueba de** proof against; -proof, e.g., **a prueba de ácidos** acidproof; **a prueba de calor** heatproof; **poner a prueba** to put to the proof, to put to the test; **prueba de aptitud** aptitude test; **prueba de consolación** (sport) consolation match; **prueba de indicios** (law) circumstantial evidence; **prueba de inteligencia** intelligence test; **prueba directa** (law) direct evidence; **prueba indiciaria** (law) circumstantial evidence; **prueba indirecta** (law) indirect evidence; **prueba mental** mental test; **prueba plena** (law) convincing proof; **pruebas de planas** (print.) page proof; **pruebas de primeras** (print.) first proof; **pruebas de segundas** (print.) galley proof; **prueba semiplena** (law) imperfect proof
**pruebista** *mf* (Am.) acrobat
**pruriginoso -sa** *adj* pruriginous
**prurigo** *m* (path.) prurigo
**prurito** *m* itch; (path.) pruritus; (fig.) eagerness, urge, itch (*to do something*); **sentir el prurito de** + *inf* to itch to + *inf*
**Prusia** *f* Prussia
**prusianismo** *m* Prussianism
**prusiano -na** *adj & mf* Prussian
**prusiato** *m* (chem.) prussiate
**prúsico -ca** *adj* prussic
**ps.** abr. of **pesos**
**P.S.** abr. of **Post Scriptum** (Lat.) **posdata**
**pseudohermafroditismo** *m* var. of **seudohermafroditismo**
**pseudomorfismo** *m* (mineral.) pseudomorphism
**pseudónimo** *m* var. of **seudónimo**
**psicastenia** *f* (path.) psychasthenia
**psicoanálisis** *m* psychoanalysis
**psicoanalista** *mf* psychoanalyst
**psicoanalítico -ca** *adj* psychoanalytic or psychoanalytical
**psicoanalizar §76** *va* to psychoanalyze
**psicodinámico -ca** *adj* psychodynamic; *f* psychodynamics
**psicofísica** *f* psychophysics
**psicognostia** *f* psychognosis
**psicología** *f* psychology; **psicología experimental** experimental psychology; **psicología infantil** child psychology
**psicológico -ca** *adj* psychologic or psychological
**psicólogo -ga** *mf* psychologist
**psicometría** *f* psychometry
**psicométrico -ca** *adj* psychometric
**psiconeurosis** *f* (*pl:* **-sis**) (path.) psychoneurosis

**psicópata** *mf* psychopath
**psicopatía** *f* psychopathy
**psicopático -ca** *adj* psychopathic
**psicopatología** *f* psychopathology
**psicosis** *f* (*pl:* **-sis**) (path.) psychosis; **psicosis de guerra** war psychosis, war scare; **psicosis maníacodepresiva** (psychopath.) manic-depressive insanity
**psicosomático -ca** *adj* psychosomatic
**psicotecnia** or **psicotécnica** *f* psychotechnology
**psicoterapia** *f* psychotherapy
**psicrómetro** *m* psychrometer
**psilosis** *f* (path.) psilosis (*fall of hair; sprue*)
**psique** *f* or **psiquis** *f* cheval glass; psyche (*soul, mind*); (*cap.*) *f* (myth.) Psyche
**psiquiatra** *mf* or **psiquíatra** *mf* psychiatrist
**psiquiatría** *f* psychiatry
**psiquiátrico -ca** *adj* psychiatric
**psiquiatro** *m* var. of **psiquiatra**
**psíquico -ca** *adj* psychic or psychical
**psitacismo** *m* psittacism
**psitacosis** *f* (path.) psittacosis, parrot disease
**P.S.M.** abr. of **por su mandato**
**psoas** *m* (anat.) psoas
**psoríasis** *f* (path.) psoriasis
**pta.** abr. of **pasta & peseta**
**pte.** abr. of **parte & presente**
**pteridófita** *f* (bot.) pteridophyte
**pterodáctilo** *m* (pal.) pterodactyl
**ptialina** *f* (path.) ptyalin
**ptialismo** *m* (path.) ptyalism
**ptolemaico -ca** *adj* Ptolemaic
**Ptolomeo** *m* var. of **Tolomeo**
**ptomaína** *f* (biochem.) ptomaine
**Pto. Rico** abr. of **Puerto Rico**
**pu** *interj* ugh!
**púa** *f* point, sharp point, prick, barb; tine, prong; needle (*of phonograph*); tooth (*of comb*); thorn; spine or quill (*of porcupine*); sting (*of pain or remorse*); (hort.) graft; (mus.) plectrum; (coll.) tricky person
**puado** *m* (set of) teeth, prongs
**puar** **§33** *va* to put teeth on (*e.g., a comb*)
**púber -bera** or **púbero -ra** *adj* pubescent; *mf* person who has attained puberty
**pubertad** *f* puberty
**pubes** *m* (*pl:* **-bes**) var. of **pubis**
**pubescencia** *f* pubescence
**pubescente** *adj* pubescent
**pubescer** **§34** *vn* to reach the age of puberty
**pubiano -na** or **púbico -ca** *adj* pubic
**pubis** *m* (*pl:* **-bis**) (anat.) pubes (*lower part of abdomen; hair covering it*); (anat.) pubis (*part of innominate bone*)
**publicación** *f* publication
**publicano** *m* (hist.) publican
**publicar** **§86** *va* to publish; to publicize; (eccl.) to publish
**publicata** *f* certificate of publication
**publicidad** *f* publicity; advertising; **en publicidad** publicly; **publicidad de lanzamiento** advance publicity
**publicista** *mf* publicist
**publicitario -ria** *adj* (pertaining to) publicity, advertising; publishing
**público -ca** *adj* public; *m* public; audience; **en público** in public; *f* public examination or defense of thesis
**pucha** *f* (Am.) small bouquet
**puchada** *f* flour poultice; hogwash; thin mortar
**puchera** *f* (coll.) stew
**pucherazo** *m* blow with a pot or kettle; **dar pucherazo** (coll.) to count votes that weren't cast
**puchero** *m* pot, kettle; stew; (coll.) daily bread; (coll.) pout, pouting; **hacer pucheros** (coll.) to pout, to screw up one's face (*in crying or weeping*); **volcar el puchero** (coll.) to count votes that weren't cast
**puches** *mpl & fpl* porridge, gruel, pap
**pucho** *m* (Am.) fag end, remnant; (Am.) stump (*of cigar*); (Am.) trifle, trinket; (Am.) baby (*youngest member of a family*)
**pude** *1st sg pret ind of* **poder**
**pudelación** *f* (found.) puddling
**pudelador** *m* (found.) puddler
**pudelaje** *m* (found.) puddling
**pudelar** *va* (found.) to puddle
**pudendo -da** *adj* ugly, shameful, obscene; private (*parts*)
**pudibundez** *f* affected modesty
**pudibundo -da** *adj* modest, shy
**pudicicia** *f* chastity; modesty
**púdico -ca** *adj* modest, shy, chaste
**pudiendo** *ger of* **poder**
**pudiente** *adj* powerful; well-off, well-to-do; **poco pudiente** not so well-off, poorer; *mf* person of means; **los pudientes** the well-to-do
**pudín** *m* pudding
**pudinga** *f* (geol.) pudding stone
**pudor** *m* modesty, shyness; virtue, chastity
**pudoroso -sa** *adj* modest, shy
**pudrición** *f* rot, rotting; **pudrición roja** plant rot
**pudridero** *m* place of decomposition; compost heap; temporary vault (*for a corpse*)
**pudrigorio** *m* (coll.) var. of **podrigorio**
**pudrimiento** *m* rot, rotting
**pudrir** (*pp:* **podrido**) *va* to rot, putrefy; to worry; *vn* to be dead and buried; *vr* to rot, putrefy; to be worried, be harassed; to languish (*e.g., in jail*)
**puebla** *f* planting the seed of a vegetable
**pueble** *m* (min.) gang of workmen
**pueblerino -na** *adj* rustic, village, plebeian
**pueblo** *m* town, village; people, nation; common people; **pueblo de Dios** or **de Israel** children of Israel
**puente** *m* bridge; (aut.) rear axle; (naut.) deck; (mus. & naut.) bridge; (mus.) tailpiece; (cards) bender, bridge; **hacer un puente de plata a** (coll.) to smooth the way for, make it easy for; **hacer puente** to take the intervening day off; **puente aéreo** airlift, air bridge; **puente basculante** bascule bridge; **puente cantilever** cantilever bridge; **puente colgante** suspension bridge; **puente de barcas** boat bridge, pontoon bridge; **puente de engrase** (aut.) grease lift, grease rack; **puente delantero** (aut.) front axle, front-axle assembly; **puente de los suspiros** Bridge of Sighs; **puente de suspensión** suspension bridge; **puente flotante** (aut.) floating axle, **puente giratorio** swing drawbridge; **puente levadizo** drawbridge, lift drawbridge; **puente suspendido** hanging scaffold; **puente transbordador** transporter bridge; **puente trasero** (aut.) rear axle, rear-axle assembly; **puente voladizo** cantilever bridge
**puentecilla** *f* (mus.) bridge; (mus.) tailpiece
**puentezuela** *f* small bridge
**puerco -ca** *adj* dirty, filthy; piggish, hoggish; coarse, mean; lewd; slovenly; *m* (zool.) hog; **puerco de mar** (zool.) sea hog; **puerco espín** or **espino** (zool.) porcupine; **puerco jabalí, montés** or **salvaje** (zool.) wild boar; **puerco marino** (zool.) dolphin; *f* (zool.) sow; (zool.) wood louse; (path.) scrofula; (fig.) slattern; (fig.) slut; (fig.) selfish woman; **puerca montés** or **salvaje** sow of wild boar
**puericia** *f* childhood
**puericultura** *f* puericulture; child care
**pueril** *adj* puerile
**puerilidad** *f* puerility, childishness
**puérpera** *f* puerpera, woman who has just given birth to a child
**puerperal** *adj* puerperal
**puerperio** *m* (obstet.) puerperium
**puerro** *m* (bot.) leek, scallion
**puerta** *f* door, doorway; gate, gateway; (*cap.*) *f* Porte (*Turkey*); **puertas** *fpl* (coll.) octroi, tax on provisions (*entering a town*); **a puerta cerrada** or **a puertas cerradas** behind closed doors; **dar a uno con la puerta en la cara** or **las narices** (coll.) to slam the door in someone's face; **de puerta en puerta** from door to door; **de puertas para adentro** indoors; **fuera de puertas** outdoors, out of doors; **Sublime Puerta** Sublime Porte (*Turkey*); **tomar la puerta** to leave, go away; **puerta abierta** (dipl.) open door; **puerta cochera** porte-cochere; **puerta de corredera** sliding door; **puerta excusada** or **puerta falsa** back door, side door; **puerta giratoria** revolving door; **puerta plegadiza** folding

door; **Puertas de Hierro** Iron Gates (*on the Danube*); **puerta trasera** back door; **puerta vidriera** glass door
**puertaventana** *f* window shutter
**puertezuela** *f* little door
**puertezuelo** *m* small port or harbor
**puerto** *m* port, harbor, haven; mountain pass; (fig.) haven, refuge; **puerto aéreo** airport; **Puerto Arturo** Port Arthur; **puerto brigantino** Corunna; **puerto de arribada** (naut.) port of call; **puerto de depósito** bonded port; **Puerto de España** Port of Spain (*in Trinidad*); **puerto de matrícula** port of registry; **puerto franco** free port; **puerto marítimo** harbor, port; **Puerto Príncipe** Port-au-Prince; **puerto seco** frontier customhouse
**puertorriqueño -ña** *adj & mf* Puerto Rican
**pues** *adv* then, well; yes, certainly; why; anyhow; **pues que** since; *conj* for, since, because, inasmuch as; *interj* (coll.) well!, then!
**puesta** *f* see **puesto**
**puestero -ra** *mf* vendor, seller (*at a booth or stand*); *m* (Am.) tender of livestock (*on a ranch*)
**puesto -ta** *pp of* **poner; puesto que** since, inasmuch as; (archaic) although ‖ *adj* placed, put, set; dressed ‖ *m* place; booth, stand; post, position; office; station; barracks; blind (*for hunters*); **puesto de socorros** first-aid station; ‖ *f* setting; laying; putting; stake (*at cards*); **a puesta del sol, a puestas del sol** at sunset; **primera puesta** (mil.) new outfit (*given to a recruit*); **puesta a masa** (aut.) grounding (*of a wire*); **puesta a punto** completion, carrying out, perfection; adjustment; keeping in shape; **puesta a tierra** (elec.) grounding; **puesta de largo** coming out, social debut; **puesta en libertad** liberation, setting free; **puesta en marcha** starting; launching
**puf** *m* pouf (*circular ottoman*); *interj* ugh!
**pufino** *m* (orn.) shearwater
**púgil** *m* pugilist
**pugilar** *adj* pugilistic; *m* Hebrew manual of the Scriptures
**pugilato** or **pugilismo** *m* pugilism
**pugilista** *m* pugilist
**pugilístico -ca** *adj* pugilistic
**pugna** *f* fight, battle; struggle, conflict; **en pugna** at issue; **en pugna con** at odds with
**pugnacidad** *f* pugnacity
**pugnante** *adj* fighting, hostile; struggling
**pugnar** *vn* to fight; to struggle; to strive, persist; **pugnar para** or **por** + *inf* to struggle to + *inf*
**pugnaz** *adj* (*pl:* **-naces**) pugnacious
**puja** *f* push, effort; bid; **sacar de la puja** (coll.) to beat, get ahead of; (coll.) to get (*someone*) out of a jam; **vender a la puja** to auction
**pujador -dora** *mf* bidder
**pujame** *m* or **pujamen** *m* (naut.) foot (*of a sail*)
**pujamiento** *m* flow of humors or blood
**pujante** *adj* mighty, puissant, vigorous
**pujanza** *f* might, puissance, vigor
**pujar** *va* to push (*e.g., a project*); to raise, bid up (*a price*); *vn* to struggle, to strain; to falter; to grope (*for words*); (coll.) to snivel
**pujavante** *m* butteris, hoof parer
**pujo** *m* (path.) tenesmus; straining; irresistible impulse (*to laugh or cry*); eagerness, strong desire; (coll.) attempt
**pulcritud** *f* neatness, tidiness; circumspection
**pulcro -cra** *adj* neat, tidy, trim; circumspect
**pulchinela** *m* punchinello; (*cap.*) *m* Punch
**pulga** *f* flea; small top (*toy*); **de malas pulgas** peppery, hot-tempered, hot-headed; **hacer de una pulga un camello** or **un elefante** (coll.) to make a mountain out of a molehill; **no aguantar pulgas** (coll.) to stand for no nonsense; **pulga de mar** (zool.) beach flea, sand hopper
**pulgada** *f* inch
**pulgar** *m* thumb; shoot left on vine; **menear los pulgares** to uncover one's cards gradually; (coll.) to do fast fingerwork; **por sus pulgares** (coll.) on one's own hook, all by oneself
**pulgarada** *f* fillip (*with thumb*); pinch (*of salt, tobacco, etc.*); inch
**pulgarcito** *m* little thumb; (*cap.*) *m* Tom Thumb
**pulgón** *m* (ent.) plant louse
**pulgoso -sa** *adj* full of fleas
**pulguera** *f* place full of fleas; wing of crossbow; (bot.) fleawort
**pulguillas** *m* (*pl:* **-llas**) (coll.) touchy fellow
**pulicán** *m* dentist's forceps
**pulidez** *f* neatness; polish
**pulido -da** *adj* pretty; neat; polished; clean, spotless
**pulidor -dora** *adj* polishing; finishing; *mf* polisher; *f* polishing machine
**pulimentar** *va* to polish
**pulimento** *m* polish; **pulimento para muebles** furniture polish
**pulir** *va* to polish; to finish; (fig.) to give a polish to; *vr* to polish; to dress up, get dressed; (fig.) to take on a polish
**pulmón** *m* (anat.) lung; **pulmón de acero** or **pulmón de hierro** iron lung; **pulmón marino** (zool.) jellyfish
**pulmonado -da** *adj* pulmonate
**pulmonar** *adj* pulmonary
**pulmonaria** *f* (bot.) lungwort
**pulmonía** *f* (path.) pneumonia; case or attack of pneumonia; **coger una pulmonía** to get pneumonia
**pulmoníaco -ca** *adj* pneumonic; *mf* person sick with pneumonia
**pulmotor** *m* pulmotor
**pulpa** *f* pulp
**pulpejo** *m* soft flesh (*of finger, ear, etc.*)
**pulpería** *f* (Am.) grocery store, general store
**pulpero** *m* octopus fisher; (Am.) grocer, storekeeper
**pulpeta** *f* slice of meat
**púlpito** *m* pulpit; (fig.) pulpit
**pulpo** *m* (zool.) octopus
**pulposo -sa** *adj* pulpy
**pulque** *m* (Am.) pulque
**pulquería** *f* (Am.) pulque tavern or bar; (Am.) pulque still
**pulquero -ra** *mf* (Am.) pulque dealer
**pulquérrimo -ma** *adj super* very or most neat or tidy; very or most circumspect
**pulsación** *f* pulsation, throb, beat; strike, striking; touch (*of pianist or typist*); (phys. & physiol.) pulsation
**pulsada** *f* pulsation, beat (*of pulse*)
**pulsador -dora** *adj* pulsating; push (*key, pedal, etc.*); *m* push button
**pulsar** *va* to play (*piano, harp, guitar*); to strike (*a key*); to feel or take the pulse of; to sound out, examine; (Am.) to feel the weight of (*by lifting*); *vn* to pulsate, throb, beat
**pulsátil** *adj* pulsatile
**pulsatila** *f* (bot.) pasqueflower
**pulsativo -va** *adj* pulsative
**pulsear** *vn* to hand-wrestle
**pulsera** *f* bracelet; wristlet, watch strap; side lock (*of hair*); (surg.) wrist bandage; **pulsera de pedida** engagement bracelet
**pulsímetro** *m* pulsimeter
**pulsista** *adj* expert on the pulse; *mf* pulse expert (*physician*)
**pulso** *m* pulse; steadiness, steady hand; tact, care, caution; (Am.) bracelet; (Am.) wrist watch; **a pulso** with hand and wrist; by main strength, the hard way; freehand (*drawing*); (Am.) straight, at one gulp; **de pulso** tactful; **sacar a pulsos** (coll.) to carry out against odds; **sin pulso** lifeless; **tomar a pulso** (Am.) to drink (*something*) straight, to drink (*something*) with one swig; **tomar el pulso a** to feel or take the pulse of; (fig.) to look into, to scrutinize
**pulsómetro** *m* pulsometer
**pulsorreactor** *m* (aer.) ram-jet engine
**pultáceo -a** *adj* pultaceous; (med.) gangrened
**pulular** *vn* to pullulate
**pulverizable** *adj* pulverizable
**pulverización** *f* pulverization; atomizing; spraying
**pulverizador -dora** *adj* pulverizing; *mf* sprayer (*person*); *m* spray, sprayer
**pulverizar** §76 *va* to pulverize; to atomize; to spray; *vr* to pulverize

**pulverulento -ta** *adj* dusty; powdery
**pulla** *f* dig, cutting remark; indecency, filthy remark; (orn.) gannet
**pullista** *mf* scoffer, giber; foul-mouthed person
**pum** *interj* bang!
**puma** *m* (zool.) puma, cougar, panther
**pumita** *f* pumice stone
**puna** *f* (Am.) bleak tableland in Andes; (Am.) mountain sickness
**punción** *f* (surg.) puncture
**puncionar** *va* (surg.) to puncture
**puncha** *f* prickle, thorn, sharp point
**punchar** *va* to prick, puncture
**punches** *mpl* (Am.) popcorn
**pundonor** *m* point of honor; dignity, face
**pundonoroso -sa** *adj* punctilious, scrupulous; haughty, dignified
**pungimiento** *m* prick; sting
**pungir §42** *va* to prick; to sting
**pungitivo -va** *adj* pricking; stinging
**punible** *adj* punishable
**punición** *f* punishment
**púnico -ca** *adj* Punic; (fig.) Punic
**punitivo -va** *adj* punitive
**punta** *f* point (*sharp end*); tip, end; butt (*of cigar*); nail; point, cape, headland; horn (*of bull*); tine, prong (*of antlers*); tip (*of tongue*); touch, tinge, trace; souring (*of wine*); (hunt.) pointing; style, graver; **puntas** *fpl* point lace; **de punta** on end; on tiptoe; **de punta en blanco** in full armor; (coll.) in full regalia; **estar de punta (con)** to be at odds (with); **hacer punta** to be or go first; to be opposed; to stand out; to knit; **sacar punta a** to put a point on, to sharpen; (coll.) to give a malicious twist to; **tener en la punta de los dedos** to have at one's finger tips; **punta de combate** war head (*of a torpedo*); **punta de chispa** (elec.) spark point; **punta de diamante** diamond point (*for cutting*); **punta de Europa** Europa Point; **punta de lanza** spearhead; (fig.) spearhead; **punta de París** wire nail; **punta de vidriar** glazier's point
**puntación** *f* pointing (*of Hebrew and Arabic letters*)
**puntada** *f* (sew.) stitch; hint; (Am.) stitch (*in the side*)
**puntal** *m* prop, support; stay, stanchion; elevation; (naut.) depth of hold; (fig.) backing, support; (Am.) bite, snack
**puntapié** *m* kick; **echar a puntapiés** (coll.) to kick out; **mandar a puntapiés** (coll.) to have an ascendancy over
**puntar** *va* to mark with dots or points; to point (*Hebrew or Arabic letters*)
**puntazo** *m* (Am.) jab, stab
**punteado -da** *adj* dotted; *m* dotting; dotted line; plucking the guitar; *f* dotting
**puntear** *va* to dot, to mark with dots or points; to pluck, to play (*a guitar*); to engrave or paint with dots; (sew.) to stitch; *vn* (naut.) to tack
**puntel** *m* pontil, punty
**punteo** *m* emphasis, great stress (*to drive home a point*); dots; (mus.) plucking
**puntera** *f* see **puntero**
**puntería** *f* aim, aiming; markmanship
**puntero -ra** *adj* sharpshooting; *m* pointer; stonecutter's chisel; hand (*of watch, clock, etc.*); punch; head, leader (*of a parade*); (mus.) finger pipe, chanter (*of bagpipe*); *f* toe, toe patch (*on shoe or stocking*); leather tip (*on shoe*); (coll.) kick
**punterola** *f* (min.) miner's pick, poll pick
**puntiagudo -da** *adj* sharp-pointed
**puntilla** *f* brad, finishing nail; narrow lace edging; point (*of fountain pen*); (carp.) tracing point; dagger; **dar la puntilla a** to stick the dagger in; (coll.) to finish off, destroy, ruin; **de** or **en puntillas** on tiptoe; **ponerse de puntillas** (coll.) to stick to one's opinion; **puntilla francesa** finishing nail
**puntillazo** *m* (coll.) kick
**puntillero** *m* puntillero, dagger man (*bullfighter who gives coup de grâce with dagger*)
**puntillo** *m* small point; punctilio; (mus.) dot, point
**puntillón** *m* (coll.) kick
**puntilloso -sa** *adj* punctilious, scrupulous
**puntiseco -ca** *adj* dry at the tips (*said of a plant*)
**puntizón** *m* (print.) frisket hole or mark
**punto** *m* point, dot; stitch, loop (*in knitting*); mesh; jot, mote; cabstand, hackstand; gun sight; hole (*in a belt*); break (*in mesh or net*); punctilio, point of honor; (gram.) period; (math., print. & sport) point; (fig.) point (*place; moment; feature; main idea; purpose; mark or quality*); **a buen punto** opportunely; **al punto** at once, instantly; **a punto** opportunely; ready; **a punto de** on the point of; **a punto fijo** precisely, with certainty; **a punto largo** roughly; **a punto que** just as, just when; **bajar de punto** to decline; **dar en el punto** to hit the nail on the head, find the trouble; **de medio punto** (arch.) semi-circular; **de punto** knitted; by the minute; **de todo punto** completely, entirely; **dos puntos** (gram.) colon; **en buen punto** fortunately; **en punto** sharp, on the dot, exactly, e.g., **son las dos en punto** it is two o'clock sharp; **en punto a** with regard to; **hasta el punto que** to the extent that; **poner los puntos sobre las íes** (coll.) to dot one's i's; **poner punto final a** to wind up, to bring to an end; **subir de punto** to grow, increase; to get worse; **tener a punto** to have ready; **punto capital** crux; **punto ciego** (anat.) blind spot; **punto de admiración** exclamation mark or point; **punto de aguja** knitting, knitwork; **punto de cadeneta** lock stitch; **punto de congelación** freezing point; **punto de costado** sharp pain across the heart; **punto de ebulición** or **ebullición** boiling point; **punto de encaje** lace; **punto de fuga** vanishing point; **punto de fusión** melting point; **punto de ganchillo** crocheting; **punto de gracia** funny side; **punto de honor** point of honor; **punto de la vista** (perspective) vanishing point; **punto de Hungría** herringbone (*in hardwood or tile floor*); **punto de malla** netting, netted fabric; **punto de media** knitwork, stockinet; **punto de mira** aim; center of attraction; **punto de partida** starting point, point of departure; **punto de rocío** (physical chem.) dew point; **punto de saturación** saturation point; **punto de vista** point of view; **¡punto en boca!** mum's the word!; **punto focal** (math.) focal point; **punto interrogante** question mark; **punto menos** almost; **punto menos que** almost; **punto muerto** dead center; (rad.) dead end; (fig.) stalemate, deadlock; **punto por punto** in detail; **puntos cardinales** cardinal points; **puntos suspensivos** suspension points; **puntos y rayas** (telg.) dots and dashes; **punto y coma** (construed as a masculine singular noun in Spanish) semicolon
**puntoso -sa** *adj* full of points; punctilious, scrupulous; haughty, dignified
**puntuación** *f* punctuation; mark, grade (*in school*); (sport) points, scoring
**puntual** *adj* punctual; certain, sure; exact; suitable
**puntualidad** *f* punctuality; certainty, sureness; exactness; suitability
**puntualizado -da** *adj* detailed, circumstantial
**puntualizar §76** *va* to fix in the memory, to fix in one's mind; to detail, to give a detailed account of; to finish, to perfect; to draw up
**puntualmente** *adv* punctually; with precision; in detail
**puntuar §33** *va & vn* to punctuate; (sport) to score
**puntuoso -sa** *adj* punctilious, scrupulous; haughty, dignified
**puntura** *f* puncture, prick; (print.) register point
**punzada** *f* prick; shooting pain; pang (*e.g., of remorse*)
**punzador -dora** *mf* puncher; *f* punching machine
**punzadura** *f* prick, puncture
**punzante** *adj* sharp, pricking; barbed, biting, caustic
**punzaorejas** *m* (*pl:* **-jas**) (ent.) earwig
**punzar §76** *va* to prick, puncture, punch; to sting; to grieve; *vn* to sting
**punzó** *adj invar & m* poppy-red, flaming red

**punzón** *m* punch; pick; graver, burin; budding horn, tenderling; tip (*of horn*); **punzón de trazar** scriber
**puñada** *f* punch; **dar de puñadas a** to strike with the fist, to punch
**puñado** *m* handful; (fig.) handful; **a puñados** in abundance, by handfuls
**puñal** *m* poniard, dagger; deep grief
**puñalada** *f* stab (*with a dagger*); blow, sudden sorrow; **coser a puñaladas** (coll.) to cut to pieces; **puñalada de misericordia** coup de grâce; **puñalada por la espalda** or **puñalada trapera** stab in the back
**puñalejo** *m* small poniard or dagger
**puñalero** *m* maker or seller of poniards or daggers
**puñera** *f* double handful
**puñetazo** *m* punch; bang with the fist; **a puñetazos** with the fists
**puñete** *m* punch; bracelet
**puño** *m* fist; grasp; fistful, handful; handle (*e.g., of umbrella*); hilt; head (*of cane*); punch; cuff; wristband; (naut.) corner (*of sail*); **a puño cerrado** with the fist; firmly; **como un puño** (coll.) whopping big; (coll.) tiny, microscopic; **de puños** strong, valiant; **de su propio puño** or **de su puño y letra** in his own hand; **meter en un puño** (coll.) to flabbergast; **por sus puños** by oneself, on one's own; **ser como un puño** (coll.) to be close-fisted; (coll.) to be small (*in stature*); **tener en un puño** to have (*someone*) scared; **un puño de casa** (coll.) a little bit of a house, a tiny house; **puño de bastón** head of a cane
**puoso -sa** *adj* jagged; rough
**pupa** *f* pimple, pustule; fever blister; (ent.) pupa; child's word to express pain; **pupa coartada** (ent.) coarctate pupa; **pupa libre** (ent.) incomplete pupa; **pupa obtecta** (ent.) true pupa
**pupal** *adj* (ent.) pupal
**pupario** *m* (ent.) puparium
**pupila** *f* see **pupilo**
**pupilaje** *m* pupilage, wardship; boarding house; board (*cost*); boarding (*e.g., of a dog*); (aut.) storage
**pupilar** *adj* pupillary (*pertaining to a ward*); (anat.) pupillary
**pupilero -ra** *mf* boarding-house keeper
**pupilo -la** *mf* boarder; orphan, ward; pupil; *f* (anat.) pupil; **tener pupila** (coll.) to be quick, to be smart
**pupinización** *f* (elec.) Pupin system
**pupitre** *m* writing desk
**puposo -sa** *adj* pimply, pustulous
**pupuso -sa** *adj* (Am.) stubby, chubby; (Am.) swollen; (Am.) proud, haughty; (Am.) rich, wealthy
**puque** *adj* rotten (*egg*); (Am.) sickly
**puquio** *m* (Am.) spring or pool of fresh, clear water
**puré** *m* purée; **puré de patatas** mashed potatoes; **puré de tomates** stewed tomatoes
**purear** *vn* (coll.) to smoke cigars
**pureza** *f* purity
**purga** *f* purge; purgative, physic; drainings; drain valve
**purgación** *f* purge, purgation; **purgaciones** *fpl* (path.) gonorrhea
**purgador -dora** *adj* purging; *mf* purger
**purgante** *adj & m* purgative
**purgar** §59 *va* to purge; to physic; to drain; to purify, refine; to expiate; to control, to check (*passions*); to clear away (*suspicion*); *vn* to drain; to atone; *vr* to take a physic; to drain; to unburden oneself
**purgativo -va** *adj* purgative
**purgatorio -ria** *adj* purgatorial; *m* (theol. & fig.) purgatory; **tener en el purgatorio** to torture, to torment
**puridad** *f* purity; secrecy; **en puridad** openly, frankly; in secret
**purificación** *f* purification
**purificadero -ra** *adj* purifying, cleansing
**purificador -dora** *adj* purifying; *m* (eccl.) purificator; (eccl.) altar napkin
**purificar** §86 *va* to purify; *vr* to purify; to become purified
**Purim** *m* (rel.) Purim
**purina** *f* (chem.) purine
**Purísima** *f* Virgin Mary
**purismo** *m* purism
**purista** *adj* purist, puristic; *mf* purist
**puritanismo** *m* Puritanism
**puritano -na** *adj* puritan; puritanic; Puritan; *mf* puritan; Puritan
**puro -ra** *adj* pure; sheer; clear (*sky*); solid (*gold*); out-and-out, outright; **de puro** completely, totally; **de puro** + *adj* because of being + *adj*; *m* cigar
**púrpura** *f* purple; (poet.) blood; **púrpura de Tiro** Tyrian purple; **púrpura visual** (biochem.) visual purple
**purpurado -da** *adj* purple; *m* (eccl.) cardinal
**purpurar** *va* to purple; to dress in purple
**purpúrea** *f* see **purpúreo**
**purpurear** *vn* to purple, to have a purple tinge
**purpúreo -a** *adj* purple; *f* (bot.) burdock
**purpurino -na** *adj* purple; *f* (chem.) purpurin; bronze powder
**purrela** *f* poor wine, small wine
**purriela** *f* (coll.) junk, piece of junk
**purulencia** *f* purulence or purulency
**purulento -ta** *adj* purulent
**pus** *adj invar* (Am.) puce (*color*); *m* pus
**puse** *1st sg pret ind of* **poner**
**pusilánime** *adj* pusillanimous
**pusilanimidad** *f* pusillanimity
**pústula** *f* (bot. & path.) pustule
**pustulación** *f* pustulation
**pustuloso -sa** *adj* pustular
**puta** *f* whore, harlot
**putaísmo** *m* whoredom, harlotry; brothel
**putañear** *vn* (coll.) to whore around, to chase after lewd women
**putañero** *adj masc* (coll.) whoring, lewd
**putativo -va** *adj* spurious; putative
**putear** *vn* (coll.) var. of **putañear**
**putero** *adj masc* (coll.) var. of **putañero**
**putesco -ca** *adj* (coll.) whorish
**putpurri** *m* (mus.) potpourri, medley
**putrefacción** *f* putrefaction
**putrefactivo -va** *adj* putrefactive
**putrefacto -ta** *adj* rotten, putrid
**putrescente** *adj* putrescent
**putrescible** *adj* putrescible
**putrescina** *f* (biochem.) putrescine
**putridez** *f* putridity, rottenness
**pútrido -da** *adj* putrid, rotten
**puya** *f* goad, steel point; spur (*of cock*); (bot.) puya
**puyazo** *m* jab or wound with a goad; (fig.) jab, dig
**puyo** *m* (Am.) woolen poncho
**puzol** *m* or **puzolana** *f* (geol.) pozzolana

**Q, q** *f* twentieth letter of the Spanish alphabet
**q.** abr. of **que**
**q.b.s.m.** abr. of **que besa su mano**
**q.b.s.p.** abr. of **que besa sus pies**
**q.d.D.g.** abr. of **que de Dios goce**
**q.D.g.** abr. of **que Dios guarde**
**q.D. tenga en s.g.** abr. of **que Dios tenga en su gracia**
**q.e** abr. of **que**
**q.e.g.e.** abr. of **que en gloria esté**
**q.e.p.d.** abr. of **que en paz descanse**
**q.e.s.m.** abr. of **que estrecha su mano**
**q.n** abr. of **quien**
**qq.** abr. of **quintales**
**q.s.g.h.** abr. of **que santa gloria haya**
**quántum** *m* (*pl:* **quanta**) (phys.) quantum
**que** *pron rel* that, which; who, whom; **el que** he who; which, the one which; who, the one who; *adv* than; *conj* that; for, because; let, e.g., **que entre** let him come in; **a que** (coll.) I bet that; **que no** and not; **que no** + *subj* without + *ger;* **que . . . que** whether . . . or
**qué** *adj & pron interr* what, which; what!; what a!; how!; **¿a qué?** why?; **sin qué ni para qué** without rhyme or reason; **¡qué de!** how much!, how many!; **¿qué más da?** what's the difference?; **¿qué tal?** how?; hello, how's everything?
**quebracho** *m* (bot.) quebracho, breakax
**quebrada** *f* see **quebrado**
**quebradero** *m* (obs.) breaker; **quebradero de cabeza** (coll.) worry, concern
**quebradizo -za** *adj* brittle, fragile; frail, delicate
**quebrado -da** *adj* weakened; bankrupt; ruptured; rough, winding; fractional; *mf* bankrupt; *m* (math.) fraction; (Am.) tobacco leaf full of holes; *f* gorge, ravine, gap; failure, bankruptcy; (Am.) brook
**quebrador -dora** *adj* breaking; *mf* breaker; lawbreaker
**quebradura** *f* breaking; fissure, slit; (path.) rupture
**quebraja** *f* crack, slit, fissure
**quebrajar** *va* to crack, to slit, to split
**quebrajoso -sa** *adj* brittle, fragile; full of cracks, splintery
**quebramiento** *m* var. of **quebrantamiento**
**quebrantable** *adj* breakable
**quebrantador -dora** *adj* breaking; crushing; *mf* breaker, crusher; *f* crusher (*machine*)
**quebrantadura** *f* var. of **quebrantamiento**
**quebrantahuesos** *m* (*pl:* **-sos**) (orn.) osprey, sea eagle; (orn.) lammergeier, bearded vulture; (coll.) bore, pest
**quebrantamiento** *m* breaking, breach; fracture, rupture; exhaustion, fatigue
**quebrantaolas** *m* (*pl:* **-las**) old ship used as a breakwater
**quebrantapiedras** *m* (*pl:* **-dras**) (bot.) burstwort
**quebrantar** *va* to break; to break in (*a colt*); to break open; to break out of; to grind, crush; to soften, mollify; (fig.) to break (*a contract, a will, the law, someone's heart*); *vr* to break; to become broken
**quebrantaterrones** *m* (*pl:* **-nes**) (coll.) clodhopper
**quebranto** *m* break, breaking; heavy loss; great sorrow; discouragement
**quebrar §18** *va* to break; to bend, to twist; to crush; to overcome; to temper, soften; to dull, darken (*the countenance*); *vn* to break; to fail; to weaken, give in; **quebrar con** to break with (*e.g., a friend*); *vr* to break; to become broken; to weaken; to become ruptured
**quebrazas** *fpl* flaws or tiny cracks in the blade of a sword
**queche** *m* smack, ketch
**quechemarín** *m* (naut.) coasting lugger
**quechua** *adj & mf* var. of **quichua**
**queda** *f* see **quedo**
**quedada** *f* stay, sojourn; (naut.) lull
**quedar** *vn* to remain; to stay; to be left; to be left over; to stop, leave off; to turn out; to be; to be found, to be located; **quedar a** + *inf* to remain + *ger*, e.g., **quedar a deber** to remain owing; **quedar bien** or **mal** to acquit oneself well or badly; **quedar en** to agree on; **quedar en** + *inf* to agree to + *inf;* **quedar en que** to agree that; **quedar por** or **sin** + *inf* to remain to be + *pp*, e.g., **aún queda más de la mitad del ferrocarril por construir** more than half of the railroad still remains to be built; *vr* to remain; to stay; to stop; to be; to be left; to put up (*e.g., at a hotel*); **quedarse con** to keep, to take; **quedarse tan fresco** (coll.) to show no offense, to be unconcerned
**quedito** *adv* softly, gently
**quedo -da** *adj* quiet, still; gentle; *f* curfew; **quedo** *adv* softly, in a low voice; gropingly; **a quedo** or **de quedo** easy, slowly
**quehacer** *m* work, task, chore
**queja** *f* complaint, lament; whine, moan; (law) complaint
**quejar** *vr* to complain, lament; to whine, moan; **quejarse de** to complain about or of; **quejarse de** + *inf* to complain of + *ger;* **quejarse de haber** + *pp* to complain of having + *pp*
**quejicoso -sa** *adj* complaining, whining, whiny
**quejido** *m* complaint, whine, moan
**quejigal** *m* or **quejigar** *m* grove of gall oaks
**quejigo** *m* (bot.) gall oak
**quejigueta** *f* (bot.) dwarf oak of Morocco and southern Spain (*Quercus humilis*)
**quejilloso -sa** *adj* complaining, whining
**quejoso -sa** *adj* complaining, querulous
**quejumbre** *f* complaining, whine, moan
**quejumbroso -sa** *adj* complaining, whining, whiny
**quela** *f* (zool.) chela
**quelícero** *m* (ent.) chelicera
**quelite** *m* (bot.) pigweed
**quelonio -nia** *adj & m* (zool.) chelonian
**quelpo** *m* (bot.) kelp
**quema** *f* fire, burning; **a quema ropa** point-blank; **de quema** distilled; **hacer quema** (Am.) to hit the mark; **huir de la quema** to get out of danger; to dodge responsibility
**quemada** *f* see **quemado**
**quemadero -ra** *adj* for burning, to be burned; *m* stake (*for burning convicts*); incinerator (*for burning dead animals or damaged food*)
**quemado -da** *adj* burned; burnt out; (Am.) angry; (Am.) colored, dark; *m* burnt brush, burnt thicket; (coll.) fire, something burning, something burnt; **oler a quemado** (coll.) to smell of fire; *f* burnt brush, burnt thicket; (Am.) fire
**quemador -dora** *adj* burning; incendiary; *mf* burner; *m* burner; **quemador de gas** gas burner; **quemador de petróleo** oil burner
**quemadura** *f* burning; burn; sunburn; scald; smut (*plant disease*)
**quemajoso -sa** *adj* burning, smarting
**quemar** *va* to burn; to scald; to kindle, set on fire; to parch, scorch; to frostbite; to sell too cheap; *vn* to burn, be hot; *vr* to burn; to be burning up; (coll.) to fret, become impatient; (coll.) to be warm, be hot (*to be about to find something sought for*)
**quemarropa; a quemarropa** point-blank

**quemazón** *f* burning; burn; intense heat; (coll.) itch, smarting; (coll.) cutting remark; (coll.) pique, anger; (hum.) bargain sale; (Am.) mirage on the pampas
**quenopodiáceo -a** *adj* (bot.) chenopodiaceous
**quenopodio** *m* (bot.) chenopod, goosefoot
**quepis** *m* (*pl:* **-pis**) (mil.) kepi
**quepo** *1st sg pres ind of* **caber**
**querargirita** *f* (mineral.) cerargyrite
**queratina** *f* (zool.) keratin
**queratógeno -na** *adj* keratogenous
**querella** *f* complaint; quarrel, dispute; (law) complaint
**querellado -da** *mf* (law) defendant
**querellador -dora** or **querellante** *adj & mf* (law) complainant
**querellar** *vr* to complain; to whine; (law) to file a complaint, bring suit
**querelloso -sa** *adj* querulous; quarrelsome
**querencia** *f* fondness, liking; attraction; love of home; haunt (*of animals*); (taur.) favorite spot or refuge (*of a bull in the arena*); (coll.) favorite spot, perch
**querencioso -sa** *adj* homing, home-returning; favorite (*haunt or spot*); (coll.) affectionate
**querendón -dona** *adj* (Am.) affectionate
**querer** *m* love, affection; liking, fondness; §70 *va* to wish, want, desire; to like; to love; **como quiera** anyhow, anyway; **como quiera que** whereas; since, inasmuch as; no matter how; **cuando quiera** any time; **donde quiera** anywhere; **que quiera, que no quiera** whether he wishes to or not; **sin querer** unwillingly; unintentionally; **querer bien** to love; **querer más** to prefer; *v aux* **querer** + *inf* to wish, want or desire to + *inf;* will + *inf;* to be about to, to be trying to + *inf*, e.g., **quiere llover** it is trying to rain; **querer decir** to mean; **querer más** + *inf* to prefer to + *inf*, would rather + *inf*
**queresa** *f* var. of **cresa**
**querido -da** *adj* dear; *mf* lover; paramour; (coll.) dearie; *f* mistress
**quermes** *m* (*pl:* **-mes**) (ent.) kermes insect; kermes (*dyestuff*); **quermes mineral** (chem.) kermes mineral
**quermés** *f* or **quermese** *f* bazaar (*for some charitable purpose*); village or country fair
**querocha** *f* var. of **cresa**
**querochar** *vn* to lay eggs (*said of bees and other insects*)
**Queronea** *f* Chaeronea
**queroseno** *m* var. of **keroseno**
**querré** *1st sg fut ind of* **querer**
**quersoneso** *m* chersonese; **el quersoneso de Tracia** the Chersonese (*Gallipoli Peninsula*)
**querub** *m* or **querube** *m* (poet.) cherub
**querúbico -ca** *adj* cherubic
**querubín** *m* (Bib., f.a. & theol.) cherub
**querva** *f* var. of **cherva**
**quesadilla** *f* cheese cake; sweet pastry
**quesear** *vn* to make cheese
**quesera** *f* see **quesero**
**quesería** *f* cheese-making season; cheese factory; cheese shop or store
**quesero -ra** *adj* caseous, cheesy; *mf* cheesemonger; cheesemaker; *f* cheese board; cheese mold; cheese tub; cheese dish; cheese factory
**quesillo** *m* heart of artichoke; **quesillo helado** brick ice cream
**quesiqués** *m* var. of **quisicosa**
**queso** *m* cheese; **queso de bola** Edam cheese; **queso de cerdo** headcheese; **queso de Edam** Edam cheese; **queso de Gruyère** Swiss cheese; **queso de higos** (Am.) fig paste; **queso de Holanda** Dutch cheese; **queso de Limburgo** Limburger; **queso de Roquefort** Roquefort cheese; **queso helado** brick ice cream; **queso parmesano** Parmesan cheese
**queteno** *m* (chem.) ketene
**quetona** *f* (chem.) ketone
**quetosa** *f* (chem.) ketose
**quetzal** *m* or **quetzale** *m* (orn.) quetzal; quetzal (*monetary unit of Guatemala*)
**quevedos** *mpl* pince-nez
**quezal** *m* (orn.) quetzal
**quiá** *interj* oh, no!
**quianti** *m* Chianti (*wine*)
**quiasma** *m* (rhet.) chiasmus; (anat. & biol.) chiasma
**quicial** *m* hinge-pole; hanging stile; pivot hole (*for hinge-pole*)
**quicialera** *f* hinge-pole; hanging stile
**quicio** *m* pivot hole (*for hinge-pole*); doorjamb; (Am.) front steps (*of a house*); **fuera de quicio** out of order; **sacar de quicio** to put out of order; **sacar de quicio** to unhinge (*a person*)
**quichua** *adj* Quechuan; *mf* Quechua; *m* Quechuan (*language*)
**quid** *m* quiddity, gist, core
**quídam** *m* (coll.) so-and-so; (coll.) nobody
**quiebra** *f* break; crack, fissure; damage, loss; bankruptcy
**quiebrahacha** *f* (bot.) breakax
**quiebro** *m* bending back at the waist; (mus.) trill; (taur.) dodge
**quien** *pron rel* who, whom; he who, she who; someone who, anyone who
**quién** *pron interr* who, whom; **¿Quién es quién?** Who's Who (*book of biographies*); **quién . . . quién** one . . . another
**quienquiera** *pron indef* anyone, anybody; **quienquiera que** whoever, whomever
**quién vive** *m* (mil.) challenge
**quiescencia** *f* (gram.) quiescence
**quiescente** *adj* (gram.) quiescent
**quietación** *f* quieting
**quietador -dora** *adj* quieting, calming; *mf* quieter
**quietar** *va & vr* var. of **aquietar**
**quiete** *f* hour of recreation (*after eating*)
**quietismo** *m* quietism
**quietista** *adj & mf* quietist
**quieto -ta** *adj* quiet, still, calm; virtuous
**quietud** *f* quiet, stillness, calm
**quijada** *f* (anat.) jaw, jawbone; (mach.) jaw
**quijal** *m* or **quijar** *m* (anat.) jaw; (anat.) grinder, molar tooth
**quijarudo -da** *adj* big-jawed
**quijera** *f* cheek strap; cheek of crossbow
**quijo** *m* (min.) quartz (*gold or silver ore*)
**quijones** *m* (*pl:* **-nes**) (bot.) aromatic herb (*Scandix australis*)
**quijotada** *f* (coll.) quixotism, quixotic deed
**quijote** *m* (arm.) cuisse; croup (*of horse*); (fig.) Quixote (*quixotic person*)
**quijotear** *vn* to act quixotically
**quijotería** *f* quixotry, quixotism
**quijotesco -ca** *adj* quixotic
**quijotil** *adj* of the Quixote (*the romance*)
**quijotismo** *m* quixotism; ridiculous pride or vanity
**quilatador** *m* assayer
**quilatar** *va* var. of **aquilatar**
**quilate** *m* carat; **quilates** *mpl* (fig.) weight in gold; **por quilates** (coll.) in small amounts, sparingly
**quilatera** *f* pearl gauge
**quilífero -ra** *adj* chyliferous
**quilificación** *f* (physiol.) chylification
**quilificar** §86 *va & vr* (physiol.) to chylify
**quilma** *f* sack, bag
**quilo** *m* (physiol.) chyle; kilo (*kilogram*); **sudar el quilo** (coll.) to slave, to be a drudge
**quilográmetro** *m* var. of **kilográmetro**
**quilogramo** *m* var. of **kilogramo**
**quilolitro** *m* var. of **kilolitro**
**quilométrico -ca** *adj* var. of **kilométrico**
**quilómetro** *m* var. of **kilómetro**
**quiloso -sa** *adj* chylous
**quilla** *f* (aer., naut. & bot.) keel; (orn.) breastbone; **dar de quilla** (naut.) to keel over; **falsa quilla** (naut.) false keel; **poner en quilla** (naut.) to put on the stocks
**quillay** *m* (bot.) soapbark tree (*of Chile*)
**quillotranza** *f* (coll.) sorrow, bitterness
**quillotrar** *va* (coll.) to incite, stir up; (coll.) to make love to; (coll.) to charm, captivate; (coll.) to consider, think over; (coll.) to adorn, deck; *vr* (coll.) to fall in love; (coll.) to deck oneself out; (coll.) to complain
**quillotro** *m* (coll.) incitement; (coll.) sign, token; (coll.) love making, love affair; (coll.) problem, puzzler; (coll.) adornment, finery; (coll.) friend, favorite
**quimafila** *f* (bot.) pipsissewa

**quimbombó** *m* (*pl:* **-boes**) var. of **quingombó**
**quimera** *f* (myth., f.a. & fig.) chimera; quarrel, dispute
**quimérico -ca** or **quimerino -na** *adj* chimeric or chimerical
**quimerista** *adj* visionary; quarrelsome; *mf* visionary; wrangler
**quimerizar** §76 *vn* to indulge in chimeras
**quimiatría** *f* chemiatry
**químico -ca** *adj* chemical; *mf* chemist; *f* chemistry; **química del carbono** organic chemistry; **química física** physical chemistry; **química fisiológica** physiological chemistry; **química inorgánica** inorganic chemistry; **química mineral** or **orgánica** organic chemistry
**quimicultura** *f* tank farming
**quimificación** *f* (physiol.) chymification
**quimificar** §86 *va* (physiol.) chymify
**quimiocirugía** *f* chemosurgery
**quimiosfera** *f* chemosphere
**quimiosíntesis** *f* chemosynthesis
**quimiotaxis** *f* (biol.) chemotaxis
**quimioterapia** *f* chemotherapy
**quimismo** *m* chemism
**quimista** *m* var. of **alquimista**
**quimo** *m* (physiol.) chyme
**quimógrafo** *m* kymograph
**quimoso -sa** *adj* chymous
**quimón** *m* kimono cotton
**quimono** *m* kimono
**quimosina** *f* (biochem.) rennin
**quina** *f* (pharm.) cinchona, Peruvian bark; keno (*in lotto*); **quinas** *fpl* quinas (*arms of Portugal*); double fives (*in dice*)
**quinal** *m* (naut.) preventer shroud
**quinaquina** *f* var. of **quina**
**quinario -ra** *adj* quinary; *m* quinary; five-day devotion
**quincajú** *m* (*pl:* **-júes**) var. of **quincayú**
**quincalla** *f* hardware; costume jewelry
**quincallería** *f* hardware business; hardware store; hardware factory; gift shop
**quincallero -ra** *mf* hardware merchant; hardware maker
**quincayú** *m* (*pl:* **-yúes**) (zool.) kinkajou
**quince** *adj* fifteen; **las quince** three P.M.; *m* fifteen; fifteenth (*in dates*); **dar quince y falta a, dar quince y raya a** (coll.) to be a thousand times better than or superior to
**quinceañero -ra** *adj* fifteen-year-old; *mf* fifteen-year-old person
**quinceavo -va** *adj* & *m* var. of **quinzavo**
**quincena** *f* see **quinceno**
**quincenal** *adj* biweekly, fortnightly
**quincenario -ria** *adj* biweekly, fortnightly; *mf* person who spends one fortnight after another in jail
**quinceno -na** *adj* fifteenth; *mf* fifteen-month-old mule; *f* two weeks, fortnight; two weeks' pay; (mus.) fifteenth (*interval and organ stop*)
**quincineta** *f* (orn.) lapwing
**quinconce** *m* (Am.) var. of **quincunce**
**quincuagena** *f* fifty
**quincuagenario -ria** *adj* & *mf* quinquagenarian
**quincuagésimo -ma** *adj* & *m* fiftieth; *f* (eccl.) Quinquagesima
**quincunce** *m* (hort.) quincunx
**quindécimo -ma** *adj* & *m* fifteenth
**quindenial** *adj* fifteen-year
**quindenio** *m* fifteen-year period, fifteen years
**quinescopio** *m* var. of **kinescopio**
**quingentésimo -ma** *adj* & *m* five-hundredth
**quingo** *m* (Am.) zigzag, twist, turn
**quingombó** *m* (*pl:* **-boes**) (bot.) okra or gumbo (*plant and fruit*)
**quiniela** *f* pelota game of five; soccer lottery; numbers game; daily double
**quinientos -tas** *adj* & *m* five hundred
**quinina** *f* (chem.) quinine
**quinismo** *m* (path.) cinchonism
**quino** *m* kino; (bot.) cinchona; (pharm.) cinchona, Peruvian bark
**quínoa** *f* (bot.) South American pigweed (*Chenopodium quinoa*)
**quínola** *f* four of a kind (*at cards*); **quínolas** *fpl* reversi (*old card game*)
**quinolillas** *fpl* var. of **quínolas**
**quinqué** *m* student lamp, oil lamp, Argand lamp; (coll.) insight, perspicacity
**quinquefolio** *m* (bot.) cinquefoil
**quinquenal** *adj* quinquennial, five-year
**quinquenervia** *f* (bot.) ribwort
**quinquenio** *m* quinquennium, five-year period
**quinquerreme** *f* quinquereme
**quinquillería** *f* var. of **quincallería**
**quinquillero -ra** *mf* var. of **quincallero**
**quinta** *f* see **quinto**
**quintacolumnista** *mf* fifth columnist
**quintador** *m* draft or induction official
**quintaesencia** *f* quintessence
**quintaesenciar** *va* to refine, purify; to extract the quintessence of
**quintal** *m* quintal (*46 kg.*); **quintal métrico** quintal (*100 kg.*)
**quintalada** *f* (naut.) primage, hat money
**quintaleño -ña** *adj* capable of holding a quintal
**quintalero -ra** *adj* weighing a quintal
**quintana** *f* villa, country house
**quintante** *m* (astr.) quintant
**quintañón -ñona** *adj* & *mf* (coll.) centenarian
**quintar** *va* to draw (*one*) out of five; (mil.) to draft, to induct; to plow for the fifth time; *vn* to reach the fifth day (*said, especially, of the moon*); to bid a fifth higher (*at an auction*)
**quintería** *f* farmhouse, grange
**quinterna** *f* keno (*in lotto*)
**quinterno** *m* quinternion (*section of five sheets of paper*); keno (*in lotto*)
**quintero** *m* farmer; farm hand
**quinteto** *m* (mus.) quintet; quintet (*group of five*)
**Quintiliano** *m* Quintilian
**quintilo** *m* quintile
**quintilla** *f* five-line stanza of eight syllables and two rhymes; any five-line stanza with two rhymes
**quintillizo -za** *mf* (coll.) quint, quintuplet
**quintillo** *m* game of ombre played by five players
**quintillón** *m* British quintillion
**quintín** *m* quintin (*fine fabric*); **armar la de San Quintín** to raise a rumpus
**quinto -ta** *adj* fifth; *m* fifth; lot (*of ground*); pasture; (mil.) draftee; *f* villa, country house; (mil.) draft, induction; five of a kind (*at cards*); (mus.) fifth; **ir a quintas** to be drafted; **redimirse de las quintas** to be exempted from the draft
**quintuplicación** *f* quintuplication
**quintuplicar** §86 *va* & *vr* to quintuple
**quíntuplo -pla** *adj* & *m* quintuple, fivefold
**quinua** *f* var. of **quínoa**
**quinzavo -va** *adj* & *m* fifteenth
**quiñón** *m* share; lot, plot (*of arable land*)
**quiñonero** *m* part owner
**quío -a** *adj* & *mf* Chian; **Quío** *f* Chios (*island*)
**quiosco** *m* kiosk, summerhouse; stand; **quiosco de periódicos** newsstand; **quiosco de música** bandstand; **quiosco de necesidad** public toilet, comfort station
**quiosquero** *m* newsstand man
**quipos** *mpl* quipu (*colored cords and knots used by ancient Peruvians instead of writing*)
**quiquiriquí** *m* (*pl:* **-quíes**) cock-a-doodle-doo; (coll.) cock of the walk
**quiragra** *f* (path.) gout in the hand
**quirinal** *adj* Quirinal; (*cap.*) *m* Quirinal
**quirófano** *m* operating room
**quirografía** *f* chirography
**quirográfico -ca** *adj* chirographic
**quirógrafo -fa** *mf* chirographer; *m* chirograph
**quiromancia** or **quiromancía** *f* chiromancy, palmistry
**quiromántico -ca** *adj* chiromantic or chiromantical, of palmistry, of palmists; *mf* chiromancer, palmist
**Quirón** *m* (myth.) Chiron
**quiropodia** *f* chiropody
**quiropodista** *mf* chiropodist
**quiropráctico -ca** *adj* chiropractic; *mf* chiropractic, chiropractor; *f* chiropractic (*method of treatment*)
**quiropractor** *m* chiropractor
**quiropraxia** *f* chiropractic (*method of treatment*)

**quiróptero -ra** *adj & m* (zool.) chiropteran
**quiroteca** *f* glove
**quirúrgico -ca** *adj* surgical
**quirurgo** *m* surgeon
**quiscal** *m* (orn.) grackle
**quiscamote** *m* (bot.) cuckoopint
**quise** *1st sg pret ind of* **querer**
**quisicosa** *f* (coll.) puzzler (*thing which puzzles*)
**quisquilla** *f* trifle, triviality, quibble; (zool.) shrimp; **quisquillas** *fpl* hairsplitting; **dejarse de quisquillas** to stop fussing; **pararse en quisquillas** to bicker, to make a fuss over nothing
**quisquillosidad** *f* triviality; touchiness; fastidiousness; hairsplitting
**quisquilloso -sa** *adj* trifling; touchy; fastidious; hairsplitting
**quistar** *vr* to get along well, to be well liked
**quiste** *m* (bot., path. & zool.) cyst
**quístico -ca** *adj* (path.) cystic
**quisto -ta** *adj* liked; **bien quisto** well-liked; well-received; **mal quisto** disliked; unwelcome
**quita** *f* see **quito**
**quitación** *f* salary, income; (law) acquittance, release
**quitador -dora** *adj* removing; *mf* remover
**quitaguas** *m* (*pl:* **-guas**) umbrella
**quitaipón** *m* var. of **quitapón**
**quitalodos** *m* (*pl:* **-dos**) scraper, foot scraper
**quitamanchas** *mf* (*pl:* **-chas**) clothes cleaner, spot remover (*person*); *m* clothes cleaner, spot remover (*material*)
**quitameriendas** *f* (*pl:* **-das**) (bot.) meadow saffron, autumn crocus
**quitamiedos** *m* (*pl:* **-dos**) handrail, railing, rope
**quitamotas** *mf* (coll.) fawner, flatterer, bootlicker
**quitanieve** *m* or **quitanieves** *m* (*pl:* **-ves**) snowplow
**quitanza** *f* quittance
**quitapelillos** *mf* (*pl:* **-llos**) (coll.) fawner, flatterer, lickspittle
**quitapesares** *m* (*pl:* **-res**) (coll.) solace, comfort; (coll.) outdoor relaxation
**quitapiedras** *m* (*pl:* **-dras**) pilot, cowcatcher
**quitapintura** *f* paint remover
**quitapón** *m* headstall ornament for mules; **de quitapón** detachable, removable
**quitar** *va* to remove; to take away; to dispel; to clear (*the table*); to free; to save (*work or effort*); to take (*time*); to parry (*in fencing*); to prevent; **quitar** + *inf* to keep (*someone*) from + *ger;* **quitar algo a algo** to take something off something, to remove something from something, e.g., **quitaron dos carros al tren en Medina del Campo** they took two cars off the train at Medina del Campo; **quitar algo a uno** to remove something from someone; to take something away from someone; *vr* to take off (*hat, article of clothing, etc.*); to tip (*one's hat*); to come out (*said of a spot or stain*); to give up (*a vice*); to withdraw; **de quita y pon** detachable, removable; **¡quita allá!** or **¡quite allá!** don't tell me!
**quitasol** *m* parasol
**quitasolillo** or **quitasolillos** *m* (*pl:* **-llos**) (bot.) marsh pennywort
**quitasueño** *m* (coll.) worry, anxiety (*that dispels sleep*)
**quite** *m* removal; hindrance; dodge, dodging; parry (*in fencing*); (taur.) attracting the bull from a man in danger
**quiteño -ña** *adj* (pertaining to) Quito; *mf* native or inhabitant of Quito
**quitina** *f* (chem.) chitin
**quitinoso -sa** *adj* chitinous
**quito -ta** *adj* free, exempt; *f* (law) acquittance, release
**quitón** *m* (hist. & zool.) chiton
**quitrín** *m* (Am.) two-wheel carriage
**quizá** or **quizás** *adv* maybe, perhaps
**quórum** *m* (*pl:* **-rum**) quorum

# R

**R, r** *f* twenty-first letter of the Spanish alphabet
**R.** abr. of **reprobado** (*en examen*), **respuesta, Reverencia** & **Reverendo**
**raba** *f* cod roe used as bait
**rabada** *f* hind quarter, rump
**rabadán** *m* head shepherd
**rabadilla** *f* (anat.) coccyx; (orn.) uropygium
**rabanal** *m* radish patch
**rabanero -ra** *adj* (coll.) short (*skirt*); (coll.) shameless, indecent; *mf* radish seller; *f* shameless woman, indecent woman; hors d'oeuvre dish, small oval dish
**rabanete** *m* small radish
**rabanillo** *m* sharpness (*of turning wine*); (bot.) jointed charlock; (coll.) sullenness; (coll.) eagerness, keenness
**rabaniza** *f* radish seed
**rábano** *m* (bot.) radish; **tomar el rábano por las hojas** (coll.) to be entirely wrong, to be on the wrong track; **rábano picante** or **rusticano** (bot.) horseradish; **rábano silvestre** (bot.) jointed charlock
**rabárbaro** *m* var. of **ruibarbo**
**rabazuz** *m* licorice extract
**rabear** *vn* to wag the tail; (naut.) to vibrate at the stern
**rabel** *m* (mus.) rebec; (hum.) backside
**rabelesiano -na** *adj* & *mf* Rabelaisian
**rabeo** *m* wagging the tail
**rabera** *f* tail end, breech; tang (*of a utensil*); handle (*of crossbow*); chaff
**raberón** *m* topped part of tree trunk
**rabí** *m* (*pl*: **-bíes**) rabbi
**rabia** *f* anger, rage; (path.) rabies; **tener rabia a** (coll.) to have a grudge against
**rabiacana** *f* (bot.) wake-robin
**rabiar** *vn* to rage, to rave; to get mad; to moan with pain; to have rabies; **a rabiar** like the deuce; **picar que rabia** to sting like the deuce; **rabiar por** to be dying for; **rabiar por** + *inf* to be dying to + *inf*
**rabiatar** *va* to tie together by the tail
**rabiazorras** *m* (coll.) east wind
**rabicán** apocopated form of **rabicano**
**rabicano -na** *adj* white-tailed
**rábico -ca** *adj* (med. & vet.) rabic
**rabicorto -ta** *adj* short-tailed; wearing a short dress
**rábido -da** *adj* var. of **rabioso**; *f* Moroccan monastery
**rabieta** *f* (coll.) tantrum, conniption
**rabihorcado** *m* (orn.) frigate bird
**rabijunco** *m* (orn.) tropic bird
**rabilargo -ga** *adj* long-tailed; *m* (orn.) blue magpie
**rabillo** *m* (bot.) leafstalk; (bot.) flower stalk; mildew spots (*on cereals*); (bot.) bearded darnel; tip; **con el rabillo del ojo** out of the corner of one's eye
**rabínico -ca** *adj* rabbinic or rabbinical
**rabinismo** *m* rabbinism
**rabinista** *mf* rabbinist
**rabino** *m* rabbi
**rabioles** *mpl* (cook.) ravioli
**rabión** *m* rapids (*in a river*)
**rabioso -sa** *adj* rabid, mad
**rabisalsera** *adj fem* (coll.) pert, flippant
**rabiza** *f* tip of fishing rod; (naut.) short piece of rope, end of rope
**rabo** *m* tail; (bot.) flower stalk; (fig.) tail, train; **con el rabo del ojo** out of the corner of one's eye; **rabo de junco** (orn.) red-billed tropic bird; **rabo de zorra** foxtail; (bot.) foxtail; **rabos de gallo** (meteor.) cocktail, mare's-tail (*cirrous clouds*); **rabo verde** (Am.) old rake
**rabón -bona** *adj* bobtail; *f* (Am.) canteen woman; **hacer rabona** (coll.) to play hooky
**rabopelado** *m* (zool.) opossum
**raboseada** or **raboseadura** *f* mussing, fretting, fraying, tampering
**rabosear** *va* to muss, fret, fray, tamper with
**raboso -sa** *adj* raggedy, frayed
**rabotada** *f* swish of the tail; (coll.) coarse remark, coarseness
**rabotear** *va* to cut off the tail of
**raboteo** *m* cropping of sheep's tails; tail-cropping time
**rabudo -da** *adj* long-tailed, large-tailed
**rábula** *m* pettifogger
**racamenta** *f* or **racamento** *m* (naut.) parral or parrel
**racel** *m* (naut.) run
**racial** *adj* racial
**racima** *f* grapes left on vines (*at vintage*)
**racimal** *adj* in bunches, in clusters
**racimar** *va* to pick (*a vine*) of grapes left after vintage; *vr* to cluster, to bunch
**racimo** *m* bunch; cluster; (bot.) raceme
**racimoso -sa** *adj* bunchy, full of bunches; (bot.) racemose
**racimudo -da** *adj* with large bunches
**raciocinación** *f* ratiocination
**raciocinar** *vn* to ratiocinate
**raciocinio** *m* reason; argument; ratiocination
**ración** *f* ration; portion; allowance; (mil.) ration; (eccl.) cathedral prebend; **ración de hambre** starvation wages, pittance
**racionabilidad** *f* reason, intelligence
**racional** *adj* rational; (math.) rational; *m* (eccl.) rational
**racionalidad** *f* rationality
**racionalismo** *m* rationalism
**racionalista** *adj* rationalistic; *mf* rationalist
**racionalización** *f* (com. & math.) rationalization
**racionalizar** §76 *va* (math.) to rationalize
**racionamiento** *m* rationing
**racionar** *va* to ration; (mil.) to ration
**racionero** *m* distributor of rations; (eccl.) prebendary
**racionista** *mf* person who lives on an allowance or ration; *m* (theat.) utility man
**racismo** *m* racism
**racista** *adj* & *mf* racist
**racha** *f* (naut.) squall, gust of wind; (coll.) streak, streak of luck; split, crack; large chip (*of wood*)
**rada** *f* (naut.) road, roadstead
**Radamanto** *m* (myth.) Rhadamanthus
**radar** *m* (elec.) radar
**radaroscopio** or **radarscopio** *m* radarscope
**radiación** *f* radiation
**radiactividad** *f* radioactivity
**radiactivo -va** *adj* radioactive
**radiado -da** *adj* radiate; (bot. & zool.) radiate; *m* (zool.) radiate
**radiador -dora** *adj* radiating; *m* radiator
**radial** *adj* radial; (Am.) (pertaining to) radio; *m* (math.) radian
**radián** *m* (math.) radian
**radiante** *adj* radiant; (phys.) radiant; (fig.) radiant (*joyful, smiling*); *m* (astr.) radiant; (math.) radian
**radiar** *va* to radio; to broadcast; to irradiate; *vn* to radiate
**radicación** *f* (math.) evolution; taking root
**radical** *adj* radical; (bot., chem., math., philol. & pol.) radical; *mf* (pol.) radical; *m* (chem., math. & philol.) radical; **radical hidroxilo** (chem.) hydroxyl radical
**radicalismo** *m* radicalism

**radicante** *adj* rooted; situated; **radicante en** (mil.) based on
**radicar** §86 *vn* to take root; to be located; *vr* to take root; to settle, settle down
**radicícola** *adj* (zool.) radicolous, radicicolous
**radicoso -sa** *adj* radicular, rooty
**radícula** *f* (bot.) radicle
**radiestesia** *f* dowsing
**radiestesista** *adj* dowsing; *mf* dowser
**radio** *m* edge, outskirts; radius (*e.g., of action*); spoke, rung (*of wheel*); (anat. & geom.) radius; (chem.) radium; *m & f* radio (*broadcasting; set; message*); **en la radio** on the radio
**radío -a** *adj* wandering
**radioactividad** *f* var. of **radiactividad**
**radioactivo -va** *adj* var. of **radiactivo**
**radioaficionado -da** *mf* radio amateur, radio fan, radio ham
**radioastronomía** *f* radioastronomy
**radiobiología** *f* radiobiology
**radiobrújula** *f* radio compass
**radiocarbono** *m* (phys.) radioactive carbon
**radiocomunicación** *f* radio communication
**radiodiagnosis** *f* or **radiodiagnóstico** *m* X-ray diagnosis
**radiodifundir** *va & vn* to broadcast, to radiobroadcast
**radiodifusión** *f* broadcasting, radiobroadcasting
**radiodifusor -sora** *adj* radiobroadcasting; *f* radiobroadcasting station
**radiodirigido -da** *adj* radio-controlled
**radioelemento** *m* (chem.) radioactive element, radioelement; **radioelemento indicador** (phys.) tracer element
**radioemisora** *f* radiobroadcasting station
**radioescucha** *mf* radio listener; radio monitor
**radioestación** *f* radio station
**radiofaro** *m* radio beacon
**radiofonema** *m* (rad. & telv.) commercial (*paid advertisement*)
**radiofonía** *f* (phys. & rad.) radiophony
**radiofónico -ca** *adj* radiophonic
**radiófono** *m* (phys. & rad.) radiophone
**radiofonógrafo** *m* radiophonograph
**radiofoto** *f* radiophoto
**radiofrecuencia** *f* (rad.) radio frequency
**radiofusión** *f* (Am.) broadcasting, radiobroadcasting
**radiogoniometría** *f* radiogoniometry
**radiogoniómetro** *m* radiogoniometer
**radiografía** *f* radiograph; radiography
**radiografiar** §90 *va* to radiograph; to wireless
**radiográfico -ca** *adj* radiographic
**radiograma** *m* radiogram
**radiogramófono** *m* radiophonograph
**radiogramola** *f* radiophonograph
**radioguía** *f* radio range beacon
**radioisótopo** *m* radioisotope
**radiolario** *m* (zool.) radiolarian
**radiolocalización** *f* radiolocation
**radiología** *f* radiology
**radiólogo -ga** *mf* radiologist
**radiómano -na** *mf* (coll.) radio fan
**radiomecánico** *m* radio serviceman
**radiomensaje** *m* radio message
**radiometría** *f* radiometry
**radiómetro** *m* radiometer
**radioonda** *f* radio wave
**radiopaco -ca** *adj* radiopaque
**radioperturbación** *f* (rad.) jamming
**radioquímica** *f* radiochemistry
**radiorrecepción** *f* reception, radio reception
**radiorreceptor -tora** *adj* receiving, radio-receiving; *m & f* radio receiver, receiving set
**radiorreparaciones** *fpl* radio repairs
**radiorreparador** *m* radio repairman
**radioscopia** *f* radioscopy
**radiosensitivo -va** *adj* radiosensitive
**radioseñal** *f* radio signal
**radioso -sa** *adj* radiant
**radiosonda** *m & f* (meteor.) radiosonde
**radioteatro** *m* theater of the air
**radiotecnia** *f* radiotechnology
**radiotécnico** *m* radiotechnician
**radiotelefonear** *va* to radiotelephone
**radiotelefonía** *f* radiotelephony
**radioteléfono** *m* radiotelephone
**radiotelegrafía** *f* radiotelegraphy, wireless
**radiotelegrafiar** §90 *va* to radiotelegraph, to wireless
**radiotelegrafista** *mf* wireless operator
**radiotelégrafo** *m* radiotelegraph
**radiotelescopio** *m* radio telescope
**radioterapia** *f* radiotherapy
**radiotermia** *f* radiothermy
**radiotorio** *m* (chem.) radiothorium
**radiotransmisión** *f* radio transmission
**radiotransmisor** *m* radio transmitter
**radiotrón** *f* radiotron
**radiovisión** *f* radiovision, television
**radioyente** *mf* radio listener
**radón** *m* (chem.) radon
**rádula** *f* (zool.) radula
**raedera** *f* scraper (*tool*)
**raedizo -za** *adj* easily scraped or scratched
**raedor -dora** *adj* scraping; *mf* scraper; *m* strickle
**raedura** *f* scraping; **raeduras** *fpl* scrapings
**raer** §71 *va* to scrape, scrape off; to smooth, to level; to wipe out, to extirpate; *vr* to become worn, become frayed, wear away
**rafa** *f* (arch.) buttress; irrigation ditch; (vet.) crack in hoof; (min.) skewback (*cut in rock*)
**Rafael** *m* Raphael
**rafaelesco -ca** *adj* Raphaelesque
**ráfaga** *f* gust, puff; gust of wind; burst (*e.g., of machine-gun fire*); light cloud (*indicating a change in the weather*); flash of light; (rad.) jingle
**rafania** *f* (path.) raphania
**rafe** *m* (arch.) eaves; (anat. & bot.) raphe
**rafear** *va* to reinforce with buttresses
**rafia** *f* (bot.) raffia (*palm and fiber*)
**Raf.l** abr. of **Rafael**
**raglán** *m* raglan
**ragua** *f* top of sugar cane
**rahez** *adj* (*pl:* **-heces**) low, vile, contemptible
**raiceja** *f* rootlet
**raicilla** *f* (bot.) radicle; rootlet
**raicita** *f* (bot.) radicle
**raído -da** *adj* threadbare; barefaced
**raigal** *adj* (pertaining to a) root
**raigambre** *f* intertwined roots; (fig.) deep-rootedness
**raigo** *1st sg pres ind of* **raer**
**raigón** *m* large root; (anat.) root (*of tooth*); **raigón del Canadá** (bot.) Kentucky coffee tree
**rail** *m* (*pl:* **raíles**) rail (*of a track*)
**raimiento** *m* scraping; barefacedness, brazenness
**Raimundo** *m* Raymond
**raíz** *f* (*pl:* **-íces**) root; (bot., gram. & math.) root; **a raíz de** close to the root of; even with; right after, hard upon; **cortar de raíz** to nip in the bud; **de raíz** by the root; completely; **echar raíces** to take root; **raíz cuadrada** (math.) square root; **raíz cúbica** (math.) cube root; **raíz de remolacha** beet root
**raja** *f* crack, split; splinter, chip; slice; coarse cloth; **hacer rajas** to divide up; **hacerse rajas** (coll.) to break to pieces
**rajá** *m* (*pl:* **-jaes**) rajah
**rajabroqueles** *m* (*pl:* **-les**) (coll.) bully
**rajadera** *f* cleaver
**rajadillo** *m* sliced sugared almonds
**rajadizo -za** *adj* easily split
**rajadura** *f* crack, split
**rajar** *va* to split, to cleave; to crack; to slice; *vn* (coll.) to boast, to lie about one's feats; (coll.) to chatter, to jabber; *vr* to split, to cleave; to crack; (slang) to give up, to back down, to break one's promise
**rajatabla; a rajatabla** (coll.) at any cost, regardless; (Am.) promptly, vigorously
**rajeta** *f* varicolored light cloth
**rajuela** *f* small crack; rough stone
**ralea** *f* kind, quality; (coll.) breed, ilk; prey (*of birds of prey*)
**ralear** *vn* to become sparse, become thin; to yield thin bunches (*said of grapevines*); to show one's real make-up or nature, to be true to form
**raleón -ona** *adj* predatory, raptorial
**raleza** *f* sparsity, thinness
**ralo -la** *adj* sparse, thin; *m* (orn.) rail
**ralladera** *f* or **rallador** *m* (cook.) grater
**ralladura** *f* mark left by grater; gratings

**rallar** *va* to grate; (coll.) to grate on, annoy
**rallo** *m* grater; scraper; rasp; sprinkling nozzle (*of water pot*); unglazed porous jug (*for cooling water by evaporation*)
**rallón** *m* arrow with a cutting crosshead (*to be shot from a crossbow*)
**rama** *f* branch, bough; (fig.) branch (*e.g., of a family, of learning*); (print.) chase; **andarse por las ramas** (coll.) to beat about the bush; **en rama** crude, raw; in the grain; (b.b.) in sheets, unbound
**ramada** *f* foliage, branches; arbor; (Am.) covering, shed
**Ramadán, el** Ramadan
**ramaje** *m* foliage, branches
**ramal** *m* strand (*e.g., of a rope*); branch; (rail.) branch line; halter
**ramalazo** *m* lash; mark left by a lash; mark left by a blow in the face; mark or spot (*caused by disease or sickness*); sharp pain; blow, sudden sorrow
**ramalear** *vn* to be easily led by the halter
**ramazón** *f* cut branches, pile of branches
**rambla** *f* dry ravine; tenter, tentering machine; boulevard, avenue
**ramblar** *m* confluence of dry ravines
**ramblazo** or **ramblizo** *m* bed of a torrent
**rameado -da** *adj* branched, flowered (*design*)
**rameal** or **rámeo -a** *adj* ramal, rameal
**ramera** *f* whore, harlot
**ramería** *f* brothel; whoredom
**ramial** *m* ramie patch, ramie field
**ramificación** *f* ramification
**ramificar** §86 *va & vr* to ramify
**ramilla** *f* sprig, twig; (fig.) small help, slight boost
**ramillete** *m* bouquet; (bot.) cluster; epergne, centerpiece; flower piece; pretty dish of sweets; collection; **ramillete de Constantinopla** (bot.) sweet william
**ramilletero -ra** *mf* maker or seller of bouquets; *m* flower vase; potted flower; *f* flower girl
**ramina** *f* ramie (*fiber*)
**ramio** *m* (bot.) ramie
**ramito** *m* small branch
**ramiza** *f* cut branches; work made of branches
**ramnáceo -a** *adj* (bot.) rhamnaceous
**ramo** *m* branch, limb; cluster, bouquet; string of onions; line (*of goods, business, etc.*); branch (*e.g., of a science*); touch, slight attack (*of a disease*); **ramo de olivo** olive branch
**ramojo** *m* brushwood, small wood, dead wood
**ramón** *m* browse; trimmed twigs; (bot.) hackberry; (*cap.*) *m* Raymond
**ramonear** *vn* to trim twigs; to browse
**ramoneo** *m* trimming twigs; trimming time; browsing
**ramoso -sa** *adj* ramous, branchy
**rampa** *f* ramp; cramp; (aer.) apron
**rampante** *adj* (her.) rampant
**rampiñete** *m* (arti.) vent drill or gimlet
**ramplón -plona** *adj* heavy, coarse (*said of shoes*); vulgar, common; *m* calk (*of horseshoe*)
**ramplonería** *f* coarseness; vulgarity
**rampojo** *m* grape stem (*with grapes removed*)
**rampollo** *m* (hort.) cutting
**Ramsés** *m* Rameses
**ramulla** *f* small branches cleaned from a tree; brushwood, small wood, dead wood
**rana** *f* (zool. & rail.) frog; **ranas** *fpl* (path.) ranula; **no ser rana** (coll.) to be adept, to be a past master; **rana arbórea** (zool.) tree frog; **rana de zarzal** (zool.) peeper; **rana marina** or **pescadora** (ichth.) angler; **rana toro** (zool.) bullfrog; **rana voladora** (zool.) flying frog
**ranacuajo** *m* var. of **renacuajo**
**rancajada** *f* uprooting
**rancajo** *m* splinter in the flesh
**ranciar** *va & vr* var. of **enranciar**
**rancidez** *f* or **ranciedad** *f* rankness, rancidity, staleness; oldness, antiquity
**rancio -cia** *adj* rank, rancid, stale; old (*wine*); old, ancient; (fig.) old, old-fashioned; *m* rancidness; rancid bacon; greasiness of cloth
**rancioso -sa** *adj* var. of **rancio**
**rancheadero** *m* settlement of huts
**ranchear** *va* (Am.) to sack, pillage; *vn & vr* to build huts, form a settlement
**rancheo** *m* (Am.) sacking, pillage
**ranchería** *f* settlement, hamlet
**ranchero** *m* messman; (Am.) rancher, ranchman
**rancho** *m* mess; messmates; camp; meeting, gathering; thatched hut; (Am.) ranch; (naut.) stock of provisions; **hacer rancho** (coll.) to make room; **hacer rancho aparte** (coll.) to go one's own way, to be a lone wolf; **rancho de Santa Bárbara** (naut.) rudder chamber
**randa** *f* lace trimming, netting; *m* (coll.) pickpocket
**randado -da** *adj* trimmed with lace
**randera** *f* lacemaker, lacewoman
**Randolfo** *m* Randolph
**ranero** *m* frogland, frog pond
**rangífero** *m* (zool.) reindeer
**rango** *m* rank; class, nature; (Am.) quality (*high social standing*); (Am.) pomp, splendor
**rangua** *f* socket, pivot bearing
**Rangún** *f* Rangoon
**raní** *f* (*pl:* **-níes**) ranee, rani
**ranilla** *f* frog (*of hoof*)
**ránula** *f* (path. & vet.) ranula
**ranunculáceo -a** *adj* (bot.) ranunculaceous
**ranúnculo** *m* (bot.) ranunculus, crowfoot; (bot.) field buttercup, blister plant
**ranura** *f* groove, slot; **a ranura y lengüeta** groove-and-tongue
**ranurador -dora** *adj* grooving; *f* grooving machine, slotting machine
**ranurar** *va* to groove, to slot
**ranzón** *m* ransom money
**raña** *f* thicket, copse; hook for catching octopuses and mollusks
**raño** *m* oyster rake; (ichth.) hogfish, scorpion fish
**rapa** *f* olive blossom
**rapabarbas** *m* (*pl:* **-bas**) (coll.) barber
**rapabolsas** *m* (*pl:* **-sas**) (coll.) pickpocket
**rapaceja** *f* lassie
**rapacejo** *m* laddie; flounce, edging
**rapacería** *f* rapacity; childishness, childish prank
**rapacidad** *f* rapacity
**rapado** *m* (Am.) shave, close haircut
**rapador -dora** *adj* scraping; *mf* scraper; *m* (coll.) barber
**rapadura** *f* shave, close haircut
**rapagón** *m* stripling, beardless young fellow
**rapamiento** *m* var. of **rapadura**
**rapante** *adj* thieving; (her.) rampant
**rapapiés** *m* (*pl:* **-piés**) snake, serpent (*kind of firecracker*)
**rapapolvo** *m* (coll.) dressing-down, sharp reprimand
**rapar** *va* to shave; to shave close, to crop; to scrape; (coll.) to snatch, filch; *vr* to shave; (Am.) to lead (*e.g., an easy life*)
**rapavelas** *m* (*pl:* **-las**) (slang) sexton, altar boy
**rapaz** (*pl:* **-paces**) *adj* thievish; rapacious; raptorial; *m* young boy, lad; **rapaces** *fpl* (zool.) Raptores
**rapaza** *f* young girl, lass
**rapazada** *f* childishness, childish prank
**rapazuelo -la** *mf* urchin, youngster
**rape** *m* (coll.) quick shave, quick haircut; (ichth.) angler; **al rape** cut very close
**rapé** *m* snuff (*tobacco*)
**rapidez** *f* rapidity
**rápido -da** *adj* rapid; *m* (rail.) express; **rápidos** *mpl* rapids (*in a river*)
**rapiego -ga** *adj* of prey (*said of a bird*)
**rapingacho** *m* (Am.) cheese omelet
**rapiña** *f* rapine; robbery, thievery
**rapiñador -dora** *adj* stealing, plundering; *mf* robber, plunderer
**rapiñar** *va* (coll.) to steal, to plunder
**rapista** *m* (coll.) barber
**rapo** *m* turnip (*root*)
**rapónchigo** *m* (bot.) rampion
**rapóntico** *m* var. of **ruipóntico**
**raposa** *f* (zool.) fox; female fox; (coll.) fox (*person*); **raposa de mar** (ichth.) thresher, thresher shark
**raposear** *vn* to be foxy, to be sly as a fox

**raposeo** *m* foxiness, cunning
**raposera** *f* fox hole, fox burrow
**raposería** *f* foxiness, cunning
**raposino -na** *adj* (pertaining to the) fox, foxy
**raposo** *m* male fox; (coll.) fox, foxy fellow; (coll.) easy-going, slipshod fellow; **raposo ferrero** (zool.) blue fox
**raposuno -na** *adj* var. of **raposino**
**rapsoda** *m* (hist.) rhapsodist
**rapsodia** *f* (mus. & lit.) rhapsody
**rapsódico -ca** *adj* rhapsodic or rhapsodical
**rapsodista** *m* (lit.) rhapsodist
**raptar** *va* to abduct; to kidnap
**rapto** *m* rapture; abduction; kidnaping; faint, swoon
**raptor -tora** *mf* kidnaper; *m* abductor, ravisher
**rapuzar** §76 *va* to trim, prune
**raque** *m* beachcombing; arrack (*liquor*); **andar** or **ir al raque** to go beachcombing
**raquear** *vn* to beachcomb
**Raquel** *f* Rachel
**raqueo** *m* beachcombing
**raqueril** *adj* beachcombing
**raquero -ra** *adj* piratical; *m* pirate; beachcomber; dock rat
**raqueta** *f* (sport) racket; (sport) battledore; (sport) battledore and shuttlecock, badminton; racket, snowshoe; rake (*of croupier*); (bot.) wall rocket
**raquetazo** *m* stroke (*with a racket*)
**raquetero -ra** *mf* racket maker or seller
**raquetón** *m* (sport) crosse (*racket used in lacrosse*)
**raquialgia** *f* (path.) rachialgia
**raquídeo -a** *adj* rachidian
**raquis** *m* (*pl:* **-quis**) (anat. & bot.) rachis
**raquítico** *adj* (path.) rachitic, rickety; rickety, flimsy, weak, miserable
**raquitis** *f* (path.) rachitis, rickets
**raquitismo** *m* (path.) rickets
**raquitomía** *f* (surg.) rachitomy
**raquítomo** *m* (surg.) rachitome
**rara** *f* see **raro**
**raramente** *adv* rarely, seldom; oddly, strangely
**rarefacción** *f* rarefaction
**rarefacer** §55 (has no compound tenses) *va & vr* to rarefy
**rarefacto -ta** *adj* rarefied, thin
**rareza** *f* rarity; rareness; queerness, funniness, oddness, strangeness; curiosity; peculiarity
**raridad** *f* rarity; (phys.) rarity, thinness, tenuity
**rarificar** §86 *va & vr* to rarefy
**raro -ra** *adj* rare; odd, strange; thin, sparse; *f* (orn.) South American passerine (*Phytotoma rara*)
**ras** *m* evenness; **a ras** close, even, flush; **a ras de** even with, flush with; **ras con ras** or **ras en ras** flush, on a level; grazing
**rasa** *f* see **raso**
**rasadura** *f* leveling with a strickle
**rasamente** *adv* clearly, openly
**rasante** *adj* grazing; flush; *f* grade line
**rasar** *va* to strickle, to smooth off with a strickle; to graze, to skim; *vr* to clear up
**rascacielos** *m* (*pl:* **-los**) skyscraper
**rascacio** *m* (ichth.) scorpene
**rascadera** *f* scraper; (coll.) currycomb
**rascador** *m* scraper; rasp; huller, sheller; ornamental hairpin
**rascadora** *f* street sweeper
**rascadura** *f* scraping; scratching, scratch
**rascalino** *m* (bot.) dodder
**rascamiento** *m* var. of **rascadura**
**rascamoño** *m* ornamental hairpin; (bot.) zinnia
**rascapiés** *m* (*pl:* **-piés**) scraper, foot scraper
**rascar** §86 *va* to scrape; to scuff; to scratch; to scrape clean; **llevar** or **tener con que rascar** (coll.) to be sorely hurt; *vn* (Am.) to itch; *vr* to pick (*a sore*); (Am.) to get drunk
**rascatripas** *mf* (*pl:* **-pas**) (coll.) scraper (*fiddler*)
**rascazón** *f* itch, itching
**rascle** *m* coral-fishing gear
**rascón -cona** *adj* sharp, acrid; *m* (orn.) rail; **rascón de agua** (orn.) crake
**rascuñar** *va* var. of **rasguñar**
**rascuño** *m* var. of **rasguño**
**rasera** *f* strike, strickle; (carp.) small plane; (cook.) spatula, turner
**rasero** *m* strike, strickle; **medir por un rasero** to treat with strict impartiality
**rasete** *m* satinet
**rasgado -da** *adj* wide-open, bright (*window*); wide-open (*mouth*); large (*eyes*); (Am.) outspoken; (Am.) generous; *m* tear, rip, rent
**rasgador -dora** *adj* tearing, ripping
**rasgadura** *f* tearing, tear, rip
**rasgar** §59 *va* to tear; to rip; *vr* to become torn
**rasgo** *m* flourish, stroke (*of pen*); trait, characteristic; feat, deed; flash of wit, bright remark; **rasgos** *mpl* features; **a grandes rasgos** in bold strokes
**rasgón** *m* tear, rip, rent
**rasgueado** *m* var. of **rasgueo**
**rasguear** *va* to thrum, to twang (*e.g., a guitar*); *vn* to make flourishes (*with a pen*)
**rasgueo** *m* thrumming, twanging (*e.g., on a guitar*)
**rasguñar** *va* to scratch; to sketch, outline
**rasguño** *m* scratch; sketch, outline
**rasguñuelo** *m* slight scratch
**rasilla** *f* camleteen; floor tile
**rasión** *f* shaving; grating
**raso -sa** *adj* smooth, flat, level, even; clear, cloudless; common, plain (*e.g., soldier*); backless (*chair*); skimming the ground; (coll.) brazen, shameless; *m* flat country; satin; **al raso** in the open air, in the open country; *f* thinness, thin spot (*in a fabric*); tableland; satin
**rasoliso** *m* satin
**raspa** *f* beard (*of ear of corn*); stalk, stem (*e.g., of a bunch of grapes*); spine, backbone (*of a fish*); cob (*with kernels removed*); shell, rind; hair or thread (*caught on tip of a pen*)
**raspador** *m* scraper
**raspadora** *f* street sweeper
**raspadura** *f* scraping; erasure; (Am.) pan sugar; **raspaduras** *fpl* scrapings
**raspaje** *m* (surg.) scraping
**raspajo** *m* grape stem (*with grapes removed*)
**raspamiento** *m* scraping
**raspante** *adj* abrasive; sharp (*wine*)
**raspar** *va* to scrape, scrape off; to scratch, scratch out; to graze; to bite (*said, e.g., of wine*); to take away, steal
**raspear** *vn* to scratch (*said of a pen*)
**raspilla** *f* (bot.) madwort, German madwort
**raspón** *m* (Am.) scratch, bruise; (Am.) scolding; (Am. coll.) involvement, complicity; (Am.) peasant's straw hat; **de raspón** askance
**rasposo -sa** *adj* rough; (Am.) stingy
**rasqueta** *f* scraper, wall scraper, shave hook; (Am.) currycomb
**rasquetear** *va* (Am.) to currycomb
**rastacueril** *adj* upstart
**rastel** *m* railing
**rastillador -dora** *mf* var. of **rastrillador**
**rastillar** *va* var. of **rastrillar**
**rastra** *f* rake; harrow; drag (*sledge for conveying heavy bodies*); string of dried fruit, string of onions; something trailing; track, trail; outcome entailing a penalty; shadow (*inseparable companion*); (naut.) drag, grapnel; **a rastra, a rastras** or **a la rastra** dragging; unwillingly; **caminar a rastras** to crawl; **llevar a rastra** to drag, to drag along; **pescar a la rastra** to trawl
**rastracueros** *m* (*pl:* **-ros**) big hide operator; upstart; boaster, show-off; sharper, adventurer
**rastrallar** *vn* var. of **restallar**
**rastreador -dora** *adj* tracking; *m* dredge; (nav.) mine sweeper
**rastrear** *va* to trail, to track, to trace; to scent; to drag; to dredge; to check into; to sell (*meat*) at the wholesale market; (nav.) to sweep (*e.g., a harbor for mines*); *vn* to rake; to skim the ground, to fly low
**rastrel** *m* var. of **ristrel**
**rastreo** *m* dragging, dredging; tracking (*e.g., of a satellite*)
**rastrero -ra** *adj* dragging, trailing; low-flying; low-hanging; abject, groveling, cringing; base, low; (bot.) creeping; *m* slaughterhouse employee; *f* (naut.) lower studding sail
**rastrillada** *f* rakeful; (Am.) track, footprint
**rastrillador -dora** *mf* raker; *f* rake (*on wheels*)
**rastrillaje** *m* raking

**rastrillar** *va* to rake; to hatchel, to comb (*flax, hemp, etc.*)
**rastrillo** *m* rake; hatchel, hackle, flax comb; battery (*of flintlock*); ward (*of key or lock*); rack (*of manger*); grating, iron gate; (fort.) portcullis; (rail.) cowcatcher
**rastro** *m* rake; harrow; trace, vestige; track, trail; scent; slaughterhouse; wholesale meat market; **el Rastro** the rag fair (*of Madrid*); **rastro de condensación** (aer.) contrail, vapor trail
**rastrojal** *m* stubble field
**rastrojar** *va* (agr.) to stubble, to clear of stubble
**rastrojera** *f* stubble field; stubble pasture; stubble-pasturing time or season
**rastrojo** *m* (agr.) stubble
**rasura** *f* shaving; scraping; **rasuras** *fpl* argol, crude tartar
**rasuración** *f* shaving; scraping
**rasurar** *va & vr* to shave
**rata** *f* (zool.) rat; female rat; female mouse; **rata blanca** (zool.) white rat; **rata de agua** (zool.) water rat; **rata de alcantarilla** (zool.) brown rat; **rata de campo** (zool.) meadow rat; **rata del trigo** (zool.) hamster; **rata de monte** or **rata silvestre** (zool.) vesper mouse; *m* (coll.) sneak thief
**ratafía** *f* ratafia or ratafee
**ratania** *f* (bot.) rhatany (*plant and root*)
**rataplán** *m* rub-a-dub
**rata por cantidad** *adv* pro rata
**ratear** *va* to decrease proportionately; to apportion, to distribute proportionately; to filch, to snitch; *vn* to crawl, to creep
**ratel** *m* (zool.) ratel
**rateo** *m* apportionment
**rateramente** *adv* basely, vilely
**ratería** *f* baseness, vileness, meanness; petty theft; petty thievery
**ratero -ra** *adj* thievish; dragging, trailing; low-flying; base, vile; *mf* sneak thief, pickpocket
**ratificación** *f* ratification
**ratificar** §86 *va* to ratify
**ratigar** §59 *va* to fasten the load in (*a cart*) with a rope
**rátigo** *m* cartload
**ratina** *f* ratiné (*fabric*)
**Ratisbona** *f* Ratisbon
**rato** *m* short time, short while, little while; nice time; long time; male rat; **a ratos** from time to time; **a ratos perdidos** in spare time, in one's leisure hours; **buen rato** pleasant time; (coll.) large amount; **de rato en rato** from time to time; **largo rato** a long time, a long while; **pasar el rato** (coll.) to waste one's time; **pasar un mal rato** to have a wretched time; **un rato** awhile
**ratón** *m* (zool.) mouse; (naut.) rock that rubs and cuts cables; **el ratón Miguelito** Mickey Mouse; **ratón almizclero** (zool.) muskrat; **ratón casero** (zool.) house mouse; **ratón de archivo** or **ratón de biblioteca** (coll.) bookworm (*person*); **ratón de campo** (zool.) field mouse
**ratona** *f* female mouse
**ratonar** *va* to eat (*e.g., cheese, bread*) full of holes (*said of a mouse*); *vr* to get sick from eating mice (*said of a cat*)
**ratonero -ra** *adj* (pertaining to a) mouse, mousy; *f* mousetrap; mousehole; nest of mice; **caer en la ratonera** (fig.) to fall into the trap
**ratonesco -ca** or **ratonil** *adj* (pertaining to a) mouse, mousy
**rauco -ca** *adj* (poet.) raucous, harsh, rough
**raudal** *m* stream, torrent; sudden abundance, plenty
**raudo -da** *adj* rapid, swift, impetuous; (poet.) whistling (*wind*)
**ravenala** *f* (bot.) traveler's tree
**ravioles** *mpl* var. of **rabioles**
**raya** *f* stripe; ray (*fine line*); stroke; dash (*in printing, writing, and telegraphy*); crease (*of trousers*); part (*in hair*); boundary line, limit; firebreak; mark, score; (arti.) rifle groove, spiral groove; (ichth.) ray; (phys.) line (*of spectrum*); **a rayas** striped; **doble raya vertical** (print.) parallels; **hacerse la raya** to part one's hair; **pasar de la raya** or **de raya** (fig.) to go too far; **tener a raya** to keep within bounds; **tres en raya** see **juego del tres en raya; raya espinosa** (ichth.) thornback; **rayas de Fraunhofer** (phys.) Fraunhofer lines
**rayadillo** *m* striped cotton duck
**rayado -da** *adj* striped; *m* ruling (*of paper*); rifling
**rayador** *m* (orn.) skimmer; (Am.) umpire; (Am.) storekeeper of company store
**rayano -na** *adj* bordering; borderline
**rayar** *va* to rule, to line (*paper*); to stripe; to scratch, score, mark; to cross out; to underscore; to rifle; *vn* to border; to stand out; to begin, arise, come forth (*said of the dawn, day, sun, light*); **rayar con** to border on; to be equal to, to match; **rayar en** to border on
**rayo** *m* ray, beam; lightning, flash of lightning; thunderbolt; spoke (*of wheel*); (fig.) thunderbolt, stroke of lightning; (fig.) wit (*person*); (fig.) live wire (*person*); (slang) eye; **echar rayos** (coll.) to blow up, hit the ceiling; **rayo lunar** moonbeam; **rayos alfa** (phys.) alpha rays; **rayos beta** (phys.) beta rays; **rayos canales** (phys.) canal rays; **rayos catódicos** (phys.) cathode rays; **rayos cósmicos** (phys.) cosmic rays; **rayos gama** (phys.) gamma rays; **rayos infrarrojos** (phys.) infrared rays; **rayo solar** or **rayo de sol** sunbeam; **rayos ultravioletas** (phys.) ultraviolet rays; **rayos X** X rays; **rayos y truenos** thunder and lightning; **rayo textorio** weaver's shuttle; **rayo violeta** violet ray; *1st sg pres ind of* **raer**
**rayón** *m* rayon
**rayoso -sa** *adj* striped
**rayuela** *f* pitching pennies
**rayuelo** *m* (orn.) snipe
**raza** *f* race; breed, strain; quality; crack, slit; ray of light (*coming through a crack*); light stripe (*in a fabric*); cleft in horse's hoof; **de raza** thoroughbred; **raza amarilla** yellow race; **raza blanca** white race; **raza cobriza** brown race; **raza negra** black race; **raza roja** red race
**razado -da** *adj* woven with light stripes
**rázago** *m* burlap, sackcloth
**razón** *f* reason; right, justice; account, story; rate (*quantity measured in proportion to something else*); (math.) ratio; **a razón de** at the rate of; **con razón o sin ella** right or wrong; rightly or wrongly; **dar la razón a** to agree with, to approve; **dar razón** to give information; **dar razón de** to give an account of; **en razón a** or **de** with regard to; **hacer la razón** to answer or return a toast; to join at table; **meter en razón** to bring to reason; **meterse en razón** to listen to reason; **no tener razón** to be wrong; **perder la razón** to lose one's reason, go out of one's mind; to hurt one's cause; **tener razón** to be right; **tomar razón de** to enter in the ledger, to record; **razón de estado** reason of state; **razón de masas** mass ratio; **razón de pie de banco** silly reason; **razón de ser** raison d'être; **razón directa** (math.) direct ratio; **razón geométrica** geometric ratio; **razón inversa** (math.) inverse ratio; **razón social** firm, firm name, trade name
**razonable** *adj* reasonable; fair, fair-sized
**razonablejo -ja** *adj* (coll.) reasonable, fair, moderate
**razonado -da** *adj* reasoned, reasoned out; itemized
**razonador -dora** *adj* reasoning; *mf* reasoner
**razonamiento** *m* reasoning
**razonar** *va* to reason, reason out; to itemize; *vn* to reason
**razzia** *f* razzia
**R.**[bí] abr. of **recibí**
**R.D.** abr. of **Real Decreto**
**Rda. M.** abr. of **Reverenda Madre**
**Rdo. P.** abr. of **Reverendo Padre**
**R.**[e] abr. of **récipe**
**re-** *prefix* (coll.) very, extremely, e.g., **rebién** very well; **redifícil** very difficult
**rea** *f* & **Rea** *f* see **reo**
**reabierto -ta** *pp of* **reabrir**
**reabrir** §17, 9 *va & vr* to reopen

**reacción** *f* reaction; (rad.) regeneration; **reacción en cadena** (phys.) chain reaction; **reacción reversible** (chem.) reversible reaction
**reaccionar** *vn* to react
**reaccionario -ria** *adj & mf* reactionary
**reacio -cia** *adj* obstinate, stubborn, fractious
**reacomodo** *m* readjustment
**reacondicionamiento** *m* reconditioning, overhauling
**reacondicionar** *va* to recondition, to overhaul
**reactancia** *f* (elec.) reactance
**reactivación** *f* reactivation
**reactivar** *va* to reactivate
**reactivo -va** *adj* reactive; *m* (chem.) reagent
**reactor** *m* (elec. & phys.) reactor; **reactor atómico** (phys.) atomic reactor; **reactor de cría** (phys.) breeder reactor; **reactor generador de energía** (phys.) power reactor; **reactor nuclear** (phys.) nuclear reactor
**reactor-generador** *m* (phys.) breeder reactor
**reactualizar §76** *va* to revive, to revitalize
**readaptar** *va* to readapt
**readmitir** *va* to readmit
**reafilar** *va* to resharpen, to regrind
**reafirmación** *f* reaffirmation
**reafirmar** *va* to reaffirm
**reagravación** *f* renewed worsening, worsening anew
**reagravar** *va* to make worse again; *vr* to get worse again
**reagrupar** *va & vr* to regroup
**reagudo -da** *adj* very sharp, keen, acute
**reajuste** *m* readjustment
**real** *adj* real; royal; fine, beautiful, handsome, splendid, first-class; royalist; *m* king's tent, general's tent (*in the field*); camp, army camp; fairground; real (*old Spanish coin; Spanish money of account equal to a quarter of a peseta*); **alzar el real** or **los reales** to break camp; **asentar los reales** to encamp; **sentar el real** or **los reales** to settle; to become entrenched
**reala** *f* var. of **rehala**
**realce** *m* embossment, raised work, relief; enhancement, lustre, splendor; emphasis; (paint.) high light; **bordar de realce** to embroider in relief; (fig.) to embroider, to exaggerate
**realegrar** *vr* to be overjoyed
**realejo** *m* hand organ
**realengo -ga** *adj* (feud.) royal; unappropriated (*land*)
**realera** *f* queen cell
**realeza** *f* royalty
**realidad** *f* reality; truth, sincerity; **en realidad** actually, in reality; **en realidad de verdad** truly, in truth; **hecho realidad** come true, e.g., **un sueño hecho realidad** a dream come true
**realimentación** *f* (elec.) feedback
**realismo** *m* realism; royalism
**realista** *adj* realistic; royalistic; (coll.) realistic (*practical*); *mf* realist; royalist; (coll.) realist (*practical person*)
**realizable** *adj* realizable, attainable; salable
**realización** *f* fulfillment, realization; accomplishment, achievement; production; sale, sellout
**realizador** *m* (mov.) producer
**realizar §76** *va* to fulfill; to carry out, accomplish; to sell, sell out; *vn* to realize (*to sell property for ready money*); *vr* to become fulfilled; to be carried out
**realquilar** *va & vn* to sublet
**realzar §76** *va* to raise, elevate; to emboss; to heighten, set off, enhance; to emphasize; (paint.) to make stand out, to brighten up
**reamar** *va* to love dearly
**reanimar** *va* to reanimate, revive, restore; *vr* to reanimate, revive, recover one's spirits
**reanudación** *f* renewal, resumption
**reanudar** *va* to renew, to resume; *vr* to be or become renewed or resumed
**reaparecer §34** *vn* to reappear
**reaparición** *f* reappearance
**reapertura** *f* reopening
**reapretar §18** *va* to press or squeeze again; to press hard, to squeeze hard
**reaprovisionar** *va* to resupply, to replenish
**rearar** *va* to plow over, plow again
**rearmamento** *m* var. of **rearme**
**rearmar** *va & vr* to rearm
**rearme** *m* rearmament
**reasegurar** *va* to reinsure
**reaseguro** *m* reinsurance
**reasentamiento** *m* resettlement
**reasentar §18** *va* to resettle
**reasumir** *va* to reassume, to resume
**reasunción** *f* reassumption, resumption
**reata** *f* rope or strap used to keep animals in single file; single file; front mule; (naut.) woolding; (Am.) rope, lasso; **de reata** in single file; (coll.) in blind submission; (coll.) right away
**reatadura** *f* tying again; tying tight; tying in single file
**reatar** *va* to tie again, to rebind; to reattach; to tie tight; to tie in single file
**reato** *m* (theol.) remaining sin (*after pardon*)
**reaventar §18** *va* to winnow again
**reavituallar** *va & vr* to revictual
**reavivar** *va* to revive
**rebaba** *f* burr, fin, rough seam, rough edge; flange, border
**rebabar** *vr* to ooze out
**rebaja** *f* rebate; lowering; diminution
**rebajado** *m* soldier on inactive service
**rebajador** *m* rabbeting plane; (phot.) bath used to tone down contrasts; **rebajador de rayos** spokeshave
**rebajamiento** *m* lowering; diminution, reduction; deduction; deflation (*of a person's opinion of himself*)
**rebajar** *va* to lower; to diminish, reduce; to underbid; to rebate, discount; to deflate (*a person; a person's pride*); (paint.) to tone down; (arch.) to depress (*an arch*); (carp.) to rabbet; (carp.) to scarf, shave down; *vr* to stoop; to humble oneself; to become deflated; to be relieved of military service; (paint.) to become toned down; **rebajarse a** + *inf* to stoop to + *inf*, to condescend to + *inf*
**rebajo** *m* rabbet, groove; offset, recess
**rebalaje** *m* stream, current
**rebalsa** *f* pool, puddle; (path.) stagnated humor
**rebalsar** *va* to dam, dam back; *vn* to become dammed; *vr* to become dammed; to be held up, become checked; to pile up, accumulate
**rebalse** *m* damming; stagnation
**rebanada** *f* slice
**rebanador -dora** *adj* slicing; *mf* slicer; *f* slicing machine
**rebanar** *va* to slice; to slice off; to cut (*something*) through
**rebanco** *m* (arch.) upper socle
**rebanear** *va* (coll.) to slice
**rebañadera** *f* grapnel
**rebañadura** *f* var. of **arrebañadura**
**rebañar** *va* to gather up; to eat up
**rebañego -ga** *adj* gregarious, herd
**rebaño** *m* flock; (fig.) flock
**rebañuelo** *m* small flock
**rebarbativo -va** *adj* surly, crabbed, forbidding
**rebasadero** *m* place for passing; (naut.) safe place for passing
**rebasar** *va* to exceed, go beyond; to overflow; (naut.) to sail past; *vn* (Am.) to escape, avoid danger; **rebasar de** (naut.) to sail past, sail beyond
**rebate** *m* fight, encounter
**rebatible** *adj* refutable; vulnerable
**rebatimiento** *m* beating; repulsion; resistance; rebuttal, refutation; rebate
**rebatiña** *f* grabbing, scramble; **andar a la rebatiña** (coll.) to scramble
**rebatir** *va* to beat again, beat hard; to repel, drive back; to check; to resist; to strengthen, reinforce; to rebut, refute; to rebate, deduct; to parry (*in fencing*)
**rebato** *m* alarm, call to arms; (fig.) alarm, excitement; (mil.) surprise attack
**rebautizar §76** *va* to rebaptize; (coll.) to rebaptize (*to give a new name to*)
**Rebeca** *f* Rebecca; (*l.c.*) *f* cardigan
**rebeco** *m* (zool.) chamois
**rebelar** *vr* to revolt, rebel; to resist; to break away
**rebelde** *adj* rebellious; stubborn; *m* rebel; (law) defaulter

**rebeldía** *f* rebelliousness; defiance, stubbornness; (law) default
**rebelión** *f* rebellion, revolt
**rebelón -lona** *adj* balky, restive
**rebellín** *m* var. of **revellín**
**rebencazo** *m* lash, blow with a whip
**rebenque** *m* whip (*for flogging galley slaves*); (naut.) ratline; (Am.) riding whip
**rebién** *adv* (coll.) very well
**rebina** *f* (agr.) third earthing-up
**rebinar** *va* (agr.) to earth up for the third time; *vn* (prov.) to meditate
**rebisabuela** *f* great-great-grandmother
**rebisabuelo** *m* great-great-grandfather
**rebisnieta** *f* great-great-granddaughter
**rebisnieto** *m* great-great-grandson
**reblandecer** **§34** *va & vr* to soften
**reblandecimiento** *m* softening; **reblandecimiento cerebral** (path.) softening of the brain
**rebobinar** *va* to rewind
**rebocillo** or **rebociño** *m* mantilla; shawl
**rebollar** *m* or **rebolledo** *m* growth of Turkey oaks
**rebollidura** *f* flaw in the bore of a gun
**rebollo** *m* (bot.) Turkey oak; (dial.) tree trunk
**rebolludo -da** *adj* thick-set; shapeless, irregular
**rebombar** *vn* to resound
**reboño** *m* mud stopped up in tailrace
**reborde** *m* flange, rim, collar
**rebosadero** *m* overflow, overflow pipe; spillway
**rebosadura** *f* or **rebosamiento** *m* overflow, overflowing
**rebosante** *adj* overflowing
**rebosar** *va* to overflow with, burst with (*e.g., joy*); to cause to overflow; *vn* to overflow, run over; to abound, be in abundance; **rebosar de** or **en** to overflow with, burst with (*e.g., joy*); to be rich in (*e.g., oil*); to have an abundance of (*e.g., money*); *vr* to overflow, run over
**rebotación** *f* (coll.) annoyance, worry, perturbation
**rebotadera** *f* nap-raising comb
**rebotadura** *f* bouncing; rebounding
**rebotar** *va* to bend (*the end or point of something*) back or over; to repel; to teasel; to change or alter in color or quality; (coll.) to annoy, worry, upset; *vn* to bounce; to bounce back, to rebound; *vr* to change in color or quality; to become annoyed, worried, upset
**rebote** *m* bounce; rebound; bump (*of airplane in rough weather*); **de rebote** indirectly
**rebotica** *f* back room (*of a drugstore; of any store*)
**rebotín** *m* second growth of mulberry leaves
**rebozar** **§76** *va* to muffle up (*one's face*); to cover with batter; to disguise (*bad news; evil intentions*); *vr* to muffle up, muffle oneself up
**rebozo** *m* muffling; muffler; shawl; disguise; **de rebozo** secretly, hiddenly; **sin rebozo** openly, frankly
**rebramar** *vn* to bellow again, to bellow loudly; to bellow back, answer with a bellow
**rebramo** *m* answering bellow
**rebrotar** *vn* to sprout, to shoot
**rebrote** *m* sprout, shoot, sucker
**rebudiar** *vn* (hunt.) to grunt (*as a wild boar at bay*)
**rebudio** *m* grunt (*of a wild boar*)
**rebufar** *vn* to snort again, to snort loudly
**rebufe** *m* snort, snorting
**rebufo** *m* expansion of air around muzzle of a gun
**rebujado -da** *adj* jumbled, entangled
**rebujal** *m* cattle in excess of fifty or a multiple of fifty; poor piece of land
**rebujar** *va* to jumble together; (naut.) to countersink; *vr* to wrap oneself all up
**rebujina** or **rebujiña** *f* (coll.) bustle, scuffle, mob
**rebujo** *m* woman's heavy veil or muffler (*for disguise*); clumsy bundle or package
**rebultado -da** *adj* bulky, massive
**rebullicio** *m* great bustle, loud uproar
**rebullir** **§26** *vn* to stir, begin to move; to give signs of life; *vr* to stir, begin to move
**rebumbar** *vn* to whistle, to whistle by (*said of a cannon ball*)
**rebumbio** *m* (coll.) noise, uproar
**reburujar** *va* (coll.) to wrap up in a bundle
**reburujón** *m* clumsy bundle or package
**rebusca** *f* searching, careful search; gleaning; leavings, refuse
**rebuscado -da** *adj* affected, unnatural, recherché
**rebuscador -dora** *adj* searching; gleaning; *mf* searcher; gleaner; dealer in gleanings
**rebuscamiento** *m* searching, careful searching; excessive elegance, affectation (*in language, bearing, etc.*)
**rebuscar** **§86** *va* to search into; to seek after; to glean
**rebusco** *m* var. of **rebusca**
**rebutir** *va* to stuff, to pack; to insert
**rebuznador -dora** *adj* braying
**rebuznar** *vn* to bray; (coll.) to talk nonsense
**rebuzno** *m* braying; (coll.) nonsense
**recabar** *va* to succeed in getting
**recadero -ra** or **recadista** *mf* messenger; *m* errand boy, deliveryman; *f* errand girl, delivery woman
**recado** *m* message; errand; gift, present; daily marketing; compliments, regards; safety, security, precaution; equipment, outfit; **a recado** or **a buen recado** in safety; **dar recados** to send regards; **enviar a un recado** to send on an errand; **mandar recado** to send word; **recado de escribir** writing materials
**recaer** **§28** *vn* to fall again, fall back; to relapse; to backslide; **recaer en** to come to, to fall to (*said, e.g., of an inheritance, an election*); **recaer sobre** to fall upon, devolve upon
**recaída** *f* relapse; backsliding
**recaigo** *1st sg pres ind of* **recaer**
**recalada** *f* (naut.) landfall (*sighting land*); (aer.) homing
**recalar** *va* to soak, saturate; *vn* (naut.) to sight land
**recalcada** *f* (naut.) listing, heeling
**recalcadamente** *adv* close, tight
**recalcadura** *f* packing, cramming, stuffing
**recalcar** **§86** *va* to press down, to squeeze; to pack, cram, stuff; to stress (*one's words*); *vn* (naut.) to list, to heel; **recalcar en** to stress, lay stress on; *vr* (coll.) to harp on the same string; (coll.) to sprawl; (coll.) to sprain (*e.g., one's wrist*)
**recalce** *m* hilling; extra felloe used instead of iron tire; underpinning
**recalcitrante** *adj* recalcitrant
**recalcitrar** *vn* to wince, back up; to balk, resist
**recalentador -dora** *adj* superheating; *m* superheater; **recalentador de vapor** superheater
**recalentamiento** *m* reheating; overheating; superheating
**recalentar** **§18** *va* to reheat, to warm over; to overheat; to superheat; to excite sexually; *vr* to overheat; to become spoiled by the heat (*said of fruit*)
**recalescencia** *f* (metal.) recalescence
**recalmón** *m* (naut.) lull (*in wind or sea*)
**recalvastro -tra** *adj* (coll.) baldpate, baldpated
**recalzar** **§76** *va* to hill (*plants*); to underpin, reinforce; to color (*a drawing or sketch*)
**recalzo** *m* extra felloe used instead of iron tire; underpinning
**recalzón** *m* extra felloe used instead of iron tire
**recamado** *m* raised embroidery
**recamador -dora** *mf* embroiderer
**recamar** *va* to embroider in relief
**recámara** *f* dressing room, wardrobe; equipage, stock of furnishings (*of house of a wealthy person*); chamber, breech (*of a gun*); (min.) blast hole; (coll.) reserve, caution; (Am.) bedroom; (Am.) bedroom furniture
**recamarera** *f* (Am.) maid, chambermaid
**recambiar** *va* to exchange again; (com.) to redraw
**recambio** *m* re-exchange; (com.) re-exchange, redraft; **de recambio** spare (*part, wheel, etc.*)
**recamo** *m* raised embroidery; frog (*button and loop on garments*)
**recancamusa** *f* (coll.) ruse, artifice, fraud

**recancanilla** *f* (coll.) hippety-hop, feigned limping of a child; (coll.) emphasis, stress; (coll.) subterfuge, evasion
**recantación** *f* recantation
**recantar** *va* to sing again; *vr* to recant
**recantón** *m* spurstone, checkstone
**recapacitar** *va* to run over in one's mind; *vn* to refresh one's memory; to think things over; **recapacitar sobre** to run over in one's mind
**recapitalización** *f* recapitalization
**recapitalizar** §76 *va* to recapitalize
**recapitulación** *f* recapitulation
**recapitular** *va & vn* to recapitulate
**recarga** *f* new charge, new tax; (elec.) recharge (*of battery*)
**recargado -da** *adj* overdone, overwrought
**recargar** §59 *va* to reload; to overload; to recharge; to overcharge; to resurface (*a road*); to increase (*e.g., tax rate*); to overadorn; (elec.) to recharge; (ins.) to load (*a premium*); *vr* (med.) to have a higher fever
**recargo** *m* new burden, increased burden; extra charge, new charge; increase (*e.g., of taxes*); penalty (*for late payment of taxes*); (med.) increased fever; **recargo al premio** (ins.) loading, margin
**recata** *f* retasting
**recatado -da** *adj* cautious, circumspect; modest, decent
**recatar** *va* to hide, conceal; to taste again; *vr* to hide; to be reserved, be afraid to take a stand; **recatarse de** + *inf* to be cautious about + *ger*
**recatear** *va* to haggle over; to sell at retail; (coll.) to avoid, to evade; *vn* to haggle
**recatería** *f* var. of **regatonería**
**recato** *m* reserve, caution; modesty, decency
**recatón -tona** *adj, mf & m* var. of **regatón**
**recatonazo** *m* blow with the tip of a lance
**recatonear** *va* var. of **regatonear**
**recatonería** *f* var. of **regatonería**
**recauchaje** *m* retreading (*of a tire*)
**recauchar** *va* to retread, to recap (*a tire*)
**recauchutaje** *m* var. of **recauchaje**
**recauchutar** *va* var. of **recauchar**
**recaudación** *f* tax collecting; sum collected; tax collector's office
**recaudador -dora** *adj* tax-collecting; *mf* collector, tax collector
**recaudamiento** *m* tax collecting; job of collector or tax collector; tax collector's district
**recaudar** *va* to gather, collect (*e.g., taxes*); to hold, guard, watch over
**recaudo** *m* tax collecting; care, precaution; bail, surety; **a recaudo** or **a buen recaudo** in safety, under guard
**recavar** *va* to dig again
**recazo** *m* guard (*of sword*); back (*of knife*)
**recebar** *va* to gravel, spread gravel over
**recebo** *m* gravel; liquid added to fill a cask or barrel
**recechar** *va* var. of **acechar**
**rececho** *m* var. of **acecho**
**recejar** *vn* to back up
**recelamiento** *m* var. of **recelo**
**recelar** *va* to fear, distrust; to get (*a mare*) in heat; *vn & vr* to fear, be afraid; **recelar de** or **recelarse de** to fear, be afraid of, distrust; **recelarse** + *inf* to be afraid of + *ger*
**recelo** *m* fear, distrust
**receloso -sa** *adj* fearful, distrustful
**recensión** *f* recension; review, book review
**recentadura** *f* leaven, leavening
**recental** *adj* sucking (*calf or lamb*)
**recentar** §18 *va* to leaven (*dough*); *vr* to become renewed
**recentín** *adj* var. of **recental**
**recentísimo -ma** *adj super* very or most recent
**receñir** §74 *va* to regird; to reëncircle; to fasten or tie again
**recepción** *f* reception; receipt; admission; (law) examination of witnesses; **recepción heterodina** (rad.) heterodyne reception; **recepción por batido** (rad.) beat reception
**receptáculo** *m* receptacle; shelter, refuge; (bot. & elec.) receptacle
**receptador -dora** *mf* receptor (*of a fugitive from justice*); receiver (*of stolen goods*)
**receptar** *va* to receive, welcome; to hide, conceal (*a fugitive from justice*); to hide, conceal, receive (*stolen goods*)
**receptividad** *f* receptivity; susceptibility (*to disease*)
**receptivo -va** *adj* receptive; susceptible (*to disease*)
**recepto** *m* shelter, place of refuge
**receptor -tora** *adj* receiving; *m* receiver; (telg., telp. & rad.) receiver, receiving set; (law & physiol.) receiver; **receptor de cabeza** headphone; **receptor de toda onda** (rad.) all-wave receiver; **receptor telefónico** (telp.) receiver (*part of phone held to ear*)
**receptoría** *f* receiver's office; (law) receivership
**recercar** §86 *va* to fence in, to fence in again; to reëncircle
**recésit** *m* rest from choir duty
**recesivo -va** *adj* (biol.) recessive
**receso** *m* separation, withdrawal; (Am.) recess (*of a legislative body*)
**receta** *f* recipe; (pharm.) prescription; (com.) order memo; (com.) amount carried forward
**recetador** *m* (pharm.) prescriptionist
**recetar** *va & vn* (pharm.) to prescribe; (coll.) to request, beg
**recetario** *m* prescription book or record; druggist's file; pharmacopoeia; recipe book
**recetor** *m* public treasurer; (law) receiver
**recetoría** *f* public treasury
**Recia, la** see **recio**
**recial** *m* rapids (*in a river*)
**reciario** *m* (hist.) retiarius
**recibí** *m* receipt; received payment
**recibidero -ra** *adj* receivable
**recibidor -dora** *adj* receiving; *mf* receiver; receiving teller; ticket collector; *m* anteroom; at-home
**recibimiento** *m* reception; welcome; anteroom; reception room; hall; parlor, salon; at-home
**recibir** *va* to receive; to welcome, to go to meet; *vn* to receive, entertain; (rad.) to receive; *vr* to be received, be admitted; **recibirse de** to graduate as, to be admitted to practice as
**recibo** *m* reception; receipt; anteroom; hall; parlor, salon; at-home; **acusar recibo de** to acknowledge receipt of; **estar de recibo** to be at home (*to callers*); **ser de recibo** to be acceptable
**recidiva** *f* relapse
**recidivismo** *m* recidivism
**recidivista** *mf* recidivist
**reciedumbre** *f* strength, vigor, endurance
**recién** *adv* (to be used only before past participles) recently, just, newly, e.g., **recién llegado** newly arrived; (Am.) recently, just now, a little while ago; (Am.) only then; *conj* (Am.) as soon as
**reciente** *adj* recent
**recientemente** *adv* recently
**recinto** *m* area, enclosure, place; (fort.) enceinte
**recio -cia** *adj* strong, robust; thick, coarse, heavy; harsh, rude; hard, bitter, arduous; severe (*weather*); swift, impetuous; **la Recia** Rhaetia; **recio** *adv* strongly; swiftly; hard; loud
**récipe** *m* (coll.) prescription; (coll.) scolding, dressing-down
**recipiendario** *m* newly inducted member
**recipiente** *adj* receiving, recipient; *m* recipient, vessel, container; receiver or bell glass (*of an air pump*)
**recíproca** *f* see **recíproco**
**reciprocación** *f* reciprocation
**reciprocar** §86 *va & vr* to reciprocate, to match
**reciprocidad** *f* reciprocity; (com.) reciprocity (*between two countries*)
**recíproco -ca** *adj* reciprocal; (gram.) reciprocal; *m* (gram.) reciprocal verb; *f* (math.) reciprocal
**recitación** *f* recitation
**recitado** *m* (mus.) recitative
**recitador -dora** *mf* reciter, elocutionist
**recital** *m* recital; (mus.) recital
**recitar** *va* to recite; to deliver (*a speech*)
**recitativo -va** *adj* recitative; (mus.) recitative
**reciura** *f* strength, vigor; severity (*of weather*)

**reclamación** *f* claim, demand; objection, remonstrance; complaint; reclamation (*protest*); (law) reclamation
**reclamante** *mf* complainer, objector, protester
**reclamar** *va* to keep calling; to claim, demand, reclaim; to decoy, lure (*a bird*); (law) to reclaim; **a reclamar** (naut.) atrip; *vn* to cry out, protest, reclaim; (poet.) to resound; *vr* to call to each other (*said of birds*)
**reclame** *m* (naut.) sheave hole; (naut.) tie block
**reclamo** *m* decoy bird; lure (*for birds*); bird call; call; allurement, attraction; ad; puff, blurb; reference; (law) reclamation; (naut.) tie block; (print.) catchword
**reclavar** *va* to nail again
**recle** *m* rest from choir duty
**reclinación** *f* reclining, recumbency; leaning
**reclinable** *adj* reclining (*seat*)
**reclinar** *va & vr* to recline; to lean
**reclinatorio** *m* prie-dieu; couch, lounge
**recluir §41** *va* to seclude, shut in; to imprison, intern; *vr* to go into seclusion; to be interned
**reclusión** *f* reclusion, seclusion; imprisonment, internment; prison, penitentiary
**recluso -sa** *adj* secluded; confined, imprisoned; *mf* prisoner; inmate
**reclusorio** *m* place of retirement
**recluta** *f* recruiting; (Am.) roundup; *m* recruit
**reclutador -dora** *adj* recruiting; *mf* recruiter
**reclutamiento** *m* recruiting, recruitment; year's recruits
**reclutar** *va* to recruit; (Am.) to round up (*cattle*)
**recobrar** *va* to recover; *vr* to recover; to come to
**recobro** *m* recovery, retrieval; pickup (*of a motor*)
**recocer §30** *va* to boil or cook again; to boil or cook to excess; to anneal; *vr* to boil or cook to excess; (fig.) to be burning up inside
**recocido -da** *adj* expert; *m & f* annealing
**recocina** *f* back kitchen
**recocho -cha** *adj* overcooked, overdone; hard-burned (*brick*)
**recodadero** *m* elbowboard, elbowchair
**recodar** *vn* to lean, lean with the elbows; to wind, twist, turn; *vr* to lean, lean on the elbows
**recodo** *m* bend, twist, turn, hook
**recogedero** *m* collector; collecting basin, drainage area
**recogedor -dora** *mf* gatherer, collector; harvester; protector, shelterer; *m* rake, scraper; collector, pan, trap
**recogegotas** *m* (*pl:* **-tas**) drip pan
**recogemigas** *m* (*pl:* **-gas**) crumb brush
**recoger §49** *va* to pick up; to gather, collect; to gather together; to harvest; to suspend; to shorten, tighten, draw in; to withdraw; to put in a safe place, to keep; to take in, to welcome; to confine, to lock up; *vr* to take shelter, take refuge; to withdraw; to retire (*to go to bed*); to go home; to retrench, cut down expenses; **recogerse en sí mismo** to withdraw within oneself
**recogido -da** *adj* cloistered, recluse; modest, bashful; moderate, temperate; *mf* inmate (*e.g., of poorhouse*); *f* harvest; collection; withdrawal; suspension; inmate of a house of correction for women; **recogida de basuras** trash collection
**recogimiento** *m* gathering, collection; harvesting; suspension; protection, sheltering; confinement; self-communion; house of correction for women
**recolar §77** *va* to strain again
**recolección** *f* compilation, summary; collection; harvest; retreat; house of retreat; recollection, spiritual meditation
**recolectar** *va* to gather, gather in; to pick (*cotton*)
**recolector** *m* collector, tax collector
**recolegir §72** *va* to gather, collect
**recoleto -ta** *adj* self-communing; cloistered, recluse; simple, plain (*in dress*); of retreat (*said, e.g., of a monastery*); *m* (eccl.) Recollect
**recomendable** *adj* commendable
**recomendación** *f* recommendation; **recomendación del alma** prayers for the dying
**recomendante** *mf* recommender
**recomendar §18** *va* to recommend; **recomendar** + *inf* to urge to + *inf*
**recomendatorio -ria** *adj* recommendatory
**recomenzar §31** *va* to recommence, to begin again
**recompensa** *f* recompense, reward
**recompensable** *adj* recompensable; worthy of reward
**recompensación** *f* var. of **recompensa**
**recompensar** *va* to recompense, reward
**recompondré** *1st sg fut ind of* **recomponer**
**recomponer §69** *va* to mend, repair; to recompose
**recompongo** *1st sg pres ind of* **recomponer**
**recomposición** *f* mending, repair; recomposition
**recompra** *f* repurchase
**recomprar** *va* to repurchase, to buy back
**recompuesto -ta** *pp of* **recomponer**
**recompuse** *1st sg pret ind of* **recomponer**
**reconcentración** *f* or **reconcentramiento** *m* concentration, gathering; concealment; deep thought, absorption
**reconcentrar** *va* to concentrate, bring together; to conceal; *vr* to gather together; to become absorbed in thought
**reconciliable** *adj* reconcilable
**reconciliación** *f* reconcilement or reconciliation
**reconciliador -dora** *adj* reconciliatory; *mf* reconciler
**reconciliar** *va* to reconcile; to confess (*a sinner*) summarily; (eccl.) to reconcile; *vr* to become reconciled; to make a slight extra confession
**reconcomer** *vr* (coll.) var. of **concomer**
**reconcomio** *m* (coll.) shrug, shrug of the shoulders; (coll.) fear, misgiving
**reconditez** *f* (*pl:* **-teces**) (coll.) obscurity, mystery
**recóndito -ta** *adj* recondite
**reconducir §38** *va* to lead back; (law) to renew (*a lease*)
**reconduje** *1st sg pret ind of* **reconducir**
**reconduzco** *1st sg pres ind of* **reconducir**
**reconfortar** *va* to comfort again; to comfort, cheer, refresh
**reconocedor -dora** *mf* examiner, inspector
**reconocer §32** *va* to recognize; to admit, to acknowledge; to examine, scrutinize; (mil.) to reconnoiter; *vn* (mil.) to reconnoiter; *vr* to be clear; to confess; to know oneself
**reconocible** *adj* recognizable
**reconocidamente** *adv* avowedly, confessedly; gratefully
**reconocido -da** *adj* recognized; grateful
**reconocimiento** *m* recognition; gratitude; admission, acknowledgment; examination; (dipl.) recognition; (mil.) reconnaissance; **reconocimiento médico** inquest
**reconozco** *1st sg pres ind of* **reconocer**
**reconquista** *f* reconquest
**reconquistar** *va* to reconquer, to reconquest; to recover
**reconsideración** *f* reconsideration
**reconsiderar** *va* to reconsider
**reconstitución** *f* reconstitution
**reconstituir §41** *va* to reconstitute
**reconstituyente** *adj & m* reconstituent, tonic
**reconstrucción** *f* reconstruction
**reconstructivo -va** *adj* reconstructive
**reconstructor -tora** *adj* reconstructive
**reconstruir §41** *va* to rebuild, to reconstruct, to recast
**recontamiento** *m* recounting, relating
**recontar §77** *va* to re-count; to recount, relate
**recontento -ta** *adj* greatly pleased; *m* great satisfaction
**reconvalecer §34** *vn* to convalesce again
**reconvención** *f* expostulation, remonstrance; (law) reconvention
**reconvendré** *1st sg fut ind of* **reconvenir**
**reconvengo** *1st sg pres ind of* **reconvenir**
**reconvenir §92** *va* to expostulate with, to remonstrate with; (law) to countercharge; **reconvenirle a uno con, de, por** or **sobre algo** to expostulate or remonstrate with someone about, for, on or upon something
**reconversión** *f* reconversion
**reconvertir §62** *va* to reconvert
**reconvine** *1st sg pret ind of* **reconvenir**

**reconviniendo** *ger of* **reconvenir**
**recopilación** *f* abridgment, summary; compilation; **Novísima Recopilación** revised code of Spanish law (1805)
**recopilador -dora** *mf* compiler
**recopilar** *va* to compile
**recoquín** *m* (coll.) chubby little fellow
**record** *m* (*pl:* **-cords**) (sport) record; **batir un record** to break a record; **establecer un record** to make a record
**recordable** *adj* memorable
**recordación** *f* recollection, remembrance
**recordar §77** *va* to remember; to remind; **recordar algo a uno** to remind someone of something; **recordar** + *inf* to remember to + *inf*, e.g., **recordó hacerlo** he remembered to do it; **recordar** + *perf inf* to remember + *ger*, e.g., **recordaba haberlo hecho** he remembered doing it; **recordar que** + *subj* to remind to + *inf*, e.g., **recuérdele Vd. que escriba** remind him to write; *vn* to remember; to get awake; to come to; **si mal no recuerdo** (coll.) if I remember correctly
**recordativo -va** *adj* reminding, reminiscent; *m* reminder
**recordatorio** *m* reminder; memento
**recordman** *m* (*pl:* **-men**) (sport) record holder
**recorredor -dora** *mf* traveler; **recorredor de la línea** (elec.) lineman; **recorredor de vía** (rail.) trackwalker
**recorrer** *va* to cross, to traverse, to go over or through; to run over; to look over, look through; to run through (*a book*); to overhaul; (print.) to justify
**recorrido** *m* trip, run, path, route; stroke (*of piston*); repair; scolding, dressing-down; **de gran recorrido** heavily traveled
**recortado -da** *adj* (bot.) notched; *m* cutout
**recortadura** *f* cutting; **recortaduras** *fpl* cuttings, trimmings
**recortar** *va* to trim, cut off, cut away; to pare off; to cut out (*figures*); to outline; *vr* to stand out, be outlined
**recorte** *m* cutting; clipping (*from a newspaper*); dodge, duck; (taur.) dodge to avoid the bull's charge; **recortes** *mpl* cuttings, trimmings; **recortes de periódico** or **de prensa** newspaper clippings
**recorvar** *va & vr* to bend, to bend over; to recurve
**recorvo -va** *adj* arched, curved, bent
**recoser** *va* to sew again; to mend
**recosido** *m* mending
**recostadero** *m* couch, lounge
**recostar §77** *va* to recline; to lean; *vr* to recline; to lean, to lean back, to sit back
**recova** *f* poultry business; poultry stand; (Am.) shed; (Am.) market; (hunt.) pack of hounds
**recovar** *va* to buy (*poultry and eggs*) for resale
**recoveco** *m* turn, bend, twist; subterfuge, trick
**recovero -ra** *mf* poultry dealer
**recre** *m* var. of **recle**
**recreable** *adj* recreative, entertaining
**recreación** *f* recreation; recess (*in school*)
**recrear** *va* to re-create; to recreate, amuse; *vr* to recreate, take recreation, amuse oneself
**recreativo -va** *adj* recreative
**recrecer §34** *va* to increase; *vn* to increase; to recur; *vr* to recover one's spirits
**recrecimiento** *m* increase, growth; recurrence; recovery
**recremento** *m* (physiol.) recrement
**recreo** *m* recreation; place of amusement; (Am.) open-air restaurant; (Am.) daytime outdoor band concert
**recría** *f* breeding in new pastures; reanimation; redemption
**recriar §90** *va* to improve (*horses, cattle, etc.*) with new pastures; to fatten away from home; to reanimate, regenerate; to redeem
**recriminación** *f* recrimination
**recriminador -dora** *mf* recriminator
**recriminar** *va* to recriminate (*an accusation*); *vn* to recriminate; **recriminar contra** to recriminate (*an accuser*); *vr* to exchange recriminations
**recriminatorio -ria** *adj* recriminatory
**recrudecer §34** *vn & vr* to break out again, flare up, get worse
**recrudecimiento** *m* or **recrudescencia** *f* recrudescence
**recrudescente** *adj* recrudescent
**recrujir** *vn* to squeak
**recruzar §76** *va & vr* to recross
**recta** *f* see **recto**
**rectal** *adj* rectal
**rectangular** *adj* rectangular
**rectángulo -la** *adj* right, right-angled; *m* (geom.) rectangle
**rectificación** *f* rectification; reboring
**rectificador -dora** *adj* rectifying; *mf* rectifier; *m* (chem. & elec.) rectifier; **rectificador de selenio** (elec.) selenium rectifier; *f* grinder
**rectificar §86** *va* to rectify; (chem. & elec.) to rectify; to rebore (*a cylinder*); to true up; *vr* to mend one's ways
**rectificativo -va** *adj* rectifying
**rectilíneo -a** *adj* rectilinear
**rectinervio -via** *adj* (bot.) rectinerved
**rectitud** *f* rectitude, righteousness, correctness; straightness
**recto -ta** *adj* straight; right (*angle*); right, just, righteous; literal (*meaning*); *m* (anat.) rectum; (anat.) rectus (*muscle*); *f* straight line; (rail.) straightaway; **recta de llegada** (sport) home stretch
**rectocele** *m* (path.) rectocele
**rector -tora** *adj* governing, directing, managing; *mf* principal, superior; *m* rector; rector or president (*of a university*)
**rectorado** *m* principalship; rectorate
**rectoral** *adj* rectorial
**rectorar** *vn* to become a rector
**rectoría** *f* principal's office; rector's office; rectorate; rectory; president's house; leadership
**rectriz** *f* (*pl:* **-trices**) (orn.) rectrix
**recua** *f* drove; multitude
**recuadrar** *va* to graticulate; to print in a box
**recuadro** *m* (arch.) square, panel; box (*section of printing enclosed in borders*)
**recubierto -ta** *pp of* **recubrir**
**recubrimiento** *m* cover, covering; capping, coating; surfacing
**recubrir §17, 9** *va* to re-cover; to cover, to cap, to coat; to recap (*a tire*); to surface
**recudimiento** *m* (law) power to collect rents
**recudir** *va* to pay (*what is due*); *vn* to come back, to revert
**recuelo** *m* strong lye; warmed-over coffee
**recuento** *m* re-count; count; inventory; **recuento de vocabulario** word count; **recuento sanguíneo** (med.) blood count
**recuentro** *m* var. of **reencuentro**
**recuerdo** *m* memory, remembrance; souvenir, memento, keepsake; **recuerdos** *mpl* regards
**recuero** *m* muleteer
**recuesta** *f* request
**recuestar** *va* to request
**recuesto** *m* slope
**reculada** *f* backing, falling back, recoil; (coll.) backing down
**recular** *vn* to back up, to fall back; to recoil (*said of a firearm*); (coll.) to back down
**reculo -la** *adj* tailless (*fowl*)
**reculones; a reculones** (coll.) backwards, backing up
**recuñar** *va* (min.) to dig by wedging
**recuperable** *adj* recoverable
**recuperación** *f* recuperation, recovery
**recuperador -dora** *adj* recuperative; *m* (mach.) recuperator; **recuperador de Cowper** (metal.) hot-blast stove
**recuperar** *va & vr* to recuperate, to recover
**recuperativo -va** *adj* recuperative
**recura** *f* comb saw
**recurar** *va* to tooth (*a comb*)
**recurrente** *adj* (anat., math. & path.) recurrent; *mf* complainant
**recurrir** *vn* to resort, have recourse; to revert
**recurso** *m* recourse; resource, resort; (law) appeal; **recursos** *mpl* resources, means; **recursos naturales** natural resources
**recusación** *f* refusal, rejection; (law) recusation, challenge
**recusar** *va* to refuse, reject; (law) to recuse, to challenge
**rechazador -dora** *adj* repelling; *mf* repeller

**rechazamiento** *m* repulsion; rejection
**rechazar §76** *va* to repel, repulse, drive back; to reject
**rechazo** *m* rebound, recoil; rejection
**rechifla** *f* catcall, hissing, hooting; (coll.) ridicule, derision
**rechiflar** *va & vn* to catcall, to hiss; *vr* to ridicule, make fun
**rechinador -dora** *adj* creaking, squeaking, grating
**rechinamiento** *m* creaking, squeaking, grating
**rechinar** *vn* to creak, squeak, grate; to gnash; to balk, be sour, act with bad grace
**rechinido** or **rechino** *m* var. of **rechinamiento**
**rechistar** *vn* to speak; **no rechistar** to not say a word
**rechoncho -cha** *adj* (coll.) chubby, tubby
**rechupete; de rechupete** (coll.) splendid, fine
**red** *f* net; netting; network, system (*of railroads, telephones, streets, etc.*); baggage rack; (opt.) grating; (fig.) net, snare; **a red barredera** (fig.) with a clean sweep; **caer en la red** (coll.) to fall into the trap; **red barredera** seine, dragnet; (fig.) dragnet; **red de alimentación** (elec.) feed line, power line; **red de araña** cobweb; **red de canalización** (elec.) distribution main, local supply circuit; **red de difracción** (opt.) diffraction grating; **red de distribución** water main, city water main; (elec.) power line, house current; **red de emisoras** radio network; **red de jorrar** or **de jorro** seine, dragnet; **red radiotransmisora** radio network; **red de salvamento** life net
**redacción** *f* redaction; writing; editing; editorial staff; newspaper office
**redactar** *va* to write up, to word; to edit, be the editor of
**redactor -tora** *mf* writer; editor, newspaper editor
**redada** *f* casting a net; catch, netful (*of fish*); (coll.) catch, haul, roundup (*e.g., of criminals*)
**redaño** *m* caul (*the great omentum*); **redaños** *mpl* strength, courage, spirit
**redar** *va* to net, to haul in
**redargución** *f* retort; (law) impugnation
**redargüir §21** *va* to retort (*an argument*); (law) to impugn
**redaya** *f* river fishing net
**redecilla** *f* small net; netting; hair net; (zool.) reticulum, honeycomb stomach
**redecir §37** *va* to say over and over again
**rededor** *m* surroundings; **al rededor** or **en rededor (de)** around
**redejón** *m* large netting
**redel** *m* (naut.) loof frame
**redención** *f* redemption; support, assistance
**redendija** *f* var. of **rendija**
**redentor -tora** *adj* redeeming, redemptive; *mf* redeemer; (*cap.*) *m* Redeemer
**redeña** *f* scoop net, dip net
**redero -ra** *adj* (pertaining to a) net, reticular; *mf* netmaker; birdcatcher who uses nets; fisherman who uses nets
**redescontar §77** *va* to rediscount
**redescubierto -ta** *pp of* **redescubrir**
**redescubrimiento** *m* rediscovery
**redescubrir §17,** 9 *va* to rediscover
**redescuento** *m* rediscount
**redevanar** *va* to rewind
**redhibición** *f* redhibition, cancellation of a purchase because of misrepresentation
**redhibir** *va* to cancel (*a purchase*) because of misrepresentation
**redhibitorio -ria** *adj* redhibitory
**redición** *f* repetition, constant repetition
**redicho -cha** *adj* (coll.) affected, overprecise (*in speech*); *pp of* **redecir**
**rediente** *m* (fort.) redan; (arch.) foliated cusp
**rediezmar** *va* to tithe a second time
**rediezmo** *m* extra tithe
**redifusión** *f* rebroadcasting
**redigo** *1st sg pres ind of* **redecir**
**redije** *1st sg pret ind of* **redecir**
**redil** *m* sheepfold
**redilar** or **redilear** *va* var. of **amajadar**
**redimible** *adj* redeemable
**redimir** *va* to redeem; to exempt; to buy back
**redingote** *m* redingote
**rediré** *1st sg fut ind of* **redecir**
**redistribución** *f* redistribution
**redistribuir §41** *va* to redistribute
**rédito** *m* income, revenue, yield
**redituable** or **reditual** *adj* income-producing
**redituar §33** *va* to yield, produce
**redivivo -va** *adj* resuscitated, revived; *mf* ghost
**redoblado -da** *adj* stocky, heavy-built; strong, heavy; (mil.) double-quick
**redobladura** *f* or **redoblamiento** *m* doubling; clinching; repeating, repetition
**redoblante** *m* (mil.) snare drum; (mil.) snare drummer
**redoblar** *va* to double; to clinch, bend back or over; to repeat, do over again; *vn* to roll a drum
**redoble** *m* doubling; clinching; repeating; roll of a drum
**redoblegar §59** *va* to double, to bend
**redoblón** *m* clinch nail, rivet
**redolente** *adj* aching, paining
**redoler §63** *vn* (coll.) to ache, to keep aching
**redolor** *m* dull pain, dull afterpain
**redoma** *f* phial, flask, balloon
**redomado -da** *adj* sly, canny; (coll.) crooked
**redonda** *f* see **redondo**
**redondamente** *adv* roundly; around; clearly, plainly, decidedly
**redondeamiento** *m* rounding; (phonet.) rounding
**redondear** *va* to round, make round; to round off; to round out; to clear (*an estate*); (phonet.) to round; *vr* to be or become well-off; to be in the clear
**redondel** *m* (coll.) circle; round cloak; ring (*arena of bull ring*)
**redondela** *f* (coll.) circle; (Am.) round mat
**redondete -ta** *adj* roundish
**redondez** *f* roundness
**redondillo -lla** *adj* (print.) roman; *f* eight-syllable quatrain with rhyme abba or abab
**redondo -da** *adj* round; clear, straightforward; definitive; pasture (*land*); (print.) roman; *m* round, ring, circle; (coll.) cash; **caer redondo** to fall senseless; **en redondo** around; clearly, plainly; *f* district, region; pasture; (mus.) whole note, semibreve; (naut.) square sail; **a la redonda** around, roundabout
**redondón** *m* large circle or sphere
**redopelo** *m* rubbing the wrong way; (coll.) row, scuffle; **a** or **al redopelo** the wrong way; (coll.) against all reason, violently; **traer al redopelo** (coll.) to ride roughshod over
**redova** *f* redowa
**redro** *m* annual ring of the horn (*of sheep or goat*); *adv* (coll.) back, behind
**redrojo** *m* small bunch of grapes remaining after vintage; late fruit, late blossom; (coll.) little runt, puny child
**redropelo** *m* var. of **redopelo**
**redroviento** *m* (hunt.) wind blowing from position of hunter in direction of the game
**redruejo** *m* var. of **redrojo**
**reducción** *f* reduction; (mach.) reducer (*to join two pipes or shafts of different sizes*); (Am.) settlement of converted Indians; **reducción al absurdo** reductio ad absurdum
**reducible** *adj* reducible
**reducido -da** *adj* reduced, diminished; small; compact; abridged
**reducimiento** *m* reduction
**reducir §38** *va* to reduce; (chem., math., surg. & phot.) to reduce; *vr* to reduce; to confine oneself, to cut down; **reducirse a** to come to, to amount to; **reducirse a** + *inf* to find oneself forced to + *inf*
**reductasa** *f* (biochem.) reductase
**reducto** *m* (fort.) redoubt
**reductor -tora** *adj* reducing; *m* reducer; (chem. & phot.) reducer
**reduje** *1st sg pret ind of* **reducir**
**redundancia** *f* redundance or redundancy
**redundante** *adj* redundant
**redundar** *vn* to overflow; to redound; **redundar en** to redound to
**reduplicación** *f* reduplication; (gram.) reduplication

**reduplicado -da** *adj* reduplicate; (bot.) reduplicate
**reduplicar §86** *va* to reduplicate
**reduvio** *m* (ent.) assassin bug
**reduzco** *1st sg pres ind of* **reducir**
**reedificación** *f* rebuilding
**reedificador -dora** *mf* rebuilder
**reedificar §86** *va* to rebuild
**reeditar** *va* to republish, to reprint
**reeducación** *f* reëducation
**reeducar §86** *va* to reëducate
**reelección** *f* reëlection
**reelecto -ta** *adj* reëlected
**reelegible** *adj* reëligible
**reelegir §72** *va* to reëlect
**reembalar** *va* to repack
**reembarcar §86** *va, vn & vr* to reëmbark, to reship
**reembarco** *m* reëmbarkation
**reembarque** *m* reshipment
**reembolsar** *va* to reimburse; to refund; *vr* to collect, to collect a debt
**reembolso** *m* reimbursement; refund; **contra reembolso** cash on delivery, collect on delivery
**reempacar §86** *va* to repack
**reempaquetar** *va* (mach.) to repack
**reemplazable** *adj* replaceable
**reemplazante** *m* replacement (*person*)
**reemplazar §76** *va* to replace
**reemplazo** *m* replacement; (mil.) substitute; (mil.) replacements
**reencaminar** *va* to reroute
**reencarnación** *f* reincarnation
**reencarnar** *va* to reincarnate; *vn & vr* to become reincarnated
**reencender §66** *va* to relight, to rekindle; to reignite
**reencuadernación** *f* (b.b.) rebinding
**reencuadernar** *va* (b.b.) to rebind
**reencuentro** *m* new meeting; collision; clash (*of troops*)
**reenganchamiento** *m* var. of **reenganche**
**reenganchar** *va & vr* to reënlist
**reenganche** *m* reënlistment; bounty for reënlisting
**reengendrador -dora** *adj* regenerating; *mf* regenerator
**reengendrar** *va* to regenerate
**reensayar** *va* to test again, to try out again; to assay again
**reensaye** *m* second assay
**reensayo** *m* second test, second tryout, retrial; new rehearsal
**reentrar** *vn* to reënter
**reenviar §90** *va* to forward; to send back
**reenvidar** *va* to raise (*the bid*)
**reenvite** *m* raised bid
**reescribir §17,** 9 *va* to rewrite
**reestrenar** *va* (theat.) to revive
**reestreno** *m* (theat.) revival
**reexamen** *m* or **reexaminación** *f* reëxamination
**reexaminar** *va* to reëxamine
**reexpedición** *f* forwarding, reshipment
**reexpedir §94** *va* to forward, to reship
**reexportación** *f* reëxport; reëxportation
**reexportar** *va* to reëxport
**refacción** *f* refection, refreshment; repair, repairs; allowance; (coll.) extra, bonus; (Am.) upkeep; (Am.) spare part
**refaccionar** *va* (Am.) to repair; (Am.) to finance
**refaccionario -nia** *adj* (com.) accruing from profits that have been plowed back
**refaccionista** *adj* (Am.) finance; *mf* (Am.) financial backer
**refajo** *m* skirt; underskirt, slip
**refalsado -da** *adj* false, deceptive
**refección** *f* refection, refreshment; repair, repairs
**refectorio** *m* refectory
**referencia** *f* reference; account, narration, report; **de referencia** in question
**referendario** *m* var. of **refrendario**
**referéndum** *m* (*pl:* **-dums**) referendum
**referente** *adj* referring; **en lo referente a** with regard to
**referible** *adj* narratable, tellable
**referido -da** *adj* said, in question, above-mentioned; **el referido** or **la referida** the said person, the person in question
**referir §62** *va* to refer; to tell, narrate, report; *vr* to refer
**refertero -ra** *adj* quarrelsome
**refigurar** *va* to imagine anew
**refilón; de refilón** askance; in passing
**refinación** *f* refining, refinement
**refinadera** *f* stone roller for kneading chocolate
**refinado -da** *adj* refined; fine, distinguished; sly, slick
**refinador** *m* refiner
**refinadura** *f* refining
**refinamiento** *m* refinement (*act of refining; elegance; improvement on something else; exaggerated sense of perfection*); refinement of cruelty
**refinar** *va* to refine; to polish (*e.g., a writing*)
**refinería** *f* refinery
**refino -na** *adj* very fine, extra fine; *m* refining; coffee, cocoa, and sugar exchange; (Am.) brandy
**refirmar** *va* to support, hold up; to ratify
**refitolero -ra** *mf* refectioner; (coll.) busybody, meddler; (Am.) fawner
**reflectar** *va* to reflect
**reflector -tora** *adj* reflecting; *m* reflector; searchlight
**refleja** *f* see **reflejo**
**reflejar** *va* to reflect; to show, reveal; to reflect on; *vn* to reflect; *vr* to be reflected
**reflejo -ja** *adj* reflected; (gram.) reflexive; (physiol.) reflex; *m* glare; reflection; reflex; (physiol.) reflex; **reflejo condicionado** (psychol.) conditioned reflex or response; **reflejo patelar** or **rotuliano** (med.) patellar reflex, knee jerk; *f* reflexion
**reflexible** *adj* reflexible
**reflexión** *f* reflection
**reflexionar** *va* to reflect on or upon; *vn* to reflect; **reflexionar en** or **sobre** to reflect on or upon
**reflexivo -va** *adj* reflective; (fig.) reflective; (gram.) reflexive; *m* (gram.) reflexive (*pronoun or verb*)
**reflexología** *f* study of conditioned reflexes, reflexology
**reflorecer §34** *vn* to blossom or flower again; to flourish again, to reflourish
**reflorecimiento** *m* new blossoming, new flowering; reflourishment
**refluente** *adj* refluent
**refluir §41** *vn* to flow back; to redound
**reflujo** *m* ebb, reflux
**refocilación** *f* cheer, exhilaration
**refocilar** *va* to cheer, exhilarate; to strengthen, fortify; *vr* to be cheered, be exhilarated; to take it easy; to abandon oneself to voluptuous living
**refocilo** *m* var. of **refocilación**
**reforestación** *f* reforestation
**reforma** *f* reform; reformation; renovation, alteration; (*cap.*) *f* (hist.) Reformation; **reforma penitenciaria** prison reform
**reformación** *f* reformation; re-formation
**reformado -da** *adj* reformed; Reformed; (archaic) retired (*soldier*); *mf* Reformed
**reformador -dora** *adj* reforming; *mf* reformer
**reformar** *va* to reform; to re-form; to mend, repair; to renovate; to revise; to reorganize; to disband (*an organization*); to drop (*an employee*); *vr* to reform; to restrain oneself, to hold oneself in check
**reformativo -va** *adj* reformative
**reformatorio -ria** *adj & m* reformatory
**reformista** *adj & mf* reformist
**reforrar** *va* to reline
**reforzado -da** *adj* reinforced; *m* tape, ribbon; braid
**reforzador** *m* (phot.) intensifier
**reforzamiento** *m* reinforcing
**reforzar §52** *va* to reinforce; to strengthen; to cheer up, encourage; (elec.) to boost; (phot.) to intensify
**refracción** *f* (phys. & opt.) refraction
**refractar** *va* to refract
**refractario -ria** *adj* refractory; rebellious

**refractivo -va** *adj* refractive
**refracto -ta** *adj* refracted
**refractómetro** *m* refractometer
**refractor -tora** *adj* refractive; *m* (opt.) refractor
**refrán** *m* proverb, saying
**refranero** *m* collection of proverbs
**refranesco -ca** *adj* proverbial (*phrases, notions, etc.*)
**refrangibilidad** *f* refrangibility
**refrangible** *adj* refrangible
**refranista** *mf* proverbialist, user of proverbs
**refregadura** *f* rubbing; rub (*mark*)
**refregamiento** *m* rubbing
**refregar §29** *va* to rub; (coll.) to upbraid, reprove
**refregón** *m* (coll.) rubbing; (coll.) rub (*mark*); gust of wind
**refreír §73 & §17,** 9 *va* to fry again, fry well, fry too much; (coll.) to bore stiff
**refrenada** *f* var. of **sofrenada**
**refrenamiento** *m* check, restraint
**refrenar** *va* to rein, curb; to check, restrain
**refrendación** *f* countersigning; legalization, authentication; visé; (coll.) repetition
**refrendar** *va* to countersign; to legalize, to authenticate; to visé; (coll.) to repeat, to take again
**refrendario** *m* countersigner
**refrendata** *f* countersignature
**refrendo** *m* countersigning; countersignature
**refrentado** *m* facing, milling
**refrentar** *va* to face, grind, mill
**refrescador -dora** *adj* refreshing; cooling
**refrescadura** *f* refreshing, refreshment; cooling
**refrescamiento** *m* var. of **refresco**
**refrescante** *adj* refreshing; cooling; refrigerant; *m* refrigerant
**refrescar §86** *va* to refresh; to renew; to cool, to refrigerate; **refrescar la memoria** to refresh the memory; *vn* to refresh; to rest up; to refresh oneself; to go out for fresh air; (naut.) to blow up (*said of the wind*); *vr* to refresh; to cool off, get cooler; to refresh oneself; to go out for fresh air; (naut.) to blow up (*said of the wind*)
**refresco** *m* refreshment; soft drink, cold drink; refreshments; **de refresco** anew; fresh (*troops*)
**refresquería** *f* (Am.) refreshment stand
**refriante** *m* refrigerant
**refriega** *f* scuffle, affray, fray
**refrigeración** *f* refrigeration; cooling; **refrigeración con aire frío** air-cooling; **refrigeración por agua** water-cooling; **refrigeración por aire** air-cooling
**refrigerador -dora** *adj* refrigerating; *m* refrigerator; ice bucket, cooler
**refrigerante** *adj* cooling, refrigerant; *m* refrigerant; refrigerator; cooler, cooling bath (*of a still*); cool drink
**refrigerar** *va* to cool; to refrigerate; to refresh; to air-condition; *vr* to cool off, become cooler
**refrigerativo -va** *adj* refrigerative
**refrigerio** *m* cool feeling; relief; refreshment, pick-me-up
**refringencia** *f* refringency
**refringente** *adj* refringent
**refringir §42** *va* to refract
**refrito -ta** *pp of* **refreír;** *m* rehash (*especially of a play*)
**refucilar** *vn* (Am.) to lighten
**refuerzo** *m* reinforcement; strengthening; bracing; aid, support; **refuerzos** *mpl* (mil.) reinforcements
**refugiado -da** *mf* refugee
**refugiar** *va* to shelter; *vr* to take refuge
**refugio** *m* refuge; hospice; shelter; haunt, retreat; safety zone (*in traffic*); **refugio antiaéreo** air-raid shelter, bomb shelter; **refugio antiatómico** fallout shelter; **refugio a prueba de bombas** bombproof shelter
**refulgencia** *f* refulgence
**refulgente** *adj* refulgent
**refulgir §42** *vn* to be refulgent, to shine
**refundición** *f* recast, recasting; revision; adaptation (*e.g., of a play*)
**refundidor -dora** *mf* recaster, adapter (*e.g., of a play*); reviser
**refundir** *va* to recast (*metals*); to recast, to adapt (*a play, a novel*); to revise (*a book*); *vn* to redound
**refunfuñador -dora** *adj* grumbling, growling
**refunfuñadura** *f* grumbling, growling
**refunfuñar** *vn* to grumble, to growl
**refunfuño** *m* var. of **refunfuñadura**
**refutación** *f* refutation
**refutar** *va* to refute
**regacear** *va* to tuck up
**regadera** *f* watering pot, watering can; irrigating ditch; sprinkler head; street sprinkler
**regadero** *m* irrigating ditch
**regadío -a** *adj* irrigable; *m* irrigable land; irrigated land
**regadizo -za** *adj* irrigable
**regador -dora** *adj* irrigating; *mf* irrigator; *f* sprinkler
**regadura** *f* irrigation; sprinkling
**regaifa** *f* cake; grooved stone of an olive-oil mill
**regajal** *m* or **regajo** *m* puddle or pool left by a stream; stream, creek
**regala** *f* (naut.) plank-sheer, gunwale
**regalado -da** *adj* delicate, dainty; pleasing, delicious; pleasant; *f* royal stable; king's horses
**regalador -dora** *adj* regaling, entertaining; *mf* regaler, entertainer
**regalamiento** *m* regalement
**regalar** *va* to give, to present; to regale; to treat; to caress, to fondle; to give away; to melt; *vr* to regale oneself; to melt
**regalejo** *m* small gift, little treat
**regalero** *m* royal purveyor of fruit and flowers
**regalía** *f* privilege, exemption, perquisite; bonus; (Am.) muff; **regalías** *fpl* regalia (*rights and privileges of king*)
**regalicia** *f* var. of **regaliz**
**regalillo** *m* small gift; fur muff
**regalismo** *m* regalism
**regalista** *mf* regalist
**regaliz** *m* or **regaliza** *f* (bot.) licorice; licorice (*candy*)
**regalo** *m* gift, present; joy, pleasure; regalement; treat, delicacy
**regalón -lona** *adj* (coll.) comfort-loving, spoiled, pampered; (coll.) soft, easy (*life*)
**regante** *m* irrigation subscriber; irrigation workman
**regañada** *f* (dial.) cookie; (Am.) growl, snarl
**regañadientes; a regañadientes** grumbling, unwillingly
**regañamiento** *m* growling, snarling; grumbling; (coll.) scolding
**regañar** *va* (coll.) to scold; *vn* to growl, snarl; to grumble; to quarrel; to split, crack open (*said, e.g., of cherries, chestnuts, bread*)
**regañir §25** *vn* to yelp, to yowl
**regaño** *m* growl, snarl; grumble; burst crust (*of a loaf of bread*); (coll.) scolding
**regañón -ñona** *adj* (coll.) grumbling, scolding; northeast (*wind*); *mf* (coll.) grumbler, scold
**regar §29** *va* to water, sprinkle; to irrigate; to strew, spread, sprinkle; to water (*a region or territory*)
**regata** *f* irrigating ditch; regatta, boat race
**regate** *m* dodge, duck; (sport) dribbling; (coll.) subterfuge
**regatear** *va* to haggle over; to begrudge; to sell at retail; (sport) to dribble; (coll.) to avoid, to evade; *vn* to haggle, to bargain; (sport) to dribble; (coll.) to duck, to dodge; (naut.) to race
**regateo** *m* haggling, bargaining
**regatería** *f* retail
**regatero -ra** *adj* retailing; (coll.) haggling; *mf* retailer
**regato** *m* var. of **regajal**
**regatón -tona** *adj* retailing; (coll.) haggling; *mf* retailer; *m* tip, ferrule
**regatonear** *va* to sell at retail
**regatonería** *f* retail; retail business
**regazar §76** *va* to tuck up
**regazo** *m* lap; (fig.) lap
**regencia** *f* regency; regentship
**regeneración** *f* regeneration; (elec.) feedback
**regenerador -dora** *adj* regenerating; *mf* regenerator; *m* (mach.) regenerator
**regenerar** *va & vr* to regenerate

**regenerativo -va** *adj* regenerative
**regenta** *f* wife of regent; directress, manageress; woman professor
**regentar** *va* to direct, to manage; to preside over; to boss
**regente** *adj* ruling, governing; regent; *mf* regent; *m* director, manager; registered pharmacist; (print.) foreman; professor
**regentear** *va* to boss, boss over
**regicida** *adj* regicidal; *mf* regicide (*person*)
**regicidio** *m* regicide (*act*)
**regidor -dora** *adj* ruling, governing; *m* alderman, councilman; *f* alderman's wife, councilman's wife; councilwoman
**regidoría** or **regiduría** *f* office or post of alderman or councilman
**régimen** *m* (*pl:* **regímenes**) regime, regimen; rate; normal rate; system, regulations, rules; flow; performance; conditions; normal operation; period (*e.g., of bad weather*); (gram.) government; **de régimen** normal, rated; **en régimen de** on the basis of; **régimen alimenticio** diet; **régimen desclorurado** salt-free diet; **régimen lácteo** milk diet; **régimen permanente** (phys.) steady state; **régimen títere** puppet regime
**regimentación** *f* regimentation
**regimental** *adj* regimental
**regimentar §18** *va* to regiment
**regimiento** *m* rule, government; aldermen, councilmen; office of alderman or councilman; (mil.) regiment; (naut.) pilot's book of rules
**Reginaldo** *m* Reginald
**regio -gia** *adj* royal, regal
**regiomontano -na** *adj* (pertaining to) Monterrey; *mf* native or inhabitant of Monterrey
**región** *f* region; **región sombra** (astr.) umbra
**regional** *adj* regional
**regionalismo** *m* regionalism
**regionalista** *adj* regionalistic, regionalist; *mf* regionalist
**regionario -ria** *adj* regionary
**regir §72** *va* to rule, govern; to control; to manage; to guide, steer; to keep (*the bowels*) open; (gram.) to govern; *vn* to prevail, be in force; to work; (naut.) to steer, steer well
**registrador -dora** *adj* registering; recording; *m* registrar, recorder; inspector; **registrador de la propiedad** recorder of deeds; **registrador de vuelo** (aer.) flight recorder; *f* cash register
**registrar** *va* to examine, to inspect, to search; to register; to record; to mark with a bookmark; (print.) to register; *vr* to register; to be recorded
**registro** *m* examination, inspection; registration, registry; recording; entry, record; bookmark; regulator (*of a watch*); inspection box; manhole; damper (*of a stove*); (mus.) stop, organ stop; (mus.) pedal; (print.) register
**regla** *f* rule; ruler; order; moderation; menstruation; **en regla** in order, in due form; **falsa regla** guide lines (*for writing*); **por regla general** as a general rule; **salir de regla** to go too far; **regla áurea** (arith.) golden rule; **regla de cálculo** slide rule; **regla del paralelogramo** (mech.) parallelogram law; **regla de oro, regla de proporción** or **regla de tres** (arith.) golden rule, rule of proportion, or rule of three
**reglable** *adj* adjustable
**reglado -da** *adj* moderate, temperate; regulated
**reglamentación** *f* regulation; rules
**reglamentar** *va* to regulate
**reglamentario -ria** *adj* regular, statutory, prescribed, (pertaining to a) regulation
**reglamento** *m* regulation; regulations
**reglar** *adj* (eccl.) regular; *va* to rule (*paper*); to regulate; *vr* to guide oneself, be guided
**regleta** *f* (print.) lead, leading
**regletear** *va* (print.) to lead, to space (*lines*)
**reglilla** *f* slide (*of slide rule*)
**reglón** *m* level (*of a mason*)
**regnícola** *adj* native; *mf* native; native writer
**regocijado -da** *adj* cheering; glad, happy, cheerful
**regocijador -dora** *adj* cheering
**regocijar** *va* to cheer, delight, rejoice; *vr* to rejoice
**regocijo** *m* cheer, joy, gladness, rejoicing
**regodear** *vr* (coll.) to take delight; (coll.) to joke, to jest
**regodeo** *m* (coll.) delight; (coll.) diversion, amusement; (coll.) joking, jesting
**regojo** *m* piece of bread left on table; little runt
**regolaje** *m* good humor, gentle nature
**regoldano -na** *adj* wild (*chestnut*)
**regoldar §19** *vn* (vulg.) to belch
**regoldo** *m* (bot.) wild chestnut
**regolfar** *vn* to flow back, surge back; *vr* to flow back, surge back; to turn, be deflected (*said of the wind*)
**regolfo** *m* eddy, whirlpool; bay, inlet
**regomar** *va* (aut.) to retread
**regona** *f* irrigation canal
**regordete -ta** *adj* chubby, plump, dumpy
**regostar** *vr* var. of **arregostar**
**regosto** *m* var. of **arregosto**
**regraciación** *f* gratitude
**regraciar** *va* to show gratitude for
**regresar** *vn* to return; **regresar a** + *inf* to return to + *inf*
**regresión** *f* regression
**regresivo -va** *adj* regressive
**regreso** *m* return; (eccl.) regress; **de regreso** back
**regruñir §25** *vn* to growl, to snarl
**reguardar** *va* (coll.) to take good care of
**regüeldo** *m* (vulg.) belch, belching
**reguera** *f* irrigating ditch
**reguero** *m* trickle, drip; track, furrow (*left by running water*); irrigating ditch; **ser un reguero de pólvora** to spread like wildfire
**reguilete** *m* var. of **rehilero**
**regulable** *adj* adjustable
**regulación** *f* regulation; control; **regulación del tono** (rad.) tone control; **regulación del volumen sonoro** (rad.) volume control
**regulado -da** *adj* regular
**regulador -dora** *adj* regulating; *mf* regulator; *m* throttle (*of locomotive*); (mach. & elec.) regulator; (mach.) governor; **reguladores** *mpl* (mus.) swell; **regulador de bolas** or **de fuerza centrífuga** (mach.) ball governor; **regulador de tensión** (elec.) voltage regulator; **regulador de volumen** (rad.) volume control
**regular** *adj* regular; fair, moderate, medium; (bot., eccl., geom., gram. & mil.) regular; **por lo regular** as a rule; *m* (eccl. & mil.) regular; *va* to regulate; to put in order; to throttle
**regularidad** *f* regularity; (rel.) strict observance of the rule
**regularización** *f* regularization; regulation
**regularizar §76** to regularize; to regulate
**regularmente** *adv* regularly; fairly, moderately
**regulativo -va** *adj* regulative
**régulo** *m* regulus; (chem. & metal.) regulus; (orn.) kinglet; (*cap.*) *m* (astr.) Regulus
**regurgitación** *f* regurgitation
**regurgitar** *vn* to regurgitate
**rehabilitación** *f* rehabilitation
**rehabilitar** *va* to rehabilitate; to renovate, to overhaul; *vr* to become rehabilitated; to get overhauled
**rehacer §55** *va* to do over, make over, remake; to rehash; to repair, renovate; *vr* to recover, to rally; to recover oneself
**rehacimiento** *m* remaking; rehash; repair, renovation
**rehago** *1st sg pres ind of* **rehacer**
**rehala** *f* flock of sheep of different owners under the care of one shepherd
**rehalero** *m* shepherd of a flock of sheep of different owners
**reharé** *1st sg fut ind of* **rehacer**
**rehartar** *va* to satiate, to cloy
**rehecho -cha** *pp of* **rehacer;** *adj* squat, broad-shouldered
**rehelear** *vn* to taste bitter
**reheleo** *m* bitterness
**rehén** *m* hostage; **llevarse en rehenes** to carry off as a hostage; **retener como rehén** to hold as a hostage; **quedar en rehenes** to be held as a hostage
**rehenchido** *m* filler, filling
**rehenchimiento** *m* refilling; stuffing, filling
**rehenchir §94&§99** *va* to refill; to stuff, to fill

**rehendija** *f* var. of **rendija**
**reherimiento** *m* repulse
**reherir §62** *va* to repulse, repel; to wound again
**reherrar §18** *va* to reshoe (*a horse*)
**rehervir §62** *va* to boil again; *vn* to boil again, to boil up; to be madly in love; to be blinded by passion; *vr* to ferment, to turn sour
**rehíce** *1st sg pret ind of* **rehacer**
**rehiladillo** *m* narrow ribbon
**rehilandera** *f* pinwheel (*toy*)
**rehilar §99** *va* to twist too hard: *vn* to quiver; to whiz, whiz by
**rehilero** or **rehilete** *m* dart (*used in game of darts*); shuttlecock; (taur.) banderilla; dig, cutting remark
**rehílo** *m* quiver, shake
**rehogar §59** *va* to cook with a slow fire in butter or oil
**rehollar §77** *va* to trample under foot; to tread again
**rehoya** *f* deep hole
**rehoyar** *vn* to hollow out an old hole for planting a tree
**rehoyo** *m* var. of **rehoya**
**rehuída** *f* fleeing, flight; backtracking (*of game*)
**rehuir §41** *va* to flee, to shrink from; to avoid, to decline; to dislike; **rehuir** + *inf* to decline to + *inf;* to dislike to + *inf; vn* to flee, to shrink; to backtrack (*said of game*); *vr* to flee, to shrink
**rehumedecer §34** *va* to wet through and through, to soak
**rehundir §99** *va* to sink; to deepen; to recast (*a metal*); to squander; *vr* to sink
**rehurtar §99** *vr* to flee in an unexpected direction (*said of game*)
**rehusar §99** *va* to refuse, turn down; **rehusar** + *inf* to refuse to + *inf*
**reidero -ra** *adj* (coll.) laughable; **reideras** *fpl* (coll.) laughing mood, spell of laughing
**reidor -dora** *adj* laughing; *mf* laugher
**reimportación** *f* reimportation, reimport
**reimportar** *va* to reimport
**reimpresión** *f* reprint, reimpression
**reimpreso -sa** *pp of* **reimprimir**
**reimprimir §17,** 9 *va* to reprint
**reina** *f* queen; queen bee; (chess & fig.) queen; **reina claudia** greengage; **reina de belleza** beauty queen; **reina de los ángeles** (ichth.) angelfish (*Angelichthys ciliaris*); **reina de los bosques** (bot.) woodruff (*Asperula odorata*); **reina de los prados** (bot.) meadowsweet; **reina de Sabá** Queen of Sheba; **reina luisa** (bot.) lemon verbena; **reina madre** queen mother; **reina Margarita** (bot.) aster, China aster; **reina mora** hopscotch; **reina regente** queen regent (*in place of absent king*); **reina reinante** queen regent, queen regnant; **reina viuda** dowager queen, queen dowager
**reinado** *m* reign; **durante el reinado de** in the reign of
**reinador -dora** *mf* ruler
**reinal** *m* twisted hemp cord
**reinante** *adj* reigning; prevailing
**reinar** *vn* to reign; to prevail
**reincidencia** *f* backsliding; repetition of an offense; relapse
**reincidente** *adj* backsliding; *mf* backslider
**reincidir** *vn* to backslide; to repeat an offense; to relapse
**reineta** *f* reinette (*type of apple*)
**reinfección** *f* reinfection
**reinfectar** *va* to reinfect
**reinflar** *va* to reinflate
**reingresar** *vn* to reënter
**reingreso** *m* reëntry
**reinita** *f* (orn.) honey creeper; (bot.) pot marigold; (Am.) glowworm, firefly; **reinita cabeza negra** (orn.) blackpoll; **reinita trepadora** (orn.) black-and-white creeper or warbler
**reino** *m* kingdom; **reino animal** animal kingdom; **reino de los cielos** kingdom of heaven; **reino mineral** mineral kingdom; **Reino Unido** United Kingdom; **reino vegetal** vegetable kingdom
**reinoculación** *f* reinoculation
**reinocular** *va & vr* to reinoculate
**reinstalación** *f* reinstatement, reinstallation
**reinstalar** *va* to reinstate, reinstall
**reintegrable** *adj* repayable
**reintegración** *f* redintegration, restoration, recovery
**reintegrar** *va* to redintegrate; to restore; to pay back; *vr* to redintegrate; to recover; to return, go back
**reintegro** *m* restoration, recovery; payment
**reinversión** *f* reinvestment
**reinvertir §62** *va* to reinvest
**reír §73** *va* to laugh at or over; *vn* to laugh; (fig.) to laugh (*said of a brook or fountain*); **reír de** to laugh at; *vr* to laugh; (coll.) to tear (*from wear or flimsiness*); **reírse de** to laugh at
**reiteración** *f* reiteration
**reiteradamente** *adv* repeatedly
**reiterar** *va* to reiterate, to repeat
**reiterativo -va** *adj* reiterative
**reivindicable** *adj* (law) repleviable
**reivindicación** *f* (law) replevin; claim, demand; recovery
**reivindicar §86** *va* (law) to replevy; to claim, demand (*e.g., one's rights*); to recover, to reclaim; to lay hold of or on
**reja** *f* grate, grating, grille; plowshare, colter; plowing; (phys.) lattice; **entre rejas** behind bars
**rejacar §86** *va* var. of **arrejacar**
**rejada** *f* var. of **arrejada**
**rejado** *m* grating
**rejal** *m* pile of bricks laid on edge and crisscross
**rejalgar** *m* (mineral.) realgar; noisome material
**rejera** *f* (naut.) mooring line, painter
**rejería** *f* ornamental ironwork
**rejero** *m* ornamental ironworker
**rejilla** *f* screen; grating; lattice, latticework; latticed window; cane, cane upholstery; (aut.) grille; (rail.) baggage netting; foot stove, foot brasier; fire grate; (rad.) grid; (elec.) grid (*of storage battery*)
**rejo** *m* sharp point; goad; hob (*for quoits*); iron frame (*of a door*); strength, vigor; (bot.) radicle
**rejón** *m* spear; dagger; (taur.) lance
**rejonazo** *m* (taur.) thrust with lance that breaks off in bull's neck
**rejoncillo** *m* (taur.) small lance
**rejoneador** *m* (taur.) rejoneador (*mounted bullfighter who breaks lance in neck of bull*)
**rejoneadora** *f* (taur.) lady rejoneador
**rejonear** *va* (taur.) to jab (*the bull*) with a lance made to break off in the bull's neck
**rejoneo** *m* (taur.) jabbing with a lance
**rejuela** *f* small grate; foot stove, foot brasier
**rejuntado** *m* (mas.) pointing
**rejuntar** *va* (mas.) to point
**rejuvenecer §34** *va* to rejuvenate; *vn & vr* to rejuvenate, become rejuvenated
**rejuvenecimiento** *m* rejuvenation
**relabra** *f* new carving
**relabrar** *va* to carve again
**relación** *f* relation; speech, long passage (*in a play*); account; list; (law) report; **relaciones** *fpl* betrothal, engagement; **en relación con** commensurate with; **falsa relación** (mus.) false relation; **relación de ciego** blind man's ballad; **relaciones públicas** public relations
**relacionado -da** *adj* related
**relacionar** *va* to relate; *vr* to relate, to be or become related
**relai** *m* or **relais** *m* (elec.) relay
**relajación** *f* relaxation; slackening, letup; laxity; rupture, hernia
**relajado -da** *adj* ruptured; debauched, dissolute, lax, loose
**relajador -dora** *adj* relaxative; *mf* relaxer
**relajadura** *f* (Am.) hernia
**relajamiento** *m* var. of **relajación**
**relajante** *adj & m* relaxative
**relajar** *va* to relax; to slacken; to debauch; *vn* to relax; *vr* to relax; to become relaxed; to become debauched; to become ruptured
**relajo -ja** *adj* (Am.) shy, aloof, gruff; (Am.) fiery, spirited; *m* (Am.) disorder, commotion; (Am.) baseness, vileness, lewdness; (Am.) joke, scorn; **echar a relajo** (Am.) to make fun of
**relamer** *va* to lick again; *vr* to lick one's lips; to gloat; to relish; to slick oneself up
**relamido -da** *adj* prim, overnice

**relámpago** *m* lightning; flash; flash of lightning; flash of wit; **relámpagos** *mpl* lightning; **relámpago de calor** heat lightning; **relámpago difuso** sheet lightning; **relámpago fotogénico** (phot.) flash bulb, flashlight
**relampagueante** *adj* lightening; flashing
**relampaguear** *vn* to lighten; to flash, to sparkle
**relampagueo** *m* lightning; flashing
**relance** *m* chance, uncertainty; second choice or lot; **de relance** by chance, unexpectedly
**relanzar** **§76** *va* to throw again, to throw hard; to repel, to repulse; to cast (*ballots*) again
**relapso -sa** *adj* backsliding; *mf* backslider; *m* relapse
**relatador -dora** *adj* relating, narrating; *mf* relater, narrator
**relatar** *va* to relate, to report; (law) to report (*a trial*)
**relatividad** *f* relativity; (phys.) relativity
**relativismo** *m* relativism
**relativo -va** *adj* relative; (gram.) relative; *m* (gram.) relative
**relato** *m* story; statement, report
**relator -tora** *adj* narrating, reporting; *mf* relator, reporter; *m* (law) court reporter
**relatoría** *f* (law) office of court reporter
**relavar** *va* to wash again
**relave** *m* second washing; **relaves** *mpl* washings (*of ore*)
**relazar** **§76** *va* to tie up
**relé** *m* var. of **relai**
**releer** **§35** *va* to reread
**relegación** *f* relegation; banishment, exile; postponement
**relegar** **§59** *va* to relegate; to banish, exile; to postpone, to shelve, to lay aside
**relej** *m* var. of **releje**
**relejar** *vn* to batter (*said of a wall*)
**releje** *m* rut, track; batter (*of a wall*); (path.) sordes
**relente** *m* night dew, light drizzle; (coll.) impudence, assurance
**relentecer** **§34** *vn & vr* to soften
**relevación** *f* relief; absolution; emphasis, enhancement, reinforcement; (law) relief
**relevante** *adj* outstanding
**relevar** *va* to emboss, make stand out in relief, make stand out; to relieve; to release; to absolve; to replace, to substitute; (mil.) to relieve; *vn* to stand out in relief
**relevo** *m* (mil.) relief; **relevos** *mpl* (sport) relay race; **relevo de mandos** (mil.) change of command
**relicario** *m* reliquary; shrine; (Am. & prov.) locket
**relicto -ta** *adj* (law) left at one's death (*said of an estate*); (biol.) relict
**relieve** *m* relief (*design standing out from surface*); prominence; (fort.) relief; **relieves** *mpl* leavings, offals; **alto relieve** high relief; **bajo relieve** bas-relief, low relief; **en relieve** in relief; **medio relieve** half relief; **poner de relieve** to point out, to emphasize, to make stand out
**religa** *f* metal added to an alloy (*to change proportion*)
**religar** **§59** *va* to tie again; to bind more tightly; to alloy again
**religión** *f* religion; **entrar en religión** to go into the church; **religión natural** natural religion; **religión revelada** revealed religion
**religionario -ria** *mf* Protestant
**religiosidad** *f* religiosity, religiousness
**religioso -sa** *adj & mf* religious
**relimar** *va* to file again
**relimpiar** *va* to clean again; to clean thoroughly
**relimpio -pia** *adj* (coll.) very clean, spick-and-span
**relinchador -dora** *adj* loud-neighing, neighing frequently
**relinchar** *vn* to neigh
**relinchido** or **relincho** *m* neigh, neighing; cry of joy
**relindo -da** *adj* very pretty
**relinga** *f* (naut.) boltrope; lead rope (*of fishing net*)
**relingar** **§59** *va* (naut.) to rope (*a sail*); to fasten the lead rope to (*a fishing net*); *vn* (naut.) to rustle
**reliquia** *f* relic; trace, vestige; ailment; (biol.) relict; **reliquia de familia** heirloom
**reló** *m* (coll.) var. of **reloj**
**reloco -ca** *adj* (coll.) downright crazy
**reloj** *m* watch; clock; meter; **relojes** *mpl* (bot.) stork's-bill; **aprender a conocer el reloj** to learn how to tell time; **como un reloj** like clockwork; **conocer el reloj** to know how to tell time; **estar como un reloj** to be in good shape; **reloj de agua** water clock; **reloj de antesala** grandfather's clock; **reloj de arena** sandglass, hourglass; **reloj de autocuerda** self-winding watch; **reloj de caja** grandfather's clock; **reloj de campana** striking clock; **reloj de carillón** chime clock; **reloj de cuclillo** or **cuco** cuckoo clock; **reloj de cuerda automática** self-winding watch or clock; **reloj de bolsillo** watch, pocket watch; **reloj de estacionamiento** parking meter; **reloj de la muerte** (ent.) deathwatch; **reloj de longitudes** box chronometer; **reloj de ocho días cuerda** eight-day clock; **reloj de péndola** pendulum clock; **reloj de pesas** weight-driven clock; **reloj de pulsera** wrist watch; **reloj de repetición** repeater, repeating watch; **reloj de segundos muertos** stop watch; **reloj de sobremesa** desk clock; **reloj de sol** sundial; **reloj despertador** alarm clock; **reloj de torre** tower clock; **reloj magistral** master clock; **reloj marino** marine chronometer; **reloj para vigilantes** watchman's clock; **reloj registrador** time clock; **reloj registrador de tarjetas** punch clock
**relojera** *f* see **relojero**
**relojería** *f* watchmaking, clockmaking; watchmaker's shop or store
**relojero -ra** *adj* (pertaining to a) watch, clock; watchmaking; *mf* watchmaker, clockmaker; *f* watchcase; watch stand; watch pocket
**reluciente** *adj* shining, flashing, brilliant
**relucir** **§60** *vn* to shine; (fig.) to shine
**reluctancia** *f* (elec.) reluctance
**reluctante** *adj* unruly, unmanageable
**reluctividad** *f* (elec.) reluctivity
**reluchar** *vn* to struggle
**relujar** *va* (Am.) to shine (*shoes*)
**relumbrante** *adj* dazzling, resplendent
**relumbrar** *vn* to shine brightly, to dazzle, to glare
**relumbre** *m* beam, sparkle; flash of bright light; taste of copper or iron (*from having been kept or cooked in copper or iron vessels*)
**relumbro** *m* var. of **relumbrón**
**relumbrón** *m* flash of bright light, dazzling brightness, glare; tinsel; **de relumbrón** showy, tawdry; flashily
**relumbroso -sa** *adj* var. of **relumbrante**
**reluzco** *1st sg pres ind of* **relucir**
**rellanar** *va* to level, smooth, or flatten again; *vr* to sprawl in one's seat
**rellano** *m* landing (*of stairs*); level stretch (*in sloping country*)
**rellenable** *adj* refillable
**rellenar** *va* to refill; to fill up; to fill, to stuff; to pad; to point (*e.g., bricks*); to fill out; (coll.) to cram, stuff; *vr* to fill up; (coll.) to cram, stuff, stuff oneself
**relleno -na** *adj* very full, packed; stuffed; *m* filling, stuffing; forcemeat; padding, wadding; (mach.) packing; (fig.) padding (*of a writing or speech*)
**remachado** *m* riveting
**remachador -dora** *adj* riveting; *mf* riveter; *f* riveting machine
**remachadura** *f* riveting
**remachar** *va* to clinch (*a driven nail*); to rivet; to confirm, to stress
**remache** *m* clinching; riveting; rivet
**remador -dora** *mf* rower
**remadura** *f* rowing
**remallar** *va* to mend (*a net or netting; a stocking or run in a stocking*)
**remalladora** *f* stocking mender (*woman or machine*)
**remamiento** *m* var. of **remadura**

**remandar** *va* to order over and over again
**remanecer §34** *vn* to show up again unexpectedly
**remanente** *adj* remanent; remnant; *m* remains, remnant, leftover
**remanga** *f* shrimp trap
**remangar §59** *va & vr* var. of **arremangar**
**remango** *m* var. of **arremango**
**remansar** *vn & vr* to dam up, to back up
**remanso** *m* dead water, backwater; still water; sluggishness
**remante** *adj* rowing; *mf* rower
**remar** *vn* to row; to toil, struggle
**remarcar §86** *va* to mark again
**rematadamente** *adv* totally, absolutely
**rematado -da** *adj* bad off, hopeless; **loco rematado** (coll.) crazy as a bedbug, raving mad
**rematamiento** *m* var. of **remate**
**rematante** *m* highest bidder
**rematar** *va* to finish off, kill off; to finish, put an end to; to put the last stitch in; to knock down (*in an auction*); *vn* to end; *vr* to come to ruin; (Am.) to get worse
**remate** *m* end; closing (*e.g., of an account*); crest, top, finial; highest bid; sale (*at an auction*); (Am.) edge, selvage; **de remate** absolutely, completely, hopelessly; **por remate** finally, in the end
**remecedor -dora** *adj* shaking, swinging; *m* worker who beats or shakes down olives from the tree
**remecer §61** *va & vr* to shake, to swing
**remedable** *adj* imitable
**remedador -dora** *adj* imitative; *mf* imitator, mimic
**remedar** *va* to imitate, copy; to ape, mimic; to mock
**remediable** *adj* remediable
**remediador -dora** *adj* remedial
**remédialotodo** *m* (*pl:* **-dos**) var. of **sánalotodo**
**remediar** *va* to remedy; to free, to save (*from danger*); to help; to prevent
**remediavagos** *m* (*pl:* **-gos**) short cut
**remedición** *f* remeasuring; remeasurement
**remedio** *m* remedy; help; recourse; amendment, correction; (law) appeal; **no hay remedio** or **más remedio** it can't be helped; **no tener más remedio que** + *inf* to not be able to help + *ger;* **no tener para un remedio** to be penniless; **no tener remedio** to be unavoidable, to be unable to be helped; **sin remedio** inevitable; **remedio heroico** desperate remedy
**remedión** *m* (theat.) substitute performance
**remedir §94** *va* to remeasure
**remedo** *m* imitation, copy; poor imitation
**remellado -da** *adj* jagged, dented; ectropic (*eye or lip*); harelipped; *mf* harelipped person
**remellar** *va* to unhair (*hides*)
**remellón -llona** *adj & mf* (coll.) var. of **remellado**
**remembranza** *f* remembrance, recollection
**remembrar** *va* var. of **rememorar**
**rememoración** *f* remembering
**rememorar** *va* to remember, recall
**rememorativo -va** *adj* commemorative
**remendado -da** *adj* spotted, patchy
**remendar §18** *va* to patch, mend, repair; to darn; to emend, correct; to touch up
**remendón -dona** *adj* mending, repairing; *mf* mender, repairer; tailor (*who does mending*); shoe mender, shoemaker
**rementir §62** *vn* to tell barefaced lies
**remero -ra** *mf* rower, paddler; *m* oarsman; *f* (orn.) flight feather
**remesa** *f* remittance; shipment
**remesar** *va* to remit; to ship; to pluck, pull out (*hair*)
**remesón** *m* plucking of hair; tuft of hair plucked out; stopping a horse in full gallop
**remeter** *va* to put back; to put in further; to tuck in (*e.g., the bedclothes*)
**remezón** *m* (Am.) tremor (*slight earthquake*)
**remiel** *m* second extraction of sugar from the cane
**remiendo** *m* patch; repair, mending; retouching; spot; emendation, correction; (print.) job printing, job work; **a remiendos** (coll.) piecemeal; **echar un remiendo a** to put a patch on; **echar un remiendo a la vida** (coll.) to take a bite to eat
**rémiges** *fpl* (orn.) remiges
**remilgado -da** *adj* prim and finicky, affected, smirking
**remilgar §59** *vr* to be prim and finicky, to smirk
**remilgo** *m* primness, overniceness, affectation
**rémington** *m* Remington gun
**reminiscencia** *f* reminiscence; (philos.) reminiscence
**remirado -da** *adj* circumspect, discreet
**remirar** *va* to look at again, to look over again, to review; to look at hard; *vr* to take great pains; to enjoy looking over; to contemplate with pleasure; **remirarse en** to take great pains with
**remisible** *adj* remissible
**remisión** *f* remission; reference; **remisión de los pecados** remission of sins
**remisivo -va** *adj* (pertaining to a) reference
**remiso -sa** *adj* lazy, indolent, sluggish
**remisor -sora** *mf* sender, shipper
**remitente** *adj* remittent; *mf* sender, shipper
**remitido** *m* personal (*in a newspaper*)
**remitir** *va* to remit; to forward, send, ship; to refer; to defer, postpone, put off; to pardon, forgive; *vn* to remit, let up; to refer *vr* to remit, let up; to defer, yield
**remo** *m* oar; leg, arm, wing; toil, labor; (sport) rowing; (sport) crew (*rowing in races*); **al remo** rowing; at hard labor; (*cap.*) *m* (myth.) Remus
**remoción** *f* removal; dismissal; modification
**remodelar** *va* (Am.) to remodel
**remojadero** *m* steeping tub, soaking vat
**remojar** *va* to soak, to steep, to dip; to celebrate with a drink
**remojo** *m* soaking, steeping, dipping; **echar en remojo** (coll.) to put off till a more opportune time
**remolacha** *f* (bot.) beet (*plant and root*); **remolacha azucarera** (bot.) sugar beet; **remolacha forrajera** (bot.) mangel-wurzel
**remolar** *m* oar maker; oar shop
**remolcador -dora** *adj* towing; *m* tug, tugboat, towboat
**remolcar §86** *va* to tow; to take in tow; to draw or take (*someone*) in
**remoler §63** *va* to grind up; (coll.) to bore; *vn* (Am.) to run around with women
**remolido** *m* (mineral.) ground ore
**remolienda** *f* (Am.) carousing
**remolimiento** *m* grinding
**remolinar** *vn & vr* to whirl about, to eddy
**remolinear** *va, vn & vr* to whirl about, to eddy
**remolino** *m* eddy, whirlpool; swirl, whirl; whirlwind; disturbance, commotion; press, throng; cowlick
**remolón -lona** *adj* soft, lazy, shirky; *mf* quitter, shirker; **hacerse el remolón** to shirk, to back down, to back out; *m* upper tusk of wild boar; point (*of horse's tooth*)
**remolonear** *vn & vr* to refuse to move, to stand still, to duck work or effort
**remolque** *m* tow (*act; what is towed; rope, chain*); (aut.) trailer; **tomar a remolque** to take in tow
**remondar** *va* to clean out, to prune again
**remonta** *f* shoe repair; patch (*on riding breeches*); restuffing of a saddle; remount cavalry; remount (*supply of horses*); remount-cavalry headquarters
**remontamiento** *m* (act of) remounting cavalry
**remontar** *va* to frighten away; to mend, repair (*a saddle, shoes, pants*); to go up (*e.g., a river*); (mil.) to remount; to elevate, raise up; *vn* to go back (*in time*); *vr* to rise, rise up; to soar; to go back (*in time*); to take to the woods (*said of a slave*)
**remonte** *m* repair, repairing; remounting; rising; soaring
**remontista** *m* (mil.) remount commissioner
**remontuar** *m* stem-winder
**remoque** *m* (coll.) gibe, cut
**remoquete** *m* punch; nickname; witticism, sarcasm; (coll.) flirting, love-making; **dar remoquete a** (coll.) to embarrass

**rémora** *f* (ichth.) remora; hindrance, obstacle, obstruction
**remordedor -dora** *adj* disturbing, causing remorse
**remorder §63** *va* to bite again; to sting, prick, cause remorse to; *vr* to show one's worry or trouble
**remordimiento** *m* remorse
**remosquear** *vr* (coll.) to become suspicious, become upset; (print.) to become blurred or smeared
**remostar** *va* to put must into (*old wine*); *vr* to rot (*said of fruit*); to taste sweet (*said of wine*)
**remostecer §34** *vr* to rot (*said of fruit*)
**remosto** *m* adding must to old wine; sweetening, sweetness (*of wine*)
**remotamente** *adv* remotely; unlikely; vaguely
**remoto -ta** *adj* remote; unlikely; **estar remoto** to be rusty (*about something once known*)
**remover §63** *va* to remove; to disturb, upset; to shake; to stir; to dismiss, discharge; *vr* to remove, move away
**removimiento** *m* var. of **remoción**
**remozamiento** *m* rejuvenation
**remozar §76** *va* to rejuvenate; *vr* to rejuvenate, become rejuvenated
**rempujar** *va* (coll.) to push, jostle; (coll.) to push (*e.g., an idea, plan*) through; (hunt.) to drive in a corner
**rempujo** *m* (coll.) push, jostle; (naut.) sailmaker's palm
**rempujón** *m* (coll.) push, shove
**remuda** *f* change, replacement; change of clothes
**remudamiento** *m* change, replacement
**remudar** *va* to change again; to change, replace; to transplant
**remugar §59** *va* var. of **rumiar**
**remullir §26** *va* to fluff, beat up (*e.g., a pillow*)
**remuneración** *f* remuneration; **remuneración por rendimiento** piece wage
**remunerador -dora** *adj* remunerating; *mf* remunerator
**remunerar** *va* to remunerate
**remunerativo -va** *adj* remunerative
**remusgar §59** *va* to guess, suspect
**remusgo** *m* guess, suspicion; sharp, cold breeze
**renacentista** *adj* (pertaining to the) Renaissance; *mf* Renaissancist
**renacer §34** *vn* to be reborn, to be born again; to bloom again; to recover
**renaciente** *adj* renascent
**renacimiento** *m* rebirth; renaissance; (*cap.*) *m* Renaissance
**renacuajo** *m* (zool.) tadpole, polliwog; (elec.) frog; (coll.) shrimp (*little fellow*)
**renadío** *m* new crop after haying
**renal** *adj* renal
**Renania** *f* Rhineland
**renano -na** *adj* Rhenish
**Renato** *m* René
**rencilla** *f* bicker, feud, quarrel
**rencilloso -sa** *adj* bickering, feuding, quarrelsome
**renco -ca** *adj* hipshot, lame
**rencor** *m* rancor
**rencoroso -sa** *adj* rancorous
**rendaje** *m* set of reins and bridles
**rendajo** *m* var. of **arrendajo**
**rendar** *va* to plow the second time; (prov.) to weed; (prov.) to imitate
**rendibú** *m* (*pl:* **-búes**) (archaic) bow, reverence, attention
**rendición** *f* surrender; submission; fatigue, exhaustion; yield; rendering (*e.g., of justice*)
**rendido -da** *adj* tired, worn out; attentive, submissive, obsequious; overcome, beaten
**rendija** *f* crack, split, slit
**rendimiento** *m* submission; obsequiousness; fatigue, exhaustion; yield; output, performance; (mech.) efficiency
**rendir §94** *va* to conquer; to subdue, to overcome; to surrender; to exhaust, wear out; to return, give back; to hand over; to yield, produce; to throw up, vomit; to render, give (*e.g., thanks*); to do (*homage*); *vn* to yield; *vr* to surrender; to yield, give in; to become exhausted, become worn out
**rene** *f* (anat.) kidney
**renegado -da** *adj* renegade; (coll.) harsh, gruff, profane; *mf* renegade; *m* ombre (*card game*)
**renegador -dora** *adj* profane; *mf* swearer
**renegar §29** *va* to deny vigorously; to abhor, to detest; *vn* to curse; to apostatize, to become a Mohammedan; (coll.) to utter insults; **renegar de** to deny; to curse; to abhor, to detest
**renegociación** *f* renegotiation
**renegón -gona** *adj* (coll.) profane; *mf* (coll.) swearer, inveterate swearer
**renegrear** *vn* to turn very black
**renegrido -da** *adj* black-and-blue
**RENFE** *f* abr. of **Red Nacional de los Ferrocarriles Españoles**
**rengífero** *m* var. of **rangífero**
**rengle** *m* or **renglera** *f* row, file, line
**renglón** *m* line (*of writing or print; of business*); **a renglón seguido** below, right after; **leer entre renglones** to read between the lines
**renglonadura** *f* ruling, ruled lines
**rengo -ga** *adj* var. of **renco**
**renguear** *vn* (Am.) to limp
**reniego** *m* curse
**reniforme** *adj* reniform
**renil** *adj* barren or spayed (*sheep*)
**renio** *m* (chem.) rhenium
**renitencia** *f* reluctance, renitency; resistance
**renitente** *adj* reluctant, renitent; resistant
**reno** *m* (zool.) reindeer
**renombrado -da** *adj* renowned, famous
**renombre** *m* renown; surname, family name
**renovable** *adj* renewable
**renovación** *f* renovation; renewal; transformation, restoration; remodeling
**renovador -dora** *adj* renewing, reviving; *mf* renovator
**renoval** *m* growth of new sprouts in a clearing
**renovar §77** *va* to renovate; to renew; to transform, to restore; to remodel; *vr* to renew, become new again
**renovero -ra** *mf* usurer, money lender
**renquear** *vn* to limp
**renta** *f* rent; annuity; income; private income; public debt; government bonds; **renta nacional** gross national product; **rentas patrimoniales** endowment income; **renta vitalicia** life annuity
**rentabilidad** *f* (econ.) yield
**rentable** *adj* income-yielding; *m* income-yielding investment
**rentado -da** *adj* enjoying an income
**rentar** *va* to produce, yield (*an income or profit*)
**rentero -ra** *adj* tributary, tax-paying; *mf* rural tenant, tenant farmer
**rentilla** *f* game played with six dice, each marked 1, 2, 3, 4, 5, or 6, on only one side
**rentista** *mf* financier; bondholder; person of independent means
**rentístico -ca** *adj* financial
**rento** *m* annual rent; farm
**rentoso -sa** *adj* income-yielding
**renuencia** *f* reluctance, unwillingness
**renuente** *adj* reluctant, unwilling
**renuevo** *m* sprout, shoot; renewal
**renuncia** *f* renunciation; resignation; (law) waiver; **hacer renuncia de** to resign (*a post*)
**renunciable** *adj* renounceable
**renunciación** *f* renunciation, renouncement
**renunciamiento** *m* renunciation
**renunciar** *va* to renounce; to resign; to renege; **renunciar una cosa en otra persona** to renounce something in favor of another person; *vn* to resign; to renege; **renunciar a** to give up (*a plan; the world*); *vr* to give up; **renunciarse a** + *inf* to give up + *ger;* **renunciarse a sí mismo** to deny oneself
**renuncio** *m* renege; slip, mistake; (coll.) lie; **coger en un renuncio** (coll.) to catch in a lie
**renvalsar** *va* to rabbet; to shave off, to plane down (*a door or window*)
**renvalso** *m* rabbet; shaving a door or window to make it fit
**reñidamente** *adv* bitterly
**reñidero** *m* cockpit, fighting pit
**reñido -da** *adj* at variance, on bad terms; bitter, hard-fought
**reñidor -dora** *adj* quarrelsome; scolding

**reñidura** *f* (coll.) scolding
**reñir §74** *va* to scold; to fight; to fight for; *vn* to quarrel, fight; to fall out, be at odds
**reo -a** *adj* guilty, criminal; **reo** *mf* offender, criminal; (law) defendant; *m* (ichth.) sea trout; **rea** *f* (law) defendant; (Am.) slattern; (*cap.*) *f* (myth.) Rhea
**reóforo** *m* (elec.) rheophore
**reojo; de reojo** askance, out of the corner of one's eye; over one's shoulder; (coll.) hostilely, scornfully
**reómetro** *m* rheometer
**reorganización** *f* reorganization
**reorganizar §76** *va & vr* to reorganize
**reorientar** *va* to reorient
**reóstato** *m* (elec.) rheostat
**repacer §34** *va* to eat up (*all the pasture*)
**repagar §59** *va* to pay too much for
**repajo** *m* field enclosed with a hedge
**repajolero -ra** *adj* var. of **pajolero**
**repanchigar** or **repantigar §59** *vr* to loll, to sprawl out in a chair
**repapilar** *vr* to glut, to stuff
**reparable** *adj* reparable; noteworthy; noticeable
**reparación** *f* repairing, repairs; reparation
**reparado -da** *adj* strengthened, supplied; squint-eyed; *f* sudden start, sudden shying away (*of a horse*)
**reparador -dora** *adj* repairing, (pertaining to) repair; restorative; faultfinding; *mf* repairer; restorative; faultfinder; *m* repairman; restorative
**reparamiento** *m* var. of **reparación** & **reparo**
**reparar** *va* to repair, to mend; to make amends for; to restore; to notice, observe; to parry; *vn* to stop; **reparar en** to notice, pay attention to; *vr* to stop; to check oneself, to refrain; (Am.) to rear
**reparativo -va** *adj* reparative
**reparista** *adj* (Am.) faultfinding
**reparo** *m* repairing, repairs; restorative; notice, observation; doubt, objection; shelter, protection; bashfulness; parry; **no tener reparos en** + *inf* to have no hesitation in + *ger;* **poner reparo a** to raise an objection to
**reparón -rona** *adj* (coll.) faultfinding; *mf* (coll.) faultfinder
**repartible** *adj* distributable
**repartición** *f* distribution; deal, dealing
**repartidamente** *adv* distributively
**repartidero -ra** *adj* to be distributed, for distribution
**repartidor -dora** *adj* distributing; *mf* distributor; assessor; dealer
**repartimiento** *m* distribution; repartition; assessment; dealing
**repartir** *va* to distribute; to assess; to deal (*cards*)
**reparto** *m* distribution; delivery; assessment; deal; (theat.) cast; (Am.) real-estate development
**repasadera** *f* (carp.) finishing plane
**repasadora** *f* wool comber (*woman*)
**repasar** *va* to repass; to retrace; to pass by or over again; to revise; to review; to mend (*clothing*); to comb (*dyed wool*); to amalgamate (*silver ore*)
**repasata** *f* (coll.) reprimand, dressing-down
**repaso** *m* review; (coll.) reprimand, dressing-down
**repastar** *va* to feed again; to have fed again; to mix again, to add more flour or water to
**repasto** *m* extra feeding
**repatriación** *f* repatriation; return home
**repatriado -da** *adj* repatriated; sent home; *mf* repatriate
**repatriar §90** *va* to repatriate; to send home; *vn & vr* to be repatriated; to go or come home
**repavimentar** *va* to repave
**repechar** *vn* to climb, to go up hill
**repeche** *adj* (Am.) fine, swell, excellent
**repecho** *m* short steep incline; **a repecho** uphill
**repeinado -da** *adj* all slicked up
**repeinar** *va* to comb again; *vr* to do one's hair, to groom one's hair
**repeladura** *f* second shearing or clipping
**repelar** *va* to pull out (*hair*); to pull out the hair of; to nibble, to nip; to clip (*e.g., the nails*); (Am.) to scold; (Am.) to anger, irritate; *vr* to feel sorry, to repent
**repelente** *adj* repellent; (Am.) grim, gruff
**repeler** *va* to repel, to repulse
**repelo** *m* twist, turn (*against the grain, nap, etc.*); crooked grain; (coll.) spat, scuffle; (coll.) aversion; (Am.) rag; **repelo de frío** chill
**repelón** *m* pull on the hair; kink (*in a stocking*); snatch; spurt; **a repelones** (coll.) little by little, with effort; **de repelón** (coll.) swiftly
**repeloso -sa** *adj* crooked-grained; (coll.) touchy, grouchy
**repeluzno** *m* (coll.) chill
**repellar** *va* to splash plaster on (*a wall*)
**repensar §18** *va* to think over again
**repente** *m* (coll.) start, sudden movement; **de repente** suddenly
**repentino -na** *adj* sudden, unexpected
**repentista** *mf* (mus.) improviser; (mus.) sight reader; improviser, extemporizer
**repentización** *f* (mus.) sight reading; improvisation, extemporization
**repentizar §76** *vn* (mus.) to perform at sight, to sight-read; to improvise
**repentón** *m* (coll.) violent start or movement
**repeor** *adj & adv* (coll.) much worse
**repercudida** *f* rebound; repercussion
**repercudir** *va, vn & vr* var. of **repercutir**
**repercusión** *f* repercussion; reflection (*of light*)
**repercusivo -va** *adj & m* (med.) repellent
**repercutir** *va* (med.) to repel; *vn* to rebound; to reëcho, reverberate; **repercutir en** to have a repercussion on; *vr* to reverberate
**repertorio** *m* repertory; repertoire
**repesar** *va* to reweigh; to weigh with great care
**repeso** *m* reweighing; weight office; reweighing charge
**repetición** *f* repetition; repeating mechanism (*of a watch*); repeating watch; (mus.) repeat
**repetidamente** *adv* repeatedly
**repetidor -dora** *adj* repeating; *m* (telp.) repeater
**repetir §94** *va* to repeat; *vn* to repeat; (path.) to repeat; *vr* to repeat oneself; (paint. & sculp.) to copy oneself
**repicar §86** *va* to chop up, to mince; to ring, to sound; to prick again, sting again; to repique (*in piquet*); *vn* to peal, ring out, resound; *vr* to boast, be conceited
**repicotear** *va* to adorn with a jagged or wavy edge
**repinaldo** *m* (hort.) delicious (*large apple*)
**repinar** *vr* to rise, to soar
**repintar** *va* to repaint; (print.) to mackle, to blur; *vn* to repaint; *vr* to paint, to use rouge; (print.) to mackle, to blur
**repinte** *m* repaint
**repique** *m* chopping, mincing; peal, ringing; repique (*in piquet*); (coll.) squabble
**repiquete** *m* lively pealing (*of bells*); brisk rapping; clash, skirmish; (naut.) short tack
**repiquetear** *va* to ring gayly; to beat away at; *vn* to resound, to peal; (mach.) to chatter, clatter; *vr* (coll.) to wrangle, to insult each other
**repiqueteo** *m* gay ringing or pealing; beating, rapping; (mach.) chatter, clatter
**repisa** *f* shelf, ledge; console, bracket; **repisa de chimenea** mantelpiece; **repisa de ventana** window sill
**repisar** *va* to tread again; to tamp, pack down; to cram, to grind into one's head
**repiso** *m* thin wine
**repizcar §86** *va* to pinch
**repizco** *m* pinch
**replantación** *f* replanting
**replantar** *va* to replant
**replantear** *va* to plan or outline again; to restate; to lay out (*a plan*)
**replanteo** *m* new plan, new outline; new layout; restatement
**repleción** *f* repletion, fullness
**replegable** *adj* folding; (aer.) retractable
**replegar §29** *va* to fold over and over; *vr* to fold, fold up; (mil.) to fall back
**repletar** *va & vr* to stuff, to cram
**repleto -ta** *adj* replete, full, loaded; fat, chubby

**réplica** *f* answer, argument, retort; (f.a.) replica; (law) replication
**replicador -dora** *adj* argumentative; *mf* arguer
**replicar §86** *va* to argue against (*e.g., an order*); *vn* to argue back, answer back, retort
**replicato** *m* answer, argument
**replicón -cona** *adj* (coll.) saucy, flip
**repliegue** *m* fold, crease; (mil.) falling back, retirement
**repoblación** *f* repopulation; restocking; afforestation
**repoblar §77** *va* to repopulate; to restock (*e.g., an aquarium*); to afforest
**repodar** *va* to prune again
**repodrir** *va & vr* var. of **repudrir** only in the *inf*
**repollar** *vn & vr* to head (*said, e.g., of a cabbage*)
**repollo** *m* (bot.) cabbage; head (*e.g., of cabbage*)
**repolludo -da** *adj* cabbage-headed, round-headed; headed (*e.g., cabbage*); chubby
**repolluelo** *m* little cabbage; little head (*of cabbage*)
**repondré** *1st sg fut ind of* **reponer**
**reponer §69** *va* to replace, to put back; to restore; to revive (*a play*); to reply, retort; *vr* to recover; to calm down
**repongo** *1st sg pres ind of* **reponer**
**reportación** *f* calm, moderation
**reportaje** *m* reporting; report, news report; **reportaje gráfico** story in pictures; **reportaje radiofónico** (rad.) newscast
**reportamiento** *m* check, restraint
**reportar** *va* to check, restrain; to get, obtain; to bring, carry; to transfer (*a drawing to a lithographic stone*); to report; *vr* to restrain or control oneself
**reporte** *m* report, news report; gossip; transfer (*drawing in lithographic crayon*)
**repórter** *m* reporter
**reporteril** *adj* reportorial
**reporterismo** *m* reporting, news reporting
**reportero -ra** *mf* reporter; **reportero gráfico** news photographer; **reportero radiofónico** (rad.) newscaster
**reportista** *mf* transferrer (*of a drawing to a lithographic stone*)
**reportorio** *m* calendar, almanac
**reposadero** *m* (metal.) iron runner
**reposado -da** *adj* reposeful; solemn, grave
**reposar** *va* to let (*food, a drink, etc.*) settle; **reposar la comida** to rest or take a nap after eating; *vn & vr* to rest; to take a nap; to lie, be at rest (*in the grave*); to settle
**reposición** *f* replacement; recovery (*e.g., of health*); (theat.) revival
**repositorio** *m* repository
**reposo** *m* rest, repose
**repostada** *f* (prov. & Am.) sharp reply, piece of abuse
**repostaje** *m* refueling
**repostar** *va, vn & vr* to stock up; to refuel
**repostería** *f* pastry shop; pastry-shop equipment; confectionery, pastry making, pastry cooking; pastry-shop employees; pantry
**repostero** *m* confectioner, pastry cook; king's butler; square cloth or cover ornamented with coat of arms
**repregunta** *f* (law) cross-examination
**repreguntar** *va* (law) to cross-examine
**reprendedor -dora** *adj & mf* var. of **reprensor**
**reprender** *va* to reprehend, to scold
**reprensible** *adj* reprehensible
**reprensión** *f* reprehension, scolding
**reprensivo -va** *adj* reproachful
**reprensor -sora** *adj* reproachful; *mf* reprehender, reproacher
**represa** *f* dam; damming; check, repression; recapture (*of a ship*)
**represalia** *f* reprisal; retaliation; **represalias** *fpl* reprisal; **tomar represalias** to make reprisals
**represaliar** *va* to make reprisals on, to retaliate on
**represar** *va* to dam; to check, repress; to recapture (*a ship*); *vr* to become dammed
**representable** *adj* representable; performable (*play*)
**representación** *f* representation; dignity, standing; performance; production; representatives; **en representación de** representing; **representación proporcional** (pol.) proportional representation
**representador -dora** *adj* representing; *mf* actor, player
**representanta** *f* actress
**representante** *adj* representing; *mf* representative; actor, player; (com.) agent, representative
**representar** *va* to represent; to show, express; to state, declare; to act, perform, play; to appear to be (*so many years old*); *vr* to imagine
**representativo -va** *adj* representative
**represión** *f* damming; repression; (psychoanal.) repression
**represivo -va** *adj* repressive
**represor -sora** *adj* repressive; *mf* represser
**reprimenda** *f* reprimand
**reprimible** *adj* repressible
**reprimir** *va* to repress
**reprobable** *adj* reprovable
**reprobación** *f* reprobation, reproval, reproof; flunk, failure
**reprobado -da** *adj* failed (*in an exam*); *mf* person who has failed; *adj & mf* var. of **réprobo**
**reprobador -dora** *adj* reproving; *mf* reprover
**reprobar §77** *va* to reprove, to reprobate; to flunk, to fail
**reprobatorio -ria** *adj* reprobative
**réprobo -ba** *adj & mf* (theol.) reprobate
**reprochable** *adj* reproachable
**reprochador -dora** *adj* reproachful; *mf* reproacher
**reprochar** *va* to reproach; **reprochar algo a alguien** to reproach someone for something
**reproche** *m* reproach
**reproducción** *f* reproduction; breeding
**reproducir §38** *va & vr* to reproduce
**reproductible** *adj* reproducible
**reproductivo -va** *adj* productive
**reproductor -tora** *adj* reproductive; reproducing; *mf* reproducer; breeder (*animal*); *m* (mach. & elec.) reproducer
**reproduje** *1st sg pret ind of* **reproducir**
**reproduzco** *1st sg pres ind of* **reproducir**
**repromisión** *f* renewed promise
**repropiar** *vr* to get balky (*said of a horse*)
**repropio -pia** *adj* balky (*horse*)
**reprueba** *f* new proof
**reps** *m* rep or repp (*fabric*)
**reptación** *f* crawl, crawling
**reptar** *vn* to crawl; to be craven, to cringe
**reptil** *adj & m* (zool. & fig.) reptile
**república** *f* republic; **la República de Platón** The Republic, The Republic of Plato; **República Árabe Unida** United Arab Republic; **república de las letras** republic of letters; **República Dominicana** Dominican Republic; **república literaria** republic of letters
**republicanismo** *m* republicanism
**republicano -na** *adj & mf* republican; *m* patriot
**repúblico** *m* prominent citizen; statesman; patriot
**repudiación** *f* repudiation
**repudiar** *va* to repudiate
**repudio** *m* repudiation (*of a wife*)
**repudrir** (*pp:* **repodrido**) *va* to rot completely; (coll.) to irritate, vex; *vr* to rot completely; (coll.) to languish, to pine away
**repuesto -ta** *pp of* **reponer;** *adj* secluded; spare, extra; *m* stock, supply; serving table; pantry; spare part; **de repuesto** spare, extra
**repugnancia** *f* repugnance or repugnancy
**repugnante** *adj* repugnant
**repugnar** *va* to conflict with; to contradict; to object to, to avoid (*e.g., work*); to revolt, to be repugnant to; *vn* to be repugnant; *vr* to conflict
**repujado -da** *adj* repoussé; *m* repoussage; repoussé
**repujar** *va* to do repoussé work on (*metal sheets*); to emboss (*e.g., leather*)
**repulgado -da** *adj* affected
**repulgar §59** *va* (sew.) to hem, to border

**repulgo** *m* (sew.) hem, border; (cook.) fancy edging (*e.g., of a pie or cake*); **repulgo de empanada** trifle, ridiculous scruple
**repulido -da** *adj* highly polished; all dolled up
**repulir** *va* to repolish; to dress up, doll up; *vr* to dress up, doll up
**repulsa** *f* rejection, refusal; reprimand
**repulsar** *va* to reject, to refuse
**repulsión** *f* repulsion; rejection, refusal; (phys.) repulsion; (fig.) repulsion (*strong dislike*)
**repulsivo -va** *adj* (phys. & fig.) repulsive
**repullo** *m* dart; start, jump
**repunta** *f* point, cape; touch, sign; (coll.) quarrel, dispute
**repuntar** *va* (Am.) to round up (*scattered animals*); *vn* to begin to appear; (naut.) to begin to rise; (naut.) to begin to ebb; *vr* to begin to turn sour; (coll.) to fall out
**repunte** *m* (naut.) rise of tide, ebb of tide
**repurgar** **§59** *va* to repurge
**repuse** *1st sg pret ind of* **reponer**
**reputación** *f* reputation, repute
**reputado -da** *adj;* **bien reputado** highly reputed; **mal reputado** of low repute
**reputar** *va* to repute; to esteem
**requebrador -dora** *adj* flirtatious; *mf* flirt
**requebrajo** *m* cheap flattery; brazen flirtation
**requebrar** **§18** *va* to break more, to recrush; to flatter; to say flattering things to, to flirt with
**requemado -da** *adj* burnt; tanned, sunburned; *m* black crepe
**requemamiento** *m* bite, sting
**requemar** *va* to burn again; to parch; to overcook; to inflame; to bite, sting (*the mouth*); *vr* to become tanned or sunburned; to smolder, to burn within
**requemazón** *f* bite, sting
**requerer** **§70** *va* (coll.) to love dearly
**requerimiento** *m* notification; request; summons; urging; checking, examination; requirement; seeking; (law) injunction
**requerir** **§62** *va* to notify; to request; to summon; to urge; to check, examine; to require; to seek, to look for; to reach for; to court, woo, make love to
**requesón** *m* cottage cheese, pot cheese; curd
**requeté** *m* Carlist volunteer; Carlist volunteer militia
**requete-** *prefix* (coll.) very, extremely, e.g., **requetebién** very well, fine; **requetesabroso** extremely tasty
**requiebro** *m* recrushing; crushed ore; flattery; flattering remarks, flirtation
**réquiem** *m* (*pl:* **réquiems**) requiem (*mass and music*)
**requilorios** *mpl* (coll.) waste of time, beating about the bush
**requintador -dora** *mf* outbidder
**requintar** *va* to outbid by a fifth; to exceed, surpass; (mus.) to raise or lower by five points
**requinto** *m* second fifth to be removed; advance of a fifth in bidding; (mus.) fife; (mus.) fifer; (mus.) small guitar
**requisa** *f* inspection; round of inspection; round (*made by jailer*); (mil.) requisition
**requisar** *va* to inspect; (mil.) to requisition
**requisición** *f* (mil.) requisition
**requisito -ta** *adj* requisite; *m* requisite, requirement; accomplishment (*in some social art or grace*); **requisito previo** prerequisite
**requives** *mpl* var. of **arrequives**
**res** *f* head of cattle; beast; **res de vientre** breeding female (*animal*)
**resaber** **§80** *va* to know thoroughly
**resabiado -da** *adj* wicked, sly, crafty; spoiled, ill-bred (*child*)
**resabiar** *va* to give a vice or bad habits to; *vr* to contract a vice or bad habits; to relish; to become displeased; to become tasteless
**resabido -da** *adj* well-known, notorious; pedantic
**resabio** *m* unpleasant aftertaste; vice, bad habit
**resabioso -sa** *adj* (Am.) sly, crafty; (Am.) wicked, vicious (*horse*)
**resabré** *1st sg fut ind of* **resaber**
**resaca** *f* surge, surf, undertow; (com.) redraft; (slang) hangover; **traer una resaca** (slang) to have a hangover
**resacar** **§86** *va* (naut.) to underrun; (hunt.) to flush out; (com.) to redraw; (coll.) to take out again, to take right out
**resalado -da** *adj* (coll.) charming, witty
**resalar** *va* to salt again
**resaldré** *1st sg fut ind of* **resalir**
**resalga** *f* brine
**resalgo** *1st sg pres ind of* **resalir**
**resalir** **§81** *vn* to jut out, project
**resalsero** *m* rough stretch of sea
**resaltar** *va* to emphasize; *vn* to bounce, rebound; to jut out, project; to stand out
**resalte** *m* projection
**resalto** *m* bounce, rebound; projection
**resaludar** *va* to return a greeting or salute to
**resalutación** *f* return greeting or salute
**resalvo** *m* sapling or staddle (*left in stubbing*)
**resallar** *va* to weed again
**resanar** *va* to retouch with gold or gilt; to repair; to patch (*a chipped wall*)
**resarcible** *adj* indemnifiable
**resarcimiento** *m* compensation, indemnification, repayment
**resarcir** **§50** *va* to make amends to (*a person*); to repay (*a harm, an insult*); to make up for, to make good (*a loss*); to mend, repair; *vr;* **resarcirse de** to make up for
**resbaladero -ra** *adj* slippery; *m* slippery place; chute; *f* slide
**resbaladizo -za** *adj* slippery; skiddy; risky; shaky, treacherous (*memory*)
**resbalador -dora** *adj* sliding; skiddy
**resbaladura** *f* mark left from sliding or slipping
**resbalamiento** *m* slide, slip; skid
**resbalar** *vn* to slide; to skid; *vr* to slide, to slip; (fig.) to slip, to misstep
**resbalera** *f* slippery place
**resbalón** *m* slide, slip; skid, skidding; misstep
**resbaloso -sa** *adj* slippery
**rescaldar** *va* var. of **escaldar**
**rescatar** *va* to ransom, redeem; to rescue; to make up for (*lost time*); to relieve; to atone for; to trade valuables for (*ordinary goods*)
**rescate** *m* ransom, redemption; rescue; salvage; ransom money; prisoner's base (*children's game*)
**rescaza** *f* (ichth.) scorpene
**rescindir** *va* to rescind
**rescisión** *f* rescission
**rescoldera** *f* (path.) heartburn
**rescoldo** *m* embers; smoldering; scruple, doubt; **arder en rescoldo** to smolder
**rescontrar** **§77** *va* (com.) to set off, to offset, to balance
**rescripto** *m* rescript
**rescuentro** *m* (com.) offset, balance
**resé** *1st sg pres ind of* **resaber**
**resecación** *f* thorough drying, desiccation
**resecar** **§86** *va* to dry up, to dry out; (surg.) to resect; *vr* to dry up, to dry out
**resección** *f* resection
**reseco -ca** *adj* very dry, too dry; very lean; *m* dry part (*of a tree; of a honeycomb*)
**reseda** *f* (bot.) mignonette; (bot.) dyer's rocket
**resedáceo -a** *adj* (bot.) resedaceous
**resegar** **§29** *va* to mow again
**reseguir** **§82** *va* to edge (*a sword*)
**resellar** *va* to reseal; to restamp; to recoin; to surcharge; *vr* to become a turncoat
**resembrar** **§18** *va* to resow, to replant
**resentido -da** *adj* resentful
**resentimiento** *m* resentment; sorrow, disappointment
**resentir** **§62** *vr* to become weakened, begin to give way; to be resentful; **resentirse de** to begin to feel the bad effects of; to resent; to suffer from; **resentirse por** to resent
**reseña** *f* sketch, outline; review (*of a book*); newspaper account; (mil.) review
**reseñar** *va* to sketch, outline; to review (*a book*); to check; (mil.) to review
**resepa** *1st sg pres subj of* **resaber**
**resequido -da** *adj* parched, dried up
**resero** *m* (Am.) cowboy, herdsman; (Am.) livestock dealer
**reserpina** *f* (pharm.) reserpine
**reserva** *f* reserve; reservation; (com. & mil.) reserve; **a reserva de** with the intention of;

**con** or **bajo la mayor reserva** in strictest confidence; **sin reserva** without reservation; **reserva de indios** (U.S.A.) Indian reservation; **reserva mental** mental reservation
**reservación** *f* reservation
**reservado -da** *adj* reserved; *m* reservation, reserved place; (rail.) reserved compartment
**reservar** *va* to reserve; to postpone; to put aside; to exempt; to conceal, keep secret; *vr* to save oneself, to bide one's time; to beware, to be distrustful
**reservista** *adj* (mil.) reserve; *mf* (mil.) reservist
**reservón -vona** *adj* (coll.) reserved, retiring, distant
**reservorio** *m* reservoir
**resfriado** *m* cold (*e.g., in the head*); watering before plowing; **resfriado común** common cold
**resfriador -dora** *adj* cooling
**resfriadura** *f* (vet.) cold
**resfriamiento** *m* cooling, refrigeration
**resfriante** *adj* cooling; *m* cooler of a still
**resfriar §90** *va* to cool, to chill; to cool off (*e.g., enthusiasm*); *vn* to turn cold; *vr* to catch cold; to cool, to chill; (fig.) to cool off, grow cold
**resfrío** *m* cold
**resguardar** *va* to defend; to protect, to shield; *vr* to take shelter; to protect oneself
**resguardo** *m* defense; protection; guard; guarantee; check, voucher; frontier guard; (naut.) wide berth, sea room
**residencia** *f* residence, residency; (educ.) residence; (law) impeachment
**residencial** *adj* residential; residentiary
**residenciar** *va* to call to account; (law) to impeach
**residente** *adj* resident, residing; *mf* resident
**residir** *vn* to reside
**residual** *adj* residual, residuary
**residuo** *m* remains, residue; residuum; (math.) remainder
**resiembra** *f* resowing, replanting
**resigna** *f* (eccl.) resignation
**resignación** *f* resignation
**resignadamente** *adv* resignedly
**resignar** *va* to resign; **resignar el mando en otra persona** to resign command to another person; *vr* to resign oneself; to become resigned; **resignarse a** + *inf* to resign oneself to + *inf*
**resiliencia** *f* (mech.) resilience
**resina** *f* resin, rosin; **resina acaroide** acaroide gum or resin
**resinación** *f* extraction of resin
**resinar** *va* to draw resin from
**resinato** *m* (chem.) resinate
**resinero -ra** *adj* (pertaining to) resin; *m* resin extractor
**resinífero -ra** *adj* resiniferous
**resinoide** *adj & m* resinoid
**resinoideo -a** *adj* resinoid
**resinoso -sa** *adj* resinous
**resistencia** *f* resistance; strength; (elec.) resistance; **oponer resistencia** to offer resistance; **resistencia al avance** (aer.) drag; **resistencia de rejilla** (rad.) grid leak; **resistencia pasiva** passive resistance
**resistente** *adj* resistant; strong, firm
**resistero** *m* hottest time of the day; heat from glare of sun; spot made hot by glare of sun
**resistibilidad** *f* resistibility
**resistible** *adj* resistible
**resistidero** *m* var. of **resistero**
**resistidor -dora** *adj* resistant
**resistir** *va* to resist (*temptation*); to bear, to stand, to withstand; *vn* to resist; **resistir a** to resist (*a contrary force, a desire to laugh*); **resistir a** + *inf* to refuse to + *inf;* to resist + *ger; vr* to resist; to struggle; to bear up; **resistirse a** + *inf* to refuse to + *inf;* to resist + *ger*
**resistividad** *f* (elec.) resistivity
**resistivo -va** *adj* resistive
**resistor** *m* (elec.) resistor
**resma** *f* ream (*of paper*)
**resmilla** *f* package of a hundred sheets of letter paper
**resnatrón** *m* (elec.) resnatron
**resobado -da** *adj* threadbare, hackneyed
**resobrar** *vn* to be greatly in excess
**resobrina** *f* grandniece, great-niece
**resobrino** *m* grandnephew, great-nephew
**resol** *m* sun's glare
**resolano -na** *adj* sunny and sheltered (*from wind*); *f* sunny and sheltered spot
**resoluble** *adj* resoluble, resolvable
**resolución** *f* resolution; **en resolución** in sum, in a word
**resolutivo -va** *adj & m* (med.) resolutive
**resoluto -ta** *adj* resolute; brief, compendious; expert, skillful
**resolvente** *adj & m* resolvent
**resolver §63 & §17, 9** *va* to resolve; to decide on; to solve; to dissolve; to analyze, divide; to sum up; **resolver** + *inf* to resolve to + *inf; vr* to resolve; **resolverse a** + *inf* to resolve to + *inf;* **resolverse en** to turn into; **resolverse por** to resolve on or upon
**resollar §77** *vn* to breathe; to breathe hard, to pant; to breathe again, breathe freely; to stop for a rest; (coll.) to show up; **no resollar** to not say a word
**resonación** *f* resounding
**resonador** *m* resonator; (telg.) sounder
**resonancia** *f* resonance; echo; (fig.) repercussion; **tener resonancia** to be bruited abroad, to be headlined
**resonante** *adj* resonant; resounding, echoing
**resonar §77** *vn* to resonate; to resound, to echo
**resoplar** *vn* to puff, to breathe hard; to snort
**resoplido** or **resoplo** *m* puffing, hard breathing; snort
**resorber** *va* to resorb
**resorcina** *f* (chem.) resorcin or resorcinol
**resorción** *f* resorption
**resorte** *m* spring; springiness; means; motive; province, scope; (Am.) rubber band; **ser del resorte de** (Am.) to be within the province of; **tocar resortes** to pull wires; **resorte espiral** coil spring
**respailar** *vn* (coll.) to scurry; **ir respailando** (coll.) to scurry along
**respaldar** *m* back (*of a seat*); *va* to indorse; (fig.) to indorse; (fig.) to back; *vr* to lean back; to sprawl, sprawl out
**respaldo** *m* back (*of a seat; of a sheet of paper*); indorsement; backing; (min.) wall of a vein
**respectar** *va* to concern; **por lo que respecta a** as far as . . . is concerned
**respectivo -va** *adj* respective
**respecto** *m* respect, reference, relation; **al respecto** in the matter; **bajo ese respecto** in that respect; **con respecto a** or **de, respecto a** or **de** with respect to, with regard to
**respeluzar §76** *va & vr* var. of **despeluzar**
**respetabilidad** *f* respectability
**respetable** *adj* respectable; **a respetable distancia** at a respectable distance; **el más respetable** the oldest
**respetador -dora** *adj* respectful
**respetar** *va* to respect
**respeto** *m* respect; consideration; spare; **campar por su respeto** or **sus respetos** to be self-centered, to be inconsiderate; **de respeto** spare, extra; **estar de respeto** to be all decked out; **ofrecer sus respetos a** to pay one's respects to
**respetuosidad** *f* respectfulness; awesomeness; humility, obedience
**respetuoso -sa** *adj* respectful; impressive, awesome; humble, obedient
**réspice** *m* (coll.) sharp reply; (coll.) sharp reproof
**respigador -dora** *mf* gleaner
**respigar §59** *va* to glean
**respigón** *m* hangnail; (vet.) sore on heel (*of horse*)
**respingado -da** *adj* upturned, turned up (*nose*)
**respingar §59** *vn* to balk, to shy; (coll.) to curl up (*said of edge of poorly made garment*); (coll.) to resist, to give in unwillingly
**respingo** *m* balking, shying; wincing; violent shaking; (coll.) gesture of revolt, gesture of revulsion
**respingón -gona** *adj* (Am.) surly, churlish; upturned, turned up (*nose*)

**respingoso -sa** *adj* balky; (coll.) gruff, sour
**respirable** *adj* breathable
**respiración** *f* respiration, breathing; ventilation
**respiradero** *m* vent, venthole (*in a barrel*); air valve; ventilation shaft; louver; breather, respite; snorkel; (coll.) organ of respiration
**respirador -dora** *adj* breathing; respiratory; *m* respirator
**respirar** *va* to breathe; (fig.) to breathe (*e.g., love, kindness*); *vn* to breathe; to leak; to breathe again, breathe freely; to breathe a sigh of relief; to catch one's breath, to stop for a rest; (coll.) to show up; to smell; **no respirar** (coll.) to not breathe a word; **sin respirar** without respite, without letup; **respirar a** to smell of
**respiratorio -ria** *adj* respiratory
**respiro** *m* breathing; respite, breather, breathing spell; reprieve, relief; extension of time (*for payment*)
**resplandecer §34** *vn* to shine; to flash, to glitter; (fig.) to shine, stand out
**resplandeciente** *adj* brilliant, radiant; resplendent
**resplandecimiento** *m* brilliance, radiance
**resplandina** *f* (coll.) sharp reproof
**resplandor** *m* brilliance, radiance; glare; resplendence; cosmetic
**respondedor -dora** *adj & mf* respondent
**responder** *va* to answer; to clear up, explain away; to answer with (*e.g., an insult*); *vn* to answer; to respond; to reëcho; to correspond, harmonize; to yield, produce; to face; to answer back, be saucy; **responder a** to answer; to match; **responder de** to answer for (*a thing*); **responder por** to answer for (*a person*)
**respondón -dona** *adj* (coll.) saucy
**responsabilidad** *f* responsibility
**responsabilizar §76** *va* to make responsible; *vr* to take the responsibility
**responsable** *adj* responsible; **responsable de** responsible for
**responsar** *va* (coll.) to scold; *vn* to say prayers for the dead
**responsear** *vn* (coll.) to say prayers for the dead
**responsivo -va** *adj* responsive
**responso** *m* (eccl.) prayer for the dead; (coll.) reprimand, scolding
**responsorio** *m* (eccl.) responsory
**respuesta** *f* answer, response; (rad.) response; **respuesta comercial** business-reply card
**resquebradura** *f* crack, split
**resquebrajadizo -za** *adj* easily cracked or split
**resquebrajadura** *f* var. of **resquebradura**
**resquebrajar** *va & vr* to crack, to split
**resquebrajo** *m* var. of **resquebradura**
**resquebrajoso -sa** *adj* var. of **resquebrajadizo**
**resquebrar §18** *va & vr* to begin to crack or split
**resquemar** *va* to bite, sting (*the tongue*); to parch; to burn (*food*); *vn* to bite, sting; *vr* to become parched; to become burned; to smolder (*to be furious without showing it*)
**resquemazón** *f* or **resquemo** *m* bite, sting (*of food*); burnt taste (*of food*); parching; burning
**resquemor** *m* sorrow, grief; bite, sting (*of food*)
**resquicio** *m* crack, chink; chance, opportunity, occasion
**resta** *f* (math.) subtraction; (math.) remainder
**restablecer §34** *va* to reëstablish, to restore; *vr* to recover
**restablecimiento** *m* reëstablishment, restoration; recovery
**restallar** *vn* to crack (*like a whip*); to crackle
**restampar** *va* to reprint, to restamp, to reëngrave
**restante** *adj* remaining; *m* rest, remainder
**restañar** *va* to stanch (*blood*); to retin; *vn* to crack (*like a whip*); to crackle; to stanch, be stanched; *vr* to stanch, be stanched
**restañasangre** *f* bloodstone
**restaño** *m* stanching, stopping; stagnation; gold cloth, silver cloth
**restar** *va* to deduct; to return (*a ball*); to reduce, take away; (math.) to subtract; **restar a** to take from; *vn* to remain, be left
**restauración** *f* restoration
**restaurador -dora** *mf* reviver; restorer
**restaurán** *m* restaurant
**restaurante** *adj* restoring; *mf* restorer; *m* restaurant; **restaurante automático** automat
**restaurar** *va* to restore; to recover
**restaurativo -va** *adj & m* restorative
**restinga** *f* (naut.) shoal, bar
**restingar** *m* (naut.) shoaly spot
**restitución** *f* restitution, return
**restituíble** *adj* returnable; restorable
**restituidor -dora** *adj* restoring; *mf* restorer
**restituir §41** *va* to return, give back; to restore; *vr* to return, come back
**restitutorio -ria** *adj* restitutory
**resto** *m* rest, remainder, residue; stakes (*at cards*); return (*of ball*); player who returns ball; (math.) remainder; **restos** *mpl* remains, mortal remains; **a resto abierto** (coll.) without limit; **echar** or **envidar el resto** to stake all, to shoot the works; (coll.) to spread oneself, to make the greatest effort; **restos de serie** remnants; **restos mortales** remains, mortal remains
**restorán** *m* restaurant
**restregadura** *f* hard rubbing or scrubbing; rub (*mark*)
**restregamiento** *m* hard rubbing or scrubbing
**restregar §29** *va* to rub or scrub hard; *vr* to rub hard
**restregón** *m* hard rub, rough rub
**restribar** *vn* to rest heavily, lean heavily
**restricción** *f* restriction, restraint; **restricción mental** mental reservation
**restrictivo -va** *adj* restrictive; (gram.) restrictive
**restricto -ta** *adj* restricted, limited
**restringa** *f* var. of **restinga**
**restringente** *adj & m* restringent
**restringir §42** *va* to restrict; to constrict, contract
**restriñimiento** *m* constriction, contraction
**restriñir §25** *va* to constrict, contract
**resucitación** *f* resuscitation
**resucitador -dora** *adj* resuscitative; *mf* resuscitator
**resucitar** *va* to resuscitate; to resurrect; (coll.) to resuscitate, revive; *vn* to resuscitate; to resurrect; (coll.) to revive
**resudación** *f* light sweat, slight perspiration; oozing
**resudamiento** *m* sweating; seepage
**resudar** *vn* to sweat or perspire slightly; to dry out; to ooze; *vr* to ooze
**resudor** *m* light sweat, slight perspiration
**resuelto -ta** *pp of* **resolver;** *adj* resolute, determined, resolved; quick, prompt
**resuello** *m* breathing; hard breathing
**resulta** *f* result; outcome; vacancy; **de resultas de** as a result of
**resultado** *m* result
**resultancia** *f* result
**resultando** *m* (law) finding
**resultante** *adj* resultant; *f* (mech.) resultant
**resultar** *vn* to result; to prove to be, to turn out to be; to become; (coll.) to please; **resultar de** to result from; to arise from; **resultar ser** to turn out to be
**resumbruno -na** *adj* yellowish black (*hawk*)
**resumen** *m* summary, recapitulation, résumé; **en resumen** in a word, to sum up
**resumidamente** *adv* in a word, to sum up
**resumidero** *m* (Am.) drain, sewer
**resumir** *va* to sum up, summarize; *vr* to be reduced, be transformed
**resupe** *1st sg pret ind of* **resaber**
**resurgimiento** *m* resurgence
**resurgir §42** *vn* to resurge; to revive; to result
**resurrección** *f* resurrection; (*cap.*) *f* (theol.) Resurrection
**resurtida** *f* rebound
**resurtir** *vn* to rebound, bounce back
**retablo** *m* series of historical paintings or carvings; (eccl.) altarpiece, retable, reredos
**retacar §86** *va* (billiards) to hit (*the ball*) twice
**retacería** *f* odds and ends (*of cloth*)

**retaco** *m* short fowling piece; short cue; (coll.) chubby fellow
**retacón -cona** *adj* (Am.) chubby
**retador -dora** *adj* challenging; *m* challenger
**retaguardia** *f* rear guard; **a retaguardia** in the rear; **picar la retaguardia** to pursue the rear guard hotly
**retahila** *f* string, line
**retajar** *va* to cut round; to trim the nib of (*a quill pen*)
**retal** *m* remnant, piece; piece of hide (*for making glue*)
**retaladrar** *va* to rebore
**retallar** *va* to retouch (*an engraving*); (arch.) to build ledges or projections in (*a wall*)
**retallecer §34** *vn* to sprout again
**retallo** *m* new sprout; (arch.) ledge, projection
**retama** *f* (bot.) Spanish broom; **retama de China** (bot.) Spanish broom; **retama de escoba** (bot.) furze; **retama de olor** (bot.) Spanish broom; **retama de tintes** or **de tintoreros** (bot.) dyeweed, woodwaxen; **retama macho** (bot.) Spanish broom; **retama negra** (bot.) furze
**retamal** *m* or **retamar** *m* growth of Spanish broom; growth of furze
**retamero -ra** *adj* broomy; furzy
**retar** *va* to challenge, to dare; (coll.) to blame, find fault with
**retardación** *f* retardation, delay; deceleration
**retardador -dora** or **-triz** (*pl:* **-trices**) *adj* retarding, delaying
**retardar** *va & vr* to retard, to slow down; to decelerate
**retardo** *m* retard, retardation, delay
**retartalillas** *fpl* flow of words, garrulity
**retasa** or **retasación** *f* reappraisement
**retasar** *va* to reappraise; to reduce the appraisement of (*an object left unsold in an auction*)
**retazar §76** *va* to tear to pieces; to separate into small flocks
**retazo** *m* remnant, piece; scrap; portion, fragment (*e.g., of a speech*)
**rete-** *prefix* (coll.) very, extremely, e.g., **retebién** very well
**retecho** *m* eaves
**retejar** *va* to repair (*a tile roof*), to retile (*a roof*); (coll.) to provide with clothing and footwear
**retejer** *va* to weave closely or tightly
**retejo** *m* roof repairing, retiling
**retel** *m* fishing net
**retemblar §18** *vn* to shake, quiver
**retén** *m* store, stock, reserve; pawl, catch; (mil.) reserve, reserve corps; *2d sg impv of* **retener**
**retención** *f* retention; stoppage (*of payment of wages, etc.*); amount withheld; (law) retainer
**retendré** *1st sg fut ind of* **retener**
**retener §85** *va* to retain, keep, withhold; to stop (*payment*); to detain, arrest
**retengo** *1st sg pres ind of* **retener**
**retenida** *f* guy; (naut.) preventer rope; (naut.) fast
**retenimiento** *m* retention
**retentar §18** *va* to threaten with a relapse
**retentiva** *f* see **retentivo**
**retentividad** *f* (phys.) retentivity
**retentivo -va** *adj* retentive; *f* retentiveness, memory
**reteñir §74** *va* to redye; *vn* to ding-dong, to jingle; to ring (*said of the ears*)
**retesamiento** *m* tightening
**retesar** *va* to draw or stretch tighter
**reteso** *m* tightening; breast, slight rise
**reticencia** *f* half-truth; evasiveness; (rhet.) reticence
**reticente** *adj* deceptive, misleading; noncommittal
**rético -ca** *adj & mf* Rhaetian; *m* Rhaetian (*language*)
**retícula** *f* reticule (*small handbag*); half-tone screen; (opt.) reticule; (*cap.*) *f* (astr.) Reticule
**reticulación** *f* reticulation
**reticulado -da** *adj* reticulate
**reticular** *adj* reticular
**retículo** *m* reticulum, network; (anat., bot. & zool.) reticulum; (opt.) reticle, spider lines
**retienta** *f* (taur.) second testing of mettle of young bull
**retina** *f* (anat.) retina
**retiniano -na** *adj* retinal
**retinitis** *f* (path.) retinitis
**retinte** *m* second dyeing; ding-dong, jingle; (coll.) tone of reproach
**retintín** *m* ding-dong, jingle; ringing (*in the ears*); (coll.) tone of reproach
**retinto -ta** *adj* dark-chestnut (*horse*)
**retiñir §25** *vn* to ding-dong, to jingle; to ring (*said of the ears*)
**retiración** *f* withdrawal; (print.) (act of) backing; (print.) form for backing
**retirada** *f* see **retirado**
**retiradamente** *adv* secretly; in seclusion
**retirado -da** *adj* far, distant; retired; *m* (mil.) retired officer; *f* retirement, withdrawal; place of refuge; dry bed (*left by changed course of stream*); (mil.) retreat, retirement; (mil.) retreat (*signal at sunset*); **emprender la retirada, batirse en retirada** or **marchar en retirada** (mil.) to beat a retreat; **en plena retirada** in full retreat
**retiramiento** *m* retirement
**retirar** *va* to retire, to withdraw; to take away; to force out; (print.) to back; *vr* to retire, to withdraw; (mil.) to retire
**retiro** *m* retirement; withdrawal; (eccl.) retreat; (mil.) retirement, pension; **retiro obrero** social security
**reto** *m* challenge, dare; threat; (Am.) insult
**retobado -da** *adj* (Am.) saucy; (Am.) stubborn; (Am.) sly, crafty
**retobar** *va* (Am.) to cover or line with hide; (Am.) to wrap in burlap, leather, or oilcloth; *vr* (Am.) to stand aloof, be unpleasant
**retocador -dora** *mf* (phot.) retoucher
**retocamiento** *m* retouching
**retocar §86** *va* to retouch; to touch up; to finish, give the finishing touch to; to play back (*a phonograph record*); (phot.) to retouch
**retoñar** *vn* to sprout, to shoot; to reappear, revive
**retoñecer §34** *vn* var. of **retoñar**
**retoño** *m* sprout, shoot, sucker
**retoque** *m* retouching; finishing touch; touch (*of sickness*)
**retor** *m* twilled cotton fabric
**rétor** *m* rhetor
**retorcedura** *f* twisting; wringing; writhing
**retorcer §87** *va* to twist; to twist together; to wring (*the hands*); (fig.) to twist, misconstrue; *vr* to twist; to writhe
**retorcido** *m* tutti-frutti
**retorcimiento** *m* var. of **retorcedura**
**retórica** *f* see **retórico**
**retoricar §86** *va* (coll.) to treat with sophistry or subtleties; *vn* to speak rhetorically; (coll.) to use sophistry or subtleties
**retórico -ca** *adj* rhetorical; *mf* rhetorician; *f* rhetoric; **retóricas** *fpl* (coll.) sophistries, subtleties
**retornamiento** *m* return
**retornar** *va* to return, give back; to back, back up; to twist again; *vn & vr* to return, go back
**retornelo** *m* (mus.) ritornello
**retorno** *m* return; barter, exchange; reward, requital; return carriage, return horse, return donkey; (naut.) leading block; **retorno eterno** (philos.) eternal recurrence; **retorno por masa** (elec.) ground return (*e.g., in an automobile or radio*); **retorno por tierra** (elec.) ground return; **retorno terrestre** (elec.) ground
**retorromano -na** *adj & m* Rhaeto-Romanic
**retorsión** *f* retorsion; retaliation; twist, misconstruction; (law) retorsion
**retorta** *f* (chem.) retort
**retortero** *m* twist, turn; **andar al retortero** (coll.) to bustle around, to worry around; **traer al retortero** (coll.) to push around, to harass; (coll.) to string along, to mislead with false promises and flattery
**retortijar** *va* to curl up, twist up
**retortijón** *m* curling up, twisting up; **retortijón de tripas** bellyache, cramps
**retostado -da** *adj* dark-brown
**retostar §77** *va* to toast again; to toast brown

**retozador -dora** *adj* var. of **retozón**
**retozadura** *f* frolicking, gamboling, romping
**retozar §76** *vn* to frolic, gambol, romp; to become aroused or inflamed
**retozo** *m* frolic, gambol, romping; **retozo de la risa** giggle, titter
**retozón -zona** *adj* frolicsome, frisky, playful
**retracción** *f* retraction
**retractable** *adj* retractable; revocable
**retractación** *f* retraction, retractation
**retractar** *va* to retract; (law) to redeem; *vr* to retract; **retractarse de** to retract, take back (*something said*)
**retráctil** *adj* retractile; (aer.) retractable
**retracto** *m* (law) prior right to purchase
**retractor -tora** *adj* retractive; *m* (surg.) retractor
**retraducir §38** *va* to retranslate
**retraduje** *1st sg pret ind of* **retraducir**
**retraduzco** *1st sg pres ind of* **retraducir**
**retraer §88** *va* to bring again, bring back; to dissuade; (law) to redeem; *vr* to withdraw, retire; to keep or stay in retirement; to take refuge; **retraerse a sagrado** to take sanctuary; **retraerse de** to withdraw from, give up, abandon
**retraído -da** *adj* solitary; reserved, shy; *mf* person who has taken sanctuary
**retraigo** *1st sg pres ind of* **retraer**
**retraimiento** *m* withdrawal, retirement; solitude; reserve, shyness; asylum, refuge; sanctum, retreat
**retraje** *1st sg pret ind of* **retraer**
**retranca** *f* breeching; (Am.) brake
**retranquear** *va* to hoist and put (*building stones*) in place
**retranqueo** *m* hoisting and placing building stones
**retranquero** *m* (Am.) brakeman
**retransmisión** *f* rebroadcasting
**retransmitir** *va* to rebroadcast
**retraqueo** *m* (arch.) setback
**retrasar** *va* to delay, retard; to put off; to set or turn back (*a watch or clock*); to slow down (*a watch or clock*); *vn* to be too slow; to be or fall behind (*e.g., in one's studies*); *vr* to delay, be late, be slow, be behind time; to be too slow; to go or be slow (*said of a watch or clock*); **retrasarse en** + *inf* to be late or slow in + *ger*
**retraso** *m* delay, slowness; lag; **tener retraso** to be late; **retraso de fase** (elec.) phase lag
**retratador -dora** *mf* var. of **retratista**
**retratar** *va* to portray; to photograph; to imitate; (fig.) to portray; *vr* to sit for a portrait or photograph; to be photographed
**retratería** *f* (Am.) photography
**retratista** *mf* portraitist, portrait painter
**retrato** *m* portrait; photograph; copy, imitation; portraiture, description; (fig.) picture; **ser el vivo retrato de** to be the living image of
**retrechar** *vn* to back, back up (*said of a horse*)
**retrechería** *f* (coll.) slyness, cunning, evasiveness
**retrechero -ra** *adj* (coll.) sly, cunning, evasive; (coll.) attractive; (Am.) shy (*horse*)
**retrepado -da** *adj* leaning backward; slanting backward
**retrepar** *vr* to lean back; to lean back in a chair
**retreta** *f* (mil.) retreat, tattoo; tattoo (*military parade and celebration after dark*); (Am.) nighttime outdoor band concert
**retrete** *m* toilet, water closet
**retretero** *m* lavatory man
**retribución** *f* repayment, reward; compensation, pay; fee
**retribuir §41** *va* to repay, reward, pay back; to pay for
**retributivo -va** *adj* rewarding
**retroactividad** *f* retroactivity
**retroactivo -va** *adj* retroactive
**retrocarga; de retrocarga** breech-loading
**retroceder** *vn* to retrocede; to back away; to back out, back down
**retrocesión** *f* retrocession
**retroceso** *m* retrocession, backing; recoil (*of a gun*); flare-up (*of a disease*)
**retrocohete** *m* retrorocket
**retrodisparo** *m* retrofiring
**retroflexión** *f* retroflexion; (path.) retroflexion
**retrogradación** *f* retrogradation; (astr.) retrogradation
**retrogradar** *vn* (astr.) to retrograde
**retrógrado -da** *adj* retrograde; (pol.) reactionary; *mf* (pol.) reactionary
**retrogresión** *f* retrogression
**retromarcha** *f* (aut.) reverse
**retronar §77** *vn* to thunder, to rumble
**retropilastra** *f* (arch.) pilaster back of a column
**retropropulsión** *f* (aer.) jet propulsion
**retropulsión** *f* (obstet. & path.) retropulsion
**retrospección** *f* retrospect, retrospection
**retrospectivo -va** *adj* retrospective
**retrotracción** *f* (law) antedating
**retrotraer §88** *va* (law) to antedate, to date back
**retrotraigo** *1st sg pres ind of* **retrotraer**
**retrotraje** *1st sg pret ind of* **retrotraer**
**retrovender** *va* (law) to sell back
**retrovendición** *f* or **retroventa** *f* (law) selling back
**retroversión** *f* (path.) retroversion
**retrovisor** *m* (aut.) rear-view mirror
**retrucar §86** *vn* to answer, to reply; (billiards) to kiss
**retruco** *m* (billiards) kiss
**retruécano** *m* pun, play on words
**retruque** *m* var. of **retruco**
**retumbante** *adj* resounding, rumbling; bombastic, high-flown
**retumbar** *vn* to resound, to rumble
**retumbo** *m* resounding, rumble, echo
**retundir** *va* to even (*the face of a wall*)
**retuso -sa** *adj* (bot.) retuse
**retuve** *1st sg pret ind of* **retener**
**reuma** *m & f* (path.) rheumatism; (path.) rheum
**reumático -ca** *adj & mf* rheumatic
**reumátide** *f* (path.) rheumatic dermatosis
**reumatismo** *m* (path.) rheumatism
**reumatoideo -a** *adj* rheumatoid
**reunificación** *f* reunification
**reunificar §86** *va* to reunify
**reunión** *f* reunion, gathering, meeting; assemblage (*of persons or things*)
**reunir §75** *va* to join, unite; to assemble, gather together, bring together; to reunite; to combine; to raise (*money*); *vr* to unite; to assemble, gather together, meet, come together; to reunite; to concur, conspire
**reuntar §75** *va* to oil again, grease again
**revacunación** *f* revaccination
**revacunar** *va* to revaccinate
**reválida** *f* final examination (*for a degree*)
**revalidación** *f* ratification, revalidation
**revalidar** *va* to ratify, revalidate; *vr* to take an examination for a degree
**revaloración** *f* (econ.) revaluation
**revalorar** *va* to revalue
**revalorización** *f* revaluation; reclamation
**revalorizar §76** *va* to revalue; to reclaim
**revancha** *f* revenge, reprisal
**revanchista** *adj & mf* revanchist
**revecero -ra** *adj* shifting; *mf* farmhand in charge of relays of oxen
**reveedor** *m* revisor, inspector
**revejecer §34** *vn & vr* to age before one's time
**revejido -da** *adj* aged before one's time
**revelación** *f* revelation
**revelado -da** *adj* revealed; *m* (phot.) development
**revelador -dora** *adj* revealing; *mf* revealer; *m* (phot.) developer
**revelamiento** *m* revealment
**revelandero -ra** *mf* fake who lays claim to divine revelation
**revelar** *va* to reveal; (phot.) to develop
**reveler** *va* (med.) to bring about revulsion in
**revellín** *m* (fort.) ravelin
**revenar** *vn* to sprout (*after a trimming, topping, or grafting*)
**revendedera** *f* var. of **revendedora**
**revendedor -dora** *mf* reseller; retailer; scalper, ticket speculator
**revender** *va* to resell; to retail
**revendré** *1st sg fut ind of* **revenir**
**revengo** *1st sg pres ind of* **revenir**
**revenido** *m* annealing

**revenimiento** *m* return (*to a previous state*); shrinking, drying out; souring; (min.) cave-in
**revenir §92** *vn* to come back; *vr* to shrink, dry out; to turn sour; to weaken, back down; (min.) to cave in
**reveno** *m* sprout (*that grows after a trimming, topping, or grafting*)
**reventa** *f* resale
**reventadero** *m* rough ground; (coll.) chore, hard task
**reventador** *m* (theat.) paid hisser
**reventar §18** *va* to smash, crush; to burst, explode, blow out; to ruin; to annoy, bore; to work (*a person*) to death; to run (*a horse*) to death; *vn* to burst, explode, blow out; to break (*said of waves*); (coll.) to burst out (*said, e.g., of anger*); (coll.) to die a violent death; (coll.) to croak (*to die*); **reventar por** + *inf* to be bursting to + *inf; vr* to burst, explode, blow out; to be worked to death; to be run to death (*said of a horse*)
**reventazón** *f* burst, bursting; blowout; dashing of waves
**reventón** *adj masc* bursting; bulging; *m* burst; steep hill; difficulty, jam; jog; (aut.) blowout
**rever §93** *va* to revise, review, inspect; (law) to retry
**reverar** *va* (naut.) to drive (*a ship*) off the sand (*said of a strong current*)
**reverberación** *f* reverberation
**reverberante** *adj* reverberant
**reverberar** *vn* to reverberate
**reverberatorio -ria** *adj* reverberatory
**reverbero** *m* reverberation; reflector; reflecting lamp; street lamp; (Am.) chafing dish
**reverdecer §34** *va* to turn green again; *vn* to turn or grow green again; to come to life again, acquire new vigor
**reverdeciente** *adj* green, turning green; fresh, renewed
**reverencia** *f* reverence; bow, curtsy; (*cap.*) *f* Reverence (*title*)
**reverenciable** *adj* worthy of reverence, worshipful
**reverenciador -dora** *adj* revering
**reverencial** *adj* reverential
**reverenciar** *va* to revere, reverence; *vn* to bow, curtsy
**reverendísimo -ma** *adj super* most reverend
**reverendo -da** *adj* reverend; (coll.) solemn, serious; **reverendas** *fpl* (eccl.) dimissory letter; fine qualities, sterling qualities
**reverente** *adj* reverent
**reversibilidad** *f* reversibility
**reversible** *adj* reversible
**reversión** *f* reversion; (biol. & law) reversion
**reverso** *m* back; wrong side; reverse (*of coin or medal*); **el reverso de la medalla** the entire opposite, the opposite in every respect
**reverter §66** *vn* to overflow
**revertir §62** *vn* to revert; (law) to revert
**revés** *m* back, reverse; backhand (*stroke*); counterstroke; wrong side; (fig.) reverse, setback; change of mood; **al revés** wrong side out, inside out; backwards, in the opposite way; **de revés** wrong side out, inside out; backwards, in the opposite way; from left to right; **el revés de la medalla** the entire opposite, the opposite in every respect
**revesa** *f* (naut.) back water, eddy
**revesado -da** *adj* complex, intricate; wild, unmanageable
**revesar** *va* to vomit
**revesino** *m* reversi (*game of cards*)
**revestimiento** *m* covering, coating, facing, lining, surfacing
**revestir §94** *va* to put on, to don; to cover, coat, face, line, surface, revet; to adorn (*a story*); to disguise; to assume, take on; **revestir con** or **de** to invest with; *vr* to put on vestments; to be haughty or proud; to be carried along; **revestirse con** or **de** to be invested with; to gird oneself with (*e.g., patience*)
**reveza** *f* var. of **revesa**
**revezar §76** *va* to replace, to spell; *vn* to alternate, work in shifts
**revezo** *m* shifting; shift; relay of a yoke of oxen, mules, etc.
**reviejo -ja** *adj* very old; *m* withered branch
**revientabuey** *m* (ent.) buprestid beetle
**reviernes** *m* Friday after Easter (*each of the first seven*)
**revine** *1st sg pret ind of* **revenir**
**reviniendo** *ger of* **revenir**
**revirado -da** *adj* twisted (*wood*)
**revirar** *va* to turn, twist; to turn over; (naut.) to veer again; *vn* (naut.) to veer again
**revisador -dora** *adj* revisory
**revisar** *va* to revise, review, check; to audit
**revisión** *f* revision, review, check
**revisionismo** *m* revisionism
**revisionista** *adj & mf* revisionist
**revisita** *f* reinspection
**revisor -sora** *adj* revisory; *mf* reviewer, examiner; (rail.) conductor, ticket collector; **revisor de cuentas** auditor
**revista** *f* see **revisto**
**revistar** *va* (mil.) to review
**revistero -ra** *mf* reviewer (*of books*); contributor, magazine writer; (Am.) editor of a review or magazine
**revisto -ta** *pp of* **rever;** *f* review (*reëxamination; survey; magazine; criticism*); (mil. & theat.) review; (law) retrial, new trial; **pasar revista a** to review, go over carefully; (mil.) to review; **suplicar en revista** (law) to appeal
**revitalizar §76** *va* to revitalize
**revividero** *m* silkworm incubator
**revivificación** *f* revivification
**revivificar §86** *va* to revivify
**revivir** *va* to revive; *vn* to revive, to be revived, to live again
**revocable** *adj* revocable
**revocación** *f* revocation
**revocador -dora** *adj* revoking; *m* plasterer
**revocadura** *f* plastering, stuccoing; (paint.) edge of canvas covered by frame
**revocar §86** *va* to revoke; to dissuade; to drive back, drive away; to plaster, to stucco; *vn* to be driven back or away
**revocatorio -ria** *adj* revocatory
**revoco** *m* plastering, stucco; driving back or away; furze cover of a charcoal basket
**revolar §77** *vn & vr* to flutter, flutter around; to fly again
**revolcadero** *m* wallowing place (*of animals*)
**revolcar §95** *va* to knock down, to roll over; (coll.) to floor; (coll.) to flunk, to fail; *vr* to wallow; to roll around; to be stubborn
**revolcón** *m* (coll.) upset, tumble
**revolear** *vn* to fly around and around
**revolotear** *va* to fling in the air; *vn* to flutter, flutter around, flit
**revoloteo** *m* flutter, fluttering
**revoltijo** or **revoltillo** *m* mass, mess, jumble; twisted mass of guts; confusion
**revoltina** *f* disturbance, uprising
**revoltón** *m* vine grub; (arch.) vault; (arch.) turn in a molding
**revoltoso -sa** *adj* mischievous; winding; complicated; riotous, rebellious; *mf* rioter, rebel
**revolución** *f* revolution
**revolucionar** *va* to incite to rebellion; to revolutionize; *vr* to revolt
**revolucionario -ria** *adj* revolutionary; *mf* revolutionist, revolutionary
**revoluto -ta** *adj* (coll.) upset; *m* (Am.) panic
**revolvedero** *m* var. of **revolcadero**
**revolvedora** *f* (Am.) mixer (*e.g., of concrete*)
**revolver §63 & §17,** 9 *va* to shake; to stir; to turn upside down; to turn around; to wrap up; to disarrange, mess up, mix up; to disturb, upset; to alienate; to retrace (*one's steps*); to swing (*a horse*) around; to revolve, turn over (*in one's mind*) ‖ *vn* to retrace one's steps; to swing around (*said, e.g., of a horseman*) ‖ *vr* to turn around; to retrace one's steps; to toss and turn; to swing around (*said, e.g., of a horseman*); to turn around; (astr.) to revolve (*in an orbit*); to turn stormy; to get rough (*said of the sea*); **revolverse a, contra** or **sobre** to turn and face (*the enemy*); to turn against
**revólver** *m* revolver
**revolvimiento** *m* revolving, revolution
**revoque** *m* plastering, stucco
**revotar** *vr* to reverse one's vote
**revuelco** *m* upset, tumble; wallowing

**revuelo** *m* second flight; flying around and around; disturbance; excitement; **de revuelo** lightly, incidentally
**revuelto -ta** *pp of* **revolver;** *adj* scrambled; easily turned (*horse*); mischievous; complicated; confused, disordered; changeable (*weather*); *f* second turn; fight, row; revolution, revolt; disturbance; turn; turning point; change
**revuelvepiedras** *m* (*pl:* **-dras**) (orn.) turnstone
**revulsar** *vn* (Am.) to vomit
**revulsión** *f* (med.) revulsion
**revulsivo -va** or **revulsorio -ria** *adj & m* revulsive
**rey** *m* king; queen bee; (cards, chess & fig.) king; (coll.) swineherd; **reyes** *mpl* king and queen; **el rey intruso** Joseph Bonaparte; **no temer rey ni roque** (coll.) to not be afraid of anything or anybody; **servir al rey** to fight for king and country; **rey de armas** earl marshal; (her.) king of arms; **rey de codornices** (orn.) corn crake; **rey de las aves** king of birds (*eagle*); **rey de los animales** king of beasts (*lion*); **rey de zarza** (orn.) wren; **Reyes Católicos** Catholic Sovereigns (*Ferdinand and Isabella*); **Reyes Magos** Magi, Three Wise Men, Wise Men of the East (*they play the rôle of Santa Claus in Latin countries*); **reyes pastores** Shepherd kings
**reyerta** *f* quarrel, wrangle
**reyezuelo** *m* kinglet; (orn.) kinglet, wren; **reyezuelo moñudo** (orn.) goldcrest
**rezado** *m* prayer; divine service
**rezador -dora** *adj* praying; *mf* prayer (*person*); *f* (ent.) praying mantis
**rezaga** *f* rear guard
**rezagado -da** *mf* straggler, laggard
**rezagar** **§59** *va* to outstrip, leave behind; to put off, postpone; *vr* to stay behind, fall behind
**rezago** *m* residue, remainder
**rezar** **§76** *va* to pray (*a prayer*); to say (*a prayer, mass, etc.*); (coll.) to say, read; (coll.) to call for, e.g., **el periódico reza agua** the newspaper calls for rain; *vn* to pray; (coll.) to grumble; (coll.) to say, read, e.g., **esta página reza así** this page reads thus; **rezar con** (coll.) to concern, to have to do with
**rezno** *m* (ent.) bot; (bot.) castor-oil plant
**rezo** *m* prayer; daily prayer; devotions
**rezón** *m* grapnel
**rezongador -dora** *adj* grumbling, growling; *mf* grumbler, growler
**rezongar** **§59** *vn* to grumble, growl
**rezonglón -glona** *adj & mf* (coll.) var. of **rezongador**
**rezongo** *m* grumbling, growling
**rezongón -gona** *adj & mf* (coll.) var. of **rezongador**
**rezumadero** *m* spot where a vessel oozes; oozing, seepage
**rezumar** *va* to ooze (*moisture*); *vn* to ooze, to seep; *vr* to ooze, to seep; to leak; (coll.) to seep out, leak out (*said, e.g., of a piece of gossip*)
**ría** *f* narrow inlet, estuary, fiord
**riacho** or **riachuelo** *m* rivulet, streamlet
**riada** *f* flood, freshet; (fig.) flood
**riba** *f* slope, embankment
**ribaldería** *f* (archaic) knavery, rascality
**ribaldo -da** *adj* (archaic) knavish, rascally; *m* (archaic) knave, rascal; bawd, procurer
**ribazo** *m* slope, embankment
**ribazón** *f* var. of **arribazón**
**ribera** *f* bank, shore, beach; riverside; dike, levee; **volar la ribera** (coll.) to be fond of wandering and adventure
**ribereño -ña** *adj* riverside, riparian; *mf* riversider, riparian
**riberiego -ga** *adj* sedentary (*sheep*); riparian
**ribero** *m* dike, levee
**ribete** *m* edge, trimming, border; addition; embellishment (*to a story*); **ribetes** *mpl* strain, streak, touch
**ribeteado -da** *adj* irritated (*eyes or eyelids*)
**ribetear** *va* to edge, trim, border, bind
**riboflavina** *f* (biochem.) riboflavin
**ricacho -cha** or **ricachón -chona** *mf* (coll.) vulgar rich person
**ricadueña** *f* (*pl:* **ricasdueñas**) (archaic) noblewoman, peeress
**ricahembra** *f* (*pl:* **ricashembras**) (archaic) var. of **ricadueña**
**Ricardo** *m* Richard
**ricial** *adj* green (*stubble field*); fresh-grown (*pasture*)
**ricino** *m* (bot.) castor-oil plant
**rico -ca** *adj* rich; dear, darling; *mf* rich person; **nuevo rico** nouveau riche
**ricohombre** *m* (*pl:* **ricoshombres**) (archaic) grandee, nobleman
**rictus** *m* (*pl:* **-tus**) convulsive grin
**ricura** *f* (coll.) richness; (coll.) excellence; (coll.) darling, sweetheart
**ridiculez** *f* ridiculousness, absurdity; touchiness
**ridiculizar** **§76** *va* to ridicule
**ridículo -la** *adj* ridiculous; touchy; *m* ridiculous situation; reticule; **poner en ridículo** to make a fool of, to expose to ridicule; **ponerse en ridículo** to make a fool of oneself
**riego** *m* irrigation; watering, sprinkling; irrigation water
**riel** *m* ingot; curtain rod; (rail.) rail
**rielar** *vn* to shimmer, to gleam; (poet.) to twinkle
**rielera** *f* ingot mold
**rienda** *f* rein; **a rienda suelta** swiftly, violently; with free rein; **aflojar las riendas a** to give rein to; **dar rienda suelta a** to give free rein to; **falsa rienda** checkrein; **soltar las riendas** to let go, to let down the bars; **tener las riendas** to draw rein; **tomar las riendas** to take the reins
**riente** *adj* laughing; bright, cheerful
**riesgo** *m* risk, danger; **a riesgo de** + *inf* at the risk of + *ger;* **correr riesgo** to run or take a risk
**riesgoso -sa** *adj* (Am.) risky
**Rif, El** Er Rif
**rifa** *f* raffle; fight, quarrel
**rifador** *m* raffler; raffle vendor; fighter
**rifadura** *f* (naut.) splitting (*of a sail*)
**rifar** *va* to raffle, to raffle off; *vn* to raffle; to fight, quarrel; *vr* (naut.) to split (*said of a sail*)
**rifeño -ña** *adj* Riffian; *mf* Riff, Riffian
**rifirrafe** *m* (coll.) squabble, row
**rifle** *m* rifle
**riflero** *m* (Am.) rifleman (*soldier*)
**rigente** *adj* (poet.) rigid
**rigidez** *f* rigidity; **rigidez cadavérica** rigor mortis
**rígido -da** *adj* rigid
**rigodón** *m* rigadoon (*dance and music*)
**rigor** *m* rigor; (path. & physiol.) rigor; **de rigor** de rigueur; **en rigor** as a matter of fact; **rigor de la muerte** rigor mortis
**rigorismo** *m* rigorism
**rigorista** *adj* rigoristic; *mf* rigorist; stickler
**rigoroso -sa** *adj* var. of **riguroso**
**rigurosidad** *f* rigorousness; severity
**riguroso -sa** *adj* rigorous; severe
**rija** *f* (path.) lachrymal fistula; fight, quarrel
**rijador -dora** *adj* var. of **rijoso**
**rijo** *m* lust, sensuality
**rijoso -sa** *adj* lustful, sensual; quarrelsome
**rilar** *vn* to shiver; *vr* to shake
**rima** *f* rhyme; heap, pile; **rimas** *fpl* poems, poetry; **octava rima** (pros.) ottava rima; **tercia rima** (pros.) terza rima; **rima femenina** (pros.) feminine rhyme; **rima masculina** (pros.) masculine rhyme; **rima perfecta** perfect rhyme
**rimador -dora** *adj* rhyming; *mf* rhymer; rhymester (*maker of poor rhymes or verse*)
**rimar** *va & vn* to rhyme
**rimbombancia** *f* resonance, echo; showiness, flashiness
**rimbombante** *adj* resounding; showy, flashy
**rimbombar** *vn* to resound, to echo
**rimbombe** *m* or **rimbombo** *m* resonance, echo; high-sounding word
**rimero** *m* heap, pile
**Rin** *m* Rhine; (*l.c.*) *m* Rhine wine
**rinal** *adj* rhinal
**rinanto** *m* (bot.) wild sage, vervain sage
**rincocéfalo -la** *adj & m* (zool.) rhynchocephalian

**rincón** *m* corner; nook, angle; patch, small piece (*e.g., of land*); bit, end; (coll.) home; **rincón de chimenea** chimney corner
**rinconada** *f* corner
**rinconera** *f* corner piece (*of furniture*); corner table; (arch.) wall between corner and window
**rinencéfalo** *m* (anat.) rhinencephalon
**ringla** *f* or **ringle** *m* (coll.) var. of **ringlera**
**ringlera** *f* row, line, tier
**ringlero** *m* ruled line (*for writing exercise*)
**ringorrango** *m* (coll.) curlicue (*in writing*); (coll.) frill, frippery
**rinitis** *f* (path.) rhinitis
**rinoceronte** *m* (zool.) rhinoceros
**rinoplastia** *f* (surg.) rhinoplasty
**rinoscopia** *f* rhinoscopy
**rinoscopio** *m* rhinoscope
**riña** *f* fight, scuffle, fray, brawl; **riña de campanario** petty local row; **riña de gallos** cockfight; **riña tumultuaria** free-for-all
**riñón** *m* (anat.) kidney; (min.) kidney ore; (cook.) kidney; (fig.) heart, center; **riñones** *mpl* back, loins; **tener recubierto** or **bien cubierto el riñón** (coll.) to be well-heeled; **riñón flotante** (path.) floating kidney
**riñonada** *f* (anat.) cortical tissue (*of kidney*); loins; kidney stew
**río** *m* river; (fig.) river (*e.g., of blood*); great flow, stream (*of people or things*); **a río revuelto** in confusion, in disorder; **pescar en río revuelto** to fish in troubled waters
**riolada** *f* (coll.) great flow, stream (*of people or things*)
**riolita** *f* (mineral.) rhyolite
**rioplatense** *adj* Platine; *mf* native or inhabitant of the Basin of the River Plate
**riostra** *f* brace, stay; guy, guy wire
**riostrar** *va* to brace, to stay
**ripia** *f* shingle; slab (*outside cut of log*)
**ripiar** *va* to fill with rubble, to riprap; *vn* to shingle
**ripio** *m* refuse, debris; rubble, debris; padding (*in writing, speech, or verse*); **no perder ripio** to not miss a word; (coll.) to not miss a trick
**ripioso -sa** *adj* rubbly; padded (*e.g., verse*)
**riqueza** *f* wealth, riches; richness; **riquezas** *fpl* wealth, riches; precious objects
**riquísimo -ma** *adj super* very or most rich
**risa** *f* laugh, laughter; **caerse** or **desternillarse de risa** to split one's sides with laughter; **dar risa a uno** to make someone laugh; **morirse de risa** to die laughing; **perderse de risas** to be convulsed with laughter; **reventar de risa** to burst with laughter; **tener la risa** to keep from laughing; **risa falsa** feigned laugh; **risa sardesca** or **sardónica** (path.) sardonic grin
**risada** *f* var. of **risotada**
**riscal** *m* cragged region
**risco** *m* cliff, crag; honey fritter
**riscoso -sa** *adj* cragged
**risibilidad** *f* risibility
**risible** *adj* risible, laughable
**risica, risilla** or **risita** *f* giggle, titter; feigned laugh, false laugh
**risol** *m* (cook.) rissole
**risotada** *f* guffaw, horse laugh, boisterous laugh
**risotear** *vn* to guffaw, to laugh boisterously
**risoteo** *m* var. of **risotada**
**ríspido -da** *adj* harsh, gruff
**rispo -pa** *adj* harsh, gruff; unruly
**ristra** *f* string of onions, string of garlic; (coll.) string, row, file
**ristre** *m* lance rest
**ristrel** *m* rail, heavy rail (*of wood*)
**risueño -ña** *adj* smiling; (fig.) smiling
**rítmico -ca** *adj* rhythmic or rhythmical; *f* rhythmics
**ritmo** *m* rhythm
**rito** *m* rite; **rito romano** Roman rite
**ritón** *m* (archeol.) rhyton
**ritornello** *m* var. of **retornelo**
**ritual** *adj & m* ritual; **ser de ritual** to be ordained by custom
**ritualidad** *f* observance of formalities
**ritualismo** *m* ritualism
**ritualista** *adj* ritualistic, ritualist; *mf* ritualist
**rival** *adj & mf* rival
**rivalidad** *f* rivalry; enmity
**rivalizar** §76 *vn* to vie, to compete; **rivalizar con** to rival
**rivera** *f* creek, brook
**riza** *f* see **rizo**
**rizado -da** *adj* curly; ripply; *m* curling; curliness; curls; pleats
**rizador** *m* curling iron; hair curler
**rizal** *m* var. of **ricial**
**rizar** §76 *va* to curl; to crimple; to ripple; *vr* to curl, be curly; to ripple
**rizo -za** *adj* curly; *m* curl, ringlet; ripple; (aer.) loop; (naut.) reef point; **hacer** or **rizar el rizo** (aer.) to loop the loop; **largar rizos** (naut.) to let out the reef; **tomar rizos** (naut.) to take in the reef; *f* barley stubble; stubbly hay left in rack (*by horses*); ravage, destruction
**rizófago -ga** *adj* (zool.) rhizophagous
**rizoforáceo -a** *adj* (bot.) rhizophoraceous
**rizoide** *adj* rhizoid; *m* (bot.) rhizoid
**rizoma** *m* (bot.) rhizome
**rizópodo** *m* (zool.) rhizopod
**rizoso -sa** *adj* curly
**rizotomía** *f* (surg.) rhizotomy
**r.**[1] abr. of **real** (*moneda*)
**R.**[1] abr. of **Real** (*del rey*)
**R.M.** abr. of **Reverenda Madre**
**Rmrz.** abr. of **Ramírez**
**R.O.** abr. of **Real Orden**
**ro** *interj* **¡ro ro!** bye-bye!, hushaby! (*lullaby word*); *m* (slang) husband
**roa** *f* (naut.) stem
**roano -na** *adj* roan
**rob** *m* fruit jelly
**robadera** *f* (agr.) harrow
**robador -dora** *adj* robbing, thieving; *mf* robber, thief
**róbalo** or **robalo** *m* (ichth.) bass, sea bass; (ichth.) snook
**robar** *va* to rob, to steal; to abduct; to sweep away, carry away; to make round, to round off; to draw (*a card or domino*); to win over; **robarle algo a alguien** to rob someone of something, to rob or steal something from someone; *vn & vr* to steal
**robellón** *m* (bot.) field mushroom
**Roberto** *m* Robert
**robezo** *m* (zool.) chamois
**robín** *m* rust
**robinete** *m* spigot, faucet, cock, valve
**robinia** *f* (bot.) locust
**robinsonismo** *m* isolation, independence, self-sufficiency
**robladero -ra** *adj* made to be clinched or riveted
**robladura** *f* clinching, riveting
**roblar** *va* to clinch, to rivet
**roble** *m* (bot.) British oak; husky person; strong thing or object; strength, bulwark; **roble ahumado** fumed oak; **roble ahorquillado** (bot.) turkey oak (*Quercus catesbaei*); **roble albero** (bot.) British oak, durmast (*Quercus sessiflora*); **roble blanco de América** (bot.) white oak (*Quercus alba*); **roble blanco de California** (bot.) valley or California oak, swamp oak; **roble borne** (bot.) pubescent oak, durmast; **roble carrasqueño** (bot.) gall oak; **roble de fruto grande** (bot.) bur oak, mossy-cup oak; **roble de hojas aliradas** (bot.) overcup oak; **roble de los pantanos** (bot.) pin oak, swamp oak; **roble escarlata** (bot.) scarlet oak; **roble negral, negro** or **villano** (bot.) pubescent oak, durmast; **roble rojo** (bot.) red oak
**robleda** *f*, **robledal** *m* or **robledo** *m* woods of oak trees
**roblizo -za** *adj* strong, hard, robust
**roblón** *m* rivet; ridge (*of tiles*)
**roblonar** *va & vn* to rivet
**robo** *m* robbery, theft; draw (*card or cards drawn*); **robo con escalo** burglary
**roboración** *f* strengthening; corroboration
**roborar** *va* to strengthen; to corroborate
**roborativo -va** *adj* strengthening; corroborative
**robot** *m* (*pl:* **-bots**) robot; (fig.) robot (*person*)
**robra** *f* var. of **alboroque**
**robustecedor -dora** *adj* strengthening

**robustecer** §76 *va* to make strong, to strengthen; *vr* to become strong
**robustez** *f* or **robusteza** *f* robustness
**robusto -ta** *adj* robust
**roca** *f* rock; **la Roca** the Rock (*Gibraltar*); **roca de respaldo** (geol. & min.) wall rock; **roca Tarpeya** Tarpeian Rock
**rocada** *f* rock (*wool or flax on distaff*)
**rocadero** *m* knob or head (*of a distaff*); conical paper hat worn as a mark of infamy
**rocador** *m* knob or head (*of a distaff*)
**rocalla** *f* pebbles; stone chips; large glass bead; (f.a.) rocaille
**rocalloso -sa** *adj* pebbly, stony
**rocambola** *f* (bot.) giant garlic, rocambole
**roce** *m* rubbing; contact, frequent contact
**rocero -ra** *adj* (dial.) too familiar (*with inferiors*); brush (*wood*)
**rociada** *f* see **rociado**
**rociadera** *f* watering can, sprinkling can, sprinkler
**rociado -da** *adj* dewy; bedewed; *m* spraying; *f* sprinkling; dew; dew-drenched grass given to a horse as medicine; shower (*of stones, bullets*); volley (*of rebukes*)
**rociador** *m* clothes sprinkler; sprayer; **rociador automático** spray bomb
**rociadura** *f* or **rociamiento** *m* sprinkling; spraying
**rociar** §90 *va* to sprinkle (*e.g., water; flowers with water*); to spray; to bedew; to scatter; *vn* to drizzle; to be dew, e.g., **rocía esta mañana** there is dew this morning
**rocín** *m* hack, nag; draft horse, work horse; (coll.) coarse, stupid fellow; (Am.) draft ox; (Am.) riding horse; **rocín matalón** thin, worn-out horse
**rocinante** *m* worn-out horse
**rocino** *m* var. of **rocín**
**rocío** *m* dew; drizzle; sprinkling; (naut.) spindrift; **rocío de sol** (bot.) sundew
**roción** *m* splash of waves
**rococó** *adj & m* (f.a.) rococo
**rocoso -sa** *adj* rocky
**rocha** *f* clearing
**rochela** *f* (Am.) noise, racket; **La Rochela** La Rochelle (*city*)
**rocho** *m* (myth) roc (*bird*)
**roda** *f* (naut.) stem
**rodaballo** *m* (ichth.) turbot; (ichth.) brill; (coll.) sly fellow; **rodaballo menor** (ichth.) brill (*Rhombus laevis*)
**rodada** *f* see **rodado**
**rodadero -ra** *adj* shaped to roll, ready to roll; easy-rolling, smooth-rolling
**rodadizo -za** *adj* easy-rolling, smooth-rolling
**rodado -da** *adj* dapple; rounded, fluent (*period*); scattered (*fragments of ore*); on wheels, rolling; *m* boulder; stray piece of ore; *f* rut, track (*left by wheel*)
**rodador -dora** *adj* rolling; *m* (ent.) mosquito; (ichth.) sunfish
**rodadura** *f* rolling; rut; tread
**rodaja** *f* disk, small wheel, caster; round slice; rowel
**rodaje** *m* wheels, set of wheels; shooting, filming (*of a moving picture, of a scene, etc.*); **en rodaje** (aut.) being broken in, being run in; (mov.) being filmed
**rodal** *m* place, spot, patch; cart with solid wheels
**rodamiento** *m* bearing; tread (*of a tire*); **rodamientos** *mpl* running gear; **rodamiento a bolas** ball bearing; **rodamiento a rodillos** roller bearing
**rodánico -ca** *adj* (pertaining to the) Rhone
**rodano -na** *adj & mf* Rhodian
**Ródano** *m* Rhone
**rodante** *adj* rolling
**rodapelo** *m* var. of **redopelo**
**rodapié** *m* baseboard; drapery around the bottom of a bed, table, etc.
**rodaplancha** *f* ward (*of a key*)
**rodar** §77 *va* to roll; to take, to shoot (*a moving picture*); to film; to screen, to project; to drag along; to roll down (*e.g., the stairs*); to turn (*a key*); (Am.) to knock down; *vn* to roll, roll along; to run (*on wheels*); to roll down; to rotate, to revolve; to tumble; to roam, wander about; to prowl; to abound; (aer.) to taxi; **echarlo todo a rodar** (coll.) to upset everything, to spoil everything; (coll.) to fly off the handle; **ir rodando** to come along all right; **rodar por** to go around through (*e.g., stores*) in vain; (coll.) to be at the beck and call of
**Rodas** *f* Rhodes
**rodeabrazo; a rodeabrazo** winding up, swinging the arm for a throw
**rodeador -dora** *adj* surrounding
**rodear** *va* to surround, go around; to turn around; (Am.) to round up; *vn* to go around; to go a roundabout way; to beat about the bush; *vr* to turn, twist, toss about
**rodela** *f* buckler, target
**rodenal** *m* growth of cluster pine trees
**rodeno -na** *adj* red, reddish; see **pino**
**rodeo** *m* surrounding; detour, roundabout way; dodge, duck; evasion, subterfuge; roundup; rodeo (*roundup; cowboy exhibition*); **andar con rodeos** to beat about the bush; **dejarse de rodeos** to stop beating about the bush
**rodero -ra** *adj* (pertaining to a) wheel; *f* track, rut (*left by a wheel*); cart or wagon road across a field
**Rodesia, la** Rhodesia
**rodete** *m* knot (*of hair*); padded ring (*for carrying an object on the head*); fifth wheel; belt pulley, band pulley; ward (*of a lock*); (hyd.) drum wheel
**rodezno** *m* horizontal water wheel; gear that meshes with millstone gear
**rodezuela** *f* small wheel
**rodilla** *f* (anat.) knee; padded ring (*for carrying an object on the head*); ward (*of a lock*); floor rag, kitchen rag, mop; **a media rodilla** on one knee; **de rodillas** kneeling, on one's knees; **doblar la rodilla** to get down on one knee; to yield, give in; **hincar la rodilla** to kneel down; to bow one's head, to humble oneself; **hincarse de rodillas** or **ponerse de rodillas** to kneel, kneel down; **rodilla de fregona** (path.) housemaid's knee
**rodillada** *f* push or blow with the knee; blow on the knee; (act of) kneeling
**rodillar** *va* to roll
**rodillazo** *m* push or blow with the knee
**rodillero -ra** *adj* (pertaining to the) knee; *f* kneepiece, genouillère (*of armor*); knee (*of garment*); kneecap, kneepad (*cover*); baggy knee (*of trousers*); knee injury (*of a horse caused by fall*); (mus.) knee swell (*of organ*)
**rodillo** *m* roller; rolling pin; road roller; inking roller; platen (*of typewriter*); **rodillo de vapor** steam roller
**rodilludo -da** *adj* big-kneed
**rodio -dia** *adj & mf* Rhodian; *m* (chem.) rhodium
**rodiota** *adj & mf* Rhodian
**rodo** *m* roller; **a rodo** in abundance
**rododafne** *f* (bot.) rosebay
**rododendro** *m* (bot.) rhododendron
**rodofíceo -a** *adj* (bot.) rhodophyceous
**Rodolfo** *m* Rudolph; Ralph
**rodomiel** *m* (pharm.) honey of rose
**rodomontada** *f* rodomontade
**rodopsina** *f* (physiol.) rhodopsin
**rodora** *f* (bot.) rhodora
**rodriga** *f* prop, stake (*for plants*)
**rodrigar** §59 *va* to prop, prop up, stake (*plants*)
**rodrigazón** *f* season for propping plants
**Rodrigo** *m* Roderick
**rodrigón** *m* prop, stake (*for plants*); (coll.) old retainer who escorts ladies
**roedor -dora** *adj* gnawing; (fig.) biting, stinging, consuming; (zool.) rodent; *m* (zool.) rodent
**roedura** *f* gnawing; nibble; place that has been nibbled
**roel** *m* (her.) bezant
**roela** *f* disk of crude gold or silver
**roentgenograma** *m* roentgenogram
**roentgenología** *f* roentgenology
**roentgenólogo -ga** *mf* roentgenologist
**roentgenoterapia** *f* roentgenotherapy
**roer** §78 *va* to gnaw, gnaw away at; to pick (*a bone*); to wear away, to wear down
**roete** *m* (pharm.) pomegranate wine

**rogación** *f* petition, request; (hist.) rogation; **rogaciones** *fpl* (eccl.) rogations
**rogado -da** *adj* fond of being coaxed
**rogante** *adj* suppliant
**rogar §79** *va & vn* to beg; to pray; **hacerse de rogar** to like to be coaxed; **rogar por** to plead for; to pray for
**rogativo -va** *adj* supplicatory; *f* (eccl.) rogation; **rogativas** *fpl* (eccl.) rogations
**rogatorio -ria** *adj* rogatory
**Rogelio** or **Rogerio** *m* Roger
**rogo** *m* (poet.) pyre
**roído -da** *adj* (coll.) miserly, stingy
**roigo** *1st sg pres ind of* **roer**
**rojal** *adj* reddish; *m* reddish earth
**rojear** *vn* to redden; to become reddish
**rojete** *m* rouge (*for face*)
**rojez** *f* redness
**rojizo -za** *adj* reddish
**rojo -ja** *adj* red; ruddy; red-haired; Red (*communist*); *mf* Red (*communist*); *m* red; **al rojo** to a red heat; **rojo cereza** cherry red (*of incandescence*); **rojo de Burdeos** Bordeaux red; **rojo de plomo** red lead; **rojo de rubia** (chem.) madder; **rojo turco** Turkey red
**rojura** *f* redness
**rol** *m* roll, list; (naut.) muster roll
**Rolando** *m* Roland
**rolar** *vn* (naut.) to veer around; (Am.) to associate
**Roldán** *m* Roland
**roldana** *f* sheave
**rolde** *m* circle, ring (*of people*)
**rolla** *f* collar of a draft horse; child's nurse
**rollar** *va* to roll, roll up
**rollizo -za** *adj* round, cylindrical; plump, stocky, stodgy, sturdy; *m* round log
**rollo** *m* roll; roller, rolling pin; round log; cylindrical stone; cylindrical pillar (*in main square of town*); yoke pad; rôle
**rollón** *m* mixed bran and flour
**rollona** *f* (coll.) nurse, child's nurse
**Roma** *f* see **romo**
**romadizar §76** *vr* to catch cold, to have a cold in the head
**romadizo** *m* cold, cold in the head
**romaico -ca** *adj & m* Romaic
**romana** *f* see **romano**
**romanador** *m* weighmaster
**romanar** *va* to weigh with a steelyard
**romance** *adj* Romance (*language*); *m* Romance language; Spanish language; romance of chivalry; octosyllabic verse with alternate lines in assonance; narrative poem in octosyllabic verse; **romances** *mpl* prattle, excuses; **en buen romance** in plain language; **hablar en romance** to speak plainly, to come to the point; **romance de ciego** ballad sung and sold on the streets by a blind man; **romance heroico** or **real** hendecasyllabic verse with alternate lines in assonance
**romancear** *va* to translate into the vernacular, to translate into Spanish
**romanceresco -ca** *adj* romantic (*event, story, imagination*)
**romancerista** *mf* romancist
**romancero -ra** *mf* romancer, romancist; *m* collection of Old Spanish romances
**romancesco -ca** *adj* novelistic; romantic
**romancillo** *m* verse of less than eight syllables with alternate lines in assonance
**romancista** *mf* romancer; writer in Spanish, writer in the vernacular (*not in Latin*)
**romanche** *m* Romansh
**romanear** *va* to weigh with a steelyard; (naut.) to balance; *vn* to weigh more
**romaneo** *m* weighing with a steelyard
**romanero** *m* weighmaster
**romanesco -ca** *adj* Roman; novelistic; romantic
**romanía; de romanía** (coll.) crestfallen
**románico -ca** *adj* Romance, Romanic (*language*); (arch.) Romanesque; *m* (arch.) Romanesque
**romanillo -lla** *adj* round-hand; (print.) roman; *f* (Am.) dining-room screen
**romanismo** *m* Romanism; Romance philology; Romance-language phenomenon (*root, idiom, characteristic*); (offensive) Romanism (*Catholic religion*)
**romanista** *mf* Romanist; (offensive) Romanist (*member of the Roman Catholic Church*)
**romanística** *f* Romance scholarship
**romanización** *f* Romanization
**romanizar §76** *va & vr* to Romanize
**romano -na** *adj* Roman; romaine (*lettuce*); *mf* Roman; *f* steelyard
**romanticismo** *m* romanticism; (*cap.*) *m* Romantic Movement
**romántico -ca** *adj* romantic; *mf* romanticist; romantic
**romanza** *f* (mus.) romance, romanza
**romanzar §76** *va* var. of **romancear**
**romaza** *f* (bot.) dock, sorrel
**rombal** *adj* (geom.) rhombic
**rombencéfalo** *m* (anat.) rhombencephalon, hindbrain
**rómbico -ca** *adj* (cryst.) rhombic
**rombo** *m* (geom.) rhomb or rhombus; diamond (*in cards*)
**romboedro** *m* (geom.) rhombohedron
**romboidal** *adj* rhomboid, rhomboidal
**romboide** *m* (geom.) rhomboid
**romeo -a** *adj* Romaean (*Byzantine Greek*)
**romeraje** *m* pilgrimage
**romeral** *m* growth of rosemary
**romería** *f* pilgrimage; gathering at a shrine on saint's day; crowd, gathering
**romeriego -ga** *adj* fond of pilgrimages
**romero -ra** *mf* pilgrim; *m* (bot.) rosemary
**romí** *adj* (*pl:* **-míes**) see **azafrán**
**romo -ma** *adj* blunt, dull; flat-nosed; (*cap.*) *f* Rome
**rompeátomos** *m* (*pl:* **-mos**) (phys.) atom smasher
**rompecabezas** *m* (*pl:* **-zas**) slung shot; riddle, puzzle; jigsaw puzzle
**rompecoches** *m* (*pl:* **-ches**) durance, everlasting (*material*)
**rompedero -ra** *adj* fragile, breakable; *f* iron punch, blacksmith's punch; powder screen
**rompedura** *f* breaking, breakage
**rompeesquinas** *m* (*pl:* **-nas**) (coll.) var. of **rompesquinas**
**rompegalas** *mf* (*pl:* **-las**) (coll.) shabby-looking person
**rompehielos** *m* (*pl:* **-los**) icebreaker, iceboat
**rompehuelgas** *mf* (*pl:* **-gas**) strikebreaker
**rompenueces** *m* (*pl:* **-ces**) nutcracker
**rompeolas** *m* (*pl:* **-las**) breakwater, mole
**romper §17, 9** *va* to break; to tear; to break through; to plow for the first time; **romper el hielo** (fig.) to break the ice; *vn* to break (*said of waves, of the dawn*); to break or burst open (*said of flowers*); to break down; **de rompe y rasga** (coll.) determined; **romper a** + *inf* to suddenly start to + *inf*, to burst out + *ger*, e.g., **romper a llorar** to burst out crying; **romper con** to break with
**rompesacos** *m* (*pl:* **-cos**) (bot.) goat grass; (bot.) lyme grass
**rompesquinas** *m* (*pl:* **-nas**) (coll.) corner loafer, corner bully
**rompible** *adj* breakable
**rompido** *m* newly broken ground
**rompiente** *m* reef, rock, shoal
**rompimiento** *m* break, breakage; breach, crack; (paint.) opening in background; (theat.) open drop scene; (min.) breakthrough
**Rómulo** *m* (myth.) Romulus
**ron** *m* (*pl:* **rones**) rum; **ron de laurel** or **de malagueta** bay rum
**ronca** *f* see **ronco**
**roncador -dora** *adj* snoring; *mf* snorer; *m* (ichth.) roncador, croaker
**roncar §86** *vn* to snore; to roar (*said of wind or sea*); to cry in rutting season; (coll.) to bully, threaten
**ronce** *m* (coll.) coaxing, cajoling
**roncear** *vn* to kill time, to fool around; (coll.) to coax, cajole; (naut.) to sail slowly
**roncería** *f* killing time, fooling around; (coll.) coaxing, cajoling; (naut.) slow sailing
**roncero -ra** *adj* poky; grouchy; (coll.) coaxing, cajoling; (naut.) slow-sailing
**ronco -ca** *adj* hoarse, raucous; *m* (ichth.) grunt; *f* rut (*season*); cry of buck in rutting season; halberd; (coll.) bullying; **echar roncas** (coll.) to bully

**roncón** *m* drone of a bagpipe
**roncha** *f* welt; black-and-blue mark; (coll.) gyp; round slice
**ronchar** *va* to crunch; *vn* to make a crunching sound (*said, e.g., of raw potatoes*); to raise welts
**ronda** *f* night patrol or round; night serenaders; round (*of visits*); (coll.) round (*of cigars or wine*); (Am.) ring-around-a-rosy; **coger la ronda a** to catch in the act; **ronda de matrícula** (nav.) press gang
**rondador** *m* night watchman; serenader; rounder; prowler
**rondalla** *f* story, tale; (dial.) serenaders
**rondar** *va* to go around, fly around; to patrol; (coll.) to hang over, threaten; (coll.) to hang around, to hound; (coll.) to court; (coll.) to go serenading (*young women*); (coll.) to go up to around, e.g., **las temperaturas rondarán los 40 grados** the temperature will go up to around forty degrees; *vn* to patrol by night, go the rounds in the night; to gad about at nighttime; to go serenading; to prowl; (mil.) to make the rounds
**rondel** *m* rondel
**rondeño -ña** *adj* (pertaining to) Ronda; *mf* native or inhabitant of Ronda; *f* (mus.) fandango of Ronda
**rondín** *m* corporal's round (*to visit sentinels*); watchman in a naval arsenal
**rondís** *m* or **rondiz** *m* face of a precious stone
**rondó** *m* (*pl:* **-dós**) rondeau; (mus.) rondo
**rondón; de rondón** brashly
**ronquear** *vn* to be hoarse
**ronquedad** *f* raucousness, harshness, hoarseness
**ronquera** *f* hoarseness (*from a cold*)
**ronquido** *m* snore, snoring; rasp, rasping sound
**ronronear** *vn* to purr (*said of a cat or airplane*)
**ronroneo** *m* purr, purring
**ronza; ir a la ronza** (naut.) to fall to leeward
**ronzal** *m* halter; (naut.) double tackle, purchase rope
**ronzar §76** *va* to crunch; (naut.) to move with a lever
**roña** *f* scab, mange; sticky dirt; pine bark; (bot.) rust; stinginess; stingy person; trickiness; moral infection; **jugar a roña or a la roña** (Am.) to play for fun (*not for money*)
**roñada** *f* (naut.) garland, grommet
**roñería** *f* (coll.) stinginess
**roñica** *mf* (coll.) skinflint
**roñoso -sa** *adj* scabby, mangy; dirty, filthy; rusty; (coll.) stingy
**ropa** *f* clothing, clothes; dry goods; **a quema ropa** point-blank; **a toca ropa** at close range; **ropa blanca** linen (*tablecloths, napkins, sheets, towels, shirts, etc.*); **ropa de cama** bed linen (*sheets, pillowcases, etc.*); bedclothes (*blankets, quilts, etc.*); **ropa de cámara** or **de levantar** dressing gown, wrapper, bath robe; **ropa dominguera** Sunday best; **ropa hecha** ready-made clothes; **ropa interior** underwear; **ropas menores** underwear; **ropa sucia** laundry (*clothes to be washed*); **ropa vieja** old clothes; stew made from leftovers
**ropaje** *m* clothes, clothing; robe, gown; drapery; language
**ropálico -ca** *adj* (pros.) rhopalic
**ropavejería** *f* old-clothes shop
**ropavejero -ra** *mf* old-clothes dealer; *m* old-clothesman
**ropería** *f* clothing business; clothing store; **ropería de viejo** old-clothes shop
**ropero -ra** *mf* ready-made clothier; wardrobe keeper; *m* wardrobe, clothes closet; charitable organization for the distribution of old clothes
**ropeta** *f* var. of **ropilla**
**ropilla** *f* doublet; **dar una ropilla a** (coll.) to scold mildly, to reprove gently
**ropón** *m* loose coat; double quilting; (Am.) woman's riding habit
**roque** *m* rook (*in chess*)
**roqueda** *f* or **roquedal** *m* rocky place or region
**roqueño -ña** *adj* rocky; hard as rock
**roquería** *f* (Am.) rookery (*of seals*)
**roquero -ra** *adj* rocky, built on rock
**roqueta** *f* (bot.) roquette, rocket salad
**roquete** *m* barbed spearhead; ramrod, rammer; (eccl.) rochet
**rorcual** *m* (zool.) rorqual, finback, razorback
**rorro** *m* (coll.) baby; (Am.) doll
**ros** *m* (mil.) Spanish shako
**rosa** *f* see **roso**
**rosáceo -a** *adj* rosaceous; (bot.) rosaceous
**rosacruz** (*pl:* **-cruces**) *adj* & *mf* Rosicrucian
**rosada** *f* see **rosado**
**rosadelfa** *f* (bot.) azalea
**rosado -da** *adj* rose; rose-colored, rosy; *f* frost
**rosal** *m* (bot.) rosebush; **rosal de China** or **rosal japonés** (bot.) japonica; **rosal de pitiminí** (bot.) crimson rambler (*plant*); **rosal perruno** or **silvestre** (bot.) dog rose
**rosaleda** or **rosalera** *f* rosary, rose garden
**Rosalía** *f* Rosalie
**rosar** *vr* to turn red, to blush
**rosariera** *f* (bot.) bead tree
**rosariero** *m* dealer in rosaries; (coll.) hypocrite
**rosario** *m* rosary; string (*e.g., of misfortunes*); chain pump; (coll.) backbone; group reciting the rosary; reciting the rosary
**rosbif** *m* (*pl:* **-bifs**) roast beef
**rosca** *f* coil, spiral; turn (*of a spiral*); twist, twisted roll; (mach.) thread; **nut and bolt**, screw and nut; fleshiness; arch ring; (Am.) padded ring (*for carrying an object on the head*); **hacer la rosca a** (coll.) to hound (*a person*); (coll.) to play up to; **hacer la rosca** or **hacer la rosca del galgo** (coll.) to curl up and go to sleep anywhere; **pasarse de rosca** to be or become stripped, to not fit (*said of a screw or nut*); to go too far, to take too much liberty; **rosca de Arquímedes** Archimedes' screw
**roscadero** *m* (dial.) large hamper
**roscado -da** *adj* threaded; spiral; *m* threading
**roscar §86** *va* to thread
**rosco** or **roscón** *m* twisted roll (*of bread*)
**Rosellón, el** the Roussillon
**róseo -a** *adj* rose, rosy
**roséola** *f* (path.) roseola, rose rash; (path.) roseola, German measles
**rosero -ra** *mf* gatherer of saffron flowers
**roseta** *f* red spot on the cheek; sprinkling nozzle (*of water pot*); (metal.) rosette; metal tip of steelyard; **rosetas** *fpl* popcorn
**rosetón** *m* (arch.) rosette; (arch.) rose window, wheel window
**rosicler** *m* pink of dawn; ruby silver
**rosicruciano -na** *adj* & *mf* Rosicrucian
**rosillo -lla** *adj* light red, pink; roan
**rosita** *f* little rose; **rositas** *fpl* popcorn; **de rositas** (coll.) free, for nothing
**rosmarino -na** *adj* light red, pink; *m* (bot.) rosemary
**rosmaro** *m* var. of **manatí**
**roso -sa** *adj* red; threadbare; **a roso y velludo** completely, without exception ‖ *f* rose (*flower*); (Am.) rosebush; rose (*rose-shaped ribbon; precious stone; perfume*); red spot (*on skin*); rose diamond; (arch.) rose, rose window; **rosas** *fpl* popcorn; **verlo todo de color de rosa** to see everything through rose-colored glasses; **rosa albardera** (bot.) peony; **rosa de China** (bot.) China rose; **rosa de Damasco** (bot.) damask rose; **rosa de güeldres** (bot.) guelder-rose; **rosa de Jericó** (bot.) rose of Jericho; **rosa de los vientos** (naut.) compass card; **rosa de pitiminí** (hort.) crimson rambler; **rosa de rejalgar** (bot.) peony; **rosa de Siria** (bot.) rose of Sharon; **rosa náutica** (naut.) compass card; **rosa montés** (bot.) peony ‖ *m* rose, pink
**rosoli** *m* rosolio (*a drink*)
**rosolí** *m* (bot.) sundew
**rosón** *m* (ent.) bot
**rosqueado -da** *adj* spiral, twisted
**rosquete** *m* coffeecake
**rosquilla** *f* coffeecake, doughnut, cruller; (ent.) grub; **saber a rosquillas** (coll.) to be gratifying, to be satisfying
**rostrado -da** *adj* rostrate
**rostral** *adj* rostral
**rostritorcido -da** or **rostrituerto -ta** *adj* (coll.) sullen, gruff, morose
**rostro** *m* beak; face; snout; (anat., naut. & zool.) rostrum; **hacer rostro a** to face up to; to face, to accept; **rostro a rostro** face to face
**rostropálido -da** *mf* paleface (*white person; so called by American Indians*)

**rota** *f* see **roto**
**rotación** *f* rotation; **rotación de cosechas** or **de cultivos** rotation of crops
**rotacismo** *m* rhotacism
**rotador -dora** *adj* rotatory; *m* (anat.) rotator
**rotar** *vn* var. of **rodar**
**rotario -ria** *adj & m* Rotarian
**rotativo -va** *adj* rotary; revolving; *m* metropolitan newspaper; *f* (print.) rotary press
**rotatorio -ria** *adj* rotatory
**roten** *m* or **rotén** *m* (bot.) rattan; rattan (*cane or staff*)
**rotífero -ra** *adj* rotiferous; *m* (zool.) rotifer
**roto -ta** *pp of* **romper;** *adj* broken, shattered; torn; ragged; debauched, licentious; *mf* (in Argentina and Peru) Chilean, poor Chilean; *f* rout, defeat; (bot.) rattan, rattan palm; (naut.) route, course; **de rota** or **de rota batida** with complete loss or destruction; all of a sudden
**rotocosido** *m* patched clothing
**rotograbado** *m* rotogravure
**rotonda** *f* rear of stagecoach; rotunda; (Am.) roundhouse
**rotor** *m* (mach. & elec.) rotor
**rótula** *f* lozenge; (anat.) kneecap, kneepan; hinge joint; knuckle
**rotulación** *f* labeling, lettering; hinge joint
**rotular** *adj* rotular; *va* to label, to title, to letter
**rotulata** *f* collection of labels or posters; (coll.) label, title, mark
**rotuliano -na** *adj* rotulian
**rotulista** *m* letterer, sign maker, sign painter
**rótulo** *m* label, title, lettering; show bill, poster
**rotunda** *f* see **rotundo**
**rotundamente** *adv* roundly, categorically
**rotundidad** *f* roundness; rotundity
**rotundo -da** *adj* round; rotund, full, sonorous; round, peremptory; *f* rotunda
**rotura** *f* breaking, breakage; breach, opening; (vet.) plaster, poultice
**roturación** *f* plowing untilled ground; newly plowed untilled ground
**roturar** *va* to plow, to break (*untilled ground*)
**roya** *f* (bot.) rust, mildew, plant rot; coir, coconut fiber
**royo** *1st sg pres ind of* **roer**
**roza** *f* grubbing, stubbing; clearing
**rozadera** *f* var. of **rozón**
**rozador -dora** *mf* stubber
**rozadura** *f* rubbing; chafing; abrasion; (bot.) punkwood
**rozagante** *adj* showy, pompous; elegant, magnificent; flowing, sweeping (*gown, robe*)
**rozamiento** *m* rubbing, friction; (mech. & fig.) friction
**rozar §76** *va* to grub, to stub; to clear (*land*); to nibble (*grass*); to cut and gather (*small branches or grass*); to scrape; to graze; to border on; *vn* to graze, graze by; *vr* to interfere (*to strike one foot against another*); to hobnob, to be close, be on close terms; to falter, stammer; to be alike; (naut.) to fret, to gall
**roznar** *va* to crunch; *vn* to bray
**roznido** *m* crunch, crunching noise; bray, braying
**rozno** *m* small donkey
**rozo** *m* grubbing, stubbing; chips, brush; **ser de buen rozo** (coll.) to have a good appetite
**rozón** *m* short, broad scythe or sickle
**R.P.** abr. of **Reverendo Padre**
**rs.** or **r.s** abr. of **reales** (*moneda*)
**R.S.** abr. of **Real Servicio**
**Rte.** abr. of **Remite**
**rúa** *f* village street; wagon road; **hacer la rúa** to walk or ride around town
**Ruán** *f* Rouen
**ruano -na** *adj* roan; *f* woolen fabric
**rubefacción** *f* rubefaction
**rubefaciente** *adj & m* (med.) rubefacient
**Rubén** *m* (Bib.) Reuben
**rúbeo -a** *adj* reddish
**rubéola** *f* (path.) German measles
**ruberoide** *m* rubberoid
**rubescente** *adj* rubescent
**rubeta** *f* (zool.) peeper, tree toad
**rubí** *m* (*pl:* **-bíes**) ruby; (horol.) ruby, jewel; (orn.) vermilion flycatcher; **rubí balaje** (mineral.) balas ruby; **rubí de Bohemia** (mineral.) rose quartz; **rubí espinela** (mineral.) ruby spinel; **rubí oriental** (mineral.) Oriental or true ruby
**rubia** *f* see **rubio**
**rubiáceo -a** *adj* (bot.) rubiaceous
**rubial** *adj* reddish (*soil or plant*); *m* madder field
**rubiales** *mf* (*pl:* **-les**) (coll.) goldilocks
**rubicán -cana** *adj* rubican
**rubicela** *f* (mineral.) rubicel
**Rubicón** *m* Rubicon; **pasar el Rubicón** to cross the Rubicon
**rubicundez** *f* rubicundity; reddishness
**rubicundo -da** *adj* rubicund; reddish
**rubidio** *m* (chem.) rubidium
**rubificar §86** *va* to redden, to dye red; (med.) to make (*the skin*) red
**rubilla** *f* (bot.) woodruff
**rubín** *m* ruby; rust
**rubinejo** *m* little ruby
**rubio -bia** *adj* golden, blond, fair; *m* blond (*man or boy*); (ichth.) red gurnard; **rubio volador** (ichth.) sea robin; *f* blonde (*girl or woman*); station wagon; (coll.) peseta; (bot.) madder (*plant and root*); **rubia platino** platinum blonde; **rubia oxigenada** peroxide blonde
**rublo** *m* ruble
**rubor** *m* bright red; flush, blush; bashfulness
**ruborizar §76** *va* to make flush, make blush; *vr* to flush, to blush
**ruboroso -sa** *adj* blushing, bashful
**rúbrica** *f* rubric; title, heading; flourish (*to a signature*); **ser de rúbrica** (coll.) to be in accordance with ritual or custom
**rubricar §86** *va* to add one's flourish to (*a document, with or without one's signature*); to sign and seal; to certify to, to attest
**rubrificar §86** *va* to rubricate, make red
**rubriquista** *m* rubrician
**rubro -bra** *adj* red; *m* (Am.) title, heading
**ruc** *m* var. of **rocho**
**ruca** *f* (bot.) rocket salad
**rucio -cia** *adj* silver-gray; (coll.) gray-haired
**ruche** *m* or **rucho** *m* (coll.) donkey
**ruda** *f* see **rudo**
**rudeza** *f* coarseness, roughness; rudeness, crudeness; dullness, stupidity; severity
**rudimental** *adj* rudimental
**rudimentario -ria** *adj* rudimentary
**rudimento** *m* rudiment
**rudo -da** *adj* coarse, rough; rude, crude; dull, stupid; hard, severe; (phonet.) rough (*breathing*); *f* (bot.) rue; **ruda cabruna** (bot.) goat's-rue; **ruda de muros** (bot.) wall rue
**rueca** *f* distaff; twist, turn; (fig.) distaff, female sex, women
**rueda** *f* wheel; caster, roller; ring, circle (*of people*); rack (*for torture*); round slice; pinwheel; turn, time; spread (*of peacock's tail*); (ichth.) sunfish; **hacer la rueda** to spread its tail (*said of a peacock*); **hacer la rueda a** (coll.) to keep after; (coll.) to flatter, play up to; **quinta rueda** fifth wheel (*superfluous person or thing*); **rueda catalina** (horol.) escapement wheel; **rueda de alfarero** potter's wheel; **rueda de andar** treadmill; **rueda de cadena** sprocket, sprocket wheel; **rueda de carro** cart wheel; **rueda de corriente media** or **de costado** breast wheel; **rueda de escape** (horol.) escapement wheel; **rueda de esmeril** emery wheel; **rueda de feria** Ferris wheel; **rueda de fuego** pinwheel; **rueda de linterna** (mach.) lantern wheel; **rueda de molino** mill wheel; **rueda dentada** gearwheel; **rueda de paletas** paddle wheel; **rueda de pecho** breast wheel; **rueda de prensa** press conference; **rueda de presos** line-up (*of suspects or criminals*); **rueda de recambio** spare wheel; **rueda de Santa Catalina** (horol.) escapement wheel; **rueda de tornillo sin fin** worm wheel; **rueda de trinquete** (mach.) ratchet wheel; **rueda directriz** (aut.) steering wheel; **rueda hidráulica** water wheel; **rueda inferior** undershot water wheel; **rueda libre** (mach.) freewheel; **rueda loca** idler wheel; **rueda motriz** (mach.) drive wheel, driving wheel, driver; **rueda superior** overshot water wheel

**ruedecilla** *f* caster, roller
**ruedero** *m* wheelwright
**ruedo** *m* turn, rotation; edge (*of something round*); round mat; skirt lining; selvage; ring (*arena of bull ring*); (box.) ring; **a todo ruedo** at all events
**ruego** *m* request, petition, entreaty; prayer
**ruezno** *m* walnut burr
**rufián -fiana** *mf* bawd, go-between; *m* pimp; scoundrel; (archaic) hired killer
**rufianear** *vn* to pander
**rufianería** *f* pandering
**rufianesco -ca** *adj* scoundrelly; *f* gang of scoundrels; scoundrelly conduct
**rufo -fa** *adj* sandy, sandy-haired, rufous; curly, curly-haired; rough, tough
**rugar** §59 *va & vr* var. of **arrugar**
**rugido** *m* roar; bellow; rumble (*of intestines*)
**ruginoso -sa** *adj* rusty
**rugir** §42 *vn* to roar; to bellow; to rumble; to be said, to come out
**rugosidad** *f* ruggedness, corrugation, rugosity
**rugoso -sa** *adj* rugged, corrugated, wrinkled, ridged
**ruibarbo** *m* (bot. & pharm.) rhubarb (*Rheum palmatum and Rheum officinale*)
**ruido** *m* noise; repercussion; row, rumpus; **hacer** or **meter ruido** to start a row; to create a stir or a sensation; **querer ruido** to be looking for a fight; **quitarse de ruidos** (coll.) to stay out of trouble; **ruidos de fondo** background noise
**ruidoso -sa** *adj* noisy, loud; sensational
**ruin** *adj* base, mean, vile; puny; small, petty, stingy; vicious (*animal*); *m* scoundrel; tip of tail of cat; **en nombrando al ruin de Roma, luego asoma** talk of the Devil and he will appear; **un ruin ido, otro venido** out of the frying pan into the fire
**ruina** *f* ruin; **estar hecho una ruina** to be a wreck (*said of a person*); **batir en ruina** (mil.) to breach, break through; **amenazar ruina** to begin to fall to pieces
**ruinar** *va & vr* var. of **arruinar**
**ruindad** *f* baseness, meanness, vileness; pettiness, stinginess; viciousness
**ruinoso -sa** *adj* ruinous; tottery, tottering; rundown, useless
**ruiponce** *m* (bot.) rampion
**ruipóntico** *m* (bot. & pharm.) rhubarb (*Rheum rhaponticum*)
**ruiseñor** *m* (orn.) nightingale
**rujada** *f* (dial.) heavy shower
**rular** *va & vn* to roll
**ruleta** *f* roulette (*game; wheel with sharp teeth*); (Am.) tape measure
**ruleteo** *m* (Am.) cruising (*in search of fares*)
**ruletero** *m* (Am.) cruiser (*taxi driver cruising in search of fares*)
**rulo** *m* ball; roller; conical stone (*of olive-oil mill*)
**rumanche** *m* Romansh
**Rumania** *f* Rumania
**rumano -na** *adj & mf* Rumanian; *m* Rumanian (*language*)
**rumazón** *f* (naut.) overcast horizon
**rumba** *f* rumba (*dance and music*)
**rumbadas** *fpl* var. of **arrumbadas**
**rumbático -ca** *adj* pompous, showy
**rumbo** *m* bearing, course, direction; (coll.) pomp, show; (coll.) generosity; (her.) rustre; **abatir el rumbo** (naut.) to fall to leeward; **con rumbo a** bound for, in the direction of; **hacer rumbo a** to head for, to sail for; **ir al rumbo** (Am.) to be on the right track; **tener mucho rumbo** to be showy, to be pompous; **rumbo a** bound for; **rumbo de la aguja** (naut.) rhumb; **rumbo verdadero** (naut.) true course
**rumbón -bona** *adj* (coll.) generous
**rumboso -sa** *adj* pompous, magnificent; (coll.) generous
**rumen** *m* (zool.) rumen
**rumí** *m* (*pl:* **-míes**) (Arab.) Christian
**rumia** or **rumiación** *f* rumination
**rumiador -dora** *adj* ruminating; *mf* ruminator
**rumiadura** *f* rumination
**rumiante** *adj* (zool. & fig.) ruminant; *m* (zool.) ruminant
**rumiar** *va & vn* to ruminate; (coll.) to ruminate, meditate
**rumión -miona** *adj* (coll.) ruminative, brooding; *mf* (coll.) brooder
**rumo** *m* first hoop of a cask or barrel
**rumor** *m* rumor; murmur, buzz (*of voices*); rumble
**rumorear** *va* to rumor, to spread by rumor; *vn* to murmur, buzz, rumble; *vr* to be rumored
**rumoroso -sa** *adj* noisy, loud, rumbling
**runa** *f* rune
**runcinado -da** *adj* (bot.) runcinate
**runfla** or **runflada** *f* (coll.) string, row; sequence (*of cards*); **echar runflas** (coll.) to bluster
**rúnico -ca** or **runo -na** *adj* runic
**runrún** *m* (coll.) rumor; (coll.) murmur, rumble; (coll.) purr; (coll.) rustle
**runrunear** *vr* to be whispered about, be bruited about; (coll.) to purr; (coll.) to rustle
**runruneo** *m* rumor, whispering; (coll.) purring; (coll.) rustling
**ruñar** *va* to croze (*a stave*)
**Ruperto** *m* Rupert
**rupestre** *adj* rupestrian
**rupia** *f* (path.) rupia; rupee
**rupicabra** or **rupicapra** *f* (zool.) chamois
**rupícola** *adj* rupicolous, growing or living on rocks; *m* (orn.) cock of the rock
**ruptor** *m* (elec.) contact breaker
**ruptura** *f* rupture, break; crack, split; fission; (fig.) rupture, break (*in friendly relations*)
**ruqueta** *f* (bot.) rocket; (bot.) hedge mustard
**rural** *adj* rural; small-town, country
**rurícola** *mf* ruralist
**rus** *m* (bot.) sumach
**rusco** *m* (bot.) butcher's-broom
**rusel** *m* woolen serge
**Rusia** *f* Russia; **la Rusia Soviética** Soviet Russia; **la Rusia Blanca** White Russia
**rusiente** *adj* candent
**rusificación** *f* Russianization
**rusificar** §86 *va* to Russianize; *vr* to become Russianized
**ruso -sa** *adj & mf* Russian; *m* Russian (*language*); ulster; **gran ruso** Great Russian; **pequeño ruso** Little Russian; **ruso blanco** White Russian
**rusófilo -la** *adj & mf* Russophile
**rusofobia** *f* Russophobia
**rusófobo -ba** *adj & mf* Russophobe
**rusojaponés -nesa** *adj* Russo-Japanese
**rúst.** abr. of **rústica**
**rusticación** *f* rustication
**rustical** *adj* rustic, rural
**rusticano -na** *adj* wild (*plant*)
**rusticar** §86 *vn* to rusticate
**rusticidad** *f* rusticity; coarseness, crudeness, clumsiness
**rústico -ca** *adj* rustic; coarse, crude, clumsy; Vulgar (*Latin*); **a la rústica** or **en rústica** paper-bound; *m* rustic, peasant
**rustiquez** *f* or **rustiqueza** *f* var. of **rusticidad**
**rustro** *m* (her.) rustre
**Rut** *f* Ruth
**ruta** *f* route; (Am.) spree; **ruta de Birmania** Burma Road
**rutabaga** *f* (bot.) rutabaga
**rutáceo -a** *adj* (bot.) rutaceous
**Rutenia** *f* Ruthenia
**rutenio** *m* (chem.) ruthenium
**ruteno -na** *adj & mf* Ruthenian; *m* Ruthenian (*language*)
**rutero -ra** *mf* var. of **rutista**
**rutilante** *adj* (poet.) shining, sparkling
**rutilar** *vn* (poet.) to shine, sparkle
**rutilo** *m* (mineral.) rutile
**rútilo -la** *adj* bright, shining, dazzling
**rutina** *f* routine; (chem.) rutin
**rutinario -ria** *adj* routine (*method; worker*); *mf* routinist
**rutinero -ra** *adj* routine (*e.g., method*); *mf* routinist
**rutista** *mf* experienced driver, driver who knows the roads; *m* long-distance teamster; road bicycle racer
**ruzafa** *f* garden, park

# S

**S, s** *f* twenty-second letter of the Spanish alphabet
**S.** abr. of **San, Santo, sobresaliente, & sur**
**S.ª** abr. of **Señora**
**s. a.** abr. of **sin año**
**sáb.** abr. of **sábado**
**Sabá** Sheba; **reina de Sabá** Queen of Sheba
**sábado** *m* Saturday; Sabbath (*of the Jews*); witches' Sabbath; **hacer sábado** to do the weekly Saturday housecleaning; **sábado de gloria** or **sábado santo** Holy Saturday
**sabalar** *m* shad net
**sabalera** *f* fire grate (*of reverberatory furnace*)
**sabalero** *m* shad fisherman
**sábalo** *m* (ichth.) shad; (Am.) tarpon
**sabana** *f* savanna or savannah
**sábana** *f* sheet; altar cloth; **pegársele a uno las sábanas** (coll.) to stay in bed late
**sabandija** *f* bug, insect, worm; (fig.) vermin (*person*); **sabandijas** *fpl* vermin
**sabanero -ra** *adj* (pertaining to a) savanna; *mf* savanna dweller; *m* (orn.) meadow lark
**sabanilla** *f* small sheet; woollen spread; napkin, kerchief, hand towel; outer altar cloth; communion cloth
**sabañón** *m* chilblain; **comer como un sabañón** (coll.) to eat like a pig
**sabatario -ria** *adj* Sabbatarian; *mf* Sabbatarian (*one who observes Saturday as Sabbath*)
**sabático -ca** *adj* (pertaining to) Saturday; (pertaining to the) Sabbath; (Jewish hist.) sabbatical
**sabatino -na** *adj* (pertaining to) Saturday; *f* Saturday mass; Saturday review, Saturday theme (*in schools*)
**sabatismo** *m* Sabbatarianism
**sabatizar** §76 *vn* to rest on Saturday, to not work on Saturday
**sabedor -dora** *adj* informed
**sabeísmo** *m* Sabaeanism
**sabela** *f* (zool.) sabella
**sabelección** *m & f* (bot.) peppergrass
**sábelotodo** *m* (*pl:* **sábelotodo**) (coll.) know-it-all, wiseacre, wise guy
**sabeo -a** *adj & mf* Sabaean
**saber** *m* knowledge, learning; **según mi leal saber y entender** to the best of my knowledge; §80 *va & vn* to know (*by reasoning or by learning*); to find out; to taste; **a saber** namely, to wit; **hacer saber** to inform, to let know; **no saber cuántas son cinco** or **no saber cuántas son dos y dos** (coll.) to not know what it's all about; **no saber cómo +** *inf* to not know how to, to be at a loss to + *inf;* **no saber dónde meterse** to not know which way to turn; **no sé cuántos** so-and-so, what's his name; **(un) no sé qué** a certain (*something*); **que yo sepa** to my knowledge, as far as I know; **¡y qué sé yo!, ¡y qué sé yo qué más!** and what not, and so forth; **saber a** to taste of, to taste like; to smack of; to know how to get to (*e.g., a person's house*); **saber a poco** to be just a taste, to taste like more; **saber cuántas son cinco** (coll.) to know a thing or two, to know what's what; **saber de** to know, know of, know about, hear of, hear from; to be aware of; **saber lo que es bueno** (coll.) to know the ropes; **saber +** *inf* to know how to, to be able to + *inf; vr* to know; **sabérselo todo** (coll.) to know it all
**sabicú** *m* (bot.) horseflesh mahogany
**sabidillo -lla** *adj & mf* (scornful) know-it-all
**sabido -da** *adj* well-informed; learned; **de sabido** certainly, surely
**sabiduría** *f* wisdom; knowledge, learning; information; **Sabiduría de Salomón** (Bib.) Wisdom of Solomon (*book of the Apocrypha*)
**sabiendas; a sabiendas** knowingly, consciously; **a sabiendas de que** knowing that
**sabihondez** *f* (coll.) affected learning, pretension to wisdom
**sabihondo -da** *adj* (coll.) know-it-all, wiseacred; *mf* (coll.) know-it-all, wiseacre
**sabina** *f* see **sabino**
**sabinar** *m* growth of savins
**sabino -na** *adj* Sabine; roan (*horse*); *mf* Sabine; *f* (bot. & pharm.) savin
**sabio -bia** *adj* wise; learned; trained (*animal*); *mf* wise person, scholar, scientist; *m* wise man, sage
**sabiondez** *f* (coll.) var. of **sabihondez**
**sabiondo -da** *adj & mf* (coll.) var. of **sabihondo**
**sablazo** *m* stroke with a saber, wound from a saber; (coll.) sponging; **dar un sablazo a** (coll.) to hit for a loan
**sable** *m* saber, cutlass; (her.) sable; (coll.) sponging
**sableador -dora** *mf* sponger; *m* saber wielder; rough soldier
**sablear** *va* (coll.) to hit for a loan, to sponge on; *vn* (coll.) to try to borrow money, to go around sponging
**sablista** *mf* (coll.) sponger
**sablón** *m* coarse sand
**saboga** *f* (ichth.) small shad
**saboneta** *f* hunting watch
**sabor** *m* taste, flavor; (fig.) flavor; **sabores** *mpl* beads on bit (*of bridle*); **a sabor** to one's taste, to one's liking
**saborcillo** *m* slight taste, touch
**saboreamiento** *m* flavoring, flavor; tasting, taste; relish, relishing
**saborear** *va* to flavor; to taste; to savor; to allure, entice; *vr* to smack one's lips; **saborearse con** to taste; to savor
**saboreo** *m* flavoring; tasting; savoring
**saborete** *m* slight flavor; slight taste
**sabotaje** *m* sabotage
**saboteador -dora** *mf* saboteur
**sabotear** *va & vn* to sabotage
**Saboya, la** Savoy
**saboyano -na** *adj & mf* Savoyard; *f* open skirt; plum pudding
**sabré** *1st sg fut ind of* **saber**
**sabroso -sa** *adj* tasty, savory, delicious; (coll.) saltish
**sabucal** *m* grove of elders
**sabuco** *m* (bot.) elder
**sabueso** *m* bloodhound, beagle; (fig.) bloodhound (*detective, sleuth*)
**sabugal** *m* var. of **sabucal**
**sabugo** *m* var. of **sabuco**
**sábulo** *m* coarse sand
**sabuloso -sa** *adj* sandy, gritty, sabulous
**saburra** *f* saburra; coat on tongue
**saburral** *adj* saburral
**saburrar** *va* to ballast with rocks and sand
**saburroso -sa** *adj* foul (*mouth or stomach*); coated (*tongue*)
**saca** *f* extraction; exportation; coarse sack; first draft, first copy; **de saca** (Am.) at full speed; **estar de saca** to be on sale; (coll.) to be marriageable
**sacabala** *f* (surg.) bullet-extracting forceps; **sacabalas** *m* (*pl:* **-las**) (arti.) bullet screw
**sacabocado** or **sacabocados** *m* (*pl:* **-dos**) ticket punch; punch; sure thing
**sacabolsas** *m* (*pl:* **-sas**) swindle
**sacabotas** *m* (*pl:* **-tas**) bootjack
**sacabrocas** *m* (*pl:* **-cas**) tack puller, nail puller
**sacabuche** *m* (bot.) strawberry tomato; (mus.) sackbut (*instrument or player*); (coll.) nincompoop; (naut.) hand pump

**sacaclavos** *m* (*pl:* **-vos**) nail puller; **sacaclavos de horquilla** claw bar
**sacacorchos** *m* (*pl:* **-chos**) corkscrew
**sacacuartos** *m* (*pl:* **-tos**) (coll.) catchpenny, bamboozle
**sacadinero** or **sacadineros** *m* (*pl:* **-ros**) (coll.) catchpenny, bamboozle; (coll.) bamboozler
**sacador -dora** *mf* (tennis) server; *m* (print.) delivery table
**sacadura** *f* (sew.) sloping cut
**sacafilásticas** *f* (*pl:* **-cas**) priming wire
**sacaliña** *f* stick, goad stick; trick, cunning
**sacamanchas** *mf* (*pl:* **-chas**) clothes cleaner, spot remover; dry cleaner; dyer
**sacamantas** *m* (*pl:* **-tas**) (coll.) delinquent-tax collector
**sacamantecas** *m* (*pl:* **-cas**) (coll.) Jack the Ripper
**sacamiento** *m* extraction; removal
**sacamolero** *m* (coll.) dentist
**sacamuelas** *mf* (*pl:* **-las**) (coll.) tooth puller; (coll.) charlatan, quack
**sacamuertos** *m* (*pl:* **-tos**) stagehand
**sacanete** *m* lansquenet (*card game*)
**sacapelotas** *m* (*pl:* **-tas**) bullet screw; (fig.) cur
**sacaperras** *m* (*pl:* **-rras**) (coll.) gambling machine
**sacapintura** *m* paint remover
**sacapotras** *m* (*pl:* **-tras**) (coll.) butcher (*surgeon*)
**sacapuntas** *m* (*pl:* **-tas**) pencil sharpener
**sacar** §86 *va* to draw, draw out, pull out; to pull up; to take out, get out; to extract, to remove; to stick out (*e.g., one's chest*); to show, bring out, publish; to find out, to solve; to elicit, draw out (*a secret*); to determine; to copy; to take (*a photograph*); to except, to exclude; to quote; to win (*a prize*); to get, obtain; to produce, invent, imitate; to serve (*a ball*); **sacar a bailar** (coll.) to drag in; **sacar adelante** to nurture, rear; **sacar a relucir** (coll.) to bring up unexpectedly; **sacar a volar** to bring out (*especially a bashful person*); **sacar de espesor** to pare down, make thin; **sacar de pobre** to lift out of poverty; **sacar de sí** to drive mad, to make crazy; **sacar en claro** or **en limpio** to deduce, to conclude clearly; to recopy clearly; **sacar mentiroso** to give the lie to
**sacarificación** *f* saccharification
**sacarificar** §86 *va* to saccharify
**sacarimetría** *f* saccharimetry
**sacarímetro** *m* saccharimeter
**sacarino -na** *adj* saccharine; *f* (chem.) saccharine
**sacaroideo -a** *adj* saccharoid
**sacarosa** *f* (chem.) saccharose, sucrose
**sacarruedas** *m* (*pl:* **-das**) (aut.) wheel puller
**sacasillas** *m* (*pl:* **-llas**) (coll.) stagehand
**sacatapón** *m* corkscrew
**sacate** *m* var. of **zacate**
**sacatrapos** *m* (*pl:* **-pos**) (arti.) wad hook, wormer
**sacerdocio** *m* priesthood
**sacerdotal** *adj* sacerdotal, priestly
**sacerdote** *m* priest; **sumo sacerdote** high priest
**sacerdotisa** *f* priestess
**sácere** *m* (bot.) maple
**saciable** *adj* satiable
**saciar** *va* to satiate
**saciedad** *f* satiety, satiation
**saciña** *f* (bot.) white willow
**sacio -cia** *adj* satiated
**saco** *m* sack, bag; sackful, bagful; pack (*e.g., of lies*); (mil.) sack, plunder, pillage; serve (*in ball games*); (anat., bot. & zool.) sac; coat; (sew.) sacque; **no echar en saco roto** (coll.) to not forget, to not overlook; **poner a saco** to plunder, to loot; **saco de noche** satchel, handbag, overnight bag; **saco terrero** (fort.) sandbag
**sacra** *f* see **sacro**
**sacramentación** *f* administration of sacraments; (theol.) transubstantiation
**sacramental** *adj* sacramental; *m* sacramental; member of an association devoted to the worship of the sacrament; *f* association devoted to the worship of the sacrament
**sacramentar** *va* to administer the sacraments to; (theol.) to transubstantiate; (coll.) to conceal, to hide; *vr* (theol.) to transubstantiate
**sacramentario -ria** *adj & mf* Sacramentarian
**sacramento** *m* sacrament; **santísimo sacramento** Holy Sacrament; **sacramento del altar** sacrament (*Eucharist*)
**sacratísimo -ma** *adj super* very or most sacred or holy
**sacre** *m* (orn. & arti.) saker; thief
**sacrificadero** *m* place for sacrifice
**sacrificador -dora** *adj* sacrificing; *mf* sacrificer
**sacrificar** §86 *va* to sacrifice; to slaughter; *vn* to sacrifice; *vr* to sacrifice, to sacrifice oneself; to devote oneself to God
**sacrificatorio -ria** *adj* sacrificial
**sacrificio** *m* sacrifice; **santo sacrificio** mass; **sacrificio del altar** Sacrifice of the Mass
**sacrilegio** *m* sacrilege
**sacrílego -ga** *adj* sacrilegious
**sacrismoche** *m* or **sacrismocho** *m* (coll.) fellow dressed in shabby black clothes
**sacrista** *m* sexton
**sacristán** *m* sacristan; sexton; hoops (*for skirt*); **ser gran sacristán** (coll.) to be crafty, to be wily; **sacristán de amén** (coll.) yes man
**sacristana** *f* sacristan's wife; sexton's wife; nun in charge of sacristy
**sacristanía** *f* office of sacristan or sexton
**sacristía** *f* sacristy; office of sacristan or sexton
**sacro -cra** *adj* sacred; (anat.) sacral; *m* (anat.) sacrum; *f* (eccl.) sacring tablet
**sacroilíaco -ca** *adj* (anat.) sacroiliac
**sacrosanto -ta** *adj* sacrosanct
**sacudido -da** *adj* indocile, intractable; determined, resolute; *f* shake, jar, jolt, jerk, bump; (elec.) shock
**sacudidor -dora** *adj* shaking, beating; *m* shaker, beater; duster; **sacudidor de alfombras** carpetbeater
**sacudidura** *f* shake (*especially to remove dust*)
**sacudimiento** *m* shaking, shake, jolt, jerk
**sacudión** *m* jolt, jerk
**sacudir** *va* to shake; to jar, jolt; to rock; to shake off, to throw off; to beat; *vr* to shake, shake oneself; to rock; to shake off; to manage to get along, to wangle through
**sacudón** *m* (Am.) jolt, jerk
**sáculo** *m* (anat.) saccule
**sachadura** *f* weeding
**sachar** *va* to weed
**sacho** *m* weeder, weeding tool
**sádico -ca** *adj* sadistic; *mf* sadist
**sadismo** *m* sadism
**saduceísmo** *m* Sadduceism
**saduceo -a** *adj* Sadducean; *mf* Sadducee, Sadducean
**saeta** *f* arrow, dart; hand (*of clock or watch*); gnomon; magnetic needle; bud of vine; sacred song; (*cap.*) *f* (astr.) Sagitta
**saetada** *f* or **saetazo** *m* arrow shot; arrow wound
**saetear** *va* var. of **asaetear**
**saetero -ra** *adj* (pertaining to an) arrow; *m* archer, bowman; *f* (fort.) loophole; narrow window
**saetilla** *f* small arrow; hand (*of watch or clock*); magnetic needle; sacred song, devotional verse; (bot.) arrowhead; (arch.) dart (*in egg-and-dart ornaments*)
**saetín** *m* millrace, flume; brad; sateen
**safari** *m* safari
**safeno -na** *adj* (anat.) saphenous
**sáfico -ca** *adj & m* Sapphic
**Safira** *f* (Bib.) Sapphira
**Safo** *f* Sappho
**saga** *f* saga; witch, sorceress
**sagacidad** *f* sagacity
**sagapeno** *m* sagapenum
**sagatí** *m* sagathy, sayette
**sagaz** *adj* (*pl:* **-gaces**) sagacious; keen-scented
**sagita** *f* (arch.) rise (*of an arch*)
**sagitado -da** *adj* (bot.) sagittate
**sagital** *adj* sagittal; (anat. & zool.) sagittal
**sagitaria** *f* (bot.) arrowhead
**sagitario** *m* bowman; (*cap.*) *m* (astr.) Sagittarius

**ságoma** *f* (arch.) pattern, templet
**sagrado -da** *adj* sacred; *m* asylum, haven, place of refuge; **acogerse a sagrado** to take sanctuary
**sagrario** *m* sacrarium, sanctuary, shrine; (eccl.) ciborium
**sagú** *m* (*pl:* **-gúes**) sago (*starch*); (bot.) sago, sago palm
**saguaro** *m* (bot.) saguaro, giant cactus
**saguino** *m* (zool.) tamarin
**ságula** *f* small frock
**saguntino -na** *adj* (pertaining to) Sagunto; *mf* native or inhabitant of Sagunto
**Sahara** *m* Sahara
**sahariano -na** *adj* (pertaining to the) Sahara; *f* tight-fitting military jacket
**sahína** *f* var. of **zahína**
**sahornar** *vr* to skin oneself, to scrape or scratch oneself
**sahorno** *m* skin abrasion, scratch
**sahuaro** *m* var. of **saguaro**
**sahumado -da** *adj* bettered, improved; (Am.) drunk
**sahumador** *m* perfuming pot, incense pot; stretcher, clothes drier
**sahumadura** *f* smoking, perfuming with smoke or incense
**sahumar** §99 *va* to smoke, to perfume with smoke or incense
**sahumerio** or **sahúmo** *m* smoking, perfuming; incense, aromatic smoke
**saica** *f* saic (*ketch used in the Levant*)
**saicar** *m* sidecar
**saín** *m* grease, fat; fish oil; greasiness, grease spot
**sainar §75** *va* to fatten
**sainete** *m* flavor, relish, spice, zest; sauce, seasoning; tidbit, delicacy; elegance; one-act farce
**sainetear** *vn* to act in a farce
**sainetero** *m* farce writer
**sainetesco -ca** *adj* farcical, burlesque
**saíno** *m* (zool.) peccary
**saja** *f* incision; leaf stalk of Manila hemp
**sajador** *m* bleeder; (surg.) scarifier (*instrument*)
**sajadura** *f* incision; slit, crack
**sajar** *va* to cut, make an incision in, tap
**sajelar** *va* to sift and clean (*clay*)
**sajía** *f* incision
**sajón -jona** *adj* & *mf* Saxon
**Sajonia** *f* Saxony
**Sajonia-Coburgo-Gotha** *f* Saxe-Coburg-Gotha
**sal** *f* salt; charm, grace; wit, wittiness; (Am.) bad luck, misfortune; **echar en sal** (coll.) to keep back; **estar hecho de sal** to be full of life, be in a good mood; **sal amoníaca, sal amoníaco** sal ammoniac; **sal ática** Attic salt; **sal común** common salt; **sal de acederas** salt of sorrel; **sal de compás** rock salt; **sal de Epsom** Epsom salt; **sal de la Higuera** Epsom salt; **sales aromáticas** smelling salts; **sal gema** rock salt; **sal marina** sea salt; **sal volátil** sal volatile; *2d sg impv of* **salir**
**sala** *f* hall; drawing room, living room, sitting room, salon, parlor; (law) bench; **hacer sala** to form a quorum (*in court*); **sala de batalla** sorting room (*in postoffice*); **sala de clase** classroom; **sala de equipajes** baggage room; **sala de enfermos** infirmary; **sala de espectáculos** auditorium; **sala de espera** waiting room; **sala de estar** living room, sitting room; **sala de fiestas** night club; **sala de gálibos** (naut.) mold loft; **sala de hospital** hospital ward; **sala de justicia** court of justice, courtroom; **sala del cine** moving-picture house; **sala de lectura** reading room; **sala de máquinas** engine room; **sala de muestras** showroom; **sala de recepción** or **recibo** reception hall; **sala de recreo** amusement parlor
**salabardo** *m* scoop net, dip net
**salacidad** *f* salacity, salaciousness
**saladar** *m* salt marsh; barren brine-soaked land
**saladero** *m* salting room, salting house
**saladillo -lla** *adj* half-salted; *m* half-salted bacon; salted peanut; *f* (bot.) saltbush
**Saladino** *m* Saladin
**salado -da** *adj* salt; salty; brine-soaked; witty, facetious; (Am.) expensive; (Am.) unfortunate; *m* (bot.) saltwort
**salador -dora** *mf* salter (*of meat, fish*); *m* salting room, salting house
**saladura** *f* salting
**salamandra** *f* salamander (*stove*); (zool. & myth.) salamander; **salamandra acuática** or **salamandra de agua** (zool.) newt, triton; **salamandra gigante** (zool.) giant salamander, hellbender
**salamandria** *f* (zool.) gecko, tarente
**salamandrino -na** *adj* (pertaining to or like the) salamander
**salamanqués -quesa** *adj* (pertaining to) Salamanca; *mf* native or inhabitant of Salamanca; *f* (zool.) gecko, tarente
**salamanquino -na** *adj* (pertaining to) Salamanca; *mf* native or inhabitant of Salamanca
**Salamina** *f* Salamis
**salangana** *f* (orn.) swift (*Collocalia esculenta*)
**salar** *va* to salt, to season or preserve with salt; to put too much salt on
**salariado** *m* payment by means of wages, remuneration in wages
**salariar** *va* to fix a salary or wages for
**salario** *m* wages, pay; **salario anual garantizado** guaranteed annual wage; **salario de hambre** starvation wages
**salaz** *adj* (*pl:* **-laces**) salacious
**salazón** *f* salting; salt meat, salt fish; salt-meat and salt-fish business
**salazonero -ra** *adj* salt-meat, salt-fish
**salbanda** *f* (min.) selvage
**salce** *m* (bot.) willow
**salceda** *f* or **salcedo** *m* willow grove, salicetum
**salcereta** *f* dicebox
**salcochar** *va* to boil in salt water
**salcocho** *m* (Am.) food boiled in salt water
**salchicha** *f* sausage; (fort.) saucisson, large fascine; (mil.) saucisson (*fuse*)
**salchichería** *f* sausage shop
**salchichero -ra** *mf* sausage maker or seller
**salchichón** *m* large sausage; (fort.) saucisson, large fascine
**saldar** *va* to settle, liquidate; to sell out, to sell out at reduced prices
**saldista** *m* liquidation broker; remnant salesman
**saldo** *m* settlement, liquidation; (com.) balance; remnant, leftover; bargain; **saldo acreedor** credit balance; **saldo deudor** debit balance
**saldré** *1st sg fut ind of* **salir**
**saledizo -za** *adj* projecting; *m* projection, ledge
**salega** *f* lick, salt lick
**salegar** *m* lick, salt lick; **§59** *vn* to lick salt
**salema** *f* (ichth.) gilthead, sheepshead
**salep** *m* salep
**salera** *f* stone or block on which salt is placed for cattle
**salero** *m* saltcellar, saltshaker; salt lick; salthouse, salt storage; (coll.) charm, grace, wit; wit (*person*)
**saleroso -sa** *adj* (coll.) salty, witty; charming, winsome, lively
**salesa** *adj* & *f* Salesian (*of Order of the Visitation*)
**salesiano -na** *adj* & *mf* Salesian (*of orders founded by Don Bosco and of Order of the Visitation*)
**saleta** *f* little hall; royal antechamber; court of appeal
**salgada** or **salgadera** *f* (bot.) orach, mountain spinach
**salgar** §59 *va* to salt (*cattle*)
**salgareño** *adj* see **pino**
**salgo** *1st sg pres ind of* **salir**
**salguera** *f* or **salguero** *m* (bot.) willow
**salicáceo -a** *adj* (bot.) salicaceous
**salicaria** *f* (bot.) loosestrife, purple loosestrife
**salicilato** *m* (chem.) salicylate
**salicílico -ca** *adj* (chem.) salicylic
**salicina** *f* (chem.) salicin
**sálico -ca** *adj* Salic
**salicor** *m* (bot.) saltwort (*Salsola soda*)
**salida** *f* see **salido**
**salidero -ra** *adj* gadabout, on the go; *m* wayout, exit
**salidizo** *m* projection, ledge

**salido -da** *adj* bulging, projecting; in heat (*said of a female*); *f* start; going out, coming out, leaving; departure; way out, exit; check (*to return to theater after intermission*); outlet; recourse, issue, outcome, result; loophole, subterfuge; pretext; outlay, expenditure; projection; outlying fields (*near city gate*); (bridge) lead; (sport) start; (mil.) sally, sortie; (naut.) sudden jerk in starting; (naut.) headway; (coll.) witticism; (com. & fig.) outlet; (elec.) output; **dar la salida** (theat.) to give the cue; **tener buenas salidas** (coll.) to be full of witty remarks; **tener salida** to sell well; to be popular with the boys (*said of young ladies*); **salida de auxilio** or **de socorro** emergency exit; **salida de baño** bathrobe, bathing wrap; **salida de pie de banco** (coll.) nonsense, piece of folly; **salida de sol** sunrise; **salida de teatro** evening wrap; **salida de teatros** after-theater party, after-theater supper; **salida de tono** (coll.) irrelevancy, impropriety; **salida lanzada** (sport) running start

**saliente** *adj* salient, projecting; outgoing, outbound; rising (*e.g., sun*); *m* east; *f* projection; shoulder (*of a bastion; of a road*)

**salífero -ra** *adj* saliferous

**salificable** *adj* (chem.) salifiable

**salificación** *f* (chem.) salification

**salificar** §86 *va* (chem.) to salify

**salimiento** *m* departure

**salín** *m* salthouse

**salina** *f* see **salino**

**salinero -ra** *adj* spotted red and white (*said of a bull*); *mf* saltmaker, salter

**salinidad** *f* salinity

**salino -na** *adj* saline; *f* salt mine; salt marsh; salt works

**salio -lia** *adj & mf* Salian

**salir** §81 *vn* to go out, come out; to leave, go away; to sail; to get out; to run out, come to an end, be over; to appear, to show, to show up; to come out, come off (*said, e.g., of a stain*); to rise (*said, e.g., of the sun*); to shoot, spring, come up; to project, stand out, stick out; to make the first move, be the first to play; to result, turn out; to be drawn (*in a lottery*); to be elected; to happen, occur; to check, come out right; (bridge) to lead; (theat.) to enter, appear; (naut.) to get ahead (*said of one boat with respect to another*); **salga lo que saliere** (coll.) come what may; **salir a** to come to, to amount to; to resemble, look like; to open into; **salir a** + *inf* to go or come out to + *inf;* **salir adelante** or **avante** to be successful, to win out; **salir al encuentro a** to go to meet; to oppose, take a stand against; to get ahead of; **salir bien en un examen** to pass an examination; **salir con** to come out with (*e.g., an unexpected remark, a claim*); **salir con bien** to be successful; **salir contra** to come out against; **salir de** to cease being; to depart from; to get rid of, to dispose of; to lose one's (*head, judgment, consciousness*); **salir disparado** to start like a shot; **salir pitando** (coll.) to start off on a mad run; (coll.) to blow up, get suddenly angry; *vr* to slip out, to escape; to slip off, to run off; to leak (*said of a liquid or its container*); to boil over; **salirse con la suya** to come out ahead, to have one's way; to carry one's point

**salitrado -da** *adj* saltpetrous

**salitral** *adj* saltpetrous; *m* saltpeter bed; saltpeter works

**salitre** *m* saltpeter (*potassium nitrate*)

**salitrera** *f* see **salitrero**

**salitrería** *f* saltpeter works

**salitrero -ra** *adj* (pertaining to) saltpeter; *mf* saltpeter refiner, saltpeter dealer; *f* saltpeter bed

**salitroso -sa** *adj* saltpetrous

**saliva** *f* saliva; **gastar saliva** (coll.) to talk in vain; to prattle; **tragar saliva** (coll.) to suffer an offense or disappointment in silence; (coll.) to be speechless

**salivación** *f* salivation

**salivajo** *m* (coll.) spit, expectoration

**salival** *adj* salivary

**salivar** *vn* to salivate

**salivazo** *m* (coll.) spit, expectoration

**saliveras** *fpl* round knobs on bits of a bridle

**salivoso -sa** *adj* salivous

**salma** *f* ton (*in reckoning displacement of vessels*); salma (*Italian, Sicilian, and Maltese measure*); light packsaddle

**salmanticense** or **salmantino -na** *adj* (pertaining to) Salamanca; *mf* native or inhabitant of Salamanca

**salmear** *vn* to sing psalms

**salmer** *m* (arch.) skewback

**salmista** *m* psalmist (*composer or cantor*); **el Salmista** (Bib.) the Psalmist

**salmo** *m* psalm; **los Salmos** (Bib.) the Psalms; **salmos penitenciales** (Bib.) penitential psalms

**salmodia** *f* psalmody; (coll.) singsong, monotonous song

**salmodiar** *va* to singsong, to sing monotonously; *vn* to sing psalms; to singsong

**salmón** *m* salmon (*color*); (ichth.) salmon; **salmón zancado** (ichth.) kelt

**salmonado -da** *adj* salmon-like; salmon (*in color*)

**salmoncillo** *m* (ichth.) samlet, parr

**salmonera** *f* salmon net

**salmonete** *m* (ichth.) red mullet

**salmorear** *va* (Am.) to lecture, to scold

**salmorejo** *m* rabbit sauce; salmi

**salmuera** *f* brine, pickle; briny moisture; salty food or drink

**salmuerar** *vr* to get sick from too much salt (*said of cattle*)

**salobral** *adj* saline (*ground*); *m* saline ground

**salobre** *adj* brackish, saltish

**salobreño -na** *adj & m* var. of **salobral**

**salobridad** *f* brackishness, saltiness

**salol** *m* (chem.) salol

**saloma** *f* (naut.) chantey

**salomador** *m* (naut.) chanteyman

**salomar** *vn* (naut.) to sing chanteys

**Salomé** *f* (Bib.) Salome

**Salomón** *m* Solomon; (fig.) Solomon

**salomónico -ca** *adj* Solomonic; (arch.) twisted (*column*)

**salón** *m* salon; drawing room; saloon (*e.g., of a steamship*); meeting room; **salón de actos** auditorium, assembly hall; **salón de baile** ballroom; **salón de belleza** beauty parlor; **salón del automóvil** automobile show; **salón del trono** throne room; **salón de pinturas** picture gallery; **salón de recreo** recreation hall; **salón de refrescos** ice-cream parlor; **salón de sesiones** assembly hall; **salón de tertulia** lounge; **salón de ventas** salesroom; **salón social** lounge

**saloncillo** *m* rest room (*e.g., of a theater*)

**salpa** *f* (ichth.) gilthead; (zool.) salpa

**salpicadero** *m* splasher, splashguard

**salpicadura** *f* splash, splashing, spattering; **salpicaduras** *fpl* indirect results

**salpicar** §86 *va* to splash, bespatter; to sprinkle; to skip through; *vn* to splash

**salpicón** *m* salmagundi; (coll.) splash, splashing; (coll.) hash, chopped mixture, hodgepodge; (Am.) cold fruit juice

**salpimentar** §18 *va* to salt and pepper; (fig.) to sweeten (*to make pleasant and agreeable*)

**salpimienta** *f* mixture of salt and pepper

**salpique** *m* splash, spatter

**salpresamiento** *m* preservation with salt

**salpresar** *va* to preserve with salt

**salpreso -sa** *adj* preserved with salt

**salpullido** *m* rash, eruption; flea bites

**salpullir** §26 *va* to cause a rash in; to splotch; *vr* to break out

**salsa** *f* sauce, dressing, gravy; **cocer en su propia salsa** to stew in one's own juice; **salsa blanca** white sauce; **salsa de ají** chili sauce; **salsa de San Bernardo** (coll.) hunger; **salsa de tomate** catsup, ketchup; **salsa francesa** French dressing; **salsa holandesa** hollandaise sauce; **salsa inglesa** Worcestershire sauce; **salsa mahonesa** or **mayonesa** mayonnaise; **salsa tártara** tartare sauce

**salsedumbre** *f* saltiness

**salsera** *f* gravy dish, gravy boat; small saucer (*to mix paints*)

**salsereta, salserilla** or **salseruela** *f* small saucer (*used especially to mix paints*)

**salsifí** *m* (*pl:* **-fíes**) (bot.) salsify; **salsifí de España** (bot.) viper's-grass; **salsifí de los prados** (bot.) yellow goatsbeard; **salsifí negro** (bot.) viper's-grass
**saltabanco** or **saltabancos** *m* (*pl:* **-cos**) quack, mountebank; prestidigitator; (coll.) trifler, nuisance
**saltabardales** *mf* (*pl:* **-les**) (coll.) wild youngster
**saltabarrancos** *mf* (*pl:* **-cos**) (coll.) jumping jack (*person*)
**saltacaballo** *m* (arch.) crossette
**saltación** *f* jumping, leaping; dance, dancing
**saltacharquillos** *mf* (*pl:* **-llos**) (coll.) youngster who goes jumping and tiptoeing about for effect
**saltadero** *m* jumping place; fountain, jet
**saltadizo -za** *adj* brittle, shattery
**saltador -dora** *adj* jumping, leaping; *mf* jumper, leaper; *m* skipping rope; **saltador del margen** margin release
**saltadura** *f* chip (*in surface of a stone*)
**saltaembanco** *m* var. of **saltabanco**
**saltamimbres** *m* (*pl:* **-bres**) (orn.) sedge warbler
**saltamontes** *m* (*pl:* **-tes**) (ent.) grasshopper
**saltante** *adj* saltant
**saltaojos** *m* (*pl:* **-jos**) (bot.) peony
**saltaparedes** *mf* (*pl:* **-des**) (coll.) var. of **saltabardales**
**saltaperico** *m* (bot.) manyroot; (Am.) snake, serpent (*kind of firework*)
**saltar** *va* to jump, jump over, leap; to skip, skip over; (naut.) to lower (*a cable*); to cover (*a female*); *vn* to jump, leap, hop, skip; to bounce, bound, fly; to shoot up, to spurt; to come loose, to come off, to slip off; to crack, break, burst; to chip; to stick out, to project; to skip a rank (*in being promoted*); to flash in the mind or memory; **saltar a la vista** or **los ojos** to be self-evident; **saltar con** to come out with (*e.g., an irrelevant remark*); **saltar de** to be kicked out of (*a job*); **saltar por** to jump over; *vr* to skip (*in reading or copying*)
**saltarelo** *m* old Spanish dance based on Italian saltarello
**saltarén** *m* guitar dance tune; (ent.) grasshopper
**saltarín -rina** *adj* dancing; *mf* dancer; *m* wild youth, restless young fellow
**saltarregla** *f* bevel square
**saltaterandate** *m* long-stitch embroidery
**saltatrás** *mf* (*pl:* **-trás**) var. of **tornatrás**
**saltatriz** *f* (*pl:* **-trices**) ballet girl, ballerina
**saltatumbas** *m* (*pl:* **-bas**) (coll.) burying parson
**salteador** *m* highwayman, holdup man
**salteadora** *f* female companion of highwaymen, moll; female robber
**salteamiento** *m* assault, holdup, highway robbery
**saltear** *va* to attack, to hold up, to waylay; to overtake suddenly, to take by surprise; to do in fits and starts, to leave for something else; to sauté
**salteo** *m* var. of **salteamiento**
**salterio** *m* (mus.) psaltery; rosary; (*cap.*) *m* Psalter
**saltero -ra** *adj* highland
**saltígrado -da** *adj* jumping (*said of animals*)
**saltimbanco** or **saltimbanqui** *m* (coll.) var. of **saltabanco**
**salto** *m* jump, leap, spring, bound; dive; skip; fall, waterfall; omission (*in reading or copying*); leapfrog; leap (*in promotion or advancement*); palpitation (*of heart*); **a saltos** by leaps; skipping; **de un salto** at one jump; **en un salto** quickly; **ir de un salto a** (Am.) to hurry over to; **por salto** (coll.) skipping, jumping around; **salto a ciegas** leap in the dark; **salto con garrocha** or **salto con pértiga** (sport) pole vault; **salto de altura** (sport) high jump; **salto de ángel** swan dive; **salto de cama** morning wrap, dressing gown; **salto de carnero** bucking; **salto de carpa** jackknife; **salto de esquí** or **con esquí** ski jump; **salto de longitud** (sport) broad jump; **salto de mal año** (coll.) sudden rise in fortune; **salto de mata** flight for fear of punishment; **salto de trucha** tumbling; **salto de vallas** (sport) leaping or clearing a hurdle; **salto de viento** (naut.) sudden shift in the wind; **salto en paracaídas** parachute jump; **salto mortal** somersault; **salto ornamental** fancy dive
**saltón -tona** *adj* jumping, hopping; projecting; bulging; *m* (ent.) grasshopper; (ent.) maggot
**salubérrimo -ma** *adj super* very or most salubrious or healthful
**salubre** *adj* salubrious, healthful
**salubridad** *f* salubrity; health, public health
**salud** *f* health; welfare; salvation; **saludes** *fpl* greetings, compliments; **¡a su salud!** to your health!; **beber a la salud de** to drink to the health of; **estar bien de salud** to be in good health; **estar mal de salud** to be in bad health; **gastar salud** to enjoy wonderful health; **vender** or **verter salud** (coll.) to radiate health; *interj* (coll.) greetings!
**saludable** *adj* healthful, wholesome; salutary
**saludador -dora** *mf* greeter, saluter; *m* quack, medicine man
**saludar** *va* to greet, salute, hail, bow to; (mil.) to salute; (mil.) to fire a salute for; (naut.) to dip the flag to; (coll.) to get a smattering of; to treat by incantation of magic; *vn* to salute; to bow
**saludo** *m* greeting, salute, bow, salutation; (mil.) salute; **saludo final** conclusion (*of a letter*)
**salumbre** *f* flower of salt
**Salustio** *m* Sallust
**salutación** *f* salutation, greeting, bow; **salutación angélica** Angelic Salutation
**salutífero -ra** *adj* var. of **saludable**
**salutista** *mf* Salvationist, member of the Salvation Army
**salva** *f* see **salvo**
**salvabarros** *m* (*pl:* **-rros**) mudguard
**salvable** *adj* savable, salvable
**salvación** *f* salvation
**salvadera** *f* sandbox (*for sprinkling sand on ink*)
**salvado** *m* bran
**salvador -dora** *adj* saving; *mf* savior, saver; lifesaver; rescuer; (*cap.*) *m* Saviour; **El Salvador** El Salvador (*country in Central America*)
**salvadoreño -ña** *adj & mf* Salvadoran
**salvaguardar** *va* to safeguard
**salvaguardia** *f* safeguard, safe-conduct; protection, shelter; *m* bodyguard, safeguard, escort; mark of protection (*on a building in wartime*)
**salvajada** *f* savagery, brutality
**salvaje** *adj* wild, uncultivated; savage; stupid; *mf* savage; dolt
**salvajería** *f* savagery
**salvajino -na** *adj* wild; savage; gamy (*said of meat*); *f* wild animal; wild animals; game (*flesh of wild animal*); wild-animal skins
**salvajismo** *m* savagery, savageness
**salvamano; a salvamano** without danger, without running any risk
**salvamanteles** *m* (*pl:* **-les**) coaster (*small tray placed under a tumbler*)
**salvamento** *m* salvation; lifesaving; rescue; rescue work; salvage; safety, place of safety
**salvamiento** *m* (archaic) var. of **salvamento**
**salvante** *adj* saving; *prep* saving, except
**salvar** *va* to save (*shipwrecked person, drowning person, lost soul, etc.*); to salvage; to avoid (*difficulty, inconvenience, etc.*); to clear (*obstacle*); to get around, to overcome (*difficulty*); to go over, to jump over; to cover, get over (*a distance*); to rise above; to except, make an exception of; to notarize (*alterations, emendations, etc.*); to prove legally the innocence of; **salvar las apariencias** to save face, to keep up appearances; *vn* to taste (*in order to prove that food or drink is not poisoned*); *vr* to save oneself; to be saved; **sálvese el que pueda** everyone for himself
**salvarsán** *m* salvarsan
**salvavidas** *m* (*pl:* **-das**) life preserver; lifeboat; fender, guard (*in front of electric cars*)
**salvedad** *f* reservation, qualification
**salvia** *f* (bot.) sage, salvia

**salvilla** *f* tray with depressions into which cups and glasses fit; (Am.) cruet stand
**salvo -va** *adj* safe; omitted, unmentioned; **a salvo** out of danger; **a salvo de** safe from; **dejar a salvo** to set aside, make an exception of; **en salvo** at liberty; out of danger; **poner a salvo** to put in a safe place; **ponerse a salvo** to seek safety, to reach safety; **quedar a salvo** to be safe, be out of danger; to be an exception; **sentirse a salvo** to feel safe ‖ **salvo** *prep* save, except for; **salvo que** unless ‖ *f* greeting, welcome; salvo; oath, solemn promise; salver, tray; ordeal (*test of innocence*); tasting (*of food before serving it, e.g., to a king*); **salva de aplausos** round or burst of applause
**salvoconducto** *m* safe-conduct
**salladura** *f* weeding
**sallar** *va* to weed; to store (*planks*) on skidding
**sallete** *m* weeder, weeding tool
**sámago** *m* sapwood
**sámara** *f* (bot.) samara
**samarilla** *f* (bot.) ironwort
**samario** *m* (chem.) samarium
**samarita** *adj & mf* Samaritan
**samaritano -na** *adj & mf* Samaritan; **el buen samaritano** (Bib.) the Good Samaritan; *m* Samaritan (*language*)
**samaruguera** *f* small-mesh fishing net
**sambenitar** *va* to put the sanbenito on (*a person*); to mark with a note of infamy; to disgrace
**sambenito** *m* sanbenito; note of infamy; disgrace
**samblaje** *m* joint, joining
**sambuca** *f* (mus.) sambuke
**samio -mia** *adj & mf* Samian
**samisén** *m* (mus.) samisen
**samoano -na** *adj & mf* Samoan
**Samos** *f* Samos
**samotracio -cia** *adj & mf* Samothracian; (*cap.*) *f* Samothrace
**samovar** *m* samovar
**sampaguita** *f* (bot.) Arabian jasmine
**sampán** *m* sampan
**sampsuco** *m* (bot.) marjoram
**Samuel** *m* Samuel
**samuga** *f* var. of **jamuga**
**samurai** *m* samurai
**san** *adj* apocopated form of **santo**, used before masculine names of saints, except Tomás, Tomé, Toribio, and Domingo
**sanable** *adj* curable
**sanador -dora** *adj* healing; *mf* healer
**sánalotodo** *m* (*pl:* **-do**) cure-all
**sanapudio** *m* (bot.) alder buckthorn; **sanapudio blanco** (bot.) cornel, red dogwood
**sanar** *va* to cure, to heal; *vn* to heal; to recover
**sanativo -va** *adj* sanative, curative
**sanatorio** *m* sanatorium, sanitarium, hospital
**sanción** *f* sanction; penalty; evil consequence; **pragmática sanción** or **sanción pragmática** pragmatic sanction
**sancionar** *va* to sanction; to penalize
**sancochado** *m* parboiling
**sancochar** *va* to parboil
**sancocho** *m* parboiled meat; (Am.) stew
**sancta** *m* fore part of tabernacle; **non sancta** *adj fem* wicked, depraved
**sanctasanctórum** *m* (*pl:* **-rum**) sanctum sanctorum; arcanum; something highly cherished
**Sanctus** *m* (*pl:* **-tus**) (eccl. & mus.) Sanctus
**sanchopancesco -ca** *adj* like Sancho Panza; credulous but shrewd and realistic
**sandalia** *f* sandal
**sandalino -na** *adj* (pertaining to) sandalwood
**sándalo** *m* (bot.) yellow sandalwood; (bot.) bergamot (*a mint*); sandalwood oil; **sándalo blanco** (bot.) sandalwood, white sandalwood; **sándalo rojo** (bot.) red sandalwood
**sandáraca** *f* sandarac (*resin; realgar*)
**sandez** *f* (*pl:* **-deces**) folly, nonsense; piece of nonsense
**sandía** *f* (bot.) watermelon (*plant and fruit*)
**sandiar** *m* watermelon patch
**sandio -dia** *adj* foolish, nonsensical, silly
**sandunga** *f* (coll.) geniality, charm
**sandunguero -ra** *adj* (coll.) genial, charming
**saneado -da** *adj* clear, unencumbered
**saneamiento** *m* guarantee; indemnification; adjustment; sanitation, drainage
**sanear** *va* to guarantee (*amends or satisfaction*); to make amends for, to indemnify; to make an adjustment for (*damages resulting from defect in thing purchased*); to make sanitary, to drain, to dry up
**sanedrín** *m* Sanhedrim
**sanfrancia** *f* (coll.) row, quarrel, dispute
**San Gotardo** *m* St. Gotthard
**sangradera** *f* (surg.) lancet; basin for blood; overflow sluice; irrigation ditch
**sangrador** *m* bloodletter; drain, outlet
**sangradura** *f* bleeding, bloodletting; inner pit of arm opposite elbow; vein incision; outlet, draining
**sangrar** *va* to bleed; to drain; to tap (*a furnace; a tree*); to draw resin from; (print.) to indent; (coll.) to filch from; (Am.) to bleed (*to draw or extort money from*); *vn* to bleed; **estar sangrando** to be new or recent; to be plain or evident; *vr* to have oneself bled; to run (*said of colors*)
**sangraza** *f* contaminated blood
**sangre** *f* blood; spirit, fire; **a sangre** by animal power, by horsepower; **a sangre caliente** impulsively; **a sangre fría** in cold blood; **a sangre y fuego** without mercy, without quarter; violently, sweeping straight ahead; **bajársele a uno la sangre a los talones** or **helársele a uno la sangre** (coll.) to have one's blood run cold; **pura sangre** *m* thoroughbred; **sangre azul** blue blood; **sangre fría** sang-froid, cold-bloodedness; **sangre torera** bullfighting in the blood
**sangría** *f* bleeding, bloodletting; outlet, draining; ditch, trench; sangaree; tap (*in a tree*); tapping (*of a furnace*); inner pit of arm opposite elbow; resin cut; pilfering; (print.) indentation; **sangría suelta** free bleeding; constant drain (*on one's resources*)
**sangriento -ta** *adj* bleeding, bloody; sanguinary; savage (*e.g., insult*); (poet.) blood-red
**sanguaza** *f* contaminated blood; red vegetable fluid
**sangüesa** *f* raspberry (*fruit*)
**sangüeso** *m* (bot.) raspberry, raspberry bush
**sanguificación** *f* (physiol.) hematosis
**sanguificar** §86 *va* to produce blood from
**sanguijolero -ra** *mf* leecher
**sanguijuela** *f* (zool.) leech; (coll.) leech (*person*); **sanguijuela borriquera** (ent.) horseleech
**sanguijuelero -ra** *mf* leecher
**sanguina** *f* see **sanguino**
**sanguinario -ria** *adj* sanguinary, bloodthirsty; *f* (bot.) bloodroot; (mineral.) bloodstone; **La Sanguinaria** Bloody Mary (*Queen of England*); **sanguinaria del Canadá** (bot.) puccoon; **sanguinaria mayor** (bot.) knotgrass; **sanguinaria menor** (bot.) whitlowwort
**sanguíneo -a** *adj* sanguineous
**sanguino -na** *adj* blood; bloody; sanguineous; blood-red; *m* (bot.) mock privet; (bot.) red dogwood; *f* sanguine (*red crayon; drawing in red crayon*)
**sanguinolencia** *f* bloodiness, sanguinolence
**sanguinolento -ta** *adj* bloody, sanguinolent
**sanguinoso -sa** *adj* sanguinous; sanguinary
**sanguiñuelo** *m* (bot.) red dogwood
**sanguisorba** *f* (bot.) burnet
**sanguisuela** or **sanguja** *f* var. of **sanguijuela**
**sanícula** *f* (bot.) sanicle, self-heal
**sanidad** *f* healthiness; healthfulness; health; sanitation; **en sanidad** in health, in good health; **sanidad pública** health department
**sanidina** *f* (mineral.) sanidine
**sanie** *f* or **sanies** *f* (path.) sanies
**sanioso -sa** *adj* (path.) sanious
**sanitario -ria** *adj* sanitary; *m* military health officer
**sanjacado** *m* sanjak
**sanjaco** *m* sanjakbeg
**sanjuanada** *f* picnic on Saint John's day
**sanjuanero -ra** *adj* ripe by Saint John's day
**sanjuanista** *m* knight of Saint John of Jerusalem
**San Lorenzo** *m* St. Lawrence (*river*)

**sanmiguelada** *f* Michaelmastide
**sanmigueleño -ña** *adj* ripe by Michaelmas
**sano -na** *adj* healthy, hale; healthful, salutary; sound; right, correct, sane; earnest, sincere; safe, sure; (coll.) whole, untouched, unharmed, unbroken; **cortar por lo sano** (coll.) to use desperate remedies; **sano de Castilla** (slang) thief in disguise; **sano y salvo** safe and sound
**San Petersburgo** St. Petersburg
**sanrafael** *m* (bot.) zinnia
**San Salvador** *f* San Salvador (*island of Bahamas; capital of El Salvador*)
**sanscritista** *mf* Sanskritist
**sánscrito -ta** *adj* & *m* Sanskrit
**sanseacabó** *interj* (coll.) finished!, O.K.!
**sanseviera** *f* (bot.) sansevieria
**sansimoniano -na** *adj* Saint-Simonian; *mf* Saint-Simonian, Saint-Simonist
**sansimonismo** *m* Saint-Simonianism
**sansirolé** *mf* (coll.) nincompoop, simpleton
**Sansón** *m* (Bib. & fig.) Samson
**santabárbara** *f* (naut.) powder magazine
**Santa Elena** St. Helena (*British island and colony in South Atlantic*)
**santaláceo -a** *adj* (bot.) santalaceous
**santanderino -na** *adj* (pertaining to) Santander; *mf* native or inhabitant of Santander
**santelmo** *m* St. Elmo's fire
**santero -ra** *adj* image-worshipping; *mf* caretaker of a sanctuary; beggar carrying saint's image; guard, watcher; (slang) friend of thieves
**Santiago** *m* James; (Bib.) Saint James; **Santiago el Mayor** (Bib.) Saint James the Greater; **Santiago el Menor** (Bib.) Saint James the Less; *interj* war cry of medieval Spaniards
**santiagueño -ña** *adj* ripe by St. James's day
**santiaguero -ra** *adj* (pertaining to) Santiago de Cuba; *mf* native or inhabitant of Santiago de Cuba
**santiagués -guesa** *adj* (pertaining to) Santiago de Compostela; *mf* native or inhabitant of Santiago de Compostela
**santiaguino -na** *adj* (pertaining to) Santiago de Chile; *mf* native or inhabitant of Santiago de Chile
**santiaguista** *adj* pertaining to the Order of St. James; *m* knight of St. James
**santiamén** *m* (coll.) jiffy, instant, twinkling of an eye; **en un santiamén** (coll.) in a jiffy
**santidad** *f* sanctity, saintliness, holiness; **su Santidad** his Holiness
**santificación** *f* sanctification
**santificador -dora** *adj* sanctifying; *mf* sanctifier
**santificar** §86 *va* to sanctify, to consecrate, to hallow; to keep (*holy days*); (coll.) to excuse, to justify; *vr* (coll.) to excuse oneself, to justify oneself
**santiguada** *f* crossing oneself, sign of the cross; (coll.) rough treatment, slap, abuse; **¡para** or **por mi santiguada!** by the rood!, upon my faith!
**santiguadero -ra** *mf* powwower, quack; *f* powwow, healing with passes and prayers
**santiguador -dora** *mf* powwower, quack
**santiguamiento** *m* var. of **santiguada**
**santiguar** §23 *va* to bless, to make the sign of the cross over; to powwow, to make passes and say prayers over; (coll.) to punish, to slap, to abuse; *vr* to make the sign of the cross, to cross oneself; (Am.) to cross oneself to express surprise
**santimonia** *f* holiness, sanctity; (bot.) chrysanthemum
**santiscario** *m* invention; **de mi santiscario** (coll.) of my own invention
**santísimo -ma** *adj super* very or most holy; livelong (*e.g., day*); *m* Holy Sacrament
**santito** *m* (coll.) sissy
**santo -ta** *adj* saint, saintly, holy, blessed; livelong (*e.g., day*); (coll.) simple, artless; **su santa voluntad** his own sweet will; **santa bofetada** fine smack in the face; **santo y bueno** well and good; *mf* saint; *m* image of a saint; saint's day (*celebrated as one's anniversary*); (coll.) picture or engraving of a saint; picture; password, watchword; **a santo de** because of; **alzarse con el santo y la limosna** (coll.) to take the pot, to walk away with the whole thing, to make a clean sweep; **dar el santo** to give the watchword; **desnudar a un santo para vestir a otro** to rob Peter to pay Paul; **írsele a uno el santo al cielo** (coll.) to forget what one was up to; **no es santo de mi devoción** (coll.) I'm not very keen on him; **tener el santo de espaldas** (taur.) to do nothing right, to have a streak of bad luck; **tener santos en la corte** to have a friend at court; **santo titular** patron saint; **santo y seña** password, watchword
**Santo Domingo** Hispaniola (*island on which are situated Haiti and the Dominican Republic*)
**santón** *m* pagan ascetic, Mohammedan ascetic, dervish; hypocrite; tycoon; sage
**santónico** *m* (bot.) santonica
**santonina** *f* (pharm.) santonin
**santoral** *m* lives of saints; choir book; calendar of saints' days
**santuario** *m* sanctuary; shrine; (Am.) buried treasure
**santucho -cha** *adj* & *mf* (coll.) var. of **santurrón**
**santulón -lona** *adj* & *mf* (Am.) var. of **santurrón**
**santurrón -rrona** *adj* sanctimonious; *mf* sanctimonious person
**santurronería** *f* sanctimony, sanctimoniousness
**saña** *f* rage, fury; cruelty
**sañoso -sa** or **sañudo -da** *adj* enraged, furious; choleric
**sao** *m* (bot.) phillyrea; (Am.) small savannah with clusters of trees and bushes
**Saona** *m* Saône
**sapidez** *f* sapidity
**sápido -da** *adj* sapid, savory
**sapiencia** *f* sapience, wisdom; (*cap.*) *f* (Bib.) Wisdom of Solomon
**sapiente** *adj* sapient, wise; *mf* wise person
**sapillo** *m* little toad; (path.) ranula
**sapina** *f* var. of **salicor**
**sapindáceo -a** *adj* (bot.) sapindaceous
**sapindo** *m* (bot.) soapberry
**sapino** *m* (bot.) fir; (bot.) savin
**sapo** *m* (zool.) toad; (ichth.) toadfish; (coll.) stuffed shirt; (coll.) beast, pest; **echar sapos y culebras** (coll.) to talk nonsense, to utter angry abuses; **sapo marino** (ichth.) angler
**saponáceo -a** *adj* saponaceous
**saponaria** *f* (bot.) soapwort, bouncing Bet
**saponificable** *adj* saponifiable
**saponificación** *f* saponification
**saponificar** §86 *va* & *vr* to saponify
**saponina** *f* (chem.) saponin
**saponita** *f* (mineral.) saponite
**saporífero -ra** *adj* saporific
**sapotáceo -a** *adj* (bot.) sapotaceous
**sapote** *m* var. of **zapote**
**sapotear** *va* (Am.) to finger, touch, feel
**sapotillo** *m* var. of **zapotillo**
**saprófago -ga** *adj* (zool.) saprophagous
**saprófito -ta** *adj* (bot.) saprophytic; *m* (biol.) saprophyte
**saque** *m* serve, service (*e.g., in tennis*); service line; server; (Am.) distillery; **tener buen saque** (coll.) to be a heavy eater and drinker
**saqueador -dora** *adj* sacking, plundering; *mf* sacker, plunderer
**saqueamiento** *m* sacking, plunder, pillage, loot
**saquear** *va* to sack, to plunder, to pillage, to pilfer, to loot
**saqueo** *m* var. of **saqueamiento**
**saquería** *f* manufacture of sacks; collection of sacks
**saquerío** *m* collection of sacks
**saquero -ra** *adj* packing (*needle*); *mf* maker or vendor of sacks or bags
**saquete** *m* small sack; (arti.) cartridge bag
**saquilada** *f* contents of a bag that is not full
**S.A.R.** abr. of **Su Alteza Real**
**Sara** *f* Sarah, Sally
**saragüete** *m* (coll.) soirée at home, informal evening party

**sarampión** *m* (path.) measles; **sarampión alemán** (path.) German measles; **sarampión negro** (path.) black measles
**sarampioso -sa** *adj* measly
**sarao** *m* soirée, evening party
**sarape** *m* (Am.) serape
**sarapia** *f* (bot.) tonka bean (*tree and fruit*)
**sarapico** *m* (orn.) curlew; (orn.) tattler, yellowlegs; (bot.) shooting star
**sarcasmo** *m* sarcasm
**sarcástico -ca** *adj* sarcastic
**sarcia** *f* load, burden
**sarcina** *f* (bact.) sarcina
**sarcocarpio** *m* (bot.) sarcocarp
**sarcocele** *m* (path.) sarcocele
**sarcocola** *f* sarcocolla (*gum*)
**sarcófago** *m* sarcophagus
**sarcolema** *m* (anat.) sarcolemma
**sarcología** *f* sarcology
**sarcoma** *m* (path.) sarcoma
**sarda** *f* see **sardo**
**sardana** *f* sardana (*Catalonian dance and music*)
**sardanapalesco -ca** *adj* Sardanapalian
**Sardanápalo** *m* Sardanapalus
**sardesco -ca** *adj* small (*said of ass, horse, etc.*); (coll.) coarse, brazen; *m* small ass, pony
**sardina** *f* (ichth.) sardine; **como sardinas en banasta** or **en lata** (coll.) packed like sardines
**sardinal** *m* sardine net
**sardinel** *m* (mas.) rowlock
**sardinero -ra** *adj* (pertaining to the) sardine; *mf* sardine dealer
**sardineta** *f* small sardine; pointed two-stripe chevron; cheese extending beyond mold
**sardio** *m* sard
**sardo -da** *adj* Sardinian; black, white, and red (*said of cattle*); *mf* Sardinian; *m* Sardinian (*language*); *f* (ichth.) horse mackerel
**sardonia** *f* (bot.) Sardinian herb
**sardónica** *f* see **sardónico**
**sardónice** *f* (mineral.) sardonyx
**sardónico -ca** *adj* sardonic (*laugh*); (Am.) sardonic, sarcastic; *f* (mineral.) sardonyx
**sardonio** *m* or **sardónique** *f* var. of **sardónica**
**sarga** *f* serge; painted wall fabric; (bot.) willow
**sargadilla** *f* (bot.) saltbush (*Suaeda splendens*)
**sargado -da** *adj* twilled, serge
**sargal** *m* willow grove
**sargatilla** *f* or **sargatillo** *m* (bot.) white willow
**sargazo** *m* (bot.) sargasso, gulfweed
**sargenta** *f* sergeant's wife; sergeant's halberd; big coarse woman
**sargentear** *va* to command as a sergeant; to boss, to manage; *vn* (coll.) to be bossy
**sargentería** *f* sergeant's drill
**sargentía** *f* sergeancy
**sargento** *m* sergeant
**sargentona** *f* big coarse woman
**sargo** m (ichth.) sargo; (ichth.) Bermuda bream, silvery porgy
**sarguero -ra** *adj* (pertaining to the) willow; *mf* painter of wall fabrics
**sarilla** *f* (bot.) marjoram
**sarmentador -dora** *mf* gatherer of vine shoots
**sarmentar §18** *vn* to gather pruned vine shoots
**sarmentazo** *m* large vine shoot; blow with a vine shoot
**sarmentera** *f* gathering vine shoots; storage of vine shoots
**sarmentillo** *m* slender vine shoot
**sarmentoso -sa** *adj* running, twining, sarmentous
**sarmiento** *m* (bot.) vine shoot, running stem, sarmentum
**sarna** *f* itch, mange, scabies; **más viejo que la sarna** (coll.) old as Methuselah; **sarna de los barberos** barber's itch
**sarnoso -sa** *adj* itchy, mangy, scabious
**sarpullido** *m* var. of **salpullido**
**sarpullir §26** *va & vr* var. of **salpullir**
**sarracénico -ca** *adj* Saracenic
**sarraceno -na** *adj & mf* Saracen
**sarracina** *f* scuffle, free fight, free-for-all; bloody brawl
**Sarre** *m* Saar (*river*); Saar or Saarland
**sarrés -rresa** *adj* (pertaining to the) Saar; *mf* Saarlander
**sarria** *f* coarse net for carrying straw
**sarrieta** *f* deep feed bag
**sarrillo** *m* death rattle; (bot.) arum
**sarro** *m* incrustation, crust; fur (*e.g., on tongue*); tartar (*on teeth*); (path.) sordes; (bot.) rust, mildew
**sarroso -sa** *adj* incrusted, crusty; full of tartar
**sarta** *f* string (*e.g., of beads*); line, file, series
**sartal** *m* string (*e.g., of beads*)
**sartén** *f* frying pan; contents of frying pan, frying panful; **saltar de la sartén y dar en las brasas** (coll.) to jump out of the frying pan into the fire; **tener la sartén por el mango** (coll.) to be in control, to have the upper hand
**sartenada** *f* contents of frying pan, frying panful
**sartenazo** *m* blow with a frying pan; (coll.) hard blow
**sartorio -ria** *adj* (anat.) sartorial
**sasafrás** *m* (bot.) sassafras (*tree and dried root bark*)
**sastra** *f* female tailor; tailor's wife
**sastre** *m* tailor
**sastrería** *f* tailoring; tailor shop
**sastresa** *f* (dial.) female tailor
**Satán** *m* or **Satanás** *m* Satan
**satánico -ca** *adj* satanic or Satanic
**satelitario -ria** *adj* (pertaining to a) satellite
**satélite** *m* (astr. & fig.) satellite; (mach.) satellite pinion; (coll.) sheriff, bailiff, constable; *adj* satellite; suburban
**satelizar §76** *va* to put into orbit; *vr* to go into orbit, to become a satellite
**satén** *m* sateen
**satinar** *va* to satin (*e.g., paper*)
**sátira** *f* satire
**satírico -ca** *adj* satiric or satirical; *mf* satirist
**satirio** *m* (zool.) water rat
**satirión** *m* (bot.) male orchis; (zool.) water rat
**satirizar §76** *va & vn* to satirize
**sátiro** *m* (myth.) satyr; satyr (*lewd man*)
**satisdación** *f* (law) bail, surety, security
**satisfacción** *f* satisfaction; **a satisfacción** satisfactorily; **a satisfacción de** to the satisfaction of
**satisfacer §55** *va & vn* to satisfy; *vr* to satisfy oneself, be satisfied, take satisfaction
**satisfaciente** *adj* satisfying
**satisfactorio -ria** *adj* satisfactory
**satisfago** *1st sg pres ind of* **satisfacer**
**satisfaré** *1st sg fut ind of* **satisfacer**
**satisfaz** *2d sg impv of* **satisfacer**
**satisfecho -cha** satisfied; conceited; *pp of* **satisfacer**
**satisfice** *1st sg pret ind of* **satisfacer**
**sativo -va** *adj* sown, cultivated
**sátrapa** *m* satrap; (coll.) crafty fellow; *adj* (coll.) crafty
**satrapía** *f* satrapy
**saturable** *adj* saturable
**saturación** *f* saturation; satiation
**saturador -dora** *adj* saturating; *mf* saturator; *m* saturator (*apparatus*)
**saturar** *va* to saturate; to satiate
**saturnal** *adj* Saturnian; Saturnalian; *f* saturnalia (*orgy*); **saturnales** *fpl* Saturnalia (*festival of Saturn*)
**saturniano -na** *adj* Saturnian (*pertaining to Saturn; pertaining to a Latin verse*); saturnine
**saturnino -na** *adj* saturnine
**saturnismo** *m* (path.) saturnism
**Saturno** *m* (myth. & astr.) Saturn
**sauce** *m* (bot.) willow; **sauce blanco** (bot.) white willow; **sauce cabruno** (bot.) sallow, goat willow; **sauce de Babilonia** or **sauce llorón** (bot.) weeping willow
**sauceda** *f*, **saucedal** *m*, or **saucera** *f* willow grove
**saucillo** *m* (bot.) knotgrass
**saúco** *m* (bot.) elder, elderberry; second hoof (*of horses*)
**Saúl** *m* (Bib.) Saul
**Saulo** *m* (Bib.) Saul (*original name of apostle Paul*)

**sauquillo** *m* (bot.) snowball, guelder-rose, cranberry tree
**saurio -ria** *adj & m* (zool.) saurian
**sausería** *f* palace larder
**sausier** *m* chief of palace larder
**sautor** *m* (her.) saltier
**sauz** *m* (*pl:* **sauces**) var. of **sauce**
**sauzal** *m* willow grove
**sauzgatillo** *m* (bot.) agnus castus, chaste tree
**savia** *f* sap (*of a plant*); (fig.) sap
**sáxeo -a** *adj* rocky, stony
**saxífraga** *f* (bot.) saxifrage
**saxifragáceo -a** *adj* (bot.) saxifragaceous
**saxifragia** *f* var. of **saxífraga**
**saxofonista** *mf* saxophonist
**saxofón** *m* or **saxófono** *m* (mus.) saxophone
**saya** *f* skirt; petticoat
**sayal** *m* sackcloth, coarse woolen cloth; skirt
**sayalería** *f* weaving of sackcloth
**sayalero -ra** *mf* weaver of sackcloth
**sayalesco -ca** *adj* sackcloth
**sayalete** *m* light flannel for undergarments
**sayete** *m* short smock
**sayo** *m* smock frock, tunic; (coll.) garment; **cortar un sayo a** (coll.) to talk behind the back of; **decir para su sayo** (coll.) to say to oneself, to say in one's sleeve
**sayón** *m* executioner; fierce-looking fellow
**sayuela** *f* serge shirt
**sazón** *f* ripeness, maturity; season; time, occasion; taste, relish, seasoning; **a la sazón** at that time; **en sazón** on time, opportunely; ripe, in season
**sazonado -da** *adj* tasty, seasoned; expressive, witty; *m* seasoning
**sazonar** *va* to ripen, to mature; to season; *vr* to ripen, to mature
**s/c** abr. of **su cuenta**
**S.C.** or **s.c.** abr. of **su casa**
**Scherezada** *f* Scheherazade
**S.D.** abr. of **se despide**
**SE** abr. of **sudeste**
**S.E.** abr. of **Su Excelencia**
**se** *pron reflex* himself, to himself; herself, to herself; itself, to itself; themselves, to themselves; yourself, to yourself; yourselves, to yourselves; oneself, to oneself; each other, to each other; *pron pers* (used before the pronouns **lo, la, los,** or **las**) to him, to her, to it, to them, to you
**sé** *1st sg pres ind of* **saber;** *2d sg impv of* **ser**
**sea** *1st sg pres subj of* **ser**
**s.e., autor** abr. of **sin editor, autor** privately printed
**sebáceo -a** *adj* sebaceous
**Sebastián** *m* Sebastian
**sebastiano** *m* var. of **sebestén**
**sebe** *f* wattle, stockade
**sebestén** *m* (bot.) sebesten (*tree and fruit*)
**sebillo** *m* light tallow
**sebo** *m* tallow; grease, fat, suet
**seboso -sa** *adj* tallowy; greasy, fatty, suety
**seca** *f* see **seco**
**secácul** *m* parsnip (*root*)
**secadal** *m* dry, barren soil; dry sand bank
**secadero -ra** *adj* dry, easily kept dry; *m* drying place, drying room
**secadillo** *m* almond meringue
**sacadío -a** *adj* capable of drying up, exhaustible
**secador -dora** *adj* drying; *m* dryer; drying place; hair dryer; *f* clothes dryer
**secamente** *adv* dryly, curtly; gruffly, harshly, sharply
**secamiento** *m* drying; drying up, withering
**secano** *m* unwatered land, dry land; dry sand bank; dryness; **cultivo de secano** dry farming
**secansa** *f* sequence (*in cards*)
**secante** *adj* drying, siccative; blotting; (geom. & trig.) secant; *m* siccative; blotting paper; *f* (geom. & trig.) secant
**secar** §86 *va* to dry, to dry up, to wipe dry; to annoy, bore, vex, tease; *vr* to dry, to get dry; to dry oneself; to get thin; to wither; to be dry, be thirsty; to run dry (*said, e.g., of a well*)
**secaral** *m* var. of **sequeral**
**secarropa** *f* clothes drier; **secarropa de travesaños** clotheshorse
**secatón -tona** *adj* (coll.) dull, inane
**secatura** *f* dullness, inanity, tiresomeness
**sección** *f* section; cross section; department (*e.g., of a store*); (arch., geom. & mil.) section; **sección cesárea** (surg.) Caesarean section; **sección cónica** (math.) conic section; **sección de captura** (phys.) capture cross section; **sección de fondo** editorial section (*of a paper*); **secciones cónicas** conic sections (*branch of geometry*); **sección transversal** cross section
**seccional** *adj* sectional (*e.g., bookcase*)
**seccionamiento** *m* sectioning
**seccionar** *va* to section
**secesión** *f* secession
**secesionismo** *m* secessionism
**secesionista** *adj & mf* secessionist
**seceso** *m* stool, excrement
**seco -ca** *adj* dry; dried, dried up, withered, dead; arid; lean, lank; plain, unadorned; cold, lukewarm, indifferent; sharp, harsh; straight (*drink*); *m* (Am.) blow, bump; **en seco** high and dry; without cause or reason; without resources; suddenly; *f* drought; dry season; (med.) desquamation; infarction (*of a gland*); dry sand bank; **a secas** merely, simply; **a secas y sin llover** (coll.) without a word of warning
**secoya** *f* (bot.) sequoia
**secreción** *f* segregation; (physiol.) secretion
**secreta** *f* see **secreto**
**secretar** *va* (physiol.) to secrete
**secretaría** *f* or **secretariado** *m* secretariat, secretaryship, office of secretary
**secretario -ria** *adj* confidential, trusted; *mf* secretary; *m* (orn.) secretary bird; *f* secretary's wife
**secretear** *vn* (coll.) to whisper, to talk confidentially
**secreteo** *m* (coll.) whispering, confidential talk
**secreter** *m* secretary (*writing desk*)
**secretina** *f* (biochem.) secretin
**secretista** *mf* naturalist; (coll.) whisperer
**secret.°** abr. of **secretario**
**secreto -ta** *adj* secret; secretive; *m* secret; secrecy; key (*combination for opening a lock*); soundboard (*of musical instrument*); hiding place, secret drawer or compartment; **en el secreto de las cosas** on the inside; **en secreto** in secret; **secreto a voces** open secret; **secreto de estado** state secret; **secreto de Pulchinela** (coll.) open secret; *f* licentiate's examination; secret investigation; (eccl.) secret (*prayer*); secret police; privy, water closet
**secretor -tora** or **secretorio -ria** *adj* (physiol.) secretory
**secta** *f* sect
**sectador -dora** *adj & mf* var. of **sectario**
**sectario -ria** *adj* sectarian, denominational; sectary; *mf* sectarian; sectary
**sectarismo** *m* sectarianism, denominationalism
**sectil** *adj* sectile
**sectilio** *m* sectile mosaic
**sector** *m* sector; (geom., math. & mil.) sector; **sector de distribución** (elec.) house current, power line
**secuacidad** *f* partisanship
**secuaz** (*pl:* **-cuaces**) *adj* partisan; *mf* partisan, follower
**secuela** *f* sequel, result; (med.) sequela, aftermath
**secuencia** *f* (eccl., mov. & mus.) sequence
**secuestración** *f* (law) sequestration
**secuestrador -dora** *adj* kidnaping; *mf* kidnaper
**secuestrar** *va* to kidnap; (law) to sequester
**secuestro** *m* kidnaping; (law) sequestration, sequestered property; (med.) sequestrum; umpire, referee
**secular** *adj* secular; centesimal, e.g., **los años seculares** the centesimal years (*1800, 1900, 2000, etc.*)
**secularidad** *f* secularity
**secularismo** *m* secularism
**secularista** *mf* secularist
**secularización** *f* secularization
**secularizar** §76 *va* to secularize; *vr* to become or to be secularized
**secundante** *mf* seconder; *m* second (*in boxing*)

**secundar** *va* to second, to back
**secundario -ria** *adj* secondary; *m* (elec.) secondary (*coil or winding*)
**secundinas** *fpl* afterbirth, secundines
**secundípara** *adj fem* secundiparous; *f* secundipara
**sed** *f* thirst; drought, dryness, need for water; (fig.) thirst; **apagar la sed, matar la sed** to quench the thirst; **tener sed** to be thirsty; **tener sed de** to be thirsty for, to thirst for
**seda** *f* silk; wild boar's bristles; **como una seda** (coll.) smooth as silk; sweet-natured; easy as pie; **de media seda** half-silk; **de toda seda** all silk; **seda conchal** choice silk; **seda encerada** dental floss; **seda floja** floss silk, untwisted silk; **seda joyante** glossy silk
**sedación** *f* soothing; (med.) sedation
**sedadera** *f* hackle for dressing flax
**sedal** *m* fish line, fishing line; (vet.) rowel
**sedalino -na** *adj* silk; silky; *f* silkaline; schappe; half-silk fabric
**sedán** *m* (aut.) sedan; **sedán de reparto** delivery truck
**sedante** *adj & m* sedative
**sedar** *va* to soothe, quiet, allay
**sedativo -va** *adj & m* (med.) sedative
**sede** *f* seat; headquarters; (eccl.) see; **Santa Sede** Holy See; **Sede apostólica** Apostolic See; **sede social** (com.) main office, headquarters
**sedear** *va* to clean with a bristle brush
**Sedecías** *m* (Bib.) Zedekiah
**sedentario -ria** *adj* sedentary
**sedente** *adj* sitting, seated
**sedeño -ña** *adj* (pertaining to) silk; bristly; *f* fine tow of flax; fine linen; fiber; horsehair fishing line
**sedera** *f* see **sedero**
**sedería** *f* silk stuff, silks; silk business; silk store
**sedero -ra** *adj* (pertaining to) silk; *mf* silk weaver; silk dealer; *f* bristle brush
**sedicente** or **sediciente** *adj* so-called, self-styled
**sedición** *f* sedition
**sedicioso -sa** *adj* seditious; *mf* seditionary
**sediento -ta** *adj* thirsty; dry (*land*); anxious, eager
**sedimentación** *f* sedimentation
**sedimentar** *va & vr* to sediment, to settle
**sedimentario -ria** *adj* sedimental or sedimentary; (geol.) sedimentary
**sedimento** *m* sediment
**sedoso -sa** *adj* silky
**seducción** *f* temptation; seduction; bribery; charm, captivation
**seducible** *adj* seducible
**seducir** §38 *va* to tempt, lead astray; to seduce; to captivate
**seductivo -va** *adj* tempting; seductive; captivating
**seductor -tora** *adj* tempting; seductive; captivating; *mf* tempter; seducer; charmer, captivator
**seduje** *1st sg pret ind of* **seducir**
**seduzco** *1st sg pres ind of* **seducir**
**sefardí** (*pl:* **-díes**) *adj* Sephardic; *mf* Sephardi; **sefardíes** *mpl* Sephardim; *m* language of the Sephardim
**sefardita** *adj* Sephardic; *mf* Sephardi
**segable** *adj* ready to be harvested
**segada** *f* harvest
**segadero -ra** *adj* ready to be harvested; *f* sickle
**segador -dora** *adj* harvesting; mowing; *m* harvester, harvestman; (ent.) harvestman, daddy longlegs; *f* harvester (*woman; machine*); mowing machine; **segadora de césped** lawn mower; **segadora trilladora** harvester-thresher, combine
**segar** §29 *va* to reap, to mow, to harvest; to cut off, to mow down; *vn* to reap, to mow, to harvest
**segazón** *f* harvest; harvest time
**seglar** *adj* secular, lay; *m* layman; *f* laywoman
**segmentación** *f* segmentation
**segmental** *adj* segmental; (arch. & zool.) segmental
**segmentario -ria** *adj* segmentary
**segmento** *m* segment; **segmento de émbolo** piston ring
**segoviano -na** or **segoviense** *adj* (pertaining to) Segovia; *mf* native or inhabitant of Segovia
**segregación** *f* segregation; (physiol.) secretion
**segregacionista** *mf* segregationist
**segregar** §59 *va* to segregate; to excommunicate; (physiol.) to secrete
**segregativo -va** *adj* segregative
**segrí** *m* heavy silk fabric
**segueta** *f* buhl saw, marquetry saw; hacksaw
**seguetear** *vn* to saw with a buhl saw
**seguida** *f* see **seguido**
**seguidamente** *adv* without interruption, successively; at once, immediately; next, next in order
**seguidero** *m* guide lines for writing
**seguidilla** *f* Spanish stanza made up of a quatrain of alternating seven-syllable and five-syllable verses, with the second and fourth verses in assonance, and of three final verses, the first and third of which are five-syllable in assonance and the second seven-syllable; **seguidillas** *fpl* (mus.) seguidillas (*air and dance*)
**seguido -da** *adj* continued, successive; straight, direct; in a row, running, e.g., **cuatro días seguidos** four days in a row, four days running; **todo seguido** straight ahead; *m* drop stitch in a stocking foot; *f* series, succession, continuation; **de seguida** without interruption, continuously; at once, immediately; in a row, e.g., **cuatro días de seguida** four days in a row; **en seguida** at once, immediately
**seguidor -dora** *adj* following; homing (*e.g., torpedo*); *mf* follower; *m* guide lines for writing
**seguimiento** *m* following, pursuit, chase, hunt; continuation
**seguir** §82 *va* to follow; to pursue; to dog, to hound; to prosecute; to continue; to bring, to institute (*e.g., a suit*); *vn* to go on, to continue; to still be, to be now; **como sigue** as follows; **seguir adelante** to go ahead; **seguir** + *ger* to keep, to continue + *ger; vr* to follow, to ensue; to issue, to spring
**según** *adv* depending on circumstances; **según que** according as; *prep* according to, as per; *conj* as, according as; **según y como, según y conforme** that depends, depending on circumstances; according as
**segunda** *f* see **segundo**
**segundar** *va* to repeat at once; *vn* to come next, to be second; to do it again
**segundario -ria** *adj* var. of **secundario**
**segundero -ra** *adj* second (*said of a crop in the same season*); *m* second hand; **segundero central** sweep second hand, sweep-second, center-second
**segundilla** *f* call bell (*in convents*)
**segundillo** *m* second serving of bread (*in a convent*)
**segundo -da** *adj* second; **de segunda mano** second-hand; **segunda intención** double meaning; double dealing; *m* second; **sin segundo** unequaled; *f* double turn (*of lock*); double meaning; (mus.) second (*part; interval*); (aut.) second
**segundogénito -ta** *adj & mf* second-born
**segundogenitura** *f* secundogeniture
**segundón** *m* second son; younger son
**seguntino -na** *adj* (pertaining to) Sigüenza; *mf* native or inhabitant of Sigüenza
**segur** *f* axe; sickle
**segurador** *m* security, bondsman
**segureja** *f* small hatchet
**seguridad** *f* security; surety; safety; certainty; sureness; confidence; assurance, guarantee; surety bond; **seguridad colectiva** collective security; **seguridad social** social security
**seguro -ra** *adj* sure, certain; secure, safe; reliable, dependable; firm, constant; steady, unfailing; **seguro** *adv* surely; *m* assurance, certainty; safety; confidence; insurance; pawl, dog, latch, stop; safety lock (*of breech mechanism*); **a buen seguro, al seguro,** or **de seguro** surely, truly; **en seguro** in safety; **irse del seguro** (coll.) to forget oneself, to cast

prudence aside; **sobre seguro** without risk; **seguro contra accidentes** accident insurance; **seguro de desocupación** unemployment insurance; **seguro de enfermedad** health insurance; **seguro de incendios** fire insurance; **seguro mutuo** mutual insurance; **seguro sobre la vida** life insurance
**segurón** *m* large axe
**seis** *adj* six; **las seis** six o'clock; *m* six; sixth (*in dates*)
**seisavado -da** *adj* hexagonal
**seisavar** *va* to make hexagonal
**seisavo -va** *adj* sixth; *m* sixth; hexagon
**seiscientos -tas** *adj & m* six hundred; **el Seiscientos** the Seventeenth Century
**seise** *m* singing and dancing choir boy (*six in all*) in Seville cathedral in certain festivals
**seiseno -na** *adj* sixth
**seisillo** *m* (mus.) sextuplet
**seísmico -ca** *adj* var. of **sísmico**
**seísmo** *m* var. of **sismo**
**selacio -cia** *adj & m* (ichth.) selachian
**selección** *f* selection; **selección natural** (biol.) natural selection
**seleccionamiento** *m* selecting, choosing
**seleccionar** *va* to select
**selecta** *f* see **selecto**
**selectividad** *f* (rad.) selectivity
**selectivo -va** *adj* selective; (rad.) selective
**selecto -ta** *adj* select, choice; *f* selection (*of works of different authors*); **selectas** *fpl* analects
**selector -tora** *adj* selective; selecting, selector; *m* (telp.) selector (*mechanism of dial telephone*)
**Selene** *f* (myth.) Selene
**selenio** *m* (chem.) selenium
**selenita** *mf* moon dweller; *f* (mineral.) selenite
**seleniuro** *m* (chem.) selenide
**selenografía** *f* selenography
**selenógrafo -fa** *mf* selenographer
**selenosis** *f* (*pl:* **-sis**) white spots on nails
**self** *f* (elec.) coil, self-induction coil
**selfactina** *f* self-acting mule (*spinning machine*)
**selva** *f* forest, woods; jungle; (Am.) selva; **Selva Negra** Black Forest (*in Germany*)
**selvático -ca** *adj* woodsy; rustic, wild
**selvatiquez** *f* woodsiness; rusticity, wildness
**selvicultura** *f* forestry
**selvoso -sa** *adj* woody, wooded, sylvan
**sellador -dora** *mf* sealer; stamper
**selladura** *f* sealing; stamping; stamp, impress
**sellaje** *m* sealing
**sellaporos** *m* (*pl:* **-ros**) (paint.) filler
**sellar** *va* to seal; to stamp; to cover, to close; to finish up
**sello** *m* seal; stamp; signet; stamp office; wafer; (fig.) seal; **echar** or **poner el sello a** to bring to perfection; **gran sello** great seal; **sello adherido** adhesive stamp; **sello aéreo** air-mail stamp; **sello de correo** postage stamp; **sello de goma** rubber stamp; **sello de Salomón** Solomon's seal; (bot.) Solomon's-seal; **sello de urgencia** special-delivery stamp; **sello fiscal** revenue stamp
**semafórico -ca** *adj* semaphoric
**semaforista** *m* (rail.) signalman
**semáforo** *m* semaphore; traffic light
**semana** *f* week; week's pay; septenary (*period of seven months, years, etc.*); **entre semana** during the week (*but not on the first or last days*); **semana de pasión** Passion Week; **semana inglesa** working week of five and a half days, working week ending Saturday noon; **semana grande, semana mayor,** or **semana santa** Holy Week; **Semana Santa** book containing Holy Week services and prayers
**semanal** *adj* weekly
**semanalmente** *adv* weekly
**semanario -ria** *adj* weekly; *m* weekly (*publication*)
**semanería** *f* week work
**semanero -ra** *adj* engaged by the week; *mf* week worker
**semanilla** *f* book containing Holy Week services and prayers
**semántico -ca** *adj* semantic; *f* semantics
**semantista** *mf* semanticist
**semasiología** *f* semasiology
**semasiológico -ca** *adj* semasiological
**semblante** *m* face, mien, countenance; look, appearance; **componer el semblante** to take on a sober look; to put on a calm appearance; **estar de mal semblante** to frown, to look grouchy; **mudar de semblante** to change color; to take on a different aspect
**semblantear** *va* (Am.) to look straight in the face
**semblanza** *f* (biographical) sketch, portrait
**sembrada** *f* sown ground
**sembradera** *f* seeder, seeding machine; sowing machine
**sembradío -a** *adj* ready for sowing, suitable for sowing
**sembrado** *m* cultivated field, sown ground; **sembrados** *mpl* grain fields
**sembrador -dora** *adj* seeding, sowing; *mf* seeder, sower; *f* seeder, seeding machine; sowing machine
**sembradura** *f* seeding, sowing
**sembrar** §18 *va* to seed; to sow; to spread, to scatter; to sprinkle; *vn* to seed; to sow
**semeja** *f* similarity, likeness, resemblance; sign, mark
**semejable** *adj* like, resembling
**semejado -da** *adj* like
**semejante** *adj* like, similar; such; (math.) like, similar; **semejantes** *adj pl* alike, e.g., **estos libros son semejantes** these books are alike; **semejante a** like, e.g., **este libro es semejante al otro** this book is like the other one; *m* resemblance, likeness; fellow, fellow man
**semejanza** *f* similarity, resemblance; simile; **a semejanza de** like, as
**semejar** *va* to resemble, to be like; *vn & vr* to be alike; **semejar a** or **semejarse a** to resemble, to be like
**Semele** *f* or **Sémele** *f* (myth.) Semele
**semen** *m* (bot. & physiol.) semen
**semencera** *f* seeding, sowing
**semencontra** *m* (pharm.) santonica
**semental** *adj* (pertaining to) seed, sowing; stud, breeding (*animal*); *m* sire; stock bull; stallion
**sementar** §18 *va* to seed, to sow
**sementera** *f* seeding, sowing; sown land; seedtime, sowing time; (fig.) hotbed
**sementero** *m* seed bag; seeding, sowing
**sementino -na** *adj* (pertaining to) seed
**semestral** *adj* (pertaining to a) semester; six-month
**semestre** *adj* semestral; six-month; *m* semester; period of six months
**semianual** *adj* semiannual
**semiárido -da** *adj* semiarid
**semiautomático -ca** *adj* semiautomatic
**semibola** *f* (bridge) little slam
**semibreve** *f* (mus.) whole note, semibreve
**semicabrón** *m* satyr
**semicadencia** *f* (mus.) semicadence
**semicapro** *m* var. of **semicabrón**
**semicilíndrico -ca** *adj* semicylindrical
**semicircular** *adj* semicircular
**semicírculo** *m* semicircle
**semicivilizado -da** *adj* semicivilized
**semiconductor -tora** *adj* (elec.) semiconducting; *m* (elec.) semiconductor
**semiconsciente** *adj* semiconscious
**semiconsonante** *adj* semiconsonantal; *f* semiconsonant
**semicoque** *m* semicoke
**semicorchea** *f* (mus.) semiquaver, sixteenth note
**semiculto -ta** *adj* (philol.) semilearned
**semidea** *f* (poet.) var. of **semidiosa**
**semideo** *m* (poet.) var. of **semidiós**
**semideponente** *adj* (gram.) semideponent
**semidiámetro** *m* (astr. & geom.) semidiameter
**semidiesel** *m* semi-Diesel engine
**semidifunto -ta** *adj* half-dead
**semidiós** *m* demigod
**semidiosa** *f* demigoddess
**semidivino -na** *adj* semidivine
**semidormido -da** *adj* half-asleep
**semieje** *m* semiaxis
**semielíptico -ca** *adj* semielliptical

**semiesfera** *f* hemisphere
**semiesférico -ca** *adj* hemispherical
**semiesquina** *f* place near the corner; **semiesquina a** around the corner from
**semifinal** *adj & f* (sport) semifinal
**semiflúido -da** *adj & m* semifluid
**semifusa** *f* (mus.) sixty-fourth note
**semigola** *f* (fort.) demigorge
**semihombre** *m* half-man; pigmy
**semilíquido -da** *adj & m* semiliquid
**semilunar** *adj* semilunar
**semilunio** *m* (astr.) half a lunation
**semilla** *f* seed; **semilla brincadora** jumping bean; **semilla de césped** grass seed
**semillero** *m* seed, seed plot; nursery; (fig.) hotbed
**seminal** *adj* seminal
**seminario** *m* seminary; seminar; seed plot; nursery; **seminario conciliar** seminary, theological seminary
**seminarista** *m* seminarist
**seminífero -ra** *adj* seminiferous
**semínima** *f* (mus.) crotchet; **semínimas** *fpl* trifles
**semínola** *adj & mf* Seminole
**semioficial** *adj* semiofficial
**semiología** *f* semeiology
**semiótico -ca** *adj* semeiotic; *f* semeiotics
**semipedal** *adj* semipedal
**semipelagianismo** *m* Semi-Pelagianism
**semipelagiano -na** *adj & m* Semi-Pelagian
**semipermeable** *adj* semipermeable
**semipleno -na** *adj* (law) incomplete, imperfect
**semipopular** *adj* semipopular
**Semíramis** *f* Semiramis
**semi-remolque** *m* semitrailer
**semirrecto -ta** *adj* (geom.) of 45 degrees
**semirrígido -da** *adj* (aer.) semirigid
**semirrubio -bia** *adj* rather blond, somewhat blond
**semisalvaje** *adj* half-savage; *mf* half savage
**semisecular** *adj* half-century
**semiseda** *f* half silk
**semiseparado -da** *adj* semidetached
**semisólido -da** *adj & m* semisolid
**semisuma** *f* half
**semita** *adj* Semitic; *mf* Semite, Semitic
**semítico -ca** *adj* Semitic; *m* Semitic (*group of languages*)
**semitismo** *m* Semitism
**semitista** *mf* Semitist
**semitono** *m* (mus.) semitone, half tone
**semitropical** *adj* semitropical
**semivivo -va** *adj* half-alive
**semivocal** *adj* semivocalic; *f* semivowel
**sémola** *f* semolina, groats
**semoviente** *adj* self-moving; **semovientes** *mpl* stock (*horses, cattle, etc.*)
**sempiterno -na** *adj* sempiternal, everlasting; *f* durance, everlasting (*a material*); (bot.) globe amaranth
**sen** *m* (bot. & pharm.) senna
**sena** *f* six (*in dice*); (bot. & pharm.) senna; **senas** *fpl* double sixes; (*cap.*) *m* Seine
**senado** *m* senate
**senadoconsulto** *m* senatus consultum
**senador -dora** *mf* senator
**senaduría** *f* senatorship
**Senaquerib** *m* Sennacherib
**senara** *f* land allowed to be worked as part wages; yield of such land; commons
**senario -ria** *adj* senary, sextuple
**senatorial** or **senatorio -ria** *adj* senatorial
**sencillez** *f* simplicity, simpleness, plainness, candor
**sencillo -lla** *adj* simple, plain, unaffected; (bot.) single; *m* change, loose change; (baseball) single
**senda** *f* path, footpath
**senderar** or **senderear** *va* to guide or lead by a path; to cut or open a path through; *vn* to take extraordinary measures
**sendero** *m* path, footpath, byway
**sendos -das** *adj pl* one each, one to each, e.g., **les dió sendos libros** he gave one book to each of them, he gave each of them a book; **hay tres circuitos recorridos por sendas corrientes** there are three circuits traversed by one current each
**séneca** *m* wise man, man of wisdom; (*cap.*) *m* Seneca
**senectud** *f* age, old age
**Senegal, el** Senegal
**senegalés -lesa** *adj & mf* Senegalese
**senescal** *m* seneschal
**senescalado** *m* seneschalsy (*territory; office*)
**senescalía** *f* seneschalsy (*office of seneschal*)
**senescencia** *f* senescence, aging
**senescente** *adj* senescent, aging
**senil** *adj* senile
**senilidad** *f* senility
**senilismo** *m* premature senility
**sénior** *m* (sport) star
**seno** *m* bosom, breast; heart; womb; lap; bay, gulf; trough (*between two waves*); cavity, hollow, recess; asylum, refuge; slack; curvature of slack sail or rope; (anat., bot., zool. & path.) sinus; (arch.) spandrel; (trig.) sine; **en el seno de** in the bosom of, in the heart of; in the midst of, in the presence of; **seno de Abrahán** Abraham's bosom; **seno verso** (trig.) versed sine
**sensación** *f* sensation; **hacer sensación** to cause a sensation
**sensacional** *adj* sensational
**sensacionalismo** *m* sensationalism; (philos.) sensationalism
**sensacionalista** *mf* (philos.) sensationalist
**sensacionismo** *m* (philos.) sensationalism
**sensacionista** *mf* (philos.) sensationalist
**sensatez** *f* good sense
**sensato -ta** *adj* sensible
**sensibilidad** *f* sensibility; sensitivity; (phot. & rad.) sensitiveness, sensitivity
**sensibilización** *f* sensitization
**sensibilizar** §76 *va* to sensitize (*e.g., the ear to music*); (phot.) to sensitize
**sensible** *adj* sensible; perceptible, noticeable, appreciable; sensitive; deplorable, lamentable; (phot. & rad.) sensitive
**sensiblería** *f* sentimentality, mawkishness
**sensiblero -ra** *adj* sentimental, mawkish
**sensitivo -va** *adj* sensitive, sense; sentient; stimulating; *f* (bot.) sensitive plant
**sensorio -ria** *adj* sensorial, sensory; *m* sensorium
**sensual** *adj* sensual, sensuous; *mf* sensualist
**sensualidad** *f* sensuality
**sensualismo** *m* sensualism; (philos.) sensualism
**sensualista** *adj & mf* sensualist; (philos.) sensualist
**sentada** *f* see **sentado**
**sentadero** *m* place to sit (*stone, board, log, etc.*)
**sentadillas; a sentadillas** sidesaddle
**sentado -da** *adj* seated; established, settled; stable, permanent; sedate, judicious; raw; (bot.) sessile; **dar por sentado** to take for granted, to consider as settled; *f* sitting; **de una sentada** at one sitting
**sentamiento** *m* settling
**sentar** §18 *va* to seat; to set, to establish; to suit, fit, become, to agree with; *vr* to sit, to sit down; to settle, to settle down; **sentarse a** (coll.) to mark the flesh of, to leave a mark on the skin of, e.g., **se me ha sentado una costura** (coll.) a seam left a mark on my skin
**sentencia** *f* sentence; (law) sentence
**sentenciador -dora** *adj* sentencing; *mf* sentencer
**sentenciar** *va* to sentence; to declare sententiously; to consign (*e.g., to the wastebasket*)
**sentencioso -sa** *adj* sententious
**senticar** *m* thicket, brambles
**sentido -da** *adj* felt, experienced; deep-felt, full of feeling, sensitive; eloquent, convincing; **darse por sentido** to show resentment, to take offense; *m* sense; meaning; direction; (geom. & mech.) sense; **aguzar el sentido** (coll.) to prick up one's ears; **con todos mis cinco sentidos** (coll.) with all my heart and soul; **costar un sentido** (coll.) to cost a fortune; **doble sentido** double-entendre; **en tal sentido** to this effect; **perder el sentido** to faint, to lose consciousness; **poner sus cinco sentidos en** (coll.) to be all eyes and ears for, to be mad about; **recobrar el sentido** to regain consciousness; **sin sentido** meaning-

less; unconscious; **tener puestos sus cinco sentidos en** (coll.) to be all eyes and ears for, to be mad about; **valer un sentido** (coll.) to be worth a fortune; **sentido común** common sense
**sentimental** *adj* sentimental
**sentimentalismo** *m* sentimentalism, sentimentality
**sentimentalista** *adj* sentimental; *mf* sentimentalist
**sentimiento** *m* sentiment; feeling; sorrow, regret
**sentina** *f* (naut.) bilge; foul, filthy place; hotbed of vice
**sentir** *m* feeling; opinion, judgment ‖ §62 *va* to feel; to hear; to regret, to be or feel sorry for; to sense; to recite (*e.g., verse*) with appropriate gestures; **dar que sentir** to give cause for regret; **sentir** + *inf* to regret to, to be or feel sorry to + *inf;* to hear + *inf*, e.g., **le sentí entrar esta mañana** I heard you come in this morning ‖ *vn* to feel; to be sorry, to feel sorry; **sin sentir** inadvertently, without being aware ‖ *vr* to feel, e.g., **me siento enfermo** I feel sick; to feel oneself to be, e.g., **me siento poeta** I feel myself to be a poet; to complain, to be resentful; to crack, be cracked; to begin to decay or rot; (naut.) to spring; **sentirse con** to feel, e.g., **me siento con mucho frío** I feel very cold; **sentirse de** to feel (*e.g., a blow*); to have a pain in, to feel sick in; to resent
**seña** *f* sign, mark, token; (mil.) password, watchword; **señas** *fpl* address; description; **dar señas de** to show signs of (*e.g., fatigue*); to describe; **hablar por señas** to talk by signs; **hacer señas** to motion; **por las señas** (coll.) to all appearances; **por señas** or **por más señas** (coll.) as a greater proof, specifically; **señas mortales** strong proof; **señas personales** personal description
**señá** *f* colloquial contraction of **señora,** commonly used before first names
**señal** *f* sign, mark, token; landmark; bookmark; trace, vestige; scar; signal; signal flag; light, traffic light; image, representation; reminder; pledge; earnest money; mark of distinction; brand; (rad.) signal; **en señal de** in proof of, in token of, as a token of; **ni señal** not a trace left; **señal de alto** stop signal; **señal de brazos** (naut.) arm signal; **señal de carretera** road sign; **señal de disco, señal de guitarra** (rail.) banjo signal; **señal de la cruz** sign of the cross; **señal del código** (naut.) code flag, code pennant; **señal de nieblas** fog signal; **señal de ocupado** (telp.) busy signal; **señal de parada** stop signal; **señal de peligro** danger signal, distress signal; **señal de tráfico** traffic sign; **señal de tramo** (rail.) block signal; **señal digital** fingerprint; **señales de dirección** (aut.) turn signals; **señales de ruta** highway signals; **señales marítimas** flags of the international code of signals; **señal horaria** time signal; **señal luminosa** traffic light; **señal para marcar** (telp.) dial tone; **señal urbana** traffic signal
**señaladamente** *adv* signally; especially
**señalado -da** *adj* signal, noted, distinguished
**señalamiento** *m* designation, pointing out; appointment, date
**señalar** *va* to mark; to show, indicate; to signal; to point at, to point out; to brand; to designate, determine, fix; to appoint; to sign and seal; to mark down (*points of score in card games*); to scar; to threaten (*a thing*); **señalar con el dedo** to point at, to point out; *vr* to distinguish oneself, to excel
**señalero** *m* signalman
**señalización** *f* (rail.) signaling; equipping with signals
**señalizar** §76 *va* to signal; to equip with signals
**señero -ra** *adj* solitary; unique
**señolear** *vn* to hunt with a decoy
**señor -ñora** *adj* ruling, master, controlling; (coll.) lordly, magnificent; (coll.) fine ‖ *m* sir, mister; gentleman; lord, master, owner; seignior; seigneur (*feudal*); (coll.) father-in-law; **señores** *mpl* Mr. and Mrs.; ladies and gentlemen: **descansar en el Señor** to rest in the Lord; **dormir en el Señor** to sleep in the Lord; **el gran señor** the Grand Turk; **el Señor** the Lord; **morir en el Señor** to die in the Lord; **muy señor mío** Dear Sir; **nuestro Señor** our Lord; **pues señor** well sir (*in telling a story*); **señor de horca y cuchillo** absolute lord, absolute master; (coll.) big shot; **Señor de los ejércitos** Lord of hosts; **señor eminentísimo** (eccl.) Eminence ‖ *f* madam, missus; lady, dame; mistress, owner; wife; (coll.) mother-in-law; **muy señora mía** Dear Madam; **Nuestra Señora** our Lady; **Nuestra Señora de los Dolores** Our Lady of Sorrows, Mary of the Sorrows; **señora de compañía** chaperon; **señora mayor** old lady, dowager
**señorada** *f* gentlemanly act, ladylike act
**señoraje** *m* seigniorage
**señoreador -dora** *adj* ruling; domineering, overbearing; *mf* ruler, master; domineering person
**señoreaje** *m* seigniorage
**señoreamiento** *m* domination, rule; mastery; seizure
**señorear** *va* to dominate, to rule; to master, to control (*e.g., passions*); to lord it over; to seize, take control of; to tower over; to excel; (coll.) to keep calling (*someone*) lord; *vn* to strut, to swagger; *vr* to control oneself; to strut, to swagger; **señorearse de** to seize, take control of
**señoría** *f* lordship, ladyship (*title and person*); rule, sway; signory (*governing body of medieval Italian city; Italian republic*)
**señorial** *adj* seigniorial, lordly; noble, majestic; feudal (*fees*)
**señoril** *adj* seignorial, lordly; majestic, haughty
**señorío** *m* seigniory; dominion, sway, rule; mastery (*e.g., of passions*); lordliness, majesty, arrogance; nobility, gentry, bon ton
**señorita** *f* young lady; miss; (coll.) mistress of the house
**señorita-torera** *f* lady bullfighter
**señoritingo** *m* (scornful) lordling
**señorito** *m* master, young gentleman, lordling; (coll.) master of the house; (scornful) playboy
**señorón -rona** *mf* (coll.) big shot, bigwig
**señuelo** *m* decoy, lure; bait; enticement
**seó** *m* (coll.) var. of **seor**
**seo** *f* (dial.) cathedral
**seor** *m* contraction of **señor**
**seora** *f* contraction of **señora**
**sepa** *1st sg pres subj of* **saber**
**sépalo** *m* (bot.) sepal
**sepancuantos** *m* (*pl:* **-tos**) (coll.) punishment, beating, scolding
**separable** *adj* separable, detachable
**separación** *f* separation
**separado -da** *adj* separate; apart; separated; **por separado** separately; under separate cover
**separador -dora** *adj* separating; *mf* separator; *m* separator (*machine; partition in storage battery*)
**separar** *va* to separate; to dismiss, discharge; *vr* to separate; to resign; (law) to waive a right
**separata** *f* offprint
**separatismo** *m* separatism
**separatista** *adj & mf* separatist
**separativo -va** *adj* separative
**sepedón** *m* (zool.) seps
**sepelio** *m* burial, interment
**sepia** *f* (zool.) sepia (*mollusk, secretion, pigment*); *m* sepia (*color; print*)
**sepsis** *f* (path.) sepsis
**septal** *adj* septal
**sept.**[e] abr. of **septiembre**
**septembrino -na** *adj* (pertaining to) September
**septena** *f* see **septeno**
**septenario -ria** *adj* septenary; *m* seven days
**septenio** *m* septennate, septennium, septenary
**septeno -na** *adj* seventh; *f* seven
**Septentrión** *m* North; (astr.) Great Bear
**septentrional** *adj* septentrional, northern
**septeto** *m* (mus.) septet
**septicemia** *f* (path.) septicemia; **septicemia hemorrágica** (vet.) hemorrhagic septicemia

**septicida** *adj* (bot.) septicidal
**séptico -ca** *adj* septic
**septiembre** *m* September
**septífrago -ga** *adj* (bot.) septifragal
**septillo** *m* (mus.) septimole
**septillón** *m* British septillion
**séptimo -ma** *adj* & *m* seventh; *f* sequence of seven (*in cards*); (mus.) seventh
**septingentésimo -ma** *adj* & *m* seven hundredth
**septisílabo -ba** *adj* seven-syllable
**septo** *m* (anat.) septum
**septuagenario -ria** *adj* & *mf* septuagenarian or septuagenary
**septuagésimo ma** *adj* & *m* seventieth; *f* (eccl.) Septuagesima, Septuagesima Sunday
**septuplicación** *f* septuplication
**septuplicar** §86 *va* to septuple
**séptuplo -pla** *adj* & *m* septuple, sevenfold
**sepulcral** *adj* sepulchral; (fig.) sepulchral
**sepulcro** *m* sepulcher, tomb, grave; (arch.) sepulcher; **santo sepulcro** Holy Sepulcher; **ser un sepulcro** to be good at keeping a secret; **sepulcro blanqueado** whited sepulcher (*hypocrite*)
**sepultar** *va* to bury, entomb; (fig.) to bury, hide away; (fig.) to bury, overwhelm, sink; *vr* to be buried (*e.g., in deep thought*)
**sepulto -ta** *adj* buried
**sepultura** *f* sepulture (*act and place*); **dar sepultura a** to bury; **estar con un pie en la sepultura** to have one foot in the grave
**sepulturera** *f* gravedigger's wife
**sepulturero** *m* gravedigger
**sequedad** *f* drought, dryness; gruffness, surliness
**sequedal** *m* or **sequeral** *m* dry, barren soil
**sequero** *m* unirrigated land; dryness; drying place
**sequeroso -sa** *adj* dried out; dry, barren
**sequete** *m* hard biscuit, hardtack; blow, bump; (coll.) gruffness, gruffness in answering
**sequía** *f* drought
**sequillo** *m* sweet biscuit
**sequío** *m* unwatered land; dryness
**séquito** *m* retinue, entourage, suite, personnel; following, popularity
**sequizo -za** *adj* dryish
**ser** *m* being; essence; life; **seres sensitivos** sentient beings; **ser humano** human being; **Ser Supremo** Supreme Being ‖ §83 *v aux* (used with past participle to form passive voice) to be, e.g., **el discurso fué aplaudido por todos** the speech was applauded by everybody ‖ *vn* to be; **a no ser por** if it were not for; **a no ser que** unless; **¡cómo es eso!** what are you up to? (*as a reproof*); **¡cómo ha de ser!** what can you expect? (*to express resignation*); **érase que se era** (coll.) once upon a time; **es a saber** to wit, namely; **es decir** that is to say; **es de creer que** it is to be believed that; **es de esperar que** it is to be hoped that; **no sea que** lest; **o sea** that is to say; **sea lo que sea** or **sea lo que fuere** be that as it may; **si yo fuera Vd.** if I were you; **un sí es, no es** a whit, a jot; **ser de** to belong to; to become of, e.g., **¿qué ha sido de él?** what has become of him; to be (*said of price, material, origin*), e.g., **el precio del sombrero es de seis dólares** the price of the watch is six dollars; **el reloj es de oro** the watch is gold; **ser de** + *inf* to be enough to + *inf;* to be to be + *pp*, e.g., **es de sentir(se) que** it is to be regretted that; **ser de lo que hay** (coll.) to be unequaled, to be among the worst; **ser de ver** to be worth seeing; **ser para** to suit, to be fitting for, to be fit for; **ser para poco** to not amount to much; **soy con Vd.** I'll be right with you; **soy yo** it is I
**sera** *f* frail, pannier without handles
**serado** *m* var. of **seraje**
**seráfico -ca** *adj* seraphic; **hacer la seráfica** to affect modesty
**serafín** *m* (Bib. & theol.) seraph; person of great beauty
**serafina** *f* fine baize
**seraje** *m* frails, panniers
**serapino** *m* sagapenum
**serba** *f* serviceberry, sorb (*fruit*)
**serbal** *m* (bot.) service tree, serviceberry (*tree*); **serbal de los cazadores** (bot.) rowan, mountain ash
**Serbia** *f* var. of **Servia**
**serbo** *m* (bot.) service tree
**serena** *f* see **sereno**
**serenar** *va* to calm; to pacify; to cool; to settle; *vn* to become calm; *vr* to become calm; to cool; to settle
**serenata** *f* serenade
**serenero** *m* woman's headpiece for protection against night air; (Am.) bandanna
**serenidad** *f* serenity, calm; (*cap.*) *f* Serenity (*title*); **serenidad del espíritu** peace of mind
**serenísimo -ma** *adj super* very or most serene, calm, or clear; serenissimo (*title of honor*)
**sereno -na** *adj* serene, calm; clear, cloudless; *m* night watchman (*who polices streets and carries keys to houses on his beat*); night dew, night air; **al sereno** in the night air; *f* serena, night love song; (coll.) night dew, night air; **a la serena** (coll.) in the night air
**serete** *m* small frail
**sergas** *fpl* deeds, exploits
**sergenta** *f* lay sister of the order of Santiago
**seriado -da** *adj* (rad.) serial
**serial** *adj* serial, seriate; *m* (rad.) serial; serial lacrimógeno
**sérico -ca** *adj* silken, seric; serous
**sericultor -tora** *mf* sericulturist
**sericultura** *f* sericulture, silk culture
**serie** *f* series; **de serie** stock, e.g., **coche de serie** stock car; **en serie** mass (*production*); (elec.) series, in series; **fuera de serie** special, unusual; outsize; **Serie Mundial** (baseball) World Series
**seriedad** *f* seriousness; reliability; sternness, severity; solemnity
**serijo** or **serillo** *m* small frail
**serio -ria** *adj* serious; reliable; stern, severe; majestic, solemn; **ir en serio** to become serious; **tomar en serio** to take seriously
**Ser.ma** or **Serma.** abr. of **Serenísima**
**Ser.mo** or **Sermo.** abr. of **Serenísimo**
**sermón** *m* sermon; (fig.) sermon; **sermón de la Montaña** (Bib.) Sermon on the Mount
**sermonar** *vn* to preach, to preach sermons
**sermoneador -dora** *adj* sermonizing
**sermonear** *va* (coll.) to sermonize; *vn* to sermonize
**sermoneo** *m* (coll.) sermonizing
**serna** *f* cultivated field
**seroja** *f* or **serojo** *m* dead leaves; brushwood
**serología** *f* serology
**serón** *m* pannier, long narrow frail; **serón caminero** horse pannier
**serondo -da** *adj* (bot.) serotinous
**serosidad** *f* (med. & physiol.) serosity
**seroso -sa** *adj* serous
**seroterapia** *f* serotherapeutics, serum therapy
**serótino -na** *adj* var. of **serondo**
**serpa** *f* (hort.) layer, runner
**serpear** *vn* var. of **serpentear**
**serpentaria** *f* (bot.) green dragon; **serpentaria virginiana** (bot.) Virginia snakeroot
**serpentario** *m* serpentarium; (orn.) secretary bird; (*cap.*) *m* (astr.) Serpent Bearer
**serpenteante** *adj* winding
**serpentear** *vn* to wind, meander; to wriggle, to squirm; to gleam, to coruscate
**serpenteo** *m* winding, meandering; wriggling; coruscation
**serpentín** *m* coil (*of a still, heater, etc.*); cock of a musket lock; **serpentín enfriador** cooling coil
**serpentino -na** *adj* serpentine; *f* coiled confetti; (mineral.) serpentine
**serpentón** *m* large serpent; (mus.) serpent (*wind instrument*)
**serpezuela** *f* little snake
**serpiente** *f* serpent; (fig.) snake, serpent (*treacherous person; Satan*); (*cap.*) *f* (astr.) Serpent; **serpiente de cascabel** (zool.) rattlesnake
**serpiginoso -sa** *adj* serpiginous
**serpigo** *m* (path.) serpigo
**serpol** *m* (bot.) wild thyme
**serpollar** *vn* to sprout, to shoot

**serpollo** *m* sprout, shoot, sucker
**serradizo -za** *adj* var. of **aserradizo**
**serrado -da** *adj* serrate
**serrador** *m* var. of **aserrador**
**serraduras** *fpl* sawdust
**serrallo** *m* seraglio
**serranía** *f* range of mountains, mountainous country
**serraniego -ga** *adj* highland, mountain
**serranil** *m* knife, dagger
**serrano -na** *adj* highland, mountain; *mf* highlander, mountaineer; *m* (ichth.) sea bass
**serrar §18** *va* to saw
**serrata** *f* (orn.) merganser (*Mergus serrator*)
**serrátil** *adj* irregular (*pulse*)
**serrato** *m* (anat.) serratus
**serrería** *f* sawmill
**serreta** *f* little saw; cavesson
**serretazo** *m* jerk on the cavesson; dressing-down, reprimand
**serrijón** *m* short chain of mountains
**serrín** *m* sawdust
**serriño -ña** *adj* mountain; (med.) high and irregular (*pulse*)
**serrón** *m* large saw; two-handed saw
**serruchar** *va* (Am.) to saw
**serrucho** *m* handsaw
**serval** *m* (zool.) serval; (bot.) service tree
**servato** *m* (bot.) hog's-fennel
**serventesio** *m* sirvente (*Provençal moral song*); quatrain with rhyme abab
**serventía** *f* (Am.) road passing through private property
**Servia** *f* see **servio**
**servible** *adj* serviceable, useful
**servicial** *adj* accommodating, obliging; *m* enema, clyster
**serviciar** *va* to collect or to pay (*cattle toll, sheepwalk dues, etc.*)
**servicio** *m* service; enema; chamber pot; (tennis) service, serve; cover (*setting at table for one person*); (Am.) toilet; **de servicio** on duty; **estar en el servicio** (coll.) to serve, to be in the service (*to be a soldier*); **hacer un flaco servicio a** (coll.) to play a dirty trick on; **servicio activo** active service; **servicio de grúa** (aut.) towing service; **servicio de mesa** set of dishes; **servicio de municionamiento** (mil.) ordnance department; **servicio de reparaciones** repair service; **servicio divino** divine service; **servicio informativo** (rad.) news service; **servicio militar** military service; **servicio secreto** secret service; **servicio social** social service
**servidero -ra** *adj* serviceable, useful; demanding
**servidor -dora** *mf* servant; humble servant; (tennis) server; **quedo de Vd. atento y seguro servidor** yours respectfully; **servidor de Vd.** your servant, at your service; *m* waiter; suitor; chamber pot; *f* waitress
**servidumbre** *f* servitude; servants, help; demand; obligation; compulsion; dominance by passion; (law) easement, servitude; **servidumbre de la gleba** serfdom; **servidumbre de luces** (law) right to not have one's windows shut off from light; **servidumbre de paso** (law) right of way; **servidumbre de vía** (rail.) right of way
**servil** *adj* servile, subservient; *m* (hist.) absolutist
**servilismo** *m* servility, subservience
**servilón -lona** *adj* servile; *m* (hist.) absolutist
**servilla** *f* pump (*low shoe*)
**servilleta** *f* napkin, serviette; **doblar la servilleta** (coll.) to die
**servilletero** *m* napkin ring
**servio -via** *adj & mf* Serbian; *m* Serbian (*language*); (*cap.*) *f* Serbia
**serviola** *f* (naut.) cathead, anchor beam
**servir §94** *va* to serve; to help, wait on; to fill (*an order*); to worship; to favor; to court (*a lady*); (tennis) to serve; **ir servido** to get one's deserts; **para servir a Vd.** at your service; **ser servido de** + *inf* to be pleased to + *inf;* **servir de** to serve (*someone*) as ‖ *vn* to serve; to be useful, to be of use; to follow suit (*in cards*); (tennis) to serve; **¿de** or **para qué sirve . . . ?** what is the good of . . . ?; **¿de** or **para qué sirve** + *inf?* what is the good of + *ger?;* **no servir para nada** to be good for nothing, to be of no use; **servir de** to serve as, to act as; to be used as; **servir para** to be used for, to be good for ‖ *vr* to help oneself, to serve oneself (*e.g., at table*); **servirse** + *inf* to have the kindness to + *inf*, to deign to + *inf;* **servirse de** to make use of; **sírvase** + *inf* please + *inf;* **¡sírvase!** please!
**serv.º** abr. of **servicio**
**servocontrol** *m* (aer.) servo control
**servocroata** *adj & mf* Serbo-Croatian; *m* Serbo-Croatian (*language*)
**servodirección** *f* (aut.) power steering
**servoembrague** *m* automatic clutch
**servofreno** *m* servo brake
**servomecanismo** *m* servomechanism
**servomotor** *m* (mach.) servomotor
**serv.ºʳ** abr. of **servidor**
**sesada** *f* brains (*of an animal*); fried brains
**sésamo** *m* (bot.) sesame; sesame (*magic word*); **¡sésamo ábrete!** open sesame!
**sesamoideo -a** *adj* sesamoid or sesamoidal
**sesear** *vn* to pronounce Spanish c and z like s
**sesenta** *adj & m* sixty
**sesentavo -va** *adj & m* sixtieth
**sesentón -tona** *adj & mf* (coll.) sexagenarian
**seseo** *m* pronunciation of Spanish c and z like s
**seseoso -sa** *adj* pronouncing Spanish c and z like s
**sesera** *f* brain; brainpan
**sesga** *f* see **sesgo**
**sesgadamente** *adv* slantingly, obliquely, on the bias
**sesgado -da** *adj* slanting, oblique; beveled
**sesgadura** *f* slant, obliquity; bevel; skew
**sesgar §59** *va* to gore, to cut (*cloth*) on the bias; to slope, bevel, slant; to skew
**sesgo -ga** *adj* slanting, sloped, oblique; beveled; severe, stern; calm, placid; *m* slope, slant, obliquity; bias, bevel; skew; compromise; turn; **al sesgo** obliquely, on the bias; *f* gore
**sésil** *adj* (bot.) sessile
**sesión** *f* session, sitting; meeting, conference; show (*each showing of a movie*); **abrir la sesión** to open the meeting; **levantar la sesión** to adjourn the meeting; **sesión continua** (mov.) continuous showing; **sesión de espiritistas** séance, spiritualistic séance
**sesionar** *vn* to be in session
**seso** *m* brain; brains, intelligence; block (*of stone, brick, or iron*) to steady a pot on the fire; **sesos** *mpl* brains (*for food*); **calentarse** or **devanarse los sesos** to rack one's brain; **levantarse la tapa de los sesos** to blow out one's brains; **perder el seso** to go crazy; **tener sorbido el seso a, tener sorbidos los sesos a** (coll.) to dominate, to have unlimited influence on; to be madly in love with; to be deeply immersed in
**sesquiáltero -ra** *adj* sesquialteral; *f* (mus.) sesquialtera (*interval; organ stop*)
**sesquipedal** *adj* sesquipedalian (*measuring a foot and a half; very long, containing many syllables*)
**sesteadero** *m* shady place where cattle rest
**sestear** *vn* to siesta, to take a siesta; to rest in the shade (*said of cattle*)
**sestil** *m* var. of **sesteadero**
**sestina** *f* sextina (*verse form*)
**sesudez** *f* braininess
**sesudo -da** *adj* brainy; wise; (Am.) stubborn
**seta** *f* bristle; toadstool
**setáceo -a** *adj* setaceous (*bristlelike*)
**setal** *m* mushroom bed or patch
**set.ᵉ** abr. of **septiembre**
**setecientos -tas** *adj & m* seven hundred; **el Setecientos** the Eighteenth Century
**setena** *f* seven
**setenar** *va* to select by lot every seventh of; to punish beyond all measure
**setenario -ria** *adj & m* var. of **septenario**
**setenta** *adj & m* seventy
**setentavo -va** *adj & m* seventieth
**setentón -tona** *adj & mf* (coll.) septuagenarian
**setiembre** *m* var. of **septiembre**
**seto** *m* fence; **seto vivo** hedge, quickset
**sétter** *m* (*pl:* **-ters**) setter (*bird dog*)

**setuní** *m* (*pl:* **-níes**) var. of **aceituní**
**seudohermafroditismo** *m* pseudohermaphroditism
**seudomorfismo** *m* (mineral.) pseudomorphism
**seudónimo -ma** *adj* pseudonymous; *m* pseudonym, pen name
**seudópodo** *m* (zool.) pseudopod or pseudopodium
**Seúl** *f* Seoul
**s.e.u.o.** abr. of **salvo error u omisión**
**severidad** *f* severity; sternness, strictness; seriousness
**Severna** *m* Severn
**severo -ra** *adj* severe; stern, strict; serious
**sevicia** *f* ferocity, great cruelty
**sevicioso -sa** *adj* ferocious, extremely cruel, brutal
**Sevilla** *f* Seville
**sevillano -na** *adj & mf* Sevillian; **sevillanas** *fpl* sevillanas (*seguidillas of Seville*)
**sexagenario -ria** *adj & mf* sexagenarian or sexagenary
**sexagesimal** *adj* sexagesimal
**sexagésimo -ma** *adj & m* sixtieth; *f* (eccl.) Sexagesima, Sexigesima Sunday
**sexángulo -la** *adj* (geom.) sexangular; *m* (geom.) sexangle
**sexcentésimo -ma** *adj & m* six hundredth
**sexenal** *adj* sexennial, six-year
**sexenio** *m* sexennium, six years
**sexmero** *m* township officer
**sexmo** *m* township
**sexo** *m* sex; **el bello sexo** the fair sex or the gentle sex; **el sexo barbudo** (Am.) the sterner or the stronger sex; **el sexo débil** the weaker sex; **el sexo feo** or **el sexo fuerte** the sterner sex or the stronger sex
**sexología** *f* sexology
**sexólogo -ga** *mf* sexologist
**sexta** *f* see **sexto**
**sextante** *m* sextant (*instrument*); (*cap.*) *m* (astr.) Sextant; **sextante de burbuja** bubble sextant
**sextavado -da** *adj* hexagonal
**sextavar** *va* to make hexagonal
**sexteto** *m* (mus.) sextet, sestet
**sextil** *adj* (astrol.) sextile
**sextilla** *f* sextain
**sextillo** *m* (mus.) sextuplet
**sextillón** *m* British sextillion
**sextina** *f* sestina (*verse form*); six-line stanza
**sexto -ta** *adj* sixth; *m* sixth; *f* sequence of six (*in cards*); (mus.) sixth; (eccl.) sext
**sextuplicación** *f* sextuplication
**sextuplicar** §86 *va & vr* to sextuple
**séxtuplo -pla** *adj & m* sextuple, sixfold
**sexual** *adj* sexual, sex
**sexualidad** *f* sexuality
**S.G.M.** abr. of **Segunda Guerra Mundial**
**shogún** *m* shogun
**shogunado** *m* shogunate
**si** *conj* if; whether; I wonder if; **como si** as if; **por si acaso** just in case; **un si es, no es** a whit, a jot, a soupçon; **si acaso** if by chance; **si no** otherwise; *m* (mus.) si
**sí** *adv* yes; indeed; (gives emphasis to verb and is often equivalent to English auxiliary verb) **él sí habla español** he does speak Spanish; **él no irá pero yo sí** he will not go but I shall; **por sí o por no** in any case; **sí que** certainly; **sí tal** yes indeed, surely; *m* yes; **dar el sí** to say yes (*especially to a proposal for marriage*); *pron reflex* (used as object of prepositions) himself, herself, itself, themselves; yourself, yourselves; oneself; each other, e.g., **independientes entre sí** independent of each other; **de por sí** separately, by oneself, in itself, by itself; **de sí** separately, in itself; **por sí y ante sí** of his own accord; **sobre sí** cautiously; haughtily
**siamés -mesa** *adj & mf* Siamese; *m* Siamese (*language*); *f* siamoise (*fabric*)
**sibarita** *adj & mf* Sybarite
**sibarítico -ca** *adj* Sybaritic
**sibaritismo** *m* sybaritism
**Siberia** *f* Siberia
**siberiano -na** *adj & mf* Siberian
**sibil** *m* cave; cellar, vault
**sibila** *f* sibyl
**sibilante** *adj* sibilant, hissing, whistling; (phonet.) sibilant
**sibilino -na** or **sibilítico -ca** *adj* sibylline; (fig.) sibylline
**siboney** *adj & mf* (Am.) Cuban
**sicalipsis** *f* spiciness, suggestiveness
**sicalíptico -ca** *adj* spicy, suggestive; ribald
**sicamor** *m* (bot.) Judas tree
**sicano -na** *adj* Sicanian
**sicario** *m* paid assassin
**sicastenia** *f* var. of **psicastenia**
**sicigia** *f* (astr.) syzygy
**Sicilia** *f* Sicily
**siciliano -na** *adj & mf* Sicilian; *m* Sicilian (*dialect*)
**siclo** *m* shekel
**sicoanálisis** *m* var. of **psicoanálisis**
**sicoanalista** *mf* var. of **psicoanalista**
**sicoanalítico -ca** *adj* var. of **psicoanalítico**
**sicoanalizar** §76 *va* var. of **psicoanalizar**
**sicodinámico -ca** *adj & f* var. of **psicodinámico**
**sicofanta** *m* or **sicofante** *m* sycophant (*informer; impostor*)
**sicofísica** *f* var. of **psicofísica**
**sicognostia** *f* var. of **psicognostia**
**sicología** *f* var. of **psicología**
**sicológico -ca** *adj* var. of **psicológico**
**sicólogo -ga** *mf* var. of **psicólogo**
**sicometría** *f* var. of **psicometría**
**sicométrico -ca** *adj* var. of **psicométrico**
**sicómoro** *m* (bot.) sycamore
**sicón** *m* (zool.) sycon
**siconeurosis** *f* (*pl:* **-sis**) var. of **psiconeurosis**
**sicono** *m* (bot.) syconium or syconus
**sicópata** *mf* var. of **psicópata**
**sicopatía** *f* var. of **psicopatía**
**sicopático -ca** *adj* var. of **psicopático**
**sicopatología** *f* var. of **psicopatología**
**sicosis** *f* (*pl:* **-sis**) (path.) psychosis; (path.) sycosis (*skin affection*)
**sicosomático -ca** *adj* var. of **psicosomático**
**sicote** *m* (prov. & Am.) personal uncleanliness, smelliness of feet
**sicotecnia** *f* var. of **psicotecnia**
**sicoterapia** *f* var. of **psicoterapia**
**sicrómetro** *m* var. of **psicrómetro**
**sículo -la** *adj & mf* Sicilian; (hist.) Siculian
**sideral** or **sidéreo -a** *adj* sidereal
**siderita** *f* (mineral.) siderite; (bot.) ironwort
**siderosa** *f* (mineral.) siderite
**siderosis** *f* (path.) siderosis
**siderurgia** *f* siderurgy; iron and steel industry
**siderúrgico -ca** *adj* siderurgical; (pertaining to) iron and steel
**sidonio -nia** *adj & mf* Sidonian
**sidra** *f* cider
**sidrería** *f* cider shop
**sidrero -ra** *adj* (pertaining to) cider
**siega** *f* reaping; harvest; crop
**siembra** *f* sowing; seed, seeding; seedtime; sown field
**siempre** *adv* always; surely; **de siempre** usual; **para siempre** or **por siempre** forever; **por siempre jamás** forever and ever; **siempre que** provided; whenever; **siempre y cuando que** provided
**siempreviva** *f* (bot.) everlasting flower; **siempreviva mayor** (bot.) houseleek; **siempreviva menor** (bot.) white stonecrop
**sien** *f* (anat.) temple
**siena** *m* sienna; **siena tostado** burnt sienna
**sienés -nesa** *adj & mf* Sienese
**sienita** *f* (mineral.) syenite
**sierpe** *f* serpent, snake; wild person; ugly-looking person; wriggler; (hort.) tiller
**sierra** *f* saw; jagged mountain range, sierra; (ichth.) sawfish; (ichth.) sierra; **sierra abrazadera** lumberman's saw; **sierra bracera** two-handed saw; **sierra de mano** handsaw; **sierra caladora** keyhole saw; **sierra circular** buzz saw, circular saw; **sierra continua** band saw; **sierra de armero** hacksaw; **sierra de bastidor** bucksaw; **sierra de cinta** band saw; **sierra de cortar metales** hacksaw; **sierra de hilo** or **hender** ripsaw; **sierra de punta** compass saw; **sierra de tras-**

**dós** backsaw; **sierra de través** crosscut saw; **sierra de vaivén** jig saw; **sierra sin fin** band saw
**siervo -va** *mf* slave; humble servant; **siervo de Dios** servant of God; (coll.) poor devil; **siervo de la gleba** serf
**sieso** *m* (anat.) fundament
**siesta** *f* siesta; sleep or rest after eating; hottest time of day; afternoon music in church; **dormir** or **echar la siesta** to siesta, to take a nap after lunch; **siesta del carnero** nap before lunch
**siete** *adj* seven; **las siete** seven o'clock; **las siete colinas** the Seven Hills (*of Rome*); **las siete maravillas del mundo** the Seven Wonders of the World; *m* seven; seventh (*in dates*); V-shaped tear; (carp.) dog clamp; **más que siete** (coll.) too much
**sieteenrama** *f* (bot.) septfoil
**sietemesino -na** *adj* born in seven months; (coll.) puny fellow; (coll.) coxcomb
**sieteñal** *adj* seven-year-old
**sífilis** *f* (path.) syphilis
**sifilítico -ca** *adj & mf* syphilitic
**sifón** *m* siphon; siphon bottle; siphon water; trap (*in a pipe*)
**sifonógamo -ma** *adj* (bot.) siphonogamic or siphonogamous; *f* (bot.) siphonogam
**sifosis** *f* var. of **cifosis**
**sifué** *m* surcingle
**sig.e** abr. of **siguiente**
**Sigfrido** *m* Siegfried
**sigilación** *f* sealing, stamping; seal, stamp; concealment
**sigilar** *va* to seal, to stamp; to conceal, keep silent
**sigilo** *m* seal; concealment, reserve; **sigilo sacramental** inviolable secrecy of the confessional
**sigilografía** *f* sigillography
**sigiloso -sa** *adj* close-lipped, tight-lipped; silent, reserved
**sigla** *f* initial (*used in an abbreviation*); abbreviation, symbol
**siglo** *m* century; world (*worldly matters or activities*); age (*long time*); period, epoch, age; times; **en** or **por los siglos de los siglos** world without end, forever and ever; **hasta la consumación de los siglos** until the end of time; **siglo de cobre** (archeol.) Age of Copper; **siglo de hierro** (myth. & fig.) iron age; **siglo de la ilustración** or **de las luces** Age of Enlightenment (*eighteenth century*); **siglo de oro** (myth. & lit.) golden age; **siglo de plata** (myth.) silver age; **siglo dorado** (myth.) golden age; **siglos medios** Middle Ages
**sigma** *f* sigma
**sigmoideo -a** *adj* sigmoid
**signáculo** *m* seal, signet
**signar** *va* to sign; to put a mark on; to make the sign of the cross over; *vr* to cross oneself
**signatario -ria** *adj & mf* signatory
**signatura** *f* library number; signature, sign, stamp, mark; signing; (print.) signature, signature mark; (eccl.) rescript granting indulgence; (mus.) signature, time signature
**significación** *f* significance; signification
**significado -da** *adj* known, well-known, important; *m* meaning, signification
**significar** §86 *va* to signify, to mean; to indicate, to point out, to make known; *vn* to signify, to be important; *vr* to be distinguished
**significativo -va** *adj* significant; significative
**signo** *m* sign (*e.g., of rain*); mark; (astr., math., med., mus. & print.) sign; scroll or flourish (*in notary's signature*); mark (*cross made instead of signature*); benediction, sign of the cross; fate, destiny; **signo de admiración** (gram.) exclamation mark; **signo de interrogación** (gram.) question mark; **signo de radicación** (math.) radical sign; **signo diacrítico** (gram.) diacritical mark
**siguapa** *f* var. of **sijú**
**siguiente** *adj* following; next
**sij** *m* (*pl:* **sijs**) Sikh
**sijú** *m* (*pl:* **-júes**) (orn.) Antillean gnome owl
**Sila** *m* Sulla (*Roman general*)
**sílaba** *f* syllable; **última sílaba** (gram.) ultima; **sílaba abierta** (phonet.) open syllable; **sílaba cerrada** (phonet.) closed syllable; **sílaba libre** (phonet.) free syllable; **sílaba trabada** (phonet.) checked syllable
**silabar** *vn* to syllable
**silabario** *m* reader with words divided in syllables; syllabary
**silabear** *va* to syllable, to syllabize, to syllabify; *vn* to syllable
**silabeo** *m* syllabication, syllabification
**silábico -ca** *adj* syllabic
**sílabo** *m* syllabus
**silba** *f* hiss, hissing
**silbador -dora** *adj* whistling; hissing; *mf* whistler; hisser
**silbante** *adj* var. of **sibilante**
**silbar** *va* to whistle (*a tune*); to blow (*a whistle*); to hiss (*an actor, a play*); *vn* to whistle; to whiz
**silbato** *m* whistle; whistling or hissing crack (*emitting air or a liquid*)
**silbido** *m* whistle, whistling, hiss; (rad.) howling, squealing; **silbido de oídos** ringing in the ears
**silbo** *m* whistle, hiss, whiz
**silbón** *m* (orn.) widgeon
**silboso -sa** *adj* whistling, hissing
**silenciador** *m* silencer (*device for firearms, internal-combustion engines, etc.*); **silenciador de ruidos** (rad.) noise suppressor
**silenciar** *va* to keep silent about, to avoid mentioning; to silence
**silenciero -ra** *mf* silencer (*person*)
**silencio** *m* silence; (mil.) taps (*signal to put out lights*); (mus.) rest; **en silencio** in silence
**silencioso -sa** *adj* silent, noiseless; still, quiet; *m* (aut.) muffler
**Sileno** *m* (myth.) Silenus
**silente** *adj* silent, still, calm, quiet
**silepsis** *f* (*pl:* **-sis**) (rhet.) syllepsis
**silero** *m* (agr.) silo
**silesiano -na** or **silesio -sia** *adj & mf* Silesian
**sílex** *m* (mineral.) silex
**sílfide** *f* (myth. & fig.) sylph
**silfo** *m* (myth.) sylph
**silga** *f* var. of **sirga**
**silgar** §59 *va* to tow (*a boat*); *vn* (naut.) to pole
**silguero** *m* (orn.) linnet
**silicato** *m* (chem.) silicate
**sílice** *f* (chem.) silica
**silíceo -a** *adj* siliceous
**silícico -ca** *adj* (chem.) silicic
**silicio** *m* (chem.) silicon
**siliciuro** *m* (chem.) silicide
**silicón** *m* (chem.) silicone
**silicosis** *f* (path.) silicosis
**silicua** *f* (bot.) silique
**silícula** *f* (bot.) silicle
**silicuoso -sa** *adj* (bot.) siliquose or siliquous
**silo** *m* (agr.) silo; cave, cavern, dark place
**Siloé** *m* (Bib.) Siloam
**silogismo** *m* syllogism
**silogístico -ca** *adj* syllogistic
**silogizar** §76 *vn* to syllogize
**silueta** *f* silhouette; **en silueta** in silhouette
**siluetear** *va* to silhouette
**siluriano -na** or **silúrico -ca** *adj & m* (geol.) Silurian
**siluro** *m* (ichth.) sheatfish; self-propelling torpedo
**silva** *f* miscellany; verse of iambic hendecasyllables intermingled with seven-syllable lines, with some verses rhymed
**Silvano** *m* Silvan, Sylvanus
**silvático -ca** *adj* var. of **selvático**
**silvestre** *adj* wild; uncultivated, rustic; (*cap.*) *m* Silvester or Sylvester
**Silvia** *f* Sylvia; **silvia blanquinegra** (orn.) black-and-white warbler
**silvicultor -tora** *mf* forester
**silvicultura** *f* forestry
**silvina** *f* (mineral.) sylvite
**silvoso -sa** *adj* var. of **selvoso**
**silla** *f* chair; saddle; (eccl.) see; **de silla a silla** tête à tête, two together in private; **silla curul** curule chair; **silla de balanza** (Am.) rocking chair; **silla de cubierta** deck chair; **silla de hamaca** (Am.) rocking chair; **silla de la reina** seat made by two people crossing hands and grasping wrists; **silla de ma-**

**nos** sedan chair; **silla de montar** saddle, riding saddle; **silla de posta** post chaise; **silla de ruedas** wheel chair; **silla de tijera** folding chair, camp stool; **silla eléctrica** electric chair; **silla giratoria** swivel chair; **Silla peligrosa** Siege Perilous (*at King Arthur's Round Table*); **silla plegadiza** folding chair; **silla poltrona** easy chair, easy armchair; **silla volante** shay (*light carriage*)
**sillar** *m* ashlar; horseback
**sillarejo** *m* small ashlar, facing ashlar
**sillera** *f* see **sillero**
**sillería** *f* set of chairs; stalls (*in a choir*); ashlar, ashlar masonry; chair factory, chair store; chairmaking, chair business
**sillero -ra** *mf* chairmaker, chair dealer; *f* (archaic) place for storing sedan chairs
**silleta** *f* little chair; bedpan; **silletas** *fpl* (prov.) sidesaddle
**silletazo** *m* blow with a chair
**silletero** *m* chairman (*one who carries people in a sedan chair or pushes them in a wheel chair*)
**silletín** *m* little chair; (dial.) stool
**sillico** *m* chamber pot
**sillín** *m* light riding saddle; harness saddle; saddle (*e.g., of bicycle*); fancy sidesaddle
**sillón** *m* armchair, easy chair; sidesaddle; **sillón de hamaca** rocking chair; **sillón de orejas** wing chair; **sillón de ruedas** wheel chair
**sima** *f* chasm, abyss; (arch.) scotia
**simbiosis** *f* (biol.) symbiosis
**simbiótico -ca** *adj* (biol.) symbiotic
**simbólico -ca** *adj* symbolic or symbolical
**simbolismo** *m* symbolism
**simbolista** *adj* symbolistic; *mf* symbolist
**simbolización** *f* symbolization
**simbolizar** §76 *va* to symbolize, to symbol
**símbolo** *m* symbol; adage; mark, device; **Símbolo Atanasiano** Athanasian Creed; **Símbolo de la fe** or **Símbolo de los Apóstoles** Apostles' Creed
**Simeón** *m* Simeon
**simetría** *f* symmetry
**simétrico -ca** *adj* symmetric or symmetrical
**simetrizar** §76 *va* to symmetrize
**simia** *f* female ape
**símico -ca** *adj* simian
**simiente** *f* seed; germ; semen; **simiente de papagayos** (bot.) bastard saffron
**simiesco -ca** *adj* apelike, apish
**símil** *adj* similar; *m* resemblance, similarity; (rhet.) simile
**similar** *adj* similar
**similicuero** *m* imitation leather
**similiseda** *f* imitation silk
**similitud** *f* similitude
**similitudinario -ria** *adj* similar
**similizar** §76 *va* to mercerize
**similor** *m* similor; **de similor** false, fake, sham
**simio** *m* (zool.) simian
**Simón** *m* Simon; (*l.c.*) *m* hack, cab; hackman
**simonía** *f* simony
**simoníaco -ca** *adj* simoniacal
**simpa** *f* (Am.) braid, plait; (Am.) tress
**simpar** *adj* unequaled, unmatched
**simpatectomía** *f* var. of **simpaticectomía**
**simpatía** *f* sympathy; fondness, liking, attachment, affection; friendliness; congeniality; **llevarse la simpatía de** to win the affection of; **tomar simpatía a** to take a liking for
**simpática** *f* see **simpático**
**simpaticectomía** *f* (surg.) sympathectomy
**simpático -ca** *adj* sympathetic; pleasant, agreeable, likable, congenial; (anat., mus., phys. & physiol.) sympathetic; **gran simpático** (anat. & physiol.) sympathetic nervous system; *f* (bot.) phlox
**simpatiquísimo -ma** *adj super* very or most sympathetic; very or most pleasant, agreeable, or congenial
**simpatizador -dora** or **simpatizante** *adj* sympathetic; *mf* sympathizer; follower, backer
**simpatizar** §76 *vn* to be congenial, to get on well together; **simpatizar con** to get on well with, to be friendly toward, to be sympathetic toward
**simpétalo -la** *adj* (bot.) sympetalous
**simple** *adj* simple; single; insipid, tasteless; *mf* simple, simpleton; *m* simple (*medicinal plant*); (pharm.) simple
**simpleza** *f* simpleness, stupidness, dullness; stupidity (*in act or word*)
**simplicidad** *f* simplicity, simpleness; simpleheartedness
**simplicísimo -ma** *adj super* very or most simple (*in all senses except that of* unwary, foolish, stupid, *for which* **simplísimo** *is used*)
**simplismo** *m* simplicity
**simplicista** *adj* simplistic; *mf* simplist, devotee of simplification
**simplificación** *f* simplification
**simplificar** §86 *va* to simplify
**simplista** *adj* simplistic, oversimplifying; *mf* simplist, person inclined to oversimplify; (med.) simplist, herbalist
**simplón -plona** *adj* simple-hearted; (coll.) simple, dull; *mf* simple-hearted person
**simposio** *m* (hist.) symposium
**simulación** *f* simulation, pretense; malingering
**simulacro** *m* simulacrum, phantom, vision; image, idol; show, semblance; pretense; sham battle; **simulacro de ataque aéreo** air-raid drill; **simulacro de combate** sham battle; **simulacro de salvamento** lifesaving drill, lifesaving test
**simuladamente** *adv* feigningly
**simulado -da** *adj* simulated, pretended, fake; (com.) pro forma
**simulador -dora** *adj* simulative; *mf* simulator; malingerer
**simular** *va* to simulate, to feign, to fake; *vn* to malinger; to pretend; **simular** + *inf* to pretend to + *inf*
**simultanear** *va* to carry out simultaneously; (educ.) to take (*courses of successive years or in different schools*) at the same time
**simultaneidad** *f* simultaneity
**simultáneo -a** *adj* simultaneous
**simún** *m* simoom or simoon
**sin** *prep* without; without counting; **sin** + *inf* without + *ger*, e.g., **salió sin despedirse** he left without saying good-by; to be + *pp*, e.g., **hay muchas necesidades urgentes sin satisfacer** there are many urgent needs to be satisfied; **sin que** + *subj* without + *ger*, e.g., **entró sin que yo le viese** he came in without my seeing him
**sinagoga** *f* synagogue
**Sinaí, el** Sinai (*peninsula*)
**sinalagmático -ca** *adj* (law) synallagmatic
**sinalefa** *f* synalepha or synaloepha
**sinapismo** *m* mustard plaster, sinapism; (coll.) nuisance, bore
**sinapsis** *f* (*pl:* **-sis**) (biol.) synapsis; (physiol.) synapsis or synapse
**sinartrosis** *f* (*pl:* **-sis**) (anat.) synarthrosis
**sincárpeo -a** *adj* (bot.) syncarpous
**sincarpo** *m* (bot.) syncarp
**sincerador -dora** *adj* exonerating; *mf* exonerator, defender
**sincerar** *va* to exonerate, vindicate; *vr* to exonerate oneself, vindicate onself; to speak frankly
**sinceridad** *f* sincerity
**sincero -ra** *adj* sincere
**sincipucio** *m* (anat.) skullcap, sinciput
**sinclástico -ca** *adj* (math.) synclastic
**sinclinal** *adj* synclinal; (geol.) synclinal; *m* (geom.) syncline
**síncopa** *f* (mus. & phonet.) syncopation, syncope
**sincopado -da** *adj* syncopated
**sincopal** *adj* syncopal
**sincopar** *va* (mus. & phonet.) to syncopate; to abridge
**síncope** *m* (path.) syncope, fainting spell; (phonet.) syncope
**sincopizar** §76 *va* to make faint, make swoon; *vr* to faint, to swoon
**sincrético -ca** *adj* syncretic
**sincretismo** *m* syncretism
**sincrisis** *f* (rhet.) syncrisis
**sincronía** *f* synchrony
**sincrónico -ca** *adj* synchronous; synchronic; (elec.) synchronous

**sincronismo** *m* synchronism
**sincronización** *f* synchronization
**sincronizador** *m* synchronizer
**sincronizar** §76 *va & vn* to synchronize
**síncrono -na** *adj* synchronous; (elec.) synchronous
**sincronoscopio** *m* (elec.) synchronoscope
**sincrotrón** *m* (phys.) synchrotron
**sindéresis** *f* discretion, good judgment; (theol.) synteresis
**sindicación** *f* syndication
**sindicado** *m* syndicate (*body of syndics*)
**sindical** *adj* syndical
**sindicalismo** *m* syndicalism; unionism, trade unionism
**sindicalista** *adj & mf* syndicalist; unionist, trade unionist
**sindicar** §86 *va* to accuse, to inform on; to put in trust; to syndicate; *vr* to syndicate
**sindicato** *m* syndicate; union, labor union, trade union
**sindicatura** *f* trusteeship; (law) receivership
**síndico** *m* syndic, trustee; (law) receiver (*in litigation over property or in a bankruptcy*)
**sindiós** (*pl:* **-diós**) *adj* godless; *mf* godless person, atheist
**síndrome** *m* (path.) syndrome
**sinécdoque** *f* (rhet.) synecdoche
**sinecura** *f* sinecure
**sinecurista** *mf* sinecurist
**sinedrio** *m* var. of **sanedrín**
**sinéresis** *f* (gram.) synaeresis
**sinergia** *f* synergy
**sinestesia** *f* (physiol. & psychol.) synesthesia
**sinfín** *m* endless number, endless amount
**sinfinidad** *f* (coll.) endless number, infinity
**sínfisis** *f* (*pl:* **-sis**) (anat. & zool.) symphysis; **sínfisis sacroilíaca** (anat.) sacroiliac joint
**sínfito** *m* (bot.) comfrey
**sinfonía** *f* symphony
**sinfónico -ca** *adj* symphonic
**sinfonista** *mf* symphonist
**Singapur** *f* Singapore
**singar** §59 *vn* (naut.) to pole
**singenésico -ca** *adj* (bot.) syngenesious
**singladura** *f* sailing, navigation; boat's speed; (naut.) day (*from noon to noon*); (naut.) day's run
**singlar** *vn* (naut.) to sail, to travel, to steer
**single** *adj* (naut.) single
**singlón** *m* (naut.) yardarm
**singular** *adj* singular; special; single; (gram.) singular; *m* (gram.) singular; **en singular** in particular
**singularidad** *f* singularity
**singularizar** §76 *va* to distinguish, to single out; to put or use in the singular (*a word which is regularly in the plural*); *vr* to distinguish oneself, to stand out; to make oneself conspicuous
**singularmente** *adv* singularly, strangely; particularly
**singulto** *m* sob; (path.) hiccup, singultus
**sinhueso** *f* (coll.) tongue
**sinicesis** *f* var. of **sinizesis**
**sínico -ca** *adj* Sinic, Sinitic
**siniestra** *f* see **siniestro**
**siniestrado -da** *adj* ill-fated; *m* victim
**siniestro -tra** *adj* sinister (*on the left; showing ill will; disastrous*); sinistral; (her.) sinister; *m* depravity, perversity; disaster, calamity; *f* left hand, left-hand side
**sinistrorso -sa** *adj* (bot.) sinistrorse
**sinizesis** *f* (gram., biol. & path.) synizesis
**sinnúmero** *m* great amount, great many
**sino** *conj* but, except; **no . . . sino** only; not . . . but; **no . . . sino que** only; **no sólo . . . sino que** not only . . . but, but also; *m* fate, destiny
**sinodal** *adj* synodal
**sinódico -ca** *adj* synodical; (astr.) synodical
**sínodo** *m* synod; (astr. & astrol.) synod
**sinojaponés -nesa** *adj* Sino-Japanese
**sinología** *f* Sinology
**sinológico -ca** *adj* Sinological
**sinólogo -ga** *mf* Sinologist
**sinonimia** *f* synonymy, synonymity; (rhet.) synonymy
**sinónimo -ma** *adj* synonymous; *m* synonym
**sinopsis** *f* (*pl:* **-sis**) synopsis
**sinóptico -ca** *adj* synoptic or synoptical
**sinovia** *f* (anat.) synovia
**sinovial** *adj* synovial
**sinovitis** *f* (path.) synovitis
**sinrazón** *f* wrong, injustice; unreason, want of reason
**sinsabor** *m* displeasure, unpleasantness; anxiety, trouble, worry
**sinsonte** *m* (orn.) mockingbird
**sinsubstancia** *mf* (coll.) trifler, good-for-nothing
**sintáctico -ca** *adj* syntactic or syntactical
**sintaxis** *f* syntax
**síntesis** *f* (*pl:* **-sis**) synthesis
**sintético -ca** *adj* synthetic or synthetical
**sintetizar** §76 *va* to synthesize
**sintoísmo** *m* Shinto, Shintoism
**sintoísta** *adj & mf* Shinto, Shintoist
**síntoma** *m* (med. & fig.) symptom
**sintomático -ca** *adj* symptomatic
**sintonía** *f* (elec.) syntony; (rad.) tuning, tune; (rad.) theme song; **sintonía afilada** (rad.) sharp tuning
**sintónico -ca** *adj* (elec.) syntonic or syntonical
**sintonina** *f* (biochem.) syntonin
**sintonizable** *adj* (rad.) tunable
**sintonización** *f* (rad.) tuning
**sintonizador -dora** *adj* (rad.) tuning; *m* (rad.) tuner
**sintonizar** §76 *va* (rad.) to tune; (rad.) to tune in; *vn* to be in tune, to harmonize
**sinuosidad** *f* sinuosity; hollow
**sinuoso -sa** *adj* sinuous, winding, wavy; evasive
**sinusitis** *f* (path.) sinusitis
**sinusoidal** *adj* sinusoidal
**sinusoide** *f* (math.) sinusoid
**sinvergüencería** *f* (coll.) brazenness, shamelessness
**sinvergüenza** *adj* (coll.) brazen, shameless; *mf* (coll.) scoundrel, rascal, shameless person
**Sión** *f* Zion
**sionista** *adj & mf* Zionist
**sionismo** *m* Zionism
**sipedón** *m* (zool.) seps
**siquiatra** *mf* var. of **psiquiatra**
**siquiatría** *f* var. of **psiquiatría**
**siquiátrico -ca** *adj* var. of **psiquiátrico**
**siquiatro** *m* var. of **psiquiatro**
**síquico -ca** *adj* var. of **psíquico**
**siquiera** *adv* at least; even; *conj* although, even though; **siquiera . . . siquiera** whether . . . or whether
**Siracusa** *f* Syracuse
**siracusano -na** *adj & mf* Syracusan
**sirena** *f* (aut., phys., myth. & fig.) siren; mermaid; **sirena de la playa** bathing beauty; **sirena de niebla** foghorn
**sirenazo** *m* blast of a siren or horn
**sirenio -nia** *adj & m* (zool.) sirenian
**sirga** *f* (naut.) towrope, towline; line for hauling in seines; **a la sirga** in tow from the shore or bank
**sirgar** §59 *va* to tow (*a boat*)
**sirgo** *m* twisted silk; silk fabric
**sirguero** *m* var. of **jilguero**
**Siria** *f* see **sirio**
**siríaco -ca** *adj* Syrian; Syriac; (astr.) Sirian; *mf* Syrian; *m* Syriac (*dialect*)
**siringa** *f* syrinx (*rustic flute; Panpipe*); (bot.) lilac; (bot.) hevea; (Am.) rubber; (Am.) drunk, spree
**siringe** *f* syrinx (*vocal organ of birds*)
**siringomielia** *f* (path.) syringomyelia
**siringotomía** *f* (surg.) syringotomy
**sirio -ria** *adj & mf* Syrian; (*cap.*) *m* (astr.) Sirius; (*cap.*) *f* Syria
**sirirí** *m* (*pl:* **-rís**) (orn.) Couch's kingbird
**sirle** *m* sheep manure, goat manure
**siro -ra** *adj & mf* Syrian
**siroco** *m* sirocco
**sirria** *f* var. of **sirle**
**sirsaca** *f* seersucker
**sirte** *f* rocky shoal; quicksand, syrtis
**sirventés** *m* sirvente (*Provençal moral song*)
**sirvienta** *f* maid, servant girl
**sirviente** *adj* serving; (law) servient; *m* servant; waiter

**sisa** *f* snitching, petty theft; sizing (*for gilding*); (sew.) dart; (archaic) excise
**sisador -dora** *adj* snitching, thieving; *mf* snitcher, petty thief
**sisallo** *m* (bot.) saltwort
**sisar** *va* to snitch, filch; to size (*for gilding*); (sew.) to take in; (archaic) to excise
**sisarcosis** *f* (anat.) syssarcosis
**sisear** *va* to hiss (*an actor, speaker, scene*); *vn* to hiss; to sizzle
**siseo** *m* hiss, hissing; sizzle, sizzling
**sisero** *m* (archaic) excise collector, exciseman
**Sísifo** *m* (myth.) Sisyphus
**sisimbrio** *m* (bot.) sisymbrium, hedge mustard
**sísmico -ca** *adj* seismic
**sismo** *m* seism, earthquake
**sismografía** *f* seismography
**sismográfico -ca** *adj* seismographic or seismographical
**sismógrafo** *m* seismograph
**sismograma** *m* seismogram
**sismología** *f* seismology
**sismológico -ca** *adj* seismologic or seismological
**sismologista** *mf* seismologist
**sismómetro** *m* seismometer
**sisón -sona** *adj* (coll.) thieving; *mf* (coll.) petty thief; *m* (orn.) little bustard
**sistáltico -ca** *adj* systaltic
**sistema** *m* system; **sistema cegesimal** or **sistema centímetro-gramo-segundo** (phys.) centimeter-gram-second system; **sistema de Copérnico** (astr.) Copernican system; **sistema de Tolomeo** (astr.) Ptolemaic system; **sistema mercantil** mercantile system; **sistema métrico** metric system; **sistema nervioso central** (anat. & physiol.) central nervous system; **sistema nervioso simpático** o **del gran simpático** (anat. & physiol.) sympathetic nervous system; **sistema periódico** (chem.) periodic system; **sistema solar** solar system
**sistemático -ca** *adj* systematic or systematical; (anat. & physiol.) systemic; *f* systematics
**sistematización** *f* systematization
**sistematizar** §76 *va* to systematize
**sístilo** *m* (arch.) systyle
**sístole** *f* (gram., biol. & physiol.) systole
**sistólico -ca** *adj* systolic
**sistro** *m* (mus.) sistrum
**sitiador -dora** *adj* besieging; *mf* besieger
**sitial** *m* chair (*seat of honor, dignity, authority, etc.*); seat
**sitibundo -da** *adj* (poet.) thirsty
**sitiar** *va* to surround, hem in; to siege, besiege
**sitio** *m* place, spot, room; location, site; country place; (Am.) cattle ranch; (Am.) taxicab stand; (mil.) siege; **dejar en el sitio** to kill on the spot; **dejar sitio a** to make room for; **levantar el sitio** (mil.) to raise the siege; **poner sitio a** (mil.) to lay siege to; **quedarse en el sitio** to die on the spot
**sito -ta** *adj* situated, located
**sitología** *f* sitology
**situación** *f* situation, position; location; **pedir situación** (aer.) to ask for bearings
**situado** *m* income, fixed income
**situar** §33 *va* to situate, locate, place; to invest, to place (*money*); *vr* to take a position; to settle; (aer.) to get one's bearings
**sixtino -na** *adj* Sistine
**Sixto** *m* Sixtus (*name of several popes*)
**s.l.** abr. of **sin lugar**
**S.l.n.a.** abr. of **sin lugar ni año**
**S.M.** abr. of **Su majestad**
**smoking** *m* (*pl:* **-kings**) tuxedo, dinner coat
**S.n** abr. of **San**
**SO** abr. of **sudoeste**
**so** *prep* under, e.g., **so pena de** under penalty of; *interj* whoa!; (coll.) you . . . !, e.g., **¡so animal!** you beast!
**soasar** *va* to roast lightly, to roast medium
**soba** *f* kneading; massage; beating, slapping
**sobacal** *adj* axillary
**sobaco** *m* (anat.) armpit, armhole; (arch.) spandrel
**sobado -da** *adj* rumpled, worn; (cook.) short; (Am.) terrific; *m* kneading
**sobadura** *f* kneading; massage
**sobajadura** *f* or **sobajamiento** *m* crushing, rumpling
**sobajar** *va* to crush, to rumple
**sobajeo** *m* crushing, rumpling
**sobanda** *f* lower curve of a cask or barrel
**sobaquera** *f* armhole (*in clothes*); shield (*for armpit*)
**sobaquina** *f* sweat under arms
**sobar** *va* to knead; to massage; to beat, to slap; to cuddle, to pet, to paw, to feel; (coll.) to annoy, be fresh to; (Am.) to tire out (*a horse*)
**sobarba** *f* noseband
**sobarbada** *f* sudden check; scolding, dressing-down
**sobarbo** *m* pallet, pawl; bucket, paddle
**sobarcar** §86 *va* to carry under the arm; to draw or slide (*clothing*) up to the armpits
**sobejos** *mpl* leavings
**sobeo** *m* thong to tie yoke to pole
**soberanamente** *adv* royally; extremely
**soberanear** *vn* to domineer, to lord it
**soberanía** *f* sovereignty; rule, sway; haughtiness
**soberano -na** *adj* sovereign; superb; *mf* sovereign; *m* sovereign (*coin*)
**soberbio -bia** *adj* proud, haughty; arrogant, presumptuous; magnificent, superb; fiery; *f* pride, haughtiness; arrogance, presumption; magnificence; frenzy
**soberbioso -sa** *adj* var. of **soberbio**
**sobermejo -ja** *adj* dark-red
**sobina** *f* wooden peg or pin
**sobo** *m* var. of **soba**
**sobón -bona** *adj* (coll.) malingering, work-dodging; (coll.) fresh, mushy, spoony
**sobordo** *m* (naut.) freight list; (naut.) bonus (*paid to crew of freighter in time of war*)
**sobornable** *adj* corrupt, purchasable
**sobornación** *f* bribing, bribery
**sobornado -da** *adj* twisted, out of shape (*said of a loaf of bread*)
**sobornador -dora** *adj* bribing; *mf* briber
**sobornal** *m* overload, extra load
**sobornar** *va* to bribe, to suborn
**soborno** *m* bribery, subornation; **soborno de testigo** (law) subornation of perjury
**sobra** *f* extra, excess, surplus; **sobras** *fpl* leavings, offal, leftovers; rubbish, trash; **de sobra** more than enough; superfluous, unnecessary
**sobradamente** *adv* excessively, too; too well; very well
**sobradar** *va* to build a garret to
**sobradillo** *m* penthouse (*sloping roof over window or door*)
**sobrado -da** *adj* excessive, abundant, more than enough; bold, daring; rich, wealthy; *m* attic, garret; **sobrado** *adv* too
**sobrancero -ra** *adj* unemployed
**sobrante** *adj* leftover, remaining, in excess, surplus; *m* leftover, surplus
**sobrar** *va* to exceed, surpass; *vn* to be more than enough, to be over and above; to be in the way; to be left, to remain
**sobrasada** *f* high-seasoned Majorcan sausage
**sobrasar** *va* to add more fire under (*a pot*)
**sobre** *prep* on, upon, over, above; about; near; after; in addition to; out of, e.g., **en nueve casos sobre diez** in nine out of ten cases; **sobre** + *inf* in addition to + *ger*; *m* envelope; address; **sobre de ventanilla** window envelope; **sobre monedero** coin container or holder (*for mailing coins*); **sobre ventana** window envelope
**sobreabundancia** *f* superabundance
**sobreabundante** *adj* superabundant
**sobreabundar** *vn* to superabound
**sobreaguar** §23 *vn & vr* to float
**sobrealiento** *m* hard breathing
**sobrealimentación** *f* overfeeding; supercharging
**sobrealimentar** *va* to overfeed; to supercharge; *vn* to overfeed
**sobreañadir** *va* to superadd
**sobreañal** *adj* over a year old
**sobrearar** *va* to plow over again
**sobrearco** *m* (arch.) relieving arch
**sobreasada** *f* var. of **sobrasada**
**sobreasar** *va* to roast again

**sobrebarato -ta** *adj* very cheap, extra cheap
**sobrebarrer** *va* to sweep lightly
**sobrebeber** *vn* to have another drink, to drink too much
**sobrecalentamiento** *m* overheating; superheating
**sobrecalentar §18** *va* to overheat; to superheat
**sobrecalza** *f* legging
**sobrecama** *f* bedspread
**sobrecaña** *f* (vet.) bony tumor on a horse's leg
**sobrecarga** *f* overload, extra load; supercharge; packing strap; added annoyance; (philately) surcharge
**sobrecargar §59** *va* to overload, to overburden; to overlay; to overcharge; (sew.) to fell; (philately) to surcharge; (aer.) to pressurize
**sobrecargo** *m* (naut.) supercargo; (Am.) purser; *f* (Am.) air hostess, stewardess
**sobrecaro -ra** *adj* very dear or expensive
**sobrecarta** *f* envelope (*for a letter*); (law) second notice
**sobreceja** *f* forehead right above eyebrows
**sobrecejo** *m* frown; **poner sobrecejo** to frown
**sobrecenar** *va* to have as a second supper; *vn* to have a second supper
**sobreceño** *m* frown
**sobrecerco** *m* (sew.) welt
**sobrecerrado -da** *adj* well closed, extra tight
**sobrecielo** *m* canopy, dais
**sobrecincha** *f* or **sobrecincho** *m* surcingle
**sobreclaustra** *f* or **sobreclaustro** *m* quarters above a cloister
**sobrecoger §49** *va* to surprise, catch; to scare, terrify; *vr* to be surprised; to be scared; **sobrecogerse de** to be seized with
**sobrecogimiento** *m* surprise, apprehension; seizure
**sobrecomida** *f* dessert
**sobrecomprimir** *va* (aer.) to pressurize
**sobrecoser** *va* (Am.) to fell, to whip
**sobrecrecer §34** *vn* to grow too much
**sobrecubierta** *f* extra cover or wrapping; jacket (*of a book*); (naut.) upper deck
**sobrecuello** *m* top collar; stock (*kind of cravat*)
**sobredicho -cha** *adj* above-mentioned
**sobrediente** *m* snaggletooth
**sobredorar** *va* to gold-plate (*especially silver*); to palliate, to extenuate
**sobreedificar §86** *va* to build on or over
**sobreempeine** *m* part of leggings covering instep
**sobreentender §66** *va & vr* var. of **sobrentender**
**sobreestadía** *f* (naut.) extra lay day, demurrage
**sobreexceder** *va* var. of **sobrexceder**
**sobreexcitación** *f* overexcitement
**sobreexcitar** *va* to overexcite; *vr* to become overexcited
**sobreexpondré** *1st sg fut ind of* **sobreexponer**
**sobreexponer §69** *va* to overexpose; (phot.) to overexpose
**sobreexpongo** *1st sg pres ind of* **sobreexponer**
**sobreexposición** *f* overexposure; (phot.) overexposure
**sobreexpuesto -ta** *pp of* **sobreexponer**
**sobreexpuse** *1st sg pret ind of* **sobreexponer**
**sobrefalda** *f* overskirt
**sobrefaz** *f* (*pl:* **-faces**) surface, outside
**sobrefrenada** *f* var. of **sofrenada**
**sobrefusión** *f* supercooling
**sobregirar** *va & vn* (com.) to overdraw
**sobregiro** *m* (com.) overdraft
**sobrehaz** *f* (*pl:* **-haces**) surface, outside; cover; superficial appearance
**sobreherido -da** *adj* slightly hurt or wounded
**sobrehilado -da** *adj* (sew.) overcast; *m* (sew.) overcast, overcasting
**sobrehilar** *va* (sew.) to overcast
**sobrehilo** *m* (sew.) overcast, overcasting
**sobrehombre** *m* superman
**sobrehueso** *m* work, trouble, annoyance; (vet.) splint (*tumor and bone*); (vet.) splint bone
**sobrehumano -na** *adj* superhuman
**sobreintendencia** *f* var. of **superintendencia**
**sobrejalma** *f* woolen blanket to put over a packsaddle
**sobrejuanete** *m* (naut.) royal mast, royal sail
**sobrejunta** *f* splice plate, butt strap
**sobrelecho** *m* (arch.) underside of stone
**sobrellave** *f* double lock
**sobrellenar** *va* to fill to overflowing
**sobrelleno -na** *adj* filled to overflowing
**sobrellevar** *va* to bear, carry; to ease (*the burden of another*); to share (*effort or trouble*); to suffer (*annoyances*) with patience; to overlook, be lenient about (*another's shortcomings*)
**sobremando** *m* (aut.) overdrive
**sobremanera** *adv* exceedingly, beyond measure
**sobremano** *f* (vet.) splint on forehoofs
**sobremantel** *m* center tablecloth
**sobremarcha** *f* (aut.) overdrive
**sobremesa** *f* tablecloth, table cover; sitting at table after eating; **de sobremesa** table, for the table; at table after eating; after-dinner
**sobremesana** *f* (naut.) mizzen topsail
**sobremodo** *adv* var. of **sobremanera**
**sobremodulación** *f* (rad.) overmodulation
**sobremundano -na** *adj* supermundane
**sobrenadante** *adj* supernatant
**sobrenadar** *vn* to float
**sobrenatural** *adj* supernatural
**sobrenaturalismo** *m* supernaturalism
**sobrenaturalizar §76** *va* to make or treat as supernatural, to supernaturalize
**sobrenjalma** *f* var. of **sobrejalma**
**sobrenombrar** *va* to surname; to nickname
**sobrenombre** *m* surname (*epithet*); nickname, agnomen
**sobrentender §66** *va* to understand; *vr* to be understood, be implied
**sobrentrenar** *va & vr* (sport) to overtrain
**sobreorgánico -ca** *adj* superorganic
**sobrepaga** *f* increased pay
**sobrepaño** *m* upper cloth
**sobreparto** *m* confinement after childbirth; indisposition after childbirth
**sobrepasar** *va* to excel, surpass, outdo; to overtake; *vr* to outdo each other; to go too far
**sobrepaso** *m* amble
**sobrepeine** *adv* (coll.) lightly, superficially, half
**sobrepelliz** *f* (*pl:* **-llices**) (eccl.) surplice
**sobrepeso** *m* overweight
**sobrepié** *m* (vet.) splint on rear hoofs
**sobreplán** *m* (naut.) rider
**sobrepondré** *1st sg fut ind of* **sobreponer**
**sobreponer §69** *va* to superpose, put on top; to superimpose; *vr* to control oneself; to triumph over adversity; **sobreponerse a** to win over, to overcome
**sobrepongo** *1st sg pres ind of* **sobreponer**
**sobreprecio** *m* extra charge, surcharge
**sobreproducción** *f* overproduction
**sobrepuerta** *f* cornice over door; door curtain, portière; overdoor, dessus de porte
**sobrepuesto -ta** *pp of* **sobreponer;** *adj* appliqué; *m* appliqué; honeycomb formed on full hive; basket or earthen jar turned upside down over hive; (Am.) patch, mend
**sobrepujamiento** *m* excellence, excelling
**sobrepujanza** *f* great power, might, strength, or vigor
**sobrepujar** *va* to excel, surpass
**sobrepuse** *1st sg pret ind of* **sobreponer**
**sobrequilla** *f* (naut.) keelson
**sobrero -ra** *adj* extra, spare
**sobrerronda** *f* var. of **contrarronda**
**sobrerropa** *f* overcoat
**sobresalario** *m* extra pay
**sobresaldré** *1st sg fut ind of* **sobresalir**
**sobresalgo** *1st sg pres ind of* **sobresalir**
**sobresaliente** *adj* projecting; outstanding, conspicuous, excellent; distinguished (*in an examination*); *mf* substitute; understudy
**sobresalir §81** *vn* to project, jut out; to stand out, excel
**sobresaltar** *va* to assail, to rush upon, to storm; to frighten, to startle; *vn* to stand out clearly; *vr* to be frightened, be startled; to start; **sobresaltarse de, con** or **por** to be frightened or startled at
**sobresalto** *m* fright, scare; start, shock; **de sobresalto** unexpectedly, suddenly

**sobresanar** *vn* to heal on the outside; to try to conceal a defect or shortcoming
**sobresano** *m* (naut.) tabling; *adv* healing on the outside; with affectation, with concealment
**sobresaturación** *f* (chem.) supersaturation
**sobresaturar** *va* to supersaturate
**sobrescribir §17,** 9 *va* to superscribe; to address (*a letter*)
**sobrescrito -ta** *adj* superscript; *pp* of **sobrescribir;** *m* superscription; address
**sobresdrújulo -la** *adj* accented on syllable preceding antepenult
**sobreseer §35** *va* (law) to supersede, to stay; *vn* to desist, yield
**sobreseguro** *adv* without risk
**sobreseimiento** *m* suspension, discontinuance; (law) stay of proceedings, supersedeas
**sobresellar** *va* to put a double seal on; to overprint
**sobresello** *m* double seal; overprint
**sobresembrar §18** *va* to sow over, sow a second time
**sobresolar §77** *va* to resole; to repave, to put a double floor on
**sobrestadía** *f* var. of **sobreestadía**
**sobrestante** *m* foreman, boss
**sobresuela** *f* new sole
**sobresueldo** *m* extra wages, extra pay
**sobresuelo** *m* pavement or floor laid over another
**sobretarde** *f* late afternoon
**sobretendón** *m* (vet.) tumor on tendon of horse's leg
**sobretensión** *f* (elec.) surge
**sobretiro** *m* offprint
**sobretodo** *m* overcoat, topcoat; *adv* especially
**sobreveedor** *m* chief overseer
**sobrevendré** *1st sg fut ind of* **sobrevenir**
**sobrevengo** *1st sg pres ind of* **sobrevenir**
**sobrevenida** *f* sudden and unexpected arrival; supervention
**sobrevenir §92** *vn* to happen, take place; to crop up, to set in, to supervene; **sobrevenir a** to come upon, to overtake
**sobreverter §66** *vr* to overflow, to run over
**sobrevesta** or **sobreveste** *f* overtunic; surcoat (*over armor*)
**sobrevestir §94** *va* to put (*a garment*) over other clothes
**sobrevidriera** *f* window screen; window grill; storm window
**sobrevienta** *f* gust of wind; rage, onslaught; start, surprise, consternation; sudden happening; **a sobrevienta** suddenly, unexpectedly
**sobreviento** *m* gust of wind; **estar** or **ponerse a sobreviento de** (naut.) to have the wind of
**sobrevine** *1st sg pret ind of* **sobrevenir**
**sobreviniendo** *ger of* **sobrevenir**
**sobrevista** *f* beaver (*of helmet*)
**sobreviviente** *adj* surviving; *mf* survivor
**sobrevivir** *vn* to survive; **sobrevivir a** to survive, outlive
**sobrexceder** *va* to exceed, excel, surpass
**sobrexcitación** *f* overexcitement
**sobrexcitar** *va* to overexcite; *vr* to become overexcited
**sobriedad** *f* sobriety, moderation
**sobrina** *f* niece
**sobrinazgo** *m* relationship of nephew or niece; nepotism
**sobrino** *m* nephew
**sobrio -bria** *adj* sober, moderate, temperate
**soca** *f* (agr.) ratoon (*of sugar cane*)
**socaire** *m* (naut.) lee; (naut.) slatch (*slack part of rope*); **al socaire de** (naut.) under the lee of; (coll.) under the shelter of; **estar** or **ponerse al socaire** (coll.) to shirk, to skulk
**socairero** *adj masc* (naut.) malingering, shirking
**socaliña** *f* swindle, swindling
**socaliñar** *va* to swindle (*e.g., money*)
**socaliñero -ra** *adj* swindling; *mf* swindler
**socalzado** *m* underpinning
**socalzar §76** *va* to underpin, to shore up
**socapa** *f* maneuver, subterfuge; **a socapa** clandestinely; cautiously
**socapiscol** *m* var. of **sochantre**
**socarra** *f* singe, scorching; craft, cunning
**socarrar** *va* to singe, scorch
**socarrén** *m* eaves
**socarrena** *f* cavity, hollow; space between two rafters
**socarrina** *f* (coll.) singeing, scorching
**socarrón -rrona** *adj* sly, cunning, crafty
**socarronería** *f* slyness, cunning, craftiness
**socava** *f* undermining; trench around base of plant or tree to hold irrigation water
**socavación** *f* undermining
**socavar** *va* to dig under, to undermine; (fig.) to undermine (*e.g., the health*)
**socavón** *m* cavern; cave-in; (min.) adit, gallery
**socaz** *m* (*pl:* **-caces**) tailrace
**sociabilidad** *f* sociability; sociality (*tendency to form social groups*)
**sociable** *adj* sociable, social; *m* sociable (*carriage*)
**social** *adj* social; (com.) (pertaining to a) company, e.g., **edificio social** company building
**socialismo** *m* socialism; **socialismo del estado** state socialism
**socialista** *adj & mf* socialist
**socialización** *f* socialization
**socializar §76** *va* to socialize
**sociedad** *f* society; company, firm; **buena sociedad** society (*fashionable people*); **hallarse en sociedad** to be in society; **sociedad anónima** (com.) stock company; **sociedad comanditaria** or **en comandita** (com.) commandite (*partnership with one or more silent partners*); **sociedad de cartera** investment trust; **sociedad de control** (com.) holding company; **sociedad de inversión** investment trust; **Sociedad de las Naciones** League of Nations; **sociedad financiera** investment trust; **sociedad limitada** (com.) limited company; **sociedad secreta** secret society
**societario -ria** *adj* labor-union; *mf* member of a labor union
**socio -cia** *mf* partner; companion; member; *m* fellow; (scornful) fellow, guy; **socio capitalista** financial partner; **socio comanditario** (com.) silent partner, sleeping partner; **socio industrial** working partner
**sociología** *f* sociology
**sociológico -ca** *adj* sociological
**sociólogo -ga** *mf* sociologist
**socolar** *va* (Am.) to clear of brush and small trees
**socolor** *m* pretext, subterfuge; **socolor de** under the pretext of
**socollada** *f* flapping (*of sails*); (naut.) pitching
**socoro** *m* (eccl.) place under the choir
**socorredor -dora** *adj* helping, aiding; *mf* helper, aid
**socorrer** *va* to succor, help, aid; to pay on account
**socorrido -da** *adj* helping, ready; well stocked; handy, useful; worn, trite, hackneyed
**socorrista** *mf* first-aider, member of a first-aid association
**socorro** *m* succor, help, aid; payment on account; (mil.) relief; **acudir en socorro de** to come to the aid of, to come to the help of
**socoyote** *m* (Am.) baby (*youngest child*)
**Sócrates** *m* Socrates
**socrático -ca** *adj* Socratic
**socrocio** *m* saffron poultice
**sochantre** *m* (eccl.) subchantor, succentor
**soda** *f* (chem.) soda; soda, soda water
**sódico -ca** *adj* (chem.) (pertaining to) sodium
**sodio** *m* (chem. sodium
**Sodoma** *f* (Bib.) Sodom
**sodomía** *f* sodomy
**sodomita** *mf* Sodomite; sodomite
**soez** *adj* (*pl:* **-eces**) base, vile, mean, crude
**sofá** *m* (*pl:* **-fás**) sofa; **sofá cama** (*pl:* **sofás cama**) day bed
**sofaldar** *va* to tuck up, to truss up; to raise, to uncover
**sofaldo** *m* tucking up, trussing up; raising
**sofí** *m* (*pl:* **-fíes**) var. of **sufí**
**Sofía** *f* Sophia; Sofia (*city*)
**sofión** *m* snort; harsh refusal; blunderbuss
**sofisma** *m* sophism
**sofismo** *m* var. of **sufismo**

**sofista** *adj* sophistic or sophistical; *m* sophist
**sofistería** *f* sophistry
**sofisticación** *f* adulteration; falsification
**sofisticar §86** *va* to adulterate; to falsify
**sofístico -ca** *adj* sophistic or sophistical
**sofito** *m* (arch.) soffit
**soflama** *f* glow, flicker; blush; deceit, cheating; hypocritical look; (coll.) speech
**soflamar** *va* to flimflam; to make blush; *vr* to scorch
**soflamero -ra** *adj* flimflamming, hypocritical; *mf* flimflammer, hypocrite
**sofocación** *f* choking, suffocation; (coll.) great annoyance, disappointment; blushing
**sofocador -dora** or **sofocante** *adj* suffocating, stifling
**sofocar §86** *va* to choke, suffocate, stifle, smother; to extinguish, quench; (coll.) to bother, harass; to make blush; *vr* to choke, suffocate; to get out of breath; to flush; **sofocarse por** to get excited over
**sofocleo -a** *adj* Sophoclean
**Sófocles** *m* Sophocles
**sofoco** *m* blush, embarrassment; **pasar un sofoco** (coll.) to get into an embarrassing situation
**sofocón** *m* (coll.) annoyance, disappointment
**Sofonías** *m* (Bib.) Zephaniah
**sofoquina** *f* (coll.) intense annoyance or disappointment
**sófora** *f* (bot.) Japanese pagoda tree
**sofreír §73 & §17,** 9 *va* to fry lightly
**sofrenada** *f* saccade, sudden checking of a horse; self-control; severe reprimand
**sofrenar** *va* to check (*a horse*) suddenly; to control (*a passion*); to reprimand severely
**sofrito -ta** *pp of* **sofreír**
**soga** *f* rope, cord, halter; (mas.) stretcher; (mas.) face (*of brick or stone*); **dar soga a** (coll.) to make fun of; **hacer soga** (coll.) to lag behind; *m* sly fellow
**soguería** *f* rope-making; rope shop; ropes
**soguero** *m* ropemaker, rope dealer; street porter
**soguilla** *f* small rope; small braid; *m* errand boy
**sois** *2d pl pres ind of* **ser**
**soja** *f* (bot.) soy, soybean
**sojuzgador -dora** *adj* subjugating; *mf* conqueror
**sojuzgar §59** *va* to subjugate, to subdue
**sol** *m* sun; sunlight; sunny side (*e.g., of bull ring*); (fig.) day; (chem. & mus.) sol.; (ichth.) sole (*Symphurus plagiusa*); sol (*Peruvian monetary unit*); **soles** *mpl* (poet.) eyes; **al sol naciente** at sunrise; (coll.) fawning on someone about to attain a position of influence; **al sol puesto** at sunset; (coll.) late, inopportunely; **arrimarse al sol que más calienta** to know on which side one's bread is buttered; **de sol a sol** from sunrise to sunset; **hacer sol** to be sunny; **morir sin sol, sin luz y sin moscas** (coll.) to die without a friend in the world; **no dejar a sol ni a sombra** (coll.) to give no rest to, to not leave in peace; **tomar el sol** to bask in the sun; (naut.) to shoot the sun, to take the sun's altitude; **sol de las Indias** (bot.) sunflower; **sol de medianoche** midnight sun; **sol medio** (astr.) mean sun
**solacear** *va* (archaic) var. of **solazar**
**solada** *f* dregs, sediment
**solado** *m* paving, tiling; pavement
**solador** *m* paver, tiler, tile man
**soladura** *f* paving, tiling; paving material; tiles
**solamente** *adv* only, solely; **solamente que** provided that, with the proviso that
**solana** *f* sunny spot; solarium, sun porch, sunroom
**solanáceo -a** *adj* (bot.) solanaceous
**solanera** *f* sunburn; hot sunny spot; hot sunshine
**solanina** *f* (chem.) solanine
**solano** *m* easterly wind; (dial.) hot stifling wind; (bot.) nightshade
**solapa** *f* lapel; pretext, pretense; flap (*of jacket of book*); (vet.) sinus (*of a small wound*); **de solapa** (coll.) sneakily
**solapado -da** *adj* overlapping; cunning, underhanded, sneaky
**solapadura** *f* (naut.) clincher work (*in the sides of a ship*)
**solapar** *va* to put lapels on; to overlap; to conceal, cover up; *vn* to overlap (*said of part of a garment*)
**solape** *m* lapel
**solapo** *m* lapel; overlapped part or piece; (coll.) chuck under chin; **a solapo** (coll.) sneakily
**solar** *adj* solar, (pertaining to the) sun; ancestral; *m* lot, plot, ground; manor house, ancestral mansion; noble lineage; **§77** *va* to pave, to floor; to sole (*a shoe*)
**solariego -ga** *adj* ancestral; manorial
**solaz** *m* (*pl:* **-laces**) solace, consolation; recreation; **a solaz** with pleasure
**solazar §76** *va* to solace, console; to amuse, divert; *vr* to be solaced or consoled; to amuse oneself, enjoy oneself
**solazo** *m* (coll.) scorching sun or sunshine
**solazoso -sa** *adj* consoling, comforting
**soldada** *f* pay, wages
**soldadesco -ca** *adj* soldier, barrack-room; **a la soldadesca** like a soldier, like soldiers; *f* soldiery; soldiership; undisciplined troops
**soldado** *m* soldier; **soldado de a caballo** cavalryman; **soldado de a pie** infantryman, foot soldier; **soldado de infantería** infantryman; **soldado de marina** marine; **soldado de primera** private first class; **soldado desconocido** unknown soldier; **soldado raso** buck private
**soldador** *m* solderer; welder; soldering iron
**soldadote** *m* gruff old campaigner
**soldadura** *f* solder; soldering; soldered joint; welding; welded joint; **soldadura al arco** arc welding; **soldadura autógena** welding; **soldadura de forja** blacksmith welding; **soldadura eléctrica** electric welding; **soldadura fuerte** hard solder; **soldadura fundente** welding compound; **soldadura oxiacetilénica** oxyacetylene welding; **soldadura por arco** arc welding; **soldadura tierna** soft solder
**soldán** *m* var. of **sultán**
**soldar §77** *va* to solder; to weld; to patch up (*a mistake*); *vr* to knit (*said of bones*)
**soleamiento** *m* sunning, basking in the sun
**solear** *va* to sun; *vr* to sun, to sun oneself
**solecismo** *m* solecism
**soledad** *f* solitude, loneliness; longing, grieving, sorrow; lonely place; mournful Andalusian tune, song, and dance
**soledoso -sa** *adj* solitary, lonely; grieving, sorrowing
**solejar** *m* sunny place
**solemne** *adj* solemn; (coll.) terrible, downright (*e.g., mistake*)
**solemnidad** *f* solemnity; formality
**solemnización** *f* solemnization
**solemnizador -dora** *adj* solemnizing; *mf* solemnizer
**solemnizar §76** *va* to solemnize
**solenoide** *m* (elec.) solenoid
**soleo** *m* gathering of fallen olives
**sóleo** *m* (anat.) soleus
**soler** *m* (naut.) underflooring; **§63** *vn* (used only in pres & imperf ind and with a following inf) to be accustomed to, e.g., **suele venir los lunes** he is accustomed to come on Monday; **suele llover en este tiempo** it generally rains at this time of the year
**solera** *f* crossbeam, entablature; lumber, timber; stone base (*for uprights*); floor (*of oven*); bottom (*of channel*); lower millstone: mother liquor (*of wine*), mother of the wine; blend of sherry; old vintage sherry; (Am.) curb; (Am.) brick, tile; **de solera** or **de rancia solera** of the good old school, of the good old times
**soleraje** *m* vintage wine
**solercia** *f* skill, zeal, shrewdness
**solería** *f* paving or flooring material; sole leather
**solerte** *adj* cunning, crafty, shrewd
**soleta** *f* patch for sole of stocking; (coll.) brazen woman; **tomar soleta** (coll.) to flee, run away, leave
**soletar** or **soletear** *va* to patch the sole of (*a stocking*)
**soletero -ra** *mf* stocking mender

**solevación** *m* rising; upheaval; revolt
**solevamiento** *m* rising; upheaval; (geol.) upthrust
**solevantado -da** *adj* worried, perturbed
**solevantamiento** *m* var. of **solevamiento**
**solevantar** *va* to raise up, to upheave; to rouse, stir up, incite; *vr* to rise up, to upheave; to become aroused, to become stirred up
**solevar** *va* to raise up, to upheave; to excite to rebellion; *vr* to rise up, to upheave; to revolt
**solfa** *f* (mus.) sol-fa; solmization; musical notation; music, harmony; (coll.) flogging; **poner en solfa** to put in a ridiculous light
**solfeador -dora** *mf* (mus.) sol-faer
**solfear** *va* (mus.) to sol-fa; (coll.) to flog, to beat; to criticize severely; *vn* (mus.) to sol-fa
**solfeo** *m* (mus.) sol-faing, solfeggio; (coll.) flogging, beating
**solferino -na** *adj* reddish-purple
**solfista** *mf* (mus.) sol-faist
**solicitación** *f* solicitation; wooing, courting; (phys.) attraction
**solicitador -dora** *adj* soliciting; attracting; *m* solicitor, agent
**solicitante** *mf* petitioner, solicitor; applicant
**solicitar** *va* to solicit, to ask for; to apply for; to seek after; to woo, to court, to attract (*e.g., attention*); to pull, to drive; to attend to; (phys.) to attract
**solícito -ta** *adj* solicitous, careful, diligent; obliging; (coll.) fond, affectionate
**solicitud** *f* solicitude; request, petition; application; **a solicitud** on request; **a solicitud de** at the request of
**solidar** *va* to harden, to make firm or solid; to establish, to prove
**solidariamente** *adj* jointly, conjointly
**solidaridad** *f* solidarity; (law) joint liability
**solidario -ria** *adj* solidary, jointly liable; jointly binding; involved; **solidario con** or **de** integral with
**solidarizar** §76 *va* to make jointly liable; *vr* to become jointly liable; to make common cause
**solideo** *m* (eccl.) calotte, zucchetto
**solidez** *f* solidity; strength, soundness; firmness, constancy; soundness of judgment; (geom.) volume
**solidificación** *f* solidification
**solidificar** §86 *va & vr* to solidify
**sólido -da** *adj* solid; strong; sound; firm; *m* solid
**soliloquiar** *vn* (coll.) to talk to oneself; to soliloquize
**soliloquio** *m* soliloquy
**solimán** *m* (alchem.) corrosive sublimate; (*cap.*) *m* Solyman
**solio** *m* throne with canopy, throne
**solípedo -da** *adj & m* (zool.) soliped
**solipsismo** *m* (philos.) solipsism
**solista** *mf* (mus.) soloist; *adj* (mus.) solo (*e.g., instrument*)
**solitario -ria** *adj* solitary; *mf* solitary, hermit, recluse; *m* solitaire (*game and diamond*); *f* post chaise; tapeworm
**sólito -ta** *adj* customary, accustomed
**soliviadura** *f* lifting; getting up partly
**soliviantar** *va* to rouse, stir up, incite; *vr* to become aroused, to become stirred up
**soliviar** *va* to lift, lift up; *vr* to rise partly, to get up partly
**solivio** *m* lifting; upward pressure; getting up partly
**solivión** *m* hard jerk to throw or pull something off or away
**solo -la** *adj* only, sole; alone; lonely; straight (*e.g., whiskey*); (mus.) solo; **a solas** alone, by oneself (*unaided*); **a mis solas** alone, by myself (*in solitude*); *m* (mus.) solo
**sólo** *adv* only, solely; **con sólo que** provided that
**solomillo** *m* sirloin
**solomo** *m* sirloin; loin of pork
**Solón** *m* Solon; (fig.) Solon
**solsticial** *adj* solstitial
**solsticio** *m* (astr.) solstice; **solsticio de invierno** or **solsticio hiemal** (astr.) winter solstice; **solsticio de verano** or **solsticio vernal** (astr.) summer solstice
**soltadizo -za** *adj* slyly let go of, easily loosened, removable, collapsible
**soltador -dora** *adj* loosening, unfastening; *mf* dropper; **soltador del margen** margin release (*of typewriter*)
**soltar** §77 *va* to untie, unfasten, loosen; to let loose, to let go, to set free; to let go of; (coll.) to let out, let slip (*a remark*); to give (*a kick or slap*); to turn on (*water*); to solve, explain; **soltar la lengua** to blow off steam; *vr* to get loose or free; to come loose, come off; to burst out; to loosen up; to acquire ease; to cast aside restraint, to thaw out, to let oneself go; **soltarse a** + *inf* to start out to + *inf*
**soltera** *f* see **soltero**
**soltería** *f* singleness; bachelorhood; celibacy
**soltero -ra** *adj* single, unmarried; *m* bachelor; *f* spinster; **de soltera** née
**solterón -rona** *adj* (coll.) old and unmarried; *m* (coll.) old bachelor; *f* (coll.) old maid, spinster, maiden lady
**soltura** *f* looseness; ease, agility, freedom; fluency; dissoluteness, licentiousness; release (*of a prisoner*)
**solubilidad** *f* solubility
**soluble** *adj* soluble
**solución** *f* solution; **solución de continuidad** solution of continuity (*break*)
**solucionar** *va* to solve, resolve
**solutivo -va** *adj & m* (med.) laxative
**soluto** *m* (chem.) solute
**solvencia** *f* settlement; solution; solvency; reliability
**solventar** *va* to settle, pay up (*what one owes*); to solve (*a difficulty*)
**solvente** *adj* solvent; reliable; (chem.) solvent; *m* (chem.) solvent
**solver** §63 & §17, 9 *va* (archaic) to solve, to explain; (obs.) to absolve
**sollado** *m* (naut.) orlop
**sollamar** *va* to scorch, to singe
**sollastre** *m* scullion (*servant; contemptible person*)
**sollastría** *f* scullery
**sollo** *m* (ichth.) sturgeon
**sollozar** §76 *vn* to sob
**sollozo** *m* sob
**soma** *f* (biol.) soma; coarse flour
**somalí** *mf* (*pl:* **-líes**) Somali
**Somalía, la** Somaliland
**somanta** *f* (coll.) drubbing, beating
**somatén** *m* (Sp. hist.) body of armed vigilantes for defense and for maintaining order; (coll.) hubbub, uproar; *interj* war cry of ancient Catalans
**somatenista** *m* vigilante (*of a somatén*)
**somático -ca** *adj* somatic
**somatología** *f* somatology
**sombra** *f* shade; shadow; shady side (*e.g., of bull ring*); parasol; darkness; ignorance; ghost, spirit, shade; grace, charm, wit; favor, protection; spot, defect; (fig.) shadow (*appearance*); (coll.) luck; (paint.) umber; **a la sombra** in the shade; (coll.) in jail; **a sombra de tejado** (coll.) stealthily, sneakingly; **hacer sombra** to cast a shadow; **hacer sombra a** to stand in the light of, to outshine; to back, to protect; **ni por sombra** by no means; without any notice; **no ser su sombra** to be but a shadow of one's former self; **no tener sombra de** to not have a bit of; **tener buena sombra** (coll.) to be likeable; to be witty; to bring good luck; **tener mala sombra** (coll.) to be disagreeable, be unpopular; to bring bad luck; **sombras chinescas** (theat.) shadow pantomime, shadow play
**sombraje** *m* sun screen made of branches and twigs
**sombrajo** *m* sun screen made of branches and twigs; (coll.) shadow (*made by getting in someone's light*); **hacer sombrajos** (coll.) to get in the light, to get in someone's light
**sombrar** *va* to shade
**sombrático -ca** or **sombrátil** *adj* shady; obscure, puzzling
**sombreado** *m* (f.a.) shading, hatching
**sombrear** *va* to shade; (f.a.) to shade
**sombrerada** *f* hatful
**sombrerazo** *m* large hat; blow with a hat; (coll.) hurried doffing of hat
**sombrerera** *f* see **sombrerero**

**sombrerería** *f* hat store; millinery shop; hat factory; hat business
**sombrerero -ra** *mf* hatter, hat maker, milliner; *f* hatter's wife; bandbox, hatbox
**sombrerete** *m* little hat; hood, bonnet (*of chimney*); spark catcher (*of locomotive*); cap (*of mushroom*); hubcap
**sombrerillo** *m* little hat; hat (*held out for alms*); cap (*of mushrooms*); (bot.) Venus's-navelwort
**sombrero** *m* hat; canopy (*of pulpit*); privilege of keeping hat on in presence of king; cap (*of mushrooms*); **pasar el sombrero** to pass the hat; **sombrero apuntado** cocked hat; **sombrero calañés** Andalusian hat with turned-up brim and low cone-shaped crown; **sombrero castoreño** beaver hat; **sombrero cordobés** low, wide-brim felt halt; **sombrero de cabrestante** (naut.) drum of the capstan; **sombrero de candil** cocked hat; **sombrero de copa** or **de copa alta** top hat, high hat; **sombrero de jipijapa** Panama hat; **sombrero del patrón** (naut.) hat money, primage; **sombrero de muelles** opera hat; **sombrero de paja** straw hat; **sombrero de pelo** (Am.) high hat; **sombrero de teja** shovel hat; **sombrero de tres picos** three-cornered hat; **sombrero flexible** soft hat; **sombrero gacho** slouch hat; **sombrero hongo** derby hat; **sombrero jarano** (Am.) sombrero; **sombrero panamá** Panama hat
**sombría** *f* see **sombrío**
**sombrilla** *f* parasol, sunshade; **sombrilla de playa** beach umbrella; **sombrilla protectora** (mil.) umbrella
**sombrío -a** *adj* shady; somber; gloomy; (f.a.) shaded; *f* shady place
**sombroso -sa** *adj* shady; shadowy, full of shadows
**somero -ra** *adj* brief, summary; slight; superficial, shallow; on the surface, just above the surface
**someter** *va* to force to yield, to subdue, to subject; to submit (*e.g., an argument; a problem for consideration or solution*); *vr* to yield, submit, surrender
**sometido -da** *adj* submissive, docile, humble
**sometimiento** *m* submission, subjection
**somier** *m* (*pl:* **-mieres**) bedspring, spring mattress
**somnambulismo** *m* var. de **sonambulismo**
**somnámbulo -la** *adj & mf* var. of **sonámbulo**
**somnífero -ra** *adj* somniferous
**somnílocuo -cua** *adj* somniloquous, sleep-talking; *mf* somniloquist, sleep talker
**somnolento -ta** *adj* sleepy, dozy, drowsy, somnolent; lazy
**somnolencia** *f* drowsiness, somnolence
**somontano -na** *adj & mf* Upper Aragonese
**somonte; de somonte** coarse, rough, unpolished
**somorgujador** *m* diver
**somorgujar** *va* to duck, to plunge, to submerge; *vn* to dive; *vr* to duck, to plunge, to submerge; to dive
**somorgujo** *m* (orn.) dabchick, grebe; **a lo somorgujo** or **a somorgujo** under the water; (coll.) secretly, stealthily; **somorgujo castaño** or **menor** (orn.) dabchick (*Podiceps ruficollis*); **somorgujo moñudo** (orn.) crested grebe
**somormujar** *va* var. of **somorgujar**
**somormujo** *m* var. of **somorgujo**
**somos** *1st pl pres ind of* **ser**
**sompesar** *va* to heft, try the weight of
**son** *m* sound, sweet sound; news, rumor; pretext, motive; manner, mode; **¿a qué son?** or **¿a son de qué?** (coll.) for what reason?; **a son de** to the sound of; **bailar a cualquier son** (coll.) to be fickle in one's likes and dislikes; **bailar al son que le tocan** (coll.) to adapt oneself to circumstances; **en son de** in the manner of, by way of, on the score of; **sin son** (coll.) without reason; *3d pl pres ind of* **ser**
**sonable** *adj* loud, noisy; noted, famous
**sonada** *f* see **sonado**
**sonadera** *f* blowing the nose
**sonadero** *m* handkerchief
**sonado -da** *adj* talked-about, bruited about; noted, famous; **hacer una que sea sonada** (coll.) to cause a scandal, to cause a lot of talk; *f* (mus.) sonata
**sonador -dora** *adj* noisemaking; *mf* noisemaker; *m* handkerchief
**sonaja** *f* jingle, metallic disk (*of tambourine*); **sonajas** *fpl* jingle hoop
**sonajero** *m* child's rattle
**sonambulismo** *m* sleepwalking, somnambulism
**sonámbulo -la** *adj* sleepwalking, somnambulistic; *mf* sleepwalker, somnambulist
**sonante** *adj* sonant, sounding, jingling; *f* (phonet.) sonorant, syllabic consonant
**sonar** *m* sonar; **§77** *va* to sound, to ring; to play (*a musical instrument*); to blow (*one's nose*); *vn* to sound, to ring; to be sounded (*said of a vowel, consonant, letter, etc.*); to strike (*said of a clock*); to be mentioned; to be reported or bruited about; to seem; (coll.) to sound familiar; (fig.) to ring, to sound (*a certain way*); **ni suena ni truena** (coll.) cuts no figure; **sonar a** to sound like, to have the appearance of; *vr* to blow one's nose; to be rumored
**sonata** *f* (mus.) sonata
**sonatina** *f* (mus.) sonatina
**sonda** *f* sounding; sounder, plummet, lead; drill; (geol.) annular borer; diamond drill; (surg.) catheter; (surg.) probe; **sonda acústica** sonic depth finder
**sondable** *adj* fathomable
**sondaje** *m* boring, drilling, sounding
**sondaleza** *f* (naut.) lead line, sounding line
**sondar** or **sondear** *va* to sound (*water, subsoil, a person, a person's intentions*); to drill, make borings in; (surg.) to sound, to probe
**sondeo** *m* sounding, probing
**sonecillo** *m* little sound, slight noise; joyous sound, merry tune
**sonería** *f* pealing of bells; set of bells, carillon; striking mechanism (*of clock*)
**sonetear** *vn* to write sonnets, to sonneteer
**sonetico** *m* light sonnet; tapping with the fingers
**sonetillo** *m* short-line sonnet
**sonetista** *mf* sonneteer
**sonetizar** **§76** *vn* to write sonnets, to sonneteer
**soneto** *m* sonnet
**sónico -ca** *adj* sonic
**sonido** *m* sound; report, rumor; literal meaning
**soniquete** *m* little sound, unpleasant sound, tapping, rapping
**sonlocado -da** *adj* mad, wild, reckless, foolish
**sonochada** *f* evening, early part of night; evening watch
**sonochar** *vn* to watch in the early part of the night
**sonómetro** *m* sonometer
**sonora** *f* see **sonoro**
**sonoridad** *f* sonority
**sonorización** *f* recording of sound effects on a film; (phonet.) voicing
**sonorizar** **§76** *va* to record sound effects on (*a film*); (phonet.) to voice; *vr* (phonet.) to voice
**sonoro -ra** *adj* sonorous; clear, loud, resounding; (phonet.) sonant; *f* (phonet.) sonant
**sonoroso -sa** *adj* (poet.) sonorous, resounding
**sonreír** **§73** *vn & vr* to smile
**sonriente** *adj* smiling; *mf* smiling person
**sonrisa** *f* smile
**sonrisueño -ña** *adj & mf* var. of **sonriente**
**sonrodar** **§77** *vr* to stick or get stuck in the mud (*said of wheels*)
**sonrojar** or **sonrojear** *va* to make blush; *vr* to blush
**sonrojo** *m* blush, blushing; word or remark that causes blushing
**sonrosado -da** *adj* rosy
**sonrosar** or **sonrosear** *va* to rose-color; to flush; *vr* to become rose-colored; to flush, to blush
**sonroseo** *m* flush, blush
**sonsaca** *f* pilfering; enticement; wresting, eliciting
**sonsacador -dora** *adj* pilfering; enticing; eliciting; *mf* pilferer; enticer; wheedler; pumper (*of secrets*)
**sonsacamiento** *m* var. of **sonsaca**

**sonsacar** §86 *va* to pilfer; to entice away; to elicit, draw out (*e.g., a secret*); **sonsacar un secreto a alguien** to elicit a secret from someone, to draw a secret out of someone
**sonsaque** *m* var. of **sonsaca**
**sonsonete** *m* rhythmical tapping; dull rumbling; singsong; smirking tone
**sonsoniche** *interj* (slang) hush!, silence!
**soñación** *f* dream; **ni por soñación** (coll.) by no means, far from it
**soñador -dora** *adj* dreamy; *mf* dreamer; (fig.) dreamer
**soñar** §77 *va* to dream; **ni soñarlo** (coll.) not even in dreams; *vn* to dream; to daydream; **soñar con** or **en** to dream of; **soñar con** or **en** + *inf* to dream of + *ger;* **soñar despierto** to daydream
**soñarrera** *f* (coll.) dreaminess; sleepiness; deep sleep
**soñera** *f* sleepiness
**soñolencia** *f* drowsiness, somnolence
**soñoliento -ta** *adj* sleepy, dozy, drowsy, somnolent; lazy; somniferous
**sopa** *f* sop (*food soaked in milk, etc.*); soup; **sopas** *fpl* slices of bread to put in soup; **a la sopa boba** (coll.) at other people's expense; **andar** or **ir a la sopa** to beg from door to door; **hecho una sopa** (coll.) soaked to the skin, sopping wet, drenched; **sopa de pastas** noodle soup; **sopa juliana** julienne
**sopaipa** *f* fritter soaked in honey
**sopalancar** §86 *va* to lift with a lever
**sopalanda** *f* student's gown
**sopanda** *f* brace; joist
**sopapear** *va* (coll.) to chuck under the chin; (coll.) to abuse
**sopapina** *f* (coll.) beating, drubbing
**sopapo** *m* chuck under the chin; (coll.) slap, blow; valve
**sopar** *va* to steep, soak
**sopear** *va* to steep, soak; to trample on; to abuse
**sopeña** *f* cavity under a rock
**sopero -ra** *adj* (pertaining to) soup; *m* soup dish; *f* soup tureen
**sopesar** *va* to heft, try the weight of
**sopetear** *va* to dunk; to abuse
**sopeteo** *m* dunking
**sopetón** *m* slap, box; toast soaked in olive oil; **de sopetón** suddenly
**sopicaldo** *m* thin soup
**sopista** *adj* poverty-stricken; *mf* beggar, object of charity; *m* student making his way on charity
**sopladero** *m* vent, air hole
**soplado -da** *adj* (coll.) overnice; (coll.) conceited, stuck up; *m* blowing; (min.) deep fissure
**soplador -dora** *adj* blowing; *m* blower; ventilator, blowing fan; vent, air hole; (zool.) blower (*whale*); *f* blower
**sopladura** *f* blowing; blowhole, air hole
**soplamocos** *m* (*pl:* **-cos**) (coll.) punch in the nose
**soplar** *va* to blow; to blow away; to blow up, to inflate; to snitch, to swipe; to prompt; to inspire (*a person; verse, poetry*); to whisper (*e.g., an answer to a pupil*); to tip, to tip off; (coll.) to squeal on; (checkers) to huff; *vn* to blow; (zool.) to blow (*said of a whale*); (coll.) to squeal; **¡sopla!** (coll.) gracious me!; *vr* to be puffed up, be conceited; (coll.) to swill, gulp, gobble
**soplete** *m* blowpipe, torch; **soplete oxiacetilénico** oxyacetylene torch; **soplete oxhídrico** oxyhydrogen torch
**soplido** *m* blowing, blast
**soplillo** *m* blowing fan, ventilator; chiffon, silk gauze; light sponge cake
**soplo** *m* blowing, blast; breath; puff, gust of wind; instant, moment; (coll.) tip (*secret information*); (coll.) squealing; (coll.) squealer; **soplo de vida** breath of life
**soplón -plona** *adj* (coll.) tattletale; *mf* (coll.) tattletale, squealer
**soplonear** *va* (coll.) to squeal on
**sopón** *m* (coll.) beggar
**soponcio** *m* swoon, faint, fainting
**sopor** *m* sleepiness, drowsiness; stupor, lethargy
**soporífero -ra** *adj* soporiferous, soporific; *m* soporific
**soporífico -ca** *adj* soporific
**soporoso -sa** *adj* sleepy; soporose
**soportable** *adj* bearable, endurable, supportable
**soportal** *m* porch, portico, arcade
**soportar** *va* to support, bear, hold up; to suffer, endure
**soporte** *m* support, bearing, rest, standard; base, stand; hanger; bracket
**soprano** *mf* soprano (*person*); *m* soprano (*voice*)
**sopuntar** *va* to put dots under (*a letter or word*)
**Sor.** abr. of **Señor**
**sor** *f* (used before names of nuns) sister
**sorber** *va* to sip, to suck; to absorb, to soak up, to swallow up; **sorber los vientos por** (coll.) to be crazy about; *vr* to overcome, get the best of
**sorbete** *m* sherbet, water ice
**sorbetera** *f* ice-cream freezer; (Am.) high hat
**sorbetón** *m* (coll.) gulp, big gulp of liquor
**sorbible** *adj* to be sipped, that can be sipped; absorbable
**sorbo** *m* sip; sipping; swallow, gulp; sniff
**Sorbona** *f* Sorbonne
**sorda** *f* see **sordo**
**sordera** *f* deafness
**sordez** *f* (phonet.) voicelessness
**sordidez** *f* sordidness
**sórdido -da** *adj* sordid
**sordina** *f* (mus.) damper; (mus.) mute; silencer; **a la sordina** silently, on the quiet
**sordino** *m* (mus.) fiddle
**sordo -da** *adj* deaf; silent, mute; muffled, dull; dull (*noise; pain*); veiled (*e.g., hostility*); deaf, indifferent; (math. & phonet.) surd; **a la sorda, a lo sordo** or **a sordas** silently, noiselessly; **sordo como una tapia** (coll.) stone-deaf, deaf as a post; *mf* deaf person; **hacerse el sordo** to pretend to be deaf; to turn a deaf ear; *f* (orn.) snipe; (naut.) hawser used for launching; (phonet.) surd
**sordomudez** *f* deaf-dumbness, deaf-muteness
**sordomudo -da** *adj* deaf and dumb, deaf-mute; *mf* deaf-mute
**sorgo** *m* (bot.) sorghum; **sorgo del Sudán** (bot.) Sudan grass
**soríasis** *f* (path.) psoriasis
**sorna** *f* slowness; sluggishness; cunning
**soro** *m* (bot.) sorus
**sorochar** *vr* (Am.) to become mountain-sick
**soroche** *m* (Am.) soroche, mountain sickness; (Am.) flush (*caused by heat, shame, etc.*); (Am.) silver-bearing lead sulfide
**sóror** *f* (eccl.) sister
**sorosis** *f* (bot.) sorosis
**sorprendente** *adj* surprising; unusual, extraordinary
**sorprender** *va* to surprise; to catch; to discover (*a secret*); **sorprender en el hecho** to catch in the act; *vr* to be surprised
**sorpresa** *f* surprise; surprise package; **coger** or **tomar de sorpresa** to take by surprise
**sorpresivamente** *adv* unexpectedly, by surprise
**sorpresivo -va** *adj* unexpected, sudden, surprising
**sorra** *f* ballast of coarse gravel; half belly of tunny
**sorregar** §29 *va* to irrigate by overflow from a higher ditch
**sorriego** *m* irrigation by overflow from a higher ditch; overflow water
**sorrostrada** *f* insolence, bluntness; **dar sorrostrada a** to insult, upbraid
**sorrostrar** *va* to insult, upbraid
**sorteamiento** *m* var. of **sorteo**
**sortear** *va* to draw or cast lots for; to choose by lot; to dodge, to evade; to duck through (*traffic*); (taur.) to choose by lot (*the bull one is to fight*); (taur.) to make passes at (*a bull*); *vn* to draw or cast lots
**sorteo** *m* drawing, casting of lots; choosing by lot; dodging, evasion; (taur.) workout, performance
**sortero -ra** *mf* soothsayer, fortuneteller
**sortiaria** *f* fortunetelling by cards
**sortija** *f* ring; curl; hoop; **sortija de sello** signet ring; **sortija solitario** solitaire (*ring*)
**sortijilla** *f* ringlet; curl
**sortijuela** *f* ringlet

**sortilegio** *m* sorcery, witchery, sortilege
**sortílego -ga** *mf* fortuneteller; *m* sorcerer; *f* sorceress
**S O S** *m* (rad.) S O S (*signal of distress*)
**sosa** *f* see **soso**
**sosaina** *adj* dull, colorless (*person*)
**sosal** *m* or **sosar** *m* field of glasswort, field of kelp
**sosegado -da** *adj* calm, quiet, peaceful
**sosegador -dora** *adj* calming, quieting; *mf* quieter, appeaser
**sosegar** §29 *va* to calm, to quiet, to allay; *vn* to become calm, to rest; *vr* to calm down, to quiet down; to become calm, to rest
**sosera** *f* see **sosero**
**sosería** *f* insipidity, tastelessness; dullness, inanity, nonsense
**sosero -ra** *adj* (bot.) soda-yielding; *f* insipidity, tastelessness; dullness, inanity, nonsense
**sosia** *m* double (*counterpart of another person*)
**sosiega** *f* rest from work; drink when resting; nightcap
**sosiego** *m* calm, quiet, serenity
**soslayar** *va* to place obliquely; to duck (*a question*); to evade (*an evil*)
**soslayo -ya** *adj* oblique, slanting; **al soslayo** or **de soslayo** obliquely, slantingly; at a slant; askance; **mirada de soslayo** side glance; **pegar de soslayo** to glance against, to hit on the slant
**soso -sa** *adj* insipid, tasteless; dull, inane; *f* (bot.) glasswort; soda ash; (chem.) soda; **sosa cáustica** (chem.) caustic soda
**sosobre** *m* or **sosobrejuanete** *m* (naut.) skysail, skysail pole
**sospecha** *f* suspicion
**sospechable** *adj* suspicious; suspect
**sospechar** *va* to suspect; *vn* to suspect, be suspicious; **sospechar de** to suspect, distrust
**sospechoso -sa** *adj* suspicious; suspect; *m* suspect
**sospesar** *va* to heft, try the weight of
**sosquín** *m* side blow; sneak blow or punch
**sostén** *m* support (*person or thing*); brassière; steadiness (*of ship*); *2d sg impv of* **sostener**
**sostendré** *1st sg fut ind of* **sostener**
**sostenedor -dora** *adj* supporting, sustaining; *mf* supporter, sustainer
**sostener** §85 *va* to support, hold up; to sustain; to maintain; to back, uphold; to bear, stand
**sostengo** *1st sg pres ind of* **sostener**
**sostenido -da** *adj & m* (mus.) sharp; **doble sostenido** (mus.) double sharp
**sostenimiento** *m* support, sustenance, maintenance
**sostuve** *1st sg pret ind of* **sostener**
**sota** *f* jack (*in cards*); jade, hussy; *m* (Am.) boss, foreman
**sotabanco** *m* attic, garret; (arch.) impost, springer, skewback
**sotabarba** *f* fringe of whiskers (*around chin from ear to ear*)
**sotacola** *f* crupper
**sotacoro** *m* var. of **socoro**
**sotalugo** *m* second hoop (*of cask or barrel*)
**sotaministro** *m* var. of **sotoministro**
**sotana** *f* soutane, cassock; (coll.) beating, drubbing
**sotanear** *va* (coll.) to beat, to drub, to reprimand harshly
**sotaní** *m* (*pl:* **-níes**) short skirt without folds
**sótano** *m* basement, cellar
**sotaventar** or **sotaventear** *vr* (naut.) to fall to leeward
**sotavento** *m* (naut.) leeward; **a sotavento** (naut.) alee, to leeward
**sotechado** *m* shed
**soteño -ña** *adj* growing in groves
**soteriología** *f* (theol.) soteriology
**soterramiento** *m* burial, inhumation
**soterraño -ña** *adj* underground, subterranean
**soterrar** §18 to bury, inhume; to hide away
**sotileza** *f* (prov.) leader (*transparent fiber of fishline*); (archaic) subtlety
**soto** *m* grove; thicket, brush
**sotoministro** *m* (eccl.) steward
**sotreta** *m* (Am.) nag
**sotrozo** *m* (mach.) key; (arti.) linchpin, axle pin; (naut.) foothook staff
**sotuer** *m* (her.) saltier
**soviet** *m* (*pl:* **-viets**) soviet
**soviético -ca** *adj* soviet, sovietic
**sovietismo** *m* sovietism
**sovietización** *f* sovietization
**sovietizar** §76 *va* to sovietize
**sovoz; a sovoz** sotto voce, in a low tone
**soy** *1st sg pres ind of* **ser**
**soya** *f* var. of **soja**
**spre.** abr. of **siempre**
**S.r** or **Sr.** abr. of **Señor**
**Sra.** abr. of **Señora**
**Sría.** abr. of **secretaría**
**Sr.ta** or **Srta.** abr. of **Señorita**
**S.S.** abr. of **Su Santidad**
**S.S.a** abr. of **Su Señoría**
**SS.mo** abr. of **Santísimo**
**SS.no** abr. of **escribano**
**S.S.S.** abr. of **su seguro servidor**
**ss. ss.** abr. of **seguros servidores**
**S.S.S. y Capellán** (coll.) formula written by priests at the end of a letter
**Sta.** abr. of **Santa**
**stajanovismo** *m* Stakhanovism
**stajanovista** *adj & mf* Stakhanovite
**Stalingrado** *f* Stalingrad
**stalinismo** *m* Stalinism
**stalinista** *adj & mf* Stalinist
**Sto.** abr. of **Santo**
**stuka** *m* Stuka (*German dive bomber*)
**su** *adj poss* his, her, its, their, your, one's
**Suabia** *f* Swabia
**suabo -ba** *adj & mf* Swabian
**suarda** *f* stain, spot; suint (*grease of wool*)
**suasorio -ria** *adj* suasive, persuasive
**suave** *adj* suave, smooth; mild, meek; gentle; (phonet.) smooth (*breathing*)
**suavidad** *f* suavity, smoothness; mildness, meekness
**suavizador -dora** *adj* smoothing, softening, mollifying; *m* razor strop
**suavizar** §76 to smooth, to ease, to sweeten, to soften, to mollify; to strop (*a razor*)
**subacetato** *m* (chem.) subacetate
**subácido -da** *adj* (chem.) subacid
**subacuático -ca** *adj* underwater, subaquatic
**subácueo -a** *adj* subaqueous
**subafluente** *m* tributary
**subagente** *m* subagent
**subalcaide** *m* deputy warden
**subalimentación** *f* undernourishment
**subalquilar** *va* var. of **subarrendar**
**subalternar** *va* to subdue, to subject
**subalterno -na** *adj & mf* subaltern, subordinate
**subálveo -a** *adj* located under the river bed; *m* place under river bed
**subantártico -ca** *adj* subantarctic
**subarrendador -dora** *mf* subletter
**subarrendar** §18 *va* to sublease; to sublet
**subarrendatario -ria** *mf* sublessor; sublessee
**subarriendo** *m* sublease
**subártico -ca** *adj* subarctic
**subasta** *f* auction, auction sale; bidding; **sacar a pública subasta** to sell at auction
**subastar** *va* to auction, sell at auction, auction off; to bid
**subatómico -ca** *adj* subatomic
**subátomo** *m* (chem. & phys.) subatom
**subcampeón -ona** *mf* (sport) runner-up
**subcentral** *f* (elec.) substation
**subclase** *f* (biol.) subclass
**subclavio -via** *adj* (anat.) subclavian
**subcolector** *m* subcollector, assistant collector
**subcomendador** *m* deputy commander (*of a military order*)
**subcomisión** *f* subcommission, subcommittee
**subconsciencia** *f* subconscious, subconsciousness
**subconsciente** *adj* subconscious
**subcontinente** *m* subcontinent
**subcontratar** *va & vn* to subcontract
**subcontratista** *mf* subcontractor
**subcontrato** *m* subcontract
**subcostal** *adj* (anat. & zool.) subcostal
**subcrítico -ca** *adj* subcritical
**subcutáneo -a** *adj* subcutaneous
**subdecano** *m* subdean
**subdelirio** *m* (path.) subdelirium

**subdesarrollado -da** *adj* underdeveloped
**subdiaconato** *m* subdeaconry
**subdiácono** *m* subdeacon
**subdirector -tora** *mf* subhead, subdirector
**súbdito -ta** *adj & mf* subject
**subdividir** *va & vr* to subdivide
**subdivisión** *f* subdivision
**subdominante** *f* (mus.) subdominant
**subduplo -pla** *adj* (math.) subdouble
**subentender** **§66** *va* to understand; *vr* be understood, be implied
**subeo** *m* var. of **sobeo**
**suberina** *f* (biochem.) suberin
**suberoso -sa** *adj* subereous
**subespecie** *f* (biol.) subspecies
**subestación** *f* (elec.) substation
**subestimar** *va* to underestimate
**subestructura** *f* substructure: (rail.) roadbed
**subexposición** *f* (phot.) underexposure
**subfamilia** *f* subfamily
**subfluvial** *adj* underriver
**subfusil** *m* submachine gun; **subfusil ametrallador** submachine gun
**subgénero** *m* (biol.) subgenus
**subgobernador** *m* lieutenant governor
**subgrupo** *m* subgroup
**subida** *f* see **subido**
**subidero -ra** *adj* climbing, for climbing; *m* way up, way to go up
**subido -da** *adj* high, fine, superior; strong, intense; bright (*color*); high, high-priced; **subido de color** off-color; *f* rise; ascent, acclivity; accession (*e.g., to the throne*)
**subidor** *m* porter; elevator, lift
**subilla** *f* awl
**subimiento** *m* rise
**subíndice** *m* subindex
**subinquilino -na** *mf* subtenant
**subinspección** *f* subinspection
**subinspector** *m* subinspector
**subintración** *f* underlapping (*of bone*); overlapping (*of fever*)
**subintrar** *vn* to come in later; to underlap (*said of a fractured bone*); to overlap (*said of onsets of fever*)
**subir** *va* to raise; to lift, to lift up; to carry up; to go up (*the stairs, a slope*); to swell, increase; (mus.) to raise the pitch of; *vn* to go up, to come up; to rise; to swell, increase; to get worse; to spread; (mus.) to rise (*said of pitch*); **subir a** + *inf* to go or come up to + *inf*; **subir a** to climb (*e.g., a tree*); **subir a** or **en** to climb to; to get in or into, to climb into; to get on, to mount; *vr* to rise; **subírsele a uno a la cabeza** to go to one's head (*said, e.g., of wine*); **subirse a** or **en** to get into
**subitáneo -a** *adj* sudden, unexpected
**súbito -ta** *adj* sudden, unexpected; hasty, impetuous; hurried; **súbito** *adv* suddenly; **de súbito** suddenly
**subjefe** *m* assistant to the chief, subhead
**subjetividad** *f* subjectivity
**subjetivismo** *m* (philos.) subjectivism
**subjetivo -va** *adj* subjective
**subjuntivo -va** *adj & m* (gram.) subjunctive
**sublevación** *f* uprising, revolt
**sublevado** *m* rebel, insurrectionist
**sublevamiento** *m* var. of **sublevación**
**sublevar** *va* to incite to rebellion; to stir up the ire of; *vr* to revolt
**sublimación** *f* sublimation
**sublimado -da** *adj* sublimated; exalted; *m* (chem.) sublimate
**sublimar** *va* to sublimate; to sublime, exalt, elevate; *vr* to be sublimated; to be sublimed, be exalted, be elevated
**sublime** *adj* sublime; **lo sublime** the sublime
**sublimidad** *f* sublimity
**subliminar** *adj & f* (psychol.) subliminal
**sublingual** *adj* (anat.) sublingual
**sublunar** *adj* sublunar or sublunary
**submarginal** *adj* submarginal
**submarinista** *mf* skin diver
**submarino -na** *adj* submarine; underwater; *m* submarine
**submaxilar** *adj* submaxillary
**submersión** *f* var. of **sumersión**
**submicroscópico -ca** *adj* submicroscopic
**submúltiplo -pla** *adj & m* (math.) submultiple
**subnormal** *adj* subnormal; *f* (geom.) subnormal
**subnota** *f* footnote to a footnote
**suboficial** *m* sergeant major; noncommissioned officer
**suborbital** *adj* suborbital
**suborden** *m* suborder
**subordinación** *f* subordination
**subordinado -da** *adj* subordinate; (gram.) subordinate, subordinating; *mf* subordinate
**subordinante** *adj* (gram.) subordinating, subordinate
**subordinar** *va* to subordinate; *vr* to be subordinated
**subprefecto** *m* subprefect
**subprefectura** *f* subprefecture
**subproducto** *m* by-product
**subrayar** *va* to underline; to emphasize
**subreino** *m* (biol.) subkingdom
**subrepción** *f* underhandedness, subreption
**subrepticio -cia** *adj* surreptitious
**subrogación** *f* substitution; (law) subrogation
**subrogar** **§59** *va* to subrogate; **subrogar con** or **por** to replace with
**subsanable** *adj* excusable; reparable
**subsanación** *f* excusal, excusing; reparation
**subsanar** *va* to excuse, overlook; to correct, repair
**subsatélite** *m* subsatellite
**subscapular** *adj* (anat.) subscapular
**subscribir** **§17**, 9 *va* to subscribe; to subscribe to, to endorse; to subscribe to or for (*e.g., bonds*); to sign; **subscribir a uno a** to enter or enroll someone for a subscription to; *vr* to subscribe; **subscribirse a** to subscribe to or for (*e.g., a journal*)
**subscripción** *f* subscription
**subscriptor -tora** *mf* subscriber
**subscrito -ta** *pp de* **subscribir**
**subscritor -tora** *mf* subscriber
**subsecretaría** *f* undersecretaryship
**subsecretario** *m* undersecretary
**subsecuente** *adj* subsequent
**subseguir** **§82** *vn & vr* to follow next; **subseguir de** to follow from
**subsidiar** *va* to subsidize
**subsidiario -ria** *adj* subsidiary; (law) ancillary
**subsidio** *m* subsidy; aid, help; **subsidio de vejez** old-age pension; **subsidio por desempleo** or **subsidios de paro** unemployment compensation
**subsiguiente** *adj* subsequent, succeeding
**subsistencia** *f* subsistence, sustenance; (philos.) subsistence
**subsistente** *adj* subsistent; persistent, lasting
**subsistir** *vn* to subsist
**subsolano** *m* east wind
**subsónico -ca** *adj* subsonic
**substancia** *f* substance; **en substancia** in substance; **substancia gris** (anat.) gray matter
**substanciación** *f* abridgment, abstraction; (law) trial
**substancial** *adj* substantial; important; nourishing
**substancialidad** *f* substantiality
**substanciar** *va* to abridge, abstract; (law) to try
**substancioso -sa** *adj* substantial; nourishing; tasty
**substantífico -ca** *adj* substantial
**substantivar** *va* (gram.) substantivize; *vr* (gram.) to become substantivized, to be used as a noun
**substantivo -va** *adj* substantive; (gram.) substantive; *m* (gram.) substantive
**substitución** *f* replacement; (alg., chem. & law) substitution
**substituíble** *adj* replaceable
**substituidor -dora** *adj* substitute, substitutional; *mf* substitute
**substituir** **§41** *va* to replace, e.g., **substituimos la mantequilla con** or **por la margarina** we replaced butter with margarine; to substitute for, take the place of, e.g., **Juan substituyó a Pedro** John substituted for Peter, John took the place of Peter; **la margarina substituyó a la mantequilla** margarine took the place of butter; *vn* to take someone's or something's place; *vr* to be replaced; to relieve each other

**substitutivo -va** *adj* substitutive; substitute; *m* substitute (*thing*); **desconfíe de substitutivos** beware of substitutes
**substituto -ta** *mf* substitute
**substracción** *f* removal, withdrawal; theft; subtraction
**substraendo** *m* (math.) subtrahend
**substraer §88** *va* to remove, to deduct; to rob, to steal; to subtract; **substraer a** to take away from; to rob from, to steal from; *vr* to withdraw; **substraerse a** to evade, to avoid, to slip away from
**substraigo** *1st sg pres ind of* **substraer**
**substraje** *1st sg pret ind of* **substraer**
**substrato** *m* substratum; (biochem.) substrate
**subsuelo** *m* subsoil
**subsumir** *va* to subsume
**subsumpción** *f* subsumption
**subtender §66** *va* (geom. & bot.) to subtend
**subtenencia** *f* second lieutenancy
**subteniente** *m* second lieutenant
**subtensa** *f* (geom.) line subtending, subtense
**subterfugio** *m* subterfuge
**subterráneo -a** *adj* subterranean, underground; *m* subterranean (*place*)
**subtitular** *va* to subtitle
**subtítulo** *m* subtitle, subhead
**subtropical** *adj* subtropical
**subtrópicos** *mpl* subtropics
**suburbano -na** *adj* outlying, adjacent (*to a city*); suburban; *mf* suburbanite
**suburbio** *m* suburb; outlying slum
**subvención** *f* subvention, subsidy
**subvencionar** *va* to subsidize
**subvendré** *1st sg fut ind of* **subvenir**
**subvengo** *1st sg pres ind of* **subvenir**
**subvenir §92** *vn* to provide; **subvenir a** to provide for (*e.g., a person's needs*); to meet, defray (*expenses*)
**subversión** *f* subversion
**subversivo -va** *adj* subversive
**subversor -sora** *adj* subversive; *mf* subverter; subversive
**subvertir §62** *va* to subvert
**subvine** *1st sg pret ind of* **subvenir**
**subviniendo** *ger of* **subvenir**
**subyacente** *adj* subjacent, underlying
**subyugación** *f* subjugation
**subyugador -dora** *adj* subjugating; *mf* subjugator
**subyugar §59** *va* to subjugate
**succínico -ca** *adj* succinic
**succino** *m* amber
**succión** *f* sucking; suction
**succionador** *m* suction cup
**succionar** *va* to suck, to suck in
**sucedáneo -a** *adj & m* substitute
**suceder** *va* to succeed, follow, be the successor of; *vn* to happen; **suceder a** to succeed to (*e.g., a throne*); **suceder con** to happen to; *vr* to follow one another, to follow one after the other
**sucedido** *m* (coll.) happening, event
**sucesión** *f* succession; issue, offspring; estate
**sucesivamente** *adv* successively; **y así sucesivamente** and so on
**sucesivo -va** *adj* successive; **en lo sucesivo** in the future
**suceso** *m* event, happening; issue, outcome; course, lapse; **sucesos de actualidad** current events
**sucesor -sora** *adj* succeeding; *mf* successor; heir
**suciedad** *f* dirt, filth; dirtiness, filthiness, filthy remark
**sucintar** *vr* to be precise, be brief
**sucinto -ta** *adj* succinct
**sucio -cia** *adj* dirty, filthy; low, base; tainted; blurred; (naut.) foul (*because of hidden rocks*); (sport) foul (*blow*); **sucio** *adv* (sport) foully, unfairly
**sucísimo -ma** *adj super* very or most dirty or filthy
**suco** *m* (archaic) juice; (Am.) muddy ground
**sucoso -sa** *adj* (archaic) juicy
**sucre** *m* sucre (*monetary unit of Ecuador*)
**suctorio -ria** *adj* suctorial
**súcubo** *adj masc* succubine; *m* succubus
**sucucho** *m* corner, nook
**súcula** *f* windlass, winch
**suculencia** *f* succulence or succulency
**suculento -ta** *adj* succulent
**sucumbir** *vn* to succumb; (law) to lose
**sucursal** *adj* branch; *f* branch, branch office
**sucusión** *f* succussation or succussion
**sudadero** *m* saddlecloth, saddle blanket; sweating room, sudatorium; handkerchief, sweat cloth; moist ground
**Sudáfrica** *f* South Africa
**sudafricano -na** *adj & mf* South African
**Sudamérica** *f* South America
**sudamericano -na** *adj & mf* South American
**Sudán** *m* Sudan; **Sudán Angloegipcio** Anglo-Egyptian Sudan
**sudanés -nesa** *adj & mf* Sudanese
**sudante** *adj* sweating; *mf* sweater (*person*)
**sudar** *va* to sweat; (coll.) to cough up; *vn* to sweat; (coll.) to sweat (*to work hard*)
**sudario** *m* shroud, winding sheet; (archaic) handkerchief, sweat cloth; (archaic) sweating room
**sudatorio -ria** *adj* sudatory; *m* (hist.) sudatorium
**sudcoreano -na** *adj & mf* South Korean
**sudeño -ña** *adj* southern
**sudestada** *f* southeaster
**sudestal** *adj* southeast; southeasterly
**sudeste** *m* southeast; southeaster (*wind*); **el Sudeste Asiático** or **de Asia** Southeast Asia; *adj* southeast; southeastern
**sudetas** *mfpl* Sudeten (*people*)
**sudetes** *mfpl* Sudeten (*people*); *mpl* Sudeten (*mountains*); **región de los Sudetes** Sudetenland
**sudista** *m* Southerner (*in U.S. Civil War*)
**sudoccidental** *adj* southwest
**sudoeste** *m* southwest; southwest wind
**sudor** *m* sweat; (fig.) sweat, toil; **sudores** (med.) sweat treatment; **chorrear de sudor** to swelter; **sudor frío** cold sweat
**sudoriento -ta** *adj* sweaty
**sudorífero -ra** *adj* sudoriferous
**sudorífico -ca** *adj & m* sudorific
**sudoríparo -ra** *adj* (anat.) sudoriparous
**sudoroso -sa** *adj* sweating, sweaty
**sudoso -sa** *adj* sweaty
**sudsudeste** *m* south-southeast
**sudsudoeste** *m* south-southwest
**sudueste** *m* var. of **sudoeste**
**Suecia** *f* Sweden; (*l.c.*) *f* suede (*leather*)
**sueco -ca** *adj* Swedish; *mf* Swede; **hacerse el sueco** (coll.) to pretend to not understand; *m* Swedish (*language*)
**suegra** *f* mother-in-law; hard crust (*of bread*)
**suegro** *m* father-in-law
**suela** *f* sole; sole leather; (ichth.) sole (*Solea vulgaris & Symphurus plagiusa*); leather tip (*of billiard cue*); horizontal beam; **suelas** *fpl* sandals; **de tres, de cuatro** or **de siete suelas** (coll.) downright; **media suela** half sole; **no llegarle a uno a la suela del zapato** (coll.) to not be able to hold a candle to someone
**suelda** *f* var. of **consuelda**
**sueldaconsuelda** *m* (bot.) snowberry (*Chiococca alba*)
**sueldacostilla** *f* (bot.) grape hyacinth
**sueldo** *m* salary, pay
**suelo** *m* ground, soil, land; floor, flooring; pavement; bottom; hoof; dregs; end; **arrastrarse por el suelo** (coll.) to crawl, to cringe; **dar consigo en el suelo** to fall down; **echar por los suelos** to ruin; **echarse por los suelos** to be excessively obsequious; **faltarle a uno el suelo** to trip, to fall; **medir el suelo** to stretch out on the ground or on the floor; (coll.) to fall flat on the ground; **no pisar en el suelo** to walk in the clouds, to walk on air; **por el suelo** or **por los suelos** cast off, cast aside; **sin suelo** unlimited; brazenly; **sobre suelo firme** on terra firma; **venir** or **venirse al suelo** to fall to the ground, to collapse, to topple; to fail; **suelo franco** loam; **suelo natal** home country
**suelto -ta** *adj* loose; free, easy; swift, agile, nimble; fluent, voluble; bold, daring; single (*copy*); blank (*verse*); odd, separate; spare; bulk; **suelto de lengua** loose-tongued; **suelto de manos** ready-fisted; *pp of* **solver;** *m*

small change; news item; *f* release; fetters (*for grazing animals*); relay (*of oxen*); **dar suelta a** to set loose; to give a recess to
**sueñecillo** *m* nap; **descabezar un sueñecillo** to take a nap
**sueño** *m* sleep, sleepiness; dream, fancy; (fig.) dream (*something beautiful*); **caerse de sueño** to be overcome with sleep; **conciliar el sueño** to manage to go to sleep; **descabezar el sueño** to doze off; **desperezar el sueño** to shake off sleep by stretching; **echar un sueño** to take a nap; **en sueños** or **entre sueños** dreaming, while dreaming; **espantar el sueño** to scare away or drive away sleep; **ni por sueños** by no means; **no dormir sueño** to not sleep a wink; **tener sueño** to be sleepy; **último sueño** last sleep (*death*); **sueño hecho realidad** dream come true; **sueños dorados** daydreams
**suero** *m* (biol. & med.) serum; **suero de la leche** serum, whey; **suero terapéutico** serum, antitoxic serum
**sueroso -sa** *adj* var. of **seroso**
**sueroterapia** *f* var. of **seroterapia**
**suerte** *f* luck, fortune, chance; piece of luck; fate, lot; augury; kind, sort; way; trick, feat; grade, quality; (print.) sort; (box.) round; (taur.) play, suerte; (Am.) lottery ticket; **buena suerte** good luck; **de esta suerte** in this way; **de suerte que** so that, with the result that; and so; **echar suertes** to draw lots, to cast lots; **mala suerte** bad luck; **por suerte** by lots; by chance; luckily; **sacar a la suerte** to draw by lots; **tener buena suerte** to be lucky; **tocarle a uno en suerte** to fall to one's lot; **suerte de banderillear** (taur.) planting darts; **suerte de matar** (taur.) death thrust; **suerte de picar** (taur.) lancing the bull
**suertero -ra** *adj* (Am.) fortunate, lucky; *mf* (Am.) vendor of lottery tickets
**sueste** *m* southwester or sou'wester (*waterproof hat*)
**suéter** *m* (*pl:* **-ters**) sweater
**Suetonio** *m* Suetonius
**suévico -ca** *adj* Suevian
**suevo -va** *adj & mf* Suevian
**sufí** *m* (*pl:* **-fíes**) Sufi
**suficiencia** *f* sufficiency; fitness, competency; adequacy; **a suficiencia** sufficiently
**suficiente** *adj* sufficient; fit, competent; adequate
**sufijo -ja** *adj* (gram.) suffixed; *m* (gram.) suffix
**sufismo** *m* Sufism
**sufra** *f* ridgeband
**sufragación** *f* defrayal or defrayment
**sufragáneo -a** *adj* suffragan
**sufragar §59** *va* to help, support, favor; to defray; *vn* (Am.) to vote
**sufragio** *m* suffrage; help, succor; (eccl.) suffrage; **en sufragio de** for the benefit of
**sufragismo** *m* woman suffrage
**sufragista** *mf* suffragist; woman-suffragist; *f* suffragette
**sufrible** *adj* sufferable
**sufridero -ra** *adj* sufferable, endurable; *f* dolly (*in riveting*); iron block or plate for placing under piece to be punched
**sufrido -da** *adj* long-suffering; serviceable (*color*); complaisant (*husband*); *m* complaisant husband
**sufridor -dora** *adj* suffering; *mf* sufferer; *m* holder-on (*in riveting gang*)
**sufriente** *adj* suffering
**sufrimiento** *m* suffering; sufferance, tolerance
**sufrir** *va* to suffer; to undergo; to support, hold up; to buck up (*a rivet*); to take (*an examination*); to tolerate; *vn* to suffer
**sufusión** *f* (path.) suffusion; (path.) cataracts
**sugerencia** *f* suggestion
**sugerente** *adj* suggestive
**sugerible** *adj* suggestible
**sugeridor -dora** *adj* suggesting
**sugerir §62** *va* to suggest; **sugerir** + *inf* to suggest + *ger*
**sugestión** *f* suggestion; (psychol.) suggestion
**sugestionable** *adj* suggestible, easily influenced
**sugestionador -dora** *adj* suggesting, suggestive, influencing
**sugestionar** *va* to suggest (*by hypnosis*); to influence
**sugestivo -va** *adj* suggestive, stimulating, striking
**suicida** *adj* suicidal; *mf* suicide (*person*)
**suicidar** *va* to force suicide on; *vr* to commit suicide
**suicidio** *m* suicide (*act*)
**suite** *f* (mus.) suite
**suizo -za** *adj & mf* Swiss; *f* fracas, row; (*cap.*) *f* Switzerland
**sujeción** *f* subjection; surrender; fastening; fastener; (rhet.) rhetorical question
**sujetador** *m* fastener, clamp, anchor, clip
**sujetahilo** *m* (elec.) binding post
**sujetapapel** *m* paper finger (*of typewriter*)
**sujetapapeles** *m* (*pl:* **-les**) paper clip
**sujetar** *va* to subject; to subdue; to fasten, hold, tighten; *vr* to subject oneself, to submit; to stick, adhere
**sujetatubos** *m* (*pl:* **-bos**) pipe clamp
**sujeto -ta** *adj* subject, liable; fastened; (Am.) able, capable; *m* (gram., med., philos., psychol. & log.) subject; fellow, individual; **buen sujeto** brick, good egg
**sulfadiacina** *f* (pharm.) sulfadiazine
**sulfanilamida** *f* (pharm.) sulfanilamide
**sulfapiridina** *f* (pharm.) sulfapyridine
**sulfarsfenamina** *f* (pharm.) sulpharsphenamine
**sulfas** *fpl* (pharm.) sulfas, sulfa drugs
**sulfatación** *f* sulfation; (elec.) sulfation
**sulfatado** *m* sulfation
**sulfatador** *m* (agr.) sprayer (*device*)
**sulfatar** *va* to sulfate; (elec.) to sulfate; (agr.) to spray (*vines*) with copper sulfate
**sulfatiazol** *m* (pharm.) sulfathiazole
**sulfato** *m* (chem.) sulfate; **sulfato de cobre** (chem.) copper sulfate; **sulfato ferroso** (chem.) ferrous sulfate
**sulfhídrico -ca** *adj* (chem.) sulfhydric or sulphydric
**sulfito** *m* (chem.) sulfite
**sulfonal** *m* (pharm.) sulfonal
**sulfonamida** *f* (chem.) sulfonamide
**sulfuración** *f* sulfuration
**sulfurar** *va* to sulfurate; to anger, to annoy; *vr* to get angry, get furious
**sulfúreo -a** *adj* sulphureous, sulphury
**sulfúrico -ca** *adj* sulfuric; (chem.) sulfuric
**sulfuro** *m* (chem.) sulfid or sulfide; **sulfuro de hidrógeno** (chem.) hydrogen sulfide; **sulfuro ferroso** (chem.) ferrous sulfide
**sulfuroso -sa** *adj* sulfurous; (chem.) sulfurous
**sultán** *m* sultan; (coll.) sheik (*great lover*)
**sultana** *f* sultana, sultaness
**sultanato** *m* sultanate (*government; territory*)
**sultanía** *f* sultanate (*territory*)
**sultánico -ca** *adj* sultanic
**sulla** *f* (bot.) sulla clover, French honeysuckle
**suma** *f* see **sumo**
**sumador -dora** *adj* adding; *mf* adder; **sumadora mecánica** adding machine
**sumamente** *adv* extremely, exceedingly
**sumando** *m* (math.) addend; added element, contribution
**sumar** *va* to add, to sum; to sum up; to amount to; *vn* to add; to amount; **sumar y restar** (arith.) to add and subtract; **suma y sigue** add and carry, carried forward; *vr* to add up; **sumarse a** to add up to; to be added to; to adhere to, to become attached to
**sumaria** *f* see **sumario**
**sumariar** *va* (law) to indict
**sumario -ria** *adj* summary; *m* summary, résumé; (law) indictment; *f* (law) indictment (*in military case*)
**sumarísimo -ma** *adj super* (law) swift, expeditious
**sumatrino -na** *adj & mf* Sumatran
**sumergible** *adj* submersible, sinkable; *m* submersible (*boat*)
**sumergimiento** *m* submersion
**sumergir §42** *va & vr* to submerge, submerse
**sumerio -ria** *adj & mf* Sumerian; *m* Sumerian (*language*)
**sumersión** *f* submersion
**sumidad** *f* top, apex, summit
**sumidero** *m* drain, sewer; sink; sump

**sumiller** *m* butler (*of royal household*)
**sumillería** *f* butlership (*in royal household*)
**suministración** *f* provision, supply
**suministrador -dora** *adj* providing, supplying; *mf* provider, supplier
**suministrar** *va* to provide, supply
**suministro** *m* provision, supply; **suministros** *mpl* (mil.) supplies; **suministro de potencia** (rad.) power supply; **suministros para oficinas** office supplies
**sumir** *va* to sink; to press down; to overwhelm; (eccl.) to swallow (*the elements of Eucharist*); *vr* to sink; to be sunken (*said, e.g., of cheeks*); (Am.) to shrink, to shrivel; (Am.) to cower; (Am.) to pull down (*e.g., a hat*)
**sumisión** *f* submission
**sumiso -sa** *adj* submissive
**sumista** *adj* compendiary; *mf* summarist; rapid calculator
**sumo -ma** *adj* high, great, extreme; supreme; **a lo sumo** at most, at the most; **de sumo** completely; **en sumo grado** exceedingly; *f* sum, addition; summary; sum and substance; summa (*of a branch of learning*); **en suma** in short, in a word
**súmulas** *fpl* compendium of logic
**sunción** *f* (eccl.) taking of Eucharistic elements (*by priest*)
**suncho** *m* hoop
**suntuario -ria** *adj* sumptuary
**suntuosidad** *f* sumptuousness, sumptuosity
**suntuoso -sa** *adj* sumptuous
**supe** *1st sg pret ind of* **saber**
**supedáneo** *m* pedestal, pedestal of a crucifix
**supeditación** *f* oppression, subjection
**supeditar** *va* to hold down, oppress, subject; *vr* to be oppressed, be held in subjection
**súper** *adj* (coll.) super (*excellent, superfine*)
**superable** *adj* superable; **difícilmente superable** hard to beat
**superabundancia** *f* superabundance
**superabundante** *adj* superabundant
**superabundar** *vn* to superabound
**superación** *f* surpassing, excelling; winning, overcoming; superiority
**superádito -ta** *adj* superadded
**superar** *va* to surpass, excel; to overcome, conquer
**superávit** *m* (com.) surplus, superavit
**superbomba** *f* superbomb
**supercapitalización** *f* overcapitalization
**supercapitalizar §76** *va* to overcapitalize
**supercarburante** *m* high-test fuel
**supercarretera** *f* superhighway
**superciliar** *adj* (anat.) superciliary
**superconductividad** *f* superconductivity
**superconductor** *m* (elec.) superconductor
**superchería** *f* fraud, deceit
**superchero -ra** *adj* fraudulent, deceitful, tricky; *mf* cheat, trickster
**superdominante** *f* (mus.) superdominant
**supereminente** *adj* supereminent
**superentender §66** *va* to superintend, to supervise
**supererogación** *f* supererogation
**supererogatorio -ria** *adj* supererogatory
**superespía** *m* superspy
**superestado** *m* superstate
**superestructura** *f* superstructure
**superfetación** *f* superfetation
**superficial** *adj* superficial; (pertaining to) surface
**superficialidad** *f* superficiality
**superficiario -ria** *adj* (law) superficiary
**superficie** *f* surface; area; outside, exterior; **superficie de caldeo** or **calefacción** heating surface; **superficie de rodadura** (aut.) tread; **superficie de sustentación** or **superficie sustentadora** (aer.) airfoil
**superfino -na** *adj* superfine
**superfluencia** *f* great abundance
**superfluidad** *f* superfluity
**superfluo -flua** *adj* superfluous
**superfortaleza** *f* (aer.) superfortress, superfort
**superfosfato** *m* (chem. & agr.) superphosphate
**superheterodino -na** *adj & m* (rad.) superheterodyne
**superhombre** *m* superman
**superhumeral** *m* (eccl.) superhumeral
**superintendencia** *f* superintendence, superintendency, supervision
**superintendente** *mf* superintendent, supervisor; **superintendente del patio** (rail.) yardmaster
**superior** *adj* superior; upper; higher; **superior a** superior to; higher than; more than, greater than, larger than; *m* superior
**superiora** *f* superioress, mother superior
**superiorato** *m* superiorship
**superioridad** *f* superiority; authorities, higher authorities
**superlación** *f* superlativeness
**superlativo -va** *adj* superlative; (gram.) superlative; *m* (gram.) superlative
**supermercado** *m* supermarket
**superno -na** *adj* supreme, highest, supernal
**supernumerario -ria** *adj* supernumerary; (mil.) (on the) reserve; *mf* supernumerary
**súpero -ra** *adj* (bot.) superior, upper
**superpista** *f* superhighway
**superpoblación** *f* overpopulation
**superpoblar §77** *va* to overpopulate
**superpondré** *1st sg fut ind of* **superponer**
**superponer §69** *va* to superpose
**superpongo** *1st sg pres ind of* **superponer**
**superposición** *f* superposition; (geom.) superposition
**superpotencia** *f* (dipl. & elec.) superpower
**superproducción** *f* overproduction; superproduction
**superpuesto -ta** *pp of* **superponer**
**superpuse** *1st sg pret ind of* **superponer**
**superreacción** *f* or **superregeneración** *f* (rad.) superregeneration
**superregenerativo -va** *adj* (rad.) superregenerative
**superscripción** *f* (pharm.) superscription
**supersensible** *adj* supersensitive
**supersónico -ca** *adj* supersonic; *f* supersonics
**superstición** *f* superstition
**supersticioso -sa** *adj* superstitious
**supérstite** *adj* (law) surviving; *mf* (law) survivor
**superstructura** *f* superstructure
**supert.te** abr. of **superintendente**
**supervención** *f* supervention
**supervendré** *1st sg fut ind of* **supervenir**
**supervengo** *1st sg pres ind of* **supervenir**
**superveniencia** *f* var. of **supervención**
**supervenir §92** *vn* var. of **sobrevenir**
**supervigilancia** *f* (Am.) superintendence, supervision
**supervigilar** *va* (Am.) to superintend, to supervise
**supervine** *1st sg pret ind of* **supervenir**
**superviniendo** *ger of* **supervenir**
**supervisar** *va* to supervise
**supervisión** *f* supervision
**supervisor** *m* supervisor
**supervivencia** *f* survival; (law) survivorship; **supervivencia de los más aptos** (biol.) survival of the fittest
**superviviente** *adj & mf* var. of **sobreviviente**
**supervoltaje** *m* (phys.) supervoltage
**super-yo** *m* (psychoanal.) superego
**supinación** *f* supination; (anat. & physiol.) supination
**supinador** *m* (anat.) supinator
**supino -na** *adj* supine; *m* (gram.) supine
**súpito -ta** *adj* sudden; (coll.) impatient; (dial.) sly, crafty; (Am.) dumfounded
**suplantación** *f* supplanting (*by treachery*); fraudulent alteration
**suplantar** *va* to supplant (*by treachery*); to alter fraudulently (*a document*)
**supleausencias** *mf* (*pl:* **-cias**) substitute
**suplefaltas** *mf* (*pl:* **-tas**) (coll.) substitute, fill-in
**suplemental** *adj* supplemental
**suplementario -ria** *adj* supplementary; (geom.) supplementary
**suplemento** *m* supplementing; supplement; excess fare; (gram.) complement; (trig.) supplement; **suplemento ilustrado** illustrated supplement (*e.g., of newspaper*)
**suplente** *adj & mf* substitute

**supletorio -ria** *adj* additional, supplementary
**súplica** *f* suppliance, supplication; petition; (law) petition; **a súplica** by request, by petition
**suplicación** *f* supplication; rolled waffle (*for making cones*); cone (*of dough*); (law) petition to a superior court against its sentence; **a suplicación** by petition
**suplicacionero -ra** *mf* waffle vendor, cone vendor
**suplicante** *adj & mf* suppliant or supplicant
**suplicar** §86 *va & vn* to supplicate, entreat, implore; (law) to petition (*a superior court*) against its sentence; **suplicar de la sentencia** (law) to petition against the sentence; **suplicar en revista** (law) to apply for a new trial
**suplicatoria** *f* (law) communication from a court to a superior court
**suplicatorio** *m* (law) communication from a court to a superior court; (law) communication from a court to the Senate or Congress requesting permission to initiate legal proceedings against a member of the legislative body
**suplicio** *m* torture; punishment, execution; place of execution; anguish; **último suplicio** capital punishment
**suplidor -dora** *adj & mf* substitute
**suplir** *va* to supplement, make up for; to replace, take the place of; to cover up (*someone's shortcomings*); (gram.) to understand
**supl.te** abr. of **suplente**
**supón** *2d sg impv of* **suponer**
**supondré** *1st sg fut ind of* **suponer**
**suponedor -dora** *mf* wrong guesser
**suponer** *m* (coll.) supposition; §69 *va* to suppose; to assume; to imply, presuppose; to entail; to cause, impose; **suponer + *inf*** to pretend to + *inf;* **suponer que sí** to suppose so; *vn* to have weight, have authority
**supongo** *1st sg pres ind of* **suponer**
**suposición** *f* supposition; distinction, high position; imposture, falsehood
**supositicio -cia** *adj* supposititious
**supositivo -va** *adj* suppositional
**supositorio** *m* suppository
**supradicho -cha** *adj* above-mentioned
**supramundano -na** *adj* supermundane
**supranacional** *adj* supranational
**supraorbital** *adj* (anat.) supraorbital
**suprarrenal** *adj* (anat.) suprarenal
**suprasensible** *adj* supersensible
**supraspina** *f* (anat.) supraspinous fossa
**supraspinoso -sa** *adj* (anat.) supraspinous
**suprema** *f* see **supremo**
**supremacía** *f* supremacy
**supremo -ma** *adj* supreme; **hora suprema** or **momento supremo** supreme moment (*death*); **sacrificio supremo** supreme sacrifice; *f* Supreme Council of the Inquisition
**supresión** *f* suppression, elimination, omission
**supresivo -va** *adj* suppressive
**supresor -sora** *adj* suppressive; *mf* suppressor
**suprimible** *adj* suppressible
**suprimir** *va* to suppress, eliminate, do away with
**suprior** *m* (eccl.) subprior
**sup.te** abr. of **suplicante**
**supuesto -ta** *pp of* **suponer;** *adj* supposed, assumed, hypothetical; **esto supuesto** this being understood; **supuesto que** since, inasmuch as; *m* assumption, hypothesis; **dar por supuesto** to take for granted; **por supuesto** of course, naturally
**supuración** *f* suppuration
**supurante** *adj* suppurating, suppurative, runny
**supurar** *vn* to suppurate
**supurativo -va** *adj & m* suppurative
**supuse** *1st sg pret ind of* **suponer**
**suputación** *f* computation, calculation
**suputar** *va* to compute, to calculate
**sur** *m* south; south wind
**surá** *m* surah (*fabric*)
**sural** *adj* (anat.) sural
**Suramérica** *f* South America
**surcador -dora** *adj* ploughing; *m* plowman; *f* plowwoman
**surcar** §86 *va* to furrow; to plough, to plough through, to cut through; to streak through
**surco** *m* furrow; wrinkle, rut, cut; groove (*e.g., of a phonograph record*); **echarse en el surco** (coll.) to lie down on the job
**surcoreano -na** *adj & mf* South Korean
**surculado -da** *adj* (bot.) single-stemmed
**súrculo** *m* (bot.) single stem
**surculoso -sa** *adj* (bot.) var. of **surculado**
**sureño -ña** *adj* southern
**surgente** *adj* spouting, spurting
**surgidero** *m* (naut.) anchorage, anchoring place
**surgimiento** *m* spouting, spurting; rise, appearance
**surgir** §42 *vn* to spout, spurt; to issue, spring up, come forth; to arise, appear; (naut.) to anchor
**suripanta** *f* (hum.) chorine; (scornful) slut, jade
**surnia** *f* (orn.) hawk owl
**suroriental** *adj* southeastern
**surrealismo** *m* surrealism
**surrealista** *adj* surrealist, surrealistic; *mf* surrealist
**sursuncorda** *m* (coll.) anonymous big shot, big so-and-so
**surtida** *f* see **surtido**
**surtidero** *m* conduit, outlet; jet, fountain
**surtido -da** *adj* assorted; *m* spouting, spurting; assortment; line, supply; **de surtido** in common use, stock; *f* side door; sally, sortie; (fort.) sally port; (naut.) slipway
**surtidor -dora** *adj* supplying, providing; *mf* supplier, provider; *m* jet, spout, fountain; **surtidor de gasolina** gasoline pump
**surtimiento** *m* provision, supply
**surtir** *va* to provide, furnish, stock; **surtir efecto** to have the desired effect, to work; *vn* to spout, spurt, shoot up
**surto -ta** *adj* quiet, still; anchored
**sus** *interj* take heart!, get going!
**Susana** *f* Susan
**suscepción** *f* assumption, reception
**susceptibilidad** *f* susceptibility; touchiness; (magnetism) susceptibility
**susceptible** *adj* susceptible; touchy
**susceptivo -va** *adj* susceptible
**suscitación** *f* stirring up, provoking
**suscitador -dora** *mf* originator, promoter
**suscitar** *va* to stir up, provoke; to raise (*doubts, a question*)
**suscribir** §17, 9 *va & vr* var. of **subscribir**
**suscripción** *f* var. of **subscripción**
**suscritor -tora** *mf* var. of **subscritor**
**susidio** *m* anxiety, uneasiness, disturbance
**susodicho -cha** *adj* above-mentioned
**suspender** *va* to hang; to suspend; to astonish, astound; to postpone; (educ.) to flunk; (educ.) to condition; *vr* to be suspended or stopped; to rear (*said of a horse*)
**suspensión** *f* suspension; amazement, astonishment; (rhet.) suspension; **suspensión de armas** suspension of arms, suspension of hostilities; **suspensión de fuegos** cease fire
**suspensivo -va** *adj* suspensive; suspension (*points*)
**suspenso -sa** *adj* suspended, hanging; baffled, bewildered; (theat.) closed; *m* (educ.) condition; **en suspenso** in suspense, suspended
**suspensores** *mpl* (Am.) suspenders
**suspensorio -ria** *adj* suspensory; *m* suspensory, supporter, jockstrap
**suspicacia** *f* suspicion, distrust; suspiciousness
**suspicaz** *adj* (*pl:* **-caces**) suspicious, distrustful
**suspirado -da** *adj* longed for
**suspirar** *vn* to sigh; **suspirar por** to sigh for, to long for, to covet
**suspiro** *m* sigh; glass whistle; ladyfinger; (bot.) morning-glory; (mus.) crotchet, quarter rest; **exhalar el último suspiro** to breathe one's last
**suspirón -rona** *adj* full of sighs
**suspiroso -sa** *adj* heavy-breathing
**sustancia** *f* var. of **substancia**
**sustanciación** *f* var. of **substanciación**
**sustancial** *adj* var. of **substancial**
**sustancialidad** *f* var. of **substancialidad**
**sustanciar** *va* var. of **substanciar**

**sustancioso -sa** *adj* var. of **substancioso**
**sustantífico -ca** *adj* var. of **substantífico**
**sustantivar** *va* var. of **substantivar**
**sustantivo -va** *adj & m* var. of **substantivo**
**sustentable** *adj* sustainable, arguable
**sustentación** *f* sustentation; support, prop; (aer.) lift; (rhet.) suspension
**sustentáculo** *m* prop, support, stay; holder
**sustentador -dora** *adj* sustaining; *mf* sustainer, support
**sustentamiento** *m* sustentation, sustenance
**sustentante** *adj* sustaining; *m* support; defender (*of a thesis*)
**sustentar** *va* to sustain, support, feed; to maintain; to defend (*a thesis*)
**sustento** *m* sustenance, support, food; maintenance
**sustitución** *f* var. of **substitución**
**sustituíble** *adj* var. of **substituíble**
**sustituir** §41 *va & vn* var. of **substituir**
**sustitutivo -va** *adj & m* var. of **substitutivo**
**sustituto -ta** *mf* var. of **substituto**
**susto** *m* scare, fright, dread; **darse un susto** to have a good scare
**sustracción** *f* var. of **substracción**
**sustraendo** *m* var. of **substraendo**
**sustraer** §88 *va & vr* var. of **substraer**
**susurración** *f* whispering, whispering gossip
**susurrador -dora** *adj* whispering; *mf* whisperer
**susurrar** *va* to whisper; *vn* to whisper, murmur, rustle, purl, hum; to be whispered about, be bruited about; *vr* to be whispered about, be bruited about
**susurrido** *m* murmur, rustle, purling, hum
**susurro** *m* whisper, murmur, rustle, purling, hum
**susurrón -rrona** *adj* (coll.) whispering; *mf* (coll.) whisperer
**sutás** *m* braid
**sutil** *adj* subtle, subtile; keen, observant
**sutileza** *f* subtlety, subtility; animal instinct; **sutileza de manos** skill, dexterity, skillful performance; slick pickpocketing
**sutilidad** *f* subtlety, subtility
**sutilizador -dora** *adj* hairsplitting; *mf* hairsplitter, quibbler
**sutilizar** §76 *va* to make thin, to taper; to file, to polish; to discuss with acuity; *vn* to split hairs, to quibble
**sutorio -ria** *adj* (pertaining to a) shoemaker
**sutura** *f* (anat., bot., surg. & zool.) suture; **sutura coronal** (anat.) coronal suture
**suyo -ya** *adj poss* of his, of hers, of yours, of theirs, e.g.,**un amigo suyo** a friend of his, of hers, etc.; *pron poss* his, hers, yours, theirs, its, one's; **de suyo** on his (her, etc.) own, on his (her, etc.) own accord: naturally, inherently; **hacer de las suyas** (coll.) to be up to one's old tricks; **los suyos** his (her, your, their) friends; his (her, etc.) men; his (her, etc.) side; **salirse con la suya** to come out ahead, to have one's way; to carry one's point; **ver la suya** (coll.) to have or get one's chance
**suzeranía** *f* (feud.) suzerainty
**suzerano** *m* (feud.) suzerain
**suzón** *m* (bot.) groundsel
**svástica** *f* swastika

# T

**T, t** *f* twenty-third letter of the Spanish alphabet
**t.** abr. of **tarde**
**ta** *interj* careful!, easy!; **¡ta, ta!** rat-a-tat!; tut, tut!
**taba** *f* anklebone; knucklebone (*of sheep*); knucklebones, dibs (*game*); (Am.) jackstones; (Am.) vent in water pipe; **calentársele a uno las tabas** (Am.) to redouble one's efforts; (Am.) to be anxious to get married; **dar** or **darse vuelta la taba** (Am.) to take a turn (*said of fate*); **darle taba a uno** to have a long-drawn-out conversation with someone; **darle** or **pegarle a uno en la taba** (Am.) to hit someone where it hurts; **menear las tabas** (coll.) to hustle about; **tomar la taba** (coll.) to start talking quickly as soon as another stops
**tabacal** *m* tobacco field
**tabacalero -ra** *adj* (pertaining to) tobacco; *mf* tobacco grower; tobacconist; tobacco twister
**tabacazo** *m* (Am.) tobacco potion (*given as poison*)
**tabaco** *m* tobacco; cigar; snuff; black rot; **tabaco cimarrón** (bot.) marijuana (*Nicotiana glauca*); **tabaco de humo** smoking tobacco; **tabaco de montaña** arnica; **tabaco de pipa** pipe tobacco; **tabaco de polvo** snuff; **tabaco en rama** leaf tobacco, wrappers; **tabaco indio** (bot.) Indian tobacco; **tabaco torcido** twisted tobacco, cigars; **tomar tabaco** to take snuff; *adj invar* (Am.) bold, determined
**tabacoso -sa** *adj* (coll.) snuffy (*addicted to use of snuff*); tobacco-stained; attacked by black rot
**tabalada** *f* (coll.) fall on the behind; (coll.) spanking
**tabalario** *m* (coll.) behind
**tabalear** *va* to rock, to shake; *vn* to drum with the fingers; *vr* to rock, to shake
**tabaleo** *m* rocking; drumming
**tabanazo** *m* (coll.) spanking; (coll.) slap (*in the face*)
**tabanco** *m* food stand; stand, stall
**tabanera** *f* place full of horseflies
**tábano** *m* (ent.) gadfly, horsefly
**tabanque** *m* treadle wheel (*of potter's wheel*)
**tabaola** *f* hubbub, uproar
**tabaque** *m* wicker basket; large tack
**tabaquera** *f* see **tabaquero**
**tabaquería** *f* cigar store, tobacco store; tobacco factory
**tabaquero -ra** *adj* (pertaining to) tobacco; *mf* tobacconist; cigar maker; *f* snuffbox; bowl (*of a tobacco pipe*)
**tabaquismo** *m* (path.) tobaccoism
**tabaquista** *mf* tobacco expert; inveterate user of tobacco
**tabardete** *m* or **tabardillo** *m* (coll.) sunstroke; (coll.) crazy annoying fellow, harum-scarum
**tabardo** *m* tabard
**tabarra** *f* (coll.) tiring speech, boring conversation, bore
**tabarrera** *f* (coll.) terrible bore
**tabasco** *f* tabasco (*sauce*); *m* (Am.) banana
**tabellar** *va* to fold (*cloth*) leaving the selvage visible; to mark with a trademark
**taberna** *f* tavern, saloon
**tabernáculo** *m* tabernacle; (*cap.*) *m* (Bib.) Tabernacle
**tabernario -ria** *adj* vulgar, low; (pertaining to a) saloon
**tabernera** *f* saloonkeeper's wife; barmaid
**tabernería** *f* saloon business
**tabernero** *m* saloonkeeper; bartender
**tabes** *f* (path.) consumption
**tabí** *m* (*pl:* **-bíes**) tabby, watered fabric
**tabica** *f* iron or copper plate; riser (*of stairs*); (arch.) covering board
**tabicar** §86 *va* to wall up; to close up
**tabicón** *m* thick partition
**tábido -da** *adj* rotted; wasted by consumption
**tabique** *m* thin wall, partition; (Am.) brick; **tabique de panderete** brick-on-edge partition; **tabique sordo** wall with air space
**tabiquería** *f* partitions
**tabiquero** *m* partition builder
**tabla** *f* board; table (*list, contents, synopsis in parallel columns, etc.*); slab (*of stone*); sheet of metal; flat diamond; wide part (*of member of body*); garden patch or bed; strip of land; land between two rows of trees; butcher shop; butcher-shop counter; box pleat; calm stretch of river; broad face of log; panel, painting on a board; (anat.) table; (Am.) cake of chocolate; **tablas** *fpl* boards (*stage*); draw, tie; barrier (*bull ring*); **a raja tabla** (coll.) at any cost, regardless; (Am.) promptly, vigorously; **cantarle a uno la tabla** (Am.) to lay down the law to someone; **en las tablas** (Am.) penniless; **escapar en una tabla** to have a narrow escape; **hacer tablas** to be tied, to be deadlocked; **hacer tabla rasa de** to do without; (Am.) to remove obstacles to; **no dar en tablas** (Am.) not to hit the nail on the head; **no saber por dónde van las tablas** to not know what is going on; **quedar tablas** to be tied, to be deadlocked; **salir a las tablas** to go upon the boards (*the stage*); **salir con las tablas** (Am.) to fail; **salvarse en una tabla** to have a narrow escape; **sobre tabla** (Am.) quickly, extemporaneously; **subir a las tablas** to go upon the boards (*the stage*); **tener tablas** to have stage presence, to be at home on the stage; **tabla de juego** gambling house, gambling stand; **tabla de conversión** conversion table; **tabla de la vaca** noisy group; **tabla de lavar** washboard; **tabla de materias** table of contents; **tabla de multiplicar** multiplication table; **tabla de planchar** ironing board; **tabla de salvación** last recourse, lifesaver; **tabla periódica** (chem.) periodic table; **tabla rasa** unpainted board; untrained mind; clean slate; **Tabla Redonda** (myth.) Round Table (*knights of King Arthur*); **tablas alfonsinas** Alphonsine Tables (*astronomical tables prepared by order of Alfonso X of Castile in 1252*); **tablas de la ley** (Bib.) tables of the law; **tablas reales** backgammon
**tablachina** *f* wooden shield
**tablacho** *m* sluice, floodgate
**tablado** *m* flooring; stage; scaffold; bottom boards of a bedstead
**tablaje** *m* boarding, planking; shed; gambling house
**tablajería** *f* gambling; butcher shop
**tablajero** *m* scaffold builder, stand builder; keeper of a gambling house; butcher
**tablar** *m* group of garden plots; calm stretch of river; sideboard (*of wagon or cart*)
**tablazo** *m* blow with a board; shoal
**tablazón** *f* boarding, planking; (naut.) decking, deck flooring
**tableado** *m* box pleat
**tablear** *va* to cut into boards; to divide (*e.g., a garden*) into plots or patches; to level or grade (*ground*) with a board or roller; to hammer into plates; to make box pleats in
**tablero** *m* board; panel; sheet (*of metal, etc.*); top, table top; timber to be sawed; checkerboard, chessboard; counter; gambling house; cutting table (*of tailor*); (wooden) blackboard; (floor) nail; floor (*of bridge*); (elec.) switchboard; (orn.) petrel; **tableros** *mpl* wooden fence or barrier around inside of bull ring; **estar en el tablero** to be exposed to public

view, to be in the limelight; **poner** or **traer al tablero** to risk; **tablero de ajedrez** chessboard; **tablero de damas** checkerboard; **tablero de instrumentos** (aut.) dashboard, instrument panel
**tableta** *f* small board; floor board; tablet, writing pad; lozenge; cake of chocolate; **tabletas** *fpl* clappers used in begging for hospitals; **estar en tabletas** to be uncertain, to be dubious (*said of the success of a thing*); **quedarse tocando tabletas** (coll.) to be disappointed, to lose all
**tableteado** *m* rattling sound
**tabletear** *vn* to rattle
**tableteo** *m* rattle, rattling
**tablilla** *f* small board; slat; shingle; bulletin board; tablet, slab; cushion of billiard table between two pockets; (surg.) splint; showcase; **tablillas de encuadernar** (b.b.) pressing boards; **tablillas de San Lázaro** clappers used in begging for hospitals
**tablón** *m* plank, heavy board; beam; strake
**tabloncillo** *m* small plank; seat in the last row (*in bull ring*)
**tabloza** *f* (painter's) palette
**tabú** *m* (*pl:* **-búes**) tabu or taboo
**tabuco** *m* hovel, shack, shanty
**tabulación** *f* tabulation
**tabulador** *m* tabulator
**tabular** *adj* tabular; *va* to tabulate
**taburete** *m* taboret, stool; small velvet-back chair without arms; **taburetes** *mpl* semicircular rows of benches in the pit (*of old Madrid theaters*); **taburete de piano** piano stool
**tac** *m* tick (*of clock, heart, etc.*)
**taca** *f* spot, stain; small closet; crucible plate
**tacada** *f* stroke (*at billiards*)
**tacamaca, tacamacha,** or **tacamahaca** *f* (bot.) tacamahac (*tree and resin*)
**tacana** *f* gray silver ore
**tacañear** *vn* to be stingy; (archaic) to be cunning
**tacañería** *f* stinginess; (archaic) cunning
**tacaño -ña** *adj* stingy, miserly; (archaic) cunning, deceitful
**tacar** §86 *va* to spot, to mark
**tacazo** *m* stroke with a cue
**taceta** *f* copper bowl for pouring olive oil from one vessel to another
**tacita** *f* little cup; demitasse
**tácito -ta** *adj* tacit; silent; (*cap.*) *m* Tacitus
**taciturnidad** *f* taciturnity; melancholy
**taciturno -na** *adj* taciturn; melancholy
**taclobo** *m* (zool.) tridacna (*bivalve and shell*)
**taco** *m* bung, plug; wad, wadding; billiard cue; popgun; rammer; pad; block; almanac pad; package; (coll.) snack, bite to eat; (coll.) drink of wine; (coll.) muddle, mess; (coll.) oath; (Am.) heel (*of shoe*); (Am.) sport; (Am.) rolled maize tortilla; **soltar tacos** (coll.) to swear; **taco de alisar** sanding block; **taco de billetes** pad or block of tickets
**tacómetro** *m* tachometer
**tacón** *m* heel (*part of shoe that raises heel of foot*)
**taconazo** *m* kick with the heel
**taconear** *va* (Am.) to fill, pack, stuff; *vn* to click the heels; to strut
**taconeo** *m* clicking of the heels (*in walking or dancing*)
**táctico -ca** *adj* tactical; *m* tactician; *f* tactics; (mil.) tactics; **gran táctica** (mil.) grand tactics
**táctil** *adj* tactile, tactual
**tactismo** *m* (biol.) taxis
**tactivo -va** *adj* tactual
**tacto** *m* (sense of) touch; skill; touch (*of piano, pianist, typewriter, or typist*); tact; **al tacto** by touch; **tacto de codos** (mil.) alignment shoulder to shoulder; (fig.) perfect union
**tacuaco -ca** *adj* (Am.) chubby
**tacha** *f* fault, defect, flaw; large tack
**tachadura** *f* erasure
**tachar** *va* to erase; to strike out; to blame, find fault with; (law) to challenge (*a witness*)
**tacho** *m* (Am.) boiler with round bottom; (Am.) evaporator, sugar pan; (Am.) tin (*sheet*); (Am.) coffee pot, tea pot; **irse al tacho** (Am.) to fail, to collapse, to die
**tachón** *m* scratch, erasure; ribbon, trimming; gimp nail, gilt-headed tack, silver-headed tack
**tachonar** *va* to adorn with ribbon or trimming; to adorn with ornamental tacks; to spangle, to stud
**tachonería** *f* ornamental work with gimp nails
**tachoso -sa** *adj* defective, faulty
**tachuela** *f* large-headed tack, hobnail; bowl; (prov.) crook, rascal; (Am.) metal warming bowl; (Am.) tin cup; (Am.) runt, half pint
**Tadeo** *m* Thaddeus
**tafanario** *m* (coll.) buttocks, behind
**tafetán** *m* taffeta; **tafetanes** *mpl* flags, colors; (coll.) finery; **tafetán adhesivo** adhesive tape; **tafetán de heridas** or **tafetán inglés** court plaster
**tafia** *f* (Am.) tafia or taffia (*rum*)
**tafilete** *m* morocco, morocco leather, shagreen; sweatband; **tafilete de Levante** Levant morocco
**tafiletear** *va* to adorn or finish with morocco leather
**tafiletería** *f* art of dressing morocco leather; morocco-leather shop
**tafón** *m* (zool.) striated sea gastropod (*Taphon striatus*)
**tafurea** *f* flat-bottomed boat for transporting horses
**tagalo -la** *mf* Tagalog; *m* Tagalog (*language*)
**tagarnina** *f* (bot.) Spanish oyster plant, golden thistle; (coll.) poor cigar
**tagarote** *m* (orn.) sparrow hawk; scrivener; (coll.) gawk; (coll.) gentleman sponger
**tagarotear** *vn* to write in a bold sweeping hand
**tagide** *adj* (poet.) of the Tagus
**tagua** *f* (bot.) ivory palm; (Am.) coot, mud hen
**taguán** *m* (zool.) flying squirrel
**taha** *f* district, region
**tahalí** *m* (*pl:* **-líes**) baldric; leather box (*to carry the Koran or Christian relics and prayers*)
**taharal** *m* var. of **tarayal**
**taheño -ña** *adj* red (*hair*); red-bearded
**tahitiano -na** *adj* & *mf* var. of **taitiano**
**tahona** *f* horse-driven flour mill; bakery
**tahonero -ra** *mf* miller; baker; *f* miller's wife; baker's wife
**tahúr -húra** *adj* gambling; cheating; *mf* gambler; cheat
**tahurería** *f* gaming house, gambling den; gambling; cheating
**taicún** *m* tycoon (*hereditary lord of Japan*)
**taifa** *f* faction, party; (coll.) bad lot, gang of bums
**tailandés -desa** *adj* & *mf* Thai; *m* Thai (*language*)
**Tailandia** *f* Thailand
**taima** *f* slyness, slickness, crookedness; (Am.) sullenness, stubbornness
**taimado -da** *adj* sly, slick, crafty; (Am.) sullen, gruff
**taimar** *vr* (Am.) to sulk, be stubborn
**taimería** *f* slyness, slickness, crookedness
**taita** m (coll.) daddy
**taitiano -na** *adj* & *mf* Tahitian
**taja** *f* cut, division; shield; saddle frame
**tajada** *f* see **tajado**
**tajadera** *f* curved chopping knife; chopping block; cold chisel
**tajadero** *m* chopping block
**tajadilla** *f* small slice; chopped lungs; (prov.) slice of orange or lemon eaten as a relish with brandy
**tajado -da** *adj* steep, sheer; *f* cut, slice; (coll.) hoarseness; (hum.) drunk; (Am.) slash, gash; **hacer tajadas** (coll.) to slash up, to cut to pieces; **sacar tajada** (coll.) to look out for number one
**tajador -dora** *adj* cutting, chopping; *mf* cutter, chopper; *m* chopping block
**tajadura** *f* cutting, slicing, chopping
**tajalápiz** *m* (*pl:* **-pices**) (Am.) pencil sharpener
**tajamar** *m* cutwater (*of bridge or ship*); (Am.) dike, dam
**tajamiento** *m* var. of **tajadura**
**tajante** *adj* cutting, sharp; incisive; complete, total; *m* butcher
**tajaplumas** *m* (*pl:* **-mas**) penknife
**tajar** *va* to cut, slice, chop; to sharpen (*pencil*)
**tajea** *f* culvert, drainpipe

**tajo** *m* cut; edge; trench; steep cliff; chopping block; block (*on which a condemned person is beheaded*); line of progress (*of gang of reapers, miners, pavers, etc.*); (*cap.*) *m* Tagus
**tajón** *m* chopping block
**tajuela** *f* three-legged rustic stool
**tajuelo** *m* three-legged rustic stool; (mach.) pillow block
**tal** *adj indef* such, such a; this; *pron indef* so-and-so; such a thing; someone; *adv* so; in such a way; **como tal** as such; **con tal (de) que** provided (that); **el tal** that; that one; that fellow, e.g., **el tal Juan** that fellow John; **no tal** no, no; **¿qué tal?** how?; hello!, how's everything?; **sí tal** yes, indeed; **un tal** a certain; one such; **tal como** just as; **tal cual** such as; an occasional, one or two, a few; so-so, middling, ordinary; **tal para cual** (coll.) two of a kind
**tala** *f* felling of trees; destruction, havoc; tipcat (*boys' game*); cat (*used in tipcat*); (mil.) abatis; (bot.) Argentine hackberry
**talabarte** *m* sword belt
**talabartería** *f* saddlery, harness shop
**talabartero** *m* saddler, harness maker
**talacha** *f*, **talache** *m* or **talacho** *m* (Am.) mattock
**taladrador -dora** *adj* boring, drilling; piercing; *mf* driller; *f* drill, drilling machine; drill press
**taladramiento** *m* boring, drilling; piercing
**taladrante** *adj* boring, drilling; piercing; (fig.) penetrating
**taladrar** *va* to bore, drill, perforate; to pierce; to punch (*a ticket*); to get to the bottom of (*a problem*)
**taladro** *m* drill; auger; drill hole; drill press; **taladro de mano** hand drill; **taladro de pecho** breast drill; **taladro de trinquete** ratchet drill; **taladro mecánico** drill press
**talamera** *f* (hunt.) tree in which a decoy is placed
**talamete** *m* (naut.) forward deck
**talámico -ca** *adj* thalamic
**tálamo** *m* bridal bed; (anat. & bot.) thalamus; **tálamo óptico** (anat.) optic thalamus
**talán** *m* ding-dong
**talanquera** *f* breastwork, parapet; cover, place of refuge; (fig.) safety; (Am.) reed fence; **desde talanquera** (coll.) without taking any chances oneself
**talante** *m* performance; mien, countenance; desire, will, pleasure; **de buen talante** in a good mood; with good grace; **de mal talante** in a bad mood; with bad grace
**talar** *adj* long (*robe or gown*); **talares** *mpl* (myth.) talaria (*of Mercury*); *va* to fell (*trees*); to destroy, lay waste; (dial. & Am.) to prune
**talásico -ca** *adj* thalassic
**talayote** *m* (archeol.) talayot (*Balearic tower-shaped stone structure*)
**talco** *m* tinsel; (mineral.) talc; **talco en polvo** talcum powder
**talcoso -sa** *adj* talcose
**talcualillo -lla** *adj* (coll.) fair, fairly good, so-so; (coll.) somewhat better (*in health*)
**taled** *m* tallith
**talega** *f* bag, sack; bagful; hair bag; diaper; **talegas** *fpl* (coll.) money, wealth
**talegalo** *m* (orn.) brush turkey, mound bird
**talego** *m* big bag, sack; (coll.) big slob; **tener talego** (coll.) to have money tucked away
**taleguilla** *f* small bag; bullfighter's breeches; **taleguilla de la sal** (coll.) daily household expenses
**talento** *m* talent
**talentoso -sa** or **talentudo -da** *adj* talented
**Tales** *m* Thales
**Talía** *f* (myth.) Thalia
**talio** *m* (chem.) thallium
**talión** *m* talion
**talionar** *va* to punish by talion
**talismán** *m* talisman
**talismánico -ca** *adj* talismanic
**talma** *f* talma (*large cape or cloak*)
**Talmud** *m* Talmud
**talmúdico -ca** *adj* Talmudic
**talmudista** *m* Talmudist
**talo** *m* (bot.) thallus
**talocha** *f* mason's float
**talófita** *f* (bot.) thallophyte
**talofítico -ca** *adj* thallophytic
**talón** *m* (anat.) heel; heel (*part of shoe or stocking that covers heel of foot*); heelpiece; (arch.) heel (*of a timber*); (arch.) talon (*molding*); (aut.) flange, lug (*on a tire*); (mus.) heel (*of violin bow*); (naut.) heel (*of keel*); (rail.) heel (*of frog*); (com.) check, voucher, coupon (*detached, e.g., from a stub*); stub (*e.g., of check*); monetary standard; **a talón** (coll.) on foot; **apretar** or **levantar los talones** (coll.) to take to one's heels; **pisarle a uno los talones** (coll.) to be at one's heels, to tail after someone; (fig.) to keep up with someone; **talón de Aquiles** Achilles' heel (*vulnerable spot*)
**talonada** *f* kick with the heels
**talonario -ria** *adj* (pertaining to a) stub; *m* stub book, checkbook
**talonazo** *m* kick with the heel
**talonear** *vn* (coll.) to dash along
**talonesco -ca** *adj* (coll.) (pertaining to the) heel
**talpa** or **talparia** *f* mole, wen, talpa
**talque** *m* tasco (*refractory clay*)
**talquita** *f* talc schist
**talud** *m* slope, talus
**talvina** *f* almond-meal porridge
**talla** *f* cut; carving; engraving; height, stature; size (*of a person, of a dress*); ransom; reward; height-measuring scale; hand (*at cards*); (naut.) purchase block; (surg.) lithotomy; **poner talla contra** to offer a reward for (*e.g., a criminal*)
**tallado -da** *adj* shaped, formed; *m* carving; engraving; grinding (*of a lens*)
**tallador -dora** *mf* carver; cutter; engraver; (Am.) dealer, banker (*at cards*); *f* cutter, cutting machine; **talladora de engranajes** (mach.) gear cutter
**talladura** *f* carving; engraving; cutting
**tallar** *adj* ready for cutting into lumber (*said of trees or woodland*); *m* woodland ready for first cutting; young growth of trees; planting of young olive trees; *va* to carve; to engrave; to cut (*a precious stone*); to measure the height of; to appraise; to deal (*cards*); to grind (*a lens*); *vn* (Am.) to chat, converse; (Am.) to make love
**tallarín** *m* noodle
**tallarola** *f* knife for cutting velvet pile
**talle** *m* shape, figure, stature; waist (*of body and of garment*); fit; outline, appearance; (Am.) bodice
**tallecer** §34 *vn & vr* to shoot, to sprout
**taller** *m* shop, workshop; mill, factory; atelier, studio; laboratory; casters (*for vinegar and oil*); (educ.) workshop; **taller agremiado** closed shop; **taller de cepillado** planing mill; **taller de reparaciones** repair shop; service station; **talleres gráficos** printing establishment; **taller franco** open shop; **taller mecánico** machine shop; **taller penitenciario** workhouse
**tallerista** *m* shopworker
**tallero -ra** *mf* (Am.) vegetable dealer
**tallista** *mf* wood carver, sculptor
**tallo** *m* stem, stalk; sprout, shoot; (Am.) cabbage; **tallos** *mpl* (Am.) greens, fresh vegetables
**tallón** *m* ransom; reward
**talludo -da** *adj* long-stalked; tall, lanky; inveterate; aging, no longer young
**tamal** *m* (Am.) tamale; (Am.) intrigue
**tamanduá** *m* (*pl:* **-duaes**) (zool.) tamandua (*arboreal anteater*)
**tamañamente** *adv* as greatly
**tamañito -ta** *adj* so small; very small; disconcerted, confused
**tamaño -ña** *adj* so big; such a big; very big, very large; **abrir tamaños ojos** to open one's eyes wide; **tamaño como** as big as; *m* size; **tamaño extra** oversize; **tamaño natural** full size
**támara** *f* (bot.) date palm; growth of date palms; **támaras** *fpl* cluster of dates; brushwood
**tamaricáceo -a** *adj* (bot.) tamaricaceous
**tamarilla** *f* (bot.) rockrose (*Cistus clusii*)
**tamarindo** *m* (bot.) tamarind (*tree and fruit*)

**tamarisco** *m* (bot.) tamarisk
**tamariz** *m* (*pl:* **-rices**) (bot.) tamarisk
**tamarrizquito -ta** or **tamarrusquito -ta** *adj* (coll.) tiny, very small
**tambaleante** *adj* staggering, tottering, reeling
**tambalear** *vn & vr* to stagger, totter, reel
**tambaleo** *m* staggering, tottering, reeling
**tambanillo** *m* (arch.) tympanum
**tambarillo** *m* chest with arched lid
**tambero -ra** *adj* (Am.) (pertaining to an) inn; (Am.) (pertaining to) cattle; *mf* (Am.) innkeeper
**también** *adv* also, too
**tambo** *m* (Am.) inn, wayside inn; (Am.) dairy; **tambo de tíos** (Am.) shindy, pandemonium
**tambor** *m* drum (*cylinder*); (arch. & mus.) drum; (sew.) tambour; sieve, screen; (anat.) eardrum; coffee roaster; (Am.) drum (*container*); **a tambor** or **con tambor batiente** with drums beating; in triumph; **bordar a tambor** to tambour; **tambor mayor** (mil.) drum major
**tambora** *f* bass drum; (Am.) drum
**tamborear** *vn* to drum with the fingers
**tamboreo** *m* drumming with the fingers
**tamboreta** *f* (orn.) tambourine
**tamborete** *m* (naut.) cap (*used in joining spars*)
**tamboril** *m* tabor, timbrel, small drum
**tamborilada** *f* or **tamborilazo** *m* (coll.) bump, bump on one's bottom; (coll.) slap on the head or shoulders
**tamborilear** *va* to extol, praise to the skies; (print.) to tap with the planer; *vn* to drum
**tamborilero** *m* taborer, drummer
**tamborilete** *m* (mus.) taboret; (print.) planer
**tamborín** *m* tabor, timbrel
**tamborino** *m* tabor, timbrel; taborer
**tamboritear** *vn* to drum
**tamboritero** *m* taborer, drummer
**tamborón** *m* big bass drum
**tambucho** *m* (naut.) hood
**Tamerlán** *m* Tamerlane
**Támesis** *m* Thames
**tamiz** *m* (*pl:* **-mices**) sieve
**tamizar** **§76** *va* to sift, to sieve
**tamo** *m* fuzz, fluff, dust
**tamojo** *m* var. of **matojo**
**tampa** *f* (Am.) tangled hair
**tampar** *va* (Am.) to tangle, confuse
**tampoco** *adv* neither, not either, e.g., **tampoco vino** or **no vino tampoco** he did not come either; **ni yo tampoco** nor I either
**tampón** *m* stamp pad
**tamposo -sa** *adj* (Am.) tangled, confused
**tamtam** *m* tom-tom
**tamujo** *m* (bot.) box-leafed broom
**tamul** *adj & mf* Tamil; *m* Tamil (*language*)
**tan.** abr. of **tangente**
**tan** *adv* so; **tan . . . como** or **cuan** as . . . as; **tan siquiera** at least; *m* boom (*of drum*)
**tanaceto** *m* (bot.) tansy
**tanagra** *f* (f.a.) Tanagra (*figurine*)
**tanato** *m* (chem.) tannate
**tanda** *f* turn; shift, relay; task; coat; layer; game, match (*especially of billiards*); lot, pack, flock; (Am.) show (*each of a continuous series of performances*); (Am.) habit, bad habit
**tándem** *m* (*pl:* **tándemes**) tandem
**tandeo** *m* distribution of irrigating water by turns
**tanganillas; en tanganillas** shaky, tottery
**tanganillo** *m* temporary prop or support
**tángara** *m* (orn.) tanager
**tangencia** *f* tangency
**tangencial** *adj* tangential
**tangente** *adj* tangent; (geom.) tangent; *f* (geom., trig. & mus.) tangent; **escapar, escaparse, irse** or **salir por la tangente** (coll.) to resort to subterfuges, to evade the issue
**Tánger** *f* Tangier
**tangerino -na** *adj & mf* Tangerine; *f* tangerine (*orange*)
**tangibilidad** *f* tangibility
**tangible** *adj* tangible
**tango** *m* tango (*dance and music*)
**tangón** *m* (naut.) outrigger, swinging boom
**tanguear** *vr* (Am.) to change parties
**tánico -ca** *adj* (chem.) tannic
**tanino** *m* (chem.) tannin
**tano -na** *adj & mf* (Am.) Neapolitan, Italian
**tanque** *m* tank; bee glue; dipper, drinking cup; (mil.) tank; **tanque del inodoro** toilet tank
**tanqueta** *f* (mil.) small tank
**tantalato** *m* (chem.) tantalate
**tantálico -ca** *adj* (chem.) tantalic
**tantalio** *m* (chem.) tantalum
**tantalita** *f* (mineral.) tantalite
**tántalo** *m* (chem.) tantalum; (orn.) wood ibis; (*cap.*) *m* (myth.) Tantalus
**tantán** *m* tom-tom; clanging (*e.g., of an anvil*)
**tantarantán** *m* rub-a-dub; (coll.) hard smack
**tanteador -dora** *mf* score keeper; *m* score board
**tantear** *va* to compare; to size up, take the measure of; to test, feel, feel out; to sketch, outline; to keep the score of; (Am.) to estimate; *vn* to keep score; (Am.) to grope, feel one's way; **¡tantee Vd.!** (Am.) fancy that!, just imagine!
**tanteo** *m* comparison; careful consideration; trial, test; feeler; trial and error; score; **al tanteo** (Am.) by sight, by guess
**tanto -ta** *adj* so much; such a big; as much; *pron* so much; as much; that; **tantos -tas** *adj & pron pl* so many; as many; **tanto** *adv* so much; so hard; so often; so long; as much; **algún tanto** somewhat, a little; **al tanto** at the same price; **al tanto de** because of; **a tanto** so far, to such a pass, to such an extent; **a tantos de** on a certain day in, on such and such a day in (*e.g., June*); **con tanto que** provided (that); **en tanto** or **entre tanto** in the meantime; **en tanto que** whereas, while; **estar al tanto de** to be or keep informed about, be aware of; **no ser para tanto** to be not so bad, to be not so serious; **otros tantos** as many others; **otro tanto** as much, the same thing; **poner al tanto de** to make aware of, to keep informed of; **por el tanto** at the same price; **por lo tanto** therefore; **por tanto** therefore, wherefore; **un tanto** somewhat, rather; **un tanto por ciento** a certain percentage; **y tantos** odd, or more, e.g., **veinte y tantos** twenty odd, twenty or more; **¡tanto bueno!** or **¡tanto bueno por aquí!** so good to see you!; **tanto como** or **cuanto** as much as; as well as; the same thing as; **tanto ... como** as much ... as; both ... and; **tantos ... como** as many . . . as; **tantos cual, cuanto** or **que** so many that; **tanto más** (or **menos**) **. . . más** (or **menos**) all the more (or less) . . . (in proportion) as . . . more (or less); **tanto más** (or **menos**) **cuanto que** all the more (or less) because; **tanto mayor (mejor, menos** or **peor)** all the more (better, less or worse); **tanto que** as soon as; *m* copy; counter, chip (*to keep score*); point (*in a score*); (Am.) part, portion; **apuntar** or **señalar los tantos** to keep score; **un tanto por cada día de trabajo** so much for each day's work
**tanza** *f* casting line
**tañedor -dora** *mf* player, musician
**tañer** **§84** *va* to play (*a musical instrument*); *vn* to drum with the fingers
**tañido** *m* sound, tone; twang (*e.g., of guitar*); ring; tang (*ringing sound*)
**tañimiento** *m* playing an instrument
**taño** *m* tanbark
**taoísmo** *m* Taoism
**taoísta** *adj & mf* Taoist
**tapa** *f* lid, cover, top, cap; head (*of a cylinder, barrel, etc.*); gate (*of sluice*); shirt front; board cover (*of book*); lift or layer (*of heel*); (aut.) valve cap; **tapas** *fpl* (coll.) appetizer, free lunch; **levantarse** or **saltarse la tapa de los sesos** to blow one's brains out; **tapas de cocina** hot appetizers
**tapaagujeros** *m* (*pl:* **-ros**) var. of **tapagujeros**
**tapabarro** *m* (Am.) mudguard
**tapaboca** *f* slap in the mouth; muffler; (coll.) squelch, squelcher; **tapabocas** *m* (*pl:* **-cas**) muffler; (arti.) tampion
**tapacete** *m* (naut.) sliding awning
**tapacubo** or **tapacubos** *m* (*pl:* **-bos**) (aut.) hubcap
**tapaculo** *m* hip (*of dog rose*)
**tapada** *f* woman who hides her face with mantle or handkerchief

**tapadera** *f* lid, cover, cap; blind (*person who shields another*)
**tapadero** *m* plug, stopper
**tapadillo** *m* woman's hiding her face with mantle or handkerchief; (mus.) flute-stop of organ; **de tapadillo** secretly, under cover
**tapadizo** *m* shed
**tapador -dora** *adj* covering; *mf* coverer; *m* lid, cover, top; plug, stopper; *f* (Am.) bottle capper
**tapadura** *f* covering; hiding; stopping, obstructing
**tapafunda** *f* flap of a holster
**tapagoteras** *m* (*pl:* **-ras**) (Am.) roofer; (Am.) roofing cement, waterproofing material
**tapagujeros** *m* (*pl:* **-ros**) (coll.) poor plasterer, awkward mason; (coll.) substitute, makeshift (*person*)
**tapajuntas** *m* (*pl:* **-tas**) strip or molding covering crack between door frame or window frame and wall; bead (*on corner to protect plaster*)
**tápalo** *m* (Am.) shawl, muffler
**tapamiento** *m* var. of **tapadura**
**tapanga** *f* (Am.) housing, trappings
**tapapecho** *m* (Am.) chuck (*of beef*)
**tapaporos** *m* (*pl:* **-ros**) primer, filler
**tapar** *va* to cover; to cover up, to hide; to conceal (*a fugitive*); to plug, stop, stop up; to shut; to obstruct (*the view*); to wrap up; (Am.) to fill (*a tooth*); (Am.) to crumple, crush; **taparlas** (prov.) to inhale (*in smoking*); *vr* to cover oneself; to wrap up, bundle up
**tapara** *f* (Am.) gourd; **vaciarse como una tapara** (Am.) to spill everything one knows
**tápara** *f* var. of **alcaparra**
**taparo** *m* (bot.) gourd tree
**taparrabo** *m* loincloth; trunks, bathing trunks
**tapera** *f* (Am.) ruins; (Am.) shack, hovel
**taperujar** *vr* (coll.) to wrap one's face all up
**taperujo** *m* (coll.) badly fitting plug; (coll.) awkward way of covering the face
**tapetado -da** *adj* dark, dark-brown
**tapete** *m* rug; runner (*of carpet, lace, etc.*); table scarf; **estar sobre el tapete** to be on the carpet (*i.e., under discussion*); **tapete verde** card table, gambling table, green table
**tapetito** *m* coaster, mat
**tapia** *f* mud wall, adobe wall
**tapiador** *m* mud-wall builder
**tapial** *m* form or mold for making mud walls; (dial. & Am.) mud wall
**tapiar** *va* to wall up, to wall in, to inclose with a wall; to close up
**tapicería** *f* tapestries; upholstery; making of tapestry; tapestry shop; upholstery shop
**tapicero** *m* tapistery maker; carpet maker; carpet layer; upholsterer
**tapido -da** *adj* closely woven
**tapiería** *f* mud walls (*of a house, enclosure, etc.*)
**tapioca** *f* tapioca
**tapir** *m* (zool.) tapir
**tapiz** *m* (*pl:* **-pices**) tapestry; **tapiz gobelino** Gobelin tapestry
**tapizado** *m* upholstery
**tapizar §76** *va* to tapestry; to upholster; to carpet; to cover
**tapón** *m* stopper, cork; cap; bottle cap; plug, bung; (elec.) fuse; (surg.) tampon; **al primer tapón, zurrapas** (coll.) off to a bad start; **tapón de algodón** (surg.) swab; **tapón de cuba** (coll.) fat, squatty person; **tapón de cubo** (aut.) hubcap; **tapón de desagüe** drain plug; **tapón de llenado** (aut.) gas-tank cap, filler cap; **tapón de radiador** (aut.) radiator cap; **tapón de tráfico** traffic jam; **tapón de vaciado** (aut.) drain plug; **tapón fusible** (elec.) plug fuse
**taponado** *m* capping, plugging
**taponamiento** *m* (surg.) tamponage
**taponar** *va* to plug, stop up; (surg.) to tampon
**taponazo** *m* pop (*of a cork*)
**taponería** *f* corks, stoppers; cork factory; cork business; cork store
**taponero -ra** *adj* (pertaining to) cork; *mf* cork maker; cork dealer
**tapsia** *f* (bot.) deadly carrot
**tapujar** *vr* (coll.) to muffle one's face, to cover one's face
**tapujo** *m* muffler, cover held over the face; (coll.) concealment, subterfuge
**taque** *m* click (*of a door as it locks or latches*); rap, knock (*at a door*)
**taqué** *m* (aut.) tappet
**taquera** *f* rack or stand for billiard cues
**taquicardia** *f* (path.) tachycardia
**taquigrafía** *f* tachygraphy; shorthand, stenography; tachygraph
**taquigrafiar §90** *va* to stenograph, take down in shorthand
**taquigráfico -ca** *adj* tachygraphic or tachygraphical; stenographic, shorthand
**taquígrafo -fa** *mf* tachygraph or tachygrapher; stenographer
**taquilita** *f* (mineral.) tachylite
**taquilla** *f* file (*for letters, papers, etc.*); ticket rack; ticket window; ticket office; box office; take, gate (*money collected for a contest, show, etc.*)· (Am.) inn, tavern
**taquillero -ra** *adj* box-office; *mf* ticket seller, ticket agent
**taquimeca** *mf* (coll.) shorthand-typist
**taquimecanógrafo -fa** *mf* shorthand-typist
**taquimetría** *f* tachymetry
**taquimétrico -ca** *adj* tachymetric
**taquímetro** *m* speedometer, tachymeter; (surv.) tachymeter
**taquín** *m* anklebone
**taquisterol** *m* (biochem.) tachysterol
**taquistoscopio** *m* tachistoscope
**tara** *f* tare (*deduction for weight*); tally (*split stick for recording transactions*); defect; allowance for weight; (Am.) noisemaker (*wooden rattle*); **menos la tara** (coll.) making due allowance for exaggeration
**tarabilla** *f* millclapper; catch (*to fasten a window*); turnbuckle; (coll.) millclapper, chatterbox; (coll.) jabber, nonsense; **soltar la tarabilla** (coll.) to talk a blue streak
**tarabita** *f* tongue (*of belt buckle*); (Am.) rope of rope railway
**taracea** *f* marquetry, inlaid work; inlaid floor
**taracear** *va* to inlay, to adorn with marquetry
**tarado -da** *adj* defective
**taragallo** *m* var. of **trangallo**
**taragontía** *f* var. of **dragontea**
**taraje** *m* var. of **taray**
**tarambana** *adj & mf* (coll.) crackpot
**tarando** *m* (zool.) reindeer
**tarángana** *f* cheap blood sausage
**tarantela** *f* tarantella (*dance and music*)
**tarántula** *f* (zool.) tarantula; (zool.) gecko, tarente
**tarantulado -da** *adj* var. of **atarantado**
**tarar** *va* to tare
**tarara** *f* or **tarará** *m* sound of trumpet
**tararear** *va & vn* to hum
**tarareo** *m* hum, humming
**tararira** *f* (coll.) noisy goings on; *mf* (coll.) blustery person
**tarasca** *f* dragon (*in Corpus Christi procession*); gluttony; (coll.) ugly wench, hag
**tarascada** *f* bite; (coll.) tart reply, rude answer
**tarascar §86** *va* to bite (*said of a dog*)
**taray** *m* (bot.) salt cedar
**tarayal** *m* growth of salt cedars
**tarazana** *f* or **tarazanal** *m* var. of **atarazana**
**tarazar §76** *va* to bite, to tear, or to lacerate with the teeth; to annoy, bother
**tarazón** *m* slice, chunk
**tarbea** *f* large hall
**tardanza** *f* slowness, delay, tardiness
**tardar** *vn* to be long; to be late; **a más tardar** at the latest; **tardar en** + *inf* to be long in + *ger;* to be late in + *ger;* **tardar . . . en** + *inf* to be . . . in + *ger* or to take . . . to + *inf*, e.g., **tardó dos horas en preparar su lección** he was two hours in preparing his lesson or he took two hours to prepare his lesson; *vr* to be long; to be late
**tarde** *adv* late; too late; **de tarde en tarde** from time to time; **hacerse tarde** to grow late; **más tarde o más temprano** sooner or later; **para luego es tarde** it's later than you think; (Am.) come on and do it, you'd better hurry up and do it; **tarde o temprano** sooner or later; *f* afternoon, evening; (fig.) evening (*of life*); **buenas tardes** good after-

noon, good evening; **de la tarde a la mañana** overnight; suddenly, in no time; unexpectedly
**tardeada** *f* (Am.) afternoon party
**tardecer** §34 *vn* to grow late, to grow dark
**tardecica** or **tardecita** *f* nightfall, dusk
**tardígrado -da** *adj* (zool.) tardigrade
**tardío -a** *adj* late, delayed, tardy; slow; **tardíos** *mpl* late crops
**tardo -da** *adj* slow; late; slow, dull, dense
**tardón -dona** *adj* (coll.) slow, poky; *mf* (coll.) poke, slow poke
**tarea** *f* task, job; work; care, worry
**tarifa** *f* tariff; price list; rate; fare; (telp.) toll; **tarifa diferencial** (rail.) differential rate; **tarifa proteccionista** protective tariff; **tarifa recargada** extra fare
**tarifar** *va* to price; *vn* to quarrel, to fall out
**tarificación** *f* price fixing
**tarima** *f* stand; platform; stool; low bench; bunk; board
**tarja** *f* shield, buckler; tally (*split stick for recording transactions*); (coll.) blow, lash; **beber sobre tarja** (coll.) to drink on tick
**tarjador -dora** *mf* tally keeper
**tarjar** *va* to tally
**tarjero -ra** *mf* tally keeper
**tarjeta** *f* card; place card; title and imprint (*on a map*); (arch.) tablet; **tarjeta de buen deseo** or **tarjeta de felicitación** greeting card; **tarjeta de felicitación de Año Nuevo** New Year's card; **tarjeta de felicitación de Pascuas** Christmas card; **tarjeta de identidad** identity card; **tarjeta de negocios** business card; **tarjeta de visita** calling card, visiting card; **tarjeta navideña** Christmas card; **tarjeta perforada** punch card, punched card; **tarjeta postal** post card, postal card; **tarjeta registradora** timecard
**tarjeteo** *m* (coll.) exchange of visiting cards
**tarjetero** *m* card case; card file, card index
**tarlatana** *f* tarlatan
**taro** *m* (bot.) taro
**tarpeyo -ya** *adj* Tarpeian; (*cap.*) *f* Tarpeia
**tarpón** *m* (ichth.) tarpon
**tarquín** *m* mire, slime, mud
**tarquinada** *f* (coll.) rape
**Tarquino** *m* Tarquin
**tarrago** *m* (bot.) meadow sage
**tarraja** *f* var. of **terraja**
**tarraya** *f* casting net
**tarrico** *m* (bot.) saltwort
**tarro** *m* jar; milk pail; (Am.) horn; (Am.) high hat
**tarsiano -na** *adj* tarsal
**tarso** *m* (anat. & zool.) tarsus; (*cap.*) *f* Tarsus
**tarta** *f* tart; pan
**tártago** *m* (bot.) caper spurge; (coll.) misfortune; (coll.) poor joke, mean trick; **tártago de Venezuela** (bot.) castor-oil plant
**tartaja** *adj* (coll.) stuttering; *mf* (coll.) stutterer
**tartajear** *vn* to stutter
**tartajeo** *m* stuttering
**tartajoso -sa** *adj* stuttering; *mf* stutterer
**tartalear** *vn* (coll.) to stagger, to sway; (coll.) to be dumbfounded, be speechless
**tartamudear** *vn* to stutter, to stammer
**tartamudeo** *m* (act of) stuttering, stammering
**tartamudez** *f* (defect of) stuttering, stammering
**tartamudo -da** *adj* stuttering, stammering; *mf* stutterer, stammerer
**tartán** *m* Scotch plaid, tartan
**tartana** *f* tartana (*two-wheeled round-top carriage of Valencia*); rickety old railroad train; (naut.) tartan
**tartanero** *m* driver of a tartana
**tartáreo -a** *adj* Tartarean
**Tartaria** *f* Tartary
**tartárico -ca** *adj* var. of **tártrico**
**tartarizar** §76 *va* to tartarize
**tártaro -ra** *adj* & *mf* Tartar; *m* (chem.) tartar; tartar (*on teeth*); **tártaro emético** (chem.) tartar emetic; (*cap.*) *m* (myth.) Tartarus (*underworld*)
**tartera** *f* pastry pan; lunch basket, dinner pail
**tartrato** *m* (chem.) tartrate
**tártrico -ca** *adj* tartaric
**tartufo** *m* hypocrite
**taruga** *f* (zool.) guemal (*Hippocamelus antisiensis*)
**tarugo** *m* wooden plug; wooden paving block; (Am.) cheat; (Am.) dolt
**tarumba** *adj* (coll.) confused, rattled; **volver tarumba** (coll.) to rattle; **volverse tarumba** (coll.) to get rattled
**tas** *m* stake (*small anvil*)
**tasa** *f* appraisal; measure, standard; rate; moderation; ceiling price
**tasación** *f* appraisal; regulation; **tasación de costas** (law) taxation
**tasadamente** *adv* with measure; scantily; (coll.) just right
**tasador -dora** *adj* appraising; *mf* appraiser; **tasador de avería** insurance adjuster
**tasajo** *m* jerked beef
**tasar** *va* to appraise; to regulate; to hold down, keep within bounds; to grudge; (law) to tax (*the costs*)
**tasca** *f* dive, joint
**tascador** *m* swingle, scutcher
**tascar** §86 *va* to swingle, to scutch; to crunch (*grass*); to champ (*the bit*)
**tasco** *m* stalk of hemp or flax (*after scutching*)
**tasconio** *m* var. of **talque**
**tasmanio -nia** *adj* & *mf* Tasmanian; (*cap.*) *f* Tasmania
**tasquera** *f* (coll.) row, quarrel
**tasquil** *m* chip, splinter (*of stone*)
**tastana** *f* hard crust (*of dry earth*); membrane (*dividing the carpels or slices of, e.g., an orange*)
**tastaz** *m* brass-polishing powder
**tasto** *m* spoiled taste (*of food*)
**tasugo** *m* (zool.) badger
**tata** *m* see **tato**; *f* see **tato**
**tatarabuelo -la** *mf* great-great-grandparent; *m* great-great-grandfather; *f* great-great-grandmother
**tataradeudo -da** *mf* remote ancestor
**tataranieto -ta** *mf* great-great-grandchild; *m* great-great-grandson; *f* great-great-granddaughter
**tátaro -ra** *adj* & *mf* Tartar, Tatar
**tatarrete** *m* (coll.) old jar
**tate** *interj* be careful!, look out!; I get it!, I get you!
**tato -ta** *adj* stammering, lisping; *m* (dial. & Am.) little brother; (zool.) armadillo; *f* (coll.) nursemaid; (dial. & Am.) little sister; **andar a tatas** (coll.) to toddle; (coll.) to go on all fours; **tata** *m* (dial. & Am.) daddy
**tatú** *m* (*pl:* **-túes**) (zool.) tatouay
**tatuaje** *m* tattoo, tattooing
**tatuar** §33 *va* & *vr* to tattoo
**taujel** *m* strip of wood, support of an arch
**taujía** *f* damascene, damascene work
**taumaturgia** *f* thaumaturgy
**taumatúrgico -ca** *adj* thaumaturgic or thaumaturgical
**taumaturgo -ga** *mf* thaumaturge, wonder-worker
**taurino -na** *adj* taurine, bullfighting; *f* (chem.) taurine
**Tauro** *m* (astr. & geog.) Taurus
**taurófilo -la** *mf* bullfight fan
**taurómaco -ca** *adj* bullfighting, tauromachian; *mf* bullfighter, tauromachian
**tauromaquia** *f* bullfighting, tauromachy
**tauromáquico -ca** *adj* bullfighting, tauromachic
**taurotraumatólogo** *m* medical expert on bullfight wounds
**tautoga** *f* (ichth.) tautog
**tautología** *f* tautology
**tautológico -ca** *adj* tautological
**tautomería** *f* (chem.) tautomerism
**tautómero** *m* (chem.) tautomer
**taxativamente** *adv* rigorously
**taxativo -va** *adj* rigorous; (law) limitative
**taxear** *vn* (aer.) to taxi
**taxi** *m* taxi, taxicab; *f* taxi dancer
**taxia** *f* (biol.) taxis
**taxidermia** *f* taxidermy
**taxidérmico -ca** *adj* taxidermal
**taxidermista** *mf* taxidermist
**taxímetro** *m* taximeter
**taxis** *f* (biol. & surg.) taxis

**taxista** *mf* taxi driver
**taxonomía** *f* taxonomy
**taxonómico -ca** *adj* taxonomic
**taxonomista** *mf* taxonomist
**taylorismo** *m* industrial management, efficiency engineering
**taz; taz a taz** on an even basis; **taz con taz** (Am.) even, tied
**taza** *f* cup; basin (*of fountain*); bowl (*of toilet*); cup guard (*of sword*)
**tazaña** *f* dragon (*in Corpus Christi procession*)
**tazar** §76 *va & vr* to fray
**tazón** *m* bowl; (prov.) basin
**T.B.O.** abr. de **tebeo** (*libro cómico*)
**te** *pron pers & reflex* (used as object of verb) thee, to thee; you, to you; thyself, to thyself; yourself, to yourself; *f* T square; tee (*pipe*)
**té** *m* (bot.) tea; (bot.) fireweed; tea (*dried leaves; drink; afternoon reception*); **té bailable** tea dance, thé dansant; **té borde** or **de Méjico** (bot.) Mexican tea; **té del Canadá** (bot.) spiceberry; **té del Paraguay** (bot.) Paraguay tea; **té de Pékoë** pekoe; **té de Pensilvania** (bot.) Oswego tea; **té de Suecia** (bot.) twinflower; **té negro** black tea; **té verde** green tea
**tea** *f* torch, firebrand
**teáceo -a** *adj* (bot.) theaceous
**teantropía** *f* theanthropism
**teatral** *adj* theatrical
**teatralidad** *f* theatricality
**teatrero -ra** *mf* (Am.) theater-goer
**teatro** *m* theater; (fig.) theater (*e.g., of war*); (fig.) scene (*e.g., of an accident*); **dar teatro a** to ballyhoo; **teatro circular** arena theater, theater-in-the-round; **teatro de estreno** first-run house; **teatro de la ópera** opera house; **teatro de repertorio** stock company; repertory theater
**teatrólogo -ga** *mf* theater critic; actor; *f* actress
**tebaico -ca** *adj* Thebaic
**tebaína** *f* (chem.) thebaine
**tebano -na** *adj & mf* Theban
**Tebas** *f* Thebes (*of Egypt; of Greece*)
**tebeo -a** *adj & mf* Theban; *m* comic book
**teca** *f* (anat. & bot.) theca; (bot.) teak (*tree and wood*); reliquary
**tecla** *f* key (*of typewriter, piano, etc.*); touchy subject; **dar en la tecla** (coll.) to get the knack of it; (coll.) to fall into a habit; **tocar una tecla** (coll.) to try to start something; (coll.) to feel one's way; **tecla de cambio** shift key; **tecla de escape** margin release; **tecla de espacios** space bar, space key; **tecla del tabulador** tabulator key; **tecla de retroceso** backspacer; **tecla muerta** dead key; **tecla tabulatoria** tabulating key
**teclado** *m* keyboard (*of typewriter, piano, etc.*); **teclado manual** (mus.) manual (*of organ*); **teclado pedalero** (mus.) pedal keyboard; **teclado universal** standard keyboard (*of typewriter*)
**tecle** *m* (naut.) single whip
**tecleado** *m* fingering
**teclear** *va* (coll.) to feel out (*a matter, deal, etc.*); *vn* to run one's fingers over the keys, to type, to play the piano; to click; (coll.) to wiggle one's fingers; (coll.) to drum, to thrum
**tecleo** *m* fingering; touch; click (*of typewriter*)
**tecnetio** *m* (chem.) technetium
**técnica** *f* see **técnico**
**tecnicidad** *f* technicality (*technical character*)
**tecnicismo** *m* technical terminology; technicality (*technical term*)
**técnico -ca** *adj* technic, technical; *m* technician; expert; *f* technic or technics (*science of an art; skill*); technique (*method; skill*)
**tecnicolor** *m* technicolor
**tecnocracia** *f* technocracy
**tecnócrata** *mf* technocrat
**tecnocrático -ca** *adj* technocratic
**tecnología** *f* technology
**tecnológico -ca** *adj* technologic or technological
**tecnólogo -ga** *mf* technologist
**tecolote** *m* (orn.) eagle owl (*of Central America*); **estar tecolote** (Am.) to be tipsy
**tectita** *f* (geol.) tektite
**tectónico -ca** *adj* tectonic; *f* tectonics
**techado** *m* roof; **bajo techado** under cover, indoors
**techador** *m* roofer
**techar** *va* to roof, put a roof on
**techo** *m* ceiling; roof, cover; (aer.) ceiling; (fig.) roof (*house, home*); (slang) lid (*hat*); **subirse al techo** (coll.) to blow one's top; **techo de paja** thatched roof; **techo de servicio** (aer.) service ceiling
**techumbre** *f* ceiling; roof
**tedero** *m* cresset, fire basket
**tedeum** *m* (*pl:* **tedeum**) Te Deum
**tediar** *va* to loathe, to be sick of
**tedio** *m* tedium, ennui, boredom
**tedioso -sa** *adj* tedious, boresome
**teelina** *f* (biochem.) theelin
**tegmen** *m* (bot. & zool.) tegmen
**tégula** *f* (zool.) tegula
**tegular** *adj* tegular
**tegumentario -ria** *adj* tegumentary
**tegumento** *m* (anat., bot. & zool.) tegument
**teína** *f* (chem.) theine
**teinada** *f* cattle shed
**teísmo** *m* theism
**teísta** *adj* theistic; *mf* theist
**teja** *f* roofing tile; shovel hat; (bot.) yew; (bot.) linden; **a teja vana** with a plain tile roof; lightly, without concern; **a toca teja** (coll.) for cash; **de tejas abajo** (coll.) in the natural order, without help from above; (coll.) here below; **de tejas arriba** (coll.) in the supernatural order; (coll.) in the other world; **teja canalón** pantile, gutter tile; **teja de cimacio** pantile; **teja de madera** shingle; **teja romana** pantile
**tejadillo** *m* top, cover
**tejado** *m* tile roof; roof; **tejado a cuatro aguas** hip roof; **tejado a dos aguas** double-sloping roof; **tejado de media agua** single-sloping roof; **tejado de vidrio** (fig.) glasshouse
**tejamaní** *m* (*pl:* **-níes**) (Am.) shake (*long shingle*)
**tejamanil** *m* (Am.) var. of **tejamaní**
**tejano -na** *adj & mf* Texan
**tejar** *m* tile works; *va* to tile, to roof with tiles
**tejaroz** *m* eaves
**Tejas** *m* Texas
**tejavana** *f* shed; building with plain tile roof; **a tejavana** lightly, without concern
**tejedera** *f* weaver (*woman*); (ent.) whirligig beetle
**tejedor -dora** *adj* weaving; (coll.) scheming; *mf* weaver; (coll.) schemer; *m* (ent.) water strider, water skipper; (orn.) weaver, weaverbird
**tejedura** *f* weaving; texture
**tejeduría** *f* (art of) weaving; weaving mill
**tejemaneje** *m* (coll.) knack, cleverness; (Am.) scheming
**tejer** *va* to weave; (fig.) to weave (*a story, a plot*); *vn* to weave; **tejer y destejer** to blow hot and cold, to back and fill
**tejera** *f* see **tejero**
**tejería** *f* tile business; tile works, tile kiln
**tejero -ra** *mf* tile maker; *f* tile works
**tejido** *m* weave, texture; web; fabric, textile; tissue; (biol.) tissue; (fig.) tissue, web; **tejido adhesivo** (elec.) friction tape; **tejido conjuntivo** or **conectivo** (anat.) connective tissue; **tejido criboso** (bot.) sieve tissue; **tejido de encaje** lace fabric; **tejido de malla** netted fabric; **tejido de media** hosiery fabric; **tejido de punto** knitted fabric, jersey
**tejo** *m* disk, weight (*in shuffleboard*); quoit; bearing, pillow block; metal disk; (bot.) yew, yew tree
**tejocote** *m* (bot.) hawthorn; haw (*fruit*)
**tejoleta** *f* broken tile; brickbat; clapper
**tejolote** *m* (Am.) stone pestle
**tejón** *m* (zool.) badger; **tejón de Australia** (zool.) wombat; **tejón de Laponia** (zool.) glutton
**tejonera** *f* burrow of badgers
**tejuela** *f* broken tile; brickbat; saddletree
**tejuelo** *m* small tile; (b.b.) label; (b.b.) lettering; (mach.) pillow block
**tela** *f* cloth, fabric; skin (*e.g., of an onion*); film; web (*of an insect*); subject, something to talk

about; (b.b.) cloth; (paint.) canvas; (hunt.) canvas enclosure; (slang) dough (*money*); **poner en tela de juicio** to question, to doubt; **tela aislante** (elec.) insulating tape, friction tape; **tela de alambre** wire screen; **tela de araña** spider web, cobweb; **tela de crin** horsehair, haircloth; **tela de esmeril** emery cloth; **tela de punto** stockinet; **tela emplástica** court plaster; **tela metálica** chicken wire; **tela polímita** fabric made of many-colored threads
**telada** *f* gang, outfit, clique
**telamón** *m* (arch.) telamon
**telangiectasia** *f* (path.) telangiectasis
**telar** *m* loom; frame; embroidery frame; (b.b.) sewing press; (theat.) gridiron
**telaraña** *f* spider web, cobweb; (fig.) cobweb (*something slight or flimsy*); **mirar las telarañas** (coll.) to be stargazing; **tener telarañas en los ojos** (coll.) to look without seeing, to be blind to what is going on
**telarañoso -sa** *adj* cobwebby, gossamery
**telautógrafo** or **teleautógrafo** *m* telautograph
**teleaudiencia** *f* television audience
**telecomunicación** *f* telecommunication
**telecontrol** *m* remote control
**telediario** *m* television newscast
**teledifundir** *va & vn* to telecast
**teledifusión** *f* telecasting; telecast; music by wire; wired wireless
**teledifusora** *f* television transmitter
**teleferaje** *m* telpherage
**teleferar** *va* to telpher
**teleférico -ca** *adj & m* telpher
**telefio** *m* (bot.) orpin
**telefonar** *va & vn* (Am.) var. of **telefonear**
**telefonazo** *m* (slang) telephone call
**telefonear** *va & vn* to telephone
**telefonema** *m* telephone message, telephone call
**telefonía** *f* telephony; **telefonía inalámbrica** or **sin hilos** wireless telephony
**telefónico -ca** *adj* telephonic
**telefonista** *mf* operator, telephonist
**teléfono** *m* telephone; **teléfono automático** dial telephone; **teléfono inalámbrico** or **sin hilos** wireless telephone; **teléfono público** pay station
**telefoto** *m* (elec.) telephote (*telectric apparatus*); *f* telephoto (*picture*)
**telefotografía** *f* telephotography; telephotograph
**telefotografiar** §90 *va & vn* to telephotograph
**telefotográfico -ca** *adj* telephoto, telephotographic
**telefotógrafo** *m* phototelegraph (*apparatus*)
**teleg.** abr. of **telégrafo** & **telegrama**
**telega** *f* telega
**telegonía** *f* (biol.) telegony
**telegrafía** *f* telegraphy; **telegrafía inalámbrica** or **sin hilos** wireless, wireless telegraphy
**telegrafiar** §90 *va & vn* to telegraph
**telegráfico -ca** *adj* telegraphic
**telegrafista** *mf* telegrapher; telegraphist
**telégrafo** *m* telegraph; **hacer telégrafos** (coll.) to talk by signs (*said especially of lovers*); **telégrafo de banderas** (nav.) wigwagging; **telégrafo de máquinas** (naut.) engine-room telegraph; **telégrafo sin hilos** wireless telegraph
**telegrama** *m* telegram
**teleguiado -da** *adj* guided by remote control
**teleimpresor** *m* teletype, teleprinter
**teleléctrico -ca** *adj* telelectric
**Telémaco** *m* (myth.) Telemachus
**telemando** *m* remote control
**telemecánico -ca** *adj* telemechanic; *m* television repairman; *f* telemechanics
**telemedición** *f* telemetering
**telemetrar** *va & vn* to telemeter
**telemetría** *f* telemetry
**telemétrico -ca** *adj* telemetric
**telémetro** *m* telemeter; (mil.) range finder
**telemisora** *f* television transmitter
**telencéfalo** *m* (anat.) telencephalon
**telendo -da** *adj* sprightly, lively, spirited
**teleobjetivo** *m* telephoto lens
**teleología** *f* teleology
**teleológico -ca** *adj* teleological
**teleósteo -a** *adj & m* (ichth.) teleost
**telépata** *mf* telepathist
**telepatía** *f* telepathy
**telepático -ca** *adj* telepathic
**telepatista** *mf* telepathist
**telequinesia** *f* telekinesis
**telera** *f* plow pin; sheepfold (*enclosed in a board fence*); jaw (*of a vise*); transom (*of gun carriage*); (naut.) rack block
**telerán** *m* (elec.) teleran
**telero** *m* stake (*of cart or truck*)
**telerreceptor** *m* television set, television receiver
**telescopaje** *m* telescoping (*of one object inside another*)
**telescopar** *va & vr* to telescope
**telescópico -ca** *adj* telescopic
**telescopio** *m* telescope; (*cap.*) *m* (astr.) Telescopium; **telescopio de espejo** reflecting telescope
**telesilla** *f* chair lift (*for skiers*)
**telesillas** *m* (*pl:* **-llas**) var. of **telesilla**
**telespectador -dora** *mf* viewer, televiewer
**telesquí** *m* ski lift, ski tow
**telestereoscopio** *m* telestereoscope
**telestesia** *f* telesthesia
**telestudio** *m* television broadcasting studio
**teleta** *f* blotting paper, blotter; sieve in a paper mill
**teletermómetro** *m* telethermometer
**teletipia** *f* teletypewriter
**teletipiadora** *f* teletype
**teletipista** *mf* teletyper
**teletipo** *m* teletype
**teletransmisora** *f* television transmitter
**teletubo** *m* (telv.) picture tube
**televidente** *mf* viewer, televiewer
**televisar** *va* to televise
**televisión** *f* television; **televisión en circuito cerrado** closed-circuit television; **televisión en colores** color television
**televiso -sa** *adj* (pertaining to) television
**televisor -sora** *adj* televising; (pertaining to) television; *m* television set; *f* television transmitter
**telilla** *f* light camelot; film
**telina** *f* (zool.) clam
**telofase** *f* (biol.) telophase
**telolecito** *adj masc* (embryol.) telolecithal
**telón** *m* (theat.) drop curtain; **telón contra incendios** (theat.) safety curtain; **telón de acero** (fig.) iron curtain; **telón de boca** (theat.) front curtain; **telón de fondo** or **foro** (theat.) backdrop; **telón de seguridad** (theat.) safety curtain
**telonero -ra** *mf* first actor in a vaudeville program
**telurato** *m* (chem.) tellurate
**telúrico -ca** *adj* telluric; (chem.) telluric
**telurio** *m* (chem.) tellurium
**telurita** *f* (mineral.) tellurite
**telurito** *m* (chem.) tellurite
**teluroso -sa** *adj* (chem.) tellurous
**telururo** *m* (chem.) telluride
**tellina** *f* (zool.) clam
**telliz** *m* (*pl:* **-llices**) horse blanket, saddle cover
**telliza** *f* bedspread, quilt
**tema** *m* theme, subject; exercise; contention; (gram.) stem; (mus.) theme; *f* persistence, insistence; fixed idea, mania; grudge; **a tema** in emulation, in competition; **tener tema** to be stubborn; **tener tema a** to have a grudge against
**temario** *m* agenda
**temático -ca** *adj* thematic; persistent, insistent; (gram.) (pertaining to the) stem
**tembladal** *m* quaking bog
**tembladero -ra** *adj* shaking, trembling; *mf* trembler; *m* quaking bog; *f* jewel mounted on a spiral spring; bowl of very thin metal or glass; (ichth.) torpedo; (bot.) large quaking grass
**temblador -dora** *adj* shaking, trembling; *mf* trembler; (rel.) trembler (*Quaker*); *m* (elec.) trembler
**temblante** *adj* shaking, trembling; *m* bracelet
**temblar** §18 *vn* to shake, tremble, quiver; to shiver; **estar temblando** to teeter

**tembleque** *adj* shaking, trembling; *m* trembler; jewel mounted on a spiral spring
**temblequear** *vn* (coll.) to shake, to tremble all the time; (coll.) to fake a tremor
**temblequeo** *m* (coll.) shaking, trembling, constant shaking, constant trembling
**tembletear** *vn* (coll.) var. of **temblequear**
**temblón -blona** *adj* (coll.) shaking, tremulous; **hacer la temblona** (coll.) to fake a tremor (*said of a beggar*); *m* (bot.) aspen
**temblor** *m* tremor, shaking, trembling, quivering; shivering; (path.) tremor; (Am.) earthquake; **temblor de tierra** earthquake
**tembloroso -sa** or **tembloso -sa** *adj* shaking, tremulous
**tembo -ba** *adj* (Am.) silly, stupid
**temedero -ra** *adj* dread, fearful
**temedor -dora** *adj* fearful, afraid
**temer** *va* to fear; *vn* to fear; **temer** + *inf* to fear to + *inf;* **temer por** to fear for
**temerario -ria** *adj* rash, reckless, hasty, foolhardy
**temeridad** *f* rashness, recklessness, temerity, foolhardiness
**temerón -rona** *adj* (coll.) blustering; *mf* (coll.) blusterer
**temeroso -sa** *adj* dread, frightful; timorous, timid; fearful
**temescal** *m* (Am.) bathhouse
**temible** *adj* dreadful, terrible, fearful
**Temístocles** *m* Themistocles
**temor** *m* fear, dread
**temoso -sa** *adj* persistent, stubborn
**tempanador** *m* beekeeper's knife (*used for removing the dome*)
**tempanar** *va* to put the head on (*a barrel*); to put the cork dome on (*a beehive*)
**témpano** *m* timbrel, small drum; drumhead, drumskin; head (*of barrel*); flitch (*of bacon*); floe (*of ice*); cork dome (*of beehive*); (arch.) tympan; (mus.) kettledrum; **témpano de hielo** iceberg
**temperación** *f* tempering
**temperadamente** *adv* temperately
**temperamental** *adj* temperamental
**temperamento** *m* temperament (*peculiar character of a person*); conciliation, compromise; weather, state of the weather; (mus.) temperament
**temperancia** *f* var. of **templanza**
**temperante** *adj* temperate (*in indulgence*); conciliatory; (Am.) abstemious; *mf* (Am.) teetotaler
**temperar** *va* to temper, to soften, to moderate, to calm; (med.) to calm; (mus.) to put in tune (*two or more instruments*); *vn* (Am.) to go to a warmer climate
**temperatísimo -ma** *adj super* very or most temperate
**temperatura** *f* temperature; weather; (path.) temperature (*i.e., high temperature, fever*); **temperatura absoluta** (phys.) absolute temperature; **temperatura del cuerpo** body temperature
**temperie** *f* weather, state of the weather
**tempero** *m* (agr.) mellowness of soil
**tempestad** *f* storm, tempest; (orn.) bluebird, western bluebird; **tempestad de arena** sandstorm; **tempestad de lluvia** rainstorm; **tempestades de risas** gales of laughter; **tempestad magnética** (phys.) magnetic storm
**tempestear** *vn* to storm, be stormy; (coll.) to storm (*to rage, become violent*)
**tempestividad** *f* opportuneness, timeliness
**tempestivo -va** *adj* opportune, timely
**tempestuoso -sa** *adj* stormy, tempestuous; (fig.) stormy, tempestuous
**templa** *f* (paint.) distemper (*pigment*); (Am.) juice in sugar pan; **templas** *fpl* (anat.) temples
**templadera** *f* head gate, sluice gate
**templado -da** *adj* temperate (*in indulgence; in climate*); (lit.) moderate (*style*); lukewarm, medium; (coll.) brave, courageous; (Am.) in love; (Am.) tipsy, drunk; (Am.) austere, severe; **bien templado** good-tempered, well-tempered; (mus.) well-tempered; **mal templado** bad-tempered
**templador** *m* (mus.) tuning key or hammer; tempering furnace
**templadura** *f* tempering; moderation; (mus.) tempering
**templanza** *f* temperance; mildness, temperateness (*of climate*)
**templar** *va* to temper; to soften; to ease; to dilute; (mus.) to temper; (naut.) to trim (*sails*) to the wind; (paint.) to blend; *vn* to warm up (*said of weather*); *vr* to temper; to be moderate; to moderate (*said of weather*); (Am.) to fall in love; (Am.) to die
**Templario** *m* Templar, Knight Templar
**temple** *m* weather, state of the weather; temper (*disposition*); humor; average; dash, boldness; temper (*hardness of steel, glass, etc.*); (mus.) tempering; (paint.) distemper (*art or process*); **al temple** (paint.) in distemper; **estar de buen temple** to be in a good humor; **estar de mal temple** to be in a bad humor
**templén** *m* temple (*of a loom*)
**templete** *m* small temple; niche, tabernacle; pavilion; bandstand
**templista** *mf* (paint.) painter in distemper
**templo** *m* temple
**témpora** *f* Ember days; **témporas** *fpl* Ember days
**temporada** *f* season; period; spell; **de temporada** temporarily; **estar de temporada** to be vacationing
**temporal** *adj* temporal; temporary; (anat. & gram.) temporal; *m* weather; spell of rainy weather; storm, tempest; (naut.) whole gale; (anat.) temporal bone; **aguantar un temporal** (naut.) to lie to
**temporalidad** *f* temporality; **temporalidades** *fpl* (eccl.) temporalities
**temporalizar** §76 *va* to secularize
**temporalmente** *adv* temporally; temporarily
**temporáneo -a** or **temporario -ria** *adj* temporary
**temporejar** *vn* (naut.) to lie to
**temporero -ra** *adj* substitute, temporary, provisional; *mf* substitute
**temporizar** §76 *vn* to temporize; to putter around
**tempranal** *adj* early-yielding (*land, crops, etc.*)
**tempranamente** *adv* early
**tempranero -ra** *adj* early
**tempranía** *f* (coll.) earliness
**tempranilla** *f* early grape
**tempranito** *adv* (coll.) pretty early
**temprano -na** *adj* early; *m* early crop; **temprano** *adv* early; **temprano y con sol** bright and early
**temulencia** *f* drunkenness, intoxication
**temulento -ta** *adj* drunk, intoxicated
**ten** *2d sg impv of* **tener; ten con ten** (coll.) caution
**tena** *f* cattle shed
**tenacear** *va* to tear the flesh of (*a person*) with nippers; to torture; *vn* to persist stubbornly
**tenacero** *m* maker, dealer, or user of pincers, pliers, or tongs
**tenacidad** *f* tenacity; (phys.) tenacity
**tenacillas** *fpl* sugar tongs; hair curler; tweezers; snuffers
**tenáculo** *m* (surg.) tenaculum
**tenada** *f* cattle shed
**tenallón** *m* (fort.) tenaillon
**tenante** *m* (her.) supporter (*of an escutcheon*)
**tenar** *adj & m* (anat.) thenar
**tenaz** *adj* (*pl:* **-naces**) tenacious
**tenaza** *f* tenace (*two high cards of a suit*); (fort.) tenaille; **tenazas** *fpl* pincers, pliers; tongs (*to carry coal, ice, wood, etc.*); pincers (*e.g., of a crab*); (dent.) forceps; **tenazas de chimenea** coal tongs, fire tongs; **tenazas de rizar** curling iron
**tenazada** *f* hold with pincers, pliers, or tongs; click of pincers or pliers, clink of tongs; hard bite
**tenazazo** *m* blow with pincers, pliers, or tongs
**tenazón; a** or **de tenazón** without taking aim; offhand
**tenazuelas** *fpl* tweezers
**tenca** *f* (ichth.) tench
**tención** *f* holding, possession
**tendajo** *m* var. of **tendejón**

**tendal** *m* awning; canvas used to catch falling olives; frame for drying clothes; clothes spread out or hung up to dry
**tendalera** *f* (coll.) litter (*on the floor or ground*)
**tendalero** *m* drying place, frame for drying clothes
**tendear** *vn* (Am.) to browse about the stores
**tendedera** *f* (Am.) clothesline
**tendedero** *m* var. of **tendalero**
**tendedor -dora** *mf* spreader, stretcher, tenter, layer, setter; person who hangs or spreads clothes to dry
**tendejón** *m* little shop; shack; shed
**tendel** *m* (mas.) chalk line, leveling line; (mas.) layer of mortar
**tendencia** *f* tendency
**tendenciosidad** *f* tendentiousness
**tendencioso -sa** *adj* tendentious
**tendente** *adj* tending
**tender** §66 *va* to spread, spread out, stretch out; to extend; to reach out; to offer, to tender; to hang out (*clothes to dry*); to coat (*e.g., with plaster*); to lay (*a cable, a track, etc.*); to throw, to build (*a bridge*); to set (*a trap*); (Am.) to lay out (*a corpse*); *vn* to tend; **tender a** + *inf* to tend to + *inf; vr* to stretch out; to throw one's cards on the table; to run at full gallop; (naut.) to swell; (coll.) to become unconcerned, neglectful
**ténder** *m* (rail.) tender
**tenderete** *m* stand, booth; (coll.) litter
**tendero -ra** *mf* storekeeper, shopkeeper; *m* tent maker
**tendezuela** *f* little shop
**tendido** *m* laying (*e.g., of a cable, of a track*); spreading (*e.g., of a curtain of smoke*); hanging, stretching (*of wires*); wires; run of lace; wash (*amount hung up to dry*); batch of bread; coat of plaster; slope of a roof, side of roof; (taur.) uncovered stand, bleachers; (dial.) clear sky; (Am.) bedclothes; **tendido aéreo** overhead wires; **tendido alto** (taur.) upper section (*of seats*); **tendido bajo** (taur.) lower section (*of seats*)
**tendinoso -sa** *adj* tendinous
**tendón** *m* (anat.) tendon; **tendón de Aquiles** (anat.) Achilles' tendon
**tendré** *1st sg fut ind of* **tener**
**tenducha** *f* or **tenducho** *m* poor little store
**tenebrario** *m* (eccl.) tenebrae hearse
**tenebrosidad** *f* darkness, gloom; obscurity
**tenebroso -sa** *adj* dark, gloomy, tenebrous; dark, shady (*e.g., deal*); obscure (*style, writer*)
**tenedero** *m* (naut.) place to anchor
**tenedor** *m* holder; bearer; fork, table fork; (sport) ball boy; **tenedor de acciones** stockholder; **tenedor de bonos** bondholder; **tenedor de libros** bookkeeper; **tenedor de una póliza** (ins.) policyholder
**teneduría** *f* bookkeeping; **teneduría de libros** bookkeeping
**tenencia** *f* tenancy, occupancy, tenure; possession; lieutenancy
**tener** §85 *va* to have; to hold; to keep; to own, possess; to consider; to esteem; to stop; to be the matter with, to ail; **no tenerlas todas consigo** (coll.) to be worried, be scared; **no tener nada que ver con** to have nothing to do with; **no tener sobre qué caerse muerto** (coll.) to not have a cent to one's name; **tener a bien** + *inf* to have the kindness to + *inf;* **tener para sí** to think, to have as one's own opinion; **tener por** to consider as; **tener que** + *inf* to have to + *inf;* **tener que ver con** to have an affair with, to have intercourse with; to have to do with, to deal with; for expressions like **tener hambre** to be hungry, see the noun; *vr* to stop; to catch oneself, to keep from falling; to consider oneself; to fit, to go; **tenerse a** to tend to, attend to; to stick to
**tenería** *f* tannery
**tenesmo** *m* (path.) tenesmus
**tengo** *1st sg pres ind of* **tener**
**tenguerengue; en tenguerengue** (coll.) teetering
**tenia** *f* (anat.) taenia; (arch.) taenia, fillet; (zool.) taenia, tapeworm
**teniasis** *f* (path.) taeniasis
**tenicida** *adj* taeniacidal; *m* taeniacide
**tenida** *f* (Am.) meeting, session
**tenienta** *f* lieutenant; lieutenant's wife
**tenientazgo** *m* lieutenancy
**teniente** *adj* holding, having, owning; immature, unripe; mean, miserly; (coll.) hard of hearing; *m* lieutenant; (mil.) lieutenant, first lieutenant; **teniente coronel** (mil.) lieutenant colonel; **teniente general** (mil.) lieutenant general
**tenífugo -ga** *adj & m* (med.) taeniafuge
**tenis** *m* (sport) tennis
**tenista** *mf* tennis player
**tenístico -ca** *adj* (pertaining to) tennis
**tenor** *m* tenor, character, import, drift; (mus.) tenor (*person; voice; instrument*); **a este tenor** like this; **a tenor de** in accordance with
**tenoriesco -ca** *adj* philandering
**tenorio** *m* lady-killer
**tenotomía** *f* (surg.) tenotomy
**tensar** *va* to tighten, to make taut
**tensible** *adj* tensible
**tensión** *f* tension; tenseness; (lit.) tenson; (mech.) stress (*molecular resistance to outside forces*): **alta tensión** (elec.) high tension; **baja tensión** (elec.) low tension; **en tensión** (elec.) in series; **tensión arterial** or **sanguínea** (med.) arterial tension; **tensión superficial** (phys.) surface tension
**tenso -sa** *adj* tense, tight, taut; tense (*person; situation*)
**tensón** *f* (lit.) tenson
**tensor -sora** *adj* tensile; *m* tension (*device*); guy; turnbuckle; (anat.) tensor
**tentación** *f* temptation
**tentaculado -da** *adj* tentacled
**tentacular** *adj* tentacular
**tentáculo** *m* (bot. & zool.) tentacle; **tentáculos** *mpl* (zool.) feelers
**tentadero** *m* (taur.) testing corral for young bulls
**tentador -dora** *adj* tempting; *m* tempter; **el tentador** the Tempter (*the Devil*); *f* temptress
**tentadura** *f* mercury test of silver ore; thrashing, drubbing
**tentalear** *va* (coll.) to feel for, to examine gropingly
**tentar** §18 *va* to touch; to feel (*e.g., one's way*); to try, to attempt; to examine; to test, try out (*a person*); to tempt; (surg.) to probe; **tentar a uno a** + *inf* to tempt someone to + *inf*
**tentaruja** *f* (coll.) mussing, rumpling
**tentativo -va** *adj* tentative; *f* attempt; preliminary examination; trial, feeler; **tentativa de delito** (law) attempt to commit a crime
**ten.**[te] abr. of **teniente**
**tente; a tente bonete** (coll.) with persistence
**tentejuela** *f* extreme effort, desperate resistance; **hasta tentejuela** (coll.) to the point of exhaustion
**tentemozo** *m* prop, support; pole prop; tumbler (*toy*): cheek strap
**tentempié** *m* (coll.) snack, bite, pick-me-up; tumbler (*toy figure*)
**tentenelaire** *mf* offspring of mulatto and quadroon; (Am.) half-breed
**tentetieso** *m* tumbler (*toy*)
**tentón** *m* (coll.) snatch; **dar un tentón a** (coll.) to snatch at
**tenue** *adj* tenuous; light, soft; faint, subdued; simple (*style*)
**tenuidad** *f* tenuity, tenuousness; trifle, triviality
**tenzón** *f* var. of **tensón**
**teñido** *m* dyeing; staining
**teñidor -dora** *mf* dyer; stainer
**teñidura** *f* dyeing; staining
**teñir** §74 *va* to color; to dye; to stain; (paint.) to darken
**teño -ña** *adj* (Am.) light-brown
**teobroma** *m* (bot.) cacao; chocolate
**teobromina** *f* (chem.) theobromine
**teocali** *m* (Am. archeol.) teocalli (*temple*)
**teocracia** *f* theocracy
**teócrata** *mf* theocrat
**teocrático -ca** *adj* theocratic
**Teócrito** *m* Theocritus
**teodicea** *f* theodicy
**teodolito** *m* theodolite
**Teodorico** *m* Theodoric

**Teodoro** *m* Theodore
**Teodosio** *m* Theodosius
**Teófilo** *m* Theophilus
**Teofrasto** *m* Theophrastus
**teogonía** *f* theogony
**teogónico -ca** *adj* theogonic
**teologal** *adj* var. of **teológico**
**teología** *f* theology; **no meterse en teologías** (coll.) to keep out of deep water
**teológico -ca** *adj* theological
**teologizar** §76 *vn* to theologize; (coll.) to prate like a theologian
**teólogo -ga** *adj* theological; *mf* theologian; divinity student, theologue
**teorema** *m* theorem
**teoría** *f* theory; **teoría atómica** (chem.) atomic theory; **teoría cuántica** or **teoría de los cuanta** (phys.) quantum theory; **teoría del conocimiento** (philos.) theory of knowledge; **teoría electromagnética** (phys.) electromagnetic theory (*of light*); **teoría electrónica** (phys.) electronic theory (*of light*); **teoría germinal** (biol. & path.) germ theory; **teoría ondulatoria** (phys.) undulatory or wave theory (*of light*); **teoría unitaria** (chem.) unitary theory
**teórico -ca** *adj* theoretic or theoretical; *mf* theoretician; theorist; *f* theory
**teorizante** *adj* theorizing; *mf* theorist, theorizer
**teorizar** §76 *va* to theorize on, to deal theoretically with; *vn* to theorize
**teoso -sa** *adj* resinous
**teosofía** *f* theosophy
**teosófico -ca** *adj* theosophic or theosophical
**teósofo -fa** *mf* theosophist
**tepe** *m* sod, turf (*used for making walls*)
**tepetate** *m* (Am.) whitish yellow rock
**tepetomate** *m* (bot.) manzanita (*Arctostaphylos tomentosa*)
**tequila** *m* (Am.) tequila (*distilled liquor*)
**terapeuta** *mf* therapeutist
**terapéutico -ca** *adj* therapeutic or therapeutical; *f* therapeutics
**terapia** *f* therapy; **terapia física** physical therapy
**teratología** *f* teratology
**teratológico -ca** *adj* teratological
**terbio** *m* (chem.) terbium
**tercena** *f* government warehouse (*especially for tobacco*); (Am.) butcher shop
**tercenista** *mf* government warehouseman; (Am.) butcher, meat dealer
**tercer** *adj* apocopated form of **tercero**, used only before masculine singular nouns and adjectives
**tercera** *f* see **tercero**
**tercería** *f* mediation; pandering, procuring; temporary occupation (*of castle, fort, etc.*); (law) right of third party
**tercerilla** *f* tercet in arte menor
**tercero -ra** *adj* third; *mf* third; mediator; go-between; *m* procuror, bawd; referee, umpire; (eccl.) tertiary; (geom.) sixtieth of a second (*of a circle*); *f* tierce (*in cards*); procuress; (mus.) third
**tercerol** *m* (naut.) third (*e.g., oar*)
**tercerola** *f* short carbine; small barrel, keg, tierce
**tercerón -rona** *mf* terceron (*offspring of white person and mulatto*)
**terceto** *m* tercet; (mus.) trio; trio (*group of three*)
**tercia** *f* see **tercio**
**terciado -da** *adj* slanting, crosswise; *m* cutlass, broadsword; broad ribbon
**tercianario -ria** *adj* suffering from tertian fever; infested with tertian fever; *mf* person suffering from tertian fever
**tercianela** *f* double-thread silk cloth
**terciano -na** *adj* tertian; *f* (path.) tertian
**terciar** *va* to place diagonally; to swing (*e.g., a weapon over one's shoulder*); to divide into three parts; to mix; to plow the third time; *vn* to intercede, to mediate; to take part; to fill in; *vr* to suit, be appropriate; to happen, take place, turn out
**terciario -ria** *adj* tertiary; (geol.) Tertiary; *m* (geol.) Tertiary
**terciazón** *f* third plowing
**tercio -cia** *adj* third; *m* third (*one of three equal parts*); pack (*carried by beast of burden*); corps, troop; harbor guild; (archaic) infantry regiment; **tercios** *mpl* tough limbs; **hacer buen tercio a** to do a good turn; **hacer mal tercio a** to do a bad turn; **hacer tercio** to fill in; **mejorado en tercio y quinto** greatly favored; *f* third; tierce (*in cards*); (eccl.) tierce
**terciopelado -da** *adj* velvety; *m* velours
**terciopelero** *m* velvet weaver
**terciopelo** *m* velvet
**terco -ca** *adj* stubborn; hard, resistant
**terebinto** *m* (bot.) terebinth
**terebrante** *adj* boring, piercing (*pain*)
**teredo** *m* (zool.) teredo
**Terencio** *m* Terence
**Teresa** *f* Theresa
**tergiversación** *f* tergiversation; slanting, twisting, perversion (*of facts, statements, etc.*)
**tergiversador -dora** *adj* tergiversating; *mf* tergiversator
**tergiversar** *va* to slant, to twist (*facts, statements, etc.*); *vn* to tergiversate
**teriaca** *f* var. of **triaca**
**teriacal** *adj* var. of **triacal**
**teriantrópico -ca** *adj* therianthropic
**teridófita** *f* (bot.) pteridophyte
**teriomórfico -ca** *adj* theriomorphic
**terliz** *m* ticking
**termal** *adj* thermal; steam (*power plant*)
**termas** *fpl* thermae, hot baths
**termatizar** §76 *va* (phys.) to thermalize or thermatize
**termia** *f* (phys.) therm
**térmico -ca** *adj* thermic; (pertaining to) temperature; steam-generated (*power*)
**terminabilidad** *f* terminability
**terminable** *adj* terminable
**terminación** *f* termination; (gram.) termination, ending
**terminacho** *m* (coll.) vulgar term; (coll.) blunder, barbarism
**terminador -dora** *adj* finishing; *mf* finisher; *f* finishing machine
**terminajo** *m* (coll.) var. of **terminacho**
**terminal** *adj* terminal; *m* (elec.) terminal; **terminales** *mpl* (Am.) bargains at end of season
**terminante** *adj* final, definitive, peremptory
**terminar** *va* to terminate, to end; to finish; *vn* to terminate, to end; **terminar por** + *inf* or **terminar** + *ger* to end by + *ger*; *vr* to terminate, to end; to lead, to issue
**terminativo -va** *adj* terminative
**terminista** *mf* phrasemaker
**término** *m* end, limit; boundary; manner, bearing; term; (arch., log. & math.) term; (*cap.*) *m* (myth.) Terminus; **en buenos términos** on good terms; in other words; **estar en buenos términos con** to be on good terms with; **llevar a término** to carry out; **pasar los términos** to go too far; **medio término** subterfuge, evasion; compromise; **poner término a** to put an end to; **por término medio** on an average; **primer término** foreground; (mov.) close-up; **segundo término** middle distance; **último término** background; **término fatal** (law) deadline; **término medio** average; compromise; (log.) middle term; **término municipal** township
**terminología** *f* terminology
**terminológico -ca** *adj* terminological
**terminote** *m* (coll.) big word
**termio** *m* (phys.) therm
**termión** *m* (phys.) thermion
**termiónico -ca** *adj* thermionic; *f* thermionics
**termistor** *m* (elec.) thermistor
**termita** *f* (chem.) thermit; (ent. & fig.) termite
**termite** *m* (ent.) termite
**termitero** *m* nest of termites
**termito** *m* (ent.) termite
**termo** *m* thermos bottle
**termobarógrafo** *m* thermobarograph
**termobarómetro** *m* thermobarometer
**termocauterio** *m* thermocautery
**termodinámico -ca** *adj* thermodynamic; *f* thermodynamics
**termoelectricidad** *f* thermoelectricity
**termoeléctrico -ca** *adj* thermoelectric or thermoelectrical

**termoelectromotor -triz** (*pl:* **-trices**) *adj* thermoelectromotive
**termoelemento** *m* (elec.) thermoelement
**termoestesia** *f* (physiol.) thermesthesia
**termofisión** *f* (phys.) thermofission
**termofusión** *f* (phys.) thermofusion
**termogénesis** *f* (physiol.) thermogenesis
**termógeno -na** *adj* thermogenetic
**termógrafo** *m* thermograph
**termoiónico -ca** *adj* var. of **termiónico**
**termolábil** *adj* (biochem.) thermolabile
**termólisis** *f* (chem. & physiol.) thermolysis
**termología** *f* thermology
**termometría** *f* thermometry
**termométrico -ca** *adj* thermometric
**termómetro** *m* thermometer; **termómetro centígrado** centigrade thermometer; **termómetro clínico** clinical thermometer; **termómetro diferencial** differential thermometer
**termomotor -triz** (*pl:* **-trices**) *adj* thermomotive; *m* heat engine
**termomultiplicador** *m* (phys.) thermomultiplier, thermopile
**termonuclear** *adj* thermonuclear
**termopar** *m* (elec.) thermocouple
**termopila** *f* (phys.) thermopile
**Termópilas, las** Thermopylae
**termoplástico -ca** *adj* thermoplastic
**termoquímico -ca** *adj* thermochemical; *f* thermochemistry
**termos** *m & f* (*pl:* **-mos**) thermos bottle; **termos de acumulación** (elec.) off-peak hot-water heater; **termos eléctrico** electric hot-water heater
**termoscopio** *m* thermoscope
**termosifón** *m* thermosiphon; boiler, hot-water boiler (*for heating rooms or water*)
**termostático -ca** *adj* thermostatic
**termóstato** *m* thermostat
**termotropismo** *m* (biol.) thermotropism
**terna** *f* three candidates presented for selection; pair of threes (*at dice*); set of dice
**ternado -da** *adj* (bot.) ternate
**ternario -ria** *adj* ternary; *m* three days' devotion
**terne** *adj* (coll.) strong, husky; (coll.) persistent, stubborn; (coll.) bullying; *m* (coll.) bully; (Am.) gaucho knife
**ternejal** *adj* (coll.) bullying; *m* (coll.) bully
**ternejo -ja** *adj* (Am.) peppy, energetic
**ternejón -jona** *adj & mf* (coll.) var. of **ternerón**
**ternera** *f* calf; veal; **ternera marina** (zool.) sea cow
**ternero** *m* bull calf
**ternerón -rona** *adj* (coll.) sentimental, easily moved; *mf* (coll.) sentimental person
**terneruela** *f* sucking calf
**terneza** *f* tenderness; fondness, love; **ternezas** *fpl* sweet nothings
**ternilla** *f* gristle
**ternilloso -sa** *adj* gristly
**ternísimo -ma** *adj super* very or most tender
**terno** *m* suit of clothes; oath, curse; set of three; tern (*in lottery*); (print.) three sheets folded together; (eccl.) group of three priests celebrating high mass; (eccl.) vestments of three priests celebrating high mass; (coll.) piece of luck; **echar ternos** to swear to curse
**ternura** *f* tenderness; fondness, love
**terpeno** *m* (chem.) terpene
**terpineol** *m* (chem.) terpineol
**Terpsícore** *f* (myth.) Terpsichore
**terquear** *vn* to be stubborn
**terquedad** *f* stubbornness, obstinacy, bullheadedness
**terracota** *f* terra cotta
**terrada** *f* bitumen
**terrado** *m* high terrace, flat roof
**terraja** *f* diestock; modeling board
**terraje** *m* land rent
**terrajero** *m* var. of **terrazguero**
**terral** *adj* land (*breeze*); *m* land breeze
**terramicina** *f* (pharm.) terramycin
**Terranova** *f* Newfoundland (*island and province*); *m* Newfoundland (*dog*)
**terraplén** *m* fill; embankment; terrace, platform; (fort.) earthwork, rampart; (fort.) terreplein
**terraplenar** *va* to fill, fill in; to embank; to terrace
**terráqueo -a** *adj* terraqueous (*globe, sphere, planet*)
**terrateniente** *mf* landholder, landowner
**terraza** *f* terrace; veranda; flat roof; border, edge (*in garden*); sidewalk café; glazed jar with two handles; (geol.) terrace
**terrazgo** *m* field for planting; land rent
**terrazguero** *m* lessee of a field for raising crops
**terrazo** *m* (paint.) ground, earth (*in a landscape*)
**terrear** *va* (Am.) to lick (*salt earth*); *vn* to be thinly sown (*said of soil, of a field, of crops*); (Am.) to drag one's feet
**terrecer** §34 *va* to frighten, terrify
**terregoso -sa** *adj* cloddy, lumpy
**terremoto** *m* earthquake
**terrenal** *adj* earthly, mundane, worldly
**terrenidad** *f* earthliness
**terreno -na** *adj* terrestrial; mundane, worldly; *m* land, ground, terrain; plot, lot, piece of land; (geol.) terrane, terrain; (sport) field, course, grounds; (fig.) field, sphere; **ceder terreno** to give ground, to yield ground; **ganar terreno** to gain ground; **medir el terreno** to see how the land lies; **minar el terreno a** to undermine the work of; **perder terreno** to lose ground; **preparar el terreno** to pave the way; **sobre el terreno** on the spot; with data in hand; **terreno de relleno** filled ground, made ground; **terreno echadizo** dump, refuse dump
**térreo -a** *adj* earthen, earthy
**terrero -ra** *adj* earthly; of earth; humble; low-flying (*bird*); *m* pile, heap (*of earth, brush, etc.*); mark, target; terrace; public square; alluvium; (min.) dump; **hacer terreros** to make love or to serenade from the street (*in front of lady's house*); *f* steep ground; frail for carrying earth; (orn.) lark
**terrestre** *adj* terrestrial, land
**terrezuela** *f* worthless piece of ground
**terribilidad** *f* terribleness
**terribilísimo -ma** *adj super* very or most terrible
**terrible** *adj* terrible; gruff, ill-tempered
**terrícola** *adj* (bot. & zool.) terricolous; *mf* earth dweller
**terrier** *m* terrier
**terrífico -ca** *adj* terrific
**terrígeno -na** *adj* earthborn
**terrino -na** *adj* earthy, terrene
**territorial** *adj* territorial
**territorialidad** *f* territoriality
**territorio** *m* territory; **territorio del Labrador** Labrador; **Territorios del Noroeste** Northwest Territories (*of Canada*)
**terromontero** *m* hill, butte
**terrón** *m* clod; lump; (coll.) small plot of ground; **terrones** *mpl* farm
**terronazo** *m* blow with a clod of earth
**terror** *m* terror; (*cap.*) *m* (hist.) Reign of Terror
**terrorífico -ca** *adj* terrific, frightful
**terrorismo** *m* terrorism, frightfulness
**terrorista** *adj* terrorist, terroristic; *mf* terrorist
**terrosidad** *f* earthiness; dirtiness
**terroso -sa** *adj* earthy; dirty
**terruño** *m* piece of ground; soil; country, native soil
**tersar** *va* to smooth, to polish, to shine
**tersidad** *f* var. of **tersura**
**Tersites** *m* (myth.) Thersites
**terso -sa** *adj* smooth, glossy, polished; smooth, limpid, flowing (*style*)
**tersura** *f* smoothness, glossiness, polish; smoothness (*of style*)
**tertulia** *f* party, social gathering; game room (*in the back of a café*); (Am.) orchestra seat; **estar de tertulia** to go to a party, to sit around and talk; **hacer tertulia** to sit around and talk; to talk (*when one should not, e.g., in class*)
**tertuliano -na** *adj* party-going; *mf* party-goer, member of a social gathering; (*cap.*) *m* Tertullian
**tertuliante** *adj* party-going; *mf* party-goer, member of a social gathering

**tertuliar** *vn* (Am.) to go to a party, to sit around and talk
**tertulio -lia** *adj & mf* var. of **tertuliante**
**tertulión** *m* big party, big gathering
**terzuelo** *m* third; (orn.) tercel, male falcon
**Tesalia, la** Thessaly
**tesaliano -na** *adj & mf* Thessalian
**tesálico -ca** *adj* Thessalian
**tesaliense, tesalio -lia** or **tésalo -la** *adj & mf* var. of **tesaliano**
**tesalonicense** *adj & mf* Thessalonian
**tesalónico -ca** *adj & mf* Thessalonian; (*cap.*) *f* Thessalonica
**tesar** *va* (naut.) to haul taut; *vn* to back, to pull back (*said of oxen*)
**tesauro** *m* thesaurus
**tesela** *f* tessera (*in mosaic work*)
**teselado -da** *adj* tessellate; *m* tessellated paving, mosaic pavement
**Teseo** *m* (myth.) Theseus
**tésera** *f* (hist.) tessera
**tesis** *f* (*pl:* **-sis**) thesis; (mus.) thesis
**tesitura** *f* attitude, state of mind; (mus.) tessitura
**teso -sa** *adj* taut, tight, tense; *m* top of a hill; rough spot (*on smooth surface*)
**tesón** *m* grit, pluck, tenacity
**tesonería** *f* obstinacy, stubbornness
**tesonero -ra** *adj* obstinate, stubborn
**tesorería** *f* treasury; treasurership
**tesorero -ra** *mf* treasurer
**tesoro** *m* treasure; treasury; treasure house; thesaurus
**Tespis** *m* Thespis
**test** *m* (educ. & psychol.) test
**testa** *f* head; front; (bot.) testa; (zool.) test or testa; (coll.) head, brains; **testa coronada** crowned head (*sovereign*); **testa de ferro** (coll.) figurehead, dummy, straw man
**testáceo -a** *adj & m* (zool.) testacean
**testación** *f* cancellation, erasure
**testado -da** *adj* testate; *f* blow with the head
**testador -dora** *mf* testator; *f* testatrix
**testadura** *f* var. of **testación**
**testaférrea** *m* or **testaferro** *m* (coll.) figurehead, dummy, straw man
**testamentaría** *f* testamentary execution; estate, inheritance; meeting of executors
**testamentario -ria** *adj* testamentary; *m* executor; *f* executrix
**testamentifacción** *f* or **testamentificación** *f* (law) power to make a will
**testamento** *m* testament, will; **Antiguo Testamento** Old Testament; **Nuevo Testamento** New Testament; **Viejo Testamento** Old Testament; **testamento nuncupativo** (law) nuncupative will
**testar** *va* (law) to seize, to attach; (obs.) to erase; (Am.) to underline; *vn* to make a testament or will
**testarada** *f* blow with the head; (coll.) stubbornness
**testarro** *m* piece of junk (*old furniture*); wreck (*sickly, useless person*)
**testarrón -rrona** *adj* (coll.) var. of **testarudo**
**testarronería** *f* (coll.) great stubbornness
**testarudez** *f* stubbornness, pig-headedness
**testarudo -da** *adj* stubborn, pig-headed
**teste** *m* (anat.) testis
**testera** *f* front; forehead (*of animal*); crownpiece (*of harness*); back seat (*of coach*); wall (*of furnace*)
**testero** *m* front; (min.) overhand stope
**testicular** *adj* testicular
**testículo** *m* (anat.) testicle
**testificación** *f* attestation, testification
**testifical** *adj* of a witness, of witnesses
**testificante** *adj* testifying
**testificar** §86 *va & vn* to testify
**testificativo -va** *adj* testificatory
**testigo** *mf* witness; **testigo auricular** auricular witness; **testigo de cargo** witness for the prosecution; **testigo de descargo** witness for the defense; **testigo de oídas** auricular witness; **testigo de vista, testigo ocular** or **testigo presencial** eyewitness; **testigos de Jehová** Jehovah's Witnesses; *m* witness (*evidence*); marker; control (*in an experiment*)
**testimonial** *adj* testificatory; **testimoniales** *fpl* (eccl.) testimonial
**testimoniar** *va* to attest, to testify to, to bear witness to
**testimoniero -ra** *adj* false, perjured; hypocritical
**testimonio** *m* testimony; false accusation; (Bib.) testimony; **en testimonio de lo cual** in testimony whereof
**test.mto** abr. of **testamento**
**test.o** abr. of **testigo**
**testolín** *m* (ichth.) spotted sea robin
**testosterona** *f* (biochem.) testosterone
**testudinal** *adj* (zool.) testudinal
**testudíneo -a** *adj* testudinous
**testudo** *m* (hist.) testudo
**testuz** *m* (*pl:* **-tuces**) nape (*of animal*); forehead (*of animal*)
**testuzo** *m* var. of **testuz**
**tesura** *f* var. of **tiesura**
**teta** *f* teat; breast; hummock, knoll; **dar la teta a** to suckle; **quitar la teta a** to wean; **teta de vaca** conical meringue
**tetada** *f* feeding, breast feeding
**tetania** *f* (path.) tetany
**tetánico -ca** *adj* tetanic
**tetanizar** §76 *va* to tetanize
**tétano** or **tétanos** *m* (path.) tetanus
**tetar** *va* to suckle
**tetartoédrico -ca** *adj* (cryst.) tetartohedral
**tetartoedro** *m* (cryst.) tetartohedron
**tetera** *f* teapot, teakettle
**tetero** *m* (Am.) nursing bottle
**tetigonia** *f* (ent.) grouse locust
**tetilla** *f* nipple (*of male; of nursing bottle*)
**Tetis** *f* (myth.) Thetis
**tetón** *m* stub (*of limb of tree*); (naut.) jutting rock
**tetraciclina** *f* (pharm.) tetracycline
**tetracloruro** *m* (chem.) tetrachloride
**tetracordal** *adj* (mus.) tetrachordal
**tetracordio** *m* (mus.) tetrachord
**tetracromía** *f* (print.) four-color process
**tetradimita** *f* (mineral.) tetradymite
**tetraédrico -ca** *adj* tetrahedral
**tetraedro** *m* (geom.) tetrahedron
**tetraetilo de plomo** *m* (chem.) tetraethyl lead
**tetragonal** *adj* tetragonal
**tetrágono** *m* (geom.) tetragon
**tetralogía** *f* (theat.) tetralogy
**tetrámetro -tra** *adj & m* tetrameter
**tetramotor** *m* (aer.) four-motor plane
**tetrapétalo -la** *adj* (bot.) tetrapetalous
**tetrarca** *m* tetrarch
**tetrarquía** *f* tetrarchy
**tetrasilábico -ca** *adj* tetrasyllabic
**tetrasílabo -ba** *adj* tetrasyllabic; *m* tetrasyllable
**tetravalente** *adj* (chem.) tetravalent
**tétrico -ca** *adj* dark, gloomy, sullen
**tetril** *m* tetryl
**tetrodo** or **tétrodo** *m* (elec.) tetrode
**tetróxido** *m* (chem.) tetroxide
**tetuaní** (*pl:* **-níes**) *adj* (pertaining to) Tetuán; *mf* native or inhabitant of Tetuán
**teucali** *m* var. of **teocali**
**teucro -cra** *adj & mf* Teucrian; (*cap.*) *m* (myth.) Teucer
**teurgia** *f* theurgy
**teúrgico -ca** *adj* theurgic or theurgical
**teurgo** *m* theurgist
**teutón -tona** *adj & mf* Teuton
**teutónico -ca** *adj* Teutonic; *m* Teutonic (*language*)
**textil** *adj & m* textile
**texto** *m* text; textbook; (print.) great primer; **el Sagrado texto** the Bible; **fuera de texto** (b.b.) tipped-in (*e.g., illustration, map*); **grabado fuera de texto** (b.b.) inset, insert
**textorio -ria** *adj* textile
**textual** *adj* textual
**textualista** *m* textualist
**textura** *f* texture; weaving; (fig.) texture (*structure*)
**textural** *adj* textural
**tez** *f* complexion
**tezado -da** *adj* tan
**ti** *pron pers* (used as object of preposition) thee; you

**tía** *f* aunt; old lady; (coll.) coarse woman; (coll.) bawd, prostitute; **no hay tu tía** (coll.) there's no use, there's no chance; **quedar** or **quedarse para tía** (coll.) to be left an old maid; **tía abuela** grandaunt, great-aunt
**tialina** *f* var. of **ptialina**
**tialismo** *m* var. of **ptialismo**
**tiamina** *f* (biochem.) thiamine
**tiara** *f* tiara
**tiazol** *m* (chem.) thiazole
**Tíber** *m* Tiber
**tiberio** *m* (coll.) noise, hubbub, uproar; (*cap.*) *m* Tiberius
**Tibet, el** Tibet
**tibetano -na** *adj & mf* Tibetan; *m* Tibetan (*language*)
**tibia** *f* see **tibio**
**tibial** *adj* tibial
**tibieza** *f* tepidity, lukewarmness; (fig.) tepidity, lukewarmness; (fig.) coolness, coldness
**tibio -bia** *adj* tepid, lukewarm; (fig.) tepid, lukewarm; *f* (anat.) tibia, shinbone; (mus.) tibia, flute, pipe
**tibor** *m* large Chinese or Japanese earthen jar; (Am.) chamber pot; (Am.) chocolate cup
**tiburón** *m* (ichth.) shark
**tic** *m* (*pl:* **tiques**) (path.) tic; **tic doloroso de la cara** (path.) tic douloureux
**Ticiano, El** Titian
**tictac** *m* tick, tick-tock
**tiemblo** *m* (bot.) aspen, aspen tree
**tiempo** *m* time; weather; stage; (gram.) tense; (mach.) cycle (*of an internal-combustion engine*); (mus.) tempo; (mus.) movement (*e.g., of a symphony*); **abrir el tiempo** to begin to clear up, to moderate; **al poco tiempo** within a short time; **alzar** or **alzarse el tiempo** to clear up; **a su tiempo** in due time; **a tiempo** in time; **a tiempo que** at the time that; **a tiempo para** + *inf* in time to + *inf;* **a tiempos** at times; **a un tiempo** at the same time; **cargarse el tiempo** to cloud over; **con tiempo** in time; **cuánto tiempo** how long; **darse buen tiempo** to have a good time; **de cuatro tiempos** (mach.) four-cycle; **de dos tiempos** (mach.) two-cycle; **de tiempo en tiempo** from time to time; **de un tiempo a esta parte** for some time, for some time now; **el Tiempo** Father Time; **engañar el tiempo** to kill time; **en los buenos tiempos** in the good old days; **en tiempo** at the right time; **en tiempo de** at the time of; **en tiempo oportuno** in due time; **entretener el tiempo** to kill time, to pass the time away; **fuera de tiempo** untimely, at the wrong time; **ganar tiempo** (coll.) to make time; (coll.) to temporize; **gastar el tiempo** to waste time; **hacer tiempo** to mark time; **hacer buen tiempo** to be clear, to be good weather; **hacer mal tiempo** to be bad weather; **medio tiempo** meantime; **mucho tiempo** a long time; **pasar el tiempo** to fritter away the time; **perder el tiempo** to waste time; **poner a mal tiempo buena cara** to make the best of a bad situation; **tomarse tiempo** to bide one's time; **tiempo de exposición** (phot.) time, exposure time; **tiempo inmemorable** time immemorial, time out of mind; **tiempo inmemorial** (law) time immemorial; **tiempo medio** (astr.) mean time; **tiempo muerto** dull season; **tiempo (solar) verdadero** (astr.) true time
**tienda** *f* store, shop; tent; tilt (*cloth cover of cart or wagon*); (naut.) awning; **abrir tienda** to set up shop; **alzar** or **levantar tienda** to shut up shop; **ir de tiendas** to go shopping; **tienda de antigüedades** antique shop; **tienda de campaña** army tent; **tienda de descuento** discount house; **tienda de modas** ladies' dress shop; **tienda de objetos de regalo** gift shop; **tienda de oxígeno** (med.) oxygen tent; **tienda de pacotilla** slopshop; **tienda de playa** beach tent; **tienda de raya** company store (*on Mexican ranch*); **tienda de ultramarinos** delicatessen store, grocery store
**tienta** *f* cleverness, shrewdness; (surg.) probe; sounding rod; (taur.) testing the mettle of a young bull or cow; **andar a tientas** to grope, to grope in the dark; (fig.) to feel one's way
**tientaguja** *f* sounding rod
**tientaparedes** *mf* (*pl:* **-des**) groper, groper in the dark
**tiento** *m* touch; blind man's stick; ropewalker's pole (*for balance*); steady hand; care, caution; (mus.) flourish (*before beginning to play*); (paint.) mahlstick, maulstick; (coll.) blow, hit; (coll.) swig; (zool.) tentacle; **andarse con tiento** to watch one's step; **a tiento** gropingly; with uncertainty; **con tiento** cautiously; **dar tiento a** to test, to try; (coll.) to take a swig from (*a bottle, a jug*); **de tiento en tiento** trying one thing after another; **perder el tiento** to lose one's touch; **por el tiento** gropingly, groping in the dark; **tener a los tientos** (Am.) to keep at hand; (Am.) to keep in sight, to keep an eye on (*a person*); **tener la vida en un tiento** (Am.) to be in great danger; **tomar el tiento a** (coll.) to examine
**tierno -na** *adj* tender; loving; tearful; soft (*e.g., cushion*)
**tierra** *f* earth; ground; dirt; land; country; (elec.) ground; **besar la tierra** (coll.) to fall flat on one's face; **caer a tierra** to fall on the ground, to fall on the floor; **dar en tierra con** to upset, overthrow, wreck, ruin; **echar en** or **por tierra** to upset, knock down; to destroy; to overthrow; **echar tierra a** to hush up; **en tierra, mar y aire** on land, on sea, and in the air; **irse a tierra** to topple, to collapse; **la tierra de nadie** (mil.) no man's land; **perder tierra** to lose one's footing; to be swept off one's feet; **poner por tierra** to demolish; **por estas tierras** in these parts; **por tierra** by land, overland; **tomar tierra** to land; to find one's way about; **venir** or **venirse a tierra** to topple, to collapse; **ver tierras** to see the world, to go traveling; **tierra adentro** inland; **tierra de batán** or **de bataneros** fuller's earth; **tierra de Hus** (Bib.) Uz; **tierra de labor** cultivated land; **tierra de ladrillos** brick clay; **tierra de pan llevar** (agr.) wheat land, cereal-growing land; **tierra de pipa** or **pipas** pipe clay; **Tierra de promisión** (Bib.) Land of Promise, Promised Land; **tierra de promisión** (fig.) promised land; **tierra de sombra** umber; **tierra firme** mainland; land, terra firma; **Tierra Firme** Spanish Main; **tierra japónica** (pharm.) terra japonica; **tierra pesada** (mineral.) heavy earth; **Tierra prometida** (Bib.) Promised Land; **tierra prometida** (fig.) promised land; **tierra rara** (chem.) rare earth; **Tierra Santa** Holy Land; **tierras antárticas** Antarctica; **tierra vegetal** vegetable mold
**tieso -sa** *adj* stiff; tight, taut, tense; strong, well; bold, enterprising; stubborn; stiff, stuck-up; **tenérselas tiesas a** or **con** (coll.) to hold one's ground with, to stand up to; **tenerse tieso** to hold tight; **tieso** *adv* hard
**tiesto -ta** *adj* stiff; tight, taut, tense; stubborn; **tiesto** *adv* hard; *m* flowerpot; broken piece of earthenware; *f* edge of headings (*of a barrel*)
**tiesura** *f* stiffness; (fig.) stiffness
**tífico -ca** *adj* typhous, typhic; typhoid
**tifo -fa** *adj* (coll.) full, satiated; *m* (path.) typhus; **tifo asiático** (path.) Asiatic cholera; **tifo de América** (path.) yellow fever; **tifo de Oriente** (path.) bubonic plague
**tifoideo -a** *adj* typhoidal; typhoid
**tifón** *m* waterspout; typhoon
**tifus** *m* (path.) typhus; (slang) free seats (*in theater*); **entrar de tifus** (slang) to get in free; **tifus exantemático** (path.) spotted fever, typhus fever; **tifus icteroides** (path.) yellow fever
**tigana** *f* (orn.) sunbird, sun bittern
**tigmotaxia** *f* (biol.) thigmotaxis
**tigmotropismo** *m* (biol.) thigmotropism
**tigra** *f* female tiger; (Am.) female jaguar
**tigre** *m* (zool.) tiger; (fig.) tiger (*bloodthirsty person*); (Am.) jaguar; **tigre de Bengala** or **tigre real** Bengal tiger
**tigresa** *f* tigress
**tigrillo** *m* (zool.) gray fox
**tigrino -na** *adj* tigerish, tigrine
**tija** *f* stem (*of key*)

**tijera** *f* scissors, shears; sawbuck, sawhorse; day's shearing (*of sheep*); gossip; **tijeras** *fpl* scissors, shears; **buena tijera** (coll.) good cutter; (coll.) good eater, trencherman; (coll.) terrible gossip; **hacer tijera** to twist the mouth (*said of a horse*)
**tijerada** *f* snip, clip, cut (*with scissors*)
**tijereta** *f* tendril (*of vine*); (ent.) earwig; (orn.) man-of-war bird; (orn.) fork-tailed flycatcher (*Milvulus tyrannus*); **tijeretas** *fpl* small scissors or shears; **¡tijeretas han de ser!** silly obstinacy!
**tijeretada** *f* or **tijeretazo** *m* var. of **tijerada**
**tijeretear** *va* to snip, clip, cut (*with scissors*); (coll.) to deal arbitrarily with (*another person's affairs*); *vn* (Am.) to gossip
**tijereteo** *m* snipping, clipping, cutting; click, clicking (*of scissors*)
**tijerilla** or **tijeruela** *f* small scissors; tendril (*of vine*)
**til** *m* (bot.) til
**tila** *f* (bot.) linden tree; flower of linden tree; linden-blossom tea; **tomar tila** (coll.) to hold one's tongue
**tílburi** *m* tilbury
**tildar** *va* to put a tilde or dash over; to erase, strike out; to brand, stigmatize; **tildar de** to brand as
**tilde** *m & f* tilde (*on letter n*); accent mark; superior dash; blemish, flaw; censure; (phonet.) til; *f* jot, tittle
**tildío** *m* (orn.) killdee
**tildón** *m* scratch, erasure
**tiliáceo -a** *adj* (bot.) tiliaceous
**tiliche** *m* (Am.) trinket; (Am.) fragment, piece
**tilichero -ra** *mf* (Am.) peddler
**tilín** *m* ting-a-ling; **hacer tilín** (coll.) to be well liked; **tener tilín** (coll.) to be appealing, be winsome
**tilio** *m* (bot.) wahoo
**tilo** *m* (bot.) linden tree
**tilla** *f* (naut.) part deck
**tillado** *m* board floor
**tillar** *va* to floor
**timador -dora** *mf* thief, swindler
**tímalo** *m* (ichth.) grayling
**timar** *va* to snitch; to swindle; *vr* (coll.) to make eyes at each other
**timba** *f* (coll.) game of chance; (coll.) gambling den; (Am.) belly
**timbal** *m* (mus.) timbal, kettledrum; (cook.) timbale
**timbalear** *vn* to play the kettledrum
**timbalero** *m* kettledrummer
**timbrado -da** *adj* stamped; **bien timbrado** sonorous (*voice*)
**timbrar** *va* to stamp; (her.) to timbre
**timbrazo** *m* loud ring (*e.g., of doorbell*)
**timbre** *m* seal, stamp; tax stamp; stamp duty or tax; bell, electric bell; snare (*of drum*); test pressure (*of boiler*); deed of glory; (her., phonet., & phys.) timbre; (Am.) postage stamp; **timbres** *mpl* (mus.) glockenspiel; **timbre adherido** adhesive stamp; **timbre nasal** twang
**timbrófilo -la** *adj & mf* philatelist
**timeleáceo -a** *adj* (bot.) thymelaeaceous
**tímico -ca** *adj* thymic (*pertaining to thyme*); thymic, thymus
**timidez** *f* timidity
**tímido -da** *adj* timid
**timo** *m* (coll.) theft, swindle; (coll.) lie; (coll.) catch phrase; (anat.) thymus; (ichth.) grayling; **dar un timo a** (coll.) to cheat, swindle, trick
**timocracia** *f* timocracy
**timocrático -ca** *adj* timocratic or timocratical
**timol** *m* (chem.) thymol
**timón** *m* beam (*of plow*); (naut. & aer.) rudder; (fig.) helm; **timón de dirección** (aer.) vertical rudder; **timón de profundidad** (aer.) elevator, horizontal rudder
**timonear** *vn* (naut.) to steer
**timonel** *m* (naut.) helmsman, steersman
**timoneo** *m* (naut.) steering
**timonera** *adj fem* (orn.) rectricial; *f* (naut.) pilot house, wheelhouse
**timorato -ta** *adj* God-fearing; timid, chicken-hearted
**Timoteo** *m* Timothy
**timpa** *f* (metal.) tymp; (metal.) hearth, grate
**timpánico -ca** *adj* (anat. & med.) tympanic
**timpanismo** *m* (path.) distention of the abdomen
**timpanítico -ca** *adj* tympanitic
**timpanitis** *f* (path.) tympanitis (*inflammation of middle ear*); (path.) tympanites (*distention caused by gas*)
**timpanizar** **§76** *vr* (path.) to become distended with gas
**tímpano** *m* (arch.) tympanum; (anat.) tympanum, eardrum; (mus.) timpano, kettledrum; (print.) tympan
**tina** *f* large earthen jar; wooden vat or tub; bathtub; juice oozing from heap of olives
**tinaco** *m* wooden vat
**tinada** *f* woodpile, fagot; cattle shed
**tinado** or **tinador** *m* cattle shed
**tinaja** *f* large earthen jar
**tinajero** *m* maker or seller of earthen water jars; stand for earthen water jars
**tinajón** *m* earthen tank (*to catch rain water*)
**tinamú** *m* (*pl:* **-múes**) (orn.) tinamou
**tincal** *m* tincal
**tincar** **§86** *va* (Am.) to fillip
**tincazo** *m* (Am.) fillip
**tinción** *f* dyeing
**tinelo** *m* servants' dining room
**tinerfeño -ña** *adj* (pertaining to) Teneriffe; *mf* native or inhabitant of Teneriffe
**tinge** *m* big black owl
**tingladillo** *m* (naut.) clinker work
**tinglado** *m* shed; temporary board floor; intrigue, trick
**tingle** *f* glazier's tool for leading window glass
**tinieblas** *fpl* darkness; (eccl.) Tenebrae
**tinillo** *m* reservoir of wine press (*for collecting must*)
**tino** *m* feel (*for things*); good aim; knack; insight, wisdom; stone tank (*in wool factory*); wine press; (bot.) laurustine; **a buen tino** (coll.) by sight, by guess; **a tino** gropingly; **coger el tino** to get the hang of it, to catch on; **sacar de tino** to wallop; to astound, confound; **sin tino** without moderation, without sense
**tinta** *f* see **tinto**
**tintaje** *m* inking (*of press or typewriter*)
**tintar** *va* to color, to tint
**tinte** *m* dye; dyeing; dyer's shop, dyeing establishment; (fig.) coloring, false appearance
**tinterazo** *m* blow with an inkwell
**tinterillada** *f* (Am.) pettifoggery
**tinterillo** *m* (coll.) clerk, lawyer's clerk; (Am.) pettifogger
**tintero** *m* inkstand, inkwell; (print.) ink fountain; **dejar en el tintero** (coll.) to forget, to overlook
**tintín** *m* clink; jingle
**tintinar** or **tintinear** *vn* to clink; to jingle
**tintineo** *m* clink, clinking; jingle, jingling
**tinto -ta** *adj* red; (Am.) dark-red; *m* red table wine; *f* ink; tint, hue; dyeing; paint (*mixed for painting*); (zool.) ink (*e.g., of squid*); **de buena tinta** (coll.) on good authority; **media tinta** (paint. & phot.) half-tone; **medias tintas** (coll.) vague notions; **tinta china** India ink; **tinta de copiar** copying ink; **tinta de imprenta** printer's ink; **tinta simpática** invisible ink, sympathetic ink
**tintóreo -a** *adj* tinctorial, dyeing
**tintorera** *f* see **tintorero**
**tintorería** *f* dyeing; dyeing establishment; dry-cleaning establishment
**tintorero -ra** *mf* dyer; dry cleaner; *f* (Am.) female shark
**tintura** *f* dye; dyeing; rouge; (pharm.) tincture; (fig.) tincture, smattering; **tintura compuesta de alcanfor** (pharm.) paregoric; **tintura de tornasol** litmus solution, litmus; **tintura de yodo** (pharm.) iodine
**tinturar** *va* to tincture; (fig.) to tincture; (fig.) to give a smattering to
**tiña** *f* (ent.) beehive spider; (path.) tinea; (path.) ringworm; (coll.) stinginess
**tiñería** *f* (coll.) stinginess
**tiñoso -sa** *adj* scabby, mangy; (coll.) stingy
**tiñuela** *f* (bot.) dodder; (zool.) shipworm

**tío** *m* uncle; (coll.) old man; (coll.) guy, fellow; **tíos** *mpl* uncle and aunt; **tío abuelo** granduncle, great-uncle
**tiocianato** *m* (chem.) thiocyanate
**tiociánico -ca** *adj* thiocyanic
**tiofeno** *m* (chem.) thiophene
**tiónico -ca** *adj* thionic
**tiosinamina** *f* (chem.) thiosinamine
**tiosulfato** *m* (chem.) thiosulfate
**tiosulfúrico -ca** *adj* thiosulfuric
**tiourea** *f* (chem.) thiourea
**tiovivo** *m* merry-go-round, carrousel
**tipejo** *m* (coll.) ridiculous fellow, sap
**tipiadora** *f* typewriter (*machine*); typist
**tipiar** *va & vn* to type, to typewrite
**tipicista** *adj* regional, local
**típico -ca** *adj* typical
**tipificar** §86 *va* to standardize
**tipismo** *m* characteristic
**tipista** *mf* typist, typewriter; linotypist
**tiple** *mf* soprano (*person*); treble-guitar player; *m* soprano (*voice*); treble guitar; (naut.) one-piece mast
**tiplisonante** *adj* (coll.) treble, soprano
**tipo** *m* type; (print.) type; rate (*of exchange, discount, interest*); type (*figure on coin or medal*); shape, figure, build; (coll.) fellow, specimen, guy; **tener buen tipo** to have a good figure; **tipo alemán** (print.) German text; **tipo de ensayo** or **de prueba** eye-test chart; **tipo impositivo** tax rate; **tipo menudo** small print
**tipocromía** *f* color printing
**tipografía** *f* typography
**tipográfico -ca** *adj* typographic or typographical
**tipógrafo** *m* typographer; type-setting machine
**tipolitografía** *f* typolithography
**tipometría** *f* typometry
**tipómetro** *m* type gauge
**tipotelégrafo** *m* var. of **teletipo**
**típula** *f* (ent.) crane fly, daddy-longlegs
**tiquete** *m* (Am.) ticket
**tiquismiquis** *mpl* (coll.) fussiness; (coll.) obsequiousness
**tiquistiquis** *m* (bot.) Philippine soapberry
**tira** *f* strip; **hecho tiras** (Am.) in rags; **sacar las tiras a** (Am.) to beat up, give a beating to; **tira de películas** film strip; **tira emplástica** (Am.) court plaster; **tiras cómicas** comics, funnies (*in the newspaper*)
**tirabala** *m* popgun
**tirabeque** *m* string pea; slingshot
**tirabotas** *m* (*pl:* **-tas**) boot hook
**tirabotón** *m* buttonhook
**tirabraguero** *m* truss (*for a rupture*)
**tirabuzón** *m* corkscrew; curl, hanging curl, corkscrew curl
**tiracantos** *m* (*pl:* **-tos**) var. of **echacantos**
**tiracol** *m* or **tiracuello** *m* baldric
**tirada** *f* see **tirado**
**tiradera** *f* long horn-tipped Indian arrow
**tiradero** *m* hunting post, shooting post
**tiradilla** *f* catgut
**tirado -da** *adj* plentiful, given away, dirt-cheap; rakish, long and low (*ship*); cursive (*handwriting*); *m* wire drawing; *f* throw; draft; distance, stretch; time, period; printing; edition, issue, run, circulation; tirade; shooting party, hunting party; (mus.) tirade; **de** or **en una tirada** at one stroke; **tirada aparte** reprint
**tirador -dora** *mf* thrower; drawer; shooter; shot, good shot; fencer; *m* knob; doorknob, pull; pull chain; (elec.) pull cord, pull chain; slingshot; ruling pen, drawing pen; (print.) pressman; **tirador apostado** sniper; **tirador certero** sharpshooter; **tirador de oro** gold wiredrawer; **tirador de plata** silver wiredrawer; **tirador emboscado** sniper
**tirafondo** *m* wood screw, lag screw; (surg.) bullet-extracting forceps
**tiraje** *m* draft; printing, edition; (phot.) printing; (phot.) focal length
**tirajo** *m* (coll.) tatter, shred
**tiralíneas** *m* (*pl:* **-as**) ruling pen
**tiramiento** *m* shooting; tension, stretching
**tiramira** *f* long, narrow range (*of mountains*); string (*of things*); distance, stretch
**tiranía** *f* tyranny
**tiranicida** *adj* tyrannicidal; *mf* tyrannicide (*person*)
**tiranicidio** *m* tyrannicide (*act*)
**tiránico -ca** *adj* tyrannic or tyrannical
**tiranizar** §76 *va & vn* to tyrannize
**tirano -na** *adj* tyrannous; *mf* tyrant; *m* (orn.) kingbird
**tirante** *adj* tense, taut, tight; (fig.) tense, strained (*relations*); *m* trace (*of harness*); brace, tie rod; tie beam; **tirantes** *mpl* suspenders; **a tirantes largos** with four horses and two coachmen
**tirantez** *f* tenseness, tautness, tightness; strain; length
**tirapié** *m* stirrup (*of shoemaker*)
**tirapo** *m* (Am.) toy pistol
**tirar** *va* to throw, cast, fling; to throw away, cast off; to shoot, fire (*e.g., a gun*); to draw, pull, stretch (*e.g., wire*); to draw (*a line*); to squander; to give (*e.g., a kick*); to print; to attract; to tear down, to knock down; (phot.) to print; **a más tirar** or **a todo tirar** at the most ‖ *vn* to draw (*said of a chimney*); to pull; to turn (*to the right, to the left*); to last; to appeal, have an appeal; **ir tirando** (coll.) to get along; **tirad** or **tirar** pull (*word on public door*); **tirar a** to shoot at; to handle (*e.g., the sword*); to shade into, e.g., **tirar a verde** to shade into green, to be greenish; **tirar a** + *inf* to tend to + *inf;* to aspire to + *inf;* **tirar de** to pull, to pull on; to draw (*a sword*); to attract; to boast of being; **tirar de largo** or **tirar por largo** (coll.) to spend lavishly; to estimate rather high than low; **tirar por su lado** to go one's own way, to fend for oneself; **tira y afloja** (coll.) give and take; (coll.) hot and cold ‖ *vr* to rush, throw oneself; to give oneself over; to lie down; **tirársela de** (Am.) to boast of
**tiratacos** *m* (*pl:* **-cos**) popgun
**tiratrón** *m* (electron.) thyratron
**tiravira** *f* parbuckle
**tirela** *f* striped cloth
**tirilla** *f* neckband (*of shirt*)
**tirio -ria** *adj & mf* Tyrian
**tiritaña** *f* thin silk cloth; (coll.) trifle
**tiritar** *vn* to shiver
**tiritón** *m* shiver
**tiritona** *f* (coll.) fake shiver
**tiro** *m* throw; shot; gun; charge, load (*of gun*); report (*of gun*); range, rifle range; trace (*of harness*); draft (*of chimney; through a window*); team (*of horses*); flight (*of stairs*); reach; length (*e.g., of piece of cloth*); pull cord, pull chain; hoisting rope; hurt, damage; theft; trick; (min.) shaft; depth of shaft; (sport) drive, shot; (fig.) shot (*marksman; remark aimed at someone*); **tiros** *mpl* sword belt; (Am.) suspenders; **a tiro** within range; within reach; **a tiro de ballesta** (coll.) at a glance, from a distance; **a tiro de fusil** within gunshot; **a tiro de piedra** within a stone's throw; **a tiros** with shots; by shooting; **al tiro** (coll.) right away; **de tiros largos** (coll.) all dressed-up; (coll.) spick-and-span; **errar el tiro** to miss the mark; **hacer tiro a** (coll.) to shoot at (*to aspire to, to aim to get*); **matar a tiros** to shoot to death; **ni a tiros** not for love nor money; **poner el tiro muy alto** to aim high, to hitch one's wagon to a star; **salir el tiro por la culata** (coll.) to backfire; **ser un buen tiro** to be a good shot, be a good marksman; **tiro al blanco** target practice; **tiro al platillo** or **al plato** trapshooting; **tiro al vuelo** trapshooting; **tiro de la pesa** (sport) shot-put; **tiro de aspiración** exhaust draft; **tiro de pichón** trapshooting; **tiro de revés** (sport) backhand drive; **tiro par** team of four mules or horses; (*cap.*) *f* Tyre
**tirocinio** *m* apprenticeship
**tiroidectomía** *f* (surg.) thyroidectomy
**tiroideo -a** *adj* thyroid
**tiroides** *adj* thyroid; *m* (anat.) thyroid (*gland, cartilage*)
**tiroidina** *f* (pharm.) thyroid, thyroid extract
**Tirol, el** the Tyrol
**tirolés -lesa** *adj & mf* Tyrolese; *m* peddler (*of toys and hardware*); *f* Tyrolienne; yodeling

**tirón** *m* tyro, novice; jerk; tug, pull; (fig.) pull (*attraction*); **de un tirón** all at once, at one stroke; **tres horas de un tirón** three hours at a stretch
**tirosina** *f* (biochem.) tyrosine
**tirosinasa** *f* (biochem.) tyrosinase
**tirotear** *va* to snipe at, to blaze away at; *vr* to fire at each other; to bicker
**tiroteo** *m* firing, shooting
**tirotricina** *f* (pharm.) tyrothricin
**tiroxina** *f* (biochem.) thyroxin
**tirreno -na** *adj* Tyrrhenian
**tirria** *f* (coll.) dislike, grudge; **tener tirria a** (coll.) to have a grudge against, to have it in for
**tirso** *m* (bot. & myth.) thyrsus
**tisana** *f* tea, infusion
**Tisbe** *f* (myth.) Thisbe
**tísico -ca** *adj* phthisical
**tisis** *f* (path.) phthisis, consumption; **tisis galopante** (path.) galloping consumption
**tisú** *m* (*pl:* **-súes**) tissue, gold or silver tissue
**tisular** *adj* (pertaining to) tissue
**tít.** abr. of **título**
**titán** *m* titan; titan crane; (*cap.*) *m* (myth.) Titan
**titanato** *m* (chem.) titanate
**Titania** *f* Titania
**titánico -ca** *adj* titanic; (chem.) titanic; (myth.) Titanic
**titanio -nia** *adj* titanic; *m* (chem.) titanium
**titanita** *f* (mineral.) titanite
**titano** *m* (chem.) titanium
**titar** *vn* (prov.) to gobble (*said of turkey*)
**títere** *m* marionette, puppet; mania, fixed idea; (coll.) whipper-snapper; (coll.) nincompoop; (fig.) puppet; **títeres** *mpl* puppet show, pantomime; acrobatics; **echar los títeres a rodar** (coll.) to tell them all where to get off at; **hacer títere a** (coll.) to fascinate, enthrall; **no dejar títere con cabeza** or **cara** (coll.) to completely upset the applecart
**titerero -ra** *mf* var. of **titiritero**
**titeretada** *f* (coll.) laxity, shabbiness, folly
**titerista** *mf* var. of **titiritero**
**tití** *m* (*pl:* **-tíes**) (zool.) marmoset
**titilación** *f* titillation; quivering; twinkling
**titilar** *va* to titillate; *vn* to quiver; to twinkle
**titileo** *m* twinkling
**titímalo** *m* (bot.) spurge
**titirimundi** *m* var. of **mundonuevo**
**titiritaina** *f* (coll.) din of wind instruments; (coll.) noisy merrymaking
**titiritar** *vn* to shake, to shiver
**titiritero -ra** *mf* puppeteer; ropewalker, acrobat, juggler
**tít.º** abr. of **título**
**tito** *m* (bot.) grass pea; chamber pot; (*cap.*) *m* Titus
**titoísmo** *m* Titoism
**titoísta** *adj & mf* Titoist
**Titono** *m* (myth.) Tithonus
**titración** *f* (chem.) titration
**titrar** *va & vn* (chem.) to titrate
**titubeante** *adj* staggering; tottering; stammering; wavering
**titubear** *vn* to stagger, totter; to stammer, stutter; to waver, hesitate; **titubear en** + *inf* to waver in + *ger*, to hesitate to + *inf*
**titubeo** *m* staggering; tottering; stammering; wavering, hesitation
**titulación** *f* (chem.) titration
**titulado -da** *adj* titled; so-called; *m* titleholder; titled person; degree holder
**titular** *adj* titular; official; *m* bearer, holder (*e.g., of a passport*); titleholder; incumbent; headline; *f* (print.) capital letter (*used in a title or headline*); *va* to title, to entitle; (chem.) to titrate; *vn* to receive a title of nobility; (chem.) to titrate; *vr* to receive a title; to be called; to call oneself
**titulillo** *m* (print.) running head, running title; **andar en titulillos** (coll.) to be a stickler
**título** *m* title; titled person; regulation; certificate; bond; diploma; degree (*granted by a university*); headline; grade, content (*of ore*); fineness (*of coinage*); strength, concentration (*of alcoholic liquors*); (chem., immun. & physiol.) titer; **títulos** *mpl* qualifications, credentials; **a título de** as a, by way of, on the score of; **a título de información** unofficially; **título de propiedad** (law) title deed
**tiza** *f* chalk
**tizna** *f* blackening
**tiznadura** *f* smudge, stain, spot
**tiznajo** *m* (coll.) smudge
**tiznar** *va* to soil with soot; to stain, to spot; to defame; *vr* to become soiled with soot; to get stained or spotted; (Am.) to get drunk
**tizne** *m & f* soot; *m* half-burned stick, firebrand
**tiznón** *m* smudge, spot of soot
**tizo** *m* brand (*partly burned piece of wood*)
**tizón** *m* brand (*partly burned piece of wood*); bunt, wheat smut; (mas.) header; (fig.) brand (*dishonor*)
**tizona** *f* (coll.) sword
**tizonada** *f* or **tizonazo** *m* blow with a firebrand; (coll.) hellfire
**tizoncillo** *m* bunt, wheat smut
**tizonear** *vn* to stir up the fire
**tizonera** *f* charcoal kiln (*made of partly burned wood*)
**tlapalería** *f* (Am.) paint store, hardware store
**tmesis** *f* (rhet.) tmesis
**tno.** abr. of **teléfono**
**T.N.T.** abr. of **trinitrotolueno**
**t.º** abr. of **tomo**
**toalla** *f* towel; pillow sham; **toalla continua** roller towel; **toalla de baño** bath towel; **toalla rusa** Turkish towel; **toalla sin fin** roller towel
**toallero** *m* towel rack
**toalleta** *f* small towel; napkin
**toar** *va* (naut.) to tow
**toba** *f* (geol.) tufa (*porous limestone*); (geol.) tuff (*volcanic rock*); (dent.) tartar; (bot.) cotton thistle; crust, cover
**tobar** *m* tufa quarry
**tobera** *f* (found.) tuyère
**Tobías** *m* Tobias
**tobillera** *adj fem* (coll.) flapperish; *f* (coll.) flapper, bobbysoxer; (coll.) subdeb; anklet; (sport) ankle support
**tobillo** *m* ankle
**tobo** *m* (Am.) bucket
**tobogán** *m* toboggan; slide, chute
**toboso -sa** *adj* tufaceous
**toca** *f* toque; headdress; veil; cornet (*headdress of Sisters of Charity*)
**tocadiscos** *m* (*pl:* **-cos**) record player; **tocadiscos automático** record changer
**tocado -da** *adj* touched (*spoiled; mentally unbalanced*); **tocado de la cabeza** (coll.) touched in the head; *m* hairdo, coiffure; headdress; topknot (*bow of ribbon worn on head*)
**tocador -dora** *mf* player, performer (*on musical instrument*); *m* boudoir; dressing table; dressing case, toilet case
**tocadura** *f* hairdo, coiffure; headdress
**tocamiento** *m* feeling, touching; inspiration
**tocante** *adj* touching; touching, moving; **tocante a** touching, concerning, with reference to
**tocar §86** *va* to feel; to touch; to touch on; to ring; to toll; to strike; to feel, to come to know, to suffer; to do (*the hair*); to touch (*with a touchstone*); (mus.) to play (*an instrument, a composition, a phonograph record*); to beat (*a drum*); (paint.) to touch up ‖ *vn* to touch; **en** or **por lo que toca a** with regard to; **tocar a** to knock at (*a door*); to behoove; to pertain to, to concern; to be related to; to fall to, to fall to the lot of; to be the turn of; to approach (*e.g., the end*); **tocar a** + *inf* to be time to + *inf*; **tocar a uno** + *inf* to be up to someone to + *inf*; **tocar en** to touch at (*a port*); to touch (*land*); to touch on; to approach, border on ‖ *vr* to put one's hat on, cover one's head; to be related (*said of two or more persons*); to touch each other; to become touched (*mentally unbalanced*); to make one's toilet; **tocarse con** to have on, to wear (*on the head*); **tocárselas** (coll.) to beat it, run away
**tocasalva** *f* var. of **salvilla**
**tocata** *f* (mus.) toccata; (coll.) drubbing, beating
**tocayo -ya** *mf* namesake
**tocía** *f* var. of **atutía**

**tocinera** *f* see **tocinero**
**tocinería** *f* bacon and pork shop or stand
**tocinero -ra** *mf* bacon and pork dealer; *f* pork-salting board or table
**tocino** *m* bacon; salt pork; (coll.) fast rope skipping; **tocino del cielo** candied yolk of egg
**tocio -cia** *adj* dwarf (*oak*)
**tocoferol** *m* (biochem.) tocopherol
**tocología** *f* tocology, obstetrics
**tocólogo -ga** *mf* tocologist, obstetrician
**tocón** *m* stump (*of tree, arm, or leg*)
**toconal** *m* ground full of stumps; olive grove of new shoots growing from stumps
**tocte** *m* (bot.) black walnut
**tocuyo** *m* (Am.) coarse cotton cloth
**tochedad** *f* roughness, coarseness, crudity
**tochimbo** *m* (Am.) smelting furnace
**tocho -cha** *adj* rough, coarse, crude; *m* (found.) bloom, billet
**tochura** *f* crudity
**todabuena** or **todasana** *f* (bot.) parkleaves, tutsan
**todavía** *adv* still, yet; **todavía no** not yet
**todo -da** *adj* all, whole, every; any; full (*e.g., speed*); *m* whole; everything; **todos** *mpl* all, everybody; **así y todo** even so, anyhow; **ante todo** first of all; **con todo** still, however; **del todo** wholly, entirely; **de todo en todo** through and through, entirely; **jugar el todo por el todo** to stake everything; **por todo** all in all; **ser el todo** (coll.) to be the whole show; **sobre todo** above all, especially; **todo el que** everybody who; **todo lo que** all that; **todos cuantos** all those who
**todopoderoso -sa** *adj* all-powerful, almighty; **el Todopoderoso** the Almighty (*God*)
**tofo** *m* (path.) tophus
**toga** *f* (hist.) toga; gown (*of professor, judge, etc.*)
**togado -da** *adj* togaed; *m* gownsman
**toisón** *m* Golden Fleece (*order*); (myth.) Golden Fleece; **toisón de oro** Golden Fleece (*order*); (myth.) Golden Fleece
**tojal** *m* growth of furze
**tojino** *m* (naut.) chock; (naut.) round, rundle (*on side of ship*); (naut.) cleat
**tojo** *m* (bot.) gorse, furze, whin
**tolanos** *mpl* short hair on back of neck; (vet.) gingivitis
**toldadura** *f* awning, awnings
**toldar** *va* to cover with an awning
**toldilla** *f* (naut.) poop, poop deck
**toldo** *m* awning; tilt (*cloth covering of cart or wagon*); pride, haughtiness
**tole** *m* hubbub, uproar; popular clamor (*against something*); **tomar el tole** (coll.) to run away, leave in a hurry; **tole tole** talk, gossip
**toledano -na** *adj & mf* Toledan
**toledo** *m* word used by the superstitious instead of thirteen
**tolerable** *adj* tolerable
**tolerancia** *f* tolerance; toleration; (mach. & med.) tolerance; tolerance (*in coinage*); **por tolerancia** on suffrance
**tolerante** *adj* tolerant
**tolerantismo** *m* toleration; tolerationism
**tolerar** *va* to tolerate
**tolete** *m* (naut.) thole, tholepin; (Am.) club, cudgel
**tolilo** *m* (chem.) tolyl
**tolmera** *f* place full of tall boulders
**tolmo** *m* tall boulder
**Tolomeo** *m* Ptolemy
**Tolón** *f* Toulon
**tolondro -dra** *adj* scatterbrained; *mf* scatterbrain; *m* bump, lump; **a topa tolondro** headlong, recklessly
**tolondrón -drona** *adj* scatterbrained; *m* bump, lump; **a tolondrones** intermittently, piecemeal
**Tolosa** *f* Toulouse; Tolosa (*town in northern Spain*)
**tolteca** *adj & mf* Toltec
**tolueno** *m* (chem.) toluene
**toluico -ca** *adj* (chem.) toluic
**toluidina** *f* (chem.) toluidine
**toluol** *m* (chem.) toluol
**tolva** *f* hopper; chute
**tolvanera** *f* dust storm, dust whirl
**tolla** *f* quagmire, soggy marsh; (Am.) drinking trough
**tollina** *f* (coll.) beating, drubbing
**tollo** *m* (hunt.) blind; quagmire; loin of stag; (ichth.) dogfish; (prov.) puddle
**tollón** *m* narrow pass, narrow road; (bot.) toyon
**tom.** abr. of **tomo**
**toma** *f* taking, assumption; seizure, capture; dose; tap; intake, inlet; (elec.) tap, outlet; (elec.) plug; (elec.) terminal; (mov.) take; **toma de antena** (rad.) antenna terminal or connection; **toma de corriente** (elec.) current collecting, current collector; (elec.) tap, outlet; (elec.) plug; **toma de posesión** installation, induction (*into a new office or position*); inauguration (*e.g., of a new president*); **toma de tierra** (aer.) landing; (rad.) ground terminal or connection; **toma directa** (aut.) high gear; **toma media** (elec.) center tap; **toma y daca** *m* give-and-take
**toma-corriente** *m* or **toma-corrientes** *m* (*pl:* **-tes**) (elec.) current collector; (elec.) tap, outlet; (elec.) plug
**tomada** *f* seizure, capture
**tomadero** *m* handle; intake, inlet
**tomador -dora** *mf* (coll.) thief; (Am.) drinker; *m* (com.) drawee; (naut.) gasket
**tomadura** *f* taking, assumption; seizure; dose
**tomaína** *f* (biochem.) ptomaine
**tomajón -jona** *adj* (coll.) thieving; *mf* (coll.) petty thief
**tomar** *va* to take; to get; to seize; to take on; to catch (*e.g., cold*); to have (*e.g., breakfast*); **tomar a** to take from; **tomar a bien** to take the right way (*i.e., in the right spirit*); **tomar a mal** to take offense at; **tomarla con** to pick at or on, to fight with; to have a grudge against; **tomarle a uno la risa** to be overcome with laughter; **tomar para sí** to take to oneself; **tomar por** to take for, e.g., **le tomé a Vd. por otra persona** I took you for someone else; **tomar prestado** to borrow; **tomar sobre sí** to take upon oneself; *vn* to take (*to the right, to the left*); **¡toma!** (coll.) why, of course!; (coll.) there you are!; *vr* to take; to have (*e.g., breakfast*); to get rusty; **tomarse con** to pick a quarrel with; **tomarse tiempo** to bide one's time
**Tomás** *m* Thomas; **Santo Tomás** Saint Thomas; **Santo Tomás de Aquino** Saint Thomas Aquinas; **un Santo Tomás** a doubting Thomas
**tomatada** *f* fried tomatoes
**tomatal** *m* tomato patch, tomato field
**tomatazo** *m* blow with a tomato
**tomate** *m* (bot.) tomato (*plant and fruit*); (coll.) tear or run (*in stocking*); (Am.) tomatillo; (Am.) cape gooseberry; **tomate de invierno** (bot.) strawberry tomato
**tomatero -ra** *adj* (pertaining to the) tomato; *mf* tomato raiser or dealer; *f* (bot.) tomato, tomato plant
**tomavistas** (*pl:* **-tas**) *adj* picture-taking; *m* motion-picture camera; cameraman
**toma y daca** *m* give-and-take
**tombac** *m* tombac, Dutch brass
**tómbola** *f* raffle, charity raffle
**tomento** *m* coarse tow; (bot.) tomentum
**tomentoso -sa** *adj* tomentose
**tomillar** *m* growth of thyme
**tomillo** *m* (bot.) thyme; **tomillo real** (bot.) savory, winter savory; **tomillo salsero** (bot.) Spanish thyme
**tomineja** *f* or **tominejo** *m* (orn.) hummingbird
**tomismo** *m* Thomism
**tomista** *adj & mf* Thomist
**tomiza** *f* esparto rope
**tomo** *m* volume (*one in a set*); bulk; importance, consequence; **de tomo y lomo** of consequence; (coll.) bulky and heavy
**tomón -mona** *adj & mf* (coll.) var. of **tomajón**
**ton.** abr. of **tonelada**
**ton** *m;* **sin ton ni son** without rhyme or reason
**tonada** *f* air, melody, song
**tonadilla** *f* light tune; (theat.) musical interlude
**tonadillero -ra** *mf* composer of musical interludes; popular singer

**tonal** *adj* tonal
**tonalidad** *f* (mus. & f.a.) tonality
**tonar** §77 *vn* (poet.) to thunder, to lighten
**tondiz** *f* var. of **tundizno**
**tonel** *m* cask, barrel; (aer.) barrel roll; (coll.) tank (*heavy drinker*)
**tonelada** *f* ton; tun (*measure equivalent to 252 gallons*); (naut.) ton; **tonelada métrica** metric ton
**tonelaje** *m* tonnage
**tonelería** *f* barrelmaking, cooperage; barrel factory; barrels, stock of barrels
**tonelero -ra** *adj* barrel, barrelmaking; *m* barrelmaker, cooper
**tonelete** *m* keg; short skirt, kilt; tutu, ballet skirt; (arm.) skirt
**tonga** *f* coat; layer; (Am.) pile
**tongada** *f* coat; layer; **en una tongada** (coll.) all at once
**tongonear** *vr* (Am.) to strut, swagger
**tongoneo** *m* (Am.) strut, swagger
**tonicidad** *f* tonicity
**tónico -ca** *adj* tonic; *m* (med.) tonic; **tónico nervioso** nerve tonic; *f* (mus.) keynote, tonic; (phonet.) tonic
**tonificación** *f* strengthening, invigoration
**tonificador -dora** or **tonificante** *adj* strengthening, invigorating
**tonificar** §86 *va* to strengthen, invigorate
**tonillo** *m* singsong; accent (*of a region*)
**tonina** *f* (ichth.) tunny; (zool.) dolphin
**tonita** *f* tonite
**tono** *m* tone; tune; (f.a., mus., phonet. & physiol.) tone; (mus.) pitch; (mus.) key; (mus.) slide (*of wind instrument*); **a este tono** like this; **a tono con** in tune with, in harmony with; **bajar el tono** to lower one's tone; **dar el tono** to set the standard; **darse tono** (coll.) to put on airs; **de buen tono** stylish, elegant; **de mal tono** vulgar; **estar a tono** (coll.) to be in style; **mudar de tono** to change one's tone; to change one's tune; **poner a tono** to tune up (*a car engine*); **subir** or **subirse de tono** to become haughty; to live in a grand style; **tono mayor** (mus.) major key; **tono menor** (mus.) minor key
**tonómetro** *m* tonometer
**Tonquín, el** Tonkin or Tongking
**tonsila** *f* (anat.) tonsil
**tonsilar** *adj* tonsillar
**tonsilectomía** *f* (surg.) tonsillectomy
**tonsilitis** *f* (path.) tonsillitis
**tonsura** *f* shearing, clipping; (eccl.) tonsure
**tonsurar** *va* to shear, to clip; (eccl.) to tonsure
**tontada** *f* silliness, nonsense
**tontaina** *adj* (coll.) foolish; *mf* (coll.) fool
**tontear** *vn* to talk nonsense, to act foolishly
**tontedad** *f*, **tontera** or **tontería** *f* foolishness, nonsense; triviality
**tontillo** *m* farthingale, hoop skirt
**tontina** *f* tontine
**tonto -ta** *adj* foolish, stupid; **a tontas y a locas** in disorder, haphazard; *mf* fool, dolt; **como tonto en vísperas** (coll.) in a brown study; **hacerse el tonto** (coll.) to play dumb; **tonto de capirote** (coll.) blockhead
**tontuna** *f* silliness, nonsense
**toña** *f* tipcat (*boys' game*); cat (*used in tipcat*)
**topacio** *m* topaz
**topada** *f* var. of **topetada**
**topadizo -za** *adj* bobbing up all the time
**topar** *va* to butt; to bump; to run into, run across, encounter; *vn* to butt; to take a bet; to come out well, to succeed; (coll.) to guess right; **tope donde tope** (coll.) strike where it may; **topar con** to run into, run across, encounter; **topar en** to run into, run across, encounter; to lie, e.g., **en eso topa la dificultad** there's where the trouble lies
**tope** *m* butt; bumper, buffer; bump, collision; encounter; top; rub, difficulty; scuffle, fight; (mach.) stop, check; (naut.) masthead; (naut.) topmast head; (naut.) topman; (rail.) bumper; **topes** *mpl* (theat.) stage to left of spectator; **ahí está el tope** there's the rub, that's the trouble; **al tope** or **a tope** end to end; flush; **estar hasta los topes** (naut.) to be loaded to the gunwales; (coll.) to be full, to be satiated; **hasta el tope** to the brim; **tope de puerta** doorstop; **tope máximo** ceiling price; *adj* top (*price*); last (*date*)
**topera** *f* molehill
**topetada** *f* butt (*e.g., given by head of a goat*); (coll.) butt (*with the head*); **darse de topetadas** (coll.) to butt each other
**topetar** *va* to butt; *vn* to butt; **topetar con** (coll.) to bump, bump into; (coll.) to run across
**topetazo** *m* var. of **topetada**
**topetear** *va & vn* var. of **topetar**
**topetón** *m* butt; bump, collision
**topetudo -da** *adj* butting (*animal*)
**topiario -ria** *adj & f* topiary
**tópico -ca** *adj* topical, local; (med.) topical; *m* topic; platitude; (med.) external local application
**topinada** *f* (coll.) blundering; (coll.) stumbling, awkwardness
**topinaria** *f* mole, wen, talpa
**topinera** *f* molehill; **beber como una topinera** to drink like a fish
**topo** *m* (zool.) mole; (coll.) blunderer; (coll.) stumbler, awkward person; top; **más ciego que un topo** blind as a bat; *adj* (coll.) blundering; (coll.) stumbly, awkward
**topografía** *f* topography
**topográfico -ca** *adj* topographic or topographical
**topógrafo -fa** *mf* topographer
**topología** *f* (anat. & math.) topology
**toponimia** *f* toponymy; (anat.) toponymy; toponymics
**toponímico -ca** *adj* toponymic
**topónimo** *m* toponym, place name
**toponomástica** *f* var. of **toponimia**
**toque** *m* touch; ring; knock; sound; beat (*of drum*); test, check; gist, point; call (*at a port*); (paint.) touch; (coll.) blow; **dar un toque a** (coll.) to put to the test; (coll.) to sound out, to feel out; **toque a muerto** toll, knell; **toque de ánimas** passing bell, burial peal; **toque de corneta** bugle call; **toque de diana** (mil.) reveille; **toque de difuntos** passing bell, burial peal; **toque de queda** curfew; **toque de retreta** (mil.) tattoo; **toque de silbato** whistle
**toqueado** *m* clapping, stamping, rapping
**toquilla** *f* triangular kerchief; knitted shawl
**tora** *f* torah; fireworks in the form of a bull; **la Tora** the Torah
**torácico -ca** *adj* thoracic
**torada** *f* drove of bulls
**toral** *adj* chief, main, principal; *m* unbleached yellow wax; mold for copper bars; copper bar
**tórax** *m* (*pl:* **-rax**) (anat. & zool.) thorax
**torbellino** *m* whirlwind; (fig.) whirlwind; (coll.) harum-scarum
**torca** *f* (geol.) crater, depression
**torce** *f* loop of necklace or chain
**torcecuello** *m* (orn.) wryneck
**torcedero -ra** *adj* crooked; *m* twister (*device*)
**torcedor -dora** *adj* twisting; *mf* twister; *m* twister, twisting machine; tobacco twister; disappointment, source of disappointment; *f* (ent.) sewer, leaf sewer
**torcedura** *f* twist, twisting; sprain; dislocation; small wine
**torcer** §87 *va* to twist; to bend; to turn; to change, turn aside; to twist up, screw up (*one's face*); to turn (*one's ankle*); to twist (*to misconstrue*); to pervert (*the ends of justice*); **andar** or **estar torcido con** (coll.) to be on the outs with; *vn* to turn (*to the right or left*); *vr* to twist; to bend; to sprain, dislocate; to turn; to turn sour; to go crooked, go astray; to turn bad, to fail; **torcérsele a uno la suerte** (Am.) to be out of luck
**torcido -da** *adj* twisted; crooked; bent; cross (*eyes*); (fig.) crooked (*person or conduct*); (Am.) unlucky; *m* curl (*of hair*); twist (*of cotton, silk, etc.*); twist of candied fruit; look of scorn; *f* wick; curlpaper
**torcijón** *m* cramps; (vet.) gripes
**torcimiento** *m* twist, twisting; roundabout way of talking
**torculado -da** *adj* screw-shaped
**tórculo** *m* press, screw press
**tordella** *f* (orn.) missel thrush
**tórdiga** *f* strip of hide or leather

**tordillo -lla** *adj* dapple-gray
**tordo -da** *adj* dapple-gray; *mf* dapple-gray horse; *m* (orn.) thrush; **tordo alirrojo** (orn.) redwing, song thrush; **tordo de agua** (orn.) water ouzel; **tordo de mar** (ichth.) red wrasse; **tordo mayor** (orn.) missel thrush
**toreador** *m* toreador; (archaic) mounted bull-fighter
**torear** *va* to fight (*bulls*); to banter, tease, string along; *vn* to fight bulls, be a bullfighter
**toreo** *m* bullfighting
**torera** *f* see **torero**
**torería** *f* bullfighters; bullfighters' guild; (Am.) boyish prank
**torero -ra** *adj* (coll.) (pertaining to) bullfighting; *mf* torero, bullfighter; *f* tight unbuttoned jacket
**torés** *m* (arch.) torus
**torete** *m* small bull; (coll.) puzzler, baffling question; (coll.) topic of conversation
**tórico -ca** *adj* toric; (chem.) thoric
**toril** *m* (taur.) bull pen
**torillo** *m* bead, small molding; dowel, pin; (coll.) topic of conversation
**torio** *m* (chem.) thorium
**toriondez** *f* rut (*of cattle*)
**toriondo -da** *adj* ruttish (*cattle*)
**torismo** *m* Toryism
**torita** *f* (mineral.) thorite
**torloroto** *m* shepherd's horn
**tormagal** *m* or **tormellera** *f* var. of **tolmera**
**tormenta** *f* storm, tempest; misfortune, adversity; turmoil
**tormentila** *f* (bot.) bloodroot, tormentil
**tormentín** *m* (naut.) jib boom
**tormento** *m* torment; torture; anguish; (hist.) tormentum
**tormentoso -sa** *adj* stormy; (naut.) storm-ridden (*ship*)
**tormera** *f* var. of **tolmera**
**tormo** *m* tall boulder; clod, clump (*of earth*)
**torna** *f* return; dam; tap; **volver las tornas** to give tit for tat; to turn the tables
**tornaboda** *f* day after wedding
**tornada** *f* return; envoy (*stanza ending a poem*); (vet.) gid, water brain
**tornadera** *f* two-pronged winnowing fork
**tornadizo -za** *adj* changeable, fickle; renegade; *mf* turncoat, renegade
**tornado** *m* (meteor.) tornado
**tornadura** *f* return
**tornaguía** *f* return receipt
**tornalecho** *m* bed canopy
**tornamiento** *m* turn, change
**tornapunta** *f* prop, brace; strut (*of a gable frame*)
**tornar** *va* to return, give back; to turn, to make; *vn* to return; to turn; **tornar a** + *inf* verb + again, e.g., **tornó a abrir la puerta** he opened the door again; *vr* to turn, to become
**tornasol** *m* (bot.) sunflower; (chem.) litmus; iridescence
**tornasolado -da** *adj* iridescent, changeable (*fabric*)
**tornasolar** *va* to make iridescent; *vr* to become iridescent
**tornátil** *adj* turned (*on a lathe*); changeable, fickle
**tornatrás** *mf* throwback, reversion (*person*); half-breed
**tornavía** *f* (rail.) turntable
**tornaviaje** *m* return trip; things brought back from a trip
**tornavirón** *m* (coll.) slap in the face, smack on the head
**tornavoz** *m* (*pl:* **-voces**) soundboard, sounding board (*to direct sound to audience*)
**torneador** *m* turner, lathe operator; tourneyer, jouster
**torneaduras** *fpl* turnings, chips (*from a lathe*)
**tornear** *va* to turn, turn up (*on a lathe*); (sport) to curve (*a ball*); *vn* to go around; to tourney; to muse, to meditate
**torneo** *m* tourney; match, tournament; turning (*on a lathe*); **torneo de tenis** tennis match
**tornería** *f* turning (*on a lathe*); lathe work; lathe shop, machine shop, turnery
**tornero** *m* turner, lathe operator
**tornillería** *f* stock of screws or bolts
**tornillero** *m* (coll.) deserter (*from army*)
**tornillo** *m* screw; bolt; vise; clamp; small lathe; (mil.) desertion; **apretar los tornillos a** (coll.) to put the screws on; **faltarle a uno un tornillo** or **tener flojos los tornillos** (coll.) to have a screw loose; **tornillo de Arquímedes** Archimedes' screw; **tornillo de mordazas** jaw vise; **tornillo de ojo** eyebolt; **tornillo de orejas** thumbscrew; **tornillo de presión** setscrew; **tornillo micrométrico** micrometric screw; **tornillo para madera** wood screw; **tornillo para metales** machine screw; **tornillo sin fin** worm gear; **tornillo tensor** turnbuckle
**torniquete** *m* bell crank; turnstile; turnbuckle (*to fasten a shutter against the wall*); (Am.) fence ratchet (*to stretch wires of fence*); (surg.) tourniquet; **dar torniquete a** to twist the meaning of
**torniscón** *m* (coll.) slap in the face, smack on the head; (coll.) sharp pinch
**torno** *m* turn, revolution; lathe; potter's wheel; vise; clamp; winch, windlass; drum; turn (*in a river*); brake (*of carriage*); revolving server (*for passing something through a wall*); **a torno** around; on a lathe; **en torno** around; in exchange; **en torno a** or **de** around; **torno de alfarero** potter's wheel; **torno de hilar** spinning wheel
**toro** *m* bull; (arch.) molding of convex profile; (anat., bot. & math.) torus; (fig.) bull (*strong, husky fellow*); **toros** *mpl* bullfight; **ciertos son los toros** (coll.) you can depend on that; **correr toros** to fight bulls; **echar** or **soltar el toro a** (coll.) to talk straight off the shoulder to; **toro corrido** (coll.) smart fellow, no easy mark; **toro de lidia** fighting bull; **toro de muerte** (taur.) bull to be fought till killed
**torófilo -la** *mf* bullfight fan
**toroide** *m* (geom.) toroid
**torón** *m* (chem.) thoron; strand (*of cable*)
**toronja** *f* grapefruit (*fruit*)
**toronjil** *m* or **toronjina** *f* (bot.) lemon balm, garden balm
**toronjo** *m* (bot.) grapefruit (*tree*)
**toroso -sa** *adj* robust, husky
**torozón** *m* annoyance, worry; (vet.) gripes
**torpe** *adj* slow, heavy; awkward; dull, stupid; bawdy, lewd; infamous; ugly, crude
**torpedeamiento** *m* var. of **torpedeo**
**torpedear** *va* (nav. & fig.) to torpedo
**torpedeo** *m* torpedoing; (fig.) torpedoing
**torpedero** *m* (nav.) torpedo boat; (Am.) shortstop
**torpedista** *m* torpedoist
**torpedo** *m* (nav., ichth. & rail.) torpedo; (aut.) open car, touring car; **torpedo aéreo** (aer.) aerial torpedo
**torpeza** *f* torpidity, slowness; awkwardness; dullness, stupidity; bawdiness, lewdness; infamy; ugliness, crudeness
**torques** *f* (*pl:* **-ques**) torque (*ancient necklace*)
**torrar** *va* to toast
**torre** *f* tower; watchtower; castle, rook (*in chess*); (arti. & nav.) turret; (prov.) country house, place in the country, farm; (Am.) chimney of sugar mill; **torre albarrana** watchtower; bartizan; **torre de Babel** Tower of Babel; **torre de burbujeo** bubble tower; **torre de control** (rail.) switch tower; **torre del homenaje** donjon, keep; stronghold; **torre de lanzamiento** launching tower; **torre de mando** (aer.) control tower; (nav.) conning tower; **torre de marfil** (fig.) ivory tower; **torre de señales** signal tower; **torre de viento** castle in the air; **torre de vigía** (naut.) crow's-nest; **torre fraccionadora** fractionating tower; **Torre inclinada** Leaning Tower; **torre maestra** donjon, keep; **torre reloj** clock tower
**torrear** *va* to fortify with towers or turrets
**torrefacción** *f* torrefaction; toasting
**torrefacto -ta** *adj* toasted
**torrejón** *m* crooked little tower
**torrencial** *adj* torrential
**torrentada** *f* flash flood
**torrente** *m* torrent (*rush of water*); (fig.) torrent
**torrentera** *f* bed of a torrent; gully

**torrentoso -sa** *adj* (Am.) torrential
**torreón** *m* (arch.) turret; fortified tower
**torrero** *m* lighthouseman
**torreta** *f* (nav.) turret; (nav.) conning tower (*of submarine*)
**torreznada** *f* large fry of bacon
**torreznero -ra** *adj* (coll.) lazy, self-indulgent; *mf* (coll.) loafer, idler
**torrezno** *m* rasher (*slice of bacon*)
**tórrido -da** *adj* torrid
**torrija** *f* slice of bread dipped in milk or wine, fried, and sweetened with sugar or honey
**torsión** *f* torsion; (mech.) torsion
**torsional** *adj* torsional
**torso** *m* torso; (f.a.) torso; (paint.) bust
**torta** *f* cake; (print.) font; (mas.) roughcast; (coll.) slap; **costar la torta un pan** (coll.) to cost a lot more than expected; **ser tortas y pan pintado** (coll.) to be not so bad; (coll.) to be a cinch; **torta a la plancha** griddlecake, hot cake
**tortada** *f* meat or chicken pie; layer of mortar; batch of mortar
**tortazo** *m* (coll.) slap, slap in the face
**tortedad** *f* twisted state
**tortero -ra** *mf* cake maker; cake dealer; *m* cake box or basket; *f* flat earthenware baking pan; round cake pan; whorl of spinning wheel
**torticero -ra** *adj* wrong, unjust
**torticolis** *m* or **tortícolis** *m* (path.) torticollis, wryneck, stiff neck
**tortilla** *f* omelet; (Am.) tortilla (*corn-meal cake*); **hacer tortilla a** (coll.) to smash or break to pieces; **volverse la tortilla** (coll.) to turn out contrary to expectations; (coll.) to turn against one, e.g., **se volvió la tortilla** fortune turned against him (her, you, etc.); **tortilla a la española** potato omelet; **tortilla a la francesa** plain omelet
**tortillo** *m* (her.) bezant
**tortillón** *m* (f.a.) stump
**tórtola** *f* (orn.) turtledove; (orn.) ringdove
**tórtolo** *m* male turtledove; (coll.) turtledove (*affectionate person*)
**tortor** *m* (naut.) twist; (naut.) heaver
**tortuga** *f* (zool.) tortoise, turtle; **tortuga gigante** (zool.) giant tortoise; **tortuga lagarto** (zool.) mud turtle, snapping turtle
**tortuguilla** *f* (ent.) Mexican bean beetle
**tortuosidad** *f* tortuosity, tortuousness
**tortuoso -sa** *adj* winding, tortuous; (fig.) tortuous, devious
**tortura** *f* twisted state; torture
**torturador -dora** *adj* torturing, torturous
**torturar** *va* to torture
**tórulo** *m* (ent.) torulus
**torva** *f* see **torvo**
**torvisca** *f* var. of **torvisco**
**torviscal** *m* field of spurge flax
**torvisco** *m* (bot.) spurge flax
**torvo -va** *adj* grim, stern, fierce; *f* rain squall, snow squall
**torzal** *m* cord, twist
**torzaldillo** *m* light cord, thin twist
**torzón** *m* var. of **torozón**
**torzonado -da** *adj* suffering from gripes
**torzuelo** *m* (orn.) tercel, male falcon
**tos** *f* (*pl:* **toses**) cough; coughing; **tos convulsiva** or **ferina** (path.) whooping cough; **tos perruna** barking cough
**tosca** *f* see **tosco**
**toscano -na** *adj & mf* Tuscan; *m* Tuscan (*language; dialect*); **la Toscana** Tuscany
**tosco -ca** *adj* coarse, rough; uncouth; *f* (geol.) tufa; (geol.) tuff
**tosegoso -sa** *adj* coughing
**toser** *va* (coll.) to equal, to beat (*especially in valor*); *vn* to cough; **toser fuerte** to boast
**tosidura** *f* coughing
**tosigar §59** *va* to poison
**tósigo** *m* poison; grief, sorrow
**tosigoso -sa** *adj* poisoned; coughing
**tosiguero** *m* (bot.) poison ivy
**tosquedad** *f* coarseness, roughness; uncouthness
**tostada** *f* see **tostado**
**tostadera** *f* toaster; roaster
**tostadero** *m* (coll.) oven (*hot place*)
**tostado -da** *adj* tan, sunburned; brown; *m* toasting; roasting; *f* piece of toast; **dar** or **pegar la** or **una tostada a** (coll.) to cheat, to trick, to harm; **no ver la tostada** (coll.) to see no good in it, to not be able to hand it a thing
**tostador -dora** *adj* toasting; roasting; burning; *mf* toaster; roaster; *m* toaster (*utensil*); roaster (*utensil*)
**tostadura** *f* toasting; roasting
**tostar §77** *va & vr* to toast; to roast; to burn; to tan
**tostón** *m* roasted chickpea; toast dipped in olive oil; roast pig; scorched piece (*of food*); Mexican silver coin worth 50 centavos
**total** *adj & m* total; overall; *adv* in a word
**totalidad** *f* totality; whole; **en su totalidad** in its entirety; **la casi totalidad de** almost all of
**totalitario -ria** *adj & mf* totalitarian
**totalitarismo** *m* totalitarianism
**totalización** *f* totalization
**totalizador** *m* totalizer; totalizator, pari-mutuel
**totalizar §76** *va* to totalize, to add up; to amount to; *vr* to add up; **totalizarse en** to add up to
**tótem** *m* (*pl:* **-tems**) totem
**totémico -ca** *adj* totemic
**totemismo** *m* totemism
**totilimundi** *m* var. of **mundonuevo**
**totipalmo -ma** *adj* (zool.) totipalmate
**totovía** *f* (orn.) crested lark
**totuma** *f* calabash (*fruit*)
**totumo** *m* (bot.) calabash tree; calabash (*fruit and vessel made with it*)
**tova** *f* var. of **totovía**
**toxalbúmina** *f* var. of **toxialbúmina**
**toxemia** *f* (path.) toxemia
**toxémico -ca** *adj* toxemic
**toxialbúmina** *f* (biochem.) toxalbumin
**toxicar §86** *va* to poison
**toxicidad** *f* toxicity
**tóxico -ca** *adj & m* toxic
**toxicogénico -ca** or **toxicógeno -na** *adj* toxicogenic
**toxicología** *f* toxicology
**toxicológico -ca** *adj* toxicological
**toxicólogo -ga** *mf* toxicologist
**toxicomanía** *f* drug addiction
**toxicómano -na** *adj* addicted to drugs; *mf* drug addict
**toxicosis** *f* (*pl:* **-sis**) (path.) toxicosis
**toxifobia** *f* var. of **toxofobia**
**toxina** *f* (bact.) toxin
**toxofobia** *f* (psychopath.) toxiphobia
**tozo -za** *adj* dwarfish, stumpy; *f* chunk of bark; log with sharp edge
**tozolada** *f* or **tozolón** *m* blow on the neck
**tozudez** *f* stubbornness
**tozudo -da** *adj* stubborn
**tozuelo** *m* thick neck (*of an animal*)
**tpo.** abr. of **tiempo**
**tr.** abr. of **transitivo**
**traba** *f* tie, bond; clasp, lock; hobble, clog, trammel; obstacle; (law) seizure, attachment; (mas.) bond
**trabacuenta** *f* mistake (*e.g., in an addition*); dispute, argument
**trabadero** *m* pastern (*of horse*)
**trabado -da** *adj* joined, connected; tied, fastened; robust, sinewy; white-footed (*i.e., having white forefeet or a white right forefoot and a white left hind foot*); (phonet.) checked (*syllable*)
**trabadura** *f* joining, uniting; bond, union
**trabajado -da** *adj* overworked, worn-out; busy; strained, forced (*e.g., style*)
**trabajador -dora** *adj* working; industrious, hard-working; *mf* worker, laborer; toiler; *m* workman, workingman; *f* workingwoman
**trabajar** *va* to work (*e.g., wood*); to till (*the soil*); to bother, disturb; to work, to drive (*a person*); *vn* to work; to strain; to warp; (naut.) to labor (*e.g., in a storm*); **trabajar en** or **por** + *inf* to strive to + *inf; vr* to strive, to exert oneself
**trabajera** *f* (coll.) bother, nuisance, chore
**trabajo** *m* work; labor (*as contrasted with capital*); trouble; (phys.) work; **trabajos** *mpl* tribulations, hardships; **trabajo a destajo** piece-

work; **trabajo a domicilio** homework (*work done in home of worker*); **trabajo a jornal** timework; **trabajo a tarea** piecework; **trabajo de campaña** or **de campo** field work; **trabajo de mucho aliento** long undertaking; endless task; **trabajo de taller** shopwork; **trabajo de zapa** underhand work; **trabajo motor** (phys.) work developed by a motor, work done by a force; **trabajo resistente** (phys.) work necessary to overcome a resistance, work done against a force; **trabajos de Hércules** (myth.) labors of Hercules; **trabajos forzados** or **forzosos** hard labor (*penal*); **costar trabajo** to take a lot of effort; **costar trabajo** + *inf* to be hard to + *inf;* **pasar trabajos** to have trouble, to have a hard time; **tomarse el trabajo de** + *inf* to take the trouble to + *inf*

**trabajoso -sa** *adj* hard, arduous, laborious; pale, sickly; labored; (Am.) unpleasant, demanding; (Am.) bothersome, annoying

**trabalenguas** *m* (*pl:* **-guas**) tongue twister, jawbreaker

**trabamiento** *m* joining, uniting

**trabanca** *f* paperhanger's table

**trabanco** *m* var. of **trangallo**

**trabar** *va* to join, unite; to catch, seize; to fasten; to fetter; to lock; to check; to thicken; to set (*a saw; the teeth of a saw*); to begin; to join (*battle*); to strike up (*a conversation, friendship, etc.*); (law) to seize, attach; (mas.) to bond; *vn* to take hold; *vr* to become entangled; to jam; to foul; **trabársele la lengua a uno** to become tongue-tied

**trabazón** *f* union; bond, connection; thickness, consistency; (mas.) bond

**trabe** *f* beam

**trabécula** *f* (anat. & bot.) trabecula

**trabilla** *f* gaiter strap; end stitch, loose stitch

**trabón** *m* fetter, hopple

**trabuca** *f* firecracker

**trabucación** *f* upset; confusion; mix-up; jumble

**trabucaire** *adj* bold, arrogant, blustering

**trabucar §86** *va* to upset, overturn; to confuse, disturb; to mix up (*words, letters, or syllables*); to jumble; *vr* to upset, overturn; to become confused; to become mixed up; to become jumbled

**trabucazo** *m* shot with a blunderbuss; (coll.) dismay

**trabuco** *m* blunderbuss; popgun; catapult; **trabuco naranjero** wide-mouthed blunderbuss

**trabujar** *va* (carp.) to plane across the grain

**trabuquete** *m* catapult; seine

**trac** *m* stage fright

**traca** *f* string of firecrackers; (naut.) strake

**tracalada** *f* (Am.) crowd, flock

**tracalero -ra** *adj* (Am.) cheating, tricky; *mf* (Am.) cheat, trickster

**tracamundana** *f* (coll.) barter; (coll.) uproar, excitement

**tracción** *f* traction; (mech.) tension; **de tracción de sangre** animal-drawn; **tracción delantera** (aut.) front drive; **tracción en cuatro ruedas** four-wheel drive

**tracería** *f* (arch.) tracery

**Tracia, la** see **tracio**

**traciano -na** *adj & mf* Thracian

**tracio -cia** *adj & mf* Thracian; **la Tracia** Thrace

**tracista** *mf* designer; schemer, trickster

**tracoma** *m* (path.) trachoma

**tracomatoso -sa** *adj* trachomatous

**tractivo -va** *adj* tractive

**tracto** *m* tract, stretch (*in space or time*)

**tractocamión** *m* tractor-trailer

**tractor** *m* tractor; **tractor de oruga** or **tractor oruga** caterpillar tractor

**tradición** *f* tradition; (law) delivery, transfer

**tradicional** *adj* traditional

**tradicionalismo** *m* traditionalism

**tradicionista** *mf* folklorist

**traducción** *f* translation; **traducción automática** machine translation

**traducianismo** *m* (theol.) traducianism

**traducible** *adj* translatable

**traducir §38** *va* to translate; to change; to express

**traductor -tora** *mf* translator

**traduje** *1st sg pret ind of* **traducir**

**traduzco** *1st sg pres ind of* **traducir**

**traedizo -za** *adj* portable, carried, brought, transported

**traedor -dora** *mf* porter, carrier, bearer

**traer §88** *va* to bring; to bring on; to draw, pull, attract; to adduce; to make, keep; to have, carry; to wear; to lead (*a good or bad life*); to hold out (*one's hands*); **traer a mal traer** (coll.) to abuse, treat roughly; **traer y llevar** (coll.) to peddle (*gossip*); *vn* to carry; **traer y llevar** (coll.) to gossip; *vr* to dress; to comport oneself; to be up to; **traérselas** (coll.) to become more and more of a problem;

**traeres** *mpl* finery

**trafagador** *m* dealer, trader

**trafagante** *adj* dealing, trading; *mf* dealer, trader

**trafagar §59** *va* to travel over or through; *vn* to traffic, to trade; to travel around; to hustle

**tráfago** *m* traffic, trade; toil, drudgery, treadmill

**trafagón -gona** *adj* (coll.) hustling, lively; (coll.) slick, tricky; *mf* (coll.) hustler, live wire

**trafalgar** *m* cotton lining

**trafalmeja** or **trafalmejas** (*pl:* **-jas**) *adj* (coll.) rattlebrained; *mf* (coll.) rattlebrain

**traficación** *f* var. of **tráfico**

**traficante** *adj* dealing, trading; *mf* dealer, trafficker; *m* tradesman

**traficar §86** *vn* to traffic, deal, trade; to travel, go about

**tráfico** *m* traffic (*trade; movement of people and vehicles*); **tráfico de negros** slave trade

**tragaaños** *mf* (Am.) well-preserved person

**tragable** *adj* swallowable

**tragacanta** *f* or **tragacanto** *m* (bot.) tragacanth (*tree and gum*)

**tragacete** *m* dart, javelin

**tragaderas** *fpl* throat; (coll.) gullibility; (coll.) tolerance, indulgence, laxity; **tener buenas tragaderas** (coll.) to be gullible

**tragadero** *m* throat; gulf, abyss; (coll.) gullibility

**tragadieces** *m* (*pl:* **-ces**) (Am.) juke box

**tragador -dora** *adj* swallowing; gluttonous; *mf* swallower; **tragador de leguas** (coll.) great walker

**tragahombres** *m* (*pl:* **-bres**) (coll.) bully

**trágala** *m;* **cantarle a uno el trágala** (coll.) to force it down one's throat

**tragaldabas** *mf* (*pl:* **-bas**) (coll.) glutton; (coll.) easy mark

**tragaleguas** *mf* (*pl:* **-guas**) (coll.) great walker

**tragaluz** *m* (*pl:* **-luces**) skylight, bull's-eye; cellar window

**tragamallas** *mf* (*pl:* **-llas**) (coll.) glutton

**tragamonedas** *m* (*pl:* **-das**) (coll.) slot machine

**tragantada** *f* swig, big swig

**tragante** *m* flue (*of reverberatory furnace*); hopper (*of blast furnace*); (dial.) flume

**tragantón -tona** *adj* (coll.) voracious, gluttonous; *mf* (coll.) big eater; (coll.) glutton; *f* (coll.) big meal, big spread; (coll.) gulp, effort to swallow; (coll.) strained belief, grudging acquiescence

**tragaperras** *m* (*pl:* **-rras**) (coll.) slot machine

**tragar §59** *va* to swallow; to swallow up; to devour, gulp down; (fig.) to swallow (*to believe too easily; to stand for, to tolerate*); to overlook; **no poder tragar** (coll.) to not be able to stomach; *vn* to swallow; *vr* to swallow up; (fig.) to swallow (*to believe too easily; to stand for, to tolerate*); to overlook

**tragasable** *m* sword swallower

**tragasantos** *mf* (*pl:* **-tos**) (coll.) churchified person

**tragasopas** *mf* (*pl:* **-pas**) (coll.) beggar

**tragavenado** *f* (zool.) anaconda (*arboreal snake of South America which crushes deer and other animals*)

**tragavino** *m* funnel

**tragavirotes** *m* (*pl:* **-tes**) (coll.) stuffed shirt

**tragazón** *f* (coll.) gluttony

**tragedia** *f* tragedy

**trágico -ca** *adj* tragic or tragical; *m* tragedian; *f* tragedienne

**tragicomedia** *f* tragicomedy
**tragicómico -ca** *adj* tragicomic or tragicomical
**trago** *m* swallow; swig; (coll.) misfortune, hard time; (anat.) tragus; (Am.) brandy; **a tragos** (coll.) slowly, by degrees; **echar un trago** (coll.) to have or take a drink
**tragón -gona** *adj* (coll.) gluttonous; *mf* (coll.) glutton
**tragonear** *va & vn* (coll.) to keep eating all the time
**tragonería** or **tragonía** *f* (coll.) gluttony
**tragontina** *f* (bot.) arum lily
**traguear** *vn* (coll.) to tipple
**trágulo** *m* (zool.) chevrotain
**traición** *f* treachery; treason; act of treason; **a traición** or **a la traición** treacherously; **hacer traición a** to betray; **alta traición** high treason
**traicionar** *va* to betray
**traicionero -ra** *adj* treacherous; traitorous, treasonous; *mf* traitor
**traído -da** *adj* threadbare; **traído y llevado** beaten about, knocked about; *f* carrying, bringing; **traída de aguas** water supply
**traidor -dora** *adj* treasonous, traitorous; treacherous; *mf* betrayer; *m* traitor; villain (*of a novel or play*); *f* traitress
**traigo** *1st sg pres ind of* **traer**
**traílla** *f* leash; lash; road scraper
**traillar** §75 *va* to scrape, to grade with a scraper
**traína** *f* deep-sea fish net; net used for fishing sardines
**trainera** *f* sardine-fishing smack; (sport) long racing rowboat
**trainerilla** *f* (sport) shell
**traíña** *f* heavy net used for catching sardines and dragging them to shore
**traite** *m* napping (*of cloth*)
**Trajano** *m* Trajan
**traje** *m* dress, costume; suit; gown; (Am.) mask; **cortar un traje a** (coll.) to gossip about; **vestir su primer traje largo** to come out, to make one's debut; **traje académico** academic costume; **traje a la medida** suit made to order; **traje a presión** pressure suit; **traje de baño** bathing suit; **traje de buzo** diving suit; **traje de calle** street clothes; **traje de ceremonia** or **de etiqueta** dress suit; full dress; evening dress; **traje de faena** working clothes; (mil.) fatigue dress; **traje de luces** bullfighter's costume; **traje de malla** tights; **traje de montar** riding habit; riding clothes; **traje de paisano** civilian clothes; **traje espacial** space suit; **traje hecho** ready-made suit or dress; **traje sastre** lady's tailor-made suit; **traje serio** formal dress; **traje talar** gown, robe (*of a priest*); *1st sg pret ind of* **traer**
**trajear** *va* to dress, clothe, costume
**trajedizo -za** *adj* well-dressed
**trajín** *m* carrying, carting; going and coming; bustle, hustle
**trajinante** *adj* carrying, carting; *m* carrier, carter, expressman
**trajinar** *va* to carry, cart, transport; (Am.) to poke into; (Am.) to deceive; *vn* to move around, bustle around; (Am.) to lose patience; *vr* (Am.) to be disappointed
**trajinería** *f* carrying, carting, cartage
**trajinero** *m* carrier, carter, expressman
**tralla** *f* whipcord; lash
**trallazo** *m* lash; crack (*of a whip*)
**trama** *f* weft or woof; tram (*twisted silk*); lay (*in ropemaking*); texture; plot, scheme; plot (*of play or novel*); blossoming, blossom (*especially of olive tree*); screen, line screen (*in photoengraving*)
**tramador -dora** *adj* weaving; plotting, scheming; *mf* weaver; plotter, schemer
**tramar** *va* to weave; to contrive; to plot, to scheme; to hatch (*a plot*); *vn* to blossom (*said especially of olive trees*)
**tramilla** *f* twine
**tramitación** *f* transaction, negotiation; steps, procedure
**tramitador -dora** *mf* transactor, negotiator
**tramitar** *va* to transact, negotiate
**trámite** *m* step, procedure; proceeding
**tramo** *m* tract, lot; stretch (*of road*); flight (*of stairs*); span (*of bridge*); level (*of canal between locks*); passage (*of writing*)
**tramojo** *m* band, cord (*used to bind a sheaf*); trouble, sorrow
**tramontano -na** *adj* tramontane; *f* north; north wind, tramontana; pride, haughtiness, vanity
**tramontar** *va* to help escape, help get away; *vn* to go over the mountains; to sink behind the mountains (*said of the sun*); *vr* to escape, get away
**tramoya** *f* stage machinery; scheme, trick, fake
**tramoyista** *adj* scheming, tricky; *mf* schemer, impostor, humbug; *m* stage machinist; scene shifter, stagehand
**trampa** *f* trap; trap door; snare, pitfall; flap (*of shop counter*); fly (*of trousers*); trick; bad debt; **armar trampa a** (coll.) to lay a trap for; **caer en la trampa** (coll.) to fall into the trap; **hacer trampas** to cheat; **llevarse la trampa** (coll.) to fall through, to come to naught; **trampa de iones** (telv.) ion trap; **trampa explosiva** (mil.) booby trap
**trampal** *m* bog, quagmire
**trampantojo** *m* (coll.) sleight of hand, trick
**trampeador -dora** *adj & mf* (coll.) var. of **tramposo**
**trampear** *va* (coll.) to trick, to swindle; *vn* (coll.) to cheat; (coll.) to shift, pull through, manage to get along
**trampería** *f* trickery, cheating, swindling
**trampero** *m* trapper
**trampilla** *f* peephole; door of coalbin; lid (*of a desk*); leaf, hinged leaf (*of table*); fly (*of trousers*)
**trampista** *adj & mf* var. of **tramposo**
**trampolín** *m* springboard, diving board; ski jump; (fig.) springboard; **trampolín de acróbata** trampoline
**tramposo -sa** *adj* tricky, crooked; *mf* trickster, cheat, swindler
**tranca** *f* beam, pole; bar, crossbar; (Am.) drunk, spree; **a trancas y barrancas** (coll.) through fire and water
**trancada** *f* big step, long stride; (prov.) blow with a cudgel; **en dos trancadas** (coll.) in a trice
**trancahilo** *m* stop knot (*on thread or cord*)
**trancanil** *m* (naut.) waterway
**trancar** §86 *va* to bar; *vn* (coll.) to stride along
**trancazo** *m* blow with a cudgel; (coll.) grippe, influenza
**trance** *m* critical moment; bad situation; trance; (law) judicial writ (*to enforce settlement of debt*); **a todo trance** at any risk, at any cost; **en trance de** in the act of; at the point of (*death*); **último trance** last stage, end (*of life*); **trance de armas** feat in arms
**trancelín** *m* (archaic) var. of **trencellín**
**tranco** *m* big step, long stride; threshold; **a trancos** (coll.) pell-mell; **en dos trancos** (coll.) in a trice
**trancha** *f* tinsmith's stake
**tranchete** *m* shoemaker's blade
**trangallo** *m* stick hung from a dog's collar to keep him from lowering his head to smell the ground
**tranquear** *vn* (coll.) to stride along
**tranquera** *f* palisade (*fence*); (Am.) gate (*opening to a field, barnyard, etc.*)
**tranquero** *m* cut stone (*for parts of doorframe*)
**tranquil** *m* plumb line
**tranquilidad** *f* tranquillity
**tranquilizador -dora** *adj* tranquilizing, calming, quieting; *m* (med.) tranquilizer
**tranquilizar** §76 *va, vn & vr* to tranquilize
**tranquilo -la** *adj* tranquil, calm
**tranquilla** *f* feeler, leader (*to elicit a reply*); bar, lug, pin
**tranquillo** *m* knack
**tranquillón** *m* maslin, mixture of wheat and rye
**transacción** *f* settlement, compromise; transaction
**transaéreo** *m* (aer.) air liner
**transalpino -na** *adj* transalpine
**transandino -na** *adj* trans-Andean
**transar** *vn* (Am.) to yield, to compromise

**transatlántico -ca** *adj* transatlantic; *m* transatlantic ship, transatlantic liner
**transbordador -dora** *adj* transshipping; transfer; *m* ferry; transporter bridge; transporter car; **transbordador funicular** funicular
**transbordar** *va* to transship; to transfer; *vn* to change trains, to transfer
**transbordo** *m* transshipment; transfer
**Transcaucasia, la** Transcaucasia
**transcendencia** *f* var. of **trascendencia**
**transcendental** *adj* var. of **trascendental**
**transcendentalismo** *m* (philos.) transcendentalism
**transcendentalista** *mf* transcendentalist
**transcendente** *adj* var. of **trascendente**
**transcender §66** *va & vn* var. of **trascender**
**transceptor** *m* (rad.) transceiver
**transcontinental** *adj* transcontinental
**transcribir §17,** 9 *va* to transcribe; (mus. & rad.) to transcribe
**transcripción** *f* transcription; (mus. & rad.) transcription
**transcripto -ta** var. of **transcrito**
**transcriptor** *m* transcriber
**transcrito -ta** *pp of* **transcribir**
**transcurrir** *vn* to pass, to elapse
**transcurso** *m* course (*of time*)
**transductor** *m* (phys.) transducer
**transepto** *m* (arch.) transept
**transeúnte** *adj* transient; transitory; *mf* transient; passer-by
**transferencia** *f* transference; (law) transfer
**transferible** *adj* transferable
**transferidor -dora** *mf* transferrer
**transferir §62** *va* to transfer; to postpone; (law) to transfer
**transfiguración** *f* transfiguration; (*cap.*) *f* (Bib. & eccl.) Transfiguration
**transfigurar** *va* to transfigure; *vr* to become transfigured
**transfijo -ja** *adj* transfixed
**transfixión** *f* transfixion; (surg.) transfixion
**transflor** *m* painting on metal (*generally green on gold*)
**transflorar** *va* to paint on metal; to copy against the light; *vn* to show through
**transflorear** *va* to paint on metal
**transformable** *adj* transformable; (aut.) convertible; *m* (aut.) convertible
**transformación** *f* transformation; transformation (*wig*)
**transformador -dora** *adj* transforming; *mf* transformer; *m* (elec.) transformer; **transformador de campanilla** (elec.) doorbell transformer; **transformador de corriente** (elec.) current transformer; **transformador de fuerza** (elec.) power transformer; **transformador de entrada** (rad.) input transformer; **transformador de núcleo de aire** (elec.) air-core transformer; **transformador de núcleo de hierro** (elec.) iron-core transformer; **transformador de poder** or **de potencia** (elec.) power transformer; **transformador de salida** (rad.) output transformer; **transformador de tensión** (elec.) voltage transformer; **transformador elevador** (elec.) step-up transformer; **transformador reductor** (elec.) step-down transformer
**transformamiento** *m* transformation
**transformar** *va* to transform; (elec., math. & phys.) to transform; *vr* to transform, to become transformed
**transformativo -va** *adj* transformative
**transformismo** *m* (biol.) transformism; (theat.) quick-change acting
**transformista** *adj* (biol.) transformist, transformistic; *mf* (biol.) transformist; (theat.) quick-change artist
**transfregar §29** *va* to rub, rumple
**transfretano -na** *adj* (located) across the strait, across the inlet
**transfretar** *va* to cross (*the sea*); *vn* to spread out, to extend
**tránsfuga** *mf* fugitive; turncoat
**tránsfugo** *m* fugitive; turncoat
**transfundición** *f* transfusion
**transfundir** *va* to transfuse; to transmit, to spread
**transfusión** *f* transfusion; **transfusión de sangre** (med.) transfusion, blood transfusion
**transfusionista** *mf* (med.) transfusionist
**transfusor -sora** *adj* transfusing; *mf* transfuser
**transgredir §53** *va* to transgress
**transgresión** *f* transgression
**transgresor -sora** *adj* transgressing; *mf* transgressor
**transiberiano -na** *adj* trans-Siberian
**transición** *f* transition
**transido -da** *adj* overcome, paralyzed; mean, cheap, stingy
**transigencia** *f* (act of) compromising; compromise
**transigente** *adj* compromising
**transigir §42** *va* to settle, to compromise; *vn* to settle, to compromise; to agree; **transigir con** to compromise on; **transigir en** + *inf* to agree to + *inf*
**Transilvania, la** Transylvania
**transilvano -na** *adj & mf* Transylvanian
**transistor** *m* (elec.) transistor
**transistorizar §76** *va* to transistorize
**transitable** *adj* passable, practicable
**transitar** *vn* to go, to walk; to travel, to journey (*sometimes with stopovers*)
**transitivo -va** *adj* transitive; (gram.) transitive
**tránsito** *m* transit; traffic; stop; passage; passing (*of a saint*); transfer; **de tránsito** in transit; transient; **hacer tránsito** to make a stop; **tránsito rodado** vehicular traffic
**transitoriedad** *f* transitoriness, transiency
**transitorio -ria** *adj* transitory
**Transjordán, el** or **Transjordania, la** Trans-Jordan or Transjordania
**translación** *f* var. of **traslación**
**transladar** *va* var. of **trasladar**
**translaticio -cia** *adj* var. of **traslaticio**
**translativo -va** *adj* var. of **traslativo**
**translimitación** *f* trespass; armed intervention
**translimitar** *va* to cross without intending to violate (*a border or frontier*); to go beyond (*any limit*)
**translinear** *vn* (law) to pass an entail from one line of heirs to another
**translucidez** *f* translucence or translucency
**translúcido -da** *adj* translucent
**translucir §60** *va, vn & vr* var. of **traslucir**
**transmarino -na** *adj* transmarine, overseas
**transmigración** *f* transmigration
**transmigrar** *vn* to transmigrate
**transmisibilidad** *f* transmissibility
**transmisible** *adj* transmissible
**transmisión** *f* transmission; **transmisión de energía** (elec.) power transmission; **transmisión del pensamiento** thought transference
**transmisor -sora** *adj* transmitting; *mf* transmitter; *m* (rad., telg. & telp.) transmitter; **transmisor de órdenes** (naut.) engine-room telegraph
**transmitir** *va & vn* to transmit
**transmontano -na** *adj* tramontane
**transmontar** *va, vn & vr* var. of **tramontar**
**transmudación** *f* or **transmudamiento** *m* var. of **transmutación**
**transmudar** *va* to move, transfer; to transmute; to persuade, convince
**transmutable** *adj* transmutable
**transmutación** *f* transmutation; (alchem. & chem.) transmutation
**transmutar** *va, vn & vr* to transmute
**transoceánico -ca** *adj* transoceanic
**transónico -ca** *adj* transonic
**transpacífico -ca** *adj* transpacific
**transpadano -na** *adj* transpadane
**transparecer §34** *vn* to show through
**transparencia** *f* transparence or transparency; slide (*for projection in a projector*)
**transparentar** *vr* to be transparent; to show through; (fig.) to become transparent
**transparente** *adj* transparent; translucent; (fig.) transparent; *m* transparency (*picture on some translucent substance*); curtain, window curtain; stained-glass window (*at back of*

*altar*); **transparente de resorte** window blind or shade
**transpiración** *f* transpiration; sweat, sweating; (bot. & physiol.) transpiration
**transpirar** *va* to transpire; to sweat; *vn* to transpire; to sweat; (fig.) to transpire (*to become known, leak out*)
**transpirenaico -ca** *adj* trans-Pyrenean
**transpondré** *1st sg fut ind of* **transponer**
**transponedor -dora** *adj* transposing; *mf* transposer
**transponer** §69 *va* to transpose; to disappear behind, to go around (*e.g., the corner*); to transplant; (alg.) to transpose; *vr* to set (*said of sun, moon, and stars*); to get sleepy
**transpongo** *1st sg pres ind of* **transponer**
**transportable** *adj* transportable
**transportación** *f* transportation, transporting
**transportador -dora** *adj* transporting; *mf* transporter; *m* conveyor; (surv.) protractor
**transportamiento** *m* transport; (fig.) transport (*e.g., of joy*)
**transportar** *va* to transport; to transfer (*a drawing, design, or pattern*); (mus.) to transpose; (elec.) to transmit; (fig.) to transport; *vr* (fig.) to be in transports, to be carried away
**transporte** *m* transport; transportation; transfer (*of a drawing, design, or pattern*); (aer. & fig.) transport; (naut.) transport, troopship; (mus.) transportation; (elec.) transmission; **transporte ilícito de armas** (law) carrying concealed weapons; **transportes en común** public conveyances
**transportista** *mf* transport worker
**transposición** *f* transposition, transposal; (mus.) transposition
**transpuesto -ta** *pp of* **transponer;** *f* var. of **traspuesta**
**transpuse** *1st sg pret ind of* **transponer**
**transterminar** *va* (law) to transfer to another jurisdiction
**transtiberino -na** *adj & mf* Trasteverine
**transubstanciación** *f* transubstantiation
**transubstancial** *adj* transubstantial
**transubstanciar** *va & vr* to transubstantiate
**transuránico -ca** *adj* (chem.) transuranic
**transuretral** *adj* transurethral
**transvasar** *va* to decant, to transvase, to pour from one vessel into another
**transverberación** *f* transfixion, transverberation
**transversal** *adj* transversal; cross (*e.g., street*); collateral
**transverso -sa** *adj* transverse
**transvestido -da** *adj & mf* transvestite
**transvestismo** or **transvestitismo** *m* transvestitism
**tranvía** *m* streetcar, trolley, trolley car; trolley line; **tranvía de sangre** horsecar
**tranviario -ria** *adj* trolley; *m* trolley or transit employee
**tranviero** *m* trolley or transit employee
**tranzadera** *f* var. of **trenzadera**
**tranzar** §76 *va* to cut, rip off; to braid, plait
**tranzón** *m* plot, lot
**trapa** *f* tramp, tramping (*of feet*); shouting, uproar; (naut.) spilling line; **trapas** *fpl* (naut.) tackle used to fasten a lifeboat on deck
**trapacear** *vn* to cheat, swindle
**trapacería** *f* cheat, swindle; fraud, deceit
**trapacero -ra** *adj* cheating, swindling; *mf* cheat, swindler
**trapacete** *m* (com.) sales book
**trapacista** *adj & mf* var. of **trapacero**
**trapajería** *f* sails of a ship; (prov.) rags, old clothes
**trapajo** *m* rag, tatter
**trapajoso -sa** *adj* ragged, tattered, torn; slovenly, untidy
**trápala** *adj* (coll.) chattering, jabbering; (coll.) cheating, false; *mf* (coll.) chatterbox, jabberer; (coll.) cheat, trickster; *m* (coll.) garrulity, loquacity; *f* noise, uproar, confusion; clatter (*of running horse*); (coll.) cheating, deceit
**trapalear** *vn* (coll.) to chatter, jabber; (coll.) to lie, cheat, deceive; to clatter along
**trapalón -lona** *adj* (coll.) cheating, tricky; *mf* (coll.) cheater, trickster
**trapatiesta** *f* (coll.) brawl, row, roughhouse
**trapaza** *f* var. of **trapacería**
**trapazar** §76 *vn* var. of **trapacear**
**trapeador** *m* (Am.) mop, floor mop
**trapear** *va* (Am.) to mop; *vn* (dial.) to snow
**trapecial** *adj* trapezial; (geom.) trapezoidal
**trapecio** *m* (sport) trapeze; (anat.) trapezium; (anat.) trapezius; (geom.) trapezoid
**trapecista** *mf* trapeze performer
**trapense** *adj & mf* Trappist
**trapería** *f* rags; rag shop
**trapero -ra** *adj* see **puñalada;** *mf* ragpicker, rag dealer; junk dealer
**trapezoedro** *m* (cryst.) trapezohedron
**trapezoidal** *adj* (geom.) trapezial
**trapezoide** *m* (anat.) trapezoid; (geom.) trapezium
**trapiche** *m* sugar mill; press, olive press; ore crusher
**trapichear** *vn* (coll.) to scheme; to deal at retail
**trapicheo** *m* (coll.) scheming
**trapichero** *m* sugar-mill worker
**trapiento -ta** *adj* ragged, raggedy
**trapillo** *m* (coll.) second-rate gallant; (coll.) soubrette; (coll.) nest egg, small nest egg (*savings*); **de trapillo** (coll.) in house clothes
**trapío** *m* (coll.) pertness, flipness; (taur.) spirit (*of bull*)
**trapisonda** *f* (coll.) brawl, uproar; (coll.) intrigue, scheming
**trapisondear** *vn* (coll.) to intrigue, to scheme
**trapisondista** *mf* (coll.) intriguer, schemer
**trapista** *adj & mf* Trappist; *m* (Am.) ragpicker, ragman
**trapito** *m* small rag; **trapitos de cristianar** (coll.) Sunday best
**trapo** *m* rag; cleaning rag; (naut.) canvas, sails; (taur.) bullfighter's bright-colored cape; (taur.) cloth (*of muleta*); (theat.) curtain; (Am.) cloth, fabric; **trapos** *mpl* (coll.) rags, duds; **a todo trapo** (naut. & fig.) full sail; **poner como un trapo** (coll.) to rake over the coals; **sacar los trapos a la colada, a relucir** or **al sol** (coll.) to wash one's dirty linen in public; **soltar el trapo** (coll.) to burst out crying, to burst out laughing; **tirar el trapo** (coll.) to withdraw, to give up; **trapos de cristianar** (coll.) Sunday best
**traque** *m* crack (*of firecracker*); fuse (*of firecracker*); **a traque barraque** (coll.) at any time, for any reason
**tráquea** *f* (anat., bot. & zool.) trachea
**traqueal** *adj* tracheal
**traquear** *va* to shake, agitate; to rattle; (coll.) to tamper with, fool with; *vn* to crackle; to rattle; (mach.) to chatter
**traqueida** *f* (bot.) tracheid
**traqueítis** *f* (path.) tracheitis
**traqueo** *m* crack, crackle; rattle; (mach.) chattering
**traqueotomía** *f* (surg.) tracheotomy
**traquetear** *va & vn* var. of **traquear**
**traqueteo** *m* var. of **traqueo**
**traquido** *m* crack (*of firecracker; of something breaking*)
**traquita** *f* (geol.) trachyte
**tras** *prep* after; behind; **tras** + *inf* after + *ger;* **tras de** behind; in addition to; *m* (coll.) behind; **¡tras, tras!** rat-a-tat!
**trasalcoba** *f* (arch.) alcove (*adjoining a bedroom*)
**trasalpino -na** *adj* var. of **transalpino**
**trasaltar** *m* space behind altar
**trasandino -na** *adj* var. of **transandino**
**trasanteanoche** *adv* three nights ago
**trasanteayer** or **trasantier** *adv* three days ago
**trasatlántico -ca** *adj* var. of **transatlántico**
**trasbarrás** *m* thump, thud
**trasbordador -dora** *adj & m* var. of **transbordador**
**trasbordar** *va* var. of **transbordar**
**trasbordo** *m* var. of **transbordo**
**trasca** *f* leather thong
**trascabo** *m* trip, tripping
**trascantón** *m* spur stone; errand boy, street porter; **a trascantón** unexpectedly; **dar trascantón a** (coll.) to shake off
**trascantonada** *f* spur stone
**trascara** *f* (hum.) backside, behind

**trascendencia** *f* penetration, keenness; importance; result, consequence; (philos.) transcendence
**trascendental** *adj* far-reaching; highly important, very serious; (philos. & math.) transcendental
**trascendente** *adj* penetrating; important; (philos. & theol.) transcendent
**trascender** **§66** *va* to go into, to dig up; *vn* to smell, be fragrant; to spread; to come to be known, to leak out
**trascendido -da** *adj* keen, perspicacious
**trascocina** *f* scullery (*room near kitchen for coarse work*)
**trascolar** **§77** *va* to strain, percolate; to take through, to take to the other side; *vr* to butt in
**trasconejar** *vr* to squat, to cower (*said of game*); to be mislaid, get lost
**trascordado -da** *adj* wrong, mistaken, confused
**trascordar** **§77** *vr* to forget, to confuse
**trascoro** *m* back choir, retrochoir
**trascorral** *m* back court, back yard; (coll.) backside
**trascorvo -va** *adj* crookkneed (*horse*)
**trascribir** **§17,** 9 *va* var. of **transcribir**
**trascripción** *f* var. of **transcripción**
**trascripto -ta** or **trascrito -ta** var. of **transcrito**
**trascuarto** *m* back room
**trascuenta** *f* mistake (*e.g., in an addition*)
**trascurrir** *vn* var. of **transcurrir**
**trascurso** *m* var. of **transcurso**
**trasdobladura** *f* trebling
**trasdoblar** *va* to treble; to fold three times
**trasdoblo** *m* triple number
**trasdós** *m* (arch.) extrados
**trasdosear** *va* (arch.) to strengthen the back of, to strengthen in the back
**trasechar** *va* to waylay, to ambush
**trasegar** **§29** *va* to upset, turn topsy-turvy; to transfer, to decant
**trasenalar** *va* to change the mark on, to put a different mark on
**trasero -ra** *adj* back, rear; *m* buttock, rump; **traseros** *mpl* (coll.) ancestors; *f* back (*of house, door, etc.*)
**trasferencia** *f* var. of **transferencia**
**trasferible** *adj* var. of **transferible**
**trasferidor -dora** *mf* var. of **transferidor**
**trasferir** **§62** *va* var. of **transferir**
**trasfiguración** *f* var. of **transfiguración**
**trasfigurar** *va & vr* var. of **transfigurar**
**trasfijo -ja** *adj* var. of **transfijo**
**trasfixión** *f* var. of **transfixión**
**trasflor** *m* var. of **transflor**
**trasflorar** *va & vn* var. of **transflorar**
**trasflorear** *va* var. of **transflorear**
**trasfollo** *m* (vet.) swollen gambrel
**trasfondo** *m* background
**trasformación** *f* var. of **transformación**
**trasformador -dora** *adj & mf* var. of **transformador**
**trasformamiento** *m* var. of **transformamiento**
**trasformar** *va & vr* var. of **transformar**
**trasformativo -va** *adj* var. of **transformativo**
**trasfregar** **§29** *va* var. of **transfregar**
**trasfretano -na** *adj* var. of **transfretano**
**trasfretar** *va & vn* var. of **transfretar**
**trásfuga** *mf* var. of **tránsfuga**
**trásfugo** *m* var. of **tránsfugo**
**trasfundición** *f* var. of **transfundición**
**trasfundir** *va* var. of **transfundir**
**trasfusión** *f* var. of **transfusión**
**trasfusor -sora** *adj & mf* var. of **transfusor**
**trasgo** *m* goblin, hobgoblin; imp (*mischievous youngster*); **dar trasgo a** to spook, to act the spook in order to frighten
**trasgredir** **§53** *va* var. of **transgredir**
**trasgresión** *f* var. of **transgresión**
**trasgresor -sora** *adj & mf* var. of **transgresor**
**trasguear** *vn* to play spook
**trasguero -ra** *mf* spook (*person who acts the spook*)
**trashoguero -ra** *adj* stay-at-home, lazy; *m* fireback; big log (*in fireplace*)
**trashojar** *va* to leaf through (*a book, a batch of papers*)
**trashumación** *f* or **trashumancia** *f* moving from winter to summer pasture, moving from summer to winter pasture
**trashumante** *adj* nomadic (*flocks*)
**trashumar** *vn* to move from winter to summer pasture, to move from summer to winter pasture (*said of sheep and shepherds*)
**trasiego** *m* upset, disorder; transfer, decantation
**trasijado -da** *adj* thin-flanked; skinny, lanky
**traslación** *f* transfer, translation; postponement; copy, transcription; (mech. & telg.) translation
**trasladable** *adj* movable, traveling
**trasladación** *f* var. of **traslación**
**trasladador -dora** *mf* carrier, mover; **trasladadora de vía** (rail.) track shifter
**trasladar** *va* to transfer, to translate; to postpone; to copy, to transcribe; to transmit; to move; (mech. & telg.) to translate; *vr* to move (*to another place, job, etc.*); to go, to betake oneself
**traslado** *m* transfer; copy, transcript; moving; (law) notification
**traslapado -da** *adj* overlapped; double-breasted
**traslapar** *va & vn* to overlap
**traslapo** *m* overlap, overlapping
**traslaticio -cia** *adj* figurative
**traslativo -va** *adj* transferring, conveying
**traslato -ta** *adj* var. of **traslaticio**
**traslator** *m* (telg. & telp.) translator
**traslinear** *vn* var. of **translinear**
**traslúcido -da** *adj* var. of **translúcido**
**traslucir** **§60** *va* to infer, to guess; *vn* to become evident, to leak out; *vr* to be translucent; to become evident, to leak out
**traslumbramiento** *m* dazzlement; sudden disappearance
**traslumbrar** *va* to dazzle; *vr* to become dazzled; to disappear suddenly, to vanish
**trasluz** *m* diffused light; glint, gleam; **al trasluz** against the light
**trasluzco** *1st sg pres ind of* **traslucir**
**trasmallo** *m* trammel net
**trasmano** *mf* second hand (*at cards*); **a trasmano** out of reach; out of the way, remote
**trasmañana** *adv* day after tomorrow
**trasmañanar** *va* to put off till tomorrow, to put off from day to day, to procrastinate
**trasmarino -na** *adj* var. of **transmarino**
**trasmatar** *va* (coll.) to wish (*someone*) dead, to kill off (*in one's mind*)
**trasmigración** *f* var. of **transmigración**
**trasmigrar** *vn* var. of **transmigrar**
**trasminante** *adj* undermining; (Am.) bitter (*cold*)
**trasminar** *va* to undermine; to permeate, to seep through; *vr* to seep, be penetrating
**trasmisibilidad** *f* var. of **transmisibilidad**
**trasmisible** *adj* var. of **transmisible**
**trasmisión** *f* var. of **transmisión**
**trasmisor -sora** *adj & mf* var. of **transmisor**
**trasmitir** *va & vn* var. of **transmitir**
**trasmochar** *va* to trim (*a tree*) for firewood
**trasmontano -na** *adj* var. of **transmontano**
**trasmontar** *va, vn & vr* var. of **tramontar**
**trasmóvil** *m* (Am.) mobile unit, radio pickup
**trasmudación** *f* or **trasmudamiento** *m* var. of **transmutación**
**trasmudar** *va* var. of **transmudar**
**trasmundo** *m* afterlife, future life
**trasmutable** *adj* var. of **transmutable**
**trasmutación** *f* var. of **transmutación**
**trasmutar** *va, vn & vr* var. of **transmutar**
**trasnochado -da** *adj* stale, spoiled (*from standing overnight*); haggard, run-down; stale, hackneyed; *f* last night; sleepless night, nightlong wakefulness; (mil.) night attack
**trasnochador -dora** *mf* nighthawk, night owl
**trasnochar** *va* to sleep over (*a problem*); *vn* to spend the night; to spend a sleepless night; to keep late hours, to stay up late
**trasnoche** *m* or **trasnocho** *m* sleepless night
**trasnombrar** *va* to change the names of
**trasnominación** *f* (rhet.) metonymy
**trasoigo** *1st sg pres ind of* **trasoír**
**trasoír** **§64** *va* to hear wrong

**trasojado -da** *adj* hollow-eyed, having rings under the eyes; careworn, emaciated
**trasoñar** **§77** *va* to imagine wrongly, to have the wrong idea about, to mistake for reality
**trasovado -da** *adj* (bot.) obovate
**traspadano -na** *adj* var. of **transpadano**
**traspalar** or **traspalear** *va* to shovel, to shovel off; to move, to transfer; (prov.) to weed (*vines*) with a hoe
**traspaleo** *m* shoveling; transfer
**traspapelar** *va* to mislay (*among one's papers*); *vr* to become mislaid
**trasparecer** **§34** *vn* var. of **transparecer**
**trasparencia** *f* var. of **transparencia**
**trasparentar** *vr* var. of **transparentar**
**trasparente** *adj & m* var. of **transparente**
**traspasador -dora** *adj* transgressing; *mf* transgressor
**traspasamiento** *m* var. of **traspaso**
**traspasar** *va* to cross, cross over; to send; to transfer; to move; to pierce, transfix; to transgress (*a law*); to pain, grieve; to pierce (*the heart with pain or grief*); *vn* (archaic) to set (*said of the sun*); *vr* to go too far
**traspaso** *m* crossing; transfer; transgression; goods transferred; cost of transfer; pain, grief; (naut.) strait
**traspatio** *m* (Am.) back yard
**traspeinar** *va* to touch up with a comb
**traspellar** *va* to close, shut
**traspié** *m* slip, stumble; trip; **dar traspiés** to stumble; (coll.) to slip, go wrong
**traspillar** *va* to close, shut; *vr* to fail, to decline
**traspintar** *va* to show (*one card*) and play another; *vr* to show through; (coll.) to turn out differently, turn out wrong, be disappointing
**traspiración** *f* var. of **transpiración**
**traspirar** *va & vn* var. of **transpirar**
**traspirenaico -ca** *adj* var. of **transpirenaico**
**trasplantable** *adj* transplantable
**trasplantación** *f* transplantation
**trasplantador -dora** *adj* transplanting; *mf* transplanter; *m* transplanter (*machine*)
**trasplantar** *va* to transplant; (surg.) to transplant; *vr* to transplant (*to admit of being transplanted*); to emigrate, settle in another country
**trasplante** *m* transplant; transplantation
**traspolar** *adj* transpolar
**traspondré** *1st sg fut ind of* **trasponer**
**trasponedor -dora** *adj & mf* var. of **transponedor**
**trasponer** **§69** *va & vr* var. of **transponer**
**traspongo** *1s sg pres ind of* **trasponer**
**traspontín** *m* small undermattress; (coll.) backside, behind
**trasportable** *adj* var. of **transportable**
**trasportación** *f* var. of **transportación**
**trasportador -dora** *adj & mf* var. of **transportador**
**trasportamiento** *m* var. of **transportamiento**
**trasportar** *va & vr* var. of **transportar**
**trasporte** *m* var. of **transporte**
**trasportín** *m* small undermattress
**trasportista** *mf* var. of **transportista**
**trasposición** *f* var. of **transposición**
**traspuesto -ta** *pp of* **trasponer;** *f* transposition; rise, elevation; back (*of house*); hiding, disappearance, flight; hiding place
**traspunte** *m* (theat.) prompter (*in the wings*)
**traspuntín** *m* small undermattress; folding seat, flap seat
**traspuse** *1st sg pret ind of* **trasponer**
**trasquero** *m* dealer in leather thongs
**trasquila** *f* lopping, cropping; shearing
**trasquilador** *m* shearer
**trasquiladura** *f* var. of **trasquila**
**trasquilar** *va* to lop, crop; to shear (*sheep*); (coll.) to lessen, reduce, curtail
**trasquilimocho -cha** *adj* (coll.) close-cropped
**trasquilón** *m* lopping, cropping; shearing; slash (*with scissors*); (coll.) swindle (*amount swindled*)
**trasroscado -da** *adj* stripped (*screw or nut*)
**trasroscar** **§86** *vr* to be or become stripped, to not fit (*said of a screw or nut*)
**trastabillar** *vn* var. of **trastrabillar**
**trastada** *f* (coll.) dirty trick
**trastajo** *m* piece of junk
**trastazo** *m* whack, blow
**traste** *m* (mus.) fret (*of guitar*); **trastes** *mpl* (Am.) dishes; **dar al traste con** to throw away, do away with, ruin, spoil; **ir fuera de trastes** (coll.) to act like a fool, to talk nonsense; **sin trastes** (coll.) without order, without method
**trasteado** *m* (mus.) set of frets
**trastear** *va* to fret (*a guitar*); to play (*a guitar*); to wave the muleta at (*the bull*); (coll.) to manage, to steer; *vn* to shove things around; to talk with sparkle
**trastejador -dora** *adj* tiling; *m* tiler
**trastejadura** *f* var. of **trastejo**
**trastejar** *va* to tile; to overhaul
**trastejo** *m* tiling; overhauling; shuffle
**trasteo** *m* waving the muleta; (coll.) management, steering
**trastera** *f* attic, lumber room
**trastería** *f* pile of junk; (coll.) mean trick
**trasterminar** *va* var. of **transterminar**
**trastesado -da** *adj* stiff, taut (*with milk*)
**trastesón** *m* fullness of milk (*of an udder*)
**trastiberino -na** *adj & mf* var. of **transtiberino**
**trastienda** *f* back room (*behind a store*); (coll.) caution, canniness; (coll.) backside, behind
**trasto** *m* piece of furniture, utensil; piece of junk; (theat.) set piece; (coll.) good-for-nothing (*person*); (coll.) nuisance (*person*); **trastos** *mpl* tools, implements, utensils; arms, weapons; junk; (taur.) muleta and sword; **trastos de pescar** fishing tackle
**trastornable** *adj* easily upset
**trastornador -dora** *adj* upsetting; *mf* upsetter; disturber, agitator
**trastornar** *va* to upset, overturn; to turn upside down; to upset, disturb; to make dizzy; to persuade
**trastorno** *m* upset; upheaval, disturbance; (path.) upset, disturbance
**trastrabado -da** *adj* with white right hind foot and left forefoot, with white left hind foot and right forefoot (*said of a horse*)
**trastrabar** *vr* to become entangled; **trastrabársele la lengua a uno** to become tongue-tied
**trastrabillar** *vn* to stumble; to stagger, reel, sway; to stammer, stutter
**trastrás** *m* (coll.) last but one (*in certain children's games*)
**trastrocamiento** *m* reversal, change
**trastrocar** **§95** *va* to turn around, to reverse, to change the nature of
**trastrueco** or **trastrueque** *m* var. of **trastrocamiento**
**trastulo** *m* toy, plaything; fun, amusement
**trastumbar** *va* to drop, let fall; to upset
**trasudación** *f* light sweat; sweating (*of an earthen vessel*)
**trasudadamente** *adv* with toil and sweat
**trasudar** *va & vn* to sweat lightly
**trasudor** *m* light sweat
**trasueño** *m* blurred dream, vague recollection
**trasuntar** *va* to copy; to abstract, sum up
**trasuntivamente** *adv* as a copy; compendiously
**trasunto** *m* copy; record; likeness, faithful image
**trasvasar** *va* var. of **transvasar**
**trasvenar** *vr* to spill; to exude through the veins
**trasver** **§93** *va* to see (*something*) on the other side; to see wrong
**trasverberación** *f* var. of **transverberación**
**trasversal** *adj* var. of **transversal**
**trasverso -sa** *adj* var. of **transverso**
**trasverter** **§66** *vn* to run over, to overflow
**trasvinar** *vr* to leak, ooze out (*said of wine*); (coll.) to become evident, to leak out
**trasvisto -ta** *pp of* **trasver**
**trasvolar** **§77** *va* to fly over
**trata** *f* trade, traffic (*in human beings*); slave trade; **trata de blancas** white slavery; **trata de esclavos** or **de negros** slave trade
**tratable** *adj* friendly, sociable; tractable, manageable
**tratadista** *mf* writer of a treatise or treatises

**tratado** *m* treatise (*book*); treaty (*agreement between nations*); agreement; **Tratado de Varsovia** Warsaw Pact
**tratador -dora** *mf* mediator
**tratamiento** *m* treatment; title; **apear el tratamiento** to leave off the title; **dar tratamiento a una persona** to give a person his title (*in speaking to him*); **¿Qué tratamiento se da a un gobernador?** How does one address a governor?; **tratamiento expectante** (med.) expectant treatment
**tratante** *m* dealer, retailer
**tratar** *va* to handle; to deal with; to treat; **tratar a uno de** to address someone as; to charge someone with being; **tratar con** or **por** (chem.) to treat with ‖ *vn* to deal; to treat; to try; **tratar con** to deal with; to have an affair with; **tratar de** to deal with; to treat of; to come in contact with; **tratar de** + *inf* to try to + *inf;* **tratar en** to deal in ‖ *vr* to deal; to behave, conduct oneself; to live (*well or badly*); **tratarse con** to have to do with; to have an affair with; **tratarse de** to deal with; to be a question of; **tratarse de** + *inf* to be a question of + *ger*
**tratero** *m* (Am.) pieceworker
**trato** *m* treatment; manner, way of acting; deal, agreement; business; title; friendly relations; communion with God; **tener buen trato** to be very nice, be very pleasant; **trato colectivo** collective bargaining; **trato de gentes** savoir-vivre; **trato doble** double-dealing; **¡trato hecho!** (coll.) it's a deal!
**trauma** *m* (path. & psychopath.) trauma
**traumaticina** *f* (pharm.) traumaticine
**traumático -ca** *adj* traumatic
**traumatismo** *m* (path.) traumatism
**traversa** *f* bolster (*of a wagon*); (fort.) traverse; (naut.) stay
**travertino** *m* (mineral.) travertine
**través** *m* bias, bend, turn; crossbeam; reverse, misfortune; (arch. & fort.) traverse; (naut.) beam (*direction at right angles to keel*); **al** or **a través de** through, across; **dar al través con** to do away with, to destroy; **de través** sidewise; **mirar de través** to squint; to look at out of the corner of one's eye; **por el través** (naut.) on the beam
**travesaño** *m* crosspiece, crosstimber; bolster (*of bed*); rung (*e.g., of a chair*)
**travesar** **§18** *va & vr* var. of **atravesar**
**travesear** *vn* to jump around, to romp, to carry on; to be witty, to sparkle; to lead a wild life
**travesero -ra** *adj* cross, transverse; *m* bolster (*of bed*); *f* cross street
**travesío -a** *adj* wandering, stray (*sheep*); cross, side (*wind*); *m* crossing, crossover; *f* crossroad; cross street; through road; path; crosswise position; crossing, voyage; distance, passage; profit or loss (*in gambling*); sailor's pay per voyage (*in merchant marine*); (fort.) traverse works; (naut.) cross wind, side wind
**travestido -da** *adj* disguised
**travesura** *f* prank, antic, mischief; wit, sparkle, keenness; slick trick
**travieso -sa** *adj* cross, transverse; keen, shrewd; restless, fidgety, naughty, mischievous; dissolute, debauched; *f* crossing, voyage; rafter, crossbeam; transverse wall; side bet; (min.) cross gallery; (rail.) tie, crosstie
**trayecto** *m* journey, passage, course
**trayectoria** *f* trajectory; path (*of a storm*)
**traza** *f* plan, design; scheme, invention; means; appearance, looks; trace, mark; footprint; streak, trait; (geom.) trace; **darse traza** (coll.) to take care of oneself, to manage; **discurrir trazas para** to contrive schemes for; **tener trazas de** to show signs of; to look like
**trazable** *adj* traceable
**trazado -da** *adj* traced, outlined; **bien trazado** well-formed, good-looking; **mal trazado** ill-formed, unattractive; *m* plan, design; outline; graph; appearance, looks; route, layout, (*e.g., of a railroad line*)
**trazador -dora** *adj* planning, designing; plotting; tracing; (chem. & phys.) tracer; *mf* planner, designer; plotter; tracer; *m* (chem. & phys.) tracer
**trazante** *adj* (chem. & phys.) tracer
**trazar** **§76** *va* to plan, design; to outline; to trace (*a curve; the characteristics of a person or thing*); to draw (*a line*); to lay out, to plot
**trazo** *m* trace (*line or figure drawn*); outline; line, stroke; (paint.) fold in drapery; **trazo magistral** heavy stroke (*of pen*)
**trazumar** *vr* to ooze, to seep
**trébedes** *mpl or fpl* trivet
**trebejar** *vn* to romp, frolic, gambol
**trebejo** *m* plaything; chess piece; **trebejos** *mpl* tools, implements, utensils
**Trebisonda** *f* Trebizond
**trébol** *m* (bot.) clover, trefoil; (arch.) trefoil; cloverleaf (*intersection*); club (*playing card*); **tréboles** *mpl* clubs (*suit of playing cards*); **trébol acuático** (bot.) buck bean; **trébol amarillo** (bot.) bird's-foot trefoil; **trébol de agua** (bot.) buck bean; **trébol de Holanda** (bot.) Dutch clover; **trébol encarnado** or **del Rosellón** (bot.) crimson clover; **trébol oloroso** or **real** (bot.) sweet clover; **trébol rampante** (bot.) white clover; **trébol rojo** (bot.) red clover; **trébol sueco** (bot.) alsike, Swedish clover
**trebolar** *m* (Am.) field of clover
**trece** *adj* thirteen; **las trece** one P.M.; *m* thirteen; thirteenth (*in dates*); **estarse, mantenerse** or **seguir en sus trece** (coll.) to be persistent; (coll.) to stick to one's opinion
**treceavo -va** *adj & m* var. of **trezavo**
**tremesino -na** *adj* thirteen-month
**trecenario** *m* thirteen days
**treceno -na** *adj* thirteenth
**trecésimo -ma** *adj & m* var. of **trigésimo**
**trecientos -tas** *adj & m* var. of **trescientos**
**trecha** *f* trick, wile
**trechear** *va* (min.) to pass along from one man to the next
**trechel** *m* spring wheat
**trecheo** *m* (min.) passing along from one man to the next
**trecho** *m* stretch (*of space or time*); while; **a trechos** at intervals; **de trecho en trecho** from place to place; from time to time; **muy de trecho en trecho** only once in a while, once in a long while
**tredécimo -ma** *adj* thirteenth
**trefe** *adj* weak, shaky; false, fake
**trefilado** *m* wiredrawing
**trefilador -dora** *mf* wiredrawer; wireworker; *f* drawplate; wiredrawing machine
**trefilaje** *m* wiredrawing
**trefilar** *va* to wiredraw
**trefilería** *f* wiredrawing; wireworks
**trefina** *f* (surg.) trephine
**trefinar** *va* (surg.) to trephine
**tregua** *f* truce; letup, respite, rest; **dar treguas** to ease up; to not be urgent; **sin tregua** without letup, without respite
**treinta** *adj* thirty; *m* thirty; thirtieth (*in dates*)
**treintaidosavo -va** *adj* thirty-second; **en treintaidosavo** thirty-twomo
**treintaidoseno -na** *adj* thirty-second
**treintanario** *m* thirty days
**treintañal** *adj* thirty-year-old
**treintavo -va** *adj & m* thirtieth
**treinteno -na** *adj* thirtieth; *f* thirty; thirtieth
**treja** *f* cushion shot
**tremadal** *m* quaking bog
**trematodo** *m* (zool.) trematode
**tremebundo -da** *adj* frightful, dreadful
**tremedal** *m* var. of **tremadal**
**tremendismo** *m* realistic movement in contemporary Spanish fiction and theater which is characterized by emphasis on suffering, horror, and violence
**tremendo -da** *adj* frightful, terrible, tremendous; awesome; (coll.) tremendous (*very great, enormous*)
**trementina** *f* turpentine
**tremer** *vn* to tremble, to shake
**tremés** or **tremesino -na** *adj* three-month-old
**tremielga** *f* (ichth.) torpedo, electric ray
**tremó** *m* (*pl:* **-mós**) pier glass, trumeau
**tremol** *m* var. of **tremó**
**tremolar** *va* to wave; to display, make a show of
**tremolina** *f* rustling; (coll.) bustle, hubbub, uproar

**tremolita** *f* (mineral.) tremolite
**trémolo** *m* (mus.) tremolo
**tremor** *m* tremor, slight tremor
**tremulante, tremulento -ta** or **trémulo -la** *adj* tremulous, quivering, flickering
**tren** *m* train (*succession, e.g., of waves*); outfit, equipment; following, retinue; show, pomp; set; way (*e.g., of life*); (mil.) train, convoy; (rail.) train; **llevar el tren** (sport) to set the pace, lead the way; **tren aerodinámico** (rail.) streamliner; **tren ascendente** (rail.) up train; **tren botijo** (rail.) excursion train; **tren carreta** (coll.) accommodation train; **tren correo** (rail.) mail train; **tren de aterrizaje** (aer.) landing gear; **tren de engranajes** (mach.) set of gears; **tren de excursión** or **de recreo** (rail.) excursion train; **tren de juguete** toy train; **tren de laminadores** train of rolls, rolling mill; **tren delantero** (aut.) front assembly; **tren de mercancías** (rail.) freight train; **tren de ondas** (phys.) wave train; **tren de ruedas** running gear; **tren descendente** (rail.) down train; **tren expreso** (rail.) express train; **tren hospital** (mil.) hospital train; **tren mixto** (rail.) mixed train; **tren ómnibus** (rail.) accommodation train; **tren rápido** (rail.) flyer, fast express; **tren trasero** (aut.) rear assembly
**trena** *f* sash; burnt silver; twist (*roll*); (prov.) jail
**trenado -da** *adj* reticulated, latticed
**trenca** *f* crosspiece (*in beehive*); main root
**trencellín** *m* (archaic) bejeweled gold or silver hatband
**trencilla** *f* braid
**trencillar** *va* to braid
**trencillo** *m* braid; (archaic) bejeweled gold or silver hatband
**treno** *m* dirge, threnody; jeremiad
**Trento** *f* Trent
**trenza** *f* braid, plait; tress; (Am.) string (*e.g., of garlic*)
**trenzadera** *f* braided cord or ribbon
**trenzado** *m* braid, plait; tress; caper (*in dancing*); prance (*of horse*); **al trenzado** carelessly
**trenzar** §76 *va* to braid, to plait; *vn* to caper, cut capers; to prance
**treo** *m* (naut.) storm lateen sail; (naut.) storm lateen yard
**treonina** *f* (biochem.) threonine
**trepa** *f* climb, climbing; drilling, boring; grain (*in polished wood*); twilled braid; (coll.) somersault; (coll.) slyness, deceit; (coll.) flogging, beating
**trepación** *f* climbing, creeping
**trepado -da** *adj* strong, husky (*animal*); *m* twilled braid; perforation (*series of holes, e.g., in stamps*)
**trepador -dora** *adj* climbing; drilling; (bot.) climbing, creeping; *mf* climber; *m* place to climb; climber (*device*); *f* drilling machine; (bot.) climber, creeper; (orn.) climber
**trepajuncos** *m* (*pl:* **-cos**) (orn.) marsh warbler
**trepanación** *f* trepanation
**trepanar** *va* (mach. & surg.) to trepan
**trépano** *m* (min. & surg.) trepan
**trepante** *adj* climbing; sly, deceitful
**trepar** *va* to climb; to drill, bore; to trim with twilled braid; *vn* to climb; (bot.) to climb, creep; **trepar por** to climb up; *vr* to lean back
**trepatroncos** *m* (*pl:* **-cos**) (orn.) blue titmouse; (orn.) nuthatch
**trepe** *m* (coll.) scolding, reprimand; **echar un trepe a** (coll.) to give a scolding to
**trepidación** *f* trepidation, vibration; (path.) trepidation (*clonus*)
**trepidar** *vn* to shake, vibrate; (Am.) to fear, hesitate, waver
**trépido -da** *adj* shaking, shivering, flickering
**tres** *adj* three; **las tres** three o'clock; *m* three; third (*in dates*); **tres en raya** see **juego del tres en raya**
**tresalbo -ba** *adj* having three white feet (*said of a horse*)
**tresañal** or **tresañejo -ja** *adj* three-year-old
**tresbolillo; a** or **al tresbolillo** (hort.) in quincunxes; (mach.) staggered
**trescientos -tas** *adj* & *m* three hundred
**tresdoblar** *va* to treble; to fold three times
**tresdoble** *adj* & *m* triple
**tresillear** *vn* (coll.) to play ombre
**tresillista** *mf* ombre player, ombre expert
**tresillo** *m* ombre (*card game*); living-room suit (*of three pieces*); ring set with three stones; (mus.) triplet
**tresnal** *m* (agr.) shock, stack
**trestanto** *adv* three times as much; *m* treble
**treta** *f* trick, scheme; feint (*in fencing*); (Am.) bad habit
**Tréveris** *f* Treves
**trezavo -va** *adj* & *m* thirteenth
**tría** *f* sorting; tease (*in fabrics*)
**triaca** *f* (old med.) theriaca; remedy, cure
**triacal** *adj* theriacal
**triache** *m* triage (*inferior grade of coffee*)
**tríada** or **tríade** *f* triad
**triadelfo -fa** *adj* (bot.) triadelphous
**triandro -dra** *adj* (bot.) triandrous
**triangulación** *f* triangulation
**triangulado -da** *adj* triangulate
**triangular** *adj* triangular; *va* to triangulate
**triángulo -la** *adj* triangular; *m* (geom., mus. & fig.) triangle; (*cap.*) *m* (astr.) Triangle
**triar** §90 *va* to sort; *vn* to swarm in and out a hive; *vr* to show teases (*said of a fabric*); (prov.) to curdle
**triásico -ca** *adj* & *m* (geol.) Triassic
**triatómico -ca** *adj* (chem.) triatomic
**triaxial** *adj* triaxial
**tríbada** *f* tribade
**tribadismo** *m* tribadism
**tribal** *adj* tribal
**tribásico -ca** *adj* (chem.) tribasic
**trib.**[1] abr. of **tribunal**
**tribraquio** *m* (pros.) tribrach
**tribu** *f* tribe
**tribual** *adj* var. of **tribal**
**tribuir** §41 *va* var. of **atribuir**
**tribulación** *f* tribulation
**tríbulo** *m* (bot.) caltrop (*Tribulus terrestris*)
**tribuna** *f* tribune, rostrum, platform; (arch.) tribune; stand, grandstand; gallery (*in a church*); parliamentary eloquence; parliament; **tribuna de la prensa** press box; **tribuna del órgano** (mus.) organ loft; **tribuna de los acusados** (law) dock
**tribunado** *m* tribunate, tribuneship
**tribunal** *m* tribunal, court; (fig.) tribunal (*of public opinion, of one's own conscience, etc.*); **tribunal de presas marítimas** prize court; **tribunal de primera instancia** court of the first instance; **tribunal de exámenes** (educ.) examining board; **Tribunal Internacional** International Court; **Tribunal Internacional de La Haya** Hague Court; **Tribunal Permanente de Arbitraje** Permanent Court of Arbitration; **Tribunal Permanente de Justicia Internacional** Permanent Court of International Justice; **Tribunal Supremo** Supreme Court; **tribunal tutelar de menores** juvenile court
**tribunicio -cia** or **tribúnico -ca** *adj* tribunitian; demagogic
**tribuno** *m* (hist.) tribune; tribune (*demagogue*)
**tributación** *f* contribution; tribute; system of taxes, taxation
**tributar** *va* to pay (*taxes, contributions, etc.*); to pay, to render (*homage, admiration, etc.*)
**tributario -ria** *adj* tributary; (pertaining to) tax; **ser tributario de** to be indebted to; *mf* tributary; *m* tributary (*stream flowing into larger one or sea*)
**tributo** *m* tribute; tax; contribution; burden
**tricenal** *adj* thirty-year
**tricentenario** *m* tercentenary, tricentennial
**tricentésimo -ma** *adj* & *m* three-hundredth
**tríceps** *m* (anat.) triceps; *adj* (anat.) tricipital
**tricésimo -ma** *adj* & *m* var. of **trigésimo**
**triciclo** *m* tricycle
**tricípite** *adj* (anat.) tricipital
**triclínico -ca** *adj* (cryst.) triclinic
**triclinio** *m* (hist.) triclinium
**tricloruro** *m* (chem.) trichloride
**tricología** *f* trichology
**tricolor** or **tricoloro -ra** *adj* tricolor
**tricorne** *adj* (poet.) three-horned
**tricornio -nia** *adj* tricorn, three-horned, three-cornered; *m* tricorn, three-cornered hat

**tricot** *m* (*pl:* **-cots**) knitted wear; jersey; sweater
**tricota** *f* (Am.) jersey
**tricotomía** *f* trichotomy
**tricotómico -ca** *adj* trichotomic
**tricótomo -ma** *adj* trichotomous
**tricotosa** *f* knitting machine
**tricroico -ca** *adj* trichroic
**tricromático -ca** *adj* trichromatic
**tricromatismo** *m* trichromatism
**tricromía** *f* three-color process; three-color photograph
**tricúspide** *adj* tricuspid; (anat.) tricuspid; *f* (anat.) tricuspid valve
**tridente** *adj* trident, tridentate; *m* trident; (hist. & myth.) trident
**tridimensional** *adj* three-dimensional, tridimensional
**triduano -na** *adj* three-day
**triduo** *m* (eccl.) triduum
**triedro -dra** *adj* trihedral; *m* (geom.) trihedron
**trienal** *adj* triennial
**trienio** *m* triennium, triennial
**trieñal** *adj* var. of **trienal**
**trifacial** *adj* trifacial
**trifásico -ca** *adj* (elec.) three-phase
**trifenilmetano** *m* (chem.) triphenylmethane
**trífido -da** *adj* trifid
**trifilar** *adj* (elec.) three-wire
**trifloro -ra** *adj* three-flowered
**trifocal** *adj* trifocal
**trifoliado -da** *adj* (bot.) trifoliate
**trifolio** *m* (bot.) trifolium
**trifoliolado -da** *adj* (bot.) trifoliolate
**triforio** *m* (arch.) triforium
**triforme** *adj* triform
**trifulca** *f* (found.) blower mechanism; (coll.) row, squabble
**trifurcación** *f* trifurcation
**trifurcado -da** *adj* trifurcate
**trifurcar** §86 *va & vr* to trifurcate
**trigal** *m* wheat field
**trigémino -na** *adj* trigeminal; trigeminous; *m* (anat.) trigeminal nerve
**trigésimo -ma** *adj & m* thirtieth
**trigla** *f* (ichth.) red mullet
**tríglifo** *m* (arch.) triglyph
**trigo** *m* (bot.) wheat (*plant and grain*); wheat field; (slang) dough, money; **echar por esos trigos** or **por los trigos de Dios** (coll.) to be off the beam; **trigo albarejo** or **albarico** summer wheat; **trigo candeal** bread wheat; **trigo de primavera** spring wheat, summer wheat; **trigo durillo** or **duro** durum; **trigo sarraceno** (bot.) buckwheat
**trigon.** abr. of **trigonometría**
**trigón** *m* (mus.) trigon
**trigonal** *adj* trigonal; (cryst.) trigonal
**trígono** *m* (astrol. & geom.) trigon
**trigonómetra** *mf* trigonometer
**trigonometría** *f* trigonometry; **trigonometría esférica** spherical trigonometry; **trigonometría plana** or **rectilínea** plane trigonometry
**trigonométrico -ca** *adj* trigonometric or trigonometrical
**trigueño -ña** *adj* darkish, olive-skinned
**triguero -ra** *adj* wheat, wheat-growing; *m* wheat dealer, grain merchant; wheat sieve, grain sieve; (orn.) meadow lark; *f* (bot.) wheat grass
**trilátero -ra** *adj* trilateral
**trilingüe** *adj* trilingual
**trilio** *m* (bot.) trillium
**trilita** *f* (chem.) TNT
**trilítero -ra** *adj* triliteral
**trilito** *m* (archeol.) trilithon
**trilobado -da** *adj* trilobate
**trilobites** *m* (*pl:* **-tes**) (pal.) trilobite
**trilocular** *adj* trilocular
**trilogía** *f* trilogy
**trilla** *f* (agr.) threshing, threshingtime; (agr.) spike-tooth harrow; (ichth.) red mullet
**trilladera** *f* (agr.) spike-tooth harrow
**trillado -da** *adj* beaten (*path*); trite, commonplace
**trillador -dora** *adj* (agr.) threshing; *mf* (agr.) thresher; *f* (agr.) threshing machine
**trilladura** *f* (agr.) threshing
**trillar** *va* (agr.) to thresh; (coll.) to frequent; to abuse, to mistreat
**trillizo -za** *mf* (coll.) triplet
**trillo** *m* (agr.) spike-tooth harrow; (agr.) threshing machine
**trillón** *m* British trillion (*a million million millions*); quintillion (*in U.S.A.*)
**trimembre** *adj* three-member
**trímero -ra** *adj* trimerous
**trimestral** *adj* trimestral or trimestrial, quarterly
**trimestre** *m* trimester, quarter; *adj* trimestral, quarterly
**trímetro** *adj masc & m* trimeter
**trimielga** *f* var. of **tremielga**
**trimotor -tora** *adj* three-motor; *m* (aer.) three-motor plane
**trinado** *m* (mus.) trill, warble
**trinador -dora** *adj* trilling, warbling; *mf* warbler
**trinar** *vn* to trill, warble, quaver; (coll.) to get angry, to be beside oneself
**trinca** *f* triad, trinity; (naut.) rope, cable; (naut.) woolding; (coll.) gang
**trincadura** *f* (naut.) big two-masted barge
**trincaesquinas** *m* (*pl:* **-nas**) pump drill
**trincafía** *f* (naut.) marline
**trincafiar** §90 *va* (naut.) to marl
**trincapiñones** *m* (*pl:* **-nes**) (coll.) scatterbrain
**trincar** §86 *va* to tie fast, to lash; to bind, bind the hands or arms of; to break up, crush; (naut.) to woold; (slang) to kill; *vn* (coll.) to drink, take a drink of liquor; (naut.) to lie to
**trincha** *f* belt, girdle; gouge
**trinchador -dora** *adj* carving; *mf* carver
**trinchante** *m* carver; carving table; carving knife
**trinchar** *va* to carve, to slice; (coll.) to settle, to settle with an air of finality
**trinche** *m* (Am.) fork
**trinchera** *f* (mil.) trench; deep cut (*for a road or railway*); trench coat
**trinchero** *m* trencher (*wooden platter*); carving table, side table
**trinchete** *m* shoemaker's blade
**trineo** *m* sleigh, sled
**trinervado -da** *adj* (bot.) triple-nerved
**tringa** *f* (orn.) sandpiper
**Trinidad** *f* (theol.) Trinity; (*l.c.*) *f* (coll.) trinity; (coll.) inseparable three
**trinitario -ria** *adj & mf* (eccl.) Trinitarian; *f* (bot.) heartsease, wild pansy; **trinitaria de Méjico** (bot.) tigerflower
**trinitrocresol** *m* (chem.) trinitrocresol
**trinitrotolueno** *m* (chem.) trinitrotoluene
**trinitrotoluol** *m* (chem.) trinitrotoluol
**trino -na** *adj* trinal, threefold; (astr.) trine; *m* (mus.) trill
**trinomio** *m* (alg.) trinomial
**trinquetada** *f* (naut.) sailing under foresail
**trinquete** *m* (mach.) pawl; (mach.) ratchet; (naut.) foremast; (naut.) foresail; (naut.) foreyard; rackets (*game*); **a cada trinquete** (coll.) at every turn
**trinquetilla** *f* (naut.) foresail, forestaysail; (naut.) small jib
**trinquis** *m* (*pl:* **-quis**) (coll.) drink, swig
**trío** *m* sorting; trio; (mus.) trio
**triodo** *m* (electron.) triode
**trióxido** *m* (chem.) trioxide
**tripa** *f* gut, intestine; belly; filler (*of cigar*); **tripas** *fpl* insides; file, dossier; **flotar tripa arriba** to float on one's back; **hacer de tripas corazón** (coll.) to pluck up courage, to put on a bold front; **tener malas tripas** to be cruel, bloodthirsty
**tripada** *f* (coll.) bellyful
**tripaflavina** *f* (pharm.) trypaflavine
**tripanosoma** *m* (zool.) trypanosome
**triparsamida** *f* (pharm.) tryparsamide
**tripartición** *f* tripartition
**tripartir** *va* to divide into three parts
**tripartito -ta** *adj* tripartite
**tripe** *m* shag (*fabric*)
**tripería** *f* tripery, tripeshop
**tripero -ra** *mf* tripe seller; *m* (coll.) bellyband
**tripétalo -la** *adj* (bot.) tripetalous
**tripicallero -ra** *mf* tripe seller, tripemonger
**tripicallos** *mpl* tripe

**tripinado -da** *adj* (bot.) tripinnate
**triplano** *m* (aer.) triplane
**triple** *adj & m* triple, treble
**tripleta** *f* three-seated tandem bicycle
**triplicación** *f* triplication
**triplicado -da** *adj* triplicate; *m* triplicate; **por triplicado** in triplicate
**triplicar** §86 *va* to treble, triple, triplicate; to do three times; *vr* to treble, triple
**tríplice** *adj* triple; (*cap.*) *f* Triple Alliance
**triplicidad** *f* triplicity
**triplo -pla** *adj & m* triple, treble
**tripo** *m* (bot.) mullein, great mullein
**trípode** *m & f* (hist.) tripod; *m* tripod (*for camera, theodolite, etc.*)
**trípol** *m* or **trípoli** *m* (mineral.) tripoli, rottenstone
**tripolino -na** or **tripolitano -na** *adj & mf* Tripolitan
**tripolizar** §76 *va* to rottenstone
**tripón -pona** *adj* (coll.) big-bellied, pot-bellied; (Am.) gluttonous
**tripsina** *f* (biochem.) trypsin
**tripso** *m* (ent.) thrips
**tríptico -ca** *adj* (physiol.) tryptic; *m* triptych (*set of three panels; hinged writing tablet*); book or treatise in three parts
**triptófano** *m* (biochem.) tryptophan
**triptongar** §59 *va* to pronounce (*three vowels*) as a triphthong
**triptongo** *m* triphthong
**tripudiar** *vn* to dance
**tripudio** *m* dance
**tripudo -da** *adj* big-bellied, pot-bellied
**tripulación** *f* crew (*of ship, plane, etc.*)
**tripulante** *m* crew member
**tripular** *va* to man (*ship, plane, etc.*); to fit out, equip; to ship on (*a certain vessel*)
**trique** *m* crack, swish; **a cada trique** (coll.) at every turn
**triquíasis** *f* (path.) trichiasis
**triquina** *f* (zool.) trichina
**triquinado -da** *adj* trichinous, trichinized
**triquinosis** *f* (path.) trichinosis
**triquinoso -sa** *adj* trichinous
**triquiñuela** *f* (coll.) chicanery, evasion, subterfuge
**triquita** *f* (petrog.) trichite
**triquitraque** *m* clatter; crack, bang, crash; cracker (*firecracker; paper roll which explodes when pulled at both ends*); **a cada triquitraque** (coll.) at every turn
**trirreme** *m* (hist.) trireme
**tris** *m* slight cracking sound; (coll.) trice; (coll.) shave, inch; (coll.) touch; **en un tris** (coll.) almost, within an ace
**trisa** *f* (ichth.) shad
**trisar** *va* (Am.) to crack, chip; *vn* to chirp
**trisca** *f* crushing sound (*made with feet*); noise, rumpus
**triscador -dora** *adj* noisy, frisky; *m* saw set
**triscar** §86 *va* to mix, to mingle; to set (*a saw*); *vn* to stamp the feet; to frisk about, romp, caper, prance
**trisecar** §86 *va* to trisect
**trisección** *f* trisection
**trisemanal** *adj* triweekly (*occurring three times a week or every three weeks*)
**trisílabo -ba** *adj* trisyllabic; *m* trisyllable
**trismo** *m* (path.) trismus, lockjaw
**trispermo -ma** *adj* (bot.) trispermous
**Tristán** *m* (myth.) Tristan or Tristram
**triste** *adj* sad; dismal, gloomy; mean, low; sorry (*e.g., figure*)
**tristeza** *f* sadness
**tristón -tona** *adj* rather sad, wistful
**tristura** *f* var. of **tristeza**
**trisulco -ca** *adj* trisulcate
**trisulfuro** *m* (chem.) trisulfide
**tritio** *m* (chem.) tritium
**tritón** *m* merman, expert swimmer; (zool.) eft, newt, triton; (*cap.*) *m* (myth.) Triton
**tritono** *m* (mus.) tritone
**trituración** *f* trituration; grinding, pounding
**triturador -dora** *adj* triturating; *mf* triturator; *f* crusher, crushing machine
**triturar** *va* to triturate; to abuse, mistreat; to grind, to pound; (fig.) to tear to pieces
**triunfada** *f* trumping (*at cards*)
**triunfador -dora** *adj* triumphant; *mf* triumpher, victor, winner
**triunfal** *adj* triumphal
**triunfante** *adj* triumphant
**triunfar** *vn* to triumph; to trump; (coll.) to be lavish, make a great show; **triunfar de** to triumph over; to trump (*opponent's card*)
**triunfo** *m* triumph; trump; trumping; **costar un triunfo** (coll.) to be a gigantic effort; **en triunfo** in triumph; **sin triunfo** no trump; **triunfo pírrico** Pyrrhic victory
**triunviral** *adj* triumviral
**triunvirato** *m* triumvirate
**triunviro** *m* triumvir
**trivalencia** *f* (chem.) trivalence or trivalency
**trivalente** *adj* (chem.) trivalent
**trivalvo -va** or **trivalvulado -da** *adj* trivalve
**trivial** *adj* trivial; trite, commonplace; beaten (*path*)
**trivialidad** *f* triviality; triteness
**trivio** *m* junction (*of three roads*); trivium (*three lower subjects of medieval seven liberal arts*)
**triza** *f* shred, fragment; (naut.) halyard; **hacer trizas** to smash to pieces, to tear to pieces
**trizar** §76 *va* to break or tear to pieces
**trocable** *adj* exchangeable
**trocada; a la trocada** in the opposite way; in exchange
**trocadamente** *adv* topsy-turvy, in reverse
**trocado** *m* change; giveaway (*game of checkers*)
**trocador -dora** *mf* exchanger, barterer
**trocaico -ca** *adj & m* trochaic
**trocamiento** *m* exchange; change
**trocánter** *m* (anat., ent. & zool.) trochanter
**trocar** *m* (surg.) trocar; §95 *va* to exchange; to barter; to confuse, distort, twist; to vomit; *vr* to change; to change seats
**trócar** *m* (surg.) trocar
**trocatinta** *f* (coll.) mistaken exchange
**trocatinte** *m* changeable color
**trocear** *va* to divide into pieces, to split up
**troceo** *m* (naut.) parrel
**trociscar** §86 *va* to make into troches or lozenges
**trocisco** *m* (pharm.) troche
**trocla** *f* pulley
**tróclea** *f* pulley; (anat.) trochlea
**troclear** *adj* (anat.) trochlear
**troclearío -ria** *adj* (bot.) trochlear
**troco** *m* (ichth.) sunfish
**trocoide** *f* (geom.) trochoid
**trocoideo -a** *adj* trochoid
**trocha** *f* trail, narrow path; (Am.) gauge (*of track*)
**trochemoche; a trochemoche** (coll.) helter-skelter, pell-mell
**trochuela** *f* narrow path
**trofeo** *m* trophy; victory, triumph
**trófico -ca** *adj* (physiol.) trophic
**trofoplasma** *m* (biol.) trophoplasm
**troglodita** *adj* troglodytic; (fig.) troglodytic (*brutal*); (fig.) gluttonous; *m* troglodyte; (fig.) troglodyte (*cruel, brutal person*); (fig.) glutton
**troglodítico -ca** *adj* troglodytic or troglodytical
**troica** *f* troika
**Troilo** *m* (myth.) Troilus
**troj** *f* or **troje** *f* granary; olive bin
**trojero** *m* granary keeper or tender
**trojezado -da** *adj* chopped up, shredded, minced
**trola** *f* (coll.) deception, lie
**trole** *m* trolley pole
**trolebús** *m* trolley bus, trackless trolley
**trolero -ra** *adj* (coll.) deceptive, false, lying; *mf* (coll.) liar
**tromba** *f* (meteor.) column, whirl (*of dust, water, etc.*); (fig.) avalanche, rush; **tromba marina** (meteor.) waterspout; **tromba terrestre** (meteor.) tornado
**trombina** *f* (biochem.) thrombin
**trombo** *m* (path.) thrombus
**trombocito** *m* (physiol.) thrombocyte
**trombón** *m* trombone (*instrument*); trombone, trombonist (*performer*); **trombón de pistones** valve trombone; **trombón de varas** slide trombone
**trombosis** *f* (path.) thrombosis
**trómel** *m* (metal.) trommel

**trompa** *f* (mus.) horn; boy's whistle (*made of onion scape*); humming top; nozzle; trunk (*of elephant*); proboscis (*of certain animals and insects*); vacuum pump; (anat.) tube, duct; (arch.) squinch arch; (found.) trompe; (hum.) proboscis (*person's nose*); (meteor.) whirl, waterspout; (Am.) cowcatcher, pilot (*of locomotive*); **a trompa tañida** at the sound of the trumpet; **a trompa y talega** (coll.) helter-skelter; **trompa de armonía** (mus.) French horn; **trompa de caza** huntinghorn; **trompa de Eustaquio** (anat.) Eustachian tube; **trompa de Falopio** (anat.) Fallopian tube; **trompa de París** or **trompa gallega** jews'-harp; *m* horn player
**trompada** *f* (coll.) blow or bump with a horn or trumpet; (coll.) bump, collision; (coll.) punch; (naut.) collision, running aground
**trompar** *vn* to spin a top
**trompazo** *m* blow with a top; blow or bump with a horn or trumpet; hard bump
**trompear** *va* (Am.) to bump; *vn* to spin a top
**trompero -ra** *adj* false, deceptive; *m* top maker, top seller
**trompeta** *f* trumpet; clarion, bugle; (aut.) axle housing; **trompeta de amor** (bot.) sunflower; *m* trumpet or trumpeter (*player*)
**trompetada** *f* (coll.) silly remark
**trompetazo** *m* trumpet blast; (coll.) silly remark
**trompetear** *va* (coll.) to trumpet; *vn* (coll.) to trumpet, to sound the trumpet
**trompeteo** *m* trumpeting
**trompetería** *f* trumpetry, trumpets; trumpets (*of organ*)
**trompetero** *m* trumpet maker; trumpeter
**trompetilla** *f* ear trumpet; (bot.) yellow elder, trumpet flower; proboscis (*of mosquito*); conical Philippine cigar; **de trompetilla** buzzing (*mosquito*); **trompetilla acústica** ear trumpet
**trompicar** **§86** *va* to trip, make stumble; (coll.) to promote (*one person*) over another; *vn* to stumble
**trompicón** *m* or **trompilladura** *f* stumble, stumbling; **a trompicones** by fits and starts
**trompillar** *va & vn* var. of **trompicar**
**trompillo** *m* (bot.) trompillo
**trompillón** *m* (arch.) keystone of a squinch arch
**trompis** *m* (*pl:* **-pis**) (coll.) punch; **andar a trompis** (coll.) to fight with the fists
**trompiza** *f* (Am.) fist fight
**trompo** *m* top (*spinning toy*); man (*at chess*); tub (*clumsy boat*); dolt; (zool.) trochid; **ponerse como un trompo** or **hecho un trompo** (coll.) to eat or drink to excess
**trompón** *m* big top; bump, collision; (bot.) daffodil; **a** or **de trompón** (coll.) helter-skelter
**trompudo -da** *adj* (Am.) thick-lipped
**trona** *f* (mineral.) trona
**tronado -da** *adj* used, worn; broke, cleaned out; *f* thunderstorm
**tronador -dora** *adj* thundering; *mf* thunderer; *f* (bot.) yellow elder
**tronamenta** *f* (Am.) thunderstorm
**tronante** *adj* thunderous
**tronar** **§77** *va* (Am.) to shoot, to execute; *vn* to thunder; (coll.) to fail, collapse, crash; **por lo que pueda tronar** (coll.) just in case; **tronar con** (coll.) to quarrel with, to break with; **tronar contra** to thunder at; **truena** it is thundering; *vr* (coll.) to fail, collapse, crash; to go to ruin
**tronca** *f* var. of **truncamiento**
**troncal** *adj* trunk
**troncar** **§86** *va* to cut off the head of; to cut, slash (*a writing, speech, etc.*)
**tronco** *m* trunk (*of human or animal body, of tree, of a line or family, of railroad, etc.*); log; team (*of horses*); (anat. & arch.) trunk; (geom.) frustum; (coll.) fathead, sap; **estar hecho un tronco** (coll.) to be knocked out; (coll.) to be sound asleep
**troncón** *m* trunk (*of human or animal body*); stump
**troncha** *f* (dial.) cinch, sinecure; (Am.) slice
**tronchar** *va* to rend, crack, shatter, split
**troncho** *m* stalk
**tronchudo -da** *adj* thick-stalked
**tronera** *f* embrasure, loophole, porthole; louver, small, narrow window; pocket (*of pool table*); *mf* harum-scarum
**tronerar** *va* var. of **atronerar**
**tronero** *m* (dial.) thunderhead
**trónica** *f* gossip
**tronido** *m* thunderclap; (prov.) show, haughtiness
**tronitoso -sa** *adj* (coll.) thundering, thunderous
**trono** *m* throne; (eccl.) shrine; **tronos** *mpl* (eccl.) thrones
**tronquista** *m* driver, teamster
**tronzador** *m* two-handed saw; crosscut saw; mechanical saw
**tronzar** **§76** *va* to shatter, break to pieces; to crosscut, to saw transversely; to pleat (*a dress*); to wear out, exhaust
**tronzo -za** *adj* with one or both ears cropped (*said of a horse*)
**troostita** *f* (metal.) troostite
**tropa** *f* troop, flock; (mil.) troops; (mil.) assembly; (Am.) troop, herd, drove; **tropas** *fpl* (mil.) troops; **en tropa** straggling, without formation; **tropa de línea** (mil.) line, regular troops; **tropas de asalto** (mil.) shock troops, storm troops; **tropas francas** (mil.) marauders, guerrillas; **tropas regulares** (mil.) regulars
**tropeína** *f* (chem.) tropeine
**tropel** *m* bustle, rush, hurry; hodgepodge, jumble; **de** or **en tropel** in a mad rush
**tropelía** *f* mad rush; precipitation; outrage; prestidigitation
**tropelista** *m* prestidigitator
**tropeolea** *f* (bot.) tropaeolum
**tropeolina** *f* (chem.) tropaeolin
**tropero** *m* (Am.) cowboy
**tropezadero** *m* stumbling place, stumbling block
**tropezador -dora** *adj* stumbling; *mf* stumbler
**tropezadura** *f* stumbling
**tropezar** **§31** *va* to hit; to strike; *vn* to stumble; to squabble, wrangle; to slip, to slip into error or wrongdoing; **tropezar con** or **en** to stumble against or over; to trip over; to run into, encounter; to come upon, meet; *vr* to interfere (*said of a horse*)
**tropezón -zona** *adj* (coll.) stumbly; *m* stumbling; stumbling place; obstacle; **tropezones** *mpl* chopped ham mixed with soup; **a tropezones** (coll.) by fits and starts; falteringly; **dar un tropezón** to stumble, to trip
**tropezoso -sa** *adj* (coll.) stumbly, faltering
**tropical** *adj* tropic or tropical
**trópico -ca** *adj* (rhet.) tropical; *m* (astr. & geog.) tropic; **trópico de Cáncer** tropic of Cancer; **trópico de Capricornio** tropic of Capricorn
**tropiezo** *m* stumble; stumbling block; slip, error, fault, guilt; cause of guilt; hitch, obstacle; squabble, wrangle
**tropina** *f* (chem.) tropine
**tropismo** *m* (biol.) tropism
**tropo** *m* (mus. & rhet.) trope
**tropoesfera** *f* var. of **troposfera**
**tropología** *f* tropology
**tropológico -ca** *adj* tropologic or tropological
**troposfera** *f* (meteor.) troposphere
**troque** *m* knot made in cloth before dyeing to show original color
**troquel** *m* die (*for stamping coins and medals*)
**troquelar** *va* to stamp in a die
**troquelero** *m* diesinker
**troqueo** *m* trochee
**troquilo** or **troquillo** *m* trochilus (*scotia*)
**trotacalles** *mf* (*pl:* **-lles**) (coll.) gadabout, loafer
**trotaconventos** *f* (*pl:* **-tos**) (coll.) procuress
**trotador -dora** *adj* trotting
**trotamundos** *m* (*pl:* **-dos**) globetrotter
**trotar** *vn* to trot; (coll.) to hustle
**trote** *m* trot; (coll.) chore; **al** or **a trote** quickly, right away; **para todo trote** (coll.) for everyday wear; **tomar el trote** (coll.) to run away, to dash off; **trote de perro** jog trot
**trotil** *m* (chem.) trotyl, trinitrotoluene
**trotón -tona** *adj* trotting; *mf* trotter; *m* horse; *f* chaperone

**trotonería** *f* constant trotting
**trotskismo** *m* Trotskyism
**trotzkista** *adj & mf* Trotskyite
**trova** *f* verse; parody; lyric; love song; (Am.) fib, lie
**trovador -dora** *adj* troubadour; *m* troubadour; poet; *f* poetess
**trovadoresco -ca** *adj* troubadour
**trovar** *va* to misconstrue; to parody; *vn* to write verse
**trovero** *m* trouvère
**trovo** *m* popular love song
**Troya** *f* Troy; **ahí, allí** or **aquí fué Troya** (coll.) all that's left is ruins; **¡arda Troya!** no matter what happens!
**troyano -na** *adj & mf* Trojan
**troza** *f* log (*of wood*); (naut.) truss
**trozar** §76 *va* to break up, to break to pieces; to cut into logs
**trozo** *m* piece, bit, fragment; block (*of wood*); excerpt, selection
**trucaje** *m* (mov.) trick photography
**trucar** §86 *vn* to pocket a ball (*at pool*)
**truco** *m* trick, device, contrivance; wrinkle; pocketing of ball; **trucos** *mpl* pool (*game*); **truco de naipes** card trick; **trucos malabares** juggling, acrobatics
**truculencia** *f* truculency
**truculento -ta** *adj* truculent
**trucha** *f* (ichth.) trout; three-legged derrick, crab; **trucha arco iris** (ichth.) rainbow trout; **trucha de mar** (ichth.) hogfish; (ichth.) sea trout; **trucha marina** (ichth.) sea trout; **trucha salmonada** (ichth.) salmon trout
**truchero -ra** *adj* (pertaining to) trout; *m* trout fisherman; trout seller
**truchimán -mana** *adj* (coll.) slick, sharp; *mf* (coll.) tricky person
**truchuela** *f* small dry codfish
**trueco** *m* var. of **trueque**
**trueno** *m* thunder, thunderclap; shot, report; (coll.) harum-scarum, wild young fellow; (bot.) wax tree (*Ligustrum lucidum*); **escapar del trueno y dar en el relámpago** to jump from the frying pan into the fire; **trueno gordo** finale (*of fireworks*); (coll.) big scandal
**trueque** *m* barter; exchange; trade-in; **trueques** *mpl* (Am.) change (*money*); **a trueque de** in exchange for, instead of
**trufa** *f* (bot.) truffle; lie, story, fib
**trufador -dora** *adj* lying, fibbing; *mf* liar, fibber
**trufar** *va* (cook.) to fill or stuff with truffles; *vn* to lie, to fib
**trufera** *f* truffle bed
**truficultura** *f* truffle growing
**truhán -hana** *adj* cheating, crooked, tricky; (coll.) clownish; *mf* cheat, crook, trickster; (coll.) clown, buffoon
**truhanada** *f* var. of **truhanería**
**truhanear** *vn* to cheat, swindle; (coll.) to play the buffoon, be clownish
**truhanería** *f* rascality, crookedness; (coll.) buffoonery; gang of crooks
**truhanesco -ca** *adj* knavish, crooked, tricky; (coll.) clownish
**truísmo** *m* truism
**truja** *f* olive bin
**trujal** *m* wine press; oil press; oil mill; soda vat (*in soapmaking*)
**trujamán -mana** *mf* interpreter; *m* adviser, expert
**trujamanear** *vn* to interpret; to counsel; to deal, to trade
**trujamanía** *f* interpreting; counseling; dealing, trading
**trujimán -mana** *mf* var. of **trujamán**
**trulla** *f* noise, bustle; crowd; trowel
**trullo** *m* (orn.) teal; vat to catch juice of pressed grapes
**truncadamente** *adv* with cuts, with omissions
**truncado -da** *adj* truncate; truncated
**truncadura** *f* (cryst.) truncation
**truncamiento** *m* truncation; curtailment
**truncar** §86 *va* to truncate; to cut off the head of; to cut, slash (*a writing, speech, etc.*); to cut off, leave unfinished
**trunco -ca** *adj* truncated
**trupial** *m* (orn.) troupial
**truquero** *m* keeper of a poolroom
**trusas** *fpl* trunk hose; (Am.) trunks
**tsetsé** *f* (ent.) tsetse
**T.S.H.** abr. of **telefonía sin hilos** & **telegrafía sin hilos**
**tu** *poss adj* thy; your
**tú** *pron pers* thou; you; **a tú por tú** (coll.) disrespectfully; **de tú por tú** intimately; **hablar, llamar** or **tratar de tú** to thou, address as thou, be on close or intimate terms with
**tuáutem** *m* (*pl:* **-temes**) (coll.) indispensable person; (coll.) sine qua non
**tuba** *f* (mus.) tuba
**Tubalcaín** *m* (Bib.) Tubal-cain
**tubercular** *adj* tubercular
**tuberculina** *f* (bact.) tuberculin
**tuberculización** *f* tubercularization
**tubérculo** *m* (anat. & bot.) tuber, tubercle; (path. & zool.) tubercle
**tuberculosis** *f* (path.) tuberculosis
**tuberculoso -sa** *adj* tuberculous; tubercular; *mf* tubercular (*person having tuberculosis*)
**tubería** *f* tubing; piping, pipes; tubeworks
**tuberosa** *f* see **tuberoso**
**tuberosidad** *f* tuberosity
**tuberoso -sa** *adj* tuberous; *f* (bot.) tuberose
**tubícola** *adj* (zool.) tubicolous
**Tubinga** *f* Tübingen
**tubo** *m* tube; pipe; (anat., elec. & rad.) tube; **tubo acústico** speaking tube; **tubo capilar** capillary, capillary tube; **tubo criboso** (bot.) sieve tube; **tubo de burbuja** bubble tube; **tubo de embocadura de flauta** (mus.) flue pipe; **tubo de ensayo** test tube; **tubo de flauta** (mus.) flue pipe; **tubo de Geissler** (elec.) Geissler tube; **tubo de humo** flue; **tubo de imagen** (telv.) picture tube; **tubo de lámpara** lamp chimney; **tubo de lengüeta** (mus.) reed pipe; **tubo de nivel** gauge glass; **tubo de órgano** (mus.) organ pipe; **tubo de radio** radio tube; **tubo de vacío** (rad.) vacuum tube; **tubo digestivo** (anat.) alimentary canal; **tubo fluorescente** fluorescent lamp; **tubo indicador** gauge glass; **tubo lanzatorpedos** (nav.) torpedo tube; **tubo radiógeno** (rad.) broadcasting tube; **tubo sonoro** chime, tubular chime; **tubo tricolor** (telv.) tricolor tube; **tubo Venturi** (hyd.) Venturi tube
**tubocurarina** *f* (chem.) tubocurarine
**tubulación** *f* tubulation
**tubulado -da** *adj* tubulate
**tubular** *adj* tubular; *m* bicycle tire
**tubuloso -sa** *adj* (bot.) tubulous
**tubulura** *f* (chem.) tubulure
**tucán** *m* (orn.) toucan; (*cap.*) *m* (astr.) Toucan (*constellation of Southern Hemisphere*)
**tucía** *f* tutty
**Tucídides** *m* Thucydides
**tudel** *m* (mus.) crook (*of bassoon*)
**tudesco -ca** *adj & mf* German
**tueca** *f* stump
**tueco** *m* stump; hollow left by wood-boring insect
**tuerca** *f* (mach.) nut; **tuerca de aletas** or **de mariposa** (mach.) wing nut; **tuerca de orejetas** (mach.) thumb nut
**tuerce** *m* twist; (Am.) misfortune
**tuercecuello** *m* (orn.) wryneck
**tuero** *m* heavy log; stick, sticks; (Am.) hide-and-seek
**tuerto -ta** *adj* twisted, crooked, bent; one-eyed; **a tuertas** (coll.) backwards, upside down; crosswise; **a tuertas o a derechas** rightly or wrongly; without reflection; **a tuerto** unjustly; **a tuerto o a derecho** rightly or wrongly; without reflection; *mf* one-eyed person; *m* wrong, harm, injustice; **tuertos** *mpl* afterpains
**tueste** *m* toast, toasting
**tuétano** *m* (anat.) marrow; (bot.) pith; **hasta los tuétanos** (coll.) through and through, head over heels
**tufarada** *f* sharp smell or odor
**tufillas** *mf* (*pl:* **-llas**) (coll.) spitfire
**tufo** *m* fume, vapor; sidelock; (geol.) tufa; (coll.) foul odor; (coll.) foul breath; **tufos** *mpl* (coll.) airs, conceit

**tufoso -sa** *adj* fumy, vaporous; foul; conceited, haughty
**tugurio** *m* shepherd's hut; hovel
**tuición** *f* protection, custody
**tuina** *f* long, loose jacket
**tuitivo -va** *adj* protective, defensive
**tul** *m* tulle
**Tula** *f* Gerty
**tularemia** *f* (path.) tularemia
**Tule** *f* Thule; **última Tule** ultima Thule; (*l.c.*) *m* (bot.) tule
**tulio** *m* (chem.) thulium; (*cap.*) *m* Tully
**tulipa** *f* (bot.) gillyflower; (bot.) small tulip; tulip-shaped glass globe; bell end (*of a pipe*)
**tulipán** *m* (bot.) tulip (*plant, bulb, and flower*); (bot.) rose of China (*Hibiscus rosa-sinensis*)
**tulipanero** or **tulipero** *m* (bot.) tulip tree
**tullecer §34** *va* to abuse, mistreat; *vn* to become crippled or paralyzed
**Tullerías** *fpl* Tuileries
**tullidez** *f* paralysis
**tullido -da** *adj* crippled, paralyzed; *mf* cripple
**tulliduras** *fpl* excreta (*of birds of prey*)
**tullimiento** *m* paralysis; abuse, mistreatment; stiff tendons
**tullir §26** *va* to cripple, paralyze; to abuse, mistreat; *vn* to excrete (*said of birds*); *vr* to become crippled or paralyzed
**tumba** *f* grave, tomb; monument, tombstone; tumble; arched top; (Am.) clearing, felling of timber
**tumbacuartillos** *mf* (*pl:* **-llos**) (coll.) old toper, rounder
**tumbadillo** *m* (naut.) roundhouse
**tumbado -da** *adj* arched, vaulted
**tumbador** *m* wrecker; feller, woodsman; wrestler; tumbler; (coll.) masher
**tumbadora** *f* tree-dozer
**tumbaga** *f* tombac (*alloy*); tombac ring; ring
**tumbagón** *m* tombac bracelet
**tumbaollas** *mf* (*pl:* **-llas**) (coll.) glutton
**tumbar** *va* to knock down, knock over; (coll.) to stun, knock out; to catch, to trick; (Am.) to clear (*land, woods*); *vn* to fall, tumble; (naut.) to capsize; *vr* (coll.) to lie down, go to bed; to ease up, to give up
**tumbilla** *f* wooden frame (*to hold a bed warmer*)
**tumbo** *m* fall, tumble, violent shaking; boom, rumble; critical moment; rise and fall of sea; rough surf; archive; **tumbo de dado** imminent danger
**tumbón -bona** *adj* (coll.) sly, wily; (coll.) lazy; *mf* (coll.) sly person; (coll.) lazy loafer; *m* coach with arched top; coffer or trunk with rounded lid
**tumbonear** *vn* (coll.) to loaf around
**tumefacción** *f* swelling, tumefaction
**tumefacer §55** (has no compound tenses) *va & vr* to swell, to tumefy
**tumefaciente** *adj* tumefacient; *m* tumefacient agent
**tumefacto -ta** *adj* swollen
**tumescencia** *f* tumescence
**tumescente** *adj* tumescent
**túmido -da** *adj* tumid, swollen; (fig.) tumid, pompous, bombastic; bulbous or onion-shaped (*arch or vault*)
**tumor** *m* (path.) tumor
**tumoral** *adj* tumorlike
**tumoroso -sa** *adj* tumorous
**tumulario -ria** *adj* tumular
**túmulo** *m* tumulus; catafalque (*with or without corpse*)
**tumulto** *m* tumult
**tumultuar §33** *va* to incite to riot, incite to make a disturbance; *vr* to riot, make a disturbance
**tumultuario -ria** *adj* tumultuary
**tumultuoso -sa** *adj* tumultuous
**tuna** *f* see **tuno**
**tunal** *m* (bot.) tuna, prickly pear; growth of prickly pears
**tunanta** *adj fem* crooked, tricky; *f* crook, rascal
**tunantada** *f* crookedness, trickiness
**tunante** *adj* bumming, loafing; crooked, tricky; *mf* bum, loafer; crook, rascal
**tunantear** *vn* to be crooked, be tricky
**tunantería** *f* crookedness, trickiness
**tunar** *vn* (coll.) to bum, to loaf
**tunda** *f* shearing of cloth; (coll.) beating, drubbing
**tundear** *va* to beat, drub, thrash
**tundente** *adj* bruising
**tundición** *f* shearing of cloth
**tundidor -dora** *adj* cloth-shearing; *mf* cloth shearer; *f* cloth-shearing machine; lawn mower
**tundidura** *f* shearing of cloth
**tundir** *va* to shear (*cloth*); to cut, to mow (*grass*); (coll.) to beat, drub, thrash
**tundizno** *m* short staple wool
**tundra** *f* tundra
**tunear** *vn* (coll.) to be crooked, be tricky
**tunecí, tunecino -na** *adj & mf* Tunisian
**túnel** *m* tunnel; **túnel aéreo** or **aerodinámico** (aer.) wind tunnel; **túnel a presión** (aer.) pressure tunnel
**tunera** *f* (bot.) prickly pear
**tunes** *mpl* (Am.) little steps, first steps
**Túnez** Tunis (*city*); Tunisia (*state*)
**túngaro** *m* (zool.) agua toad
**tungstato** *m* (chem.) tungstate
**tungsteno** *m* (chem.) tungsten
**túngstico -ca** *adj* (chem.) tungstic
**tungstita** *f* (mineral.) tungstite
**túnica** *f* tunic; (anat., bot. & zool.) tunic
**tunicado -da** *adj* tunicate; *m* (zool.) tunicate
**tunicela** *f* tunic; (eccl.) tunicle
**tunicina** *f* (biochem.) tunicin
**túnico** *m* robe, gown; (Am.) chemise
**tuno -na** *adj* crooked, tricky; *mf* crook, rascal; *f* (bot.) tuna, prickly pear (*plant and fruit*); group of students; (coll.) bumming, loafing; **correr la tuna** (coll.) to bum, to loaf
**tuntún** *m* (zool.) hookworm; **al tuntún** or **al buen tuntún** (coll.) wildly, thoughtlessly, without knowing what one is talking about
**tuntunita** *f* (Am.) tiresome repetition
**tupa** *f* stuffing, packing; (coll.) stuffing, overeating
**tupé** *m* toupee; (coll.) cheek, brass, nerve
**tupelo** *m* (bot.) tupelo
**tupí** *m* (Am.) coffee house
**tupido -da** *adj* thick, dense, heavy, compact; dull, stupid; (Am.) abundant
**tupinambo** *m* var. of **aguaturma**
**tupir** *va* to pack tight, make compact; *vr* to stuff, eat too much
**turacina** *f* (biochem.) turacin
**turaco** *m* (orn.) touraco
**turanio** *adj & mf* Turanian
**turba** *f* crowd, mob; peat, turf
**turbación** *f* disturbance, confusion
**turbadamente** *adv* confusedly, excitedly
**turbador -dora** *adj* disturbing; *mf* disturber
**turbal** *m* peat bog
**turbamiento** *m* var. of **turbación**
**turbamulta** *f* (coll.) mob, rabble
**turbante** *m* turban
**turbar** *va* to disturb, upset, trouble; to stir up; *vr* to become disturbed, to get confused or mixed up
**turbera** *f* peat bog
**turbia** *f* see **turbio**
**turbidimétrico -ca** *adj* turbidimetric
**turbidímetro** *m* turbidimeter
**túrbido -da** *adj* var. of **turbio**
**turbiedad** *f* turbidity, muddiness; confusion, obscurity
**turbieza** *f* (act of) confusing, bewildering
**turbina** *f* turbine; **turbina a vapor** steam turbine; **turbina axial** axial-flow turbine; **turbina centrífuga** outward-flow turbine; **turbina centrípeta** inward-flow turbine; **turbina de acción** impulse turbine; **turbina de gas** gas turbine; **turbina de impulsión** impulse turbine; **turbina de reacción** reaction turbine; **turbina de vapor** steam turbine; **turbina hidráulica** hydraulic turbine; **turbina límite** limit turbine; **turbina mixta** mixed-flow turbine; **turbina paralela** parallel-flow turbine; **turbina radial** radial-flow turbine
**turbinado -da** *adj* turbinate (*inversely conical*); (anat.) turbinate
**turbino** *m* (pharm.) turpeth
**turbinto** *m* (bot.) pepper tree or shrub

**turbio -bia** *adj* turbid, muddy, cloudy; troubled, confused; obscure (*language*); **de turbio en turbio** (coll.) drowsy all day (*from having been awake all night*); **turbios** *mpl* dregs, oil dregs; *f* muddiness (*of water*)
**turbión** *m* squall, heavy shower; thunderstorm; (fig.) rush, sweep; (fig.) hail (*e.g., of bullets*)
**turbit** *m* (bot.) turpeth
**turbobomba** *f* turbopump
**turbocompresor** *m* turbocompressor
**turbodínamo** *f* turbodynamo
**turboeléctrico -ca** *adj* turbine-electric
**turbogenerador** *m* turbogenerator
**turbohélice** *m* (aer.) turbo-prop
**turbomotor** *m* turbomotor
**turbonada** *f* windstorm, thunderstorm
**turbopropulsor** *m* (aer.) turbo-propeller engine
**turborreactor** *m* (aer.) turbojet; **turborreactor a postcombustión** (aer.) turbo-ram-jet
**turboso -sa** *adj* peaty, turfy
**turbosoplador** *m* turboblower
**turbosupercargador** *m* turbosupercharger
**turboventilador** *m* turbofan; turboventilator
**turbulencia** *f* turbulence or turbulency
**turbulento -ta** *adj* turbulent
**turco -ca** *adj* Turkish; (philol.) Turkic; *mf* Turk; *m* Turkish (*language*); (mil.) Turco (*Algerian tirailleur*); **el gran Turco** the Grand Turk (*the Sultan*); **gran turco** (bot.) buckwheat; *f* (coll.) jag, drunk; **coger una turca** (coll.) to go on a jag, to get drunk
**turcófilo -la** *adj & mf* Turkophile
**turcófobo -ba** *adj & mf* Turkophobe
**turcomano -na** *adj* Turkomanic; *mf* Turkoman
**turcople** *adj & mf* Turko-Greek (*of Turkish father and Greek mother*)
**túrdiga** *f* strip of hide or leather; sole of a sandal
**Turena, la** Touraine
**turf** *m* (*pl:* **turfs**) race track; horse racing; turfmen
**turfista** *adj* turfy, horsy; *m* turfman
**turfístico -ca** *adj* racing, horse-racing
**turgencia** *f* turgidity
**turgente** *adj* (path. & fig.) turgid; (poet.) raised, elevated, massive
**turgescencia** *f* turgescence
**turgescente** *adj* turgescent
**túrgido -da** *adj* (poet.) raised, elevated, massive
**turgita** *f* (mineral.) turgite
**turibular** *va* to incense with the thurible
**turibulario** *m* (eccl.) thurifer
**turíbulo** *m* (eccl.) thurible
**turiferario** *m* (eccl.) thurifer; (coll.) fawner
**turificación** *f* thurification
**turificar §86** *va & vn* to thurify
**Turín** *f* Turin
**Turingia** *f* Thuringia
**turingiano -na** *adj & mf* Thuringian
**turión** *m* (bot.) turion
**turismo** *m* touring; tourist business; touring car
**turista** *mf* tourist
**turístico -ca** *adj* touring; tourist
**Turkmenistán, el** the Turkmen Soviet Socialist Republic
**turma** *f* testicle; **turma de tierra** (bot.) truffle
**turmalina** *f* (mineral.) tourmaline
**turnar** *vn* to alternate, to take turns
**turneráceo -a** *adj* (bot.) turneraceous
**turnerita** *f* (mineral.) turnerite
**turnio -nia** *adj* squint, cross (*eyes*); squint-eyed, cross-eyed; (fig.) cross-looking, stern
**turno** *m* turn, shift; **aguardar turno** to wait one's turn; **a su turno** in his stead; **fuera de turno** out of turn; **por turno** in turn; **por turnos** by turns
**turón** *m* (zool.) fitch, polecat
**turpial** *m* var. of **trupial**
**turquear** *vr* (Am.) to be fagged out
**turquesa** *f* (mineral.) turquoise; mold; bullet mold
**turquesado -da** *adj* dark-blue
**turquesco -ca** *adj* Turkish
**Turquestán, el** Turkestan; **el Turquestán Chino** Chinese Turkestan; **el Turquestán Ruso** Russian Turkestan
**turquí** *adj* (*pl:* **-quíes**) deep-blue
**Turquía** *f* Turkey; **la Turquía de Asia** Turkey in Asia; **la Turquía de Europa** Turkey in Europe; **la Turquía Asiática** Turkey in Asia; **la Turquía Europea** Turkey in Europe
**turquino -na** *adj* var. of **turquí**
**turrar** *va* to toast, to roast, to broil
**turriculado -da** *adj* (zool.) turreted
**turrón** *m* nougat; (coll.) public office, plum; **romper el turrón** (Am.) to begin to thou each other, to begin to call each other by their first names
**turronería** *f* nougat shop
**turronero -ra** *mf* maker or seller of nougats
**Turs** *f* Tours
**turulato -ta** *adj* (coll.) stunned, dumbfounded
**turumbón** *m* (coll.) bump, bump on the head
**turuta** *f* (coll.) jag, drunk
**tus** *interj* here, here! (*to call a dog*); **sin decir tus ni mus** (coll.) without saying boo
**tusa** *f* (Am.) cigar rolled in corn husk; (Am.) corncob; (Am.) corn silk; (Am.) mane (*of horse*); (Am.) pockmark; (Am.) trollop
**tusar** *vn* (prov. & Am.) to cut, to shear
**Túsculo** *f* Tusculum
**tusícula** *f* slight cough
**tusilago** *m* (bot.) coltsfoot
**tusón** *m* fleece; unsheared sheepskin; colt under two years old
**tusona** *f* (prov.) filly under two years old
**tusor** *m* tussah (*silk*)
**tutado -da** *adj* (Am.) pock-marked
**tutar** *vr* (Am.) to become pock-marked
**tuteamiento** *m* var. of **tuteo**
**tutear** *va* to thou; to address using the second person singular; to be on close or intimate terms with; *vr* to thou each other; to address each other using the second person singular; to be on close or intimate terms with each other
**tutela** *f* guardianship, tutelage; protection
**tutelar** *adj* guardian, tutelar, tutelary; *va* to protect, take under one's wing
**tuteo** *m* thouing; addressing in the second person singular
**tutía** *f* var. of **atutía**
**tutilimundi** *m* var. of **mundonuevo**
**tutiplén; a tutiplén** (coll.) in abundance, to excess
**tutor -tora** or **-triz** (*pl:* **-trices**) *mf* guardian, protector; (law) guardian; *m* prop (*for plants*)
**tutoría** *f* guardianship, tutelage
**tutuquear** *va* (Am.) to sick (*a dog*)
**tuturuto -ta** *adj* (Am.) stunned, dumbfounded; *mf* (Am.) go-between
**tuturutú** *m* (*pl:* **-túes**) bugle call, horn call
**tuve** *1st sg pret ind of* **tener**
**tuyo -ya** *adj & pron poss* thine, yours; *f* (bot.) thuja; **tuya articulada** (bot.) sandarac; **tuya de la China** (bot.) China tree
**tuza** *f* (zool.) gopher, pocket gopher
**TV** *f* abr. of **televisión**

# U

**U, u** *f* twenty-fourth letter of the Spanish alphabet
**U.** abr. of **usted**
**u** *conj* (used for **o** before a word beginning with the vowel sound **o**) or
**uapití** *m* (*pl:* **-tíes**) (zool.) wapiti
**Ubaldo** *m* Waldo
**ubérrimo -ma** *adj super* very or most abundant or fertile
**ubicación** *f* location, situation, position
**ubicar §86** *va* (Am.) to place, locate; *vn & vr* to be located, be situated
**ubicuidad** *f* ubiquity
**ubicuo -cua** *adj* ubiquitous
**ubiquidad** *f* var. of **ubicuidad**
**ubiquitario -ria** *adj & mf* (eccl.) Ubiquitarian
**ubre** *f* teat; udder
**ubrera** *f* (path.) thrush
**ucase** *m* ukase
**-uco -ca** *suffix dim & pej* e.g., **ventanuco** ugly little window; **casuca** shack, shanty
**ucranio -nia** *adj & mf* Ukrainian; *m* Ukrainian (*language*); (*cap.*) *f* Ukraine
**-ucho -cha** *suffix dim & pej* e.g., **ventanucho** ugly little window; **casucha** shack, shanty
**uchuvito -ta** *adj* (Am.) drunk
**Ud.** abr. of **usted**
**udómetro** *m* udometer
**-udo -da** *suffix adj* -y, e.g., **carnudo** fleshy; **peludo** hairy; *suffix aug* e.g., **barbudo** long-bearded, heavy-bearded; **cabezudo** big-headed; **zancudo** long-shanked
**Uds.** abr. of **ustedes**
**-uelo -la** *suffix dim & pej* indicates smallness with or without concept of ridicule or contempt, e.g., **arroyuelo** rill; **mozuelo** young fellow; **coquetuela** vain coquette; **plazuela** small square
**-ueño -ña** *suffix adj* -ing, e.g., **halagüeño** charming; **pedigüeño** demanding; **risueño** smiling
**uesnorueste** *m* var. of **oesnoroeste**
**uessudueste** *m* var. of **oessudoeste**
**ueste** *m* var. of **oeste**
**uf** *interj* pshaw!; humph!; whew!
**ufanar** *vr* to boast; **ufanarse con** or **de** to boast of, to pride oneself on
**ufanía** *f* pride, conceit; cheer, satisfaction; smoothness, mastery
**ufano -na** *adj* proud, conceited, boastful; cheerful, satisfied; easy, smooth, masterly
**ufo; a ufo** on someone else, at someone else's expense
**ujier** *m* doorman, usher
**ulano** *m* (mil.) uhlan
**úlcera** *f* (path.) sore, ulcer; (bot.) rot; **úlcera de decúbito** bedsore; **úlcera duodenal** (path.) duodenal ulcer; **úlcera gástrica** (path.) gastric ulcer; **úlcera péptica** (path.) peptic ulcer
**ulceración** *f* ulceration
**ulcerar** *va & vr* to ulcerate, to fester
**ulceroso -sa** *adj* ulcerous
**ulema** *m* ulema
**ulero** *m* (Am.) rolling pin
**ulfilano -na** *adj* of Ulfilas (*said of an ancient mode of writing*)
**uliginoso -sa** *adj* uliginose
**Ulises** *m* (myth.) Ulysses
**ulitis** *f* (path.) ulitis
**ulmáceo -a** *adj* (bot.) ulmaceous
**ulmaria** *f* (bot.) meadowsweet
**ulna** *f* (anat.) ulna
**ulnar** *adj* ulnar
**úlster** *m* ulster
**ulterior** *adj* ulterior, later, subsequent
**ulteriormente** *adv* later, subsequently
**ultimación** *f* termination, conclusion
**últimamente** *adv* finally; recently, lately
**ultimar** *va* to end, finish, terminate, wind up
**ultimátum** *m* (*pl:* **-mátum** or **-mátumes**) ultimatum; (coll.) definitive decision
**ultimidad** *f* finality
**último -ma** *adj* last, latest; excellent, superior; most remote; lowest; final (*said, e.g., of a price*); top (*floor*); late (*hour*); **a última hora** at the eleventh hour; **a últimos de** in the latter part of (*a month*); **a la última** in the latest fashion; **estar a lo último** or **en las últimas** to be up to date, be well-informed; to be near the end, to be on one's last legs; **por último** at last, finally; **última sílaba** (gram.) ultima; **último suplicio** capital punishment
**ultra** *adv* besides
**ultraatmosférico -ca** *adj* outer (*space*)
**ultrajador -dora** *adj* insulting, offensive; *mf* insulter
**ultrajar** *va* to outrage, insult, offend
**ultraje** *m* outrage, insult, offense
**ultrajoso -sa** *adj* outrageous
**ultraliberal** *adj & mf* ultraliberal
**ultramar** *m* country overseas; ultramarine (*pigment*); **en ultramar** overseas
**ultramarino -na** *adj* ultramarine; overseas; *m* ultramarine, ultramarine blue; **ultramarinos** *mpl* delicatessen, overseas foods, groceries
**ultramicroscopia** *f* ultramicroscopy
**ultramicroscópico -ca** *adj* ultramicroscopic
**ultramicroscopio** *m* ultramicroscope
**ultramoderno -na** *adj* ultramodern
**ultramontanismo** *m* ultramontanism
**ultramontano -na** *adj & mf* ultramontane
**ultramundano -na** *adj* ultramundane, otherworldly
**ultramundo** *m* other world, future life
**ultranza; a ultranza** to the death; at any cost, unflinchingly; extreme
**ultrarradical** *adj* ultraradical
**ultrarrápido -da** *adj* ultrarapid, extra-fast
**ultrarrojo -ja** *adj* ultrared, infrared
**ultrasónico -ca** *adj* supersonic; ultrasonic; *f* ultrasonics
**ultratropical** *adj* ultratropical
**ultratumba** *adv* beyond the grave
**ultraviolado -da** or **ultravioleta** *adj* (phys.) ultraviolet
**ultravirus** *m* (*pl:* **-rus**) ultravirus
**ultrazodiacal** *adj* (astr.) ultrazodiacal
**úlula** *f* (orn.) tawny owl
**ululación** *f* howl, ululation; hoot (*of owl*); wow (*of phonograph record*)
**ululante** *adj* ululant
**ulular** *vn* to ululate; to hoot
**ululato** *m* howl, ululation; hoot (*of owl*)
**-ullo -lla** *suffix dim & pej* e.g., **zangandullo** worthless loafer; **ramulla** small wood, dead wood
**ulluco** *m* (bot.) ulluco (*South American tubercle similar to the potato*)
**umbela** *f* (bot.) umbel
**umbelado -da** *adj* umbellate
**umbelífero -ra** *adj* umbelliferous
**umbeliforme** *adj* umbellar or umbellate
**umbilicado -da** *adj* umbilicate
**umbilical** *adj* umbilical
**umbo** *m* (anat. & zool.) umbo
**umbón** *m* umbo (*of shield*)
**umbráculo** *m* shaded, airy place for plants
**umbral** *m* threshold; doorsill; (arch.) lintel (*of any opening*); (psychol., physiol. & fig.) threshold; **atravesar los umbrales** to cross the threshold; **estar en los umbrales de** to be on the threshold of; **no atravesar los umbrales** to not darken one's door

**umbralada** *f*, **umbralado** *m*, or **umbraladura** *f* (Am.) threshold
**umbralar** *va* (arch.) to put a lintel in
**umbrático -ca** *adj* umbrageous, shady
**umbrela** *f* (zool.) umbrella (*of jellyfishes*)
**umbrío -a** *adj* shady; *f* shade, shady place; shady side; **la Umbría** Umbria
**umbro -bra** *adj* & *mf* Umbrian; *m* Umbrian (*ancient Italic language*)
**umbroso -sa** *adj* umbrageous, shady
**un, una** *art indef* a, an; *adj* one (*numeral*); the form **un** is used before a masculine singular noun or an adjective + a masculine singular noun and before a feminine singular noun beginning with accented **a** or **ha;** see **uno**
**unánime** *adj* unanimous
**unanimidad** *f* unanimity
**unanimismo** *m* unanimism
**uncial** *adj* & *f* uncial
**unciforme** *adj* unciform; *m* (anat.) unciform
**uncinado -da** *adj* uncinate
**unción** *f* unction; **unciones** *fpl* treatment with mercurial ointment
**uncir** §50 *va* to yoke; to subjugate
**undante** *adj* (poet.) wavy, undulating
**undecágono** *m* undecagon
**undécimo -ma** *adj* & *m* eleventh
**undécuplo -pla** *adj* eleven times as large or as much
**undísono -na** *adj* (poet.) babbling, rippling
**undívago -ga** *adj* (poet.) wavy
**undoso -sa** *adj* waving, wavy
**undulación** *f* undulation; wave; wave motion; **undulación permanente** permanent wave
**undulante** *adj* undulant; waving
**undular** *vn* to undulate; to wriggle
**undulatorio -ria** *adj* undulatory
**Unesco** *f* Unesco
**ungido** *m* anointed; **el ungido del Señor** The Lord's Anointed
**ungimiento** *m* anointment
**ungir** §42 *va* to anoint; (eccl.) to anoint; (coll.) to dub, to name
**ungüentario -ria** *adj* unguentary; *mf* maker or dealer in unguents; *m* vessel in which unguents are kept
**ungüento** *m* unguent, ointment, salve; (fig.) salve, flattery
**unguiculado -da** *adj* ungual, unguiculate
**unguinal** *adj* ungual
**unguis** *m* (*pl:* **-guis**) (anat.) unguis or os unguis
**úngula** *f* (zool. & geom.) ungula
**ungulado -da** *adj* & *m* ungulate
**ungular** *adj* ungular
**uniato -ta** *adj* & *mf* Uniat
**uniaxial, uniáxico -ca** or **uniaxil** *adj* uniaxial
**únicamente** *adv* only, solely; uniquely
**unicameral** *adj* unicameral
**unicelular** *adj* unicellular
**unicidad** *f* unity; uniqueness
**único -ca** *adj* only, sole; unique; one, e.g., **precio único** one price
**unicolor** *adj* one-color
**unicornio -nia** *adj* unicorn; *m* (myth. & Bib.) unicorn
**unidad** *f* unit; unity; **unidad móvil** (rad.) mobile unit
**unidireccional** *adj* one-way, unidirectional
**unido -da** *adj* united; smooth; (fig.) close-knit
**unifamiliar** *adj* one-family, single-family (*e.g., house*)
**unificación** *f* unification
**unificador -dora** *adj* unifying
**unificar** §86 *va* to unify; *vr* to be or become unified
**unifloro -ra** *adj* (bot.) uniflorous
**unifoliado -da** *adj* (bot.) unifoliate
**uniformar** *va* to uniform; to clothe in uniforms; to make uniform; **uniformar una cosa a** or **con otra** to make one thing uniform with another; *vr* to become uniform
**uniforme** *adj* & *m* uniform
**uniformidad** *f* uniformity
**unigénito -ta** *adj* unigenital, only-begotten
**unilateral** *adj* unilateral
**unión** *f* union; double finger ring; (mach.) union; (*cap.*) *f* Union (*U.S.A.*); **unión aduanera** customs union; **Unión de Repúblicas Socialistas Soviéticas** Union of Soviet Socialist Republics; **Unión panamericana** Pan American Union; **Unión Soviética** Soviet Union; **Unión Sudafricana** Union of South Africa
**unionismo** *m* unionism
**unionista** *mf* unionist
**uníparo -ra** *adj* (zool. & bot.) uniparous
**unípede** *adj* uniped
**unipersonal** *adj* unipersonal; of one person, one-man (*e.g., government*); (gram.) impersonal
**unipolar** *adj* (elec.) unipolar, single-pole
**unir** *va* & *vr* to unite, join
**unisexual** *adj* unisexual
**unisón** *m* (mus.) instruments or voices in unison
**unisonancia** *f* monotony (*of an orator*); (mus.) unison
**unisonar** *vn* to sound or be in unison
**unísono -na** *adj* (mus.) unison; unisonous; **al unísono** in unison; unanimously; **al unísono de** in unison with
**unitario -ria** *adj* unitary; (pertaining to a) unit; Unitarian; *mf* Unitarian
**unitarismo** *m* (eccl.) Unitarianism
**unitivo -va** *adj* unitive
**univalencia** *f* (chem.) univalence
**univalente** *adj* (chem.) univalent
**univalvo -va** *adj* (zool.) univalve
**universal** *adj* universal; *m* (log.) universal (*each one of the five predicables*)
**universalidad** *f* universality; generality
**universalismo** *m* universalism; Universalism
**universalista** *mf* universalist; Universalist
**universalizar** §76 *va* to universalize
**universidad** *f* university
**universitario -ria** *adj* (pertaining to a) university; *mf* (Am.) university student, college student; *m* university professor
**universo -sa** *adj* universal; *m* universe; **universo aislado** (astr.) island universe
**univocación** *f* univocity
**univocar** §86 *vr* to have the same meaning
**unívoco -ca** *adj* univocal
**-uno -na** *suffix adj* -ine, e.g., **boyuno** bovine; **cervuno** cervine; **lebruno** leporine; **porcuno** porcine; -ish, e.g., **frailuno** friarish; **hombruno** mannish
**uno -na** *adj* & *pron indef* one, someone, some one; one and the same; one, they, people, e.g., **uno no sabe qué hacer aquí** one does not know what to do here; **a una** of one accord; **de una** at once; **la una** one o'clock; **somos unos** we are one; **una y no más** once is enough; **uno a otro, unos a otros** each other, one another; **uno que otro** one or more, a few; **unos -nas** some, about; a pair of, e.g., **unas gafas** a pair of glasses; **unos tirantes** a pair of suspenders; **unos cuantos** some, a few; **uno y otro** both; *m* one (*numeral*); see **un**
**untador -dora** *adj* anointing; greasing; *mf* anointer; greaser
**untadura** *f* anointing, ointment; greasing, grease
**untamiento** *m* anointing; greasing
**untar** *va* to anoint; to smear, grease; (coll.) to bribe; *vr* to get smeared; to grease oneself; (coll.) to take care of oneself, look out for oneself
**untaza** *f* fat
**unto** *m* grease; fat; ointment; salve, flattery; **unto de botas, unto de zapatos** (Am.) shoe polish; **unto de Méjico** (coll.) bribe money
**untoso -sa** *adj* var. of **untuoso**
**untuosidad** *f* greasiness, stickiness
**untuoso -sa** *adj* unctuous; greasy, sticky
**untura** *f* var. of **untadura**
**uña** *f* nail, fingernail, toenail; nail hole (*in blade of penknife*); claw; hoof, talon; sting (*of scorpion*); thorn; scab; hard tumor on eyelid; short tree stump; plectrum (*e.g., for mandolin*); (mach.) claw, gripper; (mach.) pallet (*of pawl*); fluke, bill (*of anchor*); **a uña de caballo** at full gallop, at full speed; **enseñar** or **mostrar las uñas** to show one's teeth; **ser largo de uñas** to have long fingers; **ser**

**uña y carne** (coll.) to be in cahoots, to be hand in glove; **tener en la uña** to have on the tip of one's fingers; **uña de caballo** (bot.) coltsfoot
**uñada** *f* scratch, nail scratch; nip, flip
**uñarada** *f* nail scratch
**uñate** *m* (coll.) pinch with the nail; chuckfarthing
**uñero** *m* ingrowing nail; whitlow; thumb notch
**uñeta** *f* small fingernail; stonecutter's chisel; chuckfarthing
**uñetazo** *m* nail scratch
**uñir §25** *va* (prov.) to yoke
**uñoso -sa** *adj* long-nailed, long-clawed
**upa** *interj* up, up!
**upas** *m* (bot.) upas (*tree and sap*)
**upupa** *f* (orn.) hoopoe
**ural** *adj* Ural; **los Urales** the Urals
**urálico -ca** *adj* Uralian, Uralic
**uralita** *f* (mineral.) uralite; asbestos roofing material
**uraloaltaico -ca** *adj & m* Ural-Altaic
**uranálisis** *f* (*pl:* **-sis**) urinalysis
**Urania** *f* see **uranio**
**uránico -ca** *adj* (chem.) uranic
**uranilo** *m* (chem.) uranyl
**uraninita** *f* (mineral.) uraninite
**uranio -nia** *adj* Uranian; *m* (chem.) uranium; (*cap.*) *f* (myth.) Urania
**uranismo** *m* uranism
**uranita** *f* (mineral.) uranite
**urano** *m* (chem.) uranium; (*cap.*) *m* (astr. & myth.) Uranus
**uranocircita** *f* (mineral.) uranocircite
**uranofano** *m* (mineral.) uranophane
**uranografía** *f* uranography
**uranógrafo -fa** *mf* uranographer
**uranometría** *f* uranometry
**uranosferita** *f* (mineral.) uranosphaerite
**uranospatita** *f* (mineral.) uranospathite
**uranospinita** *f* (mineral.) uranospinite
**uranotalita** *f* (mineral.) uranothallite
**uranotila** *f* (mineral.) uranotil
**uranotorita** *f* (mineral.) uranothorite
**urao** *m* (mineral.) urao, trona
**urato** *m* (chem.) urate
**urbanidad** *f* urbanity
**urbanismo** *m* city planning
**urbanista** *adj* city-planning; *m* city planner
**urbanístico -ca** *adj* urbanistic; *f* city planning
**urbanización** *f* urbanization; city planning
**urbanizar §76** *va* to urbanize; *vr* to become urbanized
**urbano -na** *adj* urban, city; urbane (*courteous, elegant*); (*cap.*) *m* Urban
**urbe** *f* big city, metropolis
**urca** *f* (naut.) hooker, dogger; (zool.) killer whale, orca
**urce** *m* (bot.) heath
**urceolado -da** *adj* urceolate
**urchilla** *f* (bot. & chem.) archil
**urdemalas** *mf* (*pl:* **-las**) (coll.) intriguer, schemer
**urdidera** *f* warper (*woman*); warping frame
**urdidor -dora** *adj* warping; scheming; *mf* warper; *f* warping frame
**urdidura** *f* warping; scheming
**urdiembre** *f* or **urdimbre** *f* warp; warping chain; scheme, scheming
**urdir** *va* to beam (*a warp*); to plot, scheme, conspire
**urdú** *m* Urdu
**urea** *f* (biochem.) urea
**uredospora** *f* (bot.) uredospore
**ureido** *m* (chem.) ureide
**uremia** *f* (path.) uremia
**urémico -ca** *adj* uremic
**urente** *adj* burning, smarting
**uréter** *m* (anat. & zool.) ureter
**uretra** *f* (anat.) urethra
**uretral** *adj* urethral
**uretritis** *f* (path.) urethritis
**uretroscopia** *f* urethroscopy
**uretroscopio** *m* urethroscope
**uretrotomía** *f* (surg.) urethrotomy
**urgencia** *f* urgency; emergency; **de urgencia** emergency; special-delivery
**urgente** *adj* urgent; special-delivery
**urgir §42** *vn* to be urgent; **urgir** + *inf* to be urgent to + *inf*
**Urías** *m* (Bib.) Uriah
**úrico -ca** *adj* (chem.) uric
**urinación** *f* urination
**urinal** *adj* urinary; *m* urinal (*place*)
**urinálisis** *f* (*pl:* **-sis**) urinalysis
**urinario -ria** *adj* urinary; *m* urinal (*place*)
**urinífero -ra** *adj* uriniferous
**urna** *f* urn; glass case; ballot box; **ir a las urnas** to go to the polls
**-uro** *suffix m* (chem.) -ide, e.g., **hidruro** hydride; **sulfuro** sulfide; (zool.) -uran, e.g., **braquiuro** brachyuran; **jifosuro** xiphosuran
**uro** *m* (zool.) aurochs; (zool.) urus
**urocisto** *m* (anat.) urocyst
**urocromo** *m* (biochem.) urochrome
**urodelo -la** *adj & m* (zool.) urodelan
**urofeína** *f* (biochem.) urophaein or urophein
**urogallo** *m* (orn.) capercaillie
**urogenital** *adj* urogenital
**urógeno -na** *adj* urogenous
**urolitiasis** *f* (path.) urolithiasis
**urolito** *m* (path.) urolith
**urología** *f* urology
**urológico -ca** *adj* urologic or urological
**urólogo -ga** *mf* urologist
**uromancia** or **uromancía** *f* divination by inspection of urine
**uropatagio** *m* (zool.) uropatagium
**uropigal** *adj* uropygial
**uropigio** *m* uropygium
**urópodo -da** *adj* (zool.) uropodal; *m* (zool.) uropod
**uropoiesis** *f* or **uropoyesis** *f* uropoiesis
**uroscopia** *f* uroscopy
**urosis** *f* (path.) urosis
**urotoxia** *f* (physiol.) urotoxy
**urraca** *f* (orn.) magpie
**ursiforme** *adj* ursiform
**ursino -na** *adj* ursine
**U.R.S.S.** abr. of **Unión de Repúblicas Socialistas Soviéticas**
**Úrsula** *f* Ursula
**ursulino -na** *adj & f* Ursuline
**urticáceo -a** *adj* (bot.) urticaceous
**urticación** *f* (med.) urtication
**urticante** *adj* urticant
**urticaria** *f* (path.) hives, urticaria, nettle rash
**urubú** *m* (*pl:* **-búes**) (orn.) black vulture
**Uruguay, el** Uruguay
**uruguayo -ya** *adj & mf* Uruguayan
**urunday** *m* (Am.) urunday (*timber tree of genus Astronium*)
**usadamente** *adv* according to custom
**usado -da** *adj* used (*customarily employed; worn, partly worn-out; accustomed*); skilled; **al usado** at usance; **poco usado** rare (*word*)
**usagre** *m* (path.) infantile impetigo; (vet.) mange
**usanza** *f* use; usage, custom
**usar** *va* to use, make use of; to follow (*a profession*); *vn* to be accustomed; **usar** + *inf* to be accustomed to + *inf*, e.g., **uso salir de paseo por la mañana** I am accustomed to go out for a walk in the morning; **usar de** to use, resort to, indulge in; **usar de la palabra** to speak, make a speech; *vr* to be the custom
**usarcé** or **usarced** *mf* (obs.) your honor
**usencia** *mf* (obs.) your reverence
**useñoría** *mf* your excellence; *m* your lordship; *f* your ladyship
**usgo** *m* loathing
**usía** *mf* your excellence; *m* your lordship; *f* your ladyship
**usier** *m* var. of **ujier**
**usina** *f* (Am.) plant, factory; (Am.) powerhouse; **usina mareamotriz** (Am.) tide-driven power plant; **usina térmica** (Am.) steam power plant
**uso** *m* use; custom, usage; habit, practice; wear, wear and tear; **al uso** according to custom; **el uso hace maestro** practice makes perfect; **en buen uso** (coll.) in good condition; **hacer uso de la palabra** to speak, to make a speech; **uso de razón** discretion, discernment
**ustaga** *f* (naut.) tie
**uste** *interj* get away!; **sin decir uste ni muste** (coll.) without saying a word

**usted** *pron pers* (used with third person of verb) you
**ustible** *adj* combustible
**ustión** *f* burning, cauterization
**ustorio -ria** *adj* burning
**usual** *adj* usual; sociable; usable
**usualmente** *adv* usually
**usuario -ria** *adj* (law) having limited use of a thing; *mf* (law) usuary; user
**usucapión** *f* (law) usucapion
**usucapir** *va* (law) to usucapt
**usufructo** *m* (law) usufruct; uses, fruits
**usufructuar** §33 *va* to usufruct; to enjoy; *vn* to be productive, be fruitful
**usura** *f* usury; interest; profit; profiteering; **pagar con usura** to pay back (*a favor, an insult, etc.*) a thousandfold
**usurar** *vn* var. of **usurear**
**usurario -ria** *adj* usurious
**usurear** *vn* to practice usury; to profiteer
**usurero -ra** *mf* usurer; profiteer
**usurpación** *f* usurpation
**usurpador -dora** *adj* usurping; *mf* usurper
**usurpar** *va* usurp
**utensilio** *m* utensil; **utensilios** *mpl* (mil.) outfit, equipment
**uterino -na** *adj* uterine
**útero** *m* (anat.) uterus, womb
**uterotomía** *f* (surg.) hysterotomy
**útil** *adj* useful; (law) lawful, legal (*time*); *m* use; tool; **útiles** *mpl* tools, equipment
**utilería** *f* (Am.) stage equipment, properties; (Am.) scenic effects
**utilero -ra** *mf* (Am.) person in charge of properties (*in a theater*); *m* (Am.) property man
**utilidad** *f* utility, usefulness; profit, earning
**utilitario -ria** *adj* utilitarian
**utilitarismo** *m* utilitarianism
**utilitarista** *adj & mf* utilitarian
**utilizable** *adj* usable, ready for use, ready for service
**utilización** *f* utilization
**utilizar** §76 *va* to utilize; *vr* to serve; **utilizarse con, de** or **en** to make use of; **utilizarse para** to be used for, to be good for
**utillaje** *m* or **utillería** *f* tools, equipment, outfit
**utopia** or **utopía** *f* utopia or Utopia
**utópico -ca** *adj* utopian or Utopian
**utopismo** *m* utopianism
**utopista** *adj & mf* utopian or Utopian
**utrera** *f* heifer between two and three years old
**utrero** *m* bull between two and three years old
**utrícula** *f* (bot.) utricle
**utricularia** *f* (bot.) bladderwort
**utrículo** *m* (anat.) utricle
**UU.** abr. of **ustedes**
**uva** *f* grape; berry of barberry; grapevine; wart on eyelid; uvular tumor; **estar hecho una uva** to be soaked, have a load on; **no entrar por uvas** to not risk interceding; **uva canilla** (bot.) white stonecrop; **uva crespa** (bot.) gooseberry; **uva de Corinto** currant; **uva de gato** (bot.) sedum, white stonecrop; **uva de playa** sea-grape berry; **uva de raposa** (bot.) nightshade; **uva espín** or **espina** (bot.) gooseberry; **uva lupina** (bot.) wolfsbane; **uva marina** (bot.) shrubby horsetail; **uva pasa** raisin; **uvas verdes** (fig.) sour grapes (*of Aesop's fable*); **uva tamínea** or **taminia** (bot.) stavesacre; **uva verga** (bot.) wolfsbane
**uvada** *f* abundance of grapes, rich crop of grapes
**uvaduz** *f* (bot.) bearberry
**uvaguemaestre** *m* (mil.) wagon master
**uval** *adj* grape-like
**uvanita** *f* (mineral.) uvanite
**uvarovita** *f* (mineral.) uvarovite
**uvate** *m* grape preserves
**uve** *f* letter V
**úvea** *f* (anat.) uvea
**uveral** *m* (Am.) growth of sea grapes
**uvero -ra** *adj* (pertaining to the) grape; *mf* grape seller; *m* (bot.) sea grape
**úvula** *f* (anat.) uvula
**uvular** *adj* (anat. & phonet.) uvular
**uvulitis** *f* (path.) uvulitis
**uxoricida** *m* uxoricide (*man*)
**uxoricidio** *m* uxoricide (*act*)
**uxorio -ria** *adj* uxorial; uxorious (*excessively fond of and doting on one's wife*)
**-uza** *suffix pej* e.g., **carnuza** coarse cheap meat; **gentuza** rabble
**uzarina** *f* (chem.) uzarin
**uzbeco -ca** *adj & mf* Uzbek or Uzbeg; *m* Uzbek or Uzbeg (*language*)
**Uzbekistán, el** Uzbekistan
**-uzco -ca** *suffix adj* -ish, e.g., **blancuzco** whitish; **negruzco** blackish

# V

**V, v** *f* twenty-fifth letter of the Spanish alphabet
**V.** abr. of **usted, véase** & **venerable**
**V.A.** abr. of **Vuestra Alteza**
**va** *3d sg pres ind of* **ir**
**vaca** *f* cow; cowhide; beef; gambling pool; **echar las vacas a** (coll.) to put the blame on; **hacer vacas** (Am.) to play truant; **vaca de la boda** (coll.) clown, laughingstock, goat; friend in need; **vaca de leche** milch cow; **vaca de San Antón** (ent.) ladybird; **vaca gruñidora** (zool.) yak; **vaca lechera** milch cow; **vaca marina** (zool.) sea cow; **vacas lecheras** dairy cattle
**vacabuey** *m* (bot.) sandpaper tree
**vacación** *f* vacation; vacancy; **vacaciones** *fpl* vacation; **estar de vacaciones** to be on vacation; **marcharse de vacaciones** to go away on a vacation, to leave for a vacation; **vacaciones retribuídas** vacations with pay
**vacacionista** *mf* vacationist
**vacada** *f* drove of cattle
**vacancia** *f* vacancy
**vacante** *adj* vacant, unoccupied; *f* vacation; vacancy
**vacar** **§86** *vn* to be vacant, to be unfilled; to be idle, to not work, to be unoccupied; **vacar a** to engage in, to attend to; **vacar de** to lack
**vacarí** *adj* (*pl* **-ríes**) cowhide, made of cowhide
**vaccíneo -a** *adj* vaccine, vaccinic
**vaccínico -ca** *adj* var. of **vaccíneo**
**vaciadero** *m* drain; drainpipe
**vaciadizo -za** *adj* cast, molded
**vaciado -da** *adj* hollow-ground; *m* cast, casting; hollow; plaster cast
**vaciador** *m* emptier; caster, molder; sharpener
**vaciamiento** *m* emptying; casting, molding
**vaciante** *m* ebb tide
**vaciar** **§90 & regular** *va* to drain, to empty; to cast, to mold; to hollow out; to sharpen on a grindstone; to transcribe; to expatiate upon; *vn* to flow, to empty; to fall (*as a flood, river, etc.*); *vr* (coll.) to blab, to spill all one knows; **vaciarse de** (coll.) to blab, to spill
**vaciedad** *f* nonsense, folly
**vacilación** *f* vacillation; unsteadiness; flickering; hesitation
**vacilada** *f* (Am.) spree, high time; (Am.) drunk
**vacilante** *adj* vacillating; unsteady; flickering; hesitant
**vacilar** *vn* to vacillate, to waver; to shake, be unsteady; to flicker; to hesitate; (Am.) to get drunk; **vacilar en** + *inf* to hesitate to + *inf*
**vacío -a** *adj* empty; hollow; idle; vain, useless, unsuccessful; lacking; proud, presumptuous; barren (*said of cattle*); *m* emptiness; vacancy; side, flank; hollow; lack; void; (phys.) vacuum; **de vacío** idle, light, unloaded; unsucessfully; **en el vacío** in vacuo; **en vacío** unsteadily; in vain; at nothing, in the air; **hacer el vacío a** to isolate, to keep people away from
**vaco -ca** *adj* vacant; *m* (coll.) ox
**vacuidad** *f* emptiness; vacuity
**vacuna** *f* see **vacuno**
**vacunación** *f* vaccination
**vacunar** *va* to vaccinate
**vacuno -na** *adj* bovine; cowhide, made of cowhide; *f* cowpox; vaccine
**vacunoterapia** *f* vaccine therapy
**vacuo -cua** *adj* empty; vacant; stupid, emptyheaded; *m* hollow; vacuum
**vacuola** *f* (biol.) vacuole
**vadeable** *adj* fordable; superable
**vadeador** *m* guide in fording streams
**vadeamiento** *m* fording
**vadear** *va* to ford; to overcome; to sound out; *vr* to behave, conduct oneself
**vademécum** *m* vade mecum; manual; school companion, school portfolio
**vadeo** *m* var. of **vadeamiento**
**vadera** *f* wide ford; (prov.) channel made by a freshet or flood
**vado** *m* ford; resource, expedient; **al vado o a la puente** (coll.) one way or another; **no hallar vado** to have no solution, to see no way out; **tentar el vado** to look into the matter, to feel one's way
**vadoso -sa** *adj* fordy, shallow, shoaly
**vagabundaje** *m* vagabondage; vagrancy
**vagabundear** *vn* to wander, to roam; to idle, to loaf around
**vagabundeo** *m* vagabondage
**vagabundo -da** *adj* vagabond; *mf* vagabond, tramp
**vagamundear** *vn* var. of **vagabundear**
**vagamundo -da** *adj & mf* var. of **vagabundo**
**vagancia** *f* vagrancy; idleness
**vagante** *adj* vagrant; (Am.) untilled
**vagar** *m* leisure, idleness; slowness; **andar de vagar** to be at leisure, to be idle; **con vagar** slowly; **§59** *vn* to wander, to roam; to lose one's way; to idle, be idle, be at leisure; to lie around (*said of a thing*); to play (*said of a smile on the face of a person*)
**vagaroso -sa** *adj* errant, wandering; flitting
**vagido** *m* (med.) vagitus
**vagina** *f* (bot. & anat.) vagina
**vaginado -da** *adj* vaginate
**vaginal** *adj* vaginal
**vaginitis** *f* (path.) vaginitis
**vagínula** *f* (bot. & zool.) vaginula
**vagneriano -na** *adj & mf* Wagnerian
**vago -ga** *adj* wandering, roaming; vagabond, idle; lazy; lax, loose; hesitating, wavering; vague; blank (*stare*); (paint.) vaporous, indistinct; *m* vagabond; **en vago** unsteadily; in vain; at nothing, in the air; **poner en vago** to tilt (*e.g., a chair*)
**vagón** *m* railroad car; moving van on flat car; **vagón cama** sleeping car; **vagón cerrado** boxcar; **vagón cisterna** tank car; **vagón cuadra** cattle van; cattle car; **vagón de carga** freight car; **vagón de cola** caboose; **vagón de mercancías** freight car; **vagón de plataforma** flatcar; **vagón de volteo** dump car; **vagón frigorífico** refrigerator car; **vagón grúa** derrick car; **vagón plano** or **raso** flatcar; **vagón salón** chair car; **vagón tanque** (rail.) tank car; **vagón tolva** hopper-bottom car; **vagón volquete** dump car
**vagonada** *f* carload
**vagoneta** *f* small car; small dump car, tip car; (Am.) delivery truck
**vagra** *f* (zool.) tapir; (naut.) ribband
**vaguada** *f* waterway, thalweg
**vagueación** *f* vagary, flight of fancy
**vaguear** *vn* to wander, to roam; to be idle, to loaf
**vaguedad** *f* vagueness; vague remark
**vaguemaestre** *m* (mil.) wagon master
**vaguido -da** *adj* dizzy, giddy; *m* dizziness, fainting spell
**vagus** *m* (anat.) vagus
**vahaje** *m* gentle breeze
**vahar** *vn* to emit fumes or vapor; to breathe forth
**vaharada** *f* exhalation, breathing
**vaharera** *f* (path.) thrush; (prov.) green melon
**vahariento -ta** *adj* vaporous
**vaharina** *f* (coll.) fume, vapor
**vahear** *vn* to emit fumes or vapor; to breathe forth
**vahído** *m* dizziness, fainting spell
**vaho** *m* vapor, fume, steam; breath

**vaina** *f* sheath, scabbard; knife case; (bot.) pod, shell, husk; (naut.) boltrope tabling, tabling (*e.g., of a flag*); (Am.) casing (*to draw string through*); (Am.) annoyance, nuisance; (Am.) luck, stroke of luck; (Am. slang) intercourse, fornication; **de vaina abierta** quick and ready; **salirse de la vaina** (Am. coll.) to get violent, to lose one's head; **vaina de haba** (Am.) trifle; *mf* (Am.) bore, wretch
**vainazas** *m* (*pl:* **-zas**) (coll.) sloppy fellow
**vainero** *m* scabbard-maker
**vainica** *f* small sheath or scabbard; hemstitch
**vainilla** *f* small pod; hemstitch; (bot.) vanilla (*plant, bean, and extract*)
**vainillar** *va* (Am.) to hemstitch
**vainillina** *f* (chem.) vanillin
**vainita** *f* (Am.) string bean
**vais** *2d pl pres ind of* **ir**
**vaivén** *m* swing, seesaw, backward and forward motion, coming and going, wavering; risk, chance; unsteadiness, inconstancy; (naut.) three-stranded rope or cable
**vajilla** *f* table service; set of dishes; dishes; **lavar la vajilla** to wash the dishes; **vajilla de oro** gold plate; **vajilla de plata** silverware, silver plate; **vajilla de porcelana** chinaware
**val** *m* apocopated form of **valle;** *2d sg impv of* **valer**
**valaco -ca** *adj & mf* Walachian; *m* Walachian (*language*); *f* (Am.) wide hair band
**Valaquia** *f* Walachia
**valar** *adj* (pertaining to a) fence, hedge, or stockade
**valdense** *adj & mf* Waldensian; **valdenses** *mpl* Waldenses
**valdepeñero -ra** *adj* (pertaining to) Valdepeñas; *mf* native or inhabitant of Valdepeñas
**valdgrave** *m* waldgrave
**valdré** *1st sg fut ind of* **valer**
**vale** *m* bond, promissory note; receipt, voucher; advance note of pardon (*in school*); farewell; (Am.) pal, chum
**valedero -ra** *adj* valid, binding
**valedor -dora** *mf* protector, defender; (Am.) friend, companion
**valedura** *f* (Am.) favor, protection
**valencia** *f* (chem.) valence, valency
**valenciano -na** *adj & mf* Valencian; *m* Valencian (*dialect*); f (Am.) cuff (*of trousers*)
**valentía** *f* valor, bravery; feat, heroic exploit; brag, boast; dash, boldness; bold stroke; **pisar de valentía** to strut
**Valentín, San** Saint Valentine
**valentino -na** *adj* Valencian
**valentísimo -ma** *adj super* very or most valiant; very or most excellent; extremely skilled or finished
**valentón -tona** *adj* arrogant, boastful; *mf* braggart, boaster; *f* bragging, boasting
**valentonada** *f* bragging, boasting
**valer** *m* worth, merit, value ‖ §89 *va* to defend, protect; to favor, patronize; to avail; to bring about, to cause; to amount to; to be worth, be valued at; to be equal to, be equivalent to; to produce, to yield; **no valer un diablo** (coll.) to be not worth a darn; **valer lo que pesa** or **valer tanto como pesa** (coll.) to be worth its (his, her, etc.) weight in gold; **valga lo que valiere** come what may; **¡válgame Dios!** so help me God!, bless my soul ‖ *vn* to have worth; to be worthy; to have force, power, authority; to be valuable; to be valid; to prevail; to hold, to count; to serve as defense; to have influence, to be in favor; **hacer valer** to make felt; to assert (*e.g., one's rights*); to make good (*e.g., a claim*); to turn to account; **más vale** it is better (to); **más vale tarde que nunca** better late than never; **valerle a uno** + *inf* to help someone to + *inf*, to get someone to + *inf*, e.g., **eso le valió ser encarcelado** that got him to be jailed, that got him jailed; **valer para** to be useful for; **valer por** to be equal to, be as good as; **vale tanto como decir** it is as much as to say ‖ *vr* to help oneself, to defend oneself; **no poder valerse** to be helpless; **valerse de** to make use of, to avail oneself of, to take advantage of; **valerse por sí mismo** to help oneself
**valeriana** *f* (bot.) valerian, setwall; (pharm.) valerian; **valeriana griega** (bot.) Greek valerian
**valerosidad** *f* bravery, valor; skill
**valeroso -sa** *adj* brave, valorous; active, effective
**valet** *m* (*pl:* **-lets**) jack (*in cards*)
**valetudinario -ria** *adj & mf* valetudinarian
**valgo** *1st sg pres ind of* **valer**
**Valhala, el** or **Valhalla, el** (myth.) Valhalla
**valí** *m* (*pl:* **-líes**) wali
**valía** *f* value, worth; favor, influence; faction, party; **a las valías** at the highest price; **mayor valía** or **plus valía** increased value, appreciation; unearned increment
**validación** *f* validation
**validar** *va* to validate
**validez** *f* validity; strength, vigor
**valido -da** *adj* valued, esteemed; influential; *m* prime minister; court favorite
**válido -da** *adj* valid; strong, robust
**valiente** *adj* valiant; fine, excellent; terrific; *m* brave fellow; bully
**valija** *f* valise; mailbag, mailpouch; **valija diplomática** diplomatic pouch
**valijero** *m* mailbag deliverer
**valimiento** *m* favor, protection; favoritism, favor at court
**valioso -sa** *adj* valuable; wealthy; influential
**valisoletano -na** *adj & mf* var. of **vallisoletano**
**valón -lona** *adj & mf* Walloon; *m* Walloon (*dialect*); **valones** *mpl* bloomers; *f* Vandyke collar
**valor** *m* value, worth; meaning, import; efficacy; equivalence; stability, steadiness; resignation; valor, courage; audacity, impudence; (mus.) value; (fig.) asset (*person, thing, or quality worth having*); **valores** *mpl* securities; **valor alimenticio** food value; **valor de rescate** (ins.) surrender value; **valor facial** face value; **valor nominal** (com.) par value, face value
**valoración** *f* valuation, appraisal
**valorar** or **valorear** *va* to value, to appraise; to enhance the value of
**valorización** *f* valorization
**valorizar** §76 *va* to valorize
**valpurgita** *f* (mineral.) walpurgite
**valquiria** *f* (myth.) Valkyrie
**vals** *m* (*pl:* **valses**) waltz
**valsar** *vn* to waltz
**valuable** *adj* ratable, appraisable
**valuación** *f* valuation, appraisal
**valuar** §33 *va* to appraise, estimate
**valuta** *f* (econ.) valuta
**valva** *f* (biol.) valve
**valviforme** *adj* valviform, valve-shaped
**válvula** *f* (anat., mach. & rad.) valve; **sin válvulas** valveless; **válvula corrediza** slide valve; **válvula de admisión** intake valve; **válvula de aguja** needle valve; **válvula de bola** ball valve; **válvula de émbolo** piston valve; **válvula de escape** exhaust valve; **válvula de escape libre** cutout; **válvula de fuerza** (rad.) power tube; **válvula de mariposa** butterfly valve; **válvula de seguridad** safety valve; **válvula en la culata** valve in the head, overhead valve; **válvula mitral** (anat.) mitral valve; **válvula tricúspide** (anat.) tricuspid valve
**valvulado -da** *adj* valvate
**valvular** *adj* valvular
**valla** *f* fence, barricade; obstacle, hindrance; (sport) hurdle; (Am.) cockpit; **valla paranieves** snow fence
**valladar** *m* fence, barricade; obstacle, hindrance
**valladear** *va* to fence, to hedge, to fence in
**vallado** *m* fence, barricade
**vallar** *adj* (pertaining to a) fence, hedge, or stockade; *va* to fence, to hedge, to fence in
**valle** *m* valley, vale; river basin; valley dwellings, valley villages; **valle de lágrimas** vale of tears; **valle de Tempe** (hist.) Vale of Tempe
**vallico** *m* var. of **ballico**
**vallisoletano -na** *adj* (pertaining to) Valladolid; *mf* native or inhabitant of Valladolid

**vamos** *1st pl pres ind & impv of* **ir;** *interj* well!; why!; come now!; let's go!; watch out!; stop!
**vampiresa** *f* vampire (*woman who preys on men*)
**vampiro** *m* vampire; (zool.) vampire; (fig.) vampire (*extortionist*)
**van** *3d pl pres ind of* **ir**
**vanadio** *m* (chem.) vanadium
**vanagloria** *f* vainglory
**vanagloriar §90 & regular** *vr* to boast; **vanagloriarse de** or **por** to boast of; **vanagloriarse de** + *inf* to boast of + *ger*
**vanaglorioso -sa** *adj* vainglorious
**vanamente** *adv* vainly
**vandálico -ca** *adj* Vandal; vandal
**vandalismo** *m* vandalism
**vándalo -la** *adj & mf* Vandal; vandal
**Vandea, la** the Vendée (*district in western France*)
**vandeano -na** *adj & mf* Vendean
**vanear** *vn* to talk idly, to talk nonsense
**vanguardia** *f* (mil. & fig.) van, vanguard; **vanguardias** *fpl* abutment (*of bridge*); **a vanguardia** in the vanguard; **estar a** or **en vanguardia** to be in the lead, to be out in front
**vanguardismo** *m* avant-garde
**vanguardista** *adj* avant-garde
**vanidad** *f* vanity; pomp; nonsense, inanity; **ajar la vanidad de** (coll.) to take down a peg; **hacer vanidad de** to boast of
**vanidoso -sa** *adj* vain, conceited
**vanilocuencia** *f* empty talk
**vanílocuo -cua** *adj* chattering, wordy; *mf* empty talker or speaker
**vaniloquio** *m* empty talk
**vanistorio** *m* (coll.) vain affectation; (coll.) affected person
**vano -na** *adj* vain; **en vano** in vain; *m* bay, opening in a wall
**vánova** *f* (dial.) bedspread
**vapor** *m* steam, vapor; mist, exhalation; vertigo, faintness; steamer, steamboat; **vapores** *mpl* gas (*belched*); hysterics; attack of blues; **al vapor** by steam; at great speed; **vapor de agua** water vapor; **vapor de paletas** or **ruedas** paddle-wheel steamboat; **vapor volandero** tramp steamer
**vapora** *f* (coll.) steam launch
**vaporable** *adj* vaporable
**vaporación** *f* evaporation
**vaporar** *va & vr* to evaporate
**vaporear** *va* to evaporate; *vn* to exhale vapors; *vr* to evaporate
**vaporización** *f* vaporization; (med.) vaporization
**vaporizador** *m* vaporizer; sprayer, atomizer
**vaporizar §76** *va & vr* to vaporize; to spray, to atomize
**vaporoso -sa** *adj* vaporous, steamy; light, diaphanous, gauzy
**vapulación** *f* or **vapulamiento** *m* whipping, flogging
**vapular** *va* to whip, to flog
**vapuleamiento** *m* var. of **vapulación**
**vapulear** *va* var. of **vapular**
**vapuleo** or **vápulo** *m* var. of **vapulación**
**vaquería** *f* drove of cattle; dairy
**vaquerizo -za** *adj* (pertaining to) cattle; *mf* cattle tender; *f* winter stable for cattle
**vaquero -ra** *adj* (pertaining to) cattle; *mf* cattle tender; *m* cowboy, cow hand
**vaqueta** *f* leather
**vaquillona** *f* (Am.) heifer
**vara** *f* twig, stick; pole, staff, rod; wand; shaft (*of carriage*); (bot.) scape; (taur.) thrust with goad; measure of length: 2.8 ft.; **entrar en vara** to gather together to feed on acorns (*said of hogs*); **tener vara alta** to have the upper hand; **vara alcándara** shaft (*of carriage*); **vara alta** upper hand, sway, authority; **vara buscadora** divining rod (*used professedly to discover water or minerals under ground*); **vara de adivinar** divining rod; **vara de Jesé** (bot.) tuberose; **vara de oro** (bot.) goldenrod; **vara de pescar** fishing rod; **vara de San José** (bot.) goldenrod; **vara mágica** divining rod
**vara-alta** *m* (coll.) boss
**varada** *f* beaching (*of a boat*); running aground; (prov.) farm workers; farming season; three-month mine work; quarterly mine earnings
**varadera** *f* (naut.) skid, skeed
**varadero** *m* shipyard, repair dock
**varadura** *f* grounding, running aground
**varal** *m* perch, long pole; horizontal pole with holes in which to fasten the upright side sticks of a cart; (coll.) tall ungainly person
**varano** *m* (zool.) monitor
**varapalo** *m* long pole; blow with stick or rod; (coll.) reverse, setback, disappointment
**varar** *va* to beach (*a boat*); *vn* to run aground; to come to a standstill (*said of business*)
**varaseto** *m* treillage, espalier
**varazo** *m* blow with a stick or pole
**varbasco** *m* (bot.) great mullein
**vardasca** *f* green twig
**vareaje** *m* beating down fruit; measuring or sale by the vara
**varear** *va* to beat, to strike; to knock (*fruit from a tree*); (taur.) to goad; to measure with a vara; to sell by the vara; *vn* to weaken, to get weak
**varec** *m* (bot.) wrack
**varejón** *m* long heavy stick
**varenga** *f* (naut.) floor timber; (naut.) headrail
**vareo** *m* beating fruit from trees
**vareta** *f* small twig or stick; lime twig for catching birds; colored stripe; cutting remark; (coll.) hint; **irse de vareta** (coll.) to have diarrhea
**varetazo** *m* stroke with a stick; side thrust with the horn (*by bull*)
**varetear** *va* to make stripes in
**varetón** *m* young stag having antlers without tines
**varga** *f* steep part of a slope
**varganal** *m* stake fence, stockade
**várgano** *m* stake (*of fence*)
**vargueño** *m* var. of **bargueño**
**variabilidad** *f* variability
**variable** *adj* variable; *f* (math.) variable
**variación** *f* variation
**variado -da** *adj* varied; variegated
**variamente** *adv* variously, diversely, differently
**variante** *adj & f* variant
**variar §90** *va* to vary, to change; *vn* to vary, to change, be different; **variar de** or **en opinión** to change one's mind
**varice** *f* or **várice** *f* (path.) varix; **varices** *fpl* (path.) varicose veins
**varicela** *f* (path.) varicella, chicken pox
**varicocele** *m* (path.) varicocele
**varicosidad** *f* varicosity (*state of being varicose; varix*)
**varicosis** *f* (path.) varicosis
**varicoso -sa** *adj* varicose
**variedad** *f* variety; **variedades** *fpl* variety, vaudeville; miscellanies
**varilarguero** *m* (taur.) picador
**varilla** *f* rod, stem, twig; wand; rib (*of umbrella, fan, etc.*); wire spoke; stay (*of corset*); (coll.) jawbone; (Am.) peddler's wares; **varillas** *fpl* frame of sieve or strainer; **varilla de virtudes, varilla mágica** magician's wand, conjurer's wand; **varilla empujadora** tappet rod; **varilla exploradora** divining rod; **varilla levantaválvula** tappet rod
**varillaje** *m* ribbing, ribs; type bars, basket of type bars (*of a typewriter*); (mech.) linkage
**varillero -ra** *mf* (Am.) peddler
**vario -ria** *adj* various, varied; inconstant; undecided; variegated; **varios -rias** *adj pl* various, several; **varios** *mpl* miscellanea, literary miscellany
**varioacoplador** *m* (rad.) variocoupler
**varioloide** *f* (path.) varioloid
**varioloso -sa** *adj* variolous; pock-marked; *mf* pock-marked person
**variómetro** *m* (elec., meteor. & rad.) variometer
**variórum** *adj & m invar* variorum
**variz** *f* (*pl:* **-rices**) var. of **varice**
**varón** *m* man, male; adult male; man of standing, man of parts; (naut.) rudder pendant; **santo varón** plain artless fellow; **Varón de Dolores** Man of Sorrows (*Jesus*); *adj* male, e.g., **hijo varón** male child

**varona** *f* woman, female; mannish woman
**varonía** *f* male issue, male descent
**varonil** *adj* manly, virile; courageous, vigorous
**varraco** *m* var. of **verraco**
**varraquear** *vn* var. of **verraquear**
**varraquera** *f* var. of **verraquera**
**Varsovia** *f* Warsaw
**varsoviano -na** *adj* (pertaining to) Warsaw; *mf* native or inhabitant of Warsaw; *f* varsoviana, varsovienne (*music and dance*)
**vas** *2d sg pres ind of* **ir**
**vasallaje** *m* vassalage; liege money
**vasallo -lla** *adj & mf* vassal
**vasar** *m* kitchen shelf, kitchen shelving
**vasco -ca** *adj & mf* Basque (*of Spain and France*); *m* Basque (*language*)
**vascón -cona** *adj & mf* Basque (*ancient*)
**vascongado -da** *adj & mf* Basque (*of Spain*); *m* Basque (*language*); **las Vascongadas** the Basque Provinces
**vascónico -ca** *adj* Basque (*ancient*)
**vascuence** *adj & m* Basque (*language*); *m* (coll.) gibberish
**vascular** *adj* (bot. & zool.) vascular
**vasculoso -sa** *adj* vasculous, vasculose
**vasectomía** *f* (surg.) vasectomy
**vaselina** *f* vaseline
**vaselinoso -sa** *adj* (coll.) full of schmaltz
**vasera** *f* kitchen shelf; glass rack, glass basket; case for carrying a glass or tumbler
**vasija** *f* vessel, receptacle, container; dish; wine casks and jars in wine cellar
**vasillo** *m* cell (*of honeycomb*); (bot.) navelwort, pennywort
**vaso** *m* glass, tumbler; glassful; receptacle; vase, flower jar; high urinal; horse's hoof; capacity; (naut.) vessel; (anat.) vas, vessel, duct; (bot.) vessel; (arch.) vase; **vaso de engrase** (mach.) grease cup; **vaso de noche** pot, chamber pot; **vaso de papel** paper cup; **vaso excretorio** chamber pot; **vaso lacrimatorio** lachrymal vase; **vaso sanguíneo** (anat.) blood vessel
**vasoligadura** *f* (surg.) vasoligation
**vasomotor -tora** *adj* (physiol.) vasomotor
**vástago** *m* twig, sapling, shoot; scion, offspring; rod, stem; **vástago de émbolo** piston rod; **vástago de válvula** valve stem
**vastedad** *f* vastness
**vasto -ta** *adj* vast
**vate** *m* poet, bard, seer
**váter** *m* (coll.) toilet, water closet
**vatiaje** *m* (elec.) wattage
**vaticano -na** *adj* (pertaining to the) Vatican; (*cap.*) *m* Vatican
**vaticinador -dora** *adj* prophesying, predicting; *mf* prophet, predicter
**vaticinante** *adj* prophesying, predicting
**vaticinar** *va* to prophesy, to predict, to vaticinate
**vaticinio** *m* prophecy, prediction
**vatídico -ca** *adj* prophetical; prophesying; *mf* prophet
**vatihorímetro** *m* (elec.) watt-hour meter
**vatímetro** *m* (elec.) wattmeter
**vatio** *m* (elec.) watt
**vatio-hora** *m* (*pl:* **vatios-hora**) (elec.) watt-hour
**vaya** *f* scoff, jest, jeer; *1st sg pres subj of* **ir**
**Vd.** abr. of **usted**
**Vds.** abr. of **ustedes**
**V.E.** abr. of **Vuestra Excelencia**
**ve** *3d sg pres ind & 2d sg impv of* **ver**
**vé** *2d sg impv of* **ir**
**vecera** *f* see **vecero**
**vecería** *f* drove (*especially of hogs*)
**vecero -ra** *adj* alternating; yielding in alternate years; *mf* person who takes turns; customer; person who waits his turn; *f* drove (*especially of hogs*)
**vecinal** *adj* (pertaining to the) neighborhood, local, vicinal
**vecinamente** *adv* nearby, near at hand
**vecindad** *f* neighborhood, vicinage, vicinity; **hacer mala vecindad** to be a bad neighbor
**vecindario** *m* neighborhood, community; population
**vecino -na** *adj* neighboring, near; similar, like; *mf* neighbor; resident, native, citizen
**vectación** *f* riding (*in vehicle*)
**vector** *m* (biol. & math.) vector
**vectorial** *adj* vector, vectorial
**veda** *f* prohibition; hindrance; closed season; (*cap.*) *m* Veda
**vedado** *m* game park, game preserve
**vedamiento** *m* prohibition; hindrance
**vedar** *va* to forbid, prohibit; to stop, hinder; to veto; **vedar** + *inf* to forbid to + *inf*
**vedegambre** *m* (bot.) hellebore
**vedeja** *f* long lock of hair; lion's mane
**védico -ca** *adj* Vedaic; *m* Vedaic (*language*)
**vedija** *f* tuft of wool; mat of hair; matted hair; (anat.) pubes
**vedijoso -sa** or **vedijudo -da** *adj* having tangled hair; tangly
**vedismo** *m* Vedism
**veedor -dora** *adj* curious, prying, spying; *mf* prier, spy, busybody; *m* supervisor, overseer; **veedor del tesoro** controller
**veeduría** *f* inspectorship; inspector's office
**vega** *f* fertile plain; (Am.) tobacco plantation; (*cap.*) *f* (astr.) Vega
**vegetación** *f* vegetation; **vegetaciones adenoideas** adenoids
**vegetal** *adj* vegetal; *m* vegetable (*plant*)
**vegetalismo** *m* var. of **vegetarianismo**
**vegetalista** *adj* var. of **vegetariano**
**vegetar** *vn* to vegetate; to grow; (fig.) to vegetate
**vegetarianismo** *m* vegetarianism
**vegetariano -na** *adj & mf* vegetarian
**vegetativo -va** *adj* vegetative
**vegoso -sa** *adj* (Am.) damp, wet (*ground*)
**veguero -ra** *adj* country; *m* farmer; (Am.) tobacco planter
**vehemencia** *f* vehemence
**vehemente** *adj* vehement
**vehicular** *adj* vehicular
**vehículo** *m* vehicle; **vehículo espacial** space vehicle; **vehículo motor** motor vehicle
**veía** *1st sg imperf ind of* **ver**
**veintavo -va** *adj & m* twentieth
**veinte** *adj* twenty; **a las veinte** (coll.) inopportunely, very late; **las veinte** eight P.M.: *m* twenty; twentieth (*in dates*)
**veintena** *f* see **veinteno**
**veintenario -ria** *adj* twenty-year-old
**veinteno -na** *adj* twentieth; *f* score, twenty
**veintenero** *m* (eccl.) succentor
**veinteñal** *adj* twenty-year
**veinticinco** *adj* twenty-five; *m* twenty-five; twenty-fifth (*in dates*)
**veinticuatreno -na** *adj* twenty-fourth
**veinticuatría** *f* (archaic) prefecture
**veinticuatro** *adj* twenty-four; **las veinticuatro** twelve midnight; *m* twenty-four; twenty-fourth (*in dates*); (archaic) prefect
**veintidós** *adj* twenty-two; **las veintidós** ten P.M.; *m* twenty-two; twenty-second (*in dates*)
**veintidoseno -na** *adj* twenty-second
**veintinueve** *adj* twenty-nine; *m* twenty-nine; twenty-ninth (*in dates*)
**veintiocheno -na** *adj* twenty-eighth
**veintiocho** *adj* twenty-eight; *m* twenty-eight; twenty-eighth (*in dates*)
**veintiséis** *adj* twenty-six; *m* twenty-six; twenty-sixth (*in dates*)
**veintiseiseno -na** *adj* twenty-sixth
**veintisiete** *adj* twenty-seven; *m* twenty-seven; twenty-seventh (*in dates*)
**veintitrés** *adj* twenty-three; **las veintitrés** eleven P.M.; *m* twenty-three; twenty-third (*in dates*)
**veintiún** *adj* apocopated form of **veintiuno,** used only before masculine nouns and adjectives
**veintiuno -na** *adj* twenty-one; **las veintiuna** nine P.M.; *m* twenty-one; twenty-first (*in dates*); *f* twenty-one (*card game*)
**vejación** *f* vexation, annoyance
**vejamen** *m* vexation, annoyance; sharp criticism
**vejar** *va* to vex, annoy; to criticize
**vejatorio -ria** *adj* vexatious, annoying
**vejestorio** *m* (coll.) old dodo; (archaic) piece of junk
**vejeta** *f* (orn.) crested lark
**vejete** *m* (coll.) little old fellow, silly old fellow
**vejez** *f* oldness; old age; peevishness of old age; platitude, old story; **a la vejez, viruelas** there's no fool like an old fool

**vejiga** *f* bladder; blister; pock mark; **vejiga de la bilis** (anat.) gall bladder; **vejiga de perro** (bot.) winter cherry; **vejiga natatoria** air bladder, swimming bladder (*of fish*)
**vejigatorio -ria** *adj* blistering; *m* blister plaster
**vejigazo** *m* blow with a bladder full of air
**vejigoso -sa** *adj* full of blisters
**vejiguilla** *f* small bladder; pustule; (bot.) winter cherry
**vela** *f* wakefulness; evening (*devoted to some pursuit*); work (*in the evening*); candle; pilgrimage; (eccl.) vigil (*before Eucharist*); sail; sailboat; awning; **a toda vela** full sail; **a vela** under sail; **a vela llena** under full sail; **dar vela** or **darse a la vela** to set sail; **en vela** awake; **estar entre dos velas** to have a sheet in the wind, to be tipsy; **hacerse a la vela** to set sail; **levantar velas** to hoist sails; to set sail; (coll.) to withdraw, give up; **tender las velas** to take advantage of wind and weather; (fig.) to make the most of an opportunity; **vela al tercio** lugsail; **vela (de) cangreja** fore-and-aft sail; **vela de cruz** square sail; **vela de estay** staysail; **vela de mesana** mizzen (sail); **vela latina** lateen sail; **vela mayor** mainsail; **vela romana** Roman candle
**velación** *f* watching, vigil, wake; (eccl.) veiling at nuptial mass
**velacho** *m* (naut.) foretopsail
**velado -da** *adj* veiled, hidden; (phot.) cloudy; *m* husband; *f* wife; vigil, watch, watching; evening, evening party, soirée
**velador -dora** *adj* watching; *m* watchman, guard; wooden candlestick; pedestal table; (Am.) night table
**veladura** *f* (paint.) velatura; (phot.) clouding (*of a film*)
**velaje** *m* or **velamen** *m* (naut.) canvas, sails
**velar** *adj & f* (phonet.) velar ‖ *va* to watch, to watch over; to guard; to keep (*guard or watch*); to wake, hold a wake over; to veil; (fig.) to veil, hide, conceal; to veil (*newly married couple*) at nuptial mass; (phot.) to fog ‖ *vn* to stay awake; to work late, to work in the evening or at night; to be solicitous; to stick out of the water (*said of rocks in sea*); to keep up all night (*said of the wind*); (eccl.) to assist by turns before the Holy Sacrament; **velar por** or **sobre** to watch over; **velar por que** to see to it that ‖ *vr* (phot.) to fog, be light-struck
**velarización** *f* (phonet.) velarization
**velarizar §76** *va* (phonet.) to velarize
**velarte** *m* broadcloth
**velatorio** *m* wake (*beside corpse*)
**veleidad** *f* caprice, whim; inconstancy, fickleness, flightiness
**veleidoso -sa** *adj* capricious, whimsical; inconstant, fickle, flighty
**velejar** *vn* (naut.) to sail with sails unfurled, to navigate under sail
**velería** *f* tallow chandler's store; sail loft
**velero -ra** *adj* (naut.) swift-sailing; fond of vigils; fond of pilgrimages; *mf* tallow chandler; *m* sailmaker; sailboat, sailer; (aer.) sailplane
**veleta** *f* vane, weathercock, weather vane; rudder, rudder vane (*of windmill*); bob (*of fishing line*); streamer, pennant; **veleta de manga** (aer.) air sleeve, air sock; *mf* weathercock (*fickle person*)
**velete** *m* small thin veil
**velicación** *f* (med.) lancing, opening
**velicar §86** *va* (med.) to lance, to open
**velicomen** *m* cup for drinking toasts
**velilla** *f* small candle
**velillo** *m* small veil; gauze embroidered with silver thread
**velís** *m* (Am.) valise
**velmez** *m* (*pl:* **-meces**) tunic worn under armor
**velo** *m* veil; white veil thrown over couple at nuptial mass; taking the veil; humeral veil; (biol.) velum; (phot.) fog; (fig.) veil (*mask, disguise*); (fig.) confusion, perplexity; **correr el velo** to pull aside the curtain, to dispel the mystery; **correr** or **echar el velo sobre** to hush up; **tomar el velo** to take the veil; **velo del paladar** (anat.) velum, soft palate; **velo de monja** nun's veiling
**velocidad** *f* velocity; speed; **en gran velocidad** (rail.) by express; **en pequeña velocidad** (rail.) by freight; **primera velocidad** (aut.) low gear; **segunda velocidad** (aut.) second; **tercera velocidad** (aut.) high gear; **velocidad con respecto al suelo** (aer.) ground speed; **velocidad de escape** escape velocity (*of a satellite*); **velocidad de régimen** working speed, steady speed; **velocidad de sincronismo** (elec.) synchronous speed; **velocidad sobremultiplicada** (aut.) overdrive
**velocímetro** *m* speedometer; velocimeter (*to measure speed of projectiles*)
**velocípedo** *m* velocipede
**velódromo** *m* velodrome
**velógrafo** *m* hectograph
**velómetro** *m* speedometer
**velón** *m* metal olive-oil lamp
**velonera** *f* lamp stand, lamp bracket
**velonero** *m* lamp maker, lamp dealer
**velorio** *m* party, gathering; wake; taking the veil; (coll.) dull party; (Am.) come-on
**velorta** *f* var. of **vilorta**
**velorto** *m* var. of **vilorto**
**veloz** *adj* (*pl:* **-loces**) swift, rapid; agile, quick
**veludillo** *m* var. of **velludillo**
**veludo** *m* plush; velvet
**vellera** *f* (archaic) depilator (*woman*)
**vellido -da** *adj* var. of **velloso**
**vello** *m* down (*on fruit and human body*); velvet (*of antlers of deer*); (anat., bot. & zool.) villus
**vellocino** *m* fleece; unsheared sheepskin
**vellón** *m* fleece; unsheared sheepskin; lock of wool; copper and silver alloy; copper coin
**vellonero** *m* gatherer of fleece
**vellora** *f* knot on wrong side of cloth
**vellorí** *m* (*pl:* **-ríes**) broadcloth of undyed wool
**vellorín** *m* var. of **vellorí**
**vellorita** *f* (bot.) cowslip; (bot.) English daisy
**vellosidad** *f* downiness, fuzziness, hairiness
**vellosilla** *f* (bot.) mouse-ear
**velloso -sa** *adj* downy, fuzzy, hairy, villous
**velludillo** *m* velveteen
**velludo -da** *adj* shaggy, hairy, fuzzy; *m* plush; velvet
**vellutero** *m* silk worker, plush worker
**ven** *2d sg impv of* **venir**
**vena** *f* vein; grain (*in stone*); (fig.) streak; (fig.) poetical inspiration; **coger a uno de vena** to find someone receptive; **darle a uno la vena** (coll.) to be bent on folly; **estar en vena** (coll.) to be all set, to be inspired; (coll.) to be sparkling with wit; **reventarse una vena** to burst a blood vessel; **vena ácigos** (anat.) azygous vein; **vena basílica** (anat.) basilic vein; **vena de agua** underground water passage; **vena de loco** fickle disposition; **vena porta** (anat.) portal vein; **vena yugular** (anat.) jugular vein
**venable** *adj* salable
**venablo** *m* javelin, dart; **echar venablos** to burst forth in angry words
**venación** *f* venation (*arrangement of veins*); (archaic) venation, venery (*hunting*)
**venadero** *m* place frequented by deer
**venado** *m* deer, stag
**venaje** *m* fountainheads (*of a river*)
**venal** *adj* salable; venal, mercenary; venous
**venalidad** *f* venality
**venático -ca** *adj* (coll.) fickle, unsteady, inconstant
**venatorio -ria** *adj* (pertaining to) hunting, venatic
**venatriz, la** (myth.) the huntress Diana
**vencedero -ra** *adj* falling due, maturing
**vencedor -dora** *adj* conquering; *mf* conqueror, victor
**vencejo** *m* band, string; (orn.) black martin, European swift
**vencer §91** *va* to conquer, vanquish; to surpass, outdo, excel; to surmount, overcome; *vn* to conquer, win out; to twist, bend, turn; (com.) to mature, fall due; to expire; to be up (*said of a period of time*); *vr* to control oneself; (Am.) to wear out, to become worthless
**vencetósigo** *m* (bot.) swallowwort, tame poison
**vencible** *adj* conquerable, superable, vincible

**vencido -da** *adj* conquered, overcome; (com.) mature, due, payable; **estar** or **ir de vencida** to be all in; to be all up; to be finished; to be past or over
**vencimiento** *m* victory; defeat, vanquishment (*state of being conquered*); (com.) maturity, expiration
**venda** *f* see **vendo**
**vendaje** *m* bandage, dressing
**vendar** *va* to bandage; to blindfold; to blind, to hoodwink
**vendaval** *m* southeasterly wind from the sea; strong wind
**vendedera** *f* saleslady, saleswoman
**vendedor -dora** *adj* selling, vending; *m* salesman; *f* saleslady, saleswoman, salesgirl
**vendehumos** *mf* (*pl:* **-mos**) (coll.) influence peddler, person who trades on his real or supposed influence
**vendeja** *f* public sale
**vender** *va* to sell; to sell out, to betray, to give away; **vender de beber** to sell drinks; **vender de comer** to sell food, to serve meals; *vn* to sell; **¡vendo, vendo, vendí!** going, going, gone!; *vr* to sell oneself; to expose oneself to danger; to sell, be for sale; to give oneself away, to show one's hand; **venderse caro** to be sold dear; to be seldom seen, to be a stranger; to be hard to see; **venderse en** to sell for (*e.g., five dollars*); **venderse por** to pretend to be
**vendetta** *f* vendetta
**vendí** *m* (*pl:* **-díes**) certificate of sale
**vendible** *adj* salable, vendible; marketable
**vendimia** *f* vintage; (fig.) rich profit
**vendimiador -dora** *mf* vintager
**vendimiar** *va* to gather (*grapes*); to reap unjustly, to reap with violence; (coll.) to kill, murder
**vendo -da** *adj* Wendish; *mf* Wend; *m* Wendish (*language*); selvage; *f* bandage; blindfold; regal fillet
**vendré** *1st sg fut ind of* **venir**
**venduta** *f* (Am.) vendue, public sale; (Am.) greengrocery
**vendutero -ra** *mf* (Am.) auctioneer; (Am.) greengrocer
**Venecia** *f* Venice (*city*); Venetia (*province or district*)
**veneciano -na** *adj & mf* Venetian; *m* Venetian (*dialect*)
**venencia** *f* tube for sampling wines
**veneno** *m* poison, venom; (fig.) bitterness
**venenosidad** *f* poisonousness
**venenoso -sa** *adj* poisonous, venomous
**venera** *f* scallop shell, cockleshell; pilgrim's scallop shell; knight's badge; spring (*of water*); **empeñar la venera** (coll.) to spare no expense, to go all out
**venerabilidad** *f* venerability
**venerabilísimo -ma** *adj super* very or most venerable
**venerable** *adj* venerable
**veneración** *f* veneration, worship
**venerador -dora** *adj* venerating, worshiping; *mf* venerator, worshiper
**venerando -da** *adj* venerable
**venerar** *va & vn* to venerate, revere; to worship
**venéreo -a** *adj* venereal; *m* venereal disease
**venero** *m* spring (*of water*); source, origin; hour mark (*on sundial*); (min.) lode
**véneto -ta** *adj & mf* Venetian; *m* sea green
**venezolanismo** *m* Venezuelanism
**venezolano -na** *adj & mf* Venezuelan
**Venezuela** *f* Venezuela
**vengable** *adj* worthy of revenge, capable of being avenged
**vengador -dora** *adj* avenging; *mf* revenger, avenger
**venganza** *f* vengeance, revenge
**vengar §59** *va* to avenge; *vr* to take revenge; **vengarse de** to take revenge for; **vengarse en** to take revenge on, to avenge oneself on
**vengativo -va** *adj* vengeful, vindictive
**vengo** *1st sg pres ind of* **venir**
**venia** *f* pardon, forgiveness; permission, leave; bow (*with head*); (law) court decree allowing minors to manage own estates; (Am.) (military) salute
**venial** *adj* venial
**venialidad** *f* veniality
**venida** *f* see **venido**
**venidero -ra** *adj* coming, future; **en lo venidero** in the future; **venideros** *mpl* successors, posterity
**venido -da** *adj* come, arrived; **bien venido** welcome; *f* coming; return; flood, freshet; impetuosity, rashness
**venir §92** *vn* to come, to go; **lo por venir** the future; **que viene** coming, next; **venga lo que viniere** come what may; **venir** + *ger* to be + *ger;* **venir a** + *inf* to come to + *inf;* to end by + *ger,* to amount to + *ger;* to happen to + *inf;* **venir a que** + *subj* to come in order that; **venir a ser** to turn out to be; **venir bien** to become, fit, suit; **venir de** + *inf* to come from + *ger,* e.g., **vengo de pagar unas cuentas** I come from paying some bills, I have just been to pay some bills; *vr* to ferment; **venirse abajo** to collapse
**venoso -sa** *adj* venous
**venta** *f* sale, selling; salesmanship; roadside inn; place in the open, unsheltered spot; **de venta** or **en venta** on sale, for sale; **hacer venta** (coll.) to invite in to have something to eat; **ser una venta** (coll.) to be a dear place; to be in the open, to be unprotected; **venta al descubierto** or **a plazo** (com.) short sale
**ventada** *f* blast, gust of wind
**ventaja** *f* advantage; extra pay; odds (*in a game*); (tennis) advantage; **llevar la ventaja a** to be ahead of; to have the advantage of
**ventajista** *mf* sharper, crook
**ventajoso -sa** *adj* advantageous
**ventalla** *f* (mach.) valve; (bot.) valve (*of capsule or legume*)
**ventalle** *m* fan; nosepiece (*of helmet*)
**ventana** *f* window (*opening in a wall; windowpane*); sash; nostril; (anat.) fenestra; **echar la casa por la ventana** (coll.) to go to a lot of expense (*to entertain or in other ways*); **tirar por la ventana** to ruin, spoil; **ventana a bisagra** or **ventana batiente** casement; **ventana de guillotina** sliding window, sash window; **ventana de la nariz** nostril; **ventana oval** (anat.) fenestra ovalis; **ventana redonda** (anat.) fenestra rotunda; **ventana salediza** bay window
**ventanaje** *m* (arch.) fenestration, windows (*of a building*)
**ventanal** *m* large window, church window
**ventanazo** *m* slamming a window, window slamming
**ventanear** *vn* (coll.) to be always at the window
**ventaneo** *m* (coll.) fondness for being at the window
**ventanero -ra** *adj* fond of being at the window; *mf* person fond of being at the window; *m* windowmaker; window gazer (*man who likes to look in windows where there are women*); *f* woman who spends a lot of time hanging out of the window; woman flirting from a window
**ventanico** *m* var. of **ventanillo**
**ventanilla** *f* small window, opening; window (*of railway car; of a bank; of an envelope*); wicket; ticket window; nostril
**ventanillo** *m* small window; peephole
**ventanuco** or **ventanucho** *m* ugly little window
**ventar §18** *va* to sniff (*said of animals*); *vn* to blow (*said of the wind*)
**ventarrón** *m* strong wind, windstorm, gale
**venteadura** *f* wind shake, split in timber caused by wind; (found.) blowhole
**ventear** *va* to sniff, to scent (*said of animals*); to air, to dry in the wind; to snoop into, to pry into; *vn* to blow (*said of the wind*); to snoop, to pry about; *vr* to split; to blister (*said of baking bricks*); to become spoiled in the air; (coll.) to break wind
**venteo** *m* sniffing, scenting; airing; snooping; venthole (*in a barrel*)
**ventero -ra** *adj* scenting (*said of animals*); *mf* innkeeper, keeper of a roadside inn
**ventilación** *f* ventilation; (fig.) airing
**ventilador** *m* ventilator; fan; (naut.) funnel; **ventilador aspirador** exhaust fan
**ventilar** *va* to ventilate; (fig.) to ventilate, to air

**ventisca** *f* blizzard; drift (*of snow*)
**ventiscar** §86 *vn* to snow and blow; to drift (*said of snow*)
**ventisco** *m* var. of **ventisca**
**ventiscoso -sa** *adj* snowy and stormy; full of snow drifts
**ventisquear** *vn* var. of **ventiscar**
**ventisquero** *m* blizzard; snowdrift; snow-capped mountain; glacier
**ventola** *f* (naut.) strong blast of wind, strong noisy blast of wind
**ventolera** *f* strong blast of wind; pinwheel; (coll.) vanity, boasting; (coll.) caprice, wild idea
**ventolina** *f* (naut.) light fresh wind, light air
**ventor -tora** *adj* scenting, hunting by scent; *m* pointer (*dog*)
**ventorrero** *m* windy spot
**ventorrillo** *m* wretched little roadhouse; lunch house in the country
**ventorro** *m* wretched little roadhouse
**ventosa** *f* see **ventoso**
**ventosear** *vn* to break wind
**ventosidad** *f* windiness; wind (*in intestines or being expelled*)
**ventoso -sa** *adj* windy; full of wind (*said of intestines*); causing wind (*in intestines*); *f* cupping glass; vacuum cup (*of tire*); (zool.) sucker; vent, air hole; **pegar una ventosa a** (coll.) to swindle
**ventral** *adj* ventral
**ventrecha** *f* belly (*of fish*)
**ventregada** *f* brood, litter; sudden abundance
**ventrera** *f* bellyband (*of man or beast*)
**ventricular** *adj* ventricular
**ventrículo** *m* (anat. & zool.) ventricle
**ventril** *m* counterpoise (*in olive-oil mill*)
**ventrílocuo -cua** *adj* ventriloquial; *mf* ventriloquist
**ventriloquia** *f* or **ventriloquismo** *m* ventriloquism
**ventrón** *m* large belly; tripe
**ventroso -sa** or **ventrudo -da** *adj* big-bellied
**ventura** *f* see **venturo**
**venturado -da** *adj* lucky, fortunate
**venturanza** *f* happiness
**venturero -ra** *adj* adventurous, vagabond; fortunate; *mf* adventurer
**venturímetro** *m* (hyd.) Venturi meter
**venturina** *f* (mineral.) aventurin or aventurine
**venturo -ra** *adj* future, coming; *f* happiness; luck, chance; risk, danger; (orn.) bluebird (*Sialia mexicana*); **a la ventura** at a venture, at random; at a risk; **por ventura** perhaps, perchance; **probar ventura** to try one's luck
**venturón** *m* stroke of luck
**venturoso -sa** *adj* lucky, fortunate
**Venus** *f* (myth.) Venus; Venus (*very beautiful woman*); *m* (astr.) Venus; (*l.c.*) *f* venery
**venustez** *f* or **venustidad** *f* beauty, gracefulness
**venusto -ta** *adj* beautiful, graceful
**venza** *f* goldbeater's skin
**veo** *1st sg pres ind of* **ver**
**ver** *m* sight; appearance; opinion; **a mi ver** in my opinion; **tener buen ver** to have a good appearance ‖ §93 *va & vn* to see; to look at; (law) to hear, to try; **a más ver** so long; **a ver** let's see; **estar por ver** to remain to be seen; **hasta más ver** good-bye, so long; **no poder ver** to not be able to bear, to despise; **no tener nada que ver con** to have nothing to do with; **ser de ver** to be worth seeing; **ver** + *inf* to see + *inf*, e.g., **vi pasar el tren** I saw the train go by; to see + *ger*, e.g., **vi llegar al médico** I saw the doctor arriving; to see + *pp*, e.g., **vi ahorcar al criminal** I saw the criminal hanged; **ver de** + *inf* to try to + *inf;* **ver venir** to see what (*someone*) is up to; to wait and see; **ver y creer** seeing is believing ‖ *vr* to be seen; to be obvious; to see oneself; to see each other; to find oneself, to be; to meet; **ya se ve** of course, certainly; **verse con** to see, to have a talk with
**vera** *f* edge, border; **veras** *fpl* truth, reality; earnestness; **a la vera de** near, beside; **de veras** in truth; in earnest; **jugar de veras** to play in earnest, to play for keeps
**veracidad** *f* veracity
**veracruzano -na** *adj* (pertaining to) Vera Cruz; *mf* native or inhabitant of Vera Cruz
**veranada** *f* summer season (for pasturing)
**veranadero** *m* summer pasture
**veranar** *vn* to summer
**veranda** *f* veranda; bay window, closed porch
**veraneante** *adj* summering, summer-vacationing; *mf* summer vacationist, summer resident
**veranear** *vn* to summer
**veraneo** *m* summering; **ir de veraneo** to summer, to go on a summer vacation
**veranero** *m* summer grazing land
**veraniego -ga** *adj* (pertaining to) summer; sickly in the summer; slight, unimportant
**veranillo** *m* Indian summer; **veranillo de San Martín** Indian summer
**verano** *m* summer; (Am.) dry season
**verascopio** *m* stereo camera; stereo viewer
**veratrina** *f* (chem.) veratrine
**veratro** *m* (bot.) hellebore
**veraz** *adj* (*pl:* **-races**) veracious
**verba** *f* loquacity, eloquence
**verbal** *adj* verbal; verb; (gram.) verbal; *m* (gram.) verbal
**verbalismo** *m* verbalism (*predominance of words over concepts*)
**verbasco** *m* (bot.) great mullein
**verbena** *f* (bot.) verbena, vervain; night festival on eve of a saint's day; evening party; soirée; fair, village or country fair; **coger la verbena** (coll.) to get up and take a walk early in the morning
**verbenáceo -a** *adj* (bot.) verbenaceous
**verbenear** *vn* to move about, to swarm; to abound
**verberación** *f* beating, striking, pounding
**verberar** *va* to beat, strike; to beat against (*said of wind and water*)
**verbigracia** verbi gratia, for example
**verbo** *m* (gram.) verb; (*cap.*) *m* (theol.) Word (*second person of Trinity*); **verbo auxiliar** (gram.) auxiliary verb
**verborragia** or **verborrea** *f* (coll.) verbosity, wordiness
**verbosidad** *f* verbosity, wordiness
**verboso -sa** *adj* verbose, wordy
**verdacho** *m* green earth, terre-verte
**verdad** *f* truth; **¿verdad?** isn't that so?; **a decir verdad** to tell the truth, as a matter of fact; **a la verdad** in truth; as a matter of fact; **decir cuatro verdades (a)** to speak one's mind (to); **en verdad** truly, really; **faltar a la verdad** to lie; **¿no es verdad?** isn't that so? Esta pregunta, que se hace muy a menudo en la conversación después de aseveraciones de todo género, se traduce al inglés de variadísimas maneras. Si la aseveración es negativa, la pregunta que equivale a **¿no es verdad?** será afirmativa, p.ej., **Vd. no trabaja. ¿No es verdad?** You are not working. Are you? Si la aseveración es afirmativa, la pregunta será negativa y se podrán usar las contracciones con 'not', p.ej., **Vd. trabaja. ¿No es verdad?** You are working. Are you not? o Aren't you? Si la aseveración contiene auxiliar, la pregunta contendrá dicho auxiliar menos el infinitivo, el participio pasado o el participio activo del verbo, p.ej., **Llegará mañana por la mañana. ¿No es verdad?** He will arrive tomorrow morning. Won't he?; **Se lo ha dicho. ¿No es verdad?** She has told you. Hasn't she? Si la aseveración no contiene auxiliar ni una forma de la cópula 'to be', la pregunta contendrá el auxiliar 'do' o 'did' menos el infinitivo del verbo, p.ej., **Vd. habla inglés. ¿No es verdad?** You speak English. Don't you?; **Fueron a Madrid. ¿No es verdad?** They went to Madrid. Didn't they? Si el sujeto de la aseveración es un nombre sustantivo, irá representado en la pregunta con un pronombre personal, p.ej., **María no bebería café. ¿No es verdad?** Mary would not drink coffee. Would she?; **ser verdad** to be true; **verdad desnuda** plain truth
**verdadero -ra** *adj* true; truthful; real
**verdal** *adj* green (although ripe)
**verdasca** *f* green twig or branch
**verde** *adj* green; young, blooming, vigorous; callow (*youth*); sharp (*reprimand*); gay, merry

(*e.g., widow, old man*); shady, off-color; smutty (*person*); **están verdes** (coll.) they're hard to reach or get; **poner verde** (coll.) to abuse, to rake over the coals; *m* green; verdure, foliage; **darse un verde** (coll.) to have a fling, to have a little change; **verde de montaña** or **de tierra** mineral green
**verdea** *f* greenish wine
**verdear** *va* to pick for sale (*grapes or olives*); *vn* to look green, to turn green
**verdeceledón** *m* celadon green
**verdecer** §34 *vn* to turn green, to grow green
**verdecillo** *m* (orn.) greenfinch; (orn.) serin
**verdegal** *m* green field
**verdegay** *adj & m* light green
**verdeguear** *vn* to grow green
**verdejo -ja** *adj* green (although ripe)
**verdemar** *m* sea green
**verdemontaña** *m* mineral green (*mineral and color*)
**verderol** *m* (orn.) greenfinch; (zool.) cockle (*Cardium edule*)
**verderón -rona** *adj* bright-green; *m* (orn.) greenfinch; (zool.) cockle (*Cardium edule*)
**verdete** *m* verdigris
**verdevejiga** *m* bladder green, sap green
**verdezuelo** *m* (orn.) greenfinch
**verdín** *m* fresh greenness (*of plants*); mold, pond scum; verdigris; green snuff
**verdina** *f* see **verdino**
**verdinal** *m* green spot
**verdinegro -gra** *adj* dark-green
**verdino -na** *adj* bright-green; *f* fresh greenness (*of plants*)
**verdinoso -sa** *adj* moldy, scummy; verdigrisy
**verdiseco -ca** *adj* half-dried
**verdolaga** *f* (bot.) purslane
**verdón** *m* (orn.) greenfinch
**verdor** *m* verdure; youth
**verdoso -sa** *adj* greenish
**verdoyo** *m* fresh greenness
**verdugada** *f* layer of bricks
**verdugado** *m* hoop skirt
**verdugal** *m* thicket, cleared and burned and now covered with growth of young shoots
**verdugazo** *m* lash with a stick
**verdugo** *m* twig, shoot, sucker; long slender rapier; scourge, lash; welt; executioner; torment; hoop (*of a ring*); layer of bricks; (orn.) shrike, butcher bird
**verdugón** *m* large twig; large welt, wale
**verduguillo** *m* wale on leaves; narrow razor; dueling rapier; earring; half-round strip or fillet; (Am.) stiletto
**verdulería** *f* greengrocery
**verdulero -ra** *mf* greengrocer; *f* foul-mouthed woman, fishwife
**verdura** *f* verdure, verdancy, greenness; smuttiness; (f.a.) verdure (*tapestry*); **verduras** *fpl* vegetables, greens
**verdusco -ca** *adj* dark-greenish
**verecundia** *f* var. of **vergüenza**
**verecundo -da** *adj* var. of **vergonzoso**
**vereda** *f* path; circular notice sent by messenger; route of traveling preachers; (Am.) sidewalk; **meter por** or **en vereda** to set aright
**veredero** *m* country messenger over a regular route
**veredicto** *m* verdict
**verga** *f* (naut.) yard; penis; steel bow (*of a crossbow*); **verga de abanico** (naut.) sprit; **verga de popa** (naut.) spanker boom; **verga mayor** (naut.) main yard; **vergas en alto** (naut.) ready to sail
**vergajo** *m* pizzle (*used as a whip*); whip
**vergel** *m* flower and fruit garden
**vergeta** *f* var. of **vergueta**
**vergeteado -da** *adj* (her.) paly
**vergonzante** *adj* bashful, shamefaced (*beggar*)
**vergonzoso -sa** *adj* bashful, shy; embarrassing; shameful; private (*parts*); *mf* bashful or shy person; *m* (zool.) armadillo (*species that rolls up in a ball when pursued*)
**verguear** *va* to whip, to flog
**vergüenza** *f* shame; bashfulness, shyness; embarrassment; dignity; public punishment; **vergüenzas** *fpl* privates, genitals; **¡qué vergüenza!** for shame!; **tener vergüenza** to be ashamed; **tener vergüenza de** + *inf* to be ashamed to + *inf;* **ser una mala vergüenza** (coll.) to be a shame, to be too bad; **vergüenza torera** (taur.) professional honor or dignity
**verguer** *m* or **verguero** *m* (prov.) high constable
**vergueta** *f* rod, stem, twig
**vergueteado -da** *adj* laid (*paper*)
**verguío -a** *adj* flexible, leathery (*said of wood*)
**vericueto** *m* rough uneven ground
**verídico -ca** *adj* truthful
**verificable** *adj* verifiable
**verificación** *f* verification; check; realization; inspection (*of water, gas, and electric meters*); (law) probate (*e.g., of a will*)
**verificador -dora** *adj* verifying; *m* meter inspector
**verificar** §86 *va* to verify, to check; to carry out; to inspect (*water, gas, and electric meters*); *vr* to be verified, to prove true; to take place
**verificativo -va** *adj* corroborative
**verija** *f* (anat.) pubes
**veril** *m* (naut.) edge of sandbank or shoal
**verilear** *vn* (naut.) to sail around a sandbank or shoal
**verisímil** *adj* likely, probable, versimilar
**verisimilitud** *f* verisimilitude, probability
**verismo** *m* verism; truthfulness, spirit of truth
**verja** *f* grating; iron fence
**vermes** *mpl* intestinal worms
**vermicida** *adj* vermicidal; *m* vermicide
**vermicular** *adj* vermicular
**vermiforme** *adj* vermiform
**vermífugo -ga** *adj & m* (med.) vermifuge
**verminoso -sa** *adj* verminous
**vermis** *m* (*pl:* **-mis**) (anat.) vermis
**vermut** *m* (*pl:* **-mutes**) vermouth
**vernación** *f* (bot.) vernation
**vernáculo -la** *adj* vernacular
**vernal** *adj* vernal, spring
**vernier** *m* (*pl:* **-nieres**) vernier
**vero** *m* vair (*fur*); **veros** *mpl* (her.) vair
**veronal** *m* veronal
**veronense** *adj & mf* Veronese
**veronés -nesa** *adj & mf* Veronese; **el Veronés** Veronese (*painter*)
**verónica** *f* (bot.) veronica; veronica (*image of face of Christ impressed on handkerchief of St. Veronica*); (taur.) veronica (*maneuver in which the bullfighter waits for the bull's attack with cape extended in both hands*)
**veroniquear** *vn* (taur.) to perform veronicas
**verosímil** *adj* var. of **verisímil**
**verraco** *m* male hog, boar
**verraquear** *vn* (coll.) to grunt, to grumble; (coll.) to keep on crying hard
**verraquera** *f* (coll.) violent crying; (Am.) drunkenness
**verriondez** *f* rut, heat; withered state; toughness
**verriondo -da** *adj* rutting, in heat; withered; poorly cooked, tough (*said of vegetables*)
**verrón** *m* var. of **verraco**
**verruga** *f* wart; (bot.) wart; (fig.) defect; (coll.) nuisance, bore
**verrugo** *m* (coll.) miser
**verrugoso -sa** *adj* warty
**versado -da** *adj* versed; **versado en** versed in, conversant with
**versal** *adj & f* capital (*letter*)
**versalilla** or **versalita** *adj fem & f* small capital (*letter*)
**Versalles** *f* Versailles
**versar** *vn* to turn, to go around; to deal; **versar acerca de** or **sobre** to deal with, to treat of; *vr* to become versed
**versátil** *adj* versatile (*fickle*); (bot. & zool.) versatile
**versatilidad** *f* versatility (*fickleness*)
**versear** *vn* (coll.) to versify
**versería** *f* verses, poems
**versicolor** *adj* many-colored, variegated
**versícula** *f* stand for choir books
**versiculario** *m* chanter of versicles; keeper of choir books
**versículo** *m* (eccl.) versicle; verse (*in Bible*)
**versificación** *f* versification
**versificador -dora** *adj* versifying; *mf* versifier, versemaker

**versificar** §86 *va & vn* to versify
**versión** *f* version; translation; (obstet.) version; **versión de los Setenta** (Bib.) Septuagint
**versista** *mf* versifier; poetaster
**verso** *m* verse; (print.) verso; **verso alejandrino** Alexandrine; **verso blanco** blank verse; **verso esdrújulo** verse whose last word is accented on antepenult; **verso libre** blank verse; **verso llano** verse whose last word is accented on penult; **versos pareados** couplet, rhymed couplet; **verso suelto** blank verse
**versta** *f* verst (*Russian measure: 3500 feet*)
**vértebra** *f* (anat. & zool.) vertebra
**vertebración** *f* vertebration
**vertebrado -da** *adj & m* vertebrate
**vertebral** *adj* vertebral
**vertedera** *f* moldboard (*of plow*)
**vertedero** *m* dumping ground, dumping place; weir, spillway
**vertedor -dora** *adj* emptying, dumping; *m* drain; weir, spillway; pan (*for articles weighed*); (naut.) boat scoop
**vertello** *m* (naut.) ball (*of parrel*)
**verter** §66 *va* to pour, to empty; to shed; to dump; to translate; *vn* to flow; *vr* to run, to empty
**vertibilidad** *f* changeableness
**vertible** *adj* changeable
**vertical** *adj* vertical; *m* (astr.) vertical circle; **primer vertical** (astr.) prime vertical; *f* vertical (*line*)
**vértice** *m* (math. & anat.) vertex
**verticilado -da** *adj* (bot. & zool.) verticillate
**verticilo** *m* (bot.) verticil, whorl
**vertiente** *adj* flowing, pouring; *m & f* slope (*e.g., of a continent or a roof*)
**vertiginoso -sa** *adj* vertiginous, dizzy, giddy
**vértigo** *m* vertigo, dizziness; fit of insanity; (vet.) vertigo, staggers
**vertimiento** *m* emptying; shedding; dumping; flowing
**vesania** *f* insanity
**vesánico -ca** *adj* insane; *mf* insane person
**vesical** *adj* vesical
**vesicante** *adj & m* vesicant
**vesícula** *f* (anat., bot., path. & zool.) vesicle; **vesícula biliar** (anat.) gall bladder; **vesícula elemental** or **orgánica** (biol.) cell
**vesiculado -da** *adj* vesiculate
**vesicular** *adj* vesicular
**vesiculoso -sa** *adj* vesiculose
**veso** *m* (zool.) polecat
**Vespasiano** *m* Vespasian
**vesperal** *adj* evening; *m* vesperal (*book*)
**Véspero** *m* Vesper
**vespertilio** *m* (zool.) vespertilio (*bat*)
**vespertino -na** *adj* vespertine, evening; *m* evening sermon; *f* evening discourse at the university; evening sermon
**Vesta** *f* (myth.) Vesta
**vestal** *adj* vestal; *f* vestal, vestal virgin
**veste** *f* (poet.) dress, clothing
**Vestfalia** *f* Westphalia
**vestfaliano -na** *adj & mf* Westphalian
**vestfálico -ca** *adj* Westphalian
**vestibular** *adj* (anat.) vestibular
**vestíbulo** *m* vestibule; (anat.) vestibule (*of ear*); (theat.) lobby, foyer
**vestido** *m* clothing; costume, suit; dress; **vestido de etiqueta** evening clothes, evening dress; **vestido de etiqueta de mujer** or **vestido de noche** evening gown; **vestido de serio** evening clothes, evening dress; **vestido de tarde-noche** cocktail dress; **vestido imperio** Empire gown
**vestidura** *f* clothing; vestment; **vestiduras** *fpl* vestments, canonicals
**vestigial** *adj* vestigial
**vestigio** *m* vestige; track, footprint; (biol.) vestige; (chem.) trace
**vestiglo** *m* horrible monster
**vestimenta** *f* clothes; vestment
**vestir** §94 *va* to clothe, to dress; to adorn, to bedeck; to cover; to disguise; to wear; to put on (*clothing*); to roughcast; **morir vestido** to die a violent death; **vestir el cargo** to look the part ‖ *vn* to dress; to be dressy (*said, e.g., of a material*); **vestir de blanco** to dress in white; **vestir de etiqueta** to dress in evening clothes; **vestir de paisano** to dress in civilian clothes ‖ *vr* to dress, to dress oneself; to be covered; to be up (*from a sick bed*); **vestirse de** to be covered with (*e.g., grass, leaves, clouds*); to assume (*e.g., importance*)
**vestuario** *m* wardrobe, apparel; dressing room, bathhouse; (mil.) uniform; (theat.) dressing room; checkroom, cloakroom
**vestugo** *m* sprout of an olive tree
**vesubiano -na** *adj* Vesuvian
**Vesubio, el** Vesuvius
**veta** *f* vein (*in the earth; in wood or stone*); stripe; **descubrir la veta de** (coll.) to be on to
**vetado -da** veined, striped
**vetar** *va* to veto
**veteado -da** *adj* veined, striped; *m* graining
**vetear** *va* to grain, to stripe
**veteranía** *f* long service, long experience
**veterano -na** *adj & mf* veteran
**veterinario -ria** *adj* veterinary; *mf* veterinary, veterinarian; *f* veterinary medicine, veterinary surgery
**vetisesgado -da** *adj* diagonal-striped
**vetiver** *m* (bot.) vetiver
**veto** *m* veto; prohibition
**vetustez** *f* great age, antiquity
**vetusto -ta** *adj* very old, ancient
**Veyos** *f* Veii
**vez** *f* (*pl:* **veces**) time; turn; drove; **a la vez** at one time, at the same time; **a la vez que** while, **alguna vez** sometimes; ever, e.g., **¿Ha estado Vd. alguna vez en España?** Have you ever been in Spain?; **a su vez** in turn; on his part; **a veces** at times, sometimes; **cada vez** every time; **cada ves más** more and more; **cada vez que** every time that; **cuántas veces** how often; **de una vez** at one time; once and for all; **de vez en cuando** once in a while; **dos veces más grande que** twice as large as; **en vez de** instead of; **esperar vez** to wait one's turn; **hacer las veces de** to serve as, to take the place of; **las más veces** in most cases, most of the time; **muchas veces** often; **otra vez** again; some other time; **pocas veces** seldom; **rara vez** or **raras veces** seldom, rarely; **repetidas veces** repeatedly, over and over again; **tal cual vez** occasionally; **tal vez** perhaps; **tomar la vez a** (coll.) to get ahead of; **una que otra vez** once in a while; **una vez** once; **una vez que** once; inasmuch as
**veza** *f* (bot.) vetch, spring vetch
**vezar** §76 *va* to accustom; *vr* to become accustomed
**vg.** abr. of **verbigracia** & **virgen**
**v.g.** & **v.gr.** abr. of **verbigracia**
**vía** *f* road, route, way; (rail.) track; rail (*of track*); gauge (*of track*); (anat.) passage, tract; (fig.) way; **cuaderna vía** stanza of mester de clerecía (*thirteenth and fourteenth centuries*) consisting of four single-rhymed Alexandrines; **estar en vías de** + *inf* to be + *ger*, to be engaged in + *ger;* **por la vía de** via; **por vía aérea** by air; **por vía bucal** by mouth, orally; **por vía de** by way of; **vía acuática** waterway; **vía aérea** airway; **vía ancha** (rail.) broad gauge; **Vía Apia** Appian Way; **vía de agua** waterway; (naut.) leak; **vía de circunvalación** (rail.) belt line; **vía ejecutiva** (law) seizure, attachment; **vía estrecha** (rail.) narrow gauge; **vía férrea** railway; **Vía Flaminia** Flaminian Way; **vía fluvial** waterway; **vía húmeda** (chem.) wet way; **Vía láctea** (astr.) Milky Way; **vía muerta** (rail.) siding; **vía normal** (rail.) standard gauge; **vía pública** thoroughfare; **vías de hecho** (Am.) violence; (Am.) assault and battery; **vías de comunicación** communications; **vías urinarias** (anat.) urinary tract; *prep* via, e.g., **vía Nueva York** via New York
**viabilidad** *f* viability; feasibility
**viable** *adj* viable; feasible
**viadera** *f* harness shaft (*of loom*)
**viador** *m* (theol.) traveler (*to the other world*)
**viaducto** *m* viaduct
**viajador -dora** *mf* traveler
**viajante** *adj* traveling; *mf* traveler; *m* traveling salesman, drummer

**viajar** *va* to sell on the road; to cover (*a certain territory*) as salesman; *vn* to travel, to journey
**viajata** *f* (coll.) journey
**viaje** *m* trip, journey, voyage; way, road; travel book; load on each trip; water supply; (arch.) obliquity; **¡buen viaje!** bon voyage!; **viaje de ida y vuelta** or **viaje redondo** round trip; **viajes por el espacio** space travel
**viajero -ra** *adj* traveling; *mf* traveler; passenger
**vial** *adj* (pertaining to a) road, highway; *m* avenue (*of trees, shrubs, etc.*)
**vialidad** *f* road service, highway service, communications
**vianda** *f* viand, food
**viandante** *mf* traveler, itinerant, stroller; tramp
**viaraza** *f* diarrhea
**viaticar** §86 *va* (eccl.) to administer the viaticum to; *vr* (eccl.) to receive the viaticum
**viático** *m* viaticum, travel allowance; (eccl.) viaticum
**víbora** *f* (zool.) viper; (fig.) viper; **víbora cornuda** (zool.) horned viper; **víbora de agua** (zool.) moccasin
**viborera** *f* (bot.) viper's bugloss, blueweed
**viborezno -na** *adj* viperous; *m* young viper
**vibración** *f* vibration
**vibrador** *m* vibrator
**vibrante** *adj* vibrant; (phonet.) trilled; (fig.) vibrant (*e.g., style*); *f* (phonet.) trilled consonant (*Spanish sound of r*)
**vibrar** *va* to vibrate; to brandish; to throw, to hurl; to roll (*the voice; the letter r*); *vn* to vibrate
**vibrátil** *adj* vibratile
**vibratorio -ria** *adj* vibrative, vibratory
**vibrio** *m* (bact.) vibrio
**vibrión** *m* (bact.) vibrion
**vibrisas** or **vibrizas** *fpl* whiskers (*e.g., of cat*); hair in the nostrils
**viburno** *m* (bot.) viburnum
**vicaria** *f* see **vicario**
**vicaría** *f* vicarage, vicarship
**vicarial** *adj* vicarial
**vicariato** *m* vicarage, vicarship
**vicario -ria** *adj* vicarious; (physiol.) vicarious; *mf* vicar; **vicario general** vicar-general; **vicarios** *mpl* (bot.) grape hyacinth; *f* assistant mother superior
**vicealmirantazgo** *m* vice-admiralty
**vicealmirante** *m* vice-admiral
**vicecanciller** *m* vice-chancellor
**viceconsiliario** *m* vice-counsellor
**vicecónsul** *m* vice-consul
**viceconsulado** *m* vice-consulate
**vicecristo** *m* vice-Christ
**vicediós** *m* vice-God
**vicegerencia** *f* vicegerency
**vicegerente** *adj* vicegerent; assistant; *m* vicegerent; assistant manager
**vicegobernador** *m* vice-governor
**vicenal** *adj* vicennial
**vicenio** *m* twenty years
**vicense** *adj* (pertaining to) Vich; *mf* native or inhabitant of Vich
**Vicente** *m* Vincent; **San Vicente** Saint Vincent (*island*)
**vicepresidencia** *f* vice-presidency
**vicepresidencial** *adj* vice-presidential
**vicepresidente -ta** *mf* vice-president; *f* wife of vice-president
**vicerrector** *m* vice-rector
**vicesecretaría** *f* vice-secretaryship
**vicesecretario -ria** *mf* vice-secretary
**vicésimo -ma** *adj & m* twentieth
**vicetesorero -ra** *mf* vice-treasurer
**viceversa** *adv* vice versa
**vicia** *f* (bot.) vetch
**viciación** *f* vitiation
**viciado -da** *adj* foul, vitiated
**viciar** *va* to vitiate, falsify, adulterate; to nullify; (law) to vitiate; *vr* to become vitiated, to give oneself up to vice; to become deeply attached; to warp, become warped
**vicio** *m* vice; viciousness; defect; overgrowth, luxuriance; **de vicio** from being spoiled; without reason, out of habit; **hablar de vicio** (coll.) to be a chatterbox, to jabber away; **quejarse de vicio** (coll.) to be a chronic complainer; **vicio de dicción** grammatical error, solecism
**vicioso -sa** *adj* vicious; faulty, defective; strong, robust; licentious; luxuriant, abundant; (coll.) spoiled (*said of a child*)
**vicisitud** *f* vicissitude
**víctima** *f* victim; **víctima propiciatoria** scapegoat
**victimar** *va* to sacrifice; (Am.) to kill, assassinate
**victo** *m* daily bread
**víctor** *m & interj* var. of **vítor**
**victorear** *va* var. of **vitorear**
**victoria** *f* victory; (bot.) victoria; victoria (*carriage*); **victoria pírrica** Pyrrhic victory
**victoriano -na** *adj & mf* Victorian
**victorioso -sa** *adj* victorious
**vicuña** *f* (zool.) vicuña (*animal, wool, and cloth*)
**vid** *f* (bot.) grapevine
**vida** *f* life; living, livelihood; life span; **con vida** alive; **darse buena vida** to enjoy life; to live comfortably; **de por vida** for life; **en mi (tu, su) vida** never; **escapar con vida** to have a narrow escape; **ganar** or **ganarse la vida** to earn one's living; **hacer por la vida** (coll.) to get a bite to eat; **hacer vida** to live together (*as man and wife*); **jugarse la vida** to take one's life in one's hands; **mudar de vida** to mend one's ways; **pasar la vida** to live frugally, to just about get along; **¡por vida!** please!; by Jove!; **quitarse la vida** to take one's life; **tener siete vidas como los gatos** to have nine lives; **vida airada** licentious living; **vida ancha** loose living; **vida canonical** or **de canónigo** (coll.) life of ease; **vida de bohemio** Bohemianism; **vida de familia** or **de hogar** home life; **vida de perros** dog's life; **vida media** (phys.) half life; **vida privada** private life
**videncia** *f* clear-sightedness; clairvoyance
**vidente** *adj* seeing; *mf* person with sight; *m* prophet, seer; *f* seeress
**vídeo** *m* video
**videofrecuencia** *f* television frequency
**videograbación** *f* video-tape recording
**videoseñal** *f* picture signal, video signal
**vidorra** *f* (prov.) life of ease
**vidorria** *f* (Am.) dog's life
**vidriado -da** *adj* brittle; glazed; *m* glazing; glazed earthenware; dishes
**vidriar** §90 & **regular** *va* to glaze; *vr* to become glazed; to become glassy
**vidriera** *f* glass window, glass door; (Am.) shopwindow, show window; **vidriera de colores** or **vidriera pintada** stained-glass window
**vidriería** *f* glasswork; glassworks; glass store
**vidriero** *m* glassworker, glazier
**vidrio** *m* glass; piece of glass; glass vessel; window pane; something delicate or brittle; touchy person; **en vidrio** in vitro; **ir al vidrio** to ride backwards (*in a coach*); **pagar los vidrios rotos** (coll.) to be the goat, to take the blame; **vidrio cilindrado** plate glass; **vidrio de aumento** magnifying glass; **vidrio de color** stained glass; **vidrio de cuarzo** quartz glass; **vidrio de plomo** flint glass; **vidrio de seguridad** safety glass; **vidrio deslustrado** ground glass; **vidrio hilado** spun glass; **vidrio pintado** stained glass; **vidrio soluble** water glass; **vidrio tallado** cut glass
**vidriosidad** *f* glassiness; brittleness; slipperiness
**vidrioso -sa** *adj* glassy, vitreous; brittle; slippery; (fig.) touchy; (fig.) glassy (*look in eyes*)
**vidual** *adj* (pertaining to a) widow; widow's; (pertaining to a) widower; widower's
**vidueño** or **viduño** *m* quality or kind of grapevine
**viejo -ja** *adj* old, ancient, antique; antiquated, old-fashioned; worn-out; *m* old man; **el viejo de la montaña** (hist.) the Old Man of the Mountain; **viejo verde** old goat, old rake; *f* old woman
**viejón -jona** *adj* (Am.) oldish
**Viena** *f* Vienna; Vienne (*French city*)
**vienense** *adj* Viennese; (pertaining to) Vienne (*France*); *mf* Viennese; native or inhabitant of Vienne

**vienés -nesa** *adj & mf* Viennese
**vientecillo** *m* breeze, light wind
**viento** *m* wind (*air in motion; strong current of air; air filled with animal odor; vanity, conceit*); air; direction, course; guy; (arti.) windage (*space between projectile and bore of gun*); (coll.) wind (*gas in stomach or bowels*); **beber los vientos por** (coll.) to turn everything upside down for; **ceñir el viento** (naut.) to sail close to the wind; **contra viento y marea** come hell and high water, against all odds; **ir viento en popa** to go very well, to get along famously; **moverse a todos vientos** to be as fickle as the wind; (coll.) to be easily led by the nose; **viento bonancible** (*naut.*) moderate breeze; **viento de cola** (aer.) tail wind; **viento de la hélice** (aer.) slip stream; **viento duro** (naut.) fresh gale; **viento flojito** (naut.) light breeze; **viento flojo** (naut.) gentle breeze; **viento frescachón** (naut.) moderate gale; **viento fresco** (naut.) strong breeze; **viento fresquito** (naut.) fresh breeze; **viento muy duro** (naut.) strong gale; **vientos alisios** trade winds; **vientos altanos** winds blowing alternately offshore and off the sea; **vientos antialisios** antitrades; **viento terral** land breeze; **viento trasero** (aer.) tail wind
**vientre** *m* belly; bowels; womb; **evacuar, exonerar** or **mover el vientre** to defecate, to stool; **vientre flojo** loose bowels
**vier.** abr. of **viernes**
**viera** *f* pilgrim's scallop shell; (zool.) scallop
**viernes** *m* (*pl:* **-nes**) Friday; **comer de viernes** to fast, to abstain from meat; **Viernes santo** Good Friday
**viero** *m* road worker
**vierteaguas** *m* (*pl:* **-guas**) flashing
**vietnamés -mesa, vietnamiano -na, vietnamiense,** or **vietnamita** *adj & mf* Viet-Namese
**viga** *f* beam, girder, joist, rafter; press; pressing of olives; **estar contando las vigas** (coll.) to gaze blankly at the ceiling
**vigencia** *f* force, operation; use, vogue; **en vigencia** in force, in effect
**vigente** *adj* effective, in force
**vigesimal** *adj* vigesimal
**vigésimo -ma** *adj* twentieth; vigesimal; *m* twentieth
**vigía** *f* watch; watchtower; (naut.) rock, reef; *m* lookout, watch; **vigía de incendios** firewarden
**vigiar §90** *va* to watch for, to lie watching
**vigilancia** *f* vigilance, watchfulness; **bajo vigilancia médica** under the care of a doctor
**vigilante** *adj* vigilant, watchful; *mf* vigilante; *m* watchman, guard; **vigilante nocturno** night watchman
**vigilar** *va* to watch over, to look out for; *vn* to watch, keep guard; **vigilar por** or **sobre** to watch over, to care for
**vigilativo -va** *adj* causing sleeplessness
**vigilia** *f* vigil; study, night study; eve; wakefulness; (mil.) watch, guard; (eccl.) vigils; **comer de vigilia** to fast, to abstain from meat; **durante la vigilia** while awake
**vigitano -na** *adj* (pertaining to) Vich; *mf* native or inhabitant of Vich
**vigor** *m* vigor; **entrar en vigor** to go into effect; **poner en vigor** to put into effect
**vigorizador -dora** *adj* invigorating; **vigorizador del cabello** hair tonic
**vigorizante** *adj* invigorating
**vigorizar §76** *va* to invigorate; to encourage; *vr* to be invigorated; to be encouraged
**vigorosidad** *f* vigorousness
**vigoroso -sa** *adj* vigorous
**vigota** *f* (naut.) deadeye
**viguería** *f* set of beams
**vigués -guesa** *adj* (pertaining to) Vigo; *mf* native or inhabitant of Vigo
**vigueta** *f* small beam, small girder
**vil** *adj* vile, base; dastardly; *mf* dastard
**vilano** *m* pappus, burr or down of the thistle
**vileza** *f* vileness; infamy
**vilipendiador -dora** *adj* scornful; vilifying; *mf* scorner; vilifier
**vilipendiar** *va* to scorn; to vilify
**vilipendio** *m* scorn; vilification
**vilipendioso -sa** *adj* contemptible
**vilo; en vilo** in the air; (fig.) up in the air (*uncertain*)
**vilordo -da** *adj* lazy, dull, slothful
**vilorta** *f* reed hoop; clasp ring of plow; washer; game like lacrosse
**vilorto** *m* reed hoop; crosse for playing vilorta; (bot.) clematis, liana
**viltrotear** *vn* (coll.) to walk the streets, to gad about
**viltrotera** *f* (coll.) gadabout (*woman*)
**villa** *f* town; villa, country or suburban house; **la Villa** or **la Villa del Manzanares** Madrid
**Villadiego** town in the province of Burgos, Spain; **coger** or **tomar las de Villadiego** to beat it, to run away
**villaje** *m* small town, village
**villanada** *f* despicable act
**villanaje** *m* peasantry; (hist.) villeinage
**villancejo** or **villancete** *m* var. of **villancico**
**villancico** *m* carol, Christmas carol; **villancico de Nochebuena** or **de Navidad** Christmas carol
**villanciquero -ra** *mf* caroler (*one who carols*)
**villanchón -chona** *adj* rustic, crude
**villanela** *f* villanelle
**villanería** *f* villainy; (hist.) villeinage
**villanesco -ca** *adj* rustic, crude, boorish
**villanía** *f* humble birth; villainy; vile remark
**villano -na** *adj* coarse, impolite; base, villainous; *mf* peasant; evil person, villain; (hist.) villain, villein
**villar** *m* village, hamlet
**villazgo** *m* village charter; village tax
**villoría** *f* hamlet, farm
**villorín** *m* var. of **vellorí**
**villorrio** *m* small country town
**vimbre** *m* (bot.) osier; wicker
**vimbrera** *f* (bot.) osier
**vinagrada** *f* vinegar water (*a drink*)
**vinagre** *m* vinegar; (coll.) grouch; **vinagre de madera** wood vinegar
**vinagrero -ra** *mf* vinegarer; *f* vinaigrette; (bot.) sorrel; (Am.) heartburn; **vinagreras** *fpl* cruet stand
**vinagreta** *f* vinegar sauce
**vinagrillo** *m* weak vinegar; vinegar lotion (*a cosmetic*)
**vinagroso -sa** *adj* vinegary (*taste or disposition*)
**vinajera** *f* (eccl.) burette, cruet; **vinajeras** *fpl* (eccl.) cruets and tray
**vinariego** *m* vineyardist
**vinario -ria** *adj* (pertaining to) wine
**vinatería** *f* wine trade; wine shop
**vinatero -ra** *adj* (pertaining to) wine; *m* wine dealer, vintner
**vinaza** *f* poor thin wine
**vinazo** *m* strong heavy wine
**vincapervinca** *f* (bot.) cut-finger, large periwinkle
**Vincenas** *f* Vincennes
**vinculable** *adj* (law) entailable
**vinculación** *f* (law) entailment; continuation
**vincular** *va* to tie, bind, unite; (law) to entail; to continue, perpetuate; to found (*e.g., hopes*)
**vínculo** *m* bond; vinculum; (law) entail
**vindicación** *f* vindication; (law) vindication
**vindicador -dora** *adj* vindicating; *mf* vindicator
**vindicar §86** *va* to avenge; to vindicate; (law) to vindicate
**vindicativo -va** *adj* vindicative; vindictive
**vindicta** *f* revenge; **vindicta pública** punishment, justice
**vine** *1st sg pret ind of* **venir**
**vínico -ca** *adj* vinic
**vinícola** *adj* (pertaining to) wine; vinegrowing; *m* vinegrower
**vinicultor -tora** *mf* vinegrower
**vinicultura** *f* vinegrowing
**viniebla** *f* (bot.) hound's-tongue
**viniendo** *ger of* **venir**
**vinífero -ra** *adj* wine-producing
**vinificación** *f* vinification
**vinilo** *m* (chem.) vinyl
**vinillo** *m* (coll.) weak wine

**vino** *m* wine; wine party, sherry reception; **bautizar** or **cristianizar el vino** to water wine; **dormir el vino** to sleep off a drunk; **tener mal vino** to be a quarrelsome drunk; **vino cubierto** dark-red wine; **vino de cuerpo** strong-bodied wine; **vino de Jerez** sherry wine; **vino de lágrima** wine from the juice exuded by ripe grapes; **vino del terruño** wine of the locality; **vino de mesa** table wine; **vino de Oporto** port wine; **vino de orujo** thin, second-run wine; **vino de pasto** table wine; **vino de postre** after-dinner wine; **vino de segunda** second-run wine; **vino de solera** old vintage wine; **vino generoso** generous, rich wine; **vino mulso** mulse; **vino seco** dry wine; **vino tinto** red table wine; *3d sg pret ind of* **venir**
**vinolencia** *f* excessive use of wine
**vinolento -ta** *adj* too fond of wine
**vinosidad** *f* vinousness
**vinoso -sa** *adj* vinous
**vinote** *m* residue in boiler after distillation of wine
**viña** *f* vineyard; **ser una viña** (coll.) to be a mine; **tener una viña** (coll.) to have a sinecure
**viñadero** *m* guard of vineyard
**viñador** *m* vinedresser, vineyardist; guard of vineyard
**viñatero** *m* (Am.) vineyardist, winegrower; (Am.) owner of a vineyard
**viñedo** *m* vineyard
**viñero -ra** *mf* owner of a vineyard
**viñeta** *f* vignette
**viola** *f* (mus. & bot.) viola; **viola de amor** (mus.) viola d'amore; *mf* viola, viola player
**violable** *adj* violable
**violáceo -a** *adj* violaceous
**violación** *f* violation
**violado -da** *adj & m* violet (*color*)
**violador -dora** *adj* violating; *mf* violator
**violar** *m* bed of violets; *va* violate; to tamper with
**violencia** *f* violence; **no violencia** nonviolence
**violentar** *va* to do violence to; to break into; *vr* to force oneself
**violento -ta** *adj* violent
**violero** *m* (ent.) mosquito
**violeta** *f* (bot.) violet; (bot.) damewort; **violeta africana** (bot.) African violet; *m* violet (*color; dye*); **violeta de genciana** gentian violet; **violeta de metilo** methyl violet; *adj invar* violet (*color and scent*)
**violetera** *f* violet vendor, flower girl
**violetero** *m* small vase
**violeto** *m* (bot.) clingstone peach
**violín** *m* violin (*instrument and performer*); bridge, cue rest (*in billiards*); **segundo violín** second violin; **violín de Ingres** avocation, hobby
**violinista** *mf* violinist
**violón** *m* (mus.) bass viol (*instrument and performer*); **estar tocando el violón** (coll.) to talk nonsense
**violoncelista** *mf* violoncellist, cellist
**violoncelo** *m* (mus.) violoncello, cello
**violonchelista** *mf* var. of **violoncelista**
**violonchelo** *m* var. of **violoncelo**
**violle** *m* violle (*photometric unit*)
**viosterol** *m* (pharm.) viosterol
**vipéreo -a** *adj* viperine
**viperino -na** *adj* viperine; (fig.) viperish; *f* (bot.) viper's bugloss, blueweed; **viperina de Virginia** (bot.) Virginia snakeroot
**vira** *f* dart; welt (*of shoe*)
**virada** *f* turn, change of direction; (naut.) tack, tacking
**virado** *m* (phot.) toning
**virador** *m* (naut.) viol; (phot.) toning bath
**virago** *f* mannish woman
**viraje** *m* turn, change of direction; (phot.) toning; **viraje en horquilla** hairpin bend, hairpin turn
**viral** *adj* viral
**virar** *va* (naut.) to wind, twist, heave; (naut.) to veer, to tack; (phot.) to tone; *vn* to turn; (naut.) to veer, to tack
**viratón** *m* large dart
**virazón** *f* sea breeze
**vireo** *m* (orn.) vireo
**víreo** *m* (orn.) golden oriole
**virescencia** *f* (bot.) virescence
**virescente** *adj* virescent
**virgen** *f* virgin; upright guide in wine or olive press; (*cap.*) *f* (astr.) Virgin; **la Santísima Virgen** the Blessed Virgin; **las islas Vírgenes** the Virgin Islands; **la Virgen María** the Virgin Mary; *adj* virgin
**virgiliano -na** *adj* Virgilian
**Virgilio** *m* Virgil
**virginal** *adj* virginal, maidenly; *m* (mus.) virginal
**virgíneo -a** *adj* virginal
**Virginia** *f* Virginia; (*l.c.*) *m* Virginia tobacco
**virginiano -na** *adj & mf* Virginian
**virginidad** *f* virginity
**virginio** *m* (chem.) virginium
**virgo** *m* virginity; (*cap.*) *m* (astr.) Virgo
**vírgula** *f* small rod; light dash; comma; (bact.) bacillus (*Vibrio comma*) causing Asiatic cholera
**virgulilla** *f* fine stroke, light dash; mark, point, sign, accent (*attached to a letter*)
**viril** *adj* virile; *m* clear glass bell; (eccl.) small monstrance within larger one
**virilidad** *f* virility
**virio** *m* (orn.) golden oriole
**viripotente** *adj* marriageable; strong, vigorous
**virol** *m* (her.) virole
**virola** *f* collar, clasp (*e.g., on a knife, sword, etc.*); check ring on a goad; (mach.) ferrule
**virolado -da** *adj* provided with a clasp; (her.) viroled
**virolento -ta** *adj* with smallpox; pock-marked; *mf* person with smallpox; pock-marked person
**virología** *f* virology
**virológico -ca** *adj* virological
**virólogo -ga** *mf* virologist
**virotazo** *m* hit or wound with an arrow
**virote** *m* iron-pointed arrow; (coll.) young single man about town; (coll.) stuffed shirt
**virotillo** *m* short upright brace
**virotismo** *m* arrogance, haughtiness
**virreina** *f* vice-queen; wife of a viceroy
**virreinal** *adj* viceregal
**virreinato** *m* viceroyalty
**virrey** *m* viceroy, vice-king
**virtual** *adj* virtual
**virtualidad** *f* virtuality
**virtud** *f* virtue; **en virtud de** by or in virtue of; **virtudes cardinales** cardinal virtues
**virtuosidad** *f* virtuousness; virtuosity
**virtuosismo** *m* virtuosity
**virtuoso -sa** *adj* virtuous; *m* virtuoso
**viruela** *f* (path.) smallpox, variola; (path.) varioloid; pock mark; **viruelas locas** (path.) chicken pox
**virulencia** *f* virulence
**virulento -ta** *adj* virulent
**virus** *m* (*pl:* **-rus**) virus
**viruta** *f* shaving (*of wood or metal*)
**virutilla** *f* thin shaving; **virutillas de acero** steel wool
**visa** *f* visa, visé
**visado** *m* visa; **visado de tránsito** transit visa
**visaje** *m* face, grimace, smirk
**visajero -ra** *adj* grimacing, making faces
**visar** *va* to visa, to visé; to endorse, to O.K.; (arti. & surv.) to sight
**visayo -ya** *adj & mf* Bisayan or Visayan
**visceral** *adj* visceral
**vísceras** *fpl* viscera
**visco** *m* (bot.) mistletoe (*Phoradendron*); birdlime; **visco quercino** (bot.) mistletoe (*Viscum album*)
**viscosa** *f* see **viscoso**
**viscosidad** *f* viscosity
**viscosilla** *f* rayon thread
**viscoso -sa** *adj* viscous; *f* viscose
**visera** *f* visor (*of helmet, cap, windshield, etc.*); eye-shade; (Am.) blinder, blinker
**visibilidad** *f* visibility
**visible** *adj* visible; evident; conspicuous
**visigodo -da** *adj* Visigothic; *mf* Visigoth
**visigótico -ca** *adj* Visigothic
**visillo** *m* window curtain, window shade
**visión** *f* vision; view; (coll.) scarecrow, sight (*person*); **ver visiones** (coll.) to be seeing things; **visión negra** blackout (*of aviators*)

**visionario -ria** *adj & mf* visionary
**visiotelefonía** *f* video telephony
**visir** *m* vizier, vizir; **gran visir** grand vizier
**visita** *f* visit; visitor; **hacer una visita** to make a call; **ir de visitas** to go calling; **pagar una visita** to return a call; **tener visita** to have callers; **visita de aspectos** medical inspection of faces of passengers; **visita de cumplido, de cumplimiento** or **de digestión** formal call; **visita de médico** (coll.) short call
**visitable** *adj* open to visitors
**visitación** *f* visitation, visit; (*cap.*) *f* Visitation
**visitador -dora** *adj* visiting; *mf* visitor, frequent visitor; inspector
**visitante** *adj* visitant; *mf* visitant; visitor; (sport) visitor
**visitar** *va* to visit; to inspect; *vr* to visit, to call on each other
**visiteo** *m* frequent exchange of visits, frequent visiting
**visitero -ra** *adj* (coll.) visiting; (coll.) fond of visits (*said of a doctor*); *mf* (coll.) visitor
**visitón** *m* (coll.) long tiresome visit
**visivo -va** *adj* visual
**vislumbrar** *va* to glimpse; to suspect, surmise; *vr* to glimmer; to loom, appear indistinctly
**vislumbre** *f* glimpse, glimmer; inkling, surmise; slight resemblance
**Visnú** *m* Vishnu
**viso** *m* sheen, gleam, glint; streak, strain; appearance; thin veneer; colored garment under transparent outer garment; eminence, height; **a dos visos** with a double purpose; **de viso** of importance, prominent
**visón** *m* (zool.) mink
**visor** *m* (aer.) bombsight; (phot.) finder; (math.) unit vector
**visorio -ria** *adj* visual; *m* inspection by an expert
**víspera** *f* eve, day before; forerunner, cause; imminence; **vísperas** *fpl* (eccl.) vespers; **en vísperas de** on the eve of; **víspera de año nuevo** New Year's Eve; **víspera de Navidad** Christmas Eve; **Vísperas sicilianas** (hist.) Sicilian Vespers
**vista** *f* see **visto**
**vistazo** *m* look, glance
**vistillas** *fpl* eminence, high spot; **irse a las vistillas** (coll.) to try to get a look at the cards of one's opponent
**visto -ta** *adj* evident, obvious; in view of, e.g., **vista la importancia del asunto** in view of the importance of the matter; **bien visto** looked on with approval; **mal visto** looked on with disapproval; **no visto** or **nunca visto** unheard-of, extraordinary; **por lo visto** evidently, as is clear from the above; **visto bueno** approved, authorized, O.K.; **visto que** whereas, inasmuch as, seeing ‖ *pp of* **ver** ‖ *f* sight, vision; view; vista; glance; appearance, comparison; purpose, design; eye, eyes; (law) trial; (law) hearing; **vistas** *fpl* windows, openings; view, outlook; conference; visible parts, parts that show; collar, cuffs, and bosom of shirt; **a la vista** (com.) at sight; **a primera vista** at first sight; **a simple vista** at a glance; with the naked eye; **a vista de** in view of, within view of, in the sight of; compared with; **con vistas a** + *inf* with a view to + *ger;* **de vista** by sight; **doble vista** second sight; **en vista de** in consideration of; **hacer la vista gorda (a)** to pretend not to see; **hasta la vista** good-bye, au revoir, so long; **medir con la vista** to size up (*a person*); **perder de vista** to lose sight of; **saltar a la vista** to be self-evident; **segunda vista** second sight; **tener a la vista** to have at hand, to have received (*a letter*); to keep one's eyes on; **torcer la vista** to squint; **vista cansada** far-sightedness; **vista corta** near-sightedness; **vista de pájaro** bird's-eye view; **vista doble** double vision; **vista en corte** cross-section view; **vista torcida** cross-eye ‖ **vista** *m* custom-house inspector
**vistosidad** *f* showiness, loudness, flashiness
**vistoso -sa** *adj* showy, loud, flashy
**Vístula** *m* Vistula
**visual** *adj* visual; *f* line of sight, visual line
**visualidad** *f* pleasure at sight of showy display
**visualización** *f* visualization
**visualizar** §76 *va* to visualize
**visuauditivo -va** *adj* audio-visual
**visura** *f* visual examination; inspection by an expert
**vitáceo -a** *adj* (bot.) vitaceous
**vital** *adj* vital
**vitalicio -cia** *adj* lifetime; (lasting for) life; (holding an office, etc. for) life; *m* life-insurance policy; lifetime pension, life annuity
**vitalicista** *mf* life annuitant
**vitalidad** *f* vitality
**vitalismo** *m* vitalism
**vitalista** *adj* vitalistic; *mf* vitalist
**vitalización** *f* vitalization
**vitalizar** §76 *va* to vitalize
**vitamina** *f* vitamine
**vitamínico -ca** *adj* vitaminic, vitamine
**vitando -da** *adj* to be avoided; odious, execrable
**vitela** *f* vellum
**vitelino -na** *adj* vitelline; *f* (biochem.) vitellin
**vitelo** *m* vitellus, yolk of an egg
**vitícola** *adj* viticultural, grape-growing; *mf* viticulturist, grape grower
**viticultor -tora** *mf* viticulturist, grape grower
**viticultura** *f* viticulture, grape growing
**vitíligo** *m* (path.) vitiligo
**vito** *m* lively Andalusian dance
**vitola** *f* calipers for bullets; cigar band; measure of size of cigars; mien, appearance
**vítor** *m* triumphal pageant; panegyric tablet; *interj* hurray!; long live!
**vitorear** *va* to cheer, to acclaim, to applaud
**vitoriano -na** *adj* (pertaining to) Vitoria; *mf* native or inhabitant of Vitoria
**vitral** *m* stained-glass window
**vitre** *m* light hempen canvas; light canvas
**vítreo -a** *adj* vitreous; glassy
**vitrificable** *adj* vitrifiable
**vitrificación** *f* vitrification
**vitrificar** §86 *va & vr* to vitrify
**vitrina** *f* showcase; display cabinet; glass case; (Am.) shopwindow
**vitriolar** *va* to vitriolize (*to throw vitriol at, to injure with vitriol*)
**vitriólico -ca** *adj* (chem.) vitriolic
**vitriolizar** §76 *va* to vitriolize (*to treat or mix with vitriol*)
**vitriolo** *m* vitriol; **vitriolo azul** blue vitriol; **vitriolo blanco** white vitriol; **vitriolo de plomo** lead sulphate
**vitualla** *f* victuals, provisions, food, abundance of food, abundance of vegetables
**vituallar** *va* to provide with food, to provision
**vituperable** *adj* vituperable
**vituperación** *f* vituperation
**vituperador -dora** *adj* vituperating; *mf* vituperator
**vituperar** *va* to vituperate
**vituperio** *m* vituperation
**vituperioso -sa** or **vituperoso -sa** *adj* vituperative
**viuda** *f* see **viudo**
**viudal** *adj* (pertaining to a) widower, widow; widower's, widow's
**viudedad** *f* widow's pension, dower
**viudez** *f* widowhood; widowerhood
**viudo -da** *adj* widowed; *m* widower; *f* widow; (bot.) mourning bride, mourning widow, sweet scabious; (orn.) whidah bird; **viuda de pecho rojo** (orn.) paradise whidah bird, paradise weaver; **viuda de marido vivo** or **viuda de paja** grass widow
**viva** *m* viva; *interj* viva!, long live!
**vivac** *m* (*pl:* **vivaques**) var. of **vivaque**
**vivacidad** *f* vigor; keenness; brightness, brilliancy
**vivandero -ra** *mf* (mil.) sutler; *f* vivandière
**vivaque** *m* bivouac; guardhouse; (Am.) police headquarters
**vivaquear** *vn* to bivouac
**vivar** *m* warren, burrow; aquarium; **vivar de garzas** heronry; *va* (Am.) to cheer, acclaim, hurrah
**vivaracho -cha** *adj* (coll.) vivacious, lively, frisky
**vivario** *m* vivarium

**vivaz** *adj* (*pl:* **-vaces**) long-lived; active, vigorous; vivacious; keen, perceptive; (bot.) perennial
**vivencia** *f* (philos.) experience
**vivera** *f* var. of **vivar**
**viveral** *m* tree nursery
**víveres** *mpl* food, victuals, provisions
**vivero** *m* tree nursery; fishpond; (fig.) hotbed
**viveza** *f* quickness, agility, briskness; ardor, vehemence; keenness, perception; brightness, brilliancy; witticism; sparkle (*in the eyes*); thoughtlessness (*in word or deed*)
**Viviana** *f* Vivian
**vividero -ra** *adj* habitable, livable
**vivido -da** *adj* based on life or experience (*said of writing*)
**vívido -da** *adj* lively; vivid
**vividor -dora** *adj* living; long-lived; thrifty; (coll.) opportunistic; *mf* liver; thrifty person; (coll.) opportunist; (slang) thief, crook; *m* sponger, hanger-on
**vivienda** *f* dwelling; housing; life, way of living; **vivienda remolque** trailer
**viviente** *adj* living
**vivificación** *f* vivification
**vivificador -dora** *adj* vivifying, life-giving
**vivificar §86** *va* to vivify, to enliven
**vivífico -ca** *adj* full of life; springing from life
**vivíparo -ra** *adj* viviparous
**vivir** *m* life; living; *va* to live (*an experience or adventure*); to live out (*e.g., one's life, one's old age*); to live in; *vn* to live; **¿quién vive?** (mil.) who goes there?; **¡viva!** viva!, long live!; **vivir de** to live on (*e.g., bread*); **vivir para ver** to live and learn; **vivir y dejar vivir** to live and let live
**vivisección** *f* vivisection
**viviseccionista** *mf* vivisectionist
**vivisector** *m* vivisector
**vivisectorio** *m* vivisectorium
**vivismo** *m* philosophy of Luis Vives
**vivo -va** *adj* alive, living; live; active, effective, in effect; vivid; intense, bright; sharp; acute, keen, deep; ingenious; expressive; quick; raw (*flesh*); modern, living (*language*); **a lo vivo** or **al vivo** vividly; effectively; **dar en lo vivo** to touch to the quick; **de viva voz** viva voce, by word of mouth; **herir en lo vivo** to cut or hurt to the quick; *mf* living person; (coll.) clever person, shrewd person; **los vivos** the living, the quick; **los vivos y los muertos** the quick and the dead; *m* edging, border; rib, corded seam; (arch.) sharp edge; (vet.) mange
**vizcacha** *f* (zool.) vizcacha or viscacha (*large South American rodent*)
**vizcainada** *f* Biscayanism; solecism
**vizcaíno -na** *adj & mf* Biscayan; *m* Biscayan (*language*)
**Vizcaya** *f* Biscay (*province of northern Spain*); **llevar hierro a Vizcaya** to carry coals to Newcastle
**vizcondado** *m* viscountcy, viscountship, or viscounty
**vizconde** *m* viscount; **vizcondes** *mpl* viscount and viscountess
**vizcondesa** *f* viscountess
**V.M.** abr. of **Vuestra Majestad**
**V.ºB.º** abr. of **visto bueno**
**vocablista** *mf* punster
**vocablo** *m* word, term; **jugar del vocablo** to pun
**vocabulario** *m* vocabulary
**vocabulista** *mf* vocabulist, lexicographer
**vocación** *f* vocation; name given to a church, chapel, or altar in dedication to the Virgin or a saint; (theol.) vocation
**vocacional** *adj* vocational
**vocal** *adj* vocal; *mf* voter, director; *f* vowel; **vocal abierta** open vowel; **vocal breve** short vowel; **vocal cerrada** close vowel; **vocal débil** weak vowel; **vocal fuerte** strong vowel; **vocal larga** long vowel; **vocal nasal** nasal vowel; **vocal posterior** back vowel
**vocálico -ca** *adj* vocalic, vowel
**vocalismo** *m* (phonet.) vocalism
**vocalista** *mf* vocalist, singer (*e.g., in a night club*)
**vocalización** *f* (mus. & phonet.) vocalization
**vocalizar §76** *va* (phonet.) to vocalize; *vn* (mus.) to vocalize; *vr* (phonet.) to vocalize
**vocativo -va** *adj & m* vocative
**voceador -dora** *adj* vociferating; *mf* vociferator; *m* town crier; (Am.) paper boy
**vocear** *va* to cry, shout, proclaim; to cheer, hail, acclaim; (coll.) to boast publicly about; *vn* to cry out, to shout
**vocejón** *m* harsh, rough voice
**vocería** *f* shouting, uproar; spokesmanship
**vocerío** *m* shouting, uproar
**vocero** *m* spokesman, mouthpiece
**vociferación** *f* vociferation
**vociferador -dora** *adj* vociferous; *mf* vociferator; barker
**vociferante** *adj & mf* vociferant
**vociferar** *va* to shout or vociferate (*e.g., insults*); to announce boastfully; *vn* to shout, to vociferate
**vocingleo** *m* or **vocinglería** *f* shouting, uproar, shrieking
**vocinglero -ra** *adj* loudmouthed; loquacious, chattering; *mf* loudmouthed person; chatterer
**vodca** *m* or **vodka** *m* vodka
**vodevil** *m* light comedy
**vodú** *m* (*pl:* **-dúes**) voodoo
**voduísmo** *m* voodooism
**voduísta** *adj* voodoo, voodooistic; *mf* voodooist
**vol.** abr. of **volumen** & **voluntad**
**volada** *f* see **volado**
**voladero -ra** *adj* flying; fleeting; floating; *m* precipice; *f* float (*of water wheel*)
**voladizo -za** *adj* projecting; *m* projection
**volado -da** *adj* (print.) superior (*letter*); **volado de genio** (Am.) quick-tempered; *m* meringue; *f* short flight; (Am.) trick; (Am.) happening
**volador -dora** *adj* flying; swinging, hanging; running, swift; *m* rocket; flying fish; (ichth.) flying gurnard
**voladura** *f* flying through the air; explosion, blast
**volandas; en volandas** in the air, flying in the air; (coll.) swiftly
**volandero -ra** *adj* ready to fly, starting to fly; hanging, swinging; accidental, unforeseen; incidental; ephemeral; unsettled; wandering; *f* (mach.) washer; grindstone; (print.) galley slice; (coll.) fib, lie
**volandillas; en volandillas** var. of **en volandas**
**volante** *adj* flying; volant; unsettled; (her.) volant; *m* shuttlecock; battledore and shuttlecock; flywheel; steering wheel; balance wheel; coining press; lackey, flunkey; outrider; folded sheet of paper, bill, note; slip (*of paper*); (sew.) ruffle; **en el volante** at the wheel (*of an auto*); **un buen volante** a good driver (*of an auto*); **volante compensador** (horol.) compensating balance; **volante de dirección** (aut.) steering wheel; **volante de reloj** (horol.) balance wheel
**volantín -tina** *adj* unsettled; *m* fish line; (Am.) kite
**volantista** *m* (coll.) man at the wheel, driver
**volantón -tona** *adj* ready to fly, starting to fly; *mf* fledgling
**volapié** *m* (taur.) suerte in which the matador moves in on the standing bull instead of awaiting the bull's charge; **a volapíe** half running, half flying; half walking, half swimming
**volar §77** *va* to fly (*to transport in an aircraft*); to blow up, to explode; to rouse (*game*); to exasperate; to blow, to fan; (print.) to raise (*a letter, number, etc.*) to the top of the line; *vn* to fly; to flutter; to fly away; to disappear rapidly; to project, to jut out; to spread rapidly (*said, e.g., of news*); to rise in the air (*said, e.g., of a steeple*); (Am.) to bluff (*in poker*); **volar a** + *inf* to fly to + *inf*; **volar sin motor** (aer.) to glide; *vr* to fly, to fly away
**volateo** *m* shooting at a flying target; **al volateo** on the wing
**volatería** *f* birdhunting with decoys; birds; random thoughts; shot in the dark; **de volatería** at random, in the dark
**volatero -ra** *adj* fickle, inconstant
**volátil** *adj* volatile
**volatilidad** *f* volatility

**volatilización** *f* volatilization
**volatilizar §76** *va* to volatilize; *vr* to volatilize; (coll.) to fade away, to disappear (*said, e.g., of money*)
**volatín** *m* ropewalker; feat of ropewalker
**volatinero -ra** *mf* ropewalker
**volatizar §76** *va* var. of **volatilizar**
**volcadero** *m* tipple
**volcán** *m* volcano; (fig.) volcano; **estar sobre un volcán** (fig.) to be on the edge of a volcano
**volcanera** *f* (orn.) wood pigeon (*Columba fasciata*)
**volcánico -ca** *adj* volcanic
**volcanismo** *m* volcanism
**volcar §95** *va* to upset, to dump; to overturn; to tip, to tilt; to make dizzy or giddy (*said of a strong odor*); to make (*a person*) change his mind; to tease, to irritate; *vn* to upset; *vr* to turn upside down; **volcarse en** to fall all over oneself in (*e.g., praises*)
**volea** *f* whippletree; (tennis) volley
**volear** *va* to volley (*a ball*); to sow (*grain*) by throwing it in the air with the hand
**voleo** *m* (tennis) volley; reeling punch or blow; **al voleo** throwing the grain in the air with the hand; **del primer voleo** or **de un voleo** (coll.) quickly, at one blow
**volframio** *m* (chem.) wolfram
**volframita** *f* (mineral.) wolframite, wolfram
**volibol** *m* volleyball
**volición** *f* volition
**volitar** *vn* to flutter
**volitivo -va** *adj* volitive, volitional
**volquear** *vr* to tumble, to roll over
**volquete** *m* dumpcart, tipcart; dump truck; dumping device
**volsco -ca** *adj & mf* Volscian
**voltaico -ca** *adj* voltaic
**voltaje** *m* (elec.) voltage
**voltámetro** *m* (phys.) voltameter
**voltamperímetro** *m* (phys.) voltammeter
**voltamperio** *m* (elec.) volt-ampere
**voltariedad** *f* fickleness, inconstancy
**voltario -ria** *adj* fickle, inconstant
**volteador -dora** *adj* tumbling; *mf* tumbler, acrobat
**voltear** *va* to upset, to roll over; to turn around; to move, transform; to build (*an arch or vaulting*); *vn* to roll over, to tumble
**voltejear** *va* to turn around; *vn* (naut.) to tack; (naut.) to maneuver
**volteo** *m* upset, rolling over; reversal; tumbling; (Am.) passage, journey; (Am.) scolding, dressing-down
**voltereta** *f* tumble, somersault; turning up card to determine trump
**volterianismo** *m* Voltairism or Voltairianism
**volteriano -na** *adj & mf* Voltairian
**volteta** *f* var. of **voltereta**
**voltímetro** *m* (elec.) voltmeter
**voltio** *m* (elec.) volt
**voltizo -za** *adj* twisted, curled; fickle, inconstant
**volubilidad** *f* volubility; fickleness, inconstancy
**voluble** *adj* voluble (*turning easily*); fickle, inconstant; (bot.) voluble, twining
**volumen** *m* volume (*book; bulk; mass, e.g., of water*); (geom.) volume; **a todo volumen** (rad.) full volume; **volumen sonoro** volume
**volumétrico -ca** *adj* volumetric
**volúmetro** *m* volumeter
**voluminoso -sa** *adj* voluminous; heavy, huge; bulky
**voluntad** *f* will; love, fondness; **a voluntad** at will; **de buena voluntad** willingly; **de mala voluntad** unwillingly; **ganarse la voluntad de** to win the favor of; **última voluntad** last wish; (law) last will and testament; **voluntad de hierro** iron will; **voluntad de poder** (philos.) will to power
**voluntariado** *m* (mil.) volunteering
**voluntariedad** *f* willfulness, self-will
**voluntario -ria** *adj* voluntary, willful; *mf* volunteer
**voluntarioso -sa** *adj* willful, self-willed; determined
**voluntarismo** *m* (philos.) voluntarism
**voluptuosidad** *f* voluptuousness
**voluptuoso -sa** *adj* voluptuous; voluptuary; *mf* voluptuary
**voluta** *f* (arch.) scroll, volute; (fig.) volute; (zool.) volute (*any of Volutidae*)
**volva** *f* (bot.) volva
**volvedor -dora** *adj* (Am.) that runs away to get back home (*said of a horse*); *m* screw driver; **volvedor de machos** tap wrench
**volver §63 & §17,** 9 *va* to turn; to turn over; to turn upside down; to turn inside out; to return, to give back, to send back; to close; to push or pull (*e.g., a door*) to; to change, transform; to make (*a person*) change his mind; to translate; to vomit; to reflect (*sound*); to plow a second time; to give (*change*) ‖ *vn* to turn; to return, come back; **volver a** + *inf* verb + again, e.g., **volvió a leer ese libro** he read that book again; **volver en sí** to come to; **volver por** to defend, to stand up for; **volver sobre** to go back on (*e.g., one's footsteps, a decision*); **volver sobre sí** to recover one's calm; to take stock of oneself or one's conduct; to recover from a loss ‖ *vr* to become; to turn, to turn sour; to return, come back; to change one's mind; **volverse atrás** to back out, to not keep one's word; **volverse contra** to turn on
**volvible** *adj* turnable, reversible
**volvo** or **vólvulo** *m* (path.) volvulus
**vómer** *m* (anat.) vomer, plowshare bone
**vomicina** *f* (chem.) vomicine
**vómico -ca** *adj* vomitive
**vomitado -da** *adj* (coll.) thin, sickly, pale
**vomitador -dora** *adj* vomiting; *mf* person who vomits
**vomitar** *va* to vomit, throw up; to belch forth; to utter (*insults, curses, etc.*); to let out (*e.g., a secret*); (coll.) to disgorge, to cough up (*something unjustly held back or stolen*); *vn* to vomit; (coll.) to disgorge
**vomitivo -va** *adj & m* vomitive
**vómito** *m* vomit, vomiting; **vómito negro** (path.) black vomit; **vómitos del embarazo** morning sickness
**vomitón -tona** *adj* vomiting (*said of a suckling child*); *f* (coll.) violent vomiting
**voquible** *m* (coll.) word
**voracidad** *f* voracity
**vorágine** *f* whirlpool, vortex
**voraz** *adj* (*pl:* **-races**) voracious; fierce, destructive
**vormela** *f* (zool.) polecat (*Putorius sarmaticus*)
**vórtice** *m* vortex; center of a cyclone
**vorticela** *f* (zool.) vorticella
**vos** *pron pers* (used as subject of verb and as object of preposition in addressing God, the Virgin Mary, a saint, or a person of high position or authority; takes plural form of verb but is singular in meaning; in popular speech in much of Spanish America is used instead of **tú**) you
**vosear** *va* to use **vos** in speaking to
**voseo** *m* use of **vos,** use of **vos** for **tú**
**Vosgos** *mpl* Vosges
**vosotros -tras** *pron pers* (used as subject of verb and object of preposition in addressing several persons each of whom would be addressed with **tú** and in the formal language of public speech, diplomatic correspondence, etc.) you
**votación** *f* voting; (total) vote; **por votación** by choice; **por votación oral** by viva-voce vote; **votación de confianza** vote of confidence; **votación por manos levantadas** show of hands
**votador -dora** *adj* voting; *mf* voter; swearer
**votante** *adj* voting; *mf* voter
**votar** *va* to vow; to vote, to vote for, to vote on; **¡voto a tal!** confound it!; goodness!; upon my soul!; *vn* to vow; to vote; to swear; *vr* to vow
**votivo -va** *adj* votive
**voto** *m* vow; curse; votive offering; vote; **votos** *mpl* wishes, good wishes; **echar votos** to swear, to curse; **hacer votos** to wish, to hope; **regular los votos** to tally the votes; **ser** or **tener voto** to have a vote; to know what one is talking about; **voto activo** right to vote; **voto de amén** or **de reata** (coll.) vote of a yes man; (coll.) yes man; **voto de calidad**

casting vote (*in case of a tie*); **voto de confianza** vote of confidence; **voto femenino** woman suffrage; **voto informativo** straw vote; **voto pasivo** eligibility; **voto secreto** secret ballot

**voy** *1st sg pres ind of* **ir**

**voz** *f* (*pl:* **voces**) voice; word; (gram. & mus.) voice; **voces** *fpl* outcry; **aclarar la voz** to clear one's throat; **alzar la voz** to raise one's voice, to lift up one's voice; **a media voz** in a low tone; with a gentle hint; **a una voz** with one voice; **a voces** shouting; **a voz en cuello** or **a voz en grito** at the top of one's voice; **correr la voz que** to be rumored that; **dar voces** to shout, to cry out; **de viva voz** viva voce, by word of mouth; **en alta voz** aloud; **en voz** verbally; (mus.) in voice; **en voz baja** in a low tone; **estar a la voz** (naut.) to be within hail, to be within hailing distance; **llevar la voz cantante** (coll.) to have the say, to be the boss; **tomar la voz** to take up the discussion; **voz activa** right to vote; (gram.) active voice; **voz de acarreo** (philol.) borrowing, loan word; **voz pasiva** eligibility; (gram.) passive voice

**vozarrón** *m* (coll.) harsh, loud voice

**voznar** *vn* to cackle

**vro.** abr. of **vuestro**

**V.S.** abr. of **Vueseñoría**

**v.[to]** abr. of **vuelto**

**vudú** *m* (*pl:* **-dúes**) var. of **vodú**

**vuduísmo** *m* var. of **voduísmo**

**vuduísta** *adj & mf* var. of **voduísta**

**vuecelencia** or **vuecencia** contraction of **vuestra excelencia** your Excellency

**vuelco** *m* upset, overturning; **dar un vuelco** to upset, to turn over; **darle a uno un vuelco el corazón** (coll.) to have a presentiment or misgiving

**vuelillo** *m* lace cuff trimming

**vuelo** *m* flight; flying; wing; spread, fullness, flare; projection; lace cuff trimming; woodland; **al vuelo** at once, in a jiffy; on the wing; scattered at random; (chess) en passant; **alzar el vuelo** to take flight; (coll.) to dash off, to leave in a hurry; **cortarle los vuelos a uno** to cut someone's wings; **de un vuelo** in a flash; in a single flight, without letup; **echar a vuelo las campanas** to ring a full peal; **en un vuelo** in a flash; in a single flight, without letup; **levantar el vuelo** to take flight; to become imaginative; to be proud, haughty; **tirar al vuelo** to shoot on the wing; **tocar al vuelo las campanas** to ring a full peal; **tomar vuelo** to progress, to grow; **vuelo a ciegas** or **vuelo ciego** (aer.) blind flying; **vuelo de distancia** (aer.) long-distance flight; **vuelo de ensayo** or **de prueba** (aer.) test flight; **vuelo espacial** space flight; **vuelo planeado** (aer.) volplane; **vuelo por instrumentos** (aer.) instrument flying; **vuelo rasante** (aer.) hedgehopping; **vuelo sin escala** (aer.) nonstop flight; **vuela sin motor** (aer.) glide, gliding; **vuelo sin parar** (aer.) nonstop flight

**vuelto -ta** *pp of* **volver;** *m* (print.) verso; (Am.) change (*money*); *f* turn, rotation, revolution; change; harshness; return; change (*money*); clock (*in stocking*); reverse, other side; repetition; burden (*of song*); beating, whipping; ploughing; cuff; cuff trimming; (arch.) interior curve; turning up a card; **a la vuelta** on returning; on the other side of the page, please turn page; **a la vuelta de** at the end of, after; at the turn of; around (*e.g., the corner*); **andar a vueltas con** to clash with; **a vuelta de** about; **a vuelta de correo** by return mail; **a vueltas de** in addition to; **dar cien vueltas a** to get far ahead of, to run rings around; **dar la vuelta** to upset; **dar la vuelta de campana** to turn somersault; **darse una vuelta a la redonda** (coll.) to tend to one's own business; **dar una vuelta** to take a stroll or walk; to make a short trip; to go and take a look; to change one's ways; **dar vuelta** to turn sour (*said of wine*); **dar vuelta a** to reverse, to turn around; **dar vueltas** to circle; to look in vain; to travel around; to keep going over the same subject; to swim, to whirl, to be dizzy; **de vuelta** on returning; **estar de vuelta** to be back; **no hay que darle vueltas** there's no use talking about it; **no tener vuelta de hoja** to be undeniable; **ponerle a uno de vuelta y media** to insult a person; **quedarse con la vuelta** to keep the change; **vuelta de braza** (naut.) timber hitch; **vuelta de cabo** (naut.) hitch; **vuelta de campana** somersault; **vuelta del mundo** trip around the world; **vuelta doble** double turn (*of lock*)

**vueludo -da** *adj* full (*said of a garment*)

**vuesarced** contraction of **vuestra merced** your Grace, your Honor

**vueseñoría** contraction of **vuestra señoría** your Lordship, your Ladyship

**vuestro -tra** (corresponds to **vos** and **vosotros**) *adj poss* your; *pron poss* yours

**vulcanio -nia** *adj* Vulcanian; vulcanian

**vulcanismo** *m* vulcanism

**vulcanista** *mf* vulcanist

**vulcanita** *f* vulcanite

**vulcanización** *f* vulcanization

**vulcanizador** *m* vulcanizer

**vulcanizar §76** *va* to vulcanize

**Vulcano** *m* (myth.) Vulcan

**vulcanología** *f* volcanology

**vulgacho** *m* mob, rabble, populace

**vulgar** *adj* vulgar; vernacular; common, ordinary; popular

**vulgaridad** *f* vulgarity, commonness; commonplace

**vulgarismo** *m* vulgarism (*in language*); (philol.) popular word, popular form

**vulgarización** *f* vulgarization; popularization

**vulgarizador -dora** *adj* vulgarizing; *mf* vulgarizer; popularizer

**vulgarizar §76** *va* to vulgarize; to popularize; to translate into the vernacular; *vr* to become common; to associate with common people, to grow vulgar

**Vulgata** *f* Vulgate

**vulgo** *m* common people; laity; *adv* vulgo, commonly

**vulnerabilidad** *f* vulnerability

**vulnerable** *adj* vulnerable

**vulneración** *f* damage to a reputation; breach (*e.g., of law*)

**vulnerar** *va* to harm, injure, damage (*e.g., a reputation*); to infringe on; to break (*a law*)

**vulnerario -ria** *adj & m* (med.) vulnerary

**vulpécula** or **vulpeja** *f* vixen, she-fox

**vulpinita** *f* (mineral.) vulpinite

**vulpino -na** *adj* vulpine; *m* (bot.) plume grass

**vultuoso -sa** *adj* bloated (*said of the face*)

**vulturno** *m* hot summer breeze

**vulva** *f* (anat.) vulva

**vulvar** *adj* vulvar

**vulvitis** *f* (path.) vulvitis

**V.V.** or **VV.** abr. of **ustedes**

**W, w** *f* called **doble v, v doble,** and **u valona** in Spanish, this letter does not belong to the Spanish alphabet
**wagneriano -na** *adj & mf* var. of **vagneriano**
**wagón** *m* var. of **vagón**
**wapití** *m* (*pl:* **-tíes**) var. of **uapití**
**wat** *m* (*pl:* **wats**) var. of **vatio**
**wáter** *m* (coll.) var. of **váter**
**water-closet** *m* (*pl:* **-sets**) toilet, water closet
**water-polista** *mf* water polo player
**water-polo** *m* (sport) var. of **polo acuático**
**wattman** *m* (*pl:* **-men**) motorman
**WC** *m* abr. of **water-closet**
**wesleyano -na** *adj & mf* Wesleyan
**Westfalia** *f* var. of **Vestfalia**
**Westfaliano -na** *adj & mf* var. of **Vestfaliano**
**whisky** *m* whiskey or whisky
**wolfram** *m* var. of **volframio**
**wulfenita** *f* (mineral.) wulfenite

# X

**X, x** *f* twenty-sixth letter of the Spanish alphabet
**xantalina** *f* (chem.) xanthaline
**xantato** *m* (chem.) xanthate
**xanteína** *f* (chem.) xanthein
**xanteno** *m* (chem.) xanthene
**xantina** *f* (chem.) xanthin; (biochem.) xanthine
**Xantipa** *f* var. of **Jantipa**
**xantocroide** *adj & mf* (anthrop.) xanthochroid
**xantodermo -ma** *mf* (anthrop.) xanthoderm
**xantofila** *f* (biochem.) xanthophyll
**xantógeno** *m* (chem.) xanthogen
**xantoma** *m* (path.) xanthoma
**xantopsia** *f* (path.) xanthopsia
**xantopsina** *f* xanthopsin
**xantosis** *f* (path.) xanthosis
**xantoxilina** *f* (chem. & pharm.) xanthoxylin
**xenia** *f* (bot.) xenia
**xeno** *m* (chem.) xenon
**xenofobia** *f* xenophobia, dislike of foreigners
**xenófobo -ba** *mf* xenophobe
**xenogénesis** *f* (biol.) xenogenesis
**xenón** *m* var. of **xeno**
**xerófito -ta** *adj* (bot.) xerophytic; *f* (bot.) xerophyte
**xeroftalmía** *f* (path.) xerophthalmia
**xifisternón** *m* (anat.) xiphisternum
**xifoides** *adj & m* (anat.) xiphoid
**xifosuro** *m* var. of **jifosuro**
**xilán** *m* (chem.) xylan
**xilema** *m* (bot.) xylem
**xileno** *m* (chem.) xylene
**xilidina** *f* (chem.) xylidine
**xilobálsamo** *m* xylobalsamum
**xilófago -ga** *adj* xylophagous
**xilófono** *m* (mus.) xylophone
**xilografía** *f* xylography (*art*); xylograph (*engraving*)
**xilográfico -ca** *adj* xylographic or xylographical
**xilógrafo -fa** *mf* xylographer
**xilol** *m* (chem.) xylol
**xilosa** *f* (chem.) xylose
**xister** *m* (surg.) xyster
**x.mo** abr. of **diezmo**
**xpiano** abr. of **cristiano**
**Xpo** abr. of **Cristo**
**xptiano** abr. of **cristiano**
**Xpto** abr. of **Cristo**
**Xptóbal** abr. of **Cristóbal**
**xucul** *m* (bot.) purslane (*of Mexico*)
**xunde** *m* (Am.) basket made of reed or palm

**Y, y** *f* twenty-seventh letter of the Spanish alphabet
**y** *conj* and
**ya** *adv* already; now; finally; at once, right away; **no ya** not only; **no . . . ya** no longer; **¡pues ya!** of course!; **ya no** no longer; **ya que** since, inasmuch as; **ya . . . ya** now . . . again, whether . . . or
**yaba** *f* (bot.) cabbage tree
**yac** *m* yak (*Tibetan ox*); (naut.) jack (*flag*)
**yacedor** *m* herdboy who drives horses out for night grazing
**yacente** *adj* recumbent, jacent; located; *m* (min.) floor of a vein
**yacer** §96 *vn* to lie; to rest, lie buried; to graze by night; **yacer con** (coll.) to lie with (*to have sexual intercourse with*)
**yacija** *f* bed, couch; grave, tomb; **ser de mala yacija** to be restless; to sleep poorly; to be a vagrant
**yacimiento** *m* bed, deposit, field
**yago** *1st sg pres ind of* **yacer**
**yagua** *f* (bot.) yagua (*palm tree: Roystonea borinqueana; broad flat stem of its leaf*)
**yaguar** *m* var. of **jaguar**
**yámbico -ca** *adj* iambic
**yambo** *m* iamb, iambus, iambic
**yanacona** *m* (Am.) serf; (Am.) sharecropper
**yanqui** *adj & mf* Yankee, American
**Yanquilandia** *f* Yankeedom
**yanquismo** *m* Yankeeism
**yantar** *m* food; *va & vn* (archaic) to eat
**yapa** *f* (Am.) lagniappe, bonus, extra, allowance; (min.) mercury added to silver ore; **de yapa** (Am.) extra, in the bargain
**yarda** *f* yard; yardstick
**yardaje** *m* yardage
**yaro** *m* (bot.) arum
**yatagán** *m* yataghan
**yate** *m* yacht
**yazco** or **yazgo** *1st sg pres ind of* **yacer**
**ye** *f* letter Y
**yedra** *f* var. of **hiedra**
**yegua** *f* mare; (Am.) cigar butt
**yeguada** *f* stud (*collection of horses; place for breeding*)
**yeguar** *adj* (pertaining to a) mare
**yegüería** *f* var. of **yeguada**
**yegüerizo -za** *adj* (pertaining to a) mare; *m* keeper of mares
**yegüero** *m* keeper of mares
**yeísmo** *m* pronunciation of Spanish **ll** like **y**
**yelmo** *m* (arm.) helmet
**yema** *f* yolk (*of egg*); candied yolk; (anat., bot. & zool.) bud; dead (*e.g., of winter*); (fig.) cream; **dar en la yema** (coll.) to hit the nail on the head; **yema del dedo** finger tip; **yema mejida** eggnog
**yemenita** *adj & mf* Yemenite
**yendo** *ger of* **ir**
**yente** *adj* going; **yentes y vinientes** frequenters, habitués
**yeral** *m* lentil field
**yerba** *f* var. of **hierba**
**yerbajo** *m* weed
**yermar** *va* to strip, lay waste, leave deserted
**yermo -ma** *adj* deserted, uninhabited, uncultivated; *m* desert, wilderness; waste land
**yerno** *m* son-in-law
**yero** *m* (bot.) tare, lentil, bitter vetch (*Ervum ervilia*)
**yerro** *m* error, mistake; **yerro de imprenta** typographical error
**yerto -ta** *adj* stiff, rigid
**yervo** *m* var. of **yero**
**yesal** *m* or **yesar** *m* gypsum pit or quarry
**yesca** *f* punk, touchwood, tinder; fuel (*for passion*); **yescas** *fpl* tinderbox
**yesería** *f* gypsum kiln; plasterer's shop; plastering
**yesero -ra** *adj* (pertaining to) gypsum; *mf* gypsum maker or dealer; plasterer
**yeso** *m* gypsum; chalk; plaster; plaster cast; **yeso blanco** finishing plaster; **yeso de París** plaster of Paris; **yeso negro** rough plaster
**yesón** *m* chunk of plaster
**yesoso -sa** *adj* gypseous; chalky
**yesquero** *m* tinder maker or dealer; tinderbox
**yeyuno** *m* (anat.) jejunum
**yezgo** *m* (bot.) danewort, dwarf elder
**yo** *pron pers* I: **soy yo** it is I; *m* ego; (philos.) I, ego
**Yocasta** *f* (myth.) Jocasta
**yod** *f* (philol.) yod
**yodado -da** *adj* iodized; sea-soaked, sea-burned
**yodato** *m* (chem.) iodate
**yodhídrico -ca** *adj* (chem.) hydriodic
**yódico -ca** *adj* (chem.) iodic
**yodismo** *m* (path.) iodism
**yodo** *m* (chem.) iodine
**yodoformo** *m* (chem.) iodoform
**yodoso -sa** *adj* (chem.) iodous
**yoduro** *m* (chem.) iodide
**yoga** *m* yoga
**yogui** *m* yogi
**yogurt** *m* yogurt
**yola** *f* (sport) shell; (sport) sailboat; (naut.) gig
**yubarta** *f* (zool.) finback
**yuca** *f* (bot.) yucca; **yuca brava** (bot.) bitter cassava; **yuca dulce** (bot.) sweet cassava
**Yucatán, el** Yucatan
**yucateco -ca** *adj* (pertaining to) Yucatan; *mf* native or inhabitant of Yucatan
**yugada** *f* day's plowing of a yoke of oxen; yoke of oxen; yoke of land
**yugo** *m* yoke; burden; marriage tie; (naut.) transom; **sacudir el yugo** to throw off the yoke; **sujetarse al yugo de** to bend under the yoke of, to yield to the ascendancy of
**Yugoeslavia** *f* Yugoslavia
**yugoeslavo -va** *adj* Yugoslav, Yugoslavic; *mf* Yugoslav
**Yugoslavia** *f* Yugoslavia
**yugoslavo -va** *adj & mf* var. of **yugoeslavo**
**yuguero** *m* plowboy, plowman
**yugular** *adj & f* (anat.) jugular; *va* to cut off, to throttle (*a disease, an epidemic*)
**Yugurta** *m* Jugurtha
**yunque** *m* anvil; (anat.) anvil, incus; long-suffering person; drudge; **estar al yunque** to be long-suffering
**yunta** *f* see **yunto**
**yuntero** *m* plowboy, plowman
**yunto -ta** *adj* close (*said of furrows*); *f* yoke (*of animals*); **yunto** *adv* close; **arar yunto** to plow close
**yusera** *f* horizontal stone base in olive-oil mill
**yusión** *f* (law) precept; (law) jussion, command
**yusivo -va** *adj* (gram.) jussive
**yute** *m* (bot.) jute (*plant, fiber, and fabric*)
**Yuturna** *f* (myth.) Juturna
**yuxtalineal** *adj* in parallel columns (*said of a translation and its original*)
**yuxtapondré** *1st sg fut ind of* **yuxtaponer**
**yuxtaponer** §69 *va* to juxtapose; *vr* to become juxtaposed
**yuxtapongo** *1st sg pres ind of* **yuxtaponer**
**yuxtaposición** *f* juxtaposition
**yuxtapuesto -ta** *pp of* **yuxtaponer**
**yuxtapuse** *1st sg pret ind of* **yuxtaponer**
**yuyo** *m* (Am.) weed; (Am.) blister between toes; **yuyos** *mpl* (Am.) greens
**yuyuba** *f* jujube

# Z

**Z, z** *f* twenty-eighth letter of the Spanish alphabet
**za** *interj* begone!, get out of here! *(said to a dog)*
**zabarcera** *f* greengrocer, dealer in fresh fruits and vegetables *(woman)*
**zabida** or **zabila** *f* (bot.) aloe
**zaborda** *f* or **zabordamiento** *m* (naut.) running aground
**zabordar** *vn* (naut.) to run aground
**zabordo** *m* var. of **zaborda**
**zaborro** *m* fat fellow, fatty
**zabucar** §86 *va* to stir by shaking
**zabullida** *f* var. of **zambullida**
**zabullidor -dora** *adj & mf* var. of **zambullidor**
**zabullidura** *f* or **zabullimiento** *m* var. of **zambullidura**
**zabullir** § 26 *va & vr* var. of **zambullir**
**zabuqueo** *m* stirring, shaking
**zaca** *f* (min.) leather bag used for bailing
**zacapela** or **zacapella** *f* shindy, row, rumpus
**Zacarías** *m* (Bib.) Zechariah; (Bib.) Zachariah
**zacate** *m* (Am.) hay, fodder; (Am.) grass; **zacate corredor** (bot.) hyssop loosestrife; **zacate de empaque** (Am.) excelsior
**zacategordura** *f* (bot.) molasses grass
**zacatín** *m* old-clothes market
**zacear** *va* to chase away (*e.g., a dog*); *vn* to lisp
**zadorija** *f* (bot.) large-flowered hypecoum
**zafa** *f* see **zafo**
**zafado -da** *adj* (Am.) alert, wide-awake; (Am.) brazen; *f* loosening, untying; freezing; lightening a ship
**zafar** *va* to adorn, bedeck; to loosen, untie; to free, to clear; to lighten *(a vessel)*; *vr* to slip away, hide away; to slip off, come off *(said of a belt)*; **zafarse de** to get out of, to dodge
**zafariche** *m* shelf for water jugs
**zafarrancho** *m* (naut.) clearing for action; clearing out, forcible evacuation; (coll.) ravage, destruction; (coll.) row, scuffle; **zafarrancho de combate** (naut.) clearing for battle
**zafiedad** *f* roughness, coarseness, crudeness, uncouthness
**zafio -fia** *adj* rough, coarse, crude, uncouth
**zafir** *m* var. of **zafiro**
**zafíreo -a** *adj* sapphire *(in color)*
**zafirino -na** *adj* sapphire *(in color)*; *f* (mineral.) sapphirine
**zafiro** *m* sapphire
**zafo -fa** *adj* intact, unhurt; (naut.) free, clear; *f* basin, bowl
**zafones** *mpl* var. of **zahones**
**zafra** *f* drip jar; oil can; ridgeband; sugar crop; sugar making; sugar-making season; (min.) rubbish, muck
**zafre** *m* (mineral.) zaffer
**zafrero** *m* (min.) mucker
**zaga** *f* rear; load carried in the rear; **a la zaga, a zaga** or **en zaga** behind; **no ir en zaga a** (coll.) to keep up with, be as good as
**zagal** *m* youth; strapping young fellow; shepherd's helper; footboy; skirt
**zagala** *f* lass, maiden; shepherdess
**zagaleja** *f* lassie
**zagalejo** *m* lad; peasant's skirt
**zagalón -lona** *mf* big youngster
**zagual** *m* paddle
**zaguán** *m* vestibule, entry
**zaguanete** *m* small vestibule; royal guard, royal escort
**zaguero -ra** *adj* rear, hind; **no quedar zaguero de** to not be behind, to keep up with; *m* backstop; *(football)* back
**zahareño -ña** *adj* wild, unsociable, intractable; haggard *(falcon)*
**zaharrón** *m* clown
**zaheridor -dora** *adj* reproachful, faultfinding; *mf* faultfinder
**zaherimiento** *m* reproach; calling down
**zaherir** §62 *va* to reproach, find fault with; to call down; to pique, to provoke
**zahína** *f* (bot.) sorghum
**zahinar** *m* sorghum field
**zahonado -da** *adj* of a different color in the front *(said of the feet of an animal)*
**zahondar** *va* to dig; *vn* to sink, sink down *(in the ground)*
**zahones** *mpl* chaps *(cowboy trousers)*; hunting breeches
**zahora** *f* (dial.) party, feast
**zahorar** *vn* (dial.) to celebrate, to feast
**zahorí** *m* (*pl:* **-ríes**) diviner, clairvoyant; keen observer
**zahorra** *f* (naut.) ballast
**zahúrda** *f* pigpen; (fig.) pigpen
**zaida** *f* (orn.) demoiselle
**zaino -na** *adj* treacherous, false; dark-chestnut *(horse)*; black *(cattle)*; vicious *(horse)*; **a lo zaino** or **de zaino** sidewise, askance
**zalá** *f* (*pl:* **-laes**) Mohammedan prayer; **hacer la zalá a** (coll.) to fawn over, bow down to
**zalagarda** *f* ambush, ambuscade; skirmish; snare, trap; (coll.) trick; (coll.) surprise disturbance *(caused by a gang of roughnecks)*; mock fight
**zalama** *f*, **zalamelé** *m* or **zalamería** *f* flattery
**zalamero -ra** *adj* flattering; *mf* flatterer
**zalea** *f* unsheared sheepskin, pelt
**zalear** *va* to drag around, to shake; to chase away *(a dog)*
**zalema** *f* (coll.) salaam
**zaleo** *m* dragging, shaking; sheepskin left by fox and brought in by shepherd to account for loss of sheep
**zaloma** *f* (naut.) var. of **saloma**
**zalona** *f* large unglazed earthen jug
**zallar** *va* (naut.) to rig out, to run out
**zamacuco** *m* (coll.) dullard; (coll.) sullen fellow; (coll.) drunkenness
**zamanca** *f* (coll.) drubbing, beating
**zamarra** *f* undressed sheepskin; shepherd's undressed sheepskin jacket
**zamarrear** *va* to shake with the teeth; (coll.) to ill-treat, abuse, knock around; to pin down, pin to the wall
**zamarreo** *m* shaking with the teeth; (coll.) ill treatment, abuse
**zamarrico** *m* sheepskin bag
**zamarrilla** *f* (bot.) poly
**zamarro** *m* lambskin, sheepskin; shepherd's undressed sheepskin jacket; (coll.) boor, rustic; (coll.) sly fellow; **zamarros** *mpl* (Am.) chaps, riding breeches
**zambaigo -ga** *adj* half Negro half Indian; (Am.) half Indian half Chinese
**zambarco** *m* breast strap *(of harness)*; strap with buckle
**zambear** *vn* to be knock-kneed
**zámbigo -ga** *adj* knock-kneed
**zambo -ba** *adj* knock-kneed; *mf* (Am.) zambo; *m* (zool.) papion
**zamboa** *f* citron *(fruit)*
**zambomba** *f* (mus.) zambomba; *interj* whew!
**zambombazo** *m* beating, clubbing
**zambombo** *m* (coll.) boor, lubber, crude fellow
**zamborondón -dona, zamborotudo -da** or **zamborrotudo -da** *adj* (coll.) awkward, clumsy, ill-shaped; (coll.) bungling; *mf* (coll.) bungler, botcher
**zambra** *f* Moorish boat; (coll.) din, uproar; (archaic) Moorish celebration, Moorish hullabaloo

**zambucar** §86 *va* (coll.) to hide away, to slip away
**zambuco** *m* (coll.) quick hiding or concealment
**zambullida** *f* dive, plunge; thrust to the breast (*in fencing*)
**zambullidor -dora** *adj* diving, plunging; *mf* diver, plunger; *m* (orn.) diver; (orn.) dabchick (*Podilymbus podiceps*)
**zambullidura** *f* or **zambullimiento** *m* diving, plunging
**zambullir** §26 *va* to duck, give a ducking to; *vr* to dive, plunge, duck under; to hide
**zambullo** *m* big chamber pot
**Zamora** *f*; **no se ganó Zamora en una hora** Rome was not built in a day
**zampa** *f* pile, bearing pile
**zampabodigos** *mf* (*pl:* **-gos**) (coll.) var. of **zampatortas**
**zampabollos** *mf* (*pl:* **-llos**) (coll.) var. of **zampatortas**
**zampacuartillos** *mf* (*pl:* **-llos**) (coll.) soak, toper
**zampalimosnas** *mf* (*pl:* **-nas**) (coll.) bum, common bum
**zampapalo** *mf* (coll.) var. of **zampatortas**
**zampar** *va* to slip away, to hide away; to gobble down; *vr* to slip away, to hide away
**zampatortas** *mf* (*pl:* **-tas**) (coll.) glutton; (coll.) boor
**zampeado** *m* (constr.) pilework and rubble, grillage
**zampear** *va* to strengthen (*soil*) with a grillage
**zampón -pona** *adj* (coll.) gluttonous; *mf* (coll.) glutton
**zampoña** *f* rustic flute, shepherd's pipe; boy's flute made of green cane; (coll.) triviality, nonsense
**zampuzar** §76 *va* to duck, give a ducking to; to slip away, to hide away
**zampuzo** *m* ducking; hiding
**zamuro** *m* (orn.) turkey buzzard
**zanahoria** *f* (bot.) carrot
**zanahoriate** *m* var. of **azanahoriate**
**zanate** *m* (Am.) grackle (*Quiscalus macrourus*)
**zanca** *f* long leg (*of bird*); (coll.) long leg, shank; horse (*of staircase*); **andar en zancas de araña** (coll.) to resort to subterfuge, to shirk; **por zancas o por barrancas** (coll.) by hook or crook
**zancada** *f* long stride; **en dos zancadas** (coll.) in a jiffy
**zancadilla** *f* trip, tripping; (coll.) booby trap, trick; **echarle la zancadilla a uno** to stick out one's foot and trip someone
**zancajear** *vn* to rush around
**zancajera** *f* footing of running board
**zancajiento -ta** *adj* var. of **zancajoso**
**zancajo** *m* heel; heel bone; heel (*of shoe or stocking*); (coll.) ugly little person; **no llegar a los zancajos** or **al zancajo a** (coll.) to not come up to, to not be the equal of; **roer los zancajos a** (coll.) to talk behind the back of
**zancajoso -sa** *adj* duck-toed; big-heeled; dirty-heeled; with the heels of one's stockings out
**zancarrón** *m* (coll.) leg bone stripped of flesh; (coll.) skinny, dirty old fellow; (coll.) ignorant teacher, teacher who does not know his subject
**zanco** *m* stilt; **en zancos** (coll.) in a lofty station
**zancón -cona** *adj* (coll.) long-shanked, long-legged
**zancudo -da** *adj* long-shanked, long-legged; (orn.) wading; *m* (Am.) mosquito; *f* (orn.) wader, wading bird
**zandía** *f* var. of **sandía**
**zanfonía** *f* hurdy-gurdy
**zangala** *f* buckram
**zangamanga** *f* (coll.) trick
**zanganada** *f* (coll.) impertinence, impropriety
**zangandongo -ga, zangandullo -lla** or **zangandungo -ga** *mf* (coll.) worthless loafer
**zanganear** *vn* (coll.) to drone, to loaf, to idle
**zángano** *m* (ent.) drone; (fig.) drone, idler, sponger
**zangarilleja** *f* slattern, trollop
**zangarrear** *vn* (coll.) to thrum a guitar
**zangarriana** *f* slight recurring indisposition; (vet.) dropsy; (coll.) gloominess, blues
**zangarullón** *m* (coll.) var. of **zangón**
**zangolotear** *va* (coll.) to jiggle; *vn* (coll.) to flit around, to fuss around; *vr* (coll.) to jiggle; (coll.) to flop around, to swing, to slam
**zangoloteo** *m* (coll.) jiggle, jiggling; (coll.) flitting, fuss, bother; (coll.) slam, rattle
**zangolotina** *f* grown girl who tries to pass as a child
**zangolotino** *m* grown boy who tries to pass as a child
**zangón** *m* (coll.) lanky young loafer
**zangotear** *va* (coll.) to jiggle, jiggle around
**zangoteo** *m* (coll.) jiggle, jiggling
**zanguango -ga** *adj* (coll.) slothful; *mf* (coll.) loafer; *f* (coll.) malingering; (coll.) flattery; **hacer la zanguanga** (coll.) to malinger
**zanguayo** *m* (coll.) sly lanky fellow
**zanja** *f* ditch, trench; (Am.) gully; **abrir las zanjas** to lay the foundations
**zanjar** *va* to dig a ditch or ditches in; to settle, clear up, expedite
**zanjón** *m* deep ditch, deep drain
**zanqueador -dora** *adj* waddling; *mf* waddler
**zanqueamiento** *m* waddling
**zanquear** *vn* to waddle; to rush around
**zanquilargo -ga** *adj* long-shanked, long-legged
**zanquilla** *mf* (coll.) short-legged little runt
**zanquituerto -ta** *adj* bandy-legged
**zanquivano -na** *adj* (coll.) spindle-shanked, spindle-legged
**zapa** *f* spade; sap, trenching; sharkskin; shagreen (*rough skin of certain sharks*); sharkskin finish (*on metal*)
**zapador** *m* (mil.) sapper
**zapalote** *m* (bot.) plantain
**zapapico** *m* mattock, pickax
**zapar** *va & vn* to mine, to excavate
**zaparrada** *f* blow with claw, clawing
**zaparrastrar** *vn* (coll.) to trail one's clothes
**zaparrastroso -sa** *adj* (coll.) ragged, shabby, filthy; *mf* (coll.) ragamuffin, tatterdemalion
**zaparrazo** *m* (coll.) var. of **zaparrada**
**zapata** *f* half boot; shoe (*of a brake; of electric car for taking current from third rail*); (naut.) shoe (*of anchor*); (naut.) false keel
**zapatazo** *m* blow with a shoe; thud, bump, bang; clatter or rattle of horse's hoofs; (naut.) flapping (*of a sail*); **mandar a zapatazos** (coll.) to have an ascendancy over; **tratar a zapatazos** (coll.) to abuse, ill-treat
**zapateado** *m* clog dance, tap dance
**zapateador -dora** *adj* clog-dancing; *mf* clog dancer
**zapatear** *va* to hit with the shoe; to tap with the feet; to touch repeatedly with the button of the foil; (coll.) to abuse, to ill-treat; *vn* to tap-dance; (naut.) to flap (*said of sails*); *vr* to hold out, hold one's own
**zapateo** *m* tapping with the feet; tap dance, tap dancing
**zapatera** *f* see **zapatero**
**zapateresco -ca** *adj* (hum.) shoemaker's, (pertaining to a) shoemaker
**zapatería** *f* shoemaking; shoe store; shoemaker's shop
**zapateril** *adj* shoemaker's, (pertaining to a) shoemaker
**zapatero -ra** *adj* hard, raw, poorly cooked; spoiled (*olive*); *mf* shoemaker; shoe dealer; **quedarse zapatero** (coll.) to not take a trick; **zapatero de viejo** or **zapatero remendón** shoemaker, shoe repairer, cobbler; *m* (ent.) water strider; (ichth.) cutlass fish; *f* shoemaker's wife
**zapateta** *f* slap on foot or shoe while jumping; *interj* upon my word!
**zapatilla** *f* slipper; pump (*low shoe*); gasket; leather washer; washer (*e.g., for a spigot*); chamois washer (*for keys of wind instrument*); leather tip or button (*of a foil*); cloven hoof; **zapatilla de baño** bath or bathing slipper; **zapatilla de la reina** (bot.) large-flowered hypecoum; **zapatilla de señorita** (bot.) lady-slipper
**zapatillazo** *m* blow with a slipper
**zapatillero -ra** *mf* maker of slippers, dealer in slippers
**zapatito** *m* little shoe; **zapatito de la reina** (bot.) butterfly pea

**zapato** *m* shoe, low shoe; **andar con zapatos de fieltro** to gumshoe; **como tres en un zapato** (coll.) like sardines; (coll.) in straits, hard up; **lamer los zapatos a** (coll.) to lick the boots of; **saber (uno) dónde le aprieta el zapato** (coll.) to know one's own mind; **zapato inglés** low shoe; **zapatos papales** overshoes
**zapatón -tona** *adj* (Am.) tough, leathery; *m* big shoe; (Am.) overshoe; **zapatones** *mpl* spurs (*for fighting cocks*)
**zapatudo -da** *adj* wearing clodhoppers; big-hoofed; big-clawed; (mach.) provided or equipped with a shoe
**zape** *interj* scat!
**zapear** *va* to chase away (*a cat*); (coll.) to scare away
**zapote** *m* (bot.) sapodilla; **zapote chico** (bot.) marmalade tree; marmalade plum
**zapotillo** *m* (bot.) marmalade tree
**zapuzar §76** *va* to duck
**zaque** *m* goatskin, wineskin; (coll.) drunk, drunkard
**zaquear** *va* to rack from one wineskin to another; to carry in wineskins
**Zaqueo** *m* (Bib.) Zaccheus
**zaquizamí** *m* (*pl:* **-míes**) garret, attic; hovel, pigpen
**zar** *m* czar
**zarabanda** *f* (mus.) saraband; noise, uproar
**zarabandista** *mf* composer of sarabands; saraband dancer; noisy person, lively person
**zarabutear** *va* (coll.) var. of **zaragutear**
**zarabutero -ra** *adj & mf* (coll.) var. of **zaragutero**
**zaragalla** *f* fine charcoal
**zaragata** *f* (coll.) row, fight, scuffle
**zaragatería** *f* rowdyism, hooliganism
**zaragatero -ra** *adj* (coll.) rowdyish; *mf* (coll.) rowdy, hooligan
**zaragatona** *f* (bot.) fleawort
**Zaragoza** *f* Saragossa
**zaragozano -na** *adj* (pertaining to) Saragossa; *mf* native or inhabitant of Saragossa
**zaragüelles** *mpl* breeches; (coll.) coarse bloomers; (dial.) drawers; (bot.) reed grass
**zaragutear** *va* (coll.) to bungle, to botch
**zaragutero -ra** *adj* (coll.) bungling; *mf* (coll.) bungler
**zaramagullón** *m* (orn.) dabchick, grebe
**zaranda** *f* sieve, screen
**zarandador -dora** *mf* sifter, winnower
**zarandajas** *fpl* (coll.) trifles, odds and ends
**zarandalí** *adj* (*pl:* **-líes**) (prov.) black-spotted (*dove*)
**zarandar** *va* to sift, to screen, to winnow; to slip or slide along; to select, pick out, separate; (coll.) to take the pick of; (coll.) to jiggle; *vr* to slip or slide along; (coll.) to jiggle
**zarandear** *va* to sift, to screen, to winnow; (coll.) to jiggle; *vr* to toil, to wear oneself out; (coll.) to jiggle
**zarandeo** *m* sifting, screening, winnowing; toiling, drudgery; (coll.) jiggle, jiggling
**zarandero -ra** *mf* var. of **zarandador**
**zarandillo** *m* small sieve, small screen; (coll.) harum-scarum; (coll.) live wire; **traerle a uno como un zarandillo** (coll.) to keep someone on the go
**zarapatel** *m* salmagundi
**zarapico** *m* (bot.) candytuft; (orn.) curlew
**zarapito** *m* (orn.) curlew
**zaratán** *m* (path.) cancer of the breast
**zaraza** *f* gingham, chintz, printed cotton; **zarazas** *fpl* animal poison (*made of powdered glass and poisonous substances*)
**zarcear** *va* to clean out (*pipes, tubes, etc.*) with brambles; *vn* to hunt in the underbrush (*said of a dog*); to rush back and forth
**zarceño -ña** *adj* brambly
**zarceta** *f* (orn.) garganey
**zarcillitos** *mpl* (bot.) quaking grass
**zarcillo** *m* eardrop; weeding hoe; (bot.) tendril; (dial.) hoop
**zarco -ca** *adj* light-blue (*eyes*)
**zarevitz** *m* czarevitch
**zargatona** *f* var. of **zaragatona**
**zariano -na** *adj* czarish
**zarigüeya** *f* (zool.) opossum
**zarina** *f* czarina
**zarismo** *m* czarism
**zarista** *mf* czarist
**zarja** *f* var. of **azarja**
**zarpa** *f* paw, claw (*of beast*); (constr.) projection of footing (*of a wall*); mud sticking to lower part of clothing; (naut.) weighing anchor
**zarpada** *f* blow with claw, clawing
**zarpar** *va* (naut.) to weigh (*anchor*); *vn* (naut.) to weigh anchor, set sail
**zarpazo** *m* blow with claw, clawing; thud, bump
**zarposo -sa** *adj* mud-splashed, mud-bespattered
**zarracatería** *f* (coll.) insincere flattery
**zarracatín** *m* (coll.) sharp dealer
**zarramplín** *m* (coll.) botcher, bungler
**zarramplinada** *f* (coll.) botch, bungle
**zarrapastra** *f* (coll.) mud sticking to lower part of clothing
**zarrapastrón -trona** or **zarrapastroso -sa** *adj & mf* (coll.) var. of **zaparrastroso**
**zarria** *f* mud sticking to clothes; thong, leather strap; rag, tatter
**zarriento -ta** or **zarrioso -sa** *adj* mud-splashed, mud-bespattered
**zarza** *f* (bot.) blackberry, blackberry bush, bramble
**zarzagán** *m* cold northeast wind
**zarzaganillo** *m* stormy northeast wind
**zarzahán** *m* striped colored silk
**zarzal** *m* blackberry patch; underbrush, brambles
**zarzamora** *f* blackberry, brambleberry (*fruit*)
**zarzaparrilla** *f* (bot.) sarsaparilla (*plant, extract, and drink*)
**zarzaparrillar** *m* sarsaparilla field
**zarzaperruna** *f* (bot.) dog rose (*plant and fruit*)
**zarzarrosa** *f* dog rose (*flower*)
**zarzo** *m* hurdle, wattle
**zarzoso -sa** *adj* brambly, bushy
**zarzuela** *f* (theat.) zarzuela (*Spanish musical comedy with alternating music and dialogue*); **zarzuela grande** three-act zarzuela
**zarzuelero -ra** *adj* (pertaining to the) zarzuela
**zarzuelista** *mf* composer of zarzuelas
**zas** *interj* bang!; **¡zas, zas!** bing, bang!
**zascandil** *m* (coll.) meddler, schemer
**zascandilear** *vn* to meddle, to scheme
**zata** or **zatara** *f* raft
**zato** *m* piece of bread
**zazo -za** or **zazoso -sa** *adj* stammering, stuttering
**Zebedeo** *m* (Bib.) Zebedee
**zedilla** *f* c cedilla; cedilla
**zéjel** *m* popular Spanish-Arabic verse form consisting of an initial theme and a number of three-line monorhymed stanzas each followed by a line in rhyme with the initial theme
**Zelanda, la** Zeeland; **Nueva Zelanda** New Zealand
**zelandés -desa** *adj & mf* var. of **celandés**
**Zelandia, la** var. of **la Zelanda**
**zenit** *m* var. of **cenit**
**Zenón** *m* Zeno
**zepelín** *m* zeppelin
**zeugma** or **zeuma** *f* (rhet.) zeugma
**Zeus** *m* (myth.) Zeus
**zigodáctilo -la** *adj & f* (orn.) zygodactyl
**zigofiláceo -a** *adj* var. of **cigofiláceo**
**zigoma** *f* var. of **cigoma**
**zigomático -ca** *adj* var. of **cigomático**
**zigomorfo -fa** *adj* (biol.) zygomorphic or zygomorphous
**zigospora** *f* (bot.) zygospore
**zigoto** *m* var. of **cigoto**
**zigzag** *m* zigzag
**zigzaguear** *vn* to zigzag
**zimasa** *f* (biochem.) zymase
**zimo** *m* var. of **cimo**
**zimógeno** *m* var. of **cimógeno**
**zimótico -ca** *adj* var. of **cimótico**
**zinc** *m* (*pl:* **zinces**) var. of **cinc**
**zipizape** *m* (coll.) scuffle, row
**zircón** *m* var. of **circón**
**zircona** *f* var. of **circona**
**zirconio** *m* var. of **circonio**
**ziriano** *m* Zyrian (*a Finno-Ugric language*)

**zis, zas** *interj* (coll.) bing, bang!
**ziszás** *m* zigzag; (fort.) zigzag intrenchment
**zoantropía** *f* (path.) zoanthropy
**zoca** *f* see **zoco**
**zócalo** *m* (arch.) socle; (rad.) socket; (Am.) center of public square
**zocatear** *vr* to become corky or pithy
**zocato -ta** *adj* corky, pithy (*fruit*); (coll.) left; (coll.) left-handed; *mf* (coll.) left-handed person
**zoclo** *m* wooden shoe, clog
**zoco -ca** *adj* (coll.) left; (coll.) left-handed; *mf* (coll.) left-handed person; *m* wooden shoe, clog; Moroccan market or market place; (arch.) socle; **andar de zocos en colodros** to go from bad to worse; *f* public square
**zodiacal** *adj* zodiacal
**zodíaco** *m* (astr.) zodiac
**zofra** *f* Moorish carpet or rug
**zoilo** *m* envious critic
**zolocho -cha** *adj* (coll.) simple, silly; *mf* (coll.) simpleton
**zollipar** *vn* (coll.) to sob
**zollipo** *m* (coll.) sob
**zoma** *f* coarse flour, middling
**zompo -pa** *adj & mf* var. of **zopo**
**zona** *f* zone; belt, girdle; **zona a batir** target area; **Zona del Canal** Canal Zone; **zona escolar** school zone; **zona glacial** frigid zone; **zona templada** temperate zone; **zona tórrida** torrid zone; **zona tropical** tropics or Tropics; *m* (path.) zona, zoster, shingles
**zonado -da** *adj* zoned (*striped*)
**zonal** *adj* zonal
**zoncería** *f* insipidity; dullness, inanity, nonsense
**zonificación** *f* zoning
**zonote** *m* (Am.) var. of **cenote**
**zonula** *f* zonule
**zonzo -za** *adj* insipid, tasteless; dull, inane; *mf* boob, simpleton; *m* (orn.) cedarbird
**zonzorrión -rriona** *adj* (coll.) dull, inane; *mf* (coll.) dullard, dolt
**zoo** *m* (coll.) zoo (*zoölogical garden*)
**zoocecidia** *f* (zool.) zoöcecidium
**zoófito** *m* (zool.) zoöphyte
**zoogeografía** *f* zoögeography
**zooglea** *f* (bact.) zoögloea
**zoografía** *f* zoögraphy
**zoología** *f* zoölogy
**zoológico -ca** *adj* zoölogical
**zoólogo -ga** *mf* zoölogist
**zoometría** *f* zoömetry
**zoométrico -ca** *adj* zoömetric
**zoomorfismo** *m* zoömorphism
**zoonosis** *f* (path.) zoönosis
**zooplancton** *m* (zool.) zoöplankton
**zooplastia** *f* (surg.) zoöplasty
**zooquímico -ca** *adj* zoöchemical; *f* zoöchemistry
**zoospora** *f* (bot.) zoöspore
**zoosporangio** *m* (bot.) zoösporangium
**zootecnia** *f* zoötechny
**zootomía** *f* zoötomy
**zootropo** *m* zoetrope (*optical toy*)
**zopas** *mf* see **zopo**
**zopenco -ca** *adj* (coll.) dull, doltish; *mf* (coll.) dullard, dolt
**zopetero** *m* slope, embankment
**zopilote** *m* (orn.) carrion crow, black vulture; **zopilote de montaña** (orn.) turkey buzzard
**zopisa** *f* pitch, tar; pine tar; ointment of pine tar and wax
**zopitas** *mf* (*pl:* **-tas**) (hum.) lisper
**zopo -pa** *adj* crippled; *mf* cripple; **zopas** *mf* (*pl:* **-pas**) (coll.) lisper
**zoqueta** *f* wooden guard to protect the left hand from the sickle
**zoquete** *m* block, chunk, end (*of wood*); bit of bread; blockhead, chump; (coll.) fat and ugly little runt
**zoquetero -ra** *mf* bum
**zoquetudo -da** *adj* coarse, rough
**zoroastriano -na** *adj & mf* Zoroastrian
**zoroástrico -ca** *adj* Zoroastrian
**zoroastrismo** *m* Zoroastrianism
**Zoroastro** *m* Zoroaster
**zorongo** *m* Aragonese kerchief (*folded like bandage around head*); flat chignon
**zorra** *f* (zool.) fox; female fox; (coll.) foxy person; prostitute; drunkenness; truck, dray; (*cap.*) *f* (astr.) Fox, Vulpecula; **pillar una zorra** (coll.) to get drunk; **zorra de mar** (ichth.) fox shark, thresher shark
**zorrastrón -trona** *adj* (coll.) crafty, tricky; *mf* (coll.) crafty person, tricky person
**zorrera** *f* see **zorrero**
**zorrería** *f* foxiness
**zorrero -ra** *adj* foxy, sly; slow, tardy; fox-hunting (*dog*); large (*shot*); (naut.) heavy-sailing; *m* royal game warden (*whose duty it was to kill foxes, wolves, birds of prey, and other harmful animals*); *f* fox hole; (coll.) confusion, worry; smoke-filled room
**zorrillo** *m* (zool.) skunk
**zorro** *m* (zool.) male fox; fox (*fur*); (coll.) fox, foxy fellow; (coll.) person who plays stupid; **zorros** *mpl* duster; **estar hecho un zorro** (coll.) to be overwhelmed with sleep; (coll.) to be dull and sullen; **hacerse el zorro** (coll.) to pretend ignorance, to pretend not to hear; **zorro azul** (zool.) blue fox; **zorro negro** (zool.) raccoon; **zorro plateado** (zool.) silver fox
**zorrocloco** *m* (coll.) sly boob; (coll.) caress
**zorronglón -glona** *adj* (coll.) grumbling; *mf* (coll.) grumbler
**zorrullo** *m* var. of **zurullo**
**zorruno -na** *adj* foxlike, foxy
**zorzal** *m* (orn.) fieldfare; sly fellow; (Am.) simpleton, boob; **zorzal marino** (ichth.) black wrasse
**zorzaleño -ña** *adj* crescent (*olive*)
**zoster** *f* (path.) zoster, shingles
**zote** *adj* simple, stupid; *mf* simpleton, dolt
**zozobra** *f* capsizing, foundering, sinking; worry, anxiety
**zozobrar** *va* to sink; to wreck (*a business*); *vn* to capsize, founder, sink; to be in jeopardy; to worry, to fret; *vr* to capsize, founder, sink
**zozobroso -sa** *adj* worried, anxious, restless
**zúa** *f* var. of **azud**
**zuavo** *m* (mil.) Zouave
**zubia** *f* drain, channel
**zucarino -na** *adj* sugary, sweet
**zueco** *m* wooden shoe, clog, sabot; wood-soled or cork-soled shoe
**zuela** *f* var. of **azuela**
**-zuelo -la** *suffix dim & pej* var. of **-uelo** and attached to polysyllables ending in **d, e, n, r,** an accented vowel, an unaccented diphthong, or an unaccented vowel in a word with a diphthong in its root, e.g., **pobrezuelo** poorish; **ladronzuelo** petty thief; **mujerzuela** woman of no account; **lengüezuela** little tongue; **piedrezuela** little stone; **huevezuelo** little egg. The radical diphthong sometimes disappears when the suffix is added, e.g., **pontezuelo** small bridge; **tendezuela** little shop; **terrezuela** worthless piece of ground
**zuingliano -na** *adj & mf* Zwinglian
**zulacar** §86 *va* to waterproof
**zulaque** *m* waterproof packing; waterproof paving material
**zulaquear** *va* var. of **zulacar**
**zulú** (*pl:* **-lús** or **-lúes**) *adj & mf* Zulu
**Zululandia** *f* Zululand
**zulla** *f* (bot.) sulla clover, French honeysuckle; (coll.) excrement (*human*)
**zullar** *vr* (coll.) to have a movement of the bowels; (coll.) to break wind
**zullenco -ca** *adj* (coll.) windy, flatulent
**zullón -llona** *adj* (coll.) windy, flatulent; *m* (coll.) wind, flatulence
**zumacal** *m* planting of sumachs
**zumacar** *m* planting of sumachs; *va* to dress or tan with sumach
**zumacaya** *f* var. of **zumaya**
**zumaque** *m* (bot.) sumach; (coll.) grape wine; **zumaque del Japón** (bot.) tree of heaven; **zumaque venenoso** (bot.) poison sumach, poison ivy
**zumaya** *f* (orn.) goatsucker; (orn.) tawny owl; (orn.) secretary bird
**zumba** *f* bell worn by leading mule; whistle (*toy made to spin on end of a string*); fun, joke; **hacer zumba a** to make fun of

**zumbador -dora** *adj* buzzing; *m* buzzer; (elec.) buzzer; (Am.) hummingbird
**zumbar** *va* to make fun of; to let have, e.g., **le zumbó una bofetada** he let him have a slap in the face; *vn* to buzz, to hum; to ring (*said of the ears*); **zumbar a** to be close to, e.g., **le zumban los sesenta años** he is close to sixty years of age; *vr* to make fun of each other; **zumbarse de** to make fun of
**zumbel** *m* string used to spin a top; (coll.) frown
**zumbido** *m* buzz, hum; (coll.) blow, smack; **zumbido de ocupación** busy signal (*of telephone*); **zumbido de oídos** (path.) ringing in the ears, tinnitus
**zumbo** *m* buzz, hum; (Am.) gourd
**zumbón -bona** *adj* funny, playful, waggish; *mf* wag, jester
**zumiento -ta** *adj* juicy
**zumillo** *m* (bot.) green dragon; (bot.) deadly carrot
**zumo** *m* juice; profit, advantage; **zumo de cepas** or **parras** (coll.) fruit of the vine, wine; **zumo de naranja** orange juice; **zumo de uva** grape juice
**zumoso -sa** *adj* juicy
**zuna** *f* Sunna or Sunnah; (dial.) treachery; (dial.) viciousness (*of a horse*)
**zunchar** *va* to band, to hoop, to fasten with a band or hoop
**zuncho** *m* band, hoop, ring; **zuncho de botalón** (naut.) boom iron
**zuño** *m* frown
**zupia** *f* dregs (*of wine*); wine full of dregs; slop; (fig.) scum, trash
**zurano -na** *adj* wild (*dove or pigeon*)
**zurcido** *m* darn, darning; **zurcido invisible** invisible mending
**zurcidor -dora** *adj* darning; *mf* darner
**zurcidura** *f* darning
**zurcir §50** *va* to darn; to strand; to join, unite; (coll.) to hatch, concoct (*a lie*), to weave (*a tissue of lies*)
**zurdazo** *m* blow with the left (*hand*); (box.) left
**zurdear** *vn* to be left-handed
**zurdería** *f* left-handedness
**zurdo -da** *adj* left; left-handed; (mach.) left-handed (*e.g., screw*); **a zurdas** with the left hand; the wrong way; *mf* left-handed person
**zurear** *vn* to coo
**zureo** *m* cooing
**zurito -ta** *adj* stock (*dove*); *f* (orn.) stock dove
**zuro -ra** *adj* wild (*dove or pigeon*); *m* stripped corncob
**zurra** *f* currying, dressing; scuffle, quarrel; grind (*long hard work or study*); drubbing, thrashing
**zurrador** *m* leather currier or dresser
**zurrapa** *f* filament, thread; (coll.) trash, rubbish; (coll.) ugly, skinny young fellow; **con zurrapas** (coll.) in an uncleanly way
**zurrapelo** *m* (coll.) dressing-down, sharp reprimand
**zurrapiento -ta** or **zurraposo -sa** *adj* dreggy, turbid, roily
**zurrar** *va* to curry, to dress (*leather*); to get the best of; to dress down; (coll.) to drub, to thrash; *vr* to have an accident, to dirty oneself; (coll.) to be scared to death
**zurriaga** *f* whip, lash; (dial.) lark (*bird*)
**zurriagar §59** *va* to whip, to horsewhip
**zurriagazo** *m* whipping, lashing; stroke of bad luck; unexpected abuse, unexpected slight
**zurriago** *m* whip, lash; strap used to spin a top
**zurriar §90** *vn* var. of **zurrir**
**zurribanda** *f* (coll.) rain of blows; (coll.) scuffle, rumpus, row
**zurriburri** *m* (coll.) cur, contemptible fellow; (coll.) gang of crooks; (coll.) uproar, confusion
**zurrido** *m* buzzing, grating noise; (coll.) blow with a stick
**zurrir** *vn* to buzz, to grate
**zurrón** *m* shepherd's leather bag; husk; placenta; **zurrón de pastor** (bot.) shepherd's-purse
**zurrona** *f* (coll.) loose, crooked woman
**zurronada** *f* bagful
**zurrusco** *m* burnt toast
**zurullo** *m* (coll.) soft roll (*of anything*); (coll.) turd
**zurumbático -ca** *adj* stunned, bewildered
**zurupeto** *m* (coll.) unregistered broker
**zutano -na** *mf* (coll.) so-and-so
**zuzo** *interj* var. of **chucho**
**zuzón** *m* (bot.) groundsel
**zuzunga** *f* strainer, colander

# CENTER SECTION — SECCIÓN CENTRAL

## BREVE HISTORIA DE LA LENGUA INGLESA

**Los orígenes del inglés.** La lengua inglesa pertenece al subgrupo germánico occidental y fué introducida por los invasores anglos y sajones en los siglos quinto y sexto en el territorio que ocupa hoy la Gran Bretaña sobre un substrato celta. En sus orígenes se entremezclan dos corrientes lingüísticas, la germánica y la latina. En su estructura gramatical se parece al alemán, el holandés y las lenguas escandinavas al paso que en su léxico ofrece mucho parecido con el latín, el francés y las otras lenguas neolatinas. Su nombre actual deriva del de la tribu de los anglos de Northumbria que vinieron de la península danesa a mediados del siglo sexto. Con el tiempo adquirió el país asimismo el nombre de *Engla-land* (tierra de los anglos). El inglés como idioma ha tenido existencia independiente por sólo mil quinientos años. Se consideran tres períodos históricos en su evolución: el inglés antiguo (450-1150), que se confunde con el llamado anglosajón, el inglés medio (1150-1500) y el inglés moderno (desde 1500).

**El inglés antiguo.** El inglés antiguo constituye una lengua homogénea y original. Se caracterizaba por sus numerosas declinaciones de substantivos y adjetivos, muy semejantes a las del alemán moderno. Por otra parte, el verbo era más simple, valiéndose solamente de dos tiempos simples, el presente y el pasado. Había, sin embargo, más de trescientos verbos fuertes (o irregulares), como **speak, spoke, spoken** del inglés moderno, a diferencia de los verbos débiles, más simples y puramente germánicos, como **talk, talked, talked** del inglés moderno. Gran parte de esta estructura gramatical, poco necesaria para la adecuada expresión de las ideas, fué eliminada durante el período del inglés medio.

Durante el período del inglés antiguo la lengua estuvo expuesta a la influencia de varias lenguas extranjeras que le dieron un número considerable de palabras nuevas. Los anglosajones, algún tiempo antes de su llegada al territorio de la Gran Bretaña, habían sostenido prolongadas guerras y más tarde establecido relaciones comerciales con los romanos, aprendiendo de ellos palabras como **caseus** (cheese), **(libras) pondo** (pound), **strata (via)** (street) y **vinum** (wine). Sus relaciones con los celtas trajeron al idioma algunas palabras del celta y otras latinas que los celtas habían aprendido durante la ocupación romana desde el año 43 al 410 de la era cristiana. Al ser convertidos al cristianismo, los ingleses adoptaron, no sólo palabras como **alb, altar, creed** y **priest**, relativas a la Iglesia, sino varios cientos de otras palabras que la elevada cultura del clero les dió a conocer. La influencia extranjera de mayor importancia durante este período fué la de los piratas escandinavos que comenzaron a saquear las costas de Inglaterra en el año 787 y que en el siglo siguiente establecieron colonias de alguna importancia en la isla. Por espacio de más de doscientos años, el inglés y las lenguas escandinavas, especialmente el danés, se hablaron conjuntamente en el nordeste de Inglaterra. Cuán estrecha fué la unión de estos elementos lingüísticos es evidente si se considera que palabras tan comunes como **knife, sister, root, skin, trust** y **window** son todas de origen danés. Aun más significativo es el hecho de que los pronombres **they, their** y **them,** la forma **are** del verbo **be** y la conjunción **though**, palabras que muy raras veces pasan de un idioma a otro, entraron a formar parte del léxico inglés. Así vemos, en el período del inglés antiguo, el comienzo de la costumbre tan marcada en la lengua inglesa, de hacer adopciones frecuentes de otros idiomas, costumbre que constituye una de las características más notables del inglés en sus épocas subsiguientes.

**El inglés medio.** En el año de 1066, Guillermo, duque de Normandía, cumplió, por medio de la conquista, su pretensión al trono de Inglaterra. La conquista normanda originó una transformación cuyo resultado fué el inglés medio, con diferentes divisiones cronológicas. Así hay el de transición o semisajón (1150-1200), el primitivo (1200-1250), el normal (1250-1400) y el tardío (1400-1500). El léxico se afrancesó con 10.000 palabras relativas a la administración, el ejército, la Iglesia, la arquitectura, el arte, la moda y la vida aristocrática, la mayor parte de las cuales están todavía en uso al paso que la gramática abandonó las leyes flexionales y sintácticas del anglosajón. A raíz de la conquista normanda el substantivo perdió todos sus casos con excepción del posesivo. Los casos se expresan por simples preposiciones; únicamente en las desinencias **-'s** y **-s'** se sigue la antigua gramática anglosajona. Las diferentes declinaciones se ordenaron bajo una sola en la cual la **s** (o **es**) forma el plural, con excepción de un pequeño número de substantivos como **man** (*pl:* **men**), **tooth** (*pl:* **teeth**) y **child** (*pl:* **children**). El adjetivo y el artículo definido perdieron sus flexiones y son hoy invariables sin consideración del género, número y caso del substantivo que modifican. Y la pérdida de las terminaciones produjo paulatinamente el abandono de los géneros gramaticales. Más de la mitad de los trescientos verbos fuertes del inglés antiguo desaparecieron durante el período del inglés medio y quedan solamente unos setenta en el inglés moderno. Para fines del período, el sistema de flexiones se había reducido poco más o menos a la forma simple actualmente en uso.

**El inglés moderno.** Durante el Renacimiento, el inglés al latinizarse substituyó al latín como lengua apropiada para materias eruditas. Y en los siglos subsiguientes los sabios continuaron recurriendo a la autoridad de los autores clásicos griegos y romanos para refinar el léxico y fijar la lengua. Los resultados no fueron siempre felices. A principios del siglo dieciocho surgió un movimiento que abogaba por el establecimiento de una academia a imitación de la Academia Francesa, pero el proyecto fracasó. A falta de academia, continúa invocándose el buen uso para resolver los problemas de corrección lingüística.

En los últimos siglos se enriqueció el léxico con muchos neologismos para expresar los nuevos conceptos de la ciencia, la tecnología y la vida modernas. Se regularizó la ortografía, que era en exceso variable y que aún está muy en desacuerdo con la pronunciación.

**La formación de palabras.** Era característica del sistema de formación de palabras en el inglés antiguo la palabra compuesta que se explica por sí misma. Muchas de estas palabras compuestas fueron reemplazadas por palabras francesas ya completamente formadas, p.ej., **bookhouse** por **library** y **treewright** por **carpenter.** Pero aún hoy se forman palabras compuestas que se explican por sí mismas, como **bridgehead, late-comer** y **nose cone.**

Hay tres maneras en que dos o más palabras pueden ser unidas en nuevas unidades del vocabulario. Primero, algunas palabras van combinadas en una unidad simple, p.ej., **steamboat** buque de vapor. Segundo, algunas van combinadas por medio de un guión, p.ej., **scissors-grinder** afilador de tijeras. Y tercero, algunas van combinadas solamente en la idea, aunque en la forma permanecen separadas, p.ej., **race track** pista de carreras.

**El uso del guión.** Existe una relación muy estrecha entre muchos nombres del tercer grupo y los adjetivos correspondientes del segundo. Esto consiste en que los nombres del tercer grupo pueden hacerse adjetivos por la simple introducción del guión, p.ej., **air raid** ataque aéreo y **air-raid shelter** refugio contra ataques aéreos. Este empleo del guión para formar adjetivos compuestos se encuentra en particular en combinaciones de adjetivos (o adverbios) y participios activos (o participios pasados), p.ej., **good-looking, high-sounding, well-meaning, high-priced, ill-gotten, well-informed.** También se encuentra en combinaciones de nombres y participios activos (o participios pasados). Tales nombres son objeto directo del participio activo, p.ej., **my beer-drinking friends** mis amigos bebedores de cerveza, pero con el participio pasado tienen la fuerza del agente con la voz pasiva, p.ej., **war-torn Europe** la Europa devastada por la guerra. En combinaciones de nombres y participios activos de verbos intransitivos, el nombre tiene fuerza adverbial, p.ej., **my church-going friends** mis amigos que van a la iglesia (es decir, que frecuentan la iglesia). Las combinaciones de nombres y participios activos pueden usarse también como nombres substantivos, p.ej., **beer-drinking** la costumbre de beber cerveza.

Se emplea asimismo el guión para formar combinaciones adjetivales de un número cardinal y un nombre que denota medida, conservando siempre la forma singular del nombre, p.ej., **a ten-mile walk** una caminata de diez millas, **a two-year course** un curso de dos años. Y tales combinaciones pueden combinarse aun más con un adjetivo que corresponda al nombre que denota medida, p.ej., **a two-mile-long race track** una pista de dos millas de largo, **a three-month-old baby** un rorro de tres meses de edad.

Queremos señalar además que hay muchos compuestos adjetivales que se escriben con guión sólo cuando van delante del nombre substantivo a que califican, p.ej., **this is a worth-while book** éste es un libro de gran mérito, pero **this book is worth while** este libro es de gran mérito.

**Variedades del inglés.** El inglés moderno ofrece variedades dialectales y regionales. Se admiten, en general, un inglés del norte, que abarca los dialectos escoceses y desciende del antiguo inglés septentrional, un inglés sudoccidental, que desciende del antiguo sajón occidental y un inglés del centro-este, que se puede considerar como el idioma predominante de la isla. Fuera de Inglaterra existen variedades dialectales y coloniales y la lengua se ha enriquecido con voces y giros indígenas. En los Estados Unidos ha adquirido ciertas características distintivas, especialmente en la pronunciación y el léxico. Al mismo tiempo hay fuerzas que tienden a disminuir las dificultades que encuentran para comprenderse los angloparlantes de diversas procedencias. Por ejemplo, la aceptación y vulgarización del cine norteamericano ha familiarizado al público británico con el idioma familiar y popular de los Estados Unidos. En resumen, se puede afirmar la unidad fundamental de la lengua inglesa. Es el lazo de unión entre la gente de origen anglosajón de muchos países y entre diversas nacionalidades y razas de todas las partes del mundo.

# RESUMEN DE GRAMÁTICA INGLESA

**§1. Símbolos fonéticos.** Pueden representarse aproximadamente todos los sonidos del idioma inglés con treinta y cuatro símbolos. En la lista que damos a continuación, cada símbolo va acompañado (1) de una palabra española o francesa que contiene un sonido (impreso en negrilla) más o menos parecido al sonido inglés referido y (2) de palabras inglesas que ejemplifican las varias grafías (también impresas en negrilla) empleadas para representar el sonido en este idioma. El signo ˈ antes de sílaba indica que tal sílaba lleva el acento principal, como en **father** [ˈfɑðər] y el signo ˌ antes de sílaba indica que tal sílaba lleva un acento menos fuerte que el principal, como en **fundamental** [ˌfʌndəˈmɛntəl].

VOCALES

| SÍMBOLO | SONIDO | GRAFÍA |
|---|---|---|
| 1. [æ] | Mucho más cerrado que la **a** de cl**a**ro. | c**a**t [kæt]<br>pl**ai**d [plæd] |
| 2. [ɑ] | Como la **a** de am**a**do. | f**a**ther [ˈfɑðər]<br>p**a**lm [pɑm]<br>w**a**s [wɑz]<br>h**ea**rth [hɑrθ]<br>s**e**rgeant [ˈsɑrdʒənt]<br>h**o**t [hɑt] |
| 3. [e] | Más cerrado que la **e** de habl**é**. Suena a menudo como si fuese seguido de [ɪ], especialmente en final de sílaba acentuada. | f**a**ce [fes]<br>r**ai**n [ren]<br>r**ay** [re]<br>g**ao**l [dʒel]<br>g**au**ge [gedʒ]<br>st**ea**k [stek]<br>v**ei**l [vel]<br>ob**ey** [oˈbe] |
| 4. [ɛ] | Como la **e** de p**e**rro. | s**e**t [sɛt]<br>**e**bb [ɛb]<br>**a**ny [ˈɛnɪ]<br>**ae**sthetic [ɛsˈθɛtɪk]<br>s**ai**d [sɛd]<br>s**ay**s [sɛz]<br>l**ea**ther [ˈlɛðər]<br>h**ei**fer [ˈhɛfər]<br>l**eo**pard [ˈlɛpərd]<br>fr**ie**nd [frɛnd]<br>f**oe**tid [ˈfɛtɪd]<br>b**u**ry [ˈbɛrɪ] |
| | En la mayor parte de las palabras en que [ɛ] va seguido de **r**, hay tendencia en algunas partes a articularlo más abiertamente y con más duración. | d**a**re [dɛr]<br>**ae**ry [ˈɛrɪ]<br>ch**ai**r [tʃɛr]<br>pr**ay**er [prɛr]<br>w**ea**r [wɛr]<br>th**e**re [ðɛr]<br>th**ei**r [ðɛr] |
| 5. [ə] | Como la **e** del artículo definido francés l**e**. | orph**a**n [ˈɔrfən]<br>m**a**chine [məˈʃin]<br>mount**ai**n [ˈmaʊntən]<br>syst**e**m [ˈsɪstəm]<br>penc**i**l [ˈpɛnsəl]<br>gall**o**p [ˈgæləp]<br>p**o**tato [pəˈteto]<br>biol**o**gy [baɪˈɔlədʒɪ]<br>aug**u**r [ˈɔgər]<br>porp**oi**se [ˈpɔrpəs]<br>curi**ou**s [ˈkjʊrɪəs] |
| 6. [i] | Como la **i** de m**i**sa. | m**e** [mi]<br>tr**ee** [tri]<br>t**ea**m [tim]<br>dec**ei**ve [dɪˈsiv]<br>k**ey** [ki]<br>p**eo**ple [ˈpipəl]<br>mach**i**ne [məˈʃin]<br>bel**ie**ve [bɪˈliv]<br>**ae**gis [ˈidʒɪs]<br>qu**ay** [ki]<br>am**oe**ba [əˈmibə] |

VOCALES

| SÍMBOLO | SONIDO | GRAFÍA |
|---|---|---|
| 7. [ɪ] | Un poco más abierto que la **i** de s**i**lba. | sit [sɪt]<br>sieve [sɪv]<br>pretty ['prɪtɪ]<br>been [bɪn]<br>beer [bɪr]<br>women ['wɪmɪn]<br>busy ['bɪzɪ]<br>build [bɪld]<br>hymn [hɪm] |
| | Encuéntrase en sílaba inacentuada. | attic ['ætɪk]<br>famine ['fæmɪn]<br>Monday ['mʌndɪ]<br>cottage ['kɑtɪdʒ]<br>carriage ['kærɪdʒ]<br>senate ['sɛnɪt]<br>coffee ['kɑfɪ]<br>foreign ['fɑrɪn]<br>money ['mʌnɪ]<br>mischief ['mɪstʃɪf]<br>chamois ['ʃæmɪ]<br>circuit ['sʌrkɪt]<br>scarlet ['skɑrlɪt] |
| 8. [o] | Más cerrado que la **o** de b**o**ca. Suena a menudo como si fuese seguido de [ʊ]. | note [not]<br>road [rod]<br>comb [kom]<br>toe [to]<br>brooch [brotʃ]<br>though [ðo]<br>know [no]<br>owe [o]<br>hautboy ['hobɔɪ]<br>beau [bo]<br>sew [so]<br>yeoman ['jomən] |
| | Cuando [o] va seguido de una **r**, se debe sobrentender que se oye [ə] después de [o] en muchas partes de los Estados Unidos, aunque el sonido [ə] no está indicado ni en la ortografía ni en la representación fonética. | floor [flor]<br>more [mor] |
| 9. [ɔ] | Más abierto que la **o** de t**o**rre. | order ['ɔrdər]<br>wrong [rɔŋ]<br>gone [gɔn]<br>broad [brɔd]<br>court [kɔrt]<br>warm [wɔrm]<br>salt [sɔlt]<br>caught [kɔt]<br>austere [ɔs'tɪr]<br>raw [rɔ] |
| 10. [u] | Como la **u** de d**u**da. | rude [rud]<br>prove [pruv]<br>do [du]<br>lose [luz]<br>tomb [tum]<br>canoe [kə'nu]<br>food [fud]<br>flue [flu]<br>fruit [frut]<br>maneuver [mə'nuvər]<br>drew [dru]<br>two [tu] |
| 11. [ʊ] | Menos cerrado que la **u** de c**u**lto. | full [fʊl]<br>bush [bʊʃ]<br>wolf [wʊlf]<br>tour [tʊr]<br>look [lʊk]<br>should [ʃʊd] |

## Diptongos

| SÍMBOLO | SONIDO | GRAFÍA |
|---|---|---|
| 12. [ʌ] | Algo parecido a **eu** en la palabra francesa s**eu**l. | c**u**p [kʌp]<br>s**u**ch [sʌtʃ]<br>s**o**n [sʌn]<br>c**o**ver [ˈkʌvər]<br>fr**o**nt [frʌnt]<br>m**o**ther [ˈmʌðər]<br>m**o**ney [ˈmʌnɪ]<br>d**oe**s [dʌz]<br>fl**oo**d [flʌd]<br>c**ou**ple [ˈkʌpəl]<br>t**wo**pence [ˈtʌpəns] |
| 13. [aɪ] | Como **ai** de habl**ái**s. | n**igh**t [naɪt]<br>t**i**me [taɪm]<br>l**ie** [laɪ]<br>**ai**sle [aɪl]<br>**aye** [aɪ]<br>h**eigh**t [haɪt]<br>**eye** [aɪ]<br>t**ie** [taɪ]<br>b**uy** [baɪ]<br>sk**y** [skaɪ]<br>l**ye** [laɪ] |
| | Cuando [aɪ] va seguido de una **r**, se debe sobrentender que se oye [ə] después de [aɪ], aunque el sonido [ə] no está indicado ni en la ortografía ni en la representación fonética. | f**i**re [faɪr]<br>t**i**re [taɪr] |
| 14. [aʊ] | Como **au** de p**au**sa. | b**ough** [baʊ]<br>s**ou**nd [saʊnd]<br>h**ow** [haʊ] |
| 15. [ɔɪ] | Como **oy** de d**oy**. | ch**oi**ce [tʃɔɪs]<br>**oi**l [ɔɪl]<br>t**oy** [tɔɪ] |
| 16. [b] | Como la **b** de cam**b**iar. | **b**ell [bɛl]<br>ho**bb**y [ˈhɑbɪ] |
| 17. [d] | Como la **d** de con**d**e. | **d**ear [dɪr]<br>la**dd**er [ˈlædər] |
| 18. [f] | Como la **f** de **f**also. | **f**ace [fes]<br>mu**ff**in [ˈmʌfɪn]<br>tou**gh** [tʌf] |
| 19. [g] | Como la **g** de **g**olpe. | **g**o [go]<br>**g**ive [gɪv]<br>a**gg**ressive [əˈgrɛsɪv]<br>e**x**act [ɛgˈzækt] |
| 20. [h] | Sonido más aspirado y más suave que el de la **j** de **j**amás. | **h**ome [hom]<br>alco**h**ol [ˈælkəhɔl]<br>**wh**o [hu] |
| 21. [j] | Como la **y** de cu**y**o. | **y**et [jɛt]<br>**u**nit [ˈjunɪt]<br>on**i**on [ˈʌnjən]<br>f**eu**d [fjud]<br>f**ew** [fju] |
| 22. [k] | Como la **c** de **c**asa. | **c**ar [kɑr]<br>a**cc**ount [əˈkaʊnt]<br>**ch**ord [kɔrd]<br>si**ck** [sɪk]<br>**k**eep [kip]<br>bo**x** [bɑks]<br>a**cq**uaint [əˈkwent] |
| 23. [l] | Como la **l** de **l**ago. | **l**ive [lɪv]<br>a**ll**ow [əˈlaʊ] |
| 24. [m] | Como la **m** de **m**anteca. | **m**ore [mor]<br>su**mm**on [ˈsʌmən] |

CONSONANTES

| SÍMBOLO | SONIDO | GRAFÍA |
|---|---|---|
| 25. [n] | Como la **n** de **n**adar. | **n**ot [nɑt]<br>ma**nn**er [ˈmænər] |
| 26. [p] | Como la **p** de ma**p**a. | **p**ay [pe]<br>a**pp**oint [əˈpɔɪnt] |
| 27. [r] | La **r** más común en la mayor parte de los Estados Unidos y en muchas partes de Inglaterra es un sonido semivocal que se articula con la punta de la lengua elevada más hacia el paladar duro que en la **r** fricativa española y aun doblada hacia atrás. Intervocálica y al final de sílaba, es muy débil y casi no se puede oír. | **r**at [ræt]<br>a**r**m [ɑrm]<br>ca**r** [kɑr]<br>ta**rr**y [ˈtærɪ] |
| | El símbolo [r] precedido de [ʌ] o [ə] representa un solo sonido, el de la llamada vocal de colorido de **r**, producido sin el sonido consonantal. Véase 40 y 41 abajo. | hu**r**t [hʌrt]<br>ea**r**ly [ˈʌrlɪ]<br>fathe**r** [ˈfɑðər]<br>pe**r**ceive [pərˈsiv] |
| 28. [s] | Como la **s** de ca**s**a. | **s**ell [sɛl]<br>**c**ent [sɛnt]<br>fa**ç**ade [fəˈsɑd]<br>bo**x** [bɑks]<br>quart**z** [kwɔrts] |
| 29. [t] | Como la **t** de car**t**a. | **t**ell [tɛl]<br>la**tt**er [ˈlætər]<br>**Th**omas [ˈtɑməs]<br>dripp**ed** [drɪpt] |
| 30. [v] | Como la **v** de la palabra francesa sa**v**oir. | **v**acate [ˈveket]<br>clo**v**er [ˈklovər]<br>o**f** [ɑv] |
| 31. [w] | Como la **u** de h**u**evo. | **w**orse [wʌrs]<br>t**w**ice [twaɪs]<br>pers**u**ade [pərˈswed]<br>q**u**een [kwin]<br>ch**o**ir [kwaɪr] |
| | Hay dos palabras que no tienen grafía para representar el sonido [w]. | one [wʌn]<br>once [wʌns] |
| 32. [z] | Como la **s** de de**s**de. | **z**est [zɛst]<br>snee**z**e [sniz]<br>bu**zz**er [ˈbʌzər]<br>bu**s**y [ˈbɪzɪ]<br>her**s** [hʌrz]<br>matche**s** [ˈmætʃɪz]<br>an**x**iety [æŋˈzaɪətɪ]<br>po**ss**ess [pəˈzɛs] |
| 33. [ð] | Como la **d** de na**d**a. | **th**en [ðɛn]<br>fa**th**er [ˈfɑðər] |
| 34. [θ] | Como la **z** de **z**orro en la pronunciación de Castilla. | **th**in [θɪn]<br>mou**th** [maʊθ]<br>e**th**er [ˈiθər] |
| 35. [ʃ] | Como **ch** de la palabra francesa **ch**emin. | **sh**eet [ʃit]<br>ma**ch**ine [məˈʃin]<br>o**c**ean [ˈoʃən]<br>vi**c**ious [ˈvɪʃəs]<br>man**s**ion [ˈmænʃən]<br>mi**ss**ion [ˈmɪʃən]<br>na**t**ion [ˈneʃən]<br>**s**ugar [ˈʃʊgər]<br>con**sc**ious [ˈkɑnʃəs]<br>an**x**ious [ˈæŋkʃəs] |
| 36. [ʒ] | Como la **j** de la palabra francesa **j**ambe. | a**z**ure [ˈæʒər]<br>gla**z**ier [ˈgleʒər]<br>plea**s**ure [ˈplɛʒər]<br>vi**s**ion [ˈvɪʒən]<br>rou**g**e [ruʒ] |
| 37. [ŋ] | Como la **n** de arra**n**car. | si**ng** [sɪŋ]<br>co**n**quer [ˈkɑŋkər]<br>a**n**xiety [æŋˈzaɪətɪ] |

## Símbolos Combinados

| SÍMBOLOS | SONIDO | GRAFÍA |
|---|---|---|
| 38. [tʃ] | Como la **ch** de mu**ch**o. | **ch**ief [tʃif]<br>mu**ch** [mʌtʃ]<br>ca**tch** [kætʃ]<br>righ**te**ous [ˈraɪtʃəs]<br>ques**ti**on [ˈkwɛstʃən]<br>na**t**ural [ˈnætʃərəl] |
| 39. [dʒ] | Como la **y** de cón**y**uge y **dj** de la palabra francesa **adj**acent. | **g**em [dʒɛm]<br>**j**ust [dʒʌst]<br>ver**d**ure [ˈvʌrdʒər]<br>sol**di**er [ˈsoldʒər]<br>bri**dg**e [brɪdʒ]<br>exa**gg**erate [ɛgˈzædʒəret]<br>**adj**ourn [əˈdʒʌrn] |
| 40. [ʌr] | El símbolo [ʌ] y el símbolo [r] que le sigue, representan en este diccionario un solo sonido, el de la llamada vocal de colorido de **r**, acentuada. Es más largo y más tenso que [ʌ]. Se produce con la lengua en la acostumbrada posición elevada para la **r** pero sin el sonido de **r**. Véase 27 arriba. | h**ur**t [hʌrt]<br>h**er**b [hʌrb]<br>**ear**ly [ˈʌrlɪ]<br>b**ir**d [bʌrd]<br>w**or**m [wʌrm]<br>c**o**lonel [ˈkʌrnəl]<br>c**our**age [ˈkʌrɪdʒ]<br>m**yr**tle [mʌrtəl] |
| 41. [ər] | El símbolo [ə] y el símbolo [r] que le sigue, representan en este diccionario un solo sonido, el de la llamada vocal de colorido de **r**, inacentuada. Se produce con la lengua en la acostumbrada posición elevada para la **r** pero sin el sonido de **r**. Véase 27 arriba. | fath**er** [ˈfɑðər]<br>li**ar** [ˈlaɪər]<br>p**er**ceive [pərˈsiv]<br>mart**yr** [ˈmɑrtər]<br>cent**re** [ˈsɛntər] |
| 42. [hw] | Como **ju** en **ju**erga pero con la **j** mucho más suave que en español. | **wh**ile [hwaɪl]<br>**wh**en [hwɛn] |
| 43. [ll] | Mucho más largo que [l] pero de carácter semejante. No tiene nada que ver con la **ll** española. | so**l**ely [ˈsollɪ]<br>coo**lly** [ˈkullɪ]<br>sou**ll**ess [ˈsollɪs] |

## Sonidos Extranjeros

| SÍMBOLO | SONIDO | GRAFÍA |
|---|---|---|
| 44. [a] | francés | **a**vant-g**a**rde [avɑ̃ˈgard] |
| 45. [ɑ̃] | francés | contret**em**ps [kõtrəˈtɑ̃] |
| 46. [æ̃] | francés | anci**en** régime [ɑ̃sjæ̃ reˈʒim] |
| 47. [õ] | francés | b**on** mot [bõˈmo] |
| 48. [ø] | francés | mili**eu** [miˈljø] |
| 49. [œ] | alemán | G**ö**ttingen [ˈgœtɪŋən] |
| 50. [y] | francés | au j**u**s [oˈʒy] |
| 51. [x] | alemán | Ma**ch**e [ˈmɑxə] |

**§2. El número.** 1. Añaden una **s** [s] para formar el plural los substantivos que terminan en uno de los siguientes sonidos consonantes sordos: [f], [k], [p], [t] y [θ].

| SONIDO FINAL | SINGULAR | PLURAL |
|---|---|---|
| [f] | **chief** [tʃif] | **chiefs** [tʃifs] |
| | **tariff** [ˈtærɪf] | **tariffs** [ˈtærɪfs] |
| | **cough** [kɔf] | **coughs** [kɔfs] |
| | **fife** [faɪf] | **fifes** [faɪfs] |
| [k] | **sack** [sæk] | **sacks** [sæks] |
| | **rake** [rek] | **rakes** [reks] |
| [p] | **cap** [kæp] | **caps** [kæps] |
| | **pipe** [paɪp] | **pipes** [paɪps] |
| [t] | **cat** [kæt] | **cats** [kæts] |
| | **fate** [fet] | **fates** [fets] |
| [θ] | **death** [dɛθ] | **deaths** [dɛθs] |

(*a*) Sin embargo, la mayor parte de los substantivos que terminan en **f** [f] y **fe** [f] cambian **f** y **fe** en **ves** [vz] para formar el plural.

| SINGULAR | PLURAL |
|---|---|
| **calf** [kæf] | **calves** [kævz] |
| **half** [hæf] | **halves** [hævz] |
| **leaf** [lif] | **leaves** [livz] |
| **thief** [θif] | **thieves** [θivz] |
| **wolf** [wʊlf] | **wolves** [wʊlvz] |
| **knife** [naɪf] | **knives** [naɪvz] |
| **life** [laɪf] | **lives** [laɪvz] |
| **wife** [waɪf] | **wives** [waɪvz] |

Los siguientes substantivos tienen el plural regular.

| SINGULAR | PLURAL |
|---|---|
| **chief** [tʃif] | **chiefs** [tʃifs] |
| **dwarf** [dwɔrf] | **dwarfs** [dwɔrfs] |
| **handkerchief** [ˈhæŋkərtʃɪf] | **handkerchiefs** [ˈhæŋkərtʃɪfs] |
| **proof** [pruf] | **proofs** [prufs] |
| **roof** [ruf] | **roofs** [rufs] |

Los siguientes substantivos tienen el plural regular e irregular.

| SINGULAR | PLURAL |
|---|---|
| **scarf** [skɑrf] | **scarfs** [skɑrfs]<br>**scarves** [skɑrvz] |
| **wharf** [hwɔrf] | **wharfs** [hwɔrfs]<br>**wharves** [hwɔrvz] |

(*b*) Añaden **s** [s] para formar el plural la mayor parte de los substantivos que terminan en **th.**

| SINGULAR | PLURAL |
|---|---|
| **breath** [brɛθ] | **breaths** [brɛθs] |
| **death** [dɛθ] | **deaths** [dɛθs] |
| **growth** [groθ] | **growths** [groθs] |
| **month** [mʌnθ] | **months** [mʌnθs] |

Algunos substantivos añaden **s** [z], cambiando el sonido de **th** a [ð].

| SINGULAR | PLURAL |
|---|---|
| **mouth** [maʊθ] | **mouths** [maʊðz] |

Y algunos forman el plural de ambos modos.

| SINGULAR | PLURAL |
|---|---|
| **oath** [oθ] | **oaths** [oθs] y [oðz] |
| **truth** [truθ] | **truths** [truθs] y [truðz] |
| **wreath** [riθ] | **wreaths** [riθs] y [riðz] |
| **youth** [juθ] | **youths** [juθs] y [juðz] |

2. Añaden una **s** [z] para formar el plural los substantivos que terminan en uno de los siguientes sonidos consonantes sonoros: [b], [d], [ð], [g], [l], [m], [n], [ŋ], [r] y [v].

| SONIDO FINAL | SINGULAR | PLURAL |
|---|---|---|
| [b] | **rib** [rɪb] | **ribs** [rɪbz] |
| | **tube** [tjub] | **tubes** [tjubz] |
| [d] | **lad** [læd] | **lads** [lædz] |
| | **side** [saɪd] | **sides** [saɪdz] |
| [ð] | **lathe** [leð] | **lathes** [leðz] |
| [g] | **pig** [pɪg] | **pigs** [pɪgz] |
| | **rogue** [rog] | **rogues** [rogz] |
| [l] | **ball** [bɔl] | **balls** [bɔlz] |
| | **tile** [taɪl] | **tiles** [taɪlz] |
| | **pebble** [ˈpɛbəl] | **pebbles** [ˈpɛbəlz] |
| [m] | **rim** [rɪm] | **rims** [rɪmz] |
| | **lamb** [læm] | **lambs** [læmz] |
| | **hymn** [hɪm] | **hymns** [hɪmz] |
| | **name** [nem] | **names** [nemz] |
| [n] | **ton** [tʌn] | **tons** [tʌnz] |
| | **bone** [bon] | **bones** [bonz] |
| [ŋ] | **bung** [bʌŋ] | **bungs** [bʌŋz] |
| | **tongue** [tʌŋ] | **tongues** [tʌŋz] |
| [r] | **bar** [bɑr] | **bars** [bɑrz] |
| | **tire** [taɪr] | **tires** [taɪrz] |
| [v] | **stove** [stov] | **stoves** [stovz] |

3. Añaden **s** [ɪz] o **es** [ɪz] para formar el plural los substantivos que terminan en uno de los siguientes sonidos consonantes africados y fricativos: [ʃ], [ʒ], [tʃ], [dʒ], [s] y [z]. Añaden **s** si la grafía termina en **e** muda, **es** si termina en consonante.

| SONIDO FINAL | SINGULAR | PLURAL |
|---|---|---|
| [ʃ] | **wish** [wɪʃ] | **wishes** [ˈwɪʃɪz] |
| [ʒ] | **mirage** [mɪˈrɑʒ] | **mirages** [mɪˈrɑʒɪz] |
| [tʃ] | **latch** [lætʃ] | **latches** [ˈlætʃɪz] |
| [dʒ] | **edge** [ɛdʒ] | **edges** [ˈɛdʒɪz] |
| [s] | **class** [klæs] | **classes** [ˈklæsɪz] |
| | **box** [bɑks] | **boxes** [ˈbɑksɪz] |
| | **case** [kes] | **cases** [ˈkesɪz] |
| [z] | **buzz** [bʌz] | **buzzes** [ˈbʌzɪz] |
| | **maze** [mez] | **mazes** [ˈmezɪz] |

El sonido [s] del substantivo **house** cambia en [z] con la adición de la **s** del plural.

| SINGULAR | PLURAL |
|---|---|
| **house** [haʊs] | **houses** [ˈhaʊzɪz] |

4. Añaden **s** [z] para formar el plural los substantivos que terminan en vocal o diptongo.

| SINGULAR | PLURAL |
|---|---|
| **sofa** [ˈsofə] | **sofas** [ˈsofəz] |
| **sea** [si] | **seas** [siz] |
| **eye** [aɪ] | **eyes** [aɪz] |
| **toe** [to] | **toes** [toz] |
| **shoe** [ʃu] | **shoes** [ʃuz] |
| **value** [ˈvæljʊ] | **values** [ˈvæljʊz] |
| **cow** [kaʊ] | **cows** [kaʊz] |
| **boy** [bɔɪ] | **boys** [bɔɪz] |

(*a*) La mayor parte de los substantivos que terminan en **o** añaden **es** [z] para formar el plural. Hay algunos que añaden **s** [z] y otros que añaden **s** [z] o **es** [z].

| SINGULAR | PLURAL |
|---|---|
| **potato** [pəˈteto] | **potatoes** [pəˈtetoz] |
| **cameo** [ˈkæmɪo] | **cameos** [ˈkæmɪoz] |
| **motto** [ˈmɑto] | **mottoes** o **mottos** [ˈmɑtoz] |

(*b*) Los substantivos que terminan en **y** cambian la **y** en **ies**, si va precedida de consonante.

| SINGULAR | PLURAL |
|---|---|
| **city** [ˈsɪtɪ] | **cities** [ˈsɪtɪz] |
| **sky** [skaɪ] | **skies** [skaɪz] |

No cambian la **y** si va precedida de vocal.

| SINGULAR | PLURAL |
|---|---|
| **toy** [tɔɪ] | **toys** [tɔɪz] |
| **key** [ki] | **keys** [kiz] |

5. Hay varios substantivos que tienen el plural enteramente irregular.

| SINGULAR | PLURAL |
|---|---|
| **man** [mæn] | **men** [mɛn] |
| **woman** [ˈwʊmən] | **women** [ˈwɪmɪn] |
| **child** [tʃaɪld] | **children** [ˈtʃɪldrən] |
| **ox** [ɑks] | **oxen** [ˈɑksən] |
| **foot** [fʊt] | **feet** [fit] |
| **goose** [gus] | **geese** [gis] |
| **tooth** [tuθ] | **teeth** [tiθ] |
| **louse** [laʊs] | **lice** [laɪs] |
| **mouse** [maʊs] | **mice** [maɪs] |

Los compuestos de estos substantivos forman el plural de la misma manera. Pero los substantivos **German, Mussulman, Roman** y **Ottoman,** que nada tienen que ver con la palabra **man,** añaden **s** para formar el plural: **Germans, Mussulmans, Romans** y **Ottomans.** Y el substantivo **Norman** también añade **s** para formar el plural: **Normans.**

6. Hay muchos substantivos que tienen como plural la misma forma del singular, p.ej., **one sheep, two sheep.** Esto se ve en los nombres de medida y de peces y también en los nombres de nacionalidad que terminan en **ese,** p.ej., **one Japanese, two Japanese.** Los siguientes substantivos de origen latino y francés también tienen como plural la misma forma y la misma pronunciación del singular: **abatis, chamois, forceps, series** y **species.** Y el plural de **corps** tiene la misma forma del singular, aunque la **s,** muda en el singular, va pronunciada en el plural: **corps** [kor] y **corps** [korz].

7. Los substantivos de origen latino que terminan en **us, a** y **um** forman el plural como en la declinación latina. Así es que **us** cambia en **i, a** en **ae,** y **um** en **a.**

| SINGULAR | PLURAL |
|---|---|
| **alumnus** [əˈlʌmnəs] | **alumni** [əˈlʌmnaɪ] |
| **alumna** [əˈlʌmnə] | **alumnae** [əˈlʌmni] |
| **addendum** [əˈdɛndəm] | **addenda** [əˈdɛndə] |

Algunos de estos substantivos tienen dos plurales, el latino y el regular, p.ej., **vertebra** con **vertebrae** y **vertebras, fungus** con **fungi** y **funguses, stratum** con **strata** y **stratums.**

8. Los substantivos de origen griego que terminan en **is** y **on** forman el plural como en la declinación griega. Así es que **is** cambia en **es** y **on** cambia en **a.**

| SINGULAR | PLURAL |
|---|---|
| **crisis** [ˈkraɪsɪs] | **crises** [ˈkraɪsiz] |
| **automaton** [ɔˈtɑmətɑn] | **automata** [ɔˈtɑmətə] |

9. Los substantivos de origen latino que terminan en **ex** e **ix** tienen dos plurales, uno como en la declinación latina y uno regular, algunas veces con sentido distinto, p.ej., **vertex** con **vertices** y **vertexes** y **matrix** con **matrices** y **matrixes.**

10. Los substantivos **cherub** y **seraph,** de origen hebreo, tienen dos plurales: **cherubim** y **cherubs, seraphim** y **seraphs.** Y hay otros plurales del tipo hebreo, p.ej., **Sephardim.**

11. Ciertos substantivos se consideran singulares aunque tienen la **s** del plural, p.ej., **gallows, measles, news.** Los substantivos acabados en **ics** pertenecen a este grupo cuando designan artes y ciencias; pero son plurales cuando tienen otro sentido, p.ej., **acoustics** es singular cuando significa acústica (*ciencia de los sonidos*) y plural cuando significa acústica arquitectural (*condiciones de un recinto para la reflexión de los sonidos*).

**§3. La comparación de los adjetivos.** Añaden **er** (o **r**) [ər] para formar el comparativo y **est** (o **st**) [ɪst] para formar el superlativo (1) los adjetivos monosílabos, (2) los adjetivos bisílabos que terminan en **er, le, ow, y** y **some** inacentuados y (3) algunos adjetivos bisílabos que terminan en sílaba acentuada.

| | | |
|---|---|---|
| **soft** | **softer** | **softest** |
| **clever** | **cleverer** | **cleverest** |
| **mellow** | **mellower** | **mellowest** |

(*a*) Si el adjetivo termina en consonante simple precedida de vocal simple acentuada, se dobla la consonante al añadir **er** y **est.**

| | | |
|---|---|---|
| **fat** | **fatter** | **fattest** |
| **sad** | **sadder** | **saddest** |
| **red** | **redder** | **reddest** |
| **dim** | **dimmer** | **dimmest** |
| **big** | **bigger** | **biggest** |
| **hot** | **hotter** | **hottest** |

(*b*) Si la vocal no es simple, no se dobla la consonante.

| | | |
|---|---|---|
| **great** | **greater** | **greatest** |
| **deep** | **deeper** | **deepest** |
| **poor** | **poorer** | **poorest** |

(*c*) Si el adjetivo termina en **e** muda, se añade simplemente **r** y **st** en la escritura pero [ər] y [ɪst] en la pronunciación.

| | | |
|---|---|---|
| **large** [lɑrdʒ] | **larger** [ˈlɑrdʒər] | **largest** [ˈlɑrdʒɪst] |
| **wise** [waɪz] | **wiser** [ˈwaɪzər] | **wisest** [ˈwaɪzɪst] |
| **handsome** [ˈhænsəm] | **handsomer** [ˈhænsəmər] | **handsomest** [ˈhænsəmɪst] |
| **polite** [pəˈlaɪt] | **politer** [pəˈlaɪtər] | **politest** [pəˈlaɪtɪst] |
| **sincere** [sɪnˈsɪr] | **sincerer** [sɪnˈsɪrər] | **sincerest** [sɪnˈsɪrɪst] |

(*d*) Si el adjetivo termina en **ng** [ŋ], se intercala el sonido [g] al añadir **er** y **est.**

| | | |
|---|---|---|
| **long** [lɔŋ] | **longer** [ˈlɔŋgər] | **longest** [ˈlɔŋgɪst] |
| **strong** [strɔŋ] | **stronger** [ˈstrɔŋgər] | **strongest** [ˈstrɔŋgɪst] |
| **young** [jʌŋ] | **younger** [ˈjʌŋgər] | **youngest** [ˈjʌŋgɪst] |

(*e*) Si el adjetivo termina en **y** precedida de consonante, se cambia la **y** en **i** al añadir **er** y **est.**

| | | |
|---|---|---|
| **holy** [ˈholɪ] | **holier** [ˈholɪər] | **holiest** [ˈholɪɪst] |
| **happy** [ˈhæpɪ] | **happier** [ˈhæpɪər] | **happiest** [ˈhæpɪɪst] |

Si la **y** va precedida de vocal, no se cambia en **i.**

| | | |
|---|---|---|
| **coy** [kɔɪ] | **coyer** [ˈkɔɪər] | **coyest** [ˈkɔɪɪst] |

Anteponen **more** para formar el comparativo y **most** para formar el superlativo los adjetivos de dos sílabas que terminan en **ful, ish** y **ous** y los adjetivos de más de dos sílabas.

| | | |
|---|---|---|
| **helpful** | **more helpful** | **most helpful** |
| **selfish** | **more selfish** | **most selfish** |
| **vicious** | **more vicious** | **most vicious** |
| **excellent** | **more excellent** | **most excellent** |

Los siguientes adjetivos tienen comparación irregular.

| | | |
|---|---|---|
| **good** }<br>**well** } | **better** | **best** |
| **bad** }<br>**ill** } | **worse** | **worst** |
| **little** | **less, lesser** | **least** |
| **much, many** | **more** | **most** |
| **far** | **farther** | **farthest** |

**§4. Presente de indicativo.** El presente de indicativo es idéntico al infinitivo con la excepción de la tercera persona del singular, que se forma añadiendo **s** o **es.**

1. Añaden una **s** [s] para formar la tercera persona del singular los verbos que terminan en uno de los siguientes sonidos consonantes sordos: [f], [k], [p], [t] y [θ].

| SONIDO FINAL | INFINITIVO | TERCERA PERSONA DEL SINGULAR |
|---|---|---|
| [f] | **doff** [dɑf] | **doffs** [dɑfs] |
| | **cough** [kɔf] | **coughs** [kɔfs] |
| | **chafe** [tʃef] | **chafes** [tʃefs] |
| [k] | **seek** [sik] | **seeks** [siks] |
| | **bake** [bek] | **bakes** [beks] |
| [p] | **sip** [sɪp] | **sips** [sɪps] |
| | **hope** [hop] | **hopes** [hops] |
| [t] | **sit** [sɪt] | **sits** [sɪts] |
| | **hate** [het] | **hates** [hets] |
| [θ] | **lath** [læθ] | **laths** [læθs] |

2. Añaden una **s** [z] para formar la tercera persona del singular los verbos que terminan en uno de los siguientes sonidos consonantes sonoros: [b], [d], [ð], [g], [l], [m], [n], [ŋ], [r] y [v].

| SONIDO FINAL | INFINITIVO | TERCERA PERSONA DEL SINGULAR |
|---|---|---|
| [b] | **sob** [sɑb] | **sobs** [sɑbz] |
| | **robe** [rob] | **robes** [robz] |
| [d] | **raid** [red] | **raids** [redz] |
| | **hide** [haɪd] | **hides** [haɪdz] |
| [ð] | **smooth** [smuð] | **smooths** [smuðz] |
| | **bathe** [beð] | **bathes** [beðz] |
| [g] | **sag** [sæg] | **sags** [sægz] |
| [l] | **kill** [kɪl] | **kills** [kɪlz] |
| | **smile** [smaɪl] | **smiles** [smaɪlz] |
| [m] | **seem** [sim] | **seems** [simz] |
| | **name** [nem] | **names** [nemz] |
| [n] | **pin** [pɪn] | **pins** [pɪnz] |
| | **sign** [saɪn] | **signs** [saɪnz] |
| | **pine** [paɪn] | **pines** [paɪnz] |
| [ŋ] | **ring** [rɪŋ] | **rings** [rɪŋz] |
| [r] | **hear** [hɪr] | **hears** [hɪrz] |
| | **care** [kɛr] | **cares** [kɛrz] |
| [v] | **rev** [rɛv] | **revs** [rɛvz] |
| | **give** [gɪv] | **gives** [gɪvz] |

3. Añaden **s** [ɪz] o **es** [ɪz] para formar la tercera persona del singular los verbos que terminan en uno de los siguientes sonidos consonantes africados y fricativos: [ʃ], [ʒ], [tʃ], [dʒ], [s], y [z]. Añaden **s** si la grafía termina en **e** muda, **es** si termina en consonante.

| SONIDO FINAL | INFINITIVO | TERCERA PERSONA DEL SINGULAR |
|---|---|---|
| [ʃ] | **wash** [wɑʃ] | **washes** [ˈwɑʃɪz] |
| | **cache** [kæʃ] | **caches** [ˈkæʃɪz] |
| [ʒ] | **massage** [məˈsɑʒ] | **massages** [məˈsɑʒɪz] |
| [tʃ] | **attach** [əˈtætʃ] | **attaches** [əˈtætʃɪz] |
| | **catch** [kætʃ] | **catches** [ˈkætʃɪz] |
| [dʒ] | **pledge** [plɛdʒ] | **pledges** [ˈplɛdʒɪz] |
| | **urge** [ʌrdʒ] | **urges** [ˈʌrdʒɪz] |
| [s] | **pass** [pæs] | **passes** [ˈpæsɪz] |
| | **race** [res] | **races** [ˈresɪz] |
| [z] | **buzz** [bʌz] | **buzzes** [ˈbʌzɪz] |
| | **praise** [prez] | **praises** [ˈprezɪz] |

4. Añaden una **s** [z] para formar la tercera persona del singular los verbos que terminan en vocal o diptongo.

| SONIDO FINAL | INFINITIVO | TERCERA PERSONA DEL SINGULAR |
|---|---|---|
| [ɑ] | **baa** [bɑ] | **baas** [bɑz] |
| [e] | **play** [ple] | **plays** [plez] |
| [i] | **see** [si] | **sees** [siz] |
| [ɔ] | **saw** [sɔ] | **saws** [sɔz] |
| [o] | **know** [no] | **knows** [noz] |
| [u] | **woo** [wu] | **woos** [wuz] |
| [aɪ] | **tie** [taɪ] | **ties** [taɪz] |
| | **sigh** [saɪ] | **sighs** [saɪz] |
| [aʊ] | **plow** [plaʊ] | **plows** [plaʊz] |
| [ɔɪ] | **toy** [tɔɪ] | **toys** [tɔɪz] |

Dos verbos que terminan en vocal añaden **es** [z] para formar la tercera persona del singular: **do** [du], **does** [dʌz] y **go** [go], **goes** [goz].

Los verbos que terminan en **y** cambian la **y** en **ies**, si va precedida de consonante.

| INFINITIVO | TERCERA PERSONA DEL SINGULAR |
|---|---|
| **carry** [ˈkærɪ] | **carries** [ˈkærɪz] |
| **satisfy** [ˈsætɪsfaɪ] | **satisfies** [ˈsætɪsfaɪz] |
| **try** [traɪ] | **tries** [traɪz] |

No cambian la **y** si va precedida de vocal.

| INFINITIVO | TERCERA PERSONA DEL SINGULAR |
|---|---|
| **pray** [pre] | **prays** [prez] |
| **buy** [baɪ] | **buys** [baɪz] |

El presente de indicativo del verbo **be** es muy irregular.

| | |
|---|---|
| **I am** [æm] | **we are** [ɑr] |
| **you are** [ɑr] | **you are** |
| **he** o **she is** [ɪz] | **they are** |

Además de **be**, cuatro verbos más tienen la tercera persona del singular irregular en la pronunciación.

| INFINITIVO | TERCERA PERSONA DEL SINGULAR |
|---|---|
| **do** [du] | **does** [dʌz] |
| **have** [hæv] | **has** [hæz] |
| **say** [se] | **says** [sɛz] |

**§5. El gerundio (participio activo).** 1. Para formar el gerundio, se añade **ing** al infinitivo, p.ej., **walk** [wɔk], **walking** [ˈwɔkɪŋ]; **eat** [it], **eating** [ˈitɪŋ].

2. Si el infinitivo termina en consonante simple precedida de vocal simple acentuada, se dobla esta consonante al añadir **ing**.

| | |
|---|---|
| **rub** [rʌb] | **rubbing** [ˈrʌbɪŋ] |
| **pad** [pæd] | **padding** [ˈpædɪŋ] |
| **beg** [bɛg] | **begging** [ˈbɛgɪŋ] |
| **dispel** [dɪsˈpɛl] | **dispelling** [dɪsˈpɛlɪŋ] |
| **trim** [trɪm] | **trimming** [ˈtrɪmɪŋ] |
| **run** [rʌn] | **running** [ˈrʌnɪŋ] |
| **sip** [sɪp] | **sipping** [ˈsɪpɪŋ] |
| **refer** [rɪˈfʌr] | **referring** [rɪˈfʌrɪŋ] |
| **bat** [bæt] | **batting** [ˈbætɪŋ] |
| **rev** [rɛv] | **revving** [ˈrɛvɪŋ] |

Si la vocal no es simple, no se dobla la consonante.

| | |
|---|---|
| **seem** [sim] | **seeming** [ˈsimɪŋ] |
| **cook** [kʊk] | **cooking** [ˈkʊkɪŋ] |
| **appear** [əˈpɪr] | **appearing** [əˈpɪrɪŋ] |
| **soak** [sok] | **soaking** [ˈsokɪŋ] |

Si la vocal no es acentuada, no se dobla la consonante.

| | |
|---|---|
| **suffer** [ˈsʌfər] | **suffering** [ˈsʌfərɪŋ] |
| **labor** [ˈlebər] | **laboring** [ˈlebərɪŋ] |

Si la consonante es **l** y la vocal no acentuada, se puede dejar la **l** simple o doblarla al añadir **ing**.

| | |
|---|---|
| **travel** [ˈtrævəl] | **traveling** [ˈtrævəlɪŋ] o **travelling** [ˈtrævəlɪŋ] |

Si el verbo termina en **e** muda, se la omite al añadir **ing**.

| | |
|---|---|
| **make** [mek] | **making** [ˈmekɪŋ] |
| **ride** [raɪd] | **riding** [ˈraɪdɪŋ] |

No se omite la **e** en los gerundios de **dye, singe** y los verbos que terminan en **oe**.

| | |
|---|---|
| **dye** [daɪ] | **dyeing** [ˈdaɪɪŋ] |
| **singe** [sɪndʒ] | **singeing** [ˈsɪndʒɪŋ] |
| **hoe** [ho] | **hoeing** [ˈho·ɪŋ] |
| **tiptoe** [ˈtɪpˌto] | **tiptoeing** [ˈtɪpˌto·ɪŋ] |

**§6. Las clases de los verbos.** Los verbos débiles son los que forman el pretérito y el participio pasado sin cambiar la vocal de la raíz y añadiendo **ed, d** o **t,** p.ej., **walk, walked, walked.** Los verbos fuertes son los que forman el pretérito y el participio pasado cambiando la vocal de la raíz y añadiendo **en, n** o **ne,** p.ej., **fly, flew, flown.** Y los verbos mixtos son los que forman el pretérito y el participio pasado cambiando la vocal de la raíz y añadiendo **d** o **t,** p.ej., **tell, told, told.**

Hay verbos débiles que no añaden **d** o **t** porque ya la tienen en el infinitivo, p.ej., **cost, cost, cost** y **spend, spent, spent.** Y hay verbos fuertes que no añaden **en, n** o **ne** en el participio pasado por haberla perdido, p.ej., **awake, awoke, awoke,** o porque ya la tienen en el infinitivo, p.ej., **spin, spun, spun.**

**§7. Los verbos débiles.** Añaden **ed** [t] o **d** [t] para formar el pretérito y el participio pasado los verbos débiles que terminan en uno de los siguientes sonidos consonantes sordos: [f], [k], [p], [s], [θ], [ʃ] y [tʃ]. La terminación se escribe **ed** si el verbo no termina en **e** muda, **d** si termina en **e** muda.

Verbos que no terminan en **e** muda.

| SONIDO FINAL | INFINITIVO | PRETÉRITO Y PARTICIPIO PASADO |
|---|---|---|
| [f] | **loaf** [lof] | **loafed** [loft] |
| | **cough** [kɔf] | **coughed** [kɔft] |
| [k] | **mock** [mɑk] | **mocked** [mɑkt] |
| [p] | **camp** [kæmp] | **camped** [kæmpt] |
| [s] | **bless** [blɛs] | **blessed** [blɛst] |
| | **mix** [mɪks] | **mixed** [mɪkst] |
| [θ] | **lath** [læθ] | **lathed** [læθt] |
| [ʃ] | **wash** [wɔʃ] | **washed** [wɔʃt] |
| [tʃ] | **patch** [pætʃ] | **patched** [pætʃt] |

Verbos que terminan en **e** muda.

| SONIDO FINAL | INFINITIVO | PRETÉRITO Y PARTICIPIO PASADO |
|---|---|---|
| [f] | **knife** [naɪf] | **knifed** [naɪft] |
| [k] | **bake** [bek] | **baked** [bekt] |
| [p] | **wipe** [waɪp] | **wiped** [waɪpt] |
| [ʃ] | **cache** [kæʃ] | **cached** [kæʃt] |

Añaden **ed** [d] o **d** [d] para formar el pretérito y el participio pasado los verbos débiles que terminan en uno de los siguientes sonidos consonantes sonoros: [b], [g], [l], [m], [n], [r], [v], [z], [ð], [ʒ], [dʒ] y [ŋ]. La terminación se escribe **ed** si el verbo no termina en **e** muda, **d** si termina en **e** muda.

Verbos que no terminan en **e** muda.

| SONIDO FINAL | INFINITIVO | PRETÉRITO Y PARTICIPIO PASADO |
|---|---|---|
| [b] | **ebb** [ɛb] | **ebbed** [ɛbd] |
| [g] | **egg** [ɛg] | **egged** [ɛgd] |
| [l] | **sail** [sel] | **sailed** [seld] |
| [m] | **storm** [stɔrm] | **stormed** [stɔrmd] |
| [n] | **lean** [lin] | **leaned** [lind] |
| [r] | **smear** [smɪr] | **smeared** [smɪrd] |
| [z] | **buzz** [bʌz] | **buzzed** [bʌzd] |
| [ð] | **smooth** [smuð] | **smoothed** [smuðd] |
| [ŋ] | **bang** [bæŋ] | **banged** [bæŋd] |

Verbos que terminan en **e** muda.

| SONIDO FINAL | INFINITIVO | PRETÉRITO Y PARTICIPIO PASADO |
|---|---|---|
| [b] | **robe** [rob] | **robed** [robd] |
| [l] | **scale** [skel] | **scaled** [skeld] |
| [m] | **name** [nem] | **named** [nemd] |
| [n] | **pine** [paɪn] | **pined** [paɪnd] |
| [r] | **care** [kɛr] | **cared** [kɛrd] |
| [v] | **move** [muv] | **moved** [muvd] |
| [z] | **praise** [prez] | **praised** [prezd] |
| [ð] | **bathe** [beð] | **bathed** [beðd] |
| [ʒ] | **massage** [mə'sɑʒ] | **massaged** [mə'sɑʒd] |
| [dʒ] | **oblige** [ə'blaɪdʒ] | **obliged** [ə'blaɪdʒd] |

Añaden **ed** [ɪd] o **d** [ɪd] para formar el pretérito y el participio pasado los verbos que terminan en [d] o [t]. La terminación se escribe **ed** si el verbo no termina en **e** muda, **d** si termina en **e** muda.

Verbos que no terminan en **e** muda.

| SONIDO FINAL | INFINITIVO | PRETÉRITO Y PARTICIPIO PASADO |
|---|---|---|
| [d] | **end** [ɛnd] | **ended** ['ɛndɪd] |
| [t] | **wait** [wet] | **waited** ['wetɪd] |

Verbos que terminan en **e** muda.

| SONIDO FINAL | INFINITIVO | PRETÉRITO Y PARTICIPIO PASADO |
|---|---|---|
| [d] | **wade** [wed] | **waded** ['wedɪd] |
| [t] | **invite** [ɪn'vaɪt] | **invited** [ɪn'vaɪtɪd] |

Añaden **ed** [d] para formar el pretérito y el participio pasado los verbos que terminan en vocal o diptongo.

| INFINITIVO | PRETÉRITO Y PARTICIPIO PASADO |
|---|---|
| **baa** [bɑ] | **baaed** [bɑd] |
| **pray** [pre] | **prayed** [pred] |
| **key** [ki] | **keyed** [kid] |
| **mow** [mo] | **mowed** [mod] |
| **woo** [wu] | **wooed** [wud] |
| **sigh** [saɪ] | **sighed** [saɪd] |
| **plow** [plaʊ] | **plowed** [plaʊd] |
| **toy** [tɔɪ] | **toyed** [tɔɪd] |

Los pretéritos y los participios pasados de dos verbos débiles que terminan en **ay** se escriben de modo irregular aunque se pronuncian regularmente.

| INFINITIVO | PRETÉRITO Y PARTICIPIO PASADO |
|---|---|
| **lay** [le] | **laid** [led] |
| **pay** [pe] | **paid** [ped] |

Los verbos débiles que terminan en **y** cambian la **y** en **ied** para formar el pretérito y el participio pasado. Si la **y** se pronuncia [aɪ], **ied** se pronuncia [aɪd]. Si la **y** se pronuncia [ɪ], **ied** se pronuncia [ɪd].

| INFINITIVO | PRETÉRITO Y PARTICIPIO PASADO |
|---|---|
| **satisfy** ['sætɪsfaɪ] | **satisfied** ['sætɪsfaɪd] |
| **try** [traɪ] | **tried** [traɪd] |
| **carry** ['kærɪ] | **carried** ['kærɪd] |
| **pity** ['pɪtɪ] | **pitied** ['pɪtɪd] |

Si el verbo termina en consonante simple precedida de vocal simple acentuada, se dobla esta consonante al añadir **ed.**

| INFINITIVO | PRETÉRITO Y PARTICIPIO PASADO |
|---|---|
| **rub** [rʌb] | **rubbed** [rʌbd] |
| **pad** [pæd] | **padded** [ˈpædɪd] |
| **beg** [bɛg] | **begged** [bɛgd] |
| **trek** [trɛk] | **trekked** [trɛkt] |
| **dispel** [dɪsˈpɛl] | **dispelled** [dɪsˈpɛld] |
| **trim** [trɪm] | **trimmed** [trɪmd] |
| **tan** [tæn] | **tanned** [tænd] |
| **sip** [sɪp] | **sipped** [sɪpt] |
| **refer** [rɪˈfʌr] | **referred** [rɪˈfʌrd] |
| **bat** [bæt] | **batted** [ˈbætɪd] |
| **rev** [rɛv] | **revved** [rɛvd] |

Si la vocal no es simple, no se dobla la consonante.

| INFINITIVO | PRETÉRITO Y PARTICIPIO PASADO |
|---|---|
| **seem** [sim] | **seemed** [simd] |
| **cook** [kʊk] | **cooked** [kʊkt] |
| **appear** [əˈpɪr] | **appeared** [əˈpɪrd] |
| **soak** [sok] | **soaked** [sokt] |

Si la vocal no va acentuada, no se dobla la consonante.

| INFINITIVO | PRETÉRITO Y PARTICIPIO PASADO |
|---|---|
| **suffer** [ˈsʌfər] | **suffered** [ˈsʌfərd] |
| **labor** [ˈlebər] | **labored** [ˈlebərd] |

Si la vocal no va acentuada y la consonante es **l**, se puede dejar la **l** simple o doblarla al añadir **ed.**

| INFINITIVO | PRETÉRITO Y PARTICIPIO PASADO |
|---|---|
| **travel** [ˈtrævəl] | **traveled** [ˈtrævəld] o **travelled** [ˈtrævəld] |

La **e** de **ed** de los participios pasados usados como adjetivos se pronuncia en todos los casos, p.ej., **blessed** [ˈblɛsɪd]; **learned** [ˈlʌrnɪd].

**§8. Los verbos débiles irregulares.** Algunos verbos débiles que terminan en **n, l** o **ll,** forman el pretérito y el participio pasado con la adición de **ed** [d] en la manera regular o con la adición de **t** y con la simplificación de **ll** en **l.**

| INFINITIVO | PRETÉRITO Y PARTICIPIO PASADO |
|---|---|
| **burn** [bʌrn] | **burned** [bʌrnd] y **burnt** [bʌrnt] |
| **spoil** [spɔɪl] | **spoiled** [spɔɪld] y **spoilt** [spɔɪlt] |
| **smell** [smɛl] | **smelled** [smɛld] y **smelt** [smɛlt] |

Algunos verbos débiles que terminan en **nd, ld** y **rd** forman el pretérito y el participio pasado cambiando la **d** final en **t.**

| INFINITIVO | PRETÉRITO Y PARTICIPIO PASADO |
|---|---|
| **bend** [bɛnd] | **bent** [bɛnt] |
| **build** [bɪld] | **built** [bɪlt] |
| **gird** [gʌrd] | **girt** [gʌrt] |

Una veintena de verbos que terminan en **d, t** o **st** no varían en la formación del pretérito y el participio pasado.

| INFINITIVO | PRETÉRITO Y PARTICIPIO PASADO |
|---|---|
| **cut** [kʌt] | **cut** [kʌt] |
| **hurt** [hʌrt] | **hurt** [hʌrt] |
| **rid** [rɪd] | **rid** [rɪd] |
| **spread** [sprɛd] | **spread** [sprɛd] |
| **cast** [kæst] | **cast** [kæst] |
| **cost** [kɔst] | **cost** [kɔst] |
| **thrust** [θrʌst] | **thrust** [θrʌst] |

**§9. Los verbos fuertes.** Damos abajo una lista de verbos fuertes que ejemplifican todas las variaciones del sonido de la vocal de la raíz en las tres partes principales.

| INFINITIVO | PRETÉRITO | PARTICIPIO PASADO |
|---|---|---|
| **hang** [hæŋ] | **hung** [hʌŋ] | **hung** [hʌŋ] |
| **lie** [laɪ] | **lay** [le] | **lain** [len] |
| **hide** [haɪd] | **hid** [hɪd] | **hidden** [ˈhɪdən] |
| **write** [raɪt] | **wrote** [rot] | **written** [ˈrɪtən] |
| **abide** [əˈbaɪd] | **abode** [əˈbod] | **abode** [əˈbod] |
| **strike** [straɪk] | **struck** [strʌk] | **struck** [strʌk] |
| **fly** [flaɪ] | **flew** [flu] | **flown** [flon] |
| **get** [gɛt] | **got** [gɑt] | **gotten** [ˈgɑtən] |
| **bear** [bɛr] | **bore** [bor] | **borne** [born] |
| **break** [brek] | **broke** [brok] | **broken** [ˈbrokən] |
| **shake** [ʃek] | **shook** [ʃʊk] | **shaken** [ˈʃekən] |
| **slay** [sle] | **slew** [slu] | **slain** [slen] |
| **bid** [bɪd] | **bade** [bæd] | **bidden** [ˈbɪdən] |
| **sing** [sɪŋ] | **sang** [sæŋ] | **sung** [sʌŋ] |
| **give** [gɪv] | **gave** [gev] | **given** [ˈgɪvən] |
| **spin** [spɪn] | **spun** [spʌn] | **spun** [spʌn] |
| **eat** [it] | **ate** [et] | **eaten** [ˈitən] |
| **see** [si] | **saw** [sɔ] | **seen** [sin] |
| **freeze** [friz] | **froze** [froz] | **frozen** [ˈfrozən] |
| **fall** [fɔl] | **fell** [fɛl] | **fallen** [ˈfɔlən] |
| **draw** [drɔ] | **drew** [dru] | **drawn** [drɔn] |
| **grow** [gro] | **grew** [gru] | **grown** [gron] |
| **run** [rʌn] | **ran** [ræn] | **run** [rʌn] |
| **come** [kʌm] | **came** [kem] | **come** [kʌm] |
| **choose** [tʃuz] | **chose** [tʃoz] | **chosen** [ˈtʃozən] |

**§10. Los verbos mixtos.** Damos abajo una lista de verbos mixtos que ejemplifican todas las variaciones del sonido de la vocal de la raíz en las tres partes principales.

| INFINITIVO | PRETÉRITO | PARTICIPIO PASADO |
|---|---|---|
| **stand** [stænd] | **stood** [stʊd] | **stood** [stʊd] |
| **catch** [kætʃ] | **caught** [kɔt] | **caught** [kɔt] |
| **slide** [slaɪd] | **slid** [slɪd] | **slid** [slɪd] |
| **fight** [faɪt] | **fought** [fɔt] | **fought** [fɔt] |
| **find** [faɪnd] | **found** [faʊnd] | **found** [faʊnd] |
| **sell** [sɛl] | **sold** [sold] | **sold** [sold] |
| **say** [se] | **said** [sɛd] | **said** [sɛd] |
| **sit** [sɪt] | **sat** [sæt] | **sat** [sæt] |
| **think** [θɪŋk] | **thought** [θɔt] | **thought** [θɔt] |
| **feed** [fid] | **fed** [fɛd] | **fed** [fɛd] |
| **teach** [titʃ] | **taught** [tɔt] | **taught** [tɔt] |
| **clothe** [kloð] | **clad** [klæd] | **clad** [klæd] |
| **hold** [hold] | **held** [hɛld] | **held** [hɛld] |
| **shoot** [ʃut] | **shot** [ʃɑt] | **shot** [ʃɑt] |
| **lose** [luz] | **lost** [lɔst] | **lost** [lɔst] |

**§11. Los verbos irregulares.** Algunos verbos tienen el pretérito y el participio pasado irregulares.

| INFINITIVO | PRETÉRITO | PARTICIPIO PASADO |
|---|---|---|
| **be** [bi] | **was** [wɑz] y **were** [wʌr] | **been** [bɪn] o [bin] |
| **do** [du] | **did** [dɪd] | **done** [dʌn] |
| **go** [go] | **went** [wɛnt] | **gone** [gɔn] o [gɑn] |
| **have** [hæv] | **had** [hæd] | **had** [hæd] |
| **make** [mek] | **made** [med] | **made** [med] |

## BRIEF HISTORY OF THE SPANISH LANGUAGE

**Vulgar Latin.** Latin as a living language was subject to constant change. While the language of the cultivated classes (Classical Latin) became more and more uniform under the conservative influences of culture, learning, and tradition, the language of the people (Vulgar Latin) became more and more altered through contact with other languages, more and more revitalized through innovation and addition, and more and more diversified as it spread with the vast Roman Empire across the continent of Europe. Classical Latin became a dead language while Vulgar Latin developed into what we now call the Neo-Latin or Romance languages.

No great literature has been handed down to us to attest the existence of Vulgar Latin. Our knowledge of it is derived from the following sources: 1) colloquialisms condemned in the works of grammarians, 2) careless mistakes of Classical Latin authors, 3) intentional colloquialisms in Classical Latin comedy, 4) the language of a few works written by poorly educated people, 5) popular forms appearing in the work of stonecutters and early scribes, 6) glosses in popular form in documents written in a more cultivated idiom, and finally, 7) the Romance languages themselves, by a comparative study of which it is possible to reconstruct hypothetically a Latin idiom which is widely different in many respects from Classical Latin.

**The Romance Languages.** The differentiation of Vulgar Latin from one region to another, which finally resulted in its transformation into the several Romance languages and their dialects, is thought to have been brought about by the following causes: 1) the varying period of Romanization, 2) the relative geographic isolation of one group from another, 3) the variation of cultural and educational conditions, 4) dialectal differences in the language of the Italic colonists, 5) the original languages encountered by the Romans in their penetration of other lands, 6) the languages of later invaders of Romanized areas, and 7) the development of separate political units. The degree of differentiation may be realized by a consideration of the large number of Romance languages and their dialects. The chief Romance languages are Spanish, Portuguese, French, Italian, Provençal-Catalan, Rhaeto-Romanic, and Rumanian.

**Castilian.** The chief Romance languages of the Iberian Peninsula were Castilian, Leonese, Navarro-Aragonese, Gallaeco-Portuguese, and Catalan. Castilian, by absorbing Leonese and Navarro-Aragonese, became the language of Spain and spread to the New World with Spanish discovery and colonization. It is important as the language of one of the world's great literatures and is spoken by over a hundred and fifty million people in Spain, Central America, South America, Mexico, the West Indies, southwestern United

States, the Philippine Islands, and many other islands of the Atlantic and Pacific.

**From Latin to Spanish.** The principal changes in the transition from Latin to Spanish were the following:

1. The diphthongization of Latin stressed short **e** to Spanish **ie,** e.g., **tenet** > **tiene, petram** > **piedra** and the diphthongization of Latin stressed short **o** to Spanish **ue,** e.g., **bonum** > **bueno, novem** > **nueve.** These changes account in part for the development of radical-changing verbs for when the vowels are not stressed they do not diphthongize. Accordingly, we have **siento** but **sentamos, duerme** but **dormimos.** And they also account for the difference in the radical vowel of such forms as **ardiente** and **ardentísimo, valiente** and **valentón.**

2. The voicing or fall of certain intervocalic consonants, e.g., **acutum** > **agudo, lupum** > **lobo, profectum** > **provecho, credo** > **creo, legalem** > **leal.**

3. The development of yod and the consequent palatalization of contiguous consonants, e.g., **meliorem** > **mejor, seniorem** > **señor, factum** > **hecho, oculum** > **ojo.**

4. The velarization of **b, p, v,** and **l,** e.g., **capitalem** > **cabdal** > **caudal, captivum** > **cautivo, civitatem** > **ciudad, alterum** > **autro** > **otro.**

5. The change of Latin initial **cl, fl,** and **pl** to Spanish **ll,** e.g., **clavem** > **llave, flammam** > **llama, plorare** > **llorar.**

6. The fall of unaccented vowels, e.g., **delicatum** > **delgado, consuturam** > **costura**; and the consequent development of new consonant groups, e.g., **hominem** > **homne** > **hombre, comitem** > **conde, judicare** > **juzgar.**

7. The partial disappearance of nominal, adjectival, and verbal inflection, e.g., the neuter gender, all cases except the accusative, many tenses, and the passive voice.

8. The emergence of word order as the prime instrument of syntax instead of inflection.

In addition to the words of popular origin, which constitute the chief wealth of the Spanish vocabulary, new Latin words have entered the language from the earliest times. These words came first through the church and the law, later through the work of scholars and men of letters, and still later through science and medicine. They have not undergone all the changes which popular words have undergone, first, because they have often entered the language after certain changes had ceased to take place, and second, because of a conscious effort to preserve their Latin form. The word **matemática** is an example of a learned word. None of its sounds has fallen, none has undergone a fundamental change.

Sometimes a learned or semilearned word already existed as a popular word. The two forms are then called doublets, e.g., **límite** and **linde, minuto** and **menudo, ración** and **razón, examen** and **enjambre.** Borrowings from dialects and other languages may also become doublets, e.g.,**jefe** (from French **chef**) and **cabo**, both from Latin **caput, juerga** (Andalusian) and **huelga**, both from the stem of Latin **follicare.**

Sometimes a popular word was modified or replaced by a Latin word from which it originally came. Such a word is called a regressive word. Thus Old Spanish **aorar** was replaced by **adorar**, Old Spanish **viesso** by **verso.**

**Non-Latin Words in Spanish.** Many languages have influenced Spanish in the course of its growth and development. But it is generally agreed that with few exceptions this influence did not go beyond vocabulary and did not affect the intrinsic character of the language.

Aside from a large number of place names only a few words, such as **izquierdo, páramo,** and **vega,** were adopted from the language of the original Iberians.

Words of Greek origin entered the language at different periods, frequently through Latin, occasionally through Arabic. The words **bodega, escuela, golpe,** and **huérfano** are popular words of Greek origin, while the words **fisiología, geografía, mecánica,** and **telégrafo** are learned words of Greek origin.

Many words were taken during the Middle Ages from the Germanic and Arabic invaders. The Germanic words were Visigothic, Swabian, and Vandal and were for the most part concerned with the waging of war and violent action, e.g., **guerra, tregua, yelmo,** and **robar.** Of Germanic origin also were many names of persons, e.g., **Elvira, Fernando,** and **Ramiro.**

The Arabic words are fairly numerous and cover practically every aspect of human activity. They give to the Spanish vocabulary an appearance which distinguishes it markedly from that of French and Italian. Here are a few examples of Arabic words: **albacea, albañil, alcalde, algodón, atalaya, noria, quilate,** and **zaguán.**

Since the thirteenth century, that is, after Spanish had passed through its formative stages, the languages from whose vocabularies it has borrowed the largest number of words are French and Italian. The words borrowed from French are, for the most part, words concerned with the church, with chivalry, diplomacy, and literature, e.g., **fraile, galán, homenaje, jardín, jaula, linaje, manjar, mensaje, monje, preste,** and **vergel,** while the words borrowed from Italian are, for the most part, words concerned with literature and the arts, e.g., **esbozo, fachada, gaceta, novela, piano,** and **soneto.**

With the discovery of America many words were adopted from Indian dialects. Some of these have not spread beyond the region of their origin, some have spread throughout Spanish America, and some have spread as far as Spain to become part of the metropolitan language, e.g., **alpaca, cacique, canoa, chocolate, huracán, maíz,** and **tomate.**

**Old and Modern Spanish.** The first traces of Spanish are found in Latin documents of the eighth century and the first great monument of Spanish literature, the Poem of the Cid, was composed in the twelfth century. As the period of Old Spanish extends to the end of the fifteenth century, the epochal year of 1492 might well be regarded as the turning point to Modern Spanish. In that year the troops of Queen Isabella completed the Reconquest by driving the Moors from Granada, the great humanist, Antonio de Nebrija, published his famous grammar of the Spanish language, and Columbus discovered the New World. Thus, the influence of the Arabs in words, thought, and action, which had been so profound and vigorous for centuries, came to an end; Spanish now began to feel the full impact of the Renaissance, which brought with it, along with new ideas and new ways to express them, the stabilizing influence of grammar, formal literature, and logic; and discovery and colonization, in carrying Spanish to new and unknown lands, introduced new scientific facts and a new view of the universe which required a richer and more flexible language for expression.

Thus the new forces to which Spanish was subjected were just as complex as those of the Middle Ages. If the language of today seems so close to that of the sixteenth century, it is because of the stabilizing influence of grammar, formal literature, and logic mentioned above. This influence was reinforced by the invention of printing, the spread of French Classicism, and the establishment of the Spanish Academy in 1713, whose emblem bears the significant legend: Limpia, fija y da esplendor. At the same time, as a result of the wide geographic spread of the Spanish-speaking regions of the globe, Spanish has grown luxuriantly in keeping pace with the developments of science, art, commerce, and industry in the nineteenth and twentieth centuries.

# OUTLINE OF SPANISH GRAMMAR

**§12. Spelling and Pronunciation.** 1. The letters of the Spanish alphabet are listed below with their names and approximate sounds in terms of equivalent English sounds. Note that **ch, ll, ñ,** and **rr** are considered to be separate single letters in Spanish and that **ch, ll,** and **ñ** (but not **rr**) are treated as separate single letters in the alphabetization of Spanish words. Thus all words beginning in **ch, ll,** and **ñ** are regularly listed after the complete listing of all words beginning in **c, l,** and **n** respectively. And thus, for example, **dúctil** is alphabetized ahead of **ducha, pelo** ahead of **pellejo,** and **vino** ahead of **viña.**

The names of all the letters are feminine and the feminine article is used before **a** and **h** in spite of the fact that they are stressed, viz., **la a** and **la h (la hache).**

| LETTER | NAME | APPROXIMATE SOUND |
|---|---|---|
| **a** | a | Like *a* in English *father,* e.g., **taza, fácil.** |
| **b** | be | At the beginning of a word and when preceded by **m**, like *b* in English *boat,* e.g., **bola, comba.** Between two vowels and when preceded by a vowel and followed by **l** or **r**, somewhat like *v* in English *voodoo* except that it is formed with both lips (not with the lower lip and the upper teeth), e.g., **caber, tabla, sobre.** It is generally silent and often dropped in spelling before **s**, e.g., **obscuro** or **oscuro, subscribir** or **suscribir.** |
| **c** | ce | When followed by **e** or **i**, like *th* in English *think* in Castilian but like *c* in English *cent* in American Spanish, e.g., **nacer, ciento.** When followed by **a, o, u,** or a consonant, like *c* in English *coal,* e.g., **canto, cola, cubo, pacto, creer.** Double **c** is always followed by **e** or **i**. This means that the first **c**, being followed by a consonant, has the sound of *c* in English *coal,* while the second **c**, being followed by **e** or **i**, has in Castilian the sound of *th* in English *think* and in American Spanish the sound of *c* in English *cent,* e.g., **accidente, lección.** |
| **ch** | che | Like *ch* in English *such,* e.g., **mucho.** |
| **d** | de | Generally, like *d* in English *dance,* e.g., **dar, conde.** Between two vowels, when preceded by a vowel and followed by **r**, and when final, like *th* in English *this,* e.g., **nada, piedra, usted.** |
| **e** | e | When ending a syllable, like *e* in English *they* (without the following sound of *y*), e.g., **dedo, menos.** When followed by a consonant in the same syllable, like *e* in English *bet,* e.g., **pérfido, celda.** |
| **f** | efe | Like *f* in English *foot,* e.g., **fonda, afectar.** |
| **g** | ge | When followed by **e** or **i**, like *h* in English *house,* e.g., **género, gitano.** When followed by **a, o, u,** or a consonant, like *g* in English *goat,* e.g., **gasto, goma, gusano, grande.** The **u** of **ue** and **ui** is silent after **g** unless marked with a diaeresis, when it has the sound of English *w,* e.g., **guerra, guía,** but **agüero, lingüístico.** |
| **h** | hache | Always silent, e.g., **hijo, alcohol.** |
| **i** | i | Like *i* in English *machine,* e.g., **línea, salido.** |
| **j** | jota | Like *h* in English *house,* e.g., **jardín, justo.** Final **j** is generally silent, e.g., **reloj.** |
| **k** | ka | Like English *k,* e.g., **kantiano, kilogramo.** |
| **l** | ele | Somewhat like *l* in English *lamb,* e.g., **bala, labio.** |
| **ll** | elle | Somewhat like *lli* in English *million* in Castilian but like *y* in English *yet* in American Spanish, e.g., **sello, llover.** |
| **m** | eme | Like *m* in English *money,* e.g., **tomar, musa.** |
| **n** | ene | Generally, like *n* in English *nut,* e.g., **andar, nombre.** But before **v**, like *m* in English *money,* e.g., **invadir, convidar.** And before hard **c** and hard **g**, like *ng* in English *singer,* e.g., **banco, manga.** |
| **ñ** | eñe | Somewhat like *ni* in English *onion,* e.g., **empeño, uña.** |
| **o** | o | When ending a syllable, like *o* in English *note* (without the following sound of *w* heard in this word), e.g., **solo, poco.** When followed by a consonant in the same syllable, like *o* in English *order,* e.g., **costa, torta.** |
| **p** | pe | Like *p* in English *path,* e.g., **puente, complicar.** It is silent in **septiembre** and **séptimo.** |
| **q** | cu | Like *c* in English *coal.* This letter is always followed by **ue** or **ui,** in which the **u** is silent, e.g., **quemar, quinta.** |
| **r** | ere | At the beginning of a word and when preceded by **l, n,** or **s**, it is strongly trilled, e.g., **ramo, malrotar, conrear, israelita.** Pronounced with a single tap of the tongue in all other positions, e.g., **pero, traigo, hablar.** |

| LETTER | NAME | APPROXIMATE SOUND |
|---|---|---|
| **rr** | erre | Strongly trilled, e.g., **perro, correr.** |
| **s** | ese | Generally, like *s* in English *see*, e.g., **secar, cosa, español.** But before a voiced consonant **(b, d,** hard **g, l, r, m, n),** like *z* in English *zero*, e.g., **esbelto, desde, rasgo, eslavo, mismo, asno.** |
| **t** | te | Like *t* in English *top*, e.g., **tejido, pata.** |
| **u** | u | Like *u* in English *rule*, e.g., **buzo, mulo.** It is silent in **gue, gui, que,** and **qui,** but not in **güe** and **güi**, e.g., **guerra, guía, quemar, quinta,** but **agüero, lingüístico.** |
| **v** | ve *or* uve (*to avoid confusion with* be) | At the beginning of a word and when preceded by **n,** like *b* in English *boat*, e.g., **vengo, invadir.** Between two vowels, somewhat like *v* in English *voodoo* except that it is formed with both lips (not with the lower lip and the upper teeth), e.g., **tuve, severo.** |
| **x** | equis | Before a consonant, like *s* in English *see*, e.g., **explicar, sexto.** Between two vowels, with the sound of *gs*, e.g., **examen, máxima**; but in some words, like *s* in English *see*, e.g., **auxilio, exacto.** In **México** (for **Méjico**) like Spanish **j.** |
| **y** | ye (*formerly* i griega) | Like *i* in English *machine*, e.g., **y** (conjunction). Before a vowel, like *y* in English *youth*, e.g., **ya, cayó.** |
| **z** | zeda *or* zeta | Like *th* in English *think* in Castilian but like *c* in English *cent* in American Spanish, e.g., **zanco, zumbar.** |

2. A diphthong is the combination into a single syllable of a vowel sound and the consonant sound of *y* (in English *yet* or English *toy*) or the consonant sound of *w* (in English *woman* or English *now*). The sound of *y* is represented in Spanish by **i** and **y, y** being used in the initial and final positions and between two vowels, the sound of *w* by **u.** Either the vowel sound or the consonant sound may come first.

It is customary to call **a, e,** and **o** strong vowels and **i (y)** and **u** weak vowels. However, in the formation of diphthongs and triphthongs containing **a, e,** and **o, i (y)** and **u** are really consonants.

Diphthongs with Vowel Sound First

| DIPHTHONG | APPROXIMATE SOUND |
|---|---|
| **ai** | Like *i* in English *night*, e.g., **traigo.** |
| **ay** | Like *i* in English *night*, e.g., **estay.** |
| **au** | Like *ou* in English *found*, e.g., **causa.** |
| **ei** | Like *ey* in English *they*, e.g., **peine.** |
| **ey** | Like *ey* in English *they*, e.g., **rey.** |
| **eu** | Like *ayw* in English *haywire*, e.g., **deuda.** |
| **oi** | Like *oy* in English *toy*, e.g., **oigo.** |
| **oy** | Like *oy* in English *toy*, e.g., **doy.** |

Diphthongs with Consonant Sound First

| DIPHTHONG | APPROXIMATE SOUND |
|---|---|
| **ia** | Like *ya* in English *yarn*, e.g., **estudiamos.** |
| **ya** | Like *ya* in English *yarn*, e.g., **vayamos.** |
| **ua** | Like *wa* in English *wad*, e.g., **cuando.** |
| **ie** | Like *ye* in English *yet*, e.g., **tierra.** |
| **ye** | Like *ye* in English *yet*, e.g., **yerno.** |
| **ue** | Like *wa* in English *wade*, e.g., **bueno.** |
| **io** | Like *yo* in English *yoke*, e.g., **naciones.** |
| **yo** | Like *yo* in English *yoke*, e.g., **yodo.** |
| **uo** | Like *uo* in English *quote*, e.g., **cuota.** |
| **iu** | Like *yu* in English *yule*, e.g., **viudo.** |
| **yu** | Like *yu* in English *yule*, e.g., **yugo.** |
| **ui** | Like *wee* in English *week*, e.g., **cuido.** |

3. A triphthong is the combination into a single syllable of the following three elements in the order given: (1) the consonant sound of *y* (represented in Spanish by **i**) or the consonant sound of *w* (represented in Spanish by **u**), (2) a vowel sound, and (3) the consonant sound of *y* (represented in Spanish by **i** or if final, by **y**) or the consonant sound of *w* (represented in Spanish by **u**).

| TRIPHTHONG | APPROXIMATE SOUND |
|---|---|
| **iai** | Like *yi* in *yipe*, e.g., **estudiáis.** |
| **iau** | Like *eow* in *meow*, e.g., **miau.** |
| **iei** | Like the English word *yea*, e.g., **estudiéis.** |
| **uai** | Like *wi* in *wine*, e.g., **continuáis.** |
| **uay** | Like *wi* in *wine*, e.g., **guay.** |
| **uau** | Like the English word *wow*, e.g., **guau.** |
| **uei** | Like *wei* in *weigh*, e.g., **continuéis.** |
| **uey** | Like *wei* in *weigh*, e.g., **buey.** |

4. Vowels, diphthongs, and triphthongs are vocalic units and words have as many syllables as they have vocalic units. Spanish words are divided into syllables according to the following principles.

(*a*) When a single consonant (including **ch, ll,** and **rr**) stands between two vocalic units it belongs to the following syllable, e.g., **ca·ja, cau·sa, bue·no, o·cho, se·llo, ca·rro.**

(*b*) When a consonant group consisting of a mute plus a liquid (i.e., of **b, c, d, f, g, p,** or **t** followed by **l** or **r**) stands between two vocalic units, the group belongs to the following syllable, e.g., **ha·blar, bu·cle, so·bre, co·fre, ma·triz.**

(*c*) When a consonant group consisting of any other pair of consonants stands between two vocalic units, the first consonant belongs to the preceding syllable, the second to the following syllable, e.g., **ac·to, en·cen·der, mas·lo, lec·ción.**

(*d*) When a consonant group consisting of more than two consonants stands between two vocalic units, the last two consonants are generally a mute plus a liquid (i.e., **b, c, d, f, g, p,** or **t** followed by **l** or **r**) and they both belong to the following syllable, e.g., **am·blar, pon·dré, ex·pli·car, com·prar.** However, if the second consonant is **s,** it belongs with the first consonant to the preceding syllable, e.g., **cons·tan·te, pers·pi·caz.**

(*e*) When no consonant stands between the two vowels, they belong to separate syllables (unless they combine to form a diphthong), e.g., **sa·e·ta, fe·o, cre·er, to·ar.** In accordance with this principle, when a letter which regularly represents the consonant element of a diphthong or triphthong has the value of a vowel, it belongs to a separate syllable and this is indicated by the written accent, e.g., **ca·í·do, ba·úl, se·rí·a, se·rí·ais.**

(*f*) When the letter **y** stands between two vowels, it forms a diphthong with the following vowel and therefore, belongs to the following syllable, e.g., **va·ya, cu·yo, le·yó.**

(*g*) Prefixes that are felt to be prefixes form separate syllables even if the division is contrary to the above principles, e.g., **ab·ro·gar, sub·le·var, des·a·sir.** But **s** in a three-consonant group is kept with the prefix, e.g., **cons·tan·te, pers·pi·caz.**

5. All Spanish words except compound nouns and adverbs ending in **mente** have but one stress. And the position of this stress is always shown by the spelling in accordance with four simple rules.

(*a*) Words ending in a vowel sound or in **n** or **s** are stressed on the syllable next to the last, e.g., **cosecha, antiguo, serio, comen, casas.**

(*b*) Words ending in a consonant except **n** or **s,** but including **y,** are stressed on the last syllable, e.g., **calor, papel, feliz, Uruguay, estoy.**

(*c*) If the stress does not fall in accordance with one or the other of the above rules, it is indicated by a written accent, e.g., **café, encendí, salís, nación, difícil, lápiz, república.**

(*d*) The stress (and the written accent) falls on the vowel element (strong vowel) of stressed diphthongs and triphthongs, e.g., **traigo, peine, cuando, bueno, habláis, continuáis.** If the letter which regularly represents the consonant element of a diphthong or triphthong has the value of a vowel, it forms a separate stressed syllable and this is indicated by the written accent, e.g., **caído, baúl, sería, seríais.**

Two words spelled alike are often distinguished by the written accent on the stressed vowel of one of them, e.g., **él** *he* and **el** *the*, **éste** *this one* and **este** *this*, **sí** *yes* and **si** *if*, **más** *more* and **mas** *but*. Interrogative and exclamatory pronouns, adjectives, and adverbs are thus distinguished from similarly spelled relative pronouns and subordinating conjunctions, e.g., **quién** and **quien, cuál** and **cual, dónde** and **donde.**

6. Spanish punctuation differs from English chiefly in the use of the inverted question mark before interrogative words and sentences and the inverted exclamation point before exclamatory words and sentences, e.g., **¿Qué hora es?, ¡Qué lástima!**

7. Capitalization is not used as much in Spanish as in English. Nouns and adjectives of nationality, religion, etc., the names of the days of the week, and the names of the months are generally not capitalized, e.g., **un español** *a Spaniard*, **el idioma español** *the Spanish language*, **un metodista** *a Methodist*, **lunes** *Monday*, **marzo** *March*.

**§13. Plural of Nouns.** Nouns ending in a vowel add **s** to form the plural, e.g., **casa** *house* and **casas** *houses*, **diente** *tooth* and **dientes** *teeth*, **tribu** *tribe* and **tribus** *tribes*. But nouns ending in accented **a, i,** or **u** add **es** to form the plural, e.g., **bajá** *pasha* and **bajaes** *pashas*, **rubí** *ruby* and **rubíes** *rubies*, **iglú** *igloo* and **iglúes** *igloos*. Nouns ending in a consonant (including **y**) add **es** to form the plural, e.g., **balcón** *balcony* and **balcones** *balconies*, **flor** *flower* and **flores** *flowers*, **mes** *month* and **meses** *months*, **rey** *king* and **reyes** *kings*. But nouns ending in **z** change this **z** to **c** and add **es**, e.g., **vez** *time* and **veces** *times*, **lápiz** *pencil* and **lápices** *pencils*. And nouns ending in **s** preceded by an unaccented vowel do not change in the plural, e.g., **crisis** *crisis* and **crisis** *crises*, **lunes** *Monday* and **lunes** *Mondays*.

The syllable stressed in the singular is always stressed in the plural except in a few words such as **carácter** and **régimen**, whose plurals are **caracteres** and **regímenes**. However, the written accent found on the last syllable of the singular of some nouns ending in **n** and **s** is not necessary in the plural and must be accordingly omitted, e.g., **acción** *action* and **acciones** *actions*, **marqués** *marquess* and **marqueses** *marquesses*.

**§14. Inflection and Comparison of Adjectives.** 1. Adjectives ending in **o** change **o** to **a** to form the feminine, e.g., **alto** and **alta** *high*. Adjectives ending in any other letter have the same form in both genders, e.g., **diferente** *different*, **difícil** *difficult*, and **belga** *Belgian*. However, adjectives of nationality ending in **l, s,** and **z,** adjectives ending in **or** (except comparatives), and adjectives ending in **án** or **ón** add **a** to form the feminine, e.g., **español** and **española** *Spanish*, **francés** and **francesa** *French*, **consolador** and **consoladora** *consoling*, **alazán** and **alazana** *sorrel*, **barrigón** and **barrigona** *big-bellied*. Comparatives ending in **or** do not change to form the feminine, e.g., **mejor** *better* and **inferior** *lower, inferior*.

Adjectives ending in a vowel form their plural by adding **s**, e.g., **alto** and **altos, alta** and **altas** *high*, **diferente** and **diferentes** *different*, **belga** and **belgas** *Belgian*. Adjectives ending in a consonant form their plural by adding **es**, e.g., **fácil** and **fáciles** *easy*, **moral** and **morales** *moral*. But adjectives ending in **z** change this **z** to **c** and add **es**, e.g., **feliz** and **felices** *happy*. When **bueno** *good*, **malo** *bad*, **primero** *first*, and **tercero** *third* are used before a masculine singular noun, they drop their final **o**, e.g., **buen libro** *good book*, **primer capítulo** *first chapter*. When **grande** *large, big, great* is used before a masculine or feminine singular noun, it drops its last syllable **de**, e.g., **gran libro** *large book*, **gran nación** *great nation*. If the noun begins with a vowel or **h**, either **gran** or **grande** may be used, e.g., **gran amigo** or **grande amigo** *great friend*. The masculine **santo** becomes **san** before all names of saints except those beginning with **Do** and **To**, e.g., **San Francisco** *Saint Francis*, but **Santo Domingo** *Saint Dominic*, **Santo Tomás** *Saint Thomas*. Before common nouns it is not shortened, e.g., **el Santo Papa** *the Holy Father*. The indefinite article **un** and the indefinite adjectives **algún** and **ningún** are formed the same way as **buen, mal, primer, tercer,** that is, by dropping the **o** of **uno, alguno,** and **ninguno.**

2. The comparative and superlative of adjectives and adverbs are formed by placing **más** before the adjective or adverb, e.g., **rico** *rich*, **más rico** *richer, richest;* **despacio** *slowly*, **más despacio** *more slowly, most slowly*. The sense generally requires the use of the definite article or a possessive adjective with the superlative in English and Spanish, e.g., **Es el alumno más inteligente de la clase** *He is the most intelligent student in the class.*

Some adjectives and adverbs have irregular comparatives and superlatives.

| POSITIVE | SUPERLATIVE |
|---|---|
| **bueno** *good, well* | **mejor** *better, best* |
| **grande** *large, big* | **mayor** *greater, greatest; older, oldest*<br>**más grande** *larger, largest* |
| **malo** *bad, ill* | **peor** *worse, worst* |
| **pequeño** *small, little* | **menor** *smaller, smallest; younger, youngest*<br>**más pequeño** *smaller, smallest* |
| **bien** *well* | **mejor** *better, best* |
| **mal** *badly, poorly* | **peor** *worse, worst* |
| **mucho** *much* | **más** *more, most* |
| **muchos** *many* | **más** *more, most* |
| **poco** *little* | **menos** *less, least* |
| **pocos** *few* | **menos** *fewer, fewest* |

The expression **más bien** means *rather*.

Comparatives and superlatives ending in **or** do not change in the feminine.

There is also an absolute superlative, which is formed by adding the ending **ísimo** to the stem of the adjective. It does not form comparisons but has intensive force equivalent to **muy** with the positive degree, e.g., **cansadísimo** *most tired, very tired;* **elocuentísimo** *most eloquent, very eloquent.*

Adjectives ending in **co** and **go** change **c** and **g** to **qu** and **gu** respectively, e.g., **rico** *rich,* **riquísimo** *very rich;* **largo** *long,* **larguísimo** *very long.* Adjectives ending in **ble** change this ending to **bilísimo,** e.g., **probable** *probable,* **probabilísimo** *very probable.* And adjectives ending in **io** show a contraction of the **i** of **io** with the **i** of **ísimo,** e.g., **limpio** *clean,* **limpísimo** *very clean.* An important exception is **frío** *cold,* **friísimo** *very cold.* And adjectives containing the accented diphthong **ie** or **ue** change **ie** to **e** and **ue** to **o** when adding **ísimo,** e.g., **ardiente** *ardent,* **ardentísimo** *very ardent;* **nuevo** *new,* **novísimo** *very new.*

**§15. Spelling-changing Verbs.** Verbs which, though regular to the ear, are irregular in spelling are called spelling-changing verbs. There are two groups, those irregular in the spelling of the stem and those irregular in the spelling of the ending. The first group consists of verbs ending in **car, gar, guar, zar; cer** preceded by a consonant; **cir** preceded by a consonant; **ger, gir, guir,** and **quir.** The second group consists of verbs of the second and third conjugations whose stems end in **ll, ñ,** or a vowel.

First Group

| MODEL | CHANGE | OCCURRENCE |
|---|---|---|
| 1. **tocar** | **c** to **qu** before **e,** e.g., **toqué** | In 1st sg. pret. ind. and whole pres. subj. |
| 2. **ligar** | **g** to **gu** before **e,** e.g., **ligué** | |
| 3. **averiguar** | **gu** to **gü** before **e,** e.g., **averigüé** | |
| 4. **rezar** | **z** to **c** before **e,** e.g., **recé** | |
| 5. **vencer** | **c** to **z** before **o** and **a,** e.g., **venzo** | In 1st sg. pres. ind. and whole pres. subj. |
| 6. **esparcir** | **c** to **z** before **o** and **a,** e.g., **esparzo** | |
| 7. **escoger** | **g** to **j** before **o** and **a,** e.g., **escojo** | |
| 8. **dirigir** | **g** to **j** before **o** and **a,** e.g., **dirijo** | |
| 9. **distinguir** | **gu** to **g** before **o** and **a,** e.g., **distingo** | |
| 10. **delinquir** | **qu** to **c** before **o** and **a,** e.g., **delinco** | |

Second Group

| MODEL | CHANGE | OCCURRENCE |
|---|---|---|
| 11. **empeller** | **i** of **ió** and **ie** falls, e.g., **empelló** | In ger., 3d sg. and 3d pl. pret. ind., whole imperf. subj. (**s**-form and **r**-form), and whole fut. subj. |
| 12. **bullir** | **i** of **ió** and **ie** falls, e.g., **bulló** | |
| 13. **tañer** | **i** of **ió** and **ie** falls, e.g., **tañó** | |
| 14. **bruñir** | **i** of **ió** and **ie** falls, e.g., **bruñó** | |
| 15. **creer** | 1. **i** of **ió** and **ie** changes to **y,** e.g., **creyó** | In ger., 3d sg. and 3 pl. pret. ind., whole imperf. subj. (**s**-form and **r**-form), and whole fut. subj. |
| | 2. stressed **i** of endings takes accent mark, e.g., **creído** | In 2d sg., 1st pl., and 2d pl. pret. ind. and past participle |
| 16. **oír** | 1. **i** of **ió** and **ie** changes to **y,** e.g., **oyó** | In ger., 3d sg. and 3d pl. pret. ind., whole imperf. subj. (**s**-form and **r**-form), and whole fut. subj. |
| | 2. stressed **i** of endings takes accent mark, e.g., **oído** | In 1st pl. pres. ind., 2d sg., 1st pl. and 2d pl. pret. ind., 2d pl. impv., and past participle |

**§16. Radical-changing Verbs.** The irregularity of radical-changing verbs consists in a change in the radical vowel in certain forms. There are four classes of these verbs. The first class consists of verbs of the first and second conjugations with radical **e** and **o**; the second class consists of verbs of the third conjugation with radical **e** and **o**; the third class consists of verbs of the third conjugation with radical **e**; and the fourth class consists of verbs of all three conjugations with radical **ai, au,** and **eu.**

FIRST CLASS

| MODEL | CHANGE | OCCURRENCE |
|---|---|---|
| 1. **acertar**<br>2. **perder**<br>3. **rodar**<br>4. **morder** | **e** stressed changes to **ie,** e.g., **acierto**<br>**e** stressed changes to **ie,** e.g., **pierdo**<br>**o** stressed changes to **ue,** e.g., **ruedo**<br>**o** stressed changes to **ue,** e.g., **muerdo** | In 1st, 2d, 3d sg. and 3d pl. pres. ind. and subj., and 2d sg. impv. |

SECOND CLASS

| MODEL | CHANGE | OCCURRENCE |
|---|---|---|
| 5. **mentir** | 1. **e** stressed changes to **ie,** e.g., **miento** | In 1st, 2d, 3d sg. and 3d pl. pres. ind. and pres. subj., and 2d sg. impv. |
| | 2. **e** unstressed and followed by an ending containing **a, ió,** or **ie** changes to **i,** e.g., **mintamos** | In ger., 1st and 2d pl. pres. subj., 3d sg. and pl. pret. ind., whole imperf. subj. (**s**-form and **r**-form), and whole future subj. |
| 6. **dormir** | 1. **o** stressed changes to **ue,** e.g., **duermo** | In 1st, 2d, 3d sg. and 3d pl. pres. ind. and pres. subj., and 2d sg. impv. |
| | 2. **o** unstressed and followed by an ending containing **a, ió,** or **ie** changes to **u,** e.g., **durmamos** | In ger., 1st and 2d pl. pres. subj., 3d sg. and pl. pret. ind., whole imperf. subj. (**s**-form and **r**-form), and whole future subj. |

THIRD CLASS

| MODEL | CHANGE | OCCURRENCE |
|---|---|---|
| 7. **vestir** | 1. **e** stressed changes to **i,** e.g., **visto** | In 1st, 2d, 3d sg. and 3d pl. pres. ind. and pres. subj., and 2d sg. impv. |
| | 2. **e** unstressed and followed by an ending containing **a, ió,** or **ie** changes to **i,** e.g., **vistamos** | In ger., 1st and 2d pl. pres. subj., 3d sg. and pl. pret. ind., whole imperf. subj. (**s**-form and **r**-form), and whole future subj. |

FOURTH CLASS

| MODEL | CHANGE | OCCURRENCE |
|---|---|---|
| 8. **reunir** | **ai, au,** and **eu** stressed change to **aí, aú,** and **eú** repectively, e.g., **reúne** | In 1st, 2d, 3d sg. and 3d pl. pres. ind. and pres. subj., and 2d sg. impv. |

9. Some verbs in **iar** and all verbs in **uar** (except those in **cuar** and **guar**) are radical-changing verbs in that the **i** or **u** with which the stem ends becomes the radical vowel in those forms in which the radical vowel is regularly stressed, namely, the whole singular and the third plural of the present indicative and the present subjunctive, and the second singular imperative. This is shown by the written accent on the **i** or **u,** e.g., **varío** from **variar, continúo** from **continuar.**

**§17. Irregular Verbs.** In addition to the irregularities of spelling-changing verbs and radical-changing verbs, there are other irregularities in certain roots, stems, and endings. These are classified below.

1. The following verbs have irregular stems in the first singular present indicative and the whole present subjunctive.

| MODEL | 1ST SG. PRES. IND. |
|---|---|
| **argüir** | **arguyo** |
| **asir** | **asgo** |
| **caber** | **quepo** |
| **caer** | **caigo** |
| **conocer** | **conozco** |
| **crecer** | **crezco** |
| **decir** | **digo** |
| **deducir** | **deduzco** |
| **destruir** | **destruyo** |
| **hacer** | **hago** |
| **lucir** | **luzco** |
| **oír** | **oigo** |
| **poner** | **pongo** |
| **raer** | **raigo**<br>**rayo** |
| **roer** | **roigo**<br>**royo** |
| **salir** | **salgo** |
| **tener** | **tengo** |
| **traer** | **traigo** |
| **valer** | **valgo** |
| **venir** | **vengo** |
| **ver** | **veo** |
| **yacer** | **yazco**<br>**yazgo**<br>**yago** |

2. The following verbs have irregular endings in the first singular present indicative and the present subjunctive cannot be derived from them.

| MODEL | 1ST SG. PRES. IND. |
|---|---|
| **dar** | **doy** |
| **estar** | **estoy** |
| **haber** | **he** |
| **ir** | **voy** |
| **saber** | **sé** |
| **ser** | **soy** |

3. The following verbs have a **y** inserted between the radical vowel and the vowel of the ending in the second and third singular and the third plural present indicative and the second singular imperative.

| MODEL | 2D SG. PRES. IND. |
|---|---|
| **argüir** | **arguyes** |
| **destruir** | **destruyes** |
| **oír** | **oyes** |

4. The following verbs have irregular imperfect indicatives.

| MODEL | 1ST SG. IMPERF. IND. |
|---|---|
| **ir** | **iba** |
| **ser** | **era** |
| **ver** | **veía** |

5. The following verbs have irregular stems in the future indicative and these stems continue through the whole conditional.

| MODEL | 1ST SG. FUT. IND. |
|---|---|
| **caber** | **cabré** |
| **decir** | **diré** |
| **haber** | **habré** |
| **hacer** | **haré** |
| **poder** | **podré** |
| **poner** | **pondré** |
| **querer** | **querré** |
| **saber** | **sabré** |
| **salir** | **saldré** |
| **tener** | **tendré** |
| **valer** | **valdré** |
| **venir** | **vendré** |

6. The following verbs have irregular radicals (vowel, stem, or both) in the whole preterit indicative, the whole imperfect subjunctive (**s**-form and **r**-form), and the whole future subjunctive. They have the further irregularity in the preterit indicative of having the stress on the radical vowel in the first and third singular forms. If the stem ends in **j**, the third plural preterit indicative, the whole imperfect subjunctive (**s**-form and **r**-form), and the whole future subjunctive have **e** instead of **ie** in the ending. The verb **placer** has these irregularities only in the forms of the third person singular. And one verb, **hacer,** has the orthographic change from **c** to **z** in the third singular preterit indicative.

| MODEL | 1ST SG. PRET. IND. |
|---|---|
| **andar** | **anduve** |
| **caber** | **cupe** |
| **decir** | **dije** (3d pl.: **dijeron**) |
| **deducir** | **deduje** (3d pl.: **dedujeron**) |
| **estar** | **estuve** |
| **haber** | **hube** |
| **hacer** | **hice** (3d sg.: **hizo**) |
| **placer** | **plugo** |
| **poder** | **pude** |
| **poner** | **puse** |
| **querer** | **quise** |
| **saber** | **supe** |
| **tener** | **tuve** |
| **traer** | **traje** (3d pl.: **trajeron**) |
| **venir** | **vine** |

7. The following verbs have irregular preterit indicatives and derived tenses.

| MODEL | 1ST SG. PRET. IND. |
|---|---|
| **dar** | **di** |
| **ir** | **fui** |
| **ser** | **fui** |

8. The following verbs have irregular second singular imperatives.

| MODEL | 2D SG. IMPV. |
|---|---|
| **decir** | **di** |
| **haber** | **hé** |
| **hacer** | **haz** |
| **ir** | **vé** |
| **poner** | **pon** |
| **salir** | **sal** |
| **ser** | **sé** |
| **tener** | **ten** |
| **valer** | **val** |
| **venir** | **ven** |
| **yacer** | **yaz** |

The compounds of **poner, tener,** and **venir** require a written accent on the second singular imperative, e.g., **supón** (of **suponer**), **retén** (of **retener**), **convén** (of **convenir**). This is true also of the compounds of **ver**, e.g., **entrevé** (of **entrever**). In addition to **benedecir (§24)** and **maldecir** (also **§24**) the compounds of **decir** have second singular imperatives in **-dice,** e.g., **desdice** (of **desdecir**). And **satisfacer** has both a regular and an irregular second singular imperative, viz., **satisface** and **satisfaz.**

9. The following verbs, some regular and some irregular, have irregular past participles. Those in standard type are compounds of those in boldface.

| MODEL | PAST PARTICIPLE | MODEL | PAST PARTICIPLE |
|---|---|---|---|
| **abrir** | **abierto** | prescribir | prescrito |
| entreabrir | entreabierto | proscribir | proscrito |
| reabrir | reabierto | reescribir | reescrito |
| **cubrir** | **cubierto** | sobrescribir | sobrescrito |
| descubrir | descubierto | subscribir | subscrito |
| encubrir | encubierto | transcribir | transcrito |
| recubrir | recubierto | **freír** | **frito** |
| redescubrir | redescubierto | refreír | refrito |
| **decir** | **dicho** | sofreír | sofrito |
| antedecir | antedicho | **hacer** | **hecho** |
| contradecir | contradicho | contrahacer | contrahecho |
| desdecir | desdicho | deshacer | deshecho |
| interdecir | interdicho | rehacer | rehecho |
| predecir | predicho | satisfacer | satisfecho |
| redecir | redicho | **imprimir** | **impreso** |
| **escribir** | **escrito** | reimprimir | reimpreso |
| adscribir | adscrito | **morir** | **muerto** |
| circunscribir | circunscrito | entremorir | entremuerto |
| describir | descrito | premorir | premuerto |
| inscribir | inscrito | **poner** | **puesto** |
| manuscribir | manuscrito | anteponer | antepuesto |

| MODEL | PAST PARTICIPLE | MODEL | PAST PARTICIPLE |
|---|---|---|---|
| componer | compuesto | yuxtaponer | yuxtapuesto |
| contraponer | contrapuesto | **proveer** | **provisto** |
| deponer | depuesto | desproveer | desprovisto |
| descomponer | descompuesto | **pudrir** | **podrido** |
| desimponer | desimpuesto | repudrir | repodrido |
| disponer | dispuesto | **romper** | **roto** |
| exponer | expuesto | **solver** | **suelto** |
| imponer | impuesto | absolver | absuelto |
| indisponer | indispuesto | disolver | disuelto |
| interponer | interpuesto | ensolver | ensuelto |
| oponer | opuesto | resolver | resuelto |
| posponer | pospuesto | **ver** | **visto** |
| predisponer | predispuesto | antever | antevisto |
| preponer | prepuesto | entrever | entrevisto |
| presuponer | presupuesto | prever | previsto |
| proponer | propuesto | rever | revisto |
| recomponer | recompuesto | trasver | trasvisto |
| reponer | repuesto | **volver** | **vuelto** |
| sobreexponer | sobreexpuesto | desenvolver | desenvuelto |
| sobreponer | sobrepuesto | desvolver | desvuelto |
| superponer | superpuesto | devolver | devuelto |
| suponer | supuesto | envolver | envuelto |
| transponer | transpuesto | revolver | revuelto |

| INFINITIVE GERUND AND PAST PARTICIPLE | PRESENT INDICATIVE | PRESENT SUBJUNCTIVE | IMPERFECT INDICATIVE | FUTURE INDICATIVE | CONDITIONAL |
|---|---|---|---|---|---|
| **§18** | | | | | |
| **acertar** | **acierto** | **acierte** | acertaba | acertaré | acertaría |
| acertando | **aciertas** | **aciertes** | acertabas | acertarás | acertarías |
| acertado | **acierta** | **acierte** | acertaba | acertará | acertaría |
| | acertamos | acertemos | acertábamos | acertaremos | acertaríamos |
| | acertáis | acertéis | acertabais | acertaréis | acertaríais |
| | **aciertan** | **acierten** | acertaban | acertarán | acertarían |
| **§19** | | | | | |
| **agorar** | **agüero** | **agüere** | agoraba | agoraré | agoraría |
| agorando | **agüeras** | **agüeres** | agorabas | agorarás | agorarías |
| agorado | **agüera** | **agüere** | agoraba | agorará | agoraría |
| | agoramos | agoremos | agorábamos | agoraremos | agoraríamos |
| | agoráis | agoréis | agorabais | agoraréis | agoraríais |
| | **agüeran** | **agüeren** | agoraban | agorarán | agorarían |
| **§20** | | | | | |
| **andar** | ando | ande | andaba | andaré | andaría |
| andando | andas | andes | andabas | andarás | andarías |
| andado | anda | ande | andaba | andará | andaría |
| | andamos | andemos | andábamos | andaremos | andaríamos |
| | andáis | andéis | andabais | andaréis | andaríais |
| | andan | anden | andaban | andarán | andarían |
| **§21** | | | | | |
| **argüir** | **arguyo** | **arguya** | argüía | argüiré | argüiría |
| **arguyendo** | **arguyes** | **arguyas** | argüías | argüirás | argüirías |
| argüido | **arguye** | **arguya** | argüía | argüirá | argüiría |
| | argüimos | **arguyamos** | argüíamos | argüiremos | argüiríamos |
| | argüís | **arguyáis** | argüíais | argüiréis | argüiríais |
| | **arguyen** | **arguyan** | argüían | argüirán | argüirían |
| **§22** | | | | | |
| **asir** | **asgo** | **asga** | asía | asiré | asiría |
| asiendo | ases | **asgas** | asías | asirás | asirías |
| asido | ase | **asga** | asía | asirá | asiría |
| | asimos | **asgamos** | asíamos | asiremos | asiríamos |
| | asís | **asgáis** | asíais | asiréis | asiríais |
| | asen | **asgan** | asían | asirán | asirían |
| **§23** | | | | | |
| **averiguar** | averiguo | **averigüe** | averiguaba | averiguaré | averiguaría |
| averiguando | averiguas | **averigües** | averiguabas | averiguarás | averiguarías |
| averiguado | averigua | **averigüe** | averiguaba | averiguará | averiguaría |
| | averiguamos | **averigüemos** | averiguábamos | averiguaremos | averiguaríamos |
| | averiguáis | **averigüéis** | averiguabais | averiguaréis | averiguaríais |
| | averiguan | **averigüen** | averiguaban | averiguarán | averiguarían |
| **§24** | | | | | |
| **bendecir** | **bendigo** | **bendiga** | bendecía | bendeciré | bendeciría |
| **bendiciendo** | **bendices** | **bendigas** | bendecías | bendecirás | bendecirías |
| bendecido | **bendice** | **bendiga** | bendecía | bendecirá | bendeciría |
| | bendecimos | **bendigamos** | bendecíamos | bendeciremos | bendeciríamos |
| | bendecís | **bendigáis** | bendecíais | bendeciréis | bendeciríais |
| | **bendicen** | **bendigan** | bendecían | bendecirán | bendecirían |
| **§25** | | | | | |
| **bruñir** | bruño | bruña | bruñía | bruñiré | bruñiría |
| **bruñendo** | bruñes | bruñas | bruñías | bruñirás | bruñirías |
| bruñido | bruñe | bruña | bruñía | bruñirá | bruñiría |
| | bruñimos | bruñamos | bruñíamos | bruñiremos | bruñiríamos |
| | bruñís | bruñáis | bruñíais | bruñiréis | bruñiríais |
| | bruñen | bruñan | bruñían | bruñirán | bruñirían |
| **§26** | | | | | |
| **bullir** | bullo | bulla | bullía | bulliré | bulliría |
| **bullendo** | bulles | bullas | bullías | bullirás | bullirías |
| bullido | bulle | bulla | bullía | bullirá | bulliría |
| | bullimos | bullamos | bullíamos | bulliremos | bulliríamos |
| | bullís | bulláis | bullíais | bulliréis | bulliríais |
| | bullen | bullan | bullían | bullirán | bullirían |
| **§27** | | | | | |
| **caber** | **quepo** | **quepa** | cabía | **cabré** | **cabría** |
| cabiendo | cabes | **quepas** | cabías | **cabrás** | **cabrías** |
| cabido | cabe | **quepa** | cabía | **cabrá** | **cabría** |
| | cabemos | **quepamos** | cabíamos | **cabremos** | **cabríamos** |
| | cabéis | **quepáis** | cabíais | **cabréis** | **cabríais** |
| | caben | **quepan** | cabían | **cabrán** | **cabrían** |

| PRETERIT INDICATIVE | IMPERF. SUBJ. s-FORM | IMPERF. SUBJ. r-FORM | FUTURE SUBJUNCTIVE | IMPERATIVE | NOTES AND REFERENCES |
|---|---|---|---|---|---|
| acerté | acertase | acertara | acertare | | **§16,** 1 |
| acertaste | acertases | acertaras | acertares | **acierta** | |
| acertó | acertase | acertara | acertare | | |
| acertamos | acertásemos | acertáramos | acertáremos | | |
| acertasteis | acertaseis | acertarais | acertareis | acertad | |
| acertaron | acertasen | acertaran | acertaren | | |
| agoré | agorase | agorara | agorare | | **Like §77 with diaeresis on u of ue** |
| agoraste | agorases | agoraras | agorares | **agüera** | |
| agoró | agorase | agorara | agorare | | |
| agoramos | agorásemos | agoráramos | agoráremos | | |
| agorasteis | agoraseis | agorarais | agorareis | agorad | |
| agoraron | agorasen | agoraran | agoraren | | |
| **anduve** | **anduviese** | **anduviera** | **anduviere** | | **§17,** 6 |
| **anduviste** | **anduvieses** | **anduvieras** | **anduvieres** | anda | |
| **anduvo** | **anduviese** | **anduviera** | **anduviere** | | |
| **anduvimos** | **anduviésemos** | **anduviéramos** | **anduviéremos** | | |
| **anduvisteis** | **anduvieseis** | **anduvierais** | **anduviereis** | andad | |
| **anduvieron** | **anduviesen** | **anduvieran** | **anduvieren** | | |
| argüí | **arguyese** | **arguyera** | **arguyere** | | **Like §41 with diaeresis on u before stressed i** |
| argüiste | **arguyeses** | **arguyeras** | **arguyeres** | **arguye** | |
| **arguyó** | **arguyese** | **arguyera** | **arguyere** | | |
| argüimos | **arguyésemos** | **arguyéramos** | **arguyéremos** | | |
| argüisteis | **arguyeseis** | **arguyerais** | **arguyereis** | argüid | |
| **arguyeron** | **arguyesen** | **arguyeran** | **arguyeren** | | |
| así | asiese | asiera | asiere | | **§17,** 1 |
| asiste | asieses | asieras | asieres | ase | |
| asió | asiese | asiera | asiere | | |
| asimos | asiésemos | asiéramos | asiéremos | | |
| asisteis | asieseis | asierais | asiereis | asid | |
| asieron | asiesen | asieran | asieren | | |
| **averigüé** | averiguase | averiguara | averiguare | | **§15,** 3 |
| averiguaste | averiguases | averiguaras | averiguares | averigua | |
| averiguó | averiguase | averiguara | averiguare | | |
| averiguamos | averiguásemos | averiguáramos | averiguáremos | | |
| averiguasteis | averiguaseis | averiguarais | averiguareis | averiguad | |
| averiguaron | averiguasen | averiguaran | averiguaren | | |
| **bendije** | **bendijese** | **bendijera** | **bendijere** | | **Like §37 except in fut. ind., cond., impv., and past participle** |
| **bendijiste** | **bendijeses** | **bendijeras** | **bendijeres** | **bendice** | |
| **bendijo** | **bendijese** | **bendijera** | **bendijere** | | |
| **bendijimos** | **bendijésemos** | **bendijéramos** | **bendijéremos** | | |
| **bendijisteis** | **bendijeseis** | **bendijerais** | **bendijereis** | bendecid | |
| **bendijeron** | **bendijesen** | **bendijeran** | **bendijeren** | | |
| bruñí | **bruñese** | **bruñera** | **bruñere** | | **§15,** 14 |
| bruñiste | **bruñeses** | **bruñeras** | **bruñeres** | bruñe | |
| **bruñó** | **bruñese** | **bruñera** | **bruñere** | | |
| bruñimos | **bruñésemos** | **bruñéramos** | **bruñéremos** | | |
| bruñisteis | **bruñeseis** | **bruñerais** | **bruñereis** | bruñid | |
| **bruñeron** | **bruñesen** | **bruñeran** | **bruñeren** | | |
| bullí | **bullese** | **bullera** | **bullere** | | **§15,** 12 |
| bulliste | **bulleses** | **bulleras** | **bulleres** | bulle | |
| **bulló** | **bullese** | **bullera** | **bullere** | | |
| bullimos | **bullésemos** | **bulléramos** | **bulléremos** | | |
| bullisteis | **bulleseis** | **bullerais** | **bullereis** | bullid | |
| **bulleron** | **bullesen** | **bulleran** | **bulleren** | | |
| **cupe** | **cupiese** | **cupiera** | **cupiere** | | **§17,** 1, 5, & 6 |
| **cupiste** | **cupieses** | **cupieras** | **cupieres** | cabe | |
| **cupo** | **cupiese** | **cupiera** | **cupiere** | | |
| **cupimos** | **cupiésemos** | **cupiéramos** | **cupiéremos** | | |
| **cupisteis** | **cupieseis** | **cupierais** | **cupiereis** | cabed | |
| **cupieron** | **cupiesen** | **cupieran** | **cupieren** | | |

| INFINITIVE GERUND AND PAST PARTICIPLE | PRESENT INDICATIVE | PRESENT SUBJUNCTIVE | IMPERFECT INDICATIVE | FUTURE INDICATIVE | CONDITIONAL |
|---|---|---|---|---|---|
| §28 | | | | | |
| **caer** | **caigo** | **caiga** | caía | caeré | caería |
| **cayendo** | caes | **caigas** | caías | caerás | caerías |
| **caído** | cae | **caiga** | caía | caerá | caería |
| | caemos | **caigamos** | caíamos | caeremos | caeríamos |
| | caéis | **caigáis** | caíais | caeréis | caeríais |
| | caen | **caigan** | caían | caerán | caerían |
| §29 | | | | | |
| **cegar** | **ciego** | **ciegue** | cegaba | cegaré | cegaría |
| cegando | **ciegas** | **ciegues** | cegabas | cegarás | cegarías |
| cegado | **ciega** | **ciegue** | cegaba | cegará | cegaría |
| | cegamos | **ceguemos** | cegábamos | cegaremos | cegaríamos |
| | cegáis | **ceguéis** | cegabais | cegaréis | cegaríais |
| | **ciegan** | **cieguen** | cegaban | cegarán | cegarían |
| §30 | | | | | |
| **cocer** | **cuezo** | **cueza** | cocía | coceré | cocería |
| cociendo | **cueces** | **cuezas** | cocías | cocerás | cocerías |
| cocido | **cuece** | **cueza** | cocía | cocerá | cocería |
| | cocemos | **cozamos** | cocíamos | coceremos | coceríamos |
| | cocéis | **cozáis** | cocíais | coceréis | coceríais |
| | **cuecen** | **cuezan** | cocían | cocerán | cocerían |
| §31 | | | | | |
| **comenzar** | **comienzo** | **comience** | comenzaba | comenzaré | comenzaría |
| comenzando | **comienzas** | **comiences** | comenzabas | comenzarás | comenzarías |
| comenzado | **comienza** | **comience** | comenzaba | comenzará | comenzaría |
| | comenzamos | **comencemos** | comenzábamos | comenzaremos | comenzaríamos |
| | comenzáis | **comencéis** | comenzabais | comenzaréis | comenzaríais |
| | **comienzan** | **comiencen** | comenzaban | comenzarán | comenzarían |
| §32 | | | | | |
| **conocer** | **conozco** | **conozca** | conocía | conoceré | conocería |
| conociendo | conoces | **conozcas** | conocías | conocerás | conocerías |
| conocido | conoce | **conozca** | conocía | conocerá | conocería |
| | conocemos | **conozcamos** | conocíamos | conoceremos | conoceríamos |
| | conocéis | **conozcáis** | conocíais | conoceréis | conoceríais |
| | conocen | **conozcan** | conocían | conocerán | conocerían |
| §33 | | | | | |
| **continuar** | **continúo** | **continúe** | continuaba | continuaré | continuaría |
| continuando | **continúas** | **continúes** | continuabas | continuarás | continuarías |
| continuado | **continúa** | **continúe** | continuaba | continuará | continuaría |
| | continuamos | continuemos | continuábamos | continuaremos | continuaríamos |
| | continuáis | continuéis | continuabais | continuaréis | continuaríais |
| | **continúan** | **continúen** | continuaban | continuarán | continuarían |
| §34 | | | | | |
| **crecer** | **crezco** | **crezca** | crecía | creceré | crecería |
| creciendo | creces | **crezcas** | crecías | crecerás | crecerías |
| crecido | crece | **crezca** | crecía | crecerá | crecería |
| | crecemos | **crezcamos** | crecíamos | creceremos | creceríamos |
| | crecéis | **crezcáis** | crecíais | creceréis | creceríais |
| | crecen | **crezcan** | crecían | crecerán | crecerían |
| §35 | | | | | |
| **creer** | creo | crea | creía | creeré | creería |
| **creyendo** | crees | creas | creías | creerás | creerías |
| **creído** | cree | crea | creía | creerá | creería |
| | creemos | creamos | creíamos | creeremos | creeríamos |
| | creéis | creáis | creíais | creeréis | creeríais |
| | creen | crean | creían | creerán | creerían |
| §36 | | | | | |
| **dar** | **doy** | **dé** | daba | daré | daría |
| dando | das | des | dabas | darás | darías |
| dado | da | **dé** | daba | dará | daría |
| | damos | demos | dábamos | daremos | daríamos |
| | dais | deis | dabais | daréis | daríais |
| | dan | den | daban | darán | darían |
| §37 | | | | | |
| **decir** | **digo** | **diga** | decía | **diré** | **diría** |
| **diciendo** | **dices** | **digas** | decías | **dirás** | **dirías** |
| **dicho** | **dice** | **diga** | decía | **dirá** | **diría** |
| | decimos | **digamos** | decíamos | **diremos** | **diríamos** |
| | decís | **digáis** | decíais | **diréis** | **diríais** |
| | **dicen** | **digan** | decían | **dirán** | **dirían** |

| PRETERIT INDICATIVE | IMPERF. SUBJ. s-FORM | IMPERF. SUBJ. r-FORM | FUTURE SUBJUNCTIVE | IMPERATIVE | NOTES AND REFERENCES |
|---|---|---|---|---|---|
| caí | **cayese** | **cayera** | **cayere** | | **§15,** 15 & **§17,** 1 |
| **caíste** | **cayeses** | **cayeras** | **cayeres** | cae | |
| **cayó** | **cayese** | **cayera** | **cayere** | | |
| **caímos** | **cayésemos** | **cayéramos** | **cayéremos** | | |
| **caísteis** | **cayeseis** | **cayerais** | **cayereis** | caed | |
| **cayeron** | **cayesen** | **cayeran** | **cayeren** | | |
| **cegué** | cegase | cegara | cegare | | Combination of **§15,** 2 & **§16,** 1 |
| cegaste | cegases | cegaras | cegares | **ciega** | |
| cegó | cegase | cegara | cegare | | |
| cegamos | cegásemos | cegáramos | cegáremos | | |
| cegasteis | cegaseis | cegarais | cegareis | cegad | |
| cegaron | cegasen | cegaran | cegaren | | |
| cocí | cociese | cociera | cociere | | Like **§87** although **c** is preceded by a vowel |
| cociste | cocieses | cocieras | cocieres | **cuece** | |
| coció | cociese | cociera | cociere | | |
| cocimos | cociésemos | cociéramos | cociéremos | | |
| cocisteis | cocieseis | cocierais | cociereis | coced | |
| cocieron | cociesen | cocieran | cocieren | | |
| **comencé** | comenzase | comenzara | comenzare | | Combination of **§15,** 4 & **§16,** 1 |
| comenzaste | comenzases | comenzaras | comenzares | **comienza** | |
| comenzó | comenzase | comenzara | comenzare | | |
| comenzamos | comenzásemos | comenzáramos | comenzáremos | | |
| comenzasteis | comenzaseis | comenzarais | comenzareis | comenzad | |
| comenzaron | comenzasen | comenzaran | comenzaren | | |
| conocí | conociese | conociera | conociere | | **§17,** 1 |
| conociste | conocieses | conocieras | conocieres | conoce | |
| conoció | conociese | conociera | conociere | | |
| conocimos | conociésemos | conociéramos | conociéremos | | |
| conocisteis | conocieseis | conocierais | conociereis | conoced | |
| conocieron | conociesen | conocieran | conocieren | | |
| continué | continuase | continuara | continuare | | **§16,** 9 |
| continuaste | continuases | continuaras | continuares | **continúa** | |
| continuó | continuase | continuara | continuare | | |
| continuamos | continuásemos | continuáramos | continuáremos | | |
| continuasteis | continuaseis | continuarais | continuareis | continuad | |
| continuaron | continuasen | continuaran | continuaren | | |
| crecí | creciese | creciera | creciere | | **§17,** 1 |
| creciste | crecieses | crecieras | crecieres | crece | |
| creció | creciese | creciera | creciere | | |
| crecimos | creciésemos | creciéramos | creciéremos | | |
| crecisteis | crecieseis | crecierais | creciereis | creced | |
| crecieron | creciesen | crecieran | crecieren | | |
| creí | **creyese** | **creyera** | **creyere** | | **§15,** 15 |
| **creíste** | **creyeses** | **creyeras** | **creyeres** | cree | |
| **creyó** | **creyese** | **creyera** | **creyere** | | |
| **creímos** | **creyésemos** | **creyéramos** | **creyéremos** | | |
| **creísteis** | **creyeseis** | **creyerais** | **creyereis** | creed | |
| **creyeron** | **creyesen** | **creyeran** | **creyeren** | | |
| **di** | **diese** | **diera** | **diere** | | **§17,** 2 & 7 |
| **diste** | **dieses** | **dieras** | **dieres** | da | |
| **dio** | **diese** | **diera** | **diere** | | |
| **dimos** | **diésemos** | **diéramos** | **diéremos** | | |
| **disteis** | **dieseis** | **dierais** | **diereis** | dad | |
| **dieron** | **diesen** | **dieran** | **dieren** | | |
| **dije** | **dijese** | **dijera** | **dijere** | | **§16,** 7 & **§17,** 1, 5, 6, 8, & 9 |
| **dijiste** | **dijeses** | **dijeras** | **dijeres** | **di** | |
| **dijo** | **dijese** | **dijera** | **dijere** | | |
| **dijimos** | **dijésemos** | **dijéramos** | **dijéremos** | | |
| **dijisteis** | **dijeseis** | **dijerais** | **dijereis** | decid | |
| **dijeron** | **dijesen** | **dijeran** | **dijeren** | | |

| INFINITIVE GERUND AND PAST PARTICIPLE | PRESENT INDICATIVE | PRESENT SUBJUNCTIVE | IMPERFECT INDICATIVE | FUTURE INDICATIVE | CONDITIONAL |
|---|---|---|---|---|---|
| §38<br>**deducir**<br>deduciendo<br>deducido | **deduzco**<br>deduces<br>deduce<br>deducimos<br>deducís<br>deducen | **deduzca**<br>**deduzcas**<br>**deduzca**<br>**deduzcamos**<br>**deduzcáis**<br>**deduzcan** | deducía<br>deducías<br>deducía<br>deducíamos<br>deducíais<br>deducían | deduciré<br>deducirás<br>deducirá<br>deduciremos<br>deduciréis<br>deducirán | deduciría<br>deducirías<br>deduciría<br>deduciríamos<br>deduciríais<br>deducirían |
| §39<br>**delinquir**<br>delinquiendo<br>delinquido | **delinco**<br>delinques<br>delinque<br>delinquimos<br>delinquís<br>delinquen | **delinca**<br>**delincas**<br>**delinca**<br>**delincamos**<br>**delincáis**<br>**delincan** | delinquía<br>delinquías<br>delinquía<br>delinquíamos<br>delinquíais<br>delinquían | delinquiré<br>delinquirás<br>delinquirá<br>delinquiremos<br>delinquiréis<br>delinquirán | delinquiría<br>delinquirías<br>delinquiría<br>delinquiríamos<br>delinquiríais<br>delinquirían |
| §40<br>**desosar**<br>desosando<br>desosado | **deshueso**<br>**deshuesas**<br>**deshuesa**<br>desosamos<br>desosáis<br>**deshuesan** | **deshuese**<br>**deshueses**<br>**deshuese**<br>desosemos<br>desoséis<br>**deshuesen** | desosaba<br>desosabas<br>desosaba<br>desosábamos<br>desosabais<br>desosaban | desosaré<br>desosarás<br>desosará<br>desosaremos<br>desosaréis<br>desosarán | desosaría<br>desosarías<br>desosaría<br>desosaríamos<br>desosaríais<br>desosarían |
| §41<br>**destruir**<br>**destruyendo**<br>destruido | **destruyo**<br>**destruyes**<br>**destruye**<br>destruimos<br>destruís<br>**destruyen** | **destruya**<br>**destruyas**<br>**destruya**<br>**destruyamos**<br>**destruyáis**<br>**destruyan** | destruía<br>destruías<br>destruía<br>destruíamos<br>destruíais<br>destruían | destruiré<br>destruirás<br>destruirá<br>destruiremos<br>destruiréis<br>destruirán | destruiría<br>destruirías<br>destruiría<br>destruiríamos<br>destruiríais<br>destruirían |
| §42<br>**dirigir**<br>dirigiendo<br>dirigido | **dirijo**<br>diriges<br>dirige<br>dirigimos<br>dirigís<br>dirigen | **dirija**<br>**dirijas**<br>**dirija**<br>**dirijamos**<br>**dirijáis**<br>**dirijan** | dirigía<br>dirigías<br>dirigía<br>dirigíamos<br>dirigíais<br>dirigían | dirigiré<br>dirigirás<br>dirigirá<br>dirigiremos<br>dirigiréis<br>dirigirán | dirigiría<br>dirigirías<br>dirigiría<br>dirigiríamos<br>dirigiríais<br>dirigirían |
| §43<br>**discernir**<br>discerniendo<br>discernido | **discierno**<br>**disciernes**<br>**discierne**<br>discernimos<br>discernís<br>**disciernen** | **discierna**<br>**disciernas**<br>**discierna**<br>discernamos<br>discernáis<br>**disciernan** | discernía<br>discernías<br>discernía<br>discerníamos<br>discerníais<br>discernían | discerniré<br>discernirás<br>discernirá<br>discerniremos<br>discerniréis<br>discernirán | discerniría<br>discernirías<br>discerniría<br>discerniríamos<br>discerniríais<br>discernirían |
| §44<br>**distinguir**<br>distinguiendo<br>distinguido | **distingo**<br>distingues<br>distingue<br>distinguimos<br>distinguís<br>distinguen | **distinga**<br>**distingas**<br>**distinga**<br>**distingamos**<br>**distingáis**<br>**distingan** | distinguía<br>distinguías<br>distinguía<br>distinguíamos<br>distinguíais<br>distinguían | distinguiré<br>distinguirás<br>distinguirá<br>distinguiremos<br>distinguiréis<br>distinguirán | distinguiría<br>distinguirías<br>distinguiría<br>distinguiríamos<br>distinguiríais<br>distinguirían |
| §45<br>**dormir**<br>**durmiendo**<br>dormido | **duermo**<br>**duermes**<br>**duerme**<br>dormimos<br>dormís<br>**duermen** | **duerma**<br>**duermas**<br>**duerma**<br>**durmamos**<br>**durmáis**<br>**duerman** | dormía<br>dormías<br>dormía<br>dormíamos<br>dormíais<br>dormían | dormiré<br>dormirás<br>dormirá<br>dormiremos<br>dormiréis<br>dormirán | dormiría<br>dormirías<br>dormiría<br>dormiríamos<br>dormiríais<br>dormirían |
| §46<br>**empeller**<br>**empellendo**<br>empellido | empello<br>empelles<br>empelle<br>empellemos<br>empelléis<br>empellen | empella<br>empellas<br>empella<br>empellamos<br>empelláis<br>empellan | empellía<br>empellías<br>empellía<br>empellíamos<br>empellíais<br>empellían | empelleré<br>empellerás<br>empellerá<br>empelleremos<br>empelleréis<br>empellerán | empellería<br>empellerías<br>empellería<br>empelleríamos<br>empelleríais<br>empellerían |

| PRETERIT INDICATIVE | IMPERF. SUBJ. s-FORM | IMPERF. SUBJ. r-FORM | FUTURE SUBJUNCTIVE | IMPERATIVE | NOTES AND REFERENCES |
|---|---|---|---|---|---|
| **deduje** | **dedujese** | **dedujera** | **dedujere** | | **§17,** 1 & 6 |
| **dedujiste** | **dedujeses** | **dedujeras** | **dedujeres** | deduce | |
| **dedujo** | **dedujese** | **dedujera** | **dedujere** | | |
| **dedujimos** | **dedujésemos** | **dedujéramos** | **dedujéremos** | | |
| **dedujisteis** | **dedujeseis** | **dedujerais** | **dedujereis** | deducid | |
| **dedujeron** | **dedujesen** | **dedujeran** | **dedujeren** | | |
| delinquí | delinquiese | delinquiera | delinquiere | | **§15,** 10 |
| delinquiste | delinquieses | delinquieras | delinquieres | delinque | |
| delinquió | delinquiese | delinquiera | delinquiere | | |
| delinquimos | delinquiésemos | delinquiéramos | delinquiéremos | | |
| delinquisteis | delinquieseis | delinquierais | delinquiereis | delinquid | |
| delinquieron | delinquiesen | delinquieran | delinquieren | | |
| desosé | desosase | desosara | desosare | | **Like §77 with h before ue as in §65** |
| desosaste | desosases | desosaras | desosares | **deshuesa** | |
| desosó | desosase | desosara | desosare | | |
| desosamos | desosásemos | desosáramos | desosáremos | | |
| desosasteis | desosaseis | desosarais | desosareis | desosad | |
| desosaron | desosasen | desosaran | desosaren | | |
| destruí | **destruyese** | **destruyera** | **destruyere** | | **§15,** 15. 1 & **§17,** 1 & 3 |
| destruiste | **destruyeses** | **destruyeras** | **destruyeres** | **destruye** | |
| **destruyó** | **destruyese** | **destruyera** | **destruyere** | | |
| destruimos | **destruyésemos** | **destruyéramos** | **destruyéremos** | | |
| destruisteis | **destruyeseis** | **destruyerais** | **destruyereis** | destruid | |
| **destruyeron** | **destruyesen** | **destruyeran** | **destruyeren** | | |
| dirigí | dirigiese | dirigiera | dirigiere | | **§15,** 8 |
| dirigiste | dirigieses | dirigieras | dirigieres | dirige | |
| dirigió | dirigiese | dirigiera | dirigiere | | |
| dirigimos | dirigiésemos | dirigiéramos | dirigiéremos | | |
| dirigisteis | dirigieseis | dirigierais | dirigiereis | dirigid | |
| dirigieron | dirigiesen | dirigieran | dirigieren | | |
| discerní | discerniese | discerniera | discerniere | | **Third conjugation with irregularities of §66** |
| discerniste | discernieses | discernieras | discernieres | **discierne** | |
| discernió | discerniese | discerniera | discerniere | | |
| discernimos | discerniésemos | discerniéramos | discerniéremos | | |
| discernisteis | discernieseis | discernierais | discerniereis | discernid | |
| discernieron | discerniesen | discernieran | discernieren | | |
| distinguí | distinguiese | distinguiera | distinguiere | | **§15,** 9 |
| distinguiste | distinguieses | distinguieras | distinguieres | distingue | |
| distinguió | distinguiese | distinguiera | distinguiere | | |
| distinguimos | distinguiésemos | distinguiéramos | distinguiéremos | | |
| distinguisteis | distinguieseis | distinguierais | distinguiereis | distinguid | |
| distinguieron | distinguiesen | distinguieran | distinguieren | | |
| dormí | **durmiese** | **durmiera** | **durmiere** | | **§16,** 6 |
| dormiste | **durmieses** | **durmieras** | **durmieres** | **duerme** | |
| **durmió** | **durmiese** | **durmiera** | **durmiere** | | |
| dormimos | **durmiésemos** | **durmiéramos** | **durmiéremos** | | |
| dormisteis | **durmieseis** | **durmierais** | **durmiereis** | dormid | |
| **durmieron** | **durmiesen** | **durmieran** | **durmieren** | | |
| empellí | **empellese** | **empellera** | **empellere** | | **§15,** 11 |
| empelliste | **empelleses** | **empelleras** | **empelleres** | empelle | |
| **empelló** | **empellese** | **empellera** | **empellere** | | |
| empellimos | **empellésemos** | **empelléramos** | **empelléremos** | | |
| empellisteis | **empelleseis** | **empellerais** | **empellereis** | empelled | |
| **empelleron** | **empellesen** | **empelleran** | **empelleren** | | |

| INFINITIVE GERUND AND PAST PARTICIPLE | PRESENT INDICATIVE | PRESENT SUBJUNCTIVE | IMPERFECT INDICATIVE | FUTURE INDICATIVE | CONDITIONAL |
|---|---|---|---|---|---|
| **§47** | | | | | |
| **erguir** | **yergo** | **yerga** | erguía | erguiré | erguiría |
| | **irgo** | **irga** | | | |
| **irguiendo** | **yergues** | **yergas** | erguías | erguirás | erguirías |
| | **irgues** | **irgas** | | | |
| erguido | **yergue** | **yerga** | erguía | erguirá | erguiría |
| | **irgue** | **irga** | | | |
| | erguimos | **irgamos** | erguíamos | erguiremos | erguiríamos |
| | erguís | **irgáis** | erguíais | erguiréis | erguiríais |
| | **yerguen** | **yergan** | erguían | erguirán | erguirían |
| | **irguen** | **irgan** | | | |
| **§48** | | | | | |
| **errar** | **yerro** | **yerre** | erraba | erraré | erraría |
| errando | **yerras** | **yerres** | errabas | errarás | errarías |
| errado | **yerra** | **yerre** | erraba | errará | erraría |
| | erramos | erremos | errábamos | erraremos | erraríamos |
| | erráis | erréis | errabais | erraréis | erraríais |
| | **yerran** | **yerren** | erraban | errarán | errarían |
| **§49** | | | | | |
| **escoger** | **escojo** | **escoja** | escogía | escogeré | escogería |
| escogiendo | escoges | **escojas** | escogías | escogerás | escogerías |
| escogido | escoge | **escoja** | escogía | escogerá | escogería |
| | escogemos | **escojamos** | escogíamos | escogeremos | escogeríamos |
| | escogéis | **escojáis** | escogíais | escogeréis | escogeríais |
| | escogen | **escojan** | escogían | escogerán | escogerían |
| **§50** | | | | | |
| **esparcir** | **esparzo** | **esparza** | esparcía | esparciré | esparciría |
| esparciendo | esparces | **esparzas** | esparcías | esparcirás | esparcirías |
| esparcido | esparce | **esparza** | esparcía | esparcirá | esparciría |
| | esparcimos | **esparzamos** | esparcíamos | esparciremos | esparciríamos |
| | esparcís | **esparzáis** | esparcíais | esparciréis | esparciríais |
| | esparcen | **esparzan** | esparcían | esparcirán | esparcirían |
| **§51** | | | | | |
| **estar** | **estoy** | **esté** | estaba | estaré | estaría |
| estando | **estás** | **estés** | estabas | estarás | estarías |
| estado | **está** | **esté** | estaba | estará | estaría |
| | estamos | estemos | estábamos | estaremos | estaríamos |
| | estáis | estéis | estabais | estaréis | estaríais |
| | **están** | **estén** | estaban | estarán | estarían |
| **§52** | | | | | |
| **forzar** | **fuerzo** | **fuerce** | forzaba | forzaré | forzaría |
| forzando | **fuerzas** | **fuerces** | forzabas | forzarás | forzarías |
| forzado | **fuerza** | **fuerce** | forzaba | forzará | forzaría |
| | forzamos | **forcemos** | forzábamos | forzaremos | forzaríamos |
| | forzáis | **forcéis** | forzabais | forzaréis | forzaríais |
| | **fuerzan** | **fuercen** | forzaban | forzarán | forzarían |
| **§53** | | | | | |
| **garantir** | | | garantía | garantiré | garantiría |
| garantiendo | | | garantías | garantirás | garantirías |
| garantido | | | garantía | garantirá | garantiría |
| | garantimos | | garantíamos | garantiremos | garantiríamos |
| | garantís | | garantíais | garantiréis | garantiríais |
| | | | garantían | garantirán | garantirían |
| **§54** | | | | | |
| **haber** | **he** | **haya** | había | **habré** | **habría** |
| habiendo | **has** | **hayas** | habías | **habrás** | **habrías** |
| habido | **ha** | **haya** | había | **habrá** | **habría** |
| | **hemos** | **hayamos** | habíamos | **habremos** | **habríamos** |
| | habéis | **hayáis** | habíais | **habréis** | **habríais** |
| | **han** | **hayan** | habían | **habrán** | **habrían** |
| **§55** | | | | | |
| **hacer** | **hago** | **haga** | hacía | **haré** | **haría** |
| haciendo | haces | **hagas** | hacías | **harás** | **harías** |
| **hecho** | hace | **haga** | hacía | **hará** | **haría** |
| | hacemos | **hagamos** | hacíamos | **haremos** | **haríamos** |
| | hacéis | **hagáis** | hacíais | **haréis** | **haríais** |
| | hacen | **hagan** | hacían | **harán** | **harían** |

| PRETERIT INDICATIVE | IMPERF. SUBJ. s-FORM | IMPERF. SUBJ. r-FORM | FUTURE SUBJUNCTIVE | IMPERATIVE | NOTES AND REFERENCES |
|---|---|---|---|---|---|
| erguí | **irguiese** | **irguiera** | **irguiere** | | §15, 9 & §16, 5 or 7 |
| erguiste | **irguieses** | **irguieras** | **irguieres** | **yergue**<br>**irgue** | |
| **irguió** | **irguiese** | **irguiera** | **irguiere** | | |
| erguimos | **irguiésemos** | **irguiéramos** | **irguiéremos** | | |
| erguisteis | **irguieseis** | **irguierais** | **irguiereis** | erguid | |
| **irguieron** | **irguiesen** | **irguieran** | **irguieren** | | |
| erré | errase | errara | errare | | Like §18 but with initial **ye** for **ie** |
| erraste | errases | erraras | errares | **yerra** | |
| erró | errase | errara | errare | | |
| erramos | errásemos | erráramos | erráremos | | |
| errasteis | erraseis | errarais | errareis | errad | |
| erraron | errasen | erraran | erraren | | |
| escogí | escogiese | escogiera | escogiere | | §15, 7 |
| escogiste | escogieses | escogieras | escogieres | escoge | |
| escogió | escogiese | escogiera | escogiere | | |
| escogimos | escogiésemos | escogiéramos | escogiéremos | | |
| escogisteis | escogieseis | escogierais | escogiereis | escoged | |
| escogieron | escogiesen | escogieran | escogieren | | |
| esparcí | esparciese | esparciera | esparciere | | §15, 6 |
| esparciste | esparcieses | esparcieras | esparcieres | esparce | |
| esparció | esparciese | esparciera | esparciere | | |
| esparcimos | esparciésemos | esparciéramos | esparciéremos | | |
| esparcisteis | esparcieseis | esparcierais | esparciereis | esparcid | |
| esparcieron | esparciesen | esparcieran | esparcieren | | |
| **estuve** | **estuviese** | **estuviera** | **estuviere** | | §17, 2 & 6 |
| **estuviste** | **estuvieses** | **estuvieras** | **estuvieres** | **está** | |
| **estuvo** | **estuviese** | **estuviera** | **estuviere** | | |
| **estuvimos** | **estuviésemos** | **estuviéramos** | **estuviéremos** | | |
| **estuvisteis** | **estuvieseis** | **estuvierais** | **estuviereis** | estad | |
| **estuvieron** | **estuviesen** | **estuvieran** | **estuvieren** | | |
| **forcé** | forzase | forzara | forzare | | Combination of §15, 4 & §16, 3 |
| forzaste | forzases | forzaras | forzares | **fuerza** | |
| forzó | forzase | forzara | forzare | | |
| forzamos | forzásemos | forzáramos | forzáremos | | |
| forzasteis | forzaseis | forzarais | forzareis | forzad | |
| forzaron | forzasen | forzaran | forzaren | | |
| garantí | garantiese | garantiera | garantiere | | Defective verb used only in forms whose endings begin with **i** |
| garantiste | garantieses | garantieras | garantieres | | |
| garantió | garantiese | garantiera | garantiere | | |
| garantimos | garantiésemos | garantiéramos | garantiéremos | | |
| garantisteis | garantieseis | garantierais | garantiereis | garantid | |
| garantieron | garantiesen | garantieran | garantieren | | |
| **hube** | **hubiese** | **hubiera** | **hubiere** | | §17, 2, 5, 6, & 8 |
| **hubiste** | **hubieses** | **hubieras** | **hubieres** | **hé** | |
| **hubo** | **hubiese** | **hubiera** | **hubiere** | | |
| **hubimos** | **hubiésemos** | **hubiéramos** | **hubiéremos** | | |
| **hubisteis** | **hubieseis** | **hubierais** | **hubiereis** | habed | |
| **hubieron** | **hubiesen** | **hubieran** | **hubieren** | | |
| **hice** | **hiciese** | **hiciera** | **hiciere** | | §17, 1, 5, 6, 8, & 9 |
| **hiciste** | **hicieses** | **hicieras** | **hicieres** | **haz** | |
| **hizo** | **hiciese** | **hiciera** | **hiciere** | | |
| **hicimos** | **hiciésemos** | **hiciéramos** | **hiciéremos** | | *1st & 3d sg pret ind of* **rehacer: rehíce, rehízo** |
| **hicisteis** | **hicieseis** | **hicierais** | **hiciereis** | haced | |
| **hicieron** | **hiciesen** | **hicieran** | **hicieren** | | |

| INFINITIVE GERUND AND PAST PARTICIPLE | PRESENT INDICATIVE | PRESENT SUBJUNCTIVE | IMPERFECT INDICATIVE | FUTURE INDICATIVE | CONDITIONAL |
|---|---|---|---|---|---|
| §56<br>**inquirir**<br>inquiriendo<br>inquirido | **inquiero**<br>**inquieres**<br>**inquiere**<br>inquirimos<br>inquirís<br>**inquieren** | **inquiera**<br>**inquieras**<br>**inquiera**<br>inquiramos<br>inquiráis<br>**inquieran** | inquiría<br>inquirías<br>inquiría<br>inquiríamos<br>inquiríais<br>inquirían | inquiriré<br>inquirirás<br>inquirirá<br>inquiriremos<br>inquiriréis<br>inquirirán | inquiriría<br>inquirirías<br>inquiriría<br>inquiriríamos<br>inquiriríais<br>inquirirían |
| §57<br>**ir**<br>**yendo**<br>ido | **voy**<br>**vas**<br>**va**<br>**vamos**<br>**vais**<br>**van** | **vaya**<br>**vayas**<br>**vaya**<br>**vayamos**<br>**vayáis**<br>**vayan** | **iba**<br>**ibas**<br>**iba**<br>**íbamos**<br>**ibais**<br>**iban** | iré<br>irás<br>irá<br>iremos<br>iréis<br>irán | iría<br>irías<br>iría<br>iríamos<br>iríais<br>irían |
| §58<br>**jugar**<br>jugando<br>jugado | **juego**<br>**juegas**<br>**juega**<br>jugamos<br>jugáis<br>**juegan** | **juegue**<br>**juegues**<br>**juegue**<br>**juguemos**<br>**juguéis**<br>**jueguen** | jugaba<br>jugabas<br>jugaba<br>jugábamos<br>jugabais<br>jugaban | jugaré<br>jugarás<br>jugará<br>jugaremos<br>jugaréis<br>jugarán | jugaría<br>jugarías<br>jugaría<br>jugaríamos<br>jugaríais<br>jugarían |
| §59<br>**ligar**<br>ligando<br>ligado | ligo<br>ligas<br>liga<br>ligamos<br>ligáis<br>ligan | **ligue**<br>**ligues**<br>**ligue**<br>**liguemos**<br>**liguéis**<br>**liguen** | ligaba<br>ligabas<br>ligaba<br>ligábamos<br>ligabais<br>ligaban | ligaré<br>ligarás<br>ligará<br>ligaremos<br>ligaréis<br>ligarán | ligaría<br>ligarías<br>ligaría<br>ligaríamos<br>ligarías<br>ligarían |
| §60<br>**lucir**<br>luciendo<br>lucido | **luzco**<br>luces<br>luce<br>lucimos<br>lucís<br>lucen | **luzca**<br>**luzcas**<br>**luzca**<br>**luzcamos**<br>**luzcáis**<br>**luzcan** | lucía<br>lucías<br>lucía<br>lucíamos<br>lucíais<br>lucían | luciré<br>lucirás<br>lucirá<br>luciremos<br>luciréis<br>lucirán | luciría<br>lucirías<br>luciría<br>luciríamos<br>luciríais<br>lucirían |
| §61<br>**mecer**<br>meciendo<br>mecido | **mezo**<br>meces<br>mece<br>mecemos<br>mecéis<br>mecen | **meza**<br>**mezas**<br>**meza**<br>**mezamos**<br>**mezáis**<br>**mezan** | mecía<br>mecías<br>mecía<br>mecíamos<br>mecíais<br>mecían | meceré<br>mecerás<br>mecerá<br>meceremos<br>meceréis<br>mecerán | mecería<br>mecerías<br>mecería<br>meceríamos<br>meceríais<br>mecerían |
| §62<br>**mentir**<br>**mintiendo**<br>mentido | **miento**<br>**mientes**<br>**miente**<br>mentimos<br>mentís<br>**mienten** | **mienta**<br>**mientas**<br>**mienta**<br>**mintamos**<br>**mintáis**<br>**mientan** | mentía<br>mentías<br>mentía<br>mentíamos<br>mentíais<br>mentían | mentiré<br>mentirás<br>mentirá<br>mentiremos<br>mentiréis<br>mentirán | mentiría<br>mentirías<br>mentiría<br>mentiríamos<br>mentiríais<br>mentirían |
| §63<br>**morder**<br>mordiendo<br>mordido | **muerdo**<br>**muerdes**<br>**muerde**<br>mordemos<br>mordéis<br>**muerden** | **muerda**<br>**muerdas**<br>**muerda**<br>mordamos<br>mordáis<br>**muerdan** | mordía<br>mordías<br>mordía<br>mordíamos<br>mordíais<br>mordían | morderé<br>morderás<br>morderá<br>morderemos<br>morderéis<br>morderán | mordería<br>morderías<br>mordería<br>morderíamos<br>morderíais<br>morderían |
| §64<br>**oír**<br>**oyendo**<br>**oído** | **oigo**<br>**oyes**<br>**oye**<br>**oímos**<br>oís<br>**oyen** | **oiga**<br>**oigas**<br>**oiga**<br>**oigamos**<br>**oigáis**<br>**oigan** | oía<br>oías<br>oía<br>oíamos<br>oíais<br>oían | oiré<br>oirás<br>oirá<br>oiremos<br>oiréis<br>oirán | oiría<br>oirías<br>oiría<br>oiríamos<br>oiríais<br>oirían |
| §65<br>**oler**<br>oliendo<br>olido | **huelo**<br>**hueles**<br>**huele**<br>olemos<br>oléis<br>**huelen** | **huela**<br>**huelas**<br>**huela**<br>olamos<br>oláis<br>**huelan** | olía<br>olías<br>olía<br>olíamos<br>olíais<br>olían | oleré<br>olerás<br>olerá<br>oleremos<br>oleréis<br>olerán | olería<br>olerías<br>olería<br>oleríamos<br>oleríais<br>olerían |

| PRETERIT INDICATIVE | IMPERF. SUBJ. s-FORM | IMPERF. SUBJ. r-FORM | FUTURE SUBJUNCTIVE | IMPERATIVE | NOTES AND REFERENCES |
|---|---|---|---|---|---|
| inquirí | inquiriese | inquiriera | inquiriere | | Third conjugation with radical **i** and irregularities of **§66** |
| inquiriste | inquirieses | inquirieras | inquirieres | **inquiere** | |
| inquirió | inquiriese | inquiriera | inquiriere | | |
| inquirimos | inquiriésemos | inquiriéramos | inquiriéremos | | |
| inquiristeis | inquirieseis | inquirierais | inquiriereis | inquirid | |
| inquirieron | inquiriesen | inquirieran | inquirieren | | |
| **fui** | **fuese** | **fuera** | **fuere** | | **§17,** 2, 4, 7, & 8 |
| **fuiste** | **fueses** | **fueras** | **fueres** | **vé** | |
| **fue** | **fuese** | **fuera** | **fuere** | | |
| **fuimos** | **fuésemos** | **fuéramos** | **fuéremos** | **vamos** | |
| **fuisteis** | **fueseis** | **fuerais** | **fuereis** | id | |
| **fueron** | **fuesen** | **fueran** | **fueren** | | |
| **jugué** | jugase | jugara | jugare | | Like **§79** but with radical **u** |
| jugaste | jugases | jugaras | jugares | **juega** | |
| jugó | jugase | jugara | jugare | | |
| jugamos | jugásemos | jugáramos | jugáremos | | |
| jugasteis | jugaseis | jugarais | jugareis | jugad | |
| jugaron | jugasen | jugaran | jugaren | | |
| **ligué** | ligase | ligara | ligare | | **§15,** 2 |
| ligaste | ligases | ligaras | ligares | liga | |
| ligó | ligase | ligara | ligare | | |
| ligamos | ligásemos | ligáramos | ligáremos | | |
| ligasteis | ligaseis | ligarais | ligareis | ligad | |
| ligaron | ligasen | ligaran | ligaren | | |
| lucí | luciese | luciera | luciere | | **§17,** 1 |
| luciste | lucieses | lucieras | lucieres | luce | |
| lució | luciese | luciera | **luciere** | | |
| lucimos | luciésemos | luciéramos | luciéremos | | |
| lucisteis | lucieseis | lucierais | luciereis | lucid | |
| lucieron | luciesen | lucieran | lucieren | | |
| mecí | meciese | meciera | meciere | | Like **§91** although **c** is preceded by a vowel |
| meciste | mecieses | mecieras | mecieres | mece | |
| meció | meciese | meciera | meciere | | |
| mecimos | meciésemos | meciéramos | meciéremos | | |
| mecisteis | mecieseis | mecierais | meciereis | meced | |
| **mecieron** | meciesen | mecieran | mecieren | | |
| mentí | **mintiese** | **mintiera** | **mintiere** | | **§16,** 5 |
| mentiste | **mintieses** | **mintieras** | **mintieres** | **miente** | |
| **mintió** | **mintiese** | **mintiera** | **mintiere** | | |
| mentimos | **mintiésemos** | **mintiéramos** | **mintiéremos** | | |
| mentisteis | **mintieseis** | **mintierais** | **mintiereis** | mentid | |
| **mintieron** | **mintiesen** | **mintieran** | **mintieren** | | |
| **mordí** | mordiese | mordiera | mordiere | | **§16,** 4 |
| mordiste | mordieses | mordieras | mordieres | **muerde** | |
| mordió | mordiese | mordiera | mordiere | | |
| mordimos | mordiésemos | mordiéramos | mordiéremos | | |
| **mordisteis** | mordieseis | mordierais | mordiereis | morded | |
| mordieron | mordiesen | mordieran | mordieren | | |
| oí | **oyese** | **oyera** | **oyere** | | **§15,** 16 & **§17,** 1 & 3 |
| **oíste** | **oyeses** | **oyeras** | **oyeres** | **oye** | |
| **oyó** | **oyese** | **oyera** | **oyere** | | |
| **oímos** | **oyésemos** | **oyéramos** | **oyéremos** | | |
| **oísteis** | **oyeseis** | **oyerais** | **oyereis** | **oíd** | |
| **oyeron** | **oyesen** | **oyeran** | **oyeren** | | |
| olí | oliese | oliera | oliere | | Like **§63** but with **h** before **ue** |
| oliste | olieses | olieras | **olieres** | **huele** | |
| olió | oliese | oliera | oliere | | |
| olimos | oliésemos | oliéramos | oliéremos | | |
| olisteis | **olieseis** | olierais | oliereis | oled | |
| olieron | oliesen | olieran | olieren | | |

| INFINITIVE GERUND AND PAST PARTICIPLE | PRESENT INDICATIVE | PRESENT SUBJUNCTIVE | IMPERFECT INDICATIVE | FUTURE INDICATIVE | CONDITIONAL |
|---|---|---|---|---|---|
| §66<br>**perder**<br>perdiendo<br>perdido | **pierdo**<br>**pierdes**<br>**pierde**<br>perdemos<br>perdéis<br>**pierden** | **pierda**<br>**pierdas**<br>**pierda**<br>perdamos<br>perdáis<br>**pierdan** | perdía<br>perdías<br>perdía<br>perdíamos<br>perdíais<br>perdían | perderé<br>perderás<br>perderá<br>perderemos<br>perderéis<br>perderán | perdería<br>perderías<br>perdería<br>perderíamos<br>perderíais<br>perderían |
| §67<br>**placer**<br><br>placiendo<br>placido | **plazco**<br>**plazgo**<br>places<br>place<br>placemos<br>placéis<br>placen | **plazca**<br>**plazga**<br>**plazcas**<br>**plazca**<br>**plazcamos**<br>**plazcáis**<br>**plazcan** | placía<br><br>placías<br>placía<br>placíamos<br>placíais<br>placían | placeré<br><br>placerás<br>placerá<br>placeremos<br>placeréis<br>placerán | placería<br><br>placerías<br>placería<br>placeríamos<br>placeríais<br>placerían |
| §68<br>**poder**<br>**pudiendo**<br>podido | **puedo**<br>**puedes**<br>**puede**<br>podemos<br>podéis<br>**pueden** | **pueda**<br>**puedas**<br>**pueda**<br>podamos<br>podáis<br>**puedan** | podía<br>podías<br>podía<br>podíamos<br>podíais<br>podían | **podré**<br>**podrás**<br>**podrá**<br>**podremos**<br>**podréis**<br>**podrán** | **podría**<br>**podrías**<br>**podría**<br>**podríamos**<br>**podríais**<br>**podrían** |
| §69<br>**poner**<br>poniendo<br>**puesto** | **pongo**<br>pones<br>pone<br>ponemos<br>ponéis<br>ponen | **ponga**<br>**pongas**<br>**ponga**<br>**pongamos**<br>**pongáis**<br>**pongan** | ponía<br>ponías<br>ponía<br>poníamos<br>poníais<br>ponían | **pondré**<br>**pondrás**<br>**pondrá**<br>**pondremos**<br>**pondréis**<br>**pondrán** | **pondría**<br>**pondrías**<br>**pondría**<br>**pondríamos**<br>**pondríais**<br>**pondrían** |
| §70<br>**querer**<br>queriendo<br>querido | **quiero**<br>**quieres**<br>**quiere**<br>queremos<br>queréis<br>**quieren** | **quiera**<br>**quieras**<br>**quiera**<br>queramos<br>queráis<br>**quieran** | quería<br>querías<br>quería<br>queríamos<br>queríais<br>querían | **querré**<br>**querrás**<br>**querrá**<br>**querremos**<br>**querréis**<br>**querrán** | **querría**<br>**querrías**<br>**querría**<br>**querríamos**<br>**querríais**<br>**querrían** |
| §71<br>**raer**<br><br>**rayendo**<br>**raído** | **raigo**<br>**rayo**<br>raes<br>rae<br>raemos<br>raéis<br>raen | **raiga**<br>**raya**<br>**raigas**<br>**raiga**<br>**raigamos**<br>**raigáis**<br>**raigan** | raía<br><br>raías<br>raía<br>raíamos<br>raíais<br>raían | raeré<br><br>raerás<br>raerá<br>raeremos<br>raeréis<br>raerán | raería<br><br>raerías<br>raería<br>raeríamos<br>raeríais<br>raerían |
| §72<br>**regir**<br>**rigiendo**<br>regido | **rijo**<br>**riges**<br>**rige**<br>regimos<br>regís<br>**rigen** | **rija**<br>**rijas**<br>**rija**<br>**rijamos**<br>**rijáis**<br>**rijan** | regía<br>regías<br>regía<br>regíamos<br>regíais<br>regían | regiré<br>regirás<br>regirá<br>regiremos<br>regiréis<br>regirán | regiría<br>regirías<br>regiría<br>regiríamos<br>regiríais<br>regirían |
| §73<br>**reír**<br>**riendo**<br>**reído** | **río**<br>**ríes**<br>**ríe**<br>**reímos**<br>reís<br>**ríen** | **ría**<br>**rías**<br>**ría**<br>**riamos**<br>**riáis**<br>**rían** | reía<br>reías<br>reía<br>reíamos<br>reíais<br>reían | reiré<br>reirás<br>reirá<br>reiremos<br>reiréis<br>reirán | reiría<br>reirías<br>reiría<br>reiríamos<br>reirías<br>reirían |
| §74<br>**reñir**<br>**riñendo**<br>reñido | **riño**<br>**riñes**<br>**riñe**<br>reñimos<br>reñís<br>**riñen** | **riña**<br>**riñas**<br>**riña**<br>**riñamos**<br>**riñáis**<br>**riñan** | reñía<br>reñías<br>reñía<br>reñíamos<br>reñíais<br>reñían | reñiré<br>reñirás<br>reñirá<br>reñiremos<br>reñiréis<br>reñirán | reñiría<br>reñirías<br>reñiría<br>reñiríamos<br>reñiríais<br>reñirían |

| PRETERIT INDICATIVE | IMPERF. SUBJ. S-FORM | IMPERF. SUBJ. R-FORM | FUTURE SUBJUNCTIVE | IMPERATIVE | NOTES AND REFERENCES |
|---|---|---|---|---|---|
| perdí | perdiese | perdiera | perdiere | | **§16,** 2 |
| perdiste | perdieses | perdieras | perdieres | **pierde** | |
| perdió | perdiese | perdiera | perdiere | | |
| perdimos | perdiésemos | perdiéramos | perdiéremos | | |
| perdisteis | perdieseis | perdierais | perdiereis | perded | |
| perdieron | perdiesen | perdieran | perdieren | | |
| plací | placiese | placiera | placiere | | **§17,** 1 & 6 |
| placiste | placieses | placieras | placieres | place | |
| plació | placiese | placiera | placiere | | |
| **plugo** | **pluguiese** | **pluguiera** | **pluguiere** | | |
| placimos | placiésemos | placiéramos | placiéremos | | |
| placisteis | placieseis | placierais | placiereis | placed | |
| placieron | placiesen | placieran | placiere | | |
| **pude** | **pudiese** | **pudiera** | **pudiere** | | **§16,** 4 & **§17,** 5 and 6; irregular **u** in gerund |
| **pudiste** | **pudieses** | **pudieras** | **pudieres** | | |
| **pudo** | **pudiese** | **pudiera** | **pudiere** | | |
| **pudimos** | **pudiésemos** | **pudiéramos** | **pudiéremos** | | |
| **pudisteis** | **pudieseis** | **pudierais** | **pudiereis** | | |
| **pudieron** | **pudiesen** | **pudieran** | **pudieren** | | |
| **puse** | **pusiese** | **pusiera** | **pusiere** | | **§17,** 1, 5, 6, 8, & 9 |
| **pusiste** | **pusieses** | **pusieras** | **pusieres** | **pon** | |
| **puso** | **pusiese** | **pusiera** | **pusiere** | | |
| **pusimos** | **pusiésemos** | **pusiéramos** | **pusiéremos** | | |
| **pusisteis** | **pusieseis** | **pusierais** | **pusiereis** | poned | |
| **pusieron** | **pusiesen** | **pusieran** | **pusieren** | | |
| **quise** | **quisiese** | **quisiera** | **quisiere** | | **§16,** 2 & **§17,** 5 & 6 |
| **quisiste** | **quisieses** | **quisieras** | **quisieres** | **quiere** | |
| **quiso** | **quisiese** | **quisiera** | **quisiere** | | |
| **quisimos** | **quisiésemos** | **quisiéramos** | **quisiéremos** | | |
| **quisisteis** | **quisieseis** | **quisierais** | **quisiereis** | quered | |
| **quisieron** | **quisiesen** | **quisieran** | **quisieren** | | |
| raí | **rayese** | **rayera** | **rayere** | | **§15,** 15 & **§17,** 1 |
| **raíste** | **rayeses** | **rayeras** | **rayeres** | rae | |
| **rayó** | **rayese** | **rayera** | **rayere** | | |
| **raímos** | **rayésemos** | **rayéramos** | **rayéremos** | | |
| **raísteis** | **rayeseis** | **rayerais** | **rayereis** | raed | |
| **rayeron** | **rayesen** | **rayeran** | **rayeren** | | |
| regí | **rigiese** | **rigiera** | **rigiere** | | Combination of **§15,** 8 & **§16,** 7 |
| registe | **rigieses** | **rigieras** | **rigieres** | **rige** | |
| **rigió** | **rigiese** | **rigiera** | **rigiere** | | |
| regimos | **rigiésemos** | **rigiéramos** | **rigiéremos** | | |
| registeis | **rigieseis** | **rigierais** | **rigiereis** | regid | |
| **rigieron** | **rigiesen** | **rigieran** | **rigieren** | | |
| reí | **riese** | **riera** | **riere** | | Like **§94** but with contraction of radical **i** and **i** of **ió** and **ie** of endings. Also **§15,** 16. 2 |
| **reíste** | **rieses** | **rieras** | **rieres** | **ríe** | |
| **rió** | **riese** | **riera** | **riere** | | |
| **reímos** | **riésemos** | **riéramos** | **riéremos** | | |
| **reísteis** | **rieseis** | **rierais** | **riereis** | **reíd** | |
| **rieron** | **riesen** | **rieran** | **rieren** | | |
| reñí | **riñese** | **riñera** | **riñere** | | Combination of **§15,** 14 & **§16,** 7 |
| reñiste | **riñeses** | **riñeras** | **riñeres** | **riñe** | |
| **riñó** | **riñese** | **riñera** | **riñere** | | |
| reñimos | **riñésemos** | **riñéramos** | **riñéremos** | | |
| reñisteis | **riñeseis** | **riñerais** | **riñereis** | reñid | |
| **riñeron** | **riñesen** | **riñeran** | **riñeren** | | |

| INFINITIVE GERUND AND PAST PARTICIPLE | PRESENT INDICATIVE | PRESENT SUBJUNCTIVE | IMPERFECT INDICATIVE | FUTURE INDICATIVE | CONDITIONAL |
|---|---|---|---|---|---|
| §75<br>**reunir**<br>reuniendo<br>reunido | **reúno**<br>**reúnes**<br>**reúne**<br>reunimos<br>reunís<br>**reúnen** | **reúna**<br>**reúnas**<br>**reúna**<br>reunamos<br>reunáis<br>**reúnan** | reunía<br>reunías<br>reunía<br>reuníamos<br>reuníais<br>reunían | reuniré<br>reunirás<br>reunirá<br>reuniremos<br>reuniréis<br>reunirán | reuniría<br>reunirías<br>reuniría<br>reuniríamos<br>reuniríais<br>reunirían |
| §76<br>**rezar**<br>rezando<br>rezado | rezo<br>rezas<br>reza<br>rezamos<br>rezáis<br>rezan | **rece**<br>**reces**<br>**rece**<br>**recemos**<br>**recéis**<br>**recen** | rezaba<br>rezabas<br>rezaba<br>rezábamos<br>rezabais<br>rezaban | rezaré<br>rezarás<br>rezará<br>rezaremos<br>rezaréis<br>rezarán | rezaría<br>rezarías<br>rezaría<br>rezaríamos<br>rezaríais<br>rezarían |
| §77<br>**rodar**<br>rodando<br>rodado | **ruedo**<br>**ruedas**<br>**rueda**<br>rodamos<br>rodáis<br>**ruedan** | **ruede**<br>**ruedes**<br>**ruede**<br>rodemos<br>rodéis<br>**rueden** | rodaba<br>rodabas<br>rodaba<br>rodábamos<br>rodabais<br>rodaban | rodaré<br>rodarás<br>rodará<br>rodaremos<br>rodaréis<br>rodarán | rodaría<br>rodarías<br>rodaría<br>rodaríamos<br>rodaríais<br>rodarían |
| §78<br>**roer**<br><br><br>**royendo**<br>**roído** | roo<br>**roigo**<br>**royo**<br>roes<br>roe<br>roemos<br>roéis<br>roen | roa<br>**roiga**<br>**roya**<br>roas<br>roa<br>roamos<br>roáis<br>roan | roía<br><br><br>roías<br>roía<br>roíamos<br>roíais<br>roían | roeré<br><br><br>roerás<br>roerá<br>roeremos<br>roeréis<br>roerán | roería<br><br><br>roerías<br>roería<br>roeríamos<br>roeríais<br>roerían |
| §79<br>**rogar**<br>rogando<br>rogado | **ruego**<br>**ruegas**<br>**ruega**<br>rogamos<br>rogáis<br>**ruegan** | **ruegue**<br>**ruegues**<br>**ruegue**<br>**roguemos**<br>**roguéis**<br>**rueguen** | rogaba<br>rogabas<br>rogaba<br>rogábamos<br>rogabais<br>rogaban | rogaré<br>rogarás<br>rogará<br>rogaremos<br>rogaréis<br>rogarán | rogaría<br>rogarías<br>rogaría<br>rogaríamos<br>rogaríais<br>rogarían |
| §80<br>**saber**<br>sabiendo<br>sabido | **sé**<br>sabes<br>sabe<br>sabemos<br>sabéis<br>saben | **sepa**<br>**sepas**<br>**sepa**<br>**sepamos**<br>**sepáis**<br>**sepan** | sabía<br>sabías<br>sabía<br>sabíamos<br>sabíais<br>sabían | **sabré**<br>**sabrás**<br>**sabrá**<br>**sabremos**<br>**sabréis**<br>**sabrán** | **sabría**<br>**sabrías**<br>**sabría**<br>**sabríamos**<br>**sabríais**<br>**sabrían** |
| §81<br>**salir**<br>saliendo<br>salido | **salgo**<br>sales<br>sale<br>salimos<br>salís<br>salen | **salga**<br>**salgas**<br>**salga**<br>**salgamos**<br>**salgáis**<br>**salgan** | salía<br>salías<br>salía<br>salíamos<br>salíais<br>salían | **saldré**<br>**saldrás**<br>**saldrá**<br>**saldremos**<br>**saldréis**<br>**saldrán** | **saldría**<br>**saldrías**<br>**saldría**<br>**saldríamos**<br>**saldríais**<br>**saldrían** |
| §82<br>**seguir**<br>**siguiendo**<br>seguido | **sigo**<br>**sigues**<br>**sigue**<br>seguimos<br>seguís<br>**siguen** | **siga**<br>**sigas**<br>**siga**<br>**sigamos**<br>**sigáis**<br>**sigan** | seguía<br>seguías<br>seguía<br>seguíamos<br>seguíais<br>seguían | seguiré<br>seguirás<br>seguirá<br>seguiremos<br>seguiréis<br>seguirán | seguiría<br>seguirías<br>seguiría<br>seguiríamos<br>seguiríais<br>seguirían |
| §83<br>**ser**<br>siendo<br>sido | **soy**<br>**eres**<br>**es**<br>**somos**<br>**sois**<br>**son** | **sea**<br>**seas**<br>**sea**<br>**seamos**<br>**seáis**<br>**sean** | **era**<br>**eras**<br>**era**<br>**éramos**<br>**erais**<br>**eran** | seré<br>serás<br>será<br>seremos<br>seréis<br>serán | sería<br>serías<br>sería<br>seríamos<br>seríais<br>serían |

| PRETERIT INDICATIVE | IMPERF. SUBJ. S-FORM | IMPERF. SUBJ. R-FORM | FUTURE SUBJUNCTIVE | IMPERATIVE | NOTES AND REFERENCES |
|---|---|---|---|---|---|
| reuní<br>reuniste<br>reunió<br>reunimos<br>reunisteis<br>reunieron | reuniese<br>reunieses<br>reuniese<br>reuniésemos<br>reunieseis<br>reuniesen | reuniera<br>reunieras<br>reuniera<br>reuniéramos<br>reunierais<br>reunieran | reuniere<br>reunieres<br>reuniere<br>reuniéremos<br>reuniereis<br>reunieren | **reúne**<br>reunid | **§16,** 8 |
| **recé**<br>rezaste<br>rezó<br>rezamos<br>rezasteis<br>rezaron | rezase<br>rezases<br>rezase<br>rezásemos<br>rezaseis<br>rezasen | rezara<br>rezaras<br>rezara<br>rezáramos<br>rezarais<br>rezaran | rezare<br>rezares<br>rezare<br>rezáremos<br>rezareis<br>rezaren | reza<br>rezad | **§15,** 4 |
| rodé<br>rodaste<br>rodó<br>rodamos<br>rodasteis<br>rodaron | rodase<br>rodases<br>rodase<br>rodásemos<br>rodaseis<br>rodasen | rodara<br>rodaras<br>rodara<br>rodáramos<br>rodarais<br>rodaran | rodare<br>rodares<br>rodare<br>rodáremos<br>rodareis<br>rodaren | **rueda**<br>rodad | **§16,** 3 |
| roí<br>**roíste**<br>**royó**<br>**roímos**<br>**roísteis**<br>**royeron** | **royese**<br>**royeses**<br>**royese**<br>**royésemos**<br>**royeseis**<br>**royesen** | **royera**<br>**royeras**<br>**royera**<br>**royéramos**<br>**royerais**<br>**royeran** | **royere**<br>**royeres**<br>**royere**<br>**royéremos**<br>**royereis**<br>**royeren** | roe<br>roed | **§15,** 15 & **§17,** 1 |
| **rogué**<br>rogaste<br>rogó<br>rogamos<br>rogasteis<br>rogaron | rogase<br>rogases<br>rogase<br>rogásemos<br>rogaseis<br>rogasen | rogara<br>rogaras<br>rogara<br>rogáramos<br>rogarais<br>rogaran | rogare<br>rogares<br>rogare<br>rogáremos<br>rogareis<br>rogaren | **ruega**<br>rogad | Combination of **§15,** 2 & **§16,** 3 |
| **supe**<br>**supiste**<br>**supo**<br>**supimos**<br>**supisteis**<br>**supieron** | **supiese**<br>**supieses**<br>**supiese**<br>**supiésemos**<br>**supieseis**<br>**supiesen** | **supiera**<br>**supieras**<br>**supiera**<br>**supiéramos**<br>**supierais**<br>**supieran** | **supiere**<br>**supieres**<br>**supiere**<br>**supiéremos**<br>**supiereis**<br>**supieren** | sabe<br>sabed | **§17,** 2, 5, & 6 |
| salí<br>saliste<br>salió<br>salimos<br>salisteis<br>salieron | saliese<br>salieses<br>saliese<br>saliésemos<br>salieseis<br>saliesen | saliera<br>salieras<br>saliera<br>saliéramos<br>salierais<br>salieran | saliere<br>salieres<br>saliere<br>saliéremos<br>saliereis<br>salieren | **sal**<br>salid | **§17,** 1, 5, & 8 |
| seguí<br>seguiste<br>**siguió**<br>seguimos<br>seguisteis<br>**siguieron** | **siguiese**<br>**siguieses**<br>**siguiese**<br>**siguiésemos**<br>**siguieseis**<br>**siguiesen** | **siguiera**<br>**siguieras**<br>**siguiera**<br>**siguiéramos**<br>**siguierais**<br>**siguieran** | **siguiere**<br>**siguieres**<br>**siguiere**<br>**siguiéremos**<br>**siguiereis**<br>**siguieren** | **sigue**<br>seguid | Combination of **§15,** 9 & **§16,** 7 |
| **fui**<br>**fuiste**<br>**fue**<br>**fuimos**<br>**fuisteis**<br>**fueron** | **fuese**<br>**fueses**<br>**fuese**<br>**fuésemos**<br>**fueseis**<br>**fuesen** | **fuera**<br>**fueras**<br>**fuera**<br>**fuéramos**<br>**fuerais**<br>**fueran** | **fuere**<br>**fueres**<br>**fuere**<br>**fuéremos**<br>**fuereis**<br>**fueren** | **sé**<br>sed | **§17,** 2, 4, 7, & 8 |

| INFINITIVE GERUND AND PAST PARTICIPLE | PRESENT INDICATIVE | PRESENT SUBJUNCTIVE | IMPERFECT INDICATIVE | FUTURE INDICATIVE | CONDITIONAL |
|---|---|---|---|---|---|
| **§84** | | | | | |
| **tañer** | taño | taña | tañía | tañeré | tañería |
| **tañendo** | tañes | tañas | tañías | tañerás | tañerías |
| tañido | tañe | taña | tañía | tañerá | tañería |
| | tañemos | tañamos | tañíamos | tañeremos | tañeríamos |
| | tañéis | tañáis | tañíais | tañeréis | tañeríais |
| | tañen | tañan | tañían | tañerán | tañerían |
| **§85** | | | | | |
| **tener** | **tengo** | **tenga** | tenía | **tendré** | **tendría** |
| teniendo | **tienes** | **tengas** | tenías | **tendrás** | **tendrías** |
| tenido | **tiene** | **tenga** | tenía | **tendrá** | **tendría** |
| | tenemos | **tengamos** | teníamos | **tendremos** | **tendríamos** |
| | tenéis | **tengáis** | teníais | **tendréis** | **tendríais** |
| | **tienen** | **tengan** | tenían | **tendrán** | **tendrían** |
| **§86** | | | | | |
| **tocar** | toco | **toque** | tocaba | tocaré | tocaría |
| tocando | tocas | **toques** | tocabas | tocarás | tocarías |
| tocado | toca | **toque** | tocaba | tocará | tocaría |
| | tocamos | **toquemos** | tocábamos | tocaremos | tocaríamos |
| | tocáis | **toquéis** | tocabais | tocaréis | tocaríais |
| | tocan | **toquen** | tocaban | tocarán | tocarían |
| **§87** | | | | | |
| **torcer** | **tuerzo** | **tuerza** | torcía | torceré | torcería |
| torciendo | **tuerces** | **tuerzas** | torcías | torcerás | torcerías |
| torcido | **tuerce** | **tuerza** | torcía | torcerá | torcería |
| | torcemos | **torzamos** | torcíamos | torceremos | torceríamos |
| | torcéis | **torzáis** | torcíais | torceréis | torceríais |
| | **tuercen** | **tuerzan** | torcían | torcerán | torcerían |
| **§88** | | | | | |
| **traer** | **traigo** | **traiga** | traía | traeré | traería |
| **trayendo** | traes | **traigas** | traías | traerás | traerías |
| **traído** | trae | **traiga** | traía | traerá | traería |
| | traemos | **traigamos** | traíamos | traeremos | traeríamos |
| | traéis | **traigáis** | traíais | traeréis | traeríais |
| | traen | **traigan** | traían | traerán | traerían |
| **§89** | | | | | |
| **valer** | **valgo** | **valga** | valía | **valdré** | **valdría** |
| valiendo | vales | **valgas** | valías | **valdrás** | **valdrías** |
| valido | vale | **valga** | valía | **valdrá** | **valdría** |
| | valemos | **valgamos** | valíamos | **valdremos** | **valdríamos** |
| | valéis | **valgáis** | valíais | **valdréis** | **valdríais** |
| | valen | **valgan** | valían | **valdrán** | **valdrían** |
| **§90** | | | | | |
| **variar** | **varío** | **varíe** | variaba | variaré | variaría |
| variando | **varías** | **varíes** | variabas | variarás | variarías |
| variado | **varía** | **varíe** | variaba | variará | variaría |
| | variamos | variemos | variábamos | variaremos | variaríamos |
| | variáis | variéis | variabais | variaréis | variaríais |
| | **varían** | **varíen** | variaban | variarán | variarían |
| **§91** | | | | | |
| **vencer** | **venzo** | **venza** | vencía | venceré | vencería |
| venciendo | vences | **venzas** | vencías | vencerás | vencerías |
| vencido | vence | **venza** | vencía | vencerá | vencería |
| | vencemos | **venzamos** | vencíamos | venceremos | venceríamos |
| | vencéis | **venzáis** | vencíais | venceréis | venceríais |
| | vencen | **venzan** | vencían | vencerán | vencerían |
| **§92** | | | | | |
| **venir** | **vengo** | **venga** | venía | **vendré** | **vendría** |
| **viniendo** | **vienes** | **vengas** | venías | **vendrás** | **vendrías** |
| venido | **viene** | **venga** | venía | **vendrá** | **vendría** |
| | venimos | **vengamos** | veníamos | **vendremos** | **vendríamos** |
| | venís | **vengáis** | veníais | **vendréis** | **vendríais** |
| | **vienen** | **vengan** | venían | **vendrán** | **vendrían** |

| PRETERIT INDICATIVE | IMPERF. SUBJ. S-FORM | IMPERF. SUBJ. R-FORM | FUTURE SUBJUNCTIVE | IMPERATIVE | NOTES AND REFERENCES |
|---|---|---|---|---|---|
| tañí<br>tañiste<br>**tañó**<br>tañimos<br>tañisteis<br>**tañeron** | **tañese**<br>**tañeses**<br>**tañese**<br>**tañésemos**<br>**tañeseis**<br>**tañesen** | **tañera**<br>**tañeras**<br>**tañera**<br>**tañéramos**<br>**tañerais**<br>**tañeran** | **tañere**<br>**tañeres**<br>**tañere**<br>**tañéremos**<br>**tañereis**<br>**tañeren** | tañe<br>tañed | **§15,** 13 |
| **tuve**<br>**tuviste**<br>**tuvo**<br>**tuvimos**<br>**tuvisteis**<br>**tuvieron** | **tuviese**<br>**tuvieses**<br>**tuviese**<br>**tuviésemos**<br>**tuvieseis**<br>**tuviesen** | **tuviera**<br>**tuvieras**<br>**tuviera**<br>**tuviéramos**<br>**tuvierais**<br>**tuvieran** | **tuviere**<br>**tuvieres**<br>**tuviere**<br>**tuviéremos**<br>**tuviereis**<br>**tuvieren** | **ten**<br>tened | **§16,** 2 & **§17,** 1, 5, 6, & 8 |
| **toqué**<br>tocaste<br>tocó<br>tocamos<br>tocasteis<br>tocaron | tocase<br>tocases<br>tocase<br>tocásemos<br>tocaseis<br>tocasen | tocara<br>tocaras<br>tocara<br>tocáramos<br>tocarais<br>tocaran | tocare<br>tocares<br>tocare<br>tocáremos<br>tocareis<br>tocaren | toca<br>tocad | **§15,** 1 |
| torcí<br>torciste<br>torció<br>torcimos<br>torcisteis<br>torcieron | torciese<br>torcieses<br>torciese<br>torciésemos<br>torcieseis<br>torciesen | torciera<br>torcieras<br>torciera<br>torciéramos<br>torcierais<br>torcieran | torciere<br>torcieres<br>torciere<br>torciéremos<br>torciereis<br>torcieren | **tuerce**<br>torced | Combination of **§15,** 5 & **§16,** 4 |
| **traje**<br>**trajiste**<br>**trajo**<br>**trajimos**<br>**trajisteis**<br>**trajeron** | **trajese**<br>**trajeses**<br>**trajese**<br>**trajésemos**<br>**trajeseis**<br>**trajesen** | **trajera**<br>**trajeras**<br>**trajera**<br>**trajéramos**<br>**trajerais**<br>**trajeran** | trajere<br>trajeres<br>trajere<br>trajéremos<br>trajereis<br>trajeron | trae<br>traed | **§15,** 15 & **§17,** 1 & 6 |
| valí<br>**valiste**<br>**valió**<br>valimos<br>valisteis<br>valieron | valiese<br>valieses<br>valiese<br>valiésemos<br>valieseis<br>valiesen | valiera<br>valieras<br>valiera<br>valiéramos<br>valierais<br>valieran | valiere<br>valieres<br>valiere<br>valiéremos<br>valiereis<br>valieren | **val** or vale<br>valed | **§17,** 1, 5 & 8 |
| varié<br>variaste<br>varió<br>variamos<br>variasteis<br>variaron | variase<br>variases<br>variase<br>variásemos<br>variaseis<br>variasen | variara<br>variaras<br>variara<br>variáramos<br>variarais<br>variaran | variare<br>variares<br>variare<br>variáremos<br>variareis<br>variaren | **varía**<br>variad | **§16,** 9 |
| vencí<br>venciste<br>venció<br>vencimos<br>vencisteis<br>vencieron | venciese<br>vencieses<br>venciese<br>venciésemos<br>vencieseis<br>venciesen | venciera<br>vencieras<br>venciera<br>venciéramos<br>vencierais<br>vencieran | venciere<br>vencieres<br>venciere<br>venciéremos<br>venciereis<br>vencieren | vence<br>venced | **§15,** 5 |
| **vine**<br>**viniste**<br>**vino**<br>**vinimos**<br>**vinisteis**<br>**vinieron** | **viniese**<br>**vinieses**<br>**viniese**<br>**viniésemos**<br>**vinieseis**<br>**viniesen** | **viniera**<br>**vinieras**<br>**viniera**<br>**viniéramos**<br>**vinierais**<br>**vinieran** | **viniere**<br>**vinieres**<br>**viniere**<br>**viniéremos**<br>**viniereis**<br>**vinieren** | **ven**<br>venid | **§16,** 5 & **§17,** 1, 5, 6, & 8 |

| INFINITIVE GERUND AND PAST PARTICIPLE | PRESENT INDICATIVE | PRESENT SUBJUNCTIVE | IMPERFECT INDICATIVE | FUTURE INDICATIVE | CONDITIONAL |
|---|---|---|---|---|---|
| §93 | | | | | |
| **ver** | **veo** | **vea** | **veía** | veré | vería |
| viendo | ves | **veas** | **veías** | verás | verías |
| **visto** | ve | **vea** | **veía** | verá | vería |
| | vemos | **veamos** | **veíamos** | veremos | veríamos |
| | veis | **veáis** | **veíais** | veréis | veríais |
| | ven | **vean** | **veían** | verán | verían |
| §94 | | | | | |
| **vestir** | **visto** | **vista** | vestía | vestiré | vestiría |
| **vistiendo** | **vistes** | **vistas** | vestías | vestirás | vestirías |
| vestido | **viste** | **vista** | vestía | vestirá | vestiría |
| | vestimos | **vistamos** | vestíamos | vestiremos | vestiríamos |
| | vestís | **vistáis** | vestíais | vestiréis | vestiríais |
| | **visten** | **vistan** | vestían | vestirán | vestirían |
| §95 | | | | | |
| **volcar** | **vuelco** | **vuelque** | volcaba | volcaré | volcaría |
| volcando | **vuelcas** | **vuelques** | volcabas | volcarás | volcarías |
| volcado | **vuelca** | **vuelque** | volcaba | volcará | volcaría |
| | volcamos | **volquemos** | volcábamos | volcaremos | volcaríamos |
| | volcáis | **volquéis** | volcabais | volcaréis | volcaríais |
| | **vuelcan** | **vuelquen** | volcaban | volcarán | volcarían |
| §96 | | | | | |
| **yacer** | **yazco** | **yazca** | yacía | yaceré | yacería |
| | **yazgo** | **yazga** | | | |
| | **yago** | **yaga** | | | |
| yaciendo | yaces | **yazcas** | yacías | yacerás | yacerías |
| yacido | yace | **yazca** | yacía | yacerá | yacería |
| | yacemos | **yazcamos** | yacíamos | yaceremos | yaceríamos |
| | yacéis | **yazcáis** | yacíais | yaceréis | yaceríais |
| | yacen | **yazcan** | yacía | yacerán | yacerían |
| §97 | | | | | |
| **arcaizar** | **arcaízo** | **arcaíce** | arcaizaba | arcaizaré | arcaizaría |
| arcaizando | **arcaízas** | **arcaíces** | arcaizabas | arcaizarás | arcaizarías |
| arcaizado | **arcaíza** | **arcaíce** | arcaizaba | arcaizará | arcaizaría |
| | arcaizamos | **arcaicemos** | arcaizábamos | arcaizaremos | arcaizaríamos |
| | arcaizáis | **arcaicéis** | arcaizabais | arcaizaréis | arcaizaríais |
| | **arcaízan** | **arcaícen** | arcaizaban | arcaizarán | arcaizarían |
| §98 | | | | | |
| **avergonzar** | **avergüenzo** | **avergüence** | avergonzaba | avergonzaré | avergonzaría |
| avergonzando | **avergüenzas** | **avergüences** | avergonzabas | avergonzarás | avergonzarías |
| avergonzado | **avergüenza** | **avergüence** | avergonzaba | avergonzará | avergonzaría |
| | avergonzamos | **avergoncemos** | avergonzábamos | avergonzaremos | avergonzaríamos |
| | avergonzáis | **avergoncéis** | avergonzabais | avergonzaréis | avergonzaríais |
| | **avergüenzan** | **avergüencen** | avergonzaban | avergonzarán | avergonzarían |
| §99 | | | | | |
| **ahusar** | **ahúso** | **ahúse** | ahusaba | ahusaré | ahusaría |
| ahusando | **ahúsas** | **ahúses** | ahusabas | ahusarás | ahusarías |
| ahusado | **ahúsa** | **ahúse** | ahusaba | ahusará | ahusaría |
| | ahusamos | ahusemos | ahusábamos | ahusaremos | ahusaríamos |
| | ahusáis | ahuséis | ahusabais | ahusaréis | ahusaríais |
| | **ahúsan** | **ahúsen** | ahusaban | ahusarán | ahusarían |

| PRETERIT INDICATIVE | IMPERF. SUBJ. s-FORM | IMPERF. SUBJ. r-FORM | FUTURE SUBJUNCTIVE | IMPERATIVE | NOTES AND REFERENCES |
|---|---|---|---|---|---|
| **vi**<br>viste<br>**vio**<br>vimos<br>visteis<br>vieron | viese<br>vieses<br>viese<br>**viésemos**<br>vieseis<br>viesen | viera<br>vieras<br>viera<br>viéramos<br>vierais<br>vieran | viere<br>vieres<br>**viere**<br>viéremos<br>viereis<br>vieren | <br>ve<br><br><br>ved | **§17,** 1, 4, & 9 |
| vestí<br>vestiste<br>**vistió**<br>vestimos<br>vestisteis<br>**vistieron** | **vistiese**<br>**vistieses**<br>**vistiese**<br>**vistiésemos**<br>**vistieseis**<br>**vistiesen** | **vistiera**<br>**vistieras**<br>**vistiera**<br>**vistiéramos**<br>**vistierais**<br>**vistieran** | **vistiere**<br>**vistieres**<br>**vistiere**<br>**vistiéremos**<br>**vistiereis**<br>**vistieren** | <br>**viste**<br><br><br>vestid | **§16,** 7 |
| **volqué**<br>volcaste<br>volcó<br>volcamos<br>volcasteis<br>volcaron | volcase<br>volcases<br>volcase<br>volcásemos<br>volcaseis<br>volcasen | volcara<br>volcaras<br>volcara<br>volcáramos<br>volcarais<br>volcaran | volcare<br>volcares<br>volcare<br>volcáremos<br>volcareis<br>volcaren | <br>**vuelca**<br><br><br>volcad | Combination of **§15,** 1 & **§16,** 3 |
| yací<br>yaciste<br>yació<br>yacimos<br>yacisteis<br>yacieron | yaciese<br>yacieses<br>yaciese<br>yaciésemos<br>yacieseis<br>yaciesen | yaciera<br>yacieras<br>yaciera<br>yaciéramos<br>yacierais<br>yacieran | yaciere<br>yacieres<br>yaciere<br>yaciéremos<br>yaciereis<br>yacieren | **yaz**<br>yace<br><br>yaced | **§17,** 1 & 8 |
| **arcaicé**<br>arcaizaste<br>arcaizó<br>arcaizamos<br>arcaizasteis<br>arcaizaron | arcaizase<br>arcaizases<br>arcaizase<br>arcaizásemos<br>arcaizaseis<br>arcaizasen | arcaizara<br>arcaizaras<br>arcaizara<br>arcaizáramos<br>arcaizarais<br>arcaizaran | arcaizare<br>arcaizares<br>arcaizare<br>arcaizáremos<br>arcaizareis<br>arcaizaren | <br>**arcaíza**<br><br><br>arcaizad | Combination of **§15,** 4 & **§16,** 8 |
| **avergoncé**<br>avergonzaste<br>avergonzó<br>avergonzamos<br>avergonzasteis<br>avergonzaron | avergonzase<br>avergonzases<br>avergonzase<br>avergonzásemos<br>avergonzaseis<br>avergonzasen | avergonzara<br>avergonzaras<br>avergonzara<br>avergonzáramos<br>avergonzarais<br>avergonzaran | avergonzare<br>avergonzares<br>avergonzare<br>avergonzáremos<br>avergonzareis<br>avergonzaren | <br>**avergüenza**<br><br>avergonzad | Combination of **§15,** 4 & **§19** |
| ahusé<br>ahusaste<br>ahusó<br>ahusamos<br>ahusasteis<br>ahusaron | ahusase<br>ahusases<br>ahusase<br>ahusásemos<br>ahusaseis<br>ahusasen | ahusara<br>ahusaras<br>ahusara<br>ahusáramos<br>ahusarais<br>ahusaran | ahusare<br>ahusares<br>ahusare<br>ahusáremos<br>ahusareis<br>ahusaren | <br>**ahúsa**<br><br><br>ahusad | Applies to verbs with radical **ahí, ahú, ehí, ehú, ohí.** See NUEVAS NORMAS 25 |

**§100. Regular Verbs.** All the tenses of model regular verbs of the three conjugations are presented on this and the three following pages. The simple tenses are on the left-hand pages, the compound tenses on the right-hand pages. And each compound tense is placed horizontally in line with the simple tense to which its auxiliary corresponds.

### Simple Tenses

The simple tenses are made from three basic stems, which for regular verbs may in turn be derived from the infinitive. These three stems are 1) the infinitive minus the ending **-ar, -er,** or **-ir,** 2) the whole infinitive itself, and 3) the third plural preterit indicative minus the last syllable **-ron.** The first of these stems is used to form the gerund, the past participle, the present indicative, the imperfect indicative, the preterit indicative, the present subjunctive, and the imperative; the second is used to form the future indicative and the conditional; and the third is used to form the imperfect subjunctive (**s**-form and **r**-form) and the future subjunctive.

| FIRST CONJUGATION | SECOND CONJUGATION | THIRD CONJUGATION |
|---|---|---|
| | INFINITIVE | |
| **habl-ar** | **com-er** | **viv-ir** |
| | GERUND | |
| habl-ando | com-iendo | viv-iendo |
| | PAST PARTICIPLE | |
| habl-ado | com-ido | viv-ido |
| | PRESENT INDICATIVE | |
| habl-o<br>habl-as<br>habl-a<br>habl-amos<br>habl-áis<br>habl-an | com-o<br>com-es<br>com-e<br>com-emos<br>com-éis<br>com-en | viv-o<br>viv-es<br>viv-e<br>viv-imos<br>viv-ís<br>viv-en |
| | IMPERFECT INDICATIVE | |
| habl-aba<br>habl-abas<br>habl-aba<br>habl-ábamos<br>habl-abais<br>habl-aban | com-ía<br>com-ías<br>com-ía<br>com-íamos<br>com-íais<br>com-ían | viv-ía<br>viv-ías<br>viv-ía<br>viv-íamos<br>viv-íais<br>viv-ían |
| | PRETERIT INDICATIVE | |
| habl-é<br>habl-aste<br>habl-ó<br>habl-amos<br>habl-asteis<br>habl-a-ron | com-í<br>com-iste<br>com-ió<br>com-imos<br>com-isteis<br>com-ie-ron | viv-í<br>viv-iste<br>viv-ió<br>viv-imos<br>viv-isteis<br>viv-ie-ron |
| | FUTURE INDICATIVE | |
| hablar-é<br>hablar-ás<br>hablar-á<br>hablar-emos<br>hablar-éis<br>hablar-án | comer-é<br>comer-ás<br>comer-á<br>comer-emos<br>comer-éis<br>comer-án | vivir-é<br>vivir-ás<br>vivir-á<br>vivir-emos<br>vivir-éis<br>vivir-án |
| | CONDITIONAL | |
| hablar-ía<br>hablar-ías<br>hablar-ía<br>hablar-íamos<br>hablar-íais<br>hablar-ían | comer-ía<br>comer-ías<br>comer-ía<br>comer-íamos<br>comer-íais<br>comer-ían | vivir-ía<br>vivir-ías<br>vivir-ía<br>vivir-íamos<br>vivir-íais<br>vivir-ían |

## Compound Tenses

**The compound tenses are made with the uninflected past participle of the verb preceded by all the simple tenses of the auxiliary haber except the imperative and the past participle, for which there are no corresponding compound tenses.**

| FIRST CONJUGATION | SECOND CONJUGATION | THIRD CONJUGATION |
|---|---|---|
| | PERFECT INFINITIVE | |
| **haber hablado** | **haber comido** | **haber vivido** |
| | COMPOUND GERUND | |
| habiendo hablado | habiendo comido | habiendo vivido |
| | | |
| | PERFECT INDICATIVE | |
| he hablado<br>has hablado<br>ha hablado<br>hemos hablado<br>habéis hablado<br>han hablado | he comido<br>has comido<br>ha comido<br>hemos comido<br>habéis comido<br>han comido | he vivido<br>has vivido<br>ha vivido<br>hemos vivido<br>habéis vivido<br>han vivido |
| | PLUPERFECT INDICATIVE | |
| había hablado<br>habías hablado<br>había hablado<br>habíamos hablado<br>habíais hablado<br>habían hablado | había comido<br>habías comido<br>había comido<br>habíamos comido<br>habíais comido<br>habían comido | había vivido<br>habías vivido<br>había vivido<br>habíamos vivido<br>habíais vivido<br>habían vivido |
| | PRETERIT PERFECT INDICATIVE | |
| hube hablado<br>hubiste hablado<br>hubo hablado<br>hubimos hablado<br>hubisteis hablado<br>hubieron hablado | hube comido<br>hubiste comido<br>hubo comido<br>hubimos comido<br>hubisteis comido<br>hubieron comido | hube vivido<br>hubiste vivido<br>hubo vivido<br>hubimos vivido<br>hubisteis vivido<br>hubieron vivido |
| | FUTURE PERFECT INDICATIVE | |
| habré hablado<br>habrás hablado<br>habrá hablado<br>habremos hablado<br>habréis hablado<br>habrán hablado | habré comido<br>habrás comido<br>habrá comido<br>habremos comido<br>habréis comido<br>habrán comido | habré vivido<br>habrás vivido<br>habrá vivido<br>habremos vivido<br>habréis vivido<br>habrán vivido |
| | CONDITIONAL PERFECT | |
| habría hablado<br>habrías hablado<br>habría hablado<br>habríamos hablado<br>habríais hablado<br>habrían hablado | habría comido<br>habrías comido<br>habría comido<br>habríamos comido<br>habríais comido<br>habrían comido | habría vivido<br>habrías vivido<br>habría vivido<br>habríamos vivido<br>habríais vivido<br>habrían vivido |

Simple Tenses

| FIRST CONJUGATION | SECOND CONJUGATION | THIRD CONJUGATION |
|---|---|---|
| | PRESENT SUBJUNCTIVE | |
| habl-e | com-a | viv-a |
| habl-es | com-as | viv-as |
| habl-e | com-a | viv-a |
| habl-emos | com-amos | viv-amos |
| habl-éis | com-áis | viv-áis |
| habl-en | com-an | viv-an |
| | IMPERF. SUBJ. **s**-FORM | |
| habla-se | comie-se | vivie-se |
| habla-ses | comie-ses | vivie-ses |
| habla-se | comie-se | vivie-se |
| hablá-semos | comié-semos | vivié-semos |
| habla-seis | comie-seis | vivie-seis |
| habla-sen | comie-sen | vivie-sen |
| | IMPERF. SUBJ. **r**-FORM | |
| habla-ra | comie-ra | vivie-ra |
| habla-ras | comie-ras | vivie-ras |
| habla-ra | comie-ra | vivie-ra |
| hablá-ramos | comié-ramos | vivié-ramos |
| habla-rais | comie-rais | vivie-rais |
| habla-ran | comie-ran | vivie-ran |
| | FUTURE SUBJUNCTIVE | |
| habla-re | comie-re | vivie-re |
| habla-res | comie-res | vivie-res |
| habla-re | comie-re | vivie-re |
| hablá-remos | comié-remos | vivié-remos |
| habla-reis | comie-reis | vivie-reis |
| habla-ren | comie-ren | vivie-ren |
| | IMPERATIVE | |
| habl-a | com-e | viv-e |
| habl-ad | com-ed | viv-id |

## Compound Tenses

| FIRST CONJUGATION | SECOND CONJUGATION | THIRD CONJUGATION |
|---|---|---|
| | PERFECT SUBJUNCTIVE | |
| haya hablado<br>hayas hablado<br>haya hablado<br>hayamos hablado<br>hayáis hablado<br>hayan hablado | haya comido<br>hayas comido<br>haya comido<br>hayamos comido<br>hayáis comido<br>hayan comido | haya vivido<br>hayas vivido<br>haya vivido<br>hayamos vivido<br>hayáis vivido<br>hayan vivido |
| | PLUPERF. SUBJ. S-FORM | |
| hubiese hablado<br>hubieses hablado<br>hubiese hablado<br>hubiésemos hablado<br>hubieseis hablado<br>hubiesen hablado | hubiese comido<br>hubieses comido<br>hubiese comido<br>hubiésemos comido<br>hubieseis comido<br>hubiesen comido | hubiese vivido<br>hubieses vivido<br>hubiese vivido<br>hubiésemos vivido<br>hubieseis vivido<br>hubiesen vivido |
| | PLUPERF. SUBJ. R-FORM | |
| hubiera hablado<br>hubieras hablado<br>hubiera hablado<br>hubiéramos hablado<br>hubierais hablado<br>hubieran hablado | hubiera comido<br>hubieras comido<br>hubiera comido<br>hubiéramos comido<br>hubierais comido<br>hubieran comido | hubiera vivido<br>hubieras vivido<br>hubiera vivido<br>hubiéramos vivido<br>hubierais vivido<br>hubieran vivido |
| | FUTURE PERFECT SUBJUNCTIVE | |
| hubiere hablado<br>hubieres hablado<br>hubiere hablado<br>hubiéremos hablado<br>hubiereis hablado<br>hubieren hablado | hubiere comido<br>hubieres comido<br>hubiere comido<br>hubiéremos comido<br>hubiereis comido<br>hubieren comido | hubiere vivido<br>hubieres vivido<br>hubiere vivido<br>hubiéremos vivido<br>hubiereis vivido<br>hubieren vivido |

**§101. Spanish and English Cognates.** The similarity of many Spanish and English words can be readily detected by noting the following equivalences in spelling, sounds, and endings.

WORDS OF GREEK ORIGIN

| EQUIVALENCES | | EXAMPLES | |
|---|---|---|---|
| SPANISH | ENGLISH | SPANISH | ENGLISH |
| **qu** followed by **e** or **i** | ch [k] followed by e, i, or y | **química**<br>**arquitectura**<br>**monarquía** | chemistry<br>architecture<br>monarchy |
| **c** followed by any other letter | ch [k] followed by any other letter | **arcaico**<br>**característico** | archaic<br>characteristic |
| **f** | ph | **filosofía**<br>**teléfono** | philosophy<br>telephone |
| **r** | rh | **retórica** | rhetoric |
| **rr** | rrh | **catarro** | catarrh |
| **t** | th | **atleta**<br>**teatro** | athlete<br>theater |
| **i** | y | **tipo**<br>**sinfonía** | type<br>symphony |
| **n** initial | pn | **neumático** | pneumatic |
| **s** initial | ps | **salmo** | psalm |
| **t** initial | pt | **tomaína** | ptomaine |

LATIN CONSONANT GROUPS

| EQUIVALENCES | | EXAMPLES | |
|---|---|---|---|
| SPANISH | ENGLISH | SPANISH | ENGLISH |
| **cc** followed by **i** + vowel | ct followed by i + vowel | **sección** | section |
| **ct** followed by **a, o, u,** or a consonant | ct followed by a, o, u, or consonant | **actor**<br>**actriz** | actor<br>actress |
| **nt** | nct | **instinto** | instinct |
| **cu** | qu | **cuarto**<br>**frecuencia** | quarter<br>frequency |
| **es** + consonant | s + consonant | **escala**<br>**estudio** | scale<br>study |

LATIN DOUBLE CONSONANTS

| EQUIVALENCES | | EXAMPLES | |
|---|---|---|---|
| SPANISH | ENGLISH | SPANISH | ENGLISH |
| **b** | bb | **abadía** | abbacy |
| **c** followed by **a, o,** or **u** | cc followed by a, o, or u | **acompañar**<br>**acusar** | accompany<br>accuse |
| **c** followed by **e** + consonant | cc followed by e + consonant | **aceptar** | accept |

### Latin Double Consonants

| EQUIVALENCES | | EXAMPLES | |
|---|---|---|---|
| SPANISH | ENGLISH | SPANISH | ENGLISH |
| **cc** followed by **e** or **i** + consonant | cc followed by e or i + consonant | **acceso**<br>**accidente** | access<br>accident |
| **d** | dd | **adición** | addition |
| **f** | ff | **efecto** | effect |
| **g** | gg | **agresivo** | aggressive |
| **l** | ll | **colegio** | college |
| **m** | mm | **recomendar** | recommend |
| **n** | nn | **anual** | annual |
| **p** | pp | **aplicar** | apply |
| **s** | ss | **clásico** | classic |
| **t** | tt | **atento** | attentive |

Latin double l sometimes corresponds to Spanish **ll,** e.g., **valle** valley and sometimes to English l, e.g., **caballería** cavalry.

If the first m of English mm belongs to the prefix com or the prefix im, the Spanish word will generally have nm, e.g., **conmoción** commotion, **inmediato** immediate.

Double n sometimes corresponds to Spanish **ñ,** e.g., **cañón** cannon.

Double r exists in both Spanish and English, e.g., **corrosión** corrosion, **irregular** irregular. In Spanish it is considered to be a single letter (**§12,** 1).

### Endings of Nouns

| EQUIVALENCES | | EXAMPLES | |
|---|---|---|---|
| SPANISH | ENGLISH | SPANISH | ENGLISH |
| **-acio** | -ace | **palacio** | palace |
| **-ada** | -ade | **mascarada** | masquerade |
| **-ador** | -ator | **orador** | orator |
| **-aje** | -age | **personaje** | personage |
| **-al** | -al | **canal** | canal |
| **-ancia** | { -ance<br>-ancy | **abundancia**<br>**constancia** | abundance<br>constancy |
| **-ante** | -ant | **instante** | instant |
| **-ario** | { -arian<br>-ary | **unitario**<br>**adversario** | unitarian<br>adversary |
| **-ato** | -ate | **sulfato** | sulfate |
| **-cia** | -cy | **aristocracia** | aristocracy |
| **-ción** | -tion | **nación** | nation |
| **-cto** | -ct | **conducto** | conduct |
| **-culo** | -cle | **círculo** | circle |
| **-dad** | -ty | **sociedad** | society |
| **-encia** | { -ence<br>-ency | **violencia**<br>**frecuencia** | violence<br>frequency |

### Endings of Nouns

| EQUIVALENCES | | EXAMPLES | |
|---|---|---|---|
| SPANISH | ENGLISH | SPANISH | ENGLISH |
| **-ente** | -ent | **accidente** | accident |
| **-gio** | -ge | **privilegio** | privilege |
| **-ia** | -y | **farmacia** | pharmacy |
| **-ía** | -y | **filosofía** | philosophy |
| **-ica** | -ic | **música** | music |
| **-icio** | -ice | **edificio** | edifice |
| **-ico** | -ic | **lógico** | logic |
| **-ina** | -ine | **doctrina** | doctrine |
| **-ión** | -ion | **religión** | religion |
| **-isco** | -isk | **asterisco** | asterisk |
| **-ismo** | -ism | **despotismo** | despotism |
| **-ista** | -ist | **artista** | artist |
| **-ita** | -ite | **fluorita** | fluorite |
| **-ito** | -ite | **sulfito** | sulfite |
| **-mento** | -ment | **suplemento** | supplement |
| **-miento** | -ment | **movimiento** | movement |
| **-monia** | -mony | **acrimonia** | acrimony |
| **-o** | -us<br>-um | **genio**<br>**museo** | genius<br>museum |
| **-oide** | -oid | **alcaloide** | alkaloid |
| **-or** | -or | **actor** | actor |
| **-orio** | -ory | **promontorio** | promontory |
| **-ota** | -ot | **patriota** | patriot |
| **-sis** | -sis | **énfasis** | emphasis |
| **-tad** | -ty | **libertad** | liberty |
| **-terio** | -tery | **misterio** | mystery |
| **-tro** | -ter | **centro** | center |
| **-tud** | -tude | **multitud** | multitude |
| **-ulo** | -ule | **glóbulo** | globule |
| **-ura** | -ure | **cultura** | culture |
| **-uro** | -ide | **cloruro** | chloride |

### Endings of Adjectives

| EQUIVALENCES | | EXAMPLES | |
|---|---|---|---|
| SPANISH | ENGLISH | SPANISH | ENGLISH |
| **-ado** | -ate | **duplicado** | duplicate |
| **-al** | -al | **natural** | natural |
| **-ano** | -an | **pagano** | pagan |
| **-áneo** | -aneous | **cutáneo** | cutaneous |
| **-ante** | -ant | **constante** | constant |

Endings of Adjectives

| Equivalences | | Examples | |
|---|---|---|---|
| SPANISH | ENGLISH | SPANISH | ENGLISH |
| **-ar** | -ar | **circular** | circular |
| **-ario** | -arious<br>-ary | **precario**<br>**ordinario** | precarious<br>ordinary |
| **-az** | -acious | **tenaz** | tenacious |
| **-ble** | -ble | **posible** | possible |
| **-cial** | -tial | **substancial** | substantial |
| **-cional** | -tional | **nacional** | national |
| **-cto** | -ct | **perfecto** | perfect |
| **-ente** | -ent | **evidente** | evident |
| **-fero** | -ferous | **carbonífero** | carboniferous |
| **-ico** | -ic<br>-ical | **público**<br>**crítico** | public<br>critical |
| **-ido** | -id | **sólido** | solid |
| **-il** | -ile | **dócil** | docile |
| **-ino** | -ine | **aquilino** | aquiline |
| **-ito** | -ite | **erudito** | erudite |
| **-ivo** | -ive | **activo** | active |
| **-no** | -nal | **eterno** | eternal |
| **-orio** | -ory | **satisfactorio** | satisfactory |
| **-oso** | -ose<br>-ous | **verboso**<br>**luminoso** | verbose<br>luminous |
| **-ulento** | -ulent | **turbulento** | turbulent |
| **-undo** | -und | **moribundo** | moribund |
| **-uro** | -ure | **maduro** | mature |

Endings of Verbs

| Equivalences | | Examples | |
|---|---|---|---|
| SPANISH | ENGLISH | SPANISH | ENGLISH |
| **-ar** | -ate | **calcular** | calculate |
| **-ducir** | -duce | **conducir** | conduce |
| **-ecer** | -ish | **establecer** | establish |
| **-ferir** | -fer | **diferir** | defer |
| **-iar** | -iate<br>-y | **afiliar**<br>**gloriar** | affiliate<br>glory |
| **-ificar** | -ify | **modificar** | modify |
| **-iguar** | -ify | **apaciguar** | pacify |
| **-izar** | -ize | **organizar** | organize |
| **-struir** | -struct | **obstruir** | obstruct |
| **-vergir** | -verge | **convergir** | converge |
| **-vertir** | -vert | **divertir** | divert |
| **-zar** | -ce | **comenzar** | commence |

# NUEVAS NORMAS DE PROSODIA Y ORTOGRAFÍA

## NUEVO TEXTO DEFINITIVO

The NUEVAS NORMAS are for the most part emendations of clauses in the Grammar of the Spanish Academy or of entries in its Dictionary. Some are optional, some prescriptive. Some have been observed for years, some have been, still are, and probably will continue to be treated unevenly in the press and other forms of publication. We give them below in slightly condensed form.

1. When the Dictionary (of the Academy) authorizes two forms of accentuation of a word, both will be included in the same entry separated by the conjunction **o**, e.g., **quiromancia** o **quiromancía.**

2. The first form is considered the more common in present-day usage but the second is as fully sanctioned and correct as the first.

3. With regard to the double forms included for the first time in the eighteenth edition of the Dictionary (1956) the order of preference shall be reversed in the following entries, thus: **pentagrama / pentágrama, reuma / reúma.**

4. The first letter of the initial groups **ps, mn, gn** may be dropped, e.g., **sicología** for **psicología.**

5. The contract forms **remplazo, remplazar, rembolso, rembolsar** may be used instead of the forms with double **e.**

6. The accent mark of the first word of a solid compound shall not be used, e.g., **asimismo, piamadre.**

7. Adverbs in **-mente** are an exception to this rule. They shall be pronounced with two accents and written with an accent if the adjective requires it, e.g., **ágilmente, cortésmente.**

8. Compounds of verb form + enclitic + object shall be written without the accent on the verb form, e.g., **sabelotodo.**

9. The stress and the written accent (if one is necessary) of each of the elements of a compound written with a hyphen shall be preserved, e.g., **hispano-belga, anglo-soviético, cántabro-astur.**

10. The infinitive ending **-uir** will continue to be written without an accent.

11. The verb **inmiscuir** may be conjugated regularly or with **y** like verbs ending in **-uir,** e.g., **inmiscuyo.**

12. A combination consisting of an accented strong vowel + an unaccented weak vowel or an unaccented weak vowel + an accented strong vowel forms a diphthong; if a written accent is required on a diphthong it shall be placed on the strong vowel. A combination in which the strong vowel is unaccented and the weak vowel accented does not form a diphthong and the written accent must always be placed on the weak vowel.

13. The diphthong **ui** shall bear the written accent only when it appears in the antepenult or at the end of the word, e.g., **casuístico, benjuí,** but not, e.g., in **casuista.**

14. Words ending in **-ay, -ey, -oy, -uy** shall be written without the accent, e.g., **taray, virrey, convoy.**

15. The monosyllables **fue, fui, dio, vio** shall be written without the accent.

16. All forms of the pronouns **éste, ése, aquél** shall be written without the accent as long as there is no risk of ambiguity.

17. When the word **aun** can be replaced by **todavía** without changing the meaning of the sentence, it shall be written with the accent and pronounced as a dissyllable, e.g., **aún está enfermo, está enfermo aún.** In all other cases, that is, when it has the meaning of **hasta, también, inclusive** (or of **siquiera** in negative sentences), it shall be written without the accent, e.g., **aun los sordos han de oírme; ni hizo nada por él ni aun lo intentó.**

18. The word **solo** used as an adverb may be written with an accent if it is necessary to avoid ambiguity.

19. The written accent shall be omitted in paroxytones ending in **-oo,** e.g., **Feijoo, Campoo.**

20. Foreign proper nouns shall be written without an accent except for accents that may be part of their spelling in the foreign language; they may be marked with an accent in the Spanish manner if their pronunciation and spelling make this feasible. Foreign place names that have become part of the Spanish language shall not be considered foreign and shall be written with the accent in accordance with the general rules.

21. The dieresis shall be required only where it is necessary to show that **u** must be pronounced in the combinations **gue** and **gui,** e.g., **pingüe, pingüino.** It may be used also by poetic license or to show some special pronunciation.

22. Compound names of nationality shall be written solid where there has been geographic or political fusion, e.g., **hispanoamericano, checoslovaco;** where there has been no fusion but rather opposition or contrast, they shall be written with a hyphen, e.g., **franco-prusiano, germano-soviético.**

23. New compounds made of two adjectives shall be written with a hyphen and only the second shall be inflected, e.g., **tratado teórico-práctico, lección teórico-práctica, cuerpos técnico-administrativos.**

24. Compounds do not have to be divided according to their components but may be divided according to the regular rules of syllabification, e.g., **no·sotros** or **nos·otros, de·samparo** or **des·amparo.** Compounds with a medial group consisting of consonant + **h** shall be divided with the **h** attached to the second element, e.g., **al·haraca, in·humación, clor·hidrato, des·hidratar.**

25. Intervocalic **h** does not prevent the vowels from becoming a diphthong, e.g., **de·sahu·cio, sahu·me·rio.** The written accent shall, therefore, be placed on a stressed weak vowel separated by **h** from an unstressed strong vowel, e.g., **vahído, búho, rehúso.**

# CONVERSION TABLES

# TABLAS DE CONVERSION

## Fahrenheit to Celsius (Centigrade)

| | | | | | | | | | |
|---|---|---|---|---|---|---|---|---|---|
| −50 | −45.5 | 18 | −7.7 | 41 | 5.0 | 64 | 17.7 | 87 | 30.5 |
| −40 | −40.0 | 19 | −7.2 | 42 | 5.5 | 65 | 18.3 | 88 | 31.0 |
| −30 | −34.4 | 20 | −6.6 | 43 | 6.1 | 66 | 18.8 | 89 | 31.5 |
| −20 | −28.8 | 21 | −6.1 | 44 | 6.6 | 67 | 19.4 | 90 | 32.1 |
| −10 | −23.3 | 22 | −5.5 | 45 | 7.2 | 68 | 20.0 | 91 | 32.6 |
| 0 | −17.7 | 23 | −5.0 | 46 | 7.7 | 69 | 20.5 | 92 | 33.2 |
| 1 | −17.2 | 24 | −4.4 | 47 | 8.3 | 70 | 21.1 | 93 | 33.7 |
| 2 | −16.6 | 25 | −3.8 | 48 | 8.8 | 71 | 21.6 | 94 | 34.3 |
| 3 | −16.1 | 26 | −3.3 | 49 | 9.4 | 72 | 22.2 | 95 | 34.8 |
| 4 | −15.5 | 27 | −2.7 | 50 | 10.0 | 73 | 22.7 | 96 | 35.4 |
| 5 | −15.0 | 28 | −2.2 | 51 | 10.5 | 74 | 23.3 | 97 | 36.0 |
| 6 | −14.4 | 29 | −1.6 | 52 | 11.1 | 75 | 23.8 | 98 | 36.5 |
| 7 | −13.8 | 30 | −1.1 | 53 | 11.6 | 76 | 24.4 | 99 | 37.1 |
| 8 | −13.3 | 31 | −0.5 | 54 | 12.2 | 77 | 25.0 | 100 | 37.6 |
| 9 | −12.7 | 32 | 0 | 55 | 12.7 | 78 | 25.5 | 125 | 51.6 |
| 10 | −12.2 | 33 | 0.5 | 56 | 13.3 | 79 | 26.1 | 150 | 65.5 |
| 11 | −11.6 | 34 | 1.1 | 57 | 13.8 | 80 | 26.6 | 175 | 79.4 |
| 12 | −11.1 | 35 | 1.6 | 58 | 14.4 | 81 | 27.2 | 200 | 93.3 |
| 13 | −10.5 | 36 | 2.2 | 59 | 15.0 | 82 | 27.7 | 250 | 121.1 |
| 14 | −10.0 | 37 | 2.7 | 60 | 15.5 | 83 | 28.3 | 300 | 148.8 |
| 15 | −9.4 | 38 | 3.3 | 61 | 16.1 | 84 | 28.8 | 350 | 176.6 |
| 16 | −8.8 | 39 | 3.8 | 62 | 16.6 | 85 | 29.4 | 400 | 204.6 |
| 17 | −8.3 | 40 | 4.4 | 63 | 17.2 | 86 | 29.9 | 450 | 232.2 |

## Grados centígrados a grados Fahrenheit

| | | | | | | | | | |
|---|---|---|---|---|---|---|---|---|---|
| −50 | −58 | 1 | 33,8 | 26 | 78,8 | 51 | 123,8 | 76 | 168,8 |
| −40 | −40 | 2 | 35,6 | 27 | 80,6 | 52 | 125,6 | 77 | 170,6 |
| −30 | −22 | 3 | 37,4 | 28 | 82,4 | 53 | 127,4 | 78 | 172,4 |
| −25 | −13 | 4 | 39,2 | 29 | 84,2 | 54 | 129,2 | 79 | 174,2 |
| −20 | −4 | 5 | 41,0 | 30 | 86,0 | 55 | 131,0 | 80 | 176,0 |
| −19 | −2,2 | 6 | 42,8 | 31 | 87,8 | 56 | 132,8 | 81 | 177,8 |
| −18 | −0,4 | 7 | 44,6 | 32 | 89,6 | 57 | 134,6 | 82 | 179,6 |
| −17,8 | 0 | 8 | 46,4 | 33 | 91,4 | 58 | 136,4 | 83 | 181,4 |
| −16 | 3,2 | 9 | 48,2 | 34 | 93,2 | 59 | 138,2 | 84 | 183,2 |
| −15 | 5 | 10 | 50,0 | 35 | 95,0 | 60 | 140,0 | 85 | 185,0 |
| −14 | 6,8 | 11 | 51,8 | 36 | 96,8 | 61 | 141,8 | 86 | 186,8 |
| −13 | 8,6 | 12 | 53,6 | 37 | 98,6 | 62 | 143,6 | 87 | 188,6 |
| −12 | 10,4 | 13 | 55,4 | 38 | 100,4 | 63 | 145,4 | 88 | 190,4 |
| −11 | 12,2 | 14 | 57,2 | 39 | 102,2 | 64 | 147,2 | 89 | 192,2 |
| −10 | 14,0 | 15 | 59,0 | 40 | 104,0 | 65 | 149,0 | 90 | 194,0 |
| −9 | 15,8 | 16 | 60,8 | 41 | 105,8 | 66 | 150,8 | 91 | 195,8 |
| −8 | 17,6 | 17 | 62,6 | 42 | 107,6 | 67 | 152,6 | 92 | 197,6 |
| −7 | 19,4 | 18 | 64,4 | 43 | 109,4 | 68 | 154,4 | 93 | 199,4 |
| −6 | 21,2 | 19 | 66,2 | 44 | 111,2 | 69 | 156,2 | 94 | 201,2 |
| −5 | 23,0 | 20 | 68,0 | 45 | 113,0 | 70 | 158,0 | 95 | 203,0 |
| −4 | 24,8 | 21 | 69,8 | 46 | 114,8 | 71 | 159,8 | 96 | 204,8 |
| −3 | 26,6 | 22 | 71,6 | 47 | 116,6 | 72 | 161,6 | 97 | 206,6 |
| −2 | 28,4 | 23 | 73,4 | 48 | 118,4 | 73 | 163,4 | 98 | 208,4 |
| −1 | 30,2 | 24 | 75,2 | 49 | 120,2 | 74 | 165,2 | 99 | 210,2 |
| 0 | 32 | 25 | 77,0 | 50 | 122,0 | 75 | 167,0 | 100 | 212,0 |

**Feet to Meters**

| | | | | | | | | | |
|---|---|---|---|---|---|---|---|---|---|
| 1 | 0.30 | 25 | 7.62 | 49 | 14.93 | 73 | 22.25 | 97 | 29.56 |
| 2 | 0.60 | 26 | 7.92 | 50 | 15.24 | 74 | 22.55 | 98 | 29.87 |
| 3 | 0.91 | 27 | 8.22 | 51 | 15.54 | 75 | 22.86 | 99 | 30.17 |
| 4 | 1.21 | 28 | 8.53 | 52 | 15.84 | 76 | 23.16 | 100 | 30.48 |
| 5 | 1.52 | 29 | 8.83 | 53 | 16.15 | 77 | 23.46 | 125 | 38.10 |
| 6 | 1.82 | 30 | 9.14 | 54 | 16.45 | 78 | 23.77 | 150 | 45.72 |
| 7 | 2.13 | 31 | 9.44 | 55 | 16.76 | 79 | 24.07 | 175 | 53.34 |
| 8 | 2.43 | 32 | 9.75 | 56 | 17.06 | 80 | 24.38 | 200 | 60.96 |
| 9 | 2.74 | 33 | 10.05 | 57 | 17.37 | 81 | 24.68 | 225 | 68.58 |
| 10 | 3.04 | 34 | 10.36 | 58 | 17.67 | 82 | 24.99 | 250 | 76.20 |
| 11 | 3.35 | 35 | 10.66 | 59 | 17.98 | 83 | 25.29 | 275 | 83.82 |
| 12 | 3.65 | 36 | 10.97 | 60 | 18.28 | 84 | 25.60 | 300 | 91.44 |
| 13 | 3.96 | 37 | 11.27 | 61 | 18.59 | 85 | 25.90 | 325 | 99.06 |
| 14 | 4.26 | 38 | 11.58 | 62 | 18.89 | 86 | 26.21 | 350 | 106.68 |
| 15 | 4.57 | 39 | 11.88 | 63 | 19.20 | 87 | 26.51 | 375 | 114.30 |
| 16 | 4.87 | 40 | 12.19 | 64 | 19.50 | 88 | 26.82 | 400 | 121.92 |
| 17 | 5.18 | 41 | 12.49 | 65 | 19.81 | 89 | 27.12 | 425 | 129.54 |
| 18 | 5.48 | 42 | 12.80 | 66 | 20.11 | 90 | 27.43 | 450 | 137.16 |
| 19 | 5.79 | 43 | 13.10 | 67 | 20.42 | 91 | 27.73 | 475 | 144.78 |
| 20 | 6.09 | 44 | 13.41 | 68 | 20.72 | 92 | 28.04 | 500 | 152.40 |
| 21 | 6.40 | 45 | 13.71 | 69 | 21.03 | 93 | 28.34 | 1000 | 304.80 |
| 22 | 6.70 | 46 | 14.02 | 70 | 21.33 | 94 | 28.65 | 2000 | 609.60 |
| 23 | 7.01 | 47 | 14.32 | 71 | 21.64 | 95 | 28.95 | 3000 | 914.40 |
| 24 | 7.31 | 48 | 14.63 | 72 | 21.94 | 96 | 29.26 | 4000 | 1219.20 |

**Metros a pies**

| | | | | | | | | | |
|---|---|---|---|---|---|---|---|---|---|
| 1 | 3,28 | 22 | 72,17 | 43 | 141,07 | 64 | 209,97 | 85 | 278,87 |
| 2 | 6,56 | 23 | 75,45 | 44 | 144,35 | 65 | 213,25 | 86 | 282,15 |
| 3 | 9,84 | 24 | 78,74 | 45 | 147,63 | 66 | 216,53 | 87 | 285,43 |
| 4 | 13,12 | 25 | 82,02 | 46 | 150,91 | 67 | 219,81 | 88 | 288,71 |
| 5 | 16,40 | 26 | 85,30 | 47 | 154,19 | 68 | 223,09 | 89 | 291,99 |
| 6 | 19,68 | 27 | 88,58 | 48 | 157,48 | 69 | 226,37 | 90 | 295,27 |
| 7 | 22,96 | 28 | 91,86 | 49 | 160,76 | 70 | 229,65 | 91 | 298,55 |
| 8 | 26,24 | 29 | 95,14 | 50 | 164,04 | 71 | 232,93 | 92 | 301,83 |
| 9 | 29,52 | 30 | 98,42 | 51 | 167,32 | 72 | 236,22 | 93 | 305,11 |
| 10 | 32,80 | 31 | 101,70 | 52 | 170,60 | 73 | 239,50 | 94 | 308,39 |
| 11 | 36,08 | 32 | 104,98 | 53 | 173,88 | 74 | 242,78 | 95 | 311,67 |
| 12 | 39,37 | 33 | 108,26 | 54 | 177,16 | 75 | 246,06 | 96 | 314,96 |
| 13 | 42,65 | 34 | 111,54 | 55 | 180,44 | 76 | 249,34 | 97 | 318,24 |
| 14 | 45,93 | 35 | 114,82 | 56 | 183,72 | 77 | 252,62 | 98 | 321,52 |
| 15 | 49,21 | 36 | 118,11 | 57 | 187,00 | 78 | 255,90 | 99 | 324,80 |
| 16 | 52,49 | 37 | 121,39 | 58 | 190,28 | 79 | 259,18 | 100 | 328,08 |
| 17 | 55,77 | 38 | 126,67 | 59 | 193,56 | 80 | 262,46 | 200 | 656,16 |
| 18 | 59,05 | 39 | 127,95 | 60 | 196,85 | 81 | 265,74 | 300 | 984,25 |
| 19 | 62,33 | 40 | 131,23 | 61 | 200,13 | 82 | 269,02 | 400 | 1312,33 |
| 20 | 65,61 | 41 | 134,51 | 62 | 203,41 | 83 | 272,30 | 500 | 1640,41 |
| 21 | 68,89 | 42 | 137,79 | 63 | 206,69 | 84 | 275,59 | 1000 | 3280,82 |

## Pounds to Kilograms

| | | | | | | | | | |
|---|---|---|---|---|---|---|---|---|---|
| 1 | .4 | 32 | 14.5 | 63 | 28.5 | 94 | 42.6 | 125 | 56.6 |
| 2 | .9 | 33 | 14.9 | 64 | 29.0 | 95 | 43.0 | 126 | 57.1 |
| 3 | 1.3 | 34 | 15.4 | 65 | 29.4 | 96 | 43.5 | 127 | 57.6 |
| 4 | 1.8 | 35 | 15.8 | 66 | 29.9 | 97 | 43.9 | 128 | 58.0 |
| 5 | 2.2 | 36 | 16.3 | 67 | 30.3 | 98 | 44.4 | 129 | 58.5 |
| 6 | 2.7 | 37 | 16.7 | 68 | 30.8 | 99 | 44.9 | 130 | 58.9 |
| 7 | 3.1 | 38 | 17.2 | 69 | 31.2 | 100 | 45.3 | 131 | 59.4 |
| 8 | 3.6 | 39 | 17.6 | 70 | 31.7 | 101 | 45.8 | 132 | 59.8 |
| 9 | 4.0 | 40 | 18.1 | 71 | 32.2 | 102 | 46.2 | 133 | 60.3 |
| 10 | 4.5 | 41 | 18.5 | 72 | 32.6 | 103 | 46.7 | 134 | 60.7 |
| 11 | 4.9 | 42 | 19.0 | 73 | 33.1 | 104 | 47.1 | 135 | 61.2 |
| 12 | 5.4 | 43 | 19.5 | 74 | 33.5 | 105 | 47.6 | 136 | 61.6 |
| 13 | 5.8 | 44 | 19.9 | 75 | 34.0 | 106 | 48.0 | 137 | 62.1 |
| 14 | 6.3 | 45 | 20.4 | 76 | 34.4 | 107 | 48.5 | 138 | 62.5 |
| 15 | 6.8 | 46 | 20.8 | 77 | 34.9 | 108 | 48.9 | 139 | 63.0 |
| 16 | 7.2 | 47 | 21.3 | 78 | 35.3 | 109 | 49.4 | 140 | 63.5 |
| 17 | 7.7 | 48 | 21.7 | 79 | 35.8 | 110 | 49.8 | 141 | 63.9 |
| 18 | 8.1 | 49 | 22.2 | 80 | 36.2 | 111 | 50.3 | 142 | 64.4 |
| 19 | 8.6 | 50 | 22.6 | 81 | 36.7 | 112 | 50.8 | 143 | 64.8 |
| 20 | 9.0 | 51 | 23.1 | 82 | 37.1 | 113 | 51.2 | 144 | 65.3 |
| 21 | 9.5 | 52 | 23.5 | 83 | 37.6 | 114 | 51.7 | 145 | 65.7 |
| 22 | 9.9 | 53 | 24.0 | 84 | 38.1 | 115 | 52.1 | 146 | 66.2 |
| 23 | 10.4 | 54 | 24.4 | 85 | 38.5 | 116 | 52.5 | 147 | 66.6 |
| 24 | 10.8 | 55 | 24.9 | 86 | 39.0 | 117 | 53.0 | 148 | 67.1 |
| 25 | 11.3 | 56 | 25.4 | 87 | 39.4 | 118 | 53.5 | 149 | 67.5 |
| 26 | 11.7 | 57 | 25.8 | 88 | 39.9 | 119 | 53.9 | 150 | 68.0 |
| 27 | 12.2 | 58 | 26.3 | 89 | 40.3 | 120 | 54.4 | 160 | 72.5 |
| 28 | 12.7 | 59 | 26.7 | 90 | 40.8 | 121 | 54.8 | 170 | 77.1 |
| 29 | 13.1 | 60 | 27.2 | 91 | 41.2 | 122 | 55.3 | 180 | 81.6 |
| 30 | 13.6 | 61 | 27.6 | 92 | 41.7 | 123 | 55.7 | 190 | 86.1 |
| 31 | 14.0 | 62 | 28.1 | 93 | 42.1 | 124 | 56.2 | 200 | 90.7 |

## Kilogramos a libras

| | | | | | | | | | |
|---|---|---|---|---|---|---|---|---|---|
| 1 | 2,2 | 21 | 46,3 | 41 | 90,3 | 61 | 134,4 | 81 | 178,5 |
| 2 | 4,4 | 22 | 48,5 | 42 | 92,5 | 62 | 136,6 | 82 | 180,7 |
| 3 | 6,6 | 23 | 50,7 | 43 | 94,8 | 63 | 138,8 | 83 | 182,9 |
| 4 | 8,8 | 24 | 52,9 | 44 | 97,0 | 64 | 141,1 | 84 | 185,1 |
| 5 | 11,0 | 25 | 55,1 | 45 | 99,2 | 65 | 143,3 | 85 | 187,3 |
| 6 | 13,2 | 26 | 57,3 | 46 | 101,4 | 66 | 145,5 | 86 | 189,6 |
| 7 | 15,4 | 27 | 59,5 | 47 | 103,6 | 67 | 147,7 | 87 | 191,8 |
| 8 | 17,6 | 28 | 61,7 | 48 | 105,8 | 68 | 149,9 | 88 | 194,0 |
| 9 | 19,8 | 29 | 63,9 | 49 | 108,0 | 69 | 152,1 | 89 | 196,2 |
| 10 | 22,0 | 30 | 66,1 | 50 | 110,2 | 70 | 154,3 | 90 | 198,4 |
| 11 | 24,2 | 31 | 68,3 | 51 | 112,4 | 71 | 156,5 | 91 | 200,6 |
| 12 | 26,4 | 32 | 70,5 | 52 | 114,6 | 72 | 158,7 | 92 | 202,8 |
| 13 | 28,6 | 33 | 72,7 | 53 | 116,8 | 73 | 160,9 | 93 | 205,0 |
| 14 | 30,8 | 34 | 74,9 | 54 | 119,0 | 74 | 163,1 | 94 | 207,2 |
| 15 | 33,0 | 35 | 77,1 | 55 | 121,2 | 75 | 165,3 | 95 | 209,4 |
| 16 | 35,2 | 36 | 79,3 | 56 | 123,4 | 76 | 167,5 | 96 | 211,6 |
| 17 | 37,4 | 37 | 81,5 | 57 | 125,6 | 77 | 169,7 | 97 | 213,8 |
| 18 | 39,6 | 38 | 83,7 | 58 | 127,8 | 78 | 171,9 | 98 | 216,0 |
| 19 | 41,8 | 39 | 85,9 | 59 | 130,6 | 79 | 174,1 | 99 | 218,2 |
| 20 | 44,0 | 40 | 88,1 | 60 | 132,2 | 80 | 176,3 | 100 | 220,4 |

Miles to Kilometers

| | | | |
|---|---|---|---|
| 1 | 1.60 | 40 | 64.37 |
| 2 | 3.21 | 50 | 80.46 |
| 3 | 4.82 | 60 | 96.55 |
| 4 | 6.43 | 70 | 112.65 |
| 5 | 8.04 | 80 | 128.74 |
| 6 | 9.65 | 90 | 144.83 |
| 7 | 11.26 | 100 | 160.93 |
| 8 | 12.87 | 200 | 321.86 |
| 9 | 14.48 | 300 | 482.79 |
| 10 | 16.09 | 400 | 643.72 |
| 20 | 32.18 | 500 | 804.65 |
| 30 | 48.27 | 1000 | 1609.30 |

Kilómetros a millas

| | | | |
|---|---|---|---|
| 1 | 0,62 | 40 | 24,85 |
| 2 | 1,24 | 50 | 31,07 |
| 3 | 1,86 | 60 | 37,28 |
| 4 | 2,48 | 70 | 43,49 |
| 5 | 3,10 | 80 | 49,71 |
| 6 | 3,72 | 90 | 55,92 |
| 7 | 4,34 | 100 | 62,14 |
| 8 | 4,97 | 200 | 124,18 |
| 9 | 5,59 | 300 | 186,42 |
| 10 | 6,21 | 400 | 248,56 |
| 20 | 12,42 | 500 | 310,70 |
| 30 | 18,64 | 1000 | 621,40 |

Gallons to Liters

| | | | |
|---|---|---|---|
| 1 | 3.7 | 21 | 79.4 |
| 2 | 7.5 | 22 | 83.2 |
| 3 | 11.3 | 23 | 87.0 |
| 4 | 15.1 | 24 | 90.8 |
| 5 | 18.9 | 25 | 94.6 |
| 6 | 22.7 | 26 | 98.4 |
| 7 | 26.4 | 27 | 102.2 |
| 8 | 30.2 | 28 | 105.9 |
| 9 | 34.0 | 29 | 109.7 |
| 10 | 37.8 | 30 | 113.5 |
| 11 | 41.6 | 31 | 117.3 |
| 12 | 45.4 | 32 | 121.1 |
| 13 | 49.2 | 33 | 124.9 |
| 14 | 52.9 | 34 | 128.7 |
| 15 | 56.7 | 35 | 132.4 |
| 16 | 60.5 | 36 | 136.2 |
| 17 | 64.3 | 37 | 140.0 |
| 18 | 68.1 | 38 | 143.8 |
| 19 | 71.9 | 39 | 147.6 |
| 20 | 75.7 | 40 | 151.4 |

Litros a galones

| | | | | | |
|---|---|---|---|---|---|
| 1 | 0,26 | 21 | 5,54 | 41 | 10,83 |
| 2 | 0,52 | 22 | 5,81 | 42 | 11,09 |
| 3 | 0,79 | 23 | 6,07 | 43 | 11,35 |
| 4 | 1,05 | 24 | 6,34 | 44 | 11,62 |
| 5 | 1,32 | 25 | 6,60 | 45 | 11,88 |
| 6 | 1,58 | 26 | 6,86 | 46 | 12,15 |
| 7 | 1,84 | 27 | 7,13 | 47 | 12,41 |
| 8 | 2,11 | 28 | 7,39 | 48 | 12,68 |
| 9 | 2,37 | 29 | 7,66 | 49 | 12,94 |
| 10 | 2,64 | 30 | 7,92 | 50 | 13,20 |
| 11 | 2,90 | 31 | 8,18 | 51 | 13,47 |
| 12 | 3,17 | 32 | 8,45 | 52 | 13,73 |
| 13 | 3,43 | 33 | 8,71 | 53 | 14,00 |
| 14 | 3,69 | 34 | 8,98 | 54 | 14,26 |
| 15 | 3,96 | 35 | 9,24 | 55 | 14,52 |
| 16 | 4,22 | 36 | 9,51 | 56 | 14,79 |
| 17 | 4,49 | 37 | 9,77 | 57 | 15,05 |
| 18 | 4,75 | 38 | 10,03 | 58 | 15,32 |
| 19 | 5,01 | 39 | 10,30 | 59 | 15,58 |
| 20 | 5,28 | 40 | 10,56 | 60 | 15,85 |

## TIRE PRESSURE — PRESIÓN DE INFLADO

| Pounds per Square Inch | Atmospheres Atmósferas | Kilogramos por centímetro cuadrado |
|---|---|---|
| 16 | 1.08 | 1,12 |
| 18 | 1.22 | 1,26 |
| 20 | 1.36 | 1,40 |
| 22 | 1.49 | 1,54 |
| 24 | 1.63 | 1,68 |
| 26 | 1.76 | 1,82 |
| 28 | 1.90 | 1,96 |
| 30 | 2.04 | 2,10 |
| 32 | 2.16 | 2,24 |
| 36 | 2.44 | 2,52 |
| 40 | 2.72 | 2,81 |
| 50 | 3.40 | 3,51 |
| 55 | 3.74 | 3,85 |
| 60 | 4.08 | 4,21 |
| 70 | 4.76 | 4,92 |

# PART II — PARTE SEGUNDA

English-Spanish

Inglés-Español

**A, a** [e] *s* (*pl:* **A's, a's** [ez]) primera letra del alfabeto inglés
**a.** abr. de **acre, acres, adjective** y **answer**
**A.** abr. de **America** y **American**
**a** [ə] o [e] *art indef* un; por, cada, a; **fifteen cents a pound** quince centavos la libra; se convierte en **an** antes de sonido vocálico, p.ej., **an orange** una naranja, **an hour** una hora
**A 1** ['e'wʌn] *adj* de primera clase, excelente
**AAA** abr. de **Agricultural Adjustment Administration**
**A.A.A.** abr. de **American Automobile Association**
**A.A.A.L.** abr. de **American Academy of Arts and Letters**
**A.A.A.S.** abr. de **American Association for the Advancement of Science**
**Aachen** ['ɑkən] *s* Aquisgrán
**aardvark** ['ɑrd,vɑrk] *s* (zool.) cerdo hormiguero
**aardwolf** ['ɑrd,wʊlf] *s* (zool.) próteles rayado
**Aaron** ['ɛrən] *s* (Bib.) Aarón
**A.B.** abr. de **Artium Baccalaureus** (Lat.) **Bachelor of Arts**
**abacá** [,ɑbɑ'kɑ] *s* (bot.) abacá (*planta y fibra textil*)
**aback** [ə'bæk] *adv* atrás; (naut.) en facha; **to be taken aback** quedar desconcertado; **to take aback** desconcertar
**abacus** ['æbəkəs] *s* (*pl:* **-cuses** o **-ci** [saɪ]) ábaco; (arch.) ábaco
**abaft** [ə'bæft] o [ə'bɑft] *adv* (naut.) a popa, en popa; *prep* (naut.) detrás de
**abalone** [,æbə'lonɪ] *s* (zool.) abalone, oreja marina
**abandon** [ə'bændən] *s* abandono; *va* abandonar; **to abandon oneself** abandonarse
**abandoned** [ə'bændənd] *adj* abandonado
**abandonment** [ə'bændənmənt] *s* abandono
**abase** [ə'bes] *va* degradar, humillar, rebajar
**abasement** [ə'besmənt] *s* degradación, humillación, rebajamiento
**abash** [ə'bæʃ] *va* azorar, avergonzar
**abashment** [ə'bæʃmənt] *s* azoramiento, avergonzamiento
**abate** [ə'bet] *va* disminuir, reducir; suprimir; anular; deducir, substraer; omitir; *vn* disminuir, moderarse
**abatement** [ə'betmənt] *s* disminución; supresión; anulación; cantidad rebajada; omisión; (law) ocupación, sin derecho, de una finca tras la muerte de su último dueño
**abatis** ['æbətɪs] *s* (*pl:* **-tis**) (fort.) abatida; barricada de alambre de púas
**A battery** *s* (rad.) batería para calentar el cátodo
**abattoir** ['æbətwɑr] *s* matadero
**abbacy** ['æbəsɪ] *s* (*pl:* **-cies**) abadía
**Abbassides** [ə'bæsaɪdz] o ['æbəsaɪdz] *spl* abasidas
**abbatial** [ə'beʃəl] *adj* abacial
**abbé** ['æbe] *s* abate
**abbess** ['æbɪs] *s* abadesa
**abbey** ['æbɪ] *s* abadía
**abbot** ['æbət] *s* abad
**abbr.** o **abbrev.** abr. de **abbreviated** y **abbreviation**
**abbreviate** [ə'brivɪet] *va* abreviar
**abbreviation** [ə,brivɪ'eʃən] *s* abreviación (*acortamiento*); abreviatura (*forma abreviada*)
**abbreviator** [ə'brivɪ,etər] *s* abreviador; (eccl.) abreviador
**A B C** [,e,bi'si] *s* abecé; **A B C's** *spl* abecedario
**A.B.C. powers** *spl* potencias A B C (*la Argentina, el Brasil, Chile*)
**abdicate** ['æbdɪket] *va & vn* abdicar
**abdication** [,æbdɪ'keʃən] *s* abdicación
**abdomen** ['æbdəmən] o [æb'domən] *s* (anat. & zool.) abdomen
**abdominal** [æb'dɑmɪnəl] *adj* abdominal
**abdominal supporter** *s* faja abdominal
**abducent** [æb'djusənt] o [æb'dusənt] *adj* (physiol.) abductor
**abduct** [æb'dʌkt] *va* raptar, secuestrar; (physiol.) abducir
**abduction** [æb'dʌkʃən] *s* rapto, secuestro; (physiol. & log.) abducción
**abductor** [æb'dʌktər] *s* raptor, secuestrador; (physiol.) abductor
**Abe** [eb] *s* nombre abreviado de **Abraham**
**abeam** [ə'bim] *adv* (naut.) de través, por el través
**abed** [ə'bɛd] *adv* en cama
**Abélard** ['æbəlɑrd] *s* Abelardo
**abele** [ə'bil] o ['ebəl] *s* (bot.) álamo blanco
**abelmosk** ['ebəl,mɑsk] *s* (bot.) abelmosco
**aberrant** [æb'ɛrənt] *adj* aberrante
**aberration** [,æbə'reʃən] *s* aberración; (astr. & opt.) aberración
**abet** [ə'bɛt] (*pret & pp:* **abetted;** *ger:* **abetting**) *va* incitar (*a una persona, especialmente al mal*); fomentar (*p.ej., el crimen*)
**abetment** [ə'bɛtmənt] *s* incitación (*especialmente al mal*); fomento (*p.ej., del crimen*)
**abetter** o **abettor** [ə'bɛtər] *s* incitador, instigador
**abeyance** [ə'beəns] *s* suspensión; **in abeyance** en suspenso
**abhor** [æb'hɔr] (*pret & pp:* **-horred;** *ger:* **-horring**) *va* aborrecer, detestar
**abhorrence** [æb'hɑrəns] o [æb'hɔrəns] *s* aborrecimiento, detestación
**abhorrent** [æb'hɑrənt] o [æb'hɔrənt] *adj* aborrecible, detestable
**abide** [ə'baɪd] (*pret & pp:* **abode** o **abided**) *va* esperar; soportar, tolerar; *vn* morar, permanecer, continuar; **to abide by** cumplir con; atenerse a
**abiding** [ə'baɪdɪŋ] *adj* permanente, perdurable
**abigail** ['æbɪgel] *s* doncella, criada confidente
**ability** [ə'bɪlɪtɪ] *s* (*pl:* **-ties**) habilidad, capacidad; talento, ingenio
**abiogenesis** [,æbɪo'dʒɛnɪsɪs] *s* abiogénesis
**abiosis** [,æbɪ'osɪs] *s* abiosis
**abiotic** [,ebaɪ'ɑtɪk] *adj* abiótico
**abirritant** [æb'ɪrɪtənt] *adj* abirritante; *s* remedio abirritante
**abirritate** [æb'ɪrɪtet] *va* (med.) abirritar
**abirritation** [æb,ɪrɪ'teʃən] *s* (med.) abirritación
**abject** ['æbdʒɛkt] o [æb'dʒɛkt] *adj* abyecto
**abjection** [æb'dʒɛkʃən] *s* abyección
**abjuration** [,æbdʒʊ'reʃən] *s* abjuración
**abjure** [æb'dʒʊr] *va* abjurar
**abjurement** [æb'dʒʊrmənt] *s* abjuración
**abl.** abr. de **ablative**
**ablactate** [æb'læktet] *va* ablactar
**ablactation** [,æblæk'teʃən] *s* ablactación
**ablation** [æb'leʃən] *s* (surg.) ablación
**ablative** ['æblətɪv] *adj & s* (gram.) ablativo
**ablative absolute** *s* (gram.) ablativo absoluto
**ablative case** *s* (gram.) ablativo
**ablaut** ['æblaʊt] *s* (phonet.) apofonía
**ablaze** [ə'blez] *adj* brillante, encendido; ardiente, anhelante; encolerizado; *adv* en llamas
**able** ['ebəl] *adj* hábil, capaz; talentoso; **to be able to** + *inf* poder + *inf*
**able-bodied** ['ebəl'bɑdɪd] *adj* sano; fornido, forzudo
**able-bodied seaman** *s* marinero experto
**ablegate** ['æblɪget] *s* (eccl.) ablegado
**ablepharia** [,æblɪ'fɛrɪə] *s* ablefaria
**ablepsia** [e'blɛpsɪə] *s* ablepsia
**abloom** [ə'blum] *adj & adv* en flor
**ablution** [æb'luʃən] *s* ablución
**ably** ['eblɪ] *adv* hábilmente; talentosamente
**abnegate** ['æbnɪget] *va* abnegar; *vn* abnegarse

**abnegation** [ˌæbnɪˈgeʃən] *s* abnegación
**abnormal** [æbˈnɔrməl] *adj* anormal
**abnormality** [ˌæbnɔrˈmælɪtɪ] *s* (*pl:* **-ties**) anormalidad
**abnormity** [æbˈnɔrmɪtɪ] *s* (*pl:* **-ties**) anomalía; monstruosidad
**aboard** [əˈbord] *adv* (naut.) a bordo; al bordo; **all aboard!** ¡ señores viajeros al tren!; **to go aboard** ir a bordo, embarcarse; **to take aboard** embarcar; *prep* en (*p.ej., el tren*); (naut.) al bordo de, al costado de
**abode** [əˈbod] *s* domicilio, morada; **to take up one's abode** adquirir o fijar domicilio, domiciliarse; *pret & pp de* **abide**
**abolish** [əˈbɑlɪʃ] *va* suprimir, eliminar
**abolition** [ˌæbəˈlɪʃən] *s* supresión, eliminación; (hist.) abolición
**abolitionism** [ˌæbəˈlɪʃənɪzəm] *s* abolicionismo
**abolitionist** [ˌæbəˈlɪʃənɪst] *s* abolicionista
**abomasum** [ˌæboˈmesəm] o **abomasus** [ˌæboˈmesəs] *s* (anat.) abomaso
**A-bomb** [ˈeˌbɑm] *s* bomba atómica
**abominable** [əˈbɑmɪnəbəl] *adj* abominable
**abominate** [əˈbɑmɪnet] *va* abominar, abominar de
**abomination** [əˌbɑmɪˈneʃən] *s* abominación
**aboriginal** [ˌæbəˈrɪdʒɪnəl] *adj & s* aborigen
**aborigines** [ˌæbəˈrɪdʒɪniz] *spl* aborígenes
**abort** [əˈbɔrt] *va & vn* abortar
**abortion** [əˈbɔrʃən] *s* aborto
**abortionist** [əˈbɔrʃənɪst] *s* abortista
**abortive** [əˈbɔrtɪv] *adj* abortivo
**abound** [əˈbaʊnd] *vn* abundar; **to abound in** o **with** abundar de o en
**about** [əˈbaʊt] *adv* casi; alrededor; aquí; acá y allá; en la dirección opuesta; uno después del otro; **to be about** estar levantado (*dícese de uno que ha estado enfermo*); **to be about to** + *inf* estar para + *inf; prep* acerca de, alrededor de; con respecto a; por, cerca de; hacia, como, a eso de, p.ej., **about six o'clock** a eso de las seis; **to be about** tratar de
**about face** *interj* (mil.) ¡ media vuelta!
**about-face** [əˈbaʊtˌfes] *s* media vuelta; cambio de opinión; [əˈbaʊtˈfes] *vn* dar media vuelta; cambiar de opinión
**above** [əˈbʌv] *adj & s* antedicho, arriba escrito; **from above** desde lo alto; de arriba; del cielo; *adv* arriba, encima; *prep* sobre, encima de, superior a, más arriba de, más alto que; **above all** sobre todo
**aboveboard** [əˈbʌvˌbord] *adj & adv* franco, francamente, sin rebozo ni disfraz
**above-cited** [əˈbʌvˌsaɪtɪd] *adj* ya citado
**aboveground** [əˈbʌvˌgraʊnd] *adj & adv* sobre la superficie de la tierra; vivo, viviente
**above-mentioned** [əˈbʌvˌmɛnʃənd] *adj* sobredicho, susodicho, dicho antes
**Abp.** abr. de **Archbishop**
**abracadabra** [ˌæbrəkəˈdæbrə] *s* abracadabra
**abrade** [əˈbred] *va* raer, desgastar por fricción
**Abraham** [ˈebrəhæm] *s* Abrahán
**Abraham's bosom** *s* seno de Abrahán
**abrasion** [əˈbreʒən] *s* abrasión, raedura; (med.) abrasión
**abrasive** [əˈbresɪv] o [əˈbrezɪv] *adj & s* abrasivo
**abreast** [əˈbrɛst] *adj & adv* de frente; **to be abreast of** o **with** correr parejas con; estar al corriente de; **to keep abreast of the times** ponerse al corriente de las cosas
**abridge** [əˈbrɪdʒ] *va* abreviar; privar
**abridgement** o **abridgment** [əˈbrɪdʒmənt] *s* abreviación; privación
**abroad** [əˈbrɔd] *adv* en el extranjero, al extranjero; en todas partes, a todas partes; fuera de casa
**abrogate** [ˈæbrəget] *va* abrogar
**abrogation** [ˌæbrəˈgeʃən] *s* abrogación
**abrupt** [əˈbrʌpt] *adj* repentino; brusco; áspero; abrupto, escarpado
**abruptness** [əˈbrʌptnɪs] *s* precipitación; brusquedad; aspereza; desigualdad
**Absalom** [ˈæbsələm] o [ˈæbsəlɑm] *s* (Bib.) Absalón
**abscess** [ˈæbsɛs] *s* (path.) absceso
**abscessed** [ˈæbsɛst] *adj* apostemado
**abscissa** [æbˈsɪsə] *s* (geom.) abscisa
**abscission** [æbˈsɪʒən] o [æbˈsɪʃən] *s* abscisión
**abscond** [æbˈskɑnd] *vn* evadirse, fugarse
**absence** [ˈæbsəns] *s* ausencia; falta de asistencia (*a la escuela, etc.*); **in the absence of** a falta de; **absence of mind** distracción
**absent** [ˈæbsənt] *adj* ausente; distraído; [æbˈsɛnt] *va* ausentar; **to absent oneself** ausentarse
**absentee** [ˌæbsənˈti] *s* absentista; ausente
**absentee ballot** *s* voto por correspondencia
**absenteeism** [ˌæbsənˈtiɪzəm] *s* absentismo, ausentismo
**absentee landlord** *s* absentista
**absentee ownership** *s* absentismo, ausentismo
**absentee voter** *s* votante por correspondencia
**absently** [ˈæbsəntlɪ] *adv* distraídamente
**absent-minded** [ˈæbsəntˈmaɪndɪd] *adj* distraído
**absent-mindedly** [ˈæbsəntˈmaɪndɪdlɪ] *adv* distraídamente
**absent-mindedness** [ˈæbsəntˈmaɪndɪdnɪs] *s* distracción
**absinth** o **absinthe** [ˈæbsɪnθ] *s* (bot.) absintio, ajenjo; absenta, ajenjo (*bebida*)
**absinthin** [æbˈsɪnθɪn] *s* (chem.) absintina
**absinthism** [ˈæbsɪnθɪzəm] o [æbˈsɪnθɪzəm] *s* (path.) absintismo
**absolute** [ˈæbsəlut] *adj & s* absoluto
**absolute alcohol** *s* alcohol absoluto
**absolutely** [ˈæbsəlutlɪ] o [ˌæbsəˈlutlɪ] *adv* absolutamente
**absolute monarchy** *s* monarquía absoluta
**absolute temperature** *s* (phys.) temperatura absoluta
**absolute zero** *s* (phys.) cero absoluto
**absolution** [ˌæbsəˈluʃən] *s* absolución
**absolutism** [ˈæbsəlutɪzəm] *s* absolutismo
**absolutist** [ˈæbsəlutɪst] *s* absolutista
**absolve** [æbˈsɑlv] o [æbˈzɑlv] *va* absolver
**absorb** [æbˈsɔrb] o [æbˈzɔrb] *va* absorber
**absorbable** [æbˈsɔrbəbəl] o [æbˈzɔrbəbəl] *adj* absorbible
**absorbed** [æbˈsɔrbd] o [æbˈzɔrbd] *adj* absorto, ensimismado
**absorbency** [æbˈsɔrbənsɪ] o [æbˈzɔrbənsɪ] *s* absorbencia
**absorbent** [æbˈsɔrbənt] o [æbˈzɔrbənt] *adj & s* absorbente
**absorbent cotton** *s* algodón hidrófilo
**absorbing** [æbˈsɔrbɪŋ] o [æbˈzɔrbɪŋ] *adj* absorbente (*interesante*)
**absorption** [æbˈsɔrpʃən] o [æbˈzɔrpʃən] *s* absorción
**abstain** [æbˈsten] *vn* abstenerse; **to abstain from** + *ger* abstenerse de + *inf*
**abstainer** [æbˈstenər] *s* abstinente
**abstemious** [æbˈstimɪəs] *adj* abstemio, abstinente
**abstention** [æbˈstɛnʃən] *s* abstención
**abstergent** [æbˈstʌrdʒənt] *adj & s* abstergente
**abstersion** [æbˈstʌrʃən] *s* abstersión
**abstersive** [æbˈstʌrsɪv] *adj* abstersivo
**abstinence** [ˈæbstɪnəns] *s* abstinencia
**abstinent** [ˈæbstɪnənt] *adj* abstinente
**abstract** [ˈæbstrækt] o [æbˈstrækt] *adj* abstracto; [ˈæbstrækt] *s* sumario, resumen; resumen analítico (*de materia científica*); **in the abstract** en abstracto; *va* resumir, compendiar; [æbˈstrækt] *va* abstraer (*una calidad*); quitar
**abstracted** [æbˈstræktɪd] *adj* abstraído
**abstraction** [æbˈstrækʃən] *s* abstracción
**abstractionism** [æbˈstrækʃənɪzəm] *s* (f.a.) abstraccionismo
**abstractionist** [æbˈstrækʃənɪst] *adj & s* (f.a.) abstraccionista
**abstruse** [æbˈstrus] *adj* abstruso
**absurd** [æbˈsʌrd] o [æbˈzʌrd] *adj* absurdo
**absurdity** [æbˈsʌrdɪtɪ] o [æbˈzʌrdɪtɪ] *s* (*pl:* **-ties**) absurdidad, absurdo
**abundance** [əˈbʌndəns] *s* abundancia
**abundant** [əˈbʌndənt] *adj* abundante
**abuse** [əˈbjus] *s* maltrato; injuria, insulto; abuso (*mal uso; costumbre injusta, injusticia*); [əˈbjuz] *va* maltratar; injuriar, insultar; abusar de (*usar mal de, p.ej., la autoridad*)
**abusive** [əˈbjusɪv] *adj* injurioso, insultante; abusivo (*que se practica por abuso*)
**abut** [əˈbʌt] (*pret & pp:* **abutted;** *ger:* **abutting**) *vn* confinar, estar contiguo; **to abut on, upon,** o **against** confinar con, terminar en
**abutment** [əˈbʌtmənt] *s* (arch.) estribo, contra-

fuerte, botarel; (carp.) empotramiento (*ensamblaje*); confinamiento, contigüidad
**Abydos** [əˈbaɪdɑs] *s* Abidos
**abysm** [əˈbɪzəm] *s* var. de **abyss**
**abysmal** [əˈbɪzməl] *adj* abismal; profundo
**abysmally** [əˈbɪzməlɪ] *adv* profundamente
**abyss** [əˈbɪs] *s* abismo
**abyssal** [əˈbɪsəl] *adj* abisal
**Abyssinia** [ˌæbɪˈsɪnɪə] *s* Abisinia
**Abyssinian** [ˌæbɪˈsɪnɪən] *adj & s* abisinio
**A.C.** o **a.c.** abr. de **alternating current**
**acacia** [əˈkeʃə] *s* (bot.) acacia; (bot.) acacia falsa (*Robinia pseudoacacia*); goma arábiga
**academic** [ˌækəˈdɛmɪk] *adj* académico (*escolar; clásico, literario; teórico; amanerado*); *s* estudiante universitario; profesor de la universidad; individuo de una sociedad de eruditos
**academical** [ˌækəˈdɛmɪkəl] *adj* var. de **academic; academicals** *spl* var. de **academic costume**
**academic costume** *s* traje de catedrático, traje académico, toga
**academic freedom** *s* libertad de cátedra
**academician** [əˌkædəˈmɪʃən] *s* académico
**academic subjects** *spl* (educ.) materias no profesionales
**academic year** *s* año escolar, año académico
**academize** [əˈkædəmaɪz] *va* academizar
**Academus** [ˌækəˈdiməs] *s* (myth.) Academo
**academy** [əˈkædəmɪ] *s* (*pl:* **-mies**) academia
**academy figure** *s* (f.a.) academia
**Acadia** [əˈkedɪə] *s* Acadia
**Acadian** [əˈkedɪən] *adj & s* acadiense
**acalephan** [ˌækəˈlɛfən] *adj & s* (zool.) acalefo
**acalycine** [eˈkælɪsɪn] o [eˈkælɪsaɪn] *adj* (bot.) acalicino
**acanthaceous** [ˌækænˈθeʃəs] *adj* (bot.) acantáceo
**acanthocephalan** [əˌkænθoˈsɛfələn] *adj & s* (zool.) acantocéfalo
**acanthopterygian** [ˌækænˌθɑptəˈrɪdʒɪən] *adj & s* (ichth.) acantopterigio
**acanthus** [əˈkænθəs] *s* (*pl:* **-thuses** o **-thi** [θaɪ]) (bot. & arch.) acanto
**acarid** [ˈækərɪd] *s* (zool.) acárido
**acaroid gum** o **resin** [ˈækərɔɪd] *s* acaroide, resina acaroide
**acarpous** [eˈkɑrpəs] *adj* (bot.) acarpo
**acarus** [ˈækərəs] *s* (*pl:* **-ri** [raɪ]) (zool.) ácaro
**acatalectic** [eˌkætəˈlɛktɪk] *adj & s* acataléctico
**acatalepsia** [eˌkætəˈlɛpsɪə] *s* (med.) acatalepsia
**acatalepsy** [eˈkætəˌlɛpsɪ] *s* (philos.) acatalepsia
**acaulescent** [ˌækɔˈlɛsənt] *adj* (bot.) acaule
**acc.** abr. de **accusative**
**accede** [ækˈsid] *vn* acceder; **to accede to** acceder a, condescender a; ascender o subir a (*p.ej., un trono*)
**accelerate** [ækˈsɛləret] *va* acelerar; *vn* acelerarse
**acceleration** [ækˌsɛləˈreʃən] *s* aceleración
**accelerator** [ækˈsɛləˌretər] *s* (aut.) acelerador
**accelerometer** [ækˌsɛləˈrɑmɪtər] *s* (aer.) acelerómetro
**accent** [ˈæksɛnt] *s* acento; [ˈæksɛnt] o [ækˈsɛnt] *va* acentuar
**accentual** [ækˈsɛntʃʊəl] *adj* acentual
**accentuate** [ækˈsɛntʃʊet] *va* acentuar
**accentuation** [ækˌsɛntʃʊˈeʃən] *s* acentuación
**accept** [ækˈsɛpt] *va* aceptar; (com.) aceptar
**acceptability** [ækˌsɛptəˈbɪlɪtɪ] *s* aceptabilidad
**acceptable** [ækˈsɛptəbəl] *adj* aceptable
**acceptably** [ækˈsɛptəblɪ] *adv* aceptablemente
**acceptance** [ækˈsɛptəns] *s* aceptación; (com.) aceptación
**acceptation** [ˌæksɛpˈteʃən] o **acception** [ækˈsɛpʃən] *s* acepción (*sentido*)
**acceptor** [ækˈsɛptər] *s* aceptador, aceptante; (com.) aceptante
**access** [ˈæksɛs] *s* acceso; (med.) acceso, ataque; aditamento, aumento
**accessary** [ækˈsɛsərɪ] *adj* var. de **accessory;** *s* (*pl:* **-ries**) var. de **accessory**
**accessibility** [ækˌsɛsɪˈbɪlɪtɪ] *s* accesibilidad
**accessible** [ækˈsɛsɪbəl] *adj* accesible
**accession** [ækˈsɛʃən] *s* accesión, consentimiento; ascenso (*a una dignidad o empleo*); aditamento, acrecentamiento; adquisición (*p. ej., de libros en una biblioteca*)
**accessory** [ækˈsɛsərɪ] *adj* accesorio; *s* (*pl:* **-ries**) accesorio; fautor, cómplice
**accessory after the fact** *s* (law) encubridor en el delito
**accessory before the fact** *s* (law) instigador de un delito
**accidence** [ˈæksɪdəns] *s* (gram.) accidentes
**accident** [ˈæksɪdənt] *s* accidente; (gram. & mus.) accidente; **by accident** por accidente
**accidental** [ˌæksɪˈdɛntəl] *adj* accidental; *s* (mus.) accidental
**accidentally** [ˌæksɪˈdɛntəlɪ] *adv* accidentalmente
**accident insurance** *s* seguro contra accidentes
**accident prevention** *s* precauciones contra accidentes
**accipiter** [ækˈsɪpɪtər] *s* (surg.) accípitre
**acclaim** [əˈklem] *s* aclamación; **to win acclaim** merecer aclamación, merecer aplausos; *va & vn* aclamar
**acclamation** [ˌækləˈmeʃən] *s* aclamación; **by acclamation** por aclamación
**acclimate** [əˈklaɪmɪt] o [ˈæklɪmet] *va* aclimatar; **to become acclimated** aclimatarse; *vn* aclimatarse
**acclimation** [ˌæklɪˈmeʃən] o **acclimatization** [əˌklaɪmətɪˈzeʃən] *s* aclimatación
**acclimatize** [əˈklaɪmətaɪz] *va & vn* var. de **acclimate**
**acclivity** [əˈklɪvɪtɪ] *s* (*pl:* **-ties**) cuesta ascendente, subida
**accolade** [ˌækəˈled] o [ˈækəled] *s* acolada, espaldarazo; elogio, premio; (arch., mus. & paleog.) acolada
**accommodate** [əˈkɑmədet] *va* acomodar; hospedar, alojar; *vn* conformarse
**accommodating** [əˈkɑməˌdetɪŋ] acomodadizo, servicial
**accommodation** [əˌkɑməˈdeʃən] *s* acomodación; hospedaje, alojamiento; (physiol.) acomodación; **accommodations** *spl* facilidades, comodidades; localidad (*p.ej., en un tren*); alojamiento, aposento (*en un hotel*)
**accommodation train** *s* tren ómnibus
**accompaniment** [əˈkʌmpənɪmənt] *s* acompañamiento; (mus.) acompañamiento
**accompanist** [əˈkʌmpənɪst] *s* acompañador, acompañante; (mus.) acompañante
**accompany** [əˈkʌmpənɪ] *va* (*pret & pp:* **-nied**) *va* acompañar; (mus.) acompañar
**accomplice** [əˈkɑmplɪs] *s* cómplice
**accomplish** [əˈkɑmplɪʃ] *va* realizar, llevar a cabo
**accomplished** [əˈkɑmplɪʃt] *adj* realizado; consumado; culto, elegante
**accomplishment** [əˈkɑmplɪʃmənt] *s* realización, ejecución, logro; **accomplishments** *spl* prendas, talentos, habilidades
**accord** [əˈkɔrd] *s* acuerdo; **in accord** de acuerdo; **in accord with** de acuerdo con; **of one's own accord** espontáneamente; **with one accord** de común acuerdo; *va* acordar, componer, conciliar; conceder, otorgar; *vn* concordar, avenirse, ponerse de acuerdo
**accordance** [əˈkɔrdəns] *s* conformidad; **in accordance with** de acuerdo con, de conformidad con
**accordant** [əˈkɔrdənt] *adj* acorde, conforme
**according** [əˈkɔrdɪŋ] *adj* acorde, conforme; **according as** según que; **according to** según, conforme a
**accordingly** [əˈkɔrdɪŋlɪ] *adv* en conformidad; por consiguiente
**accordion** [əˈkɔrdɪən] *s* acordeón; *adj* en acordeón, acordeonado
**accordionist** [əˈkɔrdɪənɪst] *s* acordeonista
**accordion pleat** *s* (sew.) pliegue acordeonado o en acordeón
**accost** [əˈkɔst] o [əˈkɑst] *va* abordar, acercarse a
**accouchement** [əˈkuʃmənt] *s* alumbramiento
**account** [əˈkaʊnt] *s* cuenta; relación, informe; importancia, monta; (com.) estado de cuenta; **by all accounts** según el decir general; **of account** de importancia; **of no account** de poca importancia; despreciable; **on account** a cuenta; **on account of** a causa de; por amor de; **on no account** de ninguna manera;

**to bring to account** pedir cuentas a; **to buy on account** comprar a plazos; **to call to account** pedir cuentas a; **to charge to the account of** cargar en cuenta a; **to give a good account of oneself** dar buena cuenta de sí; **to lose account of** perder la cuenta de; **to pay on account** pagar a buena cuenta; **to settle accounts with** ajustar cuentas con; **to take account of** tomar en cuenta; considerar; **to take account of stock** hacer inventario; **to take into account** tomar en cuenta; **to turn to account** sacar provecho de, hacer valer; *va* considerar, juzgar; *vn* echar la cuenta; **to account for** explicar; responder de, dar razón de
**accountability** [əˌkauntəˈbɪlɪtɪ] *s* responsabilidad
**accountable** [əˈkauntəbəl] *adj* responsable; explicable
**accountably** [əˈkauntəblɪ] *adv* explicablemente
**accountancy** [əˈkauntənsɪ] *s* contabilidad
**accountant** [əˈkauntənt] *s* contador, contable
**account executive** *s* (Brit.) var. de **customers' man**
**accounting** [əˈkauntɪŋ] *s* arreglo de cuentas; estado de cuentas; contabilidad
**accounts payable** *spl* (com.) cuentas a pagar
**accounts receivable** *spl* (com.) cuentas a cobrar
**accounts rendered** *spl* (com.) cuentas pasadas o rendidas
**accounts stated** *spl* (com.) cuentas convenidas
**accouter** o **accoutre** [əˈkutər] *va* aviar, equipar
**accouterments** o **accoutrements** [əˈkutərmənts] *spl* avío, equipo
**accredit** [əˈkrɛdɪt] *va* acreditar; (educ.) acreditar
**accreditation** [əˌkrɛdɪˈteʃən] *s* acreditación; (educ.) acreditación
**accretion** [əˈkriʃən] *s* acrecentamiento; (mineral. & path.) acreción
**accrual** [əˈkruəl] *s* acumulación
**accrue** [əˈkru] *vn* resultar; acumularse
**acct.** abr. de **account**
**accumulate** [əˈkjumjəlet] *va* acumular; *vn* acumularse
**accumulation** [əˌkjumjəˈleʃən] *s* acumulación
**accumulator** [əˈkjumjəˌletər] *s* acumulador; (Brit.) acumulador (*eléctrico*)
**accuracy** [ˈækjərəsɪ] *s* exactitud, precisión
**accurate** [ˈækjərɪt] *adj* exacto; seguro (*en el cálculo*)
**accursed** [əˈkʌrsɪd] o [əˈkʌrst] o **accurst** [əˈkʌrst] *adj* maldecido, maldito
**accus.** abr. de **accusative**
**accusable** [əˈkjuzəbəl] *adj* acusable
**accusation** [ˌækjəˈzeʃən] o [ˌækjuˈzeʃən] *s* acusación
**accusative** [əˈkjuzətɪv] *adj & s* (gram.) acusativo
**accusatory** [əˈkjuzəˌtorɪ] *adj* acusatorio
**accuse** [əˈkjuz] *va* acusar
**accused** [əˈkjuzd] *adj & s* acusado
**accuser** [əˈkjuzər] *s* acusador
**accusingly** [əˈkjuzɪŋlɪ] *adv* acusando
**accustom** [əˈkʌstəm] *va* acostumbrar
**accustomed** [əˈkʌstəmd] *adj* acostumbrado, de costumbre
**ace** [es] *s* as (*naipes, dados, tenis, aviación*); **to be within an ace of** + *ger* estar a dos dedos de + *inf*
**acephalous** [eˈsɛfələs] *adj* acéfalo
**aceraceous** [ˌæsəˈreʃəs] *adj* (bot.) aceráceo
**acerbate** [ˈæsərbet] *va* agriar; (fig.) exasperar
**acerbity** [əˈsʌrbɪtɪ] *s* (*pl:* **-ties**) acerbidad
**acerose** [ˈæsəros] *adj* (bot.) aceroso
**acerous** [ˈæsərəs] *adj* (bot.) aceroso; [eˈsɪrəs] *adj* (zool.) acerato (*sin cuernos*)
**acetabulum** [ˌæsɪˈtæbjələm] *s* (*pl:* **-la** [lə]) (anat., bot. & zool.) acetábulo
**acetanilid** [ˌæsɪˈtænɪlɪd] o **acetanilide** [ˌæsɪˈtænɪlɪd] o [ˌæsɪˈtænɪlaɪd] *s* (chem.) acetanilida
**acetate** [ˈæsɪtet] *s* (chem.) acetato
**acetic** [əˈsitɪk] *adj* (chem.) acético
**acetic acid** *s* (chem.) ácido acético
**acetification** [əˌsɛtɪfɪˈkeʃən] *s* acetificación
**acetify** [əˈsɛtɪfaɪ] (*pret & pp:* **-fied**) *va* acetificar; *vn* acetificarse
**acetimeter** [ˌæsɪˈtɪmɪtər] o **acetometer** [ˌæsɪˈtɑmɪtər] *s* acetímetro
**acetone** [ˈæsɪton] *s* (chem.) acetona
**acetonemia** [ˌæsɪtoˈnimɪə] *s* (path.) acetonemia
**acetonuria** [ˌæsɪtoˈnurɪə] o [ˌæsɪtoˈnjurɪə] *s* (path.) acetonuria
**acetose** [ˈæsɪtos] o **acetous** [ˈæsɪtəs] o [əˈsitəs] *adj* acetoso
**acetyl** [ˈæsɪtɪl] *s* (chem.) acetilo
**acetylene** [əˈsɛtɪlin] *s* (chem.) acetileno; *adj* acetilénico
**acetylene torch** *s* soplete oxiacetilénico
**Achaea** [əˈkiə] *s* Acaya
**Achaean** [əˈkiən] *adj & s* aqueo
**Achaia** [əˈkeə] o [əˈkaɪə] *s* var. de **Achaea**
**Achates** [əˈketiz] *s* (myth.) Acates
**ache** [ek] *s* dolor continuo, achaque; **to be full of aches and pains** estar lleno de goteras; *vn* doler, p.ej., **my head aches** me duele la cabeza; padecer dolor, estar acongojado; (coll.) suspirar, anhelar
**achene** [eˈkin] *s* (bot.) aquenio
**achenial** [eˈkinɪəl] *adj* aquénico
**Acheron** [ˈækərɑn] *s* (myth.) Aqueronte
**achievable** [əˈtʃivəbəl] *adj* acabable
**achieve** [əˈtʃiv] *va* llevar a cabo; alcanzar; ganar; *vn* tener buen éxito
**achievement** [əˈtʃivmənt] *s* realización, ejecución, logro; hazaña
**Achilles** [əˈkɪliz] *s* (myth.) Aquiles
**Achilles' heel** *s* talón de Aquiles (*sitio vulnerable*)
**Achilles' tendon** *s* (anat.) tendón de Aquiles
**achlorhydria** [eˌklorˈhaɪdrɪə] *s* (path.) aclorhidria
**achromatic** [ˌækroˈmætɪk] *adj* (opt., biol., & mus.) acromático
**achromatin** [eˈkromətɪn] *s* (biol.) acromatina
**achromatism** [eˈkromətɪzəm] *s* acromatismo
**achromatize** [eˈkromətaɪz] *va* acromatizar
**achromatosis** [eˌkroməˈtosɪs] *s* (path.) acromatosis
**achromatous** [eˈkromətəs] *adj* acromático
**acicular** [əˈsɪkjələr] *adj* acicular
**aciculate** [əˈsɪkjəlɪt] *adj* (bot. & zool.) aciculado
**acid** [ˈæsɪd] *adj* ácido; (chem.) ácido; (fig.) agrio, mordaz; *s* (chem.) ácido
**acid-forming** [ˈæsɪdˌfɔrmɪŋ] *adj* ácido; acidógeno (*dícese de los alimentos*)
**acidic** [əˈsɪdɪk] *adj* acidificante; (petrog.) ácido
**acidiferous** [ˌæsɪˈdɪfərəs] *adj* acidífero
**acidification** [əˌsɪdɪfɪˈkeʃən] *s* acidificación
**acidify** [əˈsɪdɪfaɪ] (*pret & pp:* **-fied**) *va* acidificar; *vn* acidificarse
**acidimeter** [ˌæsɪˈdɪmɪtər] *s* acidímetro
**acidity** [əˈsɪdɪtɪ] *s* (*pl:* **-ties**) acidez
**acidophil** [ˈæsɪdəˌfɪl] *adj & s* acidófilo
**acidophilus milk** [ˌæsɪˈdɑfɪləs] *s* lactobacilina
**acidosis** [ˌæsɪˈdosɪs] *s* (path.) acidosis
**acidproof** [ˈæsɪdˈpruf] *adj* inatacable por los ácidos
**acid test** *s* prueba extrema, prueba de fuego
**acidulate** [əˈsɪdjəlet] *va* acidular
**acidulous** [əˈsɪdjələs] *adj* acídulo
**ack-ack** [ˈækˌæk] *s* (slang) fuego antiaéreo; (slang) artillería antiaérea
**acknowledge** [ækˈnɑlɪdʒ] *va* admitir, confesar, reconocer; acusar (*recibo de una carta, oficios, etc.*); agradecer (*p.ej., un favor*); (law) certificar, testificar
**acknowledgment** o **acknowledgement** [ækˈnɑlɪdʒmənt] *s* admisión, confesión, reconocimiento; acuse (*de recibo*); agradecimiento; (law) certificación, testificación
**aclastic** [eˈklæstɪk] *adj* (opt.) aclástico
**acleidian** o **aclidian** [eˈklaɪdɪən] *adj & s* (anat.) acleido
**aclinic** [eˈklɪnɪk] *adj* (phys.) aclínico
**aclinic line** *s* (phys.) línea aclínica
**acme** [ˈækmɪ] *s* auge, colmo, pináculo, cima; (med.) acmé
**acne** [ˈæknɪ] *s* (path.) acne
**acology** [əˈkɑlədʒɪ] *s* acología
**acolyte** [ˈækolaɪt] *s* acólito
**acolythate** [əˈkɑlɪθet] *s* (eccl.) acolitazgo
**aconite** [ˈækənaɪt] *s* (bot.) acónito

**aconitine** [ə'kɑnɪtin] o [ə'kɑnɪtɪn] *s* (chem.) aconitina
**acorn** ['ekɔrn] o ['ekərn] *s* bellota
**acorned** ['ekɔrnd] o ['ekərnd] *adj* lleno de bellotas, cebado con bellotas; (her.) englandado
**acotyledon** [e,kɑtɪ'lidən] *s* (bot.) acotiledón
**acotyledonous** [e,kɑtɪ'lidənəs] *adj* (bot.) acotiledón o acotiledóneo
**acoustic** [ə'kustɪk] o [ə'kaʊstɪk] *adj* acústico; **acoustics** *ssg* (phys.) acústica; **acoustics** *spl* acústica arquitectural
**acoustically** [ə'kustɪkəlɪ] o [ə'kaʊstɪkəlɪ] *adv* acústicamente
**acoustical tile** *s* azulejo antisonoro
**acousticon** [ə'kustɪkɑn] o [ə'kaʊstɪkɑn] *s* (trademark) acusticón
**acquaint** [ə'kwent] *va* informar, familiarizar, poner al corriente; **to be acquainted** conocerse (*uno a otro*); **to be acquainted with** conocer; estar al corriente de; **to become acquainted** venir a conocerse; **to become acquainted with** venir a conocer; ponerse al corriente de; **to acquaint with** poner al corriente de
**acquaintance** [ə'kwentəns] *s* conocimiento; conocido (*persona*)
**acquaintanceship** [ə'kwentənsʃɪp] *s* conocimiento; trato, relaciones
**acquiesce** [,ækwɪ'ɛs] *vn* consentir, conformarse, condescender
**acquiescence** [,ækwɪ'ɛsəns] *s* consentimiento, conformidad, condescendencia, aquiescencia
**acquiescent** [,ækwɪ'ɛsənt] *adj* acomodadizo, conforme, condescendiente, aquiescente
**acquire** [ə'kwaɪr] *va* adquirir
**acquired character** *s* (biol.) carácter adquirido
**acquirement** [ə'kwaɪrmənt] *s* adquisición; **acquirements** *spl* conocimientos
**acquisition** [,ækwɪ'zɪʃən] *s* adquisición
**acquisitive** [ə'kwɪzɪtɪv] *adj* propenso a adquirir, codicioso; (law) adquisitivo
**acquisitiveness** [ə'kwɪzɪtɪvnɪs] *s* adquisividad
**acquisitive prescription** *s* (law) prescripción adquisitiva
**acquit** [ə'kwɪt] (*pret & pp:* **acquitted**; *ger:* **acquitting**) *va* absolver, exculpar; **to acquit oneself** portarse, conducirse
**acquittal** [ə'kwɪtəl] *s* absolución, exculpación; desempeño
**acquittance** [ə'kwɪtəns] *s* descargo (*de una deuda*); pago; recibo, finiquito
**acre** ['ekər] *s* acre
**acreage** ['ekərɪdʒ] *s* acreaje, superficie medida en acres
**acrid** ['ækrɪd] *adj* acre, acrimonioso; (fig.) acre, acrimonioso
**acridity** [ə'krɪdɪtɪ] *s* acritud, acrimonia; (fig.) acritud, acrimonia
**acriflavine** [,ækrɪ'flevɪn] o [,ækrɪ'flevin] *s* (pharm.) acriflavina
**acrimonious** [,ækrɪ'monɪəs] *adj* acrimonioso
**acrimony** ['ækrɪ,monɪ] *s* (*pl:* **-nies**) acrimonia
**acrobat** ['ækrəbæt] *s* acróbata
**acrobatic** [,ækrə'bætɪk] *adj* acrobático; **acrobatics** *spl* acrobacia (*ejercicios*); **acrobatics** *ssg* acrobatismo (*arte o profesión*)
**acrogen** ['ækrədʒən] *s* (bot.) acrógena
**acromegaly** [,ækro'mɛgəlɪ] *s* (path.) acromegalia
**acronym** ['ækrənɪm] *s* acrónimo
**acropolis** [ə'krɑpəlɪs] *s* acrópolis; **the Acropolis** la Acrópolis
**acrospore** ['ækrospor] *s* (bot.) acrósporo
**across** [ə'krɔs] o [ə'krɑs] *adv* a través; al otro lado; en cruz, transversalmente; *prep* a través de, al través de; al otro lado de; (elec.) en paralelo con; **to come across** encontrarse con; **to go across** atravesar; **to run across** encontrarse con; **across the way** enfrente
**across-the-board** [ə'krɔsðə'bord] o [ə'krɑsðə'bord] *adj* comprensivo, general, para todos sin excepción
**acrostic** [ə'krɔstɪk] o [ə'krɑstɪk] *s* acróstico
**acroterium** [,ækro'tɪrɪəm] *s* (*pl:* **-a** [ə]) (arch.) acrotera; (naut.) acrostolio
**acrylic** [ə'krɪlɪk] *adj* (chem.) acrílico
**acrylic acid** *s* (chem.) ácido acrílico
**act** [ækt] *s* acto, acción; (law) ley, decreto; (theat.) acto; **an act of treason** una traición; **in the act** en flagrante; *va* representar; desempeñar (*un papel*); desempeñar el papel de; aparentar; **to act the fool** hacer el bufón, hacer de bufón; **to act the part of** hacer el papel de, desempeñar el papel de; *vn* obrar, actuar, funcionar; portarse, conducirse; fingir; (theat.) hacer un papel, actuar; **to act as** actuar de; **to act as if** hacer que, hacer como que; **to act for** representar; **to act on** o **upon** actuar sobre, influir en; seguir, obedecer; **to act up** travesear; **to act up to** portarse en conformidad con; hacer zalamerías a, hacer fiestas a
**acting** ['æktɪŋ] *adj* fingidor, simulador; interino; *s* funcionamiento; simulación; (theat.) actuación, representación, desempeño de un papel
**actinic** [æk'tɪnɪk] *adj* actínico
**actinism** ['æktɪnɪzəm] *s* actinismo
**actinium** [æk'tɪnɪəm] *s* (chem.) actinio
**actinometer** [,æktɪ'nɑmɪtər] *s* actinómetro
**actinomycin** [,æktɪno'maɪsɪn] *s* (pharm.) actinomicina
**actinomycosis** [,æktɪnomaɪ'kosɪs] *s* (path.) actinomicosis
**action** ['ækʃən] *s* acción; (mach.) accionado (*mecanismo*); **actions** *spl* conducta; **in action** en acción, en marcha; **to take action** tomar medidas; (law) poner, entablar un pleito
**actionable** ['ækʃənəbəl] *adj* justiciable; procesable
**Actium** ['æktɪəm] o ['ækʃɪəm] *s* Accio
**activate** ['æktɪvet] *va* activar
**activation** [,æktɪ'veʃən] *s* activación
**activator** ['æktɪ,vetər] *s* activador; (chem.) activador
**active** ['æktɪv] *adj* activo
**active service** *s* (mil.) servicio activo
**active voice** *s* (gram.) voz activa
**activist** ['æktɪvɪst] *s* activista
**activity** [æk'tɪvɪtɪ] *s* (*pl:* **-ties**) actividad
**act of God** *s* fuerza mayor
**acton** ['æktən] *s* gambax
**actor** ['æktər] *s* actor, agente; (theat. & law) actor
**actress** ['æktrɪs] *s* (theat.) actriz; (law) actora
**Acts of the Apostles** *spl* (Bib.) Actas, Actos, o Hechos de los Apóstoles
**actual** ['æktʃʊəl] *adj* real, efectivo
**actuality** [,æktʃʊ'ælɪtɪ] *s* (*pl:* **-ties**) realidad
**actualize** ['æktʃʊəlaɪz] *va* realizar
**actually** ['æktʃʊəlɪ] *adv* en realidad
**actuarial** [,æktʃʊ'ɛrɪəl] *adj* actuario, actuarial
**actuary** ['æktʃʊ,ɛrɪ] *s* (*pl:* **-ies**) actuario, actuario de seguros
**actuate** ['æktʃʊet] *va* actuar, poner en acción; estimular, impulsar
**acuity** [ə'kjuɪtɪ] *s* agudeza, acuidad
**acumen** [ə'kjumɛn] *s* acumen, cacumen, perspicacia
**acuminate** [ə'kjumɪnet] *adj* acuminado; (bot. & zool.) acuminado; *va* aguzar; *vn* rematar en punta
**acupuncture** [,ækjə'pʌŋktʃər] *s* (surg.) acupuntura
**acute** [ə'kjut] *adj* agudo
**acute accent** *s* acento agudo
**acute angle** *s* (geom.) ángulo agudo
**acute-angled** [ə'kjut'æŋgəld] *adj* acutangulado, acutangular, acutángulo
**acuteness** [ə'kjutnɪs] *s* agudeza
**acyclic** [e'saɪklɪk] *adj* acíclico
**A.D.** abr. de **anno Domini** (Lat.) **in the year of our Lord**
**ad** [æd] *s* (coll.) anuncio
**Ada** ['edə] *s* Ada
**adage** ['ædɪdʒ] *s* adagio, refrán
**adagio** [ə'dɑdʒo] o [ə'dɑdʒɪo] *s* (*pl:* **-gios**) (mus.) adagio
**Adam** ['ædəm] *s* Adán; **not to know from Adam** (coll.) no conocer absolutamente; **the old Adam** la inclinación al pecado
**adamant** ['ædəmænt] o ['ædəmənt] *adj* diamantino, duro, inquebrantable; firme, inexorable; *s* adamas
**adamantine** [,ædə'mæntɪn], [,ædə'mæntin] o [,ædə'mæntaɪn] *adj* adamantino
**Adamic** [ə'dæmɪk] *adj* adámico
**Adam's apple** *s* nuez, nuez de la garganta, manzana de Adán

**adapt** [ə'dæpt] *va* adaptar, adecuar; refundir (*p.ej., un drama*)

**adaptability** [ə,dæptə'bɪlɪtɪ] *s* adaptabilidad

**adaptable** [ə'dæptəbəl] *adj* adaptable

**adaptation** [,ædæp'teʃən] *s* adaptación; refundición (*p.ej., de un drama*)

**adapter** [ə'dæptər] *s* adaptador; (chem.) alargadera; refundidor

**adaptive** [ə'dæptɪv] *adj* adaptante, adaptativo

**add** [æd] *va* añadir, agregar; sumar; *vn* sumar; **to add up to** subir a

**added line** *s* (mus.) línea suplementaria

**addend** ['ædɛnd] o [ə'dɛnd] *s* (math.) sumando

**addendum** [ə'dɛndəm] *s* (*pl:* **-da** [də]) complemento; (mach.) cabeza; (mach.) altura de la cabeza

**addendum circle** *s* (mach.) círculo de cabeza

**adder** ['ædər] *s* (zool.) víbora común; serpiente

**adder's-tongue** ['ædərz,tʌŋ] *s* (bot.) lengua de sierpe (*helecho*); (bot.) eritrono

**addible** ['ædɪbəl] *adj* añadible

**addict** ['ædɪkt] *s* enviciado; adicto, partidario; [ə'dɪkt] *va* enviciar; dedicar, entregar; **to addict oneself to** enviciarse en o con; dedicarse a, entregarse a

**addicted** [ə'dɪktɪd] *adj* enviciado; adicto; **addicted to** enviciado con, apasionado por

**addiction** [ə'dɪkʃən] *s* enviciamiento; adhesividad

**adding machine** *s* máquina de sumar, sumadora

**Addison's disease** ['ædɪsənz] *s* (path.) enfermedad de Addison, cirrosis hipertrófica

**addition** [ə'dɪʃən] *s* adición; **in addition** además; **in addition to** además de, a más de

**additional** [ə'dɪʃənəl] *adj* adicional

**additionally** [ə'dɪʃənəlɪ] *adv* adicionalmente

**additive** ['ædɪtɪv] *adj & s* aditivo

**addle** ['ædəl] *adj* huero; (fig.) huero; *va & vn* enhuerar

**addlebrained** ['ædəl'brend] *adj* atontado, estúpido

**address** [ə'drɛs] o ['ædrɛs] *s* dirección; (com.) consignación; [ə'drɛs] *s* discurso, alocución; destreza, habilidad; trato, maneras; **addresses** *spl* obsequios amorosos; **to deliver an address** pronunciar un discurso; *va* dirigirse a; dirigir la palabra a; dirigir (*p.ej., una alocución, una carta*); (com.) consignar; (golf) prepararse para golpear (*la pelota*); **How does one address a governor?** ¿Qué tratamiento se da a un gobernador?; **to address oneself to** dirigirse a

**addressee** [,ædrɛ'si] *s* destinatario; (com.) consignatario

**addressing machine** *s* máquina para dirigir sobres

**addressograph** [ə'drɛsəgræf] o [ə'drɛsəgrɑf] *s* (trademark) adresógrafo

**adduce** [ə'djus] o [ə'dus] *va* aducir

**adducent** [ə'djusənt] o [ə'dusənt] *adj* (physiol.) aductor

**adduct** [ə'dʌkt] *va* (physiol.) aducir

**adduction** [ə'dʌkʃən] *s* aducción; (physiol.) aducción

**adductor** [ə'dʌktər] *s* (physiol.) aductor, músculo aductor

**Adelaide** ['ædəled] *s* Adelaida

**Adeline** ['ædəlaɪn] o ['ædəlin] *s* Adelina

**Aden** ['ɑdən] o ['edən] *s* Adén

**adenia** [ə'dinɪə] *s* (path.) adenia

**adenitis** [,ædɪ'naɪtɪs] *s* (path.) adenitis

**adenoid** ['ædənɔɪd] *adj* adenoideo; **adenoids** *spl* vegetaciones adenoideas

**adenoidal** [,ædə'nɔɪdəl] *adj* adenoideo

**adenoidectomy** [,ædɪnɔɪ'dɛktəmɪ] *s* (*pl:* **-mies**) adenoidectomía

**adenoma** [,ædɪ'nomə] *s* (*pl:* **-mata** [mətə] o **-mas**) (path.) adenoma

**adept** [ə'dɛpt] *adj* experto, perito; hábil; adepto; ['ædɛpt] o [ə'dɛpt] *s* experto, perito; adepto (*en alquimia, magia, etc.*)

**adequacy** ['ædɪkwəsɪ] *s* suficiencia

**adequate** ['ædɪkwɪt] *adj* suficiente

**adhere** [æd'hɪr] *vn* adherir, adherirse; conformarse

**adherence** [æd'hɪrəns] *s* adhesión (*apoyo, fidelidad*)

**adherent** [æd'hɪrənt] *adj & s* adherente

**adhesion** [æd'hiʒən] *s* adherencia (*acción de pegarse*); adhesión (*apoyo, fidelidad*); (path.) adherencia; (phys.) adherencia o adhesión

**adhesive** [æd'hisɪv] o [æd'hizɪv] *adj & s* adhesivo

**adhesive tape** *s* tafetán adhesivo, cinta adhesiva

**ad hoc** [æd'hɑk] (Lat.) para aquello de que se trata

**adiabatic** [,ædɪə'bætɪk] *adj* adiabático

**adiaphoresis** [,ædɪ,æfo'risɪs] *s* (path.) adiaforesis

**adieu** [ə'dju] o [ə'du] *s* (*pl:* **adieus** o **adieux** [ə'djuz] o [ə'duz]) adiós; **to bid adieu to** despedirse de; *interj* ¡adiós!

**ad infinitum** [æd,ɪnfɪ'naɪtəm] *adv* a lo infinito, hasta lo infinito

**adipocere** ['ædɪpo,sɪr] *s* adipocira

**adipose** ['ædɪpos] *adj* adiposo

**adiposis** [,ædɪ'posɪs] *s* (path.) adiposis

**adiposity** [,ædɪ'pɑsɪtɪ] *s* adiposidad

**adipsia** [e'dɪpsɪə] *s* (path.) adipsia

**adit** ['ædɪt] *s* entrada; acceso; (min.) bocamina, socavón

**adjacency** [ə'dʒesənsɪ] *s* adyacencia

**adjacent** [ə'dʒesənt] *adj* adyacente

**adjacent angles** *spl* (math.) ángulos adyacentes

**adjectival** [,ædʒɪk'taɪvəl] o ['ædʒɪktɪvəl] *adj* adjetival

**adjectivally** [,ædʒɪk'taɪvəlɪ] o ['ædʒɪktɪvəlɪ] *adv* adjetivadamente

**adjective** ['ædʒɪktɪv] *adj & s* adjetivo

**adjoin** [ə'dʒɔɪn] *va* lindar con; anexar; *vn* colindar

**adjoining** [ə'dʒɔɪnɪŋ] *adj* colindante

**adjourn** [ə'dʒʌrn] *va* prorrogar, suspender, aplazar; *vn* prorrogarse, suspenderse; (coll.) trasladarse

**adjournment** [ə'dʒʌrnmənt] *s* suspensión, aplazamiento; (coll.) translación

**Adjt.** abr. de **Adjutant**

**adjudge** [ə'dʒʌdʒ] *va* decretar; sentenciar; condenar; juzgar; adjudicar (*otorgar*)

**adjudicate** [ə'dʒudɪket] *va* juzgar; *vn* juzgar (*ser juez*)

**adjudication** [ə,dʒudɪ'keʃən] *s* juicio

**adjudicator** [ə'dʒudɪ,ketər] *s* juez

**adjunct** ['ædʒʌŋkt] *adj* adjunto; *s* adjunto, ayudante; (gram.) adjunto

**adjuration** [,ædʒʊ'reʃən] *s* orden imperiosa y solemne; conjuro (*ruego encarecido*)

**adjure** [ə'dʒʊr] *va* ordenar imperiosa y solemnemente (*en nombre de Dios o mediante juramento*); conjurar (*pedir con instancia*)

**adjust** [ə'dʒʌst] *va* ajustar, arreglar; (ins.) liquidar; verificar, corregir (*un instrumento*); *vn* ajustarse, acomodarse

**adjustable** [ə'dʒʌstəbəl] *adj* ajustable, arreglable, componible

**adjuster** [ə'dʒʌstər] *s* ajustador, arreglador; (ins.) liquidador de la avería, perito en daños

**adjustment** [ə'dʒʌstmənt] *s* ajuste, arreglo, composición; (ins.) liquidación de la avería, evaluación del daño

**adjutancy** ['ædʒətənsɪ] *s* (*pl:* **-cies**) (mil.) ayudantía

**adjutant** ['ædʒətənt] *s* ayudante; (mil.) ayudante; (orn.) argala; *adj* ayudante

**adjutant bird** *s* (orn.) argala

**adjutant general** *s* (*pl:* **adjutant generals**) (mil.) ayudante general

**adjuvant** ['ædʒəvənt] *adj & s* adyuvante

**adlib** [,æd'lɪb] (*pret & pp:* **adlibbed;** *ger:* **adlibbing**) *va & vn* (coll.) improvisar

**Adm.** abr. de **Admiral**

**Admetus** [æd'mitəs] *s* (myth.) Admeto

**adminicle** [æd'mɪnɪkəl] *s* adminículo; (law) adminículo (*principio que corrobora una prueba*)

**administer** [æd'mɪnɪstər] *va* administrar; **to administer an oath** tomar juramento; *vn* ejercer el cargo de administrador; **to administer to** ayudar a (*una persona*); contribuir a (*p.ej., necesidades*)

**administration** [æd,mɪnɪs'treʃən] *s* administración

**administrative** [æd'mɪnɪs,tretɪv] *adj* administrativo

**administrator** [æd'mɪnɪs,tretər] *s* administrador; administrador judicial (*de bienes ajenos*)

**administratrix** [æd,mɪnɪs'tretrɪks] *s* (*pl:*

**-trices** [trɪsiz]) administradora judicial (*de bienes ajenos*)
**admirable** [ˈædmɪrəbəl] *adj* admirable
**admiral** [ˈædmɪrəl] *s* almirante; buque **almirante**; (ent.) ninfálido (*especialmente Vanessa atalanta y Basilarchia arthemis*)
**Admiral of the Fleet** *s* (nav.) capitán general de la armada
**admiralty** [ˈædmɪrəltɪ] *s* (*pl:* **-ties**) almirantazgo
**Admiralty Islands** *spl* islas Almirantes
**admiration** [ˌædmɪˈreʃən] *s* admiración
**admire** [ædˈmaɪr] *va* admirar; *vn* admirarse
**admirer** [ædˈmaɪrər] *s* admirador; enamorado
**admiring** [ædˈmaɪrɪŋ] *adj* admirativo, admirador
**admissibility** [ædˌmɪsɪˈbɪlɪtɪ] *s* admisibilidad
**admissible** [ædˈmɪsɪbəl] *adj* admisible
**admission** [ædˈmɪʃən] *s* admisión; ingreso (*en una escuela*); precio de entrada; **to gain admission** lograr entrar
**admit** [ædˈmɪt] (*pret & pp:* **-mitted;** *ger:* **-mitting**) *va* admitir; *vn* dar entrada; **to admit of** admitir, permitir
**admittance** [ædˈmɪtəns] *s* admisión; derecho de entrar; (elec.) admitancia; **no admittance** se prohíbe la entrada, acceso prohibido
**admittedly** [ædˈmɪtɪdlɪ] *adv* concedidamente
**admix** [ædˈmɪks] *va* mezclar
**admixture** [ædˈmɪkstʃər] *s* mezcla
**admonish** [ædˈmɑnɪʃ] *va* amonestar
**admonishment** [ædˈmɑnɪʃmənt] *s* amonestamiento, amonestación
**admonition** [ˌædməˈnɪʃən] *s* admonición
**admonitory** [ædˈmɑnɪˌtorɪ] *adj* admonitivo
**adnate** [ˈædnet] *adj* (bot. & zool.) adnato
**ad nauseam** [ædˈnɔʃɪæm] o [ædˈnɔsɪæm] (**Lat.**) hasta provocar náuseas
**adnexa** [ædˈnɛksə] *spl* (anat.) anexos
**ado** [əˈdu] *s* bulla, excitación
**adobe** [əˈdobɪ] *s* adobe; casa de adobe; *adj* adobino, de adobe
**adolescence** [ˌædəˈlɛsəns] *s* adolescencia
**adolescent** [ˌædəˈlɛsənt] *adj & s* adolescente
**Adolph** [ˈædɑlf] o [ˈedɑlf] *s* Adolfo
**Adonic** [əˈdɑnɪk] *adj & s* adónico
**Adonis** [əˈdonɪs] o [əˈdɑnɪs] *s* (myth.) Adonis; (fig.) adonis (*joven de gran belleza*)
**adopt** [əˈdɑpt] *va* adoptar
**adoptable** [əˈdɑptəbəl] *adj* adoptable
**adopter** [əˈdɑptər] *s* adoptante, adoptador
**adoption** [əˈdɑpʃən] *s* adopción
**adoptionism** [əˈdɑpʃənɪzəm] *s* adopcionismo
**adoptionist** [əˈdɑpʃənɪst] *adj & s* adopcionista
**adoptive** [əˈdɑptɪv] *adj* adoptivo
**adorable** [əˈdorəbəl] *adj* adorable; (**coll.**) adorable (*encantador, deleitoso*)
**adoration** [ˌædəˈreʃən] *s* adoración
**adore** [əˈdor] *va* adorar
**adorer** [əˈdorər] *s* adorador
**adorn** [əˈdɔrn] *va* adornar
**adornment** [əˈdɔrnmənt] *s* adorno
**adrenal** [ædˈrinəl] *adj* suprarrenal
**adrenal gland** *s* (anat.) glándula suprarrenal
**adrenalin** [ædˈrɛnəlɪn] *s* (**physiol. & pharm.**) adrenalina
**Adrian** [ˈedrɪən] *s* Adriano
**Adriatic** [ˌedrɪˈætɪk] o [ˌædrɪˈætɪk] *adj & s* Adriático
**adrift** [əˈdrɪft] *adj & adv* (naut.) al garete, a la deriva; abandonado; divagando
**adroit** [əˈdrɔɪt] *adj* diestro
**adroitness** [əˈdrɔɪtnɪs] *s* destreza
**adsorb** [ædˈsɔrb] o [ædˈzɔrb] *va* adsorber
**adsorption** [ædˈsɔrpʃən] o [ædˈzɔrpʃən] *s* adsorción
**adsorptive** [ædˈsɔrptɪv] o [ædˈzɔrptɪv] *adj* adsorbente
**adularia** [ˌædʒəˈlɛrɪə] *s* (mineral.) adularia
**adulate** [ˈædʒəlet] *va* adular
**adulation** [ˌædʒəˈleʃən] *s* adulación
**adulator** [ˈædʒəˌletər] *s* adulador
**adulatory** [ˈædʒələˌtorɪ] *adj* adulatorio
**adulatress** [ˈædʒəˌletrɪs] *s* aduladora
**adult** [əˈdʌlt] o [ˈædʌlt] *adj & s* adulto
**adult education** *s* educación de adultos
**adulterant** [əˈdʌltərənt] *adj & s* adulterante
**adulterate** [əˈdʌltəret] *va* adulterar
**adulteration** [əˌdʌltəˈreʃən] *s* adulteración
**adulterer** [əˈdʌltərər] *s* adúltero
**adulteress** [əˈdʌltərɪs] *s* adúltera
**adulterine** [əˈdʌltərɪn] o [əˈdʌltəraɪn] *adj* adulterino
**adulterize** [əˈdʌltəraɪz] *vn* adulterar
**adulterous** [əˈdʌltərəs] *adj* adúltero
**adultery** [əˈdʌltərɪ] *s* (*pl:* **-ies**) adulterio
**adulthood** [əˈdʌlthʊd] *s* edad adulta; adultez (Am.)
**adumbrate** [ædˈʌmbret] o [ˈædəmbret] *va* bosquejar; presagiar, anunciar; sombrear
**adumbration** [ˌædəmˈbreʃən] *s* bosquejo; presagio, anuncio; sombra
**adv.** abr. de **adverb, adverbial** y **advertisement**
**ad. val.** abr. de **ad valorem**
**ad valorem** [ædvəˈlorem] (Lat.) según el valor
**advance** [ædˈvæns] o [ædˈvɑns] *s* adelanto, avance; alza, aumento de precio; (mach.) avance (*del encendido, de la admisión*); **advances** *spl* propuesta, insinuación; requerimiento amoroso; propuesta indecente; **in advance** delante, al frente; por anticipado, de antemano; *adj* adelantado; anticipado; *va* adelantar; *vn* adelantar (*medrar, hacer progresos*); adelantarse (*moverse hacia adelante; irse delante*); subir (*los precios*)
**advanced** [ædˈvænst] o [ædˈvɑnst] *adj* avanzado; **advanced in years** avanzado de edad, entrado en años
**advanced standing** *s* (educ.) traspaso de matrículas, traspaso de crédito académico
**advanced studies** *spl* altos estudios
**advance guard** *s* (mil.) avanzada
**advancement** [ædˈvænsmənt] o [ædˈvɑnsmənt] *s* adelanto, anticipo; avance, mejora, subida
**advance publicity** *s* publicidad de lanzamiento
**advance sheets** *spl* (print.) hojas del autor
**advantage** [ædˈvæntɪdʒ] o [ædˈvɑntɪdʒ] *s* ventaja; **to have the advantage of** llevar la ventaja a; **to take advantage of** aprovecharse de; abusar de, engañar; **to advantage** ventajosamente; **advantage in** (tennis) ventaja dentro; **advantage out** (tennis) ventaja fuera; *va* aventajar
**advantageous** [ˌædvənˈtedʒəs] *adj* ventajoso
**advent** [ˈædvɛnt] *s* advenimiento; (*cap.*) *s* (eccl.) Adviento
**Adventism** [ˈædvɛntɪzəm] *s* adventismo
**Adventist** [ˈædvɛntɪst] *s* adventista
**adventitia** [ˌædvɛnˈtɪʃɪə] *s* (anat.) adventicia
**adventitious** [ˌædvɛnˈtɪʃəs] *adj* adventicio; (anat., biol., & med.) adventicio
**adventive** [ædˈvɛntɪv] *adj* (bot. & zool.) adventicio
**Advent Sunday** *s* domingo de Adviento, primera domínica de Adviento
**adventure** [ædˈvɛntʃər] *s* aventura; *va* aventurar; **to adventure an opinion** aventurar una opinión; *vn* aventurarse
**adventurer** [ædˈvɛntʃərər] *s* aventurero
**adventuresome** [ædˈvɛntʃərsəm] *adj* aventurero
**adventuress** [ædˈvɛntʃərɪs] *s* aventurera
**adventurous** [ædˈvɛntʃərəs] *adj* aventurero
**adverb** [ˈædvʌrb] *s* adverbio
**adverbial** [ædˈvʌrbɪəl] *adj* adverbial
**adverbialize** [ædˈvʌrbɪəlaɪz] *va* adverbializar
**adverbially** [ædˈvʌrbɪəlɪ] *adv* adverbialmente
**adversaria** [ˌædvərˈsɛrɪə] *spl* adversarios (*notas*)
**adversary** [ˈædvərˌsɛrɪ] *s* (*pl:* **-ies**) adversario; **the Adversary** el enemigo malo
**adversative** [ædˈvʌrsətɪv] *adj & s* (gram.) adversativo
**adverse** [ædˈvʌrs] o [ˈædvʌrs] *adj* adverso
**adversity** [ædˈvʌrsɪtɪ] *s* (*pl:* **-ties**) adversidad (*infortunio*)
**advert** [ædˈvʌrt] *vn* referirse, aludir
**advertent** [ædˈvʌrtənt] *adj* atento
**advertise** [ˈædvərtaɪz] o [ˌædvərˈtaɪz] *va & vn* anunciar
**advertisement** [ˌædvərˈtaɪzmənt] o [ædˈvʌrtɪzmənt] *s* anuncio
**advertiser** [ˈædvərˌtaɪzər] o [ˌædvərˈtaɪzər] *s* anunciante
**advertising** [ˈædvərˌtaɪzɪŋ] o [ˌædvərˈtaɪzɪŋ] *adj* publicitario, anunciador, de anuncios; *s* propaganda, publicidad; anuncios
**advertising agency** *s* empresa anunciadora
**advertising man** *s* empresario de publicidad

**advertising manager** *s* gerente de publicidad
**advice** [æd'vaɪs] *s* consejo (*parecer, dictamen*); noticia, aviso; **a piece of advice** un consejo
**advisability** [æd,vaɪzə'bɪlɪtɪ] *s* conveniencia, propiedad
**advisable** [æd'vaɪzəbəl] *adj* aconsejable
**advise** [æd'vaɪz] *va* aconsejar, asesorar (*dar consejo a*); avisar, informar; **to advise to** + *inf* aconsejar + *inf; vn* aconsejar; **to advise with** aconsejarse de o con
**advised** [æd'vaɪzd] *adj* premeditado, deliberado
**advisedly** [æd'vaɪzɪdlɪ] *adv* premeditadamente, deliberadamente
**advisee** [,ædvaɪ'zi] *s* aconsejado
**advisement** [æd'vaɪzmənt] *s* consideración; **to take under advisement** someter a consideración
**adviser** o **advisor** [æd'vaɪzər] *s* aconsejador, consejero, asesor
**advisory** [æd'vaɪzərɪ] *adj* consejero, asesor
**advocacy** ['ædvəkəsɪ] *s* defensa
**advocate** ['ædvəket] o ['ædvəkɪt] *s* defensor; abogado; ['ædvəket] *va* defender, abogar por
**advt.** abr. de **advertisement**
**adynamia** [,ædɪ'nemɪə] *f* (path.) adinamia
**adynamic** [,ædɪ'næmɪk] *adj* adinámico
**adz** o **adze** [ædz] *s* azuela
**aedile** ['idaɪl] *s* edil
**Aeëtes** [i'itiz] *s* (myth.) Eetes
**A.E.F.** abr. de **American Expeditionary Force**
**Aegean** [i'dʒiən] *s* Archipiélago; mar Egeo (*de los antiguos*)
**aegis** ['idʒɪs] *s* (myth. & fig.) égida
**Aegisthus** [i'dʒɪsθəs] *s* (myth.) Egisto
**Aegospotami** [,igəs'pɑtəmɪ] *s* (hist.) Egospótamos
**Aegyptus** [i'dʒɪptəs] *s* (myth.) Egipto
**Aelfric** ['ælfrɪk] *s* Aelfrico
**Aeneas** [i'niəs] *s* (myth.) Eneas
**Aeneid** [i'niɪd] *s* Eneida
**Aeolian** [i'olɪən] *adj & s* eolio; (*l.c.*) *adj* (geol.) eoliano
**aeolian harp** *s* arpa eolia
**Aeolic** [i'ɑlɪk] *adj & s* eolio (*dialecto*)
**Aeolis** ['iolɪs] *s* la Eólide
**Aeolus** ['ioləs] *s* (myth.) Éolo
**aeon** ['iən] o ['iɑn] *s* eón; (Gnosticism) eón
**aerate** ['ɛret] o ['eəret] *va* airear
**aerated** ['ɛretɪd] o ['eər,etɪd] *adj* aireado
**aeration** [ɛ'reʃən] o [,eə'reʃən] *s* aireación, aeración
**aerial** ['ɛrɪəl] o [e'ɪrɪəl] *adj* aéreo; ['ɛrɪəl] *s* (rad. & telv.) antena
**aerial beacon** *s* aerofaro
**aerialist** ['ɛrɪəlɪst] o [e'ɪrɪəlɪst] *s* volatinero, equilibrista
**aerial torpedo** *s* (aer.) torpedo aéreo
**aerie** ['ɛrɪ] o ['ɪrɪ] *s* var. de **eyrie**
**aeriferous** [ɛ'rɪfərəs] o [,eə'rɪfərəs] *adj* aerífero
**aerification** [,ɛrɪfɪ'keʃən] o [,eərɪfɪ'keʃən] *s* aerificación
**aeriform** ['ɛrɪfɔrm] o ['eərɪ,fɔrm] *adj* aeriforme; inmaterial, imaginario
**aerify** ['ɛrɪfaɪ] o ['eərɪfaɪ] (*pret & pp:* **-fied**) *va* aerificar
**aero** ['ɛro] o ['eəro] *adj* aeronáutico
**aerobatics** [,ɛro'bætɪks] o [,eəro'bætɪks] *spl* acrobacia aérea (*ejercicios*); *ssg* acrobacia aérea (*arte*)
**aerobe** ['ɛrob] o ['eərob] *s* (bact.) aerobio
**aerobic** [ɛ'robɪk] o [,eə'robɪk] *adj* (bact.) aeróbico
**aerodrome** ['ɛrədrom] o ['eərə,drom] *s* aeródromo
**aerodynamic** [,ɛrodaɪ'næmɪk] o [,eərodaɪ'næmɪk] *adj* aerodinámico; **aerodynamics** *ssg* aerodinámica
**aeroembolism** [,ɛro'ɛmbəlɪzəm] o [,eərə'ɛmbəlɪzəm] *s* (path.) aeroembolismo
**aerogram** ['ɛrəgræm] o ['eərə,græm] *s* aerograma (*despacho transmitido por vehículo aéreo; radiograma*)
**aerolite** ['ɛrolaɪt] o ['eəro,laɪt] *s* aerolito
**aerologist** [ɛ'rɑlədʒɪst] o [,eə'rɑlədʒɪst] *s* aerólogo
**aerology** [ɛ'rɑlədʒɪ] o [,eə'rɑlədʒɪ] *s* aerología
**aeromancer** ['ɛro,mænsər] o ['eəro,mænsər] *s* aeromántico
**aeromancy** ['ɛro,mænsɪ] o ['eəro,mænsɪ] *s* aeromancía
**aeromantic** [,ɛro'mæntɪk] o [,eəro'mæntɪk] *adj* aeromántico
**aeromechanic** [,ɛromɪ'kænɪk] o [,eəromɪ'kænɪk] *adj* aeromecánico; *s* mécanico de aviación; **aeromechanics** *ssg* aeromecánica
**aeromechanical** [,ɛromɪ'kænɪkəl] o [,eəromɪ'kænɪkəl] *adj* aeromecánico
**aerometer** [ɛ'rɑmɪtər] o [,eə'rɑmɪtər] *s* aerómetro
**aeronaut** ['ɛrənɔt] o ['eərə,nɔt] *s* aeronauta
**aeronautic** [,ɛrə'nɔtɪk] o [,eərə'nɔtɪk] *adj* aeronáutico; **aeronautics** *ssg* aeronáutica
**aeronautical** [,ɛrə'nɔtɪkəl] o [,eərə'nɔtɪkəl] *adj* aeronáutico
**aerophagia** [,ɛro'fedʒɪə] o [,eəro'fedʒɪə] *s* (path.) aerofagia
**aerophobia** [,ɛro'fobɪə] o [,eəro'fobɪə] *s* (path.) aerofobia
**aerophore** ['ɛrofor] o ['eəro,for] *s* (med. & min.) aeróforo
**aerophotograph** [,ɛrə'fotəgræf], [,eərə'fotəgræf], [,ɛrə'fotəgrɑf] o [,eərə'fotəgrɑf] *s* aerofotografía (*imagen*)
**aerophotography** [,ɛrəfə'tɑgrəfɪ] o [,eərəfə'tɑgrəfɪ] *s* aerofotografía (*arte*)
**aeroplane** ['ɛrəplen] o ['eərə,plen] *s* aeroplano, avión
**aeroscope** ['ɛroskop] o ['eəro,skop] *s* aeroscopio
**aerosol** ['ɛrosol] o ['eəro,sol] *s* (physical chem.) aerosol
**aerospace** ['ɛrospes] o ['eəro,spes] *adj* aéroespacial
**aerostat** ['ɛrostæt] o ['eəro,stæt] *s* aeróstato (*aparato*); aeróstata (*persona*)
**aerostatic** [,ɛro'stætɪk] o [,eəro'stætɪk] *adj* aerostático; **aerostatics** *ssg* aerostática
**aerostatical** [,ɛro'stætɪkəl] o [,eəro'stætɪkəl] *adj* aerostático
**aerostation** [,ɛro'steʃən] o [,eəro'steʃən] *s* aerostación
**aerotherapeutics** [,ɛro,θɛrə'pjutɪks] o [,eəro,θɛrə'pjutɪks] *ssg* o **aerotherapy** [,ɛro'θɛrəpɪ] o [,eəro'θɛrəpɪ] *s* aeroterapia
**aery** ['ɛrɪ] o ['ɪrɪ] *s* (*pl:* **-ies**) var. de **eyrie**
**Aeschines** ['ɛskɪniz] *s* Esquines
**Aeschylus** ['ɛskɪləs] *s* Esquilo
**Aesculapian** [,ɛskjə'lepɪən] *s* Esculapio (*cualquier médico*); *adj* de Esculapio; medicinal
**Aesculapius** [,ɛskjə'lepɪəs] *s* (myth.) Esculapio
**Aesop** ['isɑp] *s* Esopo
**Aesopian** [i'sopɪən] *adj* esópico
**aesthete** ['ɛsθit] *s* esteta
**aesthetic** [ɛs'θɛtɪk] *adj* estético; **aesthetics** *ssg* estética
**aesthetically** [ɛs'θɛtɪkəlɪ] *adv* estéticamente
**aesthetician** [,ɛsθɪ'tɪʃən] *s* estético
**aestival** ['ɛstɪvəl] o [ɛs'taɪvəl] *adj* estival
**aestivate** ['ɛstɪvet] *vn* veranear; (zool.) pasar el estío en estado de estivación
**aestivation** [,ɛstɪ'veʃən] *s* veraneo; (bot. & zool.) estivación
**aether** ['iθər] *s* éter (*los espacios celestes*); (phys.) éter (*materia hipotética*)
**aethereal** [ɪ'θɪrɪəl] *adj* etéreo; (phys.) etéreo
**aetiology** [,itɪ'ɑlədʒɪ] *s* etiología
**Aetna, Mount** ['ɛtnə] el monte Etna
**Aetolia** [i'tolɪə] *s* la Etolia
**A.F.** o **a.f.** abr. de **audio frequency**
**afar** [ə'fɑr] *adv* lejos; **from afar** de lejos, desde lejos
**affability** [,æfə'bɪlɪtɪ] *s* afabilidad
**affable** ['æfəbəl] *adj* afable
**affair** [ə'fɛr] *s* asunto, negocio; lance, episodio; amorío, aventura; encuentro, combate; **affairs** *spl* negocios
**affair of honor** *s* lance de honor
**affect** [ə'fɛkt] *va* influir en; impresionar, enternecer; aficionarse a; afectar (*poner demasiado estudio en; fingir; asumir*)
**affectation** [,æfɛk'teʃən] *s* afectación
**affected** [ə'fɛktɪd] *adj* afectado
**affecting** [ə'fɛktɪŋ] *adj* impresionante, enternecedor
**affection** [ə'fɛkʃən] *s* afecto, cariño, afección; (med.) afección
**affectionate** [ə'fɛkʃənɪt] *adj* afectuoso, cariñoso

**affective** [ə'fɛktɪv] *adj* afectivo
**afferent** ['æfərənt] *adj* (physiol.) aferente
**affiance** [ə'faɪəns] *s* palabra de casamiento; confianza; *va* dar palabra de casamiento a
**affianced** [ə'faɪənst] *adj* prometido
**affidavit** [,æfɪ'devɪt] *s* declaración jurada, acta notarial, afidávit
**affiliate** [ə'fɪlɪet] *adj* afiliado; *s* afiliado; (com.) filial; *va* afiliar; **to affiliate oneself with** afiliarse a; *vn* afiliarse; **to affiliate with** afiliarse a
**affiliation** [ə,fɪlɪ'eʃən] *s* afiliación
**affinity** [ə'fɪnɪtɪ] *s* (*pl:* **-ties**) afinidad; amante; (biol. & chem.) afinidad
**affirm** [ə'fʌrm] *va & vn* afirmar
**affirmation** [,æfər'meʃən] *s* afirmación
**affirmative** [ə'fʌrmətɪv] *adj* afirmativo; *s* afirmativa
**affix** ['æfɪks] *s* añadidura; (gram.) afijo; [ə'fɪks] *va* añadir; atribuir (*p.ej., culpa*); poner (*una firma, sello, etc.*)
**affixation** [,æfɪk'seʃən] *s* (gram.) afijación
**afflatus** [ə'fletəs] *s* aflato, ciencia infusa
**afflict** [ə'flɪkt] *va* afligir; **to be afflicted with** sufrir de
**affliction** [ə'flɪkʃən] *s* aflicción; desgracia, infortunio; achaque, mal
**afflictive** [ə'flɪktɪv] *adj* aflictivo
**affluence** ['æfluəns] *s* afluencia, abundancia; opulencia
**affluent** ['æfluənt] *adj* afluente, abundante; opulento; *s* afluente
**afflux** ['æflʌks] *s* afluencia (*acción de afluir*); (med.) aflujo
**afford** [ə'fɔrd] *va* producir, proporcionar; **to be able to afford** tener con que comprar, tener con que pagar, tener los medios para, poder permitirse
**afforest** [ə'fɑrɪst] o [ə'fɔrɪst] *va* repoblar (*con árboles jóvenes*)
**afforestation** [ə,fɑrɪs'teʃən] o [ə,fɔrɪs'teʃən] *s* repoblación forestal, aforestalación
**affranchise** [ə'fræntʃaɪz] *va* var. de **enfranchise**
**affray** [ə'fre] *s* riña, pendencia
**affricate** ['æfrɪkɪt] *s* (phonet.) africada
**affricative** [ə'frɪkətɪv] *adj* (phonet.) africado; *s* (phonet.) africada
**affront** [ə'frʌnt] *s* afrenta; *va* afrentar; arrostrar
**affusion** [ə'fjuʒən] *s* (med.) afusión
**Afghan** ['æfgən] o ['æfgæn] *adj & s* afgano; (*l.c.*) *s* manta de estambre, cubrecama de estambre
**Afghanistan** [æf'gænɪstæn] *s* el Afganistán
**afield** [ə'fild] *adv* en el campo, al campo; afuera
**afire** [ə'faɪr] *adj & adv* ardiendo
**aflame** [ə'flem] *adj & adv* en llamas
**afloat** [ə'flot] *adj & adv* a flote; a bordo; sin rumbo; inundado; en circulación
**aflutter** [ə'flʌtər] *adj & adv* en agitación
**afoot** [ə'fut] *adj & adv* a pie; en movimiento
**aforementioned** [ə'for'mɛnʃənd] o **aforesaid** [ə'for,sɛd] *adj* ya mencionado
**aforethought** [ə'for,θɔt] *adj* premeditado; *s* premeditación
**aforetime** [ə'for,taɪm] *adv* antiguamente
**a fortiori** [e,fɔrʃɪ'orɪ] (Lat.) con mayor razón
**afoul** [ə'faul] *adj & adv* en colisión; enredado; **to run afoul of** enredarse con
**afraid** [ə'fred] *adj* asustado, espantado; **to be afraid (of)** tener miedo (a o de); **to be afraid to** + *inf* tener miedo de + *inf*
**afresh** [ə'frɛʃ] *adv* de nuevo, otra vez
**Africa** ['æfrɪkə] *s* África
**African** ['æfrɪkən] *adj & s* africano
**Africanist** ['æfrɪkənɪst] *s* africanista
**African rue** *s* (bot.) alárgama
**Afrikaans** [,æfrɪ'kɑns] *s* afrikaans
**Afrikander** [,æfrɪ'kændər] *s* africander
**Afro-American** ['æfroə'mɛrɪkən] *adj & s* afroamericano
**Afro-Asian** ['æfro'eʒən] o ['æfro'eʃən] *adj* afroasiático
**aft** [æft] o [ɑft] *adj & adv* (naut.) en popa, a popa
**after** ['æftər] o ['ɑftər] *adj* siguiente; *adv* después; *prep* después de; según; al cabo de; **to run after** correr tras; **after all** al fin y al cabo; **after you!** ¡Vd. primero!; *conj* después que o después de que
**afterbirth** ['æftər,bʌrθ] o ['ɑftər,bʌrθ] *s* secundinas
**afterburner** ['æftər,bʌrnər] o ['ɑftər,bʌrnər] *s* (aer.) posquemador
**afterburning** ['æftər,bʌrnɪŋ] o ['ɑftər,bʌrnɪŋ] *s* (aer.) poscombustión
**aftercare** ['æftər,kɛr] o ['ɑftər,kɛr] *s* tratamiento postoperatorio
**afterclap** ['æftər,klæp] o ['ɑftər,klæp] *s* golpe inesperado
**aftercost** ['æftər,kɔst] o ['ɑftər,kɔst] *s* gastos adicionales, gastos de mantenimiento
**aftercrop** ['æftər,krɑp] o ['ɑftər,krɑp] *s* segunda cosecha
**afterdamp** ['æftər,dæmp] o ['ɑftər,dæmp] *s* (min.) gases de explosión
**afterdeck** ['æftər,dɛk] o ['ɑftər,dɛk] *s* (naut.) cubierta de popa
**after-dinner** ['æftər,dɪnər] o ['ɑftər,dɪnər] *adj* de sobremesa
**after-dinner speaker** *s* orador de sobremesa
**after-dinner speech** *s* discurso de sobremesa
**aftereffect** ['æftərɪ,fɛkt] o ['ɑftərɪ,fɛkt] *s* efecto resultante, consecuencia
**afterglow** ['æftər,glo] o ['ɑftər,glo] *s* brillo prolongado; resplandor crepuscular
**after-hours** ['æftər'aurz] o ['ɑftər'aurz] *adv* después del trabajo
**afterimage** ['æftər,ɪmɪdʒ] o ['ɑftər,ɪmɪdʒ] *s* postimagen
**afterlife** ['æftər,laɪf] o ['ɑftər,laɪf] *s* trasmundo, vida venidera; resto de la vida
**afterlove** ['æftər,lʌv] o ['ɑftər,lʌv] *s* segunda pasión, nuevos amores
**aftermath** ['æftərmæθ] o ['ɑftərmæθ] *s* segunda cosecha; consecuencias, consecuencias desastrosas
**aftermost** ['æftərmost] o ['ɑftərmost] *adj* último; trasero, posterior
**afternoon** ['æftər'nun] o ['ɑftər'nun] *s* tarde
**afterpains** ['æftər,penz] o ['ɑftər,penz] *spl* dolores de sobreparto, entuertos; dolor postoperatorio
**after-shaving** ['æftər,ʃevɪŋ] o ['ɑftər,ʃevɪŋ] *adj* para después de afeitarse
**aftershock** ['æftər,ʃɑk] o ['ɑftər,ʃɑk] *s* temblor secundario
**aftertaste** ['æftər,test] o ['ɑftər,test] *s* resabio, dejo, gustillo
**afterthought** ['æftər,θɔt] o ['ɑftər,θɔt] *s* idea tardía, expediente tardío, nueva ocurrencia
**aftertime** ['æftər,taɪm] o ['ɑftər,taɪm] *s* tiempo venidero
**afterward** ['æftərwərd] o ['ɑftərwərd] o **afterwards** ['æftərwərdz] o ['ɑftərwərdz] *adv* después, luego; **long afterwards** mucho tiempo después
**afterwhile** ['æftər'hwaɪl] o ['ɑftər'hwaɪl] *adv* dentro de poco
**afterworld** ['æftər,wʌrld] o ['ɑftər,wʌrld] *s* mundo futuro, vida venidera
**again** [ə'gɛn] o [ə'gen] *adv* otra vez, de nuevo; además, por otra parte; **as much again** otro tanto más; **now and again** de vez en cuando; **to** + *inf* + **again** volver a + *inf*; **again and again** repetidamente
**against** [ə'gɛnst] o [ə'genst] *prep* contra; cerca de; en contraste con; por; para; **to be against** oponerse a; **to go against the grain** desagradar, repugnar
**agalloch** [ə'gæləks] *s* (bot.) agáloco
**Agamemnon** [,ægə'mɛmnɑn] *s* (myth.) Agamenón
**agamic** [ə'gæmɪk] *adj* (biol.) ágamo
**agamogenesis** [,ægəmo'dʒɛnɪsɪs] *s* (biol.) agamogénesis
**Aganippe** [,ægə'nɪpi] *s* (myth.) Aganipe
**agape** [ə'gep] *adj & adv* con la boca abierta; abierto de par en par
**agar** ['ɑgər] o ['ægər] *s* agar-agar; (bot.) agáloco
**agar-agar** ['ɑgər'ɑgər] o ['ægər'ægər] *s* agar-agar
**agaric** ['ægərɪk] o [ə'gærɪk] *s* (bot.) agárico; (pharm.) agárico blanco
**agate** ['ægɪt] *s* (mineral.) ágata; bolilla de cristal ágata; (print.) tipo de 5½ puntos
**agateware** ['ægɪt,wɛr] *s* porcelana de imita-

ción de ágata; utensilios de hierro, de imitación de ágata
**Agatha** [ˈægəθə] *s* Ágata, Águeda
**agave** [əˈgevɪ] *s* (bot.) agave
**age** [edʒ] *s* edad; vejez, ancianidad; generación; siglo (*cien años*); (psychol.) edad mental; (coll.) siglo, eternidad (*largo tiempo*); **ages** *spl* (coll.) siglo, eternidad (*largo tiempo*); **of age** mayor de edad; **to act one's age** actuar (*una persona*) de acuerdo con su edad; **to come of age** alcanzar su mayoría de edad, llegar a mayor edad; **under age** menor de edad; *va* envejecer; *vn* envejecer o envejecerse
**aged** [ˈedʒɪd] *adj* viejo, anciano, envejecido; de la vejez; [edʒd] *adj* de la edad de
**ageless** [ˈedʒlɪs] *adj* eternamente joven
**agelong** [ˈedʒˌlɔŋ] o [ˈedʒˌlɑŋ] *adj* eterno, secular
**agency** [ˈedʒənsɪ] *s* (*pl:* **-cies**) agencia; acción, medio
**agenda** [əˈdʒɛndə] *spl* cosas que se han de hacer; *ssg* temario, agenda
**agennesis** [ˌædʒəˈnisɪs] *s* (physiol.) agenesia
**agent** [ˈedʒənt] *s* agente; (gram.) agente; (coll.) agente viajero
**agent provocateur** [æˈʒɑ̃ prɔvɔkɑˈtʌr] *s* agente provocador
**age of discretion** *s* edad de discreción
**Age of Enlightenment** *s* siglo de las luces (*siglo dieciocho*)
**ageratum** [ˌædʒəˈretəm] o [əˈdʒɛrətəm] *s* (bot.) agérato
**ageusia** [əˈgjusɪə] *s* (path.) ageusia
**agglomerant** [əˈglɑmərənt] *s* aglomerante
**agglomerate** [əˈglɑmərɪt] o [əˈglɑməret] *s* aglomeración; (geol.) aglomerado; *adj* aglomerado; [əˈglɑməret] *va* aglomerar; *vn* aglomerarse
**agglomeration** [əˌglɑməˈreʃən] *s* aglomeración
**agglutinate** [əˈglutɪnɪt] o [əˈglutɪnet] *adj* aglutinado; [əˈglutɪnet] *va* aglutinar; *vn* aglutinarse
**agglutination** [əˌglutɪˈneʃən] *s* aglutinación
**agglutinative** [əˈglutɪˌnetɪv] *adj* aglutinante
**agglutinative languages** *spl* lenguas aglutinantes
**agglutinin** [əˈglutɪnɪn] *s* (biochem.) aglutinina
**aggrandize** [ˈægrəndaɪz] o [əˈgrændaɪz] *va* agrandar, engrandecer; **to aggrandize oneself** agrandarse, engrandecerse
**aggrandizement** [əˈgrændɪzmənt] *s* agrandamiento, engrandecimiento
**aggravate** [ˈægrəvet] *va* agravar; (coll.) irritar, exasperar
**aggravating** [ˈægrəˌvetɪŋ] *adj* agravante; (coll.) irritante, exasperante
**aggravation** [ˌægrəˈveʃən] *s* agravación, agravamiento; (coll.) irritación
**aggregate** [ˈægrɪgɪt] o [ˈægrɪget] *adj & s* agregado; total; [ˈægrɪget] *va* agregar, unir, juntar; ascender a
**aggregation** [ˌægrɪˈgeʃən] *s* agregación
**aggression** [əˈgrɛʃən] *s* agresión
**aggressive** [əˈgrɛsɪv] *adj* agresivo
**aggressor** [əˈgrɛsər] *s* agresor
**aggrieve** [əˈgriv] *va* afligir, acongojar, oprimir
**aghast** [əˈgæst] o [əˈgɑst] *adj* horrorizado
**agile** [ˈædʒɪl] o [ˈædʒaɪl] *adj* ágil
**agility** [əˈdʒɪlɪtɪ] *s* agilidad
**aging** [ˈedʒɪŋ] *s* envejecimiento; añejamiento (*p.ej., del vino*)
**agio** [ˈædʒɪo] *s* (*pl:* **-os**) agio
**agitate** [ˈædʒɪtet] *va* agitar; *vn* agitar (*promover cuestiones*)
**agitation** [ˌædʒɪˈteʃən] *s* agitación
**agitator** [ˈædʒɪˌtetər] *s* agitador
**Aglaia** [əˈgleə] *s* (myth.) Aglaya
**agleam** [əˈglim] *adj & adv* reluciente
**aglitter** [əˈglɪtər] *adj & adv* rutilante
**aglow** [əˈglo] *adj & adv* fulgurante
**agnate** [ˈægnet] *adj & s* agnado
**agnation** [ægˈneʃən] *s* agnación; parentesco
**Agnes** [ˈægnɪs] *s* Inés
**agnostic** [ægˈnɑstɪk] *adj & s* agnóstico
**agnosticism** [ægˈnɑstɪsɪzəm] *s* agnosticismo
**agnus castus** [ˈægnəsˈkæstəs] *s* (bot.) agnocasto, sauzgatillo
**Agnus Dei** [ˈægnəsˈdiaɪ] *s* agnusdéi
**ago** [əˈgo] *adj & adv* hace, p.ej., **a long time ago** hace mucho tiempo
**agog** [əˈgɑg] *adj* ansioso, anhelante; curioso; *adv* con ansiedad; curiosamente; **to set agog** excitar
**agonic** [eˈgɑnɪk] *adj* (geom.) ágono
**agonic line** *s* (phys.) línea agónica
**agonistic** [ˌægəˈnɪstɪk] *adj* agonal, agonístico; **agonistics** *ssg* agonística
**agonize** [ˈægənaɪz] *va* atormentar; *vn* hacer grandes esfuerzos; retorcerse de dolor, sufrir intensamente
**agony** [ˈægənɪ] *s* (*pl:* **-nies**) agonía (*aflicción extremada; lucha postrema contra la muerte*); lucha, esfuerzos; angustia, congoja
**agony column** *s* (coll.) anuncios en un periódico relativos a parientes o amigos desaparecidos
**agora** [ˈægərə] *s* (*pl:* **-rae** [ri]) *s* ágora
**agoraphobia** [ˌægərəˈfobɪə] *s* (psychopath.) agorafobia
**agouti** [əˈgutɪ] *s* (*pl:* **-tis** o **-ties**) (zool.) acutí
**agrarian** [əˈgrɛrɪən] *adj* agrario; agrariense; *mf* agrariense
**agrarianism** [əˈgrɛrɪənɪzəm] *s* agrarianismo
**agree** [əˈgri] *vn* concordar, estar de acuerdo, ponerse de acuerdo; sentar bien; (gram.) concordar; **to agree on** convenir en; **to agree with** concordar con, estar de acuerdo con; sentar bien; (gram.) concordar con
**agreeable** [əˈgriəbəl] *adj* agradable; conforme, satisfecho
**agreement** [əˈgrimənt] *s* acuerdo, convenio; concordancia, conformidad; (gram.) concordancia; **in agreement** de acuerdo; **in agreement with** de acuerdo con
**agric.** abr. de **agriculture**
**agricultural** [ˌægrɪˈkʌltʃərəl] *adj* agrícola
**agriculturalist** [ˌægrɪˈkʌltʃərəlɪst] *s* agricultor
**agriculture** [ˈægrɪˌkʌltʃər] *s* agricultura
**agriculturist** [ˌægrɪˈkʌltʃərɪst] *s* agricultor
**agrimony** [ˈægrɪˌmonɪ] *s* (*pl:* **-nies**) (bot.) agrimonia
**Agrippa** [əˈgrɪpə] *s* Agripa
**agronomic** [ˌægrəˈnɑmɪk] *adj* agronómico
**agronomist** [əˈgrɑnəmɪst] *s* agrónomo
**agronomy** [əˈgrɑnəmɪ] *s* agronomía
**aground** [əˈgraʊnd] *adj & adv* varado, encallado; **to run aground** varar, encallar
**agt.** abr. de **agent**
**ague** [ˈegju] *s* escalofrío; fiebre intermitente
**aguish** [ˈegjuɪʃ] *adj* escalofriado; palúdico
**ah** [ɑ] *interj* ¡ah!
**aha** [ɑˈhɑ] *interj* ¡ajá!
**ahead** [əˈhɛd] *adj & adv* delante, al frente; adelante; **straight ahead** todo seguido; **to get ahead** adelantarse; **to get ahead of** adelantarse a; **to go ahead** seguir adelante; avanzar; continuar; **to send ahead** enviar por delante; **ahead of** antes de; delante de; al frente de
**ahem** [əˈhɛm] *interj* ¡eh!; ¡ejem!
**ahorse** [əˈhɔrs] *adj & adv* a caballo
**ahoy** [əˈhɔɪ] *interj* (naut.) ¡ha!; **ship ahoy!** ¡ah del barco!
**aid** [ed] *s* ayuda, auxilio; (mil.) ayudante; **to come to the aid of** acudir en socorro a; *va* ayudar; **to aid and abet** auxiliar e incitar, ser cómplice de; *vn* ayudar
**aid-de-camp** [ˈeddəˈkæmp] *s* (*pl:* **aids-de-camp**) var. de **aide-de-camp**
**aide** [ed] *s* (mil.) ayudante
**aide-de-camp** [ˈeddəˈkæmp] *s* (*pl:* **aides-de-camp**) (mil.) ayudante de campo, edecán
**aigrette** [ˈegrɛt] o [eˈgrɛt] *s* airón, penacho; (elec.) airón (*penachos en los ángulos de los cuerpos electrizados*); (orn.) garceta
**ail** [el] *va* afligir, molestar, inquietar; **what ails you?** ¿qué tiene Vd?; *vn* sufrir, estar enfermo
**ailanthus** [eˈlænθəs] *s* (bot.) ailanto
**aileron** [ˈelərɑn] *s* (aer.) alerón
**ailing** [ˈelɪŋ] *adj* enfermo, achacoso
**ailment** [ˈelmənt] *s* enfermedad, achaque
**aim** [em] *s* puntería, encaro; intento, blanco, mira; punto de mira; **to miss one's aim** errar el tiro; **to take aim** apuntar; *va* apuntar, encarar; dirigir (*p.ej., una observación*);

*vn* apuntar; intentar; **to aim to** + *inf* mirar a + *inf*

**aimless** [ˈemlɪs] *adj* sin designio, sin objeto

**ain't** [ent] (dial. & illit.) contracción de **am not** y equivalente a **am not, is not, are not, have not** y **has not**

**air** [ɛr] *s* aire; (mus.) aire; **by air** por vía aérea, en avión; **in mid air** entre cielo y tierra; **in the open air** al aire libre; **on the air** en antena, en la radio; **to fly through the air** volar por los aires; **to let the air out of** desinflar (*un neumático*); **to put on airs** darse aires; **to put on the air** (rad.) llevar a las antenas; **to walk** o **tread on air** no pisar en el suelo, estar bañado en agua de rosas; *adj* aéreo; aeronáutico; *va* airear, ventilar; radiofundir; (fig.) ventilar

**air-atomic** [ˈɛrəˈtɑmɪk] *adj* aéro-atómico

**air attack** *s* ataque aéreo

**air base** *s* base aérea

**air beacon** *s* faro aéreo

**air bends** *spl* (path.) embolia aérea

**air bladder** *s* (zool.) vejiga natatoria

**air-borne** [ˈɛr,born] *adj* (mil.) aéreo, aerotransportado; llevado por el aire

**air brake** *s* freno de aire, freno neumático

**air bridge** *s* puente aéreo

**air brush** *s* aerógrafo, pincel aéreo, pulverizador de aire comprimido

**air castle** *s* castillo en el aire

**air chamber** *s* cámara de aire

**air cock** *s* llave de admisión de aire, llave de escape de aire

**air-condition** [ˈɛrkənˈdɪʃən] *va* proveer de maquinaria acondicionadora del aire, climatizar

**air-conditioned** [ˈɛrkənˈdɪʃənd] *adj* con aire acondicionado

**air conditioner** *s* acondicionador de aire

**air conditioning** *s* acondicionamiento del aire, aire acondicionado

**air-cool** [ˈɛr,kul] *va* enfriar por aire

**air-cooling** [ˈɛr,kulɪŋ] *s* enfriamiento por aire

**air-core transformer** [ˈɛr,kor] *s* (elec.) transformador de núcleo de aire

**air corps** *s* cuerpo de aviación

**aircraft** [ˈɛr,kræft] o [ˈɛr,krɑft] *ssg* máquina de volar; *spl* máquinas de volar

**aircraft carrier** *s* portaaviones

**air cushion** *s* almohada de aire, colchón de aire

**air drill** *s* taladro neumático

**airdrome** [ˈɛr,drom] *s* aeródromo

**airdrop** [ˈɛr,drɑp] *s* (aer.) lanzamiento; (*pret & pp:* **-dropped** o **-dropt;** *ger:* **-dropping**) *va* (aer.) lanzar

**air field** *s* campo de aviación

**air fleet** *s* flotilla militar aérea

**airfoil** [ˈɛr,fɔɪl] *s* (aer.) superficie de sustentación

**air force** *s* fuerza aérea, ejército del aire

**Air Force Academy** *s* (U.S.A.) Academia General del Aire

**air frame** *s* (aer.) armadura de avión

**air gap** *s* (phys.) entrehierro

**air-ground** [ˈɛrˈgraʊnd] *adj* aeroterrestre

**air gun** *s* escopeta de aire comprimido

**air hole** *s* respiradero; (aer.) vacío; (found.) sopladura

**air hostess** *s* azafata, aeromoza

**airing** [ˈɛrɪŋ] *s* ventilación; secamiento al aire; paseo para tomar el aire; (fig.) ventilación; **to take an airing** orearse

**air lane** *s* ruta aérea

**airless** [ˈɛrlɪs] *adj* sin brisa, tranquilo

**airlift** [ˈɛr,lɪft] *s* puente aéreo; *va* transportar por puente aéreo

**air line** *s* línea aérea

**air liner** *s* avión de travesía, transaéreo

**air lock** *s* cámara intermedia (*entre presiones atmosféricas diferentes*)

**air mail** *s* correo aéreo, correo por avión

**air-mail** [ˈɛr,mel] *adj* aeropostal

**air-mail letter** *s* carta por avión, carta aérea

**air-mail pilot** *s* aviador postal

**air-mail stamp** *s* sello aéreo

**airman** [ˈɛrmən] o [ˈɛr,mæn] *s* (*pl:* **-men**) aviador; (mil.) aviador, soldado del cuerpo de aviación

**air map** *s* aeromapa

**air-minded** [ˈɛr,maɪndɪd] *adj* adicto a la aviación

**Air Ministry** *s* (Brit.) Ministerio del Aire

**air passage** *s* aire aprisionado; fuga o escape de aire

**airplane** [ˈɛr,plen] *s* avión

**airplane carrier** *s* portaaviones

**air plant** *s* (bot.) epífita

**air pocket** *s* (aer.) depresión, bolsa de aire, bache aéreo

**airport** [ˈɛr,port] *s* aeropuerto

**air power** *s* poder aéreo

**air pressure** *s* presión atmosférica

**air pump** *s* bomba de aire, máquina neumática

**air raid** *s* ataque aéreo

**air-raid alarm** [ˈɛr,red] *s* alarma aérea

**air-raid drill** *s* ejercicio antiaéreo, simulacro de ataque aéreo

**air-raid shelter** *s* abrigo antiaéreo, refugio antiaéreo

**air-raid warden** *s* vigilante contra ataques aéreos

**air-raid warning** *s* alarma aérea

**air rifle** *s* escopeta de aire comprimido, escopeta de viento

**air sac** *s* (orn.) celda para aire

**air service** *s* servicio aéreo

**air shaft** *s* respiradero

**airship** [ˈɛr,ʃɪp] *s* aeronave

**airsick** [ˈɛr,sɪk] *adj* mareado en el aire

**airsickness** [ˈɛr,sɪknɪs] *s* mareo del aire, mal de vuelo

**air sleeve** o **air sock** *s* veleta de manga

**airstrip** [ˈɛr,strɪp] *s* pista de despegue; pista de aterrizaje

**air supremacy** *s* dominio del aire

**airtight** [ˈɛrˈtaɪt] *adj* hermético, herméticamente cerrado, estanco al aire

**air-traffic control** [ˈɛr,træfɪk] *s* control de tránsito aéreo

**airwaves** [ˈɛr,wevz] *spl* ondas de radio

**airway** [ˈɛr,we] *s* aerovía, vía aérea; (min.) galería de ventilación

**airway lighting** *s* (aer.) balizaje

**air well** *s* respiradero, pozo de ventilación

**airwoman** [ˈɛr,wʊmən] *s* (*pl:* **-women**) aviadora

**airworthy** [ˈɛr,wʌrðɪ] *adj* en condiciones de vuelo

**airy** [ˈɛrɪ] *adj* (*comp:* **-ier;** *super:* **-iest**) airoso; aireado; alegre; impertinente; (coll.) afectado

**aisle** [aɪl] *s* pasillo (*en el teatro, la iglesia, etc.*); nave (*en una fábrica, tienda, etc.*); alameda, paseo; (arch.) nave lateral

**Aix-la-Chapelle** [,ekslɑʃɑˈpɛl] *s* Aquisgrán

**ajar** [əˈdʒɑr] *adj* entreabierto, entornado; en desacuerdo

**Ajax** [ˈedʒæks] *s* (myth.) Áyax

**Ajax the Less** *s* (myth.) Áyax el Pequeño

**akene** [eˈkin] *s* var. de **achene**

**akimbo** [əˈkɪmbo] *adj & adv* en jarras; **with arms akimbo** en jarras

**akin** [əˈkɪn] *adj* emparentado; semejante

**alabamine** [,æləˈbæmin] *s* (chem.) alabamio

**alabaster** [ˈælə,bæstər] o [ˈælə,bɑstər] *s* alabastro; *adj* alabastrino

**à la carte** [ɑlɑˈkɑrt] según lista, a la carta

**alacrity** [əˈlækrɪtɪ] *s* alacridad, presteza

**Aladdin** [əˈlædɪn] *s* Aladino

**Aladdin's lamp** *s* lámpara de Aladino

**à la king** [ɑlɑˈkɪŋ] con salsa de crema, harina, hongos, pimientos, etc.

**à la mode** [ɑlɑˈmod] o [,æləˈmod] a la moda; servido con helado encima

**Alaric** [ˈælərɪk] *s* Alarico

**alarm** [əˈlɑrm] *s* alarma; **to sound the alarm** dar la alarma; *va* alarmar, inquietar

**alarm clock** *s* despertador, reloj despertador

**alarming** [əˈlɑrmɪŋ] *adj* alarmante

**alarmist** [əˈlɑrmɪst] *s* alarmista

**alary** [ˈelərɪ] o [ˈælərɪ] *adj* alario

**Alas.** abr. de **Alaska**

**alas** [əˈlæs] o [əˈlɑs] *interj* ¡ay!, ¡ay de mí!

**alate** [ˈelet] *adj* alado

**alb** [ælb] *s* alba (*vestidura de lienzo blanco de sacerdote*)

**albacore** [ˈælbəkor] *s* (ichth.) albacora; (ichth.) germón (*Germo alalunga*)

**Albanian** [ælˈbenɪən] *adj & s* albanés o albano

**albatross** ['ælbətrɔs] o ['ælbətrɑs] *s* (orn.) albatros
**albeit** [ɔl'biɪt] *conj* aunque
**Albert** ['ælbərt] *s* Alberto
**Albertus Magnus** [æl'bʌrtəs 'mægnəs] *s* Alberto Magno
**Albigenses** [ˌælbɪ'dʒɛnsiz] *spl* albigenses
**Albigensian** [ˌælbɪ'dʒɛnsɪən] *adj* albigense
**albinic** [æl'bɪnɪk] *adj* albino
**albinism** ['ælbɪnɪzəm] *s* albinismo
**albino** [æl'baɪno] *s* (*pl:* **-nos**) albino
**Albion** ['ælbɪən] *s* (poet.) Albión (*Inglaterra*)
**albite** ['ælbaɪt] *s* (mineral.) albita
**albugineous** [ˌælbjə'dʒɪnɪəs] *adj* albugíneo
**albugo** [æl'bjugo] *s* (*pl:* **-gines** [dʒɪniz]) (path.) albugo
**album** ['ælbəm] *s* álbum
**albumen** [æl'bjumən] *s* (bot.) albumen; (biochem.) albúmina
**albumin** [æl'bjumɪn] *s* (biochem.) albúmina
**albuminimeter** [ælˌbjumɪ'nɪmɪtər] *s* albuminímetro
**albuminoid** [æl'bjumɪnɔɪd] *adj* albuminoideo; *s* albuminoide
**albuminous** [æl'bjumɪnəs] *adj* albuminoso
**albuminuria** [ælˌbjumɪ'njʊrɪə] o [ælˌbjumɪ'nʊrɪə] *s* (path.) albuminuria
**alburnum** [æl'bʌrnəm] *s* alborno, alburno, albura
**alcazar** ['ælkəzɑr] o [æl'kæzər] *s* alcázar
**Alcestis** [æl'sɛstɪs] *s* (myth.) Alcestes
**alchemic** [æl'kɛmɪk] o **alchemical** [æl'kɛmɪkəl] *adj* alquímico
**alchemist** ['ælkɪmɪst] *s* alquimista
**alchemy** ['ælkɪmɪ] *s* alquimia
**Alcibiades** [ˌælsɪ'baɪədiz] *s* Alcibíades
**Alcmene** [ælk'minɪ] *s* (myth.) Alcmena
**alcohol** ['ælkəhɔl] o ['ælkəhɑl] *s* alcohol
**alcoholate** ['ælkəhɔlet] o ['ælkəhɑlet] *s* (pharm.) alcoholado, alcoholato
**alcoholic** [ˌælkə'hɔlɪk] o [ˌælkə'hɑlɪk] *adj* alcohólico; (path.) alcohólico, alcoholizado; *s* (path.) alcohólico, alcoholizado
**alcoholism** ['ælkəhɔlɪzəm] o ['ælkəhɑlɪzəm] *s* (path.) alcoholismo
**alcoholization** [ˌælkəˌhɔlɪ'zeʃən] o [ˌælkəˌhɑlɪ'zeʃən] *s* alcoholización
**alcoholometer** [ˌælkəhɔ'lɑmɪtər] o [ˌælkəhɑ'lɑmɪtər] *s* alcoholímetro
**Alcoran** [ˌælko'rɑn] o [ˌælko'ræn] *s* Alcorán
**alcove** ['ælkov] *s* (arch.) trasalcoba; gabinete; cenador, glorieta
**Alcuin** ['ælkwɪn] *s* Alcuino
**Alcyone** [æl'saɪəni] *s* (astr.) Alción
**Ald.** abr. de **Alderman**
**Aldebaran** [æl'dɛbərən] *s* (astr.) Aldebarán
**aldehyde** ['ældɪhaɪd] *s* (chem.) aldehido
**alder** ['ɔldər] *s* (bot.) aliso
**alder buckthorn** *s* (bot.) arraclán, frángula
**alderman** ['ɔldərmən] *s* (*pl:* **-men**) concejal
**aldermanic** [ˌɔldər'mænɪk] *adj* de un concejal
**Alderney** ['ɔldərnɪ] *s* vaca de Alderney
**Aldine** ['ældin] o ['ældɪn] *adj* aldino
**Aldm.** abr. de **Alderman**
**ale** [el] *s* ale (*bebida semejante a la cerveza pero más obscura, espesa y amarga*)
**aleatory** ['elɪəˌtorɪ] *adj* aleatorio
**Aleck** ['ælɪk] *s* nombre abreviado de **Alexander**
**alee** [ə'li] *adv* (naut.) a sotavento
**alehouse** ['elˌhaʊs] *s* cervecería
**alembic** [ə'lɛmbɪk] *s* alambique
**Alençon** [ə'lɛnsɑn] *s* punto de Alenzón
**alepidote** [e'lɛpɪdot] *adj* (ichth.) alepídoto
**Aleppo** [ə'lɛpo] *s* Alepo
**Aleppo pine** *s* (bot.) pincarrasco
**alert** [ə'lʌrt] *adj* vigilante; vivo, listo; *s* (mil.) alerta; (aer.) alarma; **to be on the alert** estar alerta, estar sobre aviso; *va* alertar
**alertness** [ə'lʌrtnɪs] *s* vigilancia; viveza
**aleurone** [ə'luron] *s* (biochem.) aleurona
**Aleut** ['ælɪut] *s* aleutiano (*natural; idioma*)
**Aleutian** [ə'luʃən] *adj & s* aleutiano
**Aleutian Islands** *spl* islas Aleutas, islas Aleutinas
**alewife** ['elˌwaɪf] *s* (*pl:* **-wives**) tabernera; (ichth.) cervecera
**Alexander** [ˌælɪg'zændər] *s* Alejandro
**Alexander the Great** *s* Alejandro Magno
**Alexandria** [ˌælɪg'zændrɪə] *s* Alejandría
**Alexandrian** [ˌælɪg'zændrɪən] *adj* alejandrino
**Alexandrine** [ˌælɪg'zændrɪn] *adj* alejandrino; *s* alejandrino (*natural de Alejandría; verso inglés de doce sílabas y verso castellano de catorce*)
**alexia** [ə'lɛksɪə] *s* (psychopath.) alexia
**alexin** [ə'lɛksɪn] *s* (biochem.) alexina
**alexipharmic** [əˌlɛksɪ'fɑrmɪk] *adj & s* alexifármaco
**Alexis** [ə'lɛksɪs] *s* Alejo
**alfalfa** [æl'fælfə] *s* (bot.) alfalfa
**Alfred** ['ælfrɪd] *s* Alfredo
**Alfred the Great** *s* Alfredo el Grande
**alg.** abr. de **algebra**
**alga** ['ælgə] *s* (*pl:* **algae** ['ældʒi]) (bot.) alga
**algal** ['ælgəl] *adj* algáceo; *s* (bot.) alga
**algebra** ['ældʒɪbrə] *s* álgebra
**algebraic** [ˌældʒɪ'breɪk] o **algebraical** [ˌældʒɪ'breɪkəl] *adj* algebraico, algébrico
**algebraically** [ˌældʒɪ'breɪkəlɪ] *adv* algebraicamente
**algebraist** ['ældʒɪˌbreɪst] *s* algebrista
**Algeria** [æl'dʒɪrɪə] *s* Argelia
**Algerian** [æl'dʒɪrɪən] o **Algerine** [ˌældʒə'rin] *adj & s* argelino
**algid** ['ældʒɪd] *adj* frío, glacial
**algidity** [æl'dʒɪdɪtɪ] *s* frialdad
**Algiers** [æl'dʒɪrz] *s* Argel
**algology** [æl'gɑlədʒɪ] *s* algología
**Algonkian** [æl'gɑŋkɪən] *adj* (geol.) algonquino; *s* (geol.) algonquina
**Algonquian** [æl'gɑŋkɪən] o [æl'gɑŋkwɪən] *adj & s* (philol.) algonquino
**Algonquin** [æl'gɑŋkɪn] o [æl'gɑŋkwɪn] *s* algonquino
**algor** ['ælgɔr] *s* (path.) algor
**algorism** ['ælgərɪzəm] *s* (math.) algoritmia, algoritmo
**algorithmic** [ˌælgə'rɪðmɪk] *adj* algorítmico
**algous** ['ælgəs] *adj* algoso
**alias** ['elɪəs] *adv* alias; *s* alias, nombre supuesto
**alibi** ['ælɪbaɪ] *s* (*pl:* **-bis**) coartada; (coll.) excusa, pretexto, comodín; **to prove an alibi** probar la coartada
**Alice** ['ælɪs] *s* Alicia
**Alice in Wonderland** *s* Alicia en el país de las maravillas
**alidade** ['ælɪded] o **alidad** ['ælɪdæd] *s* alidada
**alien** ['eljən] o ['elɪən] *adj* extranjero; ajeno; *s* extranjero
**alienable** ['eljənəbəl] o ['elɪənəbəl] *adj* alienable, enajenable
**alienate** ['eljənet] o ['elɪənet] *va* enajenar, alienar
**alienation** [ˌeljən'eʃən] o [ˌelɪən'eʃən] *s* enajenación, alienación
**alienism** ['eljənɪzəm] o ['elɪənɪzəm] *s* extranjería; alienismo
**alienist** ['eljənɪst] o ['elɪənɪst] *s* alienista
**alien property custodian** *s* administrador de bienes de enemigos
**alight** [ə'laɪt] *adj* encendido, iluminado; (*pret & pp:* **alighted** o **alit**) *vn* bajar, apearse; **to alight on** posarse sobre; encontrarse con
**align** [ə'laɪn] *va* alinear; *vn* alinearse
**aligner** [ə'laɪnər] *s* alineador
**alignment** [ə'laɪnmənt] *s* alineación; (archeol.) alineamiento; (eng.) alineación; **in alignment** en línea; **out of alignment** fuera de alineación
**alike** [ə'laɪk] *adj* semejantes, p.ej., **these books are alike** estos libros son semejantes; **to look alike** parecerse; *adv* igualmente, del mismo modo
**aliment** ['ælɪmənt] *s* alimento
**alimentary** [ˌælɪ'mɛntərɪ] *adj* alimenticio; alimentario (*que suministra la subsistencia*)
**alimentary canal** *s* (anat.) canal o tubo digestivo, canal alimenticio
**alimentation** [ˌælɪmɛn'teʃən] *s* alimentación
**alimony** ['ælɪˌmonɪ] *s* alimentos, asistencias de divorcio o separación
**aline** [ə'laɪn] *va & vn* var. de **align**
**aliped** ['ælɪpɛd] *adj & s* alípedo
**aliphatic** [ˌælɪ'fætɪk] *adj* (chem.) alifático
**aliquant** ['ælɪkwənt] *adj* (math.) alicuanta
**aliquot** ['ælɪkwɑt] *adj* (math.) alícuota
**alish** ['elɪʃ] *adj* acervezado
**alit** [ə'lɪt] *pret & pp de* **alight**
**alive** [ə'laɪv] *adj* vivo, viviente, con vida; ac-

tivo, animado; **to look alive** darse prisa, menearse; **alive to** despierto para, sensible a; **alive with** hormigueante en
**alizarin** [ə'lɪzərɪn] *s* (chem.) alizarina
**alkalescence** [,ælkə'lɛsəns] *s* (chem.) alcalescencia
**alkalescent** [,ælkə'lɛsənt] *adj* (chem.) alcalescente
**alkali** ['ælkəlaɪ] *s* (*pl:* **-lis** o **-lies**) (chem.) álcali
**alkalimeter** [,ælkə'lɪmɪtər] *s* alcalímetro
**alkaline** ['ælkəlaɪn] o ['ælkəlɪn] *adj* alcalino
**alkaline-earth metals** ['ælkəlaɪn'ʌrθ] o ['ælkəlɪn'ʌrθ] *spl* (chem.) metales alcalinotérreos
**alkaline earths** *spl* (chem.) álcalis térreos
**alkalinity** [,ælkə'lɪnɪtɪ] *s* alcalinidad
**alkalize** ['ælkəlaɪz] *va* alcalizar
**alkaloid** ['ælkəlɔɪd] *s* alcaloide
**alkaloidal** [,ælkə'lɔɪdəl] *adj* alcalóidico
**alkalosis** [,ælkə'losɪs] *s* (physiol.) alcalosis
**alkanet** ['ælkənɛt] *s* (bot.) ancusa; (bot.) ancusa de tintes; (bot.) alcana; (chem.) ancusina
**Alkoran** [,ælko'rɑn] o [,ælko'ræn] *s* Alcorán
**all** [ɔl] *adj indef* todo, todos; todo el, todos los; *pron indef* todo; todos, todo el mundo; (tennis) iguales; **after all** sin embargo; **at all** del todo; **for all I know** que yo sepa; **for good and all** para siempre; **not at all** nada; no hay de qué; **once and for all** de una vez para siempre; **all in all** en resumen; **all of** todo el, todos los; **all that** todo lo que, todos los que; **all told** en conjunto; *adv* enteramente; **not to be all there** (slang) no estar en su juicio cabal; **to be all up with** no haber remedio para; **all at once** de golpe; **all along** desde el principio; a lo largo de, de un cabo a otro de; **all but** casi; **all in** (slang) agotado, rendido; **all of a sudden** de repente; **all off** (slang) abandonado; **all one** (coll.) igual; **all out** a ultranza; **all over** terminado; por todas partes; exactamente; **all right** está bien, bueno, corriente; **all the better** tanto mejor; **all the worse** tanto peor; **all too** excesivamente, desgraciadamente
**Allah** ['ælə] *s* Alá
**all-American** [,ɔlə'mɛrɪkən] *adj* que representa todas las partes de los Estados Unidos; exclusivamente estadunidense; (sport) seleccionado como jugador representativo nacional
**allantoid** [ə'læntɔɪd] *adj* alantoideo
**allantois** [ə'lænto·ɪs] *s* (anat.) alantoides
**all-around** ['ɔlə,raʊnd] *adj* hábil para muchas cosas
**allay** [ə'le] *va* aliviar, calmar
**all-clear** ['ɔl'klɪr] *s* cese de alarma, toque o señal de cese de alarma
**allegation** [,ælɪ'geʃən] *s* alegación; (law) alegato
**allege** [ə'lɛdʒ] *va* alegar
**allegedly** [ə'lɛdʒɪdlɪ] *adv* según se alega
**allegiance** [ə'lidʒəns] *s* lealtad, fidelidad; homenaje; **to swear allegiance to** rendir homenaje a; jurar fidelidad a
**allegoric** [,ælɪ'gɑrɪk] o [,ælɪ'gɔrɪk] o **allegorical** [,ælɪ'gɑrɪkəl] o [,ælɪ'gɔrɪkəl] *adj* alegórico
**allegorize** ['ælɪgəraɪz] *va* alegorizar
**allegory** ['ælɪ,gorɪ] *s* (*pl:* **-ries**) alegoría
**allegretto** [,ælə'grɛto] *s* (*pl:* **-tos**) (mus.) alegreto
**allegro** [ɑ'legro] o [ə'lɛgro] *s* (*pl:* **-gros**) (mus.) alegro
**alleluia** [,ælɪ'lujə] *s* aleluya; *interj* ¡ aleluya!
**allemande** [,ælə'mænd] *s* alemana o alemanda (*danza*)
**allergen** ['ælərdʒɛn] *s* (immun.) alergeno
**allergic** [ə'lʌrdʒɪk] *adj* alérgico
**allergy** ['ælərdʒɪ] *s* (*pl:* **-gies**) (path.) alergia
**alleviate** [ə'liviet] *va* aliviar
**alleviation** [ə,livɪ'eʃən] *s* alivio
**alleviative** [ə'livɪ,etɪv] *adj* aliviador
**alley** ['ælɪ] *s* callejuela, callejón; paseo arbolado, paseo de jardín; pista (*de bolera*); (tennis) espacio lateral
**alleyway** ['ælɪ,we] *s* callejuela, pasadizo
**All Fools' Day** *s* var. de **April Fools' Day**
**all fours** *spl* las cuatro patas; **on all fours** a gatas
**Allhallows** [,ɔl'hæloz] *s* día de todos los santos
**alliance** [ə'laɪəns] *s* alianza
**Alliance for Progress** *s* Alianza para el Progreso
**alligator** ['ælɪ,getər] *s* (zool.) caimán; cuero o piel de caimán o cocodrilo
**alligator gar** *s* (ichth.) pez caimán
**alligator pear** *s* aguacate
**alligator tree** *s* (bot.) ocozol
**alligator wrench** *s* llave de mandíbulas, llave dentada
**all-important** ['ɔlɪm'pɔrtənt] *adj* de toda importancia
**all-in** ['ɔl'ɪn] *adj* (Brit.) inclusivo; (Brit.) sin restricción
**alliterate** [ə'lɪtəret] *va* disponer en forma de aliteración; *vn* usar aliteración
**alliteration** [ə,lɪtə'reʃən] *s* aliteración
**alliterative** [ə'lɪtə,retɪv] *adj* aliterado
**all-knowing** ['ɔl'no·ɪŋ] *adj* omnisciente
**all-metal** ['ɔl'mɛtəl] *adj* todo de metal, todo metálico
**allocate** ['æloket] *va* asignar, señalar, distribuir
**allocation** [,ælo'keʃən] *s* asignación, distribución
**allocution** [,ælo'kjuʃən] *s* alocución
**allodium** [ə'lodɪəm] *s* (*pl:* **-a** [ə]) var. de **alodium**
**allogamy** [ə'lɑgəmɪ] *s* (bot.) alogamia
**allopath** ['ælopæθ] *s* alópata
**allopathic** [,ælo'pæθɪk] *adj* alopático
**allopathist** [ə'lɑpəθɪst] *s* var. de **allopath**
**allopathy** [ə'lɑpəθɪ] *s* alopatía
**allophone** ['ælofon] *s* miembro del fonema
**allot** [ə'lɑt] (*pret & pp:* **allotted;** *ger:* **allotting**) *va* asignar, distribuir
**allotment** [ə'lɑtmənt] *s* asignación, distribución; lote, parte, porción
**allotrope** ['ælotrop] *s* alotropo
**allotropic** [,ælo'trɑpɪk] *adj* alotrópico
**allotropism** [ə'lɑtrəpɪzəm] *s* alotropismo
**allotropy** [ə'lɑtrəpɪ] *s* alotropía
**all-out** ['ɔl'aʊt] *adj* total, acérrimo
**allover** ['ɔl,ovər] *adj* que tiene un diseño repetido sobre toda la superficie; *s* tela con diseño repetido sobre toda la superficie; diseño repetido sobre toda la superficie
**allow** [ə'laʊ] *va* dejar, permitir; admitir; conceder; poner aparte; (coll.) creer; **to allow to** + *inf* dejar + *inf*, permitir + *inf; vn* **to allow for** tener en cuenta; **to allow of** permitir; admitir
**allowable** [ə'laʊəbəl] *adj* permisible; admisible
**allowance** [ə'laʊəns] *s* permiso; concesión; asignación, pensión; ración, mesada; descuento, rebaja; tolerancia (*en el peso o en las dimensiones*); **to make allowance for** tener en cuenta
**alloy** ['ælɔɪ] o [ə'lɔɪ] *s* aleación, liga; impureza, adulteración; [ə'lɔɪ] *va* alear, ligar; adulterar
**alloy steel** *s* acero de aleación
**all-powerful** ['ɔl'paʊərfəl] *adj* todopoderoso
**all-round** ['ɔl,raʊnd] *adj* hábil para muchas cosas
**All Saints' Day** *s* día de todos los santos
**all-silk** ['ɔl,sɪlk] *adj* de pura seda
**All Souls' Day** *s* día de los difuntos
**allspice** ['ɔl,spaɪs] *s* pimienta inglesa (*fruto seco y molido*)
**allspice tree** *s* (bot.) pimienta (*Pimenta officinalis*)
**all-steel** ['ɔl'stil] *adj* todo de acero
**allude** [ə'lud] *vn* aludir
**allure** [ə'lur] *s* tentación, encanto, fascinación; *va* tentar, encantar, fascinar
**allurement** [ə'lurmənt] *s* tentación, encanto, fascinación
**alluring** [ə'lurɪŋ] *adj* tentador, encantador, fascinante
**allusion** [ə'luʒən] *s* alusión
**allusive** [ə'lusɪv] *adj* alusivo
**alluvial** [ə'luvɪəl] *adj* aluvial
**alluvion** [ə'luvɪən] *s* aluvión; (law) aluvión
**alluvium** [ə'luvɪəm] *s* (*pl:* **-ums** o **-a** [ə]) aluvión
**all-wave** ['ɔl'wev] *adj* (rad.) de toda onda, de onda universal
**all-weather** ['ɔl'wɛðər] *adj* para todo tiempo, para todas las estaciones
**all-wise** ['ɔl'waɪz] *adj* infinitamente sabio

**ally** ['ælaɪ] o [ə'laɪ] *s* (*pl:* **allies**) aliado; [ə'laɪ] (*pret & pp:* **allied**) *va* aliar; **to become allied** aliarse; **to ally oneself** aliarse; *vn* aliarse
**allyl** ['ælɪl] *s* (chem.) alilo
**allylene** ['ælɪlin] *s* (chem.) alileno
**almagest** ['ælmədʒɛst] *s* almagesto
**Alma Mater** ['ælmə'metər] o ['ɑlmə'mɑtər] *s* (myth.) alma máter; (*l.c.*) *s* alma máter (*universidad donde uno se ha graduado*)
**almanac** ['ɔlmənæk] *s* almanaque
**almighty** [ɔl'maɪtɪ] *adj* todopoderoso; (coll.) enorme, grave; **the Almighty** el Todopoderoso (*Dios*)
**almond** ['ɑmənd] o ['æmənd] *s* (bot.) almendro (*árbol*); almendra (*fruto y semilla del fruto*)
**almond brittle** *s* crocante
**almond cream** *s* crema de almendras
**almond-eyed** ['ɑmənd,aɪd] o ['æmənd,aɪd] *adj* de ojos almendrados
**almond-shaped** ['ɑmənd,ʃept] o ['æmənd,ʃept] *adj* almendrado
**almoner** ['ælmənər] o ['ɑmənər] *s* limosnero
**almonry** ['ælmənrɪ] o ['ɑmənrɪ] *s* (*pl:* **-ries**) lugar donde se reparten limosnas
**almost** ['ɔlmost] u [ɔl'most] *adv* casi
**alms** [ɑmz] *ssg & spl* limosna
**almsgiver** ['ɑmz,gɪvər] *s* limosnero
**almsgiving** ['ɑmz,gɪvɪŋ] *adj* limosnero; *s* limosna
**almshouse** ['ɑmz,haʊs] *s* casa de beneficencia, hospicio
**almsman** ['ɑmzmən] *s* (*pl:* **-men**) mendigo, pordiosero
**almswoman** ['ɑmz,wʊmən] *s* (*pl:* **-women**) mendiga, pordiosera
**almucantar** [,ælmjə'kæntər] *s* (astr.) almicantarada
**alnico** ['ælnɪko] *s* alnico (*aleación*)
**alodial** [ə'lodɪəl] *adj* (law) alodial
**alodium** [ə'lodɪəm] *s* (*pl:* **-a** [ə]) (law) alodio
**aloe** ['ælo] *s* (bot.) áloe; (bot.) maguey; **aloes** *ssg* (pharm.) áloe; palo áloe, palo de áloe
**aloes wood** *s* palo áloe, palo de áloe
**aloetic** [,ælo'ɛtɪk] *adj* aloético
**aloft** [ə'lɔft] o [ə'lɑft] *adv* arriba, en alto, en los aires; (naut.) en la arboladura; (aer.) en vuelo
**aloin** ['ælo·ɪn] *s* (chem. & pharm.) aloína
**alone** [ə'lon] *adj* solo; **let alone** sin mencionar; y mucho menos, p.ej., **he cannot speak his own language, let alone a foreign language** no puede hablar su propio idioma y mucho menos un idioma extranjero; **to leave alone** o **to let alone** no molestar a (*una persona*); no mezclarse en (*una cosa*); *adv* solamente
**along** [ə'lɔŋ] o [ə'lɑŋ] *prep* a lo largo de; **all along** de un cabo a otro de; *adv* a lo largo; adelante; conmigo, consigo, p.ej., **come along** venga Vd. conmigo; **all along** desde el principio; **to get along** irse; medrar; entenderse; **along with** junto con
**alongshore** [ə'lɔŋ,ʃor] o [ə'lɑŋ,ʃor] *adv* a la orilla, a lo largo de la costa
**alongside** [ə'lɔŋ'saɪd] o [ə'lɑŋ'saɪd] *prep* junto a, a lo largo de; (naut.) al costado de; *adv* a lo largo; (naut.) al costado, costado con costado; **to bring alongside** (naut.) acostar; **to come alongside** (naut.) acostarse; **alongside of** junto a
**aloof** [ə'luf] *adj* apartado; reservado, frío; **to keep aloof from** o **to stand aloof from** mantenerse apartado de; *adv* lejos, a distancia
**aloofness** [ə'lufnɪs] *s* apartamiento, aislamiento; reserva, frialdad
**alopecia** [,ælo'piʃɪə] *s* (path.) alopecia
**aloud** [ə'laʊd] *adv* alto, en voz alta; con voz fuerte
**alp** [ælp] *s* monte elevado
**alpaca** [æl'pækə] *s* (zool.) alpaca; alpaca (*lana y tela hecha de esta lana*)
**alpenglow** ['ælpən,glo] *s* arrebol alpestre
**alpenhorn** ['ælpən,hɔrn] *s* trompa de los Alpes
**alpenstock** ['ælpən,stɑk] *s* bastón puntiagudo de los montañeros
**alpha** ['ælfə] *s* alfa; **alpha and omega** alfa y omega
**alphabet** ['ælfəbɛt] *s* alfabeto
**alphabetic** [,ælfə'bɛtɪk] o **alphabetical** [,ælfə'bɛtɪkəl] alfabético
**alphabetically** [,ælfə'bɛtɪkəlɪ] *adv* alfabéticamente
**alphabetization** [,ælfə,bɛtɪ'zeʃən] *s* alfabetización
**alphabetize** ['ælfəbətaɪz] *va* alfabetizar
**alpha rays** *spl* (phys.) rayos alfa
**Alpheus** [æl'fiəs] *s* (myth.) Alfeo
**Alphonsine** [æl'fɑnsɪn] *adj* alfonsino
**Alphonsine Tables** *spl* tablas alfonsinas
**Alphonso** [æl'fɑnso] o [æl'fɑnzo] *s* Alfonso
**alphorn** ['ælp,hɔrn] *s* trompa de los Alpes
**alpine** ['ælpaɪn] o ['ælpɪn] *adj* alpestre; (*cap.*) *adj* alpino
**alpine chough** *s* (orn.) chova pinariega, grajo de pico amarillo
**Alpinism** ['ælpɪnɪzəm] *s* alpinismo
**Alpinist** ['ælpɪnɪst] *s* alpinista
**alpist** ['ælpɪst] *s* alpiste (*semilla*)
**Alps** [ælps] *spl* Alpes
**already** [ɔl'rɛdɪ] *adv* ya
**Alsace** ['ælses] o ['ælsæs] *s* Alsacia
**Alsace-Lorraine** ['ælseslɑ'ren] o ['ælsæslɑ'ren] *s* Alsacia-Lorena
**Alsatian** [æl'seʃən] *adj & s* alsaciano
**alsike** ['ælsaɪk] u ['ɔlsaɪk] *s* (bot.) trébol sueco
**also** ['ɔlso] *adv* también
**alt.** abr. de **alternate** y **altitude**
**Alta.** abr. de **Alberta** (*Canadá*)
**Altaic** [æl'teɪk] *adj* altaico
**altar** ['ɔltər] *s* altar; (found.) altar; **to lead to the altar** conducir al altar
**altar boy** *s* monaguillo, acólito
**altar cloth** *s* (eccl.) sabanilla, paño de altar, palia
**altarpiece** ['ɔltər,pis] *s* retablo
**altar rail** *s* comulgatorio
**alter** ['ɔltər] *va* alterar; (coll.) arreglar (*castrar*); *vn* alterarse
**alterability** [,ɔltərə'bɪlɪtɪ] *s* alterabilidad
**alterable** ['ɔltərəbəl] *adj* alterable
**alteration** [,ɔltə'reʃən] *s* alteración; reparación, compostura, reforma
**alterative** ['ɔltə,retɪv] *adj & s* (med.) alterante
**altercate** ['ɔltərket] o ['æltərket] *vn* altercar
**altercation** [,ɔltər'keʃən] o [,æltər'keʃən] *s* altercación o altercado
**alter ego** ['æltər'igo] o ['æltər'ɛgo] (Lat.) álter ego (*otro yo; amigo de confianza*)
**alternate** ['ɔltərnɪt] o ['æltərnɪt] *s* suplente; *adj* alternante; alterno; (bot. & geom.) alterno; ['ɔltərnet] o ['æltərnet] *va & vn* alternar
**alternate angles** *spl* (geom.) ángulos alternos
**alternate leaves** *spl* (bot.) hojas alternas
**alternately** ['ɔltərnɪtlɪ] o ['æltərnɪtlɪ] *adv* alternadamente, alternativamente
**alternating** ['ɔltər,netɪŋ] o ['æltər,netɪŋ] *adj* alternante, alternativo
**alternating current** *s* (elec.) corriente alterna, corriente alternativa
**alternation** [,ɔltər'neʃən] o [,æltər'neʃən] *s* alternación; (elec.) alternancia
**alternation of generations** *s* (biol.) alternancia de generaciones
**alternative** [ɔl'tʌrnətɪv] o [æl'tʌrnətɪv] *adj* alternativo; *s* alternativa
**alternative conjunction** *s* (gram.) conjunción disyuntiva
**alternator** ['ɔltər,netər] o ['æltər,netər] *s* (elec.) alternador
**althea** [æl'θiə] *s* (bot.) altea
**althorn** ['ælthɔrn] *s* trombón alto
**although** [ɔl'ðo] *conj* aunque
**altimeter** [æl'tɪmɪtər] *s* altímetro
**altimetrical** [,æltɪ'mɛtrɪkəl] *adj* altímetro
**altimetry** [æl'tɪmɪtrɪ] *s* altimetría
**altitude** ['æltɪtjud] o ['æltɪtud] *s* altitud, altura
**alto** ['ælto] *s* (*pl:* **-tos**) (mus.) alto; contralto (*mujer*)
**alto-cumulus** [,ælto'kjumjələs] *s* (meteor.) altocúmulo
**altogether** [,ɔltə'gɛðər] *adv* enteramente; en conjunto
**alto horn** *s* trombón alto
**alto-relievo** ['æltorɪ'livo] *s* (*pl:* **-vos**) alto relieve
**alto-stratus** [,ælto'stretəs] *s* (meteor.) altostrato

**altruism** ['æltruɪzəm] *s* altruísmo
**altruist** ['æltruɪst] *s* altruísta
**altruistic** [ˌæltru'ɪstɪk] *adj* altruísta
**alula** ['æljələ] *s* (*pl:* **-lae** [li]) (orn. & ent.) álula
**alum** ['æləm] *s* (chem.) alumbre
**alumina** [ə'lumɪnə] *s* (mineral.) alúmina
**aluminate** [ə'lumɪnet] *s* (chem.) aluminato
**aluminite** [ə'lumɪnaɪt] *s* (mineral.) aluminita
**aluminium** [ˌæljə'mɪnɪəm] *s* var. de **aluminum**
**aluminothermy** [ə'lumɪnoˌθʌrmɪ] *s* (metal.) aluminotermia
**aluminous** [ə'lumɪnəs] *adj* alumbroso (*que tiene alumbre*); aluminoso (*que tiene alúmina*); alumínico (*que tiene aluminio*)
**aluminum** [ə'lumɪnəm] *s* (chem.) aluminio
**aluminum bronze** *s* bronce de aluminio
**aluminum oxide** *s* (chem.) óxido de aluminio
**aluminum paint** *s* pintura de aluminio
**alumna** [ə'lʌmnə] *s* (*pl:* **-nae** [ni]) graduada
**alumni association** *s* asociación de graduados
**alumnus** [ə'lʌmnəs] *s* (*pl:* **-ni** [naɪ]) graduado
**alum rock** *s* (mineral.) piedra de alumbre
**alum schist, shale** o **slate** *s* esquisto aluminoso
**alum stone** *s* var. de **alum rock**
**alunite** ['æljənaɪt] *s* (mineral.) alunita
**alveary** ['ælvɪˌɛrɪ] *s* (*pl:* **-ies**) (anat.) alveario
**alveolar** [æl'viələr] *adj* (anat. & phonet.) alveolar
**alveolar process** *s* (anat.) apófisis alveolar
**alveolus** [æl'viələs] *s* (*pl:* **-li** [laɪ]) (anat., phonet., & zool.) alvéolo
**alvine** ['ælvɪn] o ['ælvaɪn] *adj* (med.) alvino
**always** ['ɔlwɪz] u ['ɔlwez] *adv* siempre
**alyssum** [ə'lɪsəm] *s* (bot.) alisón; (bot.) alhelicillo
**a.m.** o **A.M.** abr. de **ante meridiem** (Lat.) **before noon**
**A.M.** abr. de **Artium Magister** (Lat.) **Master of Arts**
**A.M.** o **AM** abr. de **amplitude modulation**
**Am.** abr. de **America** y **American**
**am** [æm] *primera persona del sg del pres de ind de* **be**
**A.M.A.** abr. de **American Medical Association**
**amain** [ə'men] *adv* con fuerza, con prisa, con vehemencia
**Amalekite** ['æmələkaɪt] *s* (Bib.) amalecita
**amalgam** [ə'mælgəm] *s* (chem., mineral. & fig.) amalgama
**amalgamate** [ə'mælgəmet] *va* (chem. & fig.) amalgamar; *vn* amalgamarse
**amalgamation** [əˌmælgə'meʃən] *s* amalgamación
**amalgamation process** *s* (min.) amalgamación
**amanita** [ˌæmə'naɪtə] *s* (bot.) amanita
**amanuensis** [əˌmænju'ɛnsɪs] *s* (*pl:* **-ses** [siz]) amanuense
**amaranth** ['æmərænθ] *s* (bot.) amaranto; (poet.) flor que nunca se marchita; púrpura (*color*)
**amaranthaceous** [ˌæmərænˈθeʃəs] *adj* (bot.) amarantáceo
**amaranthine** [ˌæmə'rænθɪn] o [ˌæmə'rænθaɪn] *adj* amarantino; inmarcesible, imperecedero; purpúreo
**amaryllis** [ˌæmə'rɪlɪs] *s* (bot.) amarilis; (*cap.*) *s* Amarilis (*pastora*)
**amass** [ə'mæs] *va* acumular, amontonar; amasar (*dinero, una fortuna*)
**amateur** [ˌæmə'tʌr] o ['æmətʃər] *s* aficionado; chapucero, principiante; *adj* aficionado; de afición; chapucero, principiante
**amateurish** [ˌæmə'tʌrɪʃ], ['æmətjurɪʃ] o ['æmətʃərɪʃ] *adj* superficial, chapucero
**amateurism** [ˌæmə'tʌrɪzəm], ['æmətjurɪzəm] o ['æmətʃərɪzəm] *s* estado de aficionado; chapucería
**amative** ['æmətɪv] *adj* amativo
**amatory** ['æməˌtorɪ] *adj* amatorio
**amaurosis** [ˌæmɔ'rosɪs] *s* (path.) amaurosis
**amaze** [ə'mez] *va* asombrar, pasmar, maravillar; **to be amazed at, by,** o **with** asombrarse de
**amazedly** [ə'mezɪdlɪ] *adv* con asombro, pasmadamente
**amazement** [ə'mezmənt] *s* asombro, pasmo, aturdimiento
**amazing** [ə'mezɪŋ] *adj* asombroso, pasmoso, maravilloso
**amazon** ['æməzɑn] o ['æməzən] *s* amazona (*mujer varonil*); (*cap.*) *s* Amazonas (*río*); (orn.) amazona (*loro*); (myth.) amazona
**Amazonian** [ˌæmə'zonɪən] *adj* amazónico
**amazonite** ['æməzənaɪt] *s* (mineral.) amazonita
**ambagious** [æm'bedʒəs] *adj* ambagioso
**ambassador** [æm'bæsədər] *s* embajador
**ambassadorial** [æmˌbæsə'dorɪəl] *adj* embajatorio
**ambassadorship** [æm'bæsədərˌʃɪp] *s* embajada (*dignidad, cargo, tiempo que dura el cargo*)
**ambassadress** [æm'bæsədrɪs] *s* embajadora
**amber** ['æmbər] *s* ámbar; *adj* ambarino
**ambergris** ['æmbərgris] *s* ámbar gris
**amber jack** *s* (ichth.) coronado, medregal; (ichth.) pez limón
**ambidexterity** [ˌæmbɪdɛks'tɛrɪtɪ] *s* ambidextrismo, ambidexteridad; falsedad, hipocresía
**ambidextrous** [ˌæmbɪ'dɛkstrəs] *adj* ambidextro; falso, hipócrita
**ambient** ['æmbɪənt] *adj* ambiente
**ambiguity** [ˌæmbɪ'gjuɪtɪ] *s* (*pl:* **-ties**) ambigüedad
**ambiguous** [æm'bɪgjuəs] *adj* ambiguo
**ambit** ['æmbɪt] *s* ámbito
**ambition** [æm'bɪʃən] *s* ambición
**ambitious** [æm'bɪʃəs] *adj* ambicioso
**ambivalence** [æm'bɪvələns] *s* (psychol.) ambivalencia
**ambivalent** [æm'bɪvələnt] *adj* ambivalente
**amble** ['æmbəl] *s* ambladura, paso de ambladura; *vn* amblar
**ambler** ['æmblər] *s* amblador
**amblyopia** [ˌæmblɪ'opɪə] *s* (path.) ambliopía
**ambo** ['æmbo] *s* (*pl:* **-bos**) ambón
**Ambrose** ['æmbroz] *s* Ambrosio
**Ambrose Channel** *s* el canal Ambrosio
**ambrosia** [æm'broʒə] o [æm'broʒɪə] *s* (bot., myth., & fig.) ambrosía
**ambrosial** [æm'broʒəl] o [æm'broʒɪəl] *adj* ambrosíaco
**Ambrosian** [æm'broʒən] o [æm'brozɪən] *adj* ambrosiano
**Ambrosian chant** *s* canto ambrosiano
**ambry** ['æmbrɪ] *s* (*pl:* **-bries**) armario; despensa
**ambulacral** [ˌæmbjə'lekrəl] *adj* (zool.) ambulacral
**ambulacrum** [ˌæmbjə'lekrəm] *s* (*pl:* **-kra** [krə]) (zool.) ambulacro
**ambulance** ['æmbjələns] *s* ambulancia
**ambulance driver** *s* ambulanciero
**ambulant** ['æmbjələnt] *adj* ambulante
**ambulate** ['æmbjəlet] *vn* ambular, andar, deambular
**ambulatory** ['æmbjələˌtorɪ] *adj* ambulatorio; *s* (arch.) deambulatorio
**ambuscade** [ˌæmbəs'ked] *s, va, & vn* var. de **ambush**
**ambush** ['æmbuʃ] *s* emboscada; **to fall into an ambush** caer en una emboscada; **to lie in ambush** estar emboscado; *va* emboscar, ocultar (*tropas*) para una emboscada; insidiar, poner asechanzas a; *vn* emboscarse
**ameba** [ə'mibə] *s* (*pl:* **-bas** o **-bae** [bi]) var. de **amoeba**
**ameer** [ə'mɪr] *s* amir
**Amelia** [ə'miljə] *s* Amalia
**ameliorable** [ə'miljərəbəl] *adj* mejorable
**ameliorate** [ə'miljəret] *va & vn* mejorar
**amelioration** [əˌmiljə'reʃən] *s* mejoramiento
**ameliorative** [ə'miljəˌretɪv] *adj* mejorador
**amen** ['e'mɛn] o ['ɑ'mɛn] *s & interj* amén; **to say amen to** (coll.) decir amén a (*avenirse a*)
**amenability** [əˌminə'bɪlɪtɪ] o [əˌmɛnə'bɪlɪtɪ] *s* docilidad; responsabilidad
**amenable** [ə'minəbəl] o [ə'mɛnəbəl] *adj* dócil; responsable
**amen corner** *s* banco de iglesia en donde se encuentran los fieles más ardientes y chillones (*en las iglesias protestantes*)
**amend** [ə'mɛnd] *va* enmendar; *vn* enmendarse; **amends** *spl* enmienda; **to make amends for** dar cumplida satisfacción por, enmendar

**amendment** [ə'mɛndmənt] *s* enmienda; (agr.) enmiendas

**amenity** [ə'mɛnɪtɪ] o [ə'minɪtɪ] *s* (*pl:* **-ties**) amenidad

**amenorrhea** [əˌmɛnə'riə] *s* (path.) amenorrea

**ament** ['æmənt] o ['emənt] *s* (bot.) amento (*inflorescencia*)

**amentaceous** [ˌæmən'teʃəs] *adj* (bot.) amentáceo

**amentia** [e'mɛnʃɪə] *s* demencia, locura, imbecilidad

**Amer.** abr. de **America** y **American**

**amerce** [ə'mʌrs] *va* multar; castigar

**amercement** [ə'mʌrsmənt] *s* multa; castigo

**America** [ə'mɛrɪkə] *s* América

**American** [ə'mɛrɪkən] *adj & s* americano; norteamericano, estadunidense

**Americana** [əˌmɛrɪ'kenə], [əˌmɛrɪ'kɑnə] o [əˌmɛrɪ'kænə] *spl* escritos americanos, escritos sobre cosas de América

**American aloe** *s* (bot.) maguey, pita

**American Beauty** *s* rosa encarnada de gran tamaño

**American cheese** *s* queso de Cheddar

**American eagle** *s* águila americana (*escudo de armas de los EE.UU.*)

**Americanism** [ə'mɛrɪkənɪzəm] *s* americanismo

**Americanist** [ə'mɛrɪkənɪst] *s* americanista

**Americanization** [əˌmɛrɪkənɪ'zeʃən] *s* americanización

**Americanize** [ə'mɛrɪkənaɪz] *va* americanizar; *vn* americanizarse

**American ostrich** *s* (orn.) avestruz de América, ñandú

**American plan** *s* cuartos con comidas

**americium** [ˌæmə'rɪʃɪəm] *s* (chem.) americio

**Americomania** [əˌmɛrɪko'menɪə] *s* americomanía

**Amerind** ['æmərɪnd] *s* amerindio

**Amerindian** [ˌæmə'rɪndɪən] *adj & s* amerindio

**amethyst** ['æmɪθɪst] *s* amatista

**ametropia** [ˌæmɪ'tropɪə] *s* (path.) ametropía

**amiability** [ˌemɪə'bɪlɪtɪ] *s* amabilidad

**amiable** ['emɪəbəl] *adj* amable; bonachón

**amicability** [ˌæmɪkə'bɪlɪtɪ] *s* amigabilidad

**amicable** ['æmɪkəbəl] *adj* amigable

**amice** ['æmɪs] *s* (eccl.) amito

**amid** [ə'mɪd] *prep* en medio de

**amide** ['æmɪd] o ['æmaɪd] *s* (chem.) amida

**amidine** ['æmɪdin] o ['æmɪdɪn] *s* (chem.) amidina

**amidogen** [ə'midodʒɛn] o [ə'mɪdodʒɛn] *s* (chem.) amidógeno

**amidol** ['æmɪdɑl] o ['æmɪdol] *s* (chem.) amidol

**amidship** [ə'mɪdʃɪp] o **amidships** [ə'mɪdʃɪps] *adv* en medio del navío

**amidst** [ə'mɪdst] *prep* en medio de

**amine** [ə'min] o ['æmɪn] *s* (chem.) amina

**aminic** [ə'mɪnɪk] *adj* (chem.) amínico

**amino acids** ['æmɪno] o [ə'mino] *spl* (chem.) aminoácidos

**amir** [ə'mɪr] *s* amir

**amiss** [ə'mɪs] *adj* inoportuno; malo, errado; en mal estado; *adv* inoportunamente; mal, erradamente; en mal estado; **to take amiss** llevar a mal, tomar en mala parte

**amitosis** [ˌæmɪ'tosɪs] *s* (biol.) amitosis

**amity** ['æmɪtɪ] *s* (*pl:* **-ties**) amistad, bienquerencia, armonía

**ammeter** ['æmˌmitər] o ['æmɪtər] *s* (elec.) anmetro, amperímetro

**ammonia** [ə'monɪə] *s* (chem.) amoníaco; (chem.) agua amoniacal

**ammoniac** [ə'monɪæk] *adj* amoniacal; *s* amoníaco (*goma resinosa*)

**ammoniacal** [ˌæmo'naɪəkəl] *adj* amoníaco

**ammoniacal liquor** *s* líquido amoniacal

**ammonia gas** *s* (chem.) gas amoníaco

**ammonia water** *s* (chem.) agua amoniacal

**ammonite** ['æmənaɪt] *s* (pal.) amonita; (*cap.*) *s* (Bib.) amonita

**ammonium** [ə'monɪəm] *s* (chem.) amonio; *adj* amónico

**ammonium chloride** *s* (chem.) cloruro amónico

**ammonium hydroxide** *s* (chem.) hidrato amónico

**ammonium nitrate** *s* (chem.) nitrato amónico

**ammunition** [ˌæmjə'nɪʃən] *s* munición; *va* amunicionar

**amnesia** [æm'niʒɪə] o [æm'niʒə] *s* (path.) amnesia

**amnesic** [æm'nisɪk] o [æm'nizɪk] *adj* amnésico

**amnesty** ['æmnɪstɪ] *s* (*pl:* **-ties**) amnistía; (*pret & pp:* **-tied**) *va* amnistiar

**amnion** ['æmnɪən] *s* (*pl:* **-ons** o **-a** [ə]) (anat.) amnios

**amniote** ['æmnɪot] *adj & s* (zool.) amniota

**amniotic** [ˌæmnɪ'ɑtɪk] *adj* (anat.) amniótico

**amoeba** [ə'mibə] (*pl:* **-bas** o **-bae** [bi]) (zool.) amiba

**amoebic** [ə'mibɪk] *adj* ami ıo

**amoebic dysentery** *s* (pat.. ) disentería amibiana

**amoeboid** [ə'mibɔɪd] *adj* amiboideo

**amok** [ə'mɑk] o [ə'mʌk] *adv* var. de **amuck**

**amomum** [ə'momən] *s* (bot.) amomo

**among** [ə'mʌŋ] o **amongst** [ə'mʌŋst] *prep* entre, en medio de, en el número de

**amoral** [e'mɑrəl] o [e'mɔrəl] *adj* amoral

**amorality** [ˌemə'rælɪtɪ] *s* amoralidad

**amorous** ['æmərəs] *adj* amoroso

**amorphia** [ə'mɔrfɪə] *s* amorfia

**amorphism** [ə'mɔrfɪzəm] *s* amorfismo

**amorphous** [ə'mɔrfəs] *adj* amorfo

**amortization** [ˌæmərtɪ'zeʃən] o [əˌmɔrtɪ'zeʃən] *s* amortización

**amortize** ['æmərtaɪz] o [ə'mɔrtaɪz] *va* amortizar

**amortizement** [ə'mɔrtɪzmənt] *s* amortización

**Amos** ['eməs] *s* Amós

**amount** [ə'maʊnt] *s* cantidad, importe; *vn* ascender; **to amount to** ascender a, subir a; significar

**amour** [ə'mʊr] *s* amores, amorío

**amour-propre** [ɑ'mur'prɔprə] *s* amor propio

**amp.** abr. de **ampere** y **amperage**

**ampelite** ['æmpəlaɪt] *s* (mineral.) ampelita

**ampelography** [ˌæmpə'lɑgrəfɪ] *s* ampelografía

**amperage** [æm'pɪrɪdʒ] o ['æmpɪrɪdʒ] *s* (elec.) amperaje

**ampere** ['æmpɪr] *s* (elec.) amperio

**ampere-hour** ['æmpɪr'aʊr] *s* (*pl:* **ampere-hours**) (elec.) amperio hora

**ampere turn** *s* (elec.) amperio-vuelta

**ampersand** ['æmpərsænd] *s* la cifra & que significa **and**

**amphetamine** [æm'fɛtəmin] o [æm'fɛtəmɪn] *s* (pharm.) anfetamina

**amphibian** [æm'fɪbɪən] *adj & s* (aer. & biol.) anfibio

**amphibious** [æm'fɪbɪəs] *adj* (aer., biol., & fig.) anfibio

**amphibole** ['æmfɪbol] *s* (mineral.) anfíbol

**amphibolite** [æm'fɪbolaɪt] *s* (geol.) anfibolita

**amphibological** [æmˌfɪbo'lɑdʒɪkəl] *adj* anfibológico

**amphibology** [ˌæmfɪ'bɑlədʒɪ] *s* (*pl:* **-gies**) anfibología

**amphiboly** [æm'fɪbəlɪ] *s* (*pl:* **-lies**) var. de **amphibology**

**amphibrach** ['æmfɪbræk] *s* anfíbraco

**Amphion** [æm'faɪən] *s* (myth.) Anfión

**amphipod** ['æmfɪpɑd] *adj & s* (zool.) anfípodo

**amphisbaena** [ˌæmfɪs'binə] *s* (zool.) anfisbena

**amphiscians** [æm'fɪʃɪəns] *spl* anfiscios (*habitantes de la zona tórrida*)

**amphitheater** ['æmfɪˌθiətər] *s* anfiteatro

**Amphitrite** [ˌæmfɪ'traɪtɪ] *s* (myth. & zool.) Anfitrite

**Amphitryon** [æm'fɪtrɪən] *s* (myth.) Anfitrión

**amphora** ['æmfərə] *s* (*pl:* **-rae** [ri]) ánfora

**ample** ['æmpəl] *adj* amplio; bastante, suficiente; abundante

**amplexicaul** [æm'plɛksɪkɔl] *adj* (bot.) amplexicaulo

**amplification** [ˌæmplɪfɪ'keʃən] *s* amplificación; (elec.) amplificación

**amplificative** ['æmplɪfɪˌketɪv] *adj* amplificativo

**amplifier** ['æmplɪˌfaɪər] *s* amplificador; (elec.) amplificador

**amplify** ['æmplɪfaɪ] (*pret & pp:* **-fied**) *va* amplificar; (elec.) amplificar; *vn* espaciarse (*en el discurso*)

**amplifying** ['æmplɪˌfaɪɪŋ] *adj* amplificador

**amplitude** ['æmplɪtjud] o ['æmplɪtud] *s* amplitud; (astr., elec., & mech.) amplitud

**amplitude modulation** *s* (rad.) modulación de altura o de amplitud

**amply** ['æmplɪ] *adv* ampliamente; bastante, suficientemente; abundantemente

**ampoule** [æm'pul] *s* (med.) ampolla

**ampulla** [æm'pʌlə] *s* (anat., bot., eccl., hist. & zool.) ampolla

**amputate** ['æmpjətet] *va* amputar

**amputation** [,æmpjə'teʃən] *s* amputación

**amputee** [,æmpjə'ti] *s* amputado

**amt.** abr. de **amount**

**amuck** [ə'mʌk] *adv* frenéticamente; **to run amuck** atacar a c' ras

**amulet** ['æmjəlɪt] muleto

**amuse** [ə'mjuz] *va* .vertir, entretener

**amusement** [ə'mjuzmənt] *s* diversión, entretenimiento; pasatiempo, recreación; atracción (*p.ej., en un circo*)

**amusement park** *s* parque de atracciones

**amusement tax** *s* impuesto sobre espectáculos

**amusing** [ə'mjuzɪŋ] *adj* divertido, gracioso

**Amy** ['emɪ] *s* Amata

**amygdalin** [ə'mɪgdəlɪn] *s* (chem.) amigdalina

**amygdaloid** [ə'mɪgdəlɔɪd] *adj* amigdaloideo; (mineral.) amigdaloide

**amyl** ['æmɪl] o ['emɪl] *s* (chem.) amilo; *adj* (chem.) amílico

**amylaceous** [,æmɪ'leʃəs] *adj* amiláceo

**amylase** ['æmɪles] *s* (biochem.) amilasa

**amylene** ['æmɪlin] *s* (chem.) amileno

**amylic** [ə'mɪlɪk] *adj* (chem.) amílico

**amyloid** ['æmɪlɔɪd] *adj* amiloideo

**amyloid degeneration** *s* (path.) degeneración amiloidea

**amyloidosis** [,æmɪlɔɪ'dosɪs] *s* (path.) amiloidosis

**amylopsin** [,æmɪ'lɑpsɪn] *s* (chem.) amilopsina

**an** [æn] o [ən] *art indef* (antes de sonido vocal) var. de **a**

**Anabaptism** [,ænə'bæptɪzəm] *s* anabaptismo

**Anabaptist** [,ænə'bæptɪst] *adj & s* anabaptista

**anabiosis** [,ænəbaɪ'osɪs] *s* anabiosis

**anabolic** [,ænə'bɑlɪk] *adj* anabólico

**anabolism** [ə'næbəlɪzəm] *s* (biol.) anabolismo

**anacardiaceous** [,ænə,kɑrdɪ'eʃəs] *adj* (bot.) anacardiáceo

**anacardic** [,ænə'kɑrdɪk] *adj* (chem.) anacárdico

**anachronism** [ə'nækrənɪzəm] *s* anacronismo

**anachronistic** [ə,nækrə'nɪstɪk] o **anachronous** [ə'nækrənəs] *adj* anacrónico

**anacoluthon** [,ænəko'luθɑn] *s* (*pl:* **-tha** [θə]) (gram.) anacoluto

**anaconda** [,ænə'kɑndə] *s* (zool.) anaconda

**Anacreon** [ə'nækrɪɑn] *s* Anacreonte

**Anacreontic** [ə,nækrɪ'ɑntɪk] *adj* anacreóntico

**anadromous** [ə'nædroməs] *adj* anadromo

**anaemia** [ə'nimɪə] *s* (path.) anemia

**anaemic** [ə'nimɪk] *adj* anémico

**anaerobe** [æn'ɛrob] o [æn'eərob] *s* anaerobio

**anaerobic** [,ænɛ'robɪk] o [æn,eə'robɪk] *adj* anaerobio, anaeróbico

**anaesthesia** [,ænɪs'θiʒə] o [,ænɪs'θiʒɪə] *s* anestesia

**anaesthesiologist** [,ænɪs,θizɪ'ɑlədʒɪst] *s* anestesiólogo

**anaesthesiology** [,ænɪs,θizɪ'ɑlədʒɪ] *s* anestesiología

**anaesthetic** [,ænɪs'θɛtɪk] *adj & s* anestésico

**anaesthetist** [æ'nɛsθɪtɪst] *s* anestesiador

**anaesthetize** [æ'nɛsθɪtaɪz] *va* anestesiar

**anaglyph** ['ænəglɪf] *s* anáglifo

**anagnorisis** [,ænæg'nɑrɪsɪs] *s* (rhet.) anagnórisis

**anagogics** [,ænə'gɑdʒɪks] *spl* anagoge o anagogía

**anagram** ['ænəgræm] *s* anagrama; **anagrams** *spl* anagramas (*juego*)

**anagrammatic** [,ænəgrə'mætɪk] o **anagrammatical** [,ænəgrə'mætɪkəl] *adj* anagramático

**anagrammatism** [,ænə'græmətɪzəm] *s* anagramatismo

**anal** ['enəl] *adj* (anat.) anal

**analecta** [,ænə'lɛktə] *spl* o **analects** ['ænəlɛkts] *spl* analectas

**analeptic** [,ænə'lɛptɪk] *adj* analéptico

**analgen** [æ'nældʒɛn] o **analgene** [æ'nældʒin] *s* (pharm.) analgeno

**analgesia** [,ænæl'dʒizɪə] *s* (physiol.) analgesia

**analgesic** [,ænæl'dʒizɪk] *adj & s* analgésico

**analog** ['ænəlɔg] o ['ænəlɑg] *s* var. de **analogue**

**analog computer** *s* calculadora analógica

**analogical** [,ænə'lɑdʒɪkəl] *adj* analógico

**analogous** [ə'næləgəs] *adj* análogo

**analogue** ['ænəlɔg] o ['ænəlɑg] *s* análogo; (biol.) análogo

**analogy** [ə'nælədʒɪ] *s* (*pl:* **-gies**) analogía

**analyse** ['ænəlaɪz] *va* analizar

**analyser** ['ænə,laɪzər] *s* analizador

**analysis** [ə'nælɪsɪs] *s* (*pl:* **-ses** [siz]) análisis

**analyst** ['ænəlɪst] *s* analista (*analizador; psicoanalista*)

**analytic** [,ænə'lɪtɪk] *adj* analítico; **analytics** *ssg* geometría analítica; (philos.) analítica

**analytical** [,ænə'lɪtɪkəl] *adj* analítico

**analytic geometry** *s* geometría analítica

**analyzable** ['ænə,laɪzəbəl] *adj* analizable

**analyze** ['ænəlaɪz] *va* analizar

**analyzer** ['ænə,laɪzər] *s* analizador; (opt.) analizador

**anamniotic** [æn,æmnɪ'ɑtɪk] *adj* anamriótico

**anamorphosis** [,ænə'mɔrfəsɪs] *s* (*pl:* **-ses** [siz]) anamorfosis; (biol. & bot.) anamorfosis

**Ananias** [,ænə'naɪəs] *s* (Bib.) Ananías

**anapaest** ['ænəpɛst] *s* anapesto

**anapaestic** [,ænə'pɛstɪk] *adj* anapéstico

**anapest** ['ænəpɛst] *s* anapesto

**anapestic** [,ænə'pɛstɪk] *adj* anapéstico

**anaphase** ['ænəfez] *s* (biol.) anafase

**anaphora** [ə'næfərə] *s* (rhet. & astrol.) anáfora

**anaphrodisia** [æn,æfrə'dɪzɪə] *s* (med.) anafrodisia

**anaphrodisiac** [æn,æfrə'dɪzɪæk] *adj & s* (med.) anafrodisíaco, antiafrodisíaco

**anaphylaxis** [,ænəfɪ'læksɪs] *s* (path.) anafilaxis

**anaplastic** [,ænə'plæstɪk] *adj* anaplástico

**anaplasty** ['ænə,plæstɪ] *s* (surg.) anaplastia

**anaptyxis** [,ænæp'tɪksɪs] *s* (phonet.) anaptixis

**anarch** ['ænɑrk] *s* anarquista

**anarchic** [æn'ɑrkɪk] o **anarchical** [æn'ɑrkɪkəl] *adj* anárquico

**anarchism** ['ænərkɪzəm] *s* anarquismo

**anarchist** ['ænərkɪst] *s* anarquista

**anarchistic** [,ænər'kɪstɪk] *adj* anarquista

**anarchy** ['ænərkɪ] *s* anarquía

**anasarca** [,ænə'sɑrkə] *s* (path.) anasarca

**anastatic** [,ænəs'tætɪk] *adj* anastático

**anastigmatic** [æn,æstɪg'mætɪk] *adj* (opt.) anastigmático

**anastomose** [ə'næstəmoz] *vn* anastomosarse

**anastomosis** [ə,næstə'mosɪs] *s* (*pl:* **-ses** [siz]) (anat. & biol.) anastomosis

**anastomotic** [ə,næstə'mɑtɪk] *adj* anastomótico

**anastrophe** [ə'næstrəfɪ] *s* (gram.) anástrofe

**anathema** [ə'næθɪmə] *s* anatema; persona anatematizada; persona aborrecida, cosa aborrecida

**anathematization** [ə,næθɪmətɪ'zeʃən] *s* anatematización

**anathematize** [ə'næθɪmətaɪz] *va* anatematizar

**Anatolian** [,ænə'tolɪən] *adj & s* anatolio

**anatomic** [,ænə'tɑmɪk] o **anatomical** [,ænə'tɑmɪkəl]) *adj* anatómico

**anatomist** [ə'nætəmɪst] *s* anatomista, anatómico

**anatomize** [ə'nætəmaɪz] *va* anatomizar

**anatomy** [ə'nætəmɪ] *s* (*pl:* **-mies**) anatomía

**Anaxagoras** [,ænæks'ægərəs] *s* Anaxágoras

**Anaximander** [æ,næksɪ'mændər] *s* Anaximandro

**ancestor** ['ænsɛstər] *s* antecesor, antepasado

**ancestral** [æn'sɛstrəl] *adj* ancestral

**ancestress** ['ænsɛstrɪs] *s* antecesora

**ancestry** ['ænsɛstrɪ] *s* (*pl:* **-tries**) prosapia, abolengo, alcurnia

**Anchises** [æn'kaɪsiz] *s* (myth.) Anquises

**anchor** ['æŋkər] *s* (naut.) ancla o áncora; (horol. & fig.) áncora; (dent.) anclaje; **to cast anchor** echar anclas; **to ride at anchor** estar anclado; **to weigh anchor** levar anclas; *va* (naut.) sujetar con el ancla; asegurar, sujetar, empotrar; *vn* (naut.) anclar, ancorar

**anchorage** ['æŋkərɪdʒ] *s* anclaje

**anchor escapement** *s* (horl.) escape de áncora

**anchoress** ['æŋkərɪs] *s* anacoreta

**anchoret** ['æŋkərɛt] *s* anacoreta

**anchoretic** [ˌæŋkəˈrɛtɪk] *adj* anacorético
**anchoretism** [ˈæŋkərɛtɪzəm] *s* anacoretismo
**anchorite** [ˈæŋkəraɪt] *s* anacoreta
**anchoritic** [ˌæŋkəˈrɪtɪk] *adj* anacorético
**anchoritism** [ˈæŋkəraɪtɪzəm] *s* anacoretismo
**anchorless** [ˈæŋkərlɪs] *adj* sin ancla; (fig.) inseguro, errante
**anchor ring** *s* (naut.) arganeo
**anchovy** [ˈæntʃovɪ] o [ænˈtʃovɪ] *s* (*pl:* **-vies**) (ichth.) alacha, anchoa, anchova, boquerón
**ancien régime** [ɑ̃sjɛ̃·reˈʒim] *s* antiguo régimen
**ancient** [ˈenʃənt] *adj* antiguo; **the ancients** los antiguos
**ancient history** *s* la historia antigua; (coll.) cosa vieja
**anciently** [ˈenʃəntlɪ] *adv* antiguamente
**Ancient of Days** *s* anciano de los días (*Dios*)
**ancillary** [ˈænsɪˌlɛrɪ] *adj* ancilar; auxiliar, subordinado
**ancon** [ˈæŋkɑn] *s* (*pl:* **ancones** [æŋˈkoniz]) (anat. & arch.) ancón
**and** [ænd], [ənd] o [ən] *conj* y, e; **and so on** o **and so forth** y así sucesivamente
**Andalusia** [ˌændəˈluʒə] o [ˌændəˈluʃə] *s* Andalucía
**Andalusian** [ˌændəˈluʒən] o [ˌændəˈluʃən] *adj & s* andaluz
**andalusite** [ˌændəˈlusaɪt] *s* (mineral.) andalucita
**andante** [ænˈdæntɪ] o [ɑnˈdɑnte] *s* (mus.) andante
**andantino** [ˌændænˈtino] o [ˌɑndɑnˈtino] *s* (*pl:* **-nos**) (mus.) andantino
**Andean** [ænˈdiən] o [ˈændɪən] *adj & s* andino
**Andes** [ˈændiz] *spl* Andes
**andirons** [ˈændˌaɪərnz] *spl* morillos
**Andorran** [ænˈdɔrən] *adj & s* andorrano
**Andrew** [ˈændru] *s* Andrés
**Androcles** [ˈændrokliz] *s* Ándrocles
**androecium** [ænˈdriʃɪəm] *s* (*pl:* **-a** [ə]) (bot.) androceo
**androgen** [ˈændrədʒən] *s* (biochem.) andrógeno
**androgyne** [ˈændrodʒɪn] o [ˈændrodʒaɪn] *s* andrógino; (bot.) andrógino
**androgynous** [ænˈdrɑdʒɪnəs] *adj* andrógino; (bot.) andrógino
**android** [ˈændrɔɪd] *s* androide (*autómata de forma humana*)
**Andromache** [ænˈdrɑməkɪ] *s* (myth.) Andrómaca
**Andromeda** [ænˈdrɑmɪdə] *s* (myth. & astr.) Andrómeda
**androphobia** [ˌændroˈfobɪə] *s* androfobia
**androseme** [ænˈdrɑsɪmi] *s* (bot.) androsemo
**androsphinx** [ˈændrosfɪŋks] *s* (archeol.) androsfinge
**androsterone** [ænˈdrɑstəron] *s* (biochem.) androsterona
**anecdotal** [ˈænɪkˌdotəl] *adj* anecdótico
**anecdote** [ˈænɪkdot] *s* anécdota
**anecdotist** [ˈænɪkˌdotɪst] *s* anecdotista
**anelectric** [ˌænɪˈlɛktrɪk] *adj & s* (phys.) aneléctrico
**anemia** [əˈnimɪə] *s* (path.) anemia
**anemic** [əˈnimɪk] *adj* anémico
**anemometer** [ˌænɪˈmɑmɪtər] *s* anemómetro
**anemometry** [ˌænɪˈmɑmɪtrɪ] *s* anemometría
**anemone** [əˈnɛmənɪ] *s* (bot.) anemona o anemone
**anemoscope** [əˈnɛməskop] *s* anemoscopio
**anent** [əˈnɛnt] *prep* tocante a
**anepigraphic** [ænˌɛpɪˈgræfɪk] *adj* anepigráfico
**aneroid** [ˈænərɔɪd] *adj* aneroide
**aneroid barometer** *s* barómetro aneroide
**anesthesia** [ˌænɪsˈθiʒə] o [ˌænɪsˈθiʒɪə] *s* anestesia
**anesthesiologist** [ˌænɪsˌθizɪˈɑlədʒɪst] *s* anestesiólogo
**anesthesiology** [ˌænɪsˌθizɪˈɑlədʒɪ] *s* anestesiología
**anesthetic** [ˌænɪsˈθɛtɪk] *adj & s* anestésico
**anesthetist** [æˈnɛsθɪtɪst] *s* anestesiador
**anesthetize** [æˈnɛsθɪtaɪz] *va* anestesiar
**aneurysm** [ˈænjərɪzəm] *s* (path.) aneurisma
**aneurysmatic** [ˌænjərɪzˈmætɪk] *adj* aneurismático
**anew** [əˈnju] o [əˈnu] *adv* de nuevo, nuevamente
**anfractuosity** [ænˌfræktʃuˈɑsɪtɪ] *s* (*pl:* **-ties**) anfractuosidad
**anfractuous** [ænˈfræktʃuəs] *adj* anfractuoso
**angaria** [æŋˈgɛrɪə] *s* (law) angaria
**angel** [ˈendʒəl] *s* ángel; (slang) caballo blanco (*persona que provee fondos para una empresa*)
**angel cake** *s* bizcocho blanco de harina, azúcar y clara de huevo
**angelfish** [ˈendʒəlˌfɪʃ] *s* (ichth.) angelote, ángel de mar, peje ángel; (ichth.) reina de los ángeles (*Angelichthys ciliaris*)
**angelic** [ænˈdʒɛlɪk] *adj* angélico o angelical
**angelica** [ænˈdʒɛlɪkə] *s* (bot.) angélica
**angelical** [ænˈdʒɛlɪkəl] *adj* var. de **angelic**
**Angelic Doctor** *s* doctor angélico (*Santo Tomás de Aquino*)
**Angelic Salutation** *s* salutación angélica
**angelin** [ˈændʒəlɪn] *s* (bot.) angelín, pangelín
**angel sleeve** *s* manga de ángel
**Angelus** [ˈændʒələs] *s* ángelus
**anger** [ˈæŋgər] *s* ira, cólera; *va* airar, encolerizar
**Angevin** [ˈændʒɪvɪn] *adj & s* angevino
**angina** [ænˈdʒaɪnə] o [ˈændʒɪnə] *s* (path.) angina
**angina pectoris** [ˈpɛktərɪs] *s* (path.) angina de pecho
**angiocholitis** [ˌændʒɪokoˈlaɪtɪs] *s* (path.) angiocolitis
**angiography** [ˌændʒɪˈɑgrəfɪ] *s* (anat.) angiografía
**angiology** [ˌændʒɪˈɑlədʒɪ] *s* angiología
**angiosperm** [ˈændʒɪoˌspʌrm] *s* (bot.) angiosperma
**angiospermous** [ˌændʒɪoˈspʌrməs] *adj* (bot.) angiospermo
**angle** [ˈæŋgəl] *s* ángulo; codo, ángulo de hierro, hierro en ángulo; (fig.) punto de vista; **Angles** *spl* anglos; **at an angle** en ángulo; *vn* pescar con caña; (fig.) intrigar; **to angle for** intrigar por conseguir
**angle iron** *s* hierro angular, ángulo de hierro
**angle of attack** *s* (aer.) ángulo de ataque
**angle of incidence** *s* (phys.) ángulo de incidencia
**angler** [ˈæŋglər] *s* pescador de caña; (ichth.) pejesapo; (fig.) intrigante
**anglesite** [ˈæŋgləsaɪt] *s* (mineral.) anglesita
**angleworm** [ˈæŋgəlˌwʌrm] *s* lombriz de tierra
**Anglia** [ˈæŋglɪə] *s* Anglia
**Anglian** [ˈæŋglɪən] *adj & s* anglo
**Anglican** [ˈæŋglɪkən] *adj & s* anglicano; inglés
**Anglicanism** [ˈæŋglɪkənɪzəm] *s* anglicanismo
**Anglicism** [ˈæŋglɪsɪzəm] *s* anglicismo, inglesismo
**Anglicization** [ˌæŋglɪsɪˈzeʃən] *s* anglicización
**Anglicize** [ˈæŋglɪsaɪz] *va* inglesar
**angling** [ˈæŋglɪŋ] *s* pesca con caña
**Anglo-American** [ˌæŋgloəˈmɛrɪkən] *adj & s* angloamericano, anglonorteamericano
**Anglo-Catholic** [ˌæŋgloˈkæθəlɪk] *adj & s* anglocatólico
**Anglo-Catholicism** [ˌæŋglokəˈθɑlɪsɪzəm] *s* anglocatolicismo
**Anglo-Egyptian Sudan** [ˌæŋglo·ɪˈdʒɪpʃən] *s* Sudán Angloegipcio
**Anglo-Indian** [ˌæŋgloˈɪndɪən] *adj & s* angloindio
**Anglo-Iranian** [ˌæŋgloaɪˈrenɪən] *adj & s* angloiranio
**Anglomania** [ˌæŋgloˈmenɪə] *s* anglomanía
**Anglomaniac** [ˌæŋgloˈmenɪæk] *s* anglómano
**Anglo-Norman** [ˌæŋgloˈnɔrmən] *adj & s* anglonormando
**Anglophile** [ˈæŋglofaɪl] *adj & s* anglófilo
**Anglophobe** [ˈæŋglofob] *adj & s* anglófobo
**Anglophobia** [ˌæŋgloˈfobɪə] *s* anglofobia
**Anglo-Saxon** [ˌæŋgloˈsæksən] *adj & s* anglosajón
**Angora** [æŋˈgorə] *s* angora (*gato o cabra*)
**Angora cat** *s* gato de Angora
**Angora goat** *s* cabra de Angora
**angostura** [ˌæŋgəsˈtjurə] o [ˌæŋgəsˈturə] *s* angostura (*corteza medicinal*); (pharm.) angosturina (*tónico*)
**angostura bark** *s* corteza de angostura
**angostura bitters** *spl* (trademark) (amargo de) angostura
**Angoulême** [ˌɑ̃ˌguˈlɛm] *s* Angulema
**angrily** [ˈæŋgrɪlɪ] *adv* airadamente

**angry** ['æŋgrɪ] *adj* (*comp:* **-grier;** *super:* **-griest**) enojado, airado, encolerizado; tormentoso; (path.) irritado, inflamado; **to become angry at** enojarse de (*una cosa*); **to become angry with** enojarse con o contra (*una persona*)
**angstrom** ['æŋgstrəm] *s* (phys.) angstrom
**anguish** ['æŋgwɪʃ] *s* angustia, congoja; *va* angustiar, acongojar
**angular** ['æŋgjələr] *adj* angular; anguloso (*dícese, p.ej., de las facciones*)
**angularity** [,æŋgjə'lærɪtɪ] *s* (*pl:* **-ties**) angularidad; angulosidad
**angular momentum** *s* (mech.) momento angular
**anhydrid** [æn'haɪdrɪd] o **anhydride** [æn'haɪdraɪd] o [æn'haɪdrɪd] *s* (chem.) anhídrido
**anhydrite** [æn'haɪdraɪt] *s* (mineral.) anhidrita
**anhydrous** [æn'haɪdrəs] *adj* (chem.) anhidro
**anil** ['ænɪl] *s* (bot.) añil (*planta, color y tintura*)
**anilin** ['ænɪlɪn] *s* (chem.) anilina
**aniline** ['ænɪlɪn] o ['ænɪlaɪn] *s* var. de **anilin**
**aniline dyes** *spl* colores de anilina
**anility** [ə'nɪlɪtɪ] *s* (*pl:* **-ties**) ancianidad femenil, senilidad en la mujer
**animadversion** [,ænɪmæd'vʌrʒən] o [,ænɪmæd'vʌrʃən] *s* animadversión
**animadvert** [,ænɪmæd'vʌrt] *va* reparar, observar, advertir; *vn* reparar, observar, advertir; **to animadvert on** *ó* **upon** censurar, reprochar
**animal** ['ænɪməl] *adj & s* animal
**animalcule** [,ænɪ'mælkjʊl] *s* animálculo
**animal husbandry** *s* ganadería
**animalism** ['ænɪməlɪzəm] *s* animalismo
**animalist** ['ænɪməlɪst] *s* animalista
**animalistic** [,ænɪmə'lɪstɪk] *adj* animalista
**animality** [,ænɪ'mælɪtɪ] *s* animalidad
**animalization** [,ænɪməlɪ'zeʃən] *s* animalización
**animalize** ['ænɪməlaɪz] *va* animalizar
**animal kingdom** *s* reino animal
**animal magnetism** *s* magnetismo animal
**animal spirits** *spl* ardor, vigor, vivacidad
**animate** ['ænɪmɪt] *adj* animado; ['ænɪmet] *va* animar
**animated** ['ænɪ,metɪd] *adj* animado, vivo, alegre
**animated cartoon** *s* película de dibujos, dibujo animado
**animation** [,ænɪ'meʃən] *s* animación
**animator** ['ænɪ,metər] *s* animador; (mov.) animador
**animism** ['ænɪmɪzəm] *s* animismo
**animist** ['ænɪmɪst] *s* animista
**animistic** [,ænɪ'mɪstɪk] *adj* animista
**animosity** [,ænɪ'mɑsɪtɪ] *s* (*pl:* **-ties**) animosidad
**animus** ['ænɪməs] *s* ánimo; mala voluntad, odio
**anion** ['æn,aɪən] *s* (elec.) anión
**anise** ['ænɪs] *s* (bot.) anís (*planta y semilla*)
**aniseed** ['ænɪsid] *s* grano de anís
**anisette** [,ænɪ'zɛt] *s* anisete
**anisomerous** [,ænaɪ'sɑmərəs] *adj* (bot.) anisómero
**anisometric** [æn,aɪso'mɛtrɪk] *adj* (mineral.) anisométrico
**anisophyllous** [æn,aɪso'fɪləs] *adj* (bot.) anisofilo
**ankle** ['æŋkəl] *s* tobillo
**anklebone** ['æŋkəl,bon] *s* hueso del tobillo
**ankle support** *s* (sport) tobillera
**anklet** ['æŋklɪt] *s* brazalete para el tobillo, ajorca; tobillera (*calcetín corto; abrazadera o vendaje para el tobillo*)
**ankylose** ['æŋkɪlos] *va* anquilosar; *vn* anquilosarse
**ankylosis** [,æŋkɪ'losɪs] *s* (path.) anquilosis
**Ann** [æn] o **Anna** ['ænə] *s* Ana
**annalist** ['ænəlɪst] *s* analista
**annals** ['ænəlz] *spl* anales
**Annamese** [,ænə'miz] *adj* anamita; *s* (*pl:* **-mese**) anamita
**annatto** [ɑ'nɑto] *s* (bot.) bija (*árbol y colorante*)
**annatto tree** *s* (bot.) achiote, bija
**Anne** [æn] *s* Ana
**anneal** [ə'nil] *va* recocer; (fig.) fortalecer
**annealing** [ə'nilɪŋ] *s* recocido
**annelid** ['ænəlɪd] *adj & s* (zool.) anélido
**annex** ['ænɛks] *s* anexo; pabellón (*edificio*); [ə'nɛks] *va* anexar
**annexation** [,ænɛks'eʃən] *s* anexión
**annexationism** [,ænɛks'eʃənɪzəm] *s* anexionismo
**annexationist** [,ænɛks'eʃənɪst] *adj & s* anexionista
**annihilate** [ə'naɪɪlet] *va* aniquilar
**annihilation** [ə,naɪɪ'leʃən] *s* aniquilación
**anniversary** [,ænɪ'vʌrsərɪ] *adj* aniversario; *s* (*pl:* **-ries**) aniversario
**anno Domini** ['æno'dɑmɪnaɪ] (Lat.) año de Cristo
**annonaceous** [,æno'neʃəs] *adj* anonáceo
**annotate** ['ænotet] *va* anotar
**annotation** [,æno'teʃən] *s* anotación
**annotator** ['æno,tetər] *s* anotador
**announce** [ə'naʊns] *va* anunciar
**announcement** [ə'naʊnsmənt] *s* anuncio, aviso
**announcer** [ə'naʊnsər] *s* anunciador; (rad.) locutor
**annoy** [ə'nɔɪ] *va* molestar, fastidiar
**annoyance** [ə'nɔɪəns] *s* molestia, fastidio
**annoying** [ə'nɔɪɪŋ] *adj* molesto, fastidioso
**annual** ['ænjʊəl] *adj* anual; *s* publicación anual; (bot.) planta anual
**annually** ['ænjʊəlɪ] *adv* anualmente
**annual ring** *s* (bot.) capa anual
**annuitant** [ə'njuɪtənt] o [ə'nuɪtənt] *s* censualista, rentista
**annuity** [ə'njuɪtɪ] o [ə'nuɪtɪ] *s* (*pl:* **-ties**) anualidad; renta vitalicia
**annul** [ə'nʌl] (*pret & pp:* **-nulled;** *ger:* **-nulling**) *va* anular, invalidar; revocar; destruir
**annular** ['ænjələr] *adj* anular
**annulet** ['ænjəlɪt] *s* anillejo, anillete; (her. & zool.) anillo
**annulment** [ə'nʌlmənt] *s* anulación; revocación; abolición; descasamiento
**annulus** ['ænjələs] *s* (*pl:* **-li** [laɪ] o **-luses**) (anat., arch., & bot.) anillo
**annum** ['ænəm] *s* (Lat.) año; **per annum** por año, al año
**annunciate** [ə'nʌnʃɪet] o [ə'nʌnsɪet] *va* anunciar
**annunciation** [ə,nʌnsɪ'eʃən] *s* anunciación; (*cap.*) *s* Anunciación
**annunciator** [ə'nʌnʃɪ,etər] o [ə'nʌnsɪ,etər] *s* anunciador; (elec.) cuadro indicador
**annunciator wire** *s* alambre para timbres eléctricos
**anode** ['ænod] *s* (elec.) ánodo
**anodic** [æn'ɑdɪk] *adj* anódico
**anodize** ['ænodaɪz] *va* (metal.) anodizar
**anodyne** ['ænədaɪn] *adj & s* anodino
**anodynia** [,ænə'dɪnɪə] *s* anodinia
**anoint** [ə'nɔɪnt] *va* ungir, untar; (eccl.) ungir
**anointed** [ə'nɔɪntɪd] *s* ungido
**anointment** [ə'nɔɪntmənt] *s* ungimiento, untamiento
**anomalistic** [ə,nɑmə'lɪstɪk] *adj* anomalístico
**anomalistic month** *s* (astr.) mes anomalístico
**anomalistic year** *s* (astr.) año anomalístico
**anomalous** [ə'nɑmələs] *adj* anómalo
**anomaly** [ə'nɑməlɪ] *s* (*pl:* **-lies**) anomalía
**anomuran** [,æno'mjurən] *adj & s* (zool.) anomuro
**anon.** abr. de **anonymous**
**anon** [ə'nɑn] *adv* en breve; otra vez
**anonym** ['ænənɪm] *s* anónimo
**anonymity** [,ænə'nɪmɪtɪ] *s* anonimato, anónimo; **to preserve one's anonymity** guardar o conservar el anónimo
**anonymous** [ə'nɑnɪməs] *adj* anónimo
**anopheles** [ə'nɑfəliz] *s* (*pl:* **-les**) (ent.) anofeles
**anorexia** [,æno'rɛksɪə] *s* (path.) anorexia
**anosmia** [æ'nɑzmɪə] *s* (path.) anosmia
**another** [ə'nʌðər] *adj & pron indef* otro; uno más; **one another** uno a otro, unos a otros
**anoxemia** [,ænɑks'imɪə] *s* (path.) anoxemia
**ans.** abr. de **answer**
**Anselm, Saint** ['ænsɛlm] San Anselmo
**anserine** ['ænsəraɪn] o ['ænsərɪn] *adj* ansarino; tonto, necio, mentecato
**answer** ['ænsər] o ['ɑnsər] *s* respuesta, contestación; explicación; solución (*a un problema o un enigma*); (law) contestación a la demanda; *va* responder a, contestar; resolver (*un problema o un enigma*); **to answer a purpose**

convenir a un designio; **to answer the bell, the door, the telephone** contestar el timbre, la puerta, el teléfono; *vn* responder, contestar; bastar; **to answer back** ser respondón; **to answer for** responder de (*una cosa*); responder por (*una persona*); **to answer to the name of** responder al nombre de; atender (*p.ej., un perro*) por

**answerable** ['ænsərəbəl] o ['ɑnsərəbəl] *adj* responsable; contestable; soluble

**ant** [ænt] *s* (ent.) hormiga

**antacid** [ænt'æsɪd] *adj & s* antiácido

**Antaeus** [æn'tiəs] *s* (myth.) Anteo

**antagonism** [æn'tægənɪzəm] *s* antagonismo

**antagonist** [æn'tægənɪst] *s* antagonista

**antagonistic** [æn,tægə'nɪstɪk] *adj* antagónico

**antagonize** [æn'tægənaɪz] *va* oponerse a; enemistar, enajenar

**antarctic** [ænt'ɑrktɪk] *adj* antártico; *s* tierras antárticas

**Antarctica** [ænt'ɑrktɪkə] *s* la Antártica o Antártida

**antarctic circle** *s* círculo polar antártico

**Antarctic Continent** *s* continente antártico

**Antarctic Ocean** *s* océano Antártico

**Antarctic zone** *s* zona antártica

**Antares** [æn'tɛriz] *s* (astr.) Antarés

**ant bear** *s* (zool.) oso hormiguero

**ante** ['æntɪ] *s* puesta, tanto (*en juegos de naipes*); *va* apostar; pagar; *vn* poner su apuesta; pagar su apuesta; pagar su cuota

**anteater** ['ænt,itər] *s* (zool.) oso hormiguero; (zool.) cerdo hormiguero; mamífero o pájaro que come hormigas

**ante-bellum** ['æntɪ'bɛləm] *adj* anterior a la guerra, de antes de la guerra

**antecedence** [,æntɪ'sidəns] *s* antecedencia o antecedente

**antecedent** [,æntɪ'sidənt] *adj* antecedente; *s* antecedente; (gram., log., & math.) antecedente; **antecedents** *spl* antepasados; antecedentes

**antechamber** ['æntɪ,tʃembər] *s* antecámara

**antechapel** ['æntɪ,tʃæpəl] *s* (eccl.) antecapilla

**antechoir** ['æntɪ,kwaɪr] *s* (arch.) antecoro

**antedate** ['æntɪ,det] *s* antedata; *va* antedatar; retrotraer; preceder

**antediluvian** [,æntɪdɪ'luvɪən] *adj* antediluviano

**antefix** ['æntɪfɪks] *s* (arch.) antefija

**antelope** ['æntɪlop] *s* (zool.) antílope

**antemeridian** [,æntɪmə'rɪdɪən] *adj* antemeridiano

**antenatal** [,æntɪ'netəl] *adj* antenatal

**antenna** [æn'tɛnə] *s* (*pl:* **-nae** [ni]) (ent.) antena; (*pl:* **-nas**) (rad.) antena

**antenna connection** *s* (rad.) toma de antena

**antenuptial** [,æntɪ'nʌpʃəl] *adj* antenupcial

**antependium** [,æntɪ'pɛndɪəm] *s* (*pl:* **-a** [ə]) (eccl.) antipendio

**antepenult** [,æntɪ'pinʌlt] *s* antepenúltima

**antepenultimate** [,æntɪpɪ'nʌltɪmɪt] *adj* antepenúltimo

**anterior** [æn'tɪrɪər] *adj* anterior

**anteriority** [,æntɪrɪ'ɔrɪtɪ] *s* anterioridad

**anteroom** ['æntɪ,rum] o ['æntɪ,rʊm] *s* antecámara

**anteversion** [,æntɪ'vʌrʒən] o [,æntɪ'vʌrʃən] *s* (path.) anteversión

**anthelion** [ænt'hilɪən] o [æn'θilɪən] *s* (meteor.) antelio

**anthem** ['ænθəm] *s* himno; (eccl.) antífona

**anthemion** [æn'θimɪən] *s* (*pl:* **-a** [ə]) (f.a.) antemio o antemión

**anther** ['ænθər] *s* (bot.) antera

**antheridium** [,ænθə'rɪdɪəm] *s* (*pl:* **-a** [ə]) (bot.) anteridio

**antherozoid** [,ænθərə'zo·ɪd] o ['ænθərəzɔɪd] *s* (bot.) anterozoide

**anthesis** [æn'θisɪs] *s* (bot.) antesis

**anthill** ['ænt,hɪl] *s* hormiguero

**anthocyan** [,ænθo'saɪən] o **anthocyanin** [,ænθo'saɪənɪn] *s* (biochem.) antocianina

**anthodium** [æn'θodɪəm] *s* (*pl:* **-a** [ə]) (bot.) antodio

**anthologist** [æn'θɑlədʒɪst] *s* antólogo

**anthology** [æn'θɑlədʒɪ] *s* (*pl:* **-gies**) antología

**Anthony** ['ænθənɪ] *s* Antonio

**anthophyte** ['ænθofaɪt] *s* (bot.) antofita

**anthozoans** [,ænθo'zoənz] *spl* (zool.) antozoos

**anthracene** ['ænθrəsin] *s* (chem.) antraceno

**anthracite** ['ænθrəsaɪt] *s* antracita; *adj* antracitoso

**anthracnose** [æn'θræknos] *s* (bot.) antracnosis

**anthrax** ['ænθræks] *s* (path.) ántrax

**anthropoid** ['ænθropɔɪd] *adj* antropoide; *s* (zool.) antropoideo (*mono antropoideo*)

**anthropoidal** [,ænθro'pɔɪdəl] *adj* antropoideo

**anthropological** [,ænθropə'lɑdʒɪkəl] *adj* antropológico

**anthropologist** [,ænθro'pɑlədʒɪst] *s* antropólogo

**anthropology** [,ænθro'pɑlədʒɪ] *s* antropología

**anthropometric** [,ænθropə'mɛtrɪk] o **anthropometrical** [,ænθropə'mɛtrɪkəl] *adj* antropométrico

**anthropometry** [,ænθro'pɑmɪtrɪ] *s* antropometría

**anthropomorphic** [,ænθropə'mɔrfɪk] *adj* antropomórfico

**anthropomorphism** [,ænθropə'mɔrfɪzəm] *s* antropomorfismo

**anthropomorphous** [,ænθropə'mɔrfəs] *adj* antropomorfo

**anthropophagi** [,ænθro'pɑfədʒaɪ] *spl* antropófagos

**anthropophagy** [,ænθro'pɑfədʒɪ] *s* antropofagía

**Anthropopithecus** [,ænθropopɪ'θikəs] *s* (pal.) antropopiteco

**anti** ['æntaɪ] o ['æntɪ] *s* (*pl:* **-tis**) (coll.) adversario, contrario

**anti-aircraft** [,æntɪ'ɛr,kræft] o [,æntɪ'ɛr,krɑft] *adj* antiaéreo

**anti-aircraft gun** *s* cañón antiaéreo, ametralladora antiaérea

**antialcoholism** [,æntɪ'ælkəhɔlɪzəm] o [,æntɪ'ælkəhɑlɪzəm] *s* antialcoholismo

**antiar** ['æntɪɑr] *s* antiar (*goma muy tóxica*)

**antiarin** ['æntɪərɪn] *s* (chem.) antiarina

**antibacterial** [,æntɪbæk'tɪrɪəl] *adj* antibactérico

**antibiosis** [,æntɪbaɪ'osɪs] *s* (biol.) antibiosis

**antibiotic** [,æntɪbaɪ'ɑtɪk] *adj & s* antibiótico

**antibody** ['æntɪ,bɑdɪ] *s* (*pl:* **-ies**) (bact.) anticuerpo

**anticatarrhal** [,æntɪkə'tɑrəl] *adj & s* anticatarral

**anticathode** [,æntɪ'kæθod] *s* anticátodo

**anti-Catholic** [,æntɪ'kæθəlɪk] *adj & s* anticatólico

**antichlor** ['æntɪklor] *s* (chem.) anticloro

**antichresis** [,æntɪ'krisɪs] *s* (*pl:* **-ses** [siz]) (law) anticresis

**antichretic** [,æntɪ'kritɪk] *adj* anticrético

**Antichrist** ['æntɪ,kraɪst] *s* Anticristo

**anti-Christian** [,æntɪ'krɪstʃən] *adj & s* anticristiano

**anticipate** [æn'tɪsɪpet] *va* esperar, prever; cumplir, llevar a cabo antes; anticipar, acelerar; anticiparse a; prevenir, impedir; prometerse (*p.ej., un placer*); temerse (*algo desagradable*)

**anticipation** [æn,tɪsɪ'peʃən] *s* anticipación; esperanza, previsión

**anticlerical** [,æntɪ'klɛrɪkəl] *adj* anticlerical

**anticlericalism** [,æntɪ'klɛrɪkəlɪzəm] *s* anticlericalismo

**anticlimax** [,æntɪ'klaɪmæks] *s* (rhet.) anticlímax; acontecimiento desengañador

**anticlinal** [,æntɪ'klaɪnəl] *adj* anticlinal

**anticline** ['æntɪklaɪn] *s* (geol.) anticlinal

**anticlinorium** [,æntɪklaɪ'norɪəm] *s* (*pl:* **-a** [ə]) (geol.) anticlinorio

**anticommunist** [,æntɪ'kɑmjʊnɪst] *adj & s* anticomunista

**antics** ['æntɪks] *spl* cabriolas, gracias, travesuras

**anticyclone** ['æntɪ,saɪklon] *s* (meteor.) anticiclón

**anticyclonic** [,æntɪsaɪ'klɑnɪk] *adj* anticiclonal

**antidemocratic** [,æntɪ,dɛmə'krætɪk] *adj* antidemocrático

**antidote** ['æntɪdot] *s* antídoto; (fig.) antídoto

**antiemetic** [,æntɪɪ'mɛtɪk] *adj & s* antiemético

**antifederal** [,æntɪ'fɛdərəl] *adj* antifederalista

**antifederalist** [,æntɪ'fɛdərəlɪst] *s* antifederalista

**antifreeze** [,æntɪ'friz] *s* anticongelante

**antifriction** [,æntɪ'frɪkʃən] *s* antifricción

**antifriction metal** *s* metal antifricción
**antigen** [ˈæntɪdʒən] *s* (bact.) antígeno
**antigenic** [ˌæntɪˈdʒɛnɪk] *adj* antigénico
**antiglare** [ˌæntɪˈglɛr] *adj* antideslumbrante
**Antigone** [ænˈtɪgəni] *s* (myth.) Antígone
**antigrippe** [ˌæntɪˈgrɪp] *adj* antigripal
**antihistamine** [ˌæntɪˈhɪstəmin] o [ˌæntɪˈhɪstəmɪn] *adj & s* (pharm.) antihistamínico
**anti-inflationary** [ˌæntɪɪnˈfleʃəˌnɛrɪ] *adj* antiinflacionista
**anti-Jewish** [ˌæntɪˈdʒuɪʃ] *adj* antijudío
**antiknock** [ˌæntɪˈnɑk] *adj & s* antidetonante
**antilabor** [ˌæntɪˈlebər] *adj* antiobrero
**Antillean** [ˌæntɪˈliən] o [ænˈtɪlɪən] *adj & s* antillano
**Antilles** [ænˈtɪliz] *spl* Antillas
**antilogarithm** [ˌæntɪˈlɔgərɪðəm] o [ˌæntɪˈlɑgərɪðəm] *s* (math.) antilogaritmo
**antimacassar** [ˌæntɪməˈkæsər] *s* antimacasar o paño de adorno
**antimatter** [ˈæntɪˌmætər] *s* (phys.) antimateria
**antimilitarism** [ˌæntɪˈmɪlɪtərɪzəm] *s* antimilitarismo
**antimilitarist** [ˌæntɪˈmɪlɪtərɪst] *adj & s* antimilitarista
**antimissile missile** [ˌæntɪˈmɪsɪl] *s* proyectil antiproyectil, proyectil destructor de proyectiles
**antimonarchical** [ˌæntɪməˈnɑrkɪkəl] *adj* antimonárquico
**antimonial** [ˌæntɪˈmonɪəl] *adj* (chem.) antimonial
**antimonite** [ˈæntɪˌmonaɪt] *s* (chem. & mineral.) antimonita
**antimony** [ˈæntɪˌmonɪ] *s* (chem.) antimonio
**antinode** [ˈæntɪˌnod] *s* (phys.) antinodo
**antinomic** [ˌæntɪˈnɑmɪk] *adj* antinómico
**antinomy** [ænˈtɪnəmɪ] *s* (*pl:* **-mies**) antinomia
**Antioch** [ˈæntɪɑk] *s* Antioquía
**Antiochian** [ˌæntɪˈokɪən] *adj & s* antioqueno
**Antiochus** [ænˈtaɪəkəs] *s* Antíoco
**antiparty** [ˌæntɪˈpɑrtɪ] *adj & s* antipartido
**antipasto** [ˌɑntɪˈpɑsto] *s* (*pl:* **-tos**) aperitivo, entremés
**antipathetic** [ˌæntɪpəˈθɛtɪk] o **antipathetical** [ˌæntɪpəˈθɛtɪkəl] *adj* antipático; antagónico
**antipathy** [ænˈtɪpəθɪ] *s* (*pl:* **-thies**) antipatía; cosa aborrecida, aversión
**antipersonnel** [ˌæntɪˌpʌrsəˈnɛl] *adj* (mil.) contra personal, contra las personas
**antiphlogistic** [ˌæntɪfloˈdʒɪstɪk] *adj* antiflogístico
**antiphon** [ˈæntɪfɑn] *s* (eccl.) antífona
**antiphonal** [ænˈtɪfənəl] *adj & s* antifonal
**antiphrasis** [ænˈtɪfrəsɪs] *s* (rhet.) antífrasis
**antipodal** [ænˈtɪpədˀl] *adj* antípoda
**antipode** [ˈæntɪpod] *s* antípoda (*el contrario*); **antipodes** [ænˈtɪpədiz] *spl* antípodas (*lugares y habitantes*); **Antipodes** [ænˈtɪpədiz] *spl* Antípodas (*islas*)
**antipodean** [ænˌtɪpəˈdiən] *adj* var. de **antipodal**
**antipolio** [ˌæntɪˈpolɪo] *adj* antipoliomielítico
**antipope** [ˈæntɪˌpop] *s* antipapa
**antiproton** [ˌæntɪˈprotɑn] *s* (chem. & phys.) antiprotón
**antipyretic** [ˌæntɪpaɪˈrɛtɪk] *adj & s* antipirético
**antipyrine** [ˌæntɪˈpaɪrɪn] o [ˌæntɪˈpaɪrin] *s* antipirina
**antiquarian** [ˌæntɪˈkwɛrɪən] *adj & s* anticuario
**antiquary** [ˈæntɪˌkwɛrɪ] *s* (*pl:* **-ies**) anticuario
**antiquate** [ˈæntɪkwet] *va* anticuar
**antiquated** [ˈæntɪˌkwetɪd] *adj* anticuado
**antique** [ænˈtik] *adj* antiguo; anticuado; antiguo por imitación; *s* antigualla
**antique dealer** *s* anticuario
**antique store** *s* tienda de antigüedades
**antiquity** [ænˈtɪkwɪtɪ] *s* (*pl:* **-ties**) antigüedad; **antiquities** *spl* antigüedades
**antirabic** [ˌæntɪˈræbɪk] *adj* antirrábico
**antirachitic** [ˌæntɪrəˈkɪtɪk] *adj & s* antirraquítico
**antireligious** [ˌæntɪrɪˈlɪdʒəs] *adj* antirreligioso
**antisaloon** [ˌæntɪsəˈlun] *adj* enemigo de las tabernas, antialcohólico
**antiscians** [ænˈtɪʃənz] *spl* antecos, antiscios
**antiscorbutic** [ˌæntɪskɔrˈbjutɪk] *adj & s* antiescorbútico
**anti-Semite** [ˌæntɪˈsɛmaɪt] o [ˌæntɪˈsimaɪt] *s* antisemita
**anti-Semitic** [ˌæntɪsɪˈmɪtɪk] *adj* antisemítico
**anti-Semitism** [ˌæntɪˈsɛmɪtɪzəm] *s* antisemitismo
**antisepsis** [ˌæntɪˈsɛpsɪs] *s* antisepsia o antisepsis; antiséptico
**antiseptic** [ˌæntɪˈsɛptɪk] *adj & s* antiséptico
**antiseptically** [ˌæntɪˈsɛptɪkəlɪ] *adv* antisépticamente
**antislavery** [ˌæntɪˈslevərɪ] *adj* antiesclavista
**antisocial** [ˌæntɪˈsoʃəl] *adj* antisocial
**anti-Soviet** [ˌæntɪˈsovɪɛt] *adj* antisoviético
**anti-Spanish** [ˌæntɪˈspænɪʃ] *adj* antiespañol
**antispasmodic** [ˌæntɪspæzˈmɑdɪk] *adj* antiespasmódico
**Antisthenes** [ænˈtɪsθəniz] *s* Antístenes
**antistrophe** [ænˈtɪstrəfɪ] *s* antistrofa
**antisubmarine** [ˌæntɪˈsʌbməˌrin] *adj* antisubmarino
**antitank** [ˌæntɪˈtæŋk] *adj* antitanque
**antithesis** [ænˈtɪθɪsɪs] *s* (*pl:* **-ses** [siz]) antítesis
**antithetic** [ˌæntɪˈθɛtɪk] o **antithetical** [ˌæntɪˈθɛtɪkəl] *adj* antitético
**antitoxic** [ˌæntɪˈtɑksɪk] *adj* antitóxico
**antitoxin** [ˌæntɪˈtɑksɪn] *s* (bact.) antitoxina
**antitrades** [ˈæntɪˌtredz] *spl* vientos antialisios
**antitragus** [ænˈtɪtrəgəs] *s* (*pl:* **-gi** [dʒaɪ]) (anat.) antitrago
**antitrust** [ˌæntɪˈtrʌst] *adj* anticartel
**antitwilight** [ˌæntɪˈtwaɪˌlaɪt] *s* anticrepúsculo
**antivenin** [ˌæntɪˈvɛnɪn] *s* antiveneno
**antiviral** [ˌæntɪˈvaɪrəl] *adj* antiviral, antivirulento
**antivivisectionist** [ˌæntɪˌvɪvɪˈsɛkʃənɪst] *adj & s* antiviviseccionista
**antler** [ˈæntlər] *s* cuerna, cornamenta
**antlered** [ˈæntlərd] *adj* cornudo
**ant lion** *s* (ent.) hormiga león
**Antoinette** [ˌæntwɑˈnɛt] *s* Antonieta
**Antoninus** [ˌæntəˈnaɪnəs] *s* Antonino
**Antonius** [ænˈtonɪəs] *s* Antonio
**antonomasia** [ˌæntənoˈmeʒə] *s* (rhet.) antonomasia
**antonym** [ˈæntənɪm] *s* antónimo
**antrum** [ˈæntrəm] *s* (*pl:* **-tra** [trə]) antro; (anat.) antro
**antrum of Highmore** [ˈhaɪmor] *s* (anat.) antro de Highmoro
**Antwerp** [ˈæntwərp] *s* Amberes
**anus** [ˈenəs] *s* (anat.) ano
**anvil** [ˈænvɪl] *s* yunque; (anat.) yunque
**anxiety** [æŋˈzaɪətɪ] *s* (*pl:* **-ties**) ansiedad, inquietud; anhelo
**anxiety neurosis** *s* (psychoanal.) neurosis de ansiedad
**anxious** [ˈæŋkʃəs] *adj* ansioso, inquieto; anhelante; **to be anxious to** + *inf* tener vivos deseos de + *inf*
**anxious seat** *s* ansiedad, inquietud
**any** [ˈɛnɪ] *adj indef* algún, cualquier; todo; **any place** dondequiera, en cualquier parte; **any time** cuando quiera; alguna vez; *pron indef* alguno, cualquiera; *adv* algo; **not . . . any longer** ya no; **not . . . any more** no . . . más; ya no
**anybody** [ˈɛnɪˌbɑdɪ] *pron indef* alguno, alguien, cualquiera, quienquiera; todo el mundo; **not anybody** ninguno, nadie; *s* (*pl:* **-ies**) cualquiera (*persona de poca importancia*); personaje (*persona de importancia*)
**anyhow** [ˈɛnɪhaʊ] *adv* de cualquier modo; de todos modos; sin embargo
**anyone** or **any one** [ˈɛnɪwʌn] *pron indef* alguno, alguien, cualquiera
**anything** [ˈɛnɪθɪŋ] *pron indef* algo, alguna cosa; todo cuanto; cualquier cosa; **like anything** (coll.) hasta más no poder; **not anything** nada; **anything at all** cualquier cosa que sea; **anything else** cualquier otra cosa; **anything else?** ¿algo más?
**anyway** [ˈɛnɪwe] *adv* de cualquier modo; de todos modos; por lo menos, sin embargo; sin esmero, sin orden ni concierto

**anywhere** [ˈɛnɪhwɛr] *adv* dondequiera, en cualquier parte; adondequiera, a cualquier parte; **not anywhere** en ninguna parte; a ninguna parte
**anywise** [ˈɛnɪwaɪz] *adv* de cualquier modo; del todo
**Aonian** [eˈonɪən] *adj* aonio
**aorist** [ˈeərɪst] *s* (gram.) aoristo
**aorta** [eˈɔrtə] *s* (*pl:* **-tas** o **-tae** [ti]) (anat.) aorta
**aortic** [eˈɔrtɪk] *adj* aórtico
**Ap.** abr. de **April**
**A.P.** o **AP** abr. de **Associated Press**
**apace** [əˈpes] *adv* aprisa
**apache** [əˈpɑʃ] o [əˈpæʃ] *s* (*pl:* **apache** o **apaches**) apache (*bandido, salteador*); (*cap.*) [əˈpætʃɪ] *s* apache (*piel roja*)
**apanage** [ˈæpənɪdʒ] *s* var. de **appanage**
**apart** [əˈpɑrt] *adv* aparte; en partes, en pedazos; **to come apart** desunirse; desprenderse; **to fall apart** caerse a pedazos; desunirse; (fig.) ir al desastre; **to live apart** vivir aislado; vivir separados; **to pull apart** separar por tracción; romper en dos; **to set apart** reservar, poner a un lado; **to stand apart** mantenerse apartado; **to take apart** descomponer, desarmar, desmontar; **to tear apart** romper en dos; **to tell apart** distinguir; **apart from** aparte; aparte de, a parte de; *adj* aparte, separado
**apartheid** [əˈpɑrt·haɪt] *s* política de segregación racial contra los negros en la Unión Sudafricana
**apartment** [əˈpɑrtmənt] *s* apartamento, departamento, piso
**apartment house** *s* casa de pisos, casa de departamentos
**apathetic** [ˌæpəˈθɛtɪk] *adj* apático
**apathetically** [ˌæpəˈθɛtɪkəlɪ] *adv* apáticamente
**apathy** [ˈæpəθɪ] *s* (*pl:* **-thies**) apatía
**apatite** [ˈæpətaɪt] *s* (mineral.) apatita
**ape** [ep] *s* (zool.) mono; (fig.) mona (*persona que imita a las demás*); *va* imitar, remedar
**apeak** [əˈpik] *adv* (naut.) a pique (*en posición vertical*)
**Apelles** [əˈpɛliz] *s* Apeles
**Apennines** [ˈæpənaɪnz] *spl* Apeninos
**apepsia** [eˈpɛpsɪə] *s* (path.) apepsia
**aperient** [əˈpɪrɪənt] *adj* & *s* laxante
**aperiodic** [eˌpɪrɪˈɑdɪk] *adj* aperiódico
**apéritif** [ɑperiˈtif] *s* aperitivo
**aperitive** [əˈpɛrətɪv] *adj* & *s* (med.) aperitivo
**aperture** [ˈæpərtʃər] *s* abertura, orificio
**apetalous** [eˈpɛtələs] *adj* (bot.) apétalo
**apex** [ˈepɛks] *s* (*pl:* **apexes** o **apices** [ˈæpɪsiz] o [ˈepɪsiz]) ápex o ápice; (gram. & hist.) ápex; (math.) ápice
**aphaeresis** [əˈfɛrəsɪs] *s* (gram.) aféresis
**aphanipterous** [ˌæfəˈnɪptərəs] *adj* (zool.) afaníptero
**aphasia** [əˈfeʒə] o [əˈfeʒɪə] *s* (path.) afasia
**aphelion** [æˈfilɪən] *s* (*pl:* **-ons** o **-a** [ə]) (astr.) afelio
**apheresis** [əˈfɛrəsɪs] *s* var. de **aphaeresis**
**aphid** [ˈefɪd] o [ˈæfɪd] *s* (ent.) áfido
**aphis** [ˈefɪs] *s* (*pl:* **aphides** [ˈæfɪdiz]) var. de **aphid**
**aphlogistic** [ˌefloˈdʒɪstɪk] *adj* aflogístico
**aphonia** [eˈfonɪə] *s* (path.) afonía
**aphonic** [eˈfɑnɪk] *adj* (path. & phonet.) afónico
**aphonous** [ˈæfonəs] *adj* áfono
**aphorism** [ˈæfərɪzəm] *s* aforismo
**aphoristic** [ˌæfəˈrɪstɪk] *adj* aforístico
**aphoristically** [ˌæfəˈrɪstɪkəlɪ] *adv* aforísticamente
**aphrodisia** [ˌæfrəˈdɪzɪə] *s* (path.) afrodisia
**aphrodisiac** [ˌæfrəˈdɪzɪæk] *adj* & *s* afrodisíaco
**Aphrodite** [ˌæfrəˈdaɪtɪ] *s* (myth.) Afrodita; (zool.) Afrodita (*anélido marino*)
**aphtha** [ˈæfθə] *s* (*pl:* **-thae** [θi]) (path.) afta
**aphthous** [ˈæfθəs] *adj* aftoso
**aphthous fever** *s* (vet.) fiebre aftosa
**aphyllose** [eˈfɪlos] o **aphyllous** [eˈfɪləs] *adj* áfilo
**apiary** [ˈepɪˌɛrɪ] *s* (*pl:* **-ies**) abejar, colmenar
**apical** [ˈæpɪkəl] o [ˈepɪkəl] *adj* apical; (phonet.) apical
**apiculture** [ˈepɪˌkʌltʃər] *s* apicultura
**apiculturist** [ˌepɪˈkʌltʃərɪst] *s* apicultor
**apiculus** [əˈpɪkjələs] *s* (*pl:* **-li** [laɪ]) apículo
**apiece** [əˈpis] *adv* cada uno; por persona
**apish** [ˈepɪʃ] *adj* simiesco, monesco; necio, tonto
**aplanatic** [ˌæpləˈnætɪk] *adj* (opt.) aplanético
**aplenty** [əˈplɛntɪ] *adv* en abundancia
**aplomb** [əˈplɑm] *s* aplomo, sangre fría
**apocalypse** [əˈpɑkəlɪps] *s* revelación; (*cap.*) *s* (Bib.) Apocalipsis
**apocalyptic** [əˌpɑkəˈlɪptɪk] o **apocalyptical** [əˌpɑkəˈlɪptɪkəl] *adj* apocalíptico; (fig.) apocalíptico
**apocarpous** [ˌæpəˈkɑrpəs] *adj* (bot.) apocárpico
**apocopate** [əˈpɑkəpet] *va* (gram.) apocopar
**apocope** [əˈpɑkəpɪ] *s* (gram.) apócope
**apocrypha** [əˈpɑkrɪfə] *spl* libros apócrifos; (*cap.*) *spl* Libros Apócrifos (*de la Biblia*)
**apocryphal** [əˈpɑkrɪfəl] *adj* apócrifo; (*cap.*) *adj* apócrifo
**apocynaceous** [əˌpɑsɪˈneʃəs] *adj* (bot.) apocináceo
**apodal** [ˈæpədəl] *adj* ápodo
**apodictic** [ˌæpəˈdɪktɪk] o **apodictical** [ˌæpəˈdɪktɪkəl] *adj* (log.) apodíctico
**apodosis** [əˈpɑdəsɪs] *s* (*pl:* **-ses** [siz]) (gram.) apódosis
**apogee** [ˈæpədʒi] *s* (astr. & fig.) apogeo
**apograph** [ˈæpəgræf] o [ˈæpəgrɑf] *s* apógrafo
**Apollinaris water** [əˌpɑlɪˈnɛrɪs] *s* agua de Apollinaris
**Apollo** [əˈpɑlo] *s* (myth.) Apolo
**Apollyon** [əˈpɑljən] *s* (Bib.) Apollión
**apologetic** [əˌpɑləˈdʒɛtɪk] *adj* apologético; lleno de excusas; **apologetics** *ssg* apologética
**apologetically** [əˌpɑləˈdʒɛtɪkəlɪ] *adv* excusándose, pidiendo perdón, con muchas excusas
**apologia** [ˌæpəˈlodʒɪə] *s* apología
**apologist** [əˈpɑlədʒɪst] *s* apologista
**apologize** [əˈpɑlədʒaɪz] *vn* excusarse, disculparse; apologizar; **to apologize for** disculparse de; **to apologize to** disculparse con
**apologue** [ˈæpəlɔg] o [ˈæpəlɑg] *s* apólogo
**apology** [əˈpɑlədʒɪ] *s* (*pl:* **-gies**) apología; excusa, justificación; expediente
**apomorphine** [ˌæpəˈmɔrfin] *s* (pharm.) apomorfina
**aponeurosis** [ˌæpənjuˈrosɪs] o [ˌæpənuˈrosɪs] *s* (*pl:* **-ses** [siz]) (anat.) aponeurosis
**aponeurotic** [ˌæpənjuˈrɑtɪk] o [ˌæpənuˈrɑtɪk] *adj* aponeurótico
**aponeurotome** [ˌæpəˈnjurətom] o [ˌæpəˈnurətom] *s* (surg.) aponeurótomo
**apophthegm** [ˈæpəθɛm] *s* var. de **apothegm**
**apophyge** [əˈpɑfɪdʒɪ] *s* (arch.) apófige
**apophysis** [əˈpɑfɪsɪs] *s* (*pl:* **-ses** [siz]) (anat., geol., & zool.) apófisis
**apoplectic** [ˌæpəˈplɛktɪk] *adj* & *s* apoplético
**apoplexy** [ˈæpəˌplɛksɪ] *s* (path.) apoplejía
**aport** [əˈport] *adv* (naut.) a babor
**apostasy** [əˈpɑstəsɪ] *s* (*pl:* **-sies**) apostasía
**apostate** [əˈpɑstet] o [əˈpɑstɪt] *s* apóstata
**apostatize** [əˈpɑstətaɪz] *vn* apostatar
**apostematous** [ˌæpəˈstɛmətəs] *adj* apostematoso
**apostle** [əˈpɑsəl] *s* apóstol
**Apostle of the Gentiles** *s* (Bib.) apóstol de los gentiles o las gentes
**Apostles' Creed** *s* Símbolo de los Apóstoles
**apostolate** [əˈpɑstəlet] o [əˈpɑstəlɪt] *s* apostolado
**apostolic** [ˌæpəsˈtɑlɪk] o **apostolical** [ˌæpəsˈtɑlɪkəl] *adj* apostólico
**Apostolic Fathers** *spl* Padres apostólicos
**Apostolic See** *s* Sede apostólica
**apostrophe** [əˈpɑstrəfɪ] *s* (rhet.) apóstrofe; (gram.) apóstrofo
**apostrophize** [əˈpɑstrəfaɪz] *va* apostrofar
**apothecaries' measure** *s* sistema de medidas para líquidos usado en los Estados Unidos por los boticarios
**apothecaries' weight** *s* sistema de pesos usado en los Estados Unidos y la Gran Bretaña por los boticarios
**apothecary** [əˈpɑθɪˌkɛrɪ] *s* (*pl:* **-ies**) boticario, droguero
**apothecary's jar** *s* bote de porcelana
**apothegm** [ˈæpəθɛm] *s* apotegma (*sentencia breve e instructiva*)
**apothem** [ˈæpəθɛm] *s* (geom.) apotema

**apotheosis** [əˌpɑθɪˈosɪs] o [ˌæpəˈθiəsɪs] *s* (*pl:* **-ses** [siz]) apoteosis
**apotheosize** [əˈpɑθɪosaɪz] o [ˌæpəˈθiəsaɪz] *va* deificar, endiosar
**apozem** [ˈæpəzɛm] *s* (pharm.) apócema
**appal** [əˈpɔl] (*pret & pp:* **-palled;** *ger:* **-palling**) *va* var. de **appall**
**Appalachian** [ˌæpəˈletʃən] o [ˌæpəˈlætʃən] *adj* apalache; **Appalachians** *spl* Apalaches (*montes*)
**Appalachian Mountains** *spl* montes Apalaches
**appall** [əˈpɔl] *va* espantar, aterrar; desmayar, desanimar
**appalling** [əˈpɔlɪŋ] *adj* espantoso, aterrador; desanimador
**appanage** [ˈæpənɪdʒ] *s* pertenencia, cosa accesoria; dependencia; infantado
**apparatus** [ˌæpəˈretəs] o [ˌæpəˈrætəs] *s* (*pl:* **-tus** o **-tuses**) aparato; (anat.) aparato
**apparatus criticus** [ˈkrɪtɪkəs] *s* aparato crítico
**apparel** [əˈpærəl] *s* ropa, vestido; (naut.) aparejo; (*pret & pp:* **-eled** o **-elled;** *ger:* **-eling** o **-elling**) *va* vestir, ataviar, adornar
**apparent** [əˈpærənt] o [əˈpɛrənt] *adj* aparente; manifiesto, evidente
**apparently** [əˈpærəntlɪ] o [əˈpɛrəntlɪ] *adv* aparentemente; evidentemente, por lo visto
**apparition** [ˌæpəˈrɪʃən] *s* aparición
**appeal** [əˈpil] *s* súplica, instancia; recurso; solicitud; atracción, interés; (law) apelación; *vn* ser atrayente; **to appeal for** solicitar; **to appeal from** (law) apelar de; **to appeal to** suplicar a (*una persona*); atraer a, interesar a (*una persona*); recurrir a; (law) apelar a
**appear** [əˈpɪr] *vn* aparecer; parecer; semejar; (law) comparecer
**appearance** [əˈpɪrəns] *s* aparición, aparecimiento; apariencia, aspecto; (law) comparecencia; **for appearances** por el bien parecer; **to judge by appearances** juzgar por las apariencias; **to keep up appearances** salvar las apariencias
**appease** [əˈpiz] *va* apaciguar
**appeasement** [əˈpizmənt] *s* apaciguamiento
**appeaser** [əˈpizər] *s* apaciguador
**appellant** [əˈpɛlənt] *s* (law) apelante
**appellate court** [əˈpɛlɪt] o [əˈpɛlet] *s* (law) tribunal de apelación
**appellation** [ˌæpəˈleʃən] *s* apellidamiento; nombre, título
**appellative** [æˈpɛlətɪv] *adj & s* (gram.) apelativo
**appellee** [ˌæpəˈli] *s* (law) apelado
**append** [əˈpɛnd] *va* añadir, anexar; atar
**appendage** [əˈpɛndɪdʒ] *s* apéndice; (biol.) apéndice
**appendant** [əˈpɛndənt] *adj* anexo, adjunto; accesorio; *s* apéndice; accesorio
**appendectomy** [ˌæpənˈdɛktəmɪ] *s* (*pl:* **-mies**) (surg.) apendectomía o apendicectomía
**appendicitis** [əˌpɛndɪˈsaɪtɪs] *s* (path.) apendicitis
**appendicular** [ˌæpənˈdɪkjələr] *adj* apendicular
**appendix** [əˈpɛndɪks] *s* (*pl:* **-dixes** o **-dices** [dɪsiz]) apéndice; (aer.) apéndice; (anat.) apéndice vermiforme
**apperception** [ˌæpərˈsɛpʃən] *s* (philos.) apercepción
**apperceptive** [ˌæpərˈsɛptɪv] *adj* (philos.) aperceptivo
**appertain** [ˌæpərˈten] *vn* relacionarse; **to appertain to** relacionarse con
**appetite** [ˈæpɪtaɪt] *s* apetito; **to whet the appetite** abrir el apetito
**appetizer** [ˈæpɪˌtaɪzər] *s* apetite, aperitivo
**appetizing** [ˈæpɪˌtaɪzɪŋ] *adj* apetitoso
**Appian Way** [ˈæpɪən] *s* Vía Apia
**applaud** [əˈplɔd] *va & vn* aplaudir
**applause** [əˈplɔz] *s* aplauso, aplausos
**apple** [ˈæpəl] *s* (bot.) manzano (*árbol*); manzana (*fruto*); *adj* manzanil
**apple butter** *s* mermelada de manzana espesa y condimentada con especias
**applecart** [ˈæpəlˌkɑrt] *s* carretilla para ir vendiendo manzanas por las calles; **to upset the applecart** (coll.) revolver la feria
**applejack** [ˈæpəlˌdʒæk] *s* aguardiente de manzana
**apple mint** *s* (bot.) madrastra
**apple of discord** *s* manzana de la discordia
**apple of the eye** *s* niña del ojo
**apple orchard** *s* manzanar
**apple pie** *s* pastel de manzanas
**apple-pie order** [ˈæpəlˌpaɪ] *s* condición perfecta
**apple polisher** *s* (slang) lameculos, quitamotas
**applesauce** [ˈæpəlˌsɔs] *s* mermelada de manzana; (slang) halagos insinceros; (slang) música celestial
**apple tree** *s* manzano
**apple worm** *s* gusano de la manzana
**appliance** [əˈplaɪəns] *s* artificio, dispositivo, aparato; aplicación
**applicability** [ˌæplɪkəˈbɪlɪtɪ] *s* aplicabilidad
**applicable** [ˈæplɪkəbəl] *adj* aplicable
**applicant** [ˈæplɪkənt] *s* aspirante, pretendiente, candidato, solicitante
**application** [ˌæplɪˈkeʃən] *s* aplicación; pretensión, candidatura, solicitud
**applied** [əˈplaɪd] *adj* aplicado
**appliqué** [ˌæplɪˈke] *adj* aplicado; *s* aplicación (*ornamentación sobrepuesta*); *va* aplicar sobrepuesto
**appliqué lace** *s* encaje de aplicación
**apply** [əˈplaɪ] (*pret & pp:* **-plied**) *va* aplicar; **to apply oneself** aplicarse; *vn* aplicarse (*ser pertinente*); dirigirse, recurrir; **to apply for** pedir, solicitar
**appoggiatura** [əˌpɑdʒəˈturə] *s* (mus.) apoyatura
**appoint** [əˈpɔɪnt] *va* nombrar, designar; establecer, sentar; amueblar
**appointee** [əˌpɔɪnˈti] *s* electo
**appointive** [əˈpɔɪntɪv] *adj* electivo
**appointment** [əˈpɔɪntmənt] *s* nombramiento, designación; empleo, puesto; cita
**apportion** [əˈporʃən] *va* prorratear
**apportionment** [əˈporʃənmənt] *s* prorrateo
**appose** [æˈpoz] *va* aplicar; yuxtaponer
**apposite** [ˈæpəzɪt] *adj* oportuno, conveniente, apropiado
**apposition** [ˌæpəˈzɪʃən] *s* yuxtaposición; (gram.) aposición
**appositive** [əˈpɑzɪtɪv] *adj & s* (gram.) apositivo
**appraisal** [əˈprezəl] *s* tasación, valuación, apreciación
**appraise** [əˈprez] *va* tasar, valuar, apreciar
**appraisement** [əˈprezmənt] *s* var. de **appraisal**
**appraiser** [əˈprezər] *s* tasador, apreciador
**appreciable** [əˈpriʃɪəbəl] *adj* apreciable; sensible
**appreciably** [əˈpriʃɪəblɪ] *adv* apreciablemente; sensiblemente
**appreciate** [əˈpriʃɪet] *va* apreciar; aprobar; comprender; estar agradecido por; aumentar el valor de; *vn* subir en valor
**appreciation** [əˌpriʃɪˈeʃən] *s* aprecio, apreciación; agradecimiento, reconocimiento; plusvalía, aumento en valor
**appreciative** [əˈpriʃɪˌetɪv] *adj* apreciador; agradecido
**apprehend** [ˌæprɪˈhɛnd] *va* aprehender, prender; temer; comprender
**apprehension** [ˌæprɪˈhɛnʃən] *s* aprehensión; comprensión; aprensión (*miedo, inquietud*)
**apprehensive** [ˌæprɪˈhɛnsɪv] *adj* aprensivo o aprehensivo (*receloso, miedoso*); penetrante, perspicaz
**apprentice** [əˈprɛntɪs] *s* aprendiz; *va* poner de aprendiz
**apprenticeship** [əˈprɛntɪsʃɪp] *s* aprendizaje; **to serve one's apprenticeship** hacer su aprendizaje
**apprise** o **apprize** [əˈpraɪz] *va* informar, enterar; apreciar, valuar, tasar
**approach** [əˈprotʃ] *s* acercamiento; vía de acceso, vía de entrada; proposición; enfoque (*de un problema*); **approaches** *spl* (mil.) aproches; *va* acercar (*poner más cerca*); abordar; acercarse a; parecerse a; *vn* acercarse, aproximarse
**approachability** [əˌprotʃəˈbɪlɪtɪ] *s* accesibilidad
**approachable** [əˈprotʃəbəl] *adj* abordable, accesible
**approbation** [ˌæprəˈbeʃən] *s* aprobación

**appropriable** [əˈproprɪəbəl] *adj* apropiable
**appropriate** [əˈproprɪɪt] *adj* apropiado, a propósito; [əˈproprɪet] *va* apropiarse; asignar, destinar
**appropriation** [əˌproprɪˈeʃən] *s* apropiación; asignación
**approval** [əˈpruvəl] *s* aprobación; **on approval** a prueba
**approve** [əˈpruv] *va* aprobar; probar; *vn* aprobar; **to approve of** aprobar
**approvingly** [əˈpruvɪŋlɪ] *adv* con aprobación
**approximate** [əˈprɑksɪmɪt] *adj* aproximado, aproximativo; [əˈprɑksɪmet] *va* aproximar; *vn* aproximarse
**approximately** [əˈprɑksɪmɪtlɪ] *adv* aproximadamente
**approximation** [əˌprɑksɪˈmeʃən] *s* aproximación
**appurtenance** [əˈpʌrtɪnəns] *s* pertenencia, accesorio
**appurtenant** [əˈpʌrtɪnənt] *adj* perteneciente, accesorio; *s* pertenencia, accesorio
**Apr.** abr. de **April**
**apraxia** [eˈpræksɪə] *s* (path.) apraxia
**apricot** [ˈeprɪkɑt] o [ˈæprɪkɑt] *s* (bot.) albaricoquero (*árbol*); albaricoque (*fruto*)
**April** [ˈeprɪl] *s* abril; *adj* abrileño
**April fool** *s* el que es burlado el primero de abril; **to make an April fool of** coger por inocente
**April Fools' Day** *s* primer día de abril, que corresponde al día de engañabobos o día de los santos inocentes—28 de diciembre—en que se coge por inocente a la gente
**apriorism** [ˌeprɪˈorɪzəm] *s* (philos.) apriorismo
**aprioristic** [ˌeprɪəˈrɪstɪk] *adj* apriorístico
**apriority** [ˌeprɪˈɑrɪtɪ] *s* (philos.) aprioridad
**apron** [ˈeprən] *s* delantal; mandil (*de obrero; de francmasón*); batiente (*de un dique*); (naut.) albitana; (aer.) rampa (*pavimento frente a un hangar*); **tied to the apron strings of** cosido o pegado a las faldas de
**apropos** [ˌæprəˈpo] *adj* oportuno; *adv* a propósito; **apropos of** a propósito de, acerca de
**apse** [æps] *s* (arch.) ábside
**apsidiole** [æpˈsɪdɪol] *s* (arch.) absidiolo
**apsis** [ˈæpsɪs] *s* (*pl:* **apsides** [ˈæpsɪdiz] o [æpˈsaɪdiz]) (astr.) ápside
**apsychia** [æpˈsɪkɪə] o [æpˈsaɪkɪə] *s* (med.) apsiquia
**apt** [æpt] *adj* apto; a propósito; dispuesto, propenso, tendente; **he is apt to come this morning** es fácil que venga esta mañana
**apterous** [ˈæptərəs] *adj* áptero
**aptitude** [ˈæptɪtjud] o [ˈæptɪtud] *s* aptitud
**aptitude test** *s* prueba de aptitud
**aptness** [ˈæptnɪs] *s* aptitud
**Apuleius** [ˌæpjəˈliəs] *s* Apuleyo
**apyretic** [ˌepaɪˈrɛtɪk] o [ˌæpaɪˈrɛtɪk] *adj* apirético
**apyrexia** [ˌepaɪˈrɛksɪə] o [ˌæpaɪˈrɛksɪə] *s* (path.) apirexia
**aqua** [ˈækwə] o [ˈekwə] *s* (*pl:* **aquas** o **aquae** [ˈækwi] o [ˈekwi]) (pharm.) agua
**aquacade** [ˈækwəˌked] *s* espectáculo acuático
**aqua fortis** [ˈfɔrtɪs] *s* agua fuerte (*ácido nítrico; estampa*)
**aquafortist** [ˌækwəˈfɔrtɪst] o [ˌekwəˈfɔrtɪst] *s* aguafuertista
**aqualung** [ˈækwəˌlʌŋ] *s* aparato de buceo autónomo
**aquamarine** [ˌækwəməˈrin] *s* aguamarina (*mineral y color*); *adj* de color aguamarina
**aquamarine chrysolite** *s* (mineral.) aguamarincrisolita
**aquaplane** [ˈækwəˌplen] *s* acuaplano; *vn* correr en acuaplano
**aqua regia** [ˈridʒɪə] *s* (chem.) agua regia
**aquarium** [əˈkwɛrɪəm] *s* (*pl:* **-ums** o **-a** [ə]) acuario
**Aquarius** [əˈkwɛrɪəs] *s* (astr.) Acuario
**aquatic** [əˈkwætɪk] o [əˈkwatɪk] *adj.* acuático; *s* animal acuático; planta acuática; **aquatics** *spl* (sports) deportes acuáticos
**aquatint** [ˈækwəˌtɪnt] *s* acuatinta
**aqua vitae** [ˈvaɪti] *s* licor alcohólico, aguardiente
**aqueduct** [ˈækwɪdʌkt] *s* acueducto; (anat.) acueducto
**aqueous** [ˈekwɪəs] o [ˈækwɪəs] *adj* ácueo, acuoso
**aqueous humor** *s* (anat.) humor acuoso
**aquiline** [ˈækwɪlaɪn] o [ˈækwɪlɪn] *adj* aguileño
**aquiline nose** *s* nariz aguileña
**Aquinas, Saint Thomas** [əˈkwaɪnəs] Santo Tomás de Aquino
**Aquitaine** [ˈækwɪten] *s* Aquitania
**Aquitanian** [ˌækwɪˈtenɪən] *adj & s* aquitano
**Arab** [ˈærəb] *adj* árabe; *s* árabe; caballo árabe
**arabesque** [ˌærəˈbɛsk] *adj* (f.a.) arabesco; caprichoso; *s* (f.a.) arabesco
**Arabia** [əˈrebɪə] *s* la Arabia
**Arabian** [əˈrebɪən] *adj & s* árabe
**Arabian Desert** *s* Desierto Arábigo
**Arabian jasmine** *s* (bot.) jazmín de Arabia, sampaguita
**Arabian Nights** *spl* Mil y una noches
**Arabian Sea** *s* mar Arábigo
**Arabic** [ˈærəbɪk] *adj* arábigo; *s* árabe o arábigo (*idioma*)
**arabic acid** *s* (chem.) ácido arábico
**Arabic figure** *s* cifra arábiga
**Arabic numeral** *s* número arábigo
**Arabism** [ˈærəbɪzəm] *s* arabismo
**Arabist** [ˈærəbɪst] *s* arabista
**Arabize** [ˈærəbaɪz] *va* arabizar
**arable** [ˈærəbəl] *adj* arable
**Araby** [ˈærəbɪ] *s* (poet.) Arabia
**araceous** [əˈreʃəs] *adj* (bot.) aráceo
**Arachne** [əˈræknɪ] *s* (myth.) Aracne
**arachnid** [əˈræknɪd] *s* (zool.) arácnido
**arachnidan** [əˈræknɪdən] *adj & s* (zool.) arácnido
**arachnoid** [əˈræknɔɪd] *s* (anat.) aracnoides
**Aragon** [ˈærəgɑn] *s* Aragón
**Aragonese** [ˌærəgəˈniz] *adj* aragonés; *s* (*pl:* **-nese**) aragonés
**aragonite** [əˈrægənaɪt] o [ˈærəgənaɪt] *s* (mineral.) aragonita, aragonito
**aralia** [əˈrelɪə] *s* (bot. & pharm.) aralia
**araliaceous** [əˌrelɪˈeʃəs] *adj* (bot.) araliáceo
**Aral Sea** [ˈærəl] *s* mar Aral
**Aramaean** [ˌærəˈmiən] *adj & s* arameo
**Aramaic** [ˌærəˈmeɪk] *adj & s* aramaico
**Araucan** [əˈrɔkən] *s* araucano
**Araucanian** [ˌærɔˈkenɪən] *adj & s* araucano
**araucaria** [ˌærɔˈkɛrɪə] *s* (bot.) araucaria
**arbalest** o **arbalist** [ˈɑrbəlɪst] *s* ballesta; (math.) arbalestrilla
**arbiter** [ˈɑrbɪtər] *s* árbitro
**arbitrable** [ˈɑrbɪtrəbəl] *adj* arbitrable
**arbitrage** [ˈɑrbɪtrɪdʒ] *s* arbitraje
**arbitrage of exchange** *s* arbitraje de cambio
**arbitral** [ˈɑrbɪtrəl] *adj* arbitral
**arbitrament** [ɑrˈbɪtrəmənt] *s* arbitramento
**arbitrary** [ˈɑrbɪˌtrɛrɪ] *adj* arbitrario
**arbitrate** [ˈɑrbɪtret] *va & vn* arbitrar
**arbitration** [ˌɑrbɪˈtreʃən] *s* arbitraje
**arbitrator** [ˈɑrbɪˌtretər] *s* árbitro, arbitrador
**arbitress** [ˈɑrbɪtrɪs] *s* árbitra
**arbor** [ˈɑrbər] *s* cenador, glorieta, emparrado; (mach.) árbol
**Arbor Day** *s* (U.S.A.) fiesta del árbol
**arboreal** [ɑrˈborɪəl] *adj* arbóreo
**arborescence** [ˌɑrbəˈrɛsəns] *s* arborescencia
**arborescent** [ˌɑrbəˈrɛsənt] *adj* arborescente
**arboretum** [ˌɑrbəˈritəm] *s* (*pl:* **-tums** o **-ta** [tə]) jardín botánico de árboles
**arboriculture** [ˈɑrbərɪˌkʌltʃər] *s* arboricultura
**arboriculturist** [ˈɑrbərɪˌkʌltʃərɪst] *s* arboricultor
**arboriform** [ˈɑrbərɪfɔrm] *adj* arboriforme
**arborist** [ˈɑrbərɪst] *s* arbolista
**arborization** [ˌɑrbərɪˈzeʃən] *s* (anat. & mineral.) arborización
**arbor vitae** [ˈɑrbərˈvaɪti] *s* (Bib.) árbol de la vida; (bot.) tuya, árbol de la vida; (anat.) árbol de la vida
**arbutus** [ɑrˈbjutəs] *s* (bot.) madroño; (bot.) epigea rastrera
**arc** [ɑrk] *s* (geom. & elec.) arco; (*pret & pp:* **arced** [ɑrkt] o **arcked;** *ger:* **arcing** [ˈɑrkɪŋ] o **arcking**) *vn* (elec.) formar arco
**arcade** [ɑrˈked] *s* (arch.) arcada
**Arcadia** [ɑrˈkedɪə] *s* la Arcadia
**Arcadian** [ɑrˈkedɪən] *adj* árcade, arcadio; (fig.) arcádico (*simple, campestre*); *s* árcade, arcadio

**Arcady** [ˈɑrkədɪ] *s* (poet.) la Arcadia
**arcane** [ɑrˈken] *adj* arcano
**arcanum** [ɑrˈkenəm] *s* (*pl:* **-nums** o **-na** [nə]) arcano
**arch.** abr. de **archaic, archaism, archipelago, architect, architectural** y **architecture**
**arch** [ɑrtʃ] *adj* astuto; travieso, picaresco; principal, insigne; *s* (arch. & anat.) arco; *va* arquear, enarcar; atravesar
**archaeological** [ˌɑrkɪəˈlɑdʒɪkəl] *adj* arqueológico
**archaeologist** [ˌɑrkɪˈɑlədʒɪst] *s* arqueólogo
**archaeology** [ˌɑrkɪˈɑlədʒɪ] *s* arqueología
**archaic** [ɑrˈkeɪk] *adj* arcaico
**archaism** [ˈɑrkeɪzəm] *s* arcaísmo
**archaist** [ˈɑrkeɪst] *s* arcaísta
**archaize** [ˈɑrkeaɪz] *va & vn* arcaizar
**archangel** [ˈɑrkˌendʒəl] *s* arcángel
**archangelic** [ˌɑrkænˈdʒɛlɪk] o **archangelical** [ˌɑrkænˈdʒɛlɪkəl] *adj* arcangélico
**archbishop** [ˈɑrtʃˈbɪʃəp] *s* arzobispo
**archbishopric** [ˌɑrtʃˈbɪʃəprɪk] *s* arzobispado
**archdeacon** [ˈɑrtʃˈdikən] *s* arcediano, archidiácono
**archdeaconry** [ˌɑrtʃˈdikənrɪ] *s* (*pl:* **-ries**) arcedianato
**archdiocese** [ˈɑrtʃˈdaɪəsis] o [ˈɑrtʃˈdaɪəsɪs] *s* arquidiócesis
**archducal** [ˌɑrtʃˈdjukəl] o [ˌɑrtʃˈdukəl] *adj* archiducal
**archduchess** [ˈɑrtʃˈdʌtʃɪs] *s* archiduquesa
**archduchy** [ˈɑrtʃˈdʌtʃɪ] *s* (*pl:* **-ies**) archiducado
**archduke** [ˈɑrtʃˈdjuk] o [ˈɑrtʃˈduk] *s* archiduque
**arched** [ɑrtʃt] *adj* arqueado, enarcado, combado
**archegonium** [ˌɑrkɪˈgonɪəm] *s* (*pl:* **-a** [ə]) (bot.) arquegonio
**archenemy** [ˈɑrtʃˌɛnɪmɪ] *s* (*pl:* **-mies**) archienemigo (*enemigo principal*); Satanás, el enemigo malo
**archeological** [ˌɑrkɪəˈlɑdʒɪkəl] *adj* arqueológico
**archeologist** [ˌɑrkɪˈɑlədʒɪst] *s* arqueólogo
**archeology** [ˌɑrkɪˈɑlədʒɪ] *s* arqueología
**Archeozoic** [ˌɑrkɪəˈzo·ɪk] *adj* (geol.) arqueozoico; *s* (geol.) era arqueozoica, era arcaica
**archer** [ˈɑrtʃər] *s* arquero, flechero
**archery** [ˈɑrtʃərɪ] *s* tiro de flechas, tiro de arco
**archetype** [ˈɑrkɪtaɪp] *s* arquetipo
**archfiend** [ˈɑrtʃˈfind] *s* demonio principal; Satanás, el enemigo malo
**archiepiscopal** [ˌɑrkɪɪˈpɪskəpəl] *adj* arquiepiscopal o arzobispal
**archil** [ˈɑrkɪl] *s* (bot. & chem.) orchilla
**Archimedean** [ˌɑrkɪˈmidɪən] o [ˌɑrkɪmɪˈdiən] *adj* arquimédico
**Archimedean screw** *s* rosca de Arquímedes, tornillo de Arquímedes
**Archimedes** [ˌɑrkɪˈmidiz] *s* Arquímedes
**Archimedes' screw** *s* rosca de Arquímedes, tornillo de Arquímedes
**archipelago.** [ˌɑrkɪˈpɛləgo] *s* (*pl:* **-gos** o **-goes**) archipiélago
**architect** [ˈɑrkɪtɛkt] *s* arquitecto
**architectonic** [ˌɑrkɪtɛkˈtɑnɪk] *adj* arquitectónico
**architectural** [ˌɑrkɪˈtɛktʃərəl] *adj* arquitectural
**architecture** [ˈɑrkɪˌtɛktʃər] *s* arquitectura
**architrave** [ˈɑrkɪtrev] *s* (arch.) arquitrabe
**archives** [ˈɑrkaɪvz] *spl* archivo
**archivist** [ˈɑrkɪvɪst] *s* archivero, archivista
**archivolt** [ˈɑrkɪvolt] *s* (arch.) archivolta
**archpriest** [ˈɑrtʃˈprist] *s* arcipreste
**archpriesthood** [ˌɑrtʃˈpristhʊd] *s* arciprestazgo
**archway** [ˈɑrtʃˌwe] *s* arcada
**arc lamp** *s* lámpara de arco
**arc light** *s* lámpara de arco; alumbrado de arco
**arctic** [ˈɑrktɪk] *adj* ártico; **arctics** *spl* chanclos impermeables; (*cap.*) *s* Ártico
**arctic circle** *s* círculo polar ártico
**Arctic Ocean** *s* océano Ártico
**Arctic Zone** *s* zona ártica
**Arcturus** [ɑrkˈtjʊrəs] o [ɑrkˈtʊrəs] *s* (astr.) Arturo
**arc welding** *s* soldadura de o por arco
**ardency** [ˈɑrdənsɪ] *s* ardor
**ardent** [ˈɑrdənt] *adj* ardiente
**ardent spirits** *spl* licores espirituosos
**ardor** [ˈɑrdər] *s* ardor
**ardour** [ˈɑrdər] *s* (Brit.) var. de **ardor**
**arduous** [ˈɑrdʒʊəs] o [ˈɑrdjʊəs] *adj* arduo, difícil; enérgico; escabroso, escarpado; riguroso
**are** [ɛr] o [ɑr] *s* área (*medida agraria*); [ɑr] *segunda persona del sg y primera, segunda y tercera personas del pl del pres de ind de* **be**
**area** [ˈɛrɪə] *s* área, superficie; extensión; región, comarca; zona; patio; entrada baja de un sótano
**areaway** [ˈɛrɪəˌwe] *s* entrada baja de un sótano; pasaje angosto entre edificios
**areca** [ˈærəkə] o [əˈrikə] *s* (bot.) areca (*palma y nuez*)
**arena** [əˈrinə] *s* arena o arenas
**arenaceous** [ˌærɪˈneʃəs] *adj* arenáceo
**arena theater** *s* teatro circular
**arenation** [ˌɛrɪˈneʃən] *s* (med.) arenación
**aren't** [ɑrnt] contracción de **are not**
**areola** [əˈriələ] *s* (*pl:* **-lae** [li] o **-las**) (anat., bot., path., & zool.) aréola
**areolar** [əˈriələr] *adj* areolar
**areometer** [ˌærɪˈɑmɪtər] *s* areómetro
**Areopagus** [ˌærɪˈɑpəgəs] *s* Areópago
**areostyle** [əˈriəstaɪl] *s* (arch.) areóstilo
**Ares** [ˈɛriz] *s* (myth.) Ares
**Arethusa** [ˌærɪˈθuzə] o [ˌærɪˈθusə] *s* (myth.) Aretusa
**argali** [ˈɑrgəlɪ] *s* (*pl:* **-li** o **-lis**) (zool.) argalí
**argan** [ˈɑrgən] *s* argán (*fruto*)
**argan tree** *s* (bot.) argán, erguen
**argent** [ˈɑrdʒənt] *adj* argénteo; *s* (her.) argén; (poet.) argento
**argentiferous** [ˌɑrdʒənˈtɪfərəs] *adj* argentífero
**Argentina** [ˌɑrdʒənˈtinə] *s* la Argentina
**Argentine** [ˈɑrdʒəntin] o [ˈɑrdʒəntaɪn] *adj & s* argentino; **the Argentine** la Argentina; (*l.c.*) *adj* argentino (*de plata*)
**Argentinean** [ˌɑrdʒənˈtɪnɪən] *s* argentino
**argil** [ˈɑrdʒɪl] *s* arcilla figulina
**Argive** [ˈɑrdʒaɪv] *adj & s* argivo
**Argo** [ˈɑrgo] *s* (myth.) Argos (*nave*); (astr.) Argos
**Argolic** [ɑrˈgɑlɪk] *adj* argólico
**Argolis** [ˈɑrgəlɪs] *s* la Argólide
**argon** [ˈɑrgɑn] *s* (chem.) argo o argón
**Argonaut** [ˈɑrgənɔt] *s* (myth.) argonauta; (*l.c.*) *s* (zool.) argonauta
**Argonautic** [ˌɑrgəˈnɔtɪk] *adj* (myth.) argonáutico
**Argo Navis** [ˈnevɪs] *s* (astr.) Navío Argo
**Argos** [ˈɑrgɑs] *s* Argos (*ciudad de la antigua Grecia*)
**argosy** [ˈɑrgəsɪ] *s* (*pl:* **-sies**) buque con cargamento valioso; buques valiosos
**argot** [ˈɑrgo] o [ˈɑrgət] *s* jerga
**argue** [ˈɑrgju] *va* debatir (*un proyecto*); persuadir con razones; sostener; argüir (*indicar, probar; acusar*); **to argue into** + *ger* persuadir (*a una persona*) a + *inf;* **to argue out of** + *ger* disuadir (*a una persona*) de + *inf; vn* argüir, disputar; **to argue against** argüir contra
**arguer** [ˈɑrgjʊər] *s* argumentador, argumentista
**argument** [ˈɑrgjəmənt] *s* argumento; discusión, disputa
**argumentation** [ˌɑrgjəmɛnˈteʃən] *s* argumentación
**argumentative** [ˌɑrgjəˈmɛntətɪv] *adj* argumentador; argumentativo
**Argus** [ˈɑrgəs] *s* (myth.) Argos (*monstruo*); argos (*persona muy vigilante*)
**Argus-eyed** [ˈɑrgəsˌaɪd] *adj* hecho un argos
**argyrol** [ˈɑrdʒɪrəl] *s* (trademark) argirol
**aria** [ˈɑrɪə] o [ˈɛrɪə] *s* (mus.) aria
**Ariadne** [ˌærɪˈædnɪ] *s* (myth.) Ariadna
**Arian** [ˈɛrɪən] *adj & s* arriano
**Arianism** [ˈɛrɪənɪzəm] *s* arrianismo
**arid** [ˈærɪd] *adj* árido
**aridity** [əˈrɪdɪtɪ] *s* aridez
**Aries** [ˈɛrɪiz] *m* (astr.) Aries
**aright** [əˈraɪt] *adv* acertadamente; **to set aright** rectificar
**aril** [ˈærɪl] *s* (bot.) arilo
**arillate** [ˈærɪlet] *adj* (bot.) arilado
**arise** [əˈraɪz] (*pret:* **arose;** *pp:* **arisen**) *vn*

levantarse; subir; aparecer, presentarse; **to arise from** provenir de, proceder de
**arisen** [ə'rɪzən] *pp de* **arise**
**Aristides** [,ærɪs'taɪdiz] *s* Arístides
**aristocracy** [,ærɪs'tɑkrəsɪ] *s* (*pl:* **-cies**) aristocracia
**aristocrat** [ə'rɪstəkræt] o ['ærɪstəkræt] *s* aristócrata
**aristocratic** [ə,rɪstə'krætɪk] o [,ærɪstə'krætɪk] *adj* aristocrático
**aristocratically** [ə,rɪstə'krætɪkəlɪ] o [,ærɪstə'krætɪkəlɪ] *adv* aristocráticamente
**Aristophanes** [,ærɪs'tɑfəniz] *s* Aristófanes
**Aristophanic** [,ærɪstə'fænɪk] *adj* aristofánico; *s* (rhet.) aristofánico
**Aristotelian** [,ærɪstə'tilɪən] *adj & s* aristotélico
**Aristotelianism** [,ærɪstə'tilɪənɪzəm] *s* aristotelismo
**Aristotle** ['ærɪs,tɑtəl] *s* Aristóteles
**Aristotle's lantern** *s* (zool.) linterna de Aristóteles
**arith.** abr. de **arithmetic**
**arithmetic** [ə'rɪθmətɪk] *s* aritmética
**arithmetical** [,ærɪθ'mɛtɪkəl] *adj* aritmético
**arithmetically** [,ærɪθ'mɛtɪkəlɪ] *adv* aritméticamente
**arithmetical progression** *s* progresión aritmética
**arithmetician** [ə,rɪθmə'tɪʃən] o [,ærɪθmə'tɪʃən] *s* aritmético
**arithmomania** [ə,rɪθmə'menɪə] *s* aritmomanía
**arithmometer** [,ærɪθ'mɑmɪtər] *s* aritmómetro
**Arius** [ə'raɪəs] o ['ɛrɪəs] *s* Arrio
**Ariz.** abr. de **Arizona**
**Ark.** abr. de **Arkansas**
**ark** [ɑrk] *s* (Bib.) arca de Noé; lanchón; arca, caja
**ark of the covenant** *s* (Bib.) arca de la alianza
**arkose** [ɑr'kos] *s* arcosa
**arm** [ɑrm] *s* brazo (*del cuerpo, de una silla, del mar, de la ley, etc.*); arma; ejército (*cada una de las tres ramas de las fuerzas militares*); **in arms** de pecho, de teta (*dícese de un niño*); **to arms!** ¡a las armas!; **to bear arms** llevar las armas; **to be the right arm of** ser el brazo derecho de; **to be up in arms** alzarse en armas, estar en armas; **to carry arms** tener armas consigo; **to keep at arm's length** mantener a distancia; mantenerse a distancia; **to lay down one's arms** rendir las armas; **to present arms** presentar armas; **to rise up in arms** alzarse en armas; **to take up arms** tomar (las) armas; **under arms** sobre las armas; **with arms folded** de brazos cruzados; **with open arms** con los brazos abiertos; **arm in arm** de bracero, asidos del brazo; **arm's reach** alcance del brazo; *va* armar; acorazar; *vn* armarse
**armada** [ɑr'mɑdə] o [ɑr'medə] *s* armada; **the Armada** la Armada Invencible
**armadillo** [,ɑrmə'dɪlo] *s* (*pl:* **-los**) (zool.) armadillo
**Armageddon** [,ɑrmə'gɛdən] *s* (Bib.) Armagedón (*lugar de grande y terrible conflicto*); (fig.) lucha suprema
**armament** ['ɑrməmənt] *s* armamento; *adj* armamentista
**armament race** *s* carrera de los armamentos, carrera armamentista
**armature** ['ɑrmətʃər] *s* armadura; (zool.) coraza; (elec.) armadura (*de imán, condensador, motor, etc.*); (elec.) inducido (*órgano giratorio de dínamo o motor*); (elec.) coraza alambrada
**armature winding** *s* (elec.) arrollamiento del inducido
**arm band** *s* brazal
**armchair** ['ɑrm,tʃɛr] *s* sillón, silla de brazos
**armed** [ɑrmd] *adj* armado; (her.) armado; **armed attack** ataque a mano armada
**armed forces** *spl* fuerzas armadas
**Armenia** [ɑr'minɪə] *s* Armenia
**Armenian** [ɑr'minɪən] *adj & s* armenio
**armet** ['ɑrmɛt] *s* almete
**armful** ['ɑrmfʊl] *s* brazado
**armhole** ['ɑrm,hol] *s* sobaquera; (anat.) sobaco, hueco de la axila
**armillary** ['ɑrmɪ,lɛrɪ] o [ɑr'mɪlərɪ] *adj* armilar
**armillary sphere** *s* esfera armilar
**Arminian** [ɑr'mɪnɪən] *adj & s* arminiano
**Arminianism** [ɑr'mɪnɪənɪzəm] *s* arminianismo
**Arminius** [ɑr'mɪnɪəs] *s* Arminio
**armistice** ['ɑrmɪstɪs] *s* armisticio
**armless** ['ɑrmlɪs] *adj* inerme; sin brazos
**armlet** ['ɑrmlɪt] *s* brazalete; brazal o avambrazo (*de la armadura*); pequeño brazo del mar
**armload** ['ɑrm,lod] *s* brazado
**armor** ['ɑrmər] *s* armadura; coraza, blindaje; *va* acorazar, blindar
**armor-bearer** ['ɑrmər,bɛrər] *s* armígero
**armored car** *s* (mil.) carro blindado
**armorer** ['ɑrmərər] *s* armero
**armorial** [ɑr'morɪəl] *adj* heráldico; *s* armorial
**armorial bearings** *spl* escudo de armas
**armor-piercing** ['ɑrmər,pɪrsɪŋ] *adj* perforante
**armor plate** *s* plancha de blindaje
**armor-plate** ['ɑrmər,plet] *va* acorazar, blindar
**armory** ['ɑrmərɪ] *s* (*pl:* **-ies**) armería (*fábrica de armas; arte del armero*); arsenal; cuartel; (her.) armería
**armour** ['ɑrmər] *s & va* (Brit.) var. de **armor**
**armpit** ['ɑrm,pɪt] *s* (anat.) sobaco, hueco de la axila
**armrack** ['ɑrm,ræk] *s* armero (*aparato para tener las armas*)
**armrest** ['ɑrm,rɛst] *s* apoyabrazos
**arm signal** *s* (naut.) señal de brazos
**army** ['ɑrmɪ] *s* (*pl:* **-mies**) ejército; (fig.) ejército; *adj* castrense
**army chaplain** *s* capellán de ejército, capellán castrense
**army corps** *s* (mil.) cuerpo de ejército
**arnica** ['ɑrnɪkə] *s* (bot. & pharm.) árnica
**Arnold** ['ɑrnəld] *s* Arnaldo
**aroma** [ə'romə] *s* aroma, fragancia
**aromacity** [,ærə'mæsɪtɪ] *s* aromaticidad
**aromatic** [,ærə'mætɪk] *adj* aromático; *s* (bot.) aromática; (chem. & med.) aromático
**aromatization** [ə,romətɪ'zeʃən] *s* aromatización
**aromatize** [ə'romətaɪz] *va* aromatizar
**arose** [ə'roz] *pret de* **arise**
**around** [ə'raʊnd] *adv* alrededor, a la redonda, en torno; a la vuelta; en la dirección opuesta; por todos lados; *prep* alrededor de, en torno de; cerca de; por todos lados de; a la vuelta de (*la esquina*)
**arouse** [ə'raʊz] *va* mover, excitar, incitar; despertar
**arpeggio** [ɑr'pɛdʒo] *s* (*pl:* **-gios**) (mus.) arpegio
**arrack** ['ærək] *s* raque (*aguardiente*)
**arraign** [ə'ren] *va* acusar, denunciar; (law) presentar al tribunal
**arraignment** [ə'renmənt] *s* acusación, denuncia; (law) presentación al tribunal
**arrange** [ə'rendʒ] *va* disponer, arreglar; (mus.) adaptar, refundir
**arrangement** [ə'rendʒmənt] *s* disposición, arreglo; (mus.) adaptación, refundición
**arrant** ['ærənt] *adj* redomado, consumado; descarado, infame
**arras** ['ærəs] *s* tapicería de Arrás
**array** [ə're] *s* orden; orden de batalla; adorno, atavío; *va* poner en orden; poner en orden de batalla; adornar, ataviar
**arrearage** [ə'rɪrɪdʒ] *s* demora, tardanza; deudas; reserva
**arrears** [ə'rɪrz] *spl* atrasos; trabajo no acabado; **in arrears** atrasado en pagos
**arrest** [ə'rɛst] *s* arresto, prisión; parada, detención; **under arrest** bajo arresto; *va* arrestar; parar, detener; atraer (*la atención*)
**arrester** [ə'rɛstər] *s* detenedor; (elec.) pararrayos; (elec.) apagachispas; (mach.) detenedor
**arresting** [ə'rɛstɪŋ] *adj* impresionante
**arrhizal** [ə'raɪzəl] *adj* (bot.) arrizo
**arrhythmia** [ə'rɪθmɪə] *s* (path.) arritmia
**arrhythmic** [ə'rɪðmɪk] o [ə'rɪθmɪk] *adj* arrítmico
**arris** ['ærɪs] *s* (arch.) arista
**arrival** [ə'raɪvəl] *s* llegada; llegado (*persona que llega*)
**arrive** [ə'raɪv] *vn* llegar; tener éxito; **to arrive at** llegar a

**arrogance** ['ærəgəns] *s* arrogancia
**arrogant** ['ærəgənt] *adj* arrogante
**arrogate** ['æroget] *va* arrogarse; atribuir; **to arrogate to oneself** arrogarse
**arrogation** [,æro'geʃən] *s* arrogación; atribución
**arrow** ['æro] *s* flecha
**arrowhead** ['æro,hɛd] *s* punta de flecha; (bot.) sagitaria, saetilla
**arrowroot** ['æro,rut] o ['æro,rʊt] *s* (bot.) maranta; fécula de maranta, arrurruz
**arrowweed** ['æro,wid] *s* (bot.) cachanilla
**arrowwood** ['æro,wʊd] *s* (bot.) viburno; (bot.) cachanilla; (bot.) arraclán, frángula
**arrowy** ['æro·ɪ] o ['ærəwɪ] *adj* aflechado; (fig.) veloz, cortante, penetrante
**arsenal** ['ɑrsɪnəl] *s* arsenal
**arsenate** ['ɑrsɪnet] o ['ɑrsɪnɪt] *s* (chem.) arseniato
**arsenic** ['ɑrsɪnɪk] *s* (chem. & mineral.) arsénico; [ɑr'sɛnɪk] *adj* (chem.) arsénico
**arsenic acid** *s* (chem.) ácido arsénico
**arsenical** [ɑr'sɛnɪkəl] *adj* arsenical
**arsenide** ['ɑrsɪnaɪd] o ['ɑrsɪnɪd] *s* (chem.) arseniuro
**arsenious** [ɑr'siniəs] *adj* (chem.) arsenioso
**arsenite** ['ɑrsɪnaɪt] *s* (chem.) arsenito
**arson** ['ɑrsən] *s* incendio premeditado, delito de incendio
**arsphenamine** [,ɑrsfɛnə'min] o [,ɑrsfɛ'næmɪn] *s* (pharm.) arsfenamina
**art.** abr. de **article**
**art** [ɑrt] *s* arte; *segunda persona del sg del pres de ind de* **be**
**Artaxerxes** [,ɑrtə'zɛrksiz] *s* Artajerjes
**Artemis** ['ɑrtɪmɪs] *s* (myth.) Artemis o Artemisa
**arterial** [ɑr'tɪrɪəl] *adj* arterial
**arterialization** [ɑr,tɪrɪəlɪ'zeʃən] *s* arterialización
**arterialize** [ɑr'tɪrɪəlaɪz] *va* arterializar
**arterial tension** *s* (med.) tensión arterial o sanguínea
**arteriole** [ɑr'tɪrɪol] *s* arteriola
**arteriosclerosis** [ɑr,tɪrɪosklɪ'rosɪs] *s* (path.) arteriosclerosis
**arterious** [ɑr'tɪrɪəs] *adj* arterioso
**arteritis** [,ɑrtə'raɪtɪs] *s* (path.) arteritis
**artery** ['ɑrtərɪ] *s* (*pl:* **-ies**) (anat.) arteria; (fig.) arteria (*gran vía*)
**artesian well** [ɑr'tiʒən] *s* pozo artesiano
**artful** ['ɑrtfəl] *adj* mañoso, astuto, artificioso; artificial; artístico; diestro, ingenioso
**arthritic** [ɑr'θrɪtɪk] *adj & s* artrítico
**arthritis** [ɑr'θraɪtɪs] *s* (path.) artritis
**arthromere** ['ɑrθromɪr] *s* (zool.) artrómera
**arthropod** ['ɑrθrəpɑd] *adj & s* (zool.) artrópodo
**Arthur** ['ɑrθər] *s* Arturo; **King Arthur** el rey Arturo, el rey Artús
**Arthurian** [ɑr'θʊrɪən] *adj* arturiano o artúrico
**Arthurian Cycle** *s* (lit.) ciclo de Artús
**artichoke** ['ɑrtɪtʃok] *s* (bot.) alcachofa (*planta y su piña*)
**article** ['ɑrtɪkəl] *s* artículo; **an article of clothing** una prenda; **an article of food** un alimento; **an article of furniture** un mueble; **an article of luggage** un bulto de equipaje; *va & vn* articular
**articular** [ɑr'tɪkjələr] *adj* articular
**articulate** [ɑr'tɪkjəlɪt] *adj* articulado; claro, distinto; capaz de hablar; *s* (zool.) articulado; [ɑr'tɪkjəlet] *va* articular; *vn* articularse
**articulation** [ɑr,tɪkjə'leʃən] *s* articulación; (anat., bot., zool., & phonet.) articulación
**artifact** ['ɑrtɪfækt] *s* artefacto; (biol.) artefacto
**artifice** ['ɑrtɪfɪs] *s* artificio
**artificer** [ɑr'tɪfɪsər] *s* artífice; (mil.) artificiero
**artificial** [,ɑrtɪ'fɪʃəl] *adj* artificial
**artificial insemination** *s* inseminación artificial
**artificiality** [,ɑrtɪ,fɪʃɪ'ælɪtɪ] *s* (*pl:* **-ties**) falta de naturalidad, afectación; cosa artificial
**artillerist** [ɑr'tɪlərɪst] *s* artillero
**artillery** [ɑr'tɪlərɪ] *s* artillería
**artilleryman** [ɑr'tɪlərɪmən] *s* (*pl:* **-men**) artillero
**artiodactyl** o **artiodactyle** [,ɑrtɪo'dæktɪl] *adj & s* (zool.) artiodáctilo
**artisan** ['ɑrtɪzən] *s* artesano
**artist** ['ɑrtɪst] *s* artista
**artistic** [ɑr'tɪstɪk] *adj* artístico
**artistically** [ɑr'tɪstɪkəlɪ] *adv* artísticamente
**artistry** ['ɑrtɪstrɪ] *s* arte, habilidad artística; obra del artista
**artless** ['ɑrtlɪs] *adj* sencillo, natural, sin arte; chabacano; imperito
**art paper** *s* papel cuché
**arts and crafts** *spl* artes y oficios
**arty** ['ɑrtɪ] *adj* (*comp:* **-ier;** *super:* **-iest**) (coll.) ostentosamente artístico
**arum** ['ɛrəm] *s* (bot.) aro; (bot.) aro de Etiopía
**arum lily** *s* (bot.) aro de Etiopía
**Aryan** ['ɛrɪən] o ['ɑrjən] *adj & s* ario
**as** [æz] o [əz] *pron rel* que; **the same as** el mismo que; **such as** tal cual; *adv* tan; **so as to** + *inf* para + *inf;* **as . . . as** tan . . . como; **as far as** hasta, hasta donde; **as far as he is concerned** por lo que le toca a él; **as far as I know** que yo sepa; **as for** en cuanto a; **as if** como si; **as if to** + *inf* como para + *inf;* **as long as** mientras que; ya que; **as many as** tantos como; **as much as** tanto como; **as of** en el día de; **as per** según; **as regards** en cuanto a; **as soon as** tan pronto como; **as soon as possible** cuanto antes, lo más pronto posible; **as though** como si; **as to** en cuanto a; **as well** también; **as well as** así como; **as yet** hasta ahora; *conj* como; que, ya que; a medida que; **all the more** (o **less**) **. . . (in proportion) as . . . more** (o **less**) tanto más (o menos) . . . cuanto más (o menos); **as it seems** por lo visto, según parece; **as it were** por decirlo así; *prep* por, como; **as a rule** por regla general
**asafetida** o **asafoetida** [,æsə'fɛtɪdə] *s* asafétida o asa fétida
**asarabacca** [,æsərə'bækə] *s* (bot.) asarabácara o ásaro
**asbestos** o **asbestus** [æs'bɛstəs] *s* asbesto; *adj* asbestino
**ascarid** ['æskərɪd] *s* (zool.) ascáride
**ascend** [ə'sɛnd] *va* subir (*p.ej., una cuesta*); **to ascend the throne** empuñar el cetro; *vn* ascender
**ascendance** [ə'sɛndəns] o **ascendancy** [ə'sɛndənsɪ] *s* ascendiente (*poder, influjo*); dominio, ventaja
**ascendant** [ə'sɛndənt] *adj* ascendente; predominante; *s* ascendiente (*poder, influjo*); (astrol.) ascendente; **in the ascendant** predominante, con influencia cada vez mayor, ganando poder
**ascendence** [ə'sɛndəns] o **ascendency** [ə'sɛndənsɪ] *s* var. de **ascendance**
**ascendent** [ə'sɛndənt] *adj & s* var. de **ascendant**
**ascension** [ə'sɛnʃən] *s* ascensión; (*cap.*) *s* Ascensión (*subida de Cristo; fiesta; isla en el Atlántico*)
**ascensional** [ə'sɛnʃənəl] *adj* ascensional
**Ascension Day** *s* la Ascensión, fiesta de la Ascensión
**ascent** [ə'sɛnt] *s* ascensión, subida; ascenso, promoción
**ascertain** [,æsər'ten] *va* averiguar
**ascertainable** [,æsər'tenəbəl] *adj* averiguable
**ascertainment** [,æsər'tenmənt] *s* averiguación
**ascetic** [ə'sɛtɪk] *adj* ascético; *s* asceta
**asceticism** [ə'sɛtɪsɪzəm] *s* ascetismo
**ascians** ['æʃɪənz] o ['æʃənz] *spl* ascios
**ascidian** [ə'sɪdɪən] *s* (zool.) ascidia
**ascites** [ə'saɪtiz] *s* (path.) ascitis
**Asclepius** [æs'klipɪəs] *s* (myth.) Asclepio
**ascomycete** [,æskomaɪ'sit] *s* (bot.) ascomiceto
**ascon** ['æskɑn] *s* (zool.) ascón
**ascorbic acid** [ə'skɔrbɪk] *s* (biochem.) ácido ascórbico
**ascospore** ['æskospor] *s* (bot.) ascospora
**ascot** ['æskət] *s* corbata a la inglesa
**ascribable** [ə'skraɪbəbəl] *adj* atribuible
**ascribe** [ə'skraɪb] *va* atribuir
**ascription** [ə'skrɪpʃən] *s* atribución
**ascus** ['æskəs] *s* (*pl:* **asci** ['æsaɪ]) (bot.) asca
**asepsis** [ə'sɛpsɪs] o [e'sɛpsɪs] *s* (med.) asepsia
**aseptic** [ə'sɛptɪk] o [e'sɛptɪk] *adj* aséptico
**asexual** [e'sɛkʃʊəl] *adj* asexual
**ash** [æʃ] *s* ceniza; (bot.) fresno; **ashes** *spl* ceniza, cenizas; (fig.) cenizas (*restos mortales*)

**ashamed** [ə'ʃemd] *adj* avergonzado; **to be ashamed** tener vergüenza; **to be ashamed to** + *inf* tener vergüenza de + *inf*
**ash can** *s* recipiente de hojalata para ceniza
**ashen** ['æʃən] *adj* ceniciento; fresnal
**ash fire** *s* borrajo, rescoldo
**ashlar** o **ashler** ['æʃlər] *s* sillar; sillería
**ashman** ['æʃ,mæn] *s* (*pl:* **-men**) basurero
**ashore** [ə'ʃor] *adv* en tierra, a tierra; **to come ashore** o **to go ashore** desembarcar; **to run ashore** encallar, varar
**ashpan** ['æʃ,pæn] *s* cenicero, guardacenizas
**ashpit** ['æʃ,pɪt] *s* cenizal, foso para cenizas
**ash tray** *s* cenicero
**Ash Wednesday** *s* miércoles de ceniza
**ashy** ['æʃɪ] *adj* cenizoso
**Asia** ['eʒə] o ['eʃə] *s* Asia
**Asia Minor** *s* el Asia Menor
**Asian** ['eʒən] o ['eʃən] o **Asiatic** [,eʒɪ'ætɪk] o [,eʃɪ'ætɪk] *adj & s* asiático
**Asiatic cholera** *s* (path.) cólera asiático
**Asiaticism** [,eʒɪ'ætɪsɪzəm] o [,eʃɪ'ætɪsɪzəm] *s* asiaticismo
**aside** [ə'saɪd] *adv* aparte, a un lado; **to step aside** hacerse a un lado, quitarse de en medio; **aside from** además de; *s* aparte (*observación*)
**asinine** ['æsɪnaɪn] *adj* tonto, necio
**asininity** [,æsɪ'nɪnɪtɪ] *s* (*pl:* **-ties**) asnería
**ask** [æsk] o [ɑsk] *va* pedir (*suplicar, exigir*); preguntar (*hacer preguntas a*); hacer (*una pregunta*); invitar; **to ask someone for something** pedir algo a alguien; **to ask someone something** preguntar algo a alguien; **to ask someone to** + *inf* pedir a alguien que + *subj;* invitar a alguien a + *inf; vn* pedir; preguntar; **to ask about, after** o **for** preguntar por; **to ask for** pedir; **to ask for it** (coll.) buscársela
**askance** [ə'skæns] o **askant** [ə'skænt] *adv* al sesgo, de soslayo; sospechosamente, con desdén
**askew** [ə'skju] *adj* sesgado, oblicuo; *adv* al sesgo, oblicuamente; con desdén
**asking** ['æskɪŋ] o ['ɑskɪŋ] *s* ruego, petición; **for the asking** sin más que pedirlo
**aslant** [ə'slænt] o [ə'slɑnt] *adv* oblicuamente; *prep* a través de
**asleep** [ə'slip] *adj* dormido; muerto, entumecido; **to fall asleep** dormirse
**aslope** [ə'slop] *adv* en declive
**Asmodeus** [,æzmə'diəs] o [,æsmə'diəs] *s* Asmodeo
**asp** [æsp] *s* (zool.) áspid; (poet.) tiemblo (*árbol*)
**asparagus** [ə'spærəgəs] *s* (bot.) espárrago (*planta y tallos*); espárragos (*tallos que se comen*)
**asparkle** [ə'spɑrkəl] *adj* centelleante
**aspect** ['æspɛkt] *s* aspecto; (astr., astrol. & gram.) aspecto
**aspen** ['æspən] *s* (bot.) álamo temblón, tiemblo; *adj* tremulante
**aspergillum** [,æspər'dʒɪləm] *s* (*pl:* **-la** [lə] o **-lums**) (eccl.) hisopo
**asperity** [æs'pɛrɪtɪ] *s* (*pl:* **-ties**) aspereza
**asperse** [ə'spʌrs] *va* difamar, calumniar; asperjar
**aspersion** [ə'spʌrʒən] o [ə'spʌrʃən] *s* difamación, calumnia; aspersión (*rociamiento*); **to cast aspersions on** insinuar calumnias contra
**asphalt** ['æsfɔlt] o ['æsfælt] *s* asfalto; (mineral.) asfalto; *adj* asfaltado; *va* asfaltar
**asphaltic** [æs'fɔltɪk] o [æs'fæltɪk] *adj* asfáltico
**asphaltum** [æs'fæltəm] *s* (mineral.) asfalto
**asphodel** ['æsfədɛl] *s* (bot.) asfódelo
**asphyxia** [æs'fɪksɪə] *s* (path.) asfixia
**asphyxiate** [æs'fɪksɪet] *va* asfixiar
**asphyxiation** [æs,fɪksɪ'eʃən] *s* asfixia
**aspic** ['æspɪk] *s* (zool.) áspid; manjar de gelatina, carne picada, jugo de tomate, etc.
**aspidistra** [,æspɪ'dɪstrə] *s* (bot.) aspidistra
**aspirant** [ə'spaɪrənt] o ['æspɪrənt] *s* pretendiente, candidato
**aspirate** ['æspɪrɪt] *adj* (phonet.) aspirado; *s* (phonet.) aspirada (*letra*); ['æspɪret] *va* (phonet.) aspirar
**aspiration** [,æspɪ'reʃən] *s* aspiración
**aspirator** ['æspɪ,retər] *s* aspirador
**aspire** [ə'spaɪr] *vn* aspirar; elevarse; **to aspire after** o **to** aspirar a; **to aspire to** + *inf* aspirar a + *inf*
**aspirin** ['æspɪrɪn] *s* (pharm.) aspirina
**asquint** [ə'skwɪnt] *adv* de soslayo
**ass** [æs] *s* asno; (fig.) asno
**assafetida** o **assafoetida** [,æsə'fɛtɪdə] *s* var. de **asafetida**
**assagai** ['æsəgaɪ] *s* azagaya
**assail** [ə'sel] *va* asaltar, acometer
**assailable** [ə'seləbəl] *adj* atacable
**assailant** [ə'selənt] *s* asaltador, asaltante
**assassin** [ə'sæsɪn] *s* asesino
**assassinate** [ə'sæsɪnet] *va* asesinar
**assassination** [ə,sæsɪ'neʃən] *s* asesinato
**assassin bug** *s* (ent.) reduvio
**assault** [ə'sɔlt] *s* asalto; *va* asaltar
**assault and battery** *spl* (law) vías de hecho, violencias
**assay** [ə'se] o ['æse] *s* ensaye; muestra de ensaye; [ə'se] *va* ensayar (*mineral, aleación, etc.*); apreciar
**assayer** [ə'seər] *s* ensayador, contraste, quilatador
**assemblage** [ə'sɛmblɪdʒ] *s* asamblea; reunión (*de personas o cosas*); (mach.) montaje
**assemble** [ə'sɛmbəl] *va* reunir; (mach.) armar, montar; *vn* reunirse
**assembly** [ə'sɛmblɪ] *s* (*pl:* **-blies**) asamblea; reunión (*de personas o cosas*); (mach.) montaje, armadura; (mil.) asamblea
**assembly hall** *s* aula magna, salón de sesiones, paraninfo
**assembly line** *s* línea de montaje
**assemblyman** [ə'sɛmblɪmən] *s* (*pl:* **-men**) asambleísta
**assembly plant** *s* fábrica de montaje
**assembly room** *s* sala de reunión; (mach.) taller de montaje
**assent** [ə'sɛnt] *s* asenso; *vn* asentir
**assert** [ə'sʌrt] *va* afirmar, aseverar, declarar; **to assert oneself** hacer valer sus derechos
**assertion** [ə'sʌrʃən] *s* aserción
**assertive** [ə'sʌrtɪv] *adj* asertivo; agresivo
**assess** [ə'sɛs] *va* gravar (*una propiedad inmueble*); fijar (*daños y perjuicios*); amillarar, prorratear; apreciar, estimar
**assessable** [ə'sɛsəbəl] *adj* gravable
**assessment** [ə'sɛsmənt] *s* gravamen; fijación; amillaramiento, prorrateo; apreciación, estimación
**assessor** [ə'sɛsər] *s* tasador
**asset** ['æsɛt] *s* posesión, ventaja; (fig.) valor (*persona, cosa o cualidad dignas de ser poseídas*); (com.) partida del activo; **assets** *spl* (com.) activo
**asseverate** [ə'sɛvəret] *va* aseverar
**asseveration** [ə,sɛvə'reʃən] *s* aseveración
**assibilate** [ə'sɪbɪlet] *va* (phonet.) asibilar; *vn* (phonet.) asibilarse
**assibilation** [ə,sɪbɪ'leʃən] *s* (phonet.) asibilación
**assiduity** [,æsɪ'djuɪtɪ] o [,æsɪ'duɪtɪ] *s* asiduidad
**assiduous** [ə'sɪdʒuəs] o [ə'sɪdjuəs] *adj* asiduo
**assign** [ə'saɪn] *s* (law) cesionario; *va* asignar
**assignable** [ə'saɪnəbəl] *adj* asignable
**assignat** ['æsɪgnæt] *s* asignado (*papel moneda en Francia durante la Revolución*)
**assignation** [,æsɪg'neʃən] *s* asignación; cita con una muchacha
**assignee** [,æsɪ'ni] *s* (law) cesionario
**assignment** [ə'saɪnmənt] *s* asignación, cometido; lección; (law) escritura de cesión
**assignor** [,æsɪ'nɔr] *s* (law) cesionista
**assimilable** [ə'sɪmɪləbəl] *adj* asimilable
**assimilate** [ə'sɪmɪlet] *va* asimilarse (*p.ej., los alimentos, el conocimiento*); asimilar; *vn* asimilar
**assimilation** [ə,sɪmɪ'leʃən] *s* asimilación
**assimilative** [ə'sɪmɪ,letɪv] *adj* asimilativo
**Assisi** [ə'sizɪ] *s* Asís
**assist** [ə'sɪst] *va* asistir, ayudar, socorrer, auxiliar
**assistance** [ə'sɪstəns] *s* asistencia, ayuda, socorro
**assistant** [ə'sɪstənt] *adj & s* ayudante
**assistant manager** *s* subdirector
**assistant professor** *s* ayudante de profesor, profesor agregado
**assizes** [ə'saɪzɪz] *spl* sesión del tribunal de justicia
**assn.** o **Assn.** abr. de **association**

**assoc.** abr. de **associate** y **association**
**associate** [ə'soʃɪɪt] o [ə'soʃɪet] *adj* asociado; *s* asociado, socio; [ə'soʃɪet] *va* asociar; *vn* asociarse
**associate professor** *s* profesor adjunto
**association** [ə,sosɪ'eʃən] o [ə,soʃɪ'eʃən] *s* asociación
**association football** *s* (sport) asociación o fútbol asociación
**associationism** [ə,sosɪ'eʃənɪzəm] o [ə,soʃɪ'eʃənɪzəm] *s* (psychol.) asociacionismo
**associative** [ə'soʃɪ,etɪv] *adj* asociativo
**assonance** ['æsənəns] *s* asonancia; asonante (*sonido, sílaba o letra*)
**assonanced** ['æsənənst] *adj* asonantado
**assonant** ['æsənənt] *adj & s* asonante
**assonate** ['æsənet] *vn* asonantar, asonar
**assort** [ə'sɔrt] *va* ordenar, clasificar; *vn* convenir, asociarse
**assorted** [ə'sɔrtɪd] *adj* surtido, variado; clasificado; apareado
**assortment** [ə'sɔrtmənt] *s* surtido; clasificación; clase, grupo
**asst.** o **Asst.** abr. de **assistant**
**assuage** [ə'swedʒ] *va* mitigar, aliviar
**assuagement** [ə'swedʒmənt] *s* mitigación, alivio
**assume** [ə'sum] o [ə'sjum] *va* asumir (*p.ej., el mando, responsabilidades, grandes proporciones*); adoptar; arrogarse; suponer, dar por sentado; *vn* presumir
**assumed** [ə'sumd] o [ə'sjumd] *adj* supuesto; fingido, pretendido, falso
**assuming** [ə'sumɪŋ] o [ə'sjumɪŋ] *adj* presuntuoso, presumido
**assumption** [ə'sʌmpʃən] *s* asunción; adopción; arrogación; suposición; presunción; (*cap.*) *s* (eccl.) Asunción
**Assumptionist** [ə'sʌmpʃənɪst] *s* asuncionista
**assumptive** [ə'sʌmptɪv] *adj* supuesto; arrogante, presuntuoso
**assurance** [ə'ʃurəns] *s* aseguramiento; seguridad, confianza; descaro; (com.) seguro
**assure** [ə'ʃur] *va* asegurar; (com.) asegurar
**assured** [ə'ʃurd] *adj* seguro, confiado; descarado; (com.) asegurado
**Assyria** [ə'sɪrɪə] *s* Asiria
**Assyrian** [ə'sɪrɪən] *adj & s* asirio
**Assyriologist** [ə,sɪrɪ'ɑlədʒɪst] *s* asiriólogo
**Assyriology** [ə,sɪrɪ'ɑlədʒɪ] *s* asiriología
**astatic** [e'stætɪk] *adj* astático
**astatine** ['æstətin] o ['æstətɪn] *s* (chem.) **astatino** o ástato
**aster** ['æstər] *s* (bot. & biol.) aster; (bot.) reina Margarita (*Callistephus chinensis*)
**asterisk** ['æstərɪsk] *s* asterisco
**asterism** ['æstərɪzəm] *s* (astr. & phys.) asterismo
**astern** [ə'stʌrn] *adv* (naut.) por la popa, a popa
**asteroid** ['æstərɔɪd] *adj* asteroide (*de figura de estrella*); *s* (astr.) asteroide; (bot.) asteroidea; (zool.) asteroideo, estrella de mar
**asteroidean** [,æstə'rɔɪdɪən] *adj & s* (zool.) asteroideo
**asthenia** [æs'θinɪə] *s* (path.) astenia
**asthenic** [æs'θɛnɪk] *adj & s* asténico
**asthma** ['æzmə] o ['æsmə] *s* (path.) asma
**asthmatic** [æz'mætɪk] o [æs'mætɪk] *adj & s* asmático
**astigmatic** [,æstɪg'mætɪk] *adj* astigmático
**astigmatism** [ə'stɪgmətɪzəm] *s* (med.) astigmatismo
**astigmometer** [,æstɪg'mɑmɪtər] *s* astigmómetro
**astir** [ə'stʌr] *adv* en movimiento, en actividad; levantado de la cama
**astonish** [ə'stɑnɪʃ] *va* asombrar
**astonishing** [ə'stɑnɪʃɪŋ] *adj* asombroso
**astonishment** [ə'stɑnɪʃmənt] *s* asombro
**astound** [ə'staund] *va* pasmar, aturdir
**astounding** [ə'staundɪŋ] *adj* pasmoso
**astrachan** ['æstrəkən] *s* astracán
**astraddle** [ə'strædəl] *adv* a horcajadas
**astragal** ['æstrəgəl] *s* (anat., arch. & arti.) astrágalo; (carp.) contrapilastra
**astrakhan** ['æstrəkən] *s* var. de **astrachan**
**astral** ['æstrəl] *adj* astral
**astral body** *s* (theosophy) cuerpo astral
**astral lamp** *s* lámpara astral
**astray** [ə'stre] *adv* por mal camino; **to go astray** extraviarse; **to lead astray** extraviar
**astriction** [ə'strɪkʃən] *s* astricción
**astrictive** [ə'strɪktɪv] *adj* astrictivo
**astride** [ə'straɪd] *adv* a horcajadas; *prep* a horcajadas en
**astringency** [ə'strɪndʒənsɪ] *s* astringencia; (fig.) austeridad
**astringent** [əs'trɪndʒənt] *adj* astringente; (fig.) austero; *s* astringente
**astrodome** ['æstrədom] *s* (aer.) astródomo
**astrolabe** ['æstrəleb] *s* (astr.) astrolabio
**astrologer** [ə'strɑlədʒər] *s* astrólogo
**astrological** [,æstrə'lɑdʒɪkəl] *adj* astrológico
**astrologize** [ə'strɑlədʒaɪz] *va & vn* astrologar
**astrology** [ə'strɑlədʒɪ] *s* astrología
**astronaut** ['æstrənɔt] *s* astronauta
**astronautic** [,æstrə'nɔtɪk] *adj* astronáutico; **astronautics** *ssg* astronáutica
**astronautical** [,æstrə'nɔtɪkəl] *adj* astronáutico
**astronavigation** [,æstro,nævɪ'geʃən] *s* astronavegación
**astronomer** [ə'strɑnəmər] *s* astrónomo
**astronomic** [,æstrə'nɑmɪk] o **astronomical** [,æstrə'nɑmɪkəl] *adj* astronómico; (fig.) astronómico (*extraordinariamente grande*)
**astronomical year** *s* año astronómico
**astronomy** [ə'strɑnəmɪ] *s* astronomía
**astrophotography** [,æstrəfə'tɑgrəfɪ] *s* astrofotografía
**astrophotometry** [,æstrəfo'tɑmɪtrɪ] *s* astrofotometría
**astrophysical** [,æstro'fɪzɪkəl] *adj* astrofísico
**astrophysics** [,æstro'fɪzɪks] *ssg* astrofísica
**Asturian** [æs'turɪən] *adj & s* asturiano
**astute** [æs'tjut] o [æs'tut] *adj* astuto, sagaz
**astuteness** [æs'tjutnɪs] o [æs'tutnɪs] *s* astucia
**Astyanax** [æs'taɪənæks] *s* (myth.) Astianacte
**asunder** [ə'sʌndər] *adv* a pedazos, en dos; **to tear asunder** romper en dos
**asylum** [ə'saɪləm] *s* asilo
**asymmetric** [,esɪ'mɛtrɪk] o [,æsɪ'mɛtrɪk] o **asymmetrical** [,esɪ'mɛtrɪkəl] o [,æsɪ'mɛtrɪkəl] *adj* asimétrico
**asymmetry** [e'sɪmɪtrɪ] *s* asimetría
**asymptote** ['æsɪmtot] *s* (math.) asíntota
**asynchronism** [e'sɪŋkrənɪzəm] o [e'sɪnkrənɪzəm] *s* asincronismo
**asynchronous** [e'sɪŋkrənəs] o [e'sɪnkrənəs] *adj* asincrónico
**asyndeton** [ə'sɪndətən] o [ə'sɪndɪtɑn] *s* (rhet.) asíndeton
**asystole** [e'sɪstəli] *s* (path.) asistolia
**asystolic** [,esɪs'tɑlɪk] *adj* asistólico
**at** [æt] o [ət] *prep* en, p.ej., **he was at the theater last night** estuvo en el teatro anoche; **at that time** en aquel entonces; a, p.ej., **he was waiting for me at the door** me esperaba a la puerta; **at eight o'clock** a las ocho; por, p.ej., **go in at the front door** entre Vd. por la puerta principal; **at my order** por mi orden; de, p.ej., **to be surprised at** estar sorprendido de; **to laugh at** reírse de; en casa de p.ej., **at Mary's** en casa de María; en la oficina de; en la tienda de; en el taller de; en el restaurante de
**atacamite** [ə'tækəmaɪt] *s* (mineral.) atacamita
**ataractic** [,ætə'ræktɪk] *adj* ataráxico
**ataraxia** [,ætə'ræksɪə] *s* ataraxia
**atavism** ['ætəvɪzəm] *s* (biol.) atavismo
**atavistic** [,ætə'vɪstɪk] *adj* atávico
**ataxia** [ə'tæksɪə] *s* ataxia; (path.) ataxia
**ataxic** [ə'tæksɪk] *adj & s* atáxico
**ataxy** [ə'tæksɪ] *s* var. de **ataxia**
**ate** [et] *pret de* **eat**; (*cap.*) ['etɪ] *s* (myth.) Até
**atelier** ['ætəlje] *s* taller (*de artista*)
**athanasia** [,æθə'neʒə] *s* atanasia (*inmortalidad*)
**Athanasian** [,æθə'neʒən] *adj* atanasiano
**Athanasian Creed** *s* Símbolo Atanasiano
**Athanasius, Saint** [,æθə'neʃəs] San Atanasio
**athanor** ['æθənɔr] *s* atanor, hornillo de atenor
**atheism** ['eθiɪzəm] *s* ateísmo
**atheist** ['eθiɪst] *adj & s* ateo
**atheistic** [,eθi'ɪstɪk] o **atheistical** [,eθi'ɪstɪkəl] *adj* ateo
**Athena** [ə'θinə] *s* (myth.) Atena o Atenea
**athenaeum** o **atheneum** [,æθɪ'niəm] *s* ateneo
**Athene** [ə'θinɪ] *s* var. de **Athena**

**Athenian** [əˈθiniən] *adj & s* ateniense
**Athens** [ˈæθɪnz] *s* Atenas
**atherine** [ˈæθərɪn] o [ˈæθəraɪn] *s* (ichth.) pejerrey, pez de rey
**athermancy** [eˈθʌrmənsɪ] *s* (phys.) atermancia
**athermanous** [eˈθʌrmənəs] *adj* atérmano
**atherosclerosis** [ˌæθəroskliˈrosɪs] *s* (path.) aterosclerosis
**athirst** [əˈθʌrst] *adj* sediento
**athlete** [ˈæθlit] *s* atleta
**athlete's foot** *s* (path.) pie de atleta
**athlete's heart** *s* (path.) corazón atlético
**athletic** [æθˈlɛtɪk] *adj* atlético; **athletics** *ssg* atletismo (*doctrina acerca de los ejercicios atléticos*); atlética (*arte o habilidad*); *spl* atletismo (*ejercicios atléticos*)
**athletic field** *s* campo de deportes
**at-home** [ætˈhom] *s* recepción, recibimiento
**athwart** [əˈθwɔrt] *adv* de través; *prep* por el través de; contra
**atilt** [əˈtɪlt] *adv* en posición inclinada; dando una lanzada
**atingle** [əˈtɪŋgəl] *adj* estremeciéndose
**atinkle** [əˈtɪŋkəl] *adj* tintineando
**Atlantean** [ˌætlænˈtiən] *adj* atlántico (*perteneciente al gigante Atlas o Atlante*)
**atlantes** [ætˈlæntiz] *spl* (arch.) atlantes
**Atlantic** [ætˈlæntɪk] *adj & s* Atlántico
**Atlantic Charter** *s* carta del Atlántico
**Atlantic Coast** *s* Costa del Atlántico
**Atlantic Ocean** *s* océano Atlántico
**Atlantides** [ætˈlæntɪdiz] *spl* (astr. & myth.) Atlántidas
**Atlantis** [ætˈlæntɪs] *s* Atlántida
**atlas** [ˈætləs] *s* atlas (*libro de mapas geográficos*); (anat.) atlas; (*cap.*) *s* (myth.) Atlas o Atlante
**atlas folio** *s* folio atlántico
**Atlas Mountains, the** el Atlas
**atmosphere** [ˈætməsfɪr] *s* atmósfera; (fig.) atmósfera
**atmospheric** [ˌætməsˈfɛrɪk] *adj* atmosférico; **atmospherics** *spl* (rad.) parásitos atmosféricos
**atmospheric pressure** *s* presión atmosférica
**atoll** [ˈætɑl] o [əˈtɑl] *s* atolón
**atom** [ˈætəm] *s* átomo; (chem.) átomo
**atom bomb** *s* bomba atómica
**atomic** [əˈtɑmɪk] *adj* atómico
**atomic age** *s* era atómica
**atomic air power** *s* poder aéreo atómico
**atomic bomb** *s* bomba atómica
**atomic energy** *s* (phys.) energía atómica
**atomicity** [ˌætəˈmɪsɪtɪ] *s* (chem.) atomicidad
**atomic number** *s* (chem.) número atómico
**atomic pile** *s* (phys.) pila atómica
**atomic reactor** *s* (phys.) reactor atómico
**atomic theory** *s* (chem.) teoría atómica
**atomic war** *s* guerra atómica
**atomic weapon** *s* arma atómica
**atomic weight** *s* (chem.) peso atómico
**atomism** [ˈætəmɪzəm] *s* atomismo
**atomist** [ˈætəmɪst] *s* atomista
**atomistic** [ˌætəˈmɪstɪk] *adj* atomístico; **atomistics** *ssg* atomística
**atomize** [ˈætəmaɪz] *va* atomizar
**atomizer** [ˈætəˌmaɪzər] *s* atomizador, pulverizador
**atom smasher** *s* (phys.) rompeátomos
**atomy** [ˈætəmɪ] *s* (*pl:* **-mies**) átomo; pigmeo
**atonal** [eˈtonəl] *adj* (mus.) atonal
**atonalism** [eˈtonəlɪzəm] *s* (mus.) atonalismo
**atonality** [ˌetəˈnælɪtɪ] *s* (mus.) atonalidad
**atone** [əˈton] *vn* dar reparación; **to atone for** dar reparación por; expiar
**atonement** [əˈtonmənt] *s* reparación; expiación; (theol.) redención
**atonic** [əˈtɑnɪk] *adj* (gram. & med.) átono, atónico
**atonicity** [ˌætəˈnɪsɪtɪ] o [ˌetəˈnɪsɪtɪ] *s* (med.) atonicidad
**atony** [ˈætənɪ] *s* (path. & phonet.) atonía
**atop** [əˈtɑp] *adv* encima; *prep* encima de
**atrabilious** [ˌætrəˈbɪljəs] *adj* atrabiliario
**atresia** [əˈtriʒɪə] *s* (med.) atresia
**Atreus** [ˈetrus] o [ˈetrɪəs] *s* (myth.) Atreo
**atrium** [ˈetrɪəm] *s* (*pl:* **-a** [ə]) atrio; (anat.) atrio
**atrocious** [əˈtroʃəs] *adj* atroz; (coll.) muy malo, abominable
**atrocity** [əˈtrɑsɪtɪ] *s* (*pl:* **-ties**) atrocidad
**atrophy** [ˈætrəfɪ] *s* atrofia; (*pret & pp:* **-phied**) *va* atrofiar; *vn* atrofiarse
**atropine** [ˈætrəpin] o [ˈætrəpɪn] *s* (chem. & pharm.) atropina
**Atropos** [ˈætrəpɑs] *s* (myth.) Átropos
**attach** [əˈtætʃ] *va* atar, pegar, ligar, juntar; atribuir (*p.ej., importancia*); (law) embargar, incautarse, secuestrar (*propiedad*); *vn* pertenecer
**attaché** [ˌætəˈʃe] o [əˈtæʃe] *s* agregado
**attached** [əˈtætʃt] *adj* adherido; **attached to** encariñado con, aficionado a
**attachment** [əˈtætʃmənt] *s* atadura, unión, enlace; atribución; apego, cariño; aditamento, accesorio; (law) embargo, secuestro, ejecución
**attack** [əˈtæk] *s* ataque; **an attack of pneumonia** una pulmonía, un ataque de pulmonía; *va* atacar; (chem.) atacar
**attain** [əˈten] *va* lograr, alcanzar, conseguir; *vn* alcanzar; **to attain to** alcanzar a
**attainable** [əˈtenəbəl] *adj* alcanzable, realizable
**attainder** [əˈtendər] *s* muerte civil; (obs.) deshonra
**attainment** [əˈtenmənt] *s* logro, consecución; **attainments** *spl* dotes, prendas
**attaint** [əˈtent] *s* mancha, baldón; (vet.) alcanzadura; *va* condenar a muerte civil
**attar** [ˈætər] *s* aceite esencial fragante
**attar of roses** *s* aceite esencial de rosas
**attempt** [əˈtɛmpt] *s* tentativa (*intento, prueba*); atentado; conato; *va* procurar, intentar; atentar a o contra
**attend** [əˈtɛnd] *va* atender, asistir; asistir a (*la iglesia, la escuela, etc.*); auxiliar (*a un moribundo*); *vn* atender; **to attend to** atender a
**attendance** [əˈtɛndəns] *s* asistencia, concurrencia; **to dance attendance** hacer antesala; **to dance attendance on** servir obsequiosa y constantemente
**attendant** [əˈtɛndənt] *adj & s* asistente; concomitante
**attention** [əˈtɛnʃən] *s* atención; **attentions** *spl* atenciones (*agasajo, obsequio*); **to attract attention** llamar la atención; **to call attention to** hacer presente; **to come to the attention of someone** hacérsele presente a uno; **to pay attention** hacer caso; **to stand at attention** cuadrarse (*los soldados*); *interj* ¡atención!, ¡firmes!
**attentive** [əˈtɛntɪv] *adj* atento
**attenuate** [əˈtɛnjʊet] *va* atenuar; *vn* atenuarse
**attenuation** [əˌtɛnjʊˈeʃən] *s* atenuación
**attest** [əˈtɛst] *va* atestar, atestiguar; juramentar; *vn* dar fe; **to attest to** dar fe de
**attestation** [ˌætɛsˈteʃən] *s* atestación, atestiguación
**Attic** [ˈætɪk] *adj & s* ático; (*l.c.*) *s* (anat. & arch.) ático; buharda
**Attica** [ˈætɪkə] *s* el Ática
**Atticism** [ˈætɪsɪzəm] *s* aticismo
**Atticist** [ˈætɪsɪst] *s* aticista
**Attic salt** *s* sal ática
**Attila** [ˈætɪlə] *s* Atila
**attire** [əˈtaɪr] *s* atavío, traje; *va* ataviar, vestir
**attitude** [ˈætɪtjud] o [ˈætɪtud] *s* actitud, ademán, postura; (paint. & sculp.) ademán; (aer.) posición; (fig.) actitud (*disposición de la mente*)
**attorney** [əˈtʌrnɪ] *s* procurador; abogado
**attorney at law** *s* procurador judicial
**attorney general** *s* (*pl:* **attorneys general** o **attorney generals**) procurador de síndico, procurador general; (*caps.*) *s* (U.S.A.) ministro de Justicia
**attract** [əˈtrækt] *va* atraer; llamar (*la atención*)
**attractable** [əˈtræktəbəl] *adj* atraíble
**attraction** [əˈtrækʃən] *s* atracción; atractivo (*gracia personal*)
**attractive** [əˈtræktɪv] *adj* atractivo; atrayente (*agradable, interesante*)
**attractiveness** [əˈtræktɪvnɪs] *s* atractivo
**attributable** [əˈtrɪbjətəbəl] *adj* atribuíble
**attribute** [ˈætrɪbjut] *s* atributo; (gram.) atributo; [əˈtrɪbjʊt] *va* atribuir
**attribution** [ˌætrɪˈbjuʃən] *s* atribución

**attributive** [ə'trɪbjətɪv] *adj* atributivo; (gram.) atributivo
**attrition** [ə'trɪʃən] *s* (phys. & theol.) atrición; (fig.) agotamiento, consunción
**attune** [ə'tjun] o [ə'tun] *va* acordar, afinar
**atty.** abr. de **attorney**
**at. wt.** abr. de **atomic weight**
**atypical** [e'tɪpɪkəl] *adj* atípico
**auburn** ['ɔbərn] *adj & s* castaño rojizo
**Aubusson** [oby'sõ] *s* tapiz de Aubusson
**auction** ['ɔkʃən] *s* almoneda, remate, subasta; **to put up at auction** poner en pública subasta; *va* rematar, subastar
**auction bridge** *s* bridge-remate
**auctioneer** [,ɔkʃən'ɪr] *s* pregonero, subastador; *va* rematar, subastar
**auction room** *s* sala de subastas
**audacious** [ɔ'deʃəs] *adj* audaz
**audacity** [ɔ'dæsɪtɪ] *s* (*pl:* **-ties**) audacia
**audibility** [,ɔdɪ'bɪlɪtɪ] *s* audibilidad
**audible** ['ɔdɪbəl] *adj* audible
**audience** ['ɔdɪəns] *s* audiencia; público, auditorio
**audience room** *s* audiencia (*lugar destinado para dar audiencias*)
**audio frequency** ['ɔdɪo] *s* (rad.) audiofrecuencia
**audio-frequency** [,ɔdɪo'frikwənsɪ] *adj* (rad.) de audiofrecuencia
**audiology** [,ɔdɪ'ɑlədʒɪ] *s* audiología
**audiometer** [,ɔdɪ'ɑmɪtər] *s* audímetro, audiómetro
**audion** ['ɔdɪɑn] *s* (rad.) audión
**audiophile** ['ɔdiofaɪl] *s* aficionado a la música de alta fidelidad
**audio-visual** ['ɔdɪo'vɪʒuəl] *adj* audio-visual
**audiphone** ['ɔdɪfon] *s* audífono
**audit** ['ɔdɪt] *s* (com.) intervención; *va* intervenir (*una cuenta*)
**audition** [ɔ'dɪʃən] *s* audición; *va* dar audición a
**auditor** ['ɔdɪtər] *s* oyente (*en la escuela*); (com.) interventor
**auditorium** [,ɔdɪ'torɪəm] *s* (*pl:* **-ums** o **-a** [ə]) auditorio, anfiteatro, paraninfo
**auditory** ['ɔdɪ,torɪ] *adj* auditivo; *s* (*pl:* **-ries**) auditorio, anfiteatro
**auditory canal** *s* (anat.) conducto auditivo
**auditory nerve** *s* (anat.) nervio auditivo
**Aug.** abr. de **August**
**Augean Stables** [ɔ'dʒiən] *spl* (myth.) establos de Augías
**auger** ['ɔgər] *s* barrena
**aught** [ɔt] *s* alguna cosa; cifra; nada; *adv* absolutamente; en cualquier respecto
**augite** ['ɔdʒaɪt] *s* (mineral.) augita
**augment** [ɔg'mɛnt] *va* aumentar; *vn* aumentar o aumentarse
**augmentation** [,ɔgmɛn'teʃən] *s* aumento; (her.) aumentación
**augmentative** [ɔg'mɛntətɪv] *adj & s* (gram.) aumentativo
**augmented** [ɔg'mɛntɪd] *adj* (mus.) aumentado
**au gratin** [o'grɑtən] *adv* (cook.) al gratín
**Augsburg Confession** ['ɔgzbʌrg] *s* confesión de Augsburgo
**augur** ['ɔgər] *s* augur; *va & vn* augurar; **to augur ill** ser de mal agüero; **to augur well** ser de buen agüero
**augural** ['ɔgjərəl] *adj* augural
**augurate** ['ɔgjərɪt] *s* augurado
**augury** ['ɔgjərɪ] *s* (*pl:* **-ries**) augurio
**august** [ɔ'gʌst] *adj* augusto; (*cap.*) ['ɔgəst] *s* agosto; *adj* agostero
**Augustan** [ɔ'gʌstən] *adj* augustal
**Augustan age** *s* siglo de Augusto (*de la literatura romana*); siglo de la reina Ana (*de la literatura inglesa*); siglo de Luis Catorce (*de la literatura francesa*)
**Augustine** ['ɔgəstin] u [ɔ'gʌstɪn] *s* Agustín; **Saint Augustine** San Agustín
**Augustinian** [,ɔgəs'tɪnɪən] *adj & s* agustino o agustiniano
**Augustinianism** [,ɔgəs'tɪnɪənɪzəm] *s* agustinianismo
**Augustinian Order** *s* (eccl.) orden de San Agustín
**Augustus** [ɔ'gʌstəs] *s* Augusto
**au jus** [o'ʒy] *adv* (cook.) en su jugo
**auk** [ɔk] *s* (orn.) alca
**au naturel** [onaty'rɛl] *adv* al natural
**aunt** [ænt] o [ɑnt] *s* tía
**aura** ['ɔrə] *s* (*pl:* **-ras** o **-rae** [ri]) efluvio, emanación; (med.) aura
**aural** ['ɔrəl] *adj* aural
**aureate** ['ɔrɪet] u ['ɔrɪɪt] *adj* áureo
**Aurelian** [ɔ'rilɪən] *s* Aureliano
**Aurelius, Marcus** [ɔ'rilɪəs] Marco Aurelio
**aureole** ['ɔrɪol] *s* (meteor., theol., f.a., & fig.) aureola; *va* aureolar
**aureomycin** [,ɔrɪo'maɪsɪn] *s* (pharm.) aureomicina
**au revoir** [orə'vwɑr] *interj* ¡ hasta la vista!
**auricle** ['ɔrɪkəl] *s* (anat.) aurícula
**auricula** [ɔ'rɪkjələ] *s* (*pl:* **-lae** [li] o **-las**) (bot.) aurícula
**auricular** [ɔ'rɪkjələr] *adj* auricular; (anat.) auricular
**auricular witness** *s* testigo de vista o testigo auricular
**auriculate** [ɔ'rɪkjəlɪt] *adj* (bot. & zool.) auriculado
**auriferous** [ɔ'rɪfərəs] *adj* aurífero
**Auriga** [ɔ'raɪgə] *s* (astr.) Auriga
**aurist** ['ɔrɪst] *s* aurista
**aurochs** ['ɔrɑks] *s* (zool.) uro
**aurora** [ɔ'rorə] *s* aurora; (meteor.) aurora polar; (*cap.*) *s* (myth.) Aurora
**aurora australis** [ɔs'trelɪs] *s* (meteor.) aurora austral
**aurora borealis** [,borɪ'elɪs] o [,borɪ'ælɪs] *s* (meteor.) aurora boreal
**auroral** [ɔ'rorəl] *adj* auroral
**auscultate** ['ɔskəltet] *va & vn* auscultar
**auscultation** [,ɔskəl'teʃən] *s* auscultación
**auspice** ['ɔspɪs] *s* auspicio; **under the auspices of** bajo los auspicios de
**auspicious** [ɔs'pɪʃəs] *adj* propicio, auspicioso
**austere** [ɔs'tɪr] *adj* austero
**austerity** [ɔs'tɛrɪtɪ] *s* (*pl:* **-ties**) austeridad
**Austin** ['ɔstɪn] *s* Agustín
**austral** ['ɔstrəl] *adj* austral
**Australasia** [,ɔstrəl'eʒə] u [,ɔstrəl'eʃə] *s* la Australasia
**Australasian** [,ɔstrəl'eʒən] u [,ɔstrəl'eʃən] *adj* australasiático
**Australia** [ɔs'treljə] *s* Australia
**Australian** [ɔs'treljən] *adj & s* australiano
**Australian crawl** *s* (swimming) brazada australiana
**Australian pea** *s* (bot.) caracolillo
**Austria** ['ɔstrɪə] *s* Austria
**Austria-Hungary** ['ɔstrɪə'hʌŋgərɪ] *s* Austria-Hungría
**Austrian** ['ɔstrɪən] *adj & s* austríaco
**Austro-Hungarian** [,ɔstrohʌŋ'gɛrɪən] *adj & s* austrohúngaro
**autarchic** [ɔ'tɑrkɪk] o **autarchical** [ɔ'tɑrkɪkəl] *adj* autárquico
**autarchy** ['ɔtɑrkɪ] *s* (*pl:* **-chies**) autarquía
**autarkic** [ɔ'tɑrkɪk] o **autarkical** [ɔ'tɑrkɪkəl] *adj* autárcico o autárquico
**autarky** ['ɔtɑrkɪ] *s* (*pl:* **-kies**) autarcía o autarquía (*independencia económica*)
**authentic** [ɔ'θɛntɪk] *adj* auténtico
**authentically** [ɔ'θɛntɪkəlɪ] *adv* auténticamente
**authenticate** [ɔ'θɛntɪket] *va* autenticar
**authentication** [ɔ,θɛntɪ'keʃən] *s* autenticación
**authenticity** [,ɔθɛn'tɪsɪtɪ] *s* autenticidad
**author** ['ɔθər] *s* autor
**authoress** ['ɔθərɪs] *s* autora
**authoritarian** [ɔ,θɑrɪ'tɛrɪən] u [ɔ,θɔrɪ'tɛrɪən] *adj & s* autoritario
**authoritarianism** [ɔ,θɑrɪ'tɛrɪənɪzəm] u [ɔ,θɔrɪ'tɛrɪənɪzəm] *s* autoritarismo
**authoritative** [ɔ'θɑrɪ,tetɪv] u [ɔ'θɔrɪ,tetɪv] *adj* autorizado; autoritario (*imperioso*)
**authority** [ɔ'θɑrɪtɪ] u [ɔ'θɔrɪtɪ] *s* (*pl:* **-ties**) autoridad; **on good authority** de buena tinta
**authorization** [,ɔθərɪ'zeʃən] *s* autorización
**authorize** ['ɔθəraɪz] *va* autorizar; **to authorize to** + *inf* autorizar a o para + *inf*
**Authorized Version** *s* versión autorizada (*de la Biblia*)
**authorship** ['ɔθərʃɪp] *s* profesión de autor; paternidad literaria
**auto** ['ɔto] *s* (*pl:* **-tos**) (coll.) auto
**autobiographer** [,ɔtobaɪ'ɑgrəfər] u [,ɔtobɪ'ɑgrəfər] *s* autobiógrafo
**autobiographic** [,ɔto,baɪə'græfɪk] o **autobio-**

**graphical** [ˌɔtoˌbaɪəˈgræfɪkəl] *adj* autobiográfico
**autobiography** [ˌɔtobaɪˈɑgrəfɪ] u [ˌɔtobɪˈɑgrəfɪ] *s* autobiografía
**autoblast** [ˈɔtoblæst] *s* (biol.) autoblasto
**autobus** [ˈɔtoˌbʌs] *s* autobús
**autocade** [ˈɔtoˌked] *s* caravana de automóviles
**autochthon** [ɔˈtɑkθən] *s* autóctono
**autochthonous** [ɔˈtɑkθənəs] *adj* autóctono
**autochthony** [ɔˈtɑkθənɪ] *s* autoctonía
**autoclave** [ˈɔtoklev] *s* autoclave
**autocracy** [ɔˈtɑkrəsɪ] *s* (*pl:* **-cies**) autocracia
**autocrat** [ˈɔtəkræt] *s* autócrata
**autocratic** [ˌɔtəˈkrætɪk] o **autocratical** [ˌɔtəˈkrætɪkəl] *adj* autocrático
**auto-da-fé** [ˈɔtodəˈfe] o [ˈaʊtodəˈfe] *s* (*pl:* **autos-da-fé**) auto de fe
**auto driver training school** *s* var. de **driving school**
**autofrettage** [ˌɔtoˈfrɛtɪdʒ] *s* autofretage
**autogenesis** [ˌɔtoˈdʒɛnɪsɪs] *s* autogénesis
**autogenous** [ɔˈtɑdʒɪnəs] *adj* autógeno
**autogiro** [ˌɔtoˈdʒaɪro] *s* (*pl:* **-ros**) autogiro
**autograph** [ˈɔtəgræf] u [ˈɔtəgrɑf] *adj* autógrafo (*escrito de mano de su mismo autor*); *s* autógrafo; *va* autografiar
**autographic** [ˌɔtəˈgræfɪk] o **autographical** [ˌɔtəˈgræfɪkəl] *adj* autográfico
**autograph seeker** *s* cazador de autógrafos
**autography** [ɔˈtɑgrəfɪ] *s* autografía
**autogyro** [ˌɔtoˈdʒaɪro] *s* (*pl:* **-ros**) var. de **autogiro**
**autohypnosis** [ˌɔtohɪpˈnosɪs] *s* autohipnosis
**autoinfection** [ˌɔto·ɪnˈfɛkʃən] *s* (path.) autoinfección
**autointoxication** [ˌɔto·ɪnˌtɑksɪˈkeʃən] *s* (path.) autointoxicación
**autoist** [ˈɔto·ɪst] *s* (coll.) automovilista
**automat** [ˈɔtəmæt] *s* restaurante automático, bar automático
**automate** [ˈɔtəmet] *va* automatizar
**automatic** [ˌɔtəˈmætɪk] *adj* automático
**automatically** [ˌɔtəˈmætɪkəlɪ] *adv* automáticamente
**automatic rifle** *s* fusil ametrallador
**automation** [ˌɔtəˈmeʃən] *s* automatización
**automatism** [ɔˈtɑmətɪzəm] *s* automacia, automatismo
**automaton** [ɔˈtɑmətɑn] *s* (*pl:* **-tons** o **-ta** [tə]) autómata; (fig.) autómata (*persona*)
**automobile** [ˌɔtəˈmobɪl] *adj* automóvil; automovilista; [ˌɔtəmoˈbil] u [ˌɔtəˈmobil] *s* automóvil
**automobile show** *s* salón del automóvil
**automobilist** [ˌɔtəmoˈbilɪst] u [ˌɔtəˈmobɪlɪst] *s* automovilista
**automotive** [ˌɔtəˈmotɪv] *adj* automotor
**automotive engineer** *s* autotécnico
**automotive engineering** *s* autotécnica
**autonomic** [ˌɔtəˈnɑmɪk] *adj* autonómico
**autonomist** [ɔˈtɑnəmɪst] *s* autonomista
**autonomous** [ɔˈtɑnəməs] *adj* autónomo
**autonomy** [ɔˈtɑnəmɪ] *s* autonomía
**autoplastic** [ˌɔtoˈplæstɪk] *adj* autoplástico
**autoplasty** [ˈɔtoˌplæstɪ] *s* (surg.) autoplastia
**autopsy** [ˈɔtɑpsɪ] *s* (*pl:* **-sies**) autopsia; (*pret & pp:* **-sied**) *va* autopsiar
**auto radio** *s* autorradio
**autosuggestion** [ˌɔtosəgˈdʒɛstʃən] *s* autosugestión
**autotrophic** [ˌɔtoˈtrɑfɪk] *adj* autótrofo
**autotropism** [ɔˈtɑtrəpɪzəm] *s* (bot.) autotropismo
**autotruck** [ˈɔtoˌtrʌk] *s* autocamión
**autumn** [ˈɔtəm] *s* otoño
**autumnal** [ɔˈtʌmnəl] *adj* otoñal, autumnal
**autumnal equinox** *s* (astr.) equinoccio otoñal o de otoño
**autumn crocus** *s* (bot.) cólquico
**autunite** [ˈɔtənaɪt] *s* (mineral.) autunita
**Auvergne** [oˈvʌrn], [oˈvɛrn] u [oˈvɛrnjə] *s* Auvernia
**aux.** abr. de **auxiliary**
**auxiliary** [ɔgˈzɪljərɪ] *adj* auxiliar; (gram.) auxiliar; *s* (*pl:* **-ries**) auxiliar; (gram.) auxiliar (*verbo*); **auxiliaries** *spl* tropas auxiliares
**auxiliary verb** *s* (gram.) verbo auxiliar
**auxochrome** [ˈɔksəkrom] *s* (chem.) auxocromo
**av.** abr. de **avenue, average,** y **avoirdupois**
**A.V.** abr. de **Authorized Version**

**avail** [əˈvel] *s* provecho, utilidad; *va* beneficiar; **to avail oneself of** aprovecharse de, valerse de; *vn* aprovechar
**availability** [əˌveləˈbɪlɪtɪ] *s* disponibilidad
**available** [əˈveləbəl] *adj* disponible, aprovechable; **to make available to** poner a la disposición de
**available assets** *spl* disponibilidades
**avalanche** [ˈævəlæntʃ] o [ˈævəlɑntʃ] *s* alud, avalancha; (fig.) alud, avalancha, torrente
**avant-garde** [avɑ̃ˈgard] *adj* vanguardista; *s* vanguardismo
**avant-gardist** [avɑ̃ˈgardɪst] *s* vanguardista
**avarice** [ˈævərɪs] *s* avaricia
**avaricious** [ˌævəˈrɪʃəs] *adj* avaricioso, avariento
**avast** [əˈvæst] o [əˈvɑst] *interj* (naut.) ¡ forte!
**avatar** [ˌævəˈtɑr] *s* avatar
**avaunt** [əˈvɔnt] o [əˈvɑnt] *interj* (archaic) ¡ fuera!, ¡ largo de aquí!
**Ave.** abr. de **Avenue**
**Ave Maria** [ˈɑveməˈriə] o [ˈevɪməˈraɪə] *s* avemaría
**avenge** [əˈvɛndʒ] *va* vengar; **to avenge oneself on** vengarse en
**avenger** [əˈvɛndʒər] *s* vengador
**avens** [ˈævɪnz] *s* (bot.) cariofilata, hierba de San Benito
**aventurine** [əˈvɛntʃərɪn] *s* (mineral.) venturina
**avenue** [ˈævɪnju] o [ˈævɪnu] *s* avenida
**aver** [əˈvʌr] (*pret & pp:* **averred;** *ger:* **averring**) *va* afirmar, declarar
**average** [ˈævərɪdʒ] *s* promedio, término medio; (naut.) avería; **on an average** por término medio; *adj* medio, de término medio; mediano, común, ordinario; *va* calcular el término medio de; prorratear; hacer un promedio de; ser de un promedio de, ser por término medio
**averment** [əˈvʌrmənt] *s* afirmación, declaración
**Avernus** [əˈvʌrnəs] *s* (myth.) Averno
**Averroism** [ˌævəˈro·ɪzəm] *s* averroísmo
**Averroist** [ˌævəˈro·ɪst] *s* averroísta
**averse** [əˈvʌrs] *adj* renuente, contrario
**aversion** [əˈvʌrʒən] o [əˈvʌrʃən] *s* desviación; aversión, antipatía; cosa aborrecida
**avert** [əˈvʌrt] *va* apartar, desviar, separar; impedir
**aviary** [ˈevɪˌɛrɪ] *s* (*pl:* **-ies**) avería, pajarera
**aviation** [ˌevɪˈeʃən] *s* aviación; *adj* aviatorio
**aviation medicine** *s* aeromedicina
**aviator** [ˈevɪˌetər] *s* aviador
**aviatrix** [ˌevɪˈetrɪks] *s* aviadora, aviatriz
**aviculture** [ˈevɪˌkʌltʃər] *s* avicultura
**avid** [ˈævɪd] *adj* ávido
**avidity** [əˈvɪdɪtɪ] *s* avidez
**Avignon** [ɑviˈnjõ] *s* Aviñón
**avitaminosis** [eˌvaɪtəmɪˈnosɪs] *s* (path.) avitaminosis
**avocado** [ˌævoˈkɑdo] *s* (*pl:* **-dos**) (bot.) aguacate (*árbol y fruto*)
**avocation** [ˌævəˈkeʃən] *s* diversión, distracción, ocupación accesoria
**avocet** [ˈævosɛt] *s* (orn.) avoceta
**avoid** [əˈvɔɪd] *va* evitar; (law) anular; **to avoid** + *ger* evitar + *inf*
**avoidable** [əˈvɔɪdəbəl] *adj* evitable
**avoidance** [əˈvɔɪdəns] *s* evitación; (law) anulación
**avoirdupois** [ˌævərdəˈpɔɪz] o [ˈævərdəˌpɔɪz] *s* sistema de pesos británico y estadounidense; (coll.) peso, gordura
**avoirdupois weight** *s* peso avoirdupois (*cuya unidad es la libra de dieciséis onzas, que equivale a 453,50 gramos*)
**avoset** [ˈævosɛt] *s* var. de **avocet**
**avouch** [əˈvaʊtʃ] *va* afirmar; garantizar; reconocer
**avow** [əˈvaʊ] *va* admitir, confesar
**avowal** [əˈvaʊəl] *s* admisión, confesión
**avowedly** [əˈvaʊɪdlɪ] *adv* concedidamente
**avulsion** [əˈvʌlʃən] *s* (law) avulsión
**avuncular** [əˈvʌŋkjələr] *adj* avuncular
**await** [əˈwet] *va* aguardar, esperar
**awake** [əˈwek] *adj* despierto; (*pret & pp:* **awoke** o **awaked**) *va & vn* despertar
**awaken** [əˈwekən] *va & vn* despertar
**awakening** [əˈwekənɪŋ] *adj* despertador; *s* despertamiento

**award** [əˈwɔrd] *s* concesión; recompensa, premio; condecoración; adjudicación; *va* conceder; adjudicar
**aware** [əˈwɛr] *adj* enterado; **to become aware of** enterarse de, ponerse al corriente de, darse cuenta de
**awareness** [əˈwɛrnɪs] *s* conocimiento, conciencia
**awash** [əˈwɑʃ] o [əˈwɔʃ] *adv* a flor de agua
**away** [əˈwe] *adj* ausente; distante; *adv* lejos; a lo lejos; alejándose; con ahinco; sin cesar; (sport) en campo ajeno; **to do away with** deshacerse de; matar; **to get away** escapar; **to go away** irse; **to lead away** llevar consigo; **to make away with** robar, hurtar; **to make away with oneself** darse la muerte; **to run away** fugarse; **to send away** enviar; despedir; **to take away** llevarse; quitar; **away from** lejos de; **away with you!** ¡ márchese Vd.!; ¡ lárguese Vd.!
**awe** [ɔ] *s* temor, temor reverencial; *va* infundir temor reverencial a
**aweary** [əˈwɪrɪ] *adj* (poet.) cansado, aburrido
**aweigh** [əˈwe] *adj* (naut.) levado; **with anchor aweigh** con ancla levada, levada el ancla
**awesome** [ˈɔsəm] *adj* imponente, pasmoso
**awestricken** [ˈɔˌstrɪkən] o **awestruck** [ˈɔˌstrʌk] *adj* pasmado, espantado
**awful** [ˈɔfəl] *adj* atroz, horrible, tremendo; impresionante, majestuoso; (coll.) muy malo, muy feo, enorme
**awfully** [ˈɔfəlɪ] *adv* atrozmente, horriblemente; majestuosamente; (coll.) muy, excesivamente
**awhile** [əˈhwaɪl] *adv* un rato, algún tiempo
**awkward** [ˈɔkwərd] *adj* desmañado, torpe, lerdo; embarazoso, delicado
**awkwardness** [ˈɔkwərdnɪs] *s* desmaña, torpeza; embarazo, delicadeza
**awkward squad** *s* (mil.) pelotón de los torpes
**awl** [ɔl] *s* alesna, lezna
**awn** [ɔn] *s* (bot.) arista
**awned** [ɔnd] *adj* (bot.) aristado
**awning** [ˈɔnɪŋ] *s* toldo
**awoke** [əˈwok] *pret & pp de* **awake**
**A.W.O.L.** (mil.) ausente sin licencia
**awry** [əˈraɪ] *adv* de través; equivocadamente, erradamente
**ax** o **axe** [æks] *s* hacha; **to have an ax to grind** tener algún fin interesado, tener ocultas intenciones
**axeman** [ˈæksmən] *s* (*pl:* **-men**) leñador, hachero; (mil.) hachero, gastador
**axhammer** [ˈæksˌhæmər] *s* martillo de dos filos para desbastar piedra
**axial** [ˈæksɪəl] *adj* axil, axial
**axial-flow turbine** [ˈæksɪəlˈflo] *s* turbina axial
**axil** [ˈæksɪl] *s* (bot.) axila
**axile** [ˈæksɪl] o [ˈæksaɪl] *adj* (bot.) axilar
**axilla** [ækˈsɪlə] *s* (*pl:* **-lae** [li]) (anat., bot., & zool.) axila
**axillar** [ˈæksɪlər] *adj* axilar; *s* (ent.) axilar
**axillary** [ˈæksɪˌlɛrɪ] o [ækˈsɪlərɪ] *adj* (anat., bot., & zool.) axilar
**axinite** [ˈæksɪnaɪt] *s* (mineral.) axinita
**axiology** [ˌæksɪˈɑlədʒɪ] *s* axiología
**axiom** [ˈæksɪəm] *s* axioma
**axiomatic** [ˌæksɪəˈmætɪk] *adj* axiomático
**axion** [ˈæksɪɑn] *s* (anat.) axión
**axis** [ˈæksɪs] *s* (*pl:* **axes** [ˈæksiz]) *s* eje; (math.) eje; (anat.) axis; (*cap.*) *s* Eje (*Alemania e Italia*)
**axis cylinder** *s* (anat. & physiol.) cilindroeje
**Axis nations** *spl* naciones del Eje
**axle** [ˈæksəl] *s* eje, árbol
**axletree** [ˈæksəlˌtri] *s* eje, eje de carretón
**axman** [ˈæksmən] *s* (*pl:* **-men**) leñador, hachero; (mil.) hachero, gastador
**axoid** [ˈæksɔɪd] o **axoidean** [ækˈsɔɪdɪən] *adj* (anat.) axoideo
**axolotl** [ˈæksəlɑtəl] *s* (zool.) ajolote
**axon** [ˈæksɑn] *s* (anat.) axón
**axone** [ˈækson] *s* (anat. & physiol.) axón
**axunge** [ˈæksʌndʒ] *s* enjundia
**ay** [aɪ] *adv & s* sí; [e] *adv* siempre; **for ay** por siempre; [e] *interj* ¡ ay!; **ay me!** ¡ ay de mí!
**aye** [aɪ] *adv & s* sí; [e] *adv* siempre; **for aye** por siempre
**aye-aye** [ˈaɪˌaɪ] *s* (zool.) ayeaye
**azalea** [əˈzeljə] *s* (bot.) azalea
**azarole** [ˈæzərol] *s* (bot.) acerolo (*arbusto*); acerola (*fruto*)
**azedarach** [əˈzɛdəræk] *s* (bot.) acederaque
**Azerbaijan** [ˌɑzərbaɪˈdʒɑn] *s* el Azerbeiyán
**azimuth** [ˈæzɪməθ] *s* acimut
**azimuthal** [ˈæzɪˌmʌθəl] *adj* acimutal
**azoic** [əˈzo·ɪk] *adj* (chem. & geol.) azoico
**Azores** [əˈzorz] o [ˈezorz] *spl* Azores
**azote** [ˈæzot] o [əˈzot] *s* (chem.) ázoe
**Aztec** [ˈæztɛk] *adj & s* azteca
**azure** [ˈæʒər] o [ˈeʒər] *adj* azul; *s* azul; (her.) azur, blao
**azurite** [ˈæʒəraɪt] *s* (mineral.) azurita
**azygos** [ˈæzɪgɑs] *s* (anat.) ácigos
**azygous vein** [ˈæzɪgəs] *s* (anat.) vena ácigos
**azymous** [ˈæzɪməs] *adj* ázimo

# B

**B, b** [bi] *s* (*pl:* **B's, b's** [biz]) segunda letra del alfabeto inglés
**b.** abr. de **base, bass, basso, bay, book, born, breadth** y **brother**
**B.** abr. de **bay, Bible, British** y **Brotherhood**
**B.A.** abr. de **Baccalaureus Artium** (Lat.) **Bachelor of Arts**
**baa** [bɑ] *s* be (*balido*); *vn* balar
**babbitt** ['bæbɪt] *s* metal de babbitt; *va* revestir o forrar de metal de babbitt
**Babbitt metal** *s* metal de babbitt
**babbittry** ['bæbɪtrɪ] *s* (U.S.A.) concepto de la moral y las costumbres de la clase media
**babble** ['bæbəl] *s* barboteo; charla, parloteo; murmullo (*de un arroyo*); *va* barbotar; decir indiscretamente; *vn* barbotar; charlar, parlotear; murmurar (*un arroyo*)
**babbler** ['bæblər] *s* charlatán
**babbling** ['bæblɪŋ] *adj* charlatán; murmurante; *s* charlatanería
**Babcock test** ['bæbkɑk] *s* prueba de Babcock
**babe** [beb] *s* nene, rorro; niño (*persona inocente e inexperta*)
**babel** o **Babel** ['bebəl] *s* babel
**babies'-breath** ['bebɪz,brɛθ] *s* (bot.) gipsófila
**babirusa, babiroussa** o **babirussa** [,bæbɪ'rusə] *s* (zool.) babirusa
**baboon** [bæ'bun] *s* (zool.) babuíno, mandril
**baby** ['bebɪ] *s* (*pl:* **-bies**) nene, rorro, criatura, bebé; pequeño (*de un animal*); benjamín (*el menor de una familia o un grupo*); *adj* aniñado, infantil, pequeño; (*pret & pp:* **-bied**) *va* mimar
**baby beef** *s* ternerillo para el matadero
**baby carriage** *s* cochecillo para niños, coche cuna
**baby face** *s* cara aniñada
**baby grand** *s* piano de media cola
**babyhood** ['bebɪhud] *s* infancia
**babyish** ['bebɪɪʃ] *adj* aniñado, infantil
**Babylon** ['bæbɪlən] o ['bæbɪlɑn] *s* Babilonia (*antigua ciudad; cualquier gran ciudad rica y desmoralizada*)
**Babylonia** [,bæbɪ'lonɪə] *s* Babilonia (*antiguo imperio*)
**Babylonian** [,bæbɪ'lonɪən] *adj* babilónico, babilonio; (fig.) babilónico (*fastuoso*); *s* babilonio
**Babylonian willow** *s* (bot.) sauce de Babilonia
**baby sitter** *s* (coll.) niñera por horas
**baby talk** *s* habla aniñada
**baby teeth** *s* dientes de leche
**baccalaureate** [,bækə'lɔrɪɪt] *s* bachillerato; (U.S.A.) sermón que se predica a los graduandos del bachillerato
**baccara** o **baccarat** ['bækərɑ] *s* bacará
**Bacchae** ['bæki] *spl* bacantes
**bacchanal** ['bækənəl] *adj* bacanal; *s* bacanal (*orgía*); **bacchanals** *spl* bacanales
**bacchanalia** [,bækə'nelɪə] *spl* bacanal (*orgía tumultuosa*); (*cap.*) *spl* bacanales
**bacchanalian** [,bækə'nelɪən] *adj* bacanal; *s* borracho, juerguista
**bacchant** ['bækənt] *s* sacerdote o devoto de Baco; juerguista
**bacchante** [bə'kæntɪ] o [bə'kænt] *s* bacante
**Bacchic** ['bækɪk] *adj* báquico; (*l.c.*) *adj* báquico (*borracho, desenfrenado*)
**Bacchus** ['bækəs] *s* (myth.) Baco
**bacciferous** [bæk'sɪfərəs] *adj* (bot.) bacífero
**bachelor** ['bætʃələr] *s* soltero (*hombre no casado*); bachiller (*persona que ha recibido el primer grado académico*); doncel (*joven noble*)
**bachelor-at-arms** ['bætʃələrət'ɑrmz] *s* doncel
**bachelorhood** ['bætʃələr,hud] *s* soltería
**bachelor's-button** ['bætʃələrz'bʌtən] *s* (bot.) azulejo, aciano (*Centaurea cyanus*); (bot.) margarita de los prados (*Bellis perennis*)
**bachelor's degree** *s* bachillerato
**bacillary** ['bæsɪ,lɛrɪ] *adj* bacilar
**bacillus** [bə'sɪləs] *s* (*pl:* **-li** [laɪ]) bacilo
**back** [bæk] *adj* trasero; posterior; pasado; atrasado; del interior; posterior (*diente*); (phonet.) posterior ‖ *adv* atrás, detrás; otra vez; de vuelta; hace, p.ej., **some weeks back** hace algunas semanas; **as far back as** ya en (*cierta época*); **to be back** estar de vuelta; **to come back** volver; **to go back** volver; **to go back and forth** ir y venir; **to go back on** volver sobre (*sus pasos*); (coll.) volver sobre (*p.ej., una decisión*); (coll.) faltar a (*p.ej., una promesa*); (coll.) abandonar, traicionar; **to go back to** remontarse a; **to send back** mandar para atrás, hacer volver (*a una persona*); devolver (*una cosa*); **back and forth** de una parte a otra; **back in** allá por (*cierta época*); **back of** detrás de; apoyando ‖ *s* espalda, dorso; respaldo, espaldar (*de una silla*); reverso (*de una moneda*); lomo (*de un animal, un libro o un cuchillo*); dorso (*de la mano; de un grabado, un programa, etc.*); fondo (*p.ej., de una sala*); final (*del libro*), p.ej., **you will find the passage in the back of the book** Vd. hallará el pasaje al final o hacia el final del libro; (football) defensa, zaguero; **behind one's back** a espaldas de uno; **on one's back** postrado, en cama; a cuestas; **to break the back of** deslomar, derrengar; **to get one's back up** enojarle a uno; enojarse; **to turn one's back on** volver las espaldas a; **with one's back to the wall** entre la espada y la pared; **back to back** espalda con espalda, dándose las espaldas ‖ *va* mover hacia atrás; dar marcha atrás a; respaldar (*apoyar, defender*); (naut.) engalgar (*una áncora*); (print.) retirar; **to back up** mover hacia atrás; respaldar (*apoyar, defender*); **to back water** (naut. & fig.) ciar ‖ *vn* moverse hacia atrás; dar marcha atrás; **to back and fill** zigzaguear; seguir mudando de opinión; **to back down** u **out** volverse atrás; (fig.) volverse atrás, ceder, echarse atrás
**backache** ['bæk,ek] *s* dolor de espalda
**backbite** ['bæk,baɪt] (*pret:* **-bit;** *pp:* **-bit** o **-bitten**) *va* cortar un traje a, calumniar solapadamente; *vn* murmurar (*en perjuicio de un ausente*)
**backbone** ['bæk,bon] *s* espinazo; nervura (*de un libro*); firmeza, decisión
**backbreaking** ['bæk,brekɪŋ] *adj* deslomador
**back comb** *s* peineta
**back country** *s* afueras del poblado; zona fronteriza
**backcross** ['bæk,krɔs] o ['bæk,krɑs] *s* cruzamiento retrógrado
**backdoor** ['bæk,dor] *adj* secreto, clandestino
**back door** *s* puerta excusada, falsa o trasera
**backdown** ['bæk,daun] *s* (coll.) palinodia
**backdrop** ['bæk,drɑp] *s* telón de foro
**back electromotive force** *s* (elec.) fuerza contraelectromotriz
**backer** ['bækər] *s* sostenedor, defensor; impulsor (*de un proyecto comercial*)
**backfield** ['bæk,fild] *s* (football) terreno detrás de la línea delantera; (football) defensas, zagueros, jugadores detrás de la línea delantera
**backfire** ['bæk,faɪr] *s* (aut.) petardeo; quema que se hace para evitar que se extienda un incendio; *vn* (aut.) petardear; hacer una quema para evitar que se extienda un incendio; (fig.) salir el tiro por la culata
**back formation** *s* (philol.) derivación regresiva; (philol.) derivado regresivo

**backgammon** ['bæk,gæmən] o [,bæk'gæmən] *s* chaquete
**background** ['bæk,graund] *s* fondo, último término; antecedentes, educación; olvido, obscuridad; **in the background** al fondo, en el fondo; en la obscuridad
**background music** *s* música de fondo
**background noise** *s* ruidos de fondo
**backhand** ['bæk,hænd] *s* revés; escritura inclinada a la izquierda; *adj* dado con la mano vuelta; inclinado a la izquierda
**backhanded** ['bæk,hændɪd] *adj* dado con la mano vuelta; inclinado a la izquierda; desmañado; falto de sinceridad
**backhouse** ['bæk,haus] *s* trascuarto; común o retrete (*detrás de la casa*)
**backing** ['bækɪŋ] apoyo, sostén; garantía
**backlash** ['bæk,læʃ] *s* movimiento trepidante de piezas mal articuladas; juego; contragolpe, pérdida de carrera, culateo
**backlining** ['bæk,laɪnɪŋ] *s* (b.b.) forro del lomo del libro
**backlog** ['bæk,lɔg] o ['bæk,lɑg] *s* leño trasero en un hogar; (com.) reserva, reserva de pedidos pendientes
**back number** *s* número atrasado, viejo número (*de un periódico o revista*); (coll.) persona atrasada
**back pay** *s* sueldo retrasado
**back porch** *s* galería
**back pressure** *s* contrapresión
**backsaw** ['bæk,sɔ] *s* sierra de trasdós
**back seat** *s* asiento de atrás; (fig.) puesto secundario; **to take a back seat** (fig.) ceder su puesto, perder influencia
**backset** ['bæk,sɛt] *s* revés, contrariedad; remolino
**backsheesh** o **backshish** ['bækʃiʃ] *s* propina entre los árabes y turcos
**backside** ['bæk,saɪd] *s* espalda; trasero, nalgas
**backslide** ['bæk,slaɪd] (*pret:* **-slid;** *pp:* **-slidden** o **-slid**) *vn* reincidir
**backslider** ['bæk,slaɪdər] *s* reincidente
**backspacer** ['bæk,spesər] *s* tecla de retroceso
**backspin** ['bæk,spɪn] *s* giro hacia atrás (*de una pelota o de una bola de billar*)
**backstage** ['bæk'stedʒ] *adv* (theat.) detrás del telón; (theat.) al o en el camarín de un actor o una actriz
**backstairs** ['bæk,stɛrz] *adj* indirecto, intrigante, secreto
**back stairs** *spl* escalera de servicio, escalera trasera; medios indirectos
**backstay** ['bæk,ste] *s* refuerzo de espaldar; (naut.) brandal, traversa
**backstitch** ['bæk,stɪtʃ] *s* pespunte; *va & vn* pespuntar
**backstop** ['bæk,stɑp] *s* reja o red para detener la pelota; meta, jugador que detiene la pelota
**back street** *s* callejón
**backstroke** ['bæk,strok] *s* arrastre de espalda, brazada que se emplea al nadar de espaldas; revés
**backswept wing** ['bæk,swɛpt] *s* (aer.) ala en flecha
**back swimmer** *s* (ent.) barquillero de los estanques
**back talk** *s* respuesta insolente, mala contestación
**backtrack** ['bæk,træk] *vn* volver pies atrás, retirarse
**backup** ['bæk,ʌp] *s* apoyo, sostén; retroceso, retiro; represa, estancación; acumulación; reserva; (print.) retiración; *adj* de reserva
**back vowel** *s* (phonet.) vocal posterior
**backward** ['bækwərd] *adj* vuelto hacia atrás; atrasado, tardío; tímido, retraído; *adv* atrás; de espaldas; al revés; hacia atrás; cada vez peor; **to go backward** andar de espaldas; ir hacia atrás; **to go backward and forward** ir y venir; **to read backward** leer para atrás
**backward and forward motion** *s* vaivén
**backwardness** ['bækwərdnɪs] *s* atraso, retraso, tardanza; torpeza; timidez
**backwards** ['bækwərdz] *adv* var. de **backward**
**backwash** ['bæk,wɑʃ] o ['bæk,wɔʃ] *s* agua de rechazo; (fig.) contracorriente, consecuencias
**backwater** ['bæk,wɔtər] o ['bæk,wɑtər] *s* remanso, rebalsa; contracorriente, remolino; (fig.) atraso, incultura
**backwoods** ['bæk,wudz] *spl* monte, región apartada de los centros de población
**backwoodsman** ['bæk,wudzmən] *s* (*pl:* **-men**) hombre que habita el monte
**back yard** *s* corral trasero, patio trasero
**bacon** ['bekən] *s* tocino; **to bring home the bacon** (coll.) sacarse el gordo, tener éxito
**Baconian** [be'konɪən] *adj* baconiano; *s* baconista
**Baconian theory** *s* teoría de que la obra dramática de Shakespeare fué escrita por Francisco Bacon
**bacteria** [bæk'tɪrɪə] *pl de* **bacterium**
**bacterial** [bæk'tɪrɪəl] *adj* bacteriano
**bactericidal** [bæk,tɪrɪ'saɪdəl] *adj* bactericida
**bactericide** [bæk'tɪrɪsaɪd] *s* bactericida
**bacteriological** [bæk,tɪrɪə'lɑdʒɪkəl] *adj* bacteriológico
**bacteriologist** [bæk,tɪrɪ'ɑlədʒɪst] *s* bacteriólogo
**bacteriology** [bæk,tɪrɪ'ɑlədʒɪ] *s* bacteriología
**bacteriolysis** [bæk,tɪrɪ'ɑlɪsɪs] *s* bacteriólisis
**bacteriophage** [bæk'tɪrɪəfedʒ] *s* (bact.) bacteriófago
**bacteriostasis** [bæk,tɪrɪə'stesɪs] *s* (bact.) bacteriostasis
**bacteriostatic** [bæk,tɪrɪə'stætɪk] *adj* bacteriostático
**bacterium** [bæk'tɪrɪəm] *s* (*pl:* **-a** [ə]) bacteria
**Bactrian** ['bæktrɪən] *adj & s* bactriano
**Bactrian camel** *s* (zool.) camello bactriano
**bad** [bæd] *adj* (*comp:* **worse;** *super:* **worst**) malo; incobrable (*deuda*); falso (*aplícase a la moneda*); **a bad one** un mal sujeto; **from bad to worse** de mal en peor; **not bad, not half bad** o **not so bad** bastante bueno; **to be too bad** ser lástima; **to go to the bad** caer en el mal, arruinarse; **to look bad** tener mala cara; **to the bad** en el debe (*de uno*)
**bad blood** *s* mala sangre, mala voluntad
**bad breath** *s* mal aliento
**bade** [bæd] *pret de* **bid**
**bad egg** *s* (slang) mal sujeto, calavera, buena alhaja
**bad form** *s* conducta reprobable (*por propasarse de lo que admite la buena sociedad*)
**badge** [bædʒ] *s* divisa, insignia; placa (*de metal*); (fig.) señal, símbolo
**badger** ['bædʒər] (zool.) tejón; *va* molestar, atormentar
**badinage** [,bædɪ'nɑʒ] o ['bædɪnɪdʒ] *s* broma, chanza
**Bad Lands** *spl* Tierras malas (*comarcas yermas en los estados de Nebraska y Dakota del Sur, EE.UU.*)
**badly** ['bædlɪ] *adv* mal, malamente; muy, con urgencia; gravemente
**badly off** *adj* malparado, maltrecho; muy enfermo
**badminton** ['bædmɪntən] *s* juego del volante
**badness** ['bædnɪs] *s* maldad; imperfección
**bad order** *s* desarreglo
**bad-tempered** ['bæd'tɛmpərd] *adj* de mal genio
**Baedeker** ['bedəkər] *s* Baedeker (*guía del turismo*)
**baffle** ['bæfəl] *s* (mach.) deflector; (rad.) pantalla acústica; *va* deslumbrar, confundir; *vn* luchar en vano
**bafflement** ['bæfəlmənt] *s* deslumbramiento, confusión
**baffle plate** *s* chicana, placa deflectora
**baffling** ['bæflɪŋ] *adj* deslumbrador, perplejo
**B.Ag.** abr. de **Bachelor of Agriculture**
**bag** [bæg] *s* saco, bolso; saquito de mano; bolsa (*de un vestido o tela*); rodillera (*del pantalón en las rodillas*); caza (*animales después de cazados*); (anat.) bolsita, vejiguilla; (zool.) bolsa (*del marsupial*); (baseball) almohadilla; **to be in the bag** (slang) ser cosa segura; **to be left holding the bag** (coll.) quedarse con la carga en las costillas; (*pret & pp:* **bagged;** *ger:* **bagging**) *va* ensacar; coger, cazar; (slang) robar; *vn* hacer bolsa o pliegue (*un vestido o tela*)
**bag and baggage** *adv* con todas sus pertenencias, enteramente
**bagasse** [bə'gæs] *s* bagazo
**bagatelle** [,bægə'tɛl] *s* bagatela

**baggage** ['bægɪdʒ] *s* equipaje; (mil.) bagaje
**baggage car** *s* (rail.) coche de equipajes, furgón
**baggage check** *s* talón, contraseña de equipajes
**baggage master** *s* jefe de equipajes
**baggage rack** *s* red de equipaje
**baggage room** *s* sala de equipajes
**bagging** ['bægɪŋ] *s* harpillera
**baggy** ['bægɪ] *adj* (*comp:* **-gier;** *super:* **-giest**) flojo, holgado, que hace bolsa
**bagman** ['bægmən] *s* (*pl:* **-men**) (Brit.) agente viajero
**bagnio** ['bænjo] o ['bɑnjo] *s* (*pl:* **bagnios**) baño (*cárcel mora o turca*); mancebía, casa de prostitutas
**bagpipe** ['bæg,paɪp] *s* gaita, cornamusa
**bagpiper** ['bæg,paɪpər] *s* gaitero
**B.Agr.** abr. de **Bachelor of Agriculture**
**baguet** o **baguette** [bæ'gɛt] *s* joya rectangular; (arch.) astrágalo pequeño
**bah** [bɑ] *interj* ¡bah!
**Bahama Islands** [bə'hemə] o [bə'hɑmə] *spl* islas Bahamas, islas Lucayas
**Bahamas** *spl* Bahama, archipiélago de Bahama
**bail** [bel] *s* fianza, caución; achicador; aro, zuncho; **to go bail for** salir fiador por; **to jump bail** (slang) fugarse estando bajo fianza; *va* afianzar; achicar (*la embarcación; el agua de la embarcación*); zunchar (*fijar con un zuncho*); **to bail out** salir fiador por; achicar; *vn* achicar; **to bail out** (aer.) lanzarse en paracaídas
**bailable** ['beləbəl] *adj* afianzable
**bail bond** *s* escritura de fianza
**bailiff** ['belɪf] *s* alguacil, corchete
**bailiwick** ['belɪwɪk] *s* alguacilazgo; bailía; competencia, pertenencia; **to be in the bailiwick of** ser de la pertenencia de
**bailment** ['belmənt] *s* afianzamiento; depósito
**bailsman** ['belzmən] *s* (*pl:* **-men**) fianza, fiador
**bain-marie** [,bæ̃,mɑ'ri] *s* (*pl:* **bains-marie**) baño maría
**Baird's sandpiper** [bɛrdz] *s* (orn.) chorlito unicolor, pollito de mar
**bairn** [bɛrn] *s* (Scottish) niño
**bait** [bet] *s* carnada, cebo; añagaza, señuelo; **to swallow the bait** (fig.) tragar el anzuelo; *va* cebar; azuzar, hostigar
**baize** [bez] *s* bayeta
**bake** [bek] *s* cocción al horno; cosa cocida al horno; *va* cocer al horno; **to bake on** aplicar en caliente; *vn* hornear
**baked meat** *s* carne asada al horno
**bakelite** ['bekəlaɪt] *s* (trademark) baquelita
**baker** ['bekər] *s* panadero; (orn.) hornero
**baker's dozen** *s* docena del fraile (*trece*)
**bakery** ['bekərɪ] *s* (*pl:* **-ies**) panadería
**baking** ['bekɪŋ] *s* cochura, hornada
**baking powder** *s* polvo para hornear, levadura química
**baking soda** *s* bicarbonato de sosa
**baksheesh** o **bakshish** ['bækʃiʃ] *s* propina entre los árabes y turcos
**Baku** [bɑ'ku] *s* Bakú
**bal.** abr. de **balance**
**Balaam** ['beləm] *s* (Bib.) Balaán
**balaclava helmet** [,bælə'klɑvə] *s* pasamontaña
**balalaika** [,bælə'laɪkə] *s* (mus.) balalaika
**balance** ['bæləns] *s* balanza (*instrumento para pesar*); (com.) balance; equilibrio; resto (*lo que queda*); (com.) saldo (*a favor o en contra de uno*); volante de reloj; **in the balance** en balanza; **to lose one's balance** perder el equilibrio; **to strike a balance** hacer o pasar balance; *va* balancear (*en la balanza*); equilibrar; equilibrar, nivelar (*el presupuesto*); *vn* equilibrarse; balancear (*vacilar*)
**balance beam** *s* balancín
**balanced diet** *s* régimen alimenticio bien equilibrado
**balance of payments** *s* balanza de pagos
**balance of power** *s* (dipl.) equilibrio político, equilibrio europeo
**balance of trade** *s* balanza de comercio
**balancer** ['bælənsər] *s* balanceador; balancín (*de insecto*)
**balance sheet** *s* (com.) balance, avanzo
**balance wheel** *s* volante de reloj

**balas** ['bæləs] *s* balaje (*rubí espinela*)
**balbriggan** [bæl'brɪgən] *s* tejido de algodón o de lana para medias y ropa interior
**balcony** ['bælkənɪ] *s* (*pl:* **-nies**) balcón; (theat.) galería, paraíso
**bald** [bɔld] *adj* calvo; franco, directo, sencillo, sin adornos
**baldachin** ['bældəkɪn] o ['bɔldəkɪn] *s* baldaquín, palio; (arch.) baldaquín
**bald eagle** *s* (orn.) águila de cabeza blanca
**balderdash** ['bɔldərdæʃ] *s* disparate, música celestial
**baldheaded** ['bɔld'hɛdɪd] *adj* calvo
**baldness** ['bɔldnɪs] *s* calvicie
**baldpate** ['bɔld,pet] *s* persona calva; (orn.) lavanco, mareca
**baldric** ['bɔldrɪk] *s* tahalí
**bald spot** *s* calva
**Baldwin** ['bɔldwɪn] *s* Balduíno
**baldy** ['bɔldɪ] *adj* (coll.) calvito; *s* (*pl:* **-ies**) (coll.) calvito
**bale** [bel] *s* bala (*de papel, algodón, etc.*); *va* embalar
**Balearic** [,bælɪ'ærɪk] *adj* balear
**Balearic Islands** *spl* islas Baleares
**baleen** [bə'lin] *s* ballena (*lámina córnea en la mandíbula superior de la ballena*)
**balefire** ['bel,faɪr] *s* hoguera; señal luminosa; pira funeraria
**baleful** ['belfəl] *adj* funesto, nocivo
**Balinese** [,bɑlɪ'niz] *adj* baliaga, balinés; *s* (*pl:* **-nese**) baliaga, balinés
**balk** [bɔk] *s* lomo entre surcos; viga; contratiempo, obstáculo; desliz, descuido; (billiards) cabaña; (billiards) cuadro; *va* evitar; burlar, frustrar; malograr, perder; *vn* detenerse bruscamente; emperrarse, resistirse; repropiarse (*un caballo*)
**Balkan** ['bɔlkən] *adj* balcánico; **the Balkans** los Balcanes
**Balkanize** ['bɔlkənaɪz] *va* balcanizar
**Balkan Mountains** *spl* montes Balcanes
**Balkan Peninsula** *s* Península Balcánica, Península de los Balcanes
**Balkan States** *spl* estados de los Balcanes
**balk line** *s* (sport) línea de salida; (billiards) línea o raya a la cabecera de la mesa; (billiards) línea paralela a la banda
**balky** ['bɔkɪ] *adj* (*comp:* **-ier;** *super:* **-iest**) rebelón, repropio
**ball** [bɔl] *s* bola, pelota; balón (*pelota grande*); globo, esfera; ovillo (*de hilo, lana, etc.*); yema (*del dedo*); (hort.) cepellón (*tierra pegada a las raíces*); bala (*proyectil*); baile (*festejo en que se baila*); **to carry the ball** (coll.) tener toda la responsabilidad; **to have something on the ball** (slang) tener gran capacidad o talento; **to play ball** emprender la jugada; (coll.) seguir la corriente, obrar en armonía; *va* convertir en bola; **to ball up** (slang) enredar, confundir; *vn* convertirse en bola
**ballad** ['bæləd] *s* balada; romance
**ballade** [bə'lɑd] *s* (mus.) balada
**ball and chain** *s* bola de hierro atada con una cadena; (fig.) restricción, freno
**ball-and-socket joint** ['bɔlənd'sɑkɪt] *s* (mach.) articulación esférica
**ballast** ['bæləst] *s* (naut. & aer.) lastre; (rail.) balasto; (fig.) lastre (*juicio*); *va* (naut. & aer.) lastrar; (rail.) balastar
**ball bearing** *s* juego de bolas, cojinete de bolas
**ball cock** *s* (mach.) llave de bola o flotador
**ballerina** [,bælə'rinə] *s* bailarina
**ballet** ['bæle] o [bæ'le] *s* ballet, baile
**ball float** *s* flotador esférico
**ball governor** *s* (mach.) regulador de bolas, regulador de fuerza centrífuga
**ballista** [bə'lɪstə] *s* (*pl:* **-tae** [ti]) balista
**ballistic** [bə'lɪstɪk] *adj* balístico; **ballistics** *ssg* balística
**ballistocardiogram** [bə,lɪsto'kɑrdɪo,græm] *s* balistocardiograma
**ballistocardiograph** [bə,lɪsto'kɑrdɪo,græf] o [bə,lɪsto'kɑrdɪo,grɑf] *s* balistocardiógrafo
**ballistocardiography** [bə,lɪsto,kɑrdɪ'ɑgrəfɪ] *s* balistocardiografía
**ball of fire** *s* (slang) pólvora (*persona viva, pronta y eficaz*)
**ballonet** [,bælə'nɛt] *s* globo interior (*de un dirigible*)

**balloon** [bə'lun] *s* globo; *vn* subir o viajar en un globo; hincharse como un globo
**balloon barrage** *s* barrera de globos
**balloonist** [bə'lunɪst] *s* ascensionista
**balloon tire** *s* (aut.) llanta balón
**balloon vine** *s* (bot.) farolillo
**ballot** ['bælət] *s* papeleta, balota, cédula para votar; sufragio; *vn* balotar, votar
**ballot box** *s* urna electoral; **to stuff the ballot box** echar votos fraudulentos en la urna electoral
**ball park** *s* estadio de béisbol
**ballplayer** ['bɔl,pleər] *s* pelotero, jugador de pelota; beisbolero
**ball point pen** *s* bolígrafo o polígrafo, pluma esferográfica
**ballroom** ['bɔl,rum] o ['bɔl,rʊm] *s* salón de baile, sala de fiestas
**ball valve** *s* (mach.) válvula de bola
**ballyhoo** ['bælɪhu] *s* alharaca, bombo, propaganda sensacional; ['bælihu] o [,bælɪ'hu] *va* dar teatro a, dar bombo a; *vn* hacer propaganda sensacional
**balm** [bɑm] *s* bálsamo; (bot.) toronjil; (fig.) bálsamo (*consuelo, alivio*)
**balm of Gilead** *s* (bot.) balsamea; bálsamo de Judea o de la Meca (*resina y ungüento*)
**balmy** ['bɑmɪ] *adj* (*comp:* **-ier;** *super:* **-iest**) balsámico; bonancible, suave (*tiempo*); (slang) loco
**baloney** [bə'lonɪ] *s* (slang) tonterías, música celestial
**balsa** ['bɔlsə] o ['bælsə] *s* balsa; (bot.) balsa
**balsam** ['bɔlsəm] *s* bálsamo; (fig.) bálsamo (*consuelo, alivio*); (bot.) balsamina; (bot.) abeto de la parte oriental de Norteamérica (*Abies balsamea*); (bot.) madama (*Impatiens balsamina*)
**balsam apple** *s* (bot.) balsamina
**balsam fir** *s* (bot.) abeto de la parte oriental de Norteamérica (*Abies balsamea*)
**Balt** [bɔlt] *s* balto
**Balthasar** [bæl'θezər] *s* Baltasar
**Baltic** ['bɔltɪk] *adj* báltico; *s* Báltico
**Baltic Provinces** *spl* provincias bálticas
**Baltic Sea** *s* mar Báltico
**Baltic States** *spl* países bálticos, estados bálticos
**Baltimore oriole** ['bɔltɪmor] *s* (orn.) cacique veranero
**Baluchistan** [bə,lutʃɪ'stæn] *s* el Beluchistán
**baluster** ['bæləstər] *s* balaustre
**balustrade** [,bæləs'tred] *s* balaustrada
**bambino** [bæm'bino] *s* (*pl:* **-ni** [ni]) niño pequeño; niño Jesús (*imagen*)
**bamboo** [bæm'bu] *s* (bot.) bambú (*planta y caña*)
**bamboo curtain** *s* (fig.) cortina de bambú
**bamboozle** [bæm'buzəl] *va & vn* (coll.) embaucar, engañar, confundir
**bamboozler** [bæm'buzlər] *s* (coll.) engañabobos, embaucador, engañador
**ban** [bæn] *s* prohibición; maldición; bando de destierro; **bans** *spl* amonestaciones; (*pret & pp:* **banned;** *ger:* **banning**) *va* prohibir; maldecir; excomulgar
**banal** ['benəl], [bə'næl] o ['bænəl] *adj* trivial, trillado
**banality** [bə'nælɪtɪ] *s* (*pl:* **-ties**) trivialidad
**banana** [bə'nænə] *s* (bot.) banano, bananero, plátano (*árbol*); banana, plátano (*fruto*); *adj* bananero, platanero
**banana oil** *s* acetato de amilo, esencia de pera
**Banat, the** [bɑ'nɑt] el Banato
**band** [bænd] *s* banda; cenefa; raya, filete (*línea fina*); cuadrilla (*de personas*); cintillo (*de sombrero*); anillo (*de cigarro*); liga de goma; música, banda; (min.) veta, vena; (rad.) banda; cadena, grillete; correa; *va* orlar; zunchar; rayar; reunir, abanderizar; *vn* reunirse, abanderizarse
**bandage** ['bændɪdʒ] *s* venda; *va* vendar
**bandana** o **bandanna** [bæn'dænə] *s* pañuelo de hierbas
**bandbox** ['bænd,bɑks] *s* sombrerera
**band brake** *s* freno de cinta
**bandeau** [bæn'do] o ['bændo] *s* (*pl:* **-deaux** [doz]) prendedero
**banderole** o **banderol** ['bændərol] *s* banderola, banderita
**band filter** *s* (elec.) filtro de bandas
**bandicoot** ['bændɪkut] *s* (zool.) bandicut
**bandit** ['bændɪt] *s* (*pl:* **-dits** o **-ditti** ['dɪtɪ]) bandido
**banditry** ['bændɪtrɪ] *s* banditismo, bandidaje
**bandmaster** ['bænd,mæstər] o ['bænd,mɑstər] *s* director de banda, músico mayor
**bandog** ['bæn,dɔg] o ['bæn,dɑg] *s* mastín, sabueso; perro de guarda atado
**bandoleer** o **bandolier** [,bændə'lɪr] *s* bandolera; cartuchera colgada de una bandolera
**band-pass filter** ['bænd,pæs] o ['bænd,pɑs] *s* (elec.) filtro de bandas
**band saw** *s* sierra continua, sierra de cinta, sierra sin fin
**band shell** *s* quiosco de música con cubierta en forma de concha
**bandsman** ['bændzmən] *s* (*pl:* **-men**) músico de banda
**band spread** *s* (rad.) esparcimiento de banda, ensanche de banda
**bandstand** ['bænd,stænd] *s* plataforma de banda, templete, quiosco
**bandwagon** ['bænd,wægən] *s* carro de banda de música; (coll.) partido que gana; **to climb aboard the bandwagon** (coll.) adherirse al partido que gana
**bandy** ['bændɪ] *adj* arqueado, estevado; (*pret & pp.* **-died**) *va* tirar de una parte a otra; trocar (*palabras*); *vn* contender
**bandy-legged** ['bændɪ,lɛgɪd] o ['bændɪ,lɛgd] *adj* patiestevado
**bane** [ben] *s* azote; calamidad, ruina, muerte
**baneberry** ['ben,bɛrɪ] *s* (*pl:* **-ries**) (bot.) hierba de San Cristóbal
**baneful** ['benfəl] *adj* nocivo, venenoso; funesto, mortal
**banewort** ['ben,wʌrt] *s* (bot.) belladona; (bot.) flámula
**bang** [bæŋ] *s* golpazo, ruido de un golpe; portazo; **bangs** *spl* flequillo; *adv* de repente, de golpe; con estrépito; *interj* ¡ pum!; *va* golpear con ruido, golpear con violencia; cortar (*el cabello*) en flequillo; *vn* hacer estrépito; **to bang against** dar con ruido contra
**bangle** ['bæŋgəl] *s* ajorca
**bang-up** ['bæŋ,ʌp] *adj* (slang) excelente, de primera clase
**banian** ['bænjən] *s* baniano; (bot.) baniano
**banish** ['bænɪʃ] *va* desterrar; despedir; (fig.) despedir (*p.ej., sospechas*)
**banishment** ['bænɪʃmənt] *s* destierro; despedida
**banister** ['bænɪstər] *s* balaustre; **banisters** *spl* balaustrada
**banjo** ['bændʒo] *s* (*pl:* **-jos** o **-joes**) banjo
**banjoist** ['bændʒo·ɪst] *s* banjoísta
**banjo signal** *s* (rail.) señal de guitarra, señal de disco
**bank** [bæŋk] *s* banco; banca (*en ciertos juegos*); alcancía (*vasija con una hendidura estrecha, donde se echan monedas*); ribera, margen, orilla (*de un río*); montón (*de tierra, nieve, nubes, etc.*); banda (*de la mesa de billar*); hilera; hilera de remos; teclado; (elec.) batería (*de lámparas*); (elec.) fila (*de transformadores*); (aer.) inclinación lateral (*en un viraje*); **to break the bank** hacer saltar la banca (*en el juego*); *va* amontonar; represar; cubrir (*un fuego*) con cenizas o con carbón; depositar (*dinero*); guardar (*dinero*) en un banco; poner en filas; (aer.) ladear; *vn* depositar dinero; ser banquero; (aer.) ladearse; **to bank on** (coll.) contar con
**bank acceptance** *s* giro contra un banco aceptado por éste
**bank account** *s* cuenta de banco, cuenta corriente
**bank bill** *s* cédula de banco; billete de banco
**bankbook** ['bæŋk,bʊk] *s* libreta de banco
**bank discount** *s* descuento corriente
**banker** ['bæŋkər] *s* banquero
**bank holiday** *s* día feriado para los bancos
**banking** ['bæŋkɪŋ] *adj* bancario; *s* banca
**banking house** *s* casa de banca
**banking indicator** *s* (aer.) inclinómetro
**bank note** *s* billete de banco
**bank of issue** *s* banco de emisión
**bank roll** *s* lío de papel moneda
**bankrupt** ['bæŋkrʌpt] *adj & s* bancarrotero; **to**

**go bankrupt** hacer bancarrota; *va* hacer quebrar; arruinar
**bankruptcy** ['bæŋkrʌptsɪ] o ['bæŋkrəpsɪ] *s* bancarrota, quiebra; (fig.) bancarrota (*fracaso*)
**bank vault** *s* caja fuerte
**banner** ['bænər] *s* bandera, estandarte; encabezamiento; *adj* primero, dominante
**banner cry** *s* grito de combate
**banneret** o **bannerette** [,bænə'rɛt] *s* bandereta, banderín
**banns** [bænz] *spl* amonestaciones; banas (Am.)
**banquet** ['bæŋkwɪt] *s* banquete; *va & vn* banquetear
**banquette** [bæŋ'kɛt] *s* (eng. & fort.) banqueta; acera, banqueta
**banshee** o **banshie** ['bænʃi] o [bæn'ʃi] *s* (Irish & Scottish) hada o genio cuyos lamentos bajo la ventana anuncian una muerte en la familia
**bantam** ['bæntəm] *adj* pequeño, ligero; *s* persona de pequeña talla y amiga de pelear; gallo Bantam
**bantamweight** ['bæntəm,wet] *s* (box.) peso gallo
**banter** ['bæntər] *s* burla, chanza; *va* burlarse de, chancearse con; *vn* burlar, chancear
**banteringly** ['bæntərɪŋlɪ] *adv* chanceando
**bantling** ['bæntlɪŋ] *s* chicuelo
**Bantu** ['bæntu] *adj* bantu o bantú; *s* (*pl:* **-tu** o **-tus**) bantu o bantú
**banyan** ['bænjən] *s* (bot.) baniano
**baobab** ['beobæb] *s* (bot.) baobab
**Bap.** o **Bapt.** abr. de **Baptist**
**baptism** ['bæptɪzəm] *s* bautizo o bautismo; (eccl.) bautismo
**baptismal** [bæp'tɪzməl] *adj* bautismal
**baptismal name** *s* nombre de pila
**baptism of fire** *s* bautismo de fuego
**Baptist** ['bæptɪst] *adj & s* bautista, baptista
**baptistery** ['bæptɪstərɪ] *s* (*pl:* **-ies**) baptisterio o bautisterio
**baptistry** ['bæptɪstrɪ] *s* (*pl:* **-tries**) var. de **baptistery**
**baptize** [bæp'taɪz] o ['bæptaɪz] *va* bautizar; limpiar, purificar
**baptizer** [bæp'taɪzər] *s* bautista
**bar.** abr. de **barometer, barometric, barrel** y **barrister**
**Bar.** abr. de **Baruch**
**B.Ar.** abr. de **Bachelor of Architecture**
**bar** [bɑr] *s* barra (*de metal, etc.; banco de arena; insignia militar; mostrador en un bar*); tranca (*detrás de una puerta o ventana*); reja (*de una ventana, especialmente de una cárcel*); bar (*establecimiento donde se venden licores alcohólicos para beber en el mostrador*); barrera, impedimento; raya, lista; (her.) barra; (mus.) compás; (mus.) barra, divisoria; abogacía; curia (*conjunto de abogados*); tribunal; **behind bars** entre rejas; **to be admitted to the bar** recibirse de abogado; **to tend bar** ser barman, despachar bebidas en la barra de un bar; *prep* excepto; **bar none** sin excepción; (*pret & pp:* **barred;** *ger:* **barring**) *va* barrar, barretear, atrancar; impedir, estorbar; prohibir; excluir
**Barabbas** [bə'ræbəs] *s* (Bib.) Barrabás
**barb** [bɑrb] *s* púa; lengüeta (*de un anzuelo o dardo*); barbilla (*de una pluma*); caballo de Berbería; *va* armar con púas; armar con lengüetas
**Barbados** [bɑr'bedoz] *s* la Barbada
**barbarian** [bɑr'bɛrɪən] *adj & s* bárbaro
**barbaric** [bɑr'bærɪk] *adj* bárbaro, barbárico
**barbarism** ['bɑrbərɪzəm] *s* barbaridad; (gram.) barbarismo
**barbarity** [bɑr'bærɪtɪ] *s* (*pl:* **-ties**) barbarie
**barbarous** ['bɑrbərəs] *adj* bárbaro
**Barbary** ['bɑrbərɪ] *s* Berbería
**Barbary ape** *s* (zool.) mono de Gibraltar, mona
**Barbary States** *spl* Estados Berberiscos
**barbecue** ['bɑrbəkju] *s* barbacoa, churrasco; *va* churrasquear
**barbed** [bɑrbd] *adj* armado de púas; mordaz, punzante
**barbed wire** *s* alambre de púas, espino artificial; (mil.) alambrada
**barbel** ['bɑrbəl] *s* barbilla (*alrededor de la boca de algunos peces*); (ichth.) barbo
**bar bell** *s* barra de balas
**barber** ['bɑrbər] *s* barbero, peluquero; *adj* barberil; *va* hacer la barba a
**barber pole** *s* percha (*de barbero*)
**barberry** ['bɑr,berɪ] *s* (*pl:* **-ries**) (bot.) bérbero, agracejo (*arbusto*); bérbero, agracejina (*fruto*)
**barbershop** ['bɑrbər,ʃɑp] *s* barbería, peluquería
**barber's itch** *s* sarna de los barberos
**barbette** [bɑr'bɛt] *s* (fort.) barbeta; **in barbette** a barbeta
**barbican** ['bɑrbɪkən] *s* (fort.) barbacana
**barbiturate** [bɑr'bɪtʃəret] o [,bɑrbɪ'tjʊret] *s* (chem.) barbiturato
**barbituric acid** [,bɑrbɪ'tjʊrɪk] o [,bɑrbɪ'tʊrɪk] *s* (chem.) ácido barbitúrico
**barcarole** o **barcarolle** ['bɑrkərol] *s* (mus.) barcarola
**bard** [bɑrd] *s* bardo; barda (*armadura del caballo*)
**Bard of Avon** ['evən] o ['ævən] *s* Cisne del Avon (*Shakespeare*)
**bare** [bɛr] *adj* desnudo; descubierto (*sin sombrero*); raído (*gastado por el uso*); desamueblado; mero, sencillo; sin aislar (*dícese del alambre*); **to lay bare** poner a descubierto; *va* desnudar; descubrir, manifestar
**bareback** ['bɛr,bæk] *adj* montado en pelo; *adv* en pelo, sin silla
**barefaced** ['bɛr,fest] *adj* desembozado; descarado, desvergonzado
**barefoot** ['bɛr,fʊt] *adj* descalzo; *adv* con los pies desnudos
**barefooted** ['bɛr,fʊtɪd] *adj* descalzo
**barège** [,bɑ'rɛʒ] *s* barés
**barehanded** ['bɛr,hændɪd] *adj* con las manos desnudas; desprovisto
**bareheaded** ['bɛr,hɛdɪd] *adj* descubierto; *adv* con la cabeza descubierta
**barelegged** ['bɛr,lɛgɪd] o ['bɛr,lɛgd] *adj* en pernetas
**barely** ['bɛrlɪ] *adv* solamente; apenas
**bareness** ['bɛrnɪs] *s* desnudez
**barfly** ['bɑr,flaɪ] *s* (*pl:* **-flies**) frecuentador habitual de bares o tabernas
**bargain** ['bɑrgɪn] *s* negocio, trato de compra y venta; negocio ventajoso para el comprador; ganga (*cosa comprada barato*); **at a bargain** baratísimo; **into the bargain** de añadidura; **to strike a bargain** cerrar un trato; *va* estipular; **to bargain away** vender regalado; *vn* negociar; (coll.) regatear; **to bargain for** estar dispuesto para, contar con
**bargain counter** *s* baratillo, puesto para la venta de saldos
**bargain sale** *s* venta con rebajas, liquidación
**barge** [bɑrdʒ] *s* barcaza, gabarra; *vn* moverse pesadamente; **to barge in** entrar sin pedir permiso; **to barge in on** entrar a ver sin llamar a la puerta; **to barge into** entremeterse en (*una conversación*); irrumpir en (*un cuarto*)
**bargeboard** ['bɑrdʒ,bord] *s* (arch.) guardamalleta
**bargee** [bɑr'dʒi] *s* var. de **bargeman**
**bargeman** ['bɑrdʒmən] *s* (*pl:* **-men**) gabarrero
**bar hole** *s* (naut.) bocabarra (*del cabrestante*)
**barilla** [bə'rɪlə] *s* (bot. & chem.) barrilla
**bar iron** *s* hierro en barras
**barite** ['bɛraɪt] *s* (mineral.) baritina
**baritone** ['bærɪton] *s* (mus.) barítono
**barium** ['bɛrɪəm] *s* (chem.) bario
**barium enema** *s* (med.) enema opaca, enema de bario
**bark** [bɑrk] *s* corteza (*del árbol*); ladrido (*del perro*); estampido (*del cañón*); tos; (naut.) barca, bricbarca; (poet.) barca; *va* descortezar; cubrir con una capa de corteza; curtir (*las pieles*); pelar, raspar; ladrar (*p.ej., injurias*); *vn* ladrar; (fig.) ladrar
**barkeeper** ['bɑr,kipər] *s* tabernero, cantinero, mozo que despacha bebidas alcohólicas
**barkentine** ['bɑrkəntin] *s* (naut.) barca-goleta
**barker** ['bɑrkər] *s* ladrador; descortezador; vociferador, pregonero
**barley** ['bɑrlɪ] *s* (bot.) cebada
**barleycorn** ['bɑrlɪ,kɔrn] *s* grano de cebada;

**John Barleycorn** personificación humorística de las bebidas alcohólicas
**barley sugar** *s* azúcar cande o candi
**barley water** *s* hordiate
**barm** [bɑrm] *s* jiste
**bar magnet** *s* barra imantada
**barmaid** ['bɑr,med] *s* moza de taberna
**barman** ['bɑrmən] *s* (*pl:* **-men**) (Brit.) tabernero, cantinero, barman
**Barmecide feast** ['bɑrmɪsaɪd] *s* comida fingida, sin manjares; abundancia ilusoria
**barmy** ['bɑrmɪ] *adj* (*comp:* **-ier;** *super:* **-iest**) espumoso, lleno de jiste; (coll.) alocado, cambiadizo
**barn** [bɑrn] *s* granero, pajar, troje; cuadra, establo, caballeriza; cochera
**Barnaby** ['bɑrnəbɪ] *s* Bernabé
**barnacle** ['bɑrnəkəl] *s* (zool.) cirrópodo; (zool.) anatifa (*Lepas*); (zool.) bálano (*Balanus*); (zool.) percebe (*Pollicipes*); (orn.) bernicla, ganso monjita; pegote (*persona que se pega a otra*); **barnacles** *spl* (her. & vet.) acial; (coll.) anteojos
**barnacle goose** *s* (orn.) bernicla, ganso monjita
**Barney** ['bɑrnɪ] *s* Bernardo
**barn owl** *s* (orn.) lechuza, oliva
**barnstorm** ['bɑrn,stɔrm] *vn* (coll.) dar funciones de teatro o pronunciar discursos en las aldeas o en el campo
**barnstormer** ['bɑrn,stɔrmər] *s* (coll.) cómico de la legua
**barn swallow** *s* (orn.) golondrina; (orn.) golondrina cola tijera (*Hirundo erythrogastra*)
**barnyard** ['bɑrn,jɑrd] *s* corral, patio de granja
**barnyard fowl** *spl* aves de corral
**barogram** ['bærəgræm] *s* barograma
**barograph** ['bærəgræf] o ['bærəgrɑf] *s* barógrafo
**barometer** [bə'rɑmɪtər] *s* barómetro; (fig.) barómetro
**barometric** [,bærə'mɛtrɪk] o **barometrical** [,bærə'mɛtrɪkəl] *adj* barométrico
**baron** ['bærən] *s* barón; (coll.) potentado
**baronage** ['bærənɪdʒ] *s* baronía; nobleza; **the baronage** todos los barones
**baroness** ['bærənɪs] *s* baronesa
**baronet** ['bærənɪt] *s* baronet
**baronetage** ['bærənɪtɪdʒ] *s* dignidad de baronet; **the baronetage** todos los baronets
**baronetcy** ['bærənɪtsɪ] *s* (*pl:* **-cies**) dignidad de baronet; documento que confiere la dignidad de baronet
**baronial** [bə'ronɪəl] *adj* baronial
**barony** ['bærənɪ] *s* (*pl:* **-nies**) baronía
**baroque** [bə'rok] o [bə'rɑk] *adj & s* barroco
**baroque pearl** *s* barrueco
**baroscope** ['bærəskop] *s* baroscopio
**barouche** [bə'ruʃ] *s* barrocho
**bar pin** *s* alfiler en forma de barra
**barque** [bɑrk] *s* (poet.) barca; (naut.) barca o corbeta
**barracan** ['bærəkæn] *s* barragán
**barracks** ['bærəks] *spl* barracón; (mil.) cuartel
**barracuda** [,bærə'kudə] *s* (ichth.) barracuda, picuda
**barrage** [bə'rɑʒ] *s* presa; (mil.) barrera
**barrage balloon** *s* globo de barrera
**barratry** ['bærətrɪ] *s* (law) baratería; (naut. law) baratería de capitán o de patrón
**barrel** ['bærəl] *s* barril, tonel; cañón (*de escopeta, pluma, etc.*); tambor de cabrestante; cilindro (*p.ej., del émbolo*); (*pret & pp:* **-reled** o **-relled;** *ger:* **-reling** o **-relling**) *va* embarrilar, entonelar; *vn* (slang) avanzar con gran velocidad
**barrel organ** *s* (mus.) órgano de cilindro; (mus.) órgano de manubrio, organillo
**barrel roll** *s* (aer.) tonel
**barrel vault** *s* (arch.) bóveda en cañón
**barren** ['bærən] *adj* estéril, árido; **barrens** *spl* tierra yerma
**barrenness** ['bærənnɪs] *s* esterilidad, aridez
**barrette** [bə'rɛt] *s* broche para el cabello
**barricade** [,bærɪ'ked] *s* barricada; *va* barrear
**barricado** [,bærɪ'kedo] *s* (*pl:* **-does**) var. de **barricade;** *va* var. de **barricade**
**barrier** ['bærɪər] *s* barrera
**barrier reef** *s* barrera de arrecifes
**barring** ['bɑrɪŋ] *prep* salvo, excepto, sin
**barrister** ['bærɪstər] *s* (Brit.) abogado que tiene el derecho de alegar ante cualquier tribunal; (coll.) abogado
**barroom** ['bɑr,rum] o ['bɑr,rʊm] *s* bar, cantina
**barrow** ['bæro] *s* angarillas; carretón de mano; carretilla; túmulo (*encima de una sepultura antigua*); cerdo castrado
**bar shot** *s* (nav.) palanqueta
**bar solder** *s* soldadura en barras
**barstool** ['bɑr,stul] *s* taburete de la barra de un bar
**Bart.** abr. de **baronet**
**bartender** ['bɑr,tɛndər] *s* tabernero, cantinero, barman
**barter** ['bɑrtər] *s* trueque (*de un objeto por otro*); *va* trocar; **to barter away** trocar en desventajas; vender (*su honor*); *vn* trocar
**Bartholomew** [bɑr'θɑləmju] *s* Bartolomé
**bartizan** ['bɑrtɪzən] o [,bɑrtɪ'zæn] *s* torre albarana (*en una muralla*)
**Baruch** ['bɛrək] *s* (Bib.) Baruc
**barysphere** ['bærɪsfɪr] *s* (geol.) barisfera
**baryta** [bə'raɪtə] *s* (chem.) barita
**barytone** ['bærɪton] *s* var. de **baritone**
**basal** ['besəl] *adj* basal
**basal metabolism** *s* metabolismo basal
**basalt** [bə'sɔlt] o ['bæsɔlt] *s* basalto
**basaltic** [bə'sɔltɪk] *adj* basáltico
**basanite** ['bæzənaɪt] *s* (petrog.) basanita
**bascule** ['bæskjul] *s* juego de contrapesos iguales y contrarios
**bascule bridge** *s* puente basculante
**base** [bes] *s* base; culote (*de proyectil*); (arch.) basa; (elec.) culote (*de válvula de radio o de lámpara eléctrica*); (mus.) bajo; *adj* bajo, humilde; infame, vil; tosco; bajo de ley (*dícese de los metales*); *va* basar
**baseball** ['bes,bɔl] *s* béisbol; pelota de béisbol
**baseboard** ['bes,bord] *s* rodapié
**baseborn** ['bes'bɔrn] *adj* de humilde cuna; bastardo
**baseburner** ['bes'bʌrnər] *s* horno de alimentación automática
**base hit** *s* (baseball) golpe con que el batter gana la primera base
**Basel** ['bɑzəl] *s* Basilea
**baseless** ['beslɪs] *adj* infundado
**base line** *s* línea de base; (tennis) línea de fondo
**basely** ['beslɪ] *adv* bajamente, vilmente
**baseman** ['besmən] *s* (*pl:* **-men**) (baseball) jugador de cuadro
**basement** ['besmənt] *s* sótano
**baseness** ['besnɪs] *s* bajeza, vileza
**base salary** *s* salario base
**bash** [bæʃ] *s* (coll.) golpe que quiebra; *va* (coll.) quebrar a golpes
**bashaw** [bə'ʃɔ] o ['bæʃɔ] *s* bajá; persona de campanillas
**bashful** ['bæʃfəl] *adj* tímido, vergonzoso, encogido
**bashfulness** ['bæʃfəlnɪs] *s* timidez, vergüenza, encogimiento
**basic** ['besɪk] *adj* básico; (chem.) básico
**basically** ['besɪkəlɪ] *adv* fundamentalmente
**Basic English** *s* el inglés básico
**basicity** [be'sɪsɪtɪ] *s* basicidad
**basidiomycete** [bə,sɪdɪomaɪ'sit] *s* (bot.) basidiomiceto
**basidium** [bə'sɪdɪəm] *s* (*pl:* **-a** [ə]) (bot.) basidio
**basil** ['bæzɪl] *s* (bot.) albahaca
**basilar** ['bæsɪlər] *adj* basilar
**Basilian** [bə'sɪlɪən] *adj & s* basilio
**basilica** [bə'sɪlɪkə] *s* basílica
**basilic vein** [bə'sɪlɪk] *s* (anat.) vena basílica
**basilisk** ['bæsɪlɪsk] *s* (zool. & myth.) basilisco
**basin** ['besən] *s* palangana, jofaina; tazón (*de una fuente*); cuenca (*de un río*); dársena
**basinet** ['bæsɪnɛt] *s* bacinete
**basis** ['besɪs] *s* (*pl:* **-ses** [siz]) base; **on the basis of** a base de o en base a
**bask** [bæsk] o [bɑsk] *va* asolear, calentar; *vn* asolearse, calentarse, confortarse al sol o junto al fuego
**basket** ['bæskɪt] o ['bɑskɪt] *s* cesta; cesto (*cesta grande*); canasta (*cesto con dos asas*); excusabaraja (*cesta con tapadera*); (aer.) cesto, barquilla; (sport) cesto, red

**basketball** ['bæskɪt,bɔl] o ['bɑskɪt,bɔl] *s* baloncesto, basquetbol; *adj* baloncestístico
**basketball player** *s* baloncestista
**basket-handle arch** ['bæskɪt,hændəl] o ['bɑskɪt,hændəl] *s* arco carpanel
**basket hilt** *s* cazoleta
**basketry** ['bæskɪtrɪ] o ['bɑskɪtrɪ] *s* cestería
**basket weave** *s* tejido que se parece al de una cesta
**basketwork** ['bæskɪt,wʌrk] o ['bɑskɪt,wʌrk] *s* cestería
**basking shark** *s* (ichth.) cetorrino
**Basle** [bɑl] *s* Basilea
**basque** [bæsk] *s* jubón; (*cap.*) *adj & s* vasco (*de España y Francia*); vascongado (*de España*); vascón (*de la España antigua*); vasco, vascongado, vascuence (*idioma*)
**Basque Country, the** el País Vasco
**Basque Provinces, the** las Provincias Vascongadas o las Vascongadas
**bas-relief** [,bɑrɪ'lif] o [,bæsrɪ'lif] *s* bajo relieve
**bass** [bes] *adj* (mus.) bajo; *s* (mus.) bajo; [bæs] *s* (ichth.) róbalo; (ichth.) perca; (ichth.) pomosio; (bot.) tilo; (bot.) líber
**bass clef** [bes] *s* (mus.) clave de fa
**bass drum** [bes] *s* (mus.) bombo
**basset** ['bæsɪt] *s* perro basset
**bass horn** [bes] *s* (mus.) tuba
**bassinet** [,bæsɪ'nɛt] o ['bæsɪnɛt] *s* cuna o cochecillo en forma de cesto
**basso** ['bæso] o ['bɑso] *adj* (mus.) bajo; *s* (*pl:* **-sos** o **-si** [sɪ]) (mus.) bajo
**bassoon** [bə'sun] *s* (mus.) bajón
**bassoonist** [bə'sunɪst] *s* bajonista
**basso profundo** ['bɑso pro'fʌndo] *s* (mus.) bajo profundo
**bass viol** [bes] *s* (mus.) violón, contrabajo
**basswood** ['bæs,wʊd] *s* (bot.) tilo, tilo americano
**bast** [bæst] *s* (bot.) líber
**bastard** ['bæstərd] *adj & s* bastardo
**bastardly** ['bæstərdlɪ] *adj* bastardo; bastardeado
**bastard title** *s* (print.) anteportada
**bastardy** ['bæstərdɪ] *s* bastardía
**baste** [best] *va* azotar, apalear; (sew.) hilvanar; (cook.) pringar, enlardar
**bastille** o **bastile** [bæs'til] *s* bastida (*máquina militar antigua*); bastilla (*fuerte pequeño*); prisión
**bastinado** [,bæstɪ'nedo] *s* (*pl:* **-does**) bastonada o bastonazo; bastón, porra; *va* bastonear
**bastion** ['bæstʃən] o ['bæstɪən] *s* bastión
**bastioned** ['bæstʃənd] o ['bæstɪənd] *adj* (fort.) bastionado
**bat.** abr. de **battalion** y **battery**
**bat** [bæt] *s* palo; (coll.) golpe; (slang) parranda, borrachera; (zool.) murciélago; **blind as a bat** más ciego que un topo; **right off the bat** (slang) de repente, sin deliberación; **to go on a bat** (slang) andar de parranda; (*pret & pp:* **batted;** *ger:* **batting**) *va* golpear; **without batting an eye** sin pestañear, sin inmutarse; *vn* golpear
**Bataan** [bə'tæn] *s* el Bataán
**Batavian** [bə'tevɪən] *adj & s* bátavo
**batch** [bætʃ] *s* cochura, hornada; colección; grupo; lío (*de papeles*); (coll.) soltero
**bate** [bet] *va* disminuir, suspender; **with bated breath** con aliento entrecortado; *vn* disminuirse
**bath** [bæθ] o [bɑθ] *s* baño; **to take a bath** tomar un baño
**bathe** [beð] *va* bañar; *vn* bañarse; **to go bathing** ir a bañarse
**bather** [beðər] *s* bañista
**bathhouse** ['bæθ,haʊs] o ['bɑθ,haʊs] *s* casa de baños; caseta o casilla de baños
**bathing beach** *s* playa de baños
**bathing beauty** *s* sirena de la playa
**bathing cap** *s* gorro de baño
**bathing resort** *s* estación balnearia
**bathing slipper** *s* zapatilla de baño
**bathing soap** *s* jabón de baño
**bathing suit** *s* traje de baño, bañador
**bathing trunks** *spl* taparrabo
**bath mat** *s* alfombra de baño
**batholith** ['bæθəlɪθ] *s* (geol.) batolito
**bathometer** [bə'θɑmɪtər] *s* batómetro
**bathos** ['beθɑs] *s* paso ridículo de lo sublime a lo trivial o vulgar; trivialidad; sensiblería
**bath powder** *s* polvos de baño
**bathrobe** ['bæθ,rob] o ['bɑθ,rob] *s* bata de baño, albornoz; bata, peinador
**bathroom** ['bæθ,rum] o ['bɑθ,rum] *s* baño, cuarto de baño
**bathroom fixtures** *spl* aparatos sanitarios, juego de baño
**bath salts** *spl* sales para el baño
**Bathsheba** [bæθ'ʃibə] o ['bæθʃɪbə] *s* (Bib.) Betsabé
**bath slipper** *s* zapatilla de baño
**bath soap** *s* jabón de baño
**bath sponge** *s* esponja de baño
**bath towel** *s* toalla de baño
**bathtub** ['bæθ,tʌb] o ['bɑθ,tʌb] *s* bañera, bañadera, baño
**bathybius** [bə'θɪbɪəs] *s* (zool.) batibio
**bathyscaphe** ['bæθɪskef] *s* batiscafo
**bathysphere** ['bæθɪsfɪr] *s* batisfera
**batik** [bə'tik] o ['bætɪk] *s* batik
**batiste** [bə'tist] *s* batista de Escocia; cámbric (*tejido elástico de algodón con que se hacen vendas*)
**batman** ['bætmən] *s* (*pl:* **-men**) (Brit.) ordenanza
**baton** [bæ'tɑn] o ['bætən] *s* bastón; (mus.) batuta
**batrachian** [bə'trekɪən] *adj & s* (zool.) batracio
**batsman** ['bætsmən] *s* (*pl:* **-men**) (sport) batter
**batt.** abr. de **battalion** y **battery**
**batt** [bæt] *s* hoja de algodón; algodón en hojas
**battalion** [bə'tæljən] *s* (mil. & fig.) batallón; **battalions** *spl* (mil.) fuerzas, tropas
**batten** ['bætən] *s* listón; tabla para pisos; *va* engordar; enlistonar; **to batten down the hatches** (naut.) asegurar las escotillas con listones de madera; **to batten up** cerrar con listones; *vn* engordar; medrar
**batter** ['bætər] *s* batido, pasta; talud; (baseball) bateador; *va* golpear; magullar, mellar, estropear; (baseball) batear; ataludar (*dar talud a*)
**battering ram** *s* ariete
**battery** ['bætərɪ] *s* (*pl:* **-ies**) batería; (elec.) pila; (elec.) acumulador; (elec.) batería (*dos o más pilas o acumuladores unidos entre sí*); (baseball) batería; (law) violencia
**battery charger** *s* (elec.) cargador de acumulador
**battery eliminator** *s* (rad.) eliminador de baterías
**battery tester** *s* (elec.) probador de acumuladores
**batting** ['bætɪŋ] *s* algodón en hojas; (baseball) bateo
**battle** ['bætəl] *s* batalla; **to do battle** librar batalla; *va* batallar con; *vn* batallar
**battle array** *s* orden de batalla; **in battle array** en batalla
**battleax** o **battleaxe** ['bætəl,æks] *s* hacha de armas, hacha de combate
**battle cruiser** *s* (nav.) crucero de combate
**battle cry** *s* grito de batalla, grito de combate
**battledore** ['bætəldor] *s* raqueta; **battledore and shuttlecock** volante, raqueta y volante
**battlefield** ['bætəl,fild] *s* campo de batalla
**battle front** *s* frente de combate
**battleground** ['bætəl,graʊnd] *s* campo de batalla
**battlement** ['bætəlmənt] *s* almenaje, crestería
**battle piece** *s* (paint.) batalla
**battleplane** ['bætəl,plen] *s* avión de combate
**battle royal** *s* riña promiscua; lucha hasta el último trance
**battle-scarred** ['bætəl,skɑrd] *adj* lisiado en batalla
**battleship** ['bætəl,ʃɪp] *s* acorazado
**battle stations** *spl* puestos de combate
**battology** [bə'tɑlədʒɪ] *s* batología
**battue** [bæ'tu] o [bæ'tju] *s* batida; matanza general
**batty** ['bætɪ] *adj* (*comp:* **-tier;** *super:* **-tiest**) (slang) extravagante, necio, loco
**bauble** ['bɔbəl] *s* chuchería; cetro de bufón
**Baucis** ['bɔsɪs] *s* (myth.) Baucis

**baulk** [bɔk] *s, va & vn* var. de **balk**
**bauxite** ['bɔksaɪt] o ['bozaɪt] *s* (mineral.) bauxita
**Bavaria** [bə'vɛrɪə] *s* Baviera
**Bavarian** [bə'vɛrɪən] *adj & s* bávaro
**bawd** [bɔd] *s* alcahuete o alcahueta, tercero o tercera
**bawdry** ['bɔdrɪ] *s* indecencia, obscenidad
**bawdy** ['bɔdɪ] *adj (comp:* **-ier;** *super:* **-iest)** indecente, obsceno
**bawdyhouse** ['bɔdɪ,haus] *s* mancebía, lupanar
**bawl** [bɔl] *s* voces, gritos; *va* vocear; **to bawl out** (slang) dar una calada a; *vn* vocear, gritar, chillar
**bay** [be] *s* bahía; (arch.) ventana salediza; (arch.) intercolumnio; ladrido, aullido; granero, pajar; apuro, trance; bayo; caballo bayo; (bot.) laurel; **bays** *spl* corona de laurel; lauro, fama; **at bay** acosado, acorralado, a raya; *adj* bayo; *vn* ladrar, aullar; **to bay at the moon** ladrar a la luna
**bayadere** [,bajə'dɪr] *s* bayadera (*bailarina y cantadora india*)
**Bayard, Seigneur de** ['beərd] señor de Bayardo
**bayberry** ['be,bɛrɪ] *s* (*pl:* **-ries**) (bot.) arrayán brabántico; baya del arrayán brabántico; (bot.) malagueta (*Pimenta acris*)
**Bay of Bengal** *s* golfo de Bengala
**Bay of Biscay** *s* mar Cantábrico, golfo de Vizcaya, golfo de Gascuña
**bayonet** ['beənɪt] *s* bayoneta; *va* herir con bayoneta; forzar a la bayoneta; bayonetear (Am.)
**bayonet socket** *s* (elec.) portalámparas de bayoneta
**Bayonne** [,bæ'jɔn] *s* Bayona
**bay rum** *s* ron de laurel, ron de malagueta
**bay tree** *s* (bot.) laurel
**bay window** *s* galería, mirador, ventana salediza; (slang) barriga, panza
**baywood** ['be,wud] *s* (bot.) caoba del golfo de Campeche (*Swietenia macrophylla*)
**bazaar** o **bazar** [bə'zɑr] *s* bazar; quermese, venta para reunir fondos para obras caritativas
**bazooka** [bə'zukə) *s* (mil.) bazuca (*cañón cohete portátil*)
**B.B.A.** abr. de **Bachelor of Business Administration**
**B battery** *s* (rad.) batería del circuito de la placa
**bbl.** abr. de **barrel** o **barrels**
**bbls.** abr. de **barrels**
**B.C.** abr. de **before Christ** y **British Columbia**
**B.C.E.** abr. de **Bachelor of Chemical Engineering** y **Bachelor of Civil Engineering**
**B complex** *s* (biochem.) complejo B
**bd.** abr. de **board**
**B.D.** abr. de **Bachelor of Divinity**
**bdellium** ['dɛlɪəm] *s* bedelio
**bdl.** abr. de **bundle**
**be** [bi] (*pres:* **am, is, are;** *pret:* **was, were;** *pp:* **been**) *v aux* estar, p.ej., **he is eating** está comiendo; ser, p.ej., **she is loved by everybody** es amada por todo el mundo; haber, p.ej., **he is gone** ha ido; deber, p.ej., **what are we to do?** ¿qué debemos hacer?; *v impers* ser, p.ej., **it is easy to learn Spanish** es fácil aprender el español; **so be it** o **be it so** así sea; **be that as it may** sea lo que fuere, sea como fuere; haber, p.ej., **it is foggy** hay neblina; **it is muddy** hay lodo; **it is sunny** hay sol; **there is** o **there are** hay; **what is the matter?** ¿qué hay?; **what is wrong?** ¿qué hay?; hacer, p.ej., **how is the weather?** ¿qué tiempo hace?; **it is cold** hace frío; **it is fine weather** hace buen tiempo; **it is hot** o **it is warm** hace calor; *vn* estar, p.ej., **I am tired** estoy cansado; **he is in Madrid** está en Madrid; ser, p.ej., **she is very old** es muy vieja; **I am a doctor** soy médico; tener, p.ej., **to be ashamed** tener vergüenza; **to be cold** tener frío; **to be hot** tener calor; **to be hungry** tener hambre; **to be in a hurry** tener prisa; **to be the matter with** tener p.ej., **what is the matter with you?** ¿qué tiene Vd.?; **to be right** tener razón; **to be thirsty** tener sed; **to be warm** tener calor; **to be wrong** no tener razón; **to be . . . years old** tener . . . años; **to be** futuro, p.ej., **my wife to be** mi futura esposa; **to be in** estar en casa, en la tienda, en la oficina, etc.; **to be in with** (coll.) ser muy amigo de, gozar del favor de; **to be off** irse; estar equivocado; **to be out** estar fuera de casa, estar en la calle; **to be out of** (coll.) no tener más; **to be up to** estar a la altura de, ser competente para; estar haciendo, estar urdiendo; andar en (*p.ej., travesuras*); tocar a, depender de
**beach** [bitʃ] *s* playa; *va* varar; *vn* varar, encallar
**beachcomb** ['bitʃ,kom] *vn* raquear; **to go beachcombing** andar al raque
**beachcomber** ['bitʃ,komər] *s* ola encrestada; raquero, vagabundo de las playas
**beach flea** *s* (zool.) pulga de mar
**beachhead** ['bitʃ,hɛd] *s* (mil.) cabeza de playa
**beach robe** *s* albornoz
**beach robin** *s* (U.S.A.) revuelvepiedras; (Brit.) canut (*Calidris canutus*)
**beach shoe** *s* playera
**beach umbrella** *s* parasol de playa, sombrilla de colores
**beach wagon** *s* rubia, coche rural
**beachy** ['bitʃɪ] *adj (comp:* **-ier;** *super:* **-iest)** guijoso, cascajoso
**beacon** ['bikən] *s* almenara, señal luminosa; faro; hacho (*sitio elevado cerca de la costa*); (rad.) radiofaro; (fig.) guía; *va* señalar con almenara; iluminar, guiar; *vn* brillar
**bead** [bid] *s* cuenta, abalorio; cuenta (*de rosario*); cuentecilla, mostacilla; perla; gota, burbuja; botón (*de fundente*); reborde (*borde saliente*); talón (*de neumático*); mira globular; (arch.) astrágalo; guardavivos (*moldura para proteger las esquinas*); listón separador; **beads** *spl* sarta de cuentas; rosario; **to count one's beads** rezar el rosario; **to draw a bead on** (coll.) apuntar; **to say** o **to tell one's beads** rezar el rosario; *va* adornar con abalorios; rebordear; *vn* formar reborde; burbujear
**beading** ['bidɪŋ] *s* abalorio; (arch.) astrágalo; (arch.) contero
**beadle** ['bidəl] *s* bedel; (eccl.) pertiguero
**beadsman** ['bidzmən] *s* (*pl:* **-men**) hombre que reza por otro; pobre, mendigo
**bead tree** *s* (bot.) acederaque
**beadwork** ['bid,wʌrk] *s* abalorio; (arch.) astrágalo; (arch.) contero
**beady** ['bidɪ] *adj (comp:* **-ier;** *super:* **-iest)** adornado con abalorios; que tiene apariencia de gotas brillantes; burbujeante
**beagle** ['bigəl] *s* sabueso
**beak** [bik] *s* pico; boquilla (*de un instrumento de viento*); (slang) nariz, nariz corva; mechero de gas; rostro (*del barco antiguo*); cabo, promontorio
**beaked** [bikt] *adj* picudo
**beaker** ['bikər] *s* tazón; (chem.) vaso con pequeño pico
**beakhead** ['bik,hɛd] *s* (naut.) beque
**beam** [bim] *s* viga; viga maestra; timón (*del arado*); (naut.) bao; (naut.) bao mayor; (naut.) manga (*anchura mayor*); (naut.) través (*dirección perpendicular a la de la quilla*); rayo (*de luz, de calor, de radio*); astil (*de la balanza*); balanza de cruz; (mach.) balancín; (fig.) rayo (*p.ej., de esperanza*); **on the beam** siguiendo el haz (*del radiofaro*); (naut.) por el través; (slang) siguiendo el buen camino; *va* emitir (*luz, ondas, etc.*); *vn* destellar, brillar; sonreír alegremente
**beamed** [bimd] *adj* envigado
**beaming** ['bimɪŋ] *adj* brillante, radiante; alegre, risueño
**beam sea** *s* (naut.) mar de costado
**beamy** ['bimɪ] *adj (comp:* **-ier;** *super:* **-iest)** brillante, radiante; alegre, risueño; macizo, grueso
**bean** [bin] *s* (bot.) haba (*Vicia faba*); (bot.) alubia, frijol, habichuela, judía (*Phaseolus vulgaris*), vaina del haba; haba (*simiente del café y el cacao*); (slang) cabeza; *va* (slang) golpear en la cabeza con una pelota

**beanbag** [ˈbinˌbæg] *s* saquito de habas (*que usan los niños en ciertos juegos*)
**bean ball** *s* (slang) lanzamiento a la cabeza del bateador (*en el béisbol*)
**beanpole** [ˈbinˌpol] *s* estaca para habas o frijoles; (fig.) poste de telégrafo (*persona muy alta y delgada*)
**beanstalk** [ˈbinˌstɔk] *s* tallo de haba, tallo de frijol
**bear** [bɛr] *s* oso; bajista (*en la Bolsa*); hombre ceñudo ‖ (*pret:* **bore;** *pp:* **borne**) *va* cargar; traer; llevar (*p.ej., armas, una inscripción*); apoyar, sostener; aguantar, sufrir; sentir, experimentar; dejar, permitir; producir, rendir (*p.ej., frutos, interés*); parir; referir, relatar; tener (*odio o amor*); **to bear a grudge against** guardar rencor a, tener inquina a; **to bear date** llevar fecha; **to bear in mind** tener presente, tener en cuenta; **to bear interest** devengar interés; **to bear out** apoyar, sostener; confirmar; **to bear the charges** pagar los gastos; **to bear the market** jugar a la baja; **to bear witness** dar testimonio ‖ *vn* dirigirse, seguir, volver; **to bear down** ejercer presión hacia abajo; hacer bajar por fuerza (*dícese de la mujer que está de parto*); **to bear down on** o **upon** apretar hacia abajo; contener, reprimir; correr sobre, arrojarse impetuosamente sobre; **to bear on** o **upon** referirse a; **to bear up** cobrar ánimo, no perder la esperanza; **to bear up against** resistir; arrostrar; **to bear with** ser indulgente para con, ser paciente con
**bearable** [ˈbɛrəbəl] *adj* soportable, sufrible
**bearbaiting** [ˈbɛrˌbetɪŋ] *s* deporte que consiste en echar perros a pelear con un oso encadenado
**bearberry** [ˈbɛrˌbɛrɪ] *s* (*pl:* **-ries**) (bot.) gayuba, aguavilla
**beard** [bɪrd] *s* barba; (bot.) arista; *va* mesar; retar, desafiar; poner barba a
**bearded** [ˈbɪrdɪd] *adj* barbado, barbudo; (bot.) aristado
**bearded eagle** o **vulture** *s* (orn.) águila barbuda
**bearer** [ˈbɛrər] *s* portador; (com.) portador; árbol fructífero; posesor (*de un cargo u oficio*); portaféretro
**bear garden** *s* patio de los osos; corral donde los perros pelean con un oso encadenado; merienda de negros
**bearing** [ˈbɛrɪŋ] *s* apoyo; porte, presencia, maneras; aguante, paciencia; referencia, relación; fuerza (*p.ej., de una observación*); (her.) blasón; (mach.) cojinete; **bearings** *spl* orientación; **to ask for bearings** (aer.) pedir situación; **to lose one's bearings** desorientarse
**bearish** [ˈbɛrɪʃ] *adj* osuno; ceñudo; que juega a la baja; que tiende a bajar
**bear's-ear** [ˈbɛrzˌɪr] *s* (bot.) oreja de oso
**bearskin** [ˈbɛrˌskɪn] *s* piel de oso; morrión (*gorro militar*); bayetón (*tela de lana peluda*)
**beast** [bist] *s* bestia; persona abrutada; (coll.) cosa muy mala, p.ej., **a beast of a day** un día muy malo
**beastly** [ˈbistlɪ] *adj* (*comp:* **-lier;** *super:* **-liest**) bestial; (coll.) muy malo, detestable; *adv* (coll.) muy, detestablemente
**beast of burden** *s* bestia de carga
**beast of prey** *s* animal de rapiña
**beat** [bit] *s* golpe; latido (*del corazón*); compás (*del ritmo*); marca del compás (*con la mano o el pie*); (mus.) tiempo; (phys.) batimiento; (rad.) batido; ronda (*p.ej., de un policía*); (coll.) ganador, vencedor; (slang) gorrón, embestidor; anticipación de una noticia (*por un periódico*); **off one's beat** fuera del camino trillado; **outside the beat of** fuera de la competencia de; *adj* (coll.) deslomado, derrengado; (rad.) de batido ‖ (*pret:* **beat;** *pp;* **beaten** o **beat**) *va* batir; sacudir (*una alfombra*); aventajar, ganar; (mus.) llevar (*el compás*); tocar (*un tambor*); azotar, pegar; (coll.) confundir; (coll.) engañar, estafar; **to beat a retreat** emprender la retirada; **to beat back** rechazar; **to beat down** abatir, derribar; (coll.) rebajar (*un precio*) regateando; **to beat it** (slang) largarse; **to beat off** rechazar; **to beat to death** matar a golpes; **to beat up** batir (*p.ej., huevos*); (slang) acometer, aporrear ‖ *vn* batir; latir (*el corazón*); (coll.) ganar; (naut.) barloventear; **to beat about** ir buscando; **to beat about the bush** (coll.) andarse por las ramas; **to beat against** azotar, estrellarse contra; **to beat down on** batir (*dar fuertemente en*)
**beaten** [ˈbɪtən] *adj* batido, martillado, trillado; vencido, derrotado; deslomado, derrengado; *pp de* **beat**
**beater** [ˈbitər] *s* batidor (*persona o instrumento*)
**beatific** [ˌbiəˈtɪfɪk] *adj* beatífico
**beatification** [bɪˌætɪfɪˈkeʃən] *s* beatificación
**beatify** [bɪˈætɪfaɪ] (*pret & pp:* **-fied**) beatificar
**beating** [ˈbitɪŋ] *s* golpeo; pulsación; paliza, zurra; aleteo; derrota; **to take a beating** recibir una paliza; salir derrotado; (com.) salir con pérdidas
**beatitude** [bɪˈætɪtjud] o [bɪˈætɪtud] *s* beatitud; (*cap.*) *s* beatitud (*Sumo Pontífice*); **the Beatitudes** (theol.) las bienaventuranzas
**beatnik** [ˈbitnɪk] *s* bohemio que rechaza los valores convencionales de la sociedad
**beat reception** *s* (rad.) recepción por batido
**Beatrice** [ˈbiətrɪs] *s* Beatriz
**beau** [bo] *s* (*pl:* **beaus** o **beaux** [boz]) pretendiente, cortejo; novio; petimetre, currutaco
**Beau Brummell** [ˈbrʌməl] *s* el hermoso Brummell, el Petronio, el rey de la moda; petimetre, currutaco
**beau geste** [ʒɛst] *s* (*pl:* **beaux gestes** [boˈʒɛst]) (Fr.) acción generosa; (Fr.) generosidad fingida
**beau ideal** [aɪˈdiəl] *s* bello ideal
**beau monde** [mɑnd] *s* (Fr.) gente de moda
**beauteous** [ˈbjutɪəs] *adj* bello, hermoso
**beautification** [ˌbjutɪfɪˈkeʃən] *s* embellecimiento
**beautiful** [ˈbjutɪfəl] *adj* bello, hermoso
**beautify** [ˈbjutɪfaɪ] (*pret & pp:* **-fied**) *va* embellecer, hermosear; *vn* embellecerse, hermosearse
**beauty** [ˈbjutɪ] *s* (*pl:* **-ties**) beldad, belleza (*hermosura, mujer muy hermosa*)
**beauty contest** *s* concurso de belleza
**beauty parlor** *s* salón de belleza
**beauty queen** *s* reina de belleza
**beauty sleep** *s* primer sueño (*antes de medianoche*)
**beauty spot** *s* lunar postizo, grano de belleza; sitio pintoresco
**beaver** [ˈbivər] *s* (zool.) castor; piel de castor; castor (*tejido de lana*); sombrero castoreño; sombrero de copa; sobrevista (*del morrión*); (arm.) babera, baberol; (arm.) visera
**bebeerine** [bəˈbirin] o [bəˈbɪrɪn] *s* (pharm.) bebirina
**becalm** [bɪˈkɑm] *va* serenar, calmar; **to be becalmed** (naut.) encalmarse
**became** [bɪˈkem] *pret de* **become**
**because** [bɪˈkɔz] *conj* porque; **because of** por, por causa de, a causa de, con motivo de; **because of** + *ger* por + *inf*
**beccafico** [ˌbɛkəˈfiko] *s* (*pl:* **-cos**) (orn.) becafigo
**béchamel** [beʃɑˈmɛl] *s* bechamela
**bechance** [bɪˈtʃæns] o [bɪˈtʃɑns] *vn* acontecer, suceder
**Bechuanaland** [ˌbɛtʃuˈɑnəˌlænd] o [ˌbɛkjuˈɑnəˌlænd] *s* la Bechuanalandia
**beck** [bɛk] *s* seña (*con la cabeza o la mano*); **at the beck and call of** a disposición de; completamente entregado a
**beckon** [ˈbɛkən] *s* seña (*con la cabeza o la mano*); *va* llamar con señas; atraer, tentar; *vn* hacer seña (*con la cabeza o la mano*)
**becloud** [bɪˈklaud] *va* anublar, obscurecer
**become** [bɪˈkʌm] (*pret:* **-came;** *pp:* **-come**) *va* convenir; sentar bien; *vn* hacerse, p.ej., **my brother became a doctor** mi hermano se hizo médico; **he will become rich but not happy** se hará rico pero no feliz; llegar a ser, p.ej., **he will become a general** llegará a ser general; meterse, p.ej., **he became a soldier** se metió soldado; ponerse, p.ej., **she became very ill** se puso muy enferma; volverse, p.ej., **the clouds became black** se volvieron negras las nubes; convertirse en,

p.ej., **the water became wine** se convirtió el agua en vino; (philos.) devenir; **to become of** ser de, p.ej., **what will become of me?** ¿qué será de mí?; hacerse de, p.ej., **what became of my hat?** ¿qué se ha hecho de mi sombrero?; este verbo, seguido de un adjetivo, se traduce a veces por un verbo neutro o reflexivo que corresponda al adjetivo, p.ej., **to become crazy** enloquecer; **to become useless** inutilizarse
**becoming** [bɪ'kʌmɪŋ] *adj* conveniente; que sienta bien; *s* (philos.) (el) devenir
**bed** [bɛd] *s* cama, lecho; (mas.) lecho; lecho (*del río, de la vía; asiento; capa, estrato*); (min.) yacimiento; macizo (*de jardín*); **to get up on the wrong side of the bed** levantarse por los pies de la cama; **to go to bed** acostarse; **to make the bed** hacer la cama; **to stay in bed** guardar cama; **to take to one's bed** encamarse; (*pret & pp:* **bedded;** *ger:* **bedding**) *va* acostar; dar cama a; sembrar o plantar en un macizo; poner en capas sobrepuestas; *vn* acostarse; formar una masa compacta; cohabitar, hacer vida marital
**bedabble** [bɪ'dæbəl] *va* salpicar
**bed and board** *s* techo y sustento
**bedaub** [bɪ'dɔb] *va* embadurnar; adornar vistosamente; vilipendiar; alabar con exceso
**bedaze** [bɪ'dez] *va* aturdir, atolondrar
**bedazzle** [bɪ'dæzəl] *va* deslumbrar
**bedbug** ['bɛd,bʌg] *s* (ent.) chinche
**bedchamber** ['bɛd,tʃembər] *s* alcoba, cuarto de dormir
**bedclothes** ['bɛd,kloz] *spl* ropa de cama
**bedcover** ['bɛd,kʌvər] *s* cubierta de cama
**bedding** ['bɛdɪŋ] *s* ropa de cama; paja para jergón; lecho (*asiento; capa inferior*); (geol.) estratificación
**Bede** [bid] *s* Beda; **the Venerable Bede** el venerable Beda
**bedeck** [bɪ'dɛk] *va* acicalar, adornar, engalanar
**bedevil** [bɪ'dɛvəl] (*pret & pp:* **-iled** o **-illed;** *ger:* **-iling** o **-illing**) *va* atormentar; confundir; endemoniar, hechizar
**bedevilment** [bɪ'dɛvəlmənt] *s* tormento; confusión; hechizo
**bedew** [bɪ'dju] o [bɪ'du] *va* rociar
**bedfast** ['bɛd,fæst] o ['bɛd,fɑst] *adj* postrado en cama
**bedfellow** ['bɛd,fɛlo] *s* compañero o compañera de cama; compañero, compañera
**Bedford cord** ['bɛdfərd] *s* paño Bedford
**bedgown** ['bɛd,gaʊn] *s* camisa de dormir; chaqueta (*de las mujeres del norte de Inglaterra*)
**bedight** [bɪ'daɪt] (*pret & pp:* **-dight** o **-dighted**) *va* (archaic) adornar, guarnecer
**bedim** [bɪ'dɪm] (*pret & pp:* **-dimmed;** *ger:* **-dimming**) *va* obscurecer
**bedizen** [bɪ'daɪzən] o [bɪ'dɪzən] *va* emperejilar
**bedlam** ['bɛdləm] *s* confusión, bullicio; casa de orates, manicomio
**bedlamite** ['bɛdləmaɪt] *s* loco, orate
**bed linen** *s* ropa de cama
**bed of roses** *s* canonjía, sinecura
**Bedouin** ['bɛdʊɪn] *adj* beduíno; *s* beduíno; nómada
**bedpan** ['bɛd,pæn] *s* calentador de cama; silleta
**bedpost** ['bɛd,post] *s* pilar de cama
**bedraggle** [bɪ'drægəl] *va* ensuciar o manchar arrastrando por el suelo
**bedrail** ['bɛd,rel] *s* baranda o barandilla de la cama
**bedrid** ['bɛd,rɪd] o **bedridden** ['bɛd,rɪdən] *adj* postrado en cama
**bedrock** ['bɛd,rɑk] *s* lecho de roca, roca sólida; fondo; base, fundamento
**bedroom** ['bɛd,rum] o ['bɛd,rʊm] *s* alcoba, cuarto de dormir
**bedroom suit** *s* juego de alcoba
**bedside** ['bɛd,saɪd] *s* lado de cama; cabecera; espacio entre la cama y la pared; *adj* del lado de cama; con los enfermos; práctico en cuidar a los enfermos
**bedside table** *s* velador, mesa de noche
**bedsore** ['bɛd,sor] *s* úlcera de decúbito; **to have** or **to get bedsores** decentarse
**bedspread** ['bɛd,sprɛd] *s* sobrecama
**bedspring** ['bɛd,sprɪŋ] *s* colchón de muelles
**bedstead** ['bɛd,stɛd] *s* cuja
**bedstraw** ['bɛd,strɔ] *s* paja para jergón; (bot.) amor de hortelano, cuajaleche; (bot.) pegapega (*Desmodium uncinatum*)
**bedtick** ['bɛd,tɪk] *s* cutí
**bedtime** ['bɛd,taɪm] *s* hora de acostarse
**bedtime story** *s* cuento que se dice a los niños al acostarse
**bed warmer** *s* calientacamas
**bee** [bi] *s* (ent.) abeja; reunión, tertulia; capricho extravagante; **to be busy as a bee** estar muy metido en el trabajo; **to have a bee in one's bonnet** u **one's head** tener una idea fija en la mente; ser ligero de cascos; (*cap.*) *s* nombre abreviado de **Beatrice**
**beebread** ['bi,brɛd] *s* ámago
**beech** [bitʃ] *s* (bot.) haya
**beechen** ['bitʃən] *adj* de haya, hecho de haya
**beechnut** ['bitʃ,nʌt] *s* hayuco
**beechwood** ['bitʃ,wʊd] *s* madera de haya
**bee eater** *s* (orn.) abejaruco
**beef** [bif] *s* (*pl:* **beeves** o **beefs**) carne de vaca o toro; ganado vacuno de engorde; (coll.) fuerza muscular; (coll.) peso; (*pl:* **beefs**) (slang) queja; *va* **to beef up** (coll.) reforzar; *vn* (slang) quejarse
**beef cattle** *s* ganado vacuno de engorde
**beefeater** ['bif,itər] *s* persona muy gorda; (Brit.) alabardero de palacio; (Brit.) alabardero de la Torre de Londres; (orn.) espulgabueyes, picabueyes
**bee fly** *s* (ent.) mosca abeja
**beefsteak** ['bif,stek] *s* biftec o bistec
**beef tea** *s* caldo concentrado de carne
**beefy** ['bifɪ] *adj* (*comp:* **-ier;** *super:* **-iest**) fornido, musculoso, pesado
**bee glue** *s* tanque, propóleos
**beehive** ['bi,haɪv] *s* colmena
**beekeeper** ['bi,kipər] *s* colmenero
**beeline** ['bi,laɪn] *s* línea recta; **to make a beeline for** ir en línea recta hacia
**Beelzebub** [bɪ'ɛlzɪbʌb] *s* (Bib.) Belcebú
**been** [bɪn] *pp de* **be**
**beer** [bɪr] *s* cerveza; bebida gaseosa hecha de raíces; **dark beer** cerveza parda o negra; **light beer** cerveza clara
**beer and skittles** *spl* diversión, placer
**beer garden** *s* cervecería al aire libre
**beer saloon** *s* cervecería
**beery** ['bɪrɪ] *adj* (*comp:* **-ier;** *super:* **-iest**) cervecero, de cerveza, de la cerveza
**beestings** ['bistɪŋz] *spl* calostro
**beeswax** ['biz,wæks] *s* cera de abejas; *va* encerar
**beeswing** ['biz,wɪŋ] *s* películas del oporto; viejo oporto
**beet** [bit] *s* (bot.) remolacha (*planta y raíz*)
**beetle** ['bitəl] *s* (ent.) escarabajo; martillo de madera; pisón; *adj* saliente; *va* martillar con martillo de madera; pisar con pisón; *vn* destacar, sobresalir
**beetle-browed** ['bitəl,braʊd] *adj* cejudo; (fig.) ceñudo
**beetling** ['bitlɪŋ] *adj* saliente, sobresaliente
**beet root** *s* raíz de remolacha
**beet sugar** *s* azúcar de remolacha
**befall** [bɪ'fɔl] (*pret:* **-fell;** *pp:* **-fallen**) *va* acontecer a; *vn* acontecer
**befell** [bɪ'fɛl] *pret de* **befall**
**befit** [bɪ'fɪt] (*pret & pp:* **-fitted;** *ger:* **-fitting**) *va* convenir, venir bien, cuadrar
**befitting** [bɪ'fɪtɪŋ] *adj* conveniente
**befog** [bɪ'fɑg] o [bɪ'fɔg] (*pret & pp:* **-fogged;** *ger:* **-fogging**) *va* envolver en niebla; obscurecer, confundir
**befool** [bɪ'ful] *va* engañar, embaucar
**before** [bɪ'for] *adv* delante, enfrente; antes; ya, más arriba; *prep* delante de, enfrente de; antes de; ante (*en presencia de*); *conj* antes (de) que
**beforehand** [bɪ'for,hænd] *adv* de antemano, con anticipación; *adj* hecho de antemano
**beforetime** [bɪ'for,taɪm] *adv* (archaic) en tiempos pasados
**befoul** [bɪ'faʊl] *va* ensuciar, emporcar; enredarse en
**befriend** [bɪ'frɛnd] *va* amparar, favorecer, ofrecer amistad a
**befuddle** [bɪ'fʌdəl] *va* aturdir, confundir

**beg** [bɛg] (*pret & pp:* **begged;** *ger:* **begging**) *va* rogar, pedir, solicitar; mendigar; **to beg someone for something** pedir algo a alguien; **to beg the question** dar por sentado lo mismo que se trata de probar; **to beg someone to** + *inf* pedir a alguien que + *subj; vn* mendigar; **to go begging** andar mendigando; no hallar comprador, no tener demanda; **to beg for** solicitar; **to beg off** excusarse; **to beg to** + *inf* permitirse + *inf*
**began** [bɪˈgæn] *pret de* **begin**
**beget** [bɪˈgɛt] (*pret:* **-got;** *pp:* **-gotten** o **-got;** *ger:* **-getting**) *va* engendrar
**beggar** [ˈbɛgər] *s* mendigo; pobre de solemnidad; pícaro, bribón; tipo, sujeto, individuo; *va* empobrecer, arruinar; excederse de
**beggardom** [ˈbɛgərdəm] *s* pobretería
**beggar-lice** [ˈbɛgərˌlaɪs] *ssg & spl* var. de **beggar's-lice**
**beggarly** [ˈbɛgərlɪ] *adj* pobre, miserable, mezquino, despreciable
**beggar's-lice** [ˈbɛgərzˌlaɪs] *ssg & spl* (bot.) bardana, cadillo, pegarropa (*planta y frutos espinosos que se adhieren al vestido*)
**beggar's-tick** [ˈbɛgərzˌtɪk] *s* aquenio del bidente; **beggar's-ticks** *spl* (bot.) bidente; (bot.) bardana, cadillo, pegarropa
**beggary** [ˈbɛgərɪ] *s* (*pl:* **-ies**) mendicidad; pobretería
**begin** [bɪˈgɪn] (*pret:* **-gan;** *pp:* **-gun;** *ger:* **-ginning**) *va* comenzar, empezar; *vn* comenzar, empezar; tomar principio; **to not begin to** ni por asomo, ni con mucho; **to begin by** + *ger* comenzar por + *inf;* **to begin to** + *inf* comenzar o empezar a + *inf;* **to begin** + *ger* comenzar + *ger;* **beginning with** a partir de
**beginner** [bɪˈgɪnər] *s* principiante, novicio; iniciador, originador
**beginning** [bɪˈgɪnɪŋ] *s* comienzo, principio; origen; punto de partida
**begirt** [bɪˈgʌrt] *adj* ceñido, cercado, rodeado
**begone** [bɪˈgɔn] o [bɪˈgɑn] *interj* ¡fuera!, ¡vete de aquí!
**begonia** [bɪˈgonɪə] *s* (bot.) begonia
**begoniaceous** [bɪˌgonɪˈeʃəs] *adj* (bot.) begoniáceo
**begot** [bɪˈgɑt] *pret & pp de* **beget**
**begotten** [bɪˈgɑtən] *pp de* **beget**
**begrime** [bɪˈgraɪm] *va* embarrar, tiznar
**begrudge** [bɪˈgrʌdʒ] *va* dar de mala gana; envidiar
**begrudgingly** [bɪˈgrʌdʒɪŋlɪ] *adv* de mala gana
**beguile** [bɪˈgaɪl] *va* engañar, seducir; divertir, entretener; defraudar; **to beguile the time** engañar el tiempo
**begun** [bɪˈgʌn] *pp de* **begin**
**behalf** [bɪˈhæf] o [bɪˈhɑf] *s* favor, patrocinio, interés; **in behalf of** a favor de; **on behalf of** en nombre de; a favor de
**behave** [bɪˈhev] *vn* actuar, funcionar; portarse, conducirse; portarse bien
**behavior** [bɪˈhevjər] *s* conducta, comportamiento; porte, modales; funcionamiento
**behaviorism** [bɪˈhevjərɪzəm] *s* (psychol.) comportamentismo, behaviorismo
**behaviorist** [bɪˈhevjərɪst] *s* comportamentista, behaviorista
**behavioristic** [bɪˌhevjəˈrɪstɪk] *adj* comportamentista, behaviorístico
**behead** [bɪˈhɛd] *va* descabezar
**beheld** [bɪˈhɛld] *pret & pp de* **behold**
**behemoth** [bɪˈhiməθ] o [ˈbiɪmɑθ] *s* (coll.) gigante, bestia colosal
**behind** [bɪˈhaɪnd] *s* (slang) culo, trasero; *adv* detrás; hacia atrás; más allá; con retraso; **from behind** por detrás; **to stay behind** quedarse atrás; *prep* detrás de; **to be behind the times** no estar al corriente de las cosas; **behind the back of** a espaldas de; **behind time** tarde
**behindhand** [bɪˈhaɪndˌhænd] *adv* con atraso; *adj* atrasado; tardío; atrasado en pagos
**behold** [bɪˈhold] (*pret & pp:* **-held**) *va* mirar, contemplar; *interj* ¡he aquí!
**beholden** [bɪˈholdən] *adj* obligado
**behoof** [bɪˈhuf] *s* provecho, utilidad, ventaja
**behoove** [bɪˈhuv] o **behove** [bɪˈhuv] o [bɪˈhov] *va* convenir, corresponder, tocar
**beige** [beʒ] *adj & s* beige (*amarillento*)
**being** [ˈbiɪŋ] *s* ser, ente; *adj* existente; **for the time being** por ahora, por el momento; *ger de* **be**
**bejewel** [bɪˈdʒuəl] (*pret & pp:* **-eled** o **-elled;** *ger:* **-eling** o **-elling**) *va* alhajar, enjoyar
**bejeweled** [bɪˈdʒuəld] *adj* enjoyelado, enjoyado
**bel** [bɛl] *s* (phys.) belio
**belabor** [bɪˈlebər] *va* apalear; ridiculizar
**belated** [bɪˈletɪd] *adj* atrasado; sorprendido por la noche
**belay** [bɪˈle] *va* (naut.) amarrar (*una cuerda*) dando vueltas en una cabilla; (coll.) detener
**belaying pin** *s* (naut.) cabilla de maniobra
**belch** [bɛltʃ] *s* eructo, regüeldo; *va* vomitar (*p.ej., llamas, humo, injurias*); *vn* eructar, regoldar; salir con fuerza (*llamas, humo, etc.*)
**beldam** o **beldame** [ˈbɛldəm] *s* tarasca, bruja
**beleaguer** [bɪˈligər] *va* sitiar, bloquear, cercar
**belemnite** [ˈbɛləmnaɪt] *s* (pal.) belemnita
**belfry** [ˈbɛlfrɪ] *s* (*pl:* **-fries**) campanario
**Belg.** abr. de **Belgian** y **Belgium**
**Belgian** [ˈbɛldʒən] *adj* belga, bélgico; *s* belga
**Belgian Congo** *s* el Congo Belga
**Belgium** [ˈbɛldʒəm] *s* Bélgica
**Belgrade** [bɛlˈgred] o [ˈbɛlgred] *s* Belgrado
**belie** [bɪˈlaɪ] (*pret & pp:* **-lied;** *ger:* **-lying**) *va* desmentir; calumniar, difamar; representar falsamente
**belief** [bɪˈlif] *s* creencia
**believable** [bɪˈlivəbəl] *adj* creíble
**believe** [bɪˈliv] *va* creer; *vn* creer; **to believe in** creer en (*p.ej., Dios*); aprobar; contar con
**believer** [bɪˈlivər] *s* creyente; fiel (*cristiano*)
**belike** [bɪˈlaɪk] *adv* (archaic & dial.) tal vez, probablemente
**Belisarius** [ˌbɛlɪˈsɛrɪəs] *s* Belisario
**belittle** [bɪˈlɪtəl] *va* desalabar, despreciar; empequeñecer
**Belize** [bɛˈliz] *s* Bélice
**bell** [bɛl] *s* campana; timbre (*campanilla eléctrica*); cencerro (*que se ata al pescuezo de las reses*); cascabel (*bolita hueca que contiene un pedacito de hierro*); campanada (*toque de campana*); (arch.) campana; (mus.) pabellón (*de instrumento de viento*); galardón, premio; **to bear the bell** ganar el premio, ser el primero; **to ring a bell** (coll.) sonar, p.ej., **this name rings a bell for me** este nombre me suena; *va* poner campana a; acampanar; **to bell the cat** ponerle el cascabel al gato; *vn* acampanarse; crecer (*p.ej., una flor*) en figura de campana; bramar, berrear
**Bella** [ˈbɛlə] *s* nombre abreviado de **Arabella** e **Isabella**
**belladonna** [ˌbɛləˈdɑnə] *s* (bot. & pharm.) belladona
**belladonna lily** *s* (bot.) amarilis
**bellbird** [ˈbɛlˌbʌrd] *s* (orn.) campanero
**bellboy** [ˈbɛlˌbɔɪ] *s* botones
**bell buoy** *s* (naut.) boya de campana
**belle** [bɛl] *s* beldad o belleza (*mujer muy hermosa*); buena moza
**Bellerophon** [bəˈlɛrəfɑn] *s* (myth.) Belerofonte
**belles-lettres** [ˌbɛlˈlɛtrə] *spl* bellas letras
**bellflower** [ˈbɛlˌflaʊər] *s* (bot.) campánula
**bell gable** *s* espadaña
**bell glass** *s* campana de cristal; fanal (*para resguardar una péndola, luz, etc.*)
**bellhop** [ˈbɛlˌhɑp] *s* (slang) botones
**bellicose** [ˈbɛlɪkos] *adj* belicoso
**bellicosity** [ˌbɛlɪˈkɑsɪtɪ] *s* belicosidad
**belligerence** [bəˈlɪdʒərəns] o **belligerency** [bəˈlɪdʒərənsɪ] *s* beligerancia
**belligerent** [bəˈlɪdʒərənt] *adj & s* beligerante
**bell jar** *s* var. de **bell glass**
**bellman** [ˈbɛlmən] *s* (*pl:* **-men**) pregonero de campana
**bell metal** *s* metal campanil, metal de campana, bronce de campanas
**bell-mouthed** [ˈbɛlˌmaʊðd] o [ˈbɛlˌmaʊθt] *adj* acampanado, abocinado, abocardado
**bellow** [ˈbɛlo] *s* bramido; **bellows** [ˈbɛloz] o [ˈbɛləs] *ssg o spl* fuelle; barquín (*fuelle usado en las herrerías*); (phot.) fuelle (*de la máquina fotográfica*); **bellow** [ˈbɛlo] *va* gritar, vociferar; *vn* bramar
**bellows blower** *s* entonador
**bell ringer** *s* campanero
**bell-shaped** [ˈbɛlˌʃept] *adj* acampanado

**bell tent** *s* pabellón
**bell transformer** *s* (elec.) transformador para timbres
**bellwether** [ˈbɛlˌwɛðər] *s* manso
**bell wire** *s* (elec.) alambre para timbres
**belly** [ˈbɛlɪ] *s* (*pl:* **-lies**) vientre, barriga; estómago; (*pret & pp:* **-lied**) *vn* hacer barriga; hacer bolso (*las velas*); pandearse
**bellyache** [ˈbɛlɪˌek] *s* (slang) dolor de barriga; *vn* (slang) quejarse
**bellyband** [ˈbɛlɪˌbænd] *s* ventrera; barriguera (*de las caballerías*); cincha (*para asegurar la silla a las caballerías*)
**belly dancer** *s* (coll.) bailarina ombliguista
**bellyful** [ˈbɛlɪfʊl] *s* (slang) panzada
**belong** [bɪˈlɔŋ] o [bɪˈlɑŋ] *vn* pertenecer; deber estar, p.ej., **the chair belongs in this room** la silla debe estar en este cuarto; **to belong to** pertenecer a
**belongings** [bɪˈlɔŋɪŋz] o [bɪˈlɑŋɪŋz] *spl* pertenencias; (coll.) familia; **to gather one's belongings** liar los bártulos
**beloved** [bɪˈlʌvid] o [bɪˈlʌvd] *adj* dilecto, querido, amado; *s* querido, amado
**below** [bɪˈlo] *adv* abajo; más abajo; en el infierno; bajo cero, p.ej., **ten below** diez grados bajo cero; *prep* debajo de; inferior a
**Belshazzar** [bɛlˈʃæzər] *s* (Bib.) Baltasar
**belt** [bɛlt] *s* cinto, cinturón; (aer.) correa; (mach.) correa; (geog.) faja, zona; (slang) correazo; **below the belt** (sport) de cintura abajo, sucio, suciamente; **to tighten one's belt** ceñirse; *va* ceñir; poner correa a (*una máquina*); unir con correa; (slang) golpear con correa
**belt conveyor** *s* correa transportadora, cinta de transporte
**belt course** *s* (arch.) cordón
**belt drive** *s* transmisión por correa
**belting** [ˈbɛltɪŋ] *s* correa (*material*); correaje
**belt line** *s* (rail.) línea o vía de circunvalación
**beluga** [bəˈlugə] *s* (zool.) beluga; (ichth.) esturión blanco
**belvedere** [ˌbɛlvəˈdɪr] *s* belvedere; glorieta
**bemaul** [bɪˈmɔl] *va* aporrear, maltratar a golpes
**bemazed** [bɪˈmezd] *adj* aturdido, confundido
**bemedaled** o **bemedalled** [bɪˈmɛdəld] *adj* condecorado con muchas medallas
**bemire** [bɪˈmaɪr] *va* enlodar, embarrar
**bemoan** [bɪˈmon] *va* deplorar, lamentar
**bemock** [bɪˈmɑk] *va* mofarse de, reírse de
**bemuse** [bɪˈmjuz] *va* atolondrar, aturdir, confundir, pasmar
**Ben** [bɛn] *s* nombre abreviado de **Benjamin**
**bench** [bɛntʃ] *s* banco; (law) tribunal; (law) judicatura; meseta; plataforma (*de una exposición canina*); **to be on the bench** (law) ser juez, ejercer sus funciones (*un juez*); *va* proveer de bancos; sentar en un banco; exhibir (*un perro*); poner en un tribunal; (baseball) enviar a las duchas
**bench dog** *s* perro exhibido (*en una exposición canina*)
**bencher** [ˈbɛntʃər] *s* el que trabaja en un banco; remador; frecuentador de tabernas; (Brit.) decano de un colegio de abogados
**bench mark** *s* (top.) cota, punto topográfico de referencia
**bench root** *s* (agr.) raíces trabadas
**bench show** *s* exposición canina
**bench warmer** *s* (slang) arrimón
**bench warrant** *s* (law) auto de prisión expedido por un juez o un tribunal
**bend** [bend] *s* curva; recodo (*de un camino, río, etc.*); inclinación; gaza (*lazo en el extremo de un cabo*); (her.) banda; **bends** *spl* (naut.) cinta; (coll.) enfermedad de los cajones de aire comprimido; (*pret & pp:* **bent**) *va* encorvar, combar; doblar; torcer; inclinar; dirigir; someter; (naut.) envergar (*una vela*); (naut.) entalingar (*el chicote del cable*); **to bend one's efforts** dirigir sus esfuerzos; **to bend the head** inclinar la cabeza; **to bend the head to one side** ladear la cabeza; **to bend the knee** doblar la rodilla; hincar la rodilla (*en el suelo*); *vn* encorvarse; doblarse; inclinarse; volver; someterse; **to bend down** u **over** inclinarse
**bended** [ˈbɛndɪd] (archaic) *pret & pp de* **bend; on bended knee** o **knees** arrodillado
**bender** [ˈbɛndər] *s* torcedor; (mach.) doblador (*de un tubo, carril, etc.*); (slang) juerga, jolgorio
**beneath** [bɪˈniθ] *adv* abajo, debajo; *prep* debajo de; inferior a
**benedicite** [ˌbɛnɪˈdɪsɪtɪ] *s* benedícite (*invocación*); (*cap.*) *s* (eccl.) benedícite
**benedict** [ˈbɛnɪdɪkt] *s* casado, recién casado, solterón acabado de casar; (*cap.*) *s* Benito; Benedicto (*papa*)
**Benedictine** [ˌbɛnɪˈdɪktin] o [ˌbɛnɪˈdɪktaɪn] *adj & s* benedictino; (*l.c.*) [ˌbɛnɪˈdɪktin] *s* benedictino (*licor*)
**Benedictine rule** *s* regla de San Benito
**benediction** *s* [ˌbɛnɪˈdɪkʃən] *s* bendición
**Benedictus** [ˌbɛnɪˈdɪktəs] *s* (eccl.) benedictus
**benefaction** [ˌbɛnɪˈfækʃən] *s* beneficencia; beneficio
**benefactor** [ˈbɛnɪˌfæktər] o [ˌbɛnɪˈfæktər] *s* bienhechor
**benefactress** [ˈbɛnɪˌfæktrɪs] o [ˌbɛnɪˈfæktrɪs] *s* bienhechora
**benefice** [ˈbɛnɪfɪs] *s* (eccl.) beneficio
**beneficence** [bɪˈnɛfɪsəns] *s* beneficencia; beneficio
**beneficent** [bɪˈnɛfɪsənt] *adj* benéfico, bienhechor
**beneficial** [ˌbɛnɪˈfɪʃəl] *adj* beneficioso
**beneficiary** [ˌbɛnɪˈfɪʃɪˌɛrɪ] o [ˌbɛnɪˈfɪʃərɪ] *s* (*pl:* **-ies**) beneficiario; (eccl.) beneficiado
**benefit** [ˈbɛnɪfɪt] *s* beneficio; (theat.) beneficio, **for the benefit of** a beneficio de; *va* beneficiar; *vn* beneficiar; **to benefit from** beneficiar de, aprovechar
**benevolence** [bɪˈnɛvələns] *s* benevolencia
**benevolent** [bɪˈnɛvələnt] *adj* benévolo; benéfico (*dícese, p.ej., de una institución*)
**Bengal** [bɛŋˈgɔl] *s* Bengala
**Bengalese** [ˌbɛŋgəˈliz] *adj* bengalí; *s* (*pl:* **-lese**) bengalí
**Bengali** [bɛŋˈgɔlɪ] *adj* bengalí; *s* bengalí (*habitante e idioma*); (orn.) bengalí
**bengaline** [ˈbɛŋgəlin] o [ˌbɛŋgəˈlin] *s* bengalina
**Bengal light** *s* luz de Bengala
**Bengal tiger** *s* tigre de Bengala o tigre real
**benighted** [bɪˈnaɪtɪd] *adj* sorprendido por la noche; ignorante, depravado
**benign** [bɪˈnaɪn] *adj* benigno; (path.) benigno
**benignancy** [bɪˈnɪgnənsɪ] *s* benignidad
**benignant** [bɪˈnɪgnənt] *adj* benigno; (path.) benigno
**benignity** [bɪˈnɪgnɪtɪ] *s* (*pl:* **-ties**) benignidad; bondad
**benison** [ˈbɛnɪzən] o [ˈbɛnɪsən] *s* bendición
**Benjamin** [ˈbɛndʒəmɪn] *s* Benjamín; (*l.c.*) *s* benjuí (*resina aromática*)
**benne** [ˈbɛnɪ] *s* (bot.) sésamo de la India u oriental
**bent** [bɛnt] *s* encorvadura; inclinación, propensión; (bot.) hierba amófila; (dial.) páramo, matorral; *adj* encorvado; doblado; torcido; **bent on** resuelto a, empeñado en; **bent over** cargado de espaldas; *pret & pp de* **bend**
**benthos** [ˈbɛnθɑs] *s* (biol.) bentos
**benumb** [bɪˈnʌm] *va* entorpecer
**benzedrine** [ˈbɛnzədrin] o [ˈbɛnzədrɪn] *s* (trademark) bencedrina
**benzene** [ˈbɛnzin] o [bɛnˈzin] *s* (chem.) benceno
**benzene ring** *s* (chem.) núcleo bencénico
**benzidine** [ˈbɛnzɪdin] o [ˈbɛnzɪdɪn] *s* (chem.) bencidina
**benzine** [ˈbɛnzin] o [bɛnˈzin] *s* bencina
**benzoate** [ˈbɛnzoet] *s* (chem.) benzoato
**benzoic** [bɛnˈzo·ɪk] *adj* (chem.) benzoico
**benzoic acid** *s* (chem.) ácido benzoico
**benzoin** [ˈbɛnzo·ɪn] o [ˈbɛnzɔɪn] *s* benjuí (*resina aromática*); (bot.) benzoin; (chem.) benzoína
**benzol** [ˈbɛnzɑl] *s* (chem.) benzol
**bepearl** [bɪˈpʌrl] *va* aljofarar
**bepraise** [bɪˈprez] *va* alabar con exceso, lisonjear con exageración
**bequeath** [bɪˈkwið] o [bɪˈkwiθ] *va* (law & fig.) legar
**bequeathal** [bɪˈkwiðəl] *s* manda, donación
**bequest** [bɪˈkwɛst] *s* manda; legado

**berate** [bɪ'ret] *va* zaherir, reñir, regañar
**Berber** ['bʌrbər] *adj & s* bereber
**bereave** [bɪ'riv] (*pret & pp:* **-reaved** o **-reft**) *va* despojar, privar; desconsolar, desolar
**bereavement** [bɪ'rivmənt] *s* despojo, privación; aflicción, desconsuelo, duelo
**bereft** [bɪ'rɛft] *pret & pp de* **bereave**
**beret** [bɛ'rɛ] o ['bɛrɛ] *s* boina, boina francesa
**berg** [bʌrg] *s* banquisa, iceberg
**bergamot** ['bʌrgəmɑt] *s* (bot.) bergamoto (*limero; peral*); (bot.) sándalo de agua, té de Pensilvania; bergamota (*lima; pera; aceite esencial; tabaco en polvo*); (*cap.*) *s* bérgama (*tapicería*)
**beribboned** [bɪ'rɪbənd] *adj* encintado
**beriberi** ['bɛrɪ'bɛrɪ] *s* (path.) beriberi
**beringed** [bɪ'rɪŋd] *adj* que lleva muchas sortijas
**berkelium** [bər'kilɪəm] *s* (chem.) berkelio
**berlin** [bʌr'lɪn] o ['bʌrlɪn] *s* berlina; estambre; (*cap.*) [bʌr'lɪn] *s* Berlín
**Berliner** [bʌr'lɪnər] *s* berlinés
**berm** [bʌrm] *s* (fort.) berma
**Bermuda** [bər'mjudə] *s* las Bermudas
**Bermuda onion** *s* cebolla común de las Bermudas, Tejas y California
**Bermudian** [bər'mjudɪən] *adj & s* bermudeño
**Bern** [bʌrn] o [bɛrn] *s* Berna
**Bernard** ['bʌrnərd] o [bər'nɑrd] *s* Bernardo
**Bernese** [bʌr'niz] *adj* bernés; *s* (*pl:* **-nese**) bernés
**berry** ['bɛrɪ] *s* (*pl:* **-ries**) baya; grano, haba (*simiente, p.ej., del cafeto*); polidrupa (*de la fresa, la frambuesa, etc.*); (*pret & pp:* **-ried**) *vn* coger fresas, frambuesas, grosellas, etc.; producir (*una planta*) fresas, frambuesas, grosellas, etc.
**berserk** ['bʌrsʌrk] *adj* frenético; *adv* con frenesí; **to go berserk** embestir frenéticamente a diestro y siniestro
**Bert** [bʌrt] *s* nombre abreviado de **Albert, Bertram** y **Herbert**
**berth** [bʌrθ] *s* litera (*cama fija en los buques y el ferrocarril*); (naut.) camarote (*dormitorio*); (naut.) amarradero; (naut.) dársena; puesto, empleo; **to give a wide berth to** apartarse de, evitar el encuentro de; *va & vn* (naut.) atracar
**bertha** ['bʌrθə] *s* berta (*cuello*); (*cap.*) *s* Berta; (slang) Berta (*cañón alemán*)
**Bertillon system** ['bʌrtɪlɑn] *s* bertillonaje
**Bertram** ['bʌrtrəm] *s* Beltrán
**beruffled** [bɪ'rʌfəld] *adj* adornado con volantes, fruncido
**beryl** ['bɛrɪl] *s* (mineral.) berilo
**beryllium** [bə'rɪlɪəm] *s* (chem.) berilio
**beseech** [bɪ'sitʃ] (*pret & pp:* **-sought** o **-seeched**) *va* suplicar
**beseem** [bɪ'sim] *va & vn* convenir
**beset** [bɪ'sɛt] (*pret & pp:* **-set;** *ger:* **-setting**) *va* acometer, acosar; cercar, sitiar; engastar
**besetting** [bɪ'sɛtɪŋ] *adj* constante, dominante
**beshrew** [bɪ'ʃru] *va* (archaic) echar maldiciones a
**beside** [bɪ'saɪd] *adv* además, también, por otra parte; *prep* cerca de, junto a; en comparación de; excepto, fuera de; **beside oneself** fuera de sí, **beside the point** que no viene al caso
**besides** [bɪ'saɪdz] *adv* además, también, por otra parte; *prep* además de; excepto, fuera de
**besiege** [bɪ'sidʒ] *va* asediar, sitiar; apretar, apiñar; (fig.) asediar
**besmear** [bɪ'smɪr] *va* embadurnar
**besmirch** [bɪ'smʌrtʃ] *va* ensuciar, manchar
**besom** ['bizəm] *s* escoba
**besot** [bɪ'sɑt] (*pret & pp:* **-sotted;** *ger:* **-sotting**) *va* entontecer, embrutecer; emborrachar
**besought** [bɪ'sɔt] *pret & pp de* **beseech**
**bespangle** [bɪ'spæŋgəl] *va* adornar con lentejuelas
**bespatter** [bɪ'spætər] *va* salpicar
**bespeak** [bɪ'spik] (*pret:* **-spoke;** *pp:* **-spoken** o **-spoke**) *va* apalabrar, reservar; indicar, demostrar; pedir, solicitar; (poet. & archaic) dirigir la palabra a
**bespectacled** [bɪ'spɛktəkəld] *adj* con gafas, con anteojos
**bespoke** [bɪ'spok] *pret & pp de* **bespeak**
**bespoken** [bɪ'spokən] *pp de* **bespeak**
**bespread** [bɪ'sprɛd] (*pret & pp:* **-spread**) *va* derramar, recubrir
**besprinkle** [bɪ'sprɪŋkəl] *va* rociar, salpicar; espolvorear
**Bess** [bɛs] *s* nombre abreviado de **Elizabeth**
**Bessarabia** [,bɛsə'rebɪə] *s* la Besarabia
**Bessemer converter** ['bɛsəmər] *s* convertidor Bessemer
**Bessemer process** *s* procedimiento Bessemer
**Bessemer steel** *s* acero Bessemer
**best** [bɛst] *adj super* mejor; mayor; *adv super* mejor; **had best** debería; *s* lo mejor; lo más; **all for the best** conducente al bien a la larga; **at best** a lo más; **to do one's best** hacer todo lo posible; **to get** o **to have the best of** aventajar, sobresalir; **to make the best of** salir lo mejor posible de
**bestead** [bɪ'stɛd] *adj* situado; **bestead with dangers** rodeado de peligros; *va* ayudar
**best girl** *s* (coll.) novia, amiga preferida
**bestial** ['bɛstjəl] o ['bɛstʃəl] *adj* bestial
**bestiality** [,bɛstɪ'ælɪtɪ] o [,bɛstʃɪ'ælɪtɪ] *s* bestialidad
**bestiary** ['bɛstɪ,ɛrɪ] *s* (*pl:* **-ies**) bestiario
**bestir** [bɪ'stʌr] (*pret & pp:* **-stirred;** *ger:* **-stirring**) *va* incitar, excitar; **to bestir oneself** esforzarse, menearse
**best man** *s* padrino de boda
**bestow** [bɪ'sto] *va* otorgar, conferir; emplear, dedicar
**bestowal** [bɪ'stoəl] *s* otorgamiento, donación; empleo, dedicación
**bestraddle** [bɪ'strædəl] *va* montar a horcajadas
**bestrew** [bɪ'stru] (*pret:* **-strewed;** *pp:* **-strewed** o **-strewn**) *va* desparramar, esparcir; sembrar, salpicar; estar esparcido en o por
**bestrid** [bɪ'strɪd] *pret & pp de* **bestride**
**bestridden** [bɪ'strɪdən] *pp de* **bestride**
**bestride** [bɪ'straɪd] (*pret:* **-strode** o **-strid;** *pp:* **-stridden** o **-strid**) *va* montar a horcajadas; cruzar de un tranco
**bestrode** [bɪ'strod] *pret de* **bestride**
**best seller** *s* éxito de venta; éxito de librería, libro de mayor venta; autor que más se vende
**bestud** [bɪ'stʌd] (*pret & pp:* **-studded;** *ger:* **-studding**) *va* tachonar
**bet.** abr. de **between**
**bet** [bɛt] *s* apuesta; postura (*cantidad que se apuesta*); (*pret & pp:* **bet** o **betted;** *ger:* **betting**) *va & vn* apostar; **to bet on** apostar por (*p.ej., un caballo*); **I bet** a que, apuesto a que; **you bet** (slang) ya lo creo
**beta** ['betə] o ['bitə] *s* beta
**betake** [bɪ'tek] (*pret:* **-took;** *pp:* **-taken**) *va* **to betake oneself** dirigirse; darse, aplicarse (*p.ej., al estudio*)
**betaken** [bɪ'tekən] *pp de* **betake**
**beta rays** *spl* (phys.) rayos beta
**betatron** ['betətrɑn] o ['bitətrɑn] *s* (phys.) betatrón
**betel** ['bitəl] *s* (bot.) betel
**Betelgeuse** ['bitəldʒuz] o ['bɛtəldʒʌz] *s* (astr.) Betelgeuze
**betel nut** *s* nuez de betel
**betel palm** *s* (bot.) palmera de betel
**bête noire** ['bet'nwɑr] *s* (Fr.) aversión, persona o cosa que inspira gran aversión
**Bethany** ['bɛθənɪ] *s* (Bib.) Betania
**bethel** ['bɛθəl] *s* casa de Dios, lugar santificado; iglesia o capilla para marineros; (Brit.) capilla de los disidentes
**bethink** [bɪ'θɪŋk] (*pret & pp:* **-thought**) *va* recapacitar; **to bethink oneself of** considerar, acordarse de
**Bethlehem** ['bɛθlɪəm] o ['bɛθlɪhɛm] *s* Belén
**Bethlehemite** ['bɛθlɪəmaɪt] o ['bɛθlɪhɛmaɪt] *s* betlemita
**bethought** [bɪ'θɔt] *pret & pp de* **bethink**
**Bethsaida** [bɛθ'sedə] *s* (Bib.) Betsaida
**betide** [bɪ'taɪd] *va* acontecer a; presagiar; *vn* acontecer
**betimes** [bɪ'taɪmz] *adv* temprano, pronto, con tiempo
**betoken** [bɪ'tokən] *va* indicar, anunciar, presagiar
**betony** ['bɛtənɪ] *s* (*pl:* **-nies**) (bot.) betónica
**betook** [bɪ'tʊk] *pret de* **betake**

**betray** [bɪ'tre] *va* traicionar; extraviar, violar; revelar, descubrir, mostrar
**betrayal** [bɪ'treəl] *s* traición; violación; revelación, descubrimiento
**betrayer** [bɪ'treər] *s* traicionero
**betroth** [bɪ'troð] o [bɪ'trɔθ] *va* prometer en matrimonio; **to be** o **to become betrothed** desposarse
**betrothal** [bɪ'troðəl] o [bɪ'trɔθəl] *s* desposorios, esponsales
**betrothed** [bɪ'troðd] o [bɪ'trɔθt] *s* novio, prometido
**better** ['bɛtər] *adj comp* mejor; **it is better to** + *inf* más vale + *inf;* **to grow better** mejorarse; **to make better** mejorar; *adv comp* mejor; más, p.ej., **better than a hundred** más de una centena; **had better** debería; más vale que; **to like better** preferir; **to think better of** mudar de opiníon acerca de; **you ought to know better** deberías tener vergüenza; *s* superior; ventaja; apostador; **It is changing and not for the better** Esto cambia pero no para mejorar; **This is for the better** Así es mejor, **our betters** nuestros superiores; **to get** o **to have the better of** llevar la ventaja a; *va* mejorar; aventajar; **to better oneself** mejorar su posición
**better half** *s* (hum.) cara mitad (*esposa*)
**betterment** ['bɛtərmənt] *s* mejoramiento; mejoría (*en una enfermedad*)
**better off** *adj* más acomodado, en mejores circunstancias
**bettor** ['bɛtər] *s* apostador
**Betty** ['bɛtɪ] *s* nombre abreviado de **Elizabeth**
**betulaceous** [,bɛtʃʊ'leʃəs] *adj* (bot.) betuláceo
**between** [bɪ'twin] *adv* en medio, entremedias; **in between** en medio, entremedias; *prep* entre; **between you and me** entre Vd. y yo
**between-decks** [bɪ'twin,dɛks] *s* (naut.) entrecubiertas, entrepuentes; *adv* (naut.) entre cubiertas
**between decks** *adv* (naut.) entre cubiertas
**betwixt** [bɪ'twɪkst] *adv* (archaic & poet.) en medio; **betwixt and between** entre lo uno y lo otro; *prep* (archaic & poet.) entre
**bevel** ['bɛvəl] *adj* biselado; *s* cartabón, falsa escuadra; (*pret & pp:* **-eled** o **-elled;** *ger:* **-eling** o **-elling**) *va* biselar
**bevel cut** *s* corte en bisel
**bevel edge** *s* bisel
**bevel gauge** *s* falsa escuadra
**bevel gear** *s* engranaje cónico, engranaje en bisel
**bevel protractor** *s* transportador-saltarregla
**bevel square** *s* falsa escuadra, saltarregla, baivel
**bevel wheel** *s* rueda cónica
**beverage** ['bɛvərɪdʒ] *s* bebida
**bevy** ['bɛvɪ] *s* (*pl:* **-ies**) bandada (*de aves*); grupo (*de muchachas*)
**bewail** [bɪ'wel] *va & vn* lamentar
**beware** [bɪ'wɛr] *va* guardarse de, precaverse de; *vn* tener cuidado; **to beware of** guardarse de, precaverse de; **beware!** ¡ojo!; **beware of . . .!** ¡ojo con . . .!, ¡cuidado con . . .!
**bewigged** [bɪ'wɪgd] *adj* pelucón
**bewilder** [bɪ'wɪldər] *va* aturdir, dejar perplejo
**bewilderment** [bɪ'wɪldərmənt] *s* aturdimiento, perplejidad
**bewitch** [bɪ'wɪtʃ] *va* embrujar, hechizar, encantar
**bewitching** [bɪ'wɪtʃɪŋ] *adj* hechicero, encantador
**beyond** [bɪ'jɑnd] *adv* más allá, más lejos; *prep* más allá de; además de, fuera de; no capaz de, no susceptible de; **beyond the reach of** fuera del alcance de; **beyond the seas** allende los mares; *s* **the beyond** o **the great beyond** el más allá, el otro mundo
**bezant** ['bɛzənt] o [bə'zænt] *s* bezante (*moneda*); (f.a. & her.) bezante
**bezel** ['bɛzəl] *s* bisel; faceta (*de piedra preciosa tallada*); engaste (*de una joya o una sortija*)
**bezique** [bə'zik] *s* besigue (*juego de naipes*)
**bezoar** ['bizor] *s* bezoar
**b.f.** o **bf** abr. de **bold-faced type**
**B.F.A.** abr. de **Bachelor of Fine Arts**
**bg.** abr. de **bag**
**bhang** [bæŋ] *s* (bot.) cáñamo de la India; hachich
**biangular** [baɪ'æŋgjələr] *adj* biangular
**biannual** [baɪ'ænjʊəl] *adj* semestral
**bias** ['baɪəs] *s* sesgo, diagonal; predisposición; prejuicio; (rad.) polarización negativa (*de la rejilla*); **to cut on the bias** cortar al sesgo; *adj* sesgo, diagonal; *adv* al sesgo; (*pret & pp:* **biased** o **biassed;** *ger:* **biasing** o **biassing**) *va* predisponer, prevenir
**biatomic** [,baɪə'tɑmɪk] *adj* (chem.) biatómico
**biaxial** [baɪ'æksɪəl] *adj* biaxil
**Bib.** abr. de **Bible** y **Biblical**
**bib** [bɪb] *s* babador, babero; pechera (*del delantal*)
**bib and tucker** *s* (coll.) ropa, vestido
**bibcock** ['bɪb,kɑk] *s* grifo
**bibelot** [bi'blo] o ['bɪblo] *s* objeto pequeño de lujo
**Bibl.** abr. de **Biblical** y **bibliographical**
**Bible** ['baɪbəl] *s* Biblia
**Bible Belt** *s* (U.S.A.) zona de la ortodoxia protestante
**Bible paper** *s* papel biblia
**Biblical** o **biblical** ['bɪblɪkəl] *adj* bíblico
**Biblicist** ['bɪblɪsɪst] *s* biblicista
**bibliographer** [,bɪblɪ'ɑgrəfər] *s* bibliógrafo
**bibliographic** [,bɪblɪo'græfɪk] o **bibliographical** [,bɪblɪo'græfɪkəl] *adj* bibliográfico
**bibliography** [,bɪblɪ'ɑgrəfɪ] *s* (*pl:* **-phies**) bibliografía
**bibliomania** [,bɪblɪo'menɪə] *s* bibliomanía
**bibliomaniac** [,bɪblɪo'menɪæk] *adj & s* bibliómano
**bibliophil** ['bɪblɪofɪl] o **bibliophile** ['bɪblɪofaɪl] o ['bɪblɪofɪl] *s* bibliófilo
**bibulous** ['bɪbjələs] *adj* bíbulo (*absorbente*); bebedor, borrachín
**bicameral** [baɪ'kæmərəl] *adj* bicameral
**bicarbonate** [baɪ'kɑrbənɪt] o [baɪ'kɑrbənet] *s* (chem.) bicarbonato
**bicarbonate of soda** *s* (chem.) bicarbonato sódico o de sosa
**bice** [baɪs] *s* verde mar, azul de montaña
**bicentenary** [baɪ'sɛntɪ,nɛrɪ] o [,baɪsɛn'tinərɪ] *s* (*pl:* **-ies**) bicentenario; *adj* bicentenario
**bicentennial** [,baɪsɛn'tɛnɪəl] *adj & s* bicentenario
**bicephalous** [baɪ'sɛfələs] *adj* bicéfalo
**biceps** ['baɪsɛps] *s* (anat.) bíceps
**bichlorid** [baɪ'klorɪd] o **bichloride** [baɪ'kloraɪd] o [baɪ'klorɪd] *s* (chem.) dicloruro; (chem.) cloruro mercúrico
**bichromate** [baɪ'kromet] *s* (chem.) bicromato
**bichromate cell** *s* (elec.) pila de bicromato
**bicipital** [baɪ'sɪpɪtəl] *adj* bicípite
**bicker** ['bɪkər] *s* quisquilla; charla; *vn* pararse en quisquillas; charlar; destellar
**bicolor** ['baɪ,kʌlər] o **bicolored** ['baɪ,kʌlərd] *adj* bicolor
**biconcave** [baɪ'kɑnkev] o [,baɪkɑn'kev] *adj* bicóncavo
**biconvex** [baɪ'kɑnvɛks] o [,baɪkɑn'vɛks] *adj* biconvexo
**bicuspid** [baɪ'kʌspɪd] *adj* bicúspide; (anat.) bicúspide; *s* (anat.) bicúspide
**bicuspidate** [baɪ'kʌspɪdet] *adj* bicuspidado
**bicycle** ['baɪsɪkəl] *s* bicicleta
**bicyclist** ['baɪsɪklɪst] *s* biciclista, ciclista
**bid** [bɪd] *s* oferta, postura; (bridge) envite, declaración; (*pret:* **bade** o **bid;** *pp:* **bidden;** *ger:* **bidding**) *va* mandar, ordenar; proclamar; dar (*la bienvenida*); decir (*adiós*); (*pret & pp:* **bid;** *ger:* **bidding**) *va* ofrecer; pujar, licitar; (bridge) envidar, declarar; **to bid defiance to** desafiar; **to bid up** pujar; *vn* ofrecer un precio; (bridge) envidar, declarar; **to bid fair to** + *inf* prometer + *inf*, dar indicios de + *inf*
**biddable** ['bɪdəbəl] *adj* dócil, obediente; (bridge) declarable
**bidden** ['bɪdən] *pp de* **bid**
**bidder** ['bɪdər] *s* postor; (bridge) declarante; **the highest bidder** el mejor postor
**bidding** ['bɪdɪŋ] *s* mandato; invitación; remate: (bridge) remate; **to close the bidding** (bridge) cerrar el remate; **to do the bidding of** cumplir el mandato de; **to open the bidding** (bridge) abrir el remate, abrir las declaraciones

**biddy** ['bɪdɪ] *s* (*pl:* **-dies**) pollo, gallina; (coll.) criada irlandesa
**bide** [baɪd] *va* hacer cara a; **to bide one's time** esperar la hora propicia, tomarse el tiempo; *vn* quedarse; morar
**bidentate** [baɪ'dɛntet] *adj* bidente
**biennial** [baɪ'ɛnɪəl] *adj* bienal; *s* acontecimiento bienal; planta bienal
**biennially** [baɪ'ɛnɪəlɪ] *adv* bienalmente
**biennium** [baɪ'ɛnɪəm] *s* (*pl:* **-a** [ə]) bienio
**bier** [bɪr] *s* féretro, andas
**biferous** ['bɪfərəs] *adj* (bot.) bífero
**biff** [bɪf] *s* (slang) bofetada, puñetazo; *va* (slang) dar una bofetada a, dar un puñetazo a
**bifid** ['baɪfɪd] *adj* bífido
**biflorous** [baɪ'florəs] *adj* bifloro
**bifocal** [baɪ'fokəl] *adj* bifocal; *s* lente bifocal; **bifocals** *spl* anteojos bifocales
**biform** ['baɪ,fɔrm] *adj* biforme
**bifurcate** ['baɪfərket] o [baɪ'fʌrket] *adj* bifurcado; *va* dividir en dos ramales o brazos; *vn* bifurcarse
**bifurcation** [,baɪfər'keʃən] *s* bifurcación
**big** [bɪg] *adj* (*comp:* **bigger;** *super:* **biggest**) grande; abultado; adulto; importante; engreído; preñado; **big with child** preñada; *adv* (coll.) con jactancia; **to go big** (slang) tener gran éxito; **to talk big** (slang) echar bravatas
**bigamist** ['bɪgəmɪst] *s* bígamo o bígama
**bigamous** ['bɪgəməs] *adj* bígamo
**bigamy** ['bɪgəmɪ] *s* bigamia
**big-bellied** ['bɪg,bɛlɪd] *adj* panzudo
**Big Ben** *s* campana en el reloj del Parlamento de Londres; el reloj del Parlamento
**big board** *s* (coll.) mercado de valores de Nueva York
**big-boned** ['bɪg,bond] *adj* huesudo
**big brother** *s* hermano mayor; hombre que sirve de hermano o otro; jefe de un gobierno o movimiento autoritarios
**big business** *s* (coll.) comercio acaparador
**Big Dipper** *s* (astr.) Carro mayor
**big-eared** ['bɪg,ɪrd] *adj* orejudo
**big end** *s* (mach.) cabeza de la biela
**big game** *s* caza mayor; (fig.) caza mayor
**biggish** ['bɪgɪʃ] *adj* grandote
**big gun** *s* (coll.) magnate, señorón
**big head** *s* (coll.) orgullo, envanecimiento
**big-headed** ['bɪg,hɛdɪd] *adj* cabezudo; (coll.) orgulloso, soberbio
**big-hearted** ['bɪg,hɑrtɪd] *adj* cordial, generoso
**bighorn** ['bɪg,hɔrn] *s* (zool.) carnero cimarrón de las Montañas Rocosas
**big house** *s* (slang) presidio
**bight** [baɪt] *s* codo, recodo; ensenada; gaza
**bigmouthed** ['bɪg,mauðd] o ['bɪg,mauθt] *adj* bocudo; ruidoso, hablador
**bigness** ['bɪgnɪs] *s* grandeza
**bignonia** [bɪg'nonɪə] *s* (bot.) bignonia
**big-nosed** ['bɪg,nozd] *adj* narigudo
**bigot** ['bɪgət] *s* intolerante, fanático
**bigoted** ['bɪgətɪd] *adj* intolerante, fanático
**bigotry** ['bɪgətrɪ] *s* (pl: **-ries**) intolerancia, fanatismo
**big shot** *s* (slang) personaje, señorón, persona de campanillas, señor de horca y cuchillo
**big stick** *s* palo en alto (*poder de coacción*)
**big time** *s* (slang) teatro de variedades de primera clase en las grandes ciudades; (slang) gran éxito; (slang) parranda, jaleo; **to be in the big time** (slang) asociarse con gente de influencia, tener gran éxito
**big-time** ['bɪg'taɪm] *adj* (slang) influyente, de campanillas
**big toe** *s* dedo gordo o grande del pie
**big top** *s* (coll.) techado de una tienda de circo; (coll.) circo
**big tree** *s* (bot.) secoya
**bigwig** ['bɪg,wɪg] *s* (coll.) pájaro de cuenta
**bijou** ['biʒu] *s* (*pl:* **-joux** [ʒuz]) joya; alhaja
**bijouterie** [bi'ʒutəri] *s* joyería
**bijugate** ['baɪdʒuget] o **bijugous** ['baɪdʒugəs] *adj* (bot.) biyugado
**bike** [baɪk] *s* (coll.) bici; *vn* (coll.) ir o montar en bicicleta
**bilabial** [baɪ'lebɪəl] *adj* & *s* (phonet.) bilabial
**bilabiate** [baɪ'lebɪet] *adj* (bot.) bilabiado
**bilateral** [baɪ'lætərəl] *adj* bilateral
**bilberry** ['bɪl,bɛrɪ] *s* (*pl:* **-ries**) (bot.) arándano
**bilbo** ['bɪlbo] *s* (*pl:* **-boes**) (hist.) espada, estoque; **bilboes** *spl* cepo con grillos
**bile** [baɪl] *s* (physiol. & fig.) bilis
**bile duct** *s* (anat.) conducto biliar
**bilge** [bɪldʒ] *s* (naut.) pantoque; agua de pantoque; barriga de barril; disparate, tontería; *va* combar; (naut.) desfondar; *vn* combarse; (naut.) hacer agua; (naut.) desfondarse
**bilge pump** *s* (naut.) bomba de sentina
**bilge water** *s* (naut.) agua de pantoque
**bilge ways** *spl* (naut.) anguilas
**biliary** ['bɪlɪ,ɛrɪ] *adj* biliario
**bilingual** [baɪ'lɪŋgwəl] *adj* bilingüe
**bilingualism** [baɪ'lɪŋgwəlɪzəm] *s* bilingüismo
**bilious** ['bɪljəs] *adj* bilioso; (fig.) bilioso
**bilirubin** [,bɪlɪ'rubɪn] *s* (biochem.) bilirrubina
**biliteral** [baɪ'lɪtərəl] *adj* bilítero
**biliverdin** [,bɪlɪ'vʌrdɪn] *s* (biochem.) biliverdina
**bilk** [bɪlk] *s* estafa, trampería; estafador, tramposo; *va* estafar, trampear
**bill** [bɪl] *s* cuenta, factura; billete (*que reemplaza monedas*); aviso, cartel; cartel de teatro; función de teatro; hoja suelta; cédula, escrito; proyecto de ley; (com.) giro, letra de cambio; (law) pedimento; pico (*de ave*); pica, alabarda; podadera; (naut.) uña (*de ancla*); (*cap.*) *s* nombre abreviado de **William; to fill the bill** (coll.) llenar los requisitos; **to foot the bill** (coll.) pagar la cuenta; (coll.) sufragar los gastos; *va* facturar; cargar en cuenta a; anunciar por carteles; fijar carteles en; *vn* darse el pico (*las palomas*); acariciarse (*los enamorados*); **to bill and coo** acariciarse y arrullarse (*como las palomas*)
**billboard** ['bɪl,bord] *s* cartelera
**billet** ['bɪlɪt] *s* (mil.) orden escrita de alojamiento; (mil.) lugar de alojamiento; (mil.) boleta; empleo, oficio; zoquete (*de madera*); palanquilla (*hierro de sección cuadrada*); tocho (*de hierro o acero*); *va* (mil.) alojar (*tropas*)
**billet-doux** ['bɪle'du] *s* (*pl:* **billets-doux** ['bɪle'duz]) esquela amorosa
**billfold** ['bɪl,fold] *s* billetero, cartera de bolsillo
**billhead** ['bɪl,hɛd] *s* encabezamiento de factura
**billhook** ['bɪl,huk] *s* podadera
**billiard** ['bɪljərd] *s* (coll.) carambola (*lance*); **billiards** *ssg* billar (*juego*); **to play billiards** jugar al billar
**billiard ball** *s* bola de billar
**billiard cloth** *s* paño de billar
**billiard player** *s* jugador de billar, billarista
**billiard pocket** *s* tronera de billar
**billiard table** *s* mesa de billar
**billingsgate** ['bɪlɪŋz,get] *s* lenguaje bajo y obsceno
**billion** ['bɪljən] *s* (U.S.A.) mil millones; (Brit.) billón (*un millón de millones*)
**billionaire** [,bɪljən'ɛr] *adj* & *s* billonario
**billionth** ['bɪljənθ] *adj* & *s* billonésimo
**bill of attainder** *s* (law) ley que condena a muerte civil
**bill of exchange** *s* (com.) letra de cambio
**bill of fare** *s* lista de comidas, menú
**bill of goods** *s* (com.) consignación de mercancías; **to sell a bill of goods** (coll.) dar gato por liebre
**bill of health** *s* patente de sanidad
**bill of lading** *s* (com.) conocimiento de embarque
**bill of particulars** *s* (law) declaración de hechos (*del demandante o del demandado*)
**bill of rights** *s* declaración de derechos
**bill of sale** *s* escritura de venta
**billow** ['bɪlo] *s* ondulación, oleada; *vn* ondular, hincharse
**billowy** ['bɪlo·ɪ] o ['bɪləwɪ] *adj* ondulante, hinchado
**billposter** ['bɪl,postər] *s* cartelero, fijacarteles; cartel
**billy** ['bɪlɪ] *s* (*pl:* **-lies**) cachiporra; (*cap.*) *s* nombre abreviado de **William**
**billy goat** *s* (coll.) cabrón, bode, macho cabrío
**bilocation** [,baɪlo'keʃən] *s* bilocación

**bilocular** [baɪˈlɑkjələr] *adj* bilocular
**bimetallic** [ˌbaɪmɪˈtælɪk] *adj* bimetálico; bimetalista
**bimetallism** [baɪˈmɛtəlɪzəm] *s* bimetalismo
**bimetallist** [baɪˈmɛtəlɪst] *adj & s* bimetalista
**bimonthly** [baɪˈmʌnθlɪ] *adj* bimestral o bimestre (*que se repite cada dos meses*); bimensual (*que se repite dos veces al mes*); *adv* bimestralmente; bimensualmente; *s* (*pl:* **-lies**) revista o publicación bimestre; revista o publicación bimensual
**bimotored** (baɪˈmotərd] *adj* (aer.) bimotor
**bin** [bɪn] *s* arcón, hucha; (*pret & pp:* **binned;** *ger:* **binning**) *va* guardar en arcón o hucha
**binary** [ˈbaɪnərɪ] *adj* binario
**binary star** *s* (astr.) estrella doble
**binate** [ˈbaɪnet] *adj* binado
**bination** [baɪˈneʃən] *s* (eccl.) binación
**binaural** [bɪnˈɔrəl] *adj* binaural o binauricular
**bind** [baɪnd] *s* lazo, enlace; (mus.) ligadura; (*pret & pp:* **bound**) *va* atar, ligar; unir, juntar; ceñir; enguirnaldar; ribetear; fajar; vendar (*una herida*); agavillar (*p.ej., las mieses*); encuadernar (*libros*); estreñir; contener, refrenar; obligar, precisar; escriturar; poner en aprendizaje, poner a servir; **to bind in boards** encartonar; **to bind over** (law) obligar moral o legalmente (*p.ej., a comparecer ante un juez, a mantener la paz*); *vn* atiesarse, endurecerse; agarrotarse; ser obligatorio
**binder** [ˈbaɪndər] *s* atador; (agr.) atadora, agavilladora; encuadernador; substancia aglomerante, substancia aglutinante; (mas.) perpiaño; sobretripa (*de cigarro*); (ins.) documento provisional de protección
**bindery** [ˈbaɪndərɪ] *s* (*pl:* **-ies**) encuadernación (*taller*)
**binding** [ˈbaɪndɪŋ] *adj* atador; que estriñe; obligatorio; *s* atadura; encuadernación; ribete
**binding post** *s* (elec.) borne, sujetahilo
**bindweed** [ˈbaɪndˌwid] *s* (bot.) enredadera
**bine** [baɪn] *s* sarmiento (*de la vid*); vástago de enredadera; vástago del lúpulo; lúpulo
**Binet test** [bɪˈne] *s* examen de inteligencia de Binet
**binge** [bɪndʒ] *s* (slang) jarana, borrachera; **to go on a binge** (slang) andar de jarana, tomar una borrachera
**binnacle** [ˈbɪnəkəl] *s* (naut.) bitácora
**binocle** [ˈbɪnəkəl] *s* binóculo, gemelos
**binocular** [bɪˈnɑkjələr] o [baɪˈnɑkjələr] *adj* binocular; **binoculars** *spl* prismáticos, gemelos
**binomial** [baɪˈnomɪəl] *adj* binomial, binomio; *s* (alg. & biol.) binomio
**binomial theorem** *s* (alg.) teorema binomial, binomio de Newton
**biochemical** [ˌbaɪoˈkɛmɪkəl] *adj* bioquímico
**biochemist** [ˌbaɪoˈkɛmɪst] *s* bioquímico
**biochemistry** [ˌbaɪoˈkɛmɪstrɪ] *s* bioquímica
**biodynamics** [ˌbaɪodaɪˈnæmɪks] o [ˌbaɪodɪˈnæmɪks] *ssg* biodinámica
**biog.** abr. de **biographical** y **biography**
**biogenesis** [ˌbaɪoˈdʒɛnɪsɪs] *s* (biol.) biogénesis
**biographee** [baɪˌɑgrəˈfi] o [bɪˌɑgrəˈfi] *s* biografiado
**biographer** [baɪˈɑgrəfər] o [bɪˈɑgrəfər] *s* biógrafo
**biographic** [ˌbaɪəˈgræfɪk] o **biographical** [ˌbaɪəˈgræfɪkəl] *adj* biográfico
**biography** [baɪˈɑgrəfɪ] o [bɪˈɑgrəfɪ] *s* (*pl:* **-phies**) biografía
**biol.** abr. de **biological** y **biology**
**biologic** [ˌbaɪəˈlɑdʒɪk] o **biological** [ˌbaɪəˈlɑdʒɪkəl] *adj* biológico
**biological warfare** *s* guerra biológica
**biologist** [baɪˈɑlədʒɪst] *s* biólogo
**biology** [baɪˈɑlədʒɪ] *s* biología
**biomedical** [ˌbaɪoˈmɛdɪkəl] *adj* biomédico
**biometric** [ˌbaɪoˈmɛtrɪk] o **biometrical** [ˌbaɪoˈmɛtrɪkəl] *adj* biométrico
**biometry** [baɪˈɑmɪtrɪ] *s* biometría
**biophysical** [ˌbaɪoˈfɪzɪkəl] *adj* biofísico
**biophysics** [ˌbaɪoˈfɪzɪks] *ssg* biofísica
**biopsy** [ˈbaɪɑpsɪ] *s* (med.) biopsia
**biostatic** [ˌbaɪoˈstætɪk] *adj* biostático; **biostatics** *ssg* biostática
**biostatical** [ˌbaɪoˈstætɪkəl] *adj* biostático
**biota** [baɪˈotə] *s* biota
**biotic** [baɪˈɑtɪk] o **biotical** [baɪˈɑtɪkəl] *adj* biótico
**biotite** [ˈbaɪotaɪt] *s* (mineral.) biotita
**biotype** [ˈbaɪotaɪp] *s* (biol.) biotipo
**biparous** [ˈbɪpərəs] *adj* (bot. & zool.) bíparo
**bipartisan** [baɪˈpɑrtɪzən] *adj* de (los) dos partidos políticos
**bipartite** [baɪˈpɑrtaɪt] *adj* bipartido o bipartito
**biped** [ˈbaɪpɛd] *adj & s* bípedo
**bipetalous** [baɪˈpɛtələs] *adj* (bot.) bipétalo
**bipinnate** [baɪˈpɪnet] *adj* (bot.) bipinado
**biplane** [ˈbaɪˌplen] *s* (aer.) biplano
**bipolar** [baɪˈpolər] *adj* bipolar
**birch** [bʌrtʃ] *s* (bot.) abedul; férula, palmatoria; *va* varear
**birchen** [ˈbʌrtʃən] *adj* de abedul, hecho de abedul
**bird** [bʌrd] *s* ave o pájaro; (slang) sujeto, tío, tipo; **the bird has flown** voló el golondrino; **to kill two birds with one stone** matar dos pájaros de una pedrada; **bird in the hand** pájaro en mano; **bird of ill omen** pájaro de mal agüero; **birds of a feather** pájaros de una misma pluma, gente de una calaña; *vn* andar a caza de pájaros
**bird bath** *s* baño para pájaros
**bird cage** *s* jaula
**bird call** *s* reclamo
**bird dog** *s* perro de ajeo, perro cobrador de aves
**birdie** [ˈbʌrdɪ] *s* avecilla, pajarillo
**birdlime** [ˈbʌrdˌlaɪm] *s* liga, ajonje
**birdman** [ˈbʌrdˌmæn] o [ˈbʌrdmən] *s* (*pl:* **-men**) (coll.) aviador
**bird of paradise** *s* ave del paraíso
**bird of passage** *s* ave de paso; (fig.) ave de paso
**bird of peace** *s* paloma (*que simboliza la paz*)
**bird of prey** *s* ave de rapiña
**birdseed** [ˈbʌrdˌsid] *s* alpiste, cañamones
**bird's-eye view** [ˈbʌrdzˌaɪ] *s* vista de pájaro, vista a ojo de pájaro
**bird shot** *s* perdigones
**birdwoman** [ˈbʌrdˌwʊmən] *s* (*pl:* **-women**) (coll.) aviadora o aviatriz
**birectangular** [ˌbaɪrɛkˈtæŋgjələr] *adj* birrectángulo
**birefringence** [ˌbaɪrɪˈfrɪndʒəns] *s* birrefringencia
**bireme** [ˈbaɪrim] *adj & s* birreme
**biretta** [bɪˈrɛtə] *s* birreta
**birth** [bʌrθ] *s* nacimiento; parto; camada, lechigada; linaje, alcurnia; **by birth** de nacimiento; **to give birth to** parir, dar el ser a, dar a luz
**birth certificate** *s* partida de nacimiento
**birth control** *s* control de los nacimientos, esterilidad voluntaria
**birthday** [ˈbʌrθˌde] *s* natal; cumpleaños, aniversario del nacimiento; aniversario (*de cualquier suceso*)
**birthday present** *s* cuelga, regalo de cumpleaños
**birthmark** [ˈbʌrθˌmɑrk] *s* marca de nacimiento
**birthplace** [ˈbʌrθˌples] *s* patria, suelo nativo, lugar de nacimiento, casa natal
**birth rate** *s* natalidad
**birthright** [ˈbʌrθˌraɪt] *s* derechos de nacimiento; primogenitura
**birthstone** [ˈbʌrθˌston] *s* piedra preciosa que simboliza las influencias del mes en que uno ha nacido
**birthwort** [ˈbʌrθˌwʌrt] *s* (bot.) aristoloquia
**bis** [bɪs] *adv* (mus.) bis
**Bisayan** [bɪˈsɑjən] *adj & s* bisayo o visayo
**Bisayas** [bɪˈsɑjɑs] *spl* islas Bisayas o Visayas
**Biscay** [ˈbɪske] o [ˈbɪskɪ] *s* Vizcaya
**Biscayan** [bɪsˈkeən] o [ˈbɪskeən] *adj & s* vizcaíno
**biscuit** [ˈbɪskɪt] *s* bizcocho (*pan y loza*)
**bisect** [ˈbaɪsɛkt] *s* (philately) sello cortado por la mitad; [baɪˈsɛkt] *va* dividir en dos partes; (geom.) bisecar; (philately) cortar por la mitad; *vn* empalmar (*p.ej., dos caminos*)
**bisection** [baɪˈsɛkʃən] *s* división en dos partes; (geom.) bisección
**bisector** [baɪˈsɛktər] *s* (geom.) bisectriz
**bisexual** [baɪˈsɛkʃʊəl] *adj & s* bisexual

**bishop** [ˈbɪʃəp] *s* (eccl.) obispo; alfil (*en el juego de ajedrez*)
**bishopric** [ˈbɪʃəprɪk] *s* obispado
**bishop's-weed** [ˈbɪʃəps,wid] *s* (bot.) ameos, biznaga
**bismuth** [ˈbɪzməθ] *s* (chem.) bismuto
**bismutite** [ˈbɪzmətaɪt] *s* (mineral.) bismutita
**bison** [ˈbaɪsən] o [ˈbaɪzən] *s* (zool.) bisonte
**bisque** [bɪsk] *s* sopa de cangrejos; sopa hecha con espárragos, tomates, etc., pasados por un tamiz; helado hecho con almendrados y nueces molidas; bizcocho (*loza sin barniz*)
**bissextile** [bɪˈsɛkstɪl] *adj & s* bisiesto
**bister** [ˈbɪstər] *s* (paint.) bistre
**bistort** [ˈbɪstɔrt] *s* (bot.) bistorta
**bistoury** [ˈbɪsturɪ] *s* (*pl:* **-ries**) (surg.) bisturí
**bisulfate** [baɪˈsʌlfet] *s* (chem.) bisulfato
**bisulfid** [baɪˈsʌlfɪd] o **bisulfide** [baɪˈsʌlfaɪd] o [baɪˈsʌlfɪd] *s* (chem.) bisulfuro
**bisulfite** [baɪˈsʌlfaɪt] *s* (chem.) bisulfito
**bisyllabic** [,baɪsɪˈlæbɪk] *adj* bisílabo
**bit** [bɪt] *s* pedacito, pizca, poquito; bocado (*de comida*); ratito; bocado, freno; hoja de corte; barrena; paletón (*de llave*); soldador (*punta del instrumento*); **a good bit** una buena cantidad; **not a bit** ni pizca; **to blow to bits** hacer pedazos; **to take the bit in the teeth** desbocarse; rebelarse; **two bits** (coll.) veinte y cinco centavos; **bit by bit** poco a poco; *pret de* **bite;** (*pret & pp:* **bitted;** *ger:* **bitting**) *va* enfrenar; contener, refrenar
**bitch** [bɪtʃ] *s* perra, zorra, loba; (vulg.) mujer, mujer de mal genio, ramera; (slang) queja; *va* (slang) chapucear, echar a perder; *vn* (slang) quejarse
**bite** [baɪt] *s* mordedura; picadura (*de ave o insecto*); resquemo (*sensación picante en la lengua*); bocado; tentempié, refrigerio; (print.) lardón (*blanco en la impresión*); **to take a bite** morder; comer algo; (*pret:* **bit;** *pp:* **bit** o **bitten**) *va* morder; picar (*los peces, los insectos, etc.*); resquemar (*un alimento*); comerse (*las uñas*); **to bite off** quitar mordiendo; *vn* morder; picar; resquemar; (slang) picar (*tragar el anzuelo, caer en el lazo*); **to bite at** querer morder
**biting** [ˈbaɪtɪŋ] *adj* penetrante; mordaz, picante, acre
**bit part** *s* (theat.) papel de ínfima importancia
**bit player** *s* (theat.) parte de por medio
**bitstock** [ˈbɪt,stɑk] *s* berbiquí, manubrio de taladro
**bitt** [bɪt] *s* (naut.) bita; *va* (naut.) abitar
**bitten** [ˈbɪtən] *pp de* **bite**
**bitter** [ˈbɪtər] *adj* amargo; encarnizado, p.ej., **a bitter struggle** una lucha encarnizada; **to taste bitter** ser de gusto amargo; **to the bitter end** hasta el extremo; hasta la muerte; *adv* (dial.) picantemente; **bitter cold** (dial.) frío cortante; *s* amargo, amargura; **bitters** *spl* bítter
**bitter almond** *s* (bot.) almendro amargo; almendra amarga (*semilla*)
**bitter-end** [ˈbɪtərˈɛnd] *adj* (coll.) intransigente, irreconciliable
**bitter-ender** [ˈbɪtərˈɛndər] *s* (coll.) persona intransigente, persona irreconciliable
**bitterish** [ˈbɪtərɪʃ] *adj* algo amargo
**bitterling** [ˈbɪtərlɪŋ] *s* (ichth.) bermejuela
**bittern** [ˈbɪtərn] *s* (orn.) avetoro, ave toro; agua madre de la cristalización de la sal; composición amarga de cuasia, tabaco, cocculus indicus para adulterar la cerveza
**bitterness** [ˈbɪtərnɪs] *s* amargor, amargura; encarnizamiento (*p.ej., de una lucha*)
**bitter pill** *s* lance humillante
**bittersweet** [ˈbɪtər,swit] *s* mezcla de lo dulce y lo amargo; (bot.) dulcamara; (bot.) evónimo norteamericano. *adj* dulce y amargo a la vez, agridulce; semidulce (*chocolate*)
**bitter vetch** *s* (bot.) yero, alcareña
**bitterwood** [ˈbɪtər,wʊd] *s* (bot. & pharm.) cuasia de Jamaica; (bot.) cuasia amarga; (pharm.) cuasia
**bitterwort** [ˈbɪtər,wʌrt] *s* (bot.) genciana amarilla, gencianilla; (bot.) diente de león
**bitumen** [bɪˈtjumən] o [bɪˈtumən] *s* betún
**bituminize** [bɪˈtjumɪnaɪz] o [bɪˈtumɪnaɪz] *va* embetunar, convertir en betún
**bituminous** [bɪˈtjumɪnəs] o [bɪˈtumɪnəs] *adj* bituminoso
**bituminous coal** *s* carbón bituminoso
**bivalence** [baɪˈveləns] o [ˈbɪvələns] *s* (chem.) bivalencia
**bivalent** [baɪˈvelənt] o [ˈbɪvələnt] *adj* (chem.) bivalente
**bivalve** [ˈbaɪ,vælv] *adj* bivalvo; *s* (zool.) molusco bivalvo
**bivouac** [ˈbɪvʊæk] o [ˈbɪvwæk] *s* vivaque; (*pret & pp:* **-acked;** *ger:* **-acking**) *vn* vivaquear
**biweekly** [baɪˈwiklɪ] *adj* quincenal; bisemanal; *adv* quincenalmente; bisemanalmente; *s* (*pl:* **-lies**) revista o publicación quincenal o bisemanal
**bixaceous** [bɪkˈseʃəs] *adj* (bot.) bixáceo
**biyearly** [baɪˈjɪrlɪ] *adj* semestral; *adv* semestralmente
**bizarre** [bɪˈzɑr] *adj* raro, extravagante
**bk.** abr. de **bank, block** y **book**
**bkg.** abr. de **banking**
**bkt.** abr. de **basket**
**bl.** abr. de **bale** y **barrel**
**b.l.** abr. de **bill of lading**
**B.L.** abr. de **Bachelor of Laws**
**blab** [blæb] *s* chisme, hablilla; chismoso; (*pret & pp:* **blabbed;** *ger:* **blabbing**) *va* chismear, soltar indiscretamente; *vn* chismear, vaciarse
**black** [blæk] *adj* negro; ceñudo; *adv* con ceño, p.ej., **to look black at** mirar con ceño; *s* negro; luto; *va* ennegrecer; embetunar, limpiar (*los zapatos*); **to black out** apagar (*las luces*); obscurecer (*una estancia*) contra el bombardeo aéreo; *vn* ennegrecer; **to black out** apagar las luces; desmayarse, perder el sentido; **to black up** pintarse de negro
**black amber** *s* ámbar negro
**blackamoor** [ˈblækəmʊr] *s* (offensive) negro
**black-and-blue** [ˈblækəndˈblu] *adj* amoratado, lívido, acardenalado
**black-and-blue mark** *s* cardenal
**black and white** *s* dibujo en blanco y negro; **in black and white** en blanco y negro (*por escrito*)
**black-and-white** [ˈblækəndˈhwaɪt] *adj* en blanco y negro
**black-and-white creeper** o **warbler** *s* (orn.) reinita trepadora, silvia blanquinegra
**black art** *s* magia negra, nigromancia
**blackball** [ˈblæk,bɔl] *s* bola negra; *va* bolear, dar bola negra a
**black bass** [bæs] *s* (ichth.) micróptero
**black bear** *s* (zool.) baribal; (zool.) oso del Tibet
**black-bellied plover** [ˈblæk,bɛlɪd] *s* (orn.) chorlito gris, chorlito playero
**black belt** *s* región muy fértil de los estados de Alabama y Misisipí, EE.UU.; (U.S.A.) región donde hay más negros que blancos
**blackberry** [ˈblæk,berɪ] *s* (*pl:* **-ries**) (bot.) zarza; zarzamora (*fruto*)
**blackbird** [ˈblæk,bʌrd] *s* (orn.) mirlo
**blackboard** [ˈblæk,bord] *s* pizarra, encerado
**black book** *s* lista negra
**black bread** *s* pan negro
**blackcap** [ˈblæk,kæp] *s* ave de cabeza negra; (orn.) curruca de cabeza negra; (bot.) frambuesa negra; (bot.) espadaña
**blackdamp** [ˈblæk,dæmp] *s* (min.) mofeta
**Black Death** *s* peste negra (*del siglo XIV*)
**black diamond** *s* diamante negro (*carbonado*); **black diamonds** *spl* carbón de piedra
**black drum** *s* (ichth.) corvina negra
**blacken** [ˈblækən] *va* ennegrecer; denigrar, desacreditar; *vn* ennegrecer
**black eye** *s* ojo amoratado por un golpe; (coll.) mala fama, descrédito
**black-eyed** [ˈblæk,aɪd] *adj* ojinegro
**black-eyed bean** *s* (bot.) caragilate, garrubia, judía de carete, frijol de ojos negros
**black-eyed Susan** *s* (bot.) rudbequia; (bot.) ojo de poeta, ojo de Venus (*Thunbergia alata*)
**blackface** [ˈblæk,fes] *adj* carinegro; *s* actor que se pinta de negro; pintura que se emplea para hacer el papel de negro; (print.) letra negrilla
**blackfish** [ˈblæk,fɪʃ] *s* (ichth.) tautoga; (zool.) cabeza de olla
**black flag** *s* bandera negra (*de los piratas*)

**black fly** *s* (ent.) jején (*del género Simulium*)
**Black Forest** *s* Selva Negra (*en Alemania*)
**Black Friar** *s* fraile negro (*dominico*)
**Black Friday** *s* viernes aciago; viernes santo
**black grouse** *s* (orn.) gallo de bosque
**blackguard** ['blægɑrd] *s* bribón, pillo, tunante; *va* injuriar, vilipendiar
**blackguardly** ['blægɑrdlɪ] *adj* bribón, pillo, tunante
**black-haired** ['blæk,hɛrd] *adj* pelinegro
**Black Hand** *s* mano negra
**blackhead** ['blæk,hɛd] *s* (path.) espinilla, comedón; (orn.) coquinero; (vet.) enterohepatitis infecciosa
**black-hearted** ['blæk,hɑrtɪd] *adj* malvado, perverso
**blacking** ['blækɪŋ] *s* ennegrecimiento; betún (*para dar lustre a los zapatos*)
**blackish** ['blækɪʃ] *adj* negruzco
**blackjack** ['blæk,dʒæk] *s* cachiporra con puño flexible; escudilla de metal charolado; veintiuna (*juego de naipes*); bandera negra (*de los piratas*); (bot.) roble norteamericano (*Quercus marilandica*); *va* aporrear
**black lead** [lɛd] *s* grafito, plombagina
**blackleg** ['blæk,lɛg] *s* petardista, fullero; (Brit.) esquirol; (vet.) morriña negra
**black letter** *s* (print.) letra gótica; (print.) letra negrilla
**black-letter** ['blæk,lɛtər] *adj* (print.) gótico; (print.) impreso en negrilla; aciago, infausto
**black list** *s* lista negra
**black-list** ['blæk,lɪst] *va* poner en la lista negra
**black magic** *s* magia negra, nigromancia
**blackmail** ['blæk,mel] *s* chantaje; dinero obtenido por chantaje; *va* amenazar con chantaje; arrancar dinero por chantaje a (*una persona*)
**blackmailer** ['blæk,melər] *s* chantajista
**Black Maria** [mə'raɪə] *s* (coll.) coche celular
**black mark** *s* marca negra (*de censura*); mala nota (*de los estudiantes*)
**black market** *s* estraperlo, mercado negro
**black marketeer** *s* estraperlista
**black martin** *s* (orn.) vencejo
**black measles** *s* (path.) sarampión hemorrágico, sarampión negro
**Black Monk** *s* monje negro (*benedictino*)
**blackness** ['blæknɪs] *s* negrura
**black nightshade** *s* (bot.) hierba mora
**black oak** *s* (bot.) cuercitrón
**blackout** ['blæk,aʊt] *s* apagón (*para la defensa antiaérea*); (theat.) apagamiento de luces; visión negra (*ceguera repentina y pasajera de los aviadores*); pérdida de la memoria
**black pepper** *s* (bot.) pimentero; pimienta negra (*fruto*)
**blackpoll** ['blæk,pol] *s* (orn.) reinita cabeza negra
**black pope** *s* papa negro
**black poplar** *s* (bot.) álamo negro
**black powder** *s* pólvora negra
**Black Prince** *s* Príncipe negro
**black pudding** *s* morcilla
**black race** *s* raza negra
**black sanicle** *s* (bot.) astrancia mayor
**black scoter** *s* (orn.) negreta
**Black Sea** *s* mar Negro
**black sheep** *s* oveja negra, (el) malo entre los buenos
**black shirt** *s* camisa negra (*fascista*)
**blacksmith** ['blæk,smɪθ] *s* herrero; herrador (*de caballos*)
**blacksmith welding** *s* soldadura de forja
**blacksnake** ['blæk,snek] *s* (zool.) culebra de color prieto (*Zamenis constrictor*); látigo de cuero retorcido
**black spruce** *s* (bot.) variedad de pícea (*Picea mariana*)
**blacktail** ['blæk,tel] *s* (zool.) ciervo mulo, bura
**black tea** *s* té negro
**blackthorn** ['blæk,θɔrn] *s* (bot.) espino negro, acacia bastarda, endrino; porra o bastón hecho de la rama del endrino
**black tie** *s* corbata de smoking, media etiqueta
**black top** *s* superficie bituminosa
**black vomit** *s* (path.) vómito negro
**black walnut** *s* (bot.) nogal negro
**black whale** *s* (zool.) calderón, cabeza de olla
**black widow** *s* (ent.) araña hembra (*Latrodectus mactans*)
**bladder** ['blædər] *s* (anat.) vejiga; vejiga (*saco de goma o de piel*)
**bladder green** *s* verdevejiga
**bladder senna** *s* (bot.) espantalobos
**bladderwort** ['blædər,wʌrt] *s* (bot.) utricularia
**blade** [bled] *s* hoja (*de un arma o instrumento*); espada (*arma o persona*); hojita de hierba, tallo de hierba; (bot.) lámina, limbo (*de una hoja*); aleta (*de hélice*); pala (*de remo, de la azada, etc.*); (elec.) cuchilla (*de un interruptor*); gallardo joven, buen mozo
**bladed** ['bledɪd] *adj* que tiene hoja u hojas
**bladesmith** ['bled,smɪθ] *s* espadero
**blah** [blɑ] *s* (slang) pamplina, nonada; *interj* (slang) ¡bah!
**blain** [blen] *s* ampolla, úlcera
**blamable** ['blemәbәl] *adj* culpable
**blame** [blem] *s* culpa; **to put the blame on someone for something** echar la culpa a uno de una cosa; *va* culpar; **to be to blame for** tener la culpa de
**blameless** ['blemlɪs] *adj* inculpable, intachable
**blameworthy** ['blem,wʌrðɪ] *adj* culpable
**blanch** [blæntʃ] o [blɑntʃ] *va* blanquear; blanquecer (*p.ej., la plata*); (cook. & hort.) blanquear; hacer pálido; *vn* blanquear; palidecer
**Blanch** o **Blanche** [blæntʃ] o [blɑntʃ] *s* Blanca
**blancmange** [blə'mɑnʒ] *s* manjar blanco
**bland** [blænd] *adj* blando
**blandish** ['blændɪʃ] *va* engatusar, lisonjear
**blandishment** ['blændɪʃmənt] *s* engatusamiento, lisonja
**blank** [blæŋk] *adj* en blanco (*no escrito o impreso*); blanco (*vacío, hueco*); ciego (*obstruído, cerrado*), p.ej., **blank key** llave ciega; confuso, turbado; insípido, sin interés; entero, cabal; vago, p.ej., **blank stare** mirada vaga; *s* blanco; papel blanco; formulario; cospel (*disco para hacer moneda*); tejo (*para ser estampado*); *va* esconder; borrar, cancelar; obstruir; estampar (*una chapa de metal*); (sport) impedir (*a uno*) que gane ni un solo tanto
**blank cartridge** *s* cartucho en blanco, cartucho sin bala
**blank check** *s* cheque en blanco; (fig.) carta blanca
**blanket** ['blæŋkɪt] *s* manta; capa (*p.ej., de niebla*); (fig.) manto; *adj* combinado, general, comprensivo; *va* cubrir con manta; cubrir, obscurecer; mantear; (mil. & nav.) atajar (*el fuego enemigo*) interponiendo un buque o tropas amigas; (naut.) quitar el viento a (*un buque*); (rad.) neutralizar, paralizar (*un radiorreceptor*) por medio de ondas perturbadoras
**blank signature** *s* firma en blanco
**blank verse** *s* verso blanco, libre o suelto
**blare** [blɛr] *s* fragor; son de trompetas; resplandor, color muy brillante; *va* tocar o sonar con mucho ruido; vociferar; *vn* hacer estruendo, resonar
**blarney** ['blɑrnɪ] *s* zalamerías; *va* hacer zalamerías a; *vn* hacer zalamerías
**blasé** [blɑ'ze] o ['blɑze] *adj* hastiado, indiferente
**blaspheme** [blæs'fim] *va* blasfemar contra; *vn* blasfemar; **to blaspheme against** blasfemar contra
**blasphemous** ['blæsfɪməs] *adj* blasfemo
**blasphemy** ['blæsfɪmɪ] *s* (*pl:* **-mies**) blasfemia
**blast** [blæst] o [blɑst] *s* ráfaga (*de aire o viento*); chorro (*de aire, agua, arena, etc.*); soplo (*de un fuelle*); toque o sonido (*de bocina, trompeta, pito, etc.*); carga de pólvora, carga de barreno; explosión, voladura; arruinamiento; tizón, añublo (*honguillo parásito*); **at** o **in full blast** en plena marcha; *va* volar (*p.ej., con dinamita*); arruinar; atizonar, añublar; maldecir, infamar; **to blast open** abrir con explosivos; **to blast out** arrojar (*al enemigo*) con explosivos; *vn* atizonar, añublarse
**blasted** ['blæstɪd] o ['blɑstɪd] *adj* arruinado; marchito; maldito
**blastema** [blæs'timə] *s* (*pl:* **-mata** [mətə]) (embryol.) blastema
**blast furnace** *s* alto horno

**blasting** ['blæstɪŋ] o ['blɑstɪŋ] *s* voladura; arruinamiento; atizonamiento (*de los cereales*)
**blasting cap** *s* (min.) detonador, casquete explosivo
**blasting machine** *s* explosor
**blastocoele** ['blæstəsil] *s* (embryol.) blastocele
**blastocyst** ['blæstəsɪst] *s* (embryol.) blastocisto
**blastoderm** ['blæstədʌrm] *s* (embryol.) blastodermo
**blastoff** ['blæst,ɔf] o ['blɑst,ɔf] *s* lanzamiento de cohete
**blastula** ['blæstʃulə] *s* (*pl:* **-lae** [li]) (embryol.) blástula
**blast wave** *s* onda de choque (*de una explosión nuclear*)
**blat** [blæt] (*pret & pp:* **blatted;** *ger:* **blatting**) *va* decir o soltar sin consideración y con mucho ruido; *vn* balar; hablar sin consideración y con mucho ruido
**blatancy** ['bletənsɪ] *s* vocinglería; molestia
**blatant** ['bletənt] *adj* vocinglero; molesto, intruso
**blather** ['blæðər] *s* charla, disparate; *vn* charlar
**blatherskite** ['blæðərskaɪt] *s* (coll.) hablador, charlatán
**blaze** [blez] *s* llamarada, llama muy brillante; hoguera; incendio; luz brillante; resplandor; explosión (*de cólera*); estrella (*en la frente del caballo o la vaca*); señal hecha en los árboles para servir de guía; **in a blaze** en llamas, resplandeciente; *va* encender, inflamar; marcar (*los árboles*) con cortes y señales para que sirvan de guía; publicar, proclamar; **to blaze a trail** abrir o marcar una senda; *vn* encenderse, arder con llama; resplandecer; **to blaze away** (coll.) comenzar o continuar a tirar; (coll.) seguir criticando, regañando, etc.
**blazer** ['blezər] *s* (sport) chaqueta ligera de franela o seda
**blazon** ['blezən] *s* blasón; ostentación, boato; *va* blasonar; adornar, decorar; publicar, proclamar; exhibir, mostrar
**blazonry** ['blezənrɪ] *s* blasón; decoración brillante
**bldg.** abr. de **building**
**bleach** [blitʃ] *s* blanqueo; blanquimento; *va* blanquear, blanquear al sol o con la acción química; *vn* blanquear; palidecer
**bleacher** ['blitʃər] *s* blanqueador; blanquimiento; **bleachers** *spl* (sport) gradas al aire libre
**bleachery** ['blitʃərɪ] *s* (*pl:* **-ies**) blanquería
**bleaching powder** *s* polvos de blanqueo, polvos de gas
**bleak** [blik] *adj* desierto, solitario; sombrío, triste, frío, helado
**blear** [blɪr] *adj* turbio, legañoso; *va* enturbiar; engañar
**bleareye** ['blɪr,aɪ] *s* (path.) legaña
**blear-eyed** ['blɪr,aɪd] *adj* enturbiado, legañoso; torpe de entendimiento
**bleary** ['blɪrɪ] *adj* (*comp:* **-ier;** *super:* **-iest**) turbio, legañoso
**bleat** [blit] *s* balido; *vn* balar
**bleb** [blɛb] *s* ampolla; burbuja
**bled** [blɛd] *pret & pp de* **bleed**
**bleed** [blid] (*pret & pp:* **bled**) *va* sangrar; sacar dinero a; **to bleed white** desangrar; arrancar hasta el último céntimo a; *vn* sangrar; verter su sangre, sufrir, morir; exudar (*las plantas*); llorar (*la vid*); penar, afligirse; **to bleed to death** morir de desangramiento
**bleeder** ['blidər] *s* sangrador; hemofílico; (mach.) dispositivo de sangrar
**bleeding heart** *s* (bot.) dicentra
**blemish** ['blɛmɪʃ] *s* mancha, tacha; lunar; *va* manchar
**blench** [blɛntʃ] *va* blanquear; *vn* acobardarse, recular; palidecer
**blend** [blɛnd] *s* mezcla, combinación; armonía; (*pret & pp:* **blended** o **blent**) *va* mezclar, combinar; armonizar; fusionar; *vn* mezclarse, combinarse; armonizar; fusionarse
**blende** [blɛnd] *s* (mineral.) blenda (*sulfuro de cinc*); (mineral.) sulfuro de brillo metaloideo
**blending** ['blɛndɪŋ] *s* mezcla, combinación; armonía; (philol.) cruce de palabras, fusión de voces
**blennorrhea** [,blɛnə'riə] *s* (path.) blenorrea
**blenny** ['blɛnɪ] *s* (*pl:* **-nies**) (ichth.) blenia
**blent** [blɛnt] *pret & pp de* **blend**
**blepharitis** [,blɛfə'raɪtɪs] *s* (path.) blefaritis
**bless** [blɛs] (*pret & pp:* **blessed** o **blest**) *va* bendecir; amparar, proteger; **bless my soul!** ¡válgame Dios!
**blessed** ['blɛsɪd] *adj* bendito, bienaventurado, santo, feliz; (for emphasis) santo, p.ej., **the whole blessed day** todo el santo día; maldito, p.ej., **to not know a blessed thing about the matter** no saber maldita la cosa del asunto; [blɛst] *pret & pp de* **bless**
**blessedness** ['blɛsɪdnɪs] *s* bienaventuranza, santidad, felicidad
**Blessed Virgin** *s* Santísima Virgen
**blessing** ['blɛsɪŋ] *s* bendición
**blest** [blɛst] *pret & pp de* **bless**
**blether** ['blɛðər] *s & vn* var. de **blather**
**blew** [blu] *pret de* **blow**
**blight** [blaɪt] *s* roya; (fig.) plaga, infortunio, daño grave; *va* atizonar, añublar; arruinar; frustrar (*las esperanzas*); *vn* atizonar
**blimp** [blɪmp] *s* pequeño dirigible no rígido
**blind** [blaɪnd] *adj* ciego; oculto, secreto; obscuro; (arch.) ciego (*dícese, p.ej., de una ventana o puerta*); (fig.) ciego, p.ej., **blind with anger** ciego de ira; **blind with jealousy** ciego con celos; **blind as a bat** más ciego que un topo; **blind of** o **in one eye** que no ve con un ojo, tuerto; *s* velo; venda (*para los ojos*); anteojera (*para los ojos del caballo*); disfraz, subterfugio, pretexto; estor, transparente de resorte; persiana; pantalla (*persona que encubre a otra*); (fort.) blinda; escondrijo del cazador; **to be a blind for someone** (slang) ser pantalla o tapadera de alguien; *va* cegar; deslumbrar
**blindage** ['blaɪndɪdʒ] *s* (fort.) blindaje
**blind alley** *s* callejón sin salida; (fig.) atolladero
**blind date** *s* (slang) cita a ciegas (*cita entre un muchacho y una muchacha que no se conocen*)
**blinder** ['blaɪndər] *s* anteojera
**blind flying** *s* (aer.) vuelo a ciegas
**blindfold** ['blaɪnd,fold] *adj* vendado (*de ojos*); deslumbrado; descuidado, atolondrado; *s* venda en los ojos; *va* vendar los ojos a
**blind landing** *s* (aer.) aterrizaje a ciegas
**blind man** *s* ciego
**blindman's buff** ['blaɪndmænz] *s* gallina ciega (*juego*)
**blindness** ['blaɪndnɪs] *s* ceguedad
**blind spot** *s* (anat.) punto ciego; (rad.) lugar ciego; (fig.) punto acerca de que uno, sin darse cuenta de ello, tiene pocos informes o mucho prejuicio
**blind stitch** *s* puntada invisible
**blindstitch** ['blaɪnd,stɪtʃ] *va* coser a puntadas invisibles
**blind-tool** ['blaɪnd'tul] *va* (b.b.) estampar en seco
**blind tooling** *s* (b.b.) estampación en seco
**blindworm** ['blaɪnd,wʌrm] *s* (zool.) lución
**blink** [blɪŋk] *s* mirada, vista; guiñada, parpadeo; **on the blink** (slang) incapacitado; (slang) desconcertado; *va* guiñar (*el ojo*); desconocer; señalar por luz intermitente; *vn* guiñar, parpadear; mirar con los ojos entreabiertos; oscilar (*la luz*)
**blinker** ['blɪŋkər] *s* anteojera; proyector de destellos; (naut.) señales por luz intermitente (*con el alfabeto Morse*); (slang) ojo
**blip** [blɪp] *s* (radar) bache (*indicación visual*)
**bliss** [blɪs] *s* bienaventuranza, felicidad
**blissful** ['blɪsfəl] *adj* bienaventurado, muy feliz
**blister** ['blɪstər] *s* ampolla, vejiga; *va* ampollar, avejigar; censurar acerbamente; *vn* ampollarse, avejigarse
**blister beetle** *s* (ent.) cantárida, abadejo
**blister gas** *s* gas vesicante
**blister pearl** *s* perla de ampolla
**blister plaster** *s* vejigatorio
**blithe** [blaɪð] o [blaɪθ] o **blithesome** ['blaɪðsəm] o ['blaɪθsəm] *adj* alegre, gozoso, animado
**blitz** [blɪts] *s & va* (coll.) var. de **blitzkrieg**
**blitzkrieg** ['blɪts,krig] *s* guerra relámpago; *va* atacar con guerra relámpago, arrasar por bombardeo aéreo

**blizzard** ['blɪzərd] *s* ventisca
**bloat** [blot] *va* hinchar; ahumar, curar al humo (*el arenque*); *vn* hincharse, abotagarse
**bloater** ['blotər] *s* arenque ahumado
**blob** [blɑb] *s* gota, burbuja; burujo
**bloc** [blɑk] *s* (pol.) bloque
**block** [blɑk] *s* bloque, zoquete, canto; tajo (*para partir la carne; sobre el cual se cortaba la cabeza a los reos*); plataforma en que se hace venta pública; plataforma en que se vendían los esclavos en subasta; (mach.) bloque (*de cilindros*); horma, cáliz (*pieza de madera torneada que usan los sombrereros*); polea, garrucha; (naut.) motón; (print.) bloque; (rail.) tramo; bloque (*tableta para apuntes*); cepo (*de yunque*); cuadrado; manzana (*de una ciudad*); cuadrito (*de sellos de correo*); estorbo, obstáculo; grupo, conjunto; (pol.) bloque; **blocks** *spl* piezas de madera de construcciones infantiles; **to go to the block** ir a ser decapitado; venderse en pública subasta; *va* cegar, cerrar, obstruir; bloquear; conformar (*un sombrero*); calzar (*una rueda*); parar (*una pelota, una jugada*); **to block in** o **to block out** delinear, esbozar; **to block up** cegar, tapar, taponar; apoyar mediante trozos de madera o piedra
**blockade** [blɑ'ked] *s* (mil. & naut.) bloqueo; obstrucción; **to run the blockade** (naut.) burlar, forzar o violar el bloqueo; *va* (mil. & naut.) bloquear; obstruir
**blockade runner** *s* (naut.) forzador de bloqueo
**block and tackle** *s* aparejo de poleas, polea con aparejo
**block anesthesia** *s* anestesia de bloque, anestesia regional
**blockbuster** ['blɑk,bʌstər] *s* (coll.) bomba rompemanzanas
**blockhead** ['blɑk,hɛd] *s* zoquete, zopenco, tonto
**blockhouse** ['blɑk,haus] *s* (fort.) blocao
**blockish** ['blɑkɪʃ] *adj* tonto, estúpido
**block plane** *s* cepillo de contrafibra
**block printing** *s* impresión de plancha de madera
**block signal** *s* (rail.) señal de tramo
**block system** *s* (rail.) sistema de tramos
**blocky** ['blɑkɪ] *adj* rechoncho; dividido en cuadrados alternados de luz y sombra
**blond** [blɑnd] *adj* rubio, blondo; *s* rubio (*hombre rubio*)
**blonde** [blɑnd] *adj* rubio, blondo; *s* rubia (*mujer rubia*)
**blond lace** *s* blonda
**blood** [blʌd] *s* sangre; jugo o zumo; efusión de sangre, matanza; ira, cólera; temperamento; vida; hombre animoso; libertino; caballo de pura raza; **in cold blood** a sangre fría; **to draw blood** hacer correr sangre; **to have one's blood run cold** helársele a uno la sangre
**blood bank** *s* banco de sangre
**blood brother** *s* hermano carnal; hermano por mezcla de sangre
**blood count** *s* (med.) recuento sanguíneo
**bloodcurdling** ['blʌd,kʌrdlɪŋ] *adj* horripilante, espeluznante
**blood donor** *s* donador de sangre, donante de sangre
**blood group** *s* grupo sanguíneo
**bloodguilty** ['blʌd,gɪltɪ] *adj* culpable del derramamiento de sangre, culpable de homicidio
**blood heat** *s* calor de la sangre
**bloodhound** ['blʌd,haund] *s* sabueso; (slang) sabueso (*detective*)
**bloodless** ['blʌdlɪs] *adj* exangüe, desangrado, desanimado; insensible; sin efusión de sangre
**bloodletting** ['blʌd,lɛtɪŋ] *s* sangría, flebotomía
**blood money** *s* dinero que se paga por el derramamiento de sangre; dinero que se paga como indemnización por el derramamiento de sangre
**blood orange** *s* naranja sanguínea o roja
**blood plasma** *s* plasma sanguíneo
**blood poisoning** *s* (path.) envenenamiento de la sangre (*septicemia, toxemia, piohemia*)
**blood pressure** *s* presión sanguínea, tensión arterial
**blood pudding** *s* morcilla
**blood red** *s* color rojo sangre
**blood relation** *s* pariente consanguíneo
**blood relationship** *s* consanguinidad
**blood relative** *s* var. de **blood relation**
**bloodroot** ['blʌd,rut] o ['blʌd,rut] *s* (bot.) sanguinaria del Canadá; (bot.) tormentila
**blood royal** *s* sangre real
**bloodshed** ['blʌd,ʃɛd] *s* efusión de sangre, matanza
**bloodshot** ['blʌd,ʃɑt] *adj* ensangrentado, inyectado de sangre
**bloodstained** ['blʌd,stend] *adj* manchado de sangre, homicida
**bloodstone** ['blʌd,ston] *s* (mineral.) restañasangre; (mineral.) hematites
**blood stream** *s* corriente sanguínea
**bloodsucker** ['blʌd,sʌkər] *s* (zool.) sanguijuela; (fig.) sanguijuela; (fig.) sablista, gorrista
**blood test** *s* análisis de sangre
**bloodthirsty** ['blʌd,θʌrstɪ] *adj* sanguinario
**blood transfusion** *s* transfusión sanguínea o transfusión de sangre
**blood vessel** *s* (anat.) vaso sanguíneo; **to burst a blood vessel** reventarse una vena
**bloody** ['blʌdɪ] *adj* (*comp:* **-ier**; *super:* **-iest**) sangriento; sanguíneo; (Brit. slang) maldito; *adv* (Brit. slang) muy; (*pret & pp:* **-ied**) *va* ensangrentar; herir
**Bloody Mary** *s* La Sanguinaria (*María I, reina de Inglaterra*)
**bloom** [blum] *s* florescencia, florecimiento; flor; lozanía; (found.) changote; (found.) tocho (*barra*); masa de vidrio candente; *vn* florecer; lozanear
**bloomer** ['blumər] *s* (slang) gazapatón (*en el hablar*); **bloomers** *spl* calzones cortos y holgados de mujer
**blooming** ['blumɪŋ] *adj* floreciente, lozano
**blooming mill** *s* (found.) laminadero desbastador de tochos
**bloomy** ['blumɪ] *adj* (*comp:* **-ier**; *super:* **-iest**) floreciente, lozano; lleno de polvillo
**bloop** [blup] *s* (mov.) ruido de empalme
**blossom** ['blɑsəm] *s* flor; brote, pimpollo; florescencia; **in blossom** en cierne; *vn* florecer; brotar
**blossomy** ['blɑsəmɪ] *adj* lleno de flores, lleno de botones
**blot** [blɑt] *s* borrón (*mancha de tinta*); (fig.) borrón, mancha; (*pret & pp:* **blotted**; *ger:* **blotting**) *va* borrar, emborronar; manchar; secar con papel secante; **to blot out** borrar; *vn* borrarse, emborronarse; echar borrones (*una pluma*)
**blotch** [blɑtʃ] *s* manchón; erupción (*en la piel*); *va* emborronar, cubrir con manchones; cubrir con erupciones
**blotchy** ['blɑtʃɪ] *adj* (*comp:* **-ier**; *super:* **-iest**) lleno de manchones; lleno de erupciones
**blot on the escutcheon** *s* borrón en el escudo, mancha en el honor de uno
**blotter** ['blɑtər] *s* teleta; borrador, libro borrador
**blotting paper** *s* papel secante
**blotto** ['blɑto] *adj* (slang) borracho perdido
**blouse** [blaus] o [blauz] *s* blusa
**blow** [blo] *s* golpe; soplo, soplido; ventarrón; toque, trompetazo; estocada (*cosa que ocasiona dolor*); (bot.) florescencia; (metal.) hornada; larva de mosca depositada en carne; (slang) fanfarrón; **at one blow** de un solo golpe; **to come to blows** venir a las manos; **without striking a blow** sin dar un golpe, sin esfuerzo ninguno; se traduce a menudo al español por medio del sufijo **-azo**, p.ej., **blow of a horn** bocinazo; **blow with the fist** puñetazo ‖ (*pret:* **blew**; *pp:* **blown**) *va* soplar; limpiar o vaciar a soplos; sonar o tocar (*un instrumento de viento o un silbato*); silbar (*un silbato*); volar, hacer saltar; sonarse (*las narices*); desalentar; depositar larvas en (*carne*); quemar (*un fusible*); echar (*flores*); divulgar; (slang) malgastar (*dinero*); (slang) convidar; **to blow down** derribar; **to blow in** (metal.) dar fuego a, poner a funcionar; (slang) malgastar (*dinero*); **to blow open** abrir; abrir con explosivos; **to blow out** hacer salir soplando; apagar soplando; quemar (*un fusible*); **to blow up** volar, hacer saltar; soplar, inflar; (phot.) ampliar ‖ *vn* soplar; sonar; jadear, resoplar; (zool.)

soplar (*echar agua la ballena*); quemarse (*un fusible*); abrirse (*las flores*); (slang) fanfarronear; (slang) irse, marcharse; **to blow hot and cold** estar entre sí y no; **to blow in** (slang) llegar inesperadamente; **to blow off** escaparse (*el vapor*); descargarse (*una caldera*); (slang) fanfarronear; **to blow on** (slang) delatar, traicionar; **to blow open** abrirse (*por causa del viento*); **to blow out** apagarse (*por causa del viento*); quemarse (*un fusible*); reventar (*un neumático*); **to blow over** pasar; ser olvidado; **to blow shut** cerrarse (*por causa del viento*); **to blow up** volarse, reventarse; fracasar; (slang) estallar o reventar (*de ira*)

**blower** ['bloər] *s* soplador (*persona y máquina; cetáceo*)

**blowfly** ['blo,flaɪ] *s* (*pl:* **-flies**) (ent.) moscarda

**blowgun** ['blo,gʌn] *s* cerbatana, bodoquera

**blowhole** ['blo,hol] *s* respiradero; (found.) sopladura, venteadura, escarabajo; (zool.) espiráculo; agujero en el hielo adonde vienen las ballenas, focas, etc. para respirar

**blown** [blon] *adj* agotado, desalentado; corrompido por las moscas; *pp de* **blow**

**blown glass** *s* vidrio soplado

**blowoff** ['blo,ɔf] o ['blo,ɑf] *s* escape (*p.ej., de vapor*); (slang) fanfarrón

**blowout** ['blo,aʊt] *s* reventón, estalladura; (elec.) quemadura (*de fusible*); (slang) banquete, tertulia concurrida

**blowout patch** *s* (aut.) parche para neumático

**blowpipe** ['blo,paɪp] *s* soplete; cerbatana, bodoquera

**blowtorch** ['blo,tɔrtʃ] *s* lámpara de soldar, antorcha a soplete

**blowup** ['blo,ʌp] *s* explosión; (fig.) explosión (*de ira o cólera*); (phot.) ampliación

**blowy** ['blo·ɪ] *adj* (*comp:* **-ier;** *super:* **-iest**) ventoso; ligero

**blowzy** ['blaʊzɪ] *adj* (*comp:* **-ier;** *super:* **-iest**) desaliñado, desmelenado; coloradote

**bls.** abr. de **barrels**

**blubber** ['blʌbər] *s* grasa de ballena; grasa (*de una persona o animal*); lloro ruidoso; *va* decir llorando ruidosamente; *vn* llorar con mucho ruido, llorar hasta hincharse los carrillos

**blubber lip** *s* bezo

**blucher** ['blukər] o ['blutʃər] *s* zapato de orejas sueltas

**bludgeon** ['blʌdʒən] *s* cachiporra; *va* aporrear; amedrentar, intimidar

**blue** [blu] *adj* (*comp:* **bluer;** *super:* **bluest**) azul; amoratado, lívido; abatido, triste; **to turn blue** azular; azularse; *s* azul, color azul; **the blue** el cielo; el mar; **the blues** la morriña; (*pret & pp:* **blued;** *ger:* **bluing** o **blueing**) *va* azular; añilar, dar azulete a (*la ropa blanca*); pavonar (*el hierro o el acero*); *vn* azularse

**blue baby** *s* niño azul

**Bluebeard** ['blu,bɪrd] *s* Barba Azul

**bluebell** ['blu,bɛl] *s* (bot.) campánula

**blueberry** ['blu,bɛrɪ] *s* (*pl:* **-ries**) (bot.) vaccinio

**bluebird** ['blu,bʌrd] *s* (orn.) pájaro azul (*Sialia sialis*); (orn.) tempestad, ventura (*Sialia mexicana*)

**blue-black** ['blu'blæk] *adj* negro azulado, azul obscuro

**blue blood** *s* sangre azul (*sangre noble*); (coll.) aristócrata

**blue-blooded** ['blu,blʌdɪd] *adj* de sangre azul

**bluebonnet** ['blu,bɑnɪt] *s* bonete azul; (bot.) azulejo, aciano

**blue book** *s* (coll.) anuario de la alta sociedad; (U.S.A.) registro de empleados del gobierno; (U.S.A.) librito de exámenes; (Brit.) libro azul (*que contiene documentos diplomáticos*)

**bluebottle** ['blu,bɑtəl] *s* (bot.) aciano, azulejo; (ent.) moscarda, mosca de color azul metálico

**blue cheese** *s* queso de vaca, semejante al queso de Roquefort y de fabricación norteamericana

**bluecoat** ['blu,kot] *s* policía (*que lleva uniforme azul*)

**blue devils** *spl* abatimiento, melancolía; delirio debido al abuso del alcohol

**bluefish** ['blu,fɪʃ] *s* (ichth.) pomátomo saltador, anchoa de banco

**blue flag** *s* (bot.) lirio azul

**bluegrass** ['blu,græs] o ['blu,grɑs] *s* (bot.) gramínea norteamericana de tallo verde azulado (*del género Poa*)

**blue grosbeak** *s* (orn.) alondra azul

**blue gum** *s* (bot.) eucalipto

**blueing** ['bluɪŋ] *s & ger* var. de **bluing**

**bluejacket** ['blu,dʒækɪt] *s* marinero de buque de guerra

**bluejay** ['blu,dʒe] *s* (orn.) gayo

**blue laws** *spl* (U.S.A.) leyes puritánicas severas

**blue lead** [lɛd] *s* (mineral.) galena; plomo azul (*pigmento*)

**Blue Monday** *s* lunes que precede a la Cuaresma; lunes, día triste por la necesidad de volver al trabajo

**Blue Nile** *s* Nilo Azul

**blue-pencil** ['blu'pɛnsəl] (*pret & pp:* **-ciled** o **-cilled;** *ger:* **-ciling** o **-cilling**) *va* marcar, corregir o borrar con lápiz azul

**bluepoint** ['blu,pɔɪnt] *s* ostra pequeña (*que se come cruda*)

**blueprint** ['blu,prɪnt] *s* cianotipia; cianotipo; (fig.) plan detallado; *va* copiar a la cianotipia

**blue racer** *s* (zool.) culebra de color azulado (*Coluber constrictor flaviventris*)

**blue ribbon** *s* cinta azul concedida al que gana el primer premio; divisa azul de una sociedad contra el uso del alcohol; (naut.) gallardete azul (*trofeo*); (Brit.) cinta de terciopelo azul (*de la Orden de la Jarretera*)

**blue-ribbon** ['blu'rɪbən] *adj* muy perito, muy inteligente; de capacidad especial

**blue-sky law** ['blu'skaɪ] *s* (coll.) ley para impedir la venta de acciones u obligaciones sin valor

**bluestocking** ['blu,stɑkɪŋ] *s* (coll.) marisabidilla

**bluestone** ['blu,ston] *s* arenisca azulada; (chem.) piedra azul

**blue streak** *s* (coll.) rayo; **to talk a blue streak** (coll.) soltar la tarabilla

**bluet** ['bluɪt] *s* (bot.) azulejo, aciano; (bot.) houstonia cerúlea

**blue titmouse** *s* (orn.) herrerillo, trepatroncos

**blue vitriol** *s* (chem.) vitriolo azul

**blueweed** ['blu,wid] *s* (bot.) viborera

**blue wildebeest** *s* (zool.) ñu

**blue-winged teal** ['blu,wiŋd] *s* (orn.) pato chiquito, pato zarcel

**bluff** [blʌf] *adj* escarpado; brusco, francote; *s* peñasco escarpado, risco; falsas apariencias; amenaza que no se puede realizar; fanfarrón; **to call someone's bluff** cogerle la palabra a uno; *va* tratar de engañar con falsas apariencias, tratar de intimidar con amenazas que no se pueden realizar; *vn* blufar, fanfarronear, baladronear

**bluffer** ['blʌfər] *s* fanfarrón

**bluffing** ['blʌfɪŋ] *s* fanfarronada, baladronada, faramalla

**bluing** ['bluɪŋ] *s* añil, azulete, pasta para lavandera; pavonado; *ger de* **blue**

**bluish** ['bluɪʃ] *adj* azulado, azulino

**blunder** ['blʌndər] *s* disparate, desatino, patochada; *va* chapucear, chafallar; descolgarse con, decir desatinadamente; *vn* disparatar, desatinar; **to blunder into, on** o **upon** tropezar con, hallar por accidente

**blunderbuss** ['blʌndərbʌs] *s* trabuco; desatinado (*el que habla o procede sin juicio*)

**blunderer** ['blʌndərər] *s* desatinado

**blunt** [blʌnt] *adj* embotado, despuntado; obtuso, lerdo; franco, brusco, directo; *va* embotar, despuntar; *vn* embotarse, despuntarse

**bluntness** ['blʌntnɪs] *s* embotadura; franqueza, brusquedad

**blur** [blʌr] *s* obscuridad; forma confusa; mancha, borrón; (*pret & pp:* **blurred;** *ger:* **blurring**) *va* empañar, velar; manchar; *vn* empañarse, velarse

**blurb** [blʌrb] *s* anuncio efusivo

**blurry** ['blʌrɪ] *adj* manchado, confuso, borroso; grasiento

**blurt** [blʌrt] *va* descolgarse con, soltar a tontas y a locas; **to blurt out** descolgarse con, soltar a tontas y a locas

**blush** [blʌʃ] *s* rubor, sonrojo; color de rosa; **at first blush** a primera vista; *vn* ruborizarse, sonrojarse, ponerse colorado
**blushing** ['blʌʃɪŋ] *adj* ruboroso; *s* rubor, sonrojo
**bluster** ['blʌstər] *s* borrasca ruidosa; ruido tempestuoso; tempestad de gritos; jactancia, fanfarronada; *va* hacer con gritos y violencia, decir con gritos y violencia; forzar, intimidar; conseguir por gritos y violencia; *vn* bramar, soplar con furia (*el viento*); fanfarronear, pavonearse, bravear
**blustery** ['blʌstərɪ] *adj* tempestuoso, ruidoso; fanfarrón
**blvd.** abr. de **boulevard**
**boa** ['boə] *s* (zool.) boa; boa (*prenda de pieles o plumas*)
**boa constrictor** *s* (zool.) boa, boa constrictor
**Boadicea** [,boədɪ'siə] *s* Boadicea
**boar** [bor] *s* (zool.) verraco; (zool.) jabalí (*Sus scrofa*)
**board** [bord] *s* tabla, plancha; tablero; tablilla (*para anuncios*); (elec.) cuadro; cartón; mesa; junta, consejo; pensión; canto, borde; (naut.) bordo; (naut.) bordada (*camino entre dos viradas*); **bound in boards** en cartoné, encartonado; **on board** (naut.) a bordo; en el tren; **the boards** las tablas (*la escena del teatro*); **to go by the boards** (naut.) caer por el costado del buque; fracasar; ser echado a un lado, ser abandonado; **to tread the boards** ser actor o actriz, representar un papel; *va* entablar, enmaderar; dar de comer u hospedar regularmente bajo pago; subir a (*un tren*); (naut.) embarcarse en; (naut.) abordar; *vn* hacer las comidas, hospedarse regularmente bajo pago; (naut.) dar de bordadas; (naut.) navegar de bolina
**board and lodging** *s* cuarto y comida, pensión completa
**boarder** ['bordər] *s* huésped; interno (*en una escuela*); (naut.) abordador
**board foot** *s* pie de tabla (*unidad que equivale a una tabla de un pie cuadrado y de un espesor de una pulgada*)
**boarding** ['bordɪŋ] *s* tablazón; entablado; tabique de tablas; (naut.) abordaje
**boarding house** *s* casa de huéspedes
**boarding school** *s* internado
**board measure** *s* medida de tabla (*cuya unidad es el pie de tabla*)
**Board of Admiralty** *s* (Brit.) ministerio de Marina
**board of directors** *s* directorio, junta directiva
**board of health** *s* junta de sanidad
**board of trade** *s* junta de comercio; (*caps.*) *s* (Brit.) ministerio de Comercio
**board of trustees** *s* junta de síndicos, consejo de administración
**board room** *s* sala de junta; sala del tablero indicador de las cotizaciones de bolsa
**boardwalk** ['bord,wɔk] *s* paseo entablado a la orilla del mar
**boarhound** ['bor,haund] *s* perro jabalinero
**boarish** ['borɪʃ] *adj* cochino, puerco; lascivo; cruel
**boast** [bost] *s* jactancia, baladronada; *va* jactarse de; ostentar; *vn* jactarse; **it is nothing to boast of** no es cosa para jactarse
**boastful** ['bostfəl] *adj* jactancioso
**boat** [bot] *s* barco, embarcación, nave; buque, navío; bote; barca, lancha; salsera (*vasija para la salsa*); **in the same boat** en una misma situación, corriendo los mismos peligros; **to burn one's boats** quemar las naves; *va* poner a bordo, llevar a bordo; **to boat oars** desarmar los remos; *vn* ir o pasear en bote
**boat bridge** *s* puente de barcas
**boat hook** *s* bichero
**boathouse** ['bot,haus] *s* casilla de botes
**boating** ['botɪŋ] *s* paseo en barco
**boatload** ['bot,lod] *s* barcada
**boatman** ['botmən] *s* (*pl:* **-men**) barquero; botero (*patrón*)
**boat race** *s* regata
**boatswain** ['bosən] o ['bot,swen] *s* (naut.) contramaestre
**boatswain's chair** *s* asiento colgante; (naut.) guindola
**boatswain's mate** *s* (naut.) segundo contramaestre
**bob** [bɑb] *s* sacudida, meneo brusco; cola cortada de un caballo; pelo cortado corto; lenteja (*de la péndola del reloj*); plomo (*peso de una plomada*); corcho (*de una caña de pescar*); (Brit. slang) chelín; (*cap.*) *s* nombre abreviado de **Robert**; (*pret & pp:* **bobbed**; *ger:* **bobbing**) *va* cortar corto; menear bruscamente, *vn* menearse, agitarse; **to bob at o for an apple** tratar de coger con la boca una manzana colgada de un hilo o que flota en el agua; **to bob up** dejarse ver repentina e inesperadamente; **to bob up and down** fluctuar, subir y bajar con sacudidas cortas
**bobbin** ['bɑbɪn] *s* carrete; canilla, broca (*de la máquina de coser*)
**bobbinet** [,bɑbɪ'nɛt] o ['bɑbɪnɛt] *s* bobiné
**bobbin lace** *s* encaje de bolillos
**bobby** ['bɑbɪ] *s* (*pl:* **-bies**) (Brit. slang) policía
**bobby pin** *s* horquilla de puntas apretadas para el cabello
**bobbysocks** ['bɑbɪ,sɑks] *spl* (coll.) tobilleras (*de jovencita*)
**bobbysoxer** ['bɑbɪ,sɑksər] *s* (coll.) tobillera
**bobcat** ['bɑb,kæt] *s* (zool.) lince
**bobolink** ['bɑbəlɪŋk] *s* (orn.) chambergo
**bobsled** ['bɑb,slɛd] *s* bob-sleigh; (*pret & pp:* **-sledded**; *ger:* **-sledding**) *vn* descender en bob-sleigh
**bobsleigh** ['bɑb,sle] *s & vn* var. de **bobsled**
**bobstay** ['bɑb,ste] *s* (naut.) barbiquejo
**bobtail** ['bɑb,tel] *adj* rabón; escaso, incompleto; *s* cola corta; cola cortada; animal rabón; *va* cortar muy corta la cola a
**bobwhite** ['bɑb'hwaɪt] *s* (orn.) colín de Virginia
**Boche** o **boche** [bɑʃ] o [boʃ] *s* (slang) boche (*alemán*)
**bock** [bɑk] o **bock beer** *s* cerveza de marzo (*cerveza muy fuerte de color obscuro*)
**bode** [bod] *va & vn* presagiar, prefigurar, indicar por señales; **to bode ill** ser un mal presagio; **to bode well** ser un buen presagio; *pret de* **bide**
**bodice** ['bɑdɪs] *s* almilla, jubón, corpiño; cinturón ancho
**bodiless** ['bɑdɪlɪs] *adj* incorporal, incorpóreo; sin tronco
**bodily** ['bɑdɪlɪ] *adj* corporal, corpóreo; *adv* en persona; en conjunto, todos juntos
**bodkin** ['bɑdkɪn] *s* espadilla (*para sujetar el pelo de las mujeres*); aguja de jareta; punzón (*para abrir ojales*); (obs.) daga, puñal
**Bodleian** [bɑd'liən] o ['bɑdlɪən] *s* biblioteca bodleyana (*de Oxford*)
**body** ['bɑdɪ] *s* (*pl:* **-ies**) cuerpo; tronco (*de un árbol*); nave (*de una iglesia*); caja; carrocería (*de un coche o carro*); extensión (*de agua*); masa (*de aire*); (coll.) persona; **to keep body and soul together** seguir viviendo; (*pret & pp:* **-ied**) *va* informar, dar cuerpo a; espesar (*un líquido*); **to body forth** dar forma a, representar; presagiar
**body and fender repairman** *s* (aut.) chapista carrocero, mecánico chapista
**bodyguard** ['bɑdɪ,gɑrd] *s* guardia de corps; guardaespaldas; salvaguardia
**body politic** *s* entidad política
**body snatcher** *s* ladrón de cadáveres
**body temperature** *s* temperatura del cuerpo
**Boeotia** [bi'oʃə] *s* Beocia
**Boeotian** [bi'oʃən] *adj* beocio; (fig.) beocio (*torpe, estúpido*); *s* beocio
**Boer** [bor] o [bur] *adj & s* bóer
**Boer War** *s* guerra del Transvaal
**bog** [bɑg] *s* pantano; (*pret & pp:* **bogged**; *ger:* **bogging**) *vn* atascarse, hundirse; **to bog down** atascarse, hundirse
**bog asphodel** *s* (bot.) abama
**bogey** ['bogɪ] *s* duende, demonio; coco; aversión, persona que inspira gran aversión; (golf) norma de perfección
**bogeyman** ['bogɪ,mæn] *s* (*pl:* **-men**) duende; coco
**boggle** ['bɑgəl] *s* chapucería; desatino, disparate; *vn* asustarse, vacilar; retroceder; chapucear

**boggy** ['bɑgɪ] *adj* (*comp:* **-gier**; *super:* **-giest**) pantanoso
**bogie** ['bogɪ] *s* duende, demonio; coco; aversión, persona que inspira gran aversión; (golf) norma de perfección; (Brit. rail.) bogie
**bogle** ['bogəl] o ['bɑgəl] *s* duende, demonio; coco; aversión
**bogus** ['bogəs] *adj* (U.S.A.) falso, fingido, espurio
**bogy** ['bogɪ] *s* (*pl:* **-gies**) duende, demonio; coco; aversión, persona que inspira gran aversión
**Bohemia** [bo'himɪə] *s* Bohemia
**Bohemian** [bo'himɪən] *adj & s* bohemio; (fig.) bohemio
**Bohemianism** [bo'himɪənɪzəm] *s* bohemia, vida de bohemio
**boil** [bɔɪl] *s* ebullición, hervor; cocción; (path.) divieso; **to bring to a boil** calentar (*el agua*) hasta que hierva: **to come to a boil** comenzar a hervir; *va* herventar; hacer hervir (*el agua*); **to boil down** reducir hirviendo; reducir a su más simple expresión; *vn* hervir, bullir, cocer; (fig.) hervir (*una persona*); **to boil away** consumirse (*un líquido*) a fuerza de cocer, **to boil down** reducirse hirviendo; reducirse; **to boil over** rebosar con la ebulición; **to boil up** borbollar
**boiler** ['bɔɪlər] *s* caldera; hervidor; termosifón (*para calentar agua y para calentar por medio de agua caliente*)
**boilermaker** ['bɔɪlər,mekər] *s* calderero
**boiler plate** *s* plancha de caldera
**boiler room** *s* sala de calderas
**boiler shell** *s* casco o cuerpo de caldera
**boiler tube** *s* tubería de caldera
**boiling** ['bɔɪlɪŋ] *adj* hirviente; *s* ebullición, hervor
**boiling point** *s* punto de ebullición; **at the boiling point** muy encolerizado
**boisterous** ['bɔɪstərəs] *adj* alborotado, ruidoso, turbulento, bullicioso
**Bokhara** [bo'kɑrə] *s* Bujara (*ciudad*); la Bujara (*estado*)
**Bol.** abr de **Bolivia**
**bold** [bold] *adj* audaz, osado, atrevido, arrojado; impudente, descarado; temerario; vigoroso; acantilado, escarpado; **to make bold to** + *inf* osar + *inf*, tomar la libertad de + *inf*
**boldface** ['bold,fes] *s* individuo descarado; (print.) negrilla
**boldine** ['bɑldin] o ['bɑldɪn] *s* (pharm.) boldina
**boldness** ['boldnɪs] *s* audacia, osadía, arrojo; impudencia, descaro; temeridad; vigor
**bole** [bol] *s* tronco de árbol
**bolero** [bo'lɛro] *s* (*pl:* **-ros**) bolero (*baile y música, chaquetilla de señora*)
**boletus** [bo'litəs] *s* (bot.) boleto
**Boleyn, Anne** ['bʊlɪn] Ana Bolena
**bolide** ['bolaɪd] o ['bolɪd] *s* (astr.) bólido
**Bolivia** [bo'lɪvɪə] *s* Bolivia
**Bolivian** [bo'lɪvɪən] *adj & s* boliviano
**boll** [bol] *s* (bot.) cápsula de algodón o lino
**Bollandist** ['bɑləndɪst] *s* bolandista
**bollard** ['bɑlərd] *s* (naut.) bolardo
**boll weevil** *s* (ent.) picudo, gorgojo del algodón
**bollworm** ['bol,wʌrm] *s* (zool.) larva de una mariposa que causa grandes estragos al maíz y el algodón (*Heliothis armigera*)
**Bologna** [bə'lonjə] *s* Bolonia
**boloney** [bə'lonɪ] *s* var. de **baloney**
**Bolshevik** ['bɑlʃəvɪk] o ['bolʃəvɪk] *adj* bolchevique; *s* (*pl:* **-viki** ['vikɪ] o **-viks**) bolchevique
**Bolshevism** ['bɑlʃəvɪzəm] o ['bolʃəvɪzəm] *s* bolchevismo o bolcheviquismo
**Bolshevist** ['bɑlʃəvɪst] o ['bolʃəvɪst] *adj & s* bolchevista, bolcheviquista
**Bolshevistic** o **bolshevistic** [,bɑlʃə'vɪstɪk] o [,bolʃə'vɪstɪk] *adj* bolchevista, bolcheviquista
**Bolshevization** o **bolshevization** [,bɑlʃəvɪ'zeʃən] o [,bolʃəvɪ'zeʃən] *s* bolchevización
**Bolshevize** o **bolshevize** ['bɑlʃəvaɪz] o ['bolʃəvaɪz] *va* bolchevizar
**bolster** ['bolstər] *s* almohadón; travesaño (*para la cabecera de la cama*); refuerzo, sostén, soporte; *va* apoyar con almohadón; apoyar, sostener; **to bolster up** apoyar, sostener; animar, alentar
**bolt** [bolt] *s* perno; cerrojo, pestillo, pasador; grillete; cuadrillo (*saeta*); chorro cilíndrico (*de agua*); rayo; fuga, salto repentino; rollo (*de tela o papel*); bolo alimenticio; ataque, argumento; disidencia (*de un partido político*); **to shoot one's bolt** hacer (*uno*) todo cuanto en él cabe; *adv* repentinamente; directamente; **bolt upright** enhiesto, derecho y rígido; *va* acerrojar; empernar; amarrar con grillos; deglutir de una vez; descolgarse con; cerner, cribar, tamizar; arrojar; disidir de (*un partido político*); separar, examinar, escudriñar; *vn* lanzarse, salir de repente; desbocarse (*un caballo*); disidir; **to bolt in** entrar de repente; **to bolt off** u **out** salir de repente
**bolter** ['boltər] *s* caballo desbocado; disidente (*en asuntos políticos*); criba, tamiz
**bolt from the blue** *s* rayo en cielo sin nubes; (fig.) acontecimiento inesperado
**boltrope** ['bolt,rop] *s* (naut.) relinga
**bolus** ['boləs] *s* bolo (*píldora gruesa u otra masa esférica*)
**bomb** [bɑm] *s* bomba; (fig.) acontecimiento inesperado, sorpresa inquietante; *va* bombear
**bombard** [bɑm'bɑrd] *va* bombardear; (phys.) bombardear; (fig.) asediar (*p.ej., de preguntas*)
**bombardier** [,bɑmbər'dɪr] *s* bombardero
**bombardment** [bɑm'bɑrdmənt] *s* bombardeo
**bombasine** [,bɑmbə'zin] o ['bɑmbəzin] *s* alepín
**bombast** ['bɑmbæst] *s* ampulosidad
**bombastic** [bɑm'bæstɪk] *adj* ampuloso
**bombastically** [bɑm'bæstɪkəlɪ] *adv* ampulosamente
**bombazine** [,bɑmbə'zin] o ['bɑmbəzin] *s* alepín
**bomb bay** *s* (aer.) compartimiento de las bombas
**bomb crater** *s* (mil.) embudo de bomba
**bomber** ['bɑmər] *s* bombardero (*tripulante y avión*)
**bombing** ['bɑmɪŋ] *s* bombeo, bombardeo
**bombproof** ['bɑm,pruf] *adj* a prueba de bombas
**bomb release** *s* (aer.) lanzabombas, disparador de bombas
**bombshell** ['bɑm,ʃɛl] *s* bomba; sorpresa asoladora; **to fall like a bombshell** caer como una bomba
**bomb shelter** *s* refugio antiaéreo
**bombsight** ['bɑm,saɪt] *s* (aer.) mira de bombardero, visor
**bona fide** ['bonə 'faɪdɪ] *adj & adv* de buena fe
**bonanza** [bo'nænzə] *s* (min.) bonanza; (fig.) bonanza (*prosperidad*)
**Bonapartist** ['bonə,pɑrtɪst] *s* bonapartista
**bonbon** ['bɑn,bɑn] *s* bombón
**bond** [bɑnd] *s* enlace, lazo, unión, vínculo; contrato; bono, obligación; caución, fianza; fiador; depósito de mercancías hasta el pago de los impuestos; (mas.) aparejo, trabazón; conexión eléctrica de dos carriles; **bonds** *spl* cadenas, grillos; cautiverio; **in bond** en depósito bajo fianza; *va* hipotecar; obligar por fianza; depositar (*mercancías*) hasta pago de los impuestos; enlazar, unir
**bondage** ['bɑndɪdʒ] *s* cautiverio, esclavitud, servidumbre
**bonded** ['bɑndɪd] *adj* consolidado, afianzado con bonos; depositado bajo fianza
**bonded warehouse** *s* depósito comercial
**bonderize** ['bɑndəraɪz] *va* (trademark) bonderizar
**bondholder** ['bɑnd,holdər] *s* obligacionista, tenedor de bonos
**bondmaid** ['bɑnd,med] *s* esclava
**bondman** ['bɑndmən] *s* (*pl:* **-men**) esclavo
**bond servant** *s* esclavo
**bondsman** ['bɑndzmən] *s* (*pl:* **-men**) fiador
**bondstone** ['bɑnd,ston] *s* (mas.) perpiaño
**bondwoman** ['bɑnd,wʊmən] *s* (*pl:* **-women**) esclava
**bone** [bon] *s* hueso; espina (*de los peces*); barba de ballena; armazón (*p.ej., de un buque*); **bones** *spl* esqueleto; huesos (*restos mortales*); castañuelas; (coll.) dados; **to feel in one's bones** estar seguro de (*una cosa*) sin saber por qué;

**to have a bone to pick with** tener que habérselas con; **to make no bones about** (coll.) no andarse con rodeos en; *va* desosar; quitar las espinas a; emballenar (*un corsé*); abonar con huesos molidos; *vn* (slang) estudiar con ahinco; **to bone up on** (slang) estudiar (*una cosa*) con ahinco, empollar sobre

**boneblack** [ˈbonˌblæk] *s* negro animal, carbón animal

**bone-dry** [ˈbonˈdraɪ] *adj* enteramente seco; (coll.) absolutamente abstemio; (coll.) sin venta de licor

**bonehead** [ˈbonˌhɛd] *s* (slang) mentecato, zopenco

**bone lace** *s* encaje de bolillos

**boneless** [ˈbonlɪs] *adj* mollar; desosado; sin espinas

**bone meal** *s* huesos molidos, harina de huesos

**bone of contention** *s* materia de discordia, manzana de la discordia

**boner** [ˈbonər] *s* (slang) patochada, plancha, error

**boneset** [ˈbonˌsɛt] *s* (bot.) eupatorio; (bot.) consuelda

**bonfire** [ˈbɑnˌfaɪr] *s* hoguera, fogata

**bonhomie** [ˌbɑnoˈmi] *s* bonhomía, buen natural

**Boniface** [ˈbɑnɪfes] *s* Bonifacio; (*l.c.*) *s* hostelero, dueño de una posada

**bonito** [boˈnito] *s* (*pl:* **-tos** o **-toes**) (ichth.) bonito

**bon mot** [bõˈmo] *s* (*pl:* **bons mots** [bõˈmo]) donaire, agudeza

**bonne** [bɑn] o [bʌn] *s* niñera; criada

**bonnet** [ˈbɑnɪt] *s* papalina; gorra escocesa; penacho de plumas (*de los pieles rojas norteamericanos*); (naut.) boneta; (anat. & fort.) bonete; sombrerete (*de chimenea*); (aut.) cubierta, capó; *va* cubrir (*la cabeza*)

**bonnie** o **bonny** [ˈbɑnɪ] *adj* (*comp:* **-nier;** *super:* **-niest**) (Scottish) bonito, lindo, excelente, lozano

**bonnyclabber** [ˈbɑnɪˌklæbər] *s* leche cuajada

**bonus** [ˈbonəs] *s* prima, extra, plus; (bridge) bonificación

**bon voyage** [bõvwɑˈjɑʒ] *interj* ¡buen viaje!

**bony** [ˈbonɪ] *adj* (*comp:* **-ier;** *super:* **-iest**) osudo, huesudo; óseo, huesoso; descarnado; espinoso (*pez*)

**bonze** [bɑnz] *s* bonzo (*sacerdote del culto de Buda*)

**boo** [bu] *s* abucheo; bu; **to not say boo** no decir ni chus ni mus; *interj* ¡bu!; *va* abuchear (*p.ej., a un cantante*); hacer el bu a; *vn* abuchear; hacer el bu

**boo-boo** [ˈbuˌbu] *s* (slang) patochada, plancha

**booby** [ˈbubɪ] *s* (*pl:* **-bies**) zopenco, bobalicón; el peor jugador de todos; (orn.) pato bobo

**booby hatch** *s* (naut.) tambucho; (coll.) manicomio; (slang) cárcel

**booby prize** *s* último premio, premio de consolación

**booby trap** *s* (mil.) trampa explosiva; (fig.) zancadilla (*engaño*)

**boodle** [ˈbudəl] *s* (slang) cuadrilla; (slang) dinero: (slang) soborno

**boogie-woogie** [ˈbugɪˈwugɪ] *s* bugui-bugui (*manera de tocar el piano y baile norteamericanos*)

**boohoo** [ˌbuˈhu] *s* lloro ruidoso y sollozante; *vn* llorar ruidosamente y con sollozos

**book** [buk] *s* libro; libreta (*p.ej., de la caja de ahorros*); librillo (*de papel de fumar, de panes de oro, de sellos, etc.*); libro en que se apuntan las apuestas (*en las carreras de caballos*); (bridge) conjunto de las seis primeras bazas; (com.) libro-registro; **by the book** con exactitud, según las reglas; **the Book** la Biblia; **to bring someone to book** llamar o traer a uno a capítulo; regañarle a uno; **to close the books** (com.) cerrar el borrador; **to keep books** (com.) llevar libros; **to know like a book** saber de todo en todo; conocer a fondo; *va* asentar en un libro; notar en un registro; inscribir; anotar (*un pedido, mercancías*) para despacho; reservar (*un pasaje en una embarcación*); escriturar (*a un actor para una función*)

**bookbinder** [ˈbukˌbaɪndər] *s* encuadernador

**bookbindery** [ˈbukˌbaɪndərɪ] *s* (*pl:* **-ies**) encuadernación (*taller*)

**bookbinding** [ˈbukˌbaɪndɪŋ] *s* encuadernación (*acción; arte*)

**bookcase** [ˈbukˌkes] *s* armario o estante para libros

**book end** *s* sujetalibros, apoyalibros

**bookie** [ˈbukɪ] *s* (coll.) corredor de apuestas (*en las carreras de caballos*)

**booking** [ˈbukɪŋ] *s* reservación (*de un pasaje*); escritura (*de un actor*)

**booking clerk** *s* vendedor de billetes de pasaje o teatro

**booking office** *s* despacho de pasajes

**bookish** [ˈbukɪʃ] *adj* libresco

**bookkeeper** [ˈbukˌkipər] *s* tenedor de libros

**bookkeeping** [ˈbukˌkipɪŋ] *s* teneduría de libros

**book learning** *s* ciencia libresca

**booklet** [ˈbuklɪt] *s* librete, libretín

**booklore** [ˈbukˌlor] *s* ciencia libresca

**booklover** [ˈbukˌlʌvər] *s* aficionado a los libros

**bookmaker** [ˈbukˌmekər] *s* recopilador; (print.) impresor encargado de la imposición; corredor de apuestas (*en las carreras de caballos*)

**bookmark** [ˈbukˌmɑrk] *s* registro

**bookmobile** [ˈbukmoˈbil] *s* biblioteca rodante

**Book of Common Prayer** *s* devocionario de la Iglesia anglicana

**Book of Mormon** *s* libro del Mormón, libro sagrado del mormonismo

**bookplate** [ˈbukˌplet] *s* ex libris

**bookrack** [ˈbukˌræk] *s* atril; estante

**book review** *s* reseña

**bookseller** [ˈbukˌsɛlər] *s* librero

**bookshelf** [ˈbukˌʃɛlf] *s* (*pl:* **-shelves**) estante para libros

**bookstall** [ˈbukˌstɔl] *s* puesto para la venta de libros

**bookstand** [ˈbukˌstænd] *s* atril; mostrador para libros; puesto para la venta de libros

**bookstore** [ˈbukˌstor] *s* librería

**book value** *s* (com.) valor de las acciones de una sociedad en el libro de cuenta de la sociedad

**bookworm** [ˈbukˌwʌrm] *s* polilla que roe los libros; (fig.) ratón de biblioteca

**boom** [bum] *s* trueno, estampido; auge, alza rápida, prosperidad repentina, fomento enérgico; aguilón (*de una grúa*); (naut.) botalón; (naut.) botavara (*de una vela*); (naut.) cadena de troncos, barrera de un puerto; *adj* que aumenta, crece o medra repentinamente; *va* fomentar enérgicamente; expresar con estruendo; dar (*el reloj, p.ej., las tres*) con estruendo; *vn* tronar, hacer estampido; estar en auge, medrar, estar en bonanza

**boomerang** [ˈbuməræŋ] *s* bumerang; (fig.) cosa que redunda en perjuicio del que la originó; *vn* redundar (*una cosa*) en perjuicio del que la originó

**boom iron** *s* (naut.) zuncho de botalón

**boom town** *s* pueblo que está en bonanza

**boon** [bun] *s* dicha, bendición; (archaic) favor, gracia; *adj* alegre, festivo; (archaic) bondadoso, generoso

**boon companion** *s* buen compañero

**boondocks** [ˈbunˌdɑks] *spl* (slang) monte, monte bajo; (slang) afueras del poblado

**boondoggle** [ˈbunˌdɑgəl] *s* (slang) trabajo sin provecho; *vn* (slang) trabajar sin provecho

**boor** [bur] *s* patán

**boorish** [ˈburɪʃ] *adj* grosero, chabacano

**boost** [bust] *s* empujón hacia arriba; alza (*de precios*); alabanza; ayuda; *va* empujar hacia arriba; alzar (*los precios*); alabar; ayudar

**booster** [ˈbustər] *s* aumentador de presión; detonador auxiliar; cohete de lanzamiento; (coll.) bombista, fomentador; (elec.) elevador de tensión; (med.) inyección secundaria; (rail.) propulsor

**booster battery** *s* (elec.) batería elevadora

**booster pump** *s* bomba reforzadora

**booster rocket** *s* cohete de lanzamiento

**boot** [but] *s* bota; calceta (*usada como tormento*); pesebrón (*del coche*); toldo para el cochero; **boots** *ssg* (Brit.) limpiabotas; **the boot is on the other leg** los papeles están trastrocados; **to be in the boots of** estar en el pellejo de; **to bet your boots** estar absolutamente seguro; **to boot** de añadidura; **to die with one's boots on** morir con las botas puestas, morir al pie del cañón; **to get the boot** (coll.) ser echado a la calle; **to lick the boots of** lamer los zapatos a (*adular con exceso*); **to wipe one's boots on** insultar, maltratar; *va* calzar, poner las botas a; dar un puntapié a; (slang) poner en la calle; **to boot it** ir a pie; *vn* calzarse las botas; ir a pie

**bootblack** [ˈbutˌblæk] *s* limpiabotas

**booted** [ˈbutɪd] *adj* calzado con botas

**bootee** [buˈti] *s* calzado de punto para niños; bota corta de mujer

**Boötes** [boˈotiz] *s* (astr.) Bootes

**booth** [buθ] o [buð] *s* (*pl:* **booths** [buðz]) casilla o quiosco (*de información*); cabina (*telefónica; de votación; para oír discos de fonógrafo*); puesto de feria o mercado

**boot hook** *s* tirabotas

**bootjack** [ˈbutˌdʒæk] *s* sacabotas

**bootleg** [ˈbutˌlɛg] *s* caña de bota; (slang) contrabando de licores; *adj* (slang) contrabandista; (*pret & pp:* **-legged;** *ger:* **-legging**) *va* (slang) pasar, llevar o vender (*licores*) de contrabando; *vn* (slang) contrabandear en licores

**bootlegger** [ˈbutˌlɛgər] *s* (slang) contrabandista, destilador clandestino

**bootlegging** [ˈbutˌlɛgɪŋ] *s* contrabando de licores

**bootless** [ˈbutlɪs] *adj* inútil, sin provecho

**bootlicker** [ˈbutˌlɪkər] *s* (slang) lameculos, quitamotas

**boots and saddles** *spl* (mil.) botasilla

**bootstrap** [ˈbutˌstræp] *s* elástico o tirante de la bota

**boot tree** *s* horma de bota

**booty** [ˈbutɪ] *s* (*pl:* **-ties**) botín, presa; ganancia, premio

**booze** [buz] *s* (coll.) licor; (coll.) borrachera, ataque de borrachera; *vn* (coll.) borrachear

**boozer** [ˈbuzər] *s* (coll.) borracho

**boozy** [ˈbuzɪ] *adj* (coll.) chispo; (coll.) borracho

**bop** [bɑp] (*pret & pp:* **bopped;** *ger:* **bopping**) *va* (slang) golpear, pegar

**bopeep** [boˈpip] *s* juego de niños que consiste en descubrirse los ojos rápidamente después de tenerlos tapados con las manos; **Little Bopeep** pastorcita, en un cuento de niños, que ha perdido sus ovejas

**bor.** abr. de **borough**

**boracic** [boˈræsɪk] *adj* (chem.) bórico

**boracite** [ˈborəsaɪt] *s* (mineral.) boracita

**borage** [ˈbʌrɪdʒ], [ˈbɑrɪdʒ] o [ˈbɔrɪdʒ] *s* (bot.) borraja

**borate** [ˈboret] *s* (chem.) borato

**borated** [ˈboretɪd] *adj* boratado

**borax** [ˈboræks] *s* (chem.) bórax

**Bordeaux** [bɔrˈdo] *s* Burdeos; burdeos (*vino*)

**Bordeaux mixture** *s* (hort.) caldo de Burdeos, caldo bordelés

**Bordeaux red** *s* rojo de Burdeos

**border** [ˈbɔrdər] *s* borde, margen; frontera, confín; ribete, orla; repulgo, dobladillo; arriate (*de jardín*); **borders** *spl* (theat.) bambalina; *adj* frontero; *va* limitar, deslindar, ribetear, orlar; repulgar, dobladillar; *vn* confinar; **to border on** o **upon** confinar con, rayar en; (fig.) bordear

**border clash** *s* encuentro fronterizo, choque en la frontera

**borderer** [ˈbɔrdərər] *s* habitante fronterizo

**borderland** [ˈbɔrdərˌlænd] *s* zona fronteriza; región intermedia, espacio indefinido

**borderline** [ˈbɔrderˌlaɪn] *s* frontera; *adj* fronterizo; límite, intermedio; indefinido, incierto

**bordure** [ˈbɔrdʒər] *s* (her.) bordura, bordadura

**bore** [bor] *s* barreno (*agujero*); calibre; ánima, alma (*del cañón del arma de fuego*); alesaje (*del cilindro de un motor*); machaca (*persona*); fastidio, molienda; maremoto (*grande ola al subir la marea*); *va* agujerear; barrenar; fastidiar; *vn* agujerear; adelantarse; **to bore from within** atacar por traición desde adentro; *pret de* **bear**

**boreal** [ˈborɪəl] *adj* boreal

**Boreas** [ˈborɪəs] *s* (myth.) Bóreas; bóreas (*viento del norte*)

**boredom** [ˈbordəm] *s* aburrimiento, fastidio, tedio

**borer** [ˈborər] *s* barrena, taladro; (ent.) barrenillo

**boresome** [ˈborsəm] *adj* aburrido, fastidioso, tedioso

**boric** [ˈborɪk] *adj* (chem.) bórico

**boric acid** *s* (chem.) ácido bórico

**boring** [ˈborɪŋ] *adj* aburrido, fastidioso

**born** [bɔrn] *adj* nacido; nato, innato, p.ej., **born criminal** criminal nato; **born liar** mentiroso innato; **in all my born days** (coll.) en mi vida; **to be born** nacer; **to be born again** renacer, volver a nacer

**borne** [born] *pp de* **bear**

**boron** [ˈborɑn] *s* (chem.) boro

**borough** [ˈbʌro] *s* villa; distrito administrativo de municipio

**borrow** [ˈbɑro] o [ˈbɔro] *va* pedir prestado, tomar prestado, tomar a préstamo; apropiarse, tomar para sí; **to borrow from** pedir prestado a; **to borrow trouble** darse molestia sin ningún motivo

**borrower** [ˈbɑroər] o [ˈbɔroər] *s* prestatario

**borrowing** [ˈbɑro·ɪŋ] o [ˈbɔro·ɪŋ] *s* préstamo; préstamo lingüístico

**borrow pit** *s* préstamo

**borzoi** [ˈbɔrzɔɪ] *s* barzoi (*galgo ruso*)

**boscage** [ˈbɑskɪdʒ] *s* boscaje

**bosh** [bɑʃ] *s* etalaje (*de alto horno*); (coll.) tontería, música celestial

**bosk** [bɑsk] *s* bosquecillo, maleza

**bosky** [ˈbɑskɪ] *adj* nemoroso, boscoso; frondoso, umbroso

**bo's'n** [ˈbosən] *s* var. de **boatswain**

**Bosnian** [ˈbɑznɪən] *adj & s* bosníaco o bosnio

**bosom** [ˈbuzəm] *s* seno; pechera (*de camisa*); amor, cariño; *adj* íntimo, de la mayor confianza; *va* guardar en el seno, encerrar en el pecho

**Bosporus** [ˈbɑspərəs] *s* Bósforo

**boss** [bɔs] o [bɑs] *s* (coll.) jefe, mandamás; (coll.) amo, gallo, capataz, gerente; (coll.) cacique (*en asuntos políticos*); protuberancia, figura de relieve; (arch.) crucería (*en las bóvedas góticas*); *va* (coll.) regentar, dominar; trabajar en relieve, adornar en relieve

**bossism** [ˈbɔsɪzəm] o [ˈbɑsɪzəm] *s* caciquismo, gamonalismo

**bossy** [ˈbɔsɪ] o [ˈbɑsɪ] *adj* (*comp:* **-ier;** *super:* **-iest**) mandón; adornado en relieve

**boston** [ˈbɔstən] o [ˈbɑstən] *s* bostón (*juego de naipes; vals*)

**Bostonian** [bɔsˈtonɪən] o [bɑsˈtonɪən] *adj & s* bostoniano

**Boston Tea Party** *s* (hist.) motín del té

**bostryx** [ˈbɑstrɪks] *s* (bot.) bóstrice

**bosun** [ˈbosən] *s* var. de **boatswain**

**bot** [bɑt] *s* (ent.) rezno

**botanic** [bəˈtænɪk] o **botanical** [bəˈtænɪkəl] *adj* botánico

**botanist** [ˈbɑtənɪst] *s* botanista, botánico

**botanize** [ˈbɑtənaɪz] *va* explorar la flora de; *vn* botanizar

**botany** [ˈbɑtənɪ] *s* botánica

**botch** [bɑtʃ] *s* chapucería, remiendo chapucero; *va* chapucear, remendar chapuceramente

**botchy** [ˈbɑtʃɪ] *adj* (*comp:* **-ier;** *super:* **-iest**) chapucero, mal hecho

**botfly** [ˈbɑtˌflaɪ] *s* (*pl:* **-flies**) (ent.) estro, moscardón

**both** [boθ] *adj* ambos; *pron* ambos, los dos, uno y otro; **both of** ambos; **both of them** ellos dos, los dos; **both of us** nosotros dos; *conj* a la vez; **both . . . and** tanto . . . como, así . . . como, al par . . . y; *adv* igualmente

**bother** [ˈbɑðər] *s* incomodidad, molestia; persona o cosa molesta; *va* incomodar, molestar; *vn* molestarse; **to bother about** o **with** molestarse con; **to bother to** + *inf* molestarse en + *inf*

**botheration** [ˌbɑðəˈreʃən] *s* (coll.) incomodidad, molestia; *interj* ¡caramba! (*para expresar enfado*)

**bothersome** [ˈbɑðərsəm] *adj* incómodo, molesto

**bott** [bɑt] *s* var. de **bot**

**bottle** [ˈbɑtəl] *s* botella; biberón (*para la lactancia artificial*); **the bottle** las bebidas alcohólicas; *va* embotellar; **to bottle up** embotellar

**bottle brush** *s* escobilla para limpiar botellas; (bot.) cola de rata, equiseto menor
**bottle gourd** *s* (bot.) cogorda
**bottle green** *s* verde botella
**bottle imp** *s* (phys.) diablillo de Descartes
**bottleneck** [ˈbɑtəlˌnɛk] *s* gollete, cuello de botella; embotellamiento, congestión del tráfico; embotellado, obstáculo
**bottle nose** *s* nariz hinchada por el mucho beber
**bottlenose** [ˈbɑtəlˌnoz] *s* (zool.) delfín de hocico de botella
**bottle opener** *s* abrebotellas, descapsulador; destapacorona (Am.)
**bottler** [ˈbɑtlər] *s* embotellador
**bottle rack** *s* botellero
**bottle tit** *s* (orn.) alionín, chamarón
**bottom** [ˈbɑtəm] *s* fondo; fundamento, cimiento; fundación; asiento (*de una silla*); final (*de una página*); (coll.) trasero; (naut.) fondo; (naut.) casco, nave, buque; (fig.) fondo (*lo principal*); **bottoms** *spl* hondonada; **at bottom** en el fondo, en la realidad; **to be at the bottom of** ser la causa de; ser el último de (*p.ej., la clase*); **to begin at the bottom** (fig.) empezar el oficio por abajo; **to get to the bottom of** entrar en el fondo de; **to go the bottom** irse a pique; *adj* fundamental, del fondo; (coll.) más bajo, p.ej., **the bottom price** el precio más bajo; (coll.) último, p.ej., **his bottom dollar** su último dólar; *va* fundar; profundizar; poner asiento a (*una silla*)
**bottom land** *s* hondonada
**bottomless** [ˈbɑtəmlɪs] *adj* sin fondo; sin asiento; infundado; profundo; abismal; insondable; ilimitado, inagotable
**bottomless pit, the** el abismo, el infierno
**bottomry** [ˈbɑtəmrɪ] *s* (naut.) contrato a la gruesa
**botulism** [ˈbɑtʃəlɪzəm] *s* (path.) botulismo
**bouclé** [buˈkle] *s* bouclé; *adj* de bouclé
**boudoir** [buˈdwɑr] *s* tocador, gabinete; saloncito
**bougainvillea** [ˌbugənˈvɪlɪə] *s* (bot.) buganvilla
**bough** [baʊ] *s* rama
**bought** [bɔt] *pp de* **buy**
**boughten** [ˈbɔtən] *adj* (dial.) no casero, comprado
**bougie** [ˈbudʒɪ], [ˈbuʒɪ] o [buˈʒi] *s* bujía (*vela de cera*); (surg.) bujía, candelilla
**bouillabaisse** [ˌbuljəˈbes] *s* bullabesa
**bouillon** [ˈbuljɑn] o [bʊlˈjɑn] *s* caldo
**bouillon cube** *s* cubito de caldo concentrado
**boulder** [ˈboldər] *s* guijarro grande, canto rodado
**boulevard** [ˈbʊləvɑrd] o [ˈbuləvɑrd] *s* bulevar
**boulter** [ˈboltər] *s* palangre
**bounce** [baʊns] *s* bote; jactancia; (slang) despedida; *va* hacer botar; (slang) despedir; *vn* botar; dar saltos al andar; saltar repentinamente; precipitarse ruidosamente y sin ceremonia
**bouncer** [ˈbaʊnsər] *s* cosa de gran tamaño; (coll.) fanfarrón; (slang) apagabroncas, guardián fornido que echa a la calle a los alborotadores de un café, bar, etc.
**bouncing** [ˈbaʊnsɪŋ] *adj* fuerte, frescachón
**bouncing Bess** o **Bet** *s* (bot.) jabonera
**bound** [baʊnd] *s* salto; bote (*de una pelota*); límite, margen, raya; **bounds** *spl* zona fronteriza, región, comarca; **out of bounds** fuera de los límites, más allá de los límites; **within bounds** a raya; *adj* obligado; encuadernado; estreñido; puesto en aprendizaje; (coll.) determinado, resuelto; **bound for** con destino a; **bound up in** o **with** relacionado estrechamente con; muy adicto a; absorto en; *va* limitar; deslindar; *vn* saltar; botar; confinar, rayar; *pret & pp de* **bind**
**boundary** [ˈbaʊndərɪ] *s* (*pl:* **-ries**) límite, margen, frontera
**boundary stone** *s* mojón
**bounden** [ˈbaʊndən] *adj* obligatorio; obligado
**bounder** [ˈbaʊndər] *s* advenedizo vulgar y malcriado
**boundless** [ˈbaʊndlɪs] *adj* ilimitado, infinito; vasto, inmenso
**bounteous** [ˈbaʊntɪəs] o **bountiful** [ˈbaʊntɪfəl] *adj* generoso, liberal; abundante, copioso
**bounty** [ˈbaʊntɪ] *s* (*pl:* **-ties**) generosidad, liberalidad; dádiva, regalo; premio, galardón; prima (*premio del gobierno*); (mil.) premio de enganche
**bouquet** [buˈke] o [boˈke] *s* ramo, ramillete; nariz (*perfume del vino*)
**Bourbon** [ˈbʊrbən] *s* Borbón; conservador; (*l.c.*) [ˈbʊrbən] o [ˈbʌrbən] *s* aguardiente de maíz
**Bourbonism** [ˈbʊrbənɪzəm] *s* borbonismo; conservatismo excesivo
**bourgeois** [bʊrˈʒwɑ] o [ˈbʊrʒwɑ] *adj* burgués; *s* (*pl:* **-geois** [ʒwɑ]) burgués; [bʌrˈdʒɔɪs] *s* (print.) tipo de nueve puntos
**bourgeoisie** [ˌbʊrʒwɑˈzi] *s* burguesía
**bourn** o **bourne** [born] *s* arroyo, riachuelo; [born] o [bʊrn] *s* meta; margen; límite; región, dominio
**bourse** [bʊrs] *s* bolsa
**boustrophedon** [ˌbustrəˈfidən] o [ˌbaʊstrəˈfidən] *s* bustrófedon
**bout** [baʊt] *s* encuentro; rato; ataque (*de una enfermedad*)
**boutonnière** o **boutonniere** [ˌbutəˈnjɛr] *s* flor que se lleva en el ojal
**bovine** [ˈbovaɪn] o [ˈbovɪn] *adj* bovino; lerdo, estúpido; impasible; *s* bovino
**bow** [baʊ] *s* inclinación, reverencia; (naut.) proa; **to make a bow** hacer una reverencia; **to make one's bow** presentarse; *va* inclinar (*la cabeza*); inclinarse en señal de (*p.ej., agradecimiento*); **to bow one's way in** entrar haciendo reverencias; **to bow one's way out** salir haciendo reverencias; *vn* inclinarse; ceder, someterse; **to bow and scrape** hacer reverencias profundas, mostrarse muy obsequioso; **to bow to** saludar, inclinarse delante; [bo] *s* arco; lazo, nudo; ojo (*de la llave*); (mus.) arco; *adj* arqueado; *va* (mus.) tocar con arco; *vn* arquearse; alabearse
**bow compass** [bo] *s* bigotera
**bowdlerize** [ˈbaʊdləraɪz] *va* expurgar
**bowel** [ˈbaʊəl] *s* parte del intestino; **bowels** *spl* (anat.) intestinos; (fig.) entrañas (*lo más oculto*); (archaic) entrañas (*compasión, ternura*); **to keep the bowels open** tener el vientre libre
**bowel movement** *s* evacuación del vientre
**bower** [ˈboər] *s* músico de arco; [ˈbaʊər] *s* emparrado, enramada; cenador, glorieta; (naut.) ancla de proa, ancla de servidumbre; **right bower** sota del triunfo; **left bower** sota del mismo color del triunfo; *va* emparrar
**bowerbird** [ˈbaʊərˌbʌrd] *s* (orn.) tilonorrinco
**bowery** [ˈbaʊərɪ] *adj* frondoso, emparrado, sombreado; *s* (*pl:* **-ies**) (hist.) finca, granja; (*cap.*) *s* calle y barrio de Nueva York con tabernas y hoteles de mala calidad
**bowfin** [ˈboˌfɪn] *s* (ichth.) amia
**bowie knife** [ˈbo·ɪ] o [ˈbu·ɪ] *s* cuchillo puñal
**bowknot** [ˈboˌnɑt] *s* nudo corredizo
**bowl** [bol] *s* escudilla; jofaina, palangana (*para lavarse las manos*); tazón (*de fuente*); taza (*de inodoro*); paleta (*de la cuchara*); hornillo (*de la pipa*); copa (*vaso con pie para beber*); cuenco, concavidad; anfiteatro al aire libre en forma de cuenco; bola (*en el juego de bolos*); turno (*en el juego de bolos*); **bowls** *spl* bolos (*juego*); *va* arrojar (*la bola en la vilorta*); **to bowl down** derribar; **to bowl over** tumbar; (coll.) confundir, desconcertar; *vn* jugar a los bolos; rodar; **to bowl along** rodar
**bowlder** [ˈboldər] *s* var. de **boulder**
**bowleg** [ˈboˌlɛg] *s* pierna arqueada; arqueo de las piernas
**bowlegged** [ˈboˌlɛgɪd] o [ˈboˌlɛgd] *adj* estevado, patiestevado
**bowler** [ˈbolər] *s* jugador de bolos; (Brit.) sombrero hongo
**bowline** [ˈbolɪn] o [ˈbolaɪn] *s* (naut.) bolina; as de guía; **on a bowline** (naut.) de bolina
**bowline knot** *s* as de guía
**bowling** [ˈbolɪŋ] *s* juego de bolos; *adj* bolístico
**bowling alley** *s* bolera
**bowling green** *s* bolera encespada
**bowman** [ˈbomən] *s* (*pl:* **-men**) arquero, flechero
**bow oar** [baʊ] *s* (naut.) remo de proa; (naut.) proel (*marinero*)
**bowshot** [ˈboˌʃɑt] *s* tiro de flecha, alcance de la flecha

**bowsprit** ['baʊsprɪt] o ['bosprɪt] *s* (naut.) bauprés
**bowstring** ['boˌstrɪŋ] *s* cuerda de arco; cuerda para estrangular; (*pret & pp:* **-stringed** o **-strung**) *va* estrangular con cuerda
**bowstring beam** *s* viga de cuerda y arco
**bow tie** [bo] *s* corbata de mariposa, corbata de lazo, pajarita
**bow window** [bo] *s* ventana salediza en forma de arco
**bowwow** ['baʊˌwaʊ] *s* guau guau (*ladrido del perro*); perro; *interj* ¡guau!; *vn* ladrar; gruñir, regañar
**bowwow theory** *s* (philol.) teoría de la onomatopeya
**box** [bɑks] *s* caja; casilla de establo; pescante (*asiento de cochero*); garita; bofetada; (theat.) palco; (mach.) cárter; (elec.) caja (*para llaves, tomas de corriente, etc.*); (bot.) boj; (baseball) puesto del lanzador; (baseball) puesto del cogedor; recuadro (*p.ej., en un periódico*); *va* encajonar, embalar; abofetear; **to box up** encerrar, encerrar en una caja; *vn* (sport) boxear
**boxcar** ['bɑksˌkɑr] *s* (rail.) vagón cerrado, vagón cubierto, vagón encajonado
**box couch** *s* diván arca
**box coupling** *s* (mach.) manguito, collar de acoplamiento
**box elder** *s* (bot.) negondo o negundo
**boxer** ['bɑksər] *s* embalador; (sport) boxeador; bóxer (*perro*); (*cap.*) *s* bóxer (*en China*)
**boxing** ['bɑksɪŋ] *s* embalaje; encajonamiento; madera para encajonar; marco de puerta o de ventana; (sport) boxeo; *adj* boxístico
**Boxing Day** *s* (Brit.) día festivo que se celebra, con regalos a los empleados, el primer día de trabajo después de Navidad
**boxing gloves** *spl* guantes de boxeo
**box kite** *s* cometa celular *f*
**box office** *s* despacho de localidades, contaduría, taquilla; **good box office** (slang) éxito de taquilla
**box-office** ['bɑksˌɔfɪs] o ['bɑksˌɑfɪs] *adj* de taquilla, taquillero
**box-office record** *s* marca de taquilla
**box pleat** o **plait** *s* (sew.) pliegue de tabla
**box seat** *s* (theat.) asiento de palco
**boxwood** ['bɑksˌwʊd] *s* (bot.) boj
**box wrench** *s* llave de cubo
**boy** [bɔɪ] *s* muchacho; mozo (*criado*); (coll.) hombre, compadre
**boyar** [bo'jɑr] o ['bɔɪər] o **boyard** [bo'jɑrd] o ['bɔɪərd] *s* boyardo
**boycott** ['bɔɪkɑt] *s* boicot; boicoteo; *va* boicotear
**boyhood** ['bɔɪhʊd] *s* muchachez; muchachería, muchachos; juventud masculina
**boyish** ['bɔɪɪʃ] *adj* amuchachado, muchachil
**boy scout** *s* explorador, niño explorador
**Bp.** abr. de **bishop**
**b.p.** o **B/P** abr. de **bills payable** y **boiling point**
**B.P.E.** abr. de **Bachelor of Physical Education**
**B.Ph.** abr. de **Bachelor of Philosophy**
**br.** abr. de **brand, brig** y **brother**
**Br.** abr. de **Britain** y **British**
**b.r.** o **B/R** abr. de **bills receivable**
**bra** [brɑ] *s* (coll.) portasenos, sostén
**Brabant** [brə'bænt] o ['brɑbənt] *s* Brabante
**brace** [bres] *s* riostra, tirante; apoyo; (print.) corchete; (carp.) berbiquí; (naut.) braza (*cabo para sujetar las vergas*); par; **braces** *spl* (Brit.) tirantes (*del pantalón*); *va* arriostrar; apoyar; asegurar, vigorizar; **to brace oneself** (coll.) cobrar ánimo; *vn* **to brace up** (coll.) cobrar ánimo
**brace and bit** *s* berbiquí y barrena
**bracelet** ['breslɪt] *s* brazalete, pulsera; (hum.) esposa, grillete
**bracer** ['bresər] *s* persona o cosa que fortifica; (coll.) trago fortificante; brazal de arquero
**brachial** ['brekɪəl] o ['brækɪəl] *adj* braquial
**brachiopod** ['brekɪəˌpɑd] o ['brækɪəˌpɑd] *s* (zool.) braquiópodo
**brachycephalic** [ˌbrækɪsɪ'fælɪk] *adj* (anthrop.) braquicéfalo
**brachyuran** [ˌbrækɪ'jurən] *adj & s* (zool.) braquiuro
**bracing** ['bresɪŋ] *adj* fortificante, tónico; *s* arriostramiento, refuerzo
**bracken** ['brækən] *s* (bot.) helecho común; helechal
**bracket** ['brækɪt] *s* puntal, soporte; escuadra; anaquel asegurado con ménsulas; brazo de lámpara asegurado en la pared; (arch.) ménsula, repisa; corchete o paréntesis cuadrado; clase, categoría; *va* asegurar con ménsulas; acorchetar, poner entre corchetes cuadrados; agrupar
**brackish** ['brækɪʃ] *adj* salobre
**bract** [brækt] *s* bráctea
**bractlet** ['bræktlɪt] *s* (bot.) bractéola
**brad** [bræd] *s* puntilla, clavito, clavito de ala de mosca
**bradawl** ['brædˌɔl] *s* lezna para puntillas o clavitos
**bradycardia** [ˌbrædɪ'kɑrdɪə] *s* (path.) bradicardia
**bradypepsia** [ˌbrædɪ'pɛpsɪə] *s* (path.) bradipepsia
**brae** [bre] *s* (Scottish) cuesta, pendiente
**brag** [bræg] *s* jactancia; (*pret & pp:* **bragged;** *ger:* **bragging**) *va* jactarse de; *vn* jactarse
**braggadocio** [ˌbrægə'doʃɪo] *s* (*pl:* **-os**) fanfarronada; fanfarrón
**braggart** ['brægərt] *adj & s* fanfarrón
**brahma** ['brɑmə] o ['bremə] *s* gallina brahma; (*cap.*) ['brɑmə] *s* (rel.) Brahma
**Brahman** ['brɑmən] *s* (*pl:* **-mans**) brahmán
**Brahmanism** ['brɑmənɪzəm] *s* brahmanismo
**Brahmin** ['brɑmɪn] *s* brahmán; aristócrata culto
**braid** [bred] *s* trenza, galón, pasamano, sutás; *va* trenzar, galonear, encintar
**brail** [brel] *s* (naut.) candeliza; *va* (naut.) halar por medio de candelizas
**Braille** o **braille** [brel] *s* sistema Braille; letras Braille
**brain** [bren] *s* (anat. & zool.) cerebro; **brains** *spl* cerebro, inteligencia; sesos (*que se comen*); **to beat one's brains** esforzarse por recordar algo; **to blow one's brains out** saltarse la tapa de los sesos; **to have on the brain** (coll.) tener la manía de, estar dominado por la idea de; **to rack one's brains** devanarse los sesos, romperse la cabeza; *va* descerebrar
**brain cell** *s* (anat.) neurona cerebral
**brain child** *s* parto del ingenio, obra del cerebro de uno
**brainfag** ['brenˌfæg] *s* fatiga cerebral
**brain fever** *s* (path.) fiebre cerebral
**braininess** ['breninɪs] *s* sesudez, inteligencia
**brainless** ['brenlɪs] *adj* tonto, insensato, sin sesos
**brainpan** ['brenˌpæn] *s* (anat.) cráneo
**brain sand** *s* (anat.) acérvula
**brainsick** ['brenˌsɪk] *adj* loco
**brain storm** *s* agitación repentina y transitoria; (coll.) buena idea, inspiración, hallazgo
**brain trust** *s* grupo de consejeros intelectuales
**brain washing** *s* (coll.) lavado cerebral o de cerebro
**brain wave** *s* (coll.) buena idea, inspiración, hallazgo; **brain waves** *spl* (med.) ondas encefálicas
**brain work** *s* trabajo intelectual
**brainy** ['brenɪ] *adj* (*comp:* **-ier;** *super:* **-iest**) (coll.) sesudo, inteligente
**braise** [brez] *va* (cook.) dorar (*la carne*) rápidamente y cocerla a fuego lento en una vasija bien tapada y con muy poca agua
**brake** [brek] *s* freno; agramadera; amasadera; break (*carruaje*); (bot.) helecho común; matorral; *va* frenar; agramar (*el lino o el cáñamo*); amasar (*la harina o la tierra*); *vn* trabajar como guardafrenos
**brake band** *s* (aut.) banda de freno, cinta de freno
**brake drum** *s* (aut.) tambor o campana de freno
**brake light** *s* (aut.) luz de frenado
**brake lining** *s* (aut.) forro de freno, guarnición de freno, cinta de freno
**brakeman** ['brekmən] *s* (*pl:* **-men**) (rail.) guardafrenos
**brake pedal** *s* (aut.) pedal de freno
**brake shoe** *s* zapata de freno
**brake wheel** *s* (aut.) tambor de freno

**Bramantesque** [ˌbrɑmən'tɛsk] *adj* (arch.) bramantesco
**bramble** ['bræmbəl] *s* (bot.) frambueso, zarza
**brambly** ['bræmblɪ] *adj* (*comp:* **-blier;** *super:* **-bliest**) zarzoso
**bran** [bræn] *s* afrecho, salvado
**branch** [bræntʃ] o [brɑntʃ] *s* rama (*del árbol, de un linaje; parte accesoria*); ramo (*rama de segundo orden; rama cortada del árbol; parte de una ciencia, arte, etc.*); sarmiento (*de la vid*); ramal (*de un camino, vía férrea, etc.*); brazo (*de un río, candelabro, etc.*); sucursal (*de un establecimiento, tienda, etc.*); pierna (*del compás*); *adj* dependiente; sucursal; *vn* ramificarse; **to branch off** ramificarse; bifurcarse; **to branch out** ramificarse; extenderse (*en los negocios*)
**branchia** ['bræŋkɪə] *s* (*pl:* **-chiae** [kɪi]) (ichth.) branquia
**branchial** ['bræŋkɪəl] *adj* branquial
**branchiferous** [bræŋ'kɪfərəs] *adj* branquífero
**branch line** *s* (rail.) ramal, línea de empalme
**branch office** *s* sucursal
**brand** [brænd] *s* marca (*de cualquier producto*); marca de fábrica; clase, género, especie; hierro (*que se pone a las reses*); hierro de marcar; tea; tizón (*palo a medio quemar*); (fig.) tizón (*deshonra*); (poet.) relámpago; (archaic & poet.) espada; *va* poner marca de fábrica en; imprimir de modo indeleble; herrar (*con hierro candente*); tiznar (*la reputación de una persona*); **to brand as** motejar de, tildar de
**Brandenburg** ['brændənbʌrg] *s* Brandeburgo (*ciudad, provincia y adorno militar*)
**brandied** ['brændɪd] *adj* macerado en aguardiente
**branding iron** *s* hierro de marcar
**brandish** ['brændɪʃ] *s* molinete, floreo; *va* blandear; *vn* blandear o blandearse
**brand-new** ['brænd'nju] o ['brænd'nu] *adj* flamante, nuevo flamante, nuevecito
**brandy** ['brændɪ] *s* (*pl:* **-dies**) aguardiente
**bran-new** ['bræn'nju] o ['bræn'nu] *adj* var. de **brand-new**
**brant** [brænt] *s* (orn.) branta, ganso marino; (orn.) ganso monjita atlántico; (orn.) ganso de las nieves
**brash** [bræʃ] *adj* temerario, impetuoso; insolente, respondón; (dial.) quebradizo; *s* (dial.) enfermedad repentina, sarpullido
**brasier** ['breʒər] *s* var. de **brazier**
**brasiletto** [ˌbrɑsɪ'lɛto] *s* (bot.) brasilete
**brasilin** ['bræzɪlɪn] *s* var. de **brazilin**
**brasque** [bræsk] o [brɑsk] *s* (found.) brasca; *va* (found.) brascar
**brass** [bræs] o [brɑs] *s* latón; (mach.) bronce; (mus.) cobre; (Brit. slang) dinero; (U.S. slang) los jefazos, los mandamases (*especialmente en el ejército y la marina*); color de latón; (coll.) descaro, desvergüenza; **brasses** *spl* cobre (*utensilios de cocina de cobre*); (mus.) cobres; *adj* hecho de latón; **to get down to brass tacks** (coll.) entrar en materia, ir al grano
**brassard** ['bræsɑrd] o [bræ'sɑrd] o **brassart** ['bræsərt] *s* brazal
**brass band** *s* (mus.) charanga
**brass hat** *s* (slang) espadón (*oficial de estado mayor*)
**brassie** ['bræsɪ] o ['brɑsɪ] *s* (golf) maza de madera con cabo plano de metal
**brassière** [brə'zɪr] o [ˌbræsɪ'ɛr] *s* portasenos, sostén
**brass knuckles** *spl* bóxer
**brassware** ['bræsˌwɛr] o ['brɑsˌwɛr] *s* latonería, obra de latón
**brass-wind** ['bræsˌwɪnd] o ['brɑsˌwɪnd] *adj* (mus.) de los cobres, de boquilla
**brass winds** *spl* (mus.) cobres, instrumentos de boquilla
**brasswork** ['bræsˌwʌrk] o ['brɑsˌwʌrk] *s* latonería (*arte*); **brassworks** *spl* latonería (*taller*)
**brassy** ['bræsɪ] o ['brɑsɪ] *adj* (*comp:* **-ier;** *super:* **-iest**) de latón, hecho de latón; áspero, metálico; (coll.) descarado, desvergonzado; *s* (*pl:* **-ies**) (golf) maza de madera con cabo plano de metal
**brat** [bræt] *s* (scornful) braguillas (*niño mal dispuesto*)
**brattice** ['brætɪs] *s* tabique de ventilación; *va* poner tabique de ventilación en
**bravado** [brə'vɑdo] *s* (*pl:* **-does** o **-dos**) bravata
**brave** [brev] *adj* bravo, valiente; airoso, garboso; *s* valiente; guerrero indio norteamericano; *va* arrostrar, hacer frente a; desafiar, retar
**bravery** ['brevərɪ] *s* bravura (*ánimo, valor; buen aire, apostura*); gala, atavío
**bravo** ['brɑvo] o ['brevo] *s* (*pl:* **-voes** o **-vos**) bravo (*asesino*); ['brɑvo] *s* (*pl:* **-vos**) bravo (*grito de aplauso*); *interj* ¡ bravo!
**bravura** [brə'vjʊrə] o [brə'vʊrə] *s* arrojo, brío, pujanza; (mus.) bravura
**brawl** [brɔl] *s* pendencia, reyerta; alboroto, vocerío; ruido (*de un arroyo*); *vn* armar pendencia; alborotar; correr ruidosamente (*un arroyo*)
**brawler** ['brɔlər] *s* pendenciero, alborotador
**brawn** [brɔn] *s* músculo; carne adobada de verraco
**brawny** ['brɔnɪ] *adj* (*comp:* **-ier;** *super:* **-iest**) musculoso, fornido
**bray** [bre] *s* rebuzno; *va* triturar, pulverizar; *vn* rebuznar
**Braz.** abr. de **Brazil** y **Brazilian**
**braze** [brez] *s* soldadura de latón, soldadura fuerte; *va* soldar con latón, soldar en fuerte; cubrir de latón; broncear; adornar con latón
**brazen** ['brezən] *adj* hecho de latón; bronceado; bronco, áspero; descarado, desvergonzado; *va* arrostrar descaradamente; envalentonar; **to brazen out** o **through** llevar a cabo descaradamente
**brazier** ['breʒər] *s* brasero (*vasija*); latonero
**Brazil** [brə'zɪl] *s* el Brasil
**Brazilian** [brə'zɪljən] *adj* & *s* brasileño
**brazilin** ['bræzɪlɪn] *s* (chem.) brasilina
**Brazil nut** *s* castaña de Pará, castaña del Marañón
**Brazil-nut tree** [brə'zɪl ˌnʌt] *s* (bot.) juvia, almendrón
**brazilwood** [brə'zɪlˌwʊd] *s* palo brasil, palo del Brasil
**breach** [britʃ] *s* abertura, hendidura, grieta; brecha (*en una pared o muralla*); violación; abuso (*de confianza*); *va* practicar una abertura en; abrir una brecha en
**breach of faith** *s* falta de fidelidad
**breach of peace** *s* perturbación del orden público
**breach of promise** *s* incumplimiento de promesa matrimonial
**breach of trust** *s* abuso de confianza
**bread** [brɛd] *s* pan; **on bread and water** a pan y agua; **to break bread with** sentarse a la mesa con; **to cast one's bread upon the waters** hacer el bien sin mirar a quién; **to know which side one's bread is buttered on** arrimarse al sol que más calienta; *va* (cook.) empanar (*envolver en ralladuras de pan*)
**bread and butter** *s* pan con mantequilla; (coll.) pan de cada día
**bread-and-butter** ['brɛdən'bʌtər] *adj* juvenil; práctico; prosaico; de consumo o uso general
**bread-and-butter letter** *s* carta de agradecimiento enviada después de una visita
**breadboard** ['brɛdˌbord] *s* tablero para amasar o cortar pan
**bread crumbs** *spl* pan rallado
**breaded** ['brɛdɪd] *adj* empanado
**breadfruit** ['brɛdˌfrut] *s* fruto del pan; (bot.) árbol del pan
**breadfruit tree** *s* (bot.) árbol del pan
**bread line** *s* cola del pan
**bread mold** *s* moho del pan
**breadstuff** ['brɛdˌstʌf] *s* cereales, granos, harina (*que sirven para hacer el pan*); pan
**breadth** [brɛdθ] *s* anchura; paño (*ancho de una tela*); extensión, espaciosidad; tolerancia
**breadthways** ['brɛdθˌwez] o **breadthwise** ['brɛdθˌwaɪz] *adv* a lo ancho
**breadwinner** ['brɛdˌwɪnər] *s* persona que gana el pan de la familia, sostén de la familia
**break** [brek] *s* rompimiento; interrupción; intervalo, pausa; cambio repentino; fragmento; grieta, hendidura, raja; blanco (*en los escritos*); claro (*en las nubes*); huída, evasión (*p.ej., de la cárcel*); gallo (*nota falsa en el canto*); ruptura

(*entre amigos*); (slang) disparate; (slang) suerte (*buena o mala*); (pros.) cesura; (elec.) corte, interrupción; (com.) baja (*de los precios*); **to give someone a break** abrirle a uno la puerta; **to make a break** escaparse; romper relaciones; (slang) cometer un disparate ‖ (*pret:* **broke;** *pp:* **broken**) *va* romper; domar; cambiar (*un billete*); comunicar (*p.ej., una mala noticia*); amortiguar (*p.ej., un golpe*); moderar (*la velocidad*); suspender (*relaciones*); faltar a (*la palabra, un juramento*); (mil.) degradar; (sport) batir (*un record*); (elec.) cortar (*un circuito*); (phonet.) diptongar; quebrantar (*un hábito; un testamento; la prisión o la cárcel*); romper (*una ley*); descompletar (*un juego de piezas iguales*); **to break asunder** separar en dos partes; despedazar; **to break down** analizar; **to break in** forzar (*p.ej., una puerta*); **to break oneself of a habit** deshacerse de un hábito; **to break open** abrir rompiendo; abrir con violencia, abrir por la fuerza; **to break up** desmenuzar; disolver (*p.ej., una reunión*); esparcir (*p.ej., una muchedumbre*); (coll.) desconcertar; **to break wind** ventosear ‖ *vn* romperse; romper (*las olas, el día*); quebrarse, interrumpirse; dispersarse (*la multitud*); emitirse (*un grito*); reventar; (box.) separarse; aclarar (*el tiempo*); bajar (*los precios*); (phonet.) diptongarse; romperse (*el corazón*), p.ej., **his heart is breaking** se le rompe el corazón; quebrantarse (*la salud*), p. ej., **his health is breaking** se le quebranta la salud; estallar (*la ira; una persona con ira; una noticia*); mudar (*la voz de un muchacho*); cascarse (*perder la calidad musical una voz*); cesar (*la sequía*); salir (*bien o mal*); **to break asunder** separarse; desmenuzarse; **to break away** escaparse; irse súbitamente; cambiar súbitamente; salir antes de la señal de partida; **to break down** descomponerse, desbaratarse; perder la salud; prorrumpir en llanto; **to break even** salir en paz, salir sin ganar ni perder; **to break forth** romper, salir repentinamente; brotar; exclamar; **to break in** entrar por fuerza; irrumpir, entrar de repente; irrumpir en; **to break into** forzar (*p.ej., una puerta*); allanar (*una casa*); soltarse en (*p.ej., lágrimas*); **to break into a run** empezar a correr, salir corriendo; **to break loose** desprenderse; escaparse; desencadenarse (*p.ej., la tempestad*); desbocarse (*un caballo; una persona en injurias*); **to break off** desprenderse; pararse repentinamente; **to break out** estallar (*una guerra, una tempestad*); declararse (*un incendio, una epidemia*); brotar granos (*en la piel*); romper (*en risa, en llanto*); **to break through** abrir paso por entre; abrirse paso; **to break up** desmenuzarse; disolverse, levantarse (*una reunión*); dispersarse (*la multitud*); **to break with** romper con, enemistarse con

**breakable** ['brekəbəl] *adj* rompible, quebradizo

**breakage** ['brekɪdʒ] *s* fractura, rotura; estropicio; indemnización por objetos quebrados

**breakax** o **breakaxe** ['brek,æks] *s* (bot.) quiebrahacha

**breakdown** ['brek,daʊn] *s* parada imprevista, avería repentina; pana (*de automóvil*); fracaso, mal éxito; ruptura (*p.ej., de negociaciones*); análisis; (chem.) descomposición; (med.) colapso; (U.S.A.) baile ruidoso

**breaker** ['brekər] *s* cachón (*ola*); triturador; barril pequeño; (elec.) disyuntor

**breaker points** *spl* (aut.) contactos de distribuidor

**breakfast** ['brɛkfəst] *s* desayuno; *vn* desayunar o desayunarse; **to breakfast on** desayunarse con

**breakfast food** *s* cereal para el desayuno

**breakneck** ['brek,nɛk] *adj* vertiginoso, precipitado; **at breakneck speed** a mata caballo

**break of day** *s* amanecer

**breakthrough** ['brek,θru] *s* (mil.) ruptura, brecha; (min.) rompimiento; (fig.) adelanto repentino e inesperado

**breakup** ['brek,ʌp] *s* separación; disolución, dispersión; parada, terminación; desplome; (med.) postración

**breakwater** ['brek,wɔtər] o ['brek,wɑtər] *s* rompeolas

**bream** [brim] *s* (ichth.) brema; *va* (naut.) dar fuego a (*fondos*)

**breast** [brɛst] *s* pecho, seno; pechuga (*del ave*); pechera (*de una prenda de vestir*); testera, frente, fachada; (min.) cara, frente; **to beat one's breast** darse golpes de pecho; **to make a clean breast of** reconocer con franqueza; **to make a clean breast of it** confesarlo todo; **to nurse at the breast** criar a los pechos; *va* arrostrar, acometer, embestir

**breastband** ['brɛst,bænd] *s* petral

**breastbone** ['brɛst,bon] *s* (anat.) esternón

**breast collar** *s* petral

**breast drill** *s* taladro o berbiquí de pecho

**breasthook** ['brɛst,hʊk] *s* (naut.) buzarda

**breastpin** ['brɛst,pɪn] *s* alfiler de pecho

**breastplate** ['brɛst,plet] *s* (arm.) peto; pectoral (*del sumo sacerdote hebreo*)

**breastrail** ['brɛst,rel] *s* (arch. & naut.) cairel

**breast stroke** *s* brazada de pecho

**breastsummer** ['brɛst,sʌmər] o ['brɛs,sʌmər] *s* (arch.) dintel

**breast wheel** *s* (hyd.) rueda de costado, rueda de pecho

**breastwork** ['brɛst,wʌrk] *s* (fort.) parapeto; (naut.) propao

**breath** [brɛθ] *s* respiración, aliento; hálito, soplo, perfume; respiro (*descanso, alivio*); vida, espíritu; susurro, murmullo; (phonet.) explosión; (phonet.) aspiración; **at every breath** a cada instante; **below one's breath** por lo bajo, en voz baja; **in the same breath** al mismo tiempo; **to catch one's breath** suspender un ratito la respiración, tomar aliento; **to gasp for breath** respirar anhelosamente; **to hold one's breath** contener el aliento; **to save one's breath** guardar silencio; **out of breath** sin aliento; **short of breath** corto de resuello; **under one's breath** por lo bajo, en voz baja

**breathe** [brið] *va* respirar; inspirar, infundir; desalentar; exhalar; (phonet.) aspirar; (fig.) respirar (*p.ej., amor, bondad*); **not to breathe a word** no respirar; **to breathe life into** alentar; **to breathe one's last** dar el último suspiro; *vn* respirar; soplar suavemente; **to breathe freely** respirar, cobrar aliento; **to breathe in** aspirar; **to breathe out** espirar

**breather** ['briðər] *s* respiradero; respiro, rato de descanso; ejercicio físico que hace perder la respiración

**breathing** ['briðɪŋ] *s* respiración; brisa suave, soplo de viento; (phonet.) aspiración (*de la h*); (gram.) espíritu (*en el griego*)

**breathing space** *s* lugar de descanso; rato de descanso

**breathing spell** *s* respiro, rato de descanso

**breathless** ['brɛθlɪs] *adj* falto de aliento, jadeante; intenso, vivo; muerto; sin aire, tranquilo; **to leave breathless** dejar sin aliento

**breath of life** *s* soplo de vida

**breathtaking** ['brɛθ,tekɪŋ] *adj* emocionante, imponente, conmovedor

**breccia** ['brɛtʃɪə] o ['brɛʃɪə] *s* (geol.) brecha

**bred** [brɛd] *pret & pp de* **breed**

**breech** [britʃ] *s* trasero (*del animal*); trasera (*de una cosa*); culata, recámara (*del cañón de un arma de fuego*); **breeches** ['brɪtʃɪz] *spl* calzones; (coll.) pantalones; **to wear the breeches** llevar los calzones, ponerse los pantalones (*una mujer*); [britʃ] o [brɪtʃ] *va* poner los calzones a

**breechblock** ['britʃ,blɑk] *s* cierre de cañón

**breechcloth** ['britʃ,klɔθ] o ['britʃ,klɑθ] o **breechclout** ['britʃ,klaʊt] *s* taparrabo

**breeches buoy** ['britʃɪz] *s* (naut.) boya pantalón, pantalón de salvamento

**breeching** ['brɪtʃɪŋ] o ['britʃɪŋ] *s* retranca

**breechloader** ['britʃ,lodər] *s* arma de retrocarga

**breechloading** ['britʃ,lodɪŋ] *adj* de retrocarga

**breed** [brid] *s* raza, casta (*de animales*); clase, especie; (*pret & pp:* **bred**) *va* criar; *vn* criarse

**breeder** ['bridər] *s* criador (*de animales*); reproductor (*animal*); criadero (*animal fecundo*); paridera (*hembra fecunda*); fuente, origen

**breeder reactor** *s* (phys.) reactor de cría, reactor-generador

**breeding** ['bridɪŋ] *s* cría; cría y reproducción;

crianza, modales; **bad breeding** mala crianza; **good breeding** buena crianza
**breeding ground** *s* criadero de animales
**breeding pond** *s* vivar, vivero de peces
**breeze** [briz] *s* brisa, airecillo; (coll.) agitación, alboroto
**breezy** ['brizɪ] *adj* (*comp:* **-ier;** *super:* **-iest**) airoso; animado, vivo, alegre; (coll.) ligero, vivaracho
**Brenner** ['brɛnər] *s* Brenero
**br'er** [brʌr] *s* (dial.) hermano
**brethren** ['brɛðrɪn] *spl* hermanos (*p.ej., de una hermandad*)
**Breton** ['brɛtən] *adj & s* bretón
**breve** [briv] *s* (mus.) breve; (gram.) marca curva que se pone sobre las vocales para indicar su brevedad
**brevet** [brə'vɛt] o ['brɛvɪt] *s* (mil.) comisión honoraria; *adj* (mil.) honorario; (*pret & pp:* **-veted** o **-vetted;** *ger:* **-veting** o **-vetting**) *va* (mil.) conceder una comisión honoraria a
**breviary** ['brivɪ,ɛrɪ] o ['brɛvɪ,ɛrɪ] *s* (*pl:* **-ies**) breviario; (eccl.) breviario
**brevier** [brə'vɪr] *s* (print.) breviario
**brevipennate** [,brɛvɪ'pɛnet] *adj* (orn.) brevipenne
**brevity** ['brɛvɪtɪ] *s* (*pl:* **-ties**) brevedad
**brew** [bru] *s* calderada de cerveza; mezcla; *va* bracear (*cerveza*); cocer (*tisana*); fraguar; tramar, urdir; *vn* fabricar cerveza; formarse, prepararse; amenazar (*p.ej., una tormenta*)
**brewer** ['bruər] *s* bracero, cervecero
**brewer's yeast** *s* levadura de cerveza
**brewery** ['bruərɪ] *s* (*pl:* **-ies**) cervecería, fábrica de cerveza
**briar** ['braɪər] *s* var. de **brier**
**Briareus** [braɪ'ɛrɪəs] *s* (myth.) Briareo
**briarwood** ['braɪər,wud] *s* var. de **brierwood**
**briary** ['braɪərɪ] *adj* var. de **briery**
**bribe** [braɪb] *s* soborno; *va* sobornar
**bribery** ['braɪbərɪ] *s* (*pl:* **-ies**) soborno
**bric-à-brac** o **bric-a-brac** ['brɪkə,bræk] *s* curiosidades
**brick** [brɪk] *s* ladrillo; ladrillos; (coll.) buen sujeto; *adj* de ladrillo; *va* enladrillar; **to brick up** enladrillar, tapar con ladrillos
**brickbat** ['brɪk,bæt] *s* pedazo de ladrillo; (coll.) palabra hiriente
**brick ice cream** *s* queso helado, helado al corte
**brickkiln** ['brɪk,kɪl] o ['brɪk,kɪln] *s* horno de ladrillos
**bricklayer** ['brɪk,leər] *s* ladrillador
**bricklaying** ['brɪk,leɪŋ] *s* enladrillado
**brick-red** ['brɪk,rɛd] *adj* ladrilloso, rojo ladrillo
**brickwork** ['brɪk,wʌrk] *s* enladrillado
**brickyard** ['brɪk,jɑrd] *s* ladrillal
**bridal** ['braɪdəl] *adj* nupcial; de novia, de la novia; *s* boda
**bridal wreath** *s* corona nupcial; (bot.) espirea
**bride** [braɪd] *s* novia; **the bride and groom** los novios, los recién casados
**bridegroom** ['braɪd,grum] o ['braɪd,grʊm] *s* novio
**bridesmaid** ['braɪdz,med] *s* madrina de boda
**bridewell** ['braɪdwɛl] *s* (Brit.) casa de corrección; (coll.) cárcel
**bridge** [brɪdʒ] *s* puente; (naut.) puente; (mus.) puente (*del violín*); puente dental; caballete (*de la nariz*); (billiards) violín; bridge (*juego de naipes*); **in bridge** (elec.) en paralelo; *va* tender un puente sobre; salvar (*un obstáculo*); ayudar a salir de (*una dificultad*)
**bridgeboard** ['brɪdʒ,bord] *s* (carp.) gualdera, larguero de escalera
**bridgehead** ['brɪdʒ,hɛd] *s* entrada de puente; (mil.) cabeza de puente
**Bridge of Sighs** *s* puente de los suspiros
**Bridget** ['brɪdʒɪt] *s* Brígida
**bridgework** ['brɪdʒ,wʌrk] *s* construcción de puentes; puente dental
**bridle** ['braɪdəl] *s* brida, freno; (naut.) frenillo; (fig.) freno; *va* embridar; (naut.) frenillar; (fig.) embridar; *vn* engallarse, levantar la cabeza (*en son de orgullo, desdén, resentimiento, etc.*)
**bridle path** *s* camino de herradura
**bridoon** [brɪ'dun] *s* bridón
**Brie** [bri] *s* brie (*queso*)
**brief** [brif] *adj* breve; *s* resumen; (law) escrito; (eccl.) breve; **in brief** en resumen, en pocas palabras; **to hold a brief for** abogar por; *va* resumir; dar instrucciones o consejos anticipados a; (law) alegar
**brief case** *s* portapapeles, cartera
**briefing** ['brifɪŋ] *s* instrucciones breves dadas a la tripulación de un avión de combate poco antes de emprender el vuelo
**briefless** ['briflɪs] *adj* sin pleitos, sin clientes
**briefness** ['brifnɪs] *s* brevedad
**brier** ['braɪər] *s* (bot.) zarza; (bot.) brezo blanco; (bot.) rosal silvestre; zarzal; pipa hecha de madera de brezo blanco
**brierwood** ['braɪər,wud] *s* madera de las raíces del brezo blanco; pipa hecha de madera de brezo blanco
**briery** ['braɪərɪ] *adj* zarzoso, espinoso
**Brig.** abr. de **Brigadier**
**brig** [brɪg] *s* (naut.) bergantín; (naut.) calabozo en buques de guerra
**brigade** [brɪ'ged] *s* brigada; (mil.) brigada
**brigadier** [,brɪgə'dɪr] *s* (mil.) general de brigada
**brigadier general** *s* (*pl:* **brigadier generals**) (mil.) general de brigada
**brigand** ['brɪgənd] *s* bandolero
**brigandage** ['brɪgəndɪdʒ] *s* bandolerismo
**brigandine** ['brɪgəndin] o ['brɪgəndaɪn] *s* (arm.) brigantina
**brigantine** ['brɪgəntin] o ['brɪgəntaɪn] *s* (naut.) bergantín goleta
**bright** [braɪt] *adj* brillante; claro, transparente; subido (*color*); listo, inteligente; vivo, alegre; preclaro, eximio; luminoso (*pensamiento, idea*)
**bright and early** *adv* temprano y con sol
**brighten** ['braɪtən] *va* abrillantar; avivar; alegrar; *vn* avivarse; avivar, cobrar vida; alegrarse; despejarse (*el cielo*)
**bright lights** *spl* luces brillantes del barrio de los teatros y cabarets; (aut.) faros, lámparas o luces de carretera
**brightness** ['braɪtnɪs] *s* brillantez; claridad, transparencia; inteligencia; viveza, alegría
**Bright's disease** *s* (path.) brightismo, mal de Bright
**brill** [brɪl] *s* (ichth.) rodaballo; (ichth.) rodaballo menor (*Rhombus laevis*)
**brilliance** ['brɪljəns] o **brilliancy** ['brɪljənsɪ] *s* brillantez. brillo; (fig.) brillantez, brillo
**brilliant** ['brɪljənt] *adj* brillante; (fig.) brillante; *s* brillante (*piedra brillante*); (print.) tipo de tres puntos y medio
**brilliantine** [,brɪljən'tin] o ['brɪljəntin] *s* brillantina (*aceite para los cabellos; tela lustrosa*)
**brim** [brɪm] *s* borde; labio (*de un vaso*); ala (*de sombrero*); (*pret & pp:* **brimmed;** *ger:* **brimming**) *va* llenar hasta el borde; *vn* estar de bote en bote
**brimful** ['brɪm,fʊl] *adj* lleno hasta el borde
**brimmer** ['brɪmər] *s* copa o vaso lleno
**brimstone** ['brɪm,ston] *s* azufre; mujer regañona
**brindle** ['brɪndəl] *adj* leonado mosqueado o rayado; *s* animal de color leonado mosqueado o rayado; color leonado mosqueado o rayado
**brindled** ['brɪndəld] *adj* leonado mosqueado o rayado
**brindled gnu** *s* (zool.) ñu
**brine** [braɪn] *s* salmuera; agua salobre; mar; (poet.) lágrimas; *va* remojar en salmuera
**bring** [brɪŋ] (*pret & pp:* **brought**) *va* traer; llevar (*traer consigo en la mano, el bolsillo, etc.; producir; persuadir*); hacer venir; contribuir; armar (*un pleito*); **to bring about** efectuar; **to bring around** sacar de un desmayo; persuadir; **to bring away** llevarse; **to bring back** devolver; **to bring down** bajar; abatir; (fig.) abatir, humillar; **to bring down the house** hacer venirse abajo el teatro (*con aplausos*); **to bring forth** parir; producir; poner de manifiesto; sacar, dar a luz; **to bring forward** poner de manifiesto; presentar (*un argumento*); (com.) llevar (*una suma*) a otra cuenta; **to bring home** traer a casa; conducir a casa; hacer sentir claramente, demostrar de modo concluyente; **to bring in** sacar o traer a colación (*hacer mención de*); introducir

(*p.ej., una moda*); presentar (*una cuenta*); servir (*una comida*); dar (*un fallo*); entrar (*a una persona en una sala*); **to bring into play** poner en juego; **to bring off** rescatar; exculpar· llevar a cabo; **to bring on** causar, producir; **to bring oneself to** + *inf* resignarse a + *inf;* **to bring out** sacar; demostrar; presentar al público; **to bring round** sacar de un desmayo; reanimar, curar; persuadir; ganar, convertir; **to bring suit** poner pleito; **to bring to** sacar de un desmayo; parar, detener; **to bring to bear** traer (*influencia*); asestar, apuntar, dirigir; **to bring to book** llamar o traer a capítulo, pedir cuenta a; **to bring together** reunir; confrontar; reconciliar; **to bring to pass** efectuar, realizar; **to bring up** subir; acercar, arrimar (*p.ej., una silla*); educar; sacar a colación; parar de repente; **to bring upon oneself** atraerse (*p.ej., un infortunio*)

**bringing-up** ['brɪŋɪŋ'ʌp] *s* educación

**brink** [brɪŋk] *s* borde, margen; **on the brink of** al borde de; **on the brink of** + *ger* a punto de + *inf*

**brinkmanship** ['brɪŋkmənʃɪp] *s* (coll.) práctica de llevar las cosas muy cerca de la línea fronteriza del peligro ineludible

**briny** ['braɪnɪ] *adj* (*comp:* **-ier;** *super:* **-iest**) salado, salobre; **the briny** (coll.) el mar

**briquet** o **briquette** [brɪ'kɛt] *s* briqueta (*de carbón*); comprimido, pan

**Briseis** [braɪ'siɪs] *s* (myth.) Briseida

**brisk** [brɪsk] *adj* animado, vivo; fuerte; rápido

**brisket** ['brɪskɪt] *s* pecho de animal; carne cortada del pecho de un animal

**briskness** ['brɪsknɪs] *s* animación, viveza; fuerza, vigor; rapidez

**bristle** ['brɪsəl] *s* cerda; pelusa (*que se desprende de las telas*); *va* poner cerda a; erizar (*el cabello*); *vn* erizarse; erizar las cerdas (*un animal*); encresparse, montar en cólera; cubrirse, llenarse; **to bristle with** estar erizado de (*p.ej., dificultades*)

**bristletail** ['brɪsəl,tel] *s* (ent.) lepisma

**bristly** ['brɪslɪ] *adj* (*comp:* **-tlier;** *super:* **-tliest**) cerdoso, erizado. sedeño

**Bristol board** ['brɪstəl] *s* bristol

**Brit.** abr. de **Britain** y **British**

**Britain** ['brɪtən] *s* Bretaña; la Gran Bretaña

**Britannia** [brɪ'tænɪə] *s* Bretaña; la Gran Bretaña; el Imperio Británico; (*l.c.*) *s* metal inglés, metal britannia

**britannia metal** *s* metal britannia, metal británico, metal inglés

**Britannic** [brɪ'tænɪk] *adj* británico

**Briticism** ['brɪtɪsɪzəm] *s* modismo o vocablo del inglés hablado en Inglaterra

**British** ['brɪtɪʃ] *adj* británico; **the British** los britanos

**British Columbia** *s* la Colombia Británica

**British Commonwealth of Nations** *s* Comunidad Británica de Naciones

**British East Africa** *s* el África Oriental Inglesa

**British Empire** *s* Imperio Británico

**Britisher** ['brɪtɪʃər] *s* britano

**British Guiana** *s* la Guayana Inglesa

**British Honduras** *s* la Honduras Británica

**British India** *s* la India Inglesa

**British Isles** *spl* islas Británicas

**British Malaya** *s* la Malaya Británica

**British Museum** *s* Museo Británico

**British Somaliland** *s* la Somalía Británica

**British thermal unit** *s* unidad térmica británica

**British West Africa** *s* el África Occidental Inglesa

**British West Indies** *spl* Indias Occidentales Británicas

**Briton** ['brɪtən] *s* britano

**Brittany** ['brɪtənɪ] *s* Bretaña; bretaña (*tela*)

**brittle** ['brɪtəl] *adj* quebradizo, vidrioso

**bro.** abr. de **brother**

**broach** [brotʃ] *s* asador, espetón; espita; broche, prendedero; (mach.) escariador, mandril; *va* sacar a colación; espetar; decantar, trasegar (*un líquido*); (mach.) brochar; *vn* emerger (*p.ej., una ballena, un submarino*); **to broach to** (naut.) tomar por avante

**broad** [brɔd] *adj* ancho; liberal, tolerante; general, comprensivo; lato (*sentido de una palabra*); claro, franco, sencillo; grosero, tosco; verde, libre; pleno (*día, mediodía, etc.*); (phonet.) abierto; dialectal; **as broad as it is long** que igual da que sea o que se haga de uno o de otro modo; **broad hint** insinuación clara, indirecta del padre Cobos; **broad in one's outlook** de amplias miras e ideas

**broadax** o **broadaxe** ['brɔd,æks] *s* hacha de carpintero; doladera (*de tonelero*); hacha de armas

**broadbrim** ['brɔd,brɪm] *s* sombrero de alas anchas; (*cap.*) *s* (coll.) cuáquero

**broadcast** ['brɔd,kæst] o ['brɔd,kɑst] *s* difusión, esparcimiento; radiodifusión; audición (*programa radiotelefónico*); *adj* difundido, esparcido; radiodifundido; *adv* por todas partes; (*pret & pp:* **-cast**) *va* difundir, esparcir; (*pret & pp:* **-cast** o **-casted**) *va* radiodifundir, emitir, radiar

**broadcasting** ['brɔd,kæstɪŋ] o ['brɔd,kɑstɪŋ] *adj* emisor, radiodifusor; *s* emisión, radiodifusión

**broadcasting station** *s* estación de radiodifusión, emisora, radiodifusora

**broadcloth** ['brɔd,klɔθ] o ['brɔd,klɑθ] *s* velarte

**broaden** ['brɔdən] *va* ensanchar; *vn* ensancharse

**broad-gauge** ['brɔd,gedʒ] o **broad-gauged** ['brɔd,gedʒd] *adj* de vía ancha (*de 56 y ½ pulgadas inglesas*); tolerante, de amplias miras

**broad jump** *s* (sport) salto de longitud

**broadloom** ['brɔd,lum] *adj* tejido en telar ancho y en color sólido

**broad-minded** ['brɔd'maɪndɪd] *adj* tolerante, de amplias miras

**broadness** ['brɔdnɪs] *s* anchura; tolerancia; abertura (*de una vocal*)

**broad-shouldered** ['brɔd'ʃoldərd] *adj* ancho de espaldas

**broadside** ['brɔd,saɪd] *s* (naut.) costado; batería del costado; (naut.) andanada; lado o superficie uniforme y ancha; cara de un pliego de papel; hoja suelta impresa en un solo lado; (coll.) torrente de injurias; *adv* por lo ancho; con el costado vuelto de través

**broadsword** ['brɔd,sord] *s* espada ancha, chafarote

**Brobdingnagian** ['brɑbdɪŋ'nægɪən] *adj* gigantesco, colosal, enorme; *s* gigante

**brocade** [bro'ked] *s* brocado; *va* tejer o decorar con brocado

**brocaded** [bro'kedɪd] *adj* brocado

**brocatel** [,brɑkə'tɛl] *s* brocatel (*tejido y mármol*)

**broccoli** ['brɑkəlɪ] *s* (bot.) brécol, brécoles o bróculi

**brochette** [bro'ʃɛt] *s* broqueta

**brochure** [bro'ʃur] *s* folleto

**brogan** ['brogən] *s* zapato fuerte y basto

**brogue** [brog] *s* zapato fuerte y basto; zapato basto de orejas sueltas; acento irlandés; idioma corrompido

**broil** [brɔɪl] *s* carne asada a la parrilla; camorra, pendencia; *va* asar a la parrilla; calentar con exceso; *vn* asarse (*padecer calor*)

**broiled meat** *s* carne asada a la parrilla

**broiler** ['brɔɪler] *s* parrilla; polla para asar en parrillas

**broke** [brok] *adj* (slang) sin blanca; *pret de* **break**

**broken** ['brokən] *adj* quebrado, fragoso; interrumpido. desigual, disparejo; suelto, separado; agotado, debilitado; amansado, sumiso; chapurrado; *pp de* **break**

**broken-down** ['brokən'daun] *adj* abatido, arruinado; deshecho, descompuesto

**broken-hearted** ['brokən'hɑrtɪd] *adj* acongojado, traspasado de dolor

**broken-winded** ['brokən'wɪndɪd] *adj* corto de aliento; (vet.) atacado de huélfago

**broker** ['brokər] *s* corredor

**brokerage** ['brokərɪdʒ] *s* corretaje

**bromate** ['bromet] *s* (chem.) bromato

**brome grass** [brom] *s* (bot.) bromo

**bromeliaceous** [bro,milɪ'eʃəs] *adj* (bot.) bromeliáceo

**bromic** ['bromɪk] *adj* (chem.) brómico

**bromid** ['bromɪd] o **bromide** ['bromaɪd] o

['bromɪd] *s* (chem.) bromuro; (pharm.) bromuro de potasio; (slang) trivialidad
**bromidic** [bro'mɪdɪk] *adj* (coll.) común, trivial
**bromin** ['bromɪn] o **bromine** ['bromin] o ['bromɪn] *s* (chem.) bromo
**bronchia** ['brɑŋkɪə] *spl* (anat.) bronquíolos
**bronchial** ['brɑŋkɪəl] *adj* bronquial
**bronchial tubes** *spl* (anat.) bronquios, bronquíolos
**bronchiole** ['brɑŋkɪol] *s* (anat.) bronquíolo
**bronchitic** [brɑŋ'kɪtɪk] *adj* bronquítico
**bronchitis** [brɑŋ'kaɪtɪs] *s* (path.) bronquitis
**broncho** ['brɑŋko] *s* (*pl:* **-chos**) var. de **bronco**
**bronchopneumonia** [,brɑŋkonju'monjə] o [,brɑŋkonu'monjə] *s* (path.) bronconeumonía
**bronchorrea** [,brɑŋkə'riə] *s* (path.) broncorrea
**bronchoscope** ['brɑŋkəskop] *s* broncoscopio
**bronchoscopy** [brɑŋ'kɑskəpɪ] *s* broncoscopia
**bronchus** ['brɑŋkəs] *s* (*pl:* **-chi** [kaɪ]) (anat.) bronquio; (anat.) bronquíolo
**bronco** ['brɑŋko] *s* (*pl:* **-cos**) (U.S.A.) potro cerril, potro sin domar
**broncobuster** ['brɑŋko,bʌstər] *s* chalán, picador, domador de potros
**brontosaurus** [,brɑntə'sɔrəs] *s* (pal.) brontosauro
**bronze** [brɑnz] *s* bronce (*aleación; objeto de arte; polvo*); *adj* de bronce, hecho de bronce; bronceado; *va* broncear; *vn* broncearse
**bronze age** *s* (myth.) edad de bronce; (*caps.*) *s* (archeol.) edad del bronce
**bronzesmith** ['brɑnz,smɪθ] *s* broncista
**brooch** [brotʃ] o [brutʃ] *s* alfiler de pecho, prendedero
**brood** [brud] *s* camada, cría; nidada; familia; raza, casta; *va* empollar; cobijar, albergar; *vn* enclocar, encobar; **to brood on** u **over** meditar con tristeza
**brooder** ['brudər] *s* incubadora; clueca (*gallina*); rumión
**broody** ['brudɪ] *adj* (*comp:* **-ier;** *super:* **-iest**) clueco; (fig.) triste, melancólico
**brook** [brʊk] *s* arroyo; *va* tolerar, permitir
**brooklet** ['brʊklɪt] *s* arroyuelo
**brooklime** ['brʊk,laɪm] *s* (bot.) berro de caballo; (bot.) becabunga
**brook trout** *s* (ichth.) trucha norteamericana (*Salvelinus fontinalis*)
**brookweed** ['brʊk,wid] *s* (bot.) pamplina de agua
**broom** [brum] o [brʊm] *s* escoba; (bot.) hiniesta, retama
**broomcorn** ['brum,kɔrn] o ['brʊm,kɔrn] *s* (bot.) sorgo común
**broomcorn millet** *s* (bot.) millo de escoba
**broom goosefoot** *s* (bot.) ceñiglo de jardín
**broomstick** ['brum,stɪk] o ['brʊm,stɪk] *s* palo de escoba
**bros.** abr. de **brothers**
**broth** [brɔθ] o [brɑθ] *s* caldo; (bact.) caldo de cultivo
**brothel** ['brɑθəl] o ['brɑðəl] *s* burdel
**brother** ['brʌðər] *s* hermano
**brotherhood** ['brʌðərhʊd] *s* hermandad
**brother-in-law** ['brʌðərɪn,lɔ] *s* (*pl:* **brothers-in-law**) cuñado, hermano político; concuñado
**Brother Jonathan** *s* el hermano Jonatás (*los EE.UU. o el pueblo de los EE.UU.*)
**brotherly** ['brʌðərlɪ] *adj* fraternal; amistoso, bondadoso; *adv* fraternalmente, como hermano, como hermanos
**brougham** [brum], ['bruəm] o ['broəm] *s* brougham (*carruaje; automóvil*)
**brought** [brɔt] *pret & pp de* **bring**
**brow** [braʊ] *s* frente *f;* ceja; (fig.) ceja (*de monte*); borde (*de despeñadero*); **to knit one's brow** fruncir las cejas
**browbeat** ['braʊ,bit] (*pret:* **-beat;** *pp:* **-beaten**) *va* intimidar mirando con ceño; intimidar con amenazas
**brown** [braʊn] *adj* pardo, moreno, castaño; tostado del sol; *s* pardo, color pardo; *va* poner pardo o moreno; broncear; tostar, quemar; (cook.) dorar; *vn* ponerse pardo o moreno; broncearse; tostarse, quemarse; (cook.) dorarse
**brown bear** *s* (zool.) oso pardo
**brown betty** *s* pudín de manzana y pan
**brown bread** *s* pan bazo, pan moreno
**brown coal** *s* lignito
**brown hyena** *s* (zool.) hiena parda
**Brownian movement** ['braʊnɪən] *s* (phys.) movimiento browniano
**brownie** ['braʊnɪ] *s* duende moreno y benévolo; tortita de chocolate y nueces
**brownish** ['braʊnɪʃ] *adj* pardusco
**brown race** *s* raza cobriza
**brown rat** *s* (zool.) rata de alcantarilla
**brown rice** *s* arroz no pulimentado
**brown shirt** *s* camisa parda (*nazi*)
**brownstone** ['braʊn,ston] *s* arenisca de color pardo rojizo
**brown study** *s* absorción, suspensión, pensamiento profundo
**brown sugar** *s* azúcar terciado, azúcar moreno
**brown thrasher** *s* (orn.) túrdido norteamericano (*Toxostoma rufum*)
**browse** [braʊz] *s* ramón; *va* comer (*las ramitas y las hojas de los árboles*); pacer (*la hierba*); *vn* ramonear; pacer; hojear un libro ociosamente; **to browse about** o **around** examinar ociosamente libros u obras de arte; recorrer las tiendas, más por curiosidad que por ánimo de comprar
**brucellosis** [,brusə'losɪs] *s* (path. & vet.) brucelosis
**brucine** ['brusin] o ['brusɪn] *s* (pharm.) brucina
**brucite** ['brusaɪt] *s* (mineral.) brucita
**Bruges** ['brudʒɪz] o [bruʒ] *s* Brujas
**bruin** ['bruɪn] *s* oso
**bruise** [bruz] *s* contusión, magulladura; *va* contundir, magullar; majar; *vn* contundirse, magullarse
**bruiser** ['bruzər] *s* púgil; matón
**bruit** [brut] *va* esparcir, divulgar; **to bruit about** esparcir, divulgar
**brunet** [bru'nɛt] *adj* moreno; *s* moreno (*hombre moreno*)
**brunette** [bru'nɛt] *adj* moreno; *s* morena (*mujer morena*)
**Brunhild** ['brunhɪld] *s* Brunilda
**brunt** [brʌnt] *s* fuerza, empuje; **the brunt** lo más difícil; **to bear the brunt of the battle** llevar el peso de la batalla
**brush** [brʌʃ] *s* cepillo, escobilla; brocha; pincel; cola peluda (*de un perro*); cepilladura; brochada; roce; escaramuza, encuentro; ramojo; broza (*despojo de las plantas; maleza*); (elec.) escobilla; *va* cepillar; quitar frotando; rozar; **to brush aside** echar bruscamente a un lado; **to brush up** retocar (*un cuadro*); repasar, refrescar (*la pintura de una casa*); *vn* moverse apresuradamente; **to brush by** pasar cerca de (*una persona*) sin hacer caso de ella; **to brush up on** renovar el conocimiento de (*un asunto*)
**brush discharge** *s* (elec.) efluvio
**brush holder** *s* (elec.) portaescobillas
**brush-off** ['brʌʃ,ɔf] o ['brʌʃ,ɑf] *s* (slang) despedida, desaire; **to give the brush-off to** (slang) despedir noramala, rehusar, desairar
**brush shift** *s* (elec.) decalaje de escobillas
**brushwood** ['brʌʃ,wʊd] *s* broza (*despojo de las plantas; maleza*)
**brushy** ['brʌʃɪ] *adj* (*comp:* **-ier;** *super:* **-iest**) cerdoso, peludo; zarzoso
**brusque** [brʌsk] *adj* brusco
**brusqueness** ['brʌsknɪs] *s* brusquedad
**Brussels** ['brʌsəlz] *s* Bruselas
**Brussels carpet** *s* alfombra de Bruselas
**Brussels lace** *s* encaje de Bruselas
**Brussels sprouts** *spl* (bot.) bretones, col de Bruselas
**brutal** ['brutəl] *adj* brutal
**brutality** [bru'tælɪtɪ] *s* (*pl:* **-ties**) brutalidad
**brutalize** ['brutəlaɪz] *va* brutalizar
**brute** [brut] *adj & s* bruto
**brutish** ['brutɪʃ] *adj* bruto
**Brutus** ['brutəs] *s* Bruto
**bryology** [braɪ'ɑlədʒɪ] *s* briología
**bryony** ['braɪənɪ] *s* (*pl:* **-nies**) (bot.) brionia, nueza
**bryophyte** ['braɪəfaɪt] *s* (bot.) briofita
**b.s.** abr. de **balance sheet** y **bill of sale**
**B.S.** abr. de **Baccalaureus Scientiae** (Lat.) **Bachelor of Science**

**B.S.A.** abr. de **Bachelor of Scientific Agriculture** y **Boy Scouts of America**
**B.Sc.** abr. de **Baccalaureus Scientiae** (Lat.) **Bachelor of Science**
**Bt.** abr. de **baronet**
**B.T.** o **B.Th.** abr. de **Baccalaureus Theologiae** (Lat.) **Bachelor of Theology**
**B.T.U.** abr. de **British thermal unit**
**bu.** abr. de **bushel**
**bubal** ['bjubəl] *s* (zool.) búbalo
**bubble** ['bʌbəl] *s* burbuja, borbollón; ampolla; quimera, ilusión, sueño descabellado y efímero; *vn* burbujear, borbotar; **to bubble over** desbordar, rebosar; **to bubble over with joy** desbordar o rebosar de gozo
**bubble dance** *s* baile de los globos
**bubble gum** *s* chicle de globo, chicle de burbuja, chicle hinchable
**bubble sextant** *s* sextante de burbuja
**bubble tower** *s* torre de burbujeo
**bubble tube** *s* tubo de burbuja
**bubbling** ['bʌblɪŋ] *adj* burbujeante; (fig.) efusivo; *s* burbujeo, borbollón
**bubbly** ['bʌblɪ] *adj* espumoso, efervescente
**bubo** ['bjubo] *s* (*pl:* **-boes**) (path.) buba, bubón
**buboed** ['bjubod] *adj* buboso
**bubonic** [bju'bɑnɪk] *adj* bubónico
**bubonic plague** *s* (path.) peste bubónica
**buccal** ['bʌkəl] *adj* bucal
**buccaneer** [,bʌkə'nɪr] *s* bucanero
**buccinator** ['bʌksɪ,netər] *s* (anat.) bucinador
**Bucephalus** [bju'sɛfələs] *s* Bucéfalo
**Bucharest** [,bjukə'rɛst] o [,bukə'rɛst] *s* Bucarest
**buchu** ['bjukju] o ['buku] *s* (pharm.) buchú
**buck** [bʌk] *s* (zool.) cabrón; (zool.) gamo, ciervo, conejo (*macho*); caballete, cabrilla; petimetre, pisaverde; encorvada, corveta (*de un caballo*); colada (*lejía*); (coll.) indio o negro varón; (slang) dólar; **to pass the buck** (coll.) echar la carga a otro; *va* (coll.) hacer frente a, resistir; (coll.) tirar (*al jinete*) encorvándose; (coll.) embestir, arrojarse sobre; (coll.) acornear; (mil.) castigar atando los codos, muñecas y rodillas; colar (*la ropa*); *vn* encorvarse; (elec.) ser contrario; **to buck against** embestir contra; **to buck up** (coll.) animarse, cobrar ánimo
**buckaroo** ['bʌkəru] o [,bʌkə'ru] *s* (*pl:* **-roos**) vaquero
**buck bean** *s* (bot.) trébol acuático o de agua
**buckboard** ['bʌk,bord] *s* carretón de cuatro ruedas sin muelles
**bucket** ['bʌkɪt] *s* balde, cubo; pozal (*de un pozo*); paleta (*de turbina u otra rueda*); cangilón (*de la noria*); cucharón o pala (*de excavadora*); **to kick the bucket** (slang) liar el petate, estirar la pata
**bucketful** ['bʌkɪtful] *s* balde, cubo (*contenido*)
**bucket seat** *s* (aut.) baquet
**bucket shop** *s* agencia que compra y vende acciones para otros maladministrando los intereses de éstos
**bucket wheel** *s* rueda de cangilones
**buckeye** ['bʌk,aɪ] *s* (bot.) castaño de Indias
**Buckingham Palace** ['bʌkɪŋəm] *s* palacio Buckingham
**buckle** ['bʌkəl] *s* hebilla; pandeo; *va* abrochar con hebilla; *vn* pandear; **to buckle down to** dedicarse con empeño a; **to buckle with** luchar con
**buckler** ['bʌklər] *s* escudo, broquel
**buckling** ['bʌklɪŋ] *s* pandeo
**buck private** *s* (slang) soldado raso
**buckram** ['bʌkrəm] *s* percalina, bocací; tiesura, ceremonia excesiva
**bucksaw** ['bʌk,sɔ] *s* sierra de bastidor
**buckshot** ['bʌk,ʃɑt] *s* perdigón zorrero
**buckskin** ['bʌk,skɪn] *s* ante; badana; **buckskins** *spl* calzones de ante
**buckthorn** ['bʌk,θɔrn] *s* (bot.) espino cerval
**bucktooth** ['bʌk,tuθ] *s* (*pl:* **-teeth**) diente saliente
**buckwheat** ['bʌk,hwit] *s* (bot.) alforfón, trigo sarraceno
**buckwheat cake** *s* panqué hecho de harina de trigo sarraceno
**bucolic** [bju'kɑlɪk] *adj* bucólico; *s* bucólica (*composición poética*); (hum.) pastor, campesino
**bucranium** [bju'krenɪəm] *s* (*pl:* **-a** [ə]) (arch.) bucráneo
**bud** [bʌd] *s* botón; brote; joven; niña que se pone de largo; (anat., bot. & zool.) yema; **to nip in the bud** cortar de raíz, atajar desde los principios; (*pret & pp:* **budded;** *ger:* **budding**) *va* injertar (*una yema en otra planta*); *vn* abotonar; brotar
**Buddha** ['budə] *s* Buda
**Buddhic** ['budɪk] *adj* búdico
**Buddhism** ['budɪzəm] *s* budismo
**Buddhist** ['budɪst] *adj* & *s* budista
**buddy** ['bʌdɪ] *s* (*pl:* **-dies**) (coll.) compañero; (coll.) muchachito
**budge** [bʌdʒ] *va* bullir, mover un poco; *vn* bullir, bullirse, p.ej., **he did not dare to budge** no osaba bullirse
**budgerigar** [,bʌdʒərɪ'gɑr] *s* (orn.) periquito de Australia
**budget** ['bʌdʒɪt] *s* presupuesto; acumulación, colección; *va* & *vn* presuponer
**budgetary** ['bʌdʒɪ,tɛrɪ] *adj* presupuestario
**budgie** ['bʌdʒɪ] *s* (coll.) var. de **budgerigar**
**Buenos Aires** ['bonəs'ɛriz] *s* Buenos Aires
**buff** [bʌf] *s* ante; color de ante; chaqueta de soldado hecha de ante; rueda pulidora; (coll.) piel desnuda; *adj* hecho de ante; de color de ante; *va* pulimentar con ante; pulimentar; amortiguar el choque de
**buffalo** ['bʌfəlo] *s* (*pl:* **-loes, -los** o **-lo**) (zool.) búfalo; (zool.) bisonte; piel de bisonte con pelo; *vn* (slang) confundir; (slang) impresionar
**buffalo bird** *s* (orn.) garrapatero
**buffalo grass** *s* (bot.) hierba de la pradera (*Buchloë dactyloides y Bouteloua*)
**buffalo robe** *s* piel de bisonte con pelo
**buffer** ['bʌfər] *s* tope; (rail.) tope, paragolpes; amortiguador de choques; pulidor (*persona o instrumento*)
**buffer state** *s* estado tapón, país situado entre dos naciones rivales
**buffet** [bu'fe] *s* aparador; chinero; ambigú; fonda de ferrocarril; caja (*de órgano*); ['bʌfɪt] *s* puñada; bofetada; golpe; *va* dar de puñadas; abofetear; golpear; *vn* luchar, pelear
**buffet car** [bu'fe] *s* (rail.) coche donde se sirven refrescos
**buffet lunch** [bu'fe] *s* servicio de buffet
**buffet supper** [bu'fe] *s* ambigú
**buffing wheel** *s* rueda pulidora
**buffoon** [bə'fun] *s* bufón
**buffoonery** [bə'funərɪ] *s* (*pl:* **-ies**) bufonada
**bug** [bʌg] *s* bicho, sabandija, insecto; (Brit.) chinche; microbio; (coll.) estorbo, traba; (slang) loco; (slang) manía; (slang) entusiasta
**bugaboo** ['bʌgəbu] *s* (*pl:* **-boos**) espantajo
**bugbear** ['bʌg,bɛr] *s* espantajo; aversión; coco
**bug-eyed** ['bʌg,aɪd] *adj* (slang) de ojos saltones
**buggy** ['bʌgɪ] *s* (*pl:* **-gies**) calesa de cuatro ruedas; *adj* (*comp:* **-gier;** *super:* **-giest**) lleno de bichos, sabandijas, chinches, etc.; (slang) loco
**bughouse** ['bʌg,haus] *s* (slang) casa de locos, manicomio; *adj* (slang) loco
**bugle** ['bjugəl] *s* (mus.) corneta, corneta de llaves; cañutillo (*tubido de vidrio usado en pasamanería*); (bot.) consuelda media; *va* llamar con toque de corneta; *vn* tocar la corneta
**bugle call** *s* toque de corneta
**bugle horn** *s* corneta, corneta de llaves
**bugler** ['bjuglər] *s* corneta
**bugleweed** ['bjugəl,wid] *s* marrubio acuático; (bot.) consuelda media
**bugloss** ['bjuglɑs] o ['bjuglɔs] *s* (bot.) buglosa
**buhl** [bul] *s* taracea de Boulle; mueble de Boulle
**buhl saw** *s* sierra de calar, serrezuela
**build** [bɪld] *s* estructura; talle (*del cuerpo humano*); (*pret & pp:* **built**) *va* edificar, construir, fabricar; fundar, establecer; componer; desarrollar; **to build up** componer; desarrollar; tapar, rellenar; armar; construir muchas casas en; crearse (*p.ej., una clientela*); *vn* edificar, construir; **to build on** o **upon** edificar sobre; contar con

**builder** ['bɪldər] *s* constructor; maestro de obras
**building** ['bɪldɪŋ] *s* edificio; construcción; pabellón (*p.ej., de una exposición*); *adj* de construcción, para construcciones
**building and loan association** *s* sociedad de crédito de construcción, sociedad de préstamos para edificación
**building line** *s* línea municipal, línea de edificación, alineamiento
**building lot** *s* solar
**building permit** *s* permiso de edificación
**build-up** ['bɪld,ʌp] *s* composición; (coll.) propaganda anticipada a favor de una persona o cosa
**built** [bɪlt] *prep & pp de* **build**
**built-in** ['bɪlt,ɪn] *adj* inamovible, integrante, empotrado, incorporado o montado en la construcción
**built-in antennas** (rad.) antena interior incorporada
**built-up** ['bɪlt'ʌp] *adj* compuesto, armado; aglomerado
**Bukhara** [bu'kɑrə] *s* var. de **Bokhara**
**bulb** [bʌlb] *s* (anat. & bot.) bulbo; (bot.) planta bulbosa; ampolleta, bombilla (*de luz eléctrica*); ampolleta, bola, cubeta (*del termómetro y el barómetro*); ampolla, pera (*de jeringa*); ensanche, protuberancia
**bulbil** ['bʌlbɪl] *s* (bot.) bulbillo
**bulbous** ['bʌlbəs] *adj* bulboso; ampollar
**bulbul** ['bulbul] *s* (orn.) picnonoto; (orn.) ave canora persa (*tal vez Luscinia golzii*)
**Bulgar** ['bʌlgɑr] o ['bulgɑr] *adj & s* búlgaro
**Bulgaria** [bʌl'gɛrɪə] o [bul'gɛrɪə] *s* Bulgaria
**Bulgarian** [bʌl'gɛrɪən] o [bul'gɛrɪən] *adj & s* búlgaro
**bulge** [bʌldʒ] *s* bombeo, pandeo; protuberancia; *vn* bombearse, pandearse; saltar, sobresalir
**bulging** ['bʌldʒɪŋ] *s* bombeo, pandeo; *adj* pando; protuberante
**bulgy** ['bʌldʒɪ] *adj* (*comp:* **-ier;** *super:* **-iest**) pando; protuberante
**bulk** [bʌlk] *s* bulto, volumen; grueso; **in bulk** a granel (*sin envase*); en pilas, en fardos; *adj* suelto; *va* amontonar; abultar; calcular el bulto de; *vn* abultar; hincharse; tener importancia
**bulkhead** ['bʌlk,hɛd] *s* (naut.) mamparo; escotillón; muro ribereño de contención; tabique hermético
**bulky** ['bʌlkɪ] *adj* (*comp:* **-ier;** *super:* **-iest**) abultado, grueso
**bull** [bul] *s* toro; elefante macho; macho de la ballena, la foca; (fig.) toro (*hombre muy robusto y fuerte*); alcista (*en la Bolsa*); (slang) agente de policía, detective; bula (*sello; documento pontificio*); disparate, dicho absurdo; (slang) música celestial; **to take the bull by the horns** irse a la cabeza del toro; *adj* robusto, fuerte; bramante; alcista; *va* cubrir (*el toro a la vaca*); (slang) chapucear; **to bull the market** jugar al alza; *vn* (slang) chapucear; (slang) tratar de encubrir sus desperfectos
**bulla** ['bulə] o ['bʌlə] *s* (*pl:* **-lae** [li]) bula; (path.) flictena
**bull bat** *s* (orn.) chotacabras norteamericano
**bull briar** *s* (bot.) bejuco de corona
**bulldog** ['bul,dɔg] o ['bul,dɑg] *s* dogo; *adj* porfiado, terco; valiente
**bulldoze** ['bul,doz] *va* (coll.) intimidar con amenazas o usando la violencia
**bulldozer** ['bul,dozər] *s* (coll.) valentón; (mach.) topadora, empujadora niveladora; (mach.) dobladora de ángulos
**bullet** ['bulɪt] *s* bala; plomada (*de pescador*)
**bullet-head** ['bulɪt,hɛd] *s* cabeza redonda; persona de cabeza redonda; (coll.) persona obstinada
**bullet-headed** ['bulɪt,hɛdɪd] *adj* de cabeza redonda; (coll.) obstinado
**bulletin** ['bulətɪn] *s* boletín; anuncio; anuario (*p.ej., de la universidad*)
**bulletin board** *s* tablilla o tablón de anuncios
**bulletproof** ['bulɪt,pruf] *adj* a prueba de bala
**bullfight** ['bul,faɪt] *s* toros, corrida de toros
**bullfighter** ['bul,faɪtər] *s* torero
**bullfighting** ['bul,faɪtɪŋ] *s* toreo; *adj* torero
**bullfinch** ['bul,fɪntʃ] *s* (orn.) pinzón real
**bullfrog** ['bul,frɑg] o ['bul,frɔg] *s* (zool.) rana toro
**bullhead** ['bul,hɛd] *s* persona obstinada y poco inteligente; (ichth.) amiuro; (ichth.) siluro; (orn.) chorlito
**bullheaded** ['bul,hɛdɪd] *adj* obstinado, terco; obstinado y poco inteligente
**bullion** ['buljən] *s* entorchado (*bordado del uniforme*); oro o plata en barras, lingotes de oro o plata
**bullish** ['bulɪʃ] *adj* parecido al toro; obstinado, estúpido; optimista; en alza; alcista
**bullnecked** ['bul,nɛkt] *adj* de cuello grueso
**bullock** ['bulək] *s* buey
**bull pen** *s* toril; (coll.) prevención de policía
**bull ring** *s* plaza de toros; (mach.) anillo de presión
**bull's-eye** ['bulz,aɪ] *s* centro del blanco; tiro que da en el centro del blanco; lente ojo de buey; lente con vidrio abombado; linterna sorda; (arch.) ojo de buey; (naut.) cristal de patente; (*cap.*) *s* (astr.) Ojo del Toro; **to hit the bull's-eye** o **to score a bull's-eye** hacer diana
**bull terrier** *s* bull-terrier
**bully** ['bulɪ] *s* (*pl:* **-lies**) matón, valentón; *adj* (coll.) excelente, magnífico; *interj* (coll.) ¡bravo!; (*pret & pp:* **-lied**) *va* intimidar con amenazas y gritería; **to bully someone into doing something** forzar a uno con amenazas y gritería a que haga una cosa; *vn* gallear
**bully beef** *s* carne de vaca encurtida o conservada en latas
**bullyrag** ['bulɪ,ræg] (*pret & pp:* **-ragged;** *ger:* **-ragging**) *va* atormentar, maltratar, molestar, intimidar con amenazas
**bully tree** *s* (bot.) balata
**bulrush** ['bul,rʌʃ] *s* (bot.) junco; (bot.) junco de laguna; (bot.) papiro; (bot.) anea
**bulwark** ['bulwərk] *s* (fort. & fig.) baluarte; (naut.) macarrón; *va* fortificar con baluarte; amparar, defender
**bum** [bʌm] *s* (slang) holgazán, holgazán borracho; (slang) vagabundo; (slang) sablista, mendigo; (slang) jarana, juerga, parranda; *adj* (*comp:* **bummer;** *super:* **bummest**) (slang) inferior, chapucero; (slang) inservible; **to feel bum** (slang) sentirse muy malo; (*pret & pp:* **bummed;** *ger:* **bumming**) *va* (slang) mendigar (*dinero, comidas, etc.*); *vn* (slang) holgazanear; (slang) vagabundear; (slang) beber a pote; (slang) sablear, mendigar
**bumble** ['bʌmbəl] *va* (dial.) chapucear; *vn* (dial.) zumbar (*como un abejorro*); (dial.) menearse; (dial.) chapucear
**bumblebee** ['bʌmbəl,bi] *s* (ent.) abejorro
**bumboat** ['bʌm,bot] *s* bote vivandero
**bump** [bʌmp] *s* topetón (*choque*); batacazo (*golpe al caer*); aspereza (*del terreno*); sacudida; rebote (*del avión en el aire agitado*); bollo, hinchazón; chichón (*en la cabeza*); joroba, protuberancia; *va* topar, dar contra; empujar violentamente; abollar; **to bump off** (slang) matar; *vn* chocar; dar sacudidas (*p.ej., un coche*); **to bump against** chocar contra; **to bump off** (slang) morirse
**bumper** ['bʌmpər] *s* tope; (rail.) parachoques o paratopes (*de final de línea*); (aut.) parachoques o amortiguador; copa o vaso lleno; (coll.) cosa muy grande; *adj* (coll.) muy grande, abundante
**bumping post** *s* (rail.) parachoques o paratopes
**bumpkin** ['bʌmpkɪn] *s* patán; (naut.) pescante
**bumptious** ['bʌmpʃəs] *adj* presuntuoso
**bumpy** ['bʌmpɪ] *adj* (*comp:* **-ier;** *super:* **-iest**) abollado; áspero (*terreno*); agitado (*aire*)
**bun** [bʌn] *s* bollo
**buna** ['bunə] o ['bjunə] *s* (chem.) buna
**bunch** [bʌntʃ] *s* manojo; ristra (*de tallos de ajos, cebollas, etc.*); racimo (*de uvas*); ramillete (*de flores*); manada (*de animales*); grupo (*de personas*); montón; *va* agrupar, juntar; amontonar, *vn* arracimarse
**bunchberry** ['bʌntʃ,bɛrɪ] *s* (*pl:* **-ries**) (bot.) cornejo canadiense
**bunch grass** *s* (bot.) poa
**bunchy** ['bʌntʃɪ] *adj* (*comp:* **-ier;** *super:* **-iest**) racimoso, amanojado

**bunco** ['bʌŋko] *s* (*pl:* **-cos**) (slang) estafa; banca (*juego de naipes*); *va* (slang) estafar
**buncombe** ['bʌŋkəm] *s* (coll.) discurso o lenguaje altisonante e insincero
**bundle** ['bʌndəl] *s* lío, bulto; paquete; fardo; legajo (*de papeles*); haz (*de leña, hierba, etc.*); *va* liar, atar, empaquetar, envolver; **to bundle off** u **out** despachar precipitadamente; **to bundle up** arropar; *vn* escaparse precipitadamente; meterse en cama juntos sin desnudarse (*dos amantes*); **to bundle up** arroparse
**bung** [bʌŋ] *s* bitoque; piquera (*boca para sacar el vino*); *va* atarugar; tapar con bitoque; tapar, cerrar, obstruir; (slang) abollar, magullar, machucar
**bungalow** ['bʌŋgəlo] *s* bungalow, casa de campo, de un solo piso
**bunghole** ['bʌŋ,hol] *s* piquera, boca de tonel
**bungle** ['bʌŋgəl] *s* chapucería; *va & vn* chapucear
**bungler** ['bʌŋglər] *s* chapucero
**bungling** ['bʌŋglɪŋ] *s* chapucería; *adj* chapucero
**bunion** ['bʌnjən] *s* (path.) juanete
**bunk** [bʌŋk] *s* tarima (*entablado para dormir*); (slang) habla altisonante e insincera; (slang) música celestial; *vn* (coll.) dormir en tarima, dormir, hospedarse
**bunker** ['bʌŋkər] *s* carbonera; (naut.) pañol del carbón; (golf) hoya de arena; (fort.) fortín
**bunko** ['bʌŋko] *s* (*pl:* **-kos**) var. de **bunco**; *va* var. de **bunco**
**bunkum** ['bʌŋkəm] *s* var. de **buncombe**
**bunny** ['bʌnɪ] *s* (*pl:* **-nies**) conejito; pequeña ardilla
**Bunsen burner** ['bʌnsən] *s* mechero Bunsen
**bunt** [bʌnt] *s* empellón, empujón; topetada (*con la cabeza*); (naut.) centro de una vela redonda; (baseball) golpe dado sin fuerza de modo que la pelota dé en el suelo y no vaya lejos; *va* empellar, empujar; topetar; (baseball) golpear (*la pelota*) sin fuerza de modo que dé en el suelo y no vaya lejos
**bunting** ['bʌntɪŋ] *s* lanilla para banderas; empavesado (*de un barco*); banderas colgadas como adorno; (orn.) gorrión triguero; (orn.) plectrófanes
**buntline** ['bʌntlɪn] o ['bʌntlaɪn] *s* (naut.) briol
**buoy** [bɔɪ] o ['bu·ɪ] *s* (naut.) boya; (naut.) guindola, boya salvavidas; *va* aboyar, señalar con boyas; mantener a flote; animar, alentar; **to buoy up** mantener a flote; animar, alentar
**buoyancy** ['bɔɪənsɪ] o ['bujənsɪ] *s* flotación (*facultad de flotar*); fuerza ascensional; alegría, viveza
**buoyant** ['bɔɪənt] o ['bujənt] *adj* boyante; ascensional; alegre, vivaz
**buprestid** [bju'prɛstɪd] *s* (ent.) bupresto
**bur** [bʌr] *s* erizo (*p.ej., de la castaña*); planta que tiene erizos; persona o cosa muy pegadiza; (*pret & pp:* **burred**; *ger:* **burring**) *va* quitar los erizos a
**burble** ['bʌrbəl] *s* burbujeo; charla; *vn* burbujear; charlar
**burbot** ['bʌrbət] *s* (ichth.) lota
**burden** ['bʌrdən] *s* carga; (fig.) carga; (naut.) arqueo (*capacidad de una embarcación*); (naut.) peso de la carga; tema (*de un discurso, ensayo, etc.*); estribillo (*verso*); *va* cargar; (fig.) cargar, gravar, agobiar
**burden of proof** *s* peso de la prueba
**burdensome** ['bʌrdənsəm] *adj* oneroso, gravoso, pesado
**burdock** ['bʌr,dɑk] *s* (bot.) bardana
**bureau** ['bjuro] *s* (*pl:* **-reaus** o **-reaux** [roz]) cómoda; (Brit.) escritorio, buró; oficina, dirección; negociado (*sección administrativa*); departamento del gobierno
**bureaucracy** [bju'rɑkrəsɪ] o [bju'rokrəsɪ] *s* (*pl:* **-cies**) burocracia
**bureaucrat** ['bjurokræt] *s* burócrata
**bureaucratic** [,bjuro'krætɪk] *adj* burocrático
**burette** [bju'rɛt] *s* (chem.) bureta
**burg** [bʌrg] *s* (coll.) pueblo, ciudad
**burgeon** ['bʌrdʒən] *s* (bot.) retoño; (bot.) yema; *vn* (bot.) retoñar
**burgess** ['bʌrdʒɪs] *s* vecino de una villa, pueblo, etc.; alcalde; miembro de la cámara baja de la legislatura colonial de los estados de Virginia y Maryland, EE.UU.
**burgh** [bʌrg] o ['bʌro] *s* (Scottish) villa
**burgher** ['bʌrgər] *s* vecino de una villa, pueblo, etc.; ciudadano
**burglar** ['bʌrglər] *s* escalador
**burglar alarm** *s* alarma de ladrones
**burglar insurance** *s* seguro contra robos
**burglarious** [bər'glɛrɪəs] *adj* escalador
**burglarize** ['bʌrglərаɪz] *va* (coll.) escalar para robar
**burglarproof** ['bʌrglər,pruf] *adj* a prueba de escaladores
**burglary** ['bʌrglərɪ] *s* (*pl:* **-ies**) robo con escalo
**burgle** ['bʌrgəl] *va & vn* (coll.) escalar para robar
**burgomaster** ['bʌrgo,mæstər] o ['bʌrgo,mɑstər] *s* burgomaestre
**burgonet** ['bʌrgonɛt] *s* (arm.) borgoñota, celada borgoñota
**burgrave** ['bʌrgrev] *s* burgrave
**burgraviate** [bʌr'greviɪt] *s* burgraviato
**Burgundian** [bər'gʌndɪən] *adj & s* borgoñés o borgoñón
**Burgundy** ['bʌrgəndɪ] *s* la Borgoña; borgoña (*vino*)
**burial** ['bɛrɪəl] *s* entierro
**burial ground** *s* cementerio
**burial service** *s* oficio de sepultura
**burin** ['bjurɪn] *s* buril; cincel; (fig.) buril (*estilo o modo del grabador*)
**burl** [bʌrl] *s* nudo (*en la madera*); mota (*en el paño*); *va* desmotar, despinzar
**burlap** ['bʌrlæp] *s* harpillera
**burlesque** [bər'lɛsk] *adj* extravagante; de music-hall; (lit.) festivo; *s* parodia; (theat.) music-hall; *va* parodiar
**burley** o **Burley** ['bʌrlɪ] *s* tabaco de hojas delgadas cultivado en el estado de Kentucky, EE.UU.
**burly** ['bʌrlɪ] *adj* (*comp:* **-lier**; *super:* **-liest**) membrudo, fornido
**Burma** ['bʌrmə] *s* Birmania
**Burma Road** *s* ruta de Birmania
**Burmese** [bʌr'miz] *adj* birmano; *s* (*pl:* **-mese**) birmano
**burn** [bʌrn] *s* quemadura; (Scottish) arroyo, riachuelo; (*pret & pp:* **burned** o **burnt**) *va* quemar; incendiar; inflamar (*encender; irritar*); cocer (*ladrillos*); calcinar (*minerales calcáreos*); vidriar (*la loza*); soldar o fundir (*el plomo*); (chem.) oxidar; (surg.) cauterizar; quemar (*el carbón del motor de combustión interna; el combustible para producir calor*); practicar quemando; funcionar con, p.ej., **this motor burns gasoline** este motor funciona con gasolina; **to burn out** quemar (*un cojinete, fusible, motor, transformador*); fundir (*una bombilla eléctrica*); **to burn together** reunir por fusión; **to burn up** consumir; (slang) llenar de indignación; *vn* quemarse; arder (*el fuego, el combustible*); asarse (*sentir mucho calor*); inflamarse (*encenderse; irritarse*); arder de o en deseos; (coll.) quemarse (*estar uno muy cerca de hallar lo que busca*); estar encendido, p.ej., **the light is burning in my room** la luz está encendida en mi cuarto; **to burn out** quemarse (*un fusible*); fundirse (*una bombilla eléctrica*); apagarse (*el fuego, la luz*); **to burn to death** morir quemado; **to burn to** + *inf* arder por + *inf*; **to burn with** arder de o en (*deseos, celos, etc.*); **to burn within** requemarse
**burner** ['bʌrnər] *s* quemador (*persona o aparato*); mechero
**burnet** ['bʌrnɪt] *s* (bot.) sanguisorba
**Burnett salmon** ['bʌrnɪt] *s* (ichth.) barramunda
**burning** ['bʌrnɪŋ] *s* quemadura; cocción; soldadura (*de plomo*); *adj* quemador; ardiente; (fig.) ardiente; **to be burning hot** (coll.) estar que quema; (coll.) hacer mucho calor
**burning glass** *s* espejo ustorio
**burning question** *s* cuestión batallona, cuestión palpitante
**burning shame** *s* vergüenza enorme
**burnish** ['bʌrnɪʃ] *s* bruñido; *va* bruñir; *vn* bruñirse
**burnisher** ['bʌrnɪʃər] *s* bruñidor

**burnoose** o **burnous** [bʌr'nus] o ['bʌrnus] *s* albornoz
**burnsides** ['bʌrn,saɪdz] *spl* patillas
**burnt** [bʌrnt] *pret & pp de* **burn**
**burnt almond** *s* almendra dulce tostada
**burnt offering** *s* holocausto
**burnt sienna** *s* siena tostado
**burnt umber** *s* tierra de sombra quemada
**bur oak** [bʌr] *s* (bot.) roble macrocarpo
**burr** [bʌr] *s* erizo (*p.ej., de la castaña*); planta que tiene erizos; persona o cosa muy pegadiza; rebaba (*en el borde de un corte*); fresa (*de dentista*); sonido bronco de la erre; pronunciación bronca y gutural; zumbido; *va* quitar los erizos a; quitar las rebabas a; *vn* sonar la erre con sonido bronco; hablar con pronunciación bronca y gutural; zumbar
**burrow** ['bʌro] *s* madriguera; conejera; refugio subterráneo; *va* socavar; hacer madrigueras en; *vn* amadrigarse; esconderse; buscar, hacer pesquisas
**bursa** ['bʌrsə] *s* (*pl:* **-sas** o **-sae** [si]) (anat.) bolsa
**bursar** ['bʌrsər] *s* tesorero universitario
**bursary** ['bʌrsərɪ] *s* (*pl:* **-ries**) tesorería universitaria
**bursitis** [bər'saɪtɪs] *s* (path.) bursitis
**burst** [bʌrst] *s* reventón; explosión; ráfaga (*de metralla*); salida brusca, arranque, llamarada; (*pret & pp:* **burst**) *va* reventar; quebrar; *vn* reventar, reventarse; entrar o salir repentina o violentamente; arrojarse, precipitarse; partirse (*el corazón*); **to burst into** irrumpir en (*p.ej., una habitación*); desatarse en (*amenazas, improperios, etc.*); prorrumpir en, deshacerse en (*lágrimas*); **to burst out crying** romper a llorar; **to burst out laughing** echarse a reír; **to burst with laughter** reventar de risa
**bursted** ['bʌrstɪd] *adj* (dial.) reventado
**bursted bubble** *s* burbuja deshecha, proyecto desbaratado
**burstwort** ['bʌrst,wʌrt] *s* (bot.) milgranos, quebrantapiedras
**burthen** ['bʌrðən] *s* (archaic) var. de **burden**
**bury** ['bɛrɪ] (*pret & pp:* **-ied**) *va* enterrar; (fig.) enterrar (*esconder; relegar al olvido; sobrevivir*); **to be buried in thought** estar absorto en meditación; **to bury the hatchet** envainar la espada, hacer la paz, echar pelillos a la mar
**burying beetle** *s* (ent.) enterrador, escarabajo sepulturero
**burying ground** *s* cementerio
**bus.** abr. de **business** y **bushel**
**bus** [bʌs] *s* (*pl:* **busses** o **buses**) ómnibus, autobús; autocar (*para servicio de carreteras*)
**bus bar** *s* (elec.) barra colectora
**bus boy** *s* ayudante de camarero
**busby** ['bʌzbɪ] *s* (*pl:* **-bies**) gorra de húsar
**bush.** abr. de **bushel**
**bush** [bʊʃ] *s* arbusto; matorral, monte; (mach.) buje, tejuelo, forro de metal; **to beat around the bush** andarse en chiquitas, andar con rodeos; *va* poblar de arbustos; igualar (*el terreno*) arrastrando matas; proteger con matas; poner buje o tejuelo a; *vn* crecer espeso
**bushel** ['bʊʃəl] *s* medida de capacidad para áridos, que equivale a 35,23 litros en los EE.UU. y 36,35 litros en Inglaterra; (*pret & pp:* **-eled** o **-elled**; *ger:* **-eling** o **-elling**) *va* reparar o modificar (*los vestidos*)
**bushhammer** ['bʊʃ,hæmər] *s* escoda
**bushing** ['bʊʃɪŋ] *s* (mach.) buje, tejuelo, forro de metal; (elec.) atravesador, pasatapas (*de un transformador*)
**bushman** ['bʊʃmən] *s* (*pl:* **-men**) montaraz, campesino; colonizador de la floresta australiana; (*cap.*) *s* bosquimán o bosquimano (*salvaje nómada sudafricano*)
**bushmaster** ['bʊʃ,mæstər] o ['bʊʃ,mɑstər] *s* (zool.) mapanare
**bushranger** ['bʊʃ,rendʒər] *s* montaraz; bandido australiano
**bushwhacker** ['bʊʃ,hwækər] *s* montaraz; guerrillero; guadaña para segar el arbusto, la zarza, etc.
**bushy** ['bʊʃɪ] *adj* (*comp:* **-ier;** *super:* **-iest**) espeso; peludo, lanudo; matoso; lleno de arbustos
**busily** ['bɪzɪlɪ] *adv* atareadamente, diligentemente
**business** ['bɪznɪs] *s* negocio, negocios, comercio; ocupación, empleo; cuestión, asunto; empresa; (theat.) acción; **going out of business** saldos por cambio de negocio (o por traslado); **on business** por negocios; de negocios; **to be in business** estar establecido; **to have no business** + *ger* no tener derecho a + *inf;* **to make it one's business to** + *inf* proponerse + *inf;* **to mean business** (coll.) actuar en serio, hablar en serio; **to mind one's own business** ocuparse en lo que le toca a uno, no meterse donde no le llaman a uno; **to send about one's business** echar, enviar o mandar a paseo; *adj* de negocios, comercial
**business college** *s* escuela de comercio
**business connections** *spl* relaciones comerciales
**business cycle** *s* ciclo comercial
**business deal** *s* trato comercial
**business district** *s* barrio comercial
**business expert** *s* perito mercantil
**business house** *s* casa de comercio, establecimiento mercantil
**businesslike** ['bɪznɪs,laɪk] *adj* metódico, práctico, serio, eficaz
**businessman** ['bɪznɪs,mæn] *s* (*pl:* **-men**) hombre de negocios, comerciante
**business reply card** ['bɪznɪsrɪ'plaɪ] *s* tarjeta de respuesta comercial
**business suit** *s* traje civil, traje de calle
**business trip** *s* viaje de negocios
**businesswoman** ['bɪznɪs,wʊmən] *s* (*pl:* **-women**) mujer de negocios
**busk** [bʌsk] *s* ballena (*de metal u otro material*); (dial.) corsé
**buskin** ['bʌskɪn] *s* borceguí; coturno; (fig.) drama trágico
**buskined** ['bʌskɪnd] *adj* coturnado; trágico
**busman** ['bʌsmən] *s* (*pl:* **-men**) conductor de autobús
**busman's holiday** *s* día de fiesta, pasado trabajando en trabajo igual al de todos los días
**buss** [bʌs] *s* (coll.) beso, beso sonado; *va* (coll.) besar, besar con resonancia; *vn* (coll.) dar besos; (coll.) darse besos
**bust** [bʌst] *s* busto; pecho de mujer; (slang) reventón; (slang) fracaso; (slang) borrachera, parranda; *va* (slang) hacer quebrar, arruinar; (slang) pegar, golpear; *vn* (slang) reventar; (slang) fracasar
**bustard** ['bʌstərd] *s* (orn.) avutarda (*Otis tarda*); (orn.) sisón (*Otis tetrax*)
**buster** ['bʌstər] *s* (slang) cosa muy grande, cosa extraordinaria; (coll.) muchachito
**bustle** ['bʌsəl] *s* alboroto, bullicio; polisón (*para abultar la falda por detrás*); *va* apresurar, impeler al trabajo; *vn* apresurarse ruidosamente
**bustle pipe** *s* portaviento
**bustler** ['bʌslər] *s* bullebulle
**busy** ['bɪzɪ] *adj* (*comp:* **-ier;** *super:* **-iest**) ocupado; de mucha actividad; bullicioso; entremetido, intruso; (*pret & pp:* **-ied**) *va* ocupar; **to busy oneself with** atarearse con o en
**busybody** ['bɪzɪ,bɑdɪ] *s* (*pl:* **-ies**) buscavidas, entremetido, metemuertos
**busy signal** *s* (telp.) zumbido de ocupación, señal de ocupado
**but** [bʌt] *s* pero, objeción; *adv* sólo, solamente; *prep* excepto, menos; *conj* pero, mas; sino, p.ej., **nobody knows it but John** nadie lo sabe sino Juan; sino que, p.ej., **he does not speak Spanish but he reads it very well** no habla español sino que lo lee muy bien; que no, p.ej., **she is not so tired but she can keep on talking** no está tan cansada que no pueda seguir hablando; **all but** casi; **cannot but** + *inf* no poder menos de + *inf*, no poder dejar de + *inf;* **nothing . . . but** no . . . más que; **the last but one** el penúltimo; **but for** a no ser por; **but little** muy poco
**butadiene** [,bjutə'daɪin] o [,bjutədaɪ'in] *s* (chem.) butadieno
**butane** ['bjuten] o [bju'ten] *s* (chem.) butano
**butcher** ['bʊtʃər] *s* carnicero; (fig.) carnicero (*hombre cruel y sanguinario*); *va* matar (*reses para el consumo*); dar muerte a; chapucear; *vn* ser carnicero, matar el ganado; hacer una carnicería

**butcher bird** *s* (orn.) alcaudón, verdugo, pájaro verdugo, desollador
**butcher knife** *s* cuchilla de carnicero
**butcher's-broom** ['bʊtʃərz'brum] o ['bʊtʃərz'brʊm] *s* (bot.) brusco
**butcher shop** *s* carnicería (*tienda*)
**butchery** ['bʊtʃərɪ] *s* (*pl:* **-ies**) carnicería; oficio de carnicero; matadero; (fig.) carnicería
**butene** ['bjutin] *s* (chem.) buteno
**butler** ['bʌtlər] *s* despensero, mayordomo
**butler's pantry** *s* despensa (*entre la cocina y el comedor*)
**butomaceous** [,bjuto'meʃəs] *adj* (bot.) butomáceo
**butt** [bʌt] *s* culata (*de un arma de fuego*); mocho (*de un instrumento*); tocón (*de un árbol cortado*); punta o colilla (*de cigarro*); cabezada (*golpe*); bisagra; (mach.) cabeza de biela; blanco; hazmerreír; pipa (*tonel; medida de capacidad para vinos*); **the butts** sitio para tirar al blanco; *va* topar; dar cabezadas a; acornear; apoyar; (mach.) juntar a tope; *vn* dar cabezadas; **to butt against** terminar en, confinar con; **to butt in** (slang) entremeterse; **to butt on** o **upon** terminar en, confinar con
**butte** [bjut] *s* terromontero
**butter** ['bʌtər] *s* mantequilla; **smooth as butter** como manteca; *va* untar con mantequilla, pringar con mantequilla; (coll.) adular, lisonjear
**buttercup** ['bʌtər,kʌp] *s* (bot.) ranúnculo; (bot.) botón de oro, hierba belida; (bot.) hierba velluda
**butter dish** *s* mantequera, mantequillera
**butterfat** ['bʌtər,fæt] *s* materia grasa de la leche
**butterfingers** ['bʌtər,fɪŋgərz] *s* (coll.) persona con dedos de mantequilla; (coll.) descuidado, desmañado
**butterfish** ['bʌtər,fɪʃ] *s* (ichth.) cagavino; (ichth.) blenio
**butterfly** ['bʌtər,flaɪ] *s* (*pl:* **-flies**) (ent. & fig.) mariposa
**butterfly damper** *s* mariposa reguladora de tiro
**butterfly fish** *s* (ichth.) baboso, budión; (ichth.) mariposa
**butterfly valve** *s* válvula de mariposa
**butterfly weed** *s* (bot.) seda vegetal, pelo de gato, plumerillo
**butterine** ['bʌtərin] o ['bʌtərɪn] *s* mantequilla artificial
**butteris** ['bʌtərɪs] *s* pujavante
**butter knife** *s* cuchillo mantequillero
**buttermilk** ['bʌtər,mɪlk] *s* leche de manteca
**butternut** ['bʌtər,nʌt] *s* (bot.) nogal ceniciento, nogal de Cuba; nuez de Cuba
**butter sauce** *s* mantequilla fundida
**butterscotch** ['bʌtər,skatʃ] *s* dulce de azúcar terciado con mantequilla
**butter spreader** *s* var. de **butter knife**
**buttery** ['bʌtərɪ] *adj* mantecoso; ['bʌtərɪ] o ['bʌtrɪ] *s* (*pl:* **-ies**) despensa
**butt joint** *s* junta de tope, junta de cubrejunta
**buttocks** ['bʌtəks] *spl* nalgas
**button** ['bʌtən] *s* botón; **buttons** *ssg* (coll.) botones (*mozo de hotel*); *va* abotonar; *vn* abotonarse
**buttonhole** ['bʌtən,hol] *s* ojal; *va* abrir ojales en; coser a puntadas de ojal; obligar a escuchar, detener con conversación
**buttonhole stitch** *s* puntada de ojal
**buttonhook** ['bʌtən,hʊk] *s* abotonador, abrochador
**buttonmold** ['bʌtən,mold] *s* hormilla
**buttonwood** ['bʌtən,wʊd] *s* (bot.) plátano de occidente; (bot.) botoncillo (*Conocarpus*)
**buttress** ['bʌtrɪs] *s* (arch.) contrafuerte; apoyo, refuerzo, sostén; *va* reforzar con contrafuerte, poner contrafuerte a; apoyar, reforzar, sostener
**butt weld** *s* soldadura a tope
**butyl** ['bjutɪl] *s* (chem.) butilo
**butylene** ['bjutɪlin] *s* (chem.) butileno
**butyric** [bju'tɪrɪk] *adj* (chem.) butírico
**butyric acid** *s* (chem.) ácido butírico
**butyrin** ['bjutɪrɪn] *s* (chem.) butirina
**butyrometer** [,bjutɪ'ramɪtər] *s* butirómetro
**butyrous** ['bjutɪrəs] *adj* butiroso
**buxaceous** [bʌks'eʃəs] *adj* (bot.) buxáceo
**buxom** ['bʌksəm] *adj* rollizo, frescachón
**buy** [baɪ] *s* (coll.) compra; (*pret & pp:* **bought**) *va* comprar; **to buy back** recomprar; **to buy off** comprar (*sobornar*); libertar pagando; **to buy out** comprar la parte de (*un socio*); **to buy up** acaparar
**buyer** ['baɪər] *s* comprador
**buyer's market** *s* mercado del comprador
**buzz** [bʌz] *s* zumbido; *va* expresar zumbando; (coll.) llamar por teléfono; (aer.) saludar (*a una persona*) volando muy bajo; *vn* zumbar; **to buzz about** cazcalear, andar muy ocupado; **to buzz off** cortar una conversación telefónica
**buzzard** ['bʌzərd] *s* (orn.) alfaneque, busardo, águila ratonera; (orn.) zopilote de montaña
**buzz bomb** *s* (mil.) bomba volante
**buzzer** ['bʌzər] *s* zumbador; (elec.) zumbador
**buzz saw** *s* sierra circular
**B.V.** abr. de **Beata Virgo** (Lat.) **Blessed Virgin**
**B.W.I.** abr. de **British West Indies**
**bx.** abr. de **box** o **boxes**
**bxs.** abr. de **boxes**
**by** [baɪ] *adv* cerca; a solas; más allá; aparte, a un lado; **by and by** luego, pronto, de aquí a poco; **by and large** en todo respecto, de un modo general; *prep* por; por o de (*para denotar el agente con la voz pasiva*); de (*día, noche*); (math.) por (*para indicar multiplicación*); para, p.ej., **by two o'clock** para las dos; cerca de, junto a, al lado de; **by far** con mucho; **by the by** a propósito; **by the way** de paso; a propósito
**by-and-by** ['baɪənd'baɪ] *s* porvenir
**bye** [baɪ] *s* (sport) jugador sin contrario en los juegos en que los jugadores han sido escogidos por parejas; (cricket) carrera hecha sin haber golpeado la pelota; (golf) hoyo u hoyos que se quedan sin ser jugados al fin de la partida; **by the bye** a propósito
**bye-bye** ['baɪ'baɪ] *interj* (coll.) ¡adiosito!; ¡ro ro! (*para arrullar a los niños*)
**by-election** ['baɪɪ,lɛkʃən] *s* (Brit.) elección especial para cubrir una vacante
**Byelorussian** [,bɛla'rʌʃən] *adj & s* bielorruso
**bygone** ['baɪ,gɔn] o ['baɪ,gan] *adj* pasado; *s* pasado; **let bygones be bygones** olvidemos lo pasado
**bylaw** ['baɪ,lɔ] *s* estatuto; reglamento, ley o regla secundaria
**by-line** ['baɪ,laɪn] *s* (U.S.A.) línea al comienzo de un artículo de periódico o revista dando el nombre del autor
**by-name** ['baɪ,nem] *s* sobrenombre; apodo
**by-pass** ['baɪ,pæs] o ['baɪ,pas] *s* desviación; (mach.) tubo de paso; (elec.) derivación; *va* desviar
**by-pass condenser** *s* (elec.) condensador de paso o derivación
**by-path** ['baɪ,pæθ] o ['baɪ,paθ] *s* trocha, senda
**by-play** ['baɪ,ple] *s* (theat.) acción aparte
**by-product** ['baɪ,pradəkt] *s* subproducto, derivado
**byre** [baɪr] *s* establo de vacas
**by-road** ['baɪ,rod] *s* camino apartado
**Byronic** [baɪ'ranɪk] *adj* byroniano
**byssus** ['bɪsəs] *s* (*pl:* **-suses** o **-si** [saɪ]) (hist. & zool.) biso
**bystander** ['baɪ,stændər] *s* circunstante, espectador
**by-street** ['baɪ,strit] *s* callejuela
**byway** ['baɪ,we] *s* camino apartado, camino poco frecuentado
**byword** ['baɪ,wʌrd] *s* oprobio, objeto de oprobio; refrán, proverbio; apodo
**Byzantine** ['bɪzəntin] o [bɪ'zæntin] *adj & s* bizantino
**Byzantine Empire** *s* Imperio Bizantino
**Byzantium** [bɪ'zænʃɪəm] o [bɪ'zæntɪəm] *s* Bizancio

# C

**C, c** [si] *s* (*pl:* **C's, c's** [siz]) tercera letra del alfabeto inglés
**c.** abr. de **cent** o **cents**
**C.** abr. de **centigrade**
**C.A.** abr. de **Central America**
**cab** [kæb] *s* taxi; cabriolé, coche de plaza; berlina; casilla (*de locomotora o camión*)
**cabal** [kəˈbæl] *s* cábala; (*pret & pp:* **-balled;** *ger:* **-balling**) *va & vn* tramar, maquinar
**cabala** [ˈkæbələ] o [kəˈbɑlə] *s* cábala
**cabalistic** [ˌkæbəˈlɪstɪk] *adj* cabalístico
**cabaret** [ˌkæbəˈre] o [ˈkæbəre] *s* cabaret
**cabbage** [ˈkæbɪdʒ] *s* (bot.) col; coles (*cabeza y hojas que se comen*); *va* sisar; *vn* sisar; repollar
**cabbage palm** *s* (bot.) palma real, col palma; (bot.) palmito de tierra firme
**cabby** [ˈkæbɪ] *s* (*pl:* **-bies**) (coll.) var. de **cabman**
**cab driver** *s* var. de **cabman**
**cabin** [ˈkæbɪn] *s* cabaña, choza; (naut.) camarote; (aer.) cabina; *va* apretar, encerrar; *vn* vivir en cabaña o choza
**cabin boy** *s* (naut.) mozo de cámara
**cabin class** *s* (naut.) clase de cámara
**cabinet** [ˈkæbɪnɪt] *s* escaparate, vitrina; armario; caja, estuche; caja o mueble (*p.ej., de un aparato de radio*); gabinete (*de un gobierno; colección de objetos; pieza retirada*); *adj* ministerial; digno de figurar en gabinete; secreto, reservado
**cabinetmaker** [ˈkæbɪnɪtˌmekər] *s* ebanista
**cabinetwork** [ˈkæbɪnɪtˌwʌrk] *s* ebanistería
**cable** [ˈkebəl] *s* cable; cable eléctrico; cableado eléctrico (*de un coche, radio, televisor, etc.*); cablegrama; *adj* cablegráfico; *va* cablegrafiar; atar o amarrar con cable; *vn* cablegrafiar
**cable address** *s* dirección cablegráfica
**cable car** *s* carro arrastrado por cable; tranvía de cable
**cable chain** *s* cadena de cable
**cablegram** [ˈkebəlgræm] *s* cablegrama
**cable-laid** [ˈkebəlˌled] *adj* (naut.) acalabrotado
**cable railroad** *s* andarivel
**cable ship** *s* buque cablero
**cable's length** *s* cable (*medida*)
**cable vault** *s* (elec.) caja de empalme de cables
**cableway** [ˈkebəlˌwe] *s* cable transportador, cablecarril
**cabman** [ˈkæbmən] *s* (*pl:* **-men**) cochero; taxista; conductor de automóvil de alquiler
**caboodle** [kəˈbudəl] *s* (slang) conjunto, grupo, lío
**caboose** [kəˈbus] *s* (rail.) carro o furgón de cola; (naut.) cocina (*en el puente del buque*)
**cabriolet** [ˌkæbrɪoˈle] *s* cabriolé (*carruaje y automóvil*)
**cab signal** *s* (rail.) señal en la cabina del maquinista que repite la indicación de la señal fija externa
**cabstand** [ˈkæbˌstænd] *s* punto de coches
**cacao** [kəˈkɑo] o [kəˈkeo] *s* (*pl:* **-os**) (bot.) cacao (*árbol y semilla*)
**cacao butter** *s* manteca de cacao
**cachalot** [ˈkæʃəlɑt] o [ˈkæʃəlo] *s* (zool.) cachalote
**cache** [kæʃ] *s* escondite, escondrijo; víveres escondidos; *va* depositar en un escondrijo; encubrir, ocultar
**cachectic** [kəˈkɛktɪk] o **cachectical** [kəˈkɛktɪkəl] *adj* caquéctico
**cachepot** [ˈkæʃpɑt] o [kɑʃˈpo] *s* vasija de adorno (*para ocultar una maceta tosca*)
**cache-sexe** [kɑʃˈsɛks] *s* cubresexo
**cachet** [kæˈʃe] o [ˈkæʃe] *s* sello particular; marca de distinción; carácter, originalidad; sello medicinal
**cachexia** [kəˈkɛksɪə] *s* (path.) caquexia
**cachinnate** [ˈkækɪnet] *vn* reír a carcajadas
**cachinnation** [ˌkækɪˈneʃən] *s* carcajada, risotada
**cackle** [ˈkækəl] *s* cacareo; risa aguda y sacudida; cháchara, charla; *vn* cacarear; reírse ásperamente; chacharear, charlar
**cacochymia** [ˌkækoˈkɪmɪə] *s* (path.) cacoquimia
**cacodylate** [ˈkækodɪlet] *s* (chem.) cacodilato
**cacodylic** [ˌkækoˈdɪlɪk] *adj* (chem.) cacodílico
**cacomistle** [ˈkækəˌmɪsəl] *s* (zool.) basáride
**cacophonous** [kəˈkɑfənəs] *adj* cacofónico
**cacophony** [kəˈkɑfənɪ] *s* (*pl:* **-nies**) cacofonía
**cactaceous** [kækˈteʃəs] *adj* (bot.) cactáceo
**cactus** [ˈkæktəs] *s* (*pl:* **-tuses** o **-ti** [taɪ]) (bot.) cacto
**cad** [kæd] *s* canalla, sinvergüenza, persona malcriada
**cadastral** [kəˈdæstrəl] *adj* catastral
**cadastre** [kəˈdæstər] *s* catastro
**cadaver** [kəˈdævər] *s* cadáver
**cadaverous** [kəˈdævərəs] *adj* cadavérico
**caddie** [ˈkædɪ] *s* (golf) muchacho que lleva los instrumentos de juego; (*pret & pp:* **-died;** *ger:* **-dying**) *vn* servir de muchacho de golf
**caddis** [ˈkædɪs] *s* jerguilla de lana; cinta de seda y estambre; (ent.) gusano de la paja
**caddis fly** *s* (ent.) frígano
**caddish** [ˈkædɪʃ] *adj* malcriado
**caddis worm** *s* (ent.) gusano de la paja
**caddy** [ˈkædɪ] *s* (*pl:* **-dies**) cajita, botecito o lata para té; (golf) muchacho que lleva los instrumentos de juego; (*pret & pp:* **-died;** *ger:* **-dying**) *vn* servir de muchacho de golf
**cade** [ked] *adj* manso; mimado; *s* cordero manso; animal mimado; (bot.) enebro de la miera
**cadence** [ˈkedəns] *s* cadencia; (mus.) cadencia; (mil.) cadencia del paso
**cadenza** [kəˈdɛnzə] o [kəˈdɛntsə] *s* (mus.) cadencia
**cadet** [kəˈdɛt] *s* cadete; hijo menor, hermano menor; (slang) alcahuete
**cadetship** [kəˈdɛtʃɪp] *s* grado o puesto de cadete
**cadge** [kædʒ] *va* (coll.) obtener mendigando; *vn* (coll.) mendigar, gorronear, vivir de gorra; (dial.) ir vendiendo de casa en casa
**cadi** [ˈkɑdɪ] o [ˈkedɪ] *s* (*pl:* **-dis**) cadí
**Cadmean** [kædˈmiən] *adj* cadmeo
**cadmium** [ˈkædmɪəm] *s* (chem.) cadmio
**cadmium cell** *s* (elec.) elemento de cadmio
**Cadmus** [ˈkædməs] *s* (myth.) Cadmo
**cadre** [ˈkɑdər] *s* armazón; [ˈkædrɪ] *s* (mil.) cuadro
**caduceus** [kəˈdjusɪəs] o [kəˈdusɪəs] *s* (*pl:* **-cei** [sɪaɪ]) caduceo
**caducity** [kəˈdjusɪtɪ] o [kəˈdusɪtɪ] *s* caducidad; (law) caducidad
**caducous** [kəˈdjukəs] o [kəˈdukəs] *adj* caduco; (bot. & law) caduco
**caecal** [ˈsikəl] *adj* cecal
**caecum** [ˈsikəm] *s* (*pl:* **-ca** [kə]) (anat.) intestino ciego
**Caedmon** [ˈkædmən] *s* Cedmón
**Caesar** [ˈsizər] *s* César
**Caesarea** [ˌsɛsəˈriə] o [ˌsɛzəˈriə] *s* Cesarea
**Caesarean** [sɪˈzɛrɪən] *adj* cesáreo (*imperial*); cesariano (*perteneciente a César*); (surg.) cesáreo; *s* (surg.) operación cesárea
**Caesarean operation** *s* (surg.) operación cesárea
**Caesarean section** *s* (surg.) sección cesárea
**Caesarian** [sɪˈzɛrɪən] *adj & s* var. de **Caesarean**
**caesarism** [ˈsizərɪzəm] *s* cesarismo
**caesium** [ˈsizɪəm] *s* var. de **cesium**
**caesura** [sɪˈʒurə] o [sɪˈzjurə] *s* (*pl:* **-ras** o **-rae** [ri]) (pros.) cesura
**café** [kæˈfe] *s* café, restaurante; bar; cabaret

**café au lait** [kæˈfe o ˈle] *s* (Fr.) café con leche; color de café con leche

**café society** *s* gente alegre que frecuenta los cabarets de moda

**cafeteria** [ˌkæfəˈtɪrɪə] *s* cafetería, restaurante en que uno mismo se sirve

**caffein** o **caffeine** [ˈkæfin] o [ˈkæfɪɪn] *s* (pharm.) cafeína

**caftan** [ˈkæftən] *s* cafetán o caftán

**cage** [kedʒ] *s* jaula; (elec., mach. & min.) jaula; cárcel; *va* enjaular

**cageling** [ˈkedʒlɪŋ] *s* pájaro enjaulado

**cagey** [ˈkedʒɪ] *adj* (*comp:* **cagier;** *super:* **cagiest**) (coll.) zorro, astuto

**cahoots** [kəˈhuts] *s* (slang) acuerdo, consorcio; **in cahoots** (slang) de acuerdo, asociados; **to go cahoots** (slang) entrar por partes iguales

**Caiaphas** [ˈkeəfəs] o [ˈkaɪəfəs] *s* (Bib.) Caifás

**caiman** [ˈkemən] *s* (*pl:* **-mans**) (zool.) caimán

**Cain** [ken] *s* (Bib.) Caín; **to raise Cain** (slang) armar bochinche

**caïque** [kɑˈik] *s* (naut.) caique

**cairn** [kɛrn] *s* montón de piedras que sirve de mojón, lápida, etc.

**Cairo** [ˈkaɪro] *s* El Cairo

**caisson** [ˈkesən] o [ˈkesɑn] *s* (mil.) cajón; (eng.) cajón hidráulico, cajón de aire comprimido; (naut.) cajón de suspensión; (arch.) artesón, casetón

**caisson disease** *s* (path.) enfermedad de los cajones de aire comprimido, enfermedad de los buzos

**caitiff** [ˈketɪf] *adj & s* belitre, pícaro, cobarde

**cajole** [kəˈdʒol] *va* halagar, camelar; **to cajole a person into something** conseguir por medio de halagos que una persona haga una cosa; **to cajole a person out of something** conseguir una cosa de una persona por medio de halagos

**cajolery** [kəˈdʒolərɪ] *s* (*pl:* **-ies**) halago, lisonja, camelo

**cake** [kek] *s* bollo, tortita, pastelillo; bizcocho; fritada (*p.ej., de pescado*); pan o pastilla (*de jabón, cera, etc.*); **to take the cake** (slang) ganar el premio; (slang) llevarse la mapa, ser el colmo; *vn* apelmazarse, aterronarse

**cakewalk** [ˈkekˌwɔk] *s* cake-walk; *vn* bailar el cake-walk

**Cal.** abr. de **California**

**calaba** [ˈkæləbə] *s* (bot.) calambuco, árbol de María

**calabash** [ˈkæləbæʃ] *s* (bot.) calabacera; calabaza (*fruto; botella o escudilla*); (mus.) calabazo

**calabash tree** *s* (bot.) calabacero, árbol de las calabazas, güira

**calaboose** [ˈkæləbus] *s* (coll.) calabozo

**Calabrian** [kəˈlebrɪən] *adj & s* calabrés

**calabur tree** [ˈkæləbʌr] *s* (bot.) memiso, capulín

**caladium** [kəˈledɪəm] *s* (bot.) caladio, papagayo

**calamanco** [ˌkæləˈmæŋko] *s* calamaco

**calambac** [ˈkæləmbæk] *s* calambac (*madera*)

**calamine** [ˈkæləmaɪn] o [ˈkæləmɪn] *s* (mineral.) calamina

**calamint** [ˈkæləmɪnt] *s* (bot.) calamento, calaminta

**calamistrum** [ˌkæləˈmɪstrəm] *s* (*pl:* **-tra** [trə]) (zool.) calamistro

**calamitous** [kəˈlæmɪtəs] *adj* calamitoso

**calamity** [kəˈlæmɪtɪ] *s* (*pl:* **-ties**) calamidad

**calamus** [ˈkæləməs] *s* (*pl:* **-mi** [maɪ]) (bot.) ácoro, cálamo; (pharm.) cálamo aromático

**calander** [kəˈlændər] *s* (orn.) calandria

**calash** [kəˈlæʃ] *s* carretela (*carruaje*); capota plegable; capota de señora (*de los siglos diez y ocho y diez y nueve*)

**calcareous** [kælˈkɛrɪəs] *adj* calcáreo; cálcico

**calceolaria** [ˌkælsɪəˈlɛrɪə] *s* (bot.) calceolaria

**Calchas** [ˈkælkəs] *s* (myth.) Calcas

**calcic** [ˈkælsɪk] *adj* (chem.) cálcico

**calciferous** [kælˈsɪfərəs] *adj* calcífero

**calcification** [ˌkælsɪfɪˈkeʃən] *s* calcificación

**calcify** [ˈkælsɪfaɪ] (*pret & pp:* **-fied**) *va* calcificar; *vn* calcificarse

**calcimeter** [kælˈsɪmɪtər] *s* calcímetro

**calcimine** [ˈkælsɪmaɪn] o [ˈkælsɪmɪn] *s* lechada; *va* lechar

**calcination** [ˌkælsɪˈneʃən] *s* calcinación

**calcine** [ˈkælsaɪn] *va* calcinar; *vn* calcinarse

**calcite** [ˈkælsaɪt] *s* (mineral.) calcita

**calcium** [ˈkælsɪəm] *s* (chem.) calcio

**calcium carbide** *s* (chem.) carburo de calcio

**calcium carbonate** *s* (chem.) carbonato de calcio

**calcium chloride** *s* (chem.) cloruro de calcio

**calcium cyanamide** *s* (chem.) cianamida de calcio

**calcium hydroxide** *s* (chem.) hidróxido de calcio

**calcium light** *s* luz de calcio

**calcium phosphate** *s* (chem.) fosfato cálcico

**calcium sulfate** *s* (chem.) sulfato de calcio

**calcspar** [ˈkælkˌspɑr] *s* (mineral.) espato calizo

**calculable** [ˈkælkjələbəl] *adj* calculable

**calculate** [ˈkælkjəlet] *va* calcular; **calculated to** + *inf* (coll.) aprestado para + *inf*; *vn* calcular; **to calculate on** contar con

**calculating** [ˈkælkjəˌletɪŋ] *adj* calculador; de calcular; astuto; intrigante

**calculating machine** *s* máquina de calcular, calculadora

**calculation** [ˌkælkjəˈleʃən] *s* cálculo

**calculative** [ˈkælkjəˌletɪv] *adj* calculatorio

**calculator** [ˈkælkjəˌletər] *s* calculador; calculadora (*máquina*)

**calculous** [ˈkælkjələs] *adj* (path.) calculoso

**calculus** [ˈkælkjələs] *s* (*pl:* **-li** [laɪ] o **-luses**) (math. & path.) cálculo

**Calcutta** [kælˈkʌtə] *s* Calcuta

**caldron** [ˈkɔldrən] *s* calderón

**Caledonian** [ˌkælɪˈdonɪən] *adj & s* caledonio

**calendar** [ˈkæləndər] *s* calendario; calendario escolar; programa; orden *m* del día; (law) lista de pleitos; *va* poner o entrar en el calendario; poner en la lista, reducir a lista

**calendar day** *s* día civil

**calendar month** *s* mes del año

**calendar year** *s* año civil

**calender** [ˈkæləndər] *s* calandria (*para dar lustre al papel*); *vn* calandrar (*el papel*)

**calends** [ˈkælɪndz] *spl* calendas (*primer día de cada mes*)

**calendula** [kəˈlɛndjələ] o [kəˈlɛndjʊlə] *s* (bot.) caléndula

**calenture** [ˈkæləntʃər] *s* (path.) calentura

**calf** [kæf] o [kɑf] *s* (*pl:* **calves**) ternero o ternera; cría del rinoceronete y otros animales; piel de ternero; cuero hecho de piel de ternero; pantorrilla (*de la pierna*); (coll.) bobo, mentecato; **to kill the fatted calf** preparar una fiesta para dar la bienvenida

**calf love** *s* (coll.) var. de **puppy love**

**calfskin** [ˈkæfˌskɪn] o [ˈkɑfˌskɪn] *s* piel de ternero; cuero hecho de piel de ternero

**caliber** [ˈkælɪbər] *s* calibre; (fig.) calaña (*de una persona*); (fig.) calibre (*de una cosa*)

**calibrate** [ˈkælɪbret] *va* calibrar

**calibration** [ˌkælɪˈbreʃən] *s* calibración

**calicle** [ˈkælɪkəl] *s* (anat. & zool.) calículo

**calico** [ˈkælɪko] *s* (*pl:* **-coes** o **-cos**) calicó, indiana; *adj* hecho de calicó; que tiene manchas de otro color

**calicoback** [ˈkælɪkoˌbæk] *s* (ent.) chinche de jardín

**Calif.** abr. de **California**

**calif** [ˈkelɪf] o [ˈkælɪf] *s* var. de **caliph**

**California condor** [ˌkælɪˈfɔrnɪə] *s* (orn.) cóndor de California

**Californian** [ˌkælɪˈfɔrnɪən] *adj & s* californiano

**California poppy** *s* (bot.) amapola de California, copa de oro

**californium** [ˌkælɪˈfɔrnɪəm] *s* (chem.) californio

**caliper compass** [ˈkælɪpər] *s* compás de calibres

**caliper gauge** *s* calibrador fijo

**calipers** [ˈkælɪpərz] *spl* calibrador

**caliper square** *s* pie de rey

**caliph** [ˈkelɪf] o [ˈkælɪf] *s* califa

**caliphate** [ˈkælɪfet] *s* califato

**calisaya bark** [ˌkælɪˈsejə] *s* (pharm.) calisaya

**calisthenic** [ˌkælɪsˈθɛnɪk] *adj* calisténico; **calisthenics** *spl* calistenia

**calk** [kɔk] *s* ramplón (*para las herraduras del caballo*); crampón (*para los zapatos del hombre*); callo (*de herradura*); *va* poner ramplones en; poner crampones en; calafatear

**calker** [ˈkɔkər] *s* calafate o calafateador
**calking** [ˈkɔkɪŋ] *s* calafateo
**call** [kɔl] *s* llamada; grito; invitación; visita, parada; escala (*de buque o avión*); citación (*ante un juez*); reclamo (*del ave*); balitadera (*del gamo*); (hunt.) chilla; (mil.) llamada; derecho; obligación; (coll.) demanda (*p.ej., de fondos*); **on call** disponible; (com.) a solicitud, al pedir; **within call** al alcance de la voz ‖ *va* llamar; señalar; invitar; despertar; citar; mandar; considerar, juzgar; apreciar, estimar; llamar por teléfono; convocar (*una sesión, huelga, etc.*); (sport) dar por terminada (*la partida*); (poker) exigir (*a un jugador*) la exposición de su mano; **to call aside** llamar aparte; **to call back** hacer volver; volver a llamar por teléfono; **to call down** pedir al cielo (*p.ej., favores divinos*); (slang) regañar; **to call forth** sacar (*p.ej., una respuesta*); **to call in** hacer entrar; recoger, retirar; **to call off** aplazar, dar por terminado; disuadir; **to call out** llamar (*a uno*) a que salga; desafiar; **to call together** convocar, reunir; **to call up** llamar por teléfono; recordar ‖ *vn* llamar, gritar; hacer una visita, pararse un rato; (naut.) hacer escala; **to call at** pasar por la casa o la oficina de; **to call for** ir o venir por; exigir; rezar, p.ej., **the newspaper calls for rain** el periódico reza agua; **to call on** o **upon** acudir a (*en busca de auxilio*); visitar; **to call out** llamar a gritos, gritar; **to go calling** ir de visitas
**calla** [ˈkælə] *s* (bot.) cala (*Zantedeschia aethiopica y Calla palustris*)
**calla lily** *s* (bot.) cala (*Zantedeschia aethiopica*)
**call bell** *s* timbre de llamada
**callboy** [ˈkɔlˌbɔɪ] *s* botones, mozo de hotel, paje de cámara; (theat.) avisador
**call button** *s* botón para llamar
**caller** [ˈkɔlər] *s* llamador; visita
**call girl** *s* (coll.) chica de cita
**calligraphic** [ˌkælɪˈgræfɪk] *adj* caligráfico
**calligraphy** [kəˈlɪgrəfɪ] *s* caligrafía
**calling** [ˈkɔlɪŋ] *s* invitación, convite; mandamiento; citación (*ante un juez*); vocación, profesión
**calling card** *s* tarjeta de visita
**calliope** [kəˈlaɪəpɪ] o [ˈkælɪop] *s* (mus.) órgano de vapor; (*cap.*) [kəˈlaɪəpɪ] *s* (myth.) Calíope
**calliopsis** [ˌkælɪˈɑpsɪs] *s* (bot.) coreópsida
**callipers** [ˈkælɪpərz] *spl* var. de **calipers**
**callisthenic** [ˌkælɪsˈθɛnɪk] *adj* calisténico; **callisthenics** *spl* calistenia
**Callisto** [kəˈlɪsto] *s* (myth.) Calisto
**call letters** *spl* (telg.) indicativo de llamada, letras de identificación
**call loan** *s* préstamo que debe pagarse a demanda
**call money** *s* dinero prestado que debe pagarse a demanda
**call number** *s* número de teléfono; número de clasificación (*de un libro*)
**call of the wild** *s* ansia de vagar, atracción de la vida silvestre
**callose** [ˈkælos] *s* (bot. & biochem.) callosa
**callosity** [kəˈlɑsɪtɪ] *s* (*pl:* **-ties**) callosidad; insensibilidad
**callous** [ˈkæləs] *adj* calloso; duro, insensible
**callow** [ˈkælo] *adj* joven e inexperto; desplumado (*sin plumas adecuades para volar*)
**call sign** *s* var. de **call letters**
**call slip** *s* papeleta de biblioteca
**call to arms** *s* (mil.) llamada; **to sound the call to arms** (mil.) tocar o batir llamada
**call to the colors** *s* (mil.) llamada a filas
**callus** [ˈkæləs] *s* callo
**calm** [kɑm] *s* calma; quietud, serenidad; (naut.) calma; **dead calm** calma chicha o muerta; *adj* tranquilo, bonancible; quieto, sereno; *va* calmar; *vn* calmarse; calmar, abonanzar, pacificarse (*el tiempo*)
**calmness** [ˈkɑmnɪs] *s* calma, tranquilidad
**calomel** [ˈkæləmɛl] *s* (pharm.) calomel
**calomel electrode** *s* (physical chem.) electrodo de calomel
**caloric** [kəˈlɑrɪk] o [kəˈlɔrɪk] *adj* calórico; *s* (old chem.) calórico
**caloricity** [ˌkæləˈrɪsɪtɪ] *s* (physiol.) caloricidad
**calorie** [ˈkælərɪ] *s* (phys. & physiol.) caloría; **gram calorie** o **small calorie** caloría gramo o caloría pequeña; **kilogram calorie** o **large calorie** caloría kilogramo o caloría grande
**calorific** [ˌkæləˈrɪfɪk] *adj* calorífico
**calorification** [kəˌlɑrɪfɪˈkeʃən] *s* calorificación
**calorimeter** [ˌkæləˈrɪmɪtər] *s* calorímetro
**calorimetric** [ˌkælərɪˈmɛtrɪk] o **calorimetrical** [ˌkælərɪˈmɛtrɪkəl] *adj* calorimétrico
**calorimetry** [ˌkæləˈrɪmɪtrɪ] *s* calorimetría
**calory** [ˈkælərɪ] *s* (*pl:* **-ries**) var. de **calorie**
**calotte** [kəˈlɑt] *s* casquete; (eccl.) solideo; (arch.) casquete
**caltrop** [ˈkæltrəp] *s* (bot. & mil.) abrojo
**calumba** [kəˈlʌmbə] *s* (pharm.) colombo
**calumet** [ˈkæljʊmɛt] *s* pipa larga que fuman los indios norteamericanos en las ceremonias solemnes y sobre todo en los acuerdos de paz
**calumniate** [kəˈlʌmnɪet] *va* calumniar
**calumniator** [kəˈlʌmnɪˌetər] *s* calumniador
**calumnious** [kəˈlʌmnɪəs] *adj* calumnioso
**calumny** [ˈkæləmnɪ] *s* (*pl:* **-nies**) calumnia
**Calvary** [ˈkælvərɪ] *s* (Bib.) Calvario; (*l.c.*) *s* (*pl:* **-ries**) calvario (*representación*); humilladero (*en la entrada de un pueblo*)
**calve** [kæv] o [kɑv] *va & vn* parir (*dícese de la vaca*)
**Calvin** [ˈkælvɪn] *s* Calvino
**Calvinism** [ˈkælvɪnɪzəm] *s* calvinismo
**Calvinist** [ˈkælvɪnɪst] *adj & s* calvinista
**Calvinistic** [ˌkælvɪˈnɪstɪk] *adj* calvinista
**calx** [kælks] *s* (*pl:* **calxes** o **calces** [ˈkælsiz]) residuo cenizoso de un metal o mineral calcinado; cal
**calycle** [ˈkælɪkəl] *s* (bot. & zool.) calículo
**calycular** [kəˈlɪkjələr] *adj* (bot.) calicular
**calyculus** [kəˈlɪkjələs] *s* (*pl:* **-li** [laɪ]) (anat. & zool.) calículo
**calypso** [kəˈlɪpso] *s* (*pl:* **-sos**) calipso (*canto improvisado*); (bot.) calipso; (*cap.*) *s* (myth.) Calipso
**calyx** [ˈkelɪks] o [ˈkælɪks] *s* (*pl:* **calyxes** o **calyces** [ˈkælɪsiz] o [ˈkelɪsiz]) (anat. & bot.) cáliz
**cam** [kæm] *s* (mach.) leva
**camaraderie** [ˌkɑməˈrɑdərɪ] *s* camaradería
**camarilla** [ˌkæməˈrɪlə] *s* camarilla
**camass** [ˈkæmæs] *s* (bot.) camasia
**camber** [ˈkæmbər] *s* comba, combadura; (aut.) inclinación (*de las ruedas*); convexidad (*del camino*); *va* combar, arquear; *vn* combarse, arquearse
**cambium** [ˈkæmbɪəm] *s* (bot.) cámbium o cambio
**Cambodia** [kæmˈbodɪə] *s* Camboya
**Cambodian** [kæmˈbodɪən] *adj & s* camboyano
**Cambrian** [ˈkæmbrɪən] *adj & s* cambriano o cámbrico; (geol.) cambriano o cámbrico
**cambric** [ˈkembrɪk] *s* batista
**cambric tea** *s* bebida hecha de agua caliente, leche y azúcar, y a veces un poquito de té
**Cambyses** [kæmˈbaɪsiz] *s* Cambises
**came** [kem] *pret de* **come**
**camel** [ˈkæməl] *s* (zool.) camello; (naut.) camello (*mecanismo para suspender un buque*)
**camel grass** *s* (bot.) esquenanto
**camellia** [kəˈmiljə] *s* (bot.) camelia
**camelopard** [kəˈmɛləpɑrd] o [ˈkæmələˌpɑrd] *s* (zool.) camello pardal
**camel's hair** *s* pelo de camello
**camel's-hair** [ˈkæməlzˌhɛr] *adj* de pelo de camello
**camel's-hair brush** *s* pincel de pelo de camello
**Camembert** [ˈkæməmbɛr] *s* camembert (*queso*)
**cameo** [ˈkæmɪo] *s* (*pl:* **-os**) camafeo
**camera** [ˈkæmərə] *s* cámara fotográfica; cámara apostólica; (law) sala particular del juez; **in camera** (law) en la sala particular del juez; en secreto
**camera lucida** [ˈlusɪdə] *s* (opt.) cámara clara o lúcida
**cameraman** [ˈkæmərəˌmæn] *s* (*pl:* **-men**) (mov.) cámara *m*, camarógrafo
**camera obscura** [ɑbˈskjʊrə] *s* (opt.) cámara oscura
**camera stand** *s* sostén de cámara
**Cameroons** [ˌkæməˈrunz] *s* Camerón
**Cameroun** [kɑmˈrun] *s* el Camerón francés
**camion** [ˈkæmɪən] *s* camión
**camisole** [ˈkæmɪsol] *s* camiseta de mujer; camisola (*de hombre*); cubrecorsé; camisa de fuerza

**camlet** ['kæmlɪt] *s* camelote
**camomile** ['kæməmaɪl] *s* (bot. & pharm.) camomila, manzanilla
**Camorra** [kə'mɑrə] o [kə'mɔrə] *s* Camorra
**camouflage** ['kæməflɑʒ] *s* camuflaje; *va* camuflar
**camp** [kæmp] *s* campamento, campo; **in the same camp** de acuerdo, del mismo partido; **to break camp** (mil.) levantar el campo; *vn* acampar; (coll.) alojarse transitoriamente
**campaign** [kæm'pen] *s* (mil. & fig.) campaña; *vn* hacer campaña
**campaigner** [kæm'penər] *s* persona que hace campaña o ha hecho campaña; veterano
**campanile** [,kæmpə'nilɪ] *s* campanario
**campanula** [kæm'pænjʊlə] *s* (bot.) campánula
**campanulaceous** [kæm,pænjʊ'leʃəs] *adj* (bot.) campanuláceo
**camp chair** *s* silla plegadiza
**camper** ['kæmpər] *s* acampador
**campfire** ['kæmp,faɪr] *s* hoguera de campamento; reunión de tropas, de niños exploradores, etc., alrededor de una hoguera
**camp follower** *s* vivandero u otro no combatiente que sigue al ejército
**campground** ['kæmp,graʊnd] *s* campamento
**camphor** ['kæmfər] *s* alcanfor
**camphorate** ['kæmfəret] *va* alcanforar
**camphorated oil** *s* (pharm.) aceite alcanforado
**camphor ball** *s* bola de alcanfor
**camphor tree** *s* (bot.) alcanforero, árbol del alcanfor
**camp hospital** *s* hospital de campaña
**campion** ['kæmpɪən] *s* (bot.) colleja, cruz de Malta
**camp kitchen** *s* cocina de campaña
**camp meeting** *s* campamento de devotos
**campstool** ['kæmp,stul] *s* silla ligera de tijera, catrecillo
**campus** ['kæmpəs] *s* campo, terreno, recinto (*de la universidad*)
**camshaft** ['kæm,ʃæft] o ['kæm,ʃɑft] *s* (mach.) árbol de levas, eje de levas
**Can.** abr. de **Canada** y **Canadian**
**can** [kæn] *s* lata, bote, envase; vasito para beber; (*pret & pp:* **canned;** *ger:* **canning**) *va* enlatar, envasar; (slang) despedir, echar a la calle; (*pret & cond:* **could**) *v aux* poder; saber, p.ej., **he can swim** sabe nadar
**Canaan** ['kenən] *s* (Bib.) Tierra de Canaán; (fig.) tierra de promisión
**Canaanite** ['kenənaɪt] *adj & s* (Bib.) cananeo
**Canada** ['kænədə] *s* el Canadá
**Canada balsam** *s* (bot.) bálsamo canadiense
**Canada goose** *s* (orn.) ganso de corbata
**Canada thistle** *s* (bot.) cardo negro
**Canadian** [kə'nedɪən] *adj & s* canadiense
**canaille** [kə'nel] o [kə'naɪ] *s* canalla, gentuza
**canal** [kə'næl] *s* canal *m*
**canal boat** *s* bote de canal
**canalization** [kə,nælɪ'zeʃən] o [,kænəlɪ'zeʃən] *s* canalización
**canalize** [kə'nælaɪz] o ['kænəlaɪz] *va* canalizar
**canal rays** *spl* (phys.) rayos canales
**Canal Zone** *s* Zona del Canal (*Panamá*)
**canapé** [,kænə'pe] o ['kænəpe] *s* canapé (*para excitar el apetito*)
**canard** [kə'nɑrd] o [kə'nɑr] *s* bola, embuste, noticia falsa
**Canarian** [kə'nɛrɪən] *adj & s* canario
**canary** [kə'nɛrɪ] *s* (*pl:* **-ies**) (orn.) canario; color de canario; vino de las islas Canarias; **Canaries** *spl* Canarias
**canary bird** *s* (orn.) canario
**canary grass** *s* (bot.) alpiste
**Canary Islands** *spl* islas Canarias
**canary yellow** *adj & s* amarillo canario
**canasta** [kə'næstə] *s* canasta (*juego de naipes*)
**can buoy** *s* (naut.) boya de tambor
**cancan** ['kænkæn] *s* cancán
**cancel** ['kænsəl] *s* supresión, eliminación, canceladura; (*pret & pp:* **-celed** o **-celled;** *ger:* **-celing** o **-celling**) *va* suprimir, eliminar, cancelar; matasellar, obliterar (*sellos de correo*)
**canceler** ['kænsələr] *s* matasellos
**cancellation** [,kænsə'leʃən] *s* supresión, eliminación, cancelación; obliteración (*inutilización de los sellos de correo; raya o marca de inutilización*)
**cancer** ['kænsər] *s* (path.) cáncer; (*cap.*) *s* (astr.) Cáncer
**cancerous** ['kænsərəs] *adj* canceroso
**cancroid** ['kæŋkrɔɪd] *adj* cancroideo
**candelabrum** [,kændə'lɑbrəm] o [,kændə'lebrəm] *s* (*pl:* **-bra** [brə] o **-brums**) *s* candelabro
**candescence** [kæn'dɛsəns] *s* candencia, incandescencia
**candescent** [kæn'dɛsənt] *adj* candente, incandescente
**candid** ['kændɪd] *adj* cándido; justo, imparcial
**candidacy** ['kændɪdəsɪ] *s* candidatura
**candidate** ['kændɪdet] o ['kændɪdɪt] *s* candidato; graduando
**candidature** ['kændɪ,detʃər] *s* candidatura
**candid camera** *s* máquina fotográfica de reducidas dimensiones, para poder tomar instantáneas de escenas de la vida diaria, sin llamar la atención, cámara indiscreta
**candied** ['kændɪd] *adj* convertido en azúcar; almibarado, azucarado; **candied words** palabras melosas
**candle** ['kændəl] *s* candela, bujía, vela; (eccl.) cirio; **to burn the candle at both ends** gastar locamente fuerzas y dinero, consumir la vida; **to not be able to hold a candle to** (coll.) no llegar a la suela del zapato a, no poder compararse con; *va* examinar (*huevos*) al trasluz
**candleholder** ['kændəl,holdər] *s* candelero
**candlelight** ['kændəl,laɪt] *s* luz de vela; crepúsculo
**candlelighter** ['kændəl,laɪtər] *s* encendedor de velas; acólito
**Candlemas** ['kændəlməs] *s* candelaria
**candle power** *s* bujía
**candlestick** ['kændəl,stɪk] *s* palmatoria
**candlewick** ['kændəl,wɪk] *s* pabilo, mecha de la vela
**candlewood** ['kændəl,wʊd] *s* cuelmo, tea
**candor** ['kændər] *s* candor; justicia, imparcialidad
**candour** ['kændər] *s* (Brit.) var. de **candor**
**candy** ['kændɪ] *s* (*pl:* **-dies**) bombón, confite, dulce; dulces; (*pret & pp:* **-died**) *va* confitar; almibarar, azucarar; *vn* cristalizarse
**candy box** *s* bombonera
**candytuft** ['kændɪ,tʌft] *s* (bot.) carraspique, zarapico
**cane** [ken] *s* bastón; caña (*tallo de varias plantas*); *va* bastonear; fabricar de caña; poner asiento de rejilla o de mimbre a (*una silla*)
**canebrake** ['ken,brek] *s* cañaveral
**cane seat** *s* asiento de rejilla
**cane sugar** *s* azúcar de caña
**cangue** [kæŋ] *s* canga
**can hooks** *spl* gafas
**canicular** [kə'nɪkjələr] *adj* canicular
**canine** ['kenaɪn] o ['kænaɪn] *adj* canino; *s* (anat.) canino (*colmillo*); can, perro
**canine tooth** *s* (anat.) diente canino
**Canis Major** ['kenɪs 'medʒər] *s* (astr.) Can Mayor
**Canis Minor** ['kenɪs 'maɪnər] *s* (astr.) Can Menor
**canistel** [,kænɪs'tɛl] *s* canisté o canistel (*fruto*)
**canister** ['kænɪstər] *s* bote, frasco, lata (*para té, café, tabaco, etc.*)
**canker** ['kæŋkər] *s* (path.) llaga o úlcera gangrenosa; úlcera en la boca; (bot.) cancro; (ent.) oruga; *va* ulcerar; corromper; *vn* ulcerarse; corromperse
**cankerous** ['kæŋkərəs] *adj* ulceroso, gangrenoso; ulcerativo
**canker rash** *s* (path.) escarlatina
**cankerworm** ['kæŋkər,wʌrm] *s* (ent.) oruga (*Alsophila pometaria y Paleacrita vernata*)
**canna** ['kænə] *s* (bot.) cañacoro
**cannabinaceous** [,kænəbɪ'neʃəs] *adj* (bot.) canabíneo
**cannaceous** [kə'neʃəs] *adj* (bot.) canáceo
**canned goods** *spl* conservas alimenticias
**canned music** *s* (slang) música impresa (*en discos, cintas, etc.*)
**cannel** ['kænəl] o **cannel coal** *s* carbón mate, carbón de bujía
**canner** ['kænər] *s* envasador (*persona que envasa víveres en latas*)

**cannery** ['kænərɪ] *s* (*pl:* **-ies**) fábrica de conservas alimenticias, conservera
**cannibal** ['kænɪbəl] *adj & s* caníbal
**cannibalism** ['kænɪbəlɪzəm] *s* canibalismo
**cannibalistic** [,kænɪbə'lɪstɪk] *adj* caníbal, canibalino, del canibalismo
**cannikin** ['kænɪkɪn] *s* lata o vaso pequeño de metal
**canning** ['kænɪŋ] *s* envase (*en latas*); *adj* conservero
**cannon** ['kænən] *s* cañón; cañonería, artillería (*conjunto de cañones*); (zool.) metatarso
**cannonade** [,kænə'ned] *s* cañoneo; *va* acañonear
**cannon ball** *s* bala de cañón
**cannon bone** *s* (zool.) metatarso
**cannon cracker** *s* triquitraque grande
**cannoneer** [,kænə'nɪr] *s* cañonero, artillero
**cannon fodder** *s* carne de cañón
**cannon metal** *s* metal o bronce para cañones
**cannonry** ['kænənrɪ] *s* (*pl:* **-ries**) cañoneo; cañonería
**cannon shot** *s* balas de cañón; cañonazo, tiro de cañón; alcance de un cañón
**cannot** ['kænɑt] contracción de **can not**
**cannula** ['kænjələ] *s* (*pl:* **-lae** [li]) (surg.) cánula
**cannular** ['kænjələr] *adj* canular
**canny** ['kænɪ] *adj* (*comp:* **-nier;** *super:* **-niest**) astuto, sagaz; cauteloso; parco, económico; lindo; cómodo
**canoe** [kə'nu] *s* canoa; (*pret & pp:* **-noed;** *ger:* **-noeing**) *va* llevar en canoa; *vn* pasear en canoa
**canoeist** [kə'nuɪst] *s* canoero
**canon** ['kænən] *s* canon; (Bib., eccl. & mus.) canon; canónigo (*sacerdote*); (print.) gran canon; (*cap.*) *s* (eccl.) canon (*parte de la misa que empieza Te igitur*)
**cañon** ['kænjən] *s* var. de **canyon**
**canoness** ['kænənɪs] *s* canonesa
**canonical** [kə'nɑnɪkəl] *adj* (Bib. & eccl.) canónico; aceptado, auténtico; **canonicals** *spl* vestiduras
**canonical hours** *spl* horas canónicas
**canonization** [,kænənɪ'zeʃən] *s* canonización
**canonize** ['kænənaɪz] *va* canonizar
**canon law** *s* cánones, derecho canónico
**canonry** ['kænənrɪ] *s* (*pl:* **-ries**) canonjía
**can opener** *s* abrelatas, abridor de latas
**canopy** ['kænəpɪ] *s* (*pl:* **-pies**) dosel, pabellón; sombrero (*del púlpito*); cielo (*de la cama*); conopeo (*baldaquino en forma de tienda portátil*); (arch.) doselete (*sobre las estatuas, sepulcros, etc.*); (elec.) campana; casquete (*del paracaídas*); (fig.) cielo; (*pret & pp:* **-pied**) *va* endoselar
**canopy of heaven** *s* bóveda celeste, capa del cielo
**cant** [kænt] *s* lenguaje insincero, hipocresía, gazmoñería; germanía (*de ladrones*); jerga (*de una profesión*); inclinación, sesgo; bisel, chaflán; tumbo; *adj* insincero, hipócrita, gazmoño; de una jerga; inclinado, sesgado; *va* inclinar, sesgar; arrojar, lanzar; tumbar, derribar; *vn* hablar en jerga; hablar con gazmoñería
**can't** [kænt] o [kɑnt] contracción de **can not**
**Cantab.** abr. de **Cantabrigiensis** (Lat.) **of Cambridge**
**Cantabrigian** [,kæntə'brɪdʒɪən] *adj* perteneciente a Cambridge; *s* natural o habitante de Cambridge
**cantaloup** o **cantaloupe** ['kæntəlop] *s* cantalupo
**cantankerous** [kæn'tæŋkərəs] *adj* pendenciero, quimerista, avieso
**cantata** [kən'tɑtə] *s* (mus.) cantata
**canteen** [kæn'tin] *s* cantina; cantimplora
**canter** ['kæntər] *s* medio galope; *vn* andar (*el caballo*) a medio galope
**Canterburian** [,kæntər'bjʊrɪən] *adj & s* cantuariense
**Canterbury** ['kæntər,bɛrɪ] *s* Cantórbery
**Canterbury bell** *s* (bot.) farolillo, campánula
**cantharides** [kæn'θærɪdiz] *spl* (pharm.) polvo de cantárida
**cantharis** ['kænθərɪs] *s* (*pl:* **cantharides** [kæn'θærɪdiz]) (ent.) cantárida
**cant hook** *s* palanca de gancho (*para dar vuelta a los troncos*)
**canticle** ['kæntɪkəl] *s* cántico; **Canticles** *spl* (Bib.) Cantar de los Cantares
**Canticle of Canticles** *s* (Bib.) Cantar de los Cantares
**cantilever** ['kæntɪ,lɛvər] o ['kæntɪ,livər] *s* viga voladiza; ménsula
**cantilever bridge** *s* puente cantilever, puente voladizo
**cantilever spring** *s* (aut.) muelle voladizo
**cantilever wing** *s* (aer.) ala voladiza, ala en cantilever
**cantle** ['kæntəl] *s* arzón trasero
**canto** ['kænto] *s* (*pl:* **-tos**) canto
**canton** ['kæntən] o [kæn'tɑn] *s* cantón; (her.) cantón; [kæn'tɑn] o [kæn'ton] *va* acantonar
**cantonal** ['kæntənəl] *adj* cantonal
**Canton crepe** ['kæntən] *s* burato
**Cantonese** [,kæntə'niz] *adj* cantonés; *s* (*pl:* **-ese**) cantonés
**Canton flannel** *s* moletón
**cantonment** [kæn'tɑnmənt] o ['kæntənmənt] *s* acantonamiento
**cantor** ['kæntər] o ['kæntɔr] *s* chantre; cantor principal (*de una sinagoga*)
**Canuck** [kə'nʌk] *adj & s* (slang) canadiense, francocanadiense
**canvas** ['kænvəs] *s* cañamazo, lona; (naut.) vela, lona; (naut.) velamen; (paint.) lienzo; **under canvas** (mil.) en tiendas; (naut.) con las velas izadas
**canvasback** ['kænvəs,bæk] *s* (orn.) pato pelucón
**canvass** ['kænvəs] *s* escrutinio, pesquisa, inspección; solicitación (*de votos*); *va* escudriñar; solicitar (*votos*); discutir; *vn* solicitar votos, pedidos comerciales, fondos, opiniones, etc.
**canvasser** ['kænvəsər] *s* inspector, examinador; solicitador (*de votos, pedidos comerciales, etc.*)
**canyon** ['kænjən] *s* cañón (*paso estrecho entre montañas*)
**canzonet** [,kænzə'nɛt] *s* cancioneta
**caoutchouc** ['kaʊtʃʊk] o ['kutʃʊk] *s* caucho
**cap.** abr. de **capital, capitalize** y **capital letter**
**cap** [kæp] *s* gorra, gorrilla de visera; tapa, tapón, tapita; cima, cumbre; gorra, bonete (*del traje de catedrático*); caballete (*de la chimenea*); cápsula (*de una botella o un arma de percusión*); (naut.) tamborete (*que sujeta dos palos sobrepuestos*); (bot.) sombrero o sombrerete (*de seta u hongo*); **to put on one's thinking cap** reflexionar con madurez; **to set one's cap for** (coll.) proponerse conquistar para novio; (*pret & pp:* **capped;** *ger:* **capping**) *va* cubrir con gorra; capsular (*una botella*); poner tapa a; poner cima a; poner remate a, acabar; exceder, sobrepujar; saludar descubriéndose la cabeza; **to cap the climax** ser el colmo; *vn* descubrirse en señal de reverencia
**capability** [,kepə'bɪlɪtɪ] *s* (*pl:* **-ties**) capacidad, habilidad
**capable** ['kepəbəl] *adj* capaz, hábil; **capable of** capaz de; sujeto a
**capacious** [kə'peʃəs] *adj* capaz, espacioso
**capacitance** [kə'pæsɪtəns] *s* (elec.) capacitancia
**capacitor** [kə'pæsɪtər] *s* (elec.) capacitor
**capacity** [kə'pæsɪtɪ] *s* (*pl:* **-ties**) capacidad; (elec. & phys.) capacidad
**cap and bells** *spl* gorro con campanillas (*del bufón*)
**cap and gown** *spl* toga y bonete
**cap-a-pie** o **cap-à-pie** [,kæpə'pi] *adv* de pies a cabeza
**caparison** [kə'pærɪsən] *s* caparazón; equipo, traje o vestido rico; *va* engualdrapar; vestir soberbiamente
**cape** [kep] *s* capa, esclavina; cabo, promontorio
**Cape Breton Island** ['brɪtən] o ['brɛtən] *s* la Isla del cabo Bretón
**Cape buffalo** *s* (zool.) búfalo cafre, búfalo de Cafrería
**Cape Colony** *s* la Colonia del Cabo
**Cape Horn** *s* el Cabo de Hornos
**Cape hunting dog** *s* (zool.) perro hiena
**Cape jasmine** *s* (bot.) jazmín del Cabo
**capelin** ['kæpəlɪn] *s* (ichth.) capelán
**capeline** ['kæpəlɪn] *s* (arm. & surg.) capellina

**Cape of Good Hope** *s* cabo de Buena Esperanza
**caper** ['kepər] *s* cabriola; travesura; (bot.) alcaparra; **capers** *spl* alcaparrones (*botones de la flor de la alcaparra*); **to cut capers** dar cabriolas; hacer travesuras; *vn* cabriolar
**capercaillie** [ˌkæpər'keljɪ] *s* (orn.) urogallo, grigallo
**Capernaum** [kə'pʌrnɪəm] *s* Cafarnaúm
**Capetian** [kə'piʃən] *adj & s* capetiano, capetino
**Capetown** ['kepˌtaʊn] o **Cape Town** *s* El Cabo, la Ciudad del Cabo
**Cape Verde** [vʌrd] *s* Cabo Verde
**Cape Verde Islands** *spl* islas de Cabo Verde
**capias** ['kepɪɑs] o ['kæpɪɑs] *s* (law) orden de arresto
**capillarity** [ˌkæpɪ'lærɪtɪ] *s* capilaridad
**capillary** ['kæpɪˌlɛrɪ] *adj* capilar; *s* (*pl:* **-ies**) tubo capilar; (anat.) capilar, vaso capilar
**capillary attraction** *s* (phys.) atracción capilar
**capillary tube** *s* tubo capilar
**capita** ['kæpɪtə] *pl de* **caput**
**capital** ['kæpɪtəl] *adj* capital; excelente, magnífico; *s* capital *m* (*dinero*); capital *f* (*ciudad*); (fort.) capital *f*; (arch.) capitel; (tech.) capitel (*del alambique*); **to make capital out of** sacar partido de
**capital expenditure** *s* inversión de capital para ampliar o mejorar el negocio
**capital gains** *spl* ganancias capitales
**capital goods** *spl* bienes capitales (*elementos de producción*)
**capitalism** ['kæpɪtəlɪzəm] *s* capitalismo
**capitalist** ['kæpɪtəlɪst] *adj & s* capitalista
**capitalistic** [ˌkæpɪtə'lɪstɪk] *adj* capitalista
**capitalization** [ˌkæpɪtəlɪ'zeʃən] *s* capitalización; aprovechamiento; total del capital; escritura o impresión en mayúscula
**capitalize** ['kæpɪtəlaɪz] *va* capitalizar; aprovechar; escribir o imprimir con mayúscula; *vn* capitalizar; **to capitalize on** aprovecharse de
**capital letter** *s* letra capital, letra mayúscula
**capitally** ['kæpɪtəlɪ] *adv* excelentemente, admirablemente
**capital punishment** *s* pena capital, pena de muerte
**capital ship** *s* (nav.) acorazado grande
**capital sin** *s* pecado capital, pecado mortal
**capital stock** *s* capital social
**capitate** ['kæpɪtet] *adj* (bot.) capitado
**capitation** [ˌkæpɪ'teʃən] *s* capitación
**capitol** ['kæpɪtəl] *s* capitolio; (*cap.*) *s* Capitolio
**Capitoline** ['kæpɪtəlaɪn] o [kə'pɪtəlaɪn] *adj* capitolino; *s* monte Capitolino
**capitular** [kə'pɪtʃələr] *adj* capitular
**capitulary** [kə'pɪtʃəˌlɛrɪ] *s* (*pl:* **-ies**) capitular; **capitularies** *spl* (hist.) capitulares
**capitulate** [kə'pɪtʃəlet] *vn* capitular
**capitulation** [kəˌpɪtʃə'leʃən] *s* capitulación; resumen, recapitulación
**Cap'n** ['kæpən] *s* capitán
**capnomancy** ['kæpnoˌmænsɪ] *s* capnomancia
**capon** ['kepən] o ['kepɑn] *s* capón (*pollo castrado*); capón cebado
**capote** [kə'pot] *s* capote (*capa*); capota (*cubierta de coche; sombrero sujeto con cintas*)
**Cappadocian** [ˌkæpə'doʃən] *adj & s* capadocio
**capparidaceous** [ˌkæpərɪ'deʃəs] *adj* (bot.) caparidáceo
**capriccio** [kə'prɪtʃɪo] o [kə'pritʃo] *s* (*pl:* **-cios**) travesura; capricho; (mus.) capricho
**caprice** [kə'pris] *s* capricho; veleidad, inconstancia; (mus.) capricho
**capricious** [kə'prɪʃəs] *adj* caprichoso, caprichudo
**Capricorn** ['kæprɪkɔrn] *s* (astr.) Capricornio
**caprificate** ['kæprɪfɪket] o [kə'prɪfɪket] *va* cabrahigar
**caprification** [ˌkæprɪfɪ'keʃən] *s* cabrahigadura
**caprifig** ['kæprɪˌfɪg] *s* (bot.) cabrahigo
**caprifoliaceous** [ˌkæprɪˌfolɪ'eʃəs] *adj* (bot.) caprifoliáceo
**capriole** ['kæprɪol] *s* cabriola; *vn* cabriolar
**caps.** abr. de **capital letters**
**capsaicin** [kæp'seɪsɪn] *s* (chem.) capsaicina
**cap screw** *s* tornillo de cabeza cuadrada o hexagonal
**capsicum** ['kæpsɪkəm] *s* (bot.) pimiento (*planta y fruto*)
**capsize** ['kæpsaɪz] *va* volcar; *vn* volcar; tumbar (*un barco*)
**capstan** ['kæpstən] *s* cabrestante, argüe; **to rig the capstan** guarnir el cabrestante
**capstan bar** *s* (naut.) manuella, barra del cabrestante
**capstan lathe** *s* torno revólver
**capstone** ['kæpˌston] *s* (arch.) albardilla, coronamiento; (fig.) coronamiento
**capsular** ['kæpsələr] o ['kæpsjʊlər] *adj* capsular
**capsule** ['kæpsəl] o ['kæpsjʊl] *s* (anat., bot., pharm. & zool.) cápsula; cápsula (*de un cohete espacial*)
**Capt.** abr. de **Captain**
**captain** ['kæptɪn] *s* capitán (*p.ej., de un equipo de fútbol*); (mil., naut. & nav.) capitán; *va* capitanear
**captaincy** ['kæptɪnsɪ] *s* (*pl:* **-cies**) capitanía
**captain general** *s* (*pl:* **captains general**) (mil. & Sp. hist.) capitán general
**captainship** ['kæptɪnʃɪp] *s* capitanía
**caption** ['kæpʃən] *s* título; (mov.) subtítulo; *va* intitular, poner título a
**captious** ['kæpʃəs] *adj* criticón, reparón; insidioso
**captivate** ['kæptɪvet] *va* fascinar, cautivar
**captivation** [ˌkæptɪ'veʃən] *s* fascinación
**captive** ['kæptɪv] *adj & s* cautivo
**captive balloon** *s* globo cautivo
**captivity** [kæp'tɪvɪtɪ] *s* (*pl:* **-ties**) cautiverio, cautividad
**captor** ['kæptər] *s* captor, apresador
**capture** ['kæptʃər] *s* apresamiento, captura; toma (*de una plaza*); prisionero; presa, botín; *va* apresar, capturar; tomar (*una plaza*); captar (*la confianza de uno*)
**capture cross section** *s* (phys.) sección de captura
**capuchin** ['kæpjʊtʃɪn] o ['kæpjʊʃɪn] *s* (zool.) capuchino (*mono*); (orn.) paloma capuchina; capucho (*pieza del vestido*); (*cap.*) *s* capuchino (*monje*)
**Capuchin nun** *s* capuchina
**caput** ['kepət] o ['kæpət] *s* (*pl:* **capita** ['kæpɪtə]) (Lat.) cabeza; **per capita** por cabeza, por persona
**capybara** [ˌkæpɪ'bɑrə] *s* (zool.) capibara, carpincho
**car** [kɑr] *s* coche (*carro de ferrocarril; automóvil*); caja o carro (*de ascensor*); barquilla (*de un globo aerostático*)
**carabao** [ˌkɑrə'bɑo] *s* (*pl:* **-os**) (zool.) carabao
**carabineer** o **carabinier** [ˌkærəbɪ'nɪr] *s* carabinero
**caracal** ['kærəkæl] *s* (zool.) caracal, lince de las estepas
**caracole** ['kærəkol] *s* caracol (*del caballo*); *vn* caracolear (*el caballo*)
**caracul** ['kærəkəl] *s* caracul (*piel rizada*); cordero de astracán, oveja caracul
**carafe** [kə'ræf] o [kə'rɑf] *s* garrafa
**caramel** ['kærəməl] o ['kɑrməl] *s* caramelo, azúcar quemado; confite plástico que sabe a caramelo; *va* acaramelar; *vn* acaramelarse
**caramelize** ['kærəməlaɪz] *va* acaramelizar; *vn* acaramelizarse
**carapace** ['kærəpes] *s* carapacho
**carat** ['kærət] *s* quilate
**caravan** ['kærəvæn] *s* caravana; carricoche; (Brit.) coche-habitación
**caravansary** [ˌkærə'vænsərɪ] *s* (*pl:* **-ries**) caravanera o caravansera; posada grande
**caravanserai** [ˌkærə'vænsəraɪ] o [ˌkærə'vænsəre] *s* var. de **caravansary**
**caravan site** *s* (Brit.) var. de **trailer camp**
**caravel** ['kærəvɛl] *s* (naut.) carabela
**caraway** ['kærəwe] *s* (bot.) alcaravea (*planta y simiente*)
**caraway seeds** *spl* alcaravea, carvi
**carbarn** ['kɑrˌbɑrn] *s* cochera de tranvías, cobertizo para tranvías
**carbide** ['kɑrbaɪd] o ['kɑrbɪd] *s* (chem.) carburo (*especialmente el de calcio*)
**carbine** ['kɑrbaɪn] *s* carabina
**carbineer** [ˌkɑrbɪ'nɪr] *s* var. de **carabineer**
**carbinol** ['kɑrbɪnol] o ['kɑrbɪnɑl] *s* (chem.) carbinol

**carbodynamite** [ˌkarbo'daɪnəmaɪt] *s* carbodinamita
**carbohydrate** [ˌkarbo'haɪdret] *s* (chem.) carbohidrato, hidrato de carbono
**carbolated** ['karbəˌletɪd] *adj* mezclado con ácido carbólico
**carbolic** [kar'balɪk] *adj* carbólico
**carbolic acid** *s* (chem.) ácido carbólico
**carbolineum** [ˌkarbo'lɪnɪəm] *s* (trademark) carbolíneo
**carbolize** ['karbəlaɪz] *va* mezclar o tratar con ácido carbólico
**carbon** ['karbən] *s* (chem.) carbono; (elec.) carbón (*de una pila o una lámpara de arco*); papel carbón; copia en papel carbón; (aut.) carbonilla o carboncillo (*en los cilindros*)
**carbonaceous** [ˌkarbə'neʃəs] *adj* carbonoso
**carbonado** [ˌkarbə'nedo] *s* (*pl:* **-does** o **-dos**) carne asada a la parrilla; carbonado (*diamante negro*); *va* asar a la parrilla; acuchillar
**carbonate** ['karbənet] o ['karbənɪt] *s* (chem.) carbonato; ['karbənet] *va* carbonatar
**carbon copy** *s* copia en papel carbón, copia al carbón
**carbon diamond** *s* carbonado, diamante negro
**carbon dioxide** *s* (chem.) dióxido de carbono, anhídrido carbónico
**carbon dioxide snow** *s* (chem.) nieve carbónica
**carbonic** [kar'banɪk] *adj* carbónico
**carbonic-acid gas** [kar'banɪk'æsɪd] *s* (chem.) gas carbónico, dióxido de carbono
**carboniferous** [ˌkarbə'nɪfərəs] *adj* carbonífero; (*cap.*) *adj* (geol.) carbonífero; *s* (geol.) período carbonífero; (geol.) carbonífero, formación carbonífera
**carbonization** [ˌkarbənɪ'zeʃən] *s* carbonización
**carbonize** ['karbənaɪz] *va* carbonizar; *vn* carbonizarse
**carbon monoxide** *s* (chem.) óxido de carbono, monóxido de carbono
**carbon paper** *s* papel carbón
**carbon tetrachloride** [ˌtɛtrə'kloraɪd] *s* (chem.) tetracloruro de carbono
**carbonyl** ['karbənɪl] *s* (chem.) carbonilo
**carborundum** [ˌkarbə'rʌndəm] *s* (trademark) carborundo
**carborundum detector** *s* (rad.) detector de cristales de carborundo
**carboxyl group** [kar'baksɪl] *s* (chem.) grupo carboxilo
**carboy** ['karbɔɪ] *s* bombona, garrafón
**carbuncle** ['karbʌŋkəl] *s* carbunclo o carbúnculo (*rubí o granate*); (path. & vet.) carbunco o carbunclo; grano (*tumorcillo pequeño*)
**carburet** ['karbəret] o ['karbjəret] (*pret & pp:* **-reted** o **-retted;** *ger:* **-reting** o **-retting**) *va* carburar
**carburetion** [ˌkarbə'reʃən] o [ˌkarbjə'reʃən] *s* carburación
**carburetor** o **carburettor** ['karbəˌretər] o ['karbjəˌretər] *s* carburador
**carcanet** ['karkənɛt] *s* (archaic) gargantilla o collar de piedras preciosas u oro
**carcase** o **carcass** ['karkəs] *s* cadáver (*especialmente de animal*); res muerta; esqueleto o armazón (*de una casa, un navío, etc.*); (mil.) carcasa
**Carcassonne** [ˌkarˌka'sɔn] *s* Carcasona
**carcinogen** [kar'sɪnədʒən] *s* (path.) carcinógeno
**carcinoma** [ˌkarsɪ'nomə] *s* (*pl:* **-mata** [mətə] o **-mas**) (path.) carcinoma
**card** [kard] *s* tarjeta; carta, naipe; ficha; rosa náutica; (coll.) tipo, sujeto; carda, cardencha (*para cardar lana*); **cards** *spl* naipes (*juego*); **in** u **on the cards** probable; **to cut the cards** cortar el naipe; **to deal the cards** dar las cartas; **to have a card up one's sleeve** tener otro recurso, tener ayuda en reserva; **to play cards** jugar a los naipes; **to put one's cards on the table** poner las cartas boca arriba, jugar a cartas vistas; **to shuffle the cards** barajar las cartas; *va* dar un naipe a; poner en una tarjeta o ficha; cardar (*p.ej., la lana*)
**cardamom** o **cardamum** ['kardəməm] o **cardamon** ['kardəmən] *s* (bot.) cardamomo
**cardboard** ['kardˌbord] *s* cartón
**cardboard binding** *s* encuadernación en pasta
**cardboard box** *s* cartón, caja de cartón
**card-carrying communist** ['kard'kærɪɪŋ] *s* comunista que lleva consigo la tarjeta de afiliación al partido
**card case** *s* tarjetero
**card catalogue** *s* catálogo de fichas
**carder** ['kardər] *s* cardador
**card game** *s* juego de cartas; partida de cartas
**cardia** ['kardɪə] *s* (anat.) cardias
**cardiac** ['kardɪæk] *adj* cardíaco; *s* remedio cardíaco; (coll.) cardíaco (*persona que padece del corazón*)
**cardigan** ['kardɪgən] *s* rebeca, chaqueta de lana tejida, albornoz
**cardinal** ['kardɪnəl] *adj* cardinal; *s* purpurado; (eccl. & orn.) cardenal; número cardinal
**cardinalate** ['kardɪnəlet] *s* cardenalato
**cardinal bird** *s* (orn.) cardenal
**cardinal flower** *s* (bot.) lobelia escarlata
**cardinal grosbeak** *s* (orn.) cardenal
**cardinal number** *s* número cardinal
**cardinal points** *spl* puntos cardinales
**cardinal virtues** *spl* virtudes cardinales
**card index** *s* fichero, tarjetero
**carding** ['kardɪŋ] *s* cardadura (*acción*); cardada (*porción de lana cardada*)
**cardiogram** ['kardɪoˌgræm] *s* cardiograma
**cardiograph** ['kardɪoˌgræf] o ['kardɪoˌgraf] *s* cardiógrafo
**cardiography** [ˌkardɪ'agrəfɪ] *s* cardiografía
**cardiology** [ˌkardɪ'alədʒɪ] *s* cardiología
**cardiovascular** [ˌkardɪo'væskjələr] *adj* cardiovascular
**carditis** [kar'daɪtɪs] *s* (path.) carditis
**cardoon** [kar'dun] *s* (bot.) cardo de comer
**card party** *s* tertulia de baraja
**cardsharp** ['kardˌʃarp] *s* fullero, tahur
**card table** *s* mesa de baraja
**card trick** *s* truco de naipes
**care** [kɛr] *s* cuidado, inquietud, solicitud; esmero; cargo, custodia; **to have a care** o **to take care** tener cuidado; **to take care of** cuidar, cuidar de; (coll.) tratar con, tratar de; **to take care not to** + *inf* guardarse de + *inf;* **to take care of oneself** cuidarse (*mirar por su salud; darse buena vida*); **to write in care of** escribir a manos de; **care of** suplicada en casa de; *vn* tener cuidado; interesarse; **to care about** preocuparse de o por, cuidarse de (*p.ej., el qué dirán*); **to care for** querer, amar; desear; interesarse en; cuidar de; **to care to** + *inf* tener ganas de + *inf,* cuidar de + *inf*
**careen** [kə'rin] *s* (naut.) carena; inclinación, vuelco; *va* (naut.) inclinar o volcar (*un buque*); (naut.) carenar, despalmar (*reparar o componer*); inclinar o volcar; *vn* (naut.) carenar; inclinarse o volcarse; mecerse precipitadamente
**careenage** [kə'rinɪdʒ] *s* (naut.) despalmador (*sitio*); despalmadura (*reparo o compostura*)
**career** [kə'rɪr] *s* carrera; *adj* de carrera; *vn* correr a carrera tendida
**career diplomat** *s* diplomático de carrera
**careerist** [kə'rɪrɪst] *s* profesional de carrera
**career woman** *s* (coll.) mujer que se consagra a una profesión
**carefree** ['kɛrˌfri] *adj* desenfadado, despreocupado, alegre
**careful** ['kɛrfəl] *adj* cuidadoso; esmerado (*hecho con esmero*)
**carefulness** ['kɛrfəlnɪs] *s* cuidado; esmero
**careless** ['kɛrlɪs] *adj* descuidado; inconsiderado; indiferente; alegre, sin cuidado
**carelessness** ['kɛrlɪsnɪs] *s* descuido; inconsideración; indiferencia; alegría
**caress** [kə'rɛs] *s* caricia; *va* acariciar; *vn* acariciarse
**caret** ['kærət] *s* signo de intercalación
**caretaker** ['kɛrˌtekər] *s* curador, custodio, guardián; portero; casero (*que cuida de una casa y vive en ella*)
**caretaker government** *s* gobierno provisional
**careworn** ['kɛrˌworn] *adj* agobiado de inquietud
**carfare** ['karˌfɛr] *s* pasaje (*en tren, tranvía, autobús*); pequeña cantidad de dinero
**cargo** ['kargo] *s* (*pl:* **-goes** o **-gos**) (naut.) carga, cargamento
**cargo boat** *s* barco de carga

**carhop** ['kɑr,hɑp] *s* (slang) moza de restaurante que sirve a los automovilistas en sus coches
**Carib** ['kærɪb] *s* caribe
**Caribbean** [,kærɪ'biən] o [kə'rɪbɪən] *adj* caribe; *s* mar Caribe
**Caribbean Sea** *s* mar Caribe, mar de las Antillas
**caribou** ['kærɪbu] *s* (zool.) caribú
**caricature** ['kærɪkətʃər] *s* caricatura; *va* caricaturizar
**caricaturist** ['kærɪkətʃərɪst] *s* caricaturista
**caries** ['kɛrɪz] o ['kɛrɪiz] *s* (path.) caries
**carillon** ['kærɪlɑn] o [kə'rɪljən] *s* (mus.) carillón, órgano de campanas; (*pret & pp:* **-lonned;** *ger:* **-lonning**) *vn* tocar el carillón
**carillonneur** [,kærɪlə'nʌr] *s* (mus.) campanero
**cariole** ['kærɪol] *s* carriola; carro pequeño
**carious** ['kɛrɪəs] *adj* cariado
**carking** ['kɑrkɪŋ] *adj* molesto; inquieto
**carl** o **carle** [kɑrl] *s* (archaic) campesino; (Scottish) patán, palurdo
**carline thistle** ['kɑrlɪn] *s* (bot.) ajonjera, angélica carlina
**Carlism** ['kɑrlɪzəm] *s* carlismo
**Carlist** ['kɑrlɪst] *adj & s* carlista
**carload** ['kɑr,lod] *s* vagonada, furgonada, carga de carro
**carloadings** ['kɑr,lodɪŋz] *spl* (com.) vagones cargados (*p.ej., en una semana*)
**carload lot** *s* (rail.) carro completo o entero
**Carlovingian** [,kɑrlo'vɪndʒɪən] *adj & s* carlovingio
**carmagnole** [,kɑrmə'njol] *s* carmañola (*chaqueta, canción y danza*)
**carman** ['kɑrmən] *s* (*pl:* **-men**) carretero; conductor (*de un tranvía*)
**Carmel, Mount** ['kɑrməl] *s* el monte Carmelo
**Carmelite** ['kɑrməlaɪt] *adj* carmelita, carmelitano; *s* carmelita
**carminative** [kɑr'mɪnətɪv] o ['kɑrmɪ,netɪv] *adj & s* (med.) carminativo
**carmine** ['kɑrmɪn] o ['kɑrmaɪn] *adj* carmíneo; *s* carmín (*materia colorante y color*); *va* carminar
**carminite** ['kɑrmɪnaɪt] *s* (mineral.) carminita
**carnage** ['kɑrnɪdʒ] *s* carnicería, mortandad
**carnal** ['kɑrnəl] *adj* carnal
**carnality** [kɑr'nælɪtɪ] *s* (*pl:* **-ties**) carnalidad
**carnallite** ['kɑrnəlaɪt] *s* (mineral.) carnalita
**carnation** [kɑr'neʃən] *s* (bot.) clavel, clavel reventón; encarnado; *adj* encarnado
**carnelian** [kɑr'niljən] *s* (mineral.) cornalina, cornerina
**carnification** [,kɑrnɪfɪ'keʃən] *s* (path.) carnificación
**carnival** ['kɑrnɪvəl] *s* carnaval; feria, espectáculo de atracciones; *adj* carnavalesco
**carnivore** ['kɑrnɪvor] *s* (zool. & bot.) carnívoro
**carnivorous** [kɑr'nɪvərəs] *adj* carnívoro, carnicero
**carnosine** ['kɑrnosin] *s* (chem.) carnosina
**Carnot cycle** [kɑr'no] *s* (phys.) ciclo de Carnot
**carnotite** ['kɑrnətaɪt] *s* (mineral.) carnotita
**carob** ['kærəb] *s* (bot.) algarrobo
**carol** ['kærəl] *s* canción alegre; villancico; (*pret & pp:* **-oled** u **-olled;** *ger:* **-oling** u **-olling**) *va & vn* cantar con alegría; celebrar con villancicos
**Carolina poplar** [,kærə'laɪnə] *s* (bot.) chopo de la Carolina
**Caroline** ['kærəlaɪn] o ['kærəlɪn] *s* Carolina; *adj* carolino
**Caroline Islands** *spl* islas Carolinas
**Carolingian** [,kærə'lɪndʒɪən] *adj & s* carolingio
**carom** ['kærəm] *s* carambola; rebote; *vn* carambolear; rebotar
**carotene** ['kærətin] *s* (chem.) caroteno
**carotid** [kə'rɑtɪd] *adj* carotídeo; *s* (anat.) carótida, arteria carótida
**carotid gland** *s* (anat.) glándula carótida
**carotin** ['kærətɪn] *s* var. de **carotene**
**carousal** [kə'raʊzəl] *s* jarana, gresca, borrachera
**carouse** [kə'raʊz] *s* jarana, gresca, borrachera; *vn* jaranear, emborracharse
**carousel** [,kærə'zɛl] *s* var. de **carrousel**
**carp** [kɑrp] *s* (ichth.) carpa; *vn* regañar, quejarse
**carpal** ['kɑrpəl] *adj* (anat.) carpiano; *s* (anat.) hueso del carpo
**car park** *s* (Brit.) var. de **parking lot**
**Carpathian Mountains** [kɑr'peθɪən] o **Carpathians** *spl* Cárpatos
**carpel** ['kɑrpəl] *s* (bot.) carpelo
**carpenter** ['kɑrpəntər] *s* carpintero; *vn* carpintear
**carpenter ant** *s* (ent.) hormiga carpintera
**carpenter bee** *s* (ent.) abeja carpintera
**carpentry** ['kɑrpəntrɪ] *s* carpintería
**carpet** ['kɑrpɪt] *s* alfombra; **to be on the carpet** estar sobre el tapete (*ser examinado, ser discutido*); (coll.) ser reprobado; *va* alfombrar, tapizar; (fig.) felpar (*p.ej., de hierba*)
**carpetbag** ['kɑrpɪt,bæg] *s* saco de viaje hecho de tejido de alfombra
**carpetbagger** ['kɑrpɪt,bægər] *s* aventurero, explotador; (scornful) politicastro del Norte de los EE.UU. que iba al Sur, después de la guerra entre Norte y Sur, a aprovecharse de la situación política
**carpetbeater** ['kɑrpɪt,bitər] *s* sacudidor de alfombras (*instrumento*)
**carpet beetle** *s* (ent.) polilla de los tapices
**carpet dealer** *s* alfombrista
**carpeting** ['kɑrpɪtɪŋ] *s* alfombrado; tela para alfombras
**carpet knight** *s* soldado de gabinete
**carpet maker** *s* alfombrero
**carpet moth** *s* (ent.) polilla de los paños
**carpet slipper** *s* zapatilla de fieltro
**carpet sweeper** *s* barredera de alfombras
**carping** ['kɑrpɪŋ] *adj* criticón, reparón
**carpology** [kɑr'pɑlədʒɪ] *s* carpología
**carport** ['kɑr,port] *s* alpende para automóvil
**carpus** ['kɑrpəs] *s* (*pl:* **-pi** [paɪ]) (anat.) carpo; (anat.) muñeca
**carrack** ['kærək] *s* (naut.) carraca (*galeón*)
**car radio** *s* radio para auto
**carrageen** ['kærə,gin] *s* (bot.) carragaen, musgo de Irlanda
**carrel** o **carrell** ['kærəl] *s* gabinete de estudio (*anejo a los depósitos de libros de una biblioteca*)
**car-rental service** ['kɑr'rɛntəl] *s* alquiler de coches
**carriage** ['kærɪdʒ] *s* carruaje; (arti.) cureña; (mach.) carro (*p.ej., de la máquina de escribir*); porte, continente; porte, transporte
**carriage-free** ['kærɪdʒ'fri] *adj* franco de porte
**carriage horse** *s* caballo de coche
**carriage trade** *s* clientela de personas ricas
**Carrie** ['kærɪ] *s* nombre abreviado de **Caroline**
**carrier** ['kærɪər] *s* porteador, portador; (path.) portador de gérmenes; empresa de transportes; cartero; (nav.) portaaviones; (rad.) onda portadora
**carrier-based plane** ['kærɪər,best] *s* avión con base en portaaviones
**carrier pigeon** *s* paloma de raza carrier; paloma mensajera
**carrier wave** *s* (rad.) onda portadora, onda portante
**carriole** ['kærɪol] *s* var. de **cariole**
**carrion** ['kærɪən] *s* carroña; podredumbre; inmundicia; *adj* carroño; que se alimenta de carroña; inmundo
**carrion crow** *s* (orn.) corneja; (orn.) zopilote (*Catharista atrata*)
**carronade** [,kærə'ned] *s* carronada
**carrot** ['kærət] *s* (bot.) zanahoria
**carroty** ['kærətɪ] *adj* amarillo rojizo; pelirrojo
**carrousel** [,kærə'zɛl] *s* caballitos, tiovivo
**carry** ['kærɪ] *s* (*pl:* **-ries**) alcance (*de un arma*); transporte en los hombros; trecho no navegable (*de un río*) ‖ (*pret & pp:* **-ried**) *va* llevar, traer, portar; acarrear, transportar; sostener (*una carga*); contener, comprender, incluir; ganar, lograr (*p.ej., elecciones, un premio*); ganar las elecciones en; hacer aceptar (*una proposición*); extender, llevar más lejos; influir en; llevar consigo; tener en existencia (*mercancías*); (arith.) llevar; **to carry about** llevar de un lado para otro; **to carry along** llevar consigo; **to carry away** llevarse; encantar, entusiasmar; llevar con violencia; **to carry back** devolver, restituir; **to carry**

**down** bajar; **to carry forward** llevar adelante; (com.) llevar o pasar (*en las cuentas*); **to carry into effect** llevar a cabo, poner en ejecución; **to carry off** llevarse; **to carry on** conducir, dirigir; promover; continuar; **to carry oneself** comportarse; **to carry one's point** salirse con la suya; **to carry out** realizar, llevar a cabo; **to carry over** aplazar; guardar para más tarde; pasar a otra página, cuenta, etc.; **to carry the day** quedar victorioso, ganar la palma; **to carry through** realizar, llevar a cabo; ayudar o sostener hasta el fin; **to carry up** subir; **to carry weight** ser de peso, ser de influencia; **carried forward** suma y sigue ‖ *vn* alcanzar; **to carry on** continuar; (coll.) travesear (*portarse de manera ridícula*); **to carry over** sobrar

**carryall** [ˈkærɪ,ɔl] *s* coche ligero y cubierto, de un solo caballo

**carrying charges** *spl* gastos de mantenimiento; gastos adicionales en la compra a plazos (*p.ej., intereses, seguros*)

**carry-over** [ˈkærɪ,ovər] *s* sobrante, exceso; (com.) suma anterior, suma que pasa de una página o cuenta a otra

**car-sick** [ˈkɑr,sɪk] *adj* mareado (*en un automóvil o tren*)

**cart** [kɑrt] *s* carreta; **to put the cart before the horse** empezar la casa por el tejado; *va* carretear, acarrear

**cartage** [ˈkɑrtɪdʒ] *s* carretaje, acarreo

**carte** [kɑrt] *s* lista de comidas; **à la carte** según lista, a la carta

**carte blanche** [ˈkɑrt ˈblɑnʃ] *s* carta blanca

**cartel** [kɑrˈtɛl] o [ˈkɑrtəl] *s* cartel (*escrito de desafío*); (econ., dipl. & pol.) cartel

**carter** [ˈkɑrtər] *s* carretero

**Cartesian** [kɑrˈtiʒən] *adj & s* cartesiano

**Cartesian coördinates** *spl* (math.) coordenadas cartesianas

**Cartesian devil, diver** o **imp** *s* (phys.) diablillo de Descartes

**Cartesianism** [kɑrˈtiʒənɪzəm] *s* cartesianismo

**Carthage** [ˈkɑrθɪdʒ] *s* Cartago

**Carthaginian** [,kɑrθəˈdʒɪnɪən] *adj & s* cartaginés

**cart horse** *s* caballo de tiro

**Carthusian** [kɑrˈθuʒən] *adj & s* cartujo

**cartilage** [ˈkɑrtɪlɪdʒ] *s* (anat.) cartílago

**cartilaginous** [,kɑrtɪˈlædʒɪnəs] *adj* cartilaginoso; (ichth.) cartilaginoso, cartilagíneo

**cartload** [ˈkɑrt,lod] *s* carretada

**cartographer** [kɑrˈtɑgrəfər] *s* cartógrafo

**cartographic** [,kɑrtoˈgræfɪk] *adj* cartográfico

**cartography** [kɑrˈtɑgrəfɪ] *s* cartografía

**carton** [ˈkɑrtən] *s* cartón, caja de cartón

**cartoon** [kɑrˈtun] *s* caricatura; tira cómica; cartón (*modelo de frescos, tapices, etc.*); (mov.) dibujo animado; *va* caricaturizar

**cartoonist** [kɑrˈtunɪst] *s* caricaturista

**cartouche** [kɑrˈtuʃ] *s* (arch.) cartucho, cartela

**cartridge** [ˈkɑrtrɪdʒ] *s* cartucho; cabeza (*del fonocaptor*); (phot.) rollo de películas

**cartridge belt** *s* canana, cartuchera

**cartridge box** *s* cartuchera

**cartridge case** *s* casco de cartucho

**cartridge clip** *s* peine de balas

**cartridge fuse** *s* (elec.) fusible de cartucho

**cart wheel** *s* rueda de carro; salto mortal de lado; (slang) dólar

**caruncle** [ˈkærʌŋkəl] o [kəˈrʌŋkəl] *s* (anat., bot. & zool.) carúncula

**caruncular** [kəˈrʌŋkjələr] *adj* caruncular

**carunculate** [kəˈrʌŋkjəlet] *adj* carunculado

**carve** [kɑrv] *va* trinchar (*carne*); esculpir, tallar; cincelar, grabar; **to carve out** crearse, labrarse (*p.ej., un porvenir, una fortuna*)

**carvel** [ˈkɑrvəl] *s* var. de **caravel**

**carvel-built** [ˈkɑrvəl,bɪlt] *adj* (naut.) con juntas a tope, construído a tope

**carvel joint** *s* (naut.) junta a tope

**carver** [ˈkɑrvər] *s* trinchador; trinchante (*cuchillo*); tallista (*de madera*); escultor; grabador

**carving** [ˈkɑrvɪŋ] *s* acción de trinchar; arte de trinchar; escultura; talladura; tallado, obra de talla

**carving knife** *s* trinchante

**car washer** *s* lavacoches

**caryatid** [,kærɪˈætɪd] *s* (*pl:* **-ids** o **-ides** [ɪdiz]) (arch.) cariátide

**caryophyllaceous** [,kærɪofɪˈleʃəs] *adj* (bot.) cariofiláceo

**caryopsis** [,kærɪˈɑpsɪs] *s* (*pl:* **-ses** [siz] o **-sides** [sɪdiz]) (bot.) cariópside

**casaba** [kəˈsɑbə] *s* melón de Indias

**Casbah** [ˈkɑzbɑ] *s* casba (*alcazaba y barrio musulmano de Argel y otras ciudades norteafricanas*)

**cascade** [kæsˈked] *s* cascada

**cascade amplification** *s* (elec.) amplificación en cascada

**cascade connection** *s* (elec.) conexión en cascada

**cascade control** *s* (elec.) control a cascada

**cascara** [kæsˈkɛrə] *s* (bot. & pharm.) cáscara sagrada

**cascara sagrada** [səˈgredə] *s* (pharm.) cáscara sagrada

**case** [kes] *s* caso; (gram. & med.) caso; (law) causa, pleito; argumento convincente; estuche; caja; funda, vaina; bastidor, marco (*p.ej., de una ventana*); (print.) caja; (slang) persona extravagante, persona divertida; **in case** caso que, en caso que; **in case of** en caso de; **in any case** en todo caso, de todos modos; **in no case** de ninguna manera; **in such a case** en tal caso; *adj* (gram.) casual; *va* encajonar; enfundar

**casease** [ˈkesɪes] *s* (biochem.) caseasa

**caseation** [,kesɪˈeʃən] *s* (path.) caseificación

**casebook** [ˈkes,bʊk] *s* libro de texto conteniendo casos selectos clasificados

**case ending** *s* (gram.) desinencia casual

**caseharden** [ˈkes,hɑrdən] *va* endurecer la superficie de (*p.ej., la madera*); (metal.) cementar; (fig.) volver insensible

**caseic** [ˈkesɪɪk] o [kəˈsiɪk] *adj* caseico

**casein** [ˈkesɪɪn] *s* (biochem.) caseína

**caseinogen** [,kesɪˈɪnədʒɛn] *s* (biochem.) caseinógeno

**case knife** *s* cuchillo provisto de una vaina; cuchillo de mesa

**casemate** [ˈkesmet] *s* (fort. & naut.) casamata

**casemated** [ˈkesmetɪd] *adj* acasamatado

**casement** [ˈkesmənt] *s* ventana a bisagra, ventana batiente; bastidor, marco (*de una ventana*); caja, funda; (poet.) ventana

**caseous** [ˈkesɪəs] *adj* caseoso

**caserns** o **casernes** [kəˈzʌrnz] *spl* (mil.) cuartel

**case work** *s* trabajo con casos

**cash** [kæʃ] *s* dinero contante; pago al contado; **for cash** al contado; por pago al contado; **to convert into cash** convertir en dinero efectivo; **to pay cash** pagar al contado; **cash on delivery** contra reembolso; *va* pagar al contado por; cobrar, hacer efectivo (*un cheque*); *vn* cobrar; **to cash in** (coll.) morir; **to cash in on** (coll.) sacar provecho de; (coll.) emplear útilmente

**cash and carry** *s* pago al contado con transporte por parte del comprador

**cashbook** [ˈkæʃ,bʊk] *s* libro de caja

**cashbox** [ˈkæʃ,bɑks] *s* caja

**cashew** [ˈkæʃu] o [kəˈʃu] *s* (bot.) anacardo (*planta y nuez*)

**cashew bird** *s* (orn.) paují

**cashew nut** *s* anacardo, nuez de acajú

**cashier** [kæˈʃɪr] *s* cajero; *va* destituir; degradar

**cashier's check** *s* cheque de caja

**cashier's desk** *s* caja

**cashmere** [ˈkæʃmɪr] *s* casimir o cachemir; lana muy fina de cabras; chal de lana fina de cabras; (*cap.*) *s* Cachemira

**cash on delivery** *s* entrega contra pago, pago contra reembolso

**cash on hand** *s* efectivo en caja

**cash payment** *s* pago al contado

**cash prize** *s* premio en metálico

**cash register** *s* caja registradora

**casing** [ˈkesɪŋ] *s* cubierta, caja, envoltura; tubería de revestimiento; cerco o marco (*de puerta o ventana*); (aut.) cubierta (*de neumático*); (sew.) jareta

**casino** [kəˈsino] *s* (*pl:* **-nos**) casino

**cask** [kæsk] o [kɑsk] *s* tonel, casco, pipa

**casket** [ˈkæskɪt] o [ˈkɑskɪt] *s* cajita, cofrecito; caja, ataúd

**Caspian** [ˈkæspɪən] *adj & s* caspio

**Caspian Sea** *s* mar Caspio
**casque** [kæsk] *s* capacete, casco, casquete
**cassaba** [kəˈsɑbə] *s* var. de **casaba**
**Cassandra** [kəˈsændrə] *s* (myth. & fig.) Casandra
**cassation** [kæˈseʃən] *s* (law) casación
**cassava** [kəˈsɑvə] *s* (bot.) mandioca (*planta y harina fina de su raíz*)
**casserole** [ˈkæsərol] *s* cacerola; timbal (*pastel relleno*); (chem.) cacerola
**cassia** [ˈkæʃə] o [ˈkæsɪə] *s* (bot.) casia; (pharm.) canela de la China
**cassimere** [ˈkæsɪmɪr] *s* casimir o cachemir
**cassino** [kəˈsino] *s* (*pl:* **-nos**) casino (*juego de naipes*)
**Cassiopeia** [ˌkæsɪoˈpiə] *s* (myth. & astr.) Casiopea
**cassis** [kɑˈsis] *s* (bot.) casis (*planta y licor*)
**cassiterite** [kəˈsɪtəraɪt] *s* (chem.) casiterita
**Cassius** [ˈkæʃəs] *s* Casio
**cassock** [ˈkæsək] *s* sotana, balandrán; **to doff the cassock** colgar los hábitos
**cassowary** [ˈkæsəˌwɛrɪ] *s* (*pl:* **-ies**) (orn.) casuario
**cast** [kæst] o [kɑst] *s* echada; forma, molde; pieza fundida; (theat.) reparto; aire, apariencia, semblante; clase; tinte, matiz; mirada bizca; (*pret & pp:* **cast**) *va* echar, lanzar; echar fuera, desechar; echar, volver (*los ojos*); proyectar (*una sombra*); fundir, vaciar; adicionar, calcular; (theat.) repartir (*los papeles*); echar (*balotas*); **to cast about** arrojar por todos lados; **to cast aside** desechar; **to cast away** desechar, abandonar; **to cast down** derribar; desanimar; **to cast forth** despedir, exhalar; **to cast loose** soltar; **to cast off** abandonar, echar de sí; (sew.) hacer (*la última hilera de puntadas*); **to cast on** echarse (*un vestido*) rápidamente; (sew.) empezar con (*la primera hilera de puntadas*); **to cast out** arrojar, echar fuera; despedir, desterrar; *vn* echar dados; arrojar el sedal de pescar; adicionar; **to cast about** buscar, hacer planes, revolver proyectos; **to cast off** (naut.) desamarrar
**Castalides** [kæsˈtælɪdiz] *spl* (myth.) Castálidas
**castanet** [ˌkæstəˈnɛt] *s* castañuela o castañeta
**castaway** [ˈkæstəˌwe] o [ˈkɑstəˌwe] *adj & s* náufrago; proscrito, réprobo
**caste** [kæst] o [kɑst] *s* casta; régimen de castas; **to lose caste** perder el prestigio
**castellan** [ˈkæstələn] *s* castellán o castellano
**castellated** [ˈkæstəˌletɪd] *adj* encastillado
**caster** [ˈkæstər] o [ˈkɑstər] *s* echador; fundidor, vaciador; ruedecilla de mueble; frasco para aceite, vinagre, sal, etc.; angarillas, vinagreras
**castigate** [ˈkæstɪget] *va* castigar
**castigation** [ˌkæstɪˈgeʃən] *s* castigo
**castigator** [ˈkæstɪˌgetər] *s* castigador
**Castile** [kæsˈtil] *s* Castilla
**Castile soap** *s* jabón de Castilla
**Castilian** [kæsˈtɪljən] *adj & s* castellano
**casting** [ˈkæstɪŋ] o [ˈkɑstɪŋ] *s* fundición, vaciado; pieza fundida; pesca de lanzamiento; (falc.) curalle; (theat.) reparto (*de los papeles*)
**casting line** *s* tanza, sedal
**casting net** *s* esparavel
**casting vote** *s* voto de calidad, voto decisivo (*en caso de empate*)
**cast iron** *s* hierro colado, hierro fundido
**cast-iron** [ˈkæstˈaɪərn] o [ˈkɑstˈaɪərn] *adj* hecho de hierro fundido; fuerte, endurecido; duro, inflexible
**cast-iron stomach** *s* (coll.) estómago de avestruz
**castle** [ˈkæsəl] o [ˈkɑsəl] *s* castillo; palacio (*edificio suntuoso*); (chess) roque, torre; *va & vn* (chess) enrocar
**castle in Spain** o **castle in the air** *s* castillo en el aire
**castling** [ˈkæslɪŋ] o [kɑslɪŋ] *s* (chess) enroque
**castoff** [ˈkæstˌɔf] o [ˈkɑstˌɔf] *adj* abandonado, desechado; *s* persona o cosa abandonada o desechada, plato de segunda mesa; (print.) cálculo de espacio
**castor** [ˈkæstər] o [ˈkɑstər] *s* ruedecilla de mueble; frasco para aceite, vinagre, sal, etc.; angarillas, vinagreras; sombrero de castor; castóreo (*substancia aceitosa*); (*cap.*) *s* (myth., astr. & naut.) Cástor
**Castor and Pollux** *spl* (myth., astr. & naut.) Cástor y Pólux
**castor bean** *s* (pharm.) semilla de ricino; (bot.) ricino
**castor oil** *s* aceite de ricino
**castor-oil plant** [ˈkæstərˈɔɪl] o [ˈkɑstərˈɔɪl] *s* (bot.) ricino
**castrametation** [ˌkæstrəməˈteʃən] *s* (mil.) castrametación
**castrate** [ˈkæstret] *va* castrar, capar; expurgar (*un libro*)
**castration** [kæsˈtreʃən] *s* castración, capadura; expurgación (*de un libro*)
**cast steel** *s* acero colado, acero fundido
**cast stone** *s* sillar de concreto, piedra artificial
**casual** [ˈkæʒuəl] *adj* casual; impensado, descuidado, indiferente; *s* obrero casual; persona que recibe caridad de vez en cuando; (mil.) soldado en espera de asignación
**casualty** [ˈkæʒuəltɪ] *s* (*pl:* **-ties**) accidente, desgracia; víctima; muerte; baja (*en la guerra*)
**casualty list** *s* (mil.) lista de bajas
**casuist** [ˈkæʒuɪst] *s* casuísta; sofista
**casuistic** [ˌkæʒuˈɪstɪk] o **casuistical** [ˌkæʒuˈɪstɪkəl] *adj* casuístico; sofístico
**casuistry** [ˈkæʒuɪstrɪ] *s* (*pl:* **-ries**) casuística; razonamiento hábil y falso
**casus belli** [ˈkesəs ˈbɛlaɪ] *s* casus belli, motivo de guerra
**cat.** abr. de **catalogue** y **catechism**
**cat** [kæt] *s* gato; mujer rencorosa; (ichth.) siluro, bagre, amicuro; (naut.) aparejo de gato; gato de nueve colas, azote con nueve ramales; **to bell the cat** ponerle cascabel al gato; **to let the cat out of the bag** revelar el secreto; (*pret & pp:* **catted;** *ger:* **catting**) *va* (naut.) levantar y trincar (*el ancla*)
**catabolism** [kəˈtæbəlɪzəm] *s* (biol.) catabolismo
**catachresis** [ˌkætəˈkrisɪs] *s* (*pl:* **-ses** [siz]) (rhet.) catacresis
**cataclysm** [ˈkætəklɪzəm] *s* cataclismo
**cataclysmal** [ˌkætəˈklɪzməl] o **catclysmic** [ˌkætəˈklɪzmɪk] *adj* cataclísmico
**catacomb** [ˈkætəkom] *s* catacumba
**catadioptric** [ˌkætədaɪˈɑptrɪk] *adj* (phys.) catadióptrico
**catafalque** [ˈkætəfælk] *s* catafalco
**Catalan** [ˈkætəlæn] *adj & s* catalán
**Catalan forge** o **furnace** *s* forja a la catalana
**catalase** [ˈkætəles] *s* (chem.) catalasa
**catalectic** [ˌkætəˈlɛktɪk] *adj* cataléctico
**catalepsis** [ˌkætəˈlɛpsɪs] o **catalepsy** [ˈkætəˌlɛpsɪ] *s* (path.) catalepsia
**cataleptic** [ˌkætəˈlɛptɪk] *adj & s* cataléptico
**catalog** o **catalogue** [ˈkætəlɔg] o [ˈkætəlɑg] *s* catálogo; anuario (*p.ej., de la universidad*); *va* catalogar
**catalogue card** *s* ficha catalográfica (*de una biblioteca*)
**Catalonia** [ˌkætəˈlonɪə] *s* Cataluña
**Catalonian** [ˌkætəˈlonɪən] *adj* catalán
**catalpa** [kəˈtælpə] *s* (bot.) catalpa
**catalysis** [kəˈtælɪsɪs] *s* (*pl:* **-ses** [siz]) (chem.) catálisis
**catalyst** [ˈkætəlɪst] *s* (chem.) catalizador
**catalytic** [ˌkætəˈlɪtɪk] *adj* catalítico
**catalyzer** [ˈkætəˌlaɪzər] *s* (chem.) catalizador
**catamaran** [ˌkætəməˈræn] *s* (naut.) catamarán; armadía, balsa; (coll.) persona pendenciera, mujer pendenciera
**catamount** [ˈkætəmaunt] *s* (zool.) puma; (zool.) lince, gato montés
**cataphoresis** [ˌkætəfəˈrisɪs] *s* (med. & chem.) cataforesis
**catapult** [ˈkætəpʌlt] *s* catapulta; honda; (aer.) catapulta; *va* catapultar
**cataract** [ˈkætərækt] *s* catarata; aguacero, inundación; (path.) catarata
**catarrh** [kəˈtɑr] *s* (path.) catarro
**catarrhal** [kəˈtɑrəl] *adj* catarral
**catastrophe** [kəˈtæstrəfɪ] *s* catástrofe; (theat. & geol.) catástrofe
**catastrophic** [ˌkætəˈstrɑfɪk] *adj* catastrófico
**catbird** [ˈkætˌbʌrd] *s* (orn.) pájaro gato
**catboat** [ˈkætˌbot] *s* (naut.) laúd
**catcall** [ˈkætˌkɔl] *s* rechifla; *va & vn* rechiflar
**catch** [kætʃ] *s* cogida (*de la pelota*); pestillo, cerradera; broche; presa, botín; pesca (*lo que se ha pescado*); trampa; buen partido; rondó; **catch in the voice** voz entrecortada ‖ *adj*

atractivo, llamativo; engañoso, tramposo ‖ (*pret & pp:* **caught**) *va* asir, coger, atrapar; sorprender; comprender; (sport) coger, parar; tomar (*frío*), coger (*un resfriado*); **to catch alive** cazar vivo; **to catch fire** encenderse, inflamarse; **to catch hold of** prenderse en; apoderarse de; **to catch it** (coll.) merecerse castigo, merecerse un regaño; **to catch oneself** contenerse; recobrar el equilibrio; **to catch out** (baseball) sacar fuera a (*un jugador*) cogiendo la pelota antes de que caiga ésta al suelo; **to catch up** asir, coger súbitamente; coger al vuelo; coger la palabra a; cazar (*sorprender en error o un descuido*) ‖ *vn* pegarse, transmitirse fácilmente (*una enfermedad*); enredarse, engancharse; encenderse; **to catch at** tratar de asir o coger; asir fuertemente o con anhelo; **to catch on** prender en (*p.ej., un gancho*); comprender; coger el tino; **to catch on to** ponerse al tanto de; **to catch up** emparejar, salir del atraso; ponerse al día (*en las deudas*); **to catch up with** emparejar con

**catchall** [ˈkætʃ,ɔl] *s* armario, cesto o cajón destinado a contener toda clase de objetos; vaso de seguridad

**catch basin** *s* cisterna de desagüe

**catch crop** *s* (agr.) siembra intermedia entre otras dos siembras o entre las hileras de una siembra

**catch drain** *s* cuneta

**catcher** [ˈkætʃər] *s* agarrador, cogedor; (baseball) receptor, parador, catcher

**catchfly** [ˈkætʃ,flaɪ] *s* (*pl:* **-flies**) (bot.) pegamoscas

**catching** [ˈkætʃɪŋ] *adj* contagioso; atrayente, fascinador

**catchment** [ˈkætʃmənt] *s* captación; depósito de abastecimiento

**catchment area** o **basin** *s* cuenca de captación

**catchpenny** [ˈkætʃ,pɛnɪ] *adj* barato, de pacotilla; *s* (*pl:* **-nies**) engañifa, baratija

**catchpole** o **catchpoll** [ˈkætʃ,pol] *s* alguacil, corchete

**catch question** *s* pega

**catch stitch** *s* (b.b.) punto alto y bajo; (sew.) punto espigado

**catch title** *s* título corto y expresivo

**catchup** [ˈkætʃəp] o [ˈkɛtʃəp] *s* var. de **catsup**

**catchword** [ˈkætʃ,wʌrd] *s* reclamo, lema, palabra de efecto; (print.) reclamo; (theat.) pie

**catchy** [ˈkætʃɪ] *adj* (*comp:* **-ier;** *super:* **-iest**) pegajoso, insidioso; animado, vivo

**cate** [ket] *s* (archaic) golosina

**catechetical** [,kætɪˈkɛtɪkəl] *adj* catequístico

**catechise** o **catechize** [ˈkætɪkaɪz] *va* catequizar; interrogar minuciosamente

**catechism** [ˈkætɪkɪzəm] *s* catecismo; serie de preguntas

**catechist** [ˈkætɪkɪst] *s* catequista

**catechizer** [ˈkætɪ,kaɪzər] *s* catequizador

**catechu** [ˈkætətʃu] *s* catecú

**catechumen** [,kætɪˈkjumən] *s* (eccl. & fig.) catecúmeno

**catechumenate** [,kætɪˈkjumənet] *s* catecumenado

**categorical** [,kætɪˈgɑrɪkəl] o [,kætɪˈgɔrɪkəl] *adj* categórico

**categorical imperative** *s* (philos.) imperativo categórico

**category** [ˈkætɪ,gorɪ] *s* (*pl:* **-ries**) categoría

**catenary** [ˈkætɪ,nɛrɪ] *adj* catenario; *s* (*pl:* **-ies**) (math.) catenaria

**catenate** [ˈkætɪnet] *va* encadenar, enlazar

**catenulate** [kəˈtɛnjəlet] *adj* catenular

**cater** [ˈketər] *va & vn* abastecer, proveer; **to cater for** abastecer, proveer; **to cater to** proveer a (*p.ej., el gusto popular*)

**cater-cornered** [ˈkætər,kɔrnərd] *adj* diagonal; *adv* diagonalmente

**caterer** [ˈketərər] *s* proveedor de alimentos y bebidas a domicilio, especialmente para fiestas y reuniones

**cateress** [ˈketərɪs] *s* abastecedora, proveedora

**caterpillar** [ˈkætər,pɪlər] *s* (ent.) oruga; (mach.) oruga (*mecanismo de arrastre*); (trademark) tractor de oruga

**caterpillar chain** *s* cadena de oruga

**caterpillar tractor** *s* (trademark) tractor de oruga

**caterpillar tread** *s* rodado tipo oruga

**caterwaul** [ˈkætərwɔl] *s* marramao; chillido; *vn* marramizar (*el gato*); chillar

**catfish** [ˈkæt,fɪʃ] *s* (ichth.) siluro, bagre, amiuro

**catgut** [ˈkæt,gʌt] *s* (mus.) cuerda de tripa; (surg.) catgut

**Cath.** abr. de **Catholic**

**catharsis** [kəˈθɑrsɪs] *s* (aesthetics, med. & psychoanal.) catarsis

**cathartic** [kəˈθɑrtɪk] *adj* catártico, purgante; *s* purgante

**Cathay** [kæˈθe] *s* Catay

**cathead** [ˈkæt,hɛd] *s* (naut.) serviola

**cathedra** [kəˈθidrə] o [ˈkæθɪdrə] *s* cátedra

**cathedral** [kəˈθidrəl] *s* catedral; *adj* catedral, catedralicio; episcopal

**Catherine** [ˈkæθərɪn] *s* Catalina

**catheter** [ˈkæθɪtər] *s* (surg.) catéter

**catheterization** [,kæθɪtərɪˈzeʃən] *s* (surg.) cateterismo o cateterización

**catheterize** [ˈkæθɪtəraɪz] *va* (surg.) cateterizar

**cathetometer** [,kæθɪˈtɑmɪtər] *s* (phys.) catetómetro

**cathode** [ˈkæθod] *s* (elec.) cátodo

**cathode-ray** [ˈkæθodˈre] *adj* (phys.) de rayos catódicos

**cathode rays** *spl* (phys.) rayos catódicos

**cathode-ray tube** *s* (phys.) tubo o válvula de rayos catódicos

**cathodic** [kəˈθɑdɪk] *adj* catódico

**catholic** [ˈkæθəlɪk] *adj* católico (*universal*); liberal, de amplias miras; (*cap.*) *adj & s* católico

**catholicism** [kəˈθɑlɪsɪzəm] *s* catolicidad (*universalidad*); (*cap.*) *s* catolicismo

**catholicity** [,kæθəˈlɪsɪtɪ] *s* catolicidad (*universalidad*); (*cap.*) *s* catolicidad

**catholicize** [kəˈθɑlɪsaɪz] *va* catolizar; *vn* catolizarse

**cation** [ˈkæt,aɪən] *s* (elec.) catión

**catkin** [ˈkætkɪn] *s* (bot.) amento (*inflorescencia*)

**catmint** [ˈkæt,mɪnt] *s* (bot.) hierba gatera

**cat nap** *s* siesta corta

**catnip** [ˈkætnɪp] *s* (bot.) hierba gatera

**Cato** [ˈketo] *s* Catón

**Catonian** [keˈtonɪən] *adj* catoniano

**cat-o'-nine-tails** [,kætəˈnaɪn,telz] *s* gato de nueve colas, azote con nueve ramales

**catoptric** [kəˈtɑptrɪk] *adj* catóptrico; **catoptrics** *ssg* (opt.) catóptrica

**cat-rigged** [ˈkæt,rɪgd] *adj* (naut.) aparejado como un laúd

**cat's cradle** *s* cunas, juego de la cuna

**cat's-eye** [ˈkæts,aɪ] *s* (mineral.) ojo de gato

**cat's-paw** o **catspaw** [ˈkæts,pɔ] *s* instrumento, hombre de paja, mano de gato; (naut.) soplo ligero

**cat's-tail** [ˈkæts,tel] *s* (bot.) cola de rata (*Equisetum arvense*); (bot.) viborera; (bot.) espadaña; (bot.) fleo; (meteor.) cola de gato (*cirro*)

**catsup** [ˈkætsəp] o [ˈkɛtʃəp] *s* salsa de tomate con cebollas, sal, azúcar y especias

**cat tackle** *s* (naut.) aparejo de gata

**cattail** [ˈkæt,tel] *s* (bot.) espadaña, anea (*Typha latifolia*); (bot.) anea (*Typha angustifolia*); (bot.) amento (*inflorescencia*)

**cat thyme** *s* (bot.) hierba del papa

**cattiness** [ˈkætɪnɪs] *s* gatada; chismería

**cattish** [ˈkætɪʃ] *adj* gatuno; engañoso, trampista; rencoroso, malicioso; chismoso

**cattle** [ˈkætəl] *s* ganado, ganado vacuno; gente despreciable

**cattle car** *s* vagón cuadra, vagón jaula

**cattle crossing** *s* paso de ganado

**cattleman** [ˈkætəlmən] *s* (*pl:* **-men**) ganadero

**cattle pump** *s* bomba automática para el ganado

**cattle raising** *s* ganadería

**cattle ranch** *s* hacienda de ganado

**cattle show** *s* exposición de ganado

**cattle thief** *s* ladrón de ganado

**cattle tick** *s* (ent.) garrapata

**catty** [ˈkætɪ] *adj* (*comp:* **-tier;** *super:* **-tiest**) gatesco; arisco; rencoroso, malicioso; chismoso

**Catullus** [kəˈtʌləs] *s* Catulo

**catwalk** [ˈkæt,wɔk] *s* pasadizo, pasarela

**cat whisker** *s* (rad.) bigote de gato

**Caucasian** [kɔˈkeʒən] o [kɔˈkeʃən] *adj & s*

caucásico (*blanco*); caucáseo o caucasiano (*del Cáucaso*)
**Caucasus** ['kɔkəsəs] *s* Cáucaso
**caucus** ['kɔkəs] *s* camarilla política; *vn* reunirse en camarilla política
**caudal** ['kɔdəl] *adj* (zool.) caudal
**caudate** ['kɔdet] *adj* caudato
**Caudine Forks** ['kɔdaɪn] *spl* Horcas Caudinas
**caudle** ['kɔdəl] *s* bebida caliente compuesta de azúcar, huevos, especias y vino o cerveza (*para los enfermos*)
**caught** [kɔt] *pret & pp de* **catch**
**caul** [kɔl] *s* redaño
**cauldron** ['kɔldrən] *s* var. de **caldron**
**caulescent** [kɔ'lɛsənt] *adj* (bot.) caulescente
**caulicle** ['kɔlɪkəl] *s* (bot.) caulícula
**cauliculus** [kɔ'lɪkjələs] *s* (*pl:* **-li** [laɪ]) (arch.) caulículo
**cauliflower** ['kɔlɪ,flaʊər] *s* (bot.) coliflor
**cauliflower excrescence** *s* (path.) coliflor
**caulk** [kɔk] *va* calafatear
**caulker** ['kɔkər] *s* calafate o calafateador
**causal** ['kɔzəl] *adj* causal
**causality** [kɔ'zælɪtɪ] *s* (*pl:* **-ties**) causalidad
**causation** [kɔ'zeʃən] *s* causa; causalidad (*relación de causa a efecto*)
**causative** ['kɔzətɪv] *adj* causativo (*que es causa de alguna cosa*)
**cause** [kɔz] *s* causa; causante; (law) causa; **to make common cause with** hacer causa común con; *va* causar
**causeless** ['kɔzlɪs] *adj* sin causa; infundado
**causerie** [,kozə'ri] *s* charla, plática; artículo corto
**causeway** ['kɔz,we] *s* calzada, arrecife; calzada elevada, terraplén
**caustic** ['kɔstɪk] *adj* (chem., math., opt. & fig.) cáustico; *s* (chem.) cáustico; (math. & opt.) cáustica
**caustically** ['kɔstɪkəlɪ] *adv* cáusticamente
**causticity** [kɔs'tɪsɪtɪ] *s* causticidad; (fig.) causticidad
**caustic potash** *s* (chem.) potasa cáustica
**caustic soda** *s* (chem.) sosa cáustica
**cauterization** [,kɔtərɪ'zeʃən] *s* cauterización
**cauterize** ['kɔtəraɪz] *va* cauterizar
**cautery** ['kɔtərɪ] *s* (*pl:* **-ies**) cauterio
**caution** ['kɔʃən] *s* cautela; advertencia, amonestación; (coll.) persona o cosa extraordinaria; *va* advertir, amonestar
**cautionary** ['kɔʃə,nɛrɪ] *adj* amonestador
**cautious** ['kɔʃəs] *adj* cauto, cauteloso
**Cav.** abr. de **Cavalry**
**cavalcade** [,kævəl'ked] o ['kævəlked] *s* cabalgata
**cavalier** [,kævə'lɪr] *s* caballero; galán (*que sirve de escolta a una dama*); *adj* altivo, desdeñoso; brusco, inceremonioso; desenvuelto, despreocupado
**cavalry** ['kævəlrɪ] *s* (*pl:* **-ries**) (mil.) caballería
**cavalry charge** *s* carga de caballería
**cavalryman** ['kævəlrɪmən] *s* (*pl:* **-men**) (mil.) soldado de caballería
**cavatina** [,kævə'tinə] *s* (mus.) cavatina
**cave** [kev] *s* cueva; *va* ahuecar, excavar; **to cave in** quebrar; *vn* **to cave in** derrumbarse; (coll.) ceder, rendirse
**caveat** ['kevɪæt] *s* advertencia; (law) información a un juez u otro funcionario para que suspenda algún procedimiento hasta más tarde
**cave dweller** *s* cavernícola
**cave-in** ['kev,ɪn] *s* (coll.) socavón, hundimiento, derrumbe
**cave man** *s* cavernícola, hombre de caverna; hombre grosero
**cavern** ['kævərn] *s* caverna
**cavernous** ['kævərnəs] *adj* cavernoso
**cavesson** ['kævəsən] *s* cabezón
**cavetto** [kə'vɛto] *s* (*pl:* **-ti** [tɪ] o **-tos**) (arch.) caveto, esgucio
**caviar** o **caviare** ['kævɪɑr] o ['kɑvɪɑr] *s* caviar; **caviar to the general** cosa demasiado buena para ser estimada por la gente ordinaria
**cavicorn** ['kævɪkɔrn] *adj* (zool.) cavicornio
**cavil** ['kævɪl] *s* cavilación; (*pret & pp:* **-iled** o **-illed**; *ger:* **-iling** o **-illing**) *va & vn* cavilar
**cavitation** [,kævɪ'teʃən] *s* (mach. & path.) cavitación
**cavity** ['kævɪtɪ] *s* (*pl:* **-ties**) cavidad
**cavort** [kə'vɔrt] *vn* (coll.) cabriolar
**cavy** ['kevɪ] *s* (*pl:* **-vies**) (zool.) cavia, conejillo de Indias
**caw** [kɔ] *s* graznido; *vn* graznar
**cay** [ke] o [ki] *s* cayo
**cayenne** [kaɪ'ɛn] o [ke'ɛn] *s* pimentón (*polvo*); (*cap.*) *s* Cayena
**cayenne pepper** *s* pimentón (*polvo*)
**cayman** ['kemən] *s* (*pl:* **-mans**) (zool.) caimán
**cayuse** [kaɪ'jus] *s* (U.S.A.) jaca india
**C battery** *s* (rad.) batería de rejilla
**cc.** o **c.c.** abr. de **cubic centimeter** o **cubic centimeters**
**cd.** abr. de **cord** o **cords**
**cd. ft.** abr. de **cord foot**
**cearin** ['siərɪn] *s* (pharm.) cearina
**cease** [sis] *s* cesación; **without cease** sin cesar; *va* parar, suspender; *vn* cesar; **to cease** + *ger* cesar de + *inf*
**cease fire** *s* cese de fuego, alto el fuego
**cease-fire** ['sis'faɪr] *vn* suspender hostilidades
**ceaseless** ['sislɪs] *adj* incesante, continuo
**Cecil** ['sisɪl] o ['sɛsɪl] *s* Cecilio
**Cecilia** [sɪ'sɪljə] *s* Cecilia
**Cecropia moth** [sɪ'kropɪə] *s* (ent.) mariposa del gusano de seda (*Samia cecropia*)
**cedar** ['sidər] *s* (bot.) cedro; *adj* cedrino
**cedarbird** ['sidər,bʌrd] o **cedar waxwing** *s* (orn.) filomeno, zonzo
**cedar chest** *s* cofre o arca de cedro
**cedar of Lebanon** *s* (bot.) cedro del Líbano
**cede** [sid] *va* ceder, traspasar
**cedilla** [sɪ'dɪlə] *s* cedilla
**cedrium** ['sidrɪəm] *s* cedria
**ceil** [sil] *va* forrar, revestir (*la pared o el techo interior*)
**ceiling** ['silɪŋ] *s* techo, cielo raso; (aer.) techo, cielo máximo
**ceiling price** *s* precio tope
**celadon green** ['sɛlədɑn] *s* verdeceledón
**celandine** ['sɛləndaɪn] *s* (bot.) celidonia, hierba de las golondrinas
**celebrant** ['sɛlɪbrənt] *s* celebrante (*sacerdote*)
**celebrate** ['sɛlɪbret] *va* celebrar; proclamar; festejar (*p.ej., un día de fiesta*); *vn* celebrar (*decir misa*); divertirse, festejarse, parrandear
**celebrated** ['sɛlɪ,bretɪd] *adj* célebre
**celebration** [,sɛlɪ'breʃən] *s* celebración; tertulia, diversión
**celebrator** ['sɛlɪ,bretər] *s* celebrante; contertulio; parrandista
**celebrity** [sɪ'lɛbrɪtɪ] *s* (*pl:* **-ties**) celebridad (*calidad y persona*)
**celeriac** [sɪ'lɛrɪæk] *s* (bot.) apio-nabo
**celerity** [sɪ'lɛrɪtɪ] *s* celeridad
**celery** ['sɛlərɪ] *s* (bot.) apio
**celesta** [sɪ'lɛstə] *s* (mus.) celesta; (mus.) celeste (*registro del órgano*)
**celestial** [sɪ'lɛstʃəl] *adj* celestial (*perteneciente al paraíso; perteneciente al firmamento*); celeste (*perteneciente al firmamento y a la astronomía*); (fig.) celestial (*perfecto, delicioso*); (*cap.*) *adj & s* celeste (*chino*)
**celestial body** *s* cuerpo celeste
**Celestial Empire** *s* celeste imperio, imperio celeste (*China*)
**celestial globe** *s* (astr.) globo celeste
**celestial mechanics** *s* (astr.) mecánica celeste
**celestial sphere** *s* (astr.) esfera celeste
**celibacy** ['sɛlɪbəsɪ] *s* (*pl:* **-cies**) celibato
**celibate** ['sɛlɪbɪt] o ['sɛlɪbet] *adj & s* célibe
**cell** [sɛl] *s* celda (*aposento en un convento, cárcel, etc.*); celdilla (*de los panales de las abejas*); (biol., elec. & pol.) célula; (elec.) elemento (*de una pila o acumulador*); (aer.) celda, globo (*de dirigible*); (aer.) célula (*de avión*); (bot.) celdilla (*lóculo*)
**cellar** ['sɛlər] *s* sótano, bodega
**cellarage** ['sɛlərɪdʒ] *s* sótanos, bodegas; almacenaje en una bodega
**cellarer** ['sɛlərər] *s* bodeguero
**cellaret** [,sɛlə'rɛt] *s* licorera
**celled** [sɛld] *adj* celulado
**cellist** o **'cellist** ['tʃɛlɪst] *s* violoncelista
**cello** o **'cello** ['tʃɛlo] *s* (*pl:* **-los**) (mus.) violoncelo
**celloidin** [sə'lɔɪdɪn] *s* (chem.) celoidina
**cellophane** ['sɛləfen] *s* (trademark) celofán
**cellular** ['sɛljələr] *adj* celular

**cellule** ['sɛljul] *s* celulilla; (aer.) célula (*de avión*)
**cellulitis** [ˌsɛljə'laɪtɪs] *s* (path.) celulitis
**celluloid** ['sɛljəlɔɪd] *s* (trademark) celuloide; (fig.) celuloide (*película cinematográfica*)
**cellulose** ['sɛljəlos] *s* (chem.) celulosa
**cellulous** ['sɛljələs] *adj* celuloso
**celom** ['siləm] *s* var. de **coelom**
**Celt** [sɛlt] o [kɛlt] *s* celta
**Celtiberia** [ˌsɛltɪ'bɪrɪə] *s* Celtiberia
**Celtiberian** [ˌsɛltɪ'bɪrɪən] *adj & s* celtibérico
**Celtic** ['sɛltɪk] o ['kɛltɪk] *adj* céltico; *s* celta (*idioma*)
**Celticism** ['sɛltɪsɪzəm] o ['kɛltɪsɪzəm] *s* celtismo
**Celticist** ['sɛltɪsɪst] o ['kɛltɪsɪst] *s* celtista
**cement** [sɪ'mɛnt] *s* cemento; (anat., dent. & geol.) cemento; *va* revestir de cemento; unir con cemento; (metal.) cementar; unir, pegar; consolidar (*p.ej., la amistad, la alianza*); *vn* unirse, pegarse
**cementation** [ˌsimən'teʃən] *s* (metal.) cementación
**cement block** *s* bloque de hormigón
**cement mill** *s* fábrica de cemento
**cement mixer** *s* var. de **concrete mixer**
**cemetery** ['sɛmɪˌtɛrɪ] *s* (*pl:* **-ies**) cementerio
**cen.** abr. de **central**
**Cenacle** ['sɛnəkəl] *s* Cenáculo (*sala de la última cena*)
**Cenis, Mont** [mõ sə'ni] el monte Cenís, Moncenisio
**cenobite** ['sinobaɪt] o ['sɛnobaɪt] *s* cenobita
**cenobitism** ['sinobaɪtɪzəm] o ['sɛnobaɪtɪzəm] *s* cenobitismo
**cenotaph** ['sɛnətæf] o ['sɛnətɑf] *s* cenotafio
**Cenozoic** [ˌsino'zo·ɪk] o [ˌsɛno'zo·ɪk] *adj* (geol.) cenozoico; *s* (geol.) era cenozoica, formaciones cenozoicas
**censer** ['sɛnsər] *s* incensario
**censor** ['sɛnsər] *s* censor; *va* censurar
**censorial** [sɛn'sorɪəl] *adj* censorio
**censorious** [sɛn'sorɪəs] *adj* censurista, criticón
**censorship** ['sɛnsərʃɪp] *s* censura
**censurable** ['sɛnʃərəbəl] *adj* censurable
**censure** ['sɛnʃər] *s* censura; *va* censurar
**census** ['sɛnsəs] *s* censo; **to take the census** levantar el censo; *adj* censal
**census taker** *s* enumerador censal
**census taking** *s* levantamiento del censo o de los censos
**cent.** abr. de **centigrade, central** y **century**
**cent** [sɛnt] *s* centavo
**centaur** ['sɛntɔr] *s* (myth.) centauro
**centaury** ['sɛntɔrɪ] *s* (*pl:* **-ries**) (bot.) centaura
**centenarian** [ˌsɛntɪ'nɛrɪən] *adj & s* centenario
**centenary** ['sɛntɪˌnɛrɪ] o [sɛn'tinərɪ] *adj* centenario; *s* (*pl:* **-ies**) centenario
**centennial** [sɛn'tɛnɪəl] *adj & s* centenario
**centennially** [sɛn'tɛnɪəlɪ] *adv* cada cien años
**center** ['sɛntər] *s* centro; *adj* centrista; *va* centrar; concentrar; (mil.) centrar (*fuego, ataque, etc.*); *vn* estar en el centro; concentrarse; concurrir
**centerboard** ['sɛntərˌbord] *s* (naut.) orza de deriva
**center drill** *s* broca de centrar
**center field** *s* (baseball) jardín central
**centering** ['sɛntərɪŋ] *s* centraje; (arch.) cimbra
**center of attraction** *s* (astr.) centro de atracción; (fig.) centro de interés
**center of gravity** *s* (mech.) centro de gravedad
**centerpiece** ['sɛntərˌpis] *s* centro de mesa
**center punch** *s* granete, punzón de marcar
**center service line** *s* (tennis) línea de mitad, línea de media red
**center tap** *s* (elec.) toma media, derivación central
**centesimal** [sɛn'tɛsɪməl] *adj* centesimal; *s* centésimo
**centiare** ['sɛntɪˌɛr] *s* centiárea
**centigrade** ['sɛntɪgred] *adj* centígrado
**centigrade thermometer** *s* termómetro centígrado
**centigram** o **centigramme** ['sɛntɪgræm] *s* centigramo
**centiliter** ['sɛntɪˌlitər] *s* centilitro
**centime** ['sɑntim] *s* céntimo
**centimeter** ['sɛntɪˌmitər] *s* centímetro
**centimeter-gram-second system** ['sɛntɪˌmitər'græm'sɛkənd] *s* (phys.) sistema cegesimal, sistema centímetro-gramo-segundo
**centipede** ['sɛntɪpid] *s* (zool.) ciempiés o cientopiés
**central** ['sɛntrəl] *adj* central; *s* (telp.) central; (telp.) telefonista
**Central America** *s* Centro América, la América Central
**Central American** *adj & s* centroamericano
**central heating** *s* (Brit.) calefacción central; (U.S.A.) calefacción central de un grupo de edificios
**centralism** ['sɛntrəlɪzəm] *s* centralismo
**centralist** ['sɛntrəlɪst] *adj & s* centralista
**centralization** [ˌsɛntrəlɪ'zeʃən] *s* centralización
**centralize** ['sɛntrəlaɪz] *va* centralizar; *vn* centralizarse
**centrally** ['sɛntrəlɪ] *adv* en el centro, hacia el centro
**central nervous system** *s* (anat. & physiol.) sistema nervioso central
**Central Powers** *spl* Potencias centrales
**Central time** *s* (U.S.A.) hora legal correspondiente al meridiano 90°
**centre** ['sɛntər] *s, adj, va, & vn* var. de **center**
**centric** ['sɛntrɪk] *adj* céntrico
**centrifugal** [sɛn'trɪfjugəl] *adj* centrífugo
**centrifugal force** *s* fuerza centrífuga
**centrifugal machine** *s* centrifugadora
**centrifugal pump** *s* bomba centrífuga
**centrifuge** ['sɛntrɪfjudʒ] *s* centrífuga; *va* centrifugar
**centripetal** [sɛn'trɪpɪtəl] *adj* centrípeto
**centripetal force** *s* fuerza centrípeta
**centrist** ['sɛntrɪst] *s* centrista
**centrobaric** [ˌsɛntro'bærɪk] *adj* centrobárico
**centrosome** ['sɛntrəsom] *s* (biol.) centrosoma
**centrosphere** ['sɛntrəˌsfɪr] *s* (biol.) centroesfera
**centuple** ['sɛntjupəl] o ['sɛntupəl] *adj* céntuplo; *va* centuplicar
**centurion** [sɛn'tjurɪən] o [sɛn'turɪən] *s* centurión
**century** ['sɛntʃərɪ] *s* (*pl:* **-ries**) siglo, centuria; (hist.) centuria; grupo de cien personas o cosas
**century plant** *s* (bot.) pita
**cephalic** [sɪ'fælɪk] *adj* cefálico
**cephalochordate** [ˌsɛfəlo'kɔrdet] *adj* (zool.) cefalocordado
**cephalopod** ['sɛfəloˌpɑd] *adj & s* (zool.) cefalópodo
**cephalothorax** [ˌsɛfəlo'θoræks] *s* (zool.) cefalotórax
**Cepheid** ['sɛfɪɪd] *adj* (astr.) cefeido; *s* (astr.) cefeida; **Cepheid variable** (astr.) cefeida variable
**Cepheus** ['sifjus] o ['sifɪəs] *s* (myth. & astr.) Cefeo
**ceramic** [sɪ'ræmɪk] *adj* cerámico; **ceramics** *ssg* cerámica (*arte*); *spl* cerámica (*objetos*)
**ceramist** ['sɛrəmɪst] *s* ceramista
**cerargyrite** [sɪ'rɑrdʒɪraɪt] *s* (mineral.) querargirita
**cerastes** [sɪ'ræstiz] *s* (zool.) cerasta
**cerate** ['sɪret] *s* (pharm.) cerato
**Cerberus** ['sʌrbərəs] *s* (myth. & fig.) Cancerbero
**cere** [sɪr] *s* (orn.) cera
**cereal** ['sɪrɪəl] *adj & s* cereal
**cerebellum** [ˌsɛrɪ'bɛləm] *s* (*pl:* **-lums** o **-la** [lə]) (anat.) cerebelo
**cerebral** ['sɛrɪbrəl] *adj* cerebral
**cerebral palsy** *s* (path.) parálisis cerebral infantil, diplejía espástica
**cerebrate** ['sɛrɪbret] *vn* pensar, reflexionar
**cerebration** [ˌsɛrɪ'breʃən] *s* cerebración; pensamiento
**cerebrospinal** [ˌsɛrɪbro'spaɪnəl] *adj* (anat.) cerebroespinal
**cerebrospinal meningitis** *s* (path.) meningitis cerebroespinal
**cerebrum** ['sɛrɪbrəm] *s* (*pl:* **-brums** o **-bra** [brə]) (anat.) cerebro (*encéfalo; parte anterior del encéfalo*)

**cerecloth** [ˈsɪrˌklɔθ] o [ˈsɪrˌklɑθ] *s* encerado; mortaja encerada
**cerement** [ˈsɪrmənt] *s* mortaja encerada
**ceremonial** [ˌsɛrɪˈmonɪəl] *adj* ceremonial; *s* ceremonial; (eccl.) ceremonial (*libro*)
**ceremonious** [ˌsɛrɪˈmonɪəs] *adj* ceremonioso
**ceremony** [ˈsɛrɪˌmonɪ] *s* (*pl:* **-nies**) ceremonia; **to stand on ceremony** hacer ceremonias
**Ceres** [ˈsɪriz] *s* (myth.) Ceres
**cereus** [ˈsɪrɪəs] *s* (bot.) pitahaya, acacana
**cerise** [səˈriz] o [səˈris] *s* cereza, color de cereza; *adj* de color de cereza
**cerium** [ˈsɪrɪəm] *s* (chem.) cerio
**cerium metals** *spl* (chem.) céridos
**cero** [ˈsɪro] *s* (*pl:* **-ros**) (ichth.) pintada, sierra
**ceroplastics** [ˌsɪroˈplæstɪks] o [ˌsɛroˈplæstɪks] *ssg* ceroplástica
**cerotic** [sɪˈrɑtɪk] *adj* (chem.) cerótico
**cerotic acid** *s* (chem.) ácido cerótico
**certain** [ˈsʌrtən] *adj* cierto; **a certain** cierto; **for certain** por cierto; **to be certain to** + *inf* no poder dejar de + *inf*
**certainly** [ˈsʌrtənlɪ] *adv* ciertamente, con certeza; con mucho gusto
**certainty** [ˈsʌrtəntɪ] *s* (*pl:* **-ties**) certeza o certidumbre; cosa cierta; **with certainty** a ciencia cierta
**certes** [ˈsʌrtiz] *adv* (archaic) seguramente, en verdad
**certifiable** [ˈsʌrtɪˌfaɪəbəl] *adj* certificable
**certificate** [sərˈtɪfɪkɪt] *s* certificado, certificación; título (*documento que representa valor comercial*); [sɛrˈtɪfɪket] *va* certificar
**certificate of baptism** *s* partida de bautismo
**certificate of death** *s* partida de defunción
**certificate of marriage** *s* certificado de matrimonio, partida de casamiento
**certificate of origin** *s* (com.) certificado de origen
**certification** [ˌsʌrtɪfɪˈkeʃən] *s* certificación
**certificatory** [sərˈtɪfɪkəˌtorɪ] *adj* certificatorio
**certified check** *s* (com.) cheque certificado
**certified public accountant** *s* censor jurado de cuentas, contador público titulado
**certify** [ˈsʌrtɪfaɪ] (*pret & pp:* **-fied**) *va* certificar; garantizar la calidad de
**certiorari** [ˌsʌrʃɪoˈrɛrɪ] *s* (law) auto de avocación
**certitude** [ˈsʌrtɪtjud] o [ˈsʌrtɪtud] *s* certidumbre
**cerulean** [sɪˈrulɪən] *adj* cerúleo
**cerumen** [sɪˈrumɛn] *s* (physiol.) cerumen
**ceruse** [ˈsɪrus] o [sɪˈrus] *s* (chem.) cerusa
**cerussite** [ˈsɪrəsaɪt] *s* (mineral.) cerusita
**Cervantist** [sərˈvæntɪst] *s* cervantista
**cervical** [ˈsʌrvɪkəl] *adj* cervical
**cervical rib** *s* (anat.) costilla cervical
**cervicitis** [ˌsʌrvɪˈsaɪtɪs] *s* (path.) cervicitis
**cervine** [ˈsʌrvaɪn] o [ˈsʌrvɪn] *adj* cervino
**cervix** [ˈsʌrvɪks] *s* (*pl:* **cervices** [sərˈvaɪsiz] o [ˈsʌrvɪsiz] o **cervixes**) (anat.) cerviz
**Cesarean** o **Cesarian** [sɪˈzɛrɪən] *adj & s* var. de **Caesarean**
**cesium** [ˈsizɪəm] *s* (chem.) cesio
**cespitose** [ˈsɛspɪtos] *adj* cespitoso
**cessation** [sɛˈseʃən] *s* cesación
**cessation of hostilities** *s* suspensión de hostilidades
**cession** [ˈsɛʃən] *s* cesión
**cesspool** [ˈsɛsˌpul] *s* pozo negro; sitio inmundo
**cestode** [ˈsɛstod] *s* (zool.) cestodo
**cestus** [ˈsɛstəs] *s* (hist.) cesto (*armadura de la mano*); (myth.) cinturón de Venus
**cesura** [sɪˈʒurə] o [sɪˈzjurə] *s* (*pl:* **-ras** o **-rae** [ri]) var. de **caesura**
**cetacean** [sɪˈteʃən] *adj & s* (zool.) cetáceo
**cetaceous** [sɪˈteʃəs] *adj* (zool.) cetáceo
**cetane** [ˈsiten] *s* (chem.) cetano
**cetane number** *s* (chem.) número de cetano
**cetin** [ˈsitən] *s* (chem.) cetina
**cetrarin** [sɪˈtrɛrɪn] o [ˈsɛtrərɪn] *s* (chem.) cetrarina
**Cetus** [ˈsitəs] *s* (astr.) Ballena
**cetyl** [ˈsɛtɪl] o [ˈsitɪl] *s* (chem.) cetilo
**Ceylon** [sɪˈlɑn] *s* Ceilán
**Ceylonese** [ˌsiləˈniz] *adj* ceilanés; *s* (*pl:* **-nese**) ceilanés
**cf.** abr. de **confer** (Lat.) **compare**

**c.f.i.** o **C.F.I.** abr. de **cost, freight, and insurance**
**cg.** abr. de **centigram** o **centigrams**
**c.g.s.** o **cgs** abr. de **centimeter-gram-second (system)**
**ch.** abr. de **chapter** y **church**
**chaconne** [ʃɑˈkɔn] *s* (mus.) chacona
**Chaeronea** [ˌkɛrəˈniə] *s* Queronea
**chafe** [tʃef] *s* frotamiento; desgaste; irritación; *va* frotar; escocer; desgastar, raer; irritar; *vn* desgastarse, raerse; irritarse, escocerse
**chafer** [ˈtʃefər] *s* (ent.) abejorro
**chaff** [tʃæf] o [tʃɑf] *s* barcia, aechaduras; paja menuda; broza, desperdicio; zumba, vaya, chanza ligera; *va* zumbarse de
**chaffer** [ˈtʃæfər] *s* regateo; *va* regatear; trocar (*palabras*); **to chaffer away** gastar; *vn* regatear
**chaffinch** [ˈtʃæfɪntʃ] *s* (orn.) pinzón
**chaffy** [ˈtʃæfɪ] o [ˈtʃɑfɪ] *adj* (*comp:* **-ier;** *super:* **-iest**) lleno de barcia; brozoso, inútil; chancero
**chafing dish** [ˈtʃefɪŋ] *s* cocinilla, infernillo
**chagrin** [ʃəˈgrɪn] *s* pesadumbre, desazón, disgusto; *va* apesadumbrar, desazonar, disgustar
**chain** [tʃen] *s* cadena; (chem. & rad.) cadena; *va* encadenar
**chain cable** *s* (naut.) cadena de ancla
**chain drive** *s* transmisión de cadena
**chain gang** *s* collera, cadena de presidiarios, cuerda de presos
**chain gear** *s* rueda de cadena
**chain lightning** *s* relámpagos en zigzag
**chain-link fencing** [ˈtʃenˈlɪŋk] *s* cercado eslabonado
**chain mail** *s* cota de malla
**chainman** [ˈtʃenmən] *s* (*pl:* **-men**) cadenero
**chain of mountains** *s* cordillera, cadena de montañas
**chain-pull socket** [ˈtʃenˌpʊl] *s* (elec.) portalámparas de cadena
**chain pump** *s* bomba de cadena
**chain reaction** *s* (phys.) reacción en cadena, acción eslabonada
**chain saw** *s* sierra de cadena
**chain shot** *s* (mil.) balas enramadas
**chain smoker** *s* cigarrista, fumador de un pitillo tras otro
**chain stitch** *s* punto de cadeneta
**chain-stitch** [ˈtʃenˌstɪtʃ] *va* coser empleando el punto de cadeneta
**chain store** *s* empresa con cadena de tiendas; tienda de una cadena
**chain tongs** *spl* llave de cadena
**chain wheel** *s* rueda dentada para cadena
**chair** [tʃɛr] *s* silla; cátedra (*de profesor*); silla de manos; sillón del presidente; presidente (*de una reunión*); (rail.) cojinete; **to take the chair** abrir la sesión; presidir la reunión; *va* asentar; llevar en una silla; presidir (*una reunión*)
**chair car** *s* (rail.) vagón salón
**chair lift** *s* telesilla (*para los esquiadores*)
**chairman** [ˈtʃɛrmən] *s* (*pl:* **-men**) presidente; silletero (*el que lleva una silla de manos o empuja una silla de ruedas*)
**chairmanship** [ˈtʃɛrmənʃɪp] *s* presidencia
**Chair of Saint Peter** *s* cátedra de San Pedro (*dignidad del Sumo Pontífice; silla situada en la Basílica del Vaticano*)
**chair rail** *s* guardasilla
**chairwoman** [ˈtʃɛrˌwʊmən] *s* (*pl:* **-women**) presidenta
**chaise** [ʃez] *s* calesa, calesín, silla volante
**chaise longue** [lɔŋg] *s* meridiana, chaise longue
**chalaza** [kəˈlezə] *s* (*pl:* **-zas** o **-zae** [zi]) (bot. & embryol.) chalaza
**Chalcedon** [ˈkælsɪdɑn] o [kælˈsidən] *s* Calcedonia
**chalcedony** [kælˈsɛdənɪ] o [ˈkælsɪˌdonɪ] *s* (*pl:* **-nies**) (mineral.) calcedonia
**chalcid** [ˈkælsɪd] *s* (ent.) calcídido
**chalcopyrite** [ˌkælkəˈpaɪraɪt] o [ˌkælkəˈpɪraɪt] *s* (mineral.) calcopirita
**Chaldaic** [kælˈdeɪk] *adj* caldaico, caldeo; *s* caldeo
**Chaldea** [kælˈdiə] *s* Caldea
**Chaldean** [kælˈdiən] *adj & s* caldeo; (fig.) caldeo (*astrólogo; mágico*)

**Chaldee** [kæl'di] o ['kældi] *adj & s* caldeo
**chalet** [ʃæ'le] o ['ʃæle] *s* chalet
**chalice** ['tʃælɪs] *s* (bot., eccl. & poet.) cáliz
**chalk** [tʃɔk] *s* creta; tiza (*con que se escribe en las pizarras*); *va* marcar, escribir o dibujar con tiza; mezclar o frotar con creta; enyesar; **to chalk up** apuntar; (sport) apuntar; (sport) ganar (*un tanto*); obtener (*un triunfo*)
**chalk talk** *s* conferencia esclarecida con ejemplos o dibujos hechos con tiza en una pizarra
**chalky** ['tʃɔkɪ] *adj* (*comp:* **-ier;** *super:* **-iest**) cretoso; pálido
**challenge** ['tʃælɪndʒ] *s* desafío; demanda; (mil.) quién vive; (law) recusación; *va* desafiar, retar; demandar, exigir; disputar; dudar; (mil.) dar el quién vive a; (law) recusar; **to challenge to** + *inf* desafiar a + *inf*
**challenger** ['tʃælɪndʒər] *s* desafiador, retador
**challenging** ['tʃælɪndʒɪŋ] *adj* desafiador, retador; provocador
**challie** o **challis** ['ʃælɪ] *s* chalí
**chalybeate** [kə'lɪbɪet] o [kə'lɪbɪɪt] *adj* calibeado, ferruginoso; *s* medicamento ferruginoso, agua ferruginosa
**chamber** ['tʃembər] *s* cámara; recámara (*de un arma de fuego*); (anat.) cámara; aposento, dormitorio; **chambers** *spl* oficina de abogado o juez; (Brit.) serie de cámaras que sirven de habitaciones u oficinas
**chambered** ['tʃembərd] *adj* que tiene cámara o cámaras; dividido en compartimientos
**chamberlain** ['tʃembərlɪn] *s* chambelán; tesorero
**chambermaid** ['tʃembər,med] *s* camarera
**chamber music** *s* música de cámara
**chamber of commerce** *s* cámara de comercio
**chamber orchestra** *s* orquesta de cámara
**chamber pot** *s* orinal, vaso de noche
**chambray** ['ʃæmbre] *s* cambray
**chameleon** [kə'miliən] *s* (zool. & fig.) camaleón
**chamfer** ['tʃæmfər] *s* chaflán; *va* chaflanar; acanalar, estirar
**chamois** ['ʃæmɪ] *s* (*pl:* **-ois** [ɪ]) (zool.) gamuza; gamuza (*piel*)
**champ** [tʃæmp] *s* (slang) campeón; mordisco; *va & vn* mordiscar; **to champ the bit** morder o tascar el freno
**champagne** [ʃæm'pen] *s* champaña *m* (*vino*); (*cap.*) *s* la Champaña
**champaign** [ʃæm'pen] *adj* llano y abierto; *s* campiña
**champion** ['tʃæmpɪən] *s* campeón; (fig.) campeón; paladín; *adj* campeón, p.ej., **champion cyclist** campeón ciclista; *va* defender (*a veces contra el dictamen ajeno*)
**championess** ['tʃæmpɪənɪs] *s* campeona
**championship** ['tʃæmpɪən,ʃɪp] *s* campeonato
**champlevé** [,ʃæmplə've] *s* esmalte campeado o vaciado
**Champs Elysées** [ʃɑ̃zeli'ze] *spl* Campos Elíseos (*paseo de París*)
**chance** [tʃæns] o [tʃɑns] *s* ocasión, oportunidad; posibilidad, probabilidad; casualidad; suerte, fortuna; riesgo, peligro; acontecimiento, suceso; **by chance** por acaso, por casualidad; **on the chance that** por si acaso; **the chances are even that . . .** las probabilidades corren parejas que . . .; **the chances are that . . .** (coll.) es probable que . . .; **to let the chance slip** perder la ocasión; **to look out for the main chance** estar a caza de su provecho; **to not stand a chance** no tener probabilidad; **to take a chance** probar fortuna, probar suerte; comprar un billete (*p.ej., de lotería*); **to take one's chances** aventurarse, probar fortuna; *adj* casual, imprevisto; *va* (coll.) arriesgar; *vn* acontecer, suceder; **to chance on** o **upon** tropezar con
**chancel** ['tʃænsəl] o ['tʃɑnsəl] *s* (eccl.) entrecoro
**chancellery** ['tʃænsələrɪ] o ['tʃɑnsələrɪ] *s* (*pl:* **-ies**) cancillería
**chancellor** ['tʃænsələr] o ['tʃɑnsələr] *s* canciller
**Chancellor of the Exchequer** *s* (Brit.) Canciller del echiquier, ministro de hacienda
**chancellorship** ['tʃænsələr,ʃɪp] o ['tʃɑnsələr-,ʃɪp] *s* cancillería
**chancery** ['tʃænsərɪ] o ['tʃɑnsərɪ] *s* (*pl:* **-ies**) chancillería (*tribunal de justicia*); cancillería; justicia; archivo (*de documentos públicos*); (wrestling) presa a la cabeza; **in chancery** en litigio en un tribunal de justicia; en situación muy difícil; (wrestling) debajo del brazo del contrario (*dícese de la cabeza*)
**chancre** ['ʃæŋkər] *s* (path.) chancro
**chancrous** ['ʃæŋkrəs] *adj* chancroso
**chancy** ['tʃænsɪ] o ['tʃɑnsɪ] *adj* (*comp:* **-ier;** *super:* **-iest**) (coll.) arriesgado
**chandelier** [,ʃændə'lɪr] *s* araña de luces
**chandler** ['tʃændlər] *s* cerero, velero; abacero, tendero
**chandlery** ['tʃændlərɪ] *s* (*pl:* **-ies**) cerería, velería; cirios, velas, candelas, etc.
**change** [tʃendʒ] *s* cambio, mudanza; variedad; dinero menudo, moneda suelta; vuelta (*dinero devuelto*); muda (*de ropa*); **for a change** por cambiar, por variedad; **to keep the change** quedarse con la vuelta; **to ring the changes** tocar las campanas de todas las maneras; obrar de varias maneras; **to ring the changes on** hacer (*una cosa*) de varias maneras; decir (*una cosa*) de varias maneras; *va* cambiar, mudar; reemplazar; **to change clothes** cambiar de ropa; **to change color** demudarse; **to change gears** cambiar de velocidades; **to change hands** cambiar de dueño; **to change money** cambiar moneda; **to change one's mind** cambiar de opinión; **to change one's tune** cambiar de actitud; **to change trains** cambiar de tren, transbordar; *vn* cambiar, mudar; corregirse
**'change** [tʃendʒ] *s* bolsa, lonja
**changeability** [,tʃendʒə'bɪlɪtɪ] *s* alterabilidad, mutabilidad
**changeable** ['tʃendʒəbəl] *adj* cambiable, mudable; variable; cambiadizo, inconstante
**changeful** ['tʃendʒfəl] *adj* cambiante; variable, inconstante
**changeless** ['tʃendʒlɪs] *adj* inmutable, constante
**changeling** ['tʃendʒlɪŋ] *s* niño cambiado en secreto por otro; (archaic) niño bobo, tonto o malparecido
**change of clothing** *s* muda de ropa
**change of heart** *s* conversión, cambio de sentimiento, arrepentimiento
**change of life** *s* (physiol.) menopausia
**change of time** *s* cambio de hora
**change of venue** *s* (law) cambio de tribunal (*en un proceso*)
**change of voice** *s* muda (*de los muchachos*)
**change-over** ['tʃendʒ,ovər] *s* cambio, conmutación
**channel** ['tʃænəl] *s* canal *m & f;* álveo, cauce (*de un río*); vía (*p.ej., de comunicaciones*); ranura, surco; conducto; (mil.) conducto regular; (naut.) mesa o meseta de guarnición; (rad. & telv.) canal *m;* **the Channel** el canal de la Mancha; (*pret & pp:* **-neled** o **-nelled;** *ger:* **-neling** o **-nelling**) *va* acanalar; canalizar (*p.ej., dinero, esfuerzos*)
**channel iron** *s* hierro de canal
**Channel Islands** *spl* islas Anglonormandas, islas del Canal, islas Normandas
**chant** [tʃænt] o [tʃɑnt] *s* canción; canto; salmo; *va* cantar; *vn* cantar; cantar la misma cantinela
**chanter** ['tʃæntər] o ['tʃɑntər] *s* cantor; chantre; (mus.) puntero (*de gaita*)
**chantey** ['ʃæntɪ] o ['tʃæntɪ] *s* (naut.) saloma
**chanteyman** ['ʃæntɪmən] o ['tʃæntɪmən] *s* (*pl:* **-men**) (naut.) salomador
**chanticleer** ['tʃæntɪklɪr] *s* gallo
**chantry** ['tʃæntrɪ] o ['tʃɑntrɪ] *s* (*pl:* **-tries**) capilla; dotación para decirse misas especiales en una capilla
**chanty** ['ʃæntɪ] o ['tʃæntɪ] *s* (*pl:* **-ties**) var. de **chantey**
**chaos** ['keɑs] *s* caos
**chaotic** [ke'ɑtɪk] *adj* caótico
**chaotically** [ke'ɑtɪkəlɪ] *adv* caóticamente
**chap.** abr. de **chaplain** y **chapter**
**chap** [tʃæp] o [tʃɑp] *s* mandíbula; mejilla; [tʃæp] *s* grieta, hendedura; (coll.) muchacho, chico; **chaps** *spl* zahones, chaparreras (*calzones de cuero*); (*pret & pp:* **chapped;** *ger:* **chapping**) *va* agrietar, hender, rajar; *vn* agrietarse, henderse, rajarse
**chaparral** [,tʃæpə'ræl] *s* chaparral

**chapbook** ['tʃæp,bʊk] *s* librete de cuentos, coplas, etc., que se vendía en las calles
**chapel** ['tʃæpəl] *s* capilla; oficio celebrado en una capilla; (Brit.) capilla destinada al culto de los que no pertenecen a la Iglesia establecida; imprenta; personal de la imprenta
**chapel of ease** *s* ayuda de parroquia
**chaperon** o **chaperone** ['ʃæpəron] *s* acompañanta de señoritas, señora de compañía; *va* acompañar (*una señora a una o más señoritas*)
**chaperonage** ['ʃæpə,ronɪdʒ] *s* deberes de acompañanta de señoritas
**chapfallen** ['tʃɑp,fɔlən] o ['tʃæp,fɔlən] *adj* alicaído, desanimado
**chaplain** ['tʃæplɪn] *s* capellán
**chaplaincy** ['tʃæplɪnsɪ] *s* (*pl:* **-cies**) capellanía
**chaplainship** ['tʃæplɪnʃɪp] *s* capellanía
**chaplet** ['tʃæplɪt] *s* guirnalda; gargantilla, collar; rosario; (arch.) moldura de cuentas
**chapleted** ['tʃæplɪtɪd] *adj* enguirnaldado
**chapman** ['tʃæpmən] *s* (*pl:* **-men**) (Brit.) buhonero
**chaptalization** [,ʃæptəlɪ'zeʃən] *s* (wine mfg.) captalización
**chaptalize** ['tʃæptəlaɪz] *va* captalizar
**chapter** ['tʃæptər] *s* capítulo; capítula (*pasaje de la Sagrada Escritura*)
**chapter and verse** *adv* con todos sus pelos y señales
**chapter house** *s* casa capitular; casa de una confraternidad universitaria
**char** [tʃɑr] *s* tarea de ocasión, trabajo a jornal; (*pret & pp:* **charred;** *ger:* **charring**) *va* carbonizar; socarrar (*quemar ligeramente*); *vn* hacer tareas de ocasión, trabajar a jornal; carbonizarse
**char-à-banc** ['ʃærə,bæŋ] *s* (*pl:* **-bancs** [,bæŋz]) charabán, autobús grande para excursiones
**character** ['kærɪktər] *s* carácter; personaje; (theat.) papel; (theat.) personaje; (coll.) tipo, sujeto; (bot., zool., print. & theol.) carácter; **in character** con verdad, conforme al tipo; **out of character** impropio, contrario al tipo
**character actor** *s* (theat.) actor de carácter
**character assassination** *s* calumnia hecha con propósito de destruir la confianza del público en una persona
**characteristic** [,kærɪktə'rɪstɪk] *adj* característico; *s* característica; (math. & rad.) característica
**characteristically** [,kærɪktə'rɪstɪkəlɪ] *adv* característicamente
**characterization** [,kærɪktərɪ'zeʃən] *s* caracterización
**characterize** ['kærɪktəraɪz] *va* caracterizar
**character loan** *s* préstamo sin garantía colateral
**character piece** *s* pieza breve para piano, que expresa un estado de alma o impresión simple
**character sketch** *s* semblanza; (theat.) representación de un personaje de carácter bien definido
**character study** *s* retrato literario
**character witness** *s* testigo que da testimonio de la buena reputación y la moralidad de una persona
**charactery** ['kærɪktərɪ] *s* simbolismo; símbolos, caracteres
**charade** [ʃə'red] o [ʃə'rɑd] *s* charada
**charcoal** ['tʃɑr,kol] *s* carbón de leña; carboncillo (*para dibujar*); dibujo al carbón
**charcoal burner** *s* carbonero; horno para hacer carbón de leña
**chard** [tʃɑrd] *s* (bot.) acelga
**chare** [tʃɛr] *s* tarea de ocasión, trabajo a jornal; *vn* hacer tareas de ocasión, trabajar a jornal
**charge** [tʃɑrdʒ] *s* carga (*de un arma de fuego, un horno, etc.*); cargo (*responsabilidad; acusación; cuidado, custodio; gravamen, impuesto*); encargo, orden, mando; coste, precio; (mil. & elec.) carga; (her.) blasón; **in charge** encargado; **in charge of** a cargo de (*una persona*); encargado de (*una cosa*); **to reverse the charges** (telp.) cobrar al número llamado; **to take charge of** hacerse cargo de; *va* cargar; cobrar (*cierto precio*); encargar, ordenar, mandar; embestir; (mil. & elec.) cargar; **to charge off** poner (*algo*) en cuenta restándolo como pérdida; anotar en el libro de cuentas; **to charge to the account of someone** (com.) cargarle a uno en cuenta; **to charge with** cargar de, acusar de; *vn* embestir
**chargeable** ['tʃɑrdʒəbəl] *adj* acusable; cobradero
**charge account** *s* (com.) cuenta corriente
**chargé d'affaires** [ʃɑr'ʒedæ'fɛr] *s* (*pl:* **chargés d'affaires**) encargado de negocios
**charger** ['tʃɑrdʒər] *s* cargador; caballo de guerra; (elec.) cargador (*de acumuladores*); (archaic) fuente o plato grande
**charging** ['tʃɑrdʒɪŋ] *adj* (her.) furioso
**charging rate** *s* (elec.) corriente de carga (*de un acumulador*)
**chariot** ['tʃærɪət] *s* carro romano, carro de guerra; carroza
**charioteer** [,tʃærɪə'tɪr] *s* auriga, carretero
**charism** ['kærɪzəm] *s* (theol.) carisma
**charitable** ['tʃærɪtəbəl] *adj* caritativo, benéfico
**charity** ['tʃærɪtɪ] *s* (*pl:* **-ties**) caridad
**charivari** [,ʃɑrɪ'vɑrɪ], [ʃə,rɪvə'ri] o ['ʃɪvəri] *s* cencerrada (*en particular, la dada al viudo que se vuelve a casar, la noche de bodas*); cantaleta
**charlatan** ['ʃɑrlətən] *s* charlatán (*embaidor; curandero*)
**charlatanism** ['ʃɑrlətənɪzəm] o **charlatanry** ['ʃɑrlətənrɪ] *s* charlatanismo
**Charlemagne** ['ʃɑrləmen] *s* Carlomagno
**Charles** [tʃɑrlz] *s* Carlos
**Charles's Wain** ['tʃɑrlzɪz'wen] *s* (astr.) la Osa Mayor
**Charley** o **Charlie** ['tʃɑrlɪ] *s* forma familiar de **Charles;** Carlitos (*se aplica a niños*)
**charley horse** *s* (coll.) calambre
**charlock** ['tʃɑrlɑk] *s* (bot.) mostaza silvestre
**Charlotte** ['ʃɑrlət] *s* Carlota; (*l.c.*) *s* carlota (*torta*)
**charlotte russe** ['ʃɑrlət 'rus] *s* carlota rusa (*pastel de nata*)
**charm** [tʃɑrm] *s* encanto, hechizo; dije, amuleto; **charms** *spl* hechizos (*de una mujer*); *va* encantar, hechizar
**charmer** ['tʃɑrmər] *s* encantador
**charmeuse** [ʃɑr'mʌz] *s* charmeuse (*tejido*)
**charming** ['tʃɑrmɪŋ] *adj* encantador
**charnel** ['tʃɑrnəl] *adj* sepulcral, cadavérico, horrible; *s* carnero, osario
**charnel house** *s* carnero
**Charon** ['kerɑn] *s* (myth.) Carón o Caronte
**chart** [tʃɑrt] *s* mapa geográfico; (naut.) carta de marear; lista, tabla; cuadro, diagrama; *va* poner en una carta de marear; **to chart a course** trazar o planear un derrotero
**charter** ['tʃɑrtər] *s* carta; *va* estatuir; (naut.) fletar (*un barco*); alquilar (*un autobús*)
**chartered accountant** *s* (Brit.) perito mercantil, contador perito
**charterhouse** ['tʃɑrtər,haʊs] *s* cartuja
**charter member** *s* socio fundador
**charter party** *s* (naut.) carta partida, carta de fletamento
**chartometer** [kɑr'tɑmɪtər] *s* cartómetro
**chartreuse** [ʃɑr'trʌz] *s* chartreuse
**charwoman** ['tʃɑr,wʊmən] *s* (*pl:* **-women**) criada por horas, alquilona, asistenta
**chary** ['tʃɛrɪ] *adj* (*comp:* **-ier;** *super:* **-iest**) cuidadoso; esquivo, asustado; parco; **to be chary of** ser avaro de (*p.ej., elogios*); tener miedo de (*p.ej., los extranjeros*); **to be chary of** + *ger* vacilar en + *inf*
**Charybdis** [kə'rɪbdɪs] *s* (geog. & myth.) Caribdis
**Chas.** abr. de **Charles**
**chase** [tʃes] *s* caza; persecución; ranura, muesca; (print.) rama; **to give chase** dar caza; *va* cazar; perseguir; filetear, grabar; **to chase away** ahuyentar; *vn* (coll.) precipitarse
**chaser** ['tʃesər] *s* cazador; perseguidor; avión de caza; cazasubmarinos; grabador; buril, cincel; (coll.) bebida que se toma después de un licor fuerte
**chasm** ['kæzəm] *s* grieta; abismo, desfiladero; laguna, vacío; (fig.) abismo (*entre dos personas o cosas*)
**chasseur** [ʃɑ'sʌr] *s* cazador (*soldado*); criado vestido de uniforme
**chassis** ['ʃæsɪ] o ['tʃæsɪ] *s* (*pl:* **-sis** [sɪz]) (aut. & rad.) chasis; (aer.) armazón

**chaste** [tʃest] *adj* casto; castizo, simple, sin adorno

**chasten** ['tʃesən] *va* castigar

**chaste tree** *s* (bot.) agnocasto, sauzgatillo

**chastise** [tʃæs'taɪz] *va* castigar

**chastisement** ['tʃæstɪzmənt] o [tʃæs'taɪzmənt] *s* castigo

**chastity** ['tʃæstɪtɪ] *s* castidad; casticidad, simpleza, falta de adorno

**chastity belt** *s* cinturón de castidad

**chasuble** ['tʃæzjubəl] *s* casulla

**chat** [tʃæt] *s* charla, plática; (orn.) cagaestacas; (*pret & pp:* **chatted;** *ger:* **chatting**) *vn* charlar, platicar

**chatelaine** ['ʃætəlen] *s* castellana (*señora de un castillo*); muelle, cadena con dijes o llavero que llevan las mujeres en la cintura

**chattel** ['tʃætəl] *s* bienes muebles

**chatter** ['tʃætər] *s* charla, cháchara; chirrido, rechinido; castañeteo (*de los dientes*); *vn* charlar, chacharear; chirriar, rechinar; castañetear (*los dientes*); (mach.) traquear, traquetear

**chatterbox** ['tʃætər,bɑks] *s* charlador, tarabilla

**chatty** ['tʃætɪ] *adj* (*comp:* **-tier;** *super:* **-tiest**) gárrulo, locuaz

**chauffeur** ['ʃofər] o [ʃo'fʌr] *s* chófer

**chautauqua** o **Chautauqua** [ʃə'tɔkwə] *s* (U.S.A.) reunión cultural (*que consta de conferencias, conciertos, etc., que se ofrecen durante varios días*)

**chauvinism** ['ʃovɪnɪzəm] *s* chauvinismo

**chauvinist** ['ʃovɪnɪst] *s* chauvinista

**chauvinistic** [,ʃovɪ'nɪstɪk] *adj* chauvinista

**Ch.E.** abr. de **Chemical Engineer**

**cheap** [tʃip] *adj* barato; barateado; baratero (*que vende barato*); mal pagado (*dícese del trabajo*); cursi, de mal gusto; **to feel cheap** sentirse inferior, sentir vergüenza; *adv* barato

**cheapen** ['tʃipən] *va* abaratar; *vn* abaratar, abaratarse

**cheapness** ['tʃipnɪs] *s* baratura

**cheat** [tʃit] *s* trampa, timo, fraude; trampista, timador, defraudador; *va* trampear, timar, defraudar; **to cheat someone out of something** defraudar algo a alguien

**cheater** ['tʃitər] *s* trampista, timador, defraudador

**check** [tʃɛk] *s* parada súbita; rechazo, repulsa; freno, restricción; (mach.) tope; amortiguador (*de puerta*); cheque (*de banco*); talón, contraseña (*de equipajes*); billete de reclamo; cuenta (*en un restaurante*); billete de salida, contraseña de salida (*en el teatro o cine*); comprobación, verificación; inspección; marca, señal; tela tejida a cuadros; cuadro (*de una tela tejida a cuadros*); grieta; jaque (*lance en el juego de ajedrez*); **in check** en jaque (*en el juego de ajedrez*); **to hold in check** contener, refrenar, reprimir ‖ *interj* ¡jaque! (*en el juego de ajedrez*) ‖ *va* parar súbitamente; rechazar, repulsar; refrenar, restringir; trabar; amortiguar; facturar, depositar (*equipajes*); controlar, comprobar, verificar; inspeccionar; marcar, señalar; marcar con cuadros; agrietar; jaquear, dar jaque a (*en ajedrez*); **to check off** marcar para indicar una comprobación; **to check up** comprobar, verificar ‖ *vn* pararse súbitamente; **to check in** llegar a un hotel e inscribir su nombre en el registro; (slang) morir; **to check out** despedirse en un hotel despúes de pagar la cuenta; (slang) morir

**checkbook** ['tʃɛk,bʊk] *s* libreta de cheques, libro talonario

**checked** [tʃɛkt] *adj* ajedrezado; (phonet.) trabado

**checked syllable** *s* (phonet.) sílaba trabada

**checker** ['tʃɛkər] *s* tela tejida a cuadros; cuadro (*de una tela tejida a cuadros*); ficha, pieza (*del juego de damas*); **checkers** *spl* damas, juego de damas; *va* cuadricular, dividir en cuadros, marcar con cuadros; diversificar, variar; *vn* diversificarse, variarse

**checkerberry** ['tʃɛkər,bɛrɪ] *s* (*pl:* **-ries**) (bot.) gaulteria; baya de la gaulteria; aceite de gaulteria

**checkerboard** ['tʃɛkər,bord] *s* damero

**checkered** ['tʃɛkərd] *adj* ajedrezado, escaqueado; diversificado, irregular

**check girl** *s* guardarropa (*joven encargada de custodiar vestidos, sombreros, etc.*)

**checking account** *s* cuenta corriente

**check list** *s* lista para la comprobación de nombres, etc.

**check mark** *s* marca, señal

**checkmate** ['tʃɛk,met] *s* mate o jaque mate; (fig.) derrota completa; *va* dar mate a, dar jaque mate a; (fig.) derrotar completamente

**checkpoint** ['tʃɛk,pɔɪnt] *s* punto de comprobación, punto de inspección

**checkrein** ['tʃɛk,ren] *s* engallador

**checkroom** ['tʃɛk,rum] o ['tʃɛk,rʊm] *s* guardarropa (*sitio*); (rail.) consigna

**checkup** ['tʃɛk,ʌp] *s* verificación rigurosa; reconocimiento general (*del estado de la salud de uno*); revisión (*p.ej., de un automóvil*)

**check valve** *s* válvula de retención

**checky** ['tʃɛkɪ] *adj* (her.) escacado, jaquelado

**Cheddar** ['tʃɛdər] *s* queso de Cheddar

**Che.E.** abr. de **Chemical Engineer**

**cheek** [tʃik] *s* mejilla, carrillo; (coll.) frescura, descaro, insolencia; (mach.) quijada; **to have one's tongue in one's cheek** decir una cosa queriendo decir otra

**cheekbone** ['tʃik,bon] *s* (anat.) pómulo, hueso de la mejilla

**cheek by jowl** *adv* cara a cara, lado a lado; en la mayor intimidad

**cheek pouch** *s* abazón (*de los monos*)

**cheek strap** *s* quijera (*de la cabezada del caballo*)

**cheeky** ['tʃikɪ] *adj* (*comp:* **-ier;** *super:* **-iest**) (coll.) fresco, cara dura

**cheep** [tʃip] *s* chillido (*del ave pequeña*); pío (*del pollo*); *vn* chillar; piar

**cheer** [tʃɪr] *s* alegría, ánimo, alivio; viva, aplauso; alimento; humor, estado de ánimo; **what cheer?** ¿qué tal?; *va* alegrar, animar, aliviar; vitorear, aplaudir; instar o animar con vivas o aplausos; saludar o dar la bienvenida a (*una persona*) con vivas o aplausos; *vn* alegrarse, animarse, aliviarse; **cheer up!** ¡ánimo!, ¡cobre ánimo!

**cheerful** ['tʃɪrfəl] *adj* alegre (*persona, noticia, ambiente, etc.*); pronto, complaciente

**cheerfully** ['tʃɪrfəlɪ] *adv* alegremente; de buena gana

**cheerfulness** ['tʃɪrfəlnɪs] *s* alegría; complacencia

**cheerio** ['tʃɪrɪo] *interj* (coll.) ¡qué tal!, ¡hola!; ¡adiós!, ¡hasta la vista!; ¡viva!

**cheerless** ['tʃɪrlɪs] *adj* triste, sombrío

**cheery** ['tʃɪrɪ] *adj* (*comp:* **-ier;** *super:* **-iest**) alegre (*persona, noticia, ambiente, etc.*)

**cheese** [tʃiz] *s* queso; *va* (slang) dejarse de; **cheese it!** (slang) ¡déjese de eso!; (slang) ¡cállese la boca!; (slang) ¡lárguese!

**cheesecake** ['tʃiz,kek] *s* quesadilla; (slang) fotografías de los hechizos de una mujer

**cheesecloth** ['tʃiz,klɔθ] o ['tʃiz,klɑθ] *s* estopilla

**cheeseflower** ['tʃiz,flaʊər] *s* (bot.) malva común

**cheese fly** *s* (ent.) mosca del queso

**cheese mite** *s* (ent.) ácaro del queso

**cheesemonger** ['tʃiz,mʌŋgər] *s* quesero

**cheeseparing** ['tʃiz,pɛrɪŋ] *adj* tacaño, mezquino; *s* cosa sin valor; tacañería, mezquindad

**cheese rennet** *s* (bot.) cuajaleche

**cheese skipper** *s* gusano del queso

**cheesy** ['tʃizɪ] *adj* (*comp:* **-ier;** *super:* **-iest**) caseoso; (slang) tosco, de mala calidad, sin valor

**cheetah** ['tʃitə] *s* (zool.) leopardo cazador

**chef** [ʃɛf] *s* primer cocinero, jefe de cocina

**Chefoo** ['tʃi'fu] *s* Chefú

**Cheka** ['tʃɛkɑ] *s* Checa (*policía secreta soviética*)

**chela** ['kilə] *s* (*pl:* **-lae** [li]) (zool.) quela

**chelicera** [kɪ'lɪsərə] *s* (*pl:* **-ae** [i]) (ent.) quelícero

**chelonian** [kɪ'lonɪən] *adj & s* (zool.) quelonio

**chem.** abr. de **chemical, chemist** y **chemistry**

**chemic** ['kɛmɪk] *adj* (archaic) químico, alquímico

**chemical** ['kɛmɪkəl] *adj* químico; *s* substancia química, producto químico

**chemical engineer** *s* ingeniero químico

**chemical engineering** *s* ingeniería química
**chemically** ['kɛmɪkəlɪ] *adv* químicamente
**chemical warfare** *s* guerra química
**chemise** [ʃə'miz] *s* camisa de mujer
**chemism** ['kɛmɪzəm] *s* quimismo
**chemist** ['kɛmɪst] *s* químico; (Brit.) boticario, farmacéutico
**chemistry** ['kɛmɪstrɪ] *s* química
**chemosphere** ['kɛməsfɪr] *s* quimiosfera
**chemosurgery** [,kɛmo'sʌrdʒərɪ] *s* quimiocirugía
**chemosynthesis** [,kɛmo'sɪnθɪsɪs] *s* quimiosíntesis
**chemotaxis** [,kɛmo'tæksɪs] *s* (biol.) quimiotaxis
**chemotherapy** [,kɛmo'θɛrəpɪ] *s* quimioterapia
**chemurgy** ['kɛmʌrdʒɪ] *s* química agrícola industrial
**chenille** [ʃə'nil] *s* felpilla
**chenopod** ['kinəpɑd] o ['kɛnəpɑd] *s* (bot.) quenopodio
**chenopodiaceous** [,kinə,podɪ'eʃəs] o [,kɛnə,podɪ'eʃəs] *adj* (bot.) quenopodiáceo
**cheque** ['tʃɛk] *s* (Brit.) cheque
**chequer** ['tʃɛkər] *s, va & vn* var. de **checker; chequers** *spl* var. de **checkers**
**Cherbourg** ['ʃɛrbʊrg] *s* Cherburgo
**cherish** ['tʃɛrɪʃ] *va* acariciar (*tratar con ternura; abrigar, p.ej., esperanzas*)
**cheroot** [ʃə'rut] *s* cigarro puro truncado por los dos extremos
**cherry** ['tʃɛrɪ] *s* (*pl:* **-ries**) (bot.) cerezo; cereza (*fruto; color*)
**cherry brandy** *s* aguardiente de cerezas
**cherry laurel** *s* (bot.) lauroceraso
**cherry orchard** *s* cerezal
**cherry red** *s* rojo cereza
**cherry stone** *s* hueso de cereza; (zool.) almeja redonda (*Venus mercenaria*)
**chersonese** ['kʌrsəniz] o ['kʌrsənis] *s* quersoneso; **the Chersonese** el quersoneso de Tracia (*la península de Gallípoli*)
**cherub** ['tʃɛrəb] *s* (*pl:* **-ubim** [əbɪm]) (Bib., f.a. & theol.) querubín; (*pl:* **-ubs**) niño angelical; persona de rostro regordete e inocente
**cherubic** [tʃə'rubɪk] *adj* querúbico
**chervil** ['tʃʌrvɪl] *s* (bot.) cerafolio, perifollo
**chess** [tʃɛs] *s* ajedrez
**chessboard** ['tʃɛs,bord] *s* tablero de ajedrez
**chessman** ['tʃɛs,mæn] *s* (*pl:* **-men**) pieza de ajedrez, trebejo
**chess player** *s* ajedrecista
**chess set** *s* ajedrez (*conjunto de las piezas*)
**chest** [tʃɛst] *s* (anat.) pecho; arca, cajón, cofre; cómoda, guardarropa; caja (*para dinero*); (mach.) caja
**chestnut** ['tʃɛsnʌt] *s* (bot.) castaño (*árbol y madera*); castaña (*fruto*); castaño (*color*); caballo de color castaño; (vet.) espejuelo; (coll.) broma gastada, chiste sabido por todo el mundo; **to pull someone's chestnuts out of the fire** (coll.) sacarle a uno las castañas del fuego; *adj* castaño, marrón
**chest of drawers** *s* cómoda
**chesty** ['tʃɛstɪ] *adj* (*comp:* **-ier;** *super:* **-iest**) (slang) engreído, soberbio, orgulloso
**chetah** ['tʃitə] *s* var. de **cheetah**
**cheval-de-frise** [ʃə'vældə'friz] *s* (*pl:* **chevaux-de-frise** [ʃə'vodə'friz]) erizo (*que corona lo alto de una muralla*); (mil.) caballo de frisa
**cheval glass** [ʃə'væl] *s* psique (*espejo*)
**chevalier** [,ʃɛvə'lɪr] *s* caballero
**cheviot** ['ʃɛvɪət] *s* cheviot
**chevron** ['ʃɛvrən] *s* (her.) cheurón; (mil.) insignia, galón
**chevron molding** *s* (arch.) cheurón
**chevrony** ['ʃɛvrənɪ] *adj* (her.) cheuronado
**chevrotain** ['ʃɛvrəten] o ['ʃɛvrətɪn] *s* (zool.) trágulo
**chevy** ['tʃɛvɪ] o ['tʃɪvɪ] *s* (*pl:* **-ies**) (Brit.) caza, grito de caza; (*pret & pp:* **-ied**) *va* (Brit.) cazar, perseguir; (Brit.) acosar, atormentar; *vn* (Brit.) correr, precipitarse
**chew** [tʃu] *s* mascadura; *va* mascar, masticar; **to chew the cud** rumiar; (fig.) rumiar (*meditar*); **to chew the rag** (slang) dar la lengua; *vn* mascar, masticar; (coll.) mascar tabaco
**chewing gum** *s* goma de mascar
**chewink** [tʃɪ'wɪŋk] *s* (orn.) pájaro fringílido norteamericano (*Pipilo erythrophthalmus*)
**chg.** abr. de **charge**
**chgd.** abr. de **charged**
**Chian** ['kaɪən] *adj & s* quío
**Chianti** [kɪ'ɑntɪ] o [kɪ'æntɪ] *s* quianti o chianti (*vino*)
**chiaroscuro** [kɪ,ɑrə'skjʊro] *s* (*pl:* **-ros**) (paint.) claroscuro
**chiasma** [kaɪ'æzmə] *s* (*pl:* **-mata** [mətə]) (anat. & biol.) quiasma
**chiasmus** [kaɪ'æzməs] *s* (*pl:* **-mi** [maɪ]) (rhet.) quiasma
**chibouk** o **chibouque** [tʃɪ'buk] o [tʃɪ'bʊk] *s* chibuquí
**chic** [ʃik] o [ʃɪk] *adj* elegante, gracioso; *s* chic
**chicane** [ʃɪ'ken] *s* triquiñuela, embuste; *va* defraudar; cavilar; *vn* andar con triquiñuelas
**chicanery** [ʃɪ'kenərɪ] *s* (*pl:* **-ies**) triquiñuela, embuste
**chick** [tʃɪk] *s* pollito, polluelo
**chickadee** ['tʃɪkədi] *s* (orn.) paro, paro de cabeza negra
**chickaree** ['tʃɪkəri] *s* (zool.) chicari (*ardilla norteamericana de pelaje rojizo*)
**chicken** ['tʃɪkən] *s* pollo; gallina o gallo; (fig.) pollo (*persona joven*); (fig.) polla (*mocita*); **she is no chicken** (coll.) ella ya no es muy joven; **to go to bed with the chickens** acostarse con las gallinas; *adj* joven, pequeño
**chicken cholera** *s* (vet.) cólera de las gallinas
**chicken coop** *s* gallinero
**chicken feed** *s* (slang) pequeña cantidad de dinero; (slang) calderilla, dinero menudo
**chicken-hearted** ['tʃɪkən,hɑrtɪd] *adj* gallina (*cobarde, tímido*)
**chicken pox** *s* (path.) viruelas locas, varicela
**chicken wire** *s* alambrada, tela metálica
**chickpea** ['tʃɪk,pi] *s* (bot.) garbanzo (*planta y semilla*)
**chickweed** ['tʃɪk,wid] *s* (bot.) álsine, pamplina de canarios, hierba pajarera
**chicle** ['tʃɪkəl] *s* chicle (*gomorresina*)
**chicory** ['tʃɪkərɪ] *s* (*pl:* **-ries**) (bot.) achicoria
**chid** [tʃɪd] *pret & pp de* **chide**
**chidden** ['tʃɪdən] *pp de* **chide**
**chide** [tʃaɪd] (*pret:* **chided** o **chid;** *pp:* **chided, chid** o **chidden**) *va & vn* reprobar, reprender, regañar
**chief** [tʃif] *s* jefe; cacique (*de pieles rojas*); (her.) jefe; **in chief** en jefe; *adj* principal
**chief burgess** *s* alcalde
**chief clerk** *s* oficial mayor
**chief executive** *s* jefe del estado; primer mandatario (Am.)
**chief justice** *s* presidente de sala; presidente de la corte suprema
**chiefly** ['tʃiflɪ] *adv* principalmente, mayormente; ante todo, sobre todo
**chief of staff** *s* (mil.) jefe de estado mayor
**chieftaincy** ['tʃiftənsɪ] o **chieftainship** ['tʃiftənʃɪp] *s* jefatura
**chiffon** [ʃɪ'fɑn] o ['ʃɪfɑn] *s* gasa, soplillo; **chiffons** *spl* encajes, cintas, atavíos
**chiffonier** [,ʃɪfə'nɪr] *s* cómoda alta
**chigger** ['tʃɪgər] *s* (ent.) ácaro; (ent.) garrapata; (ent.) nigua
**chignon** ['ʃinjɑn] *s* castaña, moño de pelo
**chigoe** ['tʃɪgo] *s* (ent.) nigua
**chilblain** ['tʃɪl,blen] *s* sabañón
**child** [tʃaɪld] *s* (*pl:* **children** ['tʃɪldrən]) niño; hijo; descendiente; **to be with child** estar encinta
**childbearing** ['tʃaɪld,bɛrɪŋ] *s* parto
**childbed** ['tʃaɪld,bɛd] *s* parturición
**childbirth** ['tʃaɪld,bʌrθ] *s* parto, alumbramiento
**child care** *s* puericultura
**Childermas** ['tʃɪldərməs] *s* (obs.) día de los inocentes
**childhood** ['tʃaɪldhʊd] *s* niñez, infancia
**childish** ['tʃaɪldɪʃ] *adj* aniñado, pueril
**childishness** ['tʃaɪldɪʃnɪs] *s* puerilidad
**child labor** *s* trabajo de menores
**childless** ['tʃaɪldlɪs] *adj* sin hijos
**childlike** ['tʃaɪld,laɪk] *adj* aniñado, infantil, pueril
**child prodigy** *s* niño prodigio
**child psychology** *s* psicología infantil
**children** ['tʃɪldrən] *pl de* **child**

**children of Israel** *spl* israelitas, hijos de Israel
**Children's Crusade** *s* cruzada de los Niños
**child's play** *s* juego de niños (*cosa muy fácil*)
**child welfare** *s* bienestar del niño
**chile** ['tʃɪlɪ] *s* var. de **chili;** (*cap.*) *s* Chile
**Chilean** ['tʃɪlɪən] *adj & s* chileno
**chile con carne** *s* var. de **chili con carne**
**Chile saltpeter** *s* nitro de Chile
**chili** ['tʃɪlɪ] *s* (*pl:* **-ies**) (bot.) chile (*planta y fruto*)
**chili con carne** [kɑn'kɑrnɪ] *s* chile con carne
**chili sauce** *s* ajiaco, salsa de ají
**chill** [tʃɪl] *s* frío desapacible; frialdad; calofrío, escalofrío; estremecimiento (*p.ej., que recorre una multitud*); abatimiento, desaliento; (fig.) frialdad (*falta de cordialidad*); *adj* desapaciblemente frío; (fig.) frío; (fig.) depresivo; *va* enfriar; abatir, desalentar; (metal.) enfriar; *vn* calofriarse, enfriarse
**chilli** ['tʃɪlɪ] *s* (*pl:* **-lies**) var. de **chili**
**chilly** ['tʃɪlɪ] *adj* (*comp:* **-ier;** *super:* **-iest**) frío; escalofriado, friolento; (fig.) frío
**chime** [tʃaɪm] *s* carillón, juego de campanas; tubo sonoro; repique, campaneo; armonía; conformidad; *va* repicar (*una campana o un juego de campanas*); decir en cadencia; *vn* repicar; sonar con armonía; hablar en cadencia, hablar monótonamente; estar en armonía; **to chime in** hacer coro, unisonar; (coll.) unirse, asociarse; (coll.) entremeterse; **to chime in with** armonizar con
**chime clock** *s* péndola de carillón, reloj de carillón
**chimera** o **chimaera** [kɪ'mɪrə] o [kaɪ'mɪrə] *s* (myth., f.a. & fig.) quimera
**chimeric** [kɪ'mɪrɪk] o [kaɪ'mɪrɪk] o **chimerical** [kɪ'mɪrɪkəl] o [kaɪ'mɪrɪkəl] *adj* quimérico
**chimney** ['tʃɪmnɪ] *s* chimenea; tubo de vidrio de lámpara; **to smoke like a chimney** echar más humo que una chimenea
**chimney cap** *s* caperuza, mitra de chimenea
**chimney corner** *s* rincón de chimenea
**chimney jack** *s* mitra giratoria de chimenea; reparador de altas chimeneas
**chimney piece** *s* delantera de chimenea; adorno de chimenea
**chimney pot** *s* mitra de chimenea, guardavientos
**chimney sweep** *s* limpiachimeneas, limpiador de chimenea, deshollinador
**chimney swift** *s* (orn.) vencejo americano (*Chaetura pelagica*)
**chimpanzee** [tʃɪm'pænzɪ] o [ˌtʃɪmpæn'zi] *s* (zool.) chimpancé
**Chin.** abr. de **Chinese**
**chin** [tʃɪn] *s* barba, mentón; **to keep one's chin up** (coll.) no desanimarse; (*pret & pp:* **chinned;** *ger:* **chinning**) *va* **to chin oneself** colgarse de una barra alzándose con las manos hasta tocarla con la barba; *vn* (coll.) charlar, parlotear
**china** ['tʃaɪnə] *s* china, porcelana; (*cap.*) *s* China, la China
**China aster** *s* (bot.) reina Margarita, extraña
**chinaberry** ['tʃaɪnəˌbɛrɪ] *s* (*pl:* **-ries**) (bot.) jabonero de las Antillas; (bot.) acederaque
**china closet** *s* chinero
**Chinaman** ['tʃaɪnəmən] *s* (*pl:* **-men**) chino
**China pink** *s* (bot.) clavel de China
**China rose** *s* (bot.) rosa de China, tulipán (*Hibiscus rosa-sinensis*)
**China Sea** *s* mar de la China
**China silk** *s* china
**Chinatown** ['tʃaɪnəˌtaun] *s* (U.S.A.) barrio chino
**China tree** *s* (bot.) acederaque, cinamomo, agriaz, tuya de la China
**chinaware** ['tʃaɪnəˌwɛr] *s* porcelana, vajilla de porcelana
**chincapin** ['tʃɪŋkəpɪn] *s* var. de **chinquapin**
**chinch** [tʃɪntʃ] *s* (ent.) chinche; (ent.) chinche de los cereales
**chinch bug** *s* (ent.) chinche de los cereales
**chinchilla** [tʃɪn'tʃɪlə] *s* (zool.) chinchilla (*animal y piel*); tela de lana muy espesa (*se usa para sobretodos*)
**chine** [tʃaɪn] *s* espinazo; lomo (*carne del lomo del animal*); cresta, cima (*de las montañas*)
**Chinese** [tʃaɪ'niz] *adj* chino; *s* (*pl:* **-nese**) chino
**Chinese anise** *s* (bot.) badián
**Chinese gong** *s* (mus.) batintín
**Chinese lantern** *s* linterna china
**Chinese puzzle** *s* problema muy complicado
**Chinese Turkestan** *s* el Turquestán Chino
**Chinese Wall** *s* Gran muralla de la China
**chink** [tʃɪŋk] *s* grieta, hendedura, rajadura; sonido metálico; *va* agrietar, hender, rajar; rellenar (*junturas entre ladrillos*); *vn* agrietarse, henderse, rajarse; sonar metálicamente
**chinkapin** ['tʃɪŋkəpɪn] *s* (bot.) chincapino
**chinook** [tʃɪ'nuk] o [tʃɪ'nʊk] *s* chinuco (*viento que aparece por la parte oriental de las Montañas Rocosas*); (*cap.*) *s* chinuco (*indio norteamericano; idioma*)
**chinquapin** ['tʃɪŋkəpɪn] *s* (bot.) chincapino
**chin strap** *s* barbuquejo, carrillera
**chintz** [tʃɪnts] *s* quimón, zaraza
**chiolite** ['kaɪolaɪt] *s* (mineral.) chiolita
**Chios** ['kaɪɑs] *s* Quío
**chip** [tʃɪp] *s* astilla, brizna; saltadura (*defecto en la superficie de la piedra*); raspadura (*de la corteza del pan*); pedacito (*de alimento, dulce, etc.*); ficha (*en el póker*); viruta (*de madera*); (naut.) barquilla; **chip off the old block** hijo de su padre, hijo de su madre; **chip on one's shoulder** (coll.) propensión a pendencias; (*pret & pp:* **chipped;** *ger:* **chipping**) *va* astillar, descascarillar, desconchar; picar, tajar con cincel o hacha; **to chip in** (coll.) dar, contribuir; (coll.) contribuir con su cuota; *vn* saltar, astillarse, descascarillarse, desconcharse; **to chip in** (coll.) contribuir; (coll.) pagar en la apuesta
**chip ax** *s* azuela
**chipmunk** ['tʃɪpmʌŋk] *s* (zool.) ardilla listada
**chipper** ['tʃɪpər] *adj* (coll.) alegre, jovial, vivo
**chipping sparrow** *s* (orn.) gorrión norteamericano (*Spizella passerina*)
**chippy** ['tʃɪpɪ] *s* (*pl:* **-pies**) (zool.) ardilla listada; (orn.) gorrión norteamericano (*Spizella passerina*); (slang) chica; (slang) ramera
**chirk** [tʃʌrk] *adj* (coll.) alegre, vivo; *va* (coll.) alegrar, avivar; *vn* (coll.) alegrarse, avivarse
**chirographer** [kaɪ'rɑgrəfər] *s* quirógrafo
**chirographic** [ˌkaɪro'græfɪk] *adj* quirográfico
**chirography** [kaɪ'rɑgrəfɪ] *s* quirografía
**chiromancer** ['kaɪroˌmænsər] *s* quiromántico
**chiromancy** ['kaɪroˌmænsɪ] *s* quiromancía
**chiromantic** [ˌkaɪro'mæntɪk] o **chiromantical** [ˌkaɪro'mæntɪkəl] *adj* quiromántico
**Chiron** ['kaɪrɑn] *s* (myth.) Quirón
**chiropodist** [kaɪ'rɑpədɪst] o [kɪ'rɑpədɪst] *s* quiropodista
**chiropody** [kaɪ'rɑpədɪ] o [kɪ'rɑpədɪ] *s* quiropodia
**chiropractic** [ˌkaɪro'præktɪk] *adj* quiropráctico; *s* quiropráctica (*método de tratamiento*); quiropráctico (*persona*)
**chiropractor** ['kaɪroˌpræktər] *s* quiropráctico
**chiropteran** [kaɪ'rɑptərən] *adj & s* (zool.) quiróptero
**chirp** [tʃʌrp] *s* gorjeo; chirrido (*del grillo*); *va* decir de manera chirriante; *vn* gorjear; chirriar (*el grillo*); hablar alegremente
**chirr** [tʃʌr] *s* trino agudo (*p.ej., del saltón*); *vn* trinar agudamente
**chirrup** ['tʃɪrəp] o ['tʃʌrəp] *s* gorjeo repetido; chirrido repetido; chasquido (*de la lengua*); *va* decir de manera chirriante; *vn* gorjear repetidas veces; chirriar continuamente; chascar la lengua
**chisel** ['tʃɪzəl] *s* escoplo, formón; cincel (*para labrar piedras o metales*); (*pret & pp:* **-eled** o **-elled;** *ger:* **-eling** o **-elling**) *va & vn* escoplear; cincelar (*piedras o metales*); (slang) estafar, timar
**chiseler** o **chiseller** ['tʃɪzələr] *s* escopleador; (slang) estafador, timador
**chit** [tʃɪt] *s* chiquillo; chiquilla descarada; (Brit.) carta breve, esquela
**chit-chat** ['tʃɪtˌtʃæt] *s* charla, palique; chisme, hablilla
**chitin** ['kaɪtɪn] *s* (chem.) quitina
**chitinous** ['kaɪtɪnəs] *adj* quitinoso
**chiton** ['kaɪtɑn] *s* (hist. & zool.) quitón
**chitterlings** ['tʃɪtərlɪŋz] *spl* menudos comestibles del puerco
**chivalric** ['ʃɪvəlrɪk] o [ʃɪ'vælrɪk] *adj* caba-

lleresco (*perteneciente a la caballería*); caballeroso (*propio del caballero*)
**chivalrous** [ˈʃɪvəlrəs] *adj* caballeroso (*propio del caballero*); caballeresco (*perteneciente a la caballería*)
**chivalry** [ˈʃɪvəlrɪ] *s* caballería (*especialmente de la Edad Media; conjunto de caballeros*); caballerosidad (*calidad del caballero ideal; proceederes del caballero*); caballeros, personas de consideración
**chive** [tʃaɪv] *s* (bot.) cebollino, ajo moruno
**Ch.J.** abr. de **Chief Justice**
**chlamys** [ˈklemɪs] o [ˈklæmɪs] *s* (*pl:* **-myses** o **-mydes** [mɪdiz]) clámide
**Chloe** [klo·ɪ] *s* Cloe
**chloral** [ˈklorəl] *s* (chem.) cloral; (chem.) hidrato de cloral
**chloral hydrate** *s* (chem.) hidrato de cloral
**chlorate** [ˈkloret] o [ˈklorɪt] *s* (chem.) clorato
**chloric** [ˈklorɪk] *adj* (chem.) clórico
**chloric acid** *s* (chem.) ácido clórico
**chlorid** [ˈklorɪd] o **chloride** [ˈkloraɪd] o [ˈklorɪd] *s* (chem.) cloruro; (chem.) sal del ácido clorhídrico
**chloride of lime** *s* (chem.) cloruro de cal
**chlorin** [ˈklorɪn] *s* var. de **chlorine**
**chlorinate** [ˈklorɪnet] *va* clorinar; desinfectar con cloro
**chlorination** [ˌklorɪˈneʃən] *s* clorinación; desinfección con cloro
**chlorine** [ˈklorin] o [ˈklorɪn] *s* (chem.) cloro
**Chloris** [ˈklorɪs] *s* (myth.) Cloris
**chlorite** [ˈkloraɪt] *s* (chem.) clorito; (mineral.) clorita
**chloritic** [kloˈrɪtɪk] *adj* clorítico
**chloroform** [ˈklorəfɔrm] *s* (chem.) cloroformo; *va* (med.) cloroformizar; matar aplicando cloroformo
**chloromycetin** [ˌklorəmaɪˈsitɪn] *s* (pharm.) cloromicetina
**chlorophyl** o **chlorophyll** [ˈklorəfɪl] *s* (bot. & biochem.) clorofila
**chlorophyllin** [ˌkloraˈfɪlɪn] *s* (biochem.) clorofilina
**chlorophyllous** [ˌkloraˈfɪləs] *adj* clorofílico
**chloropicrin** [ˌkloraˈpɪkrɪn] o [ˌkloraˈpaɪkrɪn] *s* (chem.) cloropicrina
**chloroplast** [ˈklorəplæst] *s* (bot.) cloroplasto
**chloroprene** [ˈklorəprin] *s* (chem.) cloropreno
**chlorosis** [kloˈrosɪs] *s* (bot. & path.) clorosis
**chlorotic** [kloˈrɑtɪk] *adj* clorótico
**chlorous** [ˈklorəs] *adj* (chem.) cloroso
**chlortetracycline** [klorˌtɛtrəˈsaɪklin] o [klorˌtɛtrəˈsaɪklɪn] *s* (pharm.) clortetraciclina
**chm.** abr. de **chairman**
**choana** [ˈkoənə] *s* (anat.) coana
**chock** [tʃɑk] *s* cuña, calzo; (naut.) choque; *adv* lo más cerca posible, lo más estrechamente posible; enteramente, completamente; *va* acuñar, calzar; afianzar o apretar con calzos; (naut.) calzar
**chock-a-block** [ˈtʃɑkəˈblɑk] *adj* (naut.) a besar; apretado
**chock-full** [ˈtʃɑkˈfʊl] *adj* colmado, de bote en bote
**chocolate** [ˈtʃɔkəlɪt] o [ˈtʃɑkəlɪt] *s* chocolate; *adj* hecho de chocolate; achocolatado, de color de chocolate
**chocolate candy** *s* confite o dulce de chocolate
**choice** [tʃɔɪs] *s* elección, selección, escogimiento; opción; lo selecto, lo más escogido; **to have no choice** no tener alternativa; *adj* selecto, escogido, excelente, superior
**choir** [kwaɪr] *s* coro; (mus., arch. & theol.) coro; *va & vn* corear
**choirboy** [ˈkwaɪrˌbɔɪ] *s* infante de coro, niño de coro
**choir desk** *s* facistol
**choir loft** *s* coro
**choirmaster** [ˈkwaɪrˌmæstər] o [ˈkwaɪrˌmɑstər] *s* jefe de coro, maestro de capilla
**choir practice** *s* ensayo de coro
**choir stall** *s* asiento del coro; **choir stalls** *spl* sillería
**choke** [tʃok] *s* estrangulación; (aut.) cierre u obturador (*del carburador*); (elec.) choque; *va* sofocar, ahogar, estrangular; reprimir, suprimir; tapar, obstruir; (aut.) obturar; **to choke back** contener, retener; **to choke down** oprimir, sujetar; atragantar; **to choke off** parar, detener; poner fin a; deshacerse de; **to choke up** tapar, obstruir; *vn* sofocarse; no poder respirar; atragantarse; **to choke on** atragantarse con; **to choke up** atragantarse; taparse, obstruirse
**chokeberry** [ˈtʃokˌbɛrɪ] *s* (*pl:* **-ries**) (bot.) amelanquier
**chokebore** [ˈtʃokˌbor] *s* (arti.) calibre estrangulado; arma de fuego de calibre estrangulado
**chokecherry** [ˈtʃokˌtʃɛrɪ] *s* (*pl:* **-ries**) (bot.) cerezo silvestre norteamericano (*Prunus virginiana*); cereza silvestre
**choke coil** *s* (elec.) bobina de choque
**chokedamp** [ˈtʃokˌdæmp] *s* (min.) mofeta
**choker** [ˈtʃokər] *s* ahogador, sofocador, estrangulador; (mach.) obturador; (elec.) bobina de reacción; (coll.) ahogador, cuello alto; (coll.) pena (*joya que se anudaba al cuello*)
**cholagogue** [ˈkɑləgɑg] *adj & s* (med.) colagogo
**cholecystectomy** [ˌkɑləsɪsˈtɛktəmɪ] *s* (*pl:* **-mies**) (surg.) colecistectomía
**cholecystostomy** [ˌkɑləsɪsˈtɑstəmɪ] *s* (*pl:* **-mies**) (surg.) colecistostomía
**choler** [ˈkɑlər] *s* cólera, ira
**cholera** [ˈkɑlərə] *s* (path.) cólera
**cholera infantum** [ɪnˈfæntəm] *s* (path.) cólera infantil
**cholera morbus** [ˈmɔrbəs] *s* (path.) cólera morbo
**cholera nostras** [ˈnɑstræs] *s* (path.) cólera nostras
**choleric** [ˈkɑlərɪk] *adj* colérico (*irascible*)
**cholerine** [ˈkɑlərɪn] o [ˈkɑləraɪn] *s* (path.) colerina
**cholesterin** [kəˈlɛstərɪn] *s* (biochem.) colesterina
**cholesterol** [kəˈlɛstərol] o [kəˈlɛstərɑl] *s* (biochem.) colesterol
**choline** [ˈkolin] o [ˈkɑlin] *s* (biochem.) colina
**cholla** [ˈtʃoljɑ] *s* (bot.) cholla
**chondriome** [ˈkɑndrɪom] *s* (biol.) condrioma
**chondriosome** [ˈkɑndrɪoˌsom] *s* (biol.) condriosoma
**chondrology** [kɑnˈdrɑlədʒɪ] *s* condrología
**choose** [tʃuz] (*pret:* **chose**; *pp:* **chosen**) *va* elegir, escoger; optar por; *vn* optar; **to choose between** optar entre (*p.ej., dos candidatos*); **to choose to** + *inf* optar por + *inf*
**choosy** [ˈtʃuzɪ] *adj* (slang) melindroso, quisquilloso
**chop** [tʃɑp] *s* golpe cortante; tajada; chuleta (*costilla con carne*); mandíbula; mejilla; marca, sello; licencia, permiso; (box.) martillazo; (coll.) grado, calidad; **chops** *spl* quijada; boca, labios; (*pret & pp:* **chopped**; *ger:* **chopping**) *va* cortar, tajar; desmenuzar; picar (*la carne*); abrirse (*paso*) cortando; arrojar, mover a tirones; **to chop off** tronchar; *vn* moverse a tirones; cambiar, variar súbito; virar (*el viento*); **to chop at** querer cortar; tratar de atrapar con la boca
**chophouse** [ˈtʃɑpˌhaʊs] *s* restaurán donde se sirven principalmente chuletas, bifteks, etc.
**chopine** [tʃoˈpin] o [ˈtʃɑpɪn] *s* chapín (*chanclo de corcho de mujer*)
**chopper** [ˈtʃɑpər] *s* hachero, tajador; hacha, hachuela; cortante (*cuchilla grande del carnicero*)
**chopping block** *s* tajo
**choppy** [ˈtʃɑpɪ] *adj* (*comp:* **-pier**; *super:* **-piest**) agitado (*mar*); variable (*viento*); cortado (*estilo*)
**chopsticks** [ˈtʃɑpˌstɪks] *spl* palillos (*de que se sirven los chinos para comer*)
**chop suey** [ˌtʃɑpˈsuɪ] *s* chopsuey (*olla china*)
**choral** [ˈkorəl] *adj* (mus.) coral; [koˈrɑl] o [ˈkorəl] *s* (mus.) coral
**chorale** [koˈrɑl] o [ˈkorəl] *s* (mus.) coral
**choral music** *s* música coreada
**choral society** *s* orfeón
**chord** [kɔrd] *s* (mus.) acorde; (aer., anat., eng. & geom.) cuerda; (fig.) cuerda sensible
**chordate** [ˈkɔrdet] *adj & s* (zool.) cordado
**chore** [tʃor] *s* faena, tarea, quehacer
**chorea** [koˈriə] *s* (path.) corea
**choreographer** [ˌkorɪˈɑgrəfər] *s* coreógrafo
**choreographic** [ˌkorɪəˈgræfɪk] *adj* coreográfico
**choreography** [ˌkorɪˈɑgrəfɪ] *s* coreografía
**choriamb** [ˈkorɪæmb] o [ˈkɑrɪæmb] *s* coriambo

**choriambic** [ˌkorɪˈæmbɪk] o [ˌkɑrɪˈæmbɪk] *adj & s* coriámbico
**choric** [ˈkorɪk] *adj* coral
**chorine** [ˈkorin] o [koˈrin] *s* (slang) corista
**chorion** [ˈkorɪɑn] *s* (embryol. & zool.) corión
**chorister** [ˈkɑrɪstər] o [ˈkɔrɪstər] *s* corista; infante o niño de coro; jefe de coro
**chorographer** [koˈrɑgrəfər] *s* corógrafo
**chorographic** [ˌkorəˈgræfɪk] o **chorographical** [ˌkorəˈgræfɪkəl] *adj* corográfico
**chorography** [koˈrɑgrəfɪ] *s* corografía
**choroid** [ˈkorɔɪd] *adj* coroideo, coroides; *s* (anat.) coroides, membrana coroides
**chortle** [ˈtʃɔrtəl] *s* resoplido alegre; *vn* resoplar alegremente
**chorus** [ˈkorəs] *s* (theat. & mus.) coro; concierto; estribillo; **in chorus** en coro; *vn* hablar o cantar en coro; contestar a una voz
**chorus girl** *s* (theat.) corista
**chorus man** *s* (theat.) corista
**chose** [tʃoz] *pret de* **choose**
**chosen** [ˈtʃozən] *adj* selecto, escogido; *pp de* **choose**
**chough** [tʃʌf] *s* (orn.) chova; (orn.) chova pinariega, grajo de pico amarillo
**chow** [tʃaʊ] *s* chao (*perro chino*); (slang) comida, alimento
**chow-chow** [ˈtʃaʊˌtʃaʊ] *s* conserva china; encurtidos con mostaza, divididos y mezclados
**chowder** [ˈtʃaʊdər] *s* sancocho de almejas o pescado, con patatas, cebollas, etc.
**chow mein** [ˌtʃaʊˈmen] *s* fideos fritos servidos con un guisado de carne, cebollas, apio, etc.
**Chr.** abr. de **Christian**
**chrestomathy** [krɛsˈtɑməθɪ] *s* (*pl:* **-thies**) crestomatía
**Chris** [krɪs] *s* nombre abreviado de **Christopher**
**chrism** [ˈkrɪzəm] *s* (eccl.) crisma
**chrismal** [ˈkrɪzməl] *adj & s* (eccl.) crismal
**chrismatory** [ˈkrɪzməˌtorɪ] *s* (*pl:* **-ries**) crismera
**chrismon** [ˈkrɪzmɑn] *s* (*pl:* **-ma** [mə]) crismón
**Christ** [kraɪst] *s* Cristo
**christcross** [ˈkrɪsˌkrɔs] o [ˈkrɪsˌkrɑs] *s* cristus
**christen** [ˈkrɪsən] *va* bautizar (*a una persona; un buque; dar nombre a*); (coll.) estrenar (*usar por primera vez*)
**Christendom** [ˈkrɪsəndəm] *s* cristiandad
**christening** [ˈkrɪsənɪŋ] *s* bautismo, bautizo
**Christian** [ˈkrɪstʃən] *adj* cristiano; (coll.) honesto, decente; *s* cristiano; (coll.) persona honesta, persona decente; Cristián (*nombre de varón*)
**Christian Brothers** *spl* hermanos de la doctrina (cristiana)
**Christian Era** *s* era cristiana, era de Cristo
**Christianity** [ˌkrɪstʃɪˈænɪtɪ] *s* cristianismo
**Christianization** [ˌkrɪstʃənɪˈzeʃən] *s* cristianización
**Christianize** [ˈkrɪstʃənaɪz] *va* cristianizar
**Christianly** [ˈkrɪstʃənlɪ] *adj* cristiano; *adv* cristianamente
**Christian name** *s* nombre de pila o de bautismo
**Christian Science** *s* ciencia cristiana
**Christian Scientist** *s* adepto de la ciencia cristiana
**Christine** [krɪsˈtin] *s* Cristina
**Christlike** [ˈkraɪstˌlaɪk] o **Christly** [ˈkraɪstlɪ] *adj* propio de Jesucristo, evangélico
**Christmas** [ˈkrɪsməs] *s* Navidad; *adj* navideño
**Christmas card** *s* tarjeta navideña, aleluya navideña, christmas
**Christmas carol** *s* villancico, villancico de Nochebuena o de Navidad
**Christmas Day** *s* Navidad, día de Navidad
**Christmas Eve** *s* víspera de Navidad, nochebuena
**Christmas gift** *s* aguinaldo, regalo de Navidad
**Christmas holidays** *spl* fiestas navideñas
**Christmas rose** *s* (bot.) eléboro negro
**Christmastide** [ˈkrɪsməsˌtaɪd] *s* tiempo de Navidad
**Christmas tree** *s* árbol de Navidad
**Christopher** [ˈkrɪstəfər] *s* Cristóbal
**Christ's-thorn** [ˈkraɪstsˌθɔrn] *s* (bot.) espina santa
**chromate** [ˈkromet] *s* (chem.) cromato

**chromatic** [kroˈmætɪk] *adj* cromático; (mus.) cromático; **chromatics** *ssg* cromática
**chromatic aberration** *s* (opt.) aberración cromática
**chromatically** [kroˈmætɪkəlɪ] *adv* cromáticamente
**chromatic scale** *s* (mus.) escala cromática
**chromatin** [ˈkromətɪn] *s* (biol.) cromatina
**chromatism** [ˈkromətɪzəm] *s* cromatismo; (bot.) cromismo
**chromatophore** [ˈkromətəˌfor] *s* (biol.) cromatóforo
**chrome** [krom] *s* (chem.) cromo; *adj* cromado; *va* cromar
**chrome green** *s* verde de cromo
**chrome red** *s* rojo de cromo
**chrome steel** *s* acerocromo
**chrome yellow** *s* amarillo de cromo
**chromic** [ˈkromɪk] *adj* (chem.) crómico
**chrominance** [ˈkromɪnəns] *s* (phys.) crominancia
**chromite** [ˈkromaɪt] *s* (chem.) cromito; (mineral.) cromita
**chromium** [ˈkromɪəm] *s* (chem.) cromo
**chromium plating** *s* cromado
**chromium steel** *s* acerocromo
**chromo** [ˈkromo] *s* (*pl:* **-mos**) cromo (*estampa*); (slang) trasto
**chromogen** [ˈkromədʒən] *s* (chem.) cromógeno
**chromogenic** [ˌkroməˈdʒɛnɪk] *adj* cromógeno
**chromolithograph** [ˌkromoˈlɪθəgræf] o [ˌkromoˈlɪθəgrɑf] *s* cromolitografía (*estampa*); *va* cromolitografiar
**chromolithographer** [ˌkromolɪˈθɑgrəfər] *s* cromolitógrafo
**chromolithographic** [ˌkromoˌlɪθəˈgræfɪk] *adj* cromolitográfico
**chromolithography** [ˌkromolɪˈθɑgrəfɪ] *s* cromolitografía
**chromophore** [ˈkroməfor] *s* (chem.) cromóforo
**chromoplasm** [ˈkroməplæzəm] *s* (biol.) cromoplasma
**chromoplast** [ˈkroməplæst] *s* (bot.) cromoplasto
**chromoscope** [ˈkroməskop] *s* (telv.) cromoscopio
**chromosome** [ˈkroməsom] *s* (biol.) cromosoma
**chromosphere** [ˈkroməsfɪr] *s* (astr.) cromosfera
**chromotypography** [ˌkromotaɪˈpɑgrəfɪ] *s* cromotipografía
**chromous** [ˈkroməs] *adj* (chem.) cromoso
**chron.** abr. de **chronological** y **chronology**
**Chron.** abr. de **Chronicles**
**chronic** [ˈkrɑnɪk] *adj* crónico
**chronically** [ˈkrɑnɪkəlɪ] *adv* crónicamente
**chronicle** [ˈkrɑnɪkəl] *s* crónica; **Chronicles** *spl* (Bib.) Crónicas (*nombre que dan los protestantes a los Paralipómenos*); *va* historiar, anotar o poner en una crónica; contar, narrar
**chronicler** [ˈkrɑnɪklər] *s* cronista
**chronograph** [ˈkrɑnəgræf] o [ˈkrɑnəgrɑf] *s* cronógrafo
**chronologic** [ˌkrɑnəˈlɑdʒɪk] o **chronological** [ˌkrɑnəˈlɑdʒɪkəl] *adj* cronológico
**chronologist** [krəˈnɑlədʒɪst] *s* cronologista o cronólogo
**chronology** [krəˈnɑlədʒɪ] *s* (*pl:* **-gies**) cronología
**chronometer** [krəˈnɑmɪtər] *s* cronómetro
**chronometry** [krəˈnɑmɪtrɪ] *s* cronometría
**chronoscope** [ˈkrɑnəskop] *s* cronoscopio
**chrysalid** [ˈkrɪsəlɪd] *s* var. de **chrysalis**
**chrysalis** [ˈkrɪsəlɪs] *s* (*pl:* **chrysalises** o **chrysalides** [krɪˈsælɪdiz]) *s* (ent.) crisálida
**chrysanthemum** [krɪˈsænθɪməm] *s* (bot.) crisantemo
**Chryseis** [kraɪˈsiɪs] *s* (myth.) Criseida
**chrysoberyl** [ˈkrɪsoˌbɛrɪl] *s* (mineral.) crisoberilo
**chrysolite** [ˈkrɪsolaɪt] *s* (mineral.) crisólito
**chrysoprase** [ˈkrɪsoprez] *s* (mineral.) crisoprasa
**Chrysostom, Saint John** [ˈkrɪsəstəm] o [krɪsˈɑstəm] San Juan Crisóstomo
**chrysotile** [ˈkrɪsətɪl] *s* (mineral.) crisotilo
**chub** [tʃʌb] *s* (ichth.) cacho
**chubby** [ˈtʃʌbɪ] *adj* (*comp:* **-bier;** *super:* **-biest**) rechoncho, gordiflón
**chuck** [tʃʌk] *s* mamola (*bajo la barbilla de una*

*persona*); echada, tirada; (mach.) mandril, portaherramienta; lomo (*tajada de carne de vaca*); *va* hacer la mamola a; arrojar
**chuck-full** [ˈtʃʌkˈfʊl] *adj* colmado, de bote en bote
**chuckhole** [ˈtʃʌkˌhol] *s* badén
**chuckle** [ˈtʃʌkəl] *s* risa ahogada; *vn* reírse ahogadamente
**chucklehead** [ˈtʃʌkəlˌhɛd] *s* (coll.) tonto, estúpido
**chug** [tʃʌg] *s* ruido explosivo corto; (*pret & pp:* **chugged;** *ger:* **chugging**) *vn* (coll.) hacer ruidos explosivos repetidos; (coll.) moverse con ruidos explosivos repetidos
**chukkar** o **chukker** [ˈtʃʌkər] *s* (sport) período en el juego de polo
**chum** [tʃʌm] *s* (coll.) compinche; (coll.) compañero de cuarto; (*pret & pp:* **chummed;** *ger:* **chumming**) *vn* (coll.) ser compinche, ser compinches; (coll.) compartir un cuarto, vivir en un mismo cuarto
**chummy** [ˈtʃʌmɪ] *adj* (*comp:* **-mier;** *super:* **-miest**) (coll.) íntimo, muy amigable
**chump** [tʃʌmp] *s* tarugo, zoquete, leño grueso; extremidad gruesa; (coll.) tonto, estúpido; (slang) cabeza
**chunk** [tʃʌŋk] *s* pedazo grueso (*p.ej., de madera*); (coll.) persona rechoncha
**chunky** [ˈtʃʌŋkɪ] *adj* (*comp:* **-ier;** *super:* **-iest**) (coll.) corto y grueso; (coll.) rechoncho
**church** [tʃʌrtʃ] *s* iglesia; **to go into the church** entrar en la iglesia (*el estado eclesiástico*); **to go to church** ir a la iglesia
**churchgoer** [ˈtʃʌrtʃˌgoər] *s* devoto, fiel; iglesiero (Am.)
**churchly** [ˈtʃʌrtʃlɪ] *adj* eclesiástico
**churchman** [ˈtʃʌrtʃmən] *s* (*pl:* **-men**) sacerdote, eclesiástico; miembro de una iglesia, feligrés
**church member** *s* miembro de una iglesia, feligrés
**church militant** *s* iglesia militante
**church music** *s* música de iglesia, música sagrada
**Church of Christ, Scientist** *s* Iglesia de la ciencia cristiana
**Church of England** *s* Iglesia de Inglaterra, Iglesia anglicana
**Church of Jesus Christ of Latter-day Saints** *s* Iglesia de Jesucristo de los santos del día final (*iglesia de los mormones*)
**Church Slavic** o **Slavonic** *s* eslavoeclesiástico (*idioma*)
**church supplies** *spl* artículos del culto
**church triumphant** *s* iglesia triunfante
**churchwarden** [ˈtʃʌrtʃˌwɔrdən] *s* capiller; (coll.) pipa de fumar larga, hecha de arcilla
**churchwoman** [ˈtʃʌrtʃˌwʊmən] *s* (*pl:* **-women**) mujer miembro de una iglesia, feligresa
**churchyard** [ˈtʃʌrtʃˌjɑrd] *s* patio de iglesia; cementerio
**churl** [tʃʌrl] *s* patán, palurdo
**churlish** [ˈtʃʌrlɪʃ] *adj* palurdo, grosero, insolente
**churn** [tʃʌrn] *s* agitación; batido; mantequera; *va* mazar (*leche*), batir en una mantequera, hacer (*mantequilla*) en una mantequera; agitar, revolver
**churr** [tʃʌr] *s & vn* var. de **chirr**
**chute** [ʃut] *s* canal o conducto inclinado; tolva; cascada, salto de agua; recial
**chutney** [ˈtʃʌtnɪ] *s* salsa picante compuesta de frutas, hierbas, pimienta, etc.
**chyle** [kaɪl] *s* (physiol.) quilo
**chyliferous** [kaɪˈlɪfərəs] *adj* quilífero
**chylification** [ˌkaɪlɪfɪˈkeʃən] *s* (physiol.) quilificación
**chylify** [ˈkaɪlɪfaɪ] (*pret & pp:* **-fied**) *va* (physiol.) quilificar; *vn* (physiol.) quilificarse
**chylous** [ˈkaɪləs] *adj* quiloso
**chyme** [kaɪm] *s* (physiol.) quimo
**chymification** [ˌkaɪmɪfɪˈkeʃən] o [ˌkɪmɪfɪˈkeʃən] *s* (physiol.) quimificación
**chymify** [ˈkaɪmɪfaɪ] (*pret & pp:* **-fied**) (physiol.) *va* quimificar
**chymous** [ˈkaɪməs] *adj* quimoso
**ciborium** [sɪˈborɪəm] *s* (*pl:* **-a** [ə]) (arch.) ciborio, baldaquín; (eccl.) copón
**cicada** [sɪˈkedə] o [sɪˈkɑdə] *s* (*pl:* **-das** o **-dae** [di]) (ent.) cigarra
**cicatrice** [ˈsɪkətrɪs] *s* var. de **cicatrix**
**cicatricle** [ˈsɪkəˌtrɪkəl] *s* (bot. & embryol.) cicatrícula
**cicatrix** [ˈsɪkətrɪks] o [sɪˈketrɪks] *s* (*pl:* **cicatrices** [ˌsɪkəˈtraɪsiz]) cicatriz; (bot.) cicatriz
**cicatrize** [ˈsɪkətraɪz] *va* cicatrizar; *vn* cicatrizarse
**cicely** [ˈsɪsəlɪ] *s* (*pl:* **-lies**) (bot.) perifollo oloroso
**Cicero** [ˈsɪsəro] *s* Cicerón
**cicerone** [ˌtʃitʃəˈrone] o [ˌsɪsəˈronɪ] *s* (*pl:* **-ni** [nɪ] o **-nes**) cicerone
**Ciceronian** [ˌsɪsəˈronɪən] *adj* ciceroniano
**cider** [ˈsaɪdər] *s* sidra
**cider press** *s* lagar para sacar el zumo de las manzanas
**c.i.f.** o **C.I.F.** abr. de **cost, insurance, and freight**
**cigar** [sɪˈgɑr] *s* cigarro, cigarro puro
**cigar band** *s* anillo (de cigarro)
**cigar case** *s* cigarrera
**cigar cutter** *s* cortacigarros, cortapuros
**cigaret** o **cigarette** [ˌsɪgəˈrɛt] *s* cigarrillo, pitillo
**cigarette case** *s* pitillera
**cigarette holder** *s* boquilla
**cigarette lighter** *s* encendedor de cigarrillos
**cigarette paper** *s* papel de fumar
**cigar holder** *s* boquilla
**cigar lighter** *s* encendedor de cigarros
**cigar store** *s* estanco, tabaquería
**cilia** [ˈsɪlɪə] *spl* cilios, pestañas; (bot. & zool.) cilios
**ciliary** [ˈsɪlɪˌɛrɪ] *adj* (anat.) ciliar
**ciliate** [ˈsɪlɪet] o [ˈsɪlɪɪt] *adj* ciliado; *s* (zool.) ciliado
**ciliated** [ˈsɪlɪˌetɪd] *adj* ciliado
**Cimmerian** [sɪˈmɪrɪən] *adj* cimerio; obscuro, sombrío; *s* cimerio
**cinch** [sɪntʃ] *s* cincha (*de una silla o albarda*); (coll.) agarro firme; (slang) breva (*cosa fácil*); *va* cinchar; (slang) agarrar
**cinchona** [sɪnˈkonə] *s* (bot.) quino, cascarillo; (pharm.) quina, cascarilla
**cinchona bark** *s* (pharm.) quina, corteza del cascarillo
**cinchonism** [ˈsɪnkənɪzəm] *s* (path.) quinismo
**cincture** [ˈsɪŋktʃər] *s* cinturón, cincho; cerco; *va* cercar
**cinder** [ˈsɪndər] *s* carbonilla, ceniza; *va* reducir a cenizas
**cinder block** *s* bloque de concreto de cenizas
**Cinderella** [ˌsɪndəˈrɛlə] *s* la Cenicienta
**cinder path** *s* sendero de cenizas
**cinder track** *s* pista de cenizas para carreras a pie
**cinema** [ˈsɪnɪmə] *s* cine
**cinematograph** [ˌsɪnɪˈmætəgræf] o [ˌsɪnɪˈmætəgrɑf] *s* cinematógrafo; *va & vn* cinematografiar
**cineraria** [ˌsɪnəˈrɛrɪə] *s* (bot.) cineraria
**cinerarium** [ˌsɪnəˈrɛrɪəm] *s* (*pl:* **-a** [ə]) lugar cinerario
**cinerary** [ˈsɪnəˌrɛrɪ] *adj* cinerario
**cingulum** [ˈsɪŋgjələm] *s* (*pl:* **-la** [lə]) cíngulo (*del alba de un sacerdote*); (anat., bot. & zool.) cíngulo
**cinnabar** [ˈsɪnəbɑr] *s* cinabrio (*mineral y color*)
**cinnamic** [sɪˈnæmɪk] o [ˈsɪnəmɪk] *adj* (chem.) cinámico
**cinnamon** [ˈsɪnəmən] *s* (bot.) canelo; canela (*corteza y especia*); *adj* acanelado
**cinquefoil** [ˈsɪŋkˌfɔɪl] *s* (bot.) cincoenrama, quinquefolio; (arch.) rosetón de cinco lóbulos
**cion** [ˈsaɪən] *s* (hort. & fig.) vástago
**cipher** [ˈsaɪfər] *s* cifra; cero; clave (*de una cifra*); monograma, cifra; (fig.) cero, cero a la izquierda; *adj* cifrado; de ningún valor, de ninguna importancia; *va* cifrar (*escribir en cifra*); numerar, calcular; *vn* numerar, calcular
**cipher device** *s* cifrador
**cipher message** *s* mensaje cifrado
**circa** [ˈsʌrkə] *prep* a eso de, cerca de, hacia
**Circassian** [sərˈkæʃən] *adj & s* circasiano
**Circe** [ˈsʌrsɪ] *s* (myth.) Circe
**circinate** [ˈsʌrsɪnet] *adj* (bot.) circinado
**circle** [ˈsʌrkəl] *s* círculo; circo; **to square the circle** cuadrar el círculo; *va* circuir, circun-

dar; dar la vuelta a; girar alrededor de; *vn* dar vueltas
**circlet** ['sʌrklɪt] *s* anillo; círculo pequeño; adorno en forma de círculo
**circuit** ['sʌrkɪt] *s* circuito; (elec.) circuito; *va* circular por; contornear; *vn* circular; hacer un circuito
**circuit breaker** *s* (elec.) disyuntor, interruptor automático
**circuit court** *s* (law) tribunal cuyos jueces administran justicia a intervalos regulares en varios lugares de un distrito
**circuitous** [sər'kjuɪtəs] *adj* tortuoso, indirecto
**circuit rider** *s* clérigo metodista que andaba de sitio en sitio para pronunciar sermones
**circuitry** ['sʌrkɪtrɪ] *s* (*pl:* **-ries**) (elec.) trazado de circuito; conjunto de los elementos de un circuito; sistema de circuitos
**circular** ['sʌrkjələr] *adj* circular; tortuoso, indirecto; *s* circular, carta circular
**circularity** [ˌsʌrkjə'lærɪtɪ] *s* circularidad
**circularize** ['sʌrkjələraɪz] *va* dirigir circulares a; dar forma circular a
**circular measure** *s* medición del círculo en grados sexagesimales
**circular saw** *s* sierra circular
**circulate** ['sʌrkjəlet] *va & vn* circular
**circulating capital** *s* (econ.) capital circulante
**circulating library** *s* biblioteca circulante
**circulation** [ˌsʌrkjə'leʃən] *s* circulación
**circulatory** ['sʌrkjələˌtorɪ] *adj* circulatorio
**circumambient** [ˌsʌrkəm'æmbɪənt] *adj* circumambiente
**circumcise** ['sʌrkəmsaɪz] *va* circuncidar
**circumcision** [ˌsʌrkəm'sɪʒən] *s* circuncisión
**circumference** [sər'kʌmfərəns] *s* circunferencia
**circumferential** [sərˌkʌmfə'rɛnʃəl] *adj* circunferencial
**circumflex** ['sʌrkəmflɛks] *adj* (anat. & gram.) circunflejo; *s* (gram.) circunflejo
**circumflex accent** *s* acento circunflejo
**circumfluent** [sər'kʌmfluənt] *adj* circunfluente
**circumfuse** [ˌsʌrkəm'fjuz] *va* difundir en derredor
**circumjacent** [ˌsʌrkəm'dʒesənt] *adj* circunyacente
**circumlocution** [ˌsʌrkəmlo'kjuʃən] *s* circunlocución, circunloquio
**circumnavigate** [ˌsʌrkəm'nævɪget] *va* circunnavegar
**circumnavigation** [ˌsʌrkəmˌnævɪ'geʃən] *s* circunnavegación
**circumnavigator** [ˌsʌrkəm'nævɪˌgetər] *s* circunnavegador
**circumpolar** [ˌsʌrkəm'polər] *adj* circumpolar
**circumscribe** [ˌsʌrkəm'skraɪb] *va* circunscribir; (geom.) circunscribir
**circumscript** ['sʌrkəmskrɪpt] *adj* circunscrito
**circumscription** [ˌsʌrkəm'skrɪpʃən] *s* circunscripción
**circumspect** ['sʌrkəmspɛkt] *adj* circunspecto
**circumspection** [ˌsʌrkəm'spɛkʃən] *s* circunspección
**circumstance** ['sʌrkəmstæns] *s* circunstancia; ostentación, ceremonia; **to be in easy circumstances** estar acomodado; **under no circumstances** de ninguna manera, no importa cuáles sean las circunstancias; **under the circumstances** en las circunstancias
**circumstantial** [ˌsʌrkəm'stænʃəl] *adj* circunstancial; circunstanciado (*detallado*)
**circumstantial evidence** *s* (law) indicios vehementes, evidencia circunstancial
**circumstantiate** [ˌsʌrkəm'stænʃɪet] *va* relatar con todas las circunstancias, probar o sostener detalladamente
**circumvallate** [ˌsʌrkəm'vælet] *va* circunvalar
**circumvallation** [ˌsʌrkəmvə'leʃən] *s* circunvalación
**circumvent** [ˌsʌrkəm'vɛnt] *va* embaucar, engañar; entrampar; evitar, desviarse de
**circumvention** [ˌsʌrkəm'vɛnʃən] *s* embaucamiento, engaño; evitación
**circumvolution** [ˌsʌrkəmvə'luʃən] *s* circunvolución
**circus** ['sʌrkəs] *s* circo; (coll.) persona o cosa muy divertida; *adj* circense
**Circus Maximus** ['mæksɪməs] *s* circo máximo
**cirque** [sʌrk] *s* circo; (geol.) circo; (poet.) anillo, círculo pequeño
**cirrhosis** [sɪ'rosɪs] *s* (path.) cirrosis
**cirrhotic** [sɪ'rɑtɪk] *adj* cirrótico
**cirriped** ['sɪrɪpɛd] *adj & s* (zool.) cirrípedo o cirrópodo
**cirro-cumulus** [ˌsɪro'kjumjələs] *s* (meteor.) cirrocúmulo
**cirro-stratus** [ˌsɪro'stretəs] *s* (meteor.) cirrostrato
**cirrus** ['sɪrəs] *s* (*pl:* **-ri** [raɪ]) (bot., zool. & meteor.) cirro
**cisalpine** [sɪs'ælpaɪn] o [sɪs'ælpɪn] *adj* cisalpino
**cisandine** [sɪs'ændaɪn] o [sɪs'ændɪn] *adj* cisandino
**cisatlantic** [ˌsɪsæt'læntɪk] *adj* cisatlántico
**cisco** ['sɪsko] *s* (*pl:* **-coes** o **-cos**) (ichth.) arenque de lago (*Leucichthys*)
**cissoid** ['sɪsɔɪd] *s* (geom.) cisoide
**cistaceous** [sɪs'teʃəs] *adj* (bot.) cistáceo
**Cistercian** [sɪs'tʌrʃən] *adj & s* cisterciense
**Cistercian Order** *s* orden *f* del Cister
**cistern** ['sɪstərn] *s* cisterna; (anat.) cisterna
**citadel** ['sɪtədəl] *s* (fort.) ciudadela
**citation** [saɪ'teʃən] o [sɪ'teʃən] *s* citación; (law) citación; (mil.) mención
**cite** [saɪt] *va* citar; (law) citar; (mil.) mencionar; mover, incitar
**cithara** ['sɪθərə] *s* (mus.) cítara (*lira griega*)
**cither** ['sɪθər] *s* (mus.) cítara (*lira griega; instrumento músico parecido a la guitarra*)
**cithern** ['sɪθərn] *s* (mus.) cítara (*instrumento músico parecido a la guitarra*)
**citified** ['sɪtɪfaɪd] *adj* urbanizado
**citizen** ['sɪtɪzən] *s* ciudadano; paisano (*el que no es militar*); *adj* ciudadano
**citizeness** ['sɪtɪzənɪs] *s* ciudadana
**citizen of the world** *s* ciudadano del mundo
**citizenry** ['sɪtɪzənrɪ] *s* ciudadanos, conjunto de ciudadanos
**citizenship** ['sɪtɪzənˌʃɪp] *s* ciudadanía
**citrate** ['sɪtret] o ['saɪtret] *s* (chem.) citrato
**citrate of magnesia** *s* (med.) citrato de magnesia
**citric** ['sɪtrɪk] *adj* (chem.) cítrico
**citric acid** *s* (chem.) ácido cítrico
**citrin** ['sɪtrɪn] *s* (biochem.) citrina
**citron** ['sɪtrən] *s* (bot.) cidro (*Citrus medica*); cidra (*fruto*); cidrada (*corteza confitada*)
**citronella** [ˌsɪtrə'nɛlə] *s* (bot.) limoncillo; esencia de limoncillo
**citron melon** *s* (bot.) sandía de carne blanca
**citrous** ['sɪtrəs] *adj* auranciáceo
**citrus** ['sɪtrəs] *adj* auranciáceo; *s* (bot.) cidro (*cualquier planta del género Citrus*); cidra (*fruto*)
**citrus fruit** *s* agrios (*fruto de cualquier planta del género Citrus*)
**cittern** ['sɪtərn] *s* var. de **cithern**
**city** ['sɪtɪ] *s* (*pl:* **-ies**) ciudad; **the City** el centro comercial, bancario y bursátil de Londres; **City** Interior o Ciudad (*palabra que se pone al sobrescrito de una carta que va al interior de la ciudad*); *adj* ciudadano; urbano
**city clerk** *s* archivero de municipio
**city council** *s* ayuntamiento
**city editor** *s* (U.S.A.) redactor de periódico encargado de las noticias locales; (Brit.) redactor de periódico encargado de las noticias comerciales y bancarias
**city fathers** *spl* concejales
**city hall** *s* ayuntamiento, casa consistorial, palacio municipal
**city limits** *spl* casco urbano
**city manager** *s* administrador municipal escogido por el ayuntamiento o por alguna comisión
**City of Brotherly Love** *s* ciudad del amor fraternal (*Filadelfia*)
**City of David** *s* ciudad de David (*Jerusalén; Belén*)
**City of God** *s* ciudad de Dios (*el paraíso*)
**City of Masts** *s* ciudad de los mástiles (*Londres*)
**City of the Seven Hills** *s* ciudad de las siete colinas (*Roma*)
**city plan** *s* plano de la ciudad
**city planner** *s* urbanista
**city planning** *s* urbanismo, urbanización

**city room** *s* redacción de un periódico (*lugar donde se redacta; conjunto de los redactores*)
**city-state** ['sɪtɪ'stet] *s* ciudad-estado
**civet** ['sɪvɪt] *s* algalia, civeto
**civet bean** (bot.) frijol iztagapa
**civet cat** *s* (zool.) algalia, civeta, gato de algalia
**civic** ['sɪvɪk] *adj* cívico; **civics** *ssg* estudio de los deberes, derechos y privilegios de los ciudadanos
**civies** ['sɪvɪz] *spl* (coll.) traje de paisano, ropas civiles; **in civies** (coll.) de paisano
**civil** ['sɪvɪl] *adj* civil
**civil defense** *s* defensa civil, protección civil
**civil disobedience** *s* desobediencia civil
**civil engineer** *s* ingeniero civil
**civil engineering** *s* ingeniería civil
**civilian** [sɪ'vɪljən] *adj* civil; *s* hombre civil, paisano
**civilian clothes** *spl* traje de paisano
**civility** [sɪ'vɪlɪtɪ] *s* (*pl:* **-ties**) civilidad
**civilization** [,sɪvɪlɪ'zeʃən] *s* civilización
**civilize** ['sɪvɪlaɪz] *va* civilizar; *vn* civilizarse
**civilized** ['sɪvɪlaɪzd] *adj* civilizado
**civil law** *s* derecho civil
**civil liberty** *s* libertad civil
**civilly** ['sɪvɪlɪ] *adv* civilmente
**civil marriage** *s* matrimonio civil
**civil rights** *s* derechos civiles
**civil servant** *s* empleado de servicio civil oficial
**civil service** *s* servicio civil oficial
**civil war** *s* guerra civil; **Civil War** *s* (U.S.A.) Guerra civil, Guerra entre Norte y Sur
**civil year** *s* año civil
**civism** ['sɪvɪzəm] *s* civismo
**civvies** ['sɪvɪz] *spl* (coll.) var. de **civies**
**clabber** ['klæbər] *s* cuajada de leche agria; *vn* cuajarse agriándose
**clack** [klæk] *s* ruido corto y agudo; charla; *vn* producir ruidos cortos y agudos; charlar
**clack valve** *s* (hyd.) chapaleta
**clad** [klæd] *pret & pp de* **clothe**
**cladoceran** [klə'dɑsərən] *adj & s* (zool.) cladócero
**cladode** ['klædod] *s* (bot.) cladodio
**claim** [klem] *s* demanda; reclamación; afirmación, declaración; (min.) pertenencia; **to jump a claim** usurpar el terreno o la mina que una persona ha denunciado; **to lay claim to** reclamar, reivindicar; *va* demandar; reclamar; afirmar, declarar; (min.) denunciar; **to claim to be** pretender ser
**claim agent** *s* agente de reclamación
**claimant** ['klemənt] *s* demandante; reclamante; (min.) denunciante; pretendiente (*al trono*)
**claim check** *s* comprobante
**clairvoyance** [klɛr'vɔɪəns] *s* clarividencia (*penetración, perspicacia; doble vista*)
**clairvoyant** [klɛr'vɔɪənt] *adj* clarividente (*perspicaz; que pretende poseer la doble vista*); *s* clarividente (*persona que pretende poseer la doble vista*)
**clam** [klæm] *s* (zool.) almeja; (coll.) chiticalla (*persona muy callada*); (*pret & pp:* **clammed;** *ger:* **clamming**) *vn* pescar almejas
**clambake** ['klæm,bek] *s* jira campestre en que se asan almejas
**clamber** ['klæmbər] *s* trepa desmañada o difícil; *vn* trepar, subir gateando
**clammy** ['klæmɪ] *adj* (*comp:* **-mier;** *super:* **-miest**) frío y húmedo
**clamor** ['klæmər] *s* clamor, clamoreo; *va & vn* clamorear
**clamorous** ['klæmərəs] *adj* clamoroso
**clamp** [klæmp] *s* abrazadera; tornillo de banco; (naut.) contradurmiente; *va* afianzar o sujetar con abrazadera; asegurar en el tornillo de banco; *vn* pisar recio; **to clamp down on** (coll.) coaccionar, apretar los tornillos a
**clamshell** ['klæm,ʃɛl] *s* concha de almeja; cucharón de almeja o de quijadas, pala de doble concha
**clamshell bucket** *s* cucharón de almeja o de quijadas, pala de doble concha
**clan** [klæn] *s* clan
**clandestine** [klæn'dɛstɪn] *adj* clandestino
**clang** [klæŋ] *s* fuerte sonido metálico como de campana; tantán (*de un yunque*); *va* hacer sonar fuertemente; *vn* sonar fuertemente
**clangor** ['klæŋgər] o ['klæŋər] *s* sonido metálico desapacible, estruendo
**clangorous** ['klæŋgərəs] o ['klæŋərəs] *adj* estrepitoso, retumbante
**clank** [klæŋk] *s* sonido metálico seco; *va* hacer sonar secamente; *vn* sonar secamente
**clannish** ['klænɪʃ] *adj* tribal; exclusivista
**clansman** ['klænzmən] *s* (*pl:* **-men**) miembro de un clan
**clap** [klæp] *s* golpe seco, estampido; trueno; palmoteo; (slang) gonorrea; (*pret & pp:* **clapped;** *ger:* **clapping**) *va* batir (*palmas*); aplaudir; poner o colocar de prisa; **to clap eyes on** (coll.) clavar la vista en; **to clap shut** cerrar de golpe; **to clap up** poner en la cárcel; *vn* estallar; palmear, palmotear
**clapboard** ['klæbərd] o ['klæp,bord] *s* chilla, tabla de chilla; *va* cubrir con tablas de chilla
**clap of thunder** *s* estampido de trueno
**clapper** ['klæpər] *s* golpeador; palmoteador; badajo (*de campana*); tarabilla, cítola; castañuelas; (coll.) lengua
**claptrap** ['klæp,træp] *s* faramalla, engañabobos; latiguillo (*de actor*); *adj* faramallón
**claque** [klæk] *s* claque
**Clare** [klɛr] *s* Clara; clarisa (*religiosa*)
**clarence** ['klærəns] *s* clarens (*coche*)
**claret** ['klærɪt] *s* clarete; rojo purpurado; (slang) sangre
**clarification** [,klærɪfɪ'keʃən] *s* clarificación
**clarifier** ['klærɪ,faɪər] *s* clarificador; clarificadora (*vasija en que se clarifica el guarapo del azúcar*)
**clarify** ['klærɪfaɪ] (*pret & pp:* **-fied**) *va* clarificar
**clarinet** [,klærɪ'nɛt] *s* (mus.) clarinete
**clarinetist** o **clarinettist** [,klærɪ'nɛtɪst] *s* clarinete o clarinetista (*músico que toca el clarinete*)
**clarion** ['klærɪən] *s* (mus.) clarín (*instrumento músico; registro del órgano*); (poet.) sonido del clarín; (poet.) sonido de clarín; *adj* claro y agudo
**clarionet** [,klærɪə'nɛt] *s* var. de **clarinet**
**clarity** ['klærɪtɪ] *s* claridad
**clary** ['klɛrɪ] *s* (*pl:* **-ies**) (bot.) amaro, esclarea
**clash** [klæʃ] *s* choque, encontrón; estruendo; *va* batir, golpear ruidosamente; *vn* chocar
**clasp** [klæsp] o [klɑsp] *s* broche, corchete; cierre; hebilla; abrazadera; abrazo; agarro; *va* abrochar, encorchetar; abrazar; agarrar, apretar (*la mano*); apretarse (*la mano*)
**clasp knife** *s* navaja (*cuya hoja puede doblarse y quedar guardada dentro del mango*)
**class.** abr. de **classical**
**class** [klæs] o [klɑs] *s* clase; (slang) excelencia; (slang) elegancia, buen tono; **the classes** las clases más altas de la sociedad; *va* clasificar; *vn* clasificarse
**classbook** ['klæs,bʊk] o ['klɑs,bʊk] *s* libro de clase; libro publicado por una clase de la escuela (*sobre todo la que está para graduarse*)
**class-conscious** ['klæs'kɑnʃəs] o ['klɑs'kɑnʃəs] *adj* consciente de su clase social
**class consciousness** *s* conciencia o conocimiento de la clase social a que uno pertenece
**class day** *s* (U.S.A.) día en que los miembros de una clase que va a graduarse celebran su graduación
**class hour** *s* (educ.) hora de clase
**classic** ['klæsɪk] *adj & s* clásico; **the classics** las obras clásicas (*de la literatura romana y griega*)
**classical** ['klæsɪkəl] *adj* clásico
**classically** ['klæsɪkəlɪ] *adv* clásicamente
**classical scholar** *s* erudito en las lenguas clásicas
**classicism** ['klæsɪsɪzəm] *s* clasicismo
**classicist** ['klæsɪsɪst] *s* clasicista
**classification** [,klæsɪfɪ'keʃən] *s* clasificación
**classification yard** *s* (rail.) patio de clasificación
**classified** ['klæsɪfaɪd] *adj* clasificado; clasificado como secreto
**classified ads** *spl* anuncios clasificados (en secciones)
**classifier** ['klæsɪ,faɪər] *s* (min.) clasificador
**classify** ['klæsɪfaɪ] (*pret & pp:* **-fied**) *va* clasificar
**class legislation** *s* legislación clasista
**classmate** ['klæs,met] o ['klɑs,met] *s* compañero de clase, condiscípulo

**classroom** ['klæs,rum] o ['klɑs,rum] *s* sala de clase
**class struggle** *s* lucha de clases
**classy** ['klæsɪ] *adj* (*comp:* **-ier;** *super:* **-iest**) (slang) elegante, de categoría
**clatter** ['klætər] *s* martilleo, estruendo confuso; algazara, gresca; trápala (*del trote de un caballo*); *va* hacer chocar ruidosamente; *vn* chocar ruidosamente; moverse o caer con estruendo confuso; hablar rápida y ruidosamente; **to clatter down the steps** bajar la escalera ruidosamente
**Claud** o **Claude** [klɔd] o **Claudius** ['klɔdɪəs] *s* Claudio
**clause** [klɔz] *s* cláusula (*disposición de un contrato u otro documento*); (gram.) oración dependiente
**claustral** ['klɔstrəl] *adj* var. de **cloistral**
**claustrophobia** [,klɔstrə'fobɪə] *s* (path.) claustrofobia
**claustrum** ['klɔstrəm] *s* (*pl:* **-tra** [trə]) (anat.) claustro
**clava** ['klevə] *s* (*pl:* **-vae** [vi]) (anat.) clava
**clavate** ['klevet] *adj* (bot. & zool.) claviforme
**clavichord** ['klævɪkɔrd] *s* (mus.) clavicordio
**clavicle** ['klævɪkəl] *s* (anat.) clavícula
**clavicular** [klə'vɪkjələr] *adj* clavicular
**claviculate** [klə'vɪkjəlet] *adj* (zool.) claviculado
**clavier** ['klævɪər] o [klə'vɪr] *s* (mus.) teclado; (mus.) teclado sin sonido para practicar; [klə'vɪr] *s* (mus.) clave, clavicordio, piano u otro instrumento musical con teclado
**claw** [klɔ] *s* (zool.) garra; (zool.) uña; (zool.) pinza (*de langosta, cangrejo, etc.*); oreja (*de martillo, llave de tuerca, etc.*); arañazo; mano, dedos; *va* agarrar; desgarrar; arañar; *vn* arañar, arañar ligeramente
**claw bar** *s* sacaclavos de horquilla
**claw clutch** *s* (mach.) embrague de garra
**claw hammer** *s* martillo de orejas, martillo sacaclavos; (coll.) frac
**clay** [kle] *s* arcilla; *va* arcillar; (agr.) arcillar
**clayey** ['kleɪ] *adj* (*comp:* **clayier;** *super:* **clayiest**) arcilloso
**claymore** ['klemor] *s* claymore (*espada escocesa*)
**clay pigeon** *s* pichón de barro (*disco de arcilla lanzado al aire en el tiro al blanco*)
**clay pipe** *s* pipa de fumar hecha de arcilla, pipa de tierra
**clay pit** *s* gredal, mina de arcilla
**clay soil** *s* terreno arcilloso
**clay stone** *s* piedra arcillosa; piedra formada a base de arcilla
**claytonia** [kle'tonɪə] *s* (bot.) claitonia
**clean** [klin] *adj* limpio; neto, distinto; completo, perfecto; liso, parejo; diestro, hábil; bien hecho, bien proporcionado; *adv* completamente, totalmente; limpio, limpiamente; **to come clean** (slang) confesarlo todo; *va* limpiar, asear; **to be cleaned out** (slang) quedar limpio (*sin dinero*); **to clean out** limpiar vaciando; limpiar (*p.ej., las ramas pequeñas de un árbol*); agotar, consumir; (slang) limpiar (*hurtando o en el juego*); **to clean up** limpiar completamente; arreglar; (mach.) alinear; (coll.) acabar, completar; (slang) sacar de ganancia; *vn* limpiarse, asearse; **to clean up** limpiarse, asearse; (coll.) llevárselo todo; (coll.) hacer mesa limpia (*en el juego*); (slang) ganar mucho dinero; **to clean up after someone** limpiar lo que alguno ha ensuciado
**clean bill of health** *s* patente limpia de sanidad; certificado de aptitud
**clean-cut** ['klin,kʌt] *adj* bien definido; bien tallado; claro, definido; de buen parecer
**cleaner** ['klinər] *s* limpiador; tintorero; quitamanchas (*persona y substancia*); **to send to the cleaners** (slang) dejar limpio, limpiarle a (*uno*) todo el dinero
**cleanhanded** ['klin'hændɪd] *adj* con las manos limpias, sin culpa
**cleaning** ['klinɪŋ] *s* limpiadura, aseo; **cleanings** *spl* limpiaduras (*desperdicios*)
**cleaning fluid** *s* quitamanchas
**cleaning rag** *s* trapo para limpiar, paño de limpiar
**cleaning rod** *s* (arti.) baqueta de limpieza
**cleaning woman** *s* criada que limpia la casa
**clean-limbed** ['klin'lɪmbd] *adj* de piernas bien proporcionadas
**cleanliness** ['klɛnlɪnɪs] *s* limpieza habitual; esmero (*en la compostura de la persona*)
**cleanly** ['klɛnlɪ] *adj* (*comp:* **-lier;** *super:* **-liest**) limpio (*que tiene el hábito de la limpieza*); ['klinlɪ] *adv* limpiamente
**cleanness** ['klinnɪs] *s* limpieza, aseo
**cleanse** [klɛnz] *va* limpiar, depurar, purificar
**clean-shaven** ['klin'ʃevən] *adj* lisamente afeitado
**cleanup** ['klin,ʌp] *s* limpieza general; (slang) gran ganancia; **to make a cleanup** (slang) hacer su pacotilla
**clear** [klɪr] *adj* claro; despejado (*sin nubes*); libre (*de culpa, deudas, estorbos, etc.*); seguro, cierto; neto, líquido; entero, completo; **clear of** libre de (*p.ej., deudas*); a distancia de; **in the clear** por dentro ‖ *adv* claro, claramente; enteramente, completamente; sin tocar, sin alcanzar; **clear through** de lado a lado ‖ *va* aclarar; clarificar; desembarazar; desmontar, rebajar (*un terreno*); salvar, saltar por encima de; pasar por un lado de, sin tocar; abonar, acreditar; absolver, probar la inocencia de; sacar (*una ganancia neta*); desocupar (*un cuarto*); (naut.) despachar en la aduana; (com.) pasar (*un cheque*) por un banco de liquidación; (com.) liquidar (*una cuenta*); **to clear a ship for action** (nav.) alistar un buque para el combate; **to clear an equation of fractions** (math.) quitar los denominadores de una ecuación; **to clear away** u **off** quitar (*estorbos u obstáculos*); desocupar; desmontar, rebajar; quitar (*la mesa*); **to clear out** limpiar, desembarazar desechando o vaciando; **to clear the way** abrir camino; **to clear up** aclarar, clarificar; arreglar, ordenar; desembarazar ‖ *vn* aclararse; clarificarse; desembarazarse; justificarse; (naut.) despacharse después de pagados los derechos de aduana; **to clear away** u **off** irse, desaparecer; **to clear out** (coll.) irse, salirse, escabullirse; **to clear up** abonanzar (*el tiempo o una situación embarazosa*); despejarse (*el cielo, el tiempo*)
**clearance** ['klɪrəns] *s* aclaración; abono, acreditación; espacio libre (*entre dos cosas que pasan la una al lado de la otra sin tocarse*); (mach.) espacio muerto (*en un cilindro*); (mach.) intersticio (*p.ej., de una turbina hidráulica*); (elec.) distancia radial (*entre el polo y el inducido*); (com.) compensación
**clearance sale** *s* venta de liquidación
**clear-cut** ['klɪr,kʌt] *adj* claro, definido; bien delineado
**clear-headed** ['klɪr'hɛdɪd] *adj* inteligente, perspicaz
**clearing** ['klɪrɪŋ] *s* claro (*en un bosque*); (com.) compensación
**clearing house** *s* (com.) cámara de compensación
**clearness** ['klɪrnɪs] *s* claridad
**clear-sighted** ['klɪr'saɪtɪd] *adj* perspicaz; (fig.) perspicaz
**clearstarch** ['klɪr,stɑrtʃ] *va* almidonar con una mezcla ligera de almidón y agua
**clearstory** ['klɪr,storɪ] *s* (*pl:* **-ries**) var. de **clerestory**
**cleat** [klit] *s* abrazadera, listón, fiador; (naut.) tojino; (naut.) cornamusa (*para amarrar cabos*); *va* enlistonar; (naut.) asegurar con o en tojino, cornamusa, etc.
**cleavage** ['klivɪdʒ] *s* hendedura, división; (biol.) segmentación del óvulo; (fig.) desunión
**cleave** [kliv] (*pret:* **cleaved, cleft** o **clove;** *pp:* **cleaved, cleft** o **cloven**) *va* hender, rajar, dividir; penetrar; abrir (*trocha en la selva*); cortar (*la cabeza*); partir (*el corazón*); hender (*las aguas un buque, los aires una flecha, las nubes un avión, etc.*); *vn* henderse, rajarse; (*pret & pp:* **cleaved**) *vn* adherirse, pegarse; ser fiel, ser leal
**cleaver** ['klivər] *s* rajadera, cortante, cuchilla de carnicero; **cleavers** *s* (*pl:* **-ers**) (bot.) presera, galio
**cleek** [klik] *s* (golf) maza de hierro para lanzamientos a distancia
**clef** [klɛf] *s* (mus.) clave
**cleft** [klɛft] *s* raja, grieta, hendedura; *adj* rajado, hendido; *pret & pp de* **cleave**

**cleft palate** *s* palatosquisis, fisura del paladar
**cleistogamous** [klaɪs'tɑgəməs] *adj* (bot.) cleistógamo
**clematis** ['klɛmətɪs] *s* (bot.) clemátide
**clemency** ['klɛmənsɪ] *s* (*pl:* **-cies**) clemencia; benignidad, suavidad
**clement** ['klɛmənt] *adj* clemente; benigno, suave; (*cap.*) *s* Clemente
**clench** [klɛntʃ] *s* agarro; *va* agarrar; cerrar o apretar (*el puño, los dientes*); remachar (*la punta de un clavo ya clavado*)
**Cleon** ['kliɑn] *s* Cleón
**clepsydra** ['klɛpsɪdrə] *s* (*pl:* **-dras** o **-drae** [dri]) reloj de agua, clepsidra
**clerestory** ['klɪr,storɪ] *s* (*pl:* **-ries**) (arch.) claraboya
**clergy** ['klʌrdʒɪ] *s* (*pl:* **-gies**) clero, clerecía
**clergyman** ['klʌrdʒɪmən] *s* (*pl:* **-men**) clérigo, sacerdote, eclesiástico, pastor
**cleric** ['klɛrɪk] *adj* clerical; *s* clérigo
**clerical** ['klɛrɪkəl] *adj* clerical; oficinesco; *s* clérigo; clerical (*partidario del clero*); **clericals** *spl* (coll.) hábitos clericales
**clerical error** *s* error de pluma
**clericalism** ['klɛrɪkəlɪzəm] *s* clericalismo
**clericalist** ['klɛrɪkəlɪst] *s* clerical
**clerical work** *s* trabajo de oficina
**clerk** [klʌrk] *s* dependiente de tienda, vendedor; oficinista, escribiente; archivero (*de municipio*); (law) escribano; lego, seglar (*en una iglesia*); (hist.) clérigo (*hombre de estudios*); *vn* trabajar como dependiente, oficinista, etc.
**clerkly** ['klʌrklɪ] *adj* (*comp:* **-lier**; *super:* **-liest**) de dependiente; clerical
**clerkship** ['klʌrkʃɪp] *s* empleo de dependiente, empleo de oficinista; (law) escribanía; secretaría
**cleveite** ['klivaɪt] *s* (mineral.) cleveíta
**clever** ['klɛvər] *adj* inteligente; hábil, diestro, mañoso
**cleverness** ['klɛvərnɪs] *s* inteligencia; habilidad, destreza, maña; gracia
**clevis** ['klɛvɪs] *s* horquilla, abrazadera
**clew** [klu] *s* indicio, pista, guía; ovillo; (naut.) puño; (naut.) anillo de hierro fijado al puño; *va* (naut.) levantar (*la vela*) sirviéndose del anillo fijado al puño
**cliché** [kli'ʃe] *s* (print.) clisé; (fig.) cliché (*frase hecha, idea gastada*)
**click** [klɪk] *s* golpecito; tecleo (*de la máquina de escribir*); piñoneo (*del arma de fuego*); taconeo; chasquido (*de la lengua*); *va* chascar (*la lengua*); **to click the heels** taconear; cuadrarse (*militarmente*); *vn* sonar con un golpecito seco; piñonear (*un arma de fuego*)
**client** ['klaɪənt] *s* cliente; cliente de abogado
**clientele** [,klaɪən'tɛl] *s* clientela
**cliff** [klɪf] *s* risco, escarpa, precipicio
**cliff dweller** *s* hombre de las rocas
**cliff dwelling** *s* casa o cueva construída en las rocas
**cliff swallow** *s* (orn.) golondrina de las rocas
**climacteric** [klaɪ'mæktərɪk] o [,klaɪmæk'tɛrɪk] *adj* climatérico; *s* climatérico o climaterio
**climactic** [klaɪ'mæktɪk] *adj* climáxico, culminante
**climate** ['klaɪmɪt] *s* clima
**climatic** [klaɪ'mætɪk] *adj* climático
**climatically** [klaɪ'mætɪkəlɪ] *adv* climáticamente
**climatology** [,klaɪmə'tɑlədʒɪ] *s* climatología
**climax** ['klaɪmæks] *s* (rhet.) clímax; colmo; **to cap the climax** ser el colmo; *va & vn* terminar
**climb** [klaɪm] *s* trepa; subida; subidero; *va* trepar, escalar, subir; *vn* trepar, escalar, subir; **to climb down** bajar a gatas; descender; (coll.) cejar, rendirse; **to climb up** trepar por
**climber** ['klaɪmər] *s* trepador; subidor; ambicioso de figurar; garfio, trepador (*clavo puntiagudo fijado en el zapato para facilitar la subida*); (bot.) trepadora, enredadera; (orn.) trepadora; **climber of hills** (aut.) subidor de cuestas
**climb indicator** *s* (aer.) ascensómetro, indicador de ascensión
**climbing belt** *s* cinturón de seguridad
**climbing fish** *s* (ichth.) anabas
**climbing irons** *spl* garfios, trepadores, crampones
**clime** [klaɪm] *s* (poet.) clima, país, región, plaga
**clinch** [klɪntʃ] *s* agarro; abrazo; remache, roblón; (box.) clincha; (naut.) entalingadura; **to be in a clinch** estar agarrados, estar abrazados; *va* agarrar; abrazar; afianzar, sujetar o fijar con firmeza; apretar (*el puño, los dientes*); remachar, roblar (*un clavo ya clavado*); afirmar, resolver decisivamente; (naut.) entalingar; *vn* abrazarse fuertemente; luchar cuerpo a cuerpo
**clincher** ['klɪntʃər] *s* remachador; clavo de remachar; (coll.) argumento decisivo; neumático de talón
**clincher tire** *s* neumático de talón
**cling** [klɪŋ] (*pret & pp:* **clung**) *vn* adherirse, pegarse
**clingstone** ['klɪŋ,ston] *s* pavía, albérchiga, peladillo; *adj* de hueso adherente, de carne pegada al hueso (*dícese del melocotón o pérsico*)
**clingy** ['klɪŋɪ] *adj* pegajoso
**clinic** ['klɪnɪk] *s* clínica
**clinical** ['klɪnɪkəl] *adj* clínico
**clinical chart** *s* hoja clínica
**clinically** ['klɪnɪkəlɪ] *adv* clínicamente
**clinical thermometer** *s* termómetro clínico
**clinician** [klɪ'nɪʃən] *s* clínico
**clink** [klɪŋk] *s* tintín (*sonido metálico ligero*); (coll.) cárcel; *va* hacer tintinar; *vn* tintinar
**clinker** ['klɪŋkər] *s* escoria de hulla; escoria de cemento; ladrillo muy duro; masa de ladrillos derretidos; *vn* formar escorias
**clinker-built** ['klɪŋkər,bɪlt] *adj* de tingladillo
**clinker work** *s* tingladillo
**clinometer** [klaɪ'nɑmɪtər] *s* clinómetro
**Clio** ['klaɪo] *s* (myth.) Clío
**clip** [klɪp] *s* tijereteo, cercenadura, esquileo; movimiento rápido; grapa, pinza; sujetapapeles, presilla de alambre; (coll.) golpe seco y súbito; **clips** *spl* tijeras; **at a good clip** a paso rápido; (*pret & pp:* **clipped**; *ger:* **clipping**) *va* tijeretear, cercenar, esquilar; cercenar (*el borde de las monedas*) dañandolas; agarrar, afianzar; recortar (*p.ej., un cupón*), acortar; (phonet.) apocopar; (coll.) golpear súbito con golpe seco; **to clip the wings of** cortar las alas a, cortar los vuelos a; *vn* moverse con rapidez
**clipped word** *s* palabra apocopada (*como* **prof** [prɑf] *por* **professor**)
**clipper** ['klɪpər] *s* cercenador; recortador; tijera, cizalla; (naut. & aer.) clíper; **clippers** *spl* maquinilla para cortar el pelo; guadañadora, tijeras podadoras
**clipper-built** ['klɪpər,bɪlt] *adj* (naut.) construído y aparejado para gran rapidez
**clipping** ['klɪpɪŋ] *s* recorte; tijereteo; esquileo; *adj* (coll.) rápido; (slang) excelente, de primera clase
**clique** [klik] *s* pandilla, compadraje, corrillo
**cliquish** ['klikɪʃ] *adj* exclusivista
**clitellum** [klɪ'tɛləm] o [klaɪ'tɛləm] *s* (*pl:* **-la** [lə]) (zool.) clitelo
**clitoris** ['klaɪtərɪs] o ['klɪtərɪs] *s* (anat.) clítoris
**clk.** abr. de **clerk** y **clock**
**cloaca** [klo'ekə] *s* (*pl:* **-cae** [si]) cloaca; (zool.) cloaca
**cloak** [klok] *s* capa, capote; disimulo, excusa; *va* encapotar; disimular, encubrir
**cloak-and-dagger** ['klokən'dægər] *adj* de capa y espada
**cloak-and-sword** ['klokənd'sord] *adj* de capa y espada
**cloak hanger** *s* cuelgacapas
**cloakroom** ['klok,rum] o ['klok,rʊm] *s* guardarropa (*sitio*); (Brit.) excusado, retrete
**clobber** ['klɑbər] *va* (slang) apalear, tundir; (slang) derrotar completamente
**cloche** [kloʃ] *s* campana de cristal; sombrero de mujer de ajuste estrecho
**clock** [klɑk] *s* reloj; cuadrado (*en las medias*); **round the clock** noche y día, todas las horas del día; **to turn the clock back** retrasar el reloj; quitarse años, fingir menos edad; remontarse al pasado; *va* registrar; (sport) cronometrar; bordar con cuadrado; *vn* **to clock in** marcar (*el obrero o el empleado*) la hora de

entrada en el reloj registrador; **to clock out** marcar (*el obrero o el empleado*) la hora de salida en el reloj registrador
**clockmaker** ['klak,mekər] *s* relojero
**clock meter** *s* (elec.) limitador de corriente
**clock tower** *s* torre reloj
**clockwise** ['klak,waɪz] *adj & adv* en el sentido de las agujas del reloj
**clockwork** ['klak,wʌrk] *s* aparato de relojería; **like clockwork** como un reloj
**clod** [klad] *s* tierra; terrón; palurdo, zoquete
**clodhopper** ['klad,hapər] *s* destripaterrones, patán; **clodhoppers** *spl* zapatos grandes y fuertes
**clog** [klag] *s* estorbo, obstáculo; traba (*para atar los pies del caballo*); chanclo, galocha; zueco (*usado en bailes*); zapateado; (*pret & pp:* **clogged;** *ger:* **clogging**) *va* atascar; estorbar; *vn* atascarse; bailar el zapateado
**clog dance** *s* zapateado
**clog dancer** *s* zapateador
**cloisonné** [,klɔɪzə'ne] *s* esmalte alveolado o tabicado
**cloister** ['klɔɪstər] *s* claustro; *va* enclaustrar
**cloistral** ['klɔɪstrəl] *adj* claustral
**clonic** ['klanɪk] *adj* clónico
**clonus** ['klonəs] *s* (path.) clono
**close** [klos] *adj* cercano, próximo; estrecho; casi igual, casi a la par, con corta distancia; cerrado, apretado; compacto (*p.ej., tejido*); exacto, estricto, riguroso; pesado, sofocante; mal ventilado; encerrado; limitado; avaro, mezquino; escaso; minucioso; reñido (*combate, carrera, etc.*); (phonet.) cerrado; **at close range** de cerca, a corta distancia ‖ *s* cercado, recinto; atrio (*de una catedral o abadía*) ‖ [kloz] *s* fin, terminación; cierre (*p.ej., de la Bolsa*); **at the close of day** a la caída de la tarde ‖ [kloz] *va* cerrar; tapar; concluir; cerrar (*un trato, un contrato*); saldar (*una cuenta*); (elec.) cerrar (*un circuito*); **to close down** cerrar completamente; **to close in** cerrar, encerrar; **to close out** vender en liquidación; saldar (*una cuenta*); **to close ranks** estrechar las distancias; (mil.) cerrar las filas; **to close up** poner más cerca; cerrar por completo; **close quote** fin de la cita ‖ *vn* cerrarse; reunirse; concordarse; (sport) luchar cuerpo a cuerpo; **to close down** cerrarse por completo; **to close in** acercarse rodeando; **to close in on** cercar, rodear; **to close up** ponerse más cerca; cerrarse por completo; cicatrizarse; **to close with** cerrar con (*p.ej., el enemigo*)
**close call** *s* (coll.) escape difícil o milagroso, escape por un pelo
**close column** *s* (mil.) columna cerrada
**close confinement** *s* prisión estrecha, estado de incomunicado
**close connection** *s* intimidad, relación estrecha; combinación de trenes sin mucho margen entre la llegada de un tren y la salida del siguiente
**close corporation** *s* (com.) sociedad anónima cuyos dignatarios son dueños de las acciones
**closed car** *s* automóvil o coche cerrado, conducción interior
**closed chapter** *s* asunto concluído
**closed circuit** *s* (elec.) circuito cerrado
**closed-circuit battery** ['klozd'sʌrkɪt] *s* (elec.) pila de circuito cerrado
**closed-circuit television** *s* televisión en circuito cerrado
**closed season** *s* veda
**closed shop** *s* taller agremiado
**closed syllable** *s* (phonet.) sílaba cerrada
**close election** *s* elección muy reñida
**close fertilization** *s* (bot.) autofecundación
**closefisted** ['klos'fɪstɪd] *adj* manicorto, cicatero, tacaño
**close-fitting** ['klos'fɪtɪŋ] *adj* ajustado, ceñido al cuerpo
**close-grained** ['klos'grend] *adj* de grano fino o cerrado
**close-hauled** ['klos'hɔld] *adj* (naut.) de bolina
**close-lipped** ['klos'lɪpt] *adj* callado, reservado
**closely** ['kloslɪ] *adv* de cerca; estrechamente; estrictamente; fielmente; sólidamente; con avaricia; **closely printed** de impresión compacta
**close-mouthed** ['klos'mauðd] o ['klos'mauθt] *adj* callado, reservado
**closeness** ['klosnɪs] *s* cercanía, proximidad; estrechez, intimidad; avaricia, tacañería; reserva, discreción; pesantez (*de la atmósfera*); falta de aire, mala ventilación; fidelidad (*de una traducción*)
**close order** *s* (mil.) formación cerrada
**close quarters** *spl* lucha casi cuerpo a cuerpo; posición muy cerrada, lugar muy estrecho
**close shave** *s* afeitado a ras; (coll.) escape difícil o milagroso, escape por un pelo
**closet** ['klazɪt] *s* armario, alacena; gabinete, retrete; gabinete privado; aposento, gabinete (*muchas veces situado debajo de la escalera*); guardarropa *m*; *va* encerrar en un gabinete para una entrevista secreta
**close to the wind** *adj* (naut.) de bolina
**close translation** *s* traducción fiel
**close-up** ['klos,ʌp] *s* vista de cerca; fotografía de cerca
**close-woven** ['klos'wovən] *adj* estrechamente tejido
**closing** ['klozɪŋ] *s* cerradura; (phonet.) cerrazón
**closure** ['kloʒər] *s* cierre; encierro; fin, término, conclusión; (phonet.) oclusión; clausura (*de un debate*)
**clot** [klat] *s* grumo, coágulo, cuajarón; (*pret & pp:* **clotted;** *ger:* **clotting**) *vn* engrumecerse, coagularse, cuajarse
**cloth** [klɔθ] o [klaθ] *s* (*pl:* **cloths** [klɔðz], [klaðz], [klɔθs] o [klaθs]) *s* tela, paño; trapo; vestidura clerical; clerecía; (b.b.) tela; (naut.) vela, lona
**clothe** [kloð] (*pret & pp:* **clothed** o **clad**) *va* vestir; trajear; cubrir, revestir; investir (*p.ej., de autoridad*); **clothes** [kloz] o [kloðz] *spl* ropa, vestidos; ropa de cama; **to change clothes** cambiar de ropa
**clothesbasket** ['kloz,bæskɪt] *s* cesto grande para ropa, cesto de la colada
**clothesbrush** ['kloz,brʌʃ] *s* cepillo de ropa
**clothes dryer** *s* secadora de ropa
**clothes hanger** *s* colgador de ropa
**clotheshorse** ['kloz,hɔrs] *s* enjugador, secarropa de travesaños
**clothesline** ['kloz,laɪn] *s* cordel para tender la ropa
**clothespin** ['kloz,pɪn] *s* alfiler de madera, pinza (*para tender la ropa*)
**clothes pole** *s* berlinga
**clothes press** *s* guardarropa, armario para guardar ropa
**clothes rack** *s* colgadero, perchero
**clothes tree** *s* percha
**clothes wringer** *s* exprimidor de ropa
**clothier** ['kloðjər] *s* fabricante de ropa; ropero; pañero
**clothing** ['kloðɪŋ] *s* ropa, vestidos; ropaje
**Clotho** ['kloθo] *s* (myth.) Cloto
**cloth of gold** *s* tela de oro
**cloth prover** *s* cuentahilos
**cloth yard** *s* yarda (*medida que equivale a 91 centímetros*)
**cloture** ['klotʃər] *s* clausura (*de un debate*)
**cloud** [klaud] *s* nube (*masa de vapores suspendida en el aire; multitud; mancha o sombra que se nota en piedras preciosas; cualquier cosa que altera la serenidad*); nubarrón (*nube grande y negra*); **in the clouds** entre las nubes, altísimo; ilusorio, quimérico; teórico; distraído, lleno de ensueños; **under a cloud** desacreditado, bajo sospecha; en aprietos; sombrío, melancólico; *va* anublar; entristecer; *vn* anublarse
**cloud bank** *s* mar de nubes
**cloudberry** ['klaud,bɛrɪ] *s* (*pl:* **-ries**) (bot.) camemoro; baya del camemoro
**cloudburst** ['klaud,bʌrst] *s* chaparrón, turbión
**cloud-capped** ['klaud,kæpt] *adj* coronado de nubes, altísimo
**cloud chamber** *s* (phys.) cámara anublada, cámara de niebla
**cloudiness** ['klaudɪnɪs] *s* nubosidad, nebulosidad
**cloudless** ['klaudlɪs] *adj* sin nubes
**cloudlet** ['klaudlɪt] *s* nube pequeña
**cloud of dust** *s* polvareda, nube de polvo
**cloud rack** *s* masa de nubes altas y algo separadas

**cloud seeding** *s* siembra de una substancia en las nubes para producir lluvia artificial
**cloudy** [ˈklaʊdɪ] *adj* (*comp:* **-ier;** *super:* **-iest**) nublado; vaporoso; turbio; obscuro, confuso; sombrío, melancólico; ceñudo; (phot.) velado; **it is cloudy** está nublado
**clough** [klʌf] o [klaʊ] *s* vallecico, cañada
**clout** [klaʊt] *s* paño blanco al cual se le tira con el arco; flechazo; (coll.) bofetada, golpe seco de mano; (archaic) trapo, paño; *va* (coll.) abofetear, dar golpe seco de mano a
**clove** [klov] *s* (bot.) clavero; clavo de especia (*flor*); (cook.) clavo; diente de ajo; *pret de* **cleave**
**clove hitch** *s* (naut.) ballestrinque
**cloven** [ˈklovən] *adj* rajado, dividido; *pp de* **cleave**
**cloven foot** *s* pie hendido
**cloven-footed** [ˈklovənˈfʊtɪd] *adj* patihendido, bisulco; diabólico
**cloven hoof** *s* pie hendido, pata hendida; **to show the cloven hoof** descubrir la oreja, sacar la pata
**cloven-hoofed** [ˈklovənˈhuft] o [ˈklovənˈhʊft] *adj* patihendido, bisulco; diabólico
**clover** [ˈklovər] *s* (bot.) trébol; **to be in clover** vivir lujosamente, gozar de una vida de abundancia
**clover dodder** *s* (bot.) epítimo, barba de capuchino
**cloverleaf** [ˈklovərˌlif] *s* (*pl:* **-leaves**) cruce en trébol (*para la circulación de automóviles*)
**Clovis** [ˈklovɪs] *s* Clodoveo
**clown** [klaʊn] *s* payaso, bufón, clown; patán; *vn* bufonear, hacer el payaso; conducirse de manera ridícula
**clownery** [ˈklaʊnərɪ] *s* (*pl:* **-ies**) payasada, bufonada
**clownish** [ˈklaʊnɪʃ] *adj* bufonesco; rústico; grosero
**cloy** [klɔɪ] *va & vn* hastiar, empalagar
**club** [klʌb] *s* clava, porra, cachiporra; (sport) bate; club, casino, círculo; trébol (*naipe que corresponde al basto*); **clubs** *spl* tréboles (*palo que corresponde al de bastos*); (*pret & pp:* **clubbed;** *ger:* **clubbing**) *va* aporrear; *vn* unirse para un mismo fin; pagar todos su escote
**club car** *s* (rail.) coche club, coche bar
**clubfoot** [ˈklʌbˌfʊt] *s* (*pl:* **-feet**) (path.) pie calcáneo, pie talo
**clubhouse** [ˈklʌbˌhaʊs] *s* casino
**clubman** [ˈklʌbmən] *s* (*pl:* **-men**) clubista (*hombre*)
**club moss** *s* (bot.) azufre vegetal, musgo terrestre
**clubwoman** [ˈklʌbˌwʊmən] *s* (*pl:* **-women**) clubista (*mujer*)
**cluck** [klʌk] *s* cloqueo, clo clo; *vn* cloquear (*la gallina*)
**clue** [klu] *s & va* var. de **clew**
**clumber** [ˈklʌmbər] *s* clumber (*perro de aguas de pies cortos y cuerpo pesado*)
**clump** [klʌmp] *s* grupo (*de árboles, arbustos, etc.*); terrón; trozo sin forma; pisada fuerte; (bact.) acúmulo; *va* formar un grupo de (*árboles, arbustos, etc.*); colocar en grupos; plantar en grupos; *vn* andar pesadamente; **to clump along** andar torpemente con pisadas fuertes
**clumpy** [ˈklʌmpɪ] *adj* lleno de grupos o montones; fuerte y torpe
**clumsy** [ˈklʌmzɪ] *adj* (*comp:* **-sier;** *super:* **-siest**) torpe, desmañado; chapucero, mal hecho; difícil, embarazoso
**clung** [klʌŋ] *pret & pp de* **cling**
**Cluniac** [ˈklunɪæk] *adj & s* cluniacense
**Cluny lace** [ˈklunɪ] *s* encaje de Cluny
**cluster** [ˈklʌstər] *s* racimo; grupo; manada; *va* agrupar, apiñar, juntar; *vn* arracimarse; agruparse, apiñarse, juntarse; **to cluster around** reunirse en torno de
**clutch** [klʌtʃ] *s* agarro, apretón fuerte; garra, uña, mano agarradora; gobierno, mando, poder; (aut.) embrague; (aut.) pedal de embrague; nidada; cría de pollos; **to fall into the clutches of** caer en las garras de; **to throw the clutch in** embragar; **to throw the clutch out** desembragar; *va* agarrar, empuñar; arrebatar
**clutch band** *s* (aut.) cinta de embrague
**clutch housing** *s* (aut.) caja de embrague
**clutch lever** *s* (aut.) palanca del embrague
**clutch pedal** *s* (aut.) pedal de embrague
**clutter** [ˈklʌtər] *s* confusión, desorden; alboroto, baraúnda; *va* poner en confusión o desorden; cubrir o llenar desordenadamente; *vn* reunirse en desorden; alborotar
**clypeus** [ˈklɪpɪəs] *s* (*pl:* **-i** [aɪ]) (archeol., bot. & zool.) clípeo
**clyster** [ˈklɪstər] *s* (med.) clistel o clister; *va* clisterizar
**Clytemnestra** [ˌklaɪtəmˈnɛstrə] *s* (myth.) Clitemnestra
**cm.** abr. de **centimeter** o **centimeters**
**cml.** abr. de **commercial**
**Cnossus** [ˈnɑsəs] *s* var. de **Knossos**
**c.o.** o **c/o** abr. de **in care of** y **carried over**
**co.** o **Co.** abr. de **Company** y **County**
**C.O.** abr. de **Commanding Officer**
**coach** [kotʃ] *s* coche, diligencia; (rail.) coche de viajeros, coche ordinario; (aut.) coche cerrado; maestro particular, preceptor; (sport) entrenador; *va* llevar en coche; aleccionar, instruir; (sport) entrenar; *vn* pasear en coche; estudiar con un preceptor; **to coach with** ser aleccionado por
**coach-and-four** [ˌkotʃəndˈfor] *s* coche o carroza de cuatro caballos
**coach box** *s* pescante
**coach dog** *s* perro dálmatico
**coach horse** *s* caballo de coche
**coach house** *s* cochera
**coaching** [ˈkotʃɪŋ] *s* lecciones particulares; (sport) entrenamiento
**coachman** [ˈkotʃmən] *s* (*pl:* **-men**) cochero
**coach stand** *s* parada o estación de coches
**coadjutor** [koˈædʒətər] o [ˌkoəˈdʒutər] *s* coadjutor
**coagulant** [koˈægjələnt] *s* coagulante
**coagulate** [koˈægjəlet] *va* coagular; *vn* coagularse
**coagulation** [koˌægjəˈleʃən] *s* coagulación
**coagulative** [koˈægjəˌletɪv] *adj* coagulador, coagulante
**coagulin** [koˈægjəlɪn] *s* (biochem.) coagulina
**coagulum** [koˈægjələm] *s* (physiol.) coágulo
**coal** [kol] *s* carbón; carbón de piedra, carbón mineral; carbón de leña; pedazo de carbón; ascua, brasa; **to haul, drag** o **rake over the coals** dar una calada a, poner como un trapo; **to heap coals of fire on one's head** avergonzarle a uno, devolviendo bien por mal; *va* proveer de carbón, cargar de carbón; *vn* proveerse de carbón, tomar carbón
**coal basin** *s* cuenca hullera
**coalbin** [ˈkolˌbɪn] *s* carbonera
**coal bunker** *s* carbonera
**coal car** *s* vagón carbonero
**coaldealer** [ˈkolˌdilər] *s* carbonero
**coaler** [ˈkolər] *s* carbonero (*obrero o comerciante*); barco carbonero, ferrocarril carbonero
**coalesce** [ˌkoəˈlɛs] *vn* unirse, incorporarse
**coalescence** [ˌkoəˈlɛsəns] *s* unión, combinación
**coal field** *s* yacimiento de carbón
**coal gas** *s* gas de hulla
**coal heaver** *s* cargador de carbón
**coaling** [ˈkolɪŋ] *adj* carbonero; *s* toma de carbón
**coaling station** *s* estación carbonera
**coalition** [ˌkoəˈlɪʃən] *s* unión, combinación; coalición
**coalitionist** [ˌkoəˈlɪʃənɪst] *s* coalicionista
**coal measures** *spl* (geol.) estratos de carbón, yacimientos de carbón
**coal mine** *s* mina de carbón, mina hullera
**coal miner** *s* minero de carbón
**coal oil** *s* aceite mineral, keroseno
**coal pipe** *s* veta delgada e irregular de hulla
**coalpit** [ˈkolˌpɪt] *s* mina de carbón
**coal scuttle** *s* cubo para carbón
**coal ship** *s* barco carbonero
**coal tar** *s* alquitrán de carbón, alquitrán de hulla
**coal titmouse** *s* (orn.) azabache
**coal tongs** *spl* tenazas de chimenea
**coalyard** [ˈkolˌjɑrd] *s* carbonería
**coaming** [ˈkomɪŋ] *s* (naut.) brazola
**coaptation** [ˌkoæpˈteʃən] *s* coaptación
**coarse** [kors] *adj* burdo, basto; grueso (*dícese,*

*por ejemplo, de la arena*); común, inferior, ordinario; grosero, rudo, vulgar
**coarse-grained** ['kors'grend] *adj* de grano grueso; tosco, grosero, rudo
**coarsen** ['korsen] *va* volver burdo, grueso o grosero; *vn* hacerse burdo, grueso o grosero
**coarseness** ['korsnɪs] *s* basteza; grosura; grosería, vulgaridad
**coast** [kost] *s* (naut.) costa; **the coast is clear** ha pasado el peligro, no hay moros en la costa; *va* costear; *vn* pasar; costear; navegar en cabotaje; deslizarse cuesta abajo (*en trineo, bicicleta u otro vehículo*); **to coast along** avanzar sin esfuerzo; **to coast to a stop** avanzar por gravedad o por impulso propio hasta pararse
**coastal** ['kostəl] *adj* costero
**coastal plain** *s* llanura costera
**coast artillery** *s* artillería de costa
**coaster** ['kostər] *s* práctico de costa; barco de cabotaje, buque costero; deslizador; trineo; montaña rusa; salvamanteles (*pieza de cristal para debajo de los vasos*)
**coaster brake** *s* freno de contrapedal (*de bicicleta*)
**coast guard** *s* (los) guardacostas, cuerpo o servicio de guardacostas; guardia (*individuo*) de los guardacostas; tercios de frontera y costas (*en España*)
**coast guard cutter** *s* guardacostas, escampavía de los guardacostas
**coasting** ['kostɪŋ] *s* (naut.) navegación costera; marcha por gravedad o por impulso propio
**coasting trade** *s* (naut.) cabotaje
**coastland** ['kost,lænd] *s* litoral
**coastline** ['kost,laɪn] *s* línea de la costa
**coastward** ['kostwərd] *adj* dirigido hacia la costa; *adv* hacia la costa
**coastwards** ['kostwərdz] *adv* hacia la costa
**coastways** ['kost,wez] *adv* a lo largo de la costa
**coastwise** ['kost,waɪz] *adj* costanero; *adv* a lo largo de la costa
**coat** [kot] *s* saco, americana, levita; abrigo, sobretodo; capa, mano (*de pintura*); lana, pelo (*de un animal*); **to turn one's coat** cambiarse la camisa, pasarse al partido opuesto; *va* proveer de saco, americana, etc.; cubrir, revestir; dar una capa o una mano de pintura a
**coated** ['kotɪd] *adj* revestido; bañado; saburroso (*dícese de la lengua*)
**coatee** [ko'ti] *s* saquete, casaquilla; vestidura exterior corta
**coat hanger** *s* colgador
**coati** [ko'ɑtɪ] *s* (*pl:* **-tis**) (zool.) coatí
**coating** ['kotɪŋ] *s* capa; revestimiento; enlucido, blanqueo; tela para casacas, abrigos, etc.
**coat of arms** *s* escudo de armas
**coat of mail** *s* cota de malla
**coat of tan** *s* solanera, atezamiento (*de la piel al sol*)
**coatroom** ['kot,rum] o ['kot,rʊm] *s* guardarropa
**coattail** ['kot,tel] *s* faldón
**coauthor** [ko'ɔθər] *s* coautor
**coax** [koks] *va* engatusar; obtener mediante caricias, halagos, etc.
**coaxial** [ko'æksɪəl] *adj* coaxial
**coaxial cable** *s* cable coaxial
**cob** [kɑb] *s* zuro (*de la mazorca del maíz*); jaca fuerte; cisne macho; **to eat corn on the cob** comer maíz en o de la mazorca
**cobalt** ['kobɔlt] *s* (chem.) cobalto
**cobalt bloom** *s* flores de cobalto, eritrita
**cobalt blue** *s* azul de cobalto
**cobaltic** [ko'bɔltɪk] *adj* (chem.) cobáltico
**cobaltite** [ko'bɔltaɪt] o ['kobɔltaɪt] *s* (mineral.) cobaltina
**cobble** ['kɑbəl] *s* guijarro; *va* empedrar con guijarros; apedazar, remendar; chalfallar; *vn* remendar zapatos
**cobbler** ['kɑblər] *s* remendón, zapatero de viejo; chapucero; pastel de frutas; bebida helada (*que contiene vino, frutas y jugo de frutas*)
**cobblestone** ['kɑbəl,ston] *s* guijarro
**cobelligerent** [,kobɪ'lɪdʒərənt] *s* cobeligerante
**Coblenz** ['koblɛnts] *s* Coblenza
**cobra** ['kobrə] *s* (zool.) cobra, culebra de anteojos
**Coburg** ['kobʌrg] *s* Coburgo
**cobweb** ['kɑb,wɛb] *s* telaraña; hilo de telaraña; (fig.) red, ardid; (fig.) telaraña (*cosa sutil de poca entidad*)
**cobwebby** ['kɑb,wɛbɪ] *adj* entelarañado, telarañoso
**coca** ['kokə] *s* (bot. & pharm.) coca
**cocain** o **cocaine** [ko'ken] o ['koken] *s* cocaína
**cocainism** [ko'kenɪzəm] *s* (path.) cocainismo
**cocainization** [ko,kenɪ'zeʃən] *s* cocainización
**cocainize** [ko'kenaɪz] *va* cocainizar
**coccobacillus** [,kɑkobə'sɪləs] *s* (bact.) cocobacilo
**coccus** ['kɑkəs] *s* (*pl:* **cocci** ['kɑksaɪ]) (bact.) coco; (bot.) carpelo; cochinilla (*materia colorante*)
**coccyx** ['kɑksɪks] *s* (*pl:* **coccyges** [kɑk'saɪdʒiz]) (anat.) cóccix
**Cochin** o **cochin** ['kotʃɪn] o ['kɑtʃɪn] *s* cochinchina (*gallina*)
**Cochin Bantam** *s* cochinchina enana (*gallina*)
**Cochin China** *s* la Cochinchina
**cochineal** [,kɑtʃɪ'nil] o ['kɑtʃɪnil] *s* cochinilla (*materia colorante*)
**cochineal insect** *s* (ent.) cochinilla
**cochlea** ['kɑklɪə] *s* (*pl:* **-ae** [i]) (anat.) cóclea, caracol
**cochlear** ['kɑklɪər] *adj* coclear
**cock** [kɑk] *s* gallo; macho de ave; espita, grifo; martillo (*de un arma de fuego*); giraldilla, veleta; jefe, caudillo; vuelta airosa hacia arriba (*de los ojos, de la nariz*); vuelta (*del ala de un sombrero*); montón (*de paja o heno*); *va* amartillar (*un arma de fuego*); enderezar, volver hacia arriba (*el ala del sombrero*); ladear (*la cabeza*); amontonar (*paja o heno*); *vn* volverse airosamente hacia arriba (*los ojos, la nariz*); contonearse, engreírse
**cockade** [kɑ'ked] *s* escarapela, cucarda
**cock-a-doodle-doo** ['kɑkə,dudəl'du] *s* quiquiriquí
**Cockaigne** [kɑ'ken] *s* tierra imaginaria de deleite y pereza
**cock-and-bull story** ['kɑkənd'bʊl] *s* cuento absurdo, exagerado o increíble
**cockatoo** [,kɑkə'tu] o ['kɑkətu] *s* (*pl:* **-toos**) (orn.) cacatúa
**cockatrice** ['kɑkətrɪs] *s* (myth.) basilisco
**cockchafer** ['kɑk,tʃefər] *s* (ent.) abejorro (*Melolontha vulgaris*)
**cockcrow** ['kɑk,kro] *s* aurora, tiempo del canto del gallo
**cocked hat** *s* sombrero de ala vuelta hacia arriba; sombrero de candil o de tres picos; **to knock into a cocked hat** (slang) arruinar, demoler o destruir completamente
**cocker** ['kɑkər] *s* cocker
**cockerel** ['kɑkərəl] *s* gallipollo
**cocker spaniel** *s* cocker
**cockeyed** ['kɑk,aɪd] *adj* bisojo, bizco; (slang) ladeado, encorvado, torcido; (slang) disparatado, extravagante
**cockfight** ['kɑk,faɪt] o **cockfighting** ['kɑk,faɪtɪŋ] *s* combate o pelea de gallos
**cockhorse** ['kɑk'hɔrs] *s* caballo mecedor
**cockle** ['kɑkəl] *s* (zool.) cardio, berberecho; (bot.) cizaña, joyo; (bot.) ballico perenne; barquichuelo; arruga, pliegue; **the cockles of the heart** las profundidades del corazón, lo íntimo del corazón; *va* arrugar, fruncir; *vn* arrugarse, fruncirse
**cockleboat** ['kɑkəl,bot] *s* barquichuelo
**cocklebur** ['kɑkəl,bʌr] *s* (bot.) cachurrera menor, bardana menor; (bot.) bardana
**cockle hat** *s* sombrero con venera (*especialmente del peregrino que va a Santiago de Compostela*)
**cockleshell** ['kɑkəl,ʃɛl] *s* concha de cardio; venera; barquichuelo; cascarón de nuez (*embarcación pequeña*)
**cockloft** ['kɑk,lɔft] o ['kɑk,lɑft] *s* desván gatero
**cockney** ['kɑknɪ] *s* habitante del barrio pobre de Londres que habla un dialecto particular; dialecto del barrio pobre de Londres
**cock of the rock** *s* (orn.) gallo de roca, rupícola anaranjado
**cock of the walk** *s* gallito del lugar
**cockpit** ['kɑk,pɪt] *s* gallera, valla (*para las*

*riñas de gallos*); (aer.) carlinga; (naut.) recámaras situadas debajo del puente (*en los buques de guerra antiguos*); sitio de muchos combates
**cockroach** [ˈkɑkˌrotʃ] *s* (ent.) cucaracha
**cock robin** *s* (orn.) petirrojo (*macho*)
**cockscomb** [ˈkɑksˌkom] *s* cresta de gallo; gorro de bufón; (bot.) cresta de gallo, moco de pavo; mequetrefe; baladrón, fanfarrón
**cocksure** [ˈkɑkˈʃʊr] *adj* completamente seguro; demasiado seguro
**cockswain** [ˈkɑksən] o [ˈkɑkswen] *s* var. de **coxswain**
**cocktail** [ˈkɑkˌtel] *s* coctel; aperitivo (*de frutas, almejas, ostras, etc.*); (meteor.) rabos de gallo (*cirro o nube cirrosa*)
**cocktail dress** *s* vestido de tarde-noche
**cocktail party** *s* coctel (*reunión donde se ofrecen cocteles*)
**cocktail shaker** *s* coctelera
**cocky** [ˈkɑkɪ] *adj* (*comp:* **-ier;** *super:* **-iest**) (coll.) arrogante, hinchado, fanfarrón
**coco** [ˈkoko] *s* (*pl:* **-cos**) (bot.) coco, cocotero
**cocoa** [ˈkoko] *s* cacao en polvo; chocolate (*bebida*); (bot.) coco, cocotero
**cocoa bean** *s* semilla del cacao
**cocoa butter** *s* manteca de cacao
**cocoanut** o **coconut** [ˈkokoˌnʌt] *s* coco (*fruto*)
**coconut butter** *s* manteca de coco
**coconut fiber** *s* bonote, coir
**coconut milk** *s* leche de coco
**coconut oil** *s* aceite de coco
**coconut palm** *s* (bot.) cocotero, coco, palma indiana
**coconut tree** *s* (bot.) cocotero, coco
**cocoon** [kəˈkun] *s* capullo
**coco plum** *s* (bot.) hicaco o icaco (*árbol y fruto*)
**Cocytus** [koˈsaɪtəs] *s* (myth.) Cocito
**c.o.d.** o **C.O.D.** abr. de **collect on delivery** (U.S.A.) y **cash on delivery** (Brit.)
**cod** [kɑd] *s* (ichth.) abadejo, bacalao
**coda** [ˈkodə] *s* (mus.) coda
**coddle** [ˈkɑdəl] *va* mimar, consentir; cocer (*huevos*) en agua caliente sin hervir
**code** [kod] *s* código; clave o cifra (*escritura secreta*); (com.) cifrario; **in code** en cifra; *va* cifrar (*escribir en cifra*); cambiar o traducir en código o clave; escribir o transmitir en código o clave
**code flag** *s* (naut.) señal del código
**codein** [ˈkodɪɪn] o **codeine** [ˈkodɪɪn] o [ˈkodin] *s* (chem.) codeína
**code of honor** *s* código de honor
**code pennant** *s* (naut.) señal del código
**code word** *s* (telg.) clave telegráfica
**codex** [ˈkodɛks] *s* (*pl:* **codices** [ˈkodɪsiz] o [ˈkɑdɪsiz]) códice
**codfish** [ˈkɑdˌfɪʃ] *s* (ichth.) abadejo, bacalao; (com.) pez palo
**codfish cake** *s* albóndiga de bacalao
**codger** [ˈkɑdʒər] *s* (coll.) tipo
**codicil** [ˈkɑdɪsɪl] *s* (law) codicilo; apéndice
**codicillary** [ˌkɑdɪˈsɪlərɪ] *adj* codicilar
**codification** [ˌkɑdɪfɪˈkeʃən] o [ˌkodɪfɪˈkeʃən] *s* codificación
**codify** [ˈkɑdɪfaɪ] o [ˈkodɪfaɪ] (*pret & pp:* **-fied**) *va* codificar
**codling** [ˈkɑdlɪŋ] *s* manzana no madura; manzana pequeña y de calidad inferior; manzana de forma larga y algo cónica; (ichth.) pescadilla; (ichth.) brótola (*Urophycis*)
**codling moth** *s* (ent.) tiña (*Carpocapsa pomonella*)
**cod liver** *s* hígado de bacalao
**cod-liver oil** [ˈkɑdˌlɪvər] *s* aceite de hígado de bacalao
**coed** o **co-ed** [ˈkoˌɛd] *s* (coll.) alumna de una escuela coeducacional
**coeducation** [ˌkoˌɛdʒəˈkeʃən] o [ˌkoˌɛdʒʊˈkeʃən] *s* coeducación
**coeducational** [ˌkoˌɛdʒəˈkeʃənəl] o [ˌkoˌɛdʒʊˈkeʃənəl] *adj* coeducacional
**coefficient** [ˌko·ɪˈfɪʃənt] *s* (math. & phys.) coeficiente; *adj* coeficiente
**coefficient of expansion** *s* (phys.) coeficiente de dilatación
**coelenterate** [sɪˈlɛntəret] *adj & s* (zool.) celenterado
**coeliac** [ˈsilɪæk] *adj* (anat.) celíaco
**coelom** [ˈsiləm] *s* (anat. & zool.) celoma
**coelomate** [siˈlomet] *adj & s* (zool.) celomado
**coenesthesis** [ˌsinɛsˈθisɪs] *s* (psychol.) cenestesia
**coenobite** [ˈsinobaɪt] o [ˈsɛnobaɪt] *s* cenobita
**coenobium** [sɪˈnobɪəm] *s* (*pl:* **-a** [ə]) (biol. & bot.) cenobio
**coequal** [koˈikwəl] *adj & s* coigual
**coerce** [koˈʌrs] *va* coactar, forzar; coercer, restringir
**coercion** [koˈʌrʃən] *s* coacción, compulsión; gobierno por fuerza; coerción, restricción
**coercive** [koˈʌrsɪv] *adj* coactivo; coercitivo
**coercive force** *s* (phys.) fuerza coercitiva
**coeternal** [ˌko·ɪˈtʌrnəl] *adj* coeterno
**coeval** [koˈivəl] *adj & s* coetáneo, contemporáneo
**coexist** [ˌkoɛgˈzɪst] *vn* coexistir
**coexistence** [ˌkoɛgˈzɪstəns] *s* coexistencia
**coexistent** [ˌkoɛgˈzɪstənt] *adj* coexistente
**coextend** [ˌkoɛksˈtɛnd] *va* extender igualmente; *vn* coextenderse
**coextension** [ˌkoɛksˈtɛnʃən] *s* coextensión
**coextensive** [ˌkoɛksˈtɛnsɪv] *adj* coextensivo
**coffee** [ˈkɔfɪ] o [ˈkɑfɪ] *s* café; (bot.) cafeto; **black coffee** café solo
**coffee bean** *s* grano de café
**coffee break** *s* rato de descanso para tomar el café
**coffee cake** *s* pastelillo o bollo que se come con el café
**coffee grinder** *s* molinillo de café
**coffee grounds** *spl* heces del café
**coffee house** *s* café
**coffee mill** *s* molinillo de café
**coffee plant** *s* (bot.) cafeto
**coffee plantation** *s* cafetal, finca cafetera
**coffee pot** *s* cafetera
**coffee shop** *s* café
**coffee table** *s* mesa de té
**coffee tree** *s* (bot.) cafeto
**coffer** [ˈkɔfər] o [ˈkɑfər] *s* cofre, arca; (arch.) artesón, casetón; (hyd.) ataguía; (fort.) cofre; **coffers** *spl* tesoro, fondos
**cofferdam** [ˈkɔfərˌdæm] o [ˈkɑfərˌdæm] *s* ataguía, caja-dique
**coffin** [ˈkɔfɪn] o [ˈkɑfɪn] *s* ataúd; *va* poner en un ataúd; encerrar estrechamente
**coffin bone** *s* (zool.) bolillo
**C. of S.** abr. de **Chief of Staff**
**cog** [kɑg] *s* diente (*de rueda dentada*); rueda dentada; (carp.) espiga; **to slip a cog** equivocarse; (*pret & pp:* **cogged;** *ger:* **cogging**) *va* poner dientes a; (carp.) ensamblar con espigas; cargar (*un dado*)
**cogency** [ˈkodʒənsɪ] *s* fuerza (*de un argumento*)
**cogent** [ˈkodʒənt] *adj* fuerte, convincente
**cogged** [kɑgd] *adj* dentado, engranado
**cogitate** [ˈkɑdʒɪtet] *va & vn* meditar, reflexionar
**cogitation** [ˌkɑdʒɪˈteʃən] *s* meditación, reflexión
**cogitative** [ˈkɑdʒɪˌtetɪv] *adj* cogitativo (*que tiene facultad de pensar*); meditabundo, reflexivo
**cognac** [ˈkonjæk] o [ˈkɑnjæk] *s* coñac
**cognate** [ˈkɑgnet] *adj & s* cognado
**cognition** [kɑgˈnɪʃən] *s* cognición (*proceso mental*)
**cognitive** [ˈkɑgnɪtɪv] *adj* cognoscitivo
**cognizable** [ˈkɑgnɪzəbəl] o [ˈkɑnɪzəbəl] *adj* cognocible; (law) justiciable
**cognizance** [ˈkɑgnɪzəns] o [ˈkɑnɪzəns] *s* conocimiento; (law) competencia; **to have** o **take cognizance of** venir en conocimiento de
**cognizant** [ˈkɑgnɪzənt] o [ˈkɑnɪzənt] *adj* sabedor; (law) competente
**cognomen** [kɑgˈnomɛn] *s* (*pl:* **-mens** o **-mina** [mɪnə]) apellido; sobrenombre; apodo
**cogon grass** [koˈgon] *s* (bot.) cisca, cogón
**cograil** [ˈkɑgˌrel] *s* cremallera
**cogwheel** [ˈkɑgˌhwil] *s* rueda dentada
**cohabit** [koˈhæbɪt] *vn* cohabitar
**cohabitation** [koˌhæbɪˈteʃən] *s* cohabitación
**coheir** [koˈɛr] *s* coheredero
**coheiress** [koˈɛrɪs] *s* coheredera
**cohere** [koˈhɪr] *vn* adherirse, pegarse; enlazarse, corresponder
**coherence** [koˈhɪrəns] o **coherency** [koˈhɪrənsɪ] *s* coherencia

**coherent** [koˈhɪrənt] *adj* coherente; (bot.) coherente
**coherer** [koˈhɪrər] *s* (rad.) cohesor
**cohesion** [koˈhiʒən] *s* cohesión; (phys.) cohesión
**cohesive** [koˈhisɪv] *adj* cohesivo; coherente
**cohobate** [ˈkohobet] *va* (chem.) cohobar
**cohort** [ˈkohɔrt] *s* cohorte; compañero
**coif** [kɔɪf] *s* cofia; (arm.) cofia; *va* cubrir con cofia
**coiffeur** [kwɑˈfʌr] *s* peluquero
**coiffure** [kwɑˈfjʊr] *s* peinado; tocado
**coign** [kɔɪn] *s* esquina saliente
**coign of vantage** *s* posición ventajosa
**coil** [kɔɪl] *s* rollo; vuelta (*de un rollo*); serpentín (*p.ej., de un alambique*); rizo (*de cabellos*); (elec.) carrete; (naut.) adujada; (naut.) aduja (*vuelta de una adujada*); (archaic) desorden; *va* arrollar, enrollar; (naut.) adujar; *vn* arrollarse, enrollarse; serpentear; andar en círculos
**coil spring** *s* resorte espiral
**coin** [kɔɪn] *s* moneda; cuña; **to pay back in his own coin** pagar en la misma moneda; *va* acuñar, troquelar; amonedar; forjar (*palabras o frases*); **to coin money** (coll.) ganar mucho dinero, enriquecerse
**coinage** [ˈkɔɪnɪdʒ] *s* acuñación; amonedación; monedas; sistema monetario; invención
**coincide** [ˌko·ɪnˈsaɪd] *vn* coincidir; ponerse de acuerdo
**coincidence** [koˈɪnsɪdəns] *s* coincidencia
**coincident** [koˈɪnsɪdənt] o **coincidental** [koˌɪnsɪˈdɛntəl] *adj* coincidente
**coiner** [ˈkɔɪnər] *s* monedero; monedero falso; inventor
**coinsurance** [ˌko·ɪnˈʃʊrəns] *s* coaseguro
**coir** [kɔɪr] *s* coir, bonote, roya
**coition** [koˈɪʃən] o **coitus** [ˈko·ɪtəs] *s* coito
**coke** [kok] *s* coque; *va & vn* coquizar
**coke oven** *s* horno de coque
**col.** abr. de **colored, colony** y **column**
**Col.** abr. de **Colonel, Colorado** y **Colossians**
**colander** [ˈkʌləndər] o [ˈkɑləndər] *s* escurridor, colador
**colchicine** [ˈkɑlkɪsin] o [ˈkɑlkɪsɪn] *s* (chem.) colquicina
**colchicum** [ˈkɑlkɪkəm] *s* (bot. & pharm.) cólquico
**Colchis** [ˈkɑlkɪs] *s* la Cólquida
**colcothar** [ˈkɑlkəθər] *s* (chem.) colcótar
**cold** [kold] *adj* frío; (fig.) frío, indiferente; (coll.) frío (*lejos de lo que se busca*); **to be cold** hacer frío (*dícese del tiempo*); tener frío (*p.ej., una persona*); *s* frío; resfriado; **to catch** o **to take cold** tomar frío, resfriarse; **to leave out in the cold** dejar colgado, menospreciar con premeditación
**cold blood** *s* sangre fría; **in cold blood** a sangre fría
**cold-blooded** [ˈkoldˈblʌdɪd] *adj* insensible; cruel, despiadado; friolento (*muy sensible al frío*); (zool.) de sangre fría
**cold chisel** *s* cortafrío
**cold cream** *s* colcrén, crema
**cold cuts** *spl* fiambres
**cold feet** *s* (coll.) miedo, desánimo
**cold frame** *s* (hort.) cajonera
**cold front** *s* (meteor.) frente frío
**cold-hearted** [ˈkoldˈhɑrtɪd] *adj* duro, insensible
**cold light** *s* luz fría
**cold meat** *s* carne fiambre
**coldness** [ˈkoldnɪs] *s* frialdad
**cold pack** *s* (med.) compresa fría
**cold-pack** [ˈkoldˈpæk] *va* aplicar una compresa fría a
**cold-rolled** [ˈkoldˈrold] *adj* laminado en frío
**cold shoulder** *s* (coll.) frialdad; **to turn a cold shoulder on** (coll.) tratar con frialdad, despedir con desaire
**cold-shoulder** [ˈkoldˈʃoldər] *va* (coll.) tratar con frialdad, despedir con desaire
**cold snap** *s* corto rato de frío agudo
**cold sore** *s* (path.) fuegos en la boca o los labios
**cold steel** *s* arma de acero, arma blanca
**cold storage** *s* conservación en cámara frigorífica
**cold-storage** [ˈkoldˈstorɪdʒ] *adj* frigorífico; *va* conservar en cámara frigorífica
**cold sweat** *s* sudor frío
**cold war** *s* guerra fría
**cold wave** *s* ola de frío; permanente en frío
**cole** [kol] *s* (bot.) naba
**colectomy** [kəˈlɛktəmɪ] *s* (*pl:* **-mies**) (surg.) colectomía
**coleopterous** [ˌkolɪˈɑptərəs] o [ˌkɑlɪˈɑptərəs] *adj* (ent.) coleóptero
**coleorhiza** [ˌkolɪəˈraɪzə] o [ˌkɑlɪəˈraɪzə] *s* (bot.) coleorriza
**coleslaw** [ˈkolˌslɔ] *s* ensalada de col
**coleus** [ˈkolɪəs] *s* (bot.) coleo
**colewort** [ˈkolˌwʌrt] *s* (bot.) col rizada, berza verde
**coli** [ˈkolaɪ] *s* (bact.) colibacilo
**colibacillosis** [ˌkolɪˌbæsɪˈlosɪs] *s* (path.) colibacilosis
**colic** [ˈkɑlɪk] *adj* (anat. & path.) cólico; *s* (path.) cólico
**colicky** [ˈkɑlɪkɪ] *adj* cólico
**coliseum** [ˌkɑlɪˈsiəm] *s* coliseo; (*cap.*) *s* Coliseo
**colitis** [koˈlaɪtɪs] *s* (path.) colitis
**coll.** abr. de **colleague, collection, collector, college** y **colloquial**
**collaborate** [kəˈlæbəret] *vn* colaborar
**collaboration** [kəˌlæbəˈreʃən] *s* colaboración
**collaborationist** [kəˌlæbəˈreʃənɪst] *s* colaboracionista
**collaborator** [kəˈlæbəˌretər] *s* colaborador
**collagen** [ˈkɑlədʒɛn] *s* (biochem.) colágeno
**collapse** [kəˈlæps] *s* hundimiento, desplome; aplastamiento; fracaso; (path. & fig.) colapso; *va* aplastar; *vn* hundirse, desplomarse; aplastarse; fracasar; postrarse, sufrir colapso
**collapse therapy** *s* colapsoterapia
**collapsible** [kəˈlæpsɪbəl] *adj* colapsible, plegable, abatible
**collapsible boat** *s* bote plegable
**collapsible target** *s* blanco abatible
**collar** [ˈkɑlər] *s* cuello; collar (*de perro, caballo, buey; raya de color que rodea el pescuezo de un animal*); (mach.) collar; **to slip the collar** escaparse, desenredarse; *va* ceñir con cuello, collar, etc.; poner cuello o collar a; agarrar por el cabezón; (coll.) coger, prender (*p.ej., a un reo*)
**collarband** [ˈkɑlərˌbænd] *s* cabezón
**collar beam** *s* (arch.) entrecinta
**collarbone** [ˈkɑlərˌbon] *s* (anat.) clavícula
**collate** [kɑˈlet] o [ˈkɑlet] *va* colacionar, cotejar, compulsar
**collateral** [kəˈlætərəl] *adj* colateral; *s* colateral (*pariente*); (com.) colateral, resguardo
**collation** [kɑˈleʃən] *s* colación (*cotejo; comida ligera*)
**collator** [kɑˈletər] o [ˈkɑletər] *s* colacionador
**colleague** [ˈkɑlig] *s* colega
**collect** [ˈkɑlɛkt] *s* (eccl.) colecta; [kəˈlɛkt] *va* acumular, reunir; coleccionar (*p.ej., sellos de correo*); colectar (*p.ej., impuestos*); cobrar (*p.ej., pasajes*); recoger (*p.ej., billetes*); suponer; **to collect oneself** recobrarse, reponerse; *vn* acumularse, reunirse; **collect on delivery** contra reembolso
**collectable** [kəˈlɛktəbəl] *adj* cobrable
**collected** [kəˈlɛktɪd] *adj* sosegado, a sangre fría
**collectible** [kəˈlɛktɪbəl] *adj* var. de **collectable**
**collection** [kəˈlɛkʃən] *s* colección; recaudación (*p.ej., de impuestos*); recogida (*p.ej., del correo*); (eccl.) colecta; montón
**collective** [kəˈlɛktɪv] *adj* colectivo; (gram.) colectivo; *s* (gram.) nombre colectivo
**collective bargaining** *s* trato colectivo entre gremios y patronos respecto a sueldos, horas y condiciones de trabajo
**collectively** [kəˈlɛktɪvlɪ] *adv* colectivamente
**collective noun** *s* (gram.) nombre colectivo
**collective security** *s* seguridad colectiva
**collectivism** [kəˈlɛktɪvɪzəm] *s* colectivismo
**collectivist** [kəˈlɛktɪvɪst] *s* colectivista
**collectivistic** [kəˌlɛktɪˈvɪstɪk] *adj* colectivista
**collectivity** [ˌkɑlɛkˈtɪvɪtɪ] *s* colectividad
**collectivization** [kəˌlɛktɪvɪˈzeʃən] *s* colectivización
**collectivize** [kəˈlɛktɪvaɪz] *va* colectivizar
**collector** [kəˈlɛktər] *s* coleccionador (*p.ej., de mapas, medallas*); recaudador (*p.ej., de impuestos*); (elec.) colector

**collectorship** [kəˈlɛktərʃɪp] *s* colecturía; distrito donde actúa el recaudador o colector
**colleen** [ˈkɑlin] o [kɑˈlin] *s* (Irish) muchacha
**college** [ˈkɑlɪdʒ] *s* colegio; colegio universitario
**College of Cardinals** *s* Colegio de cardenales
**collegian** [kəˈlidʒɪən] *s* colegial
**collegiate** [kəˈlidʒɪɪt] *adj* colegial, colegiado; universitario
**collegiate church** *s* colegiata, iglesia colegial
**collide** [kəˈlaɪd] *vn* chocar; **to collide with** chocar con
**collie** [ˈkɑlɪ] *s* collie, perro de pastor escocés
**collier** [ˈkɑljər] *s* barco carbonero; minero de carbón
**colliery** [ˈkɑljərɪ] *s* (*pl:* **-ies**) mina de carbón, hullera
**collimate** [ˈkɑlɪmet] *va* alinear; enfocar las líneas de mira de (*p.ej., un telescopio*)
**collimation** [ˌkɑlɪˈmeʃən] *s* (astr. & opt.) colimación
**collimator** [ˈkɑlɪˌmetər] *s* (opt.) colimador
**collision** [kəˈlɪʒən] *s* colisión
**collocate** [ˈkɑloket] *va* colocar, disponer, arreglar
**collocation** [ˌkɑloˈkeʃən] *s* colocación, disposición, arreglo
**collodion** [kəˈlodɪən] *s* (chem.) colodión
**colloid** [ˈkɑlɔɪd] *adj & s* (chem.) coloide
**colloidal** [kəˈlɔɪdəl] *adj* coloidal
**collop** [ˈkɑləp] *s* trocito, pedacito; tajada de carne; pliegue, doblez (*de piel en el cuerpo*)
**colloquial** [kəˈlokwɪəl] *adj* familiar, coloquial
**colloquialism** [kəˈlokwɪəlɪzəm] *s* locución familiar, palabra familiar; estilo familiar
**colloquy** [ˈkɑləkwɪ] *s* (*pl:* **-quies**) coloquio
**collude** [kəˈlud] *vn* confabularse, coludir
**collusion** [kəˈluʒən] *s* confabulación, colusión; **to be in collusion with** estar en inteligencia con
**collusive** [kəˈlusɪv] *adj* colusorio
**collyrium** [kəˈlɪrɪəm] *s* (*pl:* **-a** [ə] o **-ums**) colirio
**Colo.** abr. de **Colorado**
**colocynth** [ˈkɑləsɪnθ] *s* (bot.) coloquíntida
**cologne** [kəˈlon] *s* colonia, agua de Colonia; (*cap.*) *s* Colonia
**Colombia** [kəˈlʌmbɪə] *s* Colombia
**Colombian** [kəˈlʌmbɪən] *adj & s* colombiano
**colon** [ˈkolən] *s* (anat.) colon; (gram.) dos puntos
**colonel** [ˈkʌrnəl] *s* coronel
**colonelcy** [ˈkʌrnəlsɪ] *s* (*pl:* **-cies**) coronelía
**colonial** [kəˈlonɪəl] *adj* colonial; colonialista (*país*); *s* colono
**colonialism** [kəˈlonɪəlɪzəm] *s* colonialismo
**colonic** [kəˈlɑnɪk] *adj* colónico
**colonist** [ˈkɑlənɪst] *s* colonizador; colono
**colonization** [ˌkɑlənɪˈzeʃən] *s* colonización
**colonize** [ˈkɑlənaɪz] *va & vn* colonizar
**colonnade** [ˌkɑləˈned] *s* columnata
**colonnaded** [ˌkɑləˈnedɪd] *adj* (arch.) con columnatas
**colony** [ˈkɑlənɪ] *s* (*pl:* **-nies**) colonia
**colophon** [ˈkɑləfɑn] *s* colofón
**colophony** [ˈkɑləˌfonɪ] o [kəˈlɑfənɪ] *s* colofonia
**color** [ˈkʌlər] *s* color; **off color** descolorido; indispuesto; (slang) colorado, libre, verde; **the colors** los colores (*la bandera*); ceremonia de enarbolar la bandera por la mañana y bajarla por la noche; el ejército y la marina, el servicio militar; **to call to the colors** llamar al servicio militar; **to change color** mudar de color (*palidecer; sonrojarse*); **to give** o **to lend color to** dar impresión de probabilidad o verdad a, hacer parecer probable o verdadero; **to hoist the colors** enarbolar la bandera; **to lose color** palidecer; **to show one's colors** dejarse ver en su carácter verdadero, declarar sus opiniones o proyectos; **under color of** so color de, so pretexto de; **with flying colors** (mil.) con banderas desplegadas; con lucimiento; *va* colorar, colorear; (fig.) colorear; dar calidad distinta a; *vn* sonrojarse, encenderse
**colorable** [ˈkʌlərəbəl] *adj* plausible, admisible; especioso
**coloration** [ˌkʌləˈreʃən] *s* coloración
**coloratura** [ˌkʌlərəˈtjurə] o [ˌkʌlərəˈturə] *s* (mus.) coloratura
**colorbearer** [ˈkʌlərˌberər] *s* abanderado, portaestandarte
**color-blind** [ˈkʌlərˌblaɪnd] *adj* acromatópsico, daltoniano, ciego para los colores
**color blindness** *s* (path.) acromatopsia, daltonismo, ceguera para los colores
**color chart** *s* carta de colores, guía colorimétrica
**color company** *s* (mil.) compañía abanderada
**colored** [ˈkʌlərd] *adj* de color (*que no es blanco ni negro; que no pertenece a la raza blanca*); colorado, especioso; persuadido engañosamente
**color film** *s* película en colores
**color filter** *s* filtro cromofotográfico
**colorful** [ˈkʌlərfəl] *adj* colorido; pintoresco
**color guard** *s* (mil.) guardia de la bandera
**colorimeter** [ˌkʌləˈrɪmɪtər] *s* colorímetro
**colorimetry** [ˌkʌləˈrɪmɪtrɪ] *s* colorimetría
**coloring** [ˈkʌlərɪŋ] *s* colorido; colorante (*substancia*); (fig.) colorido
**colorist** [ˈkʌlərɪst] *s* colorista
**colorless** [ˈkʌlərlɪs] *adj* incoloro
**color line** *s* diferencia social, económica y política entre la raza blanca y las de color
**color photography** *s* fotografía en colores
**color salute** *s* (mil.) saludo con la bandera
**color sargent** *s* (mil.) sargento abanderado
**color screen** *s* (phot.) pantalla de color
**color sentinel** *s* (mil.) centinela de la bandera
**color television** *s* televisión en colores, televisión a color
**colossal** [kəˈlɑsəl] *adj* colosal
**Colosseum** [ˌkɑləˈsiəm] *s* Coliseo
**Colossian** [kəˈlɑʃən] *adj & s* colosense; **Colossians** *spl* (Bib.) Epístola a los colosenses
**colossus** [kəˈlɑsəs] *s* (*pl:* **-si** [saɪ] o **-suses**) coloso
**Colossus of Rhodes** *s* coloso de Rodas
**colostomy** [kəˈlɑstəmɪ] *s* (*pl:* **-mies**) (surg.) colostomía
**colostrum** [kəˈlɑstrəm] *s* calostro
**colour** [ˈkʌlər] *s, va & vn* (Brit.) var. de **color**
**colporteur** [ˈkɑlˌportər] *s* repartidor ambulante de escritos religiosos
**colt** [kolt] *s* potro; mozuelo sin juicio; persona joven e inexperta; (*cap.*) *s* (trademark) revólver Colt
**colter** [ˈkoltər] *s* reja del arado
**coltish** [ˈkoltɪʃ] *adj* jugetón, retozón
**coltsfoot** [ˈkoltsˌfut] *s* (*pl:* **-foots**) (bot.) uña de caballo
**columbarium** [ˌkɑləmˈberɪəm] *s* (*pl:* **-a** [ə]) columbario
**Columbia** [kəˈlʌmbɪə] *s* Colombia (*nombre dado a los EE.UU. de la América del Norte*)
**Columbian** [kəˈlʌmbɪən] *adj* colombino (*perteneciente a Cristóbal Colón*); americano
**columbine** [ˈkɑləmbaɪn] *adj* columbino; *s* (bot.) aguileña; (*cap.*) *s* Colombina
**columbium** [kəˈlʌmbɪəm] *s* (chem.) colombio
**Columbus** [kəˈlʌmbəs] *s* Colón
**Columbus Day** *s* día de la raza, fiesta de la hispanidad
**columella** [ˌkɑljəˈmɛlə] *s* (*pl:* **-lae** [li]) (arch., anat., bot. & zool.) columela
**column** [ˈkɑləm] *s* columna
**columnar** [kəˈlʌmnər] *adj* columnario
**columned** [ˈkɑləmd] *adj* con columnas
**columniation** [kəˌlʌmnɪˈeʃən] *s* (arch.) columnata
**columnist** [ˈkɑləmnɪst] o [ˈkɑləmɪst] *s* columnista
**colure** [ˈkoljʊr] *s* (astr.) coluro
**colza** [ˈkɑlzə] *s* (bot.) colza; semilla de colza
**colza oil** *s* aceite de colza
**com.** abr. de **comedy, commerce, common** y **commonly**
**Com.** abr. de **Commander, Commissioner, Committee** y **Commodore**
**coma** [ˈkomə] *s* (*pl:* **-mas**) (path.) coma; (*pl:* **-mae** [mi]) *s* (astr.) cabellera; (bot.) copete, manojo; (bot.) manojito (*de hebras sedosas en la extremidad de una semilla*)
**comatose** [ˈkɑmətos] o [ˈkomətos] *adj* comatoso
**coma vigil** *s* (path.) coma vigil
**comb** [kom] *s* peine; almohaza (*para limpiar el pelo del caballo*); cresta (*del gallo y otras aves*); panal (*de cera que forman las abejas*); cresta de ola, cima de ola; *va* peinar; cardar (*la lana*); explorar con minuciosidad, examinar por to-

das partes; rastrillar (*el lino*); *vn* encresparse y romper (*las olas*)
**combat** [ˈkɑmbæt] *s* combate; [ˈkɑmbæt] o [kəmˈbæt] (*pret & pp:* **-bated** o **-batted;** *ger:* **-bating** o **-batting**) *va* combatir; *vn* combatir, combatirse
**combatant** [ˈkɑmbətənt] *adj* combatiente; combativo; *s* combatiente
**combat car** *s* (mil.) carro de combate
**combat duty** *s* (mil.) servicio de frente
**combative** [ˈkɑmbətɪv] o [kəmˈbætɪv] *adj* combativo
**combe** o **comb** [kum] o [kom] *s* valle estrecho; hoyo profundo cercado de alturas por tres lados
**comber** [ˈkomər] *s* peinador; cardador (*de lana*); ola encrestada, ola rompiente
**combination** [ˌkɑmbɪˈneʃən] *s* combinación; combinación (*ropa interior*)
**combination faucet** *s* mezclador automático
**combination fuse** *s* espoleta de doble efecto
**combination lock** *s* cerradura de combinación
**combine** [ˈkɑmbaɪn] o [kəmˈbaɪn] *s* (coll.) combinación (*de personas reunidas para un mismo fin*); monopolio; (agr.) segadora trilladora; [kəmˈbaɪn] *va* combinar; (chem.) combinar; *vn* combinarse; (chem.) combinarse
**combings** [ˈkomɪŋz] *spl* cabellos quitados por el peine, peinadura
**combining form** *s* (gram.) elemento de compuestos
**comb perforation** *s* (philately) dentado de peine
**combustibility** [kəmˌbʌstɪˈbɪlɪtɪ] *s* combustibilidad
**combustible** [kəmˈbʌstɪbəl] *adj* combustible; ardiente, impetuoso; *s* combustible
**combustion** [kəmˈbʌstʃən] *s* combustión
**combustion chamber** *s* (mach.) cámara de combustión
**combustion engine** *s* motor de combustión
**Comdr.** abr. de **Commander**
**Comdt.** abr. de **Commandant**
**come** [kʌm] (*pret:* **came;** *pp:* **come**) *vn* venir; ir, p.ej., **I'm coming** ya voy; ascender, subir; **come!** ¡venga!, ¡mire!, ¡deténgase!; ¡estése Vd. quieto!; **come along!** ¡vamos!; **come on!** ¡vamos!; ¡adelante!; **to come about** girar, cambiar de dirección; suceder; (naut.) cambiar de amura; **to come across** atravesar; encontrarse con; (slang) entregar lo que se tiene en manos; **to come after** venir detrás de, venir después de; venir por o en busca de; **to come again** volver, venir otra vez; **to come apart** desunirse; desprenderse; caerse a pedazos; **to come around** o **round** restablecerse (*de una enfermedad*); cobrar nuevo vigor; volver en sí; ceder, rendirse; ponerse de acuerdo; girar, cambiar de dirección; **to come at** alcanzar, conseguir; arrojarse sobre; **to come away** apartarse, retirarse; **to come back** volver; retroceder; (coll.) recobrarse, rehabilitarse; **to come before** anteponerse; llegar antes; **to come between** interponerse; dividir, separar, desunir; **to come by** conseguir, obtener; **to come down** bajar; desplomarse; descender (*respecto a la posición social, el estado financiero, etc.*); ser transmitido (*de una persona a otra*); **to come down on** caer sobre, acometer de prisa; (coll.) regañar; **to come downstairs** bajar (*de un piso a otro*); **to come down with** enfermar de; **to come for** venir por, venir a buscar; **to come forth** salir; aparecer; **to come forward** avanzar; presentarse; ofrecerse a hacer algún trabajo; **to come from** venir de; provenir de; **to come in** entrar; empezar; ponerse en uso; **to come in for** obtener, recibir; **to come into** entrar; obtener, recibir; heredar; **to come into one's own** ser reconocido, hacer reconocer sus derechos; **to come off** separarse, desprenderse; acontecer; hacerse, llegar a ser; salir; conducirse; librarse; **to come on** adelantar, mejorar; encontrarse con; principiar, p.ej., **the fever came on him this morning** la fiebre le principió esta mañana; **to come out** salir; salir a luz; estrenarse, debutar; ponerse de largo; declararse; resultar; **to come out for** anunciar su apoyo de; **to come out of** dejar (*alguna actividad*); salir de (*un cuidado, negocio, etc.*); **to come out with** decir, mostrar, revelar, publicar; **to come over** asir, coger; dejarse persuadir; pasar, p.ej., **what has come over him?** ¿qué le pasó?; **to come over to** pasarse a; **to come through** salir bien, tener éxito; ganar; (slang) entregar lo que se tiene en manos; **to come to** volver en sí; (naut.) anclar; (naut.) orzar; **to come together** juntarse, reunirse; **to come to oneself** volver en sí; **to come true** resultar verdadero; hacerse realidad; realizarse; **to come up** subir; surgir; presentarse; **to come upon** encontrarse con; **to come upstairs** subir (*de un piso a otro*); **to come up to** acercarse a; subir a; estar a la altura de; **to come up with** llegar a reunirse con; proponer; **come true** hecho realidad, p.ej., **a dream come true** un sueño hecho realidad
**come-at-able** [kʌmˈætəbəl] *adj* (coll.) alcanzable, asequible
**comeback** [ˈkʌmˌbæk] *s* (coll.) rehabilitación; (slang) respuesta hábil, respuesta aguda; (slang) motivo para quejarse
**comedian** [kəˈmidɪən] *s* cómico; autor de comedias
**comedienne** [kəˌmidɪˈɛn] *s* cómica
**comedown** [ˈkʌmˌdaʊn] *s* desazón, revés, pérdida de fortuna, dignidad, etc.; humillación
**comedy** [ˈkɑmədɪ] *s* (*pl:* **-dies**) comedia, comedia cómica; comicidad (*calidad de cómico*); (fig.) comedia; **cut the comedy!** (slang) ¡basta de risas!; (slang) ¡estáte quieto!
**comedy of character** *s* comedia de carácter
**comedy of intrigue** *s* comedia de enredo
**comedy of manners** *s* comedia de costumbres
**comeliness** [ˈkʌmlɪnɪs] *s* gracia, donaire; propiedad, conveniencia
**comely** [ˈkʌmlɪ] *adj* (*comp:* **-lier;** *super:* **-liest**) gracioso, donairoso; propio, conveniente
**come-on** [ˈkʌmˌɑn] *s* (slang) añagaza (*artificio para atraer con engaño*); (slang) desafío; (slang) bobo, crédulo
**comer** [ˈkʌmər] *s* llegado, recién llegado; (coll.) persona que promete; **the first comer** el primero que se presente
**comestible** [kəˈmɛstɪbəl] *adj & s* comestible
**comet** [ˈkɑmɪt] *s* (astr.) cometa
**come-uppance** [ˌkʌmˈʌpəns] *s* (coll.) reprensión, castigo merecido
**comfit** [ˈkʌmfɪt] o [ˈkɑmfɪt] *s* confite, dulce
**comfort** [ˈkʌmfərt] *s* confort, comodidad; confortación; confortador; colcha, cobertor; (law) ayuda, sostén; *va* acomodar, dar comodidad a; confortar; (law) ayudar, sostener
**comfortable** [ˈkʌmfərtəbəl] *adj* cómodo (*aplícase a las personas o las cosas*); desahogado (*dícese de una posición, fortuna, etc.*); holgado (*que, sin ser rico, vive con bienestar*); *s* colcha, cobertor
**comforter** [ˈkʌmfərtər] *s* confortador; colcha, cobertor; bufanda de lana; **the Comforter** el Consolador (*el Espíritu Santo*)
**comforting** [ˈkʌmfərtɪŋ] *adj* confortador, confortante
**comfortless** [ˈkʌmfərtlɪs] *adj* desconsolado, inconsolable; incómodo
**comfort station** *s* lavatorio con excusado, quiosco de necesidad
**comfrey** [ˈkʌmfrɪ] *s* (bot.) consuelda, sínfito
**comic** [ˈkɑmɪk] *adj* cómico; *s* cómico (*actor; lo que es propio para hacer reír*); (coll.) periódico cómico; **comics** *spl* (coll.) tiras cómicas (*de los periódicos*)
**comical** [ˈkɑmɪkəl] *adj* cómico
**comic book** *s* tebeo
**comic opera** *s* (mus.) ópera cómica, ópera bufa
**comic relief** *s* alivio de la tensión dramática, alivio cómico (*en lo dramático*)
**comic strip** *s* tira cómica, historieta gráfica
**Cominform** [ˌkɑmɪnˈfɔrm] *s* Cominform
**coming** [ˈkʌmɪŋ] *adj* que viene, venidero; (coll.) en camino hacia la importancia o la celebridad; *s* venida, llegada; advenimiento (*de Cristo*)
**coming out** *s* (com.) emisión (*de títulos*); entrada en sociedad, puesta de largo
**coming-out party** [ˈkʌmɪŋˈaʊt] *s* recepción de una muchacha que se pone de largo
**Comintern** [ˌkɑmɪnˈtʌrn] *s* Cominterno
**comitia** [kəˈmɪʃɪə] *spl* comicios

**comity** ['kamɪtɪ] *s* (*pl:* **-ties**) cortesía
**comma** ['kamə] *s* (gram.) coma
**comma bacillus** *s* (bact.) comabacilo
**command** [kə'mænd] o [kə'mand] *s* mandato, orden; mando, dominio, imperio; (mil.) comando; comandancia (*dignidad o cargo; territorio; cuerpo de soldados, flota de buques, etc. bajo un comandante*); dominio (*p.ej., de un idioma extranjero*); alcance de vista; **to be at the command of** estar a la disposición de; **to be in command** estar al mando; **to have command of** u **over oneself** saber dominarse, tener dominio de sí mismo; **to take command** tomar el mando; *va* mandar, ordenar; (mil.) comandar; imponer; dominar; merecer (*p.ej., respeto*); *vn* mandar
**commandant** [,kamən'dænt] o [,kamən'dant] *s* comandante (*de un fuerte, arsenal, etc.*)
**commandeer** [,kamən'dɪr] *va* reclutar forzosamente; expropiar; (coll.) apoderarse de
**commander** [kə'mændər] o [kə'mandər] *s* (mil.) comandante; (nav.) capitán de fragata; comendador (*de una orden militar*)
**commander in chief** *s* jefe supremo, comandante en jefe
**commanding** [kə'mændɪŋ] o [kə'mandɪŋ] *adj* poderoso; autorizado; imponente; dominante
**commanding officer** *s* (mil.) jefe, comandante en jefe
**commandment** [kə'mændmənt] o [kə'mandmənt] *s* mandato, orden; (Bib.) mandamiento
**commando** [kə'mændo] o [kə'mando] *s* (*pl:* **-dos** o **-does**) (mil.) comando (*tropa o soldado*)
**command of the air** *s* (mil.) dominio del aire
**command performance** *s* función mandada (*por orden real, presidencial, etc.*)
**commemorable** [kə'mɛmərəbəl] *adj* conmemorable
**commemorate** [kə'mɛməret] *va* conmemorar
**commemoration** [kə,mɛmə're∫ən] *s* conmemoración; **in commemoration of** en conmemoración de
**commemorative** [kə'mɛmə,retɪv] *adj* conmemorativo
**commemoratory** [kə'mɛmərə,torɪ] *adj* conmemoratorio
**commence** [kə'mɛns] *va & vn* comenzar, empezar
**commencement** [kə'mɛnsmənt] *s* comienzo, principio; día de graduación; ceremonias de graduación
**commend** [kə'mɛnd] *va* alabar, ensalzar; recomendar; encargar, encomendar
**commendable** [kə'mɛndəbəl] *adj* loable, recomendable, meritorio
**commendam** [kə'mɛndəm] *s* (eccl.) encomienda; **in commendam** (eccl.) en encomienda
**commendation** [,kamən'de∫ən] *s* alabanza, encomio; recomendación; encargo, encomienda
**commendatory** [kə'mɛndə,torɪ] *adj* recomendatorio, laudatorio; (eccl.) comendaticio
**commensal** [kə'mɛnsəl] *s* comensal; (biol.) comensal
**commensurability** [kə,mɛn∫ərə'bɪlɪtɪ] *s* conmensurabilidad
**commensurable** [kə'mɛn∫ərəbəl] *adj* conmensurable
**commensurate** [kə'mɛn∫ərɪt] *adj* proporcionado; conmensurable; igual
**commensuration** [kə,mɛn∫ə're∫ən] *s* conmensuración
**comment** ['kamɛnt] *s* comento; comentario; observación; *vn* comentar; **to comment on** comentar
**commentary** ['kamən,tɛrɪ] *s* (*pl:* **-ies**) comentario
**commentator** ['kamən,tetər] *s* comentador, comentarista; (rad.) locutor
**commerce** ['kamərs] *s* comercio
**commercial** [kə'mʌr∫əl] *adj* comercial; *s* (rad.) anuncio comercial, programa comercial; (Brit.) agente viajero
**commercialism** [kə'mʌr∫əlɪzəm] *s* mercantilismo; costumbre de comercio; locución mercantil
**commercialization** [kə,mʌr∫əlɪ'ze∫ən] *s* comercialización
**commercialize** [kə'mʌr∫əlaɪz] *va* comercializar
**commercial traveler** *s* agente viajero
**commination** [,kamɪ'ne∫ən] *s* conminación
**commingle** [kə'mɪŋgəl] *va* mezclar; *vn* mezclarse
**comminute** ['kamɪnjut] o ['kamɪnut] *va* moler, triturar, pulverizar
**comminuted fracture** *s* (surg.) fractura conminuta
**comminution** [,kamɪ'nju∫ən] o [,kamɪ'nu∫ən] *s* molienda, trituración, pulveración; (surg.) fractura conminuta
**commiserate** [kə'mɪzəret] *va* compadecer; *vn* condolerse; **to commiserate with** condolerse de
**commiseration** [kə,mɪzə're∫ən] *s* conmiseración
**commissar** [,kamɪ'sar] *s* comisario (*en una república soviética*)
**commissariat** [,kamɪ'sɛrɪæt] *s* comisaría o comisariato
**commissary** ['kamɪ,sɛrɪ] *s* (*pl:* **-ies**) economato (*tienda*); comisario; (mil.) comisario
**commission** [kə'mɪ∫ən] *s* comisión; (mil.) nombramiento; patente; **to put in commission** poner en uso, hacer funcionar; poner (*un buque*) en servicio activo; **to put out of commission** descomponer, inutilizar; retirar (*un buque*) del servicio activo; *va* comisionar; (mil.) nombrar; poner en uso; poner (*un buque*) en servicio activo
**commissioned officer** *s* (mil. & nav.) oficial
**commissioner** [kə'mɪ∫ənər] *s* comisionado; comisario
**commissionership** [kə'mɪ∫ənər,∫ɪp] *s* cargo de comisionado
**commission government** *s* gobierno municipal dirigido por una comisión electiva
**commission merchant** *s* comisionista
**commissure** ['kamɪ∫ʊr] *s* (anat., bot. & zool.) comisura
**commit** [kə'mɪt] (*pret & pp:* **-mitted;** *ger:* **-mitting**) *va* confiar, entregar; cometer (*p.ej., un negocio a uno; un crimen, una falta*); someter (*a una comisión para su consideración*); comprometer; dar (*la palabra*); internar (*a un demente*); encomendar (*a la memoria*); **to commit oneself** declararse; comprometerse; **to commit to paper** o **to writing** poner por escrito
**commitment** [kə'mɪtmənt] *s* comisión; internación; auto de prisión; compromiso, promesa, cometido
**committal** [kə'mɪtəl] *s* comisión; entierro; compromiso, promesa
**committee** [kə'mɪtɪ] *s* comité
**committeeman** [kə'mɪtɪmən] *s* (*pl:* **-men**) comisionado
**committee of the whole** *s* comité compuesto de la totalidad de los miembros de una asamblea, un club, etc.
**commix** [ka'mɪks] *va* mezclar; *vn* mezclarse
**commixture** [ka'mɪkst∫ər] *s* conmistión
**commode** [kə'mod] *s* cómoda; lavabo; servicio, sillico
**commodious** [kə'modɪəs] *adj* cómodo, espacioso, holgado
**commodity** [kə'madɪtɪ] *s* (*pl:* **-ties**) mercancía; comodidad, cosa útil
**commodore** ['kamədor] *s* comodoro; navío del comodoro
**common** ['kamən] *adj* común; *s* campo común, ejido; **commons** *spl* estado llano; refectorio (*de un colegio*); víveres; **in common** en común; **the Commons** (Brit.) los Comunes, la Cámara de los Comunes
**commonage** ['kamənɪdʒ] *s* derecho de pastar en común; propiedad de terrenos en común; campo común; estado llano, gente común
**commonalty** ['kamənəltɪ] *s* (*pl:* **-ties**) generalidad de personas, común de las gentes; estado llano; miembros de una corporación o sociedad
**common bile duct** *s* (anat.) conducto biliar común, colédoco
**common carrier** *s* empresa de transporte público
**common cold** *s* catarro común, resfriado común
**common council** *s* ayuntamiento
**common councilman** *s* concejal

**common denominator** *s* (math. & fig.) denominador común
**common divisor** *s* (math.) común divisor
**commoner** ['kamənər] *s* plebeyo; (Brit.) miembro de la Cámara de los Comunes; (Brit.) estudiante que no tiene beca ni plaza
**common era** *s* era común, cristiana o vulgar
**common fraction** *s* (math.) fracción común, quebrado
**common gender** *s* (gram.) género común
**common law** *s* derecho consuetudinario, derecho no legislado
**common-law marriage** ['kamən'lɔ] *s* matrimonio consensual, unión matrimonial contraída sin intervención de la iglesia ni la autoridad civil
**commonly** ['kamənlɪ] *adv* comúnmente
**common noun** *s* (gram.) nombre apelativo o común
**commonplace** ['kamən,ples] *adj* común, trivial, ordinario; *s* cosa común u ordinaria; lugar común, trivialidad, observación evidente
**common pleas** *spl* (law) pleitos civiles; (law) tribunal civil
**common prayer** *s* liturgia de la Iglesia anglicana
**common room** *s* casino, sala de reunión
**common salt** *s* sal común
**common school** *s* escuela elemental
**common sense** *s* sentido común
**common-sense** ['kamən,sɛns] *adj* cuerdo, razonable
**common stock** *s* (com.) acción ordinaria, acciones ordinarias
**commonweal** ['kamən,wil] *s* bienestar general, bien público
**commonwealth** ['kamən,wɛlθ] *s* nación; república; estado (*de los Estados Unidos de América*); mancomunidad; estado libre asociado
**Commonwealth of Australia** *s* Federación Australiana
**commotion** [kə'moʃən] *s* conmoción
**communal** ['kamjunəl] o [kə'mjunəl] *adj* comunal
**communalism** ['kamjunəlɪzəm] o [kə'mjunəlɪzəm] *s* sistema de confederación de comunas
**commune** ['kamjun] *s* comunión (*trato familiar*); (eccl.) comunión; comuna; (*cap.*) *s* Comuna; [kə'mjun] *vn* conversar, comunicarse; (eccl.) comulgar
**communicable** [kə'mjunɪkəbəl] *adj* comunicable
**communicant** [kə'mjunɪkənt] *adj* comunicante; *s* comunicante; (eccl.) comulgante
**communicate** [kə'mjunɪket] *va* comunicar; (eccl.) comulgar; *vn* comunicar; comunicarse; (eccl.) comulgar
**communicating** [kə'mjunɪ,ketɪŋ] *adj* comunicador; **to be communicating** mandarse (*dos piezas de un edificio*)
**communication** [kə,mjunɪ'keʃən] *s* comunicación; **communications** *spl* comunicaciones (*teléfonos, correos, etc.*); vías de comunicación
**communicative** [kə'mjunɪ,ketɪv] *adj* comunicativo
**communion** [kə'mjunjən] *s* comunión; (*cap.*) *s* (eccl.) comunión
**communion of saints** *s* (eccl.) comunión de los santos
**communion rail** *s* comulgatorio
**Communion service** *s* oficio del sacramento de la Eucaristía
**communiqué** [kə,mjunɪ'ke] o [kə'mjunɪke] *s* comunicado, parte
**communism** ['kamjunɪzəm] *s* comunismo
**communist** ['kamjunɪst] *adj & s* comunista
**communistic** [,kamju'nɪstɪk] *adj* comunista
**Communist International** *s* Internacional Comunista
**community** [kə'mjunɪtɪ] *s* (*pl:* **-ties**) comunidad, colectividad; vecindario
**community center** *s* centro social, centro comunal
**community chest** *s* caja de beneficencia, fondos de beneficencia
**community house** *s* centro social
**communize** ['kamjunaɪz] *va* comunizar
**commutable** [kə'mjutəbəl] *adj* conmutable
**commutate** ['kamjutet] *va* (elec.) conmutar
**commutation** [,kamju'teʃən] *s* conmutación; (coll.) uso de un billete de abono; (elec. & law) conmutación
**commutation ticket** *s* billete de abono
**commutative** [kə'mjutətɪv] o ['kamju,tetɪv] *adj* conmutativo
**commutator** ['kamju,tetər] *s* (elec.) conmutador; (elec.) colector (*de dínamo*)
**commutator bar** *s* (elec.) delga
**commute** [kə'mjut] *va* conmutar; (law) conmutar; *vn* ser abonado al ferrocarril, viajar con billete de abono
**commuter** [kə'mjutər] *s* abonado al ferrocarril
**comp.** abr. de **compare, comparative, composer, composition, compositor** y **compound**
**compact** [kəm'pækt] *adj* compacto; breve, conciso; compuesto; **compact of** compuesto de; ['kampækt] *s* estuche de afeites; [kəm'pækt] *va* hacer compacto, consolidar, condensar, comprimir; componer
**companion** [kəm'pænjən] *s* compañero (*persona o cosa*); acompañador; caballero de la orden más baja; (naut.) chupeta de escala; (naut.) escalera de cámara; *va* acompañar, estar o ir en compañía de
**companionable** [kəm'pænjənəbəl] *adj* sociable, simpático
**companion-at-arms** [kəm'pænjənət'armz] *s* (*pl:* **companions-at-arms**) compañonero de armas, conmilitón
**companionate** [kəm'pænjənɪt] *adj* de compañeros, de compañerismo
**companionate marriage** *s* matrimonio de compañerismo
**companionship** [kəm'pænjənʃɪp] *s* compañerismo
**companionway** [kəm'pænjən,we] *s* (naut.) escalera de cámara
**company** ['kʌmpənɪ] *s* (*pl:* **-nies**) compañía; (com.) compañía, empresa; (mil. & theat.) compañía; compañero o compañeros; compañerismo; (coll.) huésped o huéspedes; (coll.) visita o visitas; (naut.) tripulación; **to bear company** acompañar; **to join company** incorporarse; **to be good company** ser compañero simpático, ser compañero alegre; **to keep bad company** asociarse con gente mala; **to keep company** ir juntos (*un hombre y una mujer*); **to keep company with** cortejar (*a una mujer*); recibir galanteos de (*un hombre*); **to keep good company** asociarse con gente buena; **to keep someone company** hacerle compañía a una persona; **to part company** tomar rumbos distintos; separarse; enemistarse; **to part company with** separarse de; enemistarse con; *adj* social, p.ej., **company building** edificio social
**company union** *s* gremio interno, gremio controlado por los patronos
**compar.** abr. de **comparative**
**comparable** ['kampərəbəl] *adj* comparable
**comparative** [kəm'pærətɪv] *adj* comparativo; comparado (*dícese, p.ej., de la anatomía*); (gram.) comparativo; *s* (gram.) comparativo
**comparatively** [kəm'pærətɪvlɪ] *adv* comparativamente
**comparator** ['kampə,retər] *s* (phys.) comparador
**compare** [kəm'pɛr] *s* comparación; **beyond compare** sin comparación, incomparable; *va* comparar; **not to be compared with** no ser comparable con, no poder compararse con
**comparison** [kəm'pærɪsən] *s* comparación; (gram.) comparación; **in comparison with** en comparación con, comparado con
**compartment** [kəm'partmənt] *s* compartimiento; (rail.) compartimiento, departamento
**compass** ['kʌmpəs] *s* brújula o compás; raya, confín; círculo, circunferencia; circuito, recinto, ámbito; alcance, extensión; compás (*extensión de la voz, etc.*); **compass** *s* o **compasses** *spl* compás (*para trazar curvas, etc.*); **to box the compass** (naut.) cuartear la aguja; (fig.) volver a su punto de partida; *va* contornear, rodear; circundar; maquinar, urdir; entender, comprender
**compass card** *s* (naut.) rosa náutica, rosa de los vientos
**compassion** [kəm'pæʃən] *s* compasión; **to move to compassion** mover a compasión

**compassionate** [kəmˈpæʃənɪt] *adj* compasivo
**compass needle** *s* aguja de brújula
**compass plant** *s* (bot.) planta magnética
**compass saw** *s* serrucho de calar, sierra de punta
**compaternity** [ˌkampəˈtʌrnɪtɪ] *s* compadrazgo, compaternidad
**compatibility** [kəmˌpætɪˈbɪlɪtɪ] *s* compatibilidad
**compatible** [kəmˈpætɪbəl] *adj* compatible
**compatriot** [kəmˈpetrɪət] o [kəmˈpætrɪət] *s* compatriota
**compeer** [kamˈpɪr] o [ˈkampɪr] *s* par, igual; compañero, camarada
**compel** [kəmˈpɛl] (*pret & pp:* **-pelled;** *ger:* **-pelling**) *va* compeler; imponer (*p.ej., respeto*); **to compel to** + *inf* compeler a + *inf*
**compend** [ˈkampɛnd] *s* var. de **compendium**
**compendious** [kəmˈpɛndɪəs] *adj* compendioso
**compendium** [kəmˈpɛndɪəm] *s* (*pl:* **-ums** o **-a** [ə]) compendio
**compensate** [ˈkampənset] *va & vn* compensar; **to compensate for** compensar
**compensating balance** *s* (horol.) volante compensador, balanza de compensación
**compensating pendulum** *s* compensador
**compensation** [ˌkampənˈseʃən] *s* compensación; retribución (*pago*); indemnización
**compensation balance** *s* (horol.) volante compensador
**compensation pendulum** *s* péndulo de compensación
**compensative** [ˈkampənˌsetɪv] o [kəmˈpɛnsətɪv] *adj* compensativo
**compensator** [ˈkampənˌsetər] *s* compensador
**compensatory** [kəmˈpɛnsəˌtorɪ] *adj* compensatorio
**compete** [kəmˈpit] *vn* competir
**competence** [ˈkampɪtəns] o **competency** [ˈkampɪtənsɪ] *s* competencia; (un) buen pasar; (law) competencia
**competent** [ˈkampɪtənt] *adj* competente; (law) competente
**competition** [ˌkampɪˈtɪʃən] *s* competencia; oposición (*para la obtención de un premio, cátedra, etc. por medio de un examen*); **in competition with** en competencia de
**competitive** [kəmˈpɛtɪtɪv] *adj* de concurso, de oposición
**competitor** [kəmˈpɛtɪtər] *s* competidor
**compilation** [ˌkampɪˈleʃən] *s* compilación, recopilación
**compile** [kəmˈpaɪl] *va* compilar, recopilar
**complacence** [kəmˈplesəns] o **complacency** [kəmˈplesənsɪ] *s* satisfacción de sí mismo; complacencia
**complacent** [kəmˈplesənt] *adj* complacido, satisfecho de sí mismo; complaciente
**complain** [kəmˈplen] *vn* quejarse; **to complain about** u **of** quejarse de; **to complain of** + *ger* quejarse de + *inf*
**complainant** [kəmˈplenənt] *s* querellante; (law) demandante
**complaint** [kəmˈplent] *s* queja; agravio; mal, enfermedad; (law) querella, demanda; **to lodge a complaint** hacer una reclamación
**complaisance** [kəmˈplezəns] o [ˌkampleˈzæns] *adj* complacencia, amabilidad, condescendencia
**complaisant** [kəmˈplezənt] o [ˌkampleˈzænt] *adj* complaciente, amable, condescendiente
**complement** [ˈkamplɪmənt] *s* complemento; (gram., math. & mus.) complemento; (naut.) dotación; [ˈkamplɪmɛnt] *va* complementar
**complemental** [ˌkamplɪˈmɛntəl] *adj* completivo, complementario
**complementary** [ˌkamplɪˈmɛntərɪ] *adj* complementario
**complementary angle** *s* (geom.) ángulo complementario
**complementary colors** *spl* colores complementarios
**complement fixation** *s* (bact.) fijación del complemento
**complete** [kəmˈplit] *adj* completo; *va* completar
**completeness** [kəmˈplitnɪs] *s* entereza, perfección
**completion** [kəmˈpliʃən] *s* completamiento; cumplimiento, terminación
**completory** [kəmˈplitərɪ] *s* (*pl:* **-ries**) (eccl.) completas
**complex** [kəmˈplɛks] o [ˈkamplɛks] *adj* complejo; [ˈkamplɛks] *s* complejo; (psychol.) complejo; (coll.) idea fija, prejuicio irracional
**complex fraction** *s* (math.) fracción compleja
**complexion** [kəmˈplɛkʃən] *s* complexión, tez; aspecto general, carácter
**complexity** [kəmˈplɛksɪtɪ] *s* (*pl:* **-ties**) complejidad
**complex sentence** *s* (gram.) frase compleja
**compliance** [kəmˈplaɪəns] *s* condescendencia, sumisión; complacencia, rendimiento; **in compliance with** accediendo a; de acuerdo con
**compliancy** [kəmˈplaɪənsɪ] *s* var. de **compliance**
**compliant** [kəmˈplaɪənt] *adj* condescendiente, sumiso; complaciente, servicial
**complicate** [ˈkamplɪket] *va* complicar; entrelazar, torcer juntos
**complicated** [ˈkamplɪˌketɪd] *adj* complicado
**complication** [ˌkamplɪˈkeʃən] *s* complicación
**complicity** [kəmˈplɪsɪtɪ] *s* (*pl:* **-ties**) complicidad
**compliment** [ˈkamplɪmənt] *s* alabanza, halago; cumplimiento; **to send compliments** enviar saludos; [ˈkamplɪmɛnt] *va* cumplimentar
**complimentary** [ˌkamplɪˈmɛntərɪ] *adj* lisonjero; gratuito, de regalo, de cortesía
**complimentary copy** *s* ejemplar de cortesía
**complimentary ticket** *s* billete de regalo, pase de cortesía
**complin** [ˈkamplɪn] o **compline** [ˈkamplaɪn] o [ˈkamplɪn] *s* (eccl.) completas
**complot** [ˈkamplat] *s* complot; [kəmˈplat] (*pret & pp:* **-plotted;** *ger:* **-plotting**) *vn* complotar
**comply** [kəmˈplaɪ] (*pret & pp:* **-plied**) *vn* conformarse, condescender; **to comply with** conformarse con, obrar de acuerdo con
**componé** [kamˈpone] *adj* (her.) componado
**component** [kəmˈponənt] *adj* componente; *s* componente *m;* (mech.) componente *f*
**comport** [kəmˈport] *va* acarrear; **to comport oneself** comportarse; *vn* convenir, concordar
**comportment** [kəmˈportmənt] *s* comportamiento
**compose** [kəmˈpoz] *va* componer; (mus., lit. & print.) componer; **to be composed of** constar de, estar compuesto de; *vn* componer; componerse, combinarse
**composed** [kəmˈpozd] *adj* tranquilo, sosegado
**composer** [kəmˈpozər] *s* componedor; (mus.) compositor; autor, escritor
**composing stick** *s* (print.) componedor
**composite** [kəmˈpazɪt] *adj* compuesto; (*cap.*) *adj* (arch.) compuesto; (*l.c.*) *s* compuesto; (bot.) compuesta
**composite photograph** *s* fotografía compuesta, fotografía de superposición
**composition** [ˌkampəˈzɪʃən] *s* composición
**composition of forces** *s* (mech.) composición de fuerzas
**compositor** [kəmˈpazɪtər] *s* (print.) componedor, cajista
**compost** [ˈkampost] *s* compuesto; (agr.) abono compuesto; *va* (agr.) abonar, estercolar
**composure** [kəmˈpoʒər] *s* compostura, serenidad, calma
**compote** [ˈkampot] *s* compota; compotera (*vasija*)
**compound** [ˈkampaʊnd] o [kamˈpaʊnd] *adj* compuesto; (elec. & mach.) compound; [ˈkampaʊnd] *s* compuesto; (chem.) compuesto; (gram.) vocablo compuesto, palabra compuesta; recinto; [kamˈpaʊnd] *va* componer, combinar; **to compound a felony** (law) aceptar dinero para no procesar; *vn* componerse; **to compound with** capitular con
**compound fraction** *s* (math.) fracción compuesta, quebrado compuesto
**compound fracture** *s* (surg.) fractura complicada
**compound interest** *s* interés compuesto
**compound number** *s* (math.) número compuesto
**compound sentence** *s* (gram.) oración compuesta
**comprehend** [ˌkamprɪˈhɛnd] *va* comprender

**comprehensibility** [ˌkamprɪˌhɛnsɪˈbɪlɪtɪ] *s* comprensibilidad

**comprehensible** [ˌkamprɪˈhɛnsɪbəl] *adj* comprensible

**comprehension** [ˌkamprɪˈhɛnʃən] *s* comprensión

**comprehensive** [ˌkamprɪˈhɛnsɪv] *adj* comprensivo (*que tiene la facultad de entender; que incluye o contiene*); completo, que lo abarca todo

**compress** [ˈkamprɛs] *s* (med.) compresa; compresor (*para comprimir el algodón en balas*); [kəmˈprɛs] *va* comprimir

**compressed** [kəmˈprɛst] *adj* comprimido

**compressed air** *s* aire comprimido

**compressed-air drill** [kəmˈprɛstˈɛr] *s* perforadora de aire comprimido

**compressibility** [kəmˌprɛsɪˈbɪlɪtɪ] *s* compresibilidad

**compressible** [kəmˈprɛsɪbəl] *adj* compresible

**compression** [kəmˈprɛʃən] *s* compresión

**compression ratio** *s* (mach.) índice de compresión

**compression stroke** *s* (mach.) carrera de compresión

**compressive** [kəmˈprɛsɪv] *adj* compresivo

**compressor** [kəmˈprɛsər] *s* compresor; (anat., mach. & surg.) compresor

**comprise** o **comprize** [kəmˈpraɪz] *va* abarcar, comprender, constar de

**compromise** [ˈkamprəmaɪz] *s* componenda, compromiso; (coll.) término medio; (canon law) compromiso; *va* arreglar, componer (*por medio de concesiones mutuas*); comprometer, exponer; *vn* transigir

**comprovincial** [ˌkamprəˈvɪnʃəl] *adj* (eccl.) comprovincial; *s* (eccl.) comprovincial; comprovinciano (*persona de la misma provincia*)

**comptometer** [kampˈtamɪtər] *s* (trademark) contómetro

**comptroller** [kənˈtrolər] *s* contralor, interventor

**comptrollership** [kənˈtrolərʃɪp] *s* contraloría, intervención

**compulsion** [kəmˈpʌlʃən] *s* compulsión

**compulsive** [kəmˈpʌlsɪv] *adj* compulsivo

**compulsory** [kəmˈpʌlsərɪ] *adj* obligatorio; compulsivo

**compunction** [kəmˈpʌŋkʃən] *s* compunción

**computation** [ˌkampjʊˈteʃən] *s* computación

**compute** [kəmˈpjut] *va & vn* computar, calcular

**computer** [kəmˈpjutər] *s* calculador; ordenador (*aparato*)

**comrade** [ˈkamræd] o [ˈkamrɪd] *s* camarada

**comrade in arms** *s* compañero de armas

**comradeship** [ˈkamrædʃɪp] o [ˈkamrɪdʃɪp] *s* camaradería

**con.** abr. de **conclusion, consolidated** y **contra** (Lat.) **against**

**con** [kan] contra; *s* contra (*concepto opuesto*); (*pret & pp:* **conned;** *ger:* **conning**) *va* estudiar, aprender de memoria

**conation** [koˈneʃən] *s* (psychol.) conación

**concatenate** [kanˈkætɪnet] *adj* concatenado; *va* concatenar

**concatenation** [kanˌkætɪˈneʃən] *s* concatenación

**concave** [ˈkankev] o [kanˈkev] *adj* cóncavo; [ˈkankev] *s* cóncavo

**concavity** [kanˈkævɪtɪ] *s* (*pl:* **-ties**) concavidad

**concavo-convex** [kanˈkevokanˈvɛks] *adj* cóncavoconvexo

**conceal** [kənˈsil] *va* encubrir, ocultar, disimular

**concealment** [kənˈsilmənt] *s* encubrimiento, disimulación; escondite

**concede** [kənˈsid] *va* conceder

**conceit** [kənˈsit] *s* orgullo, engreimiento; concepto, dicho ingenioso, capricho

**conceited** [kənˈsitɪd] *adj* orgulloso, engreído

**conceivable** [kənˈsivəbəl] *adj* concebible

**conceive** [kənˈsiv] *va* concebir; *vn* concebir; **to conceive of** formar concepto de

**concentrate** [ˈkansəntret] *s* substancia concentrada; (min.) gandinga; *va* concentrar; *vn* concentrarse; **to concentrate on** concentrar la atención en

**concentration** [ˌkansənˈtreʃən] *s* concentración

**concentration camp** *s* campo de concentración

**concentric** [kanˈsɛntrɪk] o **concentrical** [kanˈsɛntrɪkəl] *adj* concéntrico

**concept** [ˈkansɛpt] *s* concepto

**conception** [kənˈsɛpʃən] *s* concepción

**conceptual** [kənˈsɛptʃʊəl] *adj* conceptual

**conceptualism** [kənˈsɛptʃʊəlɪzəm] *s* (philos.) conceptualismo

**conceptualist** [kənˈsɛptʃʊəlɪst] *s* (philos.) conceptualista

**conceptualistic** [kənˌsɛptʃʊəˈlɪstɪk] *adj* (philos.) conceptualista

**concern** [kənˈsʌrn] *s* interés; inquietud; negocio, asunto importante; empresa, casa comercial, compañía; concernencia; **of concern** de interés, de importancia; *va* atañer, concernir, importar; interesar; **as concerns** respecto de; **as far as he is concerned** en cuanto le toca a él; **to concern oneself** interesarse, ocuparse; inquietarse; **to whom it may concern** a quien pueda interesar

**concerned** [kənˈsʌrnd] *adj* interesado; ocupado; inquietado

**concerning** [kənˈsʌrnɪŋ] *prep* concerniente a, respecto de

**concernment** [kənˈsʌrnmənt] *s* interés, importancia; inquietud; asunto

**concert** [ˈkansərt] *s* concierto; (mus.) concierto (*sesión musical*); **in concert** de concierto; *adj* (mus.) para conciertos; [kənˈsʌrt] *va & vn* concertar

**concerted** [kənˈsʌrtɪd] *adj* concertado; (mus.) concertante

**concert grand** *s* (mus.) gran piano para conciertos

**concertina** [ˌkansərˈtinə] *s* (mus.) concertina

**concertmaster** [ˈkansərtˌmæstər] o [ˈkansərtˌmastər] o **concertmeister** [kənˈtsɛrtˌmaɪstər] *s* (mus.) concertino

**concerto** [kanˈtʃɛrto] *s* (*pl:* **-tos** o **-ti** [ti]) (mus.) concierto, concerto (*composición*)

**concession** [kənˈsɛʃən] *s* concesión

**concessionaire** [kənˌsɛʃəˈnɛr] *s* concesionario

**concessive** [kənˈsɛsɪv] *adj* concesivo; (gram.) concesivo

**conch** [kaŋk] o [kantʃ] *s* (*pl:* **conchs** [kaŋks] o **conches** [ˈkantʃɪz]) *s* caracola; (arch.) concha

**concha** [ˈkaŋkə] *s* (*pl:* **-chae** [ki]) *s* (anat. & arch.) concha

**conchiferous** [kaŋˈkɪfərəs] *adj* conquífero

**conchoid** [ˈkaŋkɔɪd] *s* (geom.) concoide

**conchoidal** [kaŋˈkɔɪdəl] *adj* concoideo; (mineral.) concoideo

**conchologist** [kaŋˈkalədʒɪst] *s* conquiliólogo

**conchology** [kaŋˈkalədʒɪ] *s* conquiliología

**concierge** [ˌkansɪˈʌrʒ] *s* conserje

**conciliate** [kənˈsɪlɪet] *va* conciliar

**conciliation** [kənˌsɪlɪˈeʃən] *s* conciliación

**conciliative** [kənˈsɪlɪˌetɪv] *adj* conciliativo

**conciliator** [kənˈsɪlɪˌetər] *s* conciliador

**conciliatory** [kənˈsɪlɪəˌtorɪ] *adj* conciliador, conciliatorio

**concise** [kənˈsaɪs] *adj* conciso

**concision** [kənˈsɪʒən] *s* concisión

**conclave** [ˈkanklev] *s* conclave; (eccl.) conclave

**conclavist** [ˈkanklevɪst] *s* conclavista

**conclude** [kənˈklud] *va* concluir; *vn* concluir o concluirse

**conclusion** [kənˈkluʒən] *s* conclusión; despedida (*de una carta*); **in conclusion** en conclusión; **to try conclusions with** participar en una contienda con

**conclusive** [kənˈklusɪv] *adj* concluyente

**concoct** [kanˈkakt] *va* confeccionar; tramar, maquinar; forjar (*mentiras*)

**concoction** [kanˈkakʃən] *s* confección; trama, maquinación; forja (*p.ej., de mentiras*)

**concolorous** [kanˈkʌlərəs] *adj* concoloro

**concomitance** [kanˈkamɪtəns] *s* concomitancia

**concomitant** [kanˈkamɪtənt] *adj & s* concomitante

**concord** [ˈkaŋkɔrd] *s* concordia; (gram. & mus.) concordancia

**concordance** [kanˈkɔrdəns] *s* concordancia, acuerdo; concordancias (*lista de palabras con citas*)

**concordant** [kanˈkɔrdənt] *adj* concordante

**concordat** [kɑnˈkɔrdæt] *s* concordato; (eccl.) concordato
**Concord grape** *s* uva Concord
**concourse** [ˈkɑŋkors] *s* confluencia (*p.ej., de dos ríos*); concurso (*de gente*); (rail.) gran salón; bulevar, gran vía
**concrescence** [kɑnˈkrɛsəns] *s* concrescencia; (biol.) concrescencia
**concrete** [ˈkɑnkrit] o [kɑnˈkrit] *adj* concreto; de hormigón, de concreto, para concreto; cuajado, duro, sólido; *s* hormigón, concreto; *va* concretar; [kɑnˈkrit] *va* solidificar, endurecer; *vn* solidificarse, endurecerse
**concrete block** *s* bloque de hormigón
**concrete mixer** *s* mezcladora de hormigón, hormigonera
**concrete number** *s* (arith.) número concreto
**concretion** [kɑnˈkriʃən] *s* concreción; (geol. & path.) concreción
**concubinage** [kɑnˈkjubɪnɪdʒ] *s* concubinato
**concubine** [ˈkɑŋkjʊbaɪn] *s* concubina; casada de condición y derechos inferiores
**concupiscence** [kɑnˈkjupɪsəns] *s* concupiscencia
**concupiscent** [kɑnˈkjupɪsənt] *adj* concupiscente
**concupiscible** [kɑnˈkjupɪsɪbəl] *adj* concupiscible
**concur** [kənˈkʌr] (*pret & pp:* **-curred;** *ger:* **-curring**) *vn* concurrir
**concurrence** [kənˈkʌrəns] *s* concurrencia; acuerdo
**concurrent** [kənˈkʌrənt] *adj* concurrente; *s* acontecimiento concurrente
**concussion** [kənˈkʌʃən] *s* concusión; (path.) concusión
**condemn** [kənˈdɛm] *va* condenar; expropiar; **to condemn to be burned** condenar a la hoguera; **to condemn to** + *inf* condenar a + *inf*
**condemnation** [ˌkɑndɛmˈneʃən] *s* condenación; expropiación
**condemnatory** [kənˈdɛmnəˌtorɪ] *adj* condenatorio
**condensation** [ˌkɑndɛnˈseʃən] *s* condensación
**condense** [kənˈdɛns] *va* condensar; *vn* condensarse
**condensed milk** *s* leche condensada
**condenser** [kənˈdɛnsər] *s* condensador
**condescend** [ˌkɑndɪˈsɛnd] *vn* dignarse; **to condescend to** + *inf* dignarse + *inf*
**condescending** [ˌkɑndɪˈsɛndɪŋ] *adj* que trata con aire protector a inferiores, que tiene aire de superioridad
**condescension** [ˌkɑndɪˈsɛnʃən] *s* dignación, aire protector
**condign** [kənˈdaɪn] *adj* condigno, merecido (*castigo*)
**condiment** [ˈkɑndɪmənt] *s* condimento
**condisciple** [ˌkɑndɪˈsaɪpəl] *s* condiscípulo
**condition** [kənˈdɪʃən] *s* condición; **on condition that** a condición (de) que; *va* acondicionar; (educ.) suspender; (textiles) condicionar
**conditional** [kənˈdɪʃənəl] *adj* condicional; (gram.) condicional
**conditioned** [kənˈdɪʃənd] *adj* condicionado
**conditioned reflex** o **response** *s* (psychol.) reflejo condicionado
**condole** [kənˈdol] *vn* condolerse
**condolence** [kənˈdoləns] *s* condolencia
**condominium** [ˌkɑndəˈmɪnɪəm] *s* condominio
**condonation** [ˌkɑndoˈneʃən] *s* condonación
**condone** [kənˈdon] *va* condonar
**condor** [ˈkɑndər] *s* (orn.) cóndor
**condottiere** [ˌkondotˈtjɛre] *s* (*pl:* **-ri** [ri]) condotiero
**conduce** [kənˈdjus] o [kənˈdus] *vn* conducir
**conducive** [kənˈdjusɪv] o [kənˈdusɪv] *adj* conducente, contribuyente
**conduct** [ˈkɑndʌkt] *s* conducta; **to be on one's good conduct** conducirse bien; [kənˈdʌkt] *va & vn* conducir; **to conduct oneself** conducirse, comportarse
**conductance** [kənˈdʌktəns] *s* (elec.) conductancia
**conductibility** [kənˌdʌktɪˈbɪlɪtɪ] *s* conductibilidad
**conductible** [kənˈdʌktɪbəl] *adj* conductible; conductivo
**conduction** [kənˈdʌkʃən] *s* conducción; (phys. & physiol.) conducción
**conduction anesthesia** *s* anestesia de conducción, anestesia regional
**conductive** [kənˈdʌktɪv] *adj* conductivo; (phys.) conductor
**conductivity** [ˌkɑndʌkˈtɪvɪtɪ] *s* conductividad
**conductor** [kənˈdʌktər] *s* conductor, guía; (mus.) director; (phys.) conductor; (rail.) conductor, revisor; cobrador (*de billetes en un tranvía*)
**conduit** [ˈkɑndɪt] o [ˈkɑndʊɪt] *s* conducto; (elec.) conducto, canal, canal para alambres
**conduplicate** [kɑnˈdjuplɪkɪt] o [kɑnˈduplɪkɪt] *adj* (bot.) conduplicado
**condyle** [ˈkɑndɪl] *s* (anat.) cóndilo
**cone** [kon] *s* (geom. & bot.) cono; barquillo (*hoja de pasta de harina arrollada en forma de cono o cucurucho*)
**cone bearing** *s* cojinete de cono
**cone brake** *s* freno de cono
**cone clutch** *s* embrague de cono
**cone gear** *s* engranaje cónico
**cone pulley** *s* cono de poleas
**Conestoga wagon** [ˌkɑnɪsˈtogə] *s* carromato que empleaban los norteamericanos para atravesar las llanuras del oeste antes del ferrocarril transcontinental
**coney** [ˈkonɪ] *s* var. de **cony**
**confab** [ˈkɑnfæb] *s* (coll.) confabulación; (*pret & pp:* **-fabbed;** *ger:* **-fabbing**) *vn* (coll.) confabular
**confabulate** [kənˈfæbjəlet] *vn* confabular
**confabulation** [kənˌfæbjəˈleʃən] *s* confabulación
**confection** [kənˈfɛkʃən] *s* confección, hechura; confite, confitura; confección caprichosa, sombrero caprichoso
**confectioner** [kənˈfɛkʃənər] *s* confitero
**confectionery** [kənˈfɛkʃəˌnɛrɪ] *s* (*pl:* **-ies**) confitería; confituras
**confederacy** [kənˈfɛdərəsɪ] *s* (*pl:* **-cies**) confederación; cábala; (*cap.*) *s* (U.S.A.) Estados confederados
**confederate** [kənˈfɛdərɪt] *adj* confederado; *s* confederado; cómplice; [kənˈfɛdəret] *va* confederar; *vn* confederarse
**Confederate States of America** *s* (U.S.A.) Estados confederados
**confederation** [kenˌfɛdəˈreʃən] *s* confederación
**confederative** [kənˈfɛdəˌretɪv] *adj* confederativo
**confer** [kənˈfʌr] (*pret & pp:* **-ferred;** *ger:* **-ferring**) *va* conferir; *vn* conferir, conferenciar
**conferee** [ˌkɑnfəˈri] *s* conferenciante; conferido
**conference** [ˈkɑnfərəns] *s* conferencia
**conferment** [kənˈfʌrmənt] *s* otorgamiento, donación
**confess** [kənˈfɛs] *va* confesar; (eccl.) confesar (*sus pecados; a un penitente*); *vn* confesar o confesarse; (eccl.) confesar o confesarse; **to confess to** confesar o confesarse a (*Dios*); confesarse con (*un sacerdote*)
**confessedly** [kənˈfɛsɪdlɪ] *adv* reconocidamente
**confession** [kənˈfɛʃən] *s* confesión
**confessional** [kənˈfɛʃənəl] *adj* confesional; *s* confesonario; confesión, costumbre de confesar los pecados al sacerdote
**confession of faith** *s* confesión, profesión de fe
**confessor** [kənˈfɛsər] *s* confesor (*creyente; sacerdote*); confesante (*persona que confiesa delitos o pecados*)
**confetti** [kənˈfɛtɪ] *spl* confeti; serpentina (*en tiras o cintas*)
**confidant** [ˌkɑnfɪˈdænt] o [ˈkɑnfɪdænt] *s* confidente
**confidante** [ˌkɑnfɪˈdænt] o [ˈkɑnfɪdænt] *s* confidenta
**confide** [kənˈfaɪd] *va* confiar (*p.ej., algún negocio*); fiar, decir en confianza (*secretos*); *vn* confiar o confiarse; **to confide in** decir confidencias a
**confidence** [ˈkɑnfɪdəns] *s* confianza; confidencia, secreto; **in strictest confidence** bajo la mayor reserva; **to place one's confidence in** depositar su confianza en

**confidence game** *s* fraude en que el timador se gana la confianza de su víctima
**confidence man** *s* timador que se gana la confianza de su víctima
**confident** ['kɑnfɪdənt] *adj* confiado; seguro; *s* confidente, confidenta
**confidential** [,kɑnfɪ'dɛnʃəl] *adj* confidencial
**confiding** [kən'faɪdɪŋ] *adj* confiado
**configuration** [kən,fɪgjə'reʃən] *s* configuración
**confine** ['kɑnfaɪn] *s* confín; **the confines** los confines; [kən'faɪn] *va* limitar; confinar, encerrar; **to be confined** estar de parto; **to be confined to bed** tener que guardar cama, estar enfermo en cama; *vn* lindar, estar contiguos (*p.ej., dos países*)
**confinement** [kən'faɪnmənt] *s* limitación; confinamiento, encierro; parto, sobreparto
**confirm** [kən'fʌrm] *va* confirmar
**confirmation** [,kɑnfər'meʃən] *s* confirmación
**confirmative** [kən'fʌrmətɪv] *adj* confirmativo
**confirmatory** [kən'fʌrmə,torɪ] *adj* confirmatorio
**confirmed** [kən'fʌrmd] *adj* confirmado; inveterado
**confiscate** ['kɑnfɪsket] *va* confiscar
**confiscation** [,kɑnfɪs'keʃən] *s* confiscación
**confiscator** ['kɑnfɪs,ketər] *s* confiscador
**confiscatory** [kən'fɪskə,torɪ] *adj* confiscador
**confiture** ['kɑnfɪtʃʊr] *s* confitura
**conflagration** [,kɑnflə'greʃən] *s* conflagración
**conflict** ['kɑnflɪkt] *s* conflicto; incompatibilidad (*p.ej., de intereses, de horas de clase*); [kən'flɪkt] *vn* combatir; chocar, desavenirse
**conflicting** [kən'flɪktɪŋ] *adj* contradictorio; incompatible
**confluence** ['kɑnfluəns] *s* confluencia
**confluent** ['kɑnfluənt] *adj* confluente
**conflux** ['kɑnflʌks] *s* confluencia
**conform** [kən'fɔrm] *va* conformar; *vn* conformar, conformarse
**conformable** [kən'fɔrməbəl] *adj* conforme
**conformance** [kən'fɔrməns] *s* conformidad
**conformation** [,kɑnfɔr'meʃən] *s* conformación
**conformist** [kən'fɔrmɪst] *s* conformista
**conformity** [kən'fɔrmɪtɪ] *s* (*pl:* **-ties**) conformidad
**confound** [kɑn'faʊnd] *va* confundir; [kɑn'faʊnd] o ['kɑn'faʊnd] *va* condenar, maldecir; **confound it!** ¡demontre!; **confound you!** ¡vete al demonio!
**confounded** [kɑn'faʊndɪd] o ['kɑn'faʊndɪd] *adj* maldito; (coll.) aborrecible, odioso
**confraternal** [,kɑnfrə'tʌrnəl] *adj* confraternal
**confraternity** [,kɑnfrə'tʌrnɪtɪ] *s* (*pl:* **-ties**) confraternidad
**confrere** ['kɑnfrɛr] *s* colega, compañero
**confront** [kən'frʌnt] *va* encontrar cara a cara; confrontarse con, enfrentarse con, hacer frente a (*un acontecimiento, un enemigo, la necesidad*); confrontar (*poner en presencia; cotejar*)
**Confucian** [kən'fjuʃən] *adj & s* confuciano
**Confucianism** [kən'fjuʃənɪzəm] *s* confucianismo
**Confucianist** [kən'fjuʃənɪst] *adj & s* confucianista
**Confucius** [kən'fjuʃəs] *s* Confucio
**confuse** [kən'fjuz] *va* confundir
**confused** [kən'fjuzd] *adj* confuso
**confusedly** [kən'fjuzɪdlɪ] o [kən'fjuzdlɪ] *adv* confusamente
**confusion** [kən'fjuʒən] *s* confusión
**confusion of tongues** *s* (Bib.) confusión de lenguas
**confutation** [,kɑnfju'teʃən] *s* confutación
**confute** [kən'fjut] *va* confutar; anular, invalidar
**confuter** [kən'fjutər] *s* confutador
**Cong.** abr. de **Congregation, Congregational, Congregationalist** y **Congressional**
**congeal** [kən'dʒil] *va* congelar; *vn* congelarse
**congener** ['kɑndʒɪnər] *s* congénere
**congenial** [kən'dʒinjəl] *adj* congenial, simpático; compatible; agradable
**congeniality** [kən,dʒinɪ'ælɪtɪ] *s* simpatía; compatibilidad; agrado
**congenital** [kən'dʒɛnɪtəl] *adj* congénito
**conger** ['kɑŋgər] o **conger eel** *s* (ichth.) congrio
**congeries** [kɑn'dʒɪriz] o [kɑn'dʒɪrɪiz] *ssg & spl* congerie
**congest** [kən'dʒɛst] *va* apiñar, congestionar; (path.) congestionar; *vn* apiñarse, congestionarse
**congestion** [kən'dʒɛstʃən] *s* congestión; (path.) congestión
**congestive** [kən'dʒɛstɪv] *adj* congestivo
**conglomerate** [kən'glɑmərɪt] *adj & s* conglomerado; [kən'glɑməret] *va* conglomerar; *vn* conglomerarse
**conglomeration** [kən,glɑmə'reʃən] *s* conglomeración
**conglutinate** [kən'glutɪnet] *va* conglutinar; *vn* conglutinarse
**conglutination** [kən,glutɪ'neʃən] *s* conglutinación
**conglutinative** [kən'glutɪ,netɪv] *adj* conglutinativo
**Congo** ['kɑŋgo] *s* Congo
**Congoese** [,kɑŋgo'iz] *adj* congoleño o congolés; *s* (*pl:* **-ese**) congoleño o congolés
**Congo Free State** *s* Estado libre del Congo
**Congolese** [,kɑŋgo'liz] *adj* var. de **Congoese;** *s* (*pl:* **-lese**) var. de **Congoese**
**congo monkey** *s* (zool.) congo
**congo snake** *s* (zool.) anfiumo
**congratulate** [kən'grætʃəlet] *va* congratular, felicitar; **to congratulate on** congratular de o por
**congratulation** [kən,grætʃə'leʃən] *s* congratulación, felicitación, enhorabuena
**congratulatory** [kən'grætʃələ,torɪ] *adj* congratulatorio
**congregate** ['kɑŋgrɪget] *va* congregar; *vn* congregarse
**congregation** [,kɑŋgrɪ'geʃən] *s* congregación; reunión; concurso, auditorio; fieles (*de una iglesia*)
**congregational** [,kɑŋgrɪ'geʃənəl] *adj* congregacionalista; (*cap.*) *adj* congregacionalista
**congregationalism** [,kɑŋgrɪ'geʃənəlɪzəm] *s* congregacionalismo; (*cap.*) *s* congregacionalismo
**Congregationalist** [,kɑŋgrɪ'geʃənəlɪst] *adj & s* congregacionalista
**congress** ['kɑŋgrɪs] *s* congreso; diputación; (*cap.*) *s* Congreso de los EE.UU.; Congreso de los Diputados (*de las Cortes*)
**congress boot** *s* botín que tiene un trozo de materia elástica en los lados
**congressional** [kən'grɛʃənəl] *adj* congresional, de congreso; (*cap.*) *adj* congresional, del Congreso
**Congressional Record** *s* (U.S.A.) Diario de Sesiones del Congreso
**congressman** ['kɑŋgrɪsmən] *s* (*pl:* **-men**) congresista; diputado
**congresswoman** ['kɑŋgrɪs,wʊmən] *s* (*pl:* **-women**) congresista; diputada
**congruence** ['kɑŋgruəns] o **congruency** ['kɑŋgruənsɪ] *s* congruencia; (math.) congruencia
**congruent** ['kɑŋgruənt] *adj* congruente; (geom.) congruente
**congruity** [kən'gruɪtɪ] *s* (*pl:* **-ties**) congruencia; (geom.) congruencia
**congruous** ['kɑŋgruəs] *adj* congruo; (geom.) congruente
**conic** ['kɑnɪk] *adj* cónico; **conics** *ssg* curvas cónicas, secciones cónicas
**conical** ['kɑnɪkəl] *adj* cónico
**conic projection** *s* proyección cónica
**conic section** *s* (math.) sección cónica; **conic sections** *spl* secciones cónicas (*parte de la geometría*)
**conidiophore** [ko'nɪdɪə,for] *s* (bot.) conidióforo
**conidium** [ko'nɪdɪəm] *s* (*pl:* **-a** [ə]) (bot.) conidio
**conifer** ['konɪfər] o ['kɑnɪfər] *s* (bot.) conífera
**coniferous** [ko'nɪfərəs] *adj* (bot.) conífero
**conirostral** [,konɪ'rɑstrəl] *adj* (orn.) conirrostro
**conj.** abr. de **conjugation** y **conjunction**
**conjectural** [kən'dʒɛktʃərəl] *adj* conjetural
**conjecture** [kən'dʒɛktʃər] *s* conjetura; *va & vn* conjeturar
**conjoin** [kən'dʒɔɪn] *va* juntar, unir, asociar; *vn*

juntarse, unirse, asociarse; (astr.) estar en conjunción

**conjoint** [kən'dʒɔɪnt] o ['kandʒɔɪnt] *adj* conjunto

**conjointly** [kən'dʒɔɪntlɪ] o ['kandʒɔɪntlɪ] *adv* conjuntamente, de mancomún

**conjugal** ['kandʒʊgəl] *adj* conyugal

**conjugate** ['kandʒʊget] o ['kandʒʊgɪt] *adj* conjunto; (gram.) congénere; (bot. & math.) conjugado; *s* (gram.) palabra congénere; (bot.) conjugada; ['kandʒəget] *va* conjugar; (gram. & biol.) conjugar; *vn* (gram. & biol.) conjugarse

**conjugation** [,kandʒə'geʃən] *s* conjugación; (biol. & gram.) conjugación

**conjunct** [kən'dʒʌŋkt] o ['kandʒʌŋkt] *adj* conjunto

**conjunction** [kən'dʒʌŋkʃən] *s* conjunción; (astr. & gram.) conjunción

**conjunctiva** [,kandʒʌŋk'taɪvə] *s* (anat.) conjuntiva

**conjunctival** [,kandʒʌŋk'taɪvəl] *adj* conjuntival

**conjunctive** [kən'dʒʌŋktɪv] *adj* conjuntivo; conjunto; (gram.) conjuntivo; (gram.) afijo (*pronombre*); *s* (gram.) conjunción

**conjunctivitis** [kən,dʒʌŋktɪ'vaɪtɪs] *s* (path.) conjuntivitis

**conjuncture** [kən'dʒʌŋktʃər] *s* coyuntura

**conjuration** [,kandʒʊ'reʃən] *s* conjuro (*invocación supersticiosa*); magia, hechizo; (archaic) conjuro (*ruego, súplica*); (archaic) adjuración (*hecha en nombre de Dios o una cosa santa*)

**conjure** [kən'dʒʊr] *va* adjurar, conjurar (*pedir con instancia*); ['kʌndʒər] o ['kandʒər] *va* conjurar (*exorcizar; alejar, p.ej., un peligro*); evocar (*por medio de invocaciones mágicas*); hacer o efectuar por arte mágica; **to conjure away** conjurar (*exorcizar; alejar, p.ej., un peligro*); **to conjure up** evocar (*hacer aparecer por medio de invocaciones mágicas; traer a la memoria; traer a la memoria de alguien*); crear, suscitar (*p.ej., dificultades*); *vn* hacer aparecer a un demonio; practicar las artes mágicas; hacer juegos de manos

**conjurer** o **conjuror** ['kʌndʒərər] o ['kandʒərər] *s* mágico; prestidigitador; [kən'dʒʊrər] *s* conjurante (*persona que suplica*)

**Conn.** abr. de **Connecticut**

**connatural** [kə'nætʃərəl] *adj* connatural

**connect** [kə'nɛkt] *va* conectar, enlazar; conexionar, asociar, relacionar; *vn* enlazarse; conexionarse, asociarse, relacionarse; enlazar o empalmar (*p.ej., dos trenes*)

**connected** [kə'nɛktɪd] *adj* conexo; conectado; **to be connected with** estar asociado con; estar empleado por

**connecter** [kə'nɛktər] *s* var. de **connector**

**connecting rod** *s* (mach.) biela

**connection** [kə'nɛkʃən] *s* conexión; pariente; relación; comunicación; combinación, enlace, empalme (*de trenes, etc.*); (mach.) acoplamiento; **in connection with** con respecto a; juntamente con

**connective** [kə'nɛktɪv] *adj* conectivo; *s* conectador; (gram.) palabra conjuntiva

**connective tissue** *s* (anat.) tejido conjuntivo

**connector** [kə'nɛktər] *s* conectador; (elec.) conectador, enchufe

**connexion** [kə'nɛkʃən] *s* (Brit.) var. de **connection**

**conning tower** ['kanɪŋ] *s* (nav.) torre de mando; (nav.) torreta (*de un submarino*)

**conniption** [kə'nɪpʃən] *s* (coll.) rabieta

**connivance** [kə'naɪvəns] *s* connivencia, confabulación

**connive** [kə'naɪv] *vn* hacer la vista gorda, fingir ceguedad o ignorancia; cooperar secretamente; **to connive at** hacer la vista gorda respecto de; **to connive with** confabularse con

**connivent** [kə'naɪvənt] *adj* (anat. & bot.) connivente

**connoisseur** [,kanɪ'sʌr] *s* conocedor (*especialmente en materia de arte*)

**connotation** [,kano'teʃən] *s* connotación

**connotative** [kə'notətɪv] o ['kano,tetɪv] *adj* connotativo

**connote** [kə'not] *va* connotar

**connubial** [kə'njubɪəl] o [kə'nubɪəl] *adj* conyugal, connubial

**conoid** ['konɔɪd] *adj* conoide; *s* (geom.) conoide

**conoidal** [ko'nɔɪdəl] *adj* conoidal

**conquer** ['kaŋkər] *va* vencer; conquistar (*a fuerza de armas*); *vn* vencer

**conquerable** ['kaŋkərəbəl] *adj* vencible; conquistable

**conqueror** ['kaŋkərər] *s* vencedor; conquistador; **the Conqueror** el Conquistador (*Guillermo I de Inglaterra, Jaime I de Aragón, Alfonso I de Portugal*)

**conquest** ['kaŋkwɛst] *s* conquista (*acción; persona o cosa*); **the Conquest** la conquista de Inglaterra por los normandos

**conquistador** [kan'kwɪstədər] *s* conquistador (*español en las Américas en el siglo XVI*)

**Conrad** ['kanræd] *s* Conrado

**consanguineous** [,kansæŋ'gwɪnɪəs] *adj* consanguíneo

**consanguinity** [,kansæŋ'gwɪnɪtɪ] *s* consanguinidad

**conscience** ['kanʃəns] *s* conciencia; **in all conscience** en conciencia; razonablemente; seguramente

**conscience clause** *s* cláusula de conciencia

**conscience money** *s* dinero que se paga para descargar la conciencia

**conscience-stricken** ['kanʃəns,strɪkən] *adj* arrepentido, contrito, lleno de remordimientos

**conscientious** [,kanʃɪ'ɛnʃəs] *adj* concienzudo

**conscientious objector** *s* objetante de conciencia (*el que por escrúpulos de conciencia se niega a prestar servicios militares*)

**conscionable** ['kanʃənəbəl] *adj* justo, razonable

**conscious** ['kanʃəs] *adj* consciente; tímido, encogido; intencional, p.ej., **conscious lie** mentira intencional; **to be conscious** tener conocimiento; **to be conscious of** tener conciencia de; **to become conscious** volver en sí; **conscious of** consciente de (*p.ej., sus derechos*); confiado en (*p.ej., sus fuerzas*)

**consciousness** ['kanʃəsnɪs] *s* conciencia, conocimiento; **to lose consciousness** perder el conocimiento; **to regain consciousness** recobrar el conocimiento

**conscript** ['kanskrɪpt] *s* conscripto; [kən'skrɪpt] *va* reclutar; tomar para el uso del Estado

**conscript fathers** *spl* padres conscriptos

**conscription** [kən'skrɪpʃən] *s* conscripción; imposición de contribuciones, trabajos, etc., para el uso del Estado

**consecrate** ['kansɪkret] *adj* consagrado; *va* consagrar

**consecration** [,kansɪ'kreʃən] *s* consagración

**consecrator** ['kansɪ,kretər] *s* consagrante

**consecutive** [kən'sɛkjətɪv] *adj* consecutivo; consecuente; (gram.) consecutivo

**consensual** [kən'sɛnʃʊəl] *adj* (law) consensual

**consensus** [kən'sɛnsəs] *s* consenso

**consent** [kən'sɛnt] *s* consentimiento; **by common consent** según la opinión unánime; *vn* consentir; **to consent to** consentir en; **to consent to** + *inf* consentir en + *inf*

**consequence** ['kansɪkwɛns] *s* consecuencia; **in consequence** por consiguiente; **in consequence of** de resultas de; **to take the consequences** aceptar las consecuencias

**consequent** ['kansɪkwɛnt] *adj* consiguiente; *s* consecuencia; (log. & math.) consecuente

**consequential** [,kansɪ'kwɛnʃəl] *adj* consiguiente; altivo, arrogante; de consecuencia

**consequently** ['kansɪkwɛntlɪ] *adv* por consiguiente, por lo tanto

**conservation** [,kansər'veʃən] *s* conservación; conservación de los bosques, ríos, etc.; bosque bajo cuidado oficial

**conservationist** [,kansər'veʃənɪst] *s* persona que aboga por la conservación de los bosques, ríos, etc.

**conservation of energy** *s* (phys.) conservación de la energía

**conservation of mass** *s* (phys.) conservación de la masa

**conservation of matter** *s* (phys.) conservación de la materia

**conservatism** [kən'sʌrvətɪzəm] *s* conservadurismo

**conservative** [kən'sʌrvətɪv] *adj* conservativo (*que conserva*); cauteloso, moderado; (pol.) conservador; *s* preservativo; (pol.) conservador
**Conservative Party** *s* (Brit.) conservadurismo, partido conservador
**conservatoire** [kən,sʌrvə'twɑr] *s* conservatorio
**conservator** ['kɑnsər,vetər] o [kən'sʌrvətər] *s* conservador
**conservatory** [kən'sʌrvə,torɪ] *adj* conservatorio; *s* (*pl:* **-ries**) conservatorio (*establecimiento dedicado a la enseñanza de la música y las artes*); invernadero
**conserve** [kən'sʌrv] o ['kɑnsʌrv] *s* conserva, compota; [kən'sʌrv] *va* conservar
**consider** [kən'sɪdər] *va* considerar
**considerable** [kən'sɪdərəbəl] *adj* considerable
**considerably** [kən'sɪdərəblɪ] *adv* considerablemente
**considerate** [kən'sɪdərɪt] *adj* considerado, cortés, respetuoso
**consideration** [kən,sɪdə'reʃən] *s* consideración; **in consideration of** en consideración a; en cambio de; **on no consideration** bajo ningún concepto, de ninguna manera; **to take into consideration** tomar en consideración; **under consideration** en consideración; **without due consideration** sin reflexión, inconsideradamente
**considered** [kən'sɪdərd] *adj* considerado
**considering** [kən'sɪdərɪŋ] *adv* teniendo en cuenta las circunstancias; **considering that** en vista de que; *prep* en consideración a, en vista de
**consign** [kən'saɪn] *va* consignar; confiar, encomendar; (com.) consignar
**consignee** [,kɑnsaɪ'ni] *s* (com.) consignatario
**consigner** [kən'saɪnər] *s* var. de **consignor**
**consignment** [kən'saɪnmənt] *s* consignación; (com.) consignación; **on consignment** (com.) a consignación
**consignor** [kən'saɪnər] *s* (com.) consignador
**consist** [kən'sɪst] *vn* consistir; **to consist in** consistir en (*residir en, estar incluído en*); **to consist of** consistir en, constar de (*estar compuesto de*); **to consist with** concordar con
**consistence** [kən'sɪstəns] *s* var. de **consistency**
**consistency** [kən'sɪstənsɪ] *s* (*pl:* **-cies**) consistencia; consecuencia
**consistent** [kən'sɪstənt] *adj* consistente; consecuente
**consistorial** [,kɑnsɪs'torɪəl] *adj* consistorial
**consistory** [kən'sɪstərɪ] *s* (*pl:* **-ries**) consistorio
**consolation** [,kɑnsə'leʃən] *s* consolación, consuelo
**consolation match** *s* (sport) partido o match de consolación
**consolation prize** *s* premio de consuelo
**consolation race** *s* (sport) carrera de consolación
**consolatory** [kən'sɑlə,torɪ] *adj* consolatorio
**console** ['kɑnsol] *s* consola, mesa de consola; (arch., mus. & rad.) consola; [kən'sol] *va* consolar
**console table** ['kɑnsol] *s* consola, mesa de consola
**consolidate** [kən'sɑlɪdet] *va* consolidar; *vn* consolidarse
**consolidation** [kən,sɑlɪ'deʃən] *s* consolidación
**consoling** [kən'solɪŋ] *adj* consolador
**consols** ['kɑnsɑlz] o [kən'sɑlz] *spl* consolidados (*de la deuda británica*)
**consommé** [,kɑnsə'me] *s* consumado, consomé
**consonance** ['kɑnsənəns] o **consonancy** ['kɑnsənənsɪ] *s* consonancia
**consonant** ['kɑnsənənt] *adj & s* consonante
**consonantal** [,kɑnsə'næntəl] *adj* consonántico
**consort** ['kɑnsɔrt] *s* consorte (*esposo o esposa*); (naut.) buque que acompaña a otro; [kən'sɔrt] *va* asociar; *vn* asociarse; concordar
**consortium** [kən'sɔrʃɪəm] *s* (*pl:* **-tia** [ʃɪə]) consorcio
**conspectus** [kən'spɛktəs] *s* vista general; sumario, resumen
**conspicuous** [kən'spɪkjuəs] *adj* manifiesto, ostensible; conspicuo (*ilustre, insigne*); llamativo, vistoso; notable
**conspiracy** [kən'spɪrəsɪ] *s* (*pl:* **-cies**) conspiración
**conspirator** [kən'spɪrətər] *s* conspirador
**conspiratorial** [kən,spɪrə'torɪəl] *adj* conspiratorio
**conspire** [kən'spaɪr] *va* maquinar; *vn* conspirar; **to conspire to** + *inf* conspirar a o para + *inf*
**constable** ['kɑnstəbəl] o ['kʌnstəbəl] *s* policía, guardia de seguridad; condestable (*antiguo oficial superior de milicia*); guardián de un fuerte o castillo
**constabulary** [kən'stæbjə,lɛrɪ] *s* (*pl:* **-ies**) policía (*de un distrito*); guardia civil
**Constance** ['kɑnstənz] *s* Constanza (*nombre propio de mujer*)
**constancy** ['kɑnstənsɪ] *s* constancia; fidelidad, lealtad
**constant** ['kɑnstənt] *adj* constante; incesante, continuo; fiel, leal; *s* (math. & phys.) constante
**Constantine** ['kɑnstəntaɪn] o ['kɑnstəntin] *s* Constantino
**Constantinople** [,kɑnstæntɪ'nopəl] *s* Constantinopla
**constantly** ['kɑnstəntlɪ] *adv* constantemente; incesantemente, continuamente; fielmente, lealmente
**constellation** [,kɑnstə'leʃən] *s* (astr. & astrol.) constelación; cielo constelado; reunión brillante
**consternation** [,kɑnstər'neʃən] *s* consternación
**constipate** ['kɑnstɪpet] *va* estreñir
**constipated** ['kɑnstɪ,petɪd] *adj* estreñido
**constipation** [,kɑnstɪ'peʃən] *s* estreñimiento
**constituency** [kən'stɪtʃuənsɪ] *s* (*pl:* **-cies**) grupo de votantes; distrito electoral; grupo de comitentes
**constituent** [kən'stɪtʃuənt] *adj* constitutivo; (pol.) constituyente; *s* constitutivo; (pol.) elector; (law) poderdante, comitente
**constituent assembly** *s* (pol.) cortes constituyentes
**constitute** ['kɑnstɪtjut] o ['kɑnstɪtut] *va* constituir
**constitution** [,kɑnstɪ'tjuʃən] o [,kɑnstɪ'tuʃən] *s* constitución
**constitutional** [,kɑnstɪ'tjuʃənəl] o [,kɑnstɪ'tuʃənəl] *adj* constitucional
**constitutionality** [,kɑnstɪ,tjuʃən'ælɪtɪ] o [,kɑnstɪ,tuʃən'ælɪtɪ] *s* constitucionalidad
**constitutionally** [,kɑnstɪ'tjuʃənəlɪ] o [,kɑnstɪ'tuʃənəlɪ] *adv* constitucionalmente
**constitutional monarchy** *s* monarquía constitucional
**constitutive** ['kɑnstɪ,tjutɪv] o ['kɑnstɪ,tutɪv] *adj* constitutivo; constituidor
**constrain** [kən'stren] *va* constreñir, obligar; restringir, reprimir; encerrar, detener
**constrained** [kən'strend] *adj* constreñido; forzado, p.ej., **constrained smile** risa forzada
**constraint** [kən'strent] *s* constreñimiento; sujeción; encierro; embarazo, encogimiento
**constrict** [kən'strɪkt] *va* apretar, estrechar, encoger
**constriction** [kən'strɪkʃən] *s* constricción; (med.) constricción
**constrictive** [kən'strɪktɪv] *adj* constrictivo
**constrictor** [kən'strɪktər] *s* (zool.) culebra constrictora; (anat.) constrictor
**constringent** [kən'strɪndʒənt] *adj* constringente
**construct** [kən'strʌkt] *va* construir; (geom. & gram.) construir
**construction** [kən'strʌkʃən] *s* construcción; interpretación, explicación, sentido; (gram.) construcción; **under construction** en construcción
**constructional** [kən'strʌkʃənəl] *adj* estructural
**constructionist** [kən'strʌkʃənɪst] *s* interpretador
**constructive** [kən'strʌktɪv] *adj* constructor; constructivo; creador; (law) implícito
**constructor** [kən'strʌktər] *s* constructor
**construe** [kən'stru] o ['kɑnstru] *va* interpretar, explicar; deducir, inferir; traducir; (gram.) construir, analizar
**consubstantial** [,kɑnsəb'stænʃəl] *adj* consubstancial

**consubstantiality** [ˌkɑnsəbˌstænʃɪˈælɪtɪ] *s* consubstancialidad
**consubstantiation** [ˌkɑnsəbˌstænʃɪˈeʃən] *s* (theol.) consubstanciación
**consuetude** [ˈkɑnswɪtjud] o [ˈkɑnswɪtud] *s* costumbre
**consuetudinary** [ˌkɑnswɪˈtjudɪˌnɛrɪ] o [ˌkɑnswɪˈtudɪˌnɛrɪ] *adj* consuetudinario
**consul** [ˈkɑnsəl] *s* cónsul
**consular** [ˈkɑnsələr] o [ˈkɑnsjələr] *adj* consular
**consular agent** *s* agente consular
**consular invoice** *s* factura consular
**consulate** [ˈkɑnsəlɪt] o [ˈkɑnsjəlɪt] *s* consulado
**consulate general** *s* (*pl:* **consulates general**) consulado general
**consul general** *s* (*pl:* **consuls general**) cónsul general
**consulship** [ˈkɑnsəlʃɪp] *s* consulado
**consult** [kənˈsʌlt] *va & vn* consultar
**consultant** [kənˈsʌltənt] *s* consultor
**consultation** [ˌkɑnsəlˈteʃən] *s* consulta, consultación
**consultative** [kənˈsʌltətɪv] *adj* consultivo
**consumable** [kənˈsuməbəl] o [kənˈsjuməbəl] *adj* consumible
**consume** [kənˈsum] o [kənˈsjum] *va* consumir; **consumed with** preocupado con; *vn* consumirse
**consumedly** [kənˈsumɪdlɪ] o [kənˈsjumɪdlɪ] *adv* muchísimo, demasiado
**consumer** [kənˈsumər] o [kənˈsjumər] *s* consumidor
**consumer credit** *s* crédito para comprar a plazos, crédito dado al consumidor
**consumer resistence** *s* resistencia del consumidor a la venta
**consumers' goods** *spl* bienes de consumo
**consumer spending** *s* gastos de consumo
**consummate** [kənˈsʌmɪt] *adj* consumado; [ˈkɑnsəmet] *va* consumar
**consummation** [ˌkɑnsəˈmeʃən] *s* consumación
**consumption** [kənˈsʌmpʃən] *s* consunción, destrucción, extinción; consumo (*p.ej., de comestibles*); (path.) consunción
**consumptive** [kənˈsʌmptɪv] *adj* consuntivo, consumidor; (path.) tísico; *s* (path.) tísico
**cont.** abr. de **containing, contents, continent, continental, continue** y **continued**
**Cont.** abr. de **Continental**
**contact** [ˈkɑntækt] *s* contacto; (elec.) contacto; (elec.) toma de corriente; **to put in contact with** poner en contacto con; *va* (coll.) ponerse en contacto con; *vn* contactar
**contact breaker** *s* (elec.) ruptor
**contact firing** *s* (arti.) fuego de contacto
**contact goniometer** *s* goniómetro de aplicación
**contact lens** *s* lente de contacto, lente invisible
**contactor** [ˈkɑntæktər] *s* (elec.) contactor
**contact plane** *s* (mil.) aeroplano de contacto
**contact rail** *s* (elec.) carril conductor
**contagion** [kənˈtedʒən] *s* contagio
**contagious** [kənˈtedʒəs] *adj* contagioso
**contain** [kənˈten] *va* contener; (math.) ser exactamente divisible por; **to contain oneself** contenerse, refrenarse
**container** [kənˈtenər] *s* continente; envase, vasija, caja
**containment** [kənˈtenmənt] *s* refrenamiento, contención
**contaminate** [kənˈtæmɪnet] *va* contaminar
**contamination** [kənˌtæmɪˈneʃən] *s* contaminación; (philol.) cruce de palabras, contaminación
**contd.** abr. de **continued**
**contemn** [kənˈtɛm] *va* desacatar, despreciar
**contemplate** [ˈkɑntəmplet] *va & vn* contemplar; **to contemplate** + *ger* pensar + *inf*
**contemplation** [ˌkɑntəmˈpleʃən] *s* contemplación; proyecto, intención
**contemplative** [ˈkɑntəmˌpletɪv] o [kənˈtɛmplətɪv] *adj* contemplativo
**contemporaneous** [kənˌtɛmpəˈrenɪəs] *adj* contemporáneo
**contemporaneously** [kənˌtɛmpəˈrenɪəslɪ] *adv* contemporáneamente
**contemporary** [kənˈtɛmpəˌrɛrɪ] *adj* contemporáneo, coetáneo; *s* (*pl:* **-ies**) contemporáneo, coetáneo
**contempt** [kənˈtɛmpt] *s* desacato, desprecio; (law) contumacia
**contemptible** [kənˈtɛmptɪbəl] *adj* despreciable
**contempt of court** *s* menosprecio a la justicia, desacato a la autoridad del tribunal
**contemptuous** [kənˈtɛmptʃuəs] *adj* desdeñoso, despreciativo
**contend** [kənˈtɛnd] *va* sostener, mantener, defender; *vn* contender
**contender** [kənˈtɛndər] *s* contendiente, concurrente
**content** [kənˈtɛnt] *adj* contento; *s* contento; **to one's heart's content** a gusto; [ˈkɑntɛnt] *s* contenido; sustancia; cabida; volumen; **contents** [ˈkɑntɛnts] *spl* contenido; [kənˈtɛnt] *va* contentar
**contented** [kənˈtɛntɪd] *adj* contento, satisfecho
**contentedness** [kənˈtɛntɪdnɪs] *s* contentamiento, satisfacción
**contention** [kənˈtɛnʃən] *s* contención; argumento
**contentious** [kənˈtɛnʃəs] *adj* contencioso; (law) contencioso
**contentment** [kənˈtɛntmənt] *s* contento, contentamiento
**conterminous** [kɑnˈtʌrmɪnəs] *adj* contérmino; coextensivo
**contest** [ˈkɑntɛst] *s* competencia, concurso; contienda; [kənˈtɛst] *va* disputar, impugnar; tratar de conseguir; *vn* contender
**contestant** [kənˈtɛstənt] *s* contendiente
**context** [ˈkɑntɛkst] *s* contexto
**contextual** [kənˈtɛkstʃuəl] *adj* del contexto
**contexture** [kənˈtɛkstʃər] *s* contextura
**contiguity** [ˌkɑntɪˈgjuɪtɪ] *s* (*pl:* **-ties**) contigüidad; continuo
**contiguous** [kənˈtɪgjuəs] *adj* contiguo
**continence** [ˈkɑntɪnəns] *s* continencia
**continent** [ˈkɑntɪnənt] *adj* continente; *s* continente; **the Continent** la Europa continental
**continental** [ˌkɑntɪˈnɛntəl] *adj* continental; *s* papel moneda puesto en circulación durante la Revolución norteamericana; **not worth a continental** sin valor; (*cap.*) *s* habitante del continente europeo; soldado del ejército continental norteamericano durante la Revolución
**continental divide** *s* divisoria continental, parteaguas continental
**contingency** [kənˈtɪndʒənsɪ] *s* (*pl:* **-cies**) contingencia
**contingent** [kənˈtɪndʒənt] *adj* contingente; *s* contingente; (mil.) contingente
**continual** [kənˈtɪnjuəl] *adj* continuo
**continually** [kənˈtɪnjuəlɪ] *adv* continuamente, continuadamente
**continuance** [kənˈtɪnjuəns] *s* continuación; (law) aplazamiento
**continuation** [kənˌtɪnjuˈeʃən] *s* continuación
**continuative** [kənˈtɪnjuˌetɪv] *adj* (gram.) continuativo; *s* (gram.) continuativa
**continuator** [kənˈtɪnjuˌetər] *s* continuador
**continue** [kənˈtɪnju] *va* continuar; mantener, conservar; aplazar; **to be continued** continuará; **to continue** + *ger* o **to continue to** + *inf* continuar + *ger; vn* continuar; continuarse (*extenderse*)
**continued fever** *s* (path.) fiebre continua
**continued fraction** *s* (math.) fracción continua
**continuer** [kənˈtɪnjuər] *s* continuador
**continuity** [ˌkɑntɪˈnjuɪtɪ] o [ˌkɑntɪˈnuɪtɪ] *s* (*pl:* **-ties**) continuidad; (mov.) escenario; (rad.) comentarios o anuncios que se dan entre las partes de un programa
**continuous** [kənˈtɪnjuəs] *adj* continuo
**continuous current** *s* var. de **direct current**
**continuous showing** *s* (mov.) sesión continua
**continuous waves** *spl* (rad.) ondas continuas, ondas entretenidas
**continuum** [kənˈtɪnjuəm] *s* (*pl:* **-a** [ə]) continuo
**contort** [kənˈtɔrt] *va* retorcer, deformar
**contortion** [kənˈtɔrʃən] *s* contorsión
**contortionist** [kənˈtɔrʃənɪst] *s* contorsionista
**contour** [ˈkɑntur] *s* contorno
**contour chair** *s* silla de contorno
**contour line** *s* curva de nivel
**contour map** *s* plano acotado
**contourné** [kɑnˈturne] *adj* (her.) contornado

**contr.** abr. de **contract, contracted** y **contraction**
**contraband** ['kɑntrəbænd] *s* contrabando; *adj* de contrabando, contrabandista
**contrabandist** ['kɑntrə,bændɪst] *s* contrabandista
**contraband of war** *s* contrabando de guerra
**contrabass** ['kɑntrə,bes] *s* (mus.) contrabajo; *adj* (mus.) de contrabajo
**contraception** [,kɑntrə'sɛpʃən] *s* contracepción
**contraceptive** [,kɑntrə'sɛptɪv] *adj & s* contraceptivo
**contract** ['kɑntrækt] *s* contrato; contrato de matrimonio; bridge contrato; [kən'trækt] *adj* (gram.) contracto; *va* contraer; (gram.) contraer; *vn* contraerse; ['kɑntrækt] o [kən'trækt] *va* contraer (*p.ej., matrimonio*); *vn* comprometerse por contrato; **to contract for** contratar; **to contract to** + *inf* comprometerse por contrato a + *inf*
**contract bridge** ['kɑntrækt] *s* bridge contrato, bridge contratado
**contracted** [kən'træktɪd] *adj* contraído; prometido; escaso, retardado, torpe; pobre de ánimo; nada liberal
**contractible** [kən'træktɪbəl] *adj* contractable, contráctil
**contractile** [kən'træktɪl] *adj* contráctil; contractivo
**contractility** [,kɑntræk'tɪlɪtɪ] *s* contractilidad
**contraction** [kən'trækʃən] *s* contracción
**contractive** [kən'træktɪv] *adj* contractivo; contráctil
**contractor** ['kɑntræktər] o [kən'træktər] *s* contratista, contratante; empresario
**contractual** [kən'træktʃuəl] *adj* contractual
**contracture** [kən'træktʃər] *s* (arch. & path.) contractura
**contradance** ['kɑntrə,dæns] o ['kɑntrə,dɑns] *s* contradanza
**contradict** [,kɑntrə'dɪkt] *va* contradecir
**contradiction** [,kɑntrə'dɪkʃən] *s* contradicción
**contradictory** [,kɑntrə'dɪktərɪ] *adj* contradictorio; contradictor; *s* (*pl:* **-ries**) (log.) contradictoria
**contradistinction** [,kɑntrədɪs'tɪŋkʃən] *s* distinción por oposición o contraste; **in contradistinction to** a diferencia de, en contraste con
**contrail** ['kɑn,trel] *s* (aer.) estela de vapor, rastro de condensación
**contraindicant** [,kɑntrə'ɪndɪkənt] *s* (med.) contraindicante
**contraindicate** [,kɑntrə'ɪndɪket] *va* (med.) contraindicar
**contraindication** [,kɑntrə,ɪndɪ'keʃən] *s* (med.) contraindicación
**contralateral** [,kɑntrə'lætərəl] *adj* contralateral
**contralto** [kən'trælto] *s* (*pl:* **-tos**) (mus.) contralto (*voz y persona*); *adj* (mus.) de contralto, para contralto
**contraposition** [,kɑntrəpə'zɪʃən] *s* contraposición
**contraption** [kən'træpʃən] *s* (coll.) artificio, invención, dispositivo
**contrapuntal** [,kɑntrə'pʌntəl] *adj* (mus.) contrapuntístico
**contrapuntist** [,kɑntrə'pʌntɪst] *s* contrapuntista
**contrariety** [,kɑntrə'raɪətɪ] *s* (*pl:* **-ties**) contrariedad
**contrariwise** ['kɑntrɛrɪ,waɪz] *adv* en contrario; al contrario; ['kɑntrɛrɪ,waɪz] o [kən'trɛrɪ,waɪz] *adv* obstinadamente, tercamente
**contrary** ['kɑntrɛrɪ] *adj* contrario; ['kɑntrɛrɪ] o [kən'trɛrɪ] *adj* obstinado, terco; ['kɑntrɛrɪ] *adv* contrariamente, en contrario; *s* (*pl:* **-ries**) contraria (*cosa opuesta a otra*); contrario (*contradicción*); **on the contrary** al contrario; **to the contrary** en contrario
**contrary to fact sentence** *s* (gram.) oración condicional de negación implícita
**contrast** ['kɑntræst] *s* contraste; [kən'træst] *va* hacer contrastar, poner en contraste; *vn* contrastar
**contravallation** [,kɑntrəvə'leʃən] *s* (fort.) contravalación
**contravene** [,kɑntrə'vin] *va* contravenir a (*p.ej., una ley*); contradecir, oponerse a
**contravention** [,kɑntrə'vɛnʃən] *s* contravención; contradicción, oposición
**contrayerva** [,kɑntrə'jʌrvə] *s* (bot.) contrahierba
**contredanse** [kõtrə'dɑ̃s] *s* var. de **contradance**
**contretemps** [kõtrə'tɑ̃] *s* contratiempo; (mus.) contratiempo
**contribute** [kən'trɪbjut] *va & vn* contribuir; **to contribute to** + *ger* contribuir a + *inf*
**contribution** [,kɑntrɪ'bjuʃən] *s* contribución; colaboración (*a una revista, coloquio, etc.*)
**contributive** [kən'trɪbjutɪv] *adj* contribuidor
**contributor** [kən'trɪbjutər] *s* contribuidor, contribuyente
**contributory** [kən'trɪbju,torɪ] *adj* contribuidor
**contrite** ['kɑntraɪt] *adj* contrito
**contrition** [kən'trɪʃən] *s* contrición
**contrivance** [kən'traɪvəns] *s* invención; artefacto; inventiva; plan, designio
**contrive** [kən'traɪv] *va* inventar; gestionar, procurar; efectuar; maquinar; *vn* maquinar; **to contrive to** + *inf* ingeniarse a + *inf*
**control** [kən'trol] *s* gobierno, mando, dominio; dirección; derecho para intervenir; control, contrarregistro, norma de comprobación; testigo (*en un experimento de laboratorio*); (mach.) regulador; (spiritualism) comunicante; **controls** *spl* mandos; **to get under control** conseguir dominar (*p.ej., un incendio*); (*pret & pp:* **-trolled;** *ger:* **-trolling**) *va* gobernar, mandar, dominar; regular; controlar, comprobar; **to control oneself** dominarse, poseerse
**control car** *s* (aer.) barquilla de gobierno (*de un dirigible*)
**control center** *s* centro de control
**control experiment** *s* control
**controllable** [kən'troləbəl] *adj* gobernable, manejable, controlable
**controller** [kən'trolər] *s* interventor, contralor; director; (elec.) combinador; (mach.) regulador
**controllership** [kən'trolərʃɪp] *s* oficio de interventor; dirección
**controlling interest** *s* (com.) interés predominante, mayoría
**control panel** *s* (aer.) tablero de instrumentos
**control room** *s* (rad. & telv.) sala de control, sala de mando
**control stick** *s* (aer.) mango de escoba, palanca de mando
**control tower** *s* (aer.) torre de mando
**controversial** [,kɑntrə'vʌrʃəl] *adj* controvertible, disputable; contencioso
**controversialist** [,kɑntrə'vʌrʃəlɪst] *s* controversista
**controversy** ['kɑntrə,vʌrsɪ] *s* (*pl:* **-sies**) controversia
**controvert** ['kɑntrəvʌrt] o [,kɑntrə'vʌrt] *va* controvertir; contradecir; *vn* controvertir
**controvertible** [,kɑntrə'vʌrtɪbəl] *adj* controvertible
**contumacious** [,kɑntju'meʃəs] o [,kɑntu'meʃəs] *adj* contumaz
**contumacy** ['kɑntjuməsɪ] o ['kɑntuməsɪ] *s* (*pl:* **-cies**) contumacia
**contumelious** [,kɑntju'milɪəs] o [,kɑntu'milɪəs] *adj* contumelioso
**contumely** ['kɑntjumɪlɪ] o ['kɑntumɪlɪ] *s* (*pl:* **-lies**) contumelia
**contuse** [kən'tjuz] o [kən'tuz] *va* contundir, contusionar
**contusion** [kən'tjuʒən] o [kən'tuʒən] *s* contusión
**conundrum** [kə'nʌndrəm] *s* acertijo, adivinanza; problema complicado
**convalesce** [,kɑnvə'lɛs] *vn* convalecer
**convalescence** [,kɑnvə'lɛsəns] *s* convalecencia
**convalescent** [,kɑnvə'lɛsənt] *adj* convaleciente; de convalecencia; *s* convaleciente
**convalescent home** *s* clínica de reposo
**convection** [kən'vɛkʃən] *s* transporte; (phys.) convección
**convection current** *s* (elec.) corriente de convección

**convene** [kən'vin] *va* convocar; *vn* convenir, juntarse, reunirse
**convenience** [kən'vinjəns] *s* comodidad; proximidad; **at one's convenience** cuando le sea cómodo a uno; **at your earliest convenience** a su más pronta conveniencia
**conveniency** [kən'vinjənsɪ] *s* (*pl:* **-cies**) var. de **convenience**
**convenient** [kən'vinjənt] *adj* cómodo; alcanzadizo; **convenient to** (coll.) vecino a
**convent** ['kɑnvɛnt] *s* convento (*de religiosas*)
**conventicle** [kən'vɛntɪkəl] *s* conventículo
**convention** [kən'vɛnʃən] *s* convención; asamblea, congreso
**conventional** [kən'vɛnʃənəl] *adj* convencional, de convención; formalista
**conventionalism** [kən'vɛnʃənəlɪzəm] *s* convencionalismo; formalismo
**conventionality** [kən,vɛnʃə'nælɪtɪ] *s* convencionalidad; formalismo
**conventionalize** [kən'vɛnʃənəlaɪz] *va* estilizar
**conventual** [kən'vɛntʃuəl] *adj* conventual; *s* conventual (*religioso*); religiosa que vive en convento
**converge** [kən'vʌrdʒ] *va* hacer convergir; *vn* convergir
**convergence** [kən'vʌrdʒəns] o **convergency** [kən'vʌrdʒənsɪ] *s* convergencia
**convergent** [kən'vʌrdʒənt] *adj* convergente
**conversable** [kən'vʌrsəbəl] *adj* conversable; propio a la conversación
**conversant** ['kɑnvərsənt] o [kən'vʌrsənt] *adj* versado; **conversant with** versado en, al corriente de
**conversation** [,kɑnvər'seʃən] *s* conversación
**conversational** [,kɑnvər'seʃənəl] *adj* conversacional; amigo de la conversación
**conversationalist** [,kɑnvər'seʃənəlɪst] *s* conversador
**conversationally** [,kɑnvər'seʃənəlɪ] *adv* de manera propia a la conversación; en conversación
**conversation piece** *s* (paint.) cuadro de un grupo de personas de la alta sociedad; mueble de interés especial
**converse** ['kɑnvʌrs] *adj* contrario; inverso; *s* contraria; (log.) inversa; conversación; [kən'vʌrs] *vn* conversar
**conversely** ['kɑnvʌrslɪ] o [kən'vʌrslɪ] *adv* a la inversa, contrariamente
**conversion** [kən'vʌrʒən] o [kən'vʌrʃən] *s* conversión; apropiación ilícita para uso propio; (mil.) conversión (*mutación de frente*)
**conversion table** *s* tabla de conversión
**conversive** [kən'vʌrsɪv] *adj* conversivo
**convert** ['kɑnvʌrt] *s* converso, convertido; [kən'vʌrt] *va* convertir; apropiar ilícitamente para uso propio; *vn* convertirse
**converted** [kən'vʌrtɪd] *adj* converso
**converter** [kən'vʌrtər] *s* (elec.) convertidor, conmutatriz; (metal.) convertidor; (rad.) conversor; (com.) comerciante que termina la preparación de telas para la venta
**convertibility** [kən,vʌrtɪ'bɪlɪtɪ] *s* convertibilidad
**convertible** [kən'vʌrtɪbəl] *adj* convertible; (aut.) descapotable, transformable; *s* (aut.) descapotable, transformable
**convertiplane** [kən'vʌrtɪplen] *s* avión convertible, convertiplano
**convex** ['kɑnvɛks] o [kɑn'vɛks] *adj* convexo
**convexity** [kɑn'vɛksɪtɪ] *s* (*pl:* **-ties**) convexidad
**convey** [kən've] *va* conducir, transportar; transmitir (*p.ej., una corriente eléctrica*); expresar; participar; transferir, traspasar (*p.ej., bienes de una persona a otra*)
**conveyance** [kən'veəns] *s* conducción, transporte; transmisión; participación, comunicación; vehículo; traspaso de dominio; escritura de traspaso
**conveyancer** [kən'veənsər] *s* escribano que prepara escrituras de traspaso
**conveyancing** [kən'veənsɪŋ] *s* preparación de escrituras de traspaso
**conveyer** o **conveyor** [kən'veər] *s* conductor, portador; transportador
**conveyor belt** *s* correa transportadora
**conveyor chain** *s* cadena para transportador
**convict** ['kɑnvɪkt] *s* convicto; presidiario; [kən'vɪkt] *va* probar la culpabilidad de; declarar convicto a (*un acusado*); convencer de alguna culpa
**conviction** [kən'vɪkʃən] *s* convicción; (law) condena judicial
**convince** [kən'vɪns] *va* convencer
**convincible** [kən'vɪnsɪbəl] *adj* convencible
**convincing** [kən'vɪnsɪŋ] *adj* convencedor; convincente (*razón, argumento*)
**convivial** [kən'vɪvɪəl] *adj* jovial, festivo
**conviviality** [kən,vɪvɪ'ælɪtɪ] *s* (*pl:* **-ties**) jovialidad
**convocation** [,kɑnvo'keʃən] *s* convocación; asamblea
**convoke** [kɑn'vok] *va* convocar
**convolute** ['kɑnvəlut] *adj* enrollado; (bot.) convolutado
**convolution** [,kɑnvə'luʃən] *s* circunvolución, convolución; (anat.) circunvolución
**convolution of Broca** ['brokə] *s* (anat.) circunvolución de Broca
**convolvulaceous** [kən,vɑlvjə'leʃəs] *adj* (bot.) convolvuláceo
**convolvulus** [kən'vɑlvjələs] *s* (*pl:* **-luses** o **-li** [laɪ]) (bot.) convólvulo
**convoy** ['kɑnvɔɪ] *s* convoy; [kɑn'vɔɪ] *va* convoyar
**convulse** [kən'vʌls] *va* agitar; crispar, convulsionar; mover a risas convulsivas; *vn* agitarse; crisparse
**convulsion** [kən'vʌlʃən] *s* convulsión; ataque o paroxismo de risa; (path.) convulsión
**convulsive** [kən'vʌlsɪv] *adj* convulsivo; convulso
**cony** ['konɪ] *s* (*pl:* **-nies**) conejuna, pelo de conejo; (zool.) damán; (zool.) ochotona; (archaic) conejo
**coo** [ku] *s* arrullo; *va & vn* arrullar
**cooee** o **cooey** ['kuɪ] *s* grito largo y agudo
**cook** [kuk] *s* cocinero; *va* cocer, cocinar; (coll.) ajar; (slang) arruinar, echar a perder; **to cook up** preparar; (coll.) falsear, falsificar; (coll.) tramar, maquinar; *vn* cocer; cocinar (*ocuparse en cosas de cocina*)
**cookbook** ['kuk,buk] *s* libro de cocina
**cooker** ['kukər] *s* hervidor; (Brit.) cocina económica
**cookery** ['kukərɪ] *s* (*pl:* **-ies**) cocina (*arte o empleo; lugar*)
**cookhouse** ['kuk,haus] *s* cocina; cocina móvil de campaña; (naut.) fogón
**cookie** ['kukɪ] *s* var. de **cooky**
**cooking** ['kukɪŋ] *s* cocina, arte culinaria
**cooking soda** *s* (coll.) bicarbonato sódico
**cookshop** ['kuk,ʃɑp] *s* casa de comidas, pequeño restaurante
**cookstove** ['kuk,stov] *s* cocina, cocina económica
**cooky** ['kukɪ] *s* (*pl:* **-ies**) pastelito dulce, pasta seca
**cool** [kul] *adj* fresco; sereno, tranquilo; indiferente; de color azul, gris o verde; (coll.) sin calificación, sin exageración; *va* refrescar; atemplar, moderar; **to cool one's heels** (coll.) hacer antesala, estar esperando mucho tiempo; *vn* refrescarse; atemplarse, moderarse; **to cool off** refrescarse; serenarse, tranquilizarse
**coolant** ['kulənt] *s* líquido refrigerador
**cooler** ['kulər] *s* refrigerador; heladera; refrigerante; (slang) cárcel
**cool-headed** ['kul'hɛdɪd] *adj* sereno, tranquilo; juicioso, sensato
**coolie** ['kulɪ] *s* culí
**cooling** ['kulɪŋ] *s* enfriamiento; *adj* refrescante; refrigerante
**cooling coil** *s* serpentín enfriador
**cooling jacket** *s* camisa refrigerante
**cooling time** *s* (law) tiempo durante el cual se apaciguan las pasiones de los litigantes
**coolish** ['kulɪʃ] *adj* fresquito, algo fresco
**coolly** ['kulɪ] o ['kullɪ] *adv* frescamente; serenamente, tranquilamente; indiferentemente; con descaro
**coolness** ['kulnɪs] *s* frescura; tranquilidad; indiferencia
**cooly** ['kulɪ] *s* (*pl:* **-lies**) var. de **coolie**
**coomb** [kum] o [kom] *s* var. de **combe**
**coon** [kun] *s* (zool.) mapache, oso lavador; piel de mapache; (U.S.A.) miembro del partido re-

publicano en la época de la Revolución; (coll.) marrullero; (offensive) negro
**coon's age** *s* (coll.) mucho tiempo
**coop** [kup] *s* gallinero; jaula o redil para conejos u otros animales pequeños; (slang) caponera (*cárcel*); *va* encerrar en un gallinero; enjaular, emparedar
**coöp.** abr. de **coöperative**
**coöp** [ko'ɑp] o ['koɑp] *s* tienda cooperativa
**cooper** ['kupər] o ['kʊpər] *s* barrilero, tonelero; *va* fabricar o concertar (*barriles, toneles, etc.*); **to cooper out** o **up** acabar, elaborar; *vn* ser barrilero, ser tonelero
**cooperage** ['kupərɪdʒ] o ['kʊpərɪdʒ] *s* barrilería, tonelería; precio pagado por la fabricación de barriles, toneles, etc.
**coöperate** [ko'ɑpəret] *vn* cooperar; **to coöperate in** + *ger* cooperar a + *inf*
**coöperation** [ko,ɑpə'reʃən] *s* cooperación
**coöperative** [ko'ɑpə,retɪv] *adj* cooperativo; *s* cooperativa, sociedad cooperativa
**coöperative store** *s* tienda cooperativa
**coöperator** [ko'ɑpə,retər] *s* cooperador, cooperario; socio de una cooperativa
**cooper's adz** *s* doladera de tonelero
**coöpt** [ko'ɑpt] *va* cooptar
**coöptation** [,koɑp'teʃən] *s* cooptación
**coördinate** [ko'ɔrdɪnɪt] *adj* coordinado; de igual importancia; (math.) coordenado; (gram.) coordinante; *s* igual, semejante; (math.) coordenado; [ko'ɔrdɪnet] *va & vn* coordinar
**coördinate geometry** *s* geometría analítica
**coördinating conjunction** *s* (gram.) conjunción coordinante
**coördination** [ko,ɔrdɪ'neʃən] *s* coordinación
**coördinative** [ko'ɔrdɪ,netɪv] *adj* coordinativo
**coördinator** [ko'ɔrdɪ,netər] *s* coordinador
**coot** [kut] *s* (orn.) fúlica; (orn.) fúlica negra, foja; (orn.) negreta; (coll.) bobalicón
**cootie** ['kutɪ] *s* (slang) piojo
**cop** [kɑp] *s* rollo de hilos ahusado; tubo de enrollar hilos de seda u otros; (slang) polizonte; (*pret & pp:* **copped**; *ger:* **copping**) *va* (slang) coger, prender; (slang) hurtar, robar
**copaiba** [ko'pebə] o [ko'paɪbə] *s* (pharm.) copaiba
**copaiba balsam** *s* (pharm.) bálsamo de copaiba
**copal** ['kopəl] *s* copal
**copartner** [ko'pɑrtnər] *s* consocio, copartícipe
**copartnership** [ko'pɑrtnərʃɪp] *s* asociación, coparticipación
**cope** [kop] *s* (eccl.) capa pluvial; (mas.) albardilla; *va* vestir con capa pluvial; poner albardilla a, rematar con albardilla; *vn* hacer frente; **to cope with** hacer frente a, enfrentarse con
**copeck** ['kopɛk] *s* var. de **kopeck**
**Copenhagen** [,kopən'hegən] *s* Copenhague
**copepod** ['kopɪpɑd] *adj & s* (zool.) copépodo
**Copernican** [ko'pʌrnɪkən] *adj & s* copernicano
**Copernican system** *s* (astr.) sistema de Copérnico
**Copernicus** [ko'pʌrnɪkəs] *s* Copérnico
**copestone** ['kop,ston] *s* piedra de albardilla; (fig.) coronamiento
**copier** ['kɑpɪər] *s* copiador, imitador; copiante, copista
**copilot** ['ko,paɪlət] *s* (aer.) copiloto
**coping** ['kopɪŋ] *s* (mas.) albardilla
**coping saw** *s* serrucho de calar, sierra caladora
**copious** ['kopɪəs] *adj* copioso
**copper** ['kɑpər] *s* cobre; calderilla, vellón (*moneda de cobre*); caldero (*vasija*); (slang) polizonte; *adj* cobreño; cobrizo (*en el color*); *va* cubrir o revestir con cobre
**copperas** ['kɑpərəs] *s* (chem.) caparrosa verde
**copper glance** *s* (mineral.) calcosina
**copperhead** ['kɑpər,hɛd] *s* (zool.) víbora de cabeza de cobre; (*cap.*) *s* (U.S.A.) habitante de los Estados del Norte que simpatizaba con los Estados confederados del Sur
**copperplate** ['kɑpər,plet] *s* plancha de cobre (*que sirve para grabar*); grabado en lámina de cobre; grabadura en cobre; *va* grabar en cobre
**copper pyrites** *s* (mineral.) pirita de cobre
**coppersmith** ['kɑpər,smɪθ] *s* cobrero
**copper sulfate** *s* (chem.) sulfato de cobre
**coppery** ['kɑpərɪ] *adj* encobrado, cobreño; cobrizo (*en el color*)
**coppice** ['kɑpɪs] *s* var. de **copse**
**copra** ['kɑprə] *s* copra
**coproduction** [,kopro'dʌkʃən] *s* coproducción
**coprolite** ['kɑprəlaɪt] *s* (pal.) coprolito
**copse** [kɑps] *s* soto, matorral, monte bajo
**Copt** [kɑpt] *s* copto
**Coptic** ['kɑptɪk] *adj* copto, cóptico; *s* copto (*idioma*)
**Coptic Church** *s* Iglesia copta
**copula** ['kɑpjələ] *s* cópula; (anat., gram., law, log. & med.) cópula
**copulate** ['kɑpjəlet] *vn* copularse
**copulation** [,kɑpjə'leʃən] *s* copulación
**copulative** ['kɑpjə,letɪv] *adj* copulativo; *s* (gram.) palabra copulativa
**copy** ['kɑpɪ] *s* (*pl:* **-ies**) copia; modelo; ejemplar (*p.ej., de un libro*); número (*p.ej., de un periódico*); (print.) original, manuscrito, material; (*pret & pp:* **-ied**) *va* copiar; *vn* copiar; **to copy after** contrahacer
**copybook** ['kɑpɪ,bʊk] *s* cuaderno de escritura; (com.) libro copiador; *adj* común, ordinario
**copyhold** ['kɑpɪ,hold] *s* (English law) posesión en virtud de una copia del rollo del tribunal señorial; tierras poseídas en virtud de una copia del rollo señorial
**copyholder** ['kɑpɪ,holdər] *s* lector de pruebas (*el que lee en alta voz al corrector*); atendedor (*el que sigue la lectura que hace el corrector*); portacopia, sujetacuartillas (*dispositivo en que se coloca el manuscrito que se va a copiar*); (English law) poseedor en virtud de una copia del rollo señorial
**copying ink** *s* tinta de copiar
**copyist** ['kɑpɪɪst] *s* copiante, copista; copiador, imitador
**copyreader** ['kɑpɪ,ridər] *s* revisor de manuscritos
**copyright** ['kɑpɪ,raɪt] *s* (derecho de) propiedad literaria; *va* proteger solicitando la propiedad literaria; inscribir en el registro de la propiedad literaria
**copy writer** *s* escritor de anuncios
**copy writing** *s* preparación de material publicitario
**coquet** [ko'kɛt] (*pret & pp:* **-quetted**; *ger:* **-quetting**) *vn* coquetear; bromear, burlarse
**coquetry** ['kokətrɪ] o [ko'kɛtrɪ] *s* (*pl:* **-ries**) coquetería; broma, burla
**coquette** [ko'kɛt] *s* coqueta
**coquettish** [ko'kɛtɪʃ] *adj* coqueta; coquetón
**coquina** [ko'kinə] *s* coquina
**cor.** abr. de **corner, coroner, corrected, correction** y **corresponding**
**Cor.** abr. de **Corinthians** y **Coroner**
**coracle** ['kɑrəkəl] o ['kɔrəkəl] *s* (Brit.) barquilla casi redonda y en forma de canasta
**coracoid** ['kɑrəkɔɪd] o ['kɔrəkɔɪd] *adj & s* (anat.) coracoides
**coracoid process** *s* (anat.) apófisis coracoides
**coral** ['kɑrəl] o ['kɔrəl] *adj* coralino; *s* (zool.) coral (*pólipo, secreción calcárea, color, etc.*)
**coralline** ['kɑrəlɪn] o ['kɑrəlaɪn] *adj* coralino; *s* (bot. & zool.) coralina
**coral reef** *s* arrecife de coral
**Coral Sea** *s* mar del Coral
**coral snake** *s* (zool.) coral, coralillo
**corbel** ['kɔrbəl] *s* (arch.) ménsula, repisa; sostén; (*pret & pp:* **-beled** o **-belled**; *ger:* **-beling** o **-belling**) *va* proveer de ménsula o repisa; sostener por medio de una ménsula o repisa
**corbie** ['kɔrbɪ] *s* (Scotch) cuervo
**corbie gable** *s* (arch.) aguilón escalonado
**corbiestep** ['kɔrbɪ,stɛp] *s* (arch.) escalón de aguilón escalonado
**cord** [kɔrd] *s* cuerda; (anat. & elec.) cordón; corduroy; **cords** *spl* pantalones de corduroy; *va* acordonar; poner (*leña*) en cuerdas
**cordage** ['kɔrdɪdʒ] *s* cordaje, cordería; leña medida por cuerdas
**cordate** ['kɔrdet] *adj* cordiforme, cordato
**corded** ['kɔrdɪd] *adj* con cordoncillos; encordelado; hecho de cuerdas, provisto de cuerdas; puesto en cuerdas (*aplícase a la leña*)
**cordial** ['kɔrdʒəl] o ['kɔrdjəl] *adj* cordial; *s* cordial (*bebida confortante*); licor, licor tónico
**cordiality** [kɔr'dʒælɪtɪ] o [,kɔrdɪ'ælɪtɪ] *s* (*pl:* **-ties**) cordialidad
**Cordilleran** [,kɔrdɪl'jɛrən] o [kɔr'dɪlərən] *adj* cordillerano

**cordite** ['kɔrdaɪt] *s* cordita
**cordon** ['kɔrdən] *s* cordón (*cinta o cuerda ornamental*); (arch., fort., her., hort. & mil.) cordón
**Cordova** ['kɔrdovə] o [kɔr'dovə] *s* Córdoba
**Cordovan** ['kɔrdovən] o [kɔr'dovən] *adj & s* cordobés; (*l.c.*) *adj* de cordobán; *s* cordobán (*piel*)
**cord tire** *s* (aut.) neumático de cordones o de cuerdas
**corduroy** ['kɔrdərɔɪ] *s* pana, corduroy; **corduroys** *spl* pantalones de pana; traje o vestido de pana; *adj* de pana, de corduroy
**corduroy road** *s* camino de troncos
**cordwainer** ['kɔrdwenər] *s* (archaic) cordobanero; (obs.) zapatero
**cordwood** ['kɔrd,wʊd] *s* leña apilada en cuerdas; leña que se vende en cuerdas; leña cortada en trozos de a 4 pies
**core** [kor] *s* corazón (*p.ej., de ciertas frutas*); quid (*de un problema*); alma, devanador (*del ovillo*); foco (*de un absceso*); (elec.) alma (*de un cable conductor*); (elec.) núcleo (*de un electroimán*); (found.) ánima (*de un molde*); *va* quitar el corazón de (*p.ej., una manzana*)
**Corea** [ko'riə] *s* Corea
**Corean** [ko'riən] *adj & s* coreano
**coreligionist** [,korɪ'lɪdʒənɪst] *s* correligionario
**coreopsis** [,korɪ'ɑpsɪs] *s* (bot.) coreópsida
**corespondent** [,korɪs'pɑndənt] *s* (law) acusado como cómplice del demandado en un pleito de divorcio
**coriaceous** [,korɪ'eʃəs] *adj* coriáceo
**coriander** [,korɪ'ændər] *s* (bot.) cilantro o culantro
**Corinth** ['kɑrɪnθ] o ['kɔrɪnθ] *s* Corinto
**Corinthian** [kə'rɪnθɪən] *adj* corintio; *s* corintio; **Corinthians** *spl* (Bib.) Epístola de San Pablo a los corintios
**Coriolanus** [,kɑrɪə'lenəs] o [,kɔrɪə'lenəs] *s* Coriolano
**corium** ['korɪəm] *s* (*pl:* **-a** [ə]) (anat. & zool.) corión
**cork** [kɔrk] *s* corcho; corcho, tapón de corcho; tapón (*de cualquier materia*); (angling) corcho (*flotador*); *adj* corchoso (*parecido al corcho*); corchero (*perteneciente al corcho*); corchotaponero (*perteneciente a la fabricación de los tapones de corcho*); *va* tapar con corcho; encerrar; restringir; pintar con corcho quemado
**corking** ['kɔrkɪŋ] *adj* (slang) excelente, extraordinario
**cork jacket** *s* salvavidas de corcho
**cork oak** *s* (bot.) alcornoque
**corkscrew** ['kɔrk,skru] *s* sacacorchos, tirabuzón, descorchador; *adj* espiral, en forma de sacacorchos; *vn* zigzaguear; (aer.) volar en espiral
**corkscrew flower** *s* (bot.) caracol real
**cork tree** *s* var. de **cork oak**
**corkwood** ['kɔrk,wʊd] *s* (bot.) balsa o balso; (bot.) anona; (bot.) majagua (*Pariti tiliaceum*); madera de estos árboles
**corky** ['kɔrkɪ] *adj* (*comp:* **-ier;** *super:* **-iest**) corchoso; (coll.) alegre, vivaz; que sabe a corcho (*dícese del vino*)
**corm** [kɔrm] *s* (bot.) cormo
**cormophyte** ['kɔrməfaɪt] *s* (bot.) cormofita
**cormorant** ['kɔrmərənt] *s* (orn.) cormorán, corvejón, cuervo marino, mergo; (fig.) avaro, avariento; *adj* avaro, avariento
**corn** [kɔrn] *s* (U.S.A.) maíz; (England) trigo; (Scotland) avena; grano (*de maíz, trigo, etc.*); callo, clavo (*dureza de la piel*); (coll.) aguardiente de maíz; (slang) trivialidad; (slang) broma cansada o gastada; *va* acecinar, curar, salar
**cornaceous** [kɔr'neʃəs] *adj* (bot.) cornáceo
**Corn Belt** *s* (U.S.A.) zona del maíz
**corn borer** *s* (ent.) mariposa del maíz
**corn bread** *s* pan de maíz
**corncake** ['kɔrn,kek] *s* tortilla de maíz
**corncob** ['kɔrn,kɑb] *s* mazorca de maíz, carozo; pipa de fumar hecha de una mazorca de maíz
**corn cockle** *s* (bot.) neguilla, neguillón
**corn crake** *s* (orn.) guión de las codornices, rey de codornices
**corncrib** ['kɔrn,krɪb] *s* granero para maíz
**corn cure** *s* callicida
**corn cutter** *s* (U.S.A.) máquina para cortar el maíz
**corncutter** ['kɔrn,kʌtər] *s* callista, cortacallos
**cornea** ['kɔrnɪə] *s* (anat.) córnea
**corneal** ['kɔrnɪəl] *adj* corneal
**corned** [kɔrnd] *adj* acecinado
**cornel** ['kɔrnɛl] *s* (bot.) cornejo; (bot.) sanguiñuelo o sanapudio blanco
**Cornelia** [kɔr'niljə] *s* Cornelia
**cornelian** [kɔr'niljən] *s* (mineral.) cornalina
**cornelian cherry** *s* (bot.) cornejo macho
**Cornelius** [kɔr'niljəs] *s* Cornelio
**corneous** ['kɔrnɪəs] *adj* córneo
**corner** ['kɔrnər] *s* ángulo; esquina (*especialmente donde se encuentran dos calles*); rincón (*ángulo interior formado por dos o tres superficies que se encuentran; lugar retirado; parte, región*); comisura (*de los labios, los párpados, etc.*); apuro, aprieto, situación difícil; (com.) acaparamiento, monopolio; **around the corner** a la vuelta de la esquina; **out of the corner of one's eye** con el rabillo del ojo; **to cut corners** atajar; economizar acortando gastos, esfuerzos, tiempo, etc.; **to get someone in a corner** arrinconarle a uno; poner a uno en situación difícil; **to turn the corner** pasar el punto más peligroso; *adj* de esquina, p.ej., **corner room** habitación de esquina; *va* arrinconar; (com.) acaparar, monopolizar
**corner bead** *s* guardavivo
**corner block** *s* (carp.) coda
**corner chair** *s* silla de rincón
**corner cupboard** *s* rinconera (*armario*)
**cornerstone** ['kɔrnər,ston] *s* piedra angular; primera piedra (*de un nuevo edificio*); (fig.) piedra angular; **to lay the cornerstone** poner la primera piedra
**cornerways** ['kɔrnər,wez] o **cornerwise** ['kɔrnər,waɪz] *adv* diagonalmente
**cornet** [kɔr'nɛt] *s* (mus.) corneta, cornetín; ['kɔrnɛt] o [kɔr'nɛt] *s* cucurucho (*papel arrollado en forma de cono*); toca (*de las hermanas de la caridad*); (Brit.) corneta (*oficial de caballería que llevaba el estandarte*); (Brit.) helado de barquillo, cucurucho
**cornetist** o **cornettist** [kɔr'nɛtɪst] *s* (mus.) corneta, cornetín
**corn exchange** *s* bolsa de granos
**cornfield** ['kɔrn,fild] *s* (U.S.A.) maizal; (England) trigal; (Scotland) avenal
**corn flour** *s* harina de maíz
**cornflower** ['kɔrn,flaʊər] *s* (bot.) cabezuela, aciano; (bot.) neguillón; (Brit.) almidón de maíz
**corn gromwell** *s* (bot.) mijo de sol agreste
**cornhusk** ['kɔrn,hʌsk] *s* perfolla
**cornice** ['kɔrnɪs] *s* sobrepuerta; cornisa (*crestería de nieve*); (arch.) cornisa
**Cornish** ['kɔrnɪʃ] *adj* córnico; *s* córnico (*idioma*)
**Cornishman** ['kɔrnɪʃmən] *s* (*pl:* **-men**) habitante de Cornualles
**Corn Laws** *spl* (Brit.) leyes que prohibían o limitaban la importación del trigo
**corn liquor** *s* chicha
**corn meal** *s* harina de maíz
**corn on the cob** *s* maíz en la mazorca
**corn pith** *s* meollo del tallo del maíz
**corn plaster** *s* emplasto para los callos
**corn pone** *s* pan de maíz
**corn popper** *s* tostador de maíz
**corn poppy** *s* (bot.) amapola
**corn rose** *s* (bot.) amapola; (bot.) neguillón
**corn salad** *s* (bot.) valerianilla
**corn shock** *s* hacina de tallos de maíz
**corn silk** *s* cabellos, barbas del maíz
**cornstalk** ['kɔrn,stɔk] *s* tallo de maíz
**cornstarch** ['kɔrn,stɑrtʃ] *s* almidón de maíz
**corn sugar** *s* azúcar hecho de almidón de maíz
**corn syrup** *s* jarabe hecho de maíz
**cornu** ['kɔrnju] *s* (*pl:* **-nua** [njʊə]) (anat.) cuerno
**cornu ammonis** [ə'monɪs] *s* (anat. & pal.) cuerno de Amón
**cornucopia** [,kɔrnə'kopɪə] *s* cornucopia
**Cornwall** ['kɔrnwɔl] o ['kɔrnwəl] *s* Cornualles
**corn worm** *s* (ent.) gusano del maíz
**corny** ['kɔrnɪ] *adj* (*comp:* **-ier;** *super:* **-iest**)

de maíz; de trigo; calloso; (dial.) que sabe a malta; (coll.) falto de espontaneidad, muy sentimental (*dícese de la música*); (slang) muy malo, muy pesado; (slang) gastado, trillado, trivial
**corolla** [kəˈrɑlə] *s* (bot.) corola
**corollary** [ˈkɑrəˌlɛrɪ] o [ˈkɔrəˌlɛrɪ] *s* (*pl:* **-ies**) corolario; deducción; consecuencia natural
**corona** [kəˈronə] *s* (*pl:* **-nas** o **-nae** [ni]) corona; (astr., elec. & meteor.) corona
**Corona Australis** [ɔˈstrelɪs] *s* (astr.) Corona austral
**Corona Borealis** [ˌborɪˈælɪs] o [ˌborɪˈelɪs] *s* (astr.) Corona boreal
**coronach** [ˈkɔrənəx] *s* (Scotch) endecha, canto fúnebre
**coronal** [ˈkɑrənəl] o [ˈkɔrənəl] *adj* coronal; *s* corona
**coronal suture** *s* (anat.) sutura coronal
**coronary** [ˈkɑrəˌnɛrɪ] o [ˈkɔrəˌnɛrɪ] *adj* coronario
**coronary thrombosis** *s* (path.) trombosis coronaria, trombosis de las coronarias
**coronation** [ˌkɑrəˈneʃən] o [ˌkɔrəˈneʃən] *s* coronación
**coroner** [ˈkɑrənər] o [ˈkɔrənər] *s* juez de guardia, córoner
**coroner's inquest** *s* pesquisa dirigida por el juez de guardia
**coroner's jury** *s* jurado del juez de guardia
**coronet** [ˈkɑrənɛt] o [ˈkɔrənɛt] *s* corona (*que corresponde a un título nobiliario*); diadema (*que sirve de ornamento para la cabeza*); (vet.) corona (*de la cuartilla de un caballo*)
**coronium** [kəˈronɪəm] *s* (chem.) coronio
**corp.** o **Corp.** abr. de **Corporal** y **Corporation**
**corporal** [ˈkɔrpərəl] *adj* corporal; *s* (mil.) cabo; (eccl.) corporal (*lienzo*)
**corporally** [ˈkɔrpərəlɪ] *adv* corporalmente
**corporal punishment** *s* (law) castigo corporal
**corporate** [ˈkɔrpərɪt] *adj* corporativo; colectivo
**corporately** [ˈkɔrpərɪtlɪ] *adv* corporativamente; corporalmente
**corporation** [ˌkɔrpəˈreʃən] *s* corporación; sociedad anónima; (coll.) vientre abultado
**corporeal** [kɔrˈporɪəl] *adj* corpóreo; material, tangible
**corposant** [ˈkɔrpəzænt] *s* fuego de Santelmo
**corps** [kor] *s* (*pl:* **corps** [korz]) cuerpo (*conjunto de personas que obran juntamente*); (mil.) cuerpo, cuerpo de ejército
**corps area** *s* (U.S.A.) distrito militar
**corps de ballet** [kɔr də bæˈlɛ] *s* cuerpo de baile, cuerpo coreográfico
**corpse** [kɔrps] *s* cadáver (humano)
**corpulence** [ˈkɔrpjələns] o **corpulency** [ˈkɔrpjələnsɪ] *s* corpulencia
**corpulent** [ˈkɔrpjələnt] *adj* corpulento
**corpus** [ˈkɔrpəs] *s* (*pl:* **corpora** [ˈkɔrpərə]) cadáver; cuerpo (*colección de escritos, leyes, etc.*); (anat.) cuerpo
**corpus callosum** [kəˈlosəm] *s* (*pl:* **corpora callosa**) (anat.) cuerpo calloso
**Corpus Christi** [ˈkrɪstɪ] o [ˈkrɪstaɪ] *s* (eccl.) Corpus, día del Cuerpo de Cristo
**corpuscle** [ˈkɔrpʌsəl] *s* (bot., chem. & phys.) corpúsculo; (physiol.) glóbulo
**corpuscular** [kɔrˈpʌskjələr] *adj* corpuscular
**corpus delicti** [dɪˈlɪktaɪ] *s* (law) cuerpo del delito
**corpus juris** [ˈdʒurɪs] *s* cuerpo de leyes
**corpus luteum** [ˈlutɪəm] *s* (*pl:* **corpora lutea**) (embryol.) cuerpo lúteo
**corr.** abr. de **correspondence, correspondent** y **corresponding**
**corral** [kəˈræl] *s* corral; (*pret & pp:* **-ralled;** *ger:* **-ralling**) *va* acorralar
**correct** [kəˈrɛkt] *adj* correcto; cumplido (*en muestras de urbanidad*); *va* corregir
**correction** [kəˈrɛkʃən] *s* corrección
**correctional** [kəˈrɛkʃənəl] *adj & s* correccional
**corrective** [kəˈrɛktɪv] *adj & s* correctivo
**correctness** [kəˈrɛktnɪs] *s* corrección
**correlate** [ˈkɑrəlet] o [ˈkɔrəlet] *va* correlacionar; *vn* correlacionarse
**correlation** [ˌkɑrəˈleʃən] o [ˌkɔrəˈleʃən] *s* correlación
**correlative** [kəˈrɛlətɪv] *adj & s* correlativo
**correspond** [ˌkɑrɪˈspɑnd] o [ˌkɔrɪˈspɑnd] *vn* corresponder; corresponderse (*escribirse*)
**correspondence** [ˌkɑrɪˈspɑndəns] o [ˌkɔrɪˈspɑndəns] *s* correspondencia
**correspondence course** *s* curso por correspondencia
**correspondence school** *s* escuela por correspondencia
**correspondent** [ˌkɑrɪˈspɑndənt] o [ˌkɔrɪˈspɑndənt] *adj* correspondiente; *s* correspondiente, corresponsal
**corresponding** [ˌkɑrɪˈspɑndɪŋ] o [ˌkɔrɪˈspɑndɪŋ] *adj* correspondiente
**correspondingly** [ˌkɑrɪˈspɑndɪŋlɪ] o [ˌkɔrɪˈspɑndɪŋlɪ] *adv* correspondientemente
**corresponding secretary** *s* secretario que atiende la correspondencia
**corridor** [ˈkɑrɪdər] o [ˈkɔrɪdər] *s* corredor, pasillo; (pol.) corredor
**corrigendum** [ˌkɑrɪˈdʒɛndəm] o [ˌkɔrɪˈdʒɛndəm] *s* (*pl:* **-da** [də]) error por corregir (*en un manuscrito, libro, etc.*)
**corrigible** [ˈkɑrɪdʒɪbəl] o [ˈkɔrɪdʒɪbəl] *adj* corregible
**corroborant** [kəˈrɑbərənt] *adj & s* corroborante
**corroborate** [kəˈrɑbəret] *va* corroborar
**corroboration** [kəˌrɑbəˈreʃən] *s* corroboración
**corroborative** [kəˈrɑbəˌretɪv] o **corroboratory** [kəˈrɑbərəˌtorɪ] *adj* corroborativo
**corrode** [kəˈrod] *va* corroer; (fig.) corroer (*agobiar, consumir*); *vn* corroerse
**corrodible** [kəˈrodɪbəl] *adj* corrosible
**corrosion** [kəˈroʒən] *s* corrosión
**corrosive** [kəˈrosɪv] *adj & s* corrosivo
**corrosive sublimate** *s* (chem.) argento vivo sublimado, sublimado corrosivo
**corrugate** [ˈkɑrəget] o [ˈkɔrəget] *va* acanalar, ondular; corrugar (*el cartón*); arrugar
**corrugated iron** [ˈkɑrəˌgetɪd] o [ˈkɔrəˌgetɪd] *s* hierro acanalado, hierro ondulado
**corrugated paper** *s* papel corrugado
**corrugation** [ˌkɑrəˈgeʃən] o [ˌkɔrəˈgeʃən] *s* acanaladura, ondulación; corrugación; arruga
**corrupt** [kəˈrʌpt] *adj* corrompido; *va* corromper; *vn* corromperse
**corruptibility** [kəˌrʌptɪˈbɪlɪtɪ] *s* corruptibilidad
**corruptible** [kəˈrʌptɪbəl] *adj* corruptible
**corruption** [kəˈrʌpʃən] *s* corrupción
**corruptive** [kəˈrʌptɪv] *adj* corruptivo
**corsage** [kɔrˈsɑʒ] *s* corpiño, jubón; ramillete que llevan las mujeres a la cintura, el hombro, etc.
**corsair** [ˈkɔrsɛr] *s* (naut.) corsario (*pirata; barco de piratas; embarcación armada en corso*)
**corselet** [ˈkɔrslɪt] *s* coselete (*armadura*); (zool.) coselete (*tórax de los insectos*); [ˌkɔrsəˈlɛt] *s* cuerpecillo, ajustador, corsé ligero
**corset** [ˈkɔrsɪt] *s* corsé
**corset cover** *s* cubrecorsé
**Corsica** [ˈkɔrsɪkə] *s* Córcega
**Corsican** [ˈkɔrsɪkən] *adj & s* corso; **the Corsican** el Corso (*Napoleón*)
**Corsican pine** *s* (bot.) pino salgareño, pino negral
**corslet** [ˈkɔrslɪt] *s* coselete (*armadura*); (zool.) coselete (*tórax de los insectos*)
**cortege** o **cortège** [kɔrˈtɛʒ] *s* procesión; cortejo, comitiva, séquito
**cortex** [ˈkɔrtɛks] *s* (*pl:* **-tices** [tɪsiz]) (anat. & bot.) corteza
**cortical** [ˈkɔrtɪkəl] *adj* cortical
**corticate** [ˈkɔrtɪket] o **corticated** [ˈkɔrtɪˌketɪd] *adj* cortezudo, corticado
**corticotropin** [ˌkɔrtɪkoˈtropɪn] *s* (physiol. & pharm.) corticotropina
**cortisone** [ˈkɔrtɪzon] *s* (physiol. & pharm.) cortisono
**corundum** [kəˈrʌndəm] *s* (mineral.) corindón
**Corunna** [koˈrʌnə] *s* La Coruña
**coruscate** [ˈkɑrəsket] o [ˈkɔrəsket] *vn* brillar, fulgurar, relampaguear
**coruscation** [ˌkɑrəsˈkeʃən] o [ˌkɔrəsˈkeʃən] *s* brillo, fulgor, relampagueo
**corvée** [kɔrˈve] *s* prestación vecinal; trabajo impuesto por la ley
**corvet** o **corvette** [kɔrˈvɛt] *s* (naut.) corbeta
**corvine** [ˈkɔrvaɪn] o [ˈkɔrvɪn] *adj* corvino
**Corybant** [ˈkɑrɪbænt] o [ˈkɔrɪbænt] *s* (*pl:*

**-bantes** ['bæntiz]) coribante (*sacerdote de Cibeles*)
**Corybantic** [,karɪ'bæntɪk] o [,kɔrɪ'bæntɪk] *adj* de coribantes, de los coribantes
**Corycian Cave** [kə'rɪʃən] *s* gruta Coriciana
**corylaceous** [,karɪ'leʃəs] *adj* (bot.) coriláceo
**corymb** ['karɪmb] o ['kɔrɪmb] *s* (bot.) corimbo
**corymbose** [ko'rɪmbos] *adj* corimboso
**coryphaeus** [,karɪ'fiəs] *s* (*pl:* **-phaei** ['fiaɪ]) corifeo
**coryphee** [,korɪ'fe] *s* bailarina; primera bailarina
**coryza** [ko'raɪzə] *s* (path.) coriza
**cos** abr. de **cosine**
**cos** [kas] o [kɔs] *s* (bot.) lechuga Cos
**cosec** abr. de **cosecant**
**cosecant** [ko'sikənt] *s* (trig.) cosecante
**cosignatory** [ko'sɪgnə,torɪ] *adj* cosignatario; *s* (*pl:* **-ries**) cosignatario
**cosine** ['kosaɪn] *s* (trig.) coseno
**cos lettuce** *s* var. de **cos**
**cosmetic** [kaz'mɛtɪk] *adj & s* cosmético
**cosmic** ['kazmɪk] *adj* cósmico
**cosmically** ['kazmɪkəlɪ] *adv* según las leyes cósmicas; vastamente, con gran extensión
**cosmic rays** *spl* (phys.) rayos cósmicos
**cosmogonic** [,kazmə'ganɪk] o **cosmogonical** [,kazmə'ganɪkəl] *adj* cosmogónico
**cosmogony** [kaz'magənɪ] *s* (*pl:* **-nies**) cosmogonía
**cosmographer** [kaz'magrəfər] *s* cosmógrafo
**cosmographic** [,kazmə'græfɪk] o **cosmographical** [,kazmə'græfɪkəl] *adj* cosmográfico
**cosmography** [kaz'magrəfɪ] *s* cosmografía
**cosmologist** [kaz'malədʒɪst] *s* cosmólogo
**cosmology** [kaz'malədʒɪ] *s* cosmología
**cosmonaut** ['kazmənɔt] *s* cosmonauta
**cosmopolitan** [,kazmə'palɪtən] *adj & s* cosmopolita
**cosmopolitanism** [,kazmə'palɪtənɪzəm] *s* cosmopolitismo
**cosmopolite** [kaz'mapəlaɪt] *s* cosmopolita
**cosmorama** [,kazmə'ræmə] o [,kazmə'ramə] *s* cosmorama
**cosmos** ['kazməs] o ['kazmas] *s* cosmos (*universo*); (bot.) cosmos
**Cossack** ['kasæk] *adj & s* cosaco
**cosset** ['kasɪt] *s* cordero domesticado y mimado; animal domesticado y mimado; *va* mimar, acariciar
**cost** [kɔst] o [kast] *s* costa, coste, costo; **costs** *spl* (law) costas; **at cost** a precio de coste, a coste y costas; **at all costs** o **at any cost** a toda costa; (*pret & pp:* **cost**) *va & vn* costar; **cost what it may** cueste lo que cueste
**cost accounting** *s* (com.) escandallo
**costal** ['kastəl] o ['kɔstəl] *adj* (anat.) costal
**costard** ['kastərd] o ['kɔstərd] *s* variedad de manzana inglesa; (hum.) cabeza
**Costa Rican** ['kastə 'rikən] o ['kɔstə 'rikən] *adj & s* costarriqueño
**coster** ['kastər] o ['kɔstər] o **costermonger** ['kastər,mʌŋgər] o ['kɔstər,mʌŋgər] *s* (Brit.) vendedor ambulante de frutas, legumbres, pescado, etc.
**cost, insurance, and freight** *s* (com.) costo, seguro y flete
**costive** ['kastɪv] o ['kɔstɪv] *adj* estreñido
**costliness** ['kɔstlɪnɪs] o ['kastlɪnɪs] *s* carestía; suntuosidad
**costly** ['kɔstlɪ] o ['kastlɪ] *adj* (*comp:* **-lier**; *super:* **-liest**) costoso, dispendioso; suntuoso
**costmary** ['kast,mɛrɪ] o ['kɔst,mɛrɪ] *s* (bot.) hierba de Santa María, costo hortense; (bot.) hierba lombriguera
**cost of living** *s* costo de la vida
**cost-price squeeze** ['kɔst'praɪs] o ['kast'praɪs] *s* (coll.) disminución de beneficios debida a la relación estrecha entre el costo de producción y el precio resultante de la competencia
**costume** ['kastjum] o ['kastum] *s* traje; disfraz; manera de vestirse; [kas'tjum] o [kas'tum] *va* trajear, vestir
**costume ball** *s* baile de trajes
**costume jewelry** *s* joyas de fantasía, bisutería
**costumer** [kas'tjumər] o [kas'tumər] o **costumier** [kas'tjumɪər] o [kas'tumɪər] *s* sastre de máscaras, sastre de teatro, mascarero; percha
**cosy** ['kozɪ] *adj* (*comp:* **-sier**; *super:* **-siest**) var. de **cozy**; *s* (*pl:* **-sies**) var. de **cozy**
**cot** abr. de **cotangent**
**cot** [kat] *s* catre (*cama ligera*); catre de tijera; cabaña, choza; envoltura; (naut.) coy
**cotangent** [ko'tændʒənt] *s* (trig.) cotangente
**cote** [kot] *s* abrigo para aves o animales pequeños
**Côte-d'Or** [,kot'dɔr] *s* Costa de Oro (*en Francia*)
**cotenant** [ko'tɛnənt] *s* coinquilino
**coterie** ['kotərɪ] *s* grupo, círculo, cofradía; corrillo
**coterminous** [ko'tʌrmɪnəs] *adj* var. de **conterminous**
**cotillion** [kə'tɪljən] *s* cotillón
**cottage** ['katɪdʒ] *s* cabaña; casita de campo, casita en un lugar de veraneo
**cottage cheese** *s* naterón, názula, requesón
**cottage pudding** *s* pudín con salsa dulce
**cottager** ['katɪdʒər] *s* veraneante que vive en una casita de campo
**cottar** o **cotter** ['katər] *s* campesino escocés que trabaja por cuenta de algún hacendado y que recibe como parte de su remuneración una cabaña y una porción de terreno
**cotter** ['katər] o **cotter pin** *s* (mach.) chaveta
**cotton** ['katən] *s* algodón; (bot.) algodonero; cotón (*tela*); *vn* (coll.) convenir, estar de acuerdo; (coll.) aficionarse
**cotton bagging** *s* tela de algodón para sacos, sacos de tela de algodón
**cotton batting** *s* algodón en hojas
**cotton field** *s* algodonal
**cotton flannel** *s* franela de algodón
**cotton gin** *s* desmotadera de algodón
**cotton moth** *s* (ent.) mariposa del gusano del algodón
**cottonmouth** ['katən,maʊθ] *s* (zool.) mocasín, víbora de agua
**cotton picker** *s* recogedor de algodón; máquina para recolectar el algodón
**cotton plant** *s* (bot.) algodonero
**cotton plantation** *s* plantación de algodón
**cotton rose** *s* (bot.) amor al uso, flor de la vida
**cottonseed** ['katən,sid] *s* semilla de algodón
**cottonseed meal** *s* harina de las semillas del algodón
**cottonseed oil** *s* aceite de algodón
**cottontail** ['katən,tel] *s* (zool.) liebre de cola blanca
**cotton thistle** *s* (bot.) acantio, cardo borriqueño, toba
**cotton waste** *s* hilacha de algodón, desperdicios de algodón
**cottonwood** ['katən,wʊd] *s* (bot.) chopo de la Carolina; (bot.) chopo de Virginia
**cotton wool** *s* algodón en rama
**cotton worm** *s* gusano del algodón
**cottony** ['katənɪ] *adj* algodonoso
**cotton yarn** *s* hilaza de algodón
**cotyledon** [,katɪ'lidən] *s* (bot. & embryol.) cotiledón
**cotyledonous** [,katɪ'lidənəs] *adj* (bot.) cotiledóneo
**cotyloid** ['katɪlɔɪd] *adj* (anat.) cotiloideo
**couch** [kaʊtʃ] *s* canapé, sofá, yacija; cama, lecho; *va* poner en canapé, sofá o yacija; expresar; bajar o inclinar en posición de ataque; enristrar (*p.ej., una lanza*); *vn* acostarse en canapé, sofá o yacija; agacharse o esconderse para atacar
**couch grass** *s* (bot.) hierba rastrera; (bot.) grama del norte
**Couch's kingbird** *s* (orn.) burlisto grande, sirirí
**cougar** ['kugər] *s* (zool.) puma
**cough** [kɔf] o [kaf] *s* tos; *va* **to cough down** hacer callar tosiendo; **to cough up** arrojar del pecho tosiendo; (slang) dar, conceder, entregar, sudar; *vn* toser
**cough drop** *s* pastilla para la tos
**cough syrup** *s* jarabe para la tos
**could** [kud] *v aux* pude, p.ej., **I could not come yesterday** no pude venir ayer; podría, p.ej., **I could see you tomorrow** podría ver a Vd. mañana
**couldn't** ['kudənt] contracción de **could not**

**coulee** ['kulɪ] o **coulée** [ku'le] *s* cañada, quebrada; raudal de lava
**coulomb** [ku'lɑm] *s* (elec.) culombio
**coulter** ['kolter] *s* var. de **colter**
**council** ['kaʊnsəl] *s* consejo (*cuerpo consultivo y administrativo*); ayuntamiento, concejo (*de un municipio*); (eccl.) concilio
**councilman** ['kaʊnsəlmən] *s* (*pl:* **-men**) concejal
**council of state** *s* consejo de estado
**Council of Trent** *s* concilio de Trento
**council of war** *s* consejo de guerra
**councilor** o **councillor** ['kaʊnsələr] *s* conciliar; concejal
**counsel** ['kaʊnsəl] *s* consejo; deliberación; consultor, consejero; grupo de consultores o consejeros; abogado consultor; **to keep one's own counsel** ser muy reservado, no revelar su propio pensamiento; **to take counsel** tomar consejo; (*pret & pp:* **-seled** o **-selled;** *ger:* **-seling** o **-selling**) *va* aconsejar; *vn* aconsejarse
**counselor** o **counsellor** ['kaʊnsələr] *s* consejero; abogado
**count** [kaʊnt] *s* cuenta; recuento; suma, total; conde; (law) cargo (*cada falta de que se acusa a uno*); (sport) cuento de 10 segundos antes de declarar vencido a un pugilista; **to take the count** (box.) dejarse contar diez; *va* contar; **to count noses** contar personas o cabezas; **to count off** separar contando; **to count out** no incluir, no tener en cuenta; (coll.) vencer en una elección contando incorrectamente los votos; (sport) declarar vencido (*a un pugilista que no puede levantarse después de contarle los 10 segundos*); *vn* contar; tenerse en cuenta; ponerse en cuenta; valer; **to count for** valer; **to count on** contar con; **to count on** + *ger* contar + *inf*; **to count on one's fingers** contar con o por los dedos
**countable** ['kaʊntəbəl] *adj* contable
**count-down** ['kaʊnt,daʊn] *s* recuento descendente hasta cero
**countenance** ['kaʊntɪnəns] *s* semblante; apoyo, patrocinio; serenidad, compostura; **to be out of countenance** estar desconcertado, estar conturbado; **to keep one's countenance** contenerse, estar tranquilo; abstenerse de sonreír o reír; **to lose countenance** agitarse, conturbarse; **to put out of countenance** confundir, avergonzar; *va* dar su aprobación a
**counter** ['kaʊntər] *s* contador (*persona o cosa*); mostrador; ficha; pecho del caballo; (box.) contragolpe; (fencing) contra; (naut.) bovedilla; *adj* contrario, de sentido opuesto; *adv* en el sentido opuesto, al revés; **to run counter to** oponerse a; *va* oponerse a; contradecir; devolver (*p.ej., un golpe*); **to counter with** contestar (*una pregunta, proyecto*) con (*otra pregunta, proyecto, etc.*); *vn* (box.) dar un contragolpe
**counteract** [,kaʊntər'ækt] *va* contrariar, contrarrestar, neutralizar
**counteraction** [,kaʊntər'ækʃən] *s* acción contraria, contrarresto, neutralización
**counteractive** [,kaʊntər'æktɪv] *adj & s* contrario
**counterambush** [,kaʊntər'æmbʊʃ] *s* contraemboscada
**counterapproach** ['kaʊntərə,protʃ] *s* (fort.) contraaproches
**counterattack** ['kaʊntərə,tæk] *s* contraataque; [,kaʊntərə'tæk] *va & vn* contraatacar
**counterattraction** [,kaʊntərə'trækʃən] *s* atracción contraria
**counterbalance** ['kaʊntər,bæləns] *s* contrapeso, contrabalanza; (rail.) contrapeso (*de la rueda motriz de la locomotora*); [,kaʊntər'bæləns] *va* contrapesar, contrabalanzar
**counterbattery** ['kaʊntər,bætərɪ] *s* (mil.) contrabatería
**counterbrace** ['kaʊntər,bres] *s* barra de contratensión; *va* contrabracear
**countercheck** ['kaʊntər,tʃɛk] *s* oposición, obstáculo; segunda comprobación; *va* resistir, contrarrestar, estorbar; comprobar por segunda vez
**counterclaim** ['kaʊntər,klem] *s* contrarreclamación; *vn* contrarreclamar
**counterclockwise** [,kaʊntər'klɑk,waɪz] *adj* contrario a las agujas de reloj; *adv* en sentido contrario al de las agujas de reloj
**countercurrent** ['kaʊntər,kʌrənt] *s* contracorriente
**counterdike** ['kaʊntər,daɪk] *s* contradique
**counter electromotive force** *s* (elec.) fuerza contraelectromotriz
**counterespionage** ['kaʊntər,ɛspɪənɪdʒ] o ['kaʊntər,ɛspiə'nɑʒ] *s* contraespionaje
**counterfeit** ['kaʊntərfɪt] *adj* contrahecho, falsificado, fingido; *s* contrahechura, falsificación; moneda falsa; *va* contrahacer; *vn* contrahacer; contrahacerse
**counterfeiter** ['kaʊntər,fɪtər] *s* contrahacedor, falsificador; falsificador de moneda, monedero falso
**counterfeit money** *s* moneda falsa
**counterfessed** [,kaʊntər'fɛst] *adj* (her.) contrafajado
**counterflory** [,kaʊntər'florɪ] *adj* (her.) contraflorado
**counterfoil** ['kaʊntər,fɔɪl] *s* talón (*p.ej., de un cheque*)
**counterfort** ['kaʊntər,fort] *s* (arch.) contrafuerte
**counterfugue** ['kaʊntər,fjug] *s* (mus.) contrafuga
**counterguard** ['kaʊntər,gɑrd] *s* (fort.) contraguardia
**counterintelligence** ['kaʊntərɪn'tɛlɪdʒəns] *s* contrainteligencia
**counterirritant** [,kaʊntər'ɪrɪtənt] *adj & s* (med.) contrairritante
**counterirritation** ['kaʊntər,ɪrɪ'teʃən] *s* (med.) contrairritación
**counterjumper** ['kaʊntər,dʒʌmpər] *s* (slang) vendedor o dependiente de tienda
**countermand** ['kaʊntərmænd] o ['kaʊntərmɑnd] *s* contramandato, contraorden; [,kaʊntər'mænd], [,kaʊntər'mɑnd], ['kaʊntərmænd] o ['kaʊntərmɑnd] *va* contramandar; revocar, hacer volver
**countermarch** ['kaʊntər,mɑrtʃ] *s* contramarcha; *vn* contramarchar
**countermark** ['kaʊntər,mɑrk] *s* contramarca; [,kaʊntər'mɑrk] *va* contramarcar
**countermeasure** ['kaʊntər,mɛʒər] *s* paso contrario, contramedida
**countermine** ['kaʊntər,maɪn] *s* (mil.) contramina; *va* (mil. & fig.) contraminar
**counteroffensive** [,kaʊntərə'fɛnsɪv] *s* (mil.) contraofensiva
**counteropening** ['kaʊntər,opənɪŋ] *s* (surg.) contraabertura
**counterpaly** ['kaʊntər,pelɪ] *adj* (her.) contrapalado
**counterpane** ['kaʊntər,pen] *s* cubrecama
**counterpart** ['kaʊntər,pɑrt] *s* copia; duplicado; contrafigura; contraparte; (theat.) contrafigura
**counterplot** ['kaʊntər,plɑt] *s* contratreta; (*pret & pp:* **-plotted;** *ger:* **-plotting**) *va* complotar contra; contraminar
**counterpoint** ['kaʊntər,pɔɪnt] *s* (mus.) contrapunto
**counterpoise** ['kaʊntər,pɔɪz] *s* contrapeso; (rad.) contraantena; *va* contrapesar
**counterpoison** ['kaʊntər,pɔɪzən] *s* contraveneno
**counterproposal** [,kaʊntərprə'pozəl] *s* contrapropuesta
**counterquartered** [,kaʊntər'kwɔrtərd] *adj* (her.) contracuartelado
**counterreconnaissance** [,kaʊntərrɪ'kɑnɪsəns] *s* (mil.) contrarreconocimiento
**counterreformation** ['kaʊntər,rɛfər'meʃən] *s* contrarreforma
**Counter Reformation** *s* Contrarreforma
**counterrevolution** ['kaʊntər,rɛvə'luʃən] *s* contrarrevolución
**counterround** ['kaʊntər,raʊnd] *s* (mil.) contrarronda
**counterscarp** ['kaʊntər,skɑrp] *s* (fort.) contraescarpa
**countershaft** ['kaʊntər,ʃæft] o ['kaʊntər,ʃɑft] *s* (mach.) contraárbol, contraeje
**countersign** ['kaʊntər,saɪn] *s* contraseña; refrendata (*firma*); (mil.) contraseña; *va* refrendar

**countersignature** [ˌkaʊntərˈsɪgnətʃər] *s* refrendata
**countersink** [ˈkaʊntərˌsɪŋk] *s* agujero avellanado; avellanador, broca de avellanar; (*pret & pp:* **-sunk**) *va* avellanar; meter (*un tornillo*) en agujero avellanado
**countersinking bit** *s* broca de avellanar
**counterspy** [ˈkaʊntərˌspaɪ] *s* contraespía
**counterstimulant** [ˌkaʊntərˈstɪmjələnt] *s* (med.) contraestimulante
**counterstroke** [ˈkaʊntərˌstrok] *s* contragolpe
**countersunk** [ˈkaʊntərˌsʌŋk] *adj* avellanado, perdido; *pret & pp de* **countersink**
**countervail** [ˈkaʊntərˌvel] *va* contrarrestar; contrapesar, compensar; *vn* ser de fuerza igual
**counterweight** [ˈkaʊntərˌwet] *s* contrapeso
**countess** [ˈkaʊntɪs] *s* condesa
**counting house** *s* despacho, escritorio, oficina
**counting room** *s* oficina de contabilidad
**countless** [ˈkaʊntlɪs] *adj* incontable, sin cuento
**countrified** [ˈkʌntrɪfaɪd] *adj* campesino, rústico; rural
**country** [ˈkʌntrɪ] *s* (*pl:* **-tries**) país; campo (*en oposición a la ciudad*); patria (*país a que uno pertenece como ciudadano*); *adj* campestre, rural
**country club** *s* club campestre
**country cousin** *s* pariente rústico
**country-dance** [ˈkʌntrɪˌdæns] o [ˈkʌntrɪˌdɑns] *s* baile campestre; contradanza
**country estate** *s* hacienda de campo, heredad
**countryfolk** [ˈkʌntrɪˌfok] *s* gente del campo, campesinos
**country gentleman** *s* caballero de provincia, dueño acomodado de finca rural
**country house** *s* quinta, casa de campo
**country jake** *s* (coll.) patán
**country life** *s* vida campestre
**countryman** [ˈkʌntrɪmən] *s* (*pl:* **-men**) compatriota; campesino, hombre de o del campo
**country people** *spl* gente del campo
**country road** *s* camino rural
**countryseat** [ˈkʌntrɪˌsit] *s* finca, hacienda, casa de campo algo pretenciosa
**countryside** [ˈkʌntrɪˌsaɪd] *s* campiña, campo
**country-wide** [ˈkʌntrɪˌwaɪd] *adj* nacional
**countrywoman** [ˈkʌntrɪˌwʊmən] *s* (*pl:* **-women**) compatriota; campesina
**countship** [ˈkaʊntʃɪp] *s* condado
**county** [ˈkaʊntɪ] *s* (*pl:* **-ties**) partido (*distrito*); (hist.) condado
**county farm** *s* (U.S.A.) hospicio mantenido por el partido
**county seat** *s* cabeza de partido
**coup** [ku] *s* golpe, golpe maestro
**coup de grâce** [ˌkudəˈgrɑs] *s* golpe de gracia, puñalada de misericordia
**coup d'état** [ˌkudeˈtɑ] *s* golpe de estado
**coupé** [kuˈpe] o [kup] *s* cupé (*automóvil*); [kuˈpe] *s* cupé (*coche*)
**couple** [ˈkʌpəl] *s* par (*conjunto de dos cosas de la misma especie; macho y hembra*); matrimonio (*marido y mujer*); pareja (*dos personas unidas, p.ej., para un baile*); (mech.) par de fuerzas; (elec.) par voltaico; (coll.) dos más o menos; *va* juntar, unir; aparear; (coll.) casar, unir en matrimonio; *vn* juntarse, unirse; aparease; copularse
**coupler** [ˈkʌplər] *s* (mach. & rad.) acoplador; (rail.) enganche
**couplet** [ˈkʌplɪt] *s* pareado (*dos versos rimados entre sí*); par
**coupling** [ˈkʌplɪŋ] *s* junta, unión; acoplamiento; (elec.) acoplador; (rail.) enganche
**coupling box** *s* (mach.) manguito, collar de acoplamiento; (elec.) caja de empalme
**coupling pin** *s* (rail.) pasador de enganche
**coupling rod** *s* (mach.) biela de acoplamiento
**coupon** [ˈkupɑn] o [ˈkjupɑn] *s* cupón
**courage** [ˈkʌrɪdʒ] *s* valor, ánimo; firmeza, resolución; **to have the courage of one's convictions** ajustarse abiertamente con su conciencia; **to pluck up courage** hacer de tripas corazón
**courageous** [kəˈredʒəs] *adj* valiente, animoso
**courbaril** [ˈkurbərɪl] *s* (bot.) curbaril
**courbaril copal** *s* anime (*resina*)
**courier** [ˈkʌrɪər] o [ˈkʊrɪər] *s* estafeta (*mensajero*); guía
**Courland** [ˈkʊrlənd] *s* Curlandia
**course** [kors] *s* curso; asignatura; decurso; (arti.) trayectoria; (naut.) rumbo, derrota; (naut.) papahigo; (mas.) hilada; plato (*de una comida*); proceder; campo de golf; **in due course** oportunamente, a su debido tiempo; **in the course of** en el decurso de, durante; **of course** por supuesto, naturalmente; **to give course to** dar curso a (*p.ej. las lágrimas*); *va* cazar con perros; correr por; (mas.) poner en hiladas; *vn* correr; corretear; tomar parte en una carrera
**courser** [ˈkorsər] *s* (poet.) corcel
**court** [kort] *s* corte (*de un rey*); (law) corte, tribunal; patio, atrio; callejuela; pista (*p.ej., de tennis*); **in open court** en pleno tribunal; **out of court** sin merecer consideración; **to pay court to** hacer la corte a (*un magnate, una mujer, etc.*); *va* cortejar; hacer la corte a; solicitar, buscar
**court card** *s* carta de figura
**court day** *s* (law) día hábil
**courteous** [ˈkʌrtɪəs] *adj* cortés
**courtesan** [ˈkʌrtɪzən] o [ˈkortɪzən] *s* cortesana
**courtesy** [ˈkʌrtɪsɪ] *s* (*pl:* **-sies**) cortesía; **by courtesy** por cortesía
**courtezan** [ˈkʌrtɪzən] o [ˈkortɪzən] *s* var. de **courtesan**
**court hand** *s* letra de curia
**courthouse** [ˈkortˌhaʊs] *s* casa de tribunales, palacio de justicia
**courtier** [ˈkortɪər] *s* cortesano (*palaciego*); cortejador (*el que corteja*)
**court jester** *s* bufón
**courtly** [ˈkortlɪ] *adj* (*comp:* **-lier;** *super:* **-liest**) cortesano, cortés; cortejador, obsequioso
**courtly love** *s* amor cortés
**court-martial** [ˈkortˈmɑrʃəl] *s* (*pl:* **courts-martial**) consejo de guerra; juicio por el consejo de guerra; (*pret & pp:* **-tialed** o **-tialled;** *ger:* **-tialing** o **-tialling**) *va* someter a consejo de guerra
**court of record** *s* tribunal de actas perpetuas
**Court of St. James** *s* Corte de San Jaime (*corte del soberano británico*)
**court of the first instance** *s* (law) tribunal de primera instancia
**court plaster** *s* esparadrapo, tafetán inglés
**courtroom** [ˈkortˌrum] o [ˈkortˌrʊm] *s* tribunal, sala de justicia
**courtship** [ˈkortʃɪp] *s* cortejo (*acción de cortejar a una mujer*); noviazgo
**courtyard** [ˈkortˌjɑrd] *s* patio, atrio
**cousin** [ˈkʌzən] *s* primo o prima
**cousin-german** [ˈkʌzənˈdʒʌrmən] *s* (*pl:* **cousins-german**) primo hermano o prima hermana
**cousinly** [ˈkʌzənlɪ] *adj* de primo; *adv* como primo
**cousinship** [ˈkʌzənʃɪp] *s* primazgo
**cove** [kov] *s* (naut.) ensenada; escondrijo, rincón protegido; (arch.) bovedilla; (slang) mozo u hombre, tipo raro; *va* (arch.) abovedar
**covenant** [ˈkʌvənənt] *s* pacto, convenio; contrato; (Bib.) alianza; *va & vn* pactar, convenir; (*cap.*) *s* pacto firmado entre los presbiterianos escoceses y el parlamento inglés
**covenanter** [ˈkʌvənəntər] *s* contratante; (*cap.*) [ˈkʌvənəntər] o [ˌkʌvəˈnæntər] *s* Covenantario (*partidario de la liga en defensa de la religión presbiteriana*)
**Covenant of the League of Nations** *s* Pacto de la Sociedad de las Naciones
**covenant of warranty** *s* (law) cláusula de evicción de saneamiento
**Coventry** [ˈkʌvəntrɪ] o [ˈkɑvəntrɪ] *s* ciudad del condado de Warwick, Inglaterra; **to send to Coventry** evitar relaciones con
**cover** [ˈkʌvər] *s* cubierta; cubierto (*servicio de mesa para una persona*); portada (*de una revista*); **to break cover** salir al aire libre, salir a campo raso; dejarse ver; salir de la espesura; **to take cover** ocultarse; **under cover** bajo cubierto, bajo techado; secreto, oculto; disfrazado; en secreto, cubiertamente; **under cover of** a cubierto de (*p.ej., la noche*); so pretexto de, bajo la apariencia de; **under separate cover** bajo cubierta separada, por separado;

*va* cubrir; revestir; recorrer (*cierta distancia*); cubrirse (*la cabeza*); empollar; incluir; apuntar con un arma de fuego; cubrir (*el caballo a la yegua*); (mil.) cubrir (*p.ej., la retirada*); **to cover up** cubrir completamente; *vn* cubrirse; (coll.) cubrirse (*satisfacer una deuda o alcance*)
**coverage** ['kʌvərɪdʒ] *s* alcance, envergadura (*cantidad o espacio cubierto*); (ins.) agregado de los riesgos contra los cuales se contrata un seguro; reportaje
**coveralls** ['kʌvərˌɔlz] *spl* mono (*traje de faena*)
**cover charge** *s* precio del cubierto (*en los restaurantes*)
**cover crop** *s* (agr.) siembra de cubierta
**covered bridge** *s* puente cubierto
**covered wagon** *s* carro entalamado
**covered way** *s* (fort.) camino cubierto, estrada encubierta
**covered wire** *s* (elec.) alambre forrado
**cover girl** *s* (coll.) muchacha hermosa en la portada de una revista
**cover glass** *s* cubreobjeto, cubierta de vidrio (*para muestras microscópicas*)
**covering** ['kʌvərɪŋ] *s* cubierta, envoltura
**covering letter** *s* carta adjunta
**coverlet** ['kʌvərlɪt] o **coverlid** ['kʌvərlɪd] *s* cubierta, envoltura; cubrecama, sobrecama
**coversed sine** ['kovʌrst] *s* (trig.) coseno verso
**cover slip** *s* var. de **cover glass**
**covert** ['kʌvərt] *adj* cubierto; secreto, disimulado, furtivo; (law) bajo la protección del marido; *s* abrigo; guarida, escondrijo
**covert cloth** *s* tela cruzada de lana, generalmente de color pardo
**coverture** ['kʌvərtʃər] *s* cubierta; abrigo, escondrijo
**covet** ['kʌvɪt] *va & vn* codiciar
**covetous** ['kʌvɪtəs] *adj* codicioso
**covetousness** ['kʌvɪtəsnɪs] *s* codicia
**covey** ['kʌvɪ] *s* nidada, pollada; bandada; grupo (*p.ej., de muchachas*)
**cow** [kaʊ] *s* vaca; elefanta; *va* acobardar, intimidar
**coward** ['kaʊərd] *adj & s* cobarde
**cowardice** ['kaʊərdɪs] *s* cobardía
**cowardly** ['kaʊərdlɪ] *adj* cobarde; *adv* cobardemente
**cowbane** ['kaʊˌben] *s* (bot.) cicuta acuática; (bot.) cicuta mayor
**cowbell** ['kaʊˌbɛl] *s* cencerro
**cowbird** ['kaʊˌbʌrd] *s* (orn.) enmantecado, garrapatero
**cowboy** ['kaʊˌbɔɪ] *s* vaquero, gaucho, caballista
**cowboy hat** *s* sombrero de vaquero norteamericano
**cowcatcher** ['kaʊˌkætʃər] *s* (rail.) rastrillo delantero; (rail.) trompa (Am.)
**cower** ['kaʊər] *vn* agacharse
**cowfish** ['kaʊˌfɪʃ] *s* (ichth.) pez cofre
**cow hand** *s* vaquero
**cowherd** ['kaʊˌhʌrd] *s* pastor de vacas, pastor de ganado
**cowhide** ['kaʊˌhaɪd] *s* cuero; zurriago; *va* zurriagar
**cowl** [kaʊl] *s* cogulla; capucha (*parte superior de la cogulla*); (aut.) bóveda, cubretablero; (aer.) cubierta del motor; (mach.) caperuza; sombrerete de chimenea; *va* poner cogulla a, encapuchar; cubrir con tapa, tapar
**cowled** [kaʊld] *adj* encapuchado; cuculiforme
**cowlick** ['kaʊˌlɪk] *s* remolino, mechón (*que se levanta sobre la frente*)
**cowling** ['kaʊlɪŋ] *s* (aer.) cubierta del motor
**co-worker** [ko'wʌrkər] *s* coadjutor; colaborador
**cowpea** ['kaʊˌpi] *s* (bot.) caupí, frijol de maíz, frijol de vaca
**cowpox** ['kaʊˌpɑks] *s* vacuna
**cowpuncher** ['kaʊˌpʌntʃər] *s* (coll.) vaquero, gaucho
**cowrie** o **cowry** ['kaʊrɪ] *s* (*pl:* **-ries**) cauri (*concha que se usa como moneda en muchos pueblos de África*)
**cowskin** ['kaʊˌskɪn] *s* cuero
**cowslip** ['kaʊslɪp] *s* (bot.) primavera; (bot.) hierba centella
**cow tree** *s* (bot.) árbol de la leche, árbol de vaca
**cowwheat** ['kaʊˌhwit] *s* (bot.) melámpiro
**coxa** ['kɑksə] *s* (*pl:* **-ae** [i]) (anat.) coxal; (ent.) coxa
**coxal** ['kɑksəl] *adj* coxal
**coxalgia** [kɑk'sældʒɪə] *s* (path.) coxalgia
**coxalgic** [kɑk'sældʒɪk] *adj* coxálgico
**coxcomb** ['kɑksˌkom] *s* mequetrefe; baladrón, fanfarrón; cresta de gallo; gorro de bufón; (bot.) cresta de gallo
**coxcombry** ['kɑksˌkomrɪ] *s* (*pl:* **-ries**) fanfarronería; fanfarronada
**coxofemoral** [ˌkɑksə'fɛmərəl] *adj* coxofemoral
**coxswain** ['kɑksən] o ['kɑkswen] *s* (naut.) timonel
**coy** [kɔɪ] *adj* recatado, reservado; retrechero
**coyote** [kaɪ'otɪ] o ['kaɪot] *s* (zool.) coyote
**coypu** ['kɔɪpu] *s* (zool.) coipo
**coz** [kʌz] *s* (coll.) primo o prima
**cozen** ['kʌzən] *va* trampear, defraudar, engañar, entretener
**cozenage** ['kʌzənɪdʒ] *s* trampa, fraude, engaño, entretenimiento
**cozy** ['kozɪ] *adj* (*comp:* **-zier;** *super:* **-ziest**) cómodo; contento; (Brit.) sociable, charlador; *s* (*pl:* **-zies**) cubretetera
**cp.** abr. de **compare**
**c.p.** abr. de **chemically pure** y **candle power**
**C.P.** abr. de **Chemically Pure, Common Pleas, Common Prayer** y **Court of Probate**
**C.P.A.** abr. de **certified public accountant**
**cpd.** abr. de **compound**
**cr.** abr. de **credit** y **creditor**
**crab** [kræb] *s* (zool.) cangrejo; (mach.) cabria; (coll.) malhumorado, persona de mal genio; (*cap.*) *s* (astr.) Cáncer; **to catch a crab** (rowing) sacar cangrejos; (*pret & pp:* **crabbed;** *ger:* **crabbing**) *va* (coll.) criticar, censurar; (coll.) echar a perder; *vn* coger cangrejos; (coll.) regañar
**crab apple** *s* manzana silvestre (*muy estimada para hacer conservas*); (bot.) manzano silvestre
**crabbed** ['kræbɪd] *adj* avinagrado, ceñudo; enredoso, embrollado; escabroso, desigual
**crab grass** *s* (bot.) hierba rastrera; (bot.) garranchuelo (*Digitaria sanguinalis*)
**crab louse** *s* (ent.) piojo pegadizo, ladilla
**crab tree** *s* (bot.) manzano silvestre
**crack** [kræk] *s* grieta; crujido, estallido; (coll.) golpe estruendoso; (coll.) instante, momento; (slang) prueba; (slang) esfuerzo; (slang) chiste; **at the crack of dawn** al romper el alba ‖ *adj* (coll.) excelente, de primera clase; (coll.) certero (*tirador*) ‖ *va* agrietar; romper haciendo crujir; chasquear (*un látigo*); (coll.) golpear, produciendo un ruido súbito y agudo; (slang) descubrir (*un secreto*); (slang) romper, desbaratar (*una fuerza enemiga*); (slang) decir con gracejo; enloquecer; fraccionar (*petróleo*); abrir (*una caja fuerte*) por la fuerza; **to crack a book** (slang) abrir un libro para estudiarlo; **to crack a bottle** (slang) abrir una botella y beber lo que contiene; **to crack a code** llegar a descifrar un código; **to crack a joke** (slang) decir algo gracioso, decir un chiste; **to crack a smile** (slang) sonreír; **to crack up** (coll.) alabar, elogiar ‖ *vn* agrietarse; crujir; cascarse (*la voz de una persona*); enloquecerse; ceder, someterse; (slang) desbaratarse; fraccionarse (*el petróleo*); **to crack down on** (coll.) reprender severamente, castigar violentamente; **to crack up** fracasar; perder el ánimo, perder la salud; estrellarse (*un avión*)
**crackbrain** ['krækˌbren] *s* loco, mentecato
**crack-brained** ['krækˌbrend] *adj* loco, mentecato
**crackdown** ['krækˌdaʊn] *s* (coll.) reprensión severa
**cracked** [krækt] *adj* agrietado; picado (*hielo*); chillón; perjudicado; (coll.) loco, mentecato
**cracker** ['krækər] *s* galleta, galletita; triquitraque (*cohete; rollo de papel que contiene dulces y que produce una pequeña detonación cuando se arrancan las dos extremidades*); (U.S.A.) blanco de baja clase que habita una región apartada de los centros de población en los estados de Georgia y la Florida
**cracker-barrel** ['krækərˌbærəl] *adj* (coll.) sencillo, íntimo, familiar, sin concierto ni propósito fijo (*dícese de la charla de los aldeanos*)

**crackerjack** ['krækər,dʒæk] *adj* (slang) excelente, de órdago, muy hábil, muy capaz; *s* (slang) cosa excelente, individuo de gran habilidad
**crack filler** *s* relleno para hendeduras
**cracking** ['krækɪŋ] *s* fraccionamiento (*del petróleo*)
**crackle** ['krækəl] *s* crujido, crepitación; (f.a.) acabado escarchado, pintura jaspeada; (f.a.) grietado (*superficie finamente estriada*); *vn* crujir, crepitar
**crackleware** ['krækəl,wɛr] *s* (f.a.) grietado
**crackling** ['kræklɪŋ] *s* crujido, crepitación; chicharrón; chicharrón de pellejo
**cracknel** ['kræknəl] *s* coscarana, bizcocho duro y quebradizo; **cracknels** *spl* chicharrones; chicharrones de manteca
**crack of doom** *s* señal del juicio final, señal del fin del mundo
**crackpot** ['kræk,pɑt] *adj & s* (slang) excéntrico, loco, tarambana
**cracksman** ['kræksmən] *s* (*pl:* **-men**) (slang) escalador (*ladrón*)
**crack-up** ['kræk,ʌp] *s* fracaso; colisión; derrota; (coll.) colapso; (aer.) aterrizaje violento
**Cracow** ['kreko] o ['krækaʊ] *s* Cracovia
**cradle** ['kredəl] *s* cuna; (min.) artesa oscilante (*para lavar el oro*); (naut.) cuna; armazón (*de la guadaña armada*); (constr.) cuna, plataforma colgante; (surg.) tablilla (*para entablillar huesos rotos*); (telp.) horquilla (*del microteléfono*); (aut.) cojeclavos; (fig.) cuna (*lugar de nacimiento u origen*); **to rob the cradle** escoger un compañero o casarse con una persona mucho más joven; *va* meter o acostar en la cuna; acunar, mecer; (fig.) acunar (*proteger durante la infancia*); (min.) lavar (*el oro*) con artesa oscilante; (naut.) sostener por medio de una cuna; segar con guadaña armada
**cradle scythe** *s* guadaña armada
**cradlesong** ['kredəl,sɔŋ] o ['kredəl,sɑŋ] *s* arrullo, canción de cuna
**craft** [kræft] o [krɑft] *s* arte, arte manual; astucia, maña; oficio, empleo; gremio; embarcación, barco; máquina de volar; *spl* embarcaciones, barcos; máquinas de volar
**craftiness** ['kræftɪnɪs] o ['krɑftɪnɪs] *s* astucia, maña
**craftsman** ['kræftsmən] o ['krɑftsmən] *s* (*pl:* **-men**) artesano (*el que ejerce un arte mecánico*); artífice (*artista*)
**craftsmanship** ['kræftsmənʃɪp] o ['krɑftsmənʃɪp] *s* artesanía
**crafty** ['kræftɪ] o ['krɑftɪ] *adj* (*comp:* **-ier;** *super:* **-iest**) astuto, mañoso
**crag** [kræg] *s* despeñadero, peñasco, cima del despeñadero
**cragged** ['krægɪd] o **craggy** ['krægɪ] *adj* peñascoso, escarpado
**crake** [krek] *s* (orn.) guión de las codornices; (orn.) rascón de agua
**cram** [kræm] (*pret & pp:* **crammed;** *ger:* **cramming**) *va* embutir, atracar; (coll.) cargar (*la cabeza a alguien*) con datos o conocimientos; (coll.) aprender apresuradamente; *vn* atracarse; (coll.) sobrecargar la memoria con datos o conocimientos; (coll.) aprender apresuradamente (*especialmente antes de un examen*)
**crambo** ['kræmbo] *s* juego de hallar rimas o consonantes
**cramp** [kræmp] *s* grapa, laña; abrazadera, torno; aprieto; calambre (*contracción de los músculos*); *adj* apretado, restringido; nudoso, dificultoso; *va* engrapar, lañar; apretar, restringir; dar o causar calambre a; **to cramp one's style** (slang) cortarle las alas a uno, impedirle a uno manifestar su habilidad
**crampfish** ['kræmp,fɪʃ] *s* (ichth.) tremielga, torpedo
**crampon** ['kræmpən] *s* tenazas de garfios (*dispositivo de garfios y cadenas para izar cajas o sillares*); crampón (*para andar por el hielo*); (bot.) raicilla aérea trepadora
**cranberry** ['kræn,bɛrɪ] *s* (*pl:* **-ries**) (bot.) arándano agrio
**cranberry bog** *s* arandanedo
**cranberry bush** *s* (bot.) arándano agrio (*arbusto*); (bot.) mundillo, sauquillo
**cranberry tree** *s* (bot.) mundillo, sauquillo
**crane** [kren] *s* (mach.) grúa; aguilón, cigüeña o pescante de chimenea; (naut.) abanico; (orn.) grulla; (orn.) garza; *va* mover o levantar con grúa; estirar (*el cuello como hace la grulla*); *vn* estirar el cuello
**crane fly** *s* (ent.) típula
**crane's-bill** o **cranes-bill** ['krenz,bɪl] *s* (bot.) geranio, pico de grulla
**cranial** ['krenɪəl] *adj* craneal
**craniology** [,krenɪ'ɑlədʒɪ] *s* craneología
**craniometry** [,krenɪ'ɑmɪtrɪ] *s* craneometría
**craniotomy** [,krenɪ'ɑtəmɪ] *s* (*pl:* **-mies**) (surg.) craneotomía
**cranium** ['krenɪəm] *s* (*pl:* **-niums** o **-nia** [nɪə]) (anat.) cráneo
**crank** [kræŋk] *s* manivela, manubrio; idea, concepto; capricho; (coll.) maniático; (coll.) malhumorado; *adj* inestable, inseguro; *va* (aut.) hacer girar o hacer arrancar (*el motor*) con la manivela; encorvar para dar forma de manivela
**crankcase** ['kræŋk,kes] *s* (mach.) cárter del cigüeñal, cárter del motor
**crankcase service** *s* (aut.) limpieza del cárter
**crank handle** *s* mango de la manivela; (aut.) manivela de arranque
**crankshaft** ['kræŋk,ʃæft] o ['kræŋk,ʃɑft] *s* (mach.) cigüeñal, eje motor
**cranky** ['kræŋkɪ] *adj* (*comp:* **-ier;** *super:* **-iest**) caprichoso, maniático; malhumorado, irritable; inestable, inseguro; encorvado, sinuoso
**crannied** ['krænɪd] *adj* grietoso
**cranny** ['krænɪ] *s* (*pl:* **-nies**) grieta, rendija, hendedura
**crape** [krep] *s* crespón; crespón fúnebre, crespón negro, paño de tumba, gasa
**crapehanger** ['krep,hæŋər] *s* (slang) aguafiestas
**crappie** ['kræpɪ] *s* (ichth.) pomosio
**craps** [kræps] *s* juego de dados; **to shoot craps** jugar o tirar a los dados
**crapshooter** ['kræp,ʃutər] *s* jugador de dados
**crash** [kræʃ] *s* desplome; colisión; estallido, crac; fracaso; quiebra, crac financiero; lienzo grueso, cotí burdo; (aer.) aterrizaje violento; *va* romper estrepitosamente; estrellar; hacer mover o ir con fuerza y estrépito; **to crash a party** (slang) asistir a una tertulia sin invitación; **to crash the gate** (slang) colarse, colarse de gorra; *vn* desplomarse; caer, encontrar, chocar o romperse con violencia y estrépito; estallar; quebrar (*en el comercio*); aterrizar violentamente, estrellarse (*un avión*); **to crash against** o **into** estrellarse contra
**crash dive** *s* (nav.) sumersión instantánea (*de un submarino*)
**crash helmet** *s* (aer.) casco protector
**crash landing** *s* aterrizaje violento
**crash program** *s* programa intensivo
**crasis** ['kresɪs] *s* (*pl:* **-ses** [siz]) crasia, crasis; (gram.) crasis
**crass** [kræs] *adj* tosco, espeso; craso (*error*)
**crassulaceous** [,kræsjə'leʃəs] *adj* (bot.) crasuláceo
**Crassus** ['kræsəs] *s* Craso
**crate** [kret] *s* banasta, cesto, cuévano; jaula (*embalaje de tablas colocadas a cierta distancia unas de otras*); *va* embalar en jaula, embalar con tablas
**crater** ['kretər] *s* cráter; (elec. & mil.) cráter; crátera (*vasija*); (*cap.*) *s* (astr.) Cráter
**crating** ['kretɪŋ] *s* embalaje en jaulas
**cravat** [krə'væt] *s* corbata
**crave** [krev] *va* ansiar, anhelar; pedir (*indulgencia*); *vn* suplicar; **to crave after** ansiar, anhelar; **to crave for** ansiar, anhelar; pedir, pedir con insistencia
**craven** ['krevən] *adj & s* cobarde; **to cry craven** rendirse
**cravenette** [,krævə'nɛt] o [,krevə'nɛt] *s* (trademark) tela impermeable; impermeable (*sobretodo*)
**craving** ['krevɪŋ] *s* ansia, anhelo, sed
**craw** [krɔ] *s* buche
**crawfish** ['krɔ,fɪʃ] *s* (zool.) cámbaro, cangrejo de río; (zool.) langosta; *vn* (coll.) desdecirse, retroceder, ceder
**crawl** [krɔl] *s* reptación; marcha lenta; gateo; (swimming) arrastre; corral (*jaula en el agua*

*para encerrar peces, tortugas, etc.*); *vn* reptar, arrastrarse; andar o marchar paso a paso; gatear; andar furtivamente; hormiguear (*experimentar cierta sensación en la piel*); **to crawl along** andar o marchar paso a paso; **to crawl forth** u **out** avanzar o salir arrastrándose; **to crawl under** meterse debajo de; **to crawl up** trepar

**crawly** [ˈkrɔlɪ] *adj* (coll.) hormigueante

**crayfish** [ˈkreˌfɪʃ] *s* (zool.) cámbaro, cangrejo de río; (zool.) langosta

**crayon** [ˈkreən] o [ˈkreɑn] *s* creyón; dibujo al creyón; *va* dibujar con creyón

**craze** [krez] *s* moda, boga; manía, locura; estrías finas en la superficie de ciertas especies de vajilla; *va* enloquecer; estriar finamente (*la superficie de la vajilla*)

**crazy** [ˈkrezɪ] *adj* (*comp:* **-zier**; *super:* **-ziest**) loco, demente; desvencijado; achacoso, débil; loco (*que procede como loco*); **to be crazy about** (coll.) estar loco por; **to drive crazy** volver loco; **crazy as a bedbug** o **as a loon** (slang) loco de atar, loco rematado

**crazy bone** *s* hueso de la alegría

**crazy quilt** *s* centón

**crazyweed** [ˈkrezɪˌwid] *s* (bot.) loco, cascabelito

**creak** [krik] *s* chirrido, rechinamiento; *va* hacer chirriar o rechinar; *vn* chirriar, rechinar, chillar

**creaky** [ˈkrikɪ] *adj* (*comp:* **-ier**; *super:* **-iest**) chirriadero, chirriador, rechinador

**cream** [krim] *s* crema; nata y flor, crema (*p.ej., de la sociedad*); *va* proveer de crema; poner crema en; cocinar con crema o salsa de crema; desnatar (*la leche*); *vn* criar o producir nata; espumar

**cream cheese** *s* queso crema

**creamer** [ˈkrimər] *s* cremera

**creamery** [ˈkrimərɪ] *s* (*pl:* **-ies**) mantequería, quesería, lechería, granja

**cream of tartar** *s* crémor tártaro

**creamometer** [kriˈmɑmɪtər] *s* cremómetro

**cream puff** *s* bollo de crema

**cream sauce** *s* salsa de crema

**cream separator** *s* desnatadora, descremadora

**creamy** [ˈkrimɪ] *adj* (*comp:* **-ier**; *super:* **-iest**) cremoso; de color de crema

**crease** [kris] *s* arruga, pliegue; raya (*de los pantalones*); cris (*daga*); *va* arrugar, plegar; *vn* arrugarse, plegarse

**create** [kriˈet] *va* crear

**creation** [kriˈeʃən] *s* creación; **the Creation** la Creación

**creationism** [kriˈeʃənɪzəm] *s* (philos. & theol.) creacionismo

**creative** [kriˈetɪv] *adj* creador, creativo

**creator** [kriˈetər] *s* creador; **the Creator** el Creador

**creature** [ˈkritʃər] *s* criatura; (U.S.A.) animalejo, bicho; criatura (*hechura de otra persona*)

**creature comforts** *spl* cosas (*alimentos, vestidos*) que confortan el cuerpo

**crèche** [kreʃ] o [krɛʃ] *s* belén, nacimiento; casa de expósitos; guardería infantil

**credence** [ˈkridəns] *s* creencia, fe; credencia, aparador; (eccl.) credencia; **to give credence to** dar fe a, dar crédito a

**credential** [krɪˈdɛnʃəl] *adj* & *s* credencial; **credentials** *spl* credenciales; (dipl.) carta credencial

**credibility** [ˌkrɛdɪˈbɪlɪtɪ] *s* credibilidad

**credible** [ˈkrɛdɪbəl] *adj* creíble

**credit** [ˈkrɛdɪt] *s* crédito; (com. & educ.) crédito; **on credit** (com.) a crédito; **to do credit to** acreditar, dar crédito a; **to give a person credit for** concederle a una persona el mérito de; **to give credit to** creer, dar crédito a; (com.) abrir crédito a; **to take credit for** atribuirse el mérito de; *va* creer; (com. & educ.) acreditar; **to credit a person with** atribuirle a una persona el mérito de

**creditable** [ˈkrɛdɪtəbəl] *adj* honorable, estimable

**credit balance** *s* saldo acreedor

**credit card** *s* (com.) tarjeta de crédito

**credit line** *s* referencia que da el nombre del autor de un escrito que se ha reproducido

**credit man** *s* investigador de ventas al fiado

**creditor** [ˈkrɛdɪtər] *s* acreedor

**credit union** *s* asociación o banco cooperativo

**credo** [ˈkrido] o [ˈkredo] *s* (*pl:* **-dos**) credo; (mus.) credo

**credulity** [krɪˈdjulɪtɪ] o [krɪˈdulɪtɪ] *s* credulidad

**credulous** [ˈkrɛdʒələs] *adj* crédulo

**creed** [krid] *s* credo

**creek** [krik] o [krɪk] *s* arroyo; (naut.) ensenada

**creel** [kril] *s* cesta para pescados; jaula de mimbres (*para coger langostas, etc.*)

**creep** [krip] *s* arrastramiento; marcha lenta; **the creeps** (coll.) hormigueo (*en la piel*); (*pret & pp:* **crept**) *vn* arrastrarse; andar o mover cautelosa o furtivamente; gatear; trepar; desviarse; hormiguear, sentir hormigueo; **to creep forward** andar avanzando despacio; acercarse insensible o cautelosamente; **to creep in** o **into** insinuarse en; entrar cautelosa o furtivamente en; **to creep out** salir arrastrándose; salir cautelosa o furtivamente; **to creep up on** acercarse a, insensible o cautelosamente

**creepage** [ˈkripɪdʒ] *s* (elec.) fluencia, corrimiento, escurrimiento; (elec.) ascenso capilar

**creeper** [ˈkripər] *s* rastrero; (bot.) planta rastrera, planta trepadora; (orn.) trepador; **creepers** *spl* crampón, ramplón; prenda de vestir para niños (*comprende la blusa y el pantalón*)

**creeping** [ˈkripɪŋ] *s* arrastramiento; marcha lenta; desviación, deslizamiento; *adj* lento; progresivo; (bot.) rastrero

**creeping barrage** *s* (mil.) barrera de fuego móvil

**creeping paralysis** *s* (path.) parálisis progresiva

**creeping sickness** *s* (path.) ergotismo

**creepy** [ˈkripɪ] *adj* (*comp:* **-ier**; *super:* **-iest**) (coll.) hormigueante; lento; **to feel creepy** (coll.) hormiguear; (coll.) tener carne de gallina

**creese** [kris] *s* cris (*daga*)

**cremate** [ˈkrimet] o [krɪˈmet] *va* incinerar

**cremation** [krɪˈmeʃən] *s* cremación, incineración de cadáveres

**cremator** [ˈkrimetər] o [krɪˈmetər] *s* persona que incinera cadáveres; horno crematorio

**crematory** [ˈkriməˌtorɪ] o [ˈkrɛməˌtorɪ] *adj* crematorio; *s* (*pl:* **-ries**) crematorio; horno crematorio

**crème** [krɛm] *s* crema (*nata; licor espeso y dulce*)

**crème de menthe** [krɛmdəˈmɑ̃t] *s* crema de menta

**Cremona** [krɪˈmonə] *s* violín de Cremona

**crenate** [ˈkrinet] *adj* (bot.) crenato

**crenation** [krɪˈneʃən] *s* (bot.) crena, muesca; (anat.) crena

**crenelate** o **crenellate** [ˈkrɛnəlet] *va* (fort.) almenar

**Creole** [ˈkriol] *adj* & *s* criollo; (*l.c.*) *s* criollo, negro criollo

**creosol** [ˈkriəsol] *s* (chem.) creosol

**creosote** [ˈkriəsot] *s* creosota; *va* creosotar

**creosote oil** *s* aceite de creosota

**crepe** o **crêpe** [krep] *s* crespón

**crepe de Chine** [ˌkrepdəˈʃin] *s* crespón de la China

**crepitant** [ˈkrɛpɪtənt] *adj* crepitante

**crepitate** [ˈkrɛpɪtet] *vn* crepitar

**crepitation** [ˌkrɛpɪˈteʃən] *s* crepitación; (med.) crepitación

**crept** [krɛpt] *pret & pp de* **creep**

**crepuscular** [krɪˈpʌskjələr] *adj* crepuscular

**crescendo** [krəˈʃɛndo] *s* (*pl:* **-dos**) (mus.) crescendo

**crescent** [ˈkrɛsənt] *adj* creciente; *s* media luna (*figura de cuarto de luna creciente o menguante; mahometismo; imperio turco*); panecillo (*de figura de media luna*); (astr.) creciente, creciente de la luna; (her.) creciente

**cresol** [ˈkrisɑl] *s* (chem.) cresol

**cress** [krɛs] *s* (bot.) mastuerzo

**cresset** [ˈkrɛsɪt] *s* hachón, almenar, tedero

**Cressida** [ˈkrɛsɪdə] *s* (myth.) Criseida

**crest** [krɛst] *s* cresta (*copete, penacho de las aves; cima de una ola; cima, copete de una montaña; cimera sobre el morrión*); (anat., arch., bot., mach. & zool.) cresta; (her.) cimera, crista

**crested** ['krɛstɪd] *adj* crestado
**crested grebe** *s* (orn.) somorgujo moñudo
**crested lark** *s* (orn.) cochevís, cogujada, vejeta
**crestfallen** ['krɛst,fɔlən] *adj* cabizbajo, con las orejas caídas
**cretaceous** [krɪ'teʃəs] *adj* cretáceo; (*cap.*) *adj & s* (geol.) cretáceo
**Cretan** ['kritən] *adj & s* cretense
**Crete** [krit] *s* Creta
**cretin** ['kritɪn] *s* cretino
**cretinism** ['kritɪnɪzəm] *s* (path.) cretinismo
**cretonne** [krɪ'tɑn] o ['kritɑn] *s* cretona
**crevasse** [krə'væs] *s* grieta en un alud; (U.S.A.) brecha en un dique o malecón
**crevice** ['krɛvɪs] *s* grieta
**crew** [kru] *s* equipo; personal; tripulación o dotación (*de un buque o máquina de volar*); cuadrilla, banda; (sport) remo (*deporte de los remeros para carreras*); (sport) dotación (*de remeros*); *pret de* **crow**
**crew cut** *s* corte de pelo a cepillo
**crewel** ['kruəl] *s* estambre (*para bordar*)
**crew member** *s* tripulante, miembro de la tripulación
**crib** [krɪb] *s* camilla de niño; pesebre; granero; chiribitil (*cuarto muy pequeño*); (constr.) armazón de sustentación; (hyd.) cofre, cajón; (min.) brocal de entibación; (slang) chuleta (*notas que se usan a hurtadillas en un examen*); (coll.) plagio; (*pret & pp:* **cribbed;** *ger:* **cribbing**) *va* enjaular o encerrar dentro de un espacio muy pequeño; (coll.) plagiar; *vn* (slang) usar a hurtadillas claves o notas (*en un examen*)
**cribbage** ['krɪbɪdʒ] *s* juego de naipes en que se cuentan los tantos con clavijas que encajan en una tableta
**crick** [krɪk] *s* calambre; *va* hacer padecer un calambre
**cricket** ['krɪkɪt] *s* (ent.) grillo; (sport) cricquet; escabel, taburete; (coll.) juego limpio; *vn* (sport) jugar al cricquet
**cricketer** ['krɪkɪtər] *s* (sport) cricquetero
**cricoid** ['kraɪkɔɪd] *adj & s* (anat.) cricoides
**crier** ['kraɪər] *s* pregonero; baladrero; lamentador
**crime** [kraɪm] *s* crimen, delito
**Crimea** [kraɪ'miə] o [krɪ'miə] *s* Crimea
**Crimean** [kraɪ'miən] o [krɪ'miən] *adj* de Crimea
**Crimean War** *s* guerra de Crimea
**criminal** ['krɪmɪnəl] *adj & s* criminal
**criminal code** *s* (law) código penal
**criminal conversation** *s* (law) adulterio
**criminality** [,krɪmɪ'nælɪtɪ] *s* (*pl:* **-ties**) criminalidad
**criminal law** *s* derecho penal, jurisprudencia criminal
**criminally** ['krɪmɪnəlɪ] *adv* criminalmente
**criminal negligence** *s* imprudencia temeraria
**criminate** ['krɪmɪnet] *va* criminar
**crimination** [,krɪmɪ'neʃən] *s* criminación
**criminatory** ['krɪmɪnə,torɪ] *adj* acriminador
**criminological** [,krɪmɪnə'lɑdʒɪkəl] *adj* criminológico
**criminologist** [,krɪmɪ'nɑlədʒɪst] *s* criminólogo
**criminology** [,krɪmɪ'nɑlədʒɪ] *s* criminología
**crimp** [krɪmp] *s* encrespadura, rizado; arruga; rizo (*de pelo*); persona que recluta con fuerza o engaño; **to put a crimp in** (slang) estorbar, impedir; *va* encrespar, rizar; arrugar; reclutar con fuerza o engaño
**crimping iron** *s* encrespador, rizador
**crimple** ['krɪmpəl] *va* encrespar, rizar, arrugar; *vn* encresparse, rizarse, arrugarse
**crimpy** ['krɪmpɪ] *adj* (*comp:* **-ier;** *super:* **-iest**) encrespado, rizado, arrugado
**crimson** ['krɪmzən] *adj & s* carmesí; *va* teñir de carmesí; enrojecer; *vn* enrojecerse
**crimson clover** *s* (bot.) trébol encarnado, trébol del Rosellón
**cringe** [krɪndʒ] *s* adulación, bajeza; *vn* arrastrarse, reptar, encogerse
**cringle** ['krɪŋgəl] *s* (naut.) garrucho
**crinière** [,kri'njɛr] *s* (arm.) capizana
**crinkle** ['krɪŋkəl] *s* arruga, pliegue; rizo u onda (*en el agua*); susurro, crujido; *va* arrugar, plegar; *vn* arrugarse; serpentear; susurrar, crujir
**crinkly** ['krɪŋklɪ] *adj* (*comp:* **-klier;** *super:* **-kliest**) arrugado; ondulado; susurrante, crujidero
**crinoid** ['kraɪnɔɪd] o ['krɪnɔɪd] *adj & s* (zool.) crinoideo
**crinoline** ['krɪnəlɪn] o ['krɪnəlin] *s* crinolina
**cripple** ['krɪpəl] *adj & s* lisiado, baldado, estropeado; *va* lisiar, baldar, estropear; dañar, perjudicar; (naut.) desarbolar, desmantelar
**crisis** ['kraɪsɪs] *s* (*pl:* **-ses** [siz]) crisis
**crisp** [krɪsp] *adj* frágil, quebradizo; crespo, rizado; agudo; decisivo; refrescante; *va* hacer frágil o quebradizo; encrespar, rizar; ondular; *vn* encresparse, rizarse; ondularse
**crispy** ['krɪspɪ] *adj* (*comp:* **-ier;** *super:* **-iest**) var. de **crisp**
**crisscross** ['krɪs,krɔs] o ['krɪs,krɑs] *s* cruz (*figura; firma*); líneas cruzadas; cristus; juego del tres en raya; *adj* cruzado; *adv* en cruz, en forma de cruz; *va* marcar o cubrir con líneas cruzadas; *vn* entrecruzarse
**criterion** [kraɪ'tɪrɪən] *s* (*pl:* **-a** [ə] u **-ons**) criterio
**critic** ['krɪtɪk] *s* crítico; criticón (*persona que todo lo critica*)
**critical** ['krɪtɪkəl] *adj* crítico; criticón
**critical angle** *s* (aer. & opt.) ángulo crítico
**critical edition** *s* edición crítica
**critical mass** *s* (phys.) masa crítica
**critical pressure** *s* (phys.) presión crítica
**critical temperature** *s* (phys.) temperatura crítica
**criticise** ['krɪtɪsaɪz] *va & vn* var. de **criticize**
**criticism** ['krɪtɪsɪzəm] *s* crítica; (philos.) criticismo
**criticize** ['krɪtɪsaɪz] *va & vn* criticar
**critique** [krɪ'tik] *s* crítica; ensayo crítico
**croak** [krok] *s* graznido (*p.ej., del cuervo*); canto de las ranas; *va* (slang) matar; *vn* graznar (*el cuervo, el grajo, etc.*); croar (*la rana*); gruñir; presagiar el mal; (slang) reventar (*morir*)
**croaker** ['krokər] *s* gruñidor, refunfuñador; graznador; (ichth.) roncador, corvina blanca
**Croat** ['kroæt] *s* croata (*natural o habitante; idioma*)
**Croatia** [kro'eʃə] *s* Croacia
**Croatian** [kro'eʃən] *adj & s* croata
**crocein** ['krosɪɪn] *s* (chem.) croceína
**crochet** [kro'ʃe] *s* croché; (*pret & pp:* **-cheted** ['ʃed]; *ger:* **-cheting** ['ʃeɪŋ]) *va* trabajar con aguja de croché; *vn* hacer croché
**crochet needle** *s* aguja de croché, aguja de gancho
**crocin** ['krosɪn] *s* (chem.) crocina
**crock** [krɑk] *s* vasija de barro cocido, vasija de loza, cacharro
**crockery** ['krɑkərɪ] *s* loza
**crocket** ['krɑkɪt] *s* (arch.) follaje
**crocodile** ['krɑkədaɪl] *s* (zool.) cocodrilo
**crocodile tears** *spl* lágrimas de cocodrilo
**crocodilian** [,krɑkə'dɪlɪən] *adj & s* (zool.) cocodriliano
**crocus** ['krokəs] *s* (bot.) azafrán
**Croesus** ['krisəs] *s* (biog. & fig.) Creso
**croft** [krɔft] o [krɑft] *s* (Brit.) campo pequeño encerrado; (Brit.) granja muy pequeña
**crofter** ['krɔftər] o ['krɑftər] *s* (Brit.) persona que cultiva una granja muy pequeña
**Cro-Magnon** [kro'mægnɑn] *adj* (anthrop.) cromañonense; *s* (anthrop.) cromañón
**cromlech** ['krɑmlɛk] *s* crómlech o crónlech
**crone** [kron] *s* vieja acartonada
**Cronos** ['kronɑs] o **Cronus** ['kronəs] *s* (myth.) Cronos
**crony** ['kronɪ] *s* (*pl:* **-nies**) camarada, compinche
**crook** [krʊk] *s* gancho, garfio; curva, curvatura; cayado (*que usan los pastores*); (mus.) tudel (*del bajón*); (coll.) fullero, ladrón; *va* encorvar; (slang) empinar (*el codo*); *vn* encorvarse
**crooked** ['krʊkɪd] *adj* curvo, encorvado, torcido; (fig.) torcido (*dícese de una persona o su conducta*); **to go crooked** (coll.) torcerse (*desviarse del camino recto de la virtud*)
**Crookes space** [krʊks] *s* (phys.) espacio de Crookes
**Crookes tube** *s* (phys.) tubo de Crookes

**crookneck** ['kruk,nɛk] *s* (bot.) calabaza de cuello torcido
**crooknecked** ['kruk,nɛkt] *adj* de cuello torcido
**croon** [krun] *s* canturreo; *va & vn* cantar con voz suave, cantar con melancolía exagerada
**crooner** ['krunər] *s* cantor de voz suave, cantor melancólico
**crop** [krap] *s* cosecha; (fig.) cosecha (*p.ej., de mentiras*); cabellera; cabello corto; señal producida recortando las orejas a los animales; buche (*del ave*); látigo mocho, remate de látigo; (fig.) hornada (*de citas, héroes, etc.*); (*pret & pp:* **cropped;** *ger:* **cropping**) *va* sembrar y cosechar; cortar; desorejar; desmochar; esquilar, trasquilar; pacer (*la hierba*); *vn* cosechar; **to crop out** o **up** (min.) aflorar; asomar, dejarse ver, manifestarse inesperadamente
**crop dusting** *s* aerofumigación, fumigación aérea, pulverización agrícola
**cropper** ['krapər] *s* cultivador; (coll.) caída pesada; (coll.) fracaso; **to come a cropper** (coll.) caer pesadamente; (coll.) fracasar
**croquet** [kro'ke] *s* argolla, croquet (*juego*)
**croquette** [kro'kɛt] *s* croqueta
**crosier** ['kroʒər] *s* cayado, báculo pastoral; (bot.) fronda circinada (*de los helechos*)
**cross** [krɔs] o [kras] *s* cruz; cruce (*de dos caminos; de razas*); (elec.) cruzamiento; (fig.) cruz, calvario (*sufrimiento moral*); **the Cross** la Cruz, la Santa Cruz; **to make the sign of the cross** hacerse la señal de la cruz; **to take the cross** cruzarse (*alistarse en una cruzada*) ‖ *adj* transversal; travieso; cruzado (*de raza mixta*); malhumorado ‖ *va* cruzar; contrariar; frustrar; **to cross a person's path** cruzar el camino de una persona; **to cross a road** atravesar o cruzar un camino; **to cross off** u **out** borrar; **to cross oneself** hacerse la señal de la cruz; **to cross one's fingers** cruzar los dedos (*por superstición*); **to cross one's heart** hacerse la señal de la cruz sobre el corazón (*como juramento de integridad*); **to cross one's legs** cruzar las piernas; **to cross one's mind** ocurrírsele a uno; **to cross swords** cruzar las espadas (*batirse*); **to cross the Atlantic** cruzar el Atlántico; **to cross the street** atravesar o cruzar la calle; **to cross up** servir de obstáculo a ‖ *vn* cruzar; cruzarse; **to cross over** atravesar de un lado a otro
**crossbar** ['krɔs,bar] o ['kras,bar] *s* travesaño; raya o lista al través o transversal
**crossbeam** ['krɔs,bim] o ['kras,bim] *s* viga transversal
**crossbill** ['krɔs,bɪl] o ['kras,bɪl] *s* (orn.) piquituerto
**cross bond** *s* (elec.) conexión entre riel y alimentador; (mas.) aparejo cruzado
**crossbones** ['krɔs,bonz] o ['kras,bonz] *spl* huesos cruzados (*símbolo de la muerte*)
**crossbow** ['krɔs,bo] o ['kras,bo] *s* ballesta
**crossbowman** ['krɔs,bomən] o ['kras,bomən] *s* (*pl:* **-men**) ballestero
**cross bracing** *s* arriostramiento transversal
**crossbred** ['krɔs,brɛd] o ['kras,brɛd] *adj* cruzado (*de raza*)
**crossbreed** ['krɔs,brid] o ['kras,brid] *s* híbrido; (*pret & pp:* **-bred**) *va* cruzar (*animales o plantas*)
**cross-breeding** ['krɔs,bridɪŋ] o ['kras,bridɪŋ] *s* cruzamiento
**cross bun** *s* bollo marcado con la figura de una cruz (*que se come el viernes santo*)
**cross-country** ['krɔs,kʌntrɪ] o ['kras,kʌntrɪ] *adj* a campo traviesa; a través del país, transcontinental; *s* (sport) carrera a pie y a campo traviesa
**cross-country flight** *s* (aer.) vuelo a través del país
**crosscurrent** ['krɔs,kʌrənt] o ['kras,kʌrənt] *s* contracorriente; (fig.) tendencia contraria
**crosscut** ['krɔs,kʌt] o ['kras,kʌt] *adj* para cortar transversalmente; cortado transversalmente; *s* sierra de través; corte transversal; atajo (*senda*); (min.) galería transversal; (*pret & pp:* **-cut;** *ger:* **-cutting**) *va* cortar o aserrar transversalmente
**crosscut file** *s* lima de doble picadura
**crosscut saw** *s* sierra de través, tronzador
**crosse** [krɔs] o [kras] *s* (sport) raquetón (*que sirve para jugar a la crosse*)
**crossed anesthesia** *s* anestesia cruzada
**cross-examination** ['krɔsɛg,zæmɪ'neʃən] o ['krasɛg,zæmɪ'neʃən] *s* (law) repregunta; interrogatorio riguroso
**cross-examine** ['krɔsɛg'zæmɪn] o ['krasɛg'zæmɪn] *va* (law) repreguntar; interrogar rigurosamente
**cross-eye** ['krɔs,aɪ] o ['kras,aɪ] *s* (path.) estrabismo convergente, vista torcida
**cross-eyed** ['krɔs,aɪd] o ['kras,aɪd] *adj* bisojo, bizco, ojituerto
**cross-fertilization** ['krɔs,fʌrtɪlɪ'zeʃən] o ['kras,fʌrtɪlɪ'zeʃən] *s* (bot. & biol.) fertilización cruzada
**cross-fertilize** ['krɔs'fʌrtɪlaɪz] o ['kras'fʌrtɪlaɪz] *va* fecundar por fertilización cruzada; *vn* fecundarse por fertilización cruzada
**cross fire** *s* (mil.) fuego cruzado
**cross-grained** ['krɔs'grend] o ['kras'grend] *adj* de contrafibra, de contrahilo; intratable, terco
**cross hair** *s* (opt.) hilo cruzado
**crosshatch** ['krɔs,hætʃ] o ['kras,hætʃ] *va* marcar con rayitas cruzadas; *vn* marcarse con rayitas cruzadas
**crosshead** ['krɔs,hɛd] o ['kras,hɛd] *s* (mach.) cruceta
**crossing** ['krɔsɪŋ] o ['krasɪŋ] *s* cruce (*de líneas, calles, etc.*); travesía (*del mar*); vado (*de un río*); crucero, paso a nivel (*de ferrocarril*); (arch.) crucero (*sitio en que se cruzan las naves transversal y principal de una iglesia*)
**crossing gate** *s* (rail.) barrera, barrera de paso a nivel
**crossing point** *s* punto de cruce
**crossjack** ['krɔs,dʒæk] o ['kras,dʒæk] *s* (naut.) vela de mesana
**cross-legged** ['krɔs'lɛgɪd], ['kras'lɛgɪd], ['krɔs,lɛgd] o ['kras,lɛgd] *adj* con los pies cruzados; con las piernas cruzadas
**crosslet** ['krɔslɪt] o ['kraslɪt] *s* crucecita
**cross-over** ['krɔs,ovər] o ['kras,ovər] *s* crucero, traspaso; (biol.) recombinación, cruzamiento intercromosómico; (elec.) cruce de conductores
**crosspatch** ['krɔs,pætʃ] o ['kras,pætʃ] *s* (coll.) malhumorado, gruñón
**crosspiece** ['krɔs,pis] o ['kras,pis] *s* travesaño; cruceta (*de un enrejado*)
**cross-pollinate** ['krɔs'palɪnet] o ['kras'palɪnet] *va* fecundar por polinización cruzada; *vn* fecundarse por polinización cruzada
**cross-pollination** ['krɔs,palɪ'neʃən] o ['kras,palɪ'neʃən] *s* (bot.) polinización cruzada
**cross-purpose** ['krɔs'pʌrpəs] o ['kras'pʌrpəs] *s* disposición contraria, propósito contrario; **cross-purposes** *spl* juego de preguntas y respuestas en el cual se usan palabras de diferentes significados; **at cross-purposes** sin comprenderse uno a otro; oponiéndose uno a otro involuntariamente
**cross-question** ['krɔs'kwɛstʃən] o ['kras'kwɛstʃən] *s* (law) repregunta; *va* (law) repreguntar
**crossrail** ['krɔs,rel] o ['kras,rel] *s* travesaño
**cross-refer** [,krɔsrɪ'fʌr] o [,krasrɪ'fʌr] (*pret & pp:* **-ferred;** *ger:* **-ferring**) *va & vn* contrarreferir
**cross reference** *s* contrarreferencia, remisión
**crossroad** ['krɔs,rod] o ['kras,rod] *s* vía o camino transversal; vía conectadora; **crossroads** *spl* cruce, encrucijada; **at the crossroads** en el momento crítico
**crossruff** ['krɔs,rʌf] o ['kras,rʌf] *s* (cards) jugada en la cual cada compañero juega un naipe que se puede matar con el triunfo del otro
**cross sea** *s* (naut.) mar alborotada en que las olas corren en sentidos opuestos
**cross section** *s* sección transversal, corte transversal; (fig.) sección representativa (*de un grupo de personas, cosas, etc.*)
**cross spider** *s* (ent.) araña epeira
**cross-staff** ['krɔs,stæf] o ['kras,staf] *s* escuadra de agrimensor; (naut.) ballestilla
**cross-stitch** ['krɔs,stɪtʃ] o ['kras,stɪtʃ] *s* puntada cruzada; bordado hecho con puntadas cruzadas; *va* bordar o coser con puntadas cruzadas
**cross street** *s* calle de travesía, calle traviesa
**crosstie** ['krɔs,taɪ] o ['kras,taɪ] *s* (rail.) traviesa, durmiente

**crosstree** ['krɔs,tri] o ['krɑs,tri] *s* (naut.) cruceta
**cross vault** *s* (arch.) bóveda por arista
**crossway** ['krɔs,we] o ['krɑs,we] *s* var. de **crossroad**
**crossways** ['krɔs,wez] o ['krɑs,wez] o **crosswise** ['krɔs,waɪz] o ['krɑs,waɪz] *adv* al través; en cruz; mal, equivocadamente
**cross wire** *s* (opt.) hilo cruzado
**crossworder** ['krɔs,wʌrdər] o ['krɑs,wʌrdər] *s* crucigramista
**crossword puzzle** ['krɔs,wʌrd] o ['krɑs,wʌrd] *s* crucigrama
**crosswort** ['krɔs,wʌrt] o ['krɑs,wʌrt] *s* (bot.) cruciata
**crossyard** ['krɔs,jɑrd] o ['krɑs,jɑrd] *s* (naut.) palo o verga en cruz
**crotch** [krɑtʃ] *s* bifurcación; bragadura, horcajadura, entrepiernas; (naut.) pique
**crotched** [krɑtʃt] *adj* bifurcado
**crotchet** ['krɑtʃɪt] *s* capricho, rareza; ganchito; (mus.) suspiro (*pausa*); (mus.) negra
**crotchety** ['krɑtʃɪtɪ] *adj* caprichoso, excéntrico
**croton** ['krotən] *s* (bot.) crotón; (bot.) buenavista
**Croton bug** *s* (ent.) cucaracha
**croton oil** *s* aceite de crotón
**crouch** [kraʊtʃ] *s* encogimiento; posición agachada; *va* doblar o inclinar muy bajo; *vn* encogerse, agacharse; doblar las rodillas inclinándose muy bajo
**croup** [krup] *s* (path.) crup, garrotillo; anca, grupa (*del caballo*)
**croupier** ['krupɪər] *s* crupié, coime
**croupous** ['krupəs] *adj* crupal
**croupy** ['krupɪ] *adj* cruposo; crupal
**crouton** ['krutɑn] *s* cuscurro, cortezón
**crow** [kro] *s* (orn.) corneja; (orn.) grajo; (orn.) chova; barra, palanca; quiquiriquí (*del gallo*); arrullo (*de los niños pequeños*); **as the crow flies** en línea recta, por el camino más corto; **to eat crow** (coll.) cantar la palinodia; **to have a crow to pick with** (coll.) tener que habérselas con; (*pret:* **crowed** o **crew;** *pp:* **crowed**) *vn* cantar (*el gallo*); (*pret & pp:* **crowed**) *vn* bravear, jactarse; **to crow over** jactarse de
**crowbar** ['kro,bɑr] *s* palanca, pie de cabra, alzaprima
**crowd** [kraʊd] *s* gentío, afluencia, multitud; vulgo, populacho; caterva, tropel; (coll.) grupo, clase; **to follow the crowd** irse al hilo o tras el hilo de la gente (*hacer lo que hacen los otros*); *va* apretar, apiñar, atestar; empujar; **to crowd on sail** (naut.) hacer fuerza de vela; *vn* apretarse, atestarse; arremolinarse; impelerse con fuerza
**crowded** ['kraʊdɪd] *adj* apretado, apiñado, atestado; lleno, tupido
**crowfoot** ['kro,fʊt] *s* (*pl:* **-foots**) (bot.) ranúnculo; (*pl:* **-feet**) araña (*para sostener toldos*); (elec.) electrodo de cinc (*de una pila de gravedad*); (mil.) abrojo
**crown** [kraʊn] *s* corona; (dent.) corona; corona (*moneda*); (naut.) cruz (*del ancla*); copa (*de sombrero*); *adj* coronario; *va* coronar; abombar, abovedar; poner corona artificial a (*un diente*); (checkers) coronar; (slang) golpear en la cabeza
**crown colony** *s* colonia de la Corona (*colonia del imperio británico que no tiene autonomía*)
**crowned head** *s* testa coronada (*soberano*)
**crown glass** *s* crown-glass (*cristal muy puro*); vidrio en hojas circulares para ventanas
**crown lens** *s* lente convexa de crown-glass
**crown prince** *s* príncipe heredero
**crown princess** *s* consorte del príncipe heredero; princesa heredera
**crown saw** *s* sierra de corona cilíndrica
**crown sheet** *s* cielo del hogar (*de las cajas de fuego*)
**crown wheel** *s* (mach.) rueda de dientes laterales
**crownwork** ['kraʊn,wʌrk] *s* (dent.) corona artificial; (fort.) corona, obra de corona
**crow's-foot** ['kroz,fʊt] *s* (*pl:* **-feet**) pata de gallo (*arruga en el rabo del ojo*); puntada de tres puntas (*que se usa en los bordados*); (mil.) abrojo
**crow's-nest** ['kroz,nɛst] *s* (naut.) torre de vigía
**croze** [kroz] *s* gárgol, jable (*ranura*); argallera, jabladera (*serrucho*); *va* ruñar
**crozier** ['kroʒər] *s* var. de **crosier**
**crucial** ['kruʃəl] *adj* crucial, decisivo; penoso, severo; (surg.) crucial
**crucible** ['krusɪbəl] *s* crisol; (fig.) crisol
**crucible furnace** *s* horno de crisol
**crucible steel** *s* acero de crisol
**crucifer** ['krusɪfər] *s* (eccl.) crucero, crucíferario; (bot.) crucífera
**crucified** ['krusɪfaɪd] *adj* crucificado; **the Crucified** el Crucificado (*Jesucristo*)
**crucifix** ['krusɪfɪks] *s* crucifijo; cruz
**crucifixion** [,krusɪ'fɪkʃən] *s* crucifixión; (*cap.*) *s* Crucifixión
**cruciform** ['krusɪfɔrm] *adj* cruciforme
**crucify** ['krusɪfaɪ] (*pret & pp:* **-fied**) *va* crucificar; (fig.) crucificar
**crude** [krud] *adj* grosero, tosco; crudo (*no refinado; no preparado*); sin labrar
**crudity** ['krudɪtɪ] *s* (*pl:* **-ties**) grosería, tosquedad; crudeza
**cruel** ['kruəl] *adj* cruel
**cruelty** ['kruəltɪ] *s* (*pl:* **-ties**) crueldad
**cruet** ['kruɪt] *s* ampolleta, vinagrera
**cruet stand** *s* angarillas, vinagreras
**cruise** [kruz] *s* travesía, viaje por mar; excursión; (naut. & aer.) crucero; *va* (naut.) cruzar; *vn* (naut.) cruzar; (aer.) volar en crucero; (coll.) andar de un punto a otro
**cruiser** ['kruzər] *s* (nav.) crucero; aeroplano, taxi o embarcación que hace viajes de ida y vuelta
**cruising** ['kruzɪŋ] *s* (naut.) crucero; *adj* de crucero, p.ej., **cruising speed** velocidad de crucero
**cruising radius** *s* autonomía (*de un buque, avión, etc.*)
**cruller** ['krʌlər] *s* buñuelo
**crumb** [krʌm] *s* migaja (*partícula del pan; porción pequeña de cualquier cosa*); miga (*parte más blanda del pan*); *va* desmenuzar; desmigar (*el pan*); (cook.) cubrir con migajas; (coll.) limpiar (*la mesa*) de migajas; *vn* desmigarse
**crumb brush** *s* recogemigas
**crumble** ['krʌmbəl] *va* desmenuzar; *vn* desmenuzarse; desmoronarse
**crumbly** ['krʌmblɪ] *adj* (*comp:* **-blier;** *super:* **-bliest**) desmenuzable; desmoronadizo
**crumb tray** *s* bandeja en que se recogen las migajas
**crumby** ['krʌmɪ] *adj* (*comp:* **-ier;** *super:* **-iest**) lleno de migajas; blando, tierno
**crummy** ['krʌmɪ] *adj* (*comp:* **-mier;** *super:* **-miest**) (slang) desaseado, sucio; (slang) gastado, p.ej., **a crummy joke** una broma gastada
**crump** [krʌmp] *s, va & vn* var. de **crunch**
**crumpet** ['krʌmpɪt] *s* bollo blando tostado
**crumple** ['krʌmpəl] *s* arruga o pliegue que se hace aplastando una cosa; *va* arrugar, plegar, hacer contraerse en arrugas; *vn* arrugarse, plegarse, contraerse en arrugas
**crunch** [krʌntʃ] *s* roznido, mascadura; crujido; *va* ronzar, mascar ruidosamente; *vn* contraerse con ruido, crujir
**crunk** [krʌŋk] o [kruŋk] *vn* (dial.) gruir (*la grulla*)
**cruor** ['kruɔr] *s* (physiol.) crúor
**crupper** ['krʌpər] *s* baticola; anca, grupa (*del caballo*); (hum.) nalgas
**crural** ['krurəl] *adj* (anat.) crural
**crusade** [kru'sed] *s* cruzada; *vn* hacerse cruzado, abrazar una cruzada; **to crusade for** hacer campaña por
**crusader** [kru'sedər] *s* cruzado
**cruse** [kruz] o [krus] *s* ampolleta, cazuela, olla
**crush** [krʌʃ] *s* presión violenta; aplastamiento; bullaje (*de gente*); **to have a crush on** (slang) estar perdido por, perder la chaveta por (*una persona*); *va* aplastar, magullar; moler; bocartear (*el mineral*); abrumar, p.ej., **I was crushed by the news** me quedé abrumado con la noticia
**crush hat** *s* sombrero flexible; clac
**crust** [krʌst] *s* corteza; corteza de pan; corteza de papel; mendrugo; costra, escara; *va* encostrar; *vn* encostrarse

**crustacean** [krʌs'teʃən] *adj & s* crustáceo
**crustaceous** [krʌs'teʃəs] *adj* crustáceo; (zool.) crustáceo
**crusty** ['krʌstɪ] *adj* (*comp:* **-ier;** *super:* **-iest**) costroso; rudo, grosero, áspero
**crutch** [krʌtʃ] *s* muleta; (fig.) muleta
**crux** [krʌks] *s* (*pl:* **cruxes** o **cruces** ['krusiz]) punto capital; enigma, cuestión perpleja
**cry** [kraɪ] *s* (*pl:* **cries**) grito; lloro; gritería; pregón; grito de guerra; aullido (*del lobo*); bramido (*del toro*); **in full cry** en persecución inmediata; **to have a good cry** prorrumpir en lágrimas abundantes ‖ (*pret & pp:* **cried**) *va* decir a gritos; pregonar; **to cry down** gritar (*p.ej., una comedia*); despreciar, menospreciar; **to cry off** renunciar, romper (*p.ej., un acuerdo*); **to cry one's eyes** o **heart out** llorar amargamente; **to cry out** decir a gritos; pregonar o publicar en alta voz; **to cry up** alabar, elogiar; dar por importante ‖ *vn* gritar; llorar; aullar (*el lobo*); bramar (*el toro*); **to cry aloud** gritar fuertemente; llorar a gritos; **to cry for** clamar por; **to cry for joy** llorar de alegría; **to cry out** clamar; **to cry out against** clamar contra; **to cry out for** clamar, clamar por; **to cry out to** clamar a; **to cry to heaven** clamar al cielo
**crybaby** ['kraɪ,bebɪ] *s* (*pl:* **-bies**) llorón o llorona, lloraduelos
**crying** ['kraɪɪŋ] *adj* llorón; enorme, atroz
**cryogen** ['kraɪədʒən] *s* criógeno, substancia criógena
**cryogenic** [,kraɪo'dʒɛnɪk] *adj* criogénico
**cryohydrate** [,kraɪo'haɪdret] *s* (chem.) criohidrato
**cryolite** ['kraɪəlaɪt] *s* (mineral.) criolita
**cryology** [kraɪ'ɑlədʒɪ] *s* criología
**cryometer** [kraɪ'ɑmɪtər] *s* criómetro
**cryoscope** ['kraɪəskop] *s* crioscopio
**cryoscopy** [kraɪ'ɑskəpɪ] *s* crioscopia
**cryostat** ['kraɪostæt] *s* crióstato
**cryotherapy** [,kraɪo'θɛrəpɪ] *s* (med.) crioterapia
**crypt** [krɪpt] *s* cripta; (anat.) cripta
**cryptic** ['krɪptɪk] o **cryptical** ['krɪptɪkəl] *adj* secreto, misterioso
**cryptogam** ['krɪptogæm] *s* (bot.) criptógama
**cryptogamic** [,krɪpto'gæmɪk] *adj* criptogámico
**cryptogamous** [krɪp'tɑgəməs] *adj* criptógamo
**cryptogram** ['krɪptogræm] *s* criptograma
**cryptograph** ['krɪptogræf] o ['krɪptogrɑf] *s* criptógrafo (*aparato*); criptograma
**cryptographer** [krɪp'tɑgrəfər] *s* criptógrafo (*persona*)
**cryptographic** [,krɪpto'græfɪk] *adj* criptográfico
**cryptography** [krɪp'tɑgrəfɪ] *s* criptografía
**crystal** ['krɪstəl] *s* cristal (*vidrio*); abalorio, cristal; (chem., mineral. & rad.) cristal; (fig.) cristal (*agua*); cristal de reloj; cristal de roca; **as clear as crystal** tan claro como el agua; *adj* cristalino
**crystal ball** *s* bola de cristal (*que sirve para adivinar lo porvenir*)
**crystal cartridge** *s* (elec.) cápsula de cristal
**crystal detector** *s* (rad.) detector de cristal
**crystal gazing** *s* sortilegio que se hace mirando fijamente en un cristal
**crystalline** ['krɪstəlɪn] o ['krɪstəlaɪn] *adj* cristalino
**crystalline lens** *s* (anat.) cristalino
**crystallite** ['krɪstəlaɪt] *s* (mineral.) cristalito
**crystallization** [,krɪstəlɪ'zeʃən] *s* cristalización
**crystallize** ['krɪstəlaɪz] *va* cristalizar; *vn* cristalizarse
**crystallographic** [,krɪstələ'græfɪk] o **crystallographical** [,krɪstələ'græfɪkəl] *adj* cristalográfico
**crystallography** [,krɪstə'lɑgrəfɪ] *s* cristalografía
**crystalloid** ['krɪstəlɔɪd] *adj* cristaloideo; *s* cristaloide
**crystal set** *s* (rad.) receptor con detector de cristal
**crystal violet** *s* var. de **gentian violet**
**C.S.** abr. de **Christian Science** y **Civil Service**
**C.S.A.** abr. de **Confederate States Army** y **Confederate States of America**
**CSC** abr. de **Civil Service Commission**
**C.S.T.** abr. de **Central Standard Time**
**ct.** abr. de **cent**
**Ct.** abr. de **Connecticut**
**cts.** abr. de **cents**
**cu.** abr. de **cubic**
**cub** [kʌb] *s* cachorro (*de león, oso, lobo, etc.*); muchacho desmañado
**Cuban** ['kjubən] *adj & s* cubano
**Cuban lily** *s* (bot.) jacinto estrellado
**cubbyhole** ['kʌbɪ,hol] *s* chiribitil
**cube** [kjub] *s* cubo; (math.) cubo; *va* dar forma de cubo a; (math.) cubicar
**cubeb** ['kjubɛb] *s* (bot. & pharm.) cubeba; cigarrillo de cubeba
**cube root** *s* (math.) raíz cúbica
**cubic** ['kjubɪk] *adj* cúbico; (cryst. & math.) cúbico
**cubical** ['kjubɪkəl] *adj* cúbico
**cubicle** ['kjubɪkəl] *s* cubículo
**cubic measure** *s* cubicación
**cubism** ['kjubɪzəm] *s* (f.a.) cubismo
**cubist** ['kjubɪst] *adj & s* (f.a.) cubista
**cubit** ['kjubɪt] *s* codo (*medida antigua*)
**cubital** ['kjubɪtəl] *adj* cubital
**cubitus** ['kjubɪtəs] *s* (*pl:* **-ti** [taɪ]) (anat.) cúbito
**cuboid** ['kjubɔɪd] *adj* cuboideo; (anat.) cuboides; *s* cubo; (anat.) cuboides
**cub reporter** *s* (coll.) reportero novato, aprendiz de reportero
**cuckold** ['kʌkəld] *adj & s* cornudo; *va* encornudar, hacer cornudo a (*un marido*)
**cuckoo** ['kuku] *s* (orn.) cuclillo; (orn.) cuclillo de las lluvias; cucú (*canto del cuclillo*); *adj* (slang) mentecato, loco
**cuckoo clock** *s* reloj de cuclillo
**cuckoopint** ['kuku,pɪnt] *s* (bot.) aro
**cu. cm.** abr. de **cubic centimeter** o **cubic centimeters**
**cucullate** ['kjukəlet] o [kju'kʌlet] *adj* cuculiforme, cuculado
**cucumber** ['kjukʌmbər] *s* (bot.) cohombro, pepino (*planta y fruto*); **cool as a cucumber** muy fresco; sereno, tranquilo
**cucurbitaceous** [kju,kʌrbɪ'teʃəs] *adj* (bot.) cucurbitáceo
**cud** [kʌd] *s* bolo alimenticio; **to chew the cud** rumiar; (fig.) rumiar (*meditar*)
**cuddle** ['kʌdəl] *s* abrazo cariñoso; *va* abrazar con cariño; *vn* estar abrazados; arrimarse afectuosa o cómodamente
**cuddy** ['kʌdɪ] *s* (*pl:* **-dies**) pequeño cuarto; aparador; (naut.) camarote; (naut.) despensa
**cudgel** ['kʌdʒəl] *s* garrote, porra; **to take up the cudgels for** defender con vehemencia, entrar en la lucha en defensa de; (*pret & pp:* **-eled** o **-elled;** *ger:* **-eling** o **-elling**) *va* apalear, aporrear; **to cudgel one's brains** devanarse los sesos
**cue** [kju] *s* señal, indicación; papel; humor, disposición; coleta (*de cabellos*); cola (*de personas que esperan*); taco (*de billar*); (theat.) apunte; *va* trenzar
**cue rest** *s* (billiards & pool) diablo
**cuff** [kʌf] *s* puño; doblez (*del pantalón*); manilla; bofetada; *va* abofetear, dar de bofetadas
**cuff button** *s* botón del puño de la camisa
**cuff links** *spl* gemelos (*para los puños de la camisa*)
**cu. ft.** abr. de **cubic foot** o **cubic feet**
**cu. in.** abr. de **cubic inch** o **cubic inches**
**cuirass** [kwɪ'ræs] *s* (arm. & zool.) coraza; (arm.) peto (*de la coraza*); *va* armar o cubrir de coraza
**cuirassier** [,kwɪrə'sɪr] *s* coracero
**cuish** [kwɪʃ] *s* var. de **cuisse**
**cuisine** [kwɪ'zin] *s* cocina
**cuisse** [kwɪs] *s* (arm.) quijote
**cul-de-sac** ['kuldə'sæk] o ['kʌldə'sæk] *s* callejón sin salida
**culex** ['kjulɛks] *s* (*pl:* **-lices** [lɪsiz]) (ent.) mosquito común
**culinary** ['kjulɪ,nɛrɪ] *adj* culinario
**cull** [kʌl] *s* entresaca de lo inferior y sin valor; *va* entresacar, escoger, extraer
**cullet** ['kʌlɪt] *s* vidrio de desecho
**cullis** ['kʌlɪs] *s* canal de tejado

**culm** [kʌlm] *s* cisco; antracita de mala calidad; (bot.) caña, tallo (*de las gramíneas*)
**culminate** [ˈkʌlmɪnet] *vn* culminar; (astr.) culminar; **to culminate in** conducir a, terminar en
**culmination** [ˌkʌlmɪˈneʃən] *s* culminación; (astr.) culminación
**culpability** [ˌkʌlpəˈbɪlɪtɪ] *s* culpabilidad
**culpable** [ˈkʌlpəbəl] *adj* culpable
**culprit** [ˈkʌlprɪt] *s* culpado; reo
**cult** [kʌlt] *s* culto; secta, conjunto de personas que siguen la misma doctrina
**cultism** [ˈkʌltɪzəm] *s* devoción a un culto; culteranismo, cultismo
**cultist** [ˈkʌltɪst] *s* adicto a un culto; culterano
**cultivable** [ˈkʌltɪvəbəl] *adj* cultivable
**cultivate** [ˈkʌltɪvet] *va* cultivar
**cultivated** [ˈkʌltɪˌvetɪd] *adj* culto
**cultivation** [ˌkʌltɪˈveʃən] *s* cultivo (*de la tierra, las artes, la memoria, etc.*); cultura
**cultivator** [ˈkʌltɪˌvetər] *s* cultivador; cultivadora, extirpador (*máquina agrícola*)
**cultural** [ˈkʌltʃərəl] *adj* cultural
**culture** [ˈkʌltʃər] *s* cultura; (bact.) cultivo; *va* culturar; (bact.) cultivar
**cultured** [ˈkʌltʃərd] *adj* culto
**cultus** [ˈkʌltəs] *s* culto, culto religioso
**culverin** [ˈkʌlvərɪn] *s* culebrina
**culvert** [ˈkʌlvərt] *s* alcantarilla
**Cumae** [ˈkjumi] *s* Cumas
**cumber** [ˈkʌmbər] *s* estorbo, impedimento; *va* estorbar, impedir; incomodar, molestar
**cumbersome** [ˈkʌmbərsəm] o **cumbrous** [ˈkʌmbrəs] *adj* pesado, incómodo, molesto
**cumin** o **cummin** [ˈkʌmɪn] *s* (bot.) comino
**cuminseed** [ˈkʌmɪnˌsid] *s* comino
**cum laude** [kʌm ˈlɔdi] o [kum ˈlaude] (Lat.) con honor
**cummerbund** [ˈkʌmərˌbʌnd] *s* faja que se lleva con traje de etiqueta en vez de chaleco
**cumquat** [ˈkʌmkwat] *s* var. de **kumquat**
**cumulate** [ˈkjumjəlet] *va* acumular
**cumulation** [ˌkjumjəˈleʃən] *s* acumulación
**cumulative** [ˈkjumjəˌletɪv] *adj* acumulativo
**cumulo-cirrus** [ˌkjumjəloˈsɪrəs] *s* (meteor.) cumulocirro
**cumulo-nimbus** [ˌkjumjəloˈnɪmbəs] *s* (meteor.) cúmulonimbo
**cumulo-stratus** [ˌkjumjəloˈstretəs] *s* (meteor.) cumulostrato
**cumulous** [ˈkjumjələs] *adj* en forma de cúmulo; compuesto de cúmulos
**cumulus** [ˈkjumjələs] *s* (*pl:* **-li** [laɪ]) cúmulo; (meteor.) cúmulo
**cuneate** [ˈkjunɪet] o [ˈkjunɪɪt) *adj* cuneiforme; (bot.) cuneiforme, cuneado
**cuneiform** [kjuˈniɪfɔrm] o [ˈkjunɪɪˌfɔrm] *adj* cuneiforme; (anat.) cuneiforme; *s* caracteres cuneiformes; (anat.) cuneiforme
**cunner** [ˈkʌnər] *s* (ichth.) tenolabro
**cunning** [ˈkʌnɪŋ] *adj* astuto; hábil; gracioso, mono; *s* astucia
**cup** [kʌp] *s* taza, jícara; copa; bebida; (eccl.) cáliz; (eccl.) vino sagrado (*que se sirve en la misa*); (mach.) vaso de engrase; cubeta (*del barómetro*); (sport) copa; (fig.) copa (*del dolor, la desgracia, etc.*); (fig.) fortuna, suerte; (*cap.*) *s* (astr.) Copa; **in one's cups** ebrio, borracho; (*pret & pp:* **cupped;** *ger:* **cupping**) *va* ahuecar en forma de copa o taza; tomar o poner en copa, taza, etc.; aplicar ventosa a
**cupbearer** [ˈkʌpˌbɛrər] *s* copero
**cupboard** [ˈkʌbərd] *s* alacena, aparador
**cupcake** [[ˈkʌpˌkek] *s* torta hecha en una vasija de forma de copa o taza
**cupel** [ˈkjupɛl] o [kjuˈpɛl] *s* copela; (*pret & pp:* **-peled** o **-pelled;** *ger:* **-peling** o **-pelling**) *va* copelar
**cupellation** [ˌkjupəˈleʃən] *s* copelación
**cupful** [ˈkʌpful] *s* taza (*lo que contiene una taza*)
**cup grease** *s* grasa lubricante
**cupid** [ˈkjupɪd] *s* cupido (*niño alado, símbolo del amor*); (*cap.*) *s* (myth.) Cupido
**cupidity** [kjuˈpɪdɪtɪ] *s* codicia
**cupola** [ˈkjupələ] *s* (arch., anat. & nav.) cúpula; (arch.) cupulino (*remate, linterna*); (found.) cubilote
**cupping** [ˈkʌpɪŋ] *s* aplicación de ventosa
**cupping glass** *s* ventosa
**cupreous** [ˈkjuprɪəs] *adj* cobreño; cobrizo
**cupressineous** [ˌkjupreˈsɪnɪəs] *adj* (bot.) cupresíneo
**cupric** [ˈkjuprɪk] *adj* (chem.) cúprico
**cupriferous** [kjuˈprɪfərəs] *adj* cuprífero
**cuprite** [ˈkjupraɪt] *s* (mineral.) cuprita
**cupronickel** [ˌkjuproˈnɪkəl] *s* cuproníquel
**cuprous** [ˈkjuprəs] *adj* (chem.) cuproso
**cup shake** *s* acebolladura
**cupule** [ˈkjupjul] *s* (bot. & zool.) cúpula
**cupuliferous** [ˌkjupjəˈlɪfərəs] *adj* (bot.) cupulífero
**cur** [kʌr] *s* perro mestizo, perro de mala raza; drope (*hombre despreciable*)
**curability** [ˌkjurəˈbɪlɪtɪ] *s* curabilidad
**curable** [ˈkjurəbəl] *adj* curable
**curaçao** [ˌkjurəˈso] *s* curasao (*licor*); (*cap.*) *s* Curazao
**curacy** [ˈkjurəsɪ] *s* (*pl:* **-cies**) curato
**curare** [kjuˈrɑrɪ] *s* curare
**curarize** [ˈkjurəraɪz] o [kjuˈrɑraɪz] *va* curarizar
**curate** [ˈkjurɪt] *s* cura
**curative** [ˈkjurətɪv] *adj* curativo; *s* curativa
**curator** [kjuˈretər] *s* conservador
**curb** [kʌrb] *s* barbada (*del freno*); encintado (*borde de la acera*); brocal de pozo; restricción; (com.) bolsín; (vet.) corva; *va* proveer de encintado; proveer de brocal; contener, refrenar
**curb bit** *s* freno con barbada
**curbing** [ˈkʌrbɪŋ] *s* materia para construir el encintado; encintado; refrenamiento
**curb market** *s* bolsín
**curbstone** [ˈkʌrbˌston] *s* piedra de encintado; encintado; brocal de pozo
**curculio** [kʌrˈkjulɪo] *s* (*pl:* **-os**) (ent.) rincóforo
**curcuma paper** [ˈkʌrkjəmə] *s* (chem.) papel de cúrcuma
**curd** [kʌrd] *s* cuajada; *va* cuajar; *vn* cuajarse
**curdle** [ˈkʌrdəl] *va* cuajar; **to curdle the blood** causar horror u horripilación; *vn* cuajarse
**curdy** [ˈkʌrdɪ] *adj* cuajado
**cure** [kjur] *s* cura, curación; curato; *va* curar (*una enfermedad, un mal; carnes, pieles, etc.; restituir a la salud*); *vn* curar; curarse
**curé** [kjuˈre] *s* cura, párroco
**cure-all** [ˈkjurˌɔl] *s* sánalotodo, panacea
**curettage** [kjuˈrɛtɪdʒ] o [ˌkjurəˈtɑʒ] *s* (surg.) curetaje
**curette** [kjuˈrɛt] *s* (surg.) cureta
**curfew** [ˈkʌrfju] *s* queda, cubrefuego
**curia** [ˈkjurɪə] *s* (hist.) curia
**curie** [ˈkjuri] o [kjuˈri] *s* (phys.) curie
**curio** [ˈkjurɪo] *s* (*pl:* **-os**) curiosidad (*objeto curioso*)
**curiosity** [ˌkjurɪˈɑsɪtɪ] *s* (*pl:* **-ties**) curiosidad
**curiosity shop** *s* tienda de curiosidades
**curious** [ˈkjurɪəs] *adj* curioso
**curium** [ˈkjurɪəm] *s* (chem.) curio
**curl** [kʌrl] *s* bucle, rizo; tirabuzón (*rizo pendiente en espiral*); ondulación, sinuosidad; rizado; espiral (*de humo*); *va* encrespar, ensortijar, rizar; arrollar; torcer; fruncir (*los labios*); **to curl up** arrollar; *vn* encresparse, ensortijarse, rizarse; arrollarse; torcerse; **to curl up** arrollarse; tirar las piernas hacia arriba (*al acostarse*); (coll.) abatirse, desbaratarse
**curlew** [ˈkʌrlu] o [ˈkʌrlju] *s* (orn.) zarapito
**curlicue** [ˈkʌrlɪkju] *s* plumada, rasgo, ringorrango
**curling** [ˈkʌrlɪŋ] *s* (sport) curling (*juego sobre campo de hielo*)
**curling iron** *s* rizador, encrespador, maquinilla de rizar
**curlpaper** [ˈkʌrlˌpepər] *s* torcida, papelito para rizar el pelo
**curly** [ˈkʌrlɪ] *adj* (*comp:* **-ier;** *super:* **-iest**) encrespado, ensortijado, rizado; ondulado
**curly n** *s* ñ (*n con tilde*)
**curmudgeon** [kʌrˈmʌdʒən] *s* cicatero, erizo
**currant** [ˈkʌrənt] *s* pasa de Corinto; grosella; (bot.) grosellero
**currency** [ˈkʌrənsɪ] *s* (*pl:* **-cies**) moneda corriente; uso corriente; valor corriente
**current** [ˈkʌrənt] *adj* corriente; *s* corriente; (elec.) corriente
**current account** *s* (com.) cuenta corriente
**current collector** *s* (elec.) toma de corriente

**current density** *s* (elec.) densidad de corriente
**current events** *spl* actualidades, sucesos de actualidad
**current limiter** *s* (elec.) limitador de corriente, limitacorrientes
**currently** ['kʌrəntlɪ] *adv* actualmente; por lo general
**curricle** ['kʌrɪkəl] *s* carrocín
**curricular** [kə'rɪkjələr] *adj* del plan de estudios
**curriculum** [kə'rɪkjələm] *s* (*pl:* **-lums** o **-la** [lə]) *s* programa o plan de estudios
**currier** ['kʌrɪər] *s* curtidor; almohazador
**currish** ['kʌrɪʃ] *adj* perruno; gruñón, arisco, descortés
**curry** ['kʌrɪ] *s* (*pl:* **-ries**) cari (*polvo, salsa y guisado*); (*pret & pp:* **-ried**) *va* curtir (*las pieles*); almohazar (*el caballo*); preparar o sazonar con cari; **to curry favor** procurar complacer
**currycomb** ['kʌrɪ,kom] *s* almohaza; *va* almohazar
**curry powder** *s* polvo de cari
**curse** [kʌrs] *s* maldición; maleficio; calamidad; (*pret & pp:* **cursed** o **curst**) *va* maldecir; **to be cursed with** sufrir, padecer; *vn* blasfemar
**cursed** ['kʌrsɪd] o [kʌrst] *adj* maldito; aborrecible, abominable
**cursive** ['kʌrsɪv] *adj* cursivo; *s* cursiva
**cursorial** [kʌr'sorɪəl] *adj* propio para correr; que tiene piernas propias para correr
**cursory** ['kʌrsərɪ] *adj* apresurado, rápido, precipitado; superficial, de paso, por encima
**curst** [kʌrst] *adj* var. de **cursed;** *pret & pp de* **curse**
**curt** [kʌrt] *adj* corto, conciso; brusco, áspero
**curtail** [kʌr'tel] *va* acortar, abreviar, reducir; privar
**curtailment** [kʌr'telmənt] *s* acortamiento, abreviación, reducción; privación
**curtain** ['kʌrtən] *s* cortina; (theat.) telón; **to draw the curtain** correr la cortina; **to drop the curtain** (theat.) bajar el telón; *va* proveer de cortina; separar con cortina; cubrir, ocultar; **to curtain off** separar con cortina
**curtain call** *s* (theat.) aplauso de llamamiento
**curtain lecture** *s* regaño privado, reprimenda conyugal
**curtain of fire** *s* (mil.) cortina de fuego
**curtain raiser** *s* (theat.) pieza preliminar
**curtain ring** *s* anilla
**curtain rod** *s* barra de cortina, riel para cortinas
**curtation** [kʌr'teʃən] *s* (astr.) acortamiento, curtación
**curtesy** ['kʌrtəsɪ] *s* (*pl:* **-sies**) (law) título del derecho del marido a los bienes raíces de su mujer muerta
**curtsey** ['kʌrtsɪ] *s* cortesía, reverencia
**curtsy** ['kʌrtsɪ] *s* (*pl:* **-sies**) cortesía, reverencia; (*pret & pp:* **-sied**) *vn* hacer una cortesía, hacer una reverencia
**curule** ['kjurul] *adj* curul
**curule chair** *s* silla curul
**curvaceous** [kʌr'veʃəs] *adj* (coll.) curvilíneo (*dícese de una mujer*)
**curvature** ['kʌrvətʃər] *s* curvatura
**curve** [kʌrv] *s* curva; (baseball) curva; *adj* curvo; *va* encorvar; *vn* encorvarse; voltear en curva
**curvet** ['kʌrvɛt] *s* corveta; [kʌr'vɛt] o ['kʌrvɛt] (*pret & pp:* **-vetted** o **-veted;** *ger:* **-vetting** o **-veting**) *vn* corvetear
**curvilineal** [,kʌrvɪ'lɪnɪəl] o **curvilinear** [,kʌrvɪ'lɪnɪər] *adj* curvilíneo
**curvometer** [kʌr'vɑmɪtər] *s* curvímetro
**cushion** ['kʊʃən] *s* cojín, almohadón; banda o baranda (*de la mesa de billar*); (mach.) amortiguador; *va* asentar o poner sobre cojín; sostener con cojines; proteger por medio de cojines; amortiguar, someter a acción amortiguadora; acojinar (*un pistón*)
**cusk** [kʌsk] *s* (ichth.) pez marino comestible (*Brosmius brosme*); (ichth.) lota
**cusp** [kʌsp] *s* cúspide; punta (*del creciente*); (anat.) cúspide (*de un diente*)
**cuspid** ['kʌspɪd] *s* (anat.) cúspide (*diente*)
**cuspidal** ['kʌspɪdəl] *adj* de cúspide; puntiagudo
**cuspidate** ['kʌspɪdet] *adj* cuspídeo
**cuspidor** ['kʌspɪdər] *s* escupidera
**cuss** [kʌs] *s* (coll.) maldición; (coll.) tipo insignificante o impertinente; *va & vn* (coll.) maldecir
**cussed** ['kʌsɪd] *adj* (coll.) maldito; (coll.) terco
**custard** ['kʌstərd] *s* flan, natillas
**custard apple** *s* (bot.) anona; (bot.) anona blanca (*Annona squamosa*); (bot.) anona colorada, corazón, mamón, riñón (*Annona reticulata*); (bot.) papayo; papaya (*fruto*); (bot.) asimina
**custodial** [kʌs'todɪəl] *adj* del custodio, de la custodia
**custodian** [kʌs'todɪən] *s* custodio
**custodianship** [kʌs'todɪən,ʃɪp] *s* custodia
**custody** ['kʌstədɪ] *s* (*pl:* **-dies**) custodia; **in custody** en prisión; **to take into custody** arrestar, prender
**custom** ['kʌstəm] *s* costumbre; parroquia, clientela (*de una tienda*); **customs** *spl* aduana; derechos de aduana; *adj* hecho según pedido; hecho a la medida
**customary** ['kʌstəm,ɛrɪ] *adj* acostumbrado
**custom-built** ['kʌstəm,bɪlt] *adj* hecho o construído según pedido
**customer** ['kʌstəmər] *s* parroquiano, cliente; (coll.) individuo, tipo
**customers' man** *s* (coll.) empleado del corredor de bolsa que solicita y aconseja a los clientes
**customhouse** ['kʌstəm,haus] *s* aduana; *adj* aduanero
**custom-made** ['kʌstəm,med] *adj* hecho a la medida
**customs barrier** *s* barrera aduanera
**customs clearance** *s* despacho de aduana
**customs declaration** *s* declaración de aduana
**customs officer** *s* aduanero
**customs union** *s* unión aduanera
**custom tailor** *s* sastre que hace vestidos a la medida
**custom work** *s* trabajo hecho según pedido
**cut** [kʌt] *s* corte; tajada (*porción cortada*); cuchillada (*herida*); desmonte, excavación; atajo (*camino más corto*); reducción (*de precios, sueldos, etc.*); golpe cortante; hechura (*de un traje*); (tennis) golpe cortante; parte (*de las ganancias que corresponde a cada uno de los asociados en alguna empresa*); (cards) corte; (print.) estampa, grabado; (print.) clisé; (coll.) falta de asistencia (*a la clase*); (coll.) desaire; (coll.) palabra hiriente; **a cut above** (coll.) un dedo más arriba de; **cut of one's jib** (coll.) aspecto exterior de uno; *adj* cortado; tallado, labrado ‖ (*pret & pp:* **cut;** *ger:* **cutting**) *va* cortar; practicar (*p.ej., un agujero*); capar, castrar; pegar con golpe cortante; disolver; (coll.) hacer, formar, ejecutar; (coll.) faltar a, ausentarse de (*la clase*); (coll.) desairar; (coll.) herir (*con palabra hiriente*); **to cut across** cortar al través; **to cut asunder (away)** separar (quitar) cortando; **to cut back** acortar (*cortando el extremo de una cosa*); **to cut down** cortar; derribar cortando; aminorar, castigar (*gastos*); **to cut in** (elec.) intercalar, introducir (*un circuito*); **to cut off** cortar; desheredar; amputar (*p.ej., una pierna*); (elec.) cortar (*la corriente*); (aut.) cortar (*la ignición*); (aut.) cerrar (*el carburador*); **to cut open** abrir cortando; **to cut out** cortar; quitar o sacar cortando; tallar, labrar; omitir, suprimir; desbancar; soplar (*la dama a un rival*); (slang) dejarse de (*p.ej., disparates*); **to cut short** terminar de repente; chafar (*en la conversación*); **to cut teeth** endentecer; **to cut up** desmenuzar, despedazar; criticar severamente; (coll.) acongojar, afligir; **cut it out!** ¡déjese de eso!, ¡no hable más de eso! ‖ *vn* cortar; cortarse, poderse cortar; pasar rápidamente, apartarse rápidamente; salir (*los dientes*); (coll.) fumarse la clase; **to cut across** atravesar, ir a través de; **to cut back** volver de repente; **to cut in** entrar de repente; interrumpir; cortar o separar la pareja (*en el baile*); **to cut under** vender a menor precio que; **to cut up** (slang) travesear; (slang) jaranear
**cut and dried** *adj* ya dispuesto para el uso; monótono, poco interesante
**cutaneous** [kju'tenɪəs] *adj* cutáneo
**cutaway** ['kʌtə,we] o **cutaway coat** *s* chaqué
**cute** [kjut] *adj* (coll.) mono, monono; (coll.) astuto

**cut gear** *s* engranaje de dientes tallados a máquina
**cut glass** *s* cristal tallado
**cuticle** ['kjutɪkəl] *s* (anat. & bot.) cutícula
**cuticular** [kju'tɪkjələr] *adj* cuticular
**cutin** ['kjutɪn] *s* (biochem.) cutina
**cutireaction** [,kjutɪrɪ'ækʃən] *s* (med. & vet.) cutirreacción
**cutis** ['kjutɪs] *s* (anat.) dermis
**cutlass** ['kʌtləs] *s* alfanje
**cutler** ['kʌtlər] *s* cuchillero
**cutlery** ['kʌtlərɪ] *s* cuchillería; cubiertos (*cucharas, tenedores y cuchillos*); cuchillos, tijeras y otros instrumentos cortantes
**cutlet** ['kʌtlɪt] *s* chuleta; fritada de carne picada, fritada de pescado picado
**cutoff** ['kʌt,ɔf] o ['kʌt,ɑf] *s* atajo; (mach.) cierre de vapor; (mach.) cortavapor (*aparato*); (elec.) frecuencia de corte
**cutoff valve** *s* (mach.) corredera auxiliar de expansión
**cutout** ['kʌt,aʊt] *s* recortado, diseño o figura para recortar; (mach.) válvula de escape libre; (elec.) portafusible
**cutover** ['kʌt,ovər] *adj* desmontado (*terreno*)
**cutpurse** ['kʌt,pʌrs] *s* cortabolsas, carterista
**cut-rate** ['kʌt'ret] *adj* (U.S.A.) de precio reducido
**cutter** ['kʌtər] *s* cortador (*persona*); cortadora (*máquina*); freso (*de una fresadora*); (anat.) cortador (*diente incisivo*); (naut.) cúter (*embarcación de un solo palo*); (naut.) escampavía
**cutthroat** ['kʌt,θrot] *s* asesino; *adj* asesino; cruel, sanguinario; implacable
**cutting** ['kʌtɪŋ] *adj* cortante; mordaz, hiriente; *s* corte, cortadura; recorte (*de un periódico*); (hort.) esqueje, rampollo
**cuttle** ['kʌtəl] *s* var. de **cuttlefish**
**cuttlebone** ['kʌtəl,bon] *s* jibión
**cuttlefish** ['kʌtəl,fɪʃ] *s* (zool.) jibia
**cutup** ['kʌt,ʌp] *s* (slang) bromista; **cutups** *spl* diseños o figuras para recortar
**cutwater** ['kʌt,wɔtər] o ['kʌt,wɑtər] *s* espolón, tajamar (*de barco o puente*)
**cutworm** ['kʌt,wʌrm] *s* (ent.) larva de agrótida
**cuvette** [kju'vɛt] *s* (phot.) cubeta
**CW** abr. de **continuous wave**
**cwt.** abr. de **hundredweight**
**cyanamide** [saɪ'ænəmaɪd] o [,saɪə'næmaɪd] *s* (chem.) cianamida; (com.) cianamida de calcio
**cyanate** ['saɪənet] *s* (chem.) cianato
**cyanic** [saɪ'ænɪk] *adj* (chem.) ciánico; cianótico (*azulado*)
**cyanic acid** *s* (chem.) ácido ciánico
**cyanid** ['saɪənɪd] o **cyanide** ['saɪənaɪd] o ['saɪənɪd] *s* (chem.) cianuro
**cyanide of potassium** *s* (chem.) cianuro de potasio
**cyanite** ['saɪənaɪt] *s* (mineral.) cianita
**cyanogen** [saɪ'ænədʒən] *s* (chem.) cianógeno
**cyanophycean** [,saɪəno'fɪʃən] *adj* (bot.) cianofíceo; *s* (bot.) cianofícea
**cyanosis** [,saɪə'nosɪs] *s* (path.) cianosis
**cyanotic** [,saɪə'nɑtɪk] *adj* (path.) cianótico
**Cybele** ['sɪbəli] *s* (myth.) Cibeles
**cybernetics** [,saɪbər'nɛtɪks] *ssg* cibernética
**cycad** ['saɪkæd] *s* (bot.) cicadácea
**Cyclades** ['sɪklədiz] *spl* Cícladas
**cyclamen** ['sɪkləmɛn] *s* (bot.) ciclamen, pamporcino
**cyclamin** ['sɪkləmɪn] *s* (chem.) ciclamina
**cyclas** ['sɪklæs] o ['saɪklæs] *s* (*pl:* **cyclades** ['sɪklədiz]) ciclada (*de las romanas*); ciclatón (*tela de la Edad Media*)
**cycle** ['saɪkəl] *s* ciclo; bicicleta, velocípedo; (phys.) período; (mach.) tiempo (*de un motor de combustión interna*); *vn* hacer o completar un ciclo; ocurrir repetidamente en el mismo orden; andar o montar en bicicleta
**cyclic** ['saɪklɪk] o ['sɪklɪk] o **cyclical** ['saɪklɪkəl] o ['sɪklɪkəl] *adj* cíclico
**cycling** ['saɪklɪŋ] *s* ciclismo
**cyclist** ['saɪklɪst] *s* ciclista
**cycloid** ['saɪklɔɪd] *adj* cicloidal; *s* (geom.) cicloide
**cyclometer** [saɪ'klɑmɪtər] *s* ciclómetro
**cyclonal** [saɪ'klonəl] *adj* ciclonal
**cyclone** ['saɪklon] *s* ciclón
**cyclonic** [saɪ'klɑnɪk] o **cyclonical** [saɪ'klɑnɪkəl] *adj* ciclónico
**cyclopaedia** [,saɪklo'pidɪə] *s* var. de **cyclopedia**
**cyclopean** [,saɪklo'piən] *adj* ciclópeo; (*cap.*) *adj* (myth.) ciclópeo
**cyclopedia** [,saɪklo'pidɪə] *s* enciclopedia
**cyclopedic** [,saɪklo'pidɪk] *adj* enciclopédico
**cyclopentane** [,saɪklo'pɛnten] o [,sɪklo'pɛnten] *s* (chem.) ciclopentano
**Cyclopic** [saɪ'klɑpɪk] *adj* ciclópico
**cycloplegia** [,saɪklo'plidʒɪə] o [,sɪklo'plidʒɪə] *s* (path.) cicloplejía
**cyclopropane** [,saɪklo'propen] o [,sɪklo'propen] *s* (chem.) ciclopropano
**Cyclops** ['saɪklɑps] *s* (*pl:* **Cyclopes** [saɪ'klopiz]) (myth.) Cíclope
**cyclorama** [,saɪklo'ræmə] o [,saɪklo'rɑmə] *s* ciclorama
**cyclostome** ['saɪklostom] o ['sɪklostom] *s* (ichth.) ciclóstoma
**cyclotron** ['saɪklotrɑn] o ['sɪklotrɑn] *s* (phys.) ciclotrón
**Cydnus** ['sɪdnəs] *s* Cidno
**cygnet** ['sɪgnɪt] *s* (orn.) pollo de cisne
**Cygnus** ['sɪgnəs] *s* (astr.) Cisne
**cyl.** abr. de **cylinder** y **cylindrical**
**cylinder** ['sɪlɪndər] *s* cilindro; *va* proveer de cilindro o cilindros; cilindrar
**cylinder block** *s* (mach.) bloque de cilindros
**cylinder bore** *s* alesaje
**cylinder capacity** *s* cilindrada
**cylinder head** *s* tapa del cilindro (*de una máquina de vapor*); culata del cilindro (*de un motor de gasolina*)
**cylinder lock** *s* cerradura de cilindro
**cylindric** [sɪ'lɪndrɪk] o **cylindrical** [sɪ'lɪndrɪkəl] *adj* cilíndrico
**cylindroid** ['sɪlɪndrɔɪd] *adj* cilindroide; *s* (geom. & med.) cilindroide
**cymbal** ['sɪmbəl] *s* (mus.) címbalo, platillo
**cymbalist** ['sɪmbəlɪst] *s* (mus.) cimbalero, cimbalista
**cyme** [saɪm] *s* (bot.) cima
**cymene** ['saɪmin] *s* (chem.) cimeno
**cymophane** ['saɪmofen] *s* (mineral.) cimofana
**cymose** ['saɪmos] o [saɪ'mos] *adj* (bot.) cimoso
**Cymric** ['kɪmrɪk] o ['sɪmrɪk] *adj & s* címrico
**Cymry** ['kɪmrɪ] *spl* cimris
**cynic** ['sɪnɪk] *adj & s* cínico (*burlón, volteriano*); (*cap.*) *adj & s* cínico
**cynical** ['sɪnɪkəl] *adj* cínico (*burlón, volteriano*)
**cynicism** ['sɪnɪsɪzəm] *s* cinismo (*burlonería, volterianismo*); (*cap.*) *s* cinismo
**cynic spasm** *s* (path.) espasmo cínico
**cynosure** ['saɪnəʃʊr] o ['sɪnəʃʊr] *s* miradero (*objeto de la atención*); guía, norte; (*cap.*) *s* (astr.) Cinosura
**Cynthia** ['sɪnθɪə] *s* (myth.) Cintia
**cyperaceous** [,saɪpə'reʃəs] *adj* (bot.) ciperáceo
**cypher** ['saɪfər] *s, adj, va & vn* var. de **cipher**
**cypress** ['saɪprəs] *s* (bot.) ciprés; *adj* cipresino
**Cyprian** ['sɪprɪən] *adj & s* chipriota; (fig.) lujurioso
**Cypriot** ['sɪprɪət] o **Cypriote** ['sɪprɪot] *adj & s* chipriota
**cypripedium** [,sɪprɪ'pidɪəm] *s* (*pl:* **-a** [ə]) (bot.) cipripedio
**Cyprus** ['saɪprəs] *s* Chipre
**Cyrenaic** [,saɪrɪ'neɪk] o [,sɪrɪ'neɪk] *adj & s* cirenaico
**Cyrenaica** [,saɪrɪ'neɪkə] o [,sɪrɪ'neɪkə] *s* la Cirenaica
**Cyrene** [saɪ'rinɪ] *s* Cirene (*ciudad*)
**Cyril** ['sɪrɪl] *s* Cirilo
**Cyrillic** [sɪ'rɪlɪk] *adj* cirílico
**Cyrus** ['saɪrəs] *s* Ciro
**cyst** [sɪst] *s* (bot., path. & zool.) quiste
**cystic** ['sɪstɪk] *adj* (anat.) cístico; (path.) quístico
**cystic duct** *s* (anat.) cístico, conducto cístico
**cysticercosis** [,sɪstɪsər'kosɪs] *s* (path.) cisticercosis
**cysticercus** [,sɪstɪ'sʌrkəs] *s* (*pl:* **-ci** [saɪ]) (zool.) cisticerco
**cystitis** [sɪs'taɪtɪs] *s* (path.) cistitis
**cystoscope** ['sɪstoskop] *s* cistoscopio
**cystotomy** [sɪs'tɑtəmɪ] *s* (*pl:* **-mies**) (surg.) cistotomía
**cytase** ['saɪtes] *s* (biochem.) citasa

**Cytherea** [ˌsɪθəˈriə] *s* (myth.) Citerea
**Cytherean** [ˌsɪθəˈriən] *adj* citereo
**cytisine** [ˈsɪtɪsin] o [ˈsɪtɪsɪn] *s* (pharm.) citisina
**cytisus** [ˈsɪtɪsəs] *s* (*pl:* **-si** [saɪ]) (bot.) cítiso
**cytochemistry** [ˌsaɪtoˈkɛmɪstrɪ] *s* citoquímica
**cytologist** [saɪˈtɑlədʒɪst] *s* citólogo
**cytology** [saɪˈtɑlədʒɪ] *s* citología
**cytoplasm** [ˈsaɪtoplæzəm] *s* (biol.) citoplasma
**cytoplasmic** [ˌsaɪtoˈplæzmɪk] *adj* (biol.) citoplásmico
**C.Z.** abr. de **Canal Zone**
**czar** [zɑr] *s* zar; (fig.) autócrata
**czardas** [ˈtʃɑrdɑʃ] o [ˈzɑrdæs] *s* (mus.) csardas
**czarevitch** [ˈzɑrɪvɪtʃ] *s* zarevitz
**czarevna** [zɑˈrɛvnə] *s* czarevna
**czarina** [zɑˈrinə] *s* zarina
**czarism** [ˈzɑrɪzəm] *s* zarismo
**czarist** [ˈzɑrɪst] *s* zarista
**Czech** [tʃɛk] *adj & s* checo
**Czechish** [ˈtʃɛkɪʃ] *adj* checo
**Czecho-Slovak** o **Czechoslovak** [ˈtʃɛkoˈslovæk] *adj & s* checoeslovaco o checoslovaco
**Czecho-Slovakia** o **Czechoslovakia** [ˌtʃɛkosloˈvɑkɪə] o [ˌtʃɛkosloˈvækɪə] *s* Checoeslovaquia o Checoslovaquia
**Czecho-Slovakian** o **Czechoslovakian** [ˌtʃɛkosloˈvɑkɪən] o [ˌtʃɛkosloˈvækɪən] *adj & s* var. de **Czecho-Slovak**

# D

**D, d** [di] *s* (*pl:* **D's, d's** (diz]) cuarta letra del alfabeto inglés

**d.** abr. de **date, day, daughter, dead, degree, delete, diameter, died, dime, dollar** y **denarius (English penny, pence)**

**D.** abr. de **December, Democrat, Democratic, Duchess, Duke** y **Dutch**

**D.A.** abr. de **District Attorney**

**dab** [dæb] *s* golpecito, toque ligero; masa pastosa; brochazo (*hecho con pintura*); pizca; (ichth.) platija, lenguado, barbada; (*pret & pp:* **dabbed;** *ger:* **dabbing**) *va* golpear ligeramente, tocar ligeramente, frotar suavemente; embadurnar; aplicar (*pintura*) con brochazos ligeros

**dabble** [ˈdæbəl] *va* salpicar, rociar; *vn* chapotear; trabajar superficialmente; **to dabble in** mangonear en, meterse en; jugar a (*la bolsa*); especular en (*p.ej., granos*)

**dabbler** [ˈdæblər] *s* aficionado, diletante

**dabchick** [ˈdæbˌtʃɪk] *s* (orn.) zambullidor (*Podilymbus podiceps*); (orn.) somorgujo castaño o menor (*Podiceps ruficollis*)

**dabster** [ˈdæbstər] *s* (coll.) chapucero, principiante; (dial.) perito

**dace** [des] *s* (ichth.) albur, leucisco, dardo

**dachshund** [ˈdɑksˌhʊnt] o [ˈdæksˌhʊnd] *s* perro de casta alemana corto de patas y de cuerpo largo

**Dacia** [ˈdeʃə] *s* la Dacia

**Dacian** [ˈdeʃən] *adj & s* dacio

**dactyl** [ˈdæktɪl] *s* dáctilo

**dactylic** [dækˈtɪlɪk] *adj* dactílico

**dactyliography** [dækˌtɪlɪˈɑgrəfɪ] *s* dactiliografía

**dactyliology** [dækˌtɪlɪˈɑlədʒɪ] *s* dactiliología

**dactylogram** [ˈdæktɪləˌgræm] o [dækˈtɪləgræm] *s* dactilograma

**dactyloscopic** [ˌdæktɪləˈskɑpɪk] *adj* dactiloscópico

**dactyloscopy** [ˌdæktɪˈlɑskəpɪ] *s* dactiloscopia

**dad** [dæd] *s* (coll.) papá

**Dadaism** [ˈdɑdəɪzəm] *s* dadaísmo

**daddy** [ˈdædɪ] *s* (*pl:* **-dies**) (coll.) var. de **dad**

**daddy-longlegs** [ˌdædɪˈlɔŋˌlɛgz] o [ˌdædɪˈlɑŋˌlɛgz] *s* (*pl:* **-legs**) (ent.) típula; (ent.) segador; (orn.) candelero, comalteca; (*cap.*) *s* Papaíto piernas largas

**dado** [ˈdedo] *s* (*pl:* **-does**) friso; (arch.) dado

**Daedalus** [ˈdɛdələs] o [ˈdidələs] *s* (myth.) Dédalo

**daemon** [ˈdimən] *s* var. de **demon**

**daffodil** [ˈdæfədɪl] *s* (bot.) narciso trompón

**daffy** [ˈdæfɪ] *adj* (*comp:* **-ier;** *super:* **-iest**) (coll.) chiflado

**daft** [dæft] *adj* chiflado; necio

**dagger** [ˈdægər] *s* daga, puñal; (print.) cruz, obelisco; **to look daggers (at)** apuñalar con la mirada

**daguerreotype** [dəˈgɛrətaɪp] *s* daguerrotipo; *va* daguerrotipar

**dahlia** [ˈdæljə], [ˈdeljə] o [ˈdɑljə] *s* (bot.) dalia

**daily** [ˈdelɪ] *adj* diario, cotidiano; *adv* diariamente; *s* (*pl:* **-lies**) diario

**daily double** *s* apuesta doble (*en las carreras de caballos*)

**daily dozen** *spl* rato diario de gimnasia; quehaceres rutinarios

**dainty** [ˈdentɪ] *adj* (*comp:* **-tier;** *super:* **-tiest**) delicado; *s* (*pl:* **-ties**) golosina

**dairy** [ˈdɛrɪ] *s* (*pl:* **-ies**) lechería, quesería, vaquería

**dairy cattle** *s* vacas lecheras

**dairymaid** [ˈdɛrɪˌmed] *s* lechera

**dairyman** [ˈdɛrɪmən] *s* (*pl:* **-men**) lechero

**dais** [ˈde·ɪs] *s* estrado

**daisy** [ˈdezɪ] *s* (*pl:* **-sies**) (bot.) margarita; (bot.) margarita mayor; (slang) primor

**dale** [del] *s* vallecico

**dalliance** [ˈdælɪəns] *s* coquetería, frivolidad

**dally** [ˈdælɪ] (*pret & pp:* **-lied**) *vn* juguetear, retozar; tardar, holgar, perder el tiempo

**Dalmatia** [dælˈmeʃə] *s* Dalmacia

**Dalmatian** [dælˈmeʃən] *adj* dálmata, dalmático; *s* dálmata; perro dalmático

**dalmatic** [dælˈmætɪk] *s* dalmática (*vestidura*)

**Daltonism** [ˈdɔltənɪzəm] *s* (path.) daltonismo

**dam** [dæm] *s* presa, dique; madre (*de cuadrúpedos*); (dent.) dique; (found.) dama; (*pret & pp:* **dammed;** *ger:* **damming**) *va* represar, estancar; contener con diques; cerrar, tapar, obstruir

**damage** [ˈdæmɪdʒ] *s* daño, perjuicio, deterioro; desdoro (*en la reputación*); pérdida; (com.) avería; (slang) costo; **damages** *spl* daños y perjuicios; *va* dañar, perjudicar; averiar; *vn* dañarse; averiarse

**damaging** [ˈdæmɪdʒɪŋ] *adj* perjudicial; desdoroso (*p.ej., en la reputación*)

**damascene** [ˈdæməsin] o [ˌdæməˈsin] *adj* ataujiado; damasquino, damasquinado; *s* ataujía (*obra de metal adornada con embutidos de oro, plata y esmaltes*); damasquinado (*hierro o acero con líneas ondeantes; obra de metal adornada con embutidos de oro, plata y esmaltes*); *va* ataujiar; damasquinar; (*cap.*) *adj & s* damasceno

**damascene work** *s* ataujía; damasquinado

**Damascus** [dəˈmæskəs] *s* Damasco

**Damascus steel** *s* acero damasquino, acero adamascado

**damask** [ˈdæməsk] *s* damasco (*tejido*); ataujía; damasquinado; acero damasquino; *adj* adamascado; damasceno (*de Damasco*); damasquino (*dícese, p.ej., del acero*); *va* adamascar

**damask rose** *s* (bot.) rosa de Damasco

**damask steel** *s* acero damasquino, acero adamascado

**dame** [dem] *s* dama, señora; (slang) tía, mujer

**damewort** [ˈdemˌwʌrt] *s* (bot.) juliana

**damn** [dæm] *s* terno; **I don't give a damn** (slang) maldito lo que me importa; **that's not worth a damn** (slang) eso no vale un pito; *va* condenar (a pena eterna); condenar; maldecir; **to damn with faint praise** condenar por medio de alabanzas poco entusiastas; *vn* maldecir, echar ternos

**damnable** [ˈdæmnəbəl] *adj* condenable; detestable, infame, abominable

**damnation** [dæmˈneʃən] *s* damnación; (theol.) condenación

**damned** [dæmd] *adj* condenado (a pena eterna), maldito; condenado; detestable, abominable; **the damned** los condenados (a pena eterna), los malditos

**Damocles** [ˈdæməkliz] *s* (myth.) Damocles o Dámocles

**Damon** [ˈdemən] *s* (myth.) Damón

**damp** [dæmp] *adj* húmedo, mojado; *s* humedad; grisú; abatimiento, desaliento; *va* humedecer, mojar; amortecer, amortiguar; abatir, desalentar; (elec.) amortiguar (*ondas electromagnéticas*)

**damped wave** *s* (elec.) onda amortiguada

**dampen** [ˈdæmpən] humedecer; apagar, amortecer, amortiguar; abatir, desalentar; (elec.) amortiguar (*ondas electromagnéticas*); *vn* humedecerse; amortecerse

**dampener** [ˈdæmpənər] *s* (mach.) amortiguador

**damper** [ˈdæmpər] *s* registro, regulador de tiro de chimenea; llave de estufa; apagador, sordina (*del piano*); desalentador

**dampish** [ˈdæmpɪʃ] *adj* algo húmedo

**dampness** ['dæmpnɪs] *s* humedad
**damsel** ['dæmzəl] *s* damisela, señorita, muchacha
**damson** ['dæmzən] *s* (bot.) ciruelo damasceno; ciruela damascena (*fruto*)
**Danae** ['dænɪi] *s* (myth.) Dánae
**Danaides** o **Danaïdes** [də'neɪdiz] *spl* (myth.) Danaides
**Danaus** o **Danaüs** ['dæneəs] *s* (myth.) Danao
**dance** [dæns] o [dɑns] *s* baile, danza; **formal dance** baile de etiqueta; *adj* de baile, para bailar, bailable; *va* bailar, danzar (*p.ej., una polca*); *vn* bailar, danzar; (fig.) bailar, danzar; **to dance to the music** bailar al son que se toca
**danceable** ['dænsəbəl] o ['dɑnsəbəl] *adj* bailable
**dance band** *s* orquesta de jazz
**dance hall** *s* salón de baile
**dance floor** *s* pista de baile
**dance music** *s* música de baile, música bailable
**dance of death** *s* danza de la muerte
**dancer** ['dænsər] o ['dɑnsər] *s* bailador, danzador; bailarín (*profesional*)
**dancing partner** *s* pareja (de baile)
**dandelion** ['dændɪ,laɪən] *s* (bot.) amargón o diente de león
**dander** ['dændər] *s* (coll.) ira, cólera, mal genio; caspa (*escamilla a raíz de los cabellos*); **to get one's dander up** (coll.) enojarse, perder la paciencia
**dandle** ['dændəl] *va* mecer, hacer saltar sobre las rodillas; acariciar, mimar
**dandler** ['dændlər] *s* niñero
**dandruff** ['dændrəf] *s* caspa
**dandy** ['dændɪ] *s* (*pl:* **-dies**) currutaco; (slang) cosa excelente; *adj* (*comp:* **-dier;** *super:* **-diest**) currutaco; (slang) excelente, magnífico
**dandyism** ['dændɪɪzəm] *s* dandismo
**Dane** [den] *s* danés o dinamarqués
**danewort** ['den,wʌrt] *s* (bot.) actea, yezgo
**danger** ['dendʒər] *s* peligro; **out of danger** fuera de peligro
**dangerous** ['dendʒərəs] *adj* peligroso
**dangle** ['dæŋgəl] *va & vn* colgar en el aire, colgar flojamente; **to dangle after** seguir, ir tras de
**dangling** ['dæŋglɪŋ] *adj* colgante en el aire, colgante flojamente
**dangling participle** *s* (gram.) participio inconexo
**Daniel** ['dænjəl] *s* Daniel
**Danish** ['denɪʃ] *adj* danés o dinamarqués; *s* danés o dinamarqués (*idioma*); **the Danish** los daneses, los dinamarqueses
**dank** [dæŋk] *adj* liento, húmedo
**danse macabre** [dɑ̃s mɑ'kɑbrə] *s* danza macabra
**danseuse** [dɑ̃'søz] *s* bailarina
**Dantesque** [dæn'tɛsk] *adj* dantesco
**Danube** ['dænjʊb] o ['dænjub] *s* Danubio
**Danubian** [dæn'jubɪən] *adj* danubiano
**daphne** ['dæfnɪ] *s* (bot.) laurel; (bot.) adelfilla; (*cap.*) *s* (myth.) Dafne
**dapper** ['dæpər] *adj* aseado, apuesto, gallardo; vivaracho
**dapple** ['dæpəl] *s* apariencia moteada; animal rodado, caballo rodado; *adj* rodado, habado; *va* motear
**dappled** ['dæpəld] *adj* rodado, habado
**dapple gray** *s* caballo rucio rodado
**dapple-gray** ['dæpəl,gre] *adj* rucio rodado
**Dardan** ['dɑrdən] o **Dardanian** [dɑr'denɪən] *adj* dardanio o dárdano; *s* dárdano
**Dardanelles** [,dɑrdə'nɛlz] *spl* Dardanelos
**Dardanus** ['dɑrdənəs] *s* (myth.) Dárdano
**dare** [dɛr] *s* reto, provocación; *va* retar, provocar; arrostrar, resistir; *vn* atreverse; **I dare say** acaso, quizá; **to dare (to)** + *inf* atreverse a + *inf*, osar + *inf*
**daredevil** ['dɛr,dɛvəl] *adj & s* temerario
**daring** ['dɛrɪŋ] *adj* osado, atrevido; *s* osadía, atrevimiento
**Darius** [də'raɪəs] *s* Darío
**dark** [dɑrk] *adj* obscuro; trigueño, moreno; secreto, oculto; ignorante; triste, tétrico; malvado, perverso; atroz; pardo (*dícese de la cerveza*); **to become dark** o **get dark** obscurecerse; hacerse de noche, anochecer; **to keep dark** callar, tener reservado; *s* obscuridad, tinieblas; anochecer, noche; color obscuro; (paint.) sombra obscura; **in the dark** a obscuras; (fig.) a obscuras
**dark ages** o **Dark Ages** *spl* edad media; primera mitad de la edad media
**dark-complexioned** ['dɑrkkəm'plɛkʃənd] *adj* moreno
**Dark Continent** *s* Continente Negro
**darken** ['dɑrkən] *va* obscurecer; manchar; desconcertar, confundir; entristecer; *vn* obscurecerse
**darkey** ['dɑrkɪ] *s* (offensive) negro
**dark horse** *s* caballo desconocido; ganador desconocido; (pol.) candidato nombrado inesperadamente
**darkish** ['dɑrkɪʃ] *adj* algo obscuro
**dark lantern** *s* linterna sorda
**darkle** ['dɑrkəl] *va* obscurecer, volver obscuro; *vn* obscurecerse, parecer obscuro
**darkling** ['dɑrklɪŋ] *adj* obscurecido; *adv* a obscuras
**darkly** ['dɑrklɪ] *adv* obscuramente; secretamente; misteriosamente
**dark meat** *s* carne del ave fuera de la pechuga
**darkness** ['dɑrknɪs] *s* obscuridad; secreto; ignorancia; tristeza; maldad, perversidad
**darkroom** ['dɑrk,rum] o ['dɑrk,rʊm] *s* (phot.) cuarto obscuro
**darksome** ['dɑrksəm] *adj* (poet.) obscuro, sombrío
**darky** ['dɑrkɪ] *s* (*pl:* **-ies**) (offensive) negro
**darling** ['dɑrlɪŋ] *adj & s* querido; predilecto
**darn** [dɑrn] *s* zurcido; (coll.) maldición; *va & vn* zurcir; (coll.) maldecir
**darnel** ['dɑrnəl] *s* (bot.) cizaña; (bot.) ballico perenne
**darner** ['dɑrnər] *s* zurcidor; aguja de zurcir
**darning** ['dɑrnɪŋ] *s* zurcidura; cosas zurcidas; cosas por zurcir; *adj* zurcidor; de zurcir
**darning needle** *s* aguja de zurcir; (ent.) caballito del diablo
**dart** [dɑrt] *s* dardo, saeta; movimiento rápido; rehilete (*que se lanza por diversión*); aguijón (*de los insectos*); (sew.) sisa; (arch.) saetilla, dardo (*puntas de flechas que alternan con las ovas*); *vn* lanzarse, precipitarse; volar como dardo
**darter** ['dɑrtər] *s* flechador; (ichth.) eteostoma; (orn.) pájaro culebra
**dartle** ['dɑrtəl] *va* lanzar repetidamente; *vn* lanzarse repetidamente
**Darwinian** [dɑr'wɪnɪən] *adj* darviniano; *s* darvinista
**Darwinism** ['dɑrwɪnɪzəm] *s* darvinismo
**Darwinist** ['dɑrwɪnɪst] *adj* darviniano; *s* darvinista
**dash** [dæʃ] *s* rociada; arremetida, arranque; choque, colisión; revés repentino; poquito, pequeña cantidad; carrera corta; brío, espíritu; jactancia; guardafango, guardalodos; (aut.) tablero de instrumentos; raya (*en la imprenta, la escritura y la telegrafía*); **at one dash** de un golpe; **to cut a dash** hacer gran papel; *va* lanzar, tirar; quebrar, romper, estrellar; desanimar; frustrar; rociar, salpicar; mezclar; **to dash against** estampar contra; **to dash away** desechar, arrojar de sí; **to dash off** escribir de prisa; **to dash to pieces** hacer añicos, hacer mil pedazos; *vn* chocar, estrellarse (*p.ej., las olas del mar*); lanzarse; **to dash by** pasar corriendo; **to dash in** entrar como un rayo, entrar de estampía; **to dash out** salir como un rayo, salir de estampía
**dashboard** ['dæʃ,bord] *s* guardafango, guardalodos; (aut.) tablero de instrumentos
**dasher** ['dæʃər] *s* persona briosa; agitador (*de mantequera o sorbetera*)
**dashing** ['dæʃɪŋ] *adj* brioso; vistoso, ostentoso; *s* embate (*p.ej., de las olas*)
**dastard** ['dæstərd] *adj & s* vil, miserable, cobarde
**dastardly** ['dæstərdlɪ] *adj* vil, miserable, cobarde
**dat.** abr. de **dative**
**data processing** *s* tramitación automática de datos
**datary** ['detərɪ] *s* (*pl:* **-ries**) dataría (*cargo*); datario (*cardenal*)
**date** [det] *s* fecha, data; (coll.) cita; (bot.) datilera; dátil (*fruto*); **out of date** fuera de mo-

da, anticuado; **to bring up to date** poner al día; **to date** hasta la fecha; **under date of** con fecha de; **up to date** hasta la fecha; **what is the date?** ¿cuál es la fecha de hoy?; *va* fechar, datar; (coll.) tener cita o citas con; *vn* datar; llevar fecha; **to date from** datar de
**dated** [ˈdetɪd] *adj* fechado; anticuado, fuera de moda
**dateless** [ˈdetlɪs] *adj* sin fecha; sin fin; inmemorial
**date line** *s* línea (efectiva) de cambio de fecha
**date palm** *s* (bot.) palmera datilera
**date shell** *s* (zool.) dátil
**dative** [ˈdetɪv] *adj & s* (gram.) dativo
**datum** ([ˈdetəm] o [ˈdætəm] *s* (*pl:* **data** [ˈdetə] o [ˈdætə]) dato
**datum level** *s* (surv.) nivel de referencia
**datum plane** *s* (surv.) plano de referencia
**datura** [dəˈtjʊrə] *s* (bot.) datura
**dau.** abr. de **daughter**
**daub** [dɔb] *s* embadurnamiento; pintarrajo (*pintura mal hecha*); *va* embadurnar; pintarrajear; *vn* embadurnarse; pintarrajear
**dauber** [ˈdɔbər] *s* embadurnador; mal pintor
**daughter** [ˈdɔtər] *s* hija
**daughter-in-law** [ˈdɔtərɪnˌlɔ] *s* (*pl:* **daughters-in-law**) nuera
**daughterly** [ˈdɔtərlɪ] *adj* filial, como una hija
**daughter of Eve** *s* hija de Eva
**daunt** [dɔnt] o [dɑnt] *va* espantar, asustar; desanimar, acobardar
**dauntless** [ˈdɔntlɪs] o [ˈdɑntlɪs] *adj* impávido, intrépido, atrevido
**dauphin** [ˈdɔfɪn] *s* delfín
**dauphiness** [ˈdɔfɪnɪs] *s* delfina
**davenport** [ˈdævənport] *s* pequeño escritorio; sofá cama tapizado
**David** [ˈdevɪd] *s* David
**davit** [ˈdævɪt] o [ˈdevɪt] *s* (naut.) pescante, grúa de bote
**Davy Jones's locker** [ˈdevɪ ˈdʒonzɪz] *s* el fondo del mar
**Davy lamp** *s* lámpara de Davy, lámpara de seguridad para los mineros
**daw** [dɔ] *s* (orn.) corneja
**dawdle** [ˈdɔdəl] *va* malgastar (*tiempo*); *vn* malgastar el tiempo, haronear
**dawdler** [ˈdɔdlər] *s* holgazán, haragán
**dawn** [dɔn] *s* amanecer, alba, aurora; (fig.) aurora, principio, comienzo; *vn* amanecer; despuntar (*el día, la mañana, etc.*); empezar a mostrarse; **to dawn on** o **upon one** venírsele a uno a las mientes; empezar uno a comprender, p.ej., **the truth dawned on him** empezó a comprender la verdad
**day** [de] *s* día; jornada (*p.ej., de trabajo, de inquietud*); victoria, triunfo; **any day** de un día a otro, de un día para otro; **by day** de día; **by the day** a jornal; **from day to day** de día en día, de un día para otro; **the day after** el día siguiente; **the day after tomorrow** pasado mañana; **the day before** la víspera, la víspera de; **the day before yesterday** anteayer; **to call it a day** (coll.) dejar de trabajar; **to have one's day** tener sus días; **to this day** hasta el día de hoy; **to win the day** ganar la palma, ganar la victoria; **day after day** día tras día; **day by day** día por día; **day in, day out** día tras día, sin cesar; *adj* diurno
**day bed** *s* sofá cama, diván cama, canapé cama
**day book** *s* diario; (com.) libro diario; (naut.) cuaderno de bitácora
**daybreak** [ˈdeˌbrek] *s* amanecer, aurora; **at daybreak** al amanecer
**day coach** *s* (rail.) coche de viajeros
**daydream** [ˈdeˌdrim] *s* ensueño, sueño de vigilia; *vn* soñar despierto
**day laborer** *s* jornalero
**day letter** *s* telegrama diurno
**daylight** [ˈdeˌlaɪt] *s* día, luz del día; amanecer; luz, publicidad; (slang) abertura, espacio, intervalo; **in broad daylight** en pleno día; **to scare the daylights out of** (slang) pasmar de terror; **to see daylight** comprender; (coll.) ver el fin de una tarea difícil
**daylight saving** *s* aprovechamiento de la luz
**daylight-saving time** [ˈdeˌlaɪtˈsevɪŋ] *s* hora de verano
**day lily** *s* (bot.) azucena amarilla
**daylong** [ˈdeˌlɔŋ] o [ˈdeˌlɑŋ] *adj* de todo el día; *adv* todo el día
**day nursery** *s* guardería infantil
**Day of Atonement** *s* día de la expiación
**day off** *s* día de holgar o de huelga, día de vacación, asueto
**Day of Judgment** *s* día del juicio
**day of reckoning** *s* día de ajustar cuentas, día de la justicia
**day school** *s* escuela diurna; escuela de semana; externado, escuela de externos
**day shift** *s* turno diurno
**days of grace** *spl* (com.) días de gracia
**dayspring** [ˈdeˌsprɪŋ] *s* aurora, albor
**daystar** [ˈdeˌstɑr] *s* lucero del alba; (poet.) sol
**daytime** [ˈdeˌtaɪm] *s* día; **in the daytime** de día
**daze** [dez] *s* aturdimiento; deslumbramiento; **in a daze** aturdido; *va* aturdir; deslumbrar
**dazzle** [ˈdæzəl] *s* deslumbramiento, ofuscamiento; *va* deslumbrar, ofuscar
**dazzling** [ˈdæzlɪŋ] *adj* deslumbrante
**d.c.** abr. de **direct current**
**D.C.** abr. de **direct current** y **District of Columbia**
**DDT** [ˈdiˈdiˈti] *s* símbolo de **dichlorodiphenyl-trichloroethane**
**deacon** [ˈdikən] *s* diácono
**deaconess** [ˈdikənɪs] *s* diaconisa
**deaconry** [ˈdikənrɪ] *s* (*pl:* **-ries**) diaconato
**dead** [dɛd] *adj* muerto; anticuado, fuera de uso; (coll.) cansado; (sport) muerto; *adv* absolutamente, completamente; directamente; *s* época o tiempo lóbrego; **deads** *spl* (min.) escombros; **the dead** los muertos; **the dead of night** el profundo silencio de la noche; **the dead of winter** lo más frío del invierno
**dead air** *s* (rad.) interrupción del programa (*por avería*)
**dead beat** *s* (slang) gorrón; (slang) holgazán
**dead-beat** [ˈdɛdˈbit] *adj* (coll.) muerto de cansancio
**deadbeat** [ˈdɛdˌbit] *adj* (phys.) sin oscilación
**dead bolt** *s* cerrojo dormido
**dead center** *s* (mach.) punto muerto; (mach.) punta fija (*p.ej., en un torno*)
**dead-drunk** [ˈdɛdˈdrʌŋk] *adj* difunto de taberna
**dead duck** *s* (slang) persona acabada, persona sin porvenir, cosa arruinada
**deaden** [ˈdɛdən] *va* amortiguar, amortecer; insonorizar
**dead end** *s* extremo cerrado, callejón sin salida; (rad.) punto muerto; (fig.) atolladero
**dead-end** [ˈdɛdˌɛnd] *adj* sin salida; (rad.) muerto
**deadeye** [ˈdɛdˌaɪ] *s* (naut.) vigota
**dead freight** *s* (naut.) falso flete
**deadhead** [ˈdɛdˌhɛd] *s* persona exenta de pagar (*en el teatro, el ferrocarril, etc.*); (found.) mazarota; (naut.) boya de madera; (naut.) poste de amarra
**dead heat** *s* carrera indecisa
**dead key** *s* tecla muerta (*de una máquina de escribir*)
**dead language** *s* lengua muerta
**deadlatch** [ˈdɛdˌlætʃ] *s* aldaba dormida
**dead letter** *s* carta no reclamada; (fig.) letra muerta (*práctica caída en desuso, ley que ya no se cumple*)
**dead-letter office** [ˈdɛdˈlɛtər] *s* oficina de cartas no reclamadas
**deadline** [ˈdɛdˌlaɪn] *s* línea vedada; fin del plazo
**deadlock** [ˈdɛdˌlɑk] *s* cerradura dormida; estancación, callejón sin salida; *va* estancar; *vn* estancarse
**deadly** [ˈdɛdlɪ] *adj* (*comp:* **-lier;** *super:* **-liest**) mortal; fatigoso, abrumador; *adv* mortalmente; excesivamente, sumamente
**deadly carrot** *s* (bot.) tapsia
**deadly nightshade** *s* (bot.) belladona; (bot.) hierba mora
**deadly sins** *spl* siete pecados capitales
**dead march** *s* (mus.) marcha fúnebre
**dead pan** *s* (slang) semblante sin expresión
**dead point** *s* punto muerto
**dead reckoning** *s* (naut.) estima
**dead ringer** *s* segunda edición (*persona o cosa que se parece mucho a otra*)
**dead rise** *s* (naut.) delgado

**Dead Sea** *s* mar Muerto
**dead set** *adj* (coll.) muy resuelto, muy determinado
**dead-smooth file** ['dɛd,smuð] *s* lima sorda
**dead soldier** *s* (slang) botella vacía
**dead-stick landing** ['dɛd,stɪk] *s* (aer.) aterrizaje con motor muerto
**dead stop** *s* parada completa, parada en seco
**dead weight** *s* peso muerto, peso propio; carga onerosa
**deadwood** ['dɛd,wʊd] *s* leña seca; gente inútil, material inútil
**deaf** [dɛf] *adj* sordo; **as deaf as a post** sordo como una tapia; **to turn a deaf ear** hacerse sordo
**deaf and dumb** *adj* sordomudo
**deaf-and-dumb alphabet** ['dɛfənd'dʌm] *s* alfabeto para sordomudos, alfabeto dactilológico
**deaf-dumbness** ['dɛf'dʌmnɪs] *s* sordomudez
**deafen** ['dɛfən] *va* asordar, ensordecer; insonorizar (*p.ej., una pared*); apagar (*un sonido*); aturdir
**deafening** ['dɛfənɪŋ] *adj* ensordecedor; aturdidor
**deaf-mute** ['dɛf,mjut] *adj & s* sordomudo
**deafness** ['dɛfnɪs] *s* sordera
**deal** [dil] *s* negocio, negociación; (coll.) trato; reparto, repartición; mano (*p.ej., de naipes*); turno de dar (*los naipes*); parte, porción; tabla de pino, tabla de abeto; (coll.) convenio secreto; **a good deal (of)** o **a great deal (of)** mucho, p.ej., **he has a good deal of money** tiene mucho dinero; **a good deal faster** mucho más rápidamente; **it's a deal** (coll.) trato hecho; **to make a great deal of** estimar mucho; hacer fiestas a; (*pret & pp:* **dealt**) *va* asestar, dar (*un golpe*); repartir, dar (*la baraja*); *vn* negociar, comerciar; mediar, intervenir; portarse, conducirse; ser mano (*en juegos de naipes*); **to deal with** ocuparse en, entender en; tratar con, entenderse con; tratar de
**dealer** ['dilər] *s* comerciante, negociante; concesionario; repartidor (*de naipes*)
**dealing** ['dilɪŋ] *s* negocio, negociación; conducta; repartición; **dealings** *spl* negocios; relaciones de amistad
**dealt** [dɛlt] *pret & pp de* **deal**
**dean** [din] *s* decano (*de una escuela*); (eccl.) deán; (fig.) decano
**deanery** ['dinərɪ] *s* (*pl:* **-ies**) decanato
**deanship** ['dinʃɪp] *s* decanato; (eccl.) deanato o deanazgo
**dear** [dɪr] *adj* querido; caro, costoso; carero (*que vende caro*); **dear me!** ¡Dios mío!; ¡válgame Dios!; *adv* afectuosamente; caro; *s* querido
**dearie** ['dɪrɪ] *s* (coll.) queridito
**dearness** ['dɪrnɪs] *s* cariño; carestía, precio alto
**dearth** [dʌrθ] *s* carestía, escasez
**deary** ['dɪrɪ] *s* (*pl:* **-ies**) (coll.) queridito
**death** [dɛθ] *s* muerte; (*cap.*) *s* muerte (*esqueleto con una guadaña*); **to be at death's door** estar a la muerte; **to beat to death** matar a golpes; **to be bored to death** morirse de aburrimiento; **to be death on** (slang) estar loco por, amar locamente; (slang) odiar locamente; **to bleed to death** morir desangrado; **to bore to death** matar de aburrimiento; **to burn to death** morir quemado; **to choke to death** estrangular; morir atragantado; **to death** a muerte; excesivamente; **to die a violent death** morir vestido; **to do to death** dar la muerte a; **to freeze to death** morir helado; **to put to death** dar la muerte a; **to shock to death** electrocutar; **to shoot to death** matar a tiros; **to starve to death** matar de hambre; morir de hambre; **to stone to death** matar a pedradas; **to the death** a muerte; excesivamente; **to whip to death** matar a latigazos
**deathbed** ['dɛθ,bɛd] *s* lecho de muerte
**deathblow** ['dɛθ,blo] *s* golpe mortal
**death certificate** *s* fe de óbito, partida de defunción
**death cup** *s* (bot.) canaleja
**deathful** ['dɛθfəl] *adj* mortal, de muerte
**death house** *s* capilla (*de los reos de muerte*)
**deathless** ['dɛθlɪs] *adj* inmortal, eterno
**deathlike** ['dɛθ,laɪk] *adj* mortal; cadavérico
**deathly** ['dɛθlɪ] *adj* mortal, de muerte; *adv* mortalmente; excesivamente, sumamente
**death mask** *s* mascarilla (*sacada sobre el rostro de un cadáver*)
**death penalty** *s* pena de muerte
**death rate** *s* mortalidad
**death rattle** *s* estertor agónico
**death's-head** ['dɛθs,hɛd] *s* calavera
**death toll** *s* doble, toque de difuntos; número de muertos
**deathtrap** ['dɛθ,træp] *s* lugar inseguro y peligroso; situación peligrosa
**Death Valley** *s* valle de la Muerte (*en el estado de California, EE.UU.*)
**death warrant** *s* sentencia de muerte; fin de toda esperanza
**deathwatch** ['dɛθ,wɑtʃ] *s* velación de un moribundo, velación de un cadáver; guardia de un reo de muerte; (ent.) reloj de la muerte
**debacle** [de'bɑkəl] o [dɪ'bækəl] *s* desastre, catástrofe, ruina; derrota; deshielo (*de un río*); inundación violenta
**debar** [dɪ'bɑr] (*pret & pp:* **-barred;** *ger:* **-barring**) *va* excluir; prohibir
**debark** [dɪ'bɑrk] *va & vn* desembarcar
**debarkation** [,dibɑr'keʃən] *s* desembarco (*de pasajeros*); desembarque (*de mercancías*)
**debarment** [dɪ'bɑrmənt] *s* exclusión; prohibición
**debase** [dɪ'bes] *va* rebajar, degradar, envilecer; alterar, falsificar
**debasement** [dɪ'besmənt] *s* rebajamiento, degradación, envilecimiento; depreciación; alteración, falsificación
**debatable** [dɪ'betəbəl] *adj* disputable, discutible
**debate** [dɪ'bet] *s* debate, discusión; *va* debatir; *vn* debatir; deliberar
**debater** [dɪ'betər] *s* polemista, controversista
**debauch** [dɪ'bɔtʃ] *s* libertinaje; lujuria; *va* corromper, seducir; *vn* entregarse a la lujuria
**debauchee** [,dɛbɔ'ʃi] o [,dɛbɔ'tʃi] *s* libertino, disoluto
**debaucher** [dɪ'bɔtʃər] *s* corruptor, seductor
**debauchery** [dɪ'bɔtʃərɪ] *s* (*pl:* **-ies**) libertinaje; lujuria; corrupción
**debauchment** [dɪ'bɔtʃmənt] *s* corrupción, seducción
**debenture** [dɪ'bɛntʃər] *s* (com.) vale, orden de pago; (com.) obligación
**debilitate** [dɪ'bɪlɪtet] *va* debilitar
**debilitation** [dɪ,bɪlɪ'teʃən] *s* debilitación
**debility** [dɪ'bɪlɪtɪ] *s* (*pl:* **-ties**) debilidad
**debit** ['dɛbɪt] *s* (com.) debe; (com.) cargo (*entrada en el debe*); *va* (com.) debitar, adeudar, cargar
**debit balance** *s* saldo deudor
**debonair** o **debonaire** [,dɛbə'nɛr] *adj* alegre, de buen humor; cortés, urbano
**Deborah** ['dɛbərə] *s* Débora
**debouch** [dɪ'buʃ] *vn* desembocar
**debouchment** [dɪ'buʃmənt] *s* desembocadura
**débride** [de'brid] *va* (surg.) desbridar
**débridement** [de'bridmənt] *s* (surg.) desbridamiento
**debrief** [di'brif] *va* interrogar (*p.ej., a un piloto de avión*) para conseguir datos informativos
**debris** o **débris** [de'bri] o ['debri] *s* ruinas, escombros; desecho; (geol.) despojos
**debt** [dɛt] *s* deuda; (Bib.) deuda (*pecado*); **to be deeply in debt** estar lleno de deudas o trampas; **to run into debt** endeudarse
**debt of honor** *s* deuda de honor, deuda de juego
**debtor** ['dɛtər] *s* deudor
**debunk** [di'bʌŋk] *va* (slang) desenmascarar, desbaratar
**debut** o **début** [de'bju] o ['debju] *s* estreno, debut; **to make one's debut** estrenarse, debutar; presentarse en sociedad, ponerse de largo
**debutante** o **débutante** [,dɛbjʊ'tɑnt] o ['dɛbjətænt] *s* principiante, debutante; muchacha que se pone de largo
**dec.** abr. de **deceased** y **decimeter**
**Dec.** abr. de **December**
**decade** ['dɛked] *s* década, decenio
**decadence** [dɪ'kedəns] o ['dɛkədəns] o **deca-**

**dency** [dɪˈkedənsɪ] o [ˈdɛkədənsɪ] *s* decadencia; (lit.) decadentismo
**decadent** [dɪˈkedənt] o [ˈdɛkədənt] *adj* decadente; (lit.) decadentista; *s* (lit.) decadentista
**decagon** [ˈdɛkəgɑn] *adj & s* (geom.) decágono
**decagram** o **decagramme** [ˈdɛkəgræm] *s* decagramo
**decahedron** [ˌdɛkəˈhidrən] *s* (*pl:* **-drons** o **-dra** [drə]) (geom.) decaedro
**decalcomania** [dɪˌkælkəˈmenɪə] *s* calcomanía o decalcomanía
**decalescence** [ˌdikəˈlɛsəns] *s* (metal.) decalescencia
**decaliter** o **decalitre** [ˈdɛkəˌlitər] *s* decalitro
**decalog** o **decalogue** [ˈdɛkəlɔg] o [ˈdɛkəlɑg] *s* decálogo
**decalvant** [dɪˈkælvənt] *adj* (med.) decalvante
**decameter** o **decametre** [ˈdɛkəˌmitər] *s* decámetro
**decamp** [dɪˈkæmp] *vn* decampar; fugarse, escapar
**decampment** [dɪˈkæmpmənt] *s* levantamiento del campamento; fuga, escape
**decanal** [ˈdɛkənəl] o [dɪˈkenəl] *adj* de decano, del decanato
**decant** [dɪˈkænt] *va* decantar
**decantation** [ˌdikænˈteʃən] *s* decantación
**decanter** [dɪˈkæntər] *s* garrafa
**decapitate** [dɪˈkæpɪtet] *va* decapitar, descabezar
**decapitation** [dɪˌkæpɪˈteʃən] *s* decapitación, descabezamiento
**decapod** [ˈdɛkəpɑd] *adj & s* (zool.) decápodo
**decarbonate** [diˈkɑrbənet] *va* descarbonatar
**decarbonization** [diˌkɑrbənɪˈzeʃən] *s* descarburación
**decarbonize** [diˈkɑrbənaɪz] *va* descarburar
**decare** [ˈdɛkɛr] o [dɛˈkɛr] *s* decárea
**decastere** [ˈdɛkəstɪr] *s* decastéreo
**decasyllabic** [ˌdɛkəsɪˈlæbɪk] *adj* decasílabo
**decasyllable** [ˈdɛkəˌsɪləbəl] *adj & s* decasílabo
**decathlon** [dɪˈkæθlɑn] *s* (sport) decatlo
**decay** [dɪˈke] *s* podredumbre; decaimiento, descaecimiento; caries (*p.ej., de los dientes*); *va* pudrir; *vn* pudrirse; cariarse (*los dientes*); decaer
**decease** [dɪˈsis] *s* fallecimiento; *vn* fallecer
**deceased** [dɪˈsist] *adj & s* difunto, muerto
**decedent** [dɪˈsidənt] *s* difunto, muerto
**deceit** [dɪˈsit] *s* engaño; mentira, fraude; falsedad, duplicidad
**deceitful** [dɪˈsitfəl] *adj* mentiroso, engañoso
**deceivable** [dɪˈsivəbəl] *adj* engañadizo
**deceive** [dɪˈsiv] *va* engañar; *vn* mentir
**deceiver** [dɪˈsivər] *s* engañador, impostor
**decelerate** [diˈsɛləret] *va* retardar, desacelerar; *vn* retardarse, desacelerarse
**deceleration** [diˌsɛləˈreʃən] *s* retardación, desaceleración
**December** [dɪˈsɛmbər] *s* diciembre; *adj* decembrino
**decemvir** [dɪˈsɛmvər] *s* decenviro
**decemviral** [dɪˈsɛmvərəl] *adj* decenviral
**decemvirate** [dɪˈsɛmvərɪt] o [dɪˈsɛmvəret] *s* decenvirato; cuerpo de diez personas
**decency** [ˈdisənsɪ] *s* (*pl:* **-cies**) decencia, honestidad; **decencies** *spl* buenas costumbres; comodidades
**decennial** [dɪˈsɛnɪəl] *adj* decenal; *s* décimo aniversario; fiestas celebradas cada diez años
**decent** [ˈdisənt] *adj* decente, honesto
**decentralization** [diˌsɛntrəlɪˈzeʃən] *s* descentralización
**decentralize** [diˈsɛntrəlaɪz] *va* descentralizar
**deception** [dɪˈsɛpʃən] *s* decepción, engaño
**deceptive** [dɪˈsɛptɪv] *adj* engañoso
**deciare** [ˈdɛsɪɛr] *s* deciárea
**decibel** [ˈdɛsɪbɛl] *s* (phys.) decibel o decibelio
**decide** [dɪˈsaɪd] *va* decidir; *vn* decidir, decidirse; **to decide on** decidir (*p.ej., cierta gestion*); **to decide to** + *inf* decidir + *inf*, decidirse a + *inf*
**decided** [dɪˈsaɪdɪd] *adj* decidido
**decidedly** [dɪˈsaɪdɪdlɪ] *adv* decididamente
**deciduous** [dɪˈsɪdʒʊəs] o [dɪˈsɪdjʊəs] *adj* (bot. & zool.) deciduo
**decigram** o **decigramme** [ˈdɛsɪgræm] *s* decigramo
**deciliter** o **decilitre** [ˈdɛsɪˌlitər] *s* decilitro
**decillion** [dɪˈsɪljən] *s* (Brit.) decillón
**decimal** [ˈdɛsɪməl] *adj & s* decimal
**decimal fraction** *s* fracción decimal
**decimalize** [ˈdɛsɪməlaɪz] *va* decimalizar
**decimally** [ˈdɛsɪməlɪ] *adv* decimalmente
**decimal point** *s* punto decimal; coma (*usada más comúnmente en español*)
**decimate** [ˈdɛsɪmet] *va* diezmar
**decimation** [ˌdɛsɪˈmeʃən] *s* decimación
**decimeter** o **decimetre** [ˈdɛsɪˌmitər] *s* decímetro
**decipher** [dɪˈsaɪfər] *va* descifrar
**decipherable** [dɪˈsaɪfərəbəl] *adj* descifrable
**decipherer** [dɪˈsaɪfərər] *s* descifrador
**decipherment** [dɪˈsaɪfərmənt] *s* descifre
**decision** [dɪˈsɪʒən] *s* decisión
**decisive** [dɪˈsaɪsɪv] *adj* decisivo; resuelto, determinado
**decistere** [ˈdɛsɪstɪr] *s* deciestéreo
**deck** [dɛk] *s* (naut.) cubierta; baraja (*de naipes*); **on deck** (coll.) visible, listo, disponible; **to hit the deck** (slang) levantarse pronto; (slang) extenderse boca abajo; (slang) prepararse para obrar; *va* cubrir, ocultar; adornar, ataviar, engalanar, vestir
**deck chair** *s* (naut.) silla de cubierta
**deck hand** *s* (naut.) grumete, marinero de cubierta
**deck-land** [ˈdɛkˌlænd] *vn* (aer.) apontizar
**deck-landing** [ˈdɛkˌlændɪŋ] *s* (aer.) apontizaje
**deckle** [ˈdɛkəl] *s* cubierta (*bastidor*); barba (*desigualdad en los bordes del papel*)
**deckle edge** *s* barba
**deckle-edged** [ˈdɛkəlˌɛdʒd] *adj* barbado
**declaim** [dɪˈklem] *va & vn* declamar
**declaimer** [dɪˈklemər] *s* declamador
**declamation** [ˌdɛkləˈmeʃən] *s* declamación
**declamatory** [dɪˈklæməˌtorɪ] *adj* declamatorio
**declarable** [dɪˈklɛrəbəl] *adj* declarable
**declarant** [dɪˈklɛrənt] *s* declarante
**declaration** [ˌdɛkləˈreʃən] *s* declaración
**Declaration of Independence** *s* Declaración de la independencia
**declarative** [dɪˈklærətɪv] *adj* declarativo; (gram.) aseverativo, enunciativo
**declaratory** [dɪˈklærəˌtorɪ] *adj* declaratorio
**declare** [dɪˈklɛr] *va & vn* declarar
**declension** [dɪˈklɛnʃən] *s* declinación; (gram.) declinación
**declinable** [dɪˈklaɪnəbəl] *adj* declinable
**declination** [ˌdɛklɪˈneʃən] *s* declinación; (astr. & magnetism) declinación
**declinatory compass** [dɪˈklaɪnəˌtorɪ] *s* declinatorio
**declinatory plea** *s* (law) declinatoria
**decline** [dɪˈklaɪn] *s* declinación, bajada; baja (*de los precios*); bajón (*en la salud, el caudal, etc.*); ocaso (*del sol*); (coll.) consunción, tisis; **to be on the decline** (coll.) ir cabeza abajo (*decaer*); *va* rehusar, declinar; inclinar hacia abajo; (gram.) declinar; *vn* declinar; (gram.) declinar; **to decline to** + *inf* excusarse de + *inf*
**declivity** [dɪˈklɪvɪtɪ] *s* (*pl:* **-ties**) declividad
**decoct** [dɪˈkɑkt] *va* extraer por decocción
**decoction** [dɪˈkɑkʃən] *s* decocción; (pharm.) decocción
**decode** [diˈkod] *va* descifrar
**decoder** [diˈkodər] *s* descifrador
**decoding** [diˈkodɪŋ] *s* descifre
**decoherer** [ˌdikoˈhɪrər] *s* (rad.) descohesor
**décolletage** [ˌdekɑlˈtɑʒ] *s* escote o escotadura
**décolleté** [ˌdekɑlˈte] *adj* escotado (*dícese del vestido o la persona*)
**decolorization** [diˌkʌlərɪˈzeʃən] *s* decoloración
**decolorize** [diˈkʌləraɪz] *va* decolorar
**decompose** [ˌdikəmˈpoz] *va* descomponer; *vn* descomponerse
**decomposition** [ˌdikɑmpəˈzɪʃən] *s* descomposición
**decompression** [ˌdikəmˈprɛʃən] *s* descompresión
**decompression chamber** *s* cámara de descompresión
**decontaminate** [ˌdikənˈtæmɪnet] *va* descontaminar
**decontamination** [ˌdikənˌtæmɪˈneʃən] *s* descontaminación
**decontamination squad** *s* cuadrilla de descontaminación
**decontrol** [ˌdikənˈtrol] *s* supresión o termina-

ción del control; *va* suprimir o terminar el control de

**décor** [de'kɔr] *s* decoración; (theat.) decorado

**decorate** ['dɛkəret] *va* decorar; empapelar (*una pared*); pintar (*p.ej., una pared*); condecorar (*con una insignia de honor*)

**decoration** [,dɛkə'reʃən] *s* decoracion; condecoración (*insignia de honor*)

**Decoration Day** *s* (U.S.A.) día señalado para decorar las tumbas de los soldados muertos en batalla (*el 30 de mayo*)

**decorative** ['dɛkə,retɪv] *adj* decorativo

**decorator** ['dɛkə,retər] *s* decorador

**decorous** ['dɛkərəs] o [dɪ'korəs] *adj* decoroso

**decorum** [dɪ'korəm] *s* decoro

**decoy** [dɪ'kɔɪ] o ['dikɔɪ] *s* señuelo, añagaza; reclamo (*ave amaestrada*); trampa; entruchón (*persona*); [dɪ'kɔɪ] *va* atraer con señuelo; entruchar

**decrease** ['dikris] o [dɪ'kris] *s* disminución, decrecimiento; [dɪ'kris] *va* disminuir; *vn* disminuir, disminuirse, decrecer

**decree** [dɪ'kri] *s* decreto; *va* decretar

**decree law** *s* decreto-ley

**decrement** ['dɛkrɪmənt] *s* decremento, disminución; (rad.) decremento

**decremeter** [dɪ'krɛmɪtər] *s* (rad.) decrémetro

**decrepit** [dɪ'krɛpɪt] *adj* decrépito

**decrepitude** [dɪ'krɛpɪtjud] o [dɪ'krɛpɪtud] *s* decrepitud

**decrescendo** [,dekrə'ʃɛndo] *m* (*pl:* **-dos**) (mus.) decrescendo

**decretal** [dɪ'kritəl] *adj* decretal; *s* decretal; **decretals** *spl* decretales

**decretalist** [dɪ'kritəlɪst] *s* (theol.) decretalista

**decretist** [dɪ'kritɪst] *s* decretista

**decrial** [dɪ'kraɪəl] *s* vituperio; rebaja

**decry** [dɪ'kraɪ] (*pret & pp:* **-cried**) *va* vituperar; rebajar, desacreditar

**decubitus** [dɪ'kjubɪtəs] *s* (med.) decúbito; (path.) decúbito (*úlcera*)

**decumbent** [dɪ'kʌmbənt] *adj* decumbente; (bot.) decumbente

**decuple** ['dɛkjupəl] *adj & s* décuplo; *va* decuplar o decuplicar

**decurrent** [dɪ'kʌrənt] *adj* (bot.) decurrente

**decury** ['dɛkjərɪ] *s* (*pl:* **-ries**) decuria

**decussate** [dɪ'kʌsɪt] o [dɪ'kʌset] *adj* decuso o decusado; (bot.) decuso o decusado

**dedicate** ['dɛdɪket] *va* dedicar

**dedication** [,dɛdɪ'keʃən] *s* dedicación; dedicatoria (*p.ej., de un libro*)

**dedicative** ['dɛdɪ,ketɪv] *adj* dedicativo

**dedicator** ['dɛdɪ,ketər] *s* dedicante

**dedicatory** ['dɛdɪkə,torɪ] *adj* dedicatorio

**dedolation** [,dɛdə'leʃən] *s* (surg.) dedolación

**deduce** [dɪ'djus] o [dɪ'dus] *va* deducir; derivar

**deducible** [dɪ'djusɪbəl] o [dɪ'dusɪbəl] *adj* deducible

**deduct** [dɪ'dʌkt] *va* deducir

**deductible** [dɪ'dʌktɪbəl] *adj* deducible

**deduction** [dɪ'dʌkʃən] *s* deducción

**deductive** [dɪ'dʌktɪv] *adj* deductivo

**deed** [did] *s* acto, hecho; hazaña, proeza; (law) escritura; **in deed** en verdad; de obra, de hecho; *va* (law) traspasar por escritura

**deed of gift** *s* escritura de donación

**deem** [dim] *va & vn* pensar, creer, juzgar, conceptuar

**deemphasize** [di'ɛmfəsaɪz] *va* quitar importancia a

**deep** [dip] *adj* profundo; grave (*sonido*); subido (*color*); astuto; sagaz; de hondo, p.ej., **ten inches deep** diez pulgadas de hondo; **to go off the deep end** (coll.) adoptar una resolución temeraria; **deep in debt** cargado de deudas; **deep in politics** muy metido en política; **deep in thought** absorto en la meditación; **the deep** lo profundo; lo más intenso; la mar; el infierno; *adv* hondo; **deep into the night** hasta muy tarde la noche

**deep-chested** ['dip,tʃɛstɪd] *adj* ancho de pecho

**deepen** ['dipən] *va* profundizar; *vn* profundizarse

**deep-felt** ['dip,fɛlt] *adj* sentido, hondamente sentido

**deep-freeze** ['dip'friz] *s* (trademark) congeladora; (*pret:* **-froze;** *pp:* **-frozen**) *va* congelar; almacenar en congeladora

**deep-laid** ['dip,led] *adj* dispuesto con astucia

**deep mourning** *s* luto riguroso

**deep-rooted** ['dip,rutɪd] o ['dip,rʊtɪd] *adj* arraigado profundamente; afirmado, asegurado

**deep-sea** ['dip,si] *adj* de las profundidades del mar

**deep-sea fishing** *s* pesca de gran altura

**deep-sea lead** [lɛd] *s* (naut.) plomada para el sondeo profundo

**deep-seated** ['dip,sitɪd] *adj* arraigado profundamente; hundido; fijo sólidamente

**deep-set** ['dip,sɛt] *adj* puesto profundamente; fijo sólidamente

**Deep South** *s* (U.S.A.) el extremo meridional de los estados de Alabama, Georgia, Luisiana y Misisipí (*considerado como representante de la cultura y las tradiciones del Sur de los EE.UU.*)

**deepwater** ['dip,wɔtər] o ['dip,wɑtər] *adj* de gran altura

**deer** [dɪr] *s* (zool.) ciervo, venado

**deerhound** ['dɪr,haʊnd] *s* galgo escocés de pelo lanoso

**deerskin** ['dɪr,skɪn] *s* gamuza, piel de ciervo

**deerstalking** ['dɪr,stɔkɪŋ] *s* caza del venado al acecho

**def.** abr. de **defendant, deferred, defined, definite** y **definition**

**deface** [dɪ'fes] *va* desfigurar

**defacement** [dɪ'fesmənt] *s* desfiguración

**de facto** [di'fækto] *adv* de hecho; (law) de hecho

**defalcate** [dɪ'fælket] o ['difælket] *vn* desfalcar

**defalcation** [,difæl'keʃən] o [,dɛfəl'keʃən] *s* desfalco

**defamation** [,dɛfə'meʃən] o [,difə'meʃən] *s* difamación

**defamatory** [dɪ'fæmə,torɪ] *adj* difamatorio

**defame** [dɪ'fem] *va* difamar

**defamer** [dɪ'femər] *s* difamador

**default** [dɪ'fɔlt] *s* omisión, descuido; falta, incumplimiento; (law) rebeldía; **by default** (sport) por no presentarse; **in default of** por falta de; *va* dejar de cumplir; no pagar; (law) condenar en rebeldía; (sport) perder por no presentarse; *vn* faltar; (law) caer en rebeldía; (sport) perder por no presentarse

**defaulter** [dɪ'fɔltər] *s* delincuente; desfalcador; (law) rebelde

**defeat** [dɪ'fit] *s* vencimiento, derrota; *va* vencer, derrotar

**defeatism** [dɪ'fitɪzəm] *s* derrotismo

**defeatist** [dɪ'fitɪst] *adj & s* derrotista

**defecate** ['dɛfɪket] *va* defecar, clarificar; *vn* defecar

**defecation** [,dɛfɪ'keʃən] *s* defecación

**defect** [dɪ'fɛkt] o ['difɛkt] *s* defecto; [dɪ'fɛkt] *vn* desertar

**defection** [dɪ'fɛkʃən] *s* defección; fracaso, mal éxito

**defective** [dɪ'fɛktɪv] *adj* defectivo, defectuoso, deficiente; (gram.) defectivo

**defence** [dɪ'fɛns] *s* (Brit.) var. de **defense**

**defend** [dɪ'fɛnd] *va* defender; (law) defender

**defendant** [dɪ'fɛndənt] *s* (law) demandado; (law) acusado, reo

**defender** [dɪ'fɛndər] *s* defensor

**defense** [dɪ'fɛns] *s* defensa; (law & sport) defensa

**defense in depth** *s* (mil.) defensa en profundidad

**defenseless** [dɪ'fɛnslɪs] *adj* indefenso

**defense mechanism** *s* (physiol. & psychoanal.) defensa

**defensible** [dɪ'fɛnsɪbəl] *adj* defendible

**defensive** [dɪ'fɛnsɪv] *adj* defensivo; *s* defensiva; **to be on the defensive** estar a la defensiva

**defer** [dɪ'fʌr] (*pret & pp:* **-ferred;** *ger:* **-ferring**) *va* diferir, aplazar, dilatar; *vn* deferir; **to defer to** deferir a (*p.ej., el parecer de otro*)

**deference** ['dɛfərəns] *s* deferencia

**deferent** ['dɛfərənt] *adj* deferente; (anat.) deferente

**deferential** [,dɛfə'rɛnʃəl] *adj* deferente

**deferment** [dɪ'fʌrmənt] *s* aplazamiento, dilación

**defiance** [dɪ'faɪəns] *s* desafío; oposición obsti-

nada; **in defiance of** a despecho de; **to bid defiance to** o **to set at defiance** desafiar
**defiant** [dɪˈfaɪənt] *adj* desafiador; provocante
**deficiency** [dɪˈfɪʃənsɪ] *s* (*pl:* **-cies**) deficiencia, carencia; (com.) descubierto
**deficiency disease** *s* (med.) enfermedad por carencia, enfermedad carencial
**deficient** [dɪˈfɪʃənt] *adj* deficiente
**deficit** [ˈdɛfɪsɪt] *s* déficit; *adj* deficitario
**deficit spending** *s* gasto que produce déficit
**defier** [dɪˈfaɪər] *s* desafiador; provocador
**defilade** [ˌdɛfɪˈled] *s* (mil.) desenfilada; *va* (fort. & mil.) desenfilar; *vn* (fort. & mil.) desenfilarse
**defile** [dɪˈfaɪl] o [ˈdifaɪl] *s* desfiladero; [dɪˈfaɪl] *va* manchar, corromper, violar, deshonrar; *vn* desfilar
**defilement** [dɪˈfaɪlmənt] *s* corrupción, violación, deshonra
**defiler** [dɪˈfaɪlər] *s* corruptor, violador, deshonrador
**definable** [dɪˈfaɪnəbəl] *adj* definible
**define** [dɪˈfaɪn] *va* definir
**definite** [ˈdɛfɪnɪt] *adj* definido; (gram.) definido, determinado
**definite article** *s* (gram.) artículo definido, artículo determinado
**definition** [ˌdɛfɪˈnɪʃən] *s* definición; (opt.) definición
**definitive** [dɪˈfɪnɪtɪv] *adj* definitivo; *s* sentencia definitiva; (gram.) palabra limitativa
**deflagrate** [ˈdɛfləgret] *va* (chem.) hacer deflagrar; *vn* (chem.) deflagrar
**deflagration** [ˌdɛfləˈgreʃən] *s* (chem.) deflagración
**deflate** [dɪˈflet] *va* desinflar; (fig.) desinflar (*a una persona*)
**deflation** [dɪˈfleʃən] *s* desinflación; (econ.) deflación
**deflationary** [dɪˈfleʃənˌɛrɪ] *adj* deflacionista
**deflect** [dɪˈflɛkt] *va* desviar; *vn* desviarse
**deflection** [dɪˈflɛkʃən] *s* desviación, deflexión
**deflective** [dɪˈflɛktɪv] *adj* desviador
**deflector** [dɪˈflɛktər] *s* deflector; (naut.) deflector
**defloration** [ˌdɛfləˈreʃən] *s* desfloración
**deflower** [diˈflaʊər] *va* desflorar
**defoliate** [dɪˈfolɪet] *va* deshojar; *vn* deshojarse
**defoliation** [dɪˌfolɪˈeʃən] *s* defoliación
**deforce** [dɪˈfors] *va* (law) detentar
**deforcement** [dɪˈforsmənt] *s* (law) detentación
**deforciant** [dɪˈforʃənt] *s* (law) detentador
**deforest** [diˈfɑrɪst] o [diˈfɔrɪst] *va* desforestar
**deforestation** [diˌfɑrɪsˈteʃən] o [diˌfɔrɪsˈteʃən] *s* desforestación
**deform** [dɪˈfɔrm] *va* deformar
**deformation** [ˌdifɔrˈmeʃən] o [ˌdɛfərˈmeʃən] *s* deformación
**deformed** [dɪˈfɔrmd] *adj* deforme
**deformity** [dɪˈfɔrmɪtɪ] *s* (*pl:* **-ties**) deformidad
**defraud** [dɪˈfrɔd] *va* defraudar
**defrauder** [dɪˈfrɔdər] *s* defraudador
**defray** [dɪˈfre] *va* sufragar, subvenir a
**defrayal** [dɪˈfreəl] o **defrayment** [dɪˈfremənt] *s* pago, sufragación
**defrost** [diˈfrɔst] o [diˈfrɑst] *va* deshelar, descongelar
**defroster** [diˈfrɔstər] o [diˈfrɑstər] *s* desescarchador, descongelador
**defrosting** [diˈfrɔstɪŋ] o [diˈfrɑstɪŋ] *s* descongelación, deshielo
**deft** [dɛft] *adj* diestro, hábil; ligero
**deftness** [ˈdɛftnɪs] *s* destreza, habilidad; ligereza
**defunct** [dɪˈfʌŋkt] *adj* difunto
**defy** [dɪˈfaɪ] o [ˈdifaɪ] *s* (*pl:* **-fies**) (slang) desafío; [dɪˈfaɪ] (*pret & pp:* **-fied**) *va* desafiar; oponerse obstinadamente a; resistir
**deg.** abr. de **degree** o **degrees**
**degas** [diˈgæs] (*pret & pp:* **-gassed;** *ger:* **-gassing**) *va* desgasificar
**degasify** [diˈgæsɪfaɪ] (*pret & pp:* **-fied**) *va* var. de **degas**
**de Gaullist** [dəˈgolɪst] *adj & s* degaullista
**degauss** [dɪˈgaʊs] o [dɪˈgɔs] *va* desgausar
**degeneracy** [dɪˈdʒɛnərəsɪ] *s* degeneración
**degenerate** [dɪˈdʒɛnərɪt] *adj & s* degenerado; [dɪˈdʒɛnəret] *vn* degenerar
**degeneration** [dɪˌdʒɛnəˈreʃən] *s* degeneración
**degenerative** [dɪˈdʒɛnəˌretɪv] *adj* degenerativo
**deglutition** [ˌdigluˈtɪʃən] o [ˌdɛgluˈtɪʃən] *s* deglución
**degradation** [ˌdɛgrəˈdeʃən] *s* degradación; (geol.) degradación
**degrade** [dɪˈgred] *va* degradar; (geol.) degradar
**degrading** [dɪˈgredɪŋ] *adj* degradante
**degree** [dɪˈgri] *s* grado; (educ.) grado (*p.ej., de bachiller*); (gram., math. & mus.) grado; **by degrees** de grado en grado; **to a degree** algo, un poco; en sumo grado; **to take a degree** recibir un grado o título
**dehisce** [diˈhɪs] *vn* abrirse, hendirse
**dehiscence** [diˈhɪsəns] *s* (biol. & bot.) dehiscencia
**dehiscent** [diˈhɪsənt] *adj* dehiscente
**dehorn** [diˈhɔrn] *va* descornar
**dehumanization** [diˌhjumənɪˈzeʃən] *s* deshumanización
**dehumanize** [diˈhjumənaɪz] *va* deshumanizar
**dehumidifier** [ˌdihjuˈmɪdɪˌfaɪər] *s* deshumedecedor, reductor de humedad
**dehumidify** [ˌdihjuˈmɪdɪfaɪ] (*pret & pp:* **-fied**) *va* deshumedecer, deshumidificar
**dehydrate** [diˈhaɪdret] *va* deshidratar; *vn* deshidratarse
**dehydration** [ˌdihaɪˈdreʃən] *s* deshidratación
**dehypnotize** [diˈhɪpnətaɪz] *va* deshipnotizar
**deice** [diˈaɪs] *va* (aer.) deshelar
**deicer** [diˈaɪsər] *s* (aer.) deshelador
**deicidal** [ˌdiɪˈsaɪdəl] *adj* deicida
**deicide** [ˈdiɪsaɪd] *s* deicida (*persona*); deicidio (*acción*)
**deific** [diˈɪfɪk] *adj* deífico
**deification** [ˌdiɪfɪˈkeʃən] *s* deificación
**deify** [ˈdiɪfaɪ] (*pret & pp:* **-fied**) *va* deificar
**deign** [den] *va* dignarse dar o conceder; *vn* dignarse; **to deign to** + *inf* dignarse + *inf*
**deism** [ˈdiɪzəm] *s* deísmo
**deist** [ˈdiɪst] *s* deísta
**deistic** [diˈɪstɪk] o **deistical** [diˈɪstɪkəl] *adj* deísta
**deity** [ˈdiɪtɪ] *s* (*pl:* **-ties**) deidad; **the Deity** Dios
**deject** [dɪˈdʒɛkt] *va* abatir, desanimar
**dejected** [dɪˈdʒɛktɪd] *adj* abatido, desanimado
**dejection** [dɪˈdʒɛkʃən] *s* abatimiento, desánimo; (physiol.) deyección
**dekaliter** [ˈdɛkəˌlitər] *s* var. de **decaliter**
**dekameter** [ˈdɛkəˌmitər] *s* var. de **decameter**
**del.** abr. de **delegate** y **delete**
**Del.** abr. de **Delaware**
**delay** [dɪˈle] *s* dilación, retraso, tardanza; *va* dilatar, retrasar; *vn* tardar, demorarse
**delayed-action fuse** [dɪˈledˈækʃən] *s* (mil.) espoleta de explosión retardada
**delayed-time switch** [dɪˈledˈtaɪm] *s* (elec.) llave de tiempo atrasado
**dele** [ˈdilɪ] *s* (print.) dele; *va* (print.) suprimir
**delectable** [dɪˈlɛktəbəl] *adj* deleitable
**delectation** [ˌdilɛkˈteʃən] *s* delectación
**delegacy** [ˈdɛlɪgəsɪ] *s* (*pl:* **-cies**) delegación
**delegate** [ˈdɛlɪget] o [ˈdɛlɪgɪt] *s* delegado; congresista; [ˈdɛlɪget] *va* delegar
**delegation** [ˌdɛlɪˈgeʃən] *s* delegación
**delete** [dɪˈlit] *va* suprimir
**deleterious** [ˌdɛlɪˈtɪrɪəs] *adj* deletéreo
**deletion** [dɪˈliʃən] *s* supresión
**delft** [dɛlft] o **delftware** [ˈdɛlftˌwɛr] *s* porcelana de Delft
**Delian** [ˈdilɪən] *adj & s* delio
**deliberate** [dɪˈlɪbərɪt] *adj* reflexionado, pensado; circunspecto, cauto; espacioso, lento, tardo; [dɪˈlɪbəret] *va & vn* deliberar
**deliberation** [dɪˌlɪbəˈreʃən] *s* deliberación
**deliberative** [dɪˈlɪbəˌretɪv] *adj* deliberativo; deliberante
**delicacy** [ˈdɛlɪkəsɪ] *s* (*pl:* **-cies**) delicadeza; golosina (*manjar delicado*)
**delicate** [ˈdɛlɪkɪt] *adj* delicado
**delicatessen** [ˌdɛlɪkəˈtɛsən] *s* ultramarinos; tienda de ultramarinos, tienda de fiambres, ensaladas, queso, pescado ahumado, etc.
**delicious** [dɪˈlɪʃəs] *adj* delicioso, sabroso
**delight** [dɪˈlaɪt] *s* deleite, delicia; **to take delight in** deleitarse con o en; **to take delight in** + *ger* deleitarse en + *inf; va* deleitar; **to be**

**delighted to** + *inf* deleitarse en + *inf; vn* deleitarse; **to delight in** deleitarse con o en; **to delight in** + *ger* deleitarse en + *inf*
**delightful** [dɪˈlaɪtfəl] *adj* deleitoso, delicioso
**Delilah** [dɪˈlaɪlə] *s* (Bib.) Dalila
**delimit** [dɪˈlɪmɪt] *va* delimitar
**delimitation** [dɪˌlɪmɪˈteʃən] *s* delimitación
**delineate** [dɪˈlɪnɪet] *va* delinear
**delineation** [dɪˌlɪnɪˈeʃən] *s* delineación
**delineator** [dɪˈlɪnɪˌetər] *s* delineador, delineante
**delinquency** [dɪˈlɪŋkwənsɪ] *s* (*pl:* **-cies**) culpa, delincuencia; morosidad (*en el pago*)
**delinquent** [dɪˈlɪŋkwənt] *adj* culpado, delincuente; moroso (*en el pago, etc.*); debido y no pagado; *s* culpado; deudor moroso
**deliquesce** [ˌdɛlɪˈkwɛs] *vn* liquidarse lentamente, atrayendo la humedad del aire; derretirse
**deliquescence** [ˌdɛlɪˈkwɛsəns] *s* delicuescencia
**deliquescent** [ˌdɛlɪˈkwɛsənt] *adj* delicuescente
**delirious** [dɪˈlɪrɪəs] *adj* delirante; **to be delirious** delirar
**delirium** [dɪˈlɪrɪəm] *s* (*pl:* **-ums** o **-a** [ə]) delirio
**delirium tremens** [ˈtrimənz] *s* (path.) delírium tremens
**deliver** [dɪˈlɪvər] *va* librar, libertar; entregar; distribuir (*el correo*); dar, asestar, descargar (*un golpe*); lanzar (*p.ej., una pelota*); recitar, pronunciar (*un discurso*); rendir, transmitir (*energía*); partear (*a la mujer que está de parto*); **to be delivered** parir; **to deliver oneself of** aliviarse de; comunicar
**deliverance** [dɪˈlɪvərəns] *s* libramiento, liberación; rescate; profesión, dictamen; alumbramiento
**deliverer** [dɪˈlɪvərər] *s* librador, salvador; entregador; relator; distribuidor
**delivery** [dɪˈlɪvərɪ] *s* (*pl:* **-ies**) liberación; rescate; entrega; distribución (*del correo*); parto, alumbramiento; discurso, modo de expresarse
**deliveryman** [dɪˈlɪvərɪmən] *s* (*pl:* **-men**) entregador, recadero, mozo de reparto
**delivery room** *s* sala de alumbramiento (*de un hospital*)
**delivery table** *s* (print.) sacador
**delivery truck** *s* furgoneta, sedán de reparto
**dell** [dɛl] *s* vallecito, vallejuelo
**Delos** [ˈdilɑs] *s* Delos
**delouse** [diˈlaus] o [diˈlauz] *va* despiojar, espulgar
**Delphi** [ˈdɛlfaɪ] *s* Delfos
**Delphian** [ˈdɛlfɪən] *adj* délfico; ambiguo
**Delphic** [ˈdɛlfɪk] *adj* délfico; ambiguo
**Delphic oracle** *s* oráculo délfico o de Delfos
**delphinium** [dɛlˈfɪnɪəm] *s* (bot.) espuela de caballero (*Delphinium ajacis*); (bot.) consólida real (*Delphinium consolida*)
**delta** [ˈdɛltə] *s* delta
**delta connection** *s* (elec.) conexión en delta
**delta wing** *s* (aer.) ala en delta
**deltoid** [ˈdɛltɔɪd] *adj* deltoides (*triangular*); (anat.) deltoides; *s* (anat.) deltoides
**deltoid muscle** *s* (anat.) deltoides
**delude** [dɪˈlud] *va* deludir, engañar
**deluder** [dɪˈludər] *s* delusor, engañador
**deluge** [ˈdɛljudʒ] *s* diluvio; (fig.) diluvio; **the Deluge** el Diluvio; *va* inundar; **to deluge with** inundar de
**delusion** [dɪˈluʒən] *s* engaño, decepción
**delusive** [dɪˈlusɪv] o **delusory** [dɪˈlusərɪ] *adj* delusorio; ilusivo
**de luxe** [dɪˈluks] o [dɪˈlʌks] *adj & adv* de lujo
**delve** [dɛlv] *va* cavar; *vn* cavar; insudar (*afanarse*); buscar (*explorar*); **to delve into** sondear, profundizar
**Dem.** abr. de **Democrat** y **Democratic**
**demagnetization** [diˌmægnɪtɪˈzeʃən] *s* desimanación, desimantación
**demagnetize** [diˈmægnɪtaɪz] *va* desimanar, desimantar
**demagog** [ˈdɛməgɑg] *s* demagogo
**demagogic** [ˌdɛməˈgɑdʒɪk] o [ˌdɛməˈgɑgɪk] *adj* demagógico
**demagogue** [ˈdɛməgɑg] *s* var. de **demagog**
**demagoguery** [ˈdɛməˌgɑgərɪ] o **demagogy** [ˈdɛməˌgɑdʒɪ] o [ˈdɛməˌgɑgɪ] *s* demagogia
**demand** [dɪˈmænd] o [dɪˈmɑnd] *s* demanda; (com.) demanda; (law) demanda (*reclamación*); **on demand** a la presentación; **to be in demand** tener demanda; *va* demandar; pedir perentoriamente
**demanding** [dɪˈmændɪŋ] o [dɪˈmɑndɪŋ] *adj* exigente
**demarcate** [ˈdimarket] o [dɪˈmarket] *va* demarcar
**demarcation** [ˌdimɑrˈkeʃən] *s* demarcación
**démarche** [deˈmarʃ] *s* gestión, paso; (dipl.) diligencia, gestión
**demean** [dɪˈmin] *va* degradar; **to demean oneself** degradarse; portarse, conducirse; *vn* portarse, conducirse
**demeanor** [dɪˈminər] *s* porte, conducta, comportamiento
**demeanour** [dɪˈminər] *s* (Brit.) var. de **demeanor**
**demented** [dɪˈmɛntɪd] *adj* demente
**dementia** [dɪˈmɛnʃə] *s* demencia
**dementia praecox** [ˈprikɑks] *s* (path.) demencia precoz
**demerit** [diˈmɛrɪt] *s* demérito; nota de desaprobación
**demesne** [dɪˈmen] o [dɪˈmin] *s* tierra solariega; heredad; dominio; región
**Demeter** [dɪˈmitər] *s* (myth.) Deméter o Demetria
**demigod** [ˈdɛmɪˌgɑd] *s* semidiós
**demigoddess** [ˈdɛmɪˌgɑdɪs] *s* semidiosa
**demigorge** [ˈdɛmɪˌgɔrdʒ] *s* (fort.) semigola
**demijohn** [ˈdɛmɪdʒɑn] *s* damajuana
**demilitarization** [diˌmɪlɪtərɪˈzeʃən] *s* desmilitarización
**demilitarize** [diˈmɪlɪtəraɪz] *va* desmilitarizar
**demimondaine** [ˌdɛmɪmɑnˈden] *s* mujer mundana
**demimonde** [ˈdɛmɪmɑnd] *s* mujeres mundanas, mujeres de reputación equívoca
**demineralization** [diˌmɪnərəlɪˈzeʃən] *s* (med.) desmineralización
**demise** [dɪˈmaɪz] *s* fallecimiento; transmisión de la corona; (law) traslación de dominio; *va* (law) transferir, transferir por testamento o por arriendo
**demisemiquaver** [ˈdɛmɪˈsɛmɪˌkwevər] *s* (mus.) fusa
**demission** [dɪˈmɪʃən] *s* dimisión
**demit** [dɪˈmɪt] (*pret & pp:* **-mitted;** *ger:* **-mitting**) *va & vn* dimitir
**demitasse** [ˈdɛmɪˌtæs] o [ˈdɛmɪˌtɑs] *s* taza pequeña, tacita de café
**Demiurge** [ˈdɛmɪʌrdʒ] *s* (philos.) demiurgo
**demobilization** [diˌmobɪlɪˈzeʃən] *s* desmovilización
**demobilize** [diˈmobɪlaɪz] *va* desmovilizar
**democracy** [dɪˈmɑkrəsɪ] *s* (*pl:* **-cies**) democracia
**democrat** [ˈdɛməkræt] *s* demócrata
**democratic** [ˌdɛməˈkrætɪk] *adj* demócrata; democrático
**democratically** [ˌdɛməˈkrætɪkəlɪ] *adv* democráticamente
**democratization** [dɪˌmɑkrətɪˈzeʃən] *s* democratización
**democratize** [dɪˈmɑkrətaɪz] *va* democratizar; *vn* democratizarse
**Democritus** [dɪˈmɑkrɪtəs] *s* Demócrito
**demodulate** [diˈmɑdʒəlet] *va* (rad.) desmodular
**Demogorgon** [ˌdimoˈgɔrgən] o [ˌdɛmoˈgɔrgən] *s* (myth.) Demogorgón
**demographic** [ˌdiməˈgræfɪk] o **demographical** [ˌdiməˈgræfɪkəl] *adj* demográfico
**demography** [dɪˈmɑgrəfɪ] *s* demografía
**demoiselle** [ˌdɛmwɑˈzɛl] *s* damisela; (orn.) antropoide, grulla de Numidia; (ent.) caballito del diablo
**demolish** [dɪˈmɑlɪʃ] *va* demoler
**demolisher** [dɪˈmɑlɪʃər] *s* demoledor
**demolishment** [dɪˈmɑlɪʃmənt] *s* demolición
**demolition** [ˌdɛməˈlɪʃən] o [ˌdiməˈlɪʃən] *s* demolición
**demolition bomb** *s* bomba de demolición
**demolition squad** *s* cuadrilla de demolición
**demon** [ˈdimən] *s* demonio
**demonetization** [diˌmɑnɪtɪˈzeʃən] o [diˌmʌnɪtɪˈzeʃən] *s* desmonetización
**demonetize** [diˈmɑnɪtaɪz] o [diˈmʌnɪtaɪz] *va* desmonetizar
**demoniac** [dɪˈmonɪæk] *adj & s* demoníaco

**demoniacal** [ˌdiməˈnaɪəkəl] *adj* demoníaco
**demonic** [diˈmɑnɪk] *adj* demoníaco
**demonism** [ˈdimənɪzəm] *s* demonismo
**demonolatry** [ˌdimənˈɑlətrɪ] *s* demonolatría
**demonology** [ˌdimənˈɑlədʒɪ] *s* demonología
**demonomancy** [ˌdimənˈɑmənsɪ] *s* demonomancia
**demonstrability** [dɪˌmɑnstrəˈbɪlɪtɪ] o [ˌdɛmənstrəˈbɪlɪtɪ] *s* demostrabilidad
**demonstrable** [dɪˈmɑnstrəbəl] o [ˈdɛmənstrəbəl] *adj* demostrable
**demonstrably** [dɪˈmɑnstrəblɪ] o [ˈdɛmənstrəblɪ] *adv* demostrablemente
**demonstrate** [ˈdɛmənstret] *va* demostrar; *vn* manifestar
**demonstration** [ˌdɛmənˈstreʃən] *s* demostración; manifestación (*reunión pública para dar a conocer un sentimiento u opinión*)
**demonstrative** [dɪˈmɑnstrətɪv] *adj* demostrativo; (gram.) demostrativo; *s* (gram.) demostrativo
**demonstrator** [ˈdɛmənˌstretər] *s* demostrador; vehículo de demostraciones; alborotador, manifestante
**demoralization** [dɪˌmɑrəlɪˈzeʃən] o [dɪˌmɔrəlɪˈzeʃən] *s* desmoralización
**demoralize** [dɪˈmɑrəlaɪz] o [dɪˈmɔrəlaɪz] *va* desmoralizar
**demoralizing** [dɪˈmɑrəlaɪzɪŋ] o [dɪˈmɔrəlaɪzɪŋ] *adj* desmoralizador
**Demosthenes** [dɪˈmɑsθəniz] *s* Demóstenes
**demote** [dɪˈmot] *va* degradar
**demotic** [dɪˈmɑtɪk] *adj* demótico
**demotion** [dɪˈmoʃən] *s* degradación
**demount** [diˈmaʊnt] *va* desmontar
**demountable** [diˈmaʊntəbəl] *adj* desmontable
**demulcent** [dɪˈmʌlsənt] *adj* & *s* demulcente
**demulsibility** [dɪˌmʌlsɪˈbɪlɪtɪ] *s* (chem.) demulsibilidad
**demulsify** [dɪˈmʌlsɪfaɪ] (*pret* & *pp:* **-fied**) *va* (chem.) demulsionar
**demur** [dɪˈmʌr] *s* objeción; vacilación, irresolución; (*pret* & *pp:* **-murred;** *ger:* **-murring**) *vn* objetar; vacilar
**demure** [dɪˈmjʊr] *adj* recatado, modesto; gazmoño; serio, sobrio, grave
**demurrage** [dɪˈmʌrɪdʒ] *s* (com.) estadía
**demurrer** [dɪˈmʌrər] *s* objeción; persona que objeta; (law) excepción
**demy** [dɪˈmaɪ] *s* (*pl:* **-mies**) papel marquilla; becario de Magdalen College, Oxford
**Den.** abr. de **Denmark**
**den** [dɛn] *s* madriguera (*de animales o ladrones*); cuchitril (*habitación pequeña y sucia*); antro, nido (*de gente de mala conducta*); cuarto de estudio; (Bib.) fosa (*de los leones*)
**denarius** [dɪˈnɛrɪəs] *s* (*pl:* **-i** [aɪ]) denario
**denationalization** [diˌnæʃənəlɪˈzeʃən] *s* desnacionalización
**denationalize** [diˈnæʃənəlaɪz] *va* desnacionalizar
**denaturalization** [diˌnætʃərəlɪˈzeʃən] *s* desnaturalización
**denaturalize** [diˈnætʃərəlaɪz] *va* desnaturalizar
**denaturation** [diˌnetʃəˈreʃən] *s* (chem.) desnaturalización
**denature** [diˈnetʃər] *va* (chem.) desnaturalizar
**denatured alcohol** *s* alcohol desnaturalizado
**denazification** [diˌnɑtsɪfɪˈkeʃən] o [diˌnætsɪfɪˈkeʃən] *s* desnazificación
**denazify** [diˈnɑtsɪfaɪ] o [diˈnætsɪfaɪ] (*pret* & *pp:* **-fied**) *va* desnazificar
**dendriform** [ˈdɛndrɪfɔrm] *adj* dendriforme
**dendrite** [ˈdɛndraɪt] *s* (anat., physiol. & mineral.) dendrita
**dendritic** [dɛnˈdrɪtɪk] o **dendritical** [dɛnˈdrɪtɪkəl] *adj* dendrítico
**dendrography** [dɛnˈdrɑgrəfɪ] *s* dendrografía
**dendroid** [ˈdɛndrɔɪd] *adj* dendroide
**dendrometer** [dɛnˈdrɑmɪtər] *s* dendrómetro
**dengue** [ˈdɛŋge] o [ˈdɛŋgɪ] *s* (path.) dengue
**deniable** [dɪˈnaɪəbəl] *adj* negable
**denial** [dɪˈnaɪəl] *s* negación; abnegación
**denier** [dɪˈnaɪər] *s* negador
**denim** [ˈdɛnɪm] *s* dril de algodón
**Denis** [ˈdɛnɪs] *s* Dionisio; **Saint Denis** San Dionisio
**denitrification** [diˌnaɪtrɪfɪˈkeʃən] *s* desnitrificación
**denitrify** [diˈnaɪtrɪfaɪ] (*pret* & *pp:* **-fied**) *va* desnitrificar
**denizen** [ˈdɛnɪzən] *s* habitante; extranjero naturalizado; animal naturalizado, planta naturalizada, voz naturalizada
**Denmark** [ˈdɛnmɑrk] *s* Dinamarca
**den of vice** *s* nido de vicios
**denominate** [dɪˈnɑmɪnɪt] o [dɪˈnɑmɪnet] *adj* denominado; [dɪˈnɑmɪnet] *va* denominar
**denomination** [dɪˌnɑmɪˈneʃən] *s* denominación; categoría, clase; valor; (eccl.) secta, confesión
**denominational** [dɪˌnɑmɪˈneʃənəl] *adj* sectario
**denominationalism** [dɪˌnɑmɪˈneʃənəlɪzəm] *s* sectarismo
**denominative** [dɪˈnɑmɪˌnetɪv] *adj* denominativo; (gram.) denominativo; *s* (gram.) denominativo
**denominator** [dɪˈnɑmɪˌnetər] *s* denominador; (math.) denominador
**denotation** [ˌdinoˈteʃən] *s* denotación
**denotative** [dɪˈnotətɪv] *adj* denotativo
**denote** [dɪˈnot] *va* denotar
**denouement** o **dénouement** [deˈnumɑ̃] *s* desenlace
**denounce** [dɪˈnaʊns] *va* denunciar; censurar; (dipl. & min.) denunciar
**denouncement** [dɪˈnaʊnsmənt] *s* denuncia, denunciación; censura; (min.) denuncio
**denouncer** [dɪˈnaʊnsər] *s* denunciador; censurador
**de novo** [diˈnovo] (Lat.) de nuevo
**dense** [dɛns] *adj* denso; estúpido
**densimeter** [dɛnˈsɪmɪtər] *s* densímetro
**densimetry** [dɛnˈsɪmɪtrɪ] *s* densimetría
**density** [ˈdɛnsɪtɪ] *s* (*pl:* **-ties**) densidad
**dent** [dɛnt] *s* abolladura; *va* abollar; *vn* abollarse
**dental** [ˈdɛntəl] *adj* dental; (phonet.) dental; *s* (phonet.) dental
**dental floss** *s* hilo dental, seda encerada
**dentalization** [ˌdɛntəlɪˈzeʃən] *s* (phonet.) dentalización
**dentalize** [ˈdɛntəlaɪz] *va* (phonet.) dentalizar
**dental pulp** *s* (anat.) pulpa
**dental surgeon** *s* cirujano-dentista
**dentate** [ˈdɛntet] *adj* dentado
**dentex** [ˈdɛntɛks] *s* (ichth.) dentón
**denticulate** [dɛnˈtɪkjəlet] *adj* dentellado, denticulado
**denticulation** [dɛnˌtɪkjəˈleʃən] *s* denticulación
**dentifrice** [ˈdɛntɪfrɪs] *s* dentífrico
**dentil** [ˈdɛntɪl] *s* (arch.) dentellón, dentículo
**dentilabial** [ˌdɛntɪˈlebɪəl] *adj* & *s* (phonet.) dentilabial
**dentilingual** [ˌdɛntɪˈlɪŋgwəl] *adj* & *s* (phonet.) dentilingual
**dentin** [ˈdɛntɪn] o **dentine** [ˈdɛntin] o [ˈdɛntɪn] *s* (anat.) dentina
**dentiroster** [ˌdɛntɪˈrɑstər] *s* (orn.) dentirrostro
**dentirostral** [ˌdɛntɪˈrɑstrəl] *adj* dentirrostro
**dentist** [ˈdɛntɪst] *s* dentista
**dentistry** [ˈdɛntɪstrɪ] *s* dentistería, odontología
**dentition** [dɛnˈtɪʃən] *s* dentición
**denture** [ˈdɛntʃər] *s* dentadura; dentadura artificial
**denudate** [ˈdɛnjudet] o [dɪˈnjudɪt] *adj* denudado; [ˈdɛnjudet] o [dɪˈnjudet] *va* desnudar
**denudation** [ˌdɛnjuˈdeʃən] *s* denudación; desposeimiento
**denude** [dɪˈnjud] o [dɪˈnud] *va* desnudar; desposeer; *vn* desposeer
**denunciate** [dɪˈnʌnsɪet] o [dɪˈnʌnʃɪet] *va* denunciar
**denunciation** [dɪˌnʌnsɪˈeʃən] o [dɪˌnʌnʃɪˈeʃən] *s* denunciación, denuncia; censura; (dipl. & min.) denuncia
**denunciator** [dɪˈnʌnsɪˌetər] o [dɪˈnʌnʃɪˌetər] *s* denunciador
**denunciatory** [dɪˈnʌnsɪəˌtorɪ] o [dɪˈnʌnʃɪəˌtorɪ] *adj* denunciatorio
**deny** [dɪˈnaɪ] (*pret* & *pp:* **-nied**) *va* negar; **to deny having** + *pp* negar haber + *pp;* **to deny oneself** negarse a sí mismo; **to deny oneself to callers** negarse; *vn* negar
**Denys, Saint** [ˈdɛnɪs] var. de **Denis, Saint**

**deobstruent** [di'abstruənt] *adj & s* (med.) desobstruyente
**deodar** ['diodar] *s* (bot.) cedro deodara, cedro de la India
**deodorant** [di'odərənt] *adj & s* desodorante
**deodorization** [di,odərɪ'zeʃən] *s* desodorización
**deodorize** [di'odəraɪz] *va* desodorizar
**deodorizer** [di'odə,raɪzər] *s* desodorante, inodoro
**deontology** [,dian'taləd͡ʒɪ] *s* deontología
**deoxidation** [di,aksɪ'deʃən] *s* desoxidación
**deoxidizable** [di'aksɪ,daɪzəbəl] *adj* desoxidable
**deoxidize** [di'aksɪdaɪz] *va* desoxidar
**deoxidizer** [di'aksɪ,daɪzər] *s* desoxidante, desoxigenante
**deoxygenate** [di'aksɪd͡ʒənet] *va* desoxigenar
**deoxygenation** [di,aksɪd͡ʒə'neʃən] *s* desoxigenación
**deozonize** [di'ozonaɪz] *va* desozonizar
**dep.** abr. de **department, departs, deponent** y **deputy**
**depart** [dɪ'part] *va* **to depart this life** partir de esta vida; *vn* partir; fallecer, morir; apartarse, desistir
**departed** [dɪ'partɪd] *adj* difunto; pasado; *s* difunto; *spl* difuntos
**department** [dɪ'partmənt] *s* departamento; ministerio
**departmental** [,dipart'mɛntəl] *adj* departamental
**Department of Defense** *s* (U.S.A.) ministerio de Defensa Nacional
**Department of Justice** *s* (U.S.A.) ministerio de Justicia
**Department of State** *s* (U.S.A.) ministerio de Asuntos Exteriores
**Department of the Air Force** *s* (U.S.A.) ministerio del Aire
**Department of the Army** *s* (U.S.A.) ministerio del Ejército
**Department of the Interior** *s* (U.S.A.) ministerio de la Gobernación
**Department of the Lord Chancellor** *s* (Brit.) ministerio de Justicia
**Department of the Navy** *s* (U.S.A.) ministerio de Marina
**department store** *s* grandes almacenes
**departure** [dɪ'partʃər] *s* salida, partida; desviación; nuevo curso
**depend** [dɪ'pɛnd] *vn* depender; pender, colgar; **that depends** según y conforme; **to depend on** o **upon** depender de
**dependability** [dɪ,pɛndə'bɪlɪtɪ] *s* confiabilidad
**dependable** [dɪ'pɛndəbəl] *adj* confiable, seguro, fidedigno
**dependant** [dɪ'pɛndənt] *adj & s* var. de **dependent**
**dependence** [dɪ'pɛndəns] *s* dependencia
**dependency** [dɪ'pɛndənsɪ] *s* (*pl:* **-cies**) dependencia; posesión (*territorio, país*)
**dependent** [dɪ'pɛndənt] *adj* dependiente; pendiente, colgante; *s* dependiente, carga de familia, familiar dependiente
**dephase** [di'fez] *va* (elec.) defasar
**dephlegmate** [di'flɛgmet] *va* deflegmar
**depict** [dɪ'pɪkt] *va* pintar; dibujar, representar, describir
**depiction** [dɪ'pɪkʃən] *s* pintura; representación, descripción
**depilate** ['dɛpɪlet] *va* depilar
**depilation** [,dɛpɪ'leʃən] *s* depilación
**depilatory** [dɪ'pɪlə,torɪ] *adj & s* depilatorio
**deplete** [dɪ'plit] *va* agotar; depauperar
**depletion** [dɪ'pliʃən] *s* agotamiento; depauperación
**deplorable** [dɪ'plorəbəl] *adj* deplorable
**deplore** [dɪ'plor] *va* deplorar
**deploy** [dɪ'plɔɪ] *va* (mil.) desplegar; *vn* (mil.) desplegarse
**deployment** [dɪ'plɔɪmənt] *s* (mil.) despliegue
**depolarization** [di,polərɪ'zeʃən] *s* (chem. & phys.) despolarización
**depolarize** [di'poləraɪz] *va* (chem. & phys.) despolarizar
**depolarizer** [di'polə,raɪzər] *s* (chem. & phys.) despolarizador
**depone** [dɪ'pon] *va & vn* (law) deponer
**deponent** [dɪ'ponənt] *adj* (gram.) deponente; *s* (law) deponente; (gram.) verbo deponente
**depopulate** [di'papjəlet] *va* despoblar
**depopulation** [di,papjə'leʃən] *s* despoblación
**deport** [dɪ'port] *va* deportar; **to deport oneself** portarse, conducirse
**deportation** [,dipor'teʃən] *s* deportación
**deportee** [,dipor'ti] *s* deportado
**deportment** [dɪ'portmənt] *s* porte, conducta, comportamiento
**deposal** [dɪ'pozəl] *s* deposición
**depose** [dɪ'poz] *va* deponer; (law) deponer; *vn* (law) deponer
**deposit** [dɪ'pazɪt] *s* depósito; señal (*dinero que se da como anticipo*); (min.) yacimiento; **on deposit** en depósito; en el banco; *va* depositar; dar para señal; *vn* depositarse
**deposit account** *s* cuenta corriente
**depositary** [dɪ'pazɪ,tɛrɪ] *s* (*pl:* **-ies**) depositario (*persona*); depósito, almacén
**deposition** [,dɛpə'zɪʃən] o [,dipə'zɪʃən] *s* deposición; depósito; (law) deposición
**depositor** [dɪ'pazɪtər] *s* depositador, cuentacorrentista, imponente
**depository** [dɪ'pazɪ,torɪ] *adj* depositario; *s* (*pl:* **-ries**) depósito, almacén; depositario (*persona*); depositaría
**depot** ['dipo] o ['dɛpo] *s* depósito, almacén; (rail.) estación; (mil.) depósito
**depravation** [,dɛprə'veʃən] *s* depravación
**deprave** [dɪ'prev] *va* depravar
**depraved** [dɪ'prevd] *adj* depravado
**depravity** [dɪ'prævɪtɪ] *s* (*pl:* **-ties**) depravación
**deprecate** ['dɛprɪket] *va* desaprobar
**deprecation** [,dɛprɪ'keʃən] *s* desaprobación
**deprecative** ['dɛprɪ,ketɪv] *adj* deprecativo
**deprecatory** ['dɛprɪkə,torɪ] *adj* de desaprobación; deprecatorio
**depreciate** [dɪ'priʃɪet] *va* depreciar (*rebajar el valor o el precio de*); despreciar, desestimar; *vn* depreciarse
**depreciation** [dɪ,priʃɪ'eʃən] *s* depreciación (*disminución del valor*); desaprecio, desestimación
**depreciative** [dɪ'priʃɪ,etɪv] o **depreciatory** [dɪ'priʃɪə,torɪ] *adj* despreciativo
**depredate** ['dɛprɪdet] *va* depredar
**depredation** [,dɛprɪ'deʃən] *s* depredación; (law) depredación
**depress** [dɪ'prɛs] *va* deprimir; desalentar, desanimar, entristecer; bajar (*p.ej., los precios*)
**depressant** [dɪ'prɛsənt] *adj & s* (med.) deprimente
**depressed** [dɪ'prɛst] *adj* deprimido; desalentado, desanimado, entristecido; necesitado
**depression** [dɪ'prɛʃən] *s* depresión; desaliento, desanimación, entristecimiento; crisis (*económica*); (path. & meteor.) depresión
**depressive** [dɪ'prɛsɪv] *adj* depresivo; deprimente
**depressor** [dɪ'prɛsər] *s* (anat., physiol., & surg.) depresor
**deprivation** [,dɛprɪ'veʃən] *s* privación
**deprive** [dɪ'praɪv] *va* privar
**dept.** abr. de **department**
**depth** [dɛpθ] *s* profundidad; fondo (*extensión interior de un edificio*); (naut.) braceaje (*del mar*); **in the depth of** en pleno, p.ej., **in the depth of winter** en pleno invierno; **to go beyond one's depth** meterse en agua demasiado profunda; (fig.) meterse en honduras
**depth bomb** *s* bomba de profundidad
**depth charge** *s* carga de profundidad
**depurative** ['dɛpjə,retɪv] *adj & s* (med.) depurativo
**deputation** [,dɛpjə'teʃən] *s* diputación
**depute** [dɪ'pjut] *va* diputar
**deputize** ['dɛpjətaɪz] *va* diputar, delegar
**deputy** ['dɛpjətɪ] *s* (*pl:* **-ties**) diputado; *adj* teniente
**derail** [di'rel] *va* hacer descarrilar; *vn* descarrilar
**derailment** [di'relmənt] *s* descarriladura o descarrilamiento
**derange** [dɪ'rend͡ʒ] *va* desarreglar, descomponer; volver loco
**derangement** [dɪ'rend͡ʒmənt] *s* desarreglo, descompostura; locura

**derat** [di'ræt] (*pret & pp:* **-ratted;** *ger:* **-ratting**) *va* desratizar
**derby** ['dʌrbɪ] *s* (*pl:* **-bies**) sombrero hongo; (*cap.*) ['dʌrbɪ] o ['dɑrbɪ] *s* (*pl:* **-bies**) derby (*carrera de caballos que se celebra anualmente*)
**derelict** ['dɛrɪlɪkt] *adj* abandonado; negligente; *s* (naut.) derrelicto (*buque*); pelafustán
**dereliction** [ˌdɛrɪ'lɪkʃən] *s* derrelicción, abandono; negligencia; colapso (*de las fuerzas vitales*)
**deride** [dɪ'raɪd] *va* mofarse de, ridiculizar
**de rigueur** [dərɪ'gʌr] *adj & adv* de rigor
**derision** [dɪ'rɪʒən] *s* irrisión, burla
**derisive** [dɪ'raɪsɪv] *adj* mofador
**derisory** [dɪ'raɪsərɪ] *adj* mofador, burlador; ridículo, irrisorio
**derivation** [ˌdɛrɪ'veʃən] *s* derivación; (gram., math., & med.) derivación
**derivative** [dɪ'rɪvətɪv] *adj* derivativo; (gram.) derivativo, derivado; (med.) derivativo; *s* derivativo; (gram.) derivativo, derivado; (med.) derivativo; (math.) derivada
**derive** [dɪ'raɪv] *va* derivar; *vn* derivar o derivarse
**derma** ['dʌrmə] *s* (anat.) dermis; piel, cutis
**dermal** ['dʌrməl] *adj* dérmico
**dermatitis** [ˌdʌrmə'taɪtɪs] *s* (path.) dermatitis
**dermatographia** [ˌdʌrmətə'græfɪə] *s* (path.) dermatografía
**dermatography** [ˌdʌrmə'tɑgrəfɪ] *s* dermatografía (*descripción de la piel*)
**dermatological** [ˌdʌrmətə'lɑdʒɪkəl] *adj* dermatológico
**dermatologist** [ˌdʌrmə'tɑlədʒɪst] *s* dermatólogo
**dermatology** [ˌdʌrmə'tɑlədʒɪ] *s* dermatología
**dermatosis** [ˌdʌrmə'tosɪs] *s* (path.) dermatosis
**dermic** ['dʌrmɪk] *adj* dérmico
**dermis** ['dʌrmɪs] *s* (anat.) dermis
**dermographia** [ˌdʌrmə'græfɪə] o **dermographism** [dər'mɑgrəfɪzəm] *s* (path.) dermografía o dermografismo
**derogate** ['dɛrəget] *vn* desmerecer, empeorar, degenerar; **to derogate from** quitar mérito a
**derogation** [ˌdɛrə'geʃən] *s* menosprecio, desprecio; disminución, deterioración, derogación
**derogative** [dɪ'rɑgətɪv] *adj* despreciativo
**derogatory** [dɪ'rɑgəˌtorɪ] *adj* despreciativo, menospreciativo
**derout** [dɪ'raʊt] *s* derrota; *va* derrotar
**derrick** ['dɛrɪk] *s* grúa; torre de perforar (*sobre un pozo de petróleo*)
**derring-do** ['dɛrɪŋ'du] *s* proeza
**dervish** ['dʌrvɪʃ] *s* derviche
**desalt** [di'sɔlt] *va* desalar
**descant** ['dɛskænt] *s* discante; (mus.) discante; [dɛs'kænt] *va* (mus.) discantar; *vn* discantar; (mus.) discantar
**descend** [dɪ'sɛnd] *va* descender, bajar (*la escalera*); *vn* descender; (mus.) descender; **to descend from** descender de; **to descend on** o **upon** invadir, caer sobre; **to descend to** descender a, rebajarse a
**descendant** [dɪ'sɛndənt] *adj* descendente; *s* descendiente; **in the descendant** menguante, con influencia cada vez menor
**descendent** [dɪ'sɛndənt] *adj* descendente
**descent** [dɪ'sɛnt] *s* descenso (*acción de descender o bajar; caída de una situación o estado a otro inferior*); descendimiento (*acción de bajar a una persona o cosa*); descendencia (*casta, estirpe; hijos, prole*); cuesta, bajada; herencia; invasión
**describable** [dɪ'skraɪbəbəl] *adj* descriptible
**describe** [dɪ'skraɪb] *va* describir
**describer** [dɪ'skraɪbər] *s* descriptor
**description** [dɪ'skrɪpʃən] *s* descripción; género, clase, calidad
**descriptive** [dɪ'skrɪptɪv] *adj* descriptivo
**descry** [dɪ'skraɪ] (*pret & pp:* **-scried**) *va* avistar, divisar; descubrir, percibir
**desecrate** ['dɛsɪkret] *va* profanar
**desecration** [ˌdɛsɪ'kreʃən] *s* profanación
**desecrator** ['dɛsɪˌkretər] *s* profanador
**desegregate** [di'sɛgrɪget] *va* desegregar
**desegregation** [diˌsɛgrɪ'geʃən] *s* desegregación
**desensitize** [di'sɛnsɪtaɪz] *va* desensibilizar, insensibilizar; (phot.) hacer insensible a la luz
**desert** ['dɛzərt] *s* desierto; yermo; *adj* desierto; [dɪ'zʌrt] *s* merecimiento, mérito, merecido, p.ej., **he received his just deserts** llevó su merecido; *va* desertar, desertar de; *vn* desertar
**deserter** [dɪ'zɛrtər] *s* (mil. & fig.) desertor
**desertion** [dɪ'zʌrʃən] *s* deserción; abandono de cónyuge
**deserve** [dɪ'zʌrv] *va & vn* merecer; **to deserve to** + *inf* merecer + *inf*
**deservedly** [dɪ'zʌrvɪdlɪ] *adj* merecidamente
**deserving** [dɪ'zʌrvɪŋ] *adj* merecedor
**deshabille** [ˌdɛzə'bil] *s* ropa suelta, desabillé
**desiccant** ['dɛsɪkənt] *adj & s* desecante
**desiccate** ['dɛsɪket] *va* desecar; *vn* desecarse
**desiccation** [ˌdɛsɪ'keʃən] *s* desecación
**desiccative** ['dɛsɪˌketɪv] *adj* desecativo
**desiccator** ['dɛsɪˌketər] *s* desecador
**desideratum** [dɪˌsɪdə'retəm] *s* (*pl:* **-ta** [tə]) desiderátum
**design** [dɪ'zaɪn] *s* diseño, trazado (*esbozo, bosquejo*); dibujo (*delineación; disposición de detalles; arte del dibujo; objeto trabajado con arte*); designio (*plan, proyecto*); modelo; intención, mala intención; **by design** intencionalmente; **to have designs on** poner la mira en; *va* diseñar, trazar, dibujar; estudiar; idear, proyectar, proponerse; destinar (*a una persona para algún fin*); *vn* dibujar
**designate** ['dɛzɪgnet] *adj* designado; *va* señalar (*indicar por señal*); denominar (*nombrar con un título particular*); designar (*destinar para determinado fin*)
**designation** [ˌdɛzɪg'neʃən] *s* señalamiento (*indicación definida*); denominación (*nombre o título*); designación (*destinación para algún fin*)
**designedly** [dɪ'zaɪnɪdlɪ] *adv* adrede, de propósito
**designer** [dɪ'zaɪnər] *s* dibujante; proyectista; maquinador, intrigante
**designing** [dɪ'zaɪnɪŋ] *adj* maquinador, intrigante; previsor; *s* dibujo
**desirability** [dɪˌzaɪrə'bɪlɪtɪ] *s* deseabilidad
**desirable** [dɪ'zaɪrəbəl] *adj* deseable
**desire** [dɪ'zaɪr] *s* deseo; *va* desear; **to desire to** + *inf* desear + *inf*
**desirous** [dɪ'zaɪrəs] *adj* deseoso
**desist** [dɪ'zɪst] *vn* desistir
**desistance** [dɪ'zɪstəns] *s* desistimiento
**desk** [dɛsk] *s* pupitre, escritorio; atril; caja (*donde se pagan las cuentas en los hoteles*)
**desk clerk** *s* cajero (*en los hoteles*)
**desk set** *s* juego de escritorio
**desk work** *s* trabajo de escritorio; trabajo oficinesco; trabajo literario
**desolate** ['dɛsəlɪt] *adj* desolado, arruinado; desierto; solitario; infeliz, triste; lúgubre; ['dɛsəlet] *va* desolar, arruinar, arrasar; despoblar; entristecer, desconsolar
**desolation** [ˌdɛsə'leʃən] *s* desolación; soledad (*estado y lugar*)
**desolator** ['dɛsəˌletər] *s* desolador
**despair** [dɪ'spɛr] *s* desesperación; *vn* desesperar, desesperarse; **to despair of** desesperar de
**despairing** [dɪ'spɛrɪŋ] *adj* desesperado
**despatch** [dɪ'spætʃ] *s & va* var. de **dispatch**
**despatcher** [dɪ'spætʃər] *s* var. de **dispatcher**
**desperado** [ˌdɛspə'redo] o [ˌdɛspə'rɑdo] *s* (*pl:* **-does** o **-dos**) criminal desesperado
**desperate** ['dɛspərɪt] *adj* desesperado; encarnizado; heroico (*p.ej., remedio*)
**desperation** [ˌdɛspə'reʃən] *s* desesperación
**despicable** ['dɛspɪkəbəl] o [dɛs'pɪkəbəl] *adj* desdeñable, despreciable
**despise** [dɪ'spaɪz] *va* despreciar, desdeñar
**despite** [dɪ'spaɪt] *s* insulto, afrenta, odio, desafío; **in despite of** a despecho de; *prep* a despecho de, a pesar de
**despiteful** [dɪ'spaɪtfəl] *adj* malicioso, vengativo
**despoil** [dɪ'spɔɪl] *va* despojar
**despoilment** [dɪ'spɔɪlmənt] o **despoliation** [dɪˌspolɪ'eʃən] *s* despojo
**despond** [dɪ'spɑnd] *s* abatimiento; *vn* desanimarse
**despondence** [dɪ'spɑndəns] *s* desaliento, desánimo, abatimiento
**despondency** [dɪ'spɑndənsɪ] *s* (*pl:* **-cies**) var. de **despondence**

**despondent** [dɪ'spandənt] o **desponding** [dɪ'spandɪŋ] *adj* desalentado, desanimado, abatido
**despot** ['dɛspɑt] o ['dɛspət] *s* déspota
**despotic** [dɛs'pɑtɪk] *adj* despótico
**despotically** [dɛs'pɑtɪkəlɪ] *adj* despóticamente
**despotism** ['dɛspətɪzəm] *s* despotismo
**desquamate** ['dɛskwəmet] *vn* descamarse
**desquamation** [ˌdɛskwə'meʃən] *s* descamación
**dessert** [dɪ'zʌrt] *s* postre
**dessertspoon** [dɪ'zʌrtˌspun] *s* cuchara de postre
**destalinization** [diˌstalɪnɪ'zeʃən] *s* destalinización o desestalinización
**destalinize** [di'stalɪnaɪz] *va* destalinizar o desestalinizar
**destination** [ˌdɛstɪ'neʃən] *s* destinación (*acción de destinar; fin, objeto*); destino (*consignación para determinado fin; lugar a donde va una persona o cosa*)
**destine** ['dɛstɪn] *va* destinar; **to destine for** destinar para; **to destine to** + *inf* destinar (*p.ej., dinero*) a + *inf*
**destiny** ['dɛstɪnɪ] *s* (*pl:* **-nies**) destino; (*cap.*) *s* (myth.) Destino
**destitute** ['dɛstɪtjut] o ['dɛstɪtut] *adj* indigente; **destitute of** desprovisto de
**destitution** [ˌdɛstɪ'tjuʃən] o [ˌdɛstɪ'tuʃən] *s* indigencia
**destroy** [dɪ'strɔɪ] *va* destruir; matar; invalidar
**destroyer** [dɪ'strɔɪər] *s* destruidor o destructor; (nav.) destructor
**destroyer escort** *s* (nav.) destructor de escolta
**destructibility** [dɪˌstrʌktɪ'bɪlɪtɪ] *s* destructibilidad
**destructible** [dɪ'strʌktɪbəl] *adj* destruíble o destructible
**destruction** [dɪ'strʌkʃən] *s* destrucción
**destructive** [dɪ'strʌktɪv] *adj* destructivo
**desuetude** ['dɛswɪtjud] o ['dɛswɪtud] *s* desuetud, desuso
**desulfurization** [diˌsʌlfjərɪ'zeʃən] *s* desulfuración
**desulfurize** [di'sʌlfjəraɪz] *va* desulfurar
**desulphurize** [di'sʌlfjəraɪz] *va* var. de **desulfurize**
**desultory** ['dɛsəlˌtorɪ] *adj* descosido, deshilvanado
**detach** [dɪ'tætʃ] *va* separar, desprender; (mil.) destacar
**detachable** [dɪ'tætʃəbəl] *adj* separable, desmontable
**detached** [dɪ'tætʃt] *adj* separado, suelto; imparcial, desinteresado
**detachment** [dɪ'tætʃmənt] *s* separación, desprendimiento; aislamiento; imparcialidad, desinterés; (mil.) destacamento
**detail** [dɪ'tel] o ['ditel] *s* detalle, pormenor; (f.a.) detalle; (mil.) destacamento; **in detail** en detalle, detalladamente; **to go into detail** menudear; [dɪ'tel] *va* detallar; (mil.) destacar
**detain** [dɪ'ten] *va* detener
**detainer** [dɪ'tenər] *s* detenedor; (law) detentación; (law) detención ilegal; (law) auto de detención
**detainment** [dɪ'tenmənt] *s* detención
**detect** [dɪ'tɛkt] *va* detectar; (elec. & rad.) detectar
**detectable** [dɪ'tɛktəbəl] o **detectible** [dɪ'tɛktɪbəl] *adj* perceptible
**detection** [dɪ'tɛkʃən] *s* detección; (elec. & rad.) detección
**detective** [dɪ'tɛktɪv] *s* detective; *adj* detectivesco
**detective story** *s* novela policíaca, novela policial
**detector** [dɪ'tɛktər] *s* detector; (elec. & rad.) detector
**detention** [dɪ'tɛnʃən] *s* detención
**deter** [dɪ'tʌr] (*pret & pp:* **-terred;** *ger:* **-terring**) *va* refrenar, impedir, detener
**deterge** [dɪ'tʌrdʒ] *va* deterger
**detergent** [dɪ'tʌrdʒənt] *adj & s* detergente
**deteriorate** [dɪ'tɪrɪəret] *va* deteriorar; *vn* deteriorarse
**deterioration** [dɪˌtɪrɪə'reʃən] *s* deterioro o deterioración
**determinability** [dɪˌtʌrmɪnə'bɪlɪtɪ] *s* determinabilidad
**determinable** [dɪ'tʌrmɪnəbəl] *adj* determinable
**determinant** [dɪ'tʌrmɪnənt] *adj* determinante; *s* determinante; (biol., log., & math.) determinante
**determinate** [dɪ'tʌrmɪnɪt] *adj* determinado
**determination** [dɪˌtʌrmɪ'neʃən] *s* determinación
**determinative** [dɪ'tʌrmɪˌnetɪv] *adj* determinativo; (gram.) determinativo
**determine** [dɪ'tʌrmɪn] *va* determinar; *vn* determinarse
**determined** [dɪ'tʌrmɪnd] *adj* determinado, resuelto
**determinism** [dɪ'tʌrmɪnɪzəm] *s* (philos.) determinismo
**determinist** [dɪ'tʌrmɪnɪst] *adj & s* (philos.) determinista
**deterrent** [dɪ'tɛrənt] o [dɪ'tʌrənt] *adj* impeditivo, disuasivo; *s* refrenamiento, impedimento, detención; **to act as a deterrent** servir como un freno
**detersion** [dɪ'tʌrʃən] *s* detersión
**detersive** [dɪ'tʌrsɪv] *adj & s* detersivo
**detest** [dɪ'tɛst] *va* detestar
**detestable** [dɪ'tɛstəbəl] *adj* detestable
**detestation** [ˌditɛs'teʃən] *s* detestación; persona detestada, cosa detestada
**dethrone** [dɪ'θron] *va* destronar
**dethronement** [dɪ'θronmənt] *s* destronamiento
**detin** [di'tɪn] (*pret & pp:* **-tinned;** *ger:* **-tinning**) *va* desestañar; *vn* desestañarse; recuperar estaño
**detonate** ['dɛtonet] o ['ditonet] *va* hacer detonar; *vn* detonar
**detonation** [ˌdɛto'neʃən] o [ˌdito'neʃən] *s* detonación
**detonator** ['dɛtoˌnetər] o ['ditoˌnetər] *s* detonador
**detour** ['ditʊr] o [dɪ'tʊr] *s* desvío, rodeo, vuelta; manera indirecta; *va* desviar (*p.ej., el tránsito*); *vn* desviarse
**detract** [dɪ'trækt] *va* detraer, apartar; *vn* detraer; **to detract from** disminuir, rebajar; quitar atractivo, belleza, crédito, reputación, mérito, etc. a
**detraction** [dɪ'trækʃən] *s* detracción
**detractive** [dɪ'træktɪv] *adj* detractor
**detractor** [dɪ'træktər] *s* detractor
**detrain** [di'tren] *va* hacer salir del tren; *vn* salir del tren
**detrainment** [di'trenmənt] *s* salida del tren
**detriment** ['dɛtrɪmənt] *s* perjuicio, detrimento; **to the detriment of** en perjuicio de
**detrimental** [ˌdɛtrɪ'mɛntəl] *adj* perjudicial, dañoso, nocivo
**detrital** [dɪ'traɪtəl] *adj* (geol.) detrítico
**detrition** [dɪ'trɪʃən] *s* detricción
**detritus** [dɪ'traɪtəs] *s* (geol.) detrito; (fig.) restos
**Deucalion** [dju'kelɪən] o [du'kelɪən] *s* (myth.) Deucalión
**deuce** [djus] o [dus] *s* dos (*en los juegos de naipes y dados*); a dos (*en el tenis*); **the deuce!** ¡demonio!
**deuced** ['djusɪd], ['dusɪd], [djust] o [dust] *adj* diabólico, excesivo; *adv* diabólicamente, excesivamente
**deucedly** ['djusɪdlɪ] o ['dusɪdlɪ] *adv* diabólicamente, excesivamente
**Deut.** abr. de **Deuteronomy**
**deuterium** [dju'tɪrɪəm] o [du'tɪrɪəm] *s* (chem.) deuterio
**deuteron** ['djutəran] o ['dutəran] *s* (chem.) deuterión
**Deuteronomy** [ˌdjutə'ranəmɪ] o [ˌdutə'ranəmɪ] *s* (Bib.) Deuteronomio
**deuton** ['djutan] o ['dutan] *s* (chem.) deutón (*es decir, deuterión*)
**deutoplasm** ['djutoplæzəm] o ['dutoplæzəm] *s* (biol.) deutoplasma
**devaluate** [di'væljʊet] *va* desvalorizar, desvalorar
**devaluation** [diˌvælju'eʃən] *s* devaluación, desvalorización
**devalue** [di'vælju] *va* desvalorizar, desvalorar
**devastate** ['dɛvəstet] *va* devastar
**devastating** ['dɛvəsˌtetɪŋ] *adj* devastador; (slang) abrumador, arrollador

**devastation** [ˌdɛvəsˈteʃən] *s* devastación
**devastator** [ˈdɛvəsˌtetər] *s* devastador
**develop** [dɪˈvɛləp] *va* desarrollar, desenvolver; (math.) desarrollar; (phot.) desarrollar, revelar; explotar (*p.ej., una mina*); *vn* desarrollarse, desenvolverse; evolucionar; crecer
**developable** [dɪˈvɛləpəbəl] *adj* desarrollable
**developer** [dɪˈvɛləpər] *s* (phot.) revelador
**development** [dɪˈvɛləpmənt] *s* desarrollo, desenvolvimiento; explotación (*p.ej., de una mina*); nuevo cambio, acontecimiento nuevo; construcción de casas, caserío nuevo; (phot.) revelado
**developmental** [dɪˌvɛləpˈmɛntəl] *adj* evolucionista; del desarrollo; experimental
**deviate** [ˈdivɪet] *va* desviar; *vn* desviarse
**deviation** [ˌdivɪˈeʃən] *s* desviación
**deviationism** [ˌdivɪˈeʃənɪzəm] *s* desviacionismo
**deviationist** [ˌdivɪˈeʃənɪst] *s* desviacionista (*comunista que no sigue la línea del partido*)
**device** [dɪˈvaɪs] *s* dispositivo, artefacto, artificio, aparato; treta, ardid; patrón, dibujo; divisa heráldica; lema, divisa; **to leave someone to his own devices** dejar a uno que haga lo que se le antoje
**devil** [ˈdɛvəl] *s* diablo; (mach.) diablo; **between the devil and the deep blue sea** entre la espada y la pared; **like the devil** (coll.) como el diablo; **poor devil** pobre diablo; **talk of the Devil and he will appear** en nombrando al ruin de Roma, luego asoma; **the Devil** el Diablo, Satán; **the devil!** ¡diablos!; **the devil take the hindmost** quien se quede en zaga, con el diablo se las haya; **there will be the devil to pay** ahí será el diablo; **to give the devil his due** ser justo hasta con un diablo; **to raise the devil** (slang) armarla, armar un alboroto; (*pret & pp:* **-iled** o **-illed;** *ger:* **-iling** o **-illing**) *va* condimentar con picantes; (coll.) molestar, incomodar
**deviled** [ˈdɛvəld] *adj* condimentado con picantes
**deviled eggs** *spl* huevos duros rellenos con su propia yema y condimentados con picantes
**devilfish** [ˈdɛvəlˌfɪʃ] *s* (ichth.) raya, manta; (zool.) pulpo
**devil incarnate** *s* diablo encarnado
**devilish** [ˈdɛvəlɪʃ] o [ˈdɛvlɪʃ] *adj* diabólico; (coll.) diabólico (*excesivamente malo*); (coll.) excesivo; *adv* (coll.) excesivamente
**devilled** [ˈdɛvəld] *adj* var. de **deviled**
**devil-may-care** [ˈdɛvəlmeˈkɛr] *adj* atolondrado, irresponsable
**devilment** [ˈdɛvəlmənt] *s* maldad, perversidad; diablura (*travesura grande; acción temeraria*)
**devilry** [ˈdɛvəlrɪ] *s* (*pl:* **-ries**) var. de **deviltry**
**devil's advocate** *s* (eccl. & fig.) abogado del diablo
**devil's-darning-needle** [ˈdɛvəlzˈdarnɪŋˌnidəl] *s* (ent.) caballito del diablo; (bot.) peine de Venus
**Devil's Island** *s* Isla del Diablo
**deviltry** [ˈdɛvəltrɪ] *s* (*pl:* **-tries**) maldad, perversidad, crueldad; diablura (*travesura grande; acción temeraria*)
**devious** [ˈdivɪəs] *adj* apartado, desviado; tortuoso (*dícese de un camino, una persona, etc.*)
**devise** [dɪˈvaɪz] *s* (law) legado; (law) testamento; (law) propiedad legada; *va* idear, inventar, proyectar; (law) legar; *vn* formar proyectos
**devisee** [ˌdɛvɪˈze] o [dɪˌvaɪˈzi] *s* (law) legatario
**deviser** [dɪˈvaɪzər] *s* autor, inventor
**devisor** [dɪˈvaɪzər] o [dɪˈvaɪzɔr] *s* (law) testador
**devitalization** [diˌvaɪtəlɪˈzeʃən] *s* desvitalización
**devitalize** [diˈvaɪtəlaɪz] *va* desvitalizar
**devitrify** [diˈvɪtrɪfaɪ] (*pret & pp:* **-fied**) *va* desvitrificar
**devoid** [dɪˈvɔɪd] *adj* desprovisto; vacío
**devoir** [dəˈvwar] o [ˈdɛvwar] *s* cumplido, homenaje; deber, obligación
**devolution** [ˌdɛvəˈluʃən] *s* traspaso, transmisión de una persona a otra; (biol.) degeneración; (eccl.) devolución
**devolve** [dɪˈvalv] *va* transmitir, transferir; *vn* pasar, transferirse; **to devolve on, to,** o **upon** pasar a, incumbir a
**Devonian** [dɪˈvonɪən] *adj & s* devoniano; (geol.) devoniano
**Devonic** [dɪˈvanɪk] *adj* (geol.) devónico, devoniano
**devote** [dɪˈvot] *va* dedicar; **to devote oneself to** dedicarse a; **to devote oneself to** + *inf* dedicarse a + *inf*
**devoted** [dɪˈvotɪd] *adj* devoto (*afecto, aficionado*); dedicado
**devotee** [ˌdɛvəˈti] *s* devoto
**devotion** [dɪˈvoʃən] *s* devoción; dedicación (*p.ej., al estudio, al trabajo*); **devotions** *spl* preces, oraciones
**devotional** [dɪˈvoʃənəl] *adj* devoto
**devour** [dɪˈvaʊr] *va* devorar; (fig.) devorar
**devourer** [dɪˈvaʊrər] *s* devorador
**devouring** [dɪˈvaʊrɪŋ] *adj* devorador, devorante
**devout** [dɪˈvaʊt] *adj* devoto; cordial, sincero
**dew** [dju] o [du] *s* rocío; *va* rociar
**Dewar vessel** [ˈdjuər] o [ˈduər] *s* vasija de Dewar
**dewberry** [ˈdjuˌbɛrɪ] o [ˈduˌbɛrɪ] *s* (*pl:* **-ries**) (bot.) zarza; (bot.) zarza de los rastrojos (*Rubus caesius*)
**dewclaw** [ˈdjuˌklɔ] o [ˈduˌklɔ] *s* espolón, pesuño falso
**dewdrop** [ˈdjuˌdrap] o [ˈduˌdrap] *s* gota de rocío
**dewlap** [ˈdjuˌlæp] o [ˈduˌlæp] *s* papada
**dew point** *s* (physical chem.) punto de rocío
**dewy** [ˈdjuɪ] o [ˈduɪ] *adj* (*comp:* **-ier;** *super:* **-iest**) rociado; (fig.) rutilante, suave, efímero (*como el rocío*)
**dexter** [ˈdɛkstər] *adj* diestro; (her.) diestro
**dexterity** [dɛksˈtɛrɪtɪ] *s* destreza
**dexterous** [ˈdɛkstərəs] *adj* diestro
**dextral** [ˈdɛkstrəl] *adj* diestro; derecho
**dextrin** o **dextrine** [ˈdɛkstrɪn] *s* (chem.) dextrina
**dextrocardia** [ˌdɛkstroˈkardɪə] *s* (anat.) dextrocardia
**dextrogyrous** [ˌdɛkstroˈdʒaɪrəs] *adj* (phys.) dextrógiro
**dextrorotatory** [ˌdɛkstroˈrotəˌtorɪ] *adj* (phys.) dextrorrotatorio
**dextrorse** [ˈdɛkstrɔrs] o [dɛksˈtrɔrs] *adj* (bot.) dextrorso
**dextrose** [ˈdɛkstros] *s* (biochem.) dextrosa
**dextrous** [ˈdɛkstrəs] *adj* var. de **dexterous**
**D.F.** abr. de **Defender of the Faith**
**dg.** abr. de **decigram** o **decigrams**
**diabase** [ˈdaɪəbes] *s* (mineral.) diabasa
**diabetes** [ˌdaɪəˈbitɪs] o [ˌdaɪəˈbitiz] *s* (path.) diabetes
**diabetic** [ˌdaɪəˈbɛtɪk] o [ˌdaɪəˈbitɪk] *adj & s* diabético
**diabetometer** [ˌdaɪəbɪˈtamɪtər] *s* diabetómetro
**diablerie** [dɪˈablərɪ] *s* hechicería; diablura (*travesura grande; acción temeraria*); dominio de diablos
**diabolic** [ˌdaɪəˈbalɪk] o **diabolical** [ˌdaɪəˈbalɪkəl] *adj* diabólico
**diabolism** [daɪˈæbəlɪzəm] *s* diabolismo (*doctrina*); hechicería; maldad, perversidad; posesión demoníaca
**diachronic** [ˌdaɪəˈkranɪk] *adj* diacrónico
**diachrony** [daɪˈækrənɪ] *s* diacronía
**diachylon** [daɪˈækɪlan] *s* diaquilón
**diacodion** [ˌdaɪəˈkodɪən] *s* (pharm.) diacodión
**diaconal** [daɪˈækənəl] *adj* diaconal
**diaconate** [daɪˈækənɪt] o [daɪˈækənet] *s* diaconado
**diacritic** [ˌdaɪəˈkrɪtɪk] *adj* (gram. & med.) diacrítico; *s* (gram.) signo diacrítico
**diacritical** [ˌdaɪəˈkrɪtɪkəl] *adj* (gram. & med.) diacrítico
**diacritical mark** *s* (gram.) signo diacrítico
**diadelphous** [ˌdaɪəˈdɛlfəs] *adj* (bot.) diadelfo
**diadem** [ˈdaɪədɛm] *s* diadema
**diaeresis** [daɪˈɛrɪsɪs] *s* (*pl:* **-ses** [siz]) diéresis
**diagnose** [ˌdaɪəgˈnos] o [ˌdaɪəgˈnoz] *va* diagnosticar
**diagnosis** [ˌdaɪəgˈnosɪs] *s* (*pl:* **-ses** [siz]) (bot., zool. & med.) diagnosis
**diagnostic** [ˌdaɪəgˈnastɪk] *adj & s* diagnóstico
**diagnostician** [ˌdaɪəgnasˈtɪʃən] *s* médico experto en hacer el diagnóstico

**diagonal** [daɪˈægənəl] *adj & s* diagonal
**diagonal cloth** *s* diagonal
**diagonally** [daɪˈægənəlɪ] *adv* diagonalmente
**diagram** [ˈdaɪəgræm] *s* diagrama, esquema; (*pret & pp:* **-gramed** o **-grammed;** *ger:* **-graming** o **-gramming**) *va* esquematizar, dibujar en forma de diagrama
**diagrammatic** [ˌdaɪəgrəˈmætɪk] o **diagrammatical** [ˌdaɪəgrəˈmætɪkəl] *adj* diagramático
**diagrammatically** [ˌdaɪəgrəˈmætɪkəlɪ] *adv* diagramáticamente
**diagraph** [ˈdaɪəgræf] o [ˈdaɪəgrɑf] *s* diágrafo
**dial.** abr. de **dialect** y **dialectal**
**dial** [ˈdaɪəl] *s* esfera, cuadrante, muestra; (rad.) cuadrante; disco selector (*del teléfono*); (*pret & pp:* **dialed** o **dialled;** *ger:* **dialing** o **dialling**) *va* sintonizar (*el radiorreceptor o el radiotransmisor*); marcar (*el número telefónico*); llamar (*a una persona*) por teléfono automático; *vn* (telp.) marcar
**dialect** [ˈdaɪəlɛkt] *s* dialecto
**dialectal** [ˌdaɪəˈlɛktəl] *adj* dialectal
**dialectic** [ˌdaɪəˈlɛktɪk] *adj* dialéctico; dialectal; *s* dialéctica; **dialectics** *ssg* dialéctica
**dialectical** [ˌdaɪəˈlɛktɪkəl] *adj* dialéctico; dialectal
**dialectician** [ˌdaɪəlɛkˈtɪʃən] *s* dialéctico
**dialecticism** [ˌdaɪəˈlɛktɪsɪzəm] *s* dialectalismo
**dialectology** [ˌdaɪəlɛkˈtɑlədʒɪ] *s* dialectología
**dialing** o **dialling** [ˈdaɪəlɪŋ] *s* (telp.) marcaje
**diallage** [ˈdaɪəlɪdʒ] *s* (mineral.) diálaga
**dialogic** [ˌdaɪəˈlɑdʒɪk] *adj* dialogal
**dialogism** [daɪˈælədʒɪzəm] *s* (rhet.) dialogismo
**dialogist** [daɪˈælədʒɪst] *s* dialoguista (*escritor*)
**dialogue** [ˈdaɪəlɔg] o [ˈdaɪəlɑg] *s* diálogo; *va & vn* dialogar
**dial telephone** *s* teléfono automático
**dial tone** *s* (telp.) señal para marcar
**dialycarpous** [ˌdaɪəlɪˈkɑrpəs] *adj* (bot.) dialicarpelar
**dialysis** [daɪˈælɪsɪs] *s* (*pl:* **-ses** [siz]) diálisis
**dialytic** [ˌdaɪəˈlɪtɪk] *adj* dialítico
**dialyze** [ˈdaɪəlaɪz] *va* dializar
**dialyzer** [ˈdaɪəˌlaɪzər] *s* (physical chem.) dializador
**diam.** abr. de **diameter**
**diamagnetic** [ˌdaɪəmægˈnɛtɪk] *adj & s* diamagnético
**diamagnetism** [ˌdaɪəˈmægnɪtɪzəm] *s* diamagnetismo
**diamantiferous** [ˌdaɪəmənˈtɪfərəs] *adj* diamantífero
**diamat** [ˈdaɪəmæt] *s* materialismo dialéctico (*teoría de Carlos Marx y Federico Engels, basada en el método de Hegel*)
**diameter** [daɪˈæmɪtər] *s* diámetro
**diametric** [ˌdaɪəˈmɛtrɪk] o **diametrical** [ˌdaɪəˈmɛtrɪkəl] *adj* diametral
**diamond** [ˈdaɪəmənd] o [ˈdaɪmənd] *s* diamante; losange (*figura de rombo*); (baseball) losange; carró, rombo o diamante (*naipe que corresponde al oro*); **diamonds** *spl* carrós, rombos o diamantes (*palo que corresponde al de oros*); **diamond in the rough** diamante en bruto; (fig.) diamante en bruto; *adj* diamantino
**diamond cutter** *s* diamantista
**diamond edition** *s* (print.) edición diamante
**diamond wedding** *s* bodas de diamante
**Dian** [ˈdaɪæn] *s* (poet.) Diana
**Diana** [daɪˈænə] *s* (myth.) Diana
**diandrous** [daɪˈændrəs] *adj* diandro
**diapalma** [ˌdaɪəˈpælmə] *s* (pharm.) diapalma
**diapason** [ˌdaɪəˈpezən] o [ˌdaɪəˈpesən] *s* (mus.) diapasón
**diapason normal** *s* (mus.) diapasón normal
**diapedesis** [ˌdaɪəpɪˈdisɪs] *s* (physiol.) diapédesis
**diaper** [ˈdaɪəpər] *s* pañal (*de niño*); labor con motivos uniformemente repetidos; *va* labrar con motivos uniformemente repetidos; proveer con pañal, renovar el pañal de
**diaphanous** [daɪˈæfənəs] *adj* diáfano
**diaphoresis** [ˌdaɪəfoˈrisɪs] *s* (med.) diaforesis
**diaphoretic** [ˌdaɪəfoˈrɛtɪk] *adj & s* diaforético
**diaphoretical** [ˌdaɪəfoˈrɛtɪkəl] *adj* diaforético
**diaphragm** [ˈdaɪəfræm] *s* diafragma; (telp. & rad.) membrana fónica o diafragma
**diaphragmatic** [ˌdaɪəfrægˈmætɪk] *adj* diafragmático
**diaphysis** [daɪˈæfɪsɪs] *s* (*pl:* **-ses** [siz]) (anat. & bot.) diáfisis
**diapositive** [ˌdaɪəˈpɑzɪtɪv] *s* (phot.) diapositiva
**diarist** [ˈdaɪərɪst] *s* diarista
**diarrhea** o **diarrhoea** [ˌdaɪəˈriə] *s* (path.) diarrea
**diarthrosis** [ˌdaɪɑrˈθrosɪs] *s* (anat.) diartrosis
**diary** [ˈdaɪərɪ] *s* (*pl:* **-ries**) diario
**diascordium** [ˌdaɪəˈskɔrdɪəm] *s* (pharm.) diascordio
**Diaspora** [daɪˈæspərə] *s* (Bib. & fig.) Diáspora
**diaspore** [ˈdaɪəspor] *s* (mineral.) diásporo
**diastase** [ˈdaɪəstes] *s* (biochem.) diastasa
**diastasic** [ˌdaɪəˈstesɪk] *adj* (biochem. & surg.) diastásico
**diastasis** [daɪˈæstəsɪs] *s* (surg.) diastasis
**diastole** [daɪˈæstəli] *s* (physiol. & gram.) diástole
**diastolic** [ˌdaɪəˈstɑlɪk] *adj* diastólico
**diastrophism** [daɪˈæstrəfɪzəm] *s* (geol.) diastrofismo
**diastyle** [ˈdaɪəstaɪl] *s* (arch.) diástilo
**diatessaron** [ˌdaɪəˈtɛsərɑn] *s* (ancient mus., ancient pharm., & rel.) diatesarón
**diathermanous** [ˌdaɪəˈθʌrmənəs] *adj* (phys.) diatérmano
**diathermic** [ˌdaɪəˈθʌrmɪk] *adj* (med. & phys.) diatérmico
**diathermy** [ˈdaɪəˌθʌrmɪ] *s* (med.) diatermia
**diathesis** [daɪˈæθɪsɪs] *s* (med.) diátesis
**diathetic** [ˌdaɪəˈθɛtɪk] *adj* diatésico
**diatom** [ˈdaɪətɑm] *s* (bot.) diatomea
**diatomaceous** [ˌdaɪətoˈmeʃəs] *adj* diatomáceo
**diatonic** [ˌdaɪəˈtɑnɪk] *adj* (mus.) diatónico
**diatonic scale** *s* (mus.) escala diatónica
**diatribe** [ˈdaɪətraɪb] *s* diatriba
**dibasic** [daɪˈbesɪk] *adj* (chem.) dibásico
**dibble** [ˈdɪbəl] *s* plantador; *va* plantar con plantador
**dice** [daɪs] *spl* dados; cubitos (*p.ej., de zanahorias*); **to load the dice** cargar los dados; *va* perder (*dinero*) jugando a los dados; cortar (*p.ej., zanahorias*) en cubitos; *vn* jugar a los dados
**dicebox** [ˈdaɪsˌbɑks] *s* cubilete; cuchumbo (Am.)
**dicer** [ˈdaɪsər] *s* jugador de dados
**dichasium** [daɪˈkeʒɪəm] *s* (*pl:* **-a** [ə]) (bot.) dicasio
**dichloride** [daɪˈkloraɪd] o [daɪˈklorɪd] *s* (chem.) dicloruro
**dichlorodiphenyl-trichloroethane** [daɪˌklorodaɪˌfɛnɪltraɪˌkloroˈɛθen] *s* (chem.) diclorodifeniltricloroetano
**dichotomic** [ˌdaɪkəˈtɑmɪk] *adj* dicotómico
**dichotomize** [daɪˈkɑtəmaɪz] *va* dividir en dos
**dichotomous** [daɪˈkɑtəməs] *adj* dicótomo
**dichotomy** [daɪˈkɑtəmɪ] *s* (*pl:* **-mies**) dicotomía; (astr., biol., bot. & log.) dicotomía
**dichroic** [daɪˈkro·ɪk] *adj* dicroico
**dichroism** [daɪˈkro·ɪzəm] *s* dicroísmo
**dichromate** [daɪˈkromet] *s* (chem.) dicromato
**dichromatic** [ˌdaɪkroˈmætɪk] *adj* dicromático
**dichromatism** [daɪˈkromətɪzəm] *s* (path.) dicromatismo
**Dick** [dɪk] *s* nombre abreviado de **Richard**
**dickens** [ˈdɪkənz] *s* (coll.) diantre, dianche; **the dickens!** ¡diantre!, ¡dianche!
**dicker** [ˈdɪkər] *s* regateo, cambalache; *va & vn* regatear, cambalachear
**dickey** [ˈdɪkɪ] *s* camisolín, pechera postiza; cuello separado; babero de niño; (aut.) asiento del conductor; asiento descubierto detrás de un coche; (coll.) pajarito, pájaro pequeño; asno
**dicky** [ˈdɪkɪ] *s* (*pl:* **-ies**) var. de **dickey**
**diclinous** [ˈdaɪklɪnəs] o [daɪˈklaɪnəs] *adj* (bot.) diclino
**dicotyledon** [daɪˌkɑtɪˈlidən] *s* (bot.) dicotiledón
**dicotyledonous** [daɪˌkɑtɪˈlidənəs] *adj* (bot.) dicotiledóneo
**dict.** abr. de **dictionary**
**dictaphone** [ˈdɪktəfon] *s* (trademark) dictadora, dictáfono
**dictate** [ˈdɪktet] *s* mandato; **dictates** *spl* dictados; [ˈdɪktet] o [dɪkˈtet] *va & vn* dictar; mandar, disponer
**dictation** [dɪkˈteʃən] *s* dictado; mandato; **to take dictation** escribir al dictado
**dictator** [ˈdɪktetər] o [dɪkˈtetər] *s* dictador; persona que dicta cartas
**dictatorial** [ˌdɪktəˈtorɪəl] *adj* dictatorio (*per-*

*teneciente al dictador*); dictatorial (*perteneciente al dictador; imperioso, soberbio*)
**dictatorship** [ˈdɪktetər,ʃɪp] o [dɪkˈtetər,ʃɪp] *s* dictadura
**diction** [ˈdɪkʃən] *s* dicción
**dictionary** [ˈdɪkʃən,ɛrɪ] *s* (*pl:* **-ies**) diccionario
**dictograph** [ˈdɪktəgræf] o [ˈdɪktəgrɑf] *s* (trademark) dictógrafo
**dictum** [ˈdɪktəm] *s* (*pl:* **-ta** [tə]) dictamen; sentencia, aforismo; (law) fallo u opinión judicial sobre un punto no esencial al juicio principal
**did** [dɪd] *pret de* **do**
**didactic** [daɪˈdæktɪk] o [dɪˈdæktɪk] *adj* didáctico; **didactics** *ssg* didáctica
**didactical** [daɪˈdæktɪkəl] o [dɪˈdæktɪkəl] *adj* didáctico
**didacticism** [daɪˈdæktɪsɪzəm] o [dɪˈdæktɪsɪzəm] *s* método didáctico
**didactylous** [daɪˈdæktɪləs] *adj* didáctilo
**diddle** [ˈdɪdəl] *va* (coll.) estafar; (coll.) arruinar, quebrar; (coll.) perder (*el tiempo*); *vn* (coll.) zarandearse
**didelphian** [daɪˈdɛlfɪən] *adj* & *s* (zool.) didelfo
**didn't** [ˈdɪdənt] contracción de **did not**
**dido** [ˈdaɪdo] *s* (*pl:* **-dos** o **-does**) (coll.) travesura; **to cut didos** (coll.) hacer travesuras; (*cap.*) *s* (myth.) Dido
**didymium** [daɪˈdɪmɪəm] o [dɪˈdɪmɪəm] *s* (chem.) didimio
**didymous** [ˈdɪdɪməs] *adj* (bot. & zool.) dídimo
**die** [daɪ] *s* (*pl:* **dice** [daɪs]) dado; cubito (*p.ej., de zanahorias*); **the die is cast** la suerte está echada, el dado está tirado ‖ *s* (*pl:* **dies** [daɪz]) (arch.) dado; (mach.) troquel (*para acuñar monedas o estampar metales*); (mach.) hembra de terraja, cojinete de roscar ‖ (*pret & pp:* **died;** *ger:* **dieing**) *va* cortar con troquel; roscar ‖ (*pret & pp:* **died;** *ger:* **dying**) *va* morir (*p.ej., una muerte dolorosa*) ‖ *vn* morir; **to be dying to** + *inf* (coll.) morirse por + *inf;* **to die away, down** u **out** acabarse gradualmente, desaparecer gradualmente; enflaquecerse gradualmente; **to die hard** resistir hasta la muerte, rendirse de mala gana; **to die laughing** morir de risa
**die-cast** [ˈdaɪ,kæst] o [ˈdaɪ,kɑst] (*pret & pp:* **-cast**) *va* fundir a troquel
**die casting** *s* pieza fundida a troquel
**diecious** [daɪˈiʃəs] *adj* (biol. & bot.) dioico
**die-hard** [ˈdaɪ,hɑrd] *adj* & *s* intransigente
**dielectric** [,daɪɪˈlɛktrɪk] *adj* & *s* dieléctrico
**dieresis** [daɪˈɛrɪsɪs] *s* (*pl:* **-ses** [siz]) diéresis
**Diesel-electric** [ˈdizəlɪˈlɛktrɪk] *adj* dieseleléctrico
**Diesel engine** [ˈdizəl] s motor Diesel
**Dieselization** [,dizəlɪˈzeʃən] *s* dieselización
**Diesel motor** *s* motor Diesel
**diesinker** [ˈdaɪ,sɪŋkər] *s* grabador en hueco, troquelero
**diesis** [ˈdaɪɪsɪs] *s* (*pl:* **-ses** [siz]) (mus.) diesis; (print.) obelisco doble
**diestock** [ˈdaɪ,stɑk] *s* terraja, portacojinete
**diet** [ˈdaɪət] *s* dieta, régimen alimenticio; dieta (*asamblea*); **to be on a diet** estar a dieta; **to put on a diet** poner a dieta; *va* adietar; *vn* estar a dieta
**dietary** [ˈdaɪə,tɛrɪ] *adj* dietético; *s* (*pl:* **-ies**) dieta, sistema dietético; tratado sobre dietas
**dietetic** [,daɪəˈtɛtɪk] *adj* dietético; **dietetics** *ssg* dietética
**dietician** o **dietitian** [,daɪəˈtɪʃən] *s* dietista, especialista en dietética
**diff.** abr. de **difference** y **different**
**differ** [ˈdɪfər] *vn* diferenciar, discordar; diferenciarse, diferir
**difference** [ˈdɪfərəns] *s* diferencia; **it makes no difference** lo mismo da, no importa; **to not know the difference** no darse cuenta de ello; **to split the difference** partir la diferencia; **what difference does it make?** ¿qué más da?
**difference of potential** *s* (phys.) diferencia de potencial
**different** [ˈdɪfərənt] *adj* diferente
**differentia** [,dɪfəˈrɛnʃɪə] *s* (*pl:* **-ae** [i]) (log.) diferencia
**differential** [,dɪfəˈrɛnʃəl] *adj* diferencial; *s* (mach.) diferencial *m;* (math.) diferencial *f*
**differential calculus** *s* (math.) cálculo diferencial
**differential coefficient** *s* (math.) coeficiente diferencial
**differential equation** *s* (math.) ecuación diferencial
**differential gear** *s* (mach.) engranaje diferencial
**differential housing** *s* (aut.) caja del diferencial
**differential rate** *s* (rail.) tarifa diferencial
**differential thermometer** *s* termómetro diferencial
**differentiate** [,dɪfəˈrɛnʃɪet] *va* diferenciar; (math.) diferenciar; *vn* diferenciarse; (bot.) diferenciarse
**differentiation** [,dɪfə,rɛnʃɪˈeʃən] *s* diferenciación
**difficult** [ˈdɪfɪkʌlt] *adj* difícil
**difficulty** [ˈdɪfɪkʌltɪ] *s* (*pl:* **-ties**) dificultad; **difficulties** *spl* aprietos, apuros
**diffidation** [,dɪfɪˈdeʃən] *s* difidación, declaración de guerra
**diffidence** [ˈdɪfɪdəns] *s* timidez, apocamiento
**diffident** [ˈdɪfɪdənt] *adj* tímido, apocado
**diffluence** [ˈdɪflʊəns] *s* difluencia
**diffluent** [ˈdɪflʊənt] *adj* difluente
**diffract** [dɪˈfrækt] *va* difractar
**diffraction** [dɪˈfrækʃən] *s* difracción
**diffraction grating** *s* (opt.) red de difracción
**diffractive** [dɪˈfræktɪv] *adj* difractivo, difrangente
**diffuse** [dɪˈfjus] *adj* difuso; [dɪˈfjuz] *va* difundir; *vn* difundirse
**diffuser** [dɪˈfjuzər] *s* difusor
**diffusibility** [dɪ,fjuzɪˈbɪlɪtɪ] *s* difusibilidad
**diffusible** [dɪˈfjuzɪbəl] *adj* difusible
**diffusion** [dɪˈfjuʒən] *s* difusión; (anthrop., chem. & phys.) difusión
**diffusionist theory** [dɪˈfjuʒənɪst] *s* (anthrop.) difusionismo
**diffusive** [dɪˈfjusɪv] *adj* difusivo; difuso (*superabundante en palabras*)
**dig** [dɪg] *s* empuje, codazo; (coll.) pulla, puyazo, palabra hiriente; (*pret & pp:* **dug** o **digged;** *ger:* **digging**) *va* cavar, excavar; ahondar, escudriñar; **to dig up** desenterrar; (fig.) desenterrar; *vn* cavar, excavar; trabajar con azada, etc.; abrirse paso cavando; (coll.) trabajar mucho; **to dig in** (mil.) atrincherarse, afosarse; poner manos a la obra; **to dig into** (coll.) ocuparse mucho en; **to dig under** socavar
**digest** [ˈdaɪdʒɛst] *s* resumen, compendio; (law) digesto; [dɪˈdʒɛst] o [daɪˈdʒɛst] *va* (physiol. & chem.) digerir; (fig.) digerir (*meditar con cuidado, tratar de entender; sufrir con paciencia*); (fig.) resumir, compendiar; *vn* digerir, digerirse
**digester** [dɪˈdʒɛstər] o [daɪˈdʒɛstər] *s* compendiador; (med.) digestivo; digestor (*vasija cerrada a tornillo*)
**digestibility** [dɪ,dʒɛstɪˈbɪlɪtɪ] o [daɪ,dʒɛstɪˈbɪlɪtɪ] *s* digestibilidad
**digestible** [dɪˈdʒɛstɪbəl] o [daɪˈdʒɛstɪbəl] *adj* digerible, digestible
**digestion** [dɪˈdʒɛstʃən] o [daɪˈdʒɛstʃən] *s* digestión
**digestive** [dɪˈdʒɛstɪv] o [daɪˈdʒɛstɪv] *adj* & *s* digestivo
**digger** [ˈdɪgər] *s* cavador; azadón
**digger wasp** *s* (ent.) avispa cavadora
**diggings** [ˈdɪgɪŋz] *spl* excavaciones; (coll.) alojamiento
**digit** [ˈdɪdʒɪt] *s* (arith. & astr.) dígito; (hum.) dedo
**digital** [ˈdɪdʒɪtəl] *adj* digital; *s* (hum.) dedo; tecla
**digital computer** *s* calculadora numérica
**digitalin** [,dɪdʒɪˈtelɪn] o [ˈdɪdʒɪtəlɪn] *s* (chem. & pharm.) digitalina
**digitalis** [,dɪgɪˈtælɪs] o [,dɪdʒɪˈtelɪs] *s* (bot. & pharm.) digital
**digitate** [ˈdɪdʒɪtet] *adj* digitado; (bot.) digitado
**digitigrade** [ˈdɪdʒɪtɪ,gred] *adj* & *s* (zool.) digitígrado
**dignification** [,dɪgnɪfɪˈkeʃən] *s* dignificación
**dignified** [ˈdɪgnɪfaɪd] *adj* digno, grave, decoroso

**dignify** [ˈdɪgnɪfaɪ] (*pret & pp:* **-fied**) *va* dignificar; dar un título altisonante a
**dignitary** [ˈdɪgnɪˌtɛrɪ] *s* (*pl:* **-ies**) dignatario
**dignity** [ˈdɪgnɪtɪ] *s* (*pl:* **-ties**) dignidad; **to be beneath one's dignity** no estar de acuerdo con la dignidad de uno, ser impropio de la dignidad de uno; **to stand upon one's dignity** ponerse tan alto
**digram** [ˈdaɪgræm] *s* digrama
**digraph** [ˈdaɪgræf] o [ˈdaɪgrɑf] *s* digrafía, dígrafo
**digress** [dɪˈgrɛs] o [daɪˈgrɛs] *vn* divagar
**digression** [dɪˈgrɛʃən] o [daɪˈgrɛʃən] *s* digresión; (astr.) digresión
**digressive** [dɪˈgrɛsɪv] o [daɪˈgrɛsɪv] *adj* digresivo
**dihedral** [daɪˈhidrəl] *adj* (geom.) diedro
**diiamb** [ˌdaɪaɪˈæmb] *s* diyambo
**dike** [daɪk] *s* dique; zanja, arrecife; (geol.) dique; *va* contener por medio de un dique; desaguar con zanjas
**dilacerate** [dɪˈlæsəret] *va* dilacerar
**dilaceration** [dɪˌlæsəˈreʃən] *s* dilaceración
**dilapidate** [dɪˈlæpɪdet] *va* dilapidar (*malgastar*); desmantelar; *vn* desmantelarse (*abandonarse o arruinarse, p.ej., una casa*)
**dilapidated** [dɪˈlæpɪˌdetɪd] *adj* desmantelado
**dilapidation** [dɪˌlæpɪˈdeʃən] *s* dilapidación (*derroche*); desmantelamiento
**dilatability** [daɪˌletəˈbɪlɪtɪ] *s* dilatabilidad
**dilatable** [daɪˈletəbəl] *adj* dilatable
**dilatation** [ˌdɪləˈteʃən] o [ˌdaɪləˈteʃən] *s* dilatación
**dilate** [daɪˈlet] o [dɪˈlet] *va* dilatar; *vn* dilatarse
**dilation** [daɪˈleʃən] o [dɪˈleʃən] *s* dilatación
**dilative** [daɪˈletɪv] o [dɪˈletɪv] *adj* dilatativo
**dilatometer** [ˌdaɪləˈtɑmɪtər] o [ˌdɪləˈtɑmɪtər] *s* (phys.) dilatómetro
**dilator** [daɪˈletər] o [dɪˈletər] *s* (anat. & surg.) dilatador
**dilatory** [ˈdɪləˌtorɪ] *adj* tardío (*aplícase a acciones y personas*); (law) dilatorio
**dilemma** [dɪˈlɛmə] *s* dilema, disyuntiva; aprieto, conflicto; (log.) dilema
**dilettante** [ˌdɪləˈtæntɪ] *adj* diletante; *s* (*pl:* **-tes** o **-ti** [tɪ]) diletante
**dilettanteism** [ˌdɪləˈtæntɪɪzəm] or **dilettantism** [ˌdɪləˈtæntɪzəm] *s* diletantismo
**diligence** [ˈdɪlɪdʒəns] *s* diligencia
**diligent** [ˈdɪlɪdʒənt] *adj* diligente
**dill** [dɪl] *s* (bot.) eneldo
**dill pickle** *s* pepinillo encurtido sazonado con eneldo
**dillydally** [ˈdɪlɪˌdælɪ] (*pret & pp:* **-lied**) *vn* holgazanear, perder el tiempo
**diluent** [ˈdɪljuənt] *s* (med.) diluente
**dilute** [dɪˈlut] *adj* diluído; *va* diluir; *vn* diluirse
**dilution** [dɪˈluʃən] *s* dilución
**diluvial** [dɪˈluvɪəl] o **diluvian** [dɪˈluvɪən] *adj* diluviano
**dim.** abr. de **diminuendo** y **diminutive**
**dim** [dɪm] *adj* (*comp:* **dimmer;** *super:* **dimmest**) débil, mortecino; poco claro, obscuro, confuso, indistinto; lerdo, torpe; **to take a dim view of** mirar escépticamente, no entusiasmarse por; (*pret & pp:* **dimmed;** *ger:* **dimming**) *va* amortiguar, velar (*la luz*); poner a media luz (*p.ej., un faro*); obscurecer; *vn* obscurecerse
**dime** [daɪm] *s* (U.S.A.) moneda de diez centavos
**dime novel** *s* novela sensacional de ningún mérito literario
**dimension** [dɪˈmɛnʃən] *s* dimensión
**dimensional** [dɪˈmɛnʃənəl] *adj* dimensional
**dimeter** [ˈdɪmɪtər] *s* (pros.) dímetro
**dimetria** [daɪˈmitrɪə] *s* (med.) dimetría
**dimin.** abr. de **diminuendo** y **diminutive**
**diminish** [dɪˈmɪnɪʃ] *va* disminuir; *vn* disminuir, disminuirse
**diminished** [dɪˈmɪnɪʃt] *adj* (mus.) diminuto
**diminuendo** [dɪˌmɪnjuˈɛndo] *s* (*pl:* **-dos**) (mus.) diminuendo
**diminution** [ˌdɪmɪˈnjuʃən] o [ˌdɪmɪˈnuʃən] *s* diminución, disminución
**diminutive** [dɪˈmɪnjətɪv] *adj* diminuto; (gram.) diminutivo; *s* persona diminuta, cosa diminuta; (gram.) diminutivo
**dimissory letters** [ˈdɪmɪˌsorɪ] *spl* (eccl.) dimisorias
**dimity** [ˈdɪmɪtɪ] *s* (*pl:* **-ties**) cotonía
**dimmer** [ˈdɪmər] *s* amortiguador de luz; (aut.) faro, lámpara o luz de cruce
**dimorphism** [daɪˈmɔrfɪzəm] *s* dimorfismo
**dimorphous** [daɪˈmɔrfəs] *adj* dimorfo
**dimple** [ˈdɪmpəl] *s* hoyuelo; *va* formar hoyuelos en; *vn* formarse hoyuelos
**dimply** [ˈdɪmplɪ] *adj* que tiene hoyuelos
**din** [dɪn] *s* ruido ensordecedor y continuado; (*pret & pp:* **dinned;** *ger:* **dinning**) *va* atolondrar con ruido ensordecedor y continuado; repetir insistentemente; *vn* hacer un ruido ensordecedor y continuado
**Dinah** [ˈdaɪnə] *s* Dina
**Dinaric Alps** [dɪˈnærɪk] *spl* Alpes dináricos
**dine** [daɪn] *va* dar de comer a; *vn* comer; **to dine out** comer fuera de casa
**diner** [ˈdaɪnər] *s* convidado (a una comida); (rail.) coche-comedor; restaurante que se parece a un coche-comedor
**dinette** [daɪˈnɛt] *s* comedorcito, comedor pequeño junto a la cocina
**ding** [dɪŋ] *s* sonido, repique (*de campanas*); *va* repicar (*las campanas*); (coll.) repetir insistentemente; *vn* resonar
**Ding an sich** [dɪŋɑnˈzɪx] *s* (philos.) cosa en sí
**ding-dong** [ˈdɪŋˌdɔŋ] o [ˈdɪŋˌdɑŋ] *s* dindán, tintín; *va* importunar regañando; *vn* retiñir
**ding-dong theory** *s* (philol.) teoría de la invención
**dingey** [ˈdɪŋgɪ] *s* dinga
**dinghy** [ˈdɪŋgɪ] *s* (*pl:* **-ghies**) dinga
**dinginess** [ˈdɪndʒɪnɪs] *s* deslustre
**dingle** [ˈdɪŋgəl] *s* cañada pequeña
**dingo** [ˈdɪŋgo] *s* (*pl:* **-goes**) dingo (*perro salvaje*)
**dingus** [ˈdɪŋəs] *s* (slang) chisme, adminículo
**dingy** [ˈdɪndʒɪ] *adj* (*comp.* **-gier;** *super:* **-giest**) empañado, deslustrado, sucio, manchado; [ˈdɪŋgɪ] *s* (*pl:* **-gies**) dinga
**dining car** *s* (rail.) coche-comedor
**dining room** *s* comedor
**dining-room suit** [ˈdaɪnɪŋˌrum] o [ˈdaɪnɪŋˌrʊm] *s* juego de comedor
**dinkey** [ˈdɪŋkɪ] *s* (coll.) locomotora pequeña de maniobras
**dinky** [ˈdɪŋkɪ] *adj* (*comp:* **-ier;** *super:* **-iest**) (slang) diminuto, insignificante
**dinner** [ˈdɪnər] *s* comida; banquete
**dinner coat** o **dinner jacket** *s* smoking
**dinner pail** *s* fiambrera, portaviandas
**dinner set** *s* vajilla
**dinner time** *s* hora de la comida
**dinornis** [daɪˈnɔrnɪs] *s* (pal.) dinornis
**dinosaur** [ˈdaɪnəsɔr] o **dinosaurian** [ˌdaɪnəˈsɔrɪən] *s* (pal.) dinosaurio
**dinothere** [ˈdaɪnəθɪr] *s* (pal.) dinoterio
**dint** [dɪnt] *s* golpe; abolladura; fuerza; **by dint of** a fuerza de; *va* abollar
**diocesan** [daɪˈɑsɪsən] *adj & s* diocesano
**diocese** [ˈdaɪəsis] o [ˈdaɪəsɪs] *s* diócesi o diócesis
**Diocletian** [ˌdaɪəˈkliʃən] *s* Diocleciano
**diode** [ˈdaɪod] *s* (electron.) diodo
**dioecious** [daɪˈiʃəs] *adj* (biol. & bot.) dioico
**Diogenes** [daɪˈɑdʒɪniz] *s* Diógenes
**Diomede** [ˈdaɪəmid] o **Diomedes** [ˌdaɪəˈmidiz] *s* (myth.) Diomedes
**Dionysia** [ˌdaɪəˈnɪʃɪə] o [ˌdaɪəˈnɪsɪə] *spl* Dionisias, Dionisíacas (*fiestas*)
**Dionysiac** [ˌdaɪəˈnɪsɪæk] *adj* dionisíaco
**Dionysius** [ˌdaɪəˈnɪʃɪəs] *s* Dionisio
**Dionysos** o **Dionysus** [ˌdaɪəˈnaɪsəs] *s* (myth.) Dionisios o Dionisos
**diopter** [daɪˈɑptər] *s* dioptra, alidada; (opt.) dioptría (*unidad*)
**dioptric** [daɪˈɑptrɪk] *adj* dióptrico; **dioptrics** *ssg* dióptrica
**dioptrical** [daɪˈɑptrɪkəl] *adj* dióptrico
**diorama** [ˌdaɪəˈræmə] o [ˌdaɪəˈrɑmə] *s* diorama
**dioramic** [ˌdaɪəˈræmɪk] *adj* diorámico
**diorite** [ˈdaɪəraɪt] *s* (mineral.) diorita
**dioscoreaceous** [ˌdaɪɑsˌkorɪˈeʃəs] *adj* (bot.) dioscoreáceo
**Dioscuri** [ˌdaɪɑsˈkjuraɪ] *spl* (myth.) Dioscuros
**dioxide** [daɪˈɑksaɪd] o [daɪˈɑksɪd] *s* (chem.) dióxido
**dip** [dɪp] *s* inmersión, zambullida; baño corto; depresión (*p.ej., en un camino*); inclinación;

grado de inclinación; vela de sebo chorreada; (mach.) cuchara de lubricación; (geol.) buzamiento; (*pret & pp:* **dipped;** *ger:* **dipping**) *va* sumergir; sumergir para lavar o limpiar; sumergir en un tinte; sacar, levantar con cuchara, pala, etc.; bajar y alzar prontamente (*p.ej., una bandera*); *vn* sumergirse; bajar súbitamente, desaparecer súbitamente; inclinarse hacia abajo; (geol.) buzar; **to dip into** hojear, repasar (*p.ej., un libro*); empeñarse en, meterse en (*p.ej., un comercio*)
**dipetalous** [daɪˈpɛtələs] *adj* dipétalo
**diphase** [ˈdaɪˌfez] *adj* (elec.) difásico
**diphtheria** [dɪfˈθɪrɪə] *s* (path.) difteria
**diphtherial** [dɪfˈθɪrɪəl] o **diphtheritic** [ˌdɪfθəˈrɪtɪk] *adj* diftérico
**diphtheritis** [ˌdɪfθəˈraɪtɪs] *s* (path.) difteritis
**diphtheroid** [ˈdɪfθərɔɪd] *adj* difteroide
**diphthong** [ˈdɪfθɔŋ] o [ˈdɪfθɑŋ] *s* diptongo
**diphthongal** [dɪfˈθɔŋgəl] o [dɪfˈθɑŋgəl] *adj* de diptongo, del diptongo
**diphthongization** [ˌdɪfθɔŋgɪˈzeʃən] o [ˌdɪfθɑŋgɪˈzeʃən] *s* diptongación
**diphthongize** [ˈdɪfθɔŋgaɪz] o [ˈdɪfθɑŋgaɪz] *va* diptongar; *vn* diptongarse
**diphyllous** [daɪˈfɪləs] *adj* (bot.) dífilo
**diplegia** [daɪˈplidʒɪə] *s* (path.) diplejía
**diplochlamydeous** [ˌdɪpləkləˈmɪdɪəs] *adj* (bot.) diploclamídeo
**diplococcus** [ˌdɪpləˈkɑkəs] *s* (*pl:* **-cocci** [ˈkɑksaɪ]) (bact.) diplococo
**diplodocus** [dɪˈplɑdəkəs] *s* (pal.) diplodoco
**diploma** [dɪˈplomə] *s* diploma
**diplomacy** [dɪˈploməsɪ] *s* (*pl:* **-cies**) diplomacia
**diplomat** [ˈdɪpləmæt] *s* diplomático
**diplomate** [ˈdɪpləmɪt] o [ˈdɪpləmet] *s* diplomado
**diplomatic** [ˌdɪpləˈmætɪk] *adj* diplomático; **diplomatics** *ssg* diplomática (*arte de conocer los diplomas; diplomacia*)
**diplomatically** [ˌdɪpləˈmætɪkəlɪ] *adv* diplomáticamente
**diplomatic corps** *s* cuerpo diplomático
**diplomatic edition** *s* edición diplomática
**diplomatic pouch** *s* valija diplomática
**diplomatist** [dɪˈplomətɪst] *s* diplomático
**diplopia** [dɪˈplopɪə] *s* (med.) diplopía
**dipolar** [daɪˈpolər] *adj* dipolar
**dipole** [ˈdaɪˌpol] *s* (chem. & phys.) dipolo
**dipole antenna** *s* (rad.) antena dipolo
**dipper** [ˈdɪpər] *s* cazo, cucharón; cuchara (*de pala mecánica*); (orn.) zambullidor, mirlo de agua; **the Dipper** (astr.) el Carro
**dipsomania** [ˌdɪpsoˈmenɪə] *s* (path.) dipsomanía
**dipsomaniac** [ˌdɪpsoˈmenɪæk] *s* dipsomaníaco
**dipsomaniacal** [ˌdɪpsoməˈnaɪəkəl] *adj* dipsomaníaco
**dipstick** [ˈdɪpˌstɪk] *s* varilla de nivel
**dipteral** [ˈdɪptərəl] *adj* (zool. & arch.) díptero
**dipteran** [ˈdɪptərən] *adj & s* (zool.) díptero
**dipteros** [ˈdɪptərɑs] *s* (arch.) díptero (*edificio*)
**dipterous** [ˈdɪptərəs] *adj* (zool.) díptero
**diptych** [ˈdɪptɪk] *s* díptica (*tablas*); díptico (*cuadro*)
**Dircaen** [dʌrˈsiən] *adj* dirceo
**Dircaen Swan** *s* cisne dirceo (*Píndaro*)
**Dirce** [ˈdʌrsi] *s* (myth.) Dirce
**dire** [daɪr] *adj* horrendo, terrible, deplorable
**direct** [dɪˈrɛkt] o [daɪˈrɛkt] *adj* directo; sincero, franco, abierto; exacto, preciso; (gram.) directo; *va* dirigir; ordenar, mandar
**direct action** *s* acción directa
**direct current** *s* (elec.) corriente continua
**direct discourse** *s* (gram.) estilo directo
**direct distance dialing** *s* (telp.) marcaje directo a distancia
**direct hit** *s* blanco directo, impacto directo; **to score a direct hit** conseguir un impacto directo
**direction** [dɪˈrɛkʃən] o [daɪˈrɛkʃən] *s* dirección; instrucción; **in the direction of** en la dirección de, con rumbo a
**directional** [dɪˈrɛkʃənəl] o [daɪˈrɛkʃənəl] *adj* direccional
**directional antenna** *s* (rad.) antena direccional
**direction finder** *s* (rad.) radiogoniómetro
**directive** [dɪˈrɛktɪv] o [daɪˈrɛktɪv] *adj* directivo; *s* directorio, directriz
**directly** [dɪˈrɛktlɪ] o [daɪˈrɛktlɪ] *adj* directamente; inmediatamente, en seguida; exactamente, absolutamente
**directness** [dɪˈrɛktnɪs] o [daɪˈrɛktnɪs] *s* derechura
**direct object** *s* (gram.) complemento directo
**Directoire** [ˌdɪrɛkˈtwɑr] *s* Directorio
**director** [dɪˈrɛktər] o [daɪˈrɛktər] *s* director; vocal (*de un directorio*)
**directorate** [dɪˈrɛktərɪt] o [daɪˈrɛktərɪt] *s* dirección, directorio
**director-general** [dɪˈrɛktərˈdʒɛnərəl] o [daɪˈrɛktərˈdʒɛnərəl] *s* (*pl:* **director-generals**) director general
**directorial** [dɪˌrɛkˈtorɪəl] o [ˌdaɪrɛkˈtorɪəl] *adj* directoral (*del director*); directorio, directorial
**directorship** [dɪˈrɛktərʃɪp] o [daɪˈrɛktərʃɪp] *s* dirección, directorio
**directory** [dɪˈrɛktərɪ] o [daɪˈrɛktərɪ] *adj* directorio; *s* (*pl:* **-ries**) directorio (*junta directiva; libro de nombres y señas*); guía telefónica
**direct ratio** *s* (math.) razón directa
**directress** [dɪˈrɛktrɪs] o [daɪˈrɛktrɪs] *s* directora
**directrix** [dɪˈrɛktrɪks] o [daɪˈrɛktrɪks] *s* (geom.) directriz
**direct tax** *s* contribución directa
**direful** [ˈdaɪrfəl] *adj* terrible, calamitoso, espantoso
**dirge** [dʌrdʒ] *s* endecha, canto fúnebre; (eccl.) oficio de difuntos; (eccl.) misa de réquiem
**dirigible** [ˈdɪrɪdʒɪbəl] *adj & s* dirigible
**dirk** [dʌrk] *s* daga, puñal
**dirt** [dʌrt] *s* lodo, barro; polvo; tierra, suelo; bajeza, vileza; suciedad, porquería; obscenidad
**dirt-cheap** [ˈdʌrtˈtʃip] *adj* tirado, sumamente barato
**dirt farmer** *s* (coll.) agricultor practicón
**dirty** [ˈdʌrtɪ] *adj* (*comp:* **-ier;** *super:* **-iest**) enlodado, barroso; polvoriento; bajo, vil; sucio, puerco; obsceno; (*pret & pp:* **-tied**) *va* ensuciar
**dirty linen** *s* ropa sucia, ropa para lavar; **to air one's dirty linen** sacar los trapos sucios a relucir
**dirty trick** *s* (slang) perrada, perrería (*vileza*)
**disability** [ˌdɪsəˈbɪlɪtɪ] *s* (*pl:* **-ties**) inhabilidad, incapacidad; impedimento
**disable** [dɪsˈebəl] *va* inhabilitar; (law) descalificar
**disablement** [dɪsˈebəlmənt] *s* inhabilitación
**disabuse** [ˌdɪsəˈbjuz] *va* desengañar
**disaccord** [ˌdɪsəˈkɔrd] *s* desacuerdo; *vn* discordar
**disadvantage** [ˌdɪsədˈvæntɪdʒ] o [ˌdɪsədˈvɑntɪdʒ] *s* desventaja; *va* dañar, perjudicar
**disadvantageous** [dɪsˌædvənˈtedʒəs] *adj* desventajoso
**disaffect** [ˌdɪsəˈfɛkt] *va* indisponer, enemistar
**disaffected** [ˌdɪsəˈfɛktɪd] *adj* desafecto
**disaffection** [ˌdɪsəˈfɛkʃən] *s* desafección, desafecto
**disagree** [ˌdɪsəˈgri] *vn* desconvenir, desconvenirse, desavenirse; altercar, contender; **to disagree with** no estar de acuerdo con; no sentar bien a
**disagreeable** [ˌdɪsəˈgriəbəl] *adj* desagradable
**disagreeably** [ˌdɪsəˈgriəblɪ] *adv* desagradablemente
**disagreement** [ˌdɪsəˈgrimənt] *s* desacuerdo; altercado; desemejanza
**disallow** [ˌdɪsəˈlaʊ] *va* desaprobar, rechazar
**disallowance** [ˌdɪsəˈlaʊəns] *s* desaprobación, rechazamiento
**disappear** [ˌdɪsəˈpɪr] *vn* desaparecer, desaparecerse
**disappearance** [ˌdɪsəˈpɪrəns] *s* desaparecimiento, desaparición
**disappoint** [ˌdɪsəˈpɔɪnt] *va* decepcionar, desilusionar, frustrar; **to be disappointed** llevarse chasco
**disappointment** [ˌdɪsəˈpɔɪntmənt] *s* decepción, desilusión, frustración, chasco
**disapprobation** [ˌdɪsæprəˈbeʃən] o **disapproval** [ˌdɪsəˈpruvəl] *s* desaprobación
**disapprove** [ˌdɪsəˈpruv] *va & vn* desaprobar
**disapprovingly** [ˌdɪsəˈpruvɪŋlɪ] *adv* con desaprobación
**disarm** [dɪsˈɑrm] *va & vn* desarmar

**disarmament** [dɪsˈɑrməmənt] *s* desarme o desarmamiento
**disarmed** [dɪsˈɑrmd] *adj* desarmado; (her.) moznado
**disarrange** [ˌdɪsəˈrendʒ] *va* desarreglar, descomponer
**disarrangement** [ˌdɪsəˈrendʒmənt] *s* desarreglo, descomposición
**disarray** [ˌdɪsəˈre] *s* desarreglo, desorden; desatavío; *va* desarreglar, desordenar; desataviar
**disarticulate** [ˌdɪsɑrˈtɪkjəlet] *va* desarticular; (surg.) desarticular; *vn* desarticularse
**disarticulation** [ˌdɪsɑrˌtɪkjəˈleʃən] *s* desarticulación; (surg.) desarticulación
**disassemble** [ˌdɪsəˈsɛmbəl] *va* desarmar, desmontar
**disassimilate** [ˌdɪsəˈsɪmɪlet] *va* (physiol.) desasimilar
**disassimilation** [ˌdɪsəˌsɪmɪˈleʃən] *s* (physiol.) desasimilación
**disassociate** [ˌdɪsəˈsoʃɪet] *va* disociar
**disassociation** [ˌdɪsəˌsosɪˈeʃən] o [ˌdɪsəˌsoʃɪˈeʃən] *s* disociación
**disaster** [dɪzˈæstər] o [dɪzˈɑstər] *s* desastre
**disastrous** [dɪzˈæstrəs] o [dɪzˈɑstrəs] *adj* desastroso, funesto
**disavow** [ˌdɪsəˈvaʊ] *va* negar, desconocer
**disavowal** [ˌdɪsəˈvaʊəl] *s* negación, desconocimiento
**disband** [dɪsˈbænd] *va* disolver; licenciar (*tropas*); *vn* desbandarse
**disbandment** [dɪsˈbændmənt] *s* disolución; licenciamiento
**disbar** [dɪsˈbɑr] (*pret & pp:* **-barred;** *ger:* **-barring**) *va* (law) excluir del foro
**disbarment** [dɪsˈbɑrmənt] *s* (law) exclusión del foro
**disbelief** [ˌdɪsbɪˈlif] *s* incredulidad, descreimiento
**disbelieve** [ˌdɪsbɪˈliv] *va & vn* descreer
**disburden** [dɪsˈbʌrdən] *va* descargar; *vn* descargarse
**disburse** [dɪsˈbʌrs] *va* desembolsar
**disbursement** [dɪsˈbʌrsmənt] *s* desembolso
**disbursement office** *s* pagaduría
**disburser** [dɪsˈbʌrsər] *s* pagador
**disc.** abr. de **discount, discovered** y **discoverer**
**disc** [dɪsk] *s* var. de **disk**
**discalced** [dɪsˈkælst] *adj* descalzo (*fraile*)
**discard** [ˈdɪskɑrd] *s* descarte; **to put** o **to throw in the discard** (coll.) echar a un lado; [dɪsˈkɑrd] *va* descartar; *vn* descartarse
**discern** [dɪˈzʌrn] o [dɪˈsʌrn] *va & vn* discernir, percibir
**discerner** [dɪˈzʌrnər] o [dɪˈsʌrnər] *s* discernidor
**discernible** [dɪˈzʌrnɪbəl] o [dɪˈsʌrnɪbəl] *adj* discernible
**discerning** [dɪˈzʌrnɪŋ] o [dɪˈsʌrnɪŋ] *adj* discerniente, discernidor, perspicaz
**discernment** [dɪˈzʌrnmənt] o [dɪˈsʌrnmənt] *s* discernimiento, percepción, perspicacia
**discharge** [dɪsˈtʃɑrdʒ] *s* descarga; descargo (*pago de una deuda; disculpa*); cumplimiento, desempeño (*de un deber*); liberación (*de un preso*); despedida, remoción; descarga unitaria; (elec.) descarga; (med.) derrame; (mil.) certificado de licencia; *va* descargar; desempeñar (*p.ej., un deber*); libertar, soltar (*a un preso*); despedir, despachar, remover; dar de alta (*a un enfermo*); (elec.) descargar; (mil.) licenciar; *vn* descargar (*dícese de un tubo, conducto, río, etc.*); descargarse (*un arma de fuego*); correrse (*un tinte*)
**disciple** [dɪˈsaɪpəl] *s* discípulo
**discipleship** [dɪˈsaɪpəlʃɪp] *s* discipulado
**disciplinable** [ˈdɪsɪplɪnəbəl] *adj* disciplinable; castigable, punible
**disciplinal** [ˌdɪsɪˈplaɪnəl] *adj* disciplinal
**disciplinarian** [ˌdɪsɪplɪˈnɛrɪən] *adj* disciplinario; *s* ordenancista
**disciplinary** [ˈdɪsɪplɪˌnɛrɪ] *adj* disciplinario
**discipline** [ˈdɪsɪplɪn] *s* disciplina; castigo; *va* disciplinar; castigar
**discipular** [dɪˈsɪpjələr] *adj* discipular
**disclaim** [dɪsˈklem] *va* negar, desconocer; (law) renunciar
**disclaimer** [dɪsˈklemər] *s* negación, desconocimiento; (law) renuncia
**disclose** [dɪsˈkloz] *va* descubrir; revelar, divulgar, publicar
**disclosure** [dɪsˈkloʒər] *s* descubrimiento; revelación, divulgación, publicación
**discoidal** [dɪsˈkɔɪdəl] *adj* discoidal
**discolor** [dɪsˈkʌlər] *adj* (bot.) discoloro; *va* descolorar, manchar; *vn* descolorarse, mancharse
**discoloration** [dɪsˌkʌləˈreʃən] *s* descoloración, descoloramiento
**discomfit** [dɪsˈkʌmfɪt] *va* derrotar; burlar, frustrar; desconcertar
**discomfiture** [dɪsˈkʌmfɪtʃər] *s* derrota; burla, frustración; desconcierto
**discomfort** [dɪsˈkʌmfərt] *s* incomodidad; *va* incomodar
**discompose** [ˌdɪskəmˈpoz] *va* agitar, inquietar, descomponer, desconcertar
**discomposure** [ˌdɪskəmˈpoʒər] *s* agitación, inquietud, descomposición, desconcierto
**disconcert** [ˌdɪskənˈsʌrt] *va* desconcertar, agitar, confundir
**disconcerting** [ˌdɪskənˈsʌrtɪŋ] *adj* desconcertante
**disconformity** [ˌdɪskənˈfɔrmɪtɪ] *s* disconformidad
**disconnect** [ˌdɪskəˈnɛkt] *va* desunir, desacoplar; (elec. & mach.) desconectar
**disconnected** [ˌdɪskəˈnɛktɪd] *adj* inconexo, incoherente; (elec. & mach.) desconectado
**disconnection** [ˌdɪskəˈnɛkʃən] *s* desunión; desconexión
**disconsolate** [dɪsˈkɑnsəlɪt] *adj* desconsolado
**disconsolation** [dɪsˌkɑnsəˈleʃən] *s* desconsuelo
**discontent** [ˌdɪskənˈtɛnt] *adj & s* descontento; *va* descontentar
**discontented** [ˌdɪskənˈtɛntɪd] *adj* descontento
**discontentment** [ˌdɪskənˈtɛntmənt] *s* descontentamiento, descontento
**discontinuance** [ˌdɪskənˈtɪnjʊəns] o **discontinuation** [ˌdɪskənˌtɪnjʊˈeʃən] *s* descontinuación o discontinuación
**discontinue** [ˌdɪskənˈtɪnjʊ] *va* descontinuar o discontinuar
**discontinuity** [ˌdɪskɑntɪˈnjuɪtɪ] o [ˌdɪskɑntɪˈnuɪtɪ] *s* discontinuidad
**discontinuous** [ˌdɪskənˈtɪnjʊəs] *adj* descontinuo o discontinuo
**discophile** [ˈdɪskofaɪl] *s* discófilo
**discord** [ˈdɪskɔrd] *s* discordia, desacuerdo; disonancia; [dɪsˈkɔrd] *vn* discordar
**discordance** [dɪsˈkɔrdəns] o **discordancy** [dɪsˈkɔrdənsɪ] *s* discordancia; (geol.) discordancia
**discordant** [dɪsˈkɔrdənt] *adj* discordante; (geol.) discordante
**discount** [ˈdɪskaʊnt] *s* descuento; **at a discount** al descuento; mal acogido; [ˈdɪskaʊnt] o [dɪsˈkaʊnt] *va* descontar; considerar exagerado
**discountable** [dɪsˈkaʊntəbəl] *adj* descontable
**discountenance** [dɪsˈkaʊntɪnəns] *va* desaprobar; avergonzar
**discount house** *s* tienda de descuento
**discount rate** *s* tipo de descuento; tipo de redescuento
**discourage** [dɪsˈkʌrɪdʒ] *va* desalentar, desanimar; desaprobar; disuadir; **to discourage from** + *ger* disuadir de + *inf*
**discouragement** [dɪsˈkʌrɪdʒmənt] *s* desaliento, desánimo; desaprobación; disuasión
**discourse** [ˈdɪskors] o [dɪsˈkors] *s* discurso; [dɪsˈkors] *vn* discurrir
**discourteous** [dɪsˈkʌrtɪəs] *adj* descortés
**discourtesy** [dɪsˈkʌrtɪsɪ] *s* (*pl:* **-sies**) descortesía
**discover** [dɪsˈkʌvər] *va* descubrir
**discoverer** [dɪsˈkʌvərər] *s* descubridor
**discovery** [dɪsˈkʌvərɪ] *s* (*pl:* **-ies**) descubrimiento
**Discovery Day** *s* día de la raza, fiesta de la hispanidad
**discredit** [dɪsˈkrɛdɪt] *s* descrédito; *va* desacreditar; descreer
**discreditable** [dɪsˈkrɛdɪtəbəl] *adj* ignominioso, deshonroso, vergonzoso
**discreditably** [dɪsˈkrɛdɪtəblɪ] *adv* ignominiosamente, deshonrosamente, vergonzosamente
**discreet** [dɪsˈkrit] *adj* discreto (*moderado en*

*sus acciones o palabras; que incluye discreción)*
**discrepancy** [dɪsˈkrɛpənsɪ] *s* (*pl:* **-cies**) discrepancia
**discrepant** [dɪsˈkrɛpənt] *adj* discrepante
**discrete** [dɪsˈkrit] *adj* discreto (*discontinuo; que se compone de partes separadas*); (math. & med.) discreto
**discretion** [dɪsˈkrɛʃən] *s* discreción; **at discretion** a discreción
**discretional** [dɪsˈkrɛʃənəl] o **discretionary** [dɪsˈkrɛʃəˌnɛrɪ] *adj* discrecional
**discriminant** [dɪsˈkrɪmɪnənt] *adj* discriminante; *s* (math.) discriminante
**discriminate** [dɪsˈkrɪmɪnet] *va* discriminar; *vn* discriminar; hacer distinciones injustas; **to be discriminated against** ser tratado desfavorablemente; **to discriminate against** hacer distinción en perjuicio de; **to discriminate between** distinguir entre
**discriminating** [dɪsˈkrɪmɪˌnetɪŋ] *adj* distintivo, discerniente, discriminante; diferencial (*dícese de los derechos de aduana*); injusto, parcial
**discrimination** [dɪsˌkrɪmɪˈneʃən] *s* distinción, discernimiento, discriminación (*especialmente contra una persona o varias personas*)
**discriminative** [dɪsˈkrɪmɪˌnetɪv] o **discriminatory** [dɪsˈkrɪmɪnəˌtorɪ] *adj* distintivo, discerniente, discriminativo; injusto, parcial
**discrown** [dɪsˈkraʊn] *va* quitar la corona a, destronar
**discursive** [dɪsˈkʌrsɪv] *adj* digresivo, divagador
**discus** [ˈdɪskəs] *s* (sport) disco
**discuss** [dɪsˈkʌs] *va* discutir; hablar de, tratar de; (hum.) catar, probar (*un manjar, una bebida*); *vn* discutir
**discussion** [dɪsˈkʌʃən] *s* discusión
**discus thrower** *s* discóbolo
**disdain** [dɪsˈden] *s* desdén; *va* desdeñar
**disdainful** [dɪsˈdenfəl] *adj* desdeñoso
**disease** [dɪˈziz] *s* enfermedad; *adj* patógeno; *va* enfermar
**diseased** [dɪˈzizd] *adj* enfermo; morboso
**disembark** [ˌdɪsɛmˈbɑrk] *va & vn* desembarcar
**disembarkation** [dɪsˌɛmbɑrˈkeʃən] *s* desembarco (*de pasajeros*); desembarque (*de mercancías*)
**disembarrass** [ˌdɪsɛmˈbærəs] *va* desembarazar; librar de turbación
**disembodiment** [ˌdɪsɛmˈbɑdɪmənt] *s* separación del alma y el cuerpo
**disembody** [ˌdɪsɛmˈbɑdɪ] (*pret & pp:* **-ied**) *va* desencarnar; **disembodied spirit** espíritu desencarnado
**disembowel** [ˌdɪsɛmˈbaʊəl] (*pret & pp:* **-eled;** o **-elled;** *ger:* **-eling** o **-elling**) *va* desentrañar
**disembowelment** [ˌdɪsɛmˈbaʊəlmənt] *s* desentrañamiento
**disenchant** [ˌdɪsɛnˈtʃænt] o [ˌdɪsɛnˈtʃɑnt] *va* desencantar
**disenchantment** [ˌdɪsɛnˈtʃæntmənt] o [ˌdɪsɛnˈtʃɑntmənt] *s* desencantamiento o desencanto
**disencumber** [ˌdɪsɛnˈkʌmbər] *va* descombrar
**disencumbrance** [ˌdɪsɛnˈkʌmbrəns] *s* descombro
**disendow** [ˌdɪsɛnˈdaʊ] *va* privar de dotación, privar de subvención
**disendowment** [ˌdɪsɛnˈdaʊmənt] *s* privación de dotación, privación de subvención
**disenfranchise** [ˌdɪsɛnˈfræntʃaɪz] *va* var. de **disfranchise**
**disengage** [ˌdɪsɛnˈgedʒ] *va* desembarazar; desasir, desunir, desenganchar, soltar; desempeñar
**disengaged** [ˌdɪsɛnˈgedʒd] *adj* desembarazado; separado; desocupado
**disengagement** [ˌdɪsɛnˈgedʒmənt] *s* desembarazo; desasimiento; desempeño
**disentangle** [ˌdɪsɛnˈtæŋgəl] *va* desenredar
**desentanglement** [ˌdɪsɛnˈtæŋgəlmənt] *s* desenredo
**disenthrone** [ˌdɪsɛnˈθron] *va* var. de **dethrone**
**disentwine** [ˌdɪsɛnˈtwaɪn] *va* desenredar, desenmarañar
**disepalous** [daɪˈsɛpələs] *adj* (bot.) disépalo
**disestablish** [ˌdɪsɛsˈtæblɪʃ] *va* separar (*la Iglesia*) del Estado
**disestablishment** [ˌdɪsɛsˈtæblɪʃmənt] *s* separación de la Iglesia del Estado
**disesteem** [ˌdɪsɛsˈtim] *s* desestima o desestimación; *va* desestimar
**diseuse** [diˈzøz] *s* recitadora
**disfavor** [dɪsˈfevər] *s* disfavor, desgracia; *va* desfavorecer
**disfigure** [dɪsˈfɪgjər] *va* desfigurar
**disfigurement** [dɪsˈfɪgjərmənt] *s* desfiguración o desfiguramiento
**disfranchise** [dɪsˈfræntʃaɪz] *va* privar de derechos de ciudadanía
**disfranchisement** [dɪsˈfræntʃɪzmənt] *s* privación de derechos de ciudadanía
**disgorge** [dɪsˈgɔrdʒ] *va* vomitar; desembuchar (*dícese de las aves*); (fig.) vomitar (*arrojar de sí; entregar de mala gana*); *vn* vomitar; (fig.) vomitar
**disgrace** [dɪsˈgres] *s* deshonra, ignominia; desgracia, disfavor; **in disgrace** desacreditado; sin favor, en la desgracia; *va* deshonrar, desacreditar; despedir con ignominia
**disgraceful** [dɪsˈgresfəl] *adj* deshonroso, ignominioso, vergonzoso
**disgruntle** [dɪsˈgrʌntəl] *va* descontentar, disgustar, enfadar
**disgruntlement** [dɪsˈgrʌntəlmənt] *s* descontento, disgusto, enfado
**disguise** [dɪsˈgaɪz] *s* disfraz; *va* disfrazar
**disgust** [dɪsˈgʌst] *s* repugnancia, asco; *va* repugnar, dar asco a
**disgusting** [dɪsˈgʌstɪŋ] *adj* repugnante, asqueroso
**dish** [dɪʃ] *s* plato; vasija; **dishes** *spl* vajilla, vajilla de mesa; **to wash the dishes** lavar la vajilla, lavar los platos; *va* servir en un plato; formar una concavidad en; (slang) vencer, arruinar
**dishabille** [ˌdɪsəˈbil] *s* var. de **deshabille**
**disharmony** [dɪsˈhɑrmənɪ] *s* (*pl:* **-nies**) discordia, disonancia
**dishcloth** [ˈdɪʃˌklɔθ] o [ˈdɪʃˌklɑθ] *s* albero, paño de cocina
**dishearten** [dɪsˈhɑrtən] *va* abatir, desalentar, desanimar, descorazonar
**disheartening** [dɪsˈhɑrtənɪŋ] *adj* desalentador
**dishevel** [dɪˈʃɛvəl] (*pret & pp:* **-eled** o **-elled;** *ger:* **-eling** o **-elling**) *va* desgreñar, desmelenar
**dishonest** [dɪsˈɑnɪst] *adj* ímprobo, no honrado, fraudulento
**dishonesty** [dɪsˈɑnɪstɪ] *s* (*pl:* **-ties**) improbidad, falta de honradez, fraude
**dishonor** [dɪsˈɑnər] *s* deshonra, deshonor; *va* deshonrar, deshonorar; (com.) no aceptar (*un giro*); no pagar (*un cheque*)
**dishonorable** [dɪsˈɑnərəbəl] *adj* deshonroso
**dishpan** [ˈdɪʃˌpæn] *s* paila de lavar platos
**dish rack** *s* escurreplatos
**dishrag** [ˈdɪʃˌræg] *s* albero
**dishtowel** [ˈdɪʃˌtaʊəl] *s* paño para secar platos
**dishwasher** [ˈdɪʃˌwɑʃər] o [ˈdɪʃˌwɔʃər] *s* fregona; lavadora de platos o de vajilla, máquina de lavar platos, lavaplatos
**dishwater** [ˈdɪʃˌwɔtər] o [ˈdɪʃˌwɑtər] *s* agua de lavar platos
**disillusion** [ˌdɪsɪˈluʒən] *s* desilusión; *va* desilusionar
**disillusionment** [ˌdɪsɪˈluʒənmənt] *s* desilusión
**disinclination** [dɪsˌɪnklɪˈneʃən] *s* aversión, mala gana, repugnancia
**disincline** [ˌdɪsɪnˈklaɪn] *va* desinclinar; *vn* desinclinarse
**disinclined** [ˌdɪsɪnˈklaɪnd] *adj* desinclinado
**disincrust** [ˌdɪsɪnˈkrʌst] *va* desincrustar
**disincrustant** [ˌdɪsɪnˈkrʌstənt] *s* desincrustante
**disinfect** [ˌdɪsɪnˈfɛkt] *va* desinfectar, desinficionar
**disinfectant** [ˌdɪsɪnˈfɛktənt] *adj & s* desinfectante
**disinfection** [ˌdɪsɪnˈfɛkʃən] *s* desinfección
**disinfest** [ˌdɪsɪnˈfɛst] *va* desinfestar
**disingenuous** [ˌdɪsɪnˈdʒɛnjʊəs] *adj* doble, falso, disimulado
**disinherit** [ˌdɪsɪnˈhɛrɪt] *va* desheredar
**disinheritance** [ˌdɪsɪnˈhɛrɪtəns] *s* desheredación

**disintegrate** [dɪsˈɪntɪgret] *va* desagregar, desintegrar, disgregar; *vn* desagregarse, desintegrarse, disgregarse
**disintegration** [dɪsˌɪntɪˈgreʃən] *s* desagregación, desintegración, disgregación; (geol.) desagregación
**disintegrator** [dɪsˈɪntɪˌgretər] *s* disgregador
**disinter** [ˌdɪsɪnˈtʌr] (*pret & pp:* **-terred;** *ger:* **-terring**) *va* desenterrar; (fig.) desenterrar, descubrir
**disinterested** [dɪsˈɪntərɛstɪd] o [dɪsˈɪntrɪstɪd] *adj* desinteresado, imparcial
**disinterestedness** [dɪsˈɪntərɛstɪdnɪs] o [dɪsˈɪntrɪstɪdnɪs] *s* desinterés
**disinterment** [ˌdɪsɪnˈtʌrmənt] *s* desenterramiento
**disjoin** [dɪsˈdʒɔɪn] *va* desunir, separar
**disjoint** [dɪsˈdʒɔɪnt] *va* desarticular, dislocar, descoyuntar, desarreglar; *vn* desarticularse, dislocarse, descoyuntarse, desarreglarse
**disjointed** [dɪsˈdʒɔɪntɪd] *adj* desarticulado, dislocado, descoyuntado; desunido; inconexo, incoherente
**disjunction** [dɪsˈdʒʌŋkʃən] *s* disyunción; (log.) disyunción
**disjunctive** [dɪsˈdʒʌŋktɪv] *adj* disyuntivo; *s* (gram.) conjunción disyuntiva; (log.) proposición disyuntiva
**disk** [dɪsk] *s* disco; (astr., bot., & zool.) disco
**disk harrow** *s* (agr.) grada de discos
**disk jockey** *s* (rad.) locutor de un programa de discos
**dislike** [dɪsˈlaɪk] *s* aversión, antipatía; **to take a dislike for** cobrar aversión a; *va* tener aversión a, desamar
**dislocate** [ˈdɪsloket] *va* dislocar, dislocarse (*p.ej., un hueso*)
**dislocation** [ˌdɪsloˈkeʃən] *s* dislocación; (geol.) dislocación
**dislodge** [dɪsˈlɑdʒ] *va* desalojar
**dislodgment** [dɪsˈlɑdʒmənt] *s* desalojamiento
**disloyal** [dɪsˈlɔɪəl] *adj* desleal
**disloyalty** [dɪsˈlɔɪəltɪ] *s* (*pl:* **-ties**) deslealtad
**dismal** [ˈdɪzməl] *adj* obscuro, tenebroso, lúgubre; miserable, desgraciado
**Dismal Swamp** *s* Pantano maldito (*en los estados de Virginia y la Carolina del Norte, EE.UU.*)
**dismantle** [dɪsˈmæntəl] *va* desarmar, desmontar, desmantelar; desguarnecer; desamueblar; (naut.) desaparejar
**dismast** [dɪsˈmæst] o [dɪsˈmɑst] *va* (naut.) desarbolar
**dismay** [dɪsˈme] *s* consternación; *va* consternar
**dismember** [dɪsˈmɛmbər] *va* desmembrar
**dismemberment** [dɪsˈmɛmbərmənt] *s* desmembración
**dismiss** [dɪsˈmɪs] *va* despedir, destituir; dar permiso a (*una persona*) para irse; echar en olvido; (law) rechazar (*p.ej., una demanda*); (mil.) licenciar
**dismissal** [dɪsˈmɪsəl] *s* despedida, destitución; permiso para irse; (law) rechazamiento; (mil.) licenciamiento
**dismission** [dɪsˈmɪʃən] *s* var. de **dismissal**
**dismount** [dɪsˈmaʊnt] *va* desmontar; *vn* desmontar, desmontarse
**disobedience** [ˌdɪsəˈbidɪəns] *s* desobediencia
**disobedient** [ˌdɪsəˈbidɪənt] *adj* desobediente
**disobey** [ˌdɪsəˈbe] *va & vn* desobedecer
**disoblige** [ˌdɪsəˈblaɪdʒ] *va* desobligar
**disobliging** [ˌdɪsəˈblaɪdʒɪŋ] *adj* poco servicial
**disorder** [dɪsˈɔrdər] *s* desorden; *va* desordenar
**disorderly** [dɪsˈɔrdərlɪ] *adj* desordenado; alborotador; *adv* desordenadamente; turbulentamente
**disorderly conduct** *s* conducta escandalosa, perturbación del orden público
**disorderly house** *s* burdel (*casa de niñas, casa de prostitución; casa en que se falta al decoro con ruido y confusión*); casa de juego
**disorganization** [dɪsˌɔrgənɪˈzeʃən] *s* desorganización
**disorganize** [dɪsˈɔrgənaɪz] *va* desorganizar
**disorganizer** [dɪsˈɔrgəˌnaɪzər] *s* desorganizador
**disorientation** [dɪsˌorɪɛnˈteʃən] *s* (psycopath.) desorientación
**disown** [dɪsˈon] *va* desconocer, repudiar
**disparage** [dɪˈspærɪdʒ] *va* desdorar; desacreditar
**disparagement** [dɪˈspærɪdʒmənt] *s* desdoro; descrédito
**disparagingly** [dɪˈspærɪdʒɪŋlɪ] *adv* con desdoro; desacreditando
**disparate** [ˈdɪspəret] o [ˈdɪspərɪt] *adj* dispar, disparejo
**disparity** [dɪˈspærɪtɪ] *s* (*pl:* **-ties**) disparidad
**dispart** [dɪsˈpɑrt] *va* despartir; *vn* despartirse, partirse
**dispassion** [dɪsˈpæʃən] *s* desinterés, imparcialidad
**dispassionate** [dɪsˈpæʃənɪt] *adj* desapasionado
**dispatch** [dɪˈspætʃ] *s* despacho; *va* despachar; (coll.) despabilar (*alimento, una comida*)
**dispatcher** [dɪˈspætʃər] *s* despachador
**dispel** [dɪˈspɛl] (*pret & pp:* **-pelled;** *ger:* **-pelling**) *va* desvanecer, dispersar
**dispensable** [dɪˈspɛnsəbəl] *adj* dispensable; poco importante
**dispensary** [dɪˈspɛnsərɪ] *s* (*pl:* **-ries**) dispensario
**dispensation** [ˌdɪspɛnˈseʃən] *s* dispensación; designio divino, acto providencial
**dispensatory** [dɪˈspɛnsəˌtorɪ] *s* (*pl:* **-ries**) dispensatorio (*farmacopea; dispensario*)
**dispense** [dɪˈspɛns] *va* dispensar, otorgar, distribuir; eximir; administrar (*p.ej., justicia*); preparar (*medicamentos compuestos*); *vn* conceder dispensa; **to dispense with** pasar sin; deshacerse de
**dispenser** [dɪˈspɛnsər] *s* dispensador, surtidor, expedidor
**dispeople** [dɪsˈpipəl] *va* despoblar
**dispersal** [dɪˈspʌrsəl] *s* dispersión
**disperse** [dɪˈspʌrs] *va* dispersar; *vn* dispersarse
**dispersion** [dɪˈspʌrʒən] o [dɪˈspʌrʃən] *s* dispersión; (phys.) dispersión
**dispersive** [dɪˈspʌrsɪv] *adj* dispersivo
**dispireme** [daɪˈspaɪrim] *s* (biol.) dispirema
**dispirit** [dɪˈspɪrɪt] *va* desalentar, desanimar
**displace** [dɪsˈples] *va* dislocar; tomar el lugar de; destituir; desplazar (*un volumen de agua*); (chem.) reemplazar
**displaced person** *s* persona desplazada
**displacement** [dɪsˈplesmənt] *s* dislocación; cambio de situación; destitución; desplazamiento (*de un volumen de agua*); (chem.) reemplazo; (geol.) falla, quiebra; cilindrada (*de un pistón o émbolo*)
**display** [dɪˈsple] *s* despliegue; exhibición; ostentación; **on display** en exhibición; *va* desplegar; exhibir; ostentar
**display cabinet** *s* escaparate, vitrina
**display window** *s* escaparate de tienda
**displease** [dɪsˈpliz] *va* desplacer, desagradar, disgustar
**displeasing** [dɪsˈplizɪŋ] *adj* desagradable
**displeasure** [dɪsˈplɛʒər] *s* desplacer, desagrado, disgusto
**disport** [dɪˈsport] *s* diversión; *va* divertir; **to disport oneself** divertirse; *vn* divertirse; retozar, juguetear
**disposable** [dɪˈspozəbəl] *adj* disponible
**disposal** [dɪˈspozəl] *s* disposición; arreglo, ajuste; distribución; venta, liquidación; colocación; evacuación; eliminación, destrucción; **at the disposal of** a la disposición de; **to have at one's disposal** disponer de
**dispose** [dɪˈspoz] *va* disponer, arreglar, componer; mover, inducir, decidir; exponer; *vn* disponer; **to dispose of** disponer de; deshacerse de; dar; vender; comer, beber; arreglar, componer
**disposition** [ˌdɪspəˈzɪʃən] *s* disposición; índole, genio, natural; arreglo, ajuste; distribución; venta
**dispossess** [ˌdɪspəˈzɛs] *va* desposeer; desahuciar (*expulsar*)
**dispossession** [ˌdɪspəˈzɛʃən] *s* desposeimiento; desahucio (*expulsión*)
**dispraise** [dɪsˈprez] *s* censura, desaprobación; *va* censurar, desaprobar
**disproof** [dɪsˈpruf] *s* confutación, refutación
**disproportion** [ˌdɪsprəˈporʃən] *s* desproporción; *va* desproporcionar
**disproportional** [ˌdɪsprəˈporʃənəl] *adj* desproporcionado

**disproportionally** [ˌdɪsprəˈporʃənəlɪ] *adv* desproporcionadamente
**disproportionate** [ˌdɪsprəˈporʃənɪt] *adj* desproporcionado
**disproportionately** [ˌdɪsprəˈporʃənɪtlɪ] *adv* desproporcionadamente
**disprove** [dɪsˈpruv] *va* confutar, refutar
**disputable** [dɪˈspjutəbəl] *adj* disputable
**disputant** [ˈdɪspjʊtənt] *adj & s* disputador
**disputation** [ˌdɪspjʊˈteʃən] *s* disputa
**disputatious** [ˌdɪspjʊˈteʃəs] o **disputative** [dɪˈspjutətɪv] *adj* disputador
**dispute** [dɪˈspjut] *s* disputa; **beyond dispute** sin disputa; **in dispute** disputado, cuestionado; *va & vn* disputar
**disqualification** [ˌdɪsˌkwɑlɪfɪˈkeʃən]] *s* inhabilitación; descalificación; (sport) desclasificación, descalificación
**disqualify** [dɪsˈkwɑlɪfaɪ] (*pret & pp:* **-fied**) *va* inhabilitar, incapacitar; descalificar (*privar de un derecho, etc.*); (sport) desclasificar, descalificar
**disquiet** [dɪsˈkwaɪət] *s* inquietud, desasosiego; *va* inquietar, desasosegar
**disquietude** [dɪsˈkwaɪətjud] o [dɪsˈkwaɪətud] *s* inquietud
**disquisition** [ˌdɪskwɪˈzɪʃən] *s* disertación, disquisición
**disregard** [ˌdɪsrɪˈgɑrd] *s* desatención, desaire; *va* desatender, desairar; pasar por alto
**disregardful** [ˌdɪsrɪˈgɑrdfəl] *adj* desatento, negligente
**disrelish** [dɪsˈrɛlɪʃ] *s* aversión, repugnancia; *va* sentir aversión a, sentir repugnancia a
**disremember** [ˌdɪsrɪˈmɛmbər] *va* (coll.) olvidar
**disrepair** [ˌdɪsrɪˈpɛr] *s* mal estado, desconcierto
**disreputable** [dɪsˈrɛpjətəbəl] *adj* desacreditado, de mala fama; deshonroso, desdoroso, ignominioso
**disrepute** [ˌdɪsrɪˈpjut] *s* descrédito, mala fama; **in disrepute** desacreditado; **to bring into disrepute** desacreditar
**disrespect** [ˌdɪsrɪˈspɛkt] *s* desacato; *va* desacatar
**disrespectful** [ˌdɪsrɪˈspɛktfəl] *adj* irrespetuoso, desacatador
**disrobe** [dɪsˈrob] *va* desnudar; *vn* desnudarse
**disrupt** [dɪsˈrʌpt] *va* romper; desbaratar, desorganizar
**disruption** [dɪsˈrʌpʃən] *s* rompimiento; desbarate, desorganización
**disruptive** [dɪsˈrʌptɪv] *adj* rompedor; desorganizador; (elec.) disruptivo
**dissatisfaction** [ˌdɪssætɪsˈfækʃən] *s* descontento, desagrado
**dissatisfactory** [ˌdɪssætɪsˈfæktərɪ] *adj* poco satisfactorio, nada satisfactorio
**dissatisfied** [dɪsˈsætɪsfaɪd] *adj* descontento, malcontento
**dissatisfy** [dɪsˈsætɪsfaɪ] (*pret & pp:* **-fied**) *va* descontentar, desagradar
**dissect** [dɪˈsɛkt] *va* disecar; (fig.) disecar
**dissected** [dɪˈsɛktɪd] *adj* dividido; cortado en pedazos; (bot.) disecado (*dícese especialmente de algunas hojas*)
**dissection** [dɪˈsɛkʃən] *s* disección; objecto disecado; (fig.) disección (*análisis minuciosa*)
**dissector** [dɪˈsɛktər] *s* disector; instrumento para disecar
**disseize** [dɪsˈsiz] *va* (law) desposeer injustamente
**disseizin** [dɪsˈsizɪn] *s* (law) desposeimiento injusto
**dissemble** [dɪˈsɛmbəl] *va* disimular; *vn* ser hipócrita
**disseminate** [dɪˈsɛmɪnet] *va* diseminar, difundir
**dissemination** [dɪˌsɛmɪˈneʃən] *s* diseminación, difusión
**disseminator** [dɪˈsɛmɪˌnetər] *s* diseminador
**dissension** [dɪˈsɛnʃən] *s* disensión
**dissent** [dɪˈsɛnt] *s* disensión, disenso; (eccl.) disidencia; *vn* disentir; (eccl.) disidir
**dissenter** [dɪˈsɛntər] *s* disidente
**dissentient** [dɪˈsɛnʃənt] *adj & s* disidente
**dissertation** [ˌdɪsərˈteʃən] *s* disertación
**disserve** [dɪsˈsʌrv] *va* deservir
**disservice** [dɪsˈsʌrvɪs] *s* deservicio
**dissever** [dɪˈsɛvər] *va* separar, desunir
**dissidence** [ˈdɪsɪdəns] *s* disidencia
**dissident** [ˈdɪsɪdənt] *adj & s* disidente
**dissimilar** [dɪˈsɪmɪlər] *adj* disímil, disimilar, desemejante
**dissimilarity** [dɪˌsɪmɪˈlærɪtɪ] *s* (*pl:* **-ties**) disimilitud, desemejanza
**dissimilate** [dɪˈsɪmɪlet] *va* disimilar; *vn* disimilarse
**dissimilation** [dɪˌsɪmɪˈleʃən] *s* disimilación
**dissimilitude** [ˌdɪsɪˈmɪlɪtjud] o [ˌdɪsɪˈmɪlɪtud] *s* disimilitud
**dissimulate** [dɪˈsɪmjəlet] *va & vn* disimular
**dissimulation** [dɪˌsɪmjəˈleʃən] *s* disimulación
**dissipate** [ˈdɪsɪpet] *va* disipar; *vn* disiparse; entregarse a los placeres o los vicios
**dissipated** [ˈdɪsɪˌpetɪd] *adj* disipado, disoluto
**dissipation** [ˌdɪsɪˈpeʃən] *s* disipación; (fig.) disipación (*conducta de una persona que se entrega a los placeres o los vicios*); (fig.) diversión, recreo
**dissociate** [dɪˈsoʃɪet] *va* disociar; *vn* disociarse
**dissociation** [dɪˌsosɪˈeʃən] o [dɪˌsoʃɪˈeʃən] *s* disociación
**dissociative** [dɪˈsoʃɪˌetɪv] *adj* disociador
**dissolubility** [dɪˌsɑljəˈbɪlɪtɪ] *s* disolubilidad
**dissoluble** [dɪˈsɑljəbəl] *adj* disoluble
**dissolute** [ˈdɪsəlut] *adj* disoluto
**dissolution** [ˌdɪsəˈluʃən] *s* disolución (*de una familia, aparcería, gobierno, tratado, contrato, etc.*); muerte, deceso
**dissolutive** [ˈdɪsəˌlutɪv] *adj* disolutivo
**dissolve** [dɪˈzɑlv] *va* disolver; (law) disolver; *vn* disolver; disolverse
**dissolvent** [dɪˈzɑlvənt] *adj & s* disolvente
**dissonance** [ˈdɪsənəns] *s* disonancia
**dissonant** [ˈdɪsənənt] *adj* disonante
**dissuade** [dɪˈswed] *va* disuadir; **to dissuade from** + *ger* disuadir de + *inf*
**dissuasion** [dɪˈsweʒən] *s* disuasión
**dissuasive** [dɪˈswesɪv] *adj* disuasivo
**dissyllabic** [ˌdɪssɪˈlæbɪk] *adj* disílabo o disilábico
**dissyllable** [dɪˈsɪləbəl] *s* disílabo
**dissymmetric** [ˌdɪssɪˈmɛtrɪk] o **dissymetrical** [ˌdɪssɪˈmɛtrɪkəl] *adj* disimétrico
**dissymmetry** [dɪsˈsɪmɪtrɪ] *s* (*pl:* **-tries**) disimetría
**dist.** abr. de **distance, distinguish** y **district**
**distaff** [ˈdɪstæf] o [ˈdɪstɑf] *s* rueca; quehaceres de mujer; (fig.) rueca, mujeres
**distaff side** *s* lado de la madre, hembras de la familia
**distal** [ˈdɪstəl] *adj* (anat.) distal
**distance** [ˈdɪstəns] *s* distancia; (fig.) distancia (*falta de amistad, frialdad*); **at a distance** a distancia; **in the distance** a lo lejos, en lontananza; **to keep at a distance** mantener a distancia; no tratar con familiaridad; **to keep one's distance** mantenerse a distancia; *va* distanciar; dejar atrás, tomar la delantera a
**distant** [ˈdɪstənt] *adj* distante; indiferente, frío; lejano (*pariente*)
**distaste** [dɪsˈtest] *s* aversión, antipatía, disgusto
**distasteful** [dɪsˈtestfəl] *adj* desabrido, desagradable
**distemper** [dɪsˈtɛmpər] *s* enfermedad; (vet.) moquillo; tumulto, alboroto; (paint.) temple (*procedimiento*); (paint.) templa (*mezcla para desleír los colores*); (paint.) pintura al temple; *va* destemplar, desconcertar; (paint.) pintar al temple
**distend** [dɪˈstɛnd] *va* ensanchar, hinchar, distender; *vn* ensancharse, hincharse, distenderse
**distensible** [dɪsˈtɛnsɪbəl] *adj* dilatable, distensible
**distension** o **distention** [dɪsˈtɛnʃən] *s* ensanche, hinchazón, distensión
**distich** [ˈdɪstɪk] *s* dístico
**distichous** [ˈdɪstɪkəs] *adj* (bot.) dístico
**distil** o **distill** [dɪˈstɪl] (*pret & pp:* **-tilled;** *ger:* **-tilling**) *va & vn* destilar
**distillable** [dɪˈstɪləbəl] *adj* destilable
**distillate** [ˈdɪstɪlet] o [dɪˈstɪlet] *s* destilado
**distillation** [ˌdɪstɪˈleʃən] *s* destilación
**distiller** [dɪˈstɪlər] *s* destilador
**distillery** [dɪˈstɪlərɪ] *s* (*pl:* **-ies**) destilería o destilatorio

**distinct** [dɪ'stɪŋkt] *adj* distinto; inequívoco, cierto, indudable
**distinction** [dɪ'stɪŋkʃən] *s* distinción; distintivo; **in distinction from** o **to** a distinción de
**distinctive** [dɪ'stɪŋktɪv] *adj* distintivo
**distinctly** [dɪ'stɪŋktlɪ] *adv* distintamente; inequívocamente
**distinctness** [dɪ'stɪŋktnɪs] *s* distinción
**distingué** [ˌdɪstæŋ'ge] o [dɪ'stæŋge] *adj* distinguido
**distinguish** [dɪ'stɪŋgwɪʃ] *va* distinguir
**distinguishable** [dɪ'stɪŋgwɪʃəbəl] *adj* distinguible
**distinguished** [dɪ'stɪŋgwɪʃt] *adj* distinguido
**distomatous** [daɪ'stɑmətəs] o [daɪ'stomətəs] *adj* (zool.) dístomo
**distort** [dɪs'tɔrt] *va* torcer, deformar; (fig.) torcer, falsear (*p.ej., la verdad*)
**distortion** [dɪs'tɔrʃən] *s* torcimiento, deformación; (fig.) torcimiento, falseamiento, distorción; (rad.) distorsión, deformación
**distract** [dɪ'strækt] *va* distraer (*p.ej., la atención*); aturdir, confundir; enloquecer
**distraction** [dɪ'strækʃən] *s* distracción; aturdimiento, confusión; locura
**distrain** [dɪ'stren] *va & vn* (law) embargar, secuestrar, ejecutar
**distraint** [dɪ'strent] *s* (law) embargo, secuestro, ejecución
**distrait** [dɪ'stre] *adj* distraído
**distraught** [dɪ'strɔt] *adj* distraído; aturdido, confundido; loco
**distress** [dɪ'strɛs] *s* pena, dolor, angustia, aflicción; apuro, revés, infortunio, peligro; (law) embargo, secuestro; *va* apenar, angustiar, afligir; poner en aprieto; (law) embargar, secuestrar
**distressful** [dɪ'strɛsfəl] *adj* penoso, congojoso; afligido
**distressing** [dɪ'strɛsɪŋ] *adj* penoso, congojoso
**distress signal** *s* señal de socorro
**distribute** [dɪs'trɪbjut] *va* distribuir, repartir; (print.) desempastelar (*pastel*)
**distributed capacity** *s* (rad.) capacidad distribuída
**distributer** [dɪ'strɪbjətər] *s* distribuidor
**distribution** [ˌdɪstrɪ'bjuʃən] *s* distribución, repartimiento
**distributive** [dɪ'strɪbjətɪv] *adj* distributivo; *s* (gram.) distributivo (*substantivo*); (gram.) conjunción distributiva
**distributively** [dɪ'strɪbjətɪvlɪ] *adv* distributivamente
**distributor** [dɪ'strɪbjətər] *s* distribuidor; (aut.) distribuidor
**distributor points** *spl* (aut.) plaquitas del distribuidor
**district** ['dɪstrɪkt] *s* comarca, región; barrio (*de una ciudad*); distrito (*división administrativa*); *va* dividir en distritos
**district attorney** s fiscal, fiscal de distrito, acusador público
**district court** *s* tribunal de distrito; tribunal federal de primera instancia
**District of Columbia** *s* Distrito de Columbia
**distrust** [dɪs'trʌst] *s* desconfianza; *va* desconfiar de
**distrustful** [dɪs'trʌstfəl] *adj* desconfiado
**disturb** [dɪ'stʌrb] *va* disturbar, alborotar; inquietar; desordenar, revolver, descasar; perturbar (*el orden público*)
**disturbance** [dɪ'stʌrbəns] *s* disturbio, alboroto; inquietud; desorden; trastorno
**disturber** [dɪ'stʌrbər] *s* alborotador; **disturber of the peace** alborotador, perturbador del orden público
**disulfide** o **disulphide** [daɪ'sʌlfaɪd] o [daɪ'sʌlfɪd] *s* (chem.) disulfuro
**disunion** [dɪs'junjən] *s* desunión
**disunite** [ˌdɪsju'naɪt] *va* desunir; *vn* desunirse
**disuse** [dɪs'jus] *s* desuso; [dɪs'juz] *va* desusar
**ditch** [dɪtʃ] *s* zanja; (fort.) foso; **to the last ditch** hasta quemar el último cartucho; *va* zanjar; echar en una zanja; (slang) zafarse de, desembarazarse de; *vn* (aer.) amarar forzosamente
**ditch reed** *s* (bot.) carrizo
**ditheism** ['daɪθiɪzəm] *s* diteísmo
**ditheist** ['daɪθiɪst] *s* diteísta
**ditheistic** [ˌdaɪθi'ɪstɪk] *adj* diteísta
**dither** ['dɪðər] *s* (dial.) estremecimiento; **in a dither** estremecido, muy excitado; *va* (dial.) estremecer; *vn* (dial.) estremecerse
**dithyramb** ['dɪθɪræm] *s* ditirambo
**dithyrambic** [ˌdɪθɪ'ræmbɪk] *adj* ditirámbico
**ditone** ['daɪˌton] *s* (mus.) dítono
**dittany** ['dɪtənɪ] *s* (*pl:* **-nies**) (bot.) díctamo
**ditto** ['dɪto] *s* (*pl:* **-tos**) ídem; principio de comillas (*que se emplea en lugar de "ídem"*); copia, duplicado; *va* copiar, duplicar
**ditto mark** *s* principio de comillas (*que se emplea en lugar de "ídem"*)
**ditty** ['dɪtɪ] *s* (*pl:* **-ties**) cancioneta
**ditty bag** *s* saco de costura de marinero
**ditty box** *s* caja de costura de marinero
**diuresis** [ˌdaɪju'risɪs] *s* (path.) diuresis
**diuretic** [ˌdaɪju'rɛtɪk] *adj & s* (med.) diurético
**diurnal** [daɪ'ʌrnəl] *adj* diurno; diario; *s* (eccl.) diurno
**diurnally** [daɪ'ʌrnəlɪ] *adv* de día; diariamente
**diuturnal** [ˌdaɪju'tʌrnəl] *adj* diuturno
**diuturnity** [ˌdaɪju'tʌrnɪtɪ] *s* diuturnidad
**div.** abr. de **dividend, divided** y **division**
**diva** ['divə] *s* (mus.) diva
**divagate** ['daɪvəget] *vn* divagar
**divagation** [ˌdaɪvə'geʃən] *s* divagación
**divan** [dɪ'væn] *s* diván (*consejo turco y sala donde se reúne; colección de poesías*); ['daɪvæn] o [dɪ'væn] *s* diván (*canapé*); fumadero
**divaricate** [daɪ'værɪket] o [dɪ'værɪket] *adj* divergente; (bot.) divaricado; *va* dividir en dos ramales; desplegar; *vn* bifurcarse
**divarication** [daɪˌværɪ'keʃən] o [dɪˌværɪ'keʃən] *s* divaricación; divergencia (*de opiniones*)
**dive** [daɪv] *s* salto, zambullida; salto ornamental; sumersión (*de un submarino*); (aer.) picado; (coll.) tasca, casa de juego de mala fama; (*pret & pp:* **dived** o **dove**) *vn* zambullirse (*meterse debajo del agua con ímpetu; ocultarse, esconderse*); bucear (*trabajar como buzo*); sumergirse (*un submarino*); meter de repente la mano (*p.ej., en el bolsillo*); enfrascarse (*p.ej., en el trabajo, los negocios*); (aer.) picar
**dive-bomb** ['daɪvˌbɑm] *va & vn* bombardear en picado
**dive bomber** *s* (aer.) bombardero en picado, avión de bombardeo en picado
**dive bombing** *s* (aer.) bombardeo en picado
**diver** ['daɪvər] *s* zambullidor; buzo (*provisto o no de una escafandra*); (orn.) somorgujo
**diverge** [dɪ'vʌrdʒ] o [daɪ'vʌrdʒ] *vn* divergir
**divergence** [dɪ'vʌrdʒəns] o [daɪ'vʌrdʒəns] *s* divergencia
**divergency** [dɪ'vʌrdʒənsɪ] o [daɪ'vʌrdʒənsɪ] *s* (*pl:* **-cies**) var. de **divergence**
**divergent** [dɪ'vʌrdʒənt] o [daɪ'vʌrdʒənt] *adj* divergente
**divers** ['daɪvərz] *adj* diversos, varios
**diverse** [dɪ'vʌrs], [daɪ'vʌrs] o ['daɪvʌrs] *adj* diverso; variado
**diversely** [dɪ'vʌrslɪ], [daɪ'vʌrslɪ] o ['daɪvʌrslɪ] *adv* diversamente; variamente
**diver's helmet** *s* casco de escafandra
**diversification** [dɪˌvʌrsɪfɪ'keʃən] o [daɪˌvʌrsɪfɪ'keʃən] *s* diversificación
**diversiform** [dɪ'vʌrsɪfɔrm] o [daɪ'vʌrsɪfɔrm] *adj* diversiforme
**diversify** [dɪ'vʌrsɪfaɪ] o [daɪ'vʌrsɪfaɪ] (*pret & pp:* **-fied**) *va* diversificar; *vn* diversificarse
**diversion** [dɪ'vʌrʒən] o [daɪ'vʌrʒən] *s* diversión; (mil.) diversión
**diversity** [dɪ'vʌrsɪtɪ] o [daɪ'vʌrsɪtɪ] *s* (*pl:* **-ties**) diversidad
**divert** [dɪ'vʌrt] o [daɪ'vʌrt] *va* apartar, desviar; divertir, entretener; (mil.) divertir
**diverticular** [ˌdaɪvər'tɪkjələr] *adj* diverticular
**diverticulitis** [ˌdaɪvərˌtɪkjə'laɪtɪs] *s* (path.) diverticulitis
**diverticulum** [ˌdaɪvər'tɪkjələm] *s* (*pl:* **-la** [lə]) (anat. & path.) divertículo
**diverting** [dɪ'vʌrtɪŋ] o [daɪ'vʌrtɪŋ] *adj* divertido
**divertissement** [divɛrtis'mɑ̃] *s* divertimiento; (mus.) divertimiento
**divertive** [dɪ'vʌrtɪv] o [daɪ'vʌrtɪv] *adj* divertido
**divest** [dɪ'vɛst] o [daɪ'vɛst] *va* desnudar; desposeer, despojar

**divide** [dɪˈvaɪd] *s* (geog.) divisoria; *va* dividir; *vn* dividirse
**dividend** [ˈdɪvɪdɛnd] *s* (math. & com.) dividendo
**divider** [dɪˈvaɪdər] *s* divisor; **dividers** *spl* compás de división
**divination** [ˌdɪvɪˈneʃən] *s* adivinación
**divinatory** [dɪˈvɪnəˌtorɪ] *adj* adivinatorio
**divine** [dɪˈvaɪn] *s* sacerdote, predicador, clérigo; *adj* divino; (fig.) divino; *va & vn* adivinar
**divine grace** *s* (theol.) influencia, divina gracia
**divinely** [dɪˈvaɪnlɪ] *adv* divinamente
**diviner** [dɪˈvaɪnər] *s* adivinador
**divine right of kings** *s* derecho divino de los reyes
**divine service** *s* servicio divino
**diving** [ˈdaɪvɪŋ] *s* zambullida, buceo
**diving attack** *s* (aer.) ataque en picado
**diving bell** *s* campana de bucear, campana de buzo
**diving board** *s* trampolín
**diving suit** *s* escafandra o escafandro
**divining** [dɪˈvaɪnɪŋ] *adj* adivinatorio
**divining rod** *s* vara de adivinar, vara mágica; vara buscadora, varilla exploradora (*que se emplea para determinar la presencia de agua, metal o mineral subterráneos*)
**divinity** [dɪˈvɪnɪtɪ] *s* (*pl:* **-ties**) divinidad; teología; **the Divinity** Dios
**divinize** [ˈdɪvɪnaɪz] *va* divinizar
**divisibility** [dɪˌvɪzɪˈbɪlɪtɪ] *s* divisibilidad
**divisible** [dɪˈvɪzɪbəl] *adj* divisible
**division** [dɪˈvɪʒən] *s* división; (math. & mil.) división
**divisional** [dɪˈvɪʒənəl] *adj* divisional
**divisive** [dɪˈvaɪsɪv] *adj* divisivo
**divisor** [dɪˈvaɪzər] *s* (math.) divisor
**divorce** [dɪˈvors] *s* divorcio; **to get a divorce from** divorciarse de; *va* divorciar (*los cónyuges*); divorciarse de (*la mujer o el marido*); (fig.) divorciar; *vn* divorciarse
**divorcé** [dɪvorˈse] *s* hombre divorciado
**divorcee** [dɪvorˈsi] *s* persona divorciada
**divorcée** [dɪvorˈse] *s* mujer divorciada
**divorcement** [dɪˈvorsmənt] *s* divorcio
**divot** [ˈdɪvət] *s* terrón arrancado con el palo de golf
**divulge** [dɪˈvʌldʒ] *va* divulgar, publicar, revelar
**Dixie** [ˈdɪksɪ] *s* el Sur de los Estados Unidos
**dizen** [ˈdaɪzən] o [ˈdɪzən] *va* emperejilar
**dizziness** [ˈdɪzɪnɪs] *s* vértigo, desvanecimiento; aturdimiento, confusión, perplejidad
**dizzy** [ˈdɪzɪ] *adj* (*comp:* **-zier;** *super:* **-ziest**) vertiginoso; aturdido, confuso, perplejo; tonto, mentecato
**dl.** abr. de **deciliter** o **deciliters**
**D.Lit.** o **D.Litt.** abr. de **Doctor of Literature**
**dm.** abr. de **decimeter** o **decimeters**
**do.** abr. de **ditto**
**do** [du] (*pret:* **did;** *pp:* **done;** *ger:* **doing**) *va* hacer; terminar; rendir, tributar (*homenaje*); ser suficiente para; trabajar en, ocuparse de o en; resolver (*un problema*); andar, recorrer (*una distancia*); cocinar suficientemente; cumplir con (*un deber*); aprender (*una lección*); arreglar, componer (*el cuarto, la cama*); tocar (*el cabello*); pasar (*cierto tiempo*) en la cárcel; (coll.) ver, visitar (*un país extranjero*); (coll.) engañar, estafar; traducir; hacer de; **to be well done** estar bien asado; **to be done for** (coll.) estar cansado; (coll.) estar arruinado, estar destruído; (coll.) estar muerto; **to have nothing to do with** no tener nada que ver con; **to do in** (slang) apalear, azotar; (slang) rendir, vencer; (slang) despachar, matar; **to do one a world of good** sentarle a uno a las mil maravillas; **to do one's best** hacer todo lo posible; **to do over** volver a hacer; renovar; repetir; **to do over with** cubrir con, revestir con; **to do right by** tratar bien, portarse bien para con; **to do someone out of something** (coll.) defraudar algo a alguien; **to do to death** despachar, matar; **to do up** liar, empaquetar; arreglar, poner en orden; almidonar y planchar (*p.ej., una camisa*); conservar (*fruto*); (coll.) cansar, deslomar ‖ *vn* estar, hallarse, ir; conducirse, proceder; actuar, obrar; servir, ser suficiente; **how do you do?** ¿cómo está Vd.?, ¿cómo se halla Vd.?; **that will do** basta ya, eso es bastante; eso sirve; calla, no digas más; **that won't do** eso no sirve, eso no vale; **to have done** haber terminado; **to have done with** haber terminado; no tener más que ver con; **to have to do with** tratar de; **to do away with** suprimir; matar; **to do for** bastar para, servir para; **to do well in an examination** salir bien de un examen; **to do with** servirse de; **to do without** pasar sin ‖ *v aux* empléase (1) para dar énfasis a la oración, p.ej., **I do eat spinach** yo sí como espinacas; (2) para hacer una pregunta, p.ej., **Do you see me?** ¿Me ve Vd?; (3) para señalar la negación, p.ej., **He did not come** No vino; (4) para reemplazar otro verbo que va omitido, p.ej., **Do you speak Spanish? Yes, I do** ¿Habla Vd. español? Sí, lo hablo; (5) en el orden invertido después de un adverbio, p.ej., **seldom does she complain** ella rara vez se queja
**doable** [ˈduəbəl] *adj* factible
**do-all** [ˈduˌɔl] *s* factótum
**doat** [dot] *vn* var. de **dote**
**dobbin** [ˈdɑbɪn] *s* caballo lento y manso
**Docetism** [doˈsitɪzəm] *s* docetismo
**docile** [ˈdɑsɪl] *adj* dócil
**docility** [doˈsɪlɪtɪ] *s* docilidad
**docimastic** [ˌdɑsɪˈmæstɪk] *adj* docimástico
**docimasy** [ˈdɑsɪməsɪ] *s* (*pl:* **-sies**) docimasia
**dock** [dɑk] *s* muñón de cola; (naut.) dique; (naut.) muelle; (law) tribuna de los acusados; (bot.) romaza; *va* derrabar, descolar, cercenar; (naut.) poner en dique; reducir, suprimir (*el salario*); *vn* (naut.) entrar en muelle
**dockage** [ˈdɑkɪdʒ] *s* entrada en un dique; muellaje; reducción, rebaja
**docket** [ˈdɑkɪt] *s* rótulo, marbete; minuta, sumario, extracto; (law) lista de causas pendientes; (law) orden del día; **on the docket** (coll.) pendiente, entre manos, en consideración; *va* rotular; hacer la minuta de, extractar; (law) poner en la lista de causas pendientes; (law) poner en el orden del día
**dock hand** o **dock worker** *s* portuario
**dockyard** [ˈdɑkˌjɑrd] *s* (naut.) arsenal
**doctor** [ˈdɑktər] *s* médico; doctor (*en ciencias, letras, derecho, etc.*); *va* (coll.) medicinar; (coll.) alterar y adulterar; (coll.) reparar, componer, concertar; *vn* (coll.) practicar la medicina; (coll.) tomar medicinas
**doctoral** [ˈdɑktərəl] *adj* doctoral
**doctorate** [ˈdɑktərɪt] *s* doctorado
**doctrinaire** [ˌdɑktrɪˈnɛr] *adj & s* doctrinario
**doctrinairism** [ˌdɑktrɪˈnɛrɪzəm] *s* doctrinarismo
**doctrinal** [ˈdɑktrɪnəl] *adj* doctrinal
**doctrine** [ˈdɑktrɪn] *s* doctrina
**document** [ˈdɑkjəmənt] *s* documento; [ˈdɑkjəmɛnt] *va* documentar
**documental** [ˌdɑkjəˈmɛntəl] *adj* documental
**documentary** [ˌdɑkjəˈmɛntərɪ] *adj* documental; *s* (*pl:* **-ries**) (mov.) documental (*película*)
**documentation** [ˌdɑkjəmɛnˈteʃən] *s* documentación
**dodder** [ˈdɑdər] *s* (bot.) cúscuta; *vn* temblar, tambalear
**doddering** [ˈdɑdərɪŋ] *adj* sandio, chocho
**dodecagon** [doˈdɛkəgɑn] *s* (geom.) dodecágono
**dodecagonal** [ˌdodɛˈkægənəl] *adj* (geom.) dodecágono
**dodecahedron** [ˌdodɛkəˈhidrən] *s* (*pl:* **-drons** o **-dra** [drə]) (geom.) dodecaedro
**dodecahedral** [ˌdodɛkəˈhidrəl] *adj* (geom.) dodecaédrico
**Dodecanese Islands** [doˌdɛkəˈnis] *spl* Dodecaneso, islas del Dodecaneso
**dodecasyllabic** [ˌdodɛkəsɪˈlæbɪk] *adj* dodecasílabo
**dodge** [dɑdʒ] *s* regate; (fig.) regate; *va* evadir (*p.ej., un golpe*) moviéndose rápidamente a un lado; (coll.) evitar mañosamente; *vn* regatear, hurtar el cuerpo; **to dodge around the corner** voltear la esquina
**dodger** [ˈdɑdʒər] *s* persona que hace regates; trampista; anuncio pequeño; pan de maíz
**dodo** [ˈdodo] *s* (*pl:* **-dos** o **-does**) (orn.) dodo o dodó; (coll.) inocente de ideas atrasadas
**doe** [do] *s* cierva, gama; hembra del conejo, el antílope, la liebre, el canguro

**doer** ['duər] *s* hacedor
**does** [dʌz] *tercera persona del sg del pres de ind de* **do**
**doeskin** ['do,skɪn] *s* ante, piel de ante; tejido fino de lana
**doesn't** ['dʌzənt] contracción de **does not**
**doff** [dɑf] o [dɔf] *va* quitarse (*p.ej., el sombrero o chaqueta*); quitarse de encima, deshacerse de
**dog** [dɔg] o [dɑg] *s* perro; zorro, lobo (*macho*); tunante; (coll.) hombre, sujeto, individuo; fiador, asidor; morillo; (coll.) ínfulas; **to go to the dogs** darse al abandono, arruinarse; **to put on the dog** (coll.) darse ínfulas; **to teach an old dog new tricks** conseguir que un viejo cambie de ideas o hábitos; (*pret & pp:* **dogged;** *ger:* **dogging**) *va* seguir los pasos de, seguir las pisadas de, perseguir
**dogbane** ['dɔg,ben] o ['dɑg,ben] *s* (bot.) apocino
**dogberry** ['dɔg,bɛrɪ] o ['dɑg,bɛrɪ] *s* (*pl:* **-ries**) (bot.) cornejo hembra, sanguiñuelo, sanapudio blanco
**dogcart** ['dɔg,kɑrt] o ['dɑg,kɑrt] *s* carro pequeño tirado por perros; dócar (*carruaje de dos ruedas, con dos asientos colocados espalda contra espalda*)
**dogcatcher** ['dɔg,kætʃər] o ['dɑg,kætʃər] *s* lacero, perrero (*persona*); cazaperros (*animal*)
**dog clutch** *s* (mach.) embrague de mordaza
**dog days** *spl* canícula, caniculares
**doge** [dodʒ] *s* dux
**dog-ear** ['dɔg,ɪr] o ['dɑg,ɪr] *s & va* var. de **dog's-ear**
**dogfight** ['dɔg,faɪt] o ['dɑg,faɪt] *s* lucha de perros; refriega; (aer.) combate violento entre aviones pequeños y rápidos
**dogfish** ['dɔg,fɪʃ] o ['dɑg,fɪʃ] *s* (ichth.) tiburón; (ichth.) cazón
**dogged** ['dɔgɪd] o ['dɑgɪd] *adj* tenaz, terco, obstinado
**dogger** ['dɔgər] o ['dɑgər] *s* dogre (*embarcación de pesca*)
**doggerel** ['dɔgərəl] o ['dɑgərəl] *s* coplas de ciego; *adj* malo, poco artístico
**doggie** ['dɔgɪ] o ['dɑgɪ] *s* perrito
**doggy** ['dɔgɪ] o ['dɑgɪ] *s* (*pl:* **-gies**) perrito; *adj* (*comp:* **-gier;** *super:* **-giest**) emperejilado, aparatoso
**doghouse** ['dɔg,haʊs] o ['dɑg,haʊs] *s* perrera; **to be in the doghouse** (slang) estar en desgracia
**dogie** ['dogɪ] *s* ternero sin madre
**dog in the manger** *s* (coll.) el perro del hortelano
**dog Latin** *s* latinajo, latín de cocina
**dogma** ['dɔgmə] o ['dɑgmə] *s* (*pl:* **-mas** o **-mata** [mətə]) dogma
**dogmatic** [dɔg'mætɪk] o [dɑg'mætɪk] o **dogmatical** [dɔg'mætɪkəl] o [dɑg'mætɪkəl] *adj* dogmático
**dogmatism** ['dɔgmətɪzəm] o ['dɑgmətɪzəm] *s* dogmatismo
**dogmatist** ['dɔgmətɪst] o ['dɑgmətɪst] *s* dogmatizador
**dogmatize** ['dɔgmətaɪz] o ['dɑgmətaɪz] *va & vn* dogmatizar
**do-gooder** ['du,gʊdər] *s* (scornful) reformador visionario y algo tonto
**dog racing** *s* carrera de galgos
**dog rose** *s* (bot.) escaramujo (*planta y fruto*); (bot.) agavanzo (*planta*); agavanza (*fruto*); zarzarrosa (*flor*)
**dog's-ear** ['dɔgz,ɪr] o ['dɑgz,ɪr] *s* orejón (*de la hoja de un libro*); *va* doblar o plegar la punta de (*la hoja de un libro*)
**dog show** *s* exposición canina
**dog sledge** *s* rastra tirada por perros
**dog's letter** *s* letra canina (*la rr*)
**dog's life** *s* vida de perros, vida miserable
**Dog Star** *s* (astr.) Canícula; (astr.) Proción
**dog's-tooth violet** ['dɔgz,tuθ] o ['dɑgz,tuθ] *s* var. de **dogtooth violet**
**dog-tired** ['dɔg,taɪrd] o ['dɑg,taɪrd] *adj* cansadísimo
**dogtooth** ['dɔg,tuθ] o ['dɑg,tuθ] *s* (*pl:* **-teeth** [,tiθ]) (anat.) colmillo; (arch.) diente de perro
**dogtooth violet** *s* (bot.) diente de perro
**dogtrot** ['dɔg,trɑt] o ['dɑg,trɑt] *s* trote de perro
**dogwatch** ['dɔg,wɑtʃ] o ['dɑg,wɑtʃ] *s* (naut.) guardia de cuartillo
**dogwood** ['dɔg,wʊd] o ['dɑg,wʊd] *s* (bot.) cornejo
**dogy** ['dogɪ] *s* (*pl:* **-gies**) var. de **dogie**
**doily** ['dɔɪlɪ] *s* (*pl:* **-lies**) paño pequeño de adorno, pañito de adorno
**doings** ['duɪŋz] *spl* actos, hechos; conducta, proceder; (slang) actividad, tremolina
**do-it-yourself** ['duɪtjʊr'sɛlf] *adj* (slang) ideado para el que quiere hacer sus propios trabajos manuales del hogar
**doldrums** ['dɑldrəmz] *spl* (naut.) zona de calmas ecuatoriales; abatimiento, desanimación
**dole** [dol] *s* limosna; distribución en pequeñas porciones; socorro del gobierno a los desocupados; *va* dar limosna a; distribuir en pequeñas porciones; **to dole out** distribuir en pequeñas porciones
**doleful** ['dolfəl] *adj* triste, lúgubre
**dolichocephalic** [,dɑlɪkəsɪ'fælɪk] *adj* (anthrop.) dolicocéfalo
**doll** [dɑl] *s* muñeca; (fig.) muñeca (*mujer pequeñita; mozuela linda y necia*); *va* (slang) engalanar, emperejilar; *vn* (slang) engalanarse, emperejilarse; **to doll up** (slang) engalanarse, emperejilarse
**dollar** ['dɑlər] *s* dólar
**dollar diplomacy** *s* diplomacia del dólar
**dollar mark** *s* signo del dólar
**dolly** ['dɑlɪ] *s* (*pl:* **-ies**) muñequita; plataforma con rodillo, gato rodante; (mach.) sufridera
**dolman** ['dɑlmən] *s* (*pl:* **-mans**) dormán (*de los turcos, húsares, etc.*); capa de mujer de mangas perdidas
**dolmen** ['dɑlmɛn] *s* dolmen
**dolmenic** [dɑl'mɛnɪk] *adj* dolménico
**dolomite** ['dɑləmaɪt] *s* (mineral.) dolomía o dolomita
**dolomitic** [,dɑlə'mɪtɪk] *adj* dolomítico
**dolor** ['dolər] *s* (poet.) dolor
**dolorous** ['dɑlərəs] o ['dolərəs] *adj* doloroso
**dolphin** ['dɑlfɪn] *s* (zool.) delfín; (ichth.) dorado de altura; (naut.) poste de amarra; (naut.) boya de anclaje; (*cap.*) *s* (astr.) Delfín
**dolphin striker** *s* (naut.) moco del bauprés
**dolt** [dolt] *s* bobalicón, mastuerzo
**doltish** ['doltɪʃ] *adj* bobalicón, tonto
**dom.** abr. de **domestic** y **dominion**
**domain** [do'men] *s* dominio, imperio; heredad, propiedad; campo (*p.ej., de la erudición*)
**dome** [dom] *s* (arch.) domo, cúpula, cimborrio; (aut.) techo abovedado; cimborrio (*de un carro tanque, carro de riego, etc.*); *va* cubrir con un domo o cúpula; dar forma de domo o cúpula a; *vn* elevarse como un domo o cúpula
**dome light** *s* (aut.) lámpara de techo
**Domesday Book** ['dumz,de] o ['domz,de] *s* Libro del día del Juicio final (*libro que registra los nombres, extensión, valor y otros datos de todas las propiedades de Inglaterra, que Guillermo el Conquistador hizo compilar en 1086*)
**domestic** [də'mɛstɪk] *adj* doméstico; *s* doméstico (*criado que sirve en una casa*)
**domesticable** [də'mɛstɪkəbəl] *adj* domesticable
**domestically** [də'mɛstɪkəlɪ] *adv* domésticamente
**domesticate** [də'mɛstɪket] *va* domesticar; *vn* domesticarse
**domestication** [də,mɛstɪ'keʃən] *s* domesticación
**domesticity** [,domɛs'tɪsɪtɪ] *s* (*pl:* **-ties**) domesticidad; **domesticities** *spl* asuntos domésticos
**domicile** ['dɑmɪsɪl] o ['dɑmɪsaɪl] *s* domicilio; *va* domiciliar; *vn* domiciliarse
**domiciliary** [,dɑmɪ'sɪlɪ,ɛrɪ] *adj* domiciliario
**domiciliate** [,dɑmɪ'sɪlɪet] *va* domiciliar; *vn* domiciliarse
**dominance** ['dɑmɪnəns] o **dominancy** ['dɑmɪnənsɪ] *s* dominación; (biol.) dominancia
**dominant** ['dɑmɪnənt] *adj* dominante; (astrol., biol., & mus.) dominante; *s* (mus.) dominante
**dominate** ['dɑmɪnet] *va & vn* dominar
**domination** [,dɑmɪ'neʃən] *s* dominación; **dominations** *spl* dominaciones (*cuarto coro de ángeles*)
**domineer** [,dɑmɪ'nɪr] *va & vn* dominar

**domineering** [ˌdɑmɪˈnɪrɪŋ] *adj* dominante, dominador
**Dominic, Saint** [ˈdɑmɪnɪk] Santo Domingo
**Dominica** [ˌdɑmɪˈnikə] o [doˈmɪnɪkə] *s* la Dominica (*isla de las Antillas*)
**Dominican** [doˈmɪnɪkən] *adj* dominicano (*perteneciente a la orden de Santo Domingo; perteneciente a la República Dominicana*); dominico (*perteneciente a la orden de Santo Domingo*); *s* dominicano; dominico
**Dominican Republic** *s* República Dominicana
**dominie** [ˈdɑmɪnɪ] *s* dómine; [ˈdomɪnɪ] *s* cura, clérigo
**dominion** [dəˈmɪnjən] *s* dominio
**domino** [ˈdɑmɪno] *s* (*pl:* **-noes** o **-nos**) dominó (*traje que se usa en los bailes de máscara*); careta o antifaz usado con el dominó; persona que usa el dominó; ficha (*del juego de dominó*); **dominoes** *spl* dominó (*juego*)
**Domitian** [doˈmɪʃən] *s* Domiciano
**don** [dɑn] *s* caballero, señor; personaje de alta categoría; (coll.) rector, preceptor, socio (*de un colegio de las universidades de Oxford y Cambridge, Inglaterra*); (*cap.*) *s* don (*tratamiento español de cortesía que se da a los hombres y se antepone a los nombres de pila*); (*pret & pp:* **donned;** *ger:* **donning**) *va* ponerse, vestirse
**Donald** [ˈdɑnəld] *s* Donaldo
**Donald Duck** *s* el pato Donaldo
**donate** [ˈdonet] *va* dar, donar
**donation** [doˈneʃən] *s* donación, donativo
**Donatism** [ˈdɑnətɪzəm] *s* donatismo
**Donatist** [ˈdɑnətɪst] *adj & s* donatista
**done** [dʌn] *adj* hecho, acabado, terminado; (coll.) cansado, rendido; bien asado; *pp de* **do**
**donee** [ˌdoˈni] *s* donatario
**done for** *adj* (coll.) cansado; (coll.) agotado; (coll.) fuera de combate; (coll.) arruinado; (coll.) muerto
**donjon** [ˈdʌndʒən] o [ˈdɑndʒən] *s* torre del homenaje, torre maestra
**Don Juan** [dɑnˈdʒuən] *s* Don Juan (*personaje legendario que simboliza al hombre libertino; hombre libertino*)
**Don Juanism** [dɑnˈdʒuənɪzəm] *s* donjuanismo
**donkey** [ˈdɑŋkɪ] *s* burro, asno; (fig.) asno
**donkey engine** *s* pequeña máquina de vapor, máquina auxiliar
**donnish** [ˈdɑnɪʃ] *adj* profesoral; pedantesco
**Donnybrook** [ˈdɑnɪbrʊk] *s* (coll.) alboroto, riña general; (coll.) disputa acalorada y bulliciosa entre grupos contrarios
**donor** [ˈdonər] *s* donador, donante, dador
**do-nothing** [ˈduˌnʌθɪŋ] *adj* dejado, inactivo, indiferente; *s* haragán, ocioso
**don't** [dont] contracción de **do not**
**doodad** [ˈduˌdæd] *s* (coll.) chisme, adminículo; (coll.) chuchería
**doodle** [ˈdudəl] *va & vn* borrajear
**doodlebug** [ˈdudəlˌbʌg] *s* (ent.) larva de hormiga león; vara buscadora, dispositivo para determinar la presencia de minerales subterráneos; (Brit.) bomba volante
**doodlesack** [ˈdudəlˌsæk] *s* gaita escocesa
**doohickey** [ˈduˌhɪkɪ] *s* (coll.) chisme, adminículo
**doom** [dum] *s* destino, hado, suerte; ruina, perdición, muerte; condena, juicio, sentencia; juicio final; *va* predestinar a la ruina, a la muerte; condenar; sentenciar a muerte
**doom palm** *s* (bot.) duma
**doomsday** [ˈdumzˌde] *s* día del Juicio final; día del juicio
**Doomsday Book** *s* var. de **Domesday Book**
**door** [dor] *s* puerta; portezuela (*de un coche o automóvil*); hoja, batiente (*de una puerta en dos partes*); **behind closed doors** a puertas cerradas; **from door to door** de puerta en puerta; **to lay at one's door** echarle a uno la culpa de; **to show a person to the door** despedir a una persona en la puerta; pedir a una persona que salga
**doorbell** [ˈdorˌbɛl] *s* campanilla de puerta, timbre de llamada
**doorbell transformer** *s* (elec.) transformador de campanilla
**door check** *s* amortiguador, freno de puerta
**doorframe** [ˈdorˌfrem] *s* alfajía, marco de puerta, bastidor de puerta
**doorhead** [ˈdorˌhɛd] *s* dintel
**doorjamb** [ˈdorˌdʒæm] *s* jamba de puerta
**doorkeeper** [ˈdorˌkipər] *s* portero
**doorknob** [ˈdorˌnɑb] *s* pomo de puerta, tirador de puerta
**door latch** *s* pestillo
**doorman** [ˈdormən] o [ˈdorˌmæn] *s* (*pl:* **-men**) portero; abrecoches
**door mat** *s* alfombrilla
**doornail** [ˈdorˌnel] *s* clavo grande para puertas; **dead as a doornail** (coll.) absolutamente muerto
**doorplate** [ˈdorˌplet] *s* rótulo, letrero de la puerta
**doorpost** [ˈdorˌpost] *s* quicial de puerta, jamba de puerta
**door scraper** *s* limpiabarros
**doorsill** [ˈdorˌsɪl] *s* umbral
**doorstep** [ˈdorˌstɛp] *s* escalón o escalones exteriores de puerta
**doorstop** [ˈdorˌstɑp] *s* tope de puerta
**doorway** [ˈdorˌwe] *s* puerta, vano de puerta, portal
**dooryard** [ˈdorˌjɑrd] *s* patio cerca de la puerta, jardín interior
**dope** [dop] *s* grasa lubricante; material absorbente; (aer.) nobabia, barniz; (slang) narcótico, opio; (slang) informes; (slang) persona muy estúpida; *vn* (slang) aletargar o atontar con un narcótico; (slang) pronosticar
**dope fiend** *s* (slang) toxicómano
**dope sheet** *s* (slang) hoja informativa sobre los caballos que van a correr
**Doppler effect** [ˈdɑplər] *s* (phys.) efecto de Doppler
**dor** [dɔr] *s* (ent.) escarabajo estercolero
**Dorcas** [ˈdɔrkəs] *s* (Bib.) Dorcas
**Dordogne** [dɔrˈdonjə] *s* Dordoña
**Dorian** [ˈdorɪən] *adj & s* dorio
**Doric** [ˈdɑrɪk] o [ˈdɔrɪk] *adj* dórico; *s* dórico (*dialecto*)
**Doris** [ˈdorɪs] *s* la Dóride; (myth.) Doris
**dormancy** [ˈdɔrmənsɪ] *s* letargo, inactividad; latencia
**dormant** [ˈdɔrmənt] *adj* durmiente, inactivo; latente
**dormer** [ˈdɔrmər] *s* buharda o buhardilla (*ventana y su caballete*)
**dormered** [ˈdɔrmərd] *adj* (arch.) abuhardillado
**dormer window** *s* buharda o buhardilla, lumbrera
**dormitory** [ˈdɔrmɪˌtorɪ] *s* (*pl:* **-ries**) dormitorio
**dormouse** [ˈdɔrˌmaʊs] *s* (*pl:* **-mice**) (zool.) lirón; (zool.) moscardino
**Dorothy** [ˈdɔrəθɪ] o [ˈdɑrəθɪ] *s* Dorotea
**dorsal** [ˈdɔrsəl] *adj* dorsal
**dory** [ˈdorɪ] *s* (*pl:* **-ries**) bote de remos; (ichth.) gallo, ceo, pez de San Pedro
**dosage** [ˈdosɪdʒ] *s* dosificación, dosis
**dose** [dos] *s* dosis; (fig.) píldora, mal trago; **dose of patience** dosis de paciencia; *va* administrar una dosis a; mezclar; dosificar (*medicamento*); medicinar; *vn* medicinarse
**dosimeter** [doˈsɪmɪtər] *s* dosímetro
**dosimetric** [ˌdosɪˈmɛtrɪk] *adj* dosimétrico
**dosimetry** [doˈsɪmɪtrɪ] *s* dosimetría
**dossier** [ˈdɑsɪe] *s* expediente
**dot** [dɑt] *s* punto; dote; **on the dot** (coll.) en punto, a la hora exacta; (*pret & pp:* **dotted;** *ger:* **dotting**) *va* poner punto a; puntear, motear; salpicar; **to dot one's i's** poner los puntos sobre las íes (*perfeccionar una cosa minuciosamente*); **to dot the i's and cross the t's** fijar la atención en lo más insignificante
**dotage** [ˈdotɪdʒ] *s* chochera, chochez
**dotal** [ˈdotəl] *adj* dotal
**dotard** [ˈdotərd] *s* persona chocha, viejo chocho
**dote** [dot] *vn* chochear; **to dote on** o **upon** estar locamente enamorado de, idolatrar
**doting** [ˈdotɪŋ] *adj* chocho (*locamente cariñoso, locamente enamorado; que chochea de viejo*)
**dots and dashes** *spl* (telg.) puntos y rayas
**dotted line** [ˈdɑtɪd] *s* línea de puntos, línea punteada; **to sign on the dotted line** echar una firma, firmar ciegamente
**dotterel** [ˈdɑtərəl] *s* (orn.) chorlito real; (orn.) caradrida; (dial.) tonto, necio
**dotty** [ˈdɑtɪ] *adj* moteado, punteado; (coll.) trémulo, débil, vacilante; (coll.) bobo, imbécil
**double** [ˈdʌbəl] *adj* doble; *adv* doble; dos veces;

dos juntos; *s* doble; (theat. & mov.) doble; (bridge) doblo; **doubles** *spl* (tennis) juego de dobles; *va* doblar; ser el doble de; (bridge) doblar; *vn* doblarse; (theat. & mov.) doblar; (bridge) doblar; **to double back** volver atrás; **to double up** doblarse, doblarse en dos; vivir en una misma habitación, dormir en una misma cama (*dos personas*)
**double-acting** ['dʌbəl'æktɪŋ] *adj* (mach.) de doble efecto
**double-barreled** ['dʌbəl'bærəld] *adj* de dos cañones; (fig.) de dos propósitos, para dos fines
**double bass** [bes] *s* (mus.) contrabajo
**double bassoon** *s* (mus.) contrabajón
**double bed** *s* cama de matrimonio
**double boiler** *s* marmita doble, baño maría
**double bottom** *s* (naut.) doble fondo
**double-breasted** ['dʌbəl'brestɪd] *adj* traslapado, cruzado, de dos hileras de botones, de dos pechos
**double chin** *s* papada
**double consciousness** *s* (psychopath.) conciencia doble
**double cross** *s* (slang) traición hecha a un cómplice
**double-cross** ['dʌbəl'krɔs] o ['dʌbəl'krɑs] *va* (slang) traicionar (*a un socio o cómplice*)
**double-crosser** ['dʌbəl'krɔsər] o ['dʌbəl'krɑsər] *s* (slang) traidor de un cómplice
**double-cut file** ['dʌbəl,kʌt} *s* lima de doble picadura
**double dagger** *s* (print.) cruz doble, obelisco doble
**double date** *s* cita de dos parejas
**double-dealer** ['dʌbəl'dilər] *s* hombre doble, persona doble
**double-dealing** ['dʌbəl'dilɪŋ] *adj* doble; *s* trato doble, doblez, duplicidad
**double-decker** ['dʌbəl'dɛkər] *s* navío de dos cubiertas; ómnibus de dos pisos, ómnibus con imperial; cama-litera; (slang) emparedado de tres pedazos de pan
**double eagle** *s* doble águila (*antigua moneda de oro de los EE.UU.*)
**double-edged** ['dʌbəl'ɛdʒd] *adj* de dos filos, de doble filo
**double entry** *s* (com.) partida doble
**double-faced** ['dʌbəl'fest] *adj* de dos caras; doble, hipócrita
**double feature** *s* (mov.) programa doble
**double-feature** ['dʌbəl'fitʃər] *adj* (mov.) de dos películas de largo metraje
**double flat** *s* (mus.) doble bemol
**double-header** ['dʌbəl'hɛdər] *s* tren arrastrado por dos locomotoras; (baseball) dos partidos seguidos, doble juego
**double house** *s* casa con corredor central; casa doble
**double-jointed** ['dʌbəl'dʒɔɪntɪd] *adj* con articulaciones dobles
**double-lock** ['dʌbəl'lɑk] *va* cerrar con dos vueltas de llave; cerrar con dos cerrojos
**double-park** ['dʌbəl'pɑrk] *va & vn* (aut.) aparcar en doble hilera
**double play** *s* (baseball) maniobra que pone fuera a dos jugadores
**double pneumonia** *s* (path.) neumonía doble
**double-pole switch** ['dʌbəl'pol] *s* (elec.) interruptor de dos polos
**double-quick** ['dʌbəl'kwɪk] *adj & adv* (mil.) a paso ligero; *s* (mil.) paso ligero; *vn* (mil.) marchar a paso ligero
**double room** *s* habitación doble
**double sharp** *s* (mus.) doble sostenido
**double-sloping roof** ['dʌbəl'slopɪŋ] *s* tejado a dos aguas
**double-spaced** ['dʌbəl'spest] *adj* a dos espacios
**double standard** *s* norma de conducta restrictiva para la mujer, especialmente en materia sexual
**double star** *s* (astr.) estrella doble
**doublet** ['dʌblɪt] *s* jubón; doblete (*piedra falsa*); (philol.) doblete
**double tackle** *s* polea de dos ruedas acanaladas
**double talk** *s* habla ambigua para engañar; galimatías, guirigay
**double-throw switch** ['dʌbəl'θro] *s* (elec.) conmutador de doble caída
**double time** *s* pago doble por sobretiempo; (mil.) paso ligero
**doubleton** ['dʌbəltən] *s* (bridge) doblete
**double track** *s* (rail.) doble vía
**double-track** ['dʌbəl'træk] *adj* (rail.) de doble vía
**doubletree** ['dʌbəl,tri] *s* volea
**double turn** *s* segunda, vuelta doble (*de una cerradura*)
**double vision** *s* vista doble
**doubloon** [dʌb'lun] *s* doblón
**doubly** ['dʌblɪ] *adv* doblemente; dos a la vez
**doubt** [daʊt] *s* duda; **beyond doubt** sin duda; **in doubt** incierto; **no doubt** sin duda; **to call in doubt** poner en duda; **without doubt** sin duda; *va & vn* dudar; **to doubt having** + *pp* dudar haber + *pp*
**doubtable** ['daʊtəbəl] *adj* dudable
**doubter** ['daʊtər] *s* incrédulo
**doubtful** ['daʊtfəl] *adj* dudoso
**doubting Thomas, a** un Santo Tomás (*persona que lo duda todo*)
**doubtless** ['daʊtlɪs] *adj* indudable, indubitable
**douche** [duʃ] *s* ducha; jeringa; *va* duchar; *vn* ducharse
**dough** [do] *s* masa, pasta; (slang) pasta (*dinero*)
**doughboy** ['do,bɔɪ] *s* (coll.) soldado de infantería norteamericano
**doughnut** ['do,nʌt] *s* buñuelo, rosquilla
**doughty** ['daʊtɪ] *adj* (*comp:* **-tier;** *super:* **-tiest**) (hum.) bravo, valiente, esforzado
**doughy** ['do·ɪ] (*comp:* **-ier;** *super:* **-iest**) pastoso
**Douglas fir** ['dʌgləs] *s* (bot.) seudotsuga
**doum** [dum] o **doum palm** *s* (bot.) duma
**dour** [dur], [dʊr] o [daʊr] *adj* abatido, triste, melancólico; (Scottish) austero, severo, duro; (Scottish) terco, obstinado
**douse** [daʊs] *va* zambullir; empapar; (coll.) apagar (*la luz*); (coll.) quitarse (*una prenda de vestir*); arriar; (naut.) cerrar (*una porta*); *vn* zambullirse; empaparse
**dove** [dʌv] *s* (orn.) paloma; (fig.) paloma; [dov] *pret & pp* (coll.) *de* **dive**
**dovecot** ['dʌv,kɑt] o **dovecote** ['dʌv,kot] o ['dʌv,kɑt] *s* palomar
**dovetail** ['dʌv,tel] *s* (carp.) cola de milano, cola de pato, ensambladura de cola de milano, ensambladura de cola de pato; *va* machihembrar, ensamblar a cola de milano, ensamblar a cola de pato; encajar; *vn* encajar; concordar, conformar
**dowager** ['daʊədʒər] *s* viuda que goza el título o los bienes del marido, p.ej., condesa viuda, duquesa viuda, princesa viuda; (coll.) señora anciana acaudalada, matrona con pretensiones
**dowdy** ['daʊdɪ] *adj* (*comp:* **-dier;** *super:* **-diest**) basto, desaliñado; *s* (*pl:* **-dies**) mujer basta, mujer desaliñada
**dowel** ['daʊəl] *s* clavija; *va* (*pret & pp:* **-eled** o **-elled;** *ger:* **-eling** o **-elling**) enclavijar
**dower** ['daʊər] *s* viudedad; dote; prenda; *va* señalar viudedad a; dotar
**down** [daʊn] *adv* abajo; hacia abajo, para abajo; en tierra; al sur; a precio reducido; en un papel, por escrito; de pronto, al contado; **to be down on** (coll.) tener inquina a; **to get down to work** aplicarse resueltamente al trabajo; **to go down** bajar; **to lie down** acostarse; **to sit down** sentarse; **down and out** arruinado; fuera de combate; **down below** allá abajo; **down from** desde; **down in the mouth** cariacontecido; **down on one's knees** de rodillas; **down to** hasta; **down to date** hasta la fecha; hasta nuestros días; **down under** entre los antípodas; **down with . . . !** ¡abajo . . . !; *prep* bajando; abajo de; **down the river** río abajo; **down the street** calle abajo; *adj* descendente; de abajo; malo, enfermo; triste, abatido; echado, acostado; agotado (*p.ej., acumulador*); anticipado (*pago, dinero*); *s* vello (*en las frutas y el cuerpo humano*); plumón (*pluma muy fina de las aves*); baja, caída; revés de fortuna; descenso; terreno ondulado y cubierto de hierba; duna; *va* (coll.) tragar; derribar, echar por tierra; *vn* acostarse
**downcast** ['daʊn,kæst] o ['daʊn,kɑst] *adj* inclinado; abatido, desanimado

**downcomer** ['daun,kʌmər] *s* conducto de tubo descendente
**downfall** ['daun,fɔl] *s* caída, ruina; chaparrón; nevazo
**downfallen** ['daun,fɔlən] *adj* caído, arruinado
**downgrade** ['daun,gred] *adj* (coll.) pendiente, en declive; *adv* (coll.) cuesta abajo; *s* bajada; **to be on the downgrade** ir cabeza abajo (*decaer, declinar*); *va* disminuir la categoría, el sueldo, etc. de
**downhearted** ['daun,hartɪd] *adj* abatido, desanimado
**downhill** ['daun'hɪl] *adj* pendiente, en declive; peor; *adv* cuesta abajo
**down payment** *s* pago inicial, cuota de entrada
**downpour** ['daun,por] *s* chaparrón, aguacero
**downright** ['daun,raɪt] *adj* absoluto, categórico, completo; claro, patente; *adv* absolutamente, completamente
**downstairs** ['daun'stɛrz] *adj* de abajo; *adv* abajo; *s* piso inferior; piso bajo
**downstream** ['daun'strim] *adv* aguas abajo, río abajo
**downstroke** ['daun,strok] *s* (mach.) carrera descendente
**downtown** ['daun'taun] *adj* céntrico; *adv* al centro de la ciudad, en el centro de la ciudad
**down town** *s* barrios céntricos, calles céntricas
**downtrend** ['daun,trɛnd] *s* tendencia a la baja
**downtrodden** ['daun,tradən] *adj* pisoteado; oprimido, tiranizado
**downward** ['daunwərd] *adj* descendente; *adv* hacia abajo; hacia una época posterior
**downwards** ['daunwərdz] *adv* hacia abajo; hacia una época posterior
**downwind** ['daun'wɪnd] *adv* en la dirección en que sopla el viento, en sitio hacia donde sopla el viento
**downwind landing** *s* (aer.) aterrizaje con viento de cola
**downy** ['daunɪ] *adj* (*comp:* **-ier**; *super:* **-iest**) velloso (*blando como vello*); plumoso (*cubierto de plumón*)
**dowry** ['daurɪ] *s* (*pl:* **-ries**) dote
**dowse** [daus] *va & vn* var. de **douse**; [dauz] *vn* practicar la radiestesia
**doxology** [daks'alədʒɪ] *s* (*pl:* **-gies**) *s* doxología; **greater doxology** gran doxología; **lesser doxology** pequeña doxología
**doz.** abr. de **dozen** o **dozens**
**doze** [doz] *s* sueño ligero; *vn* dormitar; **to doze off** quedarse medio dormido
**dozen** ['dʌzən] *s* docena
**dozenth** ['dʌzənθ] *adj* doceno
**dozy** ['dozɪ] *adj* soñoliento
**D.P.** abr. de **displaced person**
**dpt.** abr. de **department** y **deponent**
**dr.** abr. de **debtor, drawer, dram** o **drams**
**Dr.** abr. de **debtor** y **Doctor**
**drab** [dræb] *adj* (*comp:* **drabber**; *super:* **drabbest**) gris parduzco, gris amarillento; monótono; *s* gris parduzco, gris amarillento; ramera, puta; mujer desaliñada
**drachm** [dræm] *s* dracma; (pharm.) dracma
**drachma** ['drækmə] *s* (*pl:* **-mas** o **-mae** [mi]) dracma
**Draco** ['dreko] *s* Dracón
**Draconian** [drə'konɪən] *adj* draconiano; (fig.) draconiano; (*l.c.*) *adj* draconiano
**draff** [dræf] *s* heces, poso
**draffish** ['dræfɪʃ] o **draffy** ['dræfɪ] *adj* inútil, sin valor, despreciable
**draft** [dræft] o [draft] *s* corriente de aire; tiro (*de chimenea; acción de tirar una carga*); borrador (*escrito de primera intención*); bosquejo (*primer apunte, plan, proyecto*); trago, bebida; inspiración; aire, humo inspirado; (com.) giro, letra de cambio, libranza; (naut.) calado; (mil.) quinta, conscripción; **drafts** *spl* damas, juego de damas; **on draft** a presión, servido al grifo, directo del barril; **to be exempted from the draft** redimirse de las quintas; *va* dibujar; bosquejar; hacer un borrador de; redactar (*un documento*); (mil.) quintar; **to be drafted** ir a quintas
**draft age** *s* edad de quintas
**draft beer** *s* var. de **draught beer**
**draft board** *s* junta de reclutamiento
**draft call** *s* llamada a quintas
**draft dodger** *s* (coll.) emboscado
**draftee** [,dræf'ti] o [,draf'ti] *s* (mil.) quinto, conscripto
**draft horse** *s* caballo de tiro
**drafting board** *s* tabla para dibujar
**draftsman** ['dræftsmən] o ['draftsmən] *s* (*pl:* **-men**) dibujante; redactor; peón (*del juego de damas*)
**draftsmanship** ['dræftsmənʃɪp] o ['draftsmənʃɪp] *s* arte del dibujante, labor de dibujante; redacción (*p.ej., de un proyecto de ley*)
**draft treaty** *s* proyecto de convenio
**drafty** ['dræftɪ] o ['draftɪ] *adj* (*comp:* **-ier**; *super:* **-iest**) airoso, lleno de corrientes de aire
**drag** [dræg] *s* rastra; (naut.) rastra; rastreamiento; (naut.) rastreo; narria (*para llevar arrastrando cosas de gran peso*); (aer.) resistencia al avance; (fig.) estorbo, impedimento, obstáculo; (slang) enchufe (*influencia*); (*pret & pp:* **dragged**; *ger:* **dragging**) *va* arrastrar; (naut.) rastrear; **to drag on** u **out** hacer demasiado largo, hacer demasiado lento; *vn* arrastrarse por el suelo; avanzar demasiado lentamente; decaer (*el interés*); **to drag on** u **out** avanzar demasiado lentamente, ser interminable, hilar largo
**draggle** ['drægəl] *va* ensuciar arrastrando; *vn* ensuciarse arrastrando; rezagarse, quedarse atrás
**drag link** *s* contramanivela; contrabrazo (*del mecanismo de dirección*)
**dragnet** ['dræg,nɛt] *s* red barredera; (fig.) red barredera
**dragoman** ['drægomən] *s* (*pl:* **-mans** o **-men**) dragomán
**dragon** ['drægən] *s* dragón (*animal fabuloso*); (mil.) dragoncillo (*escopeta*); (vet.) dragón (*en el ojo de un caballo*); (fig.) fiera (*persona*); mujer muy severa; *adj* dragontino
**dragoness** ['drægənɪs] *s* dragona
**dragonfly** ['drægən,flaɪ] *s* (*pl:* **-flies**) (ent.) libélula, caballito del diablo
**dragonnade** [,drægə'ned] *s* dragonada
**dragonné** ['drægəne] *adj* (her.) dragonado
**dragon's-mouth** ['drægənz,mauθ] *s* (bot.) boca de dragón
**dragon's tail** *s* (astr.) cola del dragón
**dragon tree** *s* (bot.) drago
**dragoon** [drə'gun] *s* (mil.) dragón; *va* tiranizar; **to dragoon one into working** precisar a uno a trabajar, constreñir a uno que trabaje
**dragrope** ['dræg,rop] *s* cable de arrastre; (aer.) cuerda freno
**drain** [dren] *s* dren, desaguadero (*conducto de desagüe*); consumo; (surg.) dren; desagüe; desangramiento (*desagüe completo*); (fig.) desaguadero (*ocasión de continuo gasto*); *va* drenar, desaguar; avenar (*terrenos húmedos*); desangrar; escurrir (*una vasija; un líquido*); **to drain off** u **out** desangrar; *vn* desaguar; escurrirse
**drainage** ['drenɪdʒ] *s* drenaje, desagüe, avenamiento
**drainage basin** *s* cuenca de un río
**drainboard** ['dren,bord] *s* escurridero (*mesa inclinada que sirve para escurrir platos*)
**drain cock** *s* llave de purga
**drainer** ['drenər] *s* persona que avena las tierras; colador
**drainpipe** ['dren,paɪp] *s* tubo de desagüe
**drain plug** *s* tapón de desagüe, tapón de purga: (aut.) tapón de vaciado
**drake** [drek] *s* (orn.) pato
**dram** [dræm] *s* (pharm.) dracma; trago de aguardiente; porción pequeña
**drama** ['dramə] o ['dræmə] *s* drama (*pieza de teatro; género; suceso de la vida real*)
**dramamine** ['dræməmin] *s* (trademark) dramamina
**dramatic** [drə'mætɪk] *adj* dramático; **dramatics** *ssg* (theat.) representación de aficionados; *spl* dramas presentados por aficionados
**dramatically** [drə'mætɪkəlɪ] *adv* dramáticamente
**dramatis personae** ['dræmətɪs pər'soni] *spl* personajes dramáticos
**dramatist** ['dræmətɪst] *s* dramático (*autor*)
**dramatization** [,dræmətɪ'zeʃən] *s* dramatización
**dramatize** ['dræmətaɪz] *va* dramatizar
**dramaturgic** [,dræmə'tʌrdʒɪk] *adj* dramático

**dramaturgist** ['dræmə,tʌrdʒɪst] *s* dramaturgo
**dramaturgy** ['dræmə,tʌrdʒɪ] *s* dramaturgia
**dramshop** ['dræm,ʃɑp] *s* bar, taberna
**Drang nach Osten** [drɑŋ nɑx 'ɔstən] *s* marcha hacia el este
**drank** [dræŋk] *pret de* **drink**
**drape** [drep] *s* colgadura, ropaje; *va* cubrir con colgaduras, adornar con telas colgantes; arreglar los pliegues de (*una prenda de vestir*)
**draper** ['drepər] *s* tapicero; (Brit.) pañero
**drapery** ['drepərɪ] *s* (*pl:* **-ies**) colgaduras, ropaje; (Brit.) paño, paños; (Brit.) pañería
**drastic** ['dræstɪk] *adj* drástico; (med.) drástico
**drastically** ['dræstɪkəlɪ] *adv* drásticamente, rápida y violentamente, extensamente
**draught** [dræft] o [drɑft] *s & va* var. de **draft**
**draught beer** *s* cerveza a presión
**draughtboard** ['dræft,bord] o ['drɑft,bord] *s* tablero de damas
**draughtsman** ['dræftsmən] o ['drɑftsmən] *s* (*pl:* **-men**) var. de **draftsman**
**draughty** ['dræftɪ] o ['drɑftɪ] *adj* (*comp:* **-ier;** *super:* **-iest**) var. de **drafty**
**Dravidian** [drə'vɪdɪən] *adj & s* dravidiano
**draw** [drɔ] *s* tiro (*p.ej., de una chimenea*); (coll.) función que atrae mucha gente; empate (*en un juego o contienda*); tablas (*en damas y ajedrez*); robo (*naipe o naipes que se toman de la baceta*); sorteo (*p.ej., de una lotería*); jugada, suerte (*en un juego, lotería, etc.*); barranco; piso o compuerta (*de un puente levadizo*) ‖ (*pret:* **drew;** *pp:* **drawn**) *va* tirar (*alambre, una línea; atraer*); tirar de (*arrastrar, traer hacia sí*); sacar (*p.ej., un clavo, una espada, agua, una conclusión*); aspirar, inspirar (*el aire*); atraer (*a la gente*); llamar (*la atención*); atraerse (*aplausos*); contraer, encoger; dar (*un suspiro*); correr, descorrer (*una cortina*); tender (*un arco*); cobrar (*un salario*); sacarse (*un premio*); levantar (*un puente levadizo*); preparar por infusión; empatar (*una partida*); robar (*naipes, fichas*); (com.) girar, librar; hacer (*una comparación*); (naut. & weaving) calar; (elec.) consumir (*amperios*); dibujar; redactar; **to draw a bead on** (coll.) apuntar; **to draw aside** apartar; **to draw along** arrastrar; **to draw back** hacer retroceder; **to draw forth** hacer salir; **to draw interest** devengar interés; **to draw off** sacar, extraer; trasegar (*un líquido*); retirar; **to draw on** ocasionar, producir; provocar; ponerse (*p.ej., guantes*); (com.) girar a cargo de; **to draw oneself up** enderezarse con dignidad; **to draw out** sacar; sonsacar, tirar de la lengua a; **to draw together** juntar, unir; **to draw up** extender, redactar (*un documento*); (mil.) ordenar para el combate ‖ *vn* tirar, tirar bien (*una chimenea*); contraerse, encogerse; empatar; (naut.) calar; dibujar; echar suertes; atraer mucha gente, atraer concurrencia; (com.) girar; **to draw aside** apartarse; **to draw back** retroceder, retirarse; **to draw near** acercarse; acercarse a; **to draw to a close** estar para terminar; **to draw together** juntarse, unirse; **to draw up** pararse, detenerse; **to draw up at the curb** arrimarse a la acera
**drawback** ['drɔ,bæk] *s* desventaja, inconveniente; (com.) drawback (*reembolso, p.ej., de derechos de aduana*)
**drawbridge** ['drɔ,brɪdʒ] *s* puente levadizo, puente giratorio
**drawee** [,drɔ'i] *s* (com.) girado, librado
**drawer** [drɔr] *s* cajón, gaveta; ['drɔər] *s* dibujante; (com.) girador, librador; **drawers** [drɔrz] *spl* calzoncillos
**drawing** ['drɔ·ɪŋ] *s* dibujo; sorteo (*en una lotería*)
**drawing account** *s* cuenta corriente
**drawing board** *s* tablero de dibujo
**drawing card** *s* atracción (*actor, orador, función, etc., que atraen a mucha gente*)
**drawing knife** *s* var. de **drawknife**
**drawing room** *s* sala; recepción; (rail.) departamento reservado
**drawing table** *s* mesa para dibujante
**drawknife** ['drɔ,naɪf] *s pl:* **-knives**) plana curvada, cuchilla de dos mangos
**drawl** [drɔl] *s* habla lenta y pesada; *va* pronunciar lenta y pesadamente; *vn* hablar lenta y pesadamente
**drawn** [drɔn] *pp de* **draw**
**drawn butter** *s* mantequilla derretida
**drawn work** *s* (sew.) calado
**drawplate** ['drɔ,plet] *s* (mach.) hilera
**drawshave** ['drɔ,ʃev] *s* var. de **drawknife**
**drawsheet** ['drɔ,ʃit] *s* alezo
**drawtube** ['drɔ,tjub] o ['drɔ,tub] *s* tubo telescópico (*del microscopio*)
**draw well** *s* pozo de noria
**dray** [dre] *s* carro; narria; *va* acarrear
**drayage** ['dreɪdʒ] *s* acarreo
**dray horse** *s* caballo de tiro
**drayman** ['dremən] *s* (*pl:* **-men**) acarreador, carretonero
**dread** [drɛd] *s* pavor, temor; *adj* terrible, espantoso; *va & vn* temer; **to dread to** + *inf* temer + *inf*
**dreadful** ['drɛdfəl] *adj* terrible, espantoso; (coll.) desagradable
**dreadfully** ['drɛdfəlɪ] *adv* terriblemente; (coll.) sumamente, excesivamente
**dreadnought** ['drɛd,nɔt] *s* (nav.) gran buque acorazado, dreadnought
**dream** [drim] *s* ensueño, sueño; (fig.) sueño (*cosa de gran belleza*); **dream come true** sueño hecho realidad; (*pret & pp:* **dreamed** o **dreamt**) *va* soñar; pasar (*p.ej., el día*) soñando; **to dream up** (coll.) ingeniar, imaginar; *vn* soñar; **to dream of** soñar con o en; **to dream of** + *ger* soñar con + *inf*
**dreamer** ['drimər] *s* soñador; (fig.) soñador
**dreamland** ['drim,lænd] *s* reino del ensueño; utopía; tierra de las hadas; sueño
**dreamt** [drɛmt] *pret & pp de* **dream**
**dreamy** ['drimɪ] *adj* (*comp:* **-ier;** *super:* **-iest**) soñador; lleno de sueños; vago, ligero
**dreary** ['drɪrɪ] *adj* (*comp:* **-ier;** *super:* **-iest**) triste; monótono, pesado
**dredge** [drɛdʒ] *s* draga; rastra; *va* dragar; rastrear; espolvorear
**dredger** ['drɛdʒər] *s* persona que draga; draga (*máquina o buque*); polvorera
**dredging** ['drɛdʒɪŋ] *s* dragado
**dregs** [drɛgz] *spl* heces; (fig.) heces
**drench** [drɛntʃ] *s* mojada; solución para empapar, solución para remojar; bebida; bebida purgante; *va* mojar, empapar; purgar con violencia
**drenching** ['drɛntʃɪŋ] *adj* mojador; torrencial (*lluvia*)
**Dresden** ['drɛzdən] *s* Dresde
**dress** [drɛs] *s* indumentaria; vestido; vestido exterior de mujer o niña; falda; traje de etiqueta, vestido de gala; (*pret & pp:* **dressed** o **drest**) *va* vestir; trajear; vestir de etiqueta; adornar, ataviar; preparar; peinar (*el pelo*); curar (*una herida*); adobar y curtir (*pieles*); podar (*plantas*); (naut.) empavesar; (mil.) alinear; **to dress down** (coll.) azotar, pegar; (coll.) calentar las orejas a: **to get dressed** vestirse; *vn* vestir (*ir vestido*); vestirse (*ponerse el vestido*); (mil.) alinearse; **to dress up** vestirse de etiqueta; prenderse de veinticinco alfileres
**dress ball** *s* baile de etiqueta
**dress coat** *s* frac
**dresser** ['drɛsər] *s* cómoda con espejo; aparador; **to be a good dresser** vestir con elegancia, vestir con buen gusto
**dress form** *s* maniquí
**dress goods** *spl* géneros para vestidos
**dressing** ['drɛsɪŋ] *s* aderezamiento, adorno; (cook.) aliño, salsa; (cook.) relleno; (agr.) abono; (surg.) vendaje; (coll.) regaño
**dressing-down** ['drɛsɪŋ'daun] *s* (coll.) azotamiento; (coll.) regaño, repasata
**dressing gown** *s* bata, peinador
**dressing room** *s* cuarto de vestir; (theat.) camarín
**dressing station** *s* (mil.) puesto de socorro
**dressing table** *s* tocador
**dressmaker** ['drɛs,mekər] *s* costurera, modista
**dressmaking** ['drɛs,mekɪŋ] *s* costura, modistería
**dress parade** *s* (mil.) parada
**dress rehearsal** *s* (theat.) ensayo general
**dress shirt** *s* camisa de pechera dura
**dress shop** *s* casa de modas

**dress suit** *s* traje de etiqueta
**dress tie** *s* corbata de smoking, corbata de frac
**dressy** ['drɛsɪ] *adj* (*comp:* **-ier;** *super:* **-iest**) (coll.) acicalado, aficionado a ataviarse; (coll.) elegante, vistoso
**drest** [drɛst] *pret & pp de* **dress**
**drew** [dru] *pret de* **draw**
**dribble** ['drɪbəl] *s* goteo, caída en gotas; derrame ligero; (coll.) llovizna; (sport) dribbling; *va* hacer caer gota a gota; (sport) driblar; *vn* gotear; babear; (sport) driblar
**dribbler** ['drɪblər] *s* persona que babea; (sport) jugador que dribla
**driblet** ['drɪblɪt] *s* gotita; adarme
**dried beef** [draɪd] *s* cecina
**dried fig** *s* higo paso
**drier** ['draɪər] *s* enjugador (*persona o utensilio*); desecante; secador (*para el cabello*); secadora (*máquina para secar la ropa*)
**drift** [drɪft] *s* cosa llevada por la corriente; corriente de agua, corriente de aire; montón (*de nieve, arena, etc.*); ventisca; impulsión, impulso; dirección, rumbo; tenor, sentido, significación; (geol.) terrenos de acarreo; (aer. & naut.) deriva; (min.) socavón; (rad. & telv.) desviación; *va* llevar; amontonar; (mach.) mandrilar; *vn* ser llevado por la corriente, ir arrastrado por la corriente; amontonarse; ventiscar; (aer. & naut.) derivar, ir a la deriva; (fig.) vivir sin rumbo
**driftage** ['drɪftɪdʒ] *s* cosa llevada por la corriente; (aer. & naut.) deriva
**drift angle** *s* (aer. & naut.) ángulo de deriva
**drifter** ['drɪftər] *s* vago, vagabundo
**drift ice** *s* hielo flotante, hielo acarreado por el agua
**drift meter** *s* (aer. & naut.) derivómetro
**driftpin** ['drɪft,pɪn] *s* (mach.) mandril de ensanchar
**driftwood** ['drɪft,wʊd] *s* madera flotante, madera acarreada por el agua, madera arrojada a la playa por el agua
**drill** [drɪl] *s* taladro; (agr.) sembradora mecánica; hilera de semillas sembradas en un surco; disciplina, instrucción; (mil.) ejercicio; dril (*tejido*); (zool.) dril (*mandril*); *va* taladrar; disciplinar, instruir; plantar en hileras, plantar en un surco; (mil.) enseñar el ejercicio a; *vn* (mil.) hacer el ejercicio
**drilling** ['drɪlɪŋ] *s* perforación; (mil.) ejercicio; dril (*tejido*)
**drillmaster** ['drɪl,mæstər] o ['drɪl,mɑstər] *s* maestro de ejercicios
**drill press** *s* prensa taladradora, taladro mecánico
**drily** ['draɪlɪ] *adv* secamente
**drink** [drɪŋk] *s* bebida; beber, exceso en la bebida; **the drinks are on the house!** ¡convida la casa!; **to take a drink** echar un trago; (*pret:* **drank;** *pp:* **drunk**) *va* beber; beberse (*p.ej., su sueldo*); **to drink down** beber de una vez; **to drink in** beberse (*p.ej., un libro*); beber (*las palabras de una persona*); aspirar (*aire*); *vn* beber; **to drink out of** beber de o en (*p.ej., una fuente*); **to drink to** beber a o por, brindar a o por
**drinkable** ['drɪŋkəbəl] *adj* bebible, potable
**drinker** ['drɪŋkər] *s* bebedor
**drinking** ['drɪŋkɪŋ] *s* (el) beber; *adj* de beber, para beber; bebedor
**drinking bout** *s* juerga de borrachera
**drinking cup** *s* tanque, taza para beber
**drinking fountain** *s* fuente de agua corriente para beber, fuente de beber
**drinking glass** *s* vaso para beber
**drinking horn** *s* aliara, cuerna, vaso de cuerno
**drinking song** *s* canción para beber, canción de taberna, canción báquica
**drinking trough** *s* abrevadero
**drinking water** *s* agua para beber, agua potable
**drip** [drɪp] *s* goteo; gotas; gotera (*p.ej., del techo*); tubo gotero; (arch.) alero; (*pret & pp:* **dripped** o **dript;** *ger:* **dripping**) *va* verter gota a gota, hacer gotear; *vn* caer gota a gota, gotear
**drip coffee** *s* café de maquinilla
**drip-dry** ['drɪp,draɪ] *adj* de lava y pon, p.ej., **drip-dry shirt** camisa de lava y pon
**drip feed** *s* engrase por goteo
**drip pan** *s* cubeta de goteo; (aut.) colector de aceite, recogegotas
**dripping** ['drɪpɪŋ] *s* goteo; **drippings** *spl* líquidos que gotean; pringue (*grasa que suelta la carne con el calor*)
**dripping pan** *s* grasera, pringuera
**dripstone** ['drɪp,ston] *s* (arch.) alero de piedra; carbonato cálcico de las estalactitas y estalagmitas
**dript** [drɪpt] *pret & pp de* **drip**
**drive** [draɪv] *s* calzada para coches, calzada para automóviles; paseo en coche, paseo en automóvil; energía, vigor, fuerza; urgencia, presión; campaña vigorosa; venta a bajo precio; golpe fuerte; medio de impulsión; mecanismo de dirección; mecanismo de transmisión; mecanismo de funcionamiento; **an hour's drive** una hora de coche ‖ (*pret:* **drove;** *pp:* **driven**) *va* impeler, empujar; estimular, aguijonear; compeler, forzar; clavar, hincar; actuar, mover; llevar, conducir (*p.ej., ganado*); arrear (*a las bestias*); guiar, conducir (*p.ej., un automóvil*); llevar en coche; efectuar, ejecutar; hacer excavando, hacer ahondando; obligar a trabajar mucho; (sport) golpear con gran fuerza; **to drive a good bargain** hacer un buen trato; **to drive away** ahuyentar; **to drive back** rechazar, obligar a retroceder; **to drive in** hacer entrar por fuerza; **to drive mad** volver loco; **to drive off** ahuyentar; **to drive out** echar fuera, hacer salir, expulsar ‖ *vn* ir en coche, ir en automóvil; trabajar mucho; **to drive at** tener puesta la mira en; querer decir; **to drive away** trabajar mucho; **to drive in** entrar en coche, entrar en (*un sitio*) en coche; **to drive on the right** (u **on the left**) circular por la derecha (o por la izquierda); **to drive out** salir en coche
**drive-in motion-picture theater** ['draɪv,ɪn] *s* auto-teatro (*cine al aire libre en que los espectadores motorizados ven la cinta desde los coches*)
**drive-in restaurant** *s* restaurante en que sirven a los automovilistas sin que salgan de los coches
**drivel** ['drɪvəl] *s* baba; bobería; (*pret & pp:* **-eled** o **-elled;** *ger:* **-eling** o **-elling**) *va* hacer babear; gastar (*tiempo*) tontamente; *vn* babear; bobear
**driveler** o **driveller** ['drɪvələr] *s* baboso; bobo
**driven** ['drɪvən] *pp de* **drive**
**driven well** *s* pozo abisinio
**driver** ['draɪvər] *s* conductor; cochero; maquinista (*de una locomotora*); rueda motriz (*de locomotora*); (golf) conductor; (mach.) pieza impulsora; persona despótica que fuerza a trabajar
**driver's license** *s* (aut.) permiso de conducir, carnet de conducir
**driver training school** *s* var. de **driving school**
**drive shaft** *s* (mach.) árbol de mando, árbol o eje motor
**driveway** ['draɪv,we] *s* calzada para coches; entrada para coches, calzada de acceso
**drivewell** ['draɪv,wɛl] *s* var. de **driven well**
**drive wheel** *s* (mach.) rueda motriz
**drive-yourself service** ['draɪvjʊr'sɛlf] *s* alquiler sin chófer
**driving school** *s* auto-escuela
**drizzle** ['drɪzəl] *s* llovizna; *vn* lloviznar
**drogue** [drog] *s* (aer.) paracaídas estabilizador, paracaídas desacelerador; (aer.) embudo de reaprovisionamiento en vuelo; (meteor.) cono de viento; (naut.) ancla flotante
**drogue gun** *s* (aer.) cañón eyector de paracaídas
**droll** [drol] *adj* chusco, gracioso
**drollery** ['drolərɪ] *s* (*pl:* **-ies**) chuscada, bufonería
**dromedary** ['drɑmə,dɛrɪ] *s* (*pl:* **-ies**) dromedario
**drone** [dron] *s* (ent.) zángano; (fig.) zángano; zumbido; bordón o roncón (*de la gaita*); avión radiodirigido; *va* decir monótonamente; *vn* zanganear; zumbar; hablar monótonamente
**drool** [drul] *s* baba; (slang) bobería; *vn* babear; (slang) bobear
**droop** [drup] *s* inclinación; *va* inclinar; dejar caer; *vn* inclinarse; estar pendiente, colgar;

decaer, descaecer; consumirse, marchitarse; encamarse (*las mieses*); abatirse, entristecerse
**drooping** ['drupɪŋ] *adj* caído (*dícese de los párpados, los hombros, etc.*)
**drop** [drɑp] *s* gota; pendiente (*cuesta o declive; arete*); baja, caída repentina; descenso (*de temperatura*); lanzamiento (*p.ej., de víveres desde un aeroplano*); traguito; pastilla; escotillón; horca; **drops** *spl* gotas (*medicamento*); **at the drop of a hat** al dar la señal; de buena gana, con gusto; **a drop in the bucket** cosa insignificante; **to get** o **to have the drop on** coger la delantera a, llevar la ventaja a; **drop by drop** gota a gota ❙ (*pret & pp:* **dropped** o **dropt;** *ger:* **dropping**) *va* dejar caer; hacer caer; derribar; matar; poner en tierra; bajar (*una cortina*); echar al buzón; soltar (*una palabra*) casualmente; escribir (*una esquela, unos renglones*); omitir, suprimir; abandonar, dejar; despedir; borrar de la lista (*a un alumno*); lanzar (*bombas, suministros, etc. de un avión*); escalfar (*huevos*); **to drop a hint** soltar una indirecta; **to drop anchor** echar el ancla; **to drop a line** poner unos renglones, escribir unas palabras; **to drop a subject** cambiar de asunto ❙ *vn* caer, caer de repente; dejarse caer; caer agotado, caer herido, caer muerto; bajar; cesar, terminar, parar; **to drop asleep** quedarse dormido; **to drop behind** quedarse atrás; **to drop dead** caer muerto; **to drop in, to drop over** entrar al pasar, visitar de paso; **to drop off** desaparecer; quedarse dormido; morir de repente; **to drop out** desaparecer; retirarse; darse de baja (*dejar de pertenecer voluntariamente a una sociedad, etc.*)
**drop box** *s* buzón
**drop curtain** *s* (theat.) telón
**drop-forge** ['drɑp'fordʒ] *va* forjar a martinete
**drop hammer** *s* martinete, martillo pilón
**drop kick** *s* (football) puntapié que se da a la pelota en el momento en que rebota
**drop-kick** ['drɑp,kɪk] *va* (football) dar un puntapié a (*la pelota*) en el momento en que rebota
**drop-leaf table** ['drɑp,lif] *s* mesa de hoja plegadiza
**droplet** ['drɑplɪt] *s* gotita
**droplight** ['drɑp,laɪt] *s* lámpara de extensión, lámpara colgante
**dropper** ['drɑpər] *s* cuentagotas
**dropping** ['drɑpɪŋ] *s* goteo; líquido que gotea; **droppings** *spl* excrementos de animales
**drop shutter** *s* (phot.) obturador de guillotina
**dropsical** ['drɑpsɪkəl] *adj* hidrópico
**dropsy** ['drɑpsɪ] *s* (path.) hidropesía
**dropt** [drɑpt] *pret & pp de* **drop**
**drop table** *s* mesa perezosa
**dropwort** ['drɑp,wʌrt] *s* (bot.) filipéndula
**drosera** ['drɑsərə] *s* (pharm.) drosera
**droseraceous** [,drɑsə'reʃəs] *adj* (bot.) droseráceo
**drosometer** [drə'sɑmɪtər] *s* drosómetro
**drosophila** [dro'sɑfɪlə] *s* (*pl:* **-lae** [li]) (ent.) drosófila
**dross** [drɔs] o [drɑs] *s* escoria (*de metales*); basura, desecho
**drought** [draʊt] *s* sequía (*temporada seca*); sequedad
**drought-stricken** ['draʊt,strɪkən] *adj* asolado por la sequía
**droughty** ['draʊtɪ] *adj* árido, seco
**drouth** [draʊθ] *s* var. de **drought**
**drove** [drov] *s* manada; gentío, multitud; *pret de* **drive**
**drover** ['drovər] *s* ganadero
**drown** [draʊn] *va* anegar, ahogar; apagar (*un sonido*); ahogar (*p.ej., pesares*); **to drown out** ahuyentar inundando; apagar (*un sonido, una voz*); apagar la voz de; *vn* anegarse, ahogarse, perecer ahogado
**drowse** [draʊz] *s* somnolencia, modorra; *va* adormecer; pasar (*el tiempo*) adormeciéndose; *vn* adormecerse, estar amodorrado
**drowsiness** ['draʊzɪnɪs] *s* somnolencia, modorra
**drowsy** ['draʊzɪ] *adj* (*comp:* **-sier;** *super:* **-siest**) soñoliento
**drub** [drʌb] (*pret & pp:* **drubbed;** *ger:* **drubbing**) *va* apalear, tundir; (sport) derrotar completamente
**drubbing** ['drʌbɪŋ] *s* paliza, zurra; (sport) derrota aplastante
**drudge** [drʌdʒ] *s* ganapán; yunque, esclavo del trabajo; *vn* afanarse
**drudgery** ['drʌdʒərɪ] *s* (*pl:* **-ies**) afán, trabajo penoso
**drug** [drʌg] *s* droga; narcótico; macana, artículo de comercio que queda sin fácil salida; **to be a drug on the market** ser invendible; (*pret & pp:* **drugged;** *ger:* **drugging**) *va* narcotizar; poner narcótico en; aletargar o atontar con un narcótico
**drug addict** *s* adicto a las drogas narcóticas
**drug addiction** *s* adicción a las drogas narcóticas
**drugget** ['drʌgɪt] *s* droguete
**druggist** ['drʌgɪst] *s* farmacéutico, boticario; droguero, droguista
**drug habit** *s* vicio de los narcóticos
**drug store** *s* farmacia, botica; droguería
**drug traffic** *s* contrabando de narcóticos
**druid** o **Druid** ['druɪd] *s* druida
**druidess** ['druɪdɪs] *s* druidesa
**druidic** [dru'ɪdɪk] o **druidical** [dru'ɪdɪkəl] *adj* druídico
**druidism** ['druɪdɪzəm] *s* druidismo
**drum** [drʌm] *s* tambor (*cilindro*); bidón (*p.ej., para aceite, gasolina*); (anat., arch. & mus.) tambor; (*pret & pp:* **drummed;** *ger:* **drumming**) *va* reunir a toque de tambor; **to drum a lesson into someone** meterle a uno la lección en la cabeza; **to drum out** (mil.) expulsar a toque de tambor; **to drum up** reunir a toque de tambor; reunir; **to drum up trade** fomentar ventas; *vn* tocar el tambor; teclear
**drum armature** *s* (elec.) inducido de tambor
**drumbeat** ['drʌm,bit] *s* toque de tambor
**drum corps** *s* banda de tambores
**drumfire** ['drʌm,faɪr] *s* fuego graneado
**drumfish** ['drʌm,fɪʃ] *s* (ichth.) corvina negra
**drumhead** ['drʌm,hɛd] *s* piel de tambor; (anat.) tambor
**drumhead court-martial** *s* (mil.) consejo de guerra en marcha o en el campo de batalla
**drumlin** ['drʌmlɪn] *s* (geol.) colina oval alargada, constituída por materiales detríticos de origen glacial
**drum major** *s* (mil.) tambor mayor
**drummer** ['drʌmər] *s* tambor (*persona*); (coll.) viajante
**drumstick** ['drʌm,stɪk] *s* baqueta, palillo; (coll.) muslo (*de ave cocida*)
**drunk** [drʌŋk] *adj* borracho; **to get drunk** emborracharse; *s* (slang) borracho; (slang) borrachera; *pp de* **drink**
**drunkard** ['drʌŋkərd] *s* borrachín
**drunken** ['drʌŋkən] *adj* borracho, emborrachado, embriagado
**drunken driver** *s* conductor embriagado
**drunken driving** *s* acto de conducir en estado de embriaguez; **he was arrested for drunken driving** fué arrestado por conducir en estado de embriaguez
**drunkenness** ['drʌŋkənnɪs] *s* embriaguez
**drupaceous** [dru'peʃəs] *adj* (bot.) drupáceo
**drupe** [drup] *s* (bot.) drupa
**drupelet** ['druplɪt] *s* (bot.) drupa pequeña
**druse** [druz] *s* (bot. & mineral.) drusa; (*cap.*) *s* druso
**Drusean** ['druzɪən] *adj* druso
**dry** [draɪ] *s* (coll.) prohibicionista; *adj* (*comp:* **drier;** *super:* **driest**) seco, árido; sediento; árido (*aburrido, falto de interés*); sin mantequilla (*dícese del pan*); (coll.) seco (*prohibicionista*); (*pret & pp:* **dried**) *va* secar; enjugar; **to dry up** secar rápidamente, secar completamente; *vn* secarse; **to dry up** secarse rápidamente, secarse completamente; (slang) dejar de hablar, callarse
**dryad** ['draɪæd] *s* (myth.) dríada
**dry battery** *s* (elec.) batería seca; (elec.) pila seca
**dry cell** *s* (elec.) pila seca
**dry-clean** ['draɪ,klin] *va* limpiar en seco
**dry cleaner** *s* tintorero
**dry cleaning** *s* lavado a seco, limpieza en seco
**dry-cleaning establishment** *s* tintorería
**dry dock** *s* (naut.) dique, dique de carena
**dry-dock** ['draɪ,dɑk] *va* (naut.) poner en dique de carena

**dryer** ['draɪər] *s* var. de **drier**
**dry-eyed** ['draɪ,aɪd] *adj* ojienjuto, sin lágrimas
**dry-farm** ['draɪ,fɑrm] *va* cultivar (*terrenos de secano*)
**dry farmer** *s* cultivador de terrenos de secano
**dry farming** *s* cultivo de secano
**dry goods** *spl* mercancías generales, géneros, lencería, pañería
**dry ice** *s* hielo carbónico, hielo seco o nieve carbónica
**dry law** *s* (U.S.A.) ley seca
**dryly** ['draɪlɪ] *adv* secamente
**dry measure** *s* medida para áridos
**dryness** ['draɪnɪs] *s* sequedad
**dry nurse** *s* ama seca
**dry-nurse** ['draɪ,nʌrs] *va* ser ama seca de
**dry point** *s* (f.a.) punta seca; grabado a punta seca
**dry rot** *s* (bot.) pudrición seca; (bot.) podredumbre causada por honguillos; (fig.) corrupción interna, deterioro
**dry sand** *s* (found.) arena de estufa, arena seca
**dry season** *s* estación de la seca
**dry-shod** ['draɪ,ʃɑd] *adj* a pie enjuto
**dry-stone** ['draɪ,ston] *adj* de piedra seca, de piedra en seco
**dry wash** *s* lavado secado pero no planchado
**d.s.** abr. de **days after sight** y **daylight saving**
**D.S.** abr. de **Dental Surgeon** y **Doctor of Science**
**D.Sc.** abr. de **Doctor of Science**
**D.S.C.** abr. de **Distinguished Service Cross**
**D.S.M.** abr. de **Distinguished Service Medal**
**D.S.T.** abr. de **Daylight Saving Time**
**d.t.'s** ['di'tiz] *spl* (coll.) delírium tremens; (coll.) diablos azules (Am.)
**dual** ['djuəl] o ['duəl] *adj* binario, dual; (gram.) dual; *s* (gram.) dual
**dual drive** *s* (aut.) mando doble
**dualism** ['djuəlɪzəm] o ['duəlɪzəm] *s* dualismo
**dualist** ['djuəlɪst] o ['duəlɪst] *s* dualista
**dualistic** [,djuə'lɪstɪk] o [,duə'lɪstɪk] *adj* dualista
**duality** [dju'ælɪtɪ] o [du'ælɪtɪ] *s* (*pl:* **-ties**) dualidad
**dub** [dʌb] *s* (slang) jugador desmañado; (*pret & pp:* **dubbed;** *ger:* **dubbing**) *va* apellidar, titular; armar caballero a; alisar; (mov.) doblar (*una película, generalmente en otro idioma*)
**dubiety** [dju'baɪətɪ] o [du'baɪətɪ] *s* (*pl:* **-ties**) incertidumbre; cosa dudosa
**dubious** ['djubɪəs] o ['dubɪəs] *adj* dudoso
**dubitative** ['djubɪ,tetɪv] o ['dubɪ,tetɪv] *adj* dubitativo
**dubitative conjunction** *s* (gram.) conjunción dubitativa
**ducal** ['djukəl] o ['dukəl] *adj* ducal
**ducat** ['dʌkət] *s* ducado
**duce** ['dutʃe] *s* caudillo
**duchess** ['dʌtʃɪs] *s* duquesa
**duchy** ['dʌtʃɪ] *s* (*pl:* **-ies**) ducado
**duck** [dʌk] *s* (orn.) pato; (orn.) pata; dril; terliz (*tejido*); agachada rápida (*para evitar un golpe*); zambullida (*en el agua*); (coll.) querida; **ducks** *spl* (coll.) pantalones de dril; **like water off a duck's back** sin tener ningún efecto; **to make ducks and drakes of** o **to play ducks and drakes with** malgastar, derrochar; *va* agachar rápidamente (*p.ej., la cabeza*); (coll.) evitar (*un golpe*) agachándose rápidamente; chapuzar, zambullir; *vn* agacharse; chapuzar, zambullirse; **to duck out** (slang) escaparse
**duckbill** ['dʌk,bɪl] *s* (zool.) ornitorrinco
**duck hawk** *s* (orn.) halcón peregrino patero
**ducking** ['dʌkɪŋ] *s* caza de patos silvestres; zambullida, chapuz
**ducking stool** *s* silla de chapuzar
**duckling** ['dʌklɪŋ] *s* anadeja, patito
**duckpins** ['dʌk,pɪnz] *spl* juego de bolos
**duck soup** *s* (slang) breva, ganga, cosa apreciable lograda con poco esfuerzo
**duck-toed** ['dʌk,tod] *adj* zancajoso
**duckweed** ['dʌk,wid] *s* (bot.) lenteja acuática o lenteja de agua
**duct** [dʌkt] *s* conducto, tubo, canal; (anat.) conducto
**ductile** ['dʌktɪl] *adj* dúctil; (fig.) dúctil
**ductility** [dʌk'tɪlɪtɪ] *s* (*pl:* **-ties**) ductilidad
**ductless gland** ['dʌktlɪs] *s* (anat.) glándula cerrada, glándula de secreción interna
**dud** [dʌd] *s* (coll.) prenda de vestir; (slang) bomba que no estalla, granada que no estalla; (slang) fracaso; **duds** *spl* (coll.) prendas de vestir, trapos; (coll.) pertenencias
**dude** [djud] o [dud] *s* petimetre, caballerete
**dude ranch** *s* (U.S.A.) rancho para turistas
**dudgeon** ['dʌdʒən] *s* inquina, ojeriza; **in high dudgeon** resentido, airado
**dudish** ['djudɪʃ] o ['dudɪʃ] *adj* peripuesto, lechuguino
**due** [dju] o [du] *adj* debido; pagadero; aguardado, esperado; **in due time** a su debido tiempo; **to become due** o **to fall due** vencer; **when is the train due?** ¿cuándo llega el tren?, ¿a qué hora debe llegar el tren?; **due to** debido a, ocasionado por; *adv* derecho, directamente, exactamente; *s* deuda; **dues** *spl* derechos; cuota (*de un miembro*); **to get one's due** llevar su merecido; **to give the devil his due** ser justo hasta con el diablo
**duel** ['djuəl] o ['duəl] *s* duelo; (*pret & pp:* **dueled** o **duelled;** *ger:* **dueling** o **duelling**) *va* combatir en duelo, matar en duelo; *vn* batirse en duelo
**duelist** o **duellist** ['djuəlɪst] o ['duəlɪst] *s* duelista
**duenna** [dju'ɛnə] o [du'ɛnə] *s* dueña; señora de compañía
**dues-paying** ['djuz,peɪŋ] o ['duz,peɪŋ] *adj* cotizante
**duet** [dju'ɛt] o [du'ɛt] *s* (mus.) dúo
**duettist** [dju'ɛtɪst] o [du'ɛtɪst] *s* (mus.) duetista
**duff** [dʌf] *s* pudín de harina cocido en un saco
**duffel** ['dʌfəl] *s* paño de lana basta; (coll.) pertrechos, pertrechos para acampar
**duffel bag** *s* (mil.) talego para efectos de uso personal
**duffer** ['dʌfər] *s* (coll.) estúpido, persona muy torpe, chapucero
**dug** [dʌg] *s* teta, ubre; *pret & pp de* **dig**
**dugong** ['dugɑŋ] *s* (zool.) dugón
**dugout** ['dʌg,aut] *s* (mil.) cueva de refugio, cueva de protección, defensa subterránea; piragua; (baseball) cobertizo bajo para los jugadores
**duke** [djuk] o [duk] *s* duque; **dukes** *spl* (slang) puños
**dukedom** ['djukdəm] o ['dukdəm] *s* ducado
**dulcet** ['dʌlsɪt] *adj* dulce, suave, melodioso
**dulcimer** ['dʌlsɪmər] *s* (mus.) dulcémele
**dull** [dʌl] *adj* embotado, romo, obtuso; apagado (*color*); sordo (*sonido; dolor*); insípido, insulso; aburrido, tedioso; insensible; deslustrado, deslucido; lerdo, torpe, tardo de comprensión; desanimado, inactivo, muerto (*negocios*); *va* embotar, enromar; entorpecer; deslustrar, deslucir; enfriar (*p.ej., el entusiasmo*); *vn* embotarse, enromarse; entorpecerse; deslustrarse, deslucirse
**dullard** ['dʌlərd] *s* estúpido
**dullish** ['dʌlɪʃ] *adj* algo embotado, algo obtuso; algo lerdo; algo inactivo
**dullness** ['dʌlnɪs] *s* falta de punta, embotadura; estupidez, torpeza; deslustre; pereza, pesadez; desanimación, inactividad
**dully** ['dʌllɪ] *adv* de modo obtuso; lentamente; sin brillo, sin lustre; estúpidamente
**dulness** ['dʌlnɪs] *s* var. de **dullness**
**dulse** [dʌls] *s* (bot.) rodimenia
**duly** ['djulɪ] o ['dulɪ] *adv* debidamente
**duma** ['dumɑ] *s* duma
**dumb** [dʌm] *adj* mudo; (coll.) torpe, estúpido
**dumbbell** ['dʌm,bɛl] *s* halterio (*de gimnasia*); (slang) estúpido
**dumbfound** [,dʌm'faund] *va* var. de **dumfound**
**dumb show** *s* pantomima
**dumbwaiter** ['dʌm,wetər] *s* montaplatos; estante giratorio
**dumdum bullet** ['dʌmdʌm] *s* bala dumdum
**dumfound** [,dʌm'faund] *va* confundir, pasmar, dejar sin habla
**dummy** ['dʌmɪ] *s* (*pl:* **-mies**) maniquí (*para exhibir prendas de vestir*); cabeza para pelucas; testaferro (*persona que presta su nombre en un asunto ajeno*); muerto (*en los naipes*); cartas del muerto; muñeco (*figura de hombre*);

(print.) maqueta (*libro en blanco*); (rail.) locomotora de máquina condensadora; imitación, copia; (slang) estúpido; **to be dummy** hacer de muerto (*en los naipes*); *adj* falso, fingido, simulado, de imitación; de testaferro
**dump** [dʌmp] *s* montón de basuras; basurero (*sitio en donde se amontona la basura*); terreno echadizo; (min.) terrero; (mil.) depósito de municiones; **dumps** *spl* murria; **to be down in the dumps** tener murria, estar abatido; *va* descargar, verter; (coll.) inundar el mercado con; vaciar de golpe; *vn* arrojar la basura
**dump body** *s* caja de volquete (*de un camión*)
**dump car** *s* vagón de volteo, vagón volquete
**dumpcart** [ˈdʌmp,kɑrt] *s* volquete
**dumping** [ˈdʌmpɪŋ] *s* descarga; inundación del mercado con mercancías a bajo precio
**dumpish** [ˈdʌmpɪʃ] *adj* lerdo, torpe; abatido, murrio
**dumpling** [ˈdʌmplɪŋ] *s* bola de pasta rellena de fruta o carne; bolita de pasta cocida con vapor
**dump truck** *s* camión volquete
**dumpy** [ˈdʌmpɪ] *adj* (*comp:* **-ier**; *super:* **-iest**) regordete; abatido, mohino, hosco
**dun** [dʌn] *s* acreedor importuno; apremio; color bruno; *adj* bruno, pardo; sombrío; (*pret & pp:* **dunned;** *ger:* **dunning**) *va* importunar, requerir para el pago
**dunce** [dʌns] *s* zopenco, estúpido
**dunce cap** o **dunce's cap** *s* gorro de forma de cono que se le pone al niño torpe
**dunderhead** [ˈdʌndər,hɛd] *s* bodoque
**dune** [djun] o [dun] *s* duna
**dung** [dʌŋ] *s* estiércol; *va & vn* estercolar
**dungaree** [,dʌŋgəˈri] *s* tela basta de algodón; **dungarees** *spl* pantalones de tela basta de algodón
**dungeon** [ˈdʌndʒən] *s* calabozo, mazmorra; torre del homenaje, torre maestra; *va* encalabozar
**dunghill** [ˈdʌŋ,hɪl] *s* estercolar, estercolero; lugar emporcado; persona vil
**dungy** [ˈdʌŋɪ] *adj* estercolizo
**dunk** [dʌŋk] *va & vn* sopetear, ensopar, remojar
**Dunkirk** [ˈdʌnkʌrk] o [dʌnˈkʌrk] *s* Dunquerque
**dunlin** [ˈdʌnlɪn] *s* (orn.) tringa alpina
**dunnage** [ˈdʌnɪdʒ] *s* equipaje; (naut.) abarrote, maderos de estibar
**duo** [ˈdjuo] o [ˈduo] *s* (*pl:* **duos** o **dui** [ˈdjui] o [ˈdui]) var. de **duet**
**duodecimal** [,djuoˈdɛsɪməl] o [,duoˈdɛsɪməl] *adj & s* duodecimal; **duodecimals** *spl* sistema duodecimal
**duodecimo** [,djuoˈdɛsɪmo] o [,duoˈdɛsɪmo] *adj* en dozavo; *s* (*pl:* **-mos**) libro en dozavo
**duodecuple** [,djuoˈdɛkjəpəl] o [,duoˈdɛkjəpəl] *adj* duodécuplo
**duodenal** [,djuoˈdinəl] o [,duoˈdinəl] *adj* duodenal
**duodenal ulcer** *s* (path.) úlcera duodenal
**duodenum** [,djuoˈdinəm] o [,duoˈdinəm] *s* (*pl:* **-na** [nə]) (anat.) duodeno
**dupe** [djup] o [dup] *s* primo, víctima, inocentón; *va* embaucar, engañar
**duple** [ˈdjupəl] o [ˈdupel] *adj* duplo, doble
**duplex** [ˈdjuplɛks] o [ˈduplɛks] *adj* doble, duplo, dúplice
**duplex apartment** *s* apartamiento cuyas piezas están en dos pisos
**duplex house** *s* casa para dos familias
**duplex lock** *s* cerradura de dos cilindros
**duplex process** *s* (metal.) dúplex
**duplex telegraphy** *s* dúplex
**duplicate** [ˈdjuplɪkɪt] o [ˈduplɪkɪt] *adj & s* duplicado; **in duplicate** por duplicado; en doble ejemplar; [ˈdjuplɪket] o [ˈduplɪket] *va* duplicar
**duplication** [,djuplɪˈkeʃən] o [,duplɪˈkeʃən] *s* duplicación; duplicado
**duplicator** [ˈdjuplɪ,ketər] o [ˈduplɪ,ketər] *s* duplicador, multicopista
**duplicity** [djuˈplɪsɪtɪ] o [duˈplɪsɪtɪ] *s* (*pl:* **-ties**) duplicidad
**durability** [,djurəˈbɪlɪtɪ] o [,durəˈbɪlɪtɪ] *s* (*pl:* **-ties**) durabilidad
**durable** [ˈdjurəbəl] o [ˈdurəbəl] *adj* durable, duradero
**durable goods** *spl* artículos duraderos
**duralumin** [djuˈræljəmɪn] o [duˈræljəmɪn] *s* (trademark) duraluminio
**dura mater** [ˈdjurəˈmetər] o [ˈdurəˈmetər] *s* (anat.) duramadre o duramáter
**duramen** [djuˈremɛn] o [duˈremɛn] *s* (bot.) duramen
**durance** [ˈdjurəns] o [ˈdurəns] *s* prisión, cautividad; sempiterna (*tela*)
**duration** [djuˈreʃən] o [duˈreʃən] *s* duración; **for the duration (of the war)** para el término o la duración del conflicto
**durative** [ˈdjurətɪv] o [ˈdurətɪv] *adj* durativo; (gram.) durativo
**durbar** [ˈdʌrbɑr] *s* durbar
**duress** [ˈdjurɛs], [ˈdurɛs], [djuˈrɛs] o [duˈrɛs] *s* coacción, compulsión; prisión, cautividad
**during** [ˈdjurɪŋ] o [ˈdurɪŋ] *prep* durante
**durmast** [ˈdʌrmæst] o [ˈdʌrmɑst] *s* (bot.) melojo, roble borne (*Quercus pubescens*); (bot.) roble albero (*Quercus sessiliflora*)
**durra** [ˈdurə] *s* (bot.) durra, maíz de Guinea
**durum** [ˈdjurəm] o [ˈdurəm] *s* (bot.) trigo durillo, trigo duro
**dusk** [dʌsk] *s* crepúsculo vespertino, caída de la noche; *adj* obscuro; *va* obscurecer; *vn* anochecer
**dusky** [ˈdʌskɪ] *adj* (*comp:* **-ier**; *super:* **-iest**) obscuro, negruzco; abatido, lúgubre, triste
**dust** [dʌst] *s* polvo; cenizas (*restos mortales*); cosa inútil; condición vil; (slang) dinero; **to bite the dust** morder el polvo; **to kick up a dust** armar un alboroto; **to lick the dust** morder el polvo; **to raise a dust** armar un alboroto; **to shake the dust off one's feet** irse enojado; **to throw dust in one's eyes** engañarle a uno; *va* desempolvar (*quitar el polvo a*); polvorear (*esparcir polvo sobre*); **to dust off** desempolvar; **to dust one's jacket** (slang) sacudirle el polvo a uno
**dustbin** [ˈdʌst,bɪn] *s* receptáculo para polvo, cenizas, etc.
**dust bowl** *s* cuenca de polvo
**dustcloth** [ˈdʌst,klɔθ] o [ˈdʌst,klɑθ] *s* trapo de polvo
**dust cloud** *s* polvareda, nube de polvo
**duster** [ˈdʌstər] *s* plumero, sacudidor (*mazo de plumas para quitar el polvo*); guardapolvo (*sobretodo*)
**dust jacket** *s* sobrecubierta (*de un libro encuadernado*)
**dustless** [ˈdʌstlɪs] *adj* sin polvo
**dustpan** [ˈdʌst,pæn] *s* pala de recoger la basura
**dust rag** *s* trapo del polvo
**dust storm** *s* vendaval de polvo, tolvanera
**dusty** [ˈdʌstɪ] *adj* (*comp:* **-ier**; *super:* **-iest**) polvoriento, empolvado; grisáceo
**Dutch** [dʌtʃ] *adj* holandés; (slang) alemán; *spl* holandeses; (slang) alemanes; *ssg* holandés (*idioma*); (slang) alemán (*idioma*); **in Dutch** (slang) en la desgracia; (slang) en un apuro; **to beat the Dutch** (coll.) ser sorprendente, ser extraordinario; **to go Dutch** (coll.) pagar cada uno su escote
**Dutch bond** *s* (mas.) aparejo flamenco u holandés
**Dutch Borneo** [ˈbɔrnɪo] o [ˈbornɪo] *s* el Borneo Holandés
**Dutch brass** *s* tombac
**Dutch cheese** *s* queso de Holanda; naterón
**Dutch clover** *s* (bot.) trébol de Holanda
**Dutch East Indies** *spl* Indias Orientales Holandesas
**Dutch Guiana** *s* la Guayana Holandesa
**Dutchman** [ˈdʌtʃmən] *s* (*pl:* **-men**) holandés; buque holandés; (slang) alemán
**Dutchman's-breeches** [ˈdʌtʃmənzˈbrɪtʃɪz] *ssg & spl* (bot.) dicentra
**Dutch New Guinea** *s* la Nueva Guinea Holandesa
**Dutch oven** *s* cacerola con tapa bien cerrada; horno portátil
**Dutch tile** *s* azulejo
**Dutch treat** *s* (coll.) convite a escote
**Dutch uncle** *s* (coll.) mentor muy duro
**Dutch West Indies** *spl* Indias Occidentales Holandesas
**duteous** [ˈdjutɪəs] o [ˈdutɪəs] *adj* obediente, obsequioso

**dutiable** ['djutɪəbəl] o ['dutɪəbəl] *adj* sujeto a derechos de aduana
**dutiful** ['djutɪfəl] o ['dutɪfəl] *adj* obediente, sumiso, respetuoso; concienzudo
**duty** ['djutɪ] o ['dutɪ] *s* (*pl:* **-ties**) deber, obligación; obediencia, sumisión; quehacer, tarea, faena; derechos de aduana; **off duty** libre; **on duty** de servicio; de guardia; **to do duty for** servir en lugar de; **to take up one's duties** entrar en funciones
**duty-free** ['djutɪ'fri] o ['dutɪ'fri] *adj* libre de derechos
**duumvir** [dju'ʌmvər] o [du'ʌmvər] *s* (*pl:* **-virs** o **-viri** [vɪraɪ]) duunviro
**duumviral** [dju'ʌmvərəl] o [du'ʌmvərəl] *adj* duunviral
**duumvirate** [dju'ʌmvərɪt] o [du'ʌmvərɪt] *s* duunvirato
**duvetyn** ['duvətin] *s* tejido de lana que tiene una lanilla aterciopelada
**D.V.** abr. de **Deo volente** (Lat.) **God willing**
**dwarf** [dwɔrf] *adj & s* enano; *va* impedir el desarrollo de, impedir el crecimiento de; achicar, empequeñecer; *vn* achicarse, empequeñecerse
**dwarf elder** *s* (bot.) actea, yezgo
**dwarf fan palm** *s* (bot.) palmito, palmera enana o de abanico
**dwarfish** ['dwɔrfɪʃ] *adj* enano, diminuto
**dwarf mallow** *s* (bot.) malva de hoja redonda
**dwarf star** *s* (astr.) estrella enana
**dwell** [dwɛl] (*pret & pp:* **dwelled** o **dwelt**) *vn* vivir, morar; **to dwell on** o **upon** explayarse en; hacer hincapié en
**dweller** ['dwɛlər] *s* habitante, morador
**dwelling** ['dwɛlɪŋ] *s* vivienda, morada
**dwelling house** *s* casa, domicilio
**dwelling place** *s* habitación, morada
**dwelt** [dwɛlt] *pret & pp de* **dwell**
**dwindle** ['dwɪndəl] *va* disminuir; abatir, rebajar; *vn* disminuirse; consumirse
**dwt.** abr. de **pennyweight** o **pennyweights**
**DX** o **D.X.** (rad.) abr. de **distance**
**dye** [daɪ] *s* tinte; color, matiz; **of blackest dye** u **of deepest dye** de la clase más vil; (*pret & pp:* **dyed;** *ger:* **dyeing**) *va* teñir, tinturar
**dyed-in-the-wool** ['daɪdɪnðə,wʊl] *adj* teñido en rama; (fig.) intransigente, acérrimo
**dyeing** ['daɪɪŋ] *s* tintorería; tinte, tintura; *ger de* **dye**
**dyer** ['daɪər] *s* tintorero
**dyer's-weed** ['daɪərz,wid] *s* (bot.) retama de tintes o de tintoreros (*Genista tinctoria*); (bot.) gualda (*Reseda luteola*); (bot.) hierba pastel (*Isatis tinctoria*)
**dyestuff** ['daɪ,stʌf] *s* materia de tinte, materia colorante
**dyeweed** ['daɪ,wid] *s* (bot.) retama de tintes o de tintoreros
**dyewood** ['daɪ,wʊd] *s* madera de tinte
**dying** ['daɪɪŋ] *adj* moribundo, agonizante; mortal; *ger de* **die**
**dyke** [daɪk] *s & va* var. de **dike**
**dynamic** [daɪ'næmɪk] o [dɪ'næmɪk] *adj* dinámico; (fig.) dinámico; **dynamics** *ssg* dinámica
**dynamical** [daɪ'næmɪkəl] o [dɪ'næmɪkəl] *adj* dinámico
**dynamic speaker** *s* (rad.) altoparlante dinámico
**dynamism** ['daɪnəmɪzəm] o ['dɪnəmɪzəm] *s* (philos.) dinamismo
**dynamist** ['daɪnəmɪst] o ['dɪnəmɪst] *s* dinamista
**dynamistic** [,daɪnə'mɪstɪk] o [,dɪnə'mɪstɪk] *adj* dinamista
**dynamite** ['daɪnəmaɪt] *s* dinamita; *va* dinamitar
**dynamiter** ['daɪnə,maɪtər] *s* dinamitero
**dynamo** ['daɪnəmo] *s* (*pl:* **-mos**) dínamo
**dynamoelectric** [,daɪnəmo·ɪ'lɛktrɪk] *adj* dinamoeléctrico
**dynamometer** [,daɪnə'mɑmɪtər] *s* dinamómetro
**dynamometric** [,daɪnəmo'mɛtrɪk] *adj* dinamométrico
**dynamometry** [,daɪnə'mɑmɪtrɪ] *s* (mech.) dinamometría
**dynamotor** ['daɪnə,motər] *s* (elec.) dinamotor
**dynast** ['daɪnæst] o ['daɪnəst] *s* dinasta
**dynastic** [daɪ'næstɪk] o [dɪ'næstɪk] *adj* dinástico
**dynasty** ['daɪnəstɪ] *s* (*pl:* **-ties**) dinastía
**dynatron** ['daɪnətrɑn] *s* (phys. & rad.) dinatrón
**dyne** [daɪn] *s* (phys.) dina
**dyschroa** ['dɪskroə] *s* (path.) discromía
**dyschromatopsia** [,dɪskromə'tɑpsɪə] *s* (path.) discromatopsia
**dyscrasia** [dɪs'kreʒɪə] *s* (path.) discrasia
**dysenteric** [,dɪsən'tɛrɪk] *adj* disentérico
**dysentery** ['dɪsən,tɛrɪ] *s* (path.) disentería
**dysesthesia** [,dɪsɛs'θiʒɪə] *s* (path.) disestesia
**dysfunction** [dɪs'fʌŋkʃən] *s* (med.) disfunción
**dyslalia** [dɪs'lelɪə] *s* (med.) dislalia
**dysmenorrhea** o **dysmenorrhoea** [,dɪsmɛnə'riə] *s* (path.) dismenorrea
**dyspepsia** [dɪs'pɛpsɪə] o [dɪs'pɛpʃə] *s* (path.) dispepsia
**dyspeptic** [dɪs'pɛptɪk] *adj* dispéptico; triste, melancólico; *s* dispéptico
**dyspeptically** [dɪs'pɛptɪkəlɪ] *adv* con la dispepsia; como un dispéptico; tristemente, melancólicamente
**dysphagia** [dɪs'fedʒɪə] *s* (med.) disfagía
**dysphasia** [dɪs'feʒɪə] *s* (med.) disfasia
**dyspnea** [dɪsp'niə] *s* (path.) disnea
**dysprosium** [dɪs'prosɪəm] o [dɪs'proʃɪəm] *s* (chem.) disprosio
**dystrophy** ['dɪstrəfɪ] *s* (path.) distrofia
**dysuria** [dɪs'jʊrɪə] *s* (path.) disuria
**dz.** abr. de **dozen** o **dozens**

**E, e** [i] *s* (*pl:* **E's, e's** [iz]) quinta letra del alfabeto inglés
**E.** abr. de **east, eastern** y **engineer**
**E** abr. de **east, eastern** y **Excellent**
**ea.** abr. de **each**
**each** [itʃ] *adj indef* cada; *pron indef* cada uno, cada cual; **of each other** el uno del otro, los unos de los otros, p.ej., **they took leave of each other** se despidieron los unos de los otros; **each other** nos, os, se; uno a otro, unos a otros, p.ej., **they looked at each other** se miraron uno a otro; *adv* para o por cada uno; por persona
**eager** ['igər] *adj* anhelante, ansioso; ardiente, fogoso; encarnizado (*combate*); **to be eager for** anhelar o anhelar por; **to be eager to** + *inf* anhelar + *inf*, ansiar + *inf*
**eager beaver** *s* (coll.) entusiasta diligente
**eagerness** ['igərnɪs] *s* anhelo, ansia; ardor, fogosidad; encarnizamiento
**eagle** ['igəl] *s* (orn.) águila; (fig.) águila (*emblema; moneda de oro de los EE.UU.*); (*cap.*) *s* (astr.) Águila
**eagle eye** *s* ojo avizor
**eagle-eyed** ['igəl,aɪd] *adj* de vista de águila; **to be eagle-eyed** tener vista de águila
**eagle owl** *s* (orn.) búho
**eagle ray** *s* (ichth.) águila
**eaglestone** ['igəl,ston] *s* (mineral.) etites
**eaglet** ['iglɪt] *s* (orn.) aguilucho
**eaglewood** ['igəl,wʊd] *s* (bot.) agáloco
**ear** [ɪr] *s* oreja; oído (*sentido*); asa, asidero; mazorca (*de maíz*); (bot.) espiga; **by ear** de oído; **to be all ears** (coll.) abrir tanto oído o tanto el oído, ser todo oídos; **to fall on deaf ears** no recibir atención; **to give ear to** prestar oído a; **to go in one ear and out the other** entrar por un oído y salir por el otro; **to have a good ear** tener oído, tener buen oído; **to have** o **to keep an ear to the ground** (coll.) prestar atención para estar al corriente; **to have an ear for music** tener oído para la música; **to have the ear of** gozar de la confianza de, tener influencia con; **to lend an ear** abrir los oídos, prestar el oído o los oídos; **to prick up one's ears** aguzar los oídos, aguzar las orejas; **to set by the ears** enemistar, malquistar; **to turn a deaf ear** hacerse sordo, hacer oídos de mercader; **to turn a deaf ear to** no dar oídos a; **up to one's ears** (coll.) hasta los ojos (*p.ej., en amor, en trabajo*); *vn* espigar
**earache** ['ɪr,ek] *s* dolor de oído
**eardrop** ['ɪr,drɑp] *s* arete
**eardrum** ['ɪr,drʌm] *s* (anat.) tímpano (*del oído*)
**earflap** ['ɪr,flæp] *s* orejera
**earing** ['ɪrɪŋ] *s* (naut.) empuñidura
**earl** [ʌrl] *s* conde
**earlap** ['ɪr,læp] *s* punta de la oreja; pabellón de la oreja; orejera (*de la gorra*)
**earldom** ['ʌrldəm] *s* condado
**early** ['ʌrlɪ] *adj* (*comp:* **-lier;** *super:* **-liest**) temprano; primero, antiguo; pronto, próximo, cercano; **at an early date** en fecha próxima; **the early part of** el principio de; **earlier** anterior; **early mass** misa de prima; **early times** tiempos remotos; *adv* (*comp:* **-lier;** *super:* **-liest**) temprano; al principio; en los primeros tiempos; **as early as** ya a (*cierta hora*); ya en (*cierta temporada, cierta época*); **as early as possible** lo más pronto posible; **early in** a principios de (*p.ej., el mes de febrero*); **early in the morning** muy de mañana; **one hour early** con una hora de anticipación; **to rise early** madrugar
**early bird** *s* madrugador
**earmark** ['ɪr,mɑrk] *s* marca en la oreja; señal, distintivo; *va* distinguir, designar, poner aparte (*para cierto uso*)
**earmuff** ['ɪr,mʌf] *s* orejera
**earn** [ʌrn] *va* ganar, ganarse; merecerse; obtener, conseguir, conquistar
**earnest** ['ʌrnɪst] *adj* serio; celoso, diligente; **in earnest** en serio; de veras; *s* arras, prenda
**earnest money** *s* arras
**earnestness** ['ʌrnɪstnɪs] *s* seriedad; celo, diligencia
**earning** ['ʌrnɪŋ] *s* ganancia, rédito; salario
**earphone** ['ɪr,fon] *s* casquete o teléfono de cabeza, auricular
**earpick** ['ɪr,pɪk] *s* escarbaorejas
**earring** ['ɪr,rɪŋ] *s* arete
**earshot** ['ɪr,ʃɑt] *s* alcance del oído; **within earshot** al alcance del oído
**ear-splitting** ['ɪr,splɪtɪŋ] *adj* ensordecedor
**earth** [ʌrθ] *s* tierra; mundo; madriguera; (rad.) tierra; (chem.) tierra rara; **down to earth** práctico, prosaico; **to come back to earth** bajar de las nubes; **to run to earth** cazar hasta alcanzar, buscar hasta hallar
**earthboard** ['ʌrθ,bord] *s* orejera del arado
**earthborn** ['ʌrθ,bɔrn] *adj* terrígeno; mortal, humano; de nacimiento humilde
**earthbound** ['ʌrθ,baʊnd] *adj* ligado por los intereses terrenales
**earthbred** ['ʌrθ,brɛd] *adj* humilde, bajo, vil
**earthen** ['ʌrθən] *adj* de tierra; de barro
**earthenware** ['ʌrθən,wɛr] *s* loza de barro; trastos, cacharros
**earth inductor compass** *s* (aer.) brújula de inducción terrestre
**earthling** ['ʌrθlɪŋ] *s* habitante de la tierra; persona mundana
**earthly** ['ʌrθlɪ] *adj* (*comp:* **-lier;** *super:* **-liest**) terrenal, mundano; concebible, posible; **to be of no earthly use** no servir para nada
**earthnut** ['ʌrθ,nʌt] *s* (bot.) fruto subterráneo
**earthquake** ['ʌrθ,kwek] *s* terremoto, temblor de tierra
**earth-return circuit** ['ʌrθrɪ,tʌrn] *s* (elec.) circuito de retorno por tierra
**earthward** ['ʌrθwərd] *adj & adv* hacia la tierra
**earthwards** ['ʌrθwərdz] *adv* hacia la tierra
**earthwork** ['ʌrθ,wʌrk] *s* (fort.) terraplén
**earthworm** ['ʌrθ,wʌrm] *s* (zool.) gusano o lombriz de tierra
**earthy** ['ʌrθɪ] *adj* (*comp:* **-ier;** *super:* **-iest**) terroso; basto, grosero; mundanal
**ear trumpet** *s* trompetilla acústica
**earwax** ['ɪr,wæks] *s* cera de los oídos, cerumen
**earwig** ['ɪr,wɪg] *s* (ent.) punzaorejas, tijereta
**ease** [iz] *s* facilidad; comodidad, soltura, desenvoltura, bienestar; **at ease** tranquilo, cómodo; (mil.) a discreción descanso; **to take one's ease** descansar, holgar; **with ease** con facilidad, sin esfuerzos; *va* facilitar; aliviar, mitigar; aligerar (*el peso*); aflojar, soltar; (naut.) arriar, lascar; **to ease someone of** u **out of something** (coll.) robar algo a alguien; **to ease someone out of a job** o **position** (coll.) facilitar la salida o la dimisión de una persona de un empleo o cargo; *vn* aliviarse, disminuir, aflojar; moverse lenta y suavemente
**easel** ['izəl] *s* caballete
**easement** ['izmənt] *s* alivio, comodidad; (law) servidumbre
**easily** ['izɪlɪ] *adv* fácilmente; sin duda; sobradamente, con mucho; probablemente
**easiness** ['izɪnɪs] *s* facilidad; soltura, desenvoltura; descuido, indiferencia
**east** [ist] *s* este, oriente; **down East** en o hacia la Nueva Inglaterra, EE.UU.; *adj* del este, oriental; *adv* al este
**East Berlin** *s* el Berlín-Este

**East China Sea** *s* mar Oriental, mar de la China Oriental
**Easter** [ˈistər] *s* pascua de flores, pascua florida, pascua de resurrección
**Easter egg** *s* huevo duro decorado que sirve de regalo en el día de Pascuas
**Easter Island** *s* Isla de Pascua
**easterly** [ˈistərlɪ] *adj* oriental; que viene desde el este; que va hacia el este; *adv* desde el este; hacia el este
**Easter Monday** *s* lunes de Pascua (*de resurrección*)
**eastern** [ˈistərn] *adj* oriental
**eastern cardinal** *s* (orn.) cardenal de Virginia
**Eastern Church** *s* Iglesia de Oriente
**easterner** [ˈistərnər] *s* habitante del este
**Eastern Hemisphere** *s* hemisferio oriental
**easternmost** [ˈistərnmost] *adj* (el) más oriental
**Eastern Roman Empire** *s* Imperio de Oriente
**Eastern standard time** *s* (U.S.A.) hora legal correspondiente al meridiano 75°
**Easter Sunday** *s* domingo de resurrección
**Eastertide** [ˈistər,taɪd] *s* aleluya
**East Germany** *s* la Alemania Oriental
**East India** *s* o **East Indies** *spl* Indias Orientales
**East Indian** *adj & s* indiano
**east-northeast** [ˈist,nɔrθˈist] *s* esnordeste o lesnordeste
**East Prussia** *s* la Prusia Oriental
**east-southeast** [ˈist,saʊθˈist] *s* essudeste, essueste o lesueste
**eastward** [ˈistwərd] *adj* que va hacia el este; *s* este; *adv* hacia el este
**eastwardly** [ˈistwərdlɪ] *adj* que va hacia el este; *adv* hacia el este
**eastwards** [ˈistwərdz] *adv* hacia el este
**easy** [ˈizɪ] *adj* (*comp:* **-ier;** *super:* **-iest**) fácil; cómodo, holgado; holgazán; lento, pausado, moderado; (coll.) fácil de engañar; (com.) abundante (*dinero*); **on easy street** (coll.) con el bolsillo lastrado; *adv* (coll.) fácilmente; (coll.) despacio; **to take it easy** (coll.) descansar, holgar; (coll.) no afanarse; (coll.) ir despacio; (coll.) proceder con cuidado; **easy there!** (coll.) ¡despacio!
**easy chair** *s* poltrona
**easy-going** [ˈizɪˈgo·ɪŋ] *adj* despacioso, holgazán, dejado y flojo, flojo y condescendiente
**easy mark** *s* inocentón
**easy money** *s* dinero ganado sin pena
**easy payments** *spl* facilidades de pago
**eat** [it] (*pret:* **ate;** *pp:* **eaten**) *va* comer; comerse (*producir comiendo*); **to eat away** corroer; **to eat crow** (coll.) cantar la palinodia; **to eat humble pie** humillarse cediendo; **to eat one's heart out** sufrir en silencio; **to eat one's words** retractarse, retirar sus palabras; **to eat up** devorar; destruir; *vn* comer
**eatable** [ˈitəbəl] *adj* comestible, comible; **eatables** *spl* comestibles, alimentos
**eaten** [ˈitən] *pp de* **eat**
**eater** [ˈitər] *s* comedor; comilón
**Eau de Cologne** [,o də kəˈlon] *s* agua de Colonia
**eau de vie** [,o də ˈvi] *s* aguardiente
**eaves** [ivz] *spl* alero, tejaroz, socarrén
**eaves board** *s* contrapar
**eavesdrop** [ˈivz,drɑp] (*pret & pp:* **-dropped;** *ger:* **-dropping**) *vn* escuchar a las puertas, estar de escucha
**eavesdropper** [ˈivz,drɑpər] *s* escuchador a las puertas, escuchador escondido
**ebb** [ɛb] *s* (naut.) menguante, reflujo; decadencia; **at low ebb** decaído; *vn* bajar (*la marea*); decaer
**ebb and flow** *s* flujo y reflujo
**ebb tide** *s* marea menguante
**ebenaceous** [,ɛbɪˈneʃəs] *adj* (bot.) ebenáceo
**ebonite** [ˈɛbənaɪt] *s* ebonita
**ebony** [ˈɛbənɪ] *s* (*pl:* **-ies**) (bot.) ébano (*árbol y madera*); *adj* de ébano, hecho de ébano; negro
**ebullience** [ɪˈbʌljəns] *s* ebullición; exaltación, entusiasmo
**ebullient** [ɪˈbʌljənt] *adj* hirviente; exaltado, entusiasta
**ebulliometer** [ɪ,bʌlɪˈɑmɪtər] *s* ebullómetro
**ebullioscope** [ɪˈbʌlɪə,skop] *s* ebulloscopio
**ebullition** [,ɛbəˈlɪʃən] *s* ebullición; arranque, viva emoción
**eburnation** [,ibərˈneʃən] *s* (path.) eburnación
**écarté** [,ekɑrˈte] *s* ecarté
**ecce homo** [ˈɛksɪˈhomo] *s* eccehomo (*imagen*)
**eccentric** [ɛkˈsɛntrɪk] *adj* excéntrico; *s* excéntrico; (mach.) excéntrica
**eccentrically** [ɛkˈsɛntrɪkəlɪ] *adv* excéntricamente
**eccentricity** [,ɛksɛnˈtrɪsɪtɪ] *s* (*pl:* **-ties**) excentricidad
**ecchymosis** [,ɛkɪˈmosɪs] *s* (*pl:* **-ses** [siz]) (path.) equimosis
**Eccl.** o **Eccles.** abr. de **Ecclesiastes**
**Ecclesiastes** [ɪ,klizɪˈæstiz] *s* (Bib.) el Eclesiastés
**ecclesiastic** [ɪ,klizɪˈæstɪk] *adj & s* eclesiástico
**ecclesiastical** [ɪ,klizɪˈæstɪkəl] *adj* eclesiástico
**Ecclesiasticus** [ɪ,klizɪˈæstɪkəs] *s* (Bib.) el Eclesiástico
**echelon** [ˈɛʃəlɑn] *s* escalón (*grado a que se asciende en autoridad*); (mil.) escalón; *va* (mil.) escalonar
**echidna** [ɪˈkɪdnə] *s* (zool.) equidna
**echinococcus** [ɪ,kaɪnəˈkɑkəs] *s* (*pl:* **-cocci** [ˈkɑksaɪ]) (zool.) equinococo
**echinoderm** [ɪˈkaɪnədʌrm] *s* (zool.) equinodermo
**echinus** [ɪˈkaɪnəs] *s* (*pl:* **-ni** [naɪ]) (arch. & zool.) equino
**echo** [ˈɛko] *s* (*pl:* **-oes**) eco; (*cap.*) *s* (myth.) Eco; (*l.c.*) *va* repetir (*un sonido*); imitar; *vn* hacer eco, resonar
**echoic** [ɛˈko·ɪk] *adj* ecoico
**echolalia** [,ɛkoˈlelɪə] *s* (psychol.) ecolalia
**éclair** [eˈklɛr] *s* pastelillo o bollo de crema
**eclampsia** [ɛkˈlæmpsɪə] *s* (path.) eclampsia
**éclat** [eˈklɑ] *s* brillo, resplandor; éxito brillante; renombre; aclamación
**eclectic** [ɛkˈlɛktɪk] *adj & s* ecléctico
**eclecticism** [ɛkˈlɛktɪsɪzəm] *s* eclecticismo
**eclipse** [ɪˈklɪps] *s* (astr. & fig.) eclipse; *va* (astr. & fig.) eclipsar
**ecliptic** [ɪˈklɪptɪk] *adj* eclíptico; *s* eclíptica
**ecliptical** [ɪˈklɪptɪkəl] *adj* eclíptico
**eclogue** [ˈɛklɔg] o [ˈɛklɑg] *s* égloga
**ecologist** [iˈkɑlədʒɪst] *s* ecólogo
**ecology** [iˈkɑlədʒɪ] *s* ecología
**economic** [,ikəˈnɑmɪk] o [,ɛkəˈnɑmɪk] *adj* económico; **economics** *ssg* economía política
**economical** [,ikəˈnɑmɪkəl] o [,ɛkəˈnɑmɪkəl] *adj* económico
**economically** [,ikəˈnɑmɪkəlɪ] o [,ɛkəˈnɑmɪkəlɪ] *adv* económicamente
**economist** [ɪˈkɑnəmɪst] *s* economista
**economize** [ɪˈkɑnəmaɪz] *va & vn* economizar
**economizer** [ɪˈkɑnə,maɪzər] *s* (mach.) economizador
**economy** [ɪˈkɑnəmɪ] *s* (*pl:* **-mies**) economía
**ecru** o **écru** [ˈɛkru] o [ˈekru] *adj* crudo, sin blanquear; *s* tejido sin blanquear
**ecstasy** [ˈɛkstəsɪ] *s* (*pl:* **-sies**) éxtasis
**ecstatic** [ɛkˈstætɪk] *adj* extático
**ecstatically** [ɛkˈstætɪkəlɪ] *adv* extáticamente
**ectasia** [ɛkˈteʒɪə] *s* (path.) ectasia
**ectasis** [ˈɛktəsɪs] *s* (pros.) ectasis
**ectoblast** [ˈɛktoblæst] *s* (embryol.) ectoblasto
**ectoderm** [ˈɛktodʌrm] *s* (embryol.) ectodermo
**ectoparasite** [,ɛktoˈpærəsaɪt] *s* (zool.) ectoparásito
**ectopia** [ɛkˈtopɪə] *s* (path.) ectopia
**ectoplasm** [ˈɛktoplæzəm] *s* (biol. & spiritualism) ectoplasma
**ectropion** [ɛkˈtropɪən] *s* (path.) ectropión
**Ecuador** [ˈɛkwədɔr] *s* el Ecuador
**Ecuadoran** [,ɛkwəˈdorən] o **Ecuadorian** [,ɛkwəˈdorɪən] *adj & s* ecuatoriano
**Ecuadorianism** [,ɛkwəˈdorɪənɪzəm] *s* ecuatorianismo
**ecumenic** [,ɛkjʊˈmɛnɪk] o **ecumenical** [,ɛkjʊˈmɛnɪkəl] *adj* ecuménico
**eczema** [ˈɛksɪmə] o [ɛgˈzimə] *s* (path.) eczema
**eczematous** [ɛkˈzɛmətəs] *adj* eczematoso
**ed.** abr. de **edited, edition** y **editor**
**Ed** [ɛd] *s* nombre abreviado de **Edward, Edwin, Edgar** y **Edmund**
**Edam cheese** [ˈidæm] o [ˈidəm] *s* queso de Edam, queso de Holanda
**edaphology** [,ɛdəˈfɑlədʒɪ] *s* edafología
**Edda** [ˈɛdə] *s* (lit.) edda

**eddy** [ˈɛdɪ] *s* (*pl:* **-dies**) remolino; (*pret & pp:* **-died**) *va & vn* remolinear
**eddy current** *s* (elec.) corriente parásita, corriente de Foucault
**edelweiss** [ˈedəlvaɪs] *s* (bot.) edelweiss, estrella de los Alpes, pie de león
**edema** [iˈdimə] *s* (*pl:* **-mata** [mətə]) (path.) edema
**edematous** [iˈdɛmətəs] *adj* edematoso
**Eden** [ˈidən] *s* (Bib. & fig.) edén
**Edenic** [iˈdɛnɪk] *adj* edénico
**edentate** [iˈdɛntet] *adj* desdentado; *s* (zool.) desdentado
**edge** [ɛdʒ] *s* filo (*de un instrumento cortante*); margen, borde, orilla; ángulo, esquina, punta; canto (*p.ej., de una mesa*); corte (*de cuchillo, espada o libro*); (sew.) ribete; (fig.) punta, acrimonia; (slang) ventaja; **on edge** de canto; (fig.) nervioso; **to have the edge on** (slang) llevar ventaja a; **to set on edge** poner nervioso; **to set the teeth on edge** dar dentera; **to take the edge off** embotar; (fig.) embotar ‖ *va* afilar, aguzar; bordear; (sew.) ribetear; aguijonear, incitar; abrirse (*paso*) marchando de lado; mover poco a poco de canto; **to edge out** hacer salir empujando poco a poco ‖ *vn* avanzar de lado; **to edge in** abrirse paso, lograr entrar; **to edge up** subir un poco
**edgeways** [ˈɛdʒˌwez] *adv* de filo, de canto, de lado; **to get a word in edgeways** lograr decir una palabra; **to not let a person get a word in edgeways** no dejarle a uno meter baza
**edgewise** [ˈɛdʒˌwaɪz] *adv* var. de **edgeways**
**edging** [ˈɛdʒɪŋ] *s* orla, ribete; pestaña (*encaje*)
**edgy** [ˈɛdʒɪ] *adj* angular; nervioso, irritable
**edibility** [ˌɛdɪˈbɪlɪtɪ] *s* (lo) comestible
**edible** [ˈɛdɪbəl] *adj & s* comestible
**edict** [ˈidɪkt] *s* edicto
**edification** [ˌɛdɪfɪˈkeʃən] *s* edificación (*enseñanza, beneficios espirituales*)
**edifice** [ˈɛdɪfɪs] *s* edificio
**edify** [ˈɛdɪfaɪ] (*pret & pp:* **-fied**) *va* edificar (*instruir o inspirar en materia de moral, fe, etc.*)
**edifying** [ˈɛdɪˌfaɪɪŋ] *adj* edificante
**edile** [ˈidaɪl] *s* edil
**Edinburgh** [ˈɛdɪnbərə] o [ˈɛdɪnˌbʌro] *s* Edimburgo
**edit.** abr. de **edited, edition** y **editor**
**edit** [ˈɛdɪt] *va* preparar para la imprenta; corregir para la imprenta; dirigir, redactar (*un periódico*)
**Edith** [ˈidɪθ] *s* Edita
**edition** [ɪˈdɪʃən] *s* edición
**editor** [ˈɛdɪtər] *s* director, redactor (*de un periódico o revista*); revisor (*de un manuscrito*); editor (*de artículos de fondo*)
**editorial** [ˌɛdɪˈtorɪəl] *adj* editorial; de redacción; *s* editorial, artículo de fondo
**editorialize** [ˌɛdɪˈtorɪəlaɪz] *vn* editorializar, expresar opiniones en un artículo de fondo
**editorially** [ˌɛdɪˈtorɪəlɪ] *adv* en un editorial; como en un editorial
**editorial staff** *s* redacción, cuerpo de redacción, consejo de redacción
**editor in chief** *s* jefe de redacción
**editorship** [ˈɛdɪtərˌʃɪp] *s* redacción; dirección (*de un periódico o revista*)
**Edmund** [ˈɛdmənd] *s* Edmundo
**educable** [ˈɛdʒəkəbəl] o [ˈɛdʒʊkəbəl] *adj* educable
**educate** [ˈɛdʒəket] o [ˈɛdʒʊket] *va* educar
**education** [ˌɛdʒəˈkeʃən] o [ˌɛdʒʊˈkeʃən] *s* educación, instrucción; instrucción pública
**educational** [ˌɛdʒəˈkeʃənəl] o [ˌɛdʒʊˈkeʃənəl] *adj* educacional
**educational institution** *s* centro docente
**educative** [ˈɛdʒəˌketɪv] o [ˈɛdʒʊˌketɪv] *adj* educativo
**educator** [ˈɛdʒəˌketər] o [ˈɛdʒʊˌketər] *s* educador
**educe** [ɪˈdjus] o [ɪˈdus] *va* educir
**Edward** [ˈɛdwərd] *s* Eduardo
**Edwardian** [ɛdˈwərdɪən] *adj* eduardiano
**Edwin** [ˈɛdwɪn] *s* Eduíno
**eel** [il] *s* (ichth.) anguila; (ichth.) lamprea; **to be as slippery as an eel** escurrirse como una anguila
**eelgrass** [ˈilˌgræs] o [ˈilˌgrɑs] *s* (bot.) zostera marina
**eelpot** [ˈilˌpɑt] *s* nasa para anguilas
**eelpout** [ˈilˌpaʊt] *s* (ichth.) zoarce
**eelworm** [ˈilˌwʌrm] *s* (zool.) anguílula
**e'en** [in] *adv* (poet.) var. de **even**
**e'er** [ɛr] *adv* (poet.) var. de **ever**
**eerie** o **eery** [ˈɪrɪ] o [ˈirɪ] *adj* (*comp:* **-rier;** *super:* **-riest**) misterioso, espectral; miedoso, tímido
**effect** [ɪˈfɛkt] *s* efecto; **effects** *spl* efectos; **for effect** sólo por impresionar; **in effect** en efecto, en realidad; vigente, en operación; **of no effect** sin resultado; **to feel the effect of** resentirse de; **to give effect to** activar, poner en efecto; **to go into effect** o **to take effect** hacerse vigente, ponerse en operación; **to put into effect** poner en vigor; **to the effect that** en el sentido de que; *va* efectuar
**effective** [ɪˈfɛktɪv] *adj* eficaz; vigente; impresionante; **effectives** *spl* (mil.) efectivos
**effectual** [ɪˈfɛktʃʊəl] *adj* eficaz
**effectually** [ɪˈfɛktʃʊəlɪ] *adv* eficazmente
**effectuate** [ɪˈfɛktʃʊet] *va* efectuar
**effeminacy** [ɪˈfɛmɪnəsɪ] *s* afeminación, afeminamiento
**effeminate** [ɪˈfɛmɪnɪt] *adj* afeminado; [ɪˈfɛmɪnet] *va* afeminar; *vn* afeminarse
**effemination** [ɪˌfɛmɪˈneʃən] *s* afeminación
**effendi** [ɪˈfɛndɪ] *s* (*pl:* **-dis**) efendi
**efferent** [ˈɛfərənt] *adj* (physiol.) eferente
**effervesce** [ˌɛfərˈvɛs] *vn* estar en efervescencia
**effervescence** [ˌɛfərˈvɛsəns] *s* efervescencia
**effervescent** [ˌɛfərˈvɛsənt] *adj* efervescente
**effete** [ɪˈfit] *adj* usado, gastado; estéril, infructuoso; decadente
**efficacious** [ˌɛfɪˈkeʃəs] *adj* eficaz
**efficacy** [ˈɛfɪkəsɪ] *s* (*pl:* **-cies**) eficacia
**efficiency** [ɪˈfɪʃənsɪ] *s* (*pl:* **-cies**) eficiencia; (mech.) rendimiento, efecto útil, eficiencia
**efficiency engineering** *s* taylorismo, organización científica
**efficient** [ɪˈfɪʃənt] *adj* eficiente; (mech.) de buen rendimiento
**effigy** [ˈɛfɪdʒɪ] *s* (*pl:* **-gies**) efigie; **to burn in effigy** quemar en efigie; **to hang in effigy** ahorcar en efigie
**effloresce** [ˌɛfloˈrɛs] *vn* florecer, echar flores; (chem.) eflorecerse
**efflorescence** [ˌɛfloˈrɛsəns] *s* (bot. & chem.) eflorescencia
**efflorescent** [ˌɛfloˈrɛsənt] *adj* (bot. & chem.) eflorescente
**effluence** [ˈɛflʊəns] *s* efluencia, emanación
**effluent** [ˈɛflʊənt] *adj* efluente; *s* corriente efluente
**effluvium** [ɪˈfluvɪəm] *s* (*pl:* **-via** [vɪə] o **-viums**) efluvio
**effort** [ˈɛfərt] *s* esfuerzo; obra; **to make every effort to** + *inf* hacer lo posible por + *inf*
**effrontery** [ɪˈfrʌntərɪ] *s* (*pl:* **-ies**) desfachatez, impudencia
**effulgence** [ɪˈfʌldʒəns] *s* refulgencia
**effulgent** [ɪˈfʌldʒənt] *adj* refulgente
**effuse** [ɪˈfjuz] *va* verter, derramar; *vn* emanar
**effusion** [ɪˈfjuʒən] *s* efusión; (fig.) efusión
**effusive** [ɪˈfjusɪv] *adj* efusivo; (geol. & fig.) efusivo
**eft** [ɛft] *s* (zool.) tritón; (zool.) lagartija
**e.g.** abr. de **exempli gratia** (Lat.) **for example**
**Eg.** abr. de **Egypt** y **Egyptian**
**egg** [ɛg] *s* huevo; (arch.) ova (*que alterna con el dardo*); (slang) sujeto, buen sujeto; **to have** o **to put all one's eggs in one basket** jugarlo todo a una carta; *va* mezclar o cubrir con huevos; (coll.) arrojar huevos a; **to egg on** incitar
**egg beater** *s* batidor de huevos
**egg cell** *s* (biol.) óvulo
**eggcup** [ˈɛgˌkʌp] *s* huevera
**egg glass** *s* reloj de arena de unos tres minutos para hervir huevos
**egghead** [ˈɛgˌhɛd] *s* (slang) intelectual
**eggnog** [ˈɛgˌnɑg] *s* yema mejida, caldo de la reina, ponche de huevo
**eggplant** [ˈɛgˌplænt] o [ˈɛgˌplɑnt] *s* (bot.) berenjena
**egg-shaped** [ˈɛgˌʃept] *adj* oviforme

**eggshell** [ˈɛg,ʃɛl] *s* cáscara de huevo, cascarón
**egg whisk** *s* (Brit.) var. de **egg beater**
**egis** [ˈidʒɪs] *s* var. de **aegis**
**eglantine** [ˈɛgləntaɪn] *s* (bot.) eglantina (*Rosa eglanteria y R. canina*); (bot.) rosa fétida; (bot.) madreselva
**ego** [ˈigo] o [ˈɛgo] *s* (*pl:* **-gos**) yo; (coll.) egotismo
**egocentric** [,igoˈsɛntrɪk] o [,ɛgoˈsɛntrɪk] *adj & s* egocéntrico
**egoism** [ˈigo·ɪzəm] o [ˈɛgo·ɪzəm] *s* egoísmo; egotismo
**egoist** [ˈigo·ɪst] o [ˈɛgo·ɪst] *s* egoísta; egotista
**egoistic** [,igoˈɪstɪk] o [,ɛgoˈɪstɪk] *adj* egoísta; egotista
**egotism** [ˈigotɪzəm] o [ˈɛgotɪzəm] *s* egotismo; egoísmo
**egotist** [ˈigotɪst] o [ˈɛgotɪst] *s* egotista; egoísta
**egotistic** [,igoˈtɪstɪk] o [,ɛgoˈtɪstɪk] o **egotistical** [,igoˈtɪstɪkəl] o [,ɛgoˈtɪstɪkəl] *adj* egotista; egoísta
**egregious** [ɪˈgridʒəs] *adj* (obs.) egregio; atroz, enorme
**egress** [ˈigrɛs] *s* salida
**egret** [ˈigrɛt] *s* var. de **aigrette**
**Egypt** [ˈidʒɪpt] *s* Egipto
**Egyptian** [ɪˈdʒɪpʃən] *adj & s* egipcio; gitano
**Egyptian vulture** *s* (orn.) alimoche
**Egyptological** [ɪ,dʒɪptəˈlɑdʒɪkəl] *adj* egiptológico
**Egyptologist** [,idʒɪpˈtɑlədʒɪst] *s* egiptólogo
**Egyptology** [,idʒɪpˈtɑlədʒɪ] *s* egiptología
**eh** [e] *interj* ¡eh!
**E.I.** abr. de **East Indian**
**eider** [ˈaɪdər] *s* (orn.) eíder, pato de flojel
**eider down** *s* edredón
**eider duck** *s* (orn.) eíder, pato de flojel
**eight** [et] *adj* ocho; *s* ocho; **eight o'clock** las ocho
**eight ball** *s* bola negra del juego de trucos, señalada con el número ocho; **behind the eight ball** (slang) en situación peligrosa, en situación dificultosa
**eight-cylinder** [ˈet,sɪlɪndər] *adj* (mach.) de ocho cilindros; **an eight-cylinder V motor** un ocho cilindros en V
**eight-day clock** [ˈetˈde] *s* reloj de ocho días cuerda
**eighteen** [ˈeˈtin] *adj & s* dieciocho o diez y ocho
**eighteenth** [ˈeˈtinθ] *adj* décimoctavo; dieciochavo; *s* décimoctavo; dieciochavo; dieciocho (*en las fechas*)
**eighteenth-century** [ˈeˈtinθˈsɛntʃərɪ] *adj* dieciochesco, dieciochista
**eightfold** [ˈet,fold] *adj & s* óctuple, óctuplo; *adv* ocho veces
**eighth** [etθ] *adj* octavo; *s* octavo; ocho (*en las fechas*); (mus.) octava
**eight hundred** *adj & s* ochocientos
**eightieth** [ˈetɪɪθ] *adj & s* octogésimo; ochentavo
**eighty** [ˈetɪ] *adj* ochenta; *s* (*pl:* **-ties**) ochenta
**eikon** [ˈaɪkɑn] *s* var. de **icon**
**einsteinium** [aɪnˈstaɪnɪəm] *s* (chem.) einsteinio
**Eire** [ˈɛrə] *s* Eire
**either** [ˈiðər] o [ˈaɪðər] *adj* uno u otro, cualquier . . . de los dos; cada (*de los dos*); *pron* uno u otro, cualquiera de los dos; *adv* tampoco; *conj* o sea; **either . . . or** o . . . o
**ejaculate** [ɪˈdʒækjəlet] o [iˈdʒækjʊlet] *va & vn* proferir de repente; (physiol.) eyacular
**ejaculation** [ɪ,dʒækjəˈleʃən] o [i,dʒækjʊˈleʃən] *s* exclamación; jaculatoria (*oración breve y ferviente*); (physiol.) eyaculación
**ejaculatory** [ɪˈdʒækjələ,torɪ] o [iˈdʒækjʊlə,torɪ] *adj* exclamatorio; jaculatorio (*breve y ferviente*); (physiol.) eyaculador
**ejaculatory duct** *s* (anat.) conducto eyaculador
**eject** [ɪˈdʒɛkt] *va* echar, arrojar, expulsar
**ejection** [ɪˈdʒɛkʃən] *s* expulsión; deyección (*p.ej., de un volcán*)
**ejection seat** *s* (aer.) asiento lanzable
**ejectment** [ɪˈdʒɛktmənt] *s* expulsión, exclusión
**ejector** [ɪˈdʒɛktər] *s* expulsador; (mach.) eyector; expulsor (*de arma de fuego*)
**eke** [ik] *va* aumentar con dificultad; **to eke out** ganar a duras penas
**el** [ɛl] *s* ana (*medida*); pabellón (*edificio contiguo*); (coll.) ferrocarril aéreo, ferrocarril elevado
**elaborate** [ɪˈlæbərɪt] *adj* elaborado; complicado; [ɪˈlæbəret] *va* elaborar; (physiol.) elaborar; *vn* explicarse con muchos detalles
**elaboration** [ɪ,læbəˈreʃən] *s* elaboración
**elaeagnaceous** [,ɛlɪægˈneʃəs] *adj* (bot.) eleagnáceo
**Elaine** [ɪˈlen] *s* Elena
**élan** [eˈlɑ̃] *s* entusiasmo, vivacidad
**eland** [ˈilənd] *s* (zool.) oreas
**élan vital** [viˈtɑl] *s* fuerza vital
**elapse** [ɪˈlæps] *vn* pasar, transcurrir, mediar
**elasmobranch** [ɪˈlæsməbræŋk] o [ɪˈlæzməbræŋk] *s* (ichth.) elasmobranquio
**elastic** [ɪˈlæstɪk] *adj & s* elástico
**elastically** [ɪˈlæstɪkəlɪ] *adv* elásticamente
**elasticity** [ɪ,læsˈtɪsɪtɪ] o [,ilæsˈtɪsɪtɪ] *s* elasticidad
**elastin** [ɪˈlæstɪn] *s* (biochem.) elastina
**elate** [ɪˈlet] *va* regocijar, exaltar
**elated** [ɪˈletɪd] *adj* regocijado, exaltado
**elaterin** [ɪˈlætərɪn] *s* (chem.) elaterina
**elation** [ɪˈleʃən] *s* regocijo, exaltación, viva alegría
**elbow** [ˈɛlbo] *s* codo (*del brazo o la manga*); (mach.) codo; recodo (*p.ej., de un río*); brazo (*de sillón*); **at one's elbow** a la mano, muy cerca; **out at the elbow** andrajoso; **to crook the elbow** (slang) empinar el codo; **to rub elbows with** rozarse mucho con; **up to the elbows** hasta los codos; *va* empujar codeando; **to elbow one's way through** abrirse paso codeando, abrirse paso a codazos; *vn* codear; formar recodos
**elbow bender** *s* (slang) aficionado a empinar el codo
**elbow grease** *s* (coll.) trabajo manual, duro esfuerzo, jugo de muñeca, betún de saliva, manteca de codo
**elbow patch** *s* codera
**elbow rest** *s* ménsula
**elbowroom** [ˈɛlbo,rum] o [ˈɛlbo,rʊm] *s* amplio espacio, espacio suficiente; libertad de acción
**elder** [ˈɛldər] *adj* mayor; *s* mayor; anciano; señor mayor; (eccl.) anciano; (bot.) saúco
**elderberry** [ˈɛldər,bɛrɪ] *s* (*pl:* **-ries**) (bot.) saúco; baya del saúco
**elderly** [ˈɛldərlɪ] *adj* viejo, anciano, mayor
**eldership** [ˈɛldərʃɪp] *s* señorío
**eldest** [ˈɛldɪst] *adj super* (el) más viejo, (el) mayor
**El Dorado** [ɛldəˈrɑdo] *s* (*pl:* **-dos**) Eldorado
**Eleanor** [ˈɛlənər] *s* Leonor
**Eleatic** [,ɛlɪˈætɪk] *adj & s* eleático
**elec.** abr. de **electrical** y **electricity**
**elecampane** [,ɛlɪkæmˈpen] *s* (bot.) énula campana, helenio
**elect** [ɪˈlɛkt] *adj* elegido, electo; *s* electo; **the elect** los elegidos o los escogidos (*por Dios*); los privilegiados; *va* elegir
**election** [ɪˈlɛkʃən] *s* elección; (theol.) elección, predestinación
**electioneer** [ɪ,lɛkʃəˈnɪr] *vn* solicitar votos, hacer campaña electoral
**elective** [ɪˈlɛktɪv] *adj* electivo; *s* curso o asignatura electiva
**elector** [ɪˈlɛktər] *s* elector
**electoral** [ɪˈlɛktərəl] *adj* electoral
**electoral college** *s* colegio electoral
**electorate** [ɪˈlɛktərɪt] *s* electorado
**Electra** [ɪˈlɛktrə] *s* (myth.) Electra
**Electra complex** *s* (psychoanal.) complejo de Electra
**electress** [ɪˈlɛktrɪs] *s* electriz (*mujer o viuda de un príncipe elector*); electora (*mujer que tiene derecho para elegir*)
**electric** [ɪˈlɛktrɪk] *adj* eléctrico; *s* (coll.) tranvía eléctrico, ferrocarril eléctrico
**electrical** [ɪˈlɛktrɪkəl] *adj* eléctrico
**electrical engineer** *s* ingeniero electricista
**electrical engineering** *s* electrotecnia, ingeniería electricista, ingeniería eléctrica
**electrically** [ɪˈlɛktrɪkəlɪ] *adv* eléctricamente
**electrical transcription** *s* transcripción eléctrica
**electric blanket** *s* cobija eléctrica
**electric chair** *s* silla eléctrica
**electric clock** *s* reloj eléctrico
**electric column** *s* pila voltaica

**electric eel** *s* (ichth.) anguila eléctrica
**electric eye** *s* ojo eléctrico
**electric fan** *s* ventilador eléctrico
**electric heating pad** *s* almohadilla caliente eléctrica
**electric hot-water heater** *s* termos eléctrico
**electrician** [ɪ,lɛk'trɪʃən] o [,ɛlɛk'trɪʃən] *s* electricista
**electricity** [ɪ,lɛk'trɪsɪtɪ] o [,ɛlɛk'trɪsɪtɪ] *s* electricidad
**electric percolator** *s* cafetera eléctrica
**electric-powered** [ɪ'lɛktrɪk'paʊərd] *adj* accionado eléctricamente
**electric ray** *s* (ichth.) pez eléctrico, tremielga, torpedo
**electric razor** *s* máquina de afeitar eléctrica
**electric refrigerator** *s* nevera eléctrica
**electric shaver** *s* electroafeitadora
**electric steel** *s* acero de horno eléctrico
**electric tape** *s* cinta aislante
**electric varnish** *s* barniz aislador
**electrification** [ɪ,lɛktrɪfɪ'keʃən] *s* electrificación
**electrify** [ɪ'lɛktrɪfaɪ] (*pret & pp:* **-fied**) *va* electrificar, electrizar; (fig.) electrizar
**electrocardiogram** [ɪ,lɛktro'kɑrdɪo,græm] *s* electrocardiograma
**electrocardiograph** [ɪ,lɛktro'kɑrdɪo,græf] o [ɪ,lɛktro'kɑrdɪo,grɑf] *s* electrocardiógrafo
**electrochemical** [ɪ,lɛktro'kɛmɪkəl] *adj* electroquímico
**electrochemistry** [ɪ,lɛktro'kɛmɪstrɪ] *s* electroquímica
**electro-convulsive treatment** [ɪ,lɛktrokən'vʌlsɪv] *s* electroshockterapia
**electrocute** [ɪ'lɛktrəkjut] *va* electrocutar
**electrocution** [ɪ,lɛktrə'kjuʃən] *s* electrocución
**electrode** [ɪ'lɛktrod] *s* electrodo
**electrodynamic** [ɪ,lɛktrodaɪ'næmɪk] *adj* electrodinámico; **electrodynamics** *ssg* electrodinámica
**electrolier** [ɪ,lɛktro'lɪr] *s* araña de lámparas eléctricas
**electrolysis** [ɪ,lɛk'trɑlɪsɪs] o [,ɛlɛk'trɑlɪsɪs] *s* (chem. & surg.) electrólisis; depilación con aguja electrificada
**electrolyte** [ɪ'lɛktrolaɪt] *s* electrólito
**electrolytic** [ɪ,lɛktro'lɪtɪk] *adj* electrolítico
**electrolytically** [ɪ,lɛktro'lɪtɪkəlɪ] *adv* electrolíticamente
**electrolytic condenser** *s* (rad.) condensador electrolítico
**electrolyzation** [ɪ,lɛktrəlɪ'zeʃən] *s* electrolización
**electrolyze** [ɪ'lɛktrolaɪz] *va* electrolizar
**electromagnet** [ɪ,lɛktro'mægnɪt] *s* electroimán, electro
**electromagnetic** [ɪ,lɛktromæg'nɛtɪk] *adj* electromagnético
**electromagnetic induction** *s* (elec.) inducción electromagnética
**electromagnetic speaker** *s* (rad.) altavoz o altoparlante electromagnético
**electromagnetism** [ɪ,lɛktro'mægnɪtɪzəm] *s* electromagnetismo
**electrometallurgy** [ɪ,lɛktro'mɛtəlʌrdʒɪ] *s* electrometalurgia
**electrometer** [ɪ,lɛk'trɑmɪtər] o [,ɛlɛk'trɑmɪtər] *s* electrómetro
**electrometric** [ɪ,lɛktro'mɛtrɪk] *adj* electrométrico
**electrometry** [ɪ,lɛk'trɑmɪtrɪ] o [,ɛlɛk'trɑmɪtrɪ] *s* electrometría
**electromotive** [ɪ,lɛktro'motɪv] *adj* electromotor
**electromotive force** *s* fuerza electromotriz
**electromotor** [ɪ,lɛktro'motər] *s* electromotor, motor eléctrico; aparato electrógeno
**electron** [ɪ'lɛktrɑn] *s* (phys. & chem.) electrón
**electronegative** [ɪ,lɛktro'nɛgətɪv] *adj* electronegativo
**electronic** [ɪ,lɛk'trɑnɪk] o [,ɛlɛk'trɑnɪk] *adj* electrónico; **electronics** *ssg* electrónica
**electronic brain** *s* cerebro electrónico
**electron microscope** *s* microscopio electrónico
**electron spin** *s* (phys.) giro electrónico
**electron volt** *s* (phys.) electrón voltio
**electrophonic** [ɪ,lɛktro'fɑnɪk] *adj* electrofónico
**electrophorus** [ɪ,lɛk'trɑfərəs] o [,ɛlɛk'trɑfərəs] *s* (*pl:* **-ri** [raɪ]) (phys.) electróforo
**electroplate** [ɪ'lɛktro,plet] *s* artículo galvanizado; *va* galvanizar
**electroplating** [ɪ'lɛktro,pletɪŋ] *s* galvanoplastia
**electropneumatic** [ɪ,lɛktronju'mætɪk] o [ɪ,lɛktronu'mætɪk] *adj* (mus.) electroneumático (*órgano*)
**electropositive** [ɪ,lɛktro'pɑzɪtɪv] *adj* electropositivo
**electroscope** [ɪ'lɛktrəskop] *s* (phys.) electroscopio
**electroshock** [ɪ'lɛktro,ʃɑk] *s* electrochoque
**electrostatic** [ɪ,lɛktro'stætɪk] *adj* electrostático; **electrostatics** *ssg* electrostática
**electrosurgery** [ɪ,lɛktro'sʌrdʒərɪ] *s* electrocirugía
**electrotechnical** [ɪ,lɛktro'tɛknɪkəl] *adj* electrotécnico
**electrotherapy** [ɪ,lɛktro'θɛrəpɪ] *s* electroterapia
**electrotype** [ɪ'lɛktrotaɪp] *s* electrotipo; *va* electrotipar
**electrotypy** [ɪ'lɛktro,taɪpɪ] *s* electrotipia
**electrum** [ɪ'lɛktrəm] *s* electro (*aleación*); plata alemana
**electuary** [ɪ'lɛktʃʊ,ɛrɪ] *s* (*pl:* **-ies**) electuario
**eleemosynary** [,ɛlɪ'mɑsɪ,nɛrɪ] *adj* limosnero; mendicante
**elegance** ['ɛlɪgəns] *s* elegancia
**elegancy** ['ɛlɪgənsɪ] *s* (*pl:* **-cies**) var. de **elegance**
**elegant** ['ɛlɪgənt] *adj* elegante
**elegiac** [,ɛlɪ'dʒaɪæk] o [ɛ'lidʒɪæk] *adj* elegíaco
**elegy** ['ɛlɪdʒɪ] *s* (*pl:* **-gies**) elegía
**element** ['ɛlɪmənt] *s* elemento; (anat., biol. & elec.) elemento; (chem.) elemento, cuerpo simple; **the four elements** los cuatro elementos (*fuego, agua, aire y tierra*); **the elements** los elementos (*primeros principios; las fuerzas naturales*); **to be in one's element** estar en su elemento
**elemental** [,ɛlɪ'mɛntəl] *adj* elemental
**elementary** [,ɛlɪ'mɛntərɪ] *adj* elemental
**elemi** ['ɛlɪmɪ] *s* (*pl:* **-mis**) elemí
**elephant** ['ɛlɪfənt] *s* elefante
**elephant fish** *s* (ichth.) pez elefante
**elephant grass** *s* (bot.) hierba elefante (*Pennisetum purpureum*)
**elephantiac** [,ɛlɪ'fæntɪæk] *adj & s* elefancíaco
**elephantiasis** [,ɛlɪfæn'taɪəsɪs] *s* (path.) elefantiasis
**elephantine** [,ɛlɪ'fæntɪn] o [,ɛlɪ'fæntaɪn] *adj* elefantino
**elephant seal** *s* (zool.) foca de trompa, elefante marino
**elephant's-ear** ['ɛlɪfənts,ɪr] *s* (bot.) begonia; (bot.) taro
**Eleusinian** [,ɛljʊ'sɪnɪən] *adj & s* eleusino
**Eleusinian mysteries** *spl* misterios de Eleusis
**elevate** ['ɛlɪvet] *va* elevar; regocijar
**elevated** ['ɛlɪ,vetɪd] *adj* elevado; alegre; *s* (coll.) ferrocarril aéreo, ferrocarril elevado
**elevated railroad** *s* ferrocarril aéreo, ferrocarril elevado
**elevation** [,ɛlɪ'veʃən] *s* elevación; (arch. & astr). elevación; (*cap.*) *s* (eccl.) elevación
**elevator** ['ɛlɪ,vetər] *s* ascensor, elevador; montacargas; elevador de granos; depósito de cereales; (aer.) timón de profundidad
**elevator shaft** *s* caja o pozo de ascensor
**eleven** [ɪ'lɛvən] *adj* once; *s* once; (football) once (*equipo de jugadores*); **eleven o'clock** las once
**elevenfold** [ɪ'lɛvən,fold] *adj & s* undécuplo; *adv* once veces
**eleventh** [ɪ'lɛvənθ] *adj* undécimo, onceno; onzavo; *s* undécimo, onceno; onzavo; once (*en las fechas*)
**eleventh hour** *s* último minuto
**elf** [ɛlf] *s* (*pl:* **elves**) elfo, duende; enano; niño travieso
**elfin** ['ɛlfɪn] *adj* elfino, travieso; *s* elfo
**elfish** ['ɛlfɪʃ] *adj* elfino, travieso
**elflock** ['ɛlf,lɑk] *s* greña de pelo
**Eli** ['ilaɪ] *s* (Bib.) Elí
**elicit** [ɪ'lɪsɪt] *va* sacar, sonsacar
**elicitation** [ɪ,lɪsɪ'teʃən] *s* sacamiento, sonsacamiento
**elide** [ɪ'laɪd] *va* elidir

**eligibility** [ˌɛlɪdʒɪˈbɪlɪtɪ] *s* (*pl:* **-ties**) elegibilidad
**eligible** [ˈɛlɪdʒɪbəl] *adj* elegible; admisible, aceptable
**Elijah** [ɪˈlaɪdʒə] *s* (Bib.) Elías
**eliminate** [ɪˈlɪmɪnet] *va* eliminar; (math. & physiol.) eliminar
**elimination** [ɪˌlɪmɪˈneʃən] *s* eliminación; (physiol.) eliminación
**elimination match** o **race** *s* (sport) eliminatoria
**Eliot** [ˈɛlɪət] *s* Elías
**Elisha** [ɪˈlaɪʃə] *s* (Bib.) Elíseo
**elision** [ɪˈlɪʒən] *s* elisión
**élite** o **elite** [eˈlit] *s* lo escogido, lo selecto; **the élite of society** la élite de la sociedad
**elixir** [ɪˈlɪksər] *s* elixir o elíxir
**Elizabeth** [ɪˈlɪzəbəθ] *s* Isabel
**Elizabethan** [ɪˌlɪzəˈbiθən] o [ɪˌlɪzəˈbɛθən] *adj* & *s* isabelino
**elk** [ɛlk] *s* (zool.) alce
**ell** [ɛl] *s* ana (*medida*); pabellón (*edificio contiguo*)
**Elliott** [ˈɛlɪət] *s* Elías
**ellipse** [ɪˈlɪps] *s* (geom.) elipse
**ellipsis** [ɪˈlɪpsɪs] *s* (*pl:* **-ses** [siz]) (gram.) elipsis
**ellipsograph** [ɪˈlɪpsəgræf] o [ɪˈlɪpsəgrɑf] *s* elipsógrafo
**ellipsoid** [ɪˈlɪpsɔɪd] *s* (geom.) elipsoide
**elliptic** [ɪˈlɪptɪk] o **elliptical** [ɪˈlɪptɪkəl] *adj* (geom. & gram.) elíptico
**elliptically** [ɪˈlɪptɪkəlɪ] *adv* elípticamente
**Ellis** [ˈɛlɪs] *s* Elías
**elm** [ɛlm] *s* (bot.) olmo
**elocution** [ˌɛləˈkjuʃən] *s* elocución
**elocutionary** [ˌɛləˈkjuʃənˌɛrɪ] *adj* declamatorio
**elocutionist** [ˌɛləˈkjuʃənɪst] *s* declamador, recitador
**Eloise** [ˌɛloˈiz] *s* Eloísa
**elongate** [ɪˈlɔŋget] o [ɪˈlɑŋget] *adj* alargado; *va* alargar, extender; *vn* alargarse, extenderse
**elongation** [ˌilɔŋˈgeʃən] o [ˌilɑŋˈgeʃən] *s* alargamiento, extensión; (astr.) elongación
**elope** [ɪˈlop] *vn* fugarse con un amante; huir, evadirse, escaparse
**elopement** [ɪˈlopmənt] *s* fuga con un amante; fuga, escapada
**eloquence** [ˈɛləkwəns] *s* elocuencia
**eloquent** [ˈɛləkwənt] *adj* elocuente
**El Salvador** [ɛlˈsælvədər] *s* El Salvador
**else** [ɛls] *adj* otro, diferente; más; *adv* de otro modo, de otra manera; si no; **or else** o bien
**elsewhere** [ˈɛlshwɛr] *adv* en otra parte, a otra parte
**elsewhither** [ˈɛlsˌhwɪðər] *adv* a otra parte
**elucidate** [ɪˈlusɪdet] *va* elucidar
**elucidation** [ɪˌlusɪˈdeʃən] *s* elucidación
**elude** [ɪˈlud] *va* eludir
**elusion** [ɪˈluʒən] *s* evasiva, efugio
**elusive** [ɪˈlusɪv] o **elusory** [ɪˈlusərɪ] *adj* deslumbrador, difícil de comprender; evasivo
**elver** [ˈɛlvər] *s* (ichth.) anguila joven
**elvish** [ˈɛlvɪʃ] *adj* var. de **elfish**
**Elysian** [ɪˈlɪʒən] *adj* elíseo o elisio
**Elysian Fields** *spl* (myth.) campos elíseos o elisios
**Elysium** [ɪˈlɪʒəm] o [ɪˈlɪzɪəm] *s* (myth. & fig.) Elíseo o Elisio
**elytrum** [ˈɛlɪtrəm] *s* (*pl:* **-tra** [trə]) (ent.) élitro
**Elzevir** [ˈɛlzəvər] o [ˈɛlzəvɪr] *adj* elzeviriano; *s* (bibliog. & print.) elzevir o elzevirio
**em** [ɛm] *s* (print.) eme
**em** o **'em** [əm] *pron pers pl* (coll.) var. de **them**
**emaciate** [ɪˈmeʃɪet] *va* enflaquecer; *vn* enflaquecerse
**emaciation** [ɪˌmeʃɪˈeʃən] *s* enflaquecimiento, emaciación
**emanate** [ˈɛmənet] *vn* emanar
**emanation** [ˌɛməˈneʃən] *s* emanación
**emancipate** [ɪˈmænsɪpet] *va* emancipar
**emancipation** [ɪˌmænsɪˈpeʃən] *s* emancipación
**emancipator** [ɪˈmænsɪˌpetər] *s* emancipador, libertador
**emasculate** [ɪˈmæskjəlɪt] *adj* debilitado, afeminado; [ɪˈmæskjəlet] *va* emascular; (fig.) debilitar, mutilar
**emasculation** [ɪˌmæskjəˈleʃən] *s* emasculación; (fig.) debilitación, mutilación
**embalm** [ɛmˈbɑm] *va* embalsamar (*un cadáver; el aire*); conservar, conservar en la memoria
**embalmer** [ɛmˈbɑmər] *s* embalsamador
**embalmment** [ɛmˈbɑmmənt] *s* embalsamamiento
**embank** [ɛmˈbæŋk] *va* terraplenar
**embankment** [ɛmˈbæŋkmənt] *s* terraplén
**embargo** [ɛmˈbɑrgo] *s* (*pl:* **-goes**) embargo; *va* embargar
**embark** [ɛmˈbɑrk] *va* embarcar; (fig.) embarcar, lanzar (*en una empresa*); (fig.) invertir (*dinero*) en una empresa; *vn* embarcarse
**embarkation** [ˌɛmbɑrˈkeʃən] o **embarkment** [ɛmˈbɑrkmənt] *s* embarco (*de personas*); embarque (*de mercancías*)
**embarrass** [ɛmˈbærəs] *va* avergonzar, desconcertar; embarazar, estorbar; poner en aprieto
**embarrassing** [ɛmˈbærəsɪŋ] *adj* vergonzoso, desconcertador; embarazoso
**embarrassment** [ɛmˈbærəsmənt] *s* vergüenza, desconcierto; embarazo, estorbo; apuros, dificultades
**embassador** [ɛmˈbæsədər] *s* var. de **ambassador**
**embassy** [ˈɛmbəsɪ] *s* (*pl:* **-sies**) embajada
**embattle** [ɛmˈbætəl] *va* preparar para la batalla; (fort.) almenar
**embay** [ɛmˈbe] *va* abrigar o cerrar en una bahía; encerrar
**embed** [ɛmˈbɛd] (*pret & pp:* **-bedded;** *ger:* **-bedding**) *va* hincar, encajar, empotrar, plantar
**embellish** [ɛmˈbɛlɪʃ] *va* embellecer
**embellishment** [ɛmˈbɛlɪʃmənt] *s* embellecimiento
**ember** [ˈɛmbər] *s* ascua, pavesa; **embers** *spl* rescoldo
**Ember days** *spl* témpora, témporas
**embezzle** [ɛmˈbɛzəl] *va* malversar, desfalcar
**embezzlement** [ɛmˈbɛzəlmənt] *s* malversación, desfalco
**embezzler** [ɛmˈbɛzlər] *s* malversador
**embitter** [ɛmˈbɪtər] *va* amargar
**emblazon** [ɛmˈblezən] *va* blasonar; engalanar o esmaltar con colores brillantes; (fig.) blasonar, ensalzar
**emblazonment** [ɛmˈblezənmənt] *s* var. de **emblazonry**
**emblazonry** [ɛmˈblezənrɪ] *s* (*pl:* **-ries**) blasón; adorno brillante
**emblem** [ˈɛmbləm] *s* emblema
**emblematic** [ˌɛmbləˈmætɪk] o **emblematical** [ˌɛmbləˈmætɪkəl] *adj* emblemático
**embodiment** [ɛmˈbɑdɪmənt] *s* incorporación; encarnación, personificación
**embody** [ɛmˈbɑdɪ] (*pret & pp:* **-ied**) *va* incorporar; encarnar, personificar
**embolden** [ɛmˈboldən] *va* envalentonar
**embolectomy** [ˌɛmbəˈlɛktəmɪ] *s* (*pl:* **-mies**) (surg.) embolectomía
**embolism** [ˈɛmbəlɪzəm] *s* embolismo (*para igualar el calendario*); (path.) embolia
**embolismic** [ˌɛmbəˈlɪzmɪk] *adj* embolismal o embolísmico
**embolus** [ˈɛmbələs] *s* (*pl:* **-li** [laɪ]) (path.) émbolo
**embonpoint** [ɑ̃bɔ̃ˈpwæ̃] *s* redondez de cuerpo
**embosom** [ɛmˈbʊzəm] *va* ensenar, guardar en el seno, encerrar en el pecho; envolver, abrigar, proteger cariñosamente
**emboss** [ɛmˈbɔs] o [ɛmˈbɑs] *va* abollonar; realzar, labrar de o al realce
**embossment** [ɛmˈbɔsmənt] o [ɛmˈbɑsmənt] *s* abollonadura; realce, relieve
**embouchure** [ˌɑmbuˈʃʊr] *s* desembocadura (*de un río*); embocadura (*de un instrumento músico*)
**embower** [ɛmˈbaʊər] *va* emparrar
**embrace** [ɛmˈbres] *s* abrazo; *va* abrazar; *vn* abrazarse (*dos personas*)
**embrasure** [ɛmˈbreʒər] *s* (arch.) alféizar; (fort.) aspillera, tronera; *va* aspillerar
**embrocate** [ˈɛmbroket] *va* (med.) bañar y frotar con una embrocación
**embrocation** [ˌɛmbroˈkeʃən] *s* (med.) embrocación
**embroider** [ɛmˈbrɔɪdər] *va* bordar, recamar; (fig.) bordar, embellecer
**embroidery** [ɛmˈbrɔɪdərɪ] *s* (*pl:* **-ies**) bordado, recamado

**embroidery frame** *s* bastidor para bordar

**embroil** [ɛm'brɔɪl] *va* embrollar; envolver (*p.ej., en una contienda*)

**embroilment** [ɛm'brɔɪlmənt] *s* embrollo; envolvimiento

**embrown** [ɛm'braʊn] *va* embazar, poner pardo

**embryo** ['ɛmbrɪo] *s* (*pl:* **-os**) (biol., bot. & fig.) embrión; **in embryo** en embrión; *adj* embrionario

**embryogenic** [,ɛmbrɪo'dʒɛnɪk] *adj* embriogénico

**embryogeny** [,ɛmbrɪ'ɑdʒənɪ] *s* (biol.) embriogenia

**embryologic** [,ɛmbrɪo'lɑdʒɪk] o **embryological** [,ɛmbrɪo'lɑdʒɪkəl] *adj* embriológico

**embryologist** [,ɛmbrɪ'ɑlədʒɪst] *s* embriólogo

**embryology** [,ɛmbrɪ'ɑlədʒɪ] *s* embriología

**embryonal** ['ɛmbrɪənəl] *adj* embrional

**embryonic** [,ɛmbrɪ'ɑnɪk] *adj* embrionario

**emeer** [ə'mɪr] *s* emir

**emend** [ɪ'mɛnd] *va* enmendar

**emendation** [,imɛn'deʃən] o [,ɛmɛn'deʃən] *s* enmienda

**emerald** ['ɛmərəld] *s* esmeralda; *adj* esmeraldino

**emerge** [ɪ'mʌrdʒ] *vn* emerger

**emergence** [ɪ'mʌrdʒəns] *s* emergencia; (bot.) emergencia

**emergency** [ɪ'mʌrdʒənsɪ] *s* (*pl:* **-cies**) emergencia; urgencia; caso urgente; *adj* de auxilio, de emergencia, de socorro, de fortuna, de prevención

**emergency brake** *s* freno de auxilio, freno de emergencia

**emergency exit** *s* salida de auxilio

**emergency landing** *s* (aer.) aterrizaje forzoso, aterrizaje de emergencia

**emergency landing field** *s* (aer.) campo de emergencia, aeródromo de urgencia

**emergent** [ɪ'mʌrdʒənt] *adj* emergente; urgente

**emeritus** [ɪ'mɛrɪtəs] *adj* emérito, honorario

**emeritus professor** *s* profesor honorario

**emersion** [ɪ'mʌrʒən] o [ɪ'mʌrʃən] *s* emersión; (astr.) emersión

**emery** ['ɛmərɪ] *s* esmeril

**emery cloth** *s* tela de esmeril

**emery grinder** *s* muela de esmeril

**emery paper** *s* papel de esmeril

**emery stone** *s* piedra de esmeril

**emery wheel** *s* rueda de esmeril

**emetic** [ɪ'mɛtɪk] *adj* & *s* emético

**E.M.F.** o **e.m.f.** abr. de **electromotive force**

**emigrant** ['ɛmɪgrənt] *adj* & *s* emigrante

**emigrate** ['ɛmɪgret] *vn* emigrar

**emigration** [,ɛmɪ'greʃən] *s* emigración

**émigré** [emi'gre] o ['ɛmɪgre] *s* emigrado

**Emily** ['ɛmɪlɪ] *s* Emilia

**eminence** ['ɛmɪnəns] *s* eminencia; (*cap.*) *s* (eccl.) eminencia

**éminence grise** [eminɑ̃s griz] *s* eminencia gris (*persona que tiene influencia insospechada*)

**eminency** ['ɛmɪnənsɪ] *s* (pl: **-cies**) eminencia (*dignidad, distinción*)

**eminent** ['ɛmɪnənt] *adj* eminente

**eminent domain** *s* (law) dominio eminente

**eminently** ['ɛmɪnəntlɪ] *adv* eminentemente

**emir** [ə'mɪr] *s* emir

**emissary** ['ɛmɪ,sɛrɪ] *s* (*pl:* **-ies**) emisario

**emission** [ɪ'mɪʃən] *s* emisión

**emissive** [ɪ'mɪsɪv] *adj* emisivo

**emit** [ɪ'mɪt] (*pret & pp:* **-mitted;** *ger:* **-mitting**) *va* emitir

**Emma** ['ɛmə] *s* Ema

**Emmanuel** [ɪ'mænjʊəl] *s* (Bib.) Emanuel

**emmenagogue** [ə'mɛnəgɑg] o [ə'minəgɑg] *adj* & *s* (med.) emenagogo

**emmer** ['ɛmər] *s* (bot.) escandia

**emmetrope** ['ɛmɪtrop] *s* emétrope

**emmetropia** [,ɛmɪ'tropɪə] *s* emetropía

**emollient** [ɪ'mɑljənt] *adj* & *s* emoliente

**emolument** [ɪ'mɑljəmənt] *s* emolumento

**emotion** [ɪ'moʃən] *s* emoción

**emotional** [ɪ'moʃənəl] *adj* emocional

**emotionalism** [ɪ'moʃənəlɪzəm] *s* emocionalismo

**emotive** [ɪ'motɪv] *adj* emotivo

**empanel** [ɛm'pænəl] (*pret & pp:* **-eled** o **-elled;** *ger:* **-eling** o **-elling**) *va* var. de **impanel**

**empathy** ['ɛmpəθɪ] *s* (psychol.) empatía

**Empedocles** [ɛm'pɛdəkliz] *s* Empédocles

**empennage** [,ɑ̃pɛ'nɑʒ] *s* (aer.) empenaje

**emperor** ['ɛmpərər] *s* emperador

**emphasis** ['ɛmfəsɪs] *s* (*pl:* **-ses** [siz]) énfasis

**emphasize** ['ɛmfəsaɪz] *va* dar énfasis a, acentuar; (fig.) acentuar

**emphatic** [ɛm'fætɪk] *adj* enfático

**emphatically** [ɛm'fætɪkəlɪ] *adv* enfáticamente

**emphysema** [,ɛmfɪ'simə] *s* (path.) enfisema

**emphyteusis** [,ɛmfɪ'tjusɪs] o [,ɛmfɪ'tusɪs] *s* (law) enfiteusis

**emphyteuta** [,ɛmfɪ'tjutə] o [,ɛmfɪ'tutə] *s* (*pl:* **-tae** [ti]) enfiteuta

**emphyteutic** [,ɛmfɪ'tjutɪk] o [,ɛmfɪ'tutɪk] *adj* enfitéutico

**empire** ['ɛmpaɪr] *s* imperio; (*cap.*) *adj* (f.a.) imperio, de estilo imperio

**Empire gown** *s* vestido imperio

**Empire of the Rising Sun** *s* Imperio del sol naciente (*el Japón*)

**Empire State** *s* estado de Nueva York, EE.UU.

**empiric** [ɛm'pɪrɪk] *adj* empírico; *s* empírico; curandero, charlatán

**empirical** [ɛm'pɪrɪkəl] *adj* empírico

**empiricism** [ɛm'pɪrɪsɪzəm] *s* empirismo

**empiricist** [ɛm'pɪrɪsɪst] *s* empírico, empirista; curandero, charlatán

**emplacement** [ɛm'plesmənt] *s* sitio, colocación, emplazamiento

**employ** [ɛm'plɔɪ] *s* empleo; *va* emplear

**employe, employé** o **employee** [ɛm'plɔɪi] o [,ɛmplɔɪ'i] *s* empleado

**employer** [ɛm'plɔɪər] *s* patrón

**employment** [ɛm'plɔɪmənt] *s* empleo, ocupación

**employment agency** *s* agencia de colocaciones o empleos

**emporium** [ɛm'porɪəm] *s* (*pl:* **-riums** o **-ria** [rɪə]) emporio

**empower** [ɛm'paʊər] *va* facultar, habilitar; autorizar

**empress** ['ɛmprɪs] *s* emperatriz

**emptiness** ['ɛmptɪnɪs] *s* vacío, vacuidad

**empty** ['ɛmptɪ] *adj* (*comp:* **-tier;** *super:* **-tiest**) vacío; vano, inútil; (coll.) hambriento; (*pret & pp:* **-tied**) *va* & *vn* vaciar

**empty-handed** ['ɛmptɪ'hændɪd] *adj* manivacío

**empty-headed** ['ɛmptɪ'hɛdɪd] *adj* tonto, estúpido

**empurple** [ɛm'pʌrpəl] *va* empurpurar; *vn* empurpurarse

**empyema** [,ɛmpɪ'imə] *s* (*pl:* **-mata** [mətə]) (path.) empiema

**empyreal** [ɛm'pɪrɪəl] o [,ɛmpɪ'riəl] *adj* empíreo

**empyrean** [,ɛmpɪ'riən] *adj* & *s* empíreo

**empyreuma** [,ɛmpɪ'rumə] *s* (*pl:* **-mata** [mətə] ) (chem.) empireuma

**emu** ['imju] *s* (orn.) emú

**emulate** ['ɛmjəlet] *va* & *vn* emular

**emulation** [,ɛmjə'leʃən] *s* emulación

**emulative** ['ɛmjə,letɪv] *adj* emulador

**emulator** ['ɛmjə,letər] *s* emulador

**emulgent** [ɪ'mʌldʒənt] *adj* emulgente

**emulous** ['ɛmjələs] *adj* émulo

**emulsification** [ɪ,mʌlsɪfɪ'keʃən] *s* emulsionamiento; (phot.) albuminaje, emulsionamiento

**emulsify** [ɪ'mʌlsɪfaɪ] (*pret & pp:* **-fied**) *va* emulsionar; (phot.) albuminar, emulsionar

**emulsion** [ɪ'mʌlʃən] *s* emulsión

**emulsive** [ɪ'mʌlsɪv] *adj* emulsivo

**emunctory** [ɪ'mʌŋktərɪ] *adj* emuntorio; *s* (*pl:* **-ries**) emuntorio

**en** [ɛn] *s* (print.) mitad de una eme

**enable** [ɛn'ebəl] *va* habilitar, permitir

**enact** [ɛn'ækt] *va* decretar; dar o promulgar (*una ley*); desempeñar el papel de; *vn* actuar, desempeñar un papel

**enactment** [ɛn'æktmənt] *s* ley, estatuto; promulgación (*de una ley*); representación

**enallage** [ɛn'ælədʒɪ] *s* (gram.) enálage

**enamel** [ɛn'æməl] *s* esmalte; (anat.) esmalte; (*pret & pp:* **-eled** o **-elled;** *ger:* **-eling** o **-elling**) *va* esmaltar

**enamelware** [ɛn'æməl,wɛr] *s* utensilios de cocina hechos de hierro esmaltado; enlozado (Am.)

**enamor** [ɛn'æmər] *va* enamorar

**enarthrosis** [,ɛnɑr'θrosɪs] *s* (anat.) enartrosis

**en bloc** [ɛn ˈblɑk] en bloque, en una pieza, juntos
**encamp** [ɛn ˈkæmp] *va* acampar; *vn* acampar o acamparse
**encampment** [ɛn ˈkæmpmənt] *s* campamento
**encase** [ɛn ˈkes] *va* encajonar, encerrar
**encaustic** [ɛn ˈkɔstɪk] *adj* (f.a.) encáustico; *s* (f.a.) encausto
**encaustic painting** *s* (f.a.) pintura al encausto
**encaustic tile** *s* azulejo
**enceinte** [ɛn ˈsent] *adj* encinta, preñada; *s* (fort.) recinto
**encephalic** [ˌɛnsɪ ˈfælɪk] *adj* encefálico
**encephalitis** [ɛnˌsɛfə ˈlaɪtɪs] *s* (path.) encefalitis
**encephalomyelitis** [ɛnˌsɛfəloˌmaɪə ˈlaɪtɪs] *s* (path.) encefalomielitis
**encephalon** [ɛn ˈsɛfəlɑn] *s* (*pl:* **-la** [lə]) (anat.) encéfalo
**encephalopathy** [ɛnˌsɛfə ˈlɑpəθɪ] *s* (path.) encefalopatía
**enchain** [ɛn ˈtʃen] *va* encadenar
**enchant** [ɛn ˈtʃænt] o [ɛn ˈtʃɑnt] *va* encantar
**enchanting** [ɛn ˈtʃæntɪŋ] o [ɛn ˈtʃɑntɪŋ] *adj* encantador
**enchantment** [ɛn ˈtʃæntmənt] o [ɛn ˈtʃɑntmənt] *s* encantamiento, encanto
**enchantress** [ɛn ˈtʃæntrɪs] o [ɛn ˈtʃɑntrɪs] *s* encantadora
**enchase** [ɛn ˈtʃes] *va* engastar
**encircle** [ɛn ˈsʌrkəl] *va* circuir, rodear, encerrar, circunvalar; (mil.) envolver
**encirclement** [ɛn ˈsʌrkəlmənt] *s* rodeo, circuición, encerramiento, circunvalación; (mil.) envolvimiento
**encircling** [ɛn ˈsʌrklɪŋ] *adj* (mil.) envolvente
**enclave** [ˈɛnklev] *s* (geog.) enclave; [ɛn ˈklev] *va* enclavar
**enclavement** [ɛn ˈklevmənt] *s* (med.) enclavamiento
**enclitic** [ɛn ˈklɪtɪk] *adj* (gram. & obstet.) enclítico; *s* (gram.) enclítico, partícula enclítica
**enclose** [ɛn ˈkloz] *va* cercar, encerrar, incluir; **to enclose herewith** remitir adjunto (*con una carta*)
**enclosure** [ɛn ˈkloʒər] *s* cercamiento, encerramiento, inclusión; cerca, encierro, recinto; cosa inclusa, carta inclusa, copia inclusa
**encomiast** [ɛn ˈkomɪæst] *s* encomiasta
**encomiastic** [ɛnˌkomɪ ˈæstɪk] *adj* encomiástico
**encomium** [ɛn ˈkomɪəm] *s* (*pl:* **-ums** o **-a** [ə]) encomio
**encompass** [ɛn ˈkʌmpəs] *va* abarcar, encuadrar
**encompassment** [ɛn ˈkʌmpəsmənt] *s* abarcamiento, encuadramiento
**encore** [ˈɑŋkor] *s* (theat.) bis, repetición; *interj* (theat.) ¡bis!, ¡que se repita!; *va* (theat.) pedir la repetición a o de
**encounter** [ɛn ˈkaʊntər] *s* encuentro; (mil.) encuentro; *va* encontrar, encontrarse con; *vn* encontrarse; batirse
**encourage** [ɛn ˈkʌrɪdʒ] *va* animar, alentar; fomentar; **to encourage to** + *inf* animar a, alentar a + *inf*
**encouragement** [ɛn ˈkʌrɪdʒmənt] *s* animación, ánimo; fomento; **to give encouragement to** dar ánimo o ánimos a
**encouraging** [ɛn ˈkʌrɪdʒɪŋ] *adj* animador, alentador
**encroach** [ɛn ˈkrotʃ] *vn* pasar los límites; **to encroach on** o **upon** pasar los límites de, invadir; abusar de
**encroachment** [ɛn ˈkrotʃmənt] *s* invasión; abuso
**encrust** [ɛn ˈkrʌst] *va* incrustar; *vn* incrustarse
**encumber** [ɛn ˈkʌmbər] *va* embarazar, estorbar; impedir; gravar
**encumbrance** [ɛn ˈkʌmbrəns] *s* embarazo, estorbo; impedimento; gravamen; hijo menor de edad
**ency.** o **encyc.** abr. de **encyclopedia**
**encyclical** [ɛn ˈsɪklɪkəl] o [ɛn ˈsaɪklɪkəl] *adj* circular, general; *s* encíclica
**encyclopedia** o **encyclopaedia** [ɛnˌsaɪklo ˈpidɪə] *s* enciclopedia
**encyclopedic** o **encyclopaedic** [ɛnˌsaɪklo ˈpidɪk] *adj* enciclopédico
**encyclopedism** o **encyclopaedism** [ɛnˌsaɪklo ˈpidɪzəm] *s* enciclopedismo
**encyclopedist** o **encyclopaedist** [ɛnˌsaɪklo ˈpidɪst] *s* enciclopedista
**encyst** [ɛn ˈsɪst] *va* enquistar; *vn* enquistarse
**encystment** [ɛn ˈsɪstmənt] *s* enquistamiento
**end** [ɛnd] *s* fin, límite; fines (*p.ej., del mes*); extremidad, extremo, cabo, remate; fin, objeto, mira, intento; pieza, fragmento; (football) extremo, ala; **at loose ends** en desorden; desarreglado; **at the end of** a fines de; **from one end to the other** de un extremo a otro, de cabo a cabo; **in the end** al fin; **no end of** (coll.) un sin fin de; **on end** de canto, derecho; uno después de otro; **to come out on the small end of a deal** llevarse lo peor, salir perdiendo; **to come to an end** acabarse, terminarse; **to keep one's end up** no aflojar, hacer lo que a uno le corresponde; **to make an end of** acabar con; **to make both ends meet** proveer a sus necesidades con trabajo o dificultad, pasar con lo que se tiene; **to no end** sin efecto; **to put an end to** poner fin a; **to the end that** a fin de que; **end to end** punta a punta, cabeza contra cabeza ‖ *adj* final, terminal ‖ *va* acabar, terminar ‖ *vn* acabar, terminar; desembocar (*p.ej., una calle*); **to end up** acabar, morir; **to end up as** parar en (*p.ej., ladrón*); **to end up in** ir a parar en
**end-all** [ˈɛndˌɔl] *s* punto final; golpe de gracia
**endanger** [ɛn ˈdendʒər] *va* poner en peligro
**endear** [ɛn ˈdɪr] *va* hacer querer; **to endear oneself** hacerse querer
**endearment** [ɛn ˈdɪrmənt] *s* encariñamiento; caricia, palabra cariñosa
**endeavor** [ɛn ˈdɛvər] *s* esfuerzo, empeño, conato; *vn* esforzarse, empeñarse; **to endeavor to** + *inf* esforzarse por + *inf*
**endemic** [ɛn ˈdɛmɪk] *adj* endémico; *s* endemia
**en déshabillé** [ɑ̃ dezabiˈje] a medio vestir, desaliñado, de trapillo
**ending** [ˈɛndɪŋ] *s* fin, terminación; (gram.) desinencia, terminación
**endive** [ˈɛndaɪv] o [ˈɑndiv] *s* (bot.) escarola, endibia
**endless** [ˈɛndlɪs] *adj* interminable; (mach.) continuo, sin fin
**endless chain** *s* cadena sin fin
**endless screw** *s* tornillo sin fin
**end man** *s* último hombre de una fila de hombres; (theat.) el actor a cada extremo de una fila de cómicos disfrazados de negro
**endmost** [ˈɛndmost] *adj* último, extremo
**endocarditis** [ˌɛndokɑr ˈdaɪtɪs] *s* (path.) endocarditis
**endocardium** [ˌɛndo ˈkɑrdɪəm] *s* (anat.) endocardio
**endocarp** [ˈɛndokɑrp] *s* (bot.) endocarpio
**endocrine** [ˈɛndokraɪn] o [ˈɛndokrɪn] *adj* (physiol.) endocrino; *s* (physiol.) endocrina
**endocrine gland** *s* (anat.) glándula endocrina
**endocrinology** [ˌɛndokraɪ ˈnɑlədʒɪ] o [ˌɛndokrɪ ˈnɑlədʒɪ] *s* endocrinología
**endodermis** [ˌɛndo ˈdʌrmɪs] *s* (bot.) endodermo
**endogamy** [ɛn ˈdɑgəmɪ] *s* endogamia; (biol.) endogamia
**endogenesis** [ˌɛndo ˈdʒɛnɪsɪs] *s* var. de **endogeny**
**endogenous** [ɛn ˈdɑdʒɪnəs] *adj* endógeno
**endogeny** [ɛn ˈdɑdʒɪnɪ] *s* (biol.) endogénesis
**endolymph** [ˈɛndolɪmf] *s* (anat.) endolinfa
**endomysium** [ˌɛndo ˈmɪsɪəm] o [ˌɛndo ˈmɪzɪəm] *s* (anat.) endomisio
**endoparasite** [ˌɛndo ˈpærəsaɪt] *s* (zool.) endoparásito
**endoplasm** [ˈɛndoplæzəm] *s* (biol.) endoplasma
**endorse** [ɛn ˈdɔrs] *va* endosar; apoyar, aprobar
**endorsee** [ˌɛndɔr ˈsi] *s* endosatario
**endorsement** [ɛn ˈdɔrsmənt] *s* endoso; apoyo, aprobación
**endorser** [ɛn ˈdɔrsər] *s* endosante
**endoscope** [ˈɛndoskop] *s* (med.) endoscopio
**endoskeleton** [ˌɛndo ˈskɛlɪtən] *s* (zool.) endoesqueleto
**endosmosis** [ˌɛndɑs ˈmosɪs] *s* (physical chem. & physiol.) endósmosis
**endosperm** [ˈɛndospʌrm] *s* (bot.) endospermo
**endospore** [ˈɛndospor] *s* (bot. & bact.) endospora
**endothecium** [ˌɛndo ˈθiʃɪəm] o [ˌɛndo ˈθisɪəm] *s* (*pl:* **-cia** [ʃɪə] o [sɪə]) (bot.) endotecio
**endothelium** [ˌɛndo ˈθilɪəm] *s* (*pl:* **-lia** [lɪə]) (anat.) endotelio

**endothermic** [ˌɛndo'θʌrmɪk] *adj* (chem.) endotérmico
**endow** [ɛn'daʊ] *va* dotar
**endowment** [ɛn'daʊmənt] *s* dotación; dote, prenda, gracia
**endowment insurance** *s* seguro dotal
**endowment policy** *s* póliza dotal
**end paper** *s* (b.b.) hoja de encuadernador
**end play** *s* (mach.) juego longitudinal
**end product** *s* producto final
**endue** [ɛn'dju] o [ɛn'du] *va* dotar, investir; poner, vestir
**endurance** [ɛn'djʊrəns] o [ɛn'dʊrəns] *s* aguante, paciencia, tolerancia; resistencia, duración; continuación; (sport) endurancia, resistencia, fortaleza
**endurance race** *s* (sport) carrera de resistencia
**endurance record** *s* marca de duración
**endure** [ɛn'djʊr] o [ɛn'dʊr] *va* aguantar, tolerar, endurar; *vn* durar, perdurar; continuar; sufrir con paciencia, sufrir sin rendirse
**enduring** [ɛn'djʊrɪŋ] o [ɛn'dʊrɪŋ] *adj* durable, permanente, resistente; sufrido, paciente
**end view** *s* vista de la extremidad
**endways** ['ɛndˌwez] o **endwise** ['ɛndˌwaɪz] *adv* de punta, de pie; derecho, erguido; longitudinalmente; topando
**Endymion** [ɛn'dɪmɪən] *s* (myth.) Endimión
**enema** ['ɛnɪmə] *s* (med.) enema, ayuda; lavativa, mangueta (*para echar ayudas*)
**enemy** ['ɛnɪmɪ] *s* (*pl:* **-mies**) enemigo; *adj* enemigo
**enemy alien** *s* extranjero enemigo
**enemy number one, the** el enemigo número uno
**energetic** [ˌɛnər'dʒɛtɪk] *adj* enérgico; **energetics** *ssg* energética
**energetically** [ˌɛnər'dʒɛtɪkəlɪ] *adv* enérgicamente
**energize** ['ɛnərdʒaɪz] *va* activar, excitar; *vn* obrar con energía
**energumen** [ˌɛnər'gjumɛn] *s* energúmeno
**energy** ['ɛnərdʒɪ] *s* (*pl:* **-gies**) energía
**enervate** ['ɛnərvet] *adj* enervado; *va* enervar
**enervation** [ˌɛnər'veʃən] *s* enervación
**en famille** [ɑ̃ fɑ'mi] en familia
**enfeeble** [ɛn'fibəl] *va* debilitar
**enfeeblement** [ɛn'fibəlmənt] *s* debilitación, debilidad
**enfeoff** [ɛn'fɛf] o [ɛn'fif] *va* (law) enfeudar (*dar en feudo*); (law) dar feudo a
**enfeoffment** [ɛn'fɛfmənt] o [ɛn'fifmənt] *s* (law) enfeudación
**enfilade** [ˌɛnfɪ'led] *s* enfilamiento; (mil.) enfilada; *va* enfilar; (mil.) enfilar
**enfiled** [ɛn'faɪld] *adj* (her.) enfilado
**enfleurage** [ɑ̃flʌ'rɑʒ] *s* enfloración
**enfold** [ɛn'fold] *va* envolver, arrollar, abrazar, estrechar
**enforce** [ɛn'fors] *va* hacer cumplir, poner en vigor; obtener por fuerza; imponer a la fuerza
**enforcement** [ɛn'forsmənt] *s* ejecución (*de una ley*); compulsión, coacción
**enfranchise** [ɛn'fræntʃaɪz] *va* franquear, manumitir, enfranquecer; conceder el derecho de sufragio a
**enfranchisement** [ɛn'fræntʃɪzmənt] *s* franqueo, manumisión; concesión del sufragio
**eng.** abr. de **engineer, engineering** y **engraving**
**Eng.** abr. de **England** y **English**
**engage** [ɛn'gedʒ] *va* apalabrar; ocupar, emplear; reservar, alquilar; atraer (*p.ej., la atención*); empotrar en; engranar con; trabar batalla con; **to be engaged (to be married)** estar prometido, estar comprometido para casarse; *vn* ocuparse; empeñarse, comprometerse; **to engage in** ocuparse en; empotrar en; engranar con
**engaged** [ɛn'gedʒd] *adj* prometido
**engaged column** *s* (arch.) columna embebida, columna entregada
**engagement** [ɛn'gedʒmənt] *s* ajuste, contrato, empeño; palabra de casamiento, esponsales; noviazgo; obligación; cita; (theat.) ajuste, contrato; (mil.) acción, batalla
**engagement ring** *s* anillo de compromiso, anillo de pedida
**engaging** [ɛn'gedʒɪŋ] *adj* agraciado, insinuante, simpático
**engender** [ɛn'dʒɛndər] *va* engendrar
**engine** ['ɛndʒən] *s* máquina, aparato, instrumento; motor (*p.ej., de un automóvil*); (rail.) máquina, locomotora
**engine block** *s* bloque del motor
**engine driver** *s* maquinista, conductor de locomotora
**engineer** [ˌɛndʒə'nɪr] *s* ingeniero; maquinista (*p.ej., de locomotora*); *va* construir o dirigir como ingeniero; dirigir o llevar a cabo con acierto
**engineering** [ˌɛndʒə'nɪrɪŋ] *s* ingeniería; *adj* de ingeniería, ingenieril
**engine failure** *s* avería del motor
**engine house** *s* cuartel de bomberos; casa de máquinas
**engine lathe** *s* torno de engranaje para roscar
**engineman** ['ɛndʒənmən] *s* (*pl:* **-men**) maquinista, conductor de locomotora
**engine room** *s* sala de máquinas; (naut.) cámara de las máquinas
**engine-room telegraph** ['ɛndʒənˌrum] *s* (naut.) transmisor de órdenes, telégrafo de máquinas
**engine runner** *s* var. de **engine driver**
**enginery** ['ɛndʒənrɪ] *s* maquinaria; ingenios de guerra; maña, ardid
**England** ['ɪŋglənd] *s* Inglaterra
**Englander** ['ɪŋgləndər] *s* natural inglés
**English** ['ɪŋglɪʃ] *adj* inglés; *spl* ingleses; *ssg* inglés (*idioma*); (print.) tipo de 14 puntos; (billiards) efecto; *va* traducir al inglés
**English bond** *s* (mas.) aparejo inglés
**English Channel** *s* canal de la Mancha
**English daisy** *s* (bot.) maya, vellorita, margarita de los prados
**English horn** *s* (mus.) corno o cuerno inglés
**Englishman** ['ɪŋglɪʃmən] *s* (*pl:* **-men**) inglés
**English setter** *s* perdiguero
**English sonnet** *s* soneto inglés (*rimado abab, cdcd, efef, gg*)
**English sparrow** *s* (orn.) gorrión
**English-speaking** ['ɪŋglɪʃ'spikɪŋ] *adj* de habla inglesa
**English walnut** *s* (bot.) nogal; nuez (*fruto*)
**Englishwoman** ['ɪŋglɪʃˌwʊmən] *s* (*pl:* **-women**) inglesa
**engorge** [ɛn'gordʒ] *va* atracar; *vn* atracarse
**engouled** [ɛn'guld] *adj* (her.) engolado
**engraft** [ɛn'græft] o [ɛn'grɑft] *va* (hort. & surg.) injertar; (fig.) implantar
**engrailed** [ɛn'greld] *adj* (her.) angrelado
**engrave** [ɛn'grev] *va* grabar; burilar; imprimir con grabado; (fig.) grabar (*p.ej., en la memoria*)
**engraver** *s* [ɛn'grevər] *s* grabador
**engraving** [ɛn'grevɪŋ] *s* grabado (*acción, arte, lámina y estampa*)
**engross** [ɛn'gros] *va* absorber; copiar o transcribir caligráficamente; poner en limpio, redactar en forma legal
**engrossing** [ɛn'grosɪŋ] *adj* absorbente, acaparador
**engrossment** [ɛn'grosmənt] *s* absorción, ensimismamiento; copia o transcripción caligráfica
**engulf** [ɛn'gʌlf] *va* hundir, inundar
**enhance** [ɛn'hæns] o [ɛn'hɑns] *va* realzar, engrandecer
**enhancement** [ɛn'hænsmənt] o [ɛn'hɑnsmənt] *s* realce, engrandecimiento
**enharmonic** [ˌɛnhɑr'mɑnɪk] *adj* (mus.) enarmónico
**enigma** [ɪ'nɪgmə] *s* enigma
**enigmatic** [ˌɪnɪg'mætɪk] o **enigmatical** [ˌɪnɪg'mætɪkəl] *adj* enigmático
**enjambment** o **enjambement** [ɛn'dʒæmmənt] o [ɛn'dʒæmbmənt] *s* (pros.) encabalgamiento
**enjoin** [ɛn'dʒɔɪn] *va* mandar, encargar, ordenar; **to enjoin from** prohibir, vedar
**enjoy** [ɛn'dʒɔɪ] *va* gozar (*p.ej., buena salud; la conversación*); **to enjoy** + *ger* gozarse en + *inf;* **to enjoy oneself** divertirse
**enjoyable** [ɛn'dʒɔɪəbəl] *adj* deleitable, agradable
**enjoyment** [ɛn'dʒɔɪmənt] *s* goce, placer
**enkindle** [ɛn'kɪndəl] *va* encender
**enlace** [ɛn'les] *va* enlazar, entrelazar; encerrar, rodear
**enlarge** [ɛn'lɑrdʒ] *va* agrandar, abultar, am-

pliar, ensanchar; (phot.) ampliar; *vn* agrandarse, abultarse, ampliarse, ensancharse; explayarse; exagerar; **to enlarge on** o **upon** tratar con más extensión; exagerar
**enlargement** [ɛn'lɑrdʒmənt] *s* agrandamiento, abultamiento, ampliación, ensanchamiento; (phot.) ampliación
**enlarger** [ɛn'lɑrdʒər] *s* ampliador; (phot.) ampliadora
**enlighten** [ɛn'laɪtən] *va* iluminar, ilustrar
**enlightened despotism** *s* despotismo ilustrado
**enlightenment** [ɛn'laɪtənmənt] *s* iluminación, ilustración; **the Enlightenment** el siglo de las luces (*el siglo dieciocho*)
**enlist** [ɛn'lɪst] *va* conseguir el apoyo de, emplear; alistar; *vn* poner empeño; alistarse
**enlisted man** *s* soldado raso
**enlistment** [ɛn'lɪstmənt] *s* consecución, empleo; alistamiento, enganche
**enliven** [ɛn'laɪvən] *va* avivar, vivificar
**en masse** [ɛn 'mæs] en masa
**enmesh** [ɛn'mɛʃ] *va* enredar, entrampar
**enmity** ['ɛnmɪtɪ] *s* (*pl:* **-ties**) enemistad
**ennoble** [ɛn'nobəl] *va* ennoblecer
**ennoblement** [ɛn'nobəlmənt] *s* ennoblecimiento
**ennui** ['ɑnwi] *s* tedio, fastidio, aburrimiento
**enormity** [ɪ'nɔrmɪtɪ] *s* (*pl:* **-ties**) enormidad
**enormous** [ɪ'nɔrməs] *adj* enorme
**enormously** [ɪ'nɔrməslɪ] *adv* enormemente
**enough** [ɪ'nʌf] *adj, adv & s* bastante; *interj* ¡basta!, ¡no más!
**enounce** [ɪ'naʊns] *va* enunciar; pronunciar
**enow** [ɪ'naʊ] o [ɪ'no] *adj, adv & s* (archaic) var. de **enough**
**en passant** [ɑ̃ pɑ'sɑ̃] de paso; (chess) al vuelo, al paso
**enplane** [ɛn'plen] *vn* embarcarse en un avión, salir en avión
**enquire** [ɛn'kwaɪr] *va & vn* var. de **inquire**
**enquiry** [ɛn'kwaɪrɪ] *s* (*pl:* **-ies**) var. de **inquiry**
**enrage** [ɛn'redʒ] *va* enrabiar
**en rapport** [ɑ̃ rɑ'pɔr] de acuerdo
**enrapt** [ɛn'ræpt] *adj* embelesado, transportado
**enrapture** [ɛn'ræptʃər] *va* embelesar, transportar
**enrich** [ɛn'rɪtʃ] *va* enriquecer
**enrichment** [ɛn'rɪtʃmənt] *s* enriquecimiento
**enroll** o **enrol** [ɛn'rol] (*pret & pp:* **-rolled;** *ger:* **-rolling**) *va* alistar, inscribir; redactar en forma legal; poner en limpio; enrollar, envolver; *vn* alistarse, inscribirse
**enrollment** o **enrolment** [ɛn'rolmənt] *s* alistamiento, inscripción
**en route** [ɑ̃ 'rut] o [ɑn 'rut] en camino; **en route to** camino de, con rumbo a
**ensanguine** [ɛn'sæŋgwɪn] *va* ensangrentar
**ensconce** [ɛn'skɑns] *va* esconder, poner en seguro; acomodar, situar
**ensemble** [ɑn'sɑmbəl] *s* conjunto; (mus.) grupo de músicos que tocan o cantan juntos; (mus.) ejecución por un grupo de músicos; (mus.) conjunto (*relación conveniente entre todas las partes*); traje de mujer armonioso
**enshrine** [ɛn'ʃraɪn] *va* encerrar o guardar en un relicario; abrigar, guardar con cariño y respeto
**enshrinement** [ɛn'ʃraɪnmənt] *s* encierro en un relicario; abrigo
**ensiform** ['ɛnsɪfɔrm] *adj* (anat., bot. & zool.) ensiforme
**ensign** ['ɛnsaɪn] *s* bandera, enseña; divisa, insignia; ['ɛnsən] o ['ɛnsaɪn] *s* (nav.) alférez de fragata
**ensigncy** ['ɛnsənsɪ] o ['ɛnsaɪnsɪ] o **ensignship** ['ɛnsənʃɪp] o ['ɛnsaɪnʃɪp] *s* alferazgo
**ensilage** ['ɛnsɪlɪdʒ] *s* ensilaje; *va* ensilar
**enslave** [ɛn'slev] *va* esclavizar
**enslavement** [ɛn'slevmənt] *s* esclavización
**ensnare** [ɛn'snɛr] *va* entrampar
**ensue** [ɛn'su] o [ɛn'sju] *vn* seguirse
**ensuing** [ɛn'suɪŋ] o [ɛn'sjuɪŋ] *adj* siguiente; resultante
**ensure** [ɛn'ʃʊr] *va* asegurar
**entablature** [ɛn'tæblətʃər] *s* (arch.) cornisamento
**entail** [ɛn'tel] *s* (law) vínculo; *va* ocasionar, imponer; (law) vincular
**entailment** [ɛn'telmənt] *s* (law) vinculación
**entangle** [ɛn'tæŋgəl] *va* enmarañar, enredar; *vn* enmarañarse, enredarse
**entanglement** [ɛn'tæŋgəlmənt] *s* enmarañamiento, enredo
**entasia** [ɛn'teʒɪə] *s* (path.) entasia
**entasis** ['ɛntəsɪs] *s* (arch.) éntasis
**entelechy** [ɛn'tɛləkɪ] *s* (*pl:* **-chies**) (philos.) entelequia
**entellus** [ɛn'tɛləs] *s* (zool.) entelo
**entente** [ɑn'tɑnt] *s* (dipl.) entente, trato secreto
**enter** ['ɛntər] *va* entrar en; asentar, registrar; aduanar; matricular (*a un alumno*); ingresar (*p.ej., a un menor en un asilo*); ingresar en, matricularse en; hacer miembro a; hacerse miembro de; emprender; **to enter an order** asentar un pedido; **to enter one's head** metérsele a uno en la cabeza; *vn* entrar; (theat.) entrar en escena, salir; **to enter into** entrar en; participar en; celebrar (*p.ej., un contrato*); **to enter on** o **upon** emprender; tomar posesión de
**enteralgia** [,ɛntə'rældʒɪə] *s* (path.) enteralgia
**enterectomy** [,ɛntə'rɛktəmɪ] *s* (*pl:* **-mies**) (surg.) enterectomía
**enteric** [ɛn'tɛrɪk] *adj* entérico
**enteric fever** *s* (path.) fiebre entérica
**enteritis** [,ɛntə'raɪtɪs] *s* (path.) enteritis
**enterohepatitis** [,ɛntəro,hɛpə'taɪtɪs] *s* (path.) enterohepatitis
**enterology** [,ɛntə'rɑlədʒɪ] *s* enterología
**enterostomy** [,ɛntə'rɑstəmɪ] *s* (*pl:* **-mies**) (surg.) enterostomía
**enterotomy** [,ɛntə'rɑtəmɪ] *s* (*pl:* **-mies**) (surg.) enterotomía
**enterprise** ['ɛntərpraɪz] *s* empresa; espíritu emprendedor
**enterprising** ['ɛntər,praɪzɪŋ] *adj* emprendedor
**entertain** [,ɛntər'ten] *va* entretener, divertir; recibir; festejar; abrigar (*ideas, esperanzas, etc.*); considerar; *vn* recibir; dar tertulias
**entertainer** [,ɛntər'tenər] *s* actor, vocalista, músico, etc. (*p.ej., en un café cantante*); anfitrión; festejador
**entertaining** [,ɛntər'tenɪŋ] *adj* entretenido
**entertainment** [,ɛntər'tenmənt] *s* entretenimiento, diversión; recepción; festejo; espectáculo; abrigo (*de una idea, esperanza, etc.*)
**enthrall** o **enthral** [ɛn'θrɔl] (*pret & pp:* **-thralled;** *ger:* **-thralling**) *va* encantar, dominar; esclavizar, sojuzgar
**enthrallment** o **enthralment** [ɛn'θrɔlmənt] *s* encantamiento, dominación; subyugación
**enthrone** [ɛn'θron] *va* entronizar
**enthronement** [ɛn'θronmənt] *s* entronización
**enthuse** [ɛn'θuz] o [ɛn'θjuz] *va* (coll.) entusiasmar; *vn* (coll.) entusiasmarse
**enthusiasm** [ɛn'θuzɪæzəm] o [ɛn'θjuzɪæzəm] *s* entusiasmo
**enthusiast** [ɛn'θuzɪæst] o [ɛn'θjuzɪæst] *s* entusiasta
**enthusiastic** [ɛn,θuzɪ'æstɪk] o [ɛn,θjuzɪ'æstɪk] *adj* entusiástico
**enthusiastically** [ɛn,θuzɪ'æstɪkəlɪ] o [ɛn,θjuzɪ'æstɪkəlɪ] *adv* entusiásticamente
**enthymeme** ['ɛnθɪmim] *s* (log.) entimema
**entice** [ɛn'taɪs] *va* atraer con halagos; tentar, inducir al mal; **to entice someone into** + *ger* tentar a uno a que + *subj*
**enticement** [ɛn'taɪsmənt] *s* atracción halagüeña; tentación
**entire** [ɛn'taɪr] *adj* entero; (bot.) entero, enterísimo
**entirely** [ɛn'taɪrlɪ] *adv* enteramente; solamente
**entirety** [ɛn'taɪrtɪ] *s* (*pl:* **-ties**) entereza; todo, cosa entera; **in its entirety** en su totalidad
**entitle** [ɛn'taɪtəl] *va* intitular; dar derecho a
**entity** ['ɛntɪtɪ] *s* (*pl:* **-ties**) entidad
**entomb** [ɛn'tum] *va* sepultar
**entombment** [ɛn'tummənt] *s* sepultura
**entomologic** [,ɛntəmə'lɑdʒɪk] o **entomological** [,ɛntəmə'lɑdʒɪkəl] *adj* entomológico
**entomologist** [,ɛntə'mɑlədʒɪst] *s* entomólogo
**entomology** [,ɛntə'mɑlədʒɪ] *s* entomología
**entourage** [,ɑntu'rɑʒ] *s* séquito, cortejo
**entozoan** [,ɛntə'zoən] *s* (zool.) entozoario
**entrails** ['ɛntrelz] o ['ɛntrəlz] *spl* entrañas; (fig.) entrañas (*p.ej., de la tierra*)
**entrain** [ɛn'tren] *va* despachar (*p.ej., tropas*); *vn* embarcar, salir en tren

**entrance** ['ɛntrəns] *s* entrada; ingreso; (theat.) entrada en escena; [ɛn'træns] o [ɛn'trɑns] *va* encantar, embelesar, arrebatar
**entrance examination** *s* examen de ingreso; **to take entrance examinations** examinarse de ingreso
**entrancement** [ɛn'trænsmənt] o [ɛn'trɑnsmənt] *s* encanto, embeleso
**entranceway** ['ɛntrəns,we] *s* entrada; portal, zaguán
**entrancing** [ɛn'trænsɪŋ] o [ɛn'trɑnsɪŋ] *adj* encantador, embelesador
**entrant** ['ɛntrənt] *s* entrante; principiante; (sport) concurrente
**entrap** [ɛn'træp] (*pret & pp:* **-trapped;** *ger:* **-trapping**) *va* entrampar
**entreat** [ɛn'trit] *va* rogar, suplicar
**entreaty** [ɛn'tritɪ] *s* (*pl:* **-ies**) ruego, súplica
**entree** o **entrée** ['ɑntre] *s* entrada, ingreso; (cook.) entrada, principio
**entrench** [ɛn'trɛntʃ] *va* atrincherar; establecer firmemente; *vn* atrincherarse; **to entrench on** o **upon** infringir, violar
**entrenchment** [ɛn'trɛntʃmənt] *s* atrincheramiento
**entrepôt** ['ɑntrəpo] *s* almacén; emporio, centro comercial
**entrepreneur** [,ɑntrəprə'nʌr] *s* empresario
**entresol** ['ɛntərsɑl] o ['ɑntrəsɑl] *s* entresuelo
**entropy** ['ɛntrəpɪ] *s* (*pl:* **-pies**) (thermodynamics) entropía
**entrust** [ɛn'trʌst] *va* confiar; **to entrust to** confiar a; **to entrust someone with something** confiar algo a alguien
**entry** ['ɛntrɪ] *s* (*pl:* **-tries**) entrada; (com.) entrada, partida; entrada, vestíbulo, zaguán; artículo (*cada palabra alfabetizada en un diccionario, etc.*); entrada en la aduana; rival (*en una carrera, concurso, etc.*)
**entwine** [ɛn'twaɪn] *va* entretejer, entrelazar
**entwist** [ɛn'twɪst] *va* retorcer
**enucleate** [ɪ'njuklɪet] o [ɪ'nuklɪet] *va* enuclear
**enucleation** [ɪ,njuklɪ'eʃən] o [ɪ,nuklɪ'eʃən] *s* (surg.) enucleación
**enumerate** [ɪ'njuməret] o [ɪ'numəret] *va* enumerar
**enumeration** [ɪ,njumə'reʃən] o [ɪ,numə'reʃən] *s* enumeración
**enumerative** [ɪ'njumə,retɪv] o [ɪ'numə,retɪv] *adj* enumerativo
**enumerator** [ɪ'njumə,retər] o [ɪ'numə,retər] *s* enumerador
**enunciate** [ɪ'nʌnsɪet] o [ɪ'nʌnʃɪet] *va* enunciar; pronunciar
**enunciation** [ɪ,nʌnsɪ'eʃən] o [ɪ,nʌnʃɪ'eʃən] *s* enunciación; pronunciación
**enuresis** [,ɛnjə'risɪs] *s* (path.) enuresis
**envelop** [ɛn'vɛləp] *s* sobre, cubierta; envoltura; (aer.) envoltura; (bot.) túnica, envoltura; *va* envolver
**envelope** ['ɛnvəlop] o ['ɑnvəlop] *s* sobre, cubierta; envoltura; (aer.) envoltura; (bot.) túnica, envoltura
**envelopment** [ɛn'vɛləpmənt] *s* envolvimiento; cubierta, envoltura
**envenom** [ɛn'vɛnəm] *va* envenenar
**enviable** ['ɛnvɪəbəl] *adj* envidiable
**envious** ['ɛnvɪəs] *adj* envidioso
**environ** [ɛn'vaɪrən] *va* encerrar, rodear, ceñir; **environs** [ɛn'vaɪrənz] o ['ɛnvɪrənz] *spl* alrededores, cercanías, inmediaciones
**environment** [ɛn'vaɪrənmənt] *s* encierro; medio ambiente; alrededores, cercanías, inmediaciones
**environmental** [ɛn,vaɪrən'mɛntəl] *adj* circunvecino, ambiente, ambiental
**envisage** [ɛn'vɪzɪdʒ] *va* encarar, encararse con; representarse, considerar
**envoi** ['ɛnvɔɪ] *s* tornada, despedida (*en una composición poética*)
**envoy** ['ɛnvɔɪ] *s* enviado; tornada, despedida (*en una composición poética*)
**envy** ['ɛnvɪ] *s* (*pl:* **-vies**) envidia; (*pret & pp:* **-vied**) *va* envidiar
**enwomb** [ɛn'wum] *va* sepultar, entrañar
**enwrap** [ɛn'ræp] (*pret & pp:* **-wrapped;** *ger:* **-wrapping**) *va* arropar, envolver
**enwreathe** [ɛn'rið] *va* enguirnaldar
**enzoötic** [,ɛnzo'ɑtɪk] *s* (vet.) enzootia
**enzymatic** [,ɛnzaɪ'mætɪk] o [,ɛnzɪ'mætɪk] *adj* enzímico
**enzyme** ['ɛnzaɪm] o ['ɛnzɪm] *s* (biochem.) enzima
**Eocene** ['iosin] *adj & s* (geol.) eoceno
**Eolian** [i'olɪən] *adj & s* var. de **Aeolian**
**eolithic** [,io'lɪθɪk] *adj* (archeol.) eolítico
**eon** ['iən] o ['iɑn] *s* var. de **aeon**
**Eos** ['iɑs] *s* (myth.) Eos
**eosin** ['iosɪn] *s* (chem.) eosina
**epact** ['ipækt] *s* epacta
**epaulet** o **epaulette** ['ɛpəlɛt] *s* hombrera, charretera
**ependyma** [ɛ'pɛndɪmə] *s* (anat.) epéndimo
**epenthesis** [ɛ'pɛnθɪsɪs] *s* (*pl:* **-ses** [siz]) (gram.) epéntesis
**epenthetic** [,ɛpɛn'θɛtɪk] *adj* epentético
**epergne** [ɪ'pʌrn] o [e'pɛrn] *s* centro de mesa, ramillete
**Eph.** abr. de **Ephesians**
**ephedrine** [ɪ'fɛdrɪn] o ['ɛfɪdrin] *s* (pharm.) efedrina
**ephemeral** [ɪ'fɛmərəl] *adj* efímero
**ephemerid** [ɪ'fɛmərɪd] *s* (ent.) efemérido
**ephemeris** [ɪ'fɛmərɪs] *s* (*pl:* **ephemerides** [,ɛfɪ'mɛrɪdiz]) efemérides; efemérides astronómicas
**Ephesian** [ɪ'fiʒən] *adj & s* efesino o efesio; **Ephesians** *spl* (Bib.) Epístola de San Pablo a los Efesios
**Ephesus** ['ɛfɪsəs] *s* Éfeso
**Ephraim** ['ifrɪəm] *s* (Bib.) Efraín
**epic** ['ɛpɪk] *adj* épico; *s* epopeya; (fig.) epopeya
**epical** ['ɛpɪkəl] *adj* épico
**epicalyx** [,ɛpɪ'kelɪks] o [,ɛpɪ'kælɪks] *s* (bot.) epicáliz, calículo
**epicarp** ['ɛpɪkɑrp] *s* (bot.) epicarpio
**epicedium** [,ɛpɪ'sidɪəm] *s* (*pl:* **-a** [ə]) epicedio
**epicene** ['ɛpɪsin] *adj* (gram.) epiceno
**epicenter** ['ɛpɪ,sɛntər] *s* epicentro
**epicotyl** [,ɛpɪ'kɑtɪl] *s* (bot.) epicotilo
**Epictetus** [,ɛpɪk'titəs] *s* Epicteto
**epicure** ['ɛpɪkjʊr] *s* epicúreo
**Epicurean** [,ɛpɪkjʊ'riən] *adj & s* epicúreo; (*l.c.*) *adj & s* epicúreo
**Epicureanism** [,ɛpɪkjʊ'riənɪzəm] *s* epicureísmo
**Epicurus** [,ɛpɪ'kjʊrəs] *s* Epicuro
**epicycle** ['ɛpɪ,saɪkəl] *s* (astr. & geom.) epiciclo
**epicyclic** [,ɛpɪ'saɪklɪk] o [,ɛpɪ'sɪklɪk] *adj* epicíclico
**epicycloid** [,ɛpɪ'saɪklɔɪd] *s* (geom.) epicicloide
**epidemic** [,ɛpɪ'dɛmɪk] *adj* epidémico; *s* epidemia
**epidemical** [,ɛpɪ'dɛmɪkəl] *adj* epidémico
**epidemicity** [,ɛpɪdɪ'mɪsɪtɪ] *s* epidemicidad
**epidemiologist** [,ɛpɪ,dimɪ'ɑlədʒɪst] *s* epidemiólogo
**epidemiology** [,ɛpɪ,dimɪ'ɑlədʒɪ] *s* epidemiología
**epidermal** [,ɛpɪ'dʌrməl] *adj* epidérmico
**epidermis** [,ɛpɪ'dʌrmɪs] *s* (anat.) epidermis
**epidote** ['ɛpɪdot] *s* (mineral.) epidota
**epigastric** [,ɛpɪ'gæstrɪk] *adj* epigástrico
**epigastrium** [,ɛpɪ'gæstrɪəm] *s* (anat. & zool.) epigastrio
**epigene** ['ɛpɪdʒin] *adj* (geol.) epigénico
**epiglottis** [,ɛpɪ'glɑtɪs] *s* (anat.) epiglotis
**epigram** ['ɛpɪgræm] *s* epigrama
**epigrammatic** [,ɛpɪgrə'mætɪk] *adj* epigramático
**epigrammatically** [,ɛpɪgrə'mætɪkəlɪ] *adv* epigramáticamente
**epigraph** ['ɛpɪgræf] o ['ɛpɪgrɑf] *s* epígrafe
**epigrapher** [ɪ'pɪgrəfər] *s* epigrafista
**epigraphic** [,ɛpɪ'græfɪk] *adj* epigráfico
**epigraphy** [ɪ'pɪgrəfɪ] *s* epigrafía
**epilepsy** ['ɛpɪ,lɛpsɪ] *s* (path.) epilepsia
**epileptic** [,ɛpɪ'lɛptɪk] *adj & s* epiléptico
**epilog** o **epilogue** ['ɛpɪlɔg] o ['ɛpɪlɑg] *s* epílogo
**Epiphany** [ɪ'pɪfənɪ] *s* (eccl.) Epifanía; (*l.c.*) *s* epifanía (*aparición*)
**epiphonema** [,ɛpɪfo'nimə] *s* (rhet.) epifonema
**epiphora** [ɪ'pɪfərə] *s* (path.) epifora
**epiphysis** [ɪ'pɪfɪsɪs] *s* (*pl:* **-ses** [siz]) (anat.) epífisis
**epiphyte** ['ɛpɪfaɪt] *s* (bot.) epífita
**epiphytic** [,ɛpɪ'fɪtɪk] *adj* epífito, epifítico
**Epirus** [ɪ'paɪrəs] *s* el Epiro

**Epis.** abr. de **Episcopal, Episcopalians** y **Epistle**
**Episc.** abr. de **Episcopal**
**episcopacy** [ɪˈpɪskəpəsɪ] *s* (*pl:* **-cies**) episcopado
**episcopal** [ɪˈpɪskəpəl] *adj* episcopal; (*cap.*) *adj* episcopal
**Episcopalian** [ɪˌpɪskəˈpeljən] *adj & s* episcopalista
**Episcopalianism** [ɪˌpɪskəˈpeljənɪzəm] *s* episcopalismo
**episcopalism** [ɪˈpɪskəpəlɪzəm] *s* (eccl.) episcopalismo
**episcopate** [ɪˈpɪskəpet] o [ɪˈpɪskəpɪt] *s* episcopado
**episode** [ˈɛpɪsod] *s* episodio
**episodic** [ˌɛpɪˈsɑdɪk] o **episodical** [ˌɛpɪˈsɑdɪkəl] *adj* episódico
**epispastic** [ˌɛpɪˈspæstɪk] *adj & s* (med.) epispástico
**epistaxis** [ˌɛpɪˈstæksɪs] *s* (path.) epistaxis
**epistemological** [ɪˌpɪstɪməˈlɑdʒɪkəl] *adj* epistemológico
**epistemology** [ɪˌpɪstɪˈmɑlədʒɪ] *s* epistemología
**epistle** [ɪˈpɪsəl] *s* epístola; (*cap.*) *s* (eccl.) epístola
**Epistle side** *s* (eccl.) lado de la epístola
**epistolary** [ɪˈpɪstəˌlɛrɪ] *adj* epistolar; *s* (eccl.) epistolario
**epistyle** [ˈɛpɪstaɪl] *s* (arch.) epistilo
**epitaph** [ˈɛpɪtæf] o [ˈɛpɪtɑf] *s* epitafio
**epithalamium** [ˌɛpɪθəˈlemɪəm] *s* (*pl:* **-miums** o **-mia** [mɪə]) epitalamio
**epithelial** [ˌɛpɪˈθilɪəl] *adj* epitelial
**epithelioma** [ˌɛpɪˌθilɪˈomə] *s* (*pl:* **-mata** [mətə] o **-mas**) (path.) epitelioma
**epithelium** [ˌɛpɪˈθilɪəm] *s* (*pl:* **-lia** [lɪə] o **-liums**) (anat.) epitelio
**epithem** [ˈɛpɪθɛm] *s* (med.) epítema
**epithet** [ˈɛpɪθɛt] *s* epíteto
**epitome** [ɪˈpɪtəmɪ] *s* epítome
**epitomize** [ɪˈpɪtəmaɪz] *va* epitomar
**epizoötic** [ˌɛpɪzoˈɑtɪk] *adj* epizoótico; *s* epizootia
**epoch** [ˈɛpək] o [ˈipɑk] *s* época; (astr. & geol.) época
**epochal** [ˈɛpəkəl] *adj* trascendental, memorable
**epoch-making** [ˈɛpəkˌmekɪŋ] o [ˈipɑkˌmekɪŋ] *adj* que hace época; trascendental, memorable
**epode** [ˈɛpod] *s* epoda o epodo
**eponymous** [ɛˈpɑnɪməs] *adj* epónimo
**epsilon** [ˈɛpsɪlɑn] *s* épsilon
**epsomite** [ˈɛpsəmaɪt] *s* (mineral.) epsomita
**Epsom salts** [ˈɛpsəm] *spl* sal de Epsom, sal de la Higuera
**eq.** abr. de **equal** y **equivalent**
**equability** [ˌɛkwəˈbɪlɪtɪ] o [ˌikwəˈbɪlɪtɪ] *s* igualdad, uniformidad; constancia, tranquilidad
**equable** [ˈɛkwəbəl] o [ˈikwəbəl] *adj* igual, uniforme; constante, tranquilo
**equal** [ˈikwəl] *adj* igual; **equal to** suficiente para, bastante para; a la altura de, al nivel de, con fuerzas para; *s* igual; (*pret & pp:* **equaled** o **equalled;** *ger:* **equaling** *o* **equalling**) *va* igualar (*poner igual*); igualarse a o con (*ser igual a; ponerse al nivel de*)
**equalitarian** [ɪˌkwɑlɪˈtɛrɪən] *adj & s* igualitario
**equality** [ɪˈkwɑlɪtɪ] *s* (*pl:* **-ties**) igualdad
**equalization** [ˌikwəlɪˈzeʃən] *s* igualamiento, igualación
**equalize** [ˈikwəlaɪz] *va* igualar
**equally** [ˈikwəlɪ] *adv* igualmente
**equanimity** [ˌikwəˈnɪmɪtɪ] o [ˌɛkwəˈnɪmɪtɪ] *s* ecuanimidad
**equate** [iˈkwet] *va* igualar; (math.) igualar
**equation** [iˈkweʒən] o [iˈkweʃən] *s* (math., astr. & chem.) ecuación
**equator** [iˈkwetər] *s* ecuador
**equatorial** [ˌikwəˈtorɪəl] *adj* ecuatorial; *s* (astr.) ecuatorial (*instrumento*)
**equerry** [ˈɛkwərɪ] o [ɪˈkwɛrɪ] *s* (*pl:* **-ries**) caballerizo; (Brit.) caballerizo del rey
**equestrian** [ɪˈkwɛstrɪən] *adj* ecuestre; *s* jinete
**equestrienne** [ɪˌkwɛstrɪˈɛn] *s* amazona
**equiangular** [ˌikwɪˈæŋgjələr] *adj* (geom.) equiángulo
**equid** [ˈɛkwɪd] *s* (zool.) équido
**equidistance** [ˌikwɪˈdɪstəns] *s* equidistancia
**equidistant** [ˌikwɪˈdɪstənt] *adj* equidistante
**equilateral** [ˌikwɪˈlætərəl] *adj* equilátero
**equilibrant** [ɪˈkwɪlɪbrənt] *s* (phys.) fuerza equilibrante
**equilibrate** [ˌikwɪˈlaɪbret] o [ɪˈkwɪlɪbret] *va* equilibrar
**equilibration** [ˌikwɪlaɪˈbreʃən] o [ɪˌkwɪlɪˈbreʃən] *s* equilibración
**equilibrist** [ɪˈkwɪlɪbrɪst] *s* equilibrista
**equilibrium** [ˌikwɪˈlɪbrɪəm] *s* equilibrio
**equine** [ˈikwaɪn] *adj & s* equino
**equinoctial** [ˌikwɪˈnɑkʃəl] *adj* equinoccial; *s* equinoccial, línea equinoccial; tempestad equinoccial
**equinoctial line** *s* línea equinoccial
**equinoctial point** *s* punto equinoccial
**equinox** [ˈikwɪnɑks] *s* (astr.) equinoccio
**equip** [ɪˈkwɪp] (*pret & pp:* **equipped;** *ger:* **equipping**) *va* equipar
**equipage** [ˈɛkwɪpɪdʒ] *s* equipaje, equipo; carruaje
**equipment** [ɪˈkwɪpmənt] *s* equipo; material, maquinaria, avíos; aptitud, habilitación
**equipment bond** *s* (rail.) bono respaldado por material rodante
**equipment trust** *s* (rail.) escritura fiduciaria sobre material rodante
**equipoise** [ˈikwɪpɔɪz] o [ˈɛkwɪpɔɪz] *s* equilibrio; contrapeso; *va* equilibrar; contrapesar
**equipotential** [ˌikwɪpəˈtɛnʃəl] *adj* (phys.) equipotencial
**equisetaceous** [ˌɛkwɪsɪˈteʃəs] *adj* (bot.) equisetáceo
**equisetum** [ˌɛkwɪˈsitəm] *s* (*pl:* **-tums** o **-ta** [tə]) (bot.) equiseto
**equitable** [ˈɛkwɪtəbəl] *adj* equitativo
**equitation** [ˌɛkwɪˈteʃən] *s* equitación
**equity** [ˈɛkwɪtɪ] *s* (*pl:* **-ties**) equidad; (law) equidad; (coll.) diferencia entre el valor de una propiedad y la hipoteca que la grava
**equity of redemption** *s* (law) derecho de rescate
**equivalence** [ɪˈkwɪvələns] *s* equivalencia
**equivalent** [ɪˈkwɪvələnt] *adj & s* equivalente
**equivocal** [ɪˈkwɪvəkəl] *adj* equívoco
**equivocate** [ɪˈkwɪvəket] *vn* mentir, usar palabras o frases equívocas para engañar
**equivocation** [ɪˌkwɪvəˈkeʃən] *s* equívoco
**equivocator** [ɪˈkwɪvəˌketər] *s* equivoquista
**era** [ˈɪrə] o [ˈirə] *s* era; (geol.) era
**eradicable** [ɪˈrædɪkəbəl] *adj* erradicable
**eradicate** [ɪˈrædɪket] *va* erradicar
**eradication** [ɪˌrædɪˈkeʃən] *s* erradicación
**eradicator** [ɪˈrædɪˌketər] *s* arrancarraíces; líquido para quitar grasa, aceite, tinta, etc.; líquido borratintas
**erase** [ɪˈres] *va* borrar
**erase head** *s* cabeza de borrado (*del magnetófono*)
**eraser** [ɪˈresər] *s* borrador, goma de borrar
**Erasmian** [ɪˈræzmɪən] *adj & s* erasmiano
**Erasmus** [ɪˈræzməs] *s* Erasmo
**erasure** [ɪˈreʃər] o [ɪˈreʒər] *s* borradura
**Erato** [ˈɛrəto] *s* (myth.) Erato
**erbium** [ˈʌrbɪəm] *s* (chem.) erbio
**ere** [ɛr] *prep* antes de; *conj* antes que; más bien que
**Erebus** [ˈɛrɪbəs] *s* (myth.) Erebo (*infierno*)
**erect** [ɪˈrɛkt] *adj* erguido, derecho; erizado; *va* erigir; armar, montar, instalar
**erectile** [ɪˈrɛktɪl] *adj* eréctil
**erectility** [ɪˌrɛkˈtɪlɪtɪ] o [ˌirɛkˈtɪlɪtɪ] *s* erectilidad
**erection** [ɪˈrɛkʃən] *s* erección; (physiol.) erección
**erector** [ɪˈrɛktər] *s* erector
**Erector set** *s* (trademark) mecano
**erelong** [ˌɛrˈlɔŋ] o [ˌɛrˈlɑŋ] *adv* en breve, dentro de poco
**eremite** [ˈɛrɪmaɪt] *s* eremita, ermitaño
**erepsin** [ɪˈrɛpsɪn] *s* (biochem.) erepsina
**erethism** [ˈɛrɪθɪzəm] *s* (physiol.) eretismo
**erg** [ʌrg] *s* (phys.) ergio
**ergo** [ˈʌrgo] *adv & conj* (Lat.) pues, por tanto, por consiguiente
**ergosterol** [ʌrˈgɑstərol] *s* (pharm.) ergosterol
**ergot** [ˈʌrgət] o [ˈʌrgɑt] *s* (bot. & pharm.) cornezuelo; (plant path.) ergotismo
**ergotin** [ˈʌrgətɪn] *s* (pharm.) ergotina

**ergotism** [ˈʌrgətɪzəm] *s* ergotismo (*sofistería*); (path.) ergotismo
**Eric** [ˈɛrɪk] *s* Erico
**ericaceous** [ˌɛrɪˈkeʃəs] *adj* (bot.) ericáceo
**Erin** [ˈɛrɪn] o [ˈɪrɪn] *s* (poet.) la Verde Erín
**Erinys** [ɪˈrɪnɪs] o [ɪˈraɪnɪs] *s* (*pl:* **Erinyes** [ɪˈrɪnɪiz]) (myth.) Erinia
**eristic** [ɛˈrɪstɪk] *adj* erístico; *s* erística (*arte de disputar*)
**Eritrea** [ˌɛrɪˈtriə] *s* Eritrea
**Eritrean** [ˌɛrɪˈtriən] *adj & s* eritreo
**erlking** [ˈʌrlˌkɪŋ] *s* (myth.) rey de los duendes
**ermine** [ˈʌrmɪn] *s* (zool. & her.) armiño; (fig.) toga, judicatura; **ermines** *s* (her.) contraarmiños; *adj* armiñado
**ermined** [ˈʌrmɪnd] *adj* armiñado
**erne** [ʌrn] *s* (orn.) águila marina
**Ernest** [ˈʌrnɪst] *s* Ernesto
**erode** [ɪˈrod] *va* erosionar; *vn* erosionarse
**Eros** [ˈɪrɑs], [ˈirɑs] o [ˈɛrɑs] *s* (myth.) Eros
**erosion** [ɪˈroʒən] *s* erosión; (geol.) erosión
**erosive** [ɪˈrosɪv] *adj* erosivo
**erotic** [ɪˈrɑtɪk] *adj* erótico; erotómano; *s* persona erótica, erotómano; poema erótico
**erotism** [ˈɛrətɪzəm] *s* erotismo
**erotomania** [ɪˌrotəˈmenɪə] o [ɪˌrɑtəˈmenɪə] *s* (path.) erotomanía
**err** [ʌr] *vn* marrar
**errand** [ˈɛrənd] *s* recado, mandado, comisión; **to run an errand** hacer un mandado; **to send on an errand** enviar a un recado
**errand boy** *s* mandadero, recadero
**errant** [ˈɛrənt] *adj* errante, andante; erróneo, equivocado
**errantry** [ˈɛrəntrɪ] *s* (*pl:* **-ries**) caballería andante
**erratic** [ɪˈrætɪk] *adj* irregular, inconstante; excéntrico; (geol.) errático
**erratically** [ɪˈrætɪkəlɪ] *adv* irregularmente, inconstantemente; excéntricamente
**erratum** [ɪˈretəm] o [ɪˈrɑtəm] *s* (*pl:* **-ta** [tə]) errata
**erroneous** [ɪˈronɪəs] *adj* erróneo
**error** [ˈɛrər] *s* error
**ersatz** [ɛrˈzɑts] *adj & s* sucedáneo
**Erse** [ʌrs] *adj & s* erso
**erstwhile** [ˈʌrstˌhwaɪl] *adj* antiguo, de otro tiempo; *adv* (archaic) antiguamente
**eruct** [ɪˈrʌkt] o **eructate** [ɪˈrʌktet] *va* arrojar, echar de sí, vomitar; *vn* eructar
**eructation** [ɪˌrʌkˈteʃən] o [ˌɛrəkˈteʃən] *s* eructo; vómito
**erudite** [ˈɛrʊdaɪt] o [ˈɛrjʊdaɪt] *adj* erudito
**erudition** [ˌɛrʊˈdɪʃən] o [ˌɛrjʊˈdɪʃən] *s* erudición
**erupt** [ɪˈrʌpt] *va* arrojar (*llamas, lava, etc.*); *vn* hacer erupción (*p.ej., la piel, los dientes de un niño*); erumpir (*un volcán*)
**eruption** [ɪˈrʌpʃən] *s* erupción; (path. & dent.) erupción
**eruptive** [ɪˈrʌptɪv] *adj* eruptivo
**Erymanthian boar** [ˌɛrɪˈmænθɪən] *s* (myth.) jabalí de Erimanto
**erysipelas** [ˌɛrɪˈsɪpələs] o [ˌɪrɪˈsɪpələs] *s* (path.) erisipela
**erysipeloid** [ˌɛrɪˈsɪpəlɔɪd] o [ˌɪrɪˈsɪpəlɔɪd] *s* (path.) erisipeloide
**erythema** [ˌɛrɪˈθimə] *s* (path.) eritema
**erythrin** [ɪˈrɪθrɪn] *s* (chem.) eritrina
**erythrite** [ɪˈrɪθraɪt] *s* (mineral.) eritrita
**erythroblast** [ɪˈrɪθroblæst] *s* (anat.) eritroblasto
**erythrocyte** [ɪˈrɪθrosaɪt] *s* (anat.) eritrocito
**erythroxylaceous** [ˌɛrɪˌθrɑksɪˈleʃəs] *adj* (bot.) eritroxiláceo
**Esau** [ˈisɔ] *s* (Bib.) Esaú
**escadrille** [ˌɛskəˈdrɪl] *s* (nav. & aer.) escuadrilla
**escalade** [ˌɛskəˈled] *s* escalada; *va* escalar
**escalate** [ˈɛskəlet] *va* escalarse
**escalator** [ˈɛskəˌletər] *s* (trademark) escalera mecánica, escalera móvil, escalera rodante
**escalator clause** *s* cláusula contractual de revisión de jornales por variación del costo de la vida
**escallop** [ɛsˈkɑləp] o [ɛsˈkæləp] *s* (zool.) concha de peregrino; venera (*de los peregrinos*); (sew.) festón; *va* hornear a la crema y con migajas de pan; cocer (*p.ej., ostras*) en su concha
**escapade** [ˌɛskəˈped] o [ˈɛskəped] *s* escapada; travesura, calaverada, aventura atolondrada
**escape** [ɛsˈkep] *s* escape, escapatoria; (fig.) escapatoria (*de atenciones, deberes, etc.*); *va* evitar, eludir; escapársele a uno, p.ej., **nothing escapes him** no se le escapa nada; olvidársele a uno, p.ej., **his name escapes me** se me olvida su nombre; salírsele a uno, p.ej., **a cry escaped his lips** se le salió un grito; escapar a (*p.ej., la muerte*); *vn* escapar o escaparse; **to escape from** escaparse a (*una persona*); escaparse de (*p.ej., la cárcel*)
**escape artist** *s* ilusionista que sabe desprenderse de toda suerte de ataduras y trabas
**escapee** [ˌɛskəˈpi] *s* evadido
**escape hatch** *s* escotillón de escape
**escape literature** *s* literatura de escape
**escapement** [ɛsˈkepmənt] *s* escape
**escapement wheel** *s* (horol.) rueda de escape
**escape velocity** *s* velocidad de escape (*de un satélite*)
**escape wheel** *s* var. de **escapement wheel**
**escapism** [ɛsˈkepɪzəm] *s* escapismo
**escapist** [ɛsˈkepɪst] *adj & s* escapista
**escarole** [ˈɛskərol] *s* (bot.) escarola
**escarp** [ɛsˈkɑrp] *s* escarpa; (fort.) escarpa; *va* (fort.) escarpar
**escarpment** [ɛsˈkɑrpmənt] *s* escarpa, escarpadura; (fort.) escarpa
**escharotic** [ˌɛskəˈrɑtɪk] *adj & s* (med.) escarótico
**eschatological** [ˌɛskətəˈlɑdʒɪkəl] *adj* escatológico
**eschatology** [ˌɛskəˈtɑlədʒɪ] *s* (theol.) escatología
**escheat** [ɛsˈtʃit] *s* (law) reversión al estado o al señor de bienes del que muere sin testar; (law) bienes del que muere sin testar que revierten al estado o al señor; *va* (law) transferir al estado o al señor; *vn* (law) revertir al estado o al señor (*los bienes del que muere sin testar*)
**eschew** [ɛsˈtʃu] *va* evitar
**escort** [ˈɛskɔrt] *s* escolta; (aer. & nav.) escolta; [ɛsˈkɔrt] *va* escoltar
**escort carrier** *s* (nav.) portaaviones de escolta
**escort fighter** *s* (aer.) caza de escolta
**escritoire** [ˌɛskrɪˈtwɑr] *s* escritorio
**escrow** [ɛsˈkro] o [ˈɛskro] *s* (law) plica, documento que se pone en manos de una tercera persona para entregarlo al donatario y que no tiene valor ni efecto hasta cumplidas ciertas condiciones; **in escrow** en custodia de una tercera persona
**esculent** [ˈɛskjələnt] *adj & s* comestible
**escutcheon** [ɛsˈkʌtʃən] *s* escudo de armas; escudo, escudete (*planchuela de metal delante de la cerradura*)
**Esd.** abr. de **Esdras**
**Esdras** [ˈɛzdrəs] *s* (Bib.) Esdras; (Bib.) libro de Esdras
**Eskimo** [ˈɛskɪmo] *s* (*pl:* **-mos** o **-mo**) esquimal
**Eskimoan** [ˌɛskɪˈmoən] *adj* esquimal
**Eskimo dog** *s* perro de los esquimales
**esophagus** [iˈsɑfəgəs] *s* (*pl:* **-gi** [dʒaɪ]) (anat.) esófago
**esoteric** [ˌɛsoˈtɛrɪk] *adj* esotérico
**esotropia** [ˌɛsoˈtropɪə] *s* (path.) esotropia
**esp.** abr. de **especially**
**espagnolette** [ˌɛsˌpɑˌnjoˈlɛt] *s* falleba
**espalier** [ɛsˈpæljər] *s* espaldar, espalera; planta extendida sobre el espaldar; *va* extender sobre el espaldar; proveer de espaldar
**esparto** [ɛsˈpɑrto] o **esparto grass** *s* (bot.) esparto
**espec.** abr. de **especially**
**especial** [ɛsˈpɛʃəl] *adj* especial
**especially** [ɛsˈpɛʃəlɪ] *adv* especialmente
**Esperantist** [ˌɛspəˈrɑntɪst] o [ˌɛspəˈræntɪst] *adj & s* esperantista
**Esperanto** [ˌɛspəˈrɑnto] o [ˌɛspəˈrænto] *s* esperanto
**espial** [ɛsˈpaɪəl] *s* espionaje (*acción de espiar*); observación
**espionage** [ˈɛspɪənɪdʒ] o [ˌɛspɪəˈnɑʒ] *s* espionaje
**esplanade** [ˌɛspləˈned] o [ˌɛspləˈnɑd] *s* explanada; (fort.) explanada
**espousal** [ɛsˈpaʊzəl] *s* desposorios; adhesión (*p.ej., a un dictamen*); **espousals** *spl* desposorios
**espouse** [ɛsˈpaʊz] *va* casarse con; abogar por, adherirse a (*p.ej., un dictamen*)

**esprit de corps** [ɛs'pri də 'kɔr] *s* espíritu de cuerpo, compañerismo
**espy** [ɛs'paɪ] (*pret & pp:* **-pied**) *va* divisar
**Esq.** abr. de **Esquire**
**Esquimau** ['ɛskɪmo] *s* (*pl:* **-maux** [mo] o [moz]) var. de **Eskimo**
**esquire** [ɛs'kwaɪr] *s* escudero (*paje que llevaba el escudo del caballero*); (Brit.) terrateniente de antigua heredad; (Brit.) hombre de la clase inferior a la de los caballeros; acompañante (*de una señora*); (*cap.*) *s* título de honor que se escribe después del apellido y que corresponde a Mr.
**-ess** *suffix s* -esa, p.ej., **abbess** abadesa; **countess** condesa; -isa, p.ej., **poetess** poetisa; **priestess** sacerdotisa
**essay** ['ɛse] *s* (lit.) ensayo; ['ɛse] o [ɛ'se] *s* conato, esfuerzo, ensayo; [ɛ'se] *va* ensayar (*especialmente metales, minerales*); intentar; *vn* esforzarse
**essayist** ['ɛseɪst] *s* ensayista
**essence** ['ɛsəns] *s* esencia; (chem.) esencia; **in essence** en esencia
**essential** [ɛ'sɛnʃəl] *adj & s* esencial
**essentially** [ɛ'sɛnʃəlɪ] *adv* esencialmente
**essential oil** *s* (chem.) aceite esencial
**est.** abr. de **established, estate, estimated** y **estuary**
**E.S.T.** abr. de **Eastern Standard Time**
**estab.** abr. de **established**
**establish** [ɛs'tæblɪʃ] *va* establecer
**established church** *s* iglesia oficial
**establishment** [ɛs'tæblɪʃmənt] *s* establecimiento
**estate** [ɛs'tet] *s* heredad, finca, hacienda; bienes, propiedad; bienes relictos, herencia; estado, condición; **the fourth estate** el cuarto poder (*la prensa, el periodismo*); **the three estates** los tres estados (*la nobleza, el clero y el estado llano*)
**Estates-General** [ɛs'tets'dʒɛnərəl] *spl* var. de **States-General**
**esteem** [ɛs'tim] *s* estima; *va* estimar
**ester** ['ɛstər] *s* (chem.) éster
**Esth.** abr. de **Esther**
**Esther** ['ɛstər] *s* Ester
**esthete** ['ɛsθit] *s* var. de **aesthete**
**esthetic** [ɛs'θɛtɪk] *adj* var. de **aesthetic; esthetics** *ssg* var. de **aesthetics**
**esthetically** [ɛs'θɛtɪkəlɪ] *adv* var. de **aesthetically**
**esthetician** [,ɛsθɪ'tɪʃən] *s* var. de **aesthetician**
**Esthonia** [ɛs'θonɪə] *s* var. de **Estonia**
**estimable** ['ɛstɪməbəl] *adj* estimable
**estimate** ['ɛstɪmɪt] o ['ɛstɪmet] *s* estimación; presupuesto (*p.ej., del coste de una obra*); proyecto de presupuesto; ['ɛstɪmet] *va* estimar; presuponer
**estimation** [,ɛstɪ'meʃən] *s* estimación
**estival** ['ɛstɪvəl] o [ɛs'taɪvəl] *adj* var. de **aestival**
**estivate** ['ɛstɪvet] *vn* var. de **aestivate**
**estivation** [,ɛstɪ'veʃən] *s* var. de **aestivation**
**Estonia** [ɛs'tonɪə] *s* Estonia
**Estonian** [ɛs'tonɪən] *adj & s* estonio
**estop** [ɛs'tɑp] (*pret & pp:* **-topped;** *ger:* **-topping**) *va* obstruir; impedir; (law) impedir (*a uno*) que declare en una acción lo que sea contrario a actas o manifestaciones
**estoppel** [ɛs'tɑpəl] *s* impedimento; (law) imposibilidad en que se coloca uno de declarar lo que sea contrario a actas o manifestaciones anteriores
**estrange** [ɛs'trendʒ] *va* apartar; enajenar, enemistar
**estrangement** [ɛs'trendʒmənt] *s* enajenamiento, extrañeza (*p.ej., entre amigos*)
**estray** [ɛs'tre] *s* (law) animal doméstico descarriado
**estrogen** ['ɛstrədʒən] *s* (biochem.) estrógeno
**estrone** ['ɛstron] *s* (biochem.) estrona
**estuary** ['ɛstʃu,ɛrɪ] *s* (*pl:* **-ies**) estuario; ría (*valle bajo que inunda el mar*)
**et al.** abr. de **et alii** (Lat.) **and others** y de **et alibi** (Lat.) **and elsewhere**
**etc.** abr. de **et cetera** (Lat.) **and others** y **and so forth**
**etceteras** [ɛt'sɛtərəz] *spl* adiciones, apéndices
**etch** [ɛtʃ] *va & vn* grabar al agua fuerte
**etcher** ['ɛtʃər] *s* aguafortista
**etching** ['ɛtʃɪŋ] *s* aguafuerte
**eternal** [ɪ'tʌrnəl] *adj* eterno, eternal
**Eternal City** *s* Ciudad Eterna (*Roma*)
**eternal feminine, the** (lit.) el eterno femenino
**eternal recurrence** *s* (philos.) retorno eterno
**eternity** [ɪ'tʌrnɪtɪ] *s* (*pl:* **-ties**) eternidad
**eternize** [ɪ'tʌrnaɪz] *va* eternizar
**etesian** [ɪ'tiʒən] o [ɪ'tizɪən] *adj & s* etesio
**ethane** ['ɛθen] *s* (chem.) etano
**Ethelred** ['ɛθəlrɛd] *s* Etelredo
**ether** ['iθər] *s* éter (*los espacios celestes*); (phys.) éter (*materia hipotética*); (chem.) éter ($R_2O$)
**ethereal** [ɪ'θɪrɪəl] *adj* etéreo; (phys. & chem.) etéreo
**etherealize** [ɪ'θɪrɪəlaɪz] *va* espiritualizar
**etherification** [ɪ,θɛrɪfɪ'keʃən] *s* (chem.) eterificación
**etherify** [ɪ'θɛrɪfaɪ] (*pret & pp:* **-fied**) *va* (chem.) eterificar
**etherization** [,iθərɪ'zeʃən] *s* (med.) eterización
**etherize** ['iθəraɪz] *va* (med.) eterizar; eterificar
**ethic** ['ɛθɪk] *adj* ético; **ethics** *ssg* ética
**ethical** ['ɛθɪkəl] *adj* ético
**ethically** ['ɛθɪkəlɪ] *adv* éticamente
**Ethiop** ['iθɪɑp] *adj & s* etíope
**Ethiopia** [,iθɪ'opɪə] *s* Etiopía
**Ethiopian** [,iθɪ'opɪən] *adj & s* etíope; (coll.) etíope (*de la raza negra*)
**Ethiopic** [,iθɪ'ɑpɪk] o [,iθɪ'opɪk] *adj* etiópico; *s* lengua etiópica
**ethmoid** ['ɛθmɔɪd] *adj & s* (anat.) etmoides
**ethnic** ['ɛθnɪk] o **ethnical** ['ɛθnɪkəl] *adj* étnico
**ethnographer** [ɛθ'nɑgrəfər] *s* etnógrafo
**ethnographic** [,ɛθnə'græfɪk] o **ethnographical** [,ɛθnə'græfɪkəl] *adj* etnográfico
**ethnography** [ɛθ'nɑgrəfɪ] *s* etnografía
**ethnologic** [,ɛθnə'lɑdʒɪk] o **ethnological** [,ɛθnə'lɑdʒɪkəl] *adj* etnológico
**ethnologist** [ɛθ'nɑlədʒɪst] *s* etnólogo
**ethnology** [ɛθ'nɑlədʒɪ] *s* etnología
**ethopoeia** [,iθo'pijə] *s* (rhet.) etopeya
**ethyl** ['ɛθɪl] *s* (chem.) etilo; plomo tetraetilo; (trademark) gasolina etílica
**ethyl alcohol** *s* (chem.) alcohol etílico
**ethyl chloride** *s* (chem.) cloruro de etilo
**ethylene** ['ɛθɪlin] *s* (chem.) etileno
**Ethyl gas** *s* (trademark) etilgasolina
**ethylic** [ɪ'θɪlɪk] *adj* etílico
**etiology** [,itɪ'ɑlədʒɪ] *s* var. de **aetiology**
**etiquette** ['ɛtɪkɛt] *s* etiqueta
**Etna, Mount** ['ɛtnə] el monte Etna
**Etnean** [ɛt'niən] *adj* étneo
**Eton jacket** ['itən] *s* chaqueta corta de los escolares del colegio de Eton (*Inglaterra*); chaqueta corta de mujer
**Etrurian** [ɪ'trurɪən] *adj & s* etrurio
**Etruscan** [ɪ'trʌskən] *adj & s* etrusco
**et seq.** abr. de **et sequens, et sequentes** y **et sequentia** (Lat.) **and the following**
**étude** [e'tjud] *s* (mus.) estudio
**etymological** [,ɛtɪmə'lɑdʒɪkəl] *adj* etimológico
**etymologically** [,ɛtɪmə'lɑdʒɪkəlɪ] *adv* etimológicamente
**etymologist** [,ɛtɪ'mɑlədʒɪst] *s* etimologista
**etymology** [,ɛtɪ'mɑlədʒɪ] *s* (*pl:* **-gies**) etimología
**etymon** ['ɛtɪmɑn] *s* (*pl:* **-mons** o **-ma** [mə]) (philol.) étimo o étimon
**Euboea** [ju'biə] *s* Eubea
**eucaine** [ju'ken] *s* (pharm.) eucaína
**eucalyptol** [,jukə'lɪptol] o [,jukə'lɪptɑl] *s* eucaliptol
**eucalyptus** [,jukə'lɪptəs] *s* (*pl:* **-tuses** o **-ti** [taɪ]) (bot.) eucalipto
**Eucharist** ['jukərɪst] *s* (eccl.) Eucaristía
**Eucharistic** [,jukə'rɪstɪk] *adj* eucarístico
**euchre** ['jukər] *s* juego de naipes en el que el valet del triunfo es la carta más alta; *va* vencer en el juego de euchre; (slang) ser más listo que
**Euclid** ['juklɪd] *s* Euclides
**Euclidean** [ju'klɪdɪən] *adj* euclidiano
**Euclidean space** *s* (geom.) espacio euclidiano
**eucrasia** [ju'kreʒɪə] *s* (med.) eucrasia
**eudaemonism** [ju'dimənɪzəm] *s* eudemonismo
**eudiometer** [,judɪ'ɑmɪtər] *s* eudiómetro
**Eugene** [ju'dʒin] *s* Eugenio
**Eugenia** [ju'dʒinɪə] *s* Eugenia

**eugenic** [juˈdʒɛnɪk] *adj* eugenésico; **eugenics** *ssg o spl* eugenesia
**eugenically** [juˈdʒɛnɪkəlɪ] *adv* de manera eugenésica
**eulogist** [ˈjulədʒɪst] *s* elogiador
**eulogistic** [ˌjuləˈdʒɪstɪk] *adj* elogiador, elogioso
**eulogistically** [ˌjuləˈdʒɪstɪkəlɪ] *adv* laudatoriamente
**eulogium** [juˈlodʒɪəm] *s* (*pl:* **-giums** o **-gia** [dʒɪə]) elogio
**eulogize** [ˈjulədʒaɪz] *va* elogiar
**eulogy** [ˈjulədʒɪ] *s* (*pl:* **-gies**) elogio
**Eumenides** [juˈmɛnɪdiz] *spl* (myth.) Euménides
**eunuch** [ˈjunək] *s* eunuco
**eupatorium** [ˌjupəˈtorɪəm] *s* (bot.) eupatorio
**eupepsia** [juˈpɛpsɪə] o [juˈpɛpʃə] *s* (med.) eupepsia
**eupeptic** [juˈpɛptɪk] *adj* eupéptico
**euphemism** [ˈjufɪmɪzəm] *s* eufemismo
**euphemist** [ˈjufɪmɪst] *s* persona que emplea el eufemismo
**euphemistic** [ˌjufɪˈmɪstɪk] *adj* eufemístico
**euphemistically** [ˌjufɪˈmɪstɪkəlɪ] *adv* eufemísticamente
**euphemize** [ˈjufɪmaɪz] *va* expresar con eufemismo; *vn* hacer uso del eufemismo
**euphonic** [juˈfɑnɪk] *adj* eufónico
**euphonious** [juˈfonɪəs] *adj* eufono
**euphonium** [juˈfonɪəm] *s* (mus.) eufonio (*instrumento que tiene tubos de vidrio y barras de acero*); (mus.) eufonia (*tuba*)
**euphony** [ˈjufənɪ] *s* (*pl:* **-nies**) eufonía
**euphorbia** [juˈfɔrbɪə] *s* (bot. & pharm.) euforbio
**euphorbiaceous** [juˌfɔrbɪˈeʃəs] *adj* (bot.) euforbiáceo
**euphoria** [juˈforɪə] *s* (psychol.) euforia
**euphoric** [juˈfɑrɪk] *adj* eufórico
**euphrasy** [ˈjufrəsɪ] *s* (bot.) eufrasia
**Euphrates** [juˈfretiz] *s* Éufrates
**Euphrosyne** [juˈfrɑsɪni] *s* (myth.) Eufrosina
**euphuism** [ˈjufjuɪzəm] *s* eufuísmo
**euphuist** [ˈjufjuɪst] *s* eufuísta
**euphuistic** [ˌjufjuˈɪstɪk] *adj* eufuístico
**Eur.** abr. de **Europe** y **European**
**Eurasia** [juˈreʒə] o [juˈreʃə] *s* Eurasia
**Eurasian** [juˈreʒən] o [juˈreʃən] *adj & s* eurasiano
**eureka** [juˈrikə] *interj* ¡eureka!
**eurhythmic** [juˈrɪðmɪk] *adj* (f.a.) eurítmico
**eurhythmy** [juˈrɪðmɪ] *s* (f.a.) euritmia
**Euripides** [juˈrɪpɪdiz] *s* Eurípides
**Europa** [juˈropə] *s* (myth.) Europa
**Europa Point** *s* punta de Europa
**Europe** [ˈjurəp] *s* Europa
**European** [ˌjurəˈpiən] *adj & s* europeo
**European Common Market** *s* Mercado Común Europeo
**Europeanism** [ˌjurəˈpiənɪzəm] *s* europeísmo
**Europeanize** [ˌjurəˈpiənaɪz] *va* europeizar
**European plan** *s* cuarto sin comidas
**European swift** *s* (orn.) vencejo
**europium** [juˈropɪəm] *s* (chem.) europio
**Eurydice** [juˈrɪdisi] *s* (myth.) Eurídice
**eurythmic** [juˈrɪðmɪk] *adj* var. de **eurhythmic**
**eurythmy** [juˈrɪðmɪ] *s* var. de **eurhythmy**
**Eustace** [ˈjustɪs] *s* Eustaquio
**Eustachian tube** [juˈstekɪən] o [juˈsteʃən] *s* (anat.) trompa de Eustaquio
**eustyle** [ˈjuˌstaɪl] *s* (arch.) éustilo
**Euterpe** [juˈtʌrpɪ] *s* (myth.) Euterpe
**euthanasia** [ˌjuθəˈneʒə] *s* eutanasia
**euthenics** [juˈθɛnɪks] *ssg* euténica
**Eutychian** [juˈtɪkɪən] *adj & s* eutiquiano
**Euxine Sea** [ˈjuksɪn] o [ˈjuksaɪn] *s* Ponto Euxino (*antiguo nombre del mar Negro*)
**evacuant** [ɪˈvækjuənt] *adj & s* (med.) evacuante
**evacuate** [ɪˈvækjuet] *va* evacuar; (mil.) evacuar; *vn* (mil.) evacuar
**evacuation** [ɪˌvækjuˈeʃən] *s* evacuación
**evacuee** [ɪˌvækjuˈi] *s* evacuado
**evade** [ɪˈved] *va* evadir; *vn* evadirse
**evaluate** [ɪˈvæljuet] *va* evaluar
**evaluation** [ɪˌvæljuˈeʃən] *s* evaluación
**evanesce** [ˌɛvəˈnɛs] *vn* desvanecerse
**evanescence** [ˌɛvəˈnɛsəns] *s* desvanecimiento
**evanescent** [ˌɛvəˈnɛsənt] *adj* evanescente; (bot.) evanescente
**evangel** [ɪˈvændʒəl] *s* buena nueva; evangelio (*doctrina de Jesucristo*); evangelizador; (*cap.*) *s* Evangelio (*cada uno de los cuatro primeros libros del Nuevo Testamento*)
**evangelic** [ˌivænˈdʒɛlɪk] o [ˌɛvənˈdʒɛlɪk] o **evangelical** [ˌivænˈdʒɛlɪkəl] o [ˌɛvənˈdʒəlɪkəl] *adj* evangélico
**evangelicalism** [ˌivænˈdʒɛlɪkəlɪzəm] o [ˌɛvənˈdʒɛlɪkəlɪzəm] *s* doctrina de la iglesia evangélica
**evangelism** [ɪˈvændʒəlɪzəm] *s* evangelismo
**evangelist** [ɪˈvændʒəlɪst] *s* evangelizador; (*cap.*) *s* Evangelista
**evangelistic** [ɪˌvændʒəˈlɪstɪk] *adj* evangélico
**evangelization** [ɪˌvændʒəlɪˈzeʃən] *s* evangelización
**evangelize** [ɪˈvændʒəlaɪz] *va & vn* evangelizar
**evaporable** [ɪˈvæpərəbəl] *adj* evaporable
**evaporate** [ɪˈvæpəret] *va* evaporar, vaporar; *vn* evaporarse (*convertirse en vapor; desaparecer, desvanecerse*)
**evaporated milk** [ɪˈvæpəˌretɪd] *s* leche evaporada
**evaporation** [ɪˌvæpəˈreʃən] *s* evaporación
**evaporator** [ɪˈvæpəˌretər] *s* evaporador
**evasion** [ɪˈveʒən] *s* evasiva, evasión
**evasive** [ɪˈvesɪv] *adj* evasivo
**eve** [iv] *s* víspera; (poet.) tardecita; (*cap.*) *s* Eva; **on the eve of** en vísperas de
**evection** [ɪˈvɛkʃən] *s* (astr.) evección
**even** [ˈivən] *adj* igual, llano, liso, parejo; uniforme, semejante; constante, invariable; apacible, sereno; justo, imparcial; exacto; a nivel; sin deudas; (math.) par; **to be even** estar en paz; no deber nada a nadie; **to get even with** desquitarse con; *adv* aun, hasta; también; sin embargo; igualmente; exactamente: **not even** ni . . . siquiera; **to break even** (coll.) salir sin ganar ni perder; (coll.) salir en paz (*en juego*); **even as** así como; **even if** aunque, aun cuando; **even so** así; así y todo; **even though** aunque, aun cuando; **even when** aun cuando; *s* (poet.) tardecita; *va* igualar, allanar; desquitar
**even-handed** [ˈivənˈhændɪd] *adj* justo, imparcial
**evening** [ˈivnɪŋ] *s* tarde; (fig.) tarde (*de la vida*); *adj* vespertino
**evening clothes** *spl* o **evening dress** *s* traje de etiqueta
**evening gown** *s* vestido de etiqueta de mujer, vestido de noche
**evening primrose** *s* (bot.) hierba del asno
**evening star** *s* estrella vespertina
**evening wear** *s* vestido de etiqueta
**evenness** [ˈivənnɪs] *s* igualdad; uniformidad; constancia; serenidad; imparcialidad; exactitud
**even number** *s* número par
**evensong** [ˈivənˌsɔŋ] o [ˈivənˌsɑŋ] *s* (eccl.) vísperas; canción de la tarde; (archaic) tarde, anochecher
**event** [ɪˈvɛnt] *s* acontecimiento, suceso; resultado, consecuencia; acto (*hecho público*); (sport) lucha, corrida; **at all events** o **in any event** en todo caso; **in the event of** en caso de; **in the event that** en caso que
**even-tempered** [ˈivənˈtɛmpərd] *adj* tranquilo, sereno
**eventful** [ɪˈvɛntfəl] *adj* lleno de acontecimientos; memorable
**eventide** [ˈivənˌtaɪd] *s* (poet.) caída de la tarde
**eventual** [ɪˈvɛntʃuəl] *adj* final; eventual (*posible, contingente*)
**eventuality** [ɪˌvɛntʃuˈælɪtɪ] *s* (*pl:* **-ties**) eventualidad; **for any eventuality** a todo evento
**eventually** [ɪˈvɛntʃuəlɪ] *adv* finalmente, con el tiempo
**eventuate** [ɪˈvɛntʃuet] *vn* concluir, resultar, terminarse
**ever** [ˈɛvər] *adv* siempre; por casualidad; jamás, p.ej., **Who has ever seen such a thing?** ¿Quién ha visto jamás semejante cosa?; nunca, p.ej., **the best book ever written** el mejor libro que se haya escrito nunca; **he is happier than ever** es más feliz que nunca; alguna vez, p.ej., **Have you ever been in Spain?** ¿Ha estado Vd. alguna vez en España?; **as ever** como siempre; tanto como; **be it**

**ever so** + *adj* por + *adj* + que sea; **did you ever!** ¡qué cosa!; **for ever and ever** por siempre jamás; **hardly ever** casi nunca; **not . . . ever** no . . . nunca; **scarcely ever** casi nunca; **ever and anon** de vez en cuando, una y otra vez; **ever since** desde entonces; después de que; **ever so** muy; **ever so much** muchísimo
**everglade** [ˈɛvərgled] *s* tierra baja pantanosa cubierta de altas hierbas; **Everglades** *spl* pantanos en el sur de la Florida (*E.U.A.*)
**evergreen** [ˈɛvərˌgrin] *adj* siempre verde; *s* planta siempre verde; **evergreens** *spl* ramas que se emplean para adorno
**everlasting** [ˌɛvərˈlæstɪŋ] o [ˌɛvərˈlɑstɪŋ] *adj* sempiterno, perpetuo; duradero; aburrido, cansado; *s* eternidad; sempiterna (*tela*); (bot.) siempreviva; **the Everlasting** el Eterno (*Dios*)
**evermore** [ˌɛvərˈmor] o [ˈɛvərmor] *adv* eternamente; **for evermore** para siempre jamás
**eversion** [ɪˈvʌrʃən] o [ɪˈvʌrʒən] *s* (med.) eversión
**evert** [ɪˈvʌrt] *va* volver (*p.ej., los bordes de una herida*) hacia fuera
**every** [ˈɛvrɪ] *adj* todos los, p.ej., **every day** todos los días; todo, p.ej., **every loyal American** todo fiel americano; cada, p.ej., **every time** cada vez; **every bit** (coll.) todo, p.ej., **every bit a man** todo un hombre; **every now and then** de vez en cuando; **every once in a while** una que otra vez; **every one of them** todos ellos; **every other day** cada dos días, un día sí y otro no, cada tercer día; **every which way** (coll.) por todas partes; (coll.) en desarreglo
**everybody** [ˈɛvrɪˌbɑdɪ] *pron indef* todos, todo el mundo
**everyday** [ˈɛvrɪˌde] *adj* diario, cotidiano; acostumbrado, común, ordinario; de los días de trabajo
**every man Jack** *s* cada hijo de vecino
**everyone** o **every one** [ˈɛvrɪˌwʌn] *pron indef* todos, todo el mundo, cada uno
**everything** [ˈɛvrɪˌθɪŋ] *pron indef & s* todo
**everywhere** [ˈɛvrɪˌhwɛr] *adv* en o por todas partes; a todas partes
**evict** [ɪˈvɪkt] *va* desahuciar
**eviction** [ɪˈvɪkʃən] *s* desahucio; (law) evicción
**evidence** [ˈɛvɪdəns] *s* evidencia; (law) prueba; **direct evidence** (law) prueba directa; **indirect evidence** (law) prueba indirecta; **in evidence** visible, manifiesto, notorio; *va* evidenciar
**evident** [ˈɛvɪdənt] *adj* evidente
**evidential** [ˌɛvɪˈdɛnʃəl] *adj* indicador, probatorio
**evidently** [ˈɛvɪdəntlɪ] o [ˌɛvɪˈdɛntlɪ] *adv* evidentemente, por lo visto
**evil** [ˈivəl] *adj* malo; *s* mal
**evildoer** [ˈivəlˌduər] *s* malhechor
**evildoing** [ˈivəlˌduɪŋ] *s* malhecho
**evil eye** *s* aojo, aojadura, mal de ojo
**evil-minded** [ˈivəlˈmaɪndɪd] *adj* malicioso, mal pensado
**Evil One, the** el Malo (*el demonio*)
**evince** [ɪˈvɪns] *va* mostrar, revelar, indicar
**eviscerate** [ɪˈvɪsəret] *va* desentrañar, destripar
**evisceration** [ɪˌvɪsəˈreʃən] *s* desentrañamiento, destripamiento; (surg.) evisceración
**evocation** [ˌɛvoˈkeʃən] *s* evocación
**evocative** [ɪˈvɑkətɪv] *adj* evocador
**evoke** [ɪˈvok] *va* evocar
**evolution** [ˌɛvəˈluʃən] *s* evolución; (biol., philos., mil. & nav.) evolución; (biol.) evolucionismo (*teoría*); desprendimiento (*p.ej., de calor, gases*); (math.) extracción de raíces, radicación
**evolutional** [ˌɛvəˈluʃənəl] o **evolutionary** [ˌɛvəˈluʃənˌɛrɪ] *adj* evolucionista, evolutivo
**evolutionist** [ˌɛvəˈluʃənɪst] *s & adj* evolucionista
**evolve** [ɪˈvɑlv] *va* desarrollar; desprender (*p.ej., calor, gases*); *vn* evolucionar
**evolvement** [ɪˈvɑlvmənt] *s* desarrollo; desprendimiento (*p.ej., de calor, gases*); evolución
**ewe** [ju] *s* oveja
**ewe lamb** *s* cordera
**ewer** [ˈjuər] *s* aguamanil
**ex.** abr. de **examination, examined, example, except, exchange, excursion, executed** y **executive**
**Ex.** abr. de **Exodus**
**ex** [ɛks] *prep* (com.) sin participación en; (com.) sin incluir
**exacerbate** [ɛgˈzæsərbet] o [ɛksˈæsərbet] *va* exacerbar
**exacerbation** [ɛgˌzæsərˈbeʃən] o [ɛksˌæsərˈbeʃən] *s* exacerbación
**exact** [ɛgˈzækt] *adj* exacto; *va* exigir
**exacting** [ɛgˈzæktɪŋ] *adj* exigente
**exaction** [ɛgˈzækʃən] *s* exacción
**exactitude** [ɛgˈzæktɪtjud] o [ɛgˈzæktɪtud] *s* exactitud
**exactly** [ɛgˈzæktlɪ] *adv* exactamente; en punto, p.ej., **it is exactly two o'clock** son las dos en punto
**exactness** [ɛgˈzæktnɪs] *s* var. de **exactitude**
**exact science** *s* ciencia exacta
**exaggerate** [ɛgˈzædʒəret] *va* exagerar
**exaggeration** [ɛgˌzædʒəˈreʃən] *s* exageración
**exaggerator** [ɛgˈzædʒəˌretər] *s* exagerador
**exalt** [ɛgˈzɔlt] *va* exaltar
**exaltation** [ˌɛgzɔlˈteʃən] *s* exaltación
**exam** [ɛgˈzæm] *s* (coll.) examen
**examination** [ɛgˌzæmɪˈneʃən] *s* examen; reconocimiento (*médico*); **to take an examination** sufrir un examen, examinarse; **to take an examination in** examinarse de
**examine** [ɛgˈzæmɪn] *va & vn* examinar; **to examine into** examinar, indagar, averiguar
**examinee** [ɛgˌzæmɪˈni] *s* examinando
**examiner** [ɛgˈzæmɪnər] *s* examinador
**example** [ɛgˈzæmpəl] o [ɛgˈzɑmpəl] *s* ejemplo; ejemplar (*caso que sirve de escarmiento*); problema (*p.ej., de matemáticas*); **for example** por ejemplo; **to follow the example of** seguir el ejemplo de; **to set an example** dar ejemplo
**exanimation** [ɛgˌzænɪˈmeʃən] *s* exanimación
**exanthema** [ɛkˌsænˈθimə] *s* (*pl:* **-mata** [mətə]) (path.) exantema
**exanthematic** [ɛkˌsænθɪˈmætɪk] *adj* exantemático
**exasperate** [ɛgˈzæspəret] *va* exasperar
**exasperation** [ɛgˌzæspəˈreʃən] *s* exasperación
**ex cathedra** [ɛks kəˈθidrə] o [ɛks ˈkæθɪdrə] (Lat.) ex cáthedra (*en tono doctoral y decisivo; con autoridad*)
**excavate** [ˈɛkskəvet] *va* excavar
**excavation** [ˌɛkskəˈveʃən] *s* excavación
**excavator** [ˈɛkskəˌvetər] *s* excavador (*persona*); (dent. & surg.) excavador; excavadora (*máquina*)
**exceed** [ɛkˈsid] *va* exceder; exceder de; sobrepasar (*p.ej., el límite de velocidad*); *vn* excederse
**exceeding** [ɛkˈsidɪŋ] *adj* extraordinario, extremo; *adv* (archaic) sumamente, sobremanera
**exceedingly** [ɛkˈsidɪŋlɪ] *adv* sumamente, sobremanera
**excel** [ɛkˈsɛl] (*pret & pp:* **-celled;** *ger:* **-celling**) *va* aventajar, exceder; *vn* sobresalir
**excellence** [ˈɛksələns] *s* excelencia
**excellency** [ˈɛksələnsɪ] *s* (*pl:* **-cies**) excelencia; (*cap.*) *s* Excelencia (*tratamiento*)
**excellent** [ˈɛksələnt] *adj* excelente
**excelsior** [ɛkˈsɛlsɪər] *s* virutas de madera, pajilla de madera; [ɛkˈsɛlsɪɔr] *adj* siempre más alto; lema del estado de Nueva York; *interj* ¡excelsior! (*¡más arriba!*)
**Excelsior State** *s* estado de Nueva York
**except** [ɛkˈsɛpt] *prep* excepto; **except for** sin; **except that** sin que, a menos que; *va* exceptuar; *vn* objetar, desaprobar
**exception** [ɛkˈsɛpʃən] *s* excepción; **to take exception** objetar, desaprobar; ofenderse; **with the exception of** a excepción de
**exceptionable** [ɛkˈsɛpʃənəbəl] *adj* recusable, tachable
**exceptional** [ɛkˈsɛpʃənəl] *adj* excepcional
**excerpt** [ˈɛksʌrpt] o [ɛkˈsʌrpt] *s* excerta, selección, cita; [ɛkˈsʌrpt] *va* escoger, citar; *vn* hacer selecciones
**excess** [ɛkˈsɛs] *s* exceso; (fig.) exceso (*abuso; demasía en comer y beber*); **in excess of** más que, superior a; **to excess** en exceso o por exceso; [ˈɛksɛs] o [ɛkˈsɛs] *adj* excedente, sobrante
**excess baggage** *s* exceso de equipaje
**excess fare** *s* suplemento

**excessive** [ɛkˈsɛsɪv] *adj* excesivo

**excessively** [ɛkˈsɛsɪvlɪ] *adv* excesivamente

**excess-profits tax** [ˈɛksɛsˈprɑfɪts] *s* impuesto sobre ganancias superiores al promedio durante cierto período de condiciones normales, impuesto a los beneficios extraordinarios

**excess weight** *s* exceso de peso

**exchange** [ɛksˈtʃendʒ] *s* cambio; canje (*p.ej., de prisioneros, mercancías, periódicos, credenciales*); periódico o revista de canje; (com.) cambio; (com.) bolsa, lonja; estación telefónica, central de teléfonos; **in exchange for** en cambio de; *va* cambiar; canjear; darse, hacerse (*p.ej., cortesías*); **to exchange greetings** cambiar el saludo (*dos personas*); **to exchange shots** cambiar disparos

**exchangeable** [ɛksˈtʃendʒəbəl] *adj* cambiable, canjeable

**exchange professor** *s* profesor de intercambio

**exchequer** [ɛksˈtʃɛkər] o [ˈɛkstʃɛkər] *s* tesorería; fondos; (*cap.*) *s* (Brit.) echiquier, tribunal de hacienda; (Brit.) despacho del tribunal de hacienda; (Brit.) fondos del gobierno inglés

**excipient** [ɛkˈsɪpɪənt] *s* (pharm.) excipiente

**excise** [ɛkˈsaɪz] o [ˈɛksaɪz] *s* impuesto sobre ciertas mercancías de comercio interior; (Brit.) recaudación de impuestos interiores; [ɛkˈsaɪz] *va* sacar o quitar cortando; borrar; ahuecar; someter a impuesto

**exciseman** [ɛkˈsaɪzmən] *s* (*pl:* **-men**) (Brit.) recaudador de impuestos interiores

**excise tax** *s* impuesto sobre ciertas mercancías de comercio interior

**excision** [ɛkˈsɪʒən] *s* excisión; corte (*en una composición literaria*)

**excitability** [ɛkˌsaɪtəˈbɪlɪtɪ] *s* excitabilidad

**excitable** [ɛkˈsaɪtəbəl] *adj* excitable

**excitant** [ɛkˈsaɪtənt] o [ˈɛksɪtənt] *s* (physiol.) excitante

**excitation** [ˌɛksaɪˈteʃən] o [ˌɛksɪˈteʃən] *s* excitación; (phys. & physiol.) excitación

**excitative** [ɛkˈsaɪtətɪv] *adj* excitativo

**excite** [ɛkˈsaɪt] *va* excitar; (elec. & physiol.) excitar

**excitement** [ɛkˈsaɪtmənt] *s* excitación

**exciter** [ɛkˈsaɪtər] *s* excitador; (elec.) excitador (*para sacar chispas*); (elec.) excitatriz (*para producir un campo magnético*)

**exciting** [ɛkˈsaɪtɪŋ] *adj* excitante, estimulante; emocionante, conmovedor

**exclaim** [ɛksˈklem] *va* decir con vehemencia; *vn* exclamar; **to exclaim against** o **at** clamar contra (*p.ej., la injusticia*)

**exclamation** [ˌɛkskləˈmeʃən] *s* exclamación

**exclamation mark** o **point** *s* punto de admiración

**exclamatory** [ɛksˈklæməˌtorɪ] *adj* exclamatorio

**exclude** [ɛksˈklud] *va* excluir

**exclusion** [ɛksˈkluʒən] *s* exclusión; **to the exclusion of** con exclusión de

**exclusive** [ɛksˈklusɪv] *adj* exclusivo; exclusivista; **exclusive of** fuera de, sin contar

**exclusively** [ɛksˈklusɪvlɪ] *adv* exclusivamente

**excogitate** [ɛksˈkɑdʒɪtet] *va* excogitar

**excommunicate** [ˌɛkskəˈmjunɪket] *va* excomulgar

**excommunication** [ˌɛkskəˌmjunɪˈkeʃən] *s* excomunión

**excoriate** [ɛksˈkorɪet] *va* excoriar, desollar; (fig.) vituperar

**excoriation** [ɛksˌkorɪˈeʃən] *s* excoriación, desolladura; (fig.) vituperio

**excrement** [ˈɛskrɪmənt] *s* excremento

**excremental** [ˌɛkskrɪˈmɛntəl] *adj* excremental o excrementicio

**excrescence** [ɛksˈkrɛsəns] *s* excrecencia

**excrescent** [ɛksˈkrɛsənt] *adj* excrecente

**excreta** [ɛksˈkritə] *spl* (physiol.) excreta

**excrete** [ɛksˈkrit] *va* (physiol.) excretar

**excretion** [ɛksˈkriʃən] *s* (physiol.) excreción

**excretive** [ɛksˈkritɪv] *adj* (physiol.) excrementicio

**excretory** [ˈɛkskrɪˌtorɪ] o [ɛksˈkritərɪ] *adj* (physiol.) excretorio

**excruciating** [ɛksˈkruʃɪˌetɪŋ] *adj* atroz, agudísimo (*dolor*)

**exculpate** [ˈɛkskʌlpet] o [ɛksˈkʌlpet] *va* exculpar

**exculpation** [ˌɛkskʌlˈpeʃən] *s* exculpación

**excursion** [ɛksˈkʌrʒən] o [ɛksˈkʌrʃən] *s* excursión

**excursionist** [ɛksˈkʌrʒənɪst] o [ɛksˈkʌrʃənɪst] *s* excursionista

**excursion train** *s* tren de excursión, tren botijo, tren de recreo

**excursive** [ɛksˈkʌrsɪv] *adj* divagador

**excusable** [ɛksˈkjuzəbəl] *adj* excusable

**excuse** [ɛksˈkjus] *s* excusa; **to look for an excuse** buscar excusa; [ɛksˈkjuz] *va* excusar, dispensar; **to excuse for** + *ger* dispensar que + *subj*, p.ej., **excuse me for keeping you** dispénseme que le detenga; **to excuse from** + *ger* dispensar de + *inf;* **to excuse someone for something** excusarle a uno de algo

**execrable** [ˈɛksɪkrəbəl] *adj* execrable

**execrate** [ˈɛksɪkret] *va* execrar

**execration** [ˌɛksɪˈkreʃən] *s* execración; persona o cosa aborrecidas

**executant** [ɛgˈzɛkjutənt] *s* ejecutante

**execute** [ˈɛksɪkjut] *va* ejecutar

**execution** [ˌɛksɪˈkjuʃən] *s* ejecución

**executioner** [ˌɛksɪˈkjuʃənər] *s* ejecutor de la justicia, verdugo

**executive** [ɛgˈzɛkjutɪv] *adj* ejecutivo; ejecutor; *s* ejecutor; poder ejecutivo, jefe del estado; dirigente (*p.ej., de una empresa, un centro docente*); ejecutivo (Am.)

**Executive Mansion** *s* (U.S.A.) palacio del jefe del estado; (U.S.A.) casa oficial del gobernador

**executor** [ˈɛksɪˌkjutər] *s* ejecutor; [ɛgˈzɛkjutər] *s* albacea, ejecutor testamentario

**executrix** [ɛgˈzɛkjutrɪks] *s* (*pl:* **executrices** [ɛgˌzɛkjuˈtraɪsiz] o **executrixes**) albacea, ejecutora testamentaria

**exedra** [ˈɛksɪdrə] o [ɛkˈsidrə] *s* (arch.) exedra

**exegesis** [ˌɛksɪˈdʒisɪs] *s* (*pl:* **-ses** [siz]) exégesis

**exegetic** [ˌɛksɪˈdʒɛtɪk] o **exegetical** [ˌɛksɪˈdʒɛtɪkəl] *adj* exegético

**exemplar** [ɛgˈzɛmplər] o [ɛgˈzɛmplɑr] *s* ejemplar

**exemplary** [ɛgˈzɛmplərɪ] o [ˈɛgzəmˌplɛrɪ] *adj* ejemplar

**exemplification** [ɛgˌzɛmplɪfɪˈkeʃən] *s* ejemplificación; ejemplo; (law) copia notarial

**exemplify** [ɛgˈzɛmplɪfaɪ] (*pret & pp:* **-fied**) *va* ejemplificar

**exempt** [ɛgˈzɛmpt] *adj* exento; *va* exentar, eximir; **to exempt from** + *ger* eximir de + *inf*

**exemption** [ɛgˈzɛmpʃən] *s* exención

**exequatur** [ˌɛksɪˈkwetər] *s* exequátur

**exequies** [ˈɛksɪkwɪz] *spl* exequias

**exercise** [ˈɛksərsaɪz] *s* ejercicio; uso constante; ceremonia; **to take exercise** hacer ejercicio; *va* ejercer (*una profesión, influencia, etc.*); ejercitar (*adiestrar con el ejercicio*); inquietar, preocupar; poner (*cuidado*); *vn* ejercitarse; hacer ejercicio

**exergue** [ɛgˈzʌrg] o [ˈɛksʌrg] *s* exergo

**exert** [ɛgˈzʌrt] *va* ejercer (*p.ej., una fuerza*); **to exert oneself** esforzarse

**exertion** [ɛgˈzʌrʃən] *s* ejercicio, uso constante; esfuerzo

**exeunt** [ˈɛksɪənt] (Lat.) éxeunt (*ellos salen*)

**exfoliate** [ɛksˈfolɪet] *va* exfoliar; *vn* exfoliarse

**exfoliation** [ɛksˌfolɪˈeʃən] *s* exfoliación

**exhalation** [ˌɛkshəˈleʃən] o [ˌɛgzəˈleʃən] *s* exhalación; espiración (*del aire aspirado*); evaporación

**exhale** [ɛksˈhel] o [ɛgˈzel] *va* exhalar (*gases, olores*); espirar; evaporar; *vn* exhalarse; espirar (*expeler el aire aspirado*); evaporarse

**exhaust** [ɛgˈzɔst] *s* escape; tubo de escape; *adj* de escape; aspirador; *va* agotar; hacer el vacío en, extraer el aire de; apurar (*todos los medios*); *vn* escapar, salir (*el gas, el vapor*)

**exhaust cam** *s* leva de escape

**exhaust draft** *s* tiro de aspiración

**exhaust fan** *s* ventilador aspirador

**exhaustible** [ɛgˈzɔstɪbəl] *adj* agotable

**exhaustion** [ɛgˈzɔstʃən] *s* agotamiento

**exhaustive** [ɛgˈzɔstɪv] *adj* exhaustivo, comprensivo, detallado

**exhaustless** [ɛgˈzɔstlɪs] *adj* inagotable

**exhaust manifold** *s* múltiple de escape, colector de escape

**exhaust port** *s* lumbrera de escape

**exhaust stroke** *s* carrera de escape
**exhaust valve** *s* válvula de escape
**exhibit** [ɛg'zɪbɪt] *s* exhibición; (law) documento de prueba; *va* exhibir; (law) exhibir (*un documento*); (med.) administrar (*un remedio*)
**exhibition** [,ɛksɪ'bɪʃən] *s* exhibición
**exhibitionism** [,ɛksɪ'bɪʃənɪzəm] *s* (psychol.) exhibicionismo
**exhibitionist** [,ɛksɪ'bɪʃənɪst] *s* exhibicionista
**exhibitor** o **exhibiter** [ɛg'zɪbɪtər] *s* expositor
**exhilarate** [ɛg'zɪləret] *va* excitar, alegrar, regocijar
**exhilaration** [ɛg,zɪlə'reʃən] *s* excitación, alegría, regocijo
**exhort** [ɛg'zɔrt] *va* exhortar; **to exhort to** + *inf* exhortar a + *inf*
**exhortation** [,ɛgzɔr'teʃən] o [,ɛksɔr'teʃən] *s* exhortación
**exhortative** [ɛg'zɔrtətɪv] *adj* exhortativo
**exhortatory** [ɛg'zɔrtə,torɪ] *adj* exhortatorio
**exhorter** [ɛg'zɔrtər] *s* exhortador
**exhumation** [,ɛkshju'meʃən] *s* exhumación
**exhume** [ɛks'hjum] o [ɛg'zjum] *va* exhumar
**exigence** ['ɛksɪdʒəns] *s* exigencia
**exigency** ['ɛksɪdʒənsɪ] *s* (*pl:* **-cies**) var. de **exigence**
**exigent** ['ɛksɪdʒənt] *adj* exigente
**exiguity** [,ɛksɪ'gjuɪtɪ] *s* exigüidad
**exiguous** [ɛg'zɪgjuəs] o [ɛk'sɪgjuəs] *adj* exiguo
**exile** ['ɛgzaɪl] o ['ɛksaɪl] *s* destierro; desterrado (*persona*); *va* desterrar, extrañar
**exist** [ɛg'zɪst] *vn* existir
**existence** [ɛg'zɪstəns] *s* existencia
**existent** [ɛg'zɪstənt] *adj* existente
**existentialism** [,ɛgzɪs'tɛnʃəlɪzəm] *s* (philos.) existencialismo
**existentialist** [,ɛgzɪs'tɛnʃəlɪst] *adj* & *s* existencialista
**existing** [ɛg'zɪstɪŋ] *adj* existente
**exit** ['ɛgzɪt] o ['ɛksɪt] (Lat.) éxit (*él o ella sale*); *s* salida; salida de la escena; **to make one's exit** salir, marcharse, desaparecer
**ex libris** [ɛks 'laɪbrɪs] o [ɛks 'librɪs] (Lat.) de entre los libros de; *s* (*pl:* **-bris**) ex libris
**exobiology** [,ɛksobaɪ'ɑlədʒɪ] *s* exobiología
**Exod.** abr. de **Exodus**
**exodontia** [,ɛkso'dɑnʃə] o [,ɛkso'dɑnʃɪə] *s* exodoncia
**exodus** ['ɛksədəs] *s* éxodo; (*cap.*) *s* (Bib.) Éxodo
**ex officio** [ɛks ə'fɪʃɪo] (Lat.) en virtud de autoridad o cargo
**exogamy** [ɛks'ɑgəmɪ] *s* exogamia; (biol.) exogamia
**exogenous** [ɛks'ɑdʒənəs] *adj* exógeno
**exonerate** [ɛg'zɑnəret] *va* exculpar; exonerar (*p.ej., de una obligación*)
**exoneration** [ɛg,zɑnə'reʃən] *s* exculpación; exoneración (*de una obligación*)
**exophthalmic** [,ɛksɑf'θælmɪk] *adj* exoftálmico
**exophthalmos** [,ɛksɑf'θælmɑs] *s* (path.) exoftalmía o exoftalmos
**exorable** ['ɛksərəbəl] *adj* exorable
**exorbitance** [ɛg'zɔrbɪtəns] o **exorbitancy** [ɛg'zɔrbɪtənsɪ] *s* exorbitancia
**exorbitant** [ɛg'zɔrbɪtənt] *adj* exorbitante
**exorbitantly** [ɛg'zɔrbɪtəntlɪ] *adv* exorbitantemente
**exorcise** ['ɛksɔrsaɪz] *va* exorcizar
**exorcism** ['ɛksɔrsɪzəm] *s* exorcismo
**exorcist** ['ɛksɔrsɪst] *s* exorcista
**exorcize** ['ɛksɔrsaɪz] *va* var. de **exorcise**
**exordium** [ɛg'zɔrdɪəm] o [ɛk'sɔrdɪəm] *s* (*pl:* **-diums** o **-dia** [dɪə]) exordio
**exoskeleton** [,ɛkso'skɛlɪtən] *s* (zool.) exosqueleto, dermatoesqueleto
**exosmosis** [,ɛksɑs'mosɪs] *s* (physical chem. & physiol.) exósmosis
**exosphere** ['ɛksəsfɪr] *s* exosfera
**exospore** ['ɛksospor] *s* (bot.) exospora
**exoteric** [,ɛkso'tɛrɪk] *adj* exotérico
**exothermic** [,ɛksə'θʌrmɪk] *adj* (chem.) exotérmico
**exotic** [ɛg'zɑtɪk] o [ɛks'ɑtɪk] *adj* exótico
**exoticism** [ɛg'zɑtɪsɪzəm] o [ɛks'ɑtɪsɪzəm] *s* exotismo
**exp.** abr. de **expenses, expired, export, exportation, exported, exporter** y **express**
**expand** [ɛks'pænd] *va* extender; dilatar; ampliar, ensanchar; (math.) desarrollar (*p.ej., una ecuación*); *vn* extenderse; dilatarse; ampliarse, ensancharse
**expanded metal** *s* metal desplegado
**expanse** [ɛks'pæns] *s* extención
**expansibility** [ɛks,pænsɪ'bɪlɪtɪ] *s* expansibilidad
**expansible** [ɛks'pænsɪbəl] *adj* expansible
**expansile** [ɛks'pænsɪl] *adj* expansible
**expansion** [ɛks'pænʃən] *s* expansión; (math.) desarrollo
**expansion bolt** *s* perno de expansión
**expansionism** [ɛks'pænʃənɪzəm] *s* expansionismo
**expansionist** [ɛks'pænʃənɪst] *adj* & *s* expansionista
**expansion stroke** *s* carrera de expansión
**expansive** [ɛks'pænsɪv] *adj* expansivo; (fig.) expansivo
**expatiate** [ɛks'peʃɪet] *vn* espaciarse
**expatiation** [ɛks,peʃɪ'eʃən] *s* espaciamiento
**expatriate** [ɛks'petrɪɪt] *adj* & *s* expatriado; [ɛks'petrɪet] *va* expatriar, extrañar; *vn* expatriarse
**expatriation** [ɛks,petrɪ'eʃən] *s* expatriación
**expect** [ɛks'pɛkt] *va* esperar, prometerse; (coll.) suponer
**expectance** [ɛks'pɛktəns] *s* var. de **expectancy**
**expectancy** [ɛks'pɛktənsɪ] *s* (*pl:* **-cies**) expectación, expectativa
**expectant** [ɛks'pɛktənt] *adj* expectante
**expectant mother** *s* mujer encinta, futura madre
**expectant treatment** *s* (med.) tratamiento expectante
**expectation** [,ɛkspɛk'teʃən] *s* expectación, expectativa; (med.) expectación
**expectation of life** *s* expectativa de vida
**expectorant** [ɛks'pɛktərənt] *adj* & *s* expectorante
**expectorate** [ɛks'pɛktəret] *va* & *vn* expectorar
**expectoration** [ɛks,pɛktə'reʃən] *s* expectoración
**expedience** [ɛks'pidɪəns] *s* conveniencia, utilidad, oportunidad; ventaja personal
**expediency** [ɛks'pidɪənsɪ] *s* (*pl:* **-cies**) var. de **expedience**
**expedient** [ɛks'pidɪənt] *adj* conveniente, útil, oportuno; ventajoso; egoísta; *s* expediente
**expedite** ['ɛkspɪdaɪt] *va* apresurar, facilitar, despachar
**expedition** [,ɛkspɪ'dɪʃən] *s* expedición; (fig.) expedición
**expeditionary** [,ɛkspɪ'dɪʃən,ɛrɪ] *adj* expedicionario
**expeditious** [,ɛkspɪ'dɪʃəs] *adj* expeditivo
**expel** [ɛks'pɛl] (*pret & pp:* **-pelled;** *ger:* **-pelling**) *va* expeler, expulsar; despedir
**expend** [ɛks'pɛnd] *va* expender, gastar; consumir
**expendable** [ɛks'pɛndəbəl] *adj* gastable
**expenditure** [ɛks'pɛndɪtʃər] *s* gasto; consumo
**expense** [ɛks'pɛns] *s* gasto; **expenses** *spl* gastos, expensas; **at any expense** a toda costa; **at the expense of** a expensas de; **to cover expenses** cubrir gastos; **to go to the expense of** meterse en gastos con; **to meet the expenses** hacer frente a los gastos
**expense account** *s* cuenta de gastos
**expensive** [ɛks'pɛnsɪv] *adj* caro, dispendioso; carero (*que vende caro*)
**expensively** [ɛks'pɛnsɪvlɪ] *adv* costosamente
**experience** [ɛks'pɪrɪəns] *s* experiencia (*enseñanza que se adquiere con la práctica o sólo con el vivir; cosa que uno ha experimentado, suceso en que uno ha participado*); **by experience** con su propia experiencia; *va* experimentar
**experienced** [ɛks'pɪrɪənst] *adj* experimentado
**experiential** [ɛks,pɪrɪ'ɛnʃəl] *adj* experimental
**experiment** [ɛks'pɛrɪmənt] *s* experimento o experiencia; [ɛks'pɛrɪmɛnt] *vn* experimentar
**experimental** [ɛks,pɛrɪ'mɛntəl] *adj* experimental
**experimentally** [ɛks,pɛrɪ'mɛntəlɪ] *adv* experimentalmente
**experimental psychology** *s* psicología experimental

**experimentation** [ɛks,pɛrɪmɛn'teʃən] *s* experimentación
**experimenter** [ɛks'pɛrɪmɛntər] *s* experimentador
**expert** ['ɛkspʌrt] o [ɛks'pʌrt] *adj* experto; ['ɛkspʌrt] *s* experto
**expertise** [,ɛks,pɛr'tiz] *s* pericia
**expiable** ['ɛkspɪəbəl] *adj* expiable
**expiate** ['ɛkspɪet] *va* expiar
**expiation** [,ɛkspɪ'eʃən] *s* expiación
**expiatory** ['ɛkspɪə,torɪ] *adj* expiatorio
**expiration** [,ɛkspɪ'reʃən] *s* espiración (*del aire*); expiración
**expiratory** [ɛk'spaɪrə,torɪ] *adj* (physiol.) espirador
**expire** [ɛks'paɪr] *va* expeler (*especialmente el aire*); *vn* expirar (*expeler el aire aspirado; morir; acabarse, p.ej., el plazo*)
**expiry** [ɛk'spaɪrɪ] o ['ɛkspɪrɪ] *s* (*pl:* **-ries**) expiración (*p.ej., de un contrato*)
**explain** [ɛks'plen] *va* explicar; **to explain away** apartar, descartar con explicaciones; **to explain oneself** explicarse; *vn* explicar; explicarse
**explainable** [ɛks'plenəbəl] *adj* explicable
**explanation** [,ɛksplə'neʃən] *s* explicación; **to demand an explanation** pedir explicaciones
**explanatory** [ɛks'plænə,torɪ] *adj* explicatorio, explicativo
**expletive** ['ɛksplɪtɪv] *adj* expletivo; *s* partícula expletiva; reniego, interjección
**explicable** ['ɛksplɪkəbəl] *adj* explicable
**explicate** ['ɛksplɪket] *va* explicar, exponer
**explicatory** ['ɛksplɪkə,torɪ] *adj* explicatorio
**explicit** [ɛks'plɪsɪt] *adj* explícito
**explode** [ɛks'plod] *va* volar, hacer saltar; desautorizar, refutar (*una teoría*); (phonet.) pronunciar con explosión; *vn* estallar, explotar, reventar; **to explode with laughter** echarse a reír
**exploit** ['ɛksplɔɪt] o [ɛks'plɔɪt] *s* hazaña, proeza; [ɛks'plɔɪt] *va* explotar
**exploitation** [,ɛksplɔɪ'teʃən] *s* explotación
**exploration** [,ɛksplə'reʃən] *s* exploración
**explorative** [ɛks'plorətɪv] *adj* explorativo
**exploratory** [ɛks'plorə,torɪ] *adj* exploratorio, explorador
**explore** [ɛks'plor] *va & vn* explorar
**explorer** [ɛks'plorər] *s* explorador; (med.) explorador (*instrumento*)
**explosimeter** [,ɛksplo'zɪmɪtər] *s* explosímetro
**explosion** [ɛks'ploʒən] *s* explosión; (phonet.) explosión; (fig.) refutación (*de una teoría*)
**explosive** [ɛks'plosɪv] *adj* explosivo; (phonet.) explosivo; *s* explosivo; (phonet.) explosiva
**exponent** [ɛks'ponənt] *s* exponente, expositor; representante, ejemplar, símbolo; (alg.) exponente
**exponential** [,ɛkspo'nɛnʃəl] *adj* (math.) exponencial
**export** ['ɛksport] *s* exportación (*acción o artículo*); **exports** *spl* exportación (*mercaderías que se exportan*); *adj* de exportación; [ɛks'port] o ['ɛksport] *va & vn* exportar
**exportation** [,ɛkspor'teʃən] *s* exportación
**exporter** [ɛks'portər] o ['ɛksportər] *s* exportador
**expose** [ɛks'poz] *va* exponer; desenmascarar; (phot.) exponer; (eccl.) exponer o manifestar (*el Santísimo Sacramento*)
**exposé** [,ɛkspo'ze] *s* desenmascaramiento, revelación (*p.ej., de un crimen*)
**exposition** [,ɛkspə'zɪʃən] *s* exposición; (rhet.) exposición
**expositive** [ɛks'pɑzɪtɪv] *adj* expositivo
**expositor** [ɛks'pɑzɪtər] *s* expositor
**expository** [ɛks'pɑzɪ,torɪ] *adj* expositivo, expositor
**ex post facto** [,ɛks post 'fækto] (Lat.) retroactivo
**expostulate** [ɛks'pɑstʃəlet] *vn* protestar; **to expostulate with someone about, for, on** o **upon something** reconvenirle a uno con, de, por o sobre algo
**expostulation** [ɛks,pɑstʃə'leʃən] *s* protesta, reconvención
**expostulator** [ɛks'pɑstʃə,letər] *s* amonestador
**expostulatory** [ɛks'pɑstʃələ,torɪ] *adj* amonestador
**exposure** [ɛks'poʒər] *s* exposición (*acción de exponer; situación con relación a los puntos cardinales*); desenmascaramiento; (phot.) exposición; toma (*de una fotografía*)
**exposure meter** *s* (phot.) exposímetro
**expound** [ɛks'paʊnd] *va* exponer
**expounder** [ɛks'paʊndər] *s* expositor
**ex-president** ['ɛks'prɛzɪdənt] *s* ex presidente
**express** [ɛks'prɛs] *adj* expreso (*claro, especificado; con particular intento*); expreso (*tren, carro, ascensor, etc.*); *s* expreso; **by express** (rail.) en gran velocidad; *adv* expresamente; por expreso; *va* expresar; enviar por expreso; exprimir (*extraer apretando*); **to express oneself** expresarse
**expressage** [ɛks'prɛsɪdʒ] *s* servicio del expreso; costo del expreso
**express company** *s* compañía de expreso
**expressible** [ɛks'prɛsɪbəl] *adj* decible, expresable; exprimible
**expression** [ɛks'prɛʃən] *s* expresión; (math.) expresión
**expressive** [ɛk'sprɛsɪv] *adj* expresivo
**expressly** [ɛks'prɛslɪ] *adv* expresamente
**expressman** [ɛks'prɛsmən] *s* (*pl:* **-men**) (U.S.A.) empleado del expreso
**express train** *s* tren expreso
**expressway** [ɛks'prɛs,we] *s* supercarretera
**expropriate** [ɛks'proprɪet] *va* expropiar
**expropriation** [ɛks,proprɪ'eʃən] *s* expropiación
**expugnable** [ɛks'pʌgnəbəl] *adj* expugnable
**expulsion** [ɛks'pʌlʃən] *s* expulsión
**expulsive** [ɛks'pʌlsɪv] *adj* expulsivo
**expunge** [ɛks'pʌndʒ] *va* borrar, cancelar, destruir
**expurgate** ['ɛkspərget] *va* expurgar
**expurgation** [,ɛkspər'geʃən] *s* expurgación
**expurgatory** [ɛks'pʌrgə,torɪ] *adj* expurgatorio
**exquisite** ['ɛkskwɪzɪt] o [ɛks'kwɪzɪt] *adj* exquisito; agudo, sensible
**ex-service** [,ɛks'sʌrvɪs] *adj* ex militar
**ex-serviceman** [,ɛks'sʌrvɪs,mæn] *s* (*pl:* **-men**) ex militar, ex combatiente
**extant** ['ɛkstənt] o [ɛks'tænt] *adj* existente
**extemporaneous** [ɛks,tɛmpə'renɪəs] o **extemporary** [ɛks'tɛmpə,rɛrɪ] *adj* improvisado; sin previa preparación; provisional
**extempore** [ɛks'tɛmpərɪ] *adj* improvisado; *adv* de improviso, improvisadamente
**extemporization** [ɛks,tɛmpərɪ'zeʃən] *s* improvisación
**extemporize** [ɛks'tɛmpəraɪz] *va & vn* improvisar
**extend** [ɛks'tɛnd] *va* extender; prorrogar (*p.ej., un plazo*); dar, conceder, ofrecer; *vn* extenderse
**extended** [ɛks'tɛndɪd] *adj* extendido; extenso; prolongado
**extensible** [ɛks'tɛnsɪbəl] *adj* extensible
**extensile** [ɛks'tɛnsɪl] *adj* extensible; extensor
**extension** [ɛks'tɛnʃən] *s* extensión; (telp.) extensión (*línea accesoria*); prolongación; (com.) prórroga; (mach.) alargadera; *adj* de extensión
**extension bit** *s* barrena de extensión
**extension cord** *s* (elec.) cordón de extensión
**extension ladder** *s* escalera extensible, escalera de largueros corredizos
**extension table** *s* mesa de extensión
**extensity** [ɛks'tɛnsɪtɪ] *s* extensión; (psychol.) extensión
**extensive** [ɛks'tɛnsɪv] *adj* extensivo; extenso, vasto, dilatado; (agr.) extensivo
**extensor** [ɛks'tɛnsər] *s* (anat.) extensor, músculo extensor
**extent** [ɛks'tɛnt] *s* extensión; alcance, grado; **to a certain extent** hasta cierto punto; **to a great extent** en sumo grado; **to a lesser extent** en menor grado; **to such an extent** hasta tal punto; **to that extent** hasta ese grado, hasta ahí; **to the extent that** en la medida que; hasta el punto que; **to the full extent** en toda su extensión
**extenuate** [ɛks'tɛnjʊet] *va* extenuar (*debilitar; enflaquecer*); atenuar (*aminorar, p.ej., la gravedad de un delito*)
**extenuating circumstances** *spl* circunstancias atenuantes
**extenuation** [ɛks,tɛnjʊ'eʃən] *s* extenuación (*debilitación; enflaquecimiento*); atenuación (*p.ej., de la gravedad de un delito*)

**exterior** [ɛksˈtɪrɪər] *adj & s* exterior
**exterminable** [ɛksˈtʌrmɪnəbəl] *adj* exterminable
**exterminate** [ɛksˈtʌrmɪnet] *va* exterminar
**extermination** [ɛksˌtʌrmɪˈneʃən] *s* exterminio
**exterminator** [ɛksˈtʌrmɪˌnetər] *s* exterminador (*persona o aparato*)
**external** [ɛksˈtʌrnəl] *adj* externo; (anat.) externo; **externals** *spl* exterioridad (*apariencia de las cosas*)
**externality** [ˌɛkstərˈnælɪtɪ] *s* (*pl:* **-ties**) exterioridad (*calidad de externo; cosa externa*)
**externally** [ɛksˈtʌrnəlɪ] *adv* externamente, exteriormente
**extinct** [ɛksˈtɪŋkt] *adj* extinto
**extinction** [ɛksˈtɪŋkʃən] *s* extinción
**extinctive** [ɛksˈtɪŋktɪv] *adj* extintivo; (law) extintivo
**extine** [ˈɛkstɪn] o [ˈɛkstaɪn] *s* (bot.) exina o extina (*del polen*)
**extinguish** [ɛksˈtɪŋgwɪʃ] *va* extinguir
**extinguishable** [ɛksˈtɪŋgwɪʃəbəl] *adj* extinguible
**extinguisher** [ɛksˈtɪŋgwɪʃər] *s* apagador (*persona o aparato; cono para apagar las luces*)
**extirpate** [ˈɛkstərpet] o [ɛksˈtʌrpet] *va* extirpar
**extirpation** [ˌɛkstərˈpeʃən] *s* extirpación
**extol** o **extoll** [ɛksˈtol] o [ɛksˈtɑl] (*pret & pp:* **-tolled;** *ger:* **-tolling**) *va* ensalzar
**extort** [ɛksˈtɔrt] *va* obtener por fuerza o engaño
**extortion** [ɛksˈtɔrʃən] *s* extorción; exacción (*de una promesa*)
**extortionate** [ɛksˈtɔrʃənɪt] *adj* injusto, gravoso, opresivo; excesivo
**extortioner** [ɛksˈtɔrʃənər] o **extortionist** [ɛksˈtɔrʃənɪst] *s* concusionario, desollador
**extra** [ˈɛkstrə] *adj* extra; de repuesto; *adv* extraordinariamente; *s* extra (*de un periódico; adehala, gaje, plus*); (theat.) extra; repuesto, pieza de repuesto
**extract** [ˈɛkstrækt] *s* selección, cita; (pharm.) extracto; [ɛksˈtrækt] *va* seleccionar, citar (*pasajes de un libro*); extraer; (math.) extraer (*una raíz*)
**extractable** [ɛksˈtræktəbəl] o **extractible** [ɛksˈtræktɪbəl] *adj* extractivo
**extraction** [ɛksˈtrækʃən] *s* extracción
**extractive** [ɛksˈtræktɪv] *adj* extractivo
**extractor** [ɛksˈtræktər] *s* extractor (*persona o aparato*)
**extra current** *s* (elec.) extracorriente
**extracurricular** [ˌɛkstrəkəˈrɪkjələr] *adj* extracurricular
**extraditable** [ˈɛkstrəˌdaɪtəbəl] *adj* extraditable
**extradite** [ˈɛkstrədaɪt] *va* entregar por extradición; obtener la extradición de
**extradition** [ˌɛkstrəˈdɪʃən] *s* extradición
**extrados** [ɛksˈtredɑs] *s* (arch.) extradós
**extra fare** *s* tarifa recargada, recargo de tarifa
**extrajudicial** [ˌɛkstrədʒuˈdɪʃəl] *adj* extrajudicial
**extralegal** [ˌɛkstrəˈligəl] *adj* extralegal
**extramural** [ˌɛkstrəˈmjʊrəl] *adj* extramural
**extraneous** [ɛksˈtrenɪəs] *adj* ajeno, extraño
**extraordinarily** [ɛksˈtrɔrdɪˌnɛrɪlɪ] o [ˌɛkstrəˈɔrdɪˌnɛrɪlɪ] *adv* extraordinariamente
**extraordinary** [ɛksˈtrɔrdɪˌnɛrɪ] o [ˌɛkstrəˈɔrdɪˌnɛrɪ] *adj* extraordinario
**extrapolate** [ɛksˈtræpəlet] *va & vn* (math.) extrapolar
**extrapolation** [ˌɛkstrəpoˈleʃən] o [ɛksˌtræpəˈleʃən] *s* (math.) extrapolación
**extrasensory** [ˌɛkstrəˈsɛnsərɪ] *adj* extrasensorial
**extrasystole** [ˌɛkstrəˈsɪstəlɪ] *s* (path.) extrasístole
**extraterritorial** [ˈɛkstrəˌtɛrɪˈtorɪəl] *adj* extraterritorial
**extraterritoriality** [ˈɛkstrəˌtɛrɪˌtorɪˈælɪtɪ] *s* extraterritorialidad
**extravagance** [ɛksˈtrævəgəns] *s* derroche, despilfarro, gasto excesivo; lujo excesivo; exorbitancia (*de los precios*); extravagancia
**extravagant** [ɛksˈtrævəgənt] *adj* despilfarrado, gastador; exorbitante; excesivo; extravagante
**extravaganza** [ɛksˌtrævəˈgænzə] *s* obra musical o composición literaria extravagante y fantástica
**extravasate** [ɛksˈtrævəset] *va* extravasar; *vn* (physiol.) extravasarse
**extravasation** [ɛksˌtrævəˈseʃən] *s* extravasación
**extraversion** [ˌɛkstrəˈvʌrʃən] *s* (psychol.) extraversión
**extreme** [ɛksˈtrim] *adj* extremo; *s* extremo; **in the extreme** en sumo grado; **to go from one extreme to the other** pasar de un extremo a otro; **to go to extremes** excederse, propasarse
**extremely** [ɛksˈtrimlɪ] *adv* extremamente, extremadamente
**extreme unction** *s* (eccl.) extremaunción
**extremism** [ɛksˈtrimɪzəm] *s* extremismo
**extremist** [ɛksˈtrimɪst] *s* extremista
**extremity** [ɛksˈtrɛmɪtɪ] *s* (*pl:* **-ties**) extremidad; medida extrema; extrema (*escasez grande*); **extremities** *spl* extremidades (*pies y manos*)
**extricate** [ˈɛkstrɪket] *va* librar
**extrication** [ˌɛkstrɪˈkeʃən] *s* libramiento
**extrinsic** [ɛksˈtrɪnsɪk] *adj* extrínseco
**extrinsically** [ɛksˈtrɪnsɪkəlɪ] *adv* extrínsecamente
**extrorse** [ɛksˈtrɔrs] *adj* (bot.) extrorso
**extroversion** [ˌɛkstroˈvʌrʒən] o [ˌɛkstroˈvʌrʃən] *s* (path.) extroversión; (psychol.) extraversión
**extrovert** [ˈɛkstrovʌrt] *s* extrovertido
**extrude** [ɛksˈtrud] *va* forzar o empujar hacia fuera; (metal.) estrujar; *vn* resaltar, sobresalir
**extrusion** [ɛksˈtruʒən] *s* expulsión; resalto; (metal.) estrujamiento, extrusión
**extrusive** [ɛksˈtrusɪv] *adj* expulsivo; resaltante; (geol.) efusivo
**exuberance** [ɛgˈzubərəns] o [ɛgˈzjubərəns] *s* exuberancia
**exuberancy** [ɛgˈzubərənsɪ] o [ɛgˈzjubərənsɪ] *s* (*pl:* **-cies**) var. de **exuberance**
**exuberant** [ɛgˈzubərənt] o [ɛgˈzjubərənt] *adj* exuberante
**exudate** [ˈɛksjʊdet] *s* exudado
**exudation** [ˌɛksjʊˈdeʃən] *s* exudación
**exude** [ɛgˈzud], [ɛgˈzjud] o [ɛksˈjud] *va & vn* exudar
**exult** [ɛgˈzʌlt] *vn* exultar
**exultant** [ɛgˈzʌltənt] *adj* regocijado, alborozado, ufano
**exultation** [ˌɛgzʌlˈteʃən] o [ˌɛksʌlˈteʃən] *s* exultación
**ex-voto** [ɛksˈvoto] *s* (*pl:* **-tos**) exvoto
**-ey** *suffix adj* var. de **-y**, que se usa cuando la palabra termina en **y**, p.ej., **clayey** arcilloso; **eyey** ojoso; *suffix dim* var. de **-y** en algunos nombres propios, p.ej., **Charley** Carlitos
**eyas** [ˈaɪəs] *s* halcón niego; pájaro que no ha dejado el nido
**eye** [aɪ] *s* (anat.) ojo; (fig.) ojo (*p.ej., de aguja, del queso, de una herramienta; yema o botón de las plantas; abertura redonda; mirada, vista; atención; aptitud para apreciar las cosas*); (sew.) corcheta; **an eye for an eye** ojo por ojo; **before one's eyes** delante de los ojos de uno; **in the eyes of** a los ojos de; **to catch one's eye** llamar la atención a uno; **to feast one's eyes on** deleitar la vista en; **to have an eye to** prestar atención a; vigilar; **to have an eye to the main chance** abrir los ojos; **to have one's eye on** (coll.) tener los ojos en; (coll.) echar el ojo a (*mirar con deseo*); **to keep an eye on** tener los ojos en; **to keep one's eyes open** abrir el ojo; **to lay eyes on** alcanzar a ver; **to make eyes at** hacer guiños a; **to not take one's eyes off** no quitar los ojos de; **to open one's eyes** abrir los ojos (*salir del error*); **to open someone's eyes** abrirle los ojos a uno (*desengañarle a uno*); **to roll one's eyes** poner los ojos en blanco; **to see eye to eye** estar completamente de acuerdo; **to set eyes on** (coll.) alcanzar a ver; **to shut one's eyes to** hacer la vista gorda ante; **with an eye to** con la intención de, con vistas a; **without batting an eye** sin pestañear, sin inmutarse; **with the naked eye** a simple vista; (*pret & pp:* **eyed;**

*ger:* **eying** o **eyeing**) *va* ojear; **to eye up and down** mirar de hito en hito
**eyeball** ['aɪ,bɔl] *s* globo del ojo
**eyebolt** ['aɪ,bolt] *s* perno de argolla, cáncamo de ojo
**eyebright** ['aɪ,braɪt] *s* (bot.) eufrasia
**eyebrow** ['aɪ,braʊ] *s* ceja
**eye-catching** ['aɪ,kætʃɪŋ] *adj* atrayente, llamativo, sugestivo
**eyecup** ['aɪ,kʌp] *s* ojera, lavaojos
**eyeful** ['aɪfʊl] *s* (coll.) buena ojeada
**eyeglass** ['aɪ,glæs] o ['aɪ,glɑs] *s* ocular (*del anteojo, microscopio, etc.*); ojera, lavaojos (*copita para bañar el ojo*); **eyeglasses** *spl* gafas, anteojos
**eyehole** ['aɪ,hol] *s* ojete; cuenca del ojo; atisbadero, mirilla
**eyelash** ['aɪ,læʃ] *s* pestaña
**eyeless** ['aɪlɪs] *adj* sin ojos, sin vista
**eyelet** ['aɪlɪt] *s* ojete, ojal; mirilla, atisbadero; *va* ojetear
**eyeleteer** [,aɪlɪ'tɪr] *s* punzón para abrir ojetes
**eyelet punch** *s* ojeteadora
**eyelid** ['aɪ,lɪd] *s* párpado
**eye of day, eye of the morning, eye of heaven** *s* sol
**eye opener** *s* acontecimiento asombroso, noticia inesperada e increíble; (slang) trago de licor que se toma por la mañana
**eyepiece** ['aɪ,pis] *s* ocular
**eye-shade** ['aɪ,ʃed] *s* visera
**eyeshot** ['aɪ,ʃɑt] *s* alcance de la vista
**eyesight** ['aɪ,saɪt] *s* vista; alcance de la vista
**eye socket** *s* (anat.) cuenca del ojo
**eyesore** ['aɪ,sor] *s* mácula, cosa que ofende la vista
**eyespot** ['aɪ,spɑt] *s* (zool.) mancha ocular
**eyestrain** ['aɪ,stren] *s* cansancio o irritación de los ojos
**eye-test chart** ['aɪ,tɛst] *s* gráfico para prueba oftalmométrica, tabla de graduación, tipo de ensayo o prueba
**eyetooth** ['aɪ,tuθ] *s* (*pl:* **-teeth** [,tiθ]) colmillo, diente canino; **to cut one's eyeteeth** (coll.) tener el colmillo retorcido; **to give one's eyeteeth for** (coll.) dar los ojos de la cara por
**eyewash** ['aɪ,wɑʃ] o ['aɪ,wɔʃ] *s* colirio; (slang) alabanza para engañar
**eyewinker** ['aɪ,wɪŋkər] *s* pestaña
**eyewitness** ['aɪ,wɪtnɪs] *s* testigo de vista o testigo ocular
**eyey** ['aɪ·ɪ] *adj* ojoso
**eyrie** o **eyry** ['ɛrɪ] *s* (*pl:* **-ries**) aguilera, nido de águilas; nido de ave de rapiña; nidada de aguiluchos; (fig.) morada elevada, altura
**Ezek.** abr. de **Ezekiel**
**Ezekiel** [ɪ'zikjəl] *s* (Bib.) Ecequiel o Ezequiel (*profeta y libro*)

**F, f** [ɛf] *s* (*pl:* **F's, f's** [ɛfs]) sexta letra del alfabeto inglés

**f.** abr. de **farthing, female, feminine, folio, forte** y **franc**

**F.** abr. de **Fahrenheit, French** y **Friday**

**Fabian** [ˈfebɪən] *adj* fabiano; *s* fabiano; Fabián (*nombre propio de varón*)

**fable** [ˈfebəl] *s* fábula; *va* inventar (*fábulas*); *vn* inventar fábulas, contar fábulas; fingir, mentir

**fabled** [ˈfebəld] *adj* contado en fábulas, legendario; ficticio, fingido

**fabric** [ˈfæbrɪk] *s* género, tejido, tela de uso o adorno; textura; fábrica

**fabricate** [ˈfæbrɪket] *va* fabricar

**fabrication** [ˌfæbrɪˈkeʃən] *s* fabricación; mentira

**fabricator** [ˈfæbrɪˌketər] *s* fabricante; fabricador (*p.ej., de mentiras*)

**fabrikoid** [ˈfæbrɪkɔɪd] *s* (trademark) fabricoide

**fabulist** [ˈfæbjəlɪst] *s* fabulista

**fabulous** [ˈfæbjələs] *adj* fabuloso

**façade** [fəˈsɑd] *s* fachada

**face** [fes] *s* cara; haz (*de las telas, las hojas de las plantas, etc.*); faz (*p.ej., de la tierra*); cara, dibujo (*de un naipe*); aspecto, semblante; mueca (*visaje ridículo*); esfera, muestra (*del reloj*); ancho (*de una polea*); cotillo (*del martillo*); paramento (*de un muro*); pundonor; (coll.) descaro; (com.) valor neto; (cryst. & geom.) cara; (mach.) cabeza (*de diente de rueda*); (mach.) superficie de contacto o de trabajo (*de la válvula de corredera*); (min.) cara de trabajo, fondo, frente (*p.ej., de la galería*); (print.) ojo (*relieve de las letras que produce la impresión*); (print.) carácter (*forma de las letras*); **in the face of** ante, en presencia de; a pesar de, luchando contra; **on the face of it** según las apariencias; **to keep a straight face** contener la risa; **to lose face** desprestigiarse, sufrir pérdida de prestigio; **to make a wry face** torcer el rostro (*mostrando desagrado*); **to make faces** hacer muecas; **to one's face** en la cara de uno, en la presencia de uno; **to pull a long face** poner la cara larga; **to save face** salvar las apariencias; **to set one's face against** mostrarse contrario a; **to show one's face** dejarse ver; **face to face** cara a cara, faz a faz ‖ *va* mirar hacia, volver la cara hacia; estar enfrente de; encararse con, arrostrar; forrar (*un vestido*); revestir (*un muro*); bruñir (*un metal*); acabar, alisar, labrar; **to face it out** no cejar, mantenerse firme; **to face out** sostener audazmente, insistir descaradamente en; **to face with** carear (*a uno*) con ‖ *vn* carear; volver la mirada; **to face about** volver la mirada; dar media vuelta; cambiar de opinión; **to face on** dar a, dar sobre; **to face up to** encararse con

**face card** *s* figura, naipe de figura

**face lathe** *s* torno de plato

**face lifting** *s* cirugía cosmética, decorativa o estética

**faceplate** [ˈfesˌplet] *s* (mach.) plato de mandril; (mach.) placa de recubrimiento

**face powder** *s* polvos blancos faciales

**facer** [ˈfesər] *s* puñetazo dado en la cara; revés violento e inesperado

**facet** [ˈfæsɪt] *s* faceta; (arch., zool. & fig.) faceta; *va* labrar facetas en, labrar en facetas

**facetious** [fəˈsiʃəs] *adj* chistoso, gracioso, salado

**face value** *s* valor facial; valor aparente o nominal; significado literal

**face wheel** *s* (mach.) rueda de dientes laterales

**facial** [ˈfeʃəl] *adj* facial; *s* (coll.) masaje facial

**facial angle** *s* ángulo facial

**facile** [ˈfæsɪl] *adj* fácil; vivo, listo

**facilitate** [fəˈsɪlɪtet] *va* facilitar

**facilitation** [fəˌsɪlɪˈteʃən] *s* facilitación

**facility** [fəˈsɪlɪtɪ] *s* (*pl:* **-ties**) facilidad; **facilities** *spl* facilidades (*comodidades*)

**facing** [ˈfesɪŋ] *s* encaramiento; paramento, revestimiento; (sew.) guarnición; **facings** *spl* vueltas

**facsim.** abr. de **facsimile**

**facsimile** [fækˈsɪmɪlɪ] *s* facsímile; **in facsimile** a facsímile; *adj* facsimilar; *va* facsimilar, hacer facsímile de

**fact** [fækt] *s* hecho; **in fact** de hecho, en realidad; **the fact is that** ello es que

**faction** [ˈfækʃən] *s* facción; discordia, disensión

**factional** [ˈfækʃənəl] *adj* faccionario

**factionalism** [ˈfækʃənəlɪzəm] *s* parcialidad, partidismo

**factionalist** [ˈfækʃənəlɪst] *s* faccionario

**factious** [ˈfækʃəs] *adj* faccioso

**factitious** [fækˈtɪʃəs] *adj* facticio

**factor** [ˈfæktər] *s* factor (*elemento que contribuye a producir un resultado*); (biochem., biol., law, math. & physiol.) factor; *va* (math.) dividir o descomponer en factores

**factorage** [ˈfæktərɪdʒ] *s* factoraje (*empleo de factor*); comisión pagada a un factor

**factorial** [fækˈtorɪəl] *s* (math.) factorial

**factory** [ˈfæktərɪ] *s* (*pl:* **-ries**) fábrica; factoría (*establecimiento comercial en país extranjero*)

**factotum** [fækˈtotəm] *s* factótum

**factual** [ˈfæktʃʊəl] *adj* objetivo, basado en hechos, real, verdadero

**facula** [ˈfækjələ] *s* (*pl:* **-lae** [li]) (astr.) fácula

**facultative** [ˈfækəlˌtetɪv] *adj* facultativo; (biol.) facultativo

**faculty** [ˈfækəltɪ] *s* (*pl:* **-ties**) facultad

**fad** [fæd] *s* chifladura, tema, manía; diversión favorita, novedad

**faddish** [ˈfædɪʃ] *adj* caprichoso, maniático; aficionado a novedades

**faddist** [ˈfædɪst] *s* caprichoso, maniático; aficionado a novedades

**fade** [fed] *va* marchitar; desteñir; cubrir la apuesta de (*en el juego de dados*); *vn* marchitarse; desteñirse; apagarse (*un sonido*); desvanecerse; (rad.) desvanecerse; **to fade away** desvanecerse; **to fade in** aparecer gradualmente; **to fade out** desaparecerse gradualmente

**fadeless** [ˈfedlɪs] *adj* inmarcesible

**fadeout** [ˈfedˌaʊt] *s* desaparición gradual (*de sonido o imagen*); (mov.) imagen que desaparece lentamente

**fading** [ˈfedɪŋ] *s* (rad.) fáding, desvanecimiento (*de la señal*)

**faecal** [ˈfikəl] *adj* var. de **fecal**

**faeces** [ˈfisiz] *spl* var. de **feces**

**faerie** [ˈfɛrɪ] *s* (archaic) hada; (archaic) tierra de las hadas; *adj* (archaic) de hada, de hadas

**faery** [ˈfɛrɪ] *s* (*pl:* **-ies**) (archaic) var. de **faerie;** *adj* (archaic) var. de **faerie**

**fag** [fæg] *s* yunque, esclavo del trabajo; afán, trabajo penoso; (coll.) cigarrillo, pitillo; (Brit.) alumno que sirve á los alumnos mayores; (*pret & pp:* **fagged;** *ger:* **fagging**) *va* cansar, fatigar; hacer trotar; exigir faenas groseras a; *vn* trabajar duramente, hacer faenas rudas, desfallecer de cansancio

**fagaceous** [fəˈgeʃəs] *adj* (bot.) fagáceo

**fag end** *s* cabo, final; resto, retal; sobra, desperdicio; cadillos, pezolada; flecos, hilachas; (naut.) cordón

**faggot** [ˈfægət] *s & va* var. de **fagot**

**faggoting** [ˈfægətɪŋ] *s* var. de **fagoting**

**fagot** [ˈfægət] *s* haz de leña; fajina (*haz de leña*

*ligera*); haz de barras de hierro o acero; *va* atar o liar en haces; (sew.) adornar con vainicas
**fagoting** ['fægətɪŋ] *s* (sew.) vainicas
**Fahr.** abr. de **Fahrenheit**
**Fahrenheit thermometer** ['færənhaɪt] o ['fɑrənhaɪt] *s* termómetro de Fahrenheit
**faïence** [faɪ'ɑns] o [fe'ɑns] *s* faenza
**fail** [fel] *s* falta; **without fail** sin falta; *va* faltar a, faltar a sus obligaciones a; (coll.) reprobar, suspender (*a un alumno*); (coll.) salir mal en (*un examen*); *vn* faltar; fracasar, malograrse; (coll.) salir suspendido, salir mal (*un alumno*); (com.) quebrar, hacer bancarrota; fallar (*p.ej., un motor*); **to fail to** + *inf* no poder + *inf;* no acertar a + *inf,* no llegar a + *inf;* dejar de + *inf,* p.ej., **don't fail to come** no deje Vd. de venir
**failing** ['felɪŋ] *s* falta; flaqueza; fracaso, malogro; *adj* decadente; *prep* sin, a falta de
**faille** [fel] *s* faya (*tejido de seda*); (archaic) falla (*cobertura de la cabeza que usaban las mujeres*)
**failure** ['feljər] *s* falta; fracaso, malogro; quiebra, bancarrota; fracasado; quebrado; perdigón (*alumno que pierde el curso*); **the failure to** + *inf* el dejar de + *inf*
**fain** [fen] *adj* (archaic & poet.) obligado, resignado; (archaic & poet.) dispuesto, deseoso; *adv* (archaic & poet.) gustosamente, de buena gana
**faint** [fent] *s* desmayo, desfallecimiento; **faints** *spl* productos impuros y débiles de la destilación; **to fall into a faint** desmayarse; *adj* débil; desmayado; **to be faint with** desmayarse a consecuencia de, morirse de; **to feel faint** sentirse mareado o débil; *vn* desmayarse, desfallecer; (archaic) desfallecer de ánimo
**faintheart** ['fent,hɑrt] *s* cobarde
**faint-hearted** ['fent'hɑrtɪd] *adj* cobarde, medroso
**faintness** ['fentnɪs] *s* debilidad; desmayo, desfallecimiento
**fair** [fɛr] *adj* justo; imparcial; honrado; legal; cortés; corriente, ordinario, regular; favorable, propicio; bien formado, hermoso; distinto, legible; rubio (*de pelo*); blanco (*de tez*); despejado, sereno (*cielo*); bueno, bonancible (*tiempo*); limpio; admisible; bueno, p.ej., **to be in a fair way to succeed** estar en buen camino de prosperar; **fair and square** (coll.) honrado a carta cabal; *adv* directamente; favorablemente; **to bid fair to** + *inf* prometer + *inf,* dar indicios de + *inf;* **to play fair** jugar limpio; **to speak one fair** hablarle a uno cortésmente; *s* feria; quermese, verbena; (archaic) mujer; (archaic) amada, querida
**fair ball** *s* (baseball) buen batazo, golpe bueno
**fair copy** *s* copia en limpio
**fair game** *s* caza legal; blanco u objeto legítimo
**fairground** ['fɛr,graund] *s* real (*campo donde se celebra una feria*)
**fair-haired** ['fɛr'hɛrd] *adj* pelirrubio; favorito, predilecto
**fairish** ['fɛrɪʃ] *adj* bastante bueno, bastante grande, bastante bien
**fairly** ['fɛrlɪ] *adv* justamente; imparcialmente; efectivamente; regularmente; distintamente; bastante, medianamente
**fair-minded** ['fɛr'maɪndɪd] *adj* imparcial, justo
**fairness** ['fɛrnɪs] *s* justicia; imparcialidad; honradez; legalidad; cortesía; hermosura; serenidad (*del cielo*); blancura (*de tez*); limpieza
**fair play** *s* juego limpio, proceder leal
**fair sex** *s* bello sexo
**fair-spoken** ['fɛr'spokən] *adj* cortés, bien hablado
**fair to middling** *adj* (coll.) mediano, bastante bueno
**fair-trade agreement** ['fɛr'tred] *s* convenio entre el fabricante y el comerciante en que se fija el precio mínimo de las manufacturas
**fairway** ['fɛr,we] *s* (naut.) canalizo; (golf) terreno entre tees donde no hay obstáculos
**fair-weather** ['fɛr,wɛðər] *adj* del buen tiempo; de los días prósperos; **fair-weather friend** amigo del buen viento
**fairy** ['fɛrɪ] *s* (*pl:* **-ies**) hada; *adj* de hada, de hadas, feérico
**fairy godmother** *s* hada madrina
**fairyland** [fɛrɪ,lænd] *s* tierra de las hadas; lugar hermoso y encantador
**fairy ring** *s* corro de bruja o de brujas (*círculo hecho en la hierba por ciertos hongos*)
**fairy tale** *s* cuento de hadas; (fig.) cuento de hadas, bella poesía
**fait accompli** [fɛtakõ'pli] *s* (Fr.) hecho consumado, hecho cumplido
**faith** [feθ] *s* fe; **in bad faith** de mala fe; **in good faith** de buena fe; **in faith** en verdad; **to break faith with** faltar a la palabra dada a; **to have faith in** tener fe en; **to keep faith with** cumplir la palabra dada a; **to pin one's faith on** tener puesta su esperanza en; **upon my faith!** ¡a fe mía!, ¡por mi fe!; *interj* ¡en verdad!
**faith cure** *s* curación por fe
**faithful** ['feθfəl] *adj* fiel, leal; **the faithful** los fieles, los creyentes
**faithfulness** ['feθfəlnɪs] *s* fidelidad
**faithless** ['feθlɪs] *adj* sin fe, infiel, desleal, falso
**fake** [fek] *s* (coll.) falsificación; (coll.) impostura, patraña; (coll.) farsante, impostor, patrañero; (naut.) aduja; *adj* (coll.) falso, falsificado, fingido; farsante; *va* (coll.) falsificar, fingir; (naut.) adujar; *vn* (coll.) falsificar, fingir
**faker** ['fekər] *s* (coll.) falsificador; (coll.) impostor, patrañero; (coll.) embustero; (coll.) buhonero
**fakir** [fə'kɪr] o ['fekər] *s* faquir
**Falange** ['felændʒ] *s* (pol.) Falange
**Falangist** [fə'lændʒɪst] *adj & s* falangista
**falcate** ['fælket] *adj* falcado
**falchion** ['fɔltʃən] *s* faca; (poet.) espada
**falciform** ['fælsɪfɔrm] *adj* falciforme
**falcon** ['fɔkən] o ['fɔlkən] *s* (orn.) halcón; (arti.) falcón
**falconer** ['fɔkənər] o ['fɔlkənər] *s* cetrero, halconero
**falconry** ['fɔkənrɪ] o ['fɔlkənrɪ] *s* cetrería, halconería
**falderal** ['fældə,ræl] o **falderol** ['fældə,rɑl] *s* chuchería, menudencia, retazo; disparate, tontería; estribillo de una canción que no significa nada
**faldstool** ['fɔld,stul] *s* faldistorio; facistol (*atril*)
**Falkland Islands** [,fɔklənd] *spl* islas Malvinas
**fall** [fɔl] *s* caída; catarata, salto de agua; baja (*de precios*); desembocadura (*de un río*); otoño; (naut.) tira de aparejo; (sport) partido de lucha grecorromana; **falls** *spl* cataratas, salto de agua; (naut.) aparejo de bajar o izar los botes; **the Fall** la Caída (*pecado del primer hombre*); **to ride for a fall** ir por mal camino, ir a acabar mal; *adj* otoñal; (*pret:* **fell;** *pp:* **fallen**) *vn* caer o caerse; ponerse triste (*la expresión del rostro*); **to fall aboard** (naut.) chocar con; **to fall across** dar con, encontrarse con; **to fall apart** caerse a pedazos; (fig.) ir al desastre; **to fall away** apostatar; reincidir; enflaquecer; **to fall back** (mil.) replegarse; faltar a su palabra; **to fall back on** o **upon** (mil.) replegarse hacia; echar mano de, recurrir a; **to fall backward** caer de espaldas; **to fall behind** quedarse atrás, perder terreno; **to fall down** caerse; postrarse; (slang) fracasar; **to fall due** caer o vencer (*p.ej., una letra*); **to fall flat** caer tendido, caer largo; no surtir efecto, no tener éxito; **to fall for** (slang) ser engañado por; (slang) enamorarse de; **to fall in** desplomarse (*p.ej., un techo*); caducar, terminar; ponerse de acuerdo; (mil.) ponerse en su lugar; **to fall into** abrazar, adoptar; adquirir (*p.ej., un hábito*); acceder a obrar de acuerdo con; tomar su lugar en; **to fall in upon** encontrarse con, tropezar con; visitar de repente o inesperadamente; **to fall in with** encontrarse con; trabar amistades con; conformarse con; ponerse de acuerdo con; juntarse con; **to fall off** caerse; caer de o desde; apostatar; decaer; disminuir; enemistarse; dirigirse, inclinarse; (naut.) abatir; **to fall on** asaltar, echarse sobre; encontrarse con; empezar; echar mano de, recurrir a; caer o bajar rápidamente sobre; recaer sobre; (phonet.) cargar en (*dícese del acento de una palabra*); **to fall out** caerse; desavenirse; acontecer; ve-

nir a ser, resultar; **to fall out of** caerse de (*p.ej., un árbol*); **to fall out with** reñirse con; esquinarse con; **to fall over** caerse; volcarse, venirse abajo; desertar; (slang) adular, halagar; **to fall through** fracasar, malograrse; **to fall to** venir a las manos; cerrarse por sí mismo; recaer (*la herencia, la elección, etc.*) en; tocar, corresponder a; (mil.) caer en poder de; (coll.) empezar a comer; **to fall to** + *ger* empezar a + *inf;* **to fall under** estar sujeto o subordinado a; estar entre, estar comprendido en; **to fall upon** asaltar, echarse sobre; encontrarse con; echar mano de, recurrir a; recaer sobre; **to fall within** estar dentro de; estar entre, estar comprendido en
**fallacious** [fəˈleʃəs] *adj* erróneo; delusorio; falaz (*que halaga con falsas apariencias*)
**fallacy** [ˈfæləsɪ] *s* (*pl:* **-cies**) error, falsedad; carácter erróneo; (log.) falacia
**fallal** [ˌfæˈlæl] *s* faralá, adorno excesivo; modo afectado
**fallen** [ˈfɔlən] *adj* caído; **the fallen** los caídos (*en la lucha*); *pp de* **fall**
**fallen angel** *s* ángel caído
**fall guy** *s* (slang) pato, cabeza de turco
**fallibility** [ˌfælɪˈbɪlɪtɪ] *s* falibilidad
**fallible** [ˈfælɪbəl] *adj* falible
**falling** [ˈfɔlɪŋ] *adj* cayente; (phonet.) decreciente (*diptongo*)
**falling sickness** *s* (path.) mal caduco
**falling star** *s* estrella fugaz
**fall line** *s* borde de una meseta formado por una línea de cataratas; (U.S.A.) línea que va de norte a sur, al este de los Apalaches, donde terminan los estratos duros y comienzan los terrenos blandos de la costa del este
**Fallopian tube** [fəˈlopɪən] *s* (anat.) trompa de Falopio
**fallout** [ˈfɔlˌaut] *s* caída radiactiva, precipitación radiactiva
**fallout shelter** *s* refugio antiatómico
**fallow** [ˈfælo] *adj* barbechado; flavo; **to let lie fallow** dejar en barbecho; **to lie fallow** estar en barbecho; *s* barbecho; *va* barbechar
**fallow deer** *s* (zool.) gamo, paleto
**fall wheat** *s* trigo sembrado en el otoño
**false** [fɔls] *adj* falso; postizo; *adv* falsamente; **to play false** traicionar
**false acacia** *s* (bot.) acacia falsa
**false alarm** *s* falsa alarma
**false bottom** *s* fondo falso
**false colors** *spl* bandera falsa; pretextos falsos
**false face** *s* careta, mascarilla; carantamaula (*careta fea*)
**false hair** *s* pelo postizo o falso
**false-hearted** [ˈfɔlsˈhartɪd] *adj* pérfido, traidor
**falsehood** [ˈfɔlshud] *s* falsedad
**false imprisonment** *s* detención o prisión ilegal
**false keel** *s* (naut.) falsa quilla
**false key** *s* llave falsa
**falseness** [ˈfɔlsnɪs] *s* falsedad
**false pretenses** *spl* (law) estafa, dolo
**false pride** *s* falso orgullo
**false relation** *s* (mus.) falsa relación
**false return** *s* declaración falsa
**false ribs** *spl* (anat.) costillas falsas
**false step** *s* tropiezo; (fig.) paso en falso
**false teeth** *spl* dientes postizos o falsos
**falsetto** [fɔlˈsɛto] *s* (*pl:* **-tos**) falsete (*voz*); falsetista (*persona*); **in a falsetto** de falsete; *adj* del falsete; que canta de falsete; (fig.) artificial, poco natural; *adv* de falsete
**falsification** [ˌfɔlsɪfɪˈkeʃən] *s* falsificación; mentira; refutación
**falsify** [ˈfɔlsɪfaɪ] (*pret & pp:* **-fied**) *va* falsificar; refutar; *vn* falsificar; mentir
**falsity** [ˈfɔlsɪtɪ] *s* (*pl:* **-ties**) falsedad
**falter** [ˈfɔltər] *s* vacilación; balbuceo; *va* decir titubeando; *vn* vacilar; balbucear
**falx** [fælks] *s* (*pl:* **falces** [ˈfælsiz]) (anat.) falce, hoz
**falx cerebelli** [ˌsɛrɪˈbɛlaɪ] *s* (anat.) hoz del cerebelo
**falx cerebri** [ˈsɛrɪbraɪ] *s* (anat.) hoz del cerebro
**fame** [fem] *s* fama; *va* afamar
**famed** [femd] *adj* afamado
**familiar** [fəˈmɪljər] *adj* familiar; **to be familiar to** ser familiar a; **to be familiar with** estar familiarizado con (*una persona o cosa*); tener muy sabido; *s* familiar; (eccl.) familiar
**familiarity** [fəˌmɪlɪˈærɪtɪ] *s* (*pl:* **-ties**) familiaridad; conocimiento, p.ej., **familiarity with algebra** conocimiento del álgebra
**familiarization** [fəˌmɪljərɪˈzeʃən] *s* familiarización
**familiarize** [fəˈmɪljəraɪz] *va* familiarizar; **to familiarize oneself with** familiarizarse con
**family** [ˈfæmɪlɪ] *s* (*pl:* **-lies**) familia; *adj* familiar, p.ej., **family ties** lazos familiares; **in a family way** sin ceremonia; **in the family way** (coll.) embarazada, encinta
**family circle** *s* círculo de la familia; (theat.) gallinero, paraíso
**family man** *s* padre de familia; hombre casero
**family name** *s* apellido, nombre de familia
**family physician** *s* médico de cabecera
**family skeleton** *s* cosa vergonzosa en una familia que se intenta guardar en secreto
**family tree** *s* árbol genealógico
**famine** [ˈfæmɪn] *s* hambre; carestía
**famish** [ˈfæmɪʃ] *va & vn* hambrear
**famished** [ˈfæmɪʃt] *adj* famélico
**famous** [ˈfeməs] *adj* famoso; (coll.) famoso (*excelente*)
**famulus** [ˈfæmjələs] *s* (*pl:* **-li** [laɪ]) fámulo
**fan** [fæn] *s* abanico; ventilador; aventador (*para aventar el fuego*); aventadora (*para aventar los granos*); (slang) aficionado (*a deportes, películas, etc.*); (*pret & pp:* **fanned;** *ger:* **fanning**) *va* abanicar; aventar; ahuyentar con abanico; activar o avivar (*el fuego*); excitar (*las pasiones*); azotar (*el viento, p.ej., el rostro*); abrir o extender en abanico; (slang) pegar, zurrar; (baseball) hacer golpear mal la pelota tres veces; **to fan oneself** abanicarse; *vn* abanicarse; moverse impulsado por la brisa; soplar (*el viento*); abrirse o extenderse en abanico; salir (*un camino*) en todas direcciones; (baseball) golpear mal la pelota tres veces
**fanatic** [fəˈnætɪk] *adj & s* fanático
**fanatical** [fəˈnætɪkəl] *adj* fanático
**fanaticism** [fəˈnætɪsɪzəm] *s* fanatismo
**fan belt** *s* correa de ventilador
**fan blade** *s* paleta de ventilador
**fancied** [ˈfænsɪd] *adj* imaginado, imaginario
**fancier** [ˈfænsɪər] *s* aficionado; criador aficionado (*de aves, animales, etc.*); soñador, visionario
**fanciful** [ˈfænsɪfəl] *adj* fantástico; imaginativo
**fancy** [ˈfænsɪ] *s* (*pl:* **-cies**) fantasía; antojo, capricho; afición, gusto, cariño; (mus.) fantasía; **to strike one's fancy** antojársele a uno; **to take a fancy to** prendarse de, coger cariño a; *adj* (*comp:* **-cier;** *super:* **-ciest**) fantástico; extravagante (*idea*); de fantasía, de imitación; de lujo, fino; ornamental, de adorno; primoroso; vendedor de géneros de fantasía; vendedor de géneros de lujo; criado o cultivado por afición; (*pret & pp:* **-cied**) *va* imaginar; aficionarse a; prendarse de; criar (*aves, animales, etc.*) por afición; *vn* fantasear; prendarse de amor
**fancy ball** *s* baile de trajes
**fancy dive** *s* salto ornamental
**fancy diving** *s* buceo acrobático, saltos ornamentales
**fancy dress** *s* traje de fantasía, traje de capricho
**fancy-dress ball** [ˈfænsɪˌdrɛs] *s* baile de trajes
**fancy foods** *spl* comestibles de lujo
**fancy-free** [ˈfænsɪˈfri] *adj* libre del poder del amor, no enamorado
**fancy goods** *spl* géneros de fantasía
**fancy jewelry** *s* joyas de fantasía, joyas de imitación
**fancy skater** *s* patinador de fantasía
**fancy skating** *s* patinaje de fantasía
**fancy woods** *spl* maderas preciosas
**fancywork** [ˈfænsɪˌwʌrk] *s* (sew.) labor
**fane** [fen] *s* (archaic & poet.) templo
**fanfare** [ˈfænfɛr] *s* fanfarria (*pompa excesiva; tocata de caza*); (mus.) fanfarria
**fanfaronade** [ˌfænfərəˈned] *s* fanfarronada
**fang** [fæŋ] *s* colmillo (*del lobo, las fieras, etc.*); diente (*del reptil; del tenedor, la horquilla, etc.*); raíz (*de diente*)

**fanion** ['fænjən] *s* banderola; (surv.) banderola
**fanlight** ['fæn,laɪt] *s* (arch.) abanico
**fan mail** *s* (sport) correo de hinchas; (taur.) correo de aficionados; (theat.) correo de admiradores
**Fannie** o **Fanny** ['fænɪ] *s* Paquita
**fanning mill** *s* (agr.) máquina aventadora
**fanon** ['fænən] *s* (eccl.) fanón
**fan palm** *s* (bot.) miraguano, palmera de abanico
**fan-shaped** ['fæn,ʃept] *adj* en forma de abanico
**fantail** ['fæn,tel] *s* (orn.) paloma colipava; (carp.) cola de abanico; (arch.) bovedilla; mechero de mariposa
**fan-tan** ['fæn,tæn] *s* juego chino por dinero; juego de naipes en el cual gana quien pierde sus naipes primero
**fantasia** [fæn'tɑzɪə] o [,fæntə'ziə] *s* (mus.) fantasía
**fantastic** [fæn'tæstɪk] o **fantastical** [fæn'tæstɪkəl] *adj* fantástico
**fantasy** ['fæntəzɪ] o ['fæntəsɪ] *s* (*pl:* **-sies**) fantasía; (mus.) fantasía
**fan tracery** *s* (arch.) red decorativa de bóveda de abanico
**fan vaulting** *s* (arch.) bóveda de abanico
**fan window** *s* (arch.) abanico
**fanwise** ['fæn,waɪz] *adv* en abanico
**far** [fɑr] *adj* (*comp:* **farther;** *super:* **farthest**) lejano; más lejano; largo (*viaje*); posterior; **on the far side of** del otro lado de; *adv* (*comp:* **farther;** *super:* **farthest**) lejos; más lejos; muy, p.ej., **far different** muy diferente; mucho, p.ej., **far better** mucho mejor; **as far as** hasta, hasta donde; tan lejos como; en cuanto, según que; **as far as I am concerned** por lo que a mí me toca; **as far as I know** que yo sepa, según parece; **by far** con mucho; **how far** cuán lejos, hasta dónde, hasta qué punto; **how far is it?** ¿cuánto hay de aquí?; **in so far as** en cuanto, en tanto que; **so far** hasta ahora, hasta entonces; hasta aquí, hasta ahí; **so far as** hasta, hasta donde; en cuanto, según que; **so far so good** mientras siga así, todo va bien; **that is going too far** eso es demasiado fuerte; **thus far** hasta ahora; **thus far this year** en lo que va del año; **to be far from** + *ger* estar lejos de + *inf*; **to go far** ir lejos; alcanzar para mucho; durar mucho; **to go far to** o **toward** contribuir mucho a; **far and near** o **far and wide** por todas partes; **far away** muy lejos; **far be it from me** no permita Dios; **far from** lejos de (*p.ej., la ciudad, el ánimo de uno*); **far from it** ni con mucho, muy al contrario; **far into** hasta muy adentro de; hasta muy tarde de, hasta las altas horas de (*la noche*); hasta muy avanzado (*p.ej., el verano*); **far more** mucho más; **far off** a lo lejos, a gran distancia
**farad** ['færæd] *s* (elec.) faradio
**faradic** [fə'rædɪk] *adj* farádico
**faradism** ['færədɪzəm] *s* faradismo; (med.) faradismo
**faradization** [,færədɪ'zeʃən] *s* (med.) faradización
**faradize** ['færədaɪz] *va* (med.) faradizar
**faradmeter** ['færæd,mitər] *s* (elec.) faradímetro
**farandole** ['færəndol] *s* farándola o farándula (*baile*)
**faraway** ['fɑrə,we] *adj* lejano; abstraído, preocupado
**farce** [fɑrs] *s* (theat.) farsa; (fig.) farsa, cosa de reír; *va* embutir (*un escrito*) de pasajes o citas chistosas
**farceur** [fɑr'sʌr] *s* bromista, chancero; farsante (*cómico*)
**farcical** ['fɑrsɪkəl] *adj* absurdo, ridículo, improbable; (vet.) muermoso
**far cry** *s* gran distancia, gran diferencia
**farcy** ['fɑrsɪ] *s* (vet.) muermo
**fardel** ['fɑrdəl] *s* (archaic) carga, lío, paquete
**fare** [fɛr] *s* pasaje; pasajero; alimento, comida; **to collect fares** cobrar el pasaje; *vn* acontecer, suceder; pasarlo; irle a uno (*bien o mal*), p.ej., **how did you fare?** ¿cómo le ha ido a Vd.?; vivir (*bien o mal*); comer; (archaic) ir, viajar; **to fare forth** ponerse en camino
**Far East** *s* Extremo Oriente, Lejano Oriente
**farewell** ['fɛr'wɛl] *s* despedida, adiós; salida; **to bid farewell to** o **to take farewell of** despedirse de; *adj* de despedida, p.ej., **farewell song** canción de despedida; *interj* ¡adiós!
**far-fetched** ['fɑr'fɛtʃt] *adj* forzado, traído por los pelos
**far-flung** ['fɑr'flʌŋ] *adj* extenso, vasto, de gran alcance
**farina** [fə'rinə] *s* harina; almidón; fécula; (zool.) polvo harinoso
**farinaceous** [,færɪ'neʃəs] *adj* (bot.) farináceo
**farkleberry** ['fɑrkəl,bɛrɪ] *s* (*pl:* **-ries**) (bot.) batodendrón
**farm** [fɑrm] *s* granja; terreno agrícola; plantación; *adj* agrícola; agropecuario; *va* cultivar o labrar (*la tierra*); arrendar; hacer contrato por el cuidado de (*p.ej., los indigentes*); **to farm out** ceder (*un trabajo*) por contrato; *vn* cultivar la tierra y criar animales
**farmer** ['fɑrmər] *s* granjero; agricultor, labrador
**farmerette** [,fɑrmə'rɛt] *s* (coll.) agricultora, labradora
**farmerish** ['fɑrmərɪʃ] *adj* apatanado
**Farmer-Labor Party** ['fɑrmər'lebər] *s* (U.S.A.) partido obrero-campesino
**farm hand** *s* peón, mozo de granja
**farmhouse** ['fɑrm,haʊs] *s* cortijo, alquería
**farming** ['fɑrmɪŋ] *s* agricultura, labranza
**farm produce** *s* productos del suelo
**farm school** *s* granja escuela
**farmstead** ['fɑrmstɛd] *s* granja
**farmyard** ['fɑrm,jɑrd] *s* corral de granja
**faro** ['fɛro] *s* faraón (*juego de cartas*)
**far-off** ['fɑr,ɔf] o ['fɑr,ɑf] *adj* lejano, distante
**farrago** [fə'rego] *s* (*pl:* **-goes**) fárrago
**far-reaching** ['fɑr'ritʃɪŋ] *adj* de mucho alcance
**farrier** ['færɪər] *s* herrador; albéitar
**farriery** ['færɪərɪ] *s* (*pl:* **-ies**) herrería; albeitería
**farrow** ['færo] *s* lechigada de puercos; parto de la marrana; *adj* horra (*vaca*); *va & vn* parir (*la marrana*)
**far-seeing** ['fɑr'siɪŋ] *adj* longividente; previsor, precavido
**far-sighted** ['fɑr'saɪtɪd] *adj* longividente; previsor, precavido; présbita
**far-sightedness** ['fɑr'saɪtɪdnɪs] *s* buena visión, penetración; previsión; presbicia
**farther** ['fɑrðər] *adj comp* más lejano; más, adicional; *adv comp* más lejos, más allá; además, también; **how much farther** cuánto más; **farther on** más adelante
**farthermost** ['fɑrðərmost] *adj super* más lejano (*de todos*)
**farthest** ['fɑrðɪst] *adj super* más lejano (*de todos*); último; *adv super* más lejos, a más distancia; más
**farthing** ['fɑrðɪŋ] *s* (Brit.) cuarto de penique
**farthingale** ['fɑrðɪŋgel] *s* verdugado, miriñaque
**Far West** *s* lejano oeste (*de los EE.UU.*)
**fasces** ['fæsiz] *spl* fasces
**fascia** ['fæʃɪə] *s* (*pl:* **-ae** [i]) (anat.) fascia; (arch.) faja; (surg.) faja o fascia
**fascial** ['fæʃɪəl] *adj* fascial
**fascicle** ['fæsɪkəl] *s* fascículo (*de un libro*); manojo, racimo; (anat. & bot.) fascículo
**fascicled** ['fæsɪkəld] *adj* fasciculado
**fasciculus** [fə'sɪkjələs] *s* (*pl:* **-li** [laɪ]) fascículo (*de un libro*); (anat.) fascículo
**fascinate** ['fæsɪnet] *va* fascinar; (archaic) fascinar (*aojar; hechizar*)
**fascinating** ['fæsɪ,netɪŋ] *adj* fascinador o fascinante
**fascination** [,fæsɪ'neʃən] *s* fascinación; (archaic) fascinación (*aojo*)
**fascinator** ['fæsɪ,netər] *s* fascinador; mantilla ligera de ganchillo
**fascine** [fæ'sin] *s* haz de leña, fajina; (fort.) fajina
**fascism** ['fæʃɪzəm] *s* fascismo
**fascist** ['fæʃɪst] *adj & s* fascista
**fashion** ['fæʃən] *s* moda, boga; estilo, manera; elegancia, buen tono; alta sociedad, gente de buen tono; **after** o **in a fashion** hasta cierto punto, en cierto modo, así así; **in fashion** de

moda; **out of fashion** fuera de moda, pasado de moda; **to go out of fashion** pasar de moda; *va* labrar, forjar
**fashionable** [ˈfæʃənəbəl] *adj* elegante, de moda, de buen tono
**fashion designing** *s* alta costura
**fashion piece** *s* (naut.) aleta
**fashion plate** *s* figurín (*dibujo*); (coll.) figurín, elegante (*persona*)
**fashion shop** *s* casa de modas
**fast** [fæst] o [fɑst] *s* ayuno; día de ayuno; asegurador; (naut.) cable de amarra; **to break one's fast** desayunarse; romper el ayuno; *adj* rápido, veloz; adelantado (*reloj*); disipado, disoluto; fijo; estable; fiel (*amigo*); **to pull a fast one** (slang) jugar una mala pasada; *adv* rápidamente, velozmente; firmemente; completamente; profundamente; (archaic) cerca; **fast by** cerca de; **to hold fast** mantenerse firme; **to hold fast to** agarrarse bien de; afirmarse en; **to play fast and loose** proceder de manera poco sincera; **to live fast** entregarse a los placeres o los vicios; *vn* ayunar
**fast and loose pulleys** *spl* (mach.) contramarcha (*juego de dos poleas, una fija y la otra libre o loca, que sirven para embragar o desembragar un árbol*)
**fast day** *s* día de ayuno
**fasten** [ˈfæsən] o [ˈfɑsən] *va* fijar; cerrar, cerrar con llave; atar; abrochar; ajustarse (*p.ej., el cinturón*); aplicar (*la culpa*); imprimir; *vn* fijarse; cuajarse; **to fasten on** o **upon** agarrarse o asirse a o de
**fastener** [ˈfæsənər] o [ˈfɑsənər] *s* asilla, asegurador, cierre
**fastening** [ˈfæsənɪŋ] o [ˈfɑsənɪŋ] *s* aseguramiento; asegurador (*instrumento*); cerradura; cerrojo; botón; broche; corchete
**fastidious** [fæsˈtɪdɪəs] *adj* quisquilloso; arrogante, desdeñoso
**fastigium** [fæsˈtɪdʒɪəm] *s* (*pl:* **-a** [ə]) (anat. & arch.) fastigio
**fasting** [ˈfæstɪŋ] o [ˈfɑstɪŋ] *s* ayuno
**fastness** [ˈfæstnɪs] o [ˈfɑstnɪs] *s* rapidez; adelanto (*del reloj*); disipación; estrechez (*de la amistad*); fijeza, firmeza; estabilidad o solidez (*de materias colorantes*); plaza fuerte
**fat** [fæt] *adj* (*comp:* **fatter;** *super:* **fattest**) gordo; lerdo, pesado, torpe; fuerte, poderoso; opulento; pingüe, provechoso; fértil; (aut.) caliente (*chispa*); **to get fat** engordar; *s* gordo, grasa; (chem.) grasa; **the fat of the land** lo mejor y más rico de la tierra; (*pret & pp:* **fatted;** *ger:* **fatting**) *va & vn* engordar
**fatal** [ˈfetəl] *adj* fatal
**fatalism** [ˈfetəlɪzəm] *s* fatalismo
**fatalist** [ˈfetəlɪst] *s* fatalista
**fatalistic** [ˌfetəˈlɪstɪk] *adj* fatalista
**fatality** [feˈtælɪtɪ] o [fəˈtælɪtɪ] *s* (*pl:* **-ties**) fatalidad; muerte
**fatally** [ˈfetəlɪ] *adv* fatalmente
**Fata Morgana** [ˈfɑtə mɔrˈgɑnə] *s* (meteor.) Fata Morgana; (myth.) Morgana
**fate** [fet] *s* hado; **Fates** *spl* (myth.) Parcas
**fated** [ˈfetɪd] *adj* fatal; predestinado a la ruina, la muerte, etc.
**fateful** [ˈfetfəl] *adj* fatal; fatídico
**fathead** [ˈfætˌhɛd] *s* (coll.) tronco, estúpido
**father** [ˈfɑðər] *s* padre; (eccl.) padre; tío (*tratamiento que se da a los hombres ancianos*); *va* engendrar; prohijar; servir de padre a, tratar como hijo; inventar, originar, producir; atribuir
**father confessor** *s* (eccl.) padre espiritual; confidente
**fatherhood** [ˈfɑðərhud] *s* paternidad
**father-in-law** [ˈfɑðərɪnˌlɔ] *s* (*pl:* **fathers-in-law**) suegro
**fatherland** [ˈfɑðərˌlænd] *s* patria
**fatherless** [ˈfɑðərlɪs] *adj* huérfano de padre; abandonado, sin amparo de padre
**fatherly** [ˈfɑðərlɪ] *adj* paternal; *adv* paternalmente
**Father of his Country** *s* padre de la patria (*título de honor concedido a los emperadores romanos y después a otros monarcas y príncipes y en EE.UU. a Jorge Wáshington*)
**Father of Waters** *s* padre de las aguas (*el río Misisipí*)
**fathers of the church** *spl* padres de la iglesia, santos padres
**Father Time** *s* el Tiempo (*representación del tiempo en figura de un anciano con una guadaña en una mano y un reloj de arena en la otra*)
**fathom** [ˈfæðəm] *s* (naut.) braza; *va* sondear; desenmarañar, profundizar
**fathomable** [ˈfæðəməbəl] *adj* sondable; comprensible
**fathomless** [ˈfæðəmlɪs] *adj* insondable; (fig.) insondable, incomprensible
**fatidic** [feˈtɪdɪk] o [fəˈtɪdɪk] *adj* fatídico
**fatigue** [fəˈtig] *s* fatiga; (mech. & physiol.) fatiga; (mil.) faena, trabajo distinto del manejo de las armas; *va* fatigar, cansar
**fatigue clothes** *spl* (mil.) traje de faena
**fatigue duty** *s* (mil.) faena, trabajo distinto del manejo de las armas
**fatigue party** *s* (mil.) pelotón de castigo
**fatiguing** [fəˈtigɪŋ] *adj* fatigoso
**fatling** [ˈfætlɪŋ] *s* ceboncillo
**fatness** [ˈfætnɪs] *s* gordura; graseza; fertilidad
**fatten** [ˈfætən] *va & vn* engordar
**fatty** [ˈfætɪ] *adj* (*comp:* **-tier;** *super:* **-tiest**) graso; gordiflón; (chem.) graso; (path.) grasoso; *s* (*pl:* **-ties**) (slang) gordiflón
**fatty acid** *s* (chem.) ácido graso
**fatty degeneration** *s* (path.) degeneración grasosa
**fatty heart** *s* (path.) corazón grasoso
**fatuity** [fəˈtjuɪtɪ] o [fəˈtuɪtɪ] *s* (*pl:* **-ties**) fatuidad; irrealidad, ilusión
**fatuous** [ˈfætʃuəs] *adj* fatuo; irreal, ilusivo
**faucal** [ˈfɔkəl] *adj* faucal
**fauces** [ˈfɔsiz] *spl* (anat.) fauces
**faucet** [ˈfɔsɪt] *s* grifo
**faugh** [fɔ] *interj* ¡puf!, ¡bah!
**fault** [fɔlt] *s* falta, culpa; (geol. & min.) falla; (sport) falta; (elec.) fuga de corriente, avería del circuito; **at fault** culpable; perplejo; **in fault** culpable; **it's your fault** Vd. tiene la culpa; **to a fault** excesivamente; **to find fault with** criticar, culpar; hallar defecto en; *va* culpar; (geol.) producir falla en
**faultfinder** [ˈfɔltˌfaɪndər] *s* criticón, reparón
**faultfinding** [ˈfɔltˌfaɪndɪŋ] *adj* criticón, reparón; *s* crítica, manía de criticar
**faultless** [ˈfɔltlɪs] *adj* intachable; perfecto
**faulty** [ˈfɔltɪ] *adj* (*comp:* **-ier;** *super:* **-iest**) defectuoso, imperfecto; culpable
**faun** [fɔn] *s* (myth.) fauno
**fauna** [ˈfɔnə] *s* fauna; (*cap.*) *s* (myth.) Fauna
**faunal** [ˈfɔnəl] *adj* fáunico
**Faust** [faust] *s* Fausto
**Faustian** [ˈfaustɪən] o [ˈfɔstɪən] *adj* fáustico
**faux pas** [fo ˈpɑ] *s* (*pl:* **faux pas** [fo ˈpɑ] o [fo ˈpɑz]) (Fr.) paso en falso
**favor** [ˈfevər] *s* favor; grata o atenta (*la carta de que se acusa recibo*); (fig.) favor (*regalo, señal, cinta*); **favors** *spl* favores (*de una mujer*); (fig.) regalos de fiesta (*tales como serpentinas, matracas, sombreros, panderetas*); **by your favor** con permiso de Vd.; **do me the favor of** + *ger* hágame Vd. el favor de + *inf;* **to be in favor** estar en favor (*tener buena aceptación*); **to be in favor of** estar por, ser partidario de; **to be in favor with** disfrutar del favor de, tener el apoyo de; **to be out of favor** no estar en favor; *va* favorecer; abstenerse de usar, usar con precaución; (coll.) parecerse a
**favorable** [ˈfevərəbəl] *adj* favorable
**favored** [ˈfevərd] *adj* favorecido; encarado, p.ej., **ill-favored** mal encarado; dotado, p.ej., **favored by nature** dotado por la naturaleza; **favored with beauty** dotado de hermosura
**favorite** [ˈfevərɪt] *adj* favorito, predilecto; *s* favorito
**favorite son** *s* (pol.) candidato favorito de un estado (*para la presidencia de los EE.UU.*)
**favoritism** [ˈfevərɪtɪzəm] *s* favoritismo
**favose** [ˈfevos] o [feˈvos] *adj* favoso
**favour** [ˈfevər] *s & va* (Brit.) var. de **favor**
**favus** [ˈfevəs] *s* (path.) favo
**fawn** [fɔn] *s* (zool.) cervato; corzo, gamito (*de menos de un año*); color de cervato; *vn* parir (*la cierva*); arrastrarse, reptar; hacer fiestas (*p.ej., el perro*); **to fawn on** o **upon** adular servilmente; hacer fiestas a

**fay** [fe] *s* hada; (archaic) fe; *va* empalmar, juntar; *vn* empalmarse, juntarse
**faze** [fez] *va* (coll.) inquietar, molestar, turbar, desanimar
**FBI** abr. de **Federal Bureau of Investigation**
**fealty** ['fiəltɪ] *s* (*pl:* **-ties**) homenaje; fidelidad, lealtad
**fear** [fɪr] *s* temor, miedo; **for fear of** por temor de, por miedo de; **for fear that** por miedo (de) que; **no fear** no hay peligro; **to be in fear of** tener miedo de; *va & vn* temer; **to fear for** temer por; **to fear to** + *inf* temer + *inf*
**fearful** ['fɪrfəl] *adj* medroso; (coll.) enorme, numeroso, excesivo, muy malo
**fearless** ['fɪrlɪs] *adj* intrépido, sin temor, arrojado
**fearsome** ['fɪrsəm] *adj* medroso
**feasibility** [,fizɪ'bɪlɪtɪ] *s* viabilidad
**feasible** ['fizɪbəl] *adj* viable, factible
**feast** [fist] *s* fiesta (*día; solemnidad; regocijo*); festín, banquete; *va* banquetear; *vn* banquetear; festejarse; **to feast on** regalarse con (*p.ej., golosinas*)
**feat** [fit] *s* hazaña, proeza, juego de destreza
**feather** ['fɛðər] *s* pluma; penacho (*adorno de plumas; vanidad*); condición, estado; vestido; clase, género; humor; mechón (*de pelo*); nada, p.ej., **to laugh at a feather** reírse de nada; (carp.) espiga, lengüeta; (mach.) chaveta, pestaña, soporte de refuerzo; (mach.) cuña, llave; (naut.) estela del periscopio (*del submarino*); **feathers** *spl* (poet.) alas; **in feather** plumado; **in fine, good** o **high feather** de buen humor; en buena salud; **to show the white feather** acobardarse, volver las espaldas; **feather in one's cap** timbre de honor, triunfo personal; *adj* de pluma, de plumas; leve, suave; *va* emplumar; poner pluma a (*una flecha*); cortar (*el aire*) volando; adelgazar, sutilizar; volver (*la pala del remo*) al sacarla del agua, poniéndola casi horizontal; (carp.) machihembrar; *vn* emplumecer; crecer, extenderse o moverse como pluma; volver la pala del remo al sacarla del agua, poniéndola casi horizontal
**feather bed** *s* colchón de plumas; (fig.) lecho de plumas
**featherbed** ['fɛðər,bɛd] (*pret & pp:* **-bedded;** *ger:* **-bedding**) *vn* exigir el empleo de más trabajadores de lo necesario
**featherbrain** ['fɛðər,bren] *s* cascabelero
**featherbrained** ['fɛðər,brend] *adj* cascabelero
**feather duster** *s* plumero
**feathered** ['fɛðərd] *adj* plumado; alado; ligero, veloz
**featheredge** ['fɛðər,ɛdʒ] *s* filván; bisel, canto vivo; (b.b.) barba; *adj* con filván; barbado (*papel*); *va* dejar filván en; biselar
**featheredged** ['fɛðər,ɛdʒd] *adj* con filván
**feathered hyacinth** *s* (bot.) jacinto de penacho
**feather grass** *s* (bot.) espolín
**featherless** ['fɛðərlɪs] *adj* implume
**featherstitch** ['fɛðər,stɪtʃ] *s* punto de espina, punto ruso; *va* adornar con punto de espina; *vn* hacer punto de espina
**featherweight** ['fɛðər,wet] *s* persona o cosa de muy poco peso; (box.) peso pluma; persona o cosa de poca importancia; imbécil, tonto; *adj* muy ligero; poco importante; (box.) de peso pluma
**featherwork** ['fɛðər,wʌrk] *s* arte plumaria
**feathery** ['fɛðərɪ] *adj* plumoso
**feature** ['fitʃər] *s* facción; característica, rasgo distintivo; atracción principal, película principal, artículo principal, tira cómica principal; especialidad; **features** *spl* facciones (*cara, rostro*); *va* delinear, representar; ofrecer (*como cosa principal*); (coll.) destacar, hacer resaltar; (coll.) parecerse a
**featured** ['fitʃərd] *adj* encarado, p.ej., **well-featured** bien encarado; (coll.) anunciado de modo destacado
**featureless** ['fitʃərlɪs] *adj* sin rasgos distintivos, poco interesante
**Feb.** abr. de **February**
**febrifuge** ['fɛbrɪfjudʒ] *adj & s* febrífugo
**febrile** ['fibrɪl] o ['fɛbrɪl] *adj* febril
**February** ['fɛbru,ɛrɪ] *s* febrero
**fecal** ['fikəl] *adj* fecal
**fecalith** ['fikəlɪθ] *s* (path.) fecalito
**feces** ['fisiz] *spl* heces (*excremento; poso, sedimento*)
**feckless** ['fɛklɪs] *adj* abatido, débil, sin valor
**fecula** ['fɛkjulə] *s* (*pl:* **-lae** [li]) fécula
**feculent** ['fɛkjulənt] *adj* feculento (*que tiene heces*)
**fecund** ['fikənd] o ['fɛkənd] *adj* fecundo
**fecundate** ['fikəndet] o ['fɛkəndet] *va* fecundar; (biol.) fecundar
**fecundation** [,fikən'deʃən] o [,fɛkən'deʃən] *s* fecundación; (biol.) fecundación
**fecundative** [fɪ'kʌndətɪv] *adj* fecundativo
**fecundity** [fɪ'kʌndɪtɪ] *s* fecundidad
**fed** [fɛd] *pret & pp de* **feed**
**federal** ['fɛdərəl] *adj & s* federal; (*cap.*) *s* (U.S.A.) soldado o partidario del gobierno central durante la guerra entre Norte y Sur
**federalism** ['fɛdərəlɪzəm] *s* federalismo
**federalist** ['fɛdərəlɪst] *adj & s* federalista
**federalize** ['fɛdərəlaɪz] *va* federar
**Federal Reserve Bank** *s* (U.S.A.) cada uno de los doce bancos de los distritos del sistema de Reserva Federal, establecidos para regularizar y ayudar a los bancos miembros de ese sistema
**Federal Reserve Board** *s* (U.S.A.) grupo de nueve personas elegidas por el presidente de los EE.UU. para controlar el sistema de la Reserva Federal
**Federal Reserve System** *s* (U.S.A.) sistema de la Reserva Federal
**federate** ['fɛdərɪt] o ['fɛdəret] *adj* federado; ['fɛdəret] *va* federar
**Federated Malay States** *spl* Estados Malayos Federados
**federation** [,fɛdə'reʃən] *s* federación
**federative** ['fɛdə,retɪv] *adj* federativo
**fedora** [fɪ'dorə] *s* sombrero de fieltro suave con ala vuelta
**fed up** *adj* harto; (fig.) harto; **fed up with** harto de
**fee** [fi] *s* honorarios; derechos; propina; (law) hacienda de patrimonio, herencia; (feud.) dominio; **to hold in fee** poseer, ser dueño de; *va* pagar, premiar; dar propina a
**feeble** ['fibəl] *adj* débil
**feeble-minded** ['fibəl'maɪndɪd] *adj* imbécil; irresoluto, vacilante
**feebleness** ['fibəlnɪs] *s* debilidad
**feebly** ['fiblɪ] *adv* débilmente
**feed** [fid] *s* alimento; alimentación; (coll.) comida, comida abundante; (mach.) dispositivo de alimentación, movimiento de alimentación; (*pret & pp:* **fed**) *va* alimentar; *vn* comer, alimentarse; **to feed on** o **upon** alimentarse de
**feedback** ['fid,bæk] *s* (elec.) regeneración, realimentación
**feed-back circuit** ['fid,bæk] *s* (elec.) circuito de regeneración
**feed-back coil** *s* (elec.) bobina de regeneración
**feed bag** *s* cebadera, morral
**feeder** ['fidər] *s* alimentador; fuente; afluente (*de un río*); (elec.) conductor de alimentación; (min.) filón ramal; (rail.) ramal tributario
**feedhead** ['fid,hɛd] *s* depósito de alimentación; (found.) canal de mazarota
**feed line** *s* (elec.) conductor de alimentación
**feed pump** *s* bomba alimenticia o bomba de alimentación
**feed trough** *s* artesa, comedero; (rail.) atarjea de alimentación
**feed wire** *s* (elec.) conductor de alimentación
**feel** [fil] *s* sensación; tacto; tino; (*pret & pp:* **felt**) *va* palpar, tentar; sentir; tomar (*el pulso*); resentirse de; tantear (*el camino*); **to feel out** dar un toque a, tantear; *vn* palpar; sentirse (*enfermo, obligado, etc.*); ser (*áspero, suave, etc.*) al tacto; estar (*caliente*); tener (*calor, frío, hambre, sed*); **to feel bad** sentirse mal; condolerse; **to feel cheap** avergonzarse, sentirse inferior; **to feel comfortable** sentirse a gusto; **to feel for** buscar tentando; condolerse de; **to feel like** (coll.) tener ganas de; **to feel like** + *ger* (coll.) tener ganas de + *inf;* **to feel (like) oneself** tener la salud, vigor, ánimo, etc. acostumbrados; **to feel safe** sentirse a salvo; **to feel sorry** sentir; arrepentirse; **to feel sorry for** compadecer

**feeler** ['filər] *s* persona o cosa que palpa; tentativa, tanteo (*que se hace para descubrir los sentimientos ajenos*); (mach.) calibrador de espesor, tira calibradora; **feelers** *spl* palpos, anténulas (*del insecto*); tentáculos (*del molusco y el zoófito*)
**feeling** ['filɪŋ] *s* sensación; tacto; sentimiento; parecer, opinión; presentimiento; **feelings** *spl* sensibilidad, sentimientos delicados
**feelingly** ['filɪŋlɪ] *adv* con emoción
**fee simple** *s* (law) herencia libre de condición
**feet** [fit] *pl de* **foot**
**fee tail** *s* (law) herencia cuyo derecho de sucesión está restringido a los herederos directos
**feign** [fen] *va* aparentar, fingir; *vn* fingir; **to feign to** + *inf* fingir + *inf;* **to feign to be** fingirse
**feint** [fent] *s* fingimiento; finta (*amago*); *vn* hacer una finta
**feldspar** ['fɛld,spɑr] *s* (mineral.) feldespato
**feldspathic** [fɛld'spæθɪk] o **feldspathose** ['fɛldspæθos] *adj* feldespático
**felicitate** [fɪ'lɪsɪtet] *va* felicitar
**felicitation** [fɪ,lɪsɪ'teʃən] *s* felicitación
**felicitous** [fɪ'lɪsɪtəs] *adj* feliz (*dicho, idea, etc.*); elocuente
**felicity** [fɪ'lɪsɪtɪ] *s* (*pl:* **-ties**) felicidad; aptitud o gracia de expresión; idea feliz, expresión feliz
**felid** ['filɪd] *s* (zool.) félido
**feline** ['filaɪn] *adj* (zool. & fig.) felino; *s* (zool.) felino
**fell** [fɛl] *s* tala (*de árboles*); todos los árboles cortados en una estación; (sew.) sobrecarga; pellejo; (Scotch) colina, montaña; (Scotch) páramo o brezal elevado; *adj* cruel, feroz; destructivo, mortal; *va* derribar; talar (*árboles*); (sew.) sobrecargar; *pret de* **fall**
**fellah** ['fɛlə] *s* (*pl:* **fellaheen** o **fellahin** [,fɛlə'hin] o **fellahs**) felá
**felloe** ['fɛlo] *s* aro de la rueda; pina (*pieza del aro de la rueda*)
**fellow** ['fɛlo] *s* (coll.) hombre, mozo, tipo, sujeto; (coll.) pretendiente; pícaro, pillo; compañero; igual; pareja; congénere, prójimo; miembro (*de un colegio, sociedad, etc.*); pensionista (*estudiante que disfruta una pensión o beca*)
**fellow being** *s* prójimo
**fellow citizen** *s* conciudadano
**fellow countryman** *s* compatriota
**fellow creature** *s* prójimo
**fellow feeling** *s* afinidad, compañerismo, simpatía
**fellow man** *s* prójimo
**fellow member** *s* consocio
**fellow passenger** *s* compañero de viaje
**fellow prisoner** *s* compañero de prisión
**fellowship** ['fɛloʃɪp] *s* compañerismo; coparticipación; hermandad; pensión (*para ampliar estudios*)
**fellow student** *s* condiscípulo
**fellow traveler** *s* simpatizante; compañero de viaje, comunistizante
**fellow worker** *s* compañero de trabajo
**felly** ['fɛlɪ] *s* (*pl:* **-lies**) var. de **felloe**
**felon** ['fɛlən] *adj* felón, traidor; brutal, cruel; *s* (law) delincuente de mayor cuantía; (path.) panadizo
**felonious** [fɪ'lonɪəs] *adj* felón, traidor; perverso; (law) delincuente
**felony** ['fɛlənɪ] *s* (*pl:* **-nies**) (law) delito de mayor cuantía; (feud.) felonía; **to compound a felony** (law) aceptar dinero para no procesar
**felsite** ['fɛlsaɪt] *s* (mineral.) felsita
**felspar** ['fɛl,spɑr] *s* var. de **feldspar**
**felt** [fɛlt] *s* fieltro; *adj* de fieltro; *va* fieltrar; *pret & pp de* **feel**
**felucca** [fɪ'lʌkə] *s* (naut.) falucho
**fem.** abr. de **feminine**
**female** ['fimel] *adj* femenino; hembra, p.ej., **a female fish** un pez hembra; (bot.) femenino; (bot. & mach.) hembra; *s* hembra; (bot.) hembra; (mach.) hembrilla
**feminine** ['fɛmɪnɪn] *adj* femenino; afeminado; (gram.) femenino; *s* (gram.) femenino (*género*); (gram.) palabra femenina
**feminine rhyme** *s* (pros.) rima femenina
**femininity** [,fɛmɪ'nɪnɪtɪ] *s* feminidad; bello sexo
**feminism** ['fɛmɪnɪzəm] *s* feminismo
**feminist** ['fɛmɪnɪst] *adj & s* feminista
**feministic** [,fɛmɪ'nɪstɪk] *adj* feminista
**femoral** ['fɛmərəl] *adj* femoral
**femur** ['fimər] *s* (*pl:* **femurs** o **femora** ['fɛmərə]) (anat. & ent.) fémur
**fen** [fɛn] *s* pantano
**fence** [fɛns] *s* cerca; esgrima; destreza, habilidad para el debate; alcahuete (*encubridor y vendedor de cosas robadas*); guía (*de la sierra*); **on the fence** (coll.) indeciso, irresoluto; (coll.) no comprometido; *va* cercar; defender, proteger; **to fence in** encerrar con cerca; **to fence off** separar con cerca, obstruir con cerca; **to fence out** excluir con cerca; *vn* esgrimir; defenderse con fintas o evasivas, eludir preguntas con palabras ambiguas; saltar una cerca (*el caballo*); **to fence with** eludir una contestación directa a
**fence post** *s* poste para cercas
**fencer** ['fɛnsər] *s* esgrimidor; caballo adiestrado a saltar cercas
**fencing** ['fɛnsɪŋ] *s* esgrimadura (*acción*); esgrima (*arte*); materiales para construir cercas; cercas
**fencing academy** *s* escuela de esgrima
**fencing master** *s* maestro de esgrima
**fend** [fɛnd] *va* parar, apartar; **to fend off** resguardarse de; *vn* defenderse, resistir; **to fend for oneself** (coll.) tirar por su lado, arreglárselas
**fender** ['fɛndər] *s* defensa, protección; (aut.) guardafango, guardabarros; (naut.) defensa; (rail.) trompa, quitapiedras; salvavidas (*del tranvía*); guardafuego (*de la chimenea*)
**fenestra** [fɪ'nɛstrə] *s* (*pl:* **-trae** [tri]) (anat.) ventana
**fenestra ovalis** [o'velɪs] *s* (anat.) ventana oval
**fenestra rotunda** [ro'tʌndə] *s* (anat.) ventana rotunda
**fenestration** [,fɛnɪs'treʃən] *s* (arch.) ventanaje
**Fenian** ['finɪən] *adj & s* feniano
**Fenianism** ['finɪənɪzəm] *s* fenianismo
**fennel** ['fɛnəl] *s* (bot.) hinojo (*Foeniculum vulgare*); (bot.) cáñamo
**fennelflower** ['fɛnəl,flaʊər] *s* (bot.) neguilla (*cualquier planta del género Nigella*); (bot.) toda especia (*Nigella sativa*)
**fennel giant** *s* (bot.) var. de **giant fennel**
**fenny** ['fɛnɪ] *adj* pantanoso
**fenugreek** ['fɛnjʊgrik] *s* (bot.) alholva, fenogreco
**feoff** [fɛf] o [fif] *s* var. de **fief**
**feracious** [fə'reʃəs] *adj* feraz
**feracity** [fə'ræsɪtɪ] *s* feracidad
**feral** ['fɪrəl] *adj* salvaje; feral, cruel
**fer-de-lance** [,fɛrdə'lɑ̃s] *s* (zool.) mapanare
**Ferdinand** ['fʌrdɪnænd] *s* Fernando
**ferment** ['fʌrmɛnt] *s* fermento; fermentación; (fig.) fermentación; [fər'mɛnt] *va & vn* fermentar; (fig.) fermentar
**fermentable** [fər'mɛntəbəl] *adj* fermentable
**fermentation** [,fʌrmɛn'teʃən] *s* fermentación; (fig.) fermentación
**fermentative** [fər'mɛntətɪv] *adj* fermentativo
**fermium** ['fʌrmɪəm] *s* (chem.) fermio
**fern** [fʌrn] *s* (bot.) helecho
**fernery** ['fʌrnərɪ] *s* (*pl:* **-ies**) helechal, lugar donde se crían los helechos
**ferny** ['fʌrnɪ] *adj* de helechos; abundante en helechos
**ferocious** [fɪ'roʃəs] *adj* feroz
**ferocity** [fɪ'rɑsɪtɪ] *s* (*pl:* **-ties**) ferocidad
**ferrate** ['fɛret] *s* (chem.) ferrato
**ferreous** ['fɛrɪəs] *adj* férreo
**ferret** ['fɛrɪt] *s* (zool.) hurón; *va* huronear; **to ferret out** huronear; *vn* huronear
**ferric** ['fɛrɪk] *adj* (chem.) férrico
**ferric acid** *s* (chem.) ácido férrico
**Ferris wheel** ['fɛrɪs] *s* noria, rueda de feria, gran rueda (*rueda grande y giratoria que tiene sillas en la pina, empleada en parques de recreo, ferias, etc.*)
**ferroaluminum** [,fɛroə'lumɪnəm] *s* ferroaluminio
**ferrocerium** [,fɛro'sɪrɪəm] *s* ferrocerio
**ferrochrome** ['fɛrokrom] o **ferrochromium** [,fɛro'kromɪəm] *s* ferrocromo

**ferroconcrete** [ˌfɛroˈkɑnkrit] o [ˌfɛrokɑnˈkrit] *s* ferroconcreto, ferrohormigón
**ferrocyanide** [ˌfɛroˈsaɪənaɪd] o [ˌfɛroˈsaɪənɪd] *s* (chem.) ferrocianuro
**ferromagnetic** [ˌfɛromægˈnɛtɪk] *adj* (phys.) ferromagnético
**ferromanganese** [ˌfɛroˈmæŋgənis] o [ˌfɛroˈmæŋgəniz] *s* ferromanganeso
**ferronickel** [ˌfɛroˈnɪkəl] *s* ferroníquel
**ferroprussiate** [ˌfɛroˈprʌʃɪet] o [ˌfɛroˈprʌsɪet] *s* (chem.) ferroprusiato
**ferrotungsten** [ˌfɛroˈtʌŋstən] *s* ferrotungsteno
**ferrotype** [ˈfɛrotaɪp] *s* (phot.) ferrotipo; (phot.) ferrotipia (*procedimiento*)
**ferrous** [ˈfɛrəs] *adj* ferroso; (chem.) ferroso
**ferrous sulfate** *s* (chem.) sulfato ferroso
**ferrous sulfide** *s* (chem.) sulfuro ferroso
**ferruginous** [fəˈrudʒɪnəs] *adj* ferruginoso; rojizo, herrumbroso
**ferrule** [ˈfɛrul] o [ˈfɛrəl] *s* regatón; (elec.) tapa de contacto; (mach.) virola
**ferry** [ˈfɛrɪ] *s* (*pl:* **-ries**) balsa o barco de pasar el río; balsa o barco portatrén; balsadero, embarcadero; transbordador; (*pret & pp:* **-ried**) *va* balsear (*un río*); pasar (*viajeros, mercancías o trenes de ferrocarril*) a través del río; *vn* cruzar el río en barco
**ferryboat** [ˈfɛrɪˌbot] *s* balsa o barco de pasar el río; balsa o barco portatrén
**ferryman** [ˈfɛrɪmən] *s* (*pl:* **-men**) balsero, dueño, encargado o empleado de un paso de río
**fertile** [ˈfʌrtɪl] *adj* fértil; (biol.) fecundo; (fig.) fértil
**fertility** [fərˈtɪlɪtɪ] *s* fertilidad; fecundidad
**fertilization** [ˌfʌrtɪlɪˈzeʃən] *s* fertilización; fecundación
**fertilize** [ˈfʌrtɪlaɪz] *va* fertilizar, abonar; fecundar
**fertilizer** [ˈfʌrtɪˌlaɪzər] *s* fertilizante (*persona o cosa que fertiliza; abono*)
**ferulaceous** [ˌfɛrjʊˈleʃəs] o [ˌfɛrʊˈleʃəs] *adj* (bot.) ferruláceo
**ferule** [ˈfɛrul] o [ˈfɛrəl] *s* férula; var. de **ferrule;** *va* castigar con férula
**fervency** [ˈfʌrvənsɪ] *s* fervor
**fervent** [ˈfʌrvənt] *adj* fervoroso, ferviente
**fervid** [ˈfʌrvɪd] *adj* fervoroso
**fervor** [ˈfʌrvər] *s* fervor
**fervour** [ˈfʌrvər] *s* (Brit.) var. de **fervor**
**fescue** [ˈfɛskju] *s* (bot.) cañuela; puntero
**fess** o **fesse** [fɛs] *s* (her.) faja
**festa** [ˈfɛstə] *s* fiesta
**festal** [ˈfɛstəl] *adj* festivo
**fester** [ˈfɛstər] *s* úlcera; *va* enconar, ulcerar; *vn* enconarse, ulcerarse, pudrir; (fig.) enconarse
**festival** [ˈfɛstɪvəl] *s* fiesta; festival (*especialmente musical*); *adj* festivo
**festive** [ˈfɛstɪv] *adj* festivo (*alegre, regocijado*)
**festivity** [fɛsˈtɪvɪtɪ] *s* (*pl:* **-ties**) festividad
**festoon** [fɛsˈtun] *s* festón; *va* festonear
**festooned** [fɛsˈtund] *adj* afestonado
**fetal** [ˈfitəl] *adj* fetal
**fetch** [fɛtʃ] *s* acción de ir a buscar, acción de traer; ardid, estratagema, treta; alcance, espacio, extensión; doble; aparecido, espectro; *va* ir por, traer, hacer venir; venderse a o por; proferir (*un gemido, suspiro*); cebar (*una bomba*); tomar (*aliento*); (coll.) encantar, atraer; (coll.) golpear; (dial.) alcanzar; **to fetch down** abatir; bajar; **to fetch up** elevar, levantar; descubrir, recordar; recobrar (*el tiempo perdido*); *vn* ir, moverse; **to fetch and carry** servir rastreramente; andar chismeando; realizar múltiples quehaceres de poca monta; **to fetch up** pararse; aparecer, dejarse ver
**fetching** [ˈfɛtʃɪŋ] *adj* (coll.) encantador, atractivo
**fete** o **fête** [fet] *s* fiesta; *va* festejar
**fetich** [ˈfitɪʃ] o [ˈfɛtɪʃ] *s* var. de **fetish**
**feticidal** [ˌfitɪˈsaɪdəl] *adj* feticida
**feticide** [ˈfitɪsaɪd] *s* feticidio (*acción*)
**fetid** [ˈfɛtɪd] o [ˈfitɪd] *adj* fétido
**fetidity** [fɛˈtɪdɪtɪ] o [fiˈtɪdɪtɪ] *s* fetidez
**fetish** [ˈfitɪʃ] o [ˈfɛtɪʃ] *s* fetiche
**fetishism** [ˈfitɪʃɪzəm] o [ˈfɛtɪʃɪzəm] *s* fetichismo
**fetishist** [ˈfitɪʃɪst] o [ˈfɛtɪʃɪst] *s* fetichista
**fetishistic** [ˌfitɪˈʃɪstɪk] o [ˌfɛtɪˈʃɪstɪk] *adj* fetichista
**fetlock** [ˈfɛtlɑk] *s* espolón (*prominencia*); cernejas (*pelo*)
**fetor** [ˈfitər] *s* hedor
**fetter** [ˈfɛtər] *s* grillo, grillete; *va* engrillar, encadenar; impedir, limitar
**fettle** [ˈfɛtəl] *s* condición, estado; **in fine fettle** en buena condición, bien preparado; *va* (found.) brascar
**fetus** [ˈfitəs] *s* (embryol.) feto
**feud** [fjud] *s* enemistad heredada entre familias o tribus; enemistad entre dos personas o grupos; (law) feudo
**feudal** [ˈfjudəl] *adj* feudal
**feudalism** [ˈfjudəlɪzəm] *s* feudalismo
**feudalistic** [ˌfjudəˈlɪstɪk] *adj* feudal
**feudality** [fjuˈdælɪtɪ] *s* (*pl:* **-ties**) feudalidad; feudo
**feudal system** *s* sistema feudal
**feudatory** [ˈfjudəˌtorɪ] *adj* feudatario; feudado; *s* (*pl:* **-ries**) feudatario; feudo
**feudist** [ˈfjudɪst] *s* camorrista; (law) feudista (*autor*)
**fever** [ˈfivər] *s* (path. & fig.) fiebre
**fever blister** *s* (path.) fuegos en los labios, escupidura, pupa
**fevered** [ˈfivərd] *adj* febril
**feverfew** [ˈfivərfju] *s* (bot.) matricaria
**feverish** [ˈfivərɪʃ] *adj* febril; calenturiento; febrígeno
**feverless** [ˈfivərlɪs] *adj* sin fiebre
**feverous** [ˈfivərəs] *adj* var. de **feverish**
**feverroot** [ˈfivərˌrut] o [ˈfivərˌrʊt] *s* (bot.) triosteo
**fever sore** *s* var. de **fever blister**
**few** [fju] *adj & pron indef* unos cuantos, pocos; **a few** unos cuantos; **not a few** no pocos; **quite a few** muchos; **few and far between** poquísimos
**fewness** [ˈfjunɪs] *s* corto número
**fez** [fɛz] *s* (*pl:* **fezzes**) fez
**ff.** abr. de **and the following** o **and what follows, folios** y **fortissimo**
**fiancé** [ˌfiɑnˈse] *s* novio, prometido
**fiancée** [ˌfiɑnˈse] *s* novia, prometida
**fiasco** [fɪˈæsko] *s* (*pl:* **-cos** o **-coes**) fiasco
**fiat** [ˈfaɪət] o [ˈfaɪæt] *s* fíat, autorización, mandato
**fiat money** *s* billetes sin respaldo ni garantía, emitidos por el gobierno
**fib** [fɪb] *s* mentirilla; (*pret & pp:* **fibbed;** *ger:* **fibbing**) *vn* decir mentirillas
**fibber** [ˈfɪbər] *s* mentiroso
**fiber** [ˈfaɪbər] *s* fibra; carácter, índole
**fiberboard** [ˈfaɪbərˌbord] *s* plancha o tabla de fibra
**fiberglas** [ˈfaɪbərˌglæs] o [ˈfaɪbərˌglɑs] *s* (trademark) fibravidrio, vidrio fibroso
**fibre** [ˈfaɪbər] *s* var. de **fiber**
**fibril** [ˈfaɪbrɪl] *s* (anat. & bot.) fibrilla
**fibrillation** [ˌfaɪbrɪˈleʃən] *s* (path.) fibrilación
**fibrin** [ˈfaɪbrɪn] *s* (bot.) fibrina, glutenfibrina; (physiol.) fibrina
**fibrinogen** [faɪˈbrɪnədʒən] *s* (physiol.) fibrinógeno
**fibrinous** [ˈfaɪbrɪnəs] *adj* fibrinoso
**fibrocartilage** [ˌfaɪbroˈkɑrtɪlɪdʒ] *s* (anat.) fibrocartílago
**fibroid** [ˈfaɪbrɔɪd] *adj* fibroideo; *s* (path.) fibroma, fibroide
**fibroin** [ˈfaɪbro·ɪn] *s* (biochem.) fibroína
**fibroma** [faɪˈbromə] *s* (*pl:* **-mata** [mətə] o **-mas**) (path.) fibroma
**fibrous** [ˈfaɪbrəs] *adj* fibroso
**fibula** [ˈfɪbjələ] *s* (*pl:* **-lae** [li] o **-las**) (anat.) fíbula, peroné; (archeol.) fíbula
**fibular** [ˈfɪbjələr] *adj* peroneo, fibular
**fichu** [ˈfɪʃu] *s* pañoleta
**fickle** [ˈfɪkəl] *adj* inconstante, veleidoso
**fickleness** [ˈfɪkəlnɪs] *s* inconstancia, veleidad
**fiction** [ˈfɪkʃən] *s* ficción; (law) ficción; (lit.) novelística, género novelístico; **pure fiction!** ¡puro cuento!
**fictional** [ˈfɪkʃənəl] *adj* ficcionario; (lit.) novelesco (*propio de las novelas*); (lit.) novelístico (*perteneciente a la novela*)
**fictionalize** [ˈfɪkʃənəlaɪz] *va* novelizar
**fictitious** [fɪkˈtɪʃəs] *adj* ficticio
**fid** [fɪd] *s* barra de sostén; tarugo grande de ma-

dera; burel (*para abrir cordones de los cables*); (naut.) cuña de mastelero

**fiddle** ['fɪdəl] *s* (coll.) violín; **fit as a fiddle** en buena salud; **to play second fiddle** desempeñar el papel de segundón; **to play second fiddle to** estar subordinado a; *va* (coll.) tocar (*un aire*) al violín; **to fiddle away** desperdiciar, malgastar (*dinero, tiempo, etc.*); *vn* (coll.) tocar el violín; mover los dedos o las manos rápidamente; ocuparse en fruslerías; **to fiddle with** ocuparse sin provecho en; manosear

**fiddle block** *s* (naut.) motón de dos ejes con poleas diferenciales

**fiddle bow** [bo] *s* arco de violín

**fiddle-de-dee** [,fɪdəldɪ'di] *s* disparate; *interj* ¡disparate!

**fiddle-faddle** ['fɪdəl,fædəl] *s* (coll.) disparate; *interj* (coll.) ¡disparate!; *vn* (coll.) ocuparse en fruslerías

**fiddler** ['fɪdlər] *s* (coll.) violinista

**fiddler crab** *s* (zool.) barrilete

**fiddlestick** ['fɪdəl,stɪk] *s* arco de violín; bagatela; **fiddlesticks** *interj* ¡disparate!

**fiddlestring** ['fɪdəl,strɪŋ] *s* cuerda de violín; bagatela

**fiddling** ['fɪdlɪŋ] *adj* (coll.) insignificante, trivial

**fideicommissary** [,faɪdɪaɪ'kɑmɪ,sɛrɪ] *adj* (law) fideicomisario; *s* (*pl:* **-ies**) (law) fideicomisario

**fideicommissioner** [,faɪdɪaɪkə'mɪʃənər] *s* fideicomitente

**fideicommissum** [,faɪdɪaɪkə'mɪsəm] *s* (*pl:* **-sa** [sə]) (law) fideicomiso

**fidelity** [faɪ'delɪtɪ] o [fɪ'delɪtɪ] *s* (*pl:* **-ties**) fidelidad

**fidget** ['fɪdʒɪt] *s* persona agitada, persona inquieta; *va* agitar, inquietar; *vn* agitarse, inquietarse; **to fidget with** manosear

**fidgety** ['fɪdʒɪtɪ] *adj* azogado, agitado, inquieto, revoltoso

**fid hole** *s* (naut.) ojo de la cuña de mastelero

**fiduciary** [fɪ'djuʃɪ,ɛrɪ] o [fɪ'duʃɪ,ɛrɪ] *adj* fiduciario; *s* (*pl:* **-ies**) fiduciario

**fie** [faɪ] *interj* ¡qué vergüenza!

**fief** [fif] *s* feudo

**field** [fild] *s* campo; sembrado (*tierra sembrada*); (her., phys. & sport) campo; (elec.) inductor; (elec.) campo magnético; (fig.) campo (*de varias actividades*); (baseball) jardín (*campo fuera del cuadro*); (baseball) (los) jardineros; (sport) los que participan en una carrera, partida, etc.; (sport) todos los que entran en una carrera, excepto el favorito; *va* (baseball) parar y devolver (*la pelota*)

**field artillery** *s* artillería de campaña

**field battery** *s* (mil.) batería de campaña

**field day** *s* día de ejercicios atléticos; día de ejercicios militares; día de actividad extraordinaria; día de excursión científica

**fielder** ['fildər] *s* (baseball) jardinero, jugador situado en el terreno fuera del cuadro para interceptar la pelota

**fieldfare** ['fild,fɛr] *s* (orn.) zorzal

**field judge** *s* (football) juez de línea

**field glass** *s* anteojos de campaña, gemelos de campo

**field gun** *s* cañón de campaña

**field hockey** *s* (sport) hockey sobre hierba

**field hospital** *s* (mil.) hospital de campaña o de sangre

**field kitchen** *s* (mil.) cocina de campaña

**field lark** *s* (orn.) chirlota, triguero (*Sturnella magna*); (orn.) enchilado (*Sturnella neglecta*)

**field magnet** *s* (elec.) imán inductor

**field marshal** *s* (mil.) mariscal de campo; (Brit.) capitán general de ejército

**field mouse** *s* (zool.) ratón de campo

**field officer** *s* (mil.) jefe (*coronel, teniente coronel o comandante*)

**field of honor** *s* campo del honor, terreno de honor

**fieldpiece** ['fild,pis] *s* cañón de campaña

**field trip** *s* excursión científicoescolar

**field winding** *s* (elec.) arrollamiento inductor

**fieldwork** [fild,wʌrk] *s* (fort.) obras de campo

**field work** *s* trabajo científico de campo o en el terreno

**fiend** [find] *s* diablo; fiera (*persona muy cruel*); (coll.) monomaníaco; **the Fiend** el diablo; **to be a fiend for** ser una fiera para (*p.ej., el trabajo*)

**fiendish** ['findɪʃ] *adj* diabólico

**fierce** [fɪrs] *adj* fiero, feroz; furioso (*p.ej., viento*); ardiente, vehemente; (slang) desagradable, muy malo

**fierceness** ['fɪrsnɪs] *s* fiereza, ferocidad; furia, violencia; ardor, vehemencia

**fiery** ['faɪrɪ] o ['faɪərɪ] *adj* (*comp:* **-ier;** *super:* **-iest**) ardiente, caliente

**fiery cross** *s* cruz ardiente

**fiesta** [fɪ'ɛstə] *s* fiesta

**fife** [faɪf] *s* (mus.) pífano; *vn* tocar el pífano

**fifteen** ['fɪf'tin] *adj & s* quince; **fifteen all** (tennis) quince iguales

**fifteenth** ['fɪf'tinθ] *adj* décimoquinto; quinzavo; *s* décimoquinto; quinzavo; quince (*en las fechas*)

**fifth** [fɪfθ] *adj* quinto; *s* quinto; cinco (*en las fechas*); quinto de galón (*p.ej., de whisky*); (mus.) quinta

**fifth column** *s* quinta columna

**fifth columnist** *s* quintacolumnista

**fifthly** ['fɪfθlɪ] *adv* en quinto lugar

**fifth wheel** *s* rodete (*de un coche*); quinta rueda (*persona o cosa superfluas*)

**fiftieth** ['fɪftɪɪθ] *adj & s* quincuagésimo; cincuentavo

**fifty** ['fɪftɪ] *adj* cincuenta; *s* (*pl:* **-ties**) cincuenta

**fifty-fifty** ['fɪftɪ'fɪftɪ] *adj & adv* (coll.) mitad y mitad, a medias; **to go fifty-fifty** ir a medias

**fig.** abr. de **figure, figurative** y **figuratively**

**fig** [fɪg] *s* (bot.) higuera; higo (*fruto*); breva (*higo de color purpúreo*); bledo; (coll.) traje, adorno, gala; (coll.) condición; **in fine fig** (coll.) en buena condición, entrenado; **in full fig** (coll.) de veinticuatro alfileres; **to not give a fig for** no dársele a uno un bledo de, p.ej., **I don't give a fig for that** no se me da un bledo de ello

**figeater** ['fɪg,itər] *s* (ent.) escarabajo norteamericano (*Cotinis nitida*)

**fight** [faɪt] *s* lucha, pelea; ánimo de reñir, combatividad; ánimo, brío, pujanza; **to pick a fight with** meterse con, buscar la lengua a; **to show fight** enseñar los dientes; (*pret & pp:* **fought**) *va* combatir, luchar con; alcanzar peleando; dar (*batalla*); hacer reñir (*p.ej., a los gallos*); lidiar (*al toro*); **to fight another's battles** tomar la defensa de otro; **to fight it out** decidirlo luchando; **to fight one's way** luchar por abrirse paso; *vn* luchar, pelear, lidiar; **to fight against odds** luchar con desventaja; **to fight for** luchar o pelear por; **to fight shy of** evitar, tratar de evitar

**fighter** ['faɪtər] *s* luchador, peleador; combatiente; porfiador (*persona que porfía mucho*); (aer.) avión de combate

**fighter bomber** *s* (aer.) cazabombardero

**fighter pilot** *s* (aer.) piloto de caza

**fighting** ['faɪtɪŋ] *adj* luchador, pugnante; batallador, combatiente; de pelea; de lidia; *s* lucha, pelea; riña; combate

**fighting chance** *s* (coll.) posibilidad de éxito después de larga lucha, posibilidad de recobrar la salud

**fighting cock** *s* gallo de pelea; (coll.) persona pendenciera

**fig leaf** *s* hoja de higuera; hoja de parra (*en las estatuas*); cobertura ligera

**figment** ['fɪgmənt] *s* ficción, invención

**figpecker** ['fɪg,pɛkər] *s* (orn.) papafigo

**figuline** ['fɪgjəlɪn] *adj* figulino; *s* figurilla figulina, estatua figulina

**figurant** ['fɪgjurænt] *s* (theat.) figurante

**figurante** [,fɪgjʊ'rɑnt] *s* (theat.) figuranta

**figuration** [,fɪgjə'reʃən] *s* figuración; forma, figura; (mus.) figuración

**figurative** ['fɪgjərətɪv] *adj* figurativo; figurado (*lenguaje, estilo, etc.*)

**figure** ['fɪgjər] *s* figura; (arith., geom., log. & rhet.) figura; talle (*disposición del cuerpo humano*); precio; figura, dibujo (*p.ej., en la tela*); **to be good at figures** ser listo en aritmética; **to cut a figure** hacer figura, hacer papel; **to have a good figure** tener buen tipo; **to keep one's figure** conservar la línea; *va* figurar; adornar con figuras, adornar con dibujos; ima-

ginar, suponer; calcular, computar; **to figure out** descifrar, resolver; explicarse; **to figure up** calcular, computar; *vn* figurar (*formar parte; tener autoridad o representación*); figurarse, imaginarse; **to figure on** contar con; incluir
**figured** [ˈfɪgjərd] *adj* adornado; labrado; estampado, floreado; figurado (*lenguaje*)
**figurehead** [ˈfɪgjər,hɛd] *s* (naut.) figurón de proa, mascarón de proa; (fig.) testaferro
**figure of speech** *s* (rhet.) tropo; exageración
**figure skater** *s* patinador de figura
**figure skating** *s* patinaje de figura, patinaje artístico
**figurine** [,fɪgjəˈrin] *s* figurina, figurilla
**figwort** [ˈfɪg,wʌrt] *s* (bot.) escrofularia; (bot.) celidonia menor
**Fiji** [ˈfidʒɪ] *s* Fijí (*archipiélago*); fijiano (*natural*)
**Fijian** [ˈfidʒɪən] o [fɪˈdʒiən] *adj* & *s* fijiano
**filament** [ˈfɪləmənt] *s* filamento; (bot. & elec.) filamento
**filament circuit** *s* (rad.) circuito de filamento
**filament current** *s* (rad.) corriente de filamento
**filamentous** [,fɪləˈmɛntəs] *adj* filamentoso
**filander** [fɪˈlændər] *s* (zool.) filandria
**filaria** [fɪˈlɛrɪə] *s* (*pl:* **-ae** [i]) (zool.) filaria
**filariasis** [,fɪləˈraɪəsɪs] *s* (path.) filariosis
**filbert** [ˈfɪlbərt] *s* (bot.) avellano; avellana (*fruto*)
**filch** [fɪltʃ] *va* ratear, hurtar, birlar
**file** [faɪl] *s* lima (*instrumento*); fila, hilera; archivo (*de documentos*); fichero; archivador (*carpeta*); **on file** archivado; *va* limar; poner en fila; archivar, clasificar; anotar, asentar, registrar; **to file away** archivar; *vn* desfilar; **to file by** desfilar; **to file in** entrar en fila; **to file out** salir en fila
**file brush** o **card** *s* carda para limas, cardo
**file case** *s* fichero
**file clerk** *s* fichador
**file cutter** *s* (mach.) picador de limas
**filefish** [ˈfaɪl,fɪʃ] *s* (ichth.) alútero
**filet** [fɪˈle] o [ˈfɪle] *s* filete (*lonja de carne o de pescado*); encaje o red de malla cuadrada; *va* cortar (*carne o pescado*) en filetes
**filial** [ˈfɪlɪəl] o [ˈfɪljəl] *adj* filial
**filiation** [,fɪlɪˈeʃən] *s* filiación
**filibuster** [ˈfɪlɪ,bʌstər] *s* obstruccionista (*miembro de un cuerpo legislativo que impide la aprobación de una ley por discursos largos u otros medios*); obstrucción (*de la aprobación de una ley*); filibustero (*el que lucha contra otro país sin la autorización de su propio gobierno*); *va* obstruir (*la aprobación de una ley*); *vn* obstruir la aprobación de una ley; ser filibustero, filibustear
**filicidal** [,fɪlɪˈsaɪdəl] *adj* filicida
**filicide** [ˈfɪlɪsaɪd] *s* filicidio (*acción*); filicida (*persona*)
**filiform** [ˈfɪlɪfɔrm] o [ˈfaɪlɪfɔrm] *adj* filiforme
**filigree** [ˈfɪlɪgri] *s* filigrana; *adj* afiligranado; *va* afiligranar
**filigreed** [ˈfɪlɪgrid] *adj* afiligranado
**filing** [ˈfaɪlɪŋ] *s* clasificación (*de documentos*); limadura; **filings** *spl* limaduras, limalla
**filing cabinet** *s* archivador, carpetero, clasificador
**filing card** *s* ficha
**Filipine** [ˈfɪlɪpin] *adj* filipino
**Filipino** [,fɪlɪˈpino] *adj* filipino; *s* (*pl:* **-nos**) filipino
**fill** [fɪl] *s* hartazgo; terraplén; **to have** o **get one's fill of** darse un hartazgo de (*uvas, leer, etc*). ‖ *va* llenar; rellenar; despachar, servir (*un pedido*); tapar (*un agujero*); empastar (*un diente*); inflar (*un neumático*); llenar, ocupar (*un puesto*); ocupar completamente (*un espacio*); **to be filled to overflowing** llenarse a rebosar; **to fill in** rellenar; añadir para completar, completar llenando; colmar (*lagunas*); poner al corriente; terraplenar; **to fill in on** poner al corriente de; **to fill out** ampliar, ensanchar, redondear; completar, llevar a cabo; llenar (*un formulario*); **to fill up** rellenar; (coll.) imprimir falsedades en la mente de ‖ *vn* llenarse; rellenarse; ampliarse, ensancharse, redondearse; bañarse (*los ojos*) de lágrimas; ahogarse de emoción; **to fill in** prestar sus servicios provisionalmente; terciar, hacer tercio; **to fill out** ampliarse, ensancharse, redondearse; **to fill up** atascarse, atorarse; ahogarse de emoción
**filler** [ˈfɪlər] *s* llenador; relleno; tripa (*del cigarro*); (journ.) relleno; (paint.) aparejo, imprimación
**filler cap** *s* (aut.) tapón de llenado
**filler neck** o **spout** *s* cuello de relleno
**fillet** [ˈfɪlɪt] *s* prendedero (*para asegurar el pelo*); cinta, tira, lista; (arch. & b.b.) filete; *va* filetear (*adornar con filetes*); [ˈfɪle] o [ˈfɪlɪt] *s* filete (*lonja de carne o de pescado*); encaje o red de malla cuadrada; *va* cortar (*carne o pescado*) en filetes
**filling** [ˈfɪlɪŋ] *s* relleno; tripa (*del cigarro*); trama (*del tejido*); (cook.) relleno; (dent.) empastadura (*acción*); (dent.) empaste, pasta
**filling station** *s* estación gasolinera, estación de servicio de gasolina
**fillip** [ˈfɪlɪp] *s* capirotazo; estímulo, aguijón; *va* dar un capirotazo a; tirar o impeler con un capirotazo; estimular, incitar; *vn* dar un capirotazo
**filly** [ˈfɪlɪ] *s* (*pl:* **-lies**) potra; (slang) muchacha vivaz
**film** [fɪlm] *s* película; (phot.) película; (mov.) film, película; **to shoot a film** (coll.) rodar una película; *adj* (mov.) fílmico; *va* cubrir con película; filmar, hacer una película de; *vn* cubrirse de una película; filmarse; **to film with tears** humedecerse (*los ojos*) de lágrimas
**filming** [ˈfɪlmɪŋ] *s* filmación
**film library** *s* filmoteca
**film pack** *s* (phot.) película en paquetes
**film star** *s* estrella del cine, estrella de la pantalla
**film strip** *s* tira de película
**filmy** [ˈfɪlmɪ] *adj* (*comp:* **-ier**; *super:* **-iest**) pelicular; delgadísimo, diáfano, sutil
**filose** [ˈfaɪlos] *adj* filiforme
**filter** [ˈfɪltər] *s* filtro; (elec. & opt.) filtro; *va* filtrar; *vn* filtrarse
**filterable** [ˈfɪltərəbəl] *adj* filtrable
**filter cigaret** *s* cigarrillo con filtro
**filtering** [ˈfɪltərɪŋ] *s* filtraje
**filter paper** *s* papel de filtro
**filter press** *s* filtro-prensa
**filter tip** *s* boquilla filtrónica, embocadura de filtro (*de un cigarrillo*)
**filth** [fɪlθ] *s* suciedad, inmundicia, mugre
**filthiness** [ˈfɪlθɪnɪs] *s* suciedad, inmundicia, porquería
**filthy** [ˈfɪlθɪ] *adj* (*comp:* **-ier**; *super:* **-iest**) sucio, inmundo, mugriento
**filthy lucre** *s* dinero mal ganado; (coll.) el vil metal (*dinero*)
**filtrable** [ˈfɪltrəbəl] *adj* var. de **filterable**
**filtrate** [ˈfɪltret] *s* filtrado; *va* filtrar; *vn* filtrarse
**filtration** [fɪlˈtreʃən] *s* filtración
**fin.** abr. de **financial**
**Fin.** abr. de **Finland** y **Finnish**
**fin** [fɪn] *s* aleta (*de pez, avión, etc.*); rebaba; los peces; (slang) aleta (*mano, brazo*); (*pret & pp:* **finned**; *ger:* **finning**) *va* cortar las aletas de (*un pescado*); *vn* aletear
**finagle** [fɪˈnegəl] *va* timar, trampear; conseguir por artimañas; *vn* timar, trampear
**final** [ˈfaɪnəl] *adj* final; último; decisivo, terminante; *s* cosa final; examen final; sonido final; letra final; **finals** *spl* final, p.ej., **I did not get to the finals** no llegué a la final
**finale** [fɪˈnɑlɪ] *s* final; (mus.) final, concertante
**finalism** [ˈfaɪnəlɪzəm] *s* (philos.) finalismo
**finalist** [ˈfaɪnəlɪst] *s* (philos. & sport) finalista
**finality** [faɪˈnælɪtɪ] *s* (*pl:* **-ties**) decisión, determinación; cosa final
**finalize** [ˈfaɪnəlaɪz] *va* (coll.) finalizar; (coll.) aprobar; *vn* (coll.) finalizar
**finally** [ˈfaɪnəlɪ] *adv* finalmente
**finance** [fɪˈnæns] o [ˈfaɪnæns] *s* finanzas; **finances** *spl* finanzas; *va* financiar; manejar los fondos de
**financial** [fɪˈnænʃəl] o [faɪˈnænʃəl] *adj* financiero
**financially** [fɪˈnænʃəlɪ] o [faɪˈnænʃəlɪ] *adv* financieramente
**financier** [,fɪnənˈsɪr] o [,faɪnænˈsɪr] *s* financiero

**financing** [fɪˈnænsɪŋ] o [ˈfaɪnænsɪŋ] *s* financiación
**finback** [ˈfɪn,bæk] *s* (zool.) rorcual
**finch** [fɪntʃ] *s* (orn.) pinzón
**find** [faɪnd] *s* hallazgo; (*pret & pp:* **found**) *va* hallar, encontrar; declarar, decidir; proveer; **to find oneself** encontrarse a sí mismo, descubrir sus aptitudes; **to find out** averiguar, darse cuenta de; llegar a saber cuál es el verdadero carácter de; *vn* (law) pronunciar fallo o sentencia; **to find out** informarse; **to find out about** informarse de
**finder** [ˈfaɪndər] *s* hallador; (astr.) buscador; (phot.) visor; portaobjeto cuadriculado (*del microscopio*)
**fin-de-siècle** [fæ̃dəˈsjɛkəl] *adj* finisecular
**finding** [ˈfaɪndɪŋ] *s* descubrimiento; (law) resultando; **findings** *spl* herramientas y avíos de un artesano; mercería (*alfileres, cintas, etc.*); constataciones, conclusiones
**fine** [faɪn] *adj* fino; bueno, p.ej., **fine weather** buen tiempo; magnífico; divertido (*rato*); (iron.) bueno, lindo; *adv* (coll.) muy bien; **to feel fine** (coll.) sentirse muy bien de salud; *s* multa; *va* multar
**fine arts** *spl* bellas artes
**fine-drawn** [ˈfaɪn,drɔn] *adj* estirado en un hilo finísimo; fino, sutil
**fine-grained** [ˈfaɪn,grend] *adj* de grano fino
**fineness** [ˈfaɪnnɪs] *s* fineza (*de grano, de la arena*); finura, excelencia; ley (*de las ligas de metales preciosos*)
**fineness ratio** *s* (aer.) finura
**fine print** *s* tipo menor, letra menuda
**finery** [ˈfaɪnərɪ] *s* (*pl:* **-ies**) adorno, galas, vestido de gala, atavíos
**fines herbes** [fin ˈzɛrb] *spl* hierbas finas (*aderezo de hongos, chalotes, perejil, etc. picados*)
**fine-spun** [ˈfaɪn,spʌn] *adj* estirado en hilo finísimo, hilado en hoja finísima; alambicado
**finesse** [fɪˈnɛs] *s* tino, sutileza, artificio; (bridge) impás, fineza, jugada por bajo; *va* atraer o cambiar empleando artificios; (bridge) hacer el impás con, tomar la fineza con (*cierto naipe*); *vn* valerse de artificios; (bridge) hacer un impás, hacer o tirar una fineza
**fine-tooth** [ˈfaɪn,tuθ] o **fine-toothed** [ˈfaɪn,tuθt] o [ˈfaɪn,tuðd] *adj* de dientes finos
**fine-tooth** o **fine-toothed comb** *s* peine de dientes finos; **to go over with a fine-tooth comb** o **fine-toothed comb** escudriñar minuciosamente
**finger** [ˈfɪŋgər] *s* dedo; **to burn one's fingers** cogerse los dedos; **to have a finger in the pie** tomar parte en un asunto; **to have long fingers** ser largo de uñas; **to put one's finger in the pie** meter su cucharada; **to put one's finger on** acertar; **to put one's finger on the sore spot** poner el dedo en la llaga; **to slip between the fingers** irse de entre los dedos; **to twist around one's little finger** conquistar fácilmente, manejar completamente; *va* tocar con los dedos; manosear; ejecutar con los dedos; hurtar, robar; (slang) designar, identificar; (slang) acechar, espiar, traicionar; (mus.) señalar la digitación en; (mus.) pulsar; *vn* teclear
**finger board** *s* (mus.) batidor, diapasón (*p.ej., de la guitarra*); (mus.) teclado (*del piano*)
**finger bowl** *s* lavadedos, lavafrutas
**fingerbreadth** [ˈfɪŋgər,brɛdθ] *s* dedo, anchura de un dedo
**finger dexterity** *s* (mus.) dedeo
**fingered** [ˈfɪŋgərd] *adj* con dedos; (bot. & mus.) digitado
**fingering** [ˈfɪŋgərɪŋ] *s* manoseo; obra ejecutada primorosamente con los dedos; (mus.) digitación
**fingerling** [ˈfɪŋgərlɪŋ] *s* pececillo (*del tamaño del dedo de un hombre*); cosa muy pequeña
**fingernail** [ˈfɪŋgər,nel] *s* uña
**fingernail polish** *s* esmalte para las uñas
**finger plate** *s* chapa de guarda
**finger post** *s* poste indicador (*con una mano que indica el camino*)
**fingerprint** [ˈfɪŋgər,prɪnt] *s* huella digital, dactilograma; *va* tomar las huellas digitales de
**fingerstall** [ˈfɪŋgər,stɔl] *s* dedil
**finger tip** *s* punta del dedo; **to have at one's finger tips** tener en la punta de los dedos, saber al dedillo; **to one's finger tips** al dedillo, perfectamente
**finger-tip control** [ˈfɪŋgər,tɪp] *s* mando a punta de dedo
**finger wave** *s* ondulado o peinado al agua
**finial** [ˈfɪnɪəl] *s* (arch. & f.a.) florón
**finical** [ˈfɪnɪkəl], **finicking** [ˈfɪnɪkɪŋ] o **finicky** [ˈfɪnɪkɪ] *adj* delicado, melindroso
**finish** [ˈfɪnɪʃ] *s* final; acabado; finura de ejecución; pulimento; finura, primor; (sport) llegada a la meta; (sport) línea de llegada; (sport) carrera final; **to be in at the finish** estar presente en la conclusión; **to have a rough finish** estar sin pulir, estar al natural; *va* acabar; afinar; (coll.) vencer completamente; (coll.) acabar (*matar*); (coll.) acabar con (*destruir*); **to finish off** acabar (*completar; matar*); **to finish up** acabar (*completar; consumir*); *vn* acabar; seguir el curso de una escuela de educación social para señoritas; **to finish** + *ger* acabar de + *inf*, concluir de + *inf;* **to finish by** + *ger* acabar por + *inf;* **to finish with** acabar; enemistarse con
**finished** [ˈfɪnɪʃt] *adj* acabado; pulimentado; fabricado, elaborado
**finisher** [ˈfɪnɪʃər] *s* acabador; máquina acabadora
**finishing nail** *s* alfilerillo, puntilla francesa
**finishing school** *s* escuela particular de educación social para señoritas
**finishing touch** *s* retoque, última mano
**finite** [ˈfaɪnaɪt] *adj* finito; (gram.) que expresa número, persona y tiempo determinados; **the finite** lo finito
**finite verb** *s* forma verbal flexional
**Finland** [ˈfɪnlənd] *s* Finlandia
**Finlander** [ˈfɪnləndər] *s* finlandés
**Finn** [fɪn] *s* finlandés (*natural de Finlandia*); finés (*individuo de cualquier pueblo de habla finesa*)
**finnan haddie** [ˈfɪnən ˈhædɪ] *s* eglefino ahumado
**Finnic** [ˈfɪnɪk] *adj* finés
**Finnish** [ˈfɪnɪʃ] *adj* finlandés; *s* finlandés (*idioma*)
**Finno-Ugric** [,fɪnoˈugrɪk] *adj* finoúgrio
**finny** [ˈfɪnɪ] *adj* aletado; abundante en peces
**fiord** [fjord] *s* fiord o fiordo
**fir** [fʌr] *s* (bot.) abeto
**fire** [faɪr] *s* fuego; incendio; martirio, suplicio; (fig.) fuego, fogosidad; **between two fires** entre dos fuegos; **to be on fire** estar ardiendo; **to be under enemy fire** estar expuesto al fuego del enemigo; **to catch fire** encenderse; **to catch on fire** incendiarse; **to go through fire and water** pasar las de Dios es Cristo; **to hang fire** demorarse, tardar, estar en suspenso; **to lay a fire** preparar un fuego; **to miss fire** fallar (*la escopeta; los cilindros*); fracasar; **to open fire** abrir fuego, romper el fuego; **to play with fire** jugar con fuego; **to set on fire, to set fire to** pegar fuego a; **to take fire** encenderse; **under fire** bajo el fuego del enemigo; acusado, inculpado ‖ *interj* (mil.) ¡fuego! ‖ *va* encender; incendiar (*lo que no era destinado a arder*); calentar (*el horno*); cargar (*el hogar*); encender (*la caldera*); cocer (*ladrillos*); calentar, secar al horno (*pintura, esmalte*); disparar (*un arma de fuego*); pegar (*un tiro*); lanzar (*un torpedo, una bomba*); hacer explotar (*una mina*); enrojecer; hacer (*una salva de cañonazos; un saludo nacional*); excitar (*la imaginación*); (coll.) despedir (*a un empleado*) ‖ *vn* encenderse; hacer fuego, tirar; dar explosiones (*un motor*); enrojecerse; **to fire away** (coll.) comenzar, empezar; (coll.) ponerse en marcha; **to fire on** hacer fuego sobre, hacer un disparo sobre; **to fire up** calentar el horno; cargar el hogar; encender la caldera; enfurecerse
**fire alarm** *s* alarma de incendios; avisador o timbre de incendios; **to sound the fire alarm** tocar a fuego
**firearm** [ˈfaɪr,ɑrm] *s* arma de fuego
**fireball** [ˈfaɪr,bɔl] *s* bola de fuego; bólido; rayo en bola; globo lleno de pólvora
**fire basket** *s* var. de **cresset**
**fire beetle** *s* (ent.) cucuyo
**firebird** [ˈfaɪr,bʌrd] *s* pajarillo de color ana-

ranjado subido como el cacique veranero, la piranga y el rubí
**fireboat** ['fair,bot] *s* buque con mangueras para incendios
**firebox** ['fair,bɑks] *s* caja de fuego, fogón
**firebrand** ['fair,brænd] *s* tizón; (fig.) botafuego
**firebreak** ['fair,brek] *s* raya (*para impedir la comunicación del incendio en los campos*)
**firebrick** ['fair,brɪk] *s* ladrillo refractario
**fire brigade** *s* cuerpo de bomberos
**firebug** ['fair,bʌg] *s* (coll.) incendiario
**fire clay** *s* arcilla refractaria
**fire company** *s* cuerpo de bomberos; compañía de seguros
**fire control** *s* (nav.) dirección de tiro; (mil.) conducción del fuego
**firecracker** ['fair,krækər] *s* triquitraque
**firecrest** ['fair,krɛst] *s* (orn.) abadejo
**firedamp** ['fair,dæmp] *s* (min.) grisú, mofeta
**fire department** *s* servicio de bomberos, servicio de incendios
**firedog** ['fair,dɔg] o ['fair,dɑg] *s* morillo
**fire door** *s* puerta incombustible, puerta contrafuego; boca de carga, puerta del hogar
**fire drill** *s* ejercicio o disciplina para caso de incendio
**fire-eater** ['fair,itər] *s* titiritero que finge tragarse brasas; (fig.) matamoros; (coll.) bombero muy intrépido
**fire engine** *s* bomba de incendios, coche bomba
**fire escape** *s* escalera de escape, escalera de salvamento
**fire extinguisher** *s* apagafuego, extintor
**fire fighter** *s* el que combate los incendios
**firefly** ['fair,flaɪ] *s* (*pl:* **-flies**) (ent.) bicho de luz, luciérnaga
**fire grenade** *s* extintor de granada
**fireguard** ['fair,gɑrd] *s* guardafuego; (forestry) cortafuego
**fire hose** *s* manguera contra encendios
**firehouse** ['fair,haus] *s* cuartel de bomberos, estación de incendios
**fire hydrant** *s* boca de incendio
**fire insurance** *s* seguro de incendios, seguros contra incendios
**fire irons** *spl* badil y tenazas
**fire ladder** *s* escalera de salvamento
**fireless** ['fairlɪs] *adj* sin fuego
**fireless cooker** *s* cocinilla sin fuego
**firelight** ['fair,laɪt] *s* luz de un fuego
**firelock** ['fair,lɑk] *s* pedreñal, trabuco de pedernal
**fireman** ['fairmən] *s* (*pl:* **-men**) bombero (*que apaga los incendios*); fogonero (*que cuida del fogón en las máquinas de vapor*)
**fireplace** ['fair,ples] *s* chimenea o chimenea francesa
**fire plug** *s* boca de agua
**fire pot** *s* hornillo
**fire power** *s* (mil.) potencia de fuego
**fireproof** ['fair,pruf] *adj* incombustible; *va* hacer incombustible
**fireproofing** ['fair,prufɪŋ] *s* incombustibilización; materiales refractarios
**fire sale** *s* venta de mercancías averiadas en un incendio
**fire screen** *s* pantalla de chimenea
**fire ship** *s* brulote
**fire shovel** *s* badil
**fireside** ['fair,saɪd] *s* hogar
**fireside chat** *s* (coll.) charla de chimenea
**fire station** *s* parque de incendios
**fire tongs** *spl* tenazas para coger las brasas, tenazas de chimenea
**fire tower** *s* torre con atalaya para la observación de incendios; caja de escalera de escape
**firetrap** ['fair,træp] *s* edificio que se puede encender fácilmente; edificio sin medios adecuados de escape en caso de incendio
**fire-tube boiler** ['fair,tjub] o ['fair,tub] *s* caldera tubular de humo
**fire wall** *s* cortafuego
**firewarden** ['fair,wɔrdən] *s* vigía de incendios
**firewater** ['fair,wɔtər] o ['fair,wɑtər] *s* aguardiente
**fireweed** ['fair,wid] *s* (bot.) té (*Erechtites hieracifolia*); (bot.) pascueta, hierba del burro (*Lactuca canadensis*); (bot.) hierba hedionda (*Datura stramonium*)
**firewood** ['fair,wud] *s* leña
**fireworks** ['fair,wʌrks] *spl* fuegos artificiales; (coll.) muestra de temperamento
**fire worshiper** *s* adorador del fuego, ignícola
**firing** ['fairɪŋ] *s* encendimiento; alimentación de fuego; carga de hogar; combustible, carbón, leña; cocción (*p.ej., de ladrillos*); disparo (*de un arma de fuego*); tiroteo; encendido (*de un motor de combustión interna*); (coll.) despedida (*de un empleado*)
**firing chart** *s* (arti.) cuadro de tiro
**firing line** *s* (mil.) línea de fuego, frente de batalla; **on the firing line** en vanguardia, en medio del ataque
**firing order** *s* (aut.) orden *m* del encendido
**firing pin** *s* percutor, aguja de percusión
**firing squad** *s* piquete de salvas; pelotón de fusilamiento, piquete de ejecución
**firkin** ['fʌrkɪn] *s* cuñete; medida de capacidad de 40,914 litros en Inglaterra y de 34,068 litros en EE.UU.
**firm** [fʌrm] *adj* firme; *s* razón social, firma; *va* poner firme; *vn* ponerse firme
**firmament** ['fʌrməmənt] *s* firmamento
**firman** ['fʌrmən] o [fər'mɑn] *s* (*pl:* **-mans**) firmán
**firmness** ['fʌrmnɪs] *s* firmeza
**first** [fʌrst] *adj* primero; (mus.) principal; *adv* primero (*primeramente; antes; más bien*); **first and last** bajo todos los conceptos; **first of all** ante todo; *s* primero; (aut.) primera velocidad; (mus.) voz cantante, voz principal; **firsts** *spl* (com.) artículos de primera calidad; **at first** en primer lugar; al principio; **from the first** desde el principio; **the first to** + *inf* el primero en + *inf*
**first aid** *s* primeros auxilios, cura de urgencia
**first-aid** ['fʌrst'ed] *adj* de primeros auxilios
**first-aider** [,fʌrst'edər] *s* socorrista
**first-aid kit** *s* botiquín, equipo de urgencia
**first-aid station** *s* casa de socorro
**first base** *s* (baseball) primera base *f* (*puesto*); (baseball) primera base *m* (*jugador*); **to not get to first base** (slang) no poder dar el primer paso (*en una empresa*)
**first baseman** *s* (baseball) primera base *m* (*jugador*)
**first-born** ['fʌrst,bɔrn] *adj & s* primogénito
**first class** *s* primera clase
**first-class** ['fʌrst,klæs] o ['fʌrst,klɑs] *adj* de primera clase; *adv* en primera clase
**First Day** *s* domingo (*en el lenguaje de los cuáqueros*)
**first-day cover** ['fʌrst,de] *s* (philately) sobre de primer día
**first draft** *s* borrador
**first edition** *s* edición príncipe, primera edición
**first finger** *s* dedo índice o mostrador
**first-flight cover** ['fʌrst,flaɪt] *s* (philately) sobre de primer vuelo
**first floor** *s* (U.S.A.) piso bajo; (Brit.) piso principal
**first fruits** *spl* primicia; (fig.) primicias (*primeros resultados*)
**first-hand** ['fʌrst,hænd] *adj & adv* de primera mano
**first lady of the land** *s* (U.S.A.) primera dama de la nación (*esposa del Presidente*)
**first lieutenant** *s* (mil.) teniente
**firstling** ['fʌrstlɪŋ] *s* primero (*en su clase*); primogénito; primer resultado
**firstly** ['fʌrstlɪ] *adv* primeramente, en primer lugar
**first mate** *s* (naut.) piloto
**first name** *s* nombre de pila
**first night** *s* (theat.) noche de estreno
**first-nighter** [,fʌrst'naɪtər] *s* (theat.) estrenista
**first officer** *s* (naut.) piloto
**first papers** *spl* (coll.) aplicación preliminar para la carta de naturaleza
**first person** *s* (gram.) primera persona
**first quarter** *s* cuarto creciente (*de la luna*)
**first-rate** ['fʌrst,ret] *adj* de primer orden, de mayor cuantía; (coll.) excelente; *adv* (coll.) muy bien
**first-run house** ['fʌrst,rʌn] *s* teatro de estreno
**first-string** ['fʌrst,strɪŋ] *adj* regular; de mayor cuantía, del primer rango
**first water** *s* primera calidad, primer rango

**firth** [fʌrθ] *s* estuario
**fisc** [fɪsk] *s* fisco
**fiscal** ['fɪskəl] *adj* económico, monetario; fiscal; *s* fiscal (*el que representa el ministerio en los tribunales*)
**fiscal year** *s* ejercicio, año económico
**fish** [fɪʃ] *s* pez; pescado (*pez que se saca del agua para comer; carne de pescado*); (carp.) cubrejunta; (rail.) eclisa; (naut.) jimelga; (rel.) pez (*símbolo*); (coll.) individuo, tipo; **to be like a fish out of water** estar como gallina en corral ajeno; **to be neither fish nor fowl** no ser carne ni pescado; **to drink like a fish** beber como una esponja; **to have other fish to fry** tener otras cosas que hacer; *va* pescar; pescar en (*cierto lugar*); juntar con cubrejunta; (rail.) eclisar; (naut.) enjimelgar; (elec.) pescar; **to fish out** pescar (*sacar del agua*); agotar el pescado en (*p.ej., un lago*); *vn* pescar **to fish for** buscar, tratar de conseguir con maña; **to fish for compliments** buscar alabanzas; **to go fishing** ir de pesca; **to take fishing** llevar de pesca
**fishbone** ['fɪʃ,bon] *s* espina, espina de pez
**fish bowl** *s* pecera
**fish day** *s* día de pescado
**fisher** ['fɪʃər] *s* pescador; animal pescador; embarcación de pesca; (zool.) marta del Canadá
**fisherman** ['fɪʃərmən] *s* (*pl:* **-men**) pescador; embarcación de pesca, barco pesquero
**fishery** ['fɪʃərɪ] *s* (*pl:* **-ies**) pesca (*ejercicio de los pescadores*); pesquería (*trato de los pescadores*); pesquería, pesquera (*lugar*)
**fishgig** ['fɪʃ,gɪg] *s* fisga (*arpón para pescar*)
**fish globe** *s* pecera
**fish glue** *s* cola de pescado
**fish hawk** *s* (orn.) halieto, águila pescadora
**fishhook** ['fɪʃ,hʊk] *s* anzuelo
**fishing** ['fɪʃɪŋ] *adj* pesquero; *s* pesca
**fishing ground** *s* pesquería, pesquera
**fishing reel** *s* carrete de pescar
**fishing rod** *s* caña o vara de pescar
**fishing smack** *s* barco pesquero, queche
**fishing tackle** *s* aparejo de pescar, avíos o trastos de pescar
**fish joint** *s* (rail.) junta de eclisa
**fish line** *s* sedal
**fish market** *s* pescadería
**fishmonger** ['fɪʃ,mʌŋgər] *s* pescadero
**fish oil** *s* aceite de pescado
**fishplate** ['fɪʃ,plet] *s* (rail.) eclisa
**fish pole** *s* vara de pescar
**fishpool** ['fɪʃ,pul] *s* piscina
**fish spear** *s* fisga
**fish story** *s* (coll.) burlería, patraña; **to tell fish stories** (coll.) mentir por la barba
**fishtail** ['fɪʃ,tel] *adj* de cola de pescado; *s* (aer.) coleadura; *vn* (aer.) colear
**fishtail bit** *s* barrena de cola de pescado
**fish tape** *s* (elec.) cinta pescadora
**fishwife** ['fɪʃ,waɪf] *s* (*pl:* **-wives**) pescadera; verdulera (*mujer malhablada*)
**fish wire** *s* (elec.) cinta pescadora
**fishworm** ['fɪʃ,wʌrm] *s* lombriz de tierra (*que sirve de cebo para pescar*)
**fishy** ['fɪʃɪ] *adj* (*comp:* **-ier;** *super:* **-iest**) que huele o sabe a pescado; abundante en peces; sin brillo (*dícese de los ojos*); sin visos (*dícese de las joyas*); (coll.) dudoso, inverosímil
**fissile** ['fɪsɪl] *adj* físil
**fission** ['fɪʃən] *s* escisión; (biol.) escisión; (phys.) fisión
**fissionable** ['fɪʃənəbəl] *adj* fisionable
**fissionable material** *s* (phys.) material fisionable
**fissiparous** [fɪ'sɪpərəs] *adj* fisíparo
**fissiped** ['fɪsɪpɛd] *adj* & *s* (zool.) fisípedo
**fissirostral** [,fɪsɪ'rɑstrəl] *adj* (orn.) fisirrostral
**fissure** ['fɪʃər] *s* grieta, hendedura; (anat., path. & min.) fisura; *va* hender; *vn* henderse
**fist** [fɪst] *s* puño; (print.) manecilla; (coll.) mano; (coll.) escritura; (coll.) esfuerzo; **to shake one's fist at** amenazar con el puño; *va* apuñear, dar de puñadas a; apuñar, empuñar
**fist fight** *s* pelea con los puños
**fistic** ['fɪstɪk] *adj* pugilístico
**fisticuff** ['fɪstɪ,kʌf] *s* puñetazo; **fisticuffs** *spl* pelea a puñetazos; *va* dar puñetazos a; *vn* pelear a puñetazos
**fistula** ['fɪstʃʊlə] *s* (*pl:* **-las** o **-lae** [li]) fístula; (path.) fístula
**fistular** ['fɪstʃʊlər] *adj* fistular
**fistulous** ['fɪstʃʊləs] *adj* fistuloso
**fit** [fɪt] *s* ajuste, talle; encaje (*de una pieza en otra*); ataque; acceso (*p.ej., de tos*); arranque (*de amor, cólera, etc.*); rato; **by fits and starts** a empujones; *adj* (*comp:* **fitter;** *super:* **fittest**) apto, a propósito; apropiado, conveniente; listo, preparado; adiestrado; sano, de buena salud; bueno, p.ej., **fit to eat** bueno de comer; **to be fit for** poder hacer; **to see** o **to think fit** juzgar conveniente; **to see** o **to think fit to** + *inf* tener a bien + *inf;* **fit to be tied** (coll.) impaciente; (coll.) encolerizado; (*pret & pp:* **fitted;** *ger:* **fitting**) *va* ajustar, entallar; encajar; sentar, cuadrar; cuadrar con, p.ej., **he does not fit the description** no cuadra con las señas; equipar, preparar; estar de acuerdo con (*p.ej., los hechos*); servir para; **to fit out** o **up** pertrechar, proveer de todo lo necesario; *vn* ajustar, entallar; encajar; sentar; **to fit in** caber en; encajar en; **to fit in with** concordar con; llevarse bien con
**fitch** [fɪtʃ], **fitchet** ['fɪtʃɪt] o **fitchew** ['fɪtʃu] *s* (zool.) turón, veso
**fitful** ['fɪtfəl] *adj* espasmódico, caprichoso
**fitly** ['fɪtlɪ] *adv* aptamente; acertadamente; convenientemente
**fitness** ['fɪtnɪs] *s* aptitud; conveniencia; buena salud
**fitter** ['fɪtər] *s* ajustador; montador; proveedor; (sew.) probador
**fitting** ['fɪtɪŋ] *adj* propio, apropiado; conveniente, a propósito; *s* prueba (*de una prenda de vestir*); pieza de unión (*en las tuberías*); **fittings** *spl* accesorios, avíos; herrajes; muebles
**fittingly** ['fɪtɪŋlɪ] *adv* convenientemente, a propósito
**five** [faɪv] *adj* cinco; *s* cinco; equipo de baloncesto (*compuesto de cinco jugadores*); **fives** *spl* juego de pelota (*estilo inglés*); **five o'clock** las cinco
**five-and-ten** ['faɪvənd'tɛn] o ['faɪvən'tɛn] *s* (coll.) tienda de cinco y diez centavos
**five-day week** ['faɪv,de] *s* semana laboral de cinco días
**fivefold** ['faɪv,fold] *adj* & *s* quíntuplo
**five hundred** *adj* & *s* quinientos
**five-year** ['faɪv,jɪr] *adj* quinquenal
**five-year plan** *s* plan quinquenal
**fix** [fɪks] *s* (coll.) aprieto; **in a tight fix** (coll.) en calzas prietas; **to be in a fix** (coll.) hallarse en un aprieto; (*pret & pp:* **fixed** o **fixt**) *va* fijar; arreglar, componer, reparar; calar o montar (*la bayoneta*); (phot.) fijar; (coll.) apretar las clavijas a; (coll.) castigar, pagar en la misma moneda; **to fix up** (coll.) arreglar, componer, reparar; (coll.) muñir; *vn* fijarse; **to fix on** o **upon** elegir, escoger
**fixation** [fɪks'eʃən] *s* fijación; (chem., phot., psychoanal. & psychol.) fijación
**fixation abscess** *s* (med.) absceso de fijación
**fixative** ['fɪksətɪv] *adj* & *s* fijativo
**fixed** [fɪkst] *adj* fijo
**fixed condenser** *s* (elec.) condensador fijo
**fixed idea** *s* idea fija
**fixed income** *s* renta fija
**fixedly** ['fɪksɪdlɪ] *adv* fijamente
**fixed star** *s* (astr.) estrella fija
**fixer** ['fɪksər] *s* reparador; (slang) perito en daños, liquidador de la avería; (slang) mediador entre criminales y la policía; (phot.) fijador
**fixing** ['fɪksɪŋ] *s* fijación; (phot.) fijado, fijación; **fixings** *spl* (coll.) accesorios, guarniciones
**fixing bath** *s* (phot.) fijador
**fixity** ['fɪksɪtɪ] *s* (*pl:* **-ties**) fijeza; cosa fija
**fixt** [fɪkst] *adj* var. de **fixed;** *pret & pp de* **fix**
**fixture** ['fɪkstʃər] *s* accesorio, artefacto; órgano de montaje; instalación fija; mueble fijo; brazo o sostén (*de lámpara, lavabo, etc.*); soporte de herramienta; persona que se queda mucho tiempo en un sitio, empleo, etc.; **fixtures** *spl* habilitaciones (*p.ej., de una tienda o almacén*); guarniciones de alumbrado eléctrico; aparatos sanitarios
**fixture wire** *s* (elec.) alambre para artefactos
**fiz** [fɪz] *s* ruido sibilante; gaseosa, bebida ga-

seosa; champaña; agitación, bulla; (*pret & pp:* **fizzed;** *ger:* **fizzing**) *vn* hacer un ruido sibilante
**fizgig** ['fɪz,gɪg] *s* moza casquivana y coqueta; carretilla, buscapiés; fisga (*arpón para pescar*)
**fizz** [fɪz] *s & vn* var. de **fiz**
**fizzle** ['fɪzəl] *s* chisporroteo; bocazo (*explosión que no produce efecto*); (coll.) fracaso; *vn* chisporrotear débilmente; (coll.) salir calabaza, fracasar; **to fizzle out** (coll.) chisporrotear al apagarse; (coll.) fracasar
**fizzy** ['fɪzɪ] *adj* (*comp:* **-ier;** *super:* **-iest**) que chisporrotea; efervescente
**fjord** [fjord] *s* var. de **fiord**
**fl.** abr. de **florin, flourished** y **fluid**
**Fla.** abr. de **Florida**
**flabbergast** ['flæbərgæst] *va* (coll.) pasmar, dejar sin habla
**flabby** ['flæbɪ] *adj* (*comp:* **-bier;** *super:* **-biest**) flojo, lacio
**flabellate** [flə'bɛlɪt] o [flə'bɛlet] *adj* flabelado
**flabelliform** [flə'bɛlɪfɔrm] *adj* flabeliforme
**flabellum** [flə'bɛləm] *s* (*pl:* **-la** [lə]) (eccl., bot. & zool.) flabelo
**flaccid** ['flæksɪd] *adj* fláccido
**flaccidity** [flæk'sɪdɪtɪ] *s* flaccidez
**flacon** [flɑ'kõ] *s* pomo, frasco para perfume
**flag** [flæg] *s* bandera; cola de venado; pluma larga de la pata (*de las aves*); pluma secundaria del ala (*de las aves*); piedra laminada, roca laminada; losa; (bot.) lirio; (bot.) ácoro; (*pret & pp:* **flagged;** *ger:* **flagging**) *va* hacer señales con una bandera a; hacer (*señales*) con una bandera; hacer señal de parada a (*un tren*); cazar con banderín; adornar con banderas o banderas; pavimentar o solar con losas; *vn* aflojar, falsear, flaquear, disminuir
**flag captain** *s* (nav.) capitán de bandera
**Flag Day** *s* (U.S.A.) fiesta de la bandera (*el catorce de junio*)
**flagellant** ['flædʒələnt] o [flə'dʒɛlənt] *adj & s* flagelante; (*cap.*) *s* flagelante
**flagellate** ['flædʒəlet] *adj* (bot. & biol.) flagelado; *s* (bot.) flagelado; *va* flagelar
**flagellation** [,flædʒə'leʃən] *s* flagelación
**flagellator** ['flædʒə,letər] *s* flagelador
**flagellum** [flə'dʒɛləm] *s* (*pl:* **-la** [lə] o **-lums**) flagelo; (biol.) flagelo; (bot.) brote rastrero
**flageolet** [,flædʒo'lɛt] *s* (mus.) chirimía, caramillo, dulzaina
**flagging** ['flægɪŋ] *adj* flojo, lánguido; *s* enlosado; losas
**flaggy** ['flægɪ] *adj* (*comp:* **-gier;** *super:* **-giest**) flojo, lánguido; lleno de lirios; laminado
**flagman** ['flægmən] *s* (*pl:* **-men**) abanderado; (rail.) guardavía; (rail.) guardafrenos
**flag of convenience** *s* (naut.) pabellón de conveniencia
**flag officer** *s* (nav.) jefe de escuadra
**flag of truce** *s* bandera de parlamento o de paz
**flagon** ['flægən] *s* jarro; botella que contiene unos dos litros; (bot.) ácoro bastardo, espadaña fina
**flagpole** ['flæg,pol] *s* asta de bandera; mástil para una bandera; (surv.) jalón
**flagrancy** ['flegrənsɪ] *s* enormidad, escándalo
**flagrant** ['flegrənt] *adj* enorme, escandaloso
**flagship** ['flæg,ʃɪp] *s* (nav.) capitana
**flagstaff** ['flæg,stæf] o ['flæg,stɑf] *s* (*pl:* **-staffs** o **-staves** [,stevz]) asta de bandera; mástil para una bandera
**flag station** *s* (rail.) estación de bandera, apeadero
**flagstone** ['flæg,ston] *s* piedra laminada, roca laminada; losa
**flail** [flel] *s* mayal; (mil.) mangual; *va* golpear con mayal; golpear, azotar
**flair** [flɛr] *s* instinto, penetración; disposiciones (*p.ej., para el teatro*); (hunt.) olfateo; *va* olfatear
**flak** [flæk] *s* fuego antiaéreo
**flake** [flek] *s* hojuela, escama; copo (*de nieve*); chispa; (hort.) clavel rayado; *va* formar o separar en hojuelas o escamas; cubrir con hojuelas o escamas; rayar en láminas; *vn* desprenderse en hojuelas o escamas; caer en copos pequeños
**flake white** *s* albayalde, cerusa o blanco de plomo
**flaky** ['flekɪ] *adj* (*comp:* **-ier;** *super:* **-iest**) escamoso, laminoso; desmenuzable
**flambeau** ['flæmbo] *s* (*pl:* **-beaux** [boz] o **-beaus**) antorcha; candelabro
**flamboyance** [flæm'bɔɪəns] *s* (lo) flameante; rimbombancia
**flamboyant** [flæm'bɔɪənt] *adj* flameante; (arch.) flameante, flamígero; rimbombante
**flame** [flem] *s* llama; color de llama; (slang) enamorado o enamorada; *va* iluminar con llama; hacer saber señalando con llama; tratar con la llama; flamear (*esterilizar con la llama*); *vn* llamear; inflamarse; **to flame forth, out** o **up** inflamarse; **to flame out** apagársele repentinamente la llama a (*un motor a chorro*)
**flamen** ['flemɛn] *s* (*pl:* **flamens** o **flamines** ['flæmɪniz]) (hist.) flamen
**flameout** ['flem,aut] *s* (aer.) extinción repentina de la llama de un motor a chorro
**flame thrower** *s* (mil.) lanzallamas
**flaming** ['flemɪŋ] *adj* llameante; flamante, resplandeciente; ardiente, apasionado, vehemente
**flamingo** [flə'mɪŋgo] *s* (*pl:* **-gos** o **-goes**) (orn.) flamenco
**Flaminian Way** [flə'mɪnɪən] *s* Vía Flaminia
**flammable** ['flæməbəl] *adj* inflamable
**Flanders** ['flændərz] *s* Flandes
**flange** [flændʒ] *s* pestaña; (found.) herramienta para formar pestañas; *va* hacer pestaña a; ensanchar en forma de pestaña; *vn* ensancharse en forma de pestaña
**flange coupling** *s* acoplamiento de bridas
**flange joint** *s* junta de pestañas remachadas
**flange rail** *s* riel con pestaña; riel en T
**flangeway** ['flændʒ,we] *s* canal, ranura o vía de pestaña
**flank** [flæŋk] *s* flanco; (fort., mach., mil. & nav.) flanco; *va* flanquear
**flannel** ['flænəl] *s* franela; moletón; **flannels** *spl* ropa hecha de franela; ropa interior de lana; *adj* hecho de franela
**flannelet** o **flannelette** [,flænə'lɛt] *s* moletón
**flap** [flæp] *s* falda (*parte que cae suelta de una prenda*); oreja (*del zapato*); cartera (*del bolsillo*); ala (*del sombrero*); hoja plegadiza (*de una mesa*); solapa (*de la cubierta de un libro*); faldón (*de la silla de montar*); trampa (*del mostrador de una tienda*); corbata (*de un neumático*); bofetada, cachete, golpe, palmada; lonja, rebanada; aletazo, aleteo; (phonet.) golpe de lengua (*como en la pronunciación de la r*); (*pret & pp:* **flapped;** *ger:* **flapping**) *va* golpear con ruido seco; batir o sacudir (*las alas*); *vn* aletear; flamear ruidosamente
**flapdoodle** ['flæp,dudəl] *s* (coll.) disparate, tontería
**flapjack** ['flæp,dʒæk] *s* hojuela, torta de masa frita en una plancha metálica
**flapper** ['flæpər] *s* batidor; falda; pajarito que apenas sabe volar; (coll.) tobillera; (slang) chica descarada; (slang) mano
**flare** [flɛr] *s* llamarada, destello; bengala, señal luminosa; cohete de señales; abocinamiento; vuelo (*de una falda*); *va* señalar por medio de luces o cohetes de señales; abocinar; ensanchar; *vn* arder con gran llamarada, destellar; abocinarse; **to flare out** o **up** inflamarse; recrudecer (*una enfermedad*)
**flareback** ['flɛr,bæk] *s* retroceso de la llama; (gun.) salida de gases de la culata; (fig.) réplica brusca y reprensiva; (fig.) retorno súbito y violento (*p.ej., del invierno*)
**flare-up** ['flɛr,ʌp] *s* llamarada; retroceso (*de una enfermedad*); (coll.) llamarada, arrebato de cólera
**flash** [flæʃ] *s* relámpago; instante, momento; rayo (*p.ej., de esperanza*); sentimiento o manifestación súbita y breve; acceso (*de alegría*); rasgo (*de ingenio*); ostentación; mensaje urgente enviado por radio, telégrafo, etc.; esclusa, represa; rebaba; preparación para teñir los líquidos; sonrisa; (mov.) proyección momentánea explicativa; (slang) ojeada; *va* inflamar; quemar (*pólvora*); despedir (*luz, destellos, etc.*); echar (*llamas*); (coll.) hacer ostentación de; enviar (*un mensaje*) como un rayo; despachar por radio, telégrafo, etc.; proteger (*la techumbre o parte de ella*) contra la lluvia con hoja de plomo o cinc; cubrir (*cristal*) con película de otro color; vaporizar (*el agua*) ins-

tantáneamente; *vn* relampaguear (*p.ej., los ojos*); pasar como un rayo; (coll.) alardear, fachendear
**flashback** [ˈflæʃˌbæk] *s* (mov.) episodio intercalado (*para aclarar la historia*)
**flash bulb** *s* (phot.) luz de magnesio, bombilla de destello, bombilla relámpago, relámpago fotogénico
**flash flood** *s* avenida repentina, torrentada
**flashing** [ˈflæʃɪŋ] *s* vierteaguas, despidiente de agua
**flash in the pan** *s* fogonazo sin descarga; esfuerzo o tentativa repentina y ostentosa que no tiene éxito
**flashlight** [ˈflæʃˌlaɪt] *s* fanal de destellos, luz intermitente (*de faro*); linterna eléctrica, lámpara eléctrica de bolsillo; (phot.) magnesio (*luz de magnesio; fotografía al magnesio*), relámpago fotogénico
**flashlight battery** *s* pila de linterna
**flashlight bulb** *s* bombilla de linterna, bombilla de lámpara eléctrica de bolsillo
**flashlight photography** *s* fotografía instantánea de relámpago
**flash point** *s* punto de inflamación
**flash sign** *s* anuncio intermitente
**flash welding** *s* soldadura por arco con presión
**flashy** [ˈflæʃɪ] *adj* (*comp:* **-ier;** *super:* **-iest**) relampagueante; chillón, llamativo, de relumbrón
**flask** [flæsk] o [flɑsk] *s* frasco; frasco de bolsillo; matraz, redoma; caja de moldear
**flat** [flæt] *adj* (*comp:* **flatter;** *super:* **flattest**) plano; chato (*dícese, p.ej., de la nariz, de una embarcación*); mate, deslustrado; insípido; muerto (*dícese, p.ej., de la cerveza*); desafinado, desentonado; obscuro (*sonido*); desinflado (*neumático*); redondo (*precio*); terminante; (mus.) bemol; *adv* completamente; exactamente; desafinadamente; **to fall flat** caer de plano; no surtir efecto, no tener éxito; *s* plano; barca chata; carro de plataforma; pala de remo; alma de botón; banco, bajío; pantano; piso (*de una casa de vecinos*); (mus.) bemol; (coll.) neumático desinflado; (*pret & pp:* **flatted;** *ger:* **flatting**) *va* allanar, aplanar; aplastar; achatar; deslustrar; cubrir con capa mate; quitar el lustre a (*la pintura*); bajar de tono; *vn* allanarse, aplanarse; aplastarse; achatarse; deslustrarse; aflojar, flaquear; desafinar por lo bajo
**flatboat** [ˈflætˌbot] *s* chalana
**flat-bottomed** [ˈflætˌbɑtəmd] *adj* de fondo plano (*dícese de una vasija, buque, etc.*); planudo (*buque*)
**flatcar** [ˈflætˌkɑr] *s* (rail.) vagón de plataforma, vagón plano, vagón raso, batea
**flatfish** [ˈflætˌfɪʃ] *s* (ichth.) pez pleuronecto (*p.ej., lenguado, rodaballo, platija*)
**flatfoot** [ˈflætˌfʊt] *s* (*pl:* **-feet**) pie achatado; (path.) pie plano; (slang) agente de policía
**flat-footed** [ˈflætˌfʊtɪd] *adj* de pies achatados; (coll.) inflexible
**flathead** [ˈflætˌhɛd] *s* cabeza chata (*p.ej., de un perno*); clavo de cabeza chata, tornillo de cabeza chata, perno de cabeza chata; (coll.) bobo, mentecato
**flat-headed** [ˈflætˌhɛdɪd] *adj* de cabeza chata
**flatiron** [ˈflætˌaɪərn] *s* plancha
**flat-lock seaming** [ˈflætˌlɑk] *s* (mach.) engatillado
**flatness** [ˈflætnɪs] *s* planicidad; chatedad; insipidez; deslustre; desafinación; decisión, determinación
**flatten** [ˈflætən] *va* allanar, aplanar; aplastar, chafar; arrasar; achatar; desazonar; quitar el lustre a (*la pintura*); abatir, desalentar; **to flatten out** poner horizontal; (aer.) enderezar; *vn* allanarse, aplanarse; aplastarse; achatarse; desazonarse; desalentarse; **to flatten out** ponerse horizontal; (aer.) enderezarse
**flatter** [ˈflætər] *va* lisonjear; favorecer, p.ej., **that hat flatters you** ese sombrero le favorece; **to flatter oneself** lisonjearse; *vn* lisonjear
**flatterer** [ˈflætərər] *s* lisonjero
**flattering** [ˈflætərɪŋ] *adj* lisonjero; *s* lisonja
**flattery** [ˈflætərɪ] *s* (*pl:* **-ies**) lisonja
**flattish** [ˈflætɪʃ] *adj* algo plano; algo insípido
**flattop** [ˈflætˌtɑp] *s* (nav.) portaaviones
**flatulence** [ˈflætʃələns] *s* flatulencia; hinchazón, vanidad
**flatulent** [ˈflætʃələnt] *adj* flatulento; hinchado, vanidoso
**flatus** [ˈfletəs] *s* (*pl:* **-tuses** o **-tus**) flato; golpe de viento; hinchazón (*efecto de hincharse*)
**flatware** [ˈflætˌwɛr] *s* vajilla de plata; vajilla de porcelana
**flatways** [ˈflætˌwez] o **flatwise** [ˈflætˌwaɪz] *adv* horizontalmente; con el lado plano hacia arriba, hacia adelante o en contacto
**flatwork** [ˈflætˌwʌrk] *s* ropa blanca que puede ser aprestada por medio de una mangle
**flatworm** [ˈflætˌwʌrm] *s* (zool.) gusano plano, platelminto
**flaunt** [flɔnt] o [flɑnt] *s* ostentación; *va* ostentar, hacer gala de; *vn* hacer ostentación; ondear ostentosamente
**flautist** [ˈflɔtɪst] *s* flautista
**flavor** [ˈflevər] *s* sabor; condimento; perfume; clase (*de helada*); (fig.) sabor; *va* saborear; condimentar, sazonar; aromatizar, perfumar; *vn* **to flavor of** saber a
**flavoring** [ˈflevərɪŋ] *s* condimento; perfume
**flavour** [ˈflevər] *s, va & vn* (Brit.) var. de **flavor**
**flaw** [flɔ] *s* defecto, imperfección, tacha; grieta (*algunas veces inadvertida*); ráfaga; *va* ajar; violar; agrietar; *vn* ajarse; agrietarse
**flawless** [ˈflɔlɪs] *adj* entero, perfecto, sin tacha
**flawy** [ˈflɔ·ɪ] *adj* (*comp:* **-ier;** *super:* **-iest**) defectuoso, imperfecto; agrietado; con ráfagas
**flax** [flæks] *s* (bot.) lino (*planta y fibra textil*)
**flaxen** [ˈflæksən] *adj* de lino; palizo; rubio
**flaxseed** [ˈflæksˌsid] *s* linaza
**flay** [fle] *va* desollar; desollar vivo, flagelar; hurtar, robar
**flea** [fli] *s* (ent.) pulga; **flea in one's ear** reprensión; desaire, desprecio; insinuación inesperada
**fleabane** [ˈfliˌben] *s* (bot.) erígeron; (bot.) hierba pulguera
**fleabite** [ˈfliˌbaɪt] *s* picadura de pulga; molestia insignificante
**flea-bitten** [ˈfliˌbɪtən] *adj* picado por pulgas; blanco mosqueado en colorado (*dícese, p.ej., del caballo*)
**fleam** [flim] *s* (surg.) lanceta, sangradera
**fleawort** [ˈfliˌwʌrt] *s* (bot.) pulguera, zaragatona, coniza
**flèche** [fleʃ] *s* aguja (*de campanario*); (fort.) flecha
**fleck** [flɛk] *s* punto de color o luz; vedija; copo; *va* puntear, vetear
**flection** [ˈflɛkʃən] *s* flexión; (gram.) flexión
**flectional** [ˈflɛkʃənəl] *adj* (gram.) flexional
**fled** [flɛd] *pret & pp de* **flee**
**fledge** [flɛdʒ] *va* emplumar (*p.ej., una saeta*); criar (*un pajarito*) hasta que sepa volar; *vn* emplumar, emplumecer (*echar plumas las aves*)
**fledgling** o **fledgeling** [ˈflɛdʒlɪŋ] *s* pajarito, volantón, cría; pollo, novato
**flee** [fli] (*pret & pp:* **fled**) *va & vn* huir
**fleece** [flis] *s* lana; vellón, vellocino; capa o cobertura (*p.ej., de nieve*); *va* esquilar; pelar, dejar sin blanca
**fleecy** [ˈflisɪ] *adj* (*comp:* **-ier;** *super:* **-iest**) lanudo; blanco y blando, aborregado (*como un vellón*)
**fleer** [flɪr] *s* risa falsa, mueca, pulla; *va* mirar con un gesto de desprecio; *vn* reírse o sonreírse groseramente o con desprecio
**fleet** [flit] *s* armada, marina de guerra; (naut., nav. & aer.) flota; (fig.) flota (*p.ej., de automóviles, camiones*); *adj* veloz; *vn* pasar o moverse rápidamente
**fleeting** [ˈflitɪŋ] *adj* efímero, fugaz; transitorio
**fleetness** [ˈflitnɪs] *s* velocidad
**Fleming** [ˈflɛmɪŋ] *s* flamenco
**Flemish** [ˈflɛmɪʃ] *adj* flamenco; *spl* flamencos; *ssg* flamenco (*idioma*)
**Flemish bond** *s* (mas.) aparejo flamenco u holandés
**flesh** [flɛʃ] *s* carne; gordura; género humano; familia, deudos; **in the flesh** vivo; en persona; **to lose flesh** perder carnes; **to put on flesh** cobrar carnes, echar carnes; *va* meter (*un arma blanca*) en la carne; apelambrar (*cueros*); incitar o inflamar las pasiones a; cebar (*halcones,*

*perros, etc.*) con carne; engordar; **to flesh out** suplir, completar, detallar; *vn* engordar
**flesh and blood** *s* carne y sangre; el cuerpo
**flesh-colored** ['flɛʃˌkʌlərd] *adj* encarnado, de color de carne
**flesh fly** *s* (ent.) mosca de la carne, moscarda
**fleshings** ['flɛʃɪŋz] *spl* calzas ajustadas de color de carne; raeduras de carne (*que se quitan a los pellejos antes de curtirlos*)
**fleshless** ['flɛʃlɪs] *adj* descarnado
**fleshly** ['flɛʃlɪ] *adj* (*comp:* **-lier;** *super:* **-liest**) corpóreo; carnal, sensual
**fleshpot** ['flɛʃˌpɑt] *s* olla; **fleshpots** *spl* vida regalona
**flesh wound** *s* herida superficial, herida a flor de carne
**fleshy** ['flɛʃɪ] *adj* (*comp:* **-ier;** *super:* **-iest**) carnoso; gordo
**Fletcherism** ['flɛtʃərɪzəm] *s* fletcherismo
**fleur-de-lis** [ˌflʌrdə'li] o [ˌflʌrdə'lis] *s* (*pl:* **fleurs-de-lis** [ˌflʌrdə'liz]) flor de lis (*escudo de armas de Francia*); (her.) flor de lis; (bot.) lirio de Florencia; (f.a.) flor de lis florenzada
**fleury** ['flʊrɪ] *adj* (her.) flordelisado; (her.) floronado (*dícese de una cruz*)
**flew** [flu] *pret de* **fly**
**flex** [flɛks] *va* doblar; *vn* doblarse
**flexibility** [ˌflɛksɪ'bɪlɪtɪ] *s* flexibilidad
**flexible** ['flɛksɪbəl] o **flexile** ['flɛksɪl] *adj* flexible
**flexible cord** *s* (elec.) flexible
**flexion** ['flɛkʃən] *s* var. de **flection**
**flexor** ['flɛksər] *s* (anat.) flexor, músculo flexor
**flexuous** ['flɛkʃʊəs] *adj* flexuoso
**flexure** ['flɛkʃər] *s* flexión; corvadura
**flibbertigibbet** ['flɪbərtɪˌdʒɪbɪt] *s* persona casquivana; charlador, bachiller
**flick** [flɪk] *s* golpe rápido y ligero; ruido seco; mancha pequeña, raya, salpicadura; *va* golpear rápida y ligeramente; chasquear (*un látigo*); *vn* moverse rápida y ligeramente, revolotear
**flicker** ['flɪkər] *s* luz mortecina, llama trémula; chispa; parpadeo; temblor momentáneo (*de emoción*); (orn.) picamaderos norteamericano (*Colaptes auratus*); *va* hacer brillar con luz mortecina; hacer temblar; *vn* brillar con luz mortecina, flamear con llama trémula; fluctuar, lengüetear, oscilar
**flier** ['flaɪər] *s* persona o cosa que vuela; aviador; autobús, tren o vapor rápido; (slang) empresa arriesgada, negocio arriesgado; (U.S.A.) hoja volante
**flight** [flaɪt] *s* fuga, huída; vuelo; bandada (*de pájaros*); escuadrilla (*de aviones*); trayecto (*de un avión*); tramo (*de escalera*); ímpetu, arranque (*p.ej., de la fantasía*); **to put to flight** poner en fuga; **to take flight** alzar el vuelo; **to take to flight** ponerse en fuga
**flight deck** *s* (nav.) cubierta de aterrizaje, cubierta de vuelo
**flight feather** *s* (orn.) remera
**flightiness** ['flaɪtɪnɪs] *s* frivolidad, veleidad
**flightless** ['flaɪtlɪs] *adj* incapaz de volar
**flight officer** *s* oficial de aviación
**flight path** *s* (aer.) línea de vuelo
**flight recorder** *s* (aer.) registrador de vuelo
**flighty** ['flaɪtɪ] *adj* (*comp:* **-ier;** *super:* **-iest**) frívolo, veleidoso; alocado, casquivano
**flimflam** ['flɪmˌflæm] *s* (coll.) tontería; (coll.) trampa, engaño; (*pret & pp:* **-flammed;** *ger:* **-flamming**) *va* (coll.) trampear
**flimflammer** ['flɪmˌflæmər] *s* (coll.) trampeador
**flimsy** ['flɪmzɪ] *adj* (*comp:* **-sier;** *super:* **-siest**) débil, endeble; baladí, fútil; *s* papel muy delgado que usan los repórters; informe escrito en papel delgado; (slang) billete de banco
**flinch** [flɪntʃ] *s* titubeo, vacilación; juego en que se usan naipes especiales numerados de 1 a 14; *vn* acobardarse, encogerse de miedo, desistir de miedo
**flinder** ['flɪndər] *s* astilla, fragmento
**fling** [flɪŋ] *s* echamiento violento; baile escocés de compás rápido; **to go on a fling** echar una cana al aire; **to have a fling at** ensayar (*una cosa*); escarnecer (*a una persona*); **to have one's fling** darse a los placeres mientras se puede; (*pret & pp:* **flung**) *va* arrojar, tirar; echar (*p.ej., a la cárcel, al suelo*); mandar precipitadamente (*p.ej., nuevas tropas al frente*); **to fling about** esparcir; **to fling open** abrir de golpe; **to fling out** arrojar con fuerza; hacer ondear (*una bandera*); **to fling shut** cerrar de golpe; *vn* arrojarse, lanzarse, precipitarse; cocear, corcovear
**flint** [flɪnt] *s* pedernal (*variedad de cuarzo; piedra de chispa*); cosa sumamente dura
**flint glass** *s* vidrio de plomo
**flint-hearted** ['flɪntˌhɑrtɪd] *adj* pedernalino, apedernalado
**flintlock** ['flɪntˌlɑk] *s* llave de chispa; pedreñal, trabuco de chispa
**flint paper** *s* papel de lija de pedernal
**flinty** ['flɪntɪ] *adj* (*comp:* **-ier;** *super:* **-iest**) pedernalino, de pedernal; (fig.) apedernalado, empedernido
**flip** [flɪp] *adj* (*comp:* **flipper;** *super:* **flippest**) (coll.) petulante, impertinente; *s* capirotazo, tirón; bebida de vino o cerveza caliente con azúcar y especias; (*pret & pp:* **flipped;** *ger:* **flipping**) *va* echar de un capirotazo (*p.ej., una moneda sobre el mostrador*); mover rápidamente, mover de un tirón; quitar de golpe; lanzar al aire; **to flip shut** cerrar de golpe (*p.ej., un abanico*); *vn* dar un capirotazo; moverse de un tirón; **to flip up** echar a cara o cruz
**flippancy** ['flɪpənsɪ] *s* petulancia, impertinencia, ligereza
**flippant** ['flɪpənt] *adj* petulante, impertinente, ligero
**flipper** ['flɪpər] *s* aleta (*de foca*); (slang) aleta (*mano*)
**flirt** [flʌrt] *s* coqueta; galanteador; golpe rápido, meneo rápido, tirón; *va* agitar (*p.ej., un abanico*); mover rápidamente, mover de un tirón; *vn* flirtear; coquetear (*una mujer*); galantear (*un hombre*); **to flirt with** flirtear con; acariciar (*una idea*) con poca seriedad; jugar con (*la muerte*)
**flirtation** [flʌr'teʃən] *s* flirtación, coqueteo, galanteo; amorío
**flirtatious** [flʌr'teʃəs] *adj* coqueta; de coqueteo; galanteador; de galanteo
**flirting** ['flʌrtɪŋ] *s* flirteo; coqueteo; galanteo
**flit** [flɪt] *s* movimiento rápido y ligero; (*pret & pp:* **flitted;** *ger:* **flitting**) *vn* revolotear, volar; pasar rápidamente (*p.ej., por la imaginación*)
**flitch** [flɪtʃ] *s* hoja o lonja de tocino
**flitter** ['flɪtər] *s* pedacitos de metal que sirven de adorno; (coll.) andrajo, harapo; *vn* (archaic & dial.) revolotear, lengüetear
**flittermouse** ['flɪtərˌmaʊs] *s* (*pl:* **-mice**) (zool.) murciélago
**flitting** ['flɪtɪŋ] *adj* fugaz
**flivver** ['flɪvər] *s* (slang) automóvil o avión pequeño y barato
**float** [flot] *s* flotador (*especialmente, el corcho de la caña de pescar*); boya (*corcho en las redes*); balsa; palo (*de remo*); paleta (*de rueda*); carroza alegórica, carro alegórico (*de procesiones, fiestas, etc.*); (bot. & mach.) flotador; (mas.) llana; *va* poner a flote; cubrir con agua, inundar, regar; allanar con llana; (com.) lanzar (*una empresa*); (com.) emitir; *vn* flotar
**floatability** [ˌflotə'bɪlɪtɪ] *s* flotabilidad
**floatable** ['flotəbəl] *adj* flotable
**float chamber** *s* cuba del flotador (*del carburador*)
**float-cut file** ['flotˌkʌt] *s* lima de picadura
**floater** ['flotər] *s* flotador; (coll.) persona que siempre se está mudando de domicilio o de lugar de empleo; (U.S.A.) persona que en las elecciones echa su voto en varios sitios, ilegalmente
**floating** ['flotɪŋ] *adj* flotante; no anclado; trashumante
**floating axle** *s* (mach.) eje flotante, puente flotante
**floating battery** *s* (elec.) acumulador flotante
**floating bridge** *s* pontón flotante
**floating debt** *s* deuda flotante
**floating dock** *s* dique flotante
**floating dry dock** *s* dique de carena flotante
**floating island** *s* isla flotante, isla artificial; (cook.) natillas con merengue
**floating kidney** *s* (path.) riñón flotante
**floating ribs** *spl* (anat.) costillas flotantes
**floatstone** ['flotˌston] *s* (mineral.) cuarzo esponjoso

**flocculent** ['flakjələnt] *adj* lanudo, velludo; (chem.) floculento
**flock** [flak] *s* bandada (*de aves*); rebaño (*de ganado lanar*); gentío, muchedumbre; copo (*p.ej., de lana*); borra, tamo; hatajo (*p.ej., de disparates*); sinnúmero; (fig.) rebaño (*de los fieles*); *vn* congregarse, reunirse; llegar en tropel, agolparse
**floe** [flo] *s* témpano, banquisa
**flog** [flag] (*pret & pp:* **flogged;** *ger:* **flogging**) *va* azotar
**flogging** ['flagɪŋ] *s* azotamiento
**flood** [flʌd] *s* inundación, diluvio; avenida, crecida; pleamar; (fig.) inundación, diluvio, torrente (*de luz, palabras, etc.*); (poet.) mar, lago, río; **the Flood** (Bib.) el Diluvio, el Diluvio universal; *va* inundar; abrumar; *vn* desbordar; entrar a raudales, salir a raudales
**flood control** *s* obras de defensa contra las inundaciones
**floodgate** ['flʊd,get] *s* compuerta (*de una presa*); esclusa (*de un canal*)
**floodlight** ['flʌd,laɪt] *s* faro de inundación; *va* iluminar con faro de inundación
**flood plain** *s* llanura aluvial
**flood tide** *s* (naut.) pleamar, creciente del mar, marea creciente
**floor** [flor] *s* piso, suelo; piso (*alto de escalera*); fondo (*de una piscina, del mar, etc.*); hemiciclo (*de una asamblea*); lugar donde se verifican las operaciones de compra y venta (*en las bolsas*); (naut.) varenga; **to ask for the floor** pedir la palabra; **to have the floor** tener la palabra; **to take the floor** tomar la palabra; *va* solar; entarimar; enladrillar, enlosar; derribar, echar al suelo; (coll.) abrumar, vencer; (coll.) dejar turulato, revolcar (*al adversario en controversia*)
**floorage** ['florɪdʒ] *s* superficie del piso o de los pisos
**floor board** *s* (aut.) tabla de piso
**floorcovering** ['flor,kʌvərɪŋ] *s* alfombrado: revestimiento del piso
**flooring** ['florɪŋ] *s* piso, suelo; pisos, suelos; material para pisos
**floor lamp** *s* lámpara de pie
**floor leader** *s* (U.S.A.) jefe de partido (*en la Cámara de Representantes o el Senado*)
**floor mop** *s* aljofifa, trapeador
**floor plan** *s* planta
**floor show** *s* espectáculo de cabaret
**floor slab** *s* losa de piso
**floor space** *s* área del piso o los pisos
**floor timber** *s* (naut.) varenga
**floorwalker** ['flor,wɔkər] *s* superintendente de división (*en los grandes almacenes*)
**floor wax** *s* cera de o para pisos
**flop** [flap] *s* agitación (*como de pez recién sacado del agua*); (coll.) fracaso; (coll.) caída (*de una pieza teatral*); **to take a flop** (coll.) caerse; (*pret & pp:* **flopped;** *ger:* **flopping**) *vn* agitarse (*como pez recién sacado del agua*); caerse; dejarse caer o arrojarse pesada y desmañadamente; venirse abajo; mudarse repentinamente; (coll.) salir calabaza, salir huero, fracasar; **to flop over** volcarse, dar un vuelco; cambiar de partido
**flophouse** ['flap,haʊs] *s* posada de baja categoría
**floppy** ['flapɪ] *adj* (*comp:* **-pier;** *super:* **-piest**) (coll.) dado a agitarse; colgante de modo desgarbado (*como las orejas del podenco*); flojo, holgado, flexible
**flora** ['florə] *s* flora; (*cap.*) *s* (myth.) Flora
**floral** ['florəl] *adj* floral; de flores
**floral emblem** *s* flor o planta emblemática (*de un país, una ciudad, etc.*)
**Florence** ['flarəns] o ['flɔrəns] *s* Florencia (*ciudad de Italia; nombre de mujer*)
**Florentine** ['flarəntin] o ['flɔrəntin] *adj & s* florentino
**Florentine iris** *s* (bot.) lirio de Florencia
**florescence** [flo'rɛsəns] *s* (bot.) florescencia
**florescent** [flo'rɛsənt] *adj* floreciente
**floret** ['florɪt] *s* florecilla, florecita; (bot.) flósculo
**floriculture** ['florɪ,kʌltʃər] *s* floricultura
**floriculturist** [,florɪ'kʌltʃərɪst] *s* floricultor
**florid** ['flarɪd] o ['flɔrɪd] *adj* encarnado (*dícese de la tez*); florido, elegante; (lit.) florido
**Florida** ['flarɪdə] o ['flɔrɪdə] *s* la Florida
**Florida Keys** *spl* Cayos de la Florida
**Florida moss** *s* (bot.) cabello del rey, barbas de viejo, barba española
**Floridan** ['flarɪdən] o ['flɔrɪdən] o **Floridian** [flo'rɪdɪən] *adj & s* floridano
**Florida Strait** *s* canal o estrecho de la Florida
**floriferous** [flo'rɪfərəs] *adj* florífero
**florin** ['flarɪn] o ['flɔrɪn] *s* florín (*moneda*)
**floripondio** [,florɪ'pandɪo] *s* (bot.) floripondio
**florist** ['florɪst] *s* florero, florista; floricultor
**floscule** ['flaskjʊl] *s* (bot.) flósculo
**flosculous** ['flaskjʊləs] *adj* flosculoso
**floss** [flɔs] o [flas] *s* cadarzo (*seda basta de la camisa del capullo*); seda floja (*sin torcer*); seda vegetal; (bot.) barbas, cabellos (*del maíz*)
**floss silk** *s* cadarzo; seda floja
**flossy** ['flɔsɪ] o ['flasɪ] *adj* (*comp:* **-ier;** *super:* **-iest**) len; ligero, velloso; (slang) aparatoso, vistoso, cursi
**flotation** [flo'teʃən] *s* flotación; lanzamiento (*de un buque*); (com.) lanzamiento (*de una empresa, de una emisión de valores, etc.*); (metal.) flotación
**flotilla** [flo'tɪlə] *s* flotilla
**flotsam** ['flatsəm] *s* (naut.) pecio, pecios; objetos flotantes
**flotsam and jetsam** *spl* pecios, despojos que arroja el mar a la orilla; baratijas; gente desocupada y trashumante; gente perdida
**flounce** [flaʊns] *s* sacudida rápida del cuerpo (*efecto del enojo*); vuelta rápida, torsión, tirón; (sew.) volante; *va* (sew.) adornar con volantes; *vn* andar exagerando los movimientos del cuerpo (*para mostrar enojo*); moverse violentamente, torciendo el cuerpo; **to flounce out** salir airadamente
**flounder** ['flaʊndər] *s* (ichth.) pleuronecto (*especialmente Platichthys flesus*); lenguado (*Paralichthys brasiliensis*); (ichth.) platija (*Pleuronectes platessa*); forcejeo; *vn* forcejear, andar sin poder avanzar mucho, proceder torpemente; **to flounder through** llegar tropezando al fin de
**flour** [flaʊr] *s* harina; *adj* harinero; *va* enharinar
**flour bolt** *s* cedazo, tamiz
**flourish** ['flʌrɪʃ] *s* molinete (*hecho con el bastón o espada*); plumada, rasgo; rúbrica (*hecha como parte de la firma*); alarde, ostentación; (mus.) floreo; *va* hacer molinetes con (*un bastón, una espada*); hacer alarde de; *vn* florecer; hacer molinetes; hacer rúbricas
**flourishing** ['flʌrɪʃɪŋ] *adj* floreciente
**flour mill** *s* molino de harina, molino harinero
**floury** ['flaʊrɪ] *adj* harinoso; enharinado
**flout** [flaʊt] *s* mofa, escarnio; insulto; *va* mofarse de, escarnecer; insultar; *vn* mofarse
**flow** [flo] *s* flujo; (naut.) flujo; *va* derramar; inundar; esparcir (*p.ej., pintura*) en una capa espesa; *vn* fluir; subir (*la marea*); caer o colgar (*los cabellos*); moverse o deslizarse suavemente; ondear; abundar; **to flow away** deslizarse; **to flow into** desaguar en; **to flow over** rebosar; **to flow with** abundar en, nadar en
**flower** ['flaʊər] *s* flor; (fig.) flor (*lo más escogido*); **flowers** *spl* (chem.) flor; **in flower** en flor; *va* florear, adornar con flores; *vn* florecer
**flower bed** *s* macizo, parterre
**flower beetle** *s* (ent.) cetoína
**flowered** ['flaʊərd] *adj* floreado; espolinado
**floweret** ['flaʊərɛt] *s* florecilla, florecita
**flower garden** *s* jardín de flores
**flower girl** *s* florera; damita de honor
**flowering** ['flaʊərɪŋ] *adj* floreciente; *s* florecimiento
**flowering dogwood** *s* (bot.) cornejo florido
**flowering fern** *s* (bot.) helecho florido
**flowering maple** *s* (bot.) abutilón
**flowering rush** *s* (bot.) junco florido
**flowerless** ['flaʊrlɪs] *adj* sin flores; (bot.) criptogámico
**flower of an hour** *s* (bot.) aurora común, flor de una hora
**flower piece** *s* ramillete; (f.a.) florero
**flowerpot** ['flaʊər,pat] *s* tiesto, maceta
**flowers of antimony** *spl* (chem.) flor de antimonio
**flowers of sulphur** *spl* (chem.) flor de azufre
**flower stand** *s* florero (*mueble*)

**flowery** [ˈflaʊərɪ] *adj* (*comp:* **-ier;** *super:* **-iest**) florido; (lit.) florido
**flowing** [ˈflo·ɪŋ] *adj* corriente; flotante, ondeante; fácil, flúido
**flown** [flon] *pp de* **fly**
**flow sheet** *s* gráfico de las fases de un proceso industrial
**flu** [flu] *s* (coll.) gripe
**flubdub** [ˈflʌbˌdʌb] *s* (coll.) ínfulas
**fluctuant** [ˈflʌktʃuənt] *adj* fluctuante
**fluctuate** [ˈflʌktʃuet] *vn* fluctuar
**fluctuation** [ˌflʌktʃuˈeʃən] *s* fluctuación; (biol. & med.) fluctuación
**flue** [flu] *s* cañón de chimenea, humero; tubo de humo, tubo de caldera; (mus.) tubo de embocadura de flauta (*del órgano*)
**fluency** [ˈfluənsɪ] *s* fluencia; afluencia, facundia; fluidez (*del lenguaje, estilo*)
**fluent** [ˈfluənt] *adj* fluente (*que fluye*); afluente, facundo; flúido (*lenguaje, estilo*)
**fluently** [ˈfluəntlɪ] *adv* corrientemente
**flue pipe** *s* (mus.) tubo de flauta, tubo de embocadura de flauta
**fluff** [flʌf] *s* pelusa, plumón, tamo; lanilla; copo (*de lana*); masa esponjosa (*p.ej., de crema batida*); (coll.) gazapo de actor; *va* mullir, esponjar; *vn* esponjarse
**fluffy** [ˈflʌfɪ] *adj* (*comp:* **-ier;** *super:* **-iest**) fofo, esponjoso; velloso, velludo
**fluid** [ˈfluɪd] *adj* flúido; cambiante; *s* flúido
**fluid diet** *s* régimen de alimentos líquidos
**fluid dram** *s* dracma líquida (*octava parte de la onza líquida*)
**fluidity** [fluˈɪdɪtɪ] *s* fluidez
**fluid mechanics** *ssg* mecánica de los flúidos
**fluid ounce** *s* onza líquida (*29,6 centímetros cúbicos en EE.UU. y 28,4 en Gran Bretaña*)
**fluke** [fluk] *s* uña (*de ancla, de arpón*); aleta (*de la cola de la ballena*); (ichth.) pleuronecto; (zool.) trematodo, duela del hígado; chiripa (*en el billar, suerte que se gana por casualidad; casualidad favorable*); **to win by a fluke** ganar por chiripa; *va* chiripear; *vn* chiripear; fracasar
**flume** [flum] *s* garganta profunda por cuyo fondo pasa un río o arroyo; caz, saetín; acueducto, canal de madera
**flummery** [ˈflʌmərɪ] *s* (*pl:* **-ies**) manjar blanco; pasta de harina cocida; alabanza insincera; disparates, tonterías
**flung** [flʌŋ] *pret & pp de* **fling**
**flunk** [flʌŋk] *s* (coll.) reprobación (*en un examen o asignatura*); (coll.) nota de suspenso; *va* (coll.) colgar, reprobar, dar calabazas a; perder (*un examen o asignatura*); **to flunk out** (coll.) reprobar definitivamente; *vn* (coll.) salir mal, fracasar; **to flunk out** (coll.) tener que abandonar los estudios por haber sido reprobado
**flunkey** [ˈflʌŋkɪ] *s* var. de **flunky**
**flunky** [ˈflʌŋkɪ] *s* (*pl:* **-ies**) lacayo; adulador
**flunkyism** [ˈflʌŋkɪɪzəm] *s* servilismo
**fluor** [ˈfluɔr] *s* (mineral.) fluorita
**fluoresce** [ˌfluəˈrɛs] *vn* despedir rayos de luz fluorescente
**fluorescein** [ˌfluəˈrɛsɪɪn] *s* (chem.) fluoresceína
**fluorescence** [ˌfluəˈrɛsəns] *s* fluorescencia
**fluorescent** [ˌfluəˈrɛsənt] *adj* fluorescente
**fluorescent lamp** *s* tubo fluorescente
**fluorescent lighting** *s* alumbrado fluorescente
**fluorescent screen** *s* (phys.) pantalla fluorescente
**fluoric** [fluˈɑrɪk] o [fluˈɔrɪk] *adj* fluórico
**fluorid** [ˈfluərɪd] o **fluoride** [ˈfluəraɪd] o [ˈfluərɪd] *s* (chem.) fluoruro
**fluoridate** [ˈfluərɪdet] *va* fluorizar
**fluoridation** [ˌfluərɪˈdeʃən] *s* fluorización (*del agua potable*); (geol.) fluorización
**fluorin** [ˈfluərɪn] o **fluorine** [ˈfluərin] o [ˈfluərɪn] *s* (chem.) flúor
**fluorite** [ˈfluəraɪt] *s* (mineral.) fluorita
**fluoroscope** [ˈfluərəskop] *s* fluoroscopio
**fluoroscopic** [ˌfluərəˈskɑpɪk] *adj* fluoroscópico
**fluoroscopy** [ˌfluəˈrɑskəpɪ] *s* fluoroscopia
**fluor spar** *s* (mineral.) espato flúor
**flurry** [ˈflʌrɪ] *s* (*pl:* **-ries**) ráfaga; chaparrón; nevisca; agitación, aturdimiento; (*pret & pp:* **-ried**) *va* agitar, aturdir
**flush** [flʌʃ] *s* flujo repentino; rubor, bochorno, llamarada, sonrojo; acceso (*p.ej., de alegría*); floración repentina (*p.ej., en la primavera*); vigor (*de la juventud*); chorro del inodoro; flux (*en el póker*); *adj* rasante, nivelado; enrasado, parejo; embutido; abundante, copioso; robusto, vigoroso; pródigo, próspero; rubicundo; rebosante; bien provisto; (print.) justificado; **flush with** a ras de, al mismo nivel que; *adv* ras con ras, al mismo nivel; directamente, sin errar el golpe; *va* abochornar; exaltar, regocijar; engreír; limpiar con un chorro de agua, lavar con agua a presión; hacer saltar (*una liebre*); hacer volar (*una perdiz*); *vn* abochornarse; estar encendido (*p.ej., el rostro*); fluir repentinamente; brotar; saltar o volar de repente
**flush deck** *s* (naut.) cubierta corrida
**Flushing** [ˈflʌʃɪŋ] *s* Flesinga
**flush-mounted switch** [ˈflʌʃˈmaʊntɪd] *s* (elec.) llave para embutir, llave embutida
**flush outlet** *s* (elec.) caja de enchufe embutida
**flush switch** *s* (elec.) llave para embutir, llave embutida
**flush tank** *s* depósito de limpia, tanque de inundación
**flush toilet** *s* inodoro con chorro de agua
**fluster** [ˈflʌstər] *s* confusión, aturdimiento; *va* confundir, aturdir
**flute** [flut] *s* (mus.) flauta; (mus.) flautado (*registro del órgano*); estría (*de una columna*); *va* acanalar, estriar; *vn* flautear, tocar la flauta; cantar o silbar remedando el sonido de la flauta
**fluted** [ˈflutɪd] *adj* acanalado, estriado; flauteado
**fluting** [ˈflutɪŋ] *s* acanaladura, estriadura
**flutist** [ˈflutɪst] *s* flautista
**flutter** [ˈflʌtər] *s* aleteo, revoloteo; aturdimiento, confusión, turbación; **in a flutter** aturdido; **to make a flutter** causar alboroto; *va* agitar; aturdir, confundir, turbar; *vn* aletear, revolotear; agitarse; flamear, ondear; alterarse (*el pulso*); palpitar (*el corazón*)
**fluvial** [ˈfluvɪəl] *adj* fluvial
**flux** [flʌks] *s* flujo; fusión (*estado líquido producido por el calor*); continua mudanza; (chem. & metal.) flujo o fundente; (phys. & path.) flujo; *va* fundir; unir por medio de la fusión; mezclar con un fundente; *vn* fundirse
**flux density** *s* (phys.) densidad de flujo
**fluxion** [ˈflʌkʃən] *s* flujo; (math. & path.) fluxión
**fluxmeter** [ˈflʌksˌmitər] *s* (phys.) flujómetro
**fly** [flaɪ] *s* (*pl:* **flies**) (ent.) mosca; mosca artificial (*con anzuelo de pescar escondido*); pliegue (*para cubrir botones*); bragueta (*abertura de los pantalones*); toldo que se extiende por encima de una tienda de campaña; lona que tapa la puerta de una tienda de campaña; calesín; (mach.) hélice; **on the fly** al vuelo, en el aire; **to die like flies** morir como chinches; **to hit a fly** (baseball) pegar una planchita, elevar una palomita; **flies** *spl* (theat.) bambalina ‖ (*pret:* **flew;** *pp:* **flown**) *va* hacer volar (*una cometa, un halcón*); dirigir (*un avión*); volar (*llevar en un aparato de aviación*); atravesar en avión; desplegar, llevar (*una bandera*); huir ‖ *vn* volar; huir; ondear (*una bandera*); **to fly at** lanzarse sobre; **to fly away** irse volando; escaparse; **to fly off** salir volando; desprenderse; **to fly open** abrirse de repente; **to fly over** trasvolar; **to fly shut** cerrarse de repente; **to fly to** + *inf* volar a + *inf* ‖ (*pret & pp:* **flied**) *vn* (baseball) pegar una planchita, elevar una palomita
**flyaway** [ˈflaɪəˌwe] *adj* flameante, ondeante; casquivano, frívolo
**fly ball** *s* (baseball) planchita, palomita
**flyblow** [ˈflaɪˌblo] *s* cresa; *va* llenar (*la carne*) de cresas; contaminar
**flyblown** [ˈflaɪˌblon] *adj* lleno de cresas; (fig.) contaminado, manchado, infamado
**flyboat** [ˈflaɪˌbot] *s* (naut.) filibote; buque muy rápido
**fly book** *s* cartera (*para moscas artificiales*)
**fly-by-night** [ˈflaɪbaɪˌnaɪt] *adj* indigno de confianza, poco confiable; *s* noctámbulo; (slang) persona que se escapa por la noche para evitar acreedores
**fly-casting** [ˈflaɪˌkæstɪŋ] o [ˈflaɪˌkɑstɪŋ] *s* lanzamiento de mosca (*manera de pescar*)
**flycatcher** [ˈflaɪˌkætʃər] *s* (orn.) papamoscas, cazamoscas, doral, moscareta
**flyer** [ˈflaɪər] *s* var. de **flier**

**fly-fisher** [ˈflaɪˌfɪʃər] *s* pescador que pesca con moscas artificiales
**fly-fishing** [ˈflaɪˌfɪʃɪŋ] *s* pesca con moscas artificiales
**flying** [ˈflaɪɪŋ] *adj* volante, volador; flameante, ondeante; apresurado, rápido, veloz; breve; *s* vuelo; aviación
**flying boat** *s* (aer.) hidroavión
**flying bomb** *s* bomba volante
**flying buttress** *s* (arch.) arbotante
**flying circus** *s* escuadrilla de aviones de caza; acrobacia aeronáutica
**flying colors** *spl* gran éxito, triunfo
**flying column** *s* (mil.) columna volante
**flying dragon** *s* (zool.) dragón, dragón volador
**Flying Dutchman, the** el Holandés errante; el Barco fantasma
**flying field** *s* campo de aviación
**flying fish** *s* (ichth.) volador, pez volador
**flying fortress** *s* (aer.) fortaleza volante
**flying fox** *s* (zool.) bermejizo
**flying frog** *s* (zool.) rana voladora
**flying gurnard** *s* (ichth.) pez volador
**flying jib** *s* (naut.) petifoque
**flying jib boom** *s* (naut.) botalón de petifoque
**flying machine** *s* máquina de volar
**flying saucer** *s* platillo volador o volante
**flying sickness** *s* mal de altura
**flying squadron** *s* (nav.) escuadra ligera
**flying squirrel** *s* (zool.) ardilla voladora
**fly in the ointment** *s* mosca muerta que malea el perfume (*cosa insignificante que estropea una cosa valiosa*)
**flyleaf** [ˈflaɪˌlif] *s* (*pl:* **-leaves**) (b.b.) guarda, hoja de guarda
**fly net** *s* mosquitero (*colgadura de cama*); espantamoscas (*para poner a los caballos*)
**flypaper** [ˈflaɪˌpepər] *s* matamoscas, papel pegajoso (*que se usa para coger moscas*)
**flyspeck** [ˈflaɪˌspɛk] *s* mancha de mosca; *va* manchar con manchas de mosca
**fly swatter** *s* matamoscas, paño de aporrear moscas
**flytrap** [ˈflaɪˌtræp] *s* espantamoscas (*para coger moscas*); (bot.) atrapamoscas, dionea; (bot.) apocino; (bot.) nepente
**flyweight** [ˈflaɪˌwet] *s* (box.) peso mosca
**flywheel** [ˈflaɪˌhwil] *s* volante
**fm.** abr. de **fathom**
**F.M.** o **FM** abr. de **frequency modulation**
**foal** [fol] *s* potro (*caballo*); pollino (*asno*); *va & vn* parir (*dícese de la yegua o asna*)
**foam** [fom] *s* espuma; *va* hacer espumar; *vn* espumar; espumajear
**foam extinguisher** *s* lanzaespumas, extintor de espuma
**foam rubber** *s* caucho esponjoso, espuma de caucho
**foamy** [ˈfomɪ] *adj* (*comp:* **-ier;** *super:* **-iest**) espumoso, espumajoso
**f.o.b.** o **F.O.B.** abr. de **free on board**
**fob** [fɑb] *s* faltriquera de reloj; leopoldina (*cadena del reloj de bolsillo*); dije (*de la leopoldina*); (*pret & pp:* **fobbed;** *ger:* **fobbing**) *va* embolsar; engañar; **to fob off** evadir con fraude
**focal** [ˈfokəl] *adj* focal
**focal distance** *s* (opt.) distancia focal
**focal infection** *s* (path.) infección focal
**focalization** [ˌfokəlɪˈzeʃən] *s* focalización
**focalize** [ˈfokəlaɪz] *va* enfocar
**focal length** *s* var. de **focal distance**
**focal plane** *s* (opt.) plano focal
**focal point** *s* (math.) punto focal
**focus** [ˈfokəs] *s* (*pl:* **-cuses** o **-ci** [saɪ]) enfoque (*acción de enfocar*); (math., med., phys., opt., seismol. & fig.) foco; **in focus** enfocado; **out of focus** fuera de foco, desenfocado; (*pret & pp:* **-cused** o **-cussed;** *ger:* **-cusing** o **-cussing**) *va* enfocar; fijar (*la atención*); *vn* enfocarse
**fodder** [ˈfɑdər] *s* forraje; *va* dar forraje a
**foe** [fo] *s* enemigo
**foeman** [ˈfomən] *s* (*pl:* **-men**) enemigo
**foetal** [ˈfitəl] *adj* var. de **fetal**
**foetus** [ˈfitəs] *s* var. de **fetus**
**fog** [fɑg] o [fɔg] *s* niebla; (phot.) velo; (fig.) niebla, confusión; (*pret & pp:* **fogged;** *ger:* **fogging**) *va* envolver en niebla, obscurecer; empañar; (phot.) velar; *vn* ponerse brumoso; empañarse; (phot.) velarse
**fog bank** *s* banco de nieblas
**fog bell** *s* campana de nieblas
**fogbound** [ˈfɑgˌbaʊnd] o [ˈfɔgˌbaʊnd] *adj* inmovilizado por la niebla
**fogey** [ˈfogɪ] *s* var. de **old fogey**
**foggy** [ˈfɑgɪ] o [ˈfɔgɪ] *adj* (*comp:* **-gier;** *super:* **-giest**) neblinoso, brumoso; borroso; confuso; (phot.) velado; **it is foggy** hay niebla
**foghorn** [ˈfɑgˌhɔrn] o [ˈfɔgˌhɔrn] *s* bocina de bruma, sirena de niebla; voz gritona y destemplada
**fog signal** *s* señal de nieblas
**fog whistle** *s* silbato de niebla
**fogy** [ˈfogɪ] *s* (*pl:* **-gies**) var. de **old fogey**
**foible** [ˈfɔɪbəl] *s* flaqueza, flaco, lado flaco
**foil** [fɔɪl] *s* hojuela (*de metal*); capa metálica, azogado, plateado (*de un espejo*); pan de oro o plata que se coloca bajo una piedra preciosa para que brille más; contraste, realce; florete (*espadín*); rastro, huella (*de un animal*); malogro; (arch.) lóbulo; **foils** *spl* esgrima; *va* frustrar; azogar o platear (*un espejo*); realzar; (arch.) adornar con lóbulos
**foist** [fɔɪst] *va* vender con engaño; insertar clandestinamente; **to foist something on someone** venderle a uno una cosa con engaño; lograr mediante un engaño que alguien acepte una cosa
**fol.** abr. de **folio, followed** y **following**
**fold** [fold] *s* pliegue, doblez; arruga; aprisco; rebaño, redil; iglesia; feligresía; rebaño (*de los fieles*); (geol.) pliegue, plegamiento; *va* plegar, doblar; recoger (*p.ej., un pájaro sus alas*); envolver, abrazar con ternura; apriscar; cruzar (*los brazos*); **to fold up** doblar (*p.ej., un mapa*); *vn* plegarse, doblarse; **to fold up** reducirse en tamaño doblándose; fracasar; quebrar (*en el comercio*)
**folder** [ˈfoldər] *s* plegador, doblador; plegadora mecánica, máquina de plegar; carpeta; cuadernillo, folleto, pliego
**folderol** [ˈfɑldəˌrɑl] *s* fruslería, tontería; bagatela, trivialidad
**folding** [ˈfoldɪŋ] *adj* plegable, plegadizo; plegador
**folding box** o **carton** *s* caja de cartón plegable
**folding camera** *s* cámara plegadiza, aparato fotográfico plegadizo, cámara de fuelle
**folding chair** *s* silla de tijera, silla plegadiza
**folding cot** *s* catre de tijera
**folding door** *s* puerta plegadiza; puerta corrediza; hoja o batiente de puerta
**folding machine** *s* plegadora mecánica
**folding rule** *s* metro plegadizo
**folding seat** *s* catrecillo
**foliaceous** [ˌfolɪˈeʃəs] *adj* foliáceo
**foliage** [ˈfolɪɪdʒ] *s* follaje; (arch.) follaje
**foliar** [ˈfolɪər] *adj* foliar
**foliate** [ˈfolɪɪt] o [ˈfolɪet] *adj* (bot.) foliado; [ˈfolɪet] *va* follar (*formar en hojas*); adornar con follaje; foliar (*los folios de un libro*); laminar; azogar (*un espejo*); *vn* echar hojas
**foliated** [ˈfolɪˌetɪd] *adj* follado; laminado; (arch.) lobulado
**foliation** [ˌfolɪˈeʃən] *s* foliación (*de los folios de un libro*); (bot. & geol.) foliación; (arch. & f.a.) follajería
**foliature** [ˈfolɪətʃər] *s* foliatura
**folic acid** [ˈfolɪk] *s* (biochem.) ácido fólico
**folio** [ˈfolɪo] *s* ((*pl:* **-os**) folio (*hoja de un libro*); infolio, libro en folio; (bookkeeping) folio; **in folio** en folio; *adj* en folio; *va* foliar (*los folios de un libro*)
**foliole** [ˈfolɪol] *s* (bot.) folíolo
**folk** [fok] *s* (*pl:* **folk** o **folks**) gente; (*pl:* **folks**) (archaic) gente, nación, tribu; **folks** *spl* (coll.) gente (*familia*); *adj* popular, del pueblo
**folk dance** *s* baile popular
**folk etymology** *s* etimología popular
**folklore** [ˈfokˌlor] *s* folklore
**folklorist** [ˈfokˌlorɪst] *s* folklorista
**folk music** *s* música del pueblo, música tradicional
**folk song** *s* canción popular, canción típica
**folksy** [ˈfoksɪ] *adj* (*comp:* **-sier;** *super:* **-siest**) (coll.) plebeyo; (coll.) tratable, sociable
**folk tale** *s* cuento popular

**folkway** ['fok,we] *s* costumbre tradicional de un pueblo
**follicle** ['falɪkəl] *s* (anat. & bot.) folículo
**follicular** [fə'lɪkjələr] *adj* folicular
**folliculin** [fə'lɪkjəlɪn] *s* (trademark) foliculina
**follow** ['falo] *va* seguir; seguir el hilo de (*un argumento*); interesarse en, estar al corriente de (*las noticias del día*); **to follow out** llevar hasta el fin, llevar a cabo; **to follow through** llevar hasta el fin (*una jugada o golpe*) sin flaquear ni desviarse; **to follow up** perseguir con ahinco; llevar hasta el fin; reforzar con nuevos esfuerzos o nuevas gestiones; *vn* seguir; seguirse, resultar; **as follows** como sigue(n); **it follows** síguese; **is as follows** es lo siguiente; **to follow on** seguir por el mismo camino, continuar en la misma forma
**follower** ['faloər] *s* seguidor; secuaz, partidario; imitador; criado
**following** ['falo·ɪŋ] *adj* siguiente; *s* séquito; secuaces, partidarios; **the following** el siguiente, los siguientes
**follow-up** ['falo,ʌp] *adj* consecutivo; recordativo; *s* carta recordativa, circular recordativa
**folly** ['falɪ] *s* (*pl:* **-lies**) desatino, tontería, locura; empresa temeraria
**foment** [fo'mɛnt] *va* fomentar (*p.ej., el encono*); (med.) fomentar
**fomentation** [,fomɛn'teʃən] *s* fomento; (med.) fomento, fomentación
**fomenter** [fo'mɛntər] *s* fomentador
**fond** [fand] *adj* cariñoso, afectuoso; **fond of** encariñado con (*una persona*); aficionado a; amigo de
**fondant** ['fandənt] *s* pasta de azúcar (*que se usa en la confitería*)
**fondle** ['fandəl] *va* acariciar, mimar
**fondness** ['fandnɪs] *s* cariño, afición
**fondue** [fan'du] o ['fandu] *s* flan de queso
**font** [fant] *s* pila (*de bautismo o de agua bendita*); fuente (*de bautismo; manantial de agua; origen*); (print.) fundición
**fontal** ['fantəl] *adj* fontal, fontanal
**fontanel** [,fantə'nɛl] *s* (anat.) fontanela
**food** [fud] *s* alimento, comida; (fig.) alimento, pábulo, materia; **food for thought** materia en que pensar; *adj* alimenticio
**food drop** *s* (aer.) lanzamiento de víveres
**foodstuff** ['fud,stʌf] *s* producto alimenticio, comestible
**food supplement** *s* aditivo alimenticio
**food value** *s* valor alimenticio
**foofaraw** ['fufərɔ] *s* (coll.) oropel, relumbrón; (coll.) tontería
**fool** [ful] *s* tonto, necio; bufón; víctima (*de un engaño*); **to make a fool of** poner en ridículo; **to make a fool of oneself** ponerse en ridículo; **to play the fool** hacer el tonto; *va* engañar, embaucar; **to fool away** malgastar (*tiempo, dinero*); *vn* chancear, tontear; **to fool around** (coll.) bromear, malgastar el tiempo neciamente; **to fool with** (coll.) meterse neciamente en; (coll.) ajar, manosear
**foolery** ['fulərɪ] *s* (*pl:* **-ies**) tontería, bufonada
**foolhardy** ['ful,hardɪ] *adj* (*comp:* **-dier**; *super:* **-diest**) arriesgado, temerario
**fooling** ['fulɪŋ] *s* chacota, broma; engaño; **no fooling** (coll.) sin broma, hablando en serio
**foolish** ['fulɪʃ] *adj* tonto, necio, disparatado; ridículo
**foolishness** ['fulɪʃnɪs] *s* tontería, necedad; ridiculez
**foolproof** ['ful,pruf] *adj* (coll.) a prueba de impericia, a prueba de mal trato; (coll.) cierto, infalible
**foolscap** ['fulz,kæp] *s* papel de oficio; gorro de bufón; gorro de forma de cono que se le pone al niño torpe
**fool's cap** *s* gorro de bufón; gorro de forma de cono que se le pone al niño torpe
**fool's errand** *s* caza de grillos
**fool's gold** *s* pirita amarilla
**fool's paradise** *s* felicidad que tiene por fundamento esperanzas o creencias falsas
**fool's-parsley** ['fulz,parslɪ] *s* (bot.) cicuta menor, etusa, perejil de perro
**fool's scepter** *s* cetro de locura
**foot** [fut] *s* (*pl:* **feet**) pie (*de animal, media, bota, verso, etc.; medida lineal*); (mil.) infantería; (naut.) pujamen (*de una vela*); **on foot** a pie; de pie; avanzando, haciendo progresos; **to carry off one's feet** arrebatar, cautivar; **to drag one's feet** (coll.) tardar en obrar, ir a paso de caracol (*intencionadamente*); **to have one foot in the grave** estar con un pie en la sepultura; **to put one's best foot forward** andar lo más aprisa posible; hacer grandes esfuerzos; (coll.) hacer méritos, tratar de impresionar, tratar de ganarse la buena voluntad; **to put one's foot down** (coll.) proceder con gran energía; (coll.) vedarle a otro su deseo; **to put one's foot in it** (coll.) meter la pata; (coll.) tirarse una plancha; **to trample under foot** pisotear; **to tread under foot** hollar (*pisar; despreciar; destruir*); **under foot** estorbando el paso; en el poder de uno; *va* poner el pie (o los pies) a; sumar (*una columna de guarismos*); pagar (*la cuenta*); **to foot it** andar a pie; bailar; *vn* andar a pie; bailar
**footage** ['futɪdʒ] *s* largura o distancia en pies; paga por pie de trabajo; (mov.) longitud de película en pies (*in Spanish* metraje, *i.e., length of film in meters, is used*)
**foot-and-mouth disease** ['futən'mauθ] *s* (vet.) glosopeda, fiebre aftosa
**football** ['fut,bɔl] *s* balompié, fútbol (*juego*); balón (*pelota*); (fig.) juguete; *adj* balompédico, futbolístico
**football player** *s* futbolista
**foot bath** *s* pediluvio, baño de pies
**footboard** ['fut,bord] *s* estribo; pie (*de cama*); pedal
**foot brake** *s* freno de pedal, freno de pie
**footbridge** ['fut,brɪdʒ] *s* puente para peatones, pasarela
**foot-candle** ['fut'kændəl] *s* bujía-pie o pie-bujía
**footcloth** ['fut,klɔθ] o ['fut,klaθ] *s* gualdrapa; alfombra
**footfall** ['fut,fɔl] *s* paso (*movimiento y ruido*)
**foot fault** *s* (tennis) falta de pie
**footgear** ['fut,gɪr] *s* calzado
**foothill** ['fut,hɪl] *s* falda, colina al pie de un monte o sierra
**foothold** ['fut,hold] *s* espacio en que se afirma el pie; pie, arraigo, posición establecida; **to gain a foothold** ganar pie (*p.ej., en costa enemiga*)
**footing** ['futɪŋ] *s* pie, p.ej., **he lost his footing and fell** perdió el pie y se cayó; arraigo, posición establecida; condición, estado; suma de guarismos; suma, total; (el) caminar; (el) bailar; **on a friendly footing** en relaciones amistosas; **on an equal footing** en un mismo pie de igualdad; **on a war footing** en pie de guerra
**footless** ['futlɪs] *adj* sin pies; sin fundamento; (coll.) desmañado, torpe
**footlights** ['fut,laɪts] *spl* candilejas, batería; (fig.) tablas, profesión de actor
**foot-loose** ['fut,lus] *adj* libre (*para hacer lo que a uno se le antoje*)
**footman** ['futmən] *s* (*pl:* **-men**) lacayo; soldado de a pie
**footmark** ['fut,mark] *s* huella
**footnote** ['fut,not] *s* nota al pie de una página
**footpace** ['fut,pes] *s* paso lento, paso del que camina normalmente; descanso (*de escalera*)
**footpad** ['fut,pæd] *s* salteador que camina a pie
**footpath** ['fut,pæθ] o ['fut,paθ] *s* senda para peatones
**foot-pound** ['fut,paund] *s* (mech.) librapié
**foot-poundal** ['fut,paundəl] *s* (mech.) pie-poundal
**foot-pound-second system** ['fut,paund'sɛkənd] *s* (phys.) sistema pie-libra-segundo
**footprint** ['fut,prɪnt] *s* huella
**foot race** *s* carrera a pie
**foot racing** *s* pedestrismo
**footrest** ['fut,rɛst] *s* apoyapié, descansapié
**footrope** ['fut,rop] *s* (naut.) marchapié
**foot rule** *s* regla de un pie
**foot soldier** *s* (mil.) infante, soldado de a pie
**footsore** ['fut,sor] *adj* despeado
**footsoreness** ['fut,sornɪs] *s* despeadura
**footstalk** ['fut,stɔk] *s* (bot. & zool.) pedúnculo
**footstep** ['fut,stɛp] *s* paso; **to follow** o **tread**

**in the footsteps of** seguir las huellas o los pasos de
**footstone** ['fʊt,ston] *s* lápida que se coloca al pie de una sepultura
**footstool** ['fʊt,stul] *s* escabel, escañuelo
**foot warmer** *s* calientapiés
**footway** ['fʊt,we] *s* senda para peatones; (Brit.) acera
**footwear** ['fʊt,wɛr] *s* calzado
**footwork** ['fʊt,wʌrk] *s* juego de piernas (*en los deportes o el bailar*)
**footworn** ['fʊt,wɔrn] *adj* asendereado, trillado (*camino*); despeado
**foozle** ['fuzel] *s* chambonada; (coll.) vejestorio; *va* chafallar; errar (*un golpe*) de manera chambona; *vn* chambonear
**foozler** ['fuzlər] *s* chambón
**fop** [fɑp] *s* currutaco, majadero presumido
**foppery** ['fɑpərɪ] *s* (*pl:* **-ies**) presunción de currutaco; perifollos
**foppish** ['fɑpɪʃ] *adj* alechuguinado, currutaco
**for.** abr. de **foreign** y **forestry**
**for** [fɔr] *prep* para; por; como, p.ej., **I use coal for fuel** uso carbón como combustible; en honor de; a pesar de, p.ej., **for all her intelligence** a pesar de su inteligencia; de, p.ej., **time for dinner** hora de comer; desde hace, p.ej., **I have been here for three months** estoy aquí desde hace tres meses; **O! for . . . !** ¡quién tuviera . . . !; *conj* pues, porque
**forage** ['fɑrɪdʒ] o ['fɔrɪdʒ] *s* forraje; *adj* forrajero; *va* dar forraje a; forrajear; *vn* forrajear
**forage cap** *s* (Brit.) gorra militar
**forager** ['fɑrɪdʒər] o ['fɔrɪdʒər] *s* forrajeador
**foramen** [fo'remən] *s* (*pl:* **-ramina** ['ræmɪnə] o **-ramens**) foramen; (anat. & bot.) foramen
**foraminifera** [fo,ræmɪ'nɪfərə] *spl* (zool.) foraminíferos
**forasmuch as** [,fɔrəz'mʌtʃæz] *conj* porque, puesto que, visto que
**foray** ['fɑre] o ['fɔre] *s* correría, saqueo; *va* saquear, despojar
**forbade** o **forbad** [fɔr'bæd] *pret de* **forbid**
**forbear** ['fɔrbɛr] *s* antepasado; [fɔr'bɛr] (*pret:* **-bore;** *pp:* **-borne**) *va* abstenerse de; *vn* contenerse, tener paciencia
**forbearance** [fɔr'bɛrəns] *s* abstención; dominio sobre sí mismo, paciencia
**forbid** [fɔr'bɪd] (*pret:* **-bade** o **-bad;** *pp:* **-bidden;** *ger:* **-bidding**) *va* prohibir; **God forbid!** ¡no lo permita Dios!; **to forbid to** + *inf* prohibir + *inf*
**forbidden** [fɔr'bɪdən] *pp de* **forbid**
**Forbidden City** *s* ciudad prohibida (*Lhassa, capital del Tibet; parte amurallada de Pequín*)
**forbidden fruit** *s* fruta prohibida
**forbidding** [fɔr'bɪdɪŋ] *adj* repugnante; formidable
**forbore** [fɔr'bor] *pret de* **forbear**
**forborne** [fɔr'born] *pp de* **forbear**
**force** [fors] *s* fuerza; personal; cuerpo (*de tropas, de policía, etc.*); (phys.) fuerza; **forces** *spl* (mil. & nav.) fuerzas; **by force** a la fuerza, por fuerza; **by force of** a fuerza de; **by force of habit** por la fuerza de la costumbre; **by main force** con todas sus fuerzas; **in force** en vigor, vigente; en gran número; **to join forces** coligarse, juntar diestra con diestra; **to meet force with force** oponer la fuerza a la fuerza, enfrentar la fuerza con la fuerza; *va* forzar; (agr.) forzar; **to force away** obligar a marcharse; **to force back** impeler hacia atrás, hacer retroceder; **to force down** obligar a bajar, obligar a bajarse; hacer tragar por fuerza; **to force from** echar o sacar fuera por fuerza, arrancar violentamente; **to force in** clavar o introducir por fuerza; **to force oneself** hacer esfuerzos violentos; **to force out** echar o sacar fuera por fuerza; **to force through** hacer penetrar por fuerza; llevar a cabo por fuerza; **to force to** + *inf* forzar a + *inf* o forzar a que + *subj;* **to force up** hacer subir por fuerza
**forced** [forst] *adj* forzado; (fig.) forzado (*dícese, p.ej., de una sonrisa*)
**forced air** *s* aire a presión
**forced draft** *s* tiro forzado
**forced landing** *s* (aer.) aterrizaje forzado o forzoso
**forced march** *s* (mil.) marcha forzada
**forced ventilation** *s* ventilación por presión
**force feed** *s* (mach.) alimentación forzada, lubricación a presión
**force-feeding** ['fors,fidɪŋ] *s* (med.) alimentación forzada
**forceful** ['forsfəl] *adj* eficaz, poderoso, vigoroso
**force majeure** [fɔrs mɑ'ʒœr] *s* (law) fuerza mayor
**forcemeat** ['fors,mit] *s* carne picada y condimentada que sirve de relleno
**forceps** ['fɔrsəps] *s* (*pl:* **-ceps** o **-cipes** [sɪpiz]) (obstet. & zool.) fórceps; (dent. & surg.) pinzas
**force pump** *s* bomba impelente o impulsora
**forcible** ['forsɪbəl] *adj* forzado, violentado; eficaz, poderoso, vigoroso, convincente
**forcipressure** [,fɔrsɪ'prɛʃər] *s* (surg.) forcipresión
**ford** [ford] *s* vado; *va* vadear
**fordable** ['fordəbəl] *adj* vadeable
**fore** [for] *adj* anterior, delantero; (naut.) de proa; *adv* anteriormente, antes; delante, en la delantera; (naut.) avante; *interj* (golf) ¡ojo!, ¡cuidado!; *s* cabeza, delantera, frente; **to the fore** en la delantera; destacado; dispuesto; a mano; a la vista; vivo
**fore and aft** *adv* (naut.) a proa y a popa, en proa y en popa; (naut.) de popa a proa
**fore-and-aft** ['forənd,æft] o ['forənd,ɑft] *adj* (naut.) de popa a proa
**fore-and-aft sail** *s* (naut.) vela cangreja
**forearm** ['for,ɑrm] *s* antebrazo; [for'ɑrm] *va* armar de antemano; prevenir de antemano
**forebear** ['forbɛr] *s* antepasado
**forebode** [for'bod] *va* presentir, prever con recelo; presagiar
**foreboding** [for'bodɪŋ] *s* presentimiento; presagio; *adj* presagioso, ominoso
**forebrain** ['for,bren] *s* (anat.) cerebro (*parte anterior del encéfalo*)
**forecast** ['for,kæst] o ['for,kɑst] *s* pronóstico; previsión; proyecto, plan; (*pret & pp:* **-cast** o **-casted**) *va* pronosticar; prever; proyectar
**forecastle** ['foksəl], ['for,kæsəl] o ['for,kɑsəl] *s* (naut.) castillo, castillo de proa; (naut.) camarote o camarotes en el castillo de proa (*en que se aloja la tripulación*)
**forecastle deck** *s* (naut.) castillo
**foreclose** [for'kloz] *va* excluir; impedir; (law) extinguir el derecho de redimir (*una hipoteca*); (law) privar del derecho de redimir una hipoteca
**foreclosure** [for'kloʒər] *s* (law) extinción del derecho de redimir una hipoteca
**foredoom** [for'dum] *va* predestinar a la condenación, predestinar al fracaso
**fore edge** *s* canal *f* (*de un libro*)
**forefather** ['for,fɑðər] *s* antepasado
**forefend** [for'fɛnd] *va* var. de **forfend**
**forefinger** ['for,fɪŋgər] *s* dedo índice, dedo mostrador
**forefoot** ['for,fʊt] *s* (*pl:* **-feet**) pata delantera
**forefront** ['for,frʌnt] *s* puesto delantero; sitio de mayor importancia, sitio de actividad más intensa; **in the forefront** a vanguardia
**foregather** [for'gæðər] *vn* var. de **forgather**
**forego** [for'go] (*pret:* **-went;** *pp:* **-gone**) *va* renunciar, privarse de; preceder; *vn* preceder
**foregoing** ['for,go·ɪŋ] o [for'go·ɪŋ] *adj* anterior, precedente
**foregone** ['forgɔn] o ['forgɑn] *adj* pasado, previo; [for'gɔn] o [for'gɑn] *pp de* **forego**
**foregone conclusion** *s* conclusión inevitable; decisión adoptada de antemano
**foreground** ['for,graʊnd] *s* frente, delantera; primer término, primer plano; **in the foreground** al frente; en primer término
**forehand** ['for,hænd] *s* posición delantera; posición superior; ventaja; golpe derecho; *adj* dado con la palma de la mano hacia delante
**forehanded** ['for,hændɪd] *adj* ahorrado, frugal; hecho de antemano, oportuno
**forehead** ['fɑrɪd] o ['fɔrɪd] *s* frente *f* (*de la cara*); parte delantera
**foreign** ['fɑrɪn] o ['fɔrɪn] *adj* extranjero, exterior; extraño; ajeno
**foreign affairs** *spl* asuntos exteriores
**foreign-born** ['fɑrɪn,bɔrn] o ['fɔrɪn,bɔrn]

*adj* nacido en el extranjero, extranjero de nacimiento

**foreign commerce** *s* comercio exterior

**foreigner** [ˈfɑrɪnər] o [ˈfɔrɪnər] *s* extranjero

**foreign exchange** *s* cambio exterior o extranjero; divisa

**foreignism** [ˈfɑrɪnɪzəm] o [ˈfɔrɪnɪzəm] *s* extranjerismo

**foreign legion** *s* (mil.) legión extranjera

**foreign minister** *s* ministro de asuntos exteriores

**foreign missions** *spl* (eccl.) misiones

**foreign office** *s* ministerio de asuntos exteriores; (*caps.*) *s* (Brit.) ministerio de Asuntos Exteriores

**foreign trade** *s* comercio exterior

**forejudge** [forˈdʒʌdʒ] *va* prejuzgar

**foreknew** [forˈnju] o [forˈnu] *pret de* **foreknow**

**foreknow** [forˈno] (*pret:* **-knew;** *pp:* **-known**) *va* saber con anticipación

**foreknowledge** [ˈforˌnɑlɪdʒ] o [forˈnɑlɪdʒ] *s* presciencia; (theol.) presciencia divina

**foreknown** [forˈnon] *pp de* **foreknow**

**foreland** [ˈforˌlænd] o [ˈforlənd] *s* cabo, promontorio

**foreleg** [ˈforˌlɛg] *s* brazo, pata delantera (*del cuadrúpedo*)

**forelock** [ˈforˌlɑk] *s* mechón de pelo que cae sobre la frente; copete (*del caballo*); (mach.) chaveta; **to take time by the forelock** asir, coger o tomar la ocasión por el copete, por la melena o por los cabellos

**foreman** [ˈformən] *s* (*pl:* **-men**) capataz, sobrestante, mayoral; contramaestre (*en un taller mecánico*); director, regente; (law) presidente de jurado

**foremast** [ˈforməst], [ˈforˌmæst] o [ˈforˌmɑst] *s* (naut.) palo de trinquete

**foremost** [ˈformost] *adj* delantero; primero; principal, más eminente (*de todos*); *adv* primero

**forename** [ˈforˌnem] *s* nombre de pila

**forenamed** [ˈforˌnemd] *adj* susodicho

**forenoon** [ˈforˌnun] *s* mañana; *adj* matinal

**forensic** [fəˈrɛnsɪk] *adj* forense

**foreordain** [ˌforɔrˈden] *va* preordinar

**foreordination** [ˌforɔrdɪˈneʃən] *s* preordinación

**forepart** [ˈforˌpɑrt] *s* parte delantera; principio, primera parte

**forepaw** [ˈforˌpɔ] *s* pata delantera, zarpa delantera

**forepeak** [ˈforˌpik] *s* (naut.) bodega de proa

**forequarter** [ˈforˌkwɔrtər] *s* cuarto delantero (*de la res*)

**foreran** [forˈræn] *pret de* **forerun**

**forereach** [forˈritʃ] *va* (naut.) alcanzar (*otra embarcación*); (naut.) dejar atrás (*otra embarcación*); (fig.) aventajarse a; *vn* (naut.) ganar terreno

**forerun** [forˈrʌn] (*pret:* **-ran;** *pp:* **-run**) *va* preceder; prevenir; dejar atrás

**forerunner** [ˈforˌrʌnər] o [forˈrʌnər] *s* precursor; presagio; antepasado; predecesor; **the Forerunner** el precursor de Cristo (*San Juan*)

**foresail** [ˈforsəl] o [ˈforˌsel] *s* (naut.) trinquete; (naut.) trinquetilla

**foresaw** [forˈsɔ] *pret de* **foresee**

**foresee** [forˈsi] (*pret:* **-saw;** *pp:* **-seen**) *va* prever

**foreseeable** [forˈsiəbəl] *adj* previsible

**foreshadow** [forˈʃædo] *va* presagiar, prefigurar

**foresheet** [ˈforˌʃit] *s* (naut.) escota del trinquete; **foresheets** *spl* (naut.) parte delantera de un buque abierto

**foreshore** [ˈforˌʃor] *s* playa comprendida entre los límites de pleamar y bajamar

**foreshorten** [forˈʃɔrtən] *va* (f.a.) escorzar

**foreshortening** [forˈʃɔrtənɪŋ] *s* (f.a.) escorzo

**foreshow** [forˈʃo] (*pret:* **-showed;** *pp:* **-shown**) *va* presagiar, prefigurar

**foresight** [ˈforˌsaɪt] *s* previsión, presciencia; prudencia

**foresighted** [ˈforˌsaɪtɪd] o [ˌforˈsaɪtɪd] *adj* previsor, presciente; prudente

**foreskin** [ˈforˌskɪn] *s* (anat.) prepucio

**forest** [ˈfɑrɪst] o [ˈfɔrɪst] *s* bosque; *adj* forestal; *va* plantar (*un terreno*) de árboles, convertir (*un terreno*) en bosque

**forestall** [forˈstɔl] *va* impedir, prevenir; (com.) acaparar

**forestation** [ˌfɑrɪsˈteʃən] o [ˌfɔrɪsˈteʃən] *s* silvicultura

**forestay** [ˈforˌste] *s* (naut.) estay del trinquete

**forestaysail** [ˌforˈstesəl] o [ˌforˈsteˌsel] *s* (naut.) trinquetilla

**forester** [ˈfɑrɪstər] o [ˈfɔrɪstər] *s* silvicultor; guardabosques; (zool.) canguro gigante

**forest ranger** *s* guarda forestal

**forest reserve** *s* (U.S.A.) bosque nacional

**forestry** [ˈfɑrɪstrɪ] o [ˈfɔrɪstrɪ] *s* silvicultura, dasonomía, ciencia forestal

**foretackle** [ˈforˌtækəl] *s* (naut.) aparejo del gancho del trinquete

**foretaste** [ˈforˌtest] *s* anticipación, goce anticipado; [forˈtest] *va* anticipar, catar o conocer con anticipación

**foretell** [forˈtɛl] (*pret & pp:* **-told**) *va* predecir

**foretellable** [forˈtɛləbəl] *adj* pronosticable

**forethought** [ˈforˌθɔt] *s* premeditación, providencia, prudencia

**foretoken** [ˈforˌtokən] *s* presagio; [forˈtokən] *va* presagiar

**foretold** [forˈtold] *pret & pp de* **foretell**

**foretop** [ˈfortəp] o [ˈforˌtɑp] *s* (naut.) cofa de trinquete; [ˈforˌtɑp] copete (*del caballo*)

**foretopgallant mast** [ˌfortəˈgælənt] o [ˌfortɑpˈgælənt] *s* (naut.) masterillo de juanete de proa

**foretopmast** [forˈtɑpməst] *s* (naut.) mastelero de velacho, mastelero de proa

**foretopmast staysail** *s* (naut.) contrafoque

**foretopsail** [ˌforˈtɑpsəl] o [ˌforˈtɑpˌsel] *s* (naut.) velacho

**forever** [fɔrˈɛvər] *adv* siempre; para siempre o por siempre

**forever and a day** o **forever and ever** *adv* por siempre jamás

**forevermore** [fɔrˌɛvərˈmor] *adv* por siempre, por siempre jamás

**forewarn** [forˈwɔrn] *va* prevenir con anticipación

**forewent** [forˈwɛnt] *pret de* **forego**

**foreword** [ˈforˌwʌrd] *s* advertencia, prefacio

**forfeit** [ˈfɔrfɪt] *s* multa, pena; prenda perdida; **forfeits** *spl* prendas (*juego*); *adj* perdido; *va* perder, perder el derecho a

**forfeiture** [ˈfɔrfɪtʃər] *s* multa, pena; prenda perdida

**forfend** [fɔrˈfɛnd] *va* defender, proteger; (archaic) impedir, evitar

**forgather** [fɔrˈgæðər] *vn* reunirse; encontrarse (*por casualidad*); **to forgather with** asociarse con, fraternizar con

**forgave** [fɔrˈgev] *pret de* **forgive**

**forge** [fordʒ] *s* fragua (*fogón*); herrería (*taller del herrero*); fundición (*fábrica*); *va* fraguar, forjar; falsificar (*la firma de otra persona*); (fig.) fraguar, forjar (*p.ej., mentiras*); *vn* fraguar, forjar; falsificar; **to forge ahead** avanzar despacio y con esfuerzo; **to forge ahead of** alcanzar y dejar atrás haciendo esfuerzos

**forger** [ˈfordʒər] *s* fraguador, forjador; falsificador

**forgery** [ˈfordʒərɪ] *s* (*pl:* **-ies**) falsificación; (philately) falso (*sello falsificado*)

**forget** [fɔrˈgɛt] (*pret:* **-got;** *pp:* **-gotten** o **-got;** *ger:* **-getting**) *va* olvidar, olvidarse de; olvidársele a uno, p.ej., **I forgot my passport** se me olvidó mi pasaporte; **forget it!** (coll.) ¡dejémoslo!; **to forget oneself** interesarse por los demás sin pensar en sí mismo; ser distraído; propasarse; **to forget to** + *inf* olvidar + *inf*, olvidarse de + *inf*, olvidársele a uno + *inf*, p.ej., **I forgot to close the window** se me olvidó cerrar la ventana

**forgetful** [fɔrˈgɛtfəl] *adj* olvidado, olvidadizo; descuidado

**forgetfulness** [fɔrˈgɛtfəlnɪs] *s* olvido, falta de memoria; descuido

**forget-me-not** [fɔrˈgɛtmiˌnɑt] *s* (bot.) nomeolvides

**forgettable** [fɔrˈgɛtəbəl] *adj* olvidable

**forging** [ˈfordʒɪŋ] *s* forjadura; pieza forjada

**forgivable** [fɔrˈgɪvəbəl] *adj* perdonable

**forgive** [fɔrˈgɪv] (*pret:* **-gave;** *pp:* **-given**) *va* perdonar

**forgiven** [fɔrˈgɪvən] *pp de* **forgive**

**forgiveness** [fɔrˈgɪvnɪs] *s* perdón
**forgiving** [fɔrˈgɪvɪŋ] *adj* perdonador, clemente
**forgo** [fɔrˈgo] (*pret:* **-went;** *pp:* **-gone**) *va* renunciar, privarse de
**forgone** [fɔrˈgɔn] o [fɔrˈgɑn] *pp de* **forgo**
**forgot** [fɔrˈgɑt] *pret & pp de* **forget**
**forgotten** [fɔrˈgɑtən] *pp de* **forget**
**fork** [fɔrk] *s* horca; horquilla (*de jardinero; de la bicicleta*); horqueta u horcadura (*de un árbol*); horcajo (*de dos ríos*); bieldo (*para aventar*); tenedor (*utensilio de mesa*); bifurcación; púa (*de horca*); ramal (*de ferrocarril*); afluente (*de un río*); *va* ahorquillar; cargar o hacinar con horquilla; cavar con horquilla; beldar; (chess) atacar o amenazar (*dos piezas*) a la vez; **to fork out** u **over** (slang) entregar; *vn* bifurcarse
**forked** [fɔrkt] *adj* ahorquillado, bifurcado
**forked lightning** *s* relámpago en zigzag
**fork lift truck** *s* carretilla de horquilla, montacarga de horquilla
**forlorn** [fɔrˈlɔrn] *adj* abandonado, desamparado; triste; desesperado; **forlorn of** privado de
**forlorn hope** *s* (mil.) centinela perdida; (fig.) empresa desesperada
**form** [fɔrm] *s* forma; estado; formulario; banco (*para sentarse*); grado (*en las escuelas*); encofrado (*para el hormigón*); (print.) molde; **in due form** en debida forma; **in form** en forma; (sport) en forma; *va* formar; (elec.) formar (*las placas de un acumulador*); *vn* formarse
**formal** [ˈfɔrməl] *adj* formal; de etiqueta; ceremonioso; en forma
**formal attire** *s* vestido de etiqueta
**formal call** *s* visita de cumplido
**formaldehyde** [fɔrˈmældɪhaɪd] *s* (chem.) formaldehido
**formal garden** *s* jardín de estilo francés, jardín a la francesa
**formalin** [ˈfɔrməlɪn] *s* (chem.) formalina
**formalism** [ˈfɔrməlɪzəm] *s* formalismo
**formalist** [ˈfɔrməlɪst] *s* formalista
**formalistic** [ˌfɔrməˈlɪstɪk] *adj* formalista
**formality** [fɔrˈmælɪtɪ] *s* (*pl:* **-ties**) formalidad; etiqueta, ceremonia
**formalize** [ˈfɔrməlaɪz] *va* formalizar
**formal party** *s* recepción de gala, reunión de etiqueta
**formal speech** *s* discurso de aparato
**format** [ˈfɔrmæt] *s* formato
**formate** [ˈfɔrmet] *s* (chem.) formiato
**formation** [fɔrˈmeʃən] *s* formación; (elec., geol. & mil.) formación
**formative** [ˈfɔrmətɪv] *adj* formativo
**former** [ˈfɔrmər] *adj* anterior; antiguo, pasado; primero (*de dos*); **the former** aquél; *s* formador; plantilla
**formerly** [ˈfɔrmərlɪ] *adv* antes, en otro tiempo
**form-fitting** [ˈfɔrmˈfɪtɪŋ] *adj* ajustado, ceñido al cuerpo; que se adapta bien al cuerpo
**formic** [ˈfɔrmɪk] *adj* fórmico
**formic acid** *s* (chem.) ácido fórmico
**formidable** [ˈfɔrmɪdəbəl] *adj* formidable
**formless** [ˈfɔrmlɪs] *adj* informe, sin forma
**form letter** *s* carta general
**formol** [ˈfɔrmol] o [ˈfɔrmɑl] *s* (chem.) formol
**formula** [ˈfɔrmjələ] *s* (*pl:* **-las** o **-lae** [li]) fórmula
**formulary** [ˈfɔrmjəˌlɛrɪ] *adj* formulario; *s* (*pl:* **-ies**) formulario; (pharm.) formulario
**formulate** [ˈfɔrmjəlet] *va* formular
**formulation** [ˌfɔrmjəˈleʃən] *s* formulación
**formulator** [ˈfɔrmjəˌletər] *s* formulador
**fornicate** [ˈfɔrnɪket] *vn* fornicar
**fornication** [ˌfɔrnɪˈkeʃən] *s* fornicación
**fornicator** [ˈfɔrnɪˌketər] *s* fornicador
**forsake** [fɔrˈsek] (*pret:* **-sook;** *pp:* **-saken**) *va* abandonar, desamparar; dejar, desechar
**forsaken** [fɔrˈsekən] *adj* abandonado, desamparado; *pp de* **forsake**
**forsook** [fɔrˈsʊk] *pret de* **forsake**
**forsooth** [fɔrˈsuθ] *adv* en verdad, por cierto
**forspent** [fɔrˈspɛnt] *adj* agotado de fuerzas
**forswear** [fɔrˈswɛr] (*pret:* **-swore;** *pp:* **-sworn**) *va* abjurar; negar con juramento; **to forswear oneself** perjurarse; *vn* perjurar
**forswore** [fɔrˈswor] *pret de* **forswear**
**forsworn** [fɔrˈsworn] *adj* perjuro; *pp de* **forswear**
**forsythia** [fɔrˈsɪθɪə] o [fɔrˈsaɪθɪə] *s* (bot.) forsitia
**fort** [fort] *s* fortín, fuerte; **to hold the fort** defenderse contra ataque
**forte** [fort] *s* fuerte (*afición o talento de uno*)
**forth** [forθ] *adv* adelante, delante, hacia adelante; fuera; afuera; a la vista; **and so forth** y así sucesivamente; **from this day forth** de hoy en adelante; **to go forth** salir
**forthcoming** [ˈforθˌkʌmɪŋ] o [ˌforθˈkʌmɪŋ] *adj* próximo, venidero; disponible; *s* salida, venida
**forthright** [ˈforθˌraɪt] o [ˌforθˈraɪt] *adj* derecho, sincero, extremoso, sin ambages; *adv* derecho, siempre adelante; francamente; luego, en seguida
**forthwith** [ˌforθˈwɪð] o [ˌforθˈwɪθ] *adv* inmediatamente, sin dilación
**fortieth** [ˈfɔrtɪɪθ] *adj & s* cuadragésimo; cuarentavo
**fortification** [ˌfɔrtɪfɪˈkeʃən] *s* fortificación
**fortify** [ˈfɔrtɪfaɪ] (*pret & pp:* **-fied**) *va* fortificar; encabezar (*vinos*); *vn* fortificarse
**fortitude** [ˈfɔrtɪtjud] o [ˈfɔrtɪtud] *s* fortaleza, firmeza, valor
**fortnight** [ˈfɔrtnaɪt] o [ˈfɔrtnɪt] *s* quincena, quince días
**fortnightly** [ˈfɔrtnaɪtlɪ] *adj* quincenal; *adv* quincenalmente; *s* (*pl:* **-lies**) periódico quincenal
**fortress** [ˈfɔrtrɪs] *s* fortaleza, plaza fuerte
**fortuitous** [fɔrˈtjuɪtəs] o [fɔrˈtuɪtəs] *adj* fortuito, casual
**fortuity** [fɔrˈtjuɪtɪ] o [fɔrˈtuɪtɪ] *s* (*pl:* **-ties**) fortuitez, casualidad; accidente; caso imprevisto
**fortunate** [ˈfɔrtʃənɪt] *adj* afortunado
**Fortunate Islands** *spl* (myth.) islas Afortunadas
**fortune** [ˈfɔrtʃən] *s* fortuna; **to tell one's fortune** decirle a uno la buenaventura
**fortune hunter** *s* el que quiere emparentar con una familia rica, cazador de fortunas
**fortuneteller** [ˈfɔrtʃənˌtɛlər] *s* adivino, agorero, sortílego
**forty** [ˈfɔrtɪ] *adj* cuarenta; *s* (*pl:* **-ties**) cuarenta
**forty hours' devotion** *s* (eccl.) las cuarenta horas
**Forty-Niners** [ˌfɔrtɪˈnaɪnərz] *spl* gente que fué a California en busca del oro en 1849
**forty winks** *spl* una siestecita
**forum** [ˈforəm] *s* (*pl:* **-rums** o **-ra** [rə]) (hist. & law) foro; asamblea (*en que se tratan asuntos públicos*); (fig.) tribunal (*p.ej., de la opinión pública*)
**forward** [ˈfɔrwərd] *adj* delantero; adelantado, precoz; ansioso, listo; atrevido, impertinente; de avance, p.ej., **forward step** paso de avance; *adv* adelante; hacia adelante; en la delantera; **to bring forward** aducir; **to carry forward** (coll.) pasar a cuenta nueva; **to come** o **to go forward** adelantarse; **to look forward to** esperar con placer anticipado; *va* reexpedir, hacer seguir; fomentar, patrocinar; **please forward** hágase seguir, reexpídase, dele curso; *s* (sport) delantero
**forward delivery** *s* (coll.) entrega en fecha futura
**forwarder** [ˈfɔrwərdər] *s* agente expedidor, comisionista expedidor
**forwardness** [ˈfɔrwərdnɪs] *s* adelantamiento; precocidad; ansia, ahinco; impertinencia, descaro
**forward pass** *s* (football) lanzamiento del balón en dirección de la meta del equipo contrario
**forwards** [ˈfɔrwərdz] *adv* adelante; hacia adelante; en la delantera
**forwent** [fɔrˈwɛnt] *pret de* **forgo**
**fossa** [ˈfɑsə] *s* (*pl:* **-sae** [si]) (anat.) fosa
**fosse** [fɑs] *s* foso; (fort.) foso
**fossil** [ˈfɑsɪl] *adj & s* fósil; (fig.) fósil
**fossiliferous** [ˌfɑsɪˈlɪfərəs] *adj* fosilífero
**fossilization** [ˌfɑsɪlɪˈzeʃən] *s* fosilización
**fossilize** [ˈfɑsɪlaɪz] *va* convertir en fósil; *vn* fosilizarse
**foster** [ˈfɑstər] o [ˈfɔstər] *adj* adoptivo, alle-

gado (*por la crianza y no por la sangre*); *va* fomentar; criar; cuidar con ternura
**foster brother** *s* hermano de leche, hermano de crianza
**foster child** *s* alumno, niño criado como si fuera hijo
**foster daughter** *s* hija de leche, hija adoptiva
**foster father** *s* padre adoptivo
**foster home** *s* hogar de adopción, hogar en que se asigna a un menor por orden judicial
**foster land** *s* país adoptivo
**foster mother** *s* madre adoptiva; ama de leche
**foster parent** *s* padre o madre adoptiva
**foster sister** *s* hermana de leche, hermana de crianza
**foster son** *s* hijo de leche, hijo adoptivo
**Foucault current** [fu'ko] *s* (elec.) corriente de Foucault
**fought** [fɔt] *pret & pp de* **fight**
**foul** [faʊl] *adj* asqueroso, puerco; fétido; viciado (*aire*); obsceno; pérfido; nefando; contrario (*viento*); malo (*dícese, p.ej., del tiempo*); atascado, obstruído; (baseball) fuera del cuadro; (naut.) enredado; (naut.) sin carenar; (print.) lleno de errores y correcciones; (sport) sucio, innoble; **to go, fall** o **run foul of** chocar contra; enredarse en; (fig.) enredarse con; *va* ensuciar; engrasar; atascar, obstruir; (naut.) chocar contra; (naut.) enredarse en; (naut.) cubrir (*las lapas el casco de un barco*); (baseball) volear (*la pelota*) fuera del cuadro; (sport) hacer una jugada prohibida contra; *vn* ensuciarse; engrasarse (*un motor*); (baseball) volear la pelota fuera del cuadro; (sport) hacer una jugada prohibida
**foulard** [fu'lɑrd] *s* fular
**foul ball** *s* (baseball) mal batazo, pelota que cae fuera del cuadro
**foul-mouthed** ['faʊl'maʊðd] o ['faʊl'maʊθt] *adj* deslenguado, malhablado
**foulness** ['faʊlnɪs] *s* asquerosidad, porquería; fetidez; obscenidad; perfidia; maldad
**foul play** *s* traición, violencia; (sport) juego sucio, jugada prohibida
**foul-spoken** ['faʊl'spokən] *adj* malhablado
**found** [faʊnd] *va* fundar; fundir (*un metal; una estatua*); **to found on** o **upon** fundar en o sobre; *pret & pp de* **find**
**foundation** [faʊn'deʃən] *s* fundación (*acción o efecto de fundar; donación; institución benéfica*); fundamento (*base, fondo*); (arch.) cimiento; **to dig the foundations** abrir los cimientos
**foundation stone** *s* piedra fundamental
**founder** ['faʊndər] *s* fundador; fundidor (*de metales*); (vet.) infosura, hormiguillo; *va* maltratar (*un caballo*); hundir, echar a pique; *vn* desplomarse; tropezar, despearse (*un caballo*); fracasar; hundirse, irse a fondo, irse a pique
**foundling** ['faʊndlɪŋ] *s* expósito, niño expósito
**foundling hospital** *s* casa de expósitos
**foundry** ['faʊndrɪ] *s* (*pl:* **-ries**) fundición (*acción; fábrica*)
**foundryman** ['faʊndrɪmən] *s* (*pl:* **-men**) fundidor
**fount** [faʊnt] *s* fuente
**fountain** ['faʊntən] *s* fuente
**fountainhead** ['faʊntən,hɛd] *s* nacimiento (*de un río*); (fig.) nacimiento (*origen primitivo*)
**Fountain of Youth** *s* Fuente de la juventud
**fountain pen** *s* pluma fuente, pluma estilográfica
**fountain syringe** *s* mangueta
**four** [for] *adj* cuatro; *s* cuatro; **on all fours** a cuatro pies, a gatas; igual, parejo, al mismo nivel; **four o'clock** las cuatro; **four of a kind** quínola
**four-cornered** ['for'kɔrnərd] *adj* cuadrangular
**four-cycle** ['for,saɪkəl] *adj* (mach.) de cuatro tiempos; *s* (mach.) ciclo de cuatro tiempos
**four-cylinder** ['for,sɪlɪndər] *adj* (mach.) de cuatro cilindros; **a four-cylinder motor** un cuatro cilindros
**four-dimensional** ['fordɪ'mɛnʃənəl] *adj* de cuatro dimensiones
**four flush** *s* (poker) cuatro naipes del mismo palo; bluff, finta
**four-flush** ['for,flʌʃ] *vn* (slang) bravear, fanfarronear, papelonear
**fourflusher** ['for,flʌʃər] *s* (slang) bravucón, fanfarrón, impostor, embustero
**fourfold** ['for,fold] *adj* cuádruple
**four-footed** ['for'fʊtɪd] *adj* cuadrúpedo
**four-handed** ['for'hændɪd] *adj* que tiene cuatro manos; cuadrúmano; para cuatro jugadores; (mus.) a cuatro manos
**four hundred** *adj* cuatrocientos; *s* cuatrocientos; **the four hundred** la alta sociedad
**Fourierism** ['fʊrɪərɪzəm] *s* furierismo
**four-in-hand** ['forɪn,hænd] *adj* tirado por cuatro caballos (*coche*); de nudo corredizo (*corbata*); *s* coche tirado por cuatro caballos; tiro de cuatro caballos; corbata de nudo corredizo
**four-in-hand tie** *s* corbata de nudo corredizo, corbata de pañuelo
**four-lane** ['for'len] *adj* cuadriviario
**four-leaf** ['for,lif] o **four-leaved** ['for,livd] *adj* cuadrifoliado
**four-legged** ['for'lɛgɪd] o ['for'lɛgd] *adj* de cuatro piernas; cuadrúpedo
**four-letter word** ['for'lɛtər] *s* palabra impúdica de cuatro letras (*o muy corta*)
**four-motor** ['for'motər] *adj* cuadrimotor
**four-motor plane** *s* (aer.) cuadrimotor
**four-o'clock** ['forə,klɑk] *s* (bot.) arrebolera, dondiego
**fourpence** ['forpəns] *s* cuatro peniques; moneda de cuatro peniques
**fourpenny** ['for,pɛnɪ] o ['forpənɪ] *s* (*pl:* **-nies**) cuatro peniques; moneda de cuatro peniques; *adj* de cuatro peniques
**four-poster** ['for'postər] *s* cama imperial
**fourscore** ['for'skor] *s* cuatro veintenas; *adj* ochenta
**four seas** *spl* los mares que circundan las Islas Británicas
**four-seater** ['for'sitər] *s* coche de cuatro plazas; (aer.) cuadriplaza
**foursome** ['forsəm] *s* cuatrinca; (sport) partida en la que cada uno de los dos bandos se compone de dos personas; (sport) conjunto de cuatro jugadores
**foursquare** ['for'skwɛr] *adj* cuadrado; franco, sincero; firme, constante; ['for,skwɛr] *s* cuadrado
**four-stroke cycle** ['for,strok] *s* (mach.) ciclo de cuatro tiempos
**fourteen** ['for'tin] *adj & s* catorce
**Fourteen Points, The** los catorce puntos (*del presidente Wilson*)
**fourteenth** ['for'tinθ] *adj* décimocuarto; catorzavo; *s* décimocuarto; catorzavo; catorce (*en las fechas*)
**fourth** [forθ] *adj* cuarto; *s* cuarto; cuatro (*en las fechas*); (mus.) cuarta
**fourth dimension** *s* (math.) cuarta dimensión
**fourth estate** *s* cuarto poder (*la prensa, el periodismo*)
**fourthly** ['forθlɪ] *adv* en cuarto lugar
**Fourth of July** *s* cuatro de julio (*fiesta nacional de los EE.UU.*)
**four-way** ['for,we] *adj* de cuatro direcciones, de cuatro pasos
**four-way switch** *s* (elec.) conmutador de cuatro terminales
**four-wheel** ['for'hwil] *adj* de cuatro ruedas; en las cuatro ruedas
**four-wheel brakes** *spl* (aut.) frenos en las cuatro ruedas
**four-wheel drive** *s* propulsión o tracción en cuatro ruedas
**fovea** ['fovɪə] *s* (*pl:* **-ae** [i]) fóvea; (bot.) fóvea
**fovea centralis** [sɛn'trelɪs] *s* (anat.) fóvea central
**fowl** [faʊl] *s* ave; gallo, gallina, pollo; carne de ave; *vn* cazar aves de caza
**fowler** ['faʊlər] *s* cazador de aves
**fowling piece** *s* escopeta
**fox** [fɑks] *s* (zool.) zorra; zorro (*piel*); (fig.) zorro (*persona muy taimada*); *va* engañar con astucia; descolorar, manchar
**foxglove** ['fɑks,glʌv] *s* (bot.) dedalera
**foxhole** ['fɑks,hol] *s* (mil.) pozo de lobo
**foxhound** ['fɑks,haʊnd] *s* perro raposero
**fox hunt** *s* caza de zorras
**foxiness** ['fɑksɪnɪs] *s* zorrería
**fox squirrel** *s* (zool.) ardilla negra
**foxtail** ['fɑks,tel] *s* rabo de zorra; (bot.) rabo de zorra

**foxtail grass** *s* (bot.) alopecuro
**foxtail millet** *s* (bot.) panizo
**fox terrier** *s* fox-térrier
**fox trot** *s* trote corto (*de caballo*); fox-trot (*danza y música*)
**fox-trot** ['faks,trat] (*pret & pp:* **-trotted;** *ger:* **-trotting**) *vn* ir al trote corto; bailar el fox-trot
**foxy** ['faksɪ] *adj* (*comp:* **-ier;** *super:* **-iest**) astuto, taimado; descolorado, manchado
**foyer** ['fɔɪər] o [fwa'je] *s* salón de entrada; (theat.) salón de descanso, foyer
**F.P.S.** abr. de **foot-pound-second**
**fr.** abr. de **fragment, franc** y **from**
**Fr.** abr. de **Father, France, French** y **Friday**
**Fra** [fra] *s* fray
**fracas** ['frekəs] *s* altercado, gresca, riña
**fraction** ['frækʃən] *s* fracción; pequeña porción; (math.) fracción, quebrado
**fractional** ['frækʃənəl] *adj* fraccionario; fraccionado; fraccionario (*dinero, moneda*); insignificante
**fractional distillation** *s* (chem.) destilación fraccionada
**fractionate** ['frækʃənet] *va* (chem.) fraccionar
**fractionating tower** ['frækʃə,netɪŋ] *s* torre fraccionadora
**fractionation** [,frækʃə'neʃən] *s* (chem.) fraccionamiento
**fractionize** ['frækʃənaɪz] *va* fraccionar
**fractious** ['frækʃəs] *adj* reacio, rebelón; displicente, regañón
**fracture** ['fræktʃər] *s* fractura; (geol. & surg.) fractura; *va* fracturar; *vn* fracturarse
**fraenum** ['frinəm] *s* (*pl:* **-na** [nə]) var. de **frenum**
**fragile** ['frædʒɪl] *adj* frágil
**fragility** [frə'dʒɪlɪtɪ] *s* fragilidad
**fragment** ['frægmənt] *s* fragmento
**fragmental** [fræg'mɛntəl] o **fragmentary** ['frægmən,tɛrɪ] *adj* fragmentario
**fragmentation** [,frægmən'teʃən] *s* fragmentación; (biol.) fragmentación
**fragrance** ['fregrəns] *s* fragancia
**fragrant** ['fregrənt] *adj* fragante
**frail** [frel] *adj* frágil, débil
**frailty** ['freltɪ] *s* (*pl:* **-ties**) fragilidad, debilidad
**fraise** [frez] *s* fresa (*gorguera*); (fort.) frisa; *va* (mach.) fresar
**frambesia** [fræm'biʒə] *s* (path.) frambesia
**frame** [frem] *s* armazón, esqueleto, estructura; marco (*de un cuadro, espejo, etc.*); armadura, montura (*de unas gafas*); complexión, constitución; bastidor (*para bordar*); sistema (*p.ej., de gobierno*); (mov. & telv.) encuadre; (naut.) cuaderna; *va* formar, forjar; idear; ajustar, construir; enmarcar; formular, redactar; (slang) incriminar (*a un inocente*) por medio de una estratagema; (slang) prefijar (*un resultado deseado*) por medios fraudulentos
**frame house** *s* casa de madera
**frame of mind** *s* estado de ánimo, manera de pensar
**frame of reference** *s* (math.) sistema de coordenadas o de ejes de coordenadas; puntos de referencia
**framer** ['fremər] *s* constructor; carpintero de obra de afuera; fabricante de marcos
**frame-up** ['frem,ʌp] *s* (slang) treta, estratagema para incriminar a un inocente
**framework** ['frem,wʌrk] *s* armazón, esqueleto, estructura, marco
**franc** [fræŋk] *s* franco
**France** [fræns] o [frans] *s* Francia
**Frances** ['frænsɪs] o ['fransɪs] *s* Francisca
**Franche-Comté** [frɑ̃ʃkõ'te] *s* el Franco Condado
**franchise** ['fræntʃaɪz] *s* franquicia, privilegio; sufragio
**Francis** ['frænsɪs] o ['fransɪs] *s* Francisco
**Franciscan** [fræn'sɪskən] *adj & s* franciscano
**francium** ['frænsɪəm] *s* (chem.) francio
**Franco-German** ['fræŋko'dʒʌrmən] *adj* francoalemán
**Francophile** ['fræŋkofaɪl] *adj & s* francófilo
**Francophobe** ['fræŋkofob] *adj & s* francófobo
**Franco-Prussian War** ['fræŋko'prʌʃən] *s* guerra Francoprusiana
**franc-tireur** [frɑ̃ti'rœr] *s* (*pl:* **francs-tireurs** [frɑ̃ti'rœr]) francotirador
**frangible** ['frændʒɪbəl] *adj* frangible
**frank** [fræŋk] *adj* franco; *s* carta franca, envío franco; franquicia de correos; sello indicador de franquicia; *va* franquear; (*cap.*) *s* Franco; Paco, Francho (*nombre abreviado de Francisco*)
**Frankenstein** ['fræŋkənstaɪn] *s* personaje fabuloso que crea un monstruo que no puede gobernar; cosa que llega a ser causa de la ruina de su inventor
**Frankfurt am Main** ['fraŋkfurt am 'maɪn] *s* Francfort del Main
**Frankfurt an der Oder** [an dər 'odər] *s* Francfurt del Oder
**frankfurter** ['fræŋkfərtər] *s* salchicha (*de carne de vaca y de cerdo*)
**frankincense** ['fræŋkɪnsɛns] *s* olíbano
**Frankish** ['fræŋkɪʃ] *adj* franco; *s* franco (*idioma*)
**franklin** ['fræŋklɪn] *s* (Brit.) poseedor de feudo franco (*de los siglos XIV y XV*)
**frankness** ['fræŋknɪs] *s* franqueza (*candor, sinceridad, abertura*)
**frantic** ['fræntɪk] *adj* frenético
**frantically** ['fræntɪkəlɪ] *adv* frenéticamente
**Franz Josef Land** ['frants 'jozɛf ,lænd] *s* archipiélago de Francisco José
**frappé** [fræ'pe] *adj* helado; *s* helado (*de jugo de fruta azucarado*)
**frat** [fræt] *s* (slang) club de estudiantes (*en las universidades norteamericanas*)
**fraternal** [frə'tʌrnəl] *adj* fraternal
**fraternal twins** *spl* gemelos fraternos o heterólogos
**fraternity** [frə'tʌrnɪtɪ] *s* (*pl:* **-ties**) fraternidad; cofradía; asociación secreta; (U.S.A.) club de estudiantes
**fraternization** [,frætərnɪ'zeʃən] *s* fraternización
**fraternize** ['frætərnaɪz] *vn* fraternizar
**fratricidal** [,frætrɪ'saɪdəl] o [,fretrɪ'saɪdəl] *adj* fratricida
**fratricide** ['frætrɪsaɪd] o ['fretrɪsaɪd] *s* fratricidio (*acción*); fratricida (*persona*)
**fraud** [frɔd] *s* fraude; (coll.) impostor
**fraudulence** ['frɔdʒələns] o **fraudulency** ['frɔdʒələnsɪ] *s* fraudulencia
**fraudulent** ['frɔdʒələnt] *adj* fraudulento
**fraught** [frɔt] *adj* cargado, lleno; **fraught with** cargado de, lleno de
**Fraunhofer lines** ['fraun,hofər] *spl* (phys.) rayas de Fraunhofer
**fraxinella** [,fræksɪ'nɛlə] *s* (bot.) fresnillo, díctamo blanco
**fray** [fre] *s* batalla, combate, riña; *va* desgastar, ludir; raer; *vn* raerse, deshilacharse
**frazzle** ['fræzəl] *s* condición de deshilachado; jirón; gran cansancio; **in a frazzle** deshilachado; rendido de cansancio; *va* desgastar, raer; hacer jirones; rendir de cansancio
**freak** [frik] *s* curiosidad, monstruosidad, rareza; fenómeno (*persona*); capricho, extravagancia; *adj* muy raro e inesperado
**freakish** ['frikɪʃ] *adj* muy raro; antojadizo, caprichoso
**freckle** ['frɛkəl] *s* peca; *va* motear; *vn* ponerse pecoso
**freckle-faced** ['frɛkəl,fest] *adj* pecoso
**freckly** ['frɛklɪ] *adj* pecoso
**Fred** [frɛd] o **Freddy** ['frɛdɪ] *s* Federiquito
**Frederica** [,frɛdə'rikə] *s* Federica
**Frederick** ['frɛdərɪk] *s* Federico
**free** [fri] *adj* (*comp:* **freer** ['friər]; *super:* **freest** ['friɪst]) libre; franco, gratis; liberal, generoso; **to be free with** dar abundantemente; usar de, abundantemente; **to make free with** disponer de (*una cosa*) como si fuera cosa propia; **to set free** libertar; *adv* libremente; en libertad; gratis, de balde; *va* libertar, poner en libertad; manumitir; soltar, desembarazar; exentar, eximir
**free alongside ship** *adj* libre al costado del vapor
**free and easy** *adj* despreocupado, sin ceremonia
**freeboard** ['fri,bord] *s* (naut.) francobordo, obra muerta
**freebooter** ['fri,butər] *s* pirata, forbante
**freebooting** ['fri,butɪŋ] *s* piratería

**freeborn** ['fri,bɔrn] *adj* nacido libre; propio o digno de un pueblo libre
**free city** *s* ciudad libre
**free delivery** *s* (U.S.A.) distribución gratuita del correo
**freedman** ['fridmən] *s* (*pl:* **-men**) liberto, manumiso
**freedom** ['fridəm] *s* libertad; **to receive the freedom of the city** ser recibido como ciudadano de honor
**freedom of assembly** *s* libertad de reunión
**freedom of speech** *s* libertad de palabra
**freedom of the press** *s* libertad de imprenta o de prensa
**freedom of the seas** *s* libertad de los mares
**freedom of worship** *s* libertad de cultos
**freedwoman** ['frid,wumən] *s* (*pl:* **-women**) liberta, manumisa
**free energy** *s* (phys.) energía libre
**free enterprise** *s* libertad de empresa
**free fight** *s* sarracina, riña tumultuaria
**free-for-all** ['frifər,ɔl] *adj* para todos; *s* concurso, carrera, pugna, etc. abiertas a todo el mundo; sarracina, riña tumultuaria
**free hand** *s* carta blanca, plena libertad
**freehand** ['fri,hænd] *adj* a pulso (*dícese del dibujo*)
**freehanded** ['fri,hændɪd] *adj* dadivoso, liberal
**freehold** ['fri,hold] *s* (law) feudo franco; (law) posesión de un feudo franco
**freeholder** ['fri,holdər] *s* poseedor de feudo franco
**free lance** *s* soldado mercenario; hombre despreocupado e independiente; periodista, artista u otra persona que trabaja independientemente
**free-lance** ['fri'læns] o ['fri'lɑns] *adj* mercenario; independiente; *vn* ser independiente
**free list** *s* (com.) lista de artículos exentos de derechos de aduana
**freeloader** ['fri,lodər] *s* (slang) esponja, gorrón
**free lunch** *s* tapas, tapitas
**freeman** ['frimən] *s* (*pl:* **-men**) hombre libre; ciudadano
**Freemason** ['fri,mesən] *s* francmasón
**Freemasonic** [,frimə'sɑnɪk] *adj* francmasónico
**Freemasonry** ['fri,mesənrɪ] *s* francmasonería; (*l.c.*) *s* comprensión mutua, compañerismo, simpatía natural
**free of charge** *adj* gratis, de balde
**free on board** *adj* franco a bordo
**free port** *s* puerto franco
**freesia** ['friʒə] *s* (bot.) fresia
**free silver** *s* acuñación libre de la plata
**freesilverite** [,fri'sɪlvəraɪt] *s* argentista
**free-spoken** ['fri'spokən] *adj* franco, sin reserva
**freestone** ['fri,ston] *adj* abridero, de hueso libre; *s* piedra franca; abridero, fruta abridera
**free syllable** *s* (phonet.) sílaba libre
**freethinker** ['fri'θɪŋkər] *s* librepensador
**freethinking** ['fri'θɪŋkɪŋ] *adj* librepensador; *s* librepensamiento
**free thought** *s* librepensamiento
**free trade** *s* libre cambio, librecambio
**freetrader** ['fri'tredər] *s* librecambista
**free-trading** ['fri'tredɪŋ] *adj* librecambista
**free verse** *s* poesía libre de toda traba
**freeway** ['fri,we] *s* autopista
**freewheel** ['fri'hwil] *s* (mach.) rueda libre
**freewheeling** ['fri'hwilɪŋ] *s* (mach.) marcha a rueda libre
**free will** *s* libre albedrío; propia voluntad
**freewill** ['fri'wɪl] *adj* voluntario; del libre albedrío
**freeze** [friz] *s* helada; (*pret:* **froze;** *pp:* **frozen**) *va* helar; congelar (*p.ej., los créditos*); **to freeze out** (coll.) deshacerse de (*p.ej., un rival*) quitándole la clientela; *vn* helarse; congelarse; helársele a uno la sangre (*p.ej., de miedo*); **to freeze on to** (coll.) quedar fuertemente agarrado a; **to freeze to death** morir helado, morir de frío
**freezer** ['frizər] *s* congelador; heladora, sorbetera
**freezing mixture** *s* mezcla refrigerante
**freezing point** *s* punto de congelación
**freight** [fret] *s* carga; mercancías, tren de mercancías; (naut.) flete; **by freight** por carga, como carga; (rail.) en pequeña velocidad; *va* cargar, enviar por carga
**freightage** ['fretɪdʒ] *s* carga; transporte
**freight agent** *s* (rail.) agente de carga
**freight car** *s* (rail.) vagón de carga, vagón de mercancías
**freight engine** *s* (rail.) locomotora de mercancías
**freighter** ['fretər] *s* (naut.) buque de carga, buque carguero
**freight platform** *s* (rail.) muelle
**freight station** *s* (rail.) estación de carga
**freight train** *s* mercancías, tren de mercancías
**freight yard** *s* (rail.) patio de carga
**French** [frɛntʃ] *adj* francés; *spl* franceses; *ssg* francés (*idioma*)
**French and Indian War** *s* guerra entre Francia e Inglaterra en tierras americanas
**French Canadian** *s* francocanadiense
**French-Canadian** ['frɛntʃkə'nedɪən] *adj* francocanadiense
**French chalk** *s* jaboncillo de sastre
**French Congo** *s* el Congo Francés
**French doors** *spl* puertas vidrieras dobles
**French drain** *s* desagüe de piedra en una zanja
**French dressing** *s* aliño francés, salsa francesa (*para ensaladas*)
**French Equatorial Africa** *s* el África Ecuatorial Francesa
**French fried potatoes** *spl* patatas fritas en trocitos
**French Guiana** *s* la Guayana Francesa
**French Guinea** *s* la Guinea Francesa
**French honeysuckle** *s* (bot.) zulla
**French horn** *s* (mus.) trompa de armonía
**French horsepower** *s* (mech.) caballo de fuerza, caballo de vapor (*736 vatios*)
**Frenchify** ['frɛntʃɪfaɪ] (*pret & pp:* **-fied**) *va* afrancesar
**French Indochina** *s* la Indochina Francesa
**French leave** *s* despedida a la francesa; **to take French leave** despedirse, irse o marcharse a la francesa
**Frenchman** ['frɛntʃmən] *s* (*pl:* **-men**) francés
**French marigold** *s* (bot.) damasquina, clavel de las Indias
**French Morocco** *s* el Marruecos Francés
**French telephone** *s* var. de **handset**
**French toast** *s* pan frito después de ser empapado en una mezcla de leche y huevos batidos
**French West Africa** *s* el África Occidental Francesa
**French West Indies** *spl* Antillas Francesas
**French window** *s* ventana de dos hojas de cristal
**Frenchwoman** ['frɛntʃ,wumən] *s* (*pl:* **-women**) francesa
**Frenchy** ['frɛntʃɪ] *s* (*pl:* **-chies**) (coll.) franchote
**frenum** ['frinəm] *s* (*pl:* **-na** [nə]) (anat.) frenillo
**frenzied** ['frɛnzɪd] *adj* frenético
**frenzy** ['frɛnzɪ] *s* (*pl:* **-zies**) frenesí
**freon** ['friɑn] *s* freón
**frequency** ['frikwənsɪ] *s* (*pl:* **-cies**) frecuencia
**frequency changer** *s* (elec.) cambiador de frecuencia
**frequency control** *s* (rad.) control de la frecuencia
**frequency converter** *s* (elec.) convertidor de frecuencia
**frequency curve** *s* (statistics) curva de frecuencias
**frequency distribution** *s* (statistics) distribución de frecuencias
**frequency list** *s* lista de frecuencia (*de palabras*)
**frequency meter** *s* (elec.) frecuencímetro
**frequency modulation** *s* (rad.) modulación de frecuencia, frecuencia modulada
**frequent** ['frikwənt] *adj* frecuente; [frɪ'kwɛnt] *va* frecuentar
**frequentation** [,frikwən'teʃən] *s* frecuentación
**frequentative** [frɪ'kwɛntətɪv] *adj & s* (gram.) frecuentativo
**frequenter** [frɪ'kwɛntər] *s* frecuentador

**frequently** ['frikwəntlɪ] *adv* frecuentemente, con frequencia
**fresco** ['frɛsko] *s* (*pl:* **-coes** o **-cos**) fresco (*arte; cuadro*); **in fresco** al fresco; *va* pintar al fresco
**frescoer** ['frɛskoər] *s* fresquista
**fresh** [frɛʃ] *adj* fresco; puro (*dícese del aire, agua, etc.*); dulce (*agua*); inexperto, novicio; (naut.) fresquito (*viento*); (slang) atrevido (*para con las mujeres*); (slang) fresco, desvergonzado; **fresh paint!** ¡recién pintado!, ¡ojo, mancha!; *adv* frescamente, recientemente; **I am fresh out of coffee** (coll.) el café está recién agotado
**fresh breeze** *s* (naut.) viento fresquito
**freshen** ['frɛʃən] *va* refrescar; hacer menos salado; *vn* refrescarse; refrescar (*el viento*)
**freshet** ['frɛʃɪt] *s* crecida, avenida; corriente impetuosa de agua dulce que penetra en el mar
**fresh gale** *s* (naut.) viento duro
**freshman** ['frɛʃmən] *s* (*pl:* **-men**) novato; estudiante de primer año
**freshness** ['frɛʃnɪs] *s* frescura; pureza (*del aire, agua, etc.*); (slang) frescura, descaro
**fresh-water** ['frɛʃ,wɔtər] o ['frɛʃ,wɑtər] *adj* de agua dulce; no acostumbrado a navegar; bisoño, inexperto; provinciano
**fret** [frɛt] *s* calado; (mus.) ceja o traste (*de la guitarra*); queja, displicencia; (*pret & pp:* **fretted**; *ger:* **fretting**) *va* adornar con calados; irritar; raer, gastar estregando; corroer; agitar (*el agua*); *vn* irritarse, quejarse; agitarse (*el agua*); raerse
**fretful** ['frɛtfəl] *adj* irritable, displicente, descontentadizo
**fret saw** *s* sierra de calados
**fretted** ['frɛtɪd] *adj* calado; (her.) freteado
**fretwork** ['frɛt,wʌrk] *s* calado
**Freudian** ['frɔɪdɪən] *adj & s* freudiano
**Freudianism** ['frɔɪdɪənɪzəm] *s* freudismo
**Fri.** abr. de **Friday**
**friability** [,fraɪə'bɪlɪtɪ] *s* friabilidad
**friable** ['fraɪəbəl] *adj* friable
**friar** ['fraɪər] *s* fraile; (print.) fraile
**friary** ['fraɪərɪ] *s* (*pl:* **-ies**) convento de frailes; orden de frailes
**fricassee** [,frɪkə'si] *s* fricasé; *va* guisar a la fricasé
**fricative** ['frɪkətɪv] *adj* (phonet.) fricativo; *s* (phonet.) fricativa
**friction** ['frɪkʃən] *s* fricción, rozamiento; (mech.) fricción, rozamiento; (fig.) fricción, desavenencia, rozamiento
**frictional** ['frɪkʃənəl] *adj* friccional, de fricción, de rozamiento
**friction tape** *s* (elec.) cinta aislante, tela aisladora
**Friday** ['fraɪdɪ] *s* viernes; servidor fiel y muy adicto
**fried** [fraɪd] *adj* frito
**friedcake** ['fraɪd,kek] *s* buñuelo
**fried egg** *s* huevo a la plancha
**fried potatoes** *spl* patatas fritas
**friend** [frɛnd] *s* amigo; gente de paz (*expresión con que se contesta al que pregunta ¿quién?*); (*cap.*) *s* cuáquero; **to be close friends** ser muy amigos; **to be friends with** ser amigo de; **to make friends** trabar amistades; ganarse amigos; **to make friends with** hacerse amigo de
**friend at court** *s* amigo en alto lugar; **to have a friend at court** tener el padre alcalde
**friendliness** ['frɛndlɪnɪs] *s* amigabilidad, cordialidad
**friendly** ['frɛndlɪ] *adj* (*comp:* **-lier**; *super:* **-liest**) amigable, amistoso, cordial
**Friendly Islands** *spl* islas de los Amigos
**friendship** ['frɛndʃɪp] *s* amistad
**Friesland** ['frizlənd] *s* Frisia
**frieze** [friz] *s* frisa (*tela de lana*); (arch.) friso; *va* frisar (*el paño*)
**frigate** ['frɪgɪt] *s* (naut.) fragata
**frigate bird** *s* (orn.) fragata, rabihorcado
**fright** [fraɪt] *s* susto, terror; (coll.) espantajo, mamarracho; **to take fright at** asustarse de; *va* (poet.) asustar
**frighten** ['fraɪtən] *va* asustar; espantar; **to frighten away** espantar, ahuyentar; *vn* asustar; asustarse
**frightful** ['fraɪtfəl] *adj* espantoso, horroroso; (coll.) muy feo, repugnante; (coll.) muy grande, tremendo
**frightfulness** ['fraɪtfəlnɪs] *s* espanto, horror; terrorismo
**frigid** ['frɪdʒɪd] *adj* frío; (fig.) frío (*indiferente; sin gracia*)
**frigidity** [frɪ'dʒɪdɪtɪ] *s* frialdad; (fig.) frialdad (*indiferencia, desafecto*); (path.) frialdad, frigidez (*falta de deseos sexuales*)
**frigid zone** *s* zona glacial
**frill** [frɪl] *s* lechuga, escarola; collarín (*de aves, animales*); (coll.) adorno inútil, ringorrango; (coll.) afectación (*en el vestir, el hablar, etc.*); *va* alechugar, escarolar; *vn* alechugarse
**fringe** [frɪndʒ] *s* franja, orla; borde, margen; *va* franjar, orlar; (fig.) orlar (*los árboles un camino*)
**fringe benefits** *spl* beneficios accesorios
**fringillid** [frɪn'dʒɪlɪd] *s* (orn.) fringílido
**frippery** ['frɪpərɪ] *s* (*pl:* **-ies**) cursilería; perifollos, perejiles
**Frisco** ['frɪsko] *s* (coll.) nombre abreviado de **San Francisco** (*California*)
**Frisian** ['frɪʒən] *adj & s* frisón
**frisk** [frɪsk] *va* (slang) cachear; (slang) robar con ratería; *vn* cabriolar, juguetear, retozar
**frisket** ['frɪskɪt] *s* (print.) frasqueta
**frisky** ['frɪskɪ] *adj* (*comp:* **-ier**; *super:* **-iest**) juguetón, retozón, vivaracho; fogoso (*caballo*)
**frit** [frɪt] *s* frita; (*pret & pp:* **fritted**; *ger:* **fritting**) *va* fritar (*las materias con que se fabrica el vidrio*)
**frith** [frɪθ] *s* estuario, brazo de mar
**fritillary** ['frɪtɪ,lɛrɪ] *s* (*pl:* **-ies**) (bot. & ent.) fritilaria
**fritter** ['frɪtər] *s* fruta de sartén, frisuelo; parte pequeña, fragmento; *va* desmenuzar; **to fritter away** desperdiciar o malgastar a poquitos
**frivolity** [frɪ'vɑlɪtɪ] *s* (*pl:* **-ties**) frivolidad
**frivolous** ['frɪvələs] *adj* frívolo
**friz** o **frizz** [frɪz] *s* (*pl:* **frizzes**) bucle, rizo, pelo rizado muy apretadamente; (*pret & pp:* **frizzed**; *ger:* **frizzing**) *va* rizar, rizar muy apretadamente
**frizzle** ['frɪzəl] *s* rizo pequeño y apretado; chirrido, siseo; *va* rizar apretadamente; asar o freír en parrillas; *vn* chirriar, sisear
**frizzly** ['frɪzlɪ] o **frizzy** ['frɪzɪ] *adj* muy ensortijado
**fro** [fro] *adv* atrás, hacia atrás; **to and fro** de una parte a otra, de aquí para allá
**frock** [frɑk] *s* vestido; bata, blusa; vestido talar (*de los sacerdotes*); levita; *va* vestir con vestido, bata, vestido talar, etc.
**frock coat** *s* levita
**frog** [frɑg] o [frɔg] *s* (zool. & rail.) rana; ranilla (*del casco de las caballerías*); alamar (*presilla y botón*); ronquera; (elec.) renacuajo
**frog in the throat** *s* ronquera, gallo en la garganta
**frogman** ['frɑg,mæn] o ['frɔg,mæn] *s* (*pl:* **-men**) hombre rana
**frolic** ['frɑlɪk] *s* juego alegre; travesura; jaleo, holgorio, fiesta; (*pret & pp:* **-icked**; *ger:* **-icking**) *vn* juguetear, retozar, travesear, jaranear
**frolicsome** ['frɑlɪksəm] *adj* juguetón, retozón, travieso
**from** [frɑm] o [frəm] *prep* de; desde; de parte de; según; a, p.ej., **to take something away from someone** quitar algo a alguien
**frond** [frɑnd] *s* (bot.) fronda
**frondage** ['frɑndɪdʒ] *s* frondas, frondosidad
**frondescence** [frɑn'dɛsəns] *s* (bot.) frondescencia
**frondescent** [frɑn'dɛsənt] *adj* frondescente
**front** [frʌnt] *s* frente *m & f;* frontalera (*de la brida del caballo*); pechera (*de la camisa*); principio (*de un libro*), p.ej., **you will find the passage in the front of the book** Vd. hallará el pasaje al principio o hacia el principio del libro; porción de terreno colindante con un río, calle, etc.; apariencia falsa (*de riqueza, grandeza, etc.*); ademán estudiado; (fort., mil. & pol.) frente *m;* **in front** delante, al frente, en frente; **in front of** delante de, en frente de, frente a; **to put on a front** (coll.) gastar mucho oropel; **to put up a bold front** hacer de tripas corazón (*poner buena cara a cosa desagradable*); *interj* ¡botones!;

*adj* delantero; primero; anterior (*diente*); (phonet.) anterior; *va* dar a; afrontar, arrostar; estar al frente de; poner frente o fachada a; *vn* adelantarse; **to front on** dar a; **to front towards** mirar hacia
**frontage** [ˈfrʌntɪdʒ] *s* fachada, frontera; extensión frontera; terreno frontero
**frontal** [ˈfrʌntəl] *adj* frontal; *s* frontal; (anat., arch. & eccl.) frontal
**front door** *s* puerta de entrada, puerta principal
**front drive** *s* (aut.) tracción delantera
**frontier** [frʌnˈtɪr] o [ˈfrɑntɪr] *s* frontera; *adj* fronterizo
**frontiersman** [frʌnˈtɪrzmən] *s* (*pl:* **-men**) habitante de la frontera, colonizador, explorador
**frontispiece** [ˈfrʌntɪspis] *s* portada, frontispicio (*de un libro*); (arch.) frontispicio
**frontlet** [ˈfrʌntlɪt] *s* frente de un animal; venda o adorno para la frente
**front line** *s* (mil.) línea del frente
**front matter** *s* preliminares (*de un libro*)
**front page** *s* primera plana
**front-page** [ˈfrʌntˌpedʒ] *adj* de la primera plana (*de un periódico*); muy importante
**front porch** *s* soportal
**front room** *s* cuarto que da a la calle
**front row** *s* delantera, primera fila
**front seat** *s* asiento delantero
**front steps** *spl* quicio, pretorio (*escalones en la puerta exterior de la casa*)
**front view** *s* vista de frente
**front vowel** *s* (phonet.) vocal anterior
**frost** [frɔst] o [frɑst] *s* helada (*congelación*); escarcha (*rocío helado*); (coll.) frialdad (*en el trato*); (slang) fracaso; *va* cubrir de escarcha; escarchar (*p.ej., confituras*); quemar (*el hielo las plantas*); deslustrar (*el vidrio*)
**frostbite** [ˈfrɔstˌbaɪt] o [ˈfrɑstˌbaɪt] *s* daño sufrido por causa de la helada; (*pret:* **-bit;** *pp:* **-bitten**) *va* helar; quemar (*el hielo las plantas*)
**frosted foods** *spl* var. de **frozen foods**
**frosted glass** *s* vidrio deslustrado, vidrio amolado
**frosting** [ˈfrɔstɪŋ] o [ˈfrɑstɪŋ] *s* (cook.) capa de clara de huevo y azúcar; imitación de la escarcha (*en el acabado de los metales*)
**frosty** [ˈfrɔstɪ] o [ˈfrɑstɪ] *adj* (*comp:* **-ier;** *super:* **-iest**) cubierto de escarcha; helado; escarchado; frío, poco amistoso; canoso, gris
**froth** [frɔθ] o [frɑθ] *s* espuma; frivolidad, bachillerías; *va* hacer espumar; cubrir de espuma; emitir como espuma; batir (*un líquido*) hasta que espume; *vn* espumar, echar espuma; **to froth at the mouth** espumajear, echar espumarajos por la boca
**frothy** [ˈfrɔθɪ] o [ˈfrɑθɪ] *adj* (*comp:* **-ier;** *super:* **-iest**) espumoso; frívolo
**frou-frou** [ˈfruˌfru] *s* frufrú
**froward** [ˈfrowərd] *adj* indócil, díscolo
**frown** [fraʊn] *s* ceño, entrecejo; *va* mirar con ceño; expresar (*enojo*) frunciendo el entrecejo; *vn* fruncir el entrecejo, estar de mal semblante; **to frown at** mirar con ceño; desaprobar; **to frown on** desaprobar
**frowsy** o **frowzy** [ˈfraʊzɪ] *adj* (*comp:* **-ier;** *super:* **-iest**) desaliñado, desaseado; mal peinado; maloliente
**froze** [froz] *pret de* **freeze**
**frozen** [ˈfrozən] *pp de* **freeze**
**frozen foods** *spl* viandas heladas, alimentos o comestibles congelados
**F.R.S.** abr. de **Fellow of the Royal Society**
**frt.** abr. de **freight**
**fructiferous** [frʌkˈtɪfərəs] *adj* fructífero
**fructification** [ˌfrʌktɪfɪˈkeʃən] *s* fructificación
**fructify** [ˈfrʌktɪfaɪ] (*pret & pp:* **-fied**) *va* fecundar, fertilizar; *vn* fructificar
**fructose** [ˈfrʌktos] *s* (chem.) fructosa
**fructuous** [ˈfrʌktʃuəs] *adj* fructuoso
**frugal** [ˈfrugəl] *adj* parco, comedido; escaso
**frugality** [fruˈgælɪtɪ] *s* parquedad; escasez
**frugivorous** [fruˈdʒɪvərəs] *adj* frugívoro
**fruit** [frut] *s* fruta (*p.ej., fresa, manzana, pera*); frutas, p.ej., **I like fruit** me gustan las frutas; (bot.) fruto (*parte que contiene la semilla*); (fig.) fruto (*resultado; producción*), p.ej., **the fruit of much effort** el fruto de mucho trabajo; **the fruits of the earth** los frutos de la tierra; *adj* frutal (*árbol*); frutero (*buque, plato, etc.*); *vn* frutar, dar fruto
**fruitage** [ˈfrutɪdʒ] *s* fructificación
**fruit cake** *s* torta de frutas
**fruit cup** *s* compotera de frutas picadas (*sin cocer*)
**fruit dish** *s* plato frutero
**fruiter** [ˈfrutər] *s* buque frutero; árbol frutal; cultivador de frutas
**fruiterer** [ˈfrutərər] *s* frutero; buque frutero
**fruit fly** *s* (ent.) mosca del vinagre; (ent.) mosca de las frutas, mosca mediterránea
**fruitful** [ˈfrutfəl] *adj* fructuoso, fructífero
**fruitfulness** [ˈfrutfəlnɪs] *s* fructuosidad
**fruition** [fruˈɪʃən] *s* cumplimiento, buen resultado; complacencia, goce, fruición; fructificación; **to come to fruition** lograrse cumplidamente
**fruit jar** *s* tarro para frutas
**fruit juice** *s* jugo de frutas
**fruitless** [ˈfrutlɪs] *adj* infructuoso
**fruit ranch** *s* finca dedicada a la fruticultura
**fruit salad** *s* ensalada de frutas, macedonia de frutas
**fruit stand** *s* puesto de frutas
**fruit store** *s* frutería
**fruit sugar** *s* (chem.) azúcar de fruta
**fruit tree** *s* árbol frutal
**fruitwoman** [ˈfrutˌwʊmən] *s* (*pl:* **-women**) frutera
**fruity** [ˈfrutɪ] *adj* (*comp:* **-ier;** *super:* **-iest**) que huele o sabe a fruta, de olor o sabor de fruta
**frumenty** [ˈfruməntɪ] *s* frangollo cocido con leche y condimentado con azúcar y canela
**frump** [frʌmp] *s* mujer descuidada en el vestir
**frumpish** [ˈfrʌmpɪʃ] *adj* desaliñado; malhumorado
**frumpy** [ˈfrʌmpɪ] *adj* (*comp:* **-ier;** *super:* **-iest**) var. de **frumpish**
**frustrate** [ˈfrʌstret] *va* frustrar
**frustration** [frʌsˈtreʃən] *s* frustración; desazón, desengaño
**frustule** [ˈfrʌstʃʊl] *s* (bot.) frústula
**frustum** [ˈfrʌstəm] *s* (*pl:* **-tums** o **-ta** [tə]) (geom.) tronco
**frutescent** [fruˈtɛsənt] *adj* frutescente
**fruticose** [ˈfrutɪkos] *adj* fruticoso
**fry** [fraɪ] *s* (*pl:* **fries**) fritada; *spl* pececillos; cardumen de peces pequeños; prole, hijos; (*pret & pp:* **fried**) *va* freír
**frying pan** *s* sartén; **to jump from the frying pan into the fire** saltar de la sartén y dar en las brasas, huir de las cenizas y caer en las brasas
**ft.** abr. de **foot** o **feet**
**fucaceous** [fjuˈkeʃəs] *adj* (bot.) fucáceo
**fuchsia** [ˈfjuʃə] *s* (bot.) fucsia
**fuchsin** [ˈfuksɪn] o **fuchsine** [ˈfuksɪn] o [ˈfuksin] *s* (chem.) fucsina
**fuddle** [ˈfʌdəl] *va* emborrachar; confundir
**fuddy-duddy** [ˈfʌdɪˌdʌdɪ] *adj* (coll.) atrasado, anticuado; (coll.) alharaquiento, quisquilloso; *s* (*pl:* **-dies**) (coll.) persona de ideas o costumbres atrasadas o anticuadas; (coll.) persona alharaquienta, persona quisquillosa; (coll.) tragavirotes
**fudge** [fʌdʒ] *s* dulce de chocolate (*de la consistencia de la raspadura*); *interj* ¡ tonterías!; *va* hacer de modo chapucero, hacer de modo superficial y mecánico, hacer con mala fe
**Fuegian** [fjuˈidʒɪən] *adj & s* fueguino
**fuel** [ˈfjuəl] *s* combustible; (fig.) aliciente, pábulo; (*pret & pp:* **fueled** o **fuelled;** *ger:* **fueling** o **fuelling**) *va* aprovisionar de combustible; *vn* aprovisionarse de combustible
**fuel gauge** *s* indicador de nivel del combustible
**fuel oil** *s* aceite combustible
**fuel tank** *s* depósito de combustible
**fugacious** [fjuˈgeʃəs] *adj* fugaz; (bot.) fugaz
**fugitive** [ˈfjudʒɪtɪv] *adj* fugitivo; de interés pasajero; errante, vagabundo; *s* fugitivo
**fugleman** [ˈfjugəlmən] *s* (*pl:* **-men**) (mil.) jefe de fila; (fig.) modelo (*persona digna de ser imitada*)
**fugue** [fjug] *s* (mus.) fuga
**fulcrum** [ˈfʌlkrəm] *s* (*pl:* **-crums** o **-cra** [krə]) (bot., ent., ichth. & mach.) fulcro
**-ful** *suffix adj* -oso p.ej., **frightful** espantoso;

**painful** doloroso; *suffix s* -ado, p.ej., **armful** brazado; **handful** puñado; -ada p.ej., **spoonful** cucharada; **shovelful** palada
**fulfil** o **fulfill** [fʊlˈfɪl] (*pret & pp:* **-filled;** *ger:* **-filling**) *va* cumplir (*un deseo, un plazo, una orden*); cumplir con (*una obligación*); llenar (*una condición, un requisito*); realizar
**fulfilment** o **fulfillment** [fʊlˈfɪlmənt] *s* cumplimiento, ejecución, realización
**fulgent** [ˈfʌldʒənt] *adj* fulgente
**fulgide** [ˈfʌldʒaɪd] o [ˈfʌldʒɪd] *s* (chem.) fúlgido
**fulgurate** [ˈfʌlgjəret] *vn* fulgurar
**fulgurite** [ˈfʌlgjəraɪt] *s* fulgurita
**fulgurous** [ˈfʌlgjərəs] *adj* fulguroso
**fuliginous** [fjuˈlɪdʒɪnəs] *adj* fuliginoso
**full** [fʊl] *adj* lleno; pleno; amplio, holgado (*vestido*); de etiqueta (*traje*); fuerte, sonoro (*dícese de la voz*); **full of fun** muy divertido, muy chistoso; **full of play** muy juguetón, muy retozón; **full to overflowing** lleno a rebosar; *adv* de lleno; **full many (a)** muchísimos; **full well** muy bien, perfectamente; *s* colmo, máximum; plentitud; **in full** por completo, totalmente; sin abreviar; **to the full** completamente, enteramente; *va* dar amplitud a; abatanar (*el paño*); *vn* llegar (*la Luna*) al plenilunio
**fullback** [ˈfʊlˌbæk] *s* (football) defensa, jugador trasero
**full blast** *s* pleno tiro; pleno ejercicio; toda velocidad; **at** o **in full blast** a pleno tiro; en pleno ejercicio; a toda velocidad
**full-blooded** [ˈfʊlˈblʌdɪd] *adj* vigoroso; pletórico; de raza
**full-blown** [ˈfʊlˈblon] *adj* abierto (*dícese de las flores*); maduro, desarrollado
**full-bodied** [ˈfʊlˈbɑdɪd] *adj* consistente, fuerte, espeso; aromático
**full dress** *s* traje de etiqueta; (mil.) uniforme de gala
**full-dress coat** [ˈfʊlˌdrɛs] *s* frac
**fuller** [ˈfʊlər] *s* batanero
**fuller's earth** *s* tierra de batán, tierra de bataneros
**full-faced** [ˈfʊlˈfest] *adj* carilleno; de cuadrado (*mirado frente a frente*); de rostro entero (*dícese de un retrato*)
**full-fashioned** [ˈfʊlˈfæʃənd] *adj* de costura francesa (*dícese de las medias*)
**full-fledged** [ˈfʊlˈflɛdʒd] *adj* acabado, completo; hecho y derecho, nada menos que
**full-grown** [ˈfʊlˈgron] *adj* crecido, completamente desarrollado, maduro
**full house** *s* lleno, entrada llena; (poker) fulján
**full-length mirror** [ˈfʊlˈlɛŋθ] *s* espejo de cuerpo entero, espejo de vestir
**full-length motion picture** *s* cinta de largo metraje
**full load** *s* plena carga; (aer.) peso total
**full moon** *s* luna llena, plenilunio
**full name** *s* nombre y apellidos
**fullness** [ˈfʊlnɪs] *s* (lo) lleno; plenitud, llenura
**fullness of time** *s* plenitud de los tiempos
**full of the moon** *s* lleno de la luna
**full-page** [ˈfʊlˌpedʒ] *adj* a página entera
**full powers** *spl* amplias facultades, plenos poderes
**full-rigged** [ˈfʊlˈrɪgd] *adj* pertrechado completamente; (naut.) aparejado completamente
**full sail** *adv* (naut.) a toda vela, a todo trapo; (fig.) a todo trapo
**full-sized** [ˈfʊlˈsaɪzd] *adj* de tamaño natural
**full stop** *s* parada completa; (gram.) punto final
**full swing** *s* plena operación, actividad máxima; **in full swing** en plena actividad
**full tilt** *adv* a toda velocidad
**full time** *s* las horas de costumbre, jornada ordinaria
**full-time** [ˈfʊlˌtaɪm] *adj* a tiempo completo
**full-view** [ˈfʊlˈvju] *adj* de vista completa
**full volume** *s & adv* (rad.) todo volumen
**full-wave** [ˈfʊlˌwev] *adj* (elec.) de onda completa
**fully** [ˈfʊlɪ] o [ˈfʊllɪ] *adv* completamente; llenamente, abundantemente; cabalmente, exactamente
**fulminate** [ˈfʌlmɪnet] *s* (chem.) fulminato; *va* hacer saltar, volar; fulminar (*censuras, amenazas, etc.*); *vn* fulminar; **to fulminate against** tronar contra
**fulminating powder** *s* (chem.) pólvora fulminante
**fulmination** [ˌfʌlmɪˈneʃən] *s* fulminación
**fulminic** [fʌlˈmɪnɪk] *adj* fulmínico
**fulminic acid** *s* (chem.) ácido fulmínico
**fulminous** [ˈfʌlmɪnəs] *adj* fulmíneo o fulminoso
**fulness** [ˈfʊlnɪs] *s* var. de **fullness**
**fulsome** [ˈfʊlsəm] o [ˈfʌlsəm] *adj* craso, de mal gusto; repugnante
**fumarole** [ˈfjumərol] *s* fumarola
**fumble** [ˈfʌmbəl] *s* (football) falta que consiste en dejar caer el balón; *va* manosear desmañadamente; dejar caer (*el balón o la pelota*) desmañadamente; *vn* buscar con las manos (*p.ej., en los bolsillos*); revolver papeles; andar a tientas; titubear (*en la elección o pronunciación de las palabras*)
**fume** [fjum] *s* emanación, gas, humo, vapor; mal humor, arranque de cólera; *va* ahumar; avahar; *vn* ahumar; avaharse; humear, exhalar vapores; echar pestes; **to fume at** echar pestes contra
**fumed oak** *s* roble ahumado
**fumigate** [ˈfjumɪget] *va* fumigar
**fumigation** [ˌfjumɪˈgeʃən] *s* fumigación
**fumigator** [ˈfjumɪˌgetər] *s* fumigador (*persona o aparato*)
**fumitory** [ˈfjumɪˌtorɪ] *s* (*pl:* **-ries**) (bot.) fumaria
**fun** [fʌn] *s* diversión, chacota, broma; **for fun** o **in fun** por gusto, por divertirse; **to be fun** ser divertido; **to have fun** divertirse; **to make fun of** o **to poke fun at** burlarse de, reírse de; **to play for fun** jugar de burlas
**function** [ˈfʌŋkʃən] *s* función; *vn* funcionar
**functional** [ˈfʌŋkʃənəl] *adj* funcional
**functionalism** [ˈfʌŋkʃənəlɪzəm] *s* funcionalismo
**functionary** [ˈfʌŋkʃəˌnɛrɪ] *s* (*pl:* **-ies**) funcionario
**fund** [fʌnd] *s* fondo; (fig.) fondo (*p.ej., de sabiduría*); **funds** *spl* fondos (*caudales, dinero*); *va* colocar en un fondo; consolidar (*una deuda*)
**fundable** [ˈfʌndəbəl] *adj* consolidable
**fundamental** [ˌfʌndəˈmɛntəl] *adj* fundamental; *s* fundamento; (mus.) nota fundamental
**fundamentalism** [ˌfʌndəˈmɛntəlɪzəm] *s* (rel.) fundamentalismo
**fundamentalist** [ˌfʌndəˈmɛntəlɪst] *s* (rel.) fundamentalista
**fundus** [ˈfʌndəs] *s* (anat.) fondo
**funeral** [ˈfjunərəl] *adj* funeral; *s* funeral, funerales, pompa fúnebre (*de corpore insepulto*); (slang) desgracia, mala suerte; **it's not my funeral** (slang) no corre a mi cuidado
**funeral director** *s* director de funeraria
**funeral march** *s* (mus.) marcha fúnebre
**funeral parlor** *s* funeraria
**funeral service** *s* misa de cuerpo presente
**funerary** [ˈfjunəˌrɛrɪ] *adj* funerario
**funereal** [fjuˈnɪrɪəl] *adj* funeral; fúnebre
**fungicidal** [ˌfʌndʒɪˈsaɪdəl] *adj* fungicida
**fungicide** [ˈfʌndʒɪsaɪd] *s* fungicida
**fungoid** [ˈfʌŋgɔɪd] *adj* fungoideo
**fungology** [fʌŋˈgɑlədʒɪ] *s* fungología
**fungosity** [fʌŋˈgɑsɪtɪ] *s* (*pl:* **-ties**) fungosidad; (path.) fungosidad
**fungous** [ˈfʌŋgəs] *adj* fungoso; que aparece de repente y dura poco
**fungus** [ˈfʌŋgəs] *adj* fungoso; que aparece de repente y dura poco; *s* (*pl:* **-guses** o **fungi** [ˈfʌndʒaɪ]) (bot.) hongo; (path.) hongo, fungo
**funicle** [ˈfjunɪkəl] *s* var. de **funiculus**
**funicular** [fjuˈnɪkjələr] *adj & s* funicular
**funicular railway** *s* ferrocarril funicular
**funiculate** [fjuˈnɪkjəlɪt] o [fjuˈnɪkjəlet] (bot.) *adj* funiculado
**funiculus** [fjuˈnɪkjələs] *s* (*pl:* **-li** [laɪ]) (anat., bot. & zool.) funículo
**funk** [fʌŋk] *s* (coll.) temor, temor pánico; (coll.) cobarde; **in a funk** (coll.) atemorizado; *va* (coll.) encogerse de miedo por, retraerse con temor de; (coll.) atemorizar; *vn* (coll.) encogerse de miedo, retraerse con temor
**funnel** [ˈfʌnəl] *s* embudo; (naut.) chimenea (*de un vapor*); (naut.) manguera, ventilador; (*pret & pp:* **-neled** o **-nelled;** *ger:* **-neling** o

**-nelling**) *va* verter por medio de un embudo; (fig.) concentrar
**funny** [ˈfʌnɪ] *adj* (*comp:* **-nier;** *super:* **-niest**) cómico, ridículo; divertido, chistoso; (coll.) extraño, raro; **to strike someone as funny** hacerle a uno gracia; *s* (*pl:* **-nies**) (Brit.) pequeño bote de remos de tingladillo; **funnies** *spl* (slang) tiras cómicas, páginas cómicas (*del periódico*)
**funny bone** *s* var. de **crazy bone**
**funny paper** *s* páginas cómicas (*del periódico*)
**fur.** abr. de **furlong** y **furnished**
**fur** [fʌr] *s* piel, piel con su lana o pelo; abrigo o adorno de pieles; sarro (*p.ej., en la lengua*); caza de pelo; (her.) forro; **to make the fur fly** (coll.) armar camorra, ser origen de pelotera; **to stroke a person's fur the wrong way** irritarle a una persona; *adj* de piel, de pieles; (*pret & pp:* **furred;** *ger:* **furring**) *va* guarnecer o forrar con pieles; depositar sarro en; aplicar tiras de madera a, clavar tiras de madera en; *vn* formarse incrustaciones
**furbelow** [ˈfʌrbəlo] *s* faralá, ringorrango; *va* adornar con volantes, lazos, etc.
**furbish** [ˈfʌrbɪʃ] *va* acicalar, limpiar, pulir; **to furbish up** renovar, restaurar
**furcate** [ˈfʌrket] *adj* horcado
**fur coat** *s* abrigo de pieles
**furfur** [ˈfʌrfər] *s* (*pl:* **furfures** [ˈfʌrfjuriz]) (path.) fúrfura
**furfuraceous** [ˌfʌrfjəˈreʃəs] *adj* furfuráceo; (bot.) furfuráceo
**furious** [ˈfjurɪəs] *adj* furioso
**furl** [fʌrl] *va* arrollar; (naut.) aferrar
**fur-lined** [ˈfʌrˌlaɪnd] *adj* forrado con pieles
**furlong** [ˈfʌrlɔŋ] o [ˈfʌrlɑŋ] *s* estadio
**furlough** [ˈfʌrlo] *s* (mil.) licencia; *va* (mil.) dar licencia a
**furnace** [ˈfʌrnɪs] *s* horno; calorífero (*para calentar una casa*); lugar de calor intenso; prueba penosa
**furnaceman** [ˈfʌrnɪsmən] *s* (*pl:* **-men**) hornero; hombre encargado del calorífero
**furnish** [ˈfʌrnɪʃ] *va* amueblar; proporcionar, suministrar; aducir (*pruebas*); **to furnish with** proveer de
**furnished room** *s* cuarto amueblado
**furnishings** [ˈfʌrnɪʃɪŋz] *spl* muebles, mueblaje; accesorios; artículos (*p.ej., para caballeros*)
**furniture** [ˈfʌrnɪtʃər] *s* muebles, mueblaje; arreos, avíos; (naut.) aparejo; **a piece of furniture** un mueble; **a suit of furniture** un moblaje, un mobiliario, un juego de muebles
**furniture polish** *s* pulimento para muebles
**furor** [ˈfjurɔr] *s* furor
**furrier** [ˈfʌrɪər] *s* peletero
**furriery** [ˈfʌrɪərɪ] *s* (*pl:* **-ies**) peletería
**furring** [ˈfʌrɪŋ] *s* adorno o forro de pieles; sarro; tiras de madera
**furrow** [ˈfʌro] *s* surco; *va* surcar
**furry** [ˈfʌrɪ] *adj* (*comp:* **-rier;** *super:* **-riest**) adornado con pieles; hecho de pieles; peludo; sarroso
**fur seal** *s* (zool.) oso marino (*Callorhinus alascanus*)
**further** [ˈfʌrðər] *adj comp* adicional, nuevo; más lejano; más; *adv comp* además; más lejos; *va* adelantar, promover, apoyar, fomentar
**furtherance** [ˈfʌrðərəns] *s* adelantamiento, promoción, apoyo, fomento
**furtherer** [ˈfʌrðərər] *s* promotor, patrón, fomentador
**furthermore** [ˈfʌrðərmor] *adv* además
**furthermost** [ˈfʌrðərmost] *adj super* más lejano (*de todos*)
**furthest** [ˈfʌrðɪst] *adj super* más lejano (*de todos*); más; *adv super* más lejos; más
**furtive** [ˈfʌrtɪv] *adj* furtivo
**furuncle** [ˈfjurʌŋkəl] *s* (path.) furúnculo
**fury** [ˈfjurɪ] *s* (*pl:* **-ries**) furia (*ira; violencia; prisa; persona irritada*); (*cap.*) *s* Furia; **to be in a fury** estar furioso, estar dado a los demonios; **like fury** a toda furia
**furze** [fʌrz] *s* (bot.) aliaga, aulaga, tojo; (bot.) retama de escoba
**furzy** [ˈfʌrzɪ] *adj* retamero
**fuse** [fjuz] *s* mecha; (elec.) fusible, cortacircuitos; (elec.) tapón fusible; (mil.) espoleta; **to burn** o **burn out a fuse** (elec.) quemar un fusible; *va* fundir; poner la espoleta a; (fig.) fusionar; *vn* fundirse; (fig.) fusionarse
**fuse box** *s* (elec.) caja de fusibles
**fusee** [fjuˈzi] *s* fósforo grande que no apaga el viento; (horol.) caracol, fusé; (rail.) luz de bengala que sirve de señal
**fuselage** [ˈfjuzəlɪdʒ] o [ˌfjuzəˈlɑʒ] *s* (aer.) fuselaje
**fuse link** *s* (elec.) elemento fusible
**fusel oil** [ˈfjuzəl] *s* (chem.) aceite de fusel
**fusibility** [ˌfjuzɪˈbɪlɪtɪ] *s* fusibilidad
**fusible** [ˈfjuzɪbəl] *adj* fusible o fundible
**fusiform** [ˈfjuzɪfɔrm] *adj* fusiforme
**fusileer** o **fusilier** [ˌfjuzɪˈlɪr] *s* fusilero
**fusillade** [ˌfjuzɪˈled] *s* fusilería; (fig.) andanada (*p.ej., de preguntas*); *va* atacar con una descarga de fusilería, fusilar
**fusion** [ˈfjuʒən] *s* fusión; (fig.) fusión
**fusionism** [ˈfjuʒənɪzəm] *s* (pol.) fusionismo
**fusionist** [ˈfjuʒənɪst] *adj & s* fusionista
**fuss** [fʌs] *s* alharaca, bulla innecesaria; hazañería, desvelos innecesarios; (slang) disputa por ligero motivo; **to make a fuss** hacer alharacas; **to make a fuss over** hacer fiestas a; disputar sobre; *va* molestar, inquietar, atolondrar; dejar hecho un mico; *vn* hacer alharacas, inquietarse por pequeñeces; **to fuss with** manosear
**fuss and feathers** *s* (coll.) fanfarria, magnificencia, pompa
**fussbudget** [ˈfʌsˌbʌdʒɪt] *s* (coll.) persona alharaquienta, persona quisquillosa
**fussy** [ˈfʌsɪ] *adj* (*comp:* **-ier;** *super:* **-iest**) alharaquiento; descontentadizo, exigente; melindroso; peliagudo; muy adornado; con muchos ringorrangos (*vestido*)
**fustian** [ˈfʌstʃən] *s* fustán (*tela gruesa*); pana; cultedad, follaje; *adj* de fustán; de pana; culterano, altisonante
**fustic** [ˈfʌstɪk] *s* (bot.) fustete, palo de Cuba; tintura de fustete
**fusty** [ˈfʌstɪ] *adj* (*comp:* **-ier;** *super:* **-iest**) mohoso, rancio, que huele a cosa pasada, que huele a cerrado; del tiempo de Maricastaña, pasado de moda
**fut.** abr. de **future**
**futile** [ˈfjutɪl] *adj* estéril (*inútil, vano*); fútil (*de poca importancia*)
**futility** [fjuˈtɪlɪtɪ] *s* (*pl:* **-ties**) esterilidad; futilidad
**futtock** [ˈfʌtək] *s* (naut.) genol
**future** [ˈfjutʃər] *adj* futuro; *s* futuro, porvenir; (gram.) futuro; **futures** *spl* (com.) futuros; **in the future** en lo sucesivo, en el futuro; **in the near future** en fecha próxima
**future life** *s* vida futura
**futurism** [ˈfjutʃərɪzəm] *s* futurismo
**futurist** [ˈfjutʃərɪst] *adj & s* futurista
**futuristic** [ˌfjutʃəˈrɪstɪk] *adj* futurista
**futurity** [fjuˈtjurɪtɪ] o [fjuˈturɪtɪ] *s* (*pl:* **-ties**) futuro, porvenir; estado futuro; acontecimiento futuro
**fuze** [fjuz] *s* mecha; (elec.) fusible; (mil.) espoleta; *va* poner la espoleta a
**fuzee** [fjuˈzi] *s* var. de **fusee**
**fuzz** [fʌz] *s* borra, tamo (*en los bolsillos, rincones, etc.*); pelusa, plumón, vello
**fuzzy** [ˈfʌzɪ] *adj* (*comp:* **-ier;** *super:* **-iest**) borroso; cubierto de pelusa o plumón, velloso
**fyke** [faɪk] *s* nasa para pescar
**fylfot** [ˈfɪlfɑt] *s* cruz gamada

# G

**G, g** [dʒi] *s* (*pl:* **G's, g's** [dʒiz]) séptima letra del alfabeto inglés
**g.** abr. de **gauge, gender, genitive, gram** y **guinea**
**G.** abr. de **German** y **Gulf**
**Ga.** abr. de **Georgia**
**G.A.** abr. de **General Agent** y **General Assembly**
**gab** [gæb] *s* (coll.) parleta, cotorreo; (*pret & pp:* **gabbed;** *ger:* **gabbing**) *vn* (coll.) picotear, parlotear
**gabardine** [ˈgæbərdin] *s* gabardina
**gabble** [ˈgæbəl] *s* cotorreo, parloteo; *vn* cotorrear, parlotear
**gabbler** [ˈgæblər] *s* picotero
**gaberdine** [ˈgæbərdin] *s* var. de **gabardine**
**gabion** [ˈgebɪən] *s* (fort. & hyd.) gavión
**gable** [ˈgebəl] *s* aguilón (*del tejado*); gablete, frontón (*encima de puertas o ventanas*)
**gable end** *s* hastial
**gable roof** *s* tejado de caballete, tejado de dos aguas
**gable wall** *s* pared de caballete
**Gabriel** [ˈgebrɪəl] *s* Gabriel
**gaby** [ˈgebɪ] *s* (*pl:* **-bies**) (coll.) tonto, necio
**gad** [gæd] *s* aguijada, aguijón; *interj* (archaic) ¡ pardiez!; (*pret & pp:* **gadded;** *ger:* **gadding**) *vn* callejear, andar de aquí para allá
**gadabout** [ˈgædəˌbaut] *adj* callejero; *s* cirigallo; hombre placero
**gadfly** [ˈgædˌflaɪ] *s* (*pl:* **-flies**) (ent.) tábano
**gadget** [ˈgædʒɪt] *s* (coll.) adminículo, chisme, dispositivo ingenioso
**gadid** [ˈgædɪd] *s* (ichth.) gádido
**gadolinium** [ˌgædəˈlɪnɪəm] *s* (chem.) gadolinio
**Gaea** [ˈdʒiə] *s* (myth.) Gea
**Gael** [gel] *s* gaélico (*natural o habitante celta*)
**Gaelic** [ˈgelɪk] *adj* gaélico; *s* gaélico (*idioma*)
**gaff** [gæf] *s* arpón, garfio; espolón de acero con que se calza a los gallos de pelea; (naut.) cangrejo; **to blow the gaff** (slang) revelar el secreto; **to stand the gaff** (slang) tener mucha resistencia; *va* arponear
**gaffer** [ˈgæfər] *s* vejestorio
**gafftopsail** [ˌgæfˈtɑpsəl] o [ˌgæfˈtɑpˌsel] *s* (naut.) escandalosa
**gag** [gæg] *s* mordaza; mordaza dental; (fig.) mordaza; (slang) morcilla (*añadidura que mete un actor en su papel*); (slang) chiste, payasada; (*pret & pp:* **gagged;** *ger:* **gagging**) *va* amordazar; dar bascas a; (fig.) amordazar; *vn* sentir bascas, arquear
**gage** [gedʒ] *s* gaje (*de desafío*); desafío; prenda; *va* (archaic) apostar, dar en prenda; *s & va* var. de **gauge**
**gaiety** [ˈgeɪtɪ] *s* (*pl:* **-ties**) alegría, regocijo; diversión alegre; galas
**Gaillard Cut** [ˈgelɑrd] o [gɪlˈjɑrd] *s* corte de Gaillard
**gaily** [ˈgelɪ] *adv* alegremente; vistosamente
**gain** [gen] *s* ganancia; aumento; (carp.) gárgol, ranura; (elec.) ganancia; **gains** *spl* ganancias; *va* ganar; conquistar; alcanzar; adelantarse (*p.ej., cinco minutos un reloj*); **to gain over** conquistar; *vn* ir en progreso; ganar terreno; mejorar (*un enfermo*); **to gain on** ir alcanzando
**gainer** [ˈgenər] *s* ganancioso; zambullida para cuya ejecución hay que colocarse de espaldas al agua y dar un salto mortal en el aire
**gainful** [ˈgenfəl] *adj* ganancioso
**gainsaid** [ˌgenˈsɛd] *pret & pp de* **gainsay**
**gainsay** [ˌgenˈse] (*pret & pp:* **-said** o **-sayed**) *va* contradecir, negar
**gainst** o **'gainst** [gɛnst] o [genst] *prep* (poet.) var. de **against**
**gait** [get] *s* paso, manera de andar; **at a good gait** a buen paso
**gaiter** [ˈgetər] *s* polaina corta; botina con elásticos por los lados
**gal.** abr. de **gallon** o **gallons**
**Gal.** abr. de **Galatians**
**gala** [ˈgelə] o [ˈgælə] *s* fiesta; *adj* de gala, de fiesta
**galactagogue** [gəˈlæktəgɑg] *adj & s* (med. & vet.) galactagogo
**galactic** [gəˈlæktɪk] *adj* lácteo; (astr.) galáctico
**galactite** [gəˈlæktaɪt] *s* (mineral.) galactita
**galactometer** [ˌgælækˈtɑmɪtər] *s* galactómetro
**galactose** [gəˈlæktos] *s* (chem.) galactosa
**Galahad** [ˈgæləhæd] *s* Galaad; (fig.) hombre de costumbres muy puras
**galantine** [ˈgæləntin] *s* (cook.) galantina
**Galápagos Islands** [gəˈlɑpəgos] *s* islas de (los) Galápagos
**Galatea** [ˌgæləˈtiə] *s* (myth.) Galatea
**Galatia** [gəˈleʃə] *s* Galacia
**Galatian** [gəˈleʃən] *adj & s* gálata; **Galatians** *spl* (Bib.) Epístola de San Pablo a los Gálatas
**galaxy** [ˈgæləksɪ] *s* (*pl:* **-ies**) (astr.) galaxia; grupo o reunión brillante (*de artistas, cortesanos, etc.*)
**galbanum** [ˈgælbənəm] *s* gálbano
**galbulus** [ˈgælbjələs] *s* (*pl:* **-li** [laɪ]) (bot.) gálbula
**gale** [gel] *s* ventarrón, viento muy fuerte; (coll.) explosión (*de risas*); (poet.) brisa; (bot.) mirto de Brabante; **to weather the gale** correr el temporal; (fig.) ir tirando
**Galen** [ˈgelən] *s* Galeno; (fig.) Galeno (*médico*)
**galena** [gəˈlinə] o **galenite** [gəˈlinaɪt] *s* (mineral.) galena
**Galenic** [geˈlɛnɪk] o [geˈlinɪk] *adj* galénico
**Galenism** [ˈgelɪnɪzəm] *s* galenismo
**Galicia** [gəˈlɪʃə] *s* Galicia (*de Polonia y de España*)
**Galician** [gəˈlɪʃən] *adj & s* gallego (*de España*); galiciano (*de Polonia y de España*)
**Galilean** [ˌgælɪˈliən] *adj* galileo; (phys.) de Galileo; *s* galileo; **the Galilean** el Galileo (*Jesucristo*)
**Galilee** [ˈgælɪli] *s* Galilea; (*l.c.*) *s* galilea (*pórtico*)
**galiot** [ˈgælɪət] *s* (naut.) galeota
**galipot** [ˈgælɪpɑt] *s* galipodio (*oleorresina*)
**gall** [gɔl] *s* bilis, hiel; (anat.) vejiga de la bilis, vesícula biliar; (bot.) agalla; hiel (*cosa muy amarga*); rencor, odio; rozadura, matadura; (slang) descaro; *va* lastimar rozando, hacer un desollón o desollones en; irritar, molestar grandemente; *vn* raerse
**gallant** [ˈgælənt] o [gəˈlænt] *adj* galante (*atento con las damas*); amoroso; [ˈgælənt] *adj* gallardo, valiente, noble; hazañoso; imponente; festivo, vistoso; *s* hombre valiente; galán; galanteador
**gallantry** [ˈgæləntrɪ] *s* (*pl:* **-ries**) gallardía, valor, nobleza; galantería (*para con las damas*); galanteo; (archaic) lujo, ostentación
**gall bladder** *s* (anat.) vejiga de la bilis, vesícula biliar
**galleass** [ˈgælɪæs] *s* (naut.) galeaza
**galleon** [ˈgælɪən] *s* (naut.) galeón
**gallery** [ˈgælərɪ] *s* (*pl:* **-ies**) galería; tribuna (*en las iglesias, etc.*); galería fotográfica; galería de tiro; conjunto de espectadores; (fort. min., naut. & theat.) galería; **to play to the gallery** (coll.) hablar para la galería
**galley** [ˈgælɪ] *s* (naut. & print.) galera; (naut.) fogón
**galley proof** *s* (print.) galerada, pruebas de segundas
**galley slave** *s* galeote; (fig.) esclavo del trabajo
**gallfly** [ˈgɔlˌflaɪ] *s* (*pl:* **-flies**) (ent.) cinípido
**galliard** [ˈgæljərd] *s* gallarda (*danza*)

**Gallic** [ˈgælɪk] *adj* gálico, galo; (*l.c.*) *adj* (chem.) gálico
**gallic acid** *s* (chem.) ácido gálico
**Gallican** [ˈgælɪkən] *adj* (eccl.) galicano
**Gallicanism** [ˈgælɪkənɪzəm] *s* galicanismo
**Gallicism** [ˈgælɪsɪzəm] *s* galicismo
**Gallicize** [ˈgælɪsaɪz] *va* afrancesar; *vn* afrancesarse
**galligaskins** [ˌgælɪˈgæskɪnz] *spl* calzacalzón; polainas
**gallinaceous** [ˌgælɪˈneʃəs] *adj* (orn.) gallináceo
**galling** [ˈgɔlɪŋ] *adj* irritante, ofensivo
**gallinule** [ˈgælɪnjul] o [ˈgælɪnul] *s* (orn.) polla
**gallipot** [ˈgælɪpɑt] *s* galipodio (*oleorresina*); orza (*vasija*); (coll.) boticario
**gallium** [ˈgælɪəm] *s* (chem.) galio
**gallivant** [ˈgælɪvænt] *vn* andar a placer de aquí para allá
**gallnut** [ˈgɔlˌnʌt] *s* (bot.) agalla
**gall oak** *s* (bot.) cajiga o quejigo
**Gallomania** [ˌgæloˈmenɪə] *s* galomanía
**gallon** [ˈgælən] *s* galón (*medida*)
**galloon** [gəˈlun] *s* galón (*cinta estrecha*)
**gallop** [ˈgæləp] *s* galope; paseo a galope; *va* hacer ir a galope; *vn* galopar; **to gallop through** hacer muy aprisa
**galloping** [ˈgæləpɪŋ] *adj* galopante
**galloping consumption** *s* (path.) tisis galopante
**Gallo-Roman** [ˌgæloˈromən] *adj* galorromano
**gallows** [ˈgæloz] *s* (*pl:* **-lowses** o **-lows**) horca; pena de muerte en la horca; (min.) castillete de mina
**gallows bird** *s* (coll.) carne de horca
**gallstone** [ˈgɔlˌston] *s* cálculo biliario
**gall wasp** *s* var. de **gallfly**
**galop** [ˈgæləp] *s* galopa (*baile*); *vn* galopar (*bailar la galopa*)
**galore** [gəˈlor] *adv* en abundancia
**galosh** [gəˈlɑʃ] *s* chanclo alto de goma o de tela engomada
**gals.** abr. de **gallons**
**galvanic** [gælˈvænɪk] *adj* galvánico; sorprendente
**galvanism** [ˈgælvənɪzəm] *s* galvanismo
**galvanization** [ˌgælvənɪˈzeʃən] *s* galvanización
**galvanize** [ˈgælvənaɪz] *va* galvanizar; (fig.) galvanizar
**galvanized iron** *s* hierro galvanizado
**galvanocautery** [ˌgælvanoˈkɔtərɪ] o [gælˌvænoˈkɔtərɪ] *s* (*pl:* **-ies**) (med.) galvanocauterio
**galvanometer** [ˌgælvəˈnɑmɪtər] *s* galvanómetro
**galvanometric** [ˌgælvənəˈmɛtrɪk] o [gælˌvænəˈmɛtrɪk] *adj* galvanométrico
**galvanometry** [ˌgælvəˈnɑmɪtrɪ] *s* galvanometría
**galvanoplastic** [ˌgælvanoˈplæstɪk] o [gælˌvænoˈplæstɪk] *adj* galvanoplástico; **galvanoplastics** *ssg* galvanoplástica
**galvanoplasty** [ˌgælvanoˈplæstɪ] o [gælˌvænoˈplæstɪ] *s* galvanoplastia
**galvanoscope** [ˈgælvanoˌskop] o [gælˈvænəskop] *s* galvanoscopio
**galvanotropism** [ˌgælvəˈnɑtrəpɪzəm] *s* (biol.) galvanotropismo
**gama grass** [ˈgɑmə] *s* (bot.) maicillo
**gambier** [ˈgæmbɪr] *s* (pharm.) gambir
**gambit** [ˈgæmbɪt] *s* gambito
**gamble** [ˈgæmbəl] *s* (coll.) juego, empresa arriesgada, cosa incierta; *va* jugar, aventurar en el juego; **to gamble away** perder en el juego; *vn* jugar; especular, aventurarse mucho (*p.ej., en las operaciones de bolsa*)
**gambler** [ˈgæmblər] *s* jugador; tahúr, garitero
**gambling** [ˈgæmblɪŋ] *s* juego (*por dinero*)
**gambling house** *s* casa de juego
**gambling machine** *s* máquina de apostar, sacaperras
**gambling table** *s* mesa de juego
**gamboge** [gæmˈbuʒ] o [gæmˈbodʒ] *s* gomaguta, resina de Camboya
**gambol** [ˈgæmbəl] *s* cabriola, retozo; (*pret & pp:* **-boled** o **-bolled;** *ger:* **-boling** o **-bolling**) *vn* cabriolar, retozar
**gambrel** [ˈgæmbrəl] *s* corvejón (*de caballo*); caballete de suspensión (*de los mataderos*); (arch.) techo a la holandesa
**gambrel roof** *s* (arch.) techo a la holandesa
**game** [gem] *s* juego; partida (*de juego*); tantos (*de una partida en cualquier momento*); deporte; caza; (bridge) manga; (sport) juego (*cierto número de tantos ganados*); (fig.) juego (*p.ej., de la diplomacia*); (fig.) jugada (*estratagema, treta*); (fig.) asunto, actividad; **the game is up** hemos perdido el juego, estamos frescos; **to be out of the game** estar inútil para el juego; **to make game of** burlarse de; **to play a good game** jugar muy bien, ser muy diestro; **to play the game** jugar limpio, proceder lealmente; *adj* de caza; animoso, bravo, peleón; (coll.) cojo (*dícese de la pierna*); *va* perder en el juego; *vn* jugar por dinero
**game bag** *s* morral
**game bird** *s* ave de caza
**gamecock** [ˈgemˌkɑk] *s* gallo de combate, de pelea o de riña
**game fish** *s* pez animoso y muy estimado de los pescadores deportivos
**game fowl** *s* gallo o gallina de la raza de los gallos de riña
**gamekeeper** [ˈgemˌkipər] *s* guardabosque
**game law** *s* ley que regula la caza y la pesca
**game of chance** *s* juego de azar, juego de suerte
**game preserve** *s* vedado, vedado de caza, coto
**gamesome** [ˈgemsəm] *adj* juguetón, retozón
**gamester** [ˈgemstər] *s* jugador; tahúr, garitero
**gametangium** [ˌgæmɪˈtændʒɪəm] *s* (*pl:* **-a** [ə]) (bot.) gametangio
**gamete** [ˈgæmit] o [gəˈmit] *s* (biol.) gameto
**gametogenesis** [ˌgæmɪtoˈdʒɛnɪsɪs] *s* (biol.) gametogénesis
**gametophyte** [gəˈmitəfaɪt] *s* (bot.) gametofita
**game warden** *s* guardabosque
**gaming** [ˈgemɪŋ] *s* juego (*por dinero*)
**gaming house** *s* casa de juego
**gaming table** *s* mesa de juego
**gamma** [ˈgæmə] *s* gama
**gammadion** [gəˈmedɪɑn] *s* (*pl:* **-a** [ə]) cruz gamada
**gamma globulin** *s* (physiol.) globulina gama
**gamma rays** *spl* (phys.) rayos gama
**gammer** [ˈgæmər] *s* abuelita, vieja
**gammon** [ˈgæmən] *s* extremo inferior de una lonja de tocino; jamón; (coll.) tejido de falsedades
**gamogenesis** [ˌgæmoˈdʒɛnɪsɪs] *s* (biol.) gamogénesis
**gamopetalous** [ˌgæmoˈpɛtələs] *adj* (bot.) gamopétalo
**gamophyllous** [ˌgæmoˈfɪləs] *adj* (bot.) gamofilo
**gamosepalous** [ˌgæmoˈsɛpələs] *adj* (bot.) gamosépalo
**gamp** [gæmp] *s* gran paraguas
**gamut** [ˈgæmət] *s* (mus. & fig.) gama
**gamy** [ˈgemɪ] *adj* (*comp:* **-ier;** *super:* **-iest**) salvajino; animoso, bravo, peleón
**gan** o **'gan** [gæn] *pret de* **gin** [gɪn]
**gander** [ˈgændər] *s* ganso
**gang** [gæŋ] *s* pandilla (*de pistoleros*); cuadrilla, brigada (*de braceros*); juego (*de herramientas o máquinas*); *adj* múltiple; *vn* apandillar; acuadrillarse, agavillarse; (Scotch) ir, caminar; **to gang up against** conspirar contra; atacar en cuadrilla
**gang condenser** *s* (rad.) condensador múltiple
**gangling** [ˈgæŋglɪŋ] *adj* larguirucho, larguirucho y desgarbado
**ganglion** [ˈgæŋglɪən] *s* (*pl:* **-a** [ə] o **-ons**) (anat. & path.) ganglio; (fig.) centro de actividad
**ganglionic** [ˌgæŋglɪˈɑnɪk] *adj* ganglionar
**gangly** [ˈgæŋglɪ] *adj* (coll.) var. de **gangling**
**gangplank** [ˈgæŋˌplæŋk] *s* plancha, pasarela
**gang plow** *s* arado de reja múltiple
**gangrene** [ˈgæŋgrin] *s* (path.) gangrena; *va* gangrenar; *vn* gangrenarse
**gangrenous** [ˈgæŋgrɪnəs] *adj* gangrenoso
**gangster** [ˈgæŋstər] *s* (coll.) pandillero, pistolero
**gangsterism** [ˈgæŋstərɪzəm] *s* (coll.) bandolerismo, pistolerismo, gangsterismo
**gangue** [gæŋ] *s* (min.) ganga
**gang warfare** *s* lucha entre pandillas
**gangway** [ˈgæŋˌwe] *s* (naut.) portalón (*abertura en el costado del buque*); plancha, pa-

sarela; *interj* ¡afuera!, ¡abran paso!, ¡paso libre!

**gannet** [ˈgænɪt] *s* (orn.) alcatraz, planga

**ganoid** [ˈgænɔɪd] *adj & s* (ichth.) ganoideo

**gantlet** [ˈgɑntlɪt] *s* (rail.) vía traslapada, vía de garganta; var. de **gauntlet**

**gantry** [ˈgæntrɪ] *s* (*pl:* **-tries**) caballete, poíno; puente transversal de grúa corrediza; (rail.) puente transversal de señales

**gantry crane** *s* grúa de caballete

**Ganymede** [ˈgænɪmid] *s* (myth.) Ganimedes

**gaol** [dʒel] *s* (Brit.) var. de **jail**

**gaoler** [ˈdʒelər] *s* (Brit.) var. de **jailer**

**gap** [gæp] *s* boquete (*p.ej., en una pared*); laguna (*claro, interrupción*); garganta, quebrada; (aer.) entreplanos; (fig.) sima (*entre dos puntos de vista*); (*pret & pp:* **gapped**; *ger:* **gapping**) *va* hacer brecha en; hacer muesca en

**gape** [gep] o [gæp] *s* abertura, brecha; bostezo; mirada de asombro (*con la boca abierta*); **the gapes** necesidad imperiosa de estar bostezando; enfermedad de las gallinas causada por el gusano rojo; *vn* abrirse mucho; bostezar; embobarse; **to gape at** embobarse de, con o en; **to stand gaping** embobarse

**gapeworm** [ˈgepˌwʌrm] o [ˈgæpˌwʌrm] *s* (zool.) gusano rojo

**G.A.R.** abr. de **Grand Army of the Republic**

**gar** [gɑr] *s* var. de **garfish**

**garage** [gəˈrɑʒ] *s* garage; *va* dejar en garage

**garb** [gɑrb] *s* traje, vestidura; apariencia, aspecto; *va* vestir

**garbage** [ˈgɑrbɪdʒ] *s* bazofia, basuras, desperdicios

**garbage can** *s* cubo para basuras, bote de basura

**garbage collector** *s* basurero, recogedor de bazofia, colector de basuras

**garbage disposal** *s* evacuación de basuras, remoción de basuras

**garbage truck** *s* camión basurero

**garble** [ˈgɑrbəl] *va* mutilar engañosamente (*un texto, discurso, etc.*); entresacar engañosamente (*hechos, cifras de la estadística, etc.*)

**garboard** [ˈgɑrˌbord] *s* (naut.) aparadura

**garden** [ˈgɑrdən] *s* huerto (*de hortalizas*); jardín (*de flores y plantas ornamentales*); sitio de recreo; sitio deleitoso; región fértil y cultivada; *adj* de huerto; de jardín; común, ordinario; *va* cultivar (*un terreno*) para producir hortalizas o flores; *vn* cultivar huertos o jardines

**garden balm** *s* (bot.) melisa, toronjil

**garden balsam** *s* (bot.) balsamina de jardín; (bot.) trébol oloroso

**garden city** *s* ciudad jardín

**gardener** [ˈgɑrdnər] *s* hortelano; jardinero

**gardenia** [gɑrˈdinɪə] *s* (bot.) gardenia

**gardening** [ˈgɑrdnɪŋ] *s* horticultura; jardinería

**Garden of Eden** *s* (Bib.) jardín del Edén

**garden party** *s* fiesta que se da en un jardín o parque

**garden pink** *s* (bot.) clavel coronado o clavellina de pluma

**garden rocket** *s* (bot.) juliana; (bot.) roqueta, ruca

**garden warbler** *s* (orn.) andahuertas

**garfish** [ˈgɑrˌfɪʃ] *s* (ichth.) aguja de mar, pez aguja; (ichth.) pez caimán

**garganey** [ˈgɑrgənɪ] *s* (orn.) cerceta

**Gargantuan** [gɑrˈgæntʃuən] *adj* enorme, gigantesco

**garget** [ˈgɑrgɪt] *s* (vet.) inflamación de la cabeza o la garganta del ganado; (vet.) inflamación de la ubre de las vacas; (bot.) hierba carmín

**gargle** [ˈgɑrgəl] *s* gargarismo (*líquido*); *va* enjuagarse (*la boca o la garganta*); *vn* gargarizar

**gargling** [ˈgɑrglɪŋ] *s* gárgara, gargarismo

**gargoyle** [ˈgɑrgɔɪl] *s* (arch.) gárgola

**garish** [ˈgɛrɪʃ] *adj* charro, chillón, deslumbrante

**garland** [ˈgɑrlənd] *s* guirnalda; (naut.) roñada; *va* enguirnaldar

**garlic** [ˈgɑrlɪk] *s* (bot.) ajo; ajos (*que se usan como condimento*)

**garlicky** [ˈgɑrlɪkɪ] *adj* cepáceo, aliáceo

**garlic mustard** *s* (bot.) aliaria

**garment** [ˈgɑrmənt] *s* prenda, prenda de vestir; *va* vestir

**garner** [ˈgɑrnər] *s* troj, granero; acopio, provisión; *va* entrojar; acopiar

**garnet** [ˈgɑrnɪt] *s* granate (*piedra y color*); *adj* granate

**garnish** [ˈgɑrnɪʃ] *s* adorno; (cook.) condimento de adorno; *va* adornar; (cook.) adornar (*p.ej., con perejil*); (law) notificar; (law) embargar

**garnishee** [ˌgɑrnɪˈʃi] *s* (law) persona que ha sido notificada de un entredicho; *va* (law) notificar de un entredicho; (law) embargar

**garnishment** [ˈgɑrnɪʃmənt] *s* adorno; (law) entredicho; (law) embargo de crédito; (law) emplazamiento

**garniture** [ˈgɑrnɪtʃər] *s* adorno, embellecimiento, guarnición

**Garonne** [gɑˈrɑn] *s* Garona

**garotte** [gəˈrɑt] *s & va* var. de **garrote**

**garret** [ˈgærɪt] *s* desván, buhardilla

**garrison** [ˈgærɪsən] *s* (mil.) guarnición; plaza fuerte; *va* guarnecer, guarnicionar; poner (*la tropa*) en guarnición

**garrot** [ˈgærət] *s* (orn.) clángula

**garrote** [gəˈrɑt] o [gəˈrot] o **garrotte** [gəˈrɑt] *s* estrangulación (*con robo*); garrote (*forma de ejecución de la pena de muerte; aro de hierro que sirve para tal ejecución*); *va* estrangular; estrangular para robar; agarrotar, dar garrote a

**garrulity** [gəˈrulɪtɪ] *s* garrulidad

**garrulous** [ˈgærələs] o [ˈgærjələs] *adj* gárrulo

**garter** [ˈgɑrtər] *s* liga; (*cap.*) *s* Jarretera (*orden; insignia de la orden*); *va* atar con liga

**garter snake** *s* (zool.) culebrita no venenosa (*Thamnophis*); (zool.) serpiente de coral

**garter stitch** *s* punto de media

**garth** [gɑrθ] *s* patio de claustro

**gas** [gæs] *s* gas; (coll.) gasolina; (slang) parloteo; **to cut off the gas** (aut.) cerrar el carburador; (*pret & pp:* **gassed**; *ger:* **gassing**) *va* abastecer o proveer de gas; gasear (*atacar, envenenar o asfixiar con gas*); (chem.) gasear; (coll.) abastecer o proveer de gasolina; *vn* despedir gas; (slang) parlotear

**gas attack** *s* ataque con gases

**gasbag** [ˈgæsˌbæg] *s* (aer.) cámara de gas; (slang) charlatán

**gas burner** *s* mechero de gas

**gas chamber** *s* cámara de gases

**Gascon** [ˈgæskən] *adj & s* gascón; (*l.c.*) *s* fanfarrón

**gasconade** [ˌgæskəˈned] *s* gasconada; *vn* fanfarronear

**Gasconism** [ˈgæskənɪzəm] *s* gasconismo

**Gascony** [ˈgæskənɪ] *s* Gascuña

**gas engine** *s* motor de gas

**gaseous** [ˈgæsɪəs] *adj* gaseoso

**gas fitter** *s* gasista

**gas fittings** *spl* cañerías, mecheros y accesorios de gas

**gas fixtures** *spl* guarniciones de gas

**gas generator** *s* gasógeno

**gash** [gæʃ] *s* cuchillada, chirlo; *va* acuchillar, herir con arma blanca

**gas heat** *s* calefacción por gas

**gasholder** [ˈgæsˌholdər] *s* gasómetro

**gasification** [ˌgæsɪfɪˈkeʃən] *s* gasificación

**gasiform** [ˈgæsɪfɔrm] *adj* gasiforme

**gasify** [ˈgæsɪfaɪ] (*pret & pp:* **-fied**) *va* gasificar; *vn* gasificarse

**gas jet** *s* mechero de gas; llama de mechero de gas

**gasket** [ˈgæskɪt] *s* junta, empaquetadura; (naut.) tomador

**gaslight** [ˈgæsˌlaɪt] *s* mechero de gas; luz de gas

**gas main** *s* cañería de gas, cañería maestra de gas

**gas mantle** *s* manguito de incandescencia, camiseta

**gas mask** *s* mascarilla contra gases asfixiantes, máscara contra gases, careta antigás

**gas meter** *s* contador de gas

**gasolene** o **gasoline** [ˈgæsəlin] o [ˌgæsəˈlin] *s* gasoleno o gasolina

**gasoline pump** *s* surtidor de gasolina, poste distribuidor de gasolina

**gasometer** [gæsˈɑmɪtər] *s* gasómetro

**gasp** [gæsp] o [gɑsp] *s* anhelo; grito sofocado; **at the last gasp** a punto de echar el último suspiro; *va* pronunciar con sonidos sofocados;

*vn* anhelar, sofocarse, boquear, abrir la boca de asombro
**gas pipe** *s* tubo de conducción de gas, tubería de gas
**gas producer** *s* gasógeno
**gas range** *s* cocina a gas
**gas shell** *s* (mil.) granada de gas
**gas station** *s* estación gasolinera
**gas stove** *s* cocina a gas
**gassy** [ˈgæsɪ] *adj* (*comp:* **-sier;** *super:* **-siest**) gaseoso; (coll.) hinchado
**gas tank** *s* gasómetro (municipal); (aut.) depósito de gasolina
**gas-tank cap** [ˈgæs,tæŋk] *s* (aut.) tapón de llenado
**gastight** [ˈgæs,taɪt] *adj* hermético, a prueba de gas
**gastralgia** [gæsˈtrældʒɪə] *s* (path.) gastralgia
**gastrectomy** [gæsˈtrɛktəmɪ] *s* (*pl:* **-mies**) (surg.) gastrectomía
**gastric** [ˈgæstrɪk] *adj* gástrico
**gastric juice** *s* (physiol.) jugo gástrico
**gastric ulcer** *s* (path.) úlcera gástrica
**gastritis** [gæsˈtraɪtɪs] *s* (path.) gastritis
**gastroenteritis** [,gæstro,ɛntəˈraɪtɪs] *s* (path.) gastroenteritis
**gastroenterology** [,gæstro,ɛntəˈrɑlədʒɪ] *s* gastroenterología
**gastrointestinal** [,gæstro·ɪnˈtɛstɪnəl] *adj* gastrointestinal
**gastronome** [ˈgæstrənom] o **gastronomer** [gæsˈtrɑnəmər] *s* gastrónomo
**gastronomic** [,gæstrəˈnɑmɪk] o **gastronomical** [,gæstrəˈnɑmɪkəl] *adj* gastronómico
**gastronomy** [gæsˈtrɑnəmɪ] *s* gastronomía
**gastropod** [ˈgæstrəpɑd] *adj & s* (zool.) gastrópodo
**gastrovascular** [,gæstroˈvæskjələr] *adj* gastrovascular
**gastrula** [ˈgæstrʊlə] *s* (*pl:* **-lae** [li]) (embryol.) gástrula
**gas turbine** *s* turbina de gas
**gasworker** [ˈgæs,wʌrkər] *s* gasista
**gasworks** [ˈgæs,wʌrks] *ssg o spl* fábrica de gas
**gat** [gæt] *s* (slang) arma de fuego, revólver
**gate** [get] *s* puerta (*de cercado*); portillo; (hyd.) compuerta; (rail.) barrera; entrada, taquilla, entrada de taquilla (*número de personas que asisten a un espectáculo y cantidad de dinero que pagan*); (fig.) entrada, camino, vía; **to crash the gate** (slang) colarse de gorra
**gatecrasher** [ˈget,kræʃər] *s* (slang) intruso (*persona que se cuela en alguna parte sin pagar la entrada o sin ser invitado*)
**gatekeeper** [ˈget,kipər] *s* portero; (rail.) guardabarrera
**gate-leg table** [ˈget,lɛg] o **gate-legged table** [ˈget,lɛgd] *s* mesa de hojas y patas plegadizas
**gate money** *s* entrada, taquilla (*dinero cobrado por las entradas a un espectáculo*)
**gatepost** [ˈget,post] *s* poste de una puerta de cercado
**gateway** [ˈget,we] *s* entrada, paso; (fig.) entrada, camino, vía
**gather** [ˈgæðər] *s* (sew.) frunce; *va* recoger, reunir; acumular; cosechar, recolectar; coger (*leña, flores, etc.*); calcular, deducir; cobrar (*fuerzas*); cubrirse de, llenarse de (*polvo*); recoger (*una persona sus pensamientos*); (sew.) fruncir; (b.b.) alzar; **to be gathered to one's fathers** morir y ser enterrado; **to gather speed** ir cada vez más rápidamente; **to gather up** recoger; *vn* reunirse; acumularse; condensarse; formar pus; amontonarse (*p.ej., nubes*); saltar (*p.ej., lágrimas*); **to gather oneself together** componerse, tranquilizarse y cobrar fuerzas
**gathering** [ˈgæðərɪŋ] *s* reunión; acumulación; recolección; hacinamiento; (path.) divieso, grano; (b.b.) alzado; (sew.) frunce
**Gatun Lake** [gɑˈtun] *s* lago de Gatún
**gauche** [goʃ] *adj* torpe; falto de tino
**gaucherie** [,goʃəˈri] *s* torpeza; falta de tino
**Gaucho** [ˈgaʊtʃo] *adj* gaucho, gauchesco; *s* (*pl:* **-chos**) gaucho
**gaud** [gɔd] *s* dije, adorno cursi
**gaudy** [ˈgɔdɪ] *adj* (*comp:* **-ier;** *super:* **-iest**) chillón, llamativo, vistoso, cursi
**gauge** [gedʒ] *s* norma de medida; calibre, calibrador; indicador, manómetro, nivel; plantilla; gramil (*de carpintero*); tamaño; capacidad; medidor (*p.ej., de gasolina*); (constr.) porción de tejas, tablas de ripia, etc., que queda expuesta al aire; (rail.) ancho de vía, entrevía; *va* medir; calibrar; graduar; comprobar; aforar, apreciar; (hyd.) aforar, (naut.) arquear
**gauge cock** *s* grifo del indicador, llave de prueba
**gauge glass** *s* tubo indicador, vidrio de nivel
**Gaul** [gɔl] *s* la Galia; galo (*natural*)
**Gaulish** [ˈgɔlɪʃ] *s* galo (*idioma*)
**gaultheria** [gɔlˈθɪrɪə] *s* (bot.) gaulteria
**gaunt** [gɔnt] o [gɑnt] *adj* desvaído, demacrado; triste, sombrío
**gauntlet** [ˈgɔntlɪt] o [ˈgɑntlɪt] *s* guantelete; guante con puño abocinado; puño abocinado; (surg.) guantelete; (mil. & fig.) carrera de baquetas; **to run the gauntlet** (mil. & fig.) correr baquetas o pasar por baquetas; **to take up the gauntlet** recoger el guante; **to throw down the gauntlet** arrojar el guante
**gauntleted** [ˈgɔntlɪtɪd] o [ˈgɑntlɪtɪd] *adj* enguantado con guantelete o con guante
**gauss** [gaʊs] *s* (phys.) gausio
**gauze** [gɔz] *s* gasa, cendal
**gauzy** [ˈgɔzɪ] *adj* (*comp:* **-ier;** *super:* **-iest**) diáfano, sutilísimo
**gavage** [gəˈvɑʒ] *s* gavaje
**gave** [gev] *pret de* **give**
**gavel** [ˈgævəl] *s* mazo o martillo (*de los presidentes de asambleas, etc.*)
**gavial** [ˈgevɪəl] *s* (zool.) gavial
**gavotte** [gəˈvɑt] *s* gavota (*danza y música*)
**Gawain** [ˈgɑwɪn] o [ˈgɔwɪn] *s* Galván (*de la Mesa Redonda y el Amadís de Gaula*)
**gawk** [gɔk] *s* (coll.) palurdo, papanatas; *vn* (coll.) mirar de modo impertinente; (coll.) papar moscas
**gawky** [ˈgɔkɪ] *adj* (*comp:* **-ier;** *super:* **-iest**) torpe, desgarbado, bobo
**gay** [ge] *adj* alegre, festivo; amigo de los placeres, ligero de cascos; vistoso
**gayety** [ˈgeɪtɪ] *s* (*pl:* **-ties**) var. de **gaiety**
**gay science** *s* gaya ciencia (*poesía amatoria*)
**gaz.** abr. de **gazette** y **gazetteer**
**gazabo** [gəˈzebo] *s* (*pl:* **-bos** o **-boes**) mirador (*balcón con cristales*); miranda; (slang) adefesio, mamarracho
**gaze** [gez] *s* mirada fija; *vn* mirar con fijeza
**gazebo** [gəˈzibo] *s* (*pl:* **-bos** o **-boes**) var. de **gazabo**
**gazehound** [ˈgez,haʊnd] *s* perro que sigue la caza con la vista
**gazelle** [gəˈzɛl] *s* (zool.) gacela
**gazette** [gəˈzɛt] *s* gaceta; *va* anunciar o publicar en gaceta
**gazetteer** [,gæzəˈtɪr] *s* gacetero; director de una gaceta oficial; diccionario geográfico
**G.B.** abr. de **Great Britain**
**g.c.d.** o **G.C.D.** abr. de **greatest common divisor**
**g.c.m.** o **G.C.M.** abr. de **greatest common measure**
**gear** [gɪr] *s* arneses, pertrechos, utensilios; aparato, mecanismo (*de transmisión, de gobierno, etc.*); engranaje, rueda dentada; **out of gear** desengranado; descompuesto; **to put in gear** o **to throw into gear** engranar; **to throw out of gear** desengranar; (fig.) trastornar; *va* pertrechar; engranar; *vn* engranar; funcionar (*los engranajes*); **to gear into** engranar con
**gearbox** [ˈgɪr,bɑks] *s* (mach.) caja de engranajes, cárter de engranajes; (aut.) caja de velocidades
**gear case** *s* (mach.) caja de engranajes, cárter de engranajes
**gear cutter** *s* talladora de engranajes
**gearing** [ˈgɪrɪŋ] *s* (mach.) engranaje, tren de engranajes
**gear ratio** *s* relación o razón de engranajes
**gearshift** [ˈgɪr,ʃɪft] *s* (aut.) cambio de marchas, cambio de velocidades, aparato de cambios
**gearshift lever** *s* (aut.) palanca de cambio
**gearwheel** [ˈgɪr,hwil] *s* (mach.) rueda dentada
**gecko** [ˈgɛko] *s* (*pl:* **-os** u **-oes**) (zool.) geco, salamanquesa
**gee** [dʒi] *interj* ¡caramba!; ¡a la derecha!; *va* arrear hacia la derecha; *vn* torcer o volver hacia la derecha

**geese** [gis] *pl de* **goose**
**Gehenna** [gɪˈhɛnə] *s* (Bib.) gehena
**Geiger counter** [ˈgaɪgər] *s* (phys.) contador de Geiger
**geisha** [ˈgeʃə] *s* (*pl:* **-sha** o **-shas**) geisha
**Geissler tube** [ˈgaɪslər] *s* (elec.) tubo de Geissler
**gel** [dʒɛl] *s* (chem. & phys.) gel; (*pret & pp:* **gelled;** *ger:* **gelling**) *vn* cuajarse en forma de gel
**gelatin** o **gelatine** [ˈdʒɛlətɪn] *s* gelatina
**gelatinous** [dʒɪˈlætɪnəs] *adj* gelatinoso
**gelation** [dʒɪˈleʃən] *s* gelación
**geld** [gɛld] (*pret & pp:* **gelded** o **gelt**) *va* castrar
**Gelderland** [ˈgɛldərlænd] *s* Güeldres
**gelding** [ˈgɛldɪŋ] *s* animal castrado
**gelid** [ˈdʒɛlɪd] *adj* gélido, helado, muy frío
**gelidity** [dʒəˈlɪdɪtɪ] *s* frío extremo
**gelsemium** [dʒɛlˈsimɪəm] *s* (pharm.) gelsemio
**gelt** [gɛlt] *pret & pp de* **geld**
**gem** [dʒɛm] *s* gema, piedra preciosa; (fig.) joya, preciosidad; (*pret & pp:* **gemmed;** *ger:* **gemming**) *va* adornar con piedras preciosas; tachonar (*p.ej., el cielo las estrellas*)
**gemellus** [dʒɪˈmɛləs] *s* (anat.) gemelo
**geminate** [ˈdʒɛmɪnet] *adj* geminado; *va* geminar; *vn* geminarse
**gemination** [ˌdʒɛmɪˈneʃən] *s* geminación; (phonet. & rhet.) geminación
**Gemini** [ˈdʒɛmɪnaɪ] *ssg* (astr.) Géminis o Gemelos (*constelación*); (astr.) Géminis (*signo del zodíaco*); *spl* (myth.) Cástor y Pólux
**gemma** [ˈdʒɛmə] *s* (*pl:* **-mae** [mi]) (bot. & zool.) yema
**gemmate** [ˈdʒɛmet] *adj* (bot.) gemífero; *vn* (bot.) gemificar
**gemmation** [dʒɛˈmeʃən] *s* (bot. & zool.) gemación
**gemmiferous** [dʒɛˈmɪfərəs] *adj* gemífero; (bot. & zool.) gemífero
**gemmiparous** [dʒɛˈmɪpərəs] *adj* (biol.) gemíparo
**gemmule** [ˈdʒɛmjul] *s* (bot., zool. & biol.) gémula
**gemsbok** [ˈgɛmzˌbɑk] *s* (zool.) antílope sudafricano (*Oryx gazella*)
**gen.** abr. de **gender, general, generic, genitive** y **genus**
**Gen.** abr. de **General** y **Genesis**
**gendarme** [ˈʒɑndɑrm] *s* gendarme
**gendarmerie** [ˌʒɑndɑrmˈri] *s* gendarmería
**gender** [ˈdʒɛndər] *s* (gram.) género; (coll.) sexo
**gene** [dʒin] *s* (biol.) gen; (*cap.*) *s* nombre abreviado de **Eugene**
**genealogical** [ˌdʒɛnɪəˈlɑdʒɪkəl] o [ˌdʒinɪəˈlɑdʒɪkəl] *adj* genealógico
**genealogical tree** *s* árbol genealógico
**genealogist** [ˌdʒɛnɪˈælədʒɪst] o [ˌdʒinɪˈælədʒɪst] *s* genealogista
**genealogy** [ˌdʒɛnɪˈælədʒɪ] o [ˌdʒinɪˈælədʒɪ] *s* (*pl:* **-gies**) genealogía
**general** [ˈdʒɛnərəl] *adj* general; *s* (mil.) general, oficial general; (mil.) capitán general (*grado supremo del generalato*); **in general** en general o por lo general; (*pret & pp:* **-aled** o **-alled;** *ger:* **-aling** o **-alling**) *va* mandar en calidad de general
**general anesthesia** *f* anestesia general
**General Assembly** *s* asamblea legislativa de ciertos estados de los EE.UU.; Asamblea General (*de las Naciones Unidas*)
**general average** *s* (naut.) avería gruesa
**General Court** *s* asamblea legislativa de los estados de Massachusetts y de Nuevo Hampshire, EE.UU.
**general delivery** *s* lista de correos
**general in chief** *s* (mil.) general en jefe
**generalissimo** [ˌdʒɛnərəˈlɪsɪmo] *s* (*pl:* **-mos**) generalísimo
**generality** [ˌdʒɛnəˈrælɪtɪ] *s* (*pl:* **-ties**) generalidad
**generalization** [ˌdʒɛnərəlɪˈzeʃən] *s* generalización
**generalize** [ˈdʒɛnərəlaɪz] *va & vn* generalizar
**generally** [ˈdʒɛnərəlɪ] *adv* generalmente
**general officer** *s* (mil.) oficial general
**General of the Army** *s* (mil.) capitán general de ejército
**general practitioner** *s* médico general
**general-purpose** [ˈdʒɛnərəlˈpʌrpəs] *adj* para toda clase de objetivos
**generalship** [ˈdʒɛnərəlˌʃɪp] *s* generalato; don de mando
**general staff** *s* (mil.) estado mayor general
**general store** *s* tienda de variedades
**generate** [ˈdʒɛnəret] *va* engendrar, generar; (geom.) engendrar; (elec.) generar
**generating station** *s* (elec.) central generadora, central de fuerza
**generating unit** *s* var. de **generator unit**
**generation** [ˌdʒɛnəˈreʃən] *s* generación
**generative** [ˈdʒɛnəˌretɪv] *adj* generativo
**generator** [ˈdʒɛnəˌretər] *s* generador; (elec.) generador (*dínamo*); (mach.) generador (*caldera de vapor*)
**generator unit** *s* (elec.) grupo electrógeno
**generatrix** [ˌdʒɛnəˈretrɪks] *s* (*pl:* **generatrices** [ˌdʒɛnərəˈtraɪsiz]) (elec. & geom.) generatriz
**generic** [dʒɪˈnɛrɪk] *adj* genérico
**generically** [dʒɪˈnɛrɪkəlɪ] *adv* genéricamente
**generosity** [ˌdʒɛnəˈrɑsɪtɪ] *s* (*pl:* **-ties**) generosidad
**generous** [ˈdʒɛnərəs] *adj* generoso; abundante, grande
**genesic** [dʒɪˈnɛsɪk] *adj* genésico
**genesis** [ˈdʒɛnɪsɪs] *s* (*pl:* **-ses** [siz]) génesis; (*cap.*) *s* (Bib.) el Génesis
**genet** [ˈdʒɛnɪt] *s* (zool.) jineta; jaca chica española
**genetic** [dʒɪˈnɛtɪk] *adj* genético; **genetics** *ssg* genética
**genetically** [dʒɪˈnɛtɪkəlɪ] *adv* genéticamente
**geneticist** [dʒɪˈnɛtɪsɪst] *s* genetista
**Geneva** [dʒɪˈnivə] *s* Ginebra
**Genevan** [dʒɪˈnivən] *adj & s* var. de **Genevese**
**Genevese** [ˌdʒɛnɪˈviz] *adj* ginebrés o ginebrino; calvinista; *s* (*pl:* **-vese**) ginebrés o ginebrino; calvinista
**Genevieve** [ˈdʒɛnəviv] *s* Genoveva
**genial** [ˈdʒinjəl] *adj* afable, complaciente; confortante, suave; (anat. & zool.) geniano
**geniality** [ˌdʒinɪˈælɪtɪ] *s* afabilidad, complacencia
**geniculate** [dʒɪˈnɪkjəlɪt] o [dʒɪˈnɪkjəlet] *adj* geniculado
**geniculation** [dʒɪˌnɪkjəˈleʃən] *s* geniculación
**genie** [ˈdʒinɪ] *s* var. de **jinn**
**genii** [ˈdʒinɪaɪ] *pl de* **genius**
**genipap** [ˈdʒɛnɪpæp] *s* (bot.) genipa
**genital** [ˈdʒɛnɪtəl] *adj* genital; **genitals** *spl* (anat.) genitales, órganos genitales
**genitive** [ˈdʒɛnɪtɪv] *adj & s* (gram.) genitivo
**genitourinary** [ˌdʒɛnɪtoˈjurɪˌnɛrɪ] *adj* génitourinario
**genius** [ˈdʒinjəs] o [ˈdʒinɪəs] *s* (*pl:* **geniuses**) genio (*fuerza creadora, don altísimo de invención; persona que lo posee*); (*pl:* **genii** [ˈdʒinɪaɪ]) genio (*espíritu tutelar; deidad pagana*)
**Genoa** [ˈdʒɛnoə] *s* Génova
**genocidal** [ˌdʒɛnəˈsaɪdəl] *adj* genocida
**genocide** [ˈdʒɛnəsaɪd] *s* genocidio (*acción*); genocida (*persona*)
**Genoese** [ˌdʒɛnoˈiz] *adj* genovés; *s* (*pl:* **-ese**) genovés
**genom** [ˈdʒɛnɑm] o **genome** [ˈdʒɛnom] *s* (biol.) genoma
**genotype** [ˈdʒɛnotaɪp] *s* (biol.) genotipo
**genre** [ˈʒɑnrə] *s* (f.a. & lit.) género; *adj* (f.a.) de género, p.ej., **genre painter** pintor de género
**gent.** o **Gent.** abr. de **gentleman** o **gentlemen**
**genteel** [dʒɛnˈtil] *adj* gentil, elegante; cortés, urbano; afectado, exquisito
**gentian** [ˈdʒɛnʃən] *s* (bot. & pharm.) genciana (*planta y raíz*)
**gentianaceous** [ˌdʒɛnʃɪəˈneʃəs] *adj* (bot.) gencianáceo
**gentian violet** *s* violeta de genciana
**gentile** o **Gentile** [ˈdʒɛntaɪl] *adj & s* no judío; cristiano; gentil (*pagano*); **gentile** [ˈdʒɛntɪl] o [ˈdʒɛntaɪl] *adj & s* (gram.) gentilicio
**gentility** [dʒɛnˈtɪlɪtɪ] *s* (*pl:* **-ties**) gentileza, cortesía; nobleza; **gentilities** *spl* exquisiteces
**gentle** [ˈdʒɛntəl] *adj* apacible, benévolo; suave, dulce, manso; noble, bien nacido; bueno, honrado; cortés, fino; ligero (*golpecito*); moderado, poco abrupto
**gentle breeze** *s* (naut.) viento flojo
**gentlefolk** [ˈdʒɛntəlˌfok] *s* gente bien nacida

**gentleman** ['dʒɛntəlmən] *s* (*pl:* **-men**) caballero, señor
**gentleman in waiting** *s* gentilhombre de cámara
**gentlemanly** ['dʒɛntəlmənlɪ] *adj* caballeroso
**gentleman of fortune** *s* caballero de industria
**gentleman of leisure** *s* señor que se da vida de marqués
**gentleman of the road** *s* salteador de caminos
**gentleman's agreement** *s* acuerdo verbal, pacto de caballeros
**gentleness** ['dʒɛntəlnɪs] *s* apacibilidad; suavidad, dulzura, mansedumbre; nobleza; cortesía; ligereza
**gentle sex** *s* bello sexo, sexo débil
**gentlewoman** ['dʒɛntəl,wʊmən] *s* (*pl:* **-women**) señora, dama; dama de honor
**gently** ['dʒɛntlɪ] *adv* suavemente, dulcemente, mansamente; poco a poco, despacio
**gentry** ['dʒɛntrɪ] *s* gente bien nacida; (Brit.) alta burguesía; (hum.) gente
**genuflect** ['dʒɛnjʊflɛkt] *vn* doblar las rodillas en señal de reverencia
**genuflection** o **genuflexion** [,dʒɛnjʊ'flɛkʃən] *s* genuflexión
**genuine** ['dʒɛnjʊɪn] *adj* genuino, legítimo; franco, sincero
**genuineness** ['dʒɛnjʊɪnnɪs] *s* autenticidad; sinceridad
**genus** ['dʒinəs] *s* (*pl:* **genera** ['dʒɛnərə] o **genuses**) (biol. & log.) género
**Geo.** abr. de **George**
**geocentric** [,dʒio'sɛntrɪk] o **geocentrical** [,dʒio'sɛntrɪkəl] *adj* geocéntrico
**geochemistry** [,dʒio'kɛmɪstrɪ] *s* geoquímica
**geode** ['dʒiod] *s* (geol.) geoda
**geodesic** [,dʒio'dɛsɪk] *adj* geodésico
**geodesic line** *s* (math.) línea geodésica
**geodesist** [dʒɪ'ɑdɪsɪst] *s* geodesta
**geodesy** [dʒɪ'ɑdɪsɪ] *s* geodesia
**geodetic** [,dʒio'dɛtɪk] *adj* geodésico
**Geoffrey** ['dʒɛfrɪ] *s* Geofredo
**geog.** abr. de **geographer, geographical** y **geography**
**geognosy** [dʒɪ'ɑgnəsɪ] *s* geognosia
**geographer** [dʒɪ'ɑgrəfər] *s* geógrafo
**geographic** [,dʒiə'græfɪk] o **geographical** [,dʒiə'græfɪkəl] *adj* geográfico
**geographically** [,dʒiə'græfɪkəlɪ] *adv* geográficamente
**geographical mile** *s* (naut.) milla marina, milla geográfica
**geography** [dʒɪ'ɑgrəfɪ] *s* (*pl:* **-phies**) geografía
**geoid** ['dʒiɔɪd] *s* geoide
**geol.** abr. de **geological, geologist** y **geology**
**geologic** [,dʒiə'lɑdʒɪk] o **geological** [,dʒiə'lɑdʒɪkəl] *adj* geológico
**geologically** [,dʒiə'lɑdʒɪkəlɪ] *adv* geológicamente
**geologist** [dʒɪ'ɑlədʒɪst] *s* geólogo
**geology** [dʒɪ'ɑlədʒɪ] *s* (*pl:* **-gies**) geología
**geom.** abr. de **geometrical** y **geometry**
**geomagnetic** [,dʒiomæg'nɛtɪk] *adj* geomagnético
**geomancer** ['dʒiə,mænsər] *s* geomántico
**geomancy** ['dʒiə,mænsɪ] *s* geomancía
**geomantic** [,dʒiə'mæntɪk] *adj* geomántico
**geometer** [dʒɪ'ɑmɪtər] *s* geómetra; (zool.) geómetra
**geometric** [,dʒiə'mɛtrɪk] o **geometrical** [,dʒiə'mɛtrɪkəl] *adj* geométrico
**geometrician** [dʒɪ,ɑmɪ'trɪʃən] *s* geómetra
**geometric progression** *s* progresión geométrica
**geometric ratio** *s* razón geométrica
**geometrid** [dʒɪ'ɑmɪtrɪd] *s* (ent.) geométrido
**geometrize** [dʒɪ'ɑmɪtraɪz] *va & vn* geometrizar
**geometry** [dʒɪ'ɑmɪtrɪ] *s* (*pl:* **-tries**) geometría
**geomorphology** [,dʒiəmɔr'fɑlədʒɪ] *s* geomorfología
**geophagy** [dʒɪ'ɑfədʒɪ] *s* geofagía
**geophysical** [,dʒio'fɪzɪkəl] *adj* geofísico
**geophysicist** [,dʒio'fɪzɪsɪst] *s* geofísico
**geophysics** [,dʒio'fɪzɪks] *ssg* geofísica
**geophyte** ['dʒiəfaɪt] *s* (bot.) geófita
**geopolitical** [,dʒiəpə'lɪtɪkəl] *adj* geopolítico
**geopolitics** [,dʒiə'pɑlɪtɪks] *ssg* geopolítica
**geoponic** [,dʒiə'pɑnɪk] *adj* geopónico; **geoponics** *ssg* geopónica o geoponía
**georama** [,dʒio'ræmə] o [,dʒio'rɑmə] *s* georama
**George** [dʒɔrdʒ] *s* Jorge
**georgette** [dʒɔr'dʒɛt] o **georgette crepe** *s* crespón de seda muy diáfano
**Georgia** ['dʒɔrdʒə] *s* Jorja (*nombre de mujer*)
**Georgian** ['dʒɔrdʒən] *adj & s* georgiano
**Georgiana** [,dʒɔrdʒɪ'ænə] o [,dʒɔrdʒɪ'ɑnə] *s* Georgina (*nombre de mujer*)
**georgic** ['dʒɔrdʒɪk] *s* geórgica (*poema*)
**Georgina** [dʒɔr'dʒinə] *s* var. de **Georgiana**
**geosynclinal** [,dʒiosɪn'klaɪnəl] *adj & s* (geol.) geosinclinal
**geotaxis** [,dʒio'tæksɪs] *s* geotaxia o geotactismo
**geotectonic** [,dʒiotɛk'tɑnɪk] *adj* geotectónico; **geotectonics** *ssg* geotectónica
**geothermal** [,dʒio'θʌrməl] *adj* geotérmico
**geotropic** [,dʒio'trɑpɪk] *adj* geotrópico
**geotropism** [dʒɪ'ɑtrəpɪzəm] *s* (biol.) geotropismo
**ger.** abr. de **gerund**
**Ger.** abr. de **German, Germanic** y **Germany**
**Gerald** ['dʒɛrəld] *s* Gerardo
**geraniaceous** [dʒɪ,renɪ'eʃəs] *adj* (bot.) geraniáceo
**geranium** [dʒɪ'renɪəm] *s* (bot.) geranio
**Gerard** [dʒɪ'rɑrd] o ['dʒɛrɑrd] *s* var. de **Gerald**
**gerent** ['dʒɪrənt] *s* gerente
**gerfalcon** ['dʒʌr,fɔkən] o ['dʒʌr,fɔlkən] *s* (orn.) gerifalte
**geriatrical** [,dʒɛrɪ'ætrɪkəl] *adj* geriátrico
**geriatrician** [,dʒɛrɪə'trɪʃən] *s* geriatra
**geriatrics** [,dʒɛrɪ'ætrɪks] *ssg* geriatría
**germ** [dʒʌrm] *s* (bact., biol., embryol. & fig.) germen; *adj* germinal
**german** ['dʒʌrmən] *adj* carnal (*dícese del hermano o el primo*); *s* cotillón; fiesta en que se baila el cotillón; (*cap.*) *adj* alemán; *s* (*pl:* **-mans**) alemán
**germander** [dʒər'mændər] *s* (bot.) germandrina, camedrio
**germane** [dʒər'men] *adj* relacionado, pertinente
**Germania** [dʒər'menɪə] *s* (hist. & fig.) Germania
**Germanic** [dʒər'mænɪk] *adj* germánico; *s* germánico (*grupo de lenguas*)
**Germanism** ['dʒʌrmənɪzəm] *s* germanismo
**Germanist** ['dʒʌrmənɪst] *s* germanista
**germanium** [dʒər'menɪəm] *s* (chem.) germanio
**Germanization** [,dʒʌrmənɪ'zeʃən] *s* germanización
**Germanize** ['dʒʌrmənaɪz] *va* germanizar; *vn* germanizarse
**German measles** *s* (path.) rubéola, sarampión alemán
**Germanophile** [dʒər'mænofaɪl] *adj & s* germanófilo
**Germanophobe** [dʒər'mænofob] *adj & s* germanófobo
**German script** *s* letra alemana
**German shepherd dog** *s* perro pastor alemán
**German silver** *s* melchor, plata alemana
**German text** *s* (print.) tipo alemán
**Germany** ['dʒʌrmənɪ] *s* Alemania
**germ cell** *s* (biol.) célula germen
**germicidal** [,dʒʌrmɪ'saɪdəl] *adj* germicida
**germicide** ['dʒʌrmɪsaɪd] *s* germicida
**germinal** ['dʒʌrmɪnəl] *adj* germinal
**germinant** ['dʒʌrmɪnənt] *adj* germinante
**germinate** ['dʒʌrmɪnet] *va* hacer germinar; *vn* germinar
**germination** [,dʒʌrmɪ'neʃən] *s* germinación
**germinative** ['dʒʌrmɪ,netɪv] *adj* germinativo
**germinator** ['dʒʌrmɪ,netər] *s* germinador
**germ plasm** *s* germen plasma
**germ theory** *s* (biol. & path.) teoría germinal
**germ war** o **warfare** *s* guerra bacteriana o guerra bacteriológica
**gerontology** [,dʒɛrɑn'tɑlədʒɪ] *s* gerontología
**gerrymander** ['gɛrɪ,mændər] o ['dʒɛrɪ,mændər] *s* demarcación arbitraria e injusta de los distritos electorales; [,gɛrɪ'mændər] o [,dʒɛrɪ'mændər] *va* dividir arbitrariamente (*un estado*) en distritos electorales (*para sacar ventaja de ello*); manejar injustamente (*los resortes políticos*)

**Gertrude** [ˈgʌrtrud] *s* Gertrudis
**Gerty** [ˈgʌrtɪ] *s* Tula
**gerund** [ˈdʒerənd] *s* gerundio
**gerundial** [dʒɪˈrʌndɪəl] *adj* del gerundio
**gerundive** [dʒɪˈrʌndɪv] *s* gerundino (*en gramática latina*); gerundio adjetivado
**gest** [dʒɛst] *s* (archaic) gesta
**Gestalt psychology** [gəˈʃtɑlt] *s* psicología de la forma, gestaltismo
**Gestapo** [gəˈstɑpo] *s* gestapo (*policía secreta del gobierno nazi*)
**gestation** [dʒɛsˈteʃən] *s* gestación; (fig.) gestación
**gesticulate** [dʒɛsˈtɪkjəlet] *vn* accionar, manotear
**gesticulation** [dʒɛs,tɪkjəˈleʃən] *s* manoteo, ademán
**gesticulative** [dʒɛsˈtɪkjə,letɪv] *adj* manoteador
**gesticulator** [dʒɛsˈtɪkjə,letər] *s* manoteador
**gesture** [ˈdʒɛstʃər] *s* ademán, gesto; muestra, demostración, gesto; *vn* hacer ademanes, hacer gestos
**get** [gɛt] (*pret:* **got;** *pp:* **got** o **gotten;** *ger:* **getting**) *va* obtener, recibir; conseguir; buscar, ir por; traer; tomar (*p.ej., un billete*); llevar, hacer llegar; alcanzar; proporcionar; hallar, localizar; preparar, hacer (*p.ej., la comida*); adquirir (*p.ej., destreza*); aprender de memoria; resolver (*un problema*); (coll.) comprender; (coll.) captar, conseguir sintonizar (*una estación emisora*); (slang) irritar; **let's get this over!** ¡pecho al agua!; **to have got** tener, p.ej., **I've got enough money** tengo bastante dinero; **to have got to** + *inf* tener que + *inf*, p.ej., **I've got to walk** tengo que ir a pie; **to get across** (coll.) hacer aceptar, hacer comprender; **to get back** recobrar; **to get by** conseguir que se deje pasar (*una cosa*); **to get down** descolgar; tragar; **to get going** poner en marcha; **to get in** conseguir meter (*una cosa*) en (*otra*); **to get off** quitar (*p.ej., una mancha*); quitarse (*los zapatos*); ayudar a partir o a escaparse; despachar; **to get on** ponerse (*los zapatos*); **to get out** publicar (*p.ej., un libro*); ayudar a partir o a escaparse; **to get out of** hacer confesar, lograr sacar de; **to get out of the way** quitar de en medio; **to get over** (slang) hacer aceptar, hacer comprender; conseguir pasar (*una cosa*) por encima de o más allá de (*otra*); **to get something away from someone** quitar algo a alguien; **to get through** lograr pasar (*una cosa*) por (*otra*); **to get to** + *inf* conseguir, lograr que + *subj*, p.ej., **I got him to leave** conseguí que saliese; **to get** + *pp* hacer + *inf*, p.ej., **he got his hair cut** se hizo cortar el pelo; hacer que + *subj*, p.ej., **I got him appointed** hice que le nombraran ‖ *vn* hacerse, ponerse, volverse; meterse; llegar (coll.) largarse; **to get about** mostrarse activo; estar levantado (*un convaleciente*); **to get abroad** divulgarse; **to get across** tener éxito; **to get along** marcharse; seguir andando; ir tirando; tener éxito; llevarse bien; pasarlo, p.ej., **how are you getting along?** ¿cómo lo pasa Vd.?; **to get along in years** ponerse viejo; **to get along with** congeniar con; **to get around** salir mucho, ir a todas partes; difundirse, divulgarse; eludir, pasar por alto; manejar (*a una persona*); mandarse, estar levantado (*un convaleciente*); **to get at** alcanzar, llegar hasta; averiguar, descubrir; (coll.) intimidar; (coll.) sobornar; **to get away** alejarse; conseguir marcharse; ponerse en marcha; evadirse; **to get away with** llevarse, escaparse con; (coll.) hacer impunemente; **to get away with it** (coll.) arreglárselas, quedar sin castigo; **to get back** regresar, volver; **to get back at** (slang) desquitarse con; **to get behind** quedarse atrás; apoyar; penetrar (*p.ej., la máscara de una persona*); **to get by** lograr pasar; burlar, burlar la vigilancia de; (coll.) arreglárselas; **to get going** ponerse en marcha; **to get gone** salir, irse; **to get in** conseguir entrar en; llegar (*p.ej., un tren*); volver a casa (*por la noche*); **to get into** conseguir entrar en; meterse en (*p.ej., dificultades*); **to get in with** llegar a ser amigo de, llegar a tener influencia con; **to get left** (slang) llevarse un chasco; **to get off** apearse, bajar; bajar de (*p.ej., un tranvía*); descolgarse; marcharse; escaparse; **to get off with** salir con (*p.ej., una pena leve*); **to get on** subir; subir a (*p.ej., un tranvía*); ponerse encima de; ir tirando, tener éxito; llevarse bien; **to get on with** congeniar con; tener éxito con o en; **to get out** salir; marcharse; escaparse; divulgarse; dejar un negocio, asociación, etc.; **to get out of** bajar de (*p.ej., un coche*); librarse de; evadir, escaparse de; **to get out of the way** quitarse de en medio; **to get over** atravesar, pasar por encima de, pasar más allá de; olvidar (*un disgusto*); vencer (*un obstáculo*); recobrarse de; curarse de; **to get through** pasar por entre; terminar; **to get through with** concluir de hacer; **to get to be** llegar a ser; **to get under** meterse o ponerse debajo de; **to get under way** ponerse en camino; (naut.) hacerse a la vela; **to get up** levantarse; **to get up on** subir a lo alto de; **to not get over it** (coll.) no volver de su asombro; **when I get through with you!** ¡cuando yo te deje!; **get out!** ¡aprieta! (*para expresar incredulidad*); **get up!** ¡arre! (*para arrear a las bestias*); este verbo, seguido de un adjetivo, se traduce a veces por un verbo neutro o reflexivo que corresponda al adjetivo, p.ej., **to get old** envejecer; **to get angry** enfadarse; seguido de un participio pasivo, se traduce a veces por un verbo reflexivo o por la voz pasiva, p.ej., **to get married** casarse; **to get run over** ser atropellado
**getaway** [ˈgɛtə,we] *s* escapatoria; (sport) comienzo de una carrera; (aut.) arranque, facilidad y rapidez del arranque
**Gethsemane** [gɛθˈsɛmənɪ] *s* (Bib.) Getsemaní
**get-together** [ˈgɛttʊ,gɛðər] *s* (coll.) reunión, tertulia
**get-up** [ˈgɛt,ʌp] *s* (coll.) presentación; (coll.) atavío, traje
**gewgaw** [ˈgjugɔ] *s* fruslería; adorno charro; *adj* charro, chillón
**geyser** [ˈgaɪzər] *s* géiser
**ghastly** [ˈgæstlɪ] o [ˈgɑstlɪ] *adj* (*comp:* **-lier;** *super:* **-liest**) horrible; cadavérico, espectral; *adv* horriblemente, extremadamente
**Ghent** [gɛnt] *s* Gante
**gherkin** [ˈgʌrkɪn] *s* (bot.) pepinillo (*Cucumis Anguria y fruto; pepino pequeño encurtido*)
**ghetto** [ˈgɛto] *s* (*pl:* **-tos**) ghetto, judería
**Ghibelline** [ˈgɪbəlin] *adj & s* gibelino
**ghost** [gost] *s* espectro, fantasma; alma (*de persona muerta*); alma en pena; asomo apenas perceptible; (opt.) imagen falsa; (telv.) fantasma; (coll.) escritor cuyos escritos aparecen bajo la firma de otra persona; **not a ghost of a** ni la más remota idea de, ni la más remota posibilidad de, ni sombra de; **to give up the ghost** dar, entregar o rendir el alma; *va* (coll.) componer escritos por
**ghost image** *s* (telv.) imagen fantasma, imagen falsa
**ghostly** [ˈgostlɪ] *adj* (*comp:* **-lier;** *super:* **-liest**) espectral; espiritual
**ghost story** *s* cuento de fantasmas
**ghostwrite** [ˈgost,raɪt] *va & vn* escribir bajo la firma de otra persona
**ghost writer** *s* escritor cuyos escritos aparecen bajo la firma de otra persona, colaborador anónimo
**ghoul** [gul] *s* demonio que se alimenta con la carne de los cadáveres; profanador de cadáveres, robador de cementerios; persona que se deleita con cosas brutales y horribles
**ghoulish** [ˈgulɪʃ] *adj* brutal, horrible, espantoso
**G.H.Q.** abr. de **General Headquarters**
**G.I.** [ˈdʒiˈaɪ] *adj* de munición, del ejército norteamericano; (coll.) de reglamento; (coll.) soldadesco; *s* (coll.) soldado raso (*del ejército norteamericano*)
**giant** [ˈdʒaɪənt] *adj* gigante; gigantesco; *s* gigante
**giant cactus** *s* (bot.) saguaro
**giantess** [ˈdʒaɪəntɪs] *s* giganta
**giant fennel** *s* (bot.) cañaheja
**giantism** [ˈdʒaɪəntɪzəm] *s* gigantez; (path.) gigantismo
**giant panda** *s* (zool.) panda gigante

**giant powder** *s* pólvora gigante
**giant salamander** *s* (zool.) salamandra gigante
**Giant's Causeway** *s* Calzada de los Gigantes (*en Irlanda*)
**giant's stride** *s* (sport) pasos de gigante
**giant tortoise** *s* (zool.) tortuga gigante
**gibber** ['dʒɪbər] o ['gɪbər] *s* guirigay; *vn* farfullar, parlotear
**gibberish** ['dʒɪbɛrɪʃ] o ['gɪbərɪʃ] *s* guirigay
**gibbet** ['dʒɪbɪt] *s* picota; horca; *va* empicotar; ahorcar; poner en picota, poner a la vergüenza
**gibbon** ['gɪbən] *s* (zool.) gibón
**gibbosity** [gɪ'bɑsɪtɪ] *s* (*pl:* **-ties**) gibosidad
**gibbous** ['gɪbəs] *adj* giboso
**gibe** [dʒaɪb] *s* remoque, pulla; *vn* mofarse; **to gibe at** mofarse de
**giblets** ['dʒɪblɪts] *spl* menudillos
**Gibraltar** [dʒɪ'brɔltər] *s* Gibraltar
**gid** [gɪd] *s* (vet.) modorra, tornada
**giddiness** ['gɪdɪnɪs] *s* vértigo, desvanecimiento; atolondramiento, falta de juicio
**giddy** ['gɪdɪ] *adj* (*comp:* **-dier;** *super:* **-diest**) vertiginoso; casquivano, ligero de cascos; (vet.) modorro
**Gideon** ['gɪdɪən] *s* (Bib.) Gedeón
**gift** [gɪft] *s* regalo; don, dote, prenda; *va* obsequiar; dotar
**gifted** ['gɪftɪd] *adj* de talento, talentoso
**gift horse** *s* caballo regalado, p.ej., **never look a gift horse in the mouth** a caballo regalado no se le mira el diente
**gift of gab** *s* (coll.) facundia, labia
**gift package** *s* paquete regalo
**gift shop** *s* tienda de objetos de regalo, comercio de artículos de regalo
**gift tax** *s* impuesto sobre donaciones, impuesto sobre transferencias a título gratuito
**gift-wrap** ['gɪft,ræp] (*pret & pp:* **-wrapped;** *ger:* **-wrapping**) *va* envolver en paquete regalo
**gig** [gɪg] *s* calesa (*de dos ruedas*); fisga, arpón; (naut.) falúa; (*pret & pp:* **gigged;** *ger:* **gigging**) *va & vn* pescar con fisga o arpón
**gigantean** [,dʒaɪgæn'tiən] *adj* giganteo
**gigantesque** [,dʒaɪgæn'tɛsk] *adj* gigantesco
**gigantic** [dʒaɪ'gæntɪk] *adj* gigantesco
**gigantism** ['dʒaɪgæntɪzəm] o [dʒaɪ'gæntɪzəm] *s* var. de **giantism**
**giggle** ['gɪgəl] *s* retozo de la risa; *vn* reírse nerviosamente, reír con una risilla tonta
**giggly** ['gɪglɪ] *adj* de risa fácil e inoportuna
**gigolo** ['dʒɪgəlo] *s* (*pl:* **-los**) acompañante profesional de mujeres; hombre que vive a expensas de una mujer
**gigot** ['dʒɪgət] *s* manga hueca y subida; pernil de carnero, de ternera, etc.
**Gila monster** ['hilə] *s* (zool.) monstruo de Gila
**gilbert** ['gɪlbərt] *s* (phys.) gilbertio; (*cap.*) *s* Gilberto
**gild** [gɪld] *s* gremio; asociación de carácter benéfico; (*pret & pp:* **gilded** o **gilt**) *va* dorar; dar brillo o lustre a; dar un brillo falso a
**gilder** ['gɪldər] *s* dorador
**gilding** ['gɪldɪŋ] *s* doradura; dorado
**Gilead** ['gɪlɪəd] *s* (Bib.) Galaad
**Giles** [dʒaɪlz] *s* Gil
**gill** [gɪl] *s* papada, papadilla; agalla (*de pez*); barba (*del gallo*); (bot.) hojuela o laminilla (*debajo del sombrerillo del hongo*); [dʒɪl] *s* medida para líquidos, equivalente a la cuarta parte de una pinta
**gillie** ['gɪlɪ] *s* (Scotch) ayudante o paje de un cazador o pescador; (Scotch) criado, secuaz
**gilly** ['gɪlɪ] *s* (*pl:* **-lies**) var. de **gillie**
**gillyflower** ['dʒɪlɪ,flauər] *s* (bot.) alhelí, alhelí amarillo, alhelí encarnado
**gilt** [gɪlt] *adj & s* dorado; *pret & pp de* **gild**
**gilt-edged** ['gɪlt,ɛdʒd] *adj* con cantos dorados; de toda confianza, de lo mejor que hay
**gimbals** ['dʒɪmbəlz] o ['gɪmbəlz] *spl* balancines de brújula
**gimcrack** ['dʒɪm,kræk] *s* chuchería; *adj* brillante y de poco valor, de oropel
**gimlet** ['gɪmlɪt] *s* barrena de mano
**gimlet-eyed** ['gɪmlɪt,aɪd] *adj* de ojos taladradores
**gimmick** ['gɪmɪk] *s* (slang) adminículo, dispositivo ingenioso; (slang) adminículo mágico
**gimp** [gɪmp] *s* bocadillo; (coll.) energía, vigor
**gimp nail** *s* tachón o tachuela para tapicería
**gin** o **'gin** [gɪn] (*pret:* **gan** o **'gan;** *pp:* **gun** o **'gun;** *ger:* **ginning** o **'ginning**) *va & vn* (archaic & poet.) comenzar
**gin** [dʒɪn] *s* ginebra; desmotadora de algodón; garlito, trampa; poste grúa, torno de izar; (*pret & pp:* **ginned;** *ger:* **ginning**) *va* desmotar (*algodón*); coger con garlito
**gin fiz** o **fizz** *s* ginebra con gaseosa
**ginger** ['dʒɪndʒər] *s* (bot.) jengibre (*planta, rizoma y especia*); color de jengibre; (coll.) energía, viveza; *adj* de color de jengibre
**ginger ale** o **beer** *s* cerveza de jengibre gaseosa
**gingerbread** ['dʒɪndʒər,brɛd] *s* pan de jengibre; adorno charro; *adj* recargado de adornos charros
**gingerly** ['dʒɪndʒərlɪ] *adj* cuidadoso, cauteloso; *adv* cuidadosamente, cautelosamente
**gingersnap** ['dʒɪndʒər,snæp] *s* galletita de jengibre
**gingery** ['dʒɪndʒərɪ] *adj* que sabe a jengibre; picante; de color de jengibre
**gingham** ['gɪŋəm] *s* guinga, zaraza; *adj* de guinga, de zaraza
**gingival** [dʒɪn'dʒaɪvəl] *adj* gingival
**gingivitis** [,dʒɪndʒɪ'vaɪtɪs] *s* (path.) gingivitis
**gingko** ['gɪŋko] o ['dʒɪŋko] *s* (*pl:* **-koes**) (bot.) gingo
**ginglymus** ['dʒɪŋglɪməs] o ['gɪŋglɪməs] *s* (*pl:* **-mi** [maɪ]) (anat.) gínglimo
**ginkgo** ['gɪŋko] o ['dʒɪŋko] *s* (*pl:* **-goes**) var. de **gingko**
**ginseng** ['dʒɪnsɛŋ] *s* (bot.) ginsén (*planta y raíz*)
**gipsy** ['dʒɪpsɪ] *adj* var. de **gypsy;** *s* (*pl:* **-sies**) var. de **gypsy;** (*cap.*) *s* var. de **Gypsy**
**giraffe** [dʒɪ'ræf] o [dʒɪ'rɑf] *s* (zool.) jirafa
**girandole** ['dʒɪrəndol] *s* girándula
**gird** [gʌrd] *s* (archaic) remoque; (*pret & pp:* **girded**) *va* mofarse de; *vn* mofar; (*pret & pp:* **girt** o **girded**) *va* ceñir; aprestar; dotar
**girder** ['gʌrdər] *s* viga, trabe
**girdle** ['gʌrdəl] *s* faja, ceñidor; corsé de poca anchura; *va* ceñir; circundar; ir alrededor de; quitar a (*un árbol*) una tira circular de corteza
**girl** [gʌrl] *s* niña; muchacha; criada; (coll.) novia; (coll.) mujer
**girl friend** *s* (coll.) amiguita
**girlhood** ['gʌrlhud] *s* muchachez; muchachas; juventud femenina
**girlie** ['gɪrlɪ] *s* (coll.) niña, chica
**girlish** ['gʌrlɪʃ] *adj* de niña, de muchacha, juvenil
**girl scout** *s* niña exploradora
**Girondist** [dʒɪ'rɑndɪst] *adj & s* (hist.) girondino
**girt** [gʌrt] *va* ceñir; asediar; *pret & pp de* **gird**
**girth** [gʌrθ] *s* cincha; pretina; circunferencia; *va* cinchar; ceñir
**gist** [dʒɪst] *s* enjundia, substancia, esencia
**gittern** ['gɪtərn] *s* var. de **cithern**
**give** [gɪv] *s* elasticidad ‖ (*pret:* **gave;** *pp:* **given**) *va* dar; ofrecer; causar, ocasionar (*p.ej., molestia, trabajo*); representar (*una obra dramática*); pronunciar (*un discurso*); dedicar (*sus energías o el tiempo disponible*); **to give and take** cambiar (*unas cosas por otras*) libremente; **to give away** regalar, dar de balde; revelar, divulgar; malvender; llevar (*a la novia*); (coll.) traicionar; **to give back** devolver; **to give forth** producir; divulgar; despedir, echar (*p.ej., olores*); **to give in** ceder, entregar; **to give it to** (coll.) dar una paliza a; (coll.) regañar; **to give off** despedir, echar (*p.ej., olores*); **to give oneself up** entregarse (*a las autoridades*); **to give oneself up to** entregarse a, dedicarse a; abandonarse a; **to give out** distribuir, repartir; divulgar; proclamar; despedir, echar (*p.ej., olores*); **to give over** entregar; desistir de; **to give up** entregar; abandonar, dejar (*un empleo*); renunciar; privarse de; desahuciar; **to give up** + *ger* dejar de + *inf;* privarse de + *inf;* **to give up . . . to** dedicar (*p.ej., el día entero*) a ‖ *vn* hacer regalos; prestar, dar de sí; romperse (*una cuerda*); **to give in** ceder, rendirse; consentir; **to give out** agotarse; no poder más; descomponerse; **to give up** abandonarse, darse

por vencido; **to give upon** dar a (*p.ej., un jardín*)
**give-and-take** ['gɪvənd'tek] *s* toma y daca, concesiones mutuas; conversación sazonada de burlas
**giveaway** ['gɪvə,we] *s* (coll.) revelación involuntaria; (coll.) traición, revelación intencional; (coll.) ganapierde (*modo de jugar a las damas*); **to play giveaway** jugar al o a la ganapierde
**given** ['gɪvən] *adj* dado; (math.) conocido; **given that** suponiendo que; **given to** dado a (*propenso a*); *pp de* **give**
**given name** *s* nombre de pila
**giver** ['gɪvər] *s* dador, donador
**gizzard** ['gɪzərd] *s* molleja (*de ave*); proventrículo (*de insecto*); (hum.) vientre
**Gk.** abr. de **Greek**
**glabrous** ['glebrəs] *adj* (bot. & zool.) glabro
**glacé** [glæ'se] *adj* glaseado; helado; *va* glasear (*las frutas, la piel, etc.*)
**glacial** ['gleʃəl] *adj* glacial; (chem.) glacial
**glacial epoch** *s* (geol.) época glacial
**glacial period** *s* (geol.) período glacial
**glaciate** ['gleʃɪet] *va* cubrir con heleros o con hielo glacial; congelar; someter a la acción glaciaria
**glaciation** [,gleʃɪ'eʃən] o [,glesɪ'eʃən] *s* glaciación
**glacier** ['gleʃər] *s* glaciar, helero
**glacis** ['glesɪs] o ['glæsɪs] *s* glacis; (fort.) glacis
**glad** [glæd] *adj* (*comp:* **gladder;** *super:* **gladdest**) alegre; gozoso, festivo; vistoso; **to be glad** alegrarse; **to be glad to** + *inf* alegrarse de + *inf*, tener mucho gusto en + *inf*
**gladden** ['glædən] *va* alegrar; *vn* alegrarse
**gladdon** ['glædən] *s* (bot.) íride; (bot.) espadaña, gladíolo
**glade** [gled] *s* claro, claro herboso (*en un bosque*)
**glad hand** *s* (slang) acogida efusiva
**gladiator** ['glædɪ,etər] *s* gladiador
**gladiatorial** [,glædɪə'torɪəl] *adj* gladiatorio
**gladiola** [,glædɪ'olə] o [glə'daɪələ] *s* (bot.) estoque
**gladiolus** [,glædɪ'oləs] o [glə'daɪələs] *s* (*pl:* **-luses** o **-li** [laɪ]) (bot.) estoque; [glə'daɪələs] *s* (*pl:* **-luses** o **-li** [laɪ]) (anat.) gladíolo (*mesosternón*)
**gladius** ['gledɪəs] *s* (*pl:* **-i** [aɪ]) (zool.) gladio
**gladly** ['glædlɪ] *adv* alegremente; con placer, con mucho gusto
**gladness** ['glædnɪs] *s* alegría, regocijo
**glad rags** *spl* (slang) trapos elegantes
**gladsome** ['glædsəm] *adj* alegre; festivo; agradable, delicioso
**Gladstone bag** ['glædstən] o ['glædston] *s* maleta que al abrirse se desdobla en dos mitades
**glair** [glɛr] *s* clara de huevo; aderezo o engomado hecho de clara de huevo
**glaive** [glev] *s* (hist.) alabarda; (archaic) chafarote
**glamor** ['glæmər] *s* var. de **glamour**
**glamorous** ['glæmərəs] *adj* encantador, hechicero, fascinador
**glamour** ['glæmər] *s* encanto, hechizo, fascinación
**glamour girl** *s* (slang) belleza exótica
**glamourous** ['glæmərəs] *adj* var. de **glamorous**
**glance** [glæns] o [glɑns] *s* golpe de vista, ojeada, vistazo; destello; desviación oblicua; alusión breve; **at first glance** a primera vista; **at a glance** de un vistazo; *vn* lanzar una mirada; destellar; desviarse de soslayo; **to glance at** lanzar una mirada a; mirar por encima, examinar de paso; aludir a; **to glance off** desviarse de soslayo; desviarse al chocar con; **to glance over** examinar de paso
**glancing** ['glænsɪŋ] o ['glɑnsɪŋ] *adj* de soslayo (*dícese de un golpe*)
**gland** [glænd] *s* (anat. & bot.) glándula; (mach.) casquillo del prensaestopas
**glanderous** ['glændərəs] *adj* muermoso
**glanders** ['glændərz] *s* (vet.) muermo
**glandular** ['glændʒələr] *adj* glandular
**glandulous** ['glændʒələs] *adj* glanduloso
**glare** [glɛr] *s* fulgor deslumbrante, relumbrón; luz intensa; mirada feroz y penetrante; mirada de indignación; aspecto deslumbrante; superficie lisa y brillante (*p.ej., de hielo*); *adj* liso y brillante; *va* expresar (*p.ej., indignación*) con miradas feroces; *vn* relumbrar; lanzar miradas feroces o de indignación; ser de aspecto deslumbrante
**glaring** ['glɛrɪŋ] *adj* deslumbrante, brillante; relumbrante; de miradas feroces; evidente, notorio
**glary** ['glɛrɪ] *adj* deslumbrante, brillante; alisado, resbaloso
**glass** [glæs] o [glɑs] *s* vidrio; cristal; vaso; vajilla de cristal; espejo; **glasses** *spl* anteojos, gafas; *adj* de vidrio, de cristal; *va* encerrar entre vidrios; poner vidrios a (*una ventana*); reflejar
**glass blower** *s* vidriero, soplador de vidrio
**glass blowing** *s* elaboración del vidrio mediante el soplete
**glass case** *s* vitrina
**glass cutter** *s* cortavidrios
**glass door** *s* puerta vidriera
**glassful** ['glæsfʊl] o ['glɑsfʊl] *s* vaso (*cantidad que cabe en un vaso*)
**glasshouse** ['glæs,haʊs] o ['glɑs,haʊs] *s* vidriería; invernadero; galería fotográfica; (fig.) tejado de vidrio
**glassiness** ['glæsɪnɪs] o ['glɑsɪnɪs] *s* vidriosidad
**glass snake** *s* (zool.) lución norteamericano
**glassware** ['glæs,wɛr] o ['glɑs,wɛr] *s* cristalería; vajilla de cristal
**glass wool** *s* cristal hilado, lana de vidrio, tela de vidrio
**glasswork** ['glæs,wʌrk] o ['glɑs,wʌrk] *s* vidriería, cristalería; **glassworks** *ssg o spl* vidriería, cristalería (*fábrica o taller*)
**glassworker** ['glæs,wʌrkər] o ['glɑs,wʌrkər] *s* vidriero
**glasswort** ['glæs,wʌrt] o ['glɑs,wʌrt] *s* (bot.) almajo, almajo salado, alacranera
**glassy** ['glæsɪ] o ['glɑsɪ] *adj* (*comp:* **-ier;** *super:* **-iest**) vidrioso; (fig.) de mirada fija y estúpida (*dícese de los ojos*); (fig.) vidrioso (*dícese de los ojos o la mirada*)
**Glaswegian** [glæs'widʒən] o [glɑs'widʒən] *adj* perteneciente a Glasgow; *s* natural o habitante de Glasgow
**glauberite** ['glaʊbəraɪt] o ['glɔbəraɪt] *s* (chem.) glauberita
**Glauber's salt** ['glaʊbərz] o ['glɔbərz] *s* (pharm.) sal de Glauber
**glaucoma** [glɔ'komə] *s* (path.) glaucoma
**glaucomatous** [glɔ'komətəs] o [glɔ'kɑmətəs] *adj* glaucomatoso
**glaucous** ['glɔkəs] *adj* glauco; (bot.) glauco
**glaze** [glez] *s* barniz vítreo, esmalte; superficie lisa; capa lisa y resbaladiza (*p.ej., la que produce la lluvia al congelarse*); *va* vidriar, esmaltar; lustrar (*un tejido*); poner vidrio o vidrios a (*una ventana o un marco*); cubrir con vidrio; garapiñar; *vn* vidriarse
**glazier** ['gleʒər] *s* vidriero
**glazier's point** *s* punta de vidriar
**glazing** ['glezɪŋ] *s* oficio de vidriero; trabajo de vidriero; vidrios (*puestos o que han de ponerse*); barniz vítreo, esmalte
**gleam** [glim] *s* destello, rayo de luz; luz tenue o momentánea; rayo (*de esperanza*); manifestación momentánea (*p.ej., de inteligencia*); *vn* destellar, fulgurar; brillar con luz tenue o momentánea; aparecer de repente, dejarse ver momentáneamente
**glean** [glin] *va* espigar; (fig.) espigar
**gleaner** ['glinər] *s* espigador
**gleaning** ['glinɪŋ] *s* espigadura, espigueo
**glebe** [glib] *s* (poet.) tierra, césped; (archaic) campo sembrado o labrado; (eccl.) terreno anejo a un beneficio o curato
**glee** [gli] *s* alegría, regocijo; (mus.) canción para tres o más solistas a capella
**glee club** *s* orfeón
**gleeful** ['glifəl] *adj* alegre, regocijado
**gleeman** ['glimən] *s* (*pl:* **-men**) (archaic) cantor, trovador
**gleesome** ['glisəm] *adj* var. de **gleeful**
**glen** [glɛn] *s* vallecico, valle angosto
**glengarry** [glɛn'gærɪ] *s* (*pl:* **-ries**) gorra escocesa
**glenoid** ['glinɔɪd] *adj* glenoideo

**glib** [glɪb] *adj* (*comp:* **glibber;** *super:* **glibbest**) locuaz, de mucha labia; fácil e insincero
**glide** [glaɪd] *s* deslizamiento suave, movimiento suave y silencioso; (aer.) vuelo sin motor, planeo; (mus.) ligadura; (phonet.) semivocal; *vn* deslizarse; (aer.) volar sin motor, planear; **to glide along** correr o pasar suavemente; **to glide by** pasarse (*p.ej., los años*) sin sentir
**glider** [ˈglaɪdər] *s* persona o cosa que se desliza; (aer.) deslizador, planeador
**gliding angle** *s* (aer.) ángulo de planeo
**gliding boat** *s* (aer.) hidrodeslizador
**gliding machine** *s* (aer.) deslizador, planeador
**glim** [glɪm] *s* luz (*de candil o de vela*); candil, vela; (slang) ojo
**glimmer** [ˈglɪmər] *s* luz tenue y vacilante; vislumbre; *vn* brillar con luz tenue y vacilante; vislumbrarse
**glimmering** [ˈglɪmərɪŋ] *adj* trémulo, tenue y vacilante; *s* luz tenue y vacilante; vislumbre
**glimpse** [glɪmps] *s* vislumbre, vista momentánea; manifestación momentánea; **to catch a glimpse of** vislumbrar; *va* vislumbrar, ver momentáneamente, alcanzar a ver; *vn* brillar con luz tenue y vacilante; lanzar una mirada
**glint** [glɪnt] *s* destello, rayo, relumbrón
**glioma** [glaɪˈomə] *s* (*pl:* **-mata** [mətə] o **-mas**) (path.) glioma
**glisten** [ˈglɪsən] *s* centelleo; *vn* centellear
**glitter** [ˈglɪtər] *s* brillo, resplandor; *vn* brillar, resplendecer
**glittering** [ˈglɪtərɪŋ] o **glittery** [ˈglɪtərɪ] *adj* brillante, resplandeciente
**gloaming** [ˈglomɪŋ] *s* crepúsculo vespertino, media luz del anochecer
**gloat** [glot] *vn* gozarse, relamerse; **to gloat over** gozarse en la contemplación de
**global** [ˈglobəl] *adj* globoso, esférico; mundial, global
**globate** [ˈglobet] *adj* globoso, esférico
**globe** [glob] *s* globo; globo terráqueo o terrestre (*Tierra; mapa de la Tierra en forma de bola*); (astr.) globo celeste; *va* dar forma de globo a; *vn* tomar forma de globo
**globe amaranth** *s* (bot.) sempiterna, perpetua, amarantina
**globefish** [ˈglob,fɪʃ] *s* (ichth.) orbe
**globeflower** [ˈglob,flaʊər] *s* (bot.) calderones
**globe sight** *s* mira esférica
**globetrotter** [ˈglob,trɑtər] *s* trotamundos
**globose** [ˈglobos] o **globous** [ˈglobəs] *adj* globoso
**globular** [ˈglɑbjələr] *adj* globular
**globule** [ˈglɑbjʊl] *s* glóbulo; (bot.) glóbulo
**globulin** [ˈglɑbjəlɪn] *s* (biochem.) globulina
**globulose** [ˈglɑbjəlos] *adj* globuloso
**glockenspiel** [ˈglɑkən,spil] *s* (mus.) órgano de campanas, timbres, juego de timbres
**glomerate** [ˈglɑmərɪt] *adj* aglomerado
**glomerule** [ˈglɑmərʊl] *s* (bot.) glomérula
**glomerulus** [gloˈmɛrjʊləs] o [gloˈmɛrʊləs] *s* (*pl:* **-li** [laɪ]) (anat.) glomérulo
**gloom** [glum] *s* lobreguez, tinieblas; abatimiento, tristeza; aspecto abatido, aspecto triste; *vn* obscurecerse; entristecerse, ponerse fúnebre; parecer triste
**gloomy** [ˈglumɪ] *adj* (*comp:* **-ier;** *super:* **-iest**) lóbrego (*obscuro; triste*)
**gloria** [ˈglorɪə] *s* gloria (*tejido; aureola*); canto en loor de Dios; (*cap.*) *s* (eccl.) Gloria
**glorifiable** [ˈglorɪ,faɪəbəl] *adj* glorificable
**glorification** [,glorɪfɪˈkeʃən] *s* glorificación; realce; (coll.) celebración, fiesta
**glorify** [ˈglorɪfaɪ] (*pret & pp:* **-fied**) *va* glorificar; realzar
**glorious** [ˈglorɪəs] *adj* glorioso; espléndido, excelente
**glory** [ˈglorɪ] *s* (*pl:* **-ries**) gloria; **to be in one's glory** estar en sus glorias; **to go to glory** ganar la gloria (*morirse*); (slang) fracasar, sufrir colapso; (*pret & pp:* **-ried**) *va* gloriar, glorificar; *vn* gloriarse; **to glory in** gloriarse de (*p.ej., sus hazañas*); gloriarse en (*p.ej., el Señor*)
**gloss** [glɔs] o [glɑs] *s* brillo, lustre; apariencia engañosa; glosa; glosario; glosa (*composición poética*); *va* abrillantar, lustrar; satinar, glasear; disculpar, paliar; glosar; *vn* glosar; **to gloss over** disculpar, paliar
**glossa** [ˈglɑsə] *s* (*pl:* **-sae** [si]) (zool.) glosis
**glossarial** [glɑˈsɛrɪəl] *adj* de glosario; a modo de glosario
**glossary** [ˈglɑsərɪ] *s* (*pl:* **-ries**) glosario
**glossator** [glɑˈsetər] *s* glosador
**glossectomy** [glɑˈsɛktəmɪ] *s* (*pl:* **-mies**) (surg.) glosectomía
**glossitis** [glɑˈsaɪtɪs] *s* (path.) glositis
**glossy** [ˈglɔsɪ] o [ˈglɑsɪ] *adj* (*comp:* **-ier;** *super:* **-iest**) brillante, lustroso; satinado, glaseado
**glottal** [ˈglɑtəl] *adj* glótico
**glottal stop** *s* (phonet.) choque glótico
**glottis** [ˈglɑtɪs] *s* (anat.) glotis
**glove** [glʌv] *s* guante; **to handle with gloves** manejar o tratar con sumo cuidado; **to handle without gloves** manejar o tratar sin miramientos; **to take up the glove** recoger el guante; **to throw down the glove** arrojar o echar el guante
**glove compartment** *s* (aut.) portaguantes, guantera o guantero
**glover** [ˈglʌvər] *s* guantero
**glove stretcher** *s* ensanchador, juanas
**glow** [glo] *s* resplandor (*de una cosa que arde sin llama*); brillo, esplendor (*p.ej., de los arreboles de la puesta del sol*); sensación agradable de calor corporal; color en las mejillas, color en todo el cuerpo; manifestación o señales de interés muy vivo; *vn* brillar intensamente y sin llama; manifestar calor corporal (*por el color en las mejillas o en todo el cuerpo*); tener las mejillas encendidas; estar muy animado, estar vehemente; estar anhelante (*p.ej., de interés*); arder (*p.ej., la zona tórrida*); (fig.) brillar
**glower** [ˈglaʊər] *s* ceño, mirada hosca; *vn* tener la mirada hosca; **to glower at** mirar hoscamente
**glowing** [ˈglo·ɪŋ] *adj* ardiente, encendido; radiante; entusiasta
**glowworm** [ˈglo,wʌrm] *s* (ent.) gusano de luz
**gloxinia** [glɑkˈsɪnɪə] *s* (bot.) gloxínea
**gloze** [gloz] *va* disculpar, paliar; abrillantar; *vn* glosar; brillar
**glucina** [gluˈsaɪnə] *s* (chem.) glucina
**glucinium** [gluˈsɪnɪəm] o **glucinum** [gluˈsaɪnəm] *s* (chem.) glucinio
**glucoprotein** [,glukoˈprotiɪn] o [,glukoˈprotin] *s* var. de **glycoprotein**
**glucose** [ˈglukos] *s* (biochem.) glucosa
**glucoside** [ˈglukosaɪd] o [ˈglukosɪd] *s* (chem.) glucósido
**glucosuria** [,glukoˈsʊrɪə] *s* var. de **glycosuria**
**glue** [glu] *s* cola; *va* encolar; pegar fuertemente, unir fuertemente
**glue pot** *s* cacerola para cola, pote de la cola
**gluey** [ˈgluɪ] *adj* (*comp:* **gluier;** *super:* **gluiest**) pegajoso; encolado
**glug** [glʌg] *s* gluglú (*sonido del agua*); (*pret & pp:* **glugged;** *ger:* **glugging**) *vn* hacer gluglú (*el agua*)
**glum** [glʌm] *adj* (*comp:* **glummer;** *super:* **glummest**) hosco, sombrío, tétrico
**glume** [glum] *s* (bot.) gluma
**glut** [glʌt] *s* abundancia, gran acopio; exceso, plétora; (*pret & pp:* **glutted;** *ger:* **glutting**) *va* hartar, saciar; inundar (*el mercado*); obstruir; *vn* hartarse, saciarse
**gluteal** [gluˈtiəl] o [ˈglutɪəl] *adj* (anat.) glúteo
**gluten** [ˈglutən] *s* gluten
**gluten bread** *s* pan de gluten
**gluten flour** *s* harina de gluten
**glutenous** [ˈglutɪnəs] *adj* glutenoso
**glutinous** [ˈglutɪnəs] *adj* glutinoso
**glutton** [ˈglʌtən] *s* glotón; (zool.) glotón (*Gulo gulo*); (zool.) carcayú (*Gulo luscus*)
**gluttonous** [ˈglʌtənəs] *adj* glotón
**gluttony** [ˈglʌtənɪ] *s* (*pl:* **-ies**) glotonería
**glyceric** [glɪˈsɛrɪk] o [ˈglɪsərɪk] *adj* glicérico
**glyceric acid** *s* (chem.) ácido glicérico
**glyceride** [ˈglɪsəraɪd] o [ˈglɪsərɪd] *s* (chem.) glicérido
**glycerin** o **glycerine** [ˈglɪsərɪn] *s* glicerina
**glycerol** [ˈglɪsərol] o [ˈglɪsərɑl] *s* (chem.) glicerol
**glyceryl** [ˈglɪsərɪl] *s* (chem.) glicerilo
**glycine** [ˈglaɪsin] o [glaɪˈsin] *s* (chem.) glicina
**glycogen** [ˈglaɪkədʒən] *s* (biochem.) glicógeno
**glycogenic** [,glaɪkəˈdʒɛnɪk] *adj* glicogénico

**glycol** [ˈglaɪkol] o [ˈglaɪkɑl] *s* (chem.) glicol
**glycoprotein** [ˌglaɪkoˈprotiɪn] o [ˌglaɪkoˈprotin] *s* (biochem.) glucoproteína
**glycosuria** [ˌglaɪkoˈsurɪə] *s* (path.) glucosuria
**glyph** [glɪf] *s* (arch.) glifo
**glyptography** [glɪpˈtɑgrəfɪ] *s* gliptografía
**gm.** abr. de **gram** o **grams**
**G.M.** abr. de **general manager, Grand Marshal** y **Grand Master**
**G-man** [ˈdʒiˌmæn] *s* (*pl:* **-men**) (U.S.A.) agente secreto federal
**G.M.T.** abr. de **Greenwich mean time**
**gnar** [nɑr] (*pret & pp:* **gnarred;** *ger:* **gnarring**) *vn* gruñir, refunfuñar
**gnarl** [nɑrl] *s* nudo (*en un árbol, una tabla, etc.*); *va* torcer; *vn* gruñir, refunfuñar
**gnarled** [nɑrld] *adj* nudoso, retorcido; de contrafibra; pendenciero, terco
**gnarly** [ˈnɑrlɪ] *adj* (*comp:* **-ier;** *super:* **-iest**) var. de **gnarled**
**gnash** [næʃ] *va* rechinar (*los dientes*); morder haciendo crujir los dientes; *vn* rechinar
**gnat** [næt] *s* (ent.) jején; (ent.) mosquito; **to strain at a gnat** afanarse o molestarse por pequeñeces
**gnathion** [ˈneθɪɑn] o [ˈnæθɪɑn] *s* (anat.) gnatión
**gnaw** [nɔ] (*pret:* **gnawed;** *pp:* **gnawed** o **gnawn**) *va* roer; practicar (*un agujero*) royendo; *vn* morder; **to gnaw at** roer
**gneiss** [naɪs] *s* (geol.) gneis
**gneissic** [ˈnaɪsɪk] *adj* gnéisico
**gnome** [nom] *s* gnomo; (myth.) gnomo
**gnomic** [ˈnomɪk] *adj* gnómico
**gnomon** [ˈnomɑn] *s* gnomon
**Gnostic** [ˈnɑstɪk] *adj & s* gnóstico
**Gnosticism** [ˈnɑstɪsɪzəm] *s* gnosticismo
**gnu** [nu] o [nju] *s* (zool.) gnu o ñu
**go** [go] *s* (*pl:* **goes**) ida, ir; (coll.) ánimo, energía, ímpetu; (coll.) estado, situación; (coll.) boga, furor; (coll.) ensayo; éxito; paso libre (*de la circulación de los automóviles*); **it's a go** es un trato hecho; es un gran éxito; **it's all the go** está muy en boga, hace furor; **it's no go** es inútil, es imposible; es un fracaso; **on the go** en continuo movimiento; de viaje; **this is a pretty go** estamos frescos; **to have a go at** ensayar, tentar; **to have plenty of go** estar muy animado; **to make a go of** lograr éxito en ‖ (*pret:* **went;** *pp:* **gone**) *va* ir por, llevar (*un camino*); (coll.) soportar, tolerar; (coll.) llegar hasta, aventurarse hasta; (coll.) apostar; **to go better** apostar más que; llevar la ventaja a; vencer; **to go it** (coll.) ir con gran rapidez; **to go it alone** obrar sin ayuda ‖ *vn* ir; irse, marcharse; funcionar, marchar; caminar; andar (*p.ej., desnudo, con hambre*); avanzar, seguir; correr, pasar; cundir; ponerse, volverse (*p.ej., loco*); desaparecer; estar bien; alcanzar, extenderse; venderse, tener venta; conducir, tender; surtir efecto, tener éxito; colocarse, guardarse; sonar; decirse; hacer, p.ej., **when you swim, go like this** cuando Vd. nada, haga así; **so it goes** así va el mundo; **to be going to** + *inf* o **to go to** + *inf* ir a + *inf;* **to be gone** haberse agotado; haberse gastado; haberse roto; haberse muerto; haber dejado de ser; haberse vuelto inservible; **to go** + *ger* ir de + *noun,* p.ej., **to go fishing** ir de pesca; **to go hunting** ir de caza; **to go about** andar de un sitio para otro; dar vuelta; andar (*p.ej., desnudo*); emprender (*una tarea*); ocuparse en (*los negocios de uno*); (naut.) cambiar de amura; **to go against** ir en contra de, oponerse a, chocar con; **to go ahead** seguir adelante; **to go around** andar de un sitio para otro; dar vuelta; dar vueltas; andar (*p.ej., desnudo*); alcanzar para todos; circundar; dar vueltas a, ir alrededor de; **to go at** emprender; acometer; **to go away** irse, marcharse; pasar (*p.ej., un dolor de cabeza*); **to go by** pasar, pasar por; guiarse por (*p.ej., una serie de señales*); atenerse a, regirse por; conocerse por (*un nombre, un apodo*); usar (*un nombre falso*); **to go down** bajar; hundirse (*un buque, el sol*); **to go down fighting** hundirse peleando; **to go for** ir por; favorecer; ser tenido por; pasar (*p.ej., días enteros*); (coll.) acometer; **to go get** ir por, ir a buscar; **to go in** entrar; entrar en; encajar en; caber en; **to go in for** (coll.) interesarse por, dedicarse a; **to go into** entrar en; encajar en; caber en; discutir; investigar; (aut.) poner (*p.ej., primera*); **to go in with** juntarse con, asociarse con; **to go off** irse, marcharse; estallar; dispararse; tener lugar; llevarse a cabo; **to go off very well** ser un gran éxito; **to go on** seguir adelante; ir tirando; enfurecerse; **to go on** + *ger* continuar, seguir + *ger;* **to go on with** continuar, proseguir; **to go out** salir; pasar de moda; apagarse; declararse en huelga; salir (*a tertulias, teatros, etc.*); **to go over** pasar por encima de; examinar, repasar, revisar; releer; tener éxito; **to go over to** pasarse a las filas de; **to go through** pasar por; hacer completamente, llegar al fin de; hallarse en (*una situación desagradable*); ser aprobado; disipar rápidamente, agotar (*una fortuna*); **to go through with** llevar a su término; **to go with** ir con, acompañar; salir con (*una muchacha*); hacer juego con, armonizar con; **to go without** pasarse sin, andarse sin
**goa** [ˈgoə] *s* (zool.) antílope tibetano
**goad** [god] *s* aguijada, aguijón; *va* aguijonear
**go-ahead** [ˈgoəˌhɛd] *adj* (coll.) emprendedor; *s* (coll.) señal para seguir adelante
**goal** [gol] *s* (sport & fig.) meta; (football) gol
**goalkeeper** [ˈgolˌkipər] *s* (sport) portero, guardameta
**goal line** *s* (sport) raya de la meta
**goal post** *s* (sport) poste de la meta
**goat** [got] *s* (zool.) cabra, macho cabrío; (slang) víctima inocente; **to be the goat** (slang) pagar el pato; **to get one's goat** (slang) enojar, tomar el pelo a; **to ride the goat** (coll.) recibir la iniciación en una sociedad secreta
**goatee** [goˈti] *s* perilla, pera
**goat grass** *s* (bot.) rompesacos
**goatherd** [ˈgotˌhʌrd] *s* cabrero
**goatish** [ˈgotɪʃ] *adj* cabrerizo, cabrío; lascivo, lujurioso
**goatsbeard** [ˈgotsˌbɪrd] *s* (bot.) barba cabruna; (bot.) clavaria
**goatskin** [ˈgotˌskɪn] *s* piel de cabra
**goat's-rue** [ˈgotsˌru] *s* (bot.) galega, ruda cabruna; (bot.) tefrosia
**goatsucker** [ˈgotˌsʌkər] *s* (orn.) chotacabras
**goat willow** *s* (bot.) sauce cabruno
**gob** [gɑb] *s* (coll.) masa informe y pequeña; (slang) marinero de guerra
**gobang** [goˈbæŋ] *s* juego japonés algo parecido a las damas
**gobbet** [ˈgɑbɪt] *s* pedazo; masa pequeña, terrón
**gobble** [ˈgɑbəl] *s* gluglú (*voz del pavo*); *va* engullir; **to gobble up** engullirse ávidamente; (coll.) posesionarse ávidamente de; *vn* gluglutear, gorgonear, titar (*el pavo*); engullir
**gobbledygook** [ˈgɑbəldɪˌguk] *s* (coll.) galimatías, lenguaje obscuro e incomprensible
**gobbler** [ˈgɑblər] *s* (orn.) pavo, gallipavo
**Gobelin tapestry** [ˈgɑbəlɪn] *s* tapiz gobelino
**go-between** [ˈgobɪˌtwin] *s* medianero; alcahuete; conector
**goblet** [ˈgɑblɪt] *s* copa (*con pie*)
**goblin** [ˈgɑblɪn] *s* duende, gobelino
**goby** [ˈgobɪ] *s* (*pl:* **-bies**) (ichth.) gobio
**go-by** [ˈgoˌbaɪ] *s* (coll.) desaire; **to give the go-by to** (coll.) desairar, negarse al trato de
**gocart** [ˈgoˌkɑrt] *s* cochecito para niños; andaderas; carruaje ligero
**god** [gɑd] *s* dios; (*cap.*) *s* Dios; **God forbid** no lo quiera Dios; **God grant** permita Dios; **God willing** Dios mediante
**godchild** [ˈgɑdˌtʃaɪld] *s* (*pl:* **-children**) ahijado, ahijada
**goddaughter** [ˈgɑdˌdɔtər] *s* ahijada
**goddess** [ˈgɑdɪs] *s* diosa; (fig.) diosa (*mujer sumamente bella*)
**godfather** [ˈgɑdˌfɑðər] *s* padrino
**God-fearing** [ˈgɑdˌfɪrɪŋ] *adj* timorato; devoto, pío
**Godforsaken** [ˈgɑdfərˌsekən] *adj* dejado de la mano de Dios; (coll.) descuidado, desierto, desolado
**Godfrey** [ˈgɑdfrɪ] *s* Godofredo
**God-given** [ˈgɑdˌgɪvən] *adj* que ha dado Dios; que viene como anillo al dedo
**godhead** [ˈgɑdhɛd] *s* divinidad; (*cap.*) *s* Dios
**godhood** [ˈgɑdhud] *s* divinidad

**godless** [ˈgɑdlɪs] *adj* descreído, sin religión; malvado, desalmado
**godlike** [ˈgɑd,laɪk] *adj* deiforme; propio para Dios, propio para un dios
**godliness** [ˈgɑdlɪnɪs] *s* devoción, piedad, santidad
**godly** [ˈgɑdlɪ] *adj* (*comp:* **-lier;** *super:* **-liest**) devoto, pío, piadoso; (archaic) divino
**godmother** [ˈgɑd,mʌðər] *s* madrina
**godparent** [ˈgɑd,pɛrənt] *s* padrino o madrina
**God's acre** *s* campo santo
**godsend** [ˈgɑd,sɛnd] *s* cosa llovida del cielo
**godship** [ˈgɑdʃɪp] *s* divinidad
**God's house** *s* casa de Dios (*iglesia*)
**godson** [ˈgɑd,sʌn] *s* ahijado
**Godspeed** [ˈgɑd,spid] *s* bienandanza; *interj* ¡buena suerte!, ¡feliz viaje!
**Godward** [ˈgɑdwərd] o **Godwards** [ˈgɑdwərdz] *adv* hacia Dios
**godwit** [ˈgɑdwɪt] *s* (orn.) agujeta
**goes** [goz] *tercera persona del sg del pres de ind de* **go**
**go-getter** [ˈgoˈgɛtər] *s* (slang) buscavidas, trafagón, persona emprendedora que se las sabe arreglar para todo
**goggle** [ˈgɑgəl] *adj* saltón (*dícese de los ojos*); **goggles** *spl* anteojos de camino; *vn* volver los ojos; abrir los ojos desmesuradamente; abrirse desmesuradamente (*los ojos*)
**goggle-eyed** [ˈgɑgəl,aɪd] *adj* de ojos saltones
**going** [ˈgo·ɪŋ] *s* ida, partida; estado del camino; marcha; *adj* en marcha, funcionando; (naut.) que marcha viento en popa; **going on** casi, p.ej., **it is going on two o'clock** son casi las dos; *ger de* **go**
**going concern** *s* empresa que marcha
**goings on** *spl* actividades; bulla, jarana
**goiter** [ˈgɔɪtər] *s* (path.) bocio
**gold** [gold] *s* oro; *adj* áureo, de oro; dorado
**goldbeater** [ˈgold,bitər] *s* batidor de oro, batihoja
**goldbeater's skin** *s* venza, película de tripa de buey
**gold brick** *s* (coll.) estafa, embuste; **to sell a gold brick** (coll.) vender gato por liebre
**Gold Coast** *s* Costa de Oro (*en África*)
**goldcrest** [ˈgold,krɛst] *s* (orn.) reyezuelo moñudo
**gold digger** *s* (slang) extractora de oro, buscadora de oro
**gold dust** *s* oro en polvo
**golden** [ˈgoldən] *adj* áureo, de oro; dorado; brillante; excelente; muy valioso; muy importante; muy favorable; próspero, floreciente; rubio
**golden age** *s* (myth.) edad de oro, siglo de oro; siglo de oro (*de la literatura castellana*)
**Golden Book** *s* libro de oro (*de la nobleza veneciana*)
**golden calf** *s* (Bib. & fig.) becerro de oro
**golden chain** *s* (bot.) lluvia de oro
**golden eagle** *s* (orn.) águila caudal, águila real
**goldeneye** [ˈgoldən,aɪ] *s* (orn.) clángula
**Golden Fleece** *s* toisón, toisón de oro (*orden*); (myth.) toisón de oro, vellocino de oro
**Golden Gate** *s* Puerta de Oro (*entrada de la bahía de San Francisco*)
**golden glow** *s* (bot.) rudbequia
**Golden Horn** *s* Cuerno de Oro
**golden mean** *s* justo medio
**golden oriole** *s* (orn.) oropéndola, virio
**golden pheasant** *s* (orn.) faisán dorado
**golden plover** *s* (orn.) chorlito
**goldenrod** [ˈgoldən,rɑd] *s* (bot.) vara de oro, vara de San José, plumeros amarillos
**golden rule** *s* regla de la caridad cristiana (*Todas las cosas que quisierais que los hombres hiciesen con vosotros, así también haced vosotros con ellos*); (arith.) regla áurea, regla de oro
**golden thistle** *s* (bot.) cardillo, tagarnina
**golden wedding** *s* bodas de oro
**gold-filled** [ˈgold,fɪld] *adj* revestido de oro, enchapado en oro
**goldfinch** [ˈgold,fɪntʃ] *s* (orn.) jilguero, pintacilgo
**goldfish** [ˈgold,fɪʃ] *s* pez de color, cola de cometa, carpa dorada
**gold foil** *s* pan de oro, oro batido
**goldilocks** [ˈgoldɪ,lɑks] *s* (coll.) rubiales (*persona rubia*); (bot.) ranúnculo turbante dorado; (bot.) calderones
**gold leaf** *s* pan de oro finísimo
**gold mine** *s* mina de oro; (coll.) mina, filón, Potosí; **to strike a gold mine** (fig.) encontrar una mina
**gold number** *s* (chem.) índice de oro
**gold-of-pleasure** [ˈgoldəvˈplɛʒər] *s* (bot.) camelina
**gold plate** *s* vajilla de oro
**gold-plate** [ˈgoldˈplet] *va* dorar (*cubrir con un baño de oro*)
**gold rush** *s* gran agolpamiento de exploradores en busca de veneros de oro
**goldsmith** [ˈgold,smɪθ] *s* orfebre
**gold standard** *s* patrón de oro, patrón oro
**golf** [gɑlf] *s* (sport) golf; *vn* jugar al golf
**golf club** *s* palo de golf; asociación de jugadores de golf
**golfer** [ˈgɑlfər] *s* (sport) golfista
**golf links** *spl* (sport) campo de golf
**Golgotha** [ˈgɑlgəθə] *s* (Bib.) el Gólgota
**Goliath** [goˈlaɪəθ] *s* (Bib.) Goliat
**golliwog** o **golliwogg** [ˈgɑlɪwɑg] *s* muñeca negra ridícula; persona ridícula
**golosh** [gəˈlɑʃ] *s* var. de **galosh**
**Gomorrah** o **Gomorrha** [gəˈmɑrə] o [gəˈmɔrə] *s* (Bib.) Gomorra; (fig.) lugar o centro de depravación
**gonad** [ˈgɑnæd] o [ˈgonæd] *s* (anat.) gónada
**gondola** [ˈgɑndələ] *s* góndola; (aer.) barquilla, cabina; (rail.) vagón de carga abierto, góndola
**gondolier** [,gɑndəˈlɪr] *s* gondolero
**gone** [gɔn] o [gɑn] *adj* agotado; arruinado; pasado; desaparecido; muerto; débil, desfallecido; **far gone** muy adelantado; muy comprometido; **gone on** (coll.) enamorado de; *pp de* **go**
**goneness** [ˈgɔnnɪs] o [ˈgɑnnɪs] *s* desfallecimiento, debilidad
**goner** [ˈgɔnər] o [ˈgɑnər] *s* (coll.) persona desahuciada, persona muerta, animal muerto, animal que se está muriendo, cosa echada a perder
**gonfalon** [ˈgɑnfəlɑn] *s* confalón
**gonfalonier** [,gɑnfələˈnɪr] *s* confaloniero
**gong** [gɔŋ] o [gɑŋ] *s* gongo; campana en forma de tazón
**Gongorism** [ˈgɑŋgərɪzəm] *s* gongorismo
**Gongorist** [ˈgɑŋgərɪst] *s* gongorino
**Gongoristic** [,gɑŋgəˈrɪstɪk] *adj* gongorino
**gonidium** [gəˈnɪdɪəm] *s* (*pl:* **-a** [ə]) (bot.) gonidio
**goniometer** [,gonɪˈɑmɪtər] *s* goniómetro
**goniometry** [,gonɪˈɑmɪtrɪ] *s* goniometría
**gonium** [ˈgonɪəm] *s* (*pl:* **-a** [ə]) (biol.) gonia
**gonococcus** [,gɑnəˈkɑkəs] *s* (*pl:* **-cocci** [ˈkɑksaɪ]) (bact.) gonococo
**gonophore** [ˈgɑnəfor] *s* (bot. & zool.) gonóforo
**gonorrhea** o **gonorrhoea** [,gɑnəˈriə] *s* (path.) gonorrea
**gonorrheal** [,gɑnəˈriəl] *adj* gonorreico
**goo** [gu] *s* (slang) substancia muy pegajosa
**goober** [ˈgubər] *s* (bot.) cacahuete (*planta y fruto*)
**good** [gʊd] *adj* (*comp:* **better;** *super:* **best**) bueno; **a good one** (iron.) buen chiste, buena noticia, buena jugada; **as good as** casi; **to be good at** tener talento para; **to be no good** (coll.) no servir para nada; (coll.) ser un perdido; **to hold good** seguir vigente, ser valedero; **to make good** tener éxito; probar (*un aserto*); cumplir (*sus promesas*); responder de (*los daños*); pagar o satisfacer (*una deuda*); llevar a cabo (*una evasión*); **good and** (coll.) bien, p.ej., **good and late** bien tarde; **good for** bueno para; capaz de hacer; capaz de pagar; capaz de durar o de vivir (*cierto tiempo*); *s* bien, provecho, utilidad, ventaja; **goods** *spl* efectos; géneros, mercancías; (Brit.) carga; **for good** para siempre; **for good and all** de una vez para siempre; **the good** lo bueno; los buenos; **to be up to no good** llevar mala intención; **to catch with the goods** (slang) coger con el hurto en las manos, coger en flagrante; **to deliver the goods** (slang) cumplir lo esperado, cumplir lo prometido; **to do good** hacer el bien; aprovechar; dar salud o fuerzas a; **to have** o **get the goods on** (slang) tener

la prueba de la culpa de; **to the good** de sobra, en el haber; **what is the good of . . . ?** ¿de o para qué sirve . . .?; **what is the good of** + *ger?* ¿de o para qué sirve + *inf?*
**good afternoon** *s* buenas tardes
**Good Book** *s* Biblia
**good-by** [ˌgʊdˈbaɪ] *s* (*pl:* **-bys**) adiós; *interj* ¡adiós!
**good-bye** [ˌgʊdˈbaɪ] *s* (*pl:* **-byes**) var. de **good-by;** *interj* var. de **good-by**
**good cheer** *s* alegría; buenas viandas; ánimo, valor
**good day** *s* buenos días
**good evening** *s* buenas tardes, buenas noches
**good fellow** *s* (coll.) buen chico, buen sujeto; (coll.) jaranero
**good fellowship** *s* compañerismo, camaradería
**good form** *s* buenas formas, conducta ajustada a los cánones sociales
**good-for-nothing** [ˈgʊdfərˌnʌθɪŋ] *adj* inútil, sin valor; *s* pelafustán, perdido, haragán
**Good Friday** *s* Viernes santo
**good graces** *spl* favor, amistad, estimación
**good-hearted** [ˈgʊdˈhɑrtɪd] *adj* de buen corazón
**good humor** *s* buen humor
**good-humored** [ˈgʊdˈhjuməd] o [ˈgʊdˈjuməd] *adj* de buen humor; afable, jovial
**goodish** [ˈgʊdɪʃ] *adj* bastante bueno; considerable
**goodliness** [ˈgʊdlɪnɪs] *s* excelencia; hermosura, gracia
**good liver** *s* (coll.) gastrónomo
**good-looking** [ˈgʊdˈlʊkɪŋ] *adj* guapo, bien parecido, buen mozo
**good looks** *spl* buen aspecto, hermosura
**goodly** [ˈgʊdlɪ] *adj* (*comp:* **-lier;** *super:* **-liest**) agradable, excelente; bien parecido, hermoso; considerable
**goodman** [ˈgʊdmən] o [ˈgʊdˌmæn] *s* (*pl:* **-men**) (archaic) marido, amo de casa; (archaic) tío (*título*)
**good morning** *s* buenos días
**good nature** *s* natural alegre, buen natural
**good-natured** [ˈgʊdˈnetʃərd] *adj* afable, bonachón
**Good Neighbor Policy** *s* política de la buena vecindad
**goodness** [ˈgʊdnɪs] *s* bondad; *interj* ¡válgame Dios!; **for goodness' sake!** ¡por Dios!; **thank goodness!** ¡gracias a Dios!; **goodness gracious!** ¡santo Dios!; **goodness knows!** ¡quién sabe!
**good night** *s* buenas noches
**good offices** *spl* (dipl.) buenos oficios
**Good Samaritan** *s* (Bib.) buen samaritano; persona que socorre generosamente al prójimo
**good sense** *s* sensatez
**Good Shepherd** *s* (Bib.) Buen Pastor
**good-sized** [ˈgʊdˈsaɪzd] *adj* de buen tamaño, bastante grande
**good speed** *s* adiós y buena suerte
**goods train** *s* (Brit.) mercancías, tren de mercancías
**good-tempered** [ˈgʊdˈtɛmpərd] *adj* afable, alegre, de natural apacible
**good time** *s* rato agradable; **to have a good time** pasar un buen rato, divertirse; **to make good time** llegar en poco tiempo
**good turn** *s* favor
**goodwife** [ˈgʊdˌwaɪf] *s* (*pl:* **-wives**) (archaic) ama de casa; (archaic) señá
**good will** *s* buena voluntad, buena gana; buen nombre (*de un negocio*)
**good works** *spl* buena obra, obras de misericordia
**goody** [ˈgʊdɪ] *adj* (coll.) beatuco, santurrón; *interj* (coll.) ¡qué alegría!; *s* (*pl:* **-ies**) (coll.) golosina
**goody-goody** [ˈgʊdɪˈgʊdɪ] *adj* (coll.) beatuco, santurrón; *s* (*pl:* **-ies**) beatuco, santurrón
**gooey** [ˈguɪ] *adj* (*comp:* **gooier;** *super:* **gooiest**) (slang) muy pegajoso, fangoso
**goof** [guf] *s* (slang) mentecato; *va & vn* (slang) chapucear
**goofy** [ˈgufɪ] *adj* (*comp:* **-ier;** *super:* **-iest**) (slang) mentecato
**goon** [gun] *s* (slang) terrorista de alquiler; (slang) estúpido; (slang) canalla, gamberro
**goop** [gup] *s* (slang) palurdo
**goosander** [guˈsændər] *s* (orn.) pato sierra
**goose** [gus] *s* (*pl:* **geese**) (orn.) ánsar, ganso, oca; bobo; **the goose hangs high** todo va a pedir de boca; **to cook one's goose** malbaratarle a uno los planes, perderle a uno; **to shoe the goose** holgar; emborracharse; *s* (*pl:* **gooses**) plancha de sastre
**goose barnacle** *s* (zool.) anatifa
**gooseberry** [ˈguzˌbɛrɪ] o [ˈgusˌbɛrɪ] *s* (*pl:* **-ries**) (bot.) uva crespa, uva espina, grosellero silvestre; grosella silvestre
**goose egg** *s* huevo de oca; (slang) cero
**goose flesh** *s* carne de gallina
**goosefoot** [ˈgusˌfʊt] *s* (*pl:* **-foots**) quenopodio, hierba del zorrillo
**goosegirl** [ˈgusˌgʌrl] *s* ansarera
**gooseherd** [ˈgusˌhʌrd] *s* ansarero
**gooseneck** [ˈgusˌnɛk] *s* cuello de cisne; flexo (*de una lámpara*); (naut.) gancho de botalones
**goose pimples** *spl* carne de gallina
**goose step** *s* (mil.) paso de ganso
**goose-step** [ˈgusˌstɛp] (*pret & pp:* **-stepped;** *ger:* **-stepping**) *vn* (mil.) marchar con paso de ganso
**G.O.P.** abr. de **Grand Old Party**
**gopher** [ˈgofər] *s* (zool.) ardillón, ardilla de tierra (*Spermophilus*); (zool.) tuza (*Geomys*)
**gopherwood** [ˈgofərˌwʊd] *s* (bot.) árbol tintóreo norteamericano (*Cladrastis lutea*); madera amarilla (*de Cladrastis lutea*); (Bib.) madera de gopher
**Gordian** [ˈgɔrdɪən] *adj* gordiano
**Gordian knot** *s* (myth.) nudo gordiano; **to cut the Gordian knot** (myth. & fig.) cortar el nudo gordiano
**gore** [gor] *s* sangre derramada; sangre cuajada; (sew.) nesga; *va* acornar, herir con los cuernos; (sew.) nesgar
**gorge** [gɔrdʒ] *s* garganta, desfiladero; (anat.) gorja, garganta; (arch.) garganta; atasco (*p.ej., de hielo en un río*); contenido del estómago; hartazgo, panzada; asco; indignación; (fort.) gola; *va* engullir; atiborrar; *vn* atiborrarse
**gorgeous** [ˈgɔrdʒəs] *adj* brillante, de mucho esplendor, magnífico
**gorgerin** [ˈgɔrdʒərɪn] *s* (arch.) gorguera, collarín
**gorget** [ˈgɔrdʒɪt] *s* cuello, collar; griñón, impla; (arm.) gorguera, gorjal; (mil.) gola (*insignia militar*); (surg.) gorjerete (*para fístulas*); (zool.) mancha (*en el cuello*)
**Gorgon** [ˈgɔrgən] *adj* gorgóneo; *s* (myth.) Gorgona; (*l.c.*) *s* mujer muy fea y feroz
**Gorgonian** [gɔrˈgonɪən] *adj* gorgóneo
**Gorgonzola** [ˌgɔrgənˈzolə] *s* gorgonzola (*queso*)
**gorilla** [gəˈrɪlə] *s* (zool.) gorila
**gormand** [ˈgɔrmənd] *s* var. de **gourmand**
**gormandize** [ˈgɔrməndaɪz] *va* comer glotonamente; *vn* glotonear
**gorse** [gɔrs] *s* (bot.) aulaga, tojo
**gory** [ˈgorɪ] *adj* (*comp:* **-ier;** *super:* **-iest**) ensangrentado; sangriento
**gosh** [gɑʃ] *interj* ¡caramba!
**goshawk** [ˈgɑsˌhɔk] *s* (orn.) azor, accípitre
**gosling** [ˈgɑzlɪŋ] *s* ansarino
**gospel** [ˈgɑspəl] *s* Evangelio (*doctrina y vida de Jesucristo*); evangelio (*religión cristiana; verdad indiscutible*); *adj* evangélico; (*cap.*) *s* Evangelio (*cada uno de los cuatro primeros libros del Nuevo Testamento*)
**gospeler** o **gospeller** [ˈgɑspələr] *s* (eccl.) evangelistero; fanático, sectario; (scornful) protestante, puritano
**Gospel side** *s* (eccl.) lado del evangelio
**gospel truth** *s* evangelio (*verdad indiscutible*)
**gossamer** [ˈgɑsəmər] *s* telaraña, hilo de telaraña; gasa sutilísima; tela impermeable muy delgada; impermeable de tela muy delgada; *adj* sutil, diáfano, finísimo, delgadísimo
**gossamery** [ˈgɑsəmərɪ] *adj* telarañoso
**gossip** [ˈgɑsɪp] *s* chismes, chismería; chismoso; **piece of gossip** chisme; *vn* chismear
**gossip columnist** *s* periodista chismoso
**gossipy** [ˈgɑsɪpɪ] *adj* chismoso
**gossoon** [gɑˈsun] *s* muchacho; mozo, criado
**got** [gɑt] *pret & pp de* **get**
**Goth** [gɑθ] *s* godo; (fig.) bárbaro
**Gothic** [ˈgɑθɪk] *adj* gótico; (f.a.) gótico; bár-

baro; *s* gótico (*idioma*); (f.a.) gótico; (print.) gótica, letra gótica; (*l.c.*) *s* (print.) futura, letra futura
**Gothicism** ['gɑθɪsɪzəm] *s* goticismo; (*l.c.*) *s* barbarie
**gotten** ['gɑtən] *pp de* **get**
**Göttingen** ['gœtɪŋən] *s* Gotinga
**gouache** [gwɑʃ] *s* (paint.) aguazo (*pintura*); aguada (*procedimiento; pintura*)
**gouge** [gaʊdʒ] *s* (carp.) gubia; acanaladura, estría (*hecha con gubia*); muesca, mella (*producida por un instrumento afilado o un objeto esquinado*); (coll.) estafa; *va* excavar con gubia; acanalar, estriar; mellar (*como con gubia*); sacar el ojo a; cavar (*un canal el torrente*); (coll.) estafar; **to gouge out one's eyes** sacarle a uno los ojos (*p.ej., con el pulgar*)
**goulash** ['gulɑʃ] *s* puchero húngaro, estofado húngaro (*muy condimentado*)
**gourd** [gord] o [gʊrd] *s* calabaza (*fruto; calabacino*); (bot.) calabacera; frasco
**gourmand** ['gʊrmənd] *s* goloso
**gourmet** ['gʊrme] *s* gastrónomo, buen paladar
**gout** [gaʊt] *s* (path.) gota; (archaic) gota, salpicadura (*especialmente de sangre*)
**gouty** ['gaʊtɪ] *adj* (*comp:* **-ier;** *super:* **-iest**) gotoso
**gov.** abr. de **governor** y **government**
**Gov.** abr. de **Governor**
**govern** ['gʌvərn] *va* gobernar; (gram.) regir, pedir; *vn* gobernar
**governable** ['gʌvərnəbəl] *adj* gobernable
**governance** ['gʌvərnəns] *s* gobierno
**governess** ['gʌvərnɪs] *s* aya, institutriz
**government** ['gʌvərnmənt] *s* gobierno; (gram.) régimen; **to form a government** formar ministerio; *adj* del estado
**governmental** [,gʌvərn'mɛntəl] *adj* gubernamental, gubernativo
**government in exile** *s* gobierno exilado
**governor** ['gʌvərnər] *s* gobernador; alcaide (*de cárcel, castillo, etc.*); (mach.) regulador; (coll.) padre, papá
**governor general** *s* (*pl:* **governors general**) gobernador general
**governorship** ['gʌvərnər,ʃɪp] *s* gobierno (*cargo y tiempo que dura*)
**govt.** o **Govt.** abr. de **government**
**gowan** ['gaʊən] *s* (Scotch) margarita (*flor*)
**gown** [gaʊn] *s* vestido (*de mujer*); toga (*de profesor, juez, etc.*); traje talar (*del sacerdote*); bata, peinador; camisa de dormir; conjunto de estudiantes, profesores y demás personas de la universidad; *va* poner vestido de mujer a; vestir con toga
**gownsman** ['gaʊnzmən] *s* (*pl:* **-men**) togado; paisano (*no militar*)
**G.P.O.** abr. de **General Post Office** *y* **Government Printing Office**
**gr.** abr. de **gram** o **grams, grain** o **grains** y **gross**
**Gr.** abr. de **Grecian, Greece** y **Greek**
**grab** [græb] *s* arrebatiña; presa; (coll.) robo; (mach.) gancho, gancho agarrador, arrancasondas; (mach.) pala de doble concha; (*pret & pp:* **grabbed;** *ger:* **grabbing**) *va* arrebatar; asir, agarrar; *vn* arrebatar; **to grab at** tratar de arrebatar
**grab bucket** *s* pala de doble concha
**Gracchus** ['grækəs] *s* (*pl:* **-chi** [kaɪ]) Graco
**grace** [gres] *s* gracia (*donaire; favor; perdón*); bendición de la mesa; demora; excelencia, mérito; (mus.) nota o notas de adorno; (theol.) gracia; (*cap.*) *s* Engracia (*nombre de mujer*); **the Graces** (myth.) las Gracias; **to be in the bad graces of** haber caído de la gracia de; **to be in the good graces of** estar en gracia cerca de, gozar del favor de; **to fall from grace** reincidir; **to get in the bad graces of** caer de la gracia de; **to get in the good graces of** congraciarse con; **to have the grace to** + *inf* tener la discreción de + *inf;* **to say grace** bendecir la mesa; **with bad grace** de mal talante; **with good grace** de buen talante; **Your Grace** Su Señoría, Su Señoría Ilustrísima, Su Alteza; *va* adornar, engalanar; agraciar, favorecer; (mus.) poner notas de adorno a
**graceful** ['gresfəl] *adj* gracioso, agraciado
**gracefulness** ['gresfəlnɪs] *s* graciosidad, gracia, donaire
**graceless** ['greslɪs] *adj* desgraciado (*falto de gracia o atractivo*); depravado
**grace note** *s* (mus.) apoyatura, nota de adorno
**gracile** ['græsɪl] *adj* grácil
**gracious** ['greʃəs] *adj* gracioso, graciable; benigno; misericordioso; *interj* ¡ válgame Dios!
**grackle** ['grækəl] *s* (orn.) estornino de los pastores; (orn.) quiscal
**grad.** abr. de **graduate** y **graduated**
**gradation** [gre'deʃən] *s* gradación; grado, paso, matiz; graduación
**grade** [gred] *s* grado (*estado, valor relativo; sección escolar según la edad de los alumnos*); clase, calidad; calificación, nota (*que reciben los alumnos*); pendiente; grado de pendiente; **at grade** a nivel; **down grade** cuesta abajo; (fig.) cuesta abajo; **the grades** la escuela pública elemental; **to make the grade** lograr subir la cuesta; vencer los obstáculos; **up grade** cuesta arriba; (fig.) cada vez mejor; *va* graduar, calificar, clasificar; dar nota a (*un alumno*); leer y poner nota a (*un tema*); nivelar, explanar; **to grade as** graduar de o por (*bueno, malo, etc.*); *vn* cambiarse (*pasando por una serie de gradaciones*); **to grade into** convertirse gradualmente en
**grade crossing** *s* (rail.) paso a nivel, cruce a nivel
**grade line** *s* rasante
**grader** ['gredər] *s* graduador; nivelador; niveladora (*máquina*); alumno de cierto grado, p.ej., **first grader** alumno del primer grado
**grade school** *s* escuela elemental
**gradient** ['gredɪənt] *adj* ambulante; pendiente; *s* pendiente, declive; inclinación; (math. & meteor.) gradiente
**gradin** ['gredɪn] *s* grada; (eccl.) gradilla
**gradine** [grə'din] *s* gradina
**grading** ['gredɪŋ] *s* graduación; clasificación; nivelación, explanación
**gradual** ['grædʒʊəl] *adj* gradual; *s* (eccl.) gradual
**gradually** ['grædʒʊəlɪ] *adv* paulatinamente, poco a poco
**graduate** ['grædʒʊɪt] *adj* graduado; de graduados o para graduados; *s* graduado; frasco graduado, vasija graduada; ['grædʒʊet] *va* graduar; *vn* cambiarse gradualmente; graduarse
**graduate school** *s* escuela de graduados, escuela superior
**graduate student** *s* estudiante graduado
**graduate work** *s* altos estudios, estudios avanzados para graduados de bachiller
**graduation** [,grædʒʊ'eʃən] *s* graduación; ceremonias de graduación
**graduator** ['grædʒʊ,etər] *s* (elec.) graduador, derivador
**graffito** [grə'fito] *s* (pl: **-ti** [ti]) (archeol.) grafito
**graft** [græft] o [grɑft] *s* (hort. & surg.) injerto; (coll.) malversación, soborno político, ganancia ilegal; *va & vn* (hort. & surg.) injertar; (coll.) malversar
**graftage** ['græftɪdʒ] o ['grɑftɪdʒ] *s* (hort.) injertación
**grafter** ['græftər] o ['grɑftər] *s* injertador; (coll.) malversador
**grafting** ['græftɪŋ] o ['grɑftɪŋ] *s* (hort. & surg.) injertación
**grafting knife** *s* navaja de injertar, abridor
**graham bread** ['greəm] *s* pan hecho de harina de trigo sin cerner
**graham flour** *s* harina de trigo sin cerner
**Grail** [grel] *s* Graal o Grial
**grain** [gren] *s* grano; granos; fibra (*de la madera*); vena (*de la piedra*); grano (*de una piel; de una superficie más o menos rugosa; peso*); veteado; carácter, índole; partícula; pizca, p.ej., **not a grain of truth** ni pizca de verdad; **across the grain** transversalmente a la fibra; **against the grain** contra la dirección de la fibra; **to go against the grain** hacérsele a uno cuesta arriba, p.ej., **it goes against the grain** se me hace cuesta arriba; **in the grain** en rama; **with a grain of salt** con un grano de sal; *va* granear (*la masa de pólvora; una piedra litográfica*); vetear, crispir (*la ma-*

*dera*); granular (*una piel*); teñir en rama; alimentar con cereales
**grain alcohol** *s* alcohol de grano
**grained lac** *s* laca en grano
**grain elevator** *s* elevador de granos; depósito de cereales
**grainfield** ['gren,fild] *s* sembrado de trigo (*avena, etc.*)
**graining** ['grenɪŋ] *s* veteado
**gram** [græm] *s* gramo
**gram atom** *s* (chem.) átomo-gramo
**gramercy** [grə'mʌrsɪ] *interj* (archaic) ¡ muchas gracias!; (archaic) ¡ válgame Dios!
**gramineous** [grə'mɪnɪəs] *adj* gramíneo
**graminivorous** [,græmɪ'nɪvərəs] *adj* graminívoro
**gram ion** *s* (chem.) gramión
**grammar** ['græmər] *s* gramática; *adj* de gramática
**grammarian** [grə'mɛrɪən] *s* gramático
**grammar school** *s* (U.S.A.) escuela pública elemental; (Brit.) escuela de humanidades
**grammatical** [grə'mætɪkəl] *adj* gramático, gramatical
**grammatically** [grə'mætɪkəlɪ] *adv* gramaticalmente
**gramme** [græm] *s* var. de **gram**
**gram-molecular** [,græmmə'lɛkjələr] *adj* molecular-gramo
**gram molecule** *s* (chem.) molécula-gramo
**gramophone** ['græməfon] *s* (trademark) gramófono
**Grampian Hills** ['græmpɪən] *spl* montes Grampianos
**Grampians, the** los Grampianos
**grampus** ['græmpəs] *s* (zool.) grampo; (zool.) orca
**granary** ['grænərɪ] o ['grenərɪ] *s* (*pl:* **-ries**) granero; (fig.) granero (*país*)
**grand** [grænd] *adj* grande y magnífico; grandioso, espléndido; importante, principal; excelente
**grandam** ['grændæm] o **grandame** ['grændem] *s* abuela; anciana, vieja
**Grand Army of the Republic** *s* (U.S.A.) asociación de veteranos de la guerra entre Norte y Sur
**grandaunt** ['grænd,ænt] o ['grænd,ɑnt] *s* tía abuela
**Grand Bank** *s* Gran Banco (*a lo largo de la costa de Terranova*)
**Grand Canal** *s* Gran Canal (*de la China*); Canal Grande (*de Venecia*)
**Grand Canyon** *s* Gran Cañón
**grandchild** ['grænd,tʃaɪld] *s* (*pl:* **-children**) nieto o nieta
**granddaughter** ['grænd,dɔtər] *s* nieta
**grand duchess** *s* gran duquesa
**grand duchy** *s* gran ducado
**grand duke** *s* gran duque
**grandee** [græn'di] *s* grande de España; grande, persona de campanillas
**grandeur** ['grændʒər] o ['grændʒʊr] *s* grandeza, magnificencia, esplendor
**grandfather** ['grænd,fɑðər] *s* abuelo; antepasado
**grandfatherly** ['grænd,fɑðərlɪ] *adj* de abuelo, p.ej., **grandfatherly advice** consejos de abuelo
**grandfather's clock** *s* reloj de caja
**grand guard** *s* granguardia
**grandiloquence** [græn'dɪləkwəns] *s* grandilocuencia
**grandiloquent** [græn'dɪləkwənt] *adj* grandilocuente
**grandiose** ['grændɪos] *adj* grandioso; ampuloso, hinchado
**grand jury** *s* (law) jurado de acusación
**grand larceny** *s* (law) robo de cantidad importante
**grand lodge** *s* gran oriente, gran logia (*logia masónica central*)
**grandma** ['grænd,mɑ], ['græm,mɑ] o ['græmə] *s* (coll.) abuela, abuelita
**grandmamma** ['grændmə,mɑ] *s* abuela
**grand march** *s* marcha de sarao (*que consiste en el desfile de todos los convidados*)
**grand master** *s* gran maestre; gran o grande maestro (*en la orden masónica*)
**grandmother** ['grænd,mʌðər] *s* abuela; antepasada
**grandmotherly** ['grænd,mʌðərlɪ] *adj* de abuela, p.ej., **grandmotherly advice** consejos de abuela
**grandnephew** ['grænd,nɛfju] o ['grænd,nɛvju] *s* resobrino
**grandniece** ['grænd,nis] *s* resobrina
**Grand Old Party** *s* (U.S.A.) partido republicano
**grand opera** *s* (mus.) ópera seria
**grandpa** ['grænd,pɑ], ['græm,pɑ] o ['græmpə] *s* (coll.) abuelo, abuelito
**grandpapa** ['grændpə,pɑ] *s* abuelo
**grandparent** ['grænd,pɛrənt] *s* abuelo o abuela
**grand piano** *s* gran piano, piano de cola
**grandsire** ['grænd,saɪr] *s* (archaic) abuelo; (archaic) antepasado; (archaic) viejo
**grand slam** *s* (bridge) bola, grande eslam
**grandson** ['grænd,sʌn] *s* nieto
**grandstand** ['grænd,stænd] *s* gradería cubierta, tribuna
**grandstand play** *s* (sport) jugada espectacular que hace un jugador, no para ganar sino para impresionar al público; (coll.) cosa hecha para impresionar o para granjearse aplausos
**grand strategy** *s* (mil.) alta estrategia
**grand tactics** *ssg* (mil.) gran táctica
**grand total** *s* gran total, suma de totales
**Grand Turk** *s* gran señor, gran Turco
**granduncle** ['grænd,ʌŋkəl] *s* tío abuelo
**grand vizier** *s* gran visir
**grange** [grendʒ] *s* granja; cámara agrícola
**granger** ['grendʒər] *s* granjero
**granite** ['grænɪt] *s* granito; *adj* agranitado; granítico
**graniteware** ['grænɪt,wɛr] *s* platos, tazas, utensilios, etc. de hierro con esmalte de porcelana color de granito
**granitic** [græ'nɪtɪk] *adj* granítico
**granivorous** [græ'nɪvərəs] *adj* granívoro
**grannie** o **granny** ['grænɪ] *s* (*pl:* **-nies**) (coll.) abuela, abuelita; (coll.) anciana, vieja; (coll.) malhumorado, melindroso
**granny knot** *s* gorupo
**grant** [grænt] o [grɑnt] *s* concesión; subvención; donación; transferencia de propiedad; *va* conceder, otorgar; dar (*permiso, perdón, etc.*); transferir (*el título a bienes inmuebles*); **to take for granted** dar por supuesto, dar por sentado, dar por descontado; tratar con indiferencia, no hacer caso de
**grantee** [græn'ti] o [grɑn'ti] *s* cesionario, donatario
**grant-in-aid** ['græntɪn'ed] o ['grɑntɪn'ed] *s* (*pl:* **grants-in-aid**) pensión (*auxilio pecuniario concedido para estimular conocimientos literarios, científicos, etc.*)
**grantor** [græn'tɔr] o [grɑn'tɔr] *s* cesionista, donador
**granular** ['grænjələr] *adj* granular; (path.) granuloso
**granulate** ['grænjəlet] *va* granular; granelar; *vn* granularse; (path.) granularse
**granulation** [,grænjə'leʃən] *s* granulación
**granule** ['grænjʊl] *s* gránulo; (bot. & pharm.) gránulo
**granulite** ['grænjəlaɪt] *s* (geol.) granulita
**granulose** ['grænjəlos] *s* (chem.) granulosa
**grape** [grep] *s* (bot.) vid; uva (*fruto*)
**grape arbor** *s* parral, emparrado de la vid
**grapefruit** ['grep,frut] *s* (bot.) toronjo, pamplemusa, pomelo; toronja, pamplemusa, pomelo (*fruto*)
**grape hyacinth** *s* (bot.) sueldacostilla, jacinto racimoso silvestre
**grape juice** *s* zumo de uva
**grapeshot** ['grep,ʃɑt] *s* metralla
**grape sugar** *s* azúcar de uva
**grapevine** ['grep,vaɪn] *s* (bot.) vid, parra; **by the grapevine** o **by grapevine telegraph** por vías misteriosas (*dícese de los rumores que se propalan sin que se sepa cómo*)
**graph** [græf] o [grɑf] *s* gráfica; (gram.) grafía; *va* representar mediante una gráfica, construir la gráfica de
**graphic** ['græfɪk] o **graphical** ['græfɪkəl] *adj* gráfico
**graphic arts** *spl* artes gráficas
**graphite** ['græfaɪt] *s* grafito

**graphology** [græ'fɑlədʒɪ] *s* grafología
**graphomania** [ˌgræfə'menɪə] *s* grafomanía
**graphometer** [græ'fɑmɪtər] *s* grafómetro
**graph paper** *s* papel cuadriculado
**grapnel** ['græpnəl] *s* garabato; rezón (*ancla pequeña*)
**grapple** ['græpəl] *s* asimiento; (sport) presa; rezón; garabato, arpeo; *va* asir, agarrar; apretar; luchar a brazo partido con; *vn* agarrarse; luchar a brazo partido; **to grapple for** tratar de pescar; **to grapple with** luchar a brazo partido con; tratar de resolver, tratar de vencer
**grappling hook** o **iron** *s* arpeo, garfio
**grapy** ['grepɪ] *adj* de uvas, hecho de uvas
**grasp** [græsp] o [grɑsp] *s* asimiento; alcance, mano, poder; apretón (*de la mano*); comprensión; **to have a good grasp of** saber a fondo; **within the grasp of** al alcance de; *va* asir, empuñar; apoderarse de; comprender; **grasp all, lose all** quien mucho abarca poco aprieta; *vn* extender la mano (*queriendo asir una cosa*); **to grasp at** tratar de asir o coger; aceptar con avidez
**grasping** ['græspɪŋ] o ['grɑspɪŋ] *adj* avaro, codicioso
**grass** [græs] o [grɑs] *s* hierba; césped; **to go to grass** ir al pasto; disfrutar de una temporada de descanso; acabarse, arruinarse; morirse; **to not let the grass grow under one's feet** no dormirse en las pajas; *va* apacentar; cubrir de hierba; *vn* pastar; cubrirse de hierba
**grasshopper** ['græsˌhɑpər] o ['grɑsˌhɑpər] *s* (ent.) saltamontes
**grassland** ['græsˌlænd] o ['grɑsˌlænd] *s* campo de pastoreo
**grass pea** *s* (bot.) almorta
**grass pink** *s* (bot.) clavel coronado o clavellina de pluma
**grass-roots** ['græsˌruts] o ['grɑsˌruts] *adj* (coll.) del pueblo, de la gente común
**grass seed** *s* semilla de césped
**grass snake** *s* (zool.) culebrita inofensiva que vive entre la hierba (*Natrix natrix, Liopeltis vernalis y Thamnophis sirtalis*)
**grass widow** *s* viuda de paja, viuda de marido vivo
**grass widower** *s* hombre divorciado; hombre que vive separado de su mujer
**grassy** ['græsɪ] o ['grɑsɪ] *adj* (*comp:* **-ier;** *super:* **-iest**) herboso; herbáceo
**grate** [gret] *s* reja; parrilla; *va* enrejar; hacer rechinar; rallar (*p.ej., queso*); *vn* rechinar, crujir; **to grate on** (fig.) rallar
**grateful** ['gretfəl] *adj* agradecido, reconocido; agradable, grato; confortante, refrescante
**grater** ['gretər] *s* ralladera, rallador
**gratification** [ˌgrætɪfɪ'keʃən] *s* gratificación, recompensa; complacencia, placer, satisfacción
**gratify** ['grætɪfaɪ] (*pret & pp:* **-fied**) *va* gratificar, complacer, satisfacer; (archaic) gratificar (*recompensar*)
**gratifying** ['grætɪˌfaɪɪŋ] *adj* grato, satisfactorio
**grating** ['gretɪŋ] *adj* áspero, chirriante; irritante, fastidioso; *s* enrejado; (opt.) red
**gratis** ['gretɪs] o ['grætɪs] *adj* gracioso, gratuito; *adv* gratis, de balde
**gratitude** ['grætɪtjud] o ['grætɪtud] *s* gratitud
**gratuitous** [grə'tjuɪtəs] o [grə'tuɪtəs] *adj* gratuito
**gratuity** [grə'tjuɪtɪ] o [grə'tuɪtɪ] *s* (*pl:* **-ties**) dádiva; propina, gratificación
**gratulation** [ˌgrætʃə'leʃən] *s* gratulación
**gratulatory** ['grætʃələˌtorɪ] *adj* gratulatorio
**gravamen** [grə'vemən] *s* (*pl:* **-vamens** o **-vamina** ['væmɪnə]) agravio, motivo para quejarse; (law) materia de un cargo
**grave** [grev] *adj* grave, serio, solemne; grave, bajo (*sonido*); (gram.) grave (*acento*); *s* sepulcro, sepultura; **to have one foot in the grave** estar con un pie en la sepultura; (*pret:* **graved;** *pp:* **graven** o **graved**) *va* grabar; (naut.) despalmar; (fig.) grabar (*p.ej., en la memoria*)
**grave accent** *s* acento grave
**graveclothes** ['grevˌkloz] *spl* mortaja
**gravedigger** ['grevˌdɪgər] *s* sepulturero, enterrador
**gravel** ['grævəl] *s* grava, guijo, recebo; (path.) gravela; (*pret & pp:* **-eled** o **-elled;** *ger:* **-eling** o **-elling**) *va* cubrir de grava o guijo, recebar; desconcertar, dejar perplejo
**gravelly** ['grævəlɪ] *adj* guijoso, cascajoso
**gravel pit** *s* cascajal
**gravel walk** *s* vereda de grava
**graveness** ['grevnɪs] *s* gravedad, seriedad
**graven image** ['grevən] *s* ídolo, imagen
**graver** ['grevər] *s* buril, punzón
**gravestone** ['grevˌston] *s* lápida sepulcral
**graveyard** ['grevˌjɑrd] *s* cementerio, camposanto
**gravid** ['grævɪd] *adj* grávido
**gravidity** [grə'vɪdɪtɪ] *s* gravidez
**gravimetric** [ˌgrævɪ'mɛtrɪk] o **gravimetrical** [ˌgrævɪ'mɛtrɪkəl] *adj* gravimétrico
**gravimetry** [grə'vɪmɪtrɪ] *s* gravimetría
**graving dock** *s* (naut.) dique de carena
**gravitate** ['grævɪtet] *vn* gravitar; **to gravitate to** o **toward** sentir la atracción de, tender hacia
**gravitation** [ˌgrævɪ'teʃən] *s* (phys.) gravitación; atracción, tendencia
**gravitational** [ˌgrævɪ'teʃənəl] *adj* de gravitación, gravitacional
**gravity** ['grævɪtɪ] *s* (*pl:* **-ties**) gravedad; (phys. & mus.) gravedad
**gravity cell** *s* (elec.) pila de gravedad
**gravity feed** *s* (mach.) alimentación por gravedad
**gravure** [grə'vjʊr] o ['grevjʊr] *s* fotograbado
**gravy** ['grevɪ] *s* (*pl:* **-vies**) jugo, grasa; salsa; (slang) ganga, breva
**gravy dish** o **boat** *s* salsera
**gravy train** *s* (slang) pingüe destino, enchufe
**gray** [gre] *adj* gris; cano, encanecido; viejo; lúgubre, obscuro; *s* gris; traje gris, vestido gris; tela gris; caballo tordo; media luz (*del crepúsculo*); *va* poner gris; *vn* ponerse gris; encanecer
**graybeard** ['greˌbɪrd] *s* anciano, viejo
**Gray Friar** *s* franciscano
**gray-headed** ['greˌhɛdɪd] *adj* canoso
**grayhound** ['greˌhaʊnd] *s* galgo; (fig.) galgo (*vapor transoceánico*)
**gray iron** *s* fundición gris
**grayish** ['greɪʃ] *adj* grisáceo; entrecano
**graylag** ['greˌlæg] *s* (orn.) ganso silvestre (*Anser anser*)
**grayling** ['grelɪŋ] *s* (ichth.) tímalo
**gray matter** *s* (anat.) substancia gris; (coll.) materia gris cerebral (*inteligencia*)
**gray mullet** *s* (ichth.) mújol
**gray partridge** *s* (orn.) perdiz pardilla, estarna
**gray squirrel** *s* (zool.) ardilla gris
**graywacke** ['greˌwæk] o ['greˌwækə] *s* (geol.) grauvaca
**gray wolf** *s* (zool.) lobo gris (*Canis occidentalis*)
**graze** [grez] *s* roce; arañazo, rasguño; *va* rozar; arañar, rasguñar; pacer (*la hierba*); apacentar (*el ganado*); pastar (*conducir al pasto*); *vn* pacer, pastar
**grazier** ['greʒər] *s* ganadero
**grazing** ['grezɪŋ] *s* pasto; campo de pastoreo
**Gr. Br.** o **Gr. Brit.** abr. de **Great Britain**
**grease** [gris] *s* grasa; lana en bruto y sin limpiar; (slang) lisonja, soborno; [gris] o [griz] *va* engrasar; (slang) untar, sobornar
**grease cup** [gris] *s* (mach.) vaso de engrase, caja de sebo, engrasador
**grease gun** *s* jeringa de engrase, engrasador de pistón, pistola engrasadora, bomba de engrase
**grease lift** *s* (aut.) puente de engrase
**grease pit** *s* (aut.) fosa de engrase
**greaser** ['grisər] o ['grizər] *s* engrasador; (offensive) mejicano, hispanoamericano
**grease rack** *s* var. de **grease lift**
**grease spot** *s* lámpara (*mancha de aceite o grasa*)
**greasewood** ['grisˌwʊd] *s* (bot.) arbusto quenopodiáceo (*Sarcobatus vermiculatus*)
**greasy** ['grisɪ] o ['grizɪ] *adj* (*comp:* **-ier;** *super:* **-iest**) grasiento; liso, resbaladizo
**great** [gret] *adj* grande; muy usado, muy popular; (coll.) excelente; magno, grande, p.ej., **Alexander the Great** Alejandro Magno; **Peter the Great** Pedro el Grande; **the great** los grandes

**great-aunt** ['gret,ænt] o ['gret,ɑnt] *s* tía abuela
**Great Barrier Reef** *s* Gran Barrera
**Great Basin** *s* Cuenca Grande
**Great Bear** *s* (astr.) Osa mayor
**Great Britain** *s* la Gran Bretaña
**great bustard** *s* (orn.) avutarda
**great circle** *s* (astr. & geom.) círculo máximo
**greatcoat** ['gret,kot] *s* gabán de mucho abrigo
**Great Dane** *s* mastín danés
**Great Divide** *s* divisoria continental
**Great Dog** *s* (astr.) Can mayor
**Greater Antilles** *spl* Antillas Mayores
**Greater London** *s* el Gran Londres
**Greater New York** *s* el Gran Nueva York
**greater weever** *s* (ichth.) araña, dragón, dragón marino
**greater yellowlegs** *s* (orn.) chorlo grande de patas amarillas, chorlo real
**greatest common divisor** *s* (math.) máximo común divisor
**great-grandchild** [,gret'grænd,tʃaɪld] *s* (*pl:* **-children** [,tʃɪldrən]) bisnieto, bisnieta
**great-granddaughter** [,gret'grænd,dɔtər] *s* bisnieta
**great-grandfather** [,gret'grænd,fɑðər] *s* bisabuelo
**great-grandmother** [,gret'grænd,mʌðər] *s* bisabuela
**great-grandparent** [,gret'grænd,pɛrənt] *s* bisabuelo o bisabuela
**great-grandson** [,gret'grænd,sʌn] *s* bisnieto
**great-hearted** ['gret,hɑrtɪd] *adj* generoso, noble; valiente
**great horned owl** *s* (orn.) buho americano (*Bubo virginianus*)
**Great Lakes** *spl* Grandes Lagos
**greatly** ['gretlɪ] *adv* grandemente; grandiosamente
**great mogul** *s* autócrata, magnate; **Great Mogul** *s* gran Mogol
**great mullein** *s* (bot.) gordolobo, verbasco
**great-nephew** ['gret,nɛfju] o ['gret,nɛvju] *s* resobrino
**greatness** ['gretnɪs] *s* grandeza
**great-niece** ['gret,nis] *s* resobrina
**Great Plains** *s* Pradera (*inmensas pampas de la cuenca del Misisipí y sus afluentes*)
**great primer** ['prɪmər] *s* (print.) texto
**Great Pyramid** *s* gran Pirámide
**Great Russian** *s* gran ruso
**Great Salt Lake** *s* Gran Lago Salado
**great Scott** *interj* ¡ válgame Dios!
**great seal** *s* gran sello
**Great Spirit** *s* Gran Espíritu (*dios de varias tribus de indios norteamericanos*)
**great titmouse** *s* (orn.) herrerillo
**great-uncle** ['gret,ʌŋkəl] *s* tío abuelo
**Great Wall of China** *s* Gran Muralla de la China
**Great War** *s* Gran Guerra
**Great White Way** *s* Gran Vía Blanca (*Broadway*)
**greave** [griv] *s* greba; **greaves** *spl* chicharrón
**grebe** [grib] *s* (orn.) castañero, colimbo; plumas de la pechuga del colimbo (*para adornar sombreros*)
**Grecian** ['griʃən] *adj* griego; *s* griego; helenista
**Grecian nose** *s* nariz helénica
**Grecism** ['grisɪzəm] *s* grecismo
**Grecize** ['grisaɪz] *va & vn* grecizar
**Greco-Latin** [,griko'lætɪn] o [,griko'lætən] *adj* grecolatino
**Greco-Roman** [,griko'romən] *adj* grecorromano
**Greece** [gris] *s* Grecia
**greed** [grid] *s* codicia, avaricia, glotonería
**greediness** ['gridɪnɪs] *s* codicia, avaricia, glotonería
**greedy** ['gridɪ] *adj* (*comp:* **-ier**; *super:* **-iest**) codicioso, avaro, glotón
**Greek** [grik] *adj* griego; *s* griego; **it's Greek to me** me es chino; (*l.c.*) *s* griego (*fullero*)
**Greek calends** *spl* calendas griegas (*tiempo que no ha de llegar*)
**Greek cross** *s* cruz griega
**Greek fire** *s* fuego griego
**Greek Orthodox Church** *s* Iglesia griega ortodoxa
**Greek rite** *s* rito griego
**Greek valerian** *s* (bot.) valeriana griega
**green** [grin] *adj* verde; inexperto, novato; candoroso, bobo; demudado (*por el miedo, la envidia, etc.*); *s* verde; césped, prado, terreno verdoso; (golf) terreno cubierto de césped muy fino que circunda cada agujero; **greens** *spl* verduras; ramos verdes colocados para servir de adorno
**greenback** ['grin,bæk] *s* (U.S.A.) billete de banco (*de dorso verde*)
**greenbrier** ['grin,braɪər] *s* (bot.) cocolmeca
**green corn** *s* maíz tierno
**green crab** *s* (zool.) cámbaro, cangrejo de mar
**green dragon** (bot.) dragón verde, dragontea
**green earth** *s* verdacho
**greenery** ['grinərɪ] *s* (*pl:* **-ies**) verdura; invernáculo
**green-eyed** ['grin,aɪd] *adj* de ojos verdes; celoso
**greengage** ['grin,gedʒ] *s* reina claudia, ciruela verdal
**green grasshopper** *s* (ent.) langostón
**greengrocer** ['grin,grosər] *s* verdulero
**greengrocery** ['grin,grosərɪ] *s* (*pl:* **-ies**) verdulería
**greenhorn** ['grin,hɔrn] *s* pipiolo, novato; bobo, palurdo
**greenhouse** ['grin,haus] *s* invernáculo
**greening** ['grinɪŋ] *s* variedad de manzana de color verdoso
**greenish** ['grinɪʃ] *adj* verdoso
**Greenland** ['grinlənd] *s* Groenlandia
**Greenlander** ['grinləndər] *s* groenlandés
**Greenlandic** [grin'lændɪk] *adj* groenlandés
**green manure** *s* estiércol reciente; abono vegetal
**greenness** ['grinnɪs] *s* verdura, verdor; falta de experiencia
**greenroom** ['grin,rum] o ['grin,rʊm] *s* saloncillo (*de descanso de los actores*); chismería de teatro; local para almacenar loza cruda, tela acabada de hacer, etc.
**greensand** ['grɪn,sænd] *s* arenisca verde
**green sand** *s* (found.) arena verde
**greensward** ['grin,swɔrd] *s* césped
**green table** *s* tapete verde
**green tea** *s* té verde
**green thumb** *s* don de criar plantas
**green turtle** *s* (zool.) tortuga marina de color verde (*Chelonia mydas*)
**green vegetables** *spl* verduras
**greenwing** ['grin,wɪŋ] *s* (orn.) cerceta de verano
**greenwood** ['grin,wʊd] *s* floresta, bosque frondoso
**green woodpecker** *s* (orn.) picamaderos, pájaro carpintero
**greet** [grit] *va* saludar; recibir (*p.ej., con palabras de bienvenida, con palabras airadas, con imprecaciones, etc.*); presentarse a (*los ojos de una persona*)
**greeting** ['gritɪŋ] *s* saludo, salutación; buena acogida, bienvenida; **greetings!** ¡ salud!
**greeting card** *s* tarjeta de felicitación
**gregarious** [grɪ'gɛrɪəs] *adj* gregario; sociable
**Gregorian** [grɪ'gorɪən] *adj* gregoriano
**Gregorian calendar** *s* calendario gregoriano
**Gregorian chant** *s* canto gregoriano
**Gregory** ['grɛgərɪ] *s* Gregorio
**gremial** ['grimɪəl] *s* (eccl.) gremial
**gremlin** ['grɛmlɪn] *s* hado, duende de los aviones
**grenade** [grɪ'ned] *s* granada; granada extintora
**grenadier** [,grɛnə'dɪr] *s* granadero
**grenadine** [,grɛnə'din] o ['grɛnədin] *s* granadina (*tejido; zumo*)
**grew** [gru] *pret de* **grow**
**grewsome** ['grusəm] *adj* var. de **gruesome**
**grey** [gre] *adj, s, va & vn* var. de **gray**
**greyhound** ['gre,haʊnd] *s* galgo; (fig.) galgo (*vapor transoceánico*)
**greyhound race** *s* carrera de galgos
**grid** [grɪd] *s* rejilla, parrilla; (elec. & rad.) rejilla; (Brit.) red nacional de distribución eléctrica
**grid bias** *s* (rad.) polarización de rejilla
**grid circuit** *s* (rad.) circuito de rejilla
**grid condenser** *s* (rad.) condensador de rejilla

**grid current** *s* (rad.) corriente de rejilla
**griddle** ['grɪdəl] *s* tortera, plancha; *va* cocer (*tortillas*) en una plancha
**griddlecake** ['grɪdəl,kek] *s* torta o tortita a la plancha
**gride** [graɪd] *s* rechinamiento; *va* hacer rechinar; *vn* rechinar
**gridiron** ['grɪd,aɪərn] *s* parrilla; rejilla (*parecida a una parrilla*); (U.S.A.) campo de fútbol (*marcado a manera de parrilla*); (theat.) telar
**grid leak** *s* (rad.) resistencia de rejilla, escape de rejilla
**grief** [grif] *s* aflicción, pena, pesar, quebranto; (coll.) disgusto, disgustos; **good grief!** ¡voto al chápiro!; **to come to grief** tener muchos quebrantos; fracasar, arruinarse
**grievance** ['grivəns] *s* agravio, injusticia; motivo para quejarse
**grieve** [griv] *va* afligir, apenar; *vn* afligirse, apenarse; **to grieve over** añorar
**grievous** ['grivəs] *adj* doloroso, penoso; atroz, cruel, horrible; lastimoso
**griffin** ['grɪfɪn] o **griffon** ['grɪfən] *s* (myth.) grifo
**grig** [grɪg] *s* angula (*cría de la anguila*); (ent.) grillo, saltamontes; persona vivaracha
**grill** [grɪl] *s* parrilla; ración de carne asada, ración de pescado asado; parrilla (*restaurante o comedor de hotel cuya especialidad es la carne asada o el pescado asado*); *va* emparrillar; dar tormento de fuego a; interrogar de modo muy apremiante (*a un acusado*)
**grillage** ['grɪlɪdʒ] *s* (constr.) zampeado
**grille** [grɪl] *s* reja, verja; parrilla, rejilla (*p.ej., de automóvil*)
**grillroom** ['grɪl,rum] o ['grɪl,rʊm] *s* parrilla (*restaurante o comedor de hotel cuya especialidad es la carne asada o el pescado asado*)
**grilse** [grɪls] *s* cría del salmón que habiendo pasado el invierno en el mar vuelve al agua dulce de un río
**grim** [grɪm] *adj* (*comp:* **grimmer;** *super:* **grimmest**) austero, severo; ceñudo; fiero, cruel; horrible
**grimace** [grɪ'mes] *s* mueca, sonrisa falsa o mala; *vn* hacer muecas, fruncir el hocico
**grimalkin** [grɪ'mælkɪn] o [grɪ'mɔlkɪn] *s* gato; gata vieja; vieja malévola
**grime** [graɪm] *s* mugre, tiznado; *va* ensuciar, tiznar
**grimness** ['grɪmnɪs] *s* austeridad, severidad; fiereza, crueldad; horror
**grimy** ['graɪmɪ] *adj* (*comp:* **-ier;** *super:* **-iest**) sucio, mugriento, tiznado
**grin** [grɪn] *s* sonrisa bonachona; esguince, regaño, mueca de dolor o de cólera (*mostrando los dientes*); (*pret & pp:* **grinned;** *ger:* **grinning**) *va* expresar (*p.ej., aprobación*) sonriendo bonachonamente; *vn* sonreírse bonachonamente; hacer una mueca de dolor, de cólera o de desdén (*enseñando los dientes*)
**grind** [graɪnd] *s* molienda; rechinamiento; (coll.) zurra (*trabajo o estudio continuado*); (coll.) empollón, estudiantón; (*pret & pp:* **ground**) *va* moler; afilar, amolar; tallar (*lentes*); picar (*carne*); pulverizar; hacer rechinar; dar vueltas a (*un manubrio*); **to grind out** producir (*música*) dando vueltas a un manubrio; *vn* hacer molienda; molerse; pulverizarse; rozar; rechinar; (coll.) echar los bofes
**grinder** ['graɪndər] *s* molendero; amolador; esmerilador; amoladora; esmeriladora; molino o molinillo (*para moler café, pimienta, etc.*); muela (*piedra para afilar*); (anat.) muela; **grinders** *spl* (slang) herramienta (*dientes*)
**grindstone** ['graɪnd,ston] *s* muela, piedra de amolar; **to have, keep** o **put one's nose to the grindstone** trabajar con ahinco, echar los bofes
**gringo** ['grɪŋgo] *s* (*pl:* **-gos**) (scornful) gringo (*inglés o norteamericano*)
**grip** [grɪp] *s* asimiento; agarradero; apretón (*de la mano*); modo de darse la mano (*en las asociaciones secretas*); saco de mano; dolor punzante; comprensión; (mach.) mordaza; (path.) gripe; **to come to grips (with)** luchar a brazo partido (con); arrostrarse (con), enfrentarse (con); (*pret & pp:* **gripped** o **gript;** *ger:* **gripping**) *va* asir, agarrar; apretar; tener asido, agarrarse a; absorber la atención a; *vn* agarrarse; absorber la atención
**gripe** [graɪp] *s* asimiento; sujeción; **gripes** *spl* (naut.) obenques; (path.) retortijón de tripas; *va* asir, apretar; fastidiar, molestar; dar retortijones a; (slang) molestar sobremanera; *vn* sufrir retortijones; (slang) refunfuñar, quejarse mucho
**grippe** [grɪp] *s* (path.) gripe
**gripping** ['grɪpɪŋ] *adj* conmovedor, impresionante
**gripsack** ['grɪp,sæk] *s* saco de mano, maleta
**gript** [grɪpt] *pret & pp de* **grip**
**grisaille** [grɪ'zel] *s* (f.a.) grisalla
**grisette** [grɪ'zɛt] *s* griseta (*muchacha obrera de París*)
**grisly** ['grɪzlɪ] *adj* (*comp:* **-lier;** *super:* **-liest**) espantoso, horrible, espeluznante
**grist** [grɪst] *s* harina; molienda (*cantidad que se muele de una vez*); malta molido; (coll.) acervo, acopio; **to be grist to one's mill** (coll.) serle a uno de mucho provecho
**gristle** ['grɪsəl] *s* cartílago, ternilla
**gristly** ['grɪslɪ] *adj* (*comp:* **-tlier;** *super:* **-tliest**) cartilaginoso, ternilloso
**gristmill** ['grɪst,mɪl] *s* molino harinero
**grit** [grɪt] *s* arena, guijo muy fino; asperón, arenisca silícea; tesón, ánimo, valor; **grits** *spl* farro, sémola, maíz o avena a medio moler; (*pret & pp:* **gritted;** *ger:* **gritting**) *va* cerrar fuertemente (*los dientes*); hacer rechinar (*los dientes*)
**gritrock** ['grɪt,rɑk] o **gritstone** ['grɪt,ston] *s* asperón, arenisca silícea
**gritty** ['grɪtɪ] *adj* (*comp:* **-tier;** *super:* **-tiest**) arenoso; valiente, resuelto
**grizzled** ['grɪzəld] *adj* gris; grisáceo; canoso
**grizzly** ['grɪzlɪ] *adj* (*comp:* **-zlier;** *super:* **-zliest**) gris; grisáceo; canoso; *s* (*pl:* **-zlies**) (zool.) oso gris; (min.) cribón, parrilla
**grizzly bear** *s* (zool.) oso gris
**groan** [gron] *s* gemido, quejido; *va* expresar con voz quejumbrosa; *vn* gemir, quejarse; crujir (*por exceso de peso*); estar muy cargado, p.ej., **the table groaned with good food** estaba la mesa muy cargada de platos deliciosos; estar agobiado, p.ej., **he groaned beneath his burden** estaba agobiado por la carga
**groat** [grot] *s* blanca, ardite; **groats** *spl* farro, sémola, maíz o avena a medio moler
**grocer** ['grosər] tendero de ultramarinos; abarrotero (Am.)
**grocery** ['grosərɪ] *s* (*pl:* **-ies**) tienda de ultramarinos, tienda de comestibles; abarrotería (Am.); **groceries** *spl* comestibles, víveres; abarrotes (Am.)
**grocery store** *s* tienda de ultramarinos, tienda de comestibles; abarrotería (Am.)
**grog** [grɑg] *s* grog (*ron diluído en agua; bebida espirituosa*)
**groggery** ['grɑgərɪ] *s* (*pl:* **-ies**) taberna
**groggy** ['grɑgɪ] *adj* (*comp:* **-gier;** *super:* **-giest**) (coll.) vacilante, inseguro; (coll.) atontado (*p.ej., de un golpe*); (coll.) borracho
**grogram** ['grɑgrəm] *s* cordellate, gorgorán
**grogshop** ['grɑg,ʃɑp] *s* taberna
**groin** [grɔɪn] *s* (anat.) ingle; (arch.) arista de encuentro; *va* (arch.) construir con aristas de encuentro
**grommet** ['grɑmɪt] *s* ojal; (naut.) roñada
**gromwell** ['grɑmwəl] *s* (bot.) granos de amor, mijo gris
**groom** [grum] o [grʊm] *s* novio; mozo de caballos; (Brit.) camarero, caballerizo o ayuda de cámara de la casa real; (archaic) criado; *va* asear, acicalar, poner en orden; preparar y enseñar (*a un político*) en el modo de presentarse candidato en las elecciones
**groomsman** ['grumzmən] o ['grʊmzmən] *s* (*pl:* **-men**) padrino de boda
**groove** [gruv] *s* ranura, acanaladura; garganta (*de polea*); surco (*p.ej., de un disco*); rodada (*señal que deja la rueda*); (coll.) rutina, hábito arraigado; **groove and tongue** a ranura y lengüeta; *va* ranurar, acanalar
**groove-and-tongue joint** ['gruvənd'tʌŋ] *s* (carp.) ensambladura de ranura y lengüeta
**grooving machine** *s* ranuradora
**grooving plane** *s* cepillo de ranurar

**grooving saw** *s* sierra ranuradora
**grope** [grop] *va* tentar (*p.ej., el camino en la obscuridad*); *vn* andar a tientas, palpar; pujar (*por expresarse*); **to grope for** buscar a tientas, buscar sin hallar; **to grope through** palpar (*p.ej., las tinieblas*)
**gropingly** ['gropɪŋly] *adv* a tientas; (fig.) a tientas
**grosbeak** ['gros,bik] *s* (orn.) pico duro (*Pinicola enucleator*); (orn.) degollado; (orn.) cardenal de Virginia; (orn.) cascapiñones, pico gordo (*Coccothraustes coccothraustes*)
**grosgrain** ['gro,gren] *s* gro
**gross** [gros] *adj* total; craso (*error*); grosero; grueso; denso, espeso; bruto; *s* (*pl:* **gross**) gruesa (*doce docenas*); *s* (*pl:* **grosses**) conjunto, totalidad; **in gross** o **in the gross** en grueso
**gross anatomy** *s* anatomía macroscópica
**grossly** ['groslɪ] *adv* excesivamente; groseramente; aproximadamente
**gross national product** *s* renta nacional, producto total de la economía nacional
**grossness** ['grosnɪs] *s* grosería; densidad, espesor
**gross ton** *s* tonelada gruesa (*2.240 libras o 1.016,06 kg.*)
**grossulariaceous** [,grɑsjə,lerɪ'eʃəs] *adj* (bot.) grosulariáceo
**grot** [grɑt] *s* (poet.) gruta
**grotesque** [gro'tɛsk] *adj* grotesco (*ridículo*); (f.a.) grutesco o grotesco; *s* (f.a.) grutesco o grotesco
**Grotius** ['groʃɪəs] *s* Grocio
**grotto** ['grɑto] *s* (*pl:* **-toes** o **-tos**) gruta
**grouch** [grautʃ] *s* (coll.) mal humor; (coll.) cascarrabias, vinagre (*persona*); *vn* (coll.) estar de mal humor, refunfuñar
**grouchy** ['grautʃɪ] *adj* (*comp:* **-ier**; *super:* **-iest**) (coll.) malhumorado, refunfuñador
**ground** [graund] *s* tierra; terreno; causa, fundamento; campo (*de batalla*); (elec.) tierra; (elec.) borne de conexión con tierra; (elec.) masa (*p.ej., de un automóvil*); (paint.) campo, fondo; **grounds** *spl* terreno; jardines; causa, fundamento; poso, heces; **above ground** vivo; **from the ground up** de abajo arriba; completamente; **on the ground of** con motivo de; **to be on one's own ground** estar en su elemento; **to break ground** empezar la excavación; abrir los cimientos; **to cover the ground** hacer completamente lo que hay que hacer; atravesar la distancia debida; correr mucho; **to cut the ground from under one's feet** anticiparle a uno las razones en una polémica; **to fall to the ground** fracasar, abandonarse (*un proyecto*); **to gain ground** ganar terreno; **to give ground** ceder terreno; **to hold one's ground** mantenerse firme; **to lose ground** perder terreno; **to run into the ground** (slang) abusar de (*p.ej., un recurso*); **to shift one's ground** cambiar de posición; cambiar de táctica; **to stand one's ground** mantenerse firme; **to yield ground** ceder terreno; **ground for complaint** motivo de queja ‖ *adj* a ras de tierra, terrestre; fundamental ‖ *va* poner en tierra; descansar (*armas*); cimentar, establecer, fundar; (elec.) poner a tierra; (paint.) dar campo o fondo a; **to be grounded** estar sin volar (*un avión*); **to be well grounded** ser muy versado; estar bien fundado (*un juicio*) ‖ *vn* (naut.) encallar, varar ‖ *pret & pp de* **grind**
**ground connection** *s* (rad.) toma de tierra
**ground-controlled approach** ['graundkən'trold] *s* (aer.) acceso dirigido desde tierra, aproximación controlada desde tierra
**ground crew** *s* (aer.) personal de tierra
**grounder** ['graundər] *s* (baseball) pelota rodada
**ground floor** *s* piso bajo
**ground game** *s* caza de pelo
**ground glass** *s* vidrio deslustrado
**ground hog** *s* (zool.) marmota de América
**ground ivy** *s* (bot.) hiedra terrestre
**ground lead** [lid] *s* (elec.) conductor a tierra
**groundless** ['graundlɪs] *adj* infundado
**ground line** *s* línea de tierra
**groundling** ['graundlɪŋ] *s* animal o planta terrestres; pez que habita en el fondo del mar; lector poco culto y sin gusto
**groundnut** ['graund,nʌt] *s* (bot.) chufa; (bot.) cacahuete
**ground pine** *s* (bot.) pinillo, pinillo oloroso; (bot.) licopodio
**ground plan** *s* planta (*de un edificio*); primer proyecto, proyecto fundamental
**ground return** *s* (elec.) retorno por tierra, retorno por masa
**groundsel** ['graundsəl] *s* (bot.) hierba cana, zuzón
**groundsill** ['graundsɪl] *s* (constr.) carrera inferior, solera de base
**ground speed** *s* (aer.) velocidad con respecto al suelo
**ground squirrel** *s* (zool.) tuza; (zool.) ardilla listada
**ground support** *s* (aer.) apoyo terrestre
**ground swell** *s* marejada de fondo, mar de fondo
**ground troops** *spl* (mil.) tropas terrestres
**ground water** *s* agua de pozo, agua subterránea
**ground wire** *s* (rad.) alambre de tierra, hilo de tierra; (aut.) hilo de masa
**groundwork** ['graund,wʌrk] *s* cimiento, fundamento
**group** [grup] *s* grupo; *adj* colectivo; *va* agrupar; *vn* agruparse
**grouper** ['grupər] *s* (ichth.) cabrilla, cherna, mero
**group insurance** *s* seguro a grupos
**grouse** [graus] *s* (orn.) gallo de bosque; (orn.) bonasa americana; (orn.) lagópedo de Escocia; (slang) refunfuño; *vn* (slang) refunfuñar
**grout** [graut] *s* lechada; *va* enlechar
**grove** [grov] *s* arboleda, bosquecillo
**grovel** ['grʌvəl] o ['grɑvəl] (*pret & pp:* **-eled** o **-elled**; *ger:* **-eling** o **-elling**) *vn* arrastrarse (*a los pies de un poderoso*); envilecerse, deleitarse en vilezas
**groveling** o **grovelling** ['grʌvəlɪŋ] o ['grɑvəlɪŋ] *adj* servil, rastrero
**grow** [gro] (*pret:* **grew**; *pp:* **grown**) *va* cultivar; criar; producir; dejarse (*la barba, el bigote*); *vn* crecer; desarrollarse; cultivarse; criarse; producirse; brotar, nacer; irse aumentando; hacerse, ponerse, volverse; **to grow into** hacerse, llegar a ser; **to grow on** influir cada vez más en; interesar cada vez más; **to grow out of** tener su origen en; perder (*p.ej., la costumbre*); **to grow to** adherirse a, pegarse a; llegar a, llegar a ser; **to grow together** adherirse el uno al otro; **to grow up** hacerse un adolescente, salir de la niñez; este verbo, seguido de un adjetivo, se traduce a veces por un verbo neutro o reflexivo que corresponda al adjetivo, p.ej., **to grow old** envejecer; **to grow angry** enfadarse
**grower** ['groər] *s* agricultor, cultivador; criador; planta que crece de cierto modo, p.ej., **quick grower** planta que crece rápidamente
**growing** ['gro·ɪŋ] *adj* creciente; de creces, p.ej., **growing child** muchacho de creces; *s* crecimiento; cultivo; cría
**growing pains** *spl* dolores causados (*según comúnmente se cree*) por el desarrollo rápido del cuerpo; dificultades iniciales (*p.ej., de una nueva empresa*)
**growl** [graul] *s* gruñido (*del perro*); refunfuño; *va* manifestar (*p.ej., desaprobación*) refunfuñando; *vn* gruñir (*el perro*); refunfuñar
**growler** ['graulər] *s* gruñidor; perro gruñidor; (slang) jarro en el que se trae cerveza desde la cervecería
**grown** [gron] *adj* crecido; llegado a su mayor desarrollo; adulto; cubierto de hierbas, maleza, etc.; *pp de* **grow**
**grown-up** ['gron,ʌp] *adj* adulto; serio, juicioso; *s* (*pl:* **grown-ups**) adulto
**growth** [groθ] *s* crecimiento; desarrollo; aumento; cobertura (*p.ej., forestal, herbosa*); (path.) tumor
**growth stock** *s* (com.) acción crecedera
**grub** [grʌb] *s* esclavo del trabajo; (ent.) gorgojo; (slang) condumio (*alimento, comida*); (*pret & pp:* **grubbed**; *ger:* **grubbing**) *va* arrancar (*tocones*); desmalezar (*un terreno*); *vn* cavar;

hozar (*el puerco*); emplearse en menesteres humildes
**grubby** ['grʌbɪ] *adj* (*comp:* **-bier;** *super:* **-biest**) gorgojoso; sucio, roñoso
**grubstake** ['grʌb,stek] *s* (coll.) anticipo de dinero que se da al explorador para comprar pertrechos y provisiones, pensando cobrar después de hallado el filón de mineral que se busca; *va* (coll.) subvencionar (*a un explorador*)
**Grub Street** *s* (hist.) calle de Londres habitada por escritores famélicos; escritores necesitados
**grudge** [grʌdʒ] *s* inquina, rencor; **to bear** o **to have a grudge against** tener inquina a, guardar rencor a; *va* dar de mala gana; envidiar
**grudgingly** ['grʌdʒɪŋlɪ] *adv* de mala gana
**gruel** ['gruəl] *s* avenate; (*pret & pp:* **-eled** o **-elled;** *ger:* **-eling** o **-elling**) *va* desbaratar, agotar, incapacitar
**grueling** o **gruelling** ['gruəlɪŋ] *adj* muy molesto y agotador; *s* lance muy molesto y agotador
**gruesome** ['grusəm] *adj* horrible, horripilante
**gruff** [grʌf] *adj* áspero, rudo, brusco, poco amistoso; ronco
**grum** [grʌm] *adj* (*comp:* **grummer;** *super:* **grummest**) áspero, hosco, malhumorado
**grumble** ['grʌmbəl] *s* gruñido, refunfuño; ruido sordo; *va* manifestar gruñendo o refunfuñando; *vn* gruñir, refunfuñar; producir un ruido sordo
**grume** [grum] *s* grumo
**grumpy** ['grʌmpɪ] *adj* (*comp:* **-ier;** *super:* **-iest**) gruñón, rezongón, malhumorado
**Grundy, Mrs.** ['grʌndɪ] *s* el qué dirán; **what will Mrs. Grundy say?** ¿qué dirá la gente?
**grunt** [grʌnt] *s* gruñido (*del cerdo; de una persona*); (ichth.) ronco; *va* decir entre gruñidos; *vn* gruñir
**gruyère** [grɪ'jɛr] *s* gruyère
**gryphon** ['grɪfən] o ['graɪfən] *s* var. de **griffin**
**G string** *s* cubresexo
**gt.** abr. de **great** y **gutta** (Lat.) **drop**
**Gt. Br.** o **Gt. Brit.** abr. de **Great Britain**
**g.t.c.** abr. de **good till canceled** y **good till countermanded**
**g.u.** abr. de **genitourinary**
**Guadeloupe** [,gwadə'lup] *s* Guadalupe
**guaiacol** ['gwaɪəkol] o ['gwaɪəkal] *s* (chem.) guayacol
**guaiacum** ['gwaɪəkəm] *s* (bot.) guayacán
**guanaco** [gwa'nako] *s* (*pl:* **-cos**) (zool.) guanaco
**guanidine** ['gwænɪdin] o ['gwanɪdin] *s* (chem.) guanidina
**guanine** ['gwanin] o ['guənin] *s* (chem.) guanina
**guano** ['gwano] *s* (*pl:* **-nos**) guano
**Guarani** [,gwara'ni] *adj* guaraní; *s* (*pl:* **-nis**) guaraní
**guarantee** [,gærən'ti] *s* garantía; garante; persona asegurada por una garantía; *va* garantizar
**guaranteed annual wage** *s* salario anual garantizado
**guarantor** ['gærəntɔr] *s* garante
**guaranty** ['gærəntɪ] *s* (*pl:* **-ties**) garantía; (*pret & pp:* **-tied**) *va* garantizar
**guard** [gard] *s* guarda (*acción de guardar; guarnición de la espada; persona que guarda una cosa*); guardia (*cuerpo de hombres armados; individuo de tal cuerpo; manera de defenderse en la esgrima*); salvavidas (*delante de los tranvías*); (sport) coraza; (football) guarda, defensor; **off guard** desprevenido; **on guard** prevenido, en guardia; de centinela; (fencing) en guardia; **to mount guard** montar la guardia; **under guard** a buen recado; *va* guardar; *vn* estar de centinela, hacer centinela; **to guard against** guardarse de, precaverse de; **to guard against** + *ger* guardarse de + *inf*
**guarded** ['gardɪd] *adj* guardado, protegido; cauteloso, circunspecto
**guardhouse** ['gard,haus] *s* cuartel de la guardia; cárcel militar
**guardian** ['gardɪən] *s* guardián; (law) tutor, curador; (eccl.) guardián; *adj* tutelar
**guardian angel** *s* ángel custodio, ángel de la guarda
**guardianship** ['gardɪən,ʃɪp] *s* protección; (law) tutela, curaduría; (eccl.) guardianía (*en la orden franciscana*)
**guardrail** ['gard,rel] *s* baranda; (rail.) contracarril; (naut.) barandilla
**guardroom** ['gard,rum] o ['gard,rʊm] *s* cuarto de guardia; calabozo militar
**guard ship** *s* (naut.) navío de guardia
**guardsman** ['gardzmən] *s* (*pl:* **-men**) guarda; guardia, soldado de guardia; centinela
**guard wire** *s* (elec.) alambre de guardia
**Guatemala** [,gwatɪ'malə] *s* Guatemala
**Guatemalan** [,gwatɪ'malən] *adj & s* guatemalteco
**guava** ['gwavə] *s* (bot.) guayabo (*árbol*); guayaba (*fruto*); (bot.) ingá, guamo
**guayule** [gwa'julɛ] *s* (bot.) guayule (*arbusto y caucho*)
**gubernatorial** [,gjubərnə'torɪəl] *adj* de gobernador, del gobernador
**gudgeon** ['gʌdʒən] *s* (ichth.) gobio; (mach.) gorrón; (naut.) muñonera, hembra de gorrón; bobo, mentecato; chiripa, ganga; *va* estafar
**gudgeon pin** *s* (aut.) perno de émbolo
**guelder-rose** ['gɛldər,roz] *s* (bot.) rosa de güeldres, mundillo, sauquillo
**Guelf** o **Guelph** [gwɛlf] *s* güelfo
**Guelfic** o **Guelphic** ['gwɛlfɪk] *adj* güelfo
**guerdon** ['gʌrdən] *s* (poet.) galardón
**guerilla** [gə'rɪlə] *s & adj* var. de **guerrilla**
**guernsey** ['gʌrnzɪ] *s* camiseta de punto (*de los marineros*)
**guerrilla** [gə'rɪlə] *s* guerrillero; *adj* de guerrilla, de guerrillero
**guerrilla warfare** *s* guerra de guerrillas
**guess** [gɛs] *s* conjetura, suposición; *va & vn* conjeturar, suponer; acertar, adivinar; (coll.) creer, suponer; **I guess so** (coll.) creo que sí, me parece que sí
**guessable** ['gɛsəbəl] *adj* adivinable
**guessing game** *s* juego de adivinanzas; partido de adivinanzas
**guesswork** ['gɛs,wʌrk] *s* conjetura; **by guesswork** por conjeturas
**guest** [gɛst] *s* huésped; convidado; visita; pensionista, inquilino; cliente (*de un hotel*)
**guest conductor** *s* (mus.) conductor visitante, conductor huésped
**guest of honor** *s* invitado de honor, huésped de honor
**guest room** *s* alcoba de respeto, cuarto del huésped
**guest rope** *s* (naut.) falsa amarra
**guffaw** [gʌ'fɔ] *s* risotada; *vn* risotear
**Guiana** [gɪ'anə] o [gɪ'ænə] *s* Guayana
**Guianan** [gɪ'anən] o [gɪ'ænən] *adj & s* var. de **Guianese**
**Guianese** [,gia'niz] o [,giæ'niz] *adj* guayanés; *s* (*pl:* **-nese**) guayanés
**guidance** ['gaɪdəns] *s* guía, gobierno, dirección; **for your guidance** para su gobierno
**guide** [gaɪd] *s* guía (*persona; libro o tratado*); dirección, indicación; (mil.) guía; poste indicador; (mach.) guía, guiadera; *va* guiar
**guideboard** ['gaɪd,bord] *s* señal de carretera
**guidebook** ['gaɪd,bʊk] *s* guía, guía del viajero
**guided missile** *s* (mil.) proyectil dirigido, proyectil teleguiado
**guideline** ['gaɪd,laɪn] *s* cuerda de guía; línea trazada de un cambio tipográfico a un signo en el margen; pauta, norma (*p.ej., de conducta*)
**guidepost** ['gaɪd,post] *s* poste indicador
**guide rope** *s* arrastradera (*de globo aerostático*); cuerda de guía
**guidon** ['gaɪdən] *s* (mil.) guión; (mil.) portaguión
**guild** [gɪld] *s* gremio; asociación de carácter benéfico
**guildhall** ['gɪld,hɔl] *s* casa de un gremio; casa consistorial, casa de ayuntamiento
**guildsman** ['gɪldzmən] *s* (*pl:* **-men**) gremial
**guile** [gaɪl] *s* dolo, astucia, maña
**guileful** ['gaɪlfəl] *adj* doloso, astuto, mañoso
**guileless** ['gaɪllɪs] *adj* cándido, sencillo, sincero

**guillemot** [ˈgɪlɪmɑt] *s* (orn.) uría
**guilloche** [gɪˈloʃ] *s* (f.a.) güilogis
**guillotine** [ˈgɪlətin] *s* guillotina; (surg. & law) guillotina; [ˌgɪləˈtin] *va* guillotinar
**guillotine shears** *spl* cizalla de guillotina
**guilt** [gɪlt] *s* culpa
**guiltiness** [ˈgɪltɪnɪs] *s* culpabilidad
**guiltless** [ˈgɪltlɪs] *adj* libre de culpa, inocente
**guilty** [ˈgɪltɪ] *adj* (*comp:* **-ier;** *super:* **-iest**) culpable; culpado
**guimpe** [gɪmp] o [gæmp] *s* canesú
**guinea** [ˈgɪnɪ] *s* guinea (*moneda*); gallina de Guinea; (*cap.*) *s* Guinea; *adj* guineo
**Guinea corn** *s* (bot.) maíz de Guinea
**guinea fowl** *s* pintada, gallina de Guinea
**guinea grass** *s* (bot.) gramalote, hierba de Guinea
**guinea hen** *s* var. de **guinea fowl**
**guinea pig** *s* (zool. & fig.) conejillo de Indias
**Guinever** [ˈgwɪnəvər] o **Guinevere** [ˈgwɪnəvɪr] *s* (myth.) Ginebra
**guipure** [gɪˈpjʊr] *s* guipur; guarnición de cuerdas entretejidas, con refuerzo de alambre
**guise** [gaɪz] *s* traje; semejanza, aspecto; capa, pretexto; **in the guise of** disfrazado de; **under the guise of** so capa de
**guitar** [gɪˈtɑr] *s* (mus.) guitarra
**guitarist** [gɪˈtɑrɪst] *s* guitarrista
**gulch** [gʌltʃ] *s* barranco, quebrada
**gules** [gjulz] *s* (her.) gules; *adj* (her.) de gules
**gulf** [gʌlf] *s* golfo; vorágine, torbellino
**Gulf of Aden** *s* golfo de Adén
**Gulf of Bothnia** [ˈbɑθnɪə] *s* golfo de Botnia
**Gulf of Corinth** *s* golfo de Corinto
**Gulf of Mexico** *s* golfo de Méjico
**Gulf of Oman** [oˈmɑn] *s* mar de Omán
**Gulf of Panama** *s* golfo de Panamá
**Gulf of St. Lawrence** *s* golfo de San Lorenzo
**Gulf of Venice** *s* golfo de Venecia
**Gulf States** *spl* estados de EE.UU. que confinan con el golfo de Méjico
**Gulf Stream** *s* Corriente del Golfo
**gulfweed** [ˈgʌlfˌwid] *s* (bot.) sargazo
**gull** [gʌl] *s* (orn.) gaviota; bobo; *va* engañar, estafar
**gullet** [ˈgʌlɪt] *s* garguero, gaznate; esófago
**gullibility** [ˌgʌlɪˈbɪlɪtɪ] *s* credulidad
**gullible** [ˈgʌlɪbəl] *adj* crédulo; **to be too gullible** tener buenas tragaderas
**gully** [ˈgʌlɪ] *s* (*pl:* **-lies**) arroyada, hondonada; badén (*zanja que forman las aguas llovedizas*)
**gulp** [gʌlp] *s* gorgorotada, trago; *va* engullir; **to gulp down** engullir; reprimir (*p.ej., sollozos*); *vn* estrangularse momentáneamente; no poder hablar (*por pena, susto o vergüenza*)
**gum** [gʌm] *s* goma; (bot.) gomero, árbol gomífero; (anat.) encía; chanclo de goma; (*pret & pp:* **gummed;** *ger:* **gumming**) *va* engomar; volver pegajoso; atascar, entorpecer; *vn* manar goma; volverse pegajoso
**gum ammoniac** *s* goma amoníaco
**gum arabic** *s* goma arábiga
**gumbo** [ˈgʌmbo] *s* (*pl:* **-bos**) (bot.) quingombó; sopa de quingombó; lodo muy pegajoso; dialecto criollo de la Luisiana
**gumboil** [ˈgʌmˌbɔɪl] *s* (path.) párulis, flemón
**gum boot** *s* bota de goma, bota de agua
**gumdrop** [ˈgʌmˌdrɑp] *s* pastilla de goma
**gum elastic** *s* goma elástica
**gum guttae** [ˈgʌti] *s* var. de **gamboge**
**gumma** [ˈgʌmə] *s* (*pl:* **-mata** [mətə]) (path.) goma
**gummiferous** [gʌmˈɪfərəs] *adj* gomífero
**gummosis** [gʌˈmosɪs] *s* (plant path.) gomosis
**gummy** [ˈgʌmɪ] *adj* (*comp:* **-mier;** *super:* **-miest**) gomoso
**gumption** [ˈgʌmpʃən] *s* (coll.) energía, iniciativa; (coll.) juicio, seso
**gum resin** *s* gomorresina
**gumshoe** [ˈgʌmˌʃu] *s* chanclo de goma; (slang) detective; **gumshoes** *spl* zapatos silenciosos (*con suela de goma y lo demás de lona*); (*pret & pp:* **-shoed;** *ger:* **-shoeing**) *vn* (slang) andar con zapatos de fieltro, andar espiando
**gum succory** *s* (bot.) condrila
**gum tree** *s* (bot.) gomero, árbol gomífero
**gum water** *s* aguagoma
**gumwood** [ˈgʌmˌwʊd] *s* madera de árbol gomífero
**gun** [gʌn] *s* escopeta, fusil; cañón; jeringa (*para inyectar materias blandas*); cañón (*de cemento*); cañonazo (*cada uno de los que componen una salva*); (coll.) revólver, pistola; **to spike one's guns** clavarle a uno los cañones, reducirle a uno a la impotencia; **to stick to one's guns** mantenerse en sus trece, mantenerse con la suya; (*pret & pp:* **gunned;** *ger:* **gunning**) *va* hacer fuego sobre, hacer un disparo sobre; (slang) acelerar rápidamente (*un avión, un motor*); *vn* andar a caza; hacer fuego, disparar; **to gun for** ir en busca de, tratar de conseguir; buscar para matar
**gun** o **'gun** [gʌn] *pp de* **gin** [gɪn]
**gun barrel** *s* cañón de fusil
**gunboat** [ˈgʌnˌbot] *s* cañonero, lancha cañonera
**gun carriage** *s* cureña
**guncotton** [ˈgʌnˌkɑtən] *s* pólvora de algodón, algodón pólvora, fulmicotón
**gunfire** [ˈgʌnˌfaɪr] *s* fuego (*de armas de fuego*); cañoneo, tiroteo; uso de armas de fuego
**gunlock** [ˈgʌnˌlɑk] *s* llave de fusil
**gunman** [ˈgʌnmən] *s* (*pl:* **-men**) pistolero, bandido armado
**gun metal** *s* bronce de cañón; bronce empavonado, metal pavonado
**gun-metal** [ˈgʌnˌmɛtəl] *adj* empavonado, pavonado
**gunnel** [ˈgʌnəl] *s* (ichth.) blenia; (naut.) borda, regala
**gunner** [ˈgʌnər] *s* artillero; cazador; (nav.) condestable
**gunnery** [ˈgʌnərɪ] *s* artillería
**gunning** [ˈgʌnɪŋ] *s* tiro; caza
**gunny** [ˈgʌnɪ] *s* (*pl:* **-nies**) yute; saco de yute
**gunny sack** *s* saco de yute
**gunpowder** [ˈgʌnˌpaʊdər] *s* pólvora
**gunrunner** [ˈgʌnˌrʌnər] *s* contrabandista de armas de fuego
**gunrunning** [ˈgʌnˌrʌnɪŋ] *s* contrabando de armas de fuego
**gunshot** [ˈgʌnˌʃɑt] *s* balazo, escopetazo, tiro de fusil; alcance de un fusil; **within gunshot** a tiro de fusil
**gunshot wound** *s* balazo, escopetazo
**gunsmith** [ˈgʌnˌsmɪθ] *s* armero
**gunstock** [ˈgʌnˌstɑk] *s* caja de fusil
**Gunter's chain** [ˈgʌntərz] *s* cadena de agrimensor o de Gúnter
**gunwale** [ˈgʌnəl] *s* (naut.) borda, regala
**guppy** [ˈgʌpɪ] *s* (*pl:* **-pies**) (ichth.) lebistes
**gurgle** [ˈgʌrgəl] *s* gluglú (*del agua*); gorjeo (*del niño*); *va* expresar con gorjeos, decir entre gorjeos; *vn* hacer gluglú (*el agua*); gorjearse (*el niño*)
**gurnard** [ˈgʌrnərd] o **gurnet** [ˈgʌrnɪt] *s* (ichth.) trilla; (ichth.) rubio volador
**gush** [gʌʃ] *s* borbollón, chorro; (coll.) efusión, extremos (*de cariño o entusiasmo*); *va* derramar (*p.ej., sangre*) a borbollones; *vn* surgir, salir a borbollones; (coll.) hacer extremos
**gusher** [ˈgʌʃər] *s* pozo surgente; (coll.) persona extremosa
**gushing** [ˈgʌʃɪŋ] *adj* surgente; extremoso; *s* borbollón, chorro; (coll.) efusión, extremos
**gushy** [ˈgʌʃɪ] *adj* (*comp:* **-ier;** *super:* **-iest**) efusivo, extremoso
**gusset** [ˈgʌsɪt] *s* (sew.) escudete; (constr.) esquinal, escuadra; (naut.) curvatón
**gusset plate** *s* cartabón
**gust** [gʌst] *s* ráfaga (*de viento*); bocanada (*de humo*); aguacero; explosión (*de ruido*); arrebato (*de cólera, entusiasmo, etc.*)
**gustative** [ˈgʌstətɪv] *adj* gustativo
**gustatory** [ˈgʌstəˌtorɪ] *adj* gustatorio
**Gustavus** [gʌsˈtevəs] *s* Gustavo
**Gustavus Adolphus** [əˈdɑlfəs] *s* Gustavo Adolfo
**gusto** [ˈgʌsto] *s* (*pl:* **-tos**) gusto; sumo placer, deleite, entusiasmo, satisfacción evidente; **with gusto** con sumo placer
**gusty** [ˈgʌstɪ] *adj* (*comp:* **-ier;** *super:* **-iest**) tempestuoso, impetuoso, explosivo
**gut** [gʌt] *s* tripa; cuerda de tripa; estrecho, desfiladero; **guts** *spl* tripas; (slang) agallas; (*pret & pp:* **gutted;** *ger:* **gutting**) *va* destripar; pillar lo interior de; destruir lo interior de
**gutta-percha** [ˈgʌtəˈpʌrtʃə] *s* gutapercha

**gutter** [ˈgʌtər] *s* cuneta (*al lado del camino*); arroyo (*en la calle*); canal (*en los tejados*); badén (*zanja que forman las aguas llovedizas*); acanaladura, estría; barrio bajo; *va* acanalar, estriar; *vn* acanalarse; correr, manar; gotear (*las velas*); **to gutter out** apagarse

**guttersnipe** [ˈgʌtər,snaɪp] *s* (coll.) pilluelo, hijo de la miseria

**guttiferous** [gʌˈtɪfərəs] *adj* (bot.) gutífero

**guttural** [ˈgʌtərəl] *adj* gutural; (phonet.) gutural; *s* (phonet.) sonido gutural

**guy** [gaɪ] *s* viento, cable de retén; (coll.) tipo, sujeto, tío; (coll.) adefesio, mamarracho; (*cap.*) *s* Guido; (*l.c.*) *va* sujetar con vientos; (coll.) dar vaya a, burlarse de

**guy wire** *s* viento de alambre

**guzzle** [ˈgʌzəl] *va* beber con avidez y de modo grosero; *vn* ser muy bebedor

**guzzler** [ˈgʌzlər] *s* pellejo, borrachín

**gym** [dʒɪm] *s* (coll.) gimnasio

**gymnasium** [dʒɪmˈnezɪəm] *s* (*pl:* **-ums** o **-a** [ə]) gimnasio

**gymnast** [ˈdʒɪmnæst] *s* gimnasta

**gymnastic** [dʒɪmˈnæstɪk] *adj* gimnástico; **gymnastics** *spl* gimnástica o gimnasia

**gymnosperm** [ˈdʒɪmnəspʌrm] *s* (bot.) gimnosperma

**gymnospermous** [,dʒɪmnəˈspʌrməs] *adj* gimnospermo

**gynaeceum** [,dʒɪnɪˈsiəm] o [,dʒaɪnɪˈsiəm] *s* (*pl:* **-a** [ə]) (hist.) gineceo (*departamento de las mujeres*); (bot.) gineceo

**gynaecology** [,gaɪnəˈkɑlədʒɪ], [,dʒaɪnəˈkɑlədʒɪ] o [,dʒɪnəˈkɑlədʒɪ] *s* var. de **gynecology**

**gynandrous** [dʒaɪˈnændrəs] o [dʒɪˈnændrəs] *adj* (bot.) ginandro

**gynecological** [,gaɪnəkəˈlɑdʒɪkəl], [,dʒaɪnəkəˈlɑdʒɪkəl] o [,dʒɪnəkəˈlɑdʒɪkəl] *adj* ginecológico

**gynecologist** [,gaɪnəˈkɑlədʒɪst], [,dʒaɪnəˈkɑlədʒɪst] o [,dʒɪnəˈkɑlədʒɪst] *s* ginecólogo

**gynecology** [,gaɪnəˈkɑlədʒɪ], [,dʒaɪnəˈkɑlədʒɪ] o [,dʒɪnəˈkɑlədʒɪ] *s* ginecología

**gyniatrics** [,dʒaɪnɪˈætrɪks] o [,dʒɪnɪˈætrɪks] *ssg* giniatría

**gynoecium** [dʒaɪˈnisɪəm] o [dʒɪˈnisɪəm] *s* (*pl:* **-a** [ə]) (bot.) gineceo

**gynophore** [ˈdʒaɪnəfor] o [ˈdʒɪnəfor] *s* (bot.) ginóforo

**gyp** [dʒɪp] *s* (slang) estafa, timo; (slang) estafador, timador; (*pret & pp:* **gypped;** *ger:* **gypping**) *va* (slang) estafar, timar

**gypsophila** [dʒɪpˈsɑfɪlə] *s* (bot.) gipsófila

**gypsum** [ˈdʒɪpsəm] *s* yeso

**gypsy** [ˈdʒɪpsɪ] *adj* gitano; *s* (*pl:* **-sies**) gitano; (*cap.*) *s* gitano (*idioma*)

**gypsyish** [ˈdʒɪpsɪɪʃ] *adj* gitanesco

**gypsyism** [ˈdʒɪpsɪɪzəm] *s* gitanismo

**gypsy moth** *s* (ent.) lagarta

**gyrate** [ˈdʒaɪret] o [dʒaɪˈret] *vn* girar

**gyration** [dʒaɪˈreʃən] *s* giro, vuelta

**gyratory** [ˈdʒaɪrə,torɪ] *adj* giratorio

**gyrfalcon** [ˈdʒʌr,fɔkən] o [ˈdʒʌr,fɔlkən] *s* var. de **gerfalcon**

**gyro** [ˈdʒaɪro] *s* (*pl:* **-ros**) autogiro; girocompás; giroscopio

**gyrocompass** [ˈdʒaɪro,kʌmpəs] *s* girocompás

**gyrofin** [ˈdʒaɪrəfɪn] *s* (naut.) giroaleta

**gyrometer** [dʒaɪˈrɑmɪtər] *s* girómetro

**gyron** [ˈdʒaɪrən] *s* (her.) jirón

**gyropilot** [ˈdʒaɪro,paɪlət] *s* (aer.) giropiloto

**gyroplane** [ˈdʒaɪro,plen] *s* (aer.) giroplano, giravión

**gyroscope** [ˈdʒaɪrəskop] *s* giroscopio

**gyroscopic** [,dʒaɪrəˈskɑpɪk] *adj* giroscópico

**gyrostabilizer** [,dʒaɪroˈstebɪ,laɪzər] *s* (aer. & naut.) giroestabilizador

**gyrostat** [ˈdʒaɪrəstæt] *s* giróstato

**gyrostatic** [,dʒaɪrəˈstætɪk] *adj* girostático; **gyrostatics** *ssg* girostática

**gyve** [dʒaɪv] *s* grillo; *va* encadenar con grillos

**H, h** [etʃ] *s* (*pl:* **H's, h's** ['etʃɪz]) octava letra del alfabeto inglés

**h.** abr. de **harbor, hard, height, high, hour** y **husband**

**H.** abr. de **harbor, hard, high** y **hour**

**ha** [hɑ] *interj* ¡ ha!; ¡ ja!

**Hab.** abr. de **Habakkuk**

**Habakkuk** [hə'bækək] o ['hæbəkʌk] *s* (Bib.) Habacuc

**habeas corpus** ['hebɪəs 'kɔrpəs] *s* (law) hábeas corpus

**haberdasher** ['hæbər,dæʃər] *s* camisero; mercero

**haberdashery** ['hæbər,dæʃərɪ] *s* (*pl:* **-ies**) camisería; mercería

**habergeon** ['hæbərdʒən] *s* cota de malla sin mangas; camisote

**habiliment** [hə'bɪlɪmənt] *s* ropa, vestido; **habiliments** *spl* prendas de vestir

**habit** ['hæbɪt] *s* hábito (*costumbre; inclinación adquirida por la repetición; vestido*); manera de crecer; amazona (*traje de mujer que sirve para montar a caballo*); **to be in the habit of** + *ger* acostumbrar + *inf; va* vestir

**habitable** ['hæbɪtəbəl] *adj* habitable

**habitant** ['hæbɪtənt] *s* habitante

**habitat** ['hæbɪtæt] *s* habitación (*morada, residencia*); ámbito natural; (biol.) habitación o habitat

**habitation** [,hæbɪ'teʃən] *s* habitación

**habit-forming** ['hæbɪt,fɔrmɪŋ] *adj* enviciador

**habitual** [hə'bɪtʃuəl] *adj* habitual

**habituate** [hə'bɪtʃuet] *va* habituar

**habituation** [hə,bɪtʃu'eʃən] *s* habituación

**habitué** [hə,bɪtʃu'e] o [hə,bɪtju'e] *s* habituado (*parroquiano; aficionado*)

**hachure** [hə'ʃur] o ['hæʃur] *s* plumeado; [hə'ʃur] *va* plumear

**hack** [hæk] *s* corte, cuchillada, hachazo, mella, machetazo; herramienta de cuchilla; tos seca; coche de punto, coche de alquiler; caballo de alquiler; rocín; caballo de silla; escritor mercenario; *adj* alquiladizo; trillado, gastado; mercenario; *va* cortar, acuchillar, picar, mellar; **to hack apart** partir a hachazos; *vn* dar cuchilladas; toser con tos seca; ir a caballo

**hackamore** ['hækəmor] *s* cabezada, jáquima

**hackberry** ['hæk,berɪ] *s* (*pl:* **-ries**) (bot.) almez, ramón; almeza (*fruto*)

**hackle** ['hækəl] *s* rastrillo; pluma del pescuezo (*de ciertas aves*); mosca artificial para pescar; **hackles** *spl* cerdas eréctiles del pescuezo y lomo del perro; *va* rastrillar; cortar toscamente, machetear, estropear a cuchilladas o a hachazos

**hackman** ['hækmən] *s* (*pl:* **-men**) cochero de punto

**hackmatack** ['hækmə,tæk] *s* (bot.) alerce americano (*Larix laricina*)

**hackney** ['hæknɪ] *s* caballo de silla; coche de alquiler; *adj* alquilado, de alquiler; *va* gastar, usar con exceso

**hackneyed** ['hæknɪd] *adj* gastado, muy usado, trillado

**hacksaw** ['hæk,sɔ] *s* sierra de armero, sierra de cortar metales

**had** [hæd] *pret & pp de* **have**

**haddock** ['hædək] *s* ((ichth.) eglefino (*pez parecido a la merluza*)

**Hades** ['hediz] *s* (myth. & Bib.) Hades; (*l.c.*) *s* (coll.) infierno

**hadn't** ['hædənt] contracción de **had not**

**Hadrian** ['hedrɪən] *s* Adriano

**haematic** [hi'mætɪk] *adj* var. de **hematic**

**haematin** ['hemətɪn] o ['himətɪn] *s* var. de **hematin**

**haematite** ['hemətaɪt] o ['himətaɪt] *s* var. de **hematite**

**haematocele** ['hemәto,sil] o ['himәto,sil] *s* var. de **hematocele**

**haematoma** [,himə'tomə] o [,hemə'tomə] *s* var. de **hematoma**

**haematopoiesis** [,hemәtopɔɪ'isɪs] o [,himәtopɔɪ'isɪs] *s* var. de **hematopoiesis**

**haematosis** [,himə'tosɪs] o [,hemə'tosɪs] *s* var. de **hematosis**

**haematoxylin** [,himə'tɑksɪlɪn] o [,hemə'tɑksɪlɪn] *s* var de **hematoxylin**

**haemin** ['himɪn] *s* var. de **hemin**

**haemocyanin** [,himo'saɪənɪn] o [,hemo'saɪənɪn] *s* var. de **hemocyanin**

**haemoglobin** [,himo'globɪn] o [,hemo'globɪn] *s* var. de **hemoglobin**

**haemoleucocyte** [,himə'lukəsaɪt] o [,hemə'lukəsaɪt] *s* var. de **hemoleucocyte**

**haemolysin** [,himə'laɪsɪn], [,hemə'laɪsɪn] o [hɪ'mɑlɪsɪn] *s* var. de **hemolysin**

**haemolysis** [hɪ'mɑlɪsɪs] *s* var. de **hemolysis**

**haemophilia** [,himə'fɪlɪə] o [,hemə'fɪlɪə] *s* var. de **hemophilia**

**haemophiliac** [,himə'fɪlɪæk] o [,hemə'fɪlɪæk] *s* var. de **hemophiliac**

**haemophilic** [,himə'fɪlɪk] o [,hemə'fɪlɪk] *adj* var. de **hemophilic**

**haemorrhage** ['hemərɪdʒ] *s* var. de **hemorrhage**

**haemorrhoids** ['hemərɔɪdz] *spl* var. de **hemorrhoids**

**haemostat** ['himəstæt] o ['heməstæt] *s* var. de **hemostat**

**haemostatic** [,himə'stætɪk] o [,hemə'stætɪk] *adj & s* var. de **hemostatic**

**hafnium** ['hæfnɪəm] *s* (chem.) hafnio

**haft** [hæft] o [hɑft] *s* mango, puño; *va* poner mango o puño a

**Hag.** abr. de **Haggai**

**hag** [hæg] *s* tarasca (*mujer fea y desenvuelta*); bruja

**hagfish** ['hæg,fɪʃ] *s* (ichth.) lamprea glutinosa

**Haggai** ['hægeaɪ] *s* (Bib.) Ageo

**haggard** ['hægərd] *adj* macilento, ojeroso, agobiado de inquietud; zahareño (*halcón*)

**haggis** ['hægɪs] *s* manjar escocés hecho con el estómago de carnero relleno del menudo de este animal mezclado con harina de avena

**haggle** ['hægəl] *s* regateo; *va* tajar toscamente, machetear; *vn* regatear; altercar, cavilar

**hagiographer** [,hægɪ'ɑgrəfər] o [,hedʒɪ'ɑgrəfər] *s* hagiógrafo

**hagiographic** [,hægɪə'græfɪk] o [,hedʒɪə'græfɪk] o **hagiographical** [,hægɪə'græfɪkəl] o [,hedʒɪə'græfɪkəl] *adj* hagiográfico

**hagiography** [,hægɪ'ɑgrəfɪ] o [,hedʒɪ'ɑgrəfɪ] *s* (*pl:* **-phies**) hagiografía

**hagiology** [,hægɪ'ɑlədʒɪ] o [,hedʒɪ'ɑlədʒɪ] *s* (*pl:* **-gies**) hagiología; santoral (*lista de los santos*)

**hagridden** ['hæg,rɪdən] *adj* atormentado, vejado

**Hague, The** [heg] La Haya

**Hague Court** *s* Tribunal internacional de La Haya

**hah** [hɑ] *interj* var. de **ha**

**hail** [hel] *s* saludo; viva, aplauso; llamada; granizo; **within hail** al alcance del oído; (naut.) al habla; *interj* ¡ salud!, ¡ salve!; **hail to . . . !** ¡ viva . . . !; *va* saludar; dar vivas a, acoger con vivas; aclamar; llamar; granizar (*p.ej., golpes*); (naut.) ponerse al habla con; *vn* granizar; **to hail from** venir de, ser oriundo de

**hail fellow well met** *adj* muy afable y simpático; *s* hombre muy afable y simpático

**Hail Mary** *s* avemaría

**hailstone** ['hel,ston] *s* piedra de granizo

**hailstorm** ['hel,stɔrm] *s* granizada; (fig.) granizada

**hair** [hɛr] *s* pelo; cabello; vello (*pelo corto y suave*); cerda (*pelo grueso y duro*); filamento; **to a hair** con la mayor exactitud; **to make one's hair stand on end** ponerle a uno los pelos de punta; **to not turn a hair** no inmutarse, quedarse tan fresco; **to split hairs** andar en quisquillas, pararse en pelillos; *adj* de pelo; para el cabello
**hairbreadth** ['hɛr,brɛdθ] *s* ancho de un pelo, casi nada; **to escape by a hairbreadth** librarse por un pelo, librarse milagrosamente
**hairbrush** ['hɛr,brʌʃ] *s* cepillo de cabeza
**haircloth** ['hɛr,klɔθ] o ['hɛr,klɑθ] *s* cilicio, tela de crin
**hair curler** *s* rizador, tenacillas, tenazas de rizar
**haircut** ['hɛr,kʌt] *s* corte de cabello, corte de pelo; **to get a haircut** cortarse el cabello o el pelo
**hairdo** ['hɛr,du] *s* (*pl:* **-dos**) peinado, tocado
**hairdresser** ['hɛr,drɛsər] *s* peinador, peluquero
**hair dye** *s* tinte para el pelo
**hairless** ['hɛrlɪs] *adj* pelón, calvo, sin pelo
**hairline** ['hɛr,laɪn] *s* rayita; estría filiforme
**hair net** *s* redecilla
**hairpin** ['hɛr,pɪn] *s* horquilla
**hairpin bend** *s* curva de retorno, viraje cerrado, curva de horquilla
**hair-raising** ['hɛr,rezɪŋ] *adj* (coll.) espeluznante, horripilante
**hair restorer** *s* crecepelo
**hair ribbon** *s* cinta para el cabello
**hair's-breadth** o **hairsbreadth** ['hɛrz,brɛdθ] *s* var. de **hairbreadth**
**hair set** *s* fijapeinados
**hair shirt** *s* cilicio
**hair space** *s* (print.) espacio de pelo
**hairsplitter** ['hɛr,splɪtər] *s* sutilizador, persona quisquillosa
**hairsplitting** ['hɛr,splɪtɪŋ] *adj* quisquilloso; *s* quisquillas
**hairspring** ['hɛr,sprɪŋ] *s* (horol.) espiral, pelo
**hair tonic** *s* vigorizador del cabello, tónico para el cabello
**hair trigger** *s* pelo (*de un arma de fuego*)
**hairy** ['hɛrɪ] *adj* (*comp:* **-ier;** *super:* **-iest**) peloso, peludo, cabelludo; velloso, hirsuto
**Haiti** ['hetɪ] *s* Haití
**Haitian** ['hetɪən] o ['heʃən] *adj & s* haitiano
**hake** [hek] *s* (ichth.) merluza; (ichth.) fice
**halazone** ['hæləzon] *s* (pharm.) halazona
**halberd** ['hælbərd] *s* alabarda
**halberdier** [,hælbər'dɪr] *s* alabardero
**halbert** ['hælbərt] *s* var. de **halberd**
**halcyon** ['hælsɪən] *s* (myth. & orn.) alción; *adj* apacible, tranquilo
**halcyon days** *spl* (meteor. & myth.) alciónеos; (fig.) días tranquilos, época de paz
**hale** [hel] *adj* sano, fuerte, robusto; **hale and hearty** sano y fuerte; *va* arrastrar, llevar a la fuerza
**half** [hæf] o [hɑf] *adj* medio; a medias, p.ej., **half owner** dueño a medias; **a half** medio, p.ej., **a half pound** media libra; **half a** medio, p.ej., **half an apple** media manzana; **half the** la mitad de, p.ej., **half the money** la mitad del dinero; *adv* medio, p.ej., **half asleep** medio dormido; a medio, p.ej., **half finished** a medio acabar; a medias, p.ej., **only half done** hecho solamente a medias; **not half as good as** ni la mitad de bueno que; **not half as much money as** ni la mitad del dinero que; **not half bad** bastante bueno; **half after** o **half past** y media, p.ej., **half after two** o **half past two** las dos y media; **half . . . half** medio . . . medio; *s* (*pl:* **halves**) mitad; (arith.) medio; **by half** con mucho; **by halves** a medias; **in half** por la mitad; **to go halves (with)** ir a medias (con)
**half-and-half** ['hæfənd'hæf] o ['hɑfənd'hɑf] *adj* mitad y mitad; indeterminado: *adv* a medias, p.ej., **money acquired half-and-half by two persons** dinero adquirido a medias por dos personas; *s* mezcla de leche y crema; mezcla de dos cervezas inglesas
**halfback** ['hæf,bæk] o ['hɑf,bæk] *s* (football) medio
**half-baked** ['hæf,bekt] o ['hɑf,bekt] *adj* a medio cocer; incompleto, a medio formular; inexperto, poco juicioso

**half binding** *s* (b.b.) media pasta, encuadernación a la holandesa
**half blood** *s* parentesco entre hermanos de padre o de madre
**half-blood** ['hæf,blʌd] o ['hɑf,blʌd] *s* mestizo; medio hermano o media hermana
**half-blooded** ['hæf,blʌdɪd] o ['hɑf,blʌdɪd] *adj* que tiene solamente el mismo padre o la misma madre; mestizo
**half boot** *s* bota de media caña
**half-bound** ['hæf,baʊnd] o ['hɑf,baʊnd] *adj* (b.b.) a la holandesa
**half-breed** ['hæf,brid] o ['hɑf,brid] *s* mestizo
**half brother** *s* medio hermano
**half-caste** ['hæf,kæst] o ['hɑf,kɑst] *s* mestizo; mestizo de sangre europea y asiática
**half cock** *s* posición de medio amartillado; **to go off at half cock** (coll.) hablar u obrar precipitadamente
**half-cocked** ['hæf'kɑkt] o ['hɑf'kɑkt] *adj* medio amartillado; *adv* (coll.) precipitadamente, sin preparación
**half crown** *s* (Brit.) moneda de plata de dos chelines y medio
**half dollar** *s* medio dólar
**half door** *s* compuerta, media puerta
**half dozen** *s* media docena
**half eagle** *s* (U.S.A.) moneda de oro de cinco dólares
**half fare** *s* medio billete
**half-full** ['hæf'fʊl] o ['hɑf'fʊl] *adj* mediado
**half-hearted** ['hæf,hɑrtɪd] o ['hɑf,hɑrtɪd] *adj* frío, indiferente, sin ánimo; débil
**half hitch** *s* media llave
**half holiday** *s* mañana o tarde de asueto
**half hose** *spl* calcetines
**half-hour** ['hæf'aʊr] o ['hɑf'aʊr] *s* media hora; **on the half-hour** a la media en punto, cada media hora; *adj* de media hora
**half leather** *s* var. de **half binding**
**half-length** ['hæf'lɛŋθ] o ['hɑf'lɛŋθ] *adj* de medio cuerpo
**half life** *s* (phys.) vida media, período medio (*de una substancia radiactiva*)
**half light** *s* media luz
**half-mast** ['hæf'mæst] o ['hɑf'mɑst] *s* media asta; **at half-mast** a media asta
**half moon** *s* media luna
**half mourning** *s* medio luto
**half nelson** ['nɛlsən] *s* (sport) presa empleada en la lucha a brazo partido, que consiste en pasar el brazo por debajo del sobaco del contrario, elevando después la mano para agarrarle por el cogote
**half note** *s* (mus.) nota blanca
**half pay** *s* media paga; medio sueldo
**halfpence** ['hepəns] *spl* medios peniques
**halfpenny** ['hepənɪ] o ['hepnɪ] *s* (*pl:* **-pence** o **-pennies**) medio penique; *adj* de medio penique; insignificante, de muy poco valor
**half pint** *s* media pinta (*medida*); (slang) gorgojo, mirmidón
**half round** *s* medio bocel
**half-round** ['hæf'raʊnd] o ['hɑf'raʊnd] *adj* semicircular, de forma semicircular
**half-round file** *s* mediacaña, lima de mediacaña
**half-seas over** ['hæf,siz] o ['hɑf,siz] *adj* (slang) entre dos velas, medio borracho
**half shell** *s* concha (*cada una de las dos partes del caparazón de los moluscos bivalvos*); **on the half shell** en su concha (*dícese de las ostras*); en una concha (*dícese de otros alimentos servidos así*)
**half-silk** ['hæf,sɪlk] o ['hɑf,sɪlk] *adj* de media seda
**half sister** *s* media hermana
**half sole** *s* media suela
**half-sole** ['hæf,sol] o ['hɑf,sol] *va* poner media suela a
**half sovereign** *s* (Brit.) moneda de oro de diez chelines
**half-staff** ['hæf'stæf] o ['hɑf'stɑf] *s* media asta; **at half-staff** a media asta
**half step** *s* (mus.) semitono
**half tide** *s* (naut.) media marea
**half-timbered** ['hæf,tɪmbərd] o ['hɑf,tɪmbərd] *adj* entramado, de pared entramada
**half title** *s* (print.) portadilla, anteportada, falsa portada

**half tone** *s* (mus.) semitono
**half-tone** ['hæf,ton] o ['hɑf,ton] *s* fotograbado; (paint. & phot.) media tinta
**half-tone screen** *s* retícula, trama
**half-track** ['hæf,træk] o ['hɑf,træk] *s* semitractor, media oruga
**half-truth** ['hæf,truθ] o ['hɑf,truθ] *s* (*pl:* **-truths** [,truðz] o [,truθs]) reticencia, verdad a medias
**half-wave** ['hæf,wev] o ['hɑf,wev] *adj* (elec.) de media onda
**halfway** ['hæf,we] o ['hɑf,we] *adj* a medio camino, situado a mitad del camino; hecho a medias, incompleto, insuficiente; **halfway between** a medio camino entre, a mitad de la distancia entre, equidistante de; *adv* a medio camino; **to meet halfway** partir el camino con; partir la diferencia con; hacer concesiones a; hacer concesiones mutuas; **halfway through** a la mitad de
**half-wit** ['hæf,wɪt] o ['hɑf,wɪt] *s* imbécil; necio, tonto
**half-witted** ['hæf,wɪtɪd] o ['hɑf,wɪtɪd] *adj* imbécil; necio, tonto
**half-yearly** [,hæf'jɪrlɪ] o [,hɑf'jɪrlɪ] *adj* semestral; *adv* semestralmente
**halibut** ['hælɪbət] *s* (ichth.) halibut, hipogloso
**Halicarnassus** [,hælɪkɑr'næsəs] *s* Halicarnaso
**halide** ['hælaɪd] o ['helaɪd] *adj* haloideo; *s* (chem.) haluro
**halidom** ['hælɪdəm] o **halidome** ['hælɪdom] *s* (archaic) lugar santo, santuario; (archaic) reliquia
**Haligonian** [,hælɪ'gonɪən] *adj* perteneciente a Halifax; *s* natural o habitante de Halifax
**halite** ['hælaɪt] o ['helaɪt] *s* (mineral.) halita (*sal gema*)
**halitosis** [,hælɪ'tosɪs] *s* halitosis
**halitus** ['hælɪtəs] *s* hálito
**hall** [hɔl] *s* pasillo, corredor; vestíbulo, zaguán; sala o salón (*p.ej., de conferencias*); paraninfo (*de una universidad*); edificio (*de una universidad*); (Brit.) casa señorial
**halleluiah** o **hallelujah** [,hælɪ'lujə] *s* aleluya; *interj* ¡ aleluya!
**halliard** ['hæljərd] *s* var. de **halyard**
**hallmark** ['hɔl,mɑrk] *s* marca del contraste; (fig.) sello (*distintivo*)
**hallo** [hə'lo] *s* (*pl:* **-los**) grito, llamada, grito de sorpresa; *interj* ¡ hola!; *vn* gritar
**halloa** [hə'lo] *s, interj & vn* var. de **hallo**
**Hall of Fame** *s* galería de la Fama (*galería en Nueva York que encierra bustos y placas conmemorativas de personajes célebres en la historia y la vida norteamericanas*)
**halloo** [hə'lu] *s* (*pl:* **-loos**) grita; llamada; *interj* ¡ hola!; (hunt.) ¡ sus!, ¡ busca!; *vn* gritar
**hallow** [hə'lo] *s* grita; llamada; *interj* ¡ hola!; (hunt.) ¡ sus!, ¡ busca!; *vn* gritar; ['hælo] *va* santificar (*hacer santo; honrar como santo*)
**hallowed** ['hælod] *adj* sagrado, santo; ['hæləwɪd] *adj* santificado
**Halloween** o **Hallowe'en** [,hælo'in] *s* víspera de Todos los Santos
**Hallowmas** ['hæloməs] *s* (archaic) día de Todos los Santos
**hallucinate** [hə'lusɪnet] *va* alucinar
**hallucination** [hə,lusɪ'neʃən] *s* alucinación
**hallway** ['hɔl,we] *s* pasillo, corredor; vestíbulo, zaguán
**halo** ['helo] *s* (*pl:* **-los** o **-loes**) (meteor.) halo; (f.a. & fig.) halo, aureola; *va* aureolar
**halogen** ['hælodʒən] *s* (chem.) halógeno
**halogenation** [,hælədʒɪ'neʃən] *s* halogenación
**haloid** ['hælɔɪd] o ['helɔɪd] *adj & s* (chem.) haloideo
**halophilous** [hə'lɑfɪləs] *adj* (bot.) halófilo
**halophyte** ['hæləfaɪt] s (bot.) halófita
**halophytic** [,hælə'fɪtɪk] *adj* (bot.) halófito
**halt** [hɔlt] *adj* (archaic) cojo, renco; *s* alto, parada; (archaic) cojera; **to call a halt** mandar hacer alto; **to call a halt to** atajar; **to come to a halt** pararse, interrumpirse; *va* detener, parar; *vn* hacer alto, parar; vacilar; tartamudear; (archaic) cojear, renquear
**halter** ['hɔltər] *s* cabestro, ronzal; dogal, cuerda de ahorcar; muerte en la horca; (*pl:* **halteres** [hæl'tɪriz]) balancín o halterio (*de insecto*); *va* cabestrar
**halting** ['hɔltɪŋ] *adj* cojo, renco; vacilante; imperfecto
**halve** [hæv] o [hɑv] *va* partir por la mitad, partir en dos; reducir por la mitad
**halyard** ['hæljərd] *s* (naut.) driza
**ham** [hæm] *s* pernil del cerdo; jamón (*pernil del cerdo curado*); (anat.) corva; (slang) comicastro; (slang) aficionado (*p.ej., a la radio*); **hams** *spl* nalgas
**hamadryad** [,hæmə'draɪæd] *s* (myth.) hamadríada
**hamamelidaceous** [,hæmə,milɪ'deʃəs] *adj* (bot.) hamamelidáceo
**Haman** ['hemən] *s* (Bib.) Amán
**ham and eggs** *spl* huevos con jamón
**Hamburg** ['hæmbʌrg] *s* Hamburgo
**hamburger** ['hæmbʌrgər] *s* albondigón, carne de vaca picada y frita; hamburguesa (*bocadillo o emparedado de carne de vaca picada y frita*)
**Hamburg steak** *s* albondigón, carne de vaca picada y frita en forma de tortilla
**hames** [hemz] *spl* horcate (*arreo*)
**Hamilcar** [hə'mɪlkɑr] *s* Amílcar
**Hamite** ['hæmaɪt] *s* camita, hamita
**Hamitic** [hæ'mɪtɪk] *adj* camítico
**hamlet** ['hæmlɪt] *s* aldehuela, caserío
**hammer** ['hæmər] *s* martillo; (anat.) martillo; macillo o martinete (*del piano*); **to come** o **to go under the hammer** venderse en subasta; *va* martillar; clavar (*con martillo*); hacer penetrar a martillazos; (coll.) apalear, regañar; **to hammer out** sacar a martillazos; forjar, formar a martillazos; elaborar trabajosamente; sacar en limpio a fuerza de mucho pensar o hablar; *vn* martillar; **to hammer at** trabajar asiduamente en, dedicarse con ahinco a; **to hammer away** trabajar asiduamente; **to hammer away on the same old subject** estar siempre con la misma canción
**hammer and sickle, the** la hoz y el martillo
**hammer and tongs** *adv* con violencia, con todas sus fuerzas
**hammerhead** ['hæmər,hɛd] *s* (ichth.) cornudilla, pez martillo
**hammerless** ['hæmərlɪs] *adj* sin martillo; de gatillo interior
**hammer lock** *s* (sport) presa empleada en la lucha a brazo partido, que consiste en torcer el brazo del contrario y doblarlo detrás de su espalda
**hammer mill** *s* machacadora de martillos
**hammock** ['hæmək] *s* hamaca; (naut.) coy
**hamper** ['hæmpər] *s* cesto grande (*generalmente con tapa*); *va* estorbar, embarazar, impedir
**hamster** ['hæmstər] *s* (zool.) hámster, marmota de Alemania, rata del trigo
**hamstring** ['hæm,strɪŋ] *s* (anat.) tendón de la corva; (*pret & pp:* **-strung**) *va* desjarretar; (fig.) estropear, incapacitar
**hand** [hænd] *s* mano; obrero, peón; carácter de letra, escritura, puño y letra; firma; perito; salva de aplausos; palmo menor; mano o manecilla (*de reloj*); mano (*lance entero en un juego*); juego (*conjunto de naipes en la mano*); jugador; fuente (*de una noticia*); manojo (*de tabaco*); **all hands** (naut.) toda la tripulación; (coll.) todos; **at first hand** de primera mano; de buena tinta, directamente; **at hand** a la mano (*cerca*); disponible; **by hand** a mano; **by the hand** de la mano; **in hand** en sujeción, dominado; entre manos; de contado; marchando bien; **in his own hand** de su propio puño; **in one's hands** en manos de uno; **off one's hands** desechado, despachado; **on hand** a la mano, entre manos (*cerca*); disponible; en existencia; listo; **on one's hands** en mano de uno, entre manos; **on the one hand** por una parte; **on the other hand** por otra parte; **out of hand** en seguida, luego; desbocado, desmandado; terminado; **to be at hand** obrar en mi (nuestro) poder (*una carta*); **to bear a hand** dar la mano, prestar ayuda; **to change hands** mudar de manos; **to clap hands** batir palmas; **to eat out of one's hand** aceptar dócilmente la autoridad de uno, entregarse a la voluntad de uno; **to fall into the hands of** caer en manos de; **to force one's hand** obligar a uno a hacer

lo que no quiere hacer, obligar a uno a poner de manifiesto sus intenciones; **to get one's hands on** lograr echar la garra a; **to hand** a mano; en poder de uno; **to have a hand in** tomar parte en, jugar en; **to have one's hands full** estar ocupadísimo; **to hold hands** tomarse de las manos; **to hold up one's hands** alzar las manos (*p.ej., en señal de rendición*); **to hold up the hands of** apoyar, sostener; **to join hands** darse las manos; casarse; **to keep one's hands in** seguir teniendo práctica; mantener su interés en; **to keep one's hands off** no tocar, no meterse en; **to lay hands on** tomar, coger; prender; conseguir; tener al alcance de la mano; (eccl.) imponer las manos; **to lend a hand** dar la mano, prestar ayuda; **to live from hand to mouth** vivir al día, vivir de la mano a la boca; **to not do a hand's turn** ser incapaz de mover un brazo; **to not lift a hand** no levantar paja del suelo; **to play into the hands of** hacer el caldo gordo a; **to shake hands** estrecharse la mano; **to show one's hand** descubrir su juego (*p.ej., en los naipes*); (fig.) descubrir su juego; **to take in hand** hacerse cargo de; dominar; tratar, estudiar (*una cuestión*); ensayar; **to take off one's hands** quitarle a uno de encima (*p.ej., un problema*); **to try one's hand** probar la mano; **to turn one's hand to** dedicarse a, ocuparse en; **to wash one's hands of** lavarse las manos de; **under my hand** de mi puño y letra, con mi firma, bajo mi firma; **under the hand and seal of** firmado y sellado por; **hand and glove** o **hand in glove** uña y carne; **hand in hand** de las manos, asidos de la mano; juntos; **hands up!** ¡arriba las manos!; **hand to hand** cuerpo a cuerpo ‖ *adj* de mano; manual ‖ *va* dar, pasar, entregar; poner en manos de; conducir por la mano; **to hand down** pasar de arriba abajo; transmitir; **to hand in** entregar; **to hand on** pasar a otro, transmitir; **to hand out** dar, repartir; **to hand over** entregar; **to hand up** pasar de abajo arriba

**handbag** [ˈhænd,bæg] *s* bolso de mano, faltriquera; maletilla

**hand baggage** *s* equipaje de mano

**handball** [ˈhænd,bɔl] *s* pelota; juego de pelota (*estilo norteamericano*)

**handbarrow** [ˈhænd,bæro] *s* parihuelas; carretilla de mano

**handbill** [ˈhænd,bɪl] *s* hoja volante (*que se entrega en manos de los transeúntes*)

**handbook** [ˈhænd,bʊk] *s* manual; guía (*de turistas*); registro para apuestas; sitio donde se hacen las apuestas

**hand brake** *s* freno de mano

**handbreadth** [ˈhænd,brɛdθ] *s* ancho de la mano

**handcar** [ˈhænd,kɑr] *s* (rail.) carrito de mano

**handcart** [ˈhænd,kɑrt] *s* carretilla de mano

**hand control** *s* mando a mano

**handcuff** [ˈhænd,kʌf] *s* manilla; **handcuffs** *spl* esposas; *va* poner manilla a, poner esposas a

**handful** [ˈhændfʊl] *s* puñado; (fig.) puñado (*corta cantidad*); (coll.) persona o cosa difícil de dominar

**hand glass** *s* espejo de mano; lente para leer; campana de vidrio (*que sirve de protección a una planta*)

**hand grenade** *s* granada de mano; granada extintora de mano

**handhold** [ˈhænd,hold] *s* asidero

**handicap** [ˈhændɪkæp] *s* desventaja, impedimento, obstáculo; (sport) carrera con caballos de peso igualado; (sport) carrera, lucha o torneo en que se dan ciertas ventajas a los menos aventajados; (sport) ventaja que se da o impedimento que se impone; (*pret & pp:* **-capped;** *ger:* **-capping**) *va* estorbar, poner trabas a; (sport) imponer impedimento a

**handicraft** [ˈhændɪkræft] o [ˈhændɪkrɑft] *s* destreza manual; arte mecánica

**handicraftsman** [ˈhændɪ,kræftsmən] o [ˈhændɪ,krɑftsmən] *s* (*pl:* **-men**) artesano

**handily** [ˈhændɪlɪ] *adv* diestramente; fácilmente

**handiwork** [ˈhændɪ,wʌrk] *s* obra manual; obra de las manos de uno; trabajo, producción

**handkerchief** [ˈhæŋkərtʃɪf] *s* pañuelo

**handle** [ˈhændəl] *s* asa (*de cesta, vasija, etc.*); mango (*de azadón, pala, etc.*); puño (*de bastón, paraguas, espada, etc.*); tirador (*de cajón, puerta, etc.*); manubrio (*p.ej., de organillo*); guimbalete (*de bomba de agua*); (fig.) asidero (*ocasión, pretexto*); **handles** *spl* (coll.) perejiles (*títulos o signos de dignidad*); **to fly off the handle** (slang) salirse de sus casillas, perder los estribos; *va* tocar, manosear; manejar, manipular; dirigir, gobernar, mandar; tratar; comerciar en; *vn* manejarse (*bien o mal*)

**handle bar** *s* manillar, guía (*de bicicleta*)

**handler** [ˈhændlər] *s* tratante; (box.) entrenador

**handless** [ˈhændlɪs] *adj* manco, sin mano

**handmade** [ˈhænd,med] *adj* hecho a mano

**handmaid** [ˈhænd,med] o **handmaiden** [ˈhænd,medən] *s* criada; asistenta

**hand-me-down** [ˈhændmi,daʊn] *adj* (slang) hecho de antemano; (slang) de segunda mano, barato; (slang) poco elegante, de poco gusto; *s* (slang) prenda de vestir de segunda mano

**hand organ** *s* organillo

**handout** [ˈhænd,aʊt] *s* (slang) comida que se da a un mendigo

**hand-picked** [ˈhænd,pɪkt] *adj* escogido a mano; escogido escrupulosamente; escogido con motivos ocultos

**handrail** [ˈhænd,rel] *s* barandilla, pasamano

**handsaw** [ˈhænd,sɔ] *s* serrucho, sierra de mano

**hand's-breadth** [ˈhændz,brɛdθ] *s* var. de **handbreadth**

**handsel** [ˈhændsəl] o [ˈhænsəl] *s* estrena; aguinaldo; primera paga (*de dinero*); cantidad de dinero cobrado por un tendero por la mañana; dinero cobrado por un tendero al poner una tienda nueva; indicio anticipado, goce anticipado; (*pret & pp:* **-seled** o **-selled;** *ger:* **-seling** o **-selling**) *va* dar estrena a; estrenar, inaugurar; probar (*una cosa*) antes que otro, ser el primero en probar o en tener conocimiento de

**handset** [ˈhænd,sɛt] *s* (telp.) microteléfono (*aparato con el micrófono y el auricular dispuestos a cada extremo de un mango de ebonita*)

**handshake** [ˈhænd,ʃek] *s* apretón de manos

**handsome** [ˈhænsəm] *adj* hermoso, guapo, buen mozo; liberal, considerable; donairoso, elegante

**handspike** [ˈhænd,spaɪk] *s* palanca, barra (*p.ej., del cabrestante*)

**handspring** [ˈhænd,sprɪŋ] *s* voltereta sobre las manos

**hand-to-hand** [ˈhændtʊ,hænd] *adj* cuerpo a cuerpo; de mano en mano

**hand-to-mouth** [ˈhændtʊ,maʊθ] *adj* precario, inseguro; impróvido

**hand-tooled** [ˈhændˈtuld] *adj* labrado a mano

**handwork** [ˈhænd,wʌrk] *s* obra hecha a mano, trabajo a mano

**hand-wrestle** [ˈhænd,rɛsəl] *vn* pulsear

**handwriting** [ˈhænd,raɪtɪŋ] *s* escritura; letra (*forma de letra que cada uno tiene*)

**handy** [ˈhændɪ] *adj* (*comp:* **-ier;** *super:* **-iest**) a la mano, próximo; diestro, hábil; útil; **to come in handy** venir a pelo

**handy man** *s* factótum, dije

**hang** [hæŋ] *s* caída (*p.ej., de un vestido, una cortina*); pausa; declive; tino (*destreza, acierto*); significado (*de un argumento*); **I don't care a hang** no me importa un ardite; **to get the hang of it** coger el tino ‖ (*pret & pp:* **hung**) *va* colgar; fijar (*p.ej., un letrero*); tender (*la ropa mojada para que se seque*); pegar (*el papel en una pared*); bajar, inclinar (*la cabeza, por vergüenza*); (law) hacer imposible el fallo de (*un jurado*) singularizándose en opinión contraria; **to hang out** colgar fuera; desplegar (*p.ej., una bandera por una ventana*); tender (*la ropa mojada para que se seque*); **to hang up** colgar (*p.ej., el sombrero*); estorbar, impedir los progresos de; **hang it!** ¡caramba! ‖ *vn* colgar, pender; estar fijado; inclinarse; agarrarse, estar agarrado; vacilar, estar indeciso; **to hang around** andar haraganeando, esperar sin hacer nada; rondar, no alejarse de; **to hang back** resistirse a pasar adelante; vacilar, estar indeciso; **to hang down** colgar, estar pendiente; **to hang from** colgar de (*p.ej., un clavo*); **to hang on** colgar de (*p.ej., un clavo*); depender de; estar pendiente de (*las palabras de una persona*); agarrarse; insistir, persistir, estar en sus trece; estar sin acabar de morir; **to hang on to** agarrarse a, estar agarrado a; no querer soltar, no querer deshacerse de; **to hang out** asomarse demasiado; asomarse a (*una ventana*) echando fuera el busto; (slang) alojarse, vivir; **to hang over** cernerse sobre (*amenazar*); (coll.) persistir (*como efecto de un estado anterior*); **to hang together** permanecer unidos, mantenerse unidos; tener cohesión; **to hang up** (telp.) colgar ‖ (*pret & pp:* **hanged** o **hung**) *va* ahorcar; *vn* ahorcarse

**hangar** ['hæŋər] o ['hæŋgɑr] *s* cobertizo; (aer.) hangar

**hangbird** ['hæŋ,bʌrd] *s* (orn.) pájaro de nido colgante; (orn.) cacique veranero

**hangdog** ['hæŋ,dɔg] o ['hæŋ,dɑg] *adj* avergonzado; rastrero, vil

**hanger** ['hæŋər] *s* colgador, suspensión, brazo o hierro suspensor; colgadero; anillo de suspensión; (aut.) soporte colgante

**hanger-on** ['hæŋər'ɑn] o ['hæŋər'ɔn] *s* (*pl:* **hangers-on**) secuaz, protegido; pegote; habituado, concurrente

**hanging** ['hæŋɪŋ] *adj* colgante, pendiente, suspendido; de suspensión; digno de la horca; *s* ahorcadura, muerte en la horca; **hangings** *spl* colgaduras

**hanging scaffold** *s* andamio volante, puente volante, puente suspendido

**hangman** ['hæŋmən] *s* (*pl:* **-men**) verdugo

**hangnail** ['hæŋ,nel] *s* respigón, padrastro (*de las uñas*)

**hangout** ['hæŋ,aut] *s* (slang) guarida, nidal, querencia

**hangover** ['hæŋ,ovər] *s* efecto persistente de circunstancias anteriores; (slang) resaca (*malestar que se siente al acabar de dormir la mona*)

**hank** [hæŋk] *s* madeja (*de hilo, de pelo*); (naut.) anillo

**hanker** ['hæŋkər] *vn* sentir anhelo; **to hanker after** o **for** sentir anhelo por

**hankering** ['hæŋkərɪŋ] *s* anhelo; **to have a hankering for** sentir anhelo por

**hanky-panky** ['hæŋkɪ'pæŋkɪ] *s* (coll.) superchería; (coll.) prestidigitación

**Hannibal** ['hænɪbəl] *s* Aníbal

**Hanoverian** [,hæno'vɪrɪən] *adj & s* hanoveriano

**hanse** [hæns] *s* ansa (*gremio mercantil medieval*)

**Hanseatic** [,hænsɪ'ætɪk] *adj* anseático

**Hanseatic League** *s* Liga anseática

**hansel** ['hænsəl] *s* var. de **handsel;** (*pret & pp:* **-seled** o **-selled;** *ger:* **-seling** o **-selling**) *va* var. de **handsel**

**hansom** ['hænsəm] *s* cab (*cabriolé de dos ruedas con pescante elevado por detrás*)

**hap** [hæp] *s* (archaic) destino, suerte; (archaic) acaso, lance; (*pret & pp:* **happed;** *ger:* **happing**) *vn* (archaic) acontecer

**haphazard** [,hæp'hæzərd] *adj* casual, descuidado, impensado; *adv* al acaso, al azar, a la ventura; ['hæp,hæzərd] *s* casualidad, accidente

**hapless** ['hæplɪs] *adj* desgraciado, desventurado

**haploid** ['hæplɔɪd] *adj & s* (biol.) haploide

**haplology** [hæp'lɑlədʒɪ] *s* (philol.) haplología

**haply** ['hæplɪ] *adv* por casualidad

**happen** ['hæpən] *vn* acontecer, suceder, ocurrir; resultar, p.ej., **it happened as we planned it** resultó tal como lo habíamos proyectado; pasar, p.ej., **what happened?** ¿qué pasó?; **don't let anything happen to you** que no le pase nada; dar la casualidad, p.ej., **it happens that I do not like that fellow** da la casualidad de que a mí no me gusta ese tipo; **no matter what happens** suceda lo que suceda; **to happen to** hacerse de, p.ej., **what happened to my hat?** ¿qué se ha hecho de mi sombrero?; a diferencia de los verbos acontecer, suceder, ocurrir, etc., el verbo **happen** se puede emplear en las primeras y segundas personas; **to happen in** entrar por casualidad; **to happen on** o **upon** acertar con, encontrarse con; **to happen to** + *inf* por casualidad, p.ej., **I happened to be there** me encontraba allí por casualidad; **I happened to see your name in the paper** ví por casualidad su nombre en el periódico; suceder que + *ind*, p.ej., **you happened to fall asleep** sucedió que Vd. se quedó dormido; resultar que + *ind*, p.ej., **I happen to know it** resulta que lo sé; el caso es que + *ind*, p.ej., **I don't happen to agree with you** el caso es que no estoy de acuerdo con Vd.

**happening** ['hæpənɪŋ] *s* acontecimiento, suceso

**happily** ['hæpɪlɪ] *adv* felizmente

**happiness** ['hæpɪnɪs] *s* felicidad

**happy** ['hæpɪ] *adj* (*comp:* **-pier;** *super:* **-piest**) feliz; contento; **to be happy to** + *inf* alegrarse de + *inf*, tener gusto en + *inf*

**happy event** *s* venturoso acontecimiento (*nacimiento de un niño*)

**happy-go-lucky** ['hæpɪgo'lʌkɪ] *adj* impróvido, irresponsable, imperturbable; *adv* a la buena ventura

**happy hunting grounds** *spl* tierra de caza abundante (*paraíso de los pieles rojas norteamericanos*)

**happy medium** *s* justo medio

**happy motoring** *interj* ¡feliz viaje!

**Happy New Year** *interj* ¡Feliz Año Nuevo!, ¡Próspero Año Nuevo!

**hara-kari** ['hɑrɑ'kɑrɪ] o **hara-kiri** ['hɑrɑ'kɪrɪ] *s* var. de **hari-kari**

**harangue** [hə'ræŋ] *s* arenga; *va & vn* arengar

**harass** ['hærəs] o [hə'ræs] *va* acosar, hostigar

**harassment** ['hærəsmənt] o [hə'ræsmənt] *s* acosamiento, hostigamiento

**harbinger** ['hɑrbɪndʒər] *s* precursor; anuncio, presagio; *va* anunciar, presagiar

**harbor** ['hɑrbər] *s* puerto; (fig.) puerto (*asilo, amparo*); *adj* portuario; *va* albergar; conservar o guardar (*p.ej., sentimientos de odio*); alcahuetear, encubrir (*delincuentes u objetos robados*); *vn* ir a ampararse

**harborage** ['hɑrbərɪdʒ] *s* puerto; (fig.) puerto, albergue, refugio

**harborer** ['hɑrbərər] *s* amparador; encubridor (*de delincuentes u objetos robados*)

**harbor master** *s* capitán de puerto

**harbor pilot** *s* piloto de puerto, práctico de puerto

**harbour** ['hɑrbər] *s, adj, va & vn* (Brit.) var. de **harbor**

**hard** [hɑrd] *adj* duro; difícil; asiduo (*trabajador*); crudo o duro (*dícese del agua*); fuerte (*dícese de la soldadura*); espiritoso, fuertemente alcohólico; (phonet.) gutural, velar; (phonet.) sordo; (phys.) duro (*rayo; tubo al vacío*); **to be hard on** gastar (*p.ej., zapatos*); echar a perder (*p.ej., un libro*); estar muy duro con; **to find it hard to** + *inf* hacérsele a uno cuesta arriba + *inf;* **to make it hard for** causar estorbo o trabajo a; **hard to** + *inf* malo de + *inf*, p.ej., **this lesson is hard to understand** esta lección es mala de entender; *adv* duro; mucho; fuerte; de firme, p.ej., **to drink, to rain, to work hard** beber, trabajar, llover de firme; con dificultad; con violencia; enteramente, hasta el límite; **to go hard with one** costarle a uno caro, serle a uno penoso; verse uno tratado con gran rigor (*por una culpa cometida*); **hard upon** a raíz de

**hard and fast** *adj* inflexible, riguroso; *adv* firmemente

**hard-bitten** ['hɑrd'bɪtən] *adj* duro, inflexible, terco

**hard-boiled** ['hɑrd'bɔɪld] *adj* duro, muy cocido (*huevo*); (coll.) endurecido, inflexible

**hard by** *adv* cerca; *prep* cerca de

**hard candy** *s* caramelos

**hard cash** *s* metálico, dinero contante y sonante

**hard cider** *s* sidra muy fermentada

**hard coal** *s* hulla magra, hulla seca

**hard-drawn** ['hɑrd,drɔn] *adj* (metal.) estirado en frío

**hard drinker** *s* bebedor empedernido

**hard-earned** ['hɑrd'ʌrnd] *adj* ganado a pulso

**harden** ['hɑrdən] *va* endurecer; solidificar; *vn* endurecerse; solidificarse

**hardened** ['hardənd] *adj* endurecido; empedernido
**hardening** ['hardənɪŋ] *s* endurecimiento; **hardening of the arteries** (path.) endurecimiento arterial
**hard facts** *spl* realidades
**hard-featured** ['hard'fitʃərd] *adj* de facciones duras, de semblante hosco
**hard-fisted** ['hard'fɪstɪd] *adj* de puños rudos; tacaño
**hard-fought** ['hard'fɔt] *adj* arduo, reñido
**hardhack** ['hard,hæk] *s* (bot.) espirea tomentosa
**hard-handed** ['hard'hændɪd] *adj* de manos callosas; duro, cruel, inhumano
**hard-headed** ['hard'hɛdɪd] *adj* astuto, de mucha trastienda; terco, tozudo
**hard-hearted** ['hard'hartɪd] *adj* duro de corazón
**hardihood** ['hardɪhud] *s* audacia, atrevimiento, descaro, entereza de carácter
**hardiness** ['hardɪnɪs] *s* fuerza, robustez, resistencia física; audacia, atrevimiento, descaro
**hard labor** *s* trabajos forzados
**hard lines** o **hard luck** *s* mala suerte; *interj* ¡qué mala suerte!
**hard-luck story** ['hard'lʌk] *s* (coll.) cuento de penas; **to tell a hard-luck story** (coll.) contar lástimas
**hardly** ['hardlɪ] *adv* apenas; a duras penas; casi no; difícilmente; duramente, severamente
**hardness** ['hardnɪs] *s* dureza; crudeza (*del agua*)
**hard of hearing** *adj* corto de oído, medio sordo
**hard palate** *s* (anat.) paladar duro
**hardpan** ['hard,pæn] *s* capa arcillosa y dura debajo de terreno blando; (fig.) base sólida; (fig.) fondo de realidad (*algo desagradable o poco lisonjero*)
**hard pressed** *adj* acosado; apurado, falto de caudal
**hard put to it** *adj* en apuros, en un aprieto
**hard rubber** *s* caucho duro o endurecido
**hard sauce** *s* mantequilla azucarada
**hard sell** *s* (coll.) método enérgico e insistente de anunciar o vender mercancías
**hard-set** ['hard'sɛt] *adj* en calzas prietas; resuelto; terco, inflexible
**hard-shell** ['hard,ʃɛl] *adj* de cáscara o caparazón duros; intransigente
**hard-shelled clam** ['hard,ʃɛld] *s* (zool.) almeja redonda (*Venus mercenaria*)
**hard-shelled crab** *s* cangrejo antes de la muda
**hardship** ['hardʃɪp] *s* apuro, fatiga, penalidad
**hard sledding** *s* apuros, dificultades, condiciones desfavorables
**hard soap** *s* jabón duro, jabón de piedra
**hard steel** *s* acero duro
**hardtack** ['hard,tæk] *s* galleta, sequete
**hard times** *spl* período duro, período de miseria
**hard to please** *adj* difícil de contentar
**hard up** *adj* (coll.) alcanzado, apurado
**hardware** ['hard,wɛr] *s* quincalla, objetos de metal, ferretería; herraje (*piezas metálicas para guarnecer algo*)
**hardwareman** ['hard,wɛrmən] *s* (*pl:* **-men**) quincallero, ferretero
**hardware store** *s* quincallería, ferretería
**hard water** *s* agua dura, agua cruda
**hard-won** ['hard,wʌn] *adj* ganado a pulso, conseguido con dificultad
**hardwood** ['hard,wud] *s* madera dura, madera preciosa; árbol de hojas caducas
**hardwood floor** *s* entarimado
**hardy** ['hardɪ] *adj* (*comp:* **-dier**; *super:* **-diest**) fuerte, robusto; atrevido, audaz; temerario; (bot.) resistente
**hare** [hɛr] *s* (zool.) liebre
**harebell** ['hɛr,bɛl] *s* (bot.) campánula
**harebrained** ['hɛr,brend] *adj* atolondrado, ligero de cascos
**harelip** ['hɛr,lɪp] *s* labio leporino
**harelipped** ['hɛr,lɪpt] *adj* labihendido
**harem** ['hɛrəm] *s* harem o harén
**hare's-ear** ['hɛrz,ɪr] *s* (bot.) perfoliada o perfoliata
**hari-kari** ['harɪ'karɪ] *s* harakiri
**hark** [hark] *interj* ¡oíd!; *vn* escuchar; **to hark back** (hunt.) volver sobre la pista (*dícese de la jauría*); (fig.) volver al asunto
**harken** ['harkən] *vn* escuchar, atender
**harlequin** ['harləkwɪn] *s* arlequín; *adj* arlequinesco; abigarrado; (*cap.*) *s* Arlequín
**harlequinade** [,harləkwɪ'ned] *s* arlequinada
**harlequin beetle** *s* (ent.) arlequín de Cayena
**harlequinesque** [,harləkwɪ'nɛsk] *adj* arlequinesco
**harlequin ice cream** *s* arlequín (*helado*)
**harlot** ['harlət] *s* ramera
**harlotry** ['harlətrɪ] *s* prostitución
**harm** [harm] *s* daño, perjuicio; *va* dañar, hacer daño a, perjudicar
**harmful** ['harmfəl] *adj* dañoso, perjudicial, nocivo
**harmless** ['harmlɪs] *adj* inofensivo, inocuo, inocente
**harmonic** [har'manɪk] *adj & s* (mus. & phys.) armónico; **harmonics** *ssg* (mus.) teoría musical
**harmonica** [har'manɪkə] *s* armónica
**harmonious** [har'monɪəs] *adj* armonioso
**harmonist** ['harmənɪst] *s* músico, compositor
**harmonium** [har'monɪəm] *s* (mus.) armonio
**harmonization** [,harmənɪ'zeʃən] *s* armonización
**harmonize** ['harmənaɪz] *va & vn* armonizar
**harmony** ['harmənɪ] *s* (*pl:* **-nies**) armonía
**harness** ['harnɪs] *s* guarniciones, arreos, arneses, montura; (archaic) arnés (*armadura*); **in harness** en funciones, trabajando; **to get back in the harness** volver a trabajar, volver a la rutina; **to die in the harness** morir al pie del cañón; *va* enjaezar, poner guarniciones a (*una caballería*); captar, represar (*las aguas de un río*); (archaic) armar con arnés
**harness maker** *s* guarnicionero
**harness race** *s* carrera con sulky
**Harold** ['hærəld] *s* Haroldo
**harp** [harp] *s* (mus.) arpa; *vn* tañer el arpa; **to harp on** porfiar importunamente sobre, dar en la gracia de decir
**harpist** ['harpɪst] *s* arpista
**harpoon** [har'pun] *s* arpón; *va* arponar o arponear
**harpooner** [har'punər] *s* arponero
**harpoon gun** *s* cañón lanzaarpones
**harpsichord** ['harpsɪkɔrd] *s* (mus.) clave
**harpy** ['harpɪ] *s* (*pl:* **-pies**) arpía (*persona muy codiciosa*); (*cap.*) *s* (myth.) arpía
**harpy bat** *s* (zool.) harpía
**harpy eagle** *s* (orn.) águila moneva
**harquebus** ['harkwɪbəs] *s* arcabuz
**harquebusier** [,harkwɪbəs'ɪr] *s* arcabucero
**harridan** ['hærɪdən] *s* bruja (*vieja viciosa y regañona*)
**harrier** ['hærɪər] *s* acosador, asolador; corredor por el campo; perro lebrel; (orn.) busardo
**Harriet** ['hærɪət] *s* Enriqueta
**harrow** ['hæro] *s* (agr.) grada; *va* (agr.) gradar; lacerar; atormentar, martirizar
**harrowing** ['hæro·ɪŋ] *adj* horripilante, espeluznante; *s* (agr.) gradeo
**harry** ['hærɪ] (*pret & pp:* **-ried**) *va* acosar, hostilizar, asolar; inquietar, atormentar; (*cap.*) *s* Enriquito
**harsh** [harʃ] *adj* áspero (*al tacto, al gusto, al oído; estilo*); cruel, duro
**harshness** ['harʃnɪs] *s* aspereza; crueldad, dureza
**hart** [hart] *s* (zool.) ciervo
**hartebeest** ['hartɪ,bist] o ['hart,bist] *s* (zool.) caama, ciervo del Cabo
**hartshorn** ['harts,hɔrn] *s* cuerno de ciervo; (pharm.) cuerno de ciervo
**hart's-tongue** ['harts,tʌŋ] *s* (bot.) lengua de ciervo, lengua cerval
**harum-scarum** ['hɛrəm'skɛrəm] *adj* tarambana; *adv* atolondradamente; *s* tarambana, torbellino
**haruspex** [hə'rʌspɛks] o ['hærəspɛks] *s* (*pl:* **haruspices** [hə'rʌspɪsiz]) arúspice
**harvest** ['harvɪst] *s* cosecha; (fig.) cosecha (*fruto, p.ej., de buena o mala conducta*); *va* cosechar; (fig.) recoger (*el fruto de una acción*); *vn* cosechar
**harvester** ['harvɪstər] *s* cosechero; jornalero por el agosto; segadora, máquina segadora
**harvester-thresher** ['harvɪstər'θrɛʃər] *s* segadora trilladora

**harvest home** *s* final de la cosecha; fiesta de segadores; canción de segadores
**harvestman** ['harvɪstmən] *s* (*pl:* **-men**) cosechero; jornalero por el agosto; (ent.) segador
**harvest moon** *s* plenilunio en la época de la cosecha
**harvest mouse** *s* (zool.) ratón silvestre
**has** [hæz] *tercera persona del sg del pres de ind de* **have**
**has-been** ['hæz,bɪn] *s* (coll.) persona que ya no sirve, cosa que ya no sirve
**Hasdrubal** ['hæzdrubəl] *s* Asdrúbal
**hash** [hæʃ] *s* picadillo; mezcla confusa, embrollo, lío; **to settle one's hash** (coll.) meterle a uno en cintura, acabar con uno; *va* picar, desmenuzar; embrollar; **to hash up everything** enredarlo todo
**hasheesh** o **hashish** ['hæʃiʃ] *s* hachich o hachís o haxix
**haslet** ['hæslɪt] o ['hezlɪt] *s* asadura de puerco
**hasn't** ['hæzənt] contracción de **has not**
**hasp** [hæsp] o [hasp] *s* portacandado; broche, manecilla (*para cerrar un libro*)
**hassle** ['hæsəl] *s* (coll.) disputa, controversia, pendencia
**hassock** ['hæsək] *s* cojín (*para los pies, para rezar arrodillado, etc.*); montecillo de hierbas crecientes (*en un terreno pantanoso*)
**hastate** ['hæstet] *adj* (bot.) alabardado
**haste** [hest] *s* prisa; precipitación; **in haste** de prisa; **to make haste** darse prisa
**hasten** ['hesən] *va* apresurar; apretar (*el paso*); *vn* apresurarse, darse prisa; **to hasten to** + *inf* apresurarse a + *inf*
**hasty** ['hestɪ] *adj* (*comp:* **-ier;** *super:* **-iest**) apresurado; hecho de prisa; inconsiderado; colérico
**hasty pudding** *s* gachas de harina de maíz; gachas de harina o avena
**hat** [hæt] *s* sombrero; capelo (*de cardenal*); cardenalato; sombrerillo (*para recoger las limosnas*); **to keep under one's hat** (slang) callar, no divulgar; **to pass the hat** pasar el sombrero (o la gorra); pasar el cepillo; **to take one's hat off to** (coll.) reconocer la superioridad de; **to throw one's hat in the ring** (coll.) decidirse a bajar a la arena; (*pret & pp:* **hatted;** *ger:* **hatting**) *va* dar sombrero a; cubrir con sombrero
**hatband** ['hæt,bænd] *s* cintillo (*de sombrero*)
**hat block** *s* hormillón, peana
**hatbox** ['hæt,baks] *s* sombrerera
**hatch** [hætʃ] *s* cría, nidada; salida del cascarón; trampa, escotillón; compuerta, media puerta; (f.a.) línea de sombreado; (naut.) escotilla; (naut.) cuartel (*armazón de tablas para cerrar la escotilla*); *va* sacar (*pollos*) del cascarón; empollar (*huevos*); (f.a.) sombrear, plumear; idear, maquinar, tramar; *vn* salir del huevo; empollarse
**hat-check girl** ['hæt,tʃɛk] *s* guardarropa (*joven encargada de custodiar los sombreros, etc.*)
**hatchel** ['hætʃəl] *s* rastrillo (*para limpiar el lino o el cáñamo*); (*pret & pp:* **-eled** o **-elled;** *ger:* **-eling** o **-elling**) *va* rastrillar (*lino o cáñamo*); atormentar, molestar
**hatchery** ['hætʃərɪ] *s* (*pl:* **-ies**) criadero (*p.ej., de peces*)
**hatchet** ['hætʃɪt] *s* destral; hacha de guerra (*de los pieles rojas*); **to bury the hatchet** envainar la espada, hacer la paz, echar pelillos a la mar; **to dig up the hatchet** hacer la guerra
**hatchet face** *s* cara de cuchillo
**hatchet vetch** *s* (bot.) encorvada, hierba de la segur
**hatching** ['hætʃɪŋ] *s* (f.a.) sombreado, plumeado
**hatchment** ['hætʃmənt] *s* placa cuadrada, colocada diagonalmente, en que está grabado el escudo de armas de un caballero o dama muertos
**hatchway** ['hætʃ,we] *s* escotillón (*puerta en el suelo*); (naut.) escotilla
**hate** [het] *s* odio, aborrecimiento; *va & vn* odiar, aborrecer; **to hate to** + *inf* detestar + *inf*, p.ej., **I hate to go out in the rain** detesto salir con la lluvia
**hateful** ['hetfəl] *adj* odiable, odioso; maligno, malévolo
**hatefulness** ['hetfəlnɪs] *s* odiosidad; malignidad
**hatemonger** ['het,mʌŋgər] *s* (coll.) alborotador, cizañador
**hatpin** ['hæt,pɪn] *s* pasador o aguja de sombrero
**hatrack** ['hæt,ræk] *s* percha (*para colgar sombreros*)
**hatred** ['hetrɪd] *s* odio, aborrecimiento
**hatter** ['hætər] *s* sombrerero
**Hattie** o **Hatty** ['hætɪ] *s* nombre abreviado de **Harriet**
**haubergeon** ['hɔbərdʒən] *s* var. de **habergeon**
**hauberk** ['hɔbərk] *s* camisote
**haughtiness** ['hɔtɪnɪs] *s* altanería, altivez
**haughty** ['hɔtɪ] *adj* (*comp:* **-tier;** *super:* **-tiest**) altanero, altivo
**haul** [hɔl] *s* tirón; recorrido, trayecto; redada; (fig.) redada (*p.ej., de ladrones*); *va* acarrear, transportar, arrastrar; (naut.) virar (*una nave*); **to haul up** (coll.) pedir cuentas a; (naut.) virar (*una nave*); *vn* tirar; cambiar de rumbo; **to haul off** levantar el puño (*para asestar un golpe*); retirarse; (naut.) virar (*para apartar la nave de un objeto cualquiera*); **to haul on the wind, to haul to the wind** o **to haul up** (naut.) virar para navegar ciñendo
**haulage** ['hɔlɪdʒ] *s* acarreo, transporte, arrastre; coste o gastos de acarreo
**haunch** [hɔntʃ] o [hantʃ] *s* cadera (*parte donde se unen el muslo y el tronco*); anca (*cada una de las dos partes posteriores de los animales*); pierna (*de carnero, venado, etc.*)
**haunt** [hɔnt] o [hant] *s* guarida, nidal, querencia; refugio; (dial.) fantasma, aparecido; *va* frecuentar; andar por, vagar por; perseguir (*una idea a una persona*); estar siempre en la memoria de
**haunted house** *s* casa de fantasmas
**haunting** ['hɔntɪŋ] o ['hantɪŋ] *adj* persistente, inolvidable, obsesionante
**hautboy** ['hobɔɪ] u ['obɔɪ] *s* var. de **oboe**
**hauteur** [ho'tʌr] u [o'tʌr] *s* arrogancia, altivez
**Havana** [hə'vænə] *s* La Habana; habano (*cigarro o tabaco de Cuba*)
**Havanese** [,hævə'niz] *adj* habanero; *s* (*pl:* **-nese**) habanero
**have** [hæv] (*pret & pp:* **had**) *va* tener; tomar, p.ej., **have a cigar** tome Vd. un puro; manifestar (*p.ej., respeto*); sentir (*p.ej., dolor*); conservar (*en la memoria*); tomar (*p.ej., lecciones*); decir, p.ej., **they will have it so** dicen que es así; saber, p.ej., **he has no Latin** no sabe latín; (coll.) llevar ventaja a; (slang) estafar; **there are few to be had** se consiguen difícilmente; **to have and to hold** (úsase sólo en el infinitivo) en propiedad, para ser poseído en propiedad; **to have it in for** (coll.) tener tirria a, tenérsela jurada a; **to have it out** discutir o pelear hasta poner fin al asunto; **to have it out with** emprenderla con, habérselas con; **to have on** llevar puesto; **to have to do with** tener que ver con; **to have** + *inf* hacer o mandar + *inf*, p.ej., **I had him sit down** le hice sentar; **to have** + *pp* hacer o mandar + *inf*, p.ej., **he had his watch repaired** hizo componer su reloj; **I had a suit made** mandé hacer un traje ‖ *vn* **to have at** atacar, embestir; **to have to** tener que; **to have to do with** tratar de; tener relaciones con ‖ *v aux* haber, p.ej., **I have spoken** he hablado; **I had spoken** había hablado
**havelock** ['hævlak] *s* cogotera
**haven** ['hevən] *s* puerto; buen puerto, abrigo, asilo; *va* abrigar, dar abrigo a
**have-not** ['hæv,nat] *s* (coll.) persona o nación desposeídas; **the haves and the have-nots** (coll.) los ricos y los desposeídos
**haven't** ['hævənt] contracción de **have not**
**haversack** ['hævərsæk] *s* barjuleta; (mil.) mochila
**havoc** ['hævək] *s* estrago, estragos; **to play havoc with** hacer grandes estragos en, destruir
**haw** [hɔ] *s* baya o simiente del espino; tosecilla, tos nerviosa (*al hablar*); *interj* ¡ apartа!; *va* hacer volver a la izquierda; *vn* destoserse; hablar tartaleando; doblar a la izquierda
**Hawaiian** [hə'waɪjən] *adj & s* hawaiano

**Hawaiian Islands** *spl* islas Hawai
**hawfinch** ['hɔ,fɪntʃ] *s* (orn.) cascapiñones
**haw-haw** ['hɔ,hɔ] o [hɔ'hɔ] *s* carcajada; *vn* reír a carcajadas
**hawk** [hɔk] *s* (orn.) halcón, cernícalo, gavilán, gerifalte, azor; (fig.) ave de presa (*persona*); carraspeo; esparavel; *va* pregonar (*mercancías; una noticia; un secreto*); **to hawk up** arrojar tosiendo; *vn* cazar aves con halcones; carraspear
**hawker** ['hɔkər] *s* halconero, cetrero; buhonero
**hawk-eyed** ['hɔk,aɪd] *adj* de ojos linces, de ojo avizor
**hawking** ['hɔkɪŋ] *s* halconería, cetrería
**hawklike** ['hɔk,laɪk] *adj* halconado
**hawk moth** *s* (ent.) esfinge
**hawk-nosed** ['hɔk,nozd] *adj* de nariz aguileña
**hawk owl** *s* (orn.) surnia
**hawk's-bill** o **hawksbill** ['hɔks,bɪl] o **hawksbill turtle** *s* (zool.) carey
**hawkweed** ['hɔk,wid] *s* (bot.) oreja de ratón, pelosilla
**hawse** [hɔz] *s* (naut.) escobén (*agujero*); (naut.) frente de los escobenes; (naut.) distancia entre un buque anclado y sus anclas
**hawsehole** ['hɔz,hol] *s* (naut.) escobén
**hawser** ['hɔzər] *s* (naut.) guindaleza, estacha
**hawthorn** ['hɔθɔrn] *s* (bot.) espino, oxiacanto
**hay** [he] *s* heno; **to hit the hay** (slang) acostarse; **to make hay while the sun shines** aprovechar la ocasión; *va* henear; echar heno a (*la caballería o el ganado*)
**haycock** ['he,kɑk] *s* pequeña niara de heno
**hay fever** *s* (path.) fiebre del heno
**hayfield** ['he,fild] *s* henar
**hayfork** ['he,fɔrk] *s* horca (*para levantar el heno*); elevador de heno
**hayloft** ['he,lɔft] o ['he,lɑft] *s* henil
**haymaker** ['he,mekər] *s* heneador; (slang) golpe que pone fuera de combate (*en el boxeo*)
**haymow** ['he,maʊ] *s* henil; acopio de heno (*en el henil*)
**hayrack** ['he,ræk] *s* pesebre; armazón que se monta en un carro para transportar el heno
**hayrick** ['he,rɪk] *s* almiar
**hay ride** *s* paseo de placer en un carro de heno
**hayseed** ['he,sid] *s* simiente de heno, simiente de hierbas; (coll.) patán, rústico, campesino
**haystack** ['he,stæk] *s* almiar
**haywire** ['he,waɪr] *s* alambre que se usa para el embalaje del heno; *adj* (slang) desarreglado, descompuesto; (slang) barrenado, loco
**hazard** ['hæzərd] *s* peligro, riesgo; acaso, azar; (golf) obstáculo; **at all hazards** por grande que sea el riesgo; *va* arriesgar; aventurar (*p.ej., una opinión*)
**hazardous** ['hæzərdəs] *adj* peligroso, arriesgado, aventurado
**haze** [hez] *s* calina; confusión, vaguedad, falta de claridad; *va* dar novatada a
**hazel** ['hezəl] *s* (bot.) avellano; *adj* avellanado (*de color de avellana*)
**hazelnut** ['hezəl,nʌt] *s* avellana
**hazing** ['hezɪŋ] *s* novatada
**hazy** ['hezɪ] *adj* (*comp:* **-zier**; *super:* **-ziest**) calinoso; confuso, vago, poco claro
**H-bomb** ['etʃ,bɑm] *s* bomba de hidrógeno
**H.C.** abr. de **House of Commons**
**H.C.F.** o **h.c.f.** abr. de **highest common factor**
**hd.** abr. de **head**
**hdkf.** abr. de **handkerchief**
**hdqrs.** abr. de **headquarters**
**H.E.** abr. de **His Eminence** y **His Excellency**
**he** [hi] *pron pers* (*pl:* **they**) él; *s* (*pl:* **hes**) macho, varón; *interj* ¡ji!
**head** [hɛd] *s* cabeza (*parte superior del cuerpo del hombre y el animal; razón, inteligencia; juicio, talento; parte superior de una página, de un clavo o alfiler, de un martillo; cumbre de una montaña; fuente, origen, manantial; frente de una procesión, ejército, etc.; sitio honorífico en la mesa; jefe, director; dirección; persona; res; punta de un dardo; repollo de col o de lechuga; parte grabadora o reproductora del magnetófono*); cabecera (*de cama*); encabezamiento, título; división o sección (*de un escrito*); centro (*de un divieso*); espuma (*en un vaso de cerveza*); parche (*de un tambor*); puño (*de bastón*); fondo o tapa (*de un cilindro, barril, etc.*); montera (*de la caldera de un alambique*); crisis, punto decisivo; avance, progreso; (bot.) cabezuela (*inflorescencia*); (hyd.) altura de caída; (mach.) culata (*de cilindro*); **heads** *spl* cara (*de una moneda*); **from head to foot** de pies a cabeza; **on** o **upon one's head** a responsabilidad de uno, sobre la cabeza de uno; **off** u **out of one's head** (coll.) delirante, fuera de sí, destornillado; **out of one's own head** de su cosecha, por su cabeza; **over one's head** fuera del alcance de uno; por encima de uno (*dirigiéndose a una autoridad superior*); **to be out of one's head** delirar; **to be the head** hacer cabeza (*en un negocio*); **to bother one's head about** quebrarse la cabeza con; **to come into one's head** pasarle a uno por la cabeza; **to come to a head** madurar; llegar a un punto decisivo; supurar (*un absceso*); **to eat one's head off** ser muy comilón; consumir más de lo que uno vale; **to gather head** ir en progreso; **to get something in one's head** metérsele a uno en la cabeza una cosa; **to give one his head** darle a uno rienda suelta; **to go to one's head** marearle a uno; volverle a uno el juicio; subírsele a uno a la cabeza; **to hang** o **hide one's head** caérsele a uno la cara de vergüenza; **to keep one's head** no perder la cabeza, tenerse en los estribos, mantener su sangre fría; **to keep one's head above water** mantenerse a flote; no dejarse vencer (*por las desgracias, la miseria, etc.*); **to lay** o **put heads together** consultarse (*dos o más personas*) entre sí; conspirar, confabularse, **to lose one's head** perder los estribos; **to not make head or tail of** no ver pies ni cabeza a; **to take it into one's head to** + *inf* metérsele a uno en la cabeza + *inf;* **to turn the head of** trastornar; apasionar; subirse a la cabeza, p.ej., **praise turns his head** los elogios se le suben a la cabeza; **head on** de cabeza; **head over heels** en un salto mortal; absolutamente, completamente, hasta los tuétanos; precipitadamente; **heads or tails** cara o cruz ‖ *adj* delantero, primero; más alto, superior; principal; (naut.) de proa ‖ *va* acaudillar, dirigir, mandar; aventajar, sobrepujar; estar a la cabeza de (*p.ej., la clase*); venir primero en (*p.ej., una lista*); poner cabeza a; descabezar; desmochar (*un árbol*); conducir (*un coche, un avión, etc., en cierta dirección*); **to head off** alcanzar e interceptar (*a uno que huye*); atajar (*un mal*) ‖ *vn* dirigirse; supurar (*un absceso*); repollar (*p.ej., la lechuga*); **to head towards** dirigirse hacia
**headache** ['hɛd,ek] *s* (path.) dolor de cabeza
**headband** ['hɛd,bænd] *s* venda, faja, cinta (*para la cabeza*); (b.b.) cabezada
**headboard** ['hɛd,bord] *s* cabecera de cama
**headcheese** ['hɛd,tʃiz] *s* queso de cerdo
**headdress** ['hɛd,drɛs] *s* tocado
**headed** ['hɛdɪd] *adj* que tiene cabeza; encabezado, titulado; repolludo; **headed for** con rumbo a
**header** ['hɛdər] *s* desmochador; cámara de circulación; cabeza, jefe; (carp.) brochal, embrochalado; (mas.) hilada, tizón; (coll.) caída de cabeza; **to take a header** (coll.) irse de cabeza
**header course** *s* (mas.) hilada atizonada o de cabezal
**headfirst** ['hɛd'fʌrst] o **headforemost** ['hɛd'formost] *adj* de cabeza; precipitadamente, temerariamente
**headframe** ['hɛd,frem] *s* (min.) castillete de mina
**head gate** *s* (hyd.) compuerta, paradera; (hyd.) compuerta de cabecera o de toma
**headgear** ['hɛd,gɪr] *s* sombrero (*de cualquier forma*); tocado (*de mujer*); cabezada (*de guarnición para caballo*); (football) casco de cuero
**head-hunter** ['hɛd,hʌntər] *s* cazador de cabezas
**heading** ['hɛdɪŋ] *s* encabezamiento, título; membrete; rumbo; (min.) galería de avance
**headland** ['hɛdlənd] *s* promontorio
**headledge** ['hɛd,lɛdʒ] *s* (naut.) contrabrazola
**headless** ['hɛdlɪs] *adj* acéfalo; descabezado; sin jefe o director; estúpido, tonto

**headlight** ['hɛd,laɪt] *s* (aut.) faro; (rail.) farol; (naut.) farol de tope
**headline** ['hɛd,laɪn] *s* cabecera (*de una plana de periódico*); título de página, titulillo; *va* poner cabecera a, poner título a; (slang) dar cartel a, destacar, hacer resaltar (*a un actor*)
**headliner** ['hɛd,laɪnər] *s* (slang) atracción principal (*en los anuncios de cine o teatro*)
**headlong** ['hɛd,lɔŋ] o ['hɛd,lɑŋ] *adj* de cabeza; precipitado; *adv* de cabeza; precipitadamente
**headman** ['hɛd,mæn] o ['hɛdmən] *s* (*pl:* **-men**) jefe, caudillo, cacique
**headmaster** ['hɛd'mæstər] o ['hɛd'mɑstər] *s* director (*de un colegio*)
**headmastership** ['hɛd'mæstərʃɪp] o ['hɛd'mɑstərʃɪp] *s* cargo de director (*de un colegio*)
**headmost** ['hɛdmost] *adj* delantero, primero
**head office** *s* casa matriz, oficina central
**head of hair** *s* cabellera
**head-on** [,hɛd'ɑn] o [,hɛd'ɔn] *adj* de frente, p.ej., **head-on collision** colisión de frente
**headphone** ['hɛd,fon] *s* auricular de casco, receptor de cabeza
**headpiece** ['hɛd,pis] *s* sombrero; tocado; casco, morrión, yelmo; cabeza, juicio, inteligencia; auricular de casco; cabecera de cama; (print.) cabecera, viñeta
**head pin** *s* bolo delantero (*en el juego de bolos*)
**headquarters** ['hɛd,kwɔrtərz] *ssg o spl* sede; jefatura, centro de dirección; (mil.) cuartel general
**headrace** ['hɛd,res] *s* caz de traída
**headrail** ['hɛd,rel] *s* peinazo superior de puerta; (naut.) varenga, brazal
**headrest** ['hɛd,rɛst] *s* apoyo para la cabeza
**headset** ['hɛd,sɛt] *s* auricular de casco, receptor de cabeza
**headship** ['hɛdʃɪp] *s* jefatura, dirección, mando
**headstall** ['hɛd,stɔl] *s* cabezada (*de freno*)
**headstock** ['hɛd,stɑk] *s* (mach.) cabezal (*de un torno*)
**headstone** ['hɛd,ston] *s* piedra angular; lápida sepulcral
**headstream** ['hɛd,strim] *s* afluente principal (*de un río*)
**headstrong** ['hɛd,strɔŋ] o ['hɛd,strɑŋ] *adj* cabezudo, terco, testarudo
**head tone** *s* (mus.) voz de cabeza
**headwaiter** ['hɛd'wetər] *s* encargado de comedor, jefe de camareros
**headwaters** ['hɛd,wɔtərz] o ['hɛd,wɑtərz] *spl* cabecera (*de un río*)
**headway** ['hɛd,we] *s* avance, progreso; espacio libre (*entre la cabeza y un dintel, entre un vehículo y un arco de puente, etc.*); (rail.) intervalo entre dos trenes en una misma vía; **to make headway** avanzar, adelantar, progresar
**head wind** *s* (naut.) viento de frente, viento por la proa
**headwork** ['hɛd,wʌrk] *s* trabajo intelectual
**heady** ['hɛdɪ] *adj* (*comp:* **-ier;** *super:* **-iest**) precipitado, impetuoso; cabezudo (*vino*)
**heal** [hil] *va* curar, sanar; cicatrizar; remediar (*un daño*); *vn* curar, sanar; cicatrizarse; remediarse; **to heal up** cicatrizarse
**healer** ['hilər] *s* sanador, curador
**healing** ['hilɪŋ] *adj* curativo; *s* curación
**health** [hɛlθ] *s* salud; **to be in bad health** estar mal de salud; **to be in good health** estar bien de salud; **to drink to the health of** beber a la salud de; **to enjoy wonderful health** gastar salud; **to your health!** ¡a su salud!
**health examination** *s* reconocimiento sanitario
**healthful** ['hɛlθfəl] *adj* sano, saludable
**health insurance** *s* seguro de enfermedad
**healthy** ['hɛlθɪ] *adj* (*comp:* **-ier;** *super:* **-iest**) sano (*de buena salud; saludable*)
**heap** [hip] *s* montón; (coll.) montón (*número considerable*); *va* amontonar, apilar; colmar, llenar, henchir (*p.ej., de favores, insultos*); dar generosamente; *vn* amontonarse, apilarse
**hear** [hɪr] (*pret & pp:* **heard**) *va* oír; dar audiencia a; tomar la lección a; otorgar; (law) ver; **to hear** + *ger* oír + *inf*, p.ej., **I heard the girl singing** oí cantar a la muchacha; **to hear** + *inf* oír + *inf*, p.ej., **I heard my brother come in** oí entrar a mi hermano; **to hear** + *pp* oír + *inf*, p.ej., **I heard the bell rung** oí tocar la campana; **to hear it said** oírlo decir; **to hear someone out** oír a uno hasta que concluya de hablar; *vn* oír; **he will not hear of it** no quiere ni pensar en ello, no lo permitirá de ningún modo; **to hear about** oír hablar de; **to hear from** saber de, recibir o tener noticias de; **to hear of** oír hablar de; enterarse de; **to hear tell of** oír hablar de; **to hear that** oír decir que; **hear! hear!** ¡bravo!
**heard** [hʌrd] *pret & pp de* **hear**
**hearer** [hɪrər] *s* oyente
**hearing** ['hɪrɪŋ] *s* oída (*acción*); oído (*sentido*); audiencia; (law) examen de testigos; **in the hearing of** en la presencia de; **within hearing** al alcance del oído
**hearing aid** *s* acústico, audífono, aparato auditivo
**hearken** ['hɑrkən] *vn* var. de **harken**
**hearsay** ['hɪr,se] *s* rumor, voz común; **by hearsay** de o por oídas
**hearsay evidence** *s* (law) testimonio de oídas, prueba de oídas
**hearse** [hʌrs] *s* coche fúnebre, carroza fúnebre; (eccl.) tenebrario; *va* colocar en un coche fúnebre; enterrar, sepultar
**hearsecloth** ['hʌrs,klɔθ] o ['hʌrs,klɑθ] *s* paño mortuorio
**heart** [hɑrt] *s* corazón; cogollo (*p.ej., de una lechuga*); corazón (*naipe que corresponde a la copa*); **hearts** *spl* corazones (*palo que corresponde al de copas*); **after one's heart** enteramente del gusto de uno; **at heart** verdaderamente, en el fondo; **by heart** de memoria; **dear heart** vida mía; **from one's heart** de todo corazón; **in one's heart of hearts** en lo más recóndito del corazón de uno; **near one's heart** que a uno le toca en lo más sensible, que a uno le interesa grandemente; **to break the heart of** quebrar o partir el corazón de; **to die of a broken heart** morir de pena, morir de desengaño; **to do one's heart good** alegrarle a uno el corazón; **to eat one's heart out** afligirse sobremanera, dejarse morir de tristeza; **to get to the heart of** profundizar, llegar al fondo de; **to have one's heart in one's boots** o **mouth** estar con el alma en la boca, estar muerto de miedo; **to have one's heart in one's work** esmerarse en su trabajo, trabajar con entusiasmo; **to have one's heart in the right place** tener buenas intenciones; **to lay to heart** tener presente; pensar (*una cosa*) seriamente; **to lose heart** descorazonarse; **to not have the heart to** + *inf* no tener corazón para + *inf;* **to open one's heart** descubrir el pecho; **to open one's heart to** abrirse con, descubrirse con; **to take heart** cobrar aliento; **to take the heart out of** desalentar, desanimar; **to take to heart** tomar a pecho; **to wear one's heart on one's sleeve** llevar el corazón en la mano; **with all one's heart** con toda el alma de uno; **with one's heart in one's mouth** con el credo en la boca; **heart and soul** de todo corazón, con toda el alma de uno
**heartache** ['hɑrt,ek] *s* angustia, congoja, pesar
**heart attack** *s* ataque cardíaco, ataque de corazón
**heartbeat** ['hɑrt,bit] *s* latido del corazón
**heartbreak** ['hɑrt,brek] *s* angustia, dolor abrumador
**heartbreaker** ['hɑrt,brekər] *s* ladrón de corazones; (hum.) tirabuzón (*rizo de cabello*)
**heartbreaking** ['hɑrt,brekɪŋ] *adj* angustioso
**heartbroken** ['hɑrt,brokən] *adj* acongojado, transido de dolor
**heartburn** ['hɑrt,bʌrn] *s* (path.) rescoldera; envidia, celos
**heartburning** ['hɑrt,bʌrnɪŋ] *s* envidia, celos
**heart disease** *s* enfermedad del corazón
**hearten** ['hɑrtən] *va* animar, alentar
**heart failure** *s* paro del corazón; desmayo, desfallecimiento
**heartfelt** ['hɑrt,fɛlt] *adj* cordial, sincero
**heart-free** ['hɑrt,fri] *adj* libre de amor

**hearth** [hɑrθ] *s* hogar; (metal. & fig.) hogar; (metal.) obra (*del alto horno*)

**hearth money** *s* fogaje (*tributo antiguo*)

**hearthside** ['hɑrθ,saɪd] *s* hogar

**hearthstone** ['hɑrθ,ston] *s* solera del hogar; hogar (*domicilio*)

**heartily** ['hɑrtɪlɪ] *adv* cordialmente, sinceramente; de buena gana, con entusiasmo; con buen apetito; bien, mucho, completamente

**heartiness** ['hɑrtɪnɪs] *s* cordialidad, sinceridad; buena salud, vigor; espontaneidad; entusiasmo

**heartless** ['hɑrtlɪs] *adj* cruel, empedernido; apocado, pusilánime

**heart-lung machine** ['hɑrt'lʌŋ] *s* (surg.) corazón-pulmón, aparato corazón-pulmón

**heart-rending** ['hɑrt,rɛndɪŋ] *adj* que parte el corazón, que causa mucha angustia

**heartsease** o **heart's-ease** ['hɑrts,iz] *s* serenidad de ánimo; (bot.) pensamiento, trinitaria

**heartseed** ['hɑrt,sid] *s* (bot.) farolillo

**heartsick** ['hɑrt,sɪk] *adj* desconsolado, muy abatido

**heartsore** ['hɑrt,sor] *adj* acongojado, dolorido

**heart-stricken** ['hɑrt,strɪkən] *adj* transido de dolor, angustiado

**heartstrings** ['hɑrt,strɪŋz] *spl* fibras del corazón, entretelas (*entrañas, misericordia*)

**heartthrob** ['hɑrt,θrɑb] *s* emoción vehemente

**heart-to-heart** ['hɑrttʊ,hɑrt] *adj* franco, sincero

**heart trouble** *s* enfermedad del corazón; **to have heart trouble** enfermar del corazón

**heart-whole** ['hɑrt,hol] *adj* libre de amor; cordial, sincero

**heartwood** ['hɑrt,wʊd] *s* madera de corazón

**hearty** ['hɑrtɪ] *adj* (*comp:* **-ier**; *super:* **-iest**) cordial, sincero; sano, robusto; espontáneo; nutritivo, substancioso; grande, abundante; comilón, voraz; *s* (*pl:* **-ies**) (naut.) compañero

**heat** [hit] *s* calor; calefacción; ardor, ímpetu; celo (*de las bestias*); (sport) carrera (*en las carreras de caballos*); (metal.) hornada, turno de fundición; **in heat** en celo; **to turn on the heat** (slang) aumentar la intensidad, apretar los tornillos; *adj* térmico; *va* calentar; calefaccionar; acalorar, excitar; *vn* calentarse; acalorarse, excitarse

**heat barrier** *s* var. de **thermal barrier**

**heated** ['hitɪd] *adj* acalorado

**heatedly** ['hitɪdlɪ] *adv* acaloradamente

**heat engine** *s* motor térmico

**heater** ['hitər] *s* calentador; (rad.) calefactor

**heat exchanger** [ɛks'tʃendʒər] *s* (phys.) cambiador de calor, cambiador térmico

**heath** [hiθ] *s* (bot.) brezo; brezal; **native heath** patria chica

**heathbird** ['hiθ,bʌrd] *s* (orn.) gallo de bosque

**heathen** ['hiðən] *adj* gentil, pagano; sin religión; inculto; *s* (*pl:* **-thens** o **-then**) gentil, pagano

**heathendom** ['hiðəndəm] *s* gentilidad

**heathenish** ['hiðənɪʃ] *adj* gentílico

**heathenism** ['hiðənɪzəm] *s* gentilidad; irreligión, incultura

**heathenize** ['hiðənaɪz] *va* gentilizar

**heather** ['hɛðər] *s* (bot.) brezo

**heathery** ['hɛðərɪ] *adj* brezoso; cubierto o poblado de brezos

**heathy** ['hiθɪ] *adj* brezoso

**heating** ['hitɪŋ] *adj* calentador; *s* calefacción

**heating coil** *s* (elec.) bobina térmica

**heating element** *s* (elec.) elemento calentador; (rad.) elemento de caldeo

**heating pad** *s* almohadilla caliente

**heating surface** *s* superficie de caldeo o calefacción

**heat lightning** *s* fucilazo, relámpago de calor

**heatproof** ['hit'pruf] *adj* antitérmico

**heat shield** *s* escudo térmico, blindaje térmico (*de una cápsula espacial*)

**heatstroke** ['hit,strok] *s* (path.) golpe de calor

**heat unit** *s* (phys.) unidad térmica

**heat wave** *s* (phys.) onda calorífica; (coll.) ola de calor

**heave** [hiv] *s* esfuerzo para levantar una cosa pesada, esfuerzo para levantarse; echada, tirada; henchidura (*de las olas*); jadeo; **heaves** *ssg* (vet.) huélfago; (*pret & pp:* **heaved** o **hove**) *va* levantar y lanzar (*una cosa pesada*); levantar con algún esfuerzo; exhalar (*un suspiro*); **to heave to** (naut.) poner al pairo o en facha; *vn* lanzar con esfuerzo; levantarse y bajarse alternativamente (*las olas*); palpitar (*el pecho*); combarse, elevarse; jadear; arquear, hacer esfuerzos por vomitar; **heave ho!** (naut.) ¡iza!

**heaven** ['hɛvən] *s* cielo; (*cap.*) *s* cielo (*mansión de los bienaventurados; Dios*); **heavens** *spl* cielo (*firmamento*); **for heaven's sake!** o **good heavens!** ¡válgame Dios!; **to move heaven and earth** mover cielo y tierra

**heavenly** ['hɛvənlɪ] *adj* celeste (*cuerpo*); celestial (*p.ej., mansión*); (fig.) celestial

**heavenly body** *s* astro, cuerpo celeste

**heavenly home** *s* mansión celestial, patria celestial

**heavenward** ['hɛvənwərd] *adj & adv* hacia el cielo

**heavenwards** ['hɛvənwərdz] *adv* hacia el cielo

**heaver** ['hivər] *s* (naut.) cargador; (naut.) tortor

**heavier-than-air** [,hɛvɪər θən'ɛr] *adj* (aer.) más pesado que el aire

**heaviness** ['hɛvɪnɪs] *s* pesadez; espesura; densidad; grosor (*p.ej., de una línea*); abundancia; fuerza (*p.ej., de la lluvia*); ímpetu (*de las olas*); languidez, modorra; cargazón (*en el estómago, la cabeza, etc.; en el estilo literario*); abatimiento; opresión; (com.) postración (*del mercado*)

**Heaviside layer** ['hɛvɪsaɪd] *s* (rad.) capa de Heaviside

**heavy** ['hɛvɪ] *adj* (*comp:* **-ier**; *super:* **-iest**) pesado; espeso o denso (*líquido*); denso (*tráfico*); grueso (*dícese de la tela, el papel, la mar, una línea, etc.*); tupido (*dícese de la tela, el monte, etc.*); copioso, abundante (*dícese, p.ej., de las cosechas*); recio, fuerte (*dícese de la lluvia*); fuerte (*dícese de los gastos, pérdidas, pagos, rebajas, etc.*); agravado (*dícese de los ojos*); basto (*dícese de las facciones*); fragoroso (*cañoneo*); malo, pésimo (*camino*); empinado (*dícese de una cuesta*); grande (*bebedor*); cargado (*estilo, dibujo*); abatido, cansado; triste, oprimido (*corazón*); grave, serio; sombrío; importante, considerable (*dícese de las deudas, las reparaciones*); encinta; (com.) pesado (*dícese de los géneros*); (com.) postrado (*mercado*); *adv* pesadamente; fuerte; **to hang heavy** pasar con extremada lentitud (*dícese del tiempo o las horas*); *s* (*pl:* **-ies**) (theat.) personaje perverso; **heavies** *spl* (coll.) ropa interior gruesa

**heavy-armed** ['hɛvɪ'ɑrmd] *adj* armado de armas pesadas, armado de armadura pesada

**heavy-duty** ['hɛvɪ'djutɪ] o ['hɛvɪ'dutɪ] *adj* de servicio pesado, extrafuerte; de altos derechos de aduana

**heavy earth** *s* (mineral.) tierra pesada

**heavy-eyed** ['hɛvɪ,aɪd] *adj* de ojos dormidos

**heavy-footed** ['hɛvɪ'fʊtɪd] *adj* de andar torpe o desmañado; despeado

**heavy-handed** ['hɛvɪ'hændɪd] *adj* opresor, agobiador; desmañado, torpe

**heavy-hearted** ['hɛvɪ'hɑrtɪd] *adj* acongojado, afligido, triste

**heavy hydrogen** *s* (chem.) hidrógeno pesado

**heavy industry** *s* industria pesada

**heavy-laden** ['hɛvɪ'ledən] *adj* recargado; agobiado, oprimido

**heavy-set** ['hɛvɪ'sɛt] *adj* espaldudo, costilludo

**heavy spar** *s* (mineral.) espato pesado

**heavy water** *s* (chem.) agua pesada

**heavyweight** ['hɛvɪ,wet] *s* persona que pesa mucho; persona de mucho pesquis, persona de campanillas; (box.) peso pesado, peso fuerte

**Heb.** abr. de **Hebrews**

**hebdomadal** [hɛb'dɑmədəl] *adj* hebdomadario

**Hebe** ['hibɪ] *s* (myth.) Hebe

**hebetude** ['hɛbɪtjud] o ['hɛbɪtud] *s* torpeza, estupidez

**Hebraic** [hɪ'breɪk] *adj* hebraico

**Hebraism** ['hibreɪzəm] *s* hebraísmo

**Hebraist** ['hibreɪst] *s* hebraísta; hebraizante

**Hebraistic** [,hibre'ɪstɪk] *adj* hebreo

**Hebraize** ['hibreaɪz] *va* hacer hebreo; *vn* hebraizar

**Hebrew** ['hibru] *adj & s* hebreo; **Hebrews** *spl* (Bib.) Epístola de San Pablo a los Hebreos

**Hebrew calendar** *s* calendario hebreo
**Hebrides, the** ['hɛbrɪdiz] las Hébridas
**Hecate** ['hɛkətɪ] *s* (myth.) Hécate
**hecatomb** ['hɛkətom] o ['hɛkətum] *s* hecatombe
**heckle** ['hɛkəl] *va* interrumpir (*a un orador*) con preguntas impertinentes o molestas
**hectare** ['hɛktɛr] *s* hectárea
**hectic** ['hɛktɪk] *adj* hético; (coll.) turbulento, agitado; *s* fiebre hética; rubor hético; hético (*enfermo*)
**hectocotylus** [,hɛktə'kɑtɪləs] *s* (*pl:* **-li** [laɪ]) (zool.) hectocótilo
**hectogram** o **hectogramme** ['hɛktəgræm] *s* hectogramo
**hectograph** ['hɛktəgræf] o ['hɛktəgrɑf] *s* hectógrafo; *va* copiar en el hectógrafo
**hectoliter** ['hɛktə,litər] *s* hectólitro
**hectometer** ['hɛktə,mitər] *s* hectómetro
**Hector** ['hɛktər] *s* (myth.) Héctor; (*l.c.*) *s* matón, valentón; *va & vn* atormentar o intimidar con bravatas
**Hecuba** ['hɛkjʊbə] *s* (myth.) Hécuba
**he'd** [hid] contracción de **he had** y de **he would**
**hedge** [hɛdʒ] *s* seto vivo, cerca viva; cercado, vallado; apuesta compensatoria; operación de bolsa compensatoria; *va* cercar con seto vivo; cercar con vallado; **to hedge in** encerrar, rodear; poner trabas a; *vn* eludir la respuesta, no querer comprometerse; hacer apuestas compensatorias; hacer operaciones de bolsa compensatorias (*para no perder dinero*)
**hedgehog** ['hɛdʒ,hɑg] o ['hɛdʒ,hɔg] *s* (zool.) erizo; (zool.) puerco espín
**hedgehop** ['hɛdʒ,hɑp] (*pret & pp:* **-hopped;** *ger:* **-hopping**) *vn* (aer.) volar rasando el suelo
**hedge mustard** *s* (bot.) sisimbrio; (bot.) erisimo; (bot.) epazote
**hedge nettle** *s* (bot.) ortiga hedionda
**hedgerow** ['hɛdʒ,ro] *s* cercado de arbustos o árboles pequeños
**hedge sparrow** *s* (orn.) acentor de bosque
**hedonism** ['hidənɪzəm] *s* hedonismo
**hedonist** ['hidənɪst] *s* hedonista
**heed** [hid] *s* atención, cuidado; **to take heed** poner atención; *va* atender a, hacer caso de; *vn* atender, hacer caso
**heedful** ['hidfəl] *adj* atento, cuidadoso
**heedless** ['hidlɪs] *adj* desatento, descuidado; aturdido, incauto
**heedlessness** ['hidlɪsnɪs] *s* desatención, descuido; aturdimiento, imprudencia
**heehaw** ['hi,hɔ] *s* rebuzno (*del asno*); risotada; *vn* rebuznar; risotear, reír groseramente
**heel** [hil] *s* (anat.) calcañar o talón; talón (*parte de la media o el zapato que cubre el calcañar*); tacón (*pieza semicircular del zapato debajo del calcañar*); parte inferior o trasera (*de ciertas cosas*); fin, conclusión; pedazo que queda de un pan o queso casi consumidos; (arch.) talón; (mus.) talón (*del arco del violín*); (naut.) talón (*de la quilla*); (naut.) coz o pie de palo; (rail.) talón (*de la aguja*); (slang) sinvergüenza; **at heel** a los talones; **down at the heel** con el talón muy gastado; desaliñado, mal vestido; desvalido; **out at the heels** destalonado; desaliñado, mal vestido; desvalido; **to cool one's heels** (coll.) hacer antesala, estar esperando mucho tiempo; **to heel** a los talones; **to be at one's heels** pisarle a uno los talones; **to kick one's heels** hacer antesala; esperar impacientemente; **to kick up one's heels** (slang) mostrarse alegre y retozón; (slang) morir; **to lay by the heels** echar a la cárcel, echar al cepo; **to show a clean pair of heels** o **to take to one's heels** poner pies en polvorosa, apretar los talones, batir los talones; **heels over head** patas arriba; *va* seguir de cerca; poner talón a; poner tacón a; poner espolones a (*un gallo de pelea*); *vn* seguir de cerca al amo (*dícese de los perros*); taconear (*al bailar*); (naut.) escorar
**heeler** ['hilər] *s* taconero; (slang) muñidor (*de cacique político*)
**heel lift** *s* tapa (*del tacón del zapato*)
**heelpiece** ['hil,pis] *s* talón
**heeltap** ['hil,tæp] *s* tapa (*del tacón del zapato*); vino, aguardiente, etc. que se deja en el vaso después de beber
**heft** [hɛft] *s* (coll.) influencia; **the heft of** (coll.) la mayor parte de, lo más de; *va* levantar; (coll.) sopesar (*tantear el peso de*)
**hefty** ['hɛftɪ] *adj* (*comp:* **-ier;** *super:* **-iest**) pesado; (coll.) fornido, recio
**Hegelian** [he'gelɪən] o [hi'dʒilɪən] *adj & s* hegeliano
**Hegelianism** [he'gelɪənɪzəm] o [hi'dʒilɪənɪzəm] *s* hegelianismo
**hegemony** [hɪ'dʒɛmənɪ] o ['hɛdʒɪ,monɪ] *s* (*pl:* **-nies**) hegemonía
**hegira** [hɪ'dʒaɪrə] o ['hɛdʒɪrə] *s* fuga, huída; fuga de Mahoma desde la Meca a Medina; héjira (*era de los mahometanos*)
**heifer** ['hɛfər] *s* novilla, vaquilla
**heigh** [haɪ] o [he] *interj* ¡ea! (*para animar*); ¡eh! (*para llamar*); ¡ah! (*para expresar sorpresa*)
**heigh-ho** ['haɪ'ho] o ['he'ho] *interj* ¡ay!
**height** [haɪt] *s* altura; cima (*lo más alto*); colmo (*p.ej., de la locura*); crisis (*de la fiebre*)
**heighten** ['haɪtən] *va* elevar; aumentar; realzar; intensificar; *vn* elevarse; aumentarse; realzarse; intensificarse
**heinous** ['henəs] *adj* atroz, infame, nefando
**heir** [ɛr] *s* heredero
**heir apparent** *s* (*pl:* **heirs apparent**) (law) heredero forzoso
**heirdom** ['ɛrdəm] *s* herencia
**heiress** ['ɛrɪs] *s* heredera
**heirloom** ['ɛr,lum] *s* joya de familia, reliquia de familia
**heir presumptive** *s* (*pl:* **heirs presumptive**) (law) heredero presuntivo
**heirship** ['ɛrʃɪp] *s* herencia
**hejira** [hɪ'dʒaɪrə] o ['hɛdʒɪrə] *s* var. de **hegira**
**hektare** ['hɛktɛr] *s* var. de **hectare**
**hektogram** ['hɛktəgræm] *s* var. de **hectogram**
**held** [hɛld] *pret & pp de* **hold**
**Helen** ['hɛlən] *s* Elena; (myth.) Helena (*de Troya*)
**heliacal** [hɪ'laɪəkəl] *adj* (astr.) helíaco
**helianthemum** [,hilɪ'ænθɪməm] *s* (bot.) heliantemo
**helianthin** [,hilɪ'ænθɪn] o **helianthine** [,hilɪ'ænθɪn] o [,hilɪ'ænθin] *s* heliantina
**helianthus** [,hilɪ'ænθəs] *s* (bot.) helianto
**helical** ['hɛlɪkəl] *adj* hélico
**helicoid** ['hɛlɪkɔɪd] *adj* helicoide; (bot. & zool.) helicideo; *s* (geom.) helicoide
**helicoidal** [,hɛlɪ'kɔɪdəl] *adj* helicoidal
**helicoid cyme** *s* (bot.) cima helicoidea
**Helicon** ['hɛlɪkɑn] *s* (hist., myth. & fig.) Helicón; (*l.c.*) *s* (mus.) helicón
**Heliconian** [,hɛlɪ'konɪən] *adj* heliconio
**helicopter** [,hɛlɪ'kɑptər] *s* (aer.) helicóptero
**heliocentric** [,hilɪo'sɛntrɪk] *adj* heliocéntrico
**helioengraving** ['hilɪoɛn,grevɪŋ] *s* heliograbado
**heliograph** ['hilɪo,græf] o ['hilɪo,grɑf] *s* heliógrafo; *va & vn* comunicar por medio del heliógrafo
**heliography** [,hilɪ'ɑgrəfɪ] *s* heliografía
**Helios** ['hilɪɑs] *s* (myth.) Helios
**helioscope** ['hilɪo,skop] *s* helioscopio
**heliostat** ['hilɪo,stæt] *s* helióstato
**heliotherapy** ['hilɪo,θɛrəpɪ] *s* helioterapia
**heliotrope** ['hilɪətrop] *s* (bot. & mineral.) heliotropo
**heliotropism** [,hilɪ'ɑtrəpɪzəm] *s* (biol.) heliotropismo
**heliotype** ['hilɪo,taɪp] *s* heliotipia; heliotipo
**heliport** ['hɛlɪ,port] *s* helipuerto
**helium** ['hilɪəm] *s* (chem.) helio
**helix** ['hilɪks] *s* (*pl:* **helixes** o **helices** ['hɛlɪsiz]) hélice (*espiral*); (anat., elec. & geom.) hélice; (arch.) voluta
**he'll** [hil] contracción de **he shall** y de **he will**
**hell** [hɛl] *s* infierno; madriguera (*de gente maleante*); garito; cajón de sastre; (print.) caja de letras inservibles
**Hellas** ['hɛləs] *s* Hélade (*Grecia*)
**hellbender** ['hɛl,bɛndər] *s* (zool.) salamandra gigante norteamericana; (slang) borrachera descabellada
**hell-bent** ['hɛl'bɛnt] *adj* (slang) muy resuelto,

muy determinado; **hell-bent on** (slang) empeñado en, dirigiéndose con mucho empeño a
**hellbroth** [ˈhɛlˌbrɔθ] o [ˈhɛlˌbrɑθ] *s* caldo alterado, caldo infernal
**hellcat** [ˈhɛlˌkæt] *s* bruja; arpía, mujer perversa
**helldiver** [ˈhɛlˌdaɪvər] *s* (orn.) zambullidor, acintle
**helleboraster** [ˌhɛlɪbəˈræstər] *s* (bot.) eleborastro
**hellebore** [ˈhɛlɪbor] *s* (bot. & pharm.) eléboro
**Hellene** [ˈhɛlin] *s* heleno
**Hellenic** [hɛˈlɛnɪk] o [hɛˈlinɪk] *adj* helénico
**Hellenism** [ˈhɛlənɪzəm] *s* helenismo
**Hellenist** [ˈhɛlənɪst] *s* helenista
**Hellenistic** [ˌhɛləˈnɪstɪk] *adj* helenístico
**Hellenization** [ˌhɛlənɪˈzeʃən] *s* helenización
**Hellenize** [ˈhɛlənaɪz] *va* helenizar; *vn* helenizarse
**Hellespont** [ˈhɛlɪspɑnt] *s* Helesponto
**hellfire** [ˈhɛlˌfaɪr] *s* fuego del infierno
**hellgrammite** [ˈhɛlgrəmaɪt] *s* (ent.) larva de insecto neuróptero (*Corydalis cornuta*)
**hellhound** [ˈhɛlˌhaʊnd] *s* perro de los infiernos; demonio; fiera (*persona cruel*)
**hellion** [ˈhɛljən] *s* (coll.) pícaro, bribón
**hellish** [ˈhɛlɪʃ] *adj* infernal, diabólico
**hello** [hɛˈlo] *s* (*pl:* **-los**) grito, saludo; *interj* ¡hola!, ¡qué tal!; ¡aló!, ¡diga! (*en el teléfono*); *vn* gritar, saludar
**hello girl** *s* (coll.) chica telefonista
**helm** [hɛlm] *s* (naut.) barra o caña del timón, rueda del timón; (fig.) timón; (archaic) yelmo; **to luff the helm** (naut.) tirar del timón para orzar; *va* dirigir, gobernar; (archaic) dar yelmo a, cubrir con yelmo
**helmet** [ˈhɛlmɪt] *s* casco (*de la armadura; de soldado, bombero, buzo, etc.*)
**helmeted** [ˈhɛlmɪtɪd] *adj* que lleva casco
**helminth** [ˈhɛlmɪnθ] *s* ((zool.) helminto
**helminthiasis** [ˌhɛlmɪnˈθaɪəsɪs] *s* (path.) helmintiasis
**helminthology** [ˌhɛlmɪnˈθɑlədʒɪ] *s* helmintología
**helmsman** [ˈhɛlmzmən] *s* (*pl:* **-men**) (naut.) timonel
**Héloïse** [eloˈiz] *s* Eloísa
**helot** [ˈhɛlət] o [ˈhilət] *s* ilota; (*cap.*) *s* ilota
**helotism** [ˈhɛlətɪzəm] o [ˈhilətɪzəm] *s* ilotismo
**helotry** [ˈhɛlətrɪ] o [ˈhilətrɪ] *s* ilotismo; los ilotas
**help** [hɛlp] *s* ayuda, socorro; colaboración; ración (*de alimento*); remedio, p.ej., **there is no help for it** no hay remedio para ello; ayudante; criado, criados; empleado, empleados; obreros; **by the help of** con la ayuda de; **to be a great help to** prestar servicios importantes a, ser el brazo derecho de; **to be good help** ser buen ayudante; **to come to the help of** acudir en socorro de ‖ *interj* ¡socorro! ‖ *va* ayudar, socorrer; servir; aliviar, mitigar; remediar, evitar; **it can't be helped** no hay (más) remedio; **so help me God!** ¡así Dios me salve!; **to help along** ayudar (*a uno*) para que siga su camino o para que vaya tirando; **to help down** ayudar a bajar; **to help one with his coat** ayudarle a uno a ponerse el abrigo; **to help oneself** valerse por sí mismo; servirse; **to help one to** servirle a uno (*carne, pan, etc.*); **to help out** ayudar; ayudar a salir; **to help out of** ayudar a salir de; **to help to** + *inf* o **to help** + *inf* ayudar a + *inf;* **to help up** ayudar a subir; ayudar a levantarse; **to not be able to help** + *ger* no poder menos de + *inf*, p.ej., **I couldn't help laughing** no pude menos de reír; **to not be able to help but** + *inf* (coll.) no poder menos de + *inf*, p.ej., **he cannot help but come** no puede menos de venir ‖ *vn* ayudar; servir; **to help out** ayudar
**helper** [ˈhɛlpər] *s* ayudante; apoyo; mancebo (*p.ej., en una farmacia o barbería*)
**helpful** [ˈhɛlpfəl] *adj* útil, servicial; provechoso
**helping** [ˈhɛlpɪŋ] *s* ración, porción (*de alimento*)
**helpless** [ˈhɛlplɪs] *adj* débil, impotente; desvalido; incapaz, imposibilitado
**helplessness** [ˈhɛlplɪsnɪs] *s* debilidad, impotencia; desamparo; incapacidad
**helpmate** [ˈhɛlpˌmet] o **helpmeet** [ˈhɛlpˌmit] *s* compañero; compañera (*esposa*)
**helter-skelter** [ˈhɛltərˈskɛltər] *adj, adv & s* cochite hervite
**helve** [hɛlv] *s* astil, mango
**Helvetia** [hɛlˈviʃə] *s* la Helvecia
**Helvetian** [hɛlˈviʃən] *adj & s* helvecio
**Helvetic** [hɛlˈvɛtɪk] *adj* helvético; *s* protestante suizo
**hem** [hɛm] *s* tos fingida; (sew.) bastilla, dobladillo, repulgo; *interj* ¡ejem!; (*pret & pp:* **hemmed;** *ger:* **hemming**) *va* (sew.) bastillar, dobladillar, repulgar; **to hem about, around** o **in** encerrar estrechamente; poner trabas a; **to hem out** impedir (*a uno*) que entre; *vn* destoserse; tartalear; **to hem and haw** toser y retoser; tartalear; vacilar
**hematic** [hiˈmætɪk] *adj* hemático
**hematin** [ˈhɛmətɪn] o [ˈhimətɪn] *s* (physiol.) hematina
**hematite** [ˈhɛmətaɪt] o [ˈhimətaɪt] *s* (mineral.) hematites
**hematocele** [ˈhɛmətoˌsil] o [ˈhimətoˌsil] *s* (path.) hematocele
**hematocrit** [ˈhɛmətoˌkrɪt] *s* hematócrito
**hematoma** [ˌhiməˈtomə] o [ˌhɛməˈtomə] *s* (*pl:* **-mata** [mətə] o **-mas**) (path.) hematoma
**hematopoiesis** [ˌhɛmətopɔɪˈisɪs] o [ˌhimətopɔɪˈisɪs] *s* (physiol.) hematopoyesis
**hematosis** [ˌhiməˈtosɪs] o [ˌhɛməˈtosɪs] *s* (physiol.) hematosis
**hematoxylin** [ˌhiməˈtɑksɪlɪn] o [ˌhɛməˈtɑksɪlɪn] *s* (chem.) hematoxilina
**hemelytral** [hɛˈmɛlɪtrəl] *adj* hemélitro
**hemelytron** [hɛˈmɛlɪtrɑn] o **hemelytrum** [hɛˈmɛlɪtrəm] *s* (*pl:* **-tra** [trə]) (ent.) hemélitro
**hemeralopia** [ˌhɛmərəˈlopɪə] *s* (path.) hemeralopía
**hemicellulose** [ˌhɛmɪˈsɛljəlos] *s* (chem.) hemicelulosa
**hemicrania** [ˌhɛmɪˈkrenɪə] *s* (path.) hemicránea
**hemicycle** [ˈhɛmɪˌsaɪkəl] *s* hemiciclo
**hemihedral** [ˌhɛmɪˈhidrəl] *adj* (cryst.) hemiédrico o hemiedro
**hemin** [ˈhimɪn] *s* (biochem.) hemina
**hemina** [hɪˈmaɪnə] *s* (*pl:* **-nae** [ni]) (hist.) hemina
**hemionus** [hɪˈmaɪənəs] *s* (zool.) hemíono
**hemiplegia** [ˌhɛmɪˈplidʒɪə] *s* (path.) hemiplejía
**hemipterous** [hɪˈmɪptərəs] *adj* (ent.) hemíptero
**hemisphere** [ˈhɛmɪsfɪr] *s* hemisferio
**hemispherical** [ˌhɛmɪˈsfɛrɪkəl] *adj* hemisférico
**hemispheroid** [ˌhɛmɪˈsfɪrɔɪd] *s* (geom.) hemisferoide
**hemistich** [ˈhɛmɪstɪk] *s* hemistiquio
**hemiterpene** [ˌhɛmɪˈtʌrpin] *s* (chem.) hemiterpeno
**hemline** [ˈhɛmˌlaɪn] *s* bastilla de la falda, ruedo de la falda, bajo de la falda; **in the coming season the hemline will be higher** en la próxima temporada la falda se llevará más corta
**hemlock** [ˈhɛmlɑk] *s* (bot.) cicuta; (bot.) cicuta mayor (*Conium maculatum*); (bot.) abeto del Canadá (*Tsuga canadensis*); cicuta (*veneno*)
**hemmer** [ˈhɛmər] *s* repulgador (*persona y máquina*)
**hemocyanin** [ˌhimoˈsaɪənɪn] o [ˌhɛmoˈsaɪənɪn] *s* (biochem.) hemocianina
**hemoglobin** [ˌhimoˈglobɪn] o [ˌhɛmoˈglobɪn] *s* (biochem.) hemoglobina
**hemoleucocyte** [ˌhiməˈlukəsaɪt] o [ˌhɛməˈlukəsaɪt] *s* (anat.) hemoleucocito
**hemolysin** [ˌhiməˈlaɪsɪn], [ˌhɛməˈlaɪsɪn] o [hɪˈmɑlɪsɪn] *s* (immun.) hemolisina
**hemolysis** [hɪˈmɑlɪsɪs] *s* (immun.) hemólisis
**hemophilia** [ˌhiməˈfɪlɪə] o [ˌhɛməˈfɪlɪə] *s* (path.) hemofilia
**hemophiliac** [ˌhiməˈfɪlɪæk] o [ˌhɛməˈfɪlɪæk] *s* hemofílico
**hemophilic** [ˌhiməˈfɪlɪk] o [ˌhɛməˈfɪlɪk] *adj* hemofílico
**hemoptysis** [hɪˈmɑptɪsɪs] *s* (path.) hemoptisis
**hemorrhage** [ˈhɛmərɪdʒ] *s* (path.) hemorragia
**hemorrhagic** [ˌhɛməˈrædʒɪk] *adj* hemorrágico

**hemorrhagic septicemia** *s* (vet.) septicemia hemorrágica
**hemorrhoidal** [ˌhɛməˈrɔɪdəl] *adj* hemorroidal
**hemorrhoidectomy** [ˌhɛmərɔɪˈdɛktəmɪ] *s* (*pl:* **-mies**) (surg.) hemorroidectomía
**hemorrhoids** [ˈhɛmərɔɪdz] *spl* (path.) hemorroides
**hemostat** [ˈhiməstæt] o [ˈhɛməstæt] *s* hemostato, pinza hemostática
**hemostatic** [ˌhiməˈstætɪk] o [ˌhɛməˈstætɪk] *adj & s* (med.) hemostático
**hemp** [hɛmp] *s* (bot.) cáñamo (*planta y fibra*); hachich
**hempen** [ˈhɛmpən] *adj* cañameño
**hempseed** [ˈhɛmpˌsid] *s* cañamón; (slang) carne de horca
**hemstitch** [ˈhɛmˌstɪtʃ] *s* (sew.) vainica; *va* (sew.) hacer una vainica en; *vn* (sew.) hacer vainica
**hen** [hɛn] *s* gallina
**henbane** [ˈhɛnˌben] *s* (bot.) beleño
**hence** [hɛns] *adv* de aquí; fuera de aquí; desde ahora; por lo tanto, por consiguiente; de aquí a, p.ej., **three months hence** de aquí a tres meses; **years hence** cuando hayan pasado muchos años; *interj* ¡fuera de aquí!; **hence with . . . !** ¡quítenme de delante . . . !
**henceforth** [ˌhɛnsˈforθ] o **henceforward** [ˌhɛnsˈfɔrwərd] *adv* de aquí en adelante
**henchman** [ˈhɛntʃmən] *s* (*pl:* **-men**) secuaz, servidor; muñidor
**hencoop** [ˈhɛnˌkup] o [ˈhɛnˌkʊp] *s* gallinero
**hendecagon** [hɛnˈdɛkəgɑn] *s* (geom.) endecágono
**hendecasyllabic** [ˌhɛndɛkəsɪˈlæbɪk] *adj* endecasílabo
**hendecasyllable** [ˌhɛndɛkəˈsɪləbəl] *s* endecasílabo
**hendiadys** [hɛnˈdaɪədɪs] *s* (rhet.) endíadis
**henequen** o **henequin** [ˈhɛnɪkɪn] *s* (bot.) henequén (*planta y su filamento*)
**henhouse** [ˈhɛnˌhaʊs] *s* gallinero
**henna** [ˈhɛnə] *s* (bot.) alheña, alcana (*Lawsonia inermis*); henna (*materia colorante*); color de alheña; *va* alheñarse (*el pelo*)
**hennery** [ˈhɛnərɪ] *s* (*pl:* **-ies**) gallinero
**henotheism** [ˌhɛnəˈθiɪzəm] *s* henoteísmo
**henpeck** [ˈhɛnˌpɛk] *va* importunar, tener subordinado (*al marido*)
**henpecked husband** *s* marido dominado e importunado por su mujer, marido que se deja mandar por su mujer
**Henrietta** [ˌhɛnrɪˈɛtə] *s* Enriqueta
**Henry** [ˈhɛnrɪ] *s* Enrique; (*l.c.*) *s* (*pl:* **-ries** o **-rys**) (elec.) henrio
**hep** [hɛp] *adj* (slang) enterado; **to be hep to** (slang) estar al corriente de; **to put someone hep to** (slang) poner a uno al corriente de
**heparin** [ˈhɛpərɪn] *s* (pharm.) heparina
**hepatic** [hɪˈpætɪk] *adj* hepático; de color del hígado
**hepatica** [hɪˈpætɪkə] *s* (bot.) hepática
**hepatitis** [ˌhɛpəˈtaɪtɪs] *s* (path.) hepatitis
**hepatization** [ˌhɛpətɪˈzeʃən] *s* (path.) hepatización
**hepcat** [ˈhɛpˌkæt] *s* (slang) experto en jazz, aficionado al jazz
**Hephaestus** [hɪˈfɛstəs] *s* (myth.) Hefestos
**heptagon** [ˈhɛptəgɑn] *s* (geom.) heptágono
**heptagonal** [hɛpˈtægənəl] *adj* heptagonal
**heptahedron** [ˌhɛptəˈhidrən] *s* (*pl:* **-drons** o **-dra** [drə]) (geom.) heptaedro
**heptameter** [hɛpˈtæmɪtər] *s* heptámetro
**heptane** [ˈhɛpten] *s* (chem.) heptano
**heptangular** [hɛpˈtæŋgjələr] *adj* heptangular
**heptarchy** [ˈhɛptɑrkɪ] *s* (*pl:* **-chies**) heptarquía; **the Heptarchy** la Heptarquía anglosajona
**heptasyllabic** [ˌhɛptəsɪˈlæbɪk] *adj* heptasilábico
**heptasyllable** [ˌhɛptəˈsɪləbəl] *s* heptasílabo
**Heptateuch** [ˈhɛptətjuk] o [ˈhɛptətuk] *s* (Bib.) Heptateuco
**her** [hʌr] *adj poss* su; el (o su) . . . de ella; *pron pers* la; ella; **to her** le; a ella
**Hera** [ˈhirə] o [ˈhɪrə] *s* (myth.) Hera
**Heracles** [ˈhɛrəkliz] *s* (myth.) Heracles
**Heraclitus** [ˌhɛrəˈklaɪtəs] *s* Heráclito
**Herakles** [ˈhɛrəkliz] *s* var. de **Heracles**
**herald** [ˈhɛrəld] *s* heraldo; anunciador, precursor; *va* anunciar, ser precursor de
**heraldic** [hɛˈrældɪk] *adj* heráldico
**heraldry** [ˈhɛrəldrɪ] *s* (*pl:* **-ries**) heráldica; blasón, escudo de armas; heraldía (*cargo u oficio de heraldo*); pompa heráldica, ceremonias heráldicas
**herb** [ʌrb] o [hʌrb] *s* hierba (*planta cuyo tallo nace todos los años*); hierba medicinal, hierba aromática
**herbaceous** [hʌrˈbeʃəs] *adj* herbáceo
**herbage** [ˈʌrbɪdʒ] o [ˈhʌrbɪdʒ] *s* herbaje
**herbal** [ˈhʌrbəl] o [ˈʌrbəl] *adj* herbario; *s* herbario (*libro*)
**herbalist** [ˈhʌrbəlɪst] o [ˈʌrbəlɪst] *s* herbolario, simplista
**herbarium** [hʌrˈbɛrɪəm] *s* (*pl:* **-ums** o **-a** [ə]) herbario (*colección; local*)
**herb bennet** [ˈbɛnɪt] *s* (bot.) hierba de San Benito
**herb doctor** *s* herbolario
**herbiferous** [hʌrˈbɪfərəs] *adj* herbífero
**herbivorous** [hʌrˈbɪvərəs] *adj* herbívoro
**herbman** [ˈʌrbmən] o [ˈhʌrbmən] *s* (*pl:* **-men**) herbolario
**herb mercury** *s* (bot.) mercurial
**herby** [ˈʌrbɪ] o [ˈhʌrbɪ] *adj* herboso
**Herculaneum** [ˌhʌrkjəˈlenɪəm] *s* Herculano
**Herculean** [hʌrˈkjulɪən] o [ˌhʌrkjəˈliən] *adj* hercúleo (*perteneciente a Hércules*); (*l.c.*) *adj* hercúleo (*forzudo, fornido*); laborioso, penoso
**Hercules** [ˈhʌrkjəliz] *s* (astr. & myth.) Hércules
**herd** [hʌrd] *s* manada, hato, rebaño; multitud; chusma; manadero, vaquero; *va* reunir en manada; juntar; *vn* reunirse en manada, ir en manada; ir juntos
**herd instinct** *s* instinto de rebaño
**herdsman** [ˈhʌrdzmən] *s* (*pl:* **-men**) manadero, vaquero
**here** [hɪr] *adv* aquí; acá; **that's neither here nor there** eso no viene al caso; **the here and the hereafter** esta vida y la futura; **here and there** acá y allá; **here below** acá abajo (*acá en la tierra*); **here is** o **are** aquí tiene Vd.; **here's to you!** ¡a la salud de Vd.!; *adj* presente; *interj* ¡presente!; (*cap.*) [ˈhiri] *s* (myth.) Hera
**hereabout** [ˈhɪrəˌbaʊt] o **hereabouts** [ˈhɪrəˌbaʊts] *adv* por aquí, cerca de aquí
**hereafter** [hɪrˈæftər] o [hɪrˈɑftər] *adv* de aquí en adelante; en lo futuro; en la vida futura; *s* estado futuro; **the hereafter** lo futuro; la vida futura
**hereat** [hɪrˈæt] *adv* en esto; por esto
**hereby** [hɪrˈbaɪ] *adv* por este medio; por éstas, por la presente
**hereditable** [hɪˈrɛdɪtəbəl] *adj* heredable
**hereditary** [hɪˈrɛdɪˌtɛrɪ] *adj* hereditario
**heredity** [hɪˈrɛdɪtɪ] *s* (*pl:* **-ties**) (biol.) herencia
**herein** [hɪrˈɪn] *adv* adjunto, aquí dentro; en esto, en este asunto
**hereinafter** [ˌhɪrɪnˈæftər] o [ˌhɪrɪnˈɑftər] *adv* más abajo, más adelante
**hereinbefore** [hɪrˌɪnbɪˈfor] *adv* en lo precedente; **as hereinbefore stated** como queda dicho en los párrafos precedentes
**hereinto** [hɪrˈɪntu] *adv* en esto
**hereof** [hɪrˈɑv] *adv* de esto
**hereon** [hɪrˈɑn] o [hɪrˈɔn] *adv* en esto, sobre esto
**here's** [hɪrz] contracción de **here is**
**heresiarch** [hɪˈrisɪɑrk] *s* heresiarca
**heresy** [ˈhɛrəsɪ] *s* (*pl:* **-sies**) herejía
**heretic** [ˈhɛrətɪk] *s* hereje; *adj* herético
**heretical** [hɪˈrɛtɪkəl] *adj* herético
**hereto** [hɪrˈtu] *adv* a esto, para esto
**heretofore** [ˌhɪrtʊˈfor] *adv* antes, hasta ahora
**hereunder** [hɪrˈʌndər] *adv* abajo; en virtud de esto
**hereunto** [ˌhɪrʌnˈtu] *adv* a esto, para esto
**hereupon** [ˌhɪrəˈpɑn] *adv* en esto, sobre esto; en seguida
**herewith** [hɪrˈwɪð] o [hɪrˈwɪθ] *adv* con esto; adjunto, con la presente; por este medio, de este modo
**heritable** [ˈhɛrɪtəbəl] *adj* heredable; heredero
**heritage** [ˈhɛrɪtɪdʒ] *s* herencia

**herma** ['hʌrmə] *s* (*pl:* **-mae** [mi] o **-mai** [maɪ]) (hist.) herma
**hermaphrodite** [hʌr'mæfrədaɪt] *adj & s* hermafrodita
**hermaphrodite brig** *s* (naut.) bergantín goleta
**hermaphroditic** [hʌr,mæfrə'dɪtɪk] o **hermaphroditical** [hʌr,mæfrə'dɪtɪkəl] *adj* hermafrodita
**hermaphroditism** [hʌr'mæfrədaɪtɪzəm] *s* (biol.) hermafroditismo
**hermeneutic** [,hʌrmə'njutɪk] o [,hʌrmə'nutɪk] *adj* hermenéutico; **hermeneutics** *ssg* hermenéutica
**Hermes** ['hʌrmiz] *s* (myth.) Hermes
**hermetic** [hʌr'mɛtɪk] o **hermetical** [hʌr'mɛtɪkəl] *adj* hermético
**Hermione** [hʌr'maɪənɪ] *s* (myth.) Hermíone
**hermit** ['hʌrmɪt] *s* ermitaño
**hermitage** ['hʌrmɪtɪdʒ] *s* ermita
**hermit crab** *s* (zool.) ermitaño
**hermit thrush** *s* (orn.) tordo norteamericano (*Hylocichla guttata*)
**hernia** ['hʌrnɪə] *s* (*pl:* **-as** o **-ae** [i]) (path.) hernia
**hernial** ['hʌrnɪəl] *adj* herniario
**hero** ['hɪro] *s* (*pl:* **-roes**) héroe; (*cap.*) *s* (myth.) Hero
**Herod** ['hɛrəd] *s* (Bib.) Herodes
**Herodian** [hɪ'rodɪən] *adj* herodiano
**Herodias** [hɪ'rodɪəs] *s* (Bib.) Herodías
**Herodotus** [hɪ'rɑdətəs] *s* Heródoto
**heroic** [hɪ'ro·ɪk] *adj* heroico; (med.) heroico; *s* poema heroico; **heroics** *spl* lenguaje rimbombante; acto extravagante; verso heroico
**heroic age** *s* edad heroica, tiempos heroicos
**heroical** [hɪ'ro·ɪkəl] *adj* heroico
**heroic couplet** *s* estrofa de dos versos heroicos pareados, de cinco yambos cada uno
**heroicomic** [hɪ,ro·ɪ'kɑmɪk] *adj* heroicocómico
**heroic verse** *s* verso heroico (*verso que en cada idioma se tiene por más a propósito para la poesía heroica: el pentámetro yámbico en inglés y el endecasílabo yámbico en español*)
**heroin** ['hɛro·ɪn] *s* (pharm.) heroína
**heroine** ['hɛro·ɪn] *s* heroína
**heroism** ['hɛro·ɪzəm] *s* heroísmo
**heron** ['hɛrən] *s* (orn.) garza; (orn.) garza real, airón (*Ardea cinerea*)
**heronry** ['hɛrənrɪ] *s* (*pl:* **-ries**) vivar de garzas
**heron's-bill** ['hɛrənz,bɪl] *s* (bot.) pico de cigüeña
**hero worship** *s* culto de los héroes
**herpes** ['hʌrpiz] *s* (path.) herpe
**herpetic** [hər'pɛtɪk] *adj* herpético
**herpetology** [,hʌrpɪ'tɑlədʒɪ] *s* herpetología
**herring** ['hɛrɪŋ] *s* (ichth.) arenque
**herringbone** ['hɛrɪŋ,bon] *s* espina de pescado (*en los tejidos*); punto de Hungría, espinapez (*en los entarimados*); *adj* de espina de pescado; a punto de Hungría
**herring gull** *s* (orn.) gaviota
**hers** [hʌrz] *pron poss* el suyo, el de ella; **a friend of hers** un amigo suyo
**herself** [hər'sɛlf] *pron pers* ella misma; se; sí, sí misma; **with herself** consigo
**Hertzian** ['hɛrtsɪən] *adj* (elec.) herciano o hertziano
**Hertzian wave** *s* (elec.) onda herciana o hertziana
**he's** [hiz] contracción de **he is** y de **he has**
**Hesiod** ['hisɪəd] *s* Hesíodo
**hesitance** ['hɛzɪtəns] *s* var. de **hesitancy**
**hesitancy** ['hɛzɪtənsɪ] *s* (*pl:* **-cies**) vacilación
**hesitant** ['hɛzɪtənt] *adj* vacilante
**hesitate** ['hɛzɪtet] *vn* vacilar; **don't hesitate to** + *inf* no tema + *inf*, no tenga miedo de + *inf;* **to hesitate to** + *inf* vacilar en + *inf*
**hesitatingly** ['hɛzɪ,tetɪŋlɪ] *adv* de modo vacilante
**Hesper** ['hɛspər] *s* var. de **Hesperus**
**Hesperia** [hɛs'pɪrɪə] *s* Hesperia (*España o Italia*)
**Hesperian** [hɛs'pɪrɪən] *adj* hespérido (*occidental*); hesperio (*perteneciente a España o Italia*)
**Hesperides** [hɛs'pɛrɪdiz] *spl* (myth.) Hespérides (*cuatro ninfas*); (myth.) jardín de las Hespérides (*cuyos árboles producían manzanas de oro*)
**hesperidin** [hɛs'pɛrɪdɪn] *s* (chem.) hesperidina
**hesperidium** [,hɛspə'rɪdɪəm] *s* (*pl:* **-a** [ə]) (bot.) hesperidio
**Hesperus** ['hɛspərəs] *s* Héspero (*el planeta Venus*)
**Hessian** ['hɛʃən] *adj* hesiense; *s* hesiense; soldado mercenario hesiense
**Hessian boots** *spl* botas adornadas con borlas, muy usadas en Inglaterra en el siglo XIX
**Hessian crucible** *s* crisol de arcilla muy refractaria
**Hessian fly** *s* (ent.) cecidomio
**hetaera** [hɪ'tɪrə] *s* (*pl:* **-rae** [ri]) (hist.) hetera
**hetaira** [hɪ'taɪrə] *s* (*pl:* **-rai** [raɪ]) var. de **hetaera**
**heterocercal** [,hɛtərə'sʌrkəl] *adj* (ichth.) heterocerco
**heterochlamydeous** [,hɛtərəklə'mɪdɪəs] *adj* (bot.) heteroclamídeo
**heteroclite** ['hɛtərə,klaɪt] *adj* heteróclito; *s* persona o cosa heteróclitas; (gram.) palabra heteróclita
**heterocyclic** [,hɛtərə'saɪklɪk] o [,hɛtərə'sɪklɪk] *adj* (chem.) heterocíclico
**heterodox** ['hɛtərədɑks] *adj* heterodoxo
**heterodoxy** ['hɛtərə,dɑksɪ] *s* (*pl:* **-ies**) heterodoxia
**heterodyne** ['hɛtərə,daɪn] *adj* (rad.) heterodino; *s* (rad.) heterodina (*oscilador*); *va & vn* (rad.) heterodinar
**heterodyne reception** *s* (rad.) recepción heterodina
**heteroecism** [,hɛtə'risɪzəm] *s* (biol.) heteroecia
**heterogamous** [,hɛtə'rɑgəməs] *adj* (bot.) heterógamo
**heterogamy** [,hɛtə'rɑgəmɪ] *s* heterogamia
**heterogeneity** [,hɛtərədʒɪ'niɪtɪ] *s* (*pl:* **-ties**) heterogeneidad
**heterogeneous** [,hɛtərə'dʒinɪəs] *adj* heterogéneo
**heteronym** ['hɛtərə,nɪm] *s* heterónimo
**heteronymous** [,hɛtə'rɑnɪməs] *adj* heterónimo
**heterophyllous** [,hɛtərə'fɪləs] *adj* (bot.) heterofilo
**heterophylly** ['hɛtərə,fɪlɪ] *s* (bot.) heterofilia
**heteroplasty** ['hɛtərə,plæstɪ] *s* (surg.) heteroplastia
**heterotrophic** [,hɛtərə'trɑfɪk] *adj* (biol.) heterótrofo
**hetman** ['hɛtmən] *s* (*pl:* **-mans**) hetmán (*caudillo de cosacos*)
**heuristic** [hju'rɪstɪk] *adj* heurístico
**hew** [hju] (*pret:* **hewed;** *pp:* **hewed** o **hewn**) *va* cortar, tajar; hachear; desbastar; picar (*piedra*); labrar (*madera, piedra*); **to hew down** cortar, destroncar, derribar o tumbar a hachazos; **to hew one's way through** abrirse paso a fuerza de hachazos por entre; *vn* dar hachazos; **to hew close to the line** (coll.) hilar delgado
**hewn** [hjun] *pp de* **hew**
**hex** [hɛks] *s* (coll.) bruja, hechicera; *va* (coll.) embrujar
**hexachord** ['hɛksəkɔrd] *s* (mus.) hexacordo
**hexafluoride** [,hɛksə'fluəraɪd] o [,hɛksə'fluərɪd] *s* (chem.) hexafluoruro
**hexagon** ['hɛksəgɑn] *s* (geom.) hexágono
**hexagonal** [hɛks'ægənəl] *adj* hexagonal
**hexagram** ['hɛksəgræm] *s* hexagrama
**hexahedral** [,hɛksə'hidrəl] *adj* hexaédrico
**hexahedron** [,hɛksə'hidrən] *s* (*pl:* **-drons** o **-dra** [drə]) (geom.) hexaedro
**hexameter** [hɛks'æmɪtər] *adj & s* hexámetro
**hexamethylenetetramine** [,hɛksə,mɛθɪlin,tɛtrə'min] *s* (chem.) hexametilenotetramina
**hexane** ['hɛksen] *s* (chem.) hexano
**hexangular** [hɛks'æŋgjələr] *adj* hexángulo
**hexapetalous** [,hɛksə'pɛtələs] *adj* (bot.) hexapétalo
**hexapod** ['hɛksəpɑd] *adj* hexápodo; *s* (ent.) hexápodo
**Hexateuch** ['hɛksətjuk] o ['hɛksətuk] *s* (Bib.) Hexateuco
**hexose** ['hɛksos] *s* (chem.) hexosa
**hey** [he] *interj* ¡eh!, ¡oiga!, ¡oye!

**heyday** ['he,de] *s* época de esplendor, época de mayor prosperidad, vigor, etc.
**Hezekiah** [,hezɪ'kaɪə] *s* (Bib.) Ezequías
**hf.** abr. de **half**
**hg.** abr. de **hectogram**
**H.H.** abr. de **Her Highness, His Highness** y **His Holiness**
**hhd.** abr. de **hogshead**
**H.I.** abr. de **Hawaiian Islands**
**hiatus** [haɪ'etəs] *s* (*pl:* **-tuses** o **-tus**) abertura, laguna; hiato (*en un manuscrito o texto impreso*); (anat., gram. & pros.) hiato
**hibernal** [haɪ'bʌrnəl] *adj* hibernal, invernal
**hibernate** ['haɪbərnet] *vn* invernar; (biol.) hibernar
**hibernation** [,haɪbər'neʃən] *s* invernación; (biol.) invernación, hibernación
**Hibernian** [haɪ'bʌrnɪən] *adj & s* hibernés o hiberniano
**hibiscus** [hɪ'bɪskəs] o [haɪ'bɪskəs] *s* (bot.) hibisco
**hiccough** o **hiccup** ['hɪkʌp] *s* hipo; *va* decir con hipos; *vn* hipar
**hick** [hɪk] *adj & s* (slang) campesino; (slang) palurdo
**hickey** ['hɪkɪ] *s* adminículo, chisme; (elec.) casquillo conectador, manguito sujetador; (elec.) doblador de tubos
**hickory** ['hɪkərɪ] *s* (*pl:* **-ries**) (bot.) nuez dura
**hickory nut** *s* nuez dura
**hid** [hɪd] *pret & pp de* **hide**
**hidden** ['hɪdən] *pp de* **hide;** *adj* escondido, oculto; recóndito, obscuro; secreto
**hide** [haɪd] *s* cuero, piel; **hides** *spl* corambre, curtidos; **neither hide nor hair** ni un vestigio; **to tan someone's hide** (coll.) zurrarle a uno la badana; (*pret & pp:* **hided**) *va* aporrear, medir las costillas a; (*pret:* **hid;** *pp:* **hidden** o **hid**) *va* esconder, ocultar; encubrir; disimular; *vn* esconderse, ocultarse; **to hide out** (coll.) recatarse (*en lugar apartado*)
**hide-and-seek** ['haɪdənd'sik] *s* escondite; **to play hide-and-seek** jugar al escondite
**hidebound** ['haɪd,baʊnd] *adj* que tiene la piel pegada a los huesos; dogmático, obstinado, fanático
**hideous** ['hɪdɪəs] *adj* feote; horrible, espantoso
**hideousness** ['hɪdɪəsnɪs] *s* fealdad; horribilidad
**hide-out** ['haɪd,aʊt] *s* (coll.) guarida, escondrijo, refugio
**hiding** ['haɪdɪŋ] *s* ocultación; escondite; (coll.) tunda, zurra; **in hiding** escondido, oculto; emboscado
**hidrosis** [hɪ'drosɪs] *s* (path.) hidrosis
**hie** [haɪ] (*pret & pp:* **hied;** *ger:* **hieing** o **hying**) *va* apresurar; incitar; **hie thee** date prisa; **hie thee home** apresúrate a volver a casa; *vn* correr, volar, ir volando
**hierarch** ['haɪərɑrk] *s* jerarca
**hierarchic** [,haɪə'rɑrkɪk] o **hierarchical** [,haɪə'rɑrkɪkəl] *adj* jerárquico
**hierarchize** ['haɪərɑrkaɪz] *va* jerarquizar
**hierarchy** ['haɪə,rɑrkɪ] *s* (*pl:* **-chies**) jerarquía
**hieratic** [,haɪə'rætɪk] o **hieratical** [,haɪə'rætɪkəl] *adj* hierático
**hieroglyph** ['haɪərə,glɪf] *s* jeroglífico
**hieroglyphic** [,haɪərə'glɪfɪk] *adj & s* jeroglífico
**hieroglyphical** [,haɪərə'glɪfɪkəl] *adj* jeroglífico
**Hieronymite** [,haɪə'rɑnɪmaɪt] *adj & s* jerónimo
**hierophant** ['haɪərəfænt] o [haɪ'ɛrəfænt] *s* hierofanta o hierofante
**hi-fi** ['haɪ'faɪ] *adj* (coll.) de alta fidelidad; *s* (coll.) alta fidelidad
**hi-fi fan** *s* (coll.) aficionado a la alta fidelidad
**higgle** ['hɪgəl] *vn* regatear, discutir (*sobre precios*)
**higgledy-piggledy** ['hɪgəldɪ'pɪgəldɪ] *adj* confuso, revuelto; *adv* confusamente, a río revuelto, sin orden ni concierto; *s* confusión
**high** [haɪ] *adj* alto; de alto, de altura; sumo (*pontífice*); crecido (*río*); agudo (*sonido*); fuerte (*viento*); bueno (*ánimo, humor*); altanero (*modo de proceder*); (coll.) borracho; (cook.) manido; **high and dry** en seco; plantado, abandonado, desamparado; **high and mighty** (coll.) muy arrogante; *adv* altamente, sumamente; en sumo grado; a gran precio; **to aim high** poner el tiro muy alto; **to come high** venderse caro; **to fly high** ser muy optimista; ser muy ambicioso, confiar mucho en su buena estrella; **high and low** por todas partes; **higher than** más alto que; más arriba de (*sobre*); *s* colmo; (aut.) toma directa, marcha directa; (com.) (el) precio más alto; **on high** en las alturas, en el cielo
**high altar** *s* altar mayor
**highball** ['haɪ,bɔl] *s* highball (*whisky con hielo y agua gaseosa*); *vn* (slang) avanzar o pasar con rapidez
**high-blooded** ['haɪ'blʌdɪd] *adj* de noble alcurnia
**high blood pressure** *s* (path.) hipertensión arterial
**highborn** ['haɪ,bɔrn] *adj* de ilustre cuna, linajudo
**highboy** ['haɪ,bɔɪ] *s* cómoda alta sostenida por patas altas
**highbred** ['haɪ,brɛd] *adj* de familia ilustre; cortés, fino
**highbrow** ['haɪ,braʊ] *adj* (slang) erudito, docto; (slang) de o para gente erudita; *s* (slang) erudito, docto
**high chair** *s* silla alta
**High Church** *s* alta iglesia (*rama conservadora de la Iglesia anglicana*)
**High-Church** ['haɪ,tʃʌrtʃ] *adj* ritualista
**high-colored** ['haɪ,kʌlərd] *adj* de color subido; encarnado
**high comedy** *s* alta comedia
**high command** *s* (mil.) alto mando, alto comando
**high commissioner** *s* alto comisario
**high-compression** ['haɪkəm'prɛʃən] *adj* de alta compresión
**high cost of living** *s* carestía de la vida
**high day** *s* día de fiesta
**higher criticism** *s* alta crítica (*especialmente de la Biblia*)
**higher education** *s* enseñanza superior
**higher-up** [,haɪər'ʌp] *s* (coll.) superior jerárquico
**high explosive** *s* explosivo rompedor
**highfalutin** o **highfaluting** [,haɪfə'lutən] *adj* (coll.) pomposo; (coll.) soberbio, presuntuoso
**high fashion** *s* alta costura
**high fidelity** *s* (rad.) alta fidelidad
**high-fidelity** ['haɪfaɪ'dɛlɪtɪ] o ['haɪfɪ'dɛlɪtɪ] *adj* (rad.) de alta fidelidad
**highflier** ['haɪ,flaɪər] *s* persona, cosa, pájaro de alto vuelo; extravagante; despilfarrador
**high-flown** ['haɪ,flon] *adj* ampuloso, pomposo; extravagante; soberbio, presuntuoso
**highflyer** ['haɪ,flaɪər] *s* var. de **highflier**
**high frequency** *s* (elec.) alta frecuencia
**high-frequency** ['haɪ'frikwənsɪ] *adj* (elec.) de alta frecuencia
**high-gain** ['haɪ'gen] *adj* (rad.) de alta ganancia
**high gear** *s* (aut.) toma directa, marcha directa
**High German** *s* altoalemán
**High-German** ['haɪ'dʒʌrmən] *adj* altoalemán
**high-grade** ['haɪ'gred] *adj* de calidad superior
**high hand** *s* arbitrariedad, despotismo, altanería
**high-handed** ['haɪ'hændɪd] *adj* arbitrario, despótico, altanero
**high hat** *s* sombrero de copa
**high-hat** ['haɪ'hæt] *adj* (slang) esnob; (slang) elegante, que es el colmo de la elegancia; **to be high-hat** (slang) tener mucho copete; [,haɪ'hæt] (*pret & pp:* **-hatted;** *ger:* **-hatting**) *va* (slang) desairar, tratar con desprecio estudiado
**high-heeled shoe** ['haɪ,hild] *s* zapato de tacón alto
**high horse** *s* presunción, ademán arrogante; **on a high horse** muy arrogante
**highjack** ['haɪ,dʒæk] *va* (coll.) var. de **hijack**
**highjacker** ['haɪ,dʒækər] *s* (coll.) var. de **hijacker**
**high jinks** [dʒɪŋks] *s* (coll.) jarana, jaleo, payasada
**high jump** *s* (sport) salto de altura

**highland** ['haɪlənd] *adj* de (las) tierras altas; *s* meseta, región montañosa; **highlands** *spl* tierras altas, montañas; **Highlands** *spl* región montañosa de Escocia
**highlander** ['haɪləndər] *s* montañés; (*cap.*) *s* montañés de Escocia; soldado de un regimiento de montañeses de Escocia
**Highland fling** *s* baile muy vivo de las tierras altas de Escocia
**high life** *s* alta sociedad, gran mundo
**high light** *s* (lo) más notable o interesante (*de un viaje, fiesta, etc.*); toque de luz (*de una pintura, fotografía, etc.*)
**highlight** ['haɪ,laɪt] *va* inundar de luz; (fig.) destacar
**highly** ['haɪlɪ] *adv* altamente, sumamente; en sumo grado; con aplauso general; a gran precio; **to speak highly of** decir mil bienes de
**High Mass** *s* (eccl.) misa cantada o mayor
**high-minded** ['haɪ'maɪndɪd] *adj* noble, magnánimo; arrogante, orgulloso
**highness** ['haɪnɪs] *s* altura; (*cap.*) *s* Alteza (*título*)
**high noon** *s* pleno mediodía; **at high noon** en pleno mediodía
**high-octane gasoline** [,haɪ'ɑkten] *s* gasolina de alto octanaje
**high-pass filter** ['haɪ,pæs] o ['haɪ,pɑs] *s* (elec.) filtro paso superior, filtro de paso alto
**high-pitched** ['haɪ'pɪtʃt] *adj* agudo, aflautado, chillón; escarpado; tenso, impresionable
**high-powered** ['haɪ'paʊərd] *adj* de gran potencia, de alta potencia
**high-pressure** ['haɪ'prɛʃər] *adj* de alta presión; (fig.) emprendedor, enérgico; *va* (coll.) apremiar, instar; **to high-pressure someone to do something** (coll.) instarle a uno a que haga una cosa
**high-priced** ['haɪ'praɪst] *adj* de alto costo, de precio elevado
**high priest** *s* sumo sacerdote
**high relief** *s* alto relieve
**highroad** ['haɪ,rod] *s* carretera, camino real; (fig.) camino real
**high school** *s* instituto, instituto de segunda enseñanza
**high sea** *s* mar gruesa; **high seas** *spl* alta mar
**high society** *s* alta sociedad, gran mundo
**high-sounding** ['haɪ,saʊndɪŋ] *adj* altisonante
**high-speed** ['haɪ'spid] *adj* rápido, de alta velocidad
**high-speed drill** *s* broca de alta velocidad
**high-speed steel** *s* acero rápido, acero de corte rápido
**high-spirited** ['haɪ'spɪrɪtɪd] *adj* orgulloso; animoso, valiente; fogoso (*caballo*)
**high spirits** *spl* alegría, buen humor; **in high spirits** alegre, animoso
**high-strung** ['haɪ'strʌŋ] *adj* tenso, impresionable, excitable
**high style** *s* alta costura
**hight** [haɪt] *adj* (archaic) llamado
**high tension** *s* (elec.) alta tensión
**high-tension** ['haɪ'tɛnʃən] *adj* (elec.) de alta tensión
**high terms** *s* palabras lisonjeras
**high-test** ['haɪ'tɛst] *adj* que pasa pruebas rigurosas; de alta volatilidad
**high-test fuel** *s* supercarburante
**high tide** *s* (naut.) marea alta, pleamar; (fig.) apogeo
**high time** *s* hora, p.ej., **it is high time for you to leave** ya es hora de que se marche Vd.; (slang) jarana, parranda, francachela
**high-toned** ['haɪ'tond] *adj* agudo, aflautado, chillón; noble, caballeroso; (coll.) elegante, de buen tono
**high treason** *s* alta traición
**high-up** ['haɪ'ʌp] *adj* de alto copete
**high-voltage** ['haɪ'voltɪdʒ] *adj* (elec.) de alto voltaje, de alta tensión
**high water** *s* aguas altas; marea alta, pleamar
**high-water mark** ['haɪ'wɔtər] o ['haɪ'wɑtər] *s* línea de aguas altas; línea de la marea alta; (fig.) apogeo, colmo
**highway** ['haɪ,we] *s* carretera, camino real; (fig.) camino real
**highway department** *s* servicio de tránsito de caminos
**highwayman** ['haɪ,wemən] *s* (*pl:* **-men**) bandolero, salteador de caminos
**highway robber** *s* salteador de caminos
**highway robbery** *s* salteamiento
**highway signals** *spl* señales de ruta
**high words** *spl* palabras airadas, palabras ofensivas
**H.I.H.** abr. de **His** o **(Her) Imperial Highness**
**hijack** ['haɪ,dʒæk] *va* (coll.) asaltar a un contrabandista quitándole (*el licor u otro contrabando en camino*); (coll.) asaltar (*a un contrabandista*); (coll.) robar; (coll.) apoderarse violentamente de (*un avión en vuelo*)
**hijacker** ['haɪ,dʒækər] *s* (coll.) salteador o atracador (*cuyas víctimas son otros bandidos o contrabandistas*); (coll.) robador
**hike** [haɪk] *s* (coll.) caminata; (coll.) aumento; *va* elevar de un tirón, sacar violentamente; (coll.) aumentar; *vn* (coll.) dar una caminata o caminatas, caminar por lugares agrestes
**hiker** ['haɪkər] *s* (coll.) caminante, aficionado a las caminatas
**hilarious** [hɪ'lɛrɪəs] o [haɪ'lɛrɪəs] *adj* regocijado, jubiloso
**hilarity** [hɪ'lærɪtɪ] o [haɪ'lærɪtɪ] *s* hilaridad, regocijo bullicioso
**Hilary** ['hɪlərɪ] *s* Hilario
**hill** [hɪl] *s* colina, collado, cerro; montoncillo; *va* amontonar; (agr.) acobijar, aporcar, recalzar; *vn* amontonarse
**hillbilly** ['hɪl,bɪlɪ] *s* (*pl:* **-lies**) (coll.) rústico montañés (*del sur de los EE.UU.*)
**hilling** ['hɪlɪŋ] *s* amontonamiento; (agr.) acobijo, aporcado
**hillock** ['hɪlək] *s* altozano, cerrejón
**hillside** ['hɪl,saɪd] *s* ladera
**hilly** ['hɪlɪ] *adj* (*comp:* **-ier;** *super:* **-iest**) colinoso, montuoso; empinado
**hilt** [hɪlt] *s* empuñadura, puño; **up to the hilt** completamente
**hilum** ['haɪləm] *s* (*pl:* **-la** [lə]) (anat.) hilio; (bot.) hilo
**H.I.M.** abr. de **His** o **(Her) Imperial Majesty**
**him** [hɪm] *pron pers* le, lo; él; **to him** le; a él
**Himalaya, The** [hɪ'mɑljə] o [,hɪmə'leə] el Himalaya; **The Himalayas** el Himalaya, los montes Himalaya
**Himalaya Mountains** *spl* montes Himalaya
**Himalayan** [hɪ'mɑljən] o [,hɪmə'leən] *adj* himalayo
**himself** [hɪm'sɛlf] *pron pers* él mismo; se; sí, sí mismo; **with himself** consigo
**Hind.** abr. de **Hindu, Hindustan** y **Hindustani**
**hind** [haɪnd] *adj* trasero, posterior; *s* (*pl:* **hinds** o **hind**) cierva; (*pl:* **hinds**) labriego, gañán, campesino
**hindbrain** ['haɪnd,bren] *s* (anat.) rombencéfalo; (anat.) metencéfalo
**hinder** ['haɪndər] *adj* trasero, posterior; ['hɪndər] *va* estorbar, impedir, dificultar; **to hinder from** + *ger* impedir + *inf* o impedir que + *subj*
**hindermost** ['haɪndərmost] *adj* var. de **hindmost**
**hind-foremost** ['haɪnd'formost] *adv* (dial.) con lo de atrás delante
**Hindi** ['hɪndi] *s* hindí
**hindmost** ['haɪndmost] *adj* postrero, último
**Hindoo** ['hɪndu] *adj & s* var. de **Hindu**
**hindquarter** ['haɪnd,kwɔrtər] *s* cuarto trasero
**hindrance** ['hɪndrəns] *s* estorbo, impedimento, obstáculo
**hindsight** ['haɪnd,saɪt] *s* percepción a posteriori, percepción tardía; mira posterior (*de un arma de fuego*)
**Hindu** ['hɪndu] *adj & s* hindú
**Hinduism** ['hɪnduɪzəm] *s* hinduísmo
**Hindustan** [,hɪndu'stɑn] *s* el Indostán
**Hindustani** [,hɪndu'stɑnɪ] *adj* indostánico; *s* indostaní o hindustaní (*lengua*)
**hinge** [hɪndʒ] *s* charnela, bisagra, gozne; (b.b.) cartivana; (mach.) charnela; (zool.) charnela (*de las dos valvas de los moluscos*); (fig.) punto capital, (lo) más esencial; *va* engoznar; *vn* girar sobre un gozne; **to hinge on** o **upon** depender de

**hinged** [hɪndʒd] *adj* articulado, de bisagra
**hinge joint** *s* (anat.) gínglimo
**hinny** [ˈhɪnɪ] *s* (*pl:* **-nies**) burdégano
**hint** [hɪnt] *s* indirecta, puntada, insinuación; consejo; **to take the hint** darse por aludido; *va* insinuar; indicar; *vn* echar una indirecta; echar indirectas; **to hint at** insinuar; dar a entender que se desea (*una cosa*)
**hinterland** [ˈhɪntər,lænd] *s* interior (*de un territorio colonial*); región lejana de los centros urbanos
**hip** [hɪp] *s* (anat.) cadera; escaramujo (*fruto*); lima, caballete (*arista formada por el encuentro de dos vertientes*); (arch.) lima tesa (*ángulo*); **to have someone on** o **upon the hip** tenerle a uno acorralado, tenerle a uno entre la espada y la pared; **hip and thigh** duramente, sin piedad
**hipbone** [ˈhɪp,bon] *s* (anat.) cía, hueso de la cadera
**Hipparchus** [hɪˈpɑrkəs] *s* Hiparco
**hipped** [hɪpt] *adj* renco; a cuatro aguas (*tejado*); (coll.) triste, melancólico; (coll.) enojado, ofendido; (coll.) obsesionado; **hipped on** (coll.) obsesionado por
**hippety-hoppety** [ˈhɪpɪtɪˈhɑpɪtɪ] *adv* (coll.) a coxcojita
**hippo** [ˈhɪpo] *s* (*pl:* **-pos**) (coll.) hipopótamo
**hippocampus** [,hɪpəˈkæmpəs] *s* (*pl:* **-pi** [paɪ]) (anat., ichth. & myth.) hipocampo
**hippocras** [ˈhɪpəkræs] *s* hipocrás
**Hippocrates** [hɪˈpɑkrətiz] *s* Hipócrates
**Hippocratic** [,hɪpoˈkrætɪk] *adj* hipocrático
**Hippocratic oath** *s* juramento de Hipócrates
**Hippocrene** [ˈhɪpokrin] o [,hɪpoˈkrinɪ] *s* (myth.) Hipocrene
**hippodrome** [ˈhɪpədrom] *s* hipódromo
**hippogriff** [ˈhɪpəgrɪf] *s* (myth.) hipogrifo
**Hippolytus** [hɪˈpɑlɪtəs] *s* (myth.) Hipólito
**hippopotamus** [,hɪpəˈpɑtəməs] *s* (*pl:* **-muses** o **-mi** [maɪ]) (zool.) hipopótamo
**hip rafter** *s* lima
**hip roof** *s* tejado a cuatro aguas
**hipshot** [ˈhɪp,ʃɑt] *adj* renco
**hircine** [ˈhʌrsaɪn] o [ˈhʌrsɪn] *adj* hircino
**hircocervus** [,hʌrkəˈsʌrvəs] *s* (myth.) hircocervo
**hire** [haɪr] *s* alquiler; salario; **for hire** u **on hire** de alquiler; **to work for hire** trabajar por salario; *va* alquilar (*p.ej., un coche*); ajustar (*p.ej., a un criado*); *vn* **to hire out** (coll.) alquilarse, ajustarse
**hired girl** *s* criada
**hired man** *s* (coll.) mozo de campo
**hireling** [ˈhaɪrlɪŋ] *adj* alquiladizo; mercenario; *s* alquiladizo
**hire purchase** *s* (Brit.) arriendo con opción de compra
**hirsute** [ˈhʌrsut] o [ˈhʌrsjut] *adj* hirsuto
**his** [hɪz] *adj poss* su; el (o su) . . . de él; *pron poss* el suyo, el de él; **a friend of his** un amigo suyo
**Hispania** [hɪsˈpenɪə] *s* Hispania
**Hispanic** [hɪsˈpænɪk] *adj* hispánico
**Hispanicism** [hɪsˈpænɪsɪzəm] *s* hispanismo
**Hispanicize** [hɪsˈpænɪsaɪz] *va* hispanizar
**Hispaniola** [,hɪspənˈjolə] *s* Santo Domingo (*isla dividida en dos partes: Haití y la República Dominicana*)
**hispanist** [ˈhɪspənɪst] o [hɪsˈpænɪst] *s* hispanista
**Hispano-Moresque** [hɪsˈpenomoˈrɛsk] *adj* hispanoárabe
**Hispanophile** [hɪsˈpænofaɪl] *adj & s* hispanófilo
**Hispanophobe** [hɪsˈpænofob] *adj & s* hispanófobo
**hispid** [ˈhɪspɪd] *adj* híspido
**hiss** [hɪs] *s* silbido, siseo; *va* silbar, sisear (*una escena, a un actor por malo*); expresar o manifestar (*desagrado*) con siseos; *vn* silbar, sisear
**hist.** abr. de **historian** y **history**
**hist** [hɪst] *interj* ¡ chitón!; ¡ ce!
**histamine** [ˈhɪstəmin] o [ˈhɪstəmɪn] *s* (chem.) histamina
**histidine** [ˈhɪstɪdin] o [ˈhɪstɪdɪn] *s* (chem.) histidina
**histologist** [hɪsˈtɑlədʒɪst] *s* histólogo
**histology** [hɪsˈtɑlədʒɪ] *s* histología
**histolysis** [hɪsˈtɑlɪsɪs] *s* (biol.) histólisis
**histone** [ˈhɪston] *s* (biochem.) histona
**historian** [hɪsˈtorɪən] *s* historiador
**historiated** [hɪsˈtorɪ,etɪd] *adj* (arch.) historiado
**historic** [hɪsˈtɑrɪk] o [hɪsˈtɔrɪk] o **historical** [hɪsˈtɑrɪkəl] o [hɪsˈtɔrɪkəl] *adj* histórico
**historically** [hɪsˈtɑrɪkəlɪ] o [hɪsˈtɔrɪkəlɪ] *adv* históricamente
**historicity** [,hɪstəˈrɪsɪtɪ] *s* historicidad
**historiographer** [hɪs,torɪˈɑgrəfər] *s* historiógrafo
**historiography** [hɪs,torɪˈɑgrəfɪ] *s* historiografía
**history** [ˈhɪstərɪ] *s* (*pl:* **-ries**) historia
**histrionic** [,hɪstrɪˈɑnɪk] *adj* histriónico; teatral, insincero; **histrionics** *spl* histrionismo; actitud teatral, modales teatrales o insinceros
**hit** [hɪt] *s* golpe; tiro certero, golpe bien dado; censura acerba; (coll.) éxito; (baseball) batazo; **to make a hit** (coll.) dar golpe; **to make a hit with** (coll.) caer en la gracia a; (*pret & pp:* **hit;** *ger:* **hitting**) *va* golpear, pegar; chocar con, dar con, dar contra; dar en (*p.ej., el blanco*); tropezar con (*una dificultad, un problema, etc.*); afectar mucho (*una cosa a una persona*); censurar acerbamente; ser del gusto de; **to hit it off** avenirse bien, llevarse bien; **to hit off** remedar; describir o representar con gran acierto; *vn* chocar; acertar; **to hit against** dar contra; **to hit on** o **upon** dar con (*lo que se busca*); llegar a; ocurrirse, p.ej., **how did you hit on that?** ¿ cómo se le ocurrió eso?; **hit or miss** a la buena de Dios, salga pez o salga rana
**hit-and-run** [ˈhɪtənˈrʌn] *adj* que atropella y se da a la huída, que abandona a la víctima
**hitch** [hɪtʃ] *s* tirón; cojera; broche, traba; fiador, pasador, postillo; dificultad, impedimento; obstáculo; (naut.) vuelta de cabo; **without a hitch** sin tropiezo, a pedir de boca; *va* mover a tirones, adelantar a poquitos; atar, sujetar; enganchar (*un caballo*); uncir (*bueyes*); (slang) casar; **to hitch up** enganchar (*un caballo*); uncir (*bueyes*); alzar (*p.ej., los pantalones*) de un tirón; (slang) casar; *vn* cojear; enredarse; (coll.) armonizar; **to hitch up** (slang) casarse
**hitchhike** [ˈhɪtʃ,haɪk] *vn* (coll.) hacer autostop, ir por auto-stop
**hitching post** *s* poste para atar a las cabalgaduras
**hither** [ˈhɪðər] *adv* acá, hacia acá; **hither and thither** acá y allá; *adj* citerior, de la parte de acá
**hithermost** [ˈhɪðərmost] *adj* (el) más cercano
**hitherto** [,hɪðərˈtu] o [ˈhɪðər,tu] *adv* hasta ahora, hasta aquí
**hitherward** [ˈhɪðərwərd] o **hitherwards** [ˈhɪðərwərdz] *adv* hacia acá
**Hitlerism** [ˈhɪtlərɪzəm] *s* hitlerismo
**Hitlerite** [ˈhɪtləraɪt] *s* hitleriano
**hit-or-miss** [ˈhɪtərˈmɪs] *adj* descuidado, casual, fortuito
**hit parade** *s* (rad.) los números musicales que gozan de más popularidad en la actualidad
**hit record** *s* (coll.) disco de mucho éxito
**hit-run** [ˈhɪtˈrʌn] *adj* var. de **hit-and-run**
**hit song** *s* canción de mucho éxito
**hitter** [ˈhɪtər] *s* golpeador
**Hittite** [ˈhɪtaɪt] *adj & s* heteo o hitita
**hive** [haɪv] *s* colmena; (fig.) enjambre; **hives** *spl* (path.) urticaria; *va* encorchar (*abejas*); acopiar (*miel*) en colmena; (fig.) hacer acopio de; *vn* entrar (*el enjambre*) en la colmena; vivir aglomerados
**H.J.** abr. de **hic jacet** (Lat.) **here lies**
**hl.** abr. de **hectoliter**
**hm.** abr. de **hectometer**
**H.M.** abr. de **Her Majesty** y **His Majesty**
**H.M.S.** abr. de **Her** o **(His) Majesty's Service** y **Her** o **(His) Majesty's Ship**
**ho** [ho] *interj* ¡ ah!; ¡ oiga!
**hoar** [hor] *adj* (archaic) var. de **hoary**
**hoard** [hord] *s* cúmulo; tesoro escondido; *va* atesorar; acaparar, acumular secretamente; *vn* guardar víveres, atesorar dinero
**hoarding** [ˈhordɪŋ] *s* atesoramiento; acaparamiento, acumulación secreta; (Brit.) valla de tablas provisional que encierra un edificio que se está construyendo o reparando; (Brit.) cartelera

**hoarfrost** ['hor,frɔst] o ['hor,frɑst] *s* helada blanca, escarcha
**hoarhound** ['hor,haʊnd] *s* var. de **horehound**
**hoarse** [hors] *adj* ronco
**hoarseness** ['horsnɪs] *s* ronquedad; ronquera (*afección de la laringe*)
**hoary** ['horɪ] *adj* (*comp:* **-ier;** *super:* **-iest**) cano; vetusto
**hoary-headed** ['horɪ'hɛdɪd] *adj* encanecido
**hoatzin** [ho'ætsɪn] *s* (orn.) hoazín
**hoax** [hoks] *s* mistificación, pajarota; *va* mistificar
**hob** [hɑb] *s* repisa interior de la chimenea; hito (*en el juego de tejos*); duende; (mach.) fresa; **to play** o **to raise hob** (coll.) causar trastornos; **to play hob with** (coll.) trastornar
**hobble** ['hɑbəl] *s* cojera; traba, manea; (fig.) dificultad, atolladero; *va* dejar cojo; trabar, manear; dificultar, poner trabas a; *vn* cojear; tambalear
**hobbledehoy** ['hɑbəldɪ,hɔɪ] *s* mozalbete; muchacho grandullón
**hobble skirt** *s* falda de medio paso
**hobby** ['hɑbɪ] *s* (*pl:* **-bies**) comidilla (*tema, manía*); trabajo preferido (*fuera del habitual*); **to ride a hobby** entregarse demasiado al tema favorito, distraerse mucho con la ocupación favorita
**hobbyhorse** ['hɑbɪ,hɔrs] *s* caballito (*palo en que los niños montan a caballo*); caballo mecedor
**hobgoblin** ['hɑb,gɑblɪn] *s* duende, trasgo; bu, coco
**hobnail** ['hɑb,nel] *s* tachuela; *va* clavetear con tachuelas; (fig.) atropellar
**hobnob** ['hɑb,nɑb] (*pret & pp:* **-nobbed;** *ger:* **-nobbing**) *vn* rozarse, codearse; beber juntos; **to hobnob with** codearse con
**hobo** ['hobo] *s* (*pl:* **-bos** o **-boes**) vagabundo
**Hobson's choice** ['hɑbsənz] *s* alternativa entre la cosa ofrecida o ninguna
**hock** [hɑk] *s* corvejón (*del caballo; de varias aves gallináceas*); vino del Rin; (slang) empeño; *va* desjarretar; (slang) empeñar
**hockey** ['hɑkɪ] *s* (sport) hockey, chueca
**hockey stick** *s* hockey, palo de hockey
**hocus** ['hokəs] (*pret & pp:* **-cused** o **-cussed;** *ger:* **-cusing** o **-cussing**) *va* burlar, engañar; narcotizar, atontar con drogas; echar una droga estupefaciente a (*una copa de licor*)
**hocus-pocus** ['hokəs'pokəs] *s* abracadabra; burla, engaño; juego de manos; (*pret & pp:* **-cused** o **-cussed;** *ger:* **-cusing** o **-cussing**) *va* (coll.) estafar; *vn* (coll.) estafar; (coll.) hacer juegos de manos
**hod** [hɑd] *s* capacho, cuezo (*para llevar argamasa, ladrillos, etc.*); cubo para carbón
**hod carrier** *s* peón de albañil, peón de mano
**hodden** ['hɑdən] *s* (Scotch) tejido basto de lana sin teñir
**hodgepodge** ['hɑdʒ,pɑdʒ] *s* baturrillo, ensaladilla, salpicón
**hodman** ['hɑdmən] *s* (*pl:* **-men**) peón de albañil, peón de mano; escritor mercenario
**hoe** [ho] *s* azada, azadón; (*pret & pp:* **hoed;** *ger:* **hoeing**) *va & vn* azadonar
**hoecake** ['ho,kek] *s* torta o pan de maíz
**hog** [hɑg] o [hɔg] *s* (zool.) cerdo, puerco; (coll.) cerdo, puerco; **to go the whole hog** (slang) entregarse sin reservas, llegar hasta el último límite; (*pret & pp:* **hogged;** *ger:* **hogging**) *va* (slang) tragarse lo mejor de
**hogback** ['hɑg,bæk] o ['hɔg,bæk] *s* cuchilla (*cerro escarpado*)
**hog cholera** *s* (vet.) cólera de los cerdos
**hoggish** ['hɑgɪʃ] o ['hɔgɪʃ] *adj* puerco; comilón, glotón; egoísta
**hog Latin** *s* latín de cocina
**hogmanay** ['hɑgmə'ne] *s* (Scotch) la noche vieja
**hognose snake** ['hɑg,noz] o ['hɔg,noz] *s* (zool.) heterodón (*reptil*)
**hog plum** *s* (bot.) jobo
**hog's-fennel** ['hɑgz,fɛnəl] o ['hɔgz,fɛnəl] *s* (bot.) servato
**hogshead** ['hɑgz,hɛd] o ['hɔgz,hɛd] *s* pipa que contiene de 63 a 140 galones norteamericanos; medida de capacidad que equivale a 63 galones norteamericanos, o sea 238,5 litros
**hogtie** ['hɑg,taɪ] o ['hɔg,taɪ] (*pret & pp:* **-tied;** *ger:* **-tying**) *va* atar las patas de, atar las manos y los pies de; (coll.) inmovilizar, paralizar
**hogwash** ['hɑg,wɑʃ] o ['hɔg,wɔʃ] *s* bazofia
**hoiden** ['hɔɪdən] *s* var. de **hoyden**
**hoi polloi, the** [,hɔɪ pə'lɔɪ] la gente común, las masas
**hoist** [hɔɪst] *s* (coll.) alzamiento, empujón hacia arriba; torno izador, montacargas; grúa; *va* alzar, levantar; enarbolar; izar
**hoity-toity** ['hɔɪtɪ'tɔɪtɪ] *adj* arrogante, altanero; frívolo, veleidoso; **to be hoity-toity** ponerse tan alto; *s* arrogancia, altanería; frivolidad, veleidad; *interj* ¡ caramba!
**hokey-pokey** ['hokɪ'pokɪ] *s* (coll.) abracadabra; (coll.) burla, engaño; (coll.) juego de manos; (coll.) helado barato que se vende en las calles
**hokum** ['hokəm] *s* (slang) payasadas, chistes de baja ley (*en el teatro*); (slang) sensiblerías; (slang) tonterías, música celestial
**hold** [hold] *s* agarro; asa, mango; autoridad, influencia, dominio; (mus.) calderón; (naut.) bodega; (aer.) cabina de carga; (sport) presa (*en la lucha*); **to get, lay** o **take hold of** agarrar, coger; apoderarse de; **to loosen one's hold** desasirse; **to take hold** morder (*un tornillo*) ‖ (*pret & pp:* **held**) *va* tener, guardar, retener; apoyar, sostener; agarrar, coger; sujetar (*p.ej., con un alfiler*); contener, tener cabida para; ocupar (*un cargo, puesto, etc.*); celebrar (*una reunión*); sostener (*una opinión*); juzgar, hacer (*responsable*); (mus.) sostener (*una nota*); **to hold back** detener; retener; contener, refrenar; **to hold down** tener sujeto; oprimir; (slang) mantenerse en (*un cargo, puesto, etc.*); **to hold in** refrenar; **to hold off** mantener alejado; refrenar; **to hold one's own** mantenerse firme, no perder terreno; **to hold out** extender, ofrecer; excluir; retener; **to hold over** aplazar, diferir; **to hold together** impedir que (*una cosa*) se despegue o se descomponga o se deshaga; mantener juntos; **to hold up** apoyar, sostener: detener; alzar, tener suspendido; (coll.) atracar, robar ‖ *vn* mantenerse firme o fiel; seguir vigente, ser valedero; seguir, continuar; asirse; pegarse; opinar; **to hold back** detenerse; contenerse, refrenarse; **to hold forth** arengar, declamar, perorar; **to hold in** contenerse; **to hold off** esperar; mantenerse a distancia, mostrarse frío; **to hold on** agarrarse bien, tenerse bien agarrado; aguantar; **to hold on to** agarrarse bien de, asirse de; afirmarse en; **to hold out** no cejar; ir tirando; durar; (slang) retener algo prometido o debido; **to hold out for** insistir en; **to hold over** continuar desempeñando un cargo (*cuando lo natural sería dejarlo*); **to hold to** agarrarse bien de; afirmarse en; **to hold together** no despegarse, no descomponerse, no deshacerse; mantenerse juntos; **to hold up** continuar, durar; **to hold with** convenir con, estar de acuerdo con; **hold on!** ¡ un momento!; **hold on there!** ¡ paso a paso!, ¡ ténganse todos!
**holdall** ['hold,ɔl] *s* funda
**holdback** ['hold,bæk] *s* estorbo, restricción; cejadero (*en los carruajes*); calapuerta
**holder** ['holdər] *s* posesor, tenedor; arrendatario; agarrador, cojinillo (*para coger, p.ej., un plato caliente*); boquilla (*para poner el cigarro o cigarrillo*); poseedor (*p.ej., de un récord*); titular (*p.ej., de un pasaporte*); sostén, sostenedor (*persona y cosa*); mango, puño, asa, sustentáculo; (com.) portador (*de una letra*); porta- (*en palabras compuestas españolas*), p.ej., **electrode holder** portaelectrodo
**holder-on** ['holdər'ɑn] o ['holdər'ɔn] *s* sufridor (*obrero*); sufridera
**holdfast** ['hold,fæst] o ['hold,fɑst] *s* aldabilla; agarradero; (bot.) disco adhesivo
**holding** ['holdɪŋ] *s* posesión, tenencia; terreno; **holdings** *spl* valores habidos
**holding company** *s* sociedad de control, compañía tenedora (*de valores de otras empresas*)
**holding pattern** *s* (aer.) circuito cerrado en que un avión da vueltas a una altura fija hasta recibir la orden de aterrizar
**holdover** ['hold,ovər] *s* (coll.) continuación, resto; (coll.) consecuencias; (com.) suma que

pasa de una página o cuenta a otra; (slang) malestar que se siente al acabar de dormir la mona
**holdup** ['hold,ʌp] *s* detención; (slang) atraco, asalto
**holdup man** *s* (slang) atracador
**hole** [hol] *s* agujero; cavidad, hueco, hoyo; ojo (*en el queso, pan, etc.*); guarida (*de animales; de gente maleante*); cochitril (*habitación estrecha y desaseada*); calabozo; charco, remanso (*en un río*); ancón, ensenada; (sport) agujero; (coll.) atascadero, bache (*en un camino*); (coll.) apuro, aprieto; (coll.) defecto; **in a hole** (slang) en un aprieto; **in the hole** (coll.) adeudado, perdidoso; **to burn a hole in one's pocket** írsele a uno (*el dinero*) de entre las manos; **to make a hole in** agotar gran cantidad de; **to make a hole in one** (golf) conseguir de un solo golpe desde el tee que la pelota entre en el agujero; **to pick holes in** (coll.) hallar defectos en, poner reparos a ‖ *va* agujerear; (golf) meter en el agujero ‖ *vn* encovarse; **to hole out** (golf) conseguir que la pelota entre en el agujero; **to hole up** encovarse; buscar un escondrijo, buscar un rincón cómodo; hibernar (*un animal*)
**holey** ['holɪ] *adj* agujereado, hoyoso
**holiday** ['hɑlɪde] *s* día de fiesta; vacación; *adj* de fiesta, festivo
**holiday attire** *s* trapos de cristianar
**holidays with pay** *spl* (Brit.) vacaciones retribuídas
**holiness** ['holɪnɪs] *s* santidad; **his Holiness** su Santidad
**holla** [hə'lɑ] o ['hɑlə] *s, interj, va & vn* var. de **hollo**
**Holland** ['hɑlənd] *s* Holanda; (*l.c.*) *s* tela de lino o de lino y algodón (*que se usa para fabricar transparentes, para cubrir muebles, etc.*); **Hollands** *s* ginebra holandesa
**hollandaise sauce** ['hɑlən,dez] *s* salsa holandesa
**Hollander** ['hɑləndər] *s* holandés
**Holland gin** *s* ginebra holandesa
**hollo** [hə'lo] o ['hɑlo] *s* (*pl:* **-los**) grito; saludo; grito de triunfo; *interj* ¡ah!; ¡hola!; ¡vítor!; *va* decir a gritos; *vn* gritar
**holloa** [hə'lo] o ['hɑlo] *s, interj, va & vn* var. de **hollo**
**hollow** ['hɑlo] *adj* hueco, ahuecado; ahuecado, sepulcral (*dícese de la voz*); hundido (*dícese de los ojos o las mejillas*); hambriento; falso, engañoso, insincero, sin substancia; *adv* **to beat all hollow** (coll.) vencer completamente; *s* cavidad, hueco; depresión; vallecito; hueco (*de la mano*); *va* ahuecar, excavar; **to hollow out** ahuecar, excavar
**hollow-eyed** ['hɑlo,aɪd] *adj* con los ojos hundidos, trasojado
**hollow-ground** ['hɑlo'graʊnd] *adj* afilado con cara cóncava, vaciado
**holly** ['hɑlɪ] *s* (*pl:* **-lies**) (bot.) acebo
**hollyhock** ['hɑlɪhɑk] *s* (bot.) malva arbórea, loca, real o rósea
**holm** [hom] *s* vega; isleta de río; (bot.) encina
**holmium** ['holmɪəm] *s* (chem.) holmio
**holm oak** *s* (bot.) encina
**holocaine** ['hɑləken] *s* (pharm.) holocaína
**holocaust** ['hɑləkɔst] *s* holocausto (*sacrificio; destrucción total causado por un incendio; estrago general*)
**Holocene** ['hɑləsin] *adj* (geol.) holoceno
**Holofernes** [,hɑlə'fʌrniz] *s* (Bib.) Holofernes
**holograph** ['hɑləgræf] o ['hɑləgrɑf] *adj & s* olÓgrafo
**holohedral** [,hɑlə'hidrəl] *adj* (cryst.) holoédrico
**holothurian** [,hɑlə'θʊrɪən] *s* (zool.) holoturia
**holster** ['holstər] *s* pistolera
**holy** ['holɪ] *adj* (*comp:* **-lier;** *super:* **-liest**) santo; sagrado
**Holy Alliance** *s* Santa Alianza
**Holy Bible** *s* Santa Biblia
**Holy City** *s* Ciudad Santa (*Jerusalén, Roma, la Meca, etc.*); cielo, mansión de Dios
**Holy Communion** *s* sagrada comunión
**holyday** ['holɪ,de] o **holy day** *s* (eccl.) fiesta, día de guardar, día de precepto
**holyday of obligation** *s* (eccl.) día de guardar, día de precepto
**Holy Father** *s* Padre Santo
**Holy Ghost** *s* Espíritu Santo
**Holy Grail** *s* Santo Grial
**Holy Land** *s* Tierra santa (*lugares de Palestina*)
**Holy Office** *s* Santo Oficio
**holy of holies** *s* sanctasanctórum
**holy oil** *s* santo óleo
**holy orders** *spl* (eccl.) órdenes sagradas o sagradas órdenes; **to take holy orders** ordenarse, recibir las órdenes sagradas
**Holy Roman Empire** *s* Sacro Imperio Romano-Germánico
**holy rood** *s* crucifijo; (*caps.*) *s* Santa Cruz
**Holy Sacrament** *s* santísimo sacramento
**Holy Saturday** *s* sábado de gloria, sábado santo
**Holy Scripture** *s* Sagrada Escritura
**Holy See** *s* Santa Sede
**Holy Sepulcher** *s* santo sepulcro
**Holy Spirit** *s* Espíritu Santo
**holystone** ['holɪ,ston] *s* (naut.) piedra de cubierta; *va* (naut.) limpiar con piedra y arena
**Holy Synod** *s* santo sínodo (*de la Iglesia rusa*)
**Holy Thursday** *s* Jueves Santo; (Anglican Church) fiesta de la Ascensión
**holy water** *s* agua bendita
**Holy Week** *s* semana santa
**Holy Writ** *s* Sagrada Escritura
**homage** ['hɑmɪdʒ] o ['ɑmɪdʒ] *s* homenaje (*respeto*); (feud.) homenaje, pleito homenaje
**home** [hom] *s* casa, domicilio, hogar; patria chica; asilo (*para enfermos, pobres, etc.*); patria (*p.ej., de las artes*); (biol.) habitación; (sport) meta, límite, término; **at home** en casa; en su propio país; a gusto; de recibo; al corriente; (sport) en campo propio; **away from home** fuera de casa; **make yourself at home** está Vd. en su casa, haga como si estuviera en su casa, siéntase Vd. en su casa; *adj* casero, doméstico; nativo; regional; nacional; certero, eficaz; *adv* en casa; a casa; a o en su suelo nativo; **to bring** o **to drive home** exponer de modo muy convincente; **to see home** acompañar a casa, llevar a casa; **to strike home** dar en lo vivo; *va* mandar a casa; dar domicilio a; *vn* volver a casa; habitar; buscar la querencia
**home appliances** *spl* utensilios domésticos
**homebody** ['hom,bɑdɪ] *s* (*pl:* **-ies**) hogareño; acaserado (Am.)
**homebred** ['hom,brɛd] *adj* casero; sencillo, inculto, tosco
**home-brew** ['hom'bru] *s* vino o aguardiente caseros
**home-coming** ['hom,kʌmɪŋ] *s* regreso al hogar
**home country** *s* suelo natal
**home delivery** *s* distribución a domicilio
**home economics** *s* economía doméstica
**home fleet** *s* escuadra que defiende la metrópoli inglesa
**home freezer** *s* heladora casera
**home front** *s* frente doméstico
**home-grown** ['hom'gron] *adj* casero (*dícese de las verduras y frutas*)
**homeland** ['hom,lænd] *s* patria, tierra natal; (*cap.*) *s* (Brit.) metrópoli (*a distinción de las colonias*)
**homeless** ['homlɪs] *adj* sin casa ni hogar; inhabitable, inhospedable
**home life** *s* vida de familia, vida de hogar
**homelike** ['hom,laɪk] *adj* como de casa; cómodo
**home-loving** ['hom,lʌvɪŋ] *adj* casero, hogareño; acaserado (Am.)
**homely** ['homlɪ] *adj* (*comp:* **-lier;** *super:* **-liest**) feo; sencillo, simple, llano; casero, doméstico
**homemade** ['hom'med] *adj* casero
**homemaker** ['hom,mekər] *s* ama de casa
**home office** *s* casa central, oficina o establecimiento central o principal; (*caps.*) *s* (Brit.) ministerio de la Gobernación
**homeopath** ['homɪəpæθ] o ['hɑmɪəpæθ] *s* homeópata
**homeopathic** [,homɪə'pæθɪk] o [,hɑmɪə'pæθɪk] *adj* homeopático
**homeopathist** [,homɪ'ɑpəθɪst] o [,hɑmɪ'ɑpəθɪst] *s* var. de **homeopath**

**homeopathy** [ˌhomɪˈɑpəθɪ] o [ˌhɑmɪˈɑpəθɪ] *s* homeopatía
**home plate** *s* (baseball) puesto meta
**home port** *s* puerto de origen
**Homer** [ˈhomər] *s* Homero; (*l.c.*) *s* (coll.) paloma mensajera; (baseball) jonrón
**Homeric** [hoˈmɛrɪk] *adj* homérico
**Homeric laughter** *s* risa homérica
**home rule** *s* autonomía, gobierno autónomo
**home run** *s* (baseball) cuadrangular, jonrón
**Home Secretary** *s* (Brit.) ministro de Gobernación
**homesick** [ˈhomˌsɪk] *adj* nostálgico; **to be homesick (for)** sentir nostalgia (de)
**homesickness** [ˈhomˌsɪknɪs] *s* nostalgia, morriña de la tierra
**homespun** [ˈhomˌspʌn] *adj* casero, hilado en casa; sencillo, llano; *s* cachera, tela de fabricación casera; tela que remeda la de fabricación casera
**homestead** [ˈhomstɛd] *s* heredad, casa y sus terrenos; finca rural inalienable
**homesteader** [ˈhomstɛdər] *s* dueño de una heredad; (U.S.A.) colono que ha recibido sus tierras del gobierno nacional
**home stretch** *s* último trecho, esfuerzo final (*de una carrera*)
**home town** *s* ciudad natal
**homeward** [ˈhomwərd] *adj* de regreso; *adv* hacia casa; hacia su país
**homewards** [ˈhomwərdz] *adv* hacia casa; hacia su país
**homework** [ˈhomˌwʌrk] *s* trabajo en casa, trabajo a domicilio; trabajo escolar, deber
**homey** [ˈhomɪ] *adj* (*comp:* **homier;** *super:* **homiest**) (coll.) agradable, cómodo, sosegado, íntimo
**homicidal** [ˌhɑmɪˈsaɪdəl] *adj* homicida
**homicide** [ˈhɑmɪsaɪd] *s* homicidio (*acción*); homicida (*persona*)
**homiletic** [ˌhɑmɪˈlɛtɪk] *adj* de la homilía o las homilías; exhortatorio; **homiletics** *ssg* homilética
**homiliarium** [ˌhɑmɪlɪˈɛrɪəm] *s* homiliario
**homilist** [ˈhɑmɪlɪst] *s* homilista
**homily** [ˈhɑmɪlɪ] *s* (*pl:* **-lies**) homilía
**homing** [ˈhomɪŋ] *adj* querencioso; (mil.) buscador del blanco, seguidor
**homing pigeon** *s* paloma mensajera
**hominy** [ˈhɑmɪnɪ] *s* maíz molido
**homocercal** [ˌhoməˈsʌrkəl] *adj* (ichth.) homocerco
**homochlamydeous** [ˌhomokləˈmɪdɪəs] *adj* (bot.) homoclamídeo
**homogeneity** [ˌhomodʒɪˈniɪtɪ] o [ˌhɑmodʒɪˈniɪtɪ] *s* (*pl:* **-ties**) homogeneidad
**homogeneous** [ˌhomoˈdʒinɪəs] o [ˌhɑmoˈdʒinɪəs] *adj* homogéneo
**homogenization** [hoˌmɑdʒɪnɪˈzeʃən] o [ˌhoməˌdʒinɪˈzeʃən] *s* homogenización, homogeneización
**homogenize** [hoˈmɑdʒɪnaɪz] o [ˈhomədʒənaɪz] *va* homogenizar, homogeneizar
**homogenized milk** leche homogeneizada
**homograph** [ˈhɑməgræf] o [ˈhɑməgrɑf] *s* homógrafo
**homographic** [ˌhɑməˈgræfɪk] *adj* homógrafo
**homologous** [hoˈmɑləgəs] *adj* homólogo
**homologue** [ˈhɑmələg] o [ˈhɑməlɑg] *s* cosa homóloga; (biol.) parte u órgano homólogos
**homology** [hoˈmɑlədʒɪ] *s* (*pl:* **-gies**) homología
**homonym** [ˈhɑmənɪm] *s* homónimo
**homonymous** [hoˈmɑnɪməs] *adj* homónimo
**homonymy** [hoˈmɑnɪmɪ] *s* homonimia
**homophone** [ˈhɑməfon] *s* palabra homófona; letra homófona
**homophonic** [ˌhɑməˈfɑnɪk] *adj* (mus.) homófono
**homophonous** [hoˈmɑfənəs] *adj* (phonet.) homófono
**homophony** [hoˈmɑfənɪ] o [ˈhɑməˌfonɪ] *s* (phonet. & mus.) homofonía
**homopterous** [hoˈmɑptərəs] *adj* (ent.) homóptero
**homosexual** [ˌhoməˈsɛkʃʊəl] *adj & s* homosexual
**homosexuality** [ˌhoməˌsɛkʃʊˈælɪtɪ] *s* homosexualidad

**homunculus** [hoˈmʌŋkjələs] *s* (*pl:* **-li** [laɪ]) homúnculo, hombrecillo; figurín
**hon.** abr. de **honorably** y **honorary**
**Hon.** abr. de **Honorable**
**Honduran** [hɑnˈdurən] *adj & s* hondureño
**Honduras** [hɑnˈdurəs] *s* Honduras
**hone** [hon] *s* piedra de afilar; *va* afilar con piedra
**honest** [ˈɑnɪst] *adj* honrado, recto, probo; honesto (*recatado, decente*); genuino; bien habido o bien adquirido (*dinero*)
**honesty** [ˈɑnɪstɪ] *s* honradez, rectitud, probidad; honestidad; (bot.) hierba de la plata
**honey** [ˈhʌnɪ] *s* miel; dulzura; (coll.) vida mía, querido, querida; **it's a honey** (slang) es una preciosidad; *adj* meloso, dulce; (coll.) querido; (*pret & pp:* **-eyed** o **-ied**) *va* enmelar, untar con miel, endulzar con miel; adular, lisonjear; *vn* hablar con cariño, portarse blanda y suavemente
**honeybee** [ˈhʌnɪˌbi] *s* (ent.) abeja de miel, abeja doméstica
**honeycomb** [ˈhʌnɪˌkom] *s* panal; *adj* apanalado; *va* disponer a manera de panal; acribillar; llenar, penetrar
**honeycomb coil** *s* (rad.) bobina de panal, bobina nido de abeja
**honeycomb radiator** *s* (aut.) radiador de colmena, radiador de panal
**honeycomb stomach** *s* (zool.) redecilla
**honey creeper** *s* (orn.) azucarero
**honeydew** [ˈhʌnɪˌdju] o [ˈhʌnɪˌdu] *s* liga dulce (*de ciertas plantas e insectos*); melón muy dulce, blanco y terso
**honeyed** [ˈhʌnɪd] *adj* enmelado; meloso, dulce
**honey locust** *s* (bot.) acacia de tres espinas
**honeymoon** [ˈhʌnɪˌmun] *s* luna de miel; viaje de bodas, viaje de novios; *vn* pasar la luna de miel
**honey of rose** *s* (pharm.) miel rosada, rodomiel
**honeysuckle** [ˈhʌnɪˌsʌkəl] *s* (bot.) madreselva
**honeywort** [ˈhʌnɪˌwʌrt] *s* (bot.) ceriflor; (bot.) cruciata
**honied** [ˈhʌnɪd] *adj* var. de **honeyed**
**honk** [hɑŋk] o [hɔŋk] *s* graznido (*del ganso silvestre*); pitazo, bocinazo (*del automóvil*); *va* tocar (*la bocina*); *vn* graznar; tocar la bocina, pitar
**honkytonk** [ˈhɑŋkɪtɑŋk] o [ˈhɔŋkɪtɔŋk] *s* (slang) tasca, taberna de mala muerte
**honor** [ˈɑnər] *s* honor; (*cap.*) *s* señoría (*título*); **honors** *spl* honores; (bridge) honores; **in honor of** en honor de; **to deem it an honor to** + *inf* honrarse de + *inf;* **to do** o **to show honor to** hacer honor a; **to do the honors** hacer los honores; *va* honrar; hacer honor a (*su firma*); aceptar, pagar
**honorable** [ˈɑnərəbəl] *adj* honrado (*comerciante, negocio, etc.*); honroso (*comportamiento, puesto, etc.*); honorable (*digno de ser honrado*); (*cap.*) *adj* Honorable (*título*)
**honorable mention** *s* mención honorífica, mención honrosa
**honorarium** [ˌɑnəˈrɛrɪəm] *s* (*pl:* **-ums** o **-a** [ə]) honorario
**honorary** [ˈɑnəˌrɛrɪ] *adj* honorario
**honorary doctor's degree** *s* título de doctor honorario
**honorary member** *s* miembro de honor
**honorific** [ˌɑnəˈrɪfɪk] *adj* honorífico; *s* antenombre
**honors of war** *spl* honores de la guerra
**honor system** *s* acatamiento voluntario del reglamento
**honour** [ˈɑnər] *s & va* (Brit.) var. de **honor**
**hooch** [hutʃ] *s* (slang) licor, bebida alcohólica; (slang) licor de contrabando
**-hood** *suffix s* -dad, p.ej., **brotherhood** hermandad; **falsehood** falsedad; **likelihood** probabilidad; -ez, p.ej., **childhood** niñez; **widowhood** viudez
**hood** [hud] *s* capilla; capirote (*que cubre el rostro*); capillo o capirote (*de las aves de cetrería*); muceta o capirote (*de los doctores en los actos universitarios*); sombrerete (*de chimenea*); (aut.) capó, cubierta; (naut.) tambucho; (slang) gamberro; *va* encapirotar; ocultar; encapillar (*a un halcón*)

**hooded** ['hʊdɪd] *adj* capilludo; encapirotado; encapillado (*halcón*)
**hoodlum** ['hudləm] *s* (coll.) gamberro, maleante, matón
**hoodman-blind** ['hʊdmən,blaɪnd] *s* (archaic) gallina ciega (*juego*)
**hoodoo** ['hudu] *s* vodú o vudú; (coll.) aojo, mala suerte; (coll.) cenizo o gafe; *va* aojar, traer mala suerte a
**hoodwink** ['hʊdwɪŋk] *va* vendar los ojos a; burlar, engañar, emprimar
**hooey** ['huɪ] *s* (slang) música celestial; *interj* (slang) ¡ música celestial!
**hoof** [huf] o [hʊf] *s* casco, pezuña; pata (*de caballo, toro, etc.*); (hum.) pata (*del hombre*); animal ungulado; **on the hoof** en pie (*viviente; dícese del ganado*); *va & vn* (coll.) caminar; **to hoof it** (coll.) caminar, ir a pie; (slang) bailar
**hoofbeat** ['huf,bit] o ['hʊf,bit] *s* pisada (*de animal ungulado, aludiendo al ruido*)
**hoofed** [huft] o [hʊft] *adj* ungulado
**hook** [hʊk] *s* gancho; aldabilla (*gancho para cerrar una puerta, ventana, etc.*); anzuelo (*para pescar*); enganche (*para unir*); ángulo, recodo; hoz; (baseball & golf) vuelo torcido (*de la pelota*); (box.) crochet, golpe de gancho; (mus.) rabo (*de una corchea*); (fig.) anzuelo (*trampa*); **by hook or by crook** por fas o por nefas, a todo trance; **on one's own hook** (coll.) por cuenta propia; **to get the hook** (coll.) ser silbado (*un actor*); (coll.) ser echado de patitas a la calle; **to swallow the hook** (coll.) picar en el anzuelo, tragar el anzuelo ‖ *va* enganchar; encorvar, doblar; dar forma de anzuelo a; pescar, coger (*un pez*); acornar, herir con los cuernos; (baseball) lanzar (*la pelota*) imponiéndole vuelo torcido; (box.) dar un golpe de gancho a; (coll.) birlar, robar; **to hook in** echar el gancho a; **to hook it** (slang) irse, huir; **to hook on** acoplar con; **to hook up** enganchar; sujetar con corchetes; (elec.) montar ‖ *vn* engancharse; encorvarse, doblarse; tener forma de anzuelo; **to hook on** acoplarse con
**hooka** o **hookah** ['hʊkə] o ['hukə] *s* narguile
**hook and eye** *s* corchete (*broche compuesto de macho y hembra*)
**hook and ladder** *s* carro de escaleras de incendio
**hooked** [hʊkt] *adj* ganchudo, encorvado
**hooked rug** *s* tapete de crochet (*generalmente de fabricación casera*)
**hooker** ['hʊkər] *s* (naut.) balandro; (naut.) barcarrón
**hook ladder** *s* escalera de ganchos
**hookup** ['hʊk,ʌp] *s* montaje; (rad.) montaje; (rad.) esquema de montaje; (coll.) alianza, pacto
**hookworm** ['hʊk,wʌrm] *s* (zool.) anquilostoma; (path.) anquilostomiasis, anemia de los túneles, clorosis de Egipto
**hookworm disease** *s* (path.) anquilostomiasis, anemia de los túneles, clorosis de Egipto
**hooky** ['hʊkɪ] *adj* ganchudo, encorvado; *s* **to play hooky** hacer novillos
**hooligan** ['hulɪgən] *s* gamberro
**hooliganism** ['hulɪgənɪzəm] *s* gamberrismo
**hoop** [hup] o [hʊp] *s* aro; (croquet) aro; *va* enarcar, enzunchar
**hooper** ['hupər] o ['hʊpər] *s* tonelero
**hoopoe** ['hupu] *s* (orn.) abubilla, upupa
**hoop skirt** *s* miriñaque
**hooray** [hu're] *s, interj, va & vn* var. de **hurrah**
**Hoosier** ['huʒər] *s* natural o habitante del estado de Indiana, EE.UU.
**hoot** [hut] *s* ululato, resoplido; sofión; grito; *va* dar grita a gritos; silbar, reprobar a gritos; manifestar a gritos; echar a gritos (*p.ej., a un cómico*); *vn* ulular, resoplar
**hoot owl** *s* (orn.) autillo, cárabo
**hop** [hɑp] *s* brinquito, saltito; (coll.) vuelo en avión; (coll.) sarao; (coll.) baile; (bot.) lúpulo u hombrecillo; **hops** *spl* lúpulo (*flores disecadas*); (*pret & pp:* **hopped**; *ger:* **hopping**) *va* (coll.) cruzar o saltar de un salto; (coll.) atravesar (*p.ej., el mar*) en avión; (coll.) subir a (*un tren, taxi, etc.*); mezclar el lúpulo en (*la cerveza*); *vn* brincar, saltar; avanzar a saltitos; saltar a la pata coja (*saltar en un pie*); recoger lúpulo; **to hop off** (coll.) partir en avión; (coll.) bajar de (*un tren, taxi, etc.*); **to hop on** (coll.) subir a (*un tren, taxi, etc.*)
**hope** [hop] *s* esperanza; **to hope against hope** esperar desesperando; *va & vn* esperar; **to hope for** esperar; **to hope to** + *inf* esperar + *inf*
**hope chest** *s* arca que encierra la ropa, etc., que una joven guarda para cuando se case
**hopeful** ['hopfəl] *adj* esperanzado (*que tiene esperanza*); esperanzador (*que da esperanzas*); **young hopeful** muchacho prometedor, muchacha prometedora
**hopeless** ['hoplɪs] *adj* desesperanzado, desahuciado; desesperado (*p.ej., caso*)
**hoplite** ['hɑplaɪt] *s* hoplita
**hop-o'-my-thumb** ['hɑpəmaɪ'θʌm] *s* enano, gorgojo
**hopper** ['hɑpər] *s* persona o cosa que avanza a saltitos; persona o cosa que salta a la pata coja; (ent.) saltamontes; tolva; tragante (*de un alto horno*)
**hopper-bottom car** ['hɑpər,bɑtəm] *s* (rail.) vagón tolva
**hopscotch** ['hɑp,skɑtʃ] *s* infernáculo
**hop tree** *s* (bot.) cola de zorrillo
**Horace** ['hɑrɪs] o ['hɔrɪs] *s* Horacio
**Horatian** [ho'reʃən] *adj* horaciano
**horde** [hord] *s* horda
**horehound** ['hor,haʊnd] *s* (bot.) marrubio; extracto de marrubio; dulce de marrubio
**horizon** [hə'raɪzən] *s* horizonte; (fig.) horizonte
**horizontal** [,hɑrɪ'zɑntəl] o [,hɔrɪ'zɑntəl] *adj & s* horizontal
**horizontal bars** *spl* (sport) barras horizontales
**horizontal hold** *s* (telv.) bloqueo horizontal
**horizontal rudder** *s* (aer.) timón de profundidad
**horizontal stabilizer** *s* (aer.) plano de profundidad
**hormonal** [hɔr'monəl] *adj* hormonal
**hormone** ['hɔrmon] *s* (physiol.) hormón u hormona
**horn** [hɔrn] *s* cuerno (*prolongación ósea; materia*); asta o cuerno (*del toro*); (ent.) cuerno (*antena*); (fig.) cuerno (*de la luna, del yunque, etc.*); (mus. & naut.) cuerno; (mus.) trompa de armonía; bocina (*del automóvil o el fonógrafo*); promontorio; **to blow the horn** tocar la bocina; **to blow** o **toot one's own horn** cantar sus propias alabanzas; **to draw in** o **to pull in one's horns** contenerse, volverse atrás; *adj* de cuerno; *va* acornar, dar cornadas a; proveer de cuernos; *vn* tocar un cuerno; **to horn in** (slang) entremeterse (en)
**hornbeam** ['hɔrn,bim] *s* (bot.) carpe; (bot.) lechillo, palo de barranco (*Carpinus caroliniana*)
**hornbill** ['hɔrn,bɪl] *s* (orn.) cálao
**hornblende** ['hɔrn,blɛnd] *s* (mineral.) hornablenda
**hornbook** ['hɔrn,bʊk] *s* cartel (*para enseñar a leer*); cartilla (*para aprender a leer*)
**horned** [hɔrnd] *adj* cornudo, enastado
**horned toad** *s* (zool.) lagarto cornudo
**horned viper** *s* (zool.) víbora cornuda
**hornet** ['hɔrnɪt] *s* (ent.) avispón, crabrón
**hornet's nest** *s* panal del avispón; **to stir up a hornet's nest** (coll.) armar cisco, revolver el ajo
**hornfels** ['hɔrn,fɛls] *s* (geol.) corneana
**horn lightning arrester** *s* pararrayos de cuernos
**horn of a dilemma** *s* miembro de un dilema
**horn of plenty** *s* cuerno de la abundancia
**hornpipe** ['hɔrn,paɪp] *s* (mus.) chirimía; antigua danza inglesa que ejecuta una sola persona
**hornpout** ['hɔrn,paʊt] *s* (ichth.) amiuro nebuloso
**horn-rimmed spectacles** ['hɔrn,rɪmd] *spl* anteojos de concha
**horn ring** *s* (aut.) arco de la bocina
**horn silver** *s* (mineral.) plata córnea
**hornswoggle** ['hɔrn,swɑgəl] *va* (slang) estafar, embaucar, mistificar

**hornwork** ['hɔrn,wʌrk] *s* obra de cuerno; objetos de cuerno; (fort.) hornabeque
**horny** ['hɔrnɪ] *adj* (*comp:* **-ier;** *super:* **-iest**) córneo; cornudo; calloso
**horny-handed** ['hɔrnɪ'hændɪd] *adj* con manos callosas
**horologe** ['hɑrəlodʒ] o ['hɔrəlodʒ] *s* reloj (*solar, de agua, de arena, etc.*); (eccl.) horologio
**horologer** [ho'rɑlədʒər] *s* persona entendida en horología
**horology** [ho'rɑlədʒɪ] *s* horología
**horopter** [ho'rɑptər] *s* (opt.) horópter
**horopteric** [,hɑrɑp'tɛrɪk] *adj* horoptérico
**horoscope** ['hɑrəskop] o ['hɔrəskop] *s* (astrol.) horóscopo; **to cast a horoscope** (astrol.) sacar un horóscopo
**horoscopy** [ho'rɑskəpɪ] *s* horoscopia
**horrendous** [hɑ'rɛndəs] *adj* horrendo
**horrible** ['hɑrɪbəl] o ['hɔrɪbəl] *adj* horrible; (coll.) muy desagradable, asombroso
**horrid** ['hɑrɪd] o ['hɔrɪd] *adj* horrible, horroroso; (coll.) muy desagradable
**horrify** ['hɑrɪfaɪ] o ['hɔrɪfaɪ] (*pret & pp:* **-fied**) *va* horrorizar
**horripilation** [hɑ,rɪpɪ'leʃən] *s* (path.) horripilación
**horror** ['hɑrər] o ['hɔrər] *s* horror; (coll.) horror (*atrocidad*); **horrors!** ¡qué horror!; **the horrors** melancolía, morriña; (coll.) espasmo de horror; **to have a horror of** tener horror a
**hors de combat** [ˌɔrdə'kɑmbɑ] *adv* fuera de combate
**hors d'oeuvre** [ɔr'dʌvrə] *s* (*pl:* **-vres** [vrə]) entremés
**horse** [hɔrs] *s* caballo; caballete (*de carpintero*); gualdera o zanca (*de escalera*); potro (*de gimnasio*); (mil.) caballería (*cuerpo de soldados*); **hold your horses** pare Vd. el carro (*conténgase Vd.*); **to back the wrong horse** (coll.) jugar a la carta mala; **to horse!** ¡a caballo!; **horse of another color** harina de otro costal; *adj* caballar, hípico; montado; *va* proveer de un caballo o de caballos; cargar con, llevar a cuestas; azotar; cubrir (*el caballo a la yegua*); (naut.) calafatear; (slang) acosar, fatigar; (slang) ridiculizar; *vn* andar a caballo; estar (*la yegua*) salida; **to horse around** (slang) hacer payasadas, usar de chanzas pesadas
**horseback** ['hɔrs,bæk] *s* lomo de caballo; **on horseback** a caballo; *adv* a caballo; **to ride horseback** montar a caballo
**horse bean** *s* (bot.) haba caballuna o panosa
**horse blanket** *s* manta para caballos
**horse block** *s* montadero
**horse box** *s* (Brit.) vagón de transportar caballos
**horsebreaker** ['hɔrs,brekər] *s* caballista, domador de caballos
**horsecar** ['hɔrs,kɑr] *s* tranvía de sangre; vagón o carro de transportar caballos
**horse chestnut** *s* (bot.) castaño de Indias; castaña de Indias (*fruto*)
**horse collar** *s* collera
**horse dealer** *s* chalán
**horse doctor** *s* veterinario
**horseflesh** ['hɔrs,flɛʃ] *s* carne de caballo; caballos
**horsefly** ['hɔrs,flaɪ] *s* (*pl:* **-flies**) (ent.) tábano; (ent.) mosca borriquera
**Horse Guards** *spl* (Brit.) brigada de guardias montadas; cuartel general del ejército de la Gran Bretaña
**horsehair** ['hɔrs,hɛr] *s* pelo de caballo; cerda de caballo; tela de crin; *adj* hecho de cerda de caballo; rellenado de cerda de caballo; cubierto con tela de crin
**horsehide** ['hɔrs,haɪd] *s* cuero de caballo (*curtido o sin curtir*)
**horse latitudes** *spl* latitudes de calma (*cerca del grado 30 de latitud norte o sur*)
**horse laugh** *s* risotada
**horseleech** ['hɔrs,litʃ] *s* (ent.) sanguijuela borriquera
**horseless** ['hɔrslɪs] *adj* sin caballo; automóvil
**horse mackerel** *s* (ichth.) atún; (ichth.) bonito
**horseman** ['hɔrsmən] *s* (*pl:* **-men**) jinete; caballista
**horsemanship** ['hɔrsmənʃɪp] *s* equitación, manejo
**horse marine** *s* individuo de un cuerpo legendario de soldados de marina metidos a soldados de caballería; persona fuera de su elemento natural
**horse meat** *s* carne de caballo
**horse mint** *s* (bot.) mastranzo
**horse nail** *s* clavo de herrar
**horse opera** *s* (slang) cine espeluznante que se desarrolla en el oeste de los EE.UU.
**horse pistol** *s* pistola de arzón
**horseplay** ['hɔrs,ple] *s* payasada, chanza pesada
**horsepower** ['hɔrs,pauər] *s* (mech.) caballo de vapor inglés (*746 vatios*)
**horsepower-hour** ['hɔrs,pauər'aur] *s* (mech.) caballo de fuerza hora, caballo hora
**horse race** *s* carrera de caballos
**horse racing** *s* carreras, hipismo
**horseradish** ['hɔrs,rædɪʃ] *s* (bot.) rábano picante o rusticano; raíz de rábano picante o rusticano; mostaza de los alemanes
**horse sense** *s* (coll.) sentido común
**horseshoe** ['hɔrs,ʃu] *s* herradura; **horseshoes** *spl* juego parecido al de tejos en el que se tira a un hito con herraduras
**horseshoe arch** *s* (arch.) arco de herradura
**horseshoe crab** *s* (zool.) cangrejo bayoneta
**horseshoe magnet** *s* imán de herradura
**horseshoe nail** *s* clavo de herradura, clavo de herrar
**horseshoer** ['hɔrs,ʃuər] *s* herrador; encasquillador (Am.)
**horse show** *s* concurso hípico
**horsetail** ['hɔrs,tel] *s* cola de caballo; (bot.) cola de caballo, equiseto
**horse thief** *s* cuatrero
**horse tick** *s* (ent.) mosca borriquera, hipobosco
**horse-trade** ['hɔrs,tred] *vn* (fig.) chalanear
**horse trading** *s* (fig.) chalaneo
**horse-trading** ['hɔrs,tredɪŋ] *adj* (fig.) chalanesco
**horsewhip** ['hɔrs,hwɪp] *s* látigo; (*pret & pp:* **-whipped;** *ger:* **-whipping**) *va* dar latigazos a
**horsewoman** ['hɔrs,wumən] *s* (*pl:* **-women**) amazona, caballista
**horsy** ['hɔrsɪ] *adj* (*comp:* **-ier;** *super:* **-iest**) caballar, hípico; turfista, carrerista; (slang) desmañado
**hortative** ['hɔrtətɪv] o **hortatory** ['hɔrtə,torɪ] *adj* hortatorio
**Hortense** [hɔr'tɛns] *s* Hortensia
**horticultural** [,hɔrtɪ'kʌltʃərəl] *adj* hortícola
**horticulture** ['hɔrtɪ,kʌltʃər] *s* horticultura
**horticulturist** [,hɔrtɪ'kʌltʃərɪst] *s* horticultor
**Hos.** abr. de **Hosea**
**hosanna** [ho'zænə] *s & interj* hosanna
**Hosanna Sunday** *s* domingo de ramos
**hose** [hoz] *spl* calzas; *s* (*pl:* **hose**) media; calcetín; (*pl:* **hose** o **hoses**) manguera; *va* regar o limpiar con un chorro de agua (*que sale de una manguera*)
**Hosea** [ho'ziə] o [ho'zeə] *s* (Bib.) Oseas
**hoseman** ['hozmən] *s* (*pl:* **-men**) manguero
**hosier** ['hoʒər] *s* mediero, calcetero
**hosiery** ['hoʒərɪ] *s* medias, calcetas o calcetines; géneros de punto; calcetería
**hosiery shop** *s* calcetería
**hospice** ['hɑspɪs] *s* hospicio
**hospitable** ['hɑspɪtəbəl] o [hɑs'pɪtəbəl] *adj* hospitalario
**hospital** ['hɑspɪtəl] *s* hospital
**hospitaler** ['hɑspɪtələr] *s* (Brit.) hospitalero; (hist.) hospitalario; (*cap.*) *s* (hist.) hospitalario
**hospitality** [,hɑspɪ'tælɪtɪ] *s* (*pl:* **-ties**) hospitalidad
**hospitalization** [,hɑspɪtəlɪ'zeʃən] *s* hospitalización
**hospitalize** ['hɑspɪtəlaɪz] *va* hospitalizar
**hospital ship** *s* (mil.) buque hospital
**hospital train** *s* (mil.) tren hospital
**host** [host] *s* anfitrión; huésped (*persona que hospeda a otra*); mesonero, posadero; hueste (*ejército*); multitud, sinnúmero; (bot. & zool.) huésped; (*cap.*) *s* (eccl.) hostia; **to reckon without one's host** echar la cuenta sin la huéspeda o no contar con la huéspeda
**hostage** ['hɑstɪdʒ] *s* rehén; **to be held a hostage** quedar en rehenes; **to carry off as a hostage** llevarse en rehenes; **to give hos-**

**tages to fortune** tener prendas que perder; **to hold as a hostage** retener como rehén
**hostel** [ˈhastəl] *s* parador; casa de huéspedes (*para caminantes, biciclistas, etc.*); (Brit.) residencia de estudiantes
**hostelry** [ˈhastəlrɪ] *s* (*pl:* **-ries**) parador
**hostess** [ˈhostɪs] *s* huéspeda; dueña, patrona; maestra de ceremonias (*en un cabaret*); (aer.) azafata
**hostile** [ˈhastɪl] *adj* hostil
**hostility** [hasˈtɪlɪtɪ] *s* (*pl:* **-ties**) hostilidad; **hostilities** *spl* hostilidades (*guerra*); **to cease hostilities** cesar en las hostilidades; **to start hostilities** romper las hostilidades
**hostler** [ˈhaslər] o [ˈaslər] *s* establero, mozo de cuadra, mozo de paja y cebada; (rail.) encargado de la locomotora al fin del recorrido
**hot** [hat] *adj* (*comp:* **hotter;** *super:* **hottest**) caliente (*agua, café, aire, etc.*); cálido (*clima, país, etc.; sabor*); en caliente (*remachado*); acre, picante; caluroso, apasionado; violento (*genio*); fresco, reciente (*rastro de un animal*); caliente (*en celo*); enérgico (*p.ej., perseguimiento*); muy activo; (coll.) intolerable; (coll.) caliente (*cerca de lo que se busca*); (coll.) cargado (*de electricidad*); (coll.) muy radiactivo; (slang) recién robado, recién pasado de contrabando; (slang) chic, de la última moda; **to be hot** hacer calor (*dícese del tiempo*); tener calor (*p.ej., una persona*); **to blow hot and cold** ser veleta, mudar a todos los vientos; **to make it hot for** (coll.) hostilizar; *adv* con calor; ardientemente, apasionadamente; sin piedad; **to run hot** recalentarse (*un motor, un cojinete*); **hot and heavy** airadamente; con violencia, sin piedad
**hot air** *s* (slang) palabrería, música celestial
**hot-air engine** [ˈhatˈɛr] *s* máquina de aire caliente
**hot-air furnace** *s* calorífero de aire
**hot-air heating** *s* calefacción por aire caliente
**hot and cold running water** *s* circulación de agua fría y caliente
**hot atom** *s* (phys.) átomo cálido
**hot baths** *spl* caldas, termas, baños termales
**hotbed** [ˈhat,bɛd] *s* (hort.) almajara (*abrigada artificialmente*); (fig.) sementera, semillero
**hot-blast stove** [ˈhat,blæst] o [ˈhat,blast] *s* (metal.) recuperador de Cowper
**hot-blooded** [ˈhatˈblʌdɪd] *adj* de malas pulgas; apasionado, de sangre ardiente; temerario, irreflexivo
**hotbox** [ˈhat,baks] *s* (rail.) cojinete recalentado
**hot bulb** *s* (mach.) bola caliente
**hot cake** *s* torta o tortita a la plancha; **to sell like hot cakes** (coll.) venderse como pan bendito
**hotchpotch** [ˈhatʃ,patʃ] *s* var. de **hodgepodge**
**hot cross bun** *s* bollo marcado con la figura de una cruz (*que se come el viernes santo*)
**hot dog** *s* (slang) perro caliente
**hotel** [hoˈtɛl] *s* hotel; *adj* hotelero
**hotelkeeper** [hoˈtɛl,kipər] *s* hotelero
**hotfoot** [ˈhat,fʊt] *adv* (coll.) más que de prisa; *va* (coll.) seguir o perseguir a toda prisa; **to hotfoot it** (coll.) ir más que de prisa; *vn* (coll.) ir más que de prisa
**hot-galvanize** [ˈhatˈgælvənaɪz] *va* galvanizar en caliente, cincar al fuego
**hothead** [ˈhat,hɛd] *s* persona irritable, persona de mal genio; persona temeraria o impetuosa; agitador, alborotador
**hot-headed** [ˈhatˈhɛdɪd] *adj* caliente de cascos; temerario, irreflexivo, impetuoso; agitador, alborotador
**hothouse** [ˈhat,haus] *s* invernáculo, estufa
**hot pad** *s* almohadilla caliente eléctrica
**hot plate** *s* calientaplatos, hornillo (*portátil*)
**hot-press** [ˈhat,prɛs] *s* prensa térmica; prensa de satinar papel en caliente; *va* prensar en caliente
**hot rod** *s* (slang) bólido (*automóvil desguarnecido y con motor reforzado*)
**hot seat** *s* (coll.) situación dificultosa; (coll.) situación de gran responsabilidad; (aer.) asiento lanzable; (slang) silla eléctrica
**hotshot** [ˈhat,ʃat] *adj* (slang) rápido, diestro, próspero, ostentoso, importante; *s* tren rápido de mercancías perecederas; vehículo muy rápido, avión muy rápido; obrero muy perito; deportista muy diestro (*especialmente en golpeando una pelota*); (slang) persona de muchas campanillas
**hot spot** *s* punto caliente; (coll.) cabaret
**hot springs** *spl* fuentes termales
**hotspur** [ˈhat,spʌr] *s* persona temeraria o impetuosa
**hot stuff** *s* (slang) persona extraordinaria, cosa formidable
**hot-tempered** [ˈhatˈtɛmpərd] *adj* irascible, de genio vivo y colérico
**Hottentot** [ˈhatəntat] *adj* & *s* hotentote
**hot water** *s* (coll.) lío, aprieto, dificultades
**hot-water bag** [ˈhatˈwɔtər] o [ˈhatˈwatər] *s* bolsa de agua caliente
**hot-water boiler** *s* termosifón (*para calentar agua o un edificio*)
**hot-water bottle** *s* bolsa de agua caliente
**hot-water heater** *s* calentador de agua, calentador de acumulación; calefón (Am.)
**hot-water heating** *s* calefacción por agua caliente
**hot-water tank** *s* depósito de agua caliente
**hot-wire** [ˈhat,waɪr] *adj* (elec.) de hilo caliente
**hot-wire ammeter** *s* (elec.) amperímetro de hilo caliente, amperímetro térmico
**houdah** [ˈhaudə] *s* var. de **howdah**
**hough** [hak] *s* corvejón (*del caballo; de varias aves gallináceas*)
**hound** [haund] *s* podenco; perro; canalla; **to follow the hounds** o **to ride to hounds** cazar con jauría; *va* rondar, acosar
**hound's-tongue** [ˈhaundz,tʌŋ] *s* (bot.) cinoglosa, viniebla
**houppelande** [ˈhuplænd] *s* hopalanda
**hour** [aur] *s* hora; hora actual, momento; **Hours** *spl* (myth.) Horas; **after hours** fuera de horas; **at all hours** a todas horas; muy tarde; **by the hour** por horas; **in an evil hour** en hora mala; **to keep late hours** trasnochar, acostarse tarde; **on the hour** a la hora en punto, cada hora; **to work long hours** trabajar muchas horas cada día; **hours on end** horas enteras
**hour circle** *s* (astr.) círculo horario
**hourglass** [ˈaur,glæs] o [ˈaur,glas] *s* reloj de arena
**hour hand** *s* horario
**houri** [ˈhurɪ] o [ˈhaurɪ] *s* (*pl:* **-ris**) hurí (*del paraíso de Mahoma*)
**hourly** [ˈaurlɪ] *adj* de cada hora, repetido cada hora; repetido, frecuente; *adv* cada hora; muy a menudo
**house** [haus] *s* (*pl:* **houses** [ˈhauzɪz]) casa; cámara (*legislativa*); edificio; teatro (*edificio y público*); entrada (*número de personas que asisten a un espectáculo*), p.ej., **a good house** mucha entrada; **on the house** a expensas del dueño; **to bring down the house** (coll.) hacer venirse abajo el teatro (*con aplausos*); **to clean house** hacer la limpieza de la casa; poner fin al desbarajuste (*municipal, del estado, de una casa de comercio, etc.*); **to keep house** tener casa propia; gobernar su casa; ser ama de su casa; hacer los quehaceres domésticos; **to put** o **to set one's house in order** arreglar sus asuntos; *adj* domiciliario; doméstico; de la casa; casero; [hauz] *va* alojar, hospedar; domiciliar; (agr.) entrojar; (carp. & mach.) encajar; **to house in** cubrir, encerrar; *vn* morar, albergarse
**house arrest** *s* arresto domiciliario
**houseboat** [ˈhaus,bot] *s* barco-habitación, casa flotante, embarcación en forma de casa flotante que sirve de habitación
**housebreaker** [ˈhaus,brekər] *s* escalador
**housebreaking** [ˈhaus,brekɪŋ] *s* escalo, allanamiento de morada
**housebroken** [ˈhaus,brokən] *adj* (*perro o gato*) hecho a la casa, enseñado (*a hábitos de limpieza*)
**house cleaning** *s* limpieza de la casa; (fig.) limpieza
**house coat** *s* bata
**house current** *s* (elec.) red o sector de distribución, canalización de consumo; corriente de red
**house dog** *s* perro de casa; perro de guardia
**housefly** [ˈhaus,flaɪ] *s* (*pl:* **-flies**) (ent.) mosca doméstica
**houseful** [ˈhausful] *s* casa llena, p.ej., **a**

**houseful of guests** una casa llena de convidados
**housefurnishings** ['haus,fʌrnɪʃɪŋz] *spl* ajuar, menaje, enseres domésticos
**household** ['haushold] *s* casa, familia; *adj* casero, doméstico
**household bread** *s* pan casero, pan bazo
**householder** ['haus,holdər] *s* amo o dueño de casa; jefe de familia
**household goods** *spl* enseres domésticos
**household linen** *s* var. de **flatwork**
**household word** *s* frase hecha, palabra de uso corriente
**house hunting** *s* busca de casa; **to go house hunting** ir a buscar casa
**housekeeper** ['haus,kipər] *s* mujer de casa, ama de casa; casera, ama de llaves; mujer de gobierno
**housekeeping** ['haus,kipɪŋ] *s* quehaceres domésticos; manejo doméstico, gobierno doméstico; **to set up housekeeping** poner casa
**housekeeping apartment** *s* cuarto o piso con cocina
**houseleek** ['haus,lik] *s* (bot.) hierba puntera, barba de Júpiter, siempreviva mayor
**houseline** ['haus,laɪn] *s* (naut.) piola
**housemaid** ['haus,med] *s* criada de casa
**housemaid's knee** *s* (path.) sinovitis de la rodilla, rodilla de fregona
**house meter** *s* contador de abonado
**housemother** ['haus,mʌðər] *s* mujer encargada de una residencia de alumnos
**house mouse** *s* (zool.) ratón casero
**house of assignation** *s* casa de citas
**house of cards** *s* castillo de naipes
**House of Commons** *s* (Brit.) Cámara de los Comunes
**house of correction** *s* casa de corrección
**house of God** *s* casa de Dios (*iglesia*)
**house of ill fame** o **ill repute** *s* burdel, lupanar
**House of Lords** *s* (Brit.) Cámara de los Lores
**house of prayer** *s* casa de oración
**House of Representatives** *s* (U.S.A.) Cámara de Representantes
**house of worship** *s* edificio destinado al culto
**house painter** *s* pintor de brocha gorda
**house party** *s* convite o tertulia de varios días (*especialmente en la casa de campo del anfitrión*); (los) convidados
**house physician** *s* médico residente (*de un hospital*); médico de asiento (*en un hotel*)
**house plant** *s* planta de invernadero, planta de maceta
**houseroom** ['haus,rum] o ['haus,rʊm] *s* alojamiento, cabida (*en una casa*)
**housetop** ['haus,tɑp] *s* tejado (*parte superior y exterior de la casa*); **to shout from the housetops** pregonar a los cuatro vientos
**housewares** ['haus,wɛrz] *spl* ajuar, menaje
**housewarming** ['haus,wɔrmɪŋ] *s* tertulia para celebrar el estreno de una casa; **to have a housewarming** estrenar la casa
**housewife** ['haus,waɪf] *s* (*pl:* **-wives** [,waɪvz]) ama o dueña de casa; madre de familia; ['hʌzɪf] *s* (*pl:* **-wives** [ɪvz]) estuche de costura
**housewifely** ['haus,waɪflɪ] *adj* de ama de casa, propio de un ama de casa; hacendosa
**housewifery** ['haus,waɪfərɪ] o ['haus,waɪfrɪ] *s* quehaceres domésticos, gobierno doméstico (*del ama de casa*)
**housework** ['haus,wʌrk] *s* quehaceres domésticos
**housing** ['hauzɪŋ] *s* alojamiento; abrigo, albergue; edificación (*de casas*); casas; gualdrapa (*del caballo*); (aut.) cárter; (carp.) encaje, muesca; (mach.) caja, bastidor; (naut.) piola; **housings** *spl* arreos, jaeces
**housing development** *s* colonia, viviendas nuevas
**housing shortage** *s* crisis de vivienda
**hove** [hov] *pret & pp de* **heave**
**hovel** ['hʌvəl] o ['hɑvəl] *s* casucha, choza, pocilga; cobertizo
**hover** ['hʌvər] o ['hɑvər] *va* mover (*las alas*) sin avanzar; cubrir con las alas; *vn* cernerse (*un ave*); revolotear; andar cerca; dudar, vacilar; asomar (*p.ej., una sonrisa en los labios de una persona*); estar algún tiempo (*p.ej., entre la vida y la muerte*)
**how** [hau] *adv* cómo; a cómo p.ej., **how do you sell the apples?** ¿a cómo vende Vd. las manzanas?; **how early** cuándo, a qué hora; **how else** de qué otra manera; **how far** qué distancia; a qué distancia; hasta dónde; cuánto, p.ej., **how far is it to the station?** ¿cuánto hay de aquí a la estación?; **how late** cuándo, a qué hora; **how long** cuánto, cuánto tiempo; hasta cuándo; **how many** cuántos; **how much** cuánto; lo mucho que, p.ej., **you don't know how much I have traveled in Spain** no sabe Vd. lo mucho que he viajado por España; **how now?** ¿pues qué?; **how often** cuántas veces; **how old are you?** ¿cuántos años tiene Vd.?; **how so?** ¿cómo así?; **how soon** cuándo, a qué hora; **how** + *adj* qué + *adj*, p.ej., **how beautiful she is!** ¡qué hermosa es!; cuán + *adj* o *adv.*, p.ej., **you do not know how rich he is** Vd. no sabe cuán rico es; lo + *adj*, p.ej., **do you realize how hard it is?** ¿se da Vd. cuenta de lo difícil que es?
**howbeit** [hau'biɪt] *adv* no obstante, sin embargo
**howdah** ['haudə] *s* castillo (*montura sobre un elefante*)
**how-do-you-do** ['haudəjə'du] *s* (coll.) situación enojosa; **that's a fine** (o **pretty** o **nice**) **how-do-you-do!** (coll.) ¡buena es ésa (o ésta)!
**howe'er** [hau'ɛr] *adv* var. de **however**
**however** [hau'ɛvər] *adv* sin embargo, a pesar de eso; por muy . . . que, p.ej., **however hard it is** por muy difícil que sea; por mucho . . . que, p.ej., **however cold it is** por mucho frío que haga; como quiera que, p.ej., **however you do it, do it well** como quiera que lo haga, hágalo bien; (coll.) cómo, p.ej., **however did you manage to get it?** ¿cómo se ingenió Vd. para conseguirlo?; **however much** por mucho que
**howitzer** ['hauɪtsər] *s* obús, cañón obús
**howl** [haul] *s* aullido, alarido; chillido; risa muy aguda; bramido (*del viento*); *va* decir a gritos; echar a gritos; **to howl down** imponerse a gritos a (*una persona*); *vn* aullar, dar alaridos; chillar; bramar (*el viento*); reír a más no poder
**howler** ['haulər] *s* aullador; (zool.) aullador, mono aullador; (coll.) plancha, desacierto
**howling** ['haulɪŋ] *adj* aullador; (slang) clamoroso, ruidoso (*éxito*); *s* (rad.) aullido
**howling monkey** *s* (zool.) mono aullador, mono chillón
**howsoever** [,hauso'ɛvər] *adv* como quiera que; por muy . . . que
**hoyden** ['hɔɪdən] *s* muchacha traviesa, tunantuela
**hoydenish** ['hɔɪdənɪʃ] *adj* traviesa, tunantuela
**HP, H.P., hp.** o **h.p.** abr. de **horsepower**
**hr.** abr. de **hour** o **hours**
**H.R.** abr. de **House of Representatives**
**H.R.H.** abr. de **Her Royal Highness** y **His Royal Highness**
**hrs.** abr. de **hours**
**ht.** abr. de **height**
**H.T.** abr. de **Hawaiian Territory**
**hub** [hʌb] *s* cubo (*de rueda*); (fig.) eje, centro
**hubble** ['hʌbəl] *s* elevación, prominencia, aspereza
**hubble-bubble** ['hʌbəl,bʌbəl] *s* narguile; gluglú (*de un líquido*); vocerío confuso
**hubbly** ['hʌblɪ] *adj* fragoso, quebrado, áspero
**hubbub** ['hʌbʌb] *s* alboroto, tumulto; gritería
**hubcap** ['hʌb,kæp] *s* (aut.) sombrerete, tapón de cubo, tapacubo
**huck** [hʌk] o **huckaback** ['hʌkəbæk] *s* tejido granito
**huckleberry** ['hʌkəl,bɛrɪ] *s* (*pl:* **-ries**) (bot.) planta ericácea y su baya (*Gaylussacia baccata*)
**huckster** ['hʌkstər] *s* buhonero; vendedor ambulante (*especialmente de hortalizas*); traficante despreciable; sujeto ruin; (slang) empresario de publicidad; *vn* vender por las calles; regatear
**huddle** ['hʌdəl] *s* pelotón, tropel; confusión, precipitación; (football) círculo que forman los jugadores para recibir señas; (coll.) reunión secreta; **to go into a huddle** (slang) conferenciar en secreto; *va* hacer o terminar

aprisa y mal; ponerse (*la ropa*) aprisa y mal; amontonar desordenadamente; **to huddle oneself up** arrimarse cómodamente; *vn* amontonarse; acurrucarse, arrimarse; (football) formar círculo para recibir señas

**Hudson seal** ['hʌdsən] *s* piel de almizclera teñida (*que remeda la piel de foca*)

**hue** [hju] *s* tinte, matiz, color; grita, gritería; **hue and cry** vocería de alarma o de indignación

**huff** [hʌf] *s* arrebato de cólera, enojo súbito; **in a huff** encolerizado, ofendido; *va* encolerizar, ofender; (checkers) soplar

**huffy** ['hʌfɪ] *adj* (*comp:* **-ier;** *super:* **-iest**) enojadizo, resentido

**hug** [hʌg] *s* abrazo (*de cariño, de oso, de luchador, etc.*); (*pret & pp:* **hugged;** *ger:* **hugging**) *va* abrazar, apretar con los brazos; ahogar entre los brazos (*dícese de un oso*); afirmarse en (*una opinión*); navegar muy cerca de (*la costa u orilla*); ceñirse a (*p.ej., un muro*); *vn* abrazarse; arrimarse

**huge** [hjudʒ] *adj* enorme, inmenso, descomunal

**hugger-mugger** ['hʌgər'mʌgər] *s* confusión, desorden, embrollo; *adj* confuso, embrollado, sin pies ni cabeza; *adv* desordenadamente

**Hugh** [hju] *s* Hugo

**Huguenot** ['hjugənɑt] *s* hugonote

**huh** [hʌ] *interj* ¡ eh!

**hula-hula** ['hulə'hulə] *s* baile típico de Hawai

**hulk** [hʌlk] *s* casco (*de un barco más o menos inservible*); carcamán, carraca (*buque malo y pesado*); pontón (*que sirve de cárcel*); armatoste (*máquina o mueble tosco; persona corpulenta e inútil*)

**hulking** ['hʌlkɪŋ] *adj* pesado, grueso

**hull** [hʌl] *s* casco (*de un barco o hidroavión*); armazón (*de un dirigible rígido*); vaina, hollejo (*de ciertas legumbres*); cáliz (*p.ej., de la fresa*); **hull down** (naut.) que se ven sólo las jarcias (*dícese de un barco en el horizonte*); *va* dar en el casco de (*un barco*); desvainar, deshollejar; mondar, pelar

**hullabaloo** ['hʌləbə,lu] o [,hʌləbə'lu] *s* alboroto, baraúnda, gritería, tumulto

**hullo** [hə'lo] *s* (*pl:* **-los**) var. de **hello** y **hollo;** *interj & vn* var. de **hello** y **hollo**

**hum** [hʌm] *s* tarareo, canturreo; zumbido (*de una abeja, máquina, etc.*); *interj* ¡ ejem!; (*pret & pp:* **hummed;** *ger:* **humming**) *va* tararear, canturrear; **to hum to sleep** arrullar; *vn* tararear, canturrear; zumbar; (coll.) estar muy activo; **to keep things humming** o **to make things hum** (coll.) ejecutar las cosas de una manera viva y fogosa

**human** ['hjumən] *adj & s* humano

**human being** *s* ser humano

**humane** [hju'men] *adj* humano (*compasivo, misericordioso; civilizador*)

**humanism** ['hjumənɪzəm] *s* humanismo

**humanist** ['hjumənɪst] *adj & s* humanista

**humanistic** [,hjumə'nɪstɪk] *adj* humanístico

**humanitarian** [hju,mænɪ'tɛrɪən] *adj & s* humanitario

**humanitarianism** [hju,mænɪ'tɛrɪənɪzəm] *s* humanitarismo

**humanity** [hju'mænɪtɪ] *s* (*pl:* **-ties**) humanidad; **the humanities** las humanidades

**humanize** ['hjumənaɪz] *va* humanizar; *vn* humanizarse

**humankind** ['hjumən'kaɪnd] *s* género humano

**humanly** ['hjumənlɪ] *adv* humanamente (*según las fuerzas humanas*)

**Humbert** ['hʌmbərt] *s* Humberto

**humble** ['hʌmbəl] o ['ʌmbəl] *adj* humilde; *va* humillar

**humblebee** ['hʌmbəl,bi] *s* var. de **bumblebee**

**humbleness** ['hʌmbəlnɪs] o ['ʌmbəlnɪs] *s* humildad

**humble pie** *s* empanada de menudo de venado; **to eat humble pie** someterse humildemente, reconocer el error y pedir perdón

**humbug** ['hʌm,bʌg] *s* farsa, patraña; embaucamiento; farsante, patrañero; (*pret & pp:* **-bugged;** *ger:* **-bugging**) *va* embaucar, engaitar

**humbuggery** ['hʌm,bʌgərɪ] *s* embaucamiento, engaño

**humdinger** [hʌm'dɪŋər] *s* (slang) persona extraordinaria, cosa formidable

**humdrum** ['hʌm,drʌm] *adj* monótono; *s* monotonía; charla monótona; machaca (*persona*)

**humeral** ['hjumərəl] *adj* (anat.) humeral; (anat.) braquial

**humeral veil** *s* (eccl.) humeral

**humerus** ['hjumərəs] *s* (*pl:* **-i** [aɪ]) (anat.) húmero; (anat.) brazo (*desde el hombro hasta el codo*)

**humic** ['hjumɪk] *adj* (chem.) húmico

**humid** ['hjumɪd] *adj* húmedo

**humidification** [hju,mɪdɪfɪ'keʃən] *s* humectación

**humidifier** [hju'mɪdɪ,faɪər] *s* humectador

**humidify** [hju'mɪdɪfaɪ] (*pret & pp:* **-fied**) *va* humedecer

**humidity** [hju'mɪdɪtɪ] *s* humedad

**humidor** ['hjumɪdər] *s* bote humectativo (*para tabaco de fumar*); humectador (*en la industria de hilandería*)

**humifuse** ['hjumɪfjuz] *adj* (bot.) humifuso

**humiliate** [hju'mɪlɪet] *va* humillar

**humiliating** [hju'mɪlɪ,etɪŋ] *adj* humillante

**humiliation** [hju,mɪlɪ'eʃən] *s* humillación

**humility** [hju'mɪlɪtɪ] *s* (*pl:* **-ties**) humildad

**humin** ['hjumɪn] *s* (biochem.) humina

**humming** ['hʌmɪŋ] *adj* zumbrador; (coll.) animado, vivo

**hummingbird** ['hʌmɪŋ,bʌrd] *s* (orn.) colibrí, pájaro mosca, picaflor

**hummock** ['hʌmək] *s* mogote, morón; hummock, lomo o mole de hielo

**hummocky** ['hʌməkɪ] *adj* a modo de mogote; fragoso, escabroso

**humor** ['hjumər] o ['jumər] *s* humor; humorismo; **bad humor** mal humor; **good humor** buen humor; **out of humor** de mal humor; **to be in the humor for** tener ganas de; *va* seguir el humor a; acomodarse a; manejar suavemente

**humoresque** [,hjumə'rɛsk] *s* (mus.) juguete, capricho

**humorist** ['hjumərɪst] o ['jumərɪst] *s* persona chistosa; humorista (*escritor*)

**humorous** ['hjumərəs] o ['jumərəs] *adj* chistoso, gracioso; humorístico (*escritor, dibujo*); (obs.) humoroso

**humour** ['hjumər] o ['jumər] *s & va* (Brit.) var. de **humor**

**hump** [hʌmp] *s* corcova, giba, joroba; montecillo; prominencia; (rail.) lomo, lomo de asno; *va* encorvar; **to hump it** o **to hump oneself** (slang) esforzarse, echar los bofes; *vn* encorvarse; (slang) esforzarse, echar los bofes

**humpback** ['hʌmp,bæk] *s* corcova, joroba; corcovado, jorobado; (zool.) gubarte

**humpbacked** ['hʌmp,bækt] *adj* corcovado, jorobado

**humph** [həm] *interj* ¡ bah!; ¡ uf!

**Humphrey** ['hʌmfrɪ] *s* Hunfredo

**humpty-dumpty** ['hʌmptɪ'dʌmptɪ] *adj* rechoncho

**humpy** ['hʌmpɪ] *adj* (*comp:* **-ier;** *super:* **-iest**) desigual; giboso

**hump yard** *s* (rail.) patio de lomo para maniobras por gravedad

**humus** ['hjuməs] *s* humus, mantillo

**Hun** [hʌn] *s* huno; (fig.) vándalo

**hunch** [hʌntʃ] *s* corcova, joroba; (coll.) corazonada; tajada, pedazo; *va* encorvar; mover a empujones o a tirones; *vn* encorvarse; moverse a empujones o a tirones

**hunchback** ['hʌntʃ,bæk] *s* corcova, joroba; corcovado, jorobado

**hunch-backed** ['hʌntʃ,bækt] *adj* corcovado, jorobado

**hundred** ['hʌndrəd] *adj* cien (*antes de substantivo*); ciento; **a hundred** u **one hundred** cien (*antes de substantivo*); ciento; *s* ciento, cien; **a hundred** u **one hundred** ciento, cien; **by the hundred** por cientos, a centenares; **the hundreds** las centenas (*los números 100, 200, 300, etc.*)

**Hundred Days** *spl* (hist.) Cien Días

**hundredfold** ['hʌndrəd,fold] *adj & s* céntuplo; *adv* cien veces más

**hundred-per-cent** ['hʌndrədpər'sɛnt] *adj* cabal, perfecto, puro, incontestable

**hundred-per-cent American** *s* americano cien por ciento (*americano muy patriótico*)

**hundredth** ['hʌndrədθ] *adj & s* centésimo

**hundredweight** [ˈhʌndrəd,wet] *s* centipondio, quintal
**Hundred Years' War** *s* guerra de los Cien Años
**hung** [hʌŋ] *pret & pp de* **hang**
**Hungarian** [hʌŋˈgɛrɪən] *adj & s* húngaro
**Hungary** [ˈhʌŋgərɪ] *s* Hungría
**hunger** [ˈhʌŋgər] *s* hambre; *vn* hambrear; **to hunger for** tener hambre de
**hunger march** *s* marcha del hambre
**hunger strike** *s* huelga de hambre
**hungry** [ˈhʌŋgrɪ] *adj* (*comp:* **-grier;** *super:* **-griest**) hambriento; estéril (*tierra*); **to be hungry** tener hambre; **to go hungry** pasar hambre; **hungry for** hambriento de (*p.ej., riquezas*)
**hunk** [hʌŋk] *s* (coll.) pedazo grande, buen pedazo
**hunky-dory** [,hʌŋkɪˈdorɪ] *adj* (coll.) excelente, óptimo
**hunt** [hʌnt] *s* caza; cacería, montería; partida de caza; busca; **on the hunt for** a caza de; *va* cazar; hacer la batida de (*un terreno*); emplear (*perros o caballos*) en la caza; perseguir; buscar; **to hunt down** cazar y matar, cazar y destruir; buscar (*una cosa*) hasta dar con ella; **to hunt up** rebuscar; buscar y hallar; *vn* cazar; buscar; **to go hunting** ir de caza; **to hunt for** buscar; **to hunt up and down (for)** buscar por todas partes; **to take hunting** llevar de caza
**hunter** [ˈhʌntər] *s* cazador; perro o caballo de caza; saboneta (*reloj*)
**hunting** [ˈhʌntɪŋ] *adj* cazador; de caza; *s* caza (*acción*); cacería, montería (*arte*); (elec.) movimiento oscilatorio
**hunting case** *s* caja de saboneta
**hunting dog** *s* perro de caza; (zool.) perro-hiena
**hunting ground** *s* cazadero
**huntinghorn** [ˈhʌntɪŋ,hɔrn] *s* cuerno de caza
**hunting jacket** *s* cazadora (*chaqueta*)
**hunting knife** *s* cuchillo de caza
**hunting lodge** *s* casa de montería
**hunting season** *s* tiempo de caza
**hunting watch** *s* saboneta
**huntress** [ˈhʌntrɪs] *s* cazadora (*mujer*)
**huntsman** [ˈhʌntsmən] *s* (*pl:* **-men**) cazador, montero; montero mayor
**hurdle** [ˈhʌrdəl] *s* cañizo, zarzo; narria (*para llevar los reos al patíbulo*); (sport) valla (*portátil*); (fig.) obstáculo; **hurdles** *spl* (sport) carrera de vallas; *va* cercar con zarzos; saltar por encima de, vencer
**hurdler** [ˈhʌrdlər] *s* (sport) corredor en una carrera de vallas
**hurdle race** *s* (sport) carrera de vallas
**hurdy-gurdy** [ˈhʌrdɪ,gʌrdɪ] *s* (*pl:* **-dies**) organillo; (archaic) zanfonía
**hurl** [hʌrl] *s* lanzamiento; *va* lanzar, arrojar
**hurly-burly** [ˈhʌrlɪ,bʌrlɪ] *s* (*pl:* **-ies**) alboroto, tumulto
**Huronian** [hjuˈronɪən] *adj & s* (geol.) huroniense
**hurrah** [huˈrɑ] o [huˈrɔ] o **hurray** [huˈre] *s* viva; *interj* ¡hurra!, ¡viva!; **hurrah for . . . !** ¡viva . . . !; *va* aplaudir, vitorear; *vn* dar vivas
**hurricane** [ˈhʌrɪken] *s* huracán; (naut.) huracán; *vn* huracanarse
**hurricane deck** *s* cubierta superior (*de un vapor de pasajeros*)
**hurried** [ˈhʌrɪd] *adj* apresurado; hecho de prisa
**hurry** [ˈhʌrɪ] *s* (*pl:* **-ries**) prisa; **to be in a hurry** tener prisa, estar de prisa; **to be in a hurry to** + *inf* tener prisa en o por + *inf;* **what's the hurry?** ¿qué prisa hay? ‖ (*pret & pp:* **-ried**) *va* apresurar, dar prisa a; **to hurry off** hacer marchar de prisa; **to hurry on** apresurar; **to hurry over** pasar rápidamente; hacer con precipitación o ligereza; **to hurry up** apresurar ‖ *vn* apresurarse, darse prisa; ir corriendo; **to hurry after** correr en pos de; **to hurry away** marcharse de prisa, salir precipitadamente; **to hurry back** volver de prisa, apresurarse a volver; **to hurry off** marcharse de prisa; **to hurry on** apresurarse; seguir adelante con mucha prisa; **to hurry to** + *inf* apresurarse a + *inf;* **to hurry up** apresurarse
**hurry-scurry** o **hurry-skurry** [ˈhʌrɪˈskʌrɪ] *adj* precipitado, atropellado; *adv* precipitadamente, atropelladamente; *s* precipitación, atropello
**hurt** [hʌrt] *s* daño; dolor; herida; *adj* ofendido, resentido; (*pret & pp:* **hurt**) *va* dañar, lastimar; herir; perjudicar; doler; ofender, lastimar; *vn* doler
**hurtful** [ˈhʌrtfəl] *adj* dañoso, perjudicial
**hurtle** [ˈhʌrtəl] *s* choque, fragor; *va* arrojar con violencia; chocar con; dar en o contra con gran estruendo; *vn* arrojarse con violencia; chocar; resonar con gran estruendo; pasar con gran estruendo, moverse con gran estruendo
**husband** [ˈhʌzbənd] *s* marido, esposo; *va* economizar, manejar con economía; procurar marido a; ser o pasar por marido de; (archaic) cultivar
**husbandman** [ˈhʌzbəndmən] *s* (*pl:* **-men**) granjero, agricultor
**husbandry** [ˈhʌzbəndrɪ] *s* granjería; buena dirección, buen gobierno (*de la hacienda o los recursos de uno*); economía
**hush** [hʌʃ] *s* silencio; *interj* ¡chito!, ¡chitón!; *va* callar; apaciguar; **to hush up** echar tierra a (*p.ej., un escándalo*); *vn* callar o callarse
**hushaby** [ˈhʌʃə,baɪ] *interj* ¡ro ro!
**hush-hush** [ˈhʌʃ,hʌʃ] *adj* muy secreto
**hush money** *s* dinero con que se compra el silencio de una persona
**husk** [hʌsk] *s* cáscara, hollejo, vaina; perfolla (*del maíz*); (fig.) cáscara o capa exterior; *va* descascarar, deshollejar, desvainar; espinochar (*el maíz*)
**husking** [ˈhʌskɪŋ] *s* despancación del maíz; minga para la despancación del maíz
**husking bee** *s* minga para la despancación del maíz
**husky** [ˈhʌskɪ] *adj* (*comp:* **-ier;** *super:* **-iest**) cascarudo; ronco; (coll.) fortachón, fornido; *s* (*pl:* **-ies**) (coll.) persona fornida; (*cap.*) *s* (*pl:* **-ies**) esquimal (*individuo; idioma*); perro esquimal
**hussar** [huˈzɑr] *s* (mil.) húsar
**Hussite** [ˈhʌsaɪt] *adj & s* husita
**Hussitism** [ˈhʌsaɪtɪzəm] *s* husitismo
**hussy** [ˈhʌzɪ] o [ˈhʌsɪ] *s* (*pl:* **-sies**) buena pieza, muchacha descarada; corralera (*mujer desvergonzada*)
**hustings** [ˈhʌstɪŋz] *spl* tribuna para discursos electorales; elecciones
**hustle** [ˈhʌsəl] *s* prisa; empujón; (coll.) energía, vigor; *va* apresurar, dar prisa a; empujar; echar a empellones; *vn* apresurarse, darse prisa; (coll.) menearse; (coll.) trabajar con gran ahinco
**hustler** [ˈhʌslər] *s* (coll.) trafagón, buscavidas
**hut** [hʌt] *s* casucha, choza
**hutch** [hʌtʃ] *s* conejera; hucha, arca; cabaña, choza
**huzza** [hʌˈzɑ] *s* viva; *interj* ¡vítor!; *va* vitorear; *vn* dar vivas
**hyacinth** [ˈhaɪəsɪnθ] *s* (bot. & mineral.) jacinto
**hyacinth bean** *s* (bot.) frijol caballero, frijol de Antibo
**hyacinthine** [,haɪəˈsɪnθɪn] o [,haɪəˈsɪnθaɪn] *adj* de o del jacinto; adornado con jacintos
**hyacinth of Peru** *s* (bot.) jacinto estrellado
**Hyacinthus** [,haɪəˈsɪnθəs] *s* (myth.) Jacinto
**Hyades** [ˈhaɪədiz] o **Hyads** [ˈhaɪædz] *spl* (astr. & myth.) Híadas o Híades
**hyaena** [haɪˈinə] *s* var. de **hyena**
**hyaline** [ˈhaɪəlɪn] o [ˈhaɪəlaɪn] *adj* hialino (*parecido al vidrio*); *s* (poet.) cosa vítrea o transparente; [ˈhaɪəlɪn] o [ˈhaɪəlin] *s* (biochem.) hialina
**hyaline degeneration** *s* (path.) degeneración hialina
**hyalite** [ˈhaɪəlaɪt] *s* (mineral.) hialita
**hyalitis** [,haɪəˈlaɪtɪs] *s* (path.) hialitis
**hyaloid** [ˈhaɪəlɔɪd] *adj* hialoideo; *s* (anat.) hialoides
**hyaloplasm** [ˈhaɪəloplæzəm] *s* (biol.) hialoplasma
**hybrid** [ˈhaɪbrɪd] *adj & s* híbrido
**hybridism** [ˈhaɪbrɪdɪzəm] *s* hibridismo
**hybridization** [,haɪbrɪdɪˈzeʃən] *s* hibridación
**hybridize** [ˈhaɪbrɪdaɪz] *va & vn* hibridar

**hydantoin** [haɪˈdænto·ɪn] *s* (chem.) hidantoína
**hydatid** [ˈhaɪdətɪd] *s* (path.) hidátide; *adj* hidatídico
**hydnum** [ˈhɪdnəm] *s* (bot.) hidno
**hydra** [ˈhaɪdrə] *s* (*pl:* **-dras** o **-drae** [dri]) hidra (*mal persistente*); (zool.) hidra (*pólipo*); (*cap.*) *s* (astr. & myth.) Hidra
**hydracid** [haɪˈdræsɪd] *s* (chem.) hidrácido
**hydrangea** [haɪˈdrendʒə] o [haɪˈdrændʒɪə] *s* (bot.) hortensia, hidrangea
**hydrant** [ˈhaɪdrənt] *s* boca de agua, boca de riego
**hydrargyriasis** [ˌhaɪdrɑrdʒɪˈraɪəsɪs] *s* (path.) hidrargirismo
**hydrargyrum** [haɪˈdrɑrdʒɪrəm] *s* (chem.) hidrargiro
**hydrate** [ˈhaɪdret] *s* (chem.) hidrato; *va* (chem.) hidratar; *vn* (chem.) hidratarse
**hydration** [haɪˈdreʃən] *s* (chem.) hidratación
**hydraulic** [haɪˈdrɔlɪk] *adj* hidráulico; **hydraulics** *ssg* hidráulica
**hydraulically** [haɪˈdrɔlɪkəlɪ] *adv* hidráulicamente
**hydraulic brake** *s* freno hidráulico
**hydraulic elevator** *s* ascensor hidráulico
**hydraulic jack** *s* gato hidráulico
**hydraulic lime** *s* cal hidráulica
**hydraulic mortar** *s* argamasa hidráulica
**hydraulic press** *s* prensa hidráulica
**hydraulic ram** *s* ariete hidráulico
**hydraulic turbine** *s* turbina hidráulica
**hydrazide** [ˈhaɪdrəzaɪd] o [ˈhaɪdrəzɪd] *s* (chem.) hidracida
**hydrazine** [ˈhaɪdrəzin] o [ˈhaɪdrəzɪn] *s* (chem.) hidracina
**hydric** [ˈhaɪdrɪk] *adj* (chem.) hídrico
**hydrid** [ˈhaɪdrɪd] o **hydride** [ˈhaɪdraɪd] o [ˈhaɪdrɪd] *s* (chem.) hidruro
**hydriodic** [ˌhaɪdrɪˈɑdɪk] *adj* (chem.) yodhídrico
**hydriodic acid** *s* (chem.) ácido yodhídrico
**hydrobromic** [ˌhaɪdrəˈbromɪk] *adj* (chem.) bromhídrico
**hydrobromic acid** *s* (chem.) ácido bromhídrico
**hydrocarbon** [ˌhaɪdrəˈkɑrbən] *s* (chem.) hidrocarburo
**hydrocele** [ˈhaɪdrəsil] *s* (path.) hidrocele
**hydrocephalous** [ˌhaɪdrəˈsɛfələs] *adj* hidrocéfalo
**hydrocephalus** [ˌhaɪdrəˈsɛfələs] *s* (path.) hidrocefalía
**hydrochlorate** [ˌhaɪdrəˈkloret] o [ˌhaɪdrəˈklorɪt] *s* (chem.) clorhidrato
**hydrochloric** [ˌhaɪdrəˈklorɪk] *adj* (chem.) clorhídrico
**hydrochloric acid** *s* (chem.) ácido clorhídrico
**hydrocyanic** [ˌhaɪdrosaɪˈænɪk] *adj* (chem.) cianhídrico
**hydrocyanic acid** *s* (chem.) ácido cianhídrico
**hydrodynamic** [ˌhaɪdrədaɪˈnæmɪk] o [ˌhaɪdrədɪˈnæmɪk] *adj* hidrodinámico; **hydrodynamics** *ssg* hidrodinámica
**hydroelectric** [ˌhaɪdro·ɪˈlɛktrɪk] *adj* hidroeléctrico
**hydroelectricity** [ˌhaɪdro·ɪˌlɛkˈtrɪsɪtɪ] *s* hidroelectricidad
**hydrofluoric** [ˌhaɪdrofluˈɑrɪk] o [ˌhaɪdrofluˈɔrɪk] *adj* (chem.) fluorhídrico
**hydrofluoric acid** *s* (chem.) ácido fluorhídrico
**hydrofoil** [ˈhaɪdrəˌfɔɪl] *s* superficie de reacción hidráulica, plano hidrodinámico; hidroaleta; barco que se desliza sobre hidroaletas
**hydrogel** [ˈhaɪdrəˌdʒɛl] *s* (chem.) hidrogel
**hydrogen** [ˈhaɪdrədʒən] *s* (chem.) hidrógeno
**hydrogenate** [ˈhaɪdrədʒənet] *va* (chem.) hidrogenar
**hydrogenation** [ˌhaɪdrədʒənˈeʃən] *s* (chem.) hidrogenación
**hydrogen bomb** *s* (phys.) bomba de hidrógeno
**hydrogen ion** *s* (chem.) hidrogenión, ion hidrógeno, ion de hidrógeno
**hydrogenize** [ˈhaɪdrədʒənaɪz] *va* var. de **hydrogenate**
**hydrogenous** [haɪˈdrɑdʒɪnəs] *adj* hidrogenado
**hydrogen peroxide** *s* (chem.) peróxido de hidrógeno
**hydrogen sulfide** *s* (chem.) sulfuro de hidrógeno
**hydrographer** [haɪˈdrɑgrəfər] *s* hidrógrafo
**hydrographic** [ˌhaɪdrəˈgræfɪk] *adj* hidrográfico
**hydrography** [haɪˈdrɑgrəfɪ] *s* hidrografía
**hydroid** [ˈhaɪdrɔɪd] *s* (zool.) hidroide
**hydrologist** [haɪˈdrɑlədʒɪst] *s* hidrólogo
**hydrology** [haɪˈdrɑlədʒɪ] *s* hidrología
**hydrolysis** [haɪˈdrɑlɪsɪs] *s* (*pl:* **-ses** [siz]) (chem.) hidrólisis
**hydrolytic** [ˌhaɪdrəˈlɪtɪk] *adj* hidrolítico
**hydrolyze** [ˈhaɪdrəlaɪz] *va* (chem.) hidrolizar; *vn* (chem.) hidrolizarse
**hydromancy** [ˈhaɪdrəˌmænsɪ] *s* hidromancía
**hydromantic** [ˌhaɪdrəˈmæntɪk] *adj* hidromántico
**hydromechanical** [ˌhaɪdromɪˈkænɪkəl] *adj* hidromecánico
**hydromechanics** [ˌhaɪdromɪˈkænɪks] *ssg* hidromecánica
**hydromedusa** [ˌhaɪdromɪˈdjusə] o [ˌhaɪdromɪˈdusə] *s* (*pl:* **-sae** [si]) (zool.) hidromedusa
**hydromel** [ˈhaɪdrəmɛl] *s* hidromel
**hydrometeor** [ˌhaɪdrəˈmitɪər] *s* (meteor.) hidrometeoro
**hydrometer** [haɪˈdrɑmɪtər] *s* areómetro
**hydrometric** [ˌhaɪdrəˈmɛtrɪk] o **hydrometrical** [ˌhaɪdrəˈmɛtrɪkəl] *adj* areométrico
**hydrometry** [haɪˈdrɑmɪtrɪ] *s* areometría
**hydropath** [ˈhaɪdrəpæθ] *s* hidrópata
**hydropathic** [ˌhaɪdrəˈpæθɪk] *adj* hidropático
**hydropathist** [haɪˈdrɑpəθɪst] *s* hidrópata
**hydropathy** [haɪˈdrɑpəθɪ] *s* hidropatía
**hydrophane** [ˈhaɪdrəfen] *s* (mineral.) hidrófana
**hydrophid** [ˈhaɪdrəfɪd] *s* (zool.) hidrófido
**hydrophile** [ˈhaɪdrəfaɪl] o [ˈhaɪdrəfɪl] o **hydrophilic** [ˌhaɪdrəˈfɪlɪk] *adj* (chem.) hidrófilo
**hydrophobe** [ˈhaɪdrəfob] *s* hidrófobo
**hydrophobia** [ˌhaɪdrəˈfobɪə] *s* (path.) hidrofobia
**hydrophobic** [ˌhaɪdrəˈfobɪk] *adj* hidrofóbico; hidrófobo (*que padece de hidrofobia*)
**hydrophone** [ˈhaɪdrəfon] *s* hidrófono
**hydrophyte** [ˈhaɪdrəfaɪt] *s* (bot.) hidrófita
**hydropic** [haɪˈdrɑpɪk] o **hydropical** [haɪˈdrɑpɪkəl] *adj* hidrópico
**hydroplane** [ˈhaɪdrəplen] *s* hidroplano (*buque*); (aer.) hidroplano o hidroavión
**hydroponic** [ˌhaɪdrəˈpɑnɪk] *adj* hidropónico; **hydroponics** *spl* hidroponía
**hydrops** [ˈhaɪdrɑps] o **hydropsy** [ˈhaɪˌdrɑpsɪ] *s* (path.) hidropesía
**hydroquinone** [ˌhaɪdrəkwɪˈnon] o [ˌhaɪdrəˈkwɪnon] *s* (chem.) hidroquinona
**hydrosol** [ˈhaɪdrəsɑl] o [ˈhaɪdrəsol] *s* (chem.) hidrosol
**hydrosphere** [ˈhaɪdrəsfɪr] *s* hidrosfera
**hydrostat** [ˈhaɪdrəstæt] *s* hidrostato
**hydrostatic** [ˌhaɪdrəˈstætɪk] *adj* hidrostático; **hydrostatics** *ssg* hidrostática
**hydrosulfid** [ˌhaɪdrəˈsʌlfɪd] o **hydrosulfide** [ˌhaɪdrəˈsʌlfaɪd] o [ˌhaɪdrəˈsʌlfɪd] *s* (chem.) hidrosulfuro
**hydrosulfite** [ˌhaɪdrəˈsʌlfaɪt] *s* (chem.) hidrosulfito; (chem.) hidrosulfito sódico (*agente reductor*)
**hydrotechny** [ˈhaɪdrəˌtɛknɪ] *s* hidrotecnia
**hydrotherapeutic** [ˌhaɪdroˌθɛrəˈpjutɪk] *adj* hidroterápico; **hydrotherapeutics** *ssg* hidroterapia
**hydrotherapy** [ˌhaɪdroˈθɛrəpɪ] *s* var. de **hydrotherapeutics**
**hydrothermal** [ˌhaɪdrəˈθʌrməl] *adj* hidrotérmico
**hydrothorax** [ˌhaɪdrəˈθoræks] *s* (path.) hidrotórax
**hydrotropism** [haɪˈdrɑtrəpɪzəm] *s* (biol.) hidrotropismo
**hydrous** [ˈhaɪdrəs] *adj* hidratado
**hydroxid** [haɪˈdrɑksɪd] o **hydroxide** [haɪˈdrɑksaɪd] o [haɪˈdrɑksɪd] *s* (chem.) hidróxido
**hydroxyl** [haɪˈdrɑksɪl] *s* (chem.) hidroxilo u oxhidrilo
**hydroxylamine** [haɪˌdrɑksɪləˈmin] o [haɪˌdrɑksɪlˈæmɪn] *s* (chem.) hidroxilamina
**hydroxyl radical** *s* (chem.) radical hidroxilo
**hydrozoan** [ˌhaɪdrəˈzoən] *s* (zool.) hidrozoo; *adj* hidrozoico
**hyena** [haɪˈinə] *s* (zool.) hiena

**Hygeia** [haɪˈdʒiə] *s* (myth.) Higía
**hygiene** [ˈhaɪdʒin] o [ˈhaɪdʒɪin] *s* higiene
**hygienic** [ˌhaɪdʒɪˈɛnɪk] o [haɪˈdʒinɪk] *adj* higiénico
**hygienist** [ˈhaɪdʒɪənɪst] *adj & s* higienista
**hygrometer** [haɪˈgrɑmɪtər] *s* higrómetro
**hygrometric** [ˌhaɪgrəˈmɛtrɪk] *adj* higrométrico
**hygrometry** [haɪˈgrɑmɪtrɪ] *s* higrometría
**hygroscope** [ˈhaɪgrəskop] *s* higroscopio
**hygroscopic** [ˌhaɪgrəˈskɑpɪk] *adj* higroscópico
**hying** [ˈhaɪɪŋ] *ger de* **hie**
**Hyksos** [ˈhɪksɑs] o [ˈhɪksos] *spl* (hist.) Hicsos
**hyla** [ˈhaɪlə] *s* (zool.) rubeta, rana de San Antonio
**hylozoism** [ˌhaɪləˈzo·ɪzəm] *s* (philos.) hilozoísmo
**hymen** [ˈhaɪmən] *s* (anat.) himen; (*cap.*) *s* (myth.) Himeneo
**hymeneal** [ˌhaɪməˈniəl] *adj* nupcial; *s* himeneo (*himno nupcial*)
**hymenium** [haɪˈminɪəm] *s* (*pl:* **-a** [ə] o **-ums**) (bot.) himenio
**hymenopter** [ˈhaɪməˌnɑptər] *s* (*pl:* **-tera** [tərə]) (zool.) himenóptero
**hymenopterous** [ˌhaɪməˈnɑptərəs] *adj* (zool.) himenóptero
**Hymettus** [haɪˈmɛtəs] *s* Himeto
**hymn** [hɪm] *s* himno; *va* alabar con himnos; expresar en himnos; *vn* cantar himnos
**hymnal** [ˈhɪmnəl] *s* himnario
**hymnology** [hɪmˈnɑlədʒɪ] *s* himnología; himnos
**hyoid** [ˈhaɪɔɪd] *adj* hioideo; hioides; *s* (anat.) hioides
**hyoides** [haɪˈɔɪdiz] *s* (anat.) hioides
**hyoscine** [ˈhaɪəsin] o [ˈhaɪəsɪn] *s* (trademark) hioscina (*alcaloide*)
**hyoscyamine** [ˌhaɪəˈsaɪəmin] o [ˌhaɪəˈsaɪəmɪn] *s* (chem.) hiosciamina
**hyp.** abr. de **hypotenuse** y **hypothesis**
**hypabyssal** [ˌhɪpəˈbɪsəl] *adj* (geol.) hipabisal
**hypallage** [hɪˈpælədʒi] o [haɪˈpælədʒi] *s* (rhet.) hipálage
**Hypatia** [haɪˈpeʃə] o [haɪˈpeʃɪə] *s* Hipatia
**hyperacidity** [ˌhaɪpərəˈsɪdɪtɪ] *s* hiperacidez
**hyperacusis** [ˌhaɪpərəˈkjusɪs] *s* (path.) hiperacusia o hiperacusis
**hyperaemia** [ˌhaɪpərˈimɪə] *s* (path.) var. de **hyperemia**
**hyperaesthesia** [ˌhaɪpərɪsˈθiʒə] o [ˌhaɪpərɪsˈθiʒɪə] *s* (path.) hiperestesia
**hyperbatic** [ˌhaɪpərˈbætɪk] *adj* hiperbático
**hyperbaton** [haɪˈpʌrbətɑn] *s* (*pl:* **-ta** [tə]) (gram.) hipérbaton
**hyperbola** [haɪˈpʌrbələ] *s* (geom.) hipérbola
**hyperbole** [haɪˈpʌrbəlɪ] *s* (rhet.) hipérbole
**hyperbolic** [ˌhaɪpərˈbɑlɪk] *adj* (geom. & rhet.) hiperbólico
**hyperbolism** [haɪˈpʌrbəlɪzəm] *s* (rhet.) hiperbolismo
**hyperbolize** [haɪˈpʌrbəlaɪz] *va* usar de hipérboles en; *vn* hiperbolizar
**hyperboloid** [haɪˈpʌrbəlɔɪd] *s* (geom.) hiperboloide
**hyperborean** [ˌhaɪpərˈborɪən] *adj & s* hiperbóreo; (*cap.*) *s* (myth.) hiperbóreo
**hyperchlorhydria** [ˌhaɪpərklorˈhaɪdrɪə] *s* (path.) hiperclorhidria
**hypercritical** [ˌhaɪpərˈkrɪtɪkəl] *adj* hipercrítico
**hyperdulia** [ˌhaɪpərdjuˈlaɪə] o [ˌhaɪpərduˈlaɪə] *s* (theol.) hiperdulía
**hyperemia** [ˌhaɪpərˈimɪə] *s* (path.) hiperemia
**hyperesthesia** [ˌhaɪpərɪsˈθiʒə] o [ˌhaɪpərɪsˈθiʒɪə] *s* (path.) hiperestesia
**Hyperion** [haɪˈpɪrɪən] *s* (myth.) Hiperión
**hyperkinesia** [ˌhaɪpərkɪˈniʒə] o [ˌhaɪpərkaɪˈniʒə] *s* (path.) hipercinesia
**hypermetropia** [ˌhaɪpərmɪˈtropɪə] *s* (path.) hipermetropía
**Hypermnestra** [ˌhaɪpərmˈnɛstrə] *s* (myth.) Hipermnestra
**hyperopia** [ˌhaɪpərˈopɪə] *s* (path.) hiperopía
**hyperopic** [ˌhaɪpərˈɑpɪk] *adj* hiperópico
**hyperpituitarism** [ˌhaɪpərpɪˈtjuɪtərɪzəm] o [ˌhaɪpərpɪˈtuɪtərɪzəm] *s* (path.) hiperpituitarismo
**hyperpnea** [ˌhaɪpərpˈniə] o [ˌhaɪpərˈniə] *s* (path.) hiperpnea
**hyperpyrexia** [ˌhaɪpərpaɪˈrɛksɪə] *s* (path.) hiperpirexia
**hypersensitive** [ˌhaɪpərˈsɛnsɪtɪv] *adj* extremadamente sensible; (path.) hipersensible
**hypersensitivity** [ˌhaɪpərˌsɛnsɪˈtɪvɪtɪ] *s* exceso de sensibilidad; (path.) hipersensibilidad
**hypertension** [ˌhaɪpərˈtɛnʃən] *s* (path.) hipertensión
**hyperthyroidism** [ˌhaɪpərˈθaɪrɔɪdɪzəm] *s* (path.) hipertiroidismo
**hypertonic** [ˌhaɪpərˈtɑnɪk] *adj* (chem. & physiol.) hipertónico
**hypertrophic** [ˌhaɪpərˈtrɑfɪk] *adj* hipertrófico
**hypertrophy** [ˌhaɪˈpʌrtrəfɪ] *s* (biol. & path.) hipertrofia; (*pret & pp:* **-phied**) *vn* hipertrofiarse
**hypha** [ˈhaɪfə] *s* (*pl:* **-phae** [fi]) (bot.) hifa
**hyphen** [ˈhaɪfən] *s* guión; *va* unir con guión, separar con guión
**hyphenate** [ˈhaɪfənet] *va* unir con guión, separar con guión; escribir con guión
**hyphenated American** *s* (U.S.A.) ciudadano norteamericano de nacimiento extranjero que guarda lealtad a la madre patria y cuya nacionalidad se indica con dos palabras unidas con guión, p.ej., **Anglo-American** anglonorteamericano
**hypnale** [ˈhɪpnəli] *s* (chem.) hipnal; (obs.) hipnal (*áspid*)
**Hypnos** [ˈhɪpnɑs] *s* (myth.) Hipnos
**hypnosis** [hɪpˈnosɪs] *s* (*pl:* **-ses** [siz]) hipnosis
**hypnotic** [hɪpˈnɑtɪk] *adj* hipnótico; *s* hipnótico; (med.) hipnótico (*medicamento*)
**hypnotically** [hɪpˈnɑtɪkəlɪ] *adv* hipnóticamente
**hypnotism** [ˈhɪpnətɪzəm] *s* hipnotismo
**hypnotist** [ˈhɪpnətɪst] *s* hipnotista
**hypnotization** [ˌhɪpnətɪˈzeʃən] *s* hipnotización
**hypnotize** [ˈhɪpnətaɪz] *va* hipnotizar
**hypo** [ˈhaɪpo] *s* (*pl:* **-pos**) (phot.) hipo (*hiposulfito sódico*); (slang) aguja hipodérmica, inyección hipodérmica, jeringazo
**hypoblast** [ˈhaɪpəblæst] *s* (embryol.) hipoblasto
**hypocaust** [ˈhɪpəkɔst] *s* (archeol.) hipocausto
**hypochlorite** [ˌhaɪpoˈkloraɪt] *s* (chem.) hipoclorito
**hypochlorous** [ˌhaɪpoˈklorəs] *adj* (chem.) hipocloroso
**hypochlorous acid** *s* (chem.) ácido hipocloroso
**hypochondria** [ˌhaɪpəˈkɑndrɪə] o [ˌhɪpəˈkɑndrɪə] *s* (path.) hipocondría
**hypochondriac** [ˌhaɪpəˈkɑndrɪæk] o [ˌhɪpəˈkɑndrɪæk] *adj & s* hipocondríaco
**hypochondrium** [ˌhaɪpəˈkɑndrɪəm] o [ˌhɪpəˈkɑndrɪəm] *s* (*pl:* **-a** [ə]) (anat.) hipocondrio
**hypocoristic** [ˌhɪpəkoˈrɪstɪk] *adj* hipocorístico
**hypocotyl** [ˌhaɪpoˈkɑtɪl] *s* (bot.) hipocotíleo
**hypocrisy** [hɪˈpɑkrɪsɪ] *s* (*pl:* **-sies**) hipocresía
**hypocrite** [ˈhɪpəkrɪt] *s* hipócrita
**hypocritical** [ˌhɪpəˈkrɪtɪkəl] *adj* hipócrita
**hypocycloid** [ˌhaɪpəˈsaɪklɔɪd] *s* (geom.) hipocicloide
**hypodermal** [ˌhaɪpəˈdʌrməl] *adj* (bot.) hipodermo
**hypodermic** [ˌhaɪpəˈdʌrmɪk] *adj* hipodérmico; *s* medicamento hipodérmico; inyección hipodérmica; jeringa hipodérmica
**hypodermically** [ˌhaɪpəˈdʌrmɪkəlɪ] *adv* hipodérmicamente
**hypodermic injection** *s* inyección hipodérmica
**hypodermic needle** *s* aguja hipodérmica
**hypodermic syringe** *s* jeringa hipodérmica
**hypogastric** [ˌhaɪpəˈgæstrɪk] *adj* hipogástrico
**hypogastrium** [ˌhaɪpəˈgæstrɪəm] *s* (*pl:* **-a** [ə]) (anat. & zool.) hipogastrio
**hypogene** [ˈhɪpədʒin] *adj* (geol.) hipogénico
**hypogeous** [ˌhaɪpəˈdʒiəs] *adj* (bot. & zool.) hipogeo
**hypogeum** [ˌhɪpəˈdʒiəm] *s* (*pl:* **-a** [ə]) (arch.) hipogeo
**hypoglossal** [ˌhaɪpoˈglɑsəl] *adj & s* (anat.) hipogloso
**hypoid** [ˈhaɪpɔɪd] *adj* (mach.) hipoide

**hypophosphite** [ˌhaɪpoˈfɑsfaɪt] *s* (chem.) hipofosfito
**hypophosphoric** [ˌhaɪpofɑsˈfɑrɪk] o [ˌhaɪpofɑsˈfɔrɪk] *adj* (chem.) hipofosfórico
**hypophosphoric acid** *s* (chem.) ácido hipofosfórico
**hypophosphorous** [ˌhaɪpoˈfɑsfərəs] *adj* (chem.) hipofosforoso
**hypophosphorous acid** *s* (chem.) ácido hipofosforoso
**hypophysis** [haɪˈpɑfɪsɪs] *s* (*pl:* **-ses** [siz]) (anat.) hipófisis
**hypostasis** [haɪˈpɑstəsɪs] *s* (*pl:* **-ses** [siz]) (philos. & theol.) hipóstasis
**hypostatic** [ˌhaɪpəˈstætɪk] *adj* hipostático
**hypostyle** [ˈhɪpəstaɪl] o [ˈhaɪpəstaɪl] *adj & s* (arch.) hipóstilo
**hyposulfite** [ˌhaɪpoˈsʌlfaɪt] *s* (chem.) hiposulfito (*tiosulfato; sal del ácido hiposulfuroso*)
**hyposulfurous** [ˌhaɪposʌlˈfjurəs] o [ˌhaɪpoˈsʌlfərəs] *adj* (chem.) hiposulfuroso
**hyposulfurous acid** *s* (chem.) ácido hiposulfuroso
**hypotenuse** [haɪˈpɑtɪnjus] o [haɪˈpɑtɪnus] *s* (geom.) hipotenusa
**hypothalamus** [ˌhaɪpəˈθæləməs] *s* (anat.) hipotálamo
**hypothec** [haɪˈpɑθɛk] *s* (law) hipoteca
**hypothecate** [haɪˈpɑθɪket] *va* hipotecar
**hypothecation** [haɪˌpɑθɪˈkeʃən] *s* hipotecación
**hypothenuse** [haɪˈpɑθɪnjus] o [haɪˈpɑθɪnus] *s* var. de **hypotenuse**
**hypothermia** [ˌhaɪpoˈθʌrmɪə] *s* (med.) hipotermia
**hypothesis** [haɪˈpɑθɪsɪs] *s* (*pl:* **-ses** [siz]) hipótesis
**hypothesize** [haɪˈpɑθɪsaɪz] *va* formar hipótesis de; *vn* formar hipótesis
**hypothetic** [ˌhaɪpəˈθɛtɪk] o **hypothetical** [ˌhaɪpəˈθɛtɪkəl] *adj* hipotético
**hypothyroidism** [ˌhaɪpoˈθaɪrɔɪdɪzəm] *s* (path.) hipotiroidismo
**hypotonic** [ˌhaɪpəˈtɑnɪk] *adj* (chem. & physiol.) hipotónico
**hypoxanthine** [ˌhaɪpəˈzænθin] o [ˌhaɪpəˈzænθɪn] *s* (chem.) hipoxantina
**hypsometer** [hɪpˈsɑmɪtər] *s* hipsómetro
**hypsometry** [hɪpˈsɑmɪtrɪ] *s* hipsometría
**hyson** [ˈhaɪsən] *s* té verde chino
**hyssop** [ˈhɪsəp] *s* (bot. & eccl.) hisopo; (Bib.) alcaparra (*Capparis spinosa*)
**hyssop loosestrife** *s* (bot.) hierba del toro
**hysterectomy** [ˌhɪstəˈrɛktəmɪ] *s* (*pl:* **-mies**) (surg.) histerectomía
**hysteresis** [ˌhɪstəˈrisɪs] *s* (phys.) histéresis
**hysteria** [hɪsˈtɪrɪə] *s* excitación loca; (path.) histeria
**hysteric** [hɪsˈtɛrɪk] *adj* locamente excitado; (path.) histérico; **hysterics** *spl* paroxismo histérico
**hysterical** [hɪsˈtɛrɪkəl] *adj* locamente excitado; (path.) histérico
**hysterotomy** [ˌhɪstəˈrɑtəmɪ] *s* (*pl:* **-mies**) (surg.) histerotomía
**hyther** [ˈhaɪðər] *s* (biol.) híter
**hyzone** [ˈhaɪzon] *s* (chem.) hizono

# I

**I, i** [aɪ] *s* (*pl:* **I's, i's** [aɪz]) novena letra del alfabeto inglés
**i.** abr. de **intransitive** y **island**
**I.** abr. de **Island, Islands, Isle** y **Isles**
**I** [aɪ] *pron pers* (*pl:* **we**) yo; **it is I** soy yo; *s* (*pl:* **I's** [aɪz]) (philos.) yo
**Ia.** abr. de **Iowa**
**iamb** [ˈaɪæmb] *s* yambo
**iambic** [aɪˈæmbɪk] *adj* yámbico; *s* yambo; verso yámbico
**iambus** [aɪˈæmbəs] *s* (*pl:* **-bi** [baɪ] o **-buses**) yambo
**ib.** abr. de **ibidem**
**I beam** *s* (constr.) viga I
**Iberia** [aɪˈbɪrɪə] *s* Iberia
**Iberian** [aɪˈbɪrɪən] *adj* ibérico, iberio o ibero; *s* ibero
**Iberian Peninsula** *s* Península Ibérica
**Iberism** [ˈaɪbərɪzəm] *s* iberismo
**Ibero-America** [aɪˈbɪroəˈmɛrɪkə] *s* Iberoamérica
**Ibero-American** [aɪˈbɪroəˈmɛrɪkən] *adj & s* iberoamericano
**ibex** [ˈaɪbɛks] *s* (*pl:* **ibexes** o **ibices** [ˈɪbɪsiz] o [ˈaɪbɪsiz]) (zool.) íbice, cabra montés; (zool.) cabra bezoar (*Capra aegagrus*)
**ibid.** abr. de **ibidem**
**ibidem** [ɪˈbaɪdɛm] *adv* (Lat.) ibídem (*en el mismo lugar*)
**ibis** [ˈaɪbɪs] *s* (*pl:* **ibises** o **ibis**) (orn.) ibis
**Ibsenian** [ɪbˈsinɪən] *adj & s* ibseniano
**-ic** *suffix adj* -ico, p.ej., **metallic** metálico; **public** público; **volcanic** volcánico; excepto en la terminología química, los sufijos **-ic** e **-ical** son por la mayor parte iguales e intercambiables, p.ej., **hypothetic** o **hypothetical** hipotético; **symbolic** o **symbolical** simbólico; al mismo tiempo, hay algunas palabras que tienen sentido distinto según terminan en **-ic** o **-ical,** v.g., **comic** cómico (*perteneciente a la comedia que no a la tragedia*), p.ej., **comic actor** actor cómico; **comical** cómico (*divertido, gracioso*), p.ej., **comical episode** episodio cómico; **historic** histórico (*importante en la historia*), p.ej., **historic event** acontecimiento histórico; **historical** histórico (*que trata de la historia*), p.ej., **historical novel** novela histórica; (chem.) -ico, p.ej., **cupric** cúprico; **sulfuric** sulfúrico; *suffix s* -ico, p.ej., **domestic** doméstico; **critic** crítico; -ica, p.ej., **arithmetic** aritmética; **music** música; **-ics** *suffix ssg* -ica, p.ej., **physics** física; **politics** política
**-cal** *suffix adj* -ico, p.ej., **critical** crítico; **logical** lógico; **musical** músico; para la comparación de **-ic** e **-ical,** véase **-ic**
**Icarian** [aɪˈkɛrɪən] *adj* icáreo o icario
**Icarius** [aɪˈkɛrɪəs] *s* (myth.) Icario
**Icarus** [ˈɪkərəs] *s* (myth.) Ícaro
**ICBM** abr. de **intercontinental ballistic missile**
**I.C.C.** abr. de **Interstate Commerce Commission**
**ice** [aɪs] *s* hielo; helado, sorbete; garapiña, costra de azúcar; **to break the ice** dar comienzo a una empresa difícil; romper el hielo (*quebrantar la reserva*); **to cut no ice** (coll.) no surtir efecto, no importar nada; **to skate on thin ice** buscar el peligro; usar de argumentos infundados; *adj* glacial; de hielo; *va* helar; enfriar con hielo; garapiñar (*bañar en el almíbar*); *vn* helarse; **to ice up** (aer.) helarse
**ice age** *s* (geol.) época glacial, edad del hielo
**ice bag** *s* bolsa de hielo, bolsa (de caucho) para hielo
**iceberg** [ˈaɪsˌbʌrg] *s* banquisa, iceberg
**iceboat** [ˈaɪsˌbot] *s* trineo con vela para deslizarse por el hielo; rompehielos, cortahielos
**icebound** [ˈaɪsˌbaʊnd] *adj* detenido por el hielo, rodeado de hielo
**icebox** [ˈaɪsˌbɑks] *s* nevera, fresquera
**icebreaker** [ˈaɪsˌbrekər] *s* rompehielos, cortahielos
**icecap** [ˈaɪsˌkæp] *s* manto de hielo, helero; bolsa para hielo
**ice cream** *s* helado
**ice-cream cone** [ˈaɪsˈkrim] *s* cornet de helado, cucurucho
**ice-cream freezer** *s* heladora, sorbetera, garapiñera
**ice-cream parlor** *s* heladería, salón de refrescos, botillería
**ice-cream soda** *s* agua gaseosa con helado
**ice cube** *s* cubito de hielo
**iced** [aɪst] *adj* helado; garapiñado
**ice field** *s* banquisa, bancos de hielo
**ice hockey** *s* hockey sobre patines
**icehouse** [ˈaɪsˌhaʊs] *s* nevera
**Iceland** [ˈaɪslənd] *s* Islandia
**Icelander** [ˈaɪsˌlændər] o [ˈaɪsləndər] *s* islandés
**Icelandic** [aɪsˈlændɪk] *adj* islandés; *s* islandés (*idioma*)
**Iceland moss** *s* (bot.) musgo de Islandia
**Iceland spar** *s* (mineral.) espato de Islandia
**iceman** [ˈaɪsˌmæn] *s* (*pl:* **-men**) vendedor de hielo, repartidor de hielo
**ice pack** *s* hielo flotante; aplicación de hielo empaquetado
**ice pail** *s* enfriadera
**ice pick** *s* picahielos, punzón para romper hielo
**ice plant** *s* fábrica de hielo; (bot.) escarchada
**ice sheet** *s* masa de hielo, manto de hielo
**ice skate** *s* patín de cuchilla, patín de hielo
**ice tray** *s* bandejita del hielo
**ice-up** [ˈaɪsˌʌp] *s* (aer.) formación de hielo
**ice water** *s* agua helada
**ichneumon** [ɪkˈnjumən] o [ɪkˈnumən] *s* (zool. & ent.) icneumón; (zool.) meloncillo (*Herpestes ichneumon*)
**ichneumon fly** *s* (ent.) icneumón
**ichnography** [ɪkˈnɑgrəfɪ] *s* (arch.) icnografía
**ichor** [ˈaɪkər] *s* (path.) icor (*de una úlcera*); (myth.) sangre de los dioses
**ichorous** [ˈaɪkərəs] *adj* icoroso
**ichthyol** [ˈɪkθɪol] o [ˈɪkθɪɑl] *s* (trademark) ictiol
**ichthyologic** [ˌɪkθɪəˈlɑdʒɪk] o **ichthyological** [ˌɪkθɪəˈlɑdʒɪkəl] *adj* ictiológico
**ichthyologist** [ˌɪkθɪˈɑlədʒɪst] *s* ictiólogo
**ichthyology** [ˌɪkθɪˈɑlədʒɪ] *s* ictiología
**ichthyophagist** [ˌɪkθɪˈɑfədʒɪst] *s* ictiófago
**ichthyophagous** [ˌɪkθɪˈɑfəgəs] *adj* ictiófago
**ichthyosaur** [ˈɪkθɪəˌsɔr] *s* (pal.) ictiosauro
**ichthyosaurus** [ˌɪkθɪəˈsɔrəs] *s* (*pl:* **-ri** [raɪ]) (pal.) var. de **ichthyosaur**
**ichthyosis** [ˌɪkθɪˈosɪs] *s* (path.) ictiosis
**ichthyosism** [ˈɪkθɪəsɪzəm] *s* (vet.) ictiosismo
**ichu** [ˈitʃu] *s* (bot.) icho o ichú
**-ician** *suffix s* -ico, p.ej., **logician** lógico; **musician** músico
**icicle** [ˈaɪsɪkəl] *s* carámbano
**icing** [ˈaɪsɪŋ] *s* costra de azúcar, capa de azúcar; (aer.) formación de hielo
**icon** [ˈaɪkɑn] *s* icono; (eccl.) icón
**iconoclasm** [aɪˈkɑnəklæzəm] *s* iconoclasia o iconoclasmo
**iconoclast** [aɪˈkɑnəklæst] *s* iconoclasta
**iconoclastic** [aɪˌkɑnəˈklæstɪk] *adj* iconoclasta
**iconographic** [aɪˌkɑnəˈgræfɪk] o **iconographical** [aɪˌkɑnəˈgræfɪkəl] *adj* iconográfico
**iconography** [ˌaɪkəˈnɑgrəfɪ] *s* iconografía
**iconolater** [ˌaɪkəˈnɑlətər] *s* iconólatra
**iconolatrous** [ˌaɪkəˈnɑlətrəs] *adj* iconólatra
**iconolatry** [ˌaɪkəˈnɑlətrɪ] *s* iconolatría
**iconology** [ˌaɪkəˈnɑlədʒɪ] *s* iconología

**iconomania** [aɪˌkɑnəˈmenɪə] *s* iconomanía
**iconoscope** [aɪˈkɑnəskop] *s* (trademark) iconoscopio
**iconostasion** [aɪˌkɑnəˈstesɪɑn] *s* (eccl.) iconostasio
**icosahedron** [ˌaɪkosəˈhidrən] *s* (*pl:* **-dra** [drə]) (geom.) icosaedro
**icteric** [ɪkˈtɛrɪk] *adj* ictérico
**icterus** [ˈɪktərəs] *s* (path.) ictericia
**ictus** [ˈɪktəs] *s* (*pl:* **ictuses** o **ictus**) (path. & pros.) ictus
**icy** [ˈaɪsɪ] *adj* (*comp:* **icier;** *super:* **iciest**) helado, frío; resbaladizo; (fig.) frío
**id.** abr. de **idem**
**Id.** abr. de **Idaho**
**I'd** [aɪd] contracción de **I had, I should** y **I would**
**id** [ɪd] *s* (psychoanal.) ello
**Ida.** abr. de **Idaho**
**idea** [aɪˈdiə] *s* idea
**ideal** [aɪˈdiəl] *adj & s* ideal
**idealism** [aɪˈdiəlɪzəm] *s* idealismo
**idealist** [aɪˈdiəlɪst] *adj & s* idealista
**idealistic** [aɪˌdiəlˈɪstɪk] *adj* idealista; (philos.) idealístico
**ideality** [ˌaɪdɪˈælɪtɪ] *s* (*pl:* **-ties**) idealidad
**idealization** [aɪˌdiəlɪˈzeʃən] *s* idealización
**idealize** [aɪˈdiəlaɪz] *va* idealizar
**ideally** [aɪˈdiəlɪ] *adv* idealmente
**ideation** [ˌaɪdɪˈeʃən] *s* ideación
**idem** [ˈaɪdɛm] *adj & pron* (Lat.) ídem
**identic** [aɪˈdɛntɪk] o **identical** [aɪˈdɛntɪkəl] *adj* idéntico
**identical twins** *spl* gemelos homólogos o idénticos
**identification** [aɪˌdɛntɪfɪˈkeʃən] *s* identificación
**identification tag** *s* (mil.) disco de identificación, placa de identidad
**identify** [aɪˈdɛntɪfaɪ] (*pret & pp:* **-fied**) *va* identificar
**identity** [aɪˈdɛntɪtɪ] *s* (*pl:* **-ties**) identidad
**ideogram** [ˈɪdɪoˌɡræm] o [ˈaɪdɪoˌɡræm] *s* ideograma
**ideograph** [ˈɪdɪoˌɡræf] o [ˈaɪdɪoˌɡræf] *s* ideografía
**ideographic** [ˌɪdɪoˈɡræfɪk] o [ˌaɪdɪoˈɡræfɪk] o **ideographical** [ˌɪdɪoˈɡræfɪkəl] o [ˌaɪdɪoˈɡræfɪkəl] *adj* ideográfico
**ideologic** [ˌɪdɪoˈlɑdʒɪk] o [ˌaɪdɪoˈlɑdʒɪk] o **ideological** [ˌɪdɪoˈlɑdʒɪkəl] o [ˌaɪdɪoˈlɑdʒɪkəl] *adj* ideológico
**ideologist** [ˌaɪdɪˈɑlədʒɪst] o [ˌɪdɪˈɑlədʒɪst] *s* ideólogo
**ideology** [ˌaɪdɪˈɑlədʒɪ] o [ˌɪdɪˈɑlədʒɪ] *s* (*pl:* **-gies**) ideología
**ides** [aɪdz] *spl* idus
**idiocy** [ˈɪdɪəsɪ] *s* (*pl:* **-cies**) idiotez
**idioelectric** [ˌɪdɪo·ɪˈlɛktrɪk] o **idioelectrical** [ˌɪdɪo·ɪˈlɛktrɪkəl] *adj* idioeléctrico
**idiom** [ˈɪdɪəm] *s* modismo; idioma, lenguaje, jerga; genio, índole (*de un idioma*); estilo (*de un escritor*)
**idiomatic** [ˌɪdɪəˈmætɪk] *adj* idiomático
**idiosyncrasy** [ˌɪdɪoˈsɪŋkrəsɪ] *s* (*pl:* **-sies**) idiosincrasia
**idiosyncratic** [ˌɪdɪosɪnˈkrætɪk] *adj* idiosincrásico
**idiot** [ˈɪdɪət] *s* idiota
**idiotic** [ˌɪdɪˈɑtɪk] *adj* idiota
**idiotically** [ˌɪdɪˈɑtɪkəlɪ] *adv* estúpidamente, imbécilmente
**idioticon** [ˌɪdɪˈɑtɪkɑn] *s* idiótico
**idle** [ˈaɪdəl] *adj* ocioso; **at idle moments** a ratos perdidos; **to run idle** marchar en ralentí o en vacío; *va* (mach.) hacer marchar en ralentí o en vacío; **to idle away** gastar ociosamente (*el tiempo*); *vn* estar ocioso, holgar, haraganear; (mach.) marchar en ralentí o en vacío
**idleness** [ˈaɪdəlnɪs] *s* ociosidad
**idler** [ˈaɪdlər] *s* ocioso, haragán; (mach.) polea loca, rueda loca
**idol** [ˈaɪdəl] *s* ídolo; (fig.) ídolo
**idolater** [aɪˈdɑlətər] *s* idólatra
**idolatress** [aɪˈdɑlətrɪs] *s* idólatra
**idolatrous** [aɪˈdɑlətrəs] *adj* idolátrico, idólatra
**idolatry** [aɪˈdɑlətrɪ] *s* (*pl:* **-tries**) idolatría
**idolization** [ˌaɪdəlɪˈzeʃən] *s* idolatría
**idolize** [ˈaɪdəlaɪz] *va* idolatrar

**Idomeneus** [aɪˈdɑmɪnjus] o [aɪˈdɑmɪnus] *s* (myth.) Idomeneo
**Idumaea** o **Idumea** [ˌɪdjuˈmiə] o [ˌaɪdjuˈmiə] *s* (Bib.) Idumea
**Idumaean** o **Idumean** [ˌɪdjuˈmiən] o [ˌaɪdjuˈmiən] *adj & s* idumeo
**idyl** o **idyll** [ˈaɪdəl] *s* idilio
**idyllic** [aɪˈdɪlɪk] *adj* idílico
**i.e.** abr. de **id est** (Lat.) **that is, that is to say**
**-ie** *suffix dim* var. de **-y,** p.ej., **doggie** perrito; **Annie** Anita
**if** [ɪf] *s* hipótesis; *conj* si; **if so** si es así; **if true** si es cierto
**igloo** [ˈɪɡlu] *s* iglú
**Ignatian** [ɪɡˈneʃən] *adj & s* ignaciano
**Ignatius** [ɪɡˈneʃəs] *s* Ignacio
**igneous** [ˈɪɡnɪəs] *adj* ígneo
**igniferous** [ɪɡˈnɪfərəs] *adj* ignífero
**ignifuge** [ˈɪɡnɪfjudʒ] *adj & s* ignífugo
**ignis fatuus** [ˈɪɡnɪsˈfætʃuəs] *s* (*pl:* **ignes fatui** [ˈɪɡnizˈfætʃuaɪ]) fuego fatuo
**ignite** [ɪɡˈnaɪt] *va* encender; *vn* encenderse
**igniter** [ɪɡˈnaɪtər] *s* encendedor (*persona y dispositivo*)
**ignition** [ɪɡˈnɪʃən] *s* ignición, encendido, inflamación
**ignition coil** *s* (aut.) bobina de encendido
**ignition point** *s* punto de inflamación
**ignition stroke** *s* (aut.) carrera de encendido
**ignition switch** *s* (aut.) interruptor del encendido
**ignivomous** [ɪɡˈnɪvəməs] *adj* ignívomo
**ignoble** [ɪɡˈnobəl] *adj* innoble
**ignominious** [ˌɪɡnəˈmɪnɪəs] *adj* ignominioso
**ignominy** [ˈɪɡnəmɪnɪ] *s* (*pl:* **-ies**) ignominia
**ignoramus** [ˌɪɡnəˈreməs] *s* ignorante
**ignorance** [ˈɪɡnərəns] *s* ignorancia
**ignorant** [ˈɪɡnərənt] *adj* ignorante
**ignore** [ɪɡˈnor] *va* no hacer caso de; no hacerle caso (*a una persona*); (law) rechazar
**Igorot** [ˌɪɡəˈrot] *adj & s* igorrote
**Igorrote** [ˌɪɡəˈrotɪ] *s* igorrote
**iguana** [ɪˈɡwɑnə] *s* (zool.) iguana
**iguanodont** [ɪˈɡwænədɑnt] *s* (pal.) iguanodonte
**IHS** abr. de **In Hac (Cruce) Salus** (Lat.) **In this cross salvation; In Hoc Signo Vinces** (Lat.) **In this sign shalt thou conquer;** y **Iesus Hominum Salvator** (Lat.) **Jesus, Saviour of Men**
**ikon** [ˈaɪkɑn] *s* var. de **icon**
**ileac** [ˈɪlɪæk] *adj* (anat. & path.) ilíaco
**ileocaecal** [ˌɪlɪoˈsikəl] *adj* ileocecal
**ileum** [ˈɪlɪəm] *s* (anat.) íleon
**ileus** [ˈɪlɪəs] *s* (path.) íleo
**ilex** [ˈaɪlɛks] *s* (bot.) acebo; (bot.) hierba mate; (bot.) encina
**iliac** [ˈɪlɪæk] *adj* (anat.) ilíaco; (*cap.*) *adj* (myth.) ilíaco
**Iliad** [ˈɪlɪəd] *s* Ilíada
**Ilian** [ˈɪlɪən] *adj* (myth.) iliense
**ilicaceous** [ˌaɪlɪˈkeʃəs] *adj* (bot.) ilicáceo
**Ilion** [ˈɪlɪən] *s* (myth.) Ilión
**ilium** [ˈɪlɪəm] *s* (*pl:* **-a** [ə]) (anat.) ilion; (*cap.*) *s* (myth.) Ilión
**ilk** [ɪlk] *s* jaez, especie; **of that ilk** (coll.) del mismo nombre; (coll.) de ese jaez, de esa especie
**ill.** abr. de **illustrated** y **illustration**
**Ill.** abr. de **Illinois**
**I'll** [aɪl] contracción de **I shall** y **I will**
**ill** [ɪl] *adj* (*comp:* **worse;** *super:* **worst**) malo, enfermo; *adv* mal; **to take ill** tomar a mal; caer enfermo; *s* mal, enfermedad
**ill-advised** [ˈɪlədˈvaɪzd] *adj* malaconsejado, desaconsejado
**ill at ease** *adj* incómodo, inquieto, corrido, avergonzado
**illation** [ɪˈleʃən] *s* ilación
**illative** [ˈɪlətɪv] *adj* ilativo; *s* ilativa
**ill-boding** [ˈɪlˈbodɪŋ] *adj* nefasto, aciago, ominoso
**ill-bred** [ˈɪlˈbrɛd] *adj* malcriado
**ill breeding** *s* mala crianza, malos modales
**ill-considered** [ˈɪlkənˈsɪdərd] *adj* desconsiderado
**ill-disposed** [ˈɪldɪsˈpozd] *adj* malintencionado; maldispuesto
**illegal** [ɪˈligəl] *adj* ilegal
**illegality** [ˌɪliˈɡælɪtɪ] *s* (*pl:* **-ties**) ilegalidad

**illegibility** [ˌɪlɛdʒɪˈbɪlɪtɪ] *s* (*pl:* **-ties**) ilegibilidad
**illegible** [ɪˈlɛdʒɪbəl] *adj* ilegible
**illegitimacy** [ˌɪlɪˈdʒɪtɪməsɪ] *s* ilegitimidad
**illegitimate** [ˌɪlɪˈdʒɪtɪmɪt] *adj* ilegítimo
**ill fame** *s* mala fama; reputación de inmoral
**ill-fated** [ˈɪlˈfetɪd] *adj* aciago, funesto, infausto; malogrado; siniestrado
**ill-favored** [ˈɪlˈfevərd] *adj* feo, repugnante
**ill-featured** [ˈɪlˈfitʃərd] *adj* mal agestado, de mala cara
**ill-founded** [ˈɪlˈfaʊndɪd] *adj* mal fundado
**ill-gotten** [ˈɪlˈgɑtən] *adj* mal ganado
**ill health** *s* mala salud
**ill humor** *s* mal humor
**ill-humored** [ˈɪlˈhjumərd] *adj* malhumorado
**illiberal** [ɪˈlɪbərəl] *adj* iliberal
**illiberality** [ɪˌlɪbəˈrælɪtɪ] *s* iliberalidad
**illicit** [ɪˈlɪsɪt] *adj* ilícito
**illimitable** [ɪˈlɪmɪtəbəl] *adj* ilimitable, infinito
**illinium** [ɪˈlɪnɪəm] *s* (chem.) ilinio
**illiteracy** [ɪˈlɪtərəsɪ] *s* (*pl:* **-cies**) ignorancia, incultura; analfabetismo; (gram.) barbarismo
**illiterate** [ɪˈlɪtərɪt] *adj* iliterato; analfabeto; *s* analfabeto
**ill-judged** [ˈɪlˈdʒʌdʒd] *adj* desconsiderado, imprudente
**ill-mannered** [ˈɪlˈmænərd] *adj* de malos modales
**ill nature** *s* mala disposición
**ill-natured** [ˈɪlˈnetʃərd] *adj* maldispuesto, malicioso
**illness** [ˈɪlnɪs] *s* enfermedad
**illogical** [ɪˈlɑdʒɪkəl] *adj* ilógico
**ill-omened** [ˈɪlˈomənd] *adj* malhadado
**ill-spent** [ˈɪlˈspɛnt] *adj* malgastado
**ill-starred** [ˈɪlˈstɑrd] *adj* malhadado
**ill-suited** [ˈɪlˈsutɪd] o [ˈɪlˈsjutɪd] *adj* inadecuado; incompetente
**ill temper** *s* mal genio
**ill-tempered** [ˈɪlˈtɛmpərd] *adj* de mal genio
**ill-timed** [ˈɪlˈtaɪmd] *adj* intempestivo, inoportuno
**ill-treat** [ˌɪlˈtrit] *va* maltratar
**ill treatment** *s* malos tratamientos
**ill turn** *s* mala jugada; cambio desfavorable
**illuminant** [ɪˈlumɪnənt] *adj* iluminante; *s* alumbrado
**illuminate** [ɪˈlumɪnet] *va* iluminar, alumbrar; ilustrar; (f.a.) iluminar, miniar; *vn* hacer luminarias
**Illuminati** [ɪˌlumɪˈnetaɪ] *spl* iluminados, alumbrados (*secta mística, nacida en España en el siglo XVI*)
**illuminating gas** *s* gas de alumbrado
**illuminating oil** *s* aceite de alumbrado
**illumination** [ɪˌlumɪˈneʃən] *s* iluminación
**illuminative** [ɪˈlumɪˌnetɪv] *adj* iluminativo
**illuminator** [ɪˈlumɪˌnetər] *s* iluminador
**illumine** [ɪˈlumɪn] *va* iluminar; animar, avivar; *vn* iluminarse
**Illuminism** [ɪˈlumɪnɪzəm] *s* iluminismo
**illus.** abr. de **illustrated** y **illustration**
**ill usage** *s* malos tratamientos
**ill-use** [ˌɪlˈjuz] *va* maltratar
**illusion** [ɪˈluʒən] *s* ilusión; cendal (*tela*)
**illusionist** [ɪˈluʒənɪst] *s* ilusionista, prestidigitador
**illusive** [ɪˈlusɪv] *adj* ilusivo
**illusory** [ɪˈlusərɪ] *adj* ilusorio
**illust.** abr. de **illustrated** y **illustration**
**illustrate** [ˈɪləstret] o [ɪˈlʌstret] *va* ilustrar
**illustration** [ˌɪləsˈtreʃən] *s* ilustración
**illustrative** [ɪˈlʌstrətɪv] o [ˈɪləsˌtretɪv] *adj* ilustrativo
**illustrator** [ˈɪləsˌtretər] *s* ilustrador
**illustrious** [ɪˈlʌstrɪəs] *adj* ilustre
**ill will** *s* mala voluntad, odio, inquina
**Illyria** [ɪˈlɪrɪə] *s* Iliria
**Illyrian** [ɪˈlɪrɪən] *adj & s* ilirio
**Illyric** [ɪˈlɪrɪk] *adj* ilírico
**I'm** [aɪm] contracción de **I am**
**image** [ˈɪmɪdʒ] *s* imagen; **in his own image** a su imagen; **the very image of** la propia estampa de, el vivo retrato de; *va* imaginar; representar; representar con imágenes; reflejar
**imagery** [ˈɪmɪdʒrɪ] o [ˈɪmɪdʒərɪ] *s* (*pl:* **-ries**) fantasía; imágenes; paisaje
**imaginable** [ɪˈmædʒɪnəbəl] *adj* imaginable
**imaginary** [ɪˈmædʒɪˌnɛrɪ] *adj* imaginario
**imagination** [ɪˌmædʒɪˈneʃən] *s* imaginación
**imaginative** [ɪˈmædʒɪˌnetɪv] *adj* imaginativo
**imagine** [ɪˈmædʒɪn] *va* imaginar; *vn* imaginar; (coll.) imaginarse; **to imagine** + *ger* imaginarse + *inf*
**imagist** [ˈɪmɪdʒɪst] *s* imagista o imaginista (*individuo de un grupo de poetas ingleses y norteamericanos*)
**imago** [ɪˈmego] *s* (*pl:* **imagos** o **imagines** [ɪˈmædʒɪniz]) (zool.) imago
**imam** [ɪˈmɑm] *s* imán (*título mahometano*)
**imbalm** [ɪmˈbɑm] *va* var. de **embalm**
**imbecile** [ˈɪmbɪsɪl] *adj & s* imbécil
**imbecility** [ˌɪmbɪˈsɪlɪtɪ] *s* (*pl:* **-ties**) imbecilidad
**imbed** [ɪmˈbɛd] (*pret & pp:* **-bedded;** *ger:* **-bedding**) *va* hincar, encajar, empotrar, plantar
**imbibe** [ɪmˈbaɪb] *va* beber; embeber; embeberse de o en; *vn* beber; (coll.) empinar el codo
**imbibition** [ˌɪmbɪˈbɪʃən] *s* imbibición
**imbricate** [ˈɪmbrɪket] o [ˈɪmbrɪkɪt] o **imbricated** [ˈɪmbrɪˌketɪd] *adj* imbricado
**imbrication** [ˌɪmbrɪˈkeʃən] *s* imbricación
**imbroglio** [ɪmˈbroljo] *s* (*pl:* **-glios**) embrollo
**imbrue** [ɪmˈbru] *va* mojar, mojar con sangre, ensangrentar
**imbue** [ɪmˈbju] *va* imbuir; **to imbue with** imbuir de o en
**imitable** [ˈɪmɪtəbəl] *adj* imitable
**imitate** [ˈɪmɪtet] *va* imitar
**imitation** [ˌɪmɪˈteʃən] *s* imitación; **in imitation of** a imitación de; *adj* imitación, de imitación, p.ej., **imitation jewelry** joyas imitación, joyas de imitación; imitado, p.e., **imitation pearls** perlas imitadas
**imitative** [ˈɪmɪˌtetɪv] *adj* imitativo; imitador
**imitator** [ˈɪmɪˌtetər] *s* imitador
**immaculate** [ɪˈmækjəlɪt] *adj* inmaculado
**Immaculate Conception** *s* Inmaculada Concepción
**immanence** [ˈɪmənəns] o **immanency** [ˈɪmənənsɪ] *s* inmanencia
**immanent** [ˈɪmənənt] *adj* inmanente
**Immanuel** [ɪˈmænjʊəl] *s* (Bib.) Emanuel
**immaterial** [ˌɪməˈtɪrɪəl] *adj* inmaterial; sin importancia, indiferente
**immaterialism** [ˌɪməˈtɪrɪəlɪzəm] *s* inmaterialismo
**immateriality** [ˌɪməˌtɪrɪˈælɪtɪ] *s* inmaterialidad
**immature** [ˌɪməˈtjʊr] o [ˌɪməˈtʊr] *adj* inmaturo
**immaturity** [ˌɪməˈtjʊrɪtɪ] o [ˌɪməˈtʊrɪtɪ] *s* inmadurez
**immeasurable** [ɪˈmɛʒərəbəl] *adj* inmensurable
**immeasurably** [ɪˈmɛʒərəblɪ] *adv* inmensurablemente
**immediacy** [ɪˈmidɪəsɪ] *s* inmediación
**immediate** [ɪˈmidɪɪt] *adj* inmediato
**immediately** [ɪˈmidɪɪtlɪ] *adv* inmediatamente
**immedicable** [ɪˈmɛdɪkəbəl] *adj* inmedicable
**immemorial** [ˌɪmɪˈmorɪəl] *adj* inmemorial o inmemorable
**immense** [ɪˈmɛns] *adj* inmenso; (slang) excelente
**immensely** [ɪˈmɛnslɪ] *adv* inmensamente
**immensity** [ɪˈmɛnsɪtɪ] *s* (*pl:* **-ties**) inmensidad
**immensurable** [ɪˈmɛnʃʊrəbəl] *adj* inmensurable
**immerge** [ɪˈmʌrdʒ] *va* inmergir, sumergir; *vn* inmergirse, sumergirse
**immerse** [ɪˈmʌrs] *va* inmergir, sumergir; bautizar por inmersión
**immersion** [ɪˈmʌrʃən] o [ɪˈmʌrʒən] *s* inmersión; (astr.) inmersión; bautismo por inmersión
**immigrant** [ˈɪmɪgrənt] *adj & s* inmigrante
**immigrate** [ˈɪmɪgret] *vn* inmigrar
**immigration** [ˌɪmɪˈgreʃən] *s* inmigración
**immigration quota** *s* cuota de inmigración
**imminence** [ˈɪmɪnəns] o **imminency** [ˈɪmɪnənsɪ] *s* inminencia
**imminent** [ˈɪmɪnənt] *adj* inminente
**immiscible** [ɪˈmɪsɪbəl] *adj* inmiscible
**immobile** [ɪˈmobɪl] o [ɪˈmobil] *adj* inmoble
**immobility** [ˌɪmoˈbɪlɪtɪ] *s* inmovilidad
**immobilization** [ɪˌmobɪlɪˈzeʃən] *s* inmovilización

**immobilize** [ɪ'mobɪlaɪz] *va* inmovilizar
**immoderate** [ɪ'mɑdərɪt] *adj* inmoderado
**immoderation** [ɪ,mɑdə'reʃən] *s* inmoderación
**immodest** [ɪ'mɑdɪst] *adj* inmodesto
**immodesty** [ɪ'mɑdɪstɪ] *s* inmodestia
**immolate** ['ɪmolet] *va* inmolar
**immolation** [,ɪmo'leʃən] *s* inmolación
**immolator** ['ɪmo,letər] *s* inmolador
**immoral** [ɪ'mɑrəl] o [ɪ'mɔrəl] *adj* inmoral
**immorality** [,ɪmə'rælɪtɪ] *s* (*pl:* **-ties**) inmoralidad
**immortal** [ɪ'mɔrtəl] *adj & s* inmortal
**immortality** [,ɪmɔr'tælɪtɪ] *s* inmortalidad
**immortalize** [ɪ'mɔrtəlaɪz] *va* inmortalizar
**immortelle** [,ɪmɔr'tɛl] *s* (bot.) siempreviva, perpetua
**immortification** [ɪ,mɔrtɪfɪ'keʃən] *s* inmortificación
**immortified** [ɪ'mɔrtɪfaɪd] *adj* inmortificado
**immovability** [ɪ,muvə'bɪlɪtɪ] *s* inmovilidad; impasibilidad
**immovable** [ɪ'muvəbəl] *adj* inmoble; (fig.) inmoble; impasible, insensible; (law) inmueble; **immovables** *spl* (law) inmuebles, bienes raíces
**immovable feast** *s* (eccl.) fiesta fija o inmoble
**immune** [ɪ'mjun] *adj* inmune; **immune to** inmune contra
**immunity** [ɪ'mjunɪtɪ] *s* (*pl:* **-ties**) inmunidad
**immunization** [,ɪmjənɪ'zeʃən] o [ɪ,mjunɪ'zeʃən] *s* inmunización
**immunize** ['ɪmjənaɪz] o [ɪ'mjunaɪz] *va* inmunizar
**immunologist** [,ɪmjə'nɑlədʒɪst] *s* inmunólogo
**immunology** [,ɪmjə'nɑlədʒɪ] *s* inmunología
**immure** [ɪ'mjʊr] *va* emparedar
**immurement** [ɪ'mjʊrmənt] *s* emparedamiento
**immutability** [ɪ,mjutə'bɪlɪtɪ] *s* inmutabilidad
**immutable** [ɪ'mjutəbəl] *adj* inmutable
**imp** [ɪmp] *s* diablillo; niño travieso
**impact** ['ɪmpækt] *s* impacto, choque; (fig.) impacto
**impacted** [ɪm'pæktɪd] *adj* apretado; (dent.) impactado
**impaction** [ɪm'pækʃən] *s* (dent. & med.) impacción
**impair** [ɪm'pɛr] *va* empeorar, deteriorar
**impairment** [ɪm'pɛrmənt] *s* empeoramiento, deterioro
**impale** [ɪm'pel] *va* empalar; cercar
**impalement** [ɪm'pelmənt] *s* empalamiento; cercamiento
**impalpability** [ɪm,pælpə'bɪlɪtɪ] *s* impalpabilidad
**impalpable** [ɪm'pælpəbəl] *adj* impalpable
**impanation** [,ɪmpə'neʃən] *s* (theol.) impanación
**impanel** [ɪm'pænəl] (*pret & pp:* **-eled** o **-elled;** *ger:* **-eling** o **-elling**) *va* inscribir en la lista de los jurados; elegir (*un jurado*)
**imparadise** [ɪm'pærədaɪs] *va* convertir en un paraíso; colmar de felicidad
**imparidigitate** [ɪm,pærɪ'dɪdʒɪtet] *adj* (zool.) imparidígito
**imparipinnate** [ɪm,pærɪ'pɪnet] *adj* (bot.) imparipinado
**imparisyllabic** [ɪm,pærɪsɪ'læbɪk] *adj* (gram.) imparisílabo o imparisilábico; *s* (gram.) nombre imparisílabo
**imparity** [ɪm'pærɪtɪ] *s* desigualdad, disparidad
**impart** [ɪm'pɑrt] *va* decir, hacer saber; imprimir, comunicar
**impartial** [ɪm'pɑrʃəl] *adj* imparcial
**impartiality** [,ɪmpɑrʃɪ'ælɪtɪ] *s* imparcialidad
**impassability** [ɪm,pæsə'bɪlɪtɪ] o [ɪm,pɑsə'bɪlɪtɪ] *s* impracticabilidad
**impassable** [ɪm'pæsəbəl] o [ɪm'pɑsəbəl] *adj* intransitable, impracticable
**impasse** [ɪm'pæs] o ['ɪmpæs] *s* callejón sin salida
**impassibility** [ɪm,pæsɪ'bɪlɪtɪ] *s* impasibilidad
**impassible** [ɪm'pæsɪbəl] *adj* impasible
**impassioned** [ɪm'pæʃənd] *adj* ardiente, vehemente
**impassive** [ɪm'pæsɪv] *adj* impasible
**impassivity** [,ɪmpæ'sɪvɪtɪ] *s* impasibilidad
**impaste** [ɪm'pest] *va* (f.a.) empastar
**impatience** [ɪm'peʃəns] *s* impaciencia
**impatient** [ɪm'peʃənt] *adj* impaciente

**impeach** [ɪm'pitʃ] *va* poner en tela de juicio; acusar; (law) residenciar
**impeachable** [ɪm'pitʃəbəl] *adj* censurable; (law) susceptible de ser residenciado
**impeachment** [ɪm'pitʃmənt] *s* juicio; acusación; (law) residencia
**impearl** [ɪm'pʌrl] *va* (poet.) aljofarar
**impeccability** [ɪm,pɛkə'bɪlɪtɪ] *s* impecabilidad
**impeccable** [ɪm'pɛkəbəl] *adj* impecable
**impecuniosity** [,ɪmpɪ,kjunɪ'ɑsɪtɪ] *s* inopia
**impecunious** [,ɪmpɪ'kjunɪəs] *adj* inope
**impedance** [ɪm'pidəns] *s* (elec.) impedancia
**impedance coil** *s* (elec.) bobina de impedancia
**impede** [ɪm'pid] *va* dificultar, contrariar, estorbar
**impediment** [ɪm'pɛdɪmənt] *s* impedimento; defecto; (law) impedimento
**impedimenta** [ɪm,pɛdɪ'mɛntə] *spl* equipajes; (mil.) impedimento
**impel** [ɪm'pɛl] (*pret & pp:* **-pelled;** *ger:* **-pelling**) *va* impeler, impulsar; **to impel to** + *inf* impeler o impulsar a + *inf*
**impend** [ɪm'pɛnd] *vn* pender; amenazar, ser inminente
**impending** [ɪm'pɛndɪŋ] *adj* pendiente; amenazante, inminente
**impenetrability** [ɪm,pɛnɪtrə'bɪlɪtɪ] *s* impenetrabilidad; impersuasión
**impenetrable** [ɪm'pɛnɪtrəbəl] *adj* impenetrable; impersuasible
**impenitence** [ɪm'pɛnɪtəns] *s* impenitencia
**impenitent** [ɪm'pɛnɪtənt] *adj & s* impenitente
**imper.** abr. de **imperative**
**imperative** [ɪm'pɛrətɪv] *adj* imperativo; imperioso, urgente; (gram.) imperativo; *s* imperativo; (gram.) imperativo
**imperative mood** *s* (gram.) modo imperativo
**imperceptibility** [,ɪmpər,sɛptɪ'bɪlɪtɪ] *s* imperceptibilidad
**imperceptible** [,ɪmpər'sɛptɪbəl] *adj* imperceptible
**imperceptibly** [,ɪmpər'sɛptɪblɪ] *adv* imperceptiblemente
**imperf.** abr. de **imperfect**
**imperfect** [ɪm'pʌrfɪkt] *adj* imperfecto; (gram.) imperfecto; *s* (gram.) imperfecto; (gram.) pretérito imperfecto
**imperfection** [,ɪmpər'fɛkʃən] *s* imperfección, desperfecto
**imperfective** [,ɪmpər'fɛktɪv] *adj* (gram.) imperfectivo
**imperforate** [ɪm'pʌrfəret] o [ɪm'pʌrfərɪt] *adj* imperforado; (philately) sin dentar
**imperforation** [ɪm,pʌrfə'reʃən] *s* imperforación
**imperial** [ɪm'pɪrɪəl] *adj* imperial; majestuoso, magnífico; *s* perilla; imperial (*sitio con asientos de algunos carruajes encima de la cubierta*)
**imperial eagle** *s* (orn.) águila imperial
**imperial gallon** *s* galón inglés
**imperialism** [ɪm'pɪrɪəlɪzəm] *s* imperialismo
**imperialist** [ɪm'pɪrɪəlɪst] *s* imperialista
**imperialistic** [ɪm,pɪrɪə'lɪstɪk] *adj* imperialista
**imperialistically** [ɪm,pɪrɪə'lɪstɪkəlɪ] *adv* de modo imperialista
**imperil** [ɪm'pɛrɪl] (*pret & pp:* **-iled** o **-illed;** *ger:* **-iling** o **-illing**) *va* poner en peligro
**imperious** [ɪm'pɪrɪəs] *adj* imperioso
**imperishability** [ɪm,pɛrɪʃə'bɪlɪtɪ] *s* inmortalidad, eternidad
**imperishable** [ɪm'pɛrɪʃəbəl] *adj* imperecedero
**imperium** [ɪm'pɪrɪəm] *s* (*pl:* **-a** [ə]) imperio, mandato, autoridad; (law) poder
**impermanence** [ɪm'pʌrmənəns] *s* impermanencia
**impermanent** [ɪm'pʌrmənənt] *adj* impermanente
**impermeability** [ɪm,pʌrmɪə'bɪlɪtɪ] *s* impermeabilidad
**impermeable** [ɪm'pʌrmɪəbəl] *adj* impermeable
**impermutable** [,ɪmpər'mjutəbəl] *adj* impermutable
**impers.** abr. de **impersonal**
**impersonal** [ɪm'pʌrsənəl] *adj* impersonal; (gram.) impersonal, unipersonal
**impersonality** [ɪm,pʌrsə'nælɪtɪ] *s* impersonalidad; cosa impersonal, fuerza impersonal

**impersonally** [ɪm'pʌrsənəlɪ] *adv* impersonalmente
**impersonate** [ɪm'pʌrsənet] *va* hacer el papel de; imitar; personificar
**impersonation** [ɪm,pʌrsə'neʃən] *s* papel; imitación; personificación
**impersonator** [ɪm'pʌrsə,netər] *s* representador, actor; imitador; personificador; transformista (*actor que hace mutaciones rápidas*)
**impertinence** [ɪm'pʌrtɪnəns] *s* impertinencia
**impertinency** [ɪm'pʌrtɪnənsɪ] *s* (*pl:* **-cies**) var. de **impertinence**
**impertinent** [ɪm'pʌrtɪnənt] *adj & s* impertinente
**imperturbability** [,ɪmpər,tʌrbə'bɪlɪtɪ] *s* imperturbabilidad
**imperturbable** [,ɪmpər'tʌrbəbəl] *adj* imperturbable
**impervious** [ɪm'pʌrvɪəs] *adj* impervio, impenetrable, impermeable; impersuasible, inflexible
**impetigo** [,ɪmpɪ'taɪgo] *s* (path.) impétigo
**impetuosity** [ɪm,pɛtʃʊ'ɑsɪtɪ] *s* (*pl:* **-ties**) impetuosidad
**impetuous** [ɪm'pɛtʃʊəs] *adj* impetuoso
**impetus** ['ɪmpɪtəs] *s* ímpetu
**imp. gal.** abr. de **imperial gallon**
**impiety** [ɪm'paɪətɪ] *s* (*pl:* **-ties**) impiedad
**impinge** [ɪm'pɪndʒ] *vn* incidir, chocar; **to impinge on** o **upon** incidir en; pasar los límites de
**impingement** [ɪm'pɪndʒmənt] *s* choque; infracción, violación
**impious** ['ɪmpɪəs] *adj* impío
**impish** ['ɪmpɪʃ] *adj* endiablado, travieso
**implacability** [ɪm,plekə'bɪlɪtɪ] o [ɪm,plækə'bɪlɪtɪ] *s* implacabilidad
**implacable** [ɪm'plekəbəl] o [ɪm'plækəbəl] *adj* implacable
**implant** [ɪm'plænt] *va* plantar; implantar
**implantation** [,ɪmplæn'teʃən] *s* plantación; implantación
**implement** ['ɪmplɪmənt] *s* utensilio, instrumento, herramienta; ['ɪmplɪmɛnt] *va* pertrechar; poner por obra, llevar a cabo
**implementation** [,ɪmplɪmɛn'teʃən] *s* ejecución, cumplimiento
**implicate** ['ɪmplɪket] *va* implicar, comprometer; enlazar, enredar
**implication** [,ɪmplɪ'keʃən] *s* indicación, insinuación; implicación, complicidad
**implicit** [ɪm'plɪsɪt] *adj* implícito; absoluto, ciego
**implicitly** [ɪm'plɪsɪtlɪ] *adv* implícitamente; absolutamente
**implied** [ɪm'plaɪd] *adj* implícito
**impliedly** [ɪm'plaɪɪdlɪ] *adv* implícitamente
**implore** [ɪm'plor] *va* implorar
**implosion** [ɪm'ploʒən] *s* implosión; (phonet.) implosión
**implosive** [ɪm'plosɪv] *adj* (phonet.) implosivo; *s* (phonet.) implosiva
**impluvium** [ɪm'pluvɪəm] *s* (*pl:* **-via** [vɪə]) impluvio
**imply** [ɪm'plaɪ] (*pret & pp:* **-plied**) *va* implicar, incluir en esencia, dar a entender
**impolite** [,ɪmpə'laɪt] *adj* descortés
**impolitic** [ɪm'pɑlɪtɪk] *adj* imprudente, indiscreto
**imponderability** [ɪm,pɑndərə'bɪlɪtɪ] *s* imponderabilidad
**imponderable** [ɪm'pɑndərəbəl] *adj & s* imponderable
**import** ['ɪmport] *s* importación; artículo importado; importancia; sentido, significación; [ɪm'port] o ['ɪmport] *va* importar; significar; *vn* importar
**importance** [ɪm'pɔrtəns] *s* importancia
**important** [ɪm'pɔrtənt] *adj* importante
**importation** [,ɪmpor'teʃən] *s* importación; artículo importado
**importer** [ɪm'portər] *s* importador; casa importadora
**importunate** [ɪm'pɔrtʃənɪt] *adj* importuno
**importune** [,ɪmpɔr'tjun] o [,ɪmpɔr'tun] *va* importunar
**importunity** [,ɪmpɔr'tjunɪtɪ] o [,ɪmpɔr'tunɪtɪ] *s* (*pl:* **-ties**) importunidad
**impose** [ɪm'poz] *va* imponer (*la voluntad de uno, tributos, silencio, etc.*); (print.) imponer; (eccl.) imponer (*las manos*); hacer aceptar; **to impose onself on** o **upon** hacerse aceptar por; *vn* imponerse; **to impose on** o **upon** abusar de, engañar
**imposing** [ɪm'pozɪŋ] *adj* imponente
**imposition** [,ɪmpə'zɪʃən] *s* imposición (*p.ej., de la voluntad de uno*); (print.) imposición; (eccl.) imposición; abuso, engaño
**impossibility** [ɪm,pɑsɪ'bɪlɪtɪ] *s* (*pl:* **-ties**) imposibilidad
**impossible** [ɪm'pɑsɪbəl] *adj* imposible
**impossibly** [ɪm'pɑsɪblɪ] *adv* imposiblemente
**impost** ['ɪmpost] *s* impuesto; (arch.) imposta
**impostor** [ɪm'pɑstər] *s* impostor
**impostress** [ɪm'pɑstrɪs] *s* impostora
**imposture** [ɪm'pɑstʃər] *s* impostura
**impotence** ['ɪmpətəns] o **impotency** ['ɪmpətənsɪ] *s* impotencia; (path.) impotencia
**impotent** ['ɪmpətənt] *adj* impotente; (path.) impotente
**impound** [ɪm'paʊnd] *va* acorralar, encerrar; represar, rebalsar (*agua*); (law) depositar, embargar, secuestrar
**impoverish** [ɪm'pɑvərɪʃ] *va* empobrecer
**impoverishment** [ɪm'pɑvərɪʃmənt] *s* empobrecimiento
**impower** [ɪm'paʊər] *va* facultar, habilitar; autorizar
**impracticability** [ɪm,præktɪkə'bɪlɪtɪ] *s* (*pl:* **-ties**) impracticabilidad; cosa impracticable
**impracticable** [ɪm'præktɪkəbəl] *adj* impracticable; intratable
**impractical** [ɪm'præktɪkəl] *adj* impráctico, impracticable; soñador, utópico
**imprecate** ['ɪmprɪket] *va* imprecar
**imprecation** [,ɪmprɪ'keʃən] *s* imprecación
**imprecatory** ['ɪmprɪkə,torɪ] *adj* imprecatorio
**impregnability** [ɪm,prɛgnə'bɪlɪtɪ] *s* inexpugnabilidad
**impregnable** [ɪm'prɛgnəbəl] *adj* inexpugnable
**impregnate** [ɪm'prɛgnet] *adj* imbuído; *va* empreñar; imbuir; (phys.) impregnar, empapar
**impregnation** [,ɪmprɛg'neʃən] *s* fecundación; infusión; (phys.) impregnación
**impresario** [,ɪmprɛ'sɑrɪo] *s* (*pl:* **-rios**) empresario, empresario de teatro
**imprescriptible** [,ɪmprɪ'skrɪptɪbəl] *adj* imprescriptible
**impress** ['ɪmprɛs] *s* impresión; [ɪm'prɛs] *va* imprimir; apretar; impresionar; expropiar, apoderarse de; (mil.) enganchar
**impressibility** [ɪm,prɛsɪ'bɪlɪtɪ] *s* impresionabilidad
**impressible** [ɪm'prɛsɪbəl] *adj* impresionable
**impression** [ɪm'prɛʃən] *s* impresión; (fig.) impresión
**impressionability** [ɪm,prɛʃənə'bɪlɪtɪ] *s* impresionabilidad
**impressionable** [ɪm'prɛʃənəbəl] *adj* impresionable
**impressionism** [ɪm'prɛʃənɪzəm] *s* (paint., lit. & mus.) impresionismo
**impressionist** [ɪm'prɛʃənɪst] *s* impresionista
**impressionistic** [ɪm,prɛʃə'nɪstɪk] *adj* impresionista
**impressive** [ɪm'prɛsɪv] *adv* impresionante
**impressment** [ɪm'prɛsmənt] *s* expropiación; (mil.) enganche
**imprimatur** [,ɪmprɪ'metər] *s* imprimátur; aprobación, permiso
**imprint** ['ɪmprɪnt] *s* impresión; (print.) pie de imprenta; [ɪm'prɪnt] *va* imprimir, estampar
**imprison** [ɪm'prɪzən] *va* aprisionar, encarcelar
**imprisonment** [ɪm'prɪzənmənt] *s* encarcelamiento
**improbability** [ɪm,prɑbə'bɪlɪtɪ] *s* (*pl:* **-ties**) improbabilidad
**improbable** [ɪm'prɑbəbəl] *adj* improbable
**improbably** [ɪm'prɑbəblɪ] *adv* improbablemente
**impromptu** [ɪm'prɑmptju] o [ɪm'prɑmptu] *adv* de improviso; *s* improvisación; (mus.) improvisación, impromptu
**improper** [ɪm'prɑpər] *adj* impropio; indecoroso
**improper fraction** *s* (math.) fracción impropia
**impropriety** [,ɪmprə'praɪətɪ] *s* (*pl:* **-ties**) in-

conveniencia, indecencia; impropiedad (*especialmente en el lenguaje*)
**improve** [ɪm'pruv] *va* perfeccionar, mejorar; aprovechar; *vn* perfeccionarse, mejorar, mejorarse; **to improve on** o **upon** perfeccionar, mejorar
**improvement** [ɪm'pruvmənt] *s* perfeccionamiento, mejoramiento; mejoría (*p.ej., en la salud*); reforma, renovación; aprovechamiento (*empleo útil, p.ej., del tiempo*)
**improvidence** [ɪm'prɑvɪdəns] *s* imprevisión
**improvident** [ɪm'prɑvɪdənt] *adj* imprevisor, impróvido
**improvisation** [,ɪmprəvaɪ'zeʃən] o [,ɪmprɑvɪ'zeʃən] *s* improvisación
**improvise** ['ɪmprəvaɪz] *va & vn* improvisar
**improviser** ['ɪmprə,vaɪzər] *s* improvisador
**imprudence** [ɪm'prudəns] *s* imprudencia
**imprudent** [ɪm'prudənt] *adj* imprudente
**impuberate** [ɪm'pjubəret] *adj* impúber o impúbero
**impudence** ['ɪmpjədəns] *s* impudencia, insolencia
**impudent** ['ɪmpjədənt] *adj* impudente, insolente
**impugn** [ɪm'pjun] *va* impugnar; poner en tela de juicio
**impugnable** [ɪm'pʌgnəbəl] *adj* inexpugnable
**impugnation** [,ɪmpʌg'neʃən] *s* impugnación
**impulse** ['ɪmpʌls] *s* impulso; (mech.) impulso
**impulse turbine** *s* turbina de acción, turbina de impulsión
**impulsion** [ɪm'pʌlʃən] *s* impulsión
**impulsive** [ɪm'pʌlsɪv] *adj* impulsivo
**impulsiveness** [ɪm'pʌlsɪvnɪs] *s* impulsividad
**impunity** [ɪm'pjunɪtɪ] *s* impunidad
**impure** [ɪm'pjur] *adj* impuro
**impurity** [ɪm'pjurɪtɪ] *s* (*pl:* **-ties**) impureza o impuridad
**imputable** [ɪm'pjutəbəl] *adj* imputable
**imputation** [,ɪmpjʊ'teʃən] *s* imputación
**impute** [ɪm'pjut] *va* imputar
**imputer** [ɪm'pjutər] *s* imputador
**in.** abr. de **inch** o **inches**
**in** [ɪn] *adv* dentro, adentro, hacia adentro; en casa, en su oficina; en posesión; en el poder; en su turno; **to be in** estar en casa, estar en su oficina; **to be in for** estar expuesto a, no poder evitar; **to be in with** gozar del favor de; **in here** aquí dentro; **in there** allí dentro; *adj* interior, de adentro; *prep* en, con, de, durante, dentro de, de aquí a, sobre; por, p.ej., **he traveled in Spain** viajó por España; **in so far as** en tanto que; **in that** en que, por cuanto; *s* rincón, recodo; **ins and outs** recovecos; pormenores minuciosos
**inability** [,ɪnə'bɪlɪtɪ] *s* inhabilidad, incapacidad
**inaccessibility** [,ɪnæk,sɛsɪ'bɪlɪtɪ] *s* inaccesibilidad; inasequibilidad
**inaccessible** [,ɪnæk'sɛsɪbəl] *adj* inaccesible; inasequible
**inaccessibly** [,ɪnæk'sɛsɪblɪ] *adv* inaccesiblemente; inasequiblemente
**inaccuracy** [ɪn'ækjərəsɪ] *s* (*pl:* **-cies**) inexactitud, incorrección
**inaccurate** [ɪn'ækjərɪt] *adj* inexacto, incorrecto
**inaction** [ɪn'ækʃən] *s* inacción
**inactive** [ɪn'æktɪv] *adj* inactivo
**inactivity** [,ɪnæk'tɪvɪtɪ] *s* inactividad
**inadaptability** [,ɪnə,dæptə'bɪlɪtɪ] *s* inadaptabilidad
**inadaptable** [,ɪnə'dæptəbəl] *adj* inadaptable
**inadequacy** [ɪn'ædɪkwəsɪ] *s* insuficiencia, inadecuación
**inadequate** [ɪn'ædɪkwɪt] *adj* insuficiente, inadecuado
**inadmissibility** [,ɪnəd,mɪsɪ'bɪlɪtɪ] *s* inadmisibilidad
**inadmissible** [,ɪnəd'mɪsɪbəl] *adj* inadmisible
**inadvertence** [,ɪnəd'vʌrtəns] *s* inadvertencia
**inadvertency** [,ɪnəd'vʌrtənsɪ] *s* (*pl:* **-cies**) var. de **inadvertence**
**inadvertent** [,ɪnəd'vʌrtənt] *adj* inadvertido
**inadvertently** [,ɪnəd'vʌrtəntlɪ] *adv* inadvertidamente
**inadvisable** [,ɪnəd'vaɪzəbəl] *adj* no aconsejable, imprudente
**inalienability** [ɪn,eljənə'bɪlɪtɪ] *s* inalienabilidad
**inalienable** [ɪn'eljənəbəl] *adj* inalienable, imprescindible
**inamorata** [ɪn,æmə'rɑtə] *s* amada, enamorada
**inane** [ɪn'en] *adj* inane
**inanimate** [ɪn'ænɪmɪt] *adj* inanimado
**inanition** [,ɪnə'nɪʃən] *s* inanición
**inanity** [ɪn'ænɪtɪ] *s* (*pl:* **-ties**) inanidad
**inapplicability** [ɪn,æplɪkə'bɪlɪtɪ] *s* inaplicación
**inapplicable** [ɪn'æplɪkəbəl] *adj* inaplicable
**inapposite** [ɪn'æpəzɪt] *adj* impertinente, inadecuado, inaplicable
**inappreciable** [,ɪnə'priʃɪəbəl] *adj* inapreciable
**inappreciably** [,ɪnə'priʃɪəblɪ] *adv* inapreciablemente
**inappropriate** [,ɪnə'proprɪɪt] *adj* inapropiado, no a propósito
**inapt** [ɪn'æpt] *adj* inapto
**inaptitude** [ɪn'æptɪtjud] o [ɪn'æptɪtud] *s* ineptitud
**inarticulate** [,ɪnɑr'tɪkjəlɪt] *adj* inarticulado; incapaz de expresarse
**inartistic** [,ɪnɑr'tɪstɪk] *adj* inartístico
**inartistically** [,ɪnɑr'tɪstɪkəlɪ] *adv* sin arte
**inasmuch as** [,ɪnəz'mʌtʃæz] *conj* ya que, puesto que; en cuanto, hasta donde
**inattention** [,ɪnə'tɛnʃən] *s* desatención, inatención
**inattentive** [,ɪnə'tɛntɪv] *adj* desatento, inatento
**inaudible** [ɪn'ɔdɪbəl] *adj* inaudible
**inaugural** [ɪn'ɔgjərəl] *adj* inaugural; *s* oración inaugural, discurso inaugural
**inaugurate** [ɪn'ɔgjəret] *va* inaugurar
**inauguration** [ɪn,ɔgjə'reʃən] *s* inauguración; toma de posesión
**inauspicious** [,ɪnɔ'spɪʃəs] *adj* impropicio, desfavorable
**inboard** ['ɪn,bord] *adj* (naut.) interior; *adv* (mach.) hacia dentro; (naut.) hacia dentro del casco
**inborn** ['ɪn,bɔrn] *adj* innato, ingénito
**inbound** ['ɪn,baʊnd] *adj* entrante
**inbred** ['ɪn,brɛd] *adj* ínsito, innato; engendrado sin mezcla de familias o razas; ['ɪn,brɛd] o [ɪn'brɛd] *pret & pp de* **inbreed**
**inbreed** ['ɪn,brid] o [ɪn'brid] (*pret & pp:* **-bred**) *va* engendrar sin mezclar familias ni razas
**inbreeding** ['ɪn,bridɪŋ] *s* intracruzamiento, generación sin mezcla de familias o razas
**inc.** abr. de **inclosure, included, including, inclusive, incorporated** y **increase**
**Inca** ['ɪŋkə] *s* inca; *adj* incaico
**incalculable** [ɪn'kælkjələbəl] *adj* incalculable
**Incan** ['ɪŋkən] *adj & s* inca
**incandescence** [,ɪnkən'dɛsəns] *s* incandescencia
**incandescent** [,ɪnkən'dɛsənt] *adj* incandescente
**incantation** [,ɪnkæn'teʃən] *s* conjuro
**incapability** [,ɪnkepə'bɪlɪtɪ] *s* incapacidad
**incapable** [ɪn'kepəbəl] *adj* incapaz
**incapacitate** [,ɪnkə'pæsɪtet] *va* incapacitar, inhabilitar
**incapacitation** [,ɪnkə,pæsɪ'teʃən] *s* inhabilitación
**incapacity** [,ɪnkə'pæsɪtɪ] *s* (*pl:* **-ties**) incapacidad
**incarcerate** [ɪn'kɑrsəret] *va* encarcelar
**incarceration** [ɪn,kɑrsə'reʃən] *s* encarcelación; (path.) incarceración
**incarnadine** [ɪn'kɑrnədaɪn] o [ɪn'kɑrnədin] *adj & s* encarnado; *va* volver encarnado
**incarnate** [ɪn'kɑrnɪt] o [ɪn'kɑrnet] *adj* encarnado (*en forma humana*); [ɪn'kɑrnet] *va* encarnar
**incarnation** [,ɪnkɑr'neʃən] *s* encarnación; (med.) encarnamiento; (*cap.*) *s* (theol.) encarnación
**incase** [ɪn'kes] *va* encajonar, encerrar
**incasement** [ɪn'kesmənt] *s* encajonamiento, encerramiento; caja, cobertura
**incautious** [ɪn'kɔʃəs] *adj* incauto
**incendiarism** [ɪn'sɛndɪərɪzəm] *s* incendio malicioso; (fig.) incitación al desorden
**incendiary** [ɪn'sɛndɪ,ɛrɪ] *adj* incendiario; *s* (*pl:* **-ies**) incendiario
**incendiary bomb** *s* (mil.) bomba incendiaria
**incense** ['ɪnsɛns] *s* incienso; (fig.) incienso;

*va* incensar; (fig.) incensar (*lisonjear*); [ɪn'sɛns] *va* exasperar, encolerizar
**incense burner** ['ɪnsɛns] *s* incensario
**incensory** ['ɪnsɛn,sorɪ] *s* (*pl:* **-ries**) incensario
**incentive** [ɪn'sɛntɪv] *adj & s* incentivo
**inception** [ɪn'sɛpʃən] *s* principio, comienzo
**inceptive** [ɪn'sɛptɪv] *s* (gram.) verbo incoativo; *adj* incipiente; (gram.) incoativo
**incertitude** [ɪn'sʌrtɪtjud] o [ɪn'sʌrtɪtud] *s* incertidumbre
**incessant** [ɪn'sɛsənt] *adj* incesante
**incest** ['ɪnsɛst] *s* incesto
**incestuous** [ɪn'sɛstʃuəs] *adj* incestuoso
**inch** [ɪntʃ] *s* pulgada; pizca; **by inches** pulgada por pulgada; a poquitos; **every inch** hasta los tuétanos; **inch by inch** pulgada por pulgada; a poquitos; **within an inch of** a dos dedos de; *vn* avanzar a poquitos; **to inch ahead** avanzar a poquitos
**inchmeal** ['ɪntʃ,mil] *adv* poco a poco; **by inchmeal** poco a poco
**inchoate** [ɪn'ko·ɪt] o ['ɪnkoet] *adj* incipiente, rudimental
**inchoative** [ɪn'koətɪv] *adj* incipiente, rudimental; (gram.) incoativo; *s* (gram.) verbo incoativo
**inchworm** ['ɪntʃ,wʌrm] *s* (zool.) geómetra
**incidence** ['ɪnsɪdəns] *s* incidencia; extensión (*de los efectos de una cosa*); (geom. & phys.) incidencia
**incident** ['ɪnsɪdənt] *adj* incidente; *s* incidente, incidencia
**incidental** [,ɪnsɪ'dɛntəl] *adj* incidente; obvencional; *s* elemento incidental; **incidentals** *spl* gastos menudos
**incidentally** [,ɪnsɪ'dɛntəlɪ] *adv* incidentalmente, incidentemente; a propósito
**incinerate** [ɪn'sɪnəret] *va* incinerar
**incineration** [ɪn,sɪnə'reʃən] *s* incineración
**incinerator** [ɪn'sɪnə,retər] *s* incinerador
**incipience** [ɪn'sɪpɪəns] *s* comienzo, principio
**incipient** [ɪn'sɪpɪənt] *adj* incipiente
**incise** [ɪn'saɪz] *va* cortar; grabar, tallar
**incision** [ɪn'sɪʒən] *s* incisión
**incisive** [ɪn'saɪsɪv] *adj* incisivo; (anat.) incisivo
**incisor** [ɪn'saɪzər] *s* (anat.) diente incisivo
**incisory** [ɪn'saɪsərɪ] *adj* incisorio
**incitation** [,ɪnsaɪ'teʃən] o [,ɪnsɪ'teʃən] *s* incitación
**incite** [ɪn'saɪt] *va* incitar; **to incite to** + *inf* incitar a + *inf*
**incitement** [ɪn'saɪtmənt] *s* incitamento
**incivility** [,ɪnsɪ'vɪlɪtɪ] *s* (*pl:* **-ties**) incivilidad
**incl.** abr. de **inclosure, including** y **inclusive**
**inclemency** [ɪn'klɛmənsɪ] *s* (*pl:* **-cies**) inclemencia
**inclement** [ɪn'klɛmənt] *adj* inclemente
**inclination** [,ɪnklɪ'neʃən] *s* inclinación
**incline** ['ɪnklaɪn] o [ɪn'klaɪn] *s* declive, pendiente; [ɪn'klaɪn] *va* inclinar; *vn* inclinarse
**inclined** [ɪn'klaɪnd] *adj* inclinado; **to be inclined to** + *inf* inclinarse a + *inf*
**inclined plane** *s* (mech.) plano inclinado
**inclinometer** [,ɪnklɪ'nɑmɪtər] *s* inclinómetro
**inclose** [ɪn'kloz] *va* cercar, encerrar, incluir; **to inclose herewith** remitir adjunto (*con una carta*)
**inclosure** [ɪn'kloʒər] *s* cercamiento, encerramiento, inclusión; cerca, encierro, recinto; cosa inclusa, carta inclusa, copia inclusa
**include** [ɪn'klud] *va* incluir; **to be included in** figurar en
**including** [ɪn'kludɪŋ] *prep* incluso
**inclusion** [ɪn'kluʒən] *s* inclusión; cosa inclusa, carta inclusa
**inclusion body** *s* (path.) cuerpo de inclusión
**inclusive** [ɪn'klusɪv] *adj* inclusivo; detallado, completo; **inclusive of** comprensivo de
**incog.** abr. de **incognito**
**incog** [ɪn'kɑg] *adj, s & adv* (coll.) var. de **incognito**
**incognito** [ɪn'kɑgnɪto] *adj* incógnito; *s* (*pl:* **-tos**) incógnito; *adv* de incógnito
**incoherence** [,ɪnko'hɪrəns] *s* incoherencia
**incoherency** [,ɪnko'hɪrənsɪ] *s* (*pl:* **-cies**) var. de **incoherence**
**incoherent** [,ɪnko'hɪrənt] *adj* incoherente
**incombustibility** [,ɪnkəm,bʌstɪ'bɪlɪtɪ] *s* incombustibilidad
**incombustible** [,ɪnkəm'bʌstɪbəl] *adj* incombustible; *s* substancia incombustible
**income** ['ɪnkʌm] *s* renta, utilidad, rédito
**income tax** *s* impuesto de utilidades, impuesto sobre rentas, impuesto a los réditos
**income-tax return** ['ɪnkʌm,tæks] *s* declaración de utilidades, declaración de ingresos
**incoming** ['ɪn,kʌmɪŋ] *adj* entrante; ascendente (*marea*); *s* entrada, llegada
**incommensurability** [,ɪnkə,mɛnʃərə'bɪlɪtɪ] *s* inconmensurabilidad
**incommensurable** [,ɪnkə'mɛnʃərəbəl] *adj* inconmensurable
**incommensurate** [,ɪnkə'mɛnʃərɪt] *adj* desproporcionado; inconmensurable
**incommode** [,ɪnkə'mod] *va* incomodar, desacomodar
**incommodious** [,ɪnkə'modɪəs] *adj* incómodo
**incommunicability** [,ɪnkə,mjunɪkə'bɪlɪtɪ] *s* incomunicabilidad
**incommunicable** [,ɪnkə'mjunɪkəbəl] *adj* incomunicable; inconversable
**incommunicado** [,ɪnkə,mjunɪ'kɑdo] *adj* incomunicado
**incommunicative** [,ɪnkə'mjunɪ,ketɪv] *adj* inconversable, insociable
**incomparable** [ɪn'kɑmpərəbəl] *adj* incomparable
**incompatibility** [,ɪnkəm,pætɪ'bɪlɪtɪ] *s* incompatibilidad
**incompatible** [,ɪnkəm'pætɪbəl] *adj* incompatible; desconforme
**incompetence** [ɪn'kɑmpɪtəns] o **incompetency** [ɪn'kɑmpɪtənsɪ] *s* incompetencia
**incompetent** [ɪn'kɑmpɪtənt] *adj* incompetente
**incomplete** [,ɪnkəm'plit] *adj* incompleto
**incompletely** [,ɪnkəm'plitlɪ] *adv* incompletamente
**incomplex** [,ɪnkəm'plɛks] *adj* incomplejo, incomplexo
**incomprehensibility** [,ɪnkɑmprɪ,hɛnsɪ'bɪlɪtɪ] *s* incomprehensibilidad o incomprensibilidad
**incomprehensible** [,ɪnkɑmprɪ'hɛnsɪbəl] *adj* incomprehensible o incomprensible
**incompressibility** [,ɪnkəm,prɛsɪ'bɪlɪtɪ] *s* incompresibilidad
**incompressible** [,ɪnkəm'prɛsɪbəl] *adj* incompresible
**inconceivability** [,ɪnkən,sivə'bɪlɪtɪ] *s* inconcebibilidad
**inconceivable** [,ɪnkən'sivəbəl] *adj* inconcebible
**inconceivably** [,ɪnkən'sivəblɪ] *adv* inconcebiblemente
**inconclusive** [,ɪnkən'klusɪv] *adj* inconcluyente
**inconel** ['ɪŋkənəl] *s* inconel
**incongruent** [ɪn'kɑŋgruənt] *adj* incongruente
**incongruity** [,ɪnkən'gruɪtɪ] *s* (*pl:* **-ties**) incongruencia
**incongruous** [ɪn'kɑŋgruəs] *adj* incongruo
**inconsequence** [ɪn'kɑnsɪkwɛns] *s* inconsecuencia
**inconsequent** [ɪn'kɑnsɪkwɛnt] *adj* inconsecuente
**inconsequential** [ɪn,kɑnsɪ'kwɛnʃəl] *adj* inconsecuente; de poca importancia
**inconsiderable** [,ɪnkən'sɪdərəbəl] *adj* insignificante
**inconsiderate** [,ɪnkən'sɪdərɪt] *adj* inconsiderado, desconsiderado
**inconsiderateness** [,ɪnkən'sɪdərɪtnɪs] *s* inconsideración, desconsideración
**inconsistency** [,ɪnkən'sɪstənsɪ] *s* (*pl:* **-cies**) inconsistencia, inconsecuencia
**inconsistent** [,ɪnkən'sɪstənt] *adj* inconsistente, inconsecuente
**inconsolable** [,ɪnkən'soləbəl] *adj* inconsolable
**inconsonant** [ɪn'kɑnsənənt] *adj* inconsonante
**inconspicuous** [,ɪnkən'spɪkjuəs] *adj* poco aparente; poco llamativo
**inconstancy** [ɪn'kɑnstənsɪ] *s* inconstancia
**inconstant** [ɪn'kɑnstənt] *adj* inconstante
**incontestable** [,ɪnkən'tɛstəbəl] *adj* incontestable
**incontinence** [ɪn'kɑntɪnəns] *s* incontinencia; (path.) incontinencia
**incontinent** [ɪn'kɑntɪnənt] *adj* incontinente
**incontrovertibility** [,ɪnkɑntrə,vʌrtɪ'bɪlɪtɪ] *s* incontrovertibilidad
**incontrovertible** [,ɪnkɑntrə'vʌrtɪbəl] *adj* incontrovertible

**inconvenience** [ˌɪnkən'vinjəns] *s* incomodidad, inconveniencia, molestia; *va* incomodar, molestar
**inconvenient** [ˌɪnkən'vinjənt] *adj* incómodo, inconveniente, molesto
**inconvertibility** [ˌɪnkənˌvʌrtɪ'bɪlɪtɪ] *s* inconvertibilidad
**inconvertible** [ˌɪnkən'vʌrtɪbəl] *adj* inconvertible
**inconvincible** [ˌɪnkən'vɪnsɪbəl] *adj* inconvencible
**incoördination** [ˌɪnkoˌɔrdɪ'neʃən] *s* incoordinación
**incorporate** [ɪn'kɔrpərɪt] *adj* incorporado; [ɪn'kɔrpəret] *va* incorporar; constituir en sociedad anónima; *vn* incorporarse; constituirse en sociedad anónima
**incorporation** [ɪnˌkɔrpə'reʃən] *s* incorporación; constitución en sociedad anónima
**incorporator** [ɪn'kɔrpəˌretər] *s* incorporador; fundador de una sociedad anónima
**incorporeal** [ˌɪnkɔr'porɪəl] *adj* incorpóreo, incorporal
**incorrect** [ˌɪnkə'rɛkt] *adj* incorrecto
**incorrectness** [ˌɪnkə'rɛktnɪs] *s* incorrección
**incorrigibility** [ɪnˌkɑrɪdʒɪ'bɪlɪtɪ] o [ɪnˌkɔrɪdʒɪ'bɪlɪtɪ] *s* incorregibilidad
**incorrigible** [ɪn'kɑrɪdʒɪbəl] o [ɪn'kɔrɪdʒɪbəl] *adj* incorregible
**incorrupt** [ˌɪnkə'rʌpt] *adj* incorrupto
**incorruptibility** [ˌɪnkəˌrʌptɪ'bɪlɪtɪ] *s* incorruptibilidad
**incorruptible** [ˌɪnkə'rʌptɪbəl] *adj* incorruptible
**increase** ['ɪnkris] *s* aumento; crecida, ascenso (*del agua*); ganancia, interés; hijo, hijos; productos agrícolas; **to be on the increase** ir en aumento; [ɪn'kris] *va* aumentar; multiplicar; *vn* aumentar; multiplicarse
**increasing** [ɪn'krisɪŋ] *adj* creciente
**increasingly** [ɪn'krisɪŋlɪ] *adv* cada vez más
**incredibility** [ɪnˌkrɛdɪ'bɪlɪtɪ] *s* incredibilidad
**incredible** [ɪn'krɛdɪbəl] *adj* increíble
**incredulity** [ˌɪnkrɪ'djulɪtɪ] o [ˌɪnkrɪ'dulɪtɪ] *s* incredulidad
**incredulous** [ɪn'krɛdʒələs] *adj* incrédulo
**increment** ['ɪnkrɪmənt] *s* incremento; (math.) incremento
**incriminate** [ɪn'krɪmɪnet] *va* acriminar, incriminar
**incrimination** [ɪnˌkrɪmɪ'neʃən] *s* acriminación, incriminación
**incriminatory** [ɪn'krɪmɪnəˌtorɪ] *adj* acriminador
**incrust** [ɪn'krʌst] *va* incrustar; *vn* incrustarse
**incrustation** [ˌɪnkrʌs'teʃən] *s* incrustación
**incrustive** [ɪn'krʌstɪv] *adj* incrustante
**incubate** ['ɪnkjəbet] *va & vn* incubar
**incubation** [ˌɪnkjə'beʃən] *s* incubación
**incubation period** *s* (path.) período de incubación
**incubator** ['ɪnkjəˌbetər] *s* incubadora
**incubus** ['ɪnkjəbəs] *s* (*pl:* **-buses** o **-bi** [baɪ]) íncubo; (med.) íncubo
**inculcate** [ɪn'kʌlket] o ['ɪnkʌlket] *va* inculcar
**inculcation** [ˌɪnkʌl'keʃən] *s* inculcación
**inculpable** [ɪn'kʌlpəbəl] *adj* inculpable
**inculpate** [ɪn'kʌlpet] o ['ɪnkʌlpet] *va* inculpar
**inculpation** [ˌɪnkʌl'peʃən] *s* inculpación
**incumbency** [ɪn'kʌmbənsɪ] *s* (*pl:* **-cies**) incumbencia
**incumbent** [ɪn'kʌmbənt] *adj* incumbente; (bot. & zool.) incumbente; **to be incumbent on** o **upon one** incumbirle a uno; **to be incumbent on one to** + *inf* incumbir a uno + *inf;* *s* titular, posesor; (eccl.) beneficiado
**incumber** [ɪn'kʌmbər] *va* embarazar, estorbar; impedir; gravar
**incumbrance** [ɪn'kʌmbrəns] *s* embarazo, estorbo; impedimento; gravamen; hijo menor de edad
**incunabula** [ˌɪnkjʊ'næbjələ] *spl* orígenes; incunables
**incur** [ɪn'kʌr] (*pret & pp:* **-curred;** *ger:* **-curring**) *va* incurrir en; contraer (*una deuda*)
**incurability** [ɪnˌkjʊrə'bɪlɪtɪ] *s* incurabilidad
**incurable** [ɪn'kjʊrəbəl] *adj & s* incurable
**incurious** [ɪn'kjʊrɪəs] *adj* indiferente; poco interesante
**incursion** [ɪn'kʌrʒən] o [ɪn'kʌrʃən] *s* incursión, irrupción, invasión
**incurve** ['ɪnˌkʌrv] *s* (baseball) curva adentro; [ɪn'kʌrv] *va* (baseball) encorvar hacia dentro; *vn* (baseball) encorvarse hacia dentro
**incus** ['ɪŋkəs] *s* (*pl:* **incudes** [ɪn'kjudiz]) (anat.) yunque
**incuse** [ɪn'kjuz] *adj* incuso
**ind.** abr. de **independent, indicative** y **industrial**
**Ind.** abr. de **India, Indian** y **Indiana**
**Ind** [ɪnd] *s* (poet.) India, Indias
**indebted** [ɪn'dɛtɪd] *adj* adeudado; obligado, reconocido
**indebtedness** [ɪn'dɛtɪdnɪs] *s* deuda; obligación
**indecency** [ɪn'disənsɪ] *s* (*pl:* **-cies**) indecencia, deshonestidad
**indecent** [ɪn'disənt] *adj* indecente, deshonesto
**indecent exposure** *s* exhibición impúdica, delito de exhibicionismo
**indecipherable** [ˌɪndɪ'saɪfərəbəl] *adj* indescifrable
**indecision** [ˌɪndɪ'sɪʒən] *s* indecisión
**indecisive** [ˌɪndɪ'saɪsɪv] *adj* indeciso
**indeclinable** [ˌɪndɪ'klaɪnəbəl] *adj* (gram.) indeclinable
**indecorous** [ɪn'dɛkərəs] o [ˌɪndɪ'korəs] *adj* indecoroso
**indecorum** [ˌɪndɪ'korəm] *s* indecoro
**indeed** [ɪn'did] *adv* verdaderamente, de veras, claro está; *interj* ¡ de veras!
**indef.** abr. de **indefinite**
**indefatigability** [ˌɪndɪˌfætɪgə'bɪlɪtɪ] *s* infatigabilidad
**indefatigable** [ˌɪndɪ'fætɪgəbəl] *adj* infatigable
**indefeasible** [ˌɪndɪ'fizɪbəl] *adj* inabrogable
**indefensible** [ˌɪndɪ'fɛnsɪbəl] *adj* indefendible
**indefinable** [ˌɪndɪ'faɪnəbəl] *adj* indefinible
**indefinite** [ɪn'dɛfɪnɪt] *adj* indefinido
**indefinite article** *s* (gram.) artículo indefinido
**indehiscence** [ˌɪndɪ'hɪsəns] *s* (bot.) indehiscencia
**indehiscent** [ˌɪndɪ'hɪsənt] *adj* (bot.) indehiscente
**indelibility** [ɪnˌdɛlɪ'bɪlɪtɪ] *s* indelebilidad
**indelible** [ɪn'dɛlɪbəl] *adj* indeleble
**indelible ink** *s* tinta indeleble
**indelible lead pencil** *s* lápiz tinta, lápiz violado de copiar
**indelicacy** [ɪn'dɛlɪkəsɪ] *s* (*pl:* **-cies**) indelicadeza
**indelicate** [ɪn'dɛlɪkɪt] *adj* indelicado
**indemnification** [ɪnˌdɛmnɪfɪ'keʃən] *s* indemnización
**indemnify** [ɪn'dɛmnɪfaɪ] (*pret & pp:* **-fied**) *va* indemnizar
**indemnity** [ɪn'dɛmnɪtɪ] *s* (*pl:* **-ties**) indemnización; indemnidad (***seguridad contra un daño***)
**indemonstrable** [ˌɪndɪ'mɑnstrəbəl] o [ɪn'dɛmənstrəbəl] *adj* indemostrable
**indent** ['ɪndɛnt] o [ɪn'dɛnt] *s* mella, diente, muesca; [ɪn'dɛnt] *va* mellar, dentar; (print.) sangrar; *vn* mellarse
**indentation** [ˌɪndɛn'teʃən] *s* mella, muesca; (print.) sangría
**indented** [ɪn'dɛntɪd] *adj* sangrado; (her.) endentado
**indention** [ɪn'dɛnʃən] *s* mella; (print.) sangría
**indenture** [ɪn'dɛntʃər] *s* escritura, contrato; contrato de aprendizaje, contrato de servidumbre; mella; *va* obligar por contrato
**independence** *s* [ˌɪndɪ'pɛndəns] *s* independencia
**Independence Day** *s* (U.S.A.) día de la independencia
**independency** [ˌɪndɪ'pɛndənsɪ] *s* (*pl:* **-cies**) independencia; país independente
**independent** [ˌɪndɪ'pɛndənt] *adj* independiente; **independent of** independiente de; *s* independiente
**independently** [ˌɪndɪ'pɛndəntlɪ] *adv* independientemente; **independently of** independientemente de
**indescribable** [ˌɪndɪ'skraɪbəbəl] *adj* indescriptible
**indestructibility** [ˌɪndɪˌstrʌktɪ'bɪlɪtɪ] *s* indestructibilidad
**indestructible** [ˌɪndɪ'strʌktɪbəl] *adj* indestructible

**indeterminability** [ˌɪndɪˌtʌrmɪnəˈbɪlɪtɪ] *s* indeterminabilidad
**indeterminable** [ˌɪndɪˈtʌrmɪnəbəl] *adj* indeterminable
**indeterminate** [ˌɪndɪˈtʌrmɪnɪt] *adj* indeterminado
**indetermination** [ˌɪndɪˌtʌrmɪˈneʃən] *s* indeterminación
**indeterminism** [ˌɪndɪˈtʌrmɪnɪzəm] *s* indeterminismo
**indeterminist** [ˌɪndɪˈtʌrmɪnɪst] *adj & s* indeterminista
**indeterministic** [ˌɪndɪˌtʌrmɪˈnɪstɪk] *adj* indeterminista
**indevotion** [ˌɪndɪˈvoʃən] *s* indevoción
**index** [ˈɪndɛks] *s* (*pl:* **indexes** o **indices** [ˈɪndɪsiz]) índice; (print.) manecilla; (math.) índice; (*cap.*) *s* índice de libros prohibidos; (*l.c.*) *va* poner índice a; poner en un índice
**index card** *s* ficha catalográfica (*de una biblioteca*)
**Index Expurgatorius** [ɛksˌpʌrgəˈtorɪəs] *s* (eccl.) índice expurgatorio
**index finger** *s* dedo índice
**index of refraction** *s* (phys.) índice de refracción
**index tab** *s* pestaña
**India** [ˈɪndɪə] *s* la India
**India ink** *s* tinta china
**Indiaman** [ˈɪndɪəmən] *s* (*pl:* **-men**) buque de la compañía de las Indias
**Indian** [ˈɪndɪən] *adj & s* indio
**Indian club** *s* maza de gimnasia
**Indian corn** *s* (bot.) panizo de las Indias (*planta y grano*)
**Indian cress** *s* (bot.) capuchina
**Indian Empire** *s* Imperio de las Indias
**Indian fig** *s* (bot.) nopal castellano, penco
**Indian file** *s* fila india; *adv* en fila india
**Indian giver** *s* (coll.) dador de toma y daca
**Indian heart** *s* (bot.) farolillo
**Indianism** [ˈɪndɪənɪzəm] *s* indianismo
**Indianist** [ˈɪndɪənɪst] *s* indianista
**Indian meal** *s* harina de maíz
**Indian millet** *s* (bot.) alcandía
**Indian Ocean** *s* océano Índico, mar de las Indias
**Indian pipe** *s* (bot.) monotropa
**Indian reed** *s* (bot.) caña de Indias, cañacoro
**Indian reservation** *s* (U.S.A.) reserva de indios
**Indian rice** *s* (bot.) arroz de los pieles rojas
**Indian shot** *s* var. de **Indian reed**
**Indian summer** *s* veranillo, veranillo de San Martín
**Indian Territory** *s* Gobernación de los Indios
**Indian tobacco** *s* (bot.) tabaco indio
**Indian turnip** *s* (bot.) arisema
**Indian yellow** *s* amarillo indio
**India paper** *s* papel de China
**India rubber** o **india rubber** *s* caucho
**indic.** abr. de **indicative**
**indican** [ˈɪndɪkæn] *s* (chem. & biochem.) indicán
**indicant** [ˈɪndɪkənt] *adj & s* indicante
**indicanuria** [ˌɪndɪkəˈnjʊrɪə] o [ˌɪndɪkəˈnʊrɪə] *s* (path.) indicanuria
**indicate** [ˈɪndɪket] *va* indicar
**indication** [ˌɪndɪˈkeʃən] *s* indicación
**indicative** [ɪnˈdɪkətɪv] *adj* indicativo; (gram.) indicativo; *s* (gram.) indicativo
**indicative mood** *s* (gram.) modo indicativo
**indicator** [ˈɪndɪˌketər] *s* indicador; (chem.) indicador
**indicatory** [ˈɪndɪkəˌtorɪ] *adj* indicador
**indict** [ɪnˈdaɪt] *va* (law) acusar, procesar
**indictable** [ɪnˈdaɪtəbəl] *adj* (law) denunciable, procesable
**indiction** [ɪnˈdɪkʃən] *s* indicción
**indictment** [ɪnˈdaɪtmənt] *s* (law) acusación, procesamiento; (law) auto de acusación formulado por el gran jurado
**Indies** [ˈɪndiz] *spl* Indias
**indifference** [ɪnˈdɪfərəns] *s* indiferencia
**indifferent** [ɪnˈdɪfərənt] *adj* indiferente; pasadero, mediano
**indifferentism** [ɪnˈdɪfərəntɪzəm] *s* indiferentismo
**indifferently** [ɪnˈdɪfərəntlɪ] *adv* indiferentemente; pasaderamente, medianamente; mal
**indigence** [ˈɪndɪdʒəns] *s* indigencia
**indigenous** [ɪnˈdɪdʒɪnəs] *adj* indígena; innato
**indigent** [ˈɪndɪdʒənt] *adj* indigente; **the indigent** los indigentes
**indigestibility** [ˌɪndɪˌdʒɛstɪˈbɪlɪtɪ] *s* indigestibilidad
**indigestible** [ˌɪndɪˈdʒɛstɪbəl] *adj* indigestible o indigerible
**indigestion** [ˌɪndɪˈdʒɛstʃən] *s* indigestión
**indignant** [ɪnˈdɪgnənt] *adj* indignado
**indignation** [ˌɪndɪgˈneʃən] *s* indignación
**indignation meeting** *s* reunión de protesta
**indignity** [ɪnˈdɪgnɪtɪ] *s* (*pl:* **-ties**) indignidad (*afrenta, ultraje*)
**indigo** [ˈɪndɪgo] *s* (*pl:* **-gos** o **-goes**) (bot. & chem.) índigo; añil o índigo (*del espectro solar*); *adj* de añil, azul de añil
**indigo bunting** *s* (orn.) azulejo
**indigo extract** *s* extracto de índigo, carmín de índigo
**indirect** [ˌɪndɪˈrɛkt] o [ˌɪndaɪˈrɛkt] *adj* indirecto
**indirect discourse** *s* (gram.) estilo indirecto
**indirection** [ˌɪndɪˈrɛkʃən] *s* rodeo; engaño
**indirect lighting** *s* iluminación indirecta, alumbrado reflejado
**indirect object** *s* (gram.) complemento indirecto
**indirect tax** *s* contribución indirecta
**indiscernibility** [ˌɪndɪˌzʌrnɪˈbɪlɪtɪ] o [ˌɪndɪˌsʌrnɪˈbɪlɪtɪ] *s* indiscernibilidad
**indiscernible** [ˌɪndɪˈzʌrnɪbəl] o [ˌɪndɪˈsʌrnɪbəl] *adj* indiscernible
**indiscreet** [ˌɪndɪsˈkrit] *adj* indiscreto
**indiscretion** [ˌɪndɪsˈkrɛʃən] *s* indiscreción
**indiscriminate** [ˌɪndɪsˈkrɪmɪnɪt] *adj* promiscuo; poco distintivo
**indispensability** [ˌɪndɪˌspɛnsəˈbɪlɪtɪ] *s* indispensabilidad
**indispensable** [ˌɪndɪˈspɛnsəbəl] *adj* indispensable, imprescindible
**indispose** [ˌɪndɪsˈpoz] *va* indisponer
**indisposed** [ˌɪndɪsˈpozd] *adj* maldispuesto; indispuesto (*algo enfermo*)
**indisposition** [ˌɪndɪspəˈzɪʃən] *s* desinclinación; indisposición (*enfermedad pasajera*)
**indisputability** [ɪnˌdɪspjʊtəˈbɪlɪtɪ] o [ˌɪndɪˌspjʊtəˈbɪlɪtɪ] *s* indisputabilidad
**indisputable** [ɪnˈdɪspjʊtəbəl] o [ˌɪndɪsˈpjʊtəbəl] *adj* indisputable
**indissolubility** [ˌɪndɪˌsɑljəˈbɪlɪtɪ] *s* indisolubilidad
**indissoluble** [ˌɪndɪˈsɑljəbəl] *adj* indisoluble
**indistinct** [ˌɪndɪˈstɪŋkt] *adj* indistinto
**indistinctness** [ˌɪndɪˈstɪŋktnɪs] *s* indistinción
**indistinguishable** [ˌɪndɪˈstɪŋgwɪʃəbəl] *adj* indistinguible
**indite** [ɪnˈdaɪt] *va* redactar, poner por escrito
**indium** [ˈɪndɪəm] *s* (chem.) indio
**individual** [ˌɪndɪˈvɪdʒʊəl] *adj* individual; *s* individuo; (biol.) individuo
**individualism** [ˌɪndɪˈvɪdʒʊəlɪzəm] *s* individualismo
**individualist** [ˌɪndɪˈvɪdʒʊəlɪst] *s* individualista
**individualistic** [ˌɪndɪˌvɪdʒʊəlˈɪstɪk] *adj* individualista
**individuality** [ˌɪndɪˌvɪdʒʊˈælɪtɪ] *s* (*pl:* **-ties**) individualidad; individuo
**individualize** [ˌɪndɪˈvɪdʒʊəlaɪz] *va* individualizar
**individually** [ˌɪndɪˈvɪdʒʊəlɪ] *adv* individualmente
**individuate** [ˌɪndɪˈvɪdʒʊet] *va* individuar
**individuation** [ˌɪndɪˌvɪdʒʊˈeʃən] *s* individuación
**indivisibility** [ˌɪndɪˌvɪzɪˈbɪlɪtɪ] *s* indivisibilidad
**indivisible** [ˌɪndɪˈvɪzɪbəl] *adj* indivisible
**indivision** [ˌɪndɪˈvɪʒən] *s* indivisión
**Indochina** [ˈɪndoˈtʃaɪnə] *s* la Indochina
**Indochinese** [ˈɪndotʃaɪˈniz] *adj* indochino; *s* (*pl:* **-nese**) indochino
**indoctrinate** [ɪnˈdɑktrɪnet] *va* adoctrinar, inculcar
**indoctrination** [ɪnˌdɑktrɪˈneʃən] *s* adoctrinamiento, inculcación
**Indo-European** [ˈɪndoˌjʊrəˈpiən] *adj & s* indoeuropeo

**Indo-Germanic** ['ɪndodʒʌr'mænɪk] *adj & s* indogermánico
**indole** ['ɪndol] *s* (chem.) indol
**indolence** ['ɪndələns] *s* indolencia
**indolent** ['ɪndələnt] *adj* indolente; (med.) indolente
**Indo-Malayan** ['ɪndomə'leən] *adj* indomalayo
**indomitable** [ɪn'dɑmɪtəbəl] *adj* indomable, indómito
**indomitably** [ɪn'dɑmɪtəblɪ] *adv* indómitamente
**Indonesia** [,ɪndo'niʃə] o [,ɪndo'niʒə] *s* la Indonesia
**Indonesian** [,ɪndo'niʃən] o [,ɪndo'niʒən] *adj & s* indonesio
**indoor** ['ɪn,dor] *adj* interior, de puertas adentro
**indoor aerial** *s* (rad.) antena de interior
**indoor games** *spl* diversiones caseras
**indoors** ['ɪn'dorz] *adv* dentro, en casa, bajo techado
**indophenol** [,ɪndo'finol] o [,ɪndo'finɑl] *s* (chem.) indofenol
**indorse** [ɪn'dɔrs] *va* endosar; apoyar, aprobar, respaldar
**indorsee** [,ɪndɔr'si] *s* endosatario
**indorsement** [ɪn'dɔrsmənt] *s* endoso; apoyo, aprobación
**indorser** [ɪn'dɔrsər] *s* endosante
**indoxyl** [ɪn'dɑksɪl] *s* (chem.) indoxilo
**indraft** o **indraught** ['ɪn,dræft] o ['ɪn,drɑft] *s* atracción hacia el interior; aspiración, aire aspirado; corriente entrante
**indubitable** [ɪn'djubɪtəbəl] o [ɪn'dubɪtəbəl] *adj* indubitable
**induce** [ɪn'djus] o [ɪn'dus] *va* inducir; causar, producir; (log. & elec.) inducir; **to induce to** + *inf* inducir a + *inf*
**inducement** [ɪn'djusmənt] o [ɪn'dusmənt] *s* incentivo, atractivo, estímulo
**induct** [ɪn'dʌkt] *va* instalar; introducir; iniciar; (mil.) quintar
**inductance** [ɪn'dʌktəns] *s* (elec.) inductancia
**inductee** [,ɪndʌk'ti] *s* (mil.) quinto
**inductile** [ɪn'dʌktɪl] *adj* no dúctil, inflexible
**induction** [ɪn'dʌkʃən] *s* instalación; (log. & elec.) inducción; (mil.) quinta
**induction coil** *s* (elec.) bobina de inducción, carrete de inducción
**induction motor** *s* (elec.) motor de inducción
**inductive** [ɪn'dʌktɪv] *adj* inductivo
**inductivity** [,ɪndʌk'tɪvɪtɪ] *s* inductividad
**inductor** [ɪn'dʌktər] *s* instalador; (elec.) inductor
**indue** [ɪn'dju] o [ɪn'du] *va* dotar, investir; poner, vestir
**indulge** [ɪn'dʌldʒ] *va* mimar; gratificar (*p.ej., los deseos de uno*); indulgenciar; *vn* abandonarse; **to indulge in** abandonarse a, entregarse a; permitirse el placer de, darse el lujo de
**indulgence** [ɪn'dʌldʒəns] *s* indulgencia; intemperancia, desenfreno
**indulgent** [ɪn'dʌldʒənt] *adj* indulgente
**indurate** ['ɪndjuret] o ['ɪnduret] *adj* endurecido; (med.) indurado; *va* endurecer; (med.) indurar; *vn* endurecerse
**induration** [,ɪndjʊ'reʃən] o [,ɪndʊ'reʃən] *s* induración; (med.) induración
**Indus** ['ɪndəs] *s* Indo
**indusium** [ɪn'djuzɪəm] o [ɪn'duzɪəm] *s* (bot.) indusio
**industrial** [ɪn'dʌstrɪəl] *adj* industrial
**industrialism** [ɪn'dʌstrɪəlɪzəm] *s* industrialismo
**industrialist** [ɪn'dʌstrɪəlɪst] *s* industrial
**industrialization** [ɪn,dʌstrɪəlɪ'zeʃən] *s* industrialización
**industrialize** [ɪn'dʌstrɪəlaɪz] *va* industrializar
**industrially** [ɪn'dʌstrɪəlɪ] *adv* industrialmente
**industrious** [ɪn'dʌstrɪəs] *adj* aplicado, industrioso
**industry** ['ɪndəstrɪ] *s* (*pl:* **-tries**) industria; aplicación, laboriosidad
**indwelling** ['ɪn,dwelɪŋ] *adj* interior
**-ine** *suffix adj* -uno, p.ej., **bovine** boyuno; **cervine** cervuno; **leporine** lebruno; **porcine** porcuno
**inebriate** [ɪn'ibrɪɪt] o [ɪn'ibrɪet] *s* borracho; [ɪn'ibrɪet] *va* embriagar, inebriar
**inebriation** [ɪn,ibrɪ'eʃən] o **inebriety** [,ɪnɪ'braɪətɪ] *s* embriaguez
**inedible** [ɪn'ɛdɪbəl] *adj* incomible, no comestible
**ineffability** [ɪn,ɛfə'bɪlɪtɪ] *s* inefabilidad
**ineffable** [ɪn'ɛfəbəl] *adj* inefable
**ineffaceable** [,ɪnɪ'fesəbəl] *adj* imborrable
**ineffective** [,ɪnɪ'fɛktɪv] *adj* ineficaz; incapaz
**ineffectual** [,ɪnɪ'fɛktʃʊəl] *adj* ineficaz
**inefficacious** [,ɪnɛfɪ'keʃəs] *adj* ineficaz
**inefficacy** [ɪn'ɛfɪkəsɪ] *s* ineficacia
**inefficiency** [,ɪnɪ'fɪʃənsɪ] *s* ineficiencia; mal rendimiento
**inefficient** [,ɪnɪ'fɪʃənt] *adj* ineficiente; de mal rendimiento
**inelastic** [,ɪnɪ'læstɪk] *adj* inelástico
**inelasticity** [,ɪnɪlæs'tɪsɪtɪ] *s* inelasticidad
**inelegance** [ɪn'ɛlɪgəns] *s* inelegancia
**inelegancy** [ɪn'ɛlɪgənsɪ] *s* (*pl:* **-cies**) var. de **inelegance**
**inelegant** [ɪn'ɛlɪgənt] *adj* inelegante
**ineligibility** [ɪn,ɛlɪdʒɪ'bɪlɪtɪ] *s* inelegibilidad
**ineligible** [ɪn'ɛlɪdʒɪbəl] *adj* inelegible
**ineluctable** [,ɪnɪ'lʌktəbəl] *adj* ineluctable
**inept** [ɪn'ɛpt] *adj* inepto
**ineptitude** [ɪn'ɛptɪtjud] o [ɪn'ɛptɪtud] *s* ineptitud
**inequality** [,ɪni'kwɑlɪtɪ] *s* (*pl:* **-ties**) desigualdad
**inequitable** [ɪn'ɛkwɪtəbəl] *adj* injusto
**inequity** [ɪn'ɛkwɪtɪ] *s* (*pl:* **-ties**) inequidad, injusticia
**ineradicable** [,ɪnɪ'rædɪkəbəl] *adj* inextirpable
**inert** [ɪn'ʌrt] *adj* inerte
**inert gas** *s* (chem.) gas inerte
**inertia** [ɪn'ʌrʃə] *s* inercia; (mech.) inercia; (med.) inercia de la matriz
**inertial** [ɪn'ʌrʃəl] *adj* inercial
**inescapable** [,ɪnɛs'kepəbəl] *adj* ineludible
**inestimability** [ɪn,ɛstɪmə'bɪlɪtɪ] *s* inestimabilidad
**inestimable** [ɪn'ɛstɪməbəl] *adj* inestimable
**inevitability** [ɪn,ɛvɪtə'bɪlɪtɪ] *s* inevitabilidad
**inevitable** [ɪn'ɛvɪtəbəl] *adj* inevitable
**inexact** [,ɪnɛg'zækt] *adj* inexacto
**inexcusable** [,ɪnɛks'kjuzəbəl] *adj* inexcusable, indisculpable
**inexhaustibility** [,ɪnɛg,zɔstɪ'bɪlɪtɪ] *s* (lo) inagotable
**inexhaustible** [,ɪnɛg'zɔstɪbəl] *adj* inagotable
**inexistence** [,ɪnɛg'zɪstəns] *s* inexistencia
**inexistent** [,ɪnɛg'zɪstənt] *adj* inexistente
**inexorability** [ɪn,ɛksərə'bɪlɪtɪ] *s* inexorabilidad
**inexorable** [ɪn'ɛksərəbəl] *adj* inexorable
**inexpediency** [,ɪnɛk'spidɪənsɪ] *s* imprudencia, inconveniencia, inoportunidad
**inexpedient** [,ɪnɛk'spidɪənt] *adj* imprudente, inconveniente, inoportuno
**inexpensive** [,ɪnɛk'spɛnsɪv] *adj* barato
**inexperience** [,ɪnɛk'spɪrɪəns] *s* inexperiencia
**inexperienced** [,ɪnɛk'spɪrɪənst] *adj* inexperto
**inexpert** [ɪn'ɛkspʌrt] o [,ɪnɛk'spʌrt] *adj* inexperto, imperito
**inexpiable** [ɪn'ɛkspɪəbəl] *adj* inexpiable
**inexplicable** [ɪn'ɛksplɪkəbəl] *adj* inexplicable
**inexpressible** [,ɪnɛk'sprɛsɪbəl] *adj* inexpresable
**inexpressibly** [,ɪnɛk'sprɛsɪblɪ] *adv* inexpresablemente
**inexpressive** [,ɪnɛk'sprɛsɪv] *adj* inexpresivo
**inexpugnability** [,ɪnɛk,spʌgnə'bɪlɪtɪ] *s* inexpugnabilidad
**inexpugnable** [,ɪnɛk'spʌgnəbəl] *adj* inexpugnable
**inextinguishable** [,ɪnɛk'stɪŋgwɪʃəbəl] *adj* inextinguible
**inextricability** [ɪn,ɛkstrɪkə'bɪlɪtɪ] *s* inextricabilidad
**inextricable** [ɪn'ɛkstrɪkəbəl] *adj* inextricable
**inf.** abr. de **infantry** y **infinitive**
**Inf.** abr. de **Infantry**
**infallibility** [ɪn,fælɪ'bɪlɪtɪ] *s* infalibilidad
**infallible** [ɪn'fælɪbəl] *adj* infalible
**infamous** ['ɪnfəməs] *adj* infame; (law) infamante (*pena*)
**infamy** ['ɪnfəmɪ] *s* (*pl:* **-mies**) infamia
**infancy** ['ɪnfənsɪ] *s* (*pl:* **-cies**) infancia; (fig.) infancia; (law) minoridad

**infant** [ˈɪnfənt] *s* nene, infante, criatura; (law) menor; *adj* infantil
**infanta** [ɪnˈfæntə] *s* infanta
**infante** [ɪnˈfænte] *s* infante
**infanticidal** [ɪnˈfæntɪˌsaɪdəl] *adj* infanticida
**infanticide** [ɪnˈfæntɪsaɪd] *s* infanticidio (*acción*); infanticida (*persona*)
**infantile** [ˈɪnfəntaɪl] o [ˈɪnfəntɪl] *adj* infantil; aniñado, trivial, infantil
**infantile paralysis** *s* (path.) parálisis infantil
**infantilism** [ɪnˈfæntɪlɪzəm] *s* infantilismo
**infantine** [ˈɪnfəntaɪn] o [ˈɪnfəntɪn] *adj* aniñado, infantil
**infant prodigy** *s* niño prodigio
**infantry** [ˈɪnfəntrɪ] *s* (*pl:* **-tries**) infantería
**infantryman** [ˈɪnfəntrɪmən] *s* (*pl:* **-men**) infante, soldado de infantería
**infarct** [ɪnˈfɑrkt] *s* (path.) infarto
**infarction** [ɪnˈfɑrkʃən] *s* (path.) infartación
**infatuate** [ɪnˈfætʃʊet] *adj* apasionado, amartelado; *va* apasionar, amartelar
**infatuation** [ɪnˌfætʃʊˈeʃən] *s* apasionamiento, amartelamiento
**infect** [ɪnˈfɛkt] *va* infectar, infeccionar, inficionar; influenciar
**infection** [ɪnˈfɛkʃən] *s* infección
**infectious** [ɪnˈfɛkʃəs] *adj* infeccioso
**infective** [ɪnˈfɛktɪv] *adj* infectivo
**infectivity** [ˌɪnfɛkˈtɪvɪtɪ] *s* infectividad
**infelicitous** [ˌɪnfɪˈlɪsɪtəs] *adj* infeliz, desgraciado; impropio, desacertado
**infelicity** [ˌɪnfɪˈlɪsɪtɪ] *s* (*pl:* **-ties**) infelicidad; impropiedad, desacierto
**infer** [ɪnˈfʌr] (*pret & pp:* **-ferred;** *ger:* **-ferring**) *va* inferir; (coll.) suponer, conjeturar
**inference** [ˈɪnfərəns] *s* inferencia
**inferential** [ˌɪnfəˈrɛnʃəl] *adj* ilativo
**inferior** [ɪnˈfɪrɪər] *adj & s* inferior
**inferiority** [ɪnˌfɪrɪˈɑrɪtɪ] o [ɪnˌfɪrɪˈɔrɪtɪ] *s* inferioridad
**inferiority complex** *s* complejo de inferioridad
**infernal** [ɪnˈfʌrnəl] *adj* infernal; (coll.) infernal (*muy malo, abominable*)
**infernal machine** *s* máquina infernal
**inferno** [ɪnˈfʌrno] *s* (*pl:* **-nos**) infierno
**infertile** [ɪnˈfʌrtɪl] *adj* estéril
**infertility** [ˌɪnfərˈtɪlɪtɪ] *s* esterilidad
**infest** [ɪnˈfɛst] *va* infestar
**infestation** [ˌɪnfɛsˈteʃən] *s* infestación
**infidel** [ˈɪnfɪdəl] *adj & s* infiel (*a la fe verdadera*)
**infidelity** [ˌɪnfɪˈdɛlɪtɪ] *s* (*pl:* **-ties**) infidelidad
**infield** [ˈɪnˌfild] *s* terrenos de una granja más cercanos a las casas; (baseball) losange, cuadro interior
**infielder** [ˈɪnˌfildər] *s* (baseball) jugador del cuadro interior
**infighting** [ˈɪnˌfaɪtɪŋ] *s* (box.) (el) cuerpo a cuerpo
**infiltrate** [ɪnˈfɪltret] *va* infiltrar; infiltrarse en; *vn* infiltrarse
**infiltration** [ˌɪnfɪlˈtreʃən] *s* infiltración
**infin.** abr. de **infinitive**
**infinite** [ˈɪnfɪnɪt] *adj & s* infinito; **the Infinite** el infinito (*Dios*)
**infinitely** [ˈɪnfɪnɪtlɪ] *adv* infinitamente
**infinitesimal** [ˌɪnfɪnɪˈtɛsɪməl] *adj* infinitesimal; *s* (math.) infinitésimo
**infinitesimal calculus** *s* cálculo infinitesimal
**infinitesimally small** [ˌɪnfɪnɪˈtɛsɪməlɪ] *adj* infinitamente pequeño
**infinitive** [ɪnˈfɪnɪtɪv] *adj & s* (gram.) infinitivo
**infinitude** [ɪnˈfɪnɪtjud] o [ɪnˈfɪnɪtud] *s* infinitud
**infinity** [ɪnˈfɪnɪtɪ] *s* (*pl:* **-ties**) infinidad; (math.) infinito
**infirm** [ɪnˈfʌrm] *adj* achacoso, enfermizo; inestable; inconstante; débil, flaco
**infirmary** [ɪnˈfʌrmərɪ] *s* (*pl:* **-ries**) enfermería, sala de enfermos
**infirmity** [ɪnˈfʌrmɪtɪ] *s* (*pl:* **-ties**) achaque, enfermedad; inestabilidad; inconstancia; debilidad, flaqueza
**infix** [ˈɪnfɪks] *s* (gram.) interposición; [ɪnˈfɪks] *va* clavar, encajar, empotrar
**inflame** [ɪnˈflem] *va* inflamar; *vn* inflamarse
**inflammability** [ɪnˌflæməˈbɪlɪtɪ] *s* inflamabilidad
**inflammable** [ɪnˈflæməbəl] *adj* inflamable
**inflammation** [ˌɪnfləˈmeʃən] *s* inflamación; (path.) inflamación
**inflammatory** [ɪnˈflæməˌtorɪ] *adj* incendiario; (med.) inflamatorio
**inflate** [ɪnˈflet] *va* inflar; *vn* inflarse
**inflation** [ɪnˈfleʃən] *s* inflación
**inflationary** [ɪnˈfleʃənˌɛrɪ] *adj* inflacionista, inflatorio
**inflationism** [ɪnˈfleʃənɪzəm] *s* inflacionismo
**inflationist** [ɪnˈfleʃənɪst] *s* inflacionista
**inflect** [ɪnˈflɛkt] *va* torcer, doblar; modular (*la voz*); (gram.) poner por orden las formas de, declinar (*los nombres, pronombres y adjetivos*), conjugar (*los verbos*); *vn* (gram.) experimentar o sufrir flexión
**inflection** [ɪnˈflɛkʃən] *s* inflexión; (geom. & gram.) inflexión
**inflectional** [ɪnˈflɛkʃənəl] *adj* (gram.) flexional
**inflexibility** [ɪnˌflɛksɪˈbɪlɪtɪ] *s* inflexibilidad
**inflexible** [ɪnˈflɛksɪbəl] *adj* inflexible
**inflict** [ɪnˈflɪkt] *va* infligir; **to inflict on** infligir a
**infliction** [ɪnˈflɪkʃən] *s* imposición; pena, castigo, sufrimiento
**inflorescence** [ˌɪnfloˈrɛsəns] *s* (bot.) florescencia (*época*); (bot.) inflorescencia (*disposición de las flores; conjunto de flores*)
**inflorescent** [ˌɪnfloˈrɛsənt] *adj* floreciente
**inflow** [ˈɪnˌflo] *s* afluencia; [ˌɪnˈflo] *vn* afluir
**influence** [ˈɪnfluəns] *s* influencia; *va* influenciar, influir sobre; *vn* influir
**influence peddler** *s* (coll.) vendehumos, persona que comercia en la influencia política
**influence peddling** *s* (coll.) comercio de la influencia política
**influential** [ˌɪnfluˈɛnʃəl] *adj* influyente
**influenza** [ˌɪnfluˈɛnzə] *s* (path.) influenza
**influx** [ˈɪnflʌks] *s* afluencia
**infold** [ɪnˈfold] *va* envolver, arrollar, abrazar, estrechar
**inform** [ɪnˈfɔrm] *va* informar; avisar, enterar; *vn* informar; **to inform against** informar contra
**informal** [ɪnˈfɔrməl] *adj* informal; familiar
**informality** [ˌɪnfɔrˈmælɪtɪ] *s* (*pl:* **-ties**) informalidad; sencillez, falta de ceremonia
**informant** [ɪnˈfɔrmənt] *s* informante
**information** [ˌɪnfərˈmeʃən] *s* información, informes
**informational** [ˌɪnfərˈmeʃənəl] *adj* informativo
**informative** [ɪnˈfɔrmətɪv] *adj* informativo
**informed** [ɪnˈfɔrmd] *adj* entendido; enterado; **to keep informed (about)** ponerse al corriente (de); **to keep someone informed (about)** poner a alguien al corriente (de)
**informer** [ɪnˈfɔrmər] *s* informador; delator
**infortiate** [ɪnˈfɔrʃɪɪt] *s* inforciado
**infraction** [ɪnˈfrækʃən] *s* infracción
**infra dig** [ˌɪnfrə ˈdɪg] abr. de **infra dignitatem** [ˌdɪgnɪˈtetɛm] (Lat.) por debajo de la dignidad de uno
**infrangible** [ɪnˈfrændʒɪbəl] *adj* infrangible
**infrared** [ˌɪnfrəˈrɛd] *adj & s* infrarrojo
**infrequence** [ɪnˈfrikwəns] o **infrequency** [ɪnˈfrikwənsɪ] *s* infrecuencia
**infrequent** [ɪnˈfrikwənt] *adj* infrecuente
**infringe** [ɪnˈfrɪndʒ] *va* infringir, violar; *vn* invadir; **to infringe on** o **upon** invadir, abusar de
**infringement** [ɪnˈfrɪndʒmənt] *s* infracción, violación
**infuriate** [ɪnˈfjʊrɪet] *va* enfurecer
**infuriation** [ɪnˌfjʊrɪˈeʃən] *s* enfurecimiento
**infuse** [ɪnˈfjuz] *va* infundir
**infusibility** [ɪnˌfjuzɪˈbɪlɪtɪ] *s* infusibilidad
**infusible** [ɪnˈfjuzɪbəl] *adj* infusible
**infusion** [ɪnˈfjuʒən] *s* infusión
**infusorian** [ˌɪnfjʊˈsorɪən] *adj & s* (zool.) infusorio
**-ing** *suffix adj* -ador, p.ej., **accusing** acusador; -edor, p.ej., **learning** aprendedor; -idor, p.ej., **following** seguidor; -ando, p.ej., **graduating** graduando; -ante, p.ej., **loving** amante; **Spanish-speaking** hispanohablante; -iente, p.ej., **boiling** hirviente; **following** siguiente; -ueño, p.ej., **flattering** halagüeño; **smiling** risueño; *suffix ger* -ando, p.ej., **accusing** acusando; -iendo, p.ej., **learning** aprendiendo; *suffix s* -ado, p.ej., **ironing** planchado;

**tamping** tamponado; -ería, p.ej., **barbering** barbería; **engineering** ingeniería
**ingathering** ['ɪn,gæðərɪŋ] *s* cosecha, recolección
**ingenerable** [ɪn'dʒɛnərəbəl] *adj* ingenerable
**ingenious** [ɪn'dʒinjəs] *adj* ingenioso
**ingénue** [ǣʒe'ny] *s* dama joven ingenua de la escena
**ingenuity** [,ɪndʒɪ'njuɪtɪ] o [,ɪndʒɪ'nuɪtɪ] *s* (*pl:* **-ties**) ingeniosidad
**ingenuous** [ɪn'dʒɛnjuəs] *adj* ingenuo
**ingest** [ɪn'dʒɛst] *va* injerir
**ingestion** [ɪn'dʒɛstʃən] *s* ingestión
**ingle** ['ɪŋgəl] *s* llama, fuego; chimenea, hogar
**inglenook** ['ɪŋgəl,nʊk] *s* chimenea, rincón de la chimenea
**inglorious** [ɪn'glorɪəs] *adj* sin fama; afrentoso, ignominioso
**ingoing** ['ɪn,go·ɪŋ] *adj* entrante, que llega
**ingot** ['ɪŋgət] *s* lingote
**ingraft** [ɪn'græft] o [ɪn'grɑft] *va* (hort. & surg.) injertar; (fig.) implantar
**ingrain** ['ɪn,gren] *s* lana teñida en rama, hilo teñido en rama; *adj* teñido en rama; [ɪn'gren] *va* teñir en rama
**ingrained** [ɪn'grend] *adj* profundamente arraigado
**ingrate** ['ɪngret] *s* ingrato
**ingratiate** [ɪn'greʃɪet] *va* hacer aceptable; **to ingratiate oneself with** congraciarse con
**ingratiating** [ɪn'greʃɪ,etɪŋ] *adj* congraciador
**ingratiation** [ɪn,greʃɪ'eʃən] *s* congraciamiento
**ingratitude** [ɪn'grætɪtjud] o [ɪn'grætɪtud] *s* ingratitud, desagradecimiento
**ingredient** [ɪn'gridɪənt] *s* ingrediente
**ingress** ['ɪngrɛs] *s* ingreso, entrada, acceso
**ingrowing** ['ɪn,gro·ɪŋ] *adj* que crece hacia dentro
**ingrowing nail** *s* uñero
**ingrown** ['ɪn,gron] *adj* crecido hacia dentro; introducido en la carne
**inguinal** ['ɪŋgwɪnəl] *adj* inguinal
**ingulf** [ɪn'gʌlf] *va* sumir, hundir
**ingurgitate** [ɪn'gʌrdʒɪtet] *va* ingurgitar
**ingurgitation** [ɪn,gʌrdʒɪ'teʃən] *s* ingurgitación
**inhabit** [ɪn'hæbɪt] *va* habitar, poblar
**inhabitability** [ɪn,hæbɪtə'bɪlɪtɪ] *s* habitabilidad
**inhabitable** [ɪn'hæbɪtəbəl] *adj* habitable
**inhabitant** [ɪn'hæbɪtənt] *s* habitante
**inhalant** [ɪn'helənt] *s* (med.) inhalador; medicamento inhalatorio
**inhalation** [,ɪnhə'leʃən] *s* aspiración, inspiración; (med.) inhalación; medicamento inhalado
**inhale** [ɪn'hel] *va* aspirar, inspirar; (med.) inhalar; *vn* aspirar; tragar el humo
**inhaler** [ɪn'helər] *s* (med.) inhalador; aspirador
**inharmonic** [,ɪnhɑr'mɑnɪk] *adj* inarmónico
**inharmonious** [,ɪnhɑr'monɪəs] *adj* poco armonioso, discordante
**inhere** [ɪn'hɪr] *vn* ser inherente, residir
**inherence** [ɪn'hɪrəns] *s* inherencia
**inherent** [ɪn'hɪrənt] *adj* inherente
**inherently** [ɪn'hɪrəntlɪ] *adv* inherentemente
**inherit** [ɪn'hɛrɪt] *va & vn* heredar
**inheritable** [ɪn'hɛrɪtəbəl] *adj* heredable; heredero
**inheritance** [ɪn'hɛrɪtəns] *s* herencia
**inheritance tax** *s* impuesto sobre herencias
**inheritor** [ɪn'hɛrɪtər] *s* heredero
**inhibit** [ɪn'hɪbɪt] *va* inhibir
**inhibition** [,ɪnhɪ'bɪʃən] *s* inhibición
**inhibitive** [ɪn'hɪbɪtɪv] *adj* inhibitivo
**inhibitory** [ɪn'hɪbɪ,torɪ] *adj* inhibitorio
**inhospitable** [ɪn'hɑspɪtəbəl] o [,ɪnhɑs'pɪtəbəl] *adj* inhospedable, inhospitable, inhospital o inhospitalario
**inhospitality** [ɪn,hɑspɪ'tælɪtɪ] *s* inhospitalidad
**inhuman** [ɪn'hjumən] *adj* inhumano
**inhumane** [,ɪnhju'men] *adj* inhumano, inhumanitario
**inhumanity** [,ɪnhju'mænɪtɪ] *s* (*pl:* **-ties**) inhumanidad
**inhumation** [,ɪnhjʊ'meʃən] *s* inhumación
**inhume** [ɪn'hjum] *va* inhumar
**inimical** [ɪn'ɪmɪkəl] *adj* enemigo
**inimitable** [ɪn'ɪmɪtəbəl] *adj* inimitable
**inimitably** [ɪn'ɪmɪtəblɪ] *adv* inimitablemente
**iniquitous** [ɪ'nɪkwɪtəs] *adj* inicuo
**iniquity** [ɪ'nɪkwɪtɪ] *s* (*pl:* **-ties**) iniquidad
**initial** [ɪ'nɪʃəl] *adj* inicial; *s* inicial, letra inicial; sigla (*letra inicial usada como abreviatura*); (*pret & pp:* **-tialed** o **-tialled;** *ger:* **-tialing** o **-tialling**) *va* firmar con sus iniciales; marcar (*p.ej., un pañuelo*)
**initially** [ɪ'nɪʃəlɪ] *adv* al principio
**initiate** [ɪ'nɪʃɪɪt] o [ɪ'nɪʃɪet] *s & adj* iniciado; [ɪ'nɪʃɪet] *va* iniciar
**initiation** [ɪ,nɪʃɪ'eʃən] *s* iniciación
**initiative** [ɪ'nɪʃɪətɪv] o [ɪ'nɪʃɪ,etɪv] *s* iniciativa; **to take the initiative** tomar la iniciativa
**initiator** [ɪ'nɪʃɪ,etər] *s* iniciador
**inject** [ɪn'dʒɛkt] *va* inyectar; introducir (*una advertencia*)
**injectable** [ɪn'dʒɛktəbəl] *adj* inyectable
**injection** [ɪn'dʒɛkʃən] *s* inyección
**injector** [ɪn'dʒɛktər] *s* (mach.) inyector
**injudicious** [,ɪndʒu'dɪʃəs] *adj* indiscreto, imprudente
**injunction** [ɪn'dʒʌŋkʃən] *s* mandato; (law) entredicho
**injure** ['ɪndʒər] *va* dañar, averiar; herir, lisiar, lastimar; injuriar, ofender
**injurious** [ɪn'dʒʊrɪəs] *adj* dañoso, perjudicial; injurioso, ofensivo
**injuriously** [ɪn'dʒʊrɪəslɪ] *adv* dañosamente, perjudicialmente; injuriosamente, ofensivamente
**injury** ['ɪndʒərɪ] *s* (*pl:* **-ries**) daño; herida, lesión
**injustice** [ɪn'dʒʌstɪs] *s* injusticia
**ink** [ɪŋk] *s* tinta; (zool.) tinta (*de calamar*); *va* entintar
**ink eradicator** *s* borratintas
**inkhorn** ['ɪŋk,hɔrn] *s* tintero hecho de cuerno; *adj* pedantesco
**inking** ['ɪŋkɪŋ] *s* (print.) entintado, tintaje
**inkling** ['ɪŋklɪŋ] *s* sospecha, indicio, vislumbre; insinuación
**ink sac** *s* (zool.) bolsa de la tinta
**inkstand** ['ɪŋk,stænd] *s* tintero; portatintero
**inkwell** ['ɪŋk,wɛl] *s* tintero
**inky** ['ɪŋkɪ] *adj* (*comp:* **-ier;** *super:* **-iest**) entintado; negro
**inlaid** ['ɪn,led] o [ɪn'led] *adj* embutido, taraceado; *pret & pp de* **inlay**
**inland** ['ɪnlənd] *adj* interior; ['ɪnlənd] o ['ɪn,lænd] *s* interior; *adv* tierra adentro
**Inland Sea** *s* mar del Japón
**in-law** ['ɪn,lɔ] *s* (coll.) pariente político
**inlay** ['ɪn,le] *s* embutido, taraceado; [ɪn'le] o ['ɪn,le] (*pret & pp:* **-laid**) *va* embutir, taracear
**inlet** ['ɪnlɛt] *s* entrada; ensenada; estuario
**inly** ['ɪnlɪ] *adj* interior; *adv* interiormente; completamente
**inmate** ['ɪnmet] *s* residente, asilado, recluso, desvalido; enfermo, enfermo mental; preso, presidiario
**inmost** ['ɪnmost] *adj* interior, (el) más íntimo, (el) más recóndito
**inn** [ɪn] *s* posada, mesón, fonda
**innate** ['ɪnet], [ɪn'net] o [ɪ'net] *adj* innato, ingénito
**innatism** ['ɪnnetɪzəm] *s* innatismo
**inner** ['ɪnər] *adj* interior; oculto, secreto
**Inner Mongolia** *s* la Mogolia Interior
**innermost** ['ɪnərmost] *adj* interior, (el) más íntimo
**innerspring mattress** ['ɪnər'sprɪŋ] *s* colchón de muelles interiores
**inner tube** *s* cámara, tubo interior
**innervation** [,ɪnər'veʃən] *s* inervación
**inning** ['ɪnɪŋ] *s* turno, mano, entrada
**innkeeper** ['ɪn,kipər] *s* posadero, mesonero, fondista
**innocence** ['ɪnəsəns] *s* inocencia; (bot.) houstonia cerúlea
**innocency** ['ɪnəsənsɪ] *s* (*pl:* **-cies**) inocencia
**innocent** ['ɪnəsənt] *adj & s* inocente; (*cap.*) *s* Inocencio
**innocuous** [ɪ'nɑkjuəs] *adj* innocuo
**innominate** [ɪ'nɑmɪnɪt] *adj* innominado
**innovate** ['ɪnovet] *va* innovar
**innovation** [,ɪno'veʃən] *s* innovación
**innovator** ['ɪno,vetər] *s* innovador
**innoxious** [ɪ'nɑkʃəs] *adj* innocuo

**innuendo** [ˌɪnjuˈɛndo] *s* (*pl:* **-does**) indirecta, insinuación
**innumerability** [ɪˌnjumərəˈbɪlɪtɪ] o [ɪˌnumərəˈbɪlɪtɪ] *s* innumerabilidad
**innumerable** [ɪˈnjumərəbəl] o [ɪˈnumərəbəl] *adj* innumerable
**innumerably** [ɪˈnjumərəblɪ] o [ɪˈnumərəblɪ] *adv* innumerablemente
**inobedience** [ˌɪnəˈbidɪəns] *s* desobediencia, inobediencia
**inobedient** [ˌɪnəˈbidɪənt] *adj* desobediente, inobediente
**inobservance** [ˌɪnəbˈzʌrvəns] *s* inobservancia
**inoculable** [ɪnˈɑkjələbəl] *adj* inoculable
**inoculant** [ɪnˈɑkjələnt] *s* substancia inoculante
**inoculate** [ɪnˈɑkjəlet] *va* inocular; (coll.) imbuir; *vn* inocular
**inoculation** [ɪnˌɑkjəˈleʃən] *s* inoculación
**inodorous** [ɪnˈodərəs] *adj* inodoro
**inoffensive** [ˌɪnəˈfɛnsɪv] *adj* inofensivo
**inofficious** [ˌɪnəˈfɪʃəs] *adj* inoficioso; (law) inoficioso
**inoperable** [ɪnˈɑpərəbəl] *adj* (surg.) inoperable
**inoperative** [ɪnˈɑpəˌretɪv] o [ɪnˈɑpərətɪv] *adj* inoperante
**inopportune** [ɪnˌɑpərˈtjun] o [ɪnˌɑpərˈtun] *adj* inoportuno
**inordinate** [ɪnˈɔrdɪnɪt] *adj* excesivo; desenfrenado
**inorganic** [ˌɪnɔrˈgænɪk] *adj* inorgánico
**inorganic chemistry** *s* química inorgánica
**inosculate** [ɪnˈɑskjəlet] *va* unir por anastomosis; (fig.) unir íntimamente; *vn* anastomosarse
**inpatient** [ˈɪnˌpeʃənt] *s* enfermo de dentro
**input** [ˈɪnˌpʊt] *s* gasto, consumo; dinero invertido; (mach.) potencia consumida, energía absorbida; (elec.) entrada; (elec.) circuito de entrada
**input transformer** *s* (rad.) transformador de entrada
**inquest** [ˈɪnkwɛst] *s* (law) pesquisa judicial, reconocimiento médico, levantamiento del cadáver
**inquietude** [ɪnˈkwaɪətjud] o [ɪnˈkwaɪətud] *s* inquietud
**inquire** [ɪnˈkwaɪr] *va* averiguar, inquirir; *vn* preguntar; **to inquire about, after** o **for** preguntar por; **to inquire into** averiguar, inquirir; **to inquire of** preguntar a
**inquiry** [ɪnˈkwaɪrɪ] o [ˈɪnkwɪrɪ] *s* (*pl:* **-ies**) encuesta, averiguación; pregunta
**inquisition** [ˌɪnkwɪˈzɪʃən] *s* inquisición; (*cap.*) *s* Inquisición
**inquisitive** [ɪnˈkwɪzɪtɪv] *adj* curioso
**inquisitor** [ɪnˈkwɪzɪtər] *s* inquisidor; (*cap.*) *s* (eccl.) Inquisidor
**inquisitorial** [ɪnˌkwɪzɪˈtorɪəl] *adj* inquisitorial
**in re** [ɪnˈri] (Lat.) concerniente a
**inroad** [ˈɪnˌrod] *s* incursión
**inrush** [ˈɪnˌrʌʃ] *s* afluencia; irrupción
**ins.** abr. de **inches, insulated** y **insurance**
**insalivate** [ɪnˈsælɪvet] *va* (physiol.) insalivar
**insalivation** [ɪnˌsælɪˈveʃən] *s* (physiol.) insalivación
**insalubrious** [ˌɪnsəˈlubrɪəs] *adj* insalubre
**insane** [ɪnˈsen] *adj* insano, loco
**insane asylum** *s* asilo de locos, manicomio
**insanitary** [ɪnˈsænɪˌtɛrɪ] *adj* insalubre
**insanity** [ɪnˈsænɪtɪ] *s* (*pl:* **-ties**) insania, locura
**insatiable** [ɪnˈseʃəbəl] *adj* insaciable; **insatiable for** insaciable de
**insatiably** [ɪnˈseʃəblɪ] *adv* insaciablemente
**insatiate** [ɪnˈseʃɪɪt] *adj* insaciable
**inscribe** [ɪnˈskraɪb] *va* inscribir; (geom. & fig.) inscribir; dedicar (*una obra literaria*)
**inscription** [ɪnˈskrɪpʃən] *s* inscripción; dedicatoria
**inscrutability** [ɪnˌskrutəˈbɪlɪtɪ] *s* inescrutabilidad
**inscrutable** [ɪnˈskrutəbəl] *adj* inescrutable
**insect** [ˈɪnsɛkt] *s* insecto
**insecticidal** [ɪnˈsɛktɪˌsaɪdəl] *adj* insecticida
**insecticide** [ɪnˈsɛktɪsaɪd] *adj* & *s* insecticida
**insectile** [ɪnˈsɛktɪl] *adj* insectil
**insectivore** [ɪnˈsɛktɪvor] *s* (zool.) insectívoro; (bot.) insectívora
**insectivorous** [ˌɪnsɛkˈtɪvərəs] *adj* insectívoro
**insecure** [ˌɪnsɪˈkjʊr] *adj* inseguro
**insecurity** [ˌɪnsɪˈkjʊrɪtɪ] *s* (*pl:* **-ties**) inseguridad
**inseminate** [ɪnˈsɛmɪnet] *va* sembrar; inseminar
**insemination** [ɪnˌsɛmɪˈneʃən] *s* inseminación
**insensate** [ɪnˈsɛnset] *adj* insensible (*que no experimenta sensación; cruel*); insensato (*necio, loco, ciego*)
**insensibility** [ɪnˌsɛnsɪˈbɪlɪtɪ] *s* insensibilidad; inconsciencia
**insensible** [ɪnˈsɛnsɪbəl] *adj* insensible; inconsciente
**insensitive** [ɪnˈsɛnsɪtɪv] *adj* insensible
**insentient** [ɪnˈsɛnʃɪənt] o [ɪnˈsɛnʃənt] *adj* insensible, inconsciente
**inseparability** [ɪnˌsɛpərəˈbɪlɪtɪ] *s* inseparabilidad
**inseparable** [ɪnˈsɛpərəbəl] *adj* & *s* inseparable
**insert** [ˈɪnsʌrt] *s* inserción; [ɪnˈsʌrt] *va* insertar
**insertion** [ɪnˈsʌrʃən] *s* inserción; (sew.) entredós; (bot. & zool.) inserción
**in-service** [ˈɪnˌsʌrvɪs] *adj* (educ.) en período de instrucción, adquiriendo práctica
**inset** [ˈɪnˌsɛt] *s* inserción, intercalación; [ɪnˈsɛt] o [ˈɪnˌsɛt] (*pret & pp:* **-set;** *ger:* **-setting**) *va* insertar, intercalar, encastrar, embutir
**inshore** [ˈɪnˈʃor] *adj* cercano a la orilla; *adv* cerca de la orilla; hacia la orilla
**inside** [ˈɪnˌsaɪd] *s* interior, parte de dentro; forro (*de una prenda de vestir*); **insides** *spl* (coll.) entrañas; **on the inside** (slang) en el secreto de las cosas; *adj* interior; interno; secreto; [ˌɪnˈsaɪd] *adv* dentro, hacia dentro; **to turn inside out** volver al revés; volverse al revés; **inside of** (coll.) dentro de; **inside out** al revés; *prep* dentro de
**inside information** *s* informes confidenciales
**insider** [ˌɪnˈsaɪdər] *s* socio, miembro; persona informada, persona enterada
**inside story** *s* interioridades
**inside track** *s* (sport) pista interior; (coll.) ventaja, situación favorable
**insidious** [ɪnˈsɪdɪəs] *adj* insidioso
**insight** [ˈɪnˌsaɪt] *s* penetración
**insignia** [ɪnˈsɪgnɪə] *spl* insignias
**insignificance** [ˌɪnsɪgˈnɪfɪkəns] *s* insignificancia
**insignificant** [ˌɪnsɪgˈnɪfɪkənt] *adj* insignificante
**insincere** [ˌɪnsɪnˈsɪr] *adj* insincero
**insincerity** [ˌɪnsɪnˈsɛrɪtɪ] *s* (*pl:* **-ties**) insinceridad
**insinuate** [ɪnˈsɪnjʊet] *va* insinuar; **to insinuate oneself** insinuarse
**insinuation** [ɪnˌsɪnjʊˈeʃən] *s* insinuación
**insinuative** [ɪnˈsɪnjʊˌetɪv] *adj* insinuativo
**insipid** [ɪnˈsɪpɪd] *adj* insípido
**insipidity** [ˌɪnsɪˈpɪdɪtɪ] *s* (*pl:* **-ties**) insipidez
**insist** [ɪnˈsɪst] *vn* insistir; **to insist on** o **upon** insistir en o sobre; **to insist on** + *ger* insistir en + *inf;* **to insist that** insistir en que + *subj*
**insistence** [ɪnˈsɪstəns] o **insistency** [ɪnˈsɪstənsɪ] *s* insistencia
**insistent** [ɪnˈsɪstənt] *adj* insistente; urgente
**insnare** [ɪnˈsnɛr] *va* entrampar
**insobriety** [ˌɪnsoˈbraɪətɪ] *s* intemperancia
**insofar as** [ˌɪnsoˈfɑræz] *conj* en cuanto
**insolate** [ˈɪnsolet] *va* insolar
**insolation** [ˌɪnsoˈleʃən] *s* insolación; (med. & meteor.) insolación
**insole** [ˈɪnˌsol] *s* plantilla
**insolence** [ˈɪnsələns] *s* insolencia
**insolent** [ˈɪnsələnt] *adj* insolente
**insolubility** [ɪnˌsɑljəˈbɪlɪtɪ] *s* insolubilidad
**insoluble** [ɪnˈsɑljəbəl] *adj* insoluble
**insolvable** [ɪnˈsɑlvəbəl] *adj* insoluble
**insolvency** [ɪnˈsɑlvənsɪ] *s* (*pl:* **-cies**) insolvencia
**insolvent** [ɪnˈsɑlvənt] *adj* insolvente
**insomnia** [ɪnˈsɑmnɪə] *s* insomnio
**insomuch** [ˌɪnsoˈmʌtʃ] *adv* de tal modo, hasta tal punto; **insomuch as** ya que, puesto que; **insomuch that** de tal modo que, hasta el punto que
**insouciance** [ɪnˈsusɪəns] *s* despreocupación
**insouciant** [ɪnˈsusɪənt] *adj* despreocupado

**inspect** [ɪnˈspɛkt] *va* inspeccionar; intervenir
**inspection** [ɪnˈspɛkʃən] *s* inspección; intervención
**inspector** [ɪnˈspɛktər] *s* inspector
**inspiration** [ˌɪnspɪˈreʃən] *s* inspiración
**inspirational** [ˌɪnspɪˈreʃənəl] *adj* inspirativo; inspirado
**inspiratory** [ɪnˈspaɪrəˌtorɪ] *adj* (anat.) inspirador, inspiratorio
**inspire** [ɪnˈspaɪr] *va & vn* inspirar; **to inspire to** + *inf* inspirar a + *inf*
**inspiring** [ɪnˈspaɪrɪŋ] *adj* inspirante; emocionante
**inspirit** [ɪnˈspɪrɪt] *va* alentar, animar
**inspissate** [ɪnˈspɪset] *va* espesar; *vn* espesarse
**inst.** abr. de **instant (present month)**
**Inst.** abr. de **Institute** y **Institution**
**instability** [ˌɪnstəˈbɪlɪtɪ] *s* inestabilidad
**instable** [ɪnˈstebəl] *adj* inestable
**install** [ɪnˈstɔl] *va* instalar
**installation** [ˌɪnstəˈleʃən] *s* instalación
**installment** o **instalment** [ɪnˈstɔlmənt] *s* instalación; entrega; **in installments** a plazos; por entregas
**installment plan** *s* pago a plazos, pago en abonos, compra a plazos
**instance** [ˈɪnstəns] *s* instancia, petición; ocasión; caso, ejemplo; (law) instancia; **at the instance of** a instancia de; **for instance** por ejemplo; *va* citar como ejemplo
**instant** [ˈɪnstənt] *adj* inmediato; urgente; corriente; instantáneo; *s* instante, momento; ocasión; corriente, mes corriente; **the instant** así que, tan pronto como
**instantaneous** [ˌɪnstənˈtenɪəs] *adj* instantáneo
**instanter** [ɪnˈstæntər] *adv* al instante
**instantly** [ˈɪnstəntlɪ] *adv* inmediatamente, al instante
**instate** [ɪnˈstet] *va* instalar
**instead** [ɪnˈstɛd] *adv* en lugar de otro; **instead of** en lugar de, en vez de
**instep** [ˈɪnstɛp] *s* empeine (*del pie, la media o el calzado*); parte anterior de la pata trasera (*del caballo*)
**instigate** [ˈɪnstɪget] *va* instigar
**instigation** [ˌɪnstɪˈgeʃən] *s* instigación; **at the instigation of** a instigación de
**instigator** [ˈɪnstɪˌgetər] *s* instigador
**instill** o **instil** [ɪnˈstɪl] (*pret & pp:* **-stilled;** *ger:* **-stilling**) *va* instilar
**instillation** [ˌɪnstɪˈleʃən] *s* instilación
**instinct** [ˈɪnstɪŋkt] *s* instinto; [ɪnˈstɪŋkt] *adj* animado, movido, lleno; **instinct with** animado de
**instinctive** [ɪnˈstɪŋktɪv] *adj* instintivo
**institute** [ˈɪnstɪtjut] o [ˈɪnstɪtut] *s* instituto; **institutes** *spl* (law) instituta; *va* instituir
**institution** [ˌɪnstɪˈtjuʃən] o [ˌɪnstɪˈtuʃən] *s* institución; (law) institución; uso establecido; (coll.) persona muy conocida, cosa muy conocida
**institutional** [ˌɪnstɪˈtjuʃənəl] o [ˌɪnstɪˈtuʃənəl] *adj* institucional
**instruct** [ɪnˈstrʌkt] *va* instruir
**instruction** [ɪnˈstrʌkʃən] *s* instrucción; **instructions** *spl* instrucciones, indicaciones
**instructional** [ɪnˈstrʌkʃənəl] *adj* educacional; de los instructores, para los instructores
**instructive** [ɪnˈstrʌktɪv] *adj* instructivo
**instructor** [ɪnˈstrʌktər] *s* instructor
**instructress** [ɪnˈstrʌktrɪs] *s* instructora
**instrument** [ˈɪnstrumənt] *s* instrumento; (mus.) instrumento; [ˈɪnstrumɛnt] o [ˌɪnstruˈmɛnt] *va* (mus.) instrumentar
**instrumental** [ˌɪnstruˈmɛntəl] *adj* instrumental
**instrumentalist** [ˌɪnstruˈmɛntəlɪst] *s* instrumentista
**instrumentality** [ˌɪnstrumənˈtælɪtɪ] *s* (*pl:* **-ties**) agencia, mediación
**instrumentation** [ˌɪnstrumɛnˈteʃən] *s* instrumentación
**instrument board** *s* tablero de instrumentos
**instrument flying** *s* (aer.) vuelo por instrumentos
**instrument landing** *s* (aer.) aterrizaje por instrumentos
**instrument maker** *s* instrumentista
**instrument panel** *s* (aut.) tablero de instrumentos, plancha portainstrumentos
**insubordinate** [ˌɪnsəˈbɔrdɪnɪt] *adj* insubordinado
**insubordination** [ˌɪnsəˌbɔrdɪˈneʃən] *s* insubordinación
**insubstantial** [ˌɪnsəbˈstænʃəl] *adj* insubstancial
**insubstantiality** [ˌɪnsəbˌstænʃɪˈælɪtɪ] *s* insubstancialidad
**insufferable** [ɪnˈsʌfərəbəl] *adj* insufrible
**insufficiency** [ˌɪnsəˈfɪʃənsɪ] *s* insuficiencia
**insufficient** [ˌɪnsəˈfɪʃənt] *adj* insuficiente
**insufflate** [ɪnˈsʌflet] o [ˈɪnsəflet] *va* insuflar
**insufflation** [ˌɪnsəˈfleʃən] *s* insuflación
**insular** [ˈɪnsələr] o [ˈɪnsjulər] *adj* insular; (fig.) de miras estrechas
**insularity** [ˌɪnsəˈlærɪtɪ] o [ˌɪnsjuˈlærɪtɪ] *s* insularidad; (fig.) estrechez de miras
**insulate** [ˈɪnsəlet] o [ˈɪnsjulet] *va* aislar
**insulation** [ˌɪnsəˈleʃən] o [ˌɪnsjuˈleʃən] *s* (elec.) aislamiento, aislación
**insulator** [ˈɪnsəˌletər] o [ˈɪnsjuˌletər] *s* aislador
**insulin** [ˈɪnsəlɪn] o [ˈɪnsjulɪn] *s* (trademark) insulina; *adj* insulínico
**insulin shock** *s* (path.) shock insulínico, insulismo
**insult** [ˈɪnsʌlt] *s* insulto; [ɪnˈsʌlt] *va* insultar
**insulting** [ɪnˈsʌltɪŋ] *adj* insultante
**insuperable** [ɪnˈsupərəbəl] o [ɪnˈsjupərəbəl] *adj* insuperable
**insupportable** [ˌɪnsəˈportəbəl] *adj* insoportable
**insurable** [ɪnˈʃurəbəl] *adj* asegurable
**insurance** [ɪnˈʃurəns] *s* seguro; prima (*que el asegurado paga al asegurador*)
**insurance agent** *s* agente de seguros
**insurance broker** *s* corredor de seguros
**insurance company** *s* compañía de seguros
**insurance policy** *s* póliza de seguro
**insurant** [ɪnˈʃurənt] *s* asegurado
**insure** [ɪnˈʃur] *va* asegurar
**insured** [ɪnˈʃurd] *adj & s* asegurado
**insurer** [ɪnˈʃurər] *s* asegurador
**insurgence** [ɪnˈsʌrdʒəns] o **insurgency** [ɪnˈsʌrdʒənsɪ] *s* insurrección, sublevación
**insurgent** [ɪnˈsʌrdʒənt] *adj & s* insurgente
**insurmountable** [ˌɪnsərˈmauntəbəl] *adj* insuperable
**insurrection** [ˌɪnsəˈrɛkʃən] *s* insurrección
**insurrectionary** [ˌɪnsəˈrɛkʃənˌɛrɪ] *adj* insurreccional
**insurrectionist** [ˌɪnsəˈrɛkʃənɪst] *s* insurrecto
**insusceptibility** [ˌɪnsəˌsɛptɪˈbɪlɪtɪ] *s* insusceptibilidad
**insusceptible** [ˌɪnsəˈsɛptɪbəl] *adj* insusceptible
**int.** abr. de **interest, interior, internal, international** y **intransitive**
**intact** [ɪnˈtækt] *adj* intacto, ileso, incólume
**intaglio** [ɪnˈtæljo] o [ɪnˈtɑlɪo] *s* (*pl:* **-ios**) entallo; joya entallada
**intake** [ˈɪnˌtek] *s* producto; cantidad admitida; admisión
**intake manifold** *s* múltiple de admisión, colector de admisión
**intake stroke** *s* (mach.) carrera de admisión o de aspiración
**intake valve** *s* válvula de admisión
**intangibility** [ɪnˌtændʒɪˈbɪlɪtɪ] *s* intangibilidad; incomprensibilidad
**intangible** [ɪnˈtændʒɪbəl] *adj* intangible; incomprensible
**integer** [ˈɪntɪdʒər] *s* (math.) entero, número entero; todo, cosa entera
**integrable** [ˈɪntɪgrəbəl] *adj* (math.) integrable
**integral** [ˈɪntɪgrəl] *adj* íntegro; (math.) integral; **integral with** solidario de; *s* conjunto, todo; (math.) integral
**integral calculus** *s* cálculo integral
**integral sign** *s* (math.) integral
**integrant** [ˈɪntɪgrənt] *adj* integrante
**integrate** [ˈɪntɪgret] *va* integrar; (math.) integrar
**integration** [ˌɪntɪˈgreʃən] *s* integración
**integrationist** [ˌɪntɪˈgreʃənɪst] *s* partidario de la integración racial
**integrator** [ˈɪntɪˌgretər] *s* integrador

**integrity** [ɪn'tɛgrɪtɪ] *s* integridad
**integument** [ɪn'tɛgjəmənt] *s* integumento
**intellect** ['ɪntəlɛkt] *s* intelecto; intelectual (*persona*)
**intellectual** [,ɪntə'lɛktʃuəl] *adj & s* intelectual
**intellectualism** [,ɪntə'lɛktʃuəlɪzəm] *s* intelectualismo
**intellectuality** [,ɪntə,lɛktʃu'ælɪtɪ] *s* (*pl:* **-ties**) intelectualidad
**intellectually** [,ɪntə'lɛktʃuəlɪ] *adv* intelectualmente
**intelligence** [ɪn'tɛlɪdʒəns] *s* inteligencia; información; inteligencia (*información secreta; policía secreta*)
**intelligence department** *s* departamento de inteligencia, servicio de inteligencia
**intelligence quotient** *s* cociente intelectual
**intelligence test** *s* (psychol.) prueba de inteligencia
**intelligent** [ɪn'tɛlɪdʒənt] *adj* inteligente
**intelligentsia** [ɪn,tɛlɪ'dʒɛntsɪə] o [ɪn,tɛlɪ'gɛntsɪə] *s* intelectualidad (*conjunto de los intelectuales de un país*)
**intelligibility** [ɪn,tɛlɪdʒɪ'bɪlɪtɪ] *s* inteligibilidad
**intelligible** [ɪn'tɛlɪdʒɪbəl] *adj* inteligible
**intemperance** [ɪn'tɛmpərəns] *s* intemperancia, destemplanza
**intemperate** [ɪn'tɛmpərɪt] *adj* intemperante; riguroso (*dícese del tiempo*)
**intend** [ɪn'tɛnd] *va* pensar, proponerse; destinar; querer decir; **to intend to** + *inf* pensar o proponerse + *inf*
**intendancy** [ɪn'tɛndənsɪ] *s* (*pl:* **-cies**) intendencia
**intendant** [ɪn'tɛndənt] *s* intendente
**intended** [ɪn'tɛndɪd] *adj* pensado; (coll.) prometido, prometida; *s* (coll.) prometido, prometida
**intense** [ɪn'tɛns] *adj* intenso
**intensely** [ɪn'tɛnslɪ] *adv* intensamente; sobremanera
**intensification** [ɪn,tɛnsɪfɪ'keʃən] *s* intensificación
**intensify** [ɪn'tɛnsɪfaɪ] (*pret & pp:* **-fied**) *va* intensar o intensificar; (phot.) reforzar; *vn* intensarse o intensificarse
**intensity** [ɪn'tɛnsɪtɪ] *s* (*pl:* **-ties**) intensidad
**intensive** [ɪn'tɛnsɪv] *adj* intensivo
**intent** [ɪn'tɛnt] *s* intento; acepción, sentido; **to all intents and purposes** virtualmente, en realidad; *adj* atento; resuelto; **intent on** atento a; resuelto a
**intention** [ɪn'tɛnʃən] *s* intención; acepción, sentido; **intentions** *spl* (coll.) intenciones (*con respecto al matrimonio*)
**intentional** [ɪn'tɛnʃənəl] *adj* intencional
**intentionally** [ɪn'tɛnʃənəlɪ] *adv* intencionalmente
**inter** [ɪn'tʌr] (*pret & pp:* **-terred;** *ger:* **-terring**) *va* enterrar
**interact** ['ɪntər,ækt] *s* (theat.) entreacto; [,ɪntər'ækt] *vn* obrar recíprocamente
**interaction** [,ɪntər'ækʃən] *s* interacción
**interallied** [,ɪntərə'laɪd] *adj* interaliado
**inter-American** [,ɪntərə'mɛrɪkən] *adj* interamericano
**inter-Americanism** [,ɪntərə'mɛrɪkənɪzəm] *s* interamericanismo
**inter-Andean** [,ɪntəræn'diən] *adj* interandino
**interborough** ['ɪntər,bʌro] *adj* interseccional
**interbreed** [,ɪntər'brid] (*pret & pp:* **-bred**) *va* entrecruzar; *vn* entrecruzarse
**intercadence** [,ɪntər'kedəns] *s* (med.) intercadencia
**intercalary** [ɪn'tʌrkə,lɛrɪ] *adj* intercalar
**intercalate** [ɪn'tʌrkəlet] *va* intercalar
**intercalation** [ɪn,tʌrkə'leʃən] *s* intercalación
**intercede** [,ɪntər'sid] *vn* interceder
**intercellular** [,ɪntər'sɛljələr] *adj* intercelular
**intercept** [,ɪntər'sɛpt] *va* interceptar; (geom.) cortar
**interception** [,ɪntər'sɛpʃən] *s* interceptación o intercepción
**interceptor** [,ɪntər'sɛptər] *s* interceptor; avión interceptor
**intercession** [,ɪntər'sɛʃən] *s* intercesión
**intercessor** [,ɪntər'sɛsər] o ['ɪntər,sɛsər] *s* intercesor
**intercessory** [,ɪntər'sɛsərɪ] *adj* intercesorio
**interchange** ['ɪntər,tʃendʒ] *s* intercambio; correspondencia (*en una carretera, el metro, etc.*); [,ɪntər'tʃendʒ] *va* intercambiar; alternar; *vn* intercambiarse; alternarse
**interchangeable** [,ɪntər'tʃendʒəbəl] *adj* intercambiable
**intercollegiate** [,ɪntərkə'lidʒɪɪt] *adj* interescolar, intercolegiado, interuniversitario
**intercolonial** [,ɪntərkə'lonɪəl] *adj* intercolonial
**intercolumniation** [,ɪntərkə,lʌmnɪ'eʃən] *s* (arch.) intercolumnio
**intercom** ['ɪntər,kɑm] *s* (slang) intercomunicador, aparato de intercomunicación
**intercommunicate** [,ɪntərkə'mjunɪket] *vn* intercomunicarse
**intercommunication** [,ɪntərkə,mjunɪ'keʃən] *s* intercomunicación
**interconnect** [,ɪntərkə'nɛkt] *va* interconectar
**interconnection** [,ɪntərkə'nɛkʃən] *s* interconexión
**intercontinental** [,ɪntər,kɑntɪ'nɛntəl] *adj* intercontinental
**intercostal** [,ɪntər'kɑstəl] o [,ɪntər'kɔstəl] *adj* (anat.) intercostal; *s* (anat.) músculo intercostal
**intercourse** ['ɪntərkors] *s* intercambio, comunicación, trato; comercio, cópula; **to have intercourse** juntarse
**intercross** [,ɪntər'krɔs] o [,ɪntər'krɑs] *va* entrecruzar; *vn* entrecruzarse
**intercurrent** [,ɪntər'kʌrənt] *adj* (path.) intercurrente
**intercutaneous** [,ɪntərkju'tenɪəs] *adj* intercutáneo
**interdenominational** ['ɪntərdɪ,nɑmɪ'neʃənəl] *adj* intersectario, interconfesional
**interdental** [,ɪntər'dɛntəl] *adj & s* (phonet.) interdental
**interdepartmental** ['ɪntər,dipɑrt'mɛntəl] *adj* interdepartamental
**interdependence** [,ɪntərdɪ'pɛndəns] *s* interdependencia
**interdependent** [,ɪntərdɪ'pɛndənt] *adj* interdependiente
**interdict** ['ɪntərdɪkt] *s* interdicto, entredicho; [,ɪntər'dɪkt] *va* interdecir
**interdiction** [,ɪntər'dɪkʃən] *s* interdicción, entredicho
**interdigital** [,ɪntər'dɪdʒɪtəl] *adj* interdigital
**interest** ['ɪntərɛst] o ['ɪntrɪst] *s* interés; **interests** *spl* personas interesadas; **to put out at interest** poner a interés; *va* interesar; **to be interested in** interesarse en o por; **to interest someone to** + *inf* interesarle a uno + *inf*
**interested** ['ɪntərɛstɪd] o ['ɪntrɪstɪd] *adj* interesado
**interesting** ['ɪntərɛstɪŋ] o ['ɪntrɪstɪŋ] *adj* interesante
**interfere** [,ɪntər'fɪr] *vn* oponerse; meterse, inmiscuirse; interferir, interponerse; rozarse (*el caballo un pie con el otro*); (phys.) interferir; (sport) parar una jugada; **to interfere in** meterse en; **to interfere with** estorbar, impedir, dificultar
**interference** [,ɪntər'fɪrəns] *s* oposición; ingerencia; interferencia; intervención; estorbo, impedimento; (phys. & rad.) interferencia
**interferential** [,ɪntərfɪ'rɛnʃəl] *adj* (phys.) interferencial
**interferometer** [,ɪntərfɪ'rɑmɪtər] *s* (phys.) interferómetro
**interfold** [,ɪntər'fold] *va* entrelazar
**interfoliate** [,ɪntər'folɪet] *va* interfoliar
**interfuse** [,ɪntər'fjuz] *va* entremezclar; *vn* entremezclarse
**interfusion** [,ɪntər'fjuʒən] *s* entremezcladura
**intergovernmental** [,ɪntər,gʌvərn'mɛntəl] *adj* intergubernamental
**interim** ['ɪntərɪm] *adj* interino; provisional; *s* intervalo, intermedio; **in the interim** entretanto; (*cap.*) *s* (eccl.) ínterin
**interior** [ɪn'tɪrɪər] *adj & s* interior
**interior decoration** *s* decoración interior
**interj.** abr. de **interjection**
**interjacent** [,ɪntər'dʒesənt] *adj* interyacente
**interject** [,ɪntər'dʒɛkt] *va* interponer, introducir; *vn* interponerse

**interjection** [ˌɪntərˈdʒɛkʃən] *s* interposición; exclamación; (gram.) interjección
**interjectional** [ˌɪntərˈdʒɛkʃənəl] *adj* interpuesto; exclamativo; (gram.) interjectivo
**interknit** [ˌɪntərˈnɪt] (*pret & pp:* **-knitted** o **-knit;** *ger:* **-knitting**) *va* entrelazar
**interlace** [ˈɪntərˌles] *s* entrelazado; [ˌɪntərˈles] *va* entrelazar, entretejer; *vn* entrelazarse, entretejerse
**interlard** [ˌɪntərˈlɑrd] *va* (cook.) mechar; interpolar
**interleaf** [ˈɪntərˌlif] *s* (*pl:* **-leaves**) hoja interfoliada
**interleave** [ˌɪntərˈliv] *va* interfoliar
**interlibrary loan** [ˌɪntərˈlaɪˌbrɛrɪ] o [ˌɪntərˈlaɪbrərɪ] *s* préstamo entre bibliotecas
**interline** [ˈɪntərˌlaɪn] *s* interlínea; [ˌɪntərˈlaɪn] *va* interlinear; (sew.) entretelar
**interlinear** [ˌɪntərˈlɪnɪər] *adj* interlineal
**interlineation** [ˌɪntərˌlɪnɪˈeʃən] *s* interlineación
**interlining** [ˌɪntərˈlaɪnɪŋ] *s* interlineación; [ˈɪntərˌlaɪnɪŋ] *s* (sew.) entretela
**interlink** [ˌɪntərˈlɪŋk] *va* eslabonar
**interlock** [ˌɪntərˈlɑk] *va* trabar, engargantar, enclavijar; *vn* trabarse, engargantarse, enclavijarse
**interlocking** [ˌɪntərˈlɑkɪŋ] *adj* trabado, entrelazado
**interlocking system** *s* (rail.) enclavamiento
**interlocutor** [ˌɪntərˈlɑkjətər] *s* interlocutor
**interlocutory** [ˌɪntərˈlɑkjəˌtorɪ] *adj* dialogístico; (law) interlocutorio
**interlope** [ˌɪntərˈlop] *vn* traficar sin derecho
**interloper** [ˈɪntərˌlopər] *s* intruso
**interlude** [ˈɪntərlud] *s* intervalo; (theat.) intermedio; (mus.) interludio
**interlunar** [ˌɪntərˈlunər] *adj* interlunar
**interlunation** [ˌɪntərluˈneʃən] *s* (astr.) interlunio
**intermarriage** [ˌɪntərˈmærɪdʒ] *s* casamiento entre parientes, casamiento entre personas de distintas razas
**intermarry** [ˌɪntərˈmærɪ] (*pret & pp:* **-ried**) *vn* casarse desentendiéndose del parentesco, casarse desentendiéndose de las diferencias de raza; unirse por medio del matrimonio
**intermaxillary** [ˌɪntərˈmæksɪˌlɛrɪ] *adj* intermaxilar
**intermeddle** [ˌɪntərˈmɛdəl] *vn* entrometerse
**intermediary** [ˌɪntərˈmidɪˌɛrɪ] *adj* intermediario; *s* (*pl:* **-ies**) intermediario
**intermediate** [ˌɪntərˈmidɪɪt] *adj* intermediario, intermedio; *s* intermediario; [ˌɪntərˈmidɪet] *vn* intermediar
**intermediate frequency** *s* (rad.) frecuencia intermedia
**intermediation** [ˌɪntərˌmidɪˈeʃən] *s* mediación, intervención
**interment** [ɪnˈtʌrmənt] *s* entierro
**intermezzo** [ˌɪntərˈmɛtso] o [ˌɪntərˈmɛdzo] *s* (*pl:* **-zos** o **-zi** [sɪ] o [zɪ]) intermezzo, intermedio
**interminable** [ɪnˈtʌrmɪnəbəl] *adj* interminable
**interminably** [ɪnˈtʌrmɪnəblɪ] *adv* interminablemente
**intermingle** [ˌɪntərˈmɪŋgəl] *va* entremezclar; *vn* entremezclarse
**intermission** [ˌɪntərˈmɪʃən] *s* intermisión; (path.) intermisión, intermitencia; (theat.) intermedio, entreacto
**intermit** [ˌɪntərˈmɪt] (*pret & pp:* **-mitted;** *ger:* **-mitting**) *va* intermitir
**intermittence** [ˌɪntərˈmɪtəns] o **intermittency** [ˌɪntərˈmɪtənsɪ] *s* intermitencia
**intermittent** [ˌɪntərˈmɪtənt] *adj* intermitente
**intermix** [ˌɪntərˈmɪks] *va* entremezclar; *vn* entremezclarse
**intermixture** [ˌɪntərˈmɪkstʃər] *s* entremezcladura
**intern** [ˈɪntʌrn] *s* (médico) interno de hospital; [ɪnˈtʌrn] *va* recluir, internar
**internal** [ɪnˈtʌrnəl] *adj* interno
**internal-combustion engine** [ɪnˈtʌrnəlkəmˈbʌstʃən] *s* motor de combustión interna, motor de explosión
**internally** [ɪnˈtʌrnəlɪ] *adv* internamente
**internal medicine** *s* medicina interna
**internal revenue** *s* rentas internas (*del gobierno*)
**international** [ˌɪntərˈnæʃənəl] *adj* internacional; (*cap.*) *s* Internacional (*asociación de obreros*)
**international candle** *s* (phys.) bujía internacional
**international code** *s* (telg.) código internacional
**International Court** *s* Tribunal internacional
**international date line** *s* línea internacional de cambio de fecha
**internationalism** [ˌɪntərˈnæʃənəlɪzəm] *s* internacionalismo
**internationalist** [ˌɪntərˈnæʃənəlɪst] *s* internacionalista
**internationality** [ˈɪntərˌnæʃəˈnælɪtɪ] *s* internacionalidad
**internationalization** [ˌɪntərˌnæʃənəlɪˈzeʃən] *s* internacionalización
**internationalize** [ˌɪntərˈnæʃənəlaɪz] *va* internacionalizar
**international law** *s* derecho internacional, derecho de gentes
**internationally** [ˌɪntərˈnæʃənəlɪ] *adv* internacionalmente
**interne** [ˈɪntʌrn] *s* (médico) interno de hospital
**internecine** [ˌɪntərˈnisɪn] *adj* sanguinario
**internee** [ˌɪntʌrˈni] *s* (mil.) internado
**internist** [ɪnˈtʌrnɪst] *s* (med.) internista
**internment** [ɪnˈtʌrnmənt] *s* reclusión, internación, internamiento
**internment camp** *s* campo de internamiento
**internode** [ˈɪntərˌnod] *s* internodio
**internship** [ˈɪntʌrnʃɪp] *s* residencia (*de un médico*) en un hospital
**internuncio** [ˌɪntərˈnʌnʃɪo] *s* (*pl:* **-cios**) internuncio
**interoceanic** [ˌɪntərˌoʃɪˈænɪk] *adj* interoceánico
**interocular** [ˌɪntərˈɑkjələr] *adj* interocular
**interosseous** [ˌɪntərˈɑsɪəs] *adj* interóseo
**interpage** [ˌɪntərˈpedʒ] *va* interpaginar
**interparietal** [ˌɪntərpəˈraɪətəl] *adj* (anat.) interparietal
**interparliamentary** [ˌɪntərˌpɑrlɪˈmɛntərɪ] *adj* interparlamentario
**interpellate** [ˌɪntərˈpɛlet] o [ɪnˈtʌrpɪlet] *va* interpelar
**interpellation** [ˌɪntərpɛˈleʃən] o [ɪnˌtʌrpɪˈleʃən] *s* interpelación
**interpenetrate** [ˌɪntərˈpɛnɪtret] *va* penetrar completamente; *vn* compenetrarse
**interpenetration** [ˈɪntərˌpɛnɪˈtreʃən] *s* interpenetración
**interphone** [ˈɪntərˌfon] *s* aparato de intercomunicación
**interplanetary** [ˌɪntərˈplænɪˌtɛrɪ] *adj* interplanetario
**interplay** [ˈɪntərˌple] *s* interacción
**interpolate** [ɪnˈtʌrpəlet] *va* interpolar; (math.) interpolar
**interpolation** [ɪnˌtʌrpəˈleʃən] *s* interpolación
**interpose** [ˌɪntərˈpoz] *va* interponer; *vn* interponerse
**interposition** [ˌɪntərpəˈzɪʃən] *s* interposición
**interpret** [ɪnˈtʌrprɪt] *va* interpretar
**interpretable** [ɪnˈtʌrprɪtəbəl] *adj* interpretable
**interpretation** [ɪnˌtʌrprɪˈteʃən] *s* interpretación
**interpretative** [ɪnˈtʌrprɪˌtetɪv] *adj* interpretativo
**interpreter** [ɪnˈtʌrprɪtər] *s* intérprete
**interpretive** [ɪnˈtʌrprɪtɪv] *adj* interpretativo
**interracial** [ˌɪntərˈreʃəl] *adj* interracial
**interregnum** [ˌɪntərˈrɛgnəm] *s* interregno
**interrelated** [ˌɪntərrɪˈletɪd] *adj* correlativo
**interrelation** [ˌɪntərrɪˈleʃən] *s* correlación
**interrogate** [ɪnˈtɛrəget] *va & vn* interrogar
**interrogation** [ɪnˌtɛrəˈgeʃən] *s* interrogación
**interrogation mark** o **point** *s* interrogación o signo de interrogación
**interrogative** [ˌɪntəˈrɑgətɪv] *adj* interrogativo; interrogante; *s* (gram.) interrogativo
**interrogator** [ɪnˈtɛrəˌgetər] *s* interrogante
**interrogatory** [ˌɪntəˈrɑgəˌtorɪ] *adj* interrogante; *s* (*pl:* **-ries**) interrogatorio
**interrupt** [ˌɪntəˈrʌpt] *va* interrumpir
**interruption** [ˌɪntəˈrʌpʃən] *s* interrupción
**interscholastic** [ˌɪntərskəˈlæstɪk] *adj* interescolar

**intersect** [ˌɪntər'sɛkt] *va* intersecar; *vn* intersecarse
**intersection** [ˌɪntər'sɛkʃən] *s* cruce; (geom.) intersección
**intersidereal** [ˌɪntərsaɪ'dɪrɪəl] *adj* intersideral
**interspace** ['ɪntərˌspes] *s* espacio intermedio; [ˌɪntər'spes] *va* dejar espacio entre; llenar el espacio entre; espaciar
**intersperse** [ˌɪntər'spʌrs] *va* entremezclar, intercalar, esparcir
**interspersion** [ˌɪntər'spʌrʒən] o [ˌɪntər'spʌrʃən] *s* entremezcladura, intercalación, esparcimiento
**interstage** ['ɪntərˌstedʒ] *adj* (rad.) inter-etapa
**interstate** ['ɪntərˌstet] *adj* interestadal
**interstellar** [ˌɪntər'stɛlər] *adj* interestelar
**interstice** [ɪn'tʌrstɪs] *s* intersticio
**interstitial** [ˌɪntər'stɪʃəl] *adj* intersticial
**intertribal** [ˌɪntər'traɪbəl] *adj* entre tribus
**intertrigo** [ˌɪntər'traɪgo] *s* (path.) intertrigo
**intertropical** [ˌɪntər'trɑpɪkəl] *adj* intertropical
**intertwine** [ˌɪntər'twaɪn] *va* entrelazar; *vn* entrelazarse
**intertwist** [ˌɪntər'twɪst] *va* torcer (*uno con otro*); entremezclar; *vn* torcerse uno con otro; entremezclarse
**interuniversity** [ˌɪntərˌjunɪ'vʌrsɪtɪ] *adj* interuniversitario
**interurban** [ˌɪntər'ʌrbən] *adj* interurbano
**interval** ['ɪntərvəl] *s* intervalo; (mus.) intervalo; **at intervals** de vez en cuando; de trecho en trecho
**intervene** [ˌɪntər'vin] *vn* intervenir
**intervening** [ˌɪntər'vinɪŋ] *adj* intermedio
**intervention** [ˌɪntər'vɛnʃən] *s* intervención
**interventionist** [ˌɪntər'vɛnʃənɪst] *adj & s* intervencionista
**interview** ['ɪntərvju] *s* entrevista, interviú; *va* entrevistarse con
**intervocalic** [ˌɪntərvo'kælɪk] *adj* intervocálico
**interweave** [ˌɪntər'wiv] (*pret:* **-wove** o **-weaved;** *pp:* **-woven, -wove** o **-weaved)** *va* entretejer
**interwove** [ˌɪntər'wov] *pret & pp de* **interweave**
**interwoven** [ˌɪntər'wovən] *pp de* **interweave**
**interzonal** [ˌɪntər'zonəl] o **interzone** [ˌɪntər'zon] *adj* interzonal
**intestacy** [ɪn'tɛstəsɪ] *s* falta de testamento
**intestate** [ɪn'tɛstet] o [ɪn'tɛstɪt] *adj & s* intestado
**intestinal** [ɪn'tɛstɪnəl] *adj* intestinal
**intestinal worm** *s* (zool.) lombriz intestinal
**intestine** [ɪn'tɛstɪn] *adj* intestino (*interno; doméstico*); *s* (anat.) intestino; **intestines** *spl* (anat.) intestinos
**inthrall** [ɪn'θrɔl] *va* encantar, dominar; esclavizar, sojuzgar
**inthrone** [ɪn'θron] *va* entronizar
**intimacy** ['ɪntɪməsɪ] *s* (*pl:* **-cies**) intimidad
**intimate** ['ɪntɪmɪt] *adj* íntimo; *s* amigo íntimo; ['ɪntɪmet] *va* insinuar; intimar (*hacer saber*)
**intimation** [ˌɪntɪ'meʃən] *s* insinuación; intimación (*informe, noticia*)
**intimidate** [ɪn'tɪmɪdet] *va* intimidar
**intimidation** [ɪnˌtɪmɪ'deʃən] *s* intimidación
**intine** ['ɪntɪn] o ['ɪntaɪn] *s* (bot.) intina
**intitle** [ɪn'taɪtəl] *va* intitular; dar derecho a
**into** ['ɪntu] o ['ɪntʊ] *prep* en, dentro de, hacia el interior de
**intolerability** [ɪnˌtɑlərə'bɪlɪtɪ] *s* intolerabilidad
**intolerable** [ɪn'tɑlərəbəl] *adj* intolerable
**intolerance** [ɪn'tɑlərəns] *s* intolerancia
**intolerant** [ɪn'tɑlərənt] *adj & s* intolerante
**intomb** [ɪn'tum] *va* sepultar
**intombment** [ɪn'tummənt] *s* sepultura
**intonate** ['ɪntonet] *va* entonar
**intonation** [ˌɪnto'neʃən] *s* entonación; (phonet.) entonación
**intone** [ɪn'ton] *va* entonar; salmodiar
**intoxicant** [ɪn'tɑksɪkənt] *adj* embriagador; *s* bebida alcohólica
**intoxicate** [ɪn'tɑksɪket] *va* embriagar; (med.) intoxicar, envenenar
**intoxicating** [ɪn'tɑksɪˌketɪŋ] *adj* embriagante
**intoxication** [ɪnˌtɑksɪ'keʃən] *s* embriaguez; (med.) intoxicación, envenenamiento

**intr.** abr. de **intransitive**
**intractability** [ɪnˌtræktə'bɪlɪtɪ] *s* intratabilidad
**intractable** [ɪn'træktəbəl] *adj* intratable
**intrados** [ɪn'tredɑs] *s* (arch.) intradós
**intramolecular** [ˌɪntrəmə'lɛkjələr] *adj* intramolecular
**intramural** [ˌɪntrə'mjurəl] *adj* interior; (anat.) intramural
**intramuscular** [ˌɪntrə'mʌskjələr] *adj* intramuscular
**intrans.** abr. de **intransitive**
**intransigence** [ɪn'trænsɪdʒəns] o **intransigency** [ɪn'trænsɪdʒənsɪ] *s* intransigencia
**intransigent** [ɪn'trænsɪdʒənt] *adj & s* intransigente
**intransitive** [ɪn'trænsɪtɪv] *adj* (gram.) intransitivo, neutro
**intravenous** [ˌɪntrə'vinəs] *adj* intravenoso
**intravenously** [ˌɪntrə'vinəslɪ] *adv* por vía intravenosa
**intreat** [ɪn'trit] *va* rogar, suplicar
**intrench** [ɪn'trɛntʃ] *va* atrincherar; establecer firmemente; *vn* atrincherarse; **to intrench on** o **upon** infringir, violar
**intrenchment** [ɪn'trɛntʃmənt] *s* atrincheramiento
**intrepid** [ɪn'trɛpɪd] *adj* intrépido
**intrepidity** [ˌɪntrɪ'pɪdɪtɪ] *s* intrepidez
**intricacy** ['ɪntrɪkəsɪ] *s* (*pl:* **-cies**) intrincación
**intricate** ['ɪntrɪkɪt] *adj* intrincado
**intrigue** [ɪn'trig] o ['ɪntrig] *s* intriga; intriga amorosa; [ɪn'trig] *va* intrigar, despertar la curiosidad de; *vn* intrigar; tener intrigas amorosas
**intriguer** [ɪn'trigər] *s* intrigante
**intrinsic** [ɪn'trɪnsɪk] o **intrinsical** [ɪn'trɪnsɪkəl] *adj* intrínseco
**intrinsically** [ɪn'trɪnsɪkəlɪ] *adv* intrínsecamente
**introd.** abr. de **introduction** y **introductory**
**introduce** [ˌɪntrə'djus] o [ˌɪntrə'dus] *va* introducir; presentar (*una persona a otra*)
**introducer** [ˌɪntrə'djusər] o [ˌɪntrə'dusər] *s* introductor
**introduction** [ˌɪntrə'dʌkʃən] *s* introducción; presentación
**introductory** [ˌɪntrə'dʌktərɪ] *adj* introductivo, introductor
**introductory offer** *s* ofrecimiento de presentación
**Introit** [ɪn'tro·ɪt] *s* (eccl.) introito
**introrse** [ɪn'trɔrs] *adj* (bot.) introrso
**introspection** [ˌɪntrə'spɛkʃən] *s* introspección
**introspective** [ˌɪntrə'spɛktɪv] *adj* introspectivo
**introversion** [ˌɪntrə'vʌrʒən] o [ˌɪntrə'vʌrʃən] *s* introversión
**introvert** ['ɪntrəˌvʌrt] *adj* introverso; *s* introvertido
**intrude** [ɪn'trud] *va* imponer (*su opinión a otros*); *vn* entremeterse; estorbar
**intruder** [ɪn'trudər] *s* intruso
**intrusion** [ɪn'truʒən] *s* intrusión
**intrusive** [ɪn'trusɪv] *adj* intruso
**intrust** [ɪn'trʌst] *va* confiar; **to intrust to** confiar a; **to intrust someone with something** confiar algo a alguien
**intubation** [ˌɪntjə'beʃən] *s* (med.) intubación
**intuit** ['ɪntjuɪt] o ['ɪntuɪt] *va* intuir
**intuition** [ˌɪntʊ'ɪʃən] o [ˌɪntjʊ'ɪʃən] *s* intuición
**intuitional** [ˌɪntʊ'ɪʃənəl] o [ˌɪntjʊ'ɪʃənəl] *adj* intuitivo
**intuitionism** [ˌɪntʊ'ɪʃənɪzəm] o [ˌɪntjʊ'ɪʃənɪzəm] *s* intuicionismo
**intuitive** [ɪn'tuɪtɪv] o [ɪn'tjuɪtɪv] *adj* intuitivo
**intussusception** [ˌɪntəssə'sɛpʃən] *s* (biol. & path.) intususcepción
**inulase** ['ɪnjəles] *s* (biochem.) inulasa
**inulin** ['ɪnjəlɪn] *s* (chem.) inulina
**inundate** ['ɪnʌndet] *va* inundar
**inundation** [ˌɪnʌn'deʃən] *s* inundación
**inure** [ɪn'jʊr] *va* acostumbrar, endurecer; *vn* redundar; **to inure to** redundar en
**inutility** [ˌɪnjʊ'tɪlɪtɪ] *s* (*pl:* **-ties**) inutilidad
**inv.** abr. de **invented, inventor** y **invoice**
**in vacuo** [ɪn'vækjʊo] (Lat.) en el vacío
**invade** [ɪn'ved] *va* invadir

**invader** [ɪn'vedər] *s* invasor
**invaginate** [ɪn'vædʒɪnet] *va* invaginar; *vn* invaginarse
**invagination** [ɪn,vædʒɪ'neʃən] *s* invaginación
**invalid** [ɪn'vælɪd] *adj* inválido (*nulo, de ningún valor*); ['ɪnvəlɪd] *adj & s* inválido (*por enfermo*); *va* incapacitar; matricular en el registro de inválidos
**invalidate** [ɪn'vælɪdet] *va* invalidar
**invalidation** [ɪn,vælɪ'deʃən] *s* invalidación
**invalid chair** *s* sillón para inválidos
**invalidism** ['ɪnvəlɪdɪzəm] *s* estado de inválido, estado de valetudinario
**invalidity** [,ɪnvə'lɪdɪtɪ] *s* invalidez
**invaluable** [ɪn'væljuəbəl] o [ɪn'væljəbəl] *adj* inestimable, inapreciable
**invaluably** [ɪn'væljuəblɪ] o [ɪn'væljəblɪ] *adv* inestimablemente, inapreciablemente
**invar** [ɪn'vɑr] *s* (trademark) invar (*aleación*)
**invariability** [ɪn,vɛrɪə'bɪlɪtɪ] *s* invariabilidad
**invariable** [ɪn'vɛrɪəbəl] *adj* invariable
**invariably** [ɪn'vɛrɪəblɪ] *adv* invariablemente
**invariant** [ɪn'vɛrɪənt] *adj & s* (math.) invariante
**invasion** [ɪn'veʒən] *s* invasión
**invective** [ɪn'vɛktɪv] *s* invectiva
**inveigh** [ɪn've] *vn* prorrumpir en invectivas; **to inveigh against** invectivar
**inveigle** [ɪn'vegəl] o [ɪn'vigəl] *va* engatusar; **to inveigle into** + *ger* engatusar para que + *subj*
**invent** [ɪn'vɛnt] *va* inventar
**invention** [ɪn'vɛnʃən] *s* invención; invento
**Invention of the Cross** *s* (eccl.) Invención de la Santa Cruz
**inventive** [ɪn'vɛntɪv] *adj* inventivo
**inventiveness** [ɪn'vɛntɪvnɪs] *s* inventiva
**inventor** [ɪn'vɛntər] *s* inventor
**inventory** ['ɪnvən,torɪ] *s* (*pl:* **-ries**) inventario; existencia; (*pret & pp:* **-ried**) *va* inventariar
**inverisimilitude** [ɪn,vɛrɪsɪ'mɪlɪtjud] o [,ɪn-,vɛrɪsɪ'mɪlɪtud] *s* inverisimilitud
**inverness** [,ɪnvər'nɛs] *s* macfarlán (*gabán*)
**inverse** [ɪn'vʌrs] o ['ɪnvʌrs] *adj* inverso
**inverse ratio** *s* (math.) razón inversa
**inversion** [ɪn'vʌrʒən] o [ɪn'vʌrʃən] *s* inversión
**invert** ['ɪnvʌrt] *s* (psychiatry) invertido; [ɪn-'vʌrt] *va* invertir
**invertase** [ɪn'vʌrtes] *s* (biochem.) invertasa
**invertebrate** [ɪn'vʌrtɪbret] o [ɪn'vʌrtɪbrɪt] *adj & s* invertebrado
**inverted exclamation point** *s* (gram.) principio de admiración
**inverted question mark** *s* (gram.) principio de interrogación
**invest** [ɪn'vɛst] *va* investir (*poner en posesión de una dignidad*); cubrir, envolver; sitiar, cercar; invertir (*dinero*); **to invest with** investir de o con
**investigate** [ɪn'vɛstɪget] *va* investigar
**investigation** [ɪn,vɛstɪ'geʃən] *s* investigación
**investigator** [ɪn'vɛstɪ,getər] *s* investigador
**investiture** [ɪn'vɛstɪtʃər] *s* investidura; vestidura
**investment** [ɪn'vɛstmənt] *s* investidura; vestidura; sitio, cerco; inversión (*de dinero*)
**investment capital** *s* capital de inversión
**investment trust** *s* sociedad de inversión, sociedad de cartera
**investor** [ɪn'vɛstər] *s* inversionista
**inveteracy** [ɪn'vɛtərəsɪ] *s* hábito inveterado
**inveterate** [ɪn'vɛtərɪt] *adj* inveterado, sempiterno, empedernido
**invidious** [ɪn'vɪdɪəs] *adj* odioso, abominable, injusto
**invigorate** [ɪn'vɪgəret] *va* vigorizar
**invigorating** [ɪn'vɪgə,retɪŋ] *adj* vigorizante
**invigoration** [ɪn,vɪgə'reʃən] *s* tonificación
**invincibility** [ɪn,vɪnsɪ'bɪlɪtɪ] *s* invencibilidad
**invincible** [ɪn'vɪnsɪbəl] *adj* invencible
**Invincible Armada** *s* Armada Invencible
**inviolability** [ɪn,vaɪələ'bɪlɪtɪ] *s* inviolabilidad
**inviolable** [ɪn'vaɪələbəl] *adj* inviolable
**inviolate** [ɪn'vaɪəlɪt] o [ɪn'vaɪəlet] *adj* inviolado
**invisibility** [ɪn,vɪzɪ'bɪlɪtɪ] *s* invisibilidad
**invisible** [ɪn'vɪzɪbəl] *adj* invisible; *s* ser invisible; mundo invisible
**invisible ink** *s* tinta simpática
**invisible mending** *s* zurcido invisible
**invisibly** [ɪn'vɪzɪblɪ] *adv* invisiblemente
**invitation** [,ɪnvɪ'teʃən] *s* invitación, convite
**invite** [ɪn'vaɪt] *va* convidar, invitar; **to invite to** + *inf* convidar a + *inf*
**inviting** [ɪn'vaɪtɪŋ] *adj* incitante, seductor; provocativo; apetitoso (*alimento*)
**in vitro** ['vaɪtro] (Lat.) en vidrio
**invocation** [,ɪnvə'keʃən] *s* invocación; conjuro (*p.ej., de diablos*)
**invocatory** [ɪn'vɑkə,torɪ] *adj* invocatorio
**invoice** ['ɪnvɔɪs] *s* factura; remesa; **as per invoice** según factura; *va* facturar
**invoice price** *s* precio de factura
**invoke** [ɪn'vok] *va* invocar; conjurar (*p.ej., los demonios*)
**involucrate** [,ɪnvə'lukrɪt] *adj* (bot.) involucrado
**involucre** ['ɪnvə,lukər] *s* (bot.) involucro
**involuntary** [ɪn'vɑlən,tɛrɪ] *adj* involuntario
**involute** ['ɪnvəlut] *adj* intrincado; vuelto hacia dentro; enrollado en espiral; *s* (geom.) involuta
**involution** [,ɪnvə'luʃən] *s* intrincación; involución, envolvimiento; (biol. & med.) involución; (math.) potenciación, elevación a potencias; (math.) involución (*caso particular de las formas proyectivas superpuestas*)
**involve** [ɪn'vɑlv] *va* envolver, enrollar; implicar, comprometer; enredar, enmarañar; embeber
**involvement** [ɪn'vɑlvmənt] *s* envolvimiento; complicación; implicación
**invulnerability** [ɪn,vʌlnərə'bɪlɪtɪ] *s* invulnerabilidad
**invulnerable** [ɪn'vʌlnərəbəl] *adj* invulnerable
**inward** ['ɪnwərd] *adj* interior, interno; *adv* interiormente, hacia dentro
**inward-flow turbine** ['ɪnwərd'flo] *s* turbina centrípeta
**inwardly** ['ɪnwərdlɪ] *adv* interiormente; dentro, hacia dentro
**inwardness** ['ɪnwərdnɪs] *s* esencia, fondo; espiritualidad; sinceridad
**inwards** ['ɪnwərdz] *adv* interiormente, hacia dentro; *spl* interiores, entrañas
**inweave** [ɪn'wiv] (*pret:* **-wove;** *pp:* **-woven** o **-wove**) *va* entretejer
**inwove** [ɪn'wov] *pret & pp de* **inweave**
**inwoven** [ɪn'wovən] *pp de* **inweave**
**inwrap** [ɪn'ræp] (*pret & pp:* **-wrapped;** *ger:* **-wrapping**) *va* arropar, envolver
**inwreathe** [ɪn'rið] *va* enguirnaldar
**inwrought** ['ɪn,rɔt] *adj* entremezclado; embutido, incrustado
**Io** ['aɪo] *s* (myth.) Ío
**iodate** ['aɪədet] *s* (chem.) yodato
**iodic** [aɪ'ɑdɪk] *adj* yódico
**iodid** ['aɪədɪd] o **iodide** ['aɪədaɪd] o ['aɪədɪd] *s* (chem.) yoduro
**iodin** ['aɪədɪn] o **iodine** ['aɪədaɪn], ['aɪədɪn] o ['aɪədin] *s* (chem.) yodo; (pharm.) tintura de yodo
**iodism** ['aɪədɪzəm] *s* (path.) yodismo
**iodoform** [aɪ'odəfɔrm] o [aɪ'ɑdəfɔrm] *s* (chem.) yodoformo
**iodous** [aɪ'odəs] o [aɪ'ɑdəs] *adj* (chem.) yodoso
**ion** ['aɪən] o ['aɪɑn] *s* (chem. & phys.) ion
**Ionia** [aɪ'onɪə] *s* Jonia
**Ionian** [aɪ'onɪən] *adj & s* jonio o jónico
**Ionian Islands** *spl* islas Jonias
**Ionian Sea** *s* mar Jonio
**ionic** [aɪ'ɑnɪk] *adj* (chem. & phys.) iónico; (*cap.*) *adj* jonio, jónico; (arch.) jónico
**ionium** [aɪ'onɪəm] *s* (chem.) ionio
**ionization** [,aɪənɪ'zeʃən] *s* ionización
**ionization chamber** *s* (phys.) cámara de ionización
**ionize** ['aɪənaɪz] *va* ionizar; *vn* ionizarse
**ionosphere** [aɪ'ɑnəsfɪr] *s* ionosfera
**ion trap** *s* (telv.) trampa de iones
**iota** [aɪ'otə] *s* iota (*letra griega*); ápice, jota
**iotacism** [aɪ'otəsɪzəm] *s* iotacismo
**I.O.U.** o **I O U** ['aɪ,o'ju] abr. de **I owe you;** *s* pagaré
**ipecac** ['ɪpɪkæk] *s* (bot.) ipecacuana (*planta, raíz y medicamento*)
**ipecacuanha** [,ɪpɪ,kækju'ænə] *s* var. de **ipecac**
**Iphigenia** [,ɪfɪdʒɪ'naɪə] *s* (myth.) Ifigenia

**ipse dixit** ['ɪpsɪ'dɪksɪt] *s* (*pl:* **ipse dixits**) afirmación dogmática
**I.Q.** o **IQ** abr. de **intelligence quotient**
**Ir.** abr. de **Ireland** y **Irish**
**Irak** [ɪ'rɑk] *s* var. de **Iraq**
**Iran** [ɪ'rɑn] o [aɪ'ræn] *s* el Irán
**Iranian** [aɪ'renɪən] *adj & s* iranés o iranio
**Iranian Plateau** *s* meseta del Irán
**Iraq** [ɪ'rɑk] *s* el Irak
**Iraqi** [ɪ'rɑki] *adj* iraqués; *s* (*pl:* **-qis**) iraqués
**irascibility** [ɪ,ræsɪ'bɪlɪtɪ] *s* irascibilidad
**irascible** [ɪ'ræsɪbəl] o [aɪ'ræsɪbəl] *adj* irascible
**irate** ['aɪret] o [aɪ'ret] *adj* airado
**IRBM** abr. de **intermediate range ballistic missile**
**Ire.** abr. de **Ireland**
**ire** [aɪr] *s* ira, cólera
**ireful** ['aɪrfəl] *adj* iracundo
**Ireland** ['aɪrlənd] *s* Irlanda
**Irene** [aɪ'rin] *s* Irene
**iridaceous** [,aɪrɪ'deʃəs] *adj* (bot.) iridáceo
**iridescence** [,ɪrɪ'dɛsəns] *s* iridiscencia, irisación
**iridescent** [,ɪrɪ'dɛsənt] *adj* iridiscente
**iridium** [ɪ'rɪdɪəm] o [aɪ'rɪdɪəm] *s* (chem.) iridio
**iris** ['aɪrɪs] *s* iris, arco iris; (anat. & opt.) iris; (bot.) lirio; (*cap.*) *s* (myth.) Iris; (*l.c.*) *va* irisar
**iris diaphragm** *s* (opt.) diafragma iris
**Irish** ['aɪrɪʃ] *adj* irlandés; *s* irlandés (*idioma*); whisky de Irlanda; **the Irish** los irlandeses
**Irish Free State** *s* Estado Libre de Irlanda
**Irish linen** *s* irlanda
**Irishman** ['aɪrɪʃmən] *s* (*pl:* **-men**) irlandés
**Irish moss** *s* (bot.) musgo de Irlanda
**Irish potato** *s* patata común
**Irish Sea** *s* mar de Irlanda
**Irish setter** *s* perro perdiguero de raza irlandesa
**Irish stew** *s* guisado de carne con patatas y cebollas
**Irish terrier** *s* terrier de raza irlandesa
**Irishwoman** ['aɪrɪʃ,wumən] *s* (*pl:* **-women**) irlandesa
**iritis** [aɪ'raɪtɪs] *s* (path.) iritis
**irk** [ʌrk] *va* fastidiar, molestar
**irksome** ['ʌrksəm] *adj* fastidioso, molesto
**iron** ['aɪərn] *s* hierro; plancha (*para estirar y asentar la ropa*); (golf) hierro; **irons** *spl* hierros, grilletes; **to have too many irons in the fire** tener demasiados asuntos a que atender; **to strike while the iron is hot** a hierro caliente batir de repente, aprovechar la ocasión; *adj* férreo; *va* herrar (*guarnecer de hierro*); aherrojar, poner grilletes a; poner chapas de hierro a; planchar (*la ropa*); **to iron out** (fig.) allanar
**iron age** *s* (myth. & fig.) siglo de hierro; (*caps.*) *s* (archeol.) edad del hierro
**iron-bound** ['aɪərn,baund] *adj* unido con hierro, zunchado con hierro; escabroso, rocoso; férreo, duro, inflexible
**Iron Chancellor** *s* Canciller de hierro (*Bismarck*)
**ironclad** ['aɪərn,klæd] *adj* acorazado; inabrogable; *s* acorazado
**iron constitution** *s* constitución de hierro, constitución robusta
**iron-core transformer** ['aɪərn,kor] *s* (elec.) transformador de núcleo de hierro
**Iron Cross** *s* cruz de hierro
**iron curtain** *s* (fig.) telón de acero, cortina de hierro
**iron digestion** *s* estómago de avestruz
**iron fittings** *spl* herraje
**Iron Gates** *spl* Puertas de Hierro (*en el Danubio*)
**iron-gray** ['aɪərn,gre] *adj* gris obscuro
**iron horse** *s* (coll.) caballo de hierro (*locomotora*)
**ironic** [aɪ'rɑnɪk] o **ironical** [aɪ'rɑnɪkəl] *adj* irónico
**ironing** ['aɪərnɪŋ] *s* planchado
**ironing board** *s* mesa de planchar, tabla de planchar
**iron losses** *spl* (elec.) pérdidas magnéticas
**iron lung** *s* pulmón de hierro
**ironmaster** ['aɪərn,mæstər] o ['aɪərn,mɑstər] *s* fabricante de hierro
**iron mold** *s* mancha de orín
**ironmonger** ['aɪərn,mʌŋgər] *s* (Brit.) quincallero
**ironmongery** ['aɪərn,mʌŋgərɪ] *s* (Brit.) quincalla; (Brit.) quincallería
**iron-nickel alkaline cell** ['aɪərn'nɪkəl] *s* (elec.) acumulador de ferro-níquel
**iron pyrites** *s* pirita de hierro, pirita marcial
**ironsides** ['aɪərn,saɪdz] *s* acorazado; hombre forzudo; (*cap.*) *spl* caballería de Oliverio Cromwell
**ironstone** ['aɪərn,ston] *s* mineral de hierro
**ironware** ['aɪərn,wɛr] *s* ferretería
**ironweed** ['aɪərn,wid] *s* (bot.) ambrosia; (bot.) verónica
**iron will** *s* voluntad de hierro, voluntad férrea
**iron-willed** ['aɪərn'wɪld] *adj* de voluntad férrea
**ironwood** ['aɪərn,wud] *s* (bot.) palo de hierro; (bot.) guapaque; (bot.) cambrón; (bot.) ébano de Ceilán; (bot.) palo santo
**ironwork** ['aɪərn,wʌrk] *s* herraje; **ironworks** *spl* ferrería, talleres metalúrgicos
**ironworker** ['aɪərn,wʌrkər] *s* herrero de obra, ferrón; cerrajero (*el que trabaja el hierro en frío*)
**ironwort** ['aɪərn,wʌrt] *s* (bot.) siderita, samarilla
**irony** ['aɪrənɪ] *s* (*pl:* **-nies**) ironía
**Iroquoian** [,ɪrə'kwɔɪən] *adj & s* iroqués
**Iroquois** ['ɪrəkwɔɪ] o ['ɪrəkwɔɪz] *s* (*pl:* **-quois**) iroqués
**irradiance** [ɪ'redɪəns] *s* irradiación; lustre, esplendor
**irradiate** [ɪ'redɪet] *va* irradiar; (med.) tratar con irradiación; *vn* brillar, lucir
**irradiation** [,ɪredɪ'eʃən] *s* irradiación; brillo, esplendor; (med.) irradiación
**irrational** [ɪ'ræʃənəl] *adj* irracional; (math.) irracional
**irrationality** [ɪ,ræʃə'nælɪtɪ] *s* irracionalidad
**irreclaimable** [,ɪrɪ'kleməbəl] *adj* incorregible, irredimible; inutilizable
**irreconcilable** [ɪ'rɛkən,saɪləbəl] *adj* irreconciliable; *s* intransigente
**irrecoverable** [,ɪrɪ'kʌvərəbəl] *adj* irrecuperable; irremediable
**irredeemable** [,ɪrɪ'diməbəl] *adj* irredimible
**Irredentist** [,ɪrɪ'dɛntɪst] *s* irredentista
**irreducible** [,ɪrɪ'djusɪbəl] o [,ɪrɪ'dusɪbəl] *adj* irreducible
**irrefragable** [ɪ'rɛfrəgəbəl] *adj* irrefragable
**irrefutable** [ɪ'rɛfjutəbəl] o [,ɪrɪ'fjutəbəl] *adj* irrefutable
**irregular** [ɪ'rɛgjələr] *adj* irregular; (bot., geom., gram. & mil.) irregular; *s* (mil.) irregular
**irregularity** [ɪ,rɛgjə'lærɪtɪ] *s* (*pl:* **-ties**) irregularidad
**irrelevance** [ɪ'rɛlɪvəns] *s* inaplicabilidad, impertinencia
**irrelevancy** [ɪ'rɛlɪvənsɪ] *s* (*pl:* **-cies**) var. de **irrelevance**
**irrelevant** [ɪ'rɛlɪvənt] *adj* inaplicable, impertinente
**irreligion** [,ɪrɪ'lɪdʒən] *s* irreligión
**irreligious** [,ɪrɪ'lɪdʒəs] *adj* irreligioso
**irremediable** [,ɪrɪ'midɪəbəl] *adj* irremediable
**irremissable** [,ɪrɪ'mɪsɪbəl] *adj* irremisible
**irremovable** [,ɪrɪ'muvəbəl] *adj* inamovible, irremovible
**irreparable** [ɪ'rɛpərəbəl] *adj* irreparable
**irreplaceable** [,ɪrɪ'plesəbəl] *adj* irreemplazable
**irreprehensible** [ɪ,rɛprɪ'hɛnsɪbəl] *adj* irreprensible
**irrepressible** [,ɪrɪ'prɛsɪbəl] *adj* irreprimible, incontenible
**irreproachable** [,ɪrɪ'protʃəbəl] *adj* irreprochable
**irresistible** [,ɪrɪ'zɪstɪbəl] *adj* irresistible
**irresolute** [ɪ'rɛzəlut] *adj* irresoluto
**irresolution** [,ɪrɛzə'luʃən] *s* irresolución
**irrespective** [,ɪrɪ'spɛktɪv] *adj* imparcial; **irrespective of** sin hacer caso de, prescindiendo de
**irresponsibility** [,ɪrɪ,spɑnsɪ'bɪlɪtɪ] *s* irresponsabilidad
**irresponsible** [,ɪrɪ'spɑnsɪbəl] *adj* irresponsable
**irretrievable** [,ɪrɪ'trivəbəl] *adj* irrecuperable

**irreverence** [ɪˈrɛvərəns] *s* irreverencia
**irreverent** [ɪˈrɛvərənt] *adj* irreverente
**irreversible** [ˌɪrɪˈvʌrsɪbəl] *adj* irreversible
**irrevocability** [ɪˌrɛvəkəˈbɪlɪtɪ] *s* irrevocabilidad
**irrevocable** [ɪˈrɛvəkəbəl] *adj* irrevocable
**irrigable** [ˈɪrɪgəbəl] *adj* irrigable
**irrigate** [ˈɪrɪget] *va* irrigar, regar; (med.) irrigar
**irrigation** [ˌɪrɪˈgeʃən] *s* irrigación, riego; (med.) irrigación
**irrigation channel** *s* canal de riego
**irrigator** [ˈɪrɪˌgetər] *s* irrigador
**irritability** [ˌɪrɪtəˈbɪlɪtɪ] *s* irritabilidad
**irritable** [ˈɪrɪtəbəl] *adj* irritable
**irritant** [ˈɪrɪtənt] *adj & s* irritante
**irritate** [ˈɪrɪtet] *va* irritar
**irritation** [ˌɪrɪˈteʃən] *s* irritación
**irruption** [ɪˈrʌpʃən] *s* irrupción
**irruptive** [ɪˈrʌptɪv] *adj* irruptor
**is.** abr. de **island**
**is** [ɪz] *tercera persona del sg del pres de ind de* **be; as is** tal como está
**Isaac** [ˈaɪzək] *s* Isaac
**isabelita** [ˌɪzəbəˈlitə] *s* (ichth.) isabelita
**Isabella** [ˌɪzəˈbɛlə] *s* Isabel
**Isabelline** [ˌɪzəˈbɛlɪn] o [ˌɪzəˈbɛlaɪn] *adj* isabelino
**Isaiah** [aɪˈzeə] o [aɪˈzaɪə] *s* (Bib.) Isaías
**isallobar** [aɪˈsæləbɑr] *s* (meteor.) isalóbara
**Iscariot** [ɪsˈkærɪət] *s* (Bib.) Iscariote
**ischial** [ˈɪskɪəl] *adj* (anat.) isquiático
**ischium** [ˈɪskɪəm] *s* (*pl:* **-a** [ə]) (anat.) isquión
**Iseult** [ɪˈsult] *s* (myth.) Isolda
**-ish** *suffix adj* -izco, p.ej., **whitish** blanquizco; -ujo, p.ej., **softish** blandujo; -uno, p.ej., **friarish** frailuno; **mannish** hombruno; -uzco, p.ej., **whitish** blancuzco; **blackish** negruzco; *suffix v* -ecer, p.ej., **establish** establecer; **perish** perecer
**Ishmael** [ˈɪʃmɪəl] *s* (Bib.) Ismael
**Ishmaelite** [ˈɪʃmɪəlaɪt] *s* ismaelita; (fig.) paria
**Isiac** [ˈaɪsɪæk] *adj* isíaco
**Isidore** [ˈɪzɪdor] *s* Isidoro
**Isidorian** [ˌɪzɪˈdorɪən] *adj* isidoriano
**isinglass** [ˈaɪzɪŋˌglæs] o [ˈaɪzɪŋˌglɑs] *s* colapez, cola de pescado (*gelatina*); mica
**Isis** [ˈaɪsɪs] *s* (myth.) Isis
**isl.** abr. de **island**
**Islam** [ˈɪsləm] o [ɪsˈlɑm] *s* el Islam
**Islamic** [ɪsˈlæmɪk] o [ɪsˈlɑmɪk] *adj* islámico
**Islamism** [ˈɪsləmɪzəm] *s* islamismo
**Islamite** [ˈɪsləmaɪt] *adj & s* islamista o islamita
**Islamize** [ˈɪsləmaɪz] *va* islamizar; *vn* islamizar o islamizarse
**island** [ˈaɪlənd] *s* isla; (fig.) isla (*colina; grupo de árboles*); *adj* isleño; *va* aislar; dar forma de isla a
**islander** [ˈaɪləndər] *s* isleño
**island universe** *s* (astr.) universo aislado
**isle** [aɪl] *s* isleta; isla
**Isle of Man** *s* Isla de Man
**Isle of Pines** *s* Isla de Pinos
**islet** [ˈaɪlɪt] *s* isleta
**ism** [ˈɪzəm] *s* ismo
**isn't** [ˈɪzənt] contracción de **is not**
**isobar** [ˈaɪsobɑr] *s* (chem.) isobaro; (meteor.) isobara, curva o línea isobárica
**isobaric** [ˌaɪsoˈbærɪk] *adj* isobaro, isobárico
**isocheim** [ˈaɪsokim] *s* (meteor.) isoquímena
**isocheimenal** [ˌaɪsoˈkimənəl] *adj* (meteor.) isoquímeno
**isochromatic** [ˌaɪsokroˈmætɪk] *adj* isocromático
**isochronal** [aɪˈsɑkrənəl] o **isochronous** [aɪˈsɑkrənəs] *adj* isócrono
**isoclinal** [ˌaɪsoˈklaɪnəl] *adj* isoclinal; *s* isoclina (*línea*)
**Isocrates** [aɪˈsɑkrətiz] *s* Isócrates
**isodactylous** [ˌaɪsoˈdæktɪləs] *adj* isodáctilo
**isodynamic** [ˌaɪsodaɪˈnæmɪk] o [ˌaɪsodɪˈnæmɪk] *adj* isodinámico
**isogloss** [ˈaɪsoglɔs] o [ˈaɪsoglɑs] *s* isoglosa
**isoglossal** [ˌaɪsoˈglɑsəl] *adj* isogloso
**isogonic** [ˌaɪsoˈgɑnɪk] *adj* isogónico, isógono
**isogonic line** *s* isógona
**isolate** [ˈaɪsəlet] o [ˈɪsəlet] *va* aislar
**isolation** [ˌaɪsəˈleʃən] o [ˌɪsəˈleʃən] *s* aislamiento
**isolation hospital** *s* hospital de aislamiento
**isolationism** [ˌaɪsəˈleʃənɪzəm] o [ˌɪsəˈleʃənɪzəm] *s* aislacionismo
**isolationist** [ˌaɪsəˈleʃənɪst] o [ˌɪsəˈleʃənɪst] *adj & s* aislacionista, insulista
**Isolde** [ɪˈzɔldə] o [ɪˈsold] *s* var. de **Iseult**
**isomer** [ˈaɪsomər] *s* (chem.) isómero
**isomeric** [ˌaɪsoˈmɛrɪk] o **isomerical** [ˌaɪsoˈmɛrɪkəl] *adj* (chem.) isómero o isomérico
**isomerism** [aɪˈsɑmərɪzəm] *s* (chem.) isomería o isomerismo
**isomerous** [aɪˈsɑmərəs] *adj* (anat., bot. & chem.) isómero
**isometric** [ˌaɪsoˈmɛtrɪk] o **isometrical** [ˌaɪsoˈmɛtrɪkəl] *adj* isométrico
**isomorphic** [ˌaɪsoˈmɔrfɪk] *adj* (biol., chem. & mineral.) isomorfo
**isomorphism** [ˌaɪsoˈmɔrfɪzəm] *s* (biol., chem. & mineral.) isomorfismo
**isomorphous** [ˌaɪsoˈmɔrfəs] *adj* isomorfo
**isoniazid** [ˌaɪsoˈnaɪəzɪd] *s* (pharm.) isoniacida
**isoperimetric** [ˌaɪsoˌpɛrɪˈmɛtrɪk] o **isoperimetrical** [ˌaɪsoˌpɛrɪˈmɛtrɪkəl] *adj* isoperímetro
**isopod** [ˈaɪsopɑd] *adj & s* (zool.) isópodo
**isoprene** [ˈaɪsoprin] *s* (chem.) isopreno
**isosceles** [aɪˈsɑsəliz] *adj* (geom.) isósceles
**isotheral** [aɪˈsɑθərəl] *adj* isótero
**isothere** [ˈaɪsoθɪr] *s* isótera
**isotherm** [ˈaɪsoθʌrm] *s* isoterma
**isothermal** [ˌaɪsoˈθʌrməl] *adj* isotermo
**isotope** [ˈaɪsotop] *s* (chem.) isótopo
**isotopic** [ˌaɪsoˈtɑpɪk] *adj* isotópico
**isotopy** [aɪˈsɑtəpɪ] *s* isotopia
**isotropic** [ˌaɪsoˈtrɑpɪk] *adj* (biol. & phys.) isotropo, isotrópico
**isotropous** [aɪˈsɑtrəpəs] *adj* isotropo
**isotropy** [aɪˈsɑtrəpɪ] *s* (biol. & phys.) isotropía
**Israel** [ˈɪzrɪəl] *s* Israel
**Israeli** [ɪzˈrelɪ] *adj* israelí; *s* (*pl:* **-lis** [lɪz]) israelí
**Israelite** [ˈɪzrɪəlaɪt] *adj & s* israelita
**issuance** [ˈɪʃuəns] *s* emisión
**issue** [ˈɪʃu] *s* edición, impresión, tirada; entrega, número (*de revista, periódico, etc.*); salida; emisión; flujo; beneficios, producto; réditos; consecuencia, resultado, éxito; punto en disputa, tema de discusión, problema; sucesión, prole; (med.) exutorio; **at issue** en disputa; **to face the issue** afrontar la situación; **to force the issue** forzar la solución, insistir en que se decida el asunto; **to join issue** ponerse a disputar; **to take issue with** estar en desacuerdo con, no estar de acuerdo con; *va* publicar, dar a luz; emitir, poner en circulación; expedir; *vn* salir; **to issue from** provenir de, tener su origen en; **to issue in** dar por resultado
**Istanbul** [ˌɪstɑnˈbul] *s* Istambul
**isthmian** [ˈɪsmɪən] *adj* ístmico; istmeño; *s* istmeño
**Isthmian games** *spl* juegos ístmicos
**isthmus** [ˈɪsməs] *s* istmo; (anat.) istmo
**Isthmus of Corinth** *s* istmo de Corinto
**Isthmus of Panama** *s* istmo de Panamá
**Isthmus of Suez** *s* istmo de Suez
**istle** [ˈɪstlɪ] *s* ixtle (*fibra*)
**It.** abr. de **Italian** y **Italy**
**it** [ɪt] *pron pers neuter* él, ella; lo, la; le; **this is it** ésta es la fija (*aquello que se teme o espera*); **it is raining** llueve; **it is I** soy yo
**ital.** abr. de **italic**
**Ital.** abr. de **Italian** y **Italy**
**Italian** [ɪˈtæljən] *adj & s* italiano
**Italianism** [ɪˈtæljənɪzəm] *s* italianismo
**Italianize** [ɪˈtæljənaɪz] *va* italianizar
**Italian millet** *s* (bot.) panizo
**Italian rye grass** *s* (bot.) ballico
**Italic** [ɪˈtælɪk] *adj* itálico; (*l.c.*) *adj* itálico; (print.) itálico, bastardillo; *s* (print.) letra itálica, bastardilla; **italics** *spl* (print.) letra itálica, bastardilla, letras itálicas
**italicize** [ɪˈtælɪsaɪz] *va* poner en letra bastardilla; subrayar; dar énfasis a, mediante letras bastardillas
**Italy** [ˈɪtəlɪ] *s* Italia
**itch** [ɪtʃ] *s* comezón, picazón; (path.) sarna; (fig.) comezón, prurito; *va* picar, dar comezón a; *vn* picar, sentir o tener comezón; **to itch**

**to** + *inf* tener prurito por + *inf*, sentir prurito de + *inf*
**itch mite** *s* (ent.) arador, ácaro de la sarna
**itchy** [ˈɪtʃɪ] *adj* (*comp:* **-ier;** *super:* **-iest**) picante, hormigoso; (path.) sarnoso
**itea** [ˈɪtɪə] *s* (bot.) itea
**item** [ˈaɪtəm] *s* ítem, artículo; noticia, suelto; partida (*de una cuenta*); (coll.) detalle
**itemize** [ˈaɪtəmaɪz] *va* detallar, especificar, particularizar
**iterate** [ˈɪtəret] *va* iterar
**iteration** [ˌɪtəˈreʃən] *s* iteración
**iterative** [ˈɪtəˌretɪv] o [ˈɪtərətɪv] *adj* iterativo; (gram.) frecuentativo
**Ithaca** [ˈɪθəkə] *s* Ítaca (*isla al oeste de Grecia*)
**itineracy** [aɪˈtɪnərəsɪ] o [ɪˈtɪnərəsɪ] o **itinerancy** [aɪˈtɪnərənsɪ] o [ɪˈtɪnərənsɪ] *s* peregrinación; predicadores ambulantes; jueces ambulantes
**itinerant** [aɪˈtɪnərənt] o [ɪˈtɪnərənt] *adj* ambulante; *s* viandante
**itinerary** [aɪˈtɪnəˌrɛrɪ] o [ɪˈtɪnəˌrɛrɪ] *s* (*pl:* **-ies**) itinerario; *adj* itinerario
**itinerate** [aɪˈtɪnəret] o [ɪˈtɪnəret] *va* viajar por; *vn* seguir un itinerario
**its** [ɪts] *adj poss* su; *pron poss* el suyo
**it's** [ɪts] contracción de **it is**
**itself** [ɪtˈsɛlf] *pron* mismo; sí, sí mismo; se
**I've** [aɪv] contracción de **I have**
**ivied** [ˈaɪvɪd] *adj* cubierto de hiedra
**Iviza** [iˈviθɑ] *s* Ibiza (*una de las islas Baleares*)
**ivory** [ˈaɪvərɪ] *s* (*pl:* **-ries**) marfil; **ivories** *spl* teclas del piano; bolas de billar; dados; (slang) dientes; *adj* ebúrneo, marfileño, marfilino
**ivorybill** [ˈaɪvərɪˌbɪl] *s* (orn.) pico de marfil
**ivory black** *s* negro de marfil
**Ivory Coast** *s* Costa de Marfil (*África*)
**ivory nut** *s* nuez de marfil
**ivory palm** *s* (bot.) tagua
**ivory tower** *s* (fig.) torre de marfil
**ivy** [ˈaɪvɪ] *s* (*pl:* **ivies**) (bot.) hiedra
**I.W.W.** abr. de **Industrial Workers of the World**
**Ixion** [ɪksˈaɪən] *s* (myth.) Ixión
**izzard** [ˈɪzərd] *s* (dial.) zeda (*letra*); **from A to izzard** de cabo a rabo

# J

**J, j** [dʒe] *s* (*pl:* **J's, j's** [dʒez]) décima letra del alfabeto inglés
**j.** abr. de **joule**
**J.** abr. de **Judge** y **Justice**
**Ja.** abr. de **January**
**jab** [dʒæb] *s* hurgonazo, pinchazo, piquete; codazo; (box.) golpe inverso; (*pret & pp:* **jabbed;** *ger:* **jabbing**) *va* hurgonear, pinchar; dar un codazo a; *vn* hurgonear, pinchar
**jabber** [ˈdʒæbər] *s* jerigonza; chapurreo; *va* decir precipitadamente y de modo poco inteligible; chapurrear (*un idioma*); *vn* farfullar, parlotear; chapurrear
**jabot** [ʒæˈbo] o [ˈʒæbo] *s* chorrera
**jacaranda** [ˌdʒækəˈrændə] *s* (bot.) abey, jacarandá
**jacinth** [ˈdʒesɪnθ] o [ˈdʒæsɪnθ] *s* (mineral.) jacinto
**jack** [dʒæk] *s* gato, cric; mozo, sujeto; marinero; asno, burro; liebre muy grande norteamericana; sota o valet (*en los naipes*); boliche; cantillo; torno de asador; jaquemar (*figura que da la hora en un reloj*); sacabotas; (coll.) dinero; (rad. & telp.) jack; (elec.) caja (*de enchufe*); (naut.) yac (*bandera de proa*); (*cap.*) *s* Juanillo; **jacks** *spl* cantillos, juego de los cantillos; **every man jack** todos sin excepción; *va* alzar con el gato; **to jack up** alzar con el gato; (coll.) subir, aumentar (*sueldos, precios, etc.*); (coll.) recordar su obligación a (*una persona*
**jackal** [ˈdʒækɔl] *s* (zool.) chacal; (fig.) paniaguado
**jackanapes** [ˈdʒækəneps] *s* mequetrefe
**jackass** [ˈdʒækˌæs] *s* asno, burro; (fig.) asno, burro
**jackboot** [ˈdʒækˌbut] *s* bota grande y fuerte
**jackdaw** [ˈdʒækˌdɔ] *s* (orn.) corneja
**jacket** [ˈdʒækɪt] *s* chaqueta; cubierta, envoltura; sobrecubierta (*de un libro encuadernado*); camisa (*de agua*); **to dust one's jacket** (slang) sacudirle el polvo a uno; *va* poner chaqueta a; cubrir con chaqueta; cubrir
**Jack Frost** *s* el frío (*personificado*)
**jackhammer** [ˈdʒækˌhæmər] *s* martillo perforador
**jack-in-a-box** [ˈdʒækɪnəˌbɑks] o **jack-in-the-box** [ˈdʒækɪnðəˌbɑks] *s* caja de sorpresa (*muñeco en una caja de resorte*)
**jack-in-the-pulpit** [ˈdʒækɪnðəˈpulpɪt] *s* (bot.) arisema (*Arisema triphyllum*)
**Jack Ketch** *s* el verdugo
**jackknife** [ˈdʒækˌnaɪf] *s* (*pl:* **-knives**) navaja de bolsillo; salto de carpa (*que se ejecuta tocándose los pies antes de dar en el agua*)
**jack of all trades** *s* factótum, dije, hombre apto para muchas cosas
**jack-o'-lantern** [ˈdʒækəˌlæntərn] *s* fuego fatuo; linterna que se hace colocando una vela encendida en una calabaza cortada de modo que remede las facciones humanas
**jack plane** *s* (carp.) garlopín
**jack pot** *s* (poker) jugada para la que se necesita tener un par de sotas o algo mejor; **to hit the jack pot** (slang) ponerse las botas
**jack rabbit** *s* liebre muy grande norteamericana
**jackscrew** [ˈdʒækˌskru] *s* gato de tornillo
**jacksnipe** [ˈdʒækˌsnaɪp] *s* (orn.) becada de los pantanos
**jackstone** [ˈdʒækˌston] *s* cantillo; **jackstones** *spl* cantillos, juego de los cantillos
**jackstraw** [ˈdʒækˌstrɔ] *s* pajita; **jackstraws** *spl* juego de las pajitas
**jack tar** o **Jack Tar** *s* marinero
**Jacob** [ˈdʒekəb] *s* Jacobo; (Bib.) Jacob
**Jacobean** [ˌdʒækəˈbiən] *adj* de Jacobo I de Inglaterra, del reinado de Jacobo I; *s* escritor u otro personaje del reinado de Jacobo I de Inglaterra
**jacobean lily** *s* (bot.) flor de lis
**Jacobin** [ˈdʒækəbɪn] *adj & s* jacobino
**Jacobinic** [ˌdʒækəˈbɪnɪk] o **Jacobinical** [ˌdʒækəˈbɪnɪkəl] *adj* jacobínico
**Jacobinism** [ˈdʒækəbɪnɪzəm] *s* jacobinismo
**Jacobinize** [ˈdʒækəbɪnaɪz] *va* jacobinizar
**Jacobite** [ˈdʒækəbaɪt] *s* jacobita
**Jacob's ladder** *s* (Bib.) escala de Jacob; (naut.) escala de jarcia
**Jacob's-ladder** [ˈdʒekəbzˈlædər] *s* (bot.) escala de Jacob
**Jacqueminot** [ˈdʒækmɪno] *s* rosa de color rojo intenso
**jade** [dʒed] *s* jamelgo; mujer, mujeruela; verde; (mineral.) jade; *adj* verde; *va* cansar; ahitar, saciar
**jaded** [ˈdʒedɪd] *adj* cansado; ahito, saciado
**jaeger** o **jäger** [ˈjegər] *s* (orn.) estercorario
**Jael** [ˈdʒeəl] *s* (Bib.) Jahel
**jag** [dʒæg] *s* diente, púa; **to have a jag on** (slang) estar borracho; (*pret & pp:* **jagged;** *ger:* **jagging**) *va* dentar, cortar en dientes; cortar o rasgar en sietes
**jagged** [ˈdʒægɪd] *adj* dentado; cortado o rasgado en sietes
**jaguar** [ˈdʒægwɑr] *s* (zool.) jaguar
**jail** [dʒel] *s* cárcel; **to break jail** escaparse de la cárcel; *va* encarcelar
**jailbird** [ˈdʒelˌbʌrd] *s* encarcelado, preso; malhechor que ha sido encarcelado repetidas veces
**jail delivery** *s* evasión de la cárcel; acción de sacar todos los presos de una cárcel con motivo de la vista de causa de cada uno
**jailer** o **jailor** [ˈdʒelər] *s* carcelero
**jalap** [ˈdʒæləp] *s* (bot.) jalapa
**jalopy** [dʒəˈlɑpɪ] *s* (*pl:* **-ies**) (coll.) automóvil viejo y ruinoso
**jalousie** [ˌʒæluˈzi] *s* celosía (*enrejado en las ventanas*)
**Jam.** abr. de **Jamaica**
**jam** [dʒæm] *s* compota, conserva; apiñadura, apretura; atoramiento; bloqueo, embotellamiento; (coll.) aprieto, situación peliaguda; (*pret & pp:* **jammed;** *ger:* **jamming**) *va* apiñar, apretujar; trabar; atorar; llenar y tapar apretando; machucarse (*p.ej., un dedo*); (naut.) forzar (*un buque*); (rad.) perturbar, sabotear (*un programa*); **to jam on** poner (*el freno*) con violencia; *vn* apiñarse, apretujarse; trabarse, ahorcarse; atorarse
**Jamaica** [dʒəˈmekə] *s* Jamaica; jamaica (*ron*)
**Jamaican** [dʒəˈmekən] *adj & s* jamaicano
**Jamaica quassia** *s* (bot. & pharm.) cuasia de Jamaica
**jamb** o **jambe** [dʒæm] *s* (arch.) jamba; (arm.) canillera, greba
**jambeau** [dʒæmˈbo] *s* (*pl:* **-beaux** [ˈboz]) (arm.) canillera, greba
**jamboree** [ˌdʒæmbəˈri] *s* (slang) francachela, jolgorio; congreso de Niños Exploradores
**James** [dʒemz] *s* Diego, Jacobo, Jaime, Santiago
**jamming** [ˈdʒæmɪŋ] *s* (rad.) radioperturbación, interferencia
**jam nut** *s* tuerca fiadora, contratuerca
**jam-packed** [ˈdʒæmˈpækt] *adj* (coll.) apretujado, apiñado, atestado
**jam session** *s* reunión de músicos de jazz para tocar improvisaciones
**jam weld** *s* soldadura de tope
**Jan.** abr. de **January**
**Jane** [dʒen] *s* Juana
**jangle** [ˈdʒæŋgəl] *s* cencerreo, sonido discordante; altercado, riña; *va* hacer sonar de ma-

nera discordante; *vn* cencerrear, sonar de manera discordante; altercar, reñir
**Janiculum** [dʒəˈnɪkjələm] *s* Janículo
**Janissary** o **janissary** [ˈdʒænɪˌsɛrɪ] *s* (*pl:* **-ies**) var. de **Janizary**
**janitor** [ˈdʒænɪtər] *s* portero, conserje
**janitress** [ˈdʒænɪtrɪs] *s* portera
**Janizary** o **janizary** [ˈdʒænɪˌzɛrɪ] *s* (*pl:* **-ies**) jenízaro
**Jansen** [ˈdʒænsən] *s* Jansenio
**Jansenism** [ˈdʒænsənɪzəm] *s* jansenismo
**Jansenist** [ˈdʒænsənɪst] *adj & s* jansenista
**Jansenistic** [ˌdʒænsəˈnɪstɪk] *adj* jansenista
**January** [ˈdʒænjuˌɛrɪ] *s* enero
**Janus** [ˈdʒenəs] *s* (myth.) Jano
**Janus-faced** [ˈdʒenəsˌfest] *adj* de doble cara; falso, traidor
**Jap.** abr. de **Japan** y **Japanese**
**Jap** [dʒæp] *adj & s* (slang) japonés
**Japan** [dʒəˈpæn] *s* el Japón; (*l.c.*) *s* laca japonesa; obra japonesa charolada; aceite secante japonés; (*pret & pp:* **-panned;** *ger:* **-panning**) *va* charolar con laca japonesa
**Japan current** *s* corriente del Japón
**Japanese** [ˌdʒæpəˈniz] *adj* japonés; *s* (*pl:* **-nese**) japonés
**Japanese beetle** *s* (ent.) escarabajo japonés
**Japanese lantern** *s* linterna china o veneciana
**Japanese pagoda tree** *s* (bot.) sófora
**Japanese persimmon** *s* (bot.) caqui
**Japan globeflower** *s* (bot.) mosqueta
**jape** [dʒep] *s* burla, engaño; *va* burlar, engañar; *vn* burlarse
**Japhetic** [dʒəˈfɛtɪk] *adj* jafético
**japonica** [dʒəˈpɑnɪkə] *s* (bot.) rosal de China, rosal japonés; (bot.) membrillero del Japón
**jar** [dʒɑr] *s* tarro; frasco (*p.ej., de aceitunas*); vaso, recipiente (*de acumulador*); sacudida; ruido desapacible; sorpresa desagradable; discordia; vuelta o giro; **on the jar** entreabierto, entornado; (*pret & pp:* **jarred;** *ger:* **jarring**) *va* sacudir; chocar; traquetear; *vn* sacudirse; traquetear; disputar, reñir; **to jar on** irritar
**jardiniere** [ˌdʒɑrdɪˈnɪr] *s* jardinera (*mueble*); florero (*vaso o maceta grandes*)
**jargon** [ˈdʒɑrgən] *s* jerigonza, jerga (*de los individuos de ciertos oficios, grupos, etc.; lenguaje difícil de entender*); (mineral.) jergón; *vn* hablar en jerigonza; charlar, parlotear
**jarring** [ˈdʒɑrɪŋ] *s* sacudida; discordia; *adj* discordante
**Jas.** abr. de **James**
**jasmine** [ˈdʒæsmɪn] o [ˈdʒæzmɪn] *s* (bot.) jazmín; (bot.) jazmín del Cabo; (bot.) jazmín silvestre; (bot.) lirio tricolor
**Jason** [ˈdʒesən] *s* (myth.) Jasón
**jasper** [ˈdʒæspər] *s* (mineral.) jaspe; (*cap.*) *s* Gaspar
**jaspery** [ˈdʒæspərɪ] *adj* jaspeado
**jaundice** [ˈdʒɔndɪs] o [ˈdʒɑndɪs] *s* (path.) ictericia; (fig.) negro humor, envidia, celos; *va* dar ictericia a; (fig.) avinagrar el genio a, amargar la vida a
**jaundiced** [ˈdʒɔndɪst] o [ˈdʒɑndɪst] *adj* ictericiado, aliacanado; (fig.) avinagrado
**jaunt** [dʒɔnt] o [dʒɑnt] *s* caminata, paseo, excursión; *vn* hacer una excursión de recreo
**jaunting car** *s* tílburi irlandés
**jaunty** [ˈdʒɔntɪ] o [ˈdʒɑntɪ] *adj* (*comp:* **-tier;** *super:* **-tiest**) airoso, gallardo; elegante, de buen gusto
**Javanese** [ˌdʒævəˈniz] *adj* javanés; *s* (*pl:* **-nese**) javanés
**javelin** [ˈdʒævlɪn] o [ˈdʒævəlɪn] *s* (hist. & sport) jabalina
**Javel water** [ʒəˈvɛl] *s* agua de Javel
**jaw** [dʒɔ] *s* (anat.) quijada, mandíbula; (mach.) quijada, mordaza; (mach.) mandíbula (*de una trituradora*); (slang) chismes, cháchara; **jaws** *spl* boca (*con la quijada y los dientes*); garganta, desfiladero; garras, p.ej., **into the jaws of death** a o en las garras de la muerte; *va* (slang) reñir, regañar; *vn* (slang) reñir, regañar; (slang) chismear, chacharear
**jawbone** [ˈdʒɔˌbon] *s* (anat.) quijada, mandíbula; (anat.) quijada inferior, mandíbula inferior
**jawbreaker** [ˈdʒɔˌbrekər] *s* (slang) trabalenguas; (slang) hinchabocas; (mach.) trituradora de mandíbulas
**jaw clutch** *s* (mach.) embrague de mordaza
**jaw vise** *s* tornillo de mordazas
**jay** [dʒe] *s* (orn.) arrendajo; (slang) tonto, necio
**jaywalk** [ˈdʒeˌwɔk] *vn* (coll.) cruzar la calle estúpidamente (*desentendiéndose de las ordenanzas municipales*)
**jaywalker** [ˈdʒeˌwɔkər] *s* peatón imprudente
**jazz** [dʒæz] *s* (mus.) jazz; (slang) animación, viveza; *adj* de jazz; *va* sincopar, tocar sincopadamente; (slang) animar, dar viveza a
**jazz band** *s* jazz-band, orquesta de jazz
**J.C.** abr. de **Jesus Christ** y **Julius Caesar**
**jct.** abr. de **junction**
**Je.** abr. de **June**
**jealous** [ˈdʒɛləs] *adj* celoso; envidioso; cuidadoso, solícito, vigilante
**jealousy** [ˈdʒɛləsɪ] *s* (*pl:* **-ies**) celosía, celos; celo (*esmero, interés activo*)
**Jean** [dʒin] *s* Juana; (*l.c.*) [dʒin] o [dʒen] *s* dril; **jeans** *spl* pantalones de dril, guardapolvo de dril
**Jeanne d'Arc** [ˌʒɑnˈdɑrk] *s* Juana de Arco
**Jeannette** [dʒəˈnɛt] *s* Juanita
**Jebel Musa** [ˈdʒɛbəlˈmusɑ] *s* el monte Ábila (*frente a Gibraltar*)
**jeep** [dʒip] *s* pequeño automóvil militar que se maniobra con gran facilidad y en poco espacio
**jeer** [dʒɪr] *s* befa, mofa, vaya; *va* befar; *vn* burlarse, mofarse; **to jeer at** befar, burlarse de, mofarse de
**jeeringly** [ˈdʒɪrɪŋlɪ] *adv* burlándose, con escarnio
**Jehoshaphat** [dʒɪˈhɑʃəfæt] *s* (Bib.) Josafat
**Jehovah** [dʒɪˈhovə] *s* Jehová
**Jehovah's Witnesses** *spl* testigos de Jehová
**Jehovism** [dʒɪˈhovɪzəm] *s* jehovismo
**Jehu** [ˈdʒihju] *s* (Bib.) Jehú; **like Jehu** (slang) en carrera desenfrenada, vertiginosamente; (*l.c.*) *s* (hum.) conductor, cochero (*especialmente el que va muy aprisa*)
**jejune** [dʒɪˈdʒun] *adj* seco, poco alimenticio; (fig.) árido, estéril, aburrido
**jejunum** [dʒɪˈdʒunəm] *s* (anat.) yeyuno
**jelab** [dʒəˈlɑb] *s* chilaba
**jell** [dʒɛl] *s* (coll.) jalea; *vn* (coll.) convertirse en jalea; (fig.) cuajar
**jellaba** [dʒəˈlɑbə] *s* var. de **jelab**
**jellied** [ˈdʒɛlɪd] *adj* convertido en jalea
**jellify** [ˈdʒɛlɪfaɪ] (*pret & pp:* **-fied**) *va* convertir en jalea, hacer gelatinoso; *vn* convertirse en jalea, hacerse gelatinoso
**jelly** [ˈdʒɛlɪ] *s* (*pl:* **-lies**) jalea; (*pret & pp:* **-lied**) *va* convertir en jalea; *vn* convertirse en jalea
**jellyfish** [ˈdʒɛlɪˌfɪʃ] *s* (zool.) aguamar, medusa; (coll.) calzonazos
**jennet** [ˈdʒɛnɪt] *s* jaca chica española
**jenny** [ˈdʒɛnɪ] *s* (*pl:* **-nies**) máquina de hilar de múltiples husos; hembra (*de ciertos animales*); (*cap.*) *s* nombre abreviado de **Jane**
**jenny ass** *s* asna, burra
**jenny winch** *s* grúa ligera de brazos rígidos
**jenny wren** *s* rey de zarza
**jeopard** [ˈdʒɛpərd] o **jeopardize** [ˈdʒɛpərdaɪz] *va* arriesgar, exponer, comprometer
**jeopardy** [ˈdʒɛpərdɪ] *s* riesgo, peligro
**Jephthah** [ˈdʒɛfθə] *s* (Bib.) Jefté
**Jer.** abr. de **Jeremiah**
**jerboa** [dʒərˈboə] *s* (zool.) jerbo
**jeremiad** [ˌdʒɛrɪˈmaɪæd] *s* jeremiada
**Jeremiah** [ˌdʒɛrɪˈmaɪə] o **Jeremias** [ˌdʒɛrɪˈmaɪəs] *s* (Bib.) Jeremías; (Bib.) libro de Jeremías
**Jeremian** [ˌdʒɛrɪˈmaɪən] o **Jeremianic** [ˌdʒɛrɪmaɪˈænɪk] *adj* jeremíaco
**Jericho** [ˈdʒɛrɪko] *s* (*pl:* **-chos**) Jericó; (fig.) lugar lejano
**jerk** [dʒʌrk] *s* estirón, tirón, arranque; tic, espasmo muscular; **by jerks** a tirones, a sacudidas; *va* mover de un tirón; arrojar de un tirón; decir de repente; atasajar (*carne*); *vn* avanzar a tirones, avanzar dando tumbos
**jerked beef** *s* tasajo
**jerkin** [ˈdʒʌrkɪn] *s* jubón, justillo
**jerkwater** [ˈdʒʌrkˌwɔtər] o [ˈdʒʌrkˌwɑtər] *adj* (coll.) secundario, accesorio; (coll.) de mala muerte; *s* (coll.) tren de línea secundaria, tren de ferrocarril económico
**jerky** [ˈdʒʌrkɪ] *adj* (*comp:* **-ier;** *super:* **-iest**)

desigual (*camino; estilo*); **the train was jerky** el tren andaba a tirones
**Jerome** [dʒəˈrom] o [ˈdʒɛrəm] *s* Jerónimo
**Jeronymite** [dʒɪˈrɑnɪmaɪt] *s* jerónimo
**Jerry** [ˈdʒɛrɪ] *s* nombre abreviado de **Gerald, Gerard, Jeremiah** y **Jerome**
**jerry-built** [ˈdʒɛrɪˌbɪlt] *adj* mal construído, sin solidez ni consistencia
**jersey** [ˈdʒʌrzɪ] *s* jersey; tejido de punto; (*cap.*) *s* raza jerseyesa, vaca jerseyesa
**Jerusalem** [dʒɪˈrusələm] *s* Jerusalén
**Jerusalem artichoke** *s* (bot.) ajipa, aguaturma, patata de caña, pataca
**Jerusalem sage** *s* (bot.) aguavientos, matagallos
**Jerusalem thorn** *s* (bot.) cinacina; (bot.) espina santa, espina vera
**jess** [dʒɛs] *s* pihuela (*en la pata del halcón*); *va* poner las pihuelas a
**jessamine** [ˈdʒɛsəmɪn] *s* var. de **jasmine**
**Jesse** [ˈdʒɛsɪ] *s* (Bib.) Jesé
**jest** [dʒɛst] *s* broma, chiste; cosa de risa, ridiculez; **in jest** en broma; *vn* bromear; chancearse
**jester** [ˈdʒɛstər] *s* bufón, truhán; bromista
**Jesu** [ˈdʒizju] o [ˈdʒizu] *s* (poet.) Jesús
**Jesuit** [ˈdʒɛʒʊɪt] o [ˈdʒɛzjʊɪt] *adj & s* jesuíta; (fig.) jesuíta (*intrigante*)
**Jesuitess** [ˈdʒɛʒʊɪtɪs] o [ˈdʒɛzjʊɪtɪs] *s* jesuitisa
**Jesuitic** [ˌdʒɛʒʊˈɪtɪk] o [ˌdʒɛzjʊˈɪtɪk] o **Jesuitical** [ˌdʒɛʒʊˈɪtɪkəl] o [ˌdʒɛzjʊˈɪtɪkəl] *adj* jesuítico; (*l.c.*) *adj* jesuítico (*solapado*)
**Jesuitism** [ˈdʒɛʒʊɪtɪzəm] o [ˈdʒɛzjʊɪtɪzəm] *s* jesuitismo; (*l.c.*) *s* jesuitismo (*disimulo refinado*)
**Jesus** [ˈdʒizəs] *s* Jesús
**Jesus Christ** *s* Jesucristo
**jet** [dʒɛt] *s* chorro; surtidor (*de fuente*); mechero (*de gas*); avión de chorro, avión a reacción; (mineral.) azabache; *adj* de azabache; azabachado; (*pret & pp:* **jetted;** *ger:* **jetting**) *va* echar o arrojar en chorro; *vn* chorrear, salir en chorro; volar en avión de chorro
**jet age** *s* era de los aviones de chorro
**jet-black** [ˈdʒɛtˈblæk] *adj* azabachado
**jet bomber** *s* (aer.) bombardero de reacción a chorro
**jet coal** *s* carbón de llama larga, carbón de bujía
**jet engine** *s* motor de reacción, aeropropulsor por reacción, motor a chorro
**jet fighter** *s* (aer.) caza de reacción, cazarreactor
**Jethro** [ˈdʒɛθro] *s* (Bib.) Jetró
**jetliner** [ˈdʒɛtˌlaɪnər] *s* avión de travesía con propulsión a chorro
**jet plane** *s* (aer.) avión de propulsión a chorro, avión de chorro, avión a reacción
**jet-powered** [ˈdʒɛtˌpaʊərd] *adj* propulsado por motor de reacción
**jet propulsion** *s* propulsión de escape, propulsión a chorro, propulsión por reacción
**jetsam** [ˈdʒɛtsəm] *s* (naut.) echazón; cosa desechada por inútil
**jet stream** *s* chorro del motor de reacción o el motor cohete; (meteor.) viento fuerte y veloz que circunda la tierra a la altura de 10 kilómetros y entre los 30 y 60 grados de latitud
**jettison** [ˈdʒɛtɪsən] *s* (naut.) echazón; *va* (naut.) echar al mar (*para aligerar el buque*); desechar, rechazar
**jettison gear** *s* (aer.) lanzador
**jetty** [ˈdʒɛtɪ] *s* (*pl:* **-ties**) malecón, escollera; muelle; *adj* de azabache; azabachado
**Jew** [dʒu] *s* judío
**jewel** [ˈdʒuəl] *s* piedra fina; joya, alhaja; rubí (*de un reloj*); (fig.) joya, alhaja (*persona o cosa*); (*pret & pp:* **-eled** o **-elled;** *ger:* **-eling** o **-elling**) *va* adornar con piedras preciosas; engastar con joyas; (fig.) coronar o adornar (*p.ej., de luces*)
**jewel case** *s* estuche, joyero
**jeweler** o **jeweller** [ˈdʒuələr] *s* joyero; relojero
**jewellery** [ˈdʒuəlrɪ] *s* (Brit.) var. de **jewelry**
**jewelry** [ˈdʒuəlrɪ] *s* joyería, joyas
**jewelry store** *s* joyería; relojería
**jewelweed** [ˈdʒuəlˌwid] *s* (bot.) hierba de Santa Catalina (*Impatiens biflora e I. pallida*)
**Jewess** [ˈdʒuɪs] *s* judía
**jewfish** [ˈdʒuˌfɪʃ] *s* (ichth.) cherna, mero, guasa
**Jewish** [ˈdʒuɪʃ] *adj* judío; ajudiado
**Jewry** [ˈdʒurɪ] *s* (*pl:* **-ries**) judería (*barrio; raza, pueblo*); Judea
**jews'-harp** o **jew's-harp** [ˈdʒuzˌhɑrp] *s* (mus.) birimbao
**Jew's pitch** *s* betún de Judea
**Jezebel** [ˈdʒɛzəbəl] *s* (Bib.) Jezabel; mujer depravada
**jib** [dʒɪb] *s* aguilón o pescante (*de una grúa*); (naut.) foque; **cut of one's jib** (coll.) aspecto exterior de uno; (*pret & pp:* **jibbed;** *ger:* **jibbing**) *va* (naut.) virar; *vn* andar a la pierna, plantarse (*un caballo*); (Brit.) resistirse; (naut.) virar
**jib boom** *s* (naut.) botalón de foque, tormentín
**jibe** [dʒaɪb] *s* remoque, pulla; *va* (naut.) virar; *vn* mofarse; (naut.) virar; (coll.) concordar (*dos cosas*); **to jibe at** mofarse de
**jiffy** [ˈdʒɪfɪ] *s* (*pl:* **-fies**) (coll.) periquete, santiamén; **in a jiffy** (coll.) en un periquete, en un santiamén
**jig** [dʒɪg] *s* giga (*baile y música*); anzuelo de cuchara; gálibo, plantilla; guía, montaje; (min.) criba hidráulica, cribón de vaivén; **the jig is up** (slang) ya se acabó todo, estamos perdidos; (*pret & pp:* **jigged;** *ger:* **jigging**) *va* bailar (*la giga*); mover a saltitos; mover con movimiento de vaivén; (min.) separar por vibración y lavado; *vn* bailar una giga; moverse a saltitos; oscilar en un vaivén continuo; pescar con anzuelo de cuchara
**jig bushing** *s* (mach.) buje guía
**jigger** [ˈdʒɪgər] *s* anzuelo de cuchara; rueda de alfarero; jígger (*máquina para teñir*); (elec.) transformador de oscilaciones; (ent.) ácaro; (ent.) garrapata; (ent.) nigua; (golf) jígger; (min.) criba hidráulica, cribón de vaivén; (naut.) aparejuelo (*conjunto de jarcias y velas*); (naut.) contramesana, palo de mesana; (naut.) velamen de contramesana; (coll.) cosilla, dispositivo, chisme, aparato (*cuyo nombre se ignora o se olvida*); (U.S.A.) vasito para medir el licor de un coctel (*onza y media*)
**jigger mast** *s* (naut.) contramesana, palo de mesana
**jiggle** [ˈdʒɪgəl] *s* zarandeo, zangoloteo, zangoteo; *va* zarandear, zangolotear, zangotear; *vn* zarandearse, zangolotearse, zangotearse
**jig saw** *s* sierra de vaivén
**jigsaw puzzle** [ˈdʒɪgˌsɔ] *s* rompecabezas (*figura cortada en trozos menudos que hay que recomponer*)
**jihad** [dʒɪˈhɑd] *s* guerra santa (*de los musulmanes contra pueblos que profesan distinta religión*); guerra o cruzada en pro de, o contra una religión, un principio, etc.
**jill** o **Jill** [dʒɪl] *s* muchacha; mujer, esposa; querida
**jilt** [dʒɪlt] *s* coqueta que da calabazas al galán; *va* dar calabazas a (*un galán*)
**Jim** [dʒɪm] *s* nombre abreviado de **James**
**Jim Crow** *s* (offensive) negro
**jim-crow** [ˈdʒɪmˌkro] *s* (mach.) encorvador de rieles
**Jim Crow law** *s* ley que segrega a los negros de los blancos en lugares y vehículos públicos
**jimjams** [ˈdʒɪmˌdʒæmz] *spl* (slang) nerviosidad; (slang) delírium tremens
**jimmy** [ˈdʒɪmɪ] *s* (*pl:* **-mies**) palanqueta; (*cap.*) *s* Dieguito; (*l.c.*) (*pret & pp:* **-mied**) *va* forzar con palanqueta; **to jimmy open** abrir con palanqueta
**jimson weed** o **Jimson weed** [ˈdʒɪmsən] *s* (bot.) hierba hedionda, higuera loca, manzana espinosa
**jingle** [ˈdʒɪŋgəl] *s* cascabeleo; cascabel; sonaja (*del pandero*); rima infantil; (rad.) anuncio rimado y cantado; *va* hacer sonar; *vn* cascabelear
**jinglet** [ˈdʒɪŋglɪt] *s* escrupulillo
**jingly** [ˈdʒɪŋglɪ] *adj* metálico (*sonido*)
**jingo** [ˈdʒɪŋgo] *adj* jingoísta; *s* (*pl:* **-goes**) (hist.) jingo; jingoísta; **by jingo!** (coll.) ¡caramba!
**jingoism** [ˈdʒɪŋgo·ɪzəm] *s* jingoísmo
**jingoist** [ˈdʒɪŋgo·ɪst] *adj & s* jingoísta
**jingoistic** [ˌdʒɪŋgoˈɪstɪk] *adj* jingoísta

**jinn** [dʒɪn] *s* (*pl:* **jinn** o **jinns**) genio (*espíritu fantástico*)
**jinni** o **jinnee** [dʒɪ'ni] *s* (*pl:* **jinn**) var. de **jinn**
**jinrikisha** o **jinricksha** [dʒɪn'rɪkʃə] o [dʒɪn'rɪkʃɔ] *s* jinrikischa (*pequeño carruaje chino y japonés de dos ruedas y tirado por uno o más hombres*)
**jinx** [dʒɪŋks] *s* (slang) cenizo, gafe (*persona o cosa que trae mala suerte*); *va* (slang) traer mala suerte a
**jitney** ['dʒɪtnɪ] *s* (slang) automóvil de pasaje; (slang) moneda de cinco centavos
**jitterbug** ['dʒɪtər,bʌg] *s* persona que baila de manera acrobática y entusiasta la música de jazz; (*pret & pp:* **-bugged; ***ger:* **-bugging**) *vn* bailar de manera acrobática y entusiasta la música de jazz
**jitters** ['dʒɪtərz] *spl* (slang) agitación, inquietud, nerviosidad; **to give the jitters** (slang) poner nervioso, volver loco; **to have the jitters** (slang) ponerse nervioso
**jittery** ['dʒɪtərɪ] *adj* (slang) agitado, inquieto, nervioso, loco
**jiujitsu** o **jiujutsu** [dʒu'dʒɪtsu] *s* var. de **jujitsu**
**jive** [dʒaɪv] *s* (slang) charla y bromas mientras se toca el jazz; jerga de los músicos de jazz; jazz
**Jno.** abr. de **John**
**jo** [dʒo] *s* (*pl:* **joes**) (Scotch) amante
**Joachim** ['dʒoəkɪm] *s* Joaquín
**Joan** [dʒon] *s* Juana
**Joan of Arc** ['dʒon əv 'ɑrk] o [dʒo'æn əv 'ɑrk] *s* Juana de Arco
**job** [dʒɑb] *s* obra; trabajo; tarea, quehacer; deber; oficio; destajo; agiotaje (*sobre los fondos públicos*); (print.) remiendo; (coll.) asunto; (coll.) empleo; (slang) robo; (slang) condena, período (*de prisión*); **by the job** a destajo; **on the job** (slang) en su puesto, atento a sus obligaciones; adquiriendo práctica, trabajando de aprendiz; **to be out of a job** estar desocupado, estar sin trabajo; **to lie down on the job** (slang) echarse en el surco, estirar la pierna, no trabajar por pereza o desaliento ‖ *adj* hecho a destajo; alquilado o contratado por tiempo ‖ (*cap.*)[dʒob] *s* (Bib.) Job; (Bib.) libro de Job; (fig.) job (*hombre de mucha paciencia*) ‖ [dʒɑb] (*pret & pp:* **jobbed; ***ger:* **jobbing**) *va* comprar y vender en calidad de corredor; ceder (*un trabajo*) por contrato ‖ *vn* trabajar a destajo; especular con los fondos públicos
**job analysis** *s* análisis ocupacional
**jobber** ['dʒɑbər] *s* agiotista (*a expensas del erario público*); destajero; (com.) corredor
**jobbery** ['dʒɑbərɪ] *s* agiotaje (*sobre los fondos públicos*)
**jobholder** ['dʒɑb,holdər] *s* empleado; burócrata
**jobless** ['dʒɑblɪs] *adj* desocupado, sin trabajo
**job lot** *s* lote suelto de mercancías, mercancías variadas, saldo de mercancías; sarta, letanía
**job printer** *s* impresor de remiendos
**job printing** *s* (print.) remiendo
**Job's-tears** ['dʒobz'tɪrz] *spl* (bot.) lágrimas de David o de Job
**job work** *s* var. de **job printing**
**Jocasta** [dʒo'kæstə] *s* (myth.) Yocasta
**jockey** ['dʒɑkɪ] *s* (sport) jockey; *va* (sport) montar (*un caballo*) en la pista; maniobrar (*para sacar ventaja o ganar un puesto*); embaucar; **to jockey into** + *ger* embaucar para que + *subj*, p.ej., **they jockeyed him into going into the house** le embaucaron para que entrase en la casa
**jockstrap** ['dʒɑk,stræp] *s* suspensorio (*para sostener el escroto*)
**jocose** [dʒo'kos] *adj* jocoso
**jocosity** [dʒo'kɑsɪtɪ] *s* (*pl:* **-ties**) jocosidad
**jocular** ['dʒɑkjələr] *adj* jocoso
**jocularity** [,dʒɑkjə'lærɪtɪ] *s* (*pl:* **-ties**) jocosidad
**jocund** ['dʒɑkənd] o ['dʒokənd] *adj* jocundo, alegre
**jocundity** [dʒo'kʌndɪtɪ] *s* jocundidad, alegría
**jodhpurs** ['dʒɑdpərz] o ['dʒodpʊrz] *spl* pantalones de equitación
**Joe** [dʒo] *s* Pepe; (*l.c.*) *s* (Scotch) amante
**joe-pye weed** [,dʒo'paɪ] *s* (bot.) eupatorio maculado, eupatorio purpúreo
**jog** [dʒɑg] *s* golpecito, empujoncito, sacudimiento ligero; estímulo (*a la memoria*); trote corto; paso lento; resalte, saliente; muesca cuadrada; (*pret & pp:* **jogged; ***ger:* **jogging**) *va* dar un golpecito a, empujar levemente; sacudir con el codo o la mano; estimular (*la memoria*); *vn* avanzar al trote corto, avanzar con ritmo lento; **to jog along** avanzar al trote corto, avanzar con ritmo lento
**joggle** ['dʒɑgəl] *s* traqueo; ensambladura dentada; muesca o diente (*de una ensambladura dentada*); *va* traquear; ensamblar (*con ensambladura dentada*); *vn* traquear
**jog trot** *s* trote de perro; (fig.) rutina
**John** [dʒɑn] *s* Juan; (Bib.) San Juan; (Bib.) el Evangelio según San Juan
**John Bull** *s* el inglés típico; Inglaterra
**John Doe** *s* (law) Fulano de Tal
**John Dory** *s* (*pl:* **John Dorys**) (ichth.) pez de San Pedro
**John Hancock** ['hænkɑk] *s* (coll.) la firma de uno
**Johnny** ['dʒɑnɪ] *s* Juanito
**johnnycake** ['dʒɑnɪ,kek] *s* pan de maíz
**Johnny-come-lately** ['dʒɑnɪ,kʌm'letlɪ] *s* (coll.) persona recién llegada
**Johnny-jump-up** ['dʒɑnɪ'dʒʌmp,ʌp] *s* (bot.) pensamiento, trinitaria; (bot.) violeta
**Johnny on the spot** *s* (coll.) el que llega a tiempo a todas partes; (coll.) el que está siempre presente y listo
**John of Gaunt** [gɔnt] o [gɑnt] *s* Juan de Gante
**Johnsonese** [,dʒɑnsə'niz] *s* estilo ampuloso y rimbombante
**Johnsonian** [dʒɑn'sonɪən] *adj* de Samuel Johnson y sus escritos; ampuloso y rimbombante; castizo; latinizante; difuso, dilatado
**John the Baptist** *s* San Juan Bautista
**join** [dʒɔɪn] *s* juntura, costura; *va* ensamblar, juntar, unir; unirse a, asociarse a, reunirse a; incorporarse a, ingresar en; abrazar (*un partido*); hacerse socio de (*una asociación*); alistarse en (*el ejército*); trabar (*batalla*); desaguar en, desembocar en; *vn* juntarse, unirse; confluir (*p.ej., dos ríos*)
**joiner** ['dʒɔɪnər] *s* ensamblador; ebanista; (coll.) persona que tiene la manía de incorporarse a muchas asociaciones
**joiner's gage** *s* gramil
**joinery** ['dʒɔɪnərɪ] *s* ebanistería (*arte, obras, etc. del ebanista*)
**joint** [dʒɔɪnt] *s* empalme, juntura (*p.ej., de una cañería*); artículo (*segmento interarticular*); (anat.) articulación, coyuntura; (arch.) junta; (b.b.) cartivana; (b.b.) nervura; (bot. & zool.) articulación; (carp.) ensambladura; (elec.) empalme; (geol.) grieta; tajada (*de carne*); (slang) garito; (slang) fonducho, restaurante de mala muerte; **out of joint** descoyuntado, desencajado; (fig.) en desorden, desbarajustado; **to throw out of joint** descoyuntarse (*p.ej., el brazo*); *adj* común, mutuo, unido, asociado; copartícipe; colectivo; solidario; indiviso; conjunto; *va* articular; unir, juntar; descuartizar (*p.ej., un pollo*); igualar (*los dientes de una sierra*); (carp.) ensamblar
**joint account** *s* cuenta en participación, cuenta en común
**joint author** *s* coautor
**joint box** *s* (elec.) caja de empalme, caja de conexiones
**Joint Chiefs of Staff** *spl* estado mayor conjunto
**joint committee** *s* comisión mixta
**jointer** ['dʒɔɪntər] *s* (carp.) ensambladora, juntera; igualador (*de una sierra*)
**jointer plane** *s* (carp.) garlopa
**joint fir** *s* (bot.) hierba de las coyunturas, belcho
**joint grass** *s* (bot.) gramilla; (bot.) equiseto
**jointly** ['dʒɔɪntlɪ] *adv* juntamente, en común
**joint owner** *s* condueño
**joint session** *s* sesión plena, sesión conjunta
**joint-stock company** ['dʒɔɪnt'stɑk] *s* (law) sociedad anónima
**joint tenant** *s* (law) propietario pro indiviso

**jointure** [ˈdʒɔɪntʃər] *s* (law) bienes parafernales
**joist** [dʒɔɪst] *s* viga
**joke** [dʒok] *s* broma, chiste; cosa de reír; bufón, hazmerreír; **no joke** cosa seria; **to tell a joke** contar un chiste o un chascarrillo; **to play a joke (on)** gastar una broma (a); *va* burlarse de, reírse de; **to joke one's way into** conseguir (*p.ej., un empleo*) burla burlando; *vn* bromear, chancear, hablar en broma; **no joking** o **joking aside** burlas aparte, hablando en serio
**joke book** *s* libro de chistes
**joker** [ˈdʒokər] *s* bromista, chancero; frase engañadora (*en un documento*); comodín (*naipe*)
**jollification** [ˌdʒɑlɪfɪˈkeʃən] *s* regocijo, alborozo
**jollity** [ˈdʒɑlɪtɪ] *s* (*pl:* **-ties**) alegría; diversión
**jolly** [ˈdʒɑlɪ] *adj* (*comp:* **-lier;** *super:* **-liest**) jovial, alegre; (coll.) agradable, excelente; *adv* (coll.) muy, harto; (*pret & pp:* **-lied**) *va* (coll.) dar vaya a; (coll.) seguir el humor a; (coll.) reírse de; *vn* (coll.) dar vaya
**jolly boat** *s* (naut.) bote, esquife
**Jolly Roger** *s* bandera de piratas
**jolt** [dʒolt] *s* sacudida, sacudión; *va* sacudir, traquear; *vn* traquear, dar saltos
**jolty** [ˈdʒoltɪ] *adj* (coll.) desigual (*camino*); que da saltos, que va dando tumbos
**Jonah** [ˈdʒonə] *s* (Bib.) Jonás; (Bib.) el libro de Jonás; (fig.) ave de mal agüero, persona que trae mala suerte
**Jonas** [ˈdʒonəs] *s* (Bib.) Jonás; (Bib.) el libro de Jonás
**Jonathan** [ˈdʒɑnəθən] *s* Jonatás
**jongleur** [ˈdʒɑŋglər] o [ʒõˈglœr] *s* juglar, trovador
**jonquil** [ˈdʒɑŋkwɪl] *s* (bot.) junquillo
**Jordan** [ˈdʒɔrdən] *s* Jordán (*río*); Jordania (*país*)
**Jordan almond** *s* almendra de Málaga
**Jordanian** [dʒɔrˈdenɪən] *adj & s* jordano
**jorum** [ˈdʒorəm] *s* (coll.) copa grande
**Joseph** [ˈdʒozəf] *s* José; (*l.c.*) *s* capa de montar de mujer (*del siglo XVIII*)
**Josephine** [ˈdʒozəfin] *s* Josefa o Josefina
**Joseph of Arimathea** [ˌærɪməˈθiə] *s* (Bib.) José de Arimatea
**Joseph's-coat** [ˈdʒozəfsˈkot] *s* (bot.) papagayo
**Josephus** [dʒoˈsifəs] *s* Josefo
**Josh.** abr. de **Joshua**
**josh** [dʒɑʃ] *va* (slang) dar broma a, burlarse de; *vn* (slang) dar broma, burlarse
**Joshua** [ˈdʒɑʃʊə] o [ˈdʒɑʃəwə] *s* (Bib.) Josué; (Bib.) el libro de Josué
**Josiah** [dʒoˈsaɪə] *s* (Bib.) Josías
**joss** [dʒɑs] *s* dios familiar chino, ídolo chino
**joss house** *s* templo chino
**joss stick** *s* pebete (*que queman los chinos en sus templos*)
**jostle** [ˈdʒɑsəl] *s* empellón, empujón; *va* empellar, empujar; forzar, meter a empellones; *vn* chocar; avanzar a fuerza de empujones o codazos
**jot** [dʒɑt] *s* jota (*cosa mínima*); **I don't care a jot (about)** no se me da un bledo (de); (*pret & pp:* **jotted;** *ger:* **jotting**) *va* escribir aprisa; **to jot down** apuntar
**jottings** [ˈdʒɑtɪŋz] *spl* apuntes
**joule** [dʒul] o [dʒaʊl] *s* (phys.) julio
**jounce** [dʒaʊns] *s* traqueo, sacudida; *va* traquear, sacudir; *vn* traquear, dar tumbos
**journal** [ˈdʒʌrnəl] *s* diario (*periódico; apuntes personales*); revista; (com.) libro diario; (naut.) diario de navegación; (mach.) gorrón, muñón
**journal bearing** *s* (mach.) chumacera
**journal box** *s* caja de grasa
**journalese** [ˌdʒʌrnəˈliz] *s* estilo periodístico
**journalism** [ˈdʒʌrnəlɪzəm] *s* periodismo
**journalist** [ˈdʒʌrnəlɪst] *s* periodista
**journalistic** [ˌdʒʌrnəˈlɪstɪk] *adj* periodístico
**journey** [ˈdʒʌrnɪ] *s* viaje; *vn* viajar
**journeyman** [ˈdʒʌrnɪmən] *s* (*pl:* **-men**) oficial
**joust** [dʒʌst], [dʒust] o [dʒaʊst] *s* justa, torneo; *vn* justar
**Jove** [dʒov] *s* (myth.) Jove; (poet.) Júpiter (*planeta*); **by Jove!** ¡por Dios!
**jovial** [ˈdʒovɪəl] *adj* jovial
**joviality** [ˌdʒovɪˈælɪtɪ] *s* jovialidad
**Jovian** [ˈdʒovɪən] *adj* joviano o jovio
**jowl** [dʒaʊl] *s* moflete; quijada; barba (*de ave*); papada (*del ganado*); cabeza de pescado aderezada
**joy** [dʒɔɪ] *s* alegría, regocijo; **to leap with joy** brincar o saltar de gozo; *vn* alegrarse, regocijarse
**joyance** [ˈdʒɔɪəns] *s* (archaic) alegría, júbilo
**joyful** [ˈdʒɔɪfəl] *adj* alegre (*persona; noticia*); **joyful over** gozoso con o de
**joyless** [ˈdʒɔɪlɪs] *adj* sin alegría, triste, lúgubre
**joyous** [ˈdʒɔɪəs] *adj* alegre (*persona; noticia*)
**joyousness** [ˈdʒɔɪəsnɪs] *s* alegría, regocijo
**joy ride** *s* (coll.) paseo alocado en coche (*muchas veces sin permiso del dueño*)
**joy-ride** [ˈdʒɔɪˌraɪd] (*pret:* **-rode;** *pp:* **-ridden**) *vn* (coll.) dar un paseo alocado en coche (*muchas veces sin permiso del dueño*)
**joy stick** *s* (aer.) palanca de mando
**Jozy** [ˈdʒozɪ] *s* Pepa, Pepita
**J.P.** abr. de **Justice of the Peace**
**Jr.** abr. de **Junior**
**jubbah** [ˈdʒʊbə] *s* aljuba
**jube** [ˈdʒubi] *s* (arch.) jube
**jubilance** [ˈdʒubɪləns] *s* júbilo, alborozo
**jubilant** [ˈdʒubɪlənt] *adj* jubiloso, alborozado
**Jubilate** [ˌdʒubɪˈletɪ] o [ˌdʒubɪˈlɑtɪ] *s* Salmo que empieza por esta palabra (*XCIX en la Vulgata*); jubilate (*tercer domingo después de Pascua*); (*l.c.*) [ˈdʒubɪlet] *vn* alegrarse, regocijarse
**jubilation** [ˌdʒubɪˈleʃən] *s* júbilo, regocijo, alborozo
**jubilee** [ˈdʒubɪli] *s* júbilo (*viva alegría*); aniversario; quincuagésimo aniversario; (hist. & eccl.) jubileo
**Jud.** abr. de **Judges** y **Judith**
**Judaea** [dʒuˈdiə] *s* var. de **Judea**
**Judah** [ˈdʒudə] *s* (Bib.) Judá (*hijo de Jacob; reino; tribu*)
**Judahite** [ˈdʒudəaɪt] *s* judaíta
**Judaic** [dʒuˈdeɪk] *adj* judaico
**Judaism** [ˈdʒudeɪzəm] *s* judaísmo
**Judaize** [ˈdʒudeaɪz] *va* convertir al judaísmo; hacer conforme al judaísmo; *vn* judaizar
**Judas** [ˈdʒudəs] *s* (Bib. & fig.) Judas; (Bib.) Epístola de San Judas
**Judas Iscariot** *s* (Bib.) Judas Iscariote
**Judas kiss** *s* beso de Judas
**Judas tree** *s* (bot.) árbol de Judas o de Judea, árbol del amor
**Judea** [dʒuˈdiə] *s* Judea
**Judean** [dʒuˈdiən] *adj & s* judío
**Judg.** abr. de **Judges**
**judge** [dʒʌdʒ] *s* juez; **to be a good judge of** ser buen juez en; **Judges** *spl* (Bib.) el libro de los Jueces; *va & vn* juzgar; **judging by** o **from** a juzgar por
**judge advocate** *s* (mil.) auditor de guerra; (nav.) auditor de marina
**judgeship** [ˈdʒʌdʒʃɪp] *s* judicatura
**judgment** o **judgement** [ˈdʒʌdʒmənt] *s* juicio; (law) sentencia; (law) apremio (*para compeler a uno al cumplimiento de una cosa*); (log. & theol.) juicio; **the Judgment** o **the Last Judgment** el juicio final, el juicio universal
**judgment day** *s* día del juicio
**judgment seat** *s* tribunal
**judicatory** [ˈdʒudɪkəˌtorɪ] *adj* judicial; *s* (*pl:* **-ries**) tribunal de justicia; judicatura
**judicature** [ˈdʒudɪkətʃər] *s* judicatura
**judicial** [dʒuˈdɪʃəl] *adj* judicial; juicioso
**judiciary** [dʒuˈdɪʃɪˌɛrɪ] *adj* judicial; *s* (*pl:* **-ies**) judicatura (*de una ciudad, país, etc.*); poder judicial
**judicious** [dʒuˈdɪʃəs] *adj* juicioso
**Judith** [ˈdʒudɪθ] *s* Judit; (Bib.) el libro de Judit
**judo** [ˈdʒudo] *s* judo
**Judy** [ˈdʒudɪ] *s* nombre abreviado de **Judith;** la mujer de Polichinela (*en las funciones de títeres inglesas y norteamericanas*)
**jug** [dʒʌg] *s* jarra, botija, cántaro; (slang) bote, chirona (*cárcel*); (*pret & pp:* **jugged;** *ger:* **jugging**) *va* (slang) encarcelar
**Juggernaut** [ˈdʒʌgərnɔt] *s* imagen del dios bramánico Krichna que solían sacar en procesión, colocada en un carro cuyas ruedas aplastaban a los fieles, que así se sacrificaban;

(fig.) objeto de devoción ciega; (fig.) monstruo destructor de los hombres
**juggle** [ˈdʒʌgəl] *s* juego de manos; trampa; *va* escamotear; falsear, alterar fraudulentamente (*cuentas, documentos, etc.*); *vn* hacer juegos de manos, hacer suertes; hacer trampas
**juggler** [ˈdʒʌglər] *s* jugador de manos, malabarista; impostor; (obs.) juglar, bufón
**jugglery** [ˈdʒʌglərɪ] *s* (*pl:* **-ies**) prestidigitación; decepción, fraude
**juglandaceous** [ˌdʒuglænˈdeʃəs] *adj* (bot.) juglandáceo o juglándeo
**Jugoslav** o **Jugo-Slav** [ˈjugoˈslɑv] *adj & s* var. de **Yugoslav**
**Jugoslavia** o **Jugo-Slavia** [ˈjugoˈslɑvɪə] *s* var. de **Yugoslavia**
**Jugoslavic** [ˈjugoˈslɑvɪk] *adj* var. de **Yugoslavic**
**jugular** [ˈdʒʌgjələr] o [ˈdʒugjələr] *adj & s* (anat.) yugular
**jugular vein** *s* (anat.) vena yugular
**Jugurtha** [dʒuˈgʌrθə] *s* Yugurta
**juice** [dʒus] *s* zumo, jugo; (slang) electricidad; (slang) gasolina
**juicy** [ˈdʒusɪ] *adj* (*comp:* **-ier**; *super:* **-iest**) zumoso, jugoso; (fig.) picante, sabroso; (coll.) lluvioso
**jujitsu** [dʒuˈdʒɪtsu] *s* jiu-jitsú (*arte japonés de luchar brazo a brazo sin armas*)
**jujube** [ˈdʒudʒub] *s* (bot.) azufaifo; azufaifa (*fruto*); pastilla de pasta de azufaifas; pastilla
**jujutsu** [dʒuˈdʒɪtsu] *s* var. de **jujitsu**
**juke box** [dʒuk] *s* (coll.) tocadiscos tragamonedas
**Jul.** abr. de **July**
**julep** [ˈdʒulɪp] *s* julepe (*bebida helada compuesta de whisky o aguardiente, azúcar y hojas de menta*)
**Julian** [ˈdʒuljən] *adj* juliano; *s* Juliano o Julián
**Juliana** [ˌdʒulɪˈænə] o [ˌdʒulɪˈɑnə] *s* Juliana
**Julian Alps** *spl* Alpes julianos
**Julian calendar** *s* calendario juliano
**Julian the Apostate** *s* Juliano el Apóstata
**julienne** [ˌʒulɪˈɛn] *s* sopa juliana; *adj* rajado, en rajas
**Juliet** [ˈdʒulɪɛt] *s* Julieta
**Julius** [ˈdʒuljəs] *s* Julio
**July** [dʒuˈlaɪ] *s* julio
**jumble** [ˈdʒʌmbəl] *s* masa confusa, revoltijo; bollito delgado en forma de rosca; *va* emburujar, revolver
**jumbo** [ˈdʒʌmbo] *s* (*pl:* **-bos**) elefante, coloso; *adj* enorme, colosal
**jump** [dʒʌmp] *s* salto; lanzamiento (*en paracaídas*); **to be always on the jump** (coll.) andar siempre de aquí para allí; **to get** o **to have the jump on** (slang) coger la delantera a, llevar la ventaja a; *va* saltar; hacer saltar (*a un caballo*); comer (*en las damas y el ajedrez*); salir fuera de (*el carril*); saltar a (*un tren*); *vn* saltar; lanzarse (*en paracaídas desde un avión*); saltar espacios (*la máquina de escribir*); **to jump at** saltar sobre; apresurarse a aceptar (*una invitación*); apresurarse a aprovechar (*la oportunidad*); **to jump on** saltar a (*un tren*); (slang) culpar, regañar, criticar; **to jump over** saltar por, pasar de un salto; saltar (*p.ej., la página de un libro*); **to jump to** sacar precipitadamente (*una conclusión*)
**jumper** [ˈdʒʌmpər] *s* saltador; blusa holgada de obrero; (elec.) alambre de cierre; **jumpers** *spl* traje holgado de juego para niños
**jumping bean** *s* semilla brincadora
**jumping jack** *s* títere
**jumping-off place** [ˈdʒʌmpɪŋˈɔf] o [ˈdʒʌmpɪŋˈɑf] *s* fin del camino, sitio muy remoto
**jump seat** *s* traspuntín (*de coche*); (aut.) estrapontín
**jump spark** *s* (elec.) chispa de entrehierro
**jump wire** *s* (elec.) alambre de cierre
**jumpy** [ˈdʒʌmpɪ] *adj* (*comp:* **-ier**; *super:* **-iest**) saltón; asustadizo, alborotadizo
**jun.** abr. de **junior**
**Jun.** abr. de **June** y **Junior**
**junc.** abr. de **junction**
**juncaceous** [dʒʌŋˈkeʃəs] *adj* (bot.) juncáceo
**junco** [ˈdʒʌŋko] *s* (*pl:* **-cos**) (orn.) junquito, echalumbre
**junction** [ˈdʒʌŋkʃən] *s* juntura, unión; ensambladura; confluencia (*de dos ríos*); (elec.) caja de empalme; (rail.) empalme
**junction box** *s* (elec.) caja de empalme, caja de conexiones
**juncture** [ˈdʒʌŋktʃər] *s* juntura, unión; coyuntura (*sazón, oportunidad*); **at this juncture** en esto, a esta sazón
**June** [dʒun] *s* junio
**June beetle** o **bug** *s* (ent.) escarabajo norteamericano que comienza a volar en el mes de junio (*Phyllophaga; Cotinus nitida*)
**Juneberry** [ˈdʒunˌbɛrɪ] *s* (*pl:* **-ries**) (bot.) guillomo (*arbusto y fruto*)
**jungle** [ˈdʒʌŋgəl] *s* jungla; selva, matorral impenetrable; maraña, laberinto; (slang) sitio en despoblado y casi siempre cerca de la vía del ferrocarril, donde acampan los vagos
**jungle fever** *s* (path.) fiebre de los grandes bosques
**jungle fowl** *s* (orn.) gallo salvaje; (orn.) gallo de los juncales
**junior** [ˈdʒunjər] *adj* menor, más joven; juvenil; posterior; más nuevo, más reciente; de penúltimo año; hijo, p.ej., **John Jones, Junior** Juan Jones, hijo; *s* menor; estudiante de penúltimo año
**junior college** *s* (U.S.A.) colegio que comprende los dos primeros años universitarios
**junior high school** *s* (U.S.A.) escuela intermedia (*entre la primaria y la secundaria*)
**junior partner** *s* socio menor
**juniper** [ˈdʒunɪpər] *s* (bot.) enebro común; (bot.) cedro de Virginia
**juniper berry** *s* enebrina
**juniper cedar** *s* (bot.) cedro de Virginia
**juniper-tar oil** [ˈdʒunɪpərˌtɑr] *s* aceite de cada
**junk** [dʒʌŋk] *s* chatarra, hierro viejo, ropa vieja, etc.; (slang) trastos viejos, baratijas viejas; jarcia trozada (*que se utiliza, p.ej., para estopa*); junco (*embarcación china*); (naut.) carne salada y dura; *va* (slang) echar a la basura; (slang) reducir (*una máquina*) a hierro viejo
**junk dealer** *s* chatarrero, chapucero
**Junker** [ˈjuŋkər] *s* aristócrata reaccionario prusiano
**junket** [ˈdʒʌŋkɪt] *s* manjar de leche, cuajo y azúcar; jira; viaje de recreo; *vn* ir de jira; hacer un viaje de recreo
**junkman** [ˈdʒʌŋkˌmæn] *s* (*pl:* **-men**) chatarrero, chapucero, hombre que compra y vende hierro viejo, trapos, papeles, etc.; tripulante de junco
**junk room** *s* trastera, leonera
**junk shop** *s* (coll.) tienda de trastos viejos
**junk yard** *s* chatarrería
**Juno** [ˈdʒuno] *s* (*pl:* **-nos**) (myth.) Juno; (fig.) mujer de belleza imponente
**Junoesque** [ˌdʒunoˈɛsk] *adj* imponente
**junr.** o **Junr.** abr. de **junior**
**junta** [ˈdʒʌntə] *s* junta; cábala, camarilla
**junto** [ˈdʒʌnto] *s* (*pl:* **-tos**) cábala, camarilla
**Jupiter** [ˈdʒupɪtər] *s* (astr. & myth.) Júpiter
**jural** [ˈdʒʊrəl] *adj* legal; judicial
**Jurassic** [dʒʊˈræsɪk] *adj & s* (geol.) jurásico
**Jur. D.** abr. de **juris doctor** (Lat.) **Doctor of Law**
**juridical** [dʒʊˈrɪdɪkəl] *adj* jurídico
**jurisconsult** [ˌdʒʊrɪskənˈsʌlt] o [ˌdʒʊrɪsˈkɑnsʌlt] *s* jurisconsulto
**jurisdiction** [ˌdʒʊrɪsˈdɪkʃən] *s* jurisdicción
**jurisdictional** [ˌdʒʊrɪsˈdɪkʃənəl] *adj* jurisdiccional
**jurisdictional strike** *s* huelga por jurisdicción entre gremios
**jurisprudence** [ˌdʒʊrɪsˈprudəns] *s* jurisprudencia
**jurisprudent** [ˌdʒʊrɪsˈprudənt] *s* jurisprudente
**jurist** [ˈdʒʊrɪst] *s* jurista
**juristic** [dʒʊˈrɪstɪk] *adj* jurídico
**juror** [ˈdʒʊrər] *s* jurado (*individuo*)
**jury** [ˈdʒʊrɪ] *s* (*pl:* **-ries**) jurado (*grupo*); *adj* (naut.) provisional
**jury box** *s* tribuna del jurado
**juryman** [ˈdʒʊrɪmən] *s* (*pl:* **-men**) jurado (*individuo*)
**jury mast** *s* (naut.) bandola
**jury-rigged** [ˈdʒʊrɪˌrɪgd] *adj* (naut.) de aparejo provisional

**Jus. P.** abr. de **justice of the peace**
**just** [dʒʌst] *adj* justo; **the just** los justos; *adv* justo, justamente; hace poco; apenas; casi no; no más que; sólo; (coll.) absolutamente, verdaderamente; **had just** + *pp* acababa de + *inf*, p.ej., **we had just left** acabábamos de marcharnos; **to have just** + *pp* acabar de + *inf*, p.ej., **I have just arrived** acabo de llegar; **just as** como; en el momento en que; lo mismo que; tal como; **just beyond** un poco más allá (de); **just now** ahora mismo; hace poco; **just out** acabado de aparecer, recién publicado; **just** + *pp* acabado de + *inf*, p.ej., **just received** acabado de recibir; *s* justa; *vn* justar
**justice** [ˈdʒʌstɪs] *s* justicia; premio merecido; juez; juez de paz; **to bring to justice** aprehender y condenar por justicia; **to do justice to** hacer justicia a; tratar debidamente, apreciar debidamente; **to do oneself justice** no quedar corto, hacerlo (*una persona*) lo mejor que pueda; quedar bien
**justice of the peace** *s* juez de paz
**justiceship** [ˈdʒʌstɪsʃɪp] *s* judicatura
**justifiable** [ˈdʒʌstɪˌfaɪəbəl] *adj* justificable
**justification** [ˌdʒʌstɪfɪˈkeʃən] *s* justificación; (print.) justificación
**justificatory** [dʒʌsˈtɪfɪkəˌtorɪ] *adj* justificativo
**justifier** [ˈdʒʌstɪˌfaɪər] *s* justificador, justificante
**justify** [ˈdʒʌstɪfaɪ] (*pret & pp:* **-fied**) *va* justificar; (print.) justificar
**Justinian** [dʒʌsˈtɪnɪən] *s* Justiniano
**Justinian Code** *s* código de Justiniano
**Justin Martyr** [ˈdʒʌstɪn] *s* San Justino
**justle** [ˈdʒʌsəl] *s, va & vn* var. de **jostle**
**justly** [ˈdʒʌstlɪ] *adv* justamente
**justness** [ˈdʒʌstnɪs] *s* justicia; exactitud
**jut** [dʒʌt] *s* resalto, saliente, saledizo; (*pret & pp:* **jutted**; *ger:* **jutting**) *vn* resaltar, proyectarse; **to jut out** resaltar, proyectarse
**jute** [dʒut] *s* (bot.) yute (*planta, fibra y tejido*); (*cap.*) *s* juto
**Jutland** [ˈdʒʌtlənd] *s* Jutlandia
**Jutlander** [ˈdʒʌtləndər] *s* jutlandés
**Jutlandish** [ˈdʒʌtləndɪʃ] *adj* jutlandés
**Juturna** [dʒuˈtʌrnə] *s* (myth.) Yuturna
**Juvenal** [ˈdʒuvənəl] *s* Juvenal
**juvenescence** [ˌdʒuvəˈnɛsəns] *s* rejuvenecimiento
**juvenescent** [ˌdʒuvəˈnɛsənt] *adj* rejuveneciente
**juvenile** [ˈdʒuvənɪl] o [ˈdʒuvənaɪl] *adj* juvenil; de o para jóvenes o niños; *s* joven, mocito; libro para niños; (theat.) galán joven, galancete
**juvenile court** *s* tribunal tutelar de menores
**juvenile delinquency** *s* delincuencia de menores
**juvenile lead** [lid] *s* (theat.) papel de galancete; (theat.) galancete
**juvenilia** [ˌdʒuvəˈnɪlɪə] *spl* obras de juventud
**juvenility** [ˌdʒuvəˈnɪlɪtɪ] *s* juventud, mocedad
**juxtapose** [ˌdʒʌkstəˈpoz] *va* yuxtaponer
**juxtaposition** [ˌdʒʌkstəpəˈzɪʃən] *s* yuxtaposición
**Jy.** abr. de **July**
**jynx** [dʒɪŋks] *s* encanto, hechizo; (orn.) torcecuello

# K

**K, k** [ke] *s* (*pl:* **K's, k's** [kez]) undécima letra del alfabeto inglés
**k.** abr. de **karat, kilogram** y **kopeck**
**K.** abr. de **King** y **Knight**
**Kaaba** [ˈkɑbə] *s* Caaba (*de la Meca*)
**Kaffir** o **Kafir** [ˈkæfər] o [ˈkɑfər] *adj & s* cafre; (*l.c.*) *s* (bot.) panizo negro, maíz de Guinea
**kaffir corn** o **kafir corn** *s* (bot.) panizo negro, maíz de Guinea
**kaftan** [ˈkæftən] *s* caftán
**kaiak** [ˈkaɪæk] *s* var. de **kayak**
**kail** [kel] *s* var. de **kale**
**kaiser** [ˈkaɪzər] *s* emperador
**kaki** [ˈkɑki] *s* (*pl:* **-kis**) (bot.) caqui
**kale** [kel] *s* (bot.) col, berza común (*Brassica oleracea acephala*); (slang) dinero, dinero contante y sonante
**kaleidoscope** [kəˈlaɪdəskop] *s* calidoscopio; (fig.) calidoscopio
**kaleidoscopic** [kəˌlaɪdəˈskɑpɪk] *adj* calidoscópico; (fig.) calidoscópico
**kalends** [ˈkælɪndz] *spl* var. de **calends**
**kalmia** [ˈkælmɪə] *s* (bot.) calmia
**kalsomine** [ˈkælsəmaɪn] *s & va* var. de **calcimine**
**Kamerun** [ˌkɑməˈrun] *s* var. de **Cameroons**
**kamikase** [ˌkɑmɪˈkɑzi] *s* kamikazo (*aviador suicida japonés*)
**Kan.** abr. de **Kansas**
**Kanaka** [kəˈnækə] o [ˈkænəkə] *s* hawaiano; polinesio
**kangaroo** [ˌkæŋgəˈru] *s* (zool.) canguro
**kangaroo court** *s* (coll.) tribunal irregular, tribunal desautorizado; (coll.) tribunal fingido
**kangaroo rat** *s* (zool.) rata canguro
**Kans.** abr. de **Kansas**
**Kantian** [ˈkæntɪən] *adj & s* kantiano
**Kantianism** [ˈkæntɪənɪzəm] *s* kantismo
**kaolin** o **kaoline** [ˈkeəlɪn] *s* caolín
**kapok** [ˈkepɑk] *s* capoc, lana de ceiba
**karakul** [ˈkærəkəl] *s* var. de **caracul**
**karat** [ˈkærət] *s* var. de **carat**
**Karelia** [kəˈrilɪə] *s* Carelia
**Karelian** [kəˈrilɪən] *adj & s* carelio o careliano
**karyokinesis** [ˌkærɪokɪˈnisɪs] o [ˌkærɪokaɪˈnisɪs] *s* (biol.) cariocinesis
**karyomitome** [ˌkærɪˈɑmɪtom] *s* (biol.) cariomitoma
**karyoplasm** [ˈkærɪəplæzəm] *s* (biol.) carioplasma
**karyosome** [ˈkærɪəˌsom] *s* (biol.) cariosoma
**karyotin** [ˌkærɪˈotɪn] *s* (biol.) cariotina
**Kasbah** [ˈkɑzbə] *s* var. de **Casbah**
**kashmir** y **Kashmir** [ˈkæʃmɪr] *s* var. de **cashmere** y **Cashmere**
**katabolism** [kəˈtæbəlɪzəm] *s* var. de **catabolism**
**Katherine** [ˈkæθərɪn] *s* var. de **Catherine**
**katydid** [ˈketɪdɪd] *s* (ent.) saltamontes cuyo macho emite un sonido chillón (*Microcentrum retinervis y Amblycorypha*)
**kauri** [ˈkaurɪ] *s* (*pl:* **-ris**) (bot.) kauri
**kauri resin** *s* resina o copal de kauri
**kaury** [ˈkaurɪ] *s* (*pl:* **-ries**) var. de **kauri**
**kayak** [ˈkaɪæk] *s* kayak (*embarcación*)
**kc.** abr. de **kilocycle** o **kilocycles**
**K.C.** abr. de **King's Counsel** y **Knights of Columbus**
**K.C.B.** abr. de **Knight Commander of the Bath**
**kea** [ˈkeə] o [ˈkiə] *s* (orn.) kea (*Nestor notabilis*)
**kedge** [kɛdʒ] *s* (naut.) anclote; *va* (naut.) mover con anclote; *vn* (naut.) moverse con anclote
**keel** [kil] *s* (aer., naut. & bot.) quilla; (poet.) nave; **on an even keel** (naut.) en iguales calados; (fig.) firme, estable; *va* volcar (*una embarcación*) poniéndola quilla arriba; volcar (*cualquier cosa*); *vn* (naut.) dar de quilla; volcarse; **to keel over** (naut.) dar de quilla; volcarse; caerse de repente; (coll.) desmayarse
**keelhaul** [ˈkilˌhɔl] *va* (naut.) pasar por debajo de la quilla (*por castigo*)
**keelson** [ˈkɛlsən] o [ˈkilsən] *s* (naut.) sobrequilla
**keen** [kin] *adj* agudo; mordaz; ansioso; entusiasta; **to be keen on** ser muy aficionado a (*p.ej., la lectura*); **I'm not very keen on him** no es santo de mi devoción
**keenness** [ˈkinnɪs] *s* agudeza; mordacidad; ansia, entusiasmo
**keep** [kip] *s* manutención, subsistencia; (fort.) torre del homenaje; **for keeps** (coll.) para guardar; (coll.) para siempre; **to earn one's keep** (coll.) ganarse la vida; **to play for keeps** (coll.) jugar de veras ‖ (*pret & pp:* **kept**) *va* guardar; conservar; quedarse con; tener (*criados, gallinas, huéspedes, etc.*); guardar, cumplir (*su palabra o promesa*); cultivar (*una huerta*); mantener; dirigir (*una escuela, un hotel*); llevar (*cuentas, libros; la anotación en los naipes*); celebrar (*fiestas*); mantenerse firme en (*su puesto, la silla de montar*); detener, hacer tardar (*a una persona*); **to keep away** tener apartado, impedir que venga; **to keep back** retener; reprimir; reservar (*no divulgar*); **to keep down** reprimir, sujetar; reducir (*los gastos*) al mínimo; **to keep from** + *ger* no dejar + *inf*, p.ej., **keep him from eating too much** no le deje comer demasiado; **to keep in** tener encerrado, no dejar salir; **to keep off** tener a distancia; no dejar penetrar (*p.ej., la lluvia*); evitar (*p.ej., el polvo*); **to keep on** no quitarse (*p.ej., el abrigo*); **to keep out** no dejar entrar; no dejar penetrar; **to keep someone informed (about)** poner a alguien al corriente (de); **to keep to oneself** callarse (*algo*) a sí mismo; **to keep up** mantener, conservar; **to keep** + *ger* hacer + *inf*, p.ej., **I am sorry to keep you waiting** siento hacerle esperar ‖ *vn* quedarse, permanecer; mantenerse; conservarse, durar sin dañarse; estarse, p.ej., **keep quiet** estése Vd. quieto; **to keep at** continuar en, empeñarse en (*p.ej., su trabajo*); **to keep away** mantenerse a distancia; no dejarse ver; **to keep away from** no meterse en; no dejarse ver en; no meterse con, evitar todo roce con; no probar (*p.ej., vino*); **to keep from** + *ger* abstenerse de + *inf;* **to keep informed (about)** ponerse al corriente (de); **to keep in with** (coll.) mantener amistad con, no perder el favor de; **to keep off** no acercarse a; no andar por; no pisar (*el césped*); **to keep on** continuar; no caerse de (*p.ej., un caballo*); **to keep on** + *ger* seguir + *ger;* **to keep on with** continuar con; **to keep out** no entrar; **to keep out of** no entrar en; no meterse en; evitar (*peligro*); **to keep to** adherirse estrictamente a; seguir por, llevar (*la derecha, la izquierda*); **to keep to oneself** quedarse a solas, huir de las gentes; **to keep up** continuar; no rezagarse; **to keep up with** ir al paso de; llevar el mismo tren de vida de; llevar adelante, proseguir; **to keep** + *ger* seguir + *ger*
**keeper** [ˈkipər] *s* encargado; guarda; guardabosque; archivero; guardián, custodio; protector; cerradero (*de cerrojo*); armadura, culata (*de imán*)
**keeping** [ˈkipɪŋ] *s* manutención; guarda, custodia, cuidado, cargo; guardar, p.ej., **the keeping of Lent** el guardar la cuaresma; **in keeping with** de acuerdo con, en armonía con; **in safe keeping** en lugar seguro, en bue-

nas manos; **out of keeping with** en desacuerdo con
**keepsake** ['kip,sek] *s* recuerdo
**keg** [kɛg] *s* cuñete; 100 libras de clavos
**kelp** [kɛlp] *s* (bot.) quelpo; cenizas del quelpo
**kelpie** o **kelpy** ['kɛlpɪ] *s* (*pl:* **-pies**) trasgo o duende en forma de caballo que mora en las aguas y se ocupa en ahogar a las personas o en darles aviso de que han de morir ahogadas
**kelson** ['kɛlsən] *s* var. de **keelson**
**Kelt** [kɛlt] *s* celta; (*l.c.*) *s* (ichth.) salmón zancado
**kelter** ['kɛltər] *s* var. de **kilter**
**Keltic** ['kɛltɪk] *adj & s* var. de **Celtic**
**Ken.** abr. de **Kentucky**
**ken** [kɛn] *s* alcance de la vista, alcance del saber; **beyond the ken of** fuera del alcance del saber de; (*pret & pp:* **kenned;** *ger:* **kenning**) *va* (archaic) ver, reconocer; *vn* (archaic & Brit. dial.) saber
**Kendal green** ['kɛndəl] *s* tejido de lana de Kendal (*de color verde*)
**kennel** ['kɛnəl] *s* perrera; establecimiento donde se crían los perros; jauría; (*pret & pp:* **-neled** o **-nelled;** *ger:* **-neling** o **-nelling**) *va* tener o encerrar en perrera; *vn* guarecerse en perrera
**kenning** ['kɛnɪŋ] *s* perífrasis poética, nombre metafórico (*en la literatura teutónica antigua*)
**keno** ['kino] *s* juego casero parecido a la lotería de familia
**kentledge** ['kɛntlɪdʒ] *s* (naut.) enjunque
**kepi** ['kɛpɪ] *s* (*pl:* **-is**) (mil.) quepis
**kept** [kɛpt] *pret & pp de* **keep**
**kept woman** *s* entretenida
**keramic** [kɪ'ræmɪk] *adj* var. de **ceramic; keramics** *ssg & spl* var. de **ceramics**
**keratin** ['kɛrətɪn] *s* (zool.) queratina
**keratoconus** [,kɛrəto'konəs] *s* (path.) córnea cónica
**keratogenous** [,kɛrə'tɑdʒɪnəs] *adj* queratógeno
**kerb** [kʌrb] *s* (Brit.) encintado (*de la acera*)
**kerchief** ['kʌrtʃɪf] *s* pañuelo
**kerchoo** [kə'tʃu] *interj* ¡ ah-chis!
**kerf** [kʌrf] *s* corte; trozo cortado
**kermes** ['kʌrmiz] *s* quermes (*materia colorante*); (bot.) coscoja; coscojo
**kermes mineral** *s* (chem.) quermes mineral
**kermess** ['kʌrmɛs] o **kermis** ['kʌrmɪs] *s* kermese (*fiesta generalmente con propósito caritativo*)
**kern** [kʌrn] *s* labriego irlandés; (print.) rabillo de ojo que sobresale
**kernel** ['kʌrnəl] *s* almendra (*de cualquier fruto drupáceo*); grano (*de trigo o maíz*); (fig.) medula o meollo
**kerosene** ['kɛrəsin] o [,kɛrə'sin] *s* keroseno
**kerosene lamp** *s* lámpara de petróleo
**ker-plunk** [kər'plʌŋk] *interj* ¡ pataplún!
**kersey** ['kʌrzɪ] *s* carsaya, carisea
**kestrel** ['kɛstrəl] *s* (orn.) cernícalo
**ketch** [kɛtʃ] *s* queche
**ketchup** ['kɛtʃəp] *s* var. de **catsup**
**ketene** ['kitin] *s* (chem.) queteno
**ketone** ['kiton] *s* (chem.) cetona o quetona
**ketose** ['kitos] *s* (chem.) quetosa
**kettle** ['kɛtəl] *s* caldera; cafetera; tetera; calderada (*lo que cabe en una caldera*); **kettle of fish** berenjenal, p.ej., **this is a fine kettle of fish we've got into** en buen berenjenal nos hemos metido
**kettledrum** ['kɛtəl,drʌm] *s* (mus.) timbal
**key** [ki] *s* llave; tecla (*de piano, máquina de escribir, etc.*); chaveta, clavija, cuña; (bot.) sámara; (geog.) cayo; (mus.) clave o llave; (mus.) tono; (telg.) manipulador; (fig.) persona o cosa dominante o principal; (fig.) clave o llave (*a un código, problema, secreto, etc.*); (fig.) llave (*lugar estratégico más propicio*); **off key** desafinado; desafinadamente; *adj* clave, llave, dominante; *va* afinar, templar (*con llave*); enchavetar, acuñar; arreglar; **to key up** alentar, excitar
**keyboard** ['ki,bord] *s* teclado
**key fruit** *s* (bot.) sámara, fruto alado
**keyhole** ['ki,hol] *s* ojo de la cerradura, bocallave; agujero para la llave del reloj
**keyhole saw** *s* sierra de punta, sierra caladora, sierra de calador
**key man** *s* hombre principal, hombre muy importante
**keynote** ['ki,not] *s* (mus.) tónica, nota tónica; (fig.) tónica, idea fundamental
**keynoter** ['ki'notər] *s* (coll.) miembro informante
**keynote speech** *s* discurso de apertura
**keypuncher** ['ki,pʌntʃər] *s* perforista
**key ring** *s* llavero
**key seat** *s* (mach.) cajera de cuña
**key signature** *s* (mus.) armadura
**key socket** *s* (elec.) portalámparas de llave giratoria
**keystone** ['ki,ston] *s* clave, espinazo (*de un arco*); (fig.) piedra angular
**keyway** ['ki,we] *s* (mach.) chavetera
**Key West** *s* Cayo Hueso
**key word** *s* palabra clave
**kg.** abr. de **kilogram** o **kilograms**
**K.G.** abr. de **Knight of the Garter**
**khaki** ['kɑkɪ] o ['kækɪ] *s* (*pl:* **-kis**) caqui; *adj* caqui
**khalif** ['kelɪf] o ['kælɪf] *s* var. de **caliph**
**khan** [kɑn] *s* kan (*título; sitio destinado para el reposo de las caravanas*)
**khanate** ['kɑnet] *s* kanato
**Khartoum** o **Khartum** [kɑr'tum] *s* Jartum
**khedive** [kə'div] *s* jedive
**kiang** [kɪ'æŋ] *s* (zool.) hemíono
**kibe** [kaɪb] *s* sabañón ulcerado (*en el talón*)
**kibitz** ['kɪbɪts] *vn* (coll.) dar consejos molestos a los jugadores
**kibitzer** ['kɪbɪtsər] *s* (coll.) mirón (*de una partida de juego*); (coll.) entremetido, camasquince
**kiblah** ['kɪblɑ] *s* alquibla (*punto hacia donde los musulmanes miran cuando rezan*)
**kibosh** ['kaɪbɑʃ] o [kɪ'bɑʃ] *s* (slang) música celestial; **to put the kibosh on** (slang) desbaratar, imposibilitar
**kick** [kɪk] *s* puntapié; coz (*de animal*); culatazo (*de arma de fuego*); (slang) queja, protesta; (slang) fuerza (*de una bebida*); (slang) estímulo, efecto estimulador (*de una bebida*); (slang) placer, gusto; **to get a kick out of** (slang) hallar placer en; *va* dar de puntapiés a; dar de coces a; **to kick down** echar abajo a puntapiés; **to kick in** romper a puntapiés; **to kick out** dar la patada a, echar a puntapiés a la calle; echar, despedir; **to kick up** (slang) armar (*p.ej., un bochinche*); *vn* cocear; dar culatazos, patear (*un arma de fuego*); (coll.) cocear, tirar coces, quejarse; **to kick about** (coll.) quejarse de; **to kick off** (football) dar el golpe de salida
**kickback** ['kɪk,bæk] *s* (coll.) contragolpe; (slang) devolución de cosas robadas; (slang) devolución estipulada de parte de un salario o pago, porcentaje devuelto de un salario o pago
**kickoff** ['kɪk,ɔf] o ['kɪk,ɑf] *s* (football) saque, golpe de salida, puntapié inicial
**kickshaw** ['kɪk,ʃɔ] *s* bocado delicado; bagatela, fruslería
**kid** [kɪd] *s* cabrito; cabritilla (*piel*); (coll.) chico; **kids** *spl* guantes o zapatos de cabritilla; (*pret & pp:* **kidded;** *ger:* **kidding**) *va* (slang) embromar; **to kid oneself** (slang) hacerse ilusiones; *vn* (slang) bromearse; **I was only kidding** (slang) lo decía en broma
**kidder** ['kɪdər] *s* (slang) bromista
**kid-glove** ['kɪd'glʌv] *adj* ceremonioso; quisquilloso
**kid gloves** *spl* guantes de cabritilla; **to handle with kid gloves** tratar con suma cautela y discreción
**kidnap** ['kɪdnæp] (*pret & pp:* **-naped** o **-napped;** *ger:* **-naping** o **-napping**) *va* secuestrar
**kidnaper** o **kidnapper** ['kɪd,næpər] *s* secuestrador, ladrón de niños
**kidney** ['kɪdnɪ] *s* (anat.) riñón; (cook.) riñones; carácter, natural; clase, especie
**kidney bean** *s* (bot.) judía de España, judía escarlata; (bot.) frijol, habichuela, judía
**kidney ore** *s* (min.) riñón
**kidney stone** *s* (path.) cálculo renal
**kidskin** ['kɪd,skɪn] *s* cabritilla
**kill** [kɪl] *s* matanza; ataque final (*de la jauría, el ejército, una fiera, etc.*); arroyo, riachuelo; (hunt.) caza, piezas; **for the kill** para dar muerte; para el golpe final; *va* matar (*a una*

*persona o animal; el fuego, la luz, el hambre, el tiempo, etc.*); ahogar (*un proyecto de ley*); quitar (*el sabor*); impresionar de modo irresistible; *vn* matar

**killdee** [ˈkɪl,di] o **killdeer** [ˈkɪl,dɪr] *s* (orn.) tildío, chorlito gritón peleador

**killer** [ˈkɪlər] *s* matador; (zool.) orca

**killer whale** *s* (zool.) orca

**killing** [ˈkɪlɪŋ] *s* matanza; (hunt.) caza, piezas; (coll.) gran ganancia; **to make a killing** (coll.) enriquecerse de golpe; *adj* matador; destructivo; quemador (*dícese, p.ej., de una helada*); abrumador (*trabajo*); irresistible; (coll.) de lo más ridículo

**kill-joy** [ˈkɪl,dʒɔɪ] *s* aguafiestas

**kiln** [kɪl] o [kɪln] *s* horno; *va* cocer, quemar o secar en horno

**kilo** [ˈkilo] o [ˈkɪlo] *s* (*pl:* **-los**) kilo o quilo (*kilogramo*); kilómetro o quilómetro

**kiloampere** [ˈkɪlo,æmpɪr] *s* (elec.) kiloamperio

**kilocalorie** [ˈkɪlə,kælərɪ] *s* (phys.) kilocaloría

**kilocycle** [ˈkɪlə,saɪkəl] *s* kilociclo

**kilogram** o **kilogramme** [ˈkɪləgræm] *s* kilogramo

**kilogrammeter** [ˈkɪləgræmˈmitər] *s* kilográmetro

**kiloliter** [ˈkɪlə,litər] *s* kilolitro

**kilometer** [ˈkɪlə,mitər] o [kɪˈlɑmɪtər] *s* kilómetro

**kilometric** [,kɪləˈmɛtrɪk] *adj* kilométrico

**kiloton** [ˈkɪlətʌn] *s* kilotonelada

**kilovolt** [ˈkɪlə,volt] *s* (elec.) kilovoltio

**kilowatt** [ˈkɪlə,wɑt] *s* (elec.) kilovatio

**kilowatt-hour** [ˈkɪlə,wɑtˈaʊr] *s* (*pl:* **kilowatt-hours**) (elec.) kilovatio-hora

**kilt** [kɪlt] *s* enagüillas; *va* (Scotch) arremangar; plegar

**kilter** [ˈkɪltər] *s* (coll.) buen estado, buena condición; **to be out of kilter** (coll.) estar descompuesto

**kilting** [ˈkɪltɪŋ] *s* pliegues solapados

**kimono** [kɪˈmonə] o [kɪˈmono] *s* (*pl:* **-nos**) quimono

**kin** [kɪn] *s* parentesco; parentela, familia, deudos; **near of kin** muy allegado; **next of kin** deudo más cercano, deudos más cercanos; **of kin** allegado; *adj* allegado

**kinaesthesia** [,kɪnɪsˈθiʒə] *s* cinestesia

**kind** [kaɪnd] *adj* bueno, bondadoso, amable; afectuoso (*saludo*); **to be kind to** ser bueno para con; *s* clase, especie, género, suerte; **a kind of** uno a modo de; **all kinds of** (slang) gran cantidad de; **in kind** en especie; en la misma moneda; **of a kind** de una misma clase; de mala muerte, de poco valor; **of the kind** por el estilo, semejante; **kind of** (coll.) algo, un poco, más bien, casi

**kindergarten** [ˈkɪndər,gɑrtən] *s* escuela de párvulos, jardín de la infancia

**kindergartener** o **kindergartner** [ˈkɪndər,gɑrtnər] *s* párvulo (*en las escuelas de párvulos*); parvulista (*maestro o maestra*)

**kind-hearted** [ˈkaɪndˈhɑrtɪd] *adj* de buen corazón, bondadoso

**kindle** [ˈkɪndəl] *va* encender; *vn* encenderse

**kindliness** [ˈkaɪndlɪnɪs] *s* bondad; benignidad

**kindling** [ˈkɪndlɪŋ] *s* encendimiento; leña

**kindling wood** *s* leña

**kindly** [ˈkaɪndlɪ] *adj* (*comp:* **-lier**; *super:* **-liest**) bondadoso; benigno, agradable; *adv* bondadosamente; benignamente, agradablemente; **to not take kindly to** no aceptar de buen grado, no poder sufrir

**kindness** [ˈkaɪndnɪs] *s* bondad; **have the kindness to** + *inf* tenga Vd. la bondad de + *inf*

**kindred** [ˈkɪndrɪd] *s* parentesco; parentela, familia; semejanza; *adj* allegado; semejante

**kine** [kaɪn] *spl* (archaic & dial.) vacas

**kinematic** [,kɪnɪˈmætɪk] *adj* cinemático; **kinematics** *ssg* cinemática

**kinematograph** [,kɪnɪˈmætəgræf] [,kɪnɪˈmætəgrɑf] *s* var. de **cinematograph**

**kinescope** [ˈkɪnɪskop] *s* (trademark) cinescopio

**kinesthesia** [,kɪnɪsˈθiʒə] *s* cinestesia

**kinesthetic** [,kɪnɪsˈθɛtɪk] *adj* cinestésico

**kinetic** [kɪˈnɛtɪk] o [kaɪˈnɛtɪk] *adj* cinético; **kinetics** *ssg* cinética

**kinetic energy** *s* (phys.) energía cinética, energía viva

**kinfolk** [ˈkɪn,fok] *spl* (dial.) var. de **kinsfolk**

**king** [kɪŋ] *s* rey; (cards, chess & fig.) rey; (checkers) dama; **Kings** *spl* (Bib.) el libro de los Reyes (*uno de dos libros del Antiguo Testamento protestante; uno de cuatro libros del Antiguo Testamento católico*)

**King Arthur** *s* el rey Artús

**kingbird** [ˈkɪŋ,bʌrd] *s* (orn.) tirano, pecho amarillo

**kingbolt** [ˈkɪŋ,bolt] *s* pivote central; (rail.) perno pinzote

**king crab** *s* (zool.) cangrejo bayoneta

**kingcraft** [ˈkɪŋ,kræft] o [ˈkɪŋ,krɑft] *s* arte de reinar

**kingcup** [ˈkɪŋ,kʌp] *s* (bot.) hierba velluda; (bot.) botón de oro; (bot.) hierba centella

**kingdom** [ˈkɪŋdəm] *s* reino

**kingfish** [ˈkɪŋ,fɪʃ] *s* (ichth.) pez grande comestible (*Menticirrhus nebulosus; Genyonemus lineatus; Sierra cavalla*)

**kingfisher** [ˈkɪŋ,fɪʃər] *s* (orn.) martín pescador

**King James Version** *s* traducción de la Biblia que mandó hacer el rey Jacobo de Inglaterra (*1611*)

**kinglet** [ˈkɪŋlɪt] *s* reyezuelo; (orn.) reyezuelo

**kingly** [ˈkɪŋlɪ] *adj* (*comp:* **-lier**; *super:* **-liest**) real, regio; noble, digno de un rey; *adv* regiamente; noblemente, con dignidad real

**king of arms** *s* (her.) rey de armas

**king of beasts** *s* rey de los animales (*león*)

**king of birds** *s* rey de las aves (*águila*)

**kingpin** [ˈkɪŋ,pɪn] *s* bolo de adelante (*en el juego de bolos*); pivote central; (aut.) pivote de dirección; (coll.) persona principal

**king post** *s* pendolón

**king's English** *s* inglés castizo

**king's evil** *s* escrófula

**kingship** [ˈkɪŋʃɪp] *s* dignidad real; reino (*territorio gobernado por un rey*)

**king-size** [ˈkɪŋ,saɪz] *adj* de tamaño largo (*cigarrillo*)

**king snake** *s* (zool.) coralilla

**king's ransom** *s* riquezas de Creso

**King's Speech** *s* discurso de la corona

**king truss** *s* armadura de pendolón

**kink** [kɪŋk] *s* enroscadura (*de cabo, cuerda, pelo, etc.*); tortícolis (*dolor*); chifladura, manía; *va* enroscar; *vn* enroscarse

**kinkajou** [ˈkɪŋkədʒu] *s* (zool.) quincayú, martucha

**kinky** [ˈkɪŋkɪ] *adj* (*comp:* **-ier**; *super:* **-iest**) enroscado, encarrujado

**kino** [ˈkino] *s* quino

**kino gum** *s* goma quino

**kinsfolk** [ˈkɪnz,fok] *spl* parentela, familia, deudos

**kinship** [ˈkɪnʃɪp] *s* parentesco; correspondencia, semejanza

**kinsman** [ˈkɪnzmən] *s* (*pl:* **-men**) pariente

**kinswoman** [ˈkɪnz,wʊmən] *s* (*pl:* **-women**) parienta

**kiosk** [kɪˈɑsk] o [ˈkaɪɑsk] *s* quiosco (*para vender periódicos, flores, etc.*); [kɪˈɑsk] *s* quiosco (*pabellón de gusto oriental en un jardín*)

**kip** [kɪp] *s* piel de res pequeña; kilolibra

**kipper** [ˈkɪpər] *s* macho del salmón durante o después de la época del celo; salmón o arenque acecinados o salados; *va* acecinar (*el salmón o el arenque*)

**Kirghiz** [kɪrˈgiz] *s* (*pl:* **-ghiz** o **-ghizes**) kirguís

**kirk** [kʌrk] *s* (Scotch) iglesia; **the Kirk** la iglesia nacional de Escocia (*de la secta presbiteriana*)

**kirmess** [ˈkʌrmɛs] *s* var. de **kermess**

**kirtle** [ˈkʌrtəl] *s* (archaic) falda, ropón

**kismet** [ˈkɪzmɛt] o [ˈkɪsmɛt] *s* destino, sino

**kiss** [kɪs] *s* beso; roce; pelo, retruco (*en el billar*); merengue, dulce; *va* besar; acariciar (*rozar suavemente*); **to kiss away** borrar con besos (*p.ej., las penas de otra persona*); *vn* besar; besarse; retrucar (*en el billar*)

**kisser** [ˈkɪsər] *s* besador; (slang) bozo, pico, hocico, rostro

**kissing bug** *s* (ent.) reduvio

**kit** [kɪt] *s* equipaje (*del viajero*); pertrechos o equipo (*del soldado*); avíos; herramental, cartera de herramientas; conjunto de piezas ne-

cesarias para construir una radio, un aeromodelo, etc.; balde, cubo, tineta; gatito; pequeño violín; (coll.) juego, lote, grupo; **the whole kit and caboodle** (coll.) la totalidad, el conjunto; (*cap.*) *s* abr. de **Catherine** y **Christopher**
**kitchen** [ˈkɪtʃən] *s* cocina
**kitchenette** [ˌkɪtʃəˈnɛt] *s* cocinilla, cocina pequeña
**kitchen garden** *s* huerto
**kitchenmaid** [ˈkɪtʃənˌmed] *s* pincha, ayudanta de cocina
**kitchen midden** [ˈmɪdən] *s* (anthrop.) acumulación de basura (*en o cerca de las viviendas prehistóricas*)
**kitchen police** *s* (mil.) trabajo de cocina; (mil.) pinches
**kitchen range** *s* cocina económica
**kitchen sink** *s* fregadero
**kitchenware** [ˈkɪtʃənˌwɛr] *s* chirimbolos de cocina, utensilios de cocina
**kite** [kaɪt] *s* cometa (*juguete*); (orn.) milano; *vn* (coll.) deslizarse rápidamente
**kite balloon** *s* globo cometa
**kith and kin** [kɪθ] *spl* deudos y amigos; parientes
**kitten** [ˈkɪtən] *s* gatito
**kittenish** [ˈkɪtənɪʃ] *adj* juguetón, retozón; coquetón
**kittiwake** [ˈkɪtɪwek] *s* (orn.) risa (*especie de gaviota*)
**kitty** [ˈkɪtɪ] *s* (*pl:* **-ties**) minino, gatito; polla, puesta (*en los juegos de naipes*); **kitty, kitty!** ¡miz, miz!; (*cap.*) *s* nombre abreviado de **Katherine**
**kiwi** [ˈkiwɪ] *s* (*pl:* **-wis**) (orn.) kiwi
**K.K.K.** abr. de **Ku Klux Klan**
**kl.** abr. de **kiloliter**
**klaxon** [ˈklæksən] *s* claxon
**kleptomania** [ˌklɛptoˈmenɪə] *s* cleptomanía
**kleptomaniac** [ˌklɛptoˈmenɪæk] *adj* & *s* cleptómano
**klieg light** [klig] *s* lámpara klieg
**klystron** [ˈklaɪstrən] *s* (trademark) klistrón
**km.** abr. de **kilometer** o **kilometers**
**knack** [næk] *s* tino, tranquillo; costumbre, hábito
**knapsack** [ˈnæpˌsæk] *s* mochila; *adj* de mochila, p.ej., **knapsack spray** pulverizador de mochila
**knapweed** [ˈnæpˌwid] *s* (bot.) centaura negra
**knave** [nev] *s* bribón, pícaro; sota (*en los naipes*); (archaic) criado, mozo; (archaic) villano
**knavery** [ˈnevərɪ] *s* (*pl:* **-ies**) bribonería, picardía, bellaquería
**knavish** [ˈnevɪʃ] *adj* bribón, pícaro, bellaco
**knead** [nid] *va* amasar, sobar
**knee** [ni] *s* (anat.) rodilla; codillo (*de los cuadrúpedos*); rodillera (*p.ej., de los pantalones*); ángulo, codo, escuadra; **to bring to one's knees** rendir, vencer; **to be on the knees of the gods** depender sólo de Dios o de la voluntad divina; **to go down on one's knees** caer de rodillas; **to go down on one's knees to** implorar de rodillas
**knee action** *s* (aut.) acción de rodilla, acción independiente
**knee-action wheel** [ˈniˌækʃən] *s* (aut.) rueda con acción de rodilla, rueda independiente
**knee brace** *s* esquinal
**knee breeches** *spl* pantalones cortos
**kneecap** [ˈniˌkæp] *s* (anat.) rótula, choquezuela; rodillera (*abrigo de la rodilla*)
**knee-deep** [ˈniˈdip] *adj* metido hasta las rodillas
**knee-high** [ˈniˈhaɪ] *adj* que llega hasta la rodilla
**knee-high to a grasshopper** *adj* diminuto, liliputiense
**kneehole** [ˈniˌhol] *s* hueco para introducir cómodamente las piernas
**knee jerk** *s* (med.) reflejo rotuliano o patelar
**kneel** [nil] (*pret & pp:* **knelt** o **kneeled**) *vn* arrodillarse; estar arrodillado
**kneepad** [ˈniˌpæd] *s* rodillera (*abrigo de la rodilla*)
**kneepan** [ˈniˌpæn] *s* (anat.) rótula, choquezuela
**knee swell** *s* (mus.) rodillera (*del órgano*)
**knell** [nɛl] *s* doble, toque a muerto; anuncio, mal agüero; **to toll the knell of** anunciar el fin de; *va* proclamar a toque de campana; convocar o llamar a toque de campana; *vn* doblar, tocar a muerto; sonar tristemente
**knelt** [nɛlt] *pret & pp de* **kneel**
**knew** [nju] o [nu] *pret de* **know**
**Knickerbocker** [ˈnɪkərˌbɑkər] *s* descendiente de los fundadores holandeses de Nueva York; neoyorquino; **knickerbockers** *spl* pantalones de media pierna, calzones cortos
**knickers** [ˈnɪkərz] *spl* pantalones de media pierna, calzones cortos
**knickknack** [ˈnɪkˌnæk] *s* baratija, chuchería, bujería
**knife** [naɪf] *s* (*pl:* **knives**) cuchillo; (mach.) cuchilla; **to go under the knife** (coll.) operarse; *va* acuchillar; (slang) traicionar
**knife edge** *s* filo de cuchillo; arista, filo; eje de apoyo (*de una balanza*)
**knife plug** *s* (elec.) clavija a cuchilla
**knife sharpener** *s* afilador, afilón
**knife switch** *s* (elec.) interruptor de cuchilla
**knifing** [ˈnaɪfɪŋ] *s* cuchillada
**knight** [naɪt] *s* caballero; caballo (*en el ajedrez*); *va* armar caballero
**knight-errant** [ˈnaɪtˈɛrənt] *s* (*pl:* **knights-errant**) caballero andante
**knight-errantry** [ˈnaɪtˈɛrəntrɪ] *s* (*pl:* **-ries**) caballería andante; quijotada, acción quijotesca
**knighthood** [ˈnaɪthʊd] *s* caballería
**knightly** [ˈnaɪtlɪ] *adj* caballeroso, caballeresco; *adv* caballerosamente, caballerescamente
**Knight of the Rueful Countenance** *s* Caballero de la triste figura (*Don Quijote*)
**Knights of Columbus** *spl* caballeros de Colón (*asociación fraternal católica*)
**Knight Templar** *s* (*pl:* **Knights Templars**) Templario, caballero del Temple; (*pl:* **Knights Templar**) (U.S.A.) caballero templario
**knit** [nɪt] (*pret & pp:* **knitted** o **knit**; *ger:* **knitting**) *va* trabajar a punto de aguja; enlazar, unir; fruncir (*las cejas*); *vn* hacer calceta, hacer malla; trabarse, unirse; soldarse (*un hueso*)
**knit goods** *spl* géneros de punto
**knitting** [ˈnɪtɪŋ] *s* trabajo de punto
**knitting machine** *s* máquina de hacer media, máquina de hacer punto, máquina para punto
**knitting needle** *s* aguja de media, aguja de hacer media
**knitwear** [ˈnɪtˌwɛr] *s* géneros de punto
**knob** [nɑb] *s* bulto, protuberancia; botón, tirador (*de puerta*); perilla o botón (*de aparato de radio*); colina o montaña redondeada
**knobby** [ˈnɑbɪ] *adj* (*comp:* **-bier**; *super:* **-biest**) nudoso; redondeado; montañoso
**knock** [nɑk] *s* golpe; toque, llamada; aldabonazo; golpeteo; pistoneo (*del motor de combustión interna*); (slang) censura, crítica ‖ *va* golpear; golpetear; (slang) censurar, criticar; **to knock down** derribar (*de un golpe, puñetazo, etc.*); vencer; hincar; roblar; rematar (*al mejor postor*); desarmar, desmontar (*un aparato o máquina*); **to knock off** hacer saltar a fuerza de golpes; suspender (*el trabajo*); rebajar (*del precio*); poner fin a; (slang) matar; **to knock out** agotar; (box.) poner fuera de combate; **to knock together** construir, armar o montar precipitadamente ‖ *vn* tocar, llamar; pistonear, golpear (*el motor de combustión interna*); (slang) censurar, criticar; **to knock about** (coll.) andar vagando, vagabundear; **to knock at** tocar a, llamar a (*la puerta*); **to knock against** dar contra, tropezar con; **to knock off** dejar de trabajar; (slang) morir
**knockabout** [ˈnɑkəˌbaʊt] *adj* para usos generales; turbulento, tumultuoso; *s* (naut.) yate pequeño (*sin bauprés*)
**knockdown** [ˈnɑkˌdaʊn] *adj* abrumador, irresistible; entregado en piezas sueltas (*listo para armarse o montarse*); desarmable; mínimo (*precio a que se venderá una cosa en subasta*); *s* golpe abrumador; derribo; cosa desmontada, cosa entregada en piezas (*lista para armarse o montarse*)
**knocker** [ˈnɑkər] *s* llamador; aldaba; (slang) criticón
**knock-kneed** [ˈnɑkˌnid] *adj* patizambo, zambo
**knockout** [ˈnɑkˌaʊt] *s* golpe decisivo, puñeta-

zo decisivo; (box.) (el) fuera de combate, knock-out; (elec.) agujero ciego, destapadero; (slang) real moza

**knockout drops** *spl* (slang) gotas narcóticas

**knoll** [nol] *s* mambla, otero; toque de campana; *va* anunciar a toque de campana; *vn* doblar, tocar a muerto

**Knossos** [ˈnɑsəs] *s* Cnosos

**knot** [nɑt] *s* nudo; lazo (*adorno*); lazo matrimonial; corrillo, grupo; calambre (*de un músculo*); (naut.) nudo; canut (*Calidris canutus*); chorlo rojizo (*Calidris canutus rufus*); (fig.) nudo (*enlace; punto difícil*); **to get a knot in one's throat** hacérsele a uno un nudo en la garganta; (*pret & pp:* **knotted**; *ger:* **knotting**) *va* anudar; fruncir (*las cejas*); *vn* anudarse

**knotgrass** [ˈnɑtˌgræs] o [ˈnɑtˌgrɑs] *s* (bot.) centinodia, sanguinaria mayor

**knothole** [ˈnɑtˌhol] *s* agujero (*que deja en la madera un nudo al desprenderse*)

**knotted** [ˈnɑtɪd] *adj* anudado, nudoso

**knotty** [ˈnɑtɪ] *adj* (*comp:* **-tier**; *super:* **-tiest**) nudoso; (fig.) espinoso, difícil

**knotty brake** *s* (bot.) helecho macho

**know** [no] *s* (coll.) conocimiento; **to be in the know** (coll.) estar enterado, tener informes secretos; (*pret:* **knew**; *pp:* **known**) *va & vn* saber (*tener conocimiento por medio de la razón*); conocer (*tener conocimiento por medio de los sentidos; entender, reconocer; distinguir*); **to know best** ser el mejor juez, saber lo que más conviene; **to know how to** + *inf* saber + *inf;* **to know it all** (coll.) sabérselo todo; **to know of** saber de, tener noticia de; **to know what one is doing** obrar con conocimiento de causa; **to know what's what** (coll.) saber cuántas son cinco; **to not know what it's all about** (coll.) no saber cuántas son cinco, estar a obscuras; **You ought to know better** Deberías tener vergüenza

**knowable** [ˈnoəbəl] *adj* conocible

**know-how** [ˈnoˌhaʊ] *s* destreza, habilidad, maña

**knowing** [ˈno·ɪŋ] *adj* entendido, inteligente; astuto, sutil; de inteligencia, de complicidad

**knowingly** [ˈno·ɪŋlɪ] *adv* a sabiendas; con conocimiento de causa

**know-it-all** [ˈno·ɪtˌɔl] *adj* sabidillo, sabihondo; *s* sabidillo, sabihondo, sábelotodo

**knowledge** [ˈnɑlɪdʒ] *s* el saber (*facultad*); conocimiento; conocimientos; **to be a matter of common knowledge** ser notorio; **to have a thorough knowledge of** conocer a fondo; **to my knowledge** según mi leal saber y entender; que yo sepa; **to the best of my knowledge** según mi leal saber y entender; **with full knowledge** con conocimiento de causa; **without my knowledge** sin mi noticia, sin saberlo yo

**knowledgeable** [ˈnɑlɪdʒəbəl] *adj* (coll.) conocedor, inteligente

**known** [non] *pp de* **know**

**know-nothing** [ˈnoˌnʌθɪŋ] *s* ignorante; **Know-Nothing** *s* (U.S.A.) partido político que quería alejar del gobierno a todos los individuos de nacimiento extranjero; (U.S.A.) miembro de este partido

**knuckle** [ˈnʌkəl] *s* nudillo; jarrete (*de la res*); (mach.) junta de charnela; **knuckles** *spl* bóxer; **to rap the knuckles of** dar con la badila en los nudillos a; *vn* tocar con los nudillos en el suelo; **to knuckle down** someterse, darse por vencido; trabajar con ahinco; **to knuckle under** someterse, darse por vencido

**knuckle joint** *s* (mach.) junta articulada, unión de gozne

**knurl** [nʌrl] *s* nudo, protuberancia; moleteado, gráfila; *va* moletear, cerrillar (*las piezas de moneda*)

**knurly** [ˈnʌrlɪ] *adj* (*comp:* **-ier**; *super:* **-iest**) nudoso; moleteado

**k.o.** abr. de **knockout**

**koala** [koˈɑlə] *s* (zool.) coala

**kobold** [ˈkobɑld] o [ˈkobold] *s* duende; gnomo

**kodak** [ˈkodæk] *s* (trademark) kodak; *va & vn* fotografiar con kodak

**K. of C.** abr. de **Knights of Columbus**

**kohl** [kol] *s* alcohol (*polvo negro para teñir los párpados y las pestañas*)

**kohlrabi** [ˈkolˌrɑbɪ] *s* (*pl:* **-bies**) (bot.) colirrábano

**kola** [ˈkolə] *s* (bot.) árbol de la cola; nuez de cola; (pharm.) nuez de cola

**kola nut** *s* nuez de cola

**kolinsky** [koˈlɪnskɪ] *s* (*pl:* **-skies**) (zool.) visón de Siberia (*animal y piel*)

**koodoo** [ˈkudu] *s* var. de **kudu**

**kopeck** o **kopek** [ˈkopɛk] *s* copeck (*moneda rusa*)

**Koran** [koˈrɑn] o [ˈkoræn] *s* Alcorán, Corán

**Koranic** [koˈrænɪk] *adj* alcoránico

**Koranist** [koˈrænɪst] *s* alcoranista

**Korea** [koˈriə] *s* Corea

**Korean** [koˈriən] *adj & s* coreano

**Korea Strait** *s* el estrecho de Corea

**kosher** [ˈkoʃər] *adj* autorizado por la ley judía; (slang) genuino

**kotow** [ˈkoˈtaʊ] *s & vn* var. de **kowtow**

**koumis** [ˈkumɪs] *s* var. de **kumiss**

**kowtow** [ˈkaʊˈtaʊ] o [ˈkoˈtaʊ] *s* homenaje de los chinos (*postrándose con la frente en el suelo*); *vn* arrodillarse y tocar el suelo con la frente (*en señal de homenaje*); doblegarse servilmente, humillarse

**K.P.** abr. de **Kitchen Police**

**kraal** [krɑl] *s* población de hotentotes; corral, redil (*del África austral*)

**Kremlin** [ˈkrɛmlɪn] *s* Kremlín

**kris** [kris] *s* var. de **creese**

**Kriss Kringle** [ˈkrɪs ˈkrɪŋgəl] *s* San Nicolás, Papá Noel

**kruller** [ˈkrʌlər] *s* var. de **cruller**

**krypton** [ˈkrɪptɑn] *s* (chem.) criptón

**Kt.** abr. de **Knight**

**K.T.** abr. de **Knight Templar**

**kudos** [ˈkjudɑs] *s* (coll.) renombre, gloria

**kudu** [ˈkudu] *s* (zool.) cudú

**Ku-Klux** [ˈkjuˌklʌks] o **Ku Klux Klan** [klæn] *s* asociación secreta norteamericana que combate a los negros, los judíos, los católicos y los extranjeros

**kulak** [kuˈlɑk] *s* kulak (*campesino ruso acomodado*)

**kumiss** [ˈkumɪs] *s* cumís

**kümmel** [ˈkɪməl] *s* cúmel

**kumquat** [ˈkʌmkwɑt] *s* (bot.) kumquat (*naranjo chino: Fortunella japonica; su fruto*)

**Kurd** [kʌrd] o [kurd] *s* curdo

**Kurdish** [ˈkʌrdɪʃ] o [ˈkurdɪʃ] *adj* curdo; *s* curdo (*idioma*)

**Kurdistan** [ˌkʌrdɪˈstæn] o [ˌkurdɪˈstɑn] *s* el Curdistán

**Kurile Islands** [ˈkurɪl] *spl* islas Curiles

**Kurland** [ˈkurlənd] *s* var. de **Courland**

**kw.** abr. de **kilowatt**

**K.W.H.** abr. de **kilowatt-hour**

**Ky.** abr. de **Kentucky**

**kymograph** [ˈkaɪmogræf] o [ˈkaɪmogrɑf] *s* quimógrafo

**kyphosis** [kaɪˈfosɪs] *s* (path.) cifosis

# L

**L, l** [ɛl] *s* (*pl:* **L's, l's** [ɛlz]) duodécima letra del alfabeto inglés
**l.** abr. de **liter, line, league, length,** y **lira** o **liras**
**L.** abr. de **Latin** y **Low**
**La.** abr. de **Louisiana**
**la** [lɑ] o [lə] *interj* ¡ ah!
**Lab.** abr. de **Labrador** y **Laborite**
**lab** [læb] *s* (coll.) laboratorio
**Laban** ['lebən] *s* (Bib.) Labán
**labarum** ['læbərəm] *s* (*pl:* **-ra** [rə]) lábaro; (hist.) lábaro
**labdanum** ['læbdənəm] *s* ládano
**label** ['lebəl] *s* rótulo, marbete, etiqueta; calificación, epíteto; (b.b.) tejuelo; (her.) lambel; (*pret & pp:* **-beled** o **-belled;** *ger:* **-beling** o **-belling**) *va* rotular, poner marbete o etiqueta a; calificar, apodar
**labellum** [lə'bɛləm] *s* (*pl:* **-la** [lə]) (bot.) labelo; (ent.) labela
**labial** ['lebɪəl] *adj & s* labial
**labialize** ['lebɪəlaɪz] *va* (phonet.) labializar
**labiate** ['lebɪet] o ['lebɪɪt] *adj* (anat., zool. & bot.) labiado; *s* (bot.) labiada
**labile** ['lebɪl] *adj* (chem.) lábil
**lability** [le'bɪlɪtɪ] *s* labilidad
**labiodental** [,lebɪo'dɛntəl] *adj & s* (phonet.) labiodental
**labium** ['lebɪəm] *s* (*pl:* **-a** [ə]) labio; (anat., bot. & zool.) labio
**labor** ['lebər] *s* labor, trabajo; tarea, faena; los obreros (*trabajo en contraposición de capital*); mano de obra (*trabajo de los obreros; remuneración del trabajo*); parto; **labors** *spl* esfuerzos; **to be in labor** estar de parto; *va* desarrollar (*p.ej., un concepto*) con nimiedad; *vn* trabajar; forcejar; estar de parto; trabajar (*un buque*) contra las olas y el viento; moverse penosamente; **to labor under** estar sufriendo (*p.ej., una enfermedad*); tener que luchar contra; **to labor under a mistake** estar equivocado
**laboratory** ['læbərə,torɪ] *s* (*pl:* **-ries**) laboratorio
**labor camp** *s* campo de trabajo
**Labor Day** *s* (U.S.A.) día del trabajo (*primer lunes de septiembre*)
**labored** ['lebərd] *adj* dificultoso, penoso; forzado; torpe, lento; artificial, premioso
**laborer** ['lebərər] *s* trabajador, obrero; bracero, jornalero, peón
**laborious** [lə'borɪəs] *adj* laborioso
**Laborite** ['lebəraɪt] *s* laborista
**labor-management** ['lebər'mænɪdʒmənt] *adj* obrero-patronal
**labor-saving** ['lebər,sevɪŋ] *adj* economizador de trabajo
**labors of Hercules** *spl* (myth.) trabajos de Hércules
**labor turnover** *s* número de obreros que se emplean para reemplazar a los que han dejado el trabajo; proporción entre los obreros que trabajan transitoriamente y el número total de obreros (*en una empresa*)
**labor union** *s* unión de obreros
**labour** ['lebər] *s, va & vn* (Brit.) var. de **labor**
**Labour Party** *s* (Brit.) partido laborista, laborismo británico
**Labrador** ['læbrədər] *s* el Labrador
**labradorite** ['læbrədəraɪt] o [,læbrə'doraɪt] *s* (mineral.) labradorita
**labrum** ['lebrəm] o ['læbrəm] *s* (*pl:* **-bra** [brə]) (zool.) labro
**laburnum** [lə'bʌrnəm] *s* (bot.) lluvia de oro, codeso
**labyrinth** ['læbɪrɪnθ] *s* laberinto; (anat. & mach.) laberinto; **the Labyrinth** (myth.) el laberinto de Creta
**labyrinthine** [,læbɪ'rɪnθɪn] *adj* laberíntico
**lac** [læk] *s* laca (*resina*)
**lac dye** *s* color de laca (*para usos tintóreos*)
**lace** [les] *s* encaje; cordón o lazo (*de zapato, corsé, etc.*); galón, galoncillo; *va* adornar con encaje, adornar con randas; atar (*los zapatos, el corsé, etc.*); enlazar, entrelazar; rayar (*con líneas finas*); azotar, dar una paliza a; echar licor a (*p.ej., el café*); *vn* atarse; apretarse mucho el corsé; **to lace into** arremeter contra; poner de oro y azul
**lace bug** *s* (ent.) chinche de encaje
**Lacedaemon** [,læsə'dimən] *s* la Lacedemonia
**Lacedaemonian** [,læsədɪ'monɪən] *adj & s* lacedemón o lacedemonio
**laceman** ['lesmən] *s* (*pl:* **-men**) encajero
**lacerate** ['læsəret] *va* lacerar; (fig.) herir (*p.ej., las sensibilidades de una persona*)
**laceration** [,læsə'reʃən] *s* laceración
**lacewing** ['les,wɪŋ] *s* (ent.) crisopo
**lacewoman** ['les,wumən] *s* (*pl:* **-women**) encajera
**lacework** ['les,wʌrk] *s* encaje, obra de encaje
**laches** ['lætʃɪz] *s* dejadez, flojedad, descuido; (law) culpa lata
**Lachesis** ['lækɪsɪs] *s* (myth.) Laquesis
**lachryma** ['lækrɪmə] *s* (*pl:* **-mas** o **-mae** [mi]) lágrima
**Lachryma Christi** ['krɪstɪ] o ['krɪstaɪ] *s* lácrima cristi (*vino*)
**lachrymal** ['lækrɪməl] *adj* lagrimal; (anat.) lagrimal; **lachrymals** *spl* (anat.) glándulas lagrimales
**lachrymal caruncle** *s* (anat.) carúncula lagrimal
**lachrymal gland** *s* (anat.) glándula lagrimal
**lachrymal vase** *s* vaso lacrimatorio
**lachrymatory** ['lækrɪmə,torɪ] *adj* lacrimatorio; lagrimal; *s* (*pl:* **-ries**) lacrimatorio (*vaso*); (hum.) pañuelo
**lachrymose** ['lækrɪmos] *adj* lacrimoso
**lacing** ['lesɪŋ] *s* cordón o lazo (*de zapato, corsé, etc.*); galón o galoncillo; paliza, tunda
**lacinia** [lə'sɪnɪə] *s* (*pl:* **-ae** [i] o **-as**) (bot.) lacinia
**laciniate** [lə'sɪnɪet] o [lə'sɪnɪɪt] *adj* (bot.) laciniado
**lac insect** *s* (ent.) cochinilla de la laca
**lack** [læk] *s* carencia; falta; deficiencia; **to supply the lack** suplir la falta; *va* carecer de; necesitar, faltarle a uno, hacerle a uno falta, p.ej., **I lack money** me falta dinero, me hace falta dinero; *vn* faltar
**lackadaisical** [,lækə'dezɪkəl] *adj* lánguido, indiferente
**lackaday** ['lækə,de] *interj* ¡ ay de mí!
**lackey** ['lækɪ] *s* lacayo; secuaz servil; *va* servir; doblegarse ante
**lacking** ['lækɪŋ] *adj* defectuoso; carente; falto de; **to be lacking** faltar; **lacking in** carente de, falto de; *prep* sin, no teniendo
**lackluster** ['læk,lʌstər] *adj* deslustrado, deslucido, inexpresivo
**Laconia** [lə'konɪə] *s* Laconia
**Laconian** [lə'konɪən] *adj & s* laconio
**laconic** [lə'kɑnɪk] *adj* lacónico
**laconically** [lə'kɑnɪkəlɪ] *adv* lacónicamente
**laconism** ['lækənɪzəm] *s* laconismo
**lacquer** ['lækər] *s* laca (*barniz y objeto barnizado; color*); *va* laquear, barnizar con laca
**lacquer ware** *s* lacas, objetos de laca
**lacrimal** ['lækrɪməl] *adj* var. de **lachrymal**
**lacrosse** [lə'krɔs] o [lə'krɑs] *s* (sport) crosse (*juego de pelota del Canadá*); **to play lacrosse** jugar a la crosse
**lactam** ['læktæm] *s* (biochem.) lactama
**lactase** ['læktes] *s* (biochem.) lactasa
**lactate** ['læktet] *s* (chem.) lactato

**lactation** [læk'teʃən] *s* lactancia
**lacteal** ['læktɪəl] *adj* lácteo; quilífero; *s* (anat.) vaso quilífero
**lacteous** ['læktɪəs] *adj* lácteo
**lactescence** [læk'tɛsəns] *s* lactescencia
**lactescent** [læk'tɛsənt] *adj* lactescente; (bot.) lactescente
**lactic** ['læktɪk] *adj* láctico
**lactic acid** *s* (chem.) ácido láctico
**lactiferous** [læk'tɪfərəs] *adj* lactífero
**lactoflavin** [,lækto'flevɪn] *s* lactoflavina
**lactometer** [læk'tɑmɪtər] *s* lactómetro
**lactone** ['lækton] *s* (chem.) lactona
**lactose** ['læktos] *s* (chem.) lactosa
**lacuna** [lə'kjunə] *s* (*pl:* **-nas** o **-nae** [ni]) laguna, hueco; (anat., bot. & zool.) laguna
**lacunar** [lə'kjunər] *s* (arch.) lagunar
**lacustrine** [lə'kʌstrɪn] *adj* lacustre; (geol.) lacustre
**lacy** ['lesɪ] *adj* (*comp:* **-ier**; *super:* **-iest**) de encaje; etéreo, diáfano
**lad** [læd] *s* muchacho; (coll.) hombre
**ladder** ['lædər] *s* escala, escalera; (fig.) escalón; carrera (*en las medias*)
**ladder truck** *s* carro de escaleras de incendio
**laddie** ['lædɪ] *s* (Scotch) muchacho
**lade** [led] (*pret:* **laded**; *pp:* **laden** o **laded**) *va* cargar; sacar, echar fuera, servir (*un líquido*) con cucharón; *vn* tomar cargamento
**laden** ['ledən] *adj* cargado; *pp de* **lade**
**Ladin** [lə'din] *s* ladino (*variedad de romancho*)
**lading** ['ledɪŋ] *s* carga
**Ladino** [lɑ'dino] *s* (*pl:* **-nos**) ladino (*mestizo hispanohablante; lenguaje híbrido hebreorromántico de ciertos judíos*)
**ladle** ['ledəl] s cazo, cucharón; (found.) cazo de colada, caldero de colada; *va* sacar o servir con cucharón; llevar en cucharón
**lady** ['ledɪ] *s* (*pl:* **-dies**) señora; dama
**ladybird** ['ledɪ,bʌrd] o **ladybug** ['ledɪ,bʌg] *s* (ent.) mariquita, vaca de San Antón
**lady bullfighter** *s* señorita-torera
**Lady Day** *s* (eccl.) anunciación (*25 de marzo*)
**ladyfinger** ['ledɪ,fɪŋgər] *s* melindre, bizcocho de plantilla
**lady in waiting** *s* camarera (*que sirve a una reina o princesa*)
**lady-killer** ['ledɪ,kɪlər] *s* (slang) matador de mujeres, ladrón de corazones, tenorio
**ladylike** ['ledɪ,laɪk] *adj* afeminado; delicado, elegante; **to be ladylike** ser (*una mujer*) muy dama
**ladylove** ['ledɪ,lʌv] *s* amada, amiga querida
**Lady of the Lake** *s* Doncella del Lago (*del ciclo bretón del rey Artús*)
**lady's-comb** ['ledɪz'kom] *s* (bot.) peine de Venus
**ladyship** ['ledɪʃɪp] *s* señoría (*título y persona*)
**lady-slipper** ['ledɪ,slɪpər] o **lady's-slipper** ['ledɪz,slɪpər] *s* (bot.) chapín, zapatilla de señorita
**lady's maid** *s* doncella
**lady's man** *s* perico entre ellas
**lady's-mantle** ['ledɪz'mæntəl] *s* (bot.) alquimila, estela
**lady's-thumb** ['ledɪz'θʌm] *s* (bot.) pesicaria, duraznillo
**lag** [læg] *s* retraso; (*pret & pp:* **lagged**; *ger:* **lagging**) *vn* retrasarse; quedarse atrás, rezagarse
**lagena** [lə'dʒinə] *s* (*pl:* **-nae** [ni]) (zool.) lagena
**lager** ['lɑgər] o **lager beer** *s* cerveza reposada, cerveza de conserva
**laggard** ['lægərd] *adj & s* rezagado, perezoso
**lagniappe** o **lagnappe** [læn'jæp] *s* adehala, yapa
**lagoon** [lə'gun] *s* laguna
**lag screw** *s* tirafondo
**laic** ['leɪk] *adj & s* laico
**laicization** [,leɪsɪ'zeʃən] *s* laicización
**laicize** ['leɪsaɪz] *va* laicizar
**laid** [led] *pret & pp de* **lay**; *adj* vergueteado; **laid up** almacenado, guardado; ahorrado; encamado (*por estar enfermo*); (naut.) inactivo
**lain** [len] *pp de* **lie**
**lair** [lɛr] *s* cubil, cama
**laird** [lɛrd] *s* (Scotch) dueño de tierras
**laisser faire** o **laissez faire** [,lɛse'fɛr] *s* laisser faire (*doctrina según la cual los poderes públicos deben intervenir lo menos posible en los intereses de los particulares y de las asociaciones*)
**laissez-faire** [,lɛse'fɛr] *adj* de laisser faire
**laity** ['leɪtɪ] *s* (*pl:* **-ties**) legos
**Laius** ['leəs] *s* (myth.) Layo
**lake** [lek] *s* lago; laca (*materia colorante*)
**Lake Aral** ['ærəl] *s* el lago de Aral
**Lake Country** o **Lake District** *s* región de los lagos (*en el noroeste de Inglaterra*)
**lake dweller** *s* hombre lacustre
**lake dwelling** *s* habitación lacustre
**Lake of Constance** *s* el lago de Constanza
**Lake Ontario** [ɑn'tɛrɪo] *s* el lago Ontario
**Lake poets** *spl* lakistas (*Wordsworth, Coleridge y Southey*)
**Lake Superior** *s* el lago Superior
**lake trout** *s* (ichth.) trucha de los lagos
**Lam.** abr. de **Lamentations**
**lama** ['lɑmə] *s* lama (*sacerdote del Tibet*)
**Lamaism** ['lɑməɪzəm] *s* lamaísmo
**Lamaist** ['lɑməɪst] *adj & s* lamaísta
**Lamarckian** [lə'mɑrkɪən] *adj & s* lamarquista
**Lamarckianism** [lə'mɑrkɪənɪzəm] o **Lamarckism** [lə'mɑrkɪzəm] *s* lamarquismo
**lamasery** ['lɑmə,sɛrɪ] *s* (*pl:* **-ies**) lamasería
**lamb** [læm] *s* cordero; carne de cordero; piel de cordero; (fig.) cordero (*persona inocente, humilde*); (fig.) nene; **like a lamb** inocente, humilde; inocentemente, humildemente; **the Lamb** el Cordero (*Jesucristo*); *vn* parir (*la oveja*)
**lambaste** [læm'best] *va* (slang) dar una paliza a, azotar sin piedad; (slang) dar una jabonadura a
**lamb chop** *s* chuleta de cordero
**lambent** ['læmbənt] *adj* ondulante, lamiente (*llama*); centelleante (*ingenio, estilo*); suave (*luz*)
**Lambert** ['læmbərt] *s* Lamberto
**lambkin** ['læmkɪn] *s* corderito; (fig.) nenito
**Lamb of God** *s* Cordero de Dios, Divino Cordero
**lambrequin** ['læmbrəkɪn] *s* lambrequín, guardamalleta; (her.) lambrequín
**lambskin** ['læm,skɪn] *s* corderina, piel de cordero; corderillo (*adobado con su lana*)
**lame** [lem] *adj* cojo; molido, lastimado; pobre, débil, frívolo; *va* encojar; *vn* encojarse
**lamé** [læ'me] *s* lama (*tejido*)
**lame duck** *s* (coll.) persona incapacitada; (coll.) cosa inútil; (U.S.A.) diputado que no ha sido reelegido y espera el cese venidero
**lamella** [lə'mɛlə] *s* (*pl:* **-las** o **-lae** [li]) laminilla; (bot.) laminilla
**lamellar** [lə'mɛlər] o ['læmələr] o **lamellate** ['læməlet] o [lə'mɛlet] *adj* laminar
**lamellibranch** [lə'mɛlɪbræŋk] *adj & s* (zool.) lamelibranquio
**lameness** ['lemnɪs] *s* cojera; pobreza, debilidad, imperfección
**lament** [lə'mɛnt] *s* lamento; elegía; *va* lamentar; *vn* lamentarse
**lamentable** ['læməntəbəl] *adj* lamentable
**lamentably** ['læməntəblɪ] *adv* lamentablemente
**lamentation** [,læmən'teʃən] *s* lamentación; **Lamentations** *spl* (Bib.) Lamentaciones de Jeremías
**lamia** ['lemɪə] *s* (*pl:* **-as** o **-ae** [i]) (ichth. & myth.) lamia
**lamiaceous** [,lemɪ'eʃəs] *adj* (bot.) lamiáceo
**lamina** ['læmɪnə] *s* (*pl:* **-nae** [ni] o **-nas**) lámina; (anat., bot., geol. & zool.) lámina
**laminar** ['læmɪnər] *adj* laminar
**laminate** ['læmɪnet] *adj* laminado; *va* laminar
**lamination** [,læmɪ'neʃən] *s* laminación, laminado
**laminose** ['læmɪnos] *adj* laminoso
**Lammas** ['læməs] *s* (archaic) fiesta de la recolección de la cosecha; (eccl.) fiesta de San Pedro encadenado
**lammergeier** ['læmər,gaɪər] *s* (orn.) águila barbuda
**lamp** [læmp] *s* lámpara; (poet.) antorcha; (poet.) astro; **lamps** *spl* (slang) ojos
**lampadary** ['læmpə,dɛrɪ] *s* (*pl:* **-ies**) lampadario (*sacerdote; columna con lámparas*)
**lampblack** ['læmp,blæk] *s* negro de humo
**lamp chimney** *s* tubo, tubo de lámpara
**lamp cord** *s* (elec.) cordón de lámpara

**lamp holder** *s* (elec.) portalámparas
**lamplight** [ˈlæmp,laɪt] *s* luz de lámpara
**lamplighter** [ˈlæmp,laɪtər] *s* farolero; cerilla o rollo de papel (*que sirve para encender lámparas o faroles*)
**lampoon** [læmˈpun] *s* pasquín, libelo; *va* pasquinar
**lampoonist** [læmˈpunɪst] *s* escritor de pasquines, libelista
**lamppost** [ˈlæmp,post] *s* poste de farol
**lamprey** [ˈlæmprɪ] *s* (ichth.) lamprea
**lamp shade** *s* pantalla de lámpara
**lampwick** [ˈlæmp,wɪk] *s* torcida, mecha de lámpara; (bot.) candilera
**lanate** [ˈlenet] *adj* lanado
**Lancastrian** [læŋˈkæstrɪən] *adj & s* lancasteriano
**lance** [læns] o [lɑns] *s* lanza; arpón de pesca; (surg.) lanceta; *va* alancear; (surg.) abrir con lanceta
**lance corporal** *s* (Brit.) soldado que hace las veces de cabo
**Lancelot** [ˈlænsəlɑt] o [ˈlɑnsəlɑt] *s* Lanzarote (*de la Mesa redonda*)
**lanceolate** [ˈlænsɪəlet] *adj* (bot.) lanceolado, alanceado
**lancer** [ˈlænsər] o [ˈlɑnsər] *s* lancero; **lancers** *spl* lanceros (*baile y música*)
**lance rest** *s* ristre
**lance sergeant** *s* (Brit.) cabo que hace las veces de sargento
**lancet** [ˈlænsɪt] o [ˈlɑnsɪt] *s* (surg.) lanceta; (arch.) ojiva de lanceta
**lancet arch** *s* (arch.) ojiva de lanceta
**lancewood** [ˈlæns,wʊd] o [ˈlɑns,wʊd] *s* (bot.) palo de lanza
**lancinate** [ˈlænsɪnet] *va* lancinar
**land** [lænd] *s* tierra; **by land** por tierra; **on land, on sea, and in the air** en tierra, mar y aire; **to see how the land lies** medir el terreno, ver el cariz que van tomando las cosas; *adj* terrestre; terral (*viento*); *va* desembarcar; coger (*un pez*); conducir (*un avión*) a tierra; (coll.) conseguir, obtener; *vn* desembarcar, saltar en tierra; arribar, aterrar; ir a dar, ir a parar; aterrizar (*un avión*); **to land on one's feet** caer de pies; **to land on one's head** caer de cabeza
**landau** [ˈlændɔ] o [ˈlændaʊ] *s* landó
**landaulet** o **landaulette** [,lændɔˈlɛt] *s* landolé; landolé automóvil
**land-based plane** [ˈlænd,best] *s* (aer.) avión con base en tierra
**land breeze** *s* terral
**landed** [ˈlændɪd] *adj* hacendado; que consiste en tierras; **landed property** bienes raíces
**landfall** [ˈlænd,fɔl] *s* (naut.) aterrada (*aproximación a tierra, vista de la costa*); (aer.) aterrizaje; costa o tierra vista desde el mar; tierra (*donde uno aborda*); derrumbamiento de tierra; herencia inesperada de tierras
**land grant** *s* donación de tierras
**land-grant college** o **university** [ˈlænd,grænt] o [ˈlænd,grɑnt] *s* (U.S.A.) centro docente fundado por el gobierno federal mediante una donación de tierras
**landgrave** [ˈlænd,grev] *s* landgrave o langrave
**landgraviate** [lændˈgrevɪɪt] *s* landgraviato
**landholder** [ˈlænd,holdər] *s* terrateniente
**landholding** [ˈlænd,holdɪŋ] *s* tenencia de tierra o tierras; *adj* hacendado
**landing** [ˈlændɪŋ] *s* aterraje (*de buque*); aterraje o aterrizaje (*de avión*); desembarco (*de pasajeros*); desembarcadero (*lugar para desembarcar*); desembarco o descanso (*de escalera*)
**landing beacon** *s* (aer.) radiofaro de aterrizaje
**landing craft** *s* (nav.) lancha de desembarco
**landing field** *s* (aer.) pista de aterrizaje
**landing force** *s* (nav.) compañía de desembarco
**landing gear** *s* (aer.) tren de aterrizaje
**landing net** *s* red con mango (*para sacar del agua un pez cogido en el anzuelo*)
**landing place** *s* apeadero, desembarcadero; descanso (*de escalera*)
**landing ship** *s* (nav.) buque de desembarco
**landing stage** *s* embarcadero flotante
**landing strip** *s* (aer.) faja de aterrizaje
**landlady** [ˈlænd,ledɪ] *s* (*pl:* **-dies**) dueña, casera; patrona (*de una casa de huéspedes*); mesonera, posadera
**landless** [ˈlændlɪs] *adj* sin tierras, que no posee tierras
**landlocked** [ˈlænd,lɑkt] *adj* cercado de tierra; que no tiene acceso al mar (*dícese de ciertos salmones*)
**landlord** [ˈlænd,lɔrd] *s* dueño, casero; patrón (*de una casa de huéspedes*); mesonero, posadero
**landlubber** [ˈlænd,lʌbər] *s* marinero de agua dulce; marinero matalote (*hombre de mar, torpe en su oficio*)
**landmark** [ˈlænd,mɑrk] *s* mojón (*señal en un camino que sirve de guía*); guía (*accidente del terreno que sirve de guía*); punto culminante, acontecimiento que hace época; (naut.) marca de reconocimiento
**land office** *s* oficina del catastro
**land-office business** [ˈlænd,ɔfɪs] o [ˈlænd,ɑfɪs] *s* (coll.) negocio de mucho movimiento
**land of make-believe** *s* reino de los sueños
**Land of Promise** *s* (Bib.) Tierra de promisión
**Land of the Midnight Sun** *s* tierra del sol de medianoche (*Noruega*)
**Land of the Rising Sun** *s* tierra del sol naciente (*el Japón*)
**landowner** [ˈlænd,onər] *s* terrateniente
**landownership** [ˈlænd,onərʃɪp] *s* tenencia de tierra o tierras
**land-poor** [ˈlænd,pʊr] *adj* rico de tierras y falto de dinero
**landscape** [ˈlændskep] *s* paisaje; (f.a.) paisaje; *va* ajardinar
**landscape architect** *s* arquitecto paisajista
**landscape gardener** *s* arquitecto de jardines, plantista, jardinero, adornista
**landscape painter** *s* paisajista, pintor paisajista
**landscapist** [ˈlændskepɪst] *s* paisajista
**Land's End** *s* Cabo Finisterre (*de la extremidad sudoccidental de Inglaterra*)
**landslide** [ˈlænd,slaɪd] *s* argayo, derrumbe, corrimiento; (fig.) victoria electoral arrolladora, mayoría de votos abrumadora
**landslip** [ˈlænd,slɪp] *s* (Brit.) argayo, derrumbe
**landsman** [ˈlændzmən] *s* (*pl:* **-men**) hombre de tierra; marinero matalote
**landward** [ˈlændwərd] *adj* de hacia tierra, de la parte de la tierra; *adv* hacia tierra, hacia la costa
**landwards** [ˈlændwərdz] *adv* hacia tierra, hacia la costa
**land wind** *s* terral
**lane** [len] *s* callejuela; carril (*camino muy estrecho*); faja (*de una carretera*); (aer. & naut.) derrotero, ruta, vía
**langsyne** [ˈlæŋˈsaɪn] *adv* (Scotch) hace mucho tiempo; *s* (Scotch) tiempo de antaño
**language** [ˈlæŋgwɪdʒ] *s* lenguaje; idioma, lengua (*lenguaje de un pueblo o nación*); jerga (*de un determinado grupo de personas*)
**language barrier** *s* barrera del idioma
**langued** [læŋd] *adj* (her.) linguado
**langue d'oc** [lɑ̃gˈdɑk] *s* lengua de oc, lenguadoque
**Languedocian** [,læŋgəˈdoʃən] *adj & s* languedociano
**langue d'oïl** [lɑ̃gdɔˈil] *s* lengua de oíl
**languid** [ˈlæŋgwɪd] *adj* lánguido
**languish** [ˈlæŋgwɪʃ] *vn* languidecer; afectar languidez; **to languish for** penar por, suspirar por
**languishing** [ˈlæŋgwɪʃɪŋ] *adj* lánguido; languescente
**languishment** [ˈlæŋgwɪʃmənt] *s* languidez; consumimiento; aspecto lánguido, manera lánguida
**languor** [ˈlæŋgər] *s* languidez
**languorous** [ˈlæŋgərəs] *adj* lánguido; enervante
**langur** [lʌŋˈgʊr] *s* (zool.) hanumán, mono sagrado de la India
**laniard** [ˈlænjərd] *s* var. de **lanyard**
**lank** [læŋk] *adj* descarnado, larguirucho; lacio (*cabello*)
**lanky** [ˈlæŋkɪ] *adj* (*comp:* **-ier;** *super:* **-iest**) descarnado, larguirucho
**lanner** [ˈlænər] *s* lanero (*halcón*)
**lanolin** [ˈlænəlɪn] o **lanoline** [ˈlænəlɪn] o [ˈlænəlin] *s* lanolina

**lansquenet** [ˈlænskənɛt] *s* lansquenete (*lancero de a pie; juego de naipes*)
**lantern** [ˈlæntərn] *s* linterna; linterna mágica; (arch. & mach.) linterna; (naut.) linterna (*fanal*); (zool.) linterna de Aristóteles
**lantern-jawed** [ˈlæntərnˌdʒɔd] *adj* chupado de cara
**lantern pinion** *s* (mach.) piñón de linterna
**lantern slide** *s* diapositiva, tira de vidrio
**lantern wheel** *s* (mach.) rueda de linterna
**lanthanum** [ˈlænθənəm] *s* (chem.) lantano
**lanyard** [ˈlænjərd] *s* (naut.) acollador; (arti.) cuerda y gancho de disparo
**Laocoön** [leˈɑkoɑn] *s* (myth.) Laocoonte
**Laodicean** [leˌɑdɪˈsiən] *adj* tibio e indiferente; *s* persona tibia e indiferente; cristiano tibio e indiferente
**Laotian** [leˈoʃən] *adj & s* laocio, laosiano
**lap** [læp] *s* regazo; falda; caída, doblez (*de un vestido*); traslapo; lametada; chapaleteo (*de las olas*); (mach.) recubrimiento (*de la válvula de corredera*); (sport) vuelta, etapa (*en las carreras*); **it is in the lap of the gods** eso sólo Dios lo sabe; **to live in the lap of luxury** vivir en el lujo, llevar una vida regalada; (*pret & pp:* **lapped;** *ger:* **lapping**) *va* traslapar; juntar a traslapo; envolver; beber con la lengua; lamer (*el arroyo las arenas*); (sport) llevar una vuelta o más de una vuelta de ventaja a; **to lap up** (slang) aceptar en el acto; *vn* traslapar; traslaparse (*dos o más cosas*); **to lap against** lamer (*el arroyo las arenas*); **to lap over** salir fuera; **to lap over into** extenderse hasta
**lapboard** [ˈlæpˌbord] *s* tabla faldera
**lap dog** *s* perro faldero
**lapel** [ləˈpɛl] *s* solapa
**lapful** [ˈlæpfʊl] *s* lo que cabe en el regazo, cabida del regazo
**lapidary** [ˈlæpɪˌdɛrɪ] *adj* lapidario; *s* (*pl:* **-ies**) lapidario
**lapidification** [ləˌpɪdɪfɪˈkeʃən] *s* lapidificación
**lapidify** [ləˈpɪdɪfaɪ] (*pret & pp:* **-fied**) *va* lapidificar; *vn* lapidificarse
**lapin** [ˈlæpɪn] *s* piel de conejo
**lapis lazuli** [ˈlæpɪs ˈlæzjəlaɪ] *s* (mineral.) lapislázuli
**Lapland** [ˈlæplænd] *s* Laponia
**Laplander** [ˈlæplændər] *s* lapón (*habitante*)
**Lapp** [læp] *s* lapón (*habitante; idioma*)
**lappet** [ˈlæpɪt] *s* caída, doblez, pliegue (*de un vestido*); pliegue (*de una membrana, tegumento, etc.*); lóbulo (*de la oreja*); carúncula (*de algunas aves*)
**Lappish** [ˈlæpɪʃ] *adj* lapón; *s* lapón (*idioma*)
**lap robe** *s* manta de coche
**lapse** [læps] *s* lapso (*curso de tiempo; caída en culpa o error*); recaída; (law) caducidad; *vn* caer en culpa o error; caerse; recaer; decaer, pasar (*p.ej., el entusiasmo*); (law) caducar
**lapwing** [ˈlæpˌwɪŋ] *s* (orn.) ave fría
**larboard** [ˈlɑrbərd] o [ˈlɑrbord] *s* (naut.) babor; *adj* (naut.) de babor
**larcenous** [ˈlɑrsənəs] *adj* ratero; de ratería
**larceny** [ˈlɑrsənɪ] *s* (*pl:* **-nies**) (law) ratería, hurto
**larch** [lɑrtʃ] *s* (bot.) alerce, pino salgareño, pino negral
**lard** [lɑrd] *s* manteca de puerco, cochevira; *va* (cook.) mechar; (fig.) interpolar para dar variedad o aumentar el interés
**larder** [ˈlɑrdər] *s* despensa
**lares and penates** [ˈlɛrɪz ənd pɛˈnetiz] *spl* lares y penates (*dioses domésticos de los romanos*); conjunto de objetos que dan carácter e intimidad a la casa propia u hogar
**large** [lɑrdʒ] *adj* grande; **at large** en libertad; largamente, con extensión; en general; por el estado entero (*dícese de los diputados que representan una región entera, a distinción de los que representan tan sólo una división política menos grande*); **in large** o **in the large** en grande escala
**large-hearted** [ˈlɑrdʒˈhɑrtɪd] *adj* desprendido, magnánimo
**large intestine** *s* (anat.) intestino grueso
**largely** [ˈlɑrdʒlɪ] *adj* grandemente; por la mayor parte
**largeness** [ˈlɑrdʒnɪs] *s* grandeza
**large periwinkle** *s* (bot.) vincapervinca, hierba doncella
**large-scale** [ˈlɑrdʒˌskel] *adj* en grande; grande escala, p.ej., **large-scale model** modelo grande escala
**largess** o **largesse** [ˈlɑrdʒɛs] *s* largueza (*liberalidad*); dádiva espléndida
**largo** [ˈlɑrgo] *s* (*pl:* **-gos**) (mus.) largo
**lariat** [ˈlærɪət] *s* lazo (*que sirve para enlazar caballos, toros, etc.*); cuerda o soga (*que sirve para tener atado un animal*)
**lark** [lɑrk] *s* (orn.) alondra; (orn.) chirlota (*Sturnella magna*); (coll.) parranda, travesuras; **to go on a lark** (coll.) andar de parranda, echar una cana al aire; *vn* (coll.) parrandear, hacer travesuras
**larkspur** [ˈlɑrkspʌr] *s* (bot.) consuelda (*Delphinium consolida*); consólida real, espuela de caballero (*Delphinium ajacis*)
**La Rochelle** [la roˈʃɛl] *s* La Rochela (*ciudad de Francia*)
**larrup** [ˈlærəp] *va* (coll.) zurrar, tundir
**larva** [ˈlɑrvə] *s* (*pl:* **-vae** [vi]) (ent.) larva
**larval** [ˈlɑrvəl] *adj* larval; (path.) larvado
**laryngeal** [ləˈrɪndʒɪəl] o [ˌlærɪnˈdʒiəl] *adj* laríngeo
**laryngitis** [ˌlærɪnˈdʒaɪtɪs] *s* (path.) laringitis
**laryngologist** [ˌlærɪŋˈgɑlədʒɪst] *s* laringólogo
**laryngology** [ˌlærɪŋˈgɑlədʒɪ] *s* laringología
**laryngoscope** [ləˈrɪŋgəskop] *s* laringoscopio
**laryngoscopic** [ləˌrɪŋgəˈskɑpɪk] *adj* laringoscópico
**laryngoscopy** [ˌlærɪŋˈgɑskəpɪ] *s* laringoscopia
**larynx** [ˈlærɪŋks] *s* (*pl:* **larynges** [ləˈrɪndʒiz] o **larynxes**) (anat.) laringe
**lascar** [ˈlæskər] *s* lascar (*marinero de las Indias Orientales*)
**lascivious** [ləˈsɪvɪəs] *adj* lascivo
**laserwort** [ˈlesərˌwʌrt] *s* (bot.) laserpicio
**lash** [læʃ] *s* tralla; latigazo (*golpe con el látigo; reprensión áspera*); coletazo; embate (*de las olas del mar*); (anat.) pestaña; *va* atar, trincar; azotar; agitar, sacudir; increpar, reñir; vituperar; *vn* chocar, azotar; lanzarse; pasar como un relámpago; **to lash against** chocar con, azotar; **to lash at** increpar, reñir; vituperar; **to lash down** caer con abundancia (*la lluvia*); **to lash out** dar golpes, dar coces, embestir; desatarse, descomedirse
**lashing** [ˈlæʃɪŋ] *s* atadura; (naut.) amarra; paliza, zurra; latigazo (*reprensión áspera*)
**lass** [læs] *s* muchacha; amada, amiga querida
**lassie** [ˈlæsɪ] *s* muchachita
**lassitude** [ˈlæsɪtjud] o [ˈlæsɪtud] *s* lasitud
**lasso** [ˈlæso] o [læˈsu] *s* (*pl:* **-sos** o **-soes**) lazo; *va* lazar
**last** [læst] o [lɑst] *adj* último; pasado; final; **before last** antepasado, p.ej., **the week before last** la semana antepasada; **the last to** + *inf* el último en + *inf;* **last but not least** último en orden pero no en importancia, el último pero no el ínfimo; **last but one** penúltimo; *adv* después de todos los demás; por último; por última vez; *s* última persona; última cosa; fin; horma (*en que se conforman los zapatos*); **at last** por fin; **at long last** al fin y al cabo; **stick to your last!** ¡zapatero, a tus zapatos!; **to breathe one's last** dar el último suspiro; **to see the last of** no volver a ver; **to stick to one's last** atender a sus negocios, no meterse (*uno*) en lo que no le importa; **to the last** hasta el fin; *va* fabricar (*botas, zapatos*) en la horma; *vn* durar; seguir así; p.ej., **this can't last** las cosas no pueden seguir así; resistir; dar buen resultado (*p.ej., una prenda de vestir*)
**lasting** [ˈlæstɪŋ] o [ˈlɑstɪŋ] *adj* duradero, perdurable
**Last Judgment** *s* Juicio Final
**lastly** [ˈlæstlɪ] o [ˈlɑstlɪ] *adv* finalmente, por último
**last-minute news** [ˈlæstˈmɪnɪt] o [ˈlɑstˈmɪnɪt] *s* noticias de última hora
**last name** *s* apellido
**last night** *adv* anoche
**last offices** *spl* oficio de difuntos
**last quarter** *s* cuarto menguante (*de la luna*)
**last sleep** *s* último sueño (*la muerte*)
**last straw** *s* colmo, acabóse

**Last Supper** *s* Cena, última Cena
**last will and testament** *s* (law) última voluntad
**last word** *s* última palabra; (coll.) última palabra (*última moda; lo más perfecto que hay*)
**lat.** abr. de **latitude**
**Lat.** abr. de **Latin**
**latch** [lætʃ] *s* picaporte; **on the latch** cerrado con picaporte; *va* cerrar con picaporte
**latchet** [ˈlætʃɪt] *s* (archaic) correa de zapato
**latchkey** [ˈlætʃˌki] *s* llavín, picaporte (*llave para abrir el picaporte*); llave de la puerta principal
**latchstring** [ˈlætʃˌstrɪŋ] *s* cordón de aldaba; **the latchstring is out** ya sabe Vd. que ésta es su casa
**late** [let] *adj* (*comp:* **later** o **latter;** *super:* **latest** o **last**) tardío; avanzado (*dícese de la hora*); reciente, moderno; fallecido, difunto; de fines de, p.ej., **the late nineteenth-century novel** la novela de fines del siglo diez y nueve; de última hora (*dícese de las noticias*); **to be late** ser tarde; llegar tarde (*una persona*); llegar con retraso (*p.ej., un tren*); **to be late in** + *ger* tardar en + *inf;* **of late** recientemente, últimamente; **later** posterior; *adv* (*comp:* **later;** *super:* **latest** o **last**) tarde; **late in** hacia fines de (*la semana, el año, el siglo, etc.*); **late in life** a una edad avanzada
**late-comer** [ˈletˌkʌmər] *s* recién llegado; rezagado
**lateen** [læˈtin] *adj* (naut.) latino
**lateen-rigged** [læˈtinˌrɪgd] *adj* (naut.) que tiene vela latina
**lateen sail** *s* (naut.) vela latina
**lateen yard** *s* (naut.) entena
**late-lamented** [ˈletləˈmɛntɪd] *adj* fallecido . . . que en paz descanse, p.ej., **the late-lamented professor** el fallecido profesor que en paz descanse
**lately** [ˈletlɪ] *adv* recientemente, últimamente
**latency** [ˈletənsɪ] *s* estado latente
**latent** [ˈletənt] *adj* latente
**latent period** *s* (path.) latencia
**lateral** [ˈlætərel] *adj* lateral; *s* parte lateral; ramal; (min.) galería lateral
**laterally** [ˈlætərəlɪ] *adv* lateralmente
**lateral pass** *s* (football) pase lateral (*lance que consiste en lanzar lateralmente el balón de modo que lo reciba un jugador al otro lado de la zona de juego*)
**Lateran** [ˈlætərən] *adj* lateranense; *s* San Juan de Letrán (*basílica*); palacio de Letrán
**latex** [ˈletɛks] *s* (*pl:* **latexes** o **latices** [ˈlætɪsiz]) (bot.) látex
**lath** [læθ] o [lɑθ] *s* listón; enlistonado; *va* enlistonar
**lathe** [leð] *s* torno (*para trabajar madera, hierro, etc. con movimiento circular*)
**lather** [ˈlæθər] o [ˈlɑθər] *s* (carp.) listonador; [ˈlæðər] *s* espuma de jabón; espuma de sudor; *va* enjabonar; (coll.) tundir, zurrar; *vn* espumar, echar espuma; cubrirse de espuma (*p.ej., un caballo*)
**lathery** [ˈlæðərɪ] *adj* espumoso, cubierto de espuma
**lathing** [ˈlæθɪŋ] o [ˈlɑθɪŋ] o **lathwork** [ˈlæθˌwʌrk] o [ˈlɑθˌwʌrk] *s* enlistonado
**lathy** [ˈlæθɪ] o [ˈlɑθɪ] *adj* en forma de listón; largo y delgado
**Latin** [ˈlætɪn] o [ˈlætən] *adj* latino; *s* latín (*lengua*); latino (*individuo*)
**Latin America** *s* Latinoamérica, la América Latina
**Latin American** *s* latinoamericano
**Latin-American** [ˈlætɪnəˈmɛrɪkən] *adj* latinoamericano
**Latin Church** *s* Iglesia latina
**Latin cross** *s* cruz latina
**Latinism** [ˈlætɪnɪzəm] *s* latinismo
**Latinist** [ˈlætɪnɪst] *s* latinista
**Latinity** [ləˈtɪnɪtɪ] *s* latinidad
**Latinization** [ˌlætɪnɪˈzeʃən] *s* latinización
**Latinize** [ˈlætɪnaɪz] *va* latinizar; *vn* latinizarse
**Latin Quarter** *s* Barrio Latino
**Latin Rite** *s* rito latino
**latitude** [ˈlætɪtjud] o [ˈlætɪtud] *s* latitud; (fig.) latitud (*libertad; clima, región*)
**latitudinal** [ˌlætɪˈtjudɪnəl] o [ˌlætɪˈtudɪnəl] *adj* latitudinal
**latitudinarian** [ˌlætɪˌtjudɪˈnɛrɪən] o [ˌlætɪˌtudɪˈnɛrɪən] *adj & s* latitudinario
**latitudinarianism** [ˌlætɪˌtjudɪˈnɛrɪənɪzəm] o [ˌlætɪˌtudɪˈnɛrɪənɪzəm] *s* latitudinarismo
**Latium** [ˈleʃɪəm] *s* el Lacio
**latria** [ləˈtraɪə] *s* (theol.) latría
**latrine** [ləˈtrin] *s* letrina (*en un campamento, hospital, etc.*)
**latten** [ˈlætən] *s* latón en hojas
**latter** [ˈlætər] *adj* posterior, más reciente; segundo (*de dos*); **the latter** éste; **the latter part of** la última parte de; fines de (*la semana, el mes, etc.*)
**latter-day** [ˈlætərˈde] *adj* reciente, moderno; de los últimos días
**Latter-day Saint** *s* santo de los últimos días (*mormón*)
**latterly** [ˈlætərlɪ] *adv* recientemente, últimamente
**lattice** [ˈlætɪs] *s* enrejado, celosía; (her.) celosía; (phys.) reja; *va* enrejar; poner celosía a
**lattice bridge** *s* puente de celosía
**lattice girder** *s* viga de celosía
**latticework** [ˈlætɪsˌwʌrk] *s* enrejado, celosía
**Latvia** [ˈlætvɪə] *s* Letonia o Latvia
**Latvian** [ˈlætvɪən] *adj & s* letón o latvio
**laud** [lɔd] *s* alabanza, elogio; canción laudatoria; **lauds** o **Lauds** *spl* (eccl.) laudes; *va* alabar, elogiar
**laudability** [ˌlɔdəˈbɪlɪtɪ] *s* laudabilidad
**laudable** [ˈlɔdəbəl] *adj* laudable
**laudanum** [ˈlɔdənəm] o [ˈlɔdnəm] *s* (pharm.) láudano
**laudation** [lɔˈdeʃən] *s* alabanza
**laudatory** [ˈlɔdəˌtorɪ] *adj* laudatorio
**laugh** [læf] o [lɑf] *s* risa; *va* hacer o llevar a cabo riendo; expresar riendo; **to laugh away** ahogar en risa, olvidar riendo; **to laugh off** tomar a risa; *vn* reír, reírse; (fig.) reír (*p.ej., una corriente de agua*); **to laugh out** reírse a carcajadas
**laughable** [ˈlæfəbəl] o [ˈlɑfəbəl] *adj* risible
**laughing** [ˈlæfɪŋ] o [ˈlɑfɪŋ] *adj* risueño, reidor; **to be no laughing matter** no ser cosa de juego; *s* risa, reír
**laughing gas** *s* gas exhilarante, gas hilarante
**laughing jackass** *s* (orn.) martín cazador
**laughingly** [ˈlæfɪŋlɪ] o [ˈlɑfɪŋlɪ] *adv* riendo, entre risas
**laughingstock** [ˈlæfɪŋˌstɑk] o [ˈlɑfɪŋˌstɑk] *s* hazmerreír
**laughter** [ˈlæftər] o [ˈlɑftər] *s* risa, risas
**launch** [lɔntʃ] o [lɑntʃ] *s* botadura (*de un buque*); lanzamiento (*de un cohete*); lancha automóvil; (nav.) lancha; *va* lanzar (*un dardo, un cohete, maldiciones, una ofensiva, un producto nuevo*); botar, lanzar (*un buque*); *vn* lanzarse; **to launch forth** u **out** salir, ponerse en marcha
**launcher** [ˈlɔntʃər] o [ˈlɑntʃər] *s* lanzador
**launching device** *s* instrumento de lanzamiento
**launching pad** *s* plataforma de lanzamiento
**launching silo** *s* pozo o silo de lanzamiento
**launching site** *s* puesto de lanzamiento
**launching tower** *s* torre de lanzamiento
**launder** [ˈlɔndər] o [ˈlɑndər] *va* lavar y planchar; *vn* resistir bien el lavado
**launderer** [ˈlɔndərər] o [ˈlɑndərər] *s* lavandero
**laundress** [ˈlɔndrɪs] o [ˈlɑndrɪs] *s* lavandera
**laundromat** [ˈlɔndrəmæt] o [ˈlɑndrəmæt] *s* (trademark) lavadero de autoservicio
**laundry** [ˈlɔndrɪ] o [ˈlɑndrɪ] *s* (*pl:* **-dries**) lavadero (*sitio*); lavandería (Am.); lavado de ropas; ropa sucia; ropa lavada y planchada
**laundryman** [ˈlɔndrɪmən] o [ˈlɑndrɪmən] *s* (*pl:* **-men**) lavandero
**laundrywoman** [ˈlɔndrɪˌwʊmən] o [ˈlɑndrɪˌwʊmən] *s* (*pl:* **-women**) lavandera
**lauraceous** [lɔˈreʃəs] *adj* (bot.) lauráceo
**laureate** [ˈlɔrɪɪt] *adj* laureado; *s* laureado; poeta laureado
**laureateship** [ˈlɔrɪɪtˌʃɪp] *s* dignidad de poeta laureado
**laurel** [ˈlɔrəl] o [ˈlɑrəl] *s* (bot.) laurel; (bot.) calmia; (bot.) rododendro; hojas de laurel; **laurels** *spl* laurel (*de la victoria*); **to look to one's laurels** no dormirse sobre sus laureles; **to rest** o **to sleep on one's laurels** dormirse sobre sus laureles; (*pret & pp:* **-reled** o

**-relled;** *ger:* **-reling** o **-relling**) *va* laurear, coronar de laurel
**laureled** o **laurelled** [ˈlɔrəld] o [ˈlɑrəld] *adj* laureado
**Laurence** [ˈlɔrəns] o [ˈlɑrəns] *s* Lorenzo
**Laurentian** [lɔˈrɛnʃɪən] *adj* laurentino; (geol.) laurentino; *s* (geol.) laurentino
**Laurentian Mountains** *spl* montes Laurentinos
**laurustine** [ˈlɔrəstɪn] *s* (bot.) durillo, barbadija
**Lausanne** [loˈzæn] *s* Losana
**lava** [ˈlɑvə] o [ˈlævə] *s* lava
**lava bed** *s* yacimiento de lava
**lavabo** [ləˈvebo] *s* (*pl:* **-boes**) (eccl. & hist.) lavabo; (*cap.*) *s* (eccl.) lavabo (*paño*)
**lava field** *s* terreno cubierto de lava
**lavage** [ˈlævɪdʒ] *s* lavado; (med.) lavado
**lavalier, lavaliere** o **lavallière** [ˌlævəˈlɪr] *s* pendiente (*que se lleva alrededor del cuello*)
**lavatory** [ˈlævəˌtorɪ] *s* (*pl:* **-ries**) lavabo (*cuarto*); excusado, retrete; lavamanos, lavatorio; (eccl.) lavatorio
**lave** [lev] *va* (poet.) bañar; *vn* (poet.) bañarse
**lavender** [ˈlævəndər] *s* (bot.) alhucema, espliego (*planta y flores y hojas secas*); color de alhucema; *adj* de color de alhucema
**lavender cotton** *s* (bot.) abrótano hembra
**lavender water** *s* agua de alhucema, agua de espliego
**laver** [ˈlevər] *s* (archaic) aguamanil, jofaina
**lavish** [ˈlævɪʃ] *adj* pródigo; *va* prodigar
**law** [lɔ] *s* ley; derecho (*conjunto de leyes; estudio de las leyes*); **the Law** (Bib.) la ley de Moisés; (Bib.) el Antiguo Testamento; **to enter the law** hacerse abogado; **to have the law on** (coll.) iniciar un juicio contra; **to go to law** recurrir a la ley; **to lay down the law** dar órdenes terminantes; decir cuántas son cinco; **to maintain law and order** mantener la paz; **to practice law** ejercer la profesión de abogado; **to read law** estudiar derecho (*en el bufete de un abogado*); **to take the law into one's own hands** hacerse justicia por sí mismo
**law-abiding** [ˈlɔəˌbaɪdɪŋ] *adj* observante de la ley
**lawbreaker** [ˈlɔˌbrekər] *s* infractor de la ley
**lawbreaking** [ˈlɔˌbrekɪŋ] *adj* infractor de la ley; *s* infracción de la ley
**law court** *s* tribunal de justicia
**lawful** [ˈlɔfəl] *adj* legal, lícito, legítimo, permitido
**lawgiver** [ˈlɔˌgɪvər] *s* legislador
**lawless** [ˈlɔlɪs] *adj* ilegal; desaforado, desenfrenado, licencioso; sin leyes
**lawmaker** [ˈlɔˌmekər] *s* legislador
**lawmaking** [ˈlɔˌmekɪŋ] *adj* legislativo; *s* legislación
**lawn** [lɔn] *s* césped; linón (*tela*); episcopado anglicano
**lawn mower** *s* cortacésped, tundidora de césped
**lawn tennis** *s* (sport) lawn-tennis
**law office** *s* bufete, despacho de abogado
**law of Moses** *s* ley de Moisés
**law of nations** *s* derecho de gentes
**law of the jungle** *s* ley de la selva
**law of the Medes and Persians** *s* (Bib.) ley de Media y de Persia (*ley inmutable*)
**Lawrence** [ˈlɔrəns] o [ˈlɑrəns] *s* Lorenzo
**law student** *s* estudiante de leyes, estudiante de derecho
**lawsuit** [ˈlɔˌsut] o [ˈlɔˌsjut] *s* pleito, litigio, proceso
**lawyer** [ˈlɔjər] *s* abogado
**lax** [læks] *adj* laxo (*flojo; relajado, libre*); descuidado, negligente; vago, indeterminado
**laxation** [lækˈseʃən] *s* laxación
**laxative** [ˈlæksətɪv] *adj & s* (med.) laxante
**laxity** [ˈlæksɪtɪ] *s* laxitud, flojedad; descuido, negligencia
**lay** [le] *s* disposición, situación, orientación; trama (*de un cable o cuerda*); lay (*poema, canción*); *adj* seglar, lego; lego, profano (*que carece de conocimientos en una materia*) ‖ *pret de* **lie** ‖ (*pret & pp:* **laid**) *va* poner, colocar; dejar; acostar en el suelo, dejar en el suelo; tender (*un cable*); echar (*cimientos; la culpa*); situar (*la acción de un drama*); preparar (*el fuego*); asentar (*el polvo; una vía*); poner (*huevos la gallina; la mesa una criada*); formar, proyectar, trazar (*planes*); conjurar (*un fantasma*); alisar (*la lanilla de una tela*); apostar (*dinero*); hacer (*una apuesta*); imponer (*castigos, penas, etc.*); presentar (*reclamaciones*); atribuir (*responsabilidades*); conjurar, exorcizar (*un aparecido*); (naut.) colchar o corchar (*las filásticas de un cordón o los cordones de un cabo*); **to be laid in** ser en, p.ej., **the scene is laid in New York** la escena es en Nueva York; **to lay aside, away** o **by** echar a un lado; ahorrar; **to lay bare** poner al descubierto; **to lay down** afirmar, declarar; dar (*la vida*); guardar, reservar; hacer (*una apuesta*); rendir, deponer (*las armas*); **to lay in** proveerse de, guardar, ahorrar; **to lay low** abatir, derribar; poner fuera de combate, obligar a guardar cama; matar; **to lay off** poner a un lado; despedir (*a obreros*); trazar, marcar (*en el suelo*); **to lay on** descargar (*golpes*); aplicar; distribuir (*agua, gas, etc.*); cobrar (*carnes*); **to lay oneself out** (coll.) hacer un gran esfuerzo; **to lay open** descubrir, revelar; exponer (*p.ej., a un riesgo o peligro*); **to lay out** tender, extender; jalonar; marcar (*una tarea, un trabajo*); disponer, proyectar; gastar; amortajar (*a un difunto*); **to lay over** aplazar; (slang) aventajar, superar; **to lay up** ahorrar; obligar a guardar cama; (naut.) desarmar ‖ *vn* poner (*las gallinas*); apostar; **to lay about** dar palos de ciego; **to lay down** (slang) aflojar, cejar; **to lay for** (coll.) acechar; **to lay off** (slang) parar, cesar; (slang) dejar de trabajar; (slang) dejar de molestar; **to lay on** dar palos de ciego; **to lay over** detenerse durante un viaje; **to lay to** (naut.) estar parado en la dirección del viento
**lay brother** *s* donado, lego
**lay days** *spl* (naut.) días de estadía, días de demora
**layer** [ˈleər] *s* gallina ponedora; [ˈleər] o [lɛr] *s* capa, camada; (geol.) capa, estrato; (hort.) acodo, codadura; *va* (hort.) acodar
**layerage** [ˈleərɪdʒ] *s* (hort.) acodadura
**layer cake** *s* bizcocho de varias camadas
**layette** [leˈɛt] *s* canastilla (*para el niño que ha de nacer*)
**lay figure** *s* maniquí; (fig.) maniquí
**laying** [ˈleɪŋ] *s* colocación; postura (*de huevos*); tendido (*p.ej., de un cable*); capa; primera capa (*de un enlucido*)
**laying on of hands** *s* (eccl.) imposición de manos
**laying top** *s* galapo (*usado para formar maromas*)
**layman** [ˈlemən] *s* (*pl:* **-men**) seglar, lego; lego, profano (*persona que carece de conocimientos en una materia*)
**layoff** [ˈleˌɔf] o [ˈleˌɑf] *s* despido (*de obreros*); paro forzoso
**lay of the land** *s* configuración del terreno; (fig.) cariz que van tomando las cosas
**layout** [ˈleˌaut] *s* disposición, arreglo; trazado; equipo; juego (*de herramientas, instrumentos, etc.*); conjunto de cosas exhibidas; (slang) banquete, festín
**layover** [ˈleˌovər] *s* parada intermedia
**lay sister** *s* donada
**lazar** [ˈlæzər] *s* (archaic) leproso; (archaic) mendigo enfermo
**lazaret** o **lazarette** [ˌlæzəˈrɛt] *s* var. de **lazaretto**
**lazaretto** [ˌlæzəˈrɛto] *s* (*pl:* **-tos**) lazareto; (naut.) despensa
**Lazarus** [ˈlæzərəs] *s* Lázaro
**laze** [lez] *vn* darse al ocio, holgazanear
**lazulite** [ˈlæzjəlaɪt] *s* (mineral.) lazulita
**lazy** [ˈlezɪ] *adj* (*comp:* **-zier;** *super:* **-ziest**) perezoso
**lazybones** [ˈlezɪˌbonz] *s* perezoso; **to be a lazybones** tener los huesos cansados
**lb.** abr. de **pound** o **pounds**
**lbs.** abr. de **pounds**
**l.c.** abr. de **lower case** y **loco citato** (Lat.) **in the place cited**
**l.c.m.** o **L.C.M.** abr. de **least common multiple**
**Ld.** abr. de **Lord**
**lea** [li] *s* prado

**leach** [litʃ] *s* lixiviador; *va* lixiviar; mojar; *vn* lixiviarse

**leachy** [ˈlitʃɪ] *adj* poroso

**lead** [lɛd] *s* (chem.) plomo; plomo (*pedazo de plomo; plomada de albañil; bala*); mina (*del lapicero*); (naut.) escandallo; (print.) interlínea, regleta; **leads** *spl* hojas de plomo; armaduras de plomo (*de las vidrieras*) ‖ *adj* de plomo ‖ (*pret & pp:* **leaded**) *va* emplomar; vidriar con esmalte de plomo; (print.) interlinear, regletear ‖ [lid] *s* conducta, dirección, guía; conductor, guía; ejemplo (*de otra persona*); sugestión, indicación (*con la que se guía a otra persona*); delantera, primer lugar; ventaja (*p.ej., en una carrera*); salida (*en los naipes*); traílla; pasadizo libre (*por entre masas de hielo flotante*); primer párrafo (*de un artículo de periódico*); (box.) golpe inicial (*de la ofensiva*); (elec.) conductor; (elec. & mach.) avance; (min.) filón, veta; (rad.) alambre de entrada; (theat.) papel principal; (theat.) primer galán; (theat.) dama; **to take the lead** tomar la delantera ‖ (*pret & pp:* **led**) *va* conducir, llevar; acaudillar, mandar; dirigir (*p.ej., una orquesta*); estar a la cabeza de; llevar (*buena o mala vida*); pasar (*un hilo, soga, etc.*); hacer pasar (*agua, vapor*); influenciar; dar comienzo a; salir con (*cierto naipe*); (elec. & mach.) avanzar, adelantar; **to lead to** + *inf* llevar (*a alguien*) a + *inf* ‖ *vn* enseñar el camino, ir delante; ser el primero, ser el más importante; tener el mando; cabestrear (*seguir sin repugnancia la bestia al que la lleva del cabestro*); (box.) tomar la ofensiva; (cards) salir, ser mano; (mus.) llevar la batuta; **to lead off** comenzar, empezar; **to lead on** enseñar el camino; seguir adelante; **to lead up to** conducir a

**lead acetate** [lɛd] *s* (chem.) acetato de plomo

**lead acid cell** [lɛd] *s* (elec.) acumulador de plomo-ácido

**lead-burn** [ˈlɛd,bʌrn] *va* soldar (*dos piezas de plomo*) con soldadura autógena

**lead-burning** [ˈlɛd,bʌrnɪŋ] *s* soldadura autógena del plomo

**leaden** [ˈlɛdən] *adj* de plomo; plúmbeo (*que pesa como el plomo*); plomizo (*de color de plomo*); lóbrego, triste

**leaden-eyed** [ˈlɛdən,aɪd] *adj* de ojos dormidos

**leader** [ˈlidər] *s* caudillo, jefe, líder; cabecilla, instigador; guión; guía (*caballo*); director (*p.ej., de una orquesta*); primer violín; sotileza (*parte fina del aparejo de pescar*); artículo que se ofrece a un precio muy vientajoso para despertar el interés de los compradores; artículo de fondo; (min.) guía; **leaders** *spl* (print.) puntos suspensivos

**leadership** [ˈlidərʃɪp] *s* caudillaje, dirección, jefatura, mando; dotes de mando

**lead glance** [lɛd] *s* (mineral.) galena

**leading** [ˈlidɪŋ] *adj* director; primero, principal; preeminente; *s* dirección; [ˈlɛdɪŋ] *s* hojas o tiras de plomo; armaduras de plomo (*de las vidrieras*); (print.) regletas

**leading article** *s* artículo de fondo

**leading block** *s* retorno

**leading current** *s* (elec.) corriente avanzada

**leading edge** *s* (aer.) borde de entrada o de ataque

**leading lady** *s* (theat.) dama, primera actriz

**leading man** *s* (theat.) primer galán, primer actor

**leading question** *s* pregunta capciosa, pregunta tendenciosa

**leading strings** *spl* andadores (*para sostener al niño cuando aprende a andar*)

**lead-in wire** [ˈlid,ɪn] *s* (rad.) alambre de entrada, bajada de antena

**lead pencil** [lɛd] *s* lápiz (*de grafito*)

**lead poisoning** [lɛd] *s* (path.) envenenamiento plúmbico

**lead tetraethyl** [lɛd] *s* var. de **tetraethyl lead**

**leadwort** [ˈlɛd,wʌrt] *s* (bot.) belesa, dentelaria, hierba del cáncer

**leaf** [lif] *s* (*pl:* **leaves**) hoja (*de planta, libro, mesa, muelle, puerta plegadiza, etc.; pétalo de flor*); pámpano (*de vid*); trampilla (*hoja de mesa que se levanta como trampa*); **to shake like a leaf** temblar como un azogado; **to take a leaf from the book of** seguir el ejemplo de; **to turn over a new leaf** hacer libro nuevo (*corregir sus vicios*); *va* hojear; *vn* echar hojas; **to leaf through** trashojar

**leafage** [ˈlifɪdʒ] *s* follaje

**leaf bud** *s* (bot.) yema

**leaf insect** *s* (ent.) hojaseca

**leafless** [ˈliflɪs] *adj* deshojado

**leaflet** [ˈliflɪt] *s* hojuela, hojilla; hoja suelta, hoja volante

**leaf mold** *s* (agr.) abono verde

**leaf roller** *s* (ent.) oruga de arrolladora o torcedora

**leaf sewer** [ˈsoər] *s* (ent.) arrolladora, torcedora

**leafstalk** [ˈlif,stɔk] *s* (bot.) pecíolo, rabillo (*de la hoja*)

**leafy** [ˈlifɪ] *adj* (*comp:* **-ier;** *super:* **-iest**) hojoso, hojudo, frondoso

**league** [lig] *s* legua (*medida*); liga, sociedad; **in league** asociado; **the League** la Sociedad de las Naciones; *va* asociar; *vn* asociarse, ligarse

**League of Nations** *s* Sociedad de las Naciones

**leaguer** [ˈligər] *s* miembro de una liga; (archaic) cerco, sitio; (archaic) real (*campamento de un ejército*); *va* (archaic) cercar, sitiar

**Leah** [ˈliə] *s* (Bib.) Lía

**leak** [lik] *s* gotera (*en un techo*); agua, vía de agua (*en un buque*); agujero (*por donde se escapa el agua, gas, vapor*); salida, escape, fuga (*de agua, gas, electricidad, vapor*); filtración (*de dinero*); **to spring a leak** tener un escape; (naut.) empezar a hacer agua; *va* dejar salir, dejar escapar (*el agua, gas, vapor*); *vn* tener fugas; rezumarse (*el agua*); salirse, escaparse (*el agua, gas, vapor*); filtrarse (*dinero*); (naut.) hacer agua; **to leak out** trascender (*un hecho que estaba oculto*); rezumarse (*una especie*)

**leakage** [ˈlikɪdʒ] *s* salida, escape, fuga; (com.) merma; (elec.) dispersión

**leakage conductance** *s* (elec.) perditancia

**leaky** [ˈlikɪ] *adj* (*comp:* **-ier;** *super:* **-iest**) llovedizo (*techo*); agujereado, roto; (naut.) que hace agua; (coll.) indiscreto

**lean** [lin] *s* molla, carne mollar o magra; inclinación; *adj* mollar, magro; flaco; malo, improductivo; de carestía, p.ej., **lean years** años de carestía; pobre (*mezcla de gasolina*); (*pret & pp:* **leaned** o **leant**) *va* inclinar, ladear, arrimar; *vn* inclinarse, ladearse, arrimarse; (fig.) inclinarse, propender, tender; **to lean against** apoyarse a, arrimarse a, estar arrimado a; **to lean back** retreparse, recostarse; **to lean on** apoyarse en; acodarse sobre; depender de, necesitar el apoyo de; **to lean out (of)** asomarse (a); **to lean over backward** (coll.) extremar la imparcialidad; **to lean toward** inclinarse a o hacia

**Leander** [lɪˈændər] *s* (myth.) Leandro

**leaning** [ˈlinɪŋ] *s* inclinación; (fig.) inclinación, propensión, tendencia; *adj* inclinado

**Leaning Tower** *s* Torre inclinada

**leanness** [ˈlinnɪs] *s* magrez; flaqueza; improductividad, carestía; pobreza

**leant** [lɛnt] *pret & pp de* **lean**

**lean-to** [ˈlin,tu] *adj* colgadizo; *s* (*pl:* **-tos**) colgadizo

**leap** [lip] *s* salto; **by leaps and bounds** con gran rapidez; **leap in the dark** salto a ciegas, salto en vago; (*pret & pp:* **leaped** o **leapt**) *va* saltar; *vn* saltar; dar un salto (*el corazón de uno*)

**leap day** *s* día intercalar (*en el año bisiesto y en cualquier calendario*)

**leapfrog** [ˈlip,frag] o [ˈlip,frɔg] *s* fil derecho, juego del salto; **to play leapfrog** jugar a la una la mula

**leapt** [lɛpt] o [lipt] *pret & pp de* **leap**

**leap year** *s* año bisiesto

**learn** [lʌrn] (*pret & pp:* **learned** o **learnt**) *va* aprender; saber (*una noticia*); oír decir; *vn* aprender; **to learn of** saber, tener noticia de; **to learn to** + *inf* aprender a + *inf*

**learned** [ˈlʌrnɪd] *adj* docto, erudito; (philol.) docto, culto

**learned journal** *s* publicación periódica científica

**learned society** *s* sociedad de eruditos

**learned word** *s* cultismo, voz culta

**learned world** *s* mundo de la erudición

**learner** [ˈlʌrnər] *s* aprendiz, principiante
**learning** [ˈlʌrnɪŋ] *s* aprendizaje; erudición
**learnt** [lʌrnt] *pret & pp de* **learn**
**lease** [lis] *s* arrendamiento; **to give a new lease on life to** renovar completamente, poner completamente bueno; volver a hacer feliz; *va* arrendar; *vn* arrendarse
**leasehold** [ˈlis,hold] *s* arrendamiento; bienes raíces arrendados
**leash** [liʃ] *s* traílla; pihuela (*para asegurar los pies de los halcones*); lizo; grupo de tres; **to hold in leash** dominar, reprimir; *va* atraillar
**least** [list] *adj* (el) menor, mínimo, más pequeño; *adv* menos; *s* (lo) menos, p.ej., **that is the least you can do** eso es lo menos que puede Vd. hacer; (el) menor; **at least** o **at the least** al menos, a lo menos o por lo menos; **not in the least** de ninguna manera
**least common multiple** *s* (math.) mínimo común múltiplo
**leastways** [ˈlist,wez] *adv* (coll.) var. de **leastwise**
**leastwise** [ˈlist,waɪz] *adv* por lo menos, a lo menos; de todos modos
**leather** [ˈlɛðər] *s* cuero; *adj* de cuero; *va* forrar o guarnecer con cuero; (coll.) zurrar
**leatherback** [ˈlɛðər,bæk] *s* (zool.) laúd
**leatherette** [,lɛðəˈrɛt] *s* cuero artificial, imitación cuero
**leather goods** *spl* artículos de cuero
**leathern** [ˈlɛðərn] *adj* de cuero; como de cuero
**leatherneck** [ˈlɛðər,nɛk] *s* (slang) soldado de infantería de marina de los EE.UU.
**leatheroid** [ˈlɛðərɔɪd] *s* cuero sintético
**leathery** [ˈlɛðərɪ] *adj* correoso
**leave** [liv] *s* permiso; licencia; despedida; **by your leave** con permiso de Vd.; **on leave** de permiso, con licencia; **to give leave to** dar licencia a; **to take leave (of)** despedirse (de) ‖ (*pret & pp:* **left**) *va* dejar; salir de; legar (*por testamento*); **to be left** quedarse; quedar, p.ej., **the letter was left unanswered** la carta quedó sin contestar; **to leave alone** dejar en paz, dejar tranquilo; no meterse con; no probar (*el vino*); **to leave off** dejar, cesar; no ponerse (*una prenda de vestir*); **to leave out** omitir; **to leave things as they are** dejarlo como está; **to leave to** dejar al criterio o elección de; **leave it to me!** ¡déjeme Vd. a mí! ‖ *vn* irse, marcharse; salir (*un tren, vapor, avión, etc.*); **to leave off** cesar, desistir ‖ (*pret & pp:* **leaved**) *vn* echar hojas
**leaven** [ˈlɛvən] *s* levadura; (fig.) mezcla, influencia, fuerza; *va* leudar; (fig.) penetrar, transformar, corromper
**leavening** [ˈlɛvənɪŋ] *s* levadura
**leave of absence** *s* licencia
**leave-taking** [ˈliv,tekɪŋ] *s* despedida
**leavings** [ˈlivɪŋz] *spl* desperdicios, sobras; residuos
**Lebanese** [,lɛbəˈniz] *adj* libanés; *s* (*pl:* **-nese**) libanés
**Lebanon** [ˈlɛbənən] *s* el Líbano, la República del Líbano
**Lebanon Mountains, the** el Líbano
**Lebensraum** [ˈlebəns,raum] *s* espacio vital (*de una nación*)
**lecher** [ˈlɛtʃər] *s* libertino, lujurioso
**lecherous** [ˈlɛtʃərəs] *adj* lascivo, lujurioso
**lechery** [ˈlɛtʃərɪ] *s* lascivia, lujuria
**lecithin** [ˈlɛsɪθɪn] *s* (biochem.) lecitina
**lectern** [ˈlɛktərn] *s* atril
**lection** [ˈlɛkʃən] *s* lección; (eccl.) lección
**lectionary** [ˈlɛkʃə,nɛrɪ] *s* (*pl:* **-ies**) (eccl.) leccionario
**lector** [ˈlɛktər] *s* lector
**lecture** [ˈlɛktʃər] *s* conferencia; sermoneo; *va* instruir por medio de conferencias; sermonear; *vn* dar una conferencia, dar conferencias
**lecturer** [ˈlɛktʃərər] *s* conferenciante
**led** [lɛd] *pret & pp de* **lead**
**Leda** [ˈlidə] *s* (myth.) Leda
**ledge** [lɛdʒ] *s* repisa; retallo (*en el paramento de un muro*); tongada; cama de roca; arrecife
**ledger** [ˈlɛdʒər] *s* libro mayor; losa, lápida; solera
**ledger line** *s* (mus.) línea suplementaria
**lee** [li] (naut.) socaire (*abrigo*); (naut.) sotavento; **lees** *spl* heces; *adj* (naut.) de sotavento
**leeboard** [ˈli,bord] *s* (naut.) orza de deriva
**leech** [litʃ] *s* (zool.) sanguijuela; (fig.) sanguijuela (*persona*); (naut.) grátil; (naut.) orilla de popa (*de una cangreja*); (med.) sanguijuela artificial; (archaic) médico; *va* (archaic) curar
**leek** [lik] *s* (bot.) puerro
**leer** [lɪr] *s* mirada de reojo (*con intención maligna o lujuriosa*); *va* tentar con mirada de reojo; *vn* echar una mirada o miradas de reojo (*con intención maligna o lujuriosa*)
**leery** [ˈlɪrɪ] *adj* (slang) astuto, entendido; (slang) suspicaz, receloso
**lee shore** *s* costa de sotavento
**leeward** [ˈluərd] o [ˈliwərd] *s* (naut.) sotavento; *adv* (naut.) a sotavento
**Leeward Islands** [ˈliwərd] *spl* islas de Sotavento
**leeway** [ˈli,we] *s* (naut.) deriva; (aer.) abatimiento; (coll.) libertad de acción, tiempo o dinero de sobra, sitio en que moverse
**left** [lɛft] *adj* izquierdo; (pol.) de izquierda; *s* izquierda (*mano izquierda*); (box.) zurdazo; (pol.) izquierda; **on** o **to the left** a o por la izquierda; *pret & pp de* **leave**
**left field** *s* (baseball) jardín izquierdo
**left-hand** [ˈlɛft,hænd] *adj* izquierdo; de, con o para la mano izquierda; de movimiento, funcionamiento, etc. hacia la izquierda
**left-hand drive** *s* (aut.) conducción a izquierda
**left-handed** [ˈlɛftˈhændɪd] *adj* zurdo; de la mano izquierda; para zurdos; torpe, desmañado; insincero, malicioso; irónico; (mach.) zurdo (*p.ej., tornillo*)
**left-handed marriage** *s* matrimonio de la mano izquierda
**leftish** [ˈlɛftɪʃ] *adj* izquierdizante
**leftism** [ˈlɛftɪzəm] *s* izquierdismo
**leftist** [ˈlɛftɪst] *adj & s* izquierdista
**left jab** *s* (box.) inverso de izquierda
**leftover** [ˈlɛft,ovər] *adj & s* sobrante; **leftovers** *spl* sobras
**left wing** *s* ala izquierda (*de un ejército*); (pol.) izquierda
**left-wing** [ˈlɛft,wɪŋ] *adj* izquierdista
**left-winger** [ˈlɛft,wɪŋər] *s* (coll.) izquierdista
**leg.** abr. de **legal, legislative** y **legislature**
**leg** [lɛg] *s* pierna (*de hombre o animal*); pata (*de animal, mesa, silla, etc.*); muslo (*de ave cocida*); caña (*de bota o de media*); pernera (*de pantalón*); pierna (*de un compás de dibujo*); etapa, trecho (*p.ej., de un viaje*); (elec.) circuito derivado; (geom.) cateto; **to be on one's last legs** andar de capa caída; estar al cabo, estar en las últimas; **to give a leg up** ayudar a subir; **to not have a leg to stand on** (coll.) no tener disculpa alguna; no poder aducir razón alguna en defensa de su opinión; **to pull one's leg** (coll.) tomar el pelo a, engañarle a uno; **to shake a leg** (coll.) darse prisa; (coll.) bailar; **to stretch one's legs** estirar o extender las piernas, dar un paseíto; (*pret & pp:* **legged**; *ger:* **legging**) *va* hacer con las piernas; **to leg it** (coll.) caminar, ir a pie, correr; *vn* (coll.) caminar, ir a pie, correr
**legacy** [ˈlɛgəsɪ] *s* (*pl:* **-cies**) legado
**legal** [ˈligəl] *adj* legal
**legalism** [ˈligəlɪzəm] *s* rigorismo
**legalist** [ˈligəlɪst] *s* rigorista; legista, legisperito
**legalistic** [,ligəˈlɪstɪk] *adj* legalista
**legality** [lɪˈgælɪtɪ] *s* (*pl:* **-ties**) legalidad
**legalization** [,ligəlɪˈzeʃən] *s* legalización
**legalize** [ˈligəlaɪz] *va* legalizar
**legally** [ˈligəlɪ] *adv* legalmente
**legal tender** *s* curso legal, moneda de curso legal
**legate** [ˈlɛgɪt] *s* legado
**legatee** [,lɛgəˈti] *s* (law) legatario
**legation** [lɪˈgeʃən] *s* legación
**leg bail** *s* (slang) fuga, evasión; **to give leg bail** (slang) fugarse, escaparse
**legend** [ˈlɛdʒənd] *s* leyenda
**legendary** [ˈlɛdʒən,dɛrɪ] *adj* legendario
**legerdemain** [,lɛdʒərdɪˈmen] *s* juego de manos, prestidigitación; trapacería
**leger line** [ˈlɛdʒər] *s* var. de **ledger line**
**legged** [lɛgd] o [ˈlɛgɪd] *adj* que tiene piernas o patas
**legging** [ˈlɛgɪŋ] *s* polaina
**leggy** [ˈlɛgɪ] *adj* zanquilargo
**leghorn** [ˈlɛghɔrn] o [ˈlɛgərn] *s* sombrero de pa-

ja de Italia; (*cap.*) *s* gallina Leghorn; ['lɛg-hɔrn] *s* Liorna (*ciudad*)
**legibility** [,lɛdʒɪ'bɪlɪtɪ] *s* legibilidad
**legible** ['lɛdʒɪbəl] *adj* legible
**legion** ['lidʒən] *s* legión; **to be legion** constituir legión
**legionary** ['lidʒə,nɛrɪ] *adj* legionario; *s* (*pl:* **-ies**) legionario
**legionnaire** [,lidʒə'nɛr] *s* legionario
**Legion of Honor** *s* legión de Honor
**legislate** ['lɛdʒɪslet] *va* obligar mediante legislación, hacer o llevar a cabo mediante legislación; *vn* legislar
**legislation** [,lɛdʒɪs'leʃən] *s* legislación
**legislative** ['lɛdʒɪs,letɪv] *adj* legislativo
**legislator** ['lɛdʒɪs,letər] *s* legislador
**legislature** ['lɛdʒɪs,letʃər] *s* cuerpo legislativo, asamblea legislativa
**legitim** ['lɛdʒɪtɪm] *s* (law) legítima
**legitimacy** [lɪ'dʒɪtɪməsɪ] *s* legitimidad
**legitimate** [lɪ'dʒɪtɪmɪt] *adj* legítimo; [lɪ'dʒɪtɪmet] *va* legitimar
**legitimate drama** *s* teatro serio (*a distinción del cine o el melodrama*)
**legitimation** [lɪ,dʒɪtɪ'meʃən] *s* legitimación
**legitimism** [lɪ'dʒɪtɪmɪzəm] *s* legitimismo
**legitimist** [lɪ'dʒɪtɪmɪst] *adj & s* legitimista
**legitimize** [lɪ'dʒɪtɪmaɪz] *va* legitimar
**legman** ['lɛg,mæn] *s* (*pl:* **-men**) (coll.) repórter que anda de un lugar a otro en busca de noticias; (coll.) subordinado que hace mandados y otras tareas
**leg of lamb** *s* pierna de cordero
**leg of mutton** *s* pierna de carnero
**leg-of-mutton sail** ['lɛgəv'mʌtən] *s* (naut.) vela triangular
**leg-of-mutton sleeve** *s* manga de jamón
**legume** ['lɛgjum] o [lɪ'gjum] *s* (bot.) legumbre (*planta y fruto como garbanzo, haba, etc.*); vaina (*de legumbre*)
**legumin** [lɪ'gjumɪn] *s* (biochem.) legumina
**leguminous** [lɪ'gjumɪnəs] *adj* leguminoso
**legwork** ['lɛg,wʌrk] *s* (coll.) el mucho caminar, como parte esencial de un trabajo o empleo (*especialmente de un repórter o de alguien al servicio de un repórter*)
**lehua** [le'huɑ] *s* (bot.) lehua (*planta y flor de Metrosideros polymorpha*)
**lei** ['le·ɪ] *s* guirnalda hawaiana
**leishmaniasis** [,liʃmə'naɪəsɪs] o **leishmaniosis** [liʃ,menɪ'osɪs] *s* (path.) leishmaniosis
**leisure** ['liʒər] o ['lɛʒər] *s* ocio, desocupación; **at leisure** libre, desocupado; **at one's leisure** a la conveniencia de uno; **in one's leisure** en sus ratos de ocio, en sus ratos libres; *adj* de ocio; acomodado, desocupado
**leisure classes** *s* gente acomodada
**leisured** ['liʒərd] o ['lɛʒərd] *adj* acomodado, desocupado; lento, pausado, deliberado
**leisure hours** *spl* horas de ocio, ratos perdidos
**leisurely** ['liʒərlɪ] o ['lɛʒərlɪ] *adj* lento, pausado, deliberado; *adv* despacio, sin prisa
**leitmotif** o **leitmotiv** ['laɪtmo,tif] *s* (mus.) leitmotiv, tema o motivo conductor
**lemming** ['lɛmɪŋ] *s* (zool.) conejo de Noruega
**lemnaceous** [lɛm'neʃəs] *adj* (bot.) lemnáceo
**lemniscate** [lɛm'nɪsket] *s* (geom.) lemniscata
**lemniscus** [lɛm'nɪskəs] *s* (*pl:* **-nisci** ['nɪsaɪ]) lemnisco; (anat.) lemnisco
**lemon** ['lɛmən] *s* (bot.) limonero o limón (*árbol*); limón (*fruto*); (slang) maula; *adj* de limón; limonado (*de color de limón*)
**lemonade** [,lɛmən'ed] *s* limonada
**lemon squeezer** *s* exprimidor de limón
**lemon verbena** *s* (bot.) luisa, reina luisa
**lemur** ['limər] *s* (zool.) lémur; **lemures** ['lɛmjəriz] *spl* (myth.) lémures
**lend** [lɛnd] (*pret & pp:* **lent**) *va* prestar; dar (*p.ej., color*); añadir, aumentar (*p.ej., el interés de un relato*); **to lend itself** o **to lend oneself** prestarse
**lending library** *s* biblioteca de préstamo
**Lend-Lease Act** ['lɛnd'lis] *s* ley de préstamos y arriendos
**length** [lɛŋθ] *s* largo, largura; (racing) cuerpo; **at full length** tendido cuan largo es; **at length** por fin, finalmente; largamente, extensamente; **through the length and breadth of the land** hasta los últimos rincones del país; **to go to any length** hacer cuanto esté de su parte, hacer todo lo posible; **to keep at arm's length** mantener a distancia, no querer intimar con; mantenerse a distancia; **to measure one's length** medir el suelo, caer (*uno*) cuan largo es
**lengthen** ['lɛŋθən] *va* alargar; *vn* alargarse
**lengthways** ['lɛŋθwez] o **lengthwise** ['lɛŋθwaɪz] *adj* longitudinal; *adv* longitudinalmente
**lengthy** ['lɛŋθɪ] *adj* (*comp:* **-ier**; *super:* **-iest**) largo, prolongado; difuso, prolijo
**lenience** ['linɪəns] o **leniency** ['linɪənsɪ] *s* clemencia, indulgencia, lenitud
**lenient** ['linɪənt] *adj* clemente, indulgente; (archaic) lenitivo
**Leningrad** ['lɛnɪngræd] *s* Leningrado
**Leninism** ['lɛnɪnɪzəm] *s* leninismo
**Leninist** ['lɛnɪnɪst] o **Leninite** ['lɛnɪnaɪt] *adj & s* leninista
**lenitive** ['lɛnɪtɪv] *adj & s* lenitivo; laxante
**lenity** ['lɛnɪtɪ] *s* (*pl:* **-ties**) lenidad
**lens** [lɛnz] *s* (opt. & geol.) lente; (anat.) cristalino
**Lent** [lɛnt] *s* cuaresma; (*l.c.*) *pret & pp de* **lend**
**Lenten** o **lenten** ['lɛntən] *adj* cuaresmal
**lenticel** ['lɛntɪsɛl] *s* (bot.) lentejuela
**lenticular** [lɛn'tɪkjələr] *adj* lenticular
**lentil** ['lɛntəl] *s* (bot.) lenteja (*planta y semilla*)
**l'envoi** o **l'envoy** [lɛn'vɔɪ] *s* tornada, despedida (*a una composición poética*); epílogo en prosa
**Leo** ['lio] *s* León (*nombre de varón*); (astr.) Leo o León
**Leonard** ['lɛnərd] *s* Leonardo
**Leonese** [,liə'niz] *adj* leonés; *s* (*pl:* **-nese**) leonés
**Leonid** ['liənɪd] *s* (astr.) leónida
**Leonidas** [lɪ'ɑnɪdəs] *s* Leónidas
**leonine** ['liənaɪn] *adj* leonino
**Leonora** [,liə'norə] o **Leonore** ['liənor] *s* Leonor
**leontiasis** [,liɑn'taɪəsɪs] *s* (path.) leontíasis, leonina
**leopard** ['lɛpərd] *s* (zool.) leopardo; (zool.) jaguar
**leopardess** ['lɛpərdɪs] *s* leopardo hembra
**Leopold** ['liəpold] *s* Leopoldo
**leotard** ['liətɑrd] *s* traje muy ajustado (*de los acróbatas, volatineros y bailadores*)
**leper** ['lɛpər] *s* leproso
**lepidolite** [lɪ'pɪdolaɪt] o ['lɛpɪdolaɪt] *s* (mineral.) lepidolita
**lepidopteron** [,lɛpɪ'dɑptərɑn] *s* (*pl:* **-a** [ə]) (ent.) lepidóptero
**lepidopterous** [,lɛpɪ'dɑptərəs] *adj* (ent.) lepidóptero
**lepidosiren** [,lɛpɪdo'saɪrən] *s* (ichth.) lepidosirena
**Lepidus** ['lɛpɪdəs] *s* Lépido
**leporine** ['lɛpəraɪn] o ['lɛpərɪn] *adj* leporino
**leprechaun** ['lɛprəkən] *s* (Irish) duende, gnomo
**leprosarium** [,lɛprə'sɛrɪəm] *s* leprosería
**leprosy** ['lɛprəsɪ] *s* (path.) lepra
**leprous** ['lɛprəs] *adj* leproso; escamoso
**leptophyllous** [,lɛpto'fɪləs] *adj* (bot.) leptofilo
**leptorrhine** ['lɛptərɪn] *adj* (anthrop.) leptorrino
**Lesbian** ['lɛzbɪən] *adj* lesbiano o lesbio; *s* lesbiano, lesbio; lesbia (*mujer homosexual*)
**Lesbianism** ['lɛzbɪənɪzəm] *s* lesbianismo
**lese majesty** ['liz'mædʒɪstɪ] *s* delito o crimen de lesa majestad
**lesion** ['liʒən] *s* lesión; (path. & law) lesión
**less** [lɛs] *adj* menor; *adv* menos; **at less than** en menos que; **the less . . . the less** (o **the more**) mientras menos . . . menos (o más), p.ej., **the less he works the less he earns** mientras menos trabaja menos gana; **less and less** cada vez menos; **less than** menos que; menos de lo que + *verb*; menos de + *numeral*; *prep & s* menos
**lessee** [lɛs'i] *s* arrendatario
**lessen** ['lɛsən] *va* disminuir, reducir a menos; quitar importancia a, hacer poco caso de; *vn* disminuirse; amainar (*el viento*)
**lesser** ['lɛsər] *adj* menor, más pequeño
**Lesser Antilles** *spl* Antillas Menores
**lesser bindweed** *s* (bot.) correhuela
**lesser yellowlegs** *s* (orn.) chorlo menor de

patas amarillas, chorlito pardo mayor o patiamarilla

**lesson** [ˈlɛsən] *s* lección; *va* aleccionar; sermonear, reprender

**lessor** [ˈlɛsɔr] o [lɛˈsɔr] *s* arrendador

**lest** [lɛst] *conj* no sea que, para que no, de miedo que

**let** [lɛt] *s* estorbo, obstáculo; (tennis) let (*servicio en que la pelota roza la red y cae dentro de las líneas límites*); **without let or hindrance** sin estorbo ni obstáculo ‖ (*pret & pp:* **let;** *ger:* **letting**) *va* dejar, permitir; dejar pasar; alquilar, arrendar; sacar (*sangre a un enfermo*); **to be let off** salir bien librado; **to let** se alquila, p.ej., **room to let** se alquila un cuarto; **to let** + *inf* dejar o permitir + *inf;* **to let alone** dejar en paz, dejar tranquilo; **to let be** no meterse con; no tocar; dejar en paz; **to let by** dejar pasar; **to let down** bajar; dejar bajar; dejar caer; desilusionar, traicionar, humillar; dejar plantado, dejar colgado o chasqueado; **to let fly** disparar; (fig.) disparar, soltar (*palabras injuriosas*); **to let go** soltar, desasirse de; dejar, vender; **to let good enough alone** bueno está lo bueno; **to let in** dejar entrar, dejar entrar en; **to let it go at that** no hacer o decir nada más; **to let know** hacer saber, enterar; **to let loose** soltar; **to let off** disparar; (coll.) soltar, dejar libre; **to let on** (coll.) dar a entender; **to let oneself go** entregarse a sus deseos o pasiones; emplear todas sus fuerzas o energías; **to let out** hacer saber, revelar, publicar; dejar salir; dar, soltar (*p.ej., más cuerda*); dar (*un grito*); agrandar, ensanchar (*un vestido que aprieta*); dar en arrendamiento; (coll.) despedir; **to let through** dejar pasar, dejar pasar por; **to let up** dejar subir; dejar incorporarse; dejar levantarse; **let** + *inf* que + *subj,* p.ej., **let him do it if he wants to** que lo haga si quiere; **let alone** sin mencionar; y mucho menos, p.ej., **he cannot speak his own language, let alone a foreign language** no puede hablar su propio idioma y mucho menos un idioma extranjero; **let us** + *inf* vamos a + *inf,* p.ej., **let us eat** vamos a comer, comamos ‖ *vn* alquilarse, arrendarse; **to let down** (coll.) ir más despacio; **to let fly** (slang) desatarse en improperios; **to let go** soltar, desasirse; **to let go of** soltar, desasirse de; **to let on** (coll.) fingir; **to let out** (coll.) despedirse, cerrarse (*p.ej., la escuela*); **to let up** (coll.) cesar, desistir; (coll.) disminuir, moderarse; **to let up on** largar, aflojar

**letdown** [ˈlɛtˌdaʊn] *s* aflojamiento, relajamiento; desilusión, chasco; humillación

**lethal** [ˈliθəl] *adj* letal

**lethargic** [lɪˈθɑrdʒɪk] *adj* letárgico

**lethargy** [ˈlɛθərdʒɪ] *s* (*pl:* **-gies**) letargo

**Lethe** [ˈliθɪ] *s* (myth.) Lete o Leteo (*río*); (fig.) olvido

**Lethean** [lɪˈθiən] *adj* leteo

**let's** [lɛts] contracción de **let us**

**Lett** [lɛt] *s* letón (*persona e idioma*)

**letter** [ˈlɛtər] *s* carta; letra (*del alfabeto*); patente (*para el goce de un empleo o privilegio*); (fig.) letra (*sentido material*); **letters** *spl* letras (*literatura*); **to the letter** a la letra, al pie de la letra; *va* rotular, estampar o marcar con letras

**letter box** *s* buzón

**letter carrier** *s* cartero

**letter drop** *s* buzón (*abertura por donde se echan las cartas*)

**lettered** [ˈlɛtərd] *adj* rotulado, marcado con letras; que sabe leer y escribir; letrado (*literato*)

**letter file** *s* guardacartas

**letterhead** [ˈlɛtərˌhɛd] *s* membrete; memorándum (*papel con membrete*)

**lettering** [ˈlɛtərɪŋ] *s* inscripción, letras

**letter of credit** *s* (com.) carta orden de crédito, carta de crédito

**letter paper** *s* papel de cartas

**letter-perfect** [ˈlɛtərˈpʌrfɪkt] *adj* que tiene bien aprendido su papel o su lección; exacto, correcto

**letter press** *s* prensa de copiar cartas

**letterpress** [ˈlɛtərˌprɛs] *s* (print.) texto impreso (*a distinción de los grabados, etc.*)

**letter scales** *spl* pesacartas

**letters of marque** *spl* (naut.) patente de corso o carta de marca

**letters patent** *ssg & spl* patente de privilegio

**Lettish** [ˈlɛtɪʃ] *adj* letón; *s* letón (*idioma*)

**lettre de cachet** [ˈlɛtrə də kɑˈʃɛ] *s* (hist.) carta del rey sellada (*que mandaba prisión o destierro*)

**lettuce** [ˈlɛtɪs] *s* (bot.) lechuga; lechugas (*hojas que se comen en ensalada*)

**letup** [ˈlɛtˌʌp] *s* (coll.) calma (*p.ej., en el dolor, los negocios*); **without letup** (coll.) sin cesar

**leucine** [ˈlusin] o [ˈlusɪn] *s* (biochem.) leucina

**leucite** [ˈlusaɪt] *s* (mineral.) leucita

**leuco base** [ˈluko] *s* (chem.) leucobase

**leucocyte** [ˈlukosaɪt] *s* (physiol.) leucocito

**leucocythemia** [ˌlukosaɪˈθimɪə] *s* (path.) leucocitemia

**leucocytosis** [ˌlukosaɪˈtosɪs] *s* (path.) leucocitosis

**leucoma** [luˈkomə] *s* (path.) leucoma

**leucomaine** [luˈkoməin] o [luˈkomәɪn] *s* (biochem.) leucomaína

**leucon** [ˈlukɑn] *s* (*pl:* **leucones** [luˈkoniz]) (zool.) leucón

**leucopenia** [ˌlukəˈpinɪə] *s* (path.) leucopenia

**leucoplast** [ˈlukəplæst] *s* (bot.) leucoplasto

**leucorrhea** [ˌlukəˈriə] *s* (path.) leucorrea

**leukemia** [luˈkimɪə] *s* (path.) leucemia

**Lev.** abr. de **Leviticus**

**Levant** [lɪˈvænt] *s* Levante; (*l.c.*) *s* tafilete de Levante

**Levantine** [lɪˈvæntin] o [ˈlɛvəntin] *adj* levantino; *s* levantino; buque de Levante

**Levant morocco** *s* tafilete de Levante

**levee** [ˈlɛvɪ] *s* ribero (*para contener las aguas*); desembarcadero; [ˈlɛvɪ] o [lɛˈvi] *s* besamanos; recepción

**level** [ˈlɛvəl] *s* nivel; terreno llano, llanura; tramo (*de un canal entre dos esclusas*); **to be on the level** obrar sin engaño, decir la pura verdad; ser la pura verdad; **to find its level** o **to find one's level** hallar su propio nivel; *adj* raso, llano; nivelado; a nivel; (coll.) juicioso, sensato; **one's level best** (coll.) lo mejor que uno puede; **level with** al nivel de, a flor de, a ras de; (*pret & pp:* **-eled** o **-elled;** *ger:* **-eling** o **-elling**) *va* nivelar; arrasar, echar por tierra; apuntar (*un arma de fuego*); (fig.) allanar (*dificultades*); *vn* nivelar; apuntar un arma; dirigir la mente; **to level off** (aer.) nivelarse para aterrizar

**level crossing** *s* (Brit.) paso a nivel

**level-headed** [ˈlɛvəlˈhɛdɪd] *adj* juicioso, sensato

**leveling** o **levelling** [ˈlɛvəlɪŋ] *adj* nivelador; *s* nivelación

**leveling rod** *s* (surv.) jalón de mira

**lever** [ˈlɛvər] o [ˈlivər] *s* palanca; (mach. & mech.) palanca; *va & vn* apalancar

**leverage** [ˈlɛvərɪdʒ] o [ˈlivərɪdʒ] *s* palancada; poder de una palanca; influencia, poder, ventaja

**leveret** [ˈlɛvərɪt] *s* lebratillo

**Levi** [ˈlivaɪ] *s* (Bib.) Leví

**leviathan** [lɪˈvaɪəθən] *s* (Bib. & fig.) leviatán; buque muy grande

**levigate** [ˈlɛvɪget] *va* pulverizar; pulimentar; levigar (*desleír en agua para separar la parte más leve*)

**levigation** [ˌlɛvɪˈgeʃən] *s* pulverización; pulimento; levigación

**levirate** [ˈlɛvɪrɪt] o [ˈlivɪrɪt] *s* (hist.) levirato

**levitate** [ˈlɛvɪtet] *va* elevar y mantener en el aire (*por medios espiritistas*); *vn* elevarse y flotar en el aire

**levitation** [ˌlɛvɪˈteʃən] *s* levitación

**Levite** [ˈlivaɪt] *s* (Bib.) levita

**Levitical** [lɪˈvɪtɪkəl] *adj* levítico

**Leviticus** [lɪˈvɪtɪkəs] *s* (Bib.) Levítico

**levity** [ˈlɛvɪtɪ] *s* (*pl:* **-ties**) levedad, ligereza; frivolidad

**levoglucose** [ˌlivoˈglukos] *s* (chem.) levoglucosa

**levorotatory** [ˌlivoˈrotəˌtorɪ] *adj* (chem. & opt.) levógiro

**levulin** [ˈlɛvjəlɪn] *s* (chem.) levulina

**levulinic** [ˌlɛvjəˈlɪnɪk] *adj* levulínico

**levulinic acid** *s* (chem.) ácido levulínico

**levulose** [ˈlɛvjəlos] *s* (chem.) levulosa

**levy** [ˈlɛvɪ] *s* (*pl:* **-ies**) recaudación, exacción (*de tributos, impuestos*); dinero recaudado; (mil.) leva, recluta, enganche; (*pret & pp:* **-ied**) *va* recaudar, exigir (*tributos, impuestos*); hacer (*la guerra*); (law) embargar; (mil.) reclutar, enganchar
**lewd** [lud] *adj* lascivo, lujurioso; obsceno, indecente
**lewdness** [ˈludnɪs] *s* lascivia, lujuria; obscenidad, indecencia
**Lewis** [ˈluɪs] *s* Luis
**lewisite** [ˈluɪsaɪt] *s* (mil.) lewisita
**lexical** [ˈlɛksɪkəl] *adj* léxico
**lexicographer** [ˌlɛksɪˈkɑgrəfər] *s* lexicógrafo
**lexicographic** [ˌlɛksɪkoˈgræfɪk] o **lexicographical** [ˌlɛksɪkoˈgræfɪkəl] *adj* lexicográfico
**lexicography** [ˌlɛksɪˈkɑgrəfɪ] *s* lexicografía
**lexicologic** [ˌlɛksɪkəˈlɑdʒɪk] o **lexicological** [ˌlɛksɪkəˈlɑdʒɪkəl] *adj* lexicológico
**lexicologist** [ˌlɛksɪˈkɑlədʒɪst] *s* lexicólogo
**lexicology** [ˌlɛksɪˈkɑlədʒɪ] *s* lexicología
**lexicon** [ˈlɛksɪkən] *s* léxico o lexicón
**Leyden jar** [ˈlaɪdən] *s* (elec.) botella de Leiden
**L.I.** abr. de **Long Island**
**liability** [ˌlaɪəˈbɪlɪtɪ] *s* (*pl:* **-ties**) exposición, riesgo; responsabilidad; obligación; deuda; desventaja; **liabilities** *spl* (com.) pasivo
**liability insurance** *s* seguro contra responsabilidad civil
**liable** [ˈlaɪəbəl] *adj* sujeto, expuesto; responsable, obligado
**liaison** [ˌlieˈzõ] o [ˈliəˌzɑn] *s* enlace, unión; lío, amancebamiento; (mil.) enlace, intercomunicación; (phonet.) enlace de una consonante final con la vocal inicial de la palabra siguiente
**liaison officer** *s* (mil.) oficial de enlace
**liana** [lɪˈɑnə] o [lɪˈænə] o **liane** [lɪˈɑn] *s* (bot.) bejuco, liana
**liar** [ˈlaɪər] *s* mentiroso
**Liassic** [laɪˈæsɪk] *adj & s* (geol.) liásico
**lib.** abr. de **librarian, library** y **liber** (Lat.) **book**
**libation** [laɪˈbeʃən] *s* libación; (hum.) libación (*bebida alcohólica*)
**libel** [ˈlaɪbəl] *s* libelo (*escrito infamatorio*); calumnia, difamación; (*pret & pp:* **-beled** o **-belled;** *ger:* **-beling** o **-belling**) *va* calumniar, difamar
**libeler** o **libeller** [ˈlaɪbələr] *s* libelista (*autor de un libelo*); calumniador, difamador
**libelous** o **libellous** [ˈlaɪbələs] *adj* infamador, infamatorio, calumniador
**liber** [ˈlaɪbər] *s* (bot.) líber
**liberal** [ˈlɪbərəl] *adj* liberal; tolerante, de amplias miras; (pol.) liberal; libre (*traducción*); *s* (pol.) liberal
**liberal arts** *spl* artes liberales *fpl*
**liberal education** *s* instrucción que consiste en el estudio de las artes liberales
**liberalism** [ˈlɪbərəlɪzəm] *s* liberalismo
**liberality** [ˌlɪbəˈrælɪtɪ] *s* (*pl:* **-ties**) liberalidad
**liberalization** [ˌlɪbərəlɪˈzeʃən] *s* liberalización
**liberalize** [ˈlɪbərəlaɪz] *va* liberalizar; *vn* liberalizarse
**liberal-minded** [ˈlɪbərəlˈmaɪndɪd] *adj* tolerante, de amplias miras
**liberate** [ˈlɪbəret] *va* libertar; (chem.) desprender
**liberation** [ˌlɪbəˈreʃən] *s* liberación; (chem.) desprendimiento
**liberator** [ˈlɪbəˌretər] *s* liberador, libertador
**Liberian** [laɪˈbɪrɪən] *adj & s* liberiano
**liberticidal** [lɪˌbʌrtɪˈsaɪdəl] *adj* liberticida
**liberticide** [lɪˈbʌrtɪsaɪd] *s* liberticida (*destructor de la libertad*); destrucción de la libertad
**libertine** [ˈlɪbərtin] *adj & s* libertino
**libertinism** [ˈlɪbərtɪnɪzəm] *s* libertinaje
**liberty** [ˈlɪbərtɪ] *s* (*pl:* **-ties**) libertad; (naut.) licencia, permiso; **at liberty** en libertad; libre, desocupado; **to be at liberty to** + *inf* ser libre para + *inf*, tener permiso para + *inf;* **to take the liberty to** + *inf* tomarse la libertad de + *inf;* **to take liberties** tomarse libertades (*propasarse*)
**Liberty Bell** *s* (U.S.A.) campana de la libertad
**liberty cap** *s* gorro frigio
**liberty-loving** [ˈlɪbərtɪˈlʌvɪŋ] *adj* amante de la libertad
**libidinous** [lɪˈbɪdɪnəs] *adj* libidinoso
**libido** [lɪˈbido] o [lɪˈbaɪdo] *s* (psychol.) libídine o libido
**Libra** [ˈlaɪbrə] *s* (astr.) Libra
**librarian** [laɪˈbrɛrɪən] *s* bibliotecario
**library** [ˈlaɪˌbrɛrɪ] o [ˈlaɪbrərɪ] *s* (*pl:* **-ies**) biblioteca
**library number** *s* signatura
**library school** *s* escuela de bibliotecarios
**library science** *s* bibliotecnia, biblioteconomía
**libration** [laɪˈbreʃən] *s* libración; (astr.) libración
**librettist** [lɪˈbrɛtɪst] *s* libretista
**libretto** [lɪˈbrɛto] *s* (*pl:* **-tos**) (mus.) libreto
**Libya** [ˈlɪbɪə] *s* la Libia
**Libyan** [ˈlɪbɪən] *adj* líbico o libio; *s* libio
**Libyan Desert** *s* Desierto de Libia
**lice** [laɪs] *pl de* **louse**
**license** o **licence** [ˈlaɪsəns] *s* licencia (*permiso; documento en que consta la licencia; libertad abusiva; libertinaje*); *va* licenciar
**licensee** [ˌlaɪsənˈsi] *s* concesionario, persona que obtiene licencia
**license number** *s* número de matrícula
**license plate** *s* placa de matrícula, chapa de circulación
**license-plate light** [ˈlaɪsənsˈplet] *s* luz de matrícula
**license tag** *s* var. de **license plate**
**licentiate** [laɪˈsɛnʃɪɪt] o [laɪˈsɛnʃɪet] *s* licenciado (*el que tiene licencia para ejercer una profesión; el que tiene grado de licenciado*); licencia o licenciatura (*grado*)
**licentious** [laɪˈsɛnʃəs] *adj* licencioso
**licentiousness** [laɪˈsɛnʃəsnɪs] *s* libertinaje, licencia
**lichee** [ˈlitʃi] *s* var. de **litchi**
**lichen** [ˈlaɪkən] *s* (bot. & path.) liquen
**lichenin** [ˈlaɪkənɪn] *s* (chem.) liquenina
**lichenology** [ˌlaɪkəˈnɑlədʒɪ] *s* liquenología
**lichenous** [ˈlaɪkənəs] *adj* liquenoso
**lich gate** [lɪtʃ] *s* puerta de cementerio de parroquia donde se posa en tierra el féretro mientras se espera a que venga el pastor encargado del entierro
**licit** [ˈlɪsɪt] *adj* lícito
**lick** [lɪk] *s* lamedura; lamedero, salobral; (coll.) zurra; (coll.) velocidad; (coll.) bofetón; (coll.) vestigio; (coll.) pizca; (coll.) limpión; **to give a lick and a promise to** (coll.) hacer aprisa y mal, hacer rápida y superficialmente; *va* lamer; lamerse (*p.ej., los labios*); (fig.) lamer (*dícese de las llamas*); (coll.) zurrar; (coll.) vencer; (coll.) confundir; **to lick clean** lamer hasta dejar limpio
**lickerish** [ˈlɪkərɪʃ] *adj* goloso; codicioso; lascivo
**lickspittle** [ˈlɪkˌspɪtəl] *s* quitapelillos
**licorice** [ˈlɪkərɪs] *s* (bot.) orozuz, alcazuz, regaliz; dulce de orozuz, dulce de regaliz
**lictor** [ˈlɪktər] *s* (hist.) lictor
**lid** [lɪd] *s* tapa, tapadera (*de caja, cofre, arca, etc.*); cobertera (*de olla, cazuela, etc.*); (anat.) párpado; (slang) techo (*sombrero*)
**lidless** [ˈlɪdlɪs] *adj* sin tapa, sin tapadera; sin párpados; (poet.) vigilante
**lie** [laɪ] *s* mentira; mentís (*acción de desmentir*); disposición, situación, orientación; **to catch in a lie** coger en una mentira; **to give the lie to** dar un mentís a ‖ (*pret & pp:* **lied;** *ger:* **lying**) *va* conseguir mintiendo; **to lie one's way out of** vencer (*p.ej., una dificultad*) mintiendo ‖ *vn* mentir ‖ (*pret:* **lay;** *pp:* **lain;** *ger:* **lying**) *vn* echarse, acostarse; estar echado; estar situado, hallarse; yacer, estar enterrado; (archaic) pernoctar; **to lie down** echarse, acostarse; **to lie in** depender de; consistir en; corresponder a; estar de parto; **to lie off** (naut.) guardar cierta distancia de; descansar; (slang) contenerse al principio (*de una carrera*); **to lie over** detenerse algún tiempo, esperando la hora o la ocasión de continuar el viaje; aplazarse; quedar en suspenso; **to lie to** (naut.) aguantarse a la capa; **to lie with** tocar a, corresponder a; yacer con (*tener trato carnal con*)
**lie detector** *s* detector de mentiras

**lief** [lif] *adv* de buena gana; **I would as lief** + *inf* tanto me da + *inf*
**liege** [lidʒ] *adj* feudal; vasallo; *s* señor feudal; vasallo
**Liége** [lɪ'eʒ] *s* Lieja
**liege lord** *s* señor feudal
**liegeman** ['lidʒmən] *s* (*pl:* **-men**) vasallo; (fig.) fiel secuaz
**lien** [lin] o ['liən] *s* (law) embargo preventivo, derecho de retención
**lienteric** [,laɪən'tɛrɪk] *adj* lientérico
**lientery** ['laɪən,tɛrɪ] *s* (path.) lientera o lientería
**lie of the land** *s* var. de **lay of the land**
**lieu** [lu] *s* lugar; **in lieu of** en lugar de, en vez de
**Lieut.** abr. de **Lieutenant**
**lieutenancy** [lu'tɛnənsɪ] *s* (*pl:* **-cies**) lugartenencia; (mil. & nav.) tenencia
**lieutenant** [lu'tɛnənt] *s* lugarteniente; (mil.) teniente; (nav.) teniente de navío
**lieutenant colonel** *s* (mil.) teniente coronel
**lieutenant commander** *s* (nav.) capitán de corbeta
**lieutenant general** *s* (mil.) teniente general
**lieutenant governor** *s* (U.S.A.) vicegobernador; (Brit.) lugarteniente del gobernador (*de una colonia o provincia*)
**lieutenant junior grade** *s* (nav.) alférez de navío
**lieve** [liv] *adv* var. de **lief**
**life** [laɪf] *s* (*pl:* **lives**) vida; vigencia (*de una póliza*); **as big as life** de tamaño natural; en persona; **for the life of me** a fe mía, así me maten; **for life** de por vida, por toda la vida; **from life** del natural; **the life and soul of** la alegría de (*p.ej., la fiesta*); **to come to life** volver a la vida; **to depart this life** partir o partirse de esta vida; **to have life** vivir; tener vivacidad; **to put new life into** vigorizar; **to run for one's life** salvarse por los pies, salir huyendo para que no le maten; **to see life** ver mundo; **to take one's own life** quitarse la vida; **to take one's life in one's hands** tomarse la muerte por su mano, jugarse la vida; **to the life** del natural, fielmente; *adj* vital (*perteneciente a la vida*); perpetuo; vitalicio; (f.a.) copiando el modelo vivo
**life-and-death struggle** ['laɪfən'dɛθ] *s* lucha a vida o muerte
**life annuitant** *s* vitalicista
**life annuity** *s* renta vitalicia
**life belt** *s* cinturón salvavidas
**lifeblood** ['laɪf,blʌd] *s* sangre vital; alma, nervio
**lifeboat** ['laɪf,bot] *s* bote de salvamento, bote salvavidas, salvavidas; lancha de auxilio (*en los puertos*)
**lifeboat drill** *s* (naut.) ejercicios con botes de salvamento
**lifeboat station** *s* estación de salvamento
**life buoy** *s* (naut.) boya salvavidas
**life expectancy** *s* expectación de vida
**lifeguard** ['laɪf,gɑrd] *s* empleado de una estación de salvamento
**Life Guards** *spl* (Brit.) guardia de corps
**life imprisonment** *s* cadena perpetua
**life insurance** *s* seguro sobre la vida
**life interest** *s* (law) usufructo
**lifeless** ['laɪflɪs] *adj* sin vida, muerto; exánime, desmayado; deslucido, amortiguado
**lifelike** ['laɪf,laɪk] *adj* natural, vivo
**life line** *s* cuerda salvavidas; cuerda de comunicación (*de una escafandra*); línea de la vida (*en la quiromancía*)
**lifelong** ['laɪf,lɔŋ] o ['laɪf,lɑŋ] *adj* de toda la vida; *adv* durante toda la vida; *s* toda la vida
**life net** *s* red de salvamento
**life of leisure** *s* vida de ocio
**life of Riley** ['raɪlɪ] *s* vida regalada
**life of the party** *s* (coll.) alma de la fiesta, alegría de la fiesta
**life preserver** *s* salvavidas, chaleco flotador; (Brit.) cachiporra
**lifer** ['laɪfər] *s* (slang) presidiario de por vida
**life raft** *s* balsa salvavidas
**lifesaver** ['laɪf,sevər] *s* salvador (*persona que salva la vida a otra*); empleado de una estación de salvamento; (coll.) paño de lágrimas, tabla de salvación
**lifesaving** ['laɪf,sevɪŋ] *adj* de salvamento; *s* salvamento; servicio de salvavidas
**lifesaving gun** *s* cañón lanzacabos
**life sentence** *s* condena a cadena perpetua
**life-size** ['laɪf,saɪz] *adj* de tamaño natural
**life span** *s* vida (*la duración más larga de una especie animal o vegetal*)
**lifetime** ['laɪf,taim] *s* vida, curso de la vida; *adj* vitalicio
**lifework** ['laɪf,wʌrk] *s* trabajo de toda la vida, obra principal de la vida de uno
**lift** [lɪft] *s* elevación, levantamiento; empuje hacia arriba; tapa (*del tacón del zapato*); altura de aspiración (*de una bomba*); juego de una leva; fuerza de sustentación o fuerza ascensional (*de un avión*); ayuda (*para levantar una carga*); elevación del terreno, repecho; invitación para subir a un coche que pasa; paseo en un coche que pasa; exaltación, estímulo; (Brit.) ascensor; **to give a lift to** ayudar a levantar o a levantarse; invitar (*a un peatón*) a subir a un coche; llevar en un coche; (fig.) reanimar; *va* levantar, elevar; extinguir (*una hipoteca*); quitarse (*el sombrero*); exaltar, estimular; (naut.) izar (*vergas, velas, etc.*); (coll.) robar; (coll.) plagiar; *vn* levantarse, elevarse; disiparse (*las nubes, la niebla, la obscuridad*); aparecer en el horizonte (*la tierra, cuando el navegante se aproxima a la costa*); **to lift at** tratar de levantar
**lift bridge** *s* puente levadizo
**lifter** ['lɪftər] *s* alzador; aparato de alzamiento; (mach.) leva
**lift-off** ['lɪft,ɔf] o ['lɪft,ɑf] *s* despegue vertical
**lift pump** *s* bomba aspirante
**ligament** ['lɪgəmənt] *s* ligamento; (anat. & zool.) ligamento
**ligamentous** [,lɪgə'mɛntəs] *adj* ligamentoso
**ligate** ['laɪget] *va* (surg.) ligar
**ligation** [laɪ'geʃən] *s* ligación
**ligator** [laɪ'getər] *s* (surg.) ligador
**ligature** ['lɪgətʃər] *s* ligadura; (mus.) ligado, ligadura; (print.) ligado; (surg.) ligadura; *va* ligar
**light** [laɪt] *adj* ligero, leve, liviano; ligero (*dotado de pocas armas o poca impedimenta; fino, delicado; ágil, rápido; de poca monta; superficial; impertinente; inconstante; alegre; dícese también del alimento, vino, sueño*); claro (*luminoso, brillante; que recibe mucha luz; de color poco subido; dícese tambien de la cerveza*); rubio, blondo; de tez blanca; arenoso (*suelo*); flúido (*aceite*); poco serio (*dícese, p.ej., de la lectura*); (naut.) boyante (*que no cala lo que debe calar*); **light in the head** mareado; tonto, necio; loco; **to be light on one's feet** andar con mucha agilidad; **to make light of** no dar importancia a, no tomar en serio ‖ *adv* ligeramente ‖ *s* luz; lumbre o fuego (*p.ej., para encender el cigarro*); luz o señal (*de tráfico*); luz, claro, hueco (*ventana, tronera u otra abertura en una pared*); lumbrera (*persona insigne*); (fig.) lumbre (*p.ej., del rostro de Dios*); **lights** *spl* bofes, livianos; noticias; conocimientos; (slang) ojos; **according to one's lights** según Dios le da a uno a entender, lo mejor que uno puede; **against the light** al trasluz; **in the light of** a la luz de; **in this light** desde este punto de vista; **to bring to light** sacar a luz, descubrir, revelar; **to cast light on** echar luz sobre; **to come to light** salir a luz, descubrirse; **to see the light** o **to see the light of day** salir a luz, ver la luz; caer en la cuenta; ver el cielo abierto (*descubrir el medio de salir de un apuro*); **to shed** o **throw light on** o **upon** echar luz sobre; **to strike a light** echar una yesca; encender un fósforo ‖ (*pret & pp:* **lighted** o **lit**) *va* encender (*una luz, el fuego, el cigarro, etc.*); alumbrar (*dar luz a*); iluminar (*dar luz a; adornar con muchas luces*); **to light up** iluminar ‖ *vn* encenderse; alumbrarse; bajar (*p.ej., de un coche*); posar (*las aves*); **to light into** (slang) arremeter contra; (slang) poner de oro y azul; **to light out** (slang) salir pitando, poner pies en polvorosa; **to light upon** dar con, tropezar con, hallar por casualidad
**light air** *s* (naut.) ventolina
**light alloy** *s* metal ligero de aleación

**light-armed** ['laɪt'ɑrmd] *adj* armado de armas ligeras, armado de armadura ligera
**light breeze** *s* (naut.) viento flojito
**light bulb** *s* ampolleta, bombilla
**light-complexioned** ['laɪtkəm'plɛkʃənd] *adj* de tez blanca
**lighten** ['laɪtən] *va* aligerar; alegrar, regocijar; iluminar; *vn* aligerarse; alegrarse, regocijarse; iluminarse; relampaguear; (fig.) iluminarse (*la cara de una persona*)
**lighter** ['laɪtər] *s* alumbrador; mecha (*para pegar fuego a cohetes, minas, etc.*); encendedor (*p.ej., de cigarrillos*); alijador (*barcaza*); *va* transportar en alijador
**lighterage** ['laɪtərɪdʒ] *s* alijo; gastos de alijo
**lighter-than-air** [,laɪtərθən'ɛr] *adj* (aer.) más ligero que el aire
**lightface** ['laɪt,fes] *s* (print.) tipo común
**light-fingered** ['laɪt'fɪŋgərd] *adj* largo de uñas, listo de manos
**light-foot** ['laɪt,fʊt] o **light-footed** ['laɪt'fʊtɪd] *adj* ligero de pies
**light-headed** ['laɪt'hɛdɪd] *adj* mareado; casquivano, ligero de cascos; delirante
**light-hearted** ['laɪt'hɑrtɪd] *adj* libre de cuidados, alegre
**light heavyweight** *s* (box.) peso pesado ligero, peso medio fuerte
**light horse** *s* (mil.) caballería ligera
**light-horseman** ['laɪt,hɔrsmən] *s* (*pl:* **-men**) soldado de un cuerpo de caballería ligera
**lighthouse** ['laɪt,haʊs] *s* faro
**lighthouseman** ['laɪt,haʊsmən] *s* (*pl:* **-men**) torrero
**light infantry** *s* infantería ligera
**lighting** ['laɪtɪŋ] *s* iluminación, alumbrado; encendido, encendimiento
**lighting fixtures** *spl* artefactos de alumbrado
**lightly** ['laɪtlɪ] *adv* ligeramente
**light meter** *s* (phot.) exposímetro
**light-minded** ['laɪt'maɪndɪd] *adj* tonto, atolondrado
**lightness** ['laɪtnɪs] *s* ligereza; claridad, blancura, luminosidad
**lightning** ['laɪtnɪŋ] *s* relámpagos, relampagueo; *vn* relampaguear
**lightning arrester** *s* pararrayos
**lightning bug** *s* (ent.) bicho de luz, luciérnaga
**lightning rod** *s* pararrayos, barra pararrayos
**light of the World** *s* (theol.) luz del mundo
**light opera** *s* (mus.) opereta
**lightship** ['laɪt,ʃɪp] *s* (naut.) buque fanal, buque faro
**lightsome** ['laɪtsəm] *adj* ligero (*ágil; frívolo*); alegre, festivo
**light-struck** ['laɪt,strʌk] *adj* velado (*por la acción indebida de la luz*)
**lightweight** ['laɪt,wet] *s* persona de poco peso; (box.) peso ligero, peso liviano; (coll.) pelele; *adj* ligero; de entretiempo, p.ej., **lightweight coat** abrigo de entretiempo
**light-year** ['laɪt,jɪr] *s* (astr.) año luz
**ligneous** ['lɪgnɪəs] *adj* lignario, leñoso
**lignify** ['lɪgnɪfaɪ] (*pret & pp:* **-fied**) *va* convertir en madera; *vn* lignificarse
**lignin** ['lɪgnɪn] *s* (bot.) lignina
**lignite** ['lɪgnaɪt] *s* (mineral.) lignito
**lignocellulose** [,lɪgnə'sɛljəlos] *s* lignocelulosa
**lignum vitae** ['lɪgnəm 'vaɪti] *s* (bot.) guayacán o guayaco (*árbol*); palo santo (*madera*)
**ligroin** ['lɪgro·ɪn] *s* (chem.) ligroína
**ligula** ['lɪgjələ] *s* (*pl:* **-lae** [li] o **-las**) (anat., bot. & zool.) lígula
**ligulate** ['lɪgjəlɪt] o ['lɪgjəlet] *adj* ligulado
**ligule** ['lɪgjul] *s* (bot. & zool.) lígula
**Ligurian** [lɪ'gjʊrɪən] *adj & s* ligur o ligurino
**likable** ['laɪkəbəl] *adj* simpático
**like** [laɪk] *adj* parecido, semejante, p.ej., **a like instance** un ejemplo semejante; **plants with like flowers** plantas con flores semejantes; parecido a, semejante a, p.ej., **this book is like the other one** este libro es semejante al otro; propio de, característico de; (elec.) del mismo nombre (*dícese de los polos de un imán*); **something like** algo así como; **to be like to** + *inf* (archaic & coll.) ser probable que + *subj*, p.ej., **the king is like to die** es probable que muera el rey; **to feel like** + *ger* tener ganas de + *inf;* **to look like** parecerse a; parecer que, p.ej., **it looks like rain** parece que va a llover ‖ *adv* del mismo modo; probablemente, p.ej., **like enough it will rain** probablemente lloverá; **nothing like** ni con mucho; **like mad** como un loco ‖ *prep* como ‖ *conj* (coll.) del mismo modo que; (coll.) que, p.ej., **it looks like he's right** parece que tiene razón ‖ *s* semejante; gusto, preferencia; **and the like** y cosas por el estilo; **the like** o **the likes of him** (coll.) otro semejante; **to give like for like** pagar en la misma moneda ‖ *va* gustar, p.ej., **John did not like these apples** no le gustaron a Juan estas manzanas; gustar de, p.ej., **I like music** gusto de la música; **to like better** o **best** preferir; **to like it in** estar o encontrarse a gusto en (*p.ej., el campo*); **to like to** + *inf* gustarle a uno + *inf*, p.ej., **I like to travel** me gusta viajar; gustar de + *inf*, p.ej., **I like to read** gusto de leer; **to like** (*someone*) **to** + *inf* gustar que + *subj*, p.ej., **I should like him to come to see me** me gustaría que viniese a verme ‖ *vn* querer, p.ej., **as you like** como Vd. quiera; (coll.) por poco, p.ej., **he liked to have died laughing** o **he had like to have died laughing** por poco murió de risa
**likeable** ['laɪkəbəl] *adj* var. de **likable**
**likelihood** ['laɪklɪhʊd] *s* probabilidad
**likely** ['laɪklɪ] *adj* (*comp:* **-lier**; *super:* **-liest**) probable; prometiente, prometedor; **to be likely to** + *inf* ser probable que + *subj*, p.ej., **John is likely to arrive early** es probable que Juan llegue temprano
**like-minded** ['laɪk'maɪndɪd] *adj* del mismo parecer, de natural semejante
**liken** ['laɪkən] *va* asemejar, comparar
**likeness** ['laɪknɪs] *s* parecido, semejanza; retrato; forma, aspecto; **to be a good likeness** tener un gran parecido
**likewise** ['laɪk,waɪz] *adv* asimismo, igualmente; del mismo modo; lo mismo, p.ej., **the rest did likewise** los demás hicieron lo mismo
**liking** ['laɪkɪŋ] *s* gusto, preferencia, afición, simpatía; **to be to the liking of** ser del gusto de; **to take a liking for** o **to** tomar el gusto a, aficionarse a
**lilac** ['laɪlək] *s* (bot.) lila (*arbusto y flor*); lila (*color*); *adj* de color de lila
**liliaceous** [,lɪlɪ'eʃəs] *adj* (bot.) liliáceo
**Lille** [lil] *s* Lila
**Lilliputian** [,lɪlɪ'pjuʃən] *adj & s* liliputiense
**lilt** [lɪlt] *s* música o canción alegres; paso o movimiento airosos; *va* tocar o cantar (*una melodía*) airosamente
**lily** ['lɪlɪ] *s* (*pl:* **-ies**) (bot.) azucena; (bot.) lirio de agua, cala; flor de lis (*escudo de armas de Francia*); **to gild the lily** ponerle colores al oro; *adj* de alabastro, blanco; puro, tierno; pálido
**lily family** *s* (bot.) liliáceas
**lily-livered** ['lɪlɪ,lɪvərd] *adj* cobarde, pusilánime
**lily of the valley** *s* (bot.) muguete, lirio de los valles
**lily pad** *s* hoja de nenúfar
**Lima bean** ['laɪmə] *s* (bot.) judía de la peladilla, frijol de media luna (*Phaseolus limensis*)
**Lima wood** ['limə] o ['laɪmə] *s* madera de cesalpinea tintórea
**limb** [lɪm] *s* miembro (*brazo o pierna*); rama (*de árbol*); vástago (*de una planta o una familia*); brazo (*de cruz; del mar*); (astr., bot. & surv.) limbo; **to be a limb of the devil** u **of Satan** ser maligno; ser la piel o de la piel del diablo; **to be out on a limb** (coll.) estar en un aprieto
**limber** ['lɪmbər] *s* (arti.) armón, avantrén; *adj* flexible; ágil; *va* poner flexible; agilitar; *vn* ponerse flexible; agilitarse; **to limber up** ponerse flexible; agilitarse; (fig.) humanarse (*hacerse más afable*)
**limbo** ['lɪmbo] *s* (theol.) limbo; lugar de personas o cosas olvidadas o pasadas de moda; cárcel, prisión
**limb of the law** *s* policía, guardia; abogado; juez
**Limburg** ['lɪmbʌrg] *s* Limburgo
**Limburger** ['lɪmbʌrgər] *s* queso de Limburgo
**lime** [laɪm] *s* cal; calcio; liga (*materia viscosa*); (bot.) limero agrio (*Citrus aurantifolia*); lima

agria (*fruto*); (bot.) tila o tilo; *va* encalar; (agr.) encalar; untar con liga; coger (*pájaros*) con liga
**Limean** ['limɪən] *adj & s* limeño
**lime burner** *s* calero
**limekiln** ['laɪm,kɪl] o ['laɪm,kɪln] *s* horno de cal, calera
**limelight** ['laɪm,laɪt] *s* (theat.) haz luminoso del proyector; **to be in the limelight** estar a la vista del público
**limen** ['laɪmɛn] *s* (*pl:* **-mens** o **-mina** [mɪnə]) (psychol.) umbral
**limerick** ['lɪmərɪk] *s* quintilla jocosa
**limestone** ['laɪm,ston] *s* caliza, piedra caliza; *adj* calizo
**limewater** ['laɪm,wɔtər] o ['laɪm,wɑtər] *s* agua de cal
**liminal** ['lɪmɪnəl] o ['laɪmɪnəl] *adj* (psychol.) liminal
**limit** ['lɪmɪt] *s* límite; **to be the limit** (slang) ser el colmo, ser inaguantable; **to go the limit** no dejar piedra por mover, hacer todos los esfuerzos posibles; **to know no limit** no tener límites, ser infinito; *va* limitar; **to limit to** + *ger* limitar a + *inf*
**limitation** [,lɪmɪ'teʃən] *s* limitación; (law) prescripción
**limitative** ['lɪmɪ,tetɪv] *adj* limitativo
**limited** ['lɪmɪtɪd] *adj* limitado; *s* (rail.) tren expreso con tarifa recargada
**limited company** *s* (com.) sociedad limitada
**limited monarchy** *s* monarquía constitucional
**limiter** ['lɪmɪtər] *s* limitador; (elec.) limitacorrientes
**limitless** ['lɪmɪtlɪs] *adj* ilimitado
**limit turbine** *s* turbina límite
**limn** [lɪm] *va* pintar (*un cuadro*); (fig.) pintar (*describir*)
**limnology** [lɪm'nɑlədʒɪ] *s* limnología
**limonene** ['lɪmənin] *s* (chem.) limoneno
**limonite** ['laɪmənaɪt] *s* (mineral.) limonita
**limousine** ['lɪmə,zin] o [,lɪmə'zin] *s* (aut.) limosina
**limp** [lɪmp] *s* cojera; paso cojeante; *adj* flojo; flexible; (fig.) blando, sin carácter; *vn* cojear; (fig.) cojear (*un verso*)
**limpet** ['lɪmpɪt] *s* (zool.) lapa, lápade
**limpid** ['lɪmpɪd] *adj* diáfano, cristalino; claro
**limpidity** [lɪm'pɪdɪtɪ] *s* diafanidad; claridad
**limpkin** ['lɪmpkɪn] *s* (orn.) guariao
**limy** ['laɪmɪ] *adj* (*comp:* **-ier**; *super:* **-iest**) calizo; pegajoso, viscoso; untado con liga
**linage** ['laɪnɪdʒ] *s* alineación; (print.) número de líneas
**linaloöl** [lɪ'nælool], [lɪ'næloɑl] o [,lɪnə'lul] *s* (chem.) linalol
**linchpin** ['lɪntʃ,pɪn] *s* pezonera, sotrozo
**linden** ['lɪndən] *s* (bot.) tila o tilo
**line** [laɪn] *s* línea; cuerda, cordel; sedal (*de la caña de pescar*); arruga; renglón (*línea escrita o impresa; ramo de mercancías*); ramo (*de mercancías, de negocios*); surtido; especialidad; manera (*de pensar*); (phys.) raya (*del espectro*); (slang) charla propia (*de una persona*); **lines** *spl* línea (*contorno*); (theat.) papel; versos; riendas; (mil.) línea defensiva, trincheras; **a line** unas líneas (*carta muy breve*); **all along the line** en toda la línea; por todas partes; desde cualquier punto de vista; **in line** alineado; dispuesto, preparado; **in line with** de acuerdo con; **on a line** nivelado, ras con ras; **on the line** en la línea divisoria; ni lo uno ni lo otro; **out of line** desalineado; en desacuerdo; **the line** (geog.) la línea (*el ecuador*); **to bring into line** poner de acuerdo, convencer, persuadir; **to come into line** ponerse de acuerdo, dejarse convencer o persuadir; **to draw the line at** no ir más allá de; **to fall in line** conformarse; formar cola; (mil.) alinearse en su lugar; **to fall into line** ponerse de acuerdo; **to get a line on** (coll.) llegar a conocer; **to get in line** alinearse; ponerse de acuerdo; **to get out of line** salirse de la fila; **to have a line on** (coll.) conocer, estar enterado de; **to read between the lines** leer entre líneas, leer entre renglones; **to stand in line** hacer cola; **to take a line** adoptar una actitud; **to toe the line** ponerse en la raya; obrar como se debe; **to wait in line** hacer cola (*esperar vez formando cola con otras personas*); *va* linear, rayar; arrugar (*p.ej., la cara*); alinear; formar hilera a lo largo de (*p.ej., la acera*); forrar (*p.ej., un vestido*); guarnecer (*un freno*); **to line up** (mach.) alinear; *vn* alinearse; **to line up** ponerse en fila; hacer cola
**lineage** ['lɪnɪɪdʒ] *s* linaje; alineación; (print.) número de líneas
**lineal** ['lɪnɪəl] *adj* lineal; hereditario; en línea recta
**lineally** ['lɪnɪəlɪ] *adv* en línea recta
**lineament** ['lɪnɪəmənt] *s* lineamento; **lineaments** *spl* lineamentos (*del rostro*)
**linear** ['lɪnɪər] *adj* lineal
**linear equation** *s* (alg.) ecuación de primer grado
**linearity** [,lɪnɪ'ærɪtɪ] *s* linearidad
**linear measure** *s* medida de longitud; sistema de medidas de longitud
**linear perspective** *s* perspectiva lineal
**line engraving** *s* grabado de líneas
**lineman** ['laɪnmən] *s* (*pl:* **-men**) (elec.) recorredor de la línea; (rail.) guardavía; (surv.) cadenero; (football) jugador de la línea de embestida
**linen** ['lɪnən] *s* lienzo, lino; hilo de lino; ropa blanca; *adj* de lino
**linen draper** *s* lencero
**linen drapery** *s* lencería
**line of battle** *s* línea de batalla, línea de combate
**line of circumvallation** *s* (fort.) línea de circunvalación
**line of collimation** *s* línea de colimación
**Line of Demarcation** *s* (hist.) línea de demarcación
**line of fire** *s* (mil.) línea de tiro
**line of force** *s* (phys.) línea de fuerza
**line of incidence** *s* línea de incidencia
**line of least resistance** *s* (fig.) ley del menor esfuerzo; **to follow the line of least resistance** seguir la corriente, no hacer resistencia
**line of march** *s* recorrido
**line of sight** *s* (arti. & surv.) línea de mira
**line of vision** *s* visual
**liner** ['laɪnər] *s* trazador de líneas; forrador; forro; vapor o avión de travesía; (mach.) forro tubular; (baseball) pelota rasa
**line radio** *s* (rad.) radiocomunicación por corrientes de alta frecuencia de una red alambrada
**linesman** ['laɪnzmən] *s* (*pl:* **-men**) (elec.) recorredor de la línea; (sport) juez de línea; (mil.) soldado de línea
**line squall** *s* (meteor.) línea de turbonada
**line-up** ['laɪn,ʌp] *s* formación; rueda de presos
**ling** [lɪŋ] *s* (ichth.) bacalao ling, abadejo largo; (ichth.) lota; (bot.) brezo (*Calluna vulgaris y plantas de los géneros Carex y Erica*)
**linger** ['lɪŋgər] *vn* estarse, quedarse; demorar, tardar; tardar en marcharse; tardar en morirse; **to linger over** meditar, reflexionar (*una cosa*)
**lingerie** [,lænʒə'ri] *s* lencería; lencería fina; ropa blanca de mujer
**lingering** ['lɪŋgərɪŋ] *adj* prolongado, lento
**lingo** ['lɪŋgo] *s* (*pl:* **-goes**) idioma; algarabía; jerga (*de los individuos de ciertas profesiones u oficios*)
**lingua franca** ['lɪŋgwə 'fræŋkə] *s* lengua franca
**lingual** ['lɪŋgwəl] *adj* lingual; (phonet.) lingual; *s* (phonet.) lingual
**linguist** ['lɪŋgwɪst] *s* lingüista (*el que estudia la lingüística*); poligloto (*el que sabe varias lenguas*)
**linguistic** [lɪŋ'gwɪstɪk] *adj* lingüístico; **linguistics** *ssg* lingüística
**linguistically** [lɪŋ'gwɪstɪkəlɪ] *adv* lingüísticamente
**linguistic geography** *s* geografía lingüística
**liniment** ['lɪnɪmənt] *s* linimento
**linin** ['laɪnɪn] *s* (biol. & chem.) linina
**lining** ['laɪnɪŋ] *s* forro; guarnición (*de freno*); rayado
**link** [lɪŋk] *s* eslabón; eslabón de la cadena de Gúnter (*201,2 mm*); hacha de viento; varilla de conexión; meandro de río; (fig.) eslabón;

**links** *spl* campo de golf; *va* eslabonar; *vn* eslabonarse
**linkage** [ˈlɪŋkɪdʒ] *s* eslabonamiento; (chem.) enlace; (elec.) acoplamiento inductivo; (mech.) varillaje
**linkboy** [ˈlɪŋk,bɔɪ] *s* (hist.) paje de hacha
**Linnaean** o **Linnean** [lɪˈniən] *adj* linneano
**linnet** [ˈlɪnɪt] *s* (orn.) pardillo; (orn.) jilguero
**linoleum** [lɪˈnolɪəm] *s* linóleo
**linotype** [ˈlaɪnətaɪp] *s* (trademark) linotipia; *va* componer con linotipia
**linotyper** [ˈlaɪnə,taɪpər] o **linotypist** [ˈlaɪnə,taɪpɪst] *s* linotipista
**linseed** [ˈlɪn,sid] *s* linaza
**linseed cake** *s* torta de linaza
**linseed meal** *s* harina de linaza
**linseed oil** *s* aceite de linaza
**linsey** [ˈlɪnzɪ] o **linsey-woolsey** [ˈlɪnzɪˈwʊlzɪ] *s* tela basta de lino y lana o de algodón y lana; *adj* de lino y lana, de algodón y lana; basto; ni fu ni fa
**linstock** [ˈlɪn,stɑk] *s* botafuego
**lint** [lɪnt] *s* hilacha; hilas (*para curar las llagas*)
**lintel** [ˈlɪntəl] *s* (arch.) dintel
**lion** [ˈlaɪən] *s* (zool.) león; (fig.) león (*hombre audaz y valiente*); (fig.) celebridad muy solicitada; (*cap.*) *s* (astr.) León; **to beard the lion in his den** entrar en el cubil de la fiera (*a desafiar la cólera de un jefe, etc.*); **to put one's head in the lion's mouth** meterse en la boca del lobo
**lioness** [ˈlaɪənɪs] *s* leona
**lion-hearted** [ˈlaɪən,hɑrtɪd] *adj* valiente
**lionization** [,laɪənɪˈzeʃən] *s* agasajo
**lionize** [ˈlaɪənaɪz] *va* agasajar
**lions' den** *s* (Bib.) fosa de los leones
**lion's-foot** [ˈlaɪənz,fʊt] *s* (bot.) pie de león
**lion's share** *s* parte del león
**lip** [lɪp] *s* labio; labio, pico (*de un jarro*); (mach.) labio; (mus.) boquilla o embocadura; (surg.) labio (*de una herida*); (slang) insolencias; **lips** *spl* (fig.) labios (*palabras*); **to hang on the lips of** estar pendiente de las palabras de; **to keep a stiff upper lip** no desanimarse; **to lick one's lips** lamerse los labios; (*pret & pp:* **lipped;** *ger:* **lipping**) *va* rozar con los labios; besar; lamer; murmurar; (slang) cantar; *vn* chapotear; (mus.) tocar un instrumento de viento
**lipase** [ˈlaɪpes] o [ˈlɪpes] *s* (biochem.) lipasa
**lipoma** [lɪˈpomə] *s* (*pl:* **-mata** [mətə] o **-mas**) (path.) lipoma
**lip-read** [ˈlɪp,rid] (*pret & pp:* **-read** [,rɛd]) *va & vn* leer en los labios
**lip reading** *s* lectura de los movimientos de los labios, labiolectura
**lip service** *s* jarabe de pico, homenaje de boca
**lipstick** [ˈlɪp,stɪk] *s* lápiz labial, lápiz de labios, barra de labios
**liq.** abr. de **liquid** y **liquor**
**liquate** [ˈlaɪkwet] *va* (metal.) licuar
**liquation** [laɪˈkweʃən] *s* (metal.) licuación
**liquefaction** [,lɪkwɪˈfækʃən] *s* licuefacción, liquidación
**liquefiable** [ˈlɪkwɪ,faɪəbəl] *adj* liquidable
**liquefy** [ˈlɪkwɪfaɪ] (*pret & pp:* **-fied**) *va* liquidar; *vn* liquidarse
**liquescence** [lɪˈkwɛsəns] *s* licuescencia
**liquescent** [lɪˈkwɛsənt] *adj* licuescente
**liqueur** [lɪˈkʌr] *s* licor (*bebida espiritosa preparada por mezcla de azúcar y substancias aromáticas*)
**liquid** [ˈlɪkwɪd] *adj* líquido; claro, puro (*sonido*); (com.) realizable; (phonet.) líquido; *s* líquido; (phonet.) líquida
**liquid air** *s* aire líquido
**liquidambar** [ˈlɪkwɪd,æmbər] *s* (bot.) liquidámbar (*árbol y líquido*)
**liquid ammonia** *s* (chem.) amoníaco líquido
**liquidate** [ˈlɪkwɪdet] *va* liquidar; (slang) matar (*a una persona*); *vn* liquidarse
**liquidation** [,lɪkwɪˈdeʃən] *s* liquidación
**liquidator** [ˈlɪkwɪ,detər] *s* liquidador
**liquid crystal** *s* cristal líquido
**liquid fire** *s* (mil.) fuego líquido
**liquidity** [lɪˈkwɪdɪtɪ] *s* liquidez
**liquid measure** *s* medida para líquidos; sistema de medidas para líquidos
**liquor** [ˈlɪkər] *s* licor (*bebida espiritosa; cuerpo líquido*); (pharm.) licor

**liquorice** [ˈlɪkərɪs] *s* var. de **licorice**
**Lisbon** [ˈlɪzbən] *s* Lisboa
**lisle** [laɪl] *s* hilo de Escocia
**lisp** [lɪsp] *s* ceceo; balbuceo; *vn* cecear; balbucear
**lisper** [ˈlɪspər] *s* zopas
**lissome** o **lissom** [ˈlɪsəm] *adj* flexible, elástico; ágil, ligero
**list** [lɪst] lista (*serie de palabras, nombres, etc.*); lista, tira; orilla (*de una tela*); orillo (*orilla basta*); (naut.) ladeo; **lists** *spl* liza (*campo para la lid*); barrera (*de la liza*); **to have a list** (naut.) irse a la banda, recalcar; **to enter the lists** entrar en liza, entrar en la contienda; *va* poner en una lista; hacer una lista de; registrar; alistar; orillar; (naut.) ladear, hacer recalcar; (archaic & poet.) escuchar; *vn* alistarse; (naut.) irse a la banda, recalcar; (archaic & poet.) escuchar; (archaic) querer, antojarse, p.ej., **the wind bloweth where it listeth** el viento sopla donde se le antoja
**listel** [ˈlɪstəl] *s* (arch.) listel
**listen** [ˈlɪsən] *vn* escuchar, oír; obedecer; **to listen in** escuchar a hurtadillas (*descolgando el receptor de un teléfono, sin que los interlocutores lo sepan*); escuchar por radio; **to listen to** escuchar, oír; **to listen to reason** meterse en razón
**listener** [ˈlɪsənər] *s* oyente; radioyente, radioescucha
**listening post** *s* puesto de escucha
**lister** [ˈlɪstər] *s* (agr.) arado de pala y vuelos; (agr.) arado sembrador
**listerine** [,lɪstəˈrin] o [ˈlɪstərin] *s* (trademark) listerina
**listless** [ˈlɪstlɪs] *adj* desatento, descuidado, indiferente
**listlessness** [ˈlɪstlɪsnɪs] *s* desatención, descuido, indiferencia
**list price** *s* precio de tarifa, precio de catálogo
**lit.** abr. de **liter, literature, literal** y **literally**
**lit** [lɪt] *pret & pp de* **light**
**litany** [ˈlɪtənɪ] *s* (*pl:* **-nies**) letanía; (fig.) letanía (*enumeración seguida*)
**litchi** [ˈlitʃi] *s* (bot.) litchi
**Lit.D.** abr. de **litterarum doctor** (Lat.) **Doctor of Letters**
**liter** [ˈlitər] *s* litro
**literacy** [ˈlɪtərəsɪ] *s* desanalfabetismo, capacidad de leer y escribir
**literal** [ˈlɪtərəl] *adj* literal
**literalism** [ˈlɪtərəlɪzəm] *s* literalismo
**literalist** [ˈlɪtərəlɪst] *adj & s* literalista
**literalistic** [,lɪtərəlˈɪstɪk] *adj* literalista
**literally** [ˈlɪtərəlɪ] *adv* literalmente
**literary** [ˈlɪtə,rɛrɪ] *adj* literario; literato
**literate** [ˈlɪtərɪt] *adj* que sabe leer y escribir; literato; *s* persona que sabe leer y escribir; literato
**literati** [,lɪtəˈretaɪ] o [,lɪtəˈrɑtɪ] *spl* literatos
**literatim** [,lɪtəˈretɪm] *adv* (Lat.) al pie de la letra
**literature** [ˈlɪtərətʃər] *s* literatura; (coll.) impresos, literatura de propaganda
**litharge** [ˈlɪθɑrdʒ] o [lɪˈθɑrdʒ] *s* (chem.) litargirio
**lithe** [laɪð] o **lithesome** [ˈlaɪðsəm] *adj* flexible, elástico, ágil
**lithia** [ˈlɪθɪə] *s* (chem.) litina
**lithiasis** [lɪˈθaɪəsɪs] *s* (path.) litiasis
**lithia water** *s* agua de litina
**lithic** [ˈlɪθɪk] *adj* lítico; (chem.) lítico
**lithium** [ˈlɪθɪəm] *s* (chem.) litio
**lithium hydride** *s* (chem.) hidruro de litio
**lithoclase** [ˈlɪθəkles] *s* (geol.) litoclasa
**lithograph** [ˈlɪθəgræf] o [ˈlɪθəgrɑf] *s* litografía; *va* litografiar
**lithographer** [lɪˈθɑgrəfər] *s* litógrafo
**lithographic** [,lɪθəˈgræfɪk] *adj* litográfico
**lithography** [lɪˈθɑgrəfɪ] *s* litografía
**lithoid** [ˈlɪθɔɪd] *adj* litoideo
**lithologic** [,lɪθəˈlɑdʒɪk] o **lithological** [,lɪθəˈlɑdʒɪkəl] *adj* litológico
**lithology** [lɪˈθɑlədʒɪ] *s* (geol. & med.) litología
**lithomarge** [ˈlɪθəmɑrdʒ] *s* (mineral.) litomarga
**lithophagous** [lɪˈθɑfəgəs] *adj* (zool.) litófago
**lithophotography** [,lɪθəfəˈtɑgrəfɪ] *s* litofotografía

**lithopone** ['lɪθəpon] *s* litopón
**lithosphere** ['lɪθəsfɪr] *s* litosfera
**lithotomy** [lɪ'θɑtəmɪ] *s* (*pl:* **-mies**) (surg.) litotomía
**lithotrite** ['lɪθətraɪt] *s* (surg.) litotritor
**lithotrity** [lɪ'θɑtrɪtɪ] *s* (*pl:* **-ties**) (surg.) litotricia
**Lithuania** [,lɪθʊ'enɪə] o [,lɪθjʊ'enɪə] *s* Lituania
**Lithuanian** [,lɪθʊ'enɪən] o [,lɪθjʊ'enɪən] *adj & s* lituano
**litigable** ['lɪtɪgəbəl] *adj* litigioso (*que puede ocasionar un litigio*)
**litigant** ['lɪtɪgənt] *adj & s* litigante
**litigate** ['lɪtɪget] *va & vn* litigar
**litigation** [,lɪtɪ'geʃən] *s* litigación
**litigious** [lɪ'tɪdʒəs] *adj* litigioso
**litmus** ['lɪtməs] *s* (chem.) tornasol
**litmus paper** *s* papel de tornasol
**litotes** ['laɪtətiz] o ['lɪtətiz] *s* (rhet.) lítote
**litre** ['litər] s var. de **liter**
**Litt. D.** abr. de **litterarum doctor** (Lat.) **Doctor of Literature** o **Doctor of Letters**
**litter** ['lɪtər] *s* litera (*llevada por hombres o caballerías*); camilla (*para la conducción de enfermos o heridos*); desorden, objetos en desorden; tendalera (*desorden de las cosas tendidas por el suelo*); basura (*que se recoge barriendo*); cama o paja (*que se pone en el piso de los establos*); ventregada (*conjunto de animales que nacen de una vez*); **to make a litter** dejarlo todo en desorden; *va* poner o dejar en desorden; esparcir cosas por; parir; preparar la cama de paja a (*los animales en el establo*); **to litter the floor with paper** esparcir desordenadamente papeles por el suelo; *vn* parir
**littérateur** o **litterateur** [,lɪtərə'tʌr] *s* literato
**litterbug** ['lɪtər,bʌg] s (coll.) persona que ensucia las calles tirando papeles rotos y desechados
**litter case** *s* herido que hay que transportar en camilla
**little** ['lɪtəl] *adj* (*comp:* **less, lesser** o **littler;** *super:* **least** o **littlest**) pequeño; *adv* (*comp:* **less;** *super:* **least**) poco; **little by little** poco a poco; *s* poco; **a little** un poco (de); algo; **in little** en pequeño, en pequeña escala; **not a little** muy; mucho; **to make little of** no dar importancia a, no tomar en serio; **to think little of** tener en poco; no vacilar en
**Little America** *s* la Pequeña América (*base del almirante Byrd cerca del polo sur en 1929 y 1934*)
**Little Bear** *s* (astr.) Osa menor
**little bustard** *s* (orn.) sisón
**Little Corporal** *s* Cabito (*Napoleón*)
**Little Dipper** *s* (astr.) Carro menor
**Little Dog** *s* (astr.) Can menor
**little finger** *s* dedo auricular, dedo meñique; **to twist around one's little finger** conquistar fácilmente, manejar completamente
**little hours** *spl* (eccl.) horas menores
**littleness** ['lɪtəlnɪs] *s* pequeñez
**little office** *s* (eccl.) oficio parvo
**little owl** *s* (orn.) mochuelo (*Athene noctua*)
**little people** *spl* hadas
**Little Red Ridinghood** ['raɪdɪŋ,hʊd] *s* Caperucita Roja
**Little Russian** *s* pequeño ruso
**little slam** *s* (bridge) semibola, pequeño eslam
**littoral** ['lɪtərəl] *adj & s* litoral
**liturgic** [lɪ'tʌrdʒɪk] o **liturgical** [lɪ'tʌrdʒɪkəl] *adj* litúrgico
**liturgist** ['lɪtərdʒɪst] *s* liturgista
**liturgy** ['lɪtərdʒɪ] *s* (*pl:* **-gies**) liturgia
**livable** ['lɪvəbəl] *adj* habitable; simpático; llevadero, soportable
**live** [laɪv] *adj* vivo; ardiente, encendido, en ascua; palpitante, de actualidad; natural (*música; programa*); cargado (*cartucho*); (elec.) cargado; (min.) vivo (*no separado de la cantera*) ‖ [lɪv] *va* llevar (*tal o cual vida*); vivir (*p.ej., una aventura*); obrar en conformidad con, convertir en norma de vida (*una doctrina religiosa, una filosofía, etc.*); **to live down** borrar (*una falta, un error*); **to live out** pasar (*toda la vida*); salir con vida de (*un desastre, una guerra, etc.*); vivir hasta el fin de ‖ *vn* vivir; **to live and learn** vivir para ver; **to live and let live** vivir y dejar vivir; **to live apart** vivir aislado; vivir separados; **to live high** darse buena vida; comer bien; **to live on** seguir viviendo; vivir de (*p.ej., pan*); vivir a expensas de; **to live up to** cumplir (*lo prometido*); vivir en conformidad con; **to live up to one's income** comerse todas sus rentas
**liveable** ['lɪvəbəl] *adj* var. de **livable**
**live axle** [laɪv] *s* (mach.) eje vivo
**live center** [laɪv] *s* (mach.) punta giratoria
**livelihood** ['laɪvlɪhʊd] *s* vida, subsistencia; **to earn one's livelihood** ganarse la vida
**livelong** ['lɪv,lɔŋ] o ['lɪv,lɑŋ] *adj* todo; **all the livelong day** todo el santo día
**lively** ['laɪvlɪ] *adj* (*comp:* **-lier;** *super:* **-liest**) vivo; animado, de mucho bullicio; elástico; alegre, festivo; *adv* vivamente; aprisa
**liven** ['laɪvən] *va* animar, regocijar; *vn* animarse, regocijarse
**live oak** [laɪv] *s* (bot.) roble vivo o siempre verde (*Quercus virginiana*)
**live program** [laɪv] *s* (rad.) programa vivo
**liver** ['lɪvər] *s* vividor; (anat.) hígado
**liver extract** *s* extracto de hígado
**liveried** ['lɪvərɪd] *adj* en librea
**Liverpudlian** [,lɪvər'pʌdlɪən] *adj* perteneciente a Liverpool; *mf* natural o habitante de Liverpool
**liverwort** ['lɪvər,wʌrt] *s* (bot.) hepática, hierba del hígado, hierba de la Trinidad
**liverwurst** ['lɪvər,wʊrst] *s* embutido de hígado
**livery** ['lɪvərɪ] *s* (*pl:* **-ies**) librea (*traje*); caballeriza; cochera de carruajes de alquiler; pensión de caballos; alquiler de coches, bicicletas, automóviles o embarcaciones; (fig.) librea (*señales características*)
**liveryman** ['lɪvərɪmən] *s* (*pl:* **-men**) dueño de una cochera de carruajes de alquiler; mozo de cuadra; (obs.) criado de librea
**livery stable** *s* caballeriza, cochera de carruajes de alquiler
**live steam** [laɪv] *s* vapor vivo
**livestock** ['laɪv,stɑk] *s* ganadería, ganado; *adj* ganadero
**live weight** [laɪv] *s* peso en vivo
**live wire** [laɪv] *s* (elec.) alambre cargado; (slang) trafagón, pólvora
**livid** ['lɪvɪd] *adj* lívido
**lividity** [lɪ'vɪdɪtɪ] *s* lividez
**living** ['lɪvɪŋ] *s* vida; (eccl.) beneficio; **for a living** para ganarse la vida; **to make a living** ganarse la vida; *adj* vivo, viviente; **the living** los vivos, los vivientes
**living death** *s* larga agonía, agonía que se prolonga
**living quarters** *spl* aposentos, habitaciones
**living room** *s* sala, sala de estar
**living space** *s* espacio vital (*de una nación*)
**living wage** *s* jornal suficiente para vivir
**Livy** ['lɪvɪ] *s* Livio, Tito Livio
**lizard** ['lɪzərd] *s* (zool.) lagarto; (slang) holgón
**ll.** abr. de **lines**
**llama** ['lɑmə] *s* (zool.) llama
**llano** ['lɑno] *s* (*pl:* **-nos**) llano, llanura
**LL.D.** abr. de **legum doctor** (Lat.) **Doctor of Laws**
**lo** [lo] *interj* ¡he aquí!
**loach** [lotʃ] *s* (ichth.) locha
**load** [lod] *s* carga; (elec.) carga; (slang) borrachera; **loads** *spl* (coll.) gran cantidad, gran número, muchísmos; **at full load** (elec. & mach.) con plena carga; *va* cargar (*un buque, un carro; un arma de fuego, un horno; los dados; a una persona*); recibir carga de; (ins.) recargar (*el premio*); **to load with** colmar de (*p.ej., mercedes*); agobiar de (*p.ej., tributos*); llenar de (*p.ej., reconvenciones*); *vn* cargar; cargarse; **to load up with** recibir carga de; agobiarse de
**load displacement** *s* (naut.) desplazamiento con carga
**loaded** ['lodɪd] *adj* cargado
**loaded dice** *spl* dados cargados
**load factor** *s* (elec.) factor de carga
**loading** ['lodɪŋ] *s* cargamento, embarque; (elec.) carga; (ins.) recargo al premio (*para cubrir ciertos gastos*)
**loading coil** *s* (elec.) bobina de carga
**loading zone** *s* zona de carga

**load line** *s* (naut.) línea de flotación con carga
**loadstar** [ˈlod,stɑr] *s* var. de **lodestar**
**loadstone** [ˈlod,ston] *s* piedra imán; (fig.) imán
**loaf** [lof] *s* (*pl:* **loaves**) pan; pilón (*de azúcar*); *vn* haraganear, holgazanear
**loafer** [ˈlofər] *s* haragán, holgazán, arrimón
**loaf sugar** *s* azúcar de pilón, azúcar cubicado
**loam** [lom] *s* suelo franco; (found.) tierra de moldeo; *va* cubrir o llenar de suelo franco; (found.) revestir con tierra de moldeo, rellenar de tierra de moldeo
**loamy** [ˈlomɪ] *adj* franco (*suelo*)
**loan** [lon] *s* préstamo; empréstito (*préstamo de una empresa o del Estado*); **to hit for a loan** (coll.) dar un sablazo a; *va & vn* prestar
**loan shark** *s* (coll.) usurero
**loan word** *s* (philol.) voz extranjera, préstamo lingüístico
**loath** [loθ] *adj* poco dispuesto, desinclinado; **nothing loath** dispuesto; de buena gana
**loathe** [loð] *va* abominar, detestar
**loathing** [ˈloðɪŋ] *s* abominación, asco, detestación
**loathly** [ˈloðlɪ] *adj* (lit.) asqueroso, repugnante; [ˈloθlɪ] o [ˈloðlɪ] *adv* de mala gana
**loathsome** [ˈloðsəm] *adj* asqueroso, repugnante
**lob** [lɑb] *s* (tennis) pelota voleada desde muy alto; (cricket) pelota baja, de poca velocidad; (*pret & pp:* **lobbed;** *ger:* **lobbing**) *va* (tennis) volear desde muy alto; (cricket) lanzar en trayectoria baja con poca velocidad
**lobar** [ˈlobər] *adj* lobar, lobular
**lobar pneumonia** *s* (path.) neumonía lobar
**lobate** [ˈlobet] *adj* lobado, lobulado
**lobation** [loˈbeʃən] *s* forma lobulada; lóbulo
**lobby** [ˈlɑbɪ] *s* (*pl:* **-bies**) salón de entrada, vestíbulo, foyer; cabildero, cabilderos; (*pret & pp:* **-bied**) *va* procurar ganar (*partidarios en una asamblea legislativa*); procurar ganar partidarios para (*un proyecto de ley*); *vn* cabildear
**lobbying** [ˈlɑbɪɪŋ] *s* cabildeo
**lobbyist** [ˈlɑbɪɪst] *s* cabildero
**lobe** [lob] *s* lóbulo
**lobed** [lobd] *adj* lobulado
**lobelia** [loˈbiljə] *s* (bot.) lobelia
**lobeliaceous** [lo,bilɪˈeʃəs] *adj* (bot.) lobeliáceo
**loblolly** [ˈlɑb,lɑlɪ] *s* (*pl:* **-lies**) (bot.) pino del incienso (*Pinus taeda*); pantano; gachas muy espesas
**lobotomy** [loˈbɑtəmɪ] *s* (surg.) lobotomía
**lobscouse** [ˈlɑb,skaʊs] *s* (naut.) puchero
**lobster** [ˈlɑbstər] *s* (zool.) langosta (*Palinurus*); (zool.) bogavante, cabrajo (*Homarus*)
**lobster pot** *s* langostera
**lobster thermidor** [ˈθʌrmɪdər] *s* (cook.) langosta a la Termidor
**lobular** [ˈlɑbjələr] *adj* lobular
**lobulate** [ˈlɑbjəlɪt] o [ˈlɑbjəlet] *adj* lobulado
**lobule** [ˈlɑbjul] *s* lobulillo
**local** [ˈlokəl] *adj* local; (med.) local; *s* tren ómnibus (*con paradas en todas las estaciones de la línea*); junta local (*p.ej., de una confederación de trabajadores*); noticia de interés local
**local anesthesia** *s* anestesia local
**local color** *s* (lit. & paint.) color local
**locale** [loˈkæl] *s* lugar (*considerado como teatro de ciertos acontecimientos*)
**local government** *s* gobierno local
**localism** [ˈlokəlɪzəm] *s* localismo
**locality** [loˈkælɪtɪ] *s* (*pl:* **-ties**) localidad
**localization** [,lokəlɪˈzeʃən] *s* localización
**localize** [ˈlokəlaɪz] *va* localizar
**locally** [ˈlokəlɪ] *adv* localmente
**local option** *s* jurisdicción local (*para determinar si se pueden vender bebidas alcohólicas dentro de sus límites*)
**locate** [ˈloket] o [loˈket] *va* localizar (*descubrir el paradero de*); colocar; establecer; *vn* (coll.) establecerse
**location** [loˈkeʃən] *s* localización; colocación; sitio, localidad; trazado (*p.ej., de una línea férrea*); **on location** (mov.) en exteriores
**locative** [ˈlɑkətɪv] *adj & s* (gram.) locativo
**loc. cit.** abr. de **loco citato** (Lat.) **in the place cited**
**loch** [lɑk] o [lɑx] *s* (Scotch) lago; (Scotch) ría
**lochia** [ˈlokɪə] o [ˈlɑkɪə] *spl* (obstet.) loquios
**lochial** [ˈlokɪəl] *adj* loquial
**lock** [lɑk] *s* cerradura; traba, retén; esclusa (*de un canal*); llave (*de arma de fuego*); bucle (*de pelo*); mechón; (eng.) cámara intermedia (*entre presiones atmosféricas diferentes*); (sport) presa (*en la lucha*); **locks** *spl* cabellos; **under lock and key** debajo de llave; *va* cerrar con llave; encerrar; enlazar, trabar; acuñar; hacer pasar (*un buque*) por una esclusa; **to lock in** encerrar, poner debajo de llave; **to lock out** cerrar la puerta a, dejar en la calle; dejar sin trabajo (*a los obreros para obligarles a pactar con la empresa*); **to lock up** encerrar, poner debajo de llave; encarcelar; *vn* cerrarse con llave; trabarse; pasar por una esclusa
**lockage** [ˈlɑkɪdʒ] *s* construcción de esclusas; servicio de esclusas; movimiento de buques por una esclusa; diferencia de nivel (*en un canal de esclusas*); portazgo (*de esclusa*)
**locker** [ˈlɑkər] *s* cerrador; cajón, gaveta, alacena, armario, etc., cerrados con llave
**locket** [ˈlɑkɪt] *s* guardapelo, medallón
**lockjaw** [ˈlɑk,dʒɔ] *s* (path.) trismo
**lock nut** *s* contratuerca
**lockout** [ˈlɑk,aut] *s* paro, cierre (*de una fábrica u otro establecimiento por los dueños para obligar a los obreros a pactar con la empresa*)
**locksmith** [ˈlɑk,smɪθ] *s* cerrajero
**lock step** *s* marcha en fila apretada
**lock stitch** *s* (sew.) punto encadenado (*hecho en la máquina de coser*)
**lock, stock, and barrel** *adv* (coll.) del todo, por completo
**lock tender** *s* esclusero
**lockup** [ˈlɑk,ʌp] *s* cárcel
**lock washer** *s* arandela de seguridad
**loco** [ˈloko] *s* (bot.) loco; (vet.) locoísmo; *adj* (slang) loco; *va* envenenar con el veneno del loco
**loco disease** *s* (vet.) locoísmo
**locomobile** [,lokəˈmobɪl] *adj & s* locomóvil
**locomotion** [,lokəˈmoʃən] *s* locomoción
**locomotive** [,lokəˈmotɪv] *adj* locomotor; *s* locomóvil; (rail.) locomotora
**locomotor** [,lokəˈmotər] *adj* locomotor; *s* persona, animal o cosa locomotoras
**locomotor ataxia** *s* (path.) ataxia locomotriz progresiva
**locoweed** [ˈloko,wid] *s* (bot.) loco, cascabelito
**locular** [ˈlɑkjələr] *adj* locular
**loculate** [ˈlɑkjəlet] o [ˈlɑkjəlɪt] *adj* (bot.) loculado
**loculicidal** [,lɑkjəlɪˈsaɪdəl] *adj* (bot.) loculicida
**loculus** [ˈlɑkjələs] *s* (*pl:* **-li** [laɪ]) (bot. & hist.) lóculo
**locum tenens** [ˈlokəm ˈtinɛnz] *s* interino
**locus** [ˈlokəs] *s* (*pl:* **-ci** [saɪ]) sitio, lugar; (geom.) lugar (geométrico)
**locust** [ˈlokəst] *s* (ent.) langosta, saltamontes; (ent.) cigarra; (bot.) acacia falsa
**locust bean** *s* algarroba
**locution** [loˈkjuʃən] *s* locución
**lode** [lod] *s* (min.) filón, venero
**lodestar** [ˈlod,stɑr] *s* estrella de guía; (astr.) estrella polar; (fig.) norte (*dirección o guía*)
**lodestone** [ˈlod,ston] *s* var. de **loadstone**
**lodge** [lɑdʒ] *s* casa de guarda; casa de campo; casita (*p.ej., de jardinero*); cabaña, choza; madriguera (*de castores o nutrias*); logia (*p.ej., de francmasones*); *va* alojar, hospedar; colocar, depositar; comunicar (*informes*); presentar (*una queja*); conferir (*autoridad*); *vn* alojarse, hospedarse; ir a parar, quedarse, quedar colgado
**lodgement** [ˈlɑdʒmənt] *s* var. de **lodgment**
**lodger** [ˈlɑdʒər] *s* huésped, inquilino
**lodging** [ˈlɑdʒɪŋ] *s* alojamiento, hospedaje; cobijo (*hospedaje sin manutención*); **lodgings** *spl* habitación, aposentos
**lodging house** *s* casa de huéspedes
**lodgment** [ˈlɑdʒmənt] *s* aposento, habitación, alojamiento, casa; cosa depositada; (mil.) posición ganada; (mil.) atrincheramiento hecho rápidamente en terreno recién ganado al enemigo
**loess** [ˈloɛs] o [ˈlo·ɪs] *s* loess, tierra amarilla
**loft** [lɔft] o [lɑft] *s* desván, sobrado; henal, pajar; galería (*en los teatros e iglesias*); piso al-

to (*en un almacén o edificio de oficinas*); (golf) ángulo de elevación; (golf) elevación; *va* (golf) lanzar en alto
**loftiness** ['lɔftɪnɪs] o ['lɑftɪnɪs] *s* elevación, altura; eminencia, excelsitud; altivez, orgullo
**lofty** ['lɔftɪ] o ['lɑftɪ] *adj* (*comp:* **-ier;** *super:* **-iest**) elevado, encumbrado; eminente, excelso; altivo, orgulloso
**log.** o **log** abr. de **logarithm** o **logarithmic**
**log** [lɔg] o [lɑg] *s* leño, tronco, troza; (naut.) cuaderno de bitácora; (naut.) barquilla (*de la corredera*); (naut.) corredera (*barquilla y cordel*); (aer.) diario de vuelo; **to sleep like a log** dormir como un leño; *adj* de troncos; (*pret & pp:* **logged;** *ger:* **logging**) *va* cortar en trozos; extraer madera de (*un terreno poblado de árboles*); (naut.) apuntar el nombre de (*un marinero*) en el libro de bordo, junto con el desliz que ha cometido; *vn* extraer madera de un bosque
**loganberry** ['logən,bɛrɪ] *s* (*pl:* **-ries**) (bot.) frambueso norteamericano (*Rubus loganobaccus*); frambuesa norteamericana
**loganiaceous** [lo,genɪ'eʃəs] *adj* (bot.) loganiáceo
**logarithm** ['lɔgərɪðəm] o ['lɑgərɪðəm] *s* (math.) logaritmo
**logarithmic** [,lɔgə'rɪðmɪk] o [,lɑgə'rɪðmɪk] o **logarithmical** [,lɔgə'rɪðmɪkəl] o [,lɑgə'rɪðmɪkəl] *adj* logarítmico
**logbook** ['lɔg,bʊk] o ['lɑg,bʊk] *s* (naut.) cuaderno de bitácora; (aer.) libro de vuelo
**log cabin** *s* cabaña de troncos
**log chip** *s* (naut.) barquilla
**log driver** *s* ganchero
**log driving** *s* flotaje
**logger** ['lɔgər] o ['lɑgər] *s* maderero, hachero; grúa, cargadora de troncos; tractor
**loggerhead** ['lɔgər,hɛd] o ['lɑgər,hɛd] *s* majadero, mentecato; (zool.) tortuga de mar; **to be at loggerheads** comerse unos a otros, estar reñidos
**loggia** ['lodʒə] *s* (arch.) logia
**logging** ['lɔgɪŋ] o ['lɑgɪŋ] *s* extracción de madera de los bosques
**logic** ['lɑdʒɪk] *s* lógica
**logical** ['lɑdʒɪkəl] *adj* lógico
**logician** [lo'dʒɪʃən] *s* lógico
**logistic** [lo'dʒɪstɪk] *adj* (mil.) logístico; **logistics** *ssg* (mil.) logística
**logistical** [lo'dʒɪstɪkəl] *adj* (mil.) logístico
**log line** *s* (naut.) corredera, cordel de la corredera
**logogriph** ['lɔgəgrɪf] o ['lɑgəgrɪf] *s* logogrifo
**logomachy** [lo'gɑməkɪ] *s* (*pl:* **-chies**) logomaquia
**logotype** ['lɔgətaɪp] o ['lɑgətaɪp] *s* (print.) logotipo
**log reel** *s* (naut.) carretel
**logroll** ['lɔg,rol] o ['lɑg,rol] *va* lograr que se apruebe (*un proyecto de ley*) mediante un intercambio de favores políticos; *vn* trocar favores políticos, seguir el sistema de hoy por ti y mañana por mí
**logrolling** ['lɔg,rolɪŋ] o ['lɑg,rolɪŋ] *s* intercambio de favores políticos, sistema de hoy por ti y mañana por mí; arrastre cooperativo de maderos en los bosques
**log ship** *s* var. de **log chip**
**logwood** ['lɔg,wʊd] o ['lɑg,wʊd] *s* campeche, palo campeche; (bot.) campeche (*árbol*)
**logy** ['logɪ] *adj* (*comp:* **-gier;** *super:* **-giest**) torpe, lerdo
**loin** [lɔɪn] *s* ijada, lomo; lomo (*carne de lomo del animal*); **to gird up one's loins** ceñirse los riñones (*disponerse para la acción*)
**loincloth** ['lɔɪn,klɔθ] o ['lɔɪn,klɑθ] *s* taparrabo
**Loire** [lwɑr] *s* Loira
**loiter** ['lɔɪtər] *va;* **to loiter away** malgastar (*el tiempo*); *vn* holgazanear, rezagarse, perder el tiempo
**loiterer** ['lɔɪtərər] *s* holgazán, rezagado
**loll** [lɑl] *va* colgar flojamente hacia fuera, sacar (*la lengua*) fuera de la boca; *vn* colgar flojamente hacia fuera; arrellanarse, repantigarse, estar recostado con indolencia
**Lollard** ['lɑlərd] *s* lolardo
**lollipop** ['lɑlɪpɑp] *s* paleta (*dulce con un palito que sirve de mango*)
**Lombard** ['lɑmbɑrd] o ['lɑmbərd] *adj & s* lombardo
**Lombardy** ['lɑmbərdɪ] *s* Lombardía
**Lombardy poplar** *s* (bot.) álamo de Italia, chopo lombardo
**Lombrosian** [lɑm'brozɪən] *adj* lombrosiano
**loment** ['lomɛnt] *s* (bot.) lomento
**lomentaceous** [,lomən'teʃəs] *adj* (bot.) lomentáceo
**lon.** abr. de **longitude**
**London** ['lʌndən] *s* Londres; *adj* londinense
**Londoner** ['lʌndənər] *s* londinense
**lone** [lon] *adj* solo, solitario; único; (hum.) sin cónyuge, soltero, viudo
**lone hand** *s* (cards) mano jugada sin intervención de compañero; (fig.) lobo solitario
**loneliness** ['lonlɪnɪs] *s* soledad
**lonely** ['lonlɪ] *adj* (*comp:* **-lier;** *super:* **-liest**) solitario; soledoso
**lonesome** ['lonsəm] *adj* solitario (*lugar o ambiente*); solo y triste, soledoso
**lone wolf** *s* (fig.) lobo solitario
**long.** abr. de **longitude**
**long** [lɔŋ] o [lɑŋ] *adj* (*comp:* **longer** ['lɔŋgər] o ['lɑŋgər]; *super:* **longest** ['lɔŋgɪst] o ['lɑŋgɪst]) largo; de largo, p.ej., **two feet long** dos pies de largo; (com.) alcista; (phonet.) largo; **to be long (in)** + *ger* tardar en + *inf;* **to be not long for this world** estar cercano a la muerte; *adv* (*comp:* **longer** ['lɔŋgər] o ['lɑŋgər]; *super:* **longest** ['lɔŋgɪst] o ['lɑŋgɪst]) largamente, mucho tiempo, largo tiempo; **all night long** (durante) toda la noche; **as long as** mientras; con tal de que; puesto que; **before long** dentro de poco; **how long** cuánto tiempo; cuándo; **no longer** ya no; **so long!** (coll.) ¡hasta luego!; **so long as** con tal de que; **long ago** hace mucho tiempo; **long before** mucho antes; **longer** más tiempo; **long since** desde hace mucho tiempo; *vn* anhelar, suspirar; **to long for** anhelar por; **to long to** + *inf* anhelar + *inf*
**longboat** ['lɔŋ,bot] o ['lɑŋ,bot] *s* (naut.) lancha
**longbow** ['lɔŋ,bo] o ['lɑŋ,bo] *s* arco (*disparado a mano*); **to draw the longbow** mentir por la barba (*al narrar cuentos de aventuras extraordinarias*)
**longcloth** ['lɔŋ,klɔθ] o ['lɑŋ,klɑθ] *s* tejido de algodón muy fino
**long-distance** ['lɔŋ'dɪstəns] o ['lɑŋ'dɪstəns] *adj* (telp.) de larga distancia, interurbano; *s* (telp.) central (*oficina o mujer*) de llamadas a larga distancia
**long-distance call** *s* (telp.) llamada a larga distancia
**long-distance flight** *s* (aer.) vuelo a distancia
**long dozen** *s* docena del fraile (*trece*)
**long-drawn** ['lɔŋ,drɔn] o ['lɑŋ,drɔn] *adj* muy prolongado, prolijo
**longeron** ['lɑndʒərən] *s* (aer.) larguero
**longevity** [lɑn'dʒɛvɪtɪ] *s* longevidad
**longevous** [lɑn'dʒivəs] *adj* longevo
**long face** *s* (coll.) cara triste, cara inquieta
**long green** *s* (slang) papel moneda (*de los EE.UU.*)
**longhair** ['lɔŋ,hɛr] o ['lɑŋ,hɛr] *adj* (slang) de o por la música clásica; (slang) aficionado a la música clásica; *s* (slang) aficionado a la música clásica
**longhand** ['lɔŋ,hænd] o ['lɑŋ,hænd] *s* escritura ordinaria (*a distinción de la taquigrafía*)
**long-headed** ['lɔŋ'hɛdɪd] o ['lɑŋ'hɛdɪd] *adj* dolicocéfalo; (fig.) astuto, sagaz, precavido
**longhorn** ['lɔŋ,hɔrn] o ['lɑŋ,hɔrn] *s* res vacuna de cuernos largos
**longing** ['lɔŋɪŋ] o ['lɑŋɪŋ] *s* anhelo; *adj* anhelante
**Longinus** [lɑn'dʒaɪnəs] *s* Longino
**longish** ['lɔŋɪʃ] o ['lɑŋɪʃ] *adj* algo largo, un poco largo
**longitude** ['lɑndʒɪtjud] o ['lɑndʒɪtud] *s* longitud
**longitudinal** [,lɑndʒɪ'tjudɪnəl] o [,lɑndʒɪ'tudɪnəl] *adj* longitudinal
**longitudinally** [,lɑndʒɪ'tjudɪnəlɪ] o [,lɑndʒɪ'tudɪnəlɪ] *adj* longitudinalmente
**long-lived** ['lɔŋ'laɪvd], ['lɑŋ'laɪvd], ['lɔŋ'lɪvd] o ['lɑŋ'lɪvd] *adj* duradero, de larga vida
**long measure** *s* medida de longitud

**long moss** *s* (bot.) caballo de rey
**Longobard** [ˈlɑŋgobɑrd] *adj & s* longobardo
**Long Parliament** *s* (hist.) Parlamento Largo
**long-playing record** [ˈlɔŋˈpleɪŋ] o [ˈlɑŋˈpleɪŋ] *s* disco de larga duración
**long primer** [ˈprɪmər] *s* (print.) entredós
**long-range** [ˈlɔŋˈrendʒ] o [ˈlɑŋˈrendʒ] *adj* de gran alcance, de largo alcance
**longshore** [ˈlɔŋˌʃor] o [ˈlɑŋˌʃor] *adj* de la costa; del muelle, de los muelles
**longshoreman** [ˈlɔŋˌʃormən] o [ˈlɑŋˌʃormən] *s* (*pl:* **-men**) estibador
**long-sighted** [ˈlɔŋˈsaɪtɪd] o [ˈlɑŋˈsaɪtɪd] *adj* présbita; previsor, precavido
**long-standing** [ˈlɔŋˌstændɪŋ] o [ˈlɑŋˌstændɪŋ] *adj* existente desde hace mucho tiempo
**long-suffering** [ˈlɔŋˈsʌfərɪŋ] o [ˈlɑŋˈsʌfərɪŋ] *adj* longánimo, sufrido; *s* longanimidad
**long suit** *s* (cards) palo fuerte; (fig.) fuerte
**long-tailed titmouse** [ˈlɔŋˌteld] o [ˈlɑŋˌteld] *s* (orn.) chamarón
**long-term** [ˈlɔŋˌtʌrm] o [ˈlɑŋˌtʌrm] *adj* (com.) a largo plazo
**long ton** *s* tonelada larga o gruesa (*2240 libras o 1016,06 kilogramos*)
**long-tongued** [ˈlɔŋˈtʌŋd] o [ˈlɑŋˈtʌŋd] *adj* de lengua larga; longílocuo, largo de lengua
**long wave** *s* (rad.) onda larga
**long-wave** [ˈlɔŋˌwev] o [ˈlɑŋˌwev] *adj* (rad.) de onda larga
**longways** [ˈlɔŋwez] o [ˈlɑŋwez] *adv* a lo largo, longitudinalmente
**long-winded** [ˈlɔŋˈwɪndɪd] o [ˈlɑŋˈwɪndɪd] *adj* de buenos pulmones; (fig.) palabrero, difuso, verboso
**longwise** [ˈlɔŋwaɪz] o [ˈlɑŋwaɪz] *adv* var. de **longways**
**look** [lʊk] *s* mirada; búsqueda; aspecto, apariencia; cara, aire; **looks** *spl* aspecto, apariencia; **to have a look (of)** tener un aire (de), p.ej., **to have an unfriendly look** tener un aire hostil; **to take a look at** echar una mirada a ‖ *va* expresar con la mirada; representar (*p.ej., la edad que uno tiene*); **to look over** examinar; **to look the part** vestir el cargo; **to look through** hojear, p.ej., **I didn't have time to look the book through** no tuve tiempo de hojear el libro; **to look up** buscar (*p.ej., en el diccionario*); ir a visitar, venir a ver ‖ *vn* mirar; buscar; parecer; **to look about** mirar alrededor; **to look after** mirar por, cuidar de; ocuparse en; **to look alike** parecerse; **to look at** mirar; **to look back** mirar hacia atrás; (fig.) mirar el pasado; **to look back on** o **upon** recordar, evocar; **to look down on** o **upon** mirar por encima del hombro; **to look for** buscar; creer, p.ej., **I look for rain** creo que va a llover; **to look forward to** esperar con placer anticipado, anticipar con placer; **to look ill** tener mala cara; **to look in** hacer una visita breve; **to look in on** pasar por la casa o la oficina de; **to look into** averiguar, examinar, estudiar; **to look like** parecerse a; tener trazas de; **to look on** mirar, p.ej., **he stood awhile looking on** estuvo un rato mirando; **to look on as** tener por, p.ej., **I look on him as a fool** lo tengo por muy tonto; **to look oneself** parecer el mismo; tener buena cara; **to look out** mirar por (*p.ej., la ventana*); tener cuidado; **to look out for** mirar por, cuidar de, defender; guardarse de; **to look out of** mirar por (*p.ej., la ventana*); **to look out on** dar a, p.ej., **the house looks out on the ocean** la casa da al mar; **to look through** mirar por (*p.ej., la ventana*); hojear (*p.ej., un libro*); **to look to** mirar por, cuidar de; ocuparse en; acudir a (*una persona en busca de ayuda*); **to look towards** dar a, p.ej., **the house looks towards the ocean** la casa da al mar; **to look up** (coll.) mejorar; (coll.) sentirse mejor, mejorar de salud; **to look up to** admirar, mirar con respeto; **to look well** tener buena cara; estar bien, ir bien; **look out!** ¡cuidado!, ¡ojo!
**looker-on** [ˌlʊkərˈɑn] o [ˌlʊkərˈɔn] *s* (*pl:* **lookers-on**) mirón, espectador
**look-in** [ˈlʊkˌɪn] *s* mirada, mirada adentro; (slang) oportunidad, parte de una empresa
**looking glass** *s* espejo
**lookout** [ˈlʊkˌaʊt] *s* vigilancia; vigilante; vista, perspectiva; atalaya (*hombre o torre*); (coll.) cuidado (*asunto que está a cargo de uno*); **to be on the lookout (for)** estar a la mira (de); estar a la expectativa (de)
**loom** [lum] *s* telar; (elec.) tubo fibroso flexible; (naut.) guión (*de remo*); vislumbre; *va* tejer en un telar; *vn* vislumbrarse; amenazar, parecer inevitable
**loon** [lun] *s* bobo, mequetrefe; (orn.) zambullidor (*Gavia immer*)
**loony** [ˈlunɪ] *adj* (*comp:* **-ier;** *super:* **-iest**) (slang) loco; *s* (*pl:* **-ies**) (slang) loco
**loop** [lup] *s* lazo; curva cerrada o casi cerrada; vuelta (*p.ej., de un cabo*); meandro (*p.ej., de un río*); recoveco (*p.ej., de un camino*); onda, bucle; presilla (*para asegurar un botón*); (aer.) rizo; (bact.) asa; (elec.) circuito cerrado; (rail.) ramal cerrado; **to loop the loop** (aer.) hacer o rizar el rizo; *va* hacer lazos en; doblar formando curva cerrada; enlazar; asegurar con una presilla; *vn* formar lazo o lazos; andar formando arcos (*los geómetras*); (aer.) hacer el rizo
**loop aerial** o **loop antenna** *s* (rad.) antena de cuadro
**loophole** [ˈlupˌhol] *s* aspillera, saetera, portillo; (fig.) callejuela, evasiva, efugio
**loose** [lus] *adj* flojo (*p.ej., vestido, diente, tornillo, vientre*); suelto (*p.ej., ajuste, hilo, alambre, remache, animal, lengua, vientre*); desmenuzado (*dícese de la tierra*); sueltos (*papeles sin encuadernar*); a granel, sin envase; loco (*dícese de una polea*); libre (*traducción*); poco exacto; relajado (*dícese de la vida, la moral, etc.*); fácil, frágil (*p.ej., mujer*); (paint.) bien manejado; **to become loose** aflojarse, desatarse; **to break loose** desatarse; ponerse en libertad; **to cast loose** desatar, soltar; **to cut loose** cortar las amarras de; separarse; huir, ponerse en libertad; (coll.) echar una cana al aire; **to let, set** o **turn loose** soltar; *adv* flojamente; libremente; *s* relajamiento (*en la moral*); **to be on the loose** (coll.) ser libre, estar sin trabas; (coll.) estar de juerga; *va* soltar, poner en libertad; desatar, desencadenar
**loose end** *s* cabo suelto; **at loose end** sin empleo; **at loose ends** desarreglado
**loose-jointed** [ˈlusˈdʒɔɪntɪd] *adj* de articulaciones flojas; de movimientos sueltos
**loose-leaf notebook** [ˈlusˌlif] *s* cuaderno de hojas sueltas, cuaderno de hojas cambiables
**loosen** [ˈlusən] *va* desatar, aflojar, desapretar; desasir; aflojar, laxar (*el vientre*); *vn* desatarse, aflojarse, desapretarse
**looseness** [ˈlusnɪs] *s* flojedad; soltura; relajamiento (*en la moral*)
**loosestrife** [ˈlusˌstraɪf] *s* (bot.) lisimaquia; (bot.) salicaria
**loose-tongued** [ˈlusˈtʌŋd] *adj* largo de lengua, suelto de lengua
**loot** [lut] *s* botín, presa; *va & vn* saquear, robar
**lop** [lɑp] (*pret & pp:* **lopped;** *ger:* **lopping**) *va* desmochar; podar; *vn* colgar; agitarse
**lope** [lop] *s* medio galope; paso largo; *vn* correr a medio galope; correr a paso largo
**lop-eared** [ˈlɑpˌɪrd] *adj* de orejas caídas
**lophobranch** [ˈlofəbræŋk] o [ˈlɑfəbræŋk] *adj & s* (ichth.) lofobranquio
**lopsided** [ˈlɑpˈsaɪdɪd] *adj* más pesado de un lado que de otro, ladeado, sesgado; asimétrico, desproporcionado, patituerto; (fig.) maniático
**loquacious** [loˈkweʃəs] *adj* locuaz
**loquacity** [loˈkwæsɪtɪ] *s* locuacidad
**loquat** [ˈlokwɑt] o [ˈlokwæt] *s* (bot.) níspero del Japón
**loran** [ˈlɔrən] o [ˈlorən] *s* (naut.) lorán
**lord** [lɔrd] *s* señor (*de un estado feudal; amo, dueño*); (Brit.) lord; (hum. & poet.) marido; **Lord** *s* Señor (*Dios, Jesucristo*); (Brit.) lord (*título*); **our Lord** nuestro Señor; **the Lords** los lores (*la Cámara alta del Parlamento británico*); **to die in the Lord** morir en el Señor; **to rest in the Lord** descansar en el Señor; **to sleep in the Lord** dormir en el Señor; *va* investir con la dignidad de lord; **to lord it over** imponerse a, dominar despóticamente; *vn* mandar despóticamente
**Lord Chamberlain** *s* (Brit.) camarero mayor
**lordling** [ˈlɔrdlɪŋ] *s* hidalguillo, señorito
**lordly** [ˈlɔrdlɪ] *adj* (*comp:* **-lier;** *super:* **-liest**)

señoril; espléndido, magnífico; altivo; despótico, imperioso; *adv* señorilmente; magníficamente; altivamente; imperiosamente
**Lord Mayor** *s* alcalde de la ciudad de Londres
**Lord of hosts** *s* Señor de los ejércitos
**lordosis** [lɔr'dosɪs] *s* (path.) lordosis
**Lord's Anointed, The** el ungido del Señor
**Lord's Day, the** el domingo
**lordship** ['lɔrdʃɪp] *s* señoría, excelencia; señorío
**Lord's Prayer** *s* oración dominical, padrenuestro
**lords spiritual** *spl* (Brit.) lores espirituales (*brazo eclesiástico en la Cámara alta*)
**Lord's Supper** *s* Cena, Cena del Señor; sagrada comunión
**lords temporal** *spl* (Brit.) lores temporales (*brazo de nobles en la Cámara alta*)
**lore** [lor] *s* ciencia popular, saber popular; ciencia, saber
**lorgnette** [lɔrn'jɛt] *s* impertinente o impertinentes; gemelos de teatro
**lorgnon** [lɔr'njõ] *s* gafas; lentes de nariz
**lorica** [lo'raɪkə] *s* (*pl:* **-cae** [si]) (arm. & zool.) loriga
**loris** ['lorɪs] *s* (*pl:* **-ris**) (zool.) loris
**lorn** [lɔrn] *adj* abandonado, desamparado; (archaic) arruinado, perdido
**Lorraine** [lo'ren] *s* Lorena
**Lorrainer** [lə'renər] *s* lorenés
**Lorrainese** [,lɑre'niz] *adj* lorenés
**lorry** ['lɑrɪ] o ['lɔrɪ] *s* (*pl:* **-ries**) (Brit.) vagoneta; (Brit.) carro de plataforma; (Brit.) autocamión
**lory** ['lorɪ] *s* (*pl:* **-ries**) (orn.) loro
**lose** [luz] (*pret & pp:* **lost**) *va* perder; hacer perder, p.ej., **that lost him the battle** eso le hizo perder la batalla; tener la culpa de que se pierda, p.ej., **he lost the game** él tuvo la culpa de que se perdiera el partido; no lograr salvar (*el médico al enfermo*); **to lose oneself** perderse, errar el camino; ensimismarse, abismarse (*p.ej., en la lectura*); confundirse; **to lose to** perder (*p.ej., el mercado*) en beneficio de; *vn* perder, tener una pérdida; ser o quedar vencido; retrasarse (*un reloj*)
**loser** ['luzər] *s* perdidoso
**losing** ['luzɪŋ] *adj* perdidoso; **losings** *spl* pérdidas, dinero perdido
**loss** [lɔs] o [lɑs] *s* pérdida; **to be at a loss** estar perplejo, no saber qué hacer; **to be at a loss to** + *inf* no saber cómo + *inf;* **to sell at a loss** vender con pérdida
**loss of face** *s* desprestigio, pérdida de prestigio
**lost** [lɔst] o [lɑst] *pret & pp de* **lose;** *adj* perdido; perplejo; **lost in** abismado en, embebido en; **lost to** perdido para; insensible a; inaccesible a
**lost-and-found department** ['lɔstənd'faʊnd] o ['lɑstənd'faʊnd] *s* oficina de objetos perdidos, departamento de cosas olvidadas
**lost motion** *s* movimiento perdido
**lost sheep** *s* (fig.) oveja perdida
**lot** [lɑt] *s* solar, parcela (*para construir una casa*); suerte; lote (*parte, porción*); grupo (*de personas*); (coll.) gran cantidad, gran número; (coll.) individuo, sujeto, tipo; **a lot** (coll.) mucho; (coll.) muchos; **a lot of** (coll.) mucho, muchos; **by lots** echando suertes; **to draw** o **to cast lots** echar suertes; **to cast** o **to throw in one's lot with** compartir la suerte de; **to fall to one's lot** caerle a uno en suerte; **lots of** (coll.) mucho, muchos; (*pret & pp:* **lotted;** *ger:* **lotting**) *va* repartir; asignar; dividir echando suertes, escoger echando suertes; *vn* echar suertes
**loth** [loθ] *adj* var. de **loath**
**Lothario** [lo'θɛrɪo] *s* (*pl:* **-os**) tenorio, libertino
**lotiform** ['lotɪfɔrm] *adj* lotiforme
**lotion** ['loʃən] *s* (pharm.) loción
**lotos** ['lotəs] *s* var. de **lotus**
**lottery** ['lɑtərɪ] *s* (*pl:* **-ies**) lotería
**lottery wheel** *s* rueda de lotería
**lotto** ['lɑto] *s* lotería (*juego casero*)
**lotus** ['lotəs] *s* (bot., arch. & myth.) loto
**lotus-eater** ['lotəs,itər] *s* lotófago; persona indolente y soñadora
**loud** [laʊd] *adj* alto; ruidoso; fuerte, recio; (coll.) chillón, llamativo; (coll.) charro, cursi; (coll.) apestoso, maloliente; *adv* ruidosamente; alto, en voz alta
**loudish** ['laʊdɪʃ] *adj* un poco alto, algo fuerte
**loudspeaker** ['laʊd'spikər] *s* (rad.) altavoz, altoparlante
**lough** [lɑk] o [lɑx] *s* (Irish) lago; (Irish) ría
**Louis** ['luɪ] o ['luɪs] *s* Luis
**Louisa** [lu'izə] o **Louise** [lu'iz] *s* Luisa
**Louisiana** [lu,izɪ'ænə] o [,luɪzɪ'ænə] *s* la Luisiana
**Louisianan** [lu,izɪ'ænən] o [,luɪzɪ'ænən] *adj & s* luisianense
**Louis Napoleon** ['luɪ] *s* Luis Napoleón
**Louis Phillipe** ['luɪ fɪ'lip] *s* Luis Felipe
**lounge** [laʊndʒ] *s* canapé ancho y cómodo; salón de tertulia, salón social; paso lento y perezoso; haraganería; *va* gastar ociosamente; *vn* pasearse perezosamente, repantigarse a su sabor, recostarse cómodamente, estar arrimado a la pared, un farol, etc.
**lour** [laʊr] *s* ceño; *vn* fruncir el entrecejo, poner mala cara; encapotarse o nublarse (*el cielo*)
**Lourdes** [lʊrd] *s* Lurdes
**louse** [laʊs] *s* (*pl:* **lice**) (ent.) piojo
**lousewort** ['laʊs,wʌrt] *s* (bot.) gallarito (*Pedicularis sylvatica*)
**lousy** ['laʊzɪ] *adj* (*comp:* **-ier;** *super:* **-iest**) piojoso; (slang) asqueroso, sucio; (slang) colmado (*p.ej., de riquezas*)
**lout** [laʊt] *s* patán
**loutish** ['laʊtɪʃ] *adj* patán
**Louvain** [lu'ven] *s* Lovaina
**louver** ['luvər] *s* lumbrera (*abertura por donde entran el aire y la luz*); persiana; tabla de persiana; (aut.) persiana de ventilación
**louver boards** *spl* tablas pluviales
**Louvre** ['luvrə] *s* Luvre (*museo*)
**lovable** ['lʌvəbəl] *adj* amable
**lovage** ['lʌvɪdʒ] *s* (bot.) ligústico; (bot.) levístico
**love** [lʌv] *s* amor; (tennis) cero, nada; (coll.) preciosidad, p.ej., **it's a love of a cottage** la casita es una preciosidad; (*cap.*) *s* Amor (*Cupido*); **for love** por amor, por placer; **for the love of** por el amor de; **not for love or money** ni a tiros, por nada del mundo; **to be in love (with)** estar enamorado (de); **to fall in love (with)** enamorarse (de); **to make love** hacer el amor; **to make love to** cortejar, galantear; *va* amar, querer, tener cariño a; gustar de (*p.ej., la música*); *vn* amar; enamorarse
**loveable** ['lʌvəbəl] *adj* var. de **lovable**
**love affair** *s* amores, amorío
**love apple** *s* tomate
**lovebird** ['lʌv,bʌrd] *s* (orn.) inseparable (*Agapornis*); (orn.) pupuí (*Psittacus*)
**love child** *s* hijo del amor
**love feast** *s* ágape
**love-in-a-mist** ['lʌvɪnə'mɪst] *s* (bot.) ajenuz, arañuela
**love-in-idleness** ['lʌvɪn'aɪdəlnɪs] *s* (bot.) pensamiento, trinitaria
**love knot** *s* nudo o lazo de amor
**loveless** ['lʌvlɪs] *adj* desamorado (*que no siente amor*); abandonado, sin amor
**love-lies-bleeding** ['lʌvlaɪz'blidɪŋ] *s* (bot.) amaranto rojo
**loveliness** ['lʌvlɪnɪs] *s* hermosura, belleza; preciosidad, exquisitez; (coll.) gracia, encanto
**lovelock** ['lʌv,lɑk] *s* tirabuzón (*rizo de cabello*); (archaic) rizo largo con lazo de cinta
**lovelorn** ['lʌv,lɔrn] *adj* suspirando de amor, herido de amor
**lovely** ['lʌvlɪ] *adj* (*comp:* **-lier;** *super:* **-liest**) hermoso, bello; precioso, exquisito; (coll.) gracioso, encantador
**love-maker** ['lʌv,mekər] *s* galanteador
**love-making** ['lʌv,mekɪŋ] *adj* galanteador; *s* galanteo
**love match** *s* matrimonio por amor
**love potion** *s* filtro, filtro de amor
**lover** ['lʌvər] *s* aficionado (*p.ej., a la caza*); amigo (*p.ej., del trabajo*); amante; **lovers** *spl* amantes (*hombre y mujer que se aman*)
**love seat** *s* confidente
**lovesick** ['lʌv,sɪk] *adj* enfermo de amor
**lovesickness** ['lʌv,sɪknɪs] *s* mal de amor

**love song** *s* canción de amor
**loving** [ˈlʌvɪŋ] *adj* afectuoso, cariñoso, amoroso
**loving cup** *s* copa de la amistad
**loving-kindness** [ˌlʌvɪŋˈkaɪndnɪs] *s* bondad infinita, misericordia
**low** [lo] *adj* bajo; abatido; gravemente enfermo; malo (*dícese de la dieta, la opinión, etc.*); escotado; muerto; lento (*fuego*); (phonet.) abierto; **to feel low** sentirse abatido; **to lay low** dejar tendido, derribar; matar; **to lie low** (coll.) mantenerse oculto, no dejarse ver; (coll.) no chistar; *adv* bajo; bajamente; *s* punto bajo, lugar bajo; (el) precio más bajo, precio mínimo; mugido; (aut.) primera marcha, primera velocidad; (meteor.) depresión; *vn* mugir (*la vaca*)
**low area** *s* área de baja presión barométrica
**lowborn** [ˈloˌbɔrn] *adj* de humilde cuna, plebeyo, mal nacido
**lowboy** [ˈloˌbɔɪ] *s* cómoda baja sostenida por patas cortas
**lowbred** [ˈloˌbrɛd] *adj* grosero, palurdo
**lowbrow** [ˈloˌbraʊ] *adj* (slang) ignorante; (slang) de o para gente ignorante o sin cultura; *s* (slang) ignorante
**Low Church** *s* baja iglesia (*rama no conservadora de la Iglesia anglicana*)
**Low-Church** [ˈloˈtʃʌrtʃ] *adj* no ritualista
**Low-Churchman** [ˌloˈtʃʌrtʃmən] *s* (*pl:* **-men**) protestante episcopal no ritualista
**low comedy** *s* comedia bufa, farsa
**low-cost housing** [ˈloˈkɔst] o [ˈloˈkɑst] *s* habitación popular, casas baratas
**Low Countries** *spl* Países Bajos (*Bélgica, Holanda y Luxemburgo*)
**low-country** [ˈloˌkʌntrɪ] *adj* de los Países Bajos
**low-down** [ˈloˈdaʊn] *adj* (coll.) bajo, vil; [ˈloˌdaʊn] *s* (slang) informes confidenciales, hechos verdaderos
**lower** [ˈloər] *adj* más bajo; inferior; *va & vn* bajar; [ˈlaʊər] *s* ceño; *vn* fruncir el entrecejo, poner mala cara; encapotarse o nublarse (*el cielo*)
**lower berth** [ˈloər] *s* litera baja
**Lower California** [ˈloər] *s* Baja California
**lower case** [ˈloər] *s* (print.) letra de caja baja
**lower-case** [ˈloərˌkes] *adj* (print.) de caja baja
**lowerclassman** [ˈloərˈklæsmən] o [ˈloərˈklɑsmən] *s* (*pl:* **-men**) estudiante de los dos primeros años
**Lower House** [ˈloər] *s* Cámara baja
**lowering** [ˈlaʊərɪŋ] *adj* ceñoso, ceñudo; encapotado, nublado
**lower lip** [ˈloər] *s* labio inferior
**lowermost** [ˈloərmost] *adj* (el) más bajo
**lower regions** [ˈloər] *spl* infiernos
**lower world** [ˈloər] *s* tierra; mundo subterráneo, infiernos
**low frequency** *s* (elec.) baja frecuencia
**low-frequency** [ˈloˈfrikwənsɪ] *adj* (elec.) de baja frecuencia
**low gear** *s* (aut.) primera marcha, primera velocidad
**Low German** *s* bajoalemán
**Low-German** [ˈloˈdʒʌrmən] *adj* bajoalemán
**lowland** [ˈlolənd] *adj* de tierra baja; *s* tierra baja; **Lowlands** *spl* Tierra Baja (*de Escocia*)
**Lowlander** [ˈloləndər] *s* natural de la Tierra Baja de Escocia
**Low Latin** *s* bajo latín
**lowliness** [ˈlolɪnɪs] *s* humildad
**lowly** [ˈlolɪ] *adj* (*comp:* **-lier**; *super:* **-liest**) humilde, de baja condición; *adv* humildemente
**Low Mass** *s* (eccl.) misa rezada
**low-minded** [ˈloˈmaɪndɪd] *adj* vil, ruin
**low-necked** [ˈloˈnɛkt] *adj* escotado
**low-pass filter** [ˈloˌpæs] o [ˈloˌpɑs] *s* (elec.) filtro paso inferior, filtro de paso bajo
**low-pitched** [ˈloˈpɪtʃt] *adj* de poco declive, poco pendiente; grave (*sonido*)
**low-pressure** [ˈloˈprɛʃər] *adj* de baja presión
**low relief** *s* bajo relieve
**low shoe** *s* zapato inglés (*zapato bajo que se cierra con cordones*)
**low speed** *s* baja velocidad
**low-speed** [ˈloˌspid] *adj* de baja velocidad
**low-spirited** [ˈloˈspɪrɪtɪd] *adj* abatido, desanimado
**low spirits** *spl* abatimiento, desanimación
**Low Sunday** *s* domingo de cuasimodo
**low tension** *s* (elec.) baja tensión
**low-tension** [ˈloˈtɛnʃən] *adj* (elec.) de baja tensión
**low tide** *s* bajamar, marea baja; (fig.) punto más bajo
**low visibility** *s* (aer.) poca visibilidad
**low-voltage** [ˈloˈvoltɪdʒ] *adj* (elec.) de bajo voltaje, de baja tensión
**low water** *s* estiaje (*por causa de la sequía*); marea baja; nivel mínimo (*p.ej., de un río*)
**low-water mark** [ˈloˈwɔtər] o [ˈloˈwɑtər] *s* línea de aguas mínimas, línea de bajamar; (fig.) punto más bajo
**loxodrome** [ˈlɑksədrom] *s* (naut.) loxodromia
**loxodromic** [ˌlɑksəˈdrɑmɪk] o **loxodromical** [ˌlɑksəˈdrɑmɪkəl] *adj* (naut.) loxodrómico
**loyal** [ˈlɔɪəl] *adj* leal
**loyalist** [ˈlɔɪəlɪst] *s* legitimista; (*cap.*) *s* realista (*en la guerra de la Independencia de los EE.UU.*); leal, gubernamental, republicano (*en la guerra civil de España*)
**loyalty** [ˈlɔɪəltɪ] *s* (*pl:* **-ties**) lealtad
**lozenge** [ˈlɑzɪndʒ] *s* pastilla, tableta; (geom. & her.) losange
**lozengy** [ˈlɑzɪndʒɪ] *adj* (her.) losangeado o losanjado
**LP** abr. de **long-playing**; *s* disco de larga duración, disco microsurco
**L.S.D.** o **l.s.d.** abr. de **pounds, shillings, and pence**
**Lt.** abr. de **Lieutenant**
**Ltd.** o **ltd.** abr. de **limited**
**lubber** [ˈlʌbər] *s* palurdo; marinero matalote
**lubberly** [ˈlʌbərlɪ] *adj* palurdo; *adv* palurdamente
**lubricant** [ˈlubrɪkənt] *adj & s* lubricante
**lubricate** [ˈlubrɪket] *va* lubricar
**lubrication** [ˌlubrɪˈkeʃən] *s* lubricación
**lubricator** [ˈlubrɪˌketər] *s* lubricador (*persona y aparato*)
**lubricious** [luˈbrɪʃəs] *adj* lúbrico (*libidinoso*)
**lubricity** [luˈbrɪsɪtɪ] *s* (*pl:* **-ties**) lubricidad
**lubricous** [ˈlubrɪkəs] *adj* lúbrico (*resbaladizo; libidinoso*); inconstante, incierto
**Lucan** [ˈlukən] *s* Lucano
**lucence** [ˈlusəns] o **lucency** [ˈlusənsɪ] *s* brillantez; translucidez
**lucent** [ˈlusənt] *adj* luciente; translúcido
**lucerne** [luˈsʌrn] *s* (bot.) mielga; (*cap.*) *s* Lucerna
**Lucia** [ˈluʃɪə] o [ˈluʃə] *s* Lucía
**Lucian** [ˈluʃɪən] o [ˈluʃən] *s* Luciano
**lucid** [ˈlusɪd] *adj* luciente; cristalino; lúcido (*claro en el razonamiento, estilo, etc.*); (med.) lúcido (*intervalo*)
**lucidity** [luˈsɪdɪtɪ] *s* lucidez; doble vista; (psychol.) lucidez
**lucifer** [ˈlusɪfər] *s* fósforo de fricción; (*cap.*) *s* Lucifer (*príncipe de los ángeles rebeldes; Venus, lucero del alba*)
**luciferase** [luˈsɪfəres] *s* (biochem.) luciferasa
**Luciferian** [ˌlusɪˈfɪrɪən] *adj* luciferino
**luciferin** [luˈsɪfərɪn] *s* (biochem.) luciferina
**lucifugous** [luˈsɪfjəgəs] *adj* (biol.) lucífugo
**luck** [lʌk] *s* suerte (*buena o mala*); suerte, buena suerte; **down on one's luck** (coll.) de mala suerte, de malas; **for luck** para que traiga buena suerte; **in luck** de buena suerte, de buenas; **out of luck** de mala suerte, de malas; **to bring luck** traer buena suerte; **to try one's luck** meter la mano en el cántaro, probar fortuna; **worse luck** desgraciadamente
**luckily** [ˈlʌkɪlɪ] *adv* afortunadamente
**luckless** [ˈlʌklɪs] *adj* desafortunado, malaventurado
**lucky** [ˈlʌkɪ] *adj* (*comp:* **-ier**; *super:* **-iest**) afortunado; de buen agüero; **to be lucky** tener buena suerte
**lucky hit** *s* (coll.) golpe de fortuna
**lucrative** [ˈlukrətɪv] *adj* lucrativo
**lucre** [ˈlukər] *s* (el) vil metal (*raíz de muchos males*)
**Lucrece** [luˈkris] o [ˈlukris] o **Lucretia** [luˈkriʃə] *s* Lucrecia
**Lucretius** [luˈkriʃəs] *s* Lucrecio
**lucubrate** [ˈlukjəbret] *va & vn* lucubrar

**lucubration** [ˌlukjəˈbreʃən] *s* lucubración
**Lucullian** [luˈkʌlɪən] *adj* opíparo, magnífico
**Lucullus** [luˈkʌləs] *s* Lúculo
**Lucy** [ˈlusɪ] *s* Lucía
**ludicrous** [ˈludɪkrəs] *adj* absurdo, ridículo
**lues** [ˈluiz] *s* (path.) lúes (*sífilis*)
**luff** [lʌf] *s* (naut.) orza; (naut.) orilla de proa (*de una cangreja*); (naut.) aparejo de combés; *vn* (naut.) orzar
**lug** [lʌg] *s* orejeta; estirón, esfuerzo; (naut.) vela al tercio; (*pret & pp:* **lugged;** *ger:* **lugging**) *va* arrastrar, tirar con fuerza de; (coll.) traer a colación (*especies inoportunas en una conversación*); *vn* tirar con fuerza
**luggage** [ˈlʌgɪdʒ] *s* equipaje
**luggage rack** *s* red de equipaje
**lugger** [ˈlʌgər] *s* (naut.) lugre
**lugsail** [ˈlʌgsəl] o [ˈlʌgˌsel] *s* (naut.) vela al tercio
**lugubrious** [luˈgjubrɪəs] *adj* lúgubre
**lugworm** [ˈlʌgˌwʌrm] *s* (zool.) arenícola
**Luke** [luk] *s* Lucas; (Bib.) San Lucas; (Bib.) el Evangelio según San Lucas
**lukewarm** [ˈlukˌwɔrm] *adj* tibio; (fig.) tibio
**lull** [lʌl] *s* momento de silencio, momento de calma; *va* calmar, adormecer, arrullar; *vn* calmarse; amainar (*el viento*)
**lullaby** [ˈlʌləbaɪ] *s* (*pl:* **-bies**) arrullo, canción de cuna
**Lullian** [ˈlʌlɪən] *adj* luliano o lulista
**Lullianist** [ˈlʌlɪənɪst] o **Lullist** [ˈlʌlɪst] *s* luliano o lulista
**lumbago** [lʌmˈbego] *s* (path.) lumbago
**lumbar** [ˈlʌmbər] *adj* lumbar; *s* (anat.) vértebra, arteria o nervio lumbares
**lumber** [ˈlʌmbər] *s* madera aserrada, madera de construcción; trastos viejos; *va* amontonar trastos viejos en, no dejar sitio para moverse en; *vn* cortar y aserrar madera, explotar los bosques; andar o moverse pesadamente; avanzar con ruido sordo
**lumbering** [ˈlʌmbərɪŋ] *adj* pesado, que se mueve pesadamente; *s* explotación de bosques maderables, extracción de madera
**lumberjack** [ˈlʌmbərˌdʒæk] *s* leñador, hachero
**lumberman** [ˈlʌmbərmən] *s* (*pl:* **-men**) maderero; leñador
**lumber room** *s* trastera, leonera
**lumberyard** [ˈlʌmbərˌjɑrd] *s* corral de madera, almacén de maderas, maderería
**lumbrical** [ˈlʌmbrɪkəl] *adj* (anat.) lumbrical
**lumen** [ˈlumɛn] *s* (*pl:* **-mina** [mɪnə] o **-mens**) (anat., bot. & phys.) lumen
**lumen-hour** [ˈlumɛnˈaʊr] *s* (phys.) lumen hora
**luminal** [ˈlumɪnəl] *s* (trademark) luminal
**luminary** [ˈlumɪˌnɛrɪ] *s* (*pl:* **-ies**) luminar; (fig.) luminar (*persona*)
**luminescence** [ˌlumɪˈnɛsəns] *s* luminiscencia
**luminescent** [ˌlumɪˈnɛsənt] *adj* luminiscente
**luminiferous** [ˌlumɪˈnɪfərəs] *adj* luminífero
**luminosity** [ˌlumɪˈnɑsɪtɪ] *s* (*pl:* **-ties**) luminosidad; cuerpo luminoso
**luminous** [ˈlumɪnəs] *adj* luminoso
**lummox** [ˈlʌməks] *s* (coll.) chapucero estúpido, persona torpe y estúpida
**lump** [lʌmp] *s* terrón; borujo; bulto, chichón, hinchazón; conjunto, todo; (coll.) bodoque; (coll.) persona espaldada; **in the lump** en grueso, por junto; **to get a lump in one's throat** hacérsele a uno un nudo en la garganta; *adj* en terrón, en terrones; global; *va* aterronar; aborujar; producir protuberancias en; combinar; agrupar; (coll.) aguantar, tragar (*cosa vejatoria*); *vn* aterronarse; aborujarse; abultar; andar con pasos pesados
**lumpish** [ˈlʌmpɪʃ] *adj* aterronado; torpe, pesado, estúpido, hobachón
**lump sugar** *s* azúcar en terrón
**lump sum** *s* suma total, cantidad gruesa
**lumpy** [ˈlʌmpɪ] *adj* (*comp:* **-ier;** *super:* **-iest**) aterronado; borujoso; torpe, pesado; agitado (*p.ej., mar*)
**lunacy** [ˈlunəsɪ] *s* (*pl:* **-cies**) locura
**luna moth** [ˈlunə] *s* (ent.) actias luna
**lunar** [ˈlunər] *adj* lunar
**lunar caustic** *s* cáustico lunar, piedra infernal (*nitrato de plata*)
**lunar month** *s* mes lunar
**lunar year** *s* año lunar
**lunate** [ˈlunet] *adj* lunado
**lunatic** [ˈlunətɪk] *adj* loco; de locos; necio; *s* loco
**lunatic asylum** *s* manicomio
**lunatic fringe** *s* minoría fanática (*en lo político, social, religioso, etc.*)
**lunation** [luˈneʃən] *s* (astr.) lunación
**lunch** [lʌntʃ] *s* almuerzo, merienda; colación, refacción; *vn* almorzar, merendar; tomar una colación
**lunch basket** *s* fiambrera
**lunch cloth** *s* mantelito
**luncheon** [ˈlʌntʃən] *s* almuerzo, merienda; almuerzo de ceremonia; *vn* almorzar, merendar
**luncheonette** [ˌlʌntʃəˈnɛt] *s* cantina
**lunchroom** [ˈlʌntʃˌrum] o [ˈlʌntʃˌrʊm] *s* restaurante
**lune** [lun] *s* media luna; (geom.) lúnula
**lunette** [luˈnɛt] *s* luneta (*adorno en forma de media luna*); (arch.) luneto o luneta; (fort.) luneta
**lung** [lʌŋ] *s* (anat.) pulmón
**lunge** [lʌndʒ] *s* arremetida, embestida; estocada; *vn* arremeter, embestir; dar una estocada; **to lunge at** arremeter contra
**lungwort** [ˈlʌŋˌwʌrt] *s* (bot.) pulmonaria
**lunule** [ˈlunjul] *s* (anat. & zool.) lúnula
**Lupercalia** [ˌlupərˈkelɪə] *spl* (hist.) lupercales
**lupine** [ˈlupaɪn] *adj* lupino; [ˈlupɪn] *s* (bot.) lupino, altramuz
**lupus** [ˈlupəs] *s* (path.) lupus
**lurch** [lʌrtʃ] *s* sacudida, tumbo, balanceo brusco; (naut.) bandazo; **to leave in the lurch** dejar colgado, abandonar en la estacada; *vn* dar una sacudida, dar sacudidas, dar un tumbo; (naut.) dar un bandazo
**lurcher** [ˈlʌrtʃər] *s* ladronzuelo, ratero; cazador furtivo; (Brit.) perro de caza
**lure** [lʊr] *s* cebo; señuelo; (fig.) señuelo, aliciente; *va* atraer con cebo; atraer con señuelo; (fig.) atraer, tentar, seducir; **to lure away** llevarse con señuelo; desviar (*p.ej., de su deber*); **to lure someone into** tentar a uno a que entre en; **to lure someone into** + *ger* tentar a uno a que + *subj*
**lurid** [ˈlʊrɪd] *adj* ardiente; asombroso, sensacional; espeluznante
**lurk** [lʌrk] *vn* acechar, estar oculto, moverse furtivamente
**luscious** [ˈlʌʃəs] *adj* delicioso, exquisito; rico, dulce y sabroso
**lush** [lʌʃ] *adj* jugoso, lozano; abundante; lujuriante
**Lusitanian** [ˌlusɪˈtenɪən] *adj & s* lusitano
**Lusitanism** [ˈlusɪtənɪzəm] *s* lusitanismo
**lust** [lʌst] *s* deseo vehemente, deseo desordenado; codicia; lujuria; *vn* codiciar; lujuriar; **to lust after** o **for** codiciar; apetecer contacto carnal con
**luster** [ˈlʌstər] *s* lustre, brillo; viso (*de ciertas telas*); porcelana con visos de azulejo; tela lustrosa de lana y algodón; (fig.) lustro (*fama, gloria*)
**lustful** [ˈlʌstfəl] *adj* lujurioso, lúbrico
**lustral** [ˈlʌstrəl] *adj* lustral
**lustrate** [ˈlʌstret] *va* lustrar
**lustration** [lʌsˈtreʃən] *s* lustración; (hum.) lavación, lavatorio
**lustre** [ˈlʌstər] *s* var. de **luster**
**lustrous** [ˈlʌstrəs] *adj* lustroso
**lustrum** [ˈlʌstrəm] *s* (*pl:* **-trums** o **-tra** [trə]) lustro (*cinco años*); (hist.) lustro
**lusty** [ˈlʌstɪ] *adj* (*comp:* **-ier;** *super:* **-iest**) robusto, lozano, fuerte
**lute** [lut] *s* (mus.) laúd; (chem.) lodo (*para cerrar junturas, tapar grietas, etc.*); *va* (chem.) enlodar
**lutecium** [luˈtiʃɪəm] *s* (chem.) lutecio
**luteolin** [ˈlutɪəlɪn] *s* (chem.) luteolina
**luteous** [ˈlutɪəs] *adj* lúteo
**Luther** [ˈluθər] *s* Lutero
**Lutheran** [ˈluθərən] *adj & s* luterano
**Lutheranism** [ˈluθərənɪzəm] *s* luteranismo
**lux** [lʌks] *s* (*pl:* **luces** [ˈlusiz]) (phys.) lux
**luxate** [ˈlʌkset] *va* luxar
**luxation** [lʌkˈseʃən] *s* luxación
**Luxemburg** [ˈlʌksəmbʌrg] *s* Luxemburgo
**luxuriance** [lʌgˈʒʊrɪəns] o [lʌkˈʃʊrɪəns] o **luxuriancy** [lʌgˈʒʊrɪənsɪ] o [lʌkˈʃʊrɪənsɪ] *s* lozanía

**luxuriant** [lʌg'ʒurɪənt] o [lʌk'ʃurɪənt] *adj* lozano, lujuriante; de ornamentación recargada
**luxuriate** [lʌg'ʒurɪet] o [lʌk'ʃurɪet] *vn* crecer con lozanía; entregarse al lujo; lozanear (*deleitarse*)
**luxurious** [lʌg'ʒurɪəs] o [lʌk'ʃurɪəs] *adj* lujoso
**luxury** ['lʌkʃərɪ] *s* (*pl:* **-ries**) lujo; lujuria (*concupiscencia de la carne*); *adj* de lujo
**lycanthrope** ['laɪkənθrop] o [laɪ'kænθrop] *s* licántropo
**lycanthropy** [laɪ'kænθrəpɪ] *s* licantropía
**lyceum** [laɪ'siəm] *s* liceo
**lych gate** [lɪtʃ] *s* var. de **lich gate**
**lychnis** ['lɪknɪs] *s* (bot.) licnis
**Lycia** ['lɪʃɪə] *s* Licia
**Lycian** ['lɪʃɪən] *adj & s* licio
**lycopodium** [,laɪkə'podɪəm] *s* (bot.) licopodio
**Lycurgus** [laɪ'kʌrgəs] *s* Licurgo
**lyddite** ['lɪdaɪt] *s* lidita (*explosivo*)
**Lydia** ['lɪdɪə] *s* Lidia
**Lydian** ['lɪdɪən] *adj* lidio; (mus.) lidio; (fig.) blando, afeminado, voluptuoso; *s* lidio
**lye** [laɪ] *s* lejía
**lying** ['laɪɪŋ] *s* el mentir; *adj* mentiroso; *ger de* **lie**
**lying-in** ['laɪɪŋ'ɪn] *s* parto
**lying-in hospital** *s* hospital de parturientas, casa de maternidad
**lymph** [lɪmf] *s* (anat. & physiol.) linfa
**lymphadenitis** [lɪm,fædɪ'naɪtɪs] *s* (path.) linfadenitis
**lymphangiitis** [lɪm,fændʒɪ'aɪtɪs] *s* (path.) linfangitis
**lymphatic** [lɪm'fætɪk] *adj* linfático; (fig.) linfático; *s* (anat.) vaso linfático
**lymph gland** o **node** *s* (anat.) ganglio o nódulo linfático
**lymphocyte** ['lɪmfəsaɪt] *s* (anat.) linfocito
**lyncean** [lɪn'siən] *adj* linceo
**lynch** [lɪntʃ] *va* linchar
**lynching** ['lɪntʃɪŋ] *s* linchamiento
**lynch law** *s* ley de Lynch, justicia de la soga
**lynchpin** ['lɪntʃ,pɪn] *s* var. de **linchpin**
**lynx** [lɪŋks] *s* (*pl:* **lynxes** o **lynx**) (zool.) lince; (*cap.*) *s* (astr.) Lince
**lynx-eyed** ['lɪŋks,aɪd] *adj* de ojos linces
**Lyonese** [,laɪə'niz] *adj* lionés; *s* (*pl:* **-ese**) lionés
**lyonnaise** [,laɪə'nez] *adj* (cook.) a la lionesa, p.ej., **lyonnaise potatoes** patatas a la lionesa
**Lyonnesse** [,laɪə'nɛs] *s* región fabulosa de Inglaterra que se supone hundida en el mar
**Lyons** ['laɪənz] *s* León de Francia, Lyón
**Lyra** ['laɪrə] *s* (astr.) Lira
**lyrate** ['laɪret] *adj* lirado; (bot.) lirado
**lyre** [laɪr] *s* (mus.) lira; (*cap.*) *s* (astr.) Lira
**lyrebird** ['laɪr,bʌrd] *s* (orn.) ave lira
**lyric** ['lɪrɪk] *adj* lírico; (theat.) lírico (*músico, operístico*); *s* poema lírico; (coll.) letra (*de una canción*)
**lyrical** ['lɪrɪkəl] *adj* lírico
**lyricism** ['lɪrɪsɪzəm] *s* lirismo
**Lysander** [laɪ'sændər] *s* Lisandro
**Lysenkoism** [lɪ'sɛŋko·ɪzəm] *s* lisencoísmo
**lysin** ['laɪsɪn] o **lysine** ['laɪsin] o ['laɪsɪn] *s* (biochem.) lisina
**Lysippus** [laɪ'sɪpəs] *s* Lisipo
**lysol** ['laɪsol] o ['laɪsɑl] *s* (trademark) lisol
**lyssophobia** [,lɪsə'fobɪə] *s* (psychopath.) lisofobia
**lythraceous** [lɪ'θreʃəs] o [laɪ'θreʃəs] *adj* (bot.) litráceo

# M

**M, m** [ɛm] *s* (*pl:* **M's, m's** [ɛmz]) décimotercera letra del alfabeto inglés

**m.** abr. de **mark, married, masculine, meter, midnight, mile, minim, minute, month** y **moon**

**M.** abr. de **midnight** y **Monday**

**M.A.** abr. de **Magister Artium** (Lat.) **Master of Arts**

**ma** [mɑ] *s* (coll.) mamá

**ma'am** [mæm] o [mɑm] *s* (coll.) señora

**macabre** [məˈkɑbər] *adj* macábrico o macabro

**macaco** [məˈkeko] *s* (*pl:* **-cos**) (zool.) maquí

**macadam** [məˈkædəm] *s* macadam o macadán

**macadamize** [məˈkædəmaɪz] *va* macadamizar

**macaque** [məˈkɑk] *s* (zool.) macaco

**macaroni** [ˌmækəˈronɪ] *s* (*pl:* **-nis** o **-nies**) *s* macarrones

**macaronic** [ˌmækəˈrɑnɪk] *adj* macarrónico; *s* macarronea

**macaroon** [ˌmækəˈrun] *s* almendrado, mostachón, macarrón

**Macassar oil** [məˈkæsər] *s* aceite de Macasar

**macaw** [məˈkɔ] *s* (orn.) ara, aracanga

**Maccabaeus** [ˌmækəˈbiəs] *s* (Bib.) Macabeo

**Maccabean** [ˌmækəˈbiən] *adj* de los macabeos

**Maccabees** [ˈmækəbiz] *spl* (Bib.) macabeos

**maccaboy** o **maccoboy** [ˈmækəbɔɪ] *s* macuba (*tabaco aromático*)

**mace** [mes] *s* maza; macero; macia o macis (*especia*); *va* macear

**macebearer** [ˈmesˌbɛrər] *s* macero

**macédoine** [ˌmæseˈdwɑn] *s* macedonia (*ensalada; mezcla, mezcolanza*)

**Macedon** [ˈmæsɪdɑn] *s* Macedonia (*antigua*)

**Macedonia** [ˌmæsɪˈdonɪə] *s* Macedonia

**Macedonian** [ˌmæsɪˈdonɪən] *adj & s* macedonio

**macer** [ˈmesər] *s* var. de **macebearer**

**macerate** [ˈmæsəret] *va* macerar; *vn* macerarse

**macerater** [ˈmæsəˌretər] *s* macerador

**maceration** [ˌmæsəˈreʃən] *s* maceración

**Mach** [mɑk] *s* (aer.) número Mach

**machete** [mɑˈtʃete] o [məˈʃɛt] *s* machete

**Mache unit** [ˈmɑxə] *s* (phys.) mache

**Machiavelli** [ˌmækɪəˈvɛlɪ] *s* Maquiavelo

**Machiavellian** o **Machiavelian** [ˌmækɪəˈvɛlɪən] *adj* maquiavelista; maquiavélico (*astuto, engañador*); *s* maquiavelista

**Machiavellianism** [ˌmækɪəˈvɛlɪənɪzəm] o **Machiavellism** [ˌmækɪəˈvɛlɪzəm] *s* maquiavelismo

**machicolate** [məˈtʃɪkəlet] *va* aspillerar

**machicolation** [məˌtʃɪkəˈleʃən] *s* (fort.) matacán (*balcón*); aspillera (*abertura*)

**machinate** [ˈmækɪnet] *va & vn* maquinar

**machination** [ˌmækɪˈneʃən] *s* maquinación

**machinator** [ˈmækɪˌnetər] *s* maquinador

**machine** [məˈʃin] *s* máquina; coche, automóvil; avión; camarilla (*de políticos*); (lit. & theat.) máquina; *va* trabajar a máquina

**machine age** *s* edad de la máquina

**machine gun** *s* ametralladora

**machine-gun** [məˈʃinˌgʌn] (*pret & pp:* **-gunned;** *ger:* **-gunning**) *va* ametrallar

**machine gunner** *s* ametrallador

**machine-made** [məˈʃinˌmed] *adj* hecho a máquina, labrado mecánicamente

**machinery** [məˈʃinərɪ] *s* (*pl:* **-ies**) maquinaria; (fig.) maquinaria (*p.ej., del gobierno*)

**machine screw** *s* tornillo para metales

**machine shop** *s* taller mecánico, taller de maquinaria

**machine tool** *s* máquina-herramienta

**machine translation** *s* traducción automática

**machinist** [məˈʃinɪst] *s* mecánico; maquinista; (naut.) segundo maquinista; (theat.) tramoyista

**macintosh** [ˈmækɪntɑʃ] *s* var. de **mackintosh**

**mackerel** [ˈmækərəl] *s* (ichth.) caballa, escombro

**mackerel sky** *s* cielo aborregado

**mackinaw** [ˈmækɪnɔ] *s* manta gruesa de lana con listas de varios colores; chaquetón de mucho abrigo

**mackintosh** [ˈmækɪntɑʃ] *s* impermeable; tela impermeabilizada

**mackle** [ˈmækəl] *s* (print.) maculatura (*mancha*); *va* (print.) macular, repintar; *vn* (print.) macularse, repintarse

**macle** [ˈmækəl] *s* (mineral.) macla

**macramé** [ˈmækrəme] *s* macramé

**macrobiotic** [ˌmækrəbaɪˈɑtɪk] *adj* macrobiótico; **macrobiotics** *ssg* macrobiótica

**macrocosm** [ˈmækrəkɑzəm] *s* macrocosmo

**macrocyte** [ˈmækrəsaɪt] *s* (path.) macrocito

**macrogamete** [ˌmækrogəˈmit] *s* (biol.) macrogameto

**macromolecule** [ˌmækroˈmɑlɪkjul] *s* macromolécula

**macron** [ˈmekrɑn] o [ˈmækrɑn] *s* (gram.) raya que se pone sobre las vocales para indicar su largura

**macrophysics** [ˌmækroˈfɪzɪks] *ssg* macrofísica

**macrosmatic** [ˌmækrɑzˈmætɪk] *adj* (zool.) macrosmático

**macruran** [məˈkrʊrən] *adj & s* (zool.) macruro

**macula** [ˈmækjələ] *s* (*pl:* **-lae** [li]) (anat., astr. & path.) mácula

**macule** [ˈmækjul] *s, va & vn* var. de **mackle**

**mad** [mæd] *adj* (*comp:* **madder;** *super:* **maddest**) loco; enojado, furioso; rabioso (*perro*); necio, tonto; muy aficionado; **like mad** como un loco; con todas sus fuerzas; **to be mad about** tener locura por, ser muy aficionado a; **to drive mad** volver loco, enloquecer; **to go mad** volverse loco, enloquecer; rabiar (*un perro*); **mad as a hatter** o **mad as a March hare** loco de atar

**madam** [ˈmædəm] *s* (*pl:* **madams** o **mesdames** [meˈdɑm]) señora

**madame** [ˈmædəm] o [mɑˈdɑm] *s* (*pl:* **mesdames** [meˈdɑm]) (Fr.) madama

**madapollam** [ˌmædəˈpɑləm] *s* madapolán

**madcap** [ˈmædˌkæp] *adj & s* alocado

**madden** [ˈmædən] *va* enojar, poner furioso; enloquecer

**madder** [ˈmædər] *s* (bot.) rubia (*planta y raíz*); (chem.) rojo de rubia

**madding** [ˈmædɪŋ] *adj* irritante; furioso, loco

**made** [med] *adj* hecho, fabricado; inventado; llegado (*a la meta del éxito completo*); *pret & pp de* **make**

**Madeira** [məˈdɪrə] *s* madera, vino de Madera

**Madeleine** [ˈmædəlɪn] *s* var. de **Magdalen**

**mademoiselle** [ˌmædəməˈzɛl] *s* (*pl:* **mesdemoiselles** [medmwɑˈzɛl]) (Fr.) madamisela

**made-to-order** [ˈmedtəˈɔrdər] *adj* hecho a la medida; hecho especialmente para el comprador

**made-up** [ˈmedˈʌp] *adj* hecho, completo; compuesto; ficticio; postizo; pintado (*rostro*)

**Madge** [mædʒ] *s* nombre abreviado de **Margaret**

**madhouse** [ˈmædˌhaus] *s* casa de locos, manicomio; (fig.) casa de locos, gallinero

**madly** [ˈmædlɪ] *adv* locamente; furiosamente; neciamente; desesperadamente

**madman** [ˈmædˌmæn] o [ˈmædmən] *s* (*pl:* **-men**) loco

**madness** [ˈmædnɪs] *s* locura; furia, rabia; (path.) rabia

**Madonna** [məˈdɑnə] *s* Madona; (f.a.) Madona

**Madonna lily** *s* (bot.) azucena

**madras** [ˈmædrəs] o [məˈdræs] *s* madrás

**madrepore** [ˈmædrɪpor] *s* (zool.) madrépora

**madreporic** [ˌmædrɪˈpɔrɪk] o [ˌmædrɪˈpɑrɪk] *adj* madrepórico
**madrigal** [ˈmædrɪgəl] *s* madrigal; (mus.) madrigal
**Madrilenian** [ˌmædrɪˈlinɪən] *adj & s* madrileño
**madwort** [ˈmædˌwʌrt] *s* (bot.) raspilla (*Asperugo procumbens*); (bot.) camelina
**Maecenas** [mɪˈsinəs] *s* Mecenas; (fig.) mecenas
**maelstrom** [ˈmelstrəm] *s* remolino; (fig.) remolino
**maenad** [ˈminæd] *s* (hist. & fig.) ménade
**maestro** [ˈmaɪstro] o [mɑˈɛstro] *s* (*pl:* **-tros** o **-tri** [tri]) maestro (*en cualquier arte*)
**Maffia** o **Mafia** [ˈmɑfɪɑ] *s* maffia
**mag.** abr. de **magazine**
**magazine** [ˈmægəzin] o [ˌmægəˈzin] *s* revista; almacén; cámara (*para cartuchos*); polvorín; (naut.) santabárbara; (phot.) almacén
**Magdalen** [ˈmægdələn] o [ˈmægdəlɛn] *s* Magdalena
**Magdalene** [ˈmægdəlin] o [ˌmægdəˈlini] *s* (Bib.) Santa María Magdalena; (*l.c.*) *s* (fig.) magdalena (*mujer penitente*)
**Magdalenian** [ˌmægdəˈlinɪən] *adj* (geol.) magdaleniense
**Magdeburg hemispheres** [ˈmægdəbʌrg] *spl* (phys.) hemisferios de Magdeburgo
**mage** [medʒ] *s* (archaic) mágico
**Magellan** [məˈdʒɛlən] *s* Magallanes
**Magellanic** [ˌmædʒəˈlænɪk] *adj* magallánico
**magenta** [məˈdʒɛntə] *s* magenta
**maggot** [ˈmægət] *s* (zool.) cresa; antojo, capricho
**maggoty** [ˈmægətɪ] *adj* agusanado, gusaniento; caprichoso
**Magi** [ˈmedʒaɪ] *spl* magos (*de la religión zoroástrica*); Reyes Magos
**Magian** [ˈmedʒɪən] *adj & s* mago; (*l.c.*) *adj & s* mago (*mágico*)
**magic** [ˈmædʒɪk] *adj* mágico; *s* magia; prestidigitación; **as if by magic** como por encanto
**magical** [ˈmædʒɪkəl] *adj* mágico
**magic carpet** *s* alfombra mágica
**magician** [məˈdʒɪʃən] *s* mágico; prestidigitador
**magic lantern** *s* linterna mágica
**magic square** *s* cuadrado mágico
**magisterial** [ˌmædʒɪsˈtɪrɪəl] *adj* magistral; de magistrado
**magistracy** [ˈmædʒɪstrəsɪ] *s* (*pl:* **-cies**) magistratura
**magistral** [ˈmædʒɪstrəl] *adj* magistral; (fort. & pharm.) magistral; *s* (metal.) magistral
**magistrate** [ˈmædʒɪstret] o [ˈmædʒɪstrɪt] *s* magistrado; juez
**magma** [ˈmægmə] *s* (*pl:* **-mata** [mətə] o **-mas**) magma; (geol. & pharm.) magma
**Magna Charta** o **Magna Carta** [ˈmægnə ˈkɑrtə] *s* Carta Magna
**magnanimity** [ˌmægnəˈnɪmɪtɪ] *s* (*pl:* **-ties**) magnanimidad
**magnanimous** [mægˈnænɪməs] *adj* magnánimo
**magnate** [ˈmægnet] *s* magnate
**magnesia** [mægˈniʃə] o [mægˈniʒə] *s* (chem.) magnesia; magnesio
**magnesian** [mægˈniʃən] o [mægˈniʒən] *adj* magnesiano
**magnesic** [mægˈnisɪk] *adj* magnésico
**magnesite** [ˈmægnɪsaɪt] *s* (mineral.) magnesita
**magnesium** [mægˈniʃɪəm] o [mægˈniʒɪəm] *s* (chem.) magnesio
**magnesium bronze** *s* bronce de magnesio
**magnesium light** *s* luz de magnesio
**magnet** [ˈmægnɪt] *s* (mineral., phys. & fig.) imán
**magnetic** [mægˈnɛtɪk] *adj* magnético; atrayente, cautivador
**magnetic curves** *spl* espectro magnético
**magnetic field** *s* campo magnético
**magnetic flux** *s* flujo magnético
**magnetic moment** *s* (phys.) momento magnético
**magnetic needle** *s* aguja imanada o magnética
**magnetic pole** *s* polo magnético
**magnetic storm** *s* (phys.) borrasca magnética, tempestad magnética
**magnetic tape** *s* cinta magnética
**magnetism** [ˈmægnɪtɪzəm] *s* magnetismo; magnetismo personal, don de gentes
**magnetite** [ˈmægnɪtaɪt] *s* (mineral.) magnetita
**magnetization** [ˌmægnɪtɪˈzeʃən] *s* magnetización
**magnetize** [ˈmægnɪtaɪz] *va* magnetizar; atraer, cautivar, fascinar
**magneto** [mægˈnito] *s* (*pl:* **-tos**) magneto
**magnetoelectric** [mægˌnito·ɪˈlɛktrɪk] *adj* magnetoeléctrico
**magnetometer** [ˌmægnɪˈtɑmɪtər] *s* magnetómetro
**magneton** [ˈmægnɪtɑn] *s* (phys.) magnetón
**magnetophone** [mægˈnitofon] *s* (phys.) magnetófono
**magnetosphere** [mægˈnitəsfɪr] *s* magnetosfera
**magnetron** [ˈmægnɪtrɑn] *s* (rad.) magnetrón
**magnific** [mægˈnɪfɪk] o **magnifical** [mægˈnɪfɪkəl] *adj* magnificente; grandílocuo
**Magnificat** [mægˈnɪfɪkæt] *s* magníficat
**magnification** [ˌmægnɪfɪˈkeʃən] *s* (opt.) magnificación; ampliación (*copia ampliada*); exageración
**magnificence** [mægˈnɪfɪsəns] *s* magnificencia
**magnificent** [mægˈnɪfɪsənt] *adj* magnífico
**magnifico** [mægˈnɪfɪko] *s* (*pl:* **-coes**) caballero noble de Venecia; personaje ilustre
**magnifier** [ˈmægnɪˌfaɪər] *s* magnificador; exagerador; vidrio de aumento
**magnify** [ˈmægnɪfaɪ] (*pret & pp:* **-fied**) *va* (opt.) magnificar; exagerar; (archaic) magnificar (*alabar, ensalzar*)
**magnifying glass** *s* lupa, vidrio de aumento, lente de aumento
**magniloquence** [mægˈnɪləkwəns] *s* grandilocuencia; jactancia
**magniloquent** [mægˈnɪləkwənt] *adj* grandílocuo; jactancioso
**magnitude** [ˈmægnɪtjud] o [ˈmægnɪtud] *s* magnitud; (astr. & math.) magnitud
**magnolia** [mægˈnolɪə] *s* (bot.) magnolia
**magnum** [ˈmægnəm] *s* botella de dos litros
**magnum opus** *s* obra maestra
**magpie** [ˈmægpaɪ] *s* (orn.) urraca; charlador; regañón
**maguey** [ˈmægwe] *s* (bot.) pita, maguey
**Magus** [ˈmegəs] *s* (*pl:* **-gi** [dʒaɪ]) Rey Mago
**Magyar** [ˈmægjɑr] *adj & s* magiar
**maharaja** o **maharajah** [ˌmɑhəˈrɑdʒə] *s* maharajá
**mahatma** [məˈhɑtmə] o [məˈhætmə] *s* mahatma; (theosophy) mahatma
**Mahdi** [ˈmɑdi] *s* (*pl:* **-dis**) mehedí
**mah-jongg** o **mah-jong** [ˈmɑˈdʒɑŋ] *s* mahjong (*juego chino parecido al dominó*)
**mahlstick** [ˈmɑlˌstɪk] o [ˈmɔlˌstɪk] *s* (paint.) tiento
**mahogany** [məˈhɑgənɪ] *s* (*pl:* **-nies**) (bot.) caoba; *adj* de caoba; de color de caoba
**Mahomet** [məˈhɑmɪt] *s* var. de **Mohammed**
**Mahometan** [məˈhɑmɪtən] *adj & s* var. de **Mohammedan**
**Mahometanism** [məˈhɑmɪtənɪzəm] *s* var. de **Mohammedanism**
**Mahon stock** [məˈhon] *s* (bot.) mahonesa
**mahout** [məˈhaʊt] *s* naire, cornaca
**maid** [med] *s* criada, moza; doncella (*mujer virgen; criada que se ocupa en los menesteres domésticos ajenos a la cocina*); soltera
**maiden** [ˈmedən] *s* doncella; *adj* virginal; de soltera; virgen; primero
**maidenhair** [ˈmedənˌhɛr] *s* (bot.) cabello de Venus
**maidenhead** [ˈmedənˌhɛd] *s* doncellez; (anat.) himen
**maidenhood** [ˈmedənhʊd] *s* doncellez
**maiden lady** *s* soltera, solterona
**maidenly** [ˈmedənlɪ] *adj* virginal; pudoroso
**maiden name** *s* apellido de soltera
**maiden speech** *s* primer discurso (*de un orador*)
**maiden voyage** *s* primera travesía
**maid in waiting** *s* dama
**maid of all work** *s* criada para todo, moza de servicio
**maid of honor** *s* dama, menina; doncella, menina; doncella de honor (*de una boda*)
**Maid of Orleans** *s* Doncella de Orleáns

**maidservant** ['med,sʌrvənt] *s* sirvienta, criada
**mail** [mel] *s* correspondencia; correo; vapor correo, paquebote; malla (*de la armadura*); cota (*de malla*); armadura; **by return mail** a vuelta de correo; *adj* del correo; postal; *va* enviar por correo; echar al correo; armar (*especialmente con cota de malla*)
**mailbag** ['mel,bæg] *s* valija; correo
**mailboat** ['mel,bot] *s* vapor correo, paquebote
**mailbox** ['mel,bɑks] *s* buzón
**mail car** *s* (rail.) carro correo, coche-correo
**mail carrier** *s* cartero
**mail chute** *s* buzón tubular
**mail coach** *s* diligencia (*que lleva correo*)
**mailed fist** *s* puño armado
**mailing list** *s* lista de direcciones (*de clientes*)
**mailing permit** *s* porte concertado
**mailman** ['mel,mæn] *s* (*pl:* **-men**) cartero
**mail order** *s* pedido postal
**mail-order house** ['mel,ɔrdər] *s* casa de pedidos postales; casa de ventas por correo
**mailplane** ['mel,plen] *s* avión-correo
**mail train** *s* tren correo
**maim** [mem] *va* estropear, mutilar, lisiar
**Maimonides** [maɪ'mɑnɪdiz] *s* Maimónides
**main** [men] *s* cañería, cañería maestra; (poet.) mar, océano; (archaic) tierra firme, continente; **in the main** mayormente, en su mayor parte; *adj* principal; maestro; mayor
**main clause** *s* (gram.) proposición dominante
**main course** *s* plato fuerte, plato principal; (naut.) vela mayor
**main deck** *s* (naut.) cubierta principal
**main highway** *s* carretera principal
**mainland** ['men,lænd] o ['menlənd] *s* tierra firme, continente
**main line** *s* (rail.) línea principal, tronco
**mainly** ['menlɪ] *adv* mayormente, en su mayor parte
**mainmast** ['menməst], ['men,mæst] o ['men,mɑst] *s* (naut.) palo mayor
**main office** *s* casa central, oficina central
**mainsail** ['mensəl] o ['men,sel] *s* (naut.) vela mayor
**mainsheet** ['men,ʃit] *s* (naut.) escota mayor
**mainspring** ['men,sprɪŋ] *s* (horol.) muelle real; (fig.) causa principal, origen
**mainstay** ['men,ste] *s* (naut.) estay mayor; (fig.) sostén principal
**main street** *s* calle mayor
**maintain** [men'ten] *va* mantener
**maintenance** ['mentɪnəns] *s* mantenimiento; modesto pasar; conservación, gastos de conservación, gastos de entretenimiento
**maintenance costs** *spl* gastos de conservación
**maintenance of way** *s* (rail.) conservación de la vía
**maintop** ['men,tɑp] *s* (naut.) cofa mayor o de gavia
**maintopgallant** ['mentə'gælənt] o ['men,tɑp'gælənt] *s* (naut.) mastelero de galope mayor, masterillo de mayor; (naut.) juanete mayor; (naut.) verga de juanete mayor
**maintopmast** [,men'tɑpməst] *s* (naut.) mastelero de mayor
**maintopsail** [,men'tɑpsəl] *s* (naut.) gavia, vela de gavia
**main track** *s* (rail.) vía principal
**main-traveled** o **main-travelled** ['men,trævəld] *adj* de mucho tránsito
**main yard** *s* (naut.) verga mayor
**Mainz** [maɪnts] *s* Maguncia
**maître d'hôtel** ['mɛtrədo'tɛl] *s* mayordomo; jefe de comedor; salsa de mantequilla, perejil picado y jugo de limón
**maize** [mez] *s* (bot.) maíz (*planta y grano*); color de maíz
**Maj.** abr. de **Major**
**majestic** [mə'dʒɛstɪk] o **majestical** [mə'dʒɛstɪkəl] *adj* majestuoso
**majesty** ['mædʒɪstɪ] *s* (*pl:* **-ties**) majestad; (*cap.*) *s* Majestad (*título*)
**majolica** [mə'dʒɑlɪkə] *s* mayólica
**major** ['medʒər] *adj* mayor; principal, importante; mayor de edad; (log. & mus.) mayor; *s* mayor de edad; (mil.) comandante; (educ.) asignatura o curso de especialización; (mus.) acorde, escala o intervalo mayor; *vn* (coll.) especializarse (*en una asignatura o curso*)
**major axis** *s* eje principal
**Majorca** [mə'dʒɔrkə] *s* Mallorca
**Majorcan** [mə'dʒɔrkən] *adj & s* mallorquín
**major-domo** [,medʒər'domo] *s* (*pl:* **-mos**) mayordomo
**major general** *s* (mil.) general de división
**majority** [mə'dʒɑrɪtɪ] o [mə'dʒɔrɪtɪ] *s* (*pl:* **-ties**) mayoría; (mil.) comandancia; *adj* de la mayoría, mayoritario
**major key** *s* (mus.) tono mayor
**major orders** *spl* (eccl.) órdenes mayores
**major premise** *s* (log.) premisa mayor
**major scale** *s* (mus.) escala mayor
**major surgery** *s* cirugía mayor
**make** [mek] *s* hechura; corte (*de un vestido*); marca; modelo; constitución; natural, carácter; producción total; **on the make** (slang) buscando provecho ‖ (*pret & pp:* **made**) *va* hacer; ganar (*dinero; una baza; el mayor número de tantos*); dar (*dinero una empresa*); dar (*una vuelta*); pronunciar (*un discurso*); coger (*un tren*); cometer (*un error*); adquirir (*buena reputación*); llegar a (*la meta, el puerto, etc.*); cerrar (*un circuito*); hacer (*p.ej., cien kilómetros por hora*); poner (*a uno, p.ej., nervioso*); inventar; calcular; ser causa del éxito de; ser, p.ej., **he will make a good doctor** será un buen médico; servir de; **to make** + *inf* hacer + *inf*, p.ej., **I made him leave at once** le hice salir en seguida; **to make believe** hacer creer; **to make do** hacer servir; **to make into** convertir en; **to make known** hacer saber, declarar; dar a conocer; **to make of** pensar de, sacar de, p.ej., **what do you make of this?** ¿qué saca Vd. de esto?; **to make oneself known** darse a conocer; **to make or break** hacer la fortuna o ser la ruina de; **to make out** descifrar, entender; distinguir, vislumbrar; hacer (*la cuenta que uno debe pagar*); escribir (*una receta*); llenar (*un cheque*); declarar (*peor de lo que se creía*); **to make over** rehacer (*un traje*); convertir; (com.) transferir; **to make up** juntar, reunir; preparar; confeccionar (*un medicamento*); componer; integrar; inventar (*un cuento, una disculpa*); recobrar (*el tiempo perdido*); pagar, compensar; (print.) ajustar, compaginar; este verbo, seguido de un adjetivo, se traduce a veces por un verbo activo que corresponda al adjetivo, p.ej., **to make tired** cansar; **to make sick** enfermar ‖ *vn* estar (*p.ej., seguro*); **to make to** + *inf* hacer ademán de + *inf*, dar un paso para + *inf*; **to make after** perseguir; **to make as if** fingir que, hacer como que; **to make away with** llevarse; deshacerse de; matar; **to make believe** fingir, p.ej., **he made believe he was dead** fingió estar muerto; **to make for** ir hacia; abalanzarse para coger, embestir contra; hacer, p.ej., **his presence made for a pleasant day** su presencia hizo el día agradable; contribuir a (*p.ej., la paz*); **to make of** (coll.) mostrar cariño a; **to make off** largarse; **to make off with** hacerse con, irse con, llevarse; **to make out** arreglárselas, desenvolverse; **to make toward** dirigirse a, encaminarse a; **to make up** maquillarse; componerse (*hacer las paces*); **to make up for** suplir; compensar por (*una pérdida*); **to make up to** (coll.) querer congraciarse con
**make and break** *s* (elec.) dispositivo de ruptura y contacto
**make-believe** ['mekbɪ,liv] *adj* simulado; *s* simulación, artificio, pretexto; simulador
**maker** ['mekər] *s* constructor; fabricante; (*cap.*) *s* Hacedor
**makeshift** ['mek,ʃɪft] *s* expediente; tapagujeros (*persona*); *adj* provisional, de fortuna
**make-up** ['mek,ʌp] *s* composición, constitución; cosméticos; (theat.) maquillaje; (print.) imposición
**make-up man** *s* (theat.) experto en maquillaje, maquillador
**makeweight** ['mek,wet] *s* contrapeso (*para completar el peso de carne, pescado, etc.*); (fig.) suplente
**making** ['mekɪŋ] *s* hechura; fabricación; causa del éxito (*de una persona*); material necesario (*para hacer alguna cosa*); madera (*p.ej., de estudiante, médico*); **makings** *spl* elementos,

materiales; **in the making** sin terminar, no acabado de hacer; **while in the making** mientras se está haciendo

**Malacca cane** [məˈlækə] *s* rotén (*bastón*)

**Malachi** [ˈmæləkaɪ] o **Malachias** [ˌmæləˈkaɪəs] *s* (Bib.) Malaquías

**malachite** [ˈmæləkaɪt] *s* (mineral.) malaquita

**malacology** [ˌmæləˈkɑlədʒɪ] *s* malacología

**malacopterygian** [ˌmæləˌkɑptəˈrɪdʒɪən] *adj & s* (zool.) malacopterigio

**malacostracan** [ˌmæləˈkɑstrəkən] *adj & s* (zool.) malacostráceo

**maladjusted** [ˌmæləˈdʒʌstɪd] *adj* mal ajustado; inadaptado, mal adaptado, desequilibrado

**maladjustment** [ˌmæləˈdʒʌstmənt] *s* mal ajuste; mala adaptación, desequilibrio

**maladminister** [ˌmælədˈmɪnɪstər] *va* administrar inepta, ineficaz o fraudulentamente

**maladministration** [ˌmælədˌmɪnɪsˈtreʃən] *s* administración inepta, ineficaz o fraudulenta

**maladroit** [ˌmæləˈdrɔɪt] *adj* torpe, desmañado

**malady** [ˈmælədɪ] *s* (*pl:* **-dies**) mal, enfermedad

**malaise** [mæˈlez] *s* malestar, indisposición

**malanders** [ˈmæləndərz] *spl* (vet.) ajuagas

**malapert** [ˈmæləpʌrt] *adj* descarado, insolente

**malapropism** [ˈmæləprɑpɪzəm] *s* despropósito

**malapropos** [ˌmælæprəˈpo] *adj* no a propósito; *adv* fuera de propósito

**malar** [ˈmelər] *adj & s* (anat.) malar

**malaria** [məˈlɛrɪə] *s* (path.) malaria, paludismo

**malarial** [məˈlɛrɪəl] o **malarious** [məˈlɛrɪəs] *adj* palúdico; enfermo de paludismo

**malarky** [məˈlɑrkɪ] *s* (slang) habla necia e insincera

**Malay** [ˈmele] o [məˈle] *adj & s* malayo

**Malaya** [məˈleə] *s* Malaya

**Malayan** [məˈleən] *adj & s* malayo

**Malay Archipelago** *s* archipiélago Malayo

**Malay Peninsula** *s* península Malaya o península de Malaca

**Malaysia** [məˈleʒə] o [məˈleʃə] *s* la Malasia

**Malaysian** [məˈleʒən] o [məˈleʃən] *adj & s* malasio

**Malay States** *spl* Estados Malayos

**malcontent** [ˈmælkənˌtɛnt] *adj & s* malcontento

**male** [mel] *adj* masculino; macho, p.ej., **a male weasel** una comadreja macho; varón, p.ej., **male child** hijo varón; (bot.) masculino; (bot. & mach.) macho; *s* macho; varón

**malediction** [ˌmælɪˈdɪkʃən] *s* maldición

**malefaction** [ˌmælɪˈfækʃən] *s* delito

**malefactor** [ˈmælɪˌfæktər] *s* malhechor

**male fern** *s* (bot.) helecho macho

**maleficence** [məˈlɛfɪsəns] *s* maleficencia

**maleficent** [məˈlɛfɪsənt] *adj* maléfico (*que hace daño*)

**male nurse** *s* enfermero

**malevolence** [məˈlɛvələns] *s* malevolencia

**malevolent** [məˈlɛvələnt] *adj & s* malévolo

**malfeasance** [mælˈfizəns] *s* corrupción, venalidad

**malformation** [ˌmælfɔrˈmeʃən] *s* malformación, deformidad

**malformed** [mælˈfɔrmd] *adj* malhecho, contrahecho

**malfunction** [mælˈfʌŋkʃən] *s* malfuncionamiento

**malic** [ˈmælɪk] o [ˈmelɪk] *adj* málico

**malic acid** *s* (chem.) ácido málico

**malice** [ˈmælɪs] *s* malicia, mala voluntad; (law) dolo penal, intención delictuosa; **to bear malice** guardar rencor

**malicious** [məˈlɪʃəs] *adj* malicioso (*malo, maligno*)

**malign** [məˈlaɪn] *adj* maligno; (path.) maligno; *va* calumniar

**malignance** [məˈlɪgnəns] o **malignancy** [məˈlɪgnənsɪ] *s* malignidad

**malignant** [məˈlɪgnənt] *adj* maligno; (path.) maligno

**malignity** [məˈlɪgnɪtɪ] *s* (*pl:* **-ties**) malignidad

**maline** [məˈlin] *s* tela de Malinas

**Malines** [məˈlinz] *s* Malinas; (*l.c.*) *s* tela de Malinas; encaje de Malinas

**malinger** [məˈlɪŋgər] *vn* hacerse el enfermo, fingirse enfermo

**malingerer** [məˈlɪŋgərər] *s* simulador (*persona que finge padecer una enfermedad*)

**malingering** [məˈlɪŋgərɪŋ] *s* simulación (*fingimiento de una enfermedad*)

**malison** [ˈmælɪzən] o [ˈmælɪsən] *s* (archaic) maldición

**mall** [mɔl] o [mæl] *s* alameda, paseo de árboles

**mallard** [ˈmælərd] *s* (orn.) pato silvestre, pato real, ánade salvaje

**malleability** [ˌmælɪəˈbɪlɪtɪ] *s* maleabilidad; docilidad

**malleable** [ˈmælɪəbəl] *adj* maleable; dócil, manejable

**malleolar** [məˈliələr] *adj* (anat.) maleolar

**malleolus** [məˈliələs] *s* (*pl:* **-li** [laɪ]) (anat.) maléolo

**mallet** [ˈmælɪt] *s* mazo (*martillo de madera*); (sport) mallete (*en el croquet y el polo*)

**malleus** [ˈmælɪəs] *s* (*pl:* **-i** [aɪ]) (anat.) martillo (*del oído*)

**mallow** [ˈmælo] *s* (bot.) malva

**malmsey** [ˈmɑmzɪ] *s* malvasía (*vino*)

**malnutrition** [ˌmælnjuˈtrɪʃən] o [ˌmælnuˈtrɪʃən] *s* desnutrición

**malodor** [mælˈodər] *s* olor muy malo

**malodorous** [mælˈodərəs] *adj* maloliente

**malpighiaceous** [mælˌpɪgɪˈeʃəs] *adj* (bot.) malpigiáceo

**Malpighian corpuscle** [mælˈpɪgɪən] *s* (anat.) corpúsculo de Malpighi

**malpractice** [mælˈpræktɪs] *s* malpraxis; procedimientos ilegales o criminales; mala conducta

**malt** [mɔlt] *s* malta *m*; (coll.) cerveza; *va* hacer germinar (*la cebada*); preparar con malta

**maltase** [ˈmɔltes] *s* (biochem.) maltasa

**malted milk** *s* leche preparada con malta

**Maltese** [mɔlˈtiz] *adj* maltés; *s* (*pl:* **-tese**) maltés

**Maltese cat** *s* gato maltés

**Maltese cross** *s* cruz de Malta

**malt extract** *s* extracto de malta

**malthouse** [ˈmɔltˌhaʊs] *s* cámara de germinación (*de la cebada, para la fabricación de la cerveza*)

**Malthusian** [mælˈθuʒən] *adj & s* maltusiano

**Malthusianism** [mælˈθuʒənɪzəm] *s* maltusianismo

**maltose** [ˈmɔltos] *s* (chem.) maltosa

**maltreat** [mælˈtrit] *va* maltratar

**maltreatment** [mælˈtritmənt] *s* maltratamiento, malos tratos

**maltster** [ˈmɔltstər] *s* fermentador de cebada; vendedor de malta

**malt sugar** *s* azúcar de malta

**malvaceous** [mælˈveʃəs] *adj* (bot.) malváceo

**malvasia** [ˌmælvəˈsiə] *s* malvasía (*uva y vino*)

**malversation** [ˌmælvərˈseʃən] *s* malversación

**malvoisie** [ˈmælvɔɪzɪ] *s* var. de **malmsey**

**mama** [ˈmɑmə] o [məˈmɑ] *s* mama o mamá

**mambo** [ˈmɑmbo] *s* mambo (*música y baile*); *vn* bailar el mambo

**mameluke** [ˈmæməluk] *s* mameluco (*esclavo*); (*cap.*) *s* mameluco (*soldado*)

**Mamie** [ˈmemɪ] *s* nombre abreviado de **Margaret**

**mamma** [ˈmæmə] *s* (*pl:* **-mae** [mi]) (anat.) mama; [ˈmɑmə] o [məˈmɑ] *s* mama o mamá

**mammal** [ˈmæməl] *s* (zool.) mamífero

**mammalian** [mæˈmelɪən] *adj & s* (zool.) mamífero

**mammary** [ˈmæmərɪ] *adj* mamario

**mammary gland** *s* (anat.) glándula mamaria

**mammee** [mɑˈme] o [mɑˈmi] *s* (bot.) mamey

**mammilla** [məˈmɪlə] *s* (*pl:* **-lae** [li]) (anat. & bot.) mamelón

**mammillary** [ˈmæmɪˌlɛrɪ] *adj* mamilar

**Mammon** o **mammon** [ˈmæmən] *s* (Bib.) mammón

**mammoth** [ˈmæməθ] *s* (pal.) mamut; *adj* gigantesco

**mammy** [ˈmæmɪ] *s* (*pl:* **-mies**) nodriza negra; negra vieja; mamá

**Man.** abr. de **Manitoba**

**man** [mæn] *s* (*pl:* **men**) hombre; pieza (*en el ajedrez*); pieza o peón (*en el juego de las damas*); **a man** uno, p.ej., **a man must keep his word** uno debe cumplir su palabra; **as a man** desde el punto de vista humano; **as one**

man unánimemente; **no man** nadie; **to a man** todos, sin faltar uno solo; **to become man** humanarse (*el Verbo divino*); **to be one's own man** no depender de nadie; estar sobre sí; **man alive!** ¡hombre!; **man and boy** desde la primera mocedad; **man and wife** marido y mujer; (*pret & pp:* **manned;** *ger:* **manning**) *va* proveer de gente armada, guarnecer (*una fortaleza*); tripular (*una embarcación, un coche, etc.*); servir (*los cañones*); preparar, p.ej., **to man oneself** prepararse (*p.ej., para resistir un golpe*)

**man about town** *s* hombre aficionado a los bulevares, hombre de mucho mundo

**manacle** ['mænəkəl] *s* manilla; **manacles** *spl* esposas; (fig.) estorbo; *va* poner manilla a, poner esposas a; (fig.) estorbar

**manage** ['mænɪdʒ] *va* manejar; (equit.) manejar (*un caballo*); *vn* manejarse; **to manage to** + *inf* ingeniarse a + *inf;* **to manage to get along** ingeniarse a vivir; arreglárselas

**manageability** [,mænɪdʒə'bɪlɪtɪ] *s* manejabilidad

**manageable** ['mænɪdʒəbəl] *adj* manejable

**management** ['mænɪdʒmənt] *s* dirección, gerencia, manejo; organización industrial, gestión científica, taylorismo; la parte patronal, la empresa, los dirigentes, los patronos

**manager** ['mænɪdʒər] *s* director; gerente; empresario; persona económica; (sport) manager

**managerial** [,mænə'dʒɪrɪəl] *adj* directorial, administrativo

**Manasseh** [mə'næsə] *s* (Bib.) Manasés

**man-at-arms** ['mænət'ɑrmz] *s* (*pl:* **men-at-arms**) hombre de guerra (*militar*); hombre de armas (*jinete armado de todas piezas*)

**manatee** [,mænə'ti] *s* (zool.) manatí

**manchet** ['mæntʃɪt] *s* (archaic) pan candeal

**man-child** ['mæn,tʃaɪld] *s* (*pl:* **men-children**) niño varón

**manchineel** [,mæntʃɪ'nil] *s* (bot.) manzanillo (*árbol*)

**manchineel apple** *s* manzanilla de Indias (*fruto*)

**Manchu** [mæn'tʃu] o ['mæntʃu] *adj* manchú; *s* (*pl:* **-chus**) manchú

**Manchurian** [mæn'tʃʊrɪən] *adj & s* manchuriano

**manciple** ['mænsɪpəl] *s* administrador o mayordomo (*p.ej., de un colegio*)

**Mancunian** [mæn'kjunɪən] *adj* perteneciente a Mánchester; *s* natural o habitante de Mánchester (*Inglaterra*)

**mandamus** [mæn'deməs] *s* (law) despacho

**mandarin** ['mændərɪn] *adj* mandarín; *s* mandarín; (bot.) mandarino (*árbol*); mandarina (*fruto*); (*cap.*) *s* mandarina (*lengua*)

**mandarin duck** *s* (orn.) pato mandarín

**mandarin orange** *s* naranja mandarina

**mandarin porcelain** *s* porcelana mandarina

**mandatary** ['mændə,tɛrɪ] *s* (*pl:* **-ies**) (law & dipl.) mandatario

**mandate** ['mændet] *s* mandato; (law & dipl.) mandato; (pol.) voluntad manifiesta (*de los votantes*); *va* asignar por mandato

**mandator** [mæn'detər] *s* (law) mandante

**mandatory** ['mændə,torɪ] *adj* obligatorio, preceptivo; conferido por mandato; *s* (*pl:* **-ries**) mandatario

**mandible** ['mændɪbəl] *s* (anat. & zool.) mandíbula

**mandibular** [mæn'dɪbjələr] *adj* mandibular

**mandolin** ['mændəlɪn] *s* (mus.) mandolina

**mandragora** [mæn'drægərə] *s* (bot.) mandrágora

**mandrake** ['mændrek] *s* (bot.) mandrágora; (bot.) podofilo

**mandrake apple** *s* limón silvestre, manzana de mayo

**mandrel** o **mandril** ['mændrəl] *s* (mach.) mandril

**mandrill** ['mændrɪl] *s* (zool.) mandril

**mane** [men] *s* crin (*del caballo*); melena (*del león; de una persona*)

**man-eater** ['mæn,itər] *s* caníbal; (zool.) jaquetón (*tiburón*)

**manège** [mə'nɛʒ] o [mə'neʒ] *s* (equit.) manejo (*arte*); (equit.) picadero (*sitio*); (equit.) marcha o aires (*del caballo adiestrado*)

**manes** o **Manes** ['meniz] *spl* manes

**maneuver** [mə'nuvər] *s* maniobra; (fig.) maniobra; *va* hacer maniobrar; ejecutar con maniobras, lograr con maniobras; dirigir las maniobras de; *vn* maniobrar; (fig.) maniobrar

**maneuverability** [mə,nuvərə'bɪlɪtɪ] *s* maniobrabilidad

**maneuverable** [mə'nuvərəbəl] *adj* maniobrable

**man Friday** *s* criado fidelísimo

**manful** ['mænfəl] *adj* varonil

**manganese** ['mæŋgənis] o ['mæŋgəniz] *s* (chem.) manganeso

**manganese steel** *s* acero al manganeso

**manganic** [mæn'gænɪk] *adj* mangánico

**manganic acid** *s* (chem.) ácido mangánico

**manganite** ['mæŋgənaɪt] *s* (chem.) manganita

**manganous** ['mæŋgənəs] o [mæn'gænəs] *adj* manganoso

**mange** [mendʒ] *s* sarna

**mangel-wurzel** ['mæŋgəl,wʌrzəl] *s* (bot.) remolacha forrajera

**manger** ['mendʒər] *s* pesebre

**mangle** ['mæŋgəl] *s* (mach.) mangle; *va* prensar con mangle; destrozar, lacerar; echar a perder, estropear

**mango** ['mæŋgo] *s* (*pl:* **-goes** o **-gos**) (bot.) mango

**mangonel** ['mæŋgənɛl] *s* mangano o mandrón

**mangosteen** ['mæŋgəstin] *s* (bot.) mangostán (*árbol*); mangosto (*fruto*)

**mangrove** ['mæŋgrov] *s* (bot.) mangle

**mangy** ['mendʒɪ] *adj* (*comp:* **-gier;** *super:* **-giest**) sarnoso; (fig.) roñoso, sucio

**manhandle** ['mæn,hændəl] *va* mover a brazo (*sin máquinas*); maltratar

**manhole** ['mæn,hol] *s* buzón, caja de registro (*en las calles*); agujero de hombre (*en una caldera*)

**manhole cover** *s* tapa de registro

**manhood** ['mænhʊd] *s* virilidad; masculinidad; hombres

**man-hour** ['mæn'aʊr] *s* (*pl:* **man-hours**) hora-hombre (*obra de una hora hecha por un solo hombre*)

**man hunt** *s* caza al hombre, persecución de un criminal

**mania** ['menɪə] *s* manía; (psychopath.) manía

**maniac** ['menɪæk] *adj & s* maníaco

**maniacal** [mə'naɪəkəl] *adj* maníaco

**manic** ['menɪk] o ['mænɪk] *adj* (psychopath.) maníaco

**manic-depressive insanity** ['mænɪkdɪ'prɛsɪv] *s* (psychopath.) manía-melancolía, locura de doble forma, psicosis maníacodepresiva

**Manichean** [,mænɪ'kiən] *adj & s* maniqueo

**Manicheanism** [,mænɪ'kiənɪzəm] o **Manicheism** ['mænɪ,kiɪzəm] *s* maniqueísmo

**manichord** ['mænɪkərd] *s* (mus.) manicordio o monacordio

**manicure** ['mænɪkjʊr] *s* manicura (*cuidado de las manos y las uñas*); manicuro o manicura (*persona*); *va* hacer la manicura a, hacer (*las manos o las uñas*)

**manicurist** ['mænɪ,kjʊrɪst] *s* manicuro o manicura (*persona*)

**manifest** ['mænɪfɛst] *adj* manifiesto; *s* (naut.) manifiesto; *va* manifestar

**manifestant** [,mænɪ'fɛstənt] *s* manifestante

**manifestation** [,mænɪfɛs'teʃən] *s* manifestación

**manifesto** [,mænɪ'fɛsto] *s* (*pl:* **-toes**) manifiesto, proclama

**manifold** ['mænɪfold] *adj* múltiple, variado, multiforme; *s* copia, ejemplar; (mach.) múltiple; *va* hacer o sacar varias copias de

**manikin** ['mænɪkɪn] *s* maniquí; enano

**manila** [mə'nɪlə] *s* cáñamo de Manila; papel de Manila

**Manila hemp** *s* cáñamo de Manila

**Manila paper** *s* papel de Manila

**Manila rope** *s* cuerda de cáñamo, cuerda de abacá

**manilla** [mə'nɪlə] *s* cáñamo de Manila; papel de Manila; malilla (*segunda carta en valor*)

**man in the moon** *s* cara o cuerpo de hombre imaginarios en la luna llena; persona imaginaria

**man in the street** *s* hombre de la calle (*ciudadano típico*)

**manioc** ['mænɪɑk] *s* (bot.) mandioca (*planta y harina*)
**maniple** ['mænɪpəl] *s* (hist. & eccl.) manípulo
**manipulate** [mə'nɪpjəlet] *va* manipular
**manipulation** [mə,nɪpjə'leʃən] *s* manipulación
**manipulative** [mə'nɪpjə,letɪv] *adj* de manipulación
**manipulator** [mə'nɪpjə,letər] *s* manipulador
**manito** ['mænɪto] o **manitou** ['mænɪtu] *s* espíritu, fetiche (*objeto de culto de los pieles rojas*)
**mankind** [,mæn'kaɪnd] *s* humanidad, raza humana; ['mæn,kaɪnd] *s* sexo masculino, hombres
**manlike** ['mæn,laɪk] *adj* varonil; hombruno, masculino
**manliness** ['mænlɪnɪs] *s* virilidad; masculinidad
**manly** ['mænlɪ] *adj* (*comp:* **-lier;** *super:* **-liest**) varonil; masculino
**man-made** ['mæn,med] *adj* hecho por el hombre
**man midwife** *s* comadrón, partero
**manna** ['mænə] *s* (Bib.) maná; (bot.) maná (*líquido que fluye del Fraxinus ornus y otros vegetales*); cosa llovida del cielo; **like manna from heaven** como llovido del cielo
**manna ash** *s* (bot.) orno
**manna grass** *s* (bot.) hierba del maná
**manna sugar** *s* manita
**manned spacecraft** o **spaceship** [mænd] *s* astronave tripulada
**mannequin** ['mænɪkɪn] *s* maniquí (*armazón de figura humana, que usan los sastres y costureras*); maniquí, modelo (*mujer que sirve para probar prendas de vestir*)
**manner** ['mænər] *s* manera; (f.a. & lit.) manera (*p.ej., de Rafael*); **manners** *spl* modales, maneras; costumbres; **by all manner of means** de todos modos, sin falta; **by no manner of means** de ninguna manera; **in a manner of speaking** como quien dice, como si dijéramos; **in the manner of** a la manera de; **to the manner born** avezado desde la cuna
**mannered** ['mænərd] *adj* amanerado; de modales (*buenos o malos*)
**mannerism** ['mænərɪzəm] *s* costumbre, hábito (*p.ej., de rascarse la oreja*); amaneramiento; (f.a. & lit.) manierismo
**mannerless** ['mænərlɪs] *adj* descortés
**mannerly** ['mænərlɪ] *adj* cortés, urbano; *adv* cortésmente, urbanamente
**Mannie** ['mænɪ] *s* Manolo
**mannikin** ['mænɪkɪn] *s* var. de **manikin**
**mannish** ['mænɪʃ] *adj* hombruno
**mannitol** ['mænɪtɑl] o ['mænɪtol] *s* (chem.) manita
**mannose** ['mænos] *s* (chem.) manosa
**manoeuvre** [mə'nuvər] *s, va & vn* var. de **maneuver**
**Man of Destiny** *s* hombre del destino (*Napoleón*)
**man of distinction** *s* hombre de distinción
**Man of Galilee, the** el Galileo
**man of God** *s* santo, profeta; hombre de iglesia (*clérigo*)
**man of his word** *s* hombre de palabra
**man of letters** *s* hombre de letras
**man of means** *s* hombre de dinero
**man of parts** *s* hombre de buenas prendas, hombre de talento
**man of property** *s* hombre de fondos
**man of repute** *s* hombre de fama
**Man of Sorrows** *s* Hombre de los Dolores, Varón de Dolores (*Jesucristo*)
**man of straw** *s* hombre de suposición
**man of the hour** *s* hombre del momento
**man of the world** *s* hombre de mundo
**man-of-war** [,mænəv'wɔr] *s* (*pl:* **men-of-war**) acorazado, buque de guerra
**man-of-war bird** *s* (orn.) fragata, rabihorcado
**manometer** [mə'nɑmɪtər] *s* manómetro
**manometric** [,mænə'mɛtrɪk] *adj* manométrico
**manometric capsule** *s* (phys.) cápsula manométrica
**manometric flame** *s* (phys.) llama manométrica
**man on horseback** *s* caudillo revolucionario
**manor** ['mænər] *s* feudo; finca solariega, señorío
**manor house** *s* casa solariega
**manorial** [mə'norɪəl] *adj* señorial; solariego
**man overboard** *interj* ¡hombre al agua!, ¡hombre a la mar!
**man power** *s* mano de obra, potencial humano; (mil.) fuerzas disponibles
**manrope** ['mæn,rop] *s* (naut.) guardamancebo
**mansard** ['mænsɑrd] *s* mansarda; piso de mansarda
**mansard roof** *s* mansarda
**manse** [mæns] *s* rectoría
**manservant** ['mæn,sʌrvənt] *s* (*pl:* **menservants**) criado
**mansion** ['mænʃən] *s* hotel, palacio, casa magnífica; casa solariega
**manslaughter** ['mæn,slɔtər] *s* (law) homicidio criminal pero sin premeditación
**mantel** ['mæntəl] *s* manto (*de chimenea*); mesilla, repisa de chimenea
**mantelet** ['mæntəlɛt] o ['mæntlɪt] *s* manteleta (*esclavina*); (mil.) mantelete
**mantelletta** [,mæntə'lɛtə] *s* (eccl.) mantelete
**mantelpiece** ['mæntəl,pis] *s* mesilla, repisa de chimenea
**mantilla** [mæn'tɪlə] *s* mantilla (*prenda*)
**mantis** ['mæntɪs] *s* (*pl:* **-tises** o **-tes** [tiz]) (ent.) mantis religiosa
**mantis crab** *s* (zool.) esquila
**mantissa** [mæn'tɪsə] *s* (math.) mantisa
**mantle** ['mæntəl] *s* manto (*vestido amplio a modo de capa*); capa (*p.ej., de nieve*); camiseta o manguito (*del alumbrado de gas*); (zool.) manto; *va* vestir con manto; cubrir, tapar; encubrir, ocultar; *vn* ponerse encendido (*dícese, p.ej., de las mejillas*); extenderse (*el color encendido de las mejillas*); cubrirse de algas (*las aguas estancadas*)
**mantling** ['mæntlɪŋ] *s* mesilla, repisa de chimenea; rubor, sonrojo; (her.) mantelete
**mantua** ['mæntʃuə] o ['mæntuə] *s* manto
**Mantuan** ['mæntʃuən] o ['mæntuən] *adj & s* mantuano
**Mantuan Swan** *s* cisne de Mantua (*Virgilio*)
**manual** ['mænjuəl] *adj* manual; *s* manual (*libro*); (mus.) teclado manual (*de órgano*); (mil.) ejercicio, p.ej., **manual of arms** ejercicio de armas
**manual alphabet** *s* abecedario manual
**manually** ['mænjuəlɪ] *adv* manualmente
**manual training** *s* instrucción en artes y oficios
**manubrium** [mə'njubrɪəm] o [mə'nubrɪəm] *s* (*pl:* **-a** [ə] o **-ums**) (anat., bot. & zool.) manubrio
**manufactory** [,mænjə'fæktərɪ] *s* (*pl:* **-ries**) manufactura, fábrica (*establecimiento*)
**manufacture** [,mænjə'fæktʃər] *s* fabricación; manufactura (*obra fabricada*); *va* manufacturar, fabricar; (fig.) fabricar
**manufacturer** [,mænjə'fæktʃərər] *s* fabricante
**manufacturing** [,mænjə'fæktʃərɪŋ] *adj* manufacturero; *s* fabricación
**manumission** [,mænjə'mɪʃən] *s* (law) manumisión
**manumit** [,mænjə'mɪt] (*pret & pp:* **-mitted;** *ger:* **-mitting**) *va* (law) manumitir
**manumitter** [,mænjə'mɪtər] *s* manumisor
**manure** [mə'njur] o [mə'nur] *s* estiércol; *va* estercolar
**manuscript** ['mænjəskrɪpt] *adj & s* manuscrito
**Manx** [mæŋks] *adj* manés; *s* manés (*idioma*); *spl* maneses
**Manx cat** *s* gato manés
**Manxman** ['mæŋksmən] *s* (*pl:* **-men**) manés
**many** ['mɛnɪ] *adj* (*comp:* **more;** *super:* **most**) muchos; *pron* muchos; *s* gran número; **a good many** un buen número; **a great many** un gran número; **as many as** tantos como; hasta, p.ej., **as many as ten** hasta diez; **how many** cuántos; **one too many for** la ruina de; **so many** tantos; **the many** los más; la plebe, la gente menuda; **too many** demasiados; de más, de sobra, p.ej., **one too many** uno de más, uno de sobra; **twice as many as** dos veces más que; **many a** muchos, p.ej., **many a time** muchas veces; **many another**

muchos otros; **many more** muchos más; **many of** muchos de; **many people** mucha gente
**many-colored** ['mɛnɪˌkʌlərd] *adj* multicolor
**manyplies** ['mɛnɪˌplaɪz] *s* (zool.) omaso
**manyroot** ['mɛnɪˌrut] o ['mɛnɪˌrʊt] *s* (bot.) saltaperico
**many-sided** ['mɛnɪˌsaɪdɪd] *adj* multilátero; (fig.) de muchas habilidades, de gran curiosidad intelectual, polifacético
**manzanita** [ˌmænzə'nitə] *s* (bot.) manzanita
**Maori** ['mɑorɪ] *adj* maorí; *s* (*pl:* **-ris**) maorí
**map** [mæp] *s* mapa; plano (*p.ej., de una ciudad*); (*pret & pp:* **mapped;** *ger:* **mapping**) *va* trazar el mapa de; indicar en el mapa; planear, trazar el plan de; **to map out** planear, trazar el plan de
**maple** ['mepəl] *s* (bot.) arce
**maple sugar** *s* azúcar de arce
**maple syrup** *s* jarabe de arce
**maquette** [mɑ'kɛt] *s* maqueta
**maqui** ['mɑkɪ] *s* (bot.) maqui
**Mar.** abr. de **March**
**mar** [mɑr] (*pret & pp:* **marred;** *ger:* **marring**) *va* desfigurar, estropear, echar a perder
**marabou** ['mærəbu] *s* (orn.) marabú (*ave y adorno*)
**maraschino** [ˌmærə'skino] *s* marrasquino
**maraschino cherries** *spl* guindas en conserva con sabor a marrasquino
**marasmus** [mə'ræzməs] *s* (path.) marasmo
**Marathon** ['mærəθɑn] *s* Maratón; (*l.c.*) *s* (sport) maratón, carrera de maratón
**marathon race** *s* (sport) carrera de maratón
**maraud** [mə'rɔd] *va* merodear por; *vn* merodear
**marauder** [mə'rɔdər] *s* merodeador, merodista
**marauding** [mə'rɔdɪŋ] *adj* merodeador; *s* merodeo
**maravedi** [ˌmærə'vedɪ] *s* maravedí
**marble** ['mɑrbəl] *s* mármol; canica (*bolita*); **marbles** *ssg* canica (*juego*); *adj* marmóreo; *va* marmolizar; crispir, jaspear; *vn* marmolizarse
**marcasite** ['mɑrkəsaɪt] *s* (mineral.) marcasita
**marcel** [mɑr'sɛl] *s* ondulado Marcel; (*pret & pp:* **-celled;** *ger:* **-celling**) *va* rizar (*el cabello*) a la Marcel
**Marcella** [mɑr'sɛlə] *s* Marcela
**Marcellus** [mɑr'sɛləs] *s* Marcelo
**marcescence** [mɑr'sɛsəns] *s* (bot.) marcescencia
**marcescent** [mɑr'sɛsənt] *adj* (bot.) marcescente
**march** [mɑrtʃ] *s* marcha; (mil. & mus.) marcha; (fig.) marcha (*progreso*); marca (*frontera; territorio*); **on the march** en marcha; **to steal a march on someone** ganarle a uno por la mano; (*cap.*) *s* marzo; *adj* marzal; (*l.c.*) *va* hacer marchar; llevar (*a una persona*) a donde tiene pocas ganas de ir; *vn* marchar; (mil.) marchar
**marchioness** ['mɑrʃənɪs] *s* marquesa
**marchland** ['mɑrtʃˌlænd] *s* terreno fronterizo
**marchpane** ['mɑrtʃˌpen] *s* mazapán
**marconigram** [mɑr'konɪgræm] *s* marconigrama
**Marcus** ['mɑrkəs] *s* Marco
**Mardi gras** ['mɑrdɪ 'grɑ] *s* martes de carnaval
**mare** [mɛr] *s* yegua; asna
**marekanite** [ˌmærɪ'kænaɪt] *s* (mineral.) marecanita
**mare's-nest** ['mɛrzˌnɛst] *s* parto de los montes
**mare's-tail** ['mɛrzˌtel] *s* (bot.) corregüela hembra; (bot.) cola de caballo, equiseto; rabos de gallo (*cirro o nube cirrosa*)
**Margaret** ['mɑrgərɪt] *s* Margarita
**margarin** ['mɑrdʒərɪn] o ['mɑrgərɪn] o **margarine** ['mɑrdʒərin] o ['mɑrgərin] *s* margarina
**margarite** ['mɑrgəraɪt] *s* (mineral.) margarita
**marge** [mɑrdʒ] *s* (poet.) margen
**margent** ['mɑrdʒənt] *s* (archaic) margen
**margin** ['mɑrdʒɪn] *s* margen; reserva (*para futuras contingencias*); excedente, sobrante; ganancia bruta; doble (*fianza que pide el corredor al comprador en las operaciones de bolsa*); (ins.) recargo al premio (*para cubrir ciertos gastos*)
**marginal** ['mɑrdʒɪnəl] *adj* marginal; (bot.) marginado
**marginalia** [ˌmɑrdʒɪ'nelɪə] o [ˌmɑrdʒɪ'neljə] *spl* notas marginales, apostillas
**marginally** ['mɑrdʒɪnəlɪ] *adv* al margen
**marginal note** *s* nota marginal
**marginal stop** *s* marginador, fijamárgenes (*de una máquina de escribir*)
**margin of error** *s* margen de error
**margin of safety** *s* margen de seguridad
**margin release** *s* tecla de escape, soltador del margen, llave de salto (*de una máquina de escribir*)
**margrave** ['mɑrgrev] *s* margrave
**margraviate** [mɑr'grevɪɪt] *s* margraviato
**margravine** ['mɑrgrəvin] *s* margravina
**marguerite** [ˌmɑrgə'rit] *s* (bot.) margarita; (*cap.*) *s* Margarita
**Marian** ['mærɪən] o ['mɛrɪən] *adj* mariano; *s* Mariana
**Marianne** [ˌmɛrɪ'æn] *s* Mariana
**Marie** [mə'ri] *s* María
**marigold** ['mærɪgold] *s* (bot.) maravilla, flamenquilla; (bot.) clavelón (*Targetes erecta*)
**marigraph** ['mærɪgræf] o ['mærɪgrɑf] *s* mareógrafo
**marihuana** o **marijuana** [ˌmɑrɪ'hwɑnə] *s* (bot.) mariguana (*Cannabis sativa*); mariguana falsa o maraquiana (*Nicotiana glauca*)
**marimba** [mə'rɪmbə] *s* (mus.) marimba
**marinade** [ˌmærɪ'ned] *s* escabeche; ['mærɪned] *va* escabechar, marinar
**marinate** ['mærɪnet] *va* escabechar, marinar
**marine** [mə'rin] *adj* marino, marítimo; *s* marina de guerra; marina mercante; marina (*cuadro o pintura*); infantería de marina; infante de marina, soldado de infantería de marina; **tell that to the marines** (coll.) a otro perro con ese hueso, cuénteselo a su abuela
**marine code** *s* código de señales marítimas
**Marine Corps** *s* (U.S.A.) infantería de marina
**mariner** ['mærɪnər] *s* marino, marinero
**Marion** ['mærɪən] o ['mɛrɪən] *s* Mariana (*nombre de mujer*); Mariano (*nombre de varón*)
**marionette** [ˌmærɪə'nɛt] *s* marioneta, títere, figurilla
**marish** ['mærɪʃ] *adj* (archaic & poet.) pantanoso; *s* (archaic & poet.) pantano
**Marist** ['mɛrɪst] *adj & s* (eccl.) marista
**marital** ['mærɪtəl] *adj* marital
**marital status** *s* estado civil
**maritime** ['mærɪtaɪm] o ['mærɪtɪm] *adj* marítimo
**Maritime Provinces** *spl* Provincias Marítimas (*del Canadá*)
**Marius** ['mɛrɪəs] *s* Mario
**marjoram** ['mɑrdʒərəm] *s* (bot.) orégano; (bot.) mejorana (*Majorana hortensis*)
**mark** [mɑrk] *s* marca; señal; huella; mancha; marbete, etiqueta; fin, propósito; calificación, nota (*en un examen*); blanco (*a que se tira*); signo (*señal de cruz que se usa en vez de la firma de uno*); marco (*moneda; peso*); meta; (sport) raya (*que indica el punto desde el que se ha de partir en una carrera*); (archaic) marca (*distrito fronterizo*); (*cap.*) *s* Marcos; (Bib.) Marcos; (Bib.) el Evangelio según San Marcos; **of mark** célebre, importante; **to be beside the mark** no venir al caso; **to come up to the mark** alcanzar lo que era de esperar, ser completamente satisfactorio; **to hit the mark** dar en el blanco; poner el dedo en la llaga; **to leave one's mark** dejar memoria de sí; **to make one's mark** hacerse un hombre de provecho; llegar a ser célebre; **to miss the mark** errar el tiro; **to shoot beside the mark** errar el tiro; no atinar en el punto de la dificultad; **to toe the mark** ponerse en la raya; obrar como se debe ‖ *va* marcar, señalar; indicar (*p.ej., disgusto*); distinguir; advertir, notar, poner atención a; marcar (*los tantos en un juego*); indicar el precio de, con lápiz o etiqueta; dar nota o notas a (*un alumno*); calificar (*un examen*); **to mark down** apuntar, poner por escrito; marcar a un precio más bajo; rebajar el precio de; **to mark off** u **out** indicar, señalar; separar con un guión o con una raya; **to mark out for** escoger para ‖ *vn* poner atención; dar notas (*el maestro*); quedarse marcado

**markdown** ['mɑrk,daʊn] *s* precio reducido

**marked** [mɑrkt] *adj* marcado

**marked man** *s* hombre sospechoso; futura víctima

**marker** ['mɑrkər] *s* marcador; mojón; ficha (*en los juegos*); (sport) marcador (*instrumento para señalar el terreno de juego en el tenis, etc.; aparato para señalar los tantos del billar, etc.*)

**marker light** *s* (aer.) luz de balizaje

**market** ['mɑrkɪt] *s* mercado; bolsa; **to bear the market** jugar a la baja; **to be in the market for** querer comprar; **to bull the market** jugar al alza; **to lose one's market** perder la clientela; **to play the market** jugar a la bolsa o en bolsa; **to put on the market** lanzar al mercado; *va* vender; llevar o enviar al mercado; hallar mercado para; comprar en el mercado; *vn* comerciar

**marketability** [,mɑrkɪtə'bɪlɪtɪ] *s* comercialidad

**marketable** ['mɑrkɪtəbəl] *adj* comerciable, vendible

**market basket** *s* cesta para compras

**marketeer** [,mɑrkɪ'tɪr] *s* placero

**marketing** ['mɑrkɪtɪŋ] *s* mercadotecnia, mercología; *adj* mercológico

**market place** *s* plaza del mercado

**market price** *s* precio corriente o de plaza

**market value** *s* valor en plaza

**marking** ['mɑrkɪŋ] *s* marca, señal, signo; pinta (*mancha; adorno en forma de mancha*); coloración; marchamo o marchamos (*de aduana*)

**marking gauge** *s* gramil

**marksman** ['mɑrksmən] *s* (*pl:* **-men**) tirador; **to be a good marksman** ser un buen tiro

**marksmanship** ['mɑrksmənʃɪp] *s* puntería

**markup** ['mɑrk,ʌp] *s* aumento de precio; margen de ganancia, margen de utilidad; direcciones en un manuscrito para el impresor

**marl** [mɑrl] *s* marga; *va* margar; (naut.) trincafiar

**marlin** ['mɑrlɪn] *s* (ichth.) aguja (*pez del género Makaira*)

**marline** ['mɑrlɪn] *s* (naut.) merlín, trincafía

**marlinespike** o **marlinspike** ['mɑrlɪn,spaɪk] *s* (naut.) burel, pasador

**marlpit** ['mɑrl,pɪt] *s* almarga, marguera

**marly** ['mɑrlɪ] *adj* (*comp:* **-ier;** *super:* **-iest**) margoso

**marmalade** ['mɑrməled] *s* mermelada; mermelada de naranjas

**marmalade tree** *s* (bot.) zapote chico

**marmoreal** [mɑr'morɪəl] *adj* marmóreo

**marmoset** ['mɑrməzɛt] *s* (zool.) tití

**marmot** ['mɑrmət] *s* (zool.) marmota

**maroon** [mə'run] *adj* marrón (*castaño obscuro*); *s* marrón (*castaño obscuro; esclavo fugitivo, negro descendiente de esclavos fugitivos en las Antillas y la Guayana Holandesa; bomba de anuncio*); *va* dejar abandonado, aislar (*p.ej., en una isla desierta*)

**marplot** ['mɑr,plɑt] *s* aguafiestas

**marque** [mɑrk] *s* (naut.) licencia oficial para el corso

**marquee** [mɑr'ki] *s* gran tienda de campaña; marquesina (*sobre la puerta de un hotel, etc.*)

**marquess** ['mɑrkwɪs] *s* marqués

**marquetry** ['mɑrkətrɪ] *s* (*pl:* **-tries**) marquetería (*taracea*)

**marquis** ['mɑrkwɪs] *s* marqués

**marquisate** ['mɑrkwɪzɪt] *s* marquesado

**marquise** [mɑr'kiz] *s* marquesa; marquesina (*sobre la puerta de un hotel, etc.*)

**marquisette** [,mɑrkɪ'zɛt] o [,mɑrkwɪ'zɛt] *s* tejido fino de mallas cuadradas

**marriage** ['mærɪdʒ] *s* matrimonio; maridaje (*vida de casados; unión o conformidad*)

**marriageability** [,mærɪdʒə'bɪlɪtɪ] *s* nubilidad

**marriageable** ['mærɪdʒəbəl] *adj* casadero, núbil

**marriage bed** *s* cama de recién casados

**marriage license** *s* licencia de matrimonio

**marriage portion** *s* dote

**marriage rate** *s* nupcialidad

**marriage settlement** s capitulaciones

**married** ['mærɪd] *adj* casado; conyugal; (fig.) maridado

**married life** *s* vida conyugal

**marrons** ['mærənz] *spl* marrones (*castañas confitadas*)

**marrow** ['mæro] *s* (anat. & fig.) médula

**marrowbone** ['mæro,bon] *s* hueso medular; **marrowbones** *spl* (hum.) rodillas; huesos cruzados (*símbolo de la muerte*)

**marrowfat** ['mæro,fæt] *s* guisante de semilla grande

**marrowy** ['mærəwɪ] *adj* medular, meolludo

**marry** ['mærɪ] *interj* (archaic) ¡por mi fe!, ¡válgame Dios!; (*pret & pp:* **-ried**) *va* casar; casar con o casarse con; (fig.) maridar (*unir, enlazar*); **to get married to** casar con o casarse con; *vn* casar o casarse; **to marry into** emparentar con (*p.ej., una familia rica*); **to marry the second time** casarse en segundas nupcias

**Mars** [mɑrz] *s* (astr. & myth.) Marte

**Marseillaise** [,mɑrsə'lez] *s* Marsellesa (*himno patriótico francés*)

**Marseilles** [mɑr'selz] *s* Marsella; (*l.c.*) *s* tela tupida de algodón dibujada en relieve

**marsh** [mɑrʃ] *s* pantano

**marshal** ['mɑrʃəl] *s* (mil.) mariscal; cursor de procesiones; maestro de ceremonias; magistrado de audiencias; (U.S.A.) oficial de justicia; (*pret & pp:* **-shaled** o **-shalled;** *ger:* **-shaling** *o* **-shalling**) *va* conducir con solemnidad ceremonial; ordenar (*p.ej., los hechos de un argumento*)

**marsh gas** *s* gas de los pantanos

**marsh harrier** *s* (orn.) arpella, buzo de los pantanos, busardo, borní

**marsh mallow** *s* (bot.) malvavisco

**marshmallow** ['mɑrʃ,mælo] *s* pastilla o bombón de malvavisco; pastilla o bombón de merengue blando

**marsh marigold** *s* (bot.) hierba centella

**marsh warbler** *s* (orn.) arandillo, curruca de los pantanos

**marshy** ['mɑrʃɪ] *adj* (*comp:* **-ier;** *super:* **-iest**) pantanoso; palustre

**marsupial** [mɑr'supɪəl] o [mɑr'sjupɪəl] *adj & s* (zool.) marsupial

**marsupium** [mɑr'supɪəm] o [mɑr'sjupɪəm] *s* (*pl:* **-a** [ə]) (zool.) bolsa (*de la hembra de los marsupiales*)

**Marsyas** ['mɑrsɪæs] *s* (myth.) Marsias

**mart** [mɑrt] *s* emporio, centro comercial

**marteline** ['mɑrtəlɪn] *s* martellina

**marten** ['mɑrtən] *s* (zool.) marta (*Martes martes*); (zool.) garduña (*Martes foina*)

**Martha** ['mɑrθə] *s* Marta

**martial** ['mɑrʃəl] *adj* marcial; (*cap.*) *s* Marcial

**martial law** *s* ley marcial; **to be under martial law** estar en estado de guerra

**Martian** ['mɑrʃən] *adj & s* marciano

**martin** ['mɑrtɪn] *s* (orn.) avión; (*cap.*) *s* Martín

**martinet** [,mɑrtɪ'nɛt] o ['mɑrtɪnɛt] *s* ordenancista

**martingale** ['mɑrtɪŋgel] *s* amarra, gamarra; (naut.) moco del bauprés

**Martinique** [,mɑrtɪ'nik] *s* la Martinica

**Martinmas** ['mɑrtɪnməs] *s* día de San Martín

**martlet** ['mɑrtlɪt] *s* (orn.) avión; (her.) merleta

**martyr** ['mɑrtər] *s* mártir; *va* martirizar

**martyrdom** ['mɑrtərdəm] *s* martirio

**martyrize** ['mɑrtəraɪz] *va* martirizar

**martyrology** [,mɑrtə'rɑlədʒɪ] *s* (*pl:* **-gies**) martirologio

**marvel** ['mɑrvəl] *s* maravilla; (*pret & pp:* **-veled** o **-velled;** *ger:* **-veling** o **-velling**) *vn* maravillarse; **to marvel at** maravillarse con o de

**marvel-of-Peru** ['mɑrvələvpə'ru] *s* (bot.) arrebolera, dondiego

**marvelous** o **marvellous** ['mɑrvələs] *adj* maravilloso

**Marxian** ['mɑrksɪən] *adj & s* marxista

**Marxism** ['mɑrksɪzəm] *s* marxismo

**Marxist** ['mɑrksɪst] *adj & s* var. de **Marxian**

**Mary** ['mɛrɪ] *s* María

**Mary Magdalene** *s* (Bib.) Santa María Magdalena

**marzipan** ['mɑrzɪpæn] *s* mazapán

**masc.** abr. de **masculine**

**mascara** [mæs'kærə] *s* preparación para teñir las pestañas

**mascle** ['mæskəl] *s* (her.) macle

**mascot** ['mæskɑt] *s* mascota

**masculine** ['mæskjəlɪn] *adj* masculino; hom-

bruno; (gram.) masculino; *s* (gram.) masculino (*género*); (gram.) palabra masculina
**masculine rhyme** *s* (pros.) rima masculina
**masculinity** [ˌmæskjəˈlɪnɪtɪ] *s* masculinidad, hombradía
**maser** [ˈmezər] *s* (electron.) dispositivo amplificador que sirve para captar microondas emitidas por objetos celestes lejanos, y también para generar radiaciones electromagnéticas y especialmente rayos de luz
**mash** [mæʃ] *s* masa (*mezcla espesa y blanda*); harina o afrecho amasado con agua caliente; masa de cebada (*para la elaboración de la cerveza*); *va* majar, machacar; bracear (*la cerveza*)
**mashed potatoes** *spl* patatas majadas, puré de patatas
**masher** [ˈmæʃər] *s* mano (*útil de cocina en forma de maza*); (coll.) galanteador atrevido
**mashie** o **mashy** [ˈmæʃɪ] *s* (*pl:* **-ies**) (golf) mashie
**mashie niblick** *s* (golf) mashie-morder
**mask** [mæsk] o [mɑsk] *s* máscara; mascarilla (*p.ej., de un cadáver*); máscaras, mascarada; máscara (*persona*); (phot.) desvanecedor; (arch.) mascarón; (fig.) máscara; **to take off one's mask** (fig.) quitarse la máscara; *va* enmascarar; (phot.) desvanecer; *vn* enmascararse
**masked ball** *s* baile de máscaras
**masking tape** *s* cinta para cubrir
**masochism** [ˈmæzəkɪzəm] *s* (path.) masoquismo
**masochist** [ˈmæzəkɪst] *s* masoquista
**masochistic** [ˌmæzəˈkɪstɪk] *adj* masoquista
**mason** [ˈmesən] *s* albañil; (*cap.*) *s* masón
**Mason and Dixon's Line** [ˈdɪksənz] *s* frontera entre Pensilvania y Maryland y antes considerada como la línea divisoria entre el norte y el sur de los EE.UU.
**mason bee** *s* (ent.) albañila, abeja albañila
**mason bird** *s* pájaro que hace el nido de barro
**masoned** [ˈmesənd] *adj* (her.) mazonado
**Masonic** o **masonic** [məˈsɑnɪk] *adj* masónico
**masonite** [ˈmesənaɪt] *s* (mineral.) masonita; (trademark) masonita
**masonry** [ˈmesənrɪ] *s* (*pl:* **-ries**) albañilería; (*cap.*) *s* masonería
**mason wasp** *s* (ent.) avispa de barro
**masque** [mæsk] o [mɑsk] *s* zarzuela antigua; máscaras, baile de máscaras
**masquerade** [ˌmæskəˈred] o [ˌmɑskəˈred] *s* mascarada; máscara (*traje; disfraz*); farsa; *vn* enmascararse; ser farsante
**masquerade ball** *s* baile de máscaras
**masquerader** [ˌmæskəˈredər] o [ˌmɑskəˈredər] *s* máscara (*persona*)
**Mass.** abr. de **Massachusetts**
**mass** [mæs] *s* masa; gran cantidad; bulto informe (*que se vislumbra, p.ej., entre la niebla*); macizo; mole (*cosa de gran bulto*); gran mancha (*de color en una pintura*); (phys.) masa; (eccl. & mus.) misa; **in the mass** en masa; **the masses** las masas; **to hear mass** oír misa; **to say mass** decir o cantar misa; *adj* en masa, p.ej., **mass inoculation** la inoculación en masa; (phys.) másico; *va* juntar en masa; juntar, reunir; enmasar (*tropas*); *vn* juntarse en masa; juntarse, reunirse
**massacre** [ˈmæsəkər] *s* carnicería, matanza, destrozo; *va* hacer destrozo de, degollar
**massage** [məˈsɑʒ] *s* masaje; *va* masar
**mass defect** *s* (phys.) defecto de masa
**masseter** [mæˈsitər] *s* (anat.) masetero
**masseur** [mæˈsœr] *s* masajista (*hombre*)
**masseuse** [mæˈsœz] *s* masajista (*mujer*)
**mass formation** *s* (mil.) formación en masa
**massicot** [ˈmæsɪkɑt] *s* masicote
**massive** [ˈmæsɪv] *adj* macizo, de gran mole
**mass media** *spl* medios de comunicación en grande escala (*periódicos, libros en rústica, radio, televisión, cine*)
**mass meeting** *s* mitin popular
**mass number** *s* (phys.) número másico
**mass production** *s* fabricación en serie, producción en masa o en serie
**mass ratio** *s* razón de masas
**mass spectrograph** *s* (phys.) espectrógrafo de masa o de masas
**massy** [ˈmæsɪ] *adj* (*comp:* **-ier**; *super:* **-iest**) var. de **massive**
**mast** [mæst] o [mɑst] *s* (naut.) mástil; palo (*p.ej., de una bandera*); (elec.) poste; (rad.) torre; (agr.) fabuco, bellota; **before the mast** como marinero; **to spend a mast** (naut.) perder un palo
**master** [ˈmæstər] o [ˈmɑstər] *s* patrón, dueño; amo, señor; amo (*de un perro*); maestro; perito; señorito (*título de cortesía que se da a un muchacho*); pintura o estatua de uno de los grandes maestros; (educ.) maestro; (educ.) grado de maestro; (law) juez auxiliar; (naut.) maestre; **the Master** Jesucristo; *adj* maestro; magistral; de maestro; *va* dominar, vencer; adiestrarse en, llegar a ser maestro o perito en
**master-at-arms** [ˈmæstərətˈɑrmz] o [ˈmɑstərətˈɑrmz] *s* (*pl:* **masters-at-arms**) (naut.) cabo de mar encargado de la policía y de los prisioneros
**master bedroom** *s* alcoba del jefe de familia, alcoba de respeto
**master blade** *s* hoja maestra (*de un muelle*)
**master builder** *s* arquitecto; aparejador, maestro de obras
**master clock** *s* reloj magistral
**master controller** *s* (elec.) combinador principal
**masterdom** [ˈmæstərdəm] o [ˈmɑstərdəm] *s* maestría; dominio
**masterful** [ˈmæstərfəl] o [ˈmɑstərfəl] *adj* dominante, imperioso; perito, experto, de maestro
**master hand** *s* perito; pericia de maestro
**master key** *s* llave maestra, llave de paso
**masterly** [ˈmæstərlɪ] o [ˈmɑstərlɪ] *adj* magistral; *adv* magistralmente
**master mason** *s* maestro albañil; masón de grado tres
**master mechanic** *s* maestro mecánico
**mastermind** [ˈmæstərˌmaɪnd] o [ˈmɑstərˌmaɪnd] *s* mente directora; *va* dirigir con gran acierto
**master of ceremonies** *s* maestro de ceremonias; animador (*de un café cantante*)
**masterpiece** [ˈmæstərˌpis] o [ˈmɑstərˌpis] *s* obra maestra
**master's degree** *s* maestría, grado de maestro
**mastership** [ˈmæstərʃɪp] o [ˈmɑstərʃɪp] *s* maestría; magisterio; dominio
**mastersingers** [ˈmæstərˌsɪŋərz] o [ˈmɑstərˌsɪŋərz] *spl* maestros cantores
**master stroke** *s* golpe maestro
**masterwork** [ˈmæstərˌwʌrk] o [ˈmɑstərˌwʌrk] *s* obra maestra; desempeño magistral
**masterwort** [ˈmæstərˌwʌrt] o [ˈmɑstərˌwʌrt] *s* (bot.) imperatoria; (bot.) astrancia mayor
**mastery** [ˈmæstərɪ] o [ˈmɑstərɪ] *s* (*pl:* **-ies**) maestría; dominio (*p.ej., de un idioma extranjero*)
**masthead** [ˈmæstˌhɛd] o [ˈmɑstˌhɛd] *s* (naut.) tope; membrete editorial (*de una revista, periódico, etc.*)
**mastic** [ˈmæstɪk] *s* mástique; (bot.) charneca, lentisco, almácigo
**masticate** [ˈmæstɪket] *va* masticar; (tech.) masticar (*p.ej., el caucho*)
**mastication** [ˌmæstɪˈkeʃən] *s* masticación; (tech.) masticación
**masticator** [ˈmæstɪˌketər] *s* mascador; masticador (*instrumento*)
**masticatory** [ˈmæstɪkəˌtorɪ] *adj* masticatorio; *s* (*pl:* **-ries**) masticatorio
**mastic tree** *s* (bot.) charneca, lentisco, almácigo; (bot.) ácana (*Sideroxylon mastichodendron*)
**mastiff** [ˈmæstɪf] o [ˈmɑstɪf] *s* mastín
**mastitis** [mæsˈtaɪtɪs] *s* (path.) mastitis
**mastman** [ˈmæstmən] o [ˈmɑstmən] *s* (naut.) gaviero
**mastodon** [ˈmæstədɑn] *s* (pal.) mastodonte
**mastoid** [ˈmæstɔɪd] *adj & s* (anat.) mastoides
**mastoidectomy** [ˌmæstɔɪˈdɛktəmɪ] *s* (*pl:* **-mies**) (surg.) mastoidectomía
**mastoiditis** [ˌmæstɔɪˈdaɪtɪs] *s* (path.) mastoiditis
**masturbate** [ˈmæstərbet] *vn* masturbarse
**masturbation** [ˌmæstərˈbeʃən] *s* masturbación
**masurium** [məˈsurɪəm] o [məˈsjurɪəm] *s* (chem.) masurio
**mat** [mæt] *s* estera; ruedo o esterilla (*que se coloca debajo de una fuente caliente*); felpudo

(*p.ej., de puerta*); borde de cartón (*alrededor de un cuadro y dentro del marco*); colchoncillo (*de gimnasio*); greña; entretejimiento; superficie mate; *adj* mate (*no pulido*); (*pret & pp:* **matted;** *ger:* **matting**) *va* esterar; enmarañar, entretejer, enredar; matar, deslustrar (*el brillo de un metal*); *vn* enmarañarse, entretejerse, enredarse
**matador** ['mætədɔr] *s* (taur.) matador, espada; (cards) matador
**match** [mætʃ] *s* fósforo; mecha; igual; compañero; pareja (*conjunto de dos personas o cosas*); partido (*casamiento que elegir*); (sport) match, partido; **to be a good match** ser un buen partido; **to be a match for** hacer juego con; poder con, poder vencer; **to meet one's match** hallar la horma de su zapato; *va* igualar; aparear; emparejar; medir (*sus fuerzas*); hacer juego con, responder a, p.ej., **the chair matches the table** la silla responde a la mesa; **to match someone for the drinks** jugar a uno las bebidas; *vn* hacer juego, ser parejos; **to match** a juego, p.ej., **a handkerchief to match** un pañuelo a juego
**matchbox** ['mætʃ,bɑks] *s* fosforera, cerillera
**matchless** ['mætʃlɪs] *adj* sin igual, incomparable
**matchlock** ['mætʃ,lɑk] *s* mosquete; llave de mosquete
**matchmaker** ['mætʃ,mekər] *s* fabricante de fósforos; casamentero; promotor de partidos de boxeo, de lucha, de carreras, etc.
**matchmaking** ['mætʃ,mekɪŋ] *s* fabricación de fósforos; actividad de casamentero; promoción de partidos de boxeo, de lucha, de carreras, etc.; *adj* casamentero
**matchwood** ['mætʃ,wʊd] *s* madera para hacer fósforos; astillas, fragmentos de madera
**mate** [met] *s* compañero; hermano o compañero (*p.ej., de un zapato*); cónyuge, esposo; ayudante; macho (*de una hembra*); hembra (*de un macho*); (naut.) piloto; (chess) mate; *va* aparear; casar; (chess) dar jaque mate a; **to be well mated** hacer una buena pareja; *vn* aparearse; casarse; acoplarse
**maté** o **mate** ['mɑte] *s* (bot.) mate o hierba mate; mate (*hojas e infusión*)
**mater** ['metər] o ['mɑtər] *s* (coll.) madre
**material** [mə'tɪrɪəl] *adj* material; importante; *s* material; materia; tela, género; **materials** *spl* materiales; efectos (*de escritorio*); avíos (*de fumar*)
**materialism** [mə'tɪrɪəlɪzəm] *s* materialismo
**materialist** [mə'tɪrɪəlɪst] *s* materialista
**materialistic** [mə,tɪrɪə'lɪstɪk] *adj* materialista
**materialistically** [mə,tɪrɪə'lɪstɪkəlɪ] *adv* como materialista
**materialization** [mə,tɪrɪəlɪ'zeʃən] *s* realización; encarnación (*de un espíritu*); materialización (*de las ideas*)
**materialize** [mə'tɪrɪəlaɪz] *va* realizar, convertir en realidad, dar forma a; dotar de forma visible (*a un espíritu*); materializar (*p.ej., una idea*); *vn* realizarse; tomar forma visible (*un espíritu*)
**materially** [mə'tɪrɪəlɪ] *adv* materialmente; notablemente
**materia medica** [mə'tɪrɪə 'mɛdɪkə] *s* materia médica (*cuerpos de los cuales se sacan los medicamentos; parte de la terapéutica*)
**matériel** [mə,tɪrɪ'ɛl] *s* material (*conjunto de objetos necesarios para un servicio*); (mil.) material
**maternal** [mə'tʌrnəl] *adj* materno; maternal (*propio del cariño de madre*)
**maternity** [mə'tʌrnɪtɪ] *s* maternidad; (med.) maternidad (*casa de maternidad*); *adj* de maternidad
**maternity hospital** *s* casa de maternidad
**math.** abr. de **mathematics**
**mathematical** [,mæθɪ'mætɪkəl] *adj* matemático
**mathematically** [,mæθɪ'mætɪkəlɪ] *adv* matemáticamente
**mathematical pendulum** *s* péndulo matemático
**mathematician** [,mæθɪmə'tɪʃən] *s* matemático
**mathematics** [,mæθɪ'mætɪks] *ssg* matemática o matemáticas
**Matilda** [mə'tɪldə] *s* Matilde
**matinal** ['mætɪnəl] *adj* matinal, matutino
**matinée** o **matinee** [,mætɪ'ne] o ['mætɪne] *s* matinée (*función de tarde*)
**mating season** *s* época de celo
**matins** ['mætɪnz] *spl* (eccl.) maitines; oración matinal (*en la Iglesia anglicana*); (poet.) canto matinal (*p.ej., de pájaros*)
**matrass** ['mætrəs] *s* matraz
**matriarch** ['metrɪɑrk] *s* matriarca
**matriarchal** [,metrɪ'ɑrkəl] *adj* matriarcal
**matriarchy** ['metrɪɑrkɪ] *s* (*pl:* **-chies**) matriarcado
**matricidal** [,metrɪ'saɪdəl] o [,mætrɪ'saɪdəl] *adj* matricida
**matricide** ['metrɪsaɪd] o ['mætrɪsaɪd] *s* matricidio (*acción*); matricida (*persona*)
**matriculate** [mə'trɪkjəlɪt] *adj & s* matriculado; [mə'trɪkjəlet] *va* matricular; *vn* matricularse
**matriculation** [mə,trɪkjə'leʃən] *s* matrícula
**matrimonial** [,mætrɪ'monɪəl] *adj* matrimonial
**matrimonially** [,mætrɪ'monɪəlɪ] *adv* matrimonialmente
**matrimony** ['mætrɪ,monɪ] *s* (*pl:* **-nies**) matrimonio; vida matrimonial
**matrix** ['metrɪks] o ['mætrɪks] *s* (*pl:* **matrices** ['metrɪsiz] o ['mætrɪsiz] o **matrixes**) matriz (*útero; molde; impresión de disco de fonógrafo*); (anat., biol., math. & geol.) matriz
**matron** ['metrən] *s* matrona; ama de llaves (*en un colegio, etc.*); carcelera, matrona
**matronly** ['metrənlɪ] *adj* matronal; respetable; algo gruesa
**matron of honor** *s* dama de honor (*de una boda*)
**Matt.** abr. de **Matthew**
**matte** [mæt] *s* (metal.) mata
**matter** ['mætər] *s* materia; motivo (*p.ej., de queja*); (path.) materia (*pus*); correspondencia o impresos (*enviados por correo*); (print.) material (*preparado para la prensa*); **a matter of** cosa de u obra de (*p.ej., diez minutos*); **for that matter** en cuanto a eso; **in a matter of** en cosa de; **in the matter** al respecto; **in the matter of** en materia de; **no matter** no importa; **no matter how** de cualquier modo; **no matter when** cuando quiera; **no matter where** dondequiera; **to be of no matter** no tener importancia; **to go into the matter** entrar en materia; **what is the matter?** ¿qué hay?, ¿qué pasa?; **what is the matter with him?** ¿qué tiene?, ¿qué le pasa?; *vn* importar; supurar
**Matterhorn, the** ['mætərhɔrn] el monte Cervino
**matter of course** *s* cosa de cajón; **as a matter of course** por rutina
**matter of fact** *s* hecho positivo, hecho evidente; **as a matter of fact** en honor a la verdad, en realidad
**matter-of-fact** ['mætərəv,fækt] *adj* prosaico, de poca imaginación
**matter of form** *s* cosa de pura fórmula; **as a matter of form** por fórmula
**Matthew** ['mæθju] *s* Mateo; (Bib.) San Mateo; (Bib.) el Evangelio según San Mateo
**Matthias** [mə'θaɪəs] *s* Matías
**matting** ['mætɪŋ] *s* estera
**mattock** ['mætək] *s* zapapico, azadón de peto o de pico
**mattress** ['mætrɪs] *s* colchón; (hyd.) colchón de ramaje
**maturate** ['mætʃuret] o ['mætjʊret] *va & vn* madurar
**maturation** [,mætʃʊ'reʃən] o [,mætjʊ'reʃən] *s* maduración
**mature** [mə'tjʊr] o [mə'tʊr] *adj* maduro; (com.) vencido, pagadero; (fig.) muy bien elaborado, preparado cuidadosamente; *va* madurar; elaborar o preparar cuidadosamente; *vn* madurar; (com.) vencer
**maturity** [mə'tjʊrɪtɪ] o [mə'tʊrɪtɪ] *s* madurez; perfección; (com.) vencimiento
**matutinal** [mə'tjutɪnəl] o [mə'tutɪnəl] *adj* matutinal, matutino

**matzo** ['mɑtso] *s* (*pl:* **matzos** o **matzoth** ['mɑtsoθ]) galleta de pan sin levadura

**maudlin** ['mɔdlɪn] *adj* sensiblero; chispo y lloroso

**mauger** o **maugre** ['mɔgər] *prep* (archaic) a pesar de

**maul** [mɔl] *s* machota, mazo; *va* aporrear, maltratar

**maulstick** ['mɔl,stɪk] *s* (paint.) tiento

**maunder** ['mɔndər] *vn* parlotear; andar como atontado

**maundy** ['mɔndɪ] *s* (eccl.) mandato, lavatorio

**Maundy Thursday** *s* Jueves Santo

**Maurice** ['mɔrɪs] o ['mɑrɪs] *s* Mauricio (*nombre de varón*)

**Mauritius** [mɔ'rɪʃəs] o [mɔ'rɪʃɪəs] *s* la isla Mauricio o la isla de Mauricio

**Mauser** o **mauser** ['maʊzər] *s* (trademark) máuser

**mausoleum** [,mɔsə'liəm] *s* (*pl:* **-ums** o **-a** [ə]) mausoleo

**mauve** [mov] *adj* de color de malva; *s* color de malva

**maverick** ['mævərɪk] *s* animal sin marca de hierro; becerro separado de su madre; disidente

**mavis** ['mevɪs] *s* (orn.) malvís; (orn.) cagaaceite

**mavourneen** o **mavournin** [mə'vʊrnin] *s* (Irish) vida mía

**maw** [mɔ] *s* buche (*de las aves*); vejiga de aire (*de los peces*); fauces (*de un animal devorador*)

**mawkish** ['mɔkɪʃ] *adj* empalagoso; sensiblero

**max.** abr. de **maximum**

**maxilla** [mæk'sɪlə] *s* (*pl:* **-lae** [li]) (anat. & zool.) maxila

**maxillary** ['mæksɪ,lɛrɪ] *adj* maxilar; *s* (*pl:* **-ies**) (anat.) maxilar

**maxim** ['mæksɪm] *s* máxima

**Maximilian** [,mæksɪ'mɪljən] *s* Maximiliano

**maximum** ['mæksɪməm] *adj* máximo; *s* (*pl:* **-mums** o **-ma** [mə]) máximo o máximum

**maxwell** ['mækswɛl] *s* (elec.) maxvelio

**May** [me] *s* mayo (*mes*); (*l.c.*) *v aux* poder, p.ej., **it may be** puede ser; **may I sit down?** ¿puedo sentarme?; **may you be happy!** ¡que seas feliz!

**Maya** ['mɑjə] o **Mayan** ['mɑjən] *adj & s* maya

**May apple** *s* (bot.) podofilo; limón silvestre, manzana de mayo (*fruto*)

**maybe** ['mebɪ] *adv* quizá, tal vez

**May Day** *s* primero de mayo; fiesta del primero de mayo

**Mayfair** ['me,fɛr] *s* la alta sociedad londinense

**Mayflower** ['me,flaʊər] *s* (bot. Brit.) primavera, cala, majuelo, hierba centella, etc.; (bot. U.S.A.) anemona, epigea rastrera, hepática, etc.

**May fly** *s* (ent.) mosca de mayo, mosca de un día

**mayhap** [,me'hæp] o ['mehæp] *adv* (archaic) quizá, tal vez

**mayhem** ['mehɛm] o ['meəm] *s* (law) mutilación criminal

**Maying** ['meɪŋ] *s* festejos del mes de mayo; **to go a-Maying** irse a la fiesta de mayo

**mayonnaise** [,meə'nez] *s* mayonesa, mahonesa

**mayor** ['meər] o [mɛr] *s* alcalde; intendente municipal (Am.)

**mayoralty** ['meərəltɪ] o ['mɛrəltɪ] *s* (*pl:* **-ties**) alcaldía; intendencia (Am.)

**mayoress** ['meərɪs] o ['mɛrɪs] *s* alcaldesa

**Maypole** o **maypole** ['me,pol] *s* mayo (*árbol adornado de cintas*)

**Maypole dance** *s* danza de cintas

**May queen** *s* maya (*joven que preside la fiesta de mayo*)

**Maytide** ['me,taid] o **Maytime** ['me,taɪm] *s* mes de mayo

**mayweed** ['me,wid] *s* (bot.) magarzuela, manzanilla hedionda; (bot.) matricaria

**Mazdaism** o **Mazdeism** ['mæzdəɪzəm] *s* mazdeísmo

**Mazdaist** o **Mazdeist** ['mæzdəɪst] *s* mazdeísta

**Mazdean** ['mæzdɪən] o [mæz'diən] *adj* mazdeísta

**maze** [mez] *s* laberinto

**mazourka** o **mazurka** [mə'zʌrkə] o [mə'zʊrkə] *s* (mus.) mazurca

**mazy** ['mezɪ] *adj* (*comp:* **-zier;** *super:* **-ziest**) laberíntico

**M.C.** abr. de **Master of Ceremonies** y **Member of Congress**

**Md.** abr. de **Maryland**

**M.D.** abr. de **Doctor of Medicine**

**mdse.** abr. de **merchandise**

**Me.** abr. de **Maine**

**ME.** abr. de **Middle English**

**M.E.** abr. de **Master of Engineering, Mechanical Engineer, Methodist Episcopal, Middle English** y **Mining Engineer**

**me** [mi] *pron pers* me; mí; **with me** conmigo, p.ej., **he came with me** vino conmigo

**mead** [mid] *s* aloja; (poet.) prado

**meadow** ['mɛdo] *s* henar; pradera, prado, vega

**meadow crowfoot** *s* (bot.) hierba velluda

**meadow foxtail** *s* (bot.) cola de zorra

**meadowland** ['mɛdo,lænd] *s* pradera

**meadow lark** *s* (orn.) chirlota, sabanero, triguero

**meadow sage** *s* (bot.) tarrago

**meadowsweet** ['mɛdo,swit] *s* (bot.) ulmaria, reina de los prados

**meadowy** ['mɛdo·ɪ] o ['mɛdəwɪ] *adj* pradeño, praderoso

**meager** o **meagre** ['migər] *adj* magro, flaco; pobre, escaso

**meal** [mil] *s* comida; harina

**mealtime** ['mil,taɪm] *s* hora de comer

**mealy** ['milɪ] *adj* (*comp:* **-ier;** *super:* **-iest**) panoso, harinoso; enharinado; pálido; meloso; poco sincero, falso

**mealy-mouthed** ['milɪ'maʊðd] o ['milɪ'maʊθt] *adj* meloso; poco sincero, falso

**mean** [min] *adj* medio; mediano; mezquino, tacaño; sórdido, innoble; pobre, inferior; humilde, obscuro; andrajoso, raído; vil, ruin; insignificante; mal intencionado (*dícese de las caballerías*); (coll.) malo, de mal genio, desconsiderado; (coll.) avergonzado, corrido, indigno; (coll.) indispuesto; **no mean** famoso, excelente ‖ *s* medio; promedio o término medio; (math.) media; **means** *ssg o spl* medio o medios; manera, modo; **means** *spl* bienes de fortuna, dinero, p.ej., **a man of means** un hombre de dinero; **by all means** por todos los medios posibles; sin falta; sí, por cierto; **by any means** de cualquier modo que sea; **by means of** por medio de; **by no means** de ningún modo, en ningún caso; **by some means** de alguna manera; **by this means** por este medio, de este modo; **means to an end** paso dado para lograr un fin ‖ (*pret & pp:* **meant**) *va* querer decir, significar; **to mean to** + *inf* pensar + *inf* ‖ *vn* tener intenciones (*buenas o malas*), p.ej., **he means well** tiene buenas intenciones; **to mean well by** favorecer, querer ayudar

**meander** [mɪ'ændər] *s* meandro; (f.a.) meandro; *vn* serpentear; vagar

**meander line** *s* (surv.) línea de meandro

**meandrous** [mɪ'ændrəs] *adj* meándrico

**meaning** ['minɪŋ] *adj* significativo; *s* significado, sentido

**meaningful** ['minɪŋfəl] *adj* significativo

**meaningless** ['minɪŋlɪs] *adj* sin sentido; insensato

**meanness** ['minnɪs] *s* mezquindad, tacañería; pobreza; humildad, obscuridad; vileza, ruindad; maldad; acción indigna

**mean noon** *s* (astr.) mediodía medio

**mean sun** *s* (astr.) sol medio

**meant** [mɛnt] *pret & pp de* **mean**

**meantime** ['min,taɪm] *adv* entretanto, mientras tanto; *s* ínterin, medio tiempo; **in the meantime** entretanto, mientras tanto

**mean time** *s* (astr.) tiempo medio

**meanwhile** ['min,hwaɪl] *adv & s* var. de **meantime**

**measles** ['mizəlz] *s* (path.) sarampión; (path.) rubéola; (vet.) roña de los cerdos

**measly** ['mizlɪ] *adj* (*comp:* **-slier;** *super:* **-sliest**) sarampioso; (slang) mezquino, insignificante, despreciable

**measurable** ['mɛʒərəbəl] *adj* medible, mensurable

**measurably** ['mɛʒərəblɪ] *adv* mediblemente; perceptiblemente

**measure** ['mɛʒər] *s* medida; gestión, paso;

(mus.) compás; (pros.) medida; (pros.) pie (*del verso*); (law) ley, proyecto de ley; **beyond measure** con exceso, a más no poder; **in a measure** en parte, hasta cierto punto; **in great measure** en gran parte; **to take measures** tomar las medidas necesarias; **to take one's measure** tomarle a uno las medidas, medir a uno con la vista; **to tread a measure** bailar; *va* medir; recorrer (*cierta distancia*); **to measure off** medir; **to measure out** medir; distribuir, repartir; *vn* medir
**measured** ['mɛʒərd] *adj* regular, uniforme; deliberado, hecho con reflexión; rítmico
**measureless** ['mɛʒərlɪs] *adj* inmensurable, inmenso
**measurement** ['mɛʒərmənt] *s* medida; medición
**measuring worm** *s* (zool.) geómetra
**meat** [mit] *s* carne (*de animal o de la fruta*); vianda, alimento; comida; materia (*para la reflexión*); meollo (*p.ej., de un libro*); *adj* cárnico
**meat ball** *s* albóndiga
**meat chopper** *s* picadora de carne
**meat day** *s* día de carne
**meat fly** *s* mosca de la carne
**meat grinder** *s* máquina de picar carne
**meathook** ['mit,hʊk] *s* garabato de carnicero
**meat market** *s* carnicería
**meat packing** s preparación o conservación de la carne congelada
**meat pie** *s* pastel de carne
**meatus** [mɪ'etəs] *s* (*pl:* **-tuses** o **-tus**) (anat.) meato
**meaty** ['mitɪ] *adj* (*comp:* **-ier**; *super:* **-iest**) carnoso (*de carne; que tiene consistencia de carne*); jugoso, substancioso
**mecca** o **Mecca** ['mɛkə] *s* Meca (*sitio a que se dirigen muchas personas*); (*cap.*) *s* La Meca (*ciudad*)
**Meccan** ['mɛkən] *adj & s* mecano
**mechanic** [mɪ'kænɪk] *s* mecánico; **mechanics** *ssg* mecánica (*parte de la física*); mecanismo; *spl* técnica (*de un arte o ciencia*)
**mechanical** [mɪ'kænɪkəl] *adj* mecánico, maquinal; (fig.) maquinal
**mechanical drawing** *s* dibujo mecánico
**mechanical engineer** *s* ingeniero mecánico
**mechanical engineering** *s* ingeniería mecánica
**mechanically** [mɪ'kænɪkəlɪ] *adv* mecánicamente; (fig.) maquinalmente
**mechanical pencil** *s* portaminas
**mechanical toy** *s* juguete de movimiento
**mechanician** [,mɛkə'nɪʃən] *s* mecánico
**mechanism** ['mɛkənɪzəm] *s* mecanismo; (biol. & philos.) mecanicismo
**mechanist** ['mɛkənɪst] *s* (biol. & philos.) mecanicista
**mechanistic** [,mɛkə'nɪstɪk] *adj* mecánico; (biol. & philos.) mecanicista
**mechanization** [,mɛkənɪ'zeʃən] *s* mecanización; (econ.) maquinismo
**mechanize** ['mɛkənaɪz] *va* mecanizar
**mechanotherapy** [,mɛkəno'θɛrəpɪ] *s* mecanoterapia
**Mechlin** ['mɛklɪn] *s* Malinas; encaje de Malinas
**meconium** [mɪ'konɪəm] *s* meconio
**med.** abr. de **medicinal, medicine, medieval** y **medium**
**medal** ['mɛdəl] *s* medalla
**medalist** o **medallist** ['mɛdəlɪst] *s* medallista; persona condecorada con una medalla
**medallion** [mɪ'dæljən] *s* medallón
**meddle** ['mɛdəl] *vn* entremeterse
**meddler** ['mɛdlər] *s* entremetido
**meddlesome** ['mɛdəlsəm] *adj* entremetido
**meddling** ['mɛdlɪŋ] *adj* entremetido; *s* intromisión
**Mede** [mid] *s* medo
**mediaeval** [,midɪ'ivəl] o [,mɛdɪ'ivəl] *adj* var. de **medieval**
**medial** ['midɪəl] *adj* medianero; intermedio; (phonet.) medial, interior
**medially** ['midɪəlɪ] *adv* en el centro
**medial strip** *s* faja central o divisora (*de la carretera*)
**median** ['midɪən] *adj* medio, intermedio; (bot. & zool.) medial o mediano; *s* punto medio (*en una serie*); número medio (*en una serie*); (anat.) mediano; (geom.) mediana; (*cap.*) *adj & s* medo
**median barrier** *s* barrera o valla central (*de la carretera*)
**median strip** *s* var. de **medial strip**
**mediastinum** [,midɪæs'taɪnəm] *s* (*pl:* **-na** [nə]) (anat.) mediastino
**mediate** ['midɪɪt] *adj* mediato; ['midɪet] *va* dirimir (*una contienda*); arreglar (*paces*); reconciliar; servir de mediador para efectuar (*un resultado*), entregar (*un regalo*), comunicar (*informes, etc.*); *vn* mediar
**mediation** [,midɪ'eʃən] *s* mediación; (astr., dipl. & mus.) mediación
**mediator** ['midɪ,etər] *s* mediador
**mediatorial** [,midɪə'torɪəl] o **mediatory** ['midɪə,torɪ] *adj* mediador
**medic** ['mɛdɪk] *s* (bot.) mielga; médico; (coll.) estudiante de medicina
**medicable** ['mɛdɪkəbəl] *adj* medicable
**medical** ['mɛdɪkəl] *adj* médico; de medicina, p.ej., **medical student** estudiante de medicina
**medicament** [mə'dɪkəmənt] o ['mɛdɪkəmənt] *s* medicamento
**medicaster** ['mɛdɪ,kæstər] *s* medicastro
**medicate** ['mɛdɪket] *va* medicinar (*a un enfermo*); impregnar (*p.ej., una venda*) con una substancia medicinal
**medication** [,mɛdɪ'keʃən] *s* medicación; impregnación de una venda con una substancia medicinal
**medicinal** [mɛ'dɪsɪnəl] *adj* medicinal
**medicinally** [mɛ'dɪsɪnəlɪ] *adv* medicinalmente
**medicine** ['mɛdɪsɪn] *s* medicina (*ciencia y arte*); medicina o medicamento (*remedio*); talismán (*entre los pieles rojas*); **to take one's medicine** echar el pecho al agua; hacer (*uno*) a la fuerza lo que no quiere
**medicine ball** *s* pelota medicinal
**medicine cabinet** *s* armario botiquín
**medicine dance** *s* danza sagrada (*entre los pieles rojas*)
**medicine kit** *s* botiquín
**medicine man** *s* exorcista, curandero (*entre los pieles rojas*)
**medico** ['mɛdɪko] *s* (*pl:* **-cos**) (slang) médico, cirujano, estudiante de medicina
**medicochirurgical** [,mɛdɪkokaɪ'rʌrdʒɪkəl] *adj* médicoquirúrgico
**medicolegal** [,mɛdɪko'ligəl] *adj* médicolegal
**medieval** [,midɪ'ivəl] o [,mɛdɪ'ivəl] *adj* medieval
**medieval history** *s* la historia medieval o media
**medievalism** [,midɪ'ivəlɪzəm] o [,mɛdɪ'ivəlɪzəm] *s* medievalismo
**medievalist** [,midɪ'ivəlɪst] o [,mɛdɪ'ivəlɪst] *s* medievalista
**mediocre** ['midɪ,okər] o [,midɪ'okər] *adj* mediano, mediocre
**mediocrity** [,midɪ'ɑkrɪtɪ] *s* (*pl:* **-ties**) mediocridad; medianía o mediocridad (*persona*)
**meditate** ['mɛdɪtet] *va & vn* meditar
**meditation** [,mɛdɪ'teʃən] *s* meditación
**meditative** ['mɛdɪ,tetɪv] *adj* meditativo
**Mediterranean** [,mɛdɪtə'renɪən] *adj & s* Mediterráneo
**Mediterranean Sea** *s* mar Mediterráneo
**medium** ['midɪəm] *adj* mediano, intermedio; a medio cocer, a medio asar; *s* (*pl:* **-ums** o **-a** [ə]) medio; medio o médium (*en el espiritismo*); (bot. & bact.) medio; (paint.) aceite; **through the medium of** por medio de
**mediumistic** [,midɪə'mɪstɪk] *adj* mediúmnico
**medium of exchange** *s* mediador de cambio
**medium-range** ['midɪəm'rendʒ] *adj* de alcance medio
**medium-sized** ['midɪəm'saɪzd] *adj* de tamaño mediano
**medium steel** *s* acero mediano o intermedio
**medlar** ['mɛdlər] *s* (bot.) níspero (*árbol y fruto*); níspola (*fruto*)
**medley** ['mɛdlɪ] *s* mezcolanza, revoltijo; (mus.) popurrí
**medulla** [mɪ'dʌlə] *s* (*pl:* **-lae** [li]) (anat. & bot.) medula; (anat.) medula oblonga u oblongada
**medulla oblongata** [,ɑblɑŋ'getə] *s* (anat.) medula oblonga u oblongada
**medullary** ['mɛdə,lɛrɪ] o [mɪ'dʌlərɪ] *adj* medular

**medusa** [mɪ'djusə] o [mɪ'dusə] *s* (*pl:* **-sas** o **-sae** [si]) (zool.) medusa; (*cap.*) *s* (*pl:* **-sas**) (myth.) Medusa
**meed** [mid] *s* (poet.) galardón
**meek** [mik] *adj* manso, dócil, humilde
**meekness** ['miknɪs] *s* mansedumbre, docilidad, humildad
**meerschaum** ['mɪrʃɔm] o ['mɪrʃəm] *s* (mineral.) espuma de mar; pipa de espuma de mar
**meet** [mit] *s* concurso de deportistas; concurrencia de gente (*en un lugar de luchas atléticas*); lugar de reunión; *adj* conveniente; (*pret & pp:* **met**) *va* encontrar, encontrarse con; conocer; ir a recibir; ir a esperar; satisfacer (*un pedido*); pagar, honrar (*una letra*); conformarse a (*los deseos de uno*); hacer frente a (*gastos*); cumplir (*obligaciones*); refutar (*acusaciones*); responder a (*reparos*); verse cara a cara con, batirse con; recibir (*la mirada de otra persona*); tener que aguantar (*desprecio*); tener (*mala suerte*); empalmar con (*otro tren u ómnibus*); hallar (*la muerte*); *vn* encontrarse; reunirse; conocerse; luchar, batirse; **till we meet again** hasta más ver; **to meet with** encontrarse con; reunirse con; empalmar con; tener (*un accidente*)
**meeting** ['mitɪŋ] *s* junta, sesión; asamblea, reunión; encuentro; congregación; confluencia (*de dos ríos o caminos*); desafío, duelo
**meeting house** *s* iglesia; iglesia de los disidentes; iglesia de los cuáqueros
**meeting of the minds** *s* concierto de voluntades, voluntad común
**meetly** ['mitlɪ] *adv* convenientemente
**megacycle** ['mɛgə,saɪkəl] *s* (rad.) megaciclo
**megalith** ['mɛgəlɪθ] *s* (archeol.) megalito
**megalithic** [,mɛgə'lɪθɪk] *adj* megalítico
**megalocephalous** [,mɛgəlo'sɛfələs] *adj* megalocéfalo
**megalomania** [,mɛgəlo'menɪə] *s* (psychopath.) megalomanía
**megalomaniac** [,mɛgəlo'menɪæk] *s* megalómano
**megalomaniacal** [,mɛgəloma'naɪəkəl] *adj* megalómano
**megalosaur** ['mɛgələ,sɔr] *s* (pal.) megalosaurio
**megaphone** ['mɛgəfon] *s* megáfono, portavoz
**megathere** ['mɛgəθɪr] *s* (pal.) megaterio
**megaton** ['mɛgətʌn] *s* megatón, megatonelada
**megohm** ['mɛg,om] *s* (elec.) megohmio
**megrim** ['migrɪm] *s* (path.) hemicránea, jaqueca; (archaic) antojo, capricho; **megrims** *spl* hipocondría
**Mekka** ['mɛkə] *s* var. de **Mecca**
**melancholia** [,mɛlən'kolɪə] *s* (path.) melancolía
**melancholic** [,mɛlən'kɑlɪk] *adj* melancólico; (path.) melancólico
**melancholy** ['mɛlən,kɑlɪ] *adj* melancólico; *s* (*pl:* **-ies**) melancolía
**Melanesia** [,mɛlə'niʃə] o [,mɛlə'niʒə] *s* la Melanesia
**Melanesian** [,mɛlə'niʃən] o [,mɛlə'niʒən] *adj & s* melanesio
**mélange** [me'lɑ̃ʒ] *s* mezcolanza
**melanite** ['mɛlənaɪt] *s* (mineral.) melanita
**melanoma** [,mɛlə'nomə] *s* (*pl:* **-mata** [mətə]) (path.) melanoma
**melanosis** [,mɛlə'nosɪs] *s* (path.) melanosis
**melaphyre** ['mɛləfaɪr] *s* (geol.) meláfiro
**Melbourne** ['mɛlbərn] *s* Melburna
**Melchior** ['mɛlkɪɔr] *s* Melchor
**Meleager** [,mɛlɪ'edʒər] *s* (myth.) Meleagro
**melee** o **mêlée** ['mele] o ['mɛle] *s* refriega, reyerta
**meliaceous** [,milɪ'eʃəs] *adj* (bot.) meliáceo
**melic** ['mɛlɪk] *adj* mélico
**melilot** ['mɛlɪlɑt] *s* (bot.) meliloto
**melinite** ['mɛlɪnaɪt] *s* melinita
**meliorate** ['miljəret] *va* mejorar; *vn* mejorarse
**melioration** [,miljə'reʃən] *s* mejoramiento
**mellifluence** [mɛ'lɪfluəns] *s* melifluencia
**mellifluent** [mɛ'lɪfluənt] o **mellifluous** [mɛ'lɪfluəs] *adj* melifluo
**mellow** ['mɛlo] *adj* maduro, sazonado; suave, meloso; margoso; melodioso; añejo (*vino*); *va* madurar; suavizar; *vn* madurarse; suavizarse
**melodeon** [mɪ'lodɪən] *s* (mus.) melodión
**melodic** [mɪ'lɑdɪk] *adj* melódico; **melodics** *ssg* teoría de la melodía
**melodically** [mɪ'lɑdɪkəlɪ] *adv* melódicamente
**melodious** [mɪ'lodɪəs] *adj* melodioso
**melodist** ['mɛlədɪst] *s* melodista
**melodrama** ['mɛlə,drɑmə] o ['mɛlə,dræmə] *s* melodrama; acción, literatura, discurso y escrito melodramáticos
**melodramatic** [,mɛlədrə'mætɪk] *adj* melodramático
**melodramatically** [,mɛlədrə'mætɪkəlɪ] *adv* melodramáticamente
**melody** ['mɛlədɪ] *s* (*pl:* **-dies**) melodía
**melon** ['mɛlən] *s* melón (*fruto*); **to cut a melon** (slang) repartir ganancias extraordinarias
**Melpomene** [mɛl'pɑmɪnɪ] *s* (myth.) Melpómene
**melt** [mɛlt] *s* derretimiento; (found.) hornada; *va* derretir; fundir (*metales*); disolver (*azúcar*); disipar; ablandar, aplacar; **to melt down** fundir; disolver; *vn* derretirse; fundirse; disolverse; disiparse, desaparecer; ablandarse, aplacarse; **to melt away** desvanecerse; **to melt into** convertirse gradualmente en; deshacerse en (*p.ej., lágrimas*)
**melting point** *s* punto de fusión
**melting pot** *s* crisol; (fig.) país o ciudad de mucha inmigración
**melton** ['mɛltən] *s* meltón
**member** ['mɛmbər] *s* miembro
**membered** ['mɛmbərd] *adj* (her.) membrado
**member nation** *s* (*pl:* **member nations**) nación miembro
**membership** ['mɛmbərʃɪp] *s* asociación; personal (*de un club, etc.*); número de miembros o socios
**membranaceous** [,mɛmbrə'neʃəs] *adj* membranáceo
**membrane** ['mɛmbren] *s* (bot. & zool.) membrana
**membranous** ['mɛmbrənəs] *adj* membranoso
**memento** [mɪ'mɛnto] *s* (*pl:* **-tos** o **-toes**) recordatorio, prenda de recuerdo; (*cap.*) *s* (eccl.) memento
**Memnon** ['mɛmnɑn] *s* (myth.) Memnón; estatua de Memnón en Tebas
**memo** ['mɛmo] *s* (*pl:* **-os**) (coll.) apunte, membrete; (coll.) memorándum
**memoir** ['mɛmwɑr] *s* biografía; memoria; **memoirs** *spl* memorias
**memorabilia** [,mɛmərə'bɪlɪə] *spl* cosas memorables
**memorable** ['mɛmərəbəl] *adj* memorable
**memorandum** [,mɛmə'rændəm] *s* (*pl:* **-dums** o **-da** [də]) memorándum; apunte
**memorial** [mɪ'morɪəl] *adj* conmemorativo; *s* memoráculo, monumento conmemorativo; memorial (*escrito en que se pide un favor*)
**memorial arch** *s* arco triunfal
**Memorial Day** *s* (U.S.A.) día de recordación de los caídos (*30 de mayo*)
**memorialize** [mɪ'morɪəlaɪz] *va* conmemorar; dirigir un memorial a
**memorize** ['mɛməraɪz] *va* aprender de memoria, memorizar
**memory** ['mɛmərɪ] *s* (*pl:* **-ries**) memoria; **in memory of** en memoria de; **to commit to memory** encomendar a la memoria; **within my memory** que yo recuerde; **within the memory of man** que la historia registra
**memory book** *s* libro de recuerdos
**Memphis** ['mɛmfɪs] *s* Menfis
**men** [mɛn] *pl de* **man**
**menace** ['mɛnɪs] *s* amenaza; *va & vn* amenazar
**menad** ['minæd] *s* var. de **maenad**
**ménage** o **menage** [me'nɑʒ] *s* casa, hogar; cuidado de la casa, economía doméstica
**menagerie** [mə'nædʒərɪ] o [mə'næʒərɪ] *s* colección de fieras y de animales raros; casa de fieras
**Mencius** ['mɛnʃɪəs] *s* Mencio
**mend** [mɛnd] *s* compostura; remiendo; mejora; **to be on the mend** ir mejorando; *va* componer, remendar, reparar; reformar, mejorar; *vn* mejorar o mejorarse
**mendacious** [mɛn'deʃəs] *adj* mendaz; falso
**mendacity** [mɛn'dæsɪtɪ] *s* (*pl:* **-ties**) mendacidad; mentira

**mendelevium** [ˌmɛndɪˈliviəm] *s* (chem.) mendelevio
**Mendelian** [mɛnˈdiliən] *adj* mendeliano
**Mendelianism** [mɛnˈdiliənɪzəm] o **Mendelism** [ˈmɛndəlɪzəm] *s* mendelismo
**mendicancy** [ˈmɛndɪkənsɪ] *s* mendicidad
**mendicant** [ˈmɛndɪkənt] *adj & s* mendicante
**mendicity** [mɛnˈdɪsɪtɪ] *s* var. de **mendicancy**
**mending** [ˈmɛndɪŋ] *s* remiendo, zurcido
**mending tape** *s* cinta de remendar
**Menelaus** [ˌmɛnəˈleəs] *s* (myth.) Menelao
**menfolk** [ˈmɛnˌfok] *spl* hombres
**menhaden** [mɛnˈhedən] *s* (*pl:* **-den**) (ichth.) menhaden (*Brevoortia tyrannus*)
**menhaden oil** *s* aceite de menhaden
**menhir** [ˈmɛnhɪr] *s* (archeol.) menhir
**menial** [ˈminɪəl] *adj* bajo, servil; *s* criado, doméstico
**meningeal** [mɪˈnɪndʒɪəl] *adj* meníngeo
**meninges** [mɪˈnɪndʒiz] *spl* (anat.) meninges
**meningitis** [ˌmɛnɪnˈdʒaɪtɪs] *s* (path.) meningitis
**meningococcus** [mɪˌnɪŋgəˈkɑkəs] *s* (*pl:* **-cocci** [ˈkɑksaɪ]) (bact.) meningococo
**meniscus** [mɪˈnɪskəs] *s* (*pl:* **meniscuses** o **menisci** [mɪˈnɪsaɪ]) media luna; (anat., opt. & phys.) menisco
**menispermaceous** [ˌmɛnɪspərˈmeʃəs] *adj* (bot.) menispermáceo
**Mennonite** [ˈmɛnənaɪt] *adj & s* menonita
**menopause** [ˈmɛnəpɔz] *s* (physiol.) menopausia
**menorrhagia** [ˌmɛnəˈredʒɪə] *s* (path.) menorragia
**menses** [ˈmɛnsiz] *spl* menstruo
**men's furnishings** *spl* artículos para caballeros
**Menshevik** [ˈmɛnʃəvɪk] *s* (*pl:* **Mensheviks** o **Mensheviki** [ˌmɛnʃəˈvikɪ]) menchevique
**men's room** *s* lavabo de caballeros, reservado para hombres
**menstrual** [ˈmɛnstrʊəl] *adj* mensual; (physiol.) menstrual
**menstruate** [ˈmɛnstrʊet] *vn* menstruar
**menstruation** [ˌmɛnstrʊˈeʃən] *s* menstruación
**menstruous** [ˈmɛnstrʊəs] *adj* menstruoso
**menstruum** [ˈmɛnstrʊəm] *s* (*pl:* **-ums** o **-a** [ə]) (chem.) menstruo
**mensurability** [ˌmɛnʃərəˈbɪlɪtɪ] *s* mensurabilidad
**mensurable** [ˈmɛnʃərəbəl] *adj* mensurable
**mensural** [ˈmɛnʃərəl] *adj* mensural
**mensuration** [ˌmɛnʃəˈreʃən] *s* mensuración
**mental** [ˈmɛntəl] *adj* mental
**mental age** *s* (psychol.) edad mental
**mental arithmetic** *s* cálculo mental
**mental deficiency** *s* debilidad mental
**mental disease** *s* enfermedad mental
**mental healer** *s* curador mental
**mental healing** *s* curación por el espíritu
**mental health** *s* estado mental; buen estado mental
**mental hygiene** *s* higiene mental
**mental illness** *s* enfermedad mental
**mentality** [mɛnˈtælɪtɪ] *s* (*pl:* **-ties**) mentalidad
**mentally** [ˈmɛntəlɪ] *adv* mentalmente
**mental reservation** *s* reserva mental
**mental test** *s* prueba mental
**menthol** [ˈmɛnθɑl] *s* (chem.) mentol
**mentholated** [ˈmɛnθəˌletɪd] *adj* mentolado
**mention** [ˈmɛnʃən] *s* mención; **to make mention of** hacer mención de; *va* mencionar; **don't mention it** no hay de qué; **not to mention** sin contar; además de
**mentor** [ˈmɛntər] *s* mentor; (*cap.*) *s* (myth.) Mentor
**menu** [ˈmɛnju] o [ˈmenju] *s* menú; comida
**meow** [mɪˈaʊ] *s* maullido; *vn* maullar
**Mephistopheles** [ˌmɛfɪsˈtɑfəliz] *s* Mefistófeles
**Mephistophelian** [ˌmɛfɪstəˈfiliən] *adj* mefistofélico
**mephitic** [mɪˈfɪtɪk] *adj* mefítico
**mephitis** [mɪˈfaɪtɪs] *s* mefitis
**mercantile** [ˈmʌrkəntɪl] o [ˈmʌrkəntaɪl] *adj* mercantil
**mercantile marine** *s* marina mercante
**mercantile system** *s* sistema mercantil
**mercantilism** [ˈmʌrkəntɪlɪzəm] o [ˈmʌrkəntaɪlɪzəm] *s* mercantilismo
**mercantilist** [ˈmʌrkəntɪlɪst] o [ˈmʌrkəntaɪlɪst] *adj & s* mercantilista
**Mercator's chart** [mərˈketərz] *s* (geog.) carta de Mercátor
**Mercator's projection** *s* (geog.) proyección de Mercátor
**Mercedarian** [ˌmʌrsɪˈdɛrɪən] *s* mercedario
**Mercedes** [mərˈsidiz] *s* Mercedes (*nombre de mujer*)
**mercenary** [ˈmʌrsəˌnɛrɪ] *adj* (mil. & fig.) mercenario; *s* (*pl:* **-ies**) (mil.) mercenario
**mercer** [ˈmʌrsər] *s* (Brit.) mercader de telas de seda
**mercerize** [ˈmʌrsəraɪz] *va* mercerizar
**merchandise** [ˈmʌrtʃəndaɪz] *s* mercancías; *va* comerciar o traficar en; *vn* comerciar o traficar
**merchant** [ˈmʌrtʃənt] *adj* mercante; *s* comerciante
**merchantable** [ˈmʌrtʃəntəbəl] *adj* comerciable
**merchantman** [ˈmʌrtʃəntmən] *s* (*pl:* **-men**) buque mercante
**merchant marine** *s* marina mercante
**merchant prince** *s* comerciante rico, magnate del comercio
**merchant tailor** *s* sastre comerciante
**merchant vessel** *s* buque mercante
**Mercian** [ˈmʌrʃɪən] o [ˈmʌrʃən] *adj & s* merciano
**merciful** [ˈmʌrsɪfəl] *adj* misericordioso
**merciless** [ˈmʌrsɪlɪs] *adj* desapiadado, despiadado
**mercurial** [mərˈkjʊrɪəl] *adj* mercurial; vivo, despierto; veleidoso, inconstante; (*cap.*) *adj* (astr. & myth.) mercurial; (*l.c.*) *s* (pharm.) mercurial
**mercurialism** [mərˈkjʊrɪəlɪzəm] *s* (path.) mercurialismo
**mercuric** [mərˈkjʊrɪk] *adj* (chem.) mercúrico
**mercuric chloride** *s* (chem.) cloruro mercúrico
**mercuric oxide** *s* (chem.) óxido mercúrico, óxido de mercurio
**mercurochrome** [mərˈkjʊrəˌkrom] *s* (trademark) mercurocromo
**mercurous** [mərˈkjʊrəs] o [ˈmʌrkjərəs] *adj* (chem.) mercurioso
**mercury** [ˈmʌrkjərɪ] *s* (*pl:* **-ries**) (chem.) mercurio; columna de mercurio (*del termómetro*); (*cap.*) *s* (astr. & myth.) Mercurio
**mercury-arc lamp** [ˈmʌrkjərɪˌɑrk] *s* var. de **mercury-vapor lamp**
**mercury chloride** *s* var. de **mercuric chloride**
**mercury fulminate** *s* (chem.) fulminato mercúrico
**mercury-vapor lamp** [ˈmʌrkjərɪˌvepər] *s* (elec.) lámpara de vapor de mercurio
**mercy** [ˈmʌrsɪ] *s* (*pl:* **-cies**) misericordia; merced, beneficio, favor; **to be at the mercy of** estar a la merced de
**mercy killing** *s* eutanasia
**mercy seat** *s* propiciatorio; trono de Dios
**mere** [mɪr] *adj* mero; nada más que; *s* (poet. & dial.) lago
**merely** [ˈmɪrlɪ] *adv* meramente
**meretricious** [ˌmɛrɪˈtrɪʃəs] *adj* postizo, de oropel
**merganser** [mərˈgænsər] *s* (orn.) pato sierra (*Mergus merganser*); (orn.) serrata (*Mergus serrator*)
**merge** [mʌrdʒ] *va* fusionar, enchufar (*dos negocios*); *vn* fusionarse, enchufarse; convergir (*p.ej., dos caminos*); **to merge into** convertirse gradualmente en
**merger** [ˈmʌrdʒər] *s* fusión de empresas, amalgamación comercial
**mericarp** [ˈmɛrɪkɑrp] *s* (bot.) mericarpio
**meridian** [məˈrɪdɪən] *adj* meridiano; mayor, sumo, más elevado; *s* meridiano; altura meridiana; (fig.) auge, cumbre
**meridional** [məˈrɪdɪənəl] *adj & s* meridional
**meringue** [məˈræŋ] *s* merengue
**merino** [məˈrino] *adj* merino; *s* (*pl:* **-nos**) merino (*carnero; lana; tejido*)
**meristem** [ˈmɛrɪstɛm] *s* (bot.) meristemo

**merit** ['mɛrɪt] *s* mérito, merecimiento; **merits** *spl* (law) méritos; *va & vn* merecer
**meritorious** [,mɛrɪ'torɪəs] *adj* meritorio
**merl** o **merle** [mʌrl] *s* (poet.) mirlo
**merlin** ['mʌrlɪn] *s* (orn.) esmerejón, neblí; (orn). halcón palumbario; (*cap.*) *s* Merlín
**merlon** ['mʌrlən] *s* (fort.) merlón, almena
**mermaid** ['mʌr,med] *s* sirena; (fig.) ninfa marina (*mujer muy experta en la natación*)
**merman** ['mʌr,mæn] *s* (*pl:* **-men**) tritón; (fig.) tritón (*hombre muy experto en la natación*)
**Merovingian** [,mɛro'vɪndʒɪən] *adj & s* merovingio
**merriment** ['mɛrɪmənt] *s* alegría, regocijo, alborozo
**merry** ['mɛrɪ] *adj* (*comp:* **-rier**; *super:* **-riest**) alegre, regocijado, alborozado; **to make merry** alegrarse, regocijarse
**merry-andrew** [,mɛrɪ'ændru] *s* matachín, bufón
**Merry Christmas** *interj* ¡Felices Pascuas!, ¡Felices Navidades!
**merry-go-round** ['mɛrɪgo,raund] *s* tiovivo, caballitos; fiesta continua; **merry-go-round of parties** serie ininterrumpida de fiestas o tertulias
**merrymaker** ['mɛrɪ,mekər] *s* fiestero; parrandista
**merrymaking** ['mɛrɪ,mekɪŋ] *adj* fiestero; jaranero; *s* regocijo, alborozo; jarana
**merrythought** ['mɛrɪ,θɔt] *s* hueso de la suerte
**mésalliance** [me'zælɪəns] o [meza'ljɑ̃s] *s* matrimonio con una persona de clase inferior
**mescal** [mɛs'kæl] *s* (bot.) mescal (*planta y bebida*)
**meseems** [mi'simz] *vn* (archaic) me parece
**mesencephalon** [,mɛsɛn'sɛfəlan] *s* (pl: **-la** [lə]) (anat.) mesencéfalo
**mesenchyme** ['mɛsɛŋkɪm] *s* (embryol.) mesénquima
**mesenteric** [,mɛsən'tɛrɪk] *adj* mesentérico
**mesenteritis** [mɛ,sɛntə'raɪtɪs] *s* (path.) mesenteritis
**mesentery** ['mɛsən,tɛrɪ] *s* (*pl:* **-ies**) (anat.) mesenterio
**mesh** [mɛʃ] *s* malla (*de una red*); red; (mach.) engrane; **meshes** *spl* red, celada; **in mesh** en toma, engranados; *va* enredar; (mach.) engranar; *vn* enredarse; (mach.) engranar
**mesh bag** *s* bolsa o saquillo de malla
**mesial** ['mizɪəl] o ['mɛsɪəl] *adj* mediano
**mesitylene** [mɪ'sɪtɪlin] o ['mɛsɪtɪ,lin] *s* (chem.) mesitileno
**mesmerian** [mɛs'mɪrɪən] o [mɛz'mɪrɪən] *adj & s* mesmeriano
**mesmeric** [mɛs'mɛrɪk] o [mɛz'mɛrɪk] *adj* mesmeriano
**mesmerism** ['mɛsmərɪzəm] o ['mɛzmərɪzəm] *s* mesmerismo
**mesmerist** ['mɛsmərɪst] o ['mɛzmərɪst] *s* mesmerista
**mesmerize** ['mɛsməraɪz] o ['mɛzməraɪz] *va* hipnotizar
**mesoblast** ['mɛsəblæst] o ['misəblæst] *s* (embryol.) mesoblasto
**mesocarp** ['mɛsəkarp] o ['misəkarp] *s* (bot.) mesocarpio
**mesocephalic** [,mɛsosɪ'fælɪk] o [,misosɪ'fælɪk] *adj* (anthrop.) mesocéfalo
**mesoderm** ['mɛsədʌrm] o ['misədʌrm] *s* (embryol.) mesodermo
**mesogastrium** [,mɛsə'gæstrɪəm] o [,misə'gæstrɪəm] *s* (anat. & zool.) mesogastrio
**meson** ['misan] *s* (phys.) mesón
**mesophyll** ['mɛsəfɪl] o ['misəfɪl] *s* (bot.) mesofilo
**mesophyte** ['mɛsəfaɪt] o ['misəfaɪt] *s* (bot.) mesófita
**mesorrhine** ['mɛsəraɪn] o ['misəraɪn] *adj* (anthrop.) mesorrino
**mesosphere** ['mɛzəsfɪr] *s* mesosfera
**mesothorax** [,mɛsə'θoræks] o [,misə'θoræks] *s* (*pl:* **-raxes** o **-races** [rəsiz]) (zool.) mesotórax
**mesothorium** [,mɛsə'θorɪəm] o [,mɛzə'θorɪəm] *s* (chem.) mesotorio
**mesotron** ['mɛsətran] o ['misətran] *s* (phys.) mesotrón
**Mesozoic** [,mɛsə'zo·ɪk] o [,misə'zo·ɪk] *adj & s* (geol.) mesozoico
**mesquite** [mɛs'kit] o ['mɛskit] *s* (bot.) mezquite
**mess** [mɛs] *s* fregado (*enredo*); lío, revoltijo; asco, suciedad; cochinadas; rancho (*comida para muchos; grupo de soldados que comen juntos*); cantidad; plato; bazofia; **to be in a mess** estar aviado; **to get into a mess** hacerse un lío; **to make a mess of** ensuciar; echarlo todo a rodar; *va* ensuciar; desarreglar; echar a perder, estropear; *vn* hacer rancho, comer; **to mess about** o **around** perder el tiempo, ocuparse en fruslerías
**message** ['mɛsɪdʒ] *s* mensaje; recado; buena nueva, palabras inspiradas
**messaline** [,mɛsə'lin] o ['mɛsəlin] *s* tela parecida al raso
**messenger** ['mɛsəndʒər] *s* mensajero; mandadero; precursor, presagio
**mess hall** *s* sala de rancho, salón comedor
**Messiah** [mə'saɪə] *s* (Bib. & fig.) Mesías
**Messiahship** [mə'saɪəʃɪp] *s* mesiazgo
**Messianic** [,mɛsɪ'ænɪk] *adj* mesiánico
**Messianism** [mə'saɪənɪzəm] *s* mesianismo
**mess kit** *s* utensilios de rancho
**messmate** ['mɛs,met] *s* comensal; compañero de rancho
**mess of pottage** *s* plato de lentejas, cosa de poco valor, nada
**Messrs.** ['mɛsərz] *pl de* **Mr.**
**mess table** *s* mesa de rancho
**messuage** ['mɛswɪdʒ] *s* (law) casería (*casa y edificios dependientes*)
**messy** ['mɛsɪ] *adj* (*comp:* **-ier**; *super:* **-iest**) sucio; desarreglado, desaliñado
**mestizo** [mɛs'tizo] *s* (*pl:* **-zos** o **-zoes**) mestizo
**met.** abr. de **metropolitan**
**met** [mɛt] *pret & pp de* **meet**
**metabolic** [,mɛtə'balɪk] *adj* (physiol. & zool.) metabólico
**metabolism** [mə'tæbəlɪzəm] *s* (physiol.) metabolismo
**metabolize** [mə'tæbəlaɪz] *va* transformar por metabolismo; *vn* transformarse por metabolismo
**metacarpal** [,mɛtə'karpəl] *adj & s* (anat.) metacarpiano
**metacarpus** [,mɛtə'karpəs] *s* (*pl:* **-pi** [paɪ]) (anat.) metacarpo
**metacenter** [,mɛtə'sɛntər] *s* metacentro
**metachromatism** [,mɛtə'kromətɪzəm] *s* (physical chem.) metacromatismo
**metachronism** [mɪ'tækrənɪzəm] *s* metacronismo
**metagenesis** [,mɛtə'dʒɛnɪsɪs] *s* (biol.) metagénesis
**metal** ['mɛtəl] *s* metal; vidrio en fusión; (her.) metal; (Brit.) grava (*piedra machacada para caminos*); (fig.) ánimo, brío; *adj* metálico; *va* metalizar
**metalepsis** [,mɛtə'lɛpsɪs] *s* (*pl:* **-ses** [siz]) (rhet.) metalepsis
**metaline** ['mɛtəlɪn] o ['mɛtəlin] *s* metalina (*aleación*)
**metalization** [,mɛtəlɪ'zeʃən] *s* metalización
**metalize** ['mɛtəlaɪz] *va* metalizar
**metallic** [mɪ'tælɪk] *adj* metálico
**metalliferous** [,mɛtə'lɪfərəs] *adj* metalífero
**metalline** ['mɛtəlɪn] o ['mɛtəlaɪn] *adj* metálico; que contiene sales metálicas
**metallographic** [mɪ,tælə'græfɪk] *adj* metalográfico
**metallography** [,mɛtə'lagrəfɪ] *s* metalografía
**metalloid** ['mɛtəlɔɪd] *s* (chem.) metaloide (*elemento no metálico*); (chem.) metaloide muy semejante a los metales (*antimonio, arsénico, bismuto, silicio, telurio, etc.*)
**metallotherapy** [mɪ,tælo'θɛrəpɪ] *s* metaloterapia
**metallurgic** [,mɛtə'lʌrdʒɪk] o **metallurgical** [,mɛtə'lʌrdʒɪkəl] *adj* metalúrgico
**metallurgist** ['mɛtə,lʌrdʒɪst] *s* metalúrgico o metalurgista
**metallurgy** ['mɛtə,lʌrdʒɪ] *s* metalurgia
**metal polish** *s* limpiametales
**metalwork** ['mɛtəl,wʌrk] *s* metalistería; objetos de metalistería
**metalworker** ['mɛtəl,wʌrkər] *s* metalario, metalista
**metalworking** ['mɛtəl,wʌrkɪŋ] *s* metalistería
**metamere** ['mɛtəmɪr] *s* (zool.) metámero

**metameric** [ˌmɛtəˈmɛrɪk] *adj* (chem. & zool.) metámero
**metamorphic** [ˌmɛtəˈmɔrfɪk] *adj* metamórfico
**metamorphism** [ˌmɛtəˈmɔrfɪzəm] *s* metamorfismo
**metamorphose** [ˌmɛtəˈmɔrfoz] o [ˌmɛtəˈmɔrfos] *va* metamorfosear; *vn* metamorfosearse
**metamorphosis** [ˌmɛtəˈmɔrfəsɪs] *s* (*pl:* **-ses** [siz]) metamorfosis
**metaphase** [ˈmɛtəfez] *s* (biol.) metafase
**metaphony** [mɪˈtæfənɪ] *s* (phonet.) metafonía
**metaphor** [ˈmɛtəfər] o [ˈmɛtəfɔr] *s* metáfora; **to mix metaphors** mezclar las metáforas
**metaphorical** [ˌmɛtəˈfɑrɪkəl] o [ˌmɛtəˈfɔrɪkəl] *adj* metafórico
**metaphrase** [ˈmɛtəfrez] *s* metafrasis
**metaphysical** [ˌmɛtəˈfɪzɪkəl] *adj* metafísico
**metaphysician** [ˌmɛtəfɪˈzɪʃən] *s* metafísico
**metaphysics** [ˌmɛtəˈfɪzɪks] *ssg* metafísica
**metaplasm** [ˈmɛtəplæzəm] *s* (biol.) metaplasma; (gram.) metaplasmo
**metaprotein** [ˌmɛtəˈprotiɪn] o [ˌmɛtəˈprotin] *s* (biochem.) metaproteína
**metasomatism** [ˌmɛtəˈsomətɪzəm] *s* (geol.) metasomatismo
**metastasis** [mɪˈtæstəsɪs] *s* (*pl:* **-ses** [siz]) (path.) metástasis
**metatarsal** [ˌmɛtəˈtɑrsəl] *adj & s* (anat.) metatarsiano
**metatarsus** [ˌmɛtəˈtɑrsəs] *s* (*pl:* **-si** [saɪ]) (anat. & zool.) metatarso
**metathesis** [mɪˈtæθɪsɪs] *s* (*pl:* **-ses** [siz]) (philol.) metátesis
**metathorax** [ˌmɛtəˈθoræks] *s* (*pl:* **-raxes** o **-races** [rəsiz]) (zool.) metatórax
**metazoan** [ˌmɛtəˈzoən] *s* (zool.) metazoo
**mete** [mit] *s* confín, límite; mojón; *va* repartir; (poet.) medir
**metempsychosis** [mɪˌtɛmpsɪˈkosɪs] *s* (*pl:* **-ses** [siz]) metempsicosis
**metencephalon** [ˌmɛtɛnˈsɛfəlɑn] *s* (*pl:* **-la** [lə]) (anat.) metencéfalo
**meteor** [ˈmitɪər] *s* estrella fugaz, bólido, meteorito; meteoro (*fenómeno atmosférico*)
**meteoric** [ˌmitɪˈɑrɪk] o [ˌmitɪˈɔrɪk] *adj* meteórico; (fig.) meteórico
**meteoric stone** *s* piedra meteórica
**meteorite** [ˈmitɪəraɪt] *s* meteorito
**meteorologic** [ˌmitɪərəˈlɑdʒɪk] o **meteorological** [ˌmitɪərəˈlɑdʒɪkəl] *adj* meteorológico
**meteorologist** [ˌmitɪəˈrɑlədʒɪst] *s* meteorologista
**meteorology** [ˌmitɪəˈrɑlədʒɪ] *s* meteorología
**meter** [ˈmitər] *s* metro (*unidad; verso*); (mus.) compás, tiempo; (mach.) contador, medidor; *va* medir (*con contador o medidor*)
**metering** [ˈmitərɪŋ] *s* medición
**meter reader** *s* lector (*del contador*)
**Meth.** abr. de **Methodist**
**methacrylate** [mɪˈθækrɪlet] *s* (chem.) metacrilato
**methacrylic** [ˌmɛθəˈkrɪlɪk] *adj* metacrílico
**methacrylic acid** *s* (chem.) ácido metacrílico
**methane** [ˈmɛθen] *s* (chem.) metano
**methanol** [ˈmɛθənol] o [ˈmɛθənɑl] *s* (chem.) metanol
**metheglin** [məˈθɛglɪn] *s* aloja
**methinks** [mɪˈθɪŋks] (*pret:* **methought**) *vn* (archaic) me parece
**methionine** [mɪˈθaɪənin] o [mɪˈθaɪənɪn] *s* (biochem.) metionina
**method** [ˈmɛθəd] *s* método; **there's method in his madness** es más cuerdo de lo que parece
**methodic** [mɪˈθɑdɪk] o **methodical** [mɪˈθɑdɪkəl] *adj* metódico
**Methodism** [ˈmɛθədɪzəm] *s* metodismo
**Methodist** [ˈmɛθədɪst] *adj & s* metodista
**methodize** [ˈmɛθədaɪz] *va* metodizar
**methodology** [ˌmɛθəˈdɑlədʒɪ] *s* (*pl:* **-gies**) metodología
**methought** [mɪˈθɔt] *pret de* **methinks**
**Methuselah** [mɪˈθuzələ] o [mɪˈθjuzələ] *s* (Bib. & fig.) Matusalén; **to be as old as Methuselah** vivir más años que Matusalén
**methyl** [ˈmɛθɪl] *s* (chem.) metilo
**methyl alcohol** *s* alcohol metílico
**methylamine** [ˌmɛθɪləˈmin] o [ˌmɛθɪˈlæmɪn] *s* (chem.) metilamina
**methylate** [ˈmɛθɪlet] *s* (chem.) metilato; *va* combinar con metilo o con alcohol metílico
**methylene** [ˈmɛθɪlin] *s* (chem.) metileno
**methylene blue** *s* azul de metileno
**methylic** [mɪˈθɪlɪk] *adj* (chem.) metílico
**methyl orange** *s* anaranjado de metilo
**methyl violet** *s* violeta de metilo
**meticulous** [mɪˈtɪkjələs] *adj* minucioso, meticuloso
**métier** [meˈtje] *s* oficio, profesión; fuerte (*aptitud especial de una persona*)
**metol** [ˈmitol] o [ˈmitɑl] *s* (chem.) metol
**Metonic cycle** [mɪˈtɑnɪk] *s* (astr.) ciclo de Metón
**metonym** [ˈmɛtənɪm] *s* (rhet.) palabra o expresión metonímicas
**metonymic** [ˌmɛtəˈnɪmɪk] o **metonymical** [ˌmɛtəˈnɪmɪkəl] *adj* metonímico
**metonymy** [mɪˈtɑnɪmɪ] *s* (rhet.) metonimia
**me-tooer** [ˈmiˈtuər] *s* (slang) persona que sigue al que triunfa o se pone de su parte; (slang) exitista (Am.)
**metope** [ˈmɛtəpɪ] o [ˈmɛtop] *s* (arch.) métopa
**metre** [ˈmitər] *s* metro (*unidad; verso*); (mus.) compás, tiempo
**metric** [ˈmɛtrɪk] *adj* métrico; **metrics** *spl* métrica
**metrical** [ˈmɛtrɪkəl] *adj* métrico
**metrically** [ˈmɛtrɪkəlɪ] *adv* métricamente
**metric horsepower** *s* (mech.) caballo de fuerza, caballo de vapor (*736 vatios*)
**metric system** *s* sistema métrico
**metric ton** *s* tonelada métrica (*de peso*)
**metrist** [ˈmitrɪst] o [ˈmɛtrɪst] *s* metrista
**metritis** [mɪˈtraɪtɪs] *s* (path.) metritis
**metrology** [mɪˈtrɑlədʒɪ] *s* metrología
**metronome** [ˈmɛtrənom] *s* (mus..) metrónomo
**metronomic** [ˌmɛtrəˈnɑmɪk] *adj* metronómico
**metropolis** [mɪˈtrɑpəlɪs] *s* metrópoli; (eccl.) metrópoli
**metropolitan** [ˌmɛtrəˈpɑlɪtən] *adj* metropolitano; *s* ciudadano de una gran ciudad; (eccl.) metropolitano
**metrorrhagia** [ˌmitrəˈredʒɪə] o [ˌmɛtrəˈredʒɪə] *s* (path.) metrorragia
**mettle** [ˈmɛtəl] *s* ánimo, brío; **on one's mettle** dispuesto a hacer grandes esfuerzos
**mettlesome** [ˈmɛtəlsəm] *adj* animoso, brioso
**Meuse** [mjuz] *s* Mosa
**mew** [mju] *s* jaula; halconera; maullido; (orn.) gaviota; **mews** *spl* caballeriza construída alrededor de un corral; *va* enjaular; encerrar; esconder; **to mew up** tener escondido; *vn* maullar
**mewl** [mjul] *vn* lloriquear
**Mex.** abr. de **Mexican** y **Mexico**
**Mexican** [ˈmɛksɪkən] *adj & s* mejicano
**Mexican bean beetle** *s* (ent.) tortuguilla de frijol, conchuela
**Mexican poppy** *s* (bot.) argemone mejicana, chicalote
**Mexico** [ˈmɛksɪko] *s* Méjico
**Mexico City** *s* Ciudad de Méjico
**mezereon** [mɪˈzɪrɪɑn] *s* (bot.) lauréola hembra
**mezzanine** [ˈmɛzənin] *s* entresuelo
**mezzo** [ˈmɛtso] o [ˈmɛzo] *adj* (mus.) medio, a media voz, entre fuerte y piano
**mezzo-soprano** [ˈmɛtsosəˈpræno] o [ˈmɛtsosəˈprɑno] *s* (*pl:* **-os**) mezzo-soprano
**mezzotint** [ˈmɛtsotɪnt] o [ˈmɛzotɪnt] *s* grabado al humo o a media tinta; *va* grabar al humo o a media tinta
**mfg.** abr. de **manufacturing**
**mfr.** abr. de **manufacturer**
**mg.** abr. de **milligram** o **milligrams**
**Mgr.** abr. de **Manager, Monseigneur** y **Monsignor**
**mho** [mo] *s* (elec.) mho
**mi.** abr. de **mile** o **miles**
**mi** [mi] *s* (mus.) mi
**miaow** o **miaou** [mɪˈaʊ] *s & vn* var. de **meow**
**miasma** [maɪˈæzmə] o [mɪˈæzmə] *s* (*pl:* **-mas** o **-mata** [mətə]) miasma
**miasmal** [maɪˈæzməl] o [mɪˈæzməl] o **miasmatic** [ˌmaɪæzˈmætɪk] *adj* miasmático
**mica** [ˈmaɪkə] *s* (mineral.) mica
**micaceous** [maɪˈkeʃəs] *adj* micáceo
**Micah** [ˈmaɪkə] *s* (Bib.) Miqueas
**mica schist** *s* micacita, micasquisto
**mice** [maɪs] *pl de* **mouse**

**micellar** [mɪˈsɛlər] *adj* micelar

**micelle** [mɪˈsɛl] *s* (biol. & chem.) micela

**Mich.** abr. de **Michaelmas** y **Michigan**

**Michael** [ˈmaɪkəl] *s* Miguel

**Michaelmas** [ˈmɪkəlməs] *s* fiesta de San Miguel

**Michaelmastide** [ˈmɪkəlməsˌtaɪd] *s* sanmiguelada

**Michelangelo** [ˌmaɪkəlˈændʒəlo] *s* Miguel Ángel

**Michigan** [ˈmɪʃɪgən] *s* Michigán

**Mickey Mouse** [ˈmɪkɪ] *s* el ratón Miguelito

**mickle** [ˈmɪkəl] *adj & adv* (Scotch) mucho

**microanalysis** [ˌmaɪkroəˈnælɪsɪs] *s* (*pl:* **-ses** [siz]) (chem.) microanálisis

**microbarograph** [ˌmaɪkroˈbærəgræf] o [ˌmaɪkroˈbærəgrɑf] *s* microbarógrafo

**microbe** [ˈmaɪkrob] *s* microbio

**microbial** [maɪˈkrobɪəl] *adj* microbiano

**microbic** [maɪˈkrobɪk] *adj* micróbico

**microbiological** [ˌmaɪkroˌbaɪəˈlɑdʒɪkəl] *adj* microbiológico

**microbiologist** [ˌmaɪkrobaɪˈɑlədʒɪst] *s* microbiólogo

**microbiology** [ˌmaɪkrobaɪˈɑlədʒɪ] *s* microbiología

**microcard** [ˈmaɪkrəkɑrd] *s* microficha

**microcephalic** [ˌmaɪkrosɪˈfælɪk] *adj* (anthrop. & path.) microcéfalo

**microchemistry** [ˌmaɪkroˈkɛmɪstrɪ] *s* microquímica

**microcline** [ˈmaɪkrəklaɪn] *s* (mineral.) microclina

**micrococcus** [ˌmaɪkrəˈkɑkəs] *s* (*pl:* **-cocci** [ˈkɑksaɪ]) (bact.) micrococo

**microcopy** [ˈmaɪkrəˌkɑpɪ] *s* (*pl:* **-ies**) microcopia

**microcosm** [ˈmaɪkrokɑzəm] *s* microcosmo

**microcyte** [ˈmaɪkrəsaɪt] *s* (path.) microcito

**microdissection** [ˌmaɪkrodɪˈsɛkʃən] *s* microdisección

**microdont** [ˈmaɪkrodɑnt] *adj & s* microdonte

**microfarad** [ˌmaɪkroˈfæræd] *s* (elec.) microfaradio

**microfilm** [ˈmaɪkrəfɪlm] *s* microfilm, micropelícula; *va* microfilmar

**microgamete** [ˌmaɪkrogəˈmit] *s* (biol.) microgameto

**microgram** [ˈmaɪkrogræm] *s* microgramo

**micrography** [maɪˈkrɑgrəfɪ] *s* micrografía

**microgroove** [ˈmaɪkrəgruv] *s* microsurco; (trademark) disco microsurco

**microinch** [ˈmaɪkroˌɪntʃ] *s* micropulgada

**micrometer** [maɪˈkrɑmɪtər] *s* micrómetro

**micrometer caliper** *s* pálmer, calibre micrométrico

**micrometer screw** *s* tornillo micrométrico

**micrometric** [ˌmaɪkroˈmɛtrɪk] o **micrometrical** [ˌmaɪkroˈmɛtrɪkəl] *adj* micrométrico

**micrometry** [maɪˈkrɑmɪtrɪ] *s* micrometría

**micromillimeter** [ˌmaɪkroˈmɪlɪˌmitər] *s* micromilímetro

**micromotion** [ˈmaɪkroˌmoʃən] *s* micromovimiento

**micron** [ˈmaɪkrɑn] *s* (*pl:* **-crons** o **-cra** [krə]) micra o micrón

**Micronesia** [ˌmaɪkroˈniʃə] o [ˌmaɪkroˈniʒə] *s* la Micronesia

**Micronesian** [ˌmaɪkroˈniʃən] o [ˌmaɪkroˈniʒən] *adj & s* micronesio

**microörganism** [ˌmaɪkroˈɔrgənɪzəm] *s* (bact.) microorganismo

**microphone** [ˈmaɪkrəfon] *s* micrófono

**microphotograph** [ˌmaɪkroˈfotəgræf] o [ˌmaɪkroˈfotəgrɑf] *s* microfotografía

**microphotography** [ˌmaɪkrofəˈtɑgrəfɪ] *s* microfotografía

**microphysics** [ˌmaɪkroˈfɪzɪks] *ssg* microfísica

**microphyte** [ˈmaɪkrəfaɪt] *s* (bot.) micrófito

**micropyle** [ˈmaɪkrəpaɪl] *s* (bot. & zool.) micrópilo

**microscope** [ˈmaɪkrəskop] *s* microscopio

**microscopic** [ˌmaɪkrəˈskɑpɪk] o **microscopical** [ˌmaɪkrəˈskɑpɪkəl] *adj* microscópico

**microscopically** [ˌmaɪkrəˈskɑpɪkəlɪ] *adv* microscópicamente

**microscopist** [maɪˈkrɑskəpɪst] o [ˈmaɪkrəˌskopɪst] *s* microscopista

**microscopy** [maɪˈkrɑskəpɪ] o [ˈmaɪkrəˌskopɪ] *s* microscopia

**microseism** [ˈmaɪkrosaɪzəm] *s* microsismo

**microsome** [ˈmaɪkrəsom] *s* (biol.) microsoma

**microsporangium** [ˌmaɪkrospoˈrændʒɪəm] *s* (*pl:* **-a** [ə]) (bot.) microsporangio

**microspore** [ˈmaɪkrəspor] *s* (bot.) microspora

**microsporous** [ˌmaɪkrəˈsporəs] *adj* microsporo

**microtome** [ˈmaɪkrətom] *s* micrótomo

**microwave** [ˈmaɪkroˌwev] *s* (phys.) microonda

**micturition** [ˌmɪktʃəˈrɪʃən] *s* micción, micturición

**mid** [mɪd] *adj* medio, p.ej., **in mid afternoon** a media tarde

**mid** o **'mid** [mɪd] *prep* (poet.) entre, en medio de

**Midas** [ˈmaɪdəs] *s* (myth.) Midas

**midbrain** [ˈmɪdˌbren] *s* (anat.) mesencéfalo

**midchannel** [ˌmɪdˈtʃænəl] *s* medio del canal, río o pasadizo marítimo

**midcontinent** [ˌmɪdˈkɑntɪnənt] *s* centro del continente

**midday** [ˈmɪdˌde] *s* mediodía; *adj* de mediodía

**middle** [ˈmɪdəl] *s* centro, medio; cintura (*del hombre*); **middles** *spl* (agr.) caballones, lomos; **about the middle of** a mediados de; **in the middle of** en medio de; a medio, p.ej., **in the middle of the afternoon** a media tarde; **from the middle of** desde en medio de; *adj* medio; intermedio; de en medio, p.ej., **the middle room** el cuarto de en medio

**middle age** *s* mediana edad; **Middle Ages** *spl* Edad Media

**middle-aged** [ˈmɪdəlˌedʒd] *adj* de mediana edad

**Middle America** *s* Méjico y la América Central, la parte central de las Américas

**middle class** *s* clase media, burguesía

**middle-class** [ˈmɪdəlˌklæs] o [ˈmɪdəlˌklɑs] *adj* aburguesado, de la clase media

**middle distance** *s* (paint.) segundo término

**middle ear** *s* (anat.) oído medio

**Middle East** *s* Oriente Medio

**Middle Eastern** *adj* medio-oriental

**Middle English** *s* el inglés medio

**middle finger** *s* dedo cordial, dedo de en medio, dedo del corazón

**Middle High German** *s* el medio altoalemán

**middleman** [ˈmɪdəlˌmæn] *s* (*pl:* **-men**) (com.) intermediario

**middlemost** [ˈmɪdəlmost] *adj* más céntrico, más cercano al centro

**middle passage** *s* travesía que hacían los traficantes en negros de África a las Antillas

**middle term** *s* (log.) término medio

**middle voice** *s* (gram.) voz media

**middleweight** [ˈmɪdəlˌwet] *s* persona de peso medio; (box.) peso mediano o medio

**Middle West** *s* mediooeste, llanura central (*de los EE.UU.*)

**middling** [ˈmɪdlɪŋ] *adj* mediano, regular; *adv* (coll.) medianamente; **fairly middling** (coll.) así, así; **middlings** *spl* acemite; productos de tamaño regular, o de calidad o precio intermedios; clase de algodón que sirve de base a las cotizaciones

**middy** [ˈmɪdɪ] *s* (*pl:* **-dies**) (coll.) aspirante de marina; marinera (*blusa de niño*)

**middy blouse** *s* marinera (*blusa de niño*)

**midge** [mɪdʒ] *s* (ent.) mosca pequeñita, díptero; enano

**midget** [ˈmɪdʒɪt] *s* enano

**Midianite** [ˈmɪdɪənaɪt] *s* (Bib.) madianita

**midiron** [ˈmɪdˌaɪərn] *s* (golf) mazo de hierro que se emplea cuando hay que dar a la bola un salto bastante grande

**midland** [ˈmɪdlənd] *s* interior, región central (*de un país*); *adj* del interior, de tierra adentro

**midleg** [ˈmɪdˌlɛg] *s* media pierna; (ent.) pata intermedia, pata del mesotórax; *adv* hasta la media pierna

**midmost** [ˈmɪdmost] *adj* var. de **middlemost**

**midnight** [ˈmɪdˌnaɪt] *s* medianoche; *adj* de medianoche; **to burn the midnight oil** quemarse las cejas

**midnight sun** *s* sol de medianoche

**midrange** [ˈmɪdˌrendʒ] *s* medio alcance; **gama intermedia** (*de los sonidos audibles*)

**midrib** [ˈmɪdˌrɪb] *s* (bot.) nervio medial o principal

**midriff** ['mɪdrɪf] *s* (anat.) diafragma; traje que deja descubierta parte del diafragma
**midship** ['mɪd,ʃɪp] *adj* del o en el medio del buque; **midships** *adv* en medio del buque
**midship frame** *s* (naut.) cuaderna maestra
**midshipman** ['mɪd,ʃɪpmən] *s* (*pl:* **-men**) aspirante de marina, cadete de la escuela naval; guardia marina (*en un buque naval*); (archaic) mandadero de a bordo
**midshipmite** ['mɪd,ʃɪpmaɪt] *s* (hum.) guardia marina de estatura pequeña
**midst** [mɪdst] *s* centro, medio; **in the midst of** entre, en medio de; en lo más recio de
**midst** o **'midst** [mɪdst] *prep* (poet.) var. de **amidst**
**midstream** ['mɪd,strim] *s* medio de una corriente o río; **in midstream** en pleno río
**midsummer** ['mɪd,sʌmər] *s* pleno verano; (Brit.) fines de junio, solsticio de verano; *adj* en pleno verano
**mid-Victorian** ['mɪdvɪk'torɪən] *adj* chapado a la antigua; austero, rígido; *s* contemporáneo de la reina Victoria en la época media de su reinado
**midway** ['mɪd,we] *s* mitad del camino; avenida central (*p.ej., de una exposición*); *adj* situado a mitad del camino; *adv* a mitad del camino
**midweek** ['mɪd,wik] *s* mediados de la semana; (*cap.*) *s* (Quaker) miércoles
**Midwest** ['mɪd'wɛst] *s* mediooeste, llanura central (*de los EE.UU.*)
**Midwestern** [,mɪd'wɛstərn] *adj* del mediooeste (*de los EE.UU.*)
**Midwesterner** [,mɪd'wɛstərnər] *s* habitante del mediooeste (*de los EE.UU.*)
**midwife** ['mɪd,waɪf] *s* (*pl:* **-wives**) comadrona, partera
**midwifery** ['mɪd,waɪfrɪ] *s* partería
**midwinter** ['mɪd,wɪntər] *s* pleno invierno; (Brit.) fines de diciembre, solsticio de invierno; *adj* en pleno invierno
**midyear** ['mɪd,jɪr] *adj* de mediados del año; *s* (coll.) examen de mediados del año, examen de entre semestres
**mien** [min] *s* porte, aspecto, semblante, talante
**miff** [mɪf] *s* (coll.) desavenencia, disgusto; *va* disgustar, ofender; *vn* amoscarse
**might** [maɪt] *s* fuerza, poderío; **with might and main** con todas sus fuerzas, a más no poder; *v aux* podría, ser posible, p.ej., **he might come this evening** es posible que venga esta tarde
**mightily** ['maɪtɪlɪ] *adv* poderosamente; (coll.) muchísimo
**mightiness** ['maɪtɪnɪs] *s* fuerza, poderío; grandeza
**mightn't** ['maɪtənt] contracción de **might not**
**mighty** ['maɪtɪ] *adj* (*comp:* **-ier;** *super:* **-iest**) fuerte, potente, poderoso; grandísimo; *adv* (coll.) muy, p.ej., **it's mighty hard** es muy difícil; (coll.) mucho, p.ej., **it's mighty hot** hace mucho calor
**mignon** ['mɪnjɑn] *adj* lindo, primoroso
**mignonette** [,mɪnjə'nɛt] *s* (bot.) reseda, miñoneta
**migraine** ['maɪgren] o [mɪ'gren] *s* (path.) migraña, hemicránea
**migrant** ['maɪgrənt] *adj* migratorio; *s* peregrino, nómada; planta o animal migratorios
**migrate** ['maɪgret] *vn* emigrar
**migration** [maɪ'greʃən] *s* migración
**migratory** ['maɪgrə,torɪ] *adj* migratorio
**mihrab** ['mirəb] *s* mihrab
**mikado** [mɪ'kɑdo] *s* (*pl:* **-dos**) micado
**mike** [maɪk] *s* (slang) micrófono; (*cap.*) *s* Miguelito
**mil.** abr. de **military** y **militia**
**mil** [mɪl] *s* milipulgada
**milady** o **miladi** [mɪ'ledɪ] *s* (*pl:* **-dies**) miladi
**Milan** [mɪ'læn] o ['mɪlən] *s* Milán
**Milanese** [,mɪlə'niz] *adj* milanés; *s* (*pl:* **-nese**) milanés
**milch** [mɪlk] *adj* lechero
**milch cow** *s* vaca lechera, vaca de leche
**mild** [maɪld] *adj* suave, manso; dulce; templado; leve, ligero
**mildew** ['mɪldju] o ['mɪldu] *s* (agr.) mildiú; enmohecimiento, moho; *va* enmohecer; *vn* enmohecerse
**mildly** ['maɪldlɪ] *adv* suavemente, mansamente; dulcemente; algo, un poco
**mildness** ['maɪldnɪs] *s* suavidad, mansedumbre; dulzura; templanza (*del clima*)
**mile** [maɪl] *s* milla inglesa
**mileage** ['maɪlɪdʒ] *s* número de millas, recorrido en millas; gastos de viaje (*que se pagan a tanto por milla*)
**mileage ticket** *s* billete kilométrico
**milepost** ['maɪl,post] *s* poste miliar
**Milesian** [maɪ'liʃən] o [maɪ'liʒən] *adj & s* milesio
**Milesian tales** *spl* fábulas milesias
**milestone** ['maɪl,ston] *s* piedra miliaria; (fig.) piedra miliar; **to be a milestone** hacer época
**Miletus** [maɪ'litəs] *s* Mileto
**milfoil** ['mɪlfɔɪl] *s* (bot.) milefolio
**miliary** ['mɪlɪ,ɛrɪ] o ['mɪljərɪ] *adj* miliar; (path.) miliar
**milieu** [mi'ljø] *s* medio, ambiente
**militancy** ['mɪlɪtənsɪ] *s* belicosidad; actitud o política belicosas
**militant** ['mɪlɪtənt] *adj* militante, aguerrido, belicoso; *s* militante, partidario aguerrido
**militarism** ['mɪlɪtərɪzəm] *s* militarismo
**militarist** ['mɪlɪtərɪst] *adj* militarista; *s* militarista; estratégico
**militarization** [,mɪlɪtərɪ'zeʃən] *s* militarización
**militarize** ['mɪlɪtəraɪz] *va* militarizar
**military** ['mɪlɪ,tɛrɪ] *adj* militar; *s* (los) militares
**Military Academy** *s* (U.S.A.) Academia General Militar
**military police** *s* policía militar
**military service** *s* servicio militar
**militate** ['mɪlɪtet] *vn* militar; **to militate against** militar contra
**militia** [mɪ'lɪʃə] *s* milicia
**militiaman** [mɪ'lɪʃəmən] *s* (*pl:* **-men**) miliciano
**milk** [mɪlk] *s* leche; **to cry over spilt milk** lamentar lo irremediable; *va* ordeñar; extraer; chupar; *vn* dar leche
**milk-and-water** ['mɪlkənd'wɔtər] o ['mɪlkənd'wɑtər] *adj* débil, sin carácter
**milk can** *s* lechera (*vasija*)
**milk crust** *s* (path.) lactumen
**milk diet** *s* régimen lácteo
**milker** ['mɪlkər] *s* ordeñador; ordeñadora, máquina de ordeñar; vaca, cabra, etc. lecheras
**milk fever** *s* (path.) fiebre láctea
**milking** ['mɪlkɪŋ] *s* ordeño
**milking machine** *s* ordeñadora
**milk leg** *s* (path.) flebitis de las venas de la pierna
**milkmaid** ['mɪlk,med] *s* lechera
**milkman** ['mɪlk,mæn] *s* (*pl:* **-men**) lechero
**milk of human kindness** *s* compasión, humanidad
**milk of lime** *s* lechada de cal
**milk of magnesia** *s* (pharm.) leche de magnesia
**milk pail** *s* ordeñadero
**milk powder** *s* leche en polvo
**milk shake** *s* batido de leche
**milk snake** *s* (zool.) culebrilla norteamericana (*Lampropeltis triangulum*)
**milksop** ['mɪlk,sɑp] *s* marica, calzonazos
**milk sugar** *s* azúcar de leche
**milk thistle** *s* (bot.) cardo lechero, arzolla
**milk tooth** *s* diente de leche
**milk vetch** *s* (bot.) astrágalo
**milkweed** ['mɪlk,wid] *s* (bot.) algodoncillo
**milk-white** ['mɪlk,hwaɪt] *adj* blanco como la leche
**milkwort** ['mɪlk,wʌrt] *s* (bot.) lechera amarga, polígala
**milky** ['mɪlkɪ] *adj* (*comp:* **-ier;** *super:* **-iest**) lechoso; apocado, tímido, débil
**Milky Way** *s* (astr.) Vía láctea
**mill** [mɪl] *s* molino; fábrica, taller; hilandería (*de tejidos*); ingenio (*de azúcar*); aserradero; (U.S.A.) milésima (*de dólar*); (slang) pendencia a puñetazos; **to go through the mill** (coll.) entrenarse rigurosamente; (coll.) aprender por experiencia; **to put through the mill** (coll.) poner a prueba; (coll.) someter a

un entrenamiento riguroso; *va* moler; machacar, triturar; fabricar; cerrillar o acordonar (*monedas*); fresar; batir (*chocolate*); *vn* hormiguear, arremolinarse (*una muchedumbre*); (slang) luchar a puñetazos; **to mill about** o **around** moverse en círculos

**millclapper** [ˈmɪlˌklæpər] *s* tarabilla, cítola; (dial.) tarabilla, charlador, parlanchín

**milldam** [ˈmɪlˌdæm] *s* presa de molino; represa de molino

**millenarian** [ˌmɪlɪˈnɛrɪən] *adj & s* milenario

**mill end** *s* retazo de hilandería

**millenium** [mɪˈlɛnɪəm] *s* (*pl:* **-ums** o **-a** [ə]) milenario, milenio

**millennial** [mɪˈlɛnɪəl] *adj* milenario

**millepede** [ˈmɪlɪpid] *s* (zool.) milípedo

**millepore** [ˈmɪlɪpor] *s* (zool.) milépora

**miller** [ˈmɪlər] *s* molinero; (ent.) mariposa nocturna de alas empolvadas; (mach.) fresa

**miller's-thumb** [ˈmɪlərzˈθʌm] *s* (ichth.) coto

**millesimal** [mɪˈlɛsɪməl] *adj & s* milésimo

**millet** [ˈmɪlɪt] *s* (bot.) mijo o millo; (bot.) panizo

**mill hand** *s* molinero, obrero de molino; hilandero

**milliammeter** [ˌmɪlɪˈæmˌmitər] *s* (elec.) miliamperímetro

**milliampere** [ˌmɪlɪˈæmpɪr] *s* (elec.) miliamperio

**milliard** [ˈmɪljərd] *s* mil millones

**milliary** [ˈmɪlɪˌɛrɪ] *adj* miliario

**millibar** [ˈmɪlɪbɑr] *s* milibar

**millicurie** [ˌmɪlɪˈkjuri] o [ˌmɪlɪkjuˈri] *s* (phys.) milicurie

**milligram** o **milligramme** [ˈmɪlɪgræm] *s* miligramo

**milliliter** [ˈmɪlɪˌlitər] *s* mililitro

**millimeter** [ˈmɪlɪˌmitər] *s* milímetro

**millimicron** [ˈmɪlɪˌmaɪkrɑn] *s* (*pl:* **-cra** [krə]) milimicrón

**milliner** [ˈmɪlɪnər] *s* modista de sombreros, sombrerero, sombrerera

**millinery** [ˈmɪlɪˌnɛrɪ] o [ˈmɪlɪnərɪ] *s* sombreros de señora; confección de sombreros de señora; venta de sombreros de señora

**millinery shop** *s* sombrerería (*de la modista de sombreros de señora*)

**milling** [ˈmɪlɪŋ] *s* molienda; acordonamiento; cordoncillo; fabricación; fresado

**milling machine** *s* fresadora

**million** [ˈmɪljən] *s* millón; *adj* millón de, millones de, p.ej., **two million inhabitants** dos millones de habitantes

**millionaire** [ˌmɪljənˈɛr] *adj & s* millonario

**millionfold** [ˈmɪljənˌfold] *adj* multiplicado por un millón; *adv* millón de veces

**millionth** [ˈmɪljənθ] *adj & s* millonésimo

**millipede** [ˈmɪlɪpid] *s* var. de **millepede**

**millivolt** [ˈmɪlɪˌvolt] *s* (elec.) milivoltio

**millpond** [ˈmɪlˌpɑnd] *s* represa de molino

**millrace** [ˈmɪlˌres] *s* caz; corriente del caz

**millstone** [ˈmɪlˌston] *s* muela de molino; (fig.) peso agobiador, carga agobiadora

**mill wheel** *s* rueda de molino

**millwork** [ˈmɪlˌwʌrk] *s* carpintería mecánica, materiales prefabricados de construcción; trabajo de taller, de fábrica o de molino

**millwright** [ˈmɪlˌraɪt] *s* montador de ejes, poleas, transmisiones, etc.; fabricante de molinos

**milord** [mɪˈlɔrd] *s* milord

**milt** [mɪlt] *s* (ichth.) lecha (*licor seminal y bolsa que lo contiene*); (anat.) bazo

**Miltiades** [mɪlˈtaɪədiz] *s* Milcíades

**Miltonian** [mɪlˈtonɪən] o **Miltonic** [mɪlˈtɑnɪk] *adj* miltoniano

**mimbar** [ˈmɪmbɑr] *s* almimbar (*púlpito en la mezquita*)

**mime** [maɪm] *s* mimo; *va* remedar; *vn* actuar de mimo, hacer el bufón

**mimeograph** [ˈmɪmɪəˌgræf] o [ˈmɪmɪəˌgrɑf] *s* (trademark) ciclostilo, mimeógrafo; *va* mimeografiar

**mimesis** [mɪˈmisɪs] o [maɪˈmisɪs] *s* (rhet., biol. & path.) mímesis

**mimetic** [mɪˈmɛtɪk] o [maɪˈmɛtɪk] *adj* imitativo; fingido; (biol. & mineral.) mimético

**mimic** [ˈmɪmɪk] *adj* mímico; fingido; *s* remedador; (*pret & pp:* **-icked;** *ger:* **-icking**) *va* imitar; remedar (*especialmente por burla*)

**mimicry** [ˈmɪmɪkrɪ] *s* (*pl:* **-ries**) mímica, remedo; (biol.) mimicria

**mimosaceous** [ˌmɪməˈseʃəs] o [ˌmaɪməˈseʃəs] *adj* (bot.) mimosáceo

**min.** abr. de **minimum** y **minute** o **minutes**

**minacious** [mɪˈneʃəs] *adj* amenazador

**minaret** [ˌmɪnəˈrɛt] o [ˈmɪnərɛt] *s* alminar, minarete

**minatory** [ˈmɪnəˌtorɪ] *adj* amenazador

**mince** [mɪns] *s* picadillo; *va* desmenuzar; picar (*carne*); andar con rodeos al hablar de; hacer remilgadamente; decir remilgadamente; **not to mince matters** hablar con toda franqueza, no tener pelos en la lengua; *vn* andar remilgadamente; hablar remilgadamente

**mincemeat** [ˈmɪnsˌmit] *s* cuajado (*carne picada con frutas*); **to make mincemeat of** hacer pedazos

**mince pie** *s* pastel de carne picada con frutas

**mincing** [ˈmɪnsɪŋ] *adj* remilgado; andando remilgadamente

**mind** [maɪnd] *s* mente, espíritu; juicio; ánimo; parecer; persona de gran entendimiento; **to bear in mind** tener presente; **to be in one's right mind** estar en sus cabales, estar en su juicio; **to be of one mind** estar de acuerdo (*dos o más personas*); **to be on one's mind** preocuparle a uno; **to be out of one's mind** estar fuera de juicio; **to bring** o **to call to mind** traer a las mientes; **to change one's mind** cambiar o mudar de opinión o de parecer; **to come to mind** venir a las mientes; **to go out of one's mind** volverse loco; **to have a mind to** + *inf* estar en ánimo de + *inf*, estar por + *inf;* **to have half a mind to** + *inf* inclinarse a + *inf;* **to have in mind** tener en mente, tener pensado; acordarse de; pensar en; **to have in mind to** + *inf* pensar en + *inf;* **to have on one's mind** preocuparse con; **to keep in mind** tener presente; **to know one's mind** saber lo que uno quiere; **to lose one's mind** perder el juicio; **to make up one's mind** resolverse; **to my mind** en mi opinión, a mi parecer; **to pass out of mind** caer en el olvido; **to put in mind** recordar; **to read minds** leer mentes, adivinar el pensamiento ajeno; **to say whatever comes into one's mind** decir lo que se le viene a la boca; **to set one's mind on** desear con vehemencia; **to set one's mind on** + *ger* resolverse a + *inf;* **to slip one's mind** escaparse de la memoria; **to speak one's mind** decir su parecer, hablar en plata, hablar con franqueza; **with one mind** unánimemente ‖ *va* acordarse de; tener en cuenta; fijarse en; meterse en; obedecer, guiarse por; cuidar, estar al cuidado de (*p.ej., un niño*); sentir molestia por; **do you mind the smoke?** ¿le molesta el humo?; **mind your own business** no se meta Vd. en lo que no le toca ‖ *vn* tener cuidado; fijarse; tener inconveniente; **never mind** no se moleste Vd., no importa; **now mind** fíjese Vd.

**minded** [ˈmaɪndɪd] *adj* inclinado, dispuesto

**mindful** [ˈmaɪndfəl] *adj* atento, cuidadoso; **mindful of** atento a, cuidadoso de

**mindless** [ˈmaɪndlɪs] *adj* estúpido, sin inteligencia; poco atento

**mind reader** *s* adivinador del pensamiento ajeno

**mind reading** *s* adivinación del pensamiento

**mind's eye** *s* imaginación

**mine** [maɪn] *adj poss* (archaic) mi; *pron poss* mío; el mío; **a friend of mine** un amigo mío; *s* mina; (mil., nav. & fig.) mina; **to work a mine** beneficiar una mina; *va* minar; extraer (*carbón, mineral, etc.*); beneficiar (*un terreno*); (mil., nav. & fig.) minar; *vn* minar; abrir minas; dedicarse a la minería

**mine detector** *s* detector de minas

**mine field** *s* (mil. & nav.) campo de minas

**mine layer** *s* (nav.) buque portaminas, minador

**miner** [ˈmaɪnər] *s* minero; (mil.) minador

**mineral** [ˈmɪnərəl] *adj & s* mineral

**mineral green** *s* verdemontaña (*mineral y color*)

**mineralization** [ˌmɪnərəlɪˈzeʃən] *s* mineralización

**mineralize** [ˈmɪnərəlaɪz] *va* mineralizar; *vn* buscar minerales

**mineral jelly** *s* jalea mineral (*petrolato crudo*)

**mineral kingdom** *s* reino mineral
**mineralogical** [ˌmɪnərəˈlɑdʒɪkəl] *adj* mineralógico
**mineralogically** [ˌmɪnərəˈlɑdʒɪkəlɪ] *adv* mineralógicamente
**mineralogist** [ˌmɪnəˈrælədʒɪst] *s* mineralogista
**mineralogy** [ˌmɪnəˈrælədʒɪ] *s* mineralogía
**mineral oil** *s* aceite mineral
**mineral pitch** *s* brea mineral (*asfalto*)
**mineral right** *s* (law) derecho al subsuelo, derecho para explotar yacimientos minerales
**mineral water** *s* agua mineral, agua mineromedicinal
**mineral wool** *s* lana de escoria, lana mineral
**Minerva** [mɪˈnʌrvə] *s* (myth.) Minerva
**minestrone** [ˌmɪnɛˈstrone] *s* sopa de legumbres y fideos
**mine sweeper** *s* (nav.) dragaminas, barreminas
**mine thrower** *s* (mil.) lanzaminas
**mingle** [ˈmɪŋgəl] *va* mezclar, confundir; *vn* mezclarse, confundirse; asociarse
**miniature** [ˈmɪnɪətʃər] o [ˈmɪnɪtʃər] *s* miniatura; modelo pequeño; **in miniature** en miniatura; *adj* miniatura; miniaturesco, diminuto
**miniaturist** [ˈmɪnɪətʃərɪst] o [ˈmɪnɪtʃərɪst] miniaturista
**miniaturization** [ˌmɪnɪətʃərɪˈzeʃən] o [ˌmɪnɪtʃərɪˈzeʃən] *s* miniaturización
**miniaturize** [ˈmɪnɪətʃəraiz] o [ˈmɪnɪtʃəraɪz] *va* miniaturizar
**Minié ball** [ˈmɪnɪe] o [ˈmɪnɪ] *s* bala Minié
**minim** [ˈmɪnɪm] *s* cantidad muy pequeña; mínima; (mus.) mínima; (pharm.) minim
**minimal** [ˈmɪnɪməl] *adj* mínimo
**minimization** [ˌmɪnɪmɪˈzeʃən] *s* reducción al mínimo; paliación; minimización, empequeñecimiento, menosprecio
**minimize** [ˈmɪnɪmaɪz] *va* reducir al mínimo; paliar; minimizar, empequeñecer, menospreciar
**minimum** [ˈmɪnɪməm] *adj* mínimo; *s* (*pl:* **-mums** o **-ma** [mə]) mínimo o mínimum
**minimum wage** *s* jornal mínimo
**mining** [ˈmaɪnɪŋ] *adj* minero; *s* mineraje, minería; (nav.) minado (*p.ej., de un puerto*)
**mining engineer** *s* ingeniero de minas
**minion** [ˈmɪnjən] *s* paniaguado; privado, valido; (print.) miñona; *adj* lindo, primoroso
**minion of the law** *s* esbirro, polizonte
**minister** [ˈmɪnɪstər] *s* ministro; (pol., dipl. & eccl.) ministro; *va & vn* ministrar
**Minister of Foreign Affairs** *s* (Brit.) ministro de Asuntos Exteriores
**minister of the Gospel** *s* ministro del santo Evangelio (*pastor protestante*)
**ministerial** [ˌmɪnɪsˈtɪrɪəl] *adj* ministerial; administrativo; ministrante
**minister plenipotentiary** *s* (*pl:* **ministers plenipotentiary**) ministro plenipotenciario
**minister without portfolio** *s* ministro sin cartera
**ministral** [ˈmɪnɪstrəl] *adj* ministerial
**ministrant** [ˈmɪnɪstrənt] *adj & s* ministrador, ministrante
**ministration** [ˌmɪnɪˈstreʃən] *s* ayuda, solicitud, suministración; (eccl.) ministerio
**ministry** [ˈmɪnɪstrɪ] *s* (*pl:* **-tries**) ministerio
**minitrack** [ˈmɪnɪˌtræk] *s* sistema electrónico para el rastreo de los satélites terrestres mediante radioondas captadas por una cadena mundial de radiorreceptoras
**minium** [ˈmɪnɪəm] *s* (chem.) minio
**miniver** [ˈmɪnɪvər] *s* piel de forro blanca o blanca con motas negras; (zool.) gris, ardilla de Siberia; (zool.) armiño en su piel blanca de invierno; (Brit.) piel blanca
**mink** [mɪŋk] *s* (zool.) visón; piel de visón
**mink coat** *s* abrigo de visón
**Minn.** abr. de **Minnesota**
**minnesinger** [ˈmɪnəˌsɪŋər] *s* trovador alemán
**minnow** [ˈmɪno] *s* pececillo; (ichth.) foxino; (ichth.) ciprino
**Minoan** [mɪˈnoən] *adj* minoico
**minor** [ˈmaɪnər] *adj* menor; de menor importancia; menor de edad; (log. & mus.) menor; *s* menor de edad; (educ.) asignatura o curso secundario; (mus.) acorde, escala o intervalo menor; *vn* (coll.) seguir una asignatura o curso secundario
**Minorca** [mɪˈnɔrkə] *s* Menorca
**Minorcan** [mɪˈnɔrkən] *adj & s* menorquín
**minority** [mɪˈnɑrɪtɪ] o [mɪˈnɔrɪtɪ] *s* (*pl:* **-ties**) minoría; *adj* minoritario
**minor key** *s* (mus..) tono menor
**minor orders** *spl* (eccl.) órdenes menores
**minor premise** *s* (log.) premisa menor
**minor scale** *s* (mus.) escala menor
**minor surgery** *s* cirugía menor
**Minos** [ˈmaɪnɑs] *s* (myth.) Minos
**Minotaur** [ˈmɪnətɔr] *s* (myth.) Minotauro
**minster** [ˈmɪnstər] *s* santuario de monasterio; catedral
**minstrel** [ˈmɪnstrəl] *s* ministril (*criado que con música y canto divertía a su señor*); trovador; juglar; (U.S.A.) cómico disfrazado de negro
**minstrel show** *s* función de cómicos disfrazados de negro
**minstrelsy** [ˈmɪnstrəlsɪ] *s* (*pl:* **-sies**) juglaría, poesía o música trovadorescas, cancionero; compañía de juglares o trovadores
**mint** [mɪnt] *s* (bot.) hierbabuena, menta; pastilla o bombón de menta; casa de moneda; dineral, montón de dinero; sinnúmero; fuente inagotable; *adj* sin usar, no usado; *va* acuñar; (fig.) inventar
**mintage** [ˈmɪntɪdʒ] *s* acuñación; moneda acuñada; derechos de cuño; sello, señal
**mint block** *s* (philately) cuadrito sin usar
**mint julep** *s* julepe (*bebida helada compuesta de whisky, azúcar y hojas de menta*)
**minuend** [ˈmɪnjuɛnd] *s* (math.) minuendo
**minuet** [ˌmɪnjuˈɛt] *s* minué o minuete (*baile y música*)
**minus** [ˈmaɪnəs] *s* menos (*signo*); *adj* menos; *prep* menos; falto de, sin
**minus sign** *s* signo menos
**minute** [maɪˈnjut] o [maɪˈnut] *adj* menudo, diminuto; minucioso; [ˈmɪnɪt] *s* minuto (*de hora; de grado*); instante, momento; **minutes** *spl* acta (*de una junta*); **up to the minute** al corriente; de última hora; *va* minutar; levantar acta de
**minute gun** [ˈmɪnɪt] *s* cañón que se dispara de minuto en minuto (*en señal de luto o de alarma*)
**minute hand** [ˈmɪnɪt] *s* minutero
**minutely** [maɪˈnjutlɪ] o [maɪˈnutlɪ] *adv* menudamente, minuciosamente
**minuteman** [ˈmɪnɪtˌmæn] *s* (*pl:* **-men**) (U.S.A.) miliciano de la Revolución
**minuteness** [maɪˈnjutnɪs] o [maɪˈnutnɪs] *s* menudencia, minuciosidad
**minutiae** [mɪˈnjuʃɪi] o [mɪˈnuʃɪi] *spl* minucias, detalles minuciosos
**minx** [mɪŋks] *s* moza descarada, coqueta
**Miocene** [ˈmaɪosin] *adj & s* (geol.) mioceno
**miquelet** [ˈmɪkəlɛt] *s* miquelete
**miracle** [ˈmɪrəkəl] *s* milagro; dechado (*p.ej., de paciencia*); (theat.) auto, milagro
**miracle play** *s* auto, milagro
**miraculous** [mɪˈrækjələs] *adj* milagroso
**mirage** [mɪˈrɑʒ] *s* (opt. & fig.) espejismo, miraje
**mire** [maɪr] *s* lodo, lodazal; *va* enlodar; dar con (*p.ej., caballos*) en un atolladero; *vn* atollarse, atascarse
**mirk** [mʌrk] *s* var. de **murk**
**mirky** [ˈmʌrkɪ] *adj* (*comp:* **-ier;** *super:* **-iest**) var. de **murky**
**mirror** [ˈmɪrər] *s* espejo; (aut.) retrovisor; *va* reflejar
**mirth** [mʌrθ] *s* alegría, regocijo, risa, hilaridad
**mirthful** [ˈmʌrθfəl] *adj* alegre, regocijado, reidor
**mirthless** [ˈmʌrθlɪs] *adj* abatido, triste, tétrico
**miry** [ˈmaɪrɪ] *adj* (*comp:* **-ier;** *super:* **-iest**) lodoso; pantanoso; sucio
**misadventure** [ˌmɪsədˈvɛntʃər] *s* desgracia, contratiempo
**misalignment** [ˌmɪsəˈlaɪnmənt] *s* desalineamiento
**misalliance** [ˌmɪsəˈlaɪəns] *s* alianza mal hecha; matrimonio con una persona de clase inferior
**misanthrope** [ˈmɪsənθrop] *s* misántropo

**misanthropic** [ˌmɪsən'θrɑpɪk] *adj* misantrópico
**misanthropist** [mɪs'ænθrəpɪst] *s* var. de **misanthrope**
**misanthropy** [mɪs'ænθrəpɪ] *s* misantropía
**misapplication** [ˌmɪsæplɪ'keʃən] *s* aplicación errada; mal uso
**misapply** [ˌmɪsə'plaɪ] (*pret & pp:* **-plied**) *va* aplicar mal; hacer mal uso de
**misapprehend** [ˌmɪsæprɪ'hɛnd] *va* entender mal
**misapprehension** [ˌmɪsæprɪ'hɛnʃən] *s* equivocación; mala inteligencia
**misappropriate** [ˌmɪsə'proprɪet] *va* malversar; hacer mal uso de
**misappropriation** [ˌmɪsəˌproprɪ'eʃən] *s* malversación; mal uso
**misbecome** [ˌmɪsbɪ'kʌm] (*pret:* **-came**; *pp:* **-come**) *va* no convenir a, no ser propio de, ser indigno de
**misbegotten** [ˌmɪsbɪ'gɑtən] *adj* bastardo
**misbehave** [ˌmɪsbɪ'hev] *vn* conducirse mal, portarse mal
**misbehavior** [ˌmɪsbɪ'hevjər] *s* mala conducta, mal comportamiento
**misbelief** [ˌmɪsbɪ'lif] *s* error, opinión errónea; creencia heterodoxa
**misbelieve** [ˌmɪsbɪ'liv] *va* dudar, no creer; *vn* estar en error, tener opiniones erróneas; tener creencias heterodoxas
**misbeliever** [ˌmɪsbɪ'livər] *s* persona equivocada; heterodoxo
**misbrand** [mɪs'brænd] *va* herrar falsamente; marcar falsamente
**misc.** abr. de **miscellaneous** y **miscellany**
**miscalculate** [mɪs'kælkjəlet] *va & vn* calcular mal
**miscalculation** [ˌmɪskælkjə'leʃən] *s* cálculo errado; desacierto
**miscall** [mɪs'kɔl] *va* errar el nombre de
**miscarriage** [mɪs'kærɪdʒ] *s* aborto, malparto; fracaso, malogro; extravío (*p.ej., de una carta*)
**miscarry** [mɪs'kærɪ] (*pret & pp:* **-ried**) *vn* salir mal, malograrse; extraviarse (*p.ej., una carta*); abortar
**miscegenation** [ˌmɪsɪdʒɪ'neʃən] *s* miscegenación
**miscellaneous** [ˌmɪsə'lenɪəs] *adj* misceláneo
**miscellany** ['mɪsəˌlenɪ] *s* (*pl:* **-nies**) miscelánea (*mezcla; obra*); **miscellanies** *spl* miscelánea (*obra*)
**mischance** [mɪs'tʃæns] o [mɪs'tʃɑns] *s* desgracia, infortunio, mala suerte
**mischief** ['mɪstʃɪf] *s* daño, mal; diablura; travesura; malicia; diablillo, persona traviesa
**mischief-maker** ['mɪstʃɪfˌmekər] *s* camorrista, cizañador
**mischievous** ['mɪstʃɪvəs] *adj* dañoso, malo; travieso; malicioso; enredador
**miscible** ['mɪsɪbəl] *adj* miscible
**misconceive** [ˌmɪskən'siv] *va & vn* entender mal
**misconception** [ˌmɪskən'sɛpʃən] *s* concepto erróneo; mala interpretación
**misconduct** [mɪs'kɑndʌkt] *s* mala conducta; desorden, desbarajuste; [ˌmɪskən'dʌkt] *va* administrar mal; **to misconduct oneself** conducirse mal, portarse mal
**misconstruction** [ˌmɪskən'strʌkʃən] *s* mala interpretación
**misconstrue** [ˌmɪskən'stru] o [mɪs'kɑnstru] *va* interpretar mal
**miscount** [mɪs'kaʊnt] *s* cuenta errónea; *va & vn* contar mal
**miscreant** ['mɪskrɪənt] *adj* vil, ruin; (archaic) hereje; *s* pillo, sinvergüenza; (archaic) hereje
**miscreated** [ˌmɪskri'etɪd] *adj* contrahecho, mal formado
**miscue** [mɪs'kju] *s* (billiards) pifia; (coll.) pifia, descuido; *vn* (billiards) pifiar; (theat.) equivocarse de apunte
**misdate** [mɪs'det] *s* fecha falsa o equivocada; *va* fechar falsa o equivocadamente
**misdeal** ['mɪsˌdil] *s* repartición errónea (*de naipes*); [mɪs'dil] (*pret & pp:* **-dealt**) *va & vn* dar mal, repartir mal
**misdeed** [mɪs'did] o ['mɪsˌdid] *s* malhecho, infracción
**misdemean** [ˌmɪsdɪ'min] *vn* portarse mal; (law) cometer un delito menor
**misdemeanor** [ˌmɪsdɪ'minər] *s* mala conducta; culpa; (law) delito de menor cuantía
**misdid** [mɪs'dɪd] *pret de* **misdo**
**misdirect** [ˌmɪsdɪ'rɛkt] o [ˌmɪsdaɪ'rɛkt] *va* dirigir erradamente; extraviar, hacer perder el camino a
**misdirection** [ˌmɪsdɪ'rɛkʃən] o [ˌmɪsdaɪ'rɛkʃən] *s* mala dirección, instrucciones erradas
**misdo** [mɪs'du] (*pret* **-did**; *pp:* **-done**) *va* hacer mal
**misdoing** [mɪs'duɪŋ] *s* maldad, perversidad
**misdone** [mɪs'dʌn] *pp de* **misdo**
**mise en scène** [mizɑ̃'sɛn] *s* (Fr.) puesta en escena
**misemploy** [ˌmɪsɛm'plɔɪ] *va* emplear mal
**miser** ['maɪzər] *s* avaro, verrugo
**miserable** ['mɪzərəbəl] *adj* miserable; (coll.) indispuesto, en mala salud
**Miserere** [ˌmɪzə'rɪrɪ] o [ˌmɪzə'rɛrɪ] *s* (eccl. & mus.) miserere; (*l.c.*) *s* (arch.) misericordia, coma
**misericord** [ˌmɪzərɪ'kɔrd] o [mɪ'zɛrɪkɔrd] *s* misericordia (*puñal*); (arch.) misericordia, coma (*ménsula*); (eccl.) misericordia (*sala; dispensación*)
**miserly** ['maɪzərlɪ] *adj* mísero, avariento
**misery** ['mɪzərɪ] *s* (*pl:* **-ies**) miseria; (dial.) dolor, sufrimiento
**misfeasance** [mɪs'fizəns] *s* (law) acción mala; (law) abuso de autoridad, fraude
**misfire** [mɪs'faɪr] *s* falla de tiro; falla de encendido; mechazo; *vn* no dar fuego; fallar; dar mechazo
**misfit** ['mɪsˌfɪt] *s* vestido o traje mal cortados; cosa que no encaja bien o que no sienta bien; persona desequilibrada, persona reñida con su ambiente; [mɪs'fɪt] (*pret & pp:* **-fitted**; *ger:* **-fitting**) *va* cortar mal; encajar mal, sentar mal; *vn* encajar mal, sentar mal
**misfortune** [mɪs'fɔrtʃən] *s* desventura
**misgive** [mɪs'gɪv] (*pret:* **-gave**; *pp:* **-given**) *va* hacer dudar o recelar, dar mala espina a; *vn* temer, recelar
**misgiving** [mɪs'gɪvɪŋ] *s* duda, recelo, ansiedad
**misgovern** [mɪs'gʌvərn] *va* desgobernar; administrar mal, manejar mal
**misgovernment** [mɪs'gʌvərnmənt] *s* desgobierno; mala administración, mal manejo
**misguide** [mɪs'gaɪd] *va* dirigir mal; aconsejar mal; descarriar
**misguided** [mɪs'gaɪdɪd] *adj* errado, erróneo; mal aconsejado; descarriado
**mishandle** [mɪs'hændəl] *va* manejar mal; maltratar
**mishap** ['mɪshæp] o [mɪs'hæp] *s* accidente, percance
**mishear** [mɪs'hɪr] (*pret & pp:* **-heard**) *va* oír mal
**misinform** [ˌmɪsɪn'fɔrm] *va* informar mal, dar informes erróneos o falsos a
**misinformation** [ˌmɪsɪnfər'meʃən] *s* informes erróneos o falsos
**misinterpret** [ˌmɪsɪn'tʌrprɪt] *va* interpretar mal
**misinterpretation** [ˌmɪsɪnˌtʌrprɪ'teʃən] *s* mala interpretación
**misjudge** [mɪs'dʒʌdʒ] *va & vn* juzgar mal o injustamente
**misjudgment** o **misjudgement** [mɪs'dʒʌdʒmənt] *s* juicio errado o injusto
**mislay** [mɪs'le] (*pret & pp:* **-laid**) *va* colocar mal; extraviar, perder
**mislead** [mɪs'lid] (*pret & pp:* **-led**) *va* extraviar; descarriar; engañar
**misleading** [mɪs'lidɪŋ] *adj* engañoso; de falsas apariencias
**mismanage** [mɪs'mænɪdʒ] *va* manejar mal, administrar mal
**mismanagement** [mɪs'mænɪdʒmənt] *s* mal manejo, mala administración
**mismatch** [mɪs'mætʃ] *s* unión o ayuntamiento mal hechos; casamiento desigual o mal hecho; *va* unir mal, emparejar mal, hermanar mal
**mismate** [mɪs'met] *va & vn* emparejar mal, hermanar mal; casar mal
**misname** [mɪs'nem] *va* llamar por mal nombre, equivocar el nombre de
**misnomer** [mɪs'nomər] *s* mal nombre, nombre inapropiado; nombre erróneo
**misogamic** [ˌmɪso'gæmɪk] *adj* misógamo

**misogamist** [mɪˈsɑgəmɪst] *s* misógamo
**misogamy** [mɪˈsɑgəmɪ] *s* misogamia
**misogynist** [mɪˈsɑdʒɪnɪst] *s* misógino
**misogynous** [mɪˈsɑdʒɪnəs] *adj* misógino
**misogyny** [mɪˈsɑdʒɪnɪ] *s* misoginia
**misoneism** [ˌmɪsoˈniɪzəm] *s* misoneísmo
**misoneist** [ˌmɪsoˈniɪst] *s* misoneísta
**mispickel** [ˈmɪsˌpɪkəl] *s* (mineral.) mispíquel
**misplace** [mɪsˈples] *va* colocar mal o fuera de su lugar; (coll.) extraviar, perder; dar (*amor o confianza*) a quien no lo merece
**misplacement** [mɪsˈplesmənt] *s* colocación de una cosa fuera de su lugar; extravío, pérdida
**misplay** [mɪsˈple] *s* mala jugada; *va & vn* jugar mal
**misprint** [ˈmɪsˌprɪnt] *s* errata de imprenta; [mɪsˈprɪnt] *va* imprimir mal, imprimir con erratas
**misprision** [mɪsˈprɪʒən] *s* (law) delito (*especialmente de funcionario público*); (coll.) ocultación de un delito
**misprize** [mɪsˈpraɪz] *va* menospreciar; desestimar
**mispronounce** [ˌmɪsprəˈnaʊns] *va* pronunciar mal
**mispronunciation** [ˌmɪsprəˌnʌnsɪˈeʃən] o [ˌmɪsprəˌnʌnʃɪˈeʃən] *s* pronunciación errada o inexacta
**misquotation** [ˌmɪskwoˈteʃən] *s* cita falsa o equivocada
**misquote** [mɪsˈkwot] *va* citar falsa o equivocadamente
**misread** [mɪsˈrid] (*pret & pp:* **-read** [ˈrɛd]) *va* leer mal; entender o interpretar mal
**misrepresent** [ˌmɪsrɛprɪˈzɛnt] *va* exponer o alegar falsamente; falsificar (*los hechos*); describir engañosamente
**misrepresentation** [ˌmɪsrɛprɪzɛnˈteʃən] *s* exposición falsa; falsificación; descripción falsa
**misrule** [mɪsˈrul] *s* confusión, desorden; desgobierno; *va* desgobernar
**Miss.** abr. de **Mississippi**
**miss** [mɪs] *s* falta; tiro errado; malogro, fracaso; muchacha, jovencita; (*cap.*) señorita; **a miss is as good as a mile** lo mismo da librarse por poco que por mucho; *va* echar de menos (*a una persona*); hacer falta, p.ej., **I have missed you very much** Vd. me ha hecho mucha falta; errar (*el blanco; la vocación*); perder (*el tren, la función, la oportunidad*); librarse de (*p.ej., la muerte*); no comprender, no entender; no ver; omitir; no dar con, no hallar; no encontrar; no lograr coger u obtener; escapársele a uno, p.ej., **I missed what you said** se me escapó lo que dijo Vd.; **to miss +** *ger* por poco + *ind*, p.ej., **the car just missed running over me** el coche por poco me atropella; *vn* errar el blanco; malograrse, no surtir efecto; fallar
**missal** [ˈmɪsəl] *s* (eccl.) misal
**missel thrush** [ˈmɪsəl] *s* (orn.) cagaaceite, charla
**misshape** [mɪsˈʃep] (*pret:* **-shaped;** *pp:* **-shaped** o **-shapen**) *va* deformar
**misshapen** [mɪsˈʃepən] *adj* deforme, contrahecho; *pp de* **misshape**
**missile** [ˈmɪsɪl] *adj* arrojadizo; *s* arma arrojadiza; proyectil
**missileer** [ˌmɪsɪlˈɪr] *s* var. de **missileman**
**missile gap** *s* inferioridad del proyectil, desventaja en el desarrollo del proyectil
**missileman** [ˈmɪsɪlmən] *s* (*pl:* **-men**) perito en materia de proyectiles dirigidos
**missilery** [ˈmɪsɪlrɪ] *s* ciencia de los proyectiles dirigidos
**missing** [ˈmɪsɪŋ] *adj* desaparecido; ausente; **to be missing** faltar, hacer falta; haber desaparecido
**missing link** *s* eslabón perdido, hombre mono
**missing persons** *spl* desaparecidos
**mission** [ˈmɪʃən] *s* misión; casa de misión; **missions** *spl* misiones, propagación de la fe
**missionary** [ˈmɪʃənˌɛrɪ] *adj* misional; misionero (*p.ej., espíritu*); *s* (*pl:* **-ies**) misionario; propagandista; (eccl.) misionario o misionero
**mission furniture** *s* muebles al estilo de las misiones californianas (*pesados y de roble ahumado*)
**missis** o **missus** [ˈmɪsɪz] *s* (coll.) esposa, mujer; (coll.) ama de casa
**missish** [ˈmɪsɪʃ] *adj* relamido, remilgado
**Mississippi** [ˌmɪsɪˈsɪpɪ] *s* Misisipí (*río y estado*)
**missive** [ˈmɪsɪv] *adj* misivo; *s* misiva
**Missouri** [mɪˈzʊrɪ] o [mɪˈzʊrə] *s* Misurí (*río y estado*); **from Missouri** (slang) escéptico, difícil de engañar
**misspeak** [mɪsˈspik] (*pret:* **-spoke;** *pp:* **-spoken**) *va* decir, pronunciar o hablar mal o erróneamente
**misspell** [mɪsˈspɛl] (*pret & pp:* **-spelled** o **-spelt**) *va & vn* deletrear o escribir mal
**misspelling** [mɪsˈspɛlɪŋ] *s* falta de ortografía
**misspend** [mɪsˈspɛnd] (*pret & pp:* **-spent**) *va* malgastar, desbaratar
**misspent** [mɪsˈspɛnt] *adj* malgastado, desbaratado; *pret & pp de* **misspend**
**misspoke** [mɪsˈspok] *pret de* **misspeak**
**misspoken** [mɪsˈspokən] *pp de* **misspeak**
**misstate** [mɪsˈstet] *va* relatar mal o falsamente
**misstatement** [mɪsˈstetmənt] *s* relato inexacto o falso
**misstep** [mɪsˈstɛp] *s* paso falso; resbalón (*en un delito o culpa*)
**missy** [ˈmɪsɪ] *s* (*pl:* **-ies**) (coll.) señorita, hija mía
**mist** [mɪst] *s* niebla, neblina; llovizna; velo (*p.ej., de lágrimas*); *va* empañar, velar; *vn* lloviznar; empañarse, velarse
**mistakable** [mɪsˈtekəbəl] *adj* confundible, equívoco
**mistake** [mɪsˈtek] *s* error, equivocación; culpa; decisión poco acertada; **and no mistake** sin duda alguna; **by mistake** por descuido; **to make a mistake** equivocarse; (*pret:* **-took;** *pp:* **-taken**) *va* entender mal, interpretar mal; confundir; tomar (*por otro; por lo que no es*); **to be mistaken for** equivocarse con; *vn* errar, equivocarse
**mistaken** [mɪsˈtekən] *adj* errado, erróneo; equivocado; desacertado; *pp de* **mistake**
**mistaken identity** *s* identificación equivocada
**mistakenly** [mɪsˈtekənlɪ] *adv* por error, equivocadamente
**mister** [ˈmɪstər] *s* señor; (*cap.*) *s* señor (*tratamiento de cortesía*); (*l.c.*) *va* (coll.) dar tratamiento de señor a
**mistime** [mɪsˈtaɪm] *va* hacer o decir a deshora; equivocarse al decir la hora, el día, el año, etc. de; cronometrar mal
**mistimed** [mɪsˈtaɪmd] *adj* inoportuno, intempestivo
**mistletoe** [ˈmɪsəlto] *s* (bot.) muérdago (*Viscum album*); (bot.) cabellera, visco (*Phoradendron*); (bot.) loranto
**mistook** [mɪsˈtʊk] *pret de* **mistake**
**mistral** [ˈmɪstrəl] o [mɪsˈtrɑl] *s* mistral (*viento*)
**mistranslate** [ˌmɪstrænsˈlet] o [mɪsˈtrænslet] *va* traducir mal o erróneamente
**mistranslation** [ˌmɪstrænsˈleʃən] *s* traducción errónea
**mistreat** [mɪsˈtrit] *va* maltratar
**mistreatment** [mɪsˈtritmənt] *s* maltratamiento, malos tratos
**mistress** [ˈmɪstrɪs] *s* ama de casa; señora; perita; maestra de escuela; moza, querida, manceba; (archaic) amada; (archaic & dial.) señora, señorita (*tratamiento de cortesía*); (fig.) señora (*país que gobierna, p.ej., los mares*); (*cap.*) [ˈmɪsɪz] *s* señora (*tratamiento de cortesía que se da a una mujer casada*)
**Mistress of the Seas** *s* señora de los mares (*Inglaterra*)
**mistrial** [mɪsˈtraɪəl] *s* (law) pleito o juicio viciado de nulidad
**mistrust** [mɪsˈtrʌst] *s* desconfianza; *va* desconfiar de; *vn* desconfiar
**mistrustful** [mɪsˈtrʌstfəl] *adj* desconfiado
**misty** [ˈmɪstɪ] *adj* (*comp:* **-ier;** *super:* **-iest**) brumoso, nebuloso, neblinoso; empañado; vago, indistinto
**misunderstand** [ˌmɪsʌndərˈstænd] (*pret & pp:* **-stood**) *va & vn* entender mal, no comprender
**misunderstanding** [ˌmɪsʌndərˈstændɪŋ] *s* malentendido; desavenencia
**misunderstood** [ˌmɪsʌndərˈstʊd] *adj* no bien comprendido; insuficientemente apreciado o estimado; *pret & pp de* **misunderstand**

**misusage** [mɪsˈjusɪdʒ] o [mɪsˈjuzɪdʒ] *s* mal uso, mal empleo; maltratamiento
**misuse** [mɪsˈjus] *s* mal uso, mal empleo; uso erróneo o impropio; [mɪsˈjuz] *va* emplear mal; maltratar
**misword** [mɪsˈwʌrd] *va* expresar mal, expresar con palabras impropias
**mite** [maɪt] *s* pizca; óbolo; (zool.) mita, garrapata
**miter** [ˈmaɪtər] *s* mitra (*p.ej., de obispo; cargo o dignidad de obispo*); (carp.) inglete; (carp.) junta a inglete, ensambladura de inglete; *va* conferir una mitra a, elevar al obispado; (carp.) cortar ingletes en; (carp.) juntar con junta a inglete
**miter box** *s* (carp.) caja de ingletes, caja de cortar al sesgo
**mitered** [ˈmaɪtərd] *adj* mitrado; (carp.) con junta o juntas a inglete
**miter joint** *s* (carp.) junta a inglete, ensambladura de inglete
**miter sill** *s* busco, batiente de esclusa
**Mithras** [ˈmɪθræs] *s* (myth.) Mitra
**Mithridates** [ˌmɪθrɪˈdetiz] *s* Mitridates
**mitigate** [ˈmɪtɪget] *va* mitigar; *vn* mitigarse
**mitigation** [ˌmɪtɪˈgeʃən] *s* mitigación
**mitigative** [ˈmɪtɪˌgetɪv] *adj* mitigativo
**mitigator** [ˈmɪtɪˌgetər] *s* mitigador
**mitosis** [mɪˈtosɪs] *s* (biol.) mitosis
**mitotic** [mɪˈtɑtɪk] *adj* mitósico
**mitral** [ˈmaɪtrəl] *adj* mitral; (anat.) mitral
**mitral cell** *s* (anat.) célula mitral
**mitral insufficiency** *s* (path.) insuficiencia mitral
**mitral valve** *s* (anat.) válvula mitral
**mitre** [ˈmaɪtər] *s* & *va* var. de **miter**
**mitt** [mɪt] *s* mitón (*guante que deja los dedos al descubierto*); guante con sólo el pulgar separado; guante de béisbol
**mitten** [ˈmɪtən] *s* guante con sólo el pulgar separado; **mittens** *spl* (slang) guantes de boxeo; **to get the mitten** recibir calabazas; **to give the mitten to** dar calabazas a
**mix** [mɪks] *s* mezcla; (coll.) embrollo, enredo, lío; *va* mezclar; hacer o confeccionar (*hormigón*); amasar (*una torta, un bollo*); aderezar (*ensalada*); confeccionar mezclando; **to get mixed up in** mojar en; **to get mixed with** tener que ver con; **to mix up** equivocar (*confundir completamente*); *vn* mezclarse; asociarse; granjearse amigos; entrecruzarse
**mixed** [mɪkst] *adj* mixto; mezclado; variados (*p.ej., bombones*); (coll.) confundido
**mixed chorus** *s* coro mixto
**mixed company** *s* reunión de personas de ambos sexos
**mixed drinks** *spl* bebidas mezcladas
**mixed feeling** *s* concepto vacilante
**mixed-flow turbine** [ˈmɪkstˌflo] *s* turbina mixta
**mixed marriage** *s* matrimonio mixto (*es decir, entre personas de distintas razas o religiones*)
**mixed metaphore** *s* metáfora incoherente
**mixed number** *s* (math.) número mixto
**mixed train** *s* (rail.) tren mixto
**mixer** [ˈmɪksər] *s* mezclador; mezcladora, hormigonera; persona sociable; **to be a good mixer** tener don de gentes
**mixtilineal** [ˌmɪkstɪˈlɪnɪəl] *adj* mixtilíneo
**mixture** [ˈmɪkstʃər] *s* mixtura
**mix-up** [ˈmɪksˌʌp] *s* (coll.) bullaje, bullanga; (coll.) lío, enredo; (coll.) equívoco
**mizzen** [ˈmɪzən] *s* (naut.) mesana (*vela; mástil*)
**mizzenmast** [ˈmɪzənməst], [ˈmɪzənˌmæst] o [ˈmɪzənˌmɑst] *s* (naut.) palo de mesana
**mm.** abr. de **millimeter** o **millimeters**
**mnemonic** [niˈmɑnɪk] *adj* mnemónico; **mnemonics** *ssg* mnemónica; *spl* figuras o caracteres mnemónicos
**Mnemosyne** [niˈmɑsɪni] *s* (myth.) Mnemosina o Mnemósine
**mnemotechnics** [ˌnimoˈtɛknɪks] *ssg* mnemotécnica
**mnemotechny** [ˈnimoˌtɛknɪ] *s* mnemotecnia
**mo.** abr. de **month** o **months**
**Mo.** abr. de **Missouri**
**M.O.** o **m.o.** abr. de **money order**
**Moabite** [ˈmoəbaɪt] *adj* & *s* moabita
**moan** [mon] *s* gemido; *va* expresar con gemidos; *vn* gemir
**moat** [mot] *s* (fort.) foso; *va* fosar
**mob** [mɑb] *s* gentío, muchedumbre; chusma, populacho; muchedumbre airada; (*pret* & *pp:* **mobbed;** *ger:* **mobbing**) *va* atropellar, asaltar, apoderarse de
**mobcap** [ˈmɑbˌkæp] *s* toca de mujer
**mobile** [ˈmobɪl] o [ˈmobil] *adj* móvil
**mobile unit** *s* (rad.) unidad móvil
**mobility** [moˈbɪlɪtɪ] *s* movilidad
**mobilization** [ˌmobɪlɪˈzeʃən] *s* movilización
**mobilize** [ˈmobɪlaɪz] *va* movilizar; *vn* movilizar o movilizarse
**mobster** [ˈmɑbstər] *s* (slang) bandido, malhechor
**moccasin** [ˈmɑkəsɪn] *s* mocasín o mocasina; (zool.) mocasín, víbora de agua
**moccasin flower** *s* (bot.) zapatilla de señorita
**Mocha** [ˈmokə] *s* moca, café de moca; piel de Moka (*que se usa para guantes*)
**mock** [mɑk] *s* burla, mofa, escarnio; hazmerreír; cosa despreciable; *adj* falso, fingido, simulado; *va* burlarse de, mofarse de, escarnecer; remedar; despreciar, hacer poco caso de; engañar, decepcionar; *vn* mofarse; **to mock at** mofarse de
**mock cypress** *s* (bot.) ayuga, mirabel
**mockery** [ˈmɑkərɪ] *s* (*pl:* **-ies**) burla, mofa, escarnio; hazmerreír; mal remedo; desprecio, negación (*p.ej., de la justicia*)
**mock-heroic** [ˌmɑkhɪˈro·ɪk] *adj* heroicocómico; *s* obra heroicocómica
**mockingbird** [ˈmɑkɪŋˌbʌrd] *s* (orn.) burlón, sinsonte
**mock moon** *s* (meteor.) paraselene
**mock orange** *s* (bot.) jeringuilla, celinda
**mock privet** *s* (bot.) olivillo
**mock turtle soup** *s* sopa de cabeza de ternera (*a imitación de la de tortuga*)
**mock-up** [ˈmɑkˌʌp] *s* maqueta, modelo (*generalmente en tamaño natural*)
**modal** [ˈmodəl] *adj* modal
**modal auxiliary** *s* (gram.) auxiliar modal
**modality** [moˈdælɪtɪ] *s* modalidad
**mode** [mod] *s* modo, manera; moda; (gram. & mus.) modo
**model** [ˈmɑdəl] *s* modelo; *adj* modelo, p.ej., **model city** ciudad modelo; (*pret* & *pp:* **-eled** o **-elled;** *ger:* **-eling** o **-elling**) *va* modelar; **to model after** planear según, construir a imitación de; *vn* modelar; modelarse; servir de modelo
**model airplane** *s* aeromodelo
**model airplane builder** *s* aeromodelista
**model airplane building** *s* aeromodelismo
**modeling** o **modelling** [ˈmɑdəlɪŋ] *s* modelado
**model sailing** *s* navegación de modelos a vela
**moderate** [ˈmɑdərɪt] *adj* & *s* moderado; [ˈmɑdəret] *va* moderar; *vn* moderarse
**moderate breeze** *s* (naut.) viento bonancible
**moderate gale** *s* (naut.) viento frescachón
**moderately** [ˈmɑdərɪtlɪ] *adv* moderadamente
**moderation** [ˌmɑdəˈreʃən] *s* moderación; **in moderation** con moderación
**moderator** [ˈmɑdəˌretər] *s* moderador; árbitro; presidente (*de una asamblea*); (mach., phys. & chem.) moderador
**modern** [ˈmɑdərn] *adj* & *s* moderno
**Modern English** *s* el inglés moderno
**modern history** *s* la historia moderna
**modernism** [ˈmɑdərnɪzəm] *s* modernismo; neologismo
**modernist** [ˈmɑdərnɪst] *adj* modernista; *s* modernista; neólogo
**modernistic** [ˌmɑdərˈnɪstɪk] *adj* modernista
**modernity** [moˈdʌrnɪtɪ] *s* (*pl:* **-ties**) modernidad; cosa moderna
**modernization** [ˌmɑdərnɪˈzeʃən] *s* modernización
**modernize** [ˈmɑdərnaɪz] *va* modernizar; *vn* modernizarse
**modern languages** *spl* lenguas modernas, lenguas vivas
**Modern Spanish** *s* el español moderno
**modest** [ˈmɑdɪst] *adj* modesto; moderado; sencillo
**modestly** [ˈmɑdɪstlɪ] *adv* modestamente
**modesty** [ˈmɑdɪstɪ] *s* (*pl:* **-ties**) modestia
**modicum** [ˈmɑdɪkəm] *s* cantidad módica
**modifiable** [ˈmɑdɪˌfaɪəbəl] *adj* modificable
**modification** [ˌmɑdɪfɪˈkeʃən] *s* modificación

**modifier** ['madɪ,faɪər] *s* modificador; (gram.) modificante
**modify** ['madɪfaɪ] (*pret & pp:* **-fied**) *va* modificar; *vn* modificarse
**modillion** [mo'dɪljən] *s* (arch.) modillón
**modish** ['modɪʃ] *adj* de moda, elegante
**modiste** [mo'dist] *s* modista
**modular** ['madʒələr] *adj* modular
**modulate** ['madʒəlet] *va & vn* modular
**modulation** [,madʒə'leʃən] *s* modulación
**modulator** ['madʒə,letər] *s* modulador; (rad.) modulador
**module** ['madʒul] *s* módulo (*de una medalla o moneda*); (arch., hyd. & mach.) módulo
**modulus** ['madʒələs] *s* (*pl:* **-li** [laɪ]) módulo (*norma*); (phys.) módulo
**modus** ['modəs] *s* (*pl:* **-di** [daɪ]) *s* modo
**modus operandi** [,apə'rændaɪ] *s* modo de proceder
**modus vivendi** [vɪ'vɛndaɪ] *s* modo de vivir; convenio provisional
**mofette** [mo'fɛt] *s* mofeta (*de las minas o de la actividad volcánica*)
**mogul** [mo'gʌl] o ['mogʌl] *s* magnate; locomotora mogol; (*cap.*) *s* mogol
**mohair** ['mohɛr] *s* moer o mohair
**Mohammed** [mo'hæmɪd] *s* Mahoma
**Mohammedan** [mo'hæmɪdən] *adj & s* mahometano
**Mohammedanism** [mo'hæmɪdənɪzəm] *s* mahometismo
**Mohammedanize** [mo'hæmɪdənaɪz] *va* mahometizar
**Mohican** [mo'hikən] *adj & s* mohicano
**moiety** ['mɔɪətɪ] *s* (*pl:* **-ties**) mitad; parte, porción
**moil** [mɔɪl] *s* afán, trabajo penoso; confusión, alboroto; *vn* afanarse, trabajar sin descanso
**moire** [mwar] *s* muaré
**moiré** [mwa're] o [mo're] *adj & s* muaré
**moist** [mɔɪst] *adj* húmedo; mojado
**moisten** ['mɔɪsən] *va* humedecer, mojar; *vn* humedecerse, mojarse
**moistener** ['mɔɪsənər] *s* mojador (*persona; tacita con agua para mojar sellos o para mojarse la punta de los dedos*); humectador (*para humedecer los efectos engomados*)
**moisture** ['mɔɪstʃər] *s* humedad
**mol** [mol] *s* (chem.) mol
**molal** ['moləl] *adj* (chem.) molal
**molar** ['molər] *adj* (anat., phys. & path.) molar; *s* (anat.) molar, diente molar
**molasses** [mə'læsɪz] *s* melaza
**molasses candy** *s* melcocha
**molasses grass** *s* (bot.) zacategordura
**mold** [mold] *s* molde; cosa moldeada; forma (*dada por el molde*); carácter, índole; mantillo (*tierra vegetal*); (bot.) moho; (archaic) tierra; *va* moldear; enmohecer; **to mold oneself on** amoldarse por; *vn* enmohecerse
**Moldavian** [mal'devɪən] *adj & s* moldavo
**moldboard** ['mold,bord] *s* vertedera u orejera (*del arado*)
**molder** ['moldər] *s* moldeador; *va* convertir en polvo, consumir; *vn* convertirse en polvo, consumirse
**molding** ['moldɪŋ] *s* moldeado; vaciado; moldura; (elec.) cajetín
**molding board** *s* tabla para amasar pan
**molding cutter** *s* cuchilla de moldurar
**molding machine** *s* (carp.) moldeador; (fund.) moldeadora
**molding sand** *s* arena de molde, arena de fundición
**mold loft** *s* (naut.) sala de gálibos
**moldy** ['moldɪ] *adj* (*comp:* **-ier;** *super:* **-iest**) mohoso; rancio, pasado
**mole** [mol] *s* rompeolas; dársena; lunar; (path.) mola; (zool.) topo; (hist.) mola (*harina de cebada usada en los sacrificios*)
**mole cricket** *s* (ent.) cortón, alacrán cebollero
**molecular** [mə'lɛkjələr] *adj* molecular
**molecular weight** *s* (phys.) peso molecular
**molecule** ['malɪkjul] *s* (chem. & phys.) molécula
**molehill** ['mol,hɪl] *s* topinera o topera; (fig.) pamplina, cosa de poca monta
**moleskin** ['mol,skɪn] *s* piel de topo; molesquina; **moleskins** *spl* pantalones de molesquina
**molest** [mo'lɛst] *va* molestar, incomodar; faltar al respeto a (*una mujer*)
**molestation** [,molɛs'teʃən] o [,maləs'teʃən] *s* molestia, vejación
**moll** [mal] *s* (slang) golfa, ladrona; (slang) ramera; (slang) manceba de gángster
**mollification** [,malɪfɪ'keʃən] *s* apaciguamiento, mitigación
**mollify** ['malɪfaɪ] (*pret & pp:* **-fied**) *va* apaciguar, mitigar
**mollusc** o **mollusk** ['maləsk] *s* (zool.) molusco
**Molly** ['malɪ] *s* Mariquita
**mollycoddle** ['malɪ,kadəl] *s* mantecón, marica; *va* mimar, consentir
**Moloch** ['molak] *s* (Bib.) Moloc; (*l.c.*) *s* (zool.) moloc, diablo punzante
**molt** [molt] *s* muda (*de pluma o pellejo*); *va* mudar (*la pluma, el pellejo*); *vn* mudar la pluma, mudar el pellejo
**molten** ['moltən] *adj* derretido; fundido, vaciado
**mol. wt.** abr. de **molecular weight**
**moly** ['molɪ] *s* (*pl:* **-lies**) (myth.) hierba moli; (bot.) ajo silvestre (*Allium moly*)
**molybdate** [mo'lɪbdet] *s* (chem.) molibdato
**molybdenite** [mo'lɪbdɪnaɪt] o [,malɪb'dinaɪt] *s* (mineral.) molibdenita
**molybdenous** [mo'lɪbdɪnəs] o [,malɪb'dinəs] *adj* (chem.) molibdenoso
**molybdenum** [mo'lɪbdɪnəm] o [,malɪb'dinəm] *s* (chem.) molibdeno
**molybdenum steel** *s* acero al molibdeno
**molybdic** [mo'lɪbdɪk] *adj* (chem.) molíbdico
**moment** ['momənt] *s* momento; (mech.) momento; **at any moment** de un momento a otro; **for the moment** por ahora, por lo presente; **in a moment** en un momento
**momentarily** ['momən,tɛrɪlɪ] *adv* momentáneamente; de un momento a otro
**momentary** ['momən,tɛrɪ] *adj* momentáneo
**momently** ['koməntlɪ] *adv* a cada momento; de un momento a otro; momentáneamente
**moment of inertia** *s* (mech.) momento de inercia
**momentous** [mo'mɛntəs] *adj* grave, trascendental
**momentously** [mo'mɛntəslɪ] *adv* gravemente, grandemente
**momentum** [mo'mɛntəm] *s* (*pl:* **-tums** o **-ta** [tə]) ímpetu; (mech.) cantidad de movimiento
**Momus** ['moməs] *s* (myth.) Momo; criticón, reparón
**Mon.** abr. de **Monday**
**monachal** ['manəkəl] *adj* monacal
**monachism** ['manəkɪzəm] *s* monaquismo
**monad** ['manæd] o ['monæd] *s* (biol., chem., philos. & zool.) mónada
**monadelphous** [,manə'dɛlfəs] *adj* (bot.) monadélfico
**monadism** ['manədɪzəm] o ['monədɪzəm] *s* (philos.) monadismo
**monandrous** [mo'nændrəs] *adj* monándrico; (bot.) manandro
**monandry** [mo'nændrɪ] *s* monandria; (bot.) monandria
**monarch** ['manərk] *s* monarca; (ent.) mariposa (*Danaus menippe*)
**monarchal** [mə'narkəl] *adj* monárquico
**monarchial** [mə'narkɪəl], **monarchic** [mə'narkɪk] o **monarchical** [mə'narkɪkəl] *adj* monárquico; monarquista
**monarchism** ['manərkɪzəm] *s* monarquismo
**monarchist** ['manərkɪst] *adj & s* monarquista
**monarchistic** [,manər'kɪstɪk] *adj* monarquista
**monarchy** ['manərkɪ] *s* (*pl:* **-chies**) monarquía
**monasterial** [,manəs'tɪrɪəl] *adj* monasterial
**monastery** ['manəs,tɛrɪ] *s* (*pl:* **-ies**) monasterio
**monastic** [mə'næstɪk] *adj* monástico; *s* monje
**monastical** [mə'næstɪkəl] *adj* monástico
**monasticism** [mə'næstɪsɪzəm] *s* monacato, monaquismo
**monazite** ['manəzaɪt] *s* (mineral.) monacita
**Monday** ['mʌndɪ] *s* lunes
**monecious** [mo'niʃəs] *adj* var. de **monoecious**
**Monegasque** [,manə'gask] *adj & s* monegasco
**Monel metal** [mo'nɛl] *s* (trademark) metal monel

**monetary** ['manɪ,terɪ] o ['mʌnɪ,terɪ] *adj* monetario; pecuniario
**monetization** [,manɪtɪ'zeʃən] o [,mʌnɪtɪ'zeʃen] *s* monetización
**monetize** ['manɪtaɪz] o ['mʌnɪtaɪz] *va* monetizar
**money** ['mʌnɪ] *s* dinero; **to make money** ganar dinero: dar dinero (*una empresa*); **your money or your life** la bolsa o la vida
**moneybag** ['mʌnɪ,bæg] *s* monedero, talega para dinero; **moneybags** *spl* (coll.) talegas (*riquezas*); *ssg* (coll.) tacaño, ricacho
**money belt** *s* faja para llevar moneda
**money broker** *s* numulario, cambista
**moneychanger** ['mʌnɪ,tʃendʒər] *s* cambista
**moneyed** ['mʌnɪd] *adj* adinerado, dineroso
**moneyer** ['mʌnɪər] *s* monedero
**moneylender** ['mʌnɪ,lendər] *s* prestamista
**money-maker** ['mʌnɪ,mekər] *s* acaudalador; manantial de beneficios
**money of account** *s* moneda imaginaria
**money order** *s* giro postal
**money's worth** *s* valor; **to get one's money's worth out of** sacar el valor de
**moneywort** ['mʌnɪ,wʌrt] *s* (bot.) hierba de la moneda
**monger** ['mʌŋgər] *s* tratante, traficante
**Mongol** ['maŋgal] o ['maŋgəl] *adj* & *s* mogol
**Mongolia** [maŋ'golɪə] *s* la Mogolia
**Mongolian** [maŋ'golɪən] *adj* & *s* mogol
**Mongolian idiocy** *s* idiotez mogólica
**Mongolian pheasant** *s* (orn.) faisán de Mogolia
**Mongolism** ['maŋgəlɪzəm] *s* mogolismo
**Mongoloid** ['maŋgələɪd] *adj* & *s* mogoloide
**mongoose** o **mongoos** ['maŋgus] *s* (*pl:* **-gooses**) (zool.) mangosta
**mongrel** ['mʌŋgrəl] o ['maŋgrəl] *adj* mestizo; *s* mestizo; perro mestizo, perro cruzado
**moniker** ['manɪkər] *s* signo de identificación de un vagabundo; (slang) apodo
**moniliform** [mo'nɪlɪfɔrm] *adj* moniliforme; (bot. & zool.) moniliforme
**monism** ['manɪzəm] o ['monɪzəm] *s* (philos.) monismo
**monist** ['manɪst] o ['monɪst] *adj* & *s* monista
**monistic** [mo'nɪstɪk] *adj* monista
**monition** [mo'nɪʃən] *s* admonición
**monitor** ['manɪtər] *s* monitor; (hyd., naut. & rad.) monitor; (zool.) varano; *va* (rad.) controlar (*la señal*); (rad.) escuchar (*radiotransmisiones*)
**monitorial** [,manɪ'torɪəl] *adj* monitorio
**monitorship** ['manɪtər,ʃɪp] *s* cargo de monitor
**monitory** ['manɪ,torɪ] *adj* monitorio; *s* (*pl:* **-ries**) monitorio
**monk** [mʌŋk] *s* monje
**monkey** ['mʌŋkɪ] *s* (zool.) mono; (zool.) mono pequeño (*con cola*); (fig.) mono (*persona que hace gestos monescos*); (fig.) mona (*persona que imita a las demás*); **to make a monkey of** tomar el pelo a; *va* imitar, remedar; mofarse de; *vn* tontear, hacer payasadas; **to monkey around** haraganear; **to monkey with** manosear, ajar
**monkey business** *s* (slang) conducta estrafalaria, tretas, trampas
**monkey chatter** *s* (rad.) mezcla de señales
**monkey flower** *s* (bot.) mímulo; (bot.) linaria
**monkey jacket** *s* capote de piloto; (slang) smoking
**monkey puzzle** *s* (bot.) pehuén, pino araucano
**monkeyshine** ['mʌŋkɪ,ʃaɪn] *s* (slang) monada, diablura, payasada
**monkey wrench** *s* llave inglesa; **to throw a monkey wrench into the works** (coll.) hacer fracasar el proyecto, echarlo todo a rodar
**monkhood** ['mʌŋkhʊd] *s* monacato; frailería, los monjes
**monkish** ['mʌŋkɪʃ] *adj* frailengo; (scornful) frailuno
**monk seal** *s* (zool.) foca fraile
**monkshood** ['mʌŋks,hʊd] *s* (bot.) cogulla de fraile, napelo
**monoatomic** [,manoə'tamɪk] *adj* monoatómico
**monobasic** [,manə'besɪk] *adj* (chem.) monobásico
**monocarpellary** [,manə'karpə,lerɪ] *adj* (bot.) monocarpelar
**Monoceros** [mə'nasərəs] *s* (astr.) Monócero
**monocerous** [mə'nasərəs] *adj* monócero
**monochord** ['manəkɔrd] *s* (mus.) monocordio; armonía, concordia
**monochroic** [,manə'kro·ɪk] *adj* monocroico
**monochromatic** [,manəkro'mætɪk] *adj* monocromático
**monochrome** ['manəkrom] *adj* & *s* monocromo
**monochromy** ['manə,kromɪ] *s* monocromía
**monocle** ['manəkəl] *s* monóculo
**monocled** ['manəkəld] *adj* con monóculo
**monoclinic** [,manə'klɪnɪk] *adj* (cryst.) monoclínico
**monocotyledon** [,manə,katɪ'lidən] *s* (bot.) monocotiledón
**monocular** [mə'nakjələr] *adj* monocular; monóculo (*que tiene un solo ojo*)
**monoculture** [,manə'kʌltʃər] *s* (agr.) monocultura
**monoculus** [mə'nakjələs] *s* (surg.) monóculo
**monodic** [mə'nadɪk] *adj* monódico
**monody** ['manədɪ] *s* (*pl:* **-dies**) (mus.) monodia; elegía, canto fúnebre
**monoecious** [mo'niʃəs] *adj* (bot.) monoico
**monogamic** [,manə'gæmɪk] *adj* monogámico
**monogamist** [mə'nagəmɪst] *adj* & *s* monógamo
**monogamistic** [mə,nagə'mɪstɪk] *adj* monogamista
**monogamous** [mə'nagəməs] *adj* monógamo
**monogamy** [mə'nagəmɪ] *s* monogamia; (zool.) monogamia
**monogenism** [mə'nadʒɪnɪzəm] *s* (anthrop.) monogenismo
**monogenist** [mə'nadʒɪnɪst] *s* monogenista
**monogram** ['manəgræm] *s* monograma
**monograph** ['manəgræf] o ['manəgraf] *s* monografía
**monographer** [mə'nagrəfər] *s* monografista
**monographic** [,manə'græfɪk] *adj* monográfico
**monogynous** [mə'nadʒɪnəs] *adj* (bot.) monógino
**monolith** ['manəlɪθ] *s* monolito
**monolithic** [,manə'lɪθɪk] *adj* monolítico
**monolog** ['manəlɔg] o ['manəlag] *s* var. de **monologue**
**monologist** ['manə,lɔgɪst] o ['manə,lagɪst] *s* var. de **monologuist**
**monologue** ['manəlɔg] o ['manəlag] *s* monólogo
**monologuist** ['manə,lɔgɪst] o ['manə,lagɪst] *s* monologuista; hablador que no deja meter baza a los demás
**monomania** [,manə'menɪə] *s* monomanía
**monomaniac** [,manə'menɪæk] *s* monomaníaco
**monomaniacal** [,manəmə'naɪəkəl] *adj* monomaníaco
**monometallic** [,manəmɪ'tælɪk] *adj* (chem.) monometálico; monometalista
**monometallism** [,manə'metəlɪzəm] *s* monometalismo
**monometallist** [,manə'metəlɪst] *adj* & *s* monometalista
**monomial** [mo'nomɪəl] *adj* (alg. & biol.) que consta de un solo término; *s* (alg.) monomio
**monopetalous** [,manə'petələs] *adj* (bot.) monopétalo
**monophase** ['manəfez] *adj* (elec.) monofásico
**monophonic** [,manə'fanɪk] *adj* monofónico
**monophyllous** [,manə'fɪləs] *adj* (bot.) monofilo
**Monophysite** [mə'nafɪsaɪt] *s* (rel.) monofisita
**monoplane** ['manəplen] *s* monoplano
**monoplegia** [,manə'plidʒɪə] *s* (path.) monoplejía
**monopolist** [mə'napəlɪst] *s* monopolista
**monopolistic** [mə,napə'lɪstɪk] *adj* monopolizador
**monopolization** [mə,napəlɪ'zeʃən] *s* monopolización
**monopolize** [mə'napəlaɪz] *va* monopolizar; acaparar (*p.ej., la conversación*)
**monopoly** [mə'napəlɪ] *s* (*pl:* **-lies**) monopolio
**monopteral** [mə'naptərəl] *adj* (arch.) monóptero

**monorail** [ˈmɑnərel] *s* monorriel; línea de monorriel
**monorhymed** [ˈmɑnəraɪmd] *adj* monorrimo
**monosaccharide** [ˌmɑnəˈsækəraɪd] o [ˌmɑnəˈsækərɪd] *s* (chem.) monosacárido
**monosepalous** [ˌmɑnəˈsɛpələs] *adj* (bot.) monosépalo
**monospermous** [ˌmɑnəˈspʌrməs] *adj* (bot.) monospermo
**monostrophe** [məˈnɑstrəfɪ] o [ˈmɑnəstrof] *s* monóstrofe
**monosyllabic** [ˌmɑnəsɪˈlæbɪk] *adj* monosílabo (*de una sola sílaba*); monosilábico
**monosyllable** [ˈmɑnəˌsɪləbəl] *s* monosílabo
**monotheism** [ˈmɑnəˌθiɪzəm] *s* monoteísmo
**monotheist** [ˈmɑnəˌθiɪst] *adj & s* monoteísta
**monotheistic** [ˌmɑnəθiˈɪstɪk] *adj* monoteísta
**monotone** [ˈmɑnəton] *adj* monótono; *s* monotonía
**monotonous** [məˈnɑtənəs] *adj* monótono
**monotony** [məˈnɑtənɪ] *s* monotonía
**monotreme** [ˈmɑnətrim] *adj & s* (zool.) monotrema
**monotype** [ˈmɑnətaɪp] *s* (biol.) especie única; (trademark) monotipia; carácter de monotipia; *va* componer con monotipia
**monotyper** [ˈmɑnəˌtaɪpər] *s* monotipista
**monovalent** [ˌmɑnəˈvelənt] *adj* (chem. & bact.) monovalente
**monoxide** [məˈnɑksaɪd] *s* (chem.) monóxido
**Monroe Doctrine** [mənˈro] *s* doctrina de Monroe
**Monroeism** [mənˈro·ɪzəm] *s* monroísmo
**monseigneur** o **Monseigneur** [ˌmɑnsenˈjœr] *s* (*pl:* **Messeigneurs** [ˌmɛsenˈjœr]) monseñor
**monsignor** o **Monsignor** [mɑnˈsinjər] *s* (*pl:* **Monsignors** o **Monsignori** [ˌmɔnsiˈnjori]) (eccl.) monseñor
**monsoon** [mɑnˈsun] *s* monzón
**monsoonal** [mɑnˈsunəl] *adj* monzónico
**monster** [ˈmɑnstər] *s* monstruo; *adj* monstruoso
**monstrance** [ˈmɑnstrəns] *s* (eccl.) custodia, ostensorio
**monstrosity** [mɑnˈstrɑsɪtɪ] *s* (*pl:* **-ties**) monstruosidad
**monstrous** [ˈmɑnstrəs] *adj* monstruoso; *adv* (coll.) monstruosamente
**mons Veneris** [mɑnzˈvɛnərɪs] *s* (anat.) monte de Venus
**Mont.** abr. de **Montana**
**montage** [mɑnˈtɑʒ] *s* montaje
**montane** [ˈmɑnten] *adj* montano
**montan wax** [ˈmɑntæn] *s* cera montana
**Mont Blanc** [mɑntˈblæŋk] *s* el monte Blanco
**monte** [ˈmɑntɪ] *s* monte (*juego de naipes*)
**Montenegrin** [ˌmɑntɪˈnigrɪn] *adj & s* montenegrino
**month** [mʌnθ] *s* mes
**monthly** [ˈmʌnθlɪ] *adj* mensual; *adv* mensualmente; *s* (*pl:* **-lies**) revista mensual; **monthlies** *spl* reglas
**monument** [ˈmɑnjəmənt] *s* monumento; mojón (*para fijar linderos*)
**monumental** [ˌmɑnjəˈmɛntəl] *adj* monumental
**moo** [mu] *s* mugido (*de la vaca*); *vn* mugir (*la vaca*)
**mooch** [mutʃ] *va* (slang) robar; (slang) pedir de gorra; *vn* (slang) andar a sombra de tejado
**mood** [mud] *s* humor, genio; (gram.) modo; **moods** *spl* arranques de cólera, ataques de melancolía; **to be in a bad mood** estar de mal talante; **to be in a good mood** estar de buen talante; **to be in the mood to** + *inf* estar en disposición de + *inf*
**moody** [ˈmudɪ] *adj* (*comp:* **-ier;** *super:* **-iest**) caprichoso, veleidoso; caviloso; triste, hosco
**moon** [mun] *s* luna; **to bark** o **to bay at the moon** ladrar a la luna; *vn* estar viendo visiones, andar como alma en pena
**moonbeam** [ˈmunˌbim] *s* rayo lunar
**mooncalf** [ˈmunˌkæf] o [ˈmunˌkɑf] *s* bobo, tonto, imbécil; (path.) mola (*tumor del útero*)
**moon-faced** [ˈmunˌfest] *adj* mofletudo, carirredondo
**moonlight** [ˈmunˌlaɪt] *s* claror de luna, luz de la luna; *adj* iluminado por la luna; de luz lunar
**moonlighting** [ˈmunˌlaɪtɪŋ] *s* (coll.) multiempleo
**moonlit** [ˈmunˌlɪt] *adj* iluminado por la luna
**moonrise** [ˈmunˌraɪz] *s* salida de la luna
**moonsail** [ˈmunˌsel] *s* (naut.) monterilla
**moonshine** [ˈmunˌʃaɪn] *s* luz de la luna; cháchara, pamplinas; (coll.) licor destilado ilegalmente
**moonshiner** [ˈmunˌʃaɪnər] *s* (coll.) fabricante de licor ilegal; (coll.) traficante nocturno ilegal
**moon shot** *s* lanzamiento a la Luna
**moonstone** [ˈmunˌston] *s* (mineral.) piedra de la luna
**moonstruck** [ˈmunˌstrʌk] *adj* aturdido; enloquecido
**moonwort** [ˈmunˌwʌrt] *s* (bot.) botriquio, lunaria menor; (bot.) hierba de la plata
**moony** [ˈmunɪ] *adj* (*comp:* **-ier;** *super:* **-iest**) lunar; lunado; alelado; desatento, indiferente
**moor** [mʊr] *s* brezal, páramo; (*cap.*) *s* moro; (*l.c.*) *va* (naut.) amarrar; *vn* (naut.) echar las amarras, echar las anclas
**moorage** [ˈmʊrɪdʒ] *s* (naut.) amarradura; (naut.) amarradero; (naut.) derechos de puerto
**moor cock** *s* (orn.) lagópedo de Escocia
**moorfowl** [ˈmʊrˌfaʊl] *s* (orn.) lagópedo de Escocia
**moor hen** *s* (orn.) hembra del lagópedo de Escocia; (orn.) polla
**mooring** [ˈmʊrɪŋ] *s* (naut.) amarradura; **moorings** *spl* (naut.) amarras; (naut.) amarradero
**mooring mast** *s* (aer.) antena o poste de amarre (*de un dirigible*)
**Moorish** [ˈmʊrɪʃ] *adj* moro
**Moorish arch** *s* (arch.) arco arábigo
**moorland** [ˈmʊrˌlænd] o [ˈmʊrlənd] *s* brezal
**moose** [mus] *s* (*pl:* **moose**) (zool.) alce de América
**moot** [mut] *adj* opinable, discutible; dudoso, indeciso; *s* junta, reunión; *va* discutir judicialmente; proponer para la discusión
**moot court** *s* (law) tribunal ad hoc (*en las escuelas de derecho*)
**mop** [mɑp] *s* mueca; espesura, cabellera espesa; aljofifa, estropajo; (*pret & pp:* **mopped;** *ger:* **mopping**) *va* aljofifar; enjugarse o secarse (*la frente con un pañuelo*); **to mop up** (mil.) acabar con (*el resto del enemigo*); (mil.) limpiar (*un terreno conquistado*) de combatientes dispersos; (slang) acabar con; (Brit.) beber; *vn* hacer muecas; **to mop and mow** hacer muecas
**mopboard** [ˈmɑpˌbord] *s* rodapié
**mope** [mop] *s* apático, melancólico; *vn* andar abatido, entregarse a la melancolía
**mopish** [ˈmopɪʃ] *adj* abatido, melancólico
**moppet** [ˈmɑpɪt] *s* (coll.) chiquillo; (coll.) muñeca
**moquette** [moˈkɛt] *s* moqueta
**moraceous** [moˈreʃəs] *adj* (bot.) moráceo
**moraine** [məˈren] *s* (geol.) morena
**moral** [ˈmɑrəl] o [ˈmɔrəl] *adj* moral; *s* moraleja (*p.ej., de una fábula*); **morals** *spl* moral (*ciencia de la conducta; conducta*)
**moral certainty** *s* certidumbre moral
**morale** [məˈræl] o [məˈrɑl] *s* moral (*p.ej., de las tropas*)
**moralist** [ˈmɑrəlɪst] o [ˈmɔrəlɪst] *s* moralizador; moralista
**moralistic** [ˌmɑrəˈlɪstɪk] o [ˌmɔrəˈlɪstɪk] *adj* moralizador
**morality** [məˈrælɪtɪ] *s* (*pl:* **-ties**) moralidad; (lit.) moralidad
**morality play** *s* (lit.) moralidad
**moralize** [ˈmɑrəlaɪz] o [ˈmɔrəlaɪz] *va* moralizar; deducir la moral de; *vn* moralizar
**moralizer** [ˈmɑrəˌlaɪzər] o [ˈmɔrəˌlaɪzər] *s* moralizador
**morally** [ˈmɑrəlɪ] o [ˈmɔrəlɪ] *adv* moralmente
**moral philosophy** *s* filosofía moral
**morals charge** *s* acusación por delito sexual, acusación por inmoralidades
**moral support** *s* ayuda moral
**moral victory** *s* derrota que, por razones morales, no lo es, sino victoria
**morass** [məˈræs] *s* pantano; (fig.) pantano (*dificultad, estorbo*)
**moratorium** [ˌmɑrəˈtorɪəm] o [ˌmɔrəˈtorɪəm] *s* (*pl:* **-ums** o **-a** [ə]) moratoria

**moratory** ['mɑrə,torɪ] o ['mɔrə,torɪ] *adj* moratorio

**Moravian** [mo'revɪən] *adj* moravo; *s* moravo; hermano moravo

**moray** ['more] o [mo're] *s* (ichth.) morena

**morbid** ['mɔrbɪd] *adj* morboso; malsano; horrible, espantoso

**morbidity** [mɔr'bɪdɪtɪ] *s* morbosidad

**morbific** [mɔr'bɪfɪk] o **morbifical** [mɔr'bɪfɪkəl] *adj* morbífico

**mordacious** [mɔr'deʃəs] *adj* mordaz

**mordacity** [mɔr'dæsɪtɪ] *s* mordacidad

**mordancy** ['mɔrdənsɪ] *s* mordacidad

**mordant** ['mɔrdənt] *adj* mordaz; *s* mordiente

**Mordecai** ['mɔrdɪkaɪ] *s* (Bib.) Mardoqueo

**mordent** ['mɔrdənt] *s* (mus.) mordente

**more** [mor] *adj, adv & s* más; **any more** ya no; **at more than** en más de + *numeral;* **neither more nor less** ni más ni menos; **no more** no más; ya no; se acabó; **no more, no less** ni más ni menos; **the more the merrier** cuanto más mejor, cuantos más mejor; **the more . . . the more** (o **the less**) cuanto más . . . tanto más (o menos) o mientras más . . . más (o menos), p.ej., **the more he has the more he wants** cuanto más tiene tanto más desea o mientras más tiene más desea; **more and more** más y más, cada vez más; **more or less** más o menos; poco más o menos; **more than** más que; más de lo que + *verb;* más de + *numeral*

**moreen** [mə'rin] *s* filipichín

**morel** [mə'rɛl] o ['mɑrɛl] *s* (bot.) múrgula, morilla

**moreover** [mor'ovər] *adv* además, por otra parte

**mores** ['moriz] *spl* costumbres, usos tradicionales

**Moresque** [mo'rɛsk] *adj* moro; (arch.) árabe; *s* (arch.) estilo árabe

**morganatic** [,mɔrgə'nætɪk] *adj* morganático

**morganatically** [,mɔrgə'nætɪkəlɪ] *adv* morganáticamente

**morganatic marriage** *s* matrimonio morganático

**Morgan le Fay** ['mɔrgən lə 'fe] *s* (myth.) Morgana

**morgue** [mɔrg] *s* depósito de cadáveres (*no identificados*)

**moribund** ['mɑrɪbʌnd] o ['mɔrɪbʌnd] *adj & s* moribundo

**morin** ['morɪn] *s* (chem.) morina

**morion** ['morɪɑn] *s* morrión

**Morisco** [mə'rɪsko] *adj* morisco, moro; *s* (*pl:* **-cos** o **-coes**) moro; moro de España; morisco (*en Méjico, descendiente de mulato y española o de mulata y español*)

**Mormon** ['mɔrmən] *adj* mormónico; *s* mormón; (*l.c.*) *s* (zool.) mormón

**Mormonism** ['mɔrmənɪzəm] *s* mormonismo

**morn** [mɔrn] *s* (poet.) mañana

**morning** ['mɔrnɪŋ] *s* mañana; (fig.) aurora (*principios*); **the morning after** (coll.) la mañana después de la juerga; *adj* matinal, de la mañana, de mañana

**morning coat** *s* chaqué

**morning dress** *s* traje de mañana

**morning-glory** ['mɔrnɪŋ,glorɪ] *s* (*pl:* **-ries**) (bot.) dondiego de día

**morning sickness** *s* (path.) vómitos del embarazo

**morning star** *s* lucero del alba; (bot.) pegarropa; (mil.) mangual

**Moro** ['moro] *s* (*pl:* **-ros**) moro (*malayo mahometano de las Islas Filipinas y su idioma*)

**Moroccan** [mə'rɑkən] *adj & s* marroquí o marroquín

**Morocco** [mə'rɑko] *s* Marruecos; (*l.c.*) *s* marroquí o marroquín (*tafilete*)

**moron** ['morɑn] *s* morón; (coll.) imbécil

**morose** [mə'ros] *adj* malhumorado, triste, lóbrego

**morphea** [mɔr'fiə] *s* (path.) morfea

**morpheme** ['mɔrfim] *s* (gram.) morfema

**Morpheus** ['mɔrfjus] o ['mɔrfɪəs] *s* (myth.) Morfeo

**morphia** ['mɔrfɪə] o **morphine** ['mɔrfin] *s* (chem.) morfina

**morphinism** ['mɔrfɪnɪzəm] *s* (path.) morfinismo

**morphogenesis** [,mɔrfə'dʒɛnɪsɪs] *s* morfogénesis

**morphogenic** [,mɔrfə'dʒɛnɪk] *adj* (embryol.) morfógeno

**morphologic** [,mɔrfə'lɑdʒɪk] o **morphological** [,mɔrfə'lɑdʒɪkəl] *adj* morfológico

**morphology** [mɔr'fɑlədʒɪ] *s* (biol. & gram.) morfología

**Morris** ['mɔrɪs] o ['mɑrɪs] *s* Mauricio; (*l.c.*) *s* mojiganga

**morris chair** *s* poltrona de espaldar ajustable

**morris dance** *s* mojiganga

**morrow** ['mɑro] o ['mɔro] *s* (archaic) mañana (*parte del día hasta mediodía*); mañana (*día que sigue al de hoy*); día siguiente; **on the morrow** en el día de mañana; el día siguiente

**Morse code** [mɔrs] *s* (telg.) alfabeto Morse

**morsel** ['mɔrsəl] *s* pedazo, fragmento; bocado

**mort** [mɔrt] *s* (hunt.) toque de muerte (*que se hace sonar al morir la res*); (dial.) gran cantidad, gran número

**mortal** ['mɔrtəl] *adj & s* mortal

**mortality** [mɔr'tælɪtɪ] *s* mortalidad (*calidad de mortal; número proporcional de defunciones*); mortandad (*muertes causadas por epidemia, guerra, etc.*)

**mortally** ['mɔrtəlɪ] *adv* mortalmente

**mortal sin** *s* pecado mortal

**mortar** ['mɔrtər] *s* mortero (*vasija; argamasa*); (arti.) mortero; *va* argamasar; enlucir

**mortarboard** ['mɔrtər,bord] *s* esparavel; gorro estudiantil cuadrado, birrete

**mortgage** ['mɔrgɪdʒ] *s* hipoteca; *va* hipotecar; (fig.) vender (*p.ej., el alma al diablo*)

**mortgagee** [,mɔrgɪ'dʒi] *s* acreedor hipotecario

**mortgager** o **mortgagor** ['mɔrgɪdʒər] *s* deudor hipotecario

**mortice** ['mɔrtɪs] *s & va* var. de **mortise**

**mortician** [mɔr'tɪʃən] *s* funerario, empresario de pompas fúnebres

**mortification** [,mɔrtɪfɪ'keʃən] *s* mortificación; humillación

**mortify** ['mɔrtɪfaɪ] (*pret & pp:* **-fied**) *va* mortificar; humillar; *vn* mortificarse (*un tejido u órgano del cuerpo*)

**mortise** ['mɔrtɪs] *s* (carp.) muesca, mortaja; *va* (carp.) enmuescar, amortajar

**mortise-and-tenon joint** ['mɔrtɪsənd'tɛnən] *s* (carp.) ensambladura de caja y espiga

**mortise gauge** *s* (carp.) gramil para mortajas

**mortise lock** *s* cerradura recercada, cerradura embutida

**mortiser** ['mɔrtɪsər] *s* (carp.) machihembradora (*máquina*)

**mortmain** ['mɔrtmen] *s* (law) manos muertas

**mortuary** ['mɔrtʃʊ,ɛrɪ] *adj* mortuorio; *s* (*pl:* **-ies**) depósito de cadáveres

**morula** ['mɔrjʊlə] o ['mɔrʊlə] *s* (*pl:* **-lae** [li]) (embryol.) mórula

**mos.** abr. de **months**

**Mosaic** [mo'zeɪk] *adj* mosaico (*perteneciente a Moisés*); (*l.c.*) *adj* mosaico; *s* (aer., f.a., & telv.) mosaico

**mosaic disease** *s* (plant path.) enfermedad del mosaico

**mosaic gold** *s* oro mosaico o musivo

**Mosaic law** *s* ley mosaica

**Mosaism** ['mozeɪzəm] *s* mosaísmo

**Moscow** ['mɑskaʊ] o ['mɑsko] *s* Moscú

**Moselle** [mo'zɛl] *s* Mosela

**Moses** ['mozɪz] o ['mozɪs] *s* Moisés

**Moslem** ['mɑzləm] o ['mɑsləm] *adj* musulmán, muslim; *s* (*pl:* **-lems** o **-lem**) musulmán, muslim

**mosque** [mɑsk] *s* mezquita

**mosquito** [məs'kito] *s* (*pl:* **-toes** o **-tos**) (ent.) mosquito

**mosquito fleet** *s* (slang) escuadrilla (*de barcos pequeños*)

**mosquito hawk** *s* (orn.) chotacabras; (ent.) caballito del diablo

**mosquito net** *s* mosquitero

**moss** [mɔs] o [mɑs] *s* (bot.) musgo; *va* cubrir de musgo

**moss agate** *s* (mineral.) ágata musgosa

**mossback** ['mɔs,bæk] o ['mɑs,bæk] *s* (slang) fósil (*persona de ideas anticuadas*)

**moss-grown** ['mɔs,gron] o ['mɑs,gron] *adj* musgoso; (fig.) fósil, anticuado

**moss rose** *s* (bot.) rosa musgosa
**mossy** ['mɔsɪ] o ['mɑsɪ] *adj* (*comp:* **-ier;** *super:* **-iest**) musgoso
**most** [most] *adj* más, p.ej., **the one who works hardest earns most money** el que más trabaja gana más dinero; la mayor parte de, los más de, casi todos; *adv* más, p.ej., **this tooth hurts most** esta muela duele más; **she is the most beautiful girl I know** es la muchacha más hermosa que conozco; muy, sumamente, de lo más; (coll.) casi, p.ej., **the work is most finished** el trabajo está casi terminado; *s* la mayor parte, el mayor número, los más; **at most** o **at the most** a lo más, cuando más; **to make the most of** sacar el mejor partido de; **most of** la mayor parte de, el mayor número de, los más
**most favored nation** *s* (dipl.) (la) nación más favorecida
**Most High, the** el Altísimo, el Excelso (*Dios*)
**mostly** ['mostlɪ] *adv* por la mayor parte, principalmente; casi, p.ej., **the work is mostly finished** el trabajo está casi terminado
**mote** [mot] *s* mota de polvo
**motel** [mo'tɛl] *s* motel, parador de turismo
**motet** [mo'tɛt] *s* (mus.) motete
**moth** [mɔθ] o [mɑθ] *s* (*pl:* **moths** [mɔðz], [mɑðz], [mɔθs] o [mɑθs]) (ent.) polilla; (ent.) mariposa nocturna
**moth ball** *s* bola de alcanfor, bola de naftalina (*para la polilla*)
**moth-ball fleet** ['mɔθ,bɔl] o ['mɑθ,bɔl] *s* (nav.) flota en conserva, flota en naftalina
**moth-eaten** ['mɔθ,itən] o ['mɑθ,itən] *adj* apolillado; (fig.) anticuado
**mother** ['mʌðər] *s* madre; tía (*tratamiento que se da a las mujeres ancianas*); *adj* madre, p.ej., **mother plant** planta madre; maternal, p.ej., **mother love** amor maternal; materno, p.ej., **mother tongue** lengua materna; metropolitano; *va* servir de madre a; reconocer por hijo; ser origen, causa o fuente de; reconocerse o declararse autor de
**Mother Carey's chicken** ['kerɪz] *s* (orn.) petrel de la tempestad
**mother church** *s* la santa madre iglesia; iglesia metropolitana
**mother country** *s* madre patria (*estado que ha formado una colonia y que la gobierna*); patria (*lugar de nacimiento*)
**mother earth** *s* madre tierra
**Mother Goose** *s* supuesta autora o narradora de una colección de cuentos infantiles (en España: *Cuentos de Calleja*)
**motherhood** ['mʌðərhʊd] *s* maternidad; madres, conjunto de madres
**Mother Hubbard** ['hʌbərd] *s* bata suelta (*de mujer*)
**mother-in-law** ['mʌðərɪn,lɔ] *s* (*pl:* **mothers-in-law**) suegra
**motherland** ['mʌðər,lænd] *s* patria
**motherless** ['mʌðərlɪs] *adj* huérfano de madre, sin madre
**mother liquid** o **liquor** *s* aguas madres
**mother lode** *s* (min.) veta principal
**motherly** ['mʌðərlɪ] *adj* maternal; *adv* maternalmente
**Mother of God** *s* (eccl.) madre de Dios
**mother-of-pearl** ['mʌðərəv'pʌrl] *s* nácar; *adj* nacarado
**Mother's Day** *s* (U.S.A.) día de la madre o de las madres
**mother ship** *s* (nav.) buque madre
**mother superior** *s* superiora
**mother tongue** *s* lengua materna; lengua madre o matriz (*la de que se han derivado otras*)
**mother wit** *s* inteligencia natural; chispa, ingenio
**motherwort** ['mʌðər,wʌrt] *s* (bot.) agripalma
**moth hole** *s* apolilladura
**mothy** ['mɔθɪ] o ['mɑθɪ] *adj* (*comp:* **-ier;** *super:* **-iest**) apolillado
**motif** [mo'tif] *s* (f.a. & mus.) motivo; (fig.) idea dominante
**motile** ['motɪl] *adj* movible
**motility** [mo'tɪlɪtɪ] *s* (biol.) motilidad
**motion** ['moʃən] *s* movimiento; moción (*en junta deliberante*); seña, indicación; (mus.) movimiento; **in motion** en movimiento; en marcha; **to make a motion** hacer o presentar una moción; *va* indicar a (*una persona*) con la mano, la cabeza, etc., p.ej., **he motioned me to sit down** me indicó con la mano que me sentara; *vn* hacer señas
**motionless** ['moʃənlɪs] *adj* inmoble
**motion picture** *s* película cinematográfica
**motion-picture** ['moʃən,pɪktʃər] *adj* cinematográfico
**motion-picture camera** *s* cámara cinematográfica
**motivate** ['motɪvet] *va* motivar
**motivation** [,motɪ'veʃən] *s* motivación
**motive** ['motɪv] *adj* motivo; motor; *s* motivo; (f.a. & mus.) motivo
**motive power** *s* potencia motora o motriz, fuerza motriz; conjunto de locomotoras de un ferrocarril
**motley** ['mɑtlɪ] *adj* abigarrado; mezclado, variado; *s* mezcla confusa; traje abigarrado de payaso
**motor** ['motər] *adj* motor; (anat.) motor; *s* motor; motor eléctrico; automóvil; *vn* ir, pasear o viajar en automóvil
**motor block** *s* bloque de cilindros
**motorboat** ['motər,bot] *s* autobote, gasolinera
**motorbus** ['motər,bʌs] *s* autobús, ómnibus automóvil
**motorcade** ['motər,ked] *s* caravana de automóviles
**motorcar** ['motər,kɑr] *s* automóvil; (rail.) autocarril
**motor coach** *s* coche motor, autobús
**motor converter** *s* (elec.) motor-convertidor
**motorcycle** ['motər,saɪkəl] *s* motocicleta
**motorcyclist** ['motər,saɪklɪst] *s* motociclista
**motor drive** *s* (elec.) grupo motopropulsor
**motor-driven** ['motər,drɪvən] *adj* (elec.) motopropulsor
**motordrome** ['motər,drom] *s* motódromo
**motor generator** *s* (elec.) grupo de motor y generador, motor-generador
**motoring** ['motərɪŋ] *s* motorismo, automovilismo
**motorist** ['motərɪst] *s* motorista, automovilista
**motorization** [,motərɪ'zeʃən] *s* motorización
**motorize** ['motəraɪz] *va* motorizar
**motor launch** *s* lancha automóvil
**motor lorry** *s* (Brit.) autocamión
**motorman** ['motərmən] *s* (*pl:* **-men**) conductor (*de un tranvía o de una locomotora eléctrica*)
**motor sailer** *s* (naut.) motovelero
**motor scooter** *s* motoneta
**motor ship** *s* motonave
**motor truck** *s* autocamión, camión automóvil
**motor van** *s* (Brit.) autocamión
**motor vehicle** *s* vehículo motor
**mottle** ['mɑtəl] *s* mancha o veta de color; color moteado o veteado; *va* abigarrar, jaspear, motear
**motto** ['mɑto] *s* (*pl:* **-toes** o **-tos**) lema, divisa
**mouflon** o **moufflon** ['muflɑn] *s* (zool.) musmón
**mould** [mold] *s, va & vn* var. de **mold**
**moulder** ['moldər] *s, va & vn* var. de **molder**
**moulding** ['moldɪŋ] *s* var. de **molding**
**mouldy** ['moldɪ] *adj* (*comp:* **-ier;** *super:* **-iest**) var. de **moldy**
**mound** [maʊnd] *s* montón de tierra o piedras; montecillo, montículo; (baseball) lomita, montículo; *va* amontonar; encerrar con terraplenes de defensa
**mount** [maʊnt] *s* monte; montura (*cabalgadura*); montadura (*p.ej., de una joya*); soporte; papel de soporte; cartón o tela (*en que está pegada una fotografía*); (mach.) montaje; (arti.) montajes; *va* subir (*una escalera, una cuesta, etc.*); subir a (*p.ej., la plataforma*); escalar (*p.ej., una muralla*); montar (*subir a; armar; preparar para la exhibición; engastar*); (mach.) montar; (naut.) montar (*tantos o cuantos cañones*); (mil.) montar (*la guardia*); poner a caballo; proveer de caballos; pegar (*vistas, pruebas, etc.*); *vn* montar; montarse; aumentar (*p.ej., precios, deudas*)
**mountain** ['maʊntən] *s* montaña; (fig.) montón (*cosas puestas unas encima de otras; cantidad abundante*); **to make a mountain out**

of a molehill hacer de una pulga un camello o un elefante; *adj* montañés; montañoso
**mountain ash** *s* (bot.) serbal; (bot.) serbal de los cazadores; (bot.) alfitonia
**mountain chain** *s* cadena de montañas
**mountain climber** *s* montañero, alpinista
**mountain climbing** *s* montañismo, alpinismo
**mountain cranberry** *s* (bot.) arándano encarnado
**mountain damson** *s* (bot.) aceitillo (*Simarouba amara*)
**mountain dew** *s* (slang) whisky de Escocia; (slang) whisky de contrabando
**mountaineer** [ˌmaʊntəˈnɪr] *s* montañés; alpinista, montañero; *vn* dedicarse al alpinismo
**mountaineering** [ˌmaʊntəˈnɪrɪŋ] *s* alpinismo, montañismo; *adj* montañero
**mountain goat** *s* (zool.) cabra de las Montañas Rocosas (*Oreamnos montanus*)
**mountain laurel** *s* (bot.) calmia
**mountain lion** *s* (zool.) puma, león de América
**mountainous** [ˈmaʊntənəs] *adj* montañoso; inmenso
**mountain parsley** *s* (bot.) oreoselino, perejil de monte
**mountain railroad** o **railway** *s* ferrocarril de cremallera
**mountain range** *s* cordillera, sierra
**mountain sheep** *s* (zool.) carnero cimarrón de las Montañas Rocosas
**mountain sickness** *s* mal de altura, mal de las montañas
**Mountain time** *s* (U.S.A.) hora legal correspondiente al meridiano 105°
**mountaintop** [ˈmaʊntənˌtɑp] *s* cumbre de la montaña
**mountebank** [ˈmaʊntɪbæŋk] *s* saltabanco
**mounted** [ˈmaʊntɪd] *adj* montado (*a caballo, de a caballo; armado; engastado*)
**mounting** [ˈmaʊntɪŋ] *s* montura (*de una piedra preciosa, arma, telescopio, etc.*); montaje (*de una máquina*); papel de soporte; papel o tela (*en que está pegada una fotografía*)
**mourn** [morn] *va* llorar (*la muerte de una persona*); lamentar (*una desgracia*); *vn* lamentarse; vestir de luto
**mourner** [ˈmornər] *s* doliente; penitente; plañidera
**mourners' bench** *s* banco de los penitentes (*en ciertas solemnidades religiosas*)
**mournful** [ˈmornfəl] *adj* dolorido, triste; lúgubre
**mourning** [ˈmornɪŋ] *adj* de luto; *s* luto; **to be in mourning** estar de luto
**mourning band** *s* crespón fúnebre
**mourning bride** *s* (bot.) viuda
**mourning dove** *s* (orn.) paloma triste
**mourning widow** *s* (bot.) viuda
**mouse** [maʊs] *s* (*pl:* **mice**) (zool.) ratón; (naut.) barrilete; [maʊz] *va* cazar o coger (*ratones*); husmear; (naut.) amarrar; *vn* cazar o coger ratones; andar al acecho; andar a hurtadillas
**mouse-ear** [ˈmaʊsˌɪr] *s* (bot.) pelosilla, vellosilla
**mousehole** [ˈmaʊsˌhol] *s* ratonera; pequeño agujero
**mouser** [ˈmaʊzər] *s* desmurador, gato desmurador; husmeador
**mousetrap** [ˈmaʊsˌtræp] *s* ratonera (*trampa*)
**mousing** [ˈmaʊzɪŋ] *s* (naut.) barrilete
**mousse** [mus] *s* mousse, manjar de crema batida y gelatina
**mousseline** [musˈlin] *s* (Fr.) muselina
**mousseline de laine** [də ˈlɛn] *s* (Fr.) muselina de lana
**mousseline de soie** [də ˈswɑ] *s* (Fr.) muselina de China
**moustache** [məsˈtæʃ], [məsˈtɑʃ] o [ˈmʌstæʃ] *s* var. de **mustache**
**mousy** [ˈmaʊsɪ] *adj* (*comp:* **-ier**; *super:* **-iest**) ratonesco; infestado de ratones; que huele a ratones; (fig.) silencioso
**mouth** [maʊθ] *s* (*pl:* **mouths** [maʊðz]) boca; embocadura, desembocadura (*de un río*); tragante (*de un horno de cuba*); mueca; expresión (*de un concepto*); **by mouth** por vía bucal; **down in the mouth** abatido, cariacontecido; **to be born with a silver spoon in one's mouth** nacer de pie; **to laugh on the other** o **wrong side of one's mouth** convertir la risa en llanto; **to make one's mouth water** hacerle a uno la boca agua; **to not open one's mouth** no decir esta boca es mía; [maʊð] *va* tomar en la boca, asir con los dientes; cariciar o tocar con la boca; articular (*palabras*) con rimbombancia; *vn* hablar con rimbombancia
**mouther** [ˈmaʊðər] *s* parlón
**mouthful** [ˈmaʊθfʊl] *s* bocado; (slang) abundancia de palabras
**mouth organ** *s* (mus.) armónica de boca; (mus.) flauta de Pan
**mouthpiece** [ˈmaʊθˌpis] *s* boquilla (*de un instrumento de música, de una herramienta, etc.*); bocado (*de freno*); (fig.) portavoz
**mouthwash** [ˈmaʊθˌwɑʃ] *s* enjuague, enjuagadientes
**mouthy** [ˈmaʊðɪ] o [ˈmaʊθɪ] *adj* (*comp:* **-ier**; *super:* **-iest**) deslenguado, vocinglero, ampuloso
**movable** [ˈmuvəbəl] *adj* movible; mueble; (astrol.) movible; *s* mueble; **movables** *spl* bienes muebles
**movable feast** *s* (eccl.) fiesta movible
**move** [muv] *s* movimiento; paso; mudanza (*de una casa a otra*); acción, gestión; **on the move** en movimiento; **to get a move on** (coll.) menearse, darse prisa; **to make a move** dar un paso; tomar medidas; hacer una jugada; *va* mover; evacuar, exonerar (*el vientre*); proponer; conmover, enternecer; **to move someone to** + *inf* mover a alguien a + *inf;* **to move up** adelantar (*una fecha*); *vn* moverse; caminar; desplazarse (*un viajante, los planetas, etc.*); circular; mudarse, mudar de casa; trasladarse (*p.ej., a otra ciudad*); hacer una jugada; hacer una moción; venderse, tener salida (*una mercancía*); moverse, evacuarse, exonerarse (*el vientre*); girar (*una puerta*); **to move about** moverse de acá para allá, desplazarse; **to move along** ir a gran velocidad; **to move away** apartarse; marcharse; mudar de casa; **to move forward** avanzar; **to move in** instalarse; instalarse en; alternar con, frecuentar (*p.ej., la buena sociedad*); **to move off** alejarse
**moveable** [ˈmuvəbəl] *adj* & *s* var. de **movable**
**movement** [ˈmuvmənt] *s* movimiento; evacuación (*del vientre*); aparato de relojería; (f.a. & lit.) movimiento; (mus.) movimiento (*velocidad del compás*); (mus.) tiempo (*cada una de las divisiones de una sonata, sinfonía, etc.*)
**mover** [ˈmuvər] *s* movedor; móvil; autor (*de una moción*); empleado de una casa de mudanzas
**movie** [ˈmuvɪ] *s* (coll.) película, cinta; (coll.) sala de proyección, local cinematográfico; **movies** *spl* (coll.) cine
**movie-goer** [ˈmuvɪˌgoər] *s* (coll.) aficionado al cine
**movie house** *s* (coll.) cineteatro
**movieland** [ˈmuvɪˌlænd] *s* (coll.) tierra del ensueño del cine; (coll.) cinelandia, centro principal de la producción cinematográfica
**moving** [ˈmuvɪŋ] *adj* movedor; móvil; conmovedor; *s* movimiento; mudanza (*de una casa a otra*)
**moving coil** *s* (elec.) bobina móvil
**moving day** *s* día de mudanza
**moving part** *s* (mach.) órgano móvil
**moving picture** *s* var. de **motion picture**
**moving spirit** *s* alma (*de una empresa*)
**moving staircase** o **stairway** *s* escalera automática, móvil o rodante
**moving van** *s* carro de mudanza
**mow** [mo] o [maʊ] *s* mueca; [maʊ] *s* granero; henal; montón de heno o de gavillas dentro del granero; [mo] (*pret:* **mowed;** *pp:* **mowed** o **mown**) *va* segar (*el heno, el campo*); **to mow down** segar; matar (*soldados*) con fuego graneado; *vn* segar
**mower** [ˈmoər] *s* segador; segadora mecánica, guadañadora
**mowing** [ˈmo·ɪŋ] *s* siega; prado de guadaña; *adj* segador
**mowing machine** *s* segadora mecánica, guadañadora
**Mozarab** [moˈzærəb] *s* mozárabe
**Mozarabic** [moˈzærəbɪk] *adj* mozárabe
**mozzetta** [moˈzɛtə] *s* (eccl.) muceta
**M.P.** o **MP** abr. de **Member of Parliament,**

**Metropolitan Police, Military Police** y **Mounted Police**
**mph** o **m.p.h.** abr. de **miles per hour**
**Mr.** o **Mr** ['mɪstər] *s* (*pl:* **Messrs.** ['mɛsərz]) señor (*tratamiento*)
**Mrs.** ['mɪsɪz] *s* señora (*tratamiento*)
**ms., Ms.** o **MS.** abr. de **manuscript**
**M.S.** o **M.Sc.** abr. de **Master of Science**
**Msgr.** abr. de **Monsignor**
**mss., Mss.** o **MSS.** abr. de **manuscripts**
**mt.** abr. de **mountain**
**Mt.** abr. de **Mount**
**mtn.** abr. de **mountain**
**mts.** abr. de **mountains**
**much** [mʌtʃ] *adj* (*comp:* **more;** *super:* **most**) mucho; **as much . . . as** tanto . . . como; **to be much of a** ser todo un; **too much** demasiado; *adv* (*comp:* **more;** *super:* **most**) mucho; casi, p.ej., **much the same** casi lo mismo; muy, p.ej., **much surprised** muy asombrado; **as much** tanto; otro tanto; **as much as** tanto como; **as much more** otro tanto más; **too much** demasiado; **however much** por mucho que; **how much** cuánto; **so much** tanto; **so much the better** tanto mejor; **very much** muchísimo; muy, p.ej., **very much annoyed** muy enojado; **much more** mucho más; *s* mucho; **not much of a** de poca cuantía, p.ej., **not much of a person** una persona de poca cuantía; **not much to look at** de mal aspecto, poco imponente; **to make much of** tener en mucho, dar mucha importancia a
**muchness** ['mʌtʃnɪs] *s* abundancia, gran cantidad; **much of a muchness** (coll.) casi lo mismo
**mucilage** ['mjusɪlɪdʒ] *s* mucilago
**mucilaginous** [,mjusɪ'lædʒɪnəs] *adj* mucilaginoso
**mucin** ['mjusɪn] *s* (biochem.) mucina
**muck** [mʌk] *s* estiércol húmedo; (min.) zafra; (coll.) porquería, asquerosidad; *va* estercolar; (coll.) ensuciar
**mucker** ['mʌkər] *s* (min.) zafrero; (slang) grosero
**muck-rake** ['mʌk,rek] *vn* (coll.) exponer ruindades
**muck-raker** ['mʌk,rekər] *s* (coll.) expositor de ruindades
**mucky** ['mʌkɪ] *adj* (*comp:* **-ier;** *super:* **-iest**) podrido, estercolizo; puerco, sucio
**mucoid** ['mjukɔɪd] *s* (biochem.) mucoide
**mucosa** [mju'kosə] *s* (*pl:* **-sae** [si]) (anat.) mucosa
**mucosity** [mju'kɑsɪtɪ] *s* mucosidad
**mucous** ['mjukəs] *adj* mucoso
**mucous membrane** *s* (anat.) membrana mucosa
**mucronate** ['mjukronɪt] o ['mjukronet] *adj* mucronato
**mucus** ['mjukəs] *s* moco, mucosidad
**mud** [mʌd] *s* fango, barro, lodo; (fig.) fango; **to sling mud at** (fig.) llenar de fango
**muddle** ['mʌdəl] *s* embrollo, confusión; *va* embrollar, confundir; atontar, aturdir; achispar; *vn* obrar confusamente; **to muddle through** salir del paso a duras penas; acertar de puro cachazudo
**muddlehead** ['mʌdəl,hɛd] *s* farraguista
**muddleheaded** ['mʌdəl,hɛdɪd] *adj* atontado, confuso, estúpido
**muddy** ['mʌdɪ] *adj* (*comp:* **-dier;** *super:* **-diest**) fangoso, barroso; turbio; (*pret & pp:* **-died**) *va* enturbiar; *vn* enturbiarse
**mud eel** *s* (ichth.) anguila de barro
**mudguard** ['mʌd,gɑrd] *s* guardabarros
**mud hen** *s* (orn.) polla, fúlica americana
**mudhole** ['mʌd,hol] *s* ciénaga, lodazal
**mud puppy** *s* (zool.) necturo; (zool.) ajolote; (zool.) salamandra gigante norteamericana
**mudsill** ['mʌd,sɪl] *s* madero de construcción colocado en el suelo como cimiento
**mudslinger** ['mʌd,slɪŋər] *s* (fig.) lanzador de lodo
**mud turtle** *s* (zool.) tortuga de río; (zool.) jicotea; (zool.) chiquigao, tortuga lagarto
**mud volcano** *s* (geol.) volcán de lodo
**muezzin** [mju'ɛzɪn] *s* almuecín o almuédano
**muff** [mʌf] *s* manguito; chapucería, torpeza; (baseball) falta que consiste en dejar caer torpemente la pelota; *va* chafallar, frangollar; (baseball) dejar escapar (*la pelota*)
**muffin** ['mʌfɪn] *s* bollo, mollete, panecillo
**muffle** ['mʌfəl] *s* ruido sordo o amortiguado; amortiguador de sonido; tambor de polea; mufla (*de un horno*); *va* amortiguar (*un ruido*); enfundar (*un tambor*); embozar, arropar; envolver en paños la cabeza de
**muffle furnace** *s* horno de mufla
**muffler** ['mʌflər] *s* bufanda; amortiguador de ruido; (aut.) silencioso, silenciador
**mufti** ['mʌftɪ] *s* (*pl:* **-tis**) traje de paisano; muftí (*jurisconsulto musulmán*)
**mug** [mʌg] *s* vaso con asa, pichel; (slang) hocico (*de un persona*); (slang) mueca; (*pret & pp:* **mugged;** *ger:* **mugging**) *va* (slang) fotografiar; (slang) sofocar poniendo el brazo alrededor del cuello; *vn* (slang) hacer muecas
**muggy** ['mʌgɪ] *adj* (*comp:* **-gier;** *super:* **-giest**) bochornoso, húmedo y sofocante
**mugwort** ['mʌg,wʌrt] *s* (bot.) artemisa
**mugwump** ['mʌg,wʌmp] *s* votante independiente (*sin alianzas de partido*); (U.S.A.) republicano rebelde (*de los que en las elecciones de 1884 negaron el voto al candidato oficial del partido republicano*)
**Muhammad** [mʊ'hæməd] *s* var. de **Mohammed**
**mulatto** [mjʊ'læto] o [mə'læto] *adj* mulato; *s* (*pl:* **-toes**) mulato
**mulberry** ['mʌl,bɛrɪ] *s* (*pl:* **-ries**) (bot.) morera (*Morus alba*); (bot.) moreda o moral (*Morus nigra*); mora (*fruto*); morado, color morado; *adj* morado
**mulch** [mʌltʃ] *s* (hort.) estiércol, paja y hojas; *va* (hort.) cubrir con estiércol, paja y hojas
**mulct** [mʌlkt] *s* multa; *va* multar; defraudar
**mule** [mjul] *s* mulo; babucha; hiladora mecánica alternativa; (coll.) persona terca
**mule chair** *s* artolas
**mule deer** *s* (zool.) ciervo mulo
**muleteer** [,mjulə'tɪr] *s* mulatero, arriero
**mulish** ['mjulɪʃ] *adj* terco, obstinado
**mull** [mʌl] *s* muselina clara; *va* calentar (*vino*) con especias; *vn* reflexionar; **to mull over** reflexionar sobre
**mullein** o **mullen** ['mʌlɪn] *s* (bot.) gordolobo
**muller** ['mʌlər] *s* moleta
**mullet** ['mʌlɪt] *s* (ichth.) mújol, céfalo
**mulligan** ['mʌlɪgən] *s* (slang) olla, puchero
**mulligatawny** [,mʌlɪgə'tɔnɪ] *s* sopa de arroz y carne sazonada con cari
**mullion** ['mʌljən] *s* (arch.) parteluz (*de una ventana*); (arch.) montante (*de una puerta*)
**mullioned** ['mʌljənd] *adj* (arch.) dividido por montantes
**mulse** [mʌls] *s* vino mulso
**multicellular** [,mʌltɪ'sɛljələr] *adj* multicelular
**multicolored** ['mʌltɪ,kʌlərd] *adj* multicolor
**multidentate** [,mʌltɪ'dɛntet] *adj* multidentado
**multifarious** [,mʌltɪ'fɛrɪəs] *adj* múltiple
**multiflorous** [,mʌltɪ'florəs] *adj* (bot.) multifloro
**multifold** ['mʌltɪfold] *adj* múltiple
**multiform** ['mʌltɪfɔrm] *adj* multiforme
**multigraph** ['mʌltɪgræf] o ['mʌltɪgrɑf] *s* (trademark) multígrafo; *va* multigrafiar
**multilateral** [,mʌltɪ'lætərəl] *adj* multilátero (*de muchos lados*); multilateral (*pacto, alianza*)
**multimillionaire** [,mʌltɪ,mɪljə'nɛr] *s* multimillonario
**multipara** [mʌl'tɪpərə] *s* (*pl:* **-rae** [ri]) multípara
**multiparous** [mʌl'tɪpərəs] *adj* multípara
**multiphase** ['mʌltɪfez] *adj* (elec.) polifásico
**multiple** ['mʌltɪpəl] *adj* múltiplo; (elec. & math.) múltiplo; *s* (elec. & math.) múltiplo; **in multiple** (elec.) en múltiplo
**multiple-lens camera** ['mʌltɪpəl'lɛnz] *s* (phot.) cámara múltiple
**multiple sclerosis** *s* (path.) esclerosis múltiple, esclerosis en placas
**multiplet** ['mʌltɪplɪt] *s* (phys.) multiplete
**multiplex** ['mʌltɪplɛks] *adj* múltiple; (rad. & telg.) múltiplex
**multipliable** ['mʌltɪ,plaɪəbəl] *adj* multiplicable
**multiplicand** [,mʌltɪplɪ'kænd] *s* (math.) multiplicando

**multiplication** [ˌmʌltɪplɪˈkeʃən] *s* multiplicación

**multiplication table** *s* tabla de multiplicación, tabla de multiplicar

**multiplicity** [ˌmʌltɪˈplɪsɪtɪ] *s* (*pl:* **-ties**) multiplicidad

**multiplier** [ˈmʌltɪˌplaɪər] *s* multiplicador: (math.) multiplicador

**multiply** [ˈmʌltɪplaɪ] (*pret & pp:* **-plied**) *va* multiplicar; *vn* multiplicarse

**multipolar** [ˌmʌltɪˈpolər] o **multipole** [ˈmʌltɪpol] *adj* (anat. & elec.) multipolar

**multistage** [ˈmʌltɪstedʒ] *adj* de etapas multiples, multiseccional

**multistory** [ˈmʌltɪˌstorɪ] *adj* de varios pisos

**multitude** [ˈmʌltɪtjud] o [ˈmʌltɪtud] *s* multitud

**multitudinous** [ˌmʌltɪˈtjudɪnəs] o [ˌmʌltɪˈtudɪnəs] *adj* numeroso; múltiple

**multivalence** [ˌmʌltɪˈveləns] o [mʌlˈtɪvələns] *s* (bact. & chem.) polivalencia

**multivalent** [ˌmʌltɪˈvelənt] o [mʌlˈtɪvələnt] *adj* (bact. & chem.) polivalente

**multivalve** [ˈmʌltɪˌvælv] *adj* multivalvo

**mum** [mʌm] *adj* callado; **to keep mum** estar en muda; **to keep mum about** callar; **mum's the word!** ¡punto en boca!, ¡que se guarde silencio!; *interj* ¡a callar!, ¡chitón!

**mumble** [ˈmʌmbəl] *s* mascujada; *va & vn* mascujar (*decir o hablar entre dientes; mascar mal*)

**mumbo jumbo** [ˈmʌmbo ˈdʒʌmbo] *s* (*pl:* **mumbo jumbos**) fetiche, coco; conjuro; (*caps.*) *s* genio tutelar (*entre los negros del Gambia*)

**mummer** [ˈmʌmər] *s* máscara (*persona*); cómico, histrión

**mummery** [ˈmʌmərɪ] *s* (*pl:* **-ies**) mojiganga; (fig.) mojiganga (*burla, hipocresía*)

**mummification** [ˌmʌmɪfɪˈkeʃən] *s* momificación

**mummify** [ˈmʌmɪfaɪ] (*pret & pp:* **-fied**) *va* momificar; *vn* momificarse

**mummy** [ˈmʌmɪ] *s* (*pl:* **-mies**) momia

**mumps** [mʌmps] *s* (path.) papera, parótidas

**munch** [mʌntʃ] *va* ronzar

**mundane** [ˈmʌnden] *adj* mundano

**municipal** [mjuˈnɪsɪpəl] *adj* municipal

**municipality** [mjuˌnɪsɪˈpælɪtɪ] *s* (*pl:* **-ties**) municipio

**municipalization** [mjuˌnɪsɪpəlɪˈzeʃən] *s* municipalización

**municipalize** [mjuˈnɪsɪpəlaɪz] *va* municipalizar

**munificence** [mjuˈnɪfɪsəns] *s* munificencia

**munificent** [mjuˈnɪfɪsənt] *adj* munífico

**muniment** [ˈmjunɪmənt] *s* apoyo, defensa; **muniments** *spl* (law) documentos probatorios, privilegios

**munition** [mjuˈnɪʃən] *s* munición; *adj* de municiones; *va* municionar

**munition dump** *s* depósito de municiones

**mural** [ˈmjurəl] *adj* mural; *s* pintura mural, decoración mural

**mural crown** *s* (hist.) corona mural

**murder** [ˈmʌrdər] *s* asesinato, homicidio; **murder will out** el homicidio no se encubre; toda culpa a su tiempo ha de saberse; *va* asesinar; chafallar, chapucear (*cualquier trabajo*); despachurrar, destripar (*un discurso*); cantar o tocar bárbaramente

**murderer** [ˈmʌrdərər] *s* asesino

**murderess** [ˈmʌrdərɪs] *s* asesina

**murderous** [ˈmʌrdərəs] *adj* asesino; mortal; sanguinario

**murex** [ˈmjurɛks] *s* (*pl:* **-rexes** o **-rices** [rɪsiz]) (zool.) múrice; múrice (*color de púrpura*)

**muriate** [ˈmjurɪet] o [ˈmjurɪɪt] *s* (chem.) muriato

**muriatic** [ˌmjurɪˈætɪk] *adj* muriático

**muriatic acid** *s* (chem.) ácido muriático

**murine** [ˈmjuraɪn] o [ˈmjurɪn] *adj & s* (zool.) murino

**murk** [mʌrk] *s* obscuridad, tinieblas; *adj* (poet.) obscuro, tenebroso

**murky** [ˈmʌrkɪ] *adj* (*comp:* **-ier;** *super:* **-iest**) lóbrego; calinoso, espeso

**murmur** [ˈmʌrmər] *s* murmullo; (med.) murmullo (*p.ej., del corazón*); *va & vn* murmurar

**murrain** [ˈmʌrɪn] *s* (vet.) ántrax; (vet.) fiebre aftosa; **a murrain on you!** (archaic) ¡maldito seas!

**murrhine** [ˈmʌrɪn] o [ˈmʌraɪn] *adj* múrrino

**murther** [ˈmʌrðər] *s & va* (dial.) var. de **murder**

**mus.** abr. de **museum** y **music**

**musaceous** [mjuˈzeʃəs] *adj* (bot.) musáceo

**muscadine** [ˈmʌskədɪn] o [ˈmʌskədaɪn] *s* (bot.) vid y uva del sur de los Estados Unidos (*Vitis rotundifolia*)

**muscardine** [ˈmʌskərdɪn] o [ˈmʌskərdin] *s* (zool.) muscardina

**muscarine** [ˈmʌskərin] o [ˈmʌskərɪn] *s* (chem.) muscarina

**muscat** [ˈmʌskæt] o **muscatel** [ˌmʌskəˈtɛl] *s* moscatel (*uva o vino*)

**muscle** [ˈmʌsəl] *s* (anat.) músculo; (fig.) fuerza muscular; **not to move a muscle** mantenerse inmóvil; *vn* (coll.) avanzar o entrar por fuerza

**muscle-bound** [ˈmʌsəlˌbaund] *adj* con agujetas en los músculos

**muscovado** [ˌmʌskoˈvedo] *adj & s* mascabado

**muscovite** [ˈmʌskəvaɪt] *s* (mineral.) moscovita; (*cap.*) *adj & s* moscovita

**Muscovitic** [ˌmʌskəˈvɪtɪk] *adj* moscovítico

**Muscovy** [ˈmʌskəvɪ] *s* Moscovia

**Muscovy duck** *s* (orn.) pato almizclado

**muscular** [ˈmʌskjələr] *adj* muscular (*perteneciente a los músculos*); musculoso (*que tiene muchos músculos o músculos abultados*)

**muscular dystrophy** *s* (path.) distrofia muscular progresiva

**muscularity** [ˌmʌskjəˈlærɪtɪ] *s* carnadura, musculatura, fuerza muscular

**musculature** [ˈmʌskjələtʃər] *s* musculatura

**muse** [mjuz] *s* musa; (*cap.*) *s* (myth.) Musa; (*l.c.*) *va* decir pausadamente, midiendo bien las palabras; *vn* meditar, reflexionar; **to muse on** contemplar

**musette bag** [mjuˈzɛt] *s* morral, mochila

**museum** [mjuˈziəm] *s* museo

**museum beetle** *s* (ent.) antreno, polilla de los museos de historia natural

**mush** [mʌʃ] *s* gachas; (coll.) sensiblería; marcha por la tundra nevada con un trineo tirado por perros; *vn* caminar por la tundra nevada con un trineo tirado por perros

**mushroom** [ˈmʌʃrum] o [ˈmʌʃrʊm] *s* (bot.) hongo, seta; cosa que aparece de la noche a la mañana; *adj* fungoideo; que aparece de la noche a la mañana; *vn* aparecer de la noche a la mañana; tomar la forma de hongo; esparcirse o crecer rápidamente; aplastarse; **to mushroom into** convertirse en poco tiempo en

**mushroom head** *s* (mach.) cabeza de hongo

**mushroom valve** *s* (mach.) válvula anular, válvula tipo hongo

**mushy** [ˈmʌʃɪ] *adj* (*comp:* **-ier;** *super:* **-iest**) mollar, pulposo; (coll.) sobón, sensiblero; (coll.) baboso (*para con las mujeres*); **to be mushy** (coll.) hacerse unas gachas

**music** [ˈmjuzɪk] *s* música; **to face the music** (coll.) hacer frente a las consecuencias; **to set to music** poner en música

**musical** [ˈmjuzɪkəl] *adj* musical, músico; aficionado a la música; *s* (coll.) ópera bufa, zarzuela; (coll.) velada musical, concierto casero

**musical comedy** *s* ópera bufa, zarzuela

**musicale** [ˌmjuzɪˈkæl] *s* velada musical, concierto casero

**musically** [ˈmjuzɪkəlɪ] *adv* musicalmente

**music box** *s* caja de música

**music cabinet** *s* musiquero

**music hall** *s* salón de conciertos; (Brit.) teatro de variedades, café-concierto

**musician** [mjuˈzɪʃən] *s* músico

**musicianly** [mjuˈzɪʃənlɪ] *adj* entendido en música; artístico (*respecto de las cosas de música*)

**musicianship** [mjuˈzɪʃənʃɪp] *s* musicalidad

**music lover** *s* melómano

**music of the spheres** *s* música mundana (*armonía que guardan los cuerpos celestes en su movimiento*)

**musicographer** [ˌmjuzɪˈkɑgrəfər] *s* musicógrafo

**musicological** [ˌmjuzɪkəˈlɑdʒɪkəl] *adj* musicológico

**musicologist** [ˌmjuzɪˈkɑlədʒɪst] *s* musicólogo

**musicology** [ˌmjuzɪˈkɑlədʒɪ] *s* musicología
**music paper** *s* papel de música
**music rack** *s* atril
**musing** [ˈmjuzɪŋ] *adj* pensativo, meditativo; *s* meditación, contemplación
**musk** [mʌsk] *s* almizcle; olor o perfume de almizcle
**musk beetle** *s* (ent.) macuba
**musk deer** *s* (zool.) almizclero, cabra de almizcle
**muskellunge** [ˈmʌskəlʌndʒ] *s* (ichth.) sollo norteamericano (*Esox masquinongy*)
**musket** [ˈmʌskɪt] *s* mosquete
**musketeer** [ˌmʌskɪˈtɪr] *s* mosquetero
**musketry** [ˈmʌskɪtrɪ] *s* mosquetería (*tropa; descarga*); mosquetes
**muskmelon** [ˈmʌskˌmɛlən] *s* (bot.) melón
**musk ox** *s* (zool.) buey almizclado
**muskrat** [ˈmʌskˌræt] *s* (zool.) almizclera, rata almizclera
**musk rose** *s* (bot.) rosa almizcleña
**musky** [mʌskɪ] *adj* almizcleño, almizclado
**Muslem** o **Muslim** [ˈmʌzləm] o [ˈmʌsləm] *adj & s* muslim o muslime
**muslin** [ˈmʌzlɪn] *s* muselina; *adj* de muselina
**muss** [mʌs] *s* (coll.) desaliño, desorden, confusión; *va* (coll.) desaliñar, desarreglar (*el pelo*); (coll.) chafar (*p.ej., la ropa*)
**mussel** [ˈmʌsəl] *s* (zool.) mejillón
**Mussulman** [ˈmʌsəlmən] *adj* musulmán; *s* (*pl:* **-mans**) musulmán
**mussy** [ˈmʌsɪ] *adj* (*comp:* **-ier;** *super:* **-iest**) (coll.) desaliñado, ajado
**must** [mʌst] *s* mosto (*zumo de la uva antes de fermentar*); moho; cosa indispensable; *va* enmohecer; *vn* enmohecerse; *v aux* deber, tener que; deber de; **he must be ill** estará enfermo; **he must have been ill** habrá estado enfermo
**mustache** [məsˈtæʃ], [məsˈtɑʃ] o [ˈmʌstæʃ] *s* bigote o bigotes
**mustachio** [məsˈtɑʃo] *s* (*pl:* **-chios**) var. de **mustache**
**mustachioed** [məsˈtɑʃod] *adj* abigotado, bigotudo, amostachado
**mustang** [ˈmʌstæŋ] *s* mustango
**mustard** [mʌstərd] *s* (bot.) mostaza; mostaza (*polvo o salsa*)
**mustard gas** *s* gas mostaza
**mustard oil** *s* aceite de mostaza; (chem.) esencia de mostaza
**mustard plaster** *s* sinapismo, cataplasma de mostaza
**mustard seed** *s* semilla de mostaza; mostacilla (*munición*)
**muster** [ˈmʌstər] *s* asamblea, reunión; (mil.) asamblea; (mil.) matrícula de revista; (mil.) número de oficiales y soldados en la matrícula de revista; **to pass muster** pasar revista; ser aceptable, ser aceptado; *va* llamar a asamblea; juntar o reunir para pasar revista; tomar (*resolución, ánimo, etc.*); ascender a, importar; **to muster in** (mil.) alistar; **to muster out** (mil.) dar de baja, dar la licencia absoluta a; **to muster up** tomar (*resolución, ánimo, etc.*); *vn* juntarse
**muster roll** *s* (mil.) lista de revista
**musty** [ˈmʌstɪ] *adj* (*comp:* **-tier;** *super:* **-tiest**) mohoso; que huele a cerrado; anticuado, pasado de moda
**mutability** [ˌmjutəˈbɪlɪtɪ] *s* mutabilidad
**mutable** [ˈmjutəbəl] *adj* mudable
**mutant** [ˈmjutənt] *s* (biol.) mutante
**mutarotation** [ˌmjutəroˈteʃən] *s* (chem.) mutarrotación
**mutate** [ˈmjutet] *va* mudar; *vn* sufrir mutación
**mutation** [mjuˈteʃən] *s* mutación; (biol. & phonet.) mutación
**mutational** [mjuˈteʃənəl] *adj* mutacional
**mutch** [mʌtʃ] *s* (Scotch) gorra de mujer o de niño
**mute** [mjut] *adj* mudo; (phonet.) mudo (*que no se pronuncia; oclusivo*); *s* mudo; (phonet.) letra muda; (phonet.) consonante muda; (mus.) sordina; *va* poner sordina a, ajustar la sordina a
**mutilate** [ˈmjutɪlet] *va* mutilar
**mutilation** [ˌmjutɪˈleʃən] *s* mutilación
**mutilator** [ˈmjutɪˌletər] *s* mutilador
**mutineer** [ˌmjutɪˈnɪr] *s* amotinado; *vn* amotinarse
**mutinous** [ˈmjutɪnəs] *adj* amotinado
**mutiny** [ˈmjutɪnɪ] *s* (*pl:* **-nies**) motín; (*pret & pp:* **-nied**) *vn* amotinarse
**mutism** [ˈmjutɪzəm] *s* mutismo
**mutt** [mʌt] *s* (slang) perro, perro cruzado; (slang) bobo, tonto
**mutter** [ˈmʌtər] *s* murmullo; *va & vn* murmurar
**mutton** [ˈmʌtən] *s* carnero (*carne*)
**mutton chop** *s* chuleta de carnero; (fig.) barba de boca de hacha
**mutual** [ˈmjutʃuəl] *adj* mutuo; (coll.) común
**mutual aid** *s* socorros mutuos
**mutual benefit society** *s* mutualidad, montepío
**mutual conductance** *s* (elec.) conductancia mutua
**mutual fund** *s* sociedad inversionista mutualista
**mutual inductance** *s* (elec.) inductancia mutua
**mutual induction** *s* (elec.) inducción mutua
**mutual insurance** *s* seguro mutuo
**mutualism** [ˈmjutʃuəlɪzəm] *s* mutualismo
**mutuality** [ˌmjutʃuˈælɪtɪ] *s* mutualidad
**mutual savings bank** *s* caja mutua de ahorros
**mutule** [ˈmjutʃul] *s* (arch.) mútulo
**mutuum** [ˈmjutʃuəm] *s* (*pl:* **-a** [ə]) (law) mutuo
**muzzle** [ˈmʌzəl] *s* hocico; bozal (*frenillo que se pone en el hocico*); boca (*de un arma de fuego*); *va* abozalar; (fig.) amordazar, imponer silencio a
**muzzleloader** [ˈmʌzəlˌlodər] *s* arma de antecarga
**muzzleloading** [ˈmʌzəlˌlodɪŋ] *adj* de antecarga
**muzzy** [ˈmʌzɪ] *adj* (*comp:* **-zier;** *super:* **-ziest**) (coll.) confuso, atontado; (coll.) lóbrego; (coll.) borroso
**my** [maɪ] *adj poss* mi; *interj* ¡hombre!
**myalgia** [maɪˈældʒɪə] *s* (path.) mialgia
**myasthenia** [ˌmaɪæsˈθinɪə] *s* (path.) miastenia
**mycelium** [maɪˈsilɪəm] *s* (*pl:* **-a** [ə]) (bot.) micelio
**Mycenae** [maɪˈsini] *s* Micenas
**Mycenaean** [ˌmaɪsɪˈniən] *adj* micénico
**mycologic** [ˌmaɪkəˈlɑdʒɪk] o **mycological** [ˌmaɪkəˈlɑdʒɪkəl] *adj* micológico
**mycologist** [maɪˈkɑlədʒɪst] *s* micólogo
**mycology** [maɪˈkɑlədʒɪ] *s* micología
**mycosis** [maɪˈkosɪs] *s* (path.) micosis
**mydriasis** [mɪˈdraɪəsɪs] o [maɪˈdraɪəsɪs] *s* (path.) midriasis
**mydriatic** [ˌmɪdrɪˈætɪk] *adj & s* midriático
**myelencephalon** [ˌmaɪəlɛnˈsɛfəlɑn] *s* (anat.) mielencéfalo
**myelin** [ˈmaɪəlɪn] *s* (anat.) mielina
**myelitis** [ˌmaɪəˈlaɪtɪs] *s* (path.) mielitis
**myna** [ˈmaɪnə] *s* (orn.) estornino de los pastores
**myocarditis** [ˌmaɪokɑrˈdaɪtɪs] *s* (path.) miocarditis
**myocardium** [ˌmaɪoˈkɑrdɪəm] *s* (anat.) miocardio
**myoglobin** [ˌmaɪoˈglobɪn] *s* (biochem.) mioglobina
**myograph** [ˈmaɪəgræf] o [ˈmaɪəgrɑf] *s* miógrafo
**myology** [maɪˈɑlədʒɪ] *s* miología
**myoma** [maɪˈomə] *s* (*pl:* **-mata** [mətə] o **-mas**) (path.) mioma
**myope** [ˈmaɪop] *s* miope
**myopia** [maɪˈopɪə] *s* (path.) miopía
**myopic** [maɪˈɑpɪk] *adj* miope; (fig.) miope
**myosis** [maɪˈosɪs] *s* (path.) miosis
**myosotis** [ˌmaɪəˈsotɪs] *s* (bot.) miosotis
**myriad** [ˈmɪrɪəd] *s* miríada (*diez mil; número muy grande*); *adj* miríada de; vario, múltiple
**myriapod** [ˈmɪrɪəˌpɑd] *adj & s* (zool.) miriópodo
**myricaceous** [ˌmɪrɪˈkeʃəs] *adj* (bot.) miricáceo
**myristicaceous** [mɪˌrɪstɪˈkeʃəs] *adj* (bot.) miristicáceo
**myrmecologist** [ˌmʌrmɪˈkɑlədʒɪst] *s* mirmecólogo
**myrmecology** [ˌmʌrmɪˈkɑlədʒɪ] *s* mirmecología
**myrmecophagous** [ˌmʌrmɪˈkɑfəgəs] *adj* mirmecófago

**myrmecophile** ['mʌrmɪko,faɪl] o ['mʌrmɪko,fɪl] *s* (ent.) mirmecófilo
**myrmecophilous** [,mʌrmɪ'kɑfɪləs] *adj* mirmecófilo
**myrmidon** ['mʌrmɪdɑn] *s* secuaz fiel; esbirro; (*cap.*) *s* (myth.) Mirmidón
**myrobalan** [maɪ'rɑbələn] *s* (bot.) mirobálano (*árbol y fruto*)
**myrrh** [mʌr] *s* mirra
**myrrhed** [mʌrd] *adj* mirrado
**myrrhic** ['mʌrɪk] o ['mɪrɪk] *adj* mirrino
**myrtaceous** [mʌr'teʃəs] *adj* (bot.) mirtáceo
**myrtle** ['mʌrtəl] *s* (bot.) arrayán, mirto; (bot.) pervinca, brusela
**myself** [maɪ'sɛlf] *pron pers* yo mismo; me; mí, mí mismo; **with myself** conmigo
**mystagogue** ['mɪstəgɔg] o ['mɪstəgɑg] *s* (hist.) mistagogo
**mysterious** [mɪs'tɪrɪəs] *adj* misterioso
**mystery** ['mɪstərɪ] *s* (*pl:* **-ies**) misterio; (theat.) auto, misterio; (archaic) oficio, mester; (archaic) gremio
**mystery play** *s* auto, misterio
**mystic** ['mɪstɪk] *adj & s* místico
**mystical** ['mɪstɪkəl] *adj* místico
**mysticism** ['mɪstɪsɪzəm] *s* misticismo
**mystification** [,mɪstɪfɪ'keʃən] *s* misterio; confusión, perplejidad, mixtificación
**mystify** ['mɪstɪfaɪ] (*pret & pp:* **-fied**) *va* rodear de misterio; confundir, dejar perplejo, mixtificar
**myth.** abr. de **mythology**
**myth** [mɪθ] *s* mito
**mythic** ['mɪθɪk] o **mythical** ['mɪθɪkəl] *adj* mítico
**mythological** [,mɪθə'lɑdʒɪkəl] *adj* mitológico
**mythologically** [,mɪθə'lɑdʒɪkəlɪ] *adv* mitológicamente
**mythologist** [mɪ'θɑlədʒɪst] *s* mitológico, mitologista o mitólogo
**mythology** [mɪ'θɑlədʒɪ] *s* (*pl:* **-gies**) mitología
**Mytilene** [,mɪtɪ'linɪ] *s* Mitilene
**myxedema** [,mɪksɪ'dimə] *s* (path.) mixedema
**myxomatosis** [,mɪksomə'tosɪs] *s* (vet.) mixomatosis
**myxomycete** [,mɪksomaɪ'sit] *s* (bot.) mixomiceto

# N

**N, n** [ɛn] *s* (*pl:* **N's, n's** [ɛnz]) décimocuarta letra del alfabeto inglés; (*l.c.*) *s* (alg.) n (*número indeterminado*)
**n.** abr. de **neuter, new, nominative, noon, north, northern, noun** y **number**
**N.** abr. de **Nationalist, Navy, New, Noon, Norse, North, Northern** y **November**
**N** abr. de **North** y **Northern**
**N.A.** abr. de **National Army** y **North America**
**nab** [næb] (*pret & pp:* **nabbed;** *ger:* **nabbing**) *va* (slang) coger, agarrar; (slang) prender, poner preso
**nabob** [ˈnebɑb] *s* nabab o nababo
**Naboth** [ˈnebɑθ] *s* (Bib.) Nabot
**nacelle** [næˈsɛl] *s* (aer.) barquilla o nacela
**nacre** [ˈnekər] *s* nácar
**nadir** [ˈnedər] o [ˈnedɪr] *s* (astr. & fig.) nadir
**nag** [næg] *s* caballo; caballejo, jaco; pequeño caballo de silla; (*pret & pp:* **nagged;** *ger:* **nagging**) *va* importunar regañando; *vn* regañar, ser regañón; **to nag at** importunar regañando
**Nahum** [ˈnehəm] *s* (Bib.) Nahúm
**naiad** o **Naiad** [ˈneæd] o [ˈnaɪæd] *s* (myth.) náyade; (fig.) nadadora
**nail** [nel] *s* uña (*del dedo*); clavo (*para asegurar una cosa a otra*); **on the nail** en seguida, en el acto; **to bite one's nails** comerse las uñas; **to hit the nail on the head** dar en el clavo; *va* clavar (*asegurar con clavos; fijar, p. ej., los ojos, la atención*); tachonar (*adornar con tachones*); poner término a (*p.ej., una mentira*); **to nail down** o **to nail up** clavar, cerrar con clavos
**nailbrush** [ˈnel,brʌʃ] *s* cepillo para las uñas
**nail claw** *s* arrancaclavos, sacaclavos
**nail clippers** o **nail cutters** *spl* cortaúñas
**nail extractor** *s* arrancaclavos, sacaclavos
**nail file** *s* lima de uñas, lima para las uñas
**nail hole** *s* clavera; uña (*en la hoja de un cortaplumas*)
**nail polish** *s* esmalte para las uñas, laca de uñas
**nail puller** *s* cazaclavos
**nail scissors** *ssg* o *spl* tijeras para las uñas
**nailset** [ˈnel,sɛt] *s* contrapunzón
**nail works** *s* fábrica de clavos
**nainsook** [ˈnensʊk] o [ˈnænsʊk] *s* nansú
**naïve** o **naive** [nɑˈiv] *adj* cándido, sencillo, ingenuo
**naïveté** [nɑ,ivˈte] *s* candidez, sencillez, ingenuidad
**naja** [ˈnedʒə] *s* (zool.) naja
**naked** [ˈnekɪd] *adj* desnudo; **to go naked** ir desnudo; **to strip naked** desnudar; desnudarse; **with the naked eye** a simple vista
**nakedness** [ˈnekɪdnɪs] *s* desnudez
**namby-pamby** [ˈnæmbɪˈpæmbɪ] *adj* melindroso; *s* (*pl:* **-bies**) melindroso (*persona*); melindres (*delicadeza*)
**name** [nem] *s* nombre; fama, reputación; linaje, raza; **by name** de nombre; **in the name of** a nombre de, en nombre de; **in name only** tan sólo en el nombre; **to answer to the name of** atender (*p.ej., un perro*) por; **to call names** poner como un trapo (*a una persona*); **to go by the name of** ser conocido por el nombre de; **to make a name for oneself** darse a conocer, hacerse un nombre; **what is your name?** ¿cómo se llama Vd.?; **my name is** me llamo; *va* nombrar; designar; fijar (*el precio de una cosa*)
**nameless** [ˈnemlɪs] *adj* innominado, sin nombre, anónimo; obscuro; nefando
**namely** [ˈnemlɪ] *adv* a saber
**name plate** *s* placa, letrero con nombre; placa de fabricante
**namesake** [ˈnem,sek] *s* homónimo, tocayo
**Nancy** [ˈnænsɪ] *s* Anita
**nandu** [ˈnændu] *s* (orn.) ñandú
**nankeen** o **nankin** [nænˈkin] *s* mahón o nanquín; **nankeens** *spl* pantalones de mahón
**nanny goat** [ˈnænɪ] *s* (coll.) cabra
**Naomi** [neˈomɪ] o [ˈneomɪ] (Bib.) Noemí
**nap** [næp] *s* lanilla, flojel (*pelillo que tiene el paño*); siesta, sueñecillo; **against the nap** a contrapelo, a pospelo; **to take a nap** descabezar un sueñecillo; (*pret & pp:* **napped;** *ger:* **napping**) *vn* dormir un rato; estar desprevenido; **to catch napping** coger desprevenido
**napalm** [ˈnepɑm] *s* (mil.) gelatina incendiaria
**nape** [nep] *s* nuca; **nape of the neck** nuca
**Naperian** [neˈpɪrɪən] *adj* var. de **Napierian**
**napery** [ˈnepərɪ] *s* mantelería
**Naphtali** [ˈnæftəlaɪ] *s* (Bib.) Naftalí o Neftalí
**naphtha** [ˈnæfθə] *s* nafta
**naphthalene** o **naphthaline** [ˈnæfθəlin] o **naphthalin** [ˈnæfθəlɪn] *s* (chem.) naftalina
**naphthol** [ˈnæfθɑl] *s* (chem.) naftol
**Napierian** [neˈpɪrɪən] *adj* neperiano
**napkin** [ˈnæpkɪn] *s* servilleta (*para aseo en la mesa*); pañal (*de los niños de teta*)
**napkin ring** *s* servilletero
**Naples** [ˈnepəlz] *s* Nápoles
**Napoleon** [nəˈpolɪən] *s* Napoleón; (*l.c.*) *s* napoleón (*moneda*); pastelito de crema y hojaldre
**Napoleonic** [nə,polɪˈɑnɪk] *adj* napoleónico
**Napoleonic code** *s* código napoleónico
**Narbonne** [nɑrˈbɔn] *s* Narbona
**narceine** [ˈnɑrsɪin] *s* (chem.) narceína
**narcissism** [nɑrˈsɪsɪzəm] *s* (psychoanal.) narcisismo
**narcissus** [nɑrˈsɪsəs] *s* (bot.) narciso; (*cap.*) *s* (myth.) Narciso
**narcosis** [nɑrˈkosɪs] *s* narcosis
**narcotic** [nɑrˈkɑtɪk] *s & adj* narcótico, estupefaciente
**narcotine** [ˈnɑrkətin] *s* (chem.) narcotina
**narcotism** [ˈnɑrkətɪzəm] *s* narcotismo
**narcotize** [ˈnɑrkətaɪz] *va* narcotizar
**nard** [nɑrd] *s* (bot. & pharm.) nardo
**nares** [ˈnɛriz] *spl* (anat.) narices, ventanas de la nariz
**narghile** o **nargile** [ˈnɑrgɪlɪ] *s* narguile
**narratable** [næˈretəbəl] *adj* narrable
**narrate** [næˈret] *va* narrar
**narration** [næˈreʃən] *s* narración
**narrative** [ˈnærətɪv] *adj* narrativo; *s* narrativa (*relato; habilidad en narrar*)
**narrator** [næˈretər] *s* narrador
**narrow** [ˈnæro] *adj* estrecho, angosto; intolerante; minucioso; estricto (*sentido de una palabra*); **in narrow circumstances** alcanzado, falto de recursos; **to have a narrow escape** escapar por un pelo; *s* garganta, desfiladero; **narrows** *spl* angostura, paso estrecho; *va* enangostar, estrechar, encoger, disminuir; *vn* enangostarse, estrecharse, encogerse, reducirse
**narrow gauge** *s* vía estrecha, trocha angosta
**narrow-gauge** [ˈnæro,gedʒ] *adj* de vía angosta o estrecha, de trocha angosta; intolerante
**narrow-minded** [ˈnæroˈmaɪndɪd] *adj* intolerante, poco liberal (en las ideas), de miras estrechas
**narrow-mindedness** [ˈnæroˈmaɪndɪdnɪs] *s* intolerancia, falta de liberalidad (en las ideas)
**narrowness** [ˈnæronɪs] *s* estrechez
**narrow squeak** *s* (coll.) escapada en una tabla
**narwhal** [ˈnɑrwəl] *s* (zool.) narval
**nasal** [ˈnezəl] *adj & s* nasal
**nasality** [neˈzælɪtɪ] *s* nasalidad
**nasalization** [,nezəlɪˈzeʃən] *s* nasalización; gangueo
**nasalize** [ˈnezəlaɪz] *va* nasalizar; *vn* ganguear

**nasal vowel** *s* vocal nasal
**nascent** [ˈnæsənt] o [ˈnesənt] *adj* naciente; (chem.) naciente
**nastic** [ˈnæstɪk] *adj* (plant path.) nástico
**nastiness** [ˈnæstɪnɪs] o [ˈnɑstɪnɪs] *s* suciedad, asquerosidad; molestia; desvergüenza
**nasturtium** [nəˈstʌrʃəm] *s* (bot.) capuchina, espuela de galán
**nasty** [ˈnæstɪ] o [ˈnɑstɪ] *adj* (*comp:* **-tier;** *super:* **-tiest**) sucio, asqueroso; desagradable; desvergonzado; amenazador; terrible, horrible
**nat.** abr. de **national, native** y **natural**
**natal** [ˈnetəl] *adj* natal
**natality** [neˈtælɪtɪ] *s* nacimiento; natalidad
**natant** [ˈnetənt] *adj* natátil; (bot.) natátil
**natatorial** [ˌnetəˈtorɪəl] *adj* natatorio
**natatorium** [ˌnetəˈtorɪəm] *s* (*pl:* **-ums** o **-a** [ə]) piscina de natación
**natatory** [ˈnetəˌtorɪ] *adj* natatorio
**Nathan** [ˈneθən] *s* (Bib.) Natán
**Nathanael** [nəˈθænɪəl] *s* (Bib.) Natanael
**nation** [ˈneʃən] *s* nación
**national** [ˈnæʃənəl] *adj & s* nacional
**national anthem** *s* himno nacional
**national flag** *s* bandera o pabellón nacional
**national guard** *s* milicia nacional, guardia nacional
**national holiday** *s* fiesta nacional
**nationalism** [ˈnæʃənəlɪzəm] *s* nacionalismo
**nationalist** [ˈnæʃənəlɪst] *adj & s* nacionalista
**nationalistic** [ˌnæʃənəlˈɪstɪk] *adj* nacionalista
**nationality** [ˌnæʃənˈælɪtɪ] *s* (*pl:* **-ties**) nacionalidad, naturalidad
**nationalization** [ˌnæʃənəlɪˈzeʃən] *s* nacionalización
**nationalize** [ˈnæʃənəlaɪz] *va* nacionalizar
**National Socialist Party** *s* partido nacionalsocialista
**nation-wide** [ˈneʃənˌwaɪd] *adj* por toda la nación, de toda la nación
**native** [ˈnetɪv] *adj* nativo; indígena; materno (*idioma*); **to go native** vivir como los indígenas; *s* natural; indígena
**native-born** [ˈnetɪvˌbɔrn] *adj* indígena
**native land** *s* patria
**nativity** [nəˈtɪvɪtɪ] *s* (*pl:* **-ties**) nacimiento, natividad; (astr.) horóscopo; (*cap.*) *s* natividad (*festividad en que se celebra el nacimiento de Jesucristo, de la Virgen María o de San Juan Bautista*); (f.a.) pintura de la natividad
**natl.** abr. de **national**
**Nato** [ˈneto] *s* la O.T.A.N. (*la Organización para el Tratado del Atlántico Norte*)
**natrolite** [ˈnætrəlaɪt] o [ˈnetrəlaɪt] *s* (mineral.) natrolita
**natron** [ˈnetrɑn] *s* (mineral.) natrón
**nattiness** [ˈnætɪnɪs] *s* elegancia, garbo
**natty** [ˈnætɪ] *adj* (*comp:* **-tier;** *super:* **-tiest**) elegante, garboso
**natural** [ˈnætʃərəl] *adj* natural; (mus.) natural; *s* imbécil; (coll.) cosa de éxito certero; (mus.) tono natural, nota natural; (mus.) becuadro (*signo*); (mus.) tecla blanca (*del piano*)
**natural gas** *s* gas natural, gas combustible natural
**natural history** *s* historia natural
**naturalism** [ˈnætʃərəlɪzəm] *s* naturalismo
**naturalist** [ˈnætʃərəlɪst] *s* naturalista
**naturalistic** [ˌnætʃərəˈlɪstɪk] *adj* naturalista
**naturalization** [ˌnætʃərəlɪˈzeʃən] *s* naturalización
**naturalization papers** *spl* carta de naturaleza
**naturalize** [ˈnætʃərəlaɪz] *va* naturalizar; *vn* naturalizarse (*vivir como los naturales de un país extranjero*)
**natural law** *s* ley natural
**naturally** [ˈnætʃərəlɪ] *adv* naturalmente; por supuesto
**natural magnet** *s* imán natural
**naturalness** [ˈnætʃərəlnɪs] *s* naturalidad
**natural philosophy** *s* filosofía natural
**natural religion** *s* religión natural
**natural resources** *spl* recursos naturales
**natural rights** *spl* derechos naturales
**natural science** *s* ciencia natural
**natural selection** *s* (biol.) selección natural
**natural sign** *s* (mus.) becuadro
**nature** [ˈnetʃər] *s* naturaleza; **from nature** (f.a.) del natural; **in the nature of** algo como
**nature study** *s* historia natural
**naturopathy** [ˌnetʃərˈɑpəθɪ] *s* naturopatía
**naught** [nɔt] *s* nada; cero; **to bring to naught** anular, invalidar, destruir; **to come to naught** reducirse a nada, frustrarse
**naughtiness** [ˈnɔtɪnɪs] *s* desobediencia, picardía; desvergüenza
**naughty** [ˈnɔtɪ] *adj* (*comp:* **-tier;** *super:* **-tiest**) desobediente, pícaro; desvergonzado; verde (*cuento*)
**nausea** [ˈnɔʃɪə] o [ˈnɔsɪə] *s* náusea (*mareo, basca; repugnancia, asco grande*)
**nauseate** [ˈnɔʃɪet] o [ˈnɔsɪet] *va* dar náuseas a (*marear, dar bascas a; dar asco a*); *vn* nausear, marearse
**nauseating** [ˈnɔʃɪˌetɪŋ] o [ˈnɔsɪˌetɪŋ] *adj* nauseabundo, asqueroso
**nauseous** [ˈnɔʃɪəs] o [ˈnɔsɪəs] *adj* nauseabundo
**Nausicaä** [nɔˈsɪkeə] *s* (myth.) Nausica
**nautical** [ˈnɔtɪkəl] *adj* náutico, naval
**nautical day** *s* singladura (*intervalo de 24 horas, contadas de mediodía a mediodía*)
**nautical mile** *s* milla marina
**nautics** [ˈnɔtɪks] *ssg* náutica; *spl* deportes acuáticos
**nautilus** [ˈnɔtɪləs] *s* (*pl:* **-luses** o **-li** [laɪ]) (zool.) nautilo
**nav.** abr. de **naval** y **navigation**
**naval** [ˈnevəl] *adj* naval, naval militar
**Naval Academy** *s* (U.S.A.) Escuela Naval Militar
**naval air base** *s* base aeronaval
**naval base** *s* base naval
**naval officer** *s* oficial de marina
**naval station** *s* apostadero
**Navarre** [nəˈvɑr] *s* Navarra
**Navarrese** [ˌnɑvɑˈriz] *adj* navarro; *s* (*pl:* **-rese**) navarro
**nave** [nev] *s* (arch.) nave central, nave principal; cubo (*de una rueda*)
**navel** [ˈnevəl] *s* ombligo; (fig.) centro, medio
**navel orange** *s* navel, naranja umbilicada, naranja de ombligo
**navicert** [ˈnævɪsʌrt] *s* (Brit.) pasavante
**navicula** [nəˈvɪkjələ] *s* (*pl:* **-lae** [li]) (bot.) navícula; (eccl.) naveta (*para ministrar el incienso*)
**navicular** [nəˈvɪkjələr] *adj* navicular; *s* (anat.) navicular
**navigability** [ˌnævɪgəˈbɪlɪtɪ] *s* navegabilidad (*de un río*); buen gobierno (*de un buque*)
**navigable** [ˈnævɪgəbəl] *adj* navegable (*dícese de un río, canal, etc.*); marinero, de buen gobierno
**navigate** [ˈnævɪget] *va & vn* navegar
**navigation** [ˌnævɪˈgeʃən] *s* navegación
**navigator** [ˈnævɪˌgetər] *s* navegador o navegante; oficial de derrota; tratado de náutica; (Brit.) peón
**navvy** [ˈnævɪ] *s* (*pl:* **-vies**) (Brit.) peón, bracero
**navy** [ˈnevɪ] *s* (*pl:* **-vies**) marina de guerra, flota de guerra, armada; marina (*conjunto de personas que sirven en la marina de guerra*); (archaic & poet.) armada (*reunión de buques*); color azul obscuro; *adj* azul obscuro
**navy bean** *s* (bot.) frijol blanco común
**navy blue** *s* azul de mar, azul marino
**navy-blue** [ˈnevɪˈblu] *adj* azul de mar, azul marino
**navy chaplain** *s* capellán de la armada, capellán de navío
**navy yard** *s* arsenal de puerto
**nawab** [nəˈwɔb] *s* nabab o nababo
**nay** [ne] *s* no, voto negativo; *adv* y aun, más aún; (obs.) no
**Nazarene** [ˌnæzəˈrin] *adj & s* nazareno; **the Nazarene** el Nazareno o el Divino Nazareno
**Nazareth** [ˈnæzərəθ] o [ˈnæzərɪθ] *s* Nazaret
**Nazi** [ˈnɑtsɪ] o [ˈnætsɪ] *adj* nazi o nacista; *s* (*pl:* **-zis**) nazi o nacista
**Nazify** [ˈnɑtsɪfaɪ] o [ˈnætsɪfaɪ] (*pret & pp:* **-fied**) *va* nazificar
**Nazism** [ˈnɑtsɪzəm] o [ˈnætsɪzəm] o **Naziism** [ˈnɑtsɪɪzəm] o [ˈnætsɪɪzəm] *s* nazismo
**n.b.** abr. de **nota bene** (Lat.) **note well, observe carefully**
**N.B.** abr. de **New Brunswick** y **nota bene** (Lat.) **note well, observe carefully**
**N-bomb** [ˈɛnˌbɑm] *s* bomba de neutrones

**N.C.** abr. de **North Carolina**
**N.C.O.** abr. de **noncommissioned officer**
**N.D.** o **N. Dak.** abr. de **North Dakota**
**n.e.** o **NE** abr. de **northeast** y **northeastern**
**N.E.** abr. de **New England, northeast** y **northeastern**
**Neanderthal man** [nɪ'ændərtɑl] *s* (anthrop.) hombre de Neanderthal
**neap** [nip] *s* marea muerta
**Neapolitan** [ˌniə'pɑlɪtən] *adj & s* napolitano
**Neapolitan ice cream** *s* arlequín
**Neapolitan medlar** *s* (bot.) acerolo (*arbusto*); acerola (*fruto*)
**neap tide** *s* marea muerta
**near** [nɪr] *adj* próximo, cercano; íntimo; tacaño; imitado; literal; **near** + *ger* cercano a + *inf; adv* cerca; íntimamente; **to come near** acercarse; acercarse a; *prep* cerca de; hacia, por; **to come near** + *ger* estar para + *inf*, estar en poco que + *subj; va* acercarse a; *vn* acercarse
**near beer** *s* cerveza sin alcohol
**nearby** ['nɪrˌbaɪ] *adj* próximo, cercano; *adv* cerca
**Near East** *s* Cercano Oriente, Próximo Oriente
**nearly** ['nɪrlɪ] *adv* casi; de cerca; íntimamente; tacañamente; por poco, p.ej., **he nearly fell** por poco se cae
**nearness** ['nɪrnɪs] *s* proximidad; intimidad
**near-sighted** ['nɪr'saɪtɪd] *adj* miope
**nearsightedness** ['nɪr'saɪtɪdnɪs] *s* miopía
**neat** [nit] *adj* pulcro, aseado; pulido; primoroso, diestro; puro, sin mezcla; *ssg* res vacuna; *spl* ganado vacuno
**neath** o **'neath** [niθ] *prep* (poet.) var. de **beneath**
**neatherd** ['nitˌhʌrd] *s* vaquero
**neatness** ['nitnɪs] *s* pulcritud, aseo, esmero; pulidez; primor, habilidad
**neat's-foot oil** ['nitsˌfʊt] *s* aceite de pie de buey
**neb** [nɛb] *s* pico (*del ave*); punta, extremidad; boca, nariz; hocico
**Nebuchadnezzar** [ˌnɛbjəkəd'nɛzər] *s* (Bib.) Nabucodonosor
**nebula** ['nɛbjələ] *s* (*pl:* **-lae** [li] o **-las**) (astr.) nebulosa
**nebular** ['nɛbjələr] *adj* (astr.) nebular, nebuloso
**nebular hypothesis** *s* (astr.) hipótesis nebular, hipótesis de Laplace
**nebulization** [ˌnɛbjəlɪ'zeʃən] *s* nebulización
**nebulize** ['nɛbjəlaɪz] *va & vn* nebulizar
**nebulosity** [ˌnɛbjə'lɑsɪtɪ] *s* (*pl:* **-ties**) nebulosidad; (astr.) nebulosa
**nebulous** ['nɛbjələs] *adj* nebuloso (*nubloso, brumoso, neblinoso, confuso*); (astr.) nebuloso
**necessarily** ['nɛsɪˌsɛrɪlɪ] *adv* necesariamente
**necessary** ['nɛsɪˌsɛrɪ] *adj* necesario; *s* (*pl:* **-ies**) cosa necesaria, cosa indispensable
**necessitate** [nɪ'sɛsɪtet] *va* necesitar
**necessitous** [nɪ'sɛsɪtəs] *adj* necesitado
**necessity** [nɪ'sɛsɪtɪ] *s* (*pl:* **-ties**) necesidad; **of necessity** de o por necesidad; **under the necessity of** en la necesidad de
**neck** [nɛk] *s* cuello (*del cuerpo, prenda de vestir, columna, vasija, diente, etc.*); gollete (*de botella*); mástil (*de violín o guitarra*); istmo, península; estrecho; **to break one's neck** (coll.) deslomarse, matarse trabajando; **to stick one's neck out** (coll.) descubrir el cuerpo (*exponerse a las malas resultas de un negocio*); **to win by a neck** ganar con poca ventaja; **neck and neck** parejos; **neck or nothing** a toda costa; *vn* (slang) acariciarse (*dos enamorados*)
**neckband** ['nɛkˌbænd] *s* tirilla (*de camisa*)
**neckcloth** ['nɛkˌklɔθ] o ['nɛkˌklɑθ] *s* corbata, pañuelo de cuello
**neckerchief** ['nɛkərtʃɪf] *s* pañuelo de cuello, pañoleta (*de forma triangular*)
**neckguard** ['nɛkˌgɑrd] *s* cubrenuca
**necklace** ['nɛklɪs] *s* collar (*usado como adorno*)
**necklet** ['nɛklɪt] *s* collar
**neckpiece** ['nɛkˌpis] *s* cuello de pieles
**necktie** ['nɛkˌtaɪ] *s* corbata
**necktie pin** *s* alfiler de corbata
**neckwear** ['nɛkˌwɛr] *s* prendas para el cuello
**necrology** [nɛ'krɑlədʒɪ] *s* necrología
**necromancer** ['nɛkroˌmænsər] *s* necromántico o nigromántico
**necromancy** ['nɛkroˌmænsɪ] *s* necromancia o nigromancia
**necromantic** [ˌnɛkro'mæntɪk] *adj* necromántico o nigromántico
**necropolis** [nɛ'krɑpəlɪs] *s* necrópolis
**necrosis** [nɛ'krosɪs] *s* (*pl:* **-ses** [siz]) (path. & bot.) necrosis
**nectar** ['nɛktər] *s* (myth., bot. & fig.) néctar
**nectareous** [nɛk'tɛrɪəs] *adj* nectáreo
**nectarine** ['nɛktərɪn] *adj* nectarino; [ˌnɛktə'rin] o ['nɛktərɪn] *s* bruñón (*melocotón*)
**nectary** ['nɛktərɪ] *s* (*pl:* **-ries**) (bot.) nectario
**née** o **nee** [ne] *adj* nacida o de soltera, p.ej., **Mary Wilson, née Miller** María Wilson, nacida Miller o María Wilson, de soltera Miller
**need** [nid] *s* necesidad; requisito; **to be in need** estar necesitado; **to be in need of** estar necesitado de; **to have need of** necesitar, tener necesidad de; **to have need to** + *inf* deber, necesitar, tener necesidad de + *inf; va* necesitar; **to need** + *inf* deber, tener que + *inf;* **if need be** si fuere necesario; *vn* estar necesitado; ser necesario
**needful** ['nidfəl] *adj* necesario; **the needful** lo necesario; (slang) el dinero
**needle** ['nidəl] *s* aguja (*con que se cose; del fonógrafo; obelisco*); **to look for a needle in a haystack** buscar una aguja en un pajar; *va* coser con aguja; aguijar, incitar; (coll.) añadir alcohol a (*cerveza o vino*)
**needle bath** *s* ducha en alfileres
**needlecase** ['nidəlˌkes] *s* alfiletero
**needlefish** ['nidəlˌfɪʃ] *s* (ichth.) aguja
**needleful** ['nidəlfʊl] *s* hebra
**needle gun** *s* fusil de aguja (*de Dreyse*)
**needle point** *s* bordado al pasado; encaje de mano
**needle scratch** *s* arañar de la aguja (*del fonógrafo*)
**needless** ['nidlɪs] *adj* innecesario, inútil
**needle valve** *s* válvula de aguja
**needlewoman** ['nidəlˌwʊmən] *s* (*pl:* **-women**) costurera
**needlework** ['nidəlˌwʌrk] *s* costura, labor, bordado
**needn't** ['nidənt] contracción de **need not**
**needs** [nidz] *adv* necesariamente, forzosamente
**needy** ['nidɪ] *adj* (*comp:* **-ier;** *super:* **-iest**) necesitado, indigente; **the needy** los necesitados
**ne'er** [nɛr] *adv* (poet.) var. de **never**
**ne'er-do-well** ['nɛrduˌwɛl] *adj & s* holgazán, perdido
**nefarious** [nɪ'fɛrɪəs] *adj* nefario
**negate** [nɪ'get] o ['niget] *va* negar; anular, invalidar
**negation** [nɪ'geʃən] *s* negación
**negative** ['nɛgətɪv] *adj* negativo; *s* negativa; (math.) término negativo; (elec.) electricidad negativa, borne negativo; (gram.) negación; (phot.) negativa o negativo; *va* desaprobar; inutilizar, anular
**negativism** ['nɛgətɪvɪzəm] *s* negativismo
**negatron** ['nɛgətrɑn] *s* (chem.) negatrón
**neglect** [nɪ'glɛkt] *s* negligencia, descuido, abandono; *va* descuidar, abandonar; **to neglect oneself** dejarse, descuidarse de sí mismo; **to neglect to** + *inf* dejar de, olvidarse de + *inf*
**neglectful** [nɪ'glɛktfəl] *adj* negligente, descuidado
**négligé** [negli'ʒe] o **negligee** [ˌnɛglɪ'ʒe] o ['nɛglɪʒe] *s* traje de casa, bata de mujer
**negligence** ['nɛglɪdʒəns] *s* negligencia, descuido
**negligent** ['nɛglɪdʒənt] *adj* negligente, descuidado
**negligible** ['nɛglɪdʒɪbəl] *adj* insignificante, imperceptible
**negotiability** [nɪˌgoʃɪə'bɪlɪtɪ] *s* negociabilidad
**negotiable** [nɪ'goʃɪəbəl] *adj* negociable; transitable
**negotiate** [nɪ'goʃɪet] *va* negociar; (coll.) vencer, salvar; *vn* negociar
**negotiation** [nɪˌgoʃɪ'eʃən] *s* negociación
**negotiator** [nɪ'goʃɪˌetər] *s* negociador
**Negress** ['nigrɪs] *s* (offensive) negra
**Negrito** [nɪ'grito] *s* (*pl:* **-tos** o **-toes**) negrito (*individuo de una raza parecida a la de los*

*negros, de estatura muy pequeña y de color pardo muy obscuro)*
**Negro** ['nigro] o **negro** *s* (*pl:* **-groes**) negro; *adj* negro
**Negroid** ['nigrɔɪd] *adj* negroide o negroideo
**negus** ['nigəs] *s* carraspada, sangría; (*cap.*) *s* Negus (*emperador de Abisinia*)
**Neh.** abr. de **Nehemiah**
**Nehemiah** [,niə'maɪə] *s* (Bib.) Nehemías
**neigh** [ne] *s* relincho; *vn* relinchar
**neighbor** ['nebər] *s* vecino; prójimo (*cualquier hombre respecto de otro*); *adj* vecino; *va* ser vecino de, colindar con; ser amigo de; *vn* estar cercano; tener relaciones amistosas
**neighborhood** ['nebərhʊd] *s* vecindad; **in the neighborhood of** (coll.) cerca de, casi
**neighboring** ['nebərɪŋ] *adj* vecino, colindante
**neighborly** ['nebərlɪ] *adj* buen vecino, amable
**neighbour** ['nebər] *s, adj, va & vn* (Brit.) var. de **neighbor**
**neither** ['niðər] o ['naɪðər] *pron indef* ninguno (de los dos); ni uno ni otro, ni lo uno ni lo otro; *adj indef* ninguno . . . (de los dos); **neither one** ninguno de los dos; *conj* ni; tampoco; **ni . . .** tampoco; **neither . . . nor** ni . . . ni
**nelumbo** [nɪ'lʌmbo] *s* (*pl:* **-bos**) (bot.) nelumbio
**nemathelminth** [,nɛmə'θɛlmɪnθ] *s* (zool.) nematelminto
**nematocyst** ['nɛmətəsɪst] *s* (zool.) nematocisto
**nematode** ['nɛmətod] *s* (zool.) nematoda
**Nemean** [nɪ'miən] o ['nimɪən] *adj* nemeo
**Nemean games** *spl* fiestas nemeas
**Nemean lion** *s* (myth.) león de Nemea
**nemesis** ['nɛmɪsɪs] *s* (*pl:* **-ses** [siz]) justo castigo; castigador; (*cap.*) *s* (myth.) Némesis
**Neo-Catholic** ['niə'kæθəlɪk] *adj & s* neocatólico
**Neo-Catholicism** ['niəkə'θɑlɪsɪzəm] *s* neocatolicismo
**neoclassic** [,niə'klæsɪk] *adj* neoclásico
**neoclassicism** [,niə'klæsɪsɪzəm] *s* neoclasicismo
**neoclassicist** [,niə'klæsɪsɪst] *s* neoclásico
**neodymium** [,nio'dɪmɪəm] *s* (chem.) neodimio
**Neo-Latin** [,niə'lætɪn] o [,niə'lætən] *adj* neolatino
**neolithic** [,nio'lɪθɪk] *adj* neolítico
**neologism** [ni'ɑlədʒɪzəm] *s* neologismo
**neologist** [ni'ɑlədʒɪst] *s* neologista o neólogo
**neology** [ni'ɑlədʒɪ] *s* neología
**neomycin** [,nio'maɪsɪn] *s* (pharm.) neomicina
**neon** ['niɑn] *s* (chem.) neón o neo
**neon light** *s* lámpara neón, lámpara de neo
**neophyte** ['niofaɪt] *s* neófito
**neoplasm** ['niəplæzəm] *s* (path.) neoplasia o neoplasma
**Neo-Platonism** o **Neoplatonism** [,nio'pletənɪzəm] *s* neoplatonicismo
**neoprene** ['niəprin] *s* neopreno
**neosalvarsan** [,nio'sælvərsæn] *s* (trademark) neosalvarsán
**Neo-Scholasticism** ['niəskə'læstɪsɪzəm] *s* neoescolasticismo
**neoteny** [nɪ'ɑtənɪ] *s* (biol.) neotenia
**Neo-Thomism** ['nio'tomɪzəm] o ['nio'θomɪzəm] *s* neotomismo
**neoytterbium** [,nio·ɪ'tʌrbɪəm] *s* (chem.) neoiterbio
**Neozoic** [,nio'zo·ɪk] *adj* neozoico
**Nepal** [nɪ'pɔl] *s* el Nepal
**Nepalese** [,nɛpə'liz] *adj* nepalés; *s* (*pl:* **-lese**) nepalés
**nepenthe** [nɪ'pɛnθɪ] *s* nepente (*bebida mágica*); (bot.) nepente
**nephew** ['nɛfju] o ['nɛvju] *s* sobrino
**nephoscope** ['nɛfəskop] *s* nefoscopio
**nephralgia** [nɪ'frældʒɪə] *s* (path.) nefralgia
**nephrectomy** [nɪ'frɛktəmɪ] *s* (*pl:* **-mies**) (surg.) nefrectomía
**nephridium** [nɪ'frɪdɪəm] *s* (*pl:* **-a** [ə]) (embryol.) nefridio
**nephrite** ['nɛfraɪt] *s* (mineral.) nefrita
**nephritic** [nɪ'frɪtɪk] *adj* nefrítico
**nephritis** [nɪ'fraɪtɪs] *s* (path.) nefritis
**nephrolith** ['nɛfrəlɪθ] *s* (path.) nefrolito
**nephrotomy** [nɪ'frɑtəmɪ] *s* (*pl:* **-mies**) (surg.) nefrotomía
**Nepos** ['nipɑs] o ['nɛpɑs] *s* Nepote
**nepotism** ['nɛpətɪzəm] *s* nepotismo
**Neptune** ['nɛptʃun] o ['nɛptjun] *s* (myth. & astr.) Neptuno
**Neptunian** [nɛp'tʃunɪən] o [nɛp'tjunɪən] *adj* neptúneo; (geol.) neptúnico
**neptunium** [nɛp'tʃunɪəm] o [nɛp'tjunɪəm] *s* (chem.) neptunio
**Nereid** o **nereid** ['nɪrɪɪd] *s* (myth.) nereida
**Nereus** ['nɪrus] *s* (myth.) Nereo
**Nero** ['nɪro] *s* Nerón
**nerol** ['nɪrɔl] *s* (chem.) nerol
**neroli oil** ['nɛrəlɪ] o ['nɪrəlɪ] *s* (chem.) aceite de nerolí
**nerval** ['nʌrvəl] *adj* nerval
**nervation** [nʌr'veʃən] *s* nervadura o nerviación
**nerve** [nʌrv] *s* (anat. & bot.) nervio; (ent.) nervadura; (fig.) nervio; (slang) descaro; **nerves** *spl* excitabilidad nerviosa; **to get on one's nerves** enojar, crispar o irritar los nervios a; **to strain every nerve** esforzarse lo sumo posible; *va* animar, alentar
**nerve cell** *s* (anat.) neurona; (anat.) célula nerviosa
**nerve center** *s* (anat.) centro nervioso
**nerve fiber** *s* (anat.) fibra nerviosa
**nerveless** ['nʌrvlɪs] *adj* sin nervios; enervado; cobarde
**nerve pulp** *s* (anat.) pulpa (*de los dientes*)
**nerve-racking** ['nʌrv,rækɪŋ] *adj* irritante, exasperante
**nerve tonic** *s* tónico nervioso
**nervine** ['nʌrvin] o ['nʌrvaɪn] *adj & s* nervino
**nervous** ['nʌrvəs] *adj* nervioso
**nervous breakdown** *s* crisis nerviosa, colapso nervioso
**nervousness** ['nʌrvəsnɪs] *s* nerviosidad, nerviosismo
**nervous prostration** *s* prostración nerviosa, agotamiento nervioso
**nervous shudder** *s* muerte chiquita
**nervous system** *s* (anat.) sistema nervioso
**nervure** ['nʌrvjʊr] *s* (bot. & ent.) nervadura
**nervy** ['nʌrvɪ] *adj* (*comp:* **-ier;** *super:* **-iest**) nervioso (*fuerte, vigoroso*); atrevido, audaz; (slang) descarado
**nescience** ['nɛʃəns] o ['nɛʃɪəns] *s* nesciencia
**-ness** *suffix s* -ería, p.ej., **childishness** niñería; **foolishness** tontería; -ez, p.ej., **haughtiness** altivez; **ripeness** madurez; **smallness** pequeñez; -eza, p.ej., **bigness** grandeza; **lightness** ligereza; **cleanliness** limpieza; -or, p.ej., **bitterness** amargor; **sweetness** dulzor; -ura, p.ej., **bitterness** amargura; **smoothness** lisura; los nombres que terminan en **-ness** se pueden traducir generalmente al español con el adjetivo correspondiente, precedido por **lo,** p.ej., **the pleasantness of her smile** lo agradable de su sonrisa
**Nessus** ['nɛsəs] *s* (myth.) Neso
**nest** [nɛst] *s* nido; nidal (*donde la gallina pone sus huevos*); nidada (*pajarillos en el nido*); juego (*de mesitas, cajones, etc.*); (fig.) nido (*de ladrones, de ametralladoras, etc.*); **to feather one's nest** hacer todo para enriquecerse; *va* colocar en un nido; encajar formando juego; *vn* anidar; buscar nidos
**nest egg** *s* nidal; (fig.) peculio, ahorros, reserva, buena hucha
**nestle** ['nɛsəl] *va* anidar, abrigar, poner en un nido; apretar, arrimar afectuosamente; *vn* anidar; estar abrigado como en un nido; arrimarse cómodamente; **to nestle up to** arrimarse a
**nestling** ['nɛstlɪŋ] *s* pajarillo en el nido
**Nestor** ['nɛstər] *s* (myth.) Néstor
**Nestorian** [nɛs'torɪən] *adj & s* nestoriano
**net** [nɛt] *s* red; (com.) precio neto, peso neto, ganancia líquida; *adj* neto, líquido; (*pret & pp:* **netted;** *ger:* **netting**) *va* enredar, tejer; coger con red; cubrir con red; (com.) producir (*cierta ganancia líquida*)
**nether** ['nɛðər] *adj* inferior, más bajo
**Netherlander** ['nɛðər,lændər] o ['nɛðərləndər] *s* neerlandés (*persona*)
**Netherlandish** ['nɛðər,lændɪʃ] o ['nɛðərləndɪʃ] *adj* neerlandés; *s* neerlandés (*idioma*)
**Netherlands, The** ['nɛðərləndz] los Países Bajos (*Holanda*)

**nethermost** ['nɛðərmost] *adj* (el) más bajo
**nether world** *s* infierno; (el) otro mundo
**netting** ['nɛtɪŋ] *s* red
**nettle** ['nɛtəl] *s* (bot.) ortiga; *va* irritar, provocar
**nettle rash** *s* (path.) urticaria
**nettle tree** *s* (bot.) almez
**network** ['nɛt,wʌrk] *s* red
**neume** [njum] o [num] *s* (mus.) neuma
**neuralgia** [nju'rældʒə] o [nu'rældʒə] *s* (path.) neuralgia
**neurasthenia** [,njurəs'θinɪə] o [,nurəs'θinɪə] *s* (path.) neurastenia
**neurasthenic** [,njurəs'θɛnɪk] o [,nurəs'θɛnɪk] *adj & s* neurasténico
**neurectomy** [nju'rɛktəmɪ] o [nu'rɛktəmɪ] *s* (*pl:* **-mies**) (surg.) neurectomía
**neuritis** [nju'raɪtɪs] o [nu'raɪtɪs] *s* (path.) neuritis
**neuroglia** [nju'rɑglɪə] o [nu'rɑglɪə] *s* (anat.) neuroglia
**neurological** [,njurə'lɑdʒɪkəl] o [,nurə'lɑdʒɪkəl] *adj* neurológico
**neurologist** [nju'rɑlədʒɪst] o [nu'rɑlədʒɪst] *s* neurólogo
**neurology** [nju'rɑlədʒɪ] o [nu'rɑlədʒɪ] *s* neurología
**neuron** ['njurɑn] o ['nurɑn] o **neurone** ['njuron] o ['nuron] *s* (anat.) neurona
**neuropath** ['njurəpæθ] o ['nurəpæθ] *s* neurópata
**neuropathic** [,njurə'pæθɪk] o [,nurə'pæθɪk] *adj* neuropático
**neuropathy** [nju'rɑpəθɪ] o [nu'rɑpəθɪ] *s* neuropatía
**neuropsychiatry** [,njurosaɪ'kaɪətrɪ] o [,nurosaɪ'kaɪətrɪ] *s* neuropsiquiatría
**neurosis** [nju'rosɪs] o [nu'rosɪs] *s* (*pl:* **-ses** [siz]) (path.) neurosis
**neurosurgery** [,njurə'sʌrdʒərɪ] o [,nurə'sʌrdʒərɪ] *s* cirugía nerviosa, neurocirugía
**neurosurgical** [,njurə'sʌrdʒɪkəl] o [,nurə'sʌrdʒɪkəl] *adj* neuroquirúrgico
**neurotic** [nju'rɑtɪk] o [nu'rɑtɪk] *adj & s* neurótico
**neut.** abr. de **neuter**
**neuter** ['njutər] o ['nutər] *adj* neutro; *s* (gram.) género neutro
**neutral** ['njutrəl] o ['nutrəl] *adj* neutral (*que no es de un partido ni de otro*); neutro (*que no es de un color ni de otro*); (bot., chem., elec., phonet. & zool.) neutro; *s* neutral; (aut.) punto muerto, punto neutral
**neutralism** ['njutrəlɪzəm] o ['nutrəlɪzəm] *s* neutralismo
**neutralist** ['njutrəlɪst] o ['nutrəlɪst] *adj & s* neutralista
**neutrality** [nju'trælɪtɪ] o [nu'trælɪtɪ] *s* neutralidad
**neutralization** [,njutrəlɪ'zeʃən] o [,nutrəlɪ'zeʃən] *s* neutralización
**neutralize** ['njutrəlaɪz] o ['nutrəlaɪz] *va* neutralizar
**neutrino** [nju'trino] o [nu'trino] *s* (*pl:* **-nos**) (phys.) neutrino
**neutron** ['njutrɑn] o ['nutrɑn] *s* (phys.) neutrón
**neutron bomb** *s* (phys.) bomba de neutrones, bomba neutrónica
**Nev.** abr. de **Nevada**
**never** ['nɛvər] *adv* nunca; de ningún modo, ni . . . siquiera; **never fear** no hay cuidado; **never mind** no importa
**nevermore** [,nɛvər'mor] *adv* nunca más
**nevertheless** [,nɛvərðə'lɛs] *adv* sin embargo, no obstante, a pesar de eso
**new** [nju] o [nu] *adj* nuevo
**new arrival** *s* recién llegado; recién nacido
**newborn** ['nju,bɔrn] o ['nu,bɔrn] *adj* recién nacido; renacido
**New Castile** *s* Castilla la Nueva
**Newcastle** ['nju,kæsəl] o ['nu,kæsəl] *s*; **to carry coals to Newcastle** echar agua al mar, llevar hierro a Vizcaya, cargar leña para el monte
**newcomer** ['nju,kʌmər] o ['nu,kʌmər] *s* recién venido, recién llegado
**New Covenant** *s* (Bib.) Nuevo Testamento
**New Deal** *s* (pol.) nuevo trato (*política de Franklin D. Roosevelt*)
**New Delhi** ['dɛlɪ] *s* Nueva Delhi
**newel** ['njuəl] o ['nuəl] *s* nabo (*de una escalera de caracol*); alma, núcleo (*que termina la barandilla de una escalera*)
**New England** *s* la Nueva Inglaterra
**newfangled** ['nju,fæŋgəld] o ['nu,fæŋgəld] *adj* de última moda, recién inventado
**new-fashioned** ['nju,fæʃənd] o ['nu,fæʃənd] *adj* de última moda
**Newfoundland** ['njufənd,lænd] o ['nufənd,lænd] *s* Terranova (*isla y provincia*); [nju'faundlənd] o [nu'faundlənd] *s* Terranova (*perro*)
**New Granada** [grə'nɑdə] *s* la Nueva Granada
**New Guinea** *s* la Nueva Guinea
**New Hampshire** ['hæmpʃɪr] *s* Nuevo Hampshire
**New Hebrides** *spl* Nuevas Hébridas
**newish** ['njuɪʃ] o ['nuɪʃ] *adj* algo nuevo, bastante nuevo
**New Jersey** *s* Nueva Jersey
**new look** *s* nuevo aspecto (*especialmente de las modas por el año de 1947*)
**newly** ['njulɪ] o ['nulɪ] *adv* nuevamente; **newly** + *pp* recién + *pp*
**newlywed** ['njulɪ,wɛd] o ['nulɪ,wɛd] *s* desposado, recién casado
**New Mexican** *adj & s* neomejicano, nuevomejicano
**New Mexico** *s* Nuevo Méjico
**new moon** *s* novilunio, luna nueva
**newness** ['njunɪs] o ['nunɪs] *s* novedad; falta de práctica
**New Order** *s* (pol.) Orden Nuevo
**New Orleans** ['ɔrlɪənz] *s* Nueva Orleáns
**news** [njuz] o [nuz] *ssg* noticias; **a news item** una noticia
**news agency** *s* agencia de noticias
**news beat** *s* anticipación de una noticia (*por un periódico*)
**newsboy** ['njuz,bɔɪ] o ['nuz,bɔɪ] *s* vendedor de periódicos
**newscast** ['njuz,kæst], ['njuz,kɑst], ['nuz,kæst] o ['nuz,kɑst] *s* (rad.) noticiario; *va* radiar (*noticias, sucesos*); *vn* radiar noticias
**newscaster** ['njuz,kæstər], ['njuz,kɑstər], ['nuz,kæstər] o ['nuz,kɑstər] *s* cronista de radio, reportero radiofónico
**news coverage** *s* reportaje
**newsdealer** ['njuz,dilər] o ['nuz,dilər] *s* vendedor de periódicos
**newshawk** ['njuz,hɔk] o ['nuz,hɔk] *s* (coll.) cazanoticias
**newsletter** ['njuz,lɛtər] o ['nuz,lɛtər] *s* circular noticiera
**newsmagazine** ['nuz,mægəzin] o ['nuz,mægəzin] *s* revista de noticias
**newsman** ['njuzmən] o ['nuzmən] *s* (*pl:* **-men**) noticiero
**newsmonger** ['njuz,mʌŋgər] o ['nuz,mʌŋgər] *s* portanuevas, gacetista
**New South Wales** *s* la Nueva Gales del Sur
**New Spain** *s* la Nueva España (*el Méjico de los conquistadores españoles*)
**newspaper** ['njuz,pepər] o ['nuz,pepər] *s* periódico; *adj* periodístico
**newspaper clipping** *s* recorte de periódico
**newspaperman** ['njuz,pepər,mæn] o ['nuz,pepər,mæn] *s* (*pl:* **-men**) periodista
**newspaper wrapper** *s* faja
**news photographer** *s* reportero gráfico
**newsprint** ['njuz,prɪnt] o ['nuz,prɪnt] *s* papel de periódico, papel para periódicos, papel-prensa
**newsreel** ['njuz,ril] o ['nuz,ril] *s* película noticiera, actualidades, noticiario cinematográfico
**newsroom** ['njuz,rum] o ['nuz,rum] *s* redacción de un periódico (*oficina u oficinas*); tienda de periódicos; sala de lectura de periódicos
**newsstand** ['njuz,stænd] o ['nuz,stænd] *s* quiosco de periódicos
**New Style** *s* estilo nuevo (*calendario*)
**newsweekly** ['njuz,viklɪ] o ['nuz,wiklɪ] *s* (*pl:* **-lies**) semanario de noticias
**newsworthy** ['njuz,wʌrðɪ] o ['nuz,wʌrðɪ] *adj* de gran actualidad, de interés periodístico
**newsy** ['njuzɪ] o ['nuzɪ] *s* (*pl:* **-ies**) (coll.) chiquillo vendedor de periódicos; *adj* (*comp:* **-ier;** *super:* **-iest**) (coll.) informativo

**newt** [njut] o [nut] *s* (zool.) tritón, salamandra acuática
**New Testament** *s* Nuevo Testamento
**Newtonian** [nju'tonɪən] o [nu'tonɪən] *adj* neutoniano
**New World** *s* Nuevo Mundo
**new-world** ['nju,wʌrld] o ['nu,wʌrld] *adj* del Nuevo Mundo
**new year** *s* año nuevo; (*cap.*) *s* el día de año nuevo
**New Year's** *s* el día de año nuevo
**New Year's card** *s* tarjeta de felicitación de Año Nuevo
**New Year's Day** *s* el día de año nuevo
**New Year's Eve** *s* la víspera de año nuevo, la noche vieja
**New Year's gift** *s* regalo de año nuevo
**New York** [jɔrk] *s* Nueva York; *adj* neoyorquino
**New Yorker** ['jɔrkər] *s* neoyorquino
**New Zealand** ['zilənd] *s* Nueva Zelanda; *adj* neocelandés
**New Zealander** ['ziləndər] *s* neocelandés
**next** [nɛkst] *adj* próximo, siguiente; venidero, que viene; de al lado; **next door** la casa de al lado, en la casa de al lado; **next door to** en la casa siguiente de; casi; **next of kin** pariente(s) más cercano(s); **next time** la próxima vez; *adv* luego, después, inmediatamente después; la próxima vez; **to come next** venir después, ser el que sigue; **next to** junto a; después de; el primero después de; **the next best** lo mejor después de eso; **next to nothing** casi nada
**next-door** ['nɛkst,dor] *adj* siguiente, de al lado
**nexus** ['nɛksəs] *s* nexo
**N.F.** abr. de **Newfoundland** y **Norman French**
**n.g.** abr. de **no good**
**N.G.** abr. de **National Guard** y **no good**
**N.H.** abr. de **New Hampshire**
**N.I.** abr. de **Northern Ireland**
**niacin** ['naɪəsɪn] *s* (chem.) niacina
**Niagara Falls** [naɪ'ægərə] *spl* las cataratas del Niágara
**nib** [nɪb] *s* pico (*del ave*); punta (*de la pluma de escribir*); gavilán (*cada uno de los dos lados de la punta de la pluma*)
**nibble** ['nɪbəl] *s* mordisco; *va* mordiscar; *vn* picar; **to nibble at** picar de o en
**Nibelung** ['nibəlʊŋ] *s* (myth.) nibelungo
**niblick** ['nɪblɪk] *s* (golf) niblick
**nibs** [nɪbz] *s* (hum.) personaje; **his nibs** (hum.) su Señoría
**Nicaea** [naɪ'siə] *s* Nicea
**Nicaragua** [,nɪkə'rɑgwə] *s* Nicaragua
**Nicaraguan** [,nɪkə'rɑgwən] *adj* & *s* nicaragüense o nicaragüeño
**niccolite** ['nɪkəlaɪt] *s* (mineral.) niquelina
**nice** [naɪs] *adj* fino, sutil, delicado; primoroso, pulido, refinado; dengoso, melindroso; atento, cortés, culto; escrupuloso, esmerado; simpático, agradable; complaciente; decoroso, conveniente; preciso, satisfactorio; bien, bueno; **nice and** (coll.) muy, mucho; (coll.) -ito, p.ej., **nice and early** tempranito; (*cap.*) [nis] *s* Niza
**nicely** ['naɪslɪ] *adv* con precisión; escrupulosamente; satisfactoriamente; (coll.) muy bien
**Nicene** [naɪ'sin] o ['naɪsin] *adj* & *s* niceno, de Nicea
**Nicene Council** *s* concilio de Nicea
**Nicene Creed** *s* Símbolo de Nicea
**nicety** ['naɪsətɪ] *s* (*pl:* **-ties**) precisión; sutileza; finura; **to a nicety** con la mayor precisión
**niche** [nɪtʃ] *s* hornacina, nicho; (fig.) colocación conveniente
**Nicholas** ['nɪkələs] *s* Nicolás
**nichrome** ['naɪkrom] *s* nicromo
**nick** [nɪk] *s* mella, muesca; (print.) cran; (*cap.*) *s* nombre abreviado de **Nicholas; in the nick of time** en el momento crítico; *va* mellar, hacer muescas en; cortar; acertar
**nickel** ['nɪkəl] *s* (chem.) níquel; (U.S.A.) moneda de cinco centavos; *va* niquelar
**nickel-cadmium battery** ['nɪkəl'kædmɪəm] *s* (elec.) acumulador níquel-cadmio
**nickel plate** *s* niqueladura
**nickel-plate** ['nɪkəl,plet] *va* niquelar
**nickel silver** *s* metal blanco, melchor
**nickel steel** *s* aceroníquel, acero al níquel
**nicknack** ['nɪk,næk] *s* chuchería, friolera
**nickname** ['nɪk,nem] *s* apodo; *va* apodar
**Nicol prism** ['nɪkəl] *s* (opt.) prisma de Nicol
**nicotine** ['nɪkətin] *s* nicotina
**nicotinic** [,nɪkə'tɪnɪk] *adj* nicotínico
**nicotinic acid** *s* (chem.) ácido nicotínico
**niece** [nis] *s* sobrina
**niello** [nɪ'ɛlo] *s* (*pl:* **-li** [lɪ]) niel; *va* nielar
**Nietzschean** ['nitʃɪən] *adj* & *s* nietzscheano
**Nietzscheanism** ['nitʃɪənɪzəm] o **Nietzscheism** ['nitʃɪɪzəm] *s* nietzschismo
**nifty** ['nɪftɪ] *adj* (*comp:* **-tier;** *super:* **-tiest**) (slang) elegante; (slang) excelente
**Niger** ['naɪdʒər] *s* Níger (*río*); colonia del Níger
**Nigeria** [naɪ'dʒɪrɪə] *s* Nigeria
**niggard** ['nɪgərd] *adj* & *s* tacaño
**niggardly** ['nɪgərdlɪ] *adj* tacaño; *adv* tacañamente
**nigger** ['nɪgər] *s* (offensive) negro; (offensive) defecto mecánico; (offensive) **nigger in the woodpile** (coll.) gato encerrado
**niggle** ['nɪgəl] *va* trampear; burlar, engañar; esmerarse en; recargar con adornos; *vn* ocuparse en fruslerías; agitarse, menearse; ser melindroso
**nigh** [naɪ] *adj, adv* & *prep* (archaic & dial.) var. de **near**
**night** [naɪt] *s* noche; **at** o **by night** de noche o por la noche; **to make a night of it** (coll.) divertirse hasta muy entrada la noche
**night blindness** *s* ceguera nocturna
**night-blooming cereus** ['naɪt,blumɪŋ] *s* (bot.) pitahaya
**night bolt** *s* pestillo de golpe
**nightcap** ['naɪt,kæp] *s* gorro de dormir; trago antes de acostarse, sosiega
**night clothes** *spl* traje de dormir
**night club** *s* cabaret, café cantante, café-concierto
**nightdress** ['naɪt,drɛs] *s* camisa de dormir, camisón
**night driving** *s* (aut.) conducción de noche
**nightfall** ['naɪt,fɔl] *s* anochecer, caída de la noche; **at nightfall** al anochecer
**nightgown** ['naɪt,gaʊn] *s* camisa de dormir, camisón
**nighthawk** ['naɪt,hɔk] *s* (orn.) chotacabras, chotacabras norteamericano; trasnochador, anochecedor
**night heron** *s* (orn.) martín del río, martinete
**nightingale** ['naɪtəngel] *s* (orn.) ruiseñor
**nightjar** ['naɪt,dʒɑr] *s* (orn.) chotacabras
**night lamp** *s* lamparilla o luz de noche
**night latch** *s* cerradura de resorte
**night letter** *s* carta telegráfica nocturna, telegrama nocturno
**night life** *s* vida nocturna
**night light** *s* lamparilla o luz de noche
**nightlong** ['naɪt,lɔŋ] o ['naɪt,lɑŋ] *adj* de toda la noche; *adv* durante toda la noche
**nightly** ['naɪtlɪ] *adj* nocturno; de cada noche; *adv* cada noche; de noche, por la noche
**nightmare** ['naɪt,mɛr] *s* pesadilla; (fig.) pesadilla
**nightmarish** ['naɪt,mɛrɪʃ] *adj* de pesadilla; espeluznante, horroroso
**night owl** *s* buho nocturno, lechuza nocturna; (coll.) anochecedor, noctámbulo, trasnochador
**night piece** *s* (f.a.) cuadro nocturno, escena nocturna
**night school** *s* escuela de noche, escuela nocturna
**nightshade** ['naɪt,ʃed] *s* (bot.) dulcamara; (bot.) hierba mora
**night shift** *s* turno de noche
**nightshirt** ['naɪt,ʃʌrt] *s* camisón, camisa de dormir
**night spot** *s* (coll.) var. de **night club**
**night table** *s* mesilla de noche
**nighttime** ['naɪt,taɪm] *s* noche; **in the nighttime** de noche; *adj* nocturno
**nightwalker** ['naɪt,wɔkər] *s* vagabundo nocturno, noctámbulo; ladrón nocturno; ramera callejera nocturna; somnámbulo; lombriz nocturna
**night watch** *s* sereno; guardia de noche, ronda de noche; (mil.) vigilia

**night watchman** *s* vigilante nocturno; sereno (*vigilante que vela de noche por la seguridad del vecindario*)
**nihilism** [ˈnaɪɪlɪzəm] *s* nihilismo
**nihilist** [ˈnaɪɪlɪst] *s* nihilista
**nihilistic** [ˌnaɪɪlˈɪstɪk] *adj* nihilista
**nil** [nɪl] *s* nada
**Nile** [naɪl] *s* Nilo
**nimble** [ˈnɪmbəl] *adj* ágil, ligero; vivo, listo
**nimbly** [ˈnɪmblɪ] *adv* ágilmente; vivamente
**nimbus** [ˈnɪmbəs] *s* (*pl:* **-buses** o **-bi** [baɪ]) nimbo
**Nimrod** [ˈnɪmrɑd] *s* (Bib. & fig.) Nemrod
**nincompoop** [ˈnɪnkəmpup] *s* badulaque, necio, bobo, papirote
**nine** [naɪn] *adj* nueve; **nine days' wonder** prodigio de unos días; *s* nueve; equipo de beisbol; **the Nine** (myth.) las nueve musas; **nine o'clock** las nueve
**ninefold** [ˈnaɪnˌfold] *adj* nueve veces mayor; de nueve partes; *adv* nueve veces
**nine hundred** *adj & s* novecientos
**nine hundredth** *adj & s* noningentésimo
**ninepins** [ˈnaɪnˌpɪnz] *s* juego de bolos
**nineteen** [ˈnaɪnˈtin] *adj & s* diecinueve o diez y nueve
**nineteenth** [ˈnaɪnˈtinθ] *adj* décimonono; diecinueveavo; *s* décimonono; diecinueveavo; diecinueve (*en las fechas*)
**ninetieth** [ˈnaɪntɪɪθ] *adj & s* nonagésimo, noventavo
**ninety** [ˈnaɪntɪ] *adj* noventa; *s* (*pl:* **-ties**) noventa
**Nineveh** [ˈnɪnəvə] *s* Nínive
**Ninevite** [ˈnɪnəvaɪt] *s* ninivita
**ninny** [ˈnɪnɪ] *s* (*pl:* **-nies**) mentecato, bobo
**ninth** [naɪnθ] *adj* nono, noveno; *s* nono, noveno; nueve (*en las fechas*)
**Niobe** [ˈnaɪəbɪ] *s* (myth.) Níobe
**niobium** [naɪˈobɪəm] *s* (chem.) niobio
**nip** [nɪp] *s* pellizco, mordisco; helada, escarcha, quemadura; traguito; **nip and tuck** a quién ganará; (*pret & pp:* **nipped;** *ger:* **nipping**) *va* pellizcar, mordiscar; helar, escarchar, quemar; (slang) asir, coger, robar; **to nip in the bud** atajar en el principio; *vn* beborrotear
**nipa palm** [ˈnipə] o [ˈnaɪpə] *s* (bot.) nipa
**nipper** [ˈnɪpər] *s* pinza grande (*del cangrejo*); pala (*del caballo*); (coll.) chiquillo; **nippers** *spl* tenazas, cortaalambre, alicates de corte
**nipple** [ˈnɪpəl] *s* pezón (*de las hembras*); tetilla (*de los machos; del biberón*); (mach.) entrerrosca, tubo roscado de unión
**nipplewort** [ˈnɪpəlˌwʌrt] *s* (bot.) lámpsana
**Nippon** [nɪˈpɑn] o [ˈnɪpɑn] *s* el Japón
**Nipponese** [ˌnɪpəˈniz] *adj* nipón; *s* (*pl:* **-ese**) nipón
**nippy** [ˈnɪpɪ] *adj* (*comp:* **-pier;** *super:* **-piest**) mordaz, picante; frío, helado; (Brit.) ágil, ligero
**nirvana** o **Nirvana** [nɪrˈvɑnə] *s* el nirvana
**Nisei** [ˈniˈse] *s* (*pl:* **-sei** o **-seis**) persona nacida en los EE.UU. de padres japoneses
**nit** [nɪt] *s* piojito; liendre (*huevecillo del piojo*)
**niter** [ˈnaɪtər] *s* nitro (*nitrato potásico*); nitro de Chile (*nitrato sódico*)
**niton** [ˈnaɪtɑn] *s* (chem.) nitón
**nitrate** [ˈnaɪtret] *s* nitrato; nitrato de potasio o nitrato de sodio (*empleados como abono*); *va* (chem.) nitrar
**nitration** [naɪˈtreʃən] *s* (chem.) nitración
**nitre** [ˈnaɪtər] *s* var. de **niter**
**nitric** [ˈnaɪtrɪk] *adj* (chem.) nítrico
**nitric acid** *s* (chem.) ácido nítrico
**nitride** [ˈnaɪtraɪd] o [ˈnaɪtrɪd] *s* (chem.) nitruro
**nitrification** [ˌnaɪtrɪfɪˈkeʃən] *s* nitrificación
**nitrify** [ˈnaɪtrɪfaɪ] (*pret & pp:* **-fied**) *va* nitrar; nitrificar (*por la acción de bacterias*); abonar con nitratos
**nitrile** [ˈnaɪtrɪl] o [ˈnaɪtril] *s* (chem.) nitrilo
**nitrite** [ˈnaɪtraɪt] *s* (chem.) nitrito
**nitrobacteria** [ˌnaɪtrobækˈtɪrɪə] *spl* (agr.) nitrobacterias
**nitrobenzene** [ˌnaɪtroˈbɛnzin] o [ˌnaɪtrobɛnˈzin] *s* (chem.) nitrobenceno o nitrobencina
**nitrocellulose** [ˌnaɪtroˈsɛljəlos] *s* nitrocelulosa
**nitrogen** [ˈnaɪtrədʒən] *s* (chem.) nitrógeno
**nitrogen cycle** *s* ciclo del nitrógeno
**nitrogen fixation** *s* (chem.) fijación del nitrógeno
**nitrogenous** [naɪˈtrɑdʒɪnəs] *adj* nitrogenado
**nitroglycerin** o **nitroglycerine** [ˌnaɪtroˈglɪsərɪn] *s* nitroglicerina
**nitrolic** [naɪˈtrɑlɪk] *adj* (chem.) nitrólico
**nitrolime** [ˈnaɪtroˌlaɪm] *s* nitrocal
**nitrometer** [naɪˈtrɑmɪtər] *s* nitrómetro
**nitrosyl** [naɪˈtrosɪl], [ˌnaɪtrəˈsil] o [ˈnaɪtrəsɪl] *s* (chem.) nitrosilo
**nitrous** [ˈnaɪtrəs] *adj* (chem.) nitroso
**nitrous oxide** *s* (chem.) óxido nitroso
**nitty** [ˈnɪtɪ] *adj* lendroso
**nitwit** [ˈnɪtˌwɪt] *s* (slang) bobalicón
**nix** [nɪks] *s* (myth.) espíritu de las aguas; *adv* (slang) nexo (*no*)
**nixie** [ˈnɪksɪ] *s* (myth.) ondina
**N.J.** abr. de **New Jersey**
**N.M.** o **N. Mex.** abr. de **New Mexico**
**no.** abr. de **number**
**No.** abr. de **north** y **northern**
**no** [no] *adj indef* ninguno; **with no** sin; **no admittance** no se permite la entrada; **no matter** no importa; **no parking** se prohibe estacionarse; **no smoking** se prohibe fumar; **no thoroughfare** prohibido el paso; **no use** inútil; *adv* no; **no good** de ningún valor; vil, ruin; **no longer** ya no; **no sooner** no bien
**Noah** [ˈnoə] *s* (Bib.) Noé
**Noah's Ark** *s* arca de Noé
**nob** [nɑb] *s* (slang) cabeza; (slang) persona de viso
**nobby** [ˈnɑbɪ] *adj* (*comp:* **-bier;** *super:* **-biest**) (slang) elegante; (slang) excelente
**nobelium** [noˈbilɪəm] *s* (chem.) nobelio
**Nobel prizes** [noˈbɛl] *spl* premios Nóbel
**nobiliary** [noˈbɪlɪˌɛrɪ] *adj* nobiliario
**nobiliary particle** *s* partícula nobiliaria
**nobility** [noˈbɪlɪtɪ] *s* (*pl:* **-ties**) nobleza
**noble** [ˈnobəl] *adj & s* noble
**nobleman** [ˈnobəlmən] *s* (*pl:* **-men**) noble, hidalgo
**nobleness** [ˈnobəlnɪs] *s* nobleza
**noblewoman** [ˈnobəlˌwʊmən] *s* (*pl:* **-women**) mujer noble, hidalga
**nobody** [ˈnobɑdɪ] *s* (*pl:* **-ies**) nadie (*persona insignificante*); *pron indef* nadie, ninguno; **nobody but** nadie más que; **nobody else** nadie más, ningún otro
**noctambulation** [nɑkˌtæmbjəˈleʃən] *s* noctambulación
**noctambulism** [nɑkˈtæmbjəlɪzəm] *s* noctambulismo
**nocturnal** [nɑkˈtʌrnəl] *adj* nocturno
**nocturnally** [nɑkˈtʌrnəlɪ] *adv* nocturnalmente; cada noche
**nocturne** [ˈnɑktʌrn] *s* (mus.) nocturno; (paint.) escena nocturna
**nod** [nɑd] *s* inclinación de cabeza; seña con la cabeza; cabezada (*del que duerme sentado*); (*pret & pp:* **nodded;** *ger:* **nodding**) *va* inclinar (*la cabeza*); indicar con una inclinación de cabeza; *vn* inclinar la cabeza; cabecear; dormitar
**nodal** [ˈnodəl] *adj* nodal
**noddle** [ˈnɑdəl] *s* (coll.) cabeza
**noddy** [ˈnɑdɪ] *s* (*pl:* **-dies**) bobalicón; (orn.) golondrina de mar
**node** [nod] *s* bulto, protuberancia; nudo, enredo, trama; (astr., med. & phys.) nodo; (bot.) nudo
**nodular** [ˈnɑdʒələr] *adj* nodular; (bot.) tuberculoso
**nodule** [ˈnɑdʒul] *s* nódulo; (bot.) tubérculo; (anat., geol. & min.) nódulo
**noël** [noˈɛl] o [ˈnoɛl] *s* villancico de Navidad
**noggin** [ˈnɑgɪn] *s* tacita, cubilete; octavo de litro
**nohow** [ˈnoˌhaʊ] *adv* (coll.) de ninguna manera
**noise** [nɔɪz] *s* ruido; *va* divulgar
**noiseless** [ˈnɔɪzlɪs] *adj* silencioso, sin ruido
**noisemaker** [ˈnɔɪzˌmekər] *s* persona ruidosa, parrandista; matraca
**noise suppressor** *s* (rad.) silenciador de ruidos
**noisome** [ˈnɔɪsəm] *adj* apestoso; nocivo
**noisy** [ˈnɔɪzɪ] *adj* (*comp:* **-ier;** *super:* **-iest**) ruidoso, estrepitoso
**nol-pros** [ˌnɑlˈprɑs] (*pret & pp:* **-prossed;** *ger:* **-prossing**) *va* (law) abandonar (*la acción o parte de ella*)
**nom.** abr. de **nominative**

**nomad** ['nomæd] o ['nɑmæd] *adj & s* nómada
**nomadic** [no'mædɪk] *adj* nómada
**nomadism** ['nomædɪzəm] o ['nɑmædɪzəm] *s* nomadismo
**no man's land** *s* terreno sin reclamar; (mil.) tierra de nadie
**nomenclature** ['nomən,kletʃər] o [no'mɛnklətʃər] *s* nomenclatura
**nominal** ['nɑmɪnəl] *adj* nominal; módico (*p.ej., precio*)
**nominalism** ['nɑmɪnəlɪzəm] *s* nominalismo
**nominalist** ['nɑmɪnəlɪst] *s* nominalista
**nominally** ['nɑmɪnəlɪ] *adv* nominalmente
**nominate** ['nɑmɪnet] *va* nominar; poner para candidato, elegir candidato
**nomination** [,nɑmɪ'neʃən] *s* nominación; propuesta, postulación (*de un candidato*); **to put in nomination** poner para candidato
**nominative** ['nɑmɪnətɪv] o ['nɑmɪ,netɪv] *adj* nominativo (*que lleva el nombre del propietario*); (gram.) nominativo; *s* (gram.) nominativo
**nominator** ['nɑmɪ,netər] *s* nombrador; proponedor
**nominee** [,nɑmɪ'ni] *s* nómino, propuesto (*para un cargo o empleo*)
**nonacceptance** [,nɑnæk'sɛptəns] *s* falta de aceptación
**nonage** ['nɑnɪdʒ] o ['nonɪdʒ] *s* minoridad, minoría de edad; infancia
**nonagenarian** [,nɑnədʒɪ'nɛrɪən] o [,nonədʒɪ'nɛrɪən] *adj & s* nonagenario, noventón
**nonaggression** [,nɑnə'grɛʃən] *s* no agresión
**nonagon** ['nɑnəgɑn] *s* (geom.) nonágono o eneágono
**nonalcoholic** [,nɑnælkə'hɔlɪk] o [,nɑnælkə'hɑlɪk] *adj* no alcohólico
**nonappearance** [,nɑnə'pɪrəns] *s* (law) no comparencia, contumacia
**nonattendance** [,nɑnə'tɛndəns] *s* falta de asistencia
**nonbelligerency** [,nɑnbə'lɪdʒərənsɪ] *s* no beligerancia
**nonbelligerent** [,nɑnbə'lɪdʒərənt] *adj & s* no beligerante
**nonbreakable** [nɑn'brekəbəl] *adj* irrompible
**non-Catholic** [nɑn'kæθəlɪk] *adj* acatólico
**nonce** [nɑns] *s* tiempo presente; **for the nonce** por el momento
**nonce word** *s* palabra para el caso
**nonchalance** ['nɑnʃələns] o [,nɑnʃə'lɑns] *s* descuido, indiferencia
**nonchalant** ['nɑnʃələnt] o [,nɑnʃə'lɑnt] *adj* descuidado, indiferente
**nonclerical** [nɑn'klɛrɪkəl] *adj* no oficinesco
**noncom.** abr. de **noncommissioned officer**
**noncom** ['nɑn,kɑm] *s* (coll.) clase, suboficial
**noncombatant** [nɑn'kɑmbətənt] *adj & s* no combatiente
**noncommissioned officer** [,nɑnkə'mɪʃənd] *s* clase, suboficial
**noncommittal** [,nɑnkə'mɪtəl] *adj* evasivo, reticente
**noncommitted** [,nɑnkə'mɪtɪd] *adj* no comprometido, no empeñado
**noncompliance** [,nɑnkəm'plaɪəns] *s* falta de cumplimiento
**non compos mentis** ['nɑn'kɑmpəs'mɛntɪs] *adj* falto de juicio, loco
**nonconducting** [,nɑnkən'dʌktɪŋ] *adj* no conductor, mal conductor
**nonconductor** [,nɑnkən'dʌktər] *s* mal conductor
**nonconformance** [,nɑnkən'fɔrməns] *s* disconformidad
**nonconformist** [,nɑnkən'fɔrmɪst] *s* disidente
**nonconformity** [,nɑnkən'fɔrmɪtɪ] *s* disconformidad, disidencia
**nondelivery** [,nɑndɪ'lɪvərɪ] *s* falta de entrega
**nondescript** ['nɑndɪskrɪpt] *adj* indefinido, inclasificable
**none** [non] *s* nona; **nones** *spl* (hist.) nonas; (eccl.) nona; [nʌn] *pron indef* nadie, ninguno, ningunos; **none of** ninguno de (*p.ej., los libros*); nada de (*p.ej., la leche*); **none other** ningún otro; *adv* nada, de ninguna manera; **none the less** sin embargo, no obstante
**nonentity** [nɑn'ɛntɪtɪ] *s* (*pl:* **-ties**) cosa inexistente; nulidad (*persona*)
**nonessential** [,nɑnɛ'sɛnʃəl] *adj & s* no esencial
**nonesuch** ['nʌn,sʌtʃ] *s* persona sin par, cosa sin igual
**non-Euclidean** [,nɑnju'klɪdɪən] *adj* no euclidiano
**non-Euclidean geometry** *s* geometría no euclidiana
**nonexistence** [,nɑnɛg'zɪstəns] *s* inexistencia; cosa inexistente
**nonexistent** [,nɑnɛg'zɪstənt] *adj* inexistente
**nonferrous** [nɑn'fɛrəs] *adj* no ferroso
**nonfiction** [nɑn'fɪkʃən] *s* literatura no novelesca
**nonfulfillment** [,nɑnfʊl'fɪlmənt] *s* incumplimiento
**noninflammable** [,nɑnɪn'flæməbəl] *adj* ininflamable
**noninterference** [,nɑnɪntər'fɪrəns] *s* no interferencia
**nonintervention** [,nɑnɪntər'vɛnʃən] *s* (dipl.) no intervención
**nonintoxicating** [,nɑnɪn'tɑksɪ,ketɪŋ] *adj* no embriagante
**nonjuror** [nɑn'dʒʊrər] *s* no jurante
**nonmember** [nɑn'mɛmbər] *s* no asociado, no miembro
**nonmetal** ['nɑn,mɛtəl] *s* (chem.) metaloide
**nonmetallic** [,nɑnmɪ'tælɪk] *adj* (chem.) metaloideo; no metálico
**nonmoral** [nɑn'mɑrəl] o [nɑn'mɔrəl] *adj* amoral
**nonpareil** [,nɑnpə'rɛl] *s* persona sin par, cosa sin igual; (print.) nomparell; *adj* sin par, sin igual
**nonpartisan** or **nonpartizan** [nɑn'pɑrtɪzən] *adj* independiente, imparcial
**nonpayment** [nɑn'pemənt] *s* falta de pago
**nonperformance** [,nɑnpər'fɔrməns] *s* falta de ejecución
**nonplus** ['nɑnplʌs] o [nɑn'plʌs] *s* estupefacción; (*pret & pp:* **-plused** o **-plussed;** *ger:* **-plusing** o **-plussing**) *va* dejar estupefacto, dejar perplejo, dejar pegado a la pared
**nonproductive** [,nɑnprə'dʌktɪv] *adj* no productivo
**nonprofit** [nɑn'prɑfɪt] *adj* sin beneficio, no comercial
**nonquota** [nɑn'kwotə] *adj* no cuota
**nonrefillable** [,nɑnri'fɪləbəl] *adj* irrellenable
**nonrenewable** [,nɑnrɪ'njuəbəl] o [,nɑnrɪ'nuəbəl] *adj* no renovable
**nonresidence** [nɑn'rɛzɪdəns] *s* no residencia
**nonresident** [nɑn'rɛzɪdənt] *adj & s* transeúnte
**nonresidential** [nɑn,rɛzɪ'dɛnʃəl] *adj* comercial
**nonresistance** [,nɑnrɪ'zɪstəns] *s* no resistencia; obediencia pasiva
**nonresistant** [,nɑnrɪ'zɪstənt] *adj* no resistente
**nonscientific** [nɑn,saɪən'tɪfɪk] *adj* no científico
**nonsectarian** [,nɑnsɛk'tɛrɪən] *adj* no sectario
**nonsense** ['nɑnsɛns] *s* disparate, tontería
**nonsensical** [nɑn'sɛnsɪkəl] *adj* disparatado, tonto
**non seq.** abr. de **non sequitur**
**non sequitur** [nɑn'sɛkwɪtər] *s* non séquitur (*conclusión falsa*)
**nonshatterable** [nɑn'ʃætərəbəl] *adj* inastillable
**nonskid** ['nɑn'skɪd] *adj* antideslizante, antiderrapante, antirresbaladizo
**nonstop** ['nɑn,stɑp] *adj & adv* sin parar, sin escala
**nonstop flight** *s* (aer.) vuelo sin parar
**nonsubscriber** [,nɑnsəb'skraɪbər] *s* no abonado
**nonsuit** ['nɑn,sut] o ['nɑn,sjut] *s* (law) absolución de la instancia; *va* (law) absolver de la instancia
**nonsupport** [,nɑnsə'port] *s* falta de mantenimiento, incumplimiento de la obligación de alimentos
**nontaxable** [nɑn'tæksəbəl] *adj* no sujeto a impuesto
**nonunion** [nɑn'junjən] *adj* no agremiado
**nonviolence** [nɑn'vaɪələns] *s* no violencia
**nonvoter** [nɑn'votər] *s* no votante

**noodle** ['nudəl] *s* tallarín; (slang) tonto, mentecato; (slang) cabeza
**noodle soup** *s* sopa de pastas
**nook** [nʊk] *s* rinconcito, escondrijo
**noon** [nun] o **noonday** ['nun,de] *s* mediodía; **at broad** o **high noon** en pleno mediodía; *adj* meridiano, de mediodía
**no one** o **no-one** ['no,wʌn] *pron indef* nadie, ninguno; **no one else** nadie más, ningún otro
**nooning** ['nunɪŋ] *s* mediodía; almuerzo; siesta
**noontide** ['nun,taɪd] o **noontime** ['nun,taɪm] *s* mediodía
**noose** [nus] *s* lazo corredizo; dogal (*para ahorcar a un reo*); trampa; *va* lazar, coger con lazo corredizo; coger en una trampa
**nor** [nɔr] *conj* ni; **neither . . . nor** ni . . . ni
**Nordic** ['nɔrdɪk] *adj & s* nórdico
**Norfolk Island pine** ['nɔrfək] *s* (bot.) araucaria
**norm** [nɔrm] *s* norma, pauta
**normal** ['nɔrməl] *adj* normal; *s* estado normal, nivel normal
**normalcy** ['nɔrməlsɪ] *s* normalidad
**normality** [nɔr'mælɪtɪ] *s* normalidad
**normalize** ['nɔrməlaɪz] *va* normalizar
**normally** ['nɔrməlɪ] *adv* normalmente
**normal school** *s* escuela normal
**Norman** ['nɔrmən] *adj & s* normando
**Norman Conquest** *s* conquista de Inglaterra por los normandos, conquista normanda
**Normandy** ['nɔrməndɪ] *s* Normandía
**Normanesque** [,nɔrmən'ɛsk] *adj* (arch.) normando
**Norman French** *s* normánico
**Norn** [nɔrn] *s* (myth.) Norna
**Norse** [nɔrs] *adj* nórdico; noruego; *ssg* nórdico (*antiguo idioma escandinavo*); noruego (*idioma de Noruega*); *spl* nórdicos; noruegos
**Norseman** ['nɔrsmən] *s* (*pl:* **-men**) normando (*antiguo escandinavo*)
**Norse mythology** *s* mitología nórdica
**north** [nɔrθ] *s* norte; *adj* septentrional, del norte; *adv* al norte
**North Africa** *s* Noráfrica, el África del Norte
**North African** *adj & s* norteafricano
**North America** *s* Norteamérica, la América del Norte
**North American** *adj & s* norteamericano
**North Cape** *s* el cabo Norte
**North Carolina** [,kærə'laɪnə] *s* la Carolina del Norte
**North Dakota** [də'kotə] *s* el Dakota del Norte
**northeast** [,nɔrθ'ist] *adj* nordeste, nordestal; *s* nordeste; *adv* al nordeste, hacia el nordeste
**northeaster** [,nɔrθ'istər] *s* nordeste (*viento*); nordestada (*viento fuerte*)
**northeasterly** [,nɔrθ'istərlɪ] *adj* nordestal; *adv* hacia el nordeste; desde el nordeste
**northeastern** [,nɔrθ'istərn] *adj* nordeste, nordestal
**northeastward** [,nɔrθ'istwərd] *adj* que va hacia el nordeste; *s* nordeste; *adv* hacia el nordeste
**northeastwardly** [,nɔrθ'istwərdlɪ] *adj* que va hacia el nordeste; *adv* hacia el nordeste
**northeastwards** [,nɔrθ'istwərdz] *adv* hacia el nordeste
**norther** ['nɔrðər] *s* norte, nortada (*viento*)
**northerly** ['nɔrðərlɪ] *adj* septentrional; que viene desde el norte; que va hacia el norte; *adv* desde el norte; hacia el norte
**northern** ['nɔrðərn] *adj* septentrional, norteño, nórtico
**northerner** ['nɔrðərnər] *s* septentrional, habitante del norte
**Northern Hemisphere** *s* hemisferio boreal
**Northern Ireland** *s* la Irlanda Septentrional, la Irlanda del Norte
**northern lights** *spl* aurora boreal
**northernmost** ['nɔrðərnmost] *adj* (el) más septentrional
**northern phalarope** *s* (orn.) chorlito de mar apizarrado
**North Island** *s* la Isla de Norte (*Nueva Zelanda*)
**North Korea** *s* la Corea del Norte
**North Korean** *adj & s* norcoreano
**northland** ['nɔrθlənd] *s* región septentrional; (*cap.*) *s* región boreal; Península escandinava
**northlander** ['nɔrθləndər] *s* septentrional
**North Magnetic Pole** *s* polo norte magnético
**Northman** ['nɔrθmən] *s* (*pl:* **-men**) normando (*antiguo escandinavo*); escandinavo
**north-northeast** ['nɔrθ,nɔrθ'ist] *s* nornordeste o nornoreste
**north-northwest** ['nɔrθ,nɔrθ'wɛst] *s* nornoroeste o nornorueste
**North Pole** *s* polo norte
**North Sea** *s* mar del Norte
**North Star** *s* estrella del Norte
**northward** ['nɔrθwərd] *adj* que va hacia el norte; *s* norte; *adv* hacia el norte
**northwardly** ['nɔrθwərdlɪ] *adj* que va hacia el norte; *adv* hacia el norte
**northwards** ['nɔrθwərdz] *adv* hacia el norte
**northwest** [,nɔrθ'wɛst] *adj & s* noroeste; *adv* al noroeste, hacia el noroeste
**northwester** [,nɔrθ'wɛstər] *s* noroeste (*viento*); noroestada (*viento fuerte*)
**northwesterly** [,nɔrθ'wɛstərlɪ] *adj* noroeste; *adv* hacia el noroeste; desde el noroeste
**northwestern** [,nɔrθ'wɛstərn] *adj* noroeste, nordoccidental
**Northwest Passage** *s* paso del Noroeste
**Northwest Territories** *spl* Territorios del Noroeste (*del Canadá*)
**northwestward** [,nɔrθ'wɛstwərd] *adj* que va hacia el noroeste; *s* noroeste; *adv* hacia el noroeste
**northwestwardly** [,nɔrθ'wɛstwərdlɪ] *adj* que va hacia el noroeste; *adv* hacia el noroeste
**northwestwards** [,nɔrθ'wɛstwərdz] *adv* hacia el noroeste
**north wind** *s* norte, aquilón
**Norway** ['nɔrwe] *s* Noruega
**Norway lobster** *s* (zool.) cigala
**Norway rat** *s* (zool.) rata de alcantarilla
**Norwegian** [nɔr'widʒən] *adj & s* noruego
**nos.** abr. de **numbers**
**nose** [noz] *s* nariz; (aer.) proa; **to blow one's nose** sonarse las narices; **to count noses** averiguar cuántas personas hay; **to follow one's nose** seguir todo derecho; avanzar guiándose por el instinto; **to hold one's nose** tabicarse las narices; **to lead by the nose** tener agarrado por las narices; **to look down one's nose at** (coll.) mirar por encima del hombro; **to pay through the nose** pagar un precio escandaloso; **to pick one's nose** hurgarse las narices; **to poke one's nose into** meter las narices en, meter el hocico en; **to speak through the nose** ganguear; **to thumb one's nose at** (coll.) señalar (*a una persona*) poniendo el pulgar sobre la nariz en son de burla; (coll.) tratar con sumo desprecio; **to turn up one's nose at** mirar con desprecio; **under the nose of** en las narices de, en las barbas de ‖ *va* husmear, olfatear; restregar la nariz contra; descubrir, averiguar; **to nose out** huronear; vencer con poca ventaja ‖ *vn* ventear; **to nose about** curiosear; **to nose over** (aer.) capotar; **to nose up** encabritarse (*un buque, un avión, etc.*)
**nose bag** *s* morral, cebadera
**noseband** ['noz,bænd] *s* sobarba, muserola
**nosebleed** ['noz,blid] *s* hemorragia nasal
**nose cone** *s* cono de proa (*de un cohete*)
**nose count** *s* (coll.) recuento del número de personas
**nose dive** *s* (aer.) descenso de cabeza, descenso de picado; (fig.) descenso precipitado
**nose-dive** ['noz,daɪv] *vn* (aer.) descender de cabeza, picar; (fig.) descender precipitadamente
**nosegay** ['nozge] *s* ramillete
**nose glasses** *spl* anteojos de nariz, lentes
**nosepiece** ['noz,pis] *s* sobarba, muserola; ventalle (*del yelmo*); portaobjetivo (*del microscopio*)
**nose ring** *s* nariguera
**nose wheel** *s* (aer.) rueda de proa
**nosey** ['nozɪ] *adj* var. de **nosy**
**no-show** ['no'ʃo] *s* (coll.) pasajero no presentado (*pasajero que deja de notificar la empresa que no va a ocupar la plaza reservada*)
**nosing** ['nozɪŋ] *s* vuelo de huella (*de escalera*); serpenteo, movimiento de lanzadera (*de locomotora*); tajamar (*de puente*); arista (*de moldura*)
**nostalgia** [nɑ'stældʒə] *s* nostalgia

**nostalgic** [nɑˈstældʒɪk] *adj* nostálgico
**nostril** [ˈnɑstrɪl] *s* nariz, ventana (*de la nariz*)
**nostrum** [ˈnɑstrəm] *s* remedio de charlatán; panacea
**nosy** [ˈnozɪ] *adj* (*comp:* **-ier;** *super:* **-iest**) (coll.) husmeador, curioso
**not** [nɑt] *adv* no; **to think not** creer que no; **why not?** ¿cómo no?; **not at all** de ningún modo, nada; **not yet** todavía no
**notability** [ˌnotəˈbɪlɪtɪ] *s* (*pl:* **-ties**) notabilidad
**notable** [ˈnotəbəl] *adj* notable; *s* notable, notabilidad
**notably** [ˈnotəblɪ] *adv* notablemente
**notarial** [noˈtɛrɪəl] *adj* notarial
**notarize** [ˈnotəraɪz] *va* abonar con fe notarial, dar fe notarial de
**notary** [ˈnotərɪ] *s* (*pl:* **-ries**) notario
**notary public** *s* (*pl:* **notaries public**) notario
**notation** [noˈteʃən] *s* notación
**notch** [nɑtʃ] *s* muesca, mella, corte; (U.S.A.) paso, desfiladero; (coll.) grado; *va* hacer muescas en, mellar; anotar con cortes; señalar (*los tantos*)
**note** [not] *s* nota, apunte; esquela, cartita; marca, señal; (com.) pagaré, vale; (com.) billete (*de banco*); (mus.) figura (*que fija la duración del sonido*); (mus.) nota; canto, melodía; acento, voz; **of note** notable; **to compare notes** hacer intercambio de opiniones; **to make a note of** apuntar; **to strike the right note** hacer o decir lo que conviene; **to take note of** tomar nota de; **to take notes** tomar notas; *va* notar, apuntar; marcar, señalar
**notebook** [ˈnotˌbʊk] *s* cuaderno, libro de apuntes
**noted** [ˈnotɪd] *adj* conocido, afamado
**note paper** *s* papel de cartas, papel para esquelas
**noteworthy** [ˈnotˌwʌrðɪ] *adj* notable, digno de notarse
**nothing** [ˈnʌθɪŋ] *s* nada, cero; nadería, friolera; *pron indef* nada; **for nothing** gratis, de balde; inútilmente; **that's nothing to me** eso nada me importa; **to make nothing of** no hacer caso de; no aprovecharse de; no entender; despreciar; **to think nothing of** no hacer caso de; tener por fácil; despreciar; **nothing doing** (slang) ni por pienso; **nothing else** nada más; *adv* de ninguna manera, nada; **nothing daunted** sin temor alguno; **nothing less** no menos; **nothing less than** de todo punto; **nothing like** ni con mucho
**nothingness** [ˈnʌθɪŋnɪs] *s* nada, inexistencia; nadería, friolera; insignificancia; inconsciencia, falta de conocimiento
**notice** [ˈnotɪs] *s* atención, reparo, advertencia; aviso, noticia; letrero; reseña, mención; llamada; notificación; **on short notice** con poco tiempo de aviso; **to escape one's notice** pasarle inadvertido a uno, escapársele a uno; **to give notice (that)** dar noticia (de que); **to serve notice (that)** hacer saber (que); **to take notice (of)** notar, observar, reparar; *va* notar, observar, reparar, reparar en; mencionar
**noticeable** [ˈnotɪsəbəl] *adj* sensible, perceptible; notable
**noticeably** [ˈnotɪsəblɪ] *adv* perceptiblemente
**notification** [ˌnotɪfɪˈkeʃən] *s* notificación
**notify** [ˈnotɪfaɪ] (*pret & pp:* **-fied**) *va* notificar, avisar; **to notify a person of something** notificar a una persona una cosa
**notion** [ˈnoʃən] *s* noción; capricho; **notions** *spl* mercería (*alfileres, cintas, etc.*); **to have a notion to** + *inf* pensar + *inf*, tener ganas de + *inf*
**notional** [ˈnoʃənəl] *adj* especulativo; imaginario; imaginativo, caprichoso
**notochord** [ˈnotəkɔrd] *s* (biol.) notocordio
**notoriety** [ˌnotəˈraɪɪtɪ] *s* (*pl:* **-ties**) notoriedad; mala reputación; notabilidad (*persona*)
**notorious** [noˈtorɪəs] *adj* notorio; de historia, de mala reputación
**Notre Dame** [ˌnotrəˈdɑm] *s* Nuestra Señora; Nuestra Señora de París
**no-trump** [ˈnoˈtrʌmp] *adj & s* sin triunfo; **a no-trump hand** un sin triunfo
**notwithstanding** [ˌnɑtwɪðˈstændɪŋ] o [ˌnɑtwɪθˈstændɪŋ] *adv* no obstante; *conj* a pesar de que; *prep* a pesar de
**nougat** [ˈnugət] o [ˈnugɑ] *s* turrón, nuégado
**nought** [nɔt] *s* var. de **naught**
**noumenon** [ˈnumɪnɑn] o [ˈnaʊmɪnɑn] *s* (*pl:* **-na** [nə]) (philos.) nóumeno
**noun** [naʊn] *s* nombre, substantivo; *adj* substantivo
**nourish** [ˈnʌrɪʃ] *va* nutrir, alimentar; abrigar (*pensamientos, esperanzas, etc.*)
**nourishing** [ˈnʌrɪʃɪŋ] *adj* nutritivo
**nourishment** [ˈnʌrɪʃmənt] *s* nutrimento, alimento
**nouveau riche** [nuvoˈriʃ] *s* (*pl:* **nouveaux riches** [nuvoˈriʃ]) nuevo rico
**Nov.** abr. de **November**
**nova** [ˈnovə] *s* (*pl:* **-vae** [vi] o **-vas**) (astr.) nova
**Nova Scotia** [ˈnovəˈskoʃə] *s* la Nueva Escocia
**Nova Scotian** [ˈnovəˈskoʃən] *adj & s* neoescocés
**novate** [noˈvet] o [ˈnovet] *va* (law) novar
**novation** [noˈveʃən] *s* (law) novación
**novel** [ˈnɑvəl] *s* novela; novelística (*literatura novelesca*); *adj* nuevo, insólito, original
**novelette** [ˌnɑvəlˈɛt] *s* novela corta
**novelist** [ˈnɑvəlɪst] *s* novelista
**novelistic** [ˌnɑvəlˈɪstɪk] *adj* novelesco
**novelize** [ˈnɑvəlaɪz] *va* novelizar, novelar
**novelty** [ˈnɑvəltɪ] *s* (*pl:* **-ties**) novedad, innovación; **novelties** *spl* bisutería, baratijas
**November** [noˈvɛmbər] *s* noviembre
**novena** [noˈvinə] *s* (*pl:* **-nae** [ni]) (eccl.) novena
**novice** [ˈnɑvɪs] *s* novicio, principiante; (eccl.) novicio
**noviciate** o **novitiate** [noˈvɪʃɪɪt] *s* noviciado, aprendizaje; (eccl.) noviciado
**novocaine** [ˈnovəken] *s* (trademark) novocaína
**now** [naʊ] *s* actualidad; *adv* ahora, ahora mismo; ya; entonces; **from now on** de ahora en adelante; **how now?** ¿cómo?; **just now** hace un momento; **now and again** o **now and then** de vez en cuando; **now . . . now** ora . . . ora, ya . . . ya; **now that** ya que; **now then** ahora bien; *interj* ¡vamos!
**nowadays** [ˈnaʊəˌdez] *s* actualidad; *adv* hoy en día
**noway** [ˈnowe] o **noways** [ˈnowez] *adv* de ningún modo
**nowhere** [ˈnohwɛr] *adv* en ninguna parte, a ninguna parte; **nowhere else** en ninguna otra parte
**nowise** [ˈnowaɪz] *adv* de ningún modo
**noxious** [ˈnɑkʃəs] *adj* nocivo
**nozzle** [ˈnɑzəl] *s* boquerel (*de la manguera*); rallo o roseta (*de la regadera*); cubo (*del candelero*); (slang) nariz
**N.S.** abr. de **Nova Scotia** y **New Style**
**N.S.W.** abr. de **New South Wales**
**N.T.** abr. de **New Testament** y **Northern Territory**
**nth** [ɛnθ] *adj* (math.) $n^{mo}$ (*enésimo*); **to the nth degree** (math.) elevado a la potencia n; (fig.) a lo sumo posible, lo último de potencia
**nt. wt.** abr. de **net weight**
**nuance** [njuˈɑns] o [ˈnjuɑns] *s* matiz
**nub** [nʌb] *s* protuberancia; pedazo; (coll.) meollo; **the nub of the question** lo más esencial
**nubbin** [ˈnʌbɪn] *s* pedazo; mazorca imperfecta; fruto mal desarrollado
**Nubian** [ˈnjubɪən] o [ˈnubɪən] *adj & s* nubiense
**Nubian Desert** *s* desierto de Nubia
**nubile** [ˈnjubɪl] o [ˈnubɪl] *adj* núbil
**nubility** [njuˈbɪlɪtɪ] o [nuˈbɪlɪtɪ] *s* nubilidad
**nuclear** [ˈnjuklɪər] o [ˈnuklɪər] *adj* nuclear, nucleario
**nuclear fission** *s* (phys.) fisión nuclear
**nuclear force** *s* (mil.) fuerza nuclear
**nuclear fusion** *s* (phys.) fusión nuclear
**nuclear physics** *ssg* física nuclear
**nuclear-powered** [ˈnjuklɪərˈpaʊərd] o [ˈnuklɪərˈpaʊərd] *adj* accionado por la energía nuclear
**nuclear reactor** *s* (phys.) reactor nuclear
**nuclear test ban** *s* proscripción de las pruebas nucleares
**nuclease** [ˈnjuklɪes] o [ˈnuklɪes] *s* (biochem.) nucleasa
**nucleate** [ˈnjuklɪet] o [ˈnuklɪet] *adj* nucleario; (bot.) nucleado; *va* agregar formando núcleo; *vn* formar núcleo

**nucleic** [nju'kliɪk] o [nu'kliɪk] *adj* nucleico o nucleínico
**nucleic acid** *s* (biochem.) ácido nucleico o nucleínico
**nuclein** ['njuklɪɪn] o ['nuklɪɪn] *s* (biochem.) nucleína
**nucleolus** [nju'kliələs] o [nu'kliələs] *s* (*pl:* **-li** [laɪ]) (biol.) nucléolo
**nucleon** ['njuklɪɑn] o ['nuklɪɑn] *s* (phys.) nucleón
**nucleonic** [,njuklɪ'ɑnɪk] o [,nuklɪ'ɑnɪk] *adj* nucleónico; **nucleonics** *ssg* nucleónica
**nucleus** ['njuklɪəs] o ['nuklɪəs] *s* (*pl:* **-i** [aɪ] o **-uses**) núcleo; (anat., biol., chem. & phys.) núcleo
**nude** [njud] o [nud] *adj* desnudo; *s* (f.a.) desnudo; **the nude** el desnudo; **in the nude** desnudo
**nudge** [nʌdʒ] *s* codazo suave; *va* dar un codazo suave a, empujar suavemente
**nudism** ['njudɪzəm] o ['nudɪzəm] *s* nudismo
**nudist** ['njudɪst] o ['nudɪst] *s* nudista
**nudity** ['njudɪtɪ] o ['nudɪtɪ] *s* (*pl:* **-ties**) desnudez
**nugatory** ['njugə,torɪ] o ['nugə,torɪ] *adj* insignificante, ineficaz
**nugget** ['nʌgɪt] *s* pedazo; pepita (*p.ej., de oro*); (fig.) preciosidad
**nuisance** ['njusəns] o ['nusəns] *s* molestia, estorbo, incomodidad; persona o cosa fastidiosa; **to commit a nuisance** orinar, depositar inmundicias
**nuisance tax** *s* impuesto indirecto y fastidioso
**null** [nʌl] *adj* nulo; **null and void** nulo, írrito
**nullification** [,nʌlɪfɪ'keʃən] *s* anulación, invalidación
**nullify** ['nʌlɪfaɪ] (*pret & pp:* **-fied**) *va* anular, invalidar
**nullity** ['nʌlɪtɪ] *s* (*pl:* **-ties**) nulidad
**Num.** abr. de **Numbers**
**Numantia** [nju'mænʃɪə] o [nu'mænʃɪə] *s* Numancia
**numb** [nʌm] *adj* entumecido; *va* entumecer
**number** ['nʌmbər] *s* número; (gram.) número; **numbers** *spl* muchos; (poet. & mus.) números; **Numbers** *spl* (Bib.) los Números; **a number of** varios; **beyond number** muchísimos; **to look out for number one** mirar por el número uno (*sí mismo*); **without number** sin número; *va* numerar; ascender a; **his days are numbered** tiene sus días contados o sus horas contadas; **to be numbered among** hallarse entre
**numberless** ['nʌmbərlɪs] *adj* innumerable
**numbers game** o **pool** *s* quiniela en que se apuesta a ciertas cifras de las carreras de caballos o de otros acontecimientos cotidianos
**numbness** ['nʌmnɪs] *s* entumecimiento
**numerable** ['njumərəbəl] o ['numərəbəl] *adj* numerable
**numeral** ['njumərəl] o ['numərəl] *adj* numeral; *s* número
**numerary** ['njumə,rɛrɪ] o ['numə,rɛrɪ] *adj* numerario
**numerate** ['njuməret] o ['numəret] *va* numerar; enumerar
**numeration** [,njumə'reʃən] o [,numə'reʃən] *s* numeración
**numerator** ['njumə,retər] o ['numə,retər] *s* numerador; (math.) numerador
**numeric** [nju'mɛrɪk] o [nu'mɛrɪk] o **numerical** [nju'mɛrɪkəl] o [nu'mɛrɪkəl] *adj* numérico
**numerically** [nju'mɛrɪkəlɪ] o [nu'mɛrɪkəlɪ] *adv* numéricamente
**numerous** ['njumərəs] o ['numərəs] *adj* numeroso
**Numidian** [nju'mɪdɪən] o [nu'mɪdɪən] *adj* númida, numídico; *s* númida
**Numidian crane** *s* (orn.) grulla de Numidia
**numismatic** [,njumɪz'mætɪk] o [,numɪz'mætɪk] *adj* numismático; **numismatics** *ssg* numismática
**numismatist** [nju'mɪzmətɪst] o [nu'mɪzmətɪst] *s* numismático
**numskull** ['nʌm,skʌl] *s* bodoque, mentecato
**nun** [nʌn] *s* monja, religiosa
**nunciature** ['nʌnʃɪətʃər] *s* nunciatura
**nuncio** ['nʌnʃɪo] *s* (*pl:* **-os**) nuncio o nuncio apostólico
**nuncupative will** ['nʌŋkjə,petɪv] *s* (law) testamento nuncupativo
**nunnery** ['nʌnərɪ] *s* (*pl:* **-ies**) convento de monjas
**nun's veiling** *s* velo de monja
**nuptial** ['nʌpʃəl] *adj* nupcial; **nuptials** *spl* nupcias
**nuptial mass** *s* misa de esposos, misa de velaciones
**nurse** [nʌrs] *s* enfermera; nodriza, ama de cría; niñera; protector, fomentador; **male nurse** enfermero; *va* amamantar; criar; alimentar; cuidar (*a una persona enferma*); tratar de curarse de (*p.ej., un resfriado*); cebar, fomentar (*p.ej., un sentimiento de odio*); acariciar, mimar; **to nurse at the breast** criar a los pechos; *vn* amamantarse; ser enfermera, servir de enfermera
**nurseling** ['nʌrslɪŋ] *s* var. de **nursling**
**nursemaid** ['nʌrs,med] *s* niñera
**nursery** ['nʌrsərɪ] *s* (*pl:* **-ies**) cuarto de los niños, cuarto de juegos; (agr.) semillero, criadero, plantel; (fig.) semillero
**nurserymaid** ['nʌrsərɪ,med] *s* var. de **nursemaid**
**nurseryman** ['nʌrsərɪmən] *s* (*pl:* **-men**) cultivador de semillero
**nursery rhymes** *spl* versos para niños
**nursery school** *s* escuela materna (*para niños muy pequeños*)
**nursery tales** *spl* cuentos para niños
**nursing** ['nʌrsɪŋ] *s* oficio de enfermera
**nursing bottle** *s* biberón
**nursing home** *s* clínica de reposo
**nursling** ['nʌrslɪŋ] *s* cría, niño de teta
**nurture** ['nʌrtʃər] *s* crianza, educación; alimentación, nutrimento; *va* criar, educar; alimentar, nutrir; acariciar (*p.ej., una esperanza*)
**nut** [nʌt] *s* nuez; (mach.) tuerca; diapasón (*del violín, etc.*); (slang) cabeza; (slang) estrafalario, tonto, necio; **a hard nut to crack** (coll.) hueso duro de roer, rompecabezas
**nutation** [nju'teʃən] o [nu'teʃən] *s* (astr. & bot.) nutación
**nut-brown** ['nʌt,braun] *adj* marrón, castaño, avellanado; tostado
**nutcracker** ['nʌt,krækər] *s* cascanueces; (orn.) cascanueces, nucifraga
**nut-driver** ['nʌt,draɪvər] *s* aprietatuercas
**nutgall** ['nʌt,gɔl] *s* (bot.) agalla, abogalla
**nuthatch** ['nʌt,hætʃ] *s* (orn.) trepatroncos
**nutmeat** ['nʌt,mit] *s* gajo de nuez
**nutmeg** ['nʌt,mɛg] *s* (bot.) mirística (*árbol*); nuez de especia, nuez moscada (*semilla*)
**nutria** ['njutrɪə] o ['nutrɪə] *s* (zool.) coipo; piel de coipo
**nutrient** ['njutrɪənt] o ['nutrɪənt] *adj* nutritivo; *s* nutrimento
**nutriment** ['njutrɪmənt] o ['nutrɪmənt] *s* nutrimento
**nutrition** [nju'trɪʃən] o [nu'trɪʃən] *s* nutrición, nutrimento; (biol.) nutrición
**nutritional** [nju'trɪʃənəl] o [nu'trɪʃənəl] *adj* alimenticio
**nutritious** [nju'trɪʃəs] o [nu'trɪʃəs] *adj* nutricio, nutritivo, alimentoso
**nutritive** ['njutrɪtɪv] o ['nutrɪtɪv] *adj* nutritivo; alimenticio
**nutshell** ['nʌt,ʃɛl] *s* cáscara de nuez; **in a nutshell** en pocas palabras
**nutty** ['nʌtɪ] *adj* (*comp:* **-tier;** *super:* **-tiest**) abundante en nueces; que sabe a nueces; (slang) loco; **nutty about** (slang) loco por (*p.ej., los deportes*)
**nux vomica** ['nʌks 'vɑmɪkə] *s* (bot.) nuez vómica (*árbol y semilla*)
**nuzzle** ['nʌzəl] *va* hozar, hocicar; *vn* hocicar; arrimarse cómodamente; arroparse bien
**n.w., N.W.** o **NW** abr. de **northwest**
**N.Y.** abr. de **New York State**
**N.Y.C.** abr. de **New York City**
**nyctalopia** [,nɪktə'lopɪə] *s* nictalopía
**nylon** ['naɪlɑn] *s* (trademark) nilón; **nylons** *spl* medias de nilón
**nymph** [nɪmf] *s* (myth., ent. & fig.) ninfa
**nymphomania** [,nɪmfə'menɪə] *s* (path.) ninfomanía
**nystagmus** [nɪs'tægməs] *s* (path.) nistagmo
**N.Z.** abr. de **New Zealand**

# O

**O, o** [o] *s* (*pl:* **O's, o's** [oz]) décimaquinta letra del alfabeto inglés
**O.** abr. de **Ohio**
**O** *interj* ¡Oh!; ¡oye!; ¡ay!, p.ej., **O, how pretty she is!** ¡Ay qué linda!; **O that . . .!** ¡Ojalá que . . .!
**oaf** [of] *s* tonto, zoquete; niño contrahecho
**oafish** ['ofɪʃ] *adj* tonto, torpe, pesado
**oak** [ok] *s* (bot.) roble
**oak apple** *s* gran agalla de roble
**oaken** ['okən] *adj* de roble, hecho de roble
**oak gall** *s* agalla de roble, nuez de agallas, bugalla
**oak moss** *s* (bot.) musgo de roble
**oakum** ['okəm] *s* (naut.) estopa, estopa de calafatear
**oar** [or] *s* remo; remero; **to lie** o **rest on one's oars** aguantar los remos, cesar de remar; aflojar en el trabajo, dormirse sobre sus laureles; **to put in one's oar** meter su cuchara; *va* conducir remando o a remo; *vn* remar, bogar
**oarless** ['orlɪs] *adj* sin remos; que no conoce el remo
**oarlock** ['or,lɑk] *s* (naut.) escalamera, chumacera
**oarsman** ['orzmən] *s* (*pl:* **-men**) remero
**OAS** *s* OEA (*Organización de Estados Americanos*)
**oasis** [o'esɪs] u ['oəsɪs] *s* (*pl:* **-ses** [siz]) oasis
**oat** [ot] *s* (bot.) avena; (poet.) avena (*flauta rústica*); **oats** *spl* avena (*granos*); **to feel one's oats** (slang) estar fogoso y brioso; (slang) estar muy pagado de sí mismo; **to sow one's wild oats** correrla, pasar las mocedades
**oatcake** ['ot,kek] *s* torta de harina de avena
**oaten** ['otən] *adj* hecho de harina de avena, hecho de paja de avena
**oat field** *s* avenal
**oath** [oθ] *s* (*pl:* **oaths** [oðz] u [oθs]) juramento; **on oath** bajo juramento; **to take oath** prestar juramento
**oatmeal** ['ot,mil] *s* harina de avena; gachas de avena
**ob.** abr. de **obiit** (Lat.) **died**
**obbligato** [,ablɪ'gɑto] *adj* (mus.) obligado; *s* (*pl:* **-tos**) (mus.) obligado
**obduracy** ['ɑbdjʊrəsɪ] o ['ɑbdjərəsɪ] *s* obduración
**obdurate** ['ɑbdjʊrɪt] o ['ɑbdjərɪt] *adj* obstinado, terco; empedernido
**obedience** [o'bidɪəns] *s* obediencia
**obedient** [o'bidɪənt] *adj* obediente
**obeisance** [o'besəns] u [o'bisəns] *s* saludo respetuoso; homenaje, respeto
**obelisk** ['ɑbəlɪsk] *s* obelisco
**obese** [o'bis] *adj* obeso
**obesity** [o'bisɪtɪ] u [o'bɛsɪtɪ] *s* obesidad
**obey** [o'be] *va & vn* obedecer
**obfuscate** [ɑb'fʌsket] o ['ɑbfəsket] *va* ofuscar
**obfuscation** [,ɑbfəs'keʃən] *s* ofuscación
**obiter dictum** ['ɑbɪtər 'dɪktəm] *s* (*pl:* **obiter dicta**) dictamen de carácter incidental
**obituary** [o'bɪtʃʊ,ɛrɪ] *adj* necrológico; *s* (*pl:* **-ies**) obituario; (eccl.) obituario
**obj.** abr. de **object, objection** y **objective**
**object** ['ɑbdʒɪkt] *s* objeto; mamarracho (*persona o cosa ridícula*); (gram.) objeto, complemento; **with the object of** al objeto de; [əb'dʒɛkt] *va* objetar; *vn* hacer objeciones; **to object to** hacer objeciones a, oponerse a; sentir disgusto por
**object ball** *s* mingo
**object glass** *s* (opt.) objetivo, lente objetiva
**objection** [əb'dʒɛkʃən] *s* objeción; **to have no objections to make** no tener nada que objetar; **to raise an objection to** poner reparo a
**objectionable** [əb'dʒɛkʃənəbəl] *adj* que da lugar a objeciones; desagradable; censurable, reprensible
**objective** [əb'dʒɛktɪv] *adj* objetivo; (gram.) objetivo; *s* objetivo (*fin, intento*); (opt.) objetivo
**objectivity** [,ɑbdʒɛk'tɪvɪtɪ] *s* objetividad
**object lesson** *s* lección práctica; lección de cosas
**objector** [əb'dʒɛktər] *s* objetante
**object pronoun** *s* pronombre complementario
**object teaching** *s* enseñanza objetiva
**objet d'art** [ɔbʒe 'dɑr] *s* objeto de arte
**objurgate** ['ɑbdʒərget] *va* increpar, reconvenir
**objurgation** [,ɑbdʒər'geʃən] *s* increpación, reconvención, obyurgación
**objurgatory** [əb'dʒʌrgə,torɪ] *adj* increpador
**obl.** abr. de **oblique** y **oblong**
**oblate** ['ɑblet] o [ɑb'let] *adj* (geom.) achatado por los polos; (eccl.) oblato; *s* (eccl.) oblato
**oblation** [ɑb'leʃən] *s* oblación; (eccl.) oblata (*especialmente la que se da a la fábrica de la iglesia*)
**obligate** ['ɑblɪget] *va* obligar; **to obligate oneself to** + *inf* obligarse a + *inf*
**obligation** [,ɑblɪ'geʃən] *s* obligación; **to be under obligation to** correr obligación a
**obligato** [,ɑblɪ'gɑto] *adj & s* var. de **obbligato**
**obligatory** [ə'blɪgə,torɪ] o ['ɑblɪgə,torɪ] *adj* obligatorio
**oblige** [ə'blaɪdʒ] *va* obligar; complacer; **much obliged** muchas gracias; **to be obliged for** estar agradecido por; **to be obliged to** + *inf* estar obligado a + *inf;* **to oblige to** + *inf* obligar a + *inf*
**obligee** [,ɑblɪ'dʒi] *s* obligado
**obliging** [ə'blaɪdʒɪŋ] *adj* complaciente, condescendiente, servicial
**oblique** [ə'blik] *adj* oblicuo; indirecto, evasivo, torcido; [ə'blaɪk] *vn* (mil.) oblicuar
**obliquity** [əb'lɪkwɪtɪ] *s* (*pl:* **-ties**) oblicuidad; aberración, extravío
**obliquity of the ecliptic** *s* (astr.) oblicuidad de la eclíptica
**obliterate** [ə'blɪtəret] *va* borrar; arrasar, destruir; obliterar (*un sello de correo*); (med.) obliterar
**obliteration** [ə,blɪtə'reʃən] *s* borradura; arrasamiento, destrucción; (med.) obliteración
**oblivion** [ə'blɪvɪən] *s* olvido
**oblivious** [ə'blɪvɪəs] *adj* olvidadizo, desatento, inconsciente; que causa olvido
**oblong** ['ɑblɔŋ] o ['ɑblɑŋ] *adj* oblongo, cuadrilongo; *s* cuadrilongo
**obloquy** ['ɑbləkwɪ] *s* (*pl:* **-quies**) deshonra, baldón; censura, calumnia
**obnoxious** [əb'nɑkʃəs] *adj* detestable, ofensivo, odioso
**oboe** ['obo] *s* (mus.) oboe
**oboist** ['obo·ɪst] *s* (mus.) oboe, oboísta (*músico*)
**obreptitious** [,ɑbrɛp'tɪʃəs] *adj* obrepticio
**obs.** abr. de **obsolete**
**obscene** [ɑb'sin] *adj* obsceno
**obscenity** [ɑb'sɛnɪtɪ] o [ɑb'sinɪtɪ] *s* (*pl:* **-ties**) obscenidad
**obscurant** [ɑb'skjʊrənt] *adj & s* var. de **obscurantist**
**obscurantism** [ɑb'skjʊrəntɪzəm] *s* obscurantismo
**obscurantist** [ɑb'skjʊrəntɪst] *adj & s* obscurantista
**obscuration** [,ɑbskjʊ'reʃən] *s* obscurecimiento
**obscure** [əb'skjʊr] *adj* obscuro; (phonet.) relajado, neutro; *va* obscurecer

**obscurity** [əbˈskjʊrɪtɪ] *s* (*pl:* **-ties**) obscuridad
**obsecrate** [ˈɑbsɪkret] *va* rogar, suplicar
**obsecration** [ˌɑbsɪˈkreʃən] *s* obsecración
**obsequies** [ˈɑbsɪkwɪz] *spl* exequias
**obsequious** [əbˈsikwɪəs] *adj* obsequioso, servil, rastrero
**observable** [əbˈzʌrvəbəl] *adj* observable
**observably** [əbˈzʌrvəblɪ] *adv* perceptiblemente, notablemente
**observance** [əbˈzʌrvəns] *s* observancia
**observant** [əbˈzʌrvənt] *adj* observador
**observation** [ˌɑbzərˈveʃən] *s* observación; observancia; **to escape observation** no ser observado; **to keep under observation** vigilar
**observational** [ˌɑbzərˈveʃənəl] *adj* de la observación, observacional
**observation balloon** *s* globo de observación
**observation car** *s* (rail.) vagón-mirador
**observatory** [əbˈzʌrvəˌtorɪ] *s* (*pl:* **-ries**) observatorio
**observe** [əbˈzʌrv] *va* observar (*guardar, cumplir; examinar con atención; advertir, reparar; atisbar*); guardar (*una fiesta; silencio*)
**observer** [əbˈzʌrvər] *s* observador
**observing** [əbˈzʌrvɪŋ] *adj* observador
**obsess** [əbˈsɛs] *va* obsesionar, causar obsesión a
**obsession** [əbˈsɛʃən] *s* obsesión
**obsidian** [ɑbˈsɪdɪən] *s* (mineral.) obsidiana
**obsolescence** [ˌɑbsəˈlɛsəns] *s* caída en desuso
**obsolescent** [ˌɑbsəˈlɛsənt] *adj* arcaizante, algo anticuado; **to be obsolescent** irse haciendo anticuado, ir cayendo en desuso
**obsolete** [ˈɑbsəlit] *adj* anticuado, caído en desuso, desusado; (biol.) rudimentario
**obstacle** [ˈɑbstəkəl] *s* obstáculo
**obstacle race** *s* carrera de obstáculos
**obstetric** [ɑbˈstɛtrɪk] *adj* obstétrico; **obstetrics** *ssg* obstetricia
**obstetrical** [ɑbˈstɛtrɪkəl] *adj* obstétrico
**obstetrician** [ˌɑbstɛˈtrɪʃən] *s* obstétrico, médico partero
**obstinacy** [ˈɑbstɪnəsɪ] *s* (*pl:* **-cies**) obstinación
**obstinate** [ˈɑbstɪnɪt] *adj* obstinado
**obstreperous** [əbˈstrɛpərəs] *adj* estrepitoso, turbulento, desmandado
**obstruct** [əbˈstrʌkt] *va* obstruir
**obstruction** [əbˈstrʌkʃən] *s* obstrucción
**obstructionism** [əbˈstrʌkʃənɪzəm] *s* obstruccionismo
**obstructionist** [əbˈstrʌkʃənɪst] *adj & s* obstruccionista
**obstructive** [əbˈstrʌktɪv] *adj* obstructivo
**obtain** [əbˈten] *va* obtener; *vn* existir, prevalecer
**obtainable** [əbˈtenəbəl] *adj* obtenible
**obtainment** [əbˈtenmənt] *s* obtención
**obtrude** [əbˈtrud] *va* imponer (*sus opiniones*); extender; *vn* entremeterse
**obtrusion** [əbˈtruʒən] *s* imposición; entremetimiento
**obtrusive** [əbˈtrusɪv] *adj* entremetido, intruso
**obturate** [ˈɑbtjəret] *va* obturar
**obturation** [ˌɑbtjəˈreʃən] *s* obturación
**obturator** [ˈɑbtjəˌretər] *s* obturador; (phot. & surg.) obturador
**obtuse** [əbˈtjus] o [əbˈtus] *adj* obtuso; (fig.) obtuso
**obtuse angle** *s* (geom.) ángulo obtuso
**obverse** [ɑbˈvʌrs] o [ˈɑbvʌrs] *adj* obverso; complementario; [ˈɑbvʌrs] *s* anverso; frente; complemento
**obviate** [ˈɑbvɪet] *va* obviar
**obviation** [ˌɑbvɪˈeʃən] *s* evitación
**obvious** [ˈɑbvɪəs] *adj* obvio
**ocarina** [ˌɑkəˈrinə] *s* (mus.) ocarina
**occasion** [əˈkeʒən] *s* ocasión; **on occasion** de vez en cuando; **on the occasion of** con ocasión de; **on several occasions** en varias ocasiones; **to improve the occasion** aprovechar la ocasión; *va* ocasionar
**occasional** [əˈkeʒənəl] *adj* raro, poco frecuente; alguno que otro; de circunstancia
**occasionally** [əˈkeʒənəlɪ] *adv* ocasionalmente (*de vez en cuando*)
**occident** [ˈɑksɪdənt] *s* occidente; (*cap.*) *s* Occidente
**occidental** [ˌɑksɪˈdɛntəl] *adj* occidental; (*cap.*) *adj & s* occidental
**Occidentalize** [ˌɑksɪˈdɛntəlaɪz] *va* occidentalizar
**occipital** [ɑkˈsɪpɪtəl] *adj* occipital; *s* (anat.) occipital, hueso occipital
**occipital bone** *s* (anat.) hueso occipital
**occiput** [ˈɑksɪpət] *s* (*pl:* **occipita** [ɑkˈsɪpɪtə]) (anat.) occipucio
**occlude** [əˈklud] *va* obstruir; obscurecer; (chem. & dent.) ocluir; *vn* (dent.) ocluirse
**occlusal** [əˈklusəl] *adj* (anat. & dent.) oclusal
**occlusion** [əˈkluʒən] *s* obstrucción; obscurecimiento; (chem., dent., med. & phonet.) oclusión
**occlusive** [əˈklusɪv] *adj* oclusivo; *s* (phonet.) oclusiva
**occult** [əˈkʌlt] o [ˈɑkʌlt] *adj* oculto (*misterioso; sobrenatural*)
**occultation** [ˌɑkʌlˈteʃən] *s* ocultación; (astr.) ocultación
**occultism** [əˈkʌltɪzəm] o [ˈɑkəltɪzəm] *s* ocultismo
**occultist** [əˈkʌltɪst] o [ˈɑkəltɪst] *s* ocultista
**occult sciences** *spl* ciencias ocultas
**occupancy** [ˈɑkjəpənsɪ] *s* ocupación, tenencia
**occupant** [ˈɑkjəpənt] *s* ocupante; inquilino
**occupation** [ˌɑkjəˈpeʃən] *s* ocupación; inquilinato
**occupational** [ˌɑkjəˈpeʃənəl] *adj* ocupacional
**occupational disease** *s* enfermedad profesional, enfermedad de ocupación
**occupational therapy** *s* sistema terapéutico que consiste en la enseñanza de artes y oficios
**occupy** [ˈɑkjəpaɪ] (*pret & pp:* **-pied**) *va* ocupar; habitar (*p.ej., cierta casa*)
**occur** [əˈkʌr] (*pret & pp:* **-curred;** *ger:* **-curring**) *vn* ocurrir, acontecer, suceder; encontrarse (*p.ej., una palabra en un escrito*); ocurrir (*venir a la mente*); **to occur to one to** + *inf* ocurrírsele a uno + *inf*
**occurrence** [əˈkʌrəns] *s* acontecimiento; aparición, caso
**ocean** [ˈoʃən] *s* océano; (fig.) océano (*vasta extensión de cualquier cosa*); (fig.) mar (*gran cantidad*), p.ej., **oceans of work** la mar de trabajo
**Oceania** [ˌoʃɪˈænɪə] *s* la Oceanía
**oceanic** [ˌoʃɪˈænɪk] *adj* oceánico
**Oceanica** [ˌoʃɪˈænɪkə] *s* var. de **Oceania**
**Oceanids** [oˈsiənɪdz] *spl* (myth.) Oceánidas
**ocean liner** *s* buque transoceánico
**oceanographer** [ˌoʃənˈɑgrəfər] *s* oceanógrafo
**oceanographic** [ˌoʃənəˈgræfɪk] u **oceanographical** [ˌoʃənəˈgræfɪkəl] *adj* oceanográfico
**oceanography** [ˌoʃənˈɑgrəfɪ] *s* oceanografía
**Oceanus** [oˈsiənəs] *s* (myth.) Océano
**ocellate** [ˈɑsəlet] u [oˈsɛlet] *adj* ocelado
**ocellus** [oˈsɛləs] *s* (*pl:* **-li** [laɪ]) (zool.) ocelo (*ojo simple de los anélidos; mancha redonda en las plumas de ciertas aves*)
**ocelot** [ˈosəlɑt] o [ˈɑsəlɑt] *s* (zool.) ocelote
**ocher** u **ochre** [ˈokər] *s* (mineral.) ocre; *adj* ocroso
**ocherous** [ˈokərəs] *adj* ocroso
**o'clock** [əˈklɑk] *adv* por el reloj; **it is one o'clock** es la una; **it is two o'clock** son las dos; **what o'clock is it?** ¿qué hora es?
**Oct.** abr. de **October**
**octagon** [ˈɑktəgɑn] o [ˈɑktəgən] *s* octágono
**octagonal** [ɑkˈtægənəl] *adj* octagonal, octágono
**octahedral** [ˌɑktəˈhidrəl] *adj* octaédrico
**octahedron** [ˌɑktəˈhidrən] *s* (*pl:* **-drons** o **-dra** [drə]) (geom.) octaedro
**octane** [ˈɑkten] *s* (chem.) octano
**octane number** o **rating** *s* (chem.) índice de octano
**octastyle** [ˈɑktəstaɪl] *adj* (arch.) octóstilo
**octave** [ˈɑktɪv] o [ˈɑktev] *s* (mus., pros. & eccl.) octava
**Octavian** [ɑkˈtevɪən] *s* Octaviano
**Octavius** [ɑkˈtevɪəs] *s* Octavio
**octavo** [ɑkˈtevo] o [ɑkˈtɑvo] *adj* en octavo; *s* (*pl:* **-vos**) libro en octavo
**octet** u **octette** [ɑkˈtɛt] *s* (mus.) octeto; (pros.) octava; grupo de ocho
**octillion** [ɑkˈtɪljən] *s* (Brit.) octillón
**October** [ɑkˈtobər] *s* octubre
**octogenarian** [ˌɑktodʒɪˈnɛrɪən] *adj & s* octogenario
**octopus** [ˈɑktəpəs] *s* (*pl:* **-puses** o **-pi** [paɪ]) (zool.) pulpo; (fig.) organización monopolizadora con grandes facultades para hacer daño

**octoroon** [ˌɑktəˈrun] *s* octavo (*hijo de cuarterón y blanca o de cuarterona y blanco*)
**octosyllabic** [ˌɑktosɪˈlæbɪk] *adj* octosilábico, octosílabo
**octosyllable** [ˈɑktoˌsɪləbəl] *s* octosílabo (*verso*)
**octroi** [ɑkˈtrwɑ] *s* fielato (*oficina*); consumos (*impuestos*)
**octuple** [ˈɑktjupəl] o [ˈɑktupəl] *adj & s* óctuple; *va* octuplicar; *vn* octuplicarse
**ocular** [ˈɑkjələr] *adj* ocular; *s* (opt.) ocular
**oculist** [ˈɑkjəlɪst] *s* oculista
**O.D.** abr. de **officer of the day** y **olive drab**
**odalisque** u **odalisk** [ˈodəlɪsk] *s* odalisca
**odd** [ɑd] *adj* suelto; impar (*número*); dispar (*que no hace juego*); libre, de ocio; sobrante; extraño, raro, singular; y pico o y tantos, p.ej., **two hundred odd** doscientos y pico; **odds** *ssg o spl* ventaja (*en las apuestas*); apuesta desigual; puntos de ventaja; **at odds** de monos, riñendo; **by all odds** muy probablemente, sin duda alguna; **it makes no odds** lo mismo da; **the odds are** lo probable es; la ventaja es de; **to be at odds** estar de punta, estar encontrados; **to be at odds with** estar de punta con, estar encontrado con; **to set at odds** enemistar, malquistar
**oddish** [ˈɑdɪʃ] *adj* algo raro, algo singular
**oddity** [ˈɑdɪtɪ] *s* (*pl:* **-ties**) rareza, cosa rara, ente singular
**odd jobs** *spl* extraños empleos, pequeñas tareas
**odd lot** *s* (com.) lote inferior al centenar
**oddly** [ˈɑdlɪ] *adv* extrañamente, singularmente
**oddment** [ˈɑdmənt] *s* sobra, pedazo, retal
**odd number** *s* número impar, número non
**odds and ends** *spl* trozos sobrantes, pedacitos varios, despojos, cajón de sastre
**ode** [od] *s* oda
**Odessa** [oˈdɛsə] *s* Odesa
**odeum** [oˈdiəm] *s* (*pl:* **-a** [ə]) odeón
**Odin** [ˈodɪn] *s* (myth.) Odín
**odious** [ˈodɪəs] *adj* odioso, abominable
**odium** [ˈodɪəm] *s* odio (*que una persona se conquista*); oprobio; **to bring into odium** hacer aborrecido (*a uno*); **to bring odium upon a person** hacer que una persona sea odiada
**Odoacer** [ˌodoˈesər] *s* Odoacro
**odometer** [oˈdɑmɪtər] *s* odómetro
**odontoblast** [oˈdɑntəblæst] *s* (anat.) odontoblasto
**odontocete** [oˈdɑntəsit] *adj & s* (zool.) odontoceto
**odontological** [oˌdɑntəˈlɑdʒɪkəl] *adj* odontológico
**odontologist** [ˌodɑnˈtɑlədʒɪst] *s* odontólogo
**odontology** [ˌodɑnˈtɑlədʒɪ] *s* odontología
**odor** [ˈodər] *s* olor; **to be in bad odor** tener mala fama
**odoriferous** [ˌodəˈrɪfərəs] *adj* odorífero
**odorless** [ˈodərlɪs] *adj* inodoro
**odor of sanctity** *s* olor de santidad
**odorous** [ˈodərəs] *adj* oloroso
**odour** [ˈodər] *s* (Brit.) var. de **odor**
**Odysseus** [oˈdɪsus] u [oˈdɪsɪəs] *s* (myth.) Odiseo
**Odyssey** [ˈɑdɪsɪ] *s* (myth.) Odisea; (*l.c.*) *s* (fig.) odisea
**O.E.** abr. de **Old English**
**oecumenical** [ˌɛkjuˈmɛnɪkəl] *adj* var. de **ecumenical**
**Oedipus** [ˈɛdɪpəs] o [ˈidɪpəs] *s* (myth.) Edipo
**Oedipus complex** *s* (psychoanal.) complejo de Edipo
**oenometer** [iˈnɑmɪtər] *s* enómetro
**Oenone** [iˈnonɪ] *s* (myth.) Enona
**o'er** [or] *adv & prep* (poet.) var. de **over**
**oersted** [ˈʌrstɛd] *s* (elec.) oerstedio
**oesophagus** [iˈsɑfəgəs] *s* (*pl:* **-gi** [dʒaɪ]) var. de **esophagus**
**of** [ɑv] o [əv] *prep* de, p.ej., **the top of the mountain** la cima de la montaña; a: **to smell of** oler a; **to taste of** saber a; con: **to dream of** soñar con; en; **to think of** pensar en; menos: **a quarter of two** las dos menos cuarto; por: **of a summer morning** por una mañana de verano
**off.** abr. de **office, officer** y **official**
**off** [ɔf] o [ɑf] *adj* malo, p.ej., **off day** día malo; poco probable, errado (*p.ej., en las cuentas*); en marcha; más distante, más lejano; libre, sin trabajo; quitado; apagado; cortado (*dícese, p.ej., de electricidad*); de descuento, de rebaja; de la parte del mar; de la derecha (*dícese de un caballo o buey en la yunta*); **to be . . . off** faltar para, p.ej., **the wedding is two days off** faltan dos días para la boda; *adv* fuera, a distancia, lejos; **far off** muy lejos; **to be off** ponerse en marcha, marcharse en seguida, haberse marchado; **off and on** unas veces sí y otras no, de vez en cuando; **off in the distance** allá lejos; **off of** (coll.) de; (coll.) a expensas de; *prep* fuera de (*p.ej., el camino*); de, desde; al lado de, a nivel de; (naut.) frente a, a la altura de, cerca de; libre de; **to be off** faltar a, p.ej., **a button is off his coat** a su chaqueta le falta un botón; *interj* ¡fuera!; **off with you!** ¡fuera de aquí!, ¡márchate!
**offal** [ˈɑfəl] u [ˈɔfəl] *s* carniza (*desecho de la carne*); basura, desperdicios
**offbeat** [ˈɔfˈbit] o [ˈɑfˈbit] *adj* (slang) insólito, chocante, original
**off-chance** [ˈɔfˌtʃæns], [ˈɔfˌtʃɑns], [ˈɑfˌtʃæns] o [ˈɑfˌtʃɑns] *s* posibilidad poco probable, posibilidad remota; **on the off-chance that** pensando que tal vez
**off-color** [ˈɔfˌkʌlər] o [ˈɑfˌkʌlər] *adj* desteñido; (fig.) verde, subido de color
**offend** [əˈfɛnd] *va & vn* ofender
**offender** [əˈfɛndər] *s* ofensor
**offense** [əˈfɛns] *s* ofensa; **to take offense (at)** ofenderse (de)
**offenseless** [əˈfɛnslɪs] *adj* inofensivo
**offensive** [əˈfɛnsɪv] *adj* ofensivo; *s* ofensiva; **on the offensive** en la ofensiva; **to take the offensive** tomar la ofensiva
**offer** [ˈɔfər] o [ˈɑfər] *s* ofrecimiento, oferta; *va* ofrecer; rezar (*oraciones*); oponer (*resistencia*); **to offer to** + *inf* ofrecerse a + *inf;* intentar + *inf; vn* ofrecerse
**offering** [ˈɔfərɪŋ] o [ˈɑfərɪŋ] *s* ofrecimiento; ofrenda (*en el culto divino*); oferta (*don, dádiva*)
**offertory** [ˈɔfərˌtorɪ] o [ˈɑfərˌtorɪ] *s* (*pl:* **-ries**) (eccl.) ofrenda; (eccl.) música o canto que acompaña la recaudación de la ofrenda en las iglesias protestantes; (eccl.) ofertorio (*parte de las misa y su antífona*)
**offhand** [ˈɔfˈhænd] o [ˈɑfˈhænd] *adj* hecho de improviso; brusco, desenvuelto; *adv* de corrido, de improviso, sin pensarlo; bruscamente
**offhanded** [ˈɔfˈhændɪd] o [ˈɑfˈhændɪd] *adj* hecho de improviso; brusco, desenvuelto
**office** [ˈɔfɪs] o [ˈɑfɪs] *s* oficina; oficio, función; cargo, ministerio; bufete (*de abogado*); consultorio (*de médico*); (eccl.) oficio; **offices** *spl* (Brit.) oficinas (*piezas bajas de las casas que sirven para ciertos menesteres domésticos*); **to be in office** estar en funciones; **to take office** entrar en funciones; **good offices** buenos oficios; *adj* oficinesco
**office boy** *s* mandadero
**office building** *s* edificio de oficinas
**office force** *s* personal o gente de la oficina
**officeholder** [ˈɔfɪsˌholdər] o [ˈɑfɪsˌholdər] *s* funcionario, empleado público
**office hours** *spl* horas de oficina; horas de consulta (*de un médico*)
**office manager** *s* jefe de oficina
**officer** [ˈɔfɪsər] o [ˈɑfɪsər] *s* jefe, director; dignatario; oficial (*del ejército, de una orden, sociedad, etc.*); funcionario; agente de policía; *va* mandar; proveer de jefes, proveer de oficiales
**officer of the day** *s* (mil.) jefe de día
**office seeker** *s* aspirante, pretendiente
**office supplies** *spl* artículos para escritorio, suministros para oficinas
**office work** *s* trabajo de oficina
**official** [əˈfɪʃəl] *adj* oficial; *s* jefe, director; funcionario; oficial (*p.ej., de una sociedad*)
**officialdom** [əˈfɪʃəldəm] *s* las autoridades, los círculos oficiales
**officialism** [əˈfɪʃəlɪzəm] *s* costumbres oficiales; formalismo
**officially** [əˈfɪʃəlɪ] *adv* oficialmente
**officiant** [əˈfɪʃɪənt] *s* (eccl.) oficiante
**officiate** [əˈfɪʃɪet] *vn* (eccl.) oficiar; **to officiate as** oficiar de
**officinal** [əˈfɪsɪnəl] *adj* (pharm.) oficinal; *s* (pharm.) medicamento oficinal
**officious** [əˈfɪʃəs] *adj* oficioso; (dipl.) oficioso
**offing** [ˈɔfɪŋ] o [ˈɑfɪŋ] *s* (naut.) largo, alta

mar; lontananza; **in the offing** (naut.) a lo largo, mar afuera; bastante cerca, en perspectiva
**offish** ['ɔfɪʃ] o ['ɑfɪʃ] *adj* huraño, arisco
**off-peak** ['ɔf,pik] o ['ɑf,pik] *adj* (elec.) de las horas de menos carga, en horas de valle
**off-peak heater** *s* (elec.) termos de acumulación
**off-peak load** *s* (elec.) carga en horas de valle
**offprint** ['ɔf,prɪnt] o ['ɑf,prɪnt] *s* sobretiro
**offscourings** ['ɔf,skaurɪŋz] o ['ɑf,skaurɪŋz] *spl* inmundicias; hez, gente vil
**offset** ['ɔf,sɛt] o ['ɑf,sɛt] *s* compensación; ramal; (arch.) retallo; (hort.) acodo; (mach.) codo; (print.) offset; (top.) línea perpendicular a otra principal y que se extiende a un punto exterior; *adj* (print.) de offset; [,ɔf'sɛt] o [,ɑf'sɛt] (*pret & pp:* **-set;** *ger:* **-setting**) *va* componer; oponer; (print.) imprimir por offset; *vn* imprimir por offset
**offshoot** ['ɔf,ʃut] o ['ɑf,ʃut] *s* retoño, renuevo; ramal
**offshore** ['ɔf,ʃor] o ['ɑf,ʃor] *adj* (naut.) terral, que sopla de tierra; (naut.) que se encuentra a lo largo; *adv* (naut.) a lo largo
**offshore fishing** *s* pesca de bajura
**offshore islands** *spl* islas costeras
**offside** ['ɔf,saɪd] o ['ɑf,saɪd] *adj* (sport) entre los del bando contrario; (sport) fuera de juego; **to be offside** (sport) hacer una jugada estando la pelota fuera de juego
**offspring** ['ɔf,sprɪŋ] o ['ɑf,sprɪŋ] *s* sucesión, descendencia; hijo; (fig.) producto, resultado
**off-stage** ['ɔf,stedʒ] o ['ɑf,stedʒ] *adj* (theat.) de entre bastidores
**off-the-record** ['ɔfðə'rɛkərd] o ['ɑfðə'rɛkərd] *adj* extraoficial, confidencial
**oft** [ɔft] o [ɑft] *adv* (poet.) var. de **often**
**often** ['ɔfən] o ['ɑfən] *adv* a menudo, muchas veces; **as often as** siempre que; **how often** cada cuánto, p.ej., **how often does the train stop here?** ¿cada cuánto pára el tren aquí?; cuántas veces; **not often** pocas veces, rara vez
**oftentimes** ['ɔfən,taɪmz] o ['ɑfən,taɪmz] *adv* var. de **often**
**ofttimes** ['ɔft,taɪmz] o ['ɑft,taɪmz] *adv* (poet.) var. de **often**
**ogee** [o'dʒi] u ['odʒi] *s* (arch.) cimacio, gola
**ogee arch** *s* (arch.) arco conopial
**ogival** [o'dʒaɪvəl] *adj* ojival; (arch.) ojival
**ogive** ['odʒaɪv] u [o'dʒaɪv] *s* (arch.) ojiva
**ogle** ['ogəl] *s* mirada torpe, mirada de amor; *va* ojear; echar miradas torpes a, echar miradas de amor a; *vn* mirar amorosamente
**Ogpu** ['ɑgpu] *s* Guepeu (*policía política soviética*)
**ogre** ['ogər] *s* ogro; (fig.) ogro (*persona*)
**ogreish** ['ogərɪʃ] *adj* de ogro
**ogress** ['ogrɪs] *s* ogra u ogresa
**ogrish** ['ogrɪʃ] *adj* var. de **ogreish**
**oh** u **Oh** [o] *interj* var. de **O**
**ohm** [om] *s* (elec.) ohmio
**ohmic** ['omɪk] *adj* óhmico
**ohmmeter** ['om,mitər] *s* (elec.) ohmímetro
**oho** [o'ho] *interj* ¡ajá!
**oïdium** [o'ɪdɪəm] *s* (*pl:* **-a** [ə]) (bot. & plant path.) oídio
**oil** [ɔɪl] *s* aceite; petróleo; color al óleo; óleo, pintura al óleo; **to burn the midnight oil** quemarse las cejas; **to pour oil on the fire** echar aceite en el fuego; **to pour oil on troubled waters** mojar la pólvora, aplacar las pasiones; **to strike oil** encontrar una capa de petróleo; (fig.) enriquecerse de súbito; *va* aceitar; hacer liso, suave o agradable; lisonjear; untar (*corromper, sobornar*); *vn* desleírse (*p.ej., la manteca*); proveerse de petróleo (*un buque*)
**oil beetle** *s* (ent.) aceitera, carraleja
**oilbird** ['ɔɪl,bʌrd] *s* (orn.) guácharo, papagayo de noche
**oil burner** *s* quemador de petróleo
**oil cake** *s* torta de borujo
**oilcan** ['ɔɪl,kæn] *s* aceitera
**oilcloth** ['ɔɪl,klɔθ] u ['ɔɪl,klɑθ] *s* encerado, hule
**oil color** *s* color al óleo; (paint.) pintura al óleo
**oil cup** *s* (mach.) aceitera, copilla de aceite, caja de aceite
**oiler** ['ɔɪlər] *s* aceitador (*obrero*); aceitera (*vasija*); buque petrolero
**oil field** *s* campo de petróleo
**oil filler** *s* llenador de aceite
**oil gas** *s* gas de aceite
**oil gauge** *s* indicador de aceite, indicador del nivel de aceite
**oil gun** *s* bomba de mano para lubricación
**oil hole** *s* agujero de engrase, orificio de engrase
**oil line** *s* conducto del aceite, cañería de lubricación
**oil of vitriol** *s* aceite de vitriolo
**oil of wintergreen** *s* aceite de gaulteria
**oil painting** *s* pintura al óleo, cuadro al óleo
**oil pan** *s* (aut.) colector de aceite
**oilpaper** ['ɔɪl,pepər] *s* papel encerado e impermeable
**oil pump** *s* bomba de aceite
**oilskin** ['ɔɪl,skɪn] *s* hule; **oilskins** *spl* traje de hule
**oilstone** ['ɔɪl,ston] *s* asperón de grano fino
**oil stove** *s* estufa o cocina de aceite
**oil tanker** *s* buque petrolero, buque tanque para petróleo
**oil well** *s* pozo de petróleo; (mach.) cubeta de aceite
**oily** ['ɔɪlɪ] *adj* (*comp:* **-ier;** *super:* **-iest**) aceitoso; liso, resbaladizo; zalamero
**ointment** ['ɔɪntmənt] *s* ungüento
**O.K.** u **OK** ['o'ke] *s* (coll.) aprobación; *adj* (coll.) aprobado, conforme; *adv* (coll.) está bien, muy bien, V.°B.° (*visto bueno*); (*pret & pp:* **O.K.'d** u **OK'd;** *ger:* **O.K.'ing** u **OK'ing**) *va* (coll.) aprobar
**okapi** [o'kɑpɪ] *s* (zool.) okapi
**okay** ['o'ke] *s, adj, adv & va* var. de **O.K.**
**Okla.** abr. de **Oklahoma**
**okra** ['okrə] *s* (bot.) quingombó (*planta y fruto*)
**old** [old] *adj* viejo; antiguo; añejo (*dícese, p.ej., del vino*); **of old** de antaño, antiguamente; **how old do you think he is?** ¿qué edad le echa Vd.?; **how old is . . .?** ¿cuántos años tiene . . .?; **to be . . . years old** tener . . . años; **older woman** señora de edad
**old age** *s* ancianidad, vejez; **to die of old age** morir de viejo
**old bachelor** *s* solterón
**Old Bailey** ['belɪ] *s* tribunal supremo de lo criminal en Londres
**old boy** *s* viejo; graduado; **the Old Boy** (slang) el Diablo
**Old Castile** *s* Castilla la Vieja
**old-clothesman** ['old'kloðz,mæn] *s* (*pl:* **-men**) ropavejero
**old country** *s* madre patria (*de los emigrantes o sus descendientes*)
**Old Dominion** *s* el estado de Virginia, EE.UU.
**olden** ['oldən] *adj* (poet.) antiguo
**Old English** *s* el inglés antiguo; (print.) letra gótica
**olden times** *spl* (poet.) tiempos antiguos
**old-fashioned** ['old'fæʃənd] *adj* chapado a la antigua; anticuado, fuera de moda
**old fogey** u **old fogy** *s* persona un poco ridícula por sus ideas o costumbres atrasadas
**old-fogey** u **old-fogy** ['old,fogɪ] *adj* atrasado, anticuado, fuera de moda
**Old French** *s* el francés antiguo
**Old Glory** *s* la bandera de los EE.UU.
**Old Guard** *s* (U.S.A.) bando conservador del partido republicano
**old hand** *s* perito, practicón, veterano
**Old Harry** *s* el Diablo
**Old High German** *s* el antiguo altoalemán
**oldish** ['oldɪʃ] *adj* algo viejo
**old-line** ['old,laɪn] *adj* conservador, tradicional; (com.) bien establecido, establecido desde hace muchos años
**old maid** *s* solterona
**old-maidish** [,old'medɪʃ] *adj* que parece u obra como solterona, melindroso, remilgado
**old man** *s* viejo; tío; (mach.) abrazadera de taladrar; (theol.) hombre viejo; (theat.) barba
**Old Man of the Mountain** *s* (hist.) viejo de la montaña
**old master** *s* (paint.) grande maestro; obra (de pintura) de un grande maestro
**old moon** *s* luna menguante
**Old Nick** *s* el Diablo
**Old Norse** *s* el nórdico antiguo

**old salt** *s* lobo de mar
**Old Saxon** *s* el sajón antiguo
**old school** *s* gente chapada a la antigua, gente de ideas anticuadas
**Old Spanish** *s* el español antiguo
**oldster** ['oldstər] *s* (coll.) viejo o vieja; (Brit.) guardia marina que lo es por lo menos desde hace cuatro años
**Old Style** *s* estilo antiguo (*calendario*)
**Old Testament** *s* Antiguo Testamento
**old-time** ['old,taɪm] *adj* del tiempo viejo, como en el tiempo viejo
**old-timer** ['old'taɪmər] *s* (coll.) antiguo residente, antiguo concurrente; (coll.) veterano (*en cualquier profesión o ejercicio*); (coll.) persona chapada a la antigua
**oldwife** ['old,waɪf] *s* (*pl:* **-wives**) (ichth.) cochino
**old wives' tale** *s* cuento de viejas
**old-womanish** [,old'wʊmənɪʃ] *adj* de vieja, remilgado
**Old World** *s* viejo mundo
**old-world** ['old,wʌrld] *adj* prehistórico; del tiempo viejo, de los tiempos antiguos; del viejo mundo
**oleaceous** [,olɪ'eʃəs] *adj* (bot.) oleáceo
**oleaginous** [,olɪ'ædʒɪnəs] *adj* oleaginoso
**oleander** [,olɪ'ændər] *s* (bot.) adelfa, baladre
**oleaster** [,olɪ'æstər] *s* (bot.) cinamomo (*Elaeagnus angustifolia*)
**oleate** ['olɪet] *s* (chem.) oleato
**olecranon** [o'lɛkrənɑn] u [,olə'krenɑn] *s* (anat.) olécranon
**oleic** [o'liɪk] u ['olɪɪk] *adj* (chem.) oleico
**oleic acid** *s* (chem.) ácido oleico
**oleiferous** [,olɪ'ɪfərəs] *adj* (bot.) oleífero
**olein** ['olɪɪn] *s* (chem.) oleína
**oleo** ['olɪo] *s* var. de **oleomargarin**
**oleograph** ['olɪə,græf] u ['olɪə,grɑf] *s* oleografía
**oleomargarin** [,olɪo'mɑrdʒərɪn] u [,olɪo'mɑrgərɪn] u **oleomargarine** [,olɪo'mɑrdʒərin] u [,olɪo'mɑrgərin] *s* oleomargarina
**oleometer** [,olɪ'ɑmɪtər] *s* oleómetro
**oleoresin** [,olɪo'rɛzɪn] *s* oleorresina
**olfaction** [ɑl'fækʃən] *s* olfacción
**olfactory** [ɑl'fæktərɪ] *adj* olfativo u olfatorio
**olfactory nerve** *s* (anat.) nervio olfativo
**Olga** ['ɑlgə] *s* Olga
**oligarch** ['ɑlɪgɑrk] *s* oligarca
**oligarchic** [,ɑlɪ'gɑrkɪk] u **oligarchical** [,ɑlɪ'gɑrkɪkəl] *adj* oligárquico
**oligarchy** ['ɑlɪ,gɑrkɪ] *s* (*pl:* **-chies**) oligarquía
**oligist** ['ɑlɪdʒɪst] *s* (mineral.) oligisto
**Oligocene** ['ɑlɪgosin] *adj* & *s* (geol.) oligoceno
**olivaceous** [,ɑlɪ'veʃəs] *adj* oliváceo
**olive** ['ɑlɪv] *s* (bot.) olivo, aceituno (*árbol*); aceituna (*fruto*); oliva (*color*); (anat.) oliva; *adj* aceitunado, aceitunil; verde plateado (*color de las hojas del olivo*)
**olive branch** *s* ramo de olivo; oliva (*paz*); hijo, vástago
**olive drab** *s* color oliváceo; tela de lana de color oliváceo (*que sirve para hacer los uniformes del ejército de los EE.UU.*)
**olive fly** *s* (ent.) mosca de la aceituna, mosca del olivo
**olive grove** *s* olivar
**olive oil** *s* aceite, aceite de oliva
**Oliver** ['ɑlɪvər] *s* Oliverio; Oliveros (*amigo de Roldán*)
**Olives, Mount of** el monte de los Olivos
**Olivet, Mount** ['ɑlɪvɛt] el monte Olivete
**olivine** ['ɑlɪvin] o [,ɑlɪ'vin] *s* (mineral.) olivino
**olla-podrida** [,ɑləpo'dridə] *s* (cook.) olla podrida; (fig.) mescolanza
**ology** ['ɑlədʒɪ] *s* (*pl:* **-gies**) ciencia, ramo del saber
**Olympia** [o'lɪmpɪə] *s* (geog.) Olimpia
**Olympiad** u **olympiad** [o'lɪmpɪæd] *s* Olimpíada
**Olympian** [o'lɪmpɪən] *adj* olímpico; *s* dios griego, dios del paganismo; concurrente en los Juegos olímpicos
**Olympian games** *spl* (hist.) Juegos olímpicos
**Olympic** [o'lɪmpɪk] *adj* olímpico; **Olympics** *spl* Olímpicos (*Juegos olímpicos de la Grecia antigua y los modernos*)
**Olympic games** *spl* (hist.) Juegos olímpicos; Juegos olímpicos (*modernos*)
**Olympus, Mount** [o'lɪmpəs] *s* (geog., myth. & fig.) el Olimpo
**Olynthus** [o'lɪnθəs] *s* Olinto
**omasum** [o'mesəm] *s* (*pl:* **-sa** [sə]) (zool.) omaso
**omber** ['ɑmbər] *s* hombre (*juego de naipes*)
**omega** [o'mɛgə], [o'migə] u ['omɛgə] *s* omega; fin
**omelet** u **omelette** ['ɑməlɛt] o ['ɑmlɪt] *s* tortilla (de huevos)
**omen** ['omən] *s* agüero; *va* ominar, presagiar
**omental** [o'mɛntəl] *adj* omental
**omentum** [o'mɛntəm] *s* (*pl:* **-ta** [tə]) (anat.) omento
**omicron** ['ɑmɪkrɑn] *s* ómicron
**ominous** ['ɑmɪnəs] *adj* ominoso
**omission** [o'mɪʃən] *s* omisión
**omit** [o'mɪt] (*pret* & *pp:* **omitted;** *ger:* **omitting**) *va* omitir; **to omit** + *ger* omitir + *inf*
**ommatidium** [,ɑmə'tɪdɪəm] *s* (*pl:* **-a** [ə]) (zool.) omatidio
**omnibus** ['ɑmnɪbʌs] o ['ɑmnɪbəs] *s* ómnibus; *adj* general; colecticio (*tomo*)
**omnifarious** [,ɑmnɪ'fɛrɪəs] *adj* de todo género
**omnipotence** [ɑm'nɪpətəns] *s* omnipotencia
**omnipotent** [ɑm'nɪpətənt] *adj* omnipotente
**omnipresence** [,ɑmnɪ'prɛzəns] *s* omnipresencia
**omnipresent** [,ɑmnɪ'prɛzənt] *adj* omnipresente
**omniscience** [ɑm'nɪʃəns] *s* omnisciencia
**omniscient** [ɑm'nɪʃənt] *adj* omnisciente
**omnium-gatherum** [,ɑmnɪəm'gæðərəm] *s* maremagno, mescolanza
**omnivorous** [ɑm'nɪvərəs] *adj* omnívoro
**Omphale** ['ɑmfəli] *s* (myth.) Onfala
**on** [ɑn] u [ɔn] *adj* puesto, p.ej., **with his hat on** con el sombrero puesto; principiando; en funcionamiento; encendido; conectado; **the deal is on** ya está concertado el trato; **the game is on** ya están jugando; **the race is on** allá van los corredores; **what is on at the theater this evening?** ¿qué representan esta noche? ‖ *adv* adelante; encima; **and so on** y así sucesivamente, y cosas así; **come on!** ¡anda, anda!; **farther on** más allá, más adelante; **later on** más tarde, después; **to be on to a person** (coll.) conocerle a una persona el juego; **to have on** tener puesto, llevar; **to . . . on** seguir + *ger*, p.ej., **he played on** siguió tocando; **on and on** sin cesar, sin parar, continuamente ‖ *prep* en, sobre, encima de; a, p.ej., **on foot** a pie; **on my arrival** a mi llegada; bajo, p.ej., **on my responsibility** bajo mi responsabilidad; contra, p.ej., **an attack on liberty** un ataque contra la libertad; de, p.ej., **on good authority** de buena tinta; **on a journey** de viaje; hacia, p.ej., **to march on the capital** marchar hacia la capital; por, p.ej., **on all sides** por todos lados; tras, p.ej., **defeat on defeat** derrota tras derrota; **on** + *ger* al + *inf*, p.ej., **on arriving** al llegar
**onager** ['ɑnədʒər] *s* (zool.) onagro
**Onan** ['onən] *s* (Bib.) Onán
**onanism** ['onənɪzəm] *s* onanismo
**once** [wʌns] *s* vez, una vez, p.ej., **this once** esta vez; **once is enough** basta con una vez; *adj* antiguo, que fué, p.ej., **a once friend of ours** uno amigo que fué de nosotros; *adv* una vez; antes, p.ej., **once so happy** antes tan feliz; alguna vez, p.ej., **if this once becomes known** si esto llega a saberse alguna vez; **all at once** de súbito, de repente; **at once** en seguida; a la vez, en el mismo momento; **for once** una vez por lo menos; **once and again** repetidas veces; **once for all** una vez por todas, definitivamente; **once in a while** de vez en cuando, de tarde en tarde; **once more** otra vez; más una vez; **once or twice** varias veces; **once upon a time there was** érase una vez, érase que se era; *conj* una vez que
**once-over** ['wʌns,ovər] *s* (slang) examen rápido, vistazo; **to give a thing the once-over** (coll.) examinar una cosa superficialmente
**oncology** [ɑŋ'kɑlədʒɪ] *s* oncología
**oncoming** ['ɑn,kʌmɪŋ] *adj* próximo, que viene; *s* aproximación, llegada

**ondograph** ['ɑndəgræf] o ['ɑndəgrɑf] *s* ondógrafo

**one** [wʌn] *adj* un, uno; un tal, p.ej., **one Smith** un tal Smith; único, p.ej., **one price** precio único; *s* uno; *pron* uno, p.ej., **one does not know what to do here** uno no sabe qué hacer aquí; se, p.ej., **how does one go to the station?** ¿cómo se va a la estación?; **I for one** yo por lo menos; **it's all one and the same** es lo mismo; **it's all one and the same to me** me es indiferente; **my little one** mi chiquito; **of one another** el uno del otro, los unos de los otros, p.ej., **we took leave of one another** nos despedimos el uno del otro; **the blue book and the red one** el libro azul y el rojo; **the one and only** el único; **the one that** el que, la que; **this one** éste; **that one** ése, aquél; **to make one** unir; casar; ser uno (*dícese de un grupo*); **we are one** somos unos; **one and all** todos; **one another** se, p.ej., **they greeted one another** se saludaron; uno a otro, unos a otros, p.ej., **they looked at one another** se miraron uno a otro; **one by one** uno a uno; **one o'clock** la una; **one or two** unos pocos; **one's** su, el . . . de uno

**one-act** ['wʌn,ækt] *adj* de un acto

**one-celled** ['wʌn,sɛld] *adj* (biol.) unicelular

**one-horse** ['wʌn,hɔrs] *adj* de un solo caballo, tirado por un solo caballo; (coll.) insignificante, de poca monta

**oneiromancy** [o'naɪrə,mænsɪ] *s* oniromancía

**one-man** ['wʌn,mæn] *adj* hecho por un solo hombre; de un solo hombre; para un solo hombre; apegado a un solo hombre

**one line** *s* (aut.) paso único

**oneness** ['wʌnnɪs] *s* unidad (*indivisión; singularidad; conformidad, unión*)

**one-piece** ['wʌn'pis] *adj* de una pieza

**onerous** ['ɑnərəs] *adj* oneroso; (law) oneroso

**oneself** [,wʌn'sɛlf] *pron* uno mismo; sí, sí mismo; se; **to be oneself** tener dominio de sí mismo; conducirse con naturalidad; **to come to oneself** volver en sí; **to say to oneself** decir para sí; **to talk to oneself** hablar consigo mismo; **to oneself** para sus adentros

**one-sided** ['wʌn'saɪdɪd] *adj* de un solo lado; injusto, parcial; desigual; desequilibrado, desproporcionado; unilateral

**one's self** *pron* var. de **oneself**

**one-step** ['wʌn,stɛp] *s* baile de salón con música al compás de dos por cuatro; (*pret & pp:* **-stepped;** *ger:* **-stepping**) *vn* bailar el one-step

**one-time** ['wʌn,taɪm] *adj* antiguo

**one-track** ['wʌn,træk] *adj* de carril único; (coll.) con un solo interés

**one-way** ['wʌn,we] *adj* de una sola dirección, unidireccional; (rail.) sencillo, de ida sólo

**one-way street** *s* calle de dirección única

**onion** ['ʌnjən] *s* (bot.) cebolla (*planta y bulbo*); **to know one's onions** (slang) saber más que Merlín

**onion set** *s* (bot.) cebollino

**onionskin** ['ʌnjən,skɪn] *s* papel de seda, papel cebolla

**onlooker** ['ɑn,lʊkər] *s* mirón, espectador, circunstante

**onlooking** ['ɑn,lʊkɪŋ] *adj* mirón, espectador; *s* asistencia (*a un acontecimiento*)

**only** ['onlɪ] *adj* solo, único; *adv* sólo, solamente, únicamente; no . . . más que; **if only . . .!** ¡ojalá . . .!; **only too** muy, muchísimo; **not only . . . but also** no sólo . . . sino también; **only when** solamente cuando; *conj* sólo que, pero; **only that** sólo que, pero

**only-begotten** ['onlɪbɪ'gɑtən] *adj* unigénito

**onomancy** ['ɑnə,mænsɪ] *s* onomancía

**onomastic** [,ɑnə'mæstɪk] *adj* onomástico

**onomatology** [,ɑnəmə'tɑlədʒɪ] *s* onomatología

**onomatopoeia** [,ɑnə,mætə'piə] *s* onomatopeya

**onomatopoeic** [,ɑnə,mætə'piɪk] u **onomatopoetic** [,ɑnə,mætəpo'ɛtɪk] *adj* onomatopéyico

**onrush** ['ɑn,rʌʃ] *s* arremetida, embestida; arranque, fuerza impetuosa

**onset** ['ɑn,sɛt] *s* arremetida, embestida; principio (*de una enfermedad*)

**onshore** ['ɑn,ʃor] *adj & adv* en tierra; hacia la tierra

**onside** ['ɑn,saɪd] *adj* (sport) legal, permitido; *adv* (sport) legalmente, según las reglas

**onslaught** ['ɑn,slɔt] *s* ataque furioso, embestida violenta

**Ont.** abr. de **Ontario**

**onto** ['ɑntu] *prep* a, en, sobre

**ontogeny** [ɑn'tɑdʒɪnɪ] *s* (biol.) ontogenia

**ontological** [,ɑntə'lɑdʒɪkəl] *adj* ontológico

**ontological argument** *s* (philos.) argumento ontológico

**ontologism** [ɑn'tɑlədʒɪzəm] *s* (theol.) ontologismo

**ontology** [ɑn'tɑlədʒɪ] *s* ontología

**onus** ['onəs] *s* carga, obligación, responsabilidad

**onward** ['ɑnwərd] *adj* hacia adelante; (fig.) de progreso; *adv* adelante, hacia adelante

**onwards** ['ɑnwərdz] *adv* adelante, hacia adelante

**onyx** ['ɑnɪks] *s* (mineral.) ónice u ónix

**oöcyte** ['oosaɪt] *s* (biol.) oocito

**oögonium** [,oo'gonɪəm] *s* (*pl:* **-a** [ə] o **-ums**) (bot.) oogonio

**oölite** ['oolaɪt] *s* (mineral.) oolito

**oölitic** [,oo'lɪtɪk] *adj* oolítico

**oölogy** [o'ɑlədʒɪ] *s* oología

**oomiak** ['umɪæk] *s* barca de la mujer (*de los esquimales*)

**oöphorectomy** [,oofə'rɛktəmɪ] *s* (*pl:* **-mies**) (surg.) ooforectomía

**oöphoritis** [,oofə'raɪtɪs] *s* (path.) ooforitis

**oösphere** ['oosfɪr] *s* (bot.) oosfera

**oöspore** ['oospor] *s* (bot.) oósporo

**oösporous** [o'ɑspərəs] *adj* (bot.) oósporo

**ooze** [uz] *s* chorro suave; rezumo; rezumadero; cieno, limo, lama; *va* rezumar (*humedad*); *vn* rezumar o rezumarse; manar suavemente (*p.ej., la sangre de una herida*); agotarse poco a poco

**oozy** ['uzɪ] *adj* rezumoso; cenagoso

**op.** abr. de **opera, operation, opus** y **opposite**

**opacity** [o'pæsɪtɪ] *s* (*pl:* **-ties**) opacidad; obscuridad (*del estilo*); estupidez

**opal** ['opəl] *s* (mineral.) ópalo

**opalesce** [,opə'lɛs] *vn* tener reflejos opalinos, irisar

**opalescence** [,opə'lɛsəns] *s* opalescencia

**opalescent** [,opə'lɛsənt] *adj* opalescente

**opaline** ['opəlin] u ['opəlaɪn] *adj* opalino

**opaque** [o'pek] *adj* opaco; obscuro (*estilo*); estúpido; *s* cosa opaca, substancia opaca

**op. cit.** abr. de **opere citato** (Lat.) **in the work cited**

**ope** [op] *adj, va & vn* (poet.) var. de **open**

**open** ['opən] *adj* abierto; descubierto, destapado; sin tejado; despejado; vacante; libre (*hora*); público, para todos; claro, ralo (*tejido*); extendido, desplegado (*p.ej., periódico*); templado, sin heladas (*invierno*); libre de hielo; discutible, pendiente; susceptible, expuesto; notorio, conocido o sabido de todos; liberal (*mano*); franco, abierto; (mus.) no pisado (*dícese de una cuerda*); (mus.) de cuerda no pisada (*dícese de una nota de violín*); (mil. & phonet.) abierto; (hunt.) legal (*temporada*); **to break open** o **to crack open** abrir con violencia, abrir por la fuerza; **to throw open** abrir de par en par; **open to** accesible a; expuesto a ‖ *s* abertura; claro (*en un bosque*); **in the open** al aire libre; a campo raso, al raso; en el campo; a alta mar; en alta mar; abiertamente, al descubierto ‖ *va* abrir; destapar (*una botella*); desbullar (*la ostra*); **to open up** abrir; descubrir (*p.ej., a la vista*) ‖ *vn* abrir o abrirse; estrenarse (*un drama*); expresar una opinión; llegar a ser receptivo; **to open into** desembocar en (*dícese de una calle, un río, etc.*); **to open on** dar a; **to open up** descubrirse, presentarse; descubrir el pecho

**open-air** ['opən,ɛr] *adj* al aire libre, a cielo abierto

**open-and-shut** ['opənənd'ʃʌt] *adj* (coll.) claro, manifiesto, incontestable

**open circuit** *s* (elec.) circuito abierto

**open city** *s* ciudad abierta

**open country** *s* campo raso

**open door** *s* (dipl.) puerta abierta

**opener** ['opənər] *s* abridor (*persona o cosa*); (baseball) primero de una serie de partidos

**open-eyed** ['opən,aɪd] *adj* alerta, vigilante;

con ojos asombrados; hecho con los ojos abiertos
**open face** *s* cara franca; muestra de reloj sin tapa
**open-faced** [ˈopən,fest] *adj* con la cara descubierta; de cara o mirada franca; sin tapa
**open-handed** [ˈopənˈhændɪd] *adj* maniabierto, liberal
**open-hearted** [ˈopənˈhartɪd] *adj* franco, sincero
**open-hearth furnace** [ˈopən,harθ] *s* horno de hogar abierto, horno Siemens-Martin
**open-hearth process** *s* procedimiento de solera abierta, procedimiento Siemens-Martin
**open-hearth steel** *s* acero al hogar abierto
**open house** *s* coliche; **to keep open house** agasajar o recibir a todos, gustar de tener siempre convidados en casa, tener mesa
**opening** [ˈopənɪŋ] *s* abertura; apertura (*de la escuela, el teatro, etc.*); claro (*en un bosque*); hueco, vacante (*empleo sin proveer*); hueco (*de cordón o hilera de coches*); ocasión (*p.ej., para decir algo*); (chess) apertura; (phonet.) abertura
**opening night** *s* (theat.) noche de estreno
**opening number** *s* primer número (*de un programa*)
**opening price** *s* primer curso, precio de apertura (*en la Bolsa*)
**open letter** *s* carta abierta
**open market** *s* mercado público
**open-minded** [ˈopənˈmaɪndɪd] *adj* receptivo, razonable, imparcial
**open-mouthed** [ˈopən,mauðd] u [ˈopən,mauθt] *adj* boquiabierto; voraz; clamoroso; ancho de boca
**openness** [ˈopənnɪs] *s* abertura, franqueza, sinceridad; imparcialidad, liberalidad; publicidad
**open plumbing** *s* tuberías descubiertas
**open port** *s* puerto abierto al comercio extranjero; puerto cuyas aguas no se hielan durante todo el año
**open question** *s* cuestión discutible o pendiente
**open secret** *s* secreto a voces, secreto conocido de todos
**open sesame** *interj* ¡sésamo ábrete! o ¡ábrete, sésamo! (*fórmula mágica*)
**open shop** *s* taller franco
**open trolley car** *s* jardinera
**openwork** [ˈopən,wʌrk] *s* calado
**opera** [ˈapərə] *s* (mus.) ópera
**operable** [ˈapərəbəl] *adj* operable; (surg.) operable
**opéra bouffe** [ˈapərəˈbuf] u [ɔperaˈbuf] *s* ópera bufa
**opera glasses** *spl* gemelos de teatro
**opera hat** *s* clac, sombrero de muelles
**opera house** *s* teatro de la ópera
**opera singer** *s* operista, cantante de opera
**operate** [ˈapəret] *va* actuar, hacer funcionar; efectuar, producir; dirigir, manejar; explotar; *vn* funcionar; operar (*p.ej., un medicamento*); (com., mil., nav. & surg.) operar; **to operate on** producir efecto en; (surg.) operar (*p.ej., una hernia; a un niño*); **to operate on someone for something** (surg.) operar a uno de una cosa
**operatic** [,apəˈrætɪk] *adj* operístico
**operatically** [,apəˈrætɪkəlɪ] *adv* en la ópera; a modo de ópera
**operating expenses** *spl* gastos ordinarios, gastos de explotación
**operating room** *s* (surg.) quirófano
**operating table** *s* (surg.) mesa operatoria
**operation** [,apəˈreʃən] *s* operación; funcionamiento; explotación; **in operation** funcionando; en uso, vigente
**operational** [,apəˈreʃənəl] *adj* operacional, de operación
**operative** [ˈapə,retɪv] o [ˈapərətɪv] *adj* operador, operativo; (surg.) operatorio; *s* operario; detective
**operator** [ˈapə,retər] *s* operador, maquinista; (surg. & telg.) operador; (telp.) operador, telefonista; (com.) explotador, empresario; (com.) agente, corredor de bolsa
**operculum** [oˈpʌrkjələm] *s* (*pl:* **-la** [lə] o **-lums**) (bot. & zool.) opérculo
**operetta** [,apəˈrɛtə] *s* (mus.) opereta
**Ophelia** [oˈfiljə] *s* Ofelia
**ophidian** [oˈfɪdɪən] *adj* & *s* (zool.) ofidio
**Ophir** [ˈofər] *s* (Bib.) Ofir
**ophite** [ˈafaɪt] u [ˈofaɪt] *s* (mineral.) ofita
**ophthalmia** [afˈθælmɪə] *s* (path.) oftalmía
**ophthalmic** [afˈθælmɪk] *adj* oftálmico
**ophthalmological** [af,θælməˈladʒɪkəl] *adj* oftalmológico
**ophthalmologist** [,afθælˈmalədʒɪst] *s* oftalmólogo
**ophthalmology** [,afθælˈmalədʒɪ] *s* oftalmología
**ophthalmoscope** [afˈθælməskop] *s* oftalmoscopio
**ophthalmoscopy** [,afθælˈmaskəpɪ] *s* oftalmoscopia
**opiate** [ˈopɪɪt] u [ˈopɪet] *s* opiata; calmante; *adj* opiáceo, opiático (*opiado; soporífero; calmante*)
**opine** [oˈpaɪn] *vn* opinar
**opinion** [əˈpɪnjən] *s* opinión; **in my opinion** a mi parecer; **to be of the opinion that** ser de opinión que; **to have a high opinion of** tener buen concepto de; **to have a high opinion of oneself** ser muy pagado de sí mismo
**opinionated** [əˈpɪnjə,netɪd] u **opinionative** [əˈpɪnjə,netɪv] *adj* porfiado (en su parecer), dogmático
**opium** [ˈopɪəm] *s* (pharm.) opio
**opium den** *s* fumadero de opio
**opium poppy** *s* (bot.) adormidera
**Opium War** *s* guerra del opio
**opopanax** [əˈpapənæks] *s* (pharm.) opopónaco
**opossum** [əˈpasəm] *s* (zool.) zarigüeya
**opponent** [əˈponənt] *adj* contrario; (anat.) oponente; *s* contrario, opositor; contrincante, opositor
**opportune** [,apərˈtjun] o [,apərˈtun] *adj* oportuno
**opportunism** [,apərˈtjunɪzəm] o [,apərˈtunɪzəm] *s* oportunismo
**opportunist** [,apərˈtjunɪst] o [,apərˈtunɪst] *s* oportunista
**opportunistic** [,apərtjuˈnɪstɪk] o [,apərtuˈnɪstɪk] *adj* oportunista
**opportunity** [,apərˈtjunɪtɪ] o [,apərˈtunɪtɪ] *s* (*pl:* **-ties**) oportunidad, ocasión; **to seize the opportunity** aprovechar la oportunidad
**opposable** [əˈpozəbəl] *adj* oponible
**oppose** [əˈpoz] *va* oponerse a; **to oppose something to something else** oponer una cosa a otra
**opposing** [əˈpozɪŋ] *adj* opuesto; contrario
**opposite** [ˈapəzɪt] *adj* opuesto; de enfrente, p.ej., **the house opposite** la casa de enfrente; (bot.) opuesto; *prep* enfrente de, p.ej., **he was seated opposite me** estaba sentado enfrente de mí; *s* contrario
**opposite number** *s* igual, doble (*en otro sistema u organización correspondiente*)
**opposition** [,apəˈzɪʃən] *s* oposición
**oppress** [əˈprɛs] *va* oprimir
**oppression** [əˈprɛʃən] *s* opresión
**oppressive** [əˈprɛsɪv] *adj* opresivo; sofocante, bochornoso
**oppressor** [əˈprɛsər] *s* opresor
**opprobrious** [əˈprobrɪəs] *adj* oprobioso
**opprobrium** [əˈprobrɪəm] *s* oprobio
**oppugn** [aˈpjun] *va* opugnar (*oponerse a; contradecir*)
**opsonin** [ˈapsonɪn] *s* (bact.) opsonina
**opt** [apt] *vn* optar
**optative** [ˈaptətɪv] *adj* optativo; (gram.) optativo; *s* (gram.) optativo (*modo*); (gram.) verbo optativo
**optic** [ˈaptɪk] *adj* óptico; *s* (coll.) ojo; **optics** *ssg* óptica
**optical** [ˈaptɪkəl] *adj* óptico
**optical axis** *s* (opt. & cryst.) eje óptico
**optical illusion** *s* ilusión de óptica
**optical square** *s* (surv.) escuadra de reflexión
**optician** [apˈtɪʃən] *s* óptico
**optic nerve** *s* (anat.) nervio óptico
**optic thalamus** *s* (anat.) tálamo óptico
**optimism** [ˈaptɪmɪzəm] *s* optimismo
**optimist** [ˈaptɪmɪst] *s* optimista
**optimistic** [,aptɪˈmɪstɪk] *adj* optimista
**optimistically** [,aptɪˈmɪstɪkəlɪ] *adv* con optimismo
**optimum** [ˈaptɪməm] *adj* óptimo, más favora-

ble; *s* (*pl:* **-mums** o **-ma** [mə]) cantidad óptima, grado óptimo, punto óptimo
**option** [ˈɑpʃən] *s* opción; (com.) opción
**optional** [ˈɑpʃənəl] *adj* facultativo, optativo, potestativo
**optometer** [ɑpˈtɑmɪtər] *s* optómetro
**optometrist** [ɑpˈtɑmɪtrɪst] *s* optometrista
**optometry** [ɑpˈtɑmɪtrɪ] *s* optometría
**opulence** [ˈɑpjələns] *s* opulencia
**opulent** [ˈɑpjələnt] *adj* opulento
**opus** [ˈopəs] *s* (*pl:* **opera** [ˈɑpərə]) (mus.) opus (*obra*)
**opuscule** [oˈpʌskjul] *s* opúsculo
**or** [ɔr] *conj* o, u; de otro modo
**orach** [ˈɔrətʃ] o [ˈɑrətʃ] *s* (bot.) orzaga
**oracle** [ˈɑrəkəl] u [ˈɔrəkəl] *s* oráculo; (fig.) oráculo (*persona sabia y autorizada; respuesta que da tal persona*)
**oracular** [oˈrækjələr] *adj* de oráculo; fatídico; sentencioso; ambiguo, misterioso; sabio
**oral** [ˈorəl] *adj* oral
**orally** [ˈorəlɪ] *adv* oralmente
**orang** [oˈræŋ] *s* var. de **orang-outang**
**orange** [ˈɑrɪndʒ] u [ˈɔrɪndʒ] *s* naranja (*fruto*); (bot.) naranjo (*árbol*); *adj* naranjado (*color*); naranjero
**orangeade** [ˌɑrɪndʒˈed] u [ˌɔrɪndʒˈed] *s* naranjada
**orange blossom** *s* azahar
**Orange Free State** *s* Estado Libre de Orange
**orange grove** *s* naranjal
**orange jessamine** *s* (bot.) boj de China
**orange juice** *s* zumo de naranja
**Orangeman** [ˈɑrɪndʒmən] u [ˈɔrɪndʒmən] *s* (*pl:* **-men**) orangista
**orange pekoe** *s* té negro de Ceilán o la India
**orangery** [ˈɑrɪndʒrɪ] u [ˈɔrɪndʒrɪ] *s* (*pl:* **-ries**) invernadero para naranjos
**orange squeezer** *s* exprimidera de naranjas
**orange stick** *s* limpiaúñas
**orange tree** *s* (bot.) naranjo
**orang-outang** [oˈræŋʊˌtæŋ] u **orang-utan** [oˈræŋʊˌtæn] *s* (zool.) orangután
**orate** [oˈret] u [ˈoret] *vn* (coll.) perorar
**oration** [oˈreʃən] *s* oración (*discurso*)
**orator** [ˈɑrətər] u [ˈɔrətər] *s* orador
**oratorical** [ˌɑrəˈtɑrɪkəl] u [ˌɔrəˈtɔrɪkəl] *adj* oratorio
**oratorio** [ˌɑrəˈtorɪo] u [ˌɔrəˈtorɪo] *s* (*pl:* **-os**) (mus.) oratorio
**oratory** [ˈɑrəˌtorɪ] u [ˈɔrəˌtorɪ] *s* (*pl:* **-ries**) oratoria; oratorio (*capilla*)
**orb** [ɔrb] *s* orbe; (poet.) ojo; *va* redondear; (poet.) encerrar, englobar; *vn* redondearse
**orbicular** [ɔrˈbɪkjələr] u **orbiculate** [ɔrˈbɪkjəlet] *adj* orbicular
**orbit** [ˈɔrbɪt] *s* (anat., astr., phys. & fig.) órbita; **to go into orbit** entrar en órbita; *va* poner en órbita; moverse en órbita alrededor de; *vn* moverse en órbita
**orbital** [ˈɔrbɪtəl] *adj* orbital
**orchard** [ˈɔrtʃərd] *s* huerto (*de árboles frutales*)
**orchestra** [ˈɔrkɪstrə] *s* (mus.) orquesta; (theat.) orquesta (*lugar destinado para los músicos*); (theat.) platea
**orchestral** [ɔrˈkɛstrəl] *adj* orquestal
**orchestra seat** *s* butaca de orquesta, butaca de platea
**orchestrate** [ˈɔrkɪstret] *va* orquestar
**orchestration** [ˌɔrkɪsˈtreʃən] *s* orquestación
**orchid** [ˈɔrkɪd] *s* (bot.) orquídea; *adj* purpurino
**orchidaceous** [ˌɔrkɪˈdeʃəs] *adj* orquidáceo
**orchis** [ˈɔrkɪs] *s* (bot.) órquide
**orchitis** [ɔrˈkaɪtɪs] *s* (path.) orquitis
**Orcus** [ˈɔrkəs] *s* (myth.) Orco
**ordain** [ɔrˈden] *va* ordenar (*poner en orden*); constituir; destinar; (eccl.) ordenar; **to ordain as a priest** ordenar de sacerdote; *vn* mandar, disponer
**ordeal** [ɔrˈdil] u [ˈɔrdɪəl] *s* prueba rigurosa o penosa; (hist.) ordalías, juicio de Dios
**order** [ˈɔrdər] *s* orden *m* (*sucesión metódica de las cosas; disposición metódica; paz, tranquilidad; clase, categoría*); orden *f* (*mandato; cuerpo de personas unidas por una regla común o por una distinción honorífica*); (arch., biol., gram. & math.) orden *m*; (com.) pedido; (com.) giro, libranza; (eccl.) orden *m* (*sexto sacramento*); (eccl.) orden *f* (*instituto religioso; grado del ministerio sacerdotal*); (law) provisión; (mil.) orden *f* (*mandato*); (mil.) descanso de armas; (mil.) orden *m* (*formación de la tropa*); (theol.) orden *f* (*cada uno de los nueve grados de los espíritus angélicos*); placa (*insignia de una orden*); tarea, p.ej., **a big order** una tarea peliaguda; estado, p.ej., **in good order** en buen estado; **by order of** por orden de; **in short order** pronto, en seguida; **in order** en orden; por su orden (*sucesivamente*); funcionando; en regla; conveniente, proporcionado; **in orders** revestido de funciones sacerdotales; **in order that** para que, a fin de que; **in order to** + *inf* para + *inf;* **on that order** de esa clase; **on the order of** a modo de; **out of order** desarreglado, descompuesto; mal colocado; fuera de orden (*dícese de una moción*); **till further orders** hasta nueva orden; **to call to order** abrir, llamar al orden; **to get out of order** descomponerse; **to give an order** dar una orden; (com.) hacer un pedido; **to put in order** poner en orden; componer; **to take orders** obedecer; (eccl.) ordenarse; **to the order of** (com.) a la orden de; **to order** por encargo especial; a la medida ‖ *va* ordenar; mandar; encargar, pedir (*p.ej., un coche, mercancías*); mandar hacer (*p.ej., un traje*); (eccl.) ordenar; **to order around** mandar para acá y para allá; dominar, ser muy mandón con; **to order away** despedir, mandar (*a uno*) que se marche; **to order in** mandar entrar; **to order out** mandar salir; **to order to** + *inf* mandar + *inf*, mandar que + *subj*
**order blank** *s* (com.) hoja de pedidos
**orderly** [ˈɔrdərlɪ] *adj* ordenado, gobernoso; tranquilo, obediente; *adv* ordenadamente; *s* (*pl:* **-lies**) asistente en un hospital; (mil.) ordenanza
**order of the day** *s* orden *m* del día (*en una asamblea*); (mil.) orden *f* del día; **to be the order of the day** estar a la orden del día (*eso es, a la moda, en boga*)
**Order of the Garter** *s* (Brit.) orden *f* de la Jarretera
**ordinal** [ˈɔrdɪnəl] *adj* ordinal; *s* ordinal; (eccl.) ordo
**ordinal number** *s* número ordinal
**ordinance** [ˈɔrdɪnəns] *s* ordenanza (*ley*); (arch.) ordenación; (eccl.) rito, ceremonia
**ordinarily** [ˈɔrdɪˌnɛrɪlɪ] *adv* ordinariamente
**ordinary** [ˈɔrdɪˌnɛrɪ] *adj* ordinario; *s* (*pl:* **-ies**) fonda, posada; comedor de una fonda o posada; ordinario (*juez; obispo*); (eccl.) ordinario de la misa; **in ordinary** residente; al servicio; **out of the ordinary** extraordinario, fuera de lo común
**ordinate** [ˈɔrdɪnɪt] u [ˈɔrdɪnet] *s* (geom.) ordenada
**ordination** [ˌɔrdɪˈneʃən] *s* (eccl.) ordenación
**ordnance** [ˈɔrdnəns] *s* (mil.) artillería, cañones; (mil.) pertrechos de guerra
**ordnance department** *s* (mil.) servicio de municionamiento
**Ordovician** [ˌɔrdoˈvɪʃən] *adj* & *s* (geol.) ordoviciense
**ordure** [ˈɔrdjur] u [ˈɔrdʒər] *s* excremento, inmundicia; suciedad (*dicho deshonesto*)
**Ore.** abr. de **Oregon**
**ore** [or] *s* mena, mineral metalífero
**Oread** u **oread** [ˈorɪæd] *s* (myth.) oréade
**Orestes** [oˈrɛstiz] *s* (myth.) Orestes
**organ** [ˈɔrgən] *s* (mus., physiol. & fig.) órgano
**organdy** u **organdie** [ˈɔrgəndɪ] *s* (*pl:* **-dies**) organdí
**organ-grinder** [ˈɔrgənˌgraɪndər] *s* organillero
**organic** [ɔrˈgænɪk] *adj* orgánico
**organically** [ɔrˈgænɪkəlɪ] *adv* orgánicamente
**organic chemistry** *s* química del carbono, química orgánica
**organicism** [ɔrˈgænɪsɪzəm] *s* (biol., med. & philos.) organicismo
**organicist** [ɔrˈgænɪsɪst] *adj* & *s* organicista
**organism** [ˈɔrgənɪzəm] *s* organismo; (biol.) organismo
**organist** [ˈɔrgənɪst] *s* (mus.) organista
**organization** [ˌɔrgənɪˈzeʃən] *s* organización
**organize** [ˈɔrgənaɪz] *va* organizar; *vn* organizarse
**organizer** [ˈɔrgəˌnaɪzər] *s* organizador
**organ loft** *s* (mus.) tribuna del órgano

**organography** [ˌɔrgəˈnɑgrəfɪ] *s* organografía
**organology** [ˌɔrgəˈnɑlədʒɪ] *s* organología
**organotherapy** [ˌɔrgənoˈθɛrəpɪ] *s* organoterapia
**organ pipe** *s* (mus.) tubo de órgano
**organ stop** *s* (mus.) registro de órgano
**orgasm** [ˈɔrgæzəm] *s* (physiol.) orgasmo
**orgasmic** [ɔrˈgæzmɪk] u **orgastic** [ɔrˈgæstɪk] *adj* orgástico
**orgeat** [ˈɔrʒæt] *s* horchata
**orgiastic** [ˌɔrdʒɪˈæstɪk] *adj* orgiástico
**orgy** [ˈɔrdʒɪ] *s* (*pl:* **-gies**) orgía; **orgies** *spl* orgías (*de la antigua Grecia*)
**oriel** [ˈorɪəl] *s* (arch.) camón, mirado
**Orient** [ˈorɪənt] *s* Oriente; (*l.c.*) *s* oriente (*brillo de las perlas*); (poet.) oriente (*donde nace el Sol*); *adj* naciente; (poet.) resplandeciente; (poet.) oriental, de oriente; [ˈorɪɛnt] *va* orientar; *vn* orientarse
**oriental** [ˌorɪˈɛntəl] *adj* oriental; (*cap.*) *adj & s* oriental
**Orientalism** u **orientalism** [ˌorɪˈɛntəlɪzəm] *s* orientalismo
**Orientalist** u **orientalist** [ˌorɪˈɛntəlɪst] *s* orientalista
**Orientalize** [ˌorɪˈɛntəlaɪz] *va* orientalizar
**orientate** [ˈorɪɛntet] *va* orientar; *vn* orientarse; mirar hacia el este
**orientation** [ˌorɪɛnˈteʃən] *s* orientación
**orifice** [ˈɑrɪfɪs] u [ˈɔrɪfɪs] *s* orificio
**oriflamme** [ˈɑrɪflæm] u [ˈɔrɪflæm] *s* oriflama
**orig.** abr. de **original** y **originally**
**Origen** [ˈɑrɪdʒɪn] u [ˈɔrɪdʒɪn] *s* Orígenes
**origin** [ˈɑrɪdʒɪn] u [ˈɔrɪdʒɪn] *s* origen
**original** [əˈrɪdʒɪnəl] *adj* original; originario; *s* original
**originality** [əˌrɪdʒɪˈnælɪtɪ] *s* originalidad
**originally** [əˈrɪdʒɪnəlɪ] *adv* originalmente
**original sin** *s* (theol.) pecado original
**originate** [əˈrɪdʒɪnet] *va* originar; *vn* originarse
**origination** [əˌrɪdʒɪˈneʃən] *s* creación, invención; origen
**originative** [əˈrɪdʒɪˌnetɪv] *adj* creador, inventivo
**originator** [əˈrɪdʒɪˌnetər] *s* creador, inventor
**oriole** [ˈorɪol] *s* (orn.) oriol, oropéndola
**Orion** [oˈraɪən] *s* (astr.) Orión
**orison** [ˈɑrɪzən] u [ˈɔrɪzən] *s* (archaic & poet.) oración
**Orkney Islands** [ˈɔrknɪ] *spl* Órcadas
**Orleanist** [ˈɔrlɪənɪst] *adj & s* Orleanista
**orlop** [ˈɔrlɑp] *s* (naut.) sollado
**ormolu** [ˈɔrməlu] *s* similor; oro molido (*para dorar el bronce*); bronce dorado
**ornament** [ˈɔrnəmənt] *s* ornamento; ornamentación; **ornaments** *spl* (eccl.) ornamentos; [ˈɔrnəmɛnt] *va* ornamentar
**ornamental** [ˌɔrnəˈmɛntəl] *adj* ornamental; (hort.) de adorno
**ornamentation** [ˌɔrnəmɛnˈteʃən] *s* ornamentación
**ornate** [ɔrˈnet] u [ˈɔrnet] *adj* ornado, muy ornado; florido (*estilo*)
**ornery** [ˈɔrnərɪ] *adj* (dial.) ordinario, común; (dial.) feo; (dial.) terco, displicente; (dial.) vil, ruin
**ornithological** [ˌɔrnɪθəˈlɑdʒɪkəl] *adj* ornitológico
**ornithologist** [ˌɔrnɪˈθɑlədʒɪst] *s* ornitólogo
**ornithology** [ˌɔrnɪˈθɑlədʒɪ] *s* ornitología
**ornithomancy** [ˈɔrnɪθəˌmænsɪ] *s* ornitomancía
**ornithorhyncus** [ˌɔrnɪθəˈrɪŋkəs] *s* (zool.) ornitorrinco
**orobanchaceous** [ˌɑrobæŋˈkeʃəs] *adj* (bot.) orobancáceo
**orogenic** [ˌɔrəˈdʒɛnɪk] o [ˌɑrəˈdʒɛnɪk] *adj* orogénico
**orogeny** [oˈrɑdʒənɪ] *s* orogenia
**orographic** [ˌɔrəˈgræfɪk] u **orographical** [ˌɔrəˈgræfɪkəl] *adj* orográfico
**orography** [oˈrɑgrəfɪ] *s* orografía
**orology** [oˈrɑlədʒɪ] *s* orología
**orometer** [oˈrɑmɪtər] *s* orómetro
**orotund** [ˈorətʌnd] o [ˈɑrətʌnd] *adj* rotundo (*sonoro*); rimbombante
**orotundity** [ˌorəˈtʌndɪtɪ] o [ˌɑrəˈtʌndɪtɪ] *s* rotundidad; rimbombancia
**orphan** [ˈɔrfən] *adj & s* huérfano; *va* dejar huérfano
**orphanage** [ˈɔrfənɪdʒ] *s* orfanato, asilo de huérfanos; orfandad (*estado*)
**orphan asylum** *s* asilo de huérfanos
**orphanhood** [ˈɔrfənhʊd] *s* orfandad
**Orphean** [ɔrˈfiən] *adj* órfico
**Orpheus** [ˈɔrfjus] u [ˈɔrfɪəs] *s* (myth.) Orfeo
**orphic** [ˈɔrfɪk] *adj* místico, oracular; (*cap.*) *adj* órfico; místico, oracular; dulce y suave al oído
**Orphic hymns** *spl* poesías órficas
**Orphic mysteries** *spl* fiestas órficas
**orphrey** [ˈɔrfrɪ] *s* orifrés
**orpiment** [ˈɔrpɪmənt] *s* (mineral.) oropimente
**orpine** u **orpin** [ˈɔrpɪn] *s* (bot.) hierba callera, telefio
**orrery** [ˈɑrərɪ] u [ˈɔrərɪ] *s* (*pl:* **-ies**) orrery, planetario
**orris** [ˈɑrɪs] u [ˈɔrɪs] *s* (bot.) lirio de Florencia; rizoma de lirio de Florencia; (pharm.) esencia de lirio de Florencia
**orrisroot** [ˈɑrɪsˌrut] u [ˈɔrɪsˌrut] *s* rizoma de lirio de Florencia
**orthicon** [ˈɔrθɪkɑn] *s* orticón
**orthochromatic** [ˌɔrθokroˈmætɪk] *adj* (phot.) ortocromático
**orthoclase** [ˈɔrθəkles] u [ˈɔrθəklez] *s* (mineral.) ortosa
**orthodontia** [ˌɔrθoˈdɑnʃɪə] *s* ortodoncia
**orthodox** [ˈɔrθədɑks] *adj* ortodoxo
**Orthodox Church** *s* Iglesia ortodoxa
**orthodoxy** [ˈɔrθəˌdɑksɪ] *s* ortodoxia
**orthoëpic** [ˌɔrθoˈɛpɪk] *adj* ortoépico
**orthoëpist** [ɔrˈθo·ɪpɪst] u [ˈɔrθoɛpɪst] *s* ortólogo
**orthoëpy** [ɔrˈθo·ɪpɪ] u [ˈɔrθoɛpɪ] *s* ortoepia u ortología
**orthogenesis** [ˌɔrθoˈdʒɛnɪsɪs] *s* (biol.) ortogénesis
**orthognathous** [ɔrˈθɑgnəθəs] *adj* ortognato
**orthogonal** [ɔrˈθɑgənəl] *adj* ortogonal
**orthographer** [ɔrˈθɑgrəfər] *s* ortógrafo
**orthographic** [ˌɔrθoˈgræfɪk] u **orthographical** [ˌɔrθoˈgræfɪkəl] *adj* ortográfico
**orthography** [ɔrˈθɑgrəfɪ] *s* (*pl:* **-phies**) (gram. & geom.) ortografía
**orthopaedic** u **orthopedic** [ˌɔrθoˈpidɪk] *adj* ortopédico; **orthopedics** *ssg* ortopedia
**orthopedist** [ˌɔrθoˈpidɪst] *s* ortopedista, ortopédico
**orthophony** [ɔrˈθɑfənɪ] *s* ortofonía
**orthopteran** [ɔrˈθɑptərɑn] *s* (ent.) ortóptero
**orthopterous** [ɔrˈθɑptərəs] *adj* (ent.) ortóptero
**orthorhombic** [ˌɔrθoˈrɑmbɪk] *adj* (cryst.) ortorrómbico
**orthotropism** [ɔrˈθɑtrəpɪzəm] *s* (bot.) ortotropismo
**orthotropous** [ɔrˈθɑtrəpəs] *adj* (bot.) ortótropo
**ortolan** [ˈɔrtələn] *s* (orn.) hortelano; (orn.) chambergo
**oryx** [ˈorɪks] *s* (zool.) órix
**O.S.** abr. de **Old Style**
**os** [ɑs] *s* (*pl:* **ossa** [ˈɑsə]) (anat.) hueso; (*pl:* **ora** [ˈorə]) (anat.) orificio
**Osage orange** [ˈosedʒ] *s* (bot.) maclura (*planta y fruto*)
**Oscan** [ˈɑskən] *adj & s* osco
**oscillate** [ˈɑsɪlet] *vn* oscilar; (phys.) oscilar
**oscillation** [ˌɑsɪˈleʃən] *s* oscilación
**oscillator** [ˈɑsɪˌletər] *s* oscilador; (rad.) oscilador
**oscillatory** [ˈɑsɪləˌtorɪ] *adj* oscilatorio
**oscillogram** [əˈsɪləgræm] *s* (phys.) oscilograma
**oscillograph** [əˈsɪləgræf] o [əˈsɪləgrɑf] *s* (phys.) oscilógrafo
**oscilloscope** [əˈsɪləskop] *s* (phys.) osciloscopio
**oscine** [ˈɑsɪn] o [ˈɑsaɪn] *adj* (orn.) oscino; *s* (orn.) oscina
**osculate** [ˈɑskjəlet] *va* besar; (geom.) tocar por osculación; *vn* besarse; (geom.) ser osculador
**osculation** [ˌɑskjəˈleʃən] *s* ósculo (*beso*); (geom.) osculación
**osculatory** [ˈɑskjələˌtorɪ] *adj* osculatorio; (geom.) osculador
**osculatrix** [ˌɑskjəˈletrɪks] *s* (geom.) osculatriz

**osculum** [ˈɑskjələm] *s* (*pl:* **-la** [lə]) (zool.) ósculo (*de las esponjas*)
**osier** [ˈoʒər] *s* mimbre; (bot.) mimbrera, sauce mimbrero; (bot.) cornejo
**osiery** [ˈoʒərɪ] *s* (*pl:* **-ies**) mimbreral; artículos hechos de mimbre
**Osiris** [oˈsaɪrɪs] *s* (myth.) Osiris
**Osmanli** [ɑsˈmænlɪ] *adj* osmanlí; *s* (*pl:* **-lis**) osmanlí
**osmium** [ˈɑzmɪəm] *s* (chem.) osmio
**osmosis** [ɑsˈmosɪs] *s* (chem. & physiol.) ósmosis
**osmotic** [ɑsˈmɑtɪk] *adj* osmótico
**osmotic pressure** *s* presión osmótica
**osprey** [ˈɑsprɪ] *s* (orn.) halieto, guincho
**Ossa, Mount** [ˈɑsə] el monte Osa
**osseous** [ˈɑsɪəs] *adj* óseo
**Ossian** [ˈɑʃən] o [ˈɑsɪən] *s* Osián
**Ossianic** [ˌɑʃɪˈænɪk] o [ˌɑsɪˈænɪk] *adj* osiánico
**Ossianism** [ˈɑʃənɪzəm] o [ˈɑsɪənɪzəm] *s* osianismo
**ossicle** [ˈɑsɪkəl] *s* (anat.) osículo
**ossification** [ˌɑsɪfɪˈkeʃən] *s* osificación
**ossifrage** [ˈɑsɪfrɪdʒ] *s* (orn.) osífraga
**ossify** [ˈɑsɪfaɪ] (*pret & pp:* **-fied**) *va* osificar; *vn* osificarse; volverse muy conservador
**osteitis** [ˌɑstɪˈaɪtɪs] *s* (path.) osteítis
**ostensible** [ɑsˈtɛnsɪbəl] *adj* aparente, pretendido, supuesto
**ostension** [ɑsˈtɛnʃən] *s* (eccl.) ostensión
**ostensive** [ɑsˈtɛnsɪv] *adj* ostensivo
**ostentation** [ˌɑstɛnˈteʃən] *s* ostentación
**ostentatious** [ˌɑstɛnˈteʃəs] *adj* ostentativo; ostentoso
**osteoblast** [ˈɑstɪəblæst] *s* (anat.) osteoblasto
**osteolite** [ˈɑstɪəˌlaɪt] *s* (mineral.) osteolita
**osteological** [ˌɑstɪəˈlɑdʒɪkəl] *adj* osteológico
**osteologist** [ˌɑstɪˈɑlədʒɪst] *s* osteólogo
**osteology** [ˌɑstɪˈɑlədʒɪ] *s* osteología
**osteoma** [ˌɑstɪˈomə] *s* (*pl:* **-mas** o **-mata** [mətə]) (path.) osteoma
**osteomalacia** [ˌɑstɪəməˈleʃɪə] *s* (path.) osteomalacia
**osteomyelitis** [ˌɑstɪoˌmaɪəˈlaɪtɪs] *s* (path.) osteomielitis
**osteopath** [ˈɑstɪəpæθ] *s* osteópata
**osteopathic** [ˌɑstɪəˈpæθɪk] *adj* osteopático
**osteopathist** [ˌɑstɪˈɑpəθɪst] *s* osteópata
**osteopathy** [ˌɑstɪˈɑpəθɪ] *s* osteopatía
**osteotomy** [ˌɑstɪˈɑtəmɪ] *s* (*pl:* **-mies**) (surg.) osteotomía
**ostiary** [ˈɑstɪˌɛrɪ] *s* (*pl:* **-ies**) (eccl.) ostiario
**ostler** [ˈɑslər] *s* establero, mozo de cuadra, mozo de paja y cebada; (rail.) encargado de la locomotora al fin del recorrido
**ostracism** [ˈɑstrəsɪzəm] *s* ostracismo
**ostracize** [ˈɑstrəsaɪz] *va* desterrar; excluir del trato de las gentes
**ostrich** [ˈɑstrɪtʃ] *s* (orn.) avestruz; (orn.) avestruz de América o de la pampa
**Ostrogoth** [ˈɑstrogɑθ] *adj & s* ostrogodo
**Oswego tea** [ɑsˈwigo] *s* (bot.) té de Pensilvania
**O.T.** abr. de **Old Testament**
**otacoustic** [ˌotəˈkustɪk] u [ˌotəˈkaustɪk] *adj* otacústico
**otalgia** [oˈtældʒɪə] *s* (path.) otalgia
**otalgic** [oˈtældʒɪk] *adj* otálgico
**Othello** [oˈθɛlo] *s* Otelo
**other** [ˈʌðər] *adj & pron indef* otro; *adv* otramente; **above all others** más que ningún otro; el mejor de todos; **the other day** el otro día; **the other one** el otro; **other than** otra cosa que
**otherwise** [ˈʌðərˌwaɪz] *adj* diferente; *adv* otramente, de otra manera; en otras circunstancias; fuera de eso; *conj* si no, de otro modo
**other world** *s* otro mundo (*vida eterna*)
**otherworldly** [ˈʌðərˌwʌrldlɪ] *adj* ultramundano, alejado de este mundo
**otiose** [ˈoʃɪos] u [ˈotɪos] *adj* ocioso
**otitis** [oˈtaɪtɪs] *s* (path.) otitis
**otocyst** [ˈotəsɪst] *s* (zool.) otocisto
**otolaryngology** [ˌotoˌlærɪŋˈgɑlədʒɪ] *s* otolaringología
**otologist** [oˈtɑlədʒɪst] *s* otólogo
**otology** [oˈtɑlədʒɪ] *s* otología
**otorhinolaryngologist** [ˌotəˌraɪnəˌlærɪŋˈgɑlədʒɪst] *s* otorrinolaringólogo
**otorhinolaryngology** [ˌotəˌraɪnəˌlærɪŋˈgɑlədʒɪ] *s* otorrinolaringología
**otosclerosis** [ˌotəsklɪˈrosɪs] *s* (path.) otosclerosis
**otoscope** [ˈotəskop] *s* otoscopio
**otoscopy** [oˈtɑskəpɪ] *s* otoscopia
**ottava rima** [oˈtɑvɑ ˈrimɑ] *s* (pros.) octava rima
**otter** [ˈɑtər] *s* (zool.) nutria; (zool.) nutria marina; piel de nutria
**Otto** [ˈɑto] *s* Otón
**Ottoman** [ˈɑtəmən] *adj* otomano; *s* (*pl:* **-mans**) otomano; (*l.c.*) *s* otomana (*sofá*); escañuelo con cojín; otomán (*tejido de seda*)
**Ottoman Empire** *s* Imperio otomano
**ou** [aʊ] *interj* ¡ax!
**oubliette** [ˌublɪˈɛt] *s* mazmorra; pozo profundo en una mazmorra
**ouch** [aʊtʃ] *interj* ¡ax!
**ought** [ɔt] *s* algo, alguna cosa; (coll.) cero, nada; **for ought I know** por lo que yo sepa; *v aux* se emplea para formar el modo potencial, p.ej., **he ought to go at once** debiera salir en seguida; **he ought to have gone at once** debiera haber ido en seguida
**ouija** [ˈwidʒə] *s* (trademark) tabla de escritura espiritista
**ounce** [aʊns] *s* onza; pizca
**our** [aʊr] *adj poss* nuestro
**Our Lady** *s* Nuestra Señora
**ours** [aʊrz] *pron poss* nuestro; el nuestro; **a friend of ours** un amigo nuestro
**ourself** [aʊrˈsɛlf] *pron pers* nosotros, nos (*usado por un autor, rey, etc., por ficción en vez de "mi" o "me"*)
**ourselves** [aʊrˈsɛlvz] *pron pers* nosotros mismos; nos, p.ej., **we enjoyed ourselves** nos divertimos
**-ous** *suffix adj* -oso, p.ej., **famous** famoso; **marvelous** maravilloso; (chem.) -oso, p.ej., **nitrous** nitroso; **sulfurous** sulfuroso
**ousel** [ˈuzəl] *s* var. de **ouzel**
**oust** [aʊst] *va* echar fuera, desposeer; desahuciar (*al inquilino*)
**ouster** [ˈaʊstər] *s* desposeimiento; desahucio
**out** [aʊt] *adv* afuera, fuera; al aire libre; hasta el fin; con confianza; con energía; **out and away** con mucho; **out and out** completamente; **out for** buscando; **out of** de; entre; de entre (*las manos de uno*); fuera de (*p.ej., la ciudad*); más allá de; por (*p.ej., caridad, miedo*); sin (*p.ej., dinero, trabajo*); sobre, p.ej., **in nine out of ten cases** en nueve casos sobre diez; (cards) fallo a (*un palo*); **out to** + *inf* esforzándose por + *inf; adj* fuera; fuera de juego; fuera de su sitio; echado, sacado; acabado, concluído; apagado; existente; equivocado; perdidoso; exterior; poco común (*tamaño*); divulgado; publicado; *prep* por (*p.ej., la ventana*); allá en (*p.ej., la avenida*); **out that way** por allá; *interj* ¡fuera de aquí!; *s* cesante; saliente, detalle; (print.) omisión por descuido; (baseball) jugador fuera de juego; **to be at outs** u **on the outs** estar de monos; **to be at outs** u **on the outs with** estar mal con; *va* expeler; desposeer; apagar; divulgar; (slang) poner fuera de combate; (slang) matar; (tennis) volear (*la pelota*) fuera de la pista; *vn* salir; escaparse; descubrirse; **to out with** (coll.) divulgar, revelar
**out-and-out** [ˈaʊtəndˌaʊt] *adj* perfecto, verdadero, rematado
**outbalance** [aʊtˈbæləns] *va* pesar más que; aventajar, sobreexceder
**outbid** [aʊtˈbɪd] (*pret:* **-bid;** *pp:* **-bid** o **-bidden;** *ger:* **-bidding**) *va* licitar más que (*otra persona*); (bridge) sobrepasar
**outboard** [ˈaʊtˌbord] *adj & adv* fuera de borda
**outboard motor** *s* motor fuera de borda, motor de fuera
**outbound** [ˈaʊtˌbaʊnd] *adj* saliente, de salida
**outbrave** [aʊtˈbrev] *va* arrostrar; aventajar en valentía
**outbreak** [ˈaʊtˌbrek] *s* tumulto, motín; arranque (*de ira*); estallido (*p.ej., de una guerra*); brote (*de una epidemia*)
**outbuild** [aʊtˈbɪld] (*pret & pp:* **-built**) *va* hacer construcciones más imponentes o mejores que las de
**outbuilding** [ˈaʊtˌbɪldɪŋ] *s* dependencia accesoria

**outburst** ['aʊt,bʌrst] *s* explosión, arranque; **outburst of laughter** carcajada
**outcast** ['aʊt,kæst] o ['aʊt,kɑst] *adj* desterrado, excluído, rechazado; *s* paria
**outclass** [aʊt'klæs] o [aʊt'klɑs] *va* aventajar, ser muy superior a
**outcome** ['aʊt,kʌm] *s* resultado
**outcrop** ['aʊt,krɑp] *s* (min.) crestón, afloramiento; [aʊt'krɑp] (*pret & pp:* **-cropped;** *ger:* **-cropping**) *vn* asomar; (min.) aflorar
**outcry** ['aʊt,kraɪ] *s* (*pl:* **-cries**) grito; gritería, clamoreo; subasta, venta pública
**outcurve** ['aʊt,kʌrv] *s* (baseball) curva fuera
**outdated** [aʊt'detɪd] *adj* fuera de moda, anticuado
**outdid** [aʊt'dɪd] *pret de* **outdo**
**outdistance** [aʊt'dɪstəns] *va* dejar atrás, distanciar, rezagar
**outdo** [aʊt'du] (*pret:* **-did;** *pp:* **-done**) *va* exceder; **to outdo oneself** excederse a sí mismo
**outdone** [aʊt'dʌn] *pp de* **outdo**
**outdoor** ['aʊt,dor] *adj* al aire libre; fuera del hospital
**outdoors** [,aʊt'dorz] *adv* al aire libre, fuera de casa; *s* aire libre, campo raso
**outer** ['aʊtər] *adj* exterior, externo
**Outer Mongolia** *s* la Mogolia Exterior
**outermost** ['aʊtərmost] *adj* extremo, último; (el) más exterior
**outer space** s espacio exterior; espacio extraatmosférico
**outface** [aʊt'fes] *va* intimidar mirando con ceño, dominar con los ojos; arrostrar
**outfield** ['aʊt,fild] *s* (baseball) jardín
**outfielder** ['aʊt,fildər] *s* (baseball) jardinero
**outfit** ['aʊtfɪt] *s* equipo (*de ropas, etc.; de obreros, etc.*); traje (*completo*); juego de herramientas; cuerpo (*de soldados*); (com.) compañía; ajuar (*de novia*); (*pret & pp:* **-fitted;** *ger:* **-fitting**) *va* equipar
**outfitter** ['aʊt,fɪtər] *s* habilitador; abastecedor; armador
**outflank** [aʊt'flæŋk] *va* (mil.) flanquear; (fig.) burlar (*a un contrario*)
**outflow** ['aʊt,flo] *s* efusión, derrame, flujo; (fig.) efusión
**outgeneral** [aʊt'dʒɛnərəl] (*pret & pp:* **-aled** o **-alled;** *ger:* **-aling** o **-alling**) *va* exceder en táctica militar; vencer por medio de evoluciones geniales
**outgo** ['aʊt,go] *s* (*pl:* **-goes**) gasto
**outgoing** ['aʊt,go·ɪŋ] *adj* saliente, de salida; exteriorista (*p.ej., índole, naturaleza*); *s* salida
**outgrew** [aʊt'gru] *pret de* **outgrow**
**outgrow** [aʊt'gro] (*pret:* **-grew;** *pp:* **-grown**) *va* crecer más que; ser ya grande para; ser ya viejo para; ser ya más apto que; dejar (*las cosas de los niños; a los amigos de la niñez, etc.*); *vn* extenderse
**outgrowth** ['aʊt,groθ] *s* excrecencia, bulto; nacimiento (*p.ej., de las hojas en la primavera*); consecuencia, resultado
**outguess** [aʊt'gɛs] *va* burlar a fuerza de ingenio; llevar la ventaja a
**outhouse** ['aʊt,haʊs] *s* dependencia accesoria; letrina situada fuera de la casa
**outing** ['aʊtɪŋ] *s* caminata, excursión al campo
**outing flannel** *s* moletón
**outlander** ['aʊt,lændər] *s* extranjero; forastero
**outlandish** [aʊt'lændɪʃ] *adj* estrafalario; de aspecto extranjero; de acento extranjero
**outlast** [aʊt'læst] o [aʊt'lɑst] *va* durar más que; sobrevivir a
**outlaw** ['aʊt,lɔ] *s* forajido, bandido; prófugo, proscrito; *va* privar de la protección de las leyes; proscribir; declarar ilegal
**outlawry** ['aʊt,lɔrɪ] *s* (*pl:* **-ries**) bandolerismo; privación de la protección de las leyes; proscripción
**outlay** ['aʊt,le] *s* desembolso; [aʊt'le] (*pret & pp:* **-laid**) *va* desembolsar
**outlet** ['aʊtlɛt] *s* salida; desaguadero; orificio de salida; (elec.) caja de enchufe, toma, receptáculo tomacorriente; (com. & fig.) salida
**outlet box** *s* (elec.) caja de salida, caja de enchufe
**outline** ['aʊt,laɪn] *s* contorno; trazado; esquema; esbozo, bosquejo; compendio; **in outline** en silueta; a grandes rasgos, en sus líneas generales; *va* contornar; trazar; trazar el esquema de; esbozar, bosquejar; compendiar
**outlive** [aʊt'lɪv] *va* sobrevivir a; durar más que
**outlook** ['aʊt,lʊk] *s* perspectiva; expectativa; concepto de la vida, punto de vista; atalaya
**outlying** ['aʊt,laɪɪŋ] *adj* remoto, circundante, de las afueras
**outmaneuver** u **outmanoeuvre** [,aʊtmə'nuvər] *va* ser mejor estratega que; vencer por ser mejor estratega
**outmatch** [aʊt'mætʃ] *va* aventajar, exceder, mostrarse superior a
**outmoded** [aʊt'modɪd] *adj* fuera de moda, anticuado
**outmost** ['aʊtmost] *adj* var. de **outermost**
**outnumber** [aʊt'nʌmbər] *va* exceder en número, ser más que, ser más numeroso que
**out-of-date** ['aʊtəv'det] *adj* fuera de moda, anticuado
**out-of-door** ['aʊtəv'dor] *adj* al aire libre
**out-of-doors** ['aʊtəv'dorz] *adj* al aire libre; *adv* afuera, fuera de la casa, al aire libre; *s* aire libre, campo raso
**out-of-print** ['aʊtəv'prɪnt] *adj* agotado
**out-of-the-way** ['aʊtəvðə'we] *adj* remoto, en sitio apartado; poco usual, poco común
**outpatient** ['aʊt,peʃənt] *s* enfermo de fuera (*enfermo no hospitalizado que recibe cuidados de un dispensario*)
**outpoint** [aʊt'pɔɪnt] *va* (sport) exceder en el número de tantos ganados; (naut.) ceñir más el viento que
**outpost** ['aʊt,post] *s* (mil.) avanzada; (mil.) puesto avanzado; (mil.) fortín de la frontera; (fig.) avanzada; (fig.) portaestandarte
**outpour** ['aʊt,por] *s* chorro, chorreo; [aʊt'por] *va* verter; hacer salir profusamente; *vn* chorrear; salir profusamente
**outpouring** ['aʊt,porɪŋ] *s* chorro, efusión; (fig.) efusión
**output** ['aʊt,pʊt] *s* producción, rendimiento; capacidad; (mech.) rendimiento de trabajo, efecto útil; (elec.) salida; (elec.) circuito de salida
**output stage** *s* (rad.) etapa de salida
**output transformer** *s* (rad.) transformador de salida
**outrage** ['aʊtredʒ] *s* atrocidad; violación; ultraje; *va* maltratar, violentar; violar; ultrajar; escandalizar
**outrageous** [aʊt'redʒəs] *adj* atroz; violento; ultrajoso
**outran** [aʊt'ræn] *pret de* **outrun**
**outrank** [aʊt'ræŋk] *va* exceder en rango o grado, ser de categoría superior a
**outré** [u'tre] o ['utre] *adj* extremoso, extravagante, raro
**outreach** [aʊt'ritʃ] *va* pasar más allá de, exceder; extender; *vn* extenderse
**outridden** [aʊt'rɪdən] *pp de* **outride**
**outride** [aʊt'raɪd] (*pret:* **-rode;** *pp:* **-ridden**) *va* galopar más que; manejar el caballo mejor que; (naut.) correr (*un temporal*)
**outrider** ['aʊt,raɪdər] *s* volante, carretista; (Brit.) viajante de comercio
**outrigger** ['aʊt,rɪgər] *s* (naut.) botalón, botavara, tangón; (naut.) balancín (*de una canoa*); (naut.) portarremos exterior; (naut.) bote con portarremos exteriores
**outright** ['aʊt,raɪt] *adj* cabal, completo, total; franco, sincero, sin rodeos; hacia adelante; *adv* enteramente; de una vez; abiertamente, sin rodeos; luego, en seguida
**outrode** [aʊt'rod] *pret de* **outride**
**outrun** [aʊt'rʌn] (*pret:* **-ran;** *pp:* **-run;** *ger:* **-running**) *va* dejar atrás; correr más aprisa que; exceder; pasar los límites de
**outsell** [aʊt'sɛl] (*pret & pp:* **-sold**) *va* vender más, más caro o más aprisa que; venderse más, más caro o más aprisa que
**outset** ['aʊt,sɛt] *s* principio; **at the outset** o **from the outset** al principio, a los principios, de primero
**outshine** [aʊt'ʃaɪn] (*pret & pp:* **outshone**) *va* brillar más que, exceder en brillantez; (fig.) eclipsar
**outshone** [aʊt'ʃon] *pret & pp de* **outshine**
**outshoot** ['aʊt,ʃut] *s* saliente; ramal; [aʊt'ʃut] (*pret & pp:* **-shot**) *va* ser mejor tirador que; tirar más lejos que; *vn* extenderse, sobresalir
**outshot** [aʊt'ʃɑt] *pret & pp de* **outshoot**

**outside** [ˈaʊtˈsaɪd] *adj* exterior; superficial; ajeno, de otras personas; más liberal, más optimista; (el) máximo (*precio*); *s* exterior; apariencia; **at the outside** a lo más, a lo sumo; **on the outside** por fuera; *adv* fuera, afuera; **outside of** fuera de; *prep* fuera de; más allá de; (coll.) a excepción de
**outsider** [ˌaʊtˈsaɪdər] *s* forastero; intruso; (sport) caballo que no figura entre los favoritos
**outsize** [ˈaʊtˌsaɪz] *s* prenda hecha de tamaño extraordinario; *adj* de tamaño extraordinario
**outskirts** [ˈaʊtˌskʌrts] *spl* afueras
**outsold** [aʊtˈsold] *pret & pp de* **outsell**
**outspoken** [ˈaʊtˈspokən] *adj* boquifresco, franco
**outspread** [ˈaʊtˌsprɛd] *adj* extendido; [aʊtˈsprɛd] (*pret & pp:* **-spread**) *va* extender; *vn* extenderse
**outstanding** [aʊtˈstændɪŋ] *adj* saliente, saledizo; destacado, distinguido, sobresaliente; prominente; (com.) pendiente, sin pagar, sin cobrar
**outstay** [aʊtˈste] (*pret & pp:* **-stayed** o **-staid**) *va* quedarse más tiempo que; quedarse más tiempo de lo que permite (*la cortesía o la licencia que uno tiene*)
**outstretched** [ˈaʊtˌstrɛtʃt] *adj* extendido, abierto
**outstrip** [aʊtˈstrɪp] (*pret & pp:* **-stripped; ger: -stripping**) *va* pasar, dejar atrás; aventajar, adelantar, adelantarse de
**outtalk** [aʊtˈtɔk] *va* hablar más que, ser más hablador que
**outvote** [aʊtˈvot] *va* vencer en las elecciones; disponer de más votantes que
**outward** [ˈaʊtwərd] *adj* exterior, externo; *adv* exteriormente, hacia fuera
**outward-flow turbine** [ˈaʊtwərdˈflo] *s* turbina centrífuga
**outwardly** [ˈaʊtwərdlɪ] *adv* exteriormente; superficialmente; al parecer; fuera, hacia fuera
**outwards** [ˈaʊtwərdz] *adv* exteriormente, hacia fuera
**outwear** [aʊtˈwɛr] (*pret:* **-wore;** *pp:* **-worn**) *va* durar más que; gastar, romper por uso excesivo; curarse de (*penas*) con el tiempo
**outweigh** [aʊtˈwe] *va* pesar más que; contrapesar, compensar
**outwit** [aʊtˈwɪt] (*pret & pp:* **-witted;** *ger:* **-witting**) *va* burlar, sobrepujar en astucia, ser más listo que
**outwore** [aʊtˈwor] *pret de* **outwear**
**outwork** [ˈaʊtˌwʌrk] *s* (fort.) obra exterior; [aʊtˈwʌrk] *va* trabajar más o más aprisa que
**outworn** [ˈaʊtˌworn] *adj* ajado, usado, desgastado; anticuado, viejo; [aʊtˈworn] *pp de* **outwear**
**ouzel** [ˈuzəl] *s* (orn.) mirlo; (orn.) mirlo de agua
**oval** [ˈovəl] *adj* oval, ovalado; *s* óvalo
**ovally** [ˈovəlɪ] *adv* en figura de óvalo, de modo que forma óvalo
**ovarian** [oˈvɛrɪən] *adj* ovárico
**ovariotomy** [oˌvɛrɪˈɑtəmɪ] *s* (*pl:* **-mies**) (surg.) ovariotomía
**ovaritis** [ˌovəˈraɪtɪs] *s* (path.) ovaritis
**ovary** [ˈovərɪ] *s* (*pl:* **-ries**) (anat. & bot.) ovario
**ovate** [ˈovet] *adj* aovado, ovado
**ovation** [oˈveʃən] *s* ovación
**oven** [ˈʌvən] *s* horno
**ovenbird** [ˈʌvənˌbʌrd] *s* (orn.) hornero; (orn.) seiuro
**over** [ˈovər] *adv* encima, por encima; al otro lado, a la otra orilla; hacia abajo; al revés; patas arriba; otra vez, de nuevo; de añadidura; acá, p.ej., **hand over the money** déme acá el dinero; allá, p.ej., **over in Europe** allá en Europa; **to be all over** haber pasado, haberse acabado; **over again** una vez más; **over against** enfrente de; a distinción de; en contraste con; **over and over** una y otra vez, repetidas veces; **over here** acá; **over there** allá; *adj* superior, de más autoridad; adicional; excesivo; acabado, concluído; *prep* sobre, encima de, por encima de; por (*un terreno o país*); de un extremo a otro de; al otro lado de; más allá de; desde (*un sitio elevado*); más de (*cierto número*); acerca de; por causa de; durante; **over and above** además de, en exceso de; *s* exceso
**overabundance** [ˌovərəˈbʌndəns] *s* sobreabundancia
**overact** [ˌovərˈækt] *va* exagerar (*un papel*)
**overactive** [ˌovərˈæktɪv] *adj* demasiado activo
**overall** [ˈovərˌɔl] *adj* cabal, completo; extremo, total; **overalls** *spl* pantalones de trabajo; polainas impermeables
**overarch** [ˌovərˈɑrtʃ] *va* abovedar; *vn* formar bóveda
**overate** [ˌovərˈet] *pret de* **overeat**
**overawe** [ˌovərˈɔ] *va* imponer respeto a, intimidar
**overbalance** [ˌovərˈbæləns] *s* exceso de peso o valor; falta de equilibrio; *va* pesar más que; valer más que; llevar la ventaja a; derribar
**overbear** [ˌovərˈbɛr] (*pret:* **-bore;** *pp:* **-borne**) *va* dominar, oprimir; no hacer caso de; echar por tierra, derribar
**overbearing** [ˌovərˈbɛrɪŋ] *adj* altanero, despótico, imperioso
**overbid** [ˌovərˈbɪd] (*pret:* **-bid;** *pp:* **-bid** o **-bidden;** *ger:* **-bidding**) *va* ofrecer más de lo que vale (*un objeto*); licitar más que (*otra persona*); *vn* (bridge) declarar demasiado
**overblown** [ˈovərˌblon] *adj* deshojado, marchito, pasado; lleno (*de cosas traídas por el viento*)
**overboard** [ˈovərˌbord] *adj* al agua; **man overboard!** ¡hombre al agua!; **to throw overboard** arrojar, echar o tirar por la borda; (coll.) arrojar, echar o tirar (*p.ej., a un amigo, las ambiciones de uno, los escrúpulos de uno*) por la borda
**overbore** [ˌovərˈbor] *pret de* **overbear**
**overborne** [ˌovərˈborn] *pp de* **overbear**
**overburden** [ˌovərˈbʌrdən] *va* cargar de modo excesivo
**overcame** [ˌovərˈkem] *pret de* **overcome**
**overcapitalization** [ˈovərˌkæpɪtəlɪˈzeʃən] *s* supercapitalización
**overcapitalize** [ˌovərˈkæpɪtəlaɪz] *va* supercapitalizar
**overcast** [ˈovərˌkæst] u [ˈovərˌkɑst] *adj* nublado, encapotado; (sew.) sobrehilado; *s* cielo encapotado; (sew.) sobrehilado; (*pret & pp:* **-cast**) *va* nublar; (sew.) sobrehilar; *vn* nublarse
**overcharge** [ˈovərˌtʃɑrdʒ] *s* cargo excesivo, recargo de precio; sobrecarga; (elec.) carga excesiva; [ˌovərˈtʃɑrdʒ] *va* estafar, hacer pagar mucho más del valor, cargar demasiado en la cuenta a; cargar . . . de más, p.ej., **you have overcharged me one dollar** me ha cargado Vd. un dólar de más; sobrecargar; (elec.) poner una carga excesiva a
**overcloud** [ˌovərˈklaʊd] *va* anublar; *vn* anublarse
**overcoat** [ˈovərˌkot] *s* abrigo, gabán, sobretodo
**overcome** [ˌovərˈkʌm] (*pret:* **-came;** *pp:* **-come**) *va* vencer; rendir; superar (*dificultades*)
**overconfidence** [ˌovərˈkɑnfɪdəns] *s* confianza excesiva
**overcritical** [ˌovərˈkrɪtɪkəl] *adj* hipercrítico
**overcrowd** [ˌovərˈkraʊd] *va* atestar, apiñar; poblar con exceso
**overcrowding** [ˌovərˈkraʊdɪŋ] *s* exceso de habitantes
**overcup oak** [ˈovərˌkʌp] *s* (bot.) roble de hojas aliradas
**overdevelop** [ˌovərdɪˈvɛləp] *va* desarrollar demasiado; (phot.) revelar demasiado
**overdid** [ˌovərˈdɪd] *pret de* **overdo**
**overdo** [ˌovərˈdu] (*pret:* **-did;** *pp:* **-done**) *va* exagerar; agobiar; asurar, requemar; *vn* cansarse mucho, excederse en el trabajo
**overdone** [ˌovərˈdʌn] *pp de* **overdo**
**overdose** [ˈovərˌdos] *s* dosis excesiva; [ˌovərˈdos] *va* dar una dosis excesiva a
**overdraft** [ˈovərˌdræft] u [ˈovərˌdrɑft] *s* (com.) sobregiro, giro en descubierto
**overdraw** [ˌovərˈdrɔ] (*pret:* **-drew;** *pp:* **-drawn**) *va & vn* (com.) sobregirar
**overdress** [ˈovərˌdrɛs] *s* sobreveste; [ˌovərˈdrɛs] *va* engalanar o ataviar con exceso; *vn* engalanarse o ataviarse con exceso
**overdrew** [ˌovərˈdru] *pret de* **overdraw**

**overdrive** [ˈovərˌdraɪv] *s* (aut.) sobremarcha, velocidad sobremultiplicada
**overdue** [ˈovərˈdju] u [ˈovərˈdu] *adj* atrasado (*p.ej., en el pago de una cuenta, en llegar al tiempo debido*); vencido y no pagado
**overeat** [ˌovərˈit] (*pret:* **-ate;** *pp:* **-eaten**) *va & vn* comer con exceso
**overemphasize** [ˌovərˈɛmfəsaɪz] *va* acentuar demasiado, acentuar demasiado la importancia de
**overestimate** [ˈovərˈɛstɪmɪt] *s* apreciación o estimación excesiva; presupuesto excesivo; [ˌovərˈɛstɪmet] *va* avaluar o estimar en valor excesivo; tener un concepto demasiado favorable de; **to overestimate one's strength** creerse (*uno*) más fuerte de lo que es
**overexcite** [ˌovərɛkˈsaɪt] *va* sobreexcitar
**overexcitement** [ˌovərɛkˈsaɪtmənt] *s* sobrexcitación
**overexert** [ˌovərɛgˈzʌrt] *va* ejercer de modo excesivo; **to overexert oneself** darse demasiado trabajo, hacer esfuerzo excesivo
**overexertion** [ˌovərɛgˈzʌrʃən] *s* esfuerzo excesivo
**overexpand** [ˌovərɛksˈpænd] *va* ensanchar o extender con exceso; *vn* ensancharse o extenderse con exceso
**overexpose** [ˌovərɛksˈpoz] *va* sobreexponer; (phot.) sobreexponer
**overexposure** [ˌovərɛksˈpoʒər] *s* sobreexposición; (phot.) sobreexposición
**overfed** [ˌovərˈfɛd] *pret & pp de* **overfeed**
**overfeed** [ˌovərˈfid] (*pret & pp:* **-fed**) *va* sobrealimentar; *vn* sobrealimentarse
**overfill** [ˌovərˈfɪl] *va* sobrellenar
**overflow** [ˈovərˌflo] *s* desbordamiento, rebosamiento; derrames; rebosadero, caño de reboso; [ˌovərˈflo] *vn* desbordar, rebosar; **to overflow with joy** rebosar de alegría
**overflowing** [ˌovərˈflo·ɪŋ] *s* desbordamiento, rebosamiento; **to overflowing** a rebosar, hasta derramarse; en suma abundancia; *adj* desbordante
**overflow pipe** *s* caño de reboso
**overgrew** [ˌovərˈgru] *pret de* **overgrow**
**overgrow** [ˌovərˈgro] (*pret:* **-grew;** *pp:* **-grown**) *va* cubrir, entapizar; crecer más que; ser ya grande para; ser ya viejo para; ser ya más apto que; dejar (*las cosas de los niños; a los amigos de la niñez, etc.*); *vn* crecer con demasiada rapidez
**overgrown** [ˌovərˈgron] *adj* demasiado grande para su edad; **overgrown boy** muchachón; *pp de* **overgrow**
**overgrowth** [ˈovərˌgroθ] *s* crecimiento excesivo; maleza, vegetación exuberante
**overhand** [ˈovərˌhænd] *adj* (sew.) sobrehilado; (sport) voleado por lo alto; *adv* (sew.) con costura sobrehilada; por lo alto; palma abajo; *va* (sew.) sobrehilar
**overhang** [ˈovərˌhæŋ] *s* alcance, proyección; alero (*del tejado*); vuelo (*de cualquier fábrica*); [ˌovərˈhæŋ] (*pret & pp:* **-hung**) *va* sobresalir por encima de, estar pendiente o colgando sobre, salir fuera del nivel de; amenazar; *vn* estar pendiente, estar colgando
**overhaul** [ˌovərˈhɔl] *va* examinar, registrar, revisar; ir alcanzando, alcanzar; componer, rehabilitar, reacondicionar
**overhead** [ˌovərˈhɛd] *adv* por encima de la cabeza; en lo alto, arriba; [ˈovərˌhɛd] *adj* de arriba; aéreo, elevado; general, de conjunto; *s* gastos generales
**overhead railway** *s* (Brit.) ferrocarril aéreo
**overhead valve** *s* válvula en la culata
**overhear** [ˌovərˈhɪr] (*pret & pp:* **-heard**) *va* oír por casualidad; acertar a oír, alcanzar a oír
**overheard** [ˌovərˈhʌrd] *pret & pp de* **overhear**
**overheat** [ˌovərˈhit] *va* recalentar; *vn* recalentarse
**overhung** [ˌovərˈhʌŋ] *pret & pp de* **overhang**
**overindulge** [ˌovərɪnˈdʌldʒ] *va* mimar demasiado; dedicarse con exceso a; tomar con exceso; *vn* darse demasiada buena vida
**overindulgence** [ˌovərɪnˈdʌldʒəns] *s* exceso, excesos; indulgencia o lenidad excesiva
**overjoy** [ˌovərˈdʒɔɪ] *va* arrebatar de alegría; **to be overjoyed** no caber de contento

**overladen** [ˌovərˈledən] *adj* sobrecargado
**overlaid** [ˌovərˈled] *pret & pp de* **overlay**
**overlain** [ˌovərˈlen] *pp de* **overlie**
**overland** [ˈovərˌlænd] u [ˈovərlənd] *adj & adv* por tierra, por vía terrestre
**overlap** [ˈovərˌlæp] *s* solapadura; solapo; imbricación; [ˌovərˈlæp] (*pret & pp:* **-lapped;** *ger:* **-lapping**) *va* solapar, traslapar; *vn* solapar, traslapar; traslaparse (*dos o más cosas*); suceder (*dos hechos*) en parte al mismo tiempo
**overlay** [ˈovərˌle] *s* capa sobrepuesta; hoja sobrepuesta; incrustación; [ˌovərˈle] (*pret & pp:* **-laid**) *va* cubrir; sobrecargar; incrustar; *pret de* **overlie**
**overleap** [ˌovərˈlip] *va* saltar por encima de
**overlie** [ˌovərˈlaɪ] (*pret:* **-lay;** *pp:* **-lain;** *ger:* **-lying**) *va* descansar sobre; sofocar (*a un niño*) echándosele encima
**overload** [ˈovərˌlod] *s* sobrecarga; [ˌovərˈlod] *va* sobrecargar
**overlong** [ˈovərˈlɔŋ] u [ˈovərˈlɑŋ] *adj* demasiado largo; *adv* mucho tiempo, demasiado tiempo
**overlook** [ˌovərˈlʊk] *va* dominar con la vista; pasar por alto, no hacer caso de; perdonar, tolerar; espiar, vigilar; cuidar de, dirigir; dar a, p.ej., **the window overlooks the garden** la ventana da al jardín
**overlord** [ˈovərˌlɔrd] *s* jefe supremo; [ˌovərˈlɔrd] *va* dominar despóticamente, imponerse a
**overlordship** [ˈovərˌlɔrdʃɪp] *s* jefatura suprema
**overly** [ˈovərlɪ] *adv* (coll.) excesivamente, demasiado
**overlying** [ˌovərˈlaɪɪŋ] *ger de* **overlie**
**overman** [ˈovərmən] *s* (*pl:* **-men**) capataz; árbitro; [ˈovərˌmæn] *s* sobrehombre
**overmaster** [ˌovərˈmæstər] u [ˌovərˈmɑstər] *va* dominar, sojuzgar
**overmatch** [ˌovərˈmætʃ] *va* sobrepujar
**overmodulation** [ˈovərˌmɑdʒəˈleʃən] *s* (rad.) sobremodulación
**overmuch** [ˈovərˈmʌtʃ] *s* demasía, exceso; *adj & adv* demasiado
**overnice** [ˈovərˈnaɪs] *adj* melindroso, remilgado
**overnight** [ˌovərˈnaɪt] *adv* toda la noche; de la tarde a la mañana, durante la noche; **to stay overnight** pasar la noche; [ˈovərˌnaɪt] *adj* de noche; de una sola noche; de la noche anterior; *s* la noche anterior
**overnight bag** *s* maletín, saco de noche (*para viajes cortos*)
**overpaid** [ˌovərˈped] *pret & pp de* **overpay**
**overpass** [ˈovərˌpæs] u [ˈovərˌpɑs] *s* viaducto; [ˌovərˈpæs] u [ˌovərˈpɑs] (*pret & pp:* **-passed** o **-past**) *va* atravesar, salvar; aventajar, exceder; pasar por alto, no hacer caso de
**overpay** [ˌovərˈpe] (*pret & pp:* **-paid**) *va* pagar con exceso
**overpayment** [ˌovərˈpemənt] *s* pago excesivo, exceso de pago
**overpeopled** [ˌovərˈpipəld] *adj* excesivamente poblado
**overplay** [ˌovərˈple] *va* (theat.) exagerar (*un papel*); aventajar, exceder; vencer
**overplus** [ˈovərplʌs] *s* sobrante, superávit
**overpopulate** [ˌovərˈpɑpjəlet] *va* superpoblar
**overpopulation** [ˈovərˌpɑpjəˈleʃən] *s* superpoblación
**overpower** [ˌovərˈpaʊər] *va* dominar, supeditar, subyugar; colmar, dejar estupefacto
**overpowering** [ˌovərˈpaʊərɪŋ] *adj* abrumador, arrollador, irresistible
**overproduction** [ˌovərprəˈdʌkʃən] *s* superproducción, sobreproducción
**overproud** [ˈovərˈpraʊd] *adj* orgulloso en exceso
**overran** [ˌovərˈræn] *pret de* **overrun**
**overrate** [ˌovərˈret] *va* exagerar el valor de, apreciar o valuar en más de lo que vale (*una persona o cosa*)
**overreach** [ˌovərˈritʃ] *va* ir más allá de, extenderse más allá de; engañar con astucias; **to overreach oneself** aventurarse más allá de sus fuerzas, pasarse de listo; *vn* ir más allá de lo necesario, extenderse demasiado; alcanzarse (*un caballo*)
**overridden** [ˌovərˈrɪdən] *pp de* **override**

**override** [ˌovərˈraɪd] (*pret:* **-rode;** *pp:* **-ridden**) *va* recorrer; atropellar; desentenderse de, no hacer caso de; anular, invalidar; fatigar, reventar (*p.ej., un caballo*)
**overripe** [ˈovərˈraɪp] *adj* demasiado maduro, pachucho, papandujo
**overrode** [ˌovərˈrod] *pret de* **override**
**overrule** [ˌovərˈrul] *va* anular, invalidar; vencer, triunfar de; (law) denegar
**overrun** [ˌovərˈrʌn] (*pret:* **-ran;** *pp:* **-run;** *ger:* **-running**) *va* cubrir enteramente; infestar; exceder; **to overrun one's time** quedarse más de lo justo; hablar más de lo justo
**oversaw** [ˌovərˈsɔ] *pret de* **oversee**
**overscore** [ˈovərˌskor] *s* (bridge) exceso sobre lo declarado; [ˌovərˈskor] *va* poner una virgulilla o raya sobre; *vn* (bridge) ganar sobre lo declarado
**oversea** [ˈovərˌsi] *adj* de ultramar; [ˌovərˈsi] *adv* allende los mares, en ultramar
**overseas** [ˈovərˌsiz] *adj* var. de **oversea;** [ˌovərˈsiz] *adv* var. de **oversea**
**oversee** [ˌovərˈsi] (*pret:* **-saw;** *pp:* **-seen**) *va* dirigir, superentender, fiscalizar
**overseer** [ˈovərˌsiər] *s* director, superintendente
**oversell** [ˌovərˈsɛl] (*pret & pp:* **-sold**) *va* excederse en la venta de; vender (*efectos no disponibles*)
**overset** [ˈovərˌsɛt] *s* vuelco; [ˌovərˈsɛt] (*pret & pp:* **-set;** *ger:* **-setting**) *va* volcar; (fig.) derrocar; *vn* volcar
**overshadow** [ˌovərˈʃædo] *va* sombrear; (fig.) eclipsar
**overshoe** [ˈovərˌʃu] *s* chanclo, zapatón
**overshoot** [ˌovərˈʃut] (*pret & pp:* **-shot**) *va* tirar por encima de o más allá de; **to overshoot oneself** o **to overshoot the mark** pasar de la raya, excederse; *vn* pasar de la raya, excederse
**overshot** [ˈovərˌʃɑt] *adj* que tiene saliente la mandíbula superior; de corriente alta; [ˌovərˈʃɑt] *pret & pp de* **overshoot**
**overshot water wheel** *s* rueda (hidráulica) de corriente alta o de cajones
**overside** [ˈovərˌsaɪd] *adj* (naut.) por la borda, por encima de la regala; [ˌovərˈsaɪd] *adv* (naut.) por la borda, por encima de la regala
**oversight** [ˈovərˌsaɪt] *s* inadvertencia, descuido; vigilancia, cuidado
**oversize** [ˈovərˌsaɪz] *s* tamaño extra; cosa de tamaño extra; *adj* extragrande, de tamaño extra
**overskirt** [ˈovərˌskʌrt] *s* sobrefalda (*falda corta*); refajo
**oversleep** [ˌovərˈslip] (*pret & pp:* **-slept**) *vn* dormir demasiado tarde, no despertar
**oversold** [ˌovərˈsold] *pret & pp de* **oversell**
**overspread** [ˌovərˈsprɛd] (*pret & pp:* **-spread**) *va* extenderse sobre
**overstate** [ˌovərˈstet] *va* exagerar
**overstatement** [ˌovərˈstetmənt] *s* exageración
**overstay** [ˌovərˈste] (*pret & pp:* **-stayed** o **-staid**) *va* quedarse más tiempo de lo que permite (*la licencia que uno tiene*)
**overstep** [ˌovərˈstɛp] (*pret & pp:* **-stepped;** *ger:* **-stepping**) *va* exceder, traspasar
**overstock** [ˈovərˌstɑk] *s* surtido excesivo; existencias excesivas; [ˌovərˈstɑk] *va* abarrotar; **to be overstocked with** tener existencias excesivas de
**overstrung** [ˈovərˈstrʌŋ] *adj* demasiado impresionable, demasiado excitable
**overstuff** [ˌovərˈstʌf] *va* atestar; rellenar (*un cojín, almohada, etc.*)
**oversubscribe** [ˌovərsəbˈskraɪb] *va* contribuir más de lo pedido a (*p.ej., una recaudación de carácter benéfico*); subscribir (*un empréstito*) en exceso de lo disponible
**oversubscription** [ˌovərsəbˈskrɪpʃən] *s* contribución en exceso de lo pedido; subscripción en exceso de lo disponible
**oversupply** [ˈovərsəˌplaɪ] *s* (*pl:* **-plies**) provisión excesiva; [ˌovərsəˈplaɪ] (*pret & pp:* **-plied**) *va* proveer en exceso
**overt** [ˈovʌrt] u [oˈvʌrt] *adj* abierto, manifiesto; premeditado
**overtake** [ˌovərˈtek] (*pret:* **-took;** *pp:* **-taken**) *va* alcanzar; sobrepasar; sorprender; sobrevenir a
**overtask** [ˌovərˈtæsk] u [ˌovərˈtɑsk] *va* atarear demasiado, oprimir con trabajo
**overtax** [ˌovərˈtæks] *va* oprimir con tributos; agotar (*las fuerzas de uno*); exceder los límites de (*p.ej., la credulidad de uno*)
**over-the-counter** [ˈovərðəˈkaʊntər] *adj* vendido directamente al comprador (*y no en el mercado bursátil*); vendido en tienda al por mayor
**overthrew** [ˌovərˈθru] *pret de* **overthrow**
**overthrow** [ˈovərˌθro] *s* derrocamiento (*p.ej., del gobierno*); trastorno (*p.ej., de los proyectos de uno*); [ˌovərˈθro] (*pret:* **-threw;** *pp:* **-thrown**) *va* derrocar; trastornar
**overtime** [ˈovərˌtaɪm] *adj & adv* en exceso de las horas regulares; *s* tiempo suplementario, horas extraordinarias de trabajo; [ˌovərˈtaɪm] *va* (phot.) sobreexponer
**overtone** [ˈovərˌton] *s* armónico; **overtones** *spl* insinuación
**overtook** [ˌovərˈtuk] *pret de* **overtake**
**overtop** [ˌovərˈtɑp] (*pret & pp:* **-topped;** *ger:* **-topping**) *va* descollar sobre; sobresalir entre
**overtrain** [ˌovərˈtren] *va* (sport) sobrentrenar; *vn* (sport) sobrentrenarse
**overtrump** [ˈovərˌtrʌmp] *s* contrafallo; [ˌovərˈtrʌmp] *va & vn* contrafallar
**overture** [ˈovərtʃər] *s* insinuación, proposición; (mus.) obertura
**overturn** [ˈovərˌtʌrn] *s* vuelco; (com.) movimiento de mercancías; [ˌovərˈtʌrn] *va* volcar; trastornar; derrocar (*el gobierno*); *vn* volcar; trastornarse
**overwatch** [ˌovərˈwɔtʃ] *va* vigilar; cansar a fuerza de vigilias
**overweening** [ˌovərˈwinɪŋ] *adj* arrogante, presuntuoso
**overweigh** [ˌovərˈwe] *va* pesar más que; contrapesar, compensar; prevalecer contra; oprimir
**overweight** [ˈovərˌwet] *adj* excesivamente gordo o grueso; *s* sobrepeso; exceso de peso; peso de añadidura; [ˌovərˈwet] *va* sobrecargar; abrumar con trabajo, responsabilidades, etc.
**overwhelm** [ˌovərˈhwɛlm] *va* abrumar; inundar; anonadar; colmar (*p.ej., de favores, regalos*)
**overwhelming** [ˌovərˈhwɛlmɪŋ] *adj* abrumador, arrollador, irresistible
**overwork** [ˈovərˌwʌrk] *s* trabajo excesivo, exceso de trabajo; trabajo fuera de las horas regulares; [ˌovərˈwʌrk] (*pret & pp:* **-worked** o **-wrought**) *va* hacer trabajar demasiado; oprimir con trabajo; *vn* darse con exceso al trabajo, trabajar demasiado
**overworked** [ˌovərˈwʌrkt] *adj* atrabajado
**overwrite** [ˌovərˈraɪt] (*pret:* **-wrote;** *pp:* **-written**) *va* escribir sobre (*una superficie*); escribir encima de; escribir acerca de; refundir; escribir en un estilo acicalado; [ˈovərˌraɪt] *va* (com.) garantizar comisión a (*un representante general*) sobre ventas hechas por un agente regional
**overwrought** [ˌovərˈrɔt] *adj* atrabajado, abrumado de trabajo; sobrexcitado; muy ornamentado, recargado de ornamentación; *pret & pp de* **overwork**
**oviculum** [oˈvɪkjələm] *s* (*pl:* **-la** [lə]) (arch.) ovículo
**Ovid** [ˈɑvɪd] *s* Ovidio
**oviduct** [ˈovɪdʌkt] *s* (anat.) oviducto
**oviform** [ˈovɪfɔrm] *adj* oviforme
**ovine** [ˈovaɪn] u [ˈovɪn] *adj & s* ovino
**oviparous** [oˈvɪpərəs] *adj* ovíparo
**oviposit** [ˌovɪˈpɑzɪt] *vn* desovar
**ovipositor** [ˌovɪˈpɑzɪtər] *s* (zool.) oviscapto
**ovoid** [ˈovɔɪd] *adj* ovoide, ovoideo; *s* cuerpo ovoideo
**ovolo** [ˈovəlo] *s* (*pl:* **-li** [li]) (arch.) óvolo
**ovoviviparous** [ˌovovaɪˈvɪpərəs] *adj* ovovivíparo
**ovular** [ˈovjələr] *adj* ovular
**ovulation** [ˌovjəˈleʃən] *s* (biol.) ovulación
**ovule** [ˈovjul] *s* (biol. & bot.) óvulo
**ovum** [ˈovəm] *s* (*pl:* **ova** [ˈovə]) (biol.) huevo
**ow** [aʊ] *interj* ¡ax!
**owe** [o] *va* deber; *vn* tener deudas
**owing** [ˈo·ɪŋ] *adj* adeudado; debido, pagadero; **owing to** debido a, por causa de

**owl** [aʊl] *s* (orn.) búho, lechuza, mochuelo
**owlet** [ˈaʊlɪt] *s* búho, lechuza o mochuelo pequeños; hijuelo del búho, la lechuza o el mochuelo
**owlish** [ˈaʊlɪʃ] *adj* de búho; que se da aires de sabio
**own** [on] *adj* propio, p.ej., **my own brother** mi propio hermano; *s* suyo, lo suyo; **on one's own** (coll.) por su propia cuenta, sin depender de nadie; por su cabeza (*sin tomar consejo*); (coll.) de su cabeza (*de su propio ingenio o invención*); **to come into one's own** entrar en posesión de lo suyo; tener el éxito merecido, recibir el honor merecido; **to have nothing of one's own** no tener (*uno*) nada que pueda llamar suyo; **to hold one's own** no aflojar, no cejar, mantenerse firme; *va* poseer; reconocer; *vn* confesar; **to own up** (coll.) confesar de plano; **to own up to** (coll.) confesar de plano (*una culpa, un delito, etc.*)
**owner** [ˈonər] *s* amo, dueño, poseedor, propietario
**ownership** [ˈonərʃɪp] *s* posesión, propiedad
**owner's license** *s* (aut.) permiso de circulación
**ox** [ɑks] *s* (*pl:* **oxen**) (zool.) buey; **to work like an ox** trabajar como un buey
**oxalate** [ˈɑksəlet] *s* (chem.) oxalato
**oxalic** [ɑksˈælɪk] *adj* oxálico
**oxalic acid** *s* (chem.) ácido oxálico
**oxalidaceous** [ɑks,ælɪˈdeʃəs] *adj* (bot.) oxalidáceo
**oxalis** [ˈɑksəlɪs] *s* (bot.) aleluya, acedera menor, acederilla
**oxazine** [ˈɑksəzin] o [ˈɑksəzɪn] *s* (chem.) oxacina
**oxbow** [ˈɑks,bo] *s* collera de yugo; recodo de un río; terreno encerrado en un recodo de río
**oxcart** [ˈɑks,kɑrt] *s* carreta de bueyes
**oxen** [ˈɑksən] *pl de* **ox**
**oxeye** [ˈɑks,aɪ] *s* (bot.) hierba amarilla; (bot.) margarita mayor; (bot.) ojo de buey; (bot.) rudbequia
**ox-eyed** [ˈɑks,aɪd] *adj* de ojos rasgados, de ojos grandes
**oxeye daisy** *s* (bot.) hierba amarilla; (bot.) margarita mayor
**oxford** [ˈɑksfərd] *s* oxford (*tela*); zapato de estilo Oxford; color negro agrisado
**Oxford gray** *s* color negro agrisado
**Oxfordian** [ɑksˈfordɪən] *adj & s* oxfordiano; (geol.) oxfordiense
**Oxford movement** *s* movimiento religioso de Oxford
**oxheart** [ˈɑks,hɑrt] *s* cereza de color casi negro y de forma de corazón
**oxhide** [ˈɑks,haɪd] *s* cuero de buey
**oxid** [ˈɑksɪd] *s* var. de **oxide**
**oxidase** [ˈɑksɪdes] o [ˈɑksɪdez] *s* (biochem.) oxidasa
**oxidation** [,ɑksɪˈdeʃən] *s* oxidación
**oxide** [ˈɑksaɪd] *s* (chem.) óxido
**oxide blue** *s* azul de cobalto
**oxide of iron** *s* (chem.) óxido de hierro
**oxide yellow** *s* óxido amarillo
**oxidimetry** [,ɑksɪˈdɪmɪtrɪ] *s* oxidimetría
**oxidizable** [ˈɑksɪ,daɪzəbəl] *adj* oxidable
**oxidization** [,ɑksɪdɪˈzeʃən] *s* var. of **oxidation**
**oxidize** [ˈɑksɪdaɪz] *va* oxidar; *vn* oxidarse
**oxidizer** [ˈɑksɪ,daɪzər] *s* (chem.) oxidante
**oxidizing flame** *s* (chem.) llama oxidante
**oxime** [ˈɑksim] o [ˈɑksɪm] *s* (chem.) oxima
**oxlip** [ˈɑks,lɪp] *s* (bot.) hierba de San Pablo mayor
**oxman** [ˈɑksmən] *s* (*pl:* **-men**) boyero
**Oxonian** [ɑksˈonɪən] *adj & s* oxoniense
**oxonium** [ɑksˈonɪəm] *s* (chem.) oxonio
**oxozone** [ˈɑksozon] *s* (chem.) oxozono
**oxpecker** [ˈɑks,pɛkər] *s* (orn.) espulgabueyes, picabueyes
**oxtail soup** [ˈɑks,tel] *s* sopa de cola de buey
**oxtongue** [ˈɑks,tʌŋ] *s* (bot.) lengua de buey
**oxyacetylene** [,ɑksɪəˈsɛtɪlin] *adj* oxiacetilénico
**oxyacetylene torch** *s* soplete oxiacetilénico
**oxyacetylene welding** *s* soldadura oxiacetilénica
**oxyblepsia** [,ɑksɪˈblɛpsɪə] *s* oxiblepsia
**oxybromide** [,ɑksɪˈbromaɪd] o [,ɑksɪˈbromɪd] *s* (chem.) oxibromuro
**oxychloride** [,ɑksɪˈkloraɪd] o [,ɑksɪˈklorɪd] *s* (chem.) oxicloruro
**oxycyanide** [,ɑksɪˈsaɪənaɪd] o [,ɑksɪˈsaɪənɪd] *s* (chem.) oxicianuro
**oxygen** [ˈɑksɪdʒən] *s* (chem.) oxígeno
**oxygenate** [ˈɑksɪdʒənet] *va* (chem.) oxigenar
**oxygenation** [,ɑksɪdʒəˈneʃən] *s* oxigenación
**oxygen-hydrogen welding** [ˈɑksɪdʒənˈhaɪdrədʒən] *s* soldadura oxhídrica
**oxygenize** [ˈɑksɪdʒənaɪz] *va* oxigenar
**oxygen mask** *s* máscara de oxígeno
**oxygen tent** *s* (med.) tienda de oxígeno, cámara de oxígeno
**oxyhemoglobin** [,ɑksɪ,himəˈglobɪn] *s* (biochem.) oxihemoglobina
**oxyhydrogen** [,ɑksɪˈhaɪdrədʒən] *adj* (chem.) oxhídrico; *s* (chem.) gas oxhídrico
**oxyhydrogen torch** *s* soplete oxhídrico
**oxymel** [ˈɑksɪmɛl] *s* (pharm.) ojimel
**oxyntic** [ɑksˈɪntɪk] *adj* oxíntico
**oxysulfide** [,ɑksɪˈsʌlfaɪd] o [,ɑksɪˈsʌlfɪd] *s* (chem.) oxisulfuro
**oxytocic** [,ɑksɪˈtosɪk] o [,ɑksɪˈtɑsɪk] *adj & s* (med.) oxitócico
**oxytone** [ˈɑksɪton] *adj & s* (phonet.) oxítono
**oyez** u **oyes** [ˈojɛs] u [oˈjɛs] *interj* (law) ¡oíd! (*voz de los ujieres*)
**oyster** [ˈɔɪstər] *s* (zool.) ostra; (slang) chiticalla (*persona muy callada*); *adj* ostrero
**oyster bed** *s* ostrero, ostral
**oyster catcher** *s* (orn.) ostrero
**oyster cocktail** *s* ostras de entremés, ostras en su concha
**oyster crab** *s* (zool.) pinotero
**oyster cracker** *s* galletita salada
**oyster culture** *s* ostricultura
**oysterer** [ˈɔɪstərər] *s* ostrero
**oyster farm** *s* ostrero, ostral, criadero ostrícola
**oyster farmer** *s* ostricultor
**oyster fork** *s* desbullador
**oysterhouse** [ˈɔɪstər,haʊs] *s* ostrería
**oyster knife** *s* abreostras
**oysterman** [ˈɔɪstərmən] *s* (*pl:* **-men**) ostrero
**oyster opener** *s* desbullador (*persona*)
**oyster plant** *s* (bot.) salsifí; (bot.) mertensia marítima
**oyster plover** *s* var. de **oyster catcher**
**oyster rake** *s* raño
**oyster shell** *s* desbulla, concha de ostra
**oyster soup** *s* sopa de ostras
**oyster tree** *s* (bot.) mangle
**oysterwoman** [ˈɔɪstər,wʊmən] *s* (*pl:* **-women**) ostrera
**oz.** abr. de **ounce** u **ounces**
**ozena** [oˈzinə] *s* (path.) ocena
**ozocerite** [oˈzokəraɪt] u [,ozoˈsɪraɪt] *s* (mineral.) ozocerita u ozoquerita
**ozone** [ˈozon] *s* (chem.) ozono; (coll.) aire fresco; **to get some ozone** (coll.) tomar el fresco
**ozone layer** *s* (meteor.) capa de ozono, ozonosfera
**ozone paper** *s* (chem.) papel de ozono
**ozonide** [ˈozonaɪd] u [ˈozonɪd] *s* (chem.) ozonuro
**ozoniferous** [,ozoˈnɪfərəs] *adj* ozonífero
**ozonization** [,ozonɪˈzeʃən] *s* ozonización
**ozonize** [ˈozonaɪz] *va* ozonizar; *vn* ozonizarse
**ozonolysis** [,ozoˈnɑlɪsɪs] *s* (chem.) ozonolisis
**ozonometer** [,ozoˈnɑmɪtər] *s* ozonómetro
**ozonoscope** [oˈzonəskop] *s* ozonoscopio
**ozonosphere** [oˈzonəsfɪr] *s* ozonosfera
**ozostomia** [,ozɑsˈtomɪə] *s* ozostomía
**ozs.** abr. de **ounces**

# P

**P, p** [pi] *s* (*pl:* **P's, p's** [piz]) décimasexta letra del alfabeto inglés; **mind your P's and Q's!** ¡tenga Vd. cuidado!, ¡ande Vd. con cuidado con lo que dice!
**p.** abr. de **page** y **participle**
**p.a.** abr. de **participial adjective, per annum** y **press agent**
**Pa.** abr. de **Pennsylvania**
**P.A.** abr. de **Passenger Agent, Post Adjutant, power of attorney** y **Purchasing Agent**
**pa** [pɑ] *s* (coll.) papá
**pabulum** ['pæbjələm] *s* pábulo
**Pac.** abr. de **Pacific**
**pace** [pes] *s* paso; aire (*manera de andar del caballo*); portante (*manera de andar del caballo en la cual mueve a un tiempo la mano y el pie del mismo lado*); **at a slow pace** a paso lento; **to keep pace with** ir, andar o avanzar al mismo paso que; **to put through one's paces** poner (*a uno*) a prueba; dar (*a uno*) ocasión de lucirse; **to set the pace** llevar el tren, establecer el paso; dar el ejemplo; **to set the pace for** marcar la pauta a; *va* establecer el paso para; medir a pasos; recorrer a pasos; **to pace the floor** pasearse desesperadamente por la habitación; *vn* andar a pasos regulares; amblar (*andar al paso portante*)
**pacemaker** ['pes,mekər] *s* establecedor del paso; ejemplo; (med.) marcapaso (*regulador del latido cardíaco*)
**pacer** ['pesər] *s* establecedor del paso; persona que anda a pasos regulares; caballo amblador
**pacha** [pə'ʃɑ] o ['pæʃə] *s* var. de **pasha**
**pachyderm** ['pækɪdʌrm] *s* (zool.) paquidermo; (fig.) tronco (*persona insensible*)
**pachysandra** [,pækɪ'sændrə] *s* (bot.) paquisandra
**pacific** [pə'sɪfɪk] *adj* pacífico; (*cap.*) *adj & s* Pacífico (*océano*)
**pacifically** [pə'sɪfɪkəlɪ] *adv* pacíficamente
**pacification** [,pæsɪfɪ'keʃən] *s* pacificación
**pacificatory** [pə'sɪfɪkə,torɪ] *adj* pacificador
**Pacific Coast** *s* Costa del Pacífico
**Pacific Ocean** *s* océano Pacífico
**Pacific time** *s* (U.S.A.) hora legal correspondiente al meridiano 120°
**pacifier** ['pæsɪ,faɪər] *s* pacificador; chupete (*para los niños*)
**pacifism** ['pæsɪfɪzəm] *s* pacifismo
**pacifist** ['pæsɪfɪst] *adj & s* pacifista
**pacifistic** [,pæsɪ'fɪstɪk] *adj* pacifista
**pacify** ['pæsɪfaɪ] (*pret & pp:* **-fied**) *va* pacificar
**pack** [pæk] *s* lío, fardo; paquete; cantidad empaquetada; perrada, jauría; manada; cuadrilla; pandilla (*de malhechores*); saco, sarta, montón (*p.ej., de mentiras*); baraja (*de naipes*); cajetilla (*de cigarrillos*); témpano (*de hielo flotante*); mochila, morral (*de los caminantes*); (med.) compresa; *va* empaquetar; embaular; encajonar; hacer (*el baúl, la maleta*); conservar en latas; apretar, atestar, llenar; cargar (*una acémila*); escoger o nombrar de modo fraudulento, llenar de partidarios (*p.ej., un jurado*); (coll.) llevar a cuestas; (mach.) empaquetar; **to be packed in** estar o ir como sardinas en banasta; **to pack down** apretar, comprimir; apisonar; **to pack in** empaquetar (*gente en un local*); **to pack up** empaquetar; *vn* empaquetarse; encajonarse; empaquetarse fácilmente; hacer el baúl, hacer la maleta; consolidarse, endurecerse, formar masa compacta; **to pack up** liar el petate, hacer la pacotilla
**package** ['pækɪdʒ] *s* paquete; *va* empaquetar
**pack animal** *s* acémila, animal de carga
**packer** ['pækər] *s* empaquetador, embaulador; empaquetadora (*máquina*); portador; dueño de una fábrica de conservas alimenticias
**packet** ['pækɪt] *s* paquete; paquebote
**packet boat** *s* paquebote
**pack horse** *s* caballo de carga
**packing** ['pækɪŋ] *s* empaque, embalaje; envase; preparación de conservas alimenticias; (mach.) estopa, empaquetadura o guarnición; relleno (*para hacer impermeable al agua*)
**packing box** *s* caja de embalaje o de embalar; (mach.) prensa estopa
**packing case** *s* caja de embalaje o de embalar
**packing effect** *s* (phys.) efecto de empaquetamiento
**packing house** *s* frigorífico, fábrica para envasar o enlatar comestibles
**packing slip** *s* hoja de embalaje
**packman** ['pækmən] *s* (*pl:* **-men**) buhonero
**pack mule** *s* mula de carga
**pack needle** *s* aguja de embalar, aguja saquera
**pack rat** *s* (zool.) rata norteamericana (*Neotoma cinerea*)
**packsaddle** ['pæk,sædəl] *s* albarda
**packthread** ['pæk,θrɛd] *s* bramante
**pack train** *s* recua
**pact** [pækt] *s* pacto
**paction** ['pækʃən] *s* pacto
**pad** [pæd] *s* cojincillo; almohadilla; sillín; bloc (*de papel*); tampón (*para entintar sellos*); pisada (*ruido*); jaca, caballo de camino; hoja (*de planta acuática*); peto, plastrón; pata (*de perro, zorra, etc.*); eminencia hipotenar (*del pie de ciertos animales*); plataforma (*de lanzamiento de cohete*); (*pret & pp:* **padded;** *ger:* **padding**) *va* rellenar (*p.ej., con algodón*); acolchar; meter mucho ripio en (*un escrito*); *vn* andar, caminar; caminar despacio y pesadamente; andar con un trotecito ligero
**padding** ['pædɪŋ] *s* relleno; (fig.) relleno, ripio (*en un escrito, discurso o verso*)
**paddle** ['pædəl] *s* canalete, zagual; pala (*de una rueda*); paseo en embarcación impulsada con canalete; palo (*para apalear a una persona, la ropa, etc.*); batidor; *va* impulsar con canalete; apalear; **to paddle one's own canoe** (coll.) bastarse a sí mismo; *vn* remar con canalete; remar suavemente; chapotear, guachapear
**paddle box** *s* caja que cubre la parte superior de la rueda de paletas
**paddlefish** ['pædəl,fɪʃ] *s* (ichth.) pez hoja
**paddle wheel** *s* rueda de paletas
**paddle-wheel steamer** ['pædəl,hwil] *s* buque de ruedas, vapor de ruedas
**paddock** ['pædək] *s* dehesa; pesaje, cercado para caballos de carrera (*en los hipódromos*)
**paddy** ['pædɪ] *s* (*pl:* **-dies**) arroz; arroz sin cosechar; palay, arroz con cáscara; (*cap.*) *s* irlandés; nombre abreviado de **Patrick**
**paddy wagon** *s* (slang) camión de policía
**paddywhack** ['pædɪ,hwæk] *s* (U.S.A. coll.) paliza; (Brit. coll.) mal genio, cólera
**padlock** ['pæd,lɑk] *s* candado; *va* cerrar con candado; condenar (*una habitación*)
**padre** ['pɑdrɪ] *s* padre (*especialmente sacerdote*); (mil.) páter
**paean** ['piən] *s* canto triunfal, himno de gloria; (hist.) peán
**pagan** ['pegən] *adj & s* pagano
**pagandom** ['pegəndəm] *s* gentilidad
**paganism** ['pegənɪzəm] *s* paganismo
**paganize** ['pegənaɪz] *va & vn* paganizar
**page** [pedʒ] *s* página; paje; escudero; botones; (fig.) página; *va* paginar; buscar llamando (*en un hotel, club, etc.*)
**pageant** ['pædʒənt] *s* fiesta pública, espectáculo público, pompa; representación al aire libre en una serie de cuadros; boato, bambolla
**pageantry** ['pædʒəntrɪ] *s* (*pl:* **-ries**) pompa; boato, bambolla
**page proof** *s* (print.) pruebas de planas

**pagination** [ˌpædʒɪ'neʃən] *s* paginación
**pagoda** [pə'godə] *s* pagoda
**paid** [ped] *adj* asalariado; pagado; hecho efectivo; *pret & pp de* **pay**
**paid-up** ['ped'ʌp] *adj* terminado de pagar, libre
**pail** [pel] *s* balde, cubo
**pailful** ['pelfʊl] *s* balde, cubo (*contenido*)
**paillasse** [pæl'jæs] o ['pæljæs] *s* colchón de paja, jergón
**pain** [pen] *s* dolor; **pains** *spl* esmero, trabajo; dolores de parto; **on pain of** so pena de; **to be in pain** estar con dolor, tener dolores; **to take pains** esmerarse; **to take pains to** + *inf* poner mucho cuidado en + *inf;* **to take pains not to** + *inf* guardarse de + *inf; va & vn* doler
**pained** [pend] *adj* apenado, afligido
**painful** ['penfəl] *adj* doloroso; penoso
**painkiller** ['penˌkɪlər] *s* (coll.) remedio contra el dolor
**painless** ['penlɪs] *adj* indoloro, sin dolor; fácil, sin trabajo
**pain reliever** *s* calmante del dolor
**painstaking** ['penzˌtekɪŋ] *adj* esmerado
**paint** [pent] *s* pintura; colorete (*afeite*); *va* pintar; *vn* pintar, ser pintor; pintarse, repintarse
**paintbox** ['pentˌbɑks] *s* caja de colores, caja de pinturas
**paintbrush** ['pentˌbrʌʃ] *s* brocha, pincel
**painted lady** *s* (bot.) judía de España, judía escarlata
**painter** ['pentər] *s* pintor; (naut.) rejera, amarra; (zool.) puma
**Painter's Easel** *s* (astr.) Caballete del pintor
**painting** ['pentɪŋ] *s* pintura
**paint remover** *s* sacapintura, quitapintura
**pair** [pɛr] *s* par; (pol.) par de diputados apareados para abstenerse de votar; (pol.) convenio para abstenerse de votar; parejas (*dos naipes iguales*); *va* aparear, parear; **to pair off** aparear; *vn* aparearse; **to pair off** aparearse; (pol.) aparearse (*dos diputados*) para abstenerse de votar
**pair of glasses** *s* gafas; **a pair of glasses** unas gafas
**pair of mustaches** *s* bigotes
**pair of scissors** *s* tijeras
**pair of spectacles** *s* anteojos, gafas
**pair of suspenders** *s* tirantes
**pair of trousers** *s* pantalones
**paisley** ['pezlɪ] *s* tela de Paisley; prenda de tela de Paisley
**pajamas** [pə'dʒɑməz] o [pə'dʒæməz] *spl* pijama
**Pakistan** ['pækɪstæn] o ['pɑkɪstɑn] *s* el Paquistán
**Pakistani** [ˌpækɪ'stænɪ] o [ˌpɑkɪ'stɑnɪ] *adj & s* pakistano o pakistaní
**pal** [pæl] *s* (slang) compañero; (*pret & pp:* **palled;** *ger:* **palling**) *vn* (slang) ser compañeros; **to pal around with** (slang) ser compañero de
**palace** ['pælɪs] *s* palacio
**paladin** ['pælədɪn] *s* paladín
**palaestra** [pə'lɛstrə] *s* palestra
**palankeen** o **palanquin** [ˌpælən'kin] *s* palanquín
**palatable** ['pælətəbəl] *adj* sabroso, apetitoso
**palatal** ['pælətəl] *adj* palatal; (phonet.) palatal; *s* (phonet.) palatal
**palatalization** [ˌpælətəlɪ'zeʃən] *s* palatalización
**palatalize** ['pælətəlaɪz] *va* palatalizar; *vn* palatalizarse
**palate** ['pælɪt] *s* (anat.) paladar; (fig.) paladar (*gusto; gastrónomo*)
**palatial** [pə'leʃəl] *adj* magnífico, suntuoso
**palatinate** [pə'lætɪnet] o [pə'lætɪnɪt] *s* palatinado; (*cap.*) *s* Palatinado
**palatine** ['pælətaɪn] *adj* palatino; *s* señor palatino, conde palatino; (*cap.*) *adj & s* palatino; **the Palatine** el Palatino
**Palatine Hill** *s* monte Palatino
**palaver** [pə'lævər] o [pə'lɑvər] *s* plática, conferencia; charla, palabrería; parlamento entre exploradores y bárbaros; lisonja, zalamería; *vn* charlar; parlamentar (*exploradores y bárbaros*); lagotear
**pale** [pel] *adj* pálido; *s* estaca; palizada; (her.) palo; límite, término; **outside the pale of** fuera de los límites de; *va* empalizar; *vn* palidecer
**paleface** ['pelˌfes] *s* rostropálido (*así llamaban los pieles rojas a los de piel blanca*)
**paleness** ['pelnɪs] *s* palidez
**paleobotany** [ˌpelɪo'bɑtənɪ] *s* paleobotánica
**paleographer** [ˌpelɪ'ɑgrəfər] *s* paleógrafo
**paleographic** [ˌpelɪo'græfɪk] *adj* paleográfico
**paleography** [ˌpelɪ'ɑgrəfɪ] *s* paleografía
**paleolithic** [ˌpelɪo'lɪθɪk] *adj* paleolítico
**paleontologist** [ˌpelɪɑn'tɑlədʒɪst] *s* paleontólogo
**paleontology** [ˌpelɪɑn'tɑlədʒɪ] *s* paleontología
**Paleozoic** [ˌpelɪo'zo·ɪk] *adj & s* (geol.) paleozoico
**Palestine** ['pælɪstaɪn] *s* Palestina
**Palestinian** [ˌpælɪs'tɪnɪən] *adj & s* palestino
**palette** ['pælɪt] *s* (paint.) paleta
**palette knife** *s* espátula
**palfrey** ['pɔlfrɪ] *s* palafrén
**Pali** ['pɑlɪ] *adj & s* pali
**palimpsest** ['pælɪmpsɛst] *s* palimpsesto
**palindrome** ['pælɪndrom] *s* palíndromo, capicúa
**paling** ['pelɪŋ] *s* estaca; estacada
**palingenesis** [ˌpælɪn'dʒɛnɪsɪs] *s* palingenesia
**palingenetic** [ˌpælɪndʒɪ'nɛtɪk] *adj* palingenésico
**palinode** ['pælɪnod] *s* palinodia
**palisade** ['pælɪsed] *s* estaca; estacada, empalizada; acantilado; *va* encerrar con estacada o empalizada
**palisander** [ˌpælɪ'sændər] *s* (bot.) palisandro
**palish** ['pelɪʃ] *adj* paliducho
**pall** [pɔl] *s* paño de ataúd, paño mortuorio; capa (*p.e.j., de humo*); (eccl.) palia; hijuela (*para cubrir el cáliz*); *va* hartar, saciar; quitar el sabor a; *vn* perder el sabor; **to pall on** hartar, saciar, dejar de gustar a
**palladium** [pə'ledɪəm] *s* (*pl:* **-a** [ə]) (chem.) paladio; paladión (*defensa, sostén*); (*cap.*) *s* (myth.) Paladión
**Pallas** ['pæləs] *s* (myth.) Palas
**Pallas Athene** *s* (myth.) Palas Atenea
**pallbearer** ['pɔlˌbɛrər] *s* acompañante de un cadáver; portaféretro, portador del féretro
**pallet** ['pælɪt] *s* jergón; paleta o llana (*de alfarero*); (mach.) uña (*de un trinquete*); (paint.) paleta
**palliate** ['pælɪet] *va* paliar
**palliation** [ˌpælɪ'eʃən] *s* paliación
**palliative** ['pælɪˌetɪv] *adj & s* paliativo
**pallid** ['pælɪd] *adj* pálido
**pallium** ['pælɪəm] *s* (*pl:* **-ums** o **-a** [ə]) (anat., eccl. & hist.) palio; (eccl.) palia
**pall-mall** ['pɛl'mɛl] *s* mallo (*juego y terreno*)
**pallor** ['pælər] *s* palidez, palor
**palm** [pɑm] *s* palma (*de la mano*); palmo (*medida*); (bot.) palma (*árbol y hoja*); (fig.) palma; **to bear the palm** o **to carry off the palm** llevarse la palma; **to grease the palm of** (slang) untar la mano a; **to have an itching palm** (coll.) ser cicatero, ser pesetero; **to yield the palm to** reconocer por vencedor; *va* esconder en la mano; escamotear (*una carta*); **to palm something off on someone** encajarle una cosa a uno
**palmaceous** [pæl'meʃəs] *adj* (bot.) palmáceo
**palma Christi** ['pælmə 'krɪstaɪ] *s* (bot.) palmacristi
**palmary** ['pælmərɪ] *adj* principal, supremo
**palmate** ['pælmet] *adj* palmeado; (bot. & zool.) palmeado
**palmation** [pæl'meʃən] *s* disposición o estructura palmeada; forma o parte palmeada
**Palm Beach** *s* (trademark) palmiche (*tela*)
**palmer** ['pɑmər] *s* palmero (*peregrino de Tierra Santa*); peregrino; fullero, tahur
**palmer worm** *s* (ent.) polilla del manzano
**palmetto** [pæl'mɛto] *s* (*pl:* **-tos** o **-toes**) (bot.) palmito
**palmiped** ['pælmɪpɛd] *adj & s* (zool.) palmípedo
**palmist** ['pɑmɪst] *s* quiromántico
**palmistry** ['pɑmɪstrɪ] *s* quiromancía
**palmitate** ['pælmɪtet] *s* (chem.) palmitato
**palm leaf** *s* palma, hoja de la palmera
**palm oil** *s* aceite de palma; (slang) propina; (slang) soborno

**Palm Sunday** *s* día de ramos, domingo de ramos
**palm wax** *s* cera de palma
**palmy** ['pɑmɪ] *adj* (*comp:* **-ier;** *super:* **-iest**) abundante en palmeras; sombreado por palmeras; floreciente, próspero, glorioso
**palp** [pælp] *s* palpo
**palpability** [,pælpə'bɪlɪtɪ] *s* palpabilidad
**palpable** ['pælpəbəl] *adj* palpable
**palpate** ['pælpet] *va* (med.) palpar
**palpation** [pæl'peʃən] *s* (med.) palpación
**palpebral** ['pælpɪbrəl] *adj* palpebral
**palpitate** ['pælpɪtet] *vn* palpitar
**palpitation** [,pælpɪ'teʃən] *s* palpitación
**palpus** ['pælpəs] *s* (*pl:* **-pi** [paɪ]) palpo
**palsy** ['pɔlzɪ] *s* (*pl:* **-sies**) (path.) perlesía; (*pret & pp:* **-sied**) *va* paralizar
**palter** ['pɔltər] *vn* hablar u obrar sin sinceridad; regatear; estafar, petardear
**paltry** ['pɔltrɪ] *adj* (*comp:* **-trier;** *super:* **-triest**) vil, ruin, mezquino, baladí
**paly** ['pelɪ] *adj* (poet.) algo pálido; (her.) palado
**Pamela** ['pæmələ] *s* Pamela
**pampa** ['pæmpə] *s* pampa; **the Pampas** La Pampa
**pampas grass** *s* (bot.) carrizo de las pampas
**pampean** [pæm'piən] *adj & s* pampero
**pamper** ['pæmpər] *va* mimar, consentir
**pamphlet** ['pæmflɪt] *s* folleto
**pamphleteer** [,pæmflɪ'tɪr] *s* folletista; *vn* publicar folletos, lanzar folletos
**Pamphylia** [pæm'fɪlɪə] *s* Panfilia
**pan** [pæn] *s* cacerola, cazuela, sartén; caldera, perol; cubeta (*usada, p.ej., en la fotografía*); cazoleta (*de arma de fuego*); (min.) gamella; capa arcillosa y dura debajo de terreno blando; (*cap.*) *s* (myth.) Pan; (*l.c.*) (*pret & pp:* **panned;** *ger:* **panning**) *va* cocer, freír; separar (*el oro*) en la gamella; (coll.) criticar ásperamente; *vn* separar el oro en la gamella; dar oro; **to pan out** (coll.) resultar; **to pan out well** (coll.) tener éxito, dar buen resultado
**panacea** [,pænə'siə] *s* panacea
**panache** [pə'næʃ] o [pə'nɑʃ] *s* penacho
**Panama** ['pænəmɑ] o [,pænə'mɑ] *s* Panamá; (*l.c.*) *s* panamá (*sombrero*)
**Panama Canal** *s* canal de Panamá
**Panama Canal Zone** *s* Zona del Canal
**Panama hat** *s* panamá
**Panamanian** [,pænə'menɪən] o [,pænə'mɑnɪən] *adj & s* panameño
**Pan-American** [,pænə'mɛrɪkən] *adj* panamericano
**Pan-Americanism** [,pænə'mɛrɪkənɪzəm] *s* panamericanismo
**Pan American Union** *s* Unión panamericana
**Pan-Arabian** [,pænə'rebɪən] *adj* panarábico
**Panathenaea** [,pænæθɪ'niə] *spl* (hist.) Panateneas
**pancake** ['pæn,kek] *s* panqueque, hojuela; (aer.) aterrizaje hecho de plano; *vn* (aer.) aterrizar de plano, desplomarse
**Pancake Day** *s* martes de Carnaval
**pancake landing** *s* (aer.) aterrizaje en desplome, aterrizaje aplastado
**Pancake Tuesday** *s* var. de **Pancake Day**
**panchromatic** [,pænkro'mætɪk] *adj* pancromático
**pancreas** ['pænkrɪəs] *s* (anat.) páncreas
**pancreatic** [,pænkrɪ'ætɪk] *adj* pancreático
**pancreatic juice** *s* (physiol.) jugo pancreático
**pancreatin** ['pænkrɪətɪn] o ['pæŋkrɪətɪn] *s* (biochem.) pancreatina
**panda** ['pændə] *s* (zool.) panda
**pandanaceous** [,pændə'neʃəs] *adj* (bot.) pandanáceo
**pandect** ['pændɛkt] *s* digesto; **pandects** *spl* recopilación (*de leyes*); **Pandects** *spl* Pandectas
**pandemic** [pæn'dɛmɪk] *adj* pandémico; *s* pandemia
**pandemonium** [,pændɪ'monɪəm] *s* pandemónium o pandemonio; alboroto diabólico, gresca de todos los demonios
**pander** ['pændər] *s* alcahuete; *vn* alcahuetear; **to pander to** gratificar
**Pandora** [pæn'dorə] *s* (myth.) Pandora
**Pandora's box** *s* caja de Pandora
**pandowdy** [pæn'daudɪ] *s* (*pl:* **-dies**) pastel de manzana hecho en vasija honda
**pane** [pen] *s* cristal, vidrio, hoja de vidrio
**panegyric** [,pænɪ'dʒɪrɪk] *s* panegírico
**panegyrical** [,pænɪ'dʒɪrɪkəl] *adj* panegírico
**panegyrist** [,pænɪ'dʒɪrɪst] o ['pænɪ,dʒɪrɪst] *s* panegirista
**panegyrize** ['pænɪdʒɪraɪz] *va* panegirizar
**panel** ['pænəl] *s* panel, entrepaño, cuarterón; tabla (*cuadro pintado en una tabla*); pequeño grupo de personas en discusión cara al público; (aut. & elec.) tablero, panel; (law) lista (*de personas que pueden servir como jurados o para algún otro fin*); (mach.) tablero, plancha; (sew.) paño; (*pret & pp:* **-eled** o **-elled;** *ger:* **-eling** o **-elling**) *va* adornar con cuarterones, labrar en cuarterones; artesonar (*un techo o bóveda*)
**panelboard** ['pænəl,bord] *s* cuadro de mandos
**panel discussion** *s* coloquio ante un auditorio
**paneling** o **panelling** ['pænəlɪŋ] *s* entrepaños, cuarterones; artesonado (*de un techo o bóveda*)
**panelist** ['pænəlɪst] *s* coloquiante ante un auditorio
**panel lights** *spl* (aut.) luces del tablero
**panentheism** [,pæn'ɛnθiɪzəm] *s* (theol.) panenteísmo
**pane of glass** *s* hoja de vidrio
**panetella** [[pænə'tɛlə] *s* panetela (*cigarro*)
**pang** [pæŋ] *s* dolor agudo; punzada (*de remordimiento*); agonía (*de la muerte*)
**pangenesis** [pæn'dʒɛnɪsɪs] *s* (biol.) pangénesis
**Pan-German** [,pæn'dʒʌrmən] *adj* pangermanista; *s* (*pl:* **-mans**) pangermanista
**Pan-Germanic** [,pændʒər'mænɪk] *adj* pangermanista
**Pan-Germanism** [,pæn'dʒʌrmənɪzəm] *s* pangermanismo
**pangolin** [pæŋ'golɪn] *s* (zool.) pangolín
**panhandle** ['pæn,hændəl] *s* mango de sartén; (U.S.A.) faja angosta de territorio de un estado que entra en el de otro; *vn* (slang) mendigar, pedir limosna
**panhandler** ['pæn,hændlər] *s* (slang) mendigo, pordiosero
**Panhellenic** o **panhellenic** [,pænhɛ'lɛnɪk] o [,pænhɛ'linɪk] *adj* panhelénico
**Panhellenism** [pæn'hɛlənɪzəm] *s* panhelenismo
**panic** ['pænɪk] *adj & s* pánico; (*pret & pp:* **-icked;** *ger:* **-icking**) *va* sobrecoger de pánico; *vn* sobrecogerse de pánico
**panic grass** *s* (bot.) mijo común
**panicky** ['pænɪkɪ] *adj* pánico; asustadizo
**panicle** ['pænɪkəl] *s* (bot.) panícula, panoja
**panicled** ['pænɪkəld] *adj* (bot.) apanojado
**panic-stricken** ['pænɪk,strɪkən] *adj* muerto de miedo, paralizado de pánico, sobrecogido de terror
**paniculate** [pə'nɪkjəlet] *adj* (bot.) paniculado
**panification** [,pænɪfɪ'keʃən] *s* panificación
**Pan-Islamic** [,pænɪs'læmɪk] o [,pænɪs'lɑmɪk] *adj* panislamista
**Pan-Islamism** [,pæn'ɪsləmɪzəm] *s* panislamismo
**Pan-Islamist** [,pæn'ɪsləmɪst] *s* panislamista
**panjandrum** [pæn'dʒændrəm] *s* (hum.) persona de campanillas; (hum.) ceremonia exagerada
**pannicular** [pə'nɪkjələr] *adj* panicular
**panniculus** [pə'nɪkjələs] *s* (anat.) panículo
**pannier** ['pænɪər] *s* serón, cuévano; tontillo
**pannikin** ['pænɪkɪn] *s* cacillo; cubilete, copa
**panocha** [pə'notʃə] *s* panocha (*azúcar, melcocha*)
**panoplied** ['pænəplɪd] *adj* armado de pies a cabeza
**panoply** ['pænəplɪ] *s* (*pl:* **-plies**) panoplia; traje ceremonial
**panorama** [,pænə'ræmə] o [,pænə'rɑmə] s panorama
**panoramic** [,pænə'ræmɪk] *adj* panorámico
**panoramically** [,pænə'ræmɪkəlɪ] *adv* panorámicamente
**Panpipe** ['pæn,paɪp] *s* (mus.) flauta de Pan
**Pan-Slav** [,pæn'slɑv] o **Pan-Slavic** [,pæn'slɑvɪk] *adj* paneslavista
**Pan-Slavism** [,pæn'slɑvɪzəm] *s* paneslavismo
**Pan's pipes** *s* (mus.) flauta de Pan
**pansy** ['pænzɪ] *s* (*pl:* **-sies**) (bot.) pensamiento
**pant** [pænt] *s* jadeo; palpitación; resoplido (*de

*una máquina de vapor*); **pants** *spl* (coll.) pantalones; **to wear the pants** (coll.) calzarse o ponerse los pantalones; *vn* jadear: palpitar; **to pant for** anhelar, desear con vehemencia
**Pantagruelian** [ˌpæntəgruˈɛlɪən] o **Pantagruelic** [ˌpæntəgruˈɛlɪk] *adj* pantagruélico
**pantalets** o **pantalettes** [ˌpæntəˈlɛts] *spl* pantalones de mujer que asomaban debajo de la falda
**pantaloon** [ˌpæntəˈlun] *s* bufón, gracioso; **pantaloons** *spl* pantalones
**pantechnicon** [pænˈtɛknɪkən] *s* (Brit.) camión de mudanzas; (Brit.) almacén o depósito de muebles
**pantheism** [ˈpænθiɪzəm] *s* panteísmo
**pantheist** [ˈpænθiɪst] *s* panteísta
**pantheistic** [ˌpænθiˈɪstɪk] *adj* panteístico
**pantheistically** [ˌpænθiˈɪstɪkəlɪ] *adv* según la doctrina del panteísmo
**pantheon** [ˈpænθɪɑn] o [pænˈθiən] *s* panteón
**panther** [ˈpænθər] *s* (zool.) pantera; (zool.) puma
**panties** [ˈpæntɪz] *spl* braguitas
**pantile** [ˈpænˌtaɪl] *s* teja romana, teja de cimacio; teja canalón
**pantograph** [ˈpæntəgræf] o [ˈpæntəgrɑf] *s* pantógrafo; (elec.) pantógrafo
**pantomime** [ˈpæntəmaɪm] *s* pantomima; *va* expresar o representar por arte pantomímico
**pantomimic** [ˌpæntəˈmɪmɪk] *adj* pantomímico
**pantomimist** [ˈpæntəˌmaɪmɪst] *s* pantomimo
**pantothenic** [ˌpæntəˈθɛnɪk] *adj* pantoténico
**pantothenic acid** *s* (biochem.) ácido pantoténico
**pantry** [ˈpæntrɪ] *s* (*pl:* **-tries**) despensa
**pantywaist** [ˈpæntɪˌwest] *s* (slang) alfeñique, santito; *adj* (slang) afeminado, aniñado
**panzer** [ˈpænzər] *adj* (mil.) armado, blindado
**pap** [pæp] *s* papilla o papas
**papa** [ˈpɑpə] o [pəˈpɑ] *s* papá
**papable** [ˈpepəbəl] *adj* papable
**papacy** [ˈpepəsɪ] *s* (*pl:* **-cies**) papado, pontificado
**papain** [pəˈpeɪn] o [ˈpepəɪn] *s* (biochem.) papaína
**papal** [ˈpepəl] *adj* papal
**papal nuncio** *s* nuncio, nuncio apostólico
**Papal States** *spl* Estados pontificios
**papaveraceous** [pəˌpævəˈreʃəs] *adj* (bot.) papaveráceo
**papaw** [ˈpɔpɔ] o [pəˈpɔ] *s* (bot.) asimina; (bot.) papayo; papaya (*fruto*)
**papaya** [pəˈpɑjə] *s* (bot.) papayo; papaya (*fruto*)
**paper** [ˈpepər] *s* papel; periódico; papel o paño (*p.ej., de agujas*); *va* empapelar
**paperback** [ˈpepərˌbæk] *s* libro en rústica
**paper blockade** *s* bloqueo en el papel
**paper-bound** [ˈpepərˌbaund] *adj* en rústica
**paper clip** *s* abrazadera para papeles, sujetapapeles
**paper cone** *s* cucurucho
**paper cup** *s* vaso de papel
**paper-cup dispenser** [ˈpepərˌkʌp] *s* portavasos de papel
**paper cutter** *s* cortapapeles; guillotina
**paper finger** *s* aprietapapeles (*de la máquina de escribir*)
**paper flower** *s* flor de mano, flor artificial
**paper hanger** *s* empapelador, papelista, pegador
**paper knife** *s* cortapapeles
**paper mill** *s* fábrica de papel
**paper money** *s* papel moneda
**paper mulberry** *s* (bot.) papelero
**paper nautilus** *s* (zool.) argonauta
**paper profits** *spl* ganancias no realizadas sobre valores no vendidos
**paper tape** *s* cinta perforada
**paperweight** [ˈpepərˌwet] *s* pisapapeles
**paper work** *s* preparación o comprobación de escritos (*archivos, avisos, exámenes de alumnos, etc.*)
**papery** [ˈpepərɪ] *adj* parecido al papel, fino o delgado como el papel
**papier-mâché** [ˈpepərməˈʃe] *s* cartón piedra; *adj* de cartón piedra
**papilionaceous** [pəˌpɪlɪəˈneʃəs] *adj* (bot.) papilionáceo
**papilla** [pəˈpɪlə] *s* (*pl:* **-lae** [li]) (anat. & bot.) papila
**papillary** [ˈpæpɪˌlɛrɪ] o [pəˈpɪlərɪ] *adj* papilar
**papilloma** [ˌpæpɪˈlomə] *s* (*pl:* **-mata** [mətə] o **-mas**) (path.) papiloma
**papillose** [ˈpæpɪlos] *adj* lleno de papilas
**papion** [ˈpepɪɑn] *s* (zool.) papión
**papist** [ˈpepɪst] *adj* & *s* (scornful) papista
**papistic** [peˈpɪstɪk] o [pəˈpɪstɪk] o **papistical** [peˈpɪstɪkəl] o [pəˈpɪstɪkəl] *adj* (scornful) papístico
**papistry** [ˈpepɪstrɪ] *s* (scornful) papismo
**pappus** [ˈpæpəs] *s* (*pl:* **-pi** [paɪ]) (bot.) papo, vilano
**pappy** [ˈpæpɪ] *adj* (*comp:* **-pier;** *super:* **-piest**) mollar, jugoso; *s* (*pl:* **-pies**) (slang) papá
**paprika** [pæˈprikə] o [ˈpæprɪkə] *s* pimentón
**Papua** [ˈpæpjuə] *s* la Papuasia
**Papuan** [ˈpæpjuən] *adj* & *s* papú
**papule** [ˈpæpjul] *s* (path.) pápula
**papulose** [ˈpæpjəlos] *adj* papuloso
**papyraceous** [ˌpæpɪˈreʃəs] *adj* papiráceo
**papyrus** [pəˈpaɪrəs] *s* (*pl:* **-ri** [raɪ]) (bot.) papiro; papiro (*lámina del tallo de esta planta; hoja de papiro escrita*)
**par.** abr. de **paragraph, parallel, parenthesis** y **parish**
**par** [pɑr] *adj* a la par; nominal; normal; *s* (com.) paridad; (com.) valor nominal; (golf) norma de perfección; **above par** (com.) sobre la par; (com.) con beneficio, con premio; **at par** (com.) a la par; **below par** o **under par** (com.) bajo la par; (com.) con pérdida, con quebranto; (coll.) indispuesto; **to be on a par with** correr parejas con
**parable** [ˈpærəbəl] *s* parábola
**parabola** [pəˈræbələ] *s* (geom.) parábola
**parabolic** [ˌpærəˈbɑlɪk] *adj* parabólico; (geom.) parabólico
**paraboloid** [pəˈræbəlɔɪd] *s* (geom.) paraboloide
**Paracelsus** [ˌpærəˈsɛlsəs] *s* Paracelso
**paracentesis** [ˌpærəsenˈtisɪs] *s* (surg.) paracentesis
**parachronism** [pæˈrækrənɪzəm] *s* paracronismo
**parachute** [ˈpærəʃut] *s* paracaídas; *vn* lanzarse en paracaídas; **to parachute to safety** salvarse en paracaídas
**parachute jump** *s* salto en paracaídas
**parachutist** [ˈpærəˌʃutɪst] *s* paracaidista
**Paraclete** [ˈpærəklit] *s* paráclito
**parade** [pəˈred] *s* desfile; paseo; ostentación; **parade rest** (mil.) en su lugar descanso; *va* ostentar, pasear (*p.ej., una bandera*); (mil.) convocar a una revista; *vn* desfilar, pasar por las calles; (mil.) formar en parada
**parade ground** *s* (mil.) plaza de armas
**paradichlorobenzene** [ˌpærədaɪˌkloroˈbɛnzin] *s* (chem.) paradiclorobenceno
**paradigm** [ˈpærədɪm] o [ˈpærədaɪm] *s* (gram. & fig.) paradigma
**paradise** [ˈpærədaɪs] *s* paraíso; (slang) paraíso (*en el teatro*); (hort.) manzano enano de San Juan o del paraíso
**paradisiacal** [ˌpærədɪˈsaɪəkəl] *adj* paradisíaco
**paradox** [ˈpærədɑks] *s* paradoja; persona o cosa incomprensibles
**paradoxical** [ˌpærəˈdɑksɪkəl] *adj* paradójico
**paraffin** [ˈpærəfɪn] o **paraffine** [ˈpærəfɪn] o [ˈpærəfin] *s* parafina
**paragoge** [ˌpærəˈgodʒɪ] *s* (gram.) paragoge
**paragogic** [ˌpærəˈgɑdʒɪk] *adj* paragógico
**paragon** [ˈpærəgɑn] *s* dechado; (print.) parangona
**paragraph** [ˈpærəgræf] o [ˈpærəgrɑf] *s* párrafo; suelto o gacetilla (*en un periódico*); *va* dividir en párrafos; escribir sueltos o gacetillas sobre
**paragrapher** [ˈpærəˌgræfər] o [ˈpærəˌgrɑfər] *s* gacetillero
**paragraphia** [ˌpærəˈgræfɪə] *s* (path.) paragrafía
**Paraguay** [ˈpærəgwe] o [ˈpærəgwaɪ] *s* el Paraguay
**Paraguayan** [ˌpærəˈgweən] o [ˌpærəˈgwaɪən] *adj* & *s* paraguayano o paraguayo
**Paraguay tea** *s* (bot.) hierba del Paraguay
**parakeet** [ˈpærəkit] *s* (orn.) perico, periquito

**paraldehyde** [pəˈrældɪhaɪd] *s* (chem.) paraldehido
**Paralipomena** [ˌpærəlɪˈpɑmɪnə] *spl* (Bib.) paralipómenos; (*l.c.*) *spl* cosas omitidas u olvidadas
**paralipsis** [ˌpærəˈlɪpsɪs] *s* (*pl:* **-ses** [siz]) (rhet.) paralipsis
**parallactic** [ˌpærəˈlæktɪk] *adj* paraláctico
**parallax** [ˈpærəlæks] *s* paralaje
**parallel** [ˈpærəlɛl] *adj* paralelo; (elec.) en paralelo; **to run parallel to** andar o ir en línea paralela a; *s* (geom. & fort.) paralela; (geom.) plano paralelo; (geog. & fig.) paralelo; **parallels** *spl* (print.) doble raya vertical; **in parallel** (elec.) en paralelo; (*pret & pp:* **-leled** o **-lelled;** *ger:* **-leling** o **-lelling**) *va* ser paralelo a; poner en dirección paralela; correr parejas con; hallar una cosa semejante a; paralelizar (*hacer la comparación entre*)
**parallel bars** *spl* (sport) paralelas, barras paralelas
**parallelepiped** [ˌpærəˌlɛlɪˈpaɪpɪd] o **parallelepipedon** [ˌpærəˌlɛlɪˈpɪpɪdɑn] *s* (geom.) paralelepípedo
**parallel-flow turbine** [ˈpærəlɛlˈflo] *s* turbina paralela
**parallelism** [ˈpærəlɛlɪzəm] *s* paralelismo
**parallel motion** *s* (mach.) mecanismo de movimiento paralelo; (mus.) movimiento paralelo
**parallelogram** [ˌpærəˈlɛləgræm] *s* (geom.) paralelogramo
**parallelogram law** *s* (mech.) regla del paralelogramo
**parallel postulate** *s* (math.) postulado de las paralelas
**paralogism** [pəˈrælədʒɪzəm] *s* paralogismo
**paralogize** [pəˈrælədʒaɪz] *vn* paralogizarse
**paralysis** [pəˈrælɪsɪs] *s* (*pl:* **-ses** [siz]) (path. & fig.) parálisis
**paralysis agitans** [ˈædʒɪtænz] *s* (path.) parálisis agitante
**paralytic** [ˌpærəˈlɪtɪk] *adj & s* paralítico
**paralyzation** [ˌpærəlɪˈzeʃən] *s* paralización
**paralyze** [ˈpærəlaɪz] *va* paralizar; (fig.) paralizar
**paramagnetic** [ˌpærəmægˈnɛtɪk] *adj* paramagnético
**paramagnetism** [ˌpærəˈmægnɪtɪzəm] *s* paramagnetismo
**paramecium** [ˌpærəˈmiʃɪəm] o [ˌpærəˈmisɪəm] *s* (*pl:* **-a** [ə]) (zool.) paramecio
**parameter** [pəˈræmɪtər] *s* (math.) parámetro
**paramount** [ˈpærəmaʊnt] *adj* capital, supremo, principalísimo
**paramour** [ˈpærəmʊr] *s* querido o querida
**paranoia** [ˌpærəˈnɔɪə] *s* (path.) paranoia
**paranoiac** [ˌpærəˈnɔɪæk] *adj & s* paranoico
**parapet** [ˈpærəpɛt] *s* parapeto; (fort.) parapeto
**paraphernalia** [ˌpærəfərˈnelɪə] *spl* bienes personales, trastos, atavíos; (law) bienes parafernales
**paraphrase** [ˈpærəfrez] *s* paráfrasis; *va* parafrasear
**paraphrast** [ˈpærəfræst] *s* parafraste
**paraphrastic** [ˌpærəˈfræstɪk] *adj* parafrástico
**paraphrastically** [ˌpærəˈfræstɪkəlɪ] *adv* parafrásticamente
**paraplegia** [ˌpærəˈplidʒɪə] *s* (path.) paraplejía
**paraplegic** [ˌpærəˈplɛdʒɪk] o [ˌpærəˈplidʒɪk] *adj & s* parapléjico
**parapsychology** [ˌpærəsaɪˈkɑlədʒɪ] *s* parapsicología
**parasang** [ˈpærəsæŋ] *s* parasanga
**parasceve** [ˈpærəsiv] *s* parasceve
**paraselene** [ˌpærəsɪˈlinɪ] *s* (*pl:* **-nae** [ni]) (meteor.) paraselene
**parasite** [ˈpærəsaɪt] *s* (biol. & fig.) parásito
**parasitic** [ˌpærəˈsɪtɪk] o **parasitical** [ˌpærəˈsɪtɪkəl] *adj* parasítico o parasitario
**parasiticide** [ˌpærəˈsɪtɪsaɪd] *adj & s* parasiticida
**parasitism** [ˈpærəˌsaɪtɪzəm] *s* parasitismo
**parasitological** [ˌpærəˌsaɪtəˈlɑdʒɪkəl] *adj* parasitológico
**parasitologist** [ˌpærəsaɪˈtɑlədʒɪst] *s* parasitólogo
**parasitology** [ˌpærəsaɪˈtɑlədʒɪ] *s* parasitología
**parasol** [ˈpærəsɔl] o [ˈpærəsɑl] *s* quitasol, parasol
**parasympathetic** [ˌpærəˌsɪmpəˈθɛtɪk] *adj & s* (anat. & physiol.) parasimpático
**parasynthesis** [ˌpærəˈsɪnθɪsɪs] *s* (gram.) parasíntesis
**parathyroid** [ˌpærəˈθaɪrɔɪd] *adj & s* (anat.) paratiroides
**parathyroid glands** *spl* (anat.) glándulas paratiroides
**paratrooper** [ˈpærəˌtrupər] *s* (mil.) paracaidista
**paratroops** [ˈpærətrups] *spl* (mil.) tropas paracaidistas
**paratyphoid** [ˌpærəˈtaɪfɔɪd] *adj* paratifoide
**paratyphoid fever** *s* (path.) fiebre paratifoidea
**parboil** [ˈpɑrbɔɪl] *va* sancochar; calentar con exceso
**parbuckle** [ˈpɑrˌbʌkəl] *s* tiravira
**Parcae** [ˈpɑrsi] *spl* (myth.) Parcas
**parcel** [ˈpɑrsəl] *s* paquete, lío, atado; solar, lote; hatajo (*p.ej., de embustes*); pandilla (*p.ej., de embusteros*); (*pret & pp:* **-celed** o **-celled;** *ger:* **-celing** o **-celling**) *va* empaquetar, embalar; parcelar (*el terreno*); **to parcel out** repartir
**parceling** o **parcelling** [ˈpɑrsəlɪŋ] *s* parcelación (*del terreno*); (naut.) entreforro, fajadura
**parcel post** *s* paquetes postales (*servicio*)
**parch** [pɑrtʃ] *va* tostar; abrasar; agostar (*las plantas*); *vn* tostarse; abrasarse, sufrir con el calor
**parcheesi** o **parchesi** [pɑrˈtʃizɪ] *s* parchesí
**parchment** [ˈpɑrtʃmənt] *s* pergamino; pergamino de imitación
**parchment paper** *s* papel pergamino
**pard** [pɑrd] *s* (slang) compadre, amigote; (archaic) pardo, leopardo
**pardi** o **pardie** [pɑrˈdi] *interj* (archaic) en verdad, por cierto
**pardon** [ˈpɑrdən] *s* perdón; indulto (*gracia concedida, p.ej., por el Estado*); **I beg your pardon** dispense Vd.; *va* perdonar, dispensar; **pardon me** dispense Vd.
**pardonable** [ˈpɑrdənəbəl] *adj* perdonable
**pardonably** [ˈpɑrdənəblɪ] *adv* disculpablemente
**pardon board** *s* junta de perdones
**pardoner** [ˈpɑrdənər] *s* perdonador; (eccl.) perdonador
**pare** [pɛr] *va* mondar (*fruta*); pelar (*patatas*); cortar (*callos, uñas, etc.*); despalmar (*la palma córnea de los animales*); adelgazar, sacar de espesor; reducir (*p.ej., gastos*)
**paregoric** [ˌpærɪˈgɑrɪk] o [ˌpærɪˈgɔrɪk] *adj* paregórico, calmante; *s* (pharm.) elixir paregórico, tintura compuesta de alcanfor
**paren.** abr. de **parenthesis**
**parenchyma** [pəˈrɛŋkɪmə] *s* (anat. & bot.) parénquima
**parenchymatous** [ˌpærɛŋˈkɪmətəs] *adj* parenquimatoso
**parent** [ˈpɛrənt] *s* padre o madre; autor, fuente, origen; **parents** *spl* padres (*padre y madre*); *adj* madre, principal
**parentage** [ˈpɛrəntɪdʒ] *s* paternidad o maternidad; abolengo, linaje
**parental** [pəˈrɛntəl] *adj* parental, de padre y madre
**parent company** *s* compañía matriz
**parenteral** [pæˈrɛntərəl] *adj* parenteral
**parenthesis** [pəˈrɛnθɪsɪs] *s* (*pl:* **-ses** [siz]) (gram. & fig.) paréntesis; **in parentheses** dentro de un paréntesis o entre paréntesis
**parenthesize** [pəˈrɛnθɪsaɪz] *va* poner entre paréntesis; insertar entre paréntesis; interrumpir (*un discurso*) con muchos paréntesis
**parenthetic** [ˌpærənˈθɛtɪk] o **parenthetical** [ˌpærənˈθɛtɪkəl] *adj* parentético; explicativo; digresivo
**parenthetically** [ˌpærənˈθɛtɪkəlɪ] *adv* por paréntesis
**parenthood** [ˈpɛrənthʊd] *s* paternidad o maternidad
**paresis** [pəˈrisɪs] o [ˈpærɪsɪs] *s* (path.) paresia o paresis
**paretic** [pəˈrɛtɪk] o [pəˈritɪk] *adj & s* parético

**par excellence** [pɑr 'ɛksələns] o [pɑr ɛksɛ-'lɑ̃s] (Fr.) por excelencia
**parfait** [pɑr'fe] *s* helado hecho sin agitación, de crema batida muy dulce
**parget** ['pɑrdʒɪt] *s* enlucido; molduras de yeso; *va* enlucir; adornar con molduras de yeso
**parheliacal** [,pɑrhɪ'laɪəkəl] *adj* parhélico
**parheliacal ring** *s* (meteor.) círculo parhélico
**parhelic** [pɑr'hilɪk] *adj* var. de **parheliacal**
**parhelic circle** *s* var. de **parheliacal ring**
**parhelion** [pɑr'hilɪən] *s* (*pl:* **-a** [ə]) (meteor.) parhelio
**pariah** [pə'raɪə] o ['pɑrɪə] *s* paria
**Parian** ['pɛrɪən] *adj* pario; *s* pario; porcelana paria
**parietal** [pə'raɪətəl] *adj* parietal; interior; (anat., bot. & zool.) parietal; *s* (anat.) parietal
**pari-mutuel** ['pærɪ'mjutʃʊəl] *s* apuesta mutua; totalizador, aparato para registro de apuestas mutuas
**paring** ['pɛrɪŋ] *s* peladura, raspadura; cáscara; **parings** *spl* espalmadura, despalmadura (*del casco de los animales*)
**paring knife** *s* cuchillo para mondar
**paripinnate** [,pærɪ'pɪnet] *adj* (bot.) paripinado
**Paris** ['pærɪs] *s* París; (myth.) Paris
**Paris green** *s* verde de París, verde de Schweinfurt
**parish** ['pærɪʃ] *s* parroquia; jurisdicción o subdivisión (*del estado de Luisiana, EE.UU.*); (Brit.) distrito civil; *adj* parroquial
**parishioner** [pə'rɪʃənər] *s* parroquiano, feligrés
**Parisian** [pə'rɪʒən] *adj & s* parisiense
**parisyllabic** [,pærɪsɪ'læbɪk] *adj* parisilábico o parisílabo
**parity** ['pærɪtɪ] *s* paridad
**park** [pɑrk] *s* parque; (mil.) parque; (Brit.) parque (*destinado a las fieras*); *va* (aut.) estacionar (*p.ej., en la calle por poco tiempo*); (aut.) aparcar, parquear (*p.ej., en una estación de aparcamiento por un largo plazo*); (mil.) aparcar, parquear; (coll.) colocar, dejar; *vn* (aut.) estacionar; (aut.) aparcar, parquear
**parka** ['pɑrkə] *s* especie de zamarra de los esquimales; chaqueta de lana con capucha (*que llevan los esquiadores y otros deportistas*)
**Parker Kalon screw** ['pɑrkər 'kelɑn] *s* (trademark) tornillo Parker (*especie de tornillo que labra la rosca por sí mismo*)
**parking** ['pɑrkɪŋ] *s* terreno poblado de árboles y plantas; césped (*y a veces árboles*) plantado entre las dos vías de la carretera o por los dos lados de ella; (aut.) estacionamiento; (aut. & mil.) aparcamiento; **no parking** se prohibe estacionarse
**parking brake** *s* (aut.) freno de estacionamiento
**parking light** *s* (aut.) luz de estacionamiento, población o situación
**parking lot** *s* (aut.) parque, parque de estacionamiento
**parking meter** *s* (aut.) reloj de estacionamiento
**parking station** *s* (aut.) estación de aparcamiento
**parking ticket** *s* aviso de multa (*por estacionar un auto indebidamente*)
**Parkinson's disease** ['pɑrkɪnsənz] *s* (path.) enfermedad de Parkinson, parálisis agitante
**parkleaves** ['pɑrk,livz] *s* (bot.) todabuena
**parkway** ['pɑrk,we] *s* gran vía adornada con árboles
**parlance** ['pɑrləns] *s* lenguaje
**parley** ['pɑrlɪ] *s* parlamento; *vn* parlamentar
**parliament** ['pɑrlɪmənt] *s* parlamento
**parliamentarian** [,pɑrlɪmɛn'tɛrɪən] *s* parlamentario; (*cap.*) *s* (hist.) Parlamentario
**parliamentarism** [,pɑrlɪ'mɛntərɪzəm] *s* parlamentarismo
**parliamentary** [,pɑrlɪ'mɛntərɪ] *adj* parlamentario
**parlor** ['pɑrlər] *s* sala; parlatorio, locutorio; salón (*p. ej., de belleza*); *adj* de gabinete
**parlor car** *s* (rail.) coche-salón
**parlor games** *spl* diversiones de salón, juegos de sociedad
**parlous** ['pɑrləs] *adj* (archaic & dial.) peligroso; (archaic & dial.) terrible, enorme; (archaic & dial.) astuto; *adv* (archaic & dial.) enormemente, sumamente
**Parmenides** [pɑr'mɛnɪdiz] *s* Parménides
**Parmesan** [,pɑrmɪ'zæn] *adj* parmesano; *s* parmesano (*natural; queso*)
**Parmesan cheese** *s* queso parmesano
**Parnassian** [pɑr'næsɪən] *adj* parnasiano
**Parnassus** [pɑr'næsəs] *s* parnaso (*colección de poesías*); el Parnaso; **Mount Parnassus** el monte Parnaso; **to try to climb Parnassus** hacer pinos en poesía
**parochial** [pə'rokɪəl] *adj* parroquial; estrecho, limitado
**parochialism** [pə'rokɪəlɪzəm] *s* parroquialidad; estrechez de miras, intolerancia
**parochial school** *s* escuela parroquial
**parodist** ['pærədɪst] *s* parodista
**parody** ['pærədɪ] *s* (*pl:* **-dies**) parodia; (*pret & pp:* **-died**) *va* parodiar
**parole** [pə'rol] *s* palabra de honor; libertad bajo palabra, remisión condicional de la pena, régimen de libertad provisional; **on parole** bajo el régimen de libertad provisional; *va* dejar libre bajo palabra
**parolee** [pə,ro'li] *s* delincuente bajo el régimen de libertad vigilada
**paronomasia** [,pærənə'meʒɪə] *s* paronomasia
**paronym** ['pærənɪm] *s* parónimo
**paronymous** [pə'rɑnɪməs] *adj* parónimo
**paronymy** [pə'rɑnɪmɪ] *s* paronimia
**paroquet** ['pærəkɛt] *s* var. de **parakeet**
**parotid** [pə'rɑtɪd] *adj* (anat.) parotídeo; *s* (anat.) parótida
**parotitic** [,pærə'tɪtɪk] *adj* (path.) parotídeo
**paroxysm** ['pærəksɪzəm] *s* paroxismo; (path.) paroxismo
**paroxysmal** [,pærək'sɪzməl] *adj* paroxismal
**paroxytone** [pær'ɑksɪton] *adj & s* (phonet.) paroxítono
**parquet** [pɑr'ke] o [pɑr'kɛt] *s* entarimado; (theat.) platea; (*pret & pp:* **-queted** ['ked] o ['kɛtɪd]; *ger:* **-queting** ['keɪŋ] o ['kɛtɪŋ]) *va* entarimar
**parquet circle** *s* (theat.) anfiteatro debajo de la galería
**parquetry** ['pɑrkɪtrɪ] *s* mosaico de madera, obra de entarimado
**parr** [pɑr] *s* (ichth.) alevín, esguín
**parrakeet** ['pærəkit] *s* var. de **parakeet**
**parral** o **parrel** ['pærəl] *s* (naut.) racamenta o racamento
**parricidal** [,pærɪ'saɪdəl] *adj* parricida
**parricide** ['pærɪsaɪd] *s* parricidio (*acción*); parricida (*persona*)
**parrot** ['pærət] *s* (orn.) papagayo, loro; (fig.) papagayo; *va* repetir o imitar como loro
**parrot disease** o **parrot fever** *s* (path.) psitacosis
**parrot fish** *s* (ichth.) pez-papagayo
**parry** ['pærɪ] *s* (*pl:* **-ries**) parada, quite; (fig.) defensa; (*pret & pp:* **-ried**) *va* parar; (fig.) defenderse de
**parry of** o **in carte** o **quarte** [kɑrt] *s* (fencing) parada en cuarta
**parry of** o **in prime** *s* (fencing) parada en primera
**parry of** o **in seconde** [sɪ'kɑnd] *s* (fencing) parada en segunda
**parry of** o **in tierce** *s* (fencing) parada en tercera
**parse** [pɑrs] *va* analizar (*una oración*) gramaticalmente; describir (*una palabra*) gramaticalmente
**Parsee** o **Parsi** ['pɑrsi] *s* parsi
**Parseeism** ['pɑrsiɪzəm] *s* parsismo
**Parsic** ['pɑrsɪk] *adj* parsi
**parsimonious** [,pɑrsɪ'monɪəs] *adj* parsimonioso
**parsimony** ['pɑrsɪ,monɪ] *s* parsimonia
**parsley** ['pɑrslɪ] *s* (bot.) perejil (*planta y hojas*)
**parsnip** ['pɑrsnɪp] *s* (bot.) chirivía (*planta y raíz*)
**parson** ['pɑrsən] *s* cura, párroco; clérigo; pastor protestante
**parsonage** ['pɑrsənɪdʒ] *s* rectoría
**part.** abr. de **participle** y **particular**
**part** [pɑrt] *s* parte; pieza (*de una máquina*); (theat. & mus.) parte; raya (*en los cabellos*); **parts** *spl* partes, prendas, dotes; partes, partes

vergonzosas; **foreign parts** países extranjeros; **for my (his) part** por mi (su) parte; **for the most part** por lo general, por la mayor parte; **in good part** en buena parte (*sin ofenderse*); **in part** en parte; **on the part of** de la parte de; **to do one's part** cumplir con su obligación; **to look the part** vestir el cargo; **to take part in** tomar parte en; **to take the part of** tomar el partido de, defender; desempeñar el papel de; **part and parcel** parte esencial, elemento esencial, parte inseparable; *va* dividir, partir, separar; **to part company** separarse; **to part the hair** hacerse la raya; *vn* separarse; **to part from** separarse de, despedirse de; **to part with** deshacerse de, abandonar; despedirse de; *adj* parcial; *adv* parte, en parte

**partake** [pɑr'tek] (*pret:* **-took;** *pp:* **-taken**) *va* compartir; comer; beber; *vn* participar; **to partake in** participar en; **to partake of** participar de; tener algo de; comer; beber; **will you partake?** ¿gusta Vd.?

**parterre** [pɑr'tɛr] *s* parterre (*de jardín*); (theat.) anfiteatro debajo de la galería

**parthenogenesis** [,pɑrθɪno'dʒɛnɪsɪs] *s* (biol.) partenogénesis

**parthenogenetic** [,pɑrθɪnodʒɪ'nɛtɪk] *adj* partenogenético

**Parthenon** ['pɑrθɪnɑn] *s* Partenón

**Parthia** ['pɑrθɪə] *s* Partia

**Parthian** ['pɑrθɪən] *adj & s* parto

**Parthian shot** *s* la flecha del parto

**partial** ['pɑrʃəl] *adj* parcial; aficionado

**partial eclipse** *s* (astr.) eclipse parcial

**partiality** [,pɑrʃɪ'ælɪtɪ] *s* (*pl:* **-ties**) parcialidad; afición

**partially** ['pɑrʃəlɪ] *adv* parcialmente

**participant** [pɑr'tɪsɪpənt] *adj & s* partícipe

**participate** [pɑr'tɪsɪpet] *vn* participar; **to participate in** participar en

**participation** [pɑr,tɪsɪ'peʃən] *s* participación

**participator** [pɑr'tɪsɪ,petər] *s* partícipe

**participial** [,pɑrtɪ'sɪpɪəl] *adj* participial

**participially** [,pɑrtɪ'sɪpɪəlɪ] *adv* a modo de participio

**participle** ['pɑrtɪsɪpəl] *s* (gram.) participio

**particle** ['pɑrtɪkəl] *s* partícula; (eccl. & gram.) partícula; (chem. & phys.) corpúsculo, partícula

**parti-colored** ['pɑrtɪ,kʌlərd] *adj* abigarrado, jaspeado; (fig.) diversificado, variado

**particular** [pər'tɪkjələr] *adj* particular; difícil, exigente, quisquilloso; esmerado; minucioso, detallado; **that particular book** ese libro y no otro; *s* particular (*punto, asunto*); **in particular** en particular

**particularity** [pər,tɪkjə'lærɪtɪ] *s* (*pl:* **-ties**) particularidad; quisquillosidad; esmero; minuciosidad

**particularization** [pər,tɪkjələrɪ'zeʃən] *s* particularización

**particularize** [pər'tɪkjələraɪz] *va & vn* particularizar

**particularly** [pər'tɪkjələrlɪ] *adv* particularmente; minuciosamente, detalladamente

**partile** ['pɑrtɪl] o ['pɑrtaɪl] *adj* (astrol.) partil

**parting** ['pɑrtɪŋ] *s* partida; separación, punto de separación; **to come to the parting of the ways** llegar al momento de separarse, no poder permanecer más tiempo asociados; *adj* de despedida; que declina (*dícese del día*)

**parting strip** *s* (carp.) listón separador; faja central o divisora (*del camino*)

**partisan** ['pɑrtɪzən] *adj & s* partidario, partidista; (mil.) partisano

**partisanship** ['pɑrtɪzənʃɪp] *s* parcialidad, partidismo

**partition** [pɑr'tɪʃən] *s* partición, distribución; división; parte, porción; tabique; *va* repartir; dividir en cuartos, aposentos, etc.; tabicar

**partitive** ['pɑrtɪtɪv] *adj* partitivo; (gram.) partitivo; *s* (gram.) palabra partitiva, caso partitivo

**partizan** ['pɑrtɪzən] *adj & s* var. de **partisan**

**partner** ['pɑrtnər] *s* compañero; cónyuge (*marido o mujer*); pareja (*compañero o compañera en los bailes*); (com.) socio

**partnership** ['pɑrtnərʃɪp] *s* asociación; consorcio, vida en común; (com.) sociedad, asociación comercial

**part of speech** *s* (gram.) parte de la oración, parte del discurso

**partook** [pɑr'tʊk] *pret de* **partake**

**part owner** *s* condueño

**partridge** ['pɑrtrɪdʒ] *s* (orn.) perdiz; (orn.) perdiz pardilla; (orn.) perdiz blanca; (orn.) colín de Virginia; (orn.) bonasa americana

**partridgeberry** ['pɑrtrɪdʒ,bɛrɪ] *s* (*pl:* **-ries**) (bot.) planta rubiácea norteamericana (*Mitchella repens*); (bot.) gaulteria del Canadá

**part-time** ['pɑrt,taɪm] *adj* por horas, parcial

**parturient** [pɑr'tjʊrɪənt] o [pɑr'tʊrɪənt] *adj* parturiente; prolífico, lleno (*p.ej., de ideas*)

**parturition** [,pɑrtjʊ'rɪʃən] o [,pɑrtʃʊ'rɪʃən] *s* parturición

**part way** *adv* en parte; parte de la distancia

**party** ['pɑrtɪ] *s* (*pl:* **-ties**) *s* convite, reunión, fiesta, tertulia, recepción; partida (*de campo, caza, pesca, etc.; de gente armada*); grupo; (pol.) partido; parte, cómplice, interesado; (law) parte; (coll.) persona, individuo; **to be a party to** tener parte en, estar interesado en; **to join the party** agregarse a la partida; afiliarse al partido; *adj* de partido; de gala

**party boss** *s* jefe de partido (comunista)

**party-colored** ['pɑrtɪ,kʌlərd] *adj* var. de **parti-colored**

**party girl** *s* chica de vida alegre

**party-goer** ['pɑrtɪ,goər] *s* tertuliano; fiestero

**party line** *s* linde o lindero (*entre dos inmuebles*); (telp.) línea compartida; línea del partido (*política del partido comunista*)

**party liner** *s* secuaz del partido comunista

**party politics** *ssg* política de partido

**party wall** *s* medianería, pared medianera

**party wire** *s* (telp.) línea compartida

**par value** *s* (com.) valor nominal, valor a la par

**parvenu** ['pɑrvənju] o ['pɑrvənu] *adj & s* advenedizo

**paschal** ['pæskəl] *adj* pascual

**paschal candle** *s* (eccl.) cirio pascual

**paschal lamb** *s* cordero pascual

**pasha** [pə'ʃɑ] o ['pæʃə] *s* bajá

**pasqueflower** ['pæsk,flaʊər] *s* (bot.) pulsatila

**pasquinade** [,pæskwɪ'ned] *s* pasquín; *va* pasquinar

**pass.** abr. de **passenger** y **passive**

**pass** [pæs] o [pɑs] *s* paso; pase (*permiso; billete gratuito; movimiento de las manos en el mesmerismo*); aprobación (*en un examen*); nota de aprobado ‖ (*pret:* **passed;** *pp:* **passed** o **past**) *va* pasar; pasar de largo (*una luz roja*); aprobar (*un proyecto de ley; un examen; a un alumno*); ser aprobado en (*un examen*); dejar atrás; cruzarse con; expresar (*una opinión*); pronunciar (*una sentencia*); dar (*la palabra*); dejar sin protestar; no pagar (*un dividendo*); evacuar; **to pass along** o **around** pasar de uno a otro; **to pass by** no fijarse en, pasar por alto, no hacer caso de; **to pass each other** cruzarse; **to pass off** colar, pasar, hacer aceptar (*p.ej., moneda falsa*); disimular (*p.ej., una ofensa con una risa*); **to pass on** pasar, transmitir; **to pass out** distribuir; **to pass over** omitir, pasar por alto; excusar; desdeñar; dejar sin protestar; postergar (*a un empleado*); **to pass over in silence** pasar en silencio; **to pass through** pasar por, hacer pasar por ‖ *vn* pasar; pasarse (*introducirse*); aprobar; **to bring to pass** llevar a cabo; **to come to pass** suceder; **to let pass** no hacer caso de; **to pass along** pasar de largo; pasar por (*p.ej., la calle*); **to pass as** pasar por; **to pass away** pasar; **to pass beyond** pasar de, ir más allá de; **to pass by** pasar, pasar de largo; pasar cerca de; **to pass for** pasar por; **to pass off** pasar (*una enfermedad, una tempestad, etc.*); tener lugar; **to pass on** pasar; formar juicio sobre; **to pass out** salir; (slang) desmayarse; **to pass over** atravesar, pasar por; **to pass over to** pasarse a (*p.ej., el enemigo*); **to pass through** atravesar, pasar por

**passable** ['pæsəbəl] o ['pɑsəbəl] *adj* pasadero; corriente (*moneda*); promulgable (*ley*)

**passably** ['pæsəblɪ] o ['pɑsəblɪ] *adv* pasaderamente

**passacaglia** [,pɑsɑ'kɑljɑ] *s* (mus.) pasacalle

**passage** ['pæsɪdʒ] *s* paso, pasaje; transcurso (*del tiempo*); lance, encuentro personal; intercambio (*p.ej., de confidencias*); evacuación (*del vientre*); (mus.) pasaje
**passage at** u **of arms** *s* combate, lucha
**passageway** ['pæsɪdʒ,we] *s* pasillo, pasadizo; callejón, pasaje
**passant** ['pæsənt] *adj* (her.) pasante
**passbook** ['pæs,bʊk] o ['pɑs,bʊk] *s* cartilla, libreta de banco
**passementerie** [pæs'mɛntrɪ] *s* pasamanería
**passenger** ['pæsəndʒər] *s* pasajero
**passenger car** *s* (rail.) coche de viajeros; (aut.) coche de paseo o de turismo
**passenger engine** *s* (rail.) locomotora de viajeros
**passenger miles** *spl* (rail. & aer.) millas-pasajeros, pasajeros-milla
**passenger pigeon** *s* (orn.) paloma emigrante
**passe partout** [,pæs pɑr'tu] *s* paspartú, marco de vidrio y cartón; papel engomado que sirve para pegar el vidrio al cartón; llave maestra
**passer-by** ['pæsər'baɪ] o ['pɑsər'baɪ] *s* (*pl:* **passers-by**) transeúnte
**passifloraceous** [,pæsɪflo'reʃəs] *adj* (bot.) pasifloráceo
**passing** ['pæsɪŋ] o ['pɑsɪŋ] *adj* pasajero; corriente; de aprobado; *s* paso (*acción de pasar; trance de la muerte*); aprobación (*en un examen*); **in passing** de paso, al pasar; *adv* (archaic) muy, sumamente
**passing bell** *s* toque de difuntos
**passion** ['pæʃən] *s* pasión; (*cap.*) *s* (rel. & f.a.) Pasión; **to have a passion for** tener pasión por
**passional** ['pæʃənəl] *adj* pasional
**passionate** ['pæʃənɪt] *adj* apasionado; ardiente, vehemente; colérico
**passionflower** ['pæʃən,flaʊər] *s* (bot.) pasionaria (*planta*); granadilla (*flor*)
**passionfruit** ['pæʃən,frut] *s* granadilla
**passionless** ['pæʃənlɪs] *adj* sin pasión, frío
**Passion Play** *s* drama de la Pasión
**Passion Sunday** *s* domingo de lázaro o de pasión
**Passion Week** *s* semana de pasión
**passive** ['pæsɪv] *adj* pasivo; (gram.) pasivo; *s* (gram.) voz pasiva, verbo pasivo, construcción pasiva
**passive immunity** *s* (immun.) inmunidad pasiva
**passively** ['pæsɪvlɪ] *adv* pasivamente; (gram.) pasivamente
**passive resistance** *s* resistencia pasiva
**passive voice** *s* (gram.) voz pasiva
**passivity** [pæ'sɪvɪtɪ] *s* pasividad
**passkey** ['pæs,ki] o ['pɑs,ki] *s* llave de paso; llavín
**Passover** ['pæs,ovər] o ['pɑs,ovər] *s* pascua (*de los hebreos*)
**passport** ['pæs,port] o ['pɑs,port] *s* pasaporte; (fig.) pasaporte
**password** ['pæs,wʌrd] o ['pɑs,wʌrd] *s* santo y seña
**past** [pæst] o [pɑst] *adj* pasado; último; que fué, p.ej., **past president** presidente que fué; acabado, concluído; (gram.) pasado; **he has been here for some years past** está aquí desde hace algunos años; *adv* más allá; por delante; *prep* más allá de; más de; por delante de; fuera de; después de, p.ej., **past two o'clock** después de las dos; **past belief** increíble; **past cure** incurable; **past hope** sin esperanza; **past recovery** incurable, sin remedio; *s* pasado; (gram.) pasado; *pp de* **pass**
**past absolute** *s* (gram.) pretérito indefinido (*pasado absoluto*)
**paste** [pest] *s* pasta (*masa blanda para hacer pasteles, etc.*); engrudo; (mineral. & ceramics) pasta; *va* engrudar, pegar con engrudo; (slang) pegar (*golpear*); **to paste together** juntar con engrudo
**pasteboard** ['pest,bord] *s* cartón; (slang) naipe
**pastel** [pæs'tɛl] o ['pæstɛl] *s* pastel (*lápiz*); pastel, pintura al pastel; matiz suave de un color; ensayo breve; *adj* claro, suave (*matiz*)
**pastelist** ['pæstɛlɪst] o [pæs'tɛlɪst] *s* pastelista
**paster** ['pestər] *s* engrudador; papel engomado
**pastern** ['pæstərn] *s* cuartilla
**pasteurization** [,pæstərɪ'zeʃən] *s* pasterización
**pasteurize** ['pæstəraɪz] *va* pasterizar
**pasteurized milk** *s* leche pasterizada
**pastil** ['pæstɪl] o **pastille** [pæs'til] *s* pastilla; pastel (*lápiz; pasta de que se forman los pasteles*)
**pastime** ['pæs,taɪm] o ['pɑs,taɪm] *s* pasatiempo
**past master** *s* ex maestre, maestre que fué (*de una logia*); maestro sobresaliente, experto
**pastor** ['pæstər] o ['pɑstər] *s* pastor (*eclesiástico*)
**pastoral** ['pæstərəl] o ['pɑstərəl] *adj* pastoral; *s* (eccl. & mus.) pastoral; (lit.) pastoral (*drama*); (lit.) pastorela (*composición lírica*)
**pastorale** [,pæstə'rɑlɪ] *s* (*pl:* **-li** [li] o **-les**) (mus.) pastoral
**pastorally** ['pæstərəlɪ] o ['pɑstərəlɪ] *adv* pastoralmente, pastorilmente
**pastorate** ['pæstərɪt] o ['pɑstərɪt] *s* rectorado, curato; clero, pastores
**pastose** [pæs'tos] o ['pæstos] *adj* (paint.) pastoso
**pastourelle** [,pɑs,tʊ'rɛl] *s* (lit.) pastorela
**past participle** *s* (gram.) participio pasivo o de pretérito
**past perfect** *s* (gram.) pluscuamperfecto
**pastry** ['pestrɪ] *s* (*pl:* **-tries**) pastelería
**pastry cook** *s* pastelero, repostero
**pastry shop** *s* pastelería
**pastry tube** *s* carretilla, pintadera
**pasturage** ['pæstʃərɪdʒ] o ['pɑstʃərɪdʒ] *s* pasto (*pasturaje, pastura, pastoreo*)
**pasture** ['pæstʃər] o ['pɑstʃər] *s* pasto, pastura, dehesa; *va* apacentar, pastorear; pacer
**pasty** ['pestɪ] *adj* (*comp:* **-ier**; *super:* **-iest**) pastoso; flojo, fofo, pálido; ['pæstɪ] o ['pɑstɪ] *s* (*pl:* **-ies**) (Brit.) pastel de carne o pescado
**pat** [pæt] *adj* bueno, apto; *adv* a propósito; firme; **to have** o **to know pat** (coll.) saber al dedillo; **to stand pat** (coll.) mantenerse firme; *s* golpecito, palmadita; ruido de pasos ligeros; pastelillo (*p.ej., de mantequilla*); (*cap.*) *s* nombre abreviado de **Patricia;** (*l.c.*) (*pret & pp:* **patted;** *ger:* **patting**) *va* dar golpecitos a, dar palmaditas a; formar a golpecitos de la mano; acariciar con la mano; **to pat on the back** elogiar, cumplimentar; *vn* andar con un trotecito ligero
**patagium** [pə'tedʒɪəm] *s* (*pl:* **-a** [ə]) (zool.) patagio
**Patagonian** [,pætə'gonɪən] *adj* & *s* patagón
**patch** [pætʃ] *s* remiendo; parche; terreno, pedazo de terreno; mancha; lunar postizo; *va* remendar; **to patch up** componer (*una desavenencia*); arreglar o componer lo mejor posible (*una cosa descompuesta*); chafallar, hacer aprisa y mal
**patchouli** ['pætʃʊlɪ] o [pə'tʃulɪ] *s* (bot.) pachulí
**patch pocket** *s* bolsillo de parche
**patch test** *s* (med.) alergodiagnóstico con parches de lino o papel secante
**patchwork** ['pætʃ,wʌrk] *s* labor u obra de retacitos; chapucería; cuadros (*p.ej., de sembrados y bosques vistos desde un avión*)
**patchwork quilt** *s* colcha de retacitos
**patchy** ['pætʃɪ] *adj* (*comp:* **-ier**; *super:* **-iest**) muy remendado; desigual, irregular
**pate** [pet] *s* mollera
**pâté** [pɑ'te] *s* pastel de carne o pescado; pasta de carne
**pâté de foie gras** [də fwɑ 'grɑ] *s* pasta o pastelillo de hígado de ganso
**patella** [pə'tɛlə] *s* (*pl:* **-las** o **-lae** [li]) (anat.) rótula, patela; (archeol.) patela; (bot.) patélula; (zool.) patela
**patellar** [pə'tɛlər] *adj* (anat.) rotular, rotuliano, patelar
**patellar reflex** *s* (med.) reflejo rotuliano o patelar
**paten** ['pætən] *s* platillo u hoja de metal; (eccl.) patena
**patency** ['petənsɪ] o ['pætənsɪ] *s* evidencia, claridad
**patent** ['petənt] o ['pætənt] *adj* patente; abierto; ['pætənt] *adj* patentado; de patente; *s* patente, patente de invención; propiedad industrial; **to take out a patent** obtener una pa-

tente; **patent applied for** se ha solicitado patente; *va* patentar
**patent agent** ['pætənt] *s* agente de patentes
**patentee** [,pætən'ti] *s* poseedor de patente
**patent law** ['pætənt] *s* ley de patentes
**patent leather** ['pætənt] *s* charol
**patently** ['petəntlɪ] o ['pætəntlɪ] *adv* patentemente; abiertamente
**patent medicine** ['pætənt] *s* medicamento de patente, específico
**patent office** ['pætənt] *s* oficina de patentes
**patent rights** ['pætənt] *s* derechos de patente
**paterfamilias** [,petərfə'mɪlɪəs] *s* (*pl:* **patresfamilias** [,petrizfə'mɪlɪəs]) *s* cabeza de familia; (Roman law) páter familias
**paternal** [pə'tʌrnəl] *adj* paterno; paternal (*propio del cariño de padre*)
**paternalism** [pə'tʌrnəlɪzəm] *s* paternalismo
**paternalistic** [pə,tʌrnə'lɪstɪk] *adj* paternal
**paternity** [pə'tʌrnɪtɪ] *s* paternidad
**paternoster** ['petər'nɑstər] o ['pætər'nɑstər] *s* padrenuestro, paternóster
**path** [pæθ] o [pɑθ] *s* senda, sendero; curso, trayectoria; órbita (*de un astro*)
**pathetic** [pə'θɛtɪk] o **pathetical** [pə'θɛtɪkəl] *adj* patético
**pathetically** [pə'θɛtɪkəlɪ] *adv* patéticamente
**pathetic fallacy** *s* atribución de los sentimientos humanos a la naturaleza inanimada
**pathfinder** ['pæθ,faɪndər] o ['pɑθ,faɪndər] *s* baquiano; explorador
**pathless** ['pæθlɪs] o ['pɑθlɪs] *adj* sin caminos, no hollado, desconocido
**pathogenesis** [,pæθə'dʒɛnɪsɪs] o **pathogeny** [pə'θɑdʒɪnɪ] *s* patogénesis o patogenia
**pathogenic** [,pæθə'dʒɛnɪk] *adj* patógeno (*que produce enfermedades*); patogénico
**pathogenic organism** *s* (biol.) organismo patógeno
**pathologic** [,pæθə'lɑdʒɪk] o **pathological** [,pæθə'lɑdʒɪkəl] *adj* patológico
**pathologist** [pə'θɑlədʒɪst] *s* patólogo
**pathology** [pə'θɑlədʒɪ] *s* (*pl:* **-gies**) patología
**pathos** ['peθɑs] *s* patetismo
**pathway** ['pæθ,we] o ['pɑθ,we] *s* var. de **path**
**patience** ['peʃəns] *s* paciencia; solitario (*juego de naipes*); **to get out of patience** perder la paciencia
**patient** ['peʃənt] *adj* paciente; *s* paciente, enfermo; (gram.) paciente
**patin** ['pætən] *s* var. de **paten**
**patina** ['pætɪnə] *s* pátina
**patine** ['pætən] *s* var. de **paten**
**patio** ['pɑtɪo] *s* (*pl:* **-os**) patio; (metal.) patio, incorporadero
**patio process** *s* (metal.) método del patio
**patois** ['pætwɑ] *s* (*pl:* **patois** ['pætwɑz]) patuá o patués
**patriarch** ['petrɪɑrk] *s* patriarca
**patriarchal** [,petrɪ'ɑrkəl] *adj* patriarcal
**patriarchate** ['petrɪɑrkɪt] *s* patriarcado
**patriarchy** ['petrɪɑrkɪ] *s* (*pl:* **-chies**) patriarcado
**patrician** [pə'trɪʃən] *adj & s* patricio
**patriciate** [pə'trɪʃɪet] *s* patriciado
**patricidal** [,pætrɪ'saɪdəl] *adj* parricida
**patricide** ['pætrɪsaɪd] *s* parricidio (*acción*); parricida (*persona*)
**Patrick** ['pætrɪk] *s* Patricio
**patrimonial** [,pætrɪ'monɪəl] *adj* patrimonial
**patrimony** ['pætrɪ,monɪ] *s* (*pl:* **-nies**) patrimonio
**patriot** ['petrɪət] o ['pætrɪət] *s* patriota
**patriotic** [,petrɪ'ɑtɪk] o [,pætrɪ'ɑtɪk] *adj* patriótico
**patriotically** [,petrɪ'ɑtɪkəlɪ] o [,pætrɪ'ɑtɪkəlɪ] *adv* patrióticamente
**patriotism** ['petrɪətɪzəm] o ['pætrɪətɪzəm] *s* patriotismo
**patristic** [pə'trɪstɪk] *adj* patrístico; **patristics** *ssg* patrística
**Patroclus** [pə'trokləs] *s* (myth.) Patroclo
**patrol** [pə'trol] *s* ronda; (aer., mil. & nav.) patrulla; (*pret & pp:* **-trolled;** *ger:* **-trolling**) *va & vn* rondar; (aer., mil. & nav.) patrullar
**patrolman** [pə'trolmən] *s* (*pl:* **-men**) rondador, guardia municipal, vigilante de policía
**patrology** [pə'trɑlədʒɪ] *s* patrología
**patrol wagon** *s* camión de policía, coche de patrulla
**patron** ['petrən] o ['pætrən] *adj* tutelar, patrocinador; *s* parroquiano; patrocinador, patrono; (eccl.) patrono
**patronage** ['petrənɪdʒ] o ['pætrənɪdʒ] *s* trato, clientela; patrocinio; aire protector; prebendas, favores políticos; prestigio político
**patronal** ['petrənəl] o ['pætrənəl] *adj* patronal
**patroness** ['petrənɪs] o ['pætrənɪs] *s* parroquiana; patrocinadora; madrina; (eccl.) santa patrona
**patronize** ['petrənaɪz] o ['pætrənaɪz] *va* ser parroquiano de (*un tendero*); comprar de costumbre en (*una tienda*); patrocinar; tratar con aire protector
**patronizing** ['petrə,naɪzɪŋ] o ['pætrə,naɪzɪŋ] *adj* que trata con aire protector a inferiores; protector (*aire, conducta, etc.*)
**patron saint** *s* patrón, santo titular
**patronymic** [,pætrə'nɪmɪk] *adj & s* patronímico
**patroon** [pə'trun] *s* encomendero holandés en las colonias norteamericanas
**patten** ['pætən] *s* almadreña, chanclo, zueco
**patter** ['pætər] *s* golpeteo (*p.ej., de las pisaditas de un niño*); chapaleteo (*de la lluvia*); charla, parloteo; jerga (*lenguaje especial*); *va* repetir rápidamente y sin pensar; murmurar (*p.ej., el padrenuestro*); *vn* golpetear; charlar, parlotear
**pattern** ['pætərn] *s* patrón, modelo; *va* modelar; **to pattern after** ajustar al modelo de; **to pattern oneself after** imitar, seguir en todo el ejemplo de
**patternmaker** ['pætərn,mekər] *s* carpintero modelista
**patternmaking** ['pætərn,mekɪŋ] *s* carpintería de modelos, modelaje
**patty** ['pætɪ] *s* (*pl:* **-ties**) pastelito; pastilla
**patty pan** *s* tortera para hacer pastelitos
**P.A.U.** abr. de **Pan American Union**
**paucity** ['pɔsɪtɪ] *s* corto número; falta, escasez, insuficiencia
**Paul** [pɔl] *s* Pablo
**pauldron** ['pɔldrən] *s* (arm.) hombrera
**Pauline** ['pɔlaɪn] *adj* paulino; [pɔ'lin] *s* Paulina
**Paulinist** ['pɔlɪnɪst] *adj & s* paulinista
**Paul Jones** [dʒonz] *s* bolanchera (*danza*)
**paulownia** [pɔ'lonɪə] *s* (bot.) paulonia
**paunch** [pɔntʃ] *s* panza; (zool.) panza (*de los rumiantes*)
**paunchy** ['pɔntʃɪ] *adj* panzudo
**pauper** ['pɔpər] *s* pobre, indigente
**pauperism** ['pɔpərɪzəm] *s* pauperismo
**pauperize** ['pɔpəraɪz] *va* depauperar
**pause** [pɔz] *s* pausa; (gram. & mus.) pausa; **to give pause to** dar que pensar a; *vn* hacer pausa, detenerse brevemente; vacilar
**pavan** o **pavane** ['pævən] *s* pavana (*danza y música*)
**pave** [pev] *va* pavimentar; **to pave the way for** preparar el terreno a, abrir el camino a
**pavement** ['pevmənt] *s* pavimento
**pavilion** [pə'vɪljən] *s* pabellón; (anat. & arch.) pabellón; *va* cobijar o proveer de pabellón
**paving** ['pevɪŋ] *s* pavimentación; pavimento
**paving block** *s* adoquín
**paw** [pɔ] *s* pata; garra, zarpa; (coll.) mano (*del hombre*); *va* dar zarpazos a, restregar con las uñas; golpear (*el suelo los caballos*); (coll.) manosear; (coll.) sobar (*manosear con demasiada familiaridad*); *vn* piafar (*el caballo*)
**pawl** [pɔl] *s* (mach.) trinquete; (naut.) linguete
**pawl bitt** *s* (naut.) bita de linguete
**pawn** [pɔn] *s* peón (*de ajedrez*); (fig.) instrumento (*en manos de otra persona*); (fig.) víctima; prenda; **in pawn** en prenda; *va* empeñar, dar en prenda
**pawnbroker** ['pɔn,brokər] *s* prestamista
**pawnshop** ['pɔn,ʃɑp] *s* empeño, casa de empeños, monte de piedad
**pawn ticket** *s* papeleta de empeño
**pawpaw** ['pɔpɔ] *s* var. de **papaw**
**pax** [pæks] *s* (eccl.) paz (*ceremonia y patena*)
**pay** [pe] *s* paga, sueldo; galardón, recompensa; fuente de sueldos; castigo merecido; **bad pay** mala paga (*persona*); **good pay** buena paga (*persona*); **in the pay of** al servicio de; **poor pay** mala paga (*persona*) ‖ (*pret & pp:* **paid**)

*va* pagar; prestar o poner (*atención*); dar (*cumplidos*); dar (*dinero una actividad comercial*); dar dinero a, dar grandes ingresos a, ser provechoso a; pagar en la misma moneda, pagar con creces; sufrir (*el castigo de una ofensa*); hacer (*una visita*); cubrir (*los gastos*); **to pay back** devolver; pagar en la misma moneda; **to pay for** pagar, p.ej., **I will pay him for it** se lo pagaré; recompensar, p.ej., **I will pay him well for it** se lo recompensaré muy bien; **to pay off** pagar y despedir (*a un empleado*); pagar todo lo adeudado a; vengarse de; redimir (*una hipoteca*); **to pay out** desembolsar ‖ *vn* pagar; ser provechoso, valer la pena; (naut.) virar a sotavento; **to pay for** pagar, pagar por (*una cosa*); **to pay up** pagar todo lo adeudado; **pay as you enter** pague a la entrada; **pay as you go** pagar el impuesto de utilidades con descuentos anticipados; **pay as you leave** pague a la salida ‖ (*pret & pp:* **payed**) *va* (naut.) ir dando (*cuerda*); **to pay away** u **out** (naut.) ir dando (*cuerda*)

**payable** ['peəbəl] *adj* pagadero

**pay boost** *s* (coll.) aumento de salario

**paycheck** ['pe,tʃək] *s* cheque en pago del sueldo; sueldo

**payday** ['pe,de] *s* día de pago

**pay dirt** *s* (min.) grava provechosa, terreno aurífero

**payee** [pe'i] *s* (com.) portador, tenedor (*p.ej., de un giro*)

**pay envelope** *s* sobre con el jornal; jornal, salario

**payer** ['peər] *s* pagador

**paying teller** *s* pagador (*de un banco*)

**pay load** *s* carga útil

**paymaster** ['pe,mæstər] o ['pe,mɑstər] *s* pagador, contador, habilitado

**paymaster's office** *s* pagaduría

**payment** ['pemənt] *s* pago; castigo; **to make payment** efectuar el pago

**paynim** o **Paynim** ['penɪm] *adj & s* (archaic) gentil, pagano; (archaic) sarraceno, mahometano

**pay-off** ['pe,ɔf] o ['pe,ɑf] *s* paga; (coll.) arreglo, resultado

**payola** [pe'olə] *s* (slang) pago clandestino por un servicio comercial, pago por un servicio ilícito

**pay roll** *s* nómina, hoja de paga; paga (*de todos los empleados u obreros*)

**pay station** *s* teléfono público

**payt.** abr. de **payment**

**pc.** abr. de **piece**

**p.c.** abr. de **percent** y **post card**

**pd.** abr. de **paid**

**p.d.** abr. de **per diem** y **potential difference**

**P.D.** abr. de **Police Department** y **per diem**

**P.E.** abr. de **Protestant Episcopal**

**pea** [pi] *s* (bot.) guisante (*planta y semilla*); **as like as two peas** parecidos como dos gotas de agua

**peace** [pis] *s* paz; **to hold** o **keep one's peace** callar; **to keep the peace** mantener la paz; **to make peace with** hacer las paces con

**peaceable** ['pisəbəl] *adj* pacífico

**peaceful** ['pisfəl] *adj* tranquilo, pacífico

**peaceful penetration** *s* (pol.) penetración pacífica

**peace-loving** ['pis'lʌvɪŋ] *adj* amante de la paz

**peacemaker** ['pis,mekər] *s* pacificador, iris de paz

**peace offensive** *s* ofensiva de paz

**peace offering** *s* sacrificio propiciatorio; prenda de paz

**peace officer** *s* agente del orden público, guardia municipal

**peace of mind** *s* serenidad del espíritu

**peace pipe** *s* pipa ceremonial (*de los pieles rojas*)

**peach** [pitʃ] *s* (bot.) melocotonero, duraznero; melocotón, durazno (*fruto*); (slang) persona o cosa admirables; (slang) real moza; color de melocotón; *adj* de color de melocotón; *vn* (slang) cantar; **to peach on** (slang) denunciar, hacerse delator de

**peachy** ['pitʃɪ] *adj* (*comp:* **-ier**; *super:* **-iest**) de melocotón; (slang) estupendo, magnífico

**pea coal** *s* antracita de ½ a 1 y 1⁄16 pulgada

**peacock** ['pi,kɑk] *s* (orn.) pavo real, pavón; (fig.) pinturero; (*cap.*) *s* (astr.) Pavón

**peacock blue** *s* verde azulado

**peacock butterfly** *s* (ent.) ojo de pavo real (*Vanessa io*)

**peacock fish** *s* (ichth.) papagayo, loro de mar

**peafowl** ['pi,faul] *s* (orn.) pavo real o pava real

**pea green** *s* verde claro

**peahen** ['pi,hɛn] *s* (orn.) pava real

**pea jacket** *s* chaqueta de marinero

**peak** [pik] *s* cima, cumbre, pico; punta, extremo; máximo, punto culminante; visera (*de gorra*); cresta (*de una curva*); (elec.) pico; (naut.) penol (*de la verga*); (naut.) pico (*de vela*); *va* (naut.) enarbolar, levantar (*una verga contra el mástil*)

**peaked** [pikt] *adj* afilado (*dícese de la nariz, el rostro, etc.*); ['pikɪd] *adj* enjuto, delgado

**peak factor** *s* (elec.) factor de punta, factor de cresta

**peak load** *s* (elec.) carga de punta

**peak traffic** *s* afluencia máxima, movimiento máximo

**peal** [pil] *s* fragor, estruendo; repique (*de campanas*); juego de campanas; *va* lanzar (*un mensaje*) con repiqueteo sonoro; *vn* repicar; resonar

**peal of laughter** *s* carcajada

**peal of thunder** *s* trueno

**peanut** ['pi,nʌt] *s* (bot.) cacahuete, aráquida, maní (*planta y fruto*)

**peanut brittle** *s* guirlache o crocante de cacahuetes

**peanut butter** *s* manteca de cacahuete

**peanut candy** *s* var. de **peanut brittle**

**peanut oil** *s* aceite de cacahuete

**peanut vendor** *s* cacahuetero, manicero

**pear** [pɛr] *s* (bot.) peral; pera (*fruto*)

**pearl** [pʌrl] *s* margarita, perla; color de perla; flujo o murmullo (*del agua al correr*); (fig.) perla (*persona o cosa*); (pharm. & f.a.) perla; inversión de la puntada al tejer; guarnición rizada de tela, encaje o cinta; **to cast pearls before swine** echar margaritas a los cerdos o los puercos; *adj* perlino, aperlado; granoso, granular; *va* aljofarar; tejer invirtiendo la puntada; bordar u orlar con guarnición rizada; *vn* aljofararse; pescar perlas

**pearlash** ['pʌrl,æʃ] *s* cenizas de perla

**pearl barley** *s* cebada perlada

**pearl button** *s* botón de madreperla

**pearl gray** *s* color de perla, gris de perla

**pearl oyster** *s* (zool.) madreperla, ostra perlera

**pearly** ['pʌrlɪ] *adj* (*comp:* **-ier**; *super:* **-iest**) aperlado; nacarado; aljofarado

**pearly nautilus** *s* (zool.) nautilo

**pearmain** ['pɛrmen] *s* (bot.) pero

**pear-shaped** ['pɛr,ʃept] *adj* piriforme

**peart** [pɪrt] *adj* (dial.) alegre, jovial, vivo

**peasant** ['pɛzənt] *adj & s* campesino, rústico, labrador

**peasantry** ['pɛzəntrɪ] *s* paisanaje, gente del campo

**peascod** o **peasecod** ['piz,kɑd] *s* vaina de los guisantes

**peashooter** ['pi,ʃutər] *s* cerbatana, bodoquera

**pea soup** *s* sopa de guisantes, puré de guisantes; (coll.) neblina espesa y amarillenta

**peat** [pit] *s* turba

**peat bog** *s* turbal o turbera

**peaty** ['pitɪ] *adj* turboso

**peavey** ['pivɪ] *s* palanca puntiaguda con gancho

**peavy** ['pivɪ] *s* (*pl:* **-vies**) var. de **peavey**

**pebble** ['pɛbəl] *s* china, guija; *va* agranelar (*cuero*)

**pebbly** ['pɛblɪ] *adj* guijoso

**pecan** [pɪ'kɑn] o [pɪ'kæn] *s* (bot.) pacana, nuez encarcelada (*árbol y fruto*)

**peccadillo** [,pɛkə'dɪlo] *s* (*pl:* **-loes** o **-los**) pecadillo, pecado leve

**peccary** ['pɛkərɪ] *s* (*pl:* **-ries**) (zool.) pecarí, baquira

**peck** [pɛk] *s* medida de áridos (*nueve litros*); gran cantidad, montón; picotazo; (coll.) beso dado de mala gana; **a peck of trouble** mil dificultades, la mar de disgustos; *va* picotear; **to peck holes in** horadar a picotazos; *vn* picotear; (coll.) rezongar; (coll.) comer melindrosamente; **to peck at** (coll.) comer melindrosamente; querer picar, hacer un amago a (*otra ave*) con el pico; censurar constantemente

**pecker** ['pɛkər] *s* picoteador; rezongador; persona que come melindrosamente

**pecten** ['pɛktən] *s* (zool.) pectén, peine

**pectin** ['pɛktɪn] *s* (chem.) pectina

**pectinate** ['pɛktɪnet] *adj* pectinado

**pectineus** [pɛk'tɪnɪəs] *s* (anat.) pectíneo

**pectinibranchian** [,pɛktɪnɪ'bræŋkɪən] *adj* (zool.) pectinibranquio

**pectoral** ['pɛktərəl] *adj* pectoral; *s* pectoral; (pharm.) pectoral

**pectoral cross** *s* (eccl.) pectoral

**peculate** ['pɛkjəlet] *va & vn* malversar

**peculation** [,pɛkjə'leʃən] *s* peculado

**peculator** ['pɛkjə,letər] *s* malversador

**peculiar** [pɪ'kjuljər] *adj* peculiar; singular; excéntrico

**peculiarity** [pɪ,kjulɪ'ærɪtɪ] *s* (*pl:* **-ties**) peculiaridad; singularidad; excentricidad, rasgo característico

**peculiarly** [pɪ'kjuljərlɪ] *adv* peculiarmente; singularmente; excéntricamente

**pecuniary** [pɪ'kjunɪ,ɛrɪ] *adj* pecuniario

**pedagog** ['pɛdəgɑg] *s* var. de **pedagogue**

**pedagogic** [,pɛdə'gɑdʒɪk] o **pedagogical** [,pɛdə'gɑdʒɪkəl] *adj* pedagógico

**pedagogically** [,pɛdə'gɑdʒɪkəlɪ] *adv* pedagógicamente

**pedagogue** ['pɛdəgɑg] *s* pedagogo; dómine, pedante

**pedagogy** ['pɛdə,godʒɪ] o ['pɛdə,gɑdʒɪ] *s* pedagogía

**pedal** ['pɛdəl] o ['pidəl] *adj* del pie; ['pɛdəl] *s* pedal; (mus.) pedal; (*pret & pp:* **-aled** o **-alled**; *ger:* **-aling** o **-alling**) *va* impulsar pedaleando; *vn* pedalear

**pedal board** *s* (mus.) pedalero

**pedal brake** *s* freno de pedal, freno de pie

**pedal keyboard** *s* (mus.) pedalero, teclado pedalero

**pedant** ['pɛdənt] *s* pedante

**pedantic** [pɪ'dæntɪk] *adj* pedantesco

**pedantically** [pɪ'dæntɪkəlɪ] *adv* pedantescamente

**pedantry** ['pɛdəntrɪ] *s* (*pl:* **-ries**) pedantería

**pedate** ['pɛdet] *adj* (bot.) pedato

**peddle** ['pɛdəl] *va* ir vendiendo de puerta en puerta; traer y llevar (*chismes*); vender (*favores*); *vn* ser buhonero, vender menudencias por las calles

**peddler** ['pɛdlər] *s* buhonero

**pederast** ['pɛdəræst] o ['pidəræst] *s* pederasta

**pederasty** ['pɛdə,ræstɪ] o ['pidə,ræstɪ] *s* pederastia

**pedestal** ['pɛdɪstəl] *s* pedestal; (mus.) cubeta (*del arpa*)

**pedestal box** *s* (mach.) caja de engrase

**pedestal lamp** *s* lámpara de pie

**pedestal table** *s* velador

**pedestrian** [pɪ'dɛstrɪən] *adj* pedestre; (fig.) pedestre; *s* peatón

**pedestrianism** [pɪ'dɛstrɪənɪzəm] *s* pedestrismo

**pediatric** [,pidɪ'ætrɪk] o [,pɛdɪ'ætrɪk] *adj* pediátrico; **pediatrics** *ssg* pediatría

**pediatrician** [,pidɪə'trɪʃən] o [,pɛdɪə'trɪʃən] *s* pedíatra

**pedicel** ['pɛdɪsəl] *s* (bot. & zool.) pedicelo

**pedicle** ['pɛdɪkəl] *s* (bot.) pedículo

**pedicular** [pɪ'dɪkjələr] *adj* pedicular

**pedicure** ['pɛdikjʊr] *s* pedicuro (*persona*); quiropedia

**pedigree** ['pɛdɪgri] *s* árbol genealógico, linaje; ascendencia

**pedigreed** ['pɛdɪgrid] *adj* de pura raza

**pediment** ['pɛdɪmənt] *s* (arch.) frontón

**pedipalpus** [,pɛdɪ'pælpəs] *s* (*pl:* **-pi** [paɪ]) (zool.) pedipalpo

**pedlar** ['pɛdlər] *s* var. de **peddler**

**pedometer** [pɪ'dɑmɪtər] *s* podómetro

**peduncle** [pɪ'dʌŋkəl] *s* (anat., bot. & zool.) pedúnculo

**peduncular** [pɪ'dʌŋkjələr] *adj* peduncular

**pedunculate** [pɪ'dʌŋkjəlet] *adj* pedunculado

**peek** [pik] *s* mirada rápida y furtiva; **to take a peek at** echar una mirada rápida y furtiva a; *vn* mirar, mirar a hurtadillas

**peel** [pil] *s* cáscara, corteza, hollejo, telilla; pala (*de horno*); (print.) colgador; **a piece of lemon peel** una cascarita de limón; *va* pelar; **to keep one's eyes peeled** (slang) estar ojo alerta; **to peel off** pelar, arrancar pelando; *vn* pelarse; desconcharse; (slang) desnudarse

**peeling** ['pilɪŋ] *s* peladura

**peen** [pin] *s* peña (*del martillo*)

**peep** [pip] *s* mirada por una rendija o a hurtadillas; rendija (*por la cual se mira*); pío (*de la cría del ave*); **at the peep of day** al despuntar el día; *va* asomar; **to peep out** asomar; descubrir (*un secreto*); *vn* mirar por una rendija o a hurtadillas; asomar; piar (*los pollos*)

**peeper** ['pipər] *s* atisbador, mirador; mirón; (coll.) ojo; (zool.) rubeta

**peephole** ['pip,hol] *s* atisbadero, mirilla, ventanillo

**Peeping Tom** *s* el mirón Tom; mirón

**peep show** *s* mundonuevo; (slang) vistas sicalípticas

**peer** [pɪr] *s* par; *vn* mirar fijando la vista de cerca; asomar, aparecer; **to peer at** mirar con fijeza, mirar con ojos de miope; **to peer into** mirar hacia lo interior de, mirar lo que hay dentro de

**peerage** ['pɪrɪdʒ] *s* paría; guía de la nobleza

**peeress** ['pɪrɪs] *s* paresa

**peerless** ['pɪrlɪs] *adj* sin par, incomparable

**peeve** [piv] *s* cojijo; *va* (coll.) enojar, irritar

**peevish** ['pivɪʃ] *adj* cojijoso, displicente

**peevishness** ['pivɪʃnɪs] *s* displicencia, quejumbre

**peg** [pɛg] *s* clavija, claveta, estaquilla; escarpia, colgador; grado; (Brit.) trago, traguito; **to take down a peg** bajar los humos a, obligar a guardar más moderación o más cortesía; (*pret & pp:* **pegged;** *ger:* **pegging**) *va* enclavijar; marcar o señalar con clavijas; (com.) fijar, estabilizar (*precios*); (coll.) lanzar (*una pelota*); (surv.) jalonar; *vn* trabajar con ahinco; **to peg away** afanarse, trabajar con ahinco; **to peg away at** afanarse en

**Pegasus** ['pɛgəsəs] *s* (myth. & astr.) Pegaso

**pegbox** ['pɛg,bɑks] *s* (mus.) clavijero (*p.ej., de la guitarra*)

**Peggy** ['pɛgɪ] *s* nombre abreviado de **Margaret**

**peg ladder** *s* escalera de papagayo

**peg leg** *s* pata de palo; (slang) pata de palo (*persona*)

**pegmatite** ['pɛgmətaɪt] *s* (petrog.) pegmatita

**peg top** *s* peonza; **peg tops** *spl* pantalones anchos de caderas y perniles ajustados

**peg-top** ['pɛg,tɑp] *adj* en forma de peonza

**P.E.I.** abr. de **Prince Edward Island**

**peignoir** [pen'wɑr] o ['penwɑr] *s* peinador, bata de señora

**Peiping** ['pe'pɪŋ] *s* Peipín

**Peiraeus** [paɪ'riəs] *s* el Pireo

**pejorative** ['pidʒə,retɪv] o [pɪ'dʒɔrətɪv] *adj* (gram.) despectivo, peyorativo

**pekin** ['pi'kɪn] *s* pequín; (*cap.*) *s* Pequín

**Pekinese** [,pikɪ'niz] *adj* pekinés; *s* (*pl:* **-ese**) pekinés (*natural de Pequín; perro*)

**Pekingese** [,pikɪŋ'iz] *adj & s* var. de **Pekinese**

**pekoe** ['pico] *s* té de Pékoë

**pelage** ['pɛlɪdʒ] *s* pelaje

**pelagic** [pɪ'lædʒɪk] *adj* pelágico

**Pelasgian** [pɪ'læzdʒɪən] *adj & s* pelasgo

**Pelée, Mount** [pə'le] el monte Pelado

**pelerine** [,pɛlə'rin] *s* esclavina, pelerina

**Peleus** ['piljus] o ['pilɪəs] *s* (myth.) Peleo

**pelf** [pɛlf] *s* dinero mal ganado, riquezas mal ganadas

**pelican** ['pɛlɪkən] *s* (orn.) pelícano

**Pelion** ['pilɪən] *s* el Pelión; **to heap Pelion upon Ossa** levantar el Pelión sobre el Osa, superponer el Pelión al Osa

**pelisse** [pə'lis] *s* pelliza

**pellagra** [pə'legrə] o [pə'lægrə] *s* (path.) pelagra

**pellagrous** [pə'legrəs] o [pə'lægrəs] *adj* pelagroso

**pellet** ['pɛlɪt] *s* pelotilla, pella; píldora; bolita; perdigón

**pellicle** ['pɛlɪkəl] *s* película

**pellicular** [pə'lɪkjələr] *adj* pelicular

**pellitory** ['pɛlɪ,torɪ] *s* (*pl:* **-ries**) (bot. & pharm.) pelitre; (bot.) caracolera
**pell-mell** ['pɛl'mɛl] *adj* confuso, tumultuoso; *adv* atropelladamente; **to run pell-mell** salir pitando, salvarse por pies; *s* batahola, confusión, desorden
**pellucid** [pə'lusɪd] *adj* diáfano; claro, evidente
**Peloponnesian** [,pɛləpə'niʃən] o [,pɛləpə'niʒən] *adj* & *s* peloponense
**Peloponnesian War** *s* guerra del Peloponeso
**Peloponnesos** o **Peloponnesus** [,pɛləpə'nisəs] *s* Peloponeso
**Pelops** ['pilɑps] *s* (myth.) Pélope
**pelota** [pɛ'lotə] *s* (sport) pelota vasca
**pelt** [pɛlt] *s* pellejo; golpe violento; golpeo violento; velocidad; (hum.) pellejo (*de una persona*); *va* golpear violentamente; apedrear; tirar; *vn* golpear violentamente; caer con fuerza (*el granizo, la lluvia, etc.*); apresurarse
**peltry** ['pɛltrɪ] *s* (*pl:* **-ries**) pellejería, corambre; pellejo
**pelvic** ['pɛlvɪk] *adj* pelviano
**pelvimeter** [pɛl'vɪmɪtər] *s* pelvímetro
**pelvis** ['pɛlvɪs] *s* (*pl:* **-ves** [viz]) (anat.) pelvis
**pemmican** ['pɛmɪkən] *s* penmicán
**pemphigus** ['pɛmfɪgəs] o [pɛm'faɪgəs] *s* (path.) pénfigo
**pen.** abr. de **peninsula**
**pen** [pɛn] *s* pluma; corral, redil; (fig.) pluma; **to live by one's pen** vivir de la pluma; (*pret & pp:* **penned;** *ger:* **penning**) *va* escribir (*con pluma*); redactar; (*pret & pp:* **penned** o **pent;** *ger:* **penning**) *va* acorralar, encerrar
**penal** ['pinəl] *adj* penal; penable
**penal code** *s* código penal
**penalize** ['pinəlaɪz] o ['pɛnəlaɪz] *va* penar (*un acto, a una persona*); (sport) aplicar una sanción a
**penal servitude** *s* pena de trabajos forzados, pena de reclusión
**penalty** ['pɛnəltɪ] *s* (*pl:* **-ties**) pena; (sport) sanción (*que se aplica a ciertas faltas del juego*); (law) penalidad; recargo (*que paga el contribuyente moroso*); **under penalty of** so pena de
**penance** ['pɛnəns] *s* penitencia; **to do penance** hacer penitencia
**penates** o **Penates** [pɛ'netiz] *spl* penates
**pence** [pɛns] *spl* peniques
**penchant** ['pɛnʃənt] *s* afición, inclinación, tendencia
**pencil** ['pɛnsəl] *s* lápiz; lápiz de color; pincel fino; (fig.) pincel (*modo de pintar*); haz (*de rayos, de luz, etc.*); (*pret & pp:* **-ciled** o **-cilled;** *ger:* **-ciling** o **-cilling**) *va* escribir con lápiz, marcar con lápiz; (med.) pincelar
**pencil sharpener** *s* sacapuntas, afilalápices
**pendant** o **pendent** ['pɛndənt] *adj* pendiente; sobresaliente; (fig.) pendiente; *s* pinjante, medallón; pendiente (*arete*); araña (*de luces*); (arch.) pinjante
**pendentive** [pɛn'dɛntɪv] *s* (arch.) pechina
**pending** ['pɛndɪŋ] *adj* pendiente; *prep* hasta; durante
**pendragon** o **Pendragon** [pɛn'drægən] *s* jefe supremo de los antiguos británicos
**pendulous** ['pɛndʒələs] *adj* colgante, pendiente; oscilante
**pendulum** ['pɛndʒələm] o ['pɛndjələm] *s* péndulo; péndola (*de un reloj*)
**pendulum bob** *s* lenteja
**Penelope** [pɪ'nɛləpɪ] *s* (myth.) Penélope
**peneplain** ['pinɪ,plen] *s* (geol.) penillanura
**penetrability** [,pɛnɪtrə'bɪlɪtɪ] *s* penetrabilidad
**penetrable** ['pɛnɪtrəbəl] *adj* penetrable
**penetrate** ['pɛnɪtret] *va* & *vn* penetrar
**penetrating** ['pɛnɪ,tretɪŋ] *adj* penetrante; (fig.) penetrante
**penetration** [,pɛnɪ'treʃən] *s* penetración; (fig.) penetración
**penetrative** ['pɛnɪ,tretɪv] *adj* penetrante, penetrativo
**penguin** ['pɛŋgwɪn] *s* (orn.) pingüino, pájaro bobo
**penholder** ['pɛn,holdər] *s* portaplumas (*mango*); plumero (*caja*)
**penicillin** [,pɛnɪ'sɪlɪn] *s* (pharm.) penicilina
**peninsula** [pə'nɪnsələ] o [pə'nɪnsjʊlə] *s* península
**peninsular** [pə'nɪnsələr] o [pə'nɪnsjʊlər] *adj* & *s* peninsular
**penis** ['pinɪs] *s* (*pl:* **-nes** [niz] o **-nises**) (anat.) pene
**penitence** ['pɛnɪtəns] *s* penitencia
**penitent** ['pɛnɪtənt] *adj* & *s* penitente
**penitential** [,pɛnɪ'tɛnʃəl] *adj* penitencial; *s* (eccl.) penitencial
**penitentially** [,pɛnɪ'tɛnʃəlɪ] *adv* de modo penitencial; por vía de penitencia
**penitential psalms** *spl* (Bib.) salmos penitenciales
**penitentiary** [,pɛnɪ'tɛnʃərɪ] *adj* penitencial; penable; penitenciario; *s* (*pl:* **-ries**) penitenciaría, presidio; (eccl.) penitenciaría (*tribunal*); (eccl.) penitenciario (*presbítero*)
**penknife** ['pɛn,naɪf] *s* (*pl:* **-knives**) navaja, cortaplumas
**penman** ['pɛnmən] *s* (*pl:* **-men**) pendolista; escritor
**penmanship** ['pɛnmənʃɪp] *s* caligrafía; letra (*de una persona*)
**Penn.** o **Penna.** abr. de **Pennsylvania**
**penna** ['pɛnə] *s* (*pl:* **-nae** [ni]) (orn.) pena
**pen name** *s* seudónimo
**pennant** ['pɛnənt] *s* gallardete
**pennate** ['pɛnet] *adj* pennado
**penniless** ['pɛnɪlɪs] *adj* pelón, sin dinero
**penninervate** [,pɛnɪ'nʌrvet] (bot.) penninervio
**pennon** ['pɛnən] *s* pendón
**Pennsylvania** [,pɛnsɪl'venɪə] *s* Pensilvania
**Pennsylvania Dutch** *spl* descendientes de los colonizadores alemanes en Pensilvania; *ssg* dialecto alemán hablado en Pensilvania
**Pennsylvanian** [,pɛnsɪl'venɪən] *adj* & *s* pensilvano
**penny** ['pɛnɪ] *s* (*pl:* **-nies**) (U.S.A.) centavo; **a pretty penny** (coll.) un dineral, un ojo de la cara; **to turn an honest penny** ganar honradamente algún dinero; (*pl:* **pence**) (Brit.) penique
**pennyroyal** [,pɛnɪ'rɔɪəl] *s* (bot.) poleo
**pennyweight** ['pɛnɪ,wet] *s* peso de 24 granos
**penny-wise** ['pɛnɪ'waɪz] *adj* tacaño; **penny-wise and pound-foolish** tacaño en lo pequeño, derrochador en lo grande
**pennyworth** ['pɛnɪ,wʌrθ] *s* valor de un penique; pizca, pequeña cantidad
**penological** [,pinə'lɑdʒɪkəl] *adj* penológico
**penologist** [pi'nɑlədʒɪst] *s* penologista o penólogo
**penology** [pi'nɑlədʒɪ] *s* penología
**pen pal** *s* (coll.) amigo por correspondencia
**pen point** *s* punta de la pluma; plumilla or puntilla (*de la plumafuente*)
**pensile** ['pɛnsɪl] *adj* pensil
**pension** ['pɛnʃən] *s* pensión, jubilación; *va* pensionar, jubilar
**pensioner** ['pɛnʃənər] *s* pensionado, pensionista, alimentista
**pension fund** *s* caja de jubilaciones
**pensive** ['pɛnsɪv] *adj* pensativo; melancólico
**penstock** ['pɛn,stɑk] *s* (hyd.) tubo en carga; (hyd.) compuerta de esclusa; (hyd.) canal de carga
**pent** [pɛnt] *adj* acorralado, encerrado; *pret* & *pp de* **pen**
**pentacle** ['pɛntəkəl] *s* pentaclo
**pentadactyl** o **pentadactyle** [,pɛntə'dæktɪl] *adj* pentadáctilo
**pentagon** ['pɛntəgɑn] *s* (geom.) pentágono; **the Pentagon** el Pentágono (*edificio del Ministerio de Defensa en Wáshington*)
**pentagonal** [pɛn'tægənəl] *adj* pentagonal
**pentahedron** [,pɛntə'hidrən] *s* (*pl:* **-drons** o **-dra** [drə]) (geom.) pentaedro
**pentamerous** [pɛn'tæmərəs] *adj* (bot. & zool.) pentámero
**pentameter** [pɛn'tæmɪtər] *adj* & *s* pentámetro
**pentane** ['pɛnten] *s* (chem.) pentano
**pentarchy** ['pɛntɑrkɪ] *s* (*pl:* **-chies**) pentarquía
**pentasyllabic** [,pɛntəsɪ'læbɪk] *adj* pentasílabo
**Pentateuch** ['pɛntətjuk] o ['pɛntətuk] *s* (Bib.) Pentateuco
**pentathlon** [pɛn'tæθlɑn] *s* (sport) péntatlo
**pentatonic** [,pɛntə'tɑnɪk] *adj* pentatónico
**pentavalent** [,pɛntə'velənt] o [pɛn'tævələnt] (chem.) pentavalente

**Pentecost** ['pɛntɪkɑst] o ['pɛntɪkɔst] *s* Pentecostés
**Pentecostal** o **pentecostal** [,pɛntɪ'kɑstəl] o [,pɛntɪ'kɔstəl] *adj* de Pentecostés
**penthouse** ['pɛnt,haʊs] *adj* colgadizo; *s* colgadizo; alpende; casa de azotea
**pentode** ['pɛntod] *s* (elec.) pentodo o péntodo
**pentosan** ['pɛntəsæn] *s* (chem.) pentosana
**pentose** ['pɛntos] *s* (chem.) pentosa
**pent roof** *s* tejado colgadizo
**pent-up** ['pɛnt,ʌp] *adj* contenido, reprimido
**penult** ['pinʌlt] o [pɪ'nʌlt] *s* (phonet.) penúltima
**penultimate** [pɪ'nʌltɪmɪt] *adj* penúltimo; *s* (phonet.) penúltima
**penumbra** [pɪ'nʌmbrə] *s* (*pl:* **-brae** [bri] o **-bras**) penumbra
**penurious** [pɪ'njʊrɪəs] o [pɪ'nʊrɪəs] *adj* tacaño, mezquino
**penury** ['pɛnjərɪ] *s* pobreza, miseria; penuria (*escasez*)
**penwiper** ['pɛn,waɪpər] *s* limpiaplumas
**peonage** ['piənɪdʒ] *s* condición de peón; esclavitud económica de los peones
**peony** ['piənɪ] *s* (*pl:* **-nies**) (bot.) peonía
**people** ['pipəl] *spl* gente; personas, p.ej., **a hundred people** un centenar de personas; gente del pueblo, gente común; se, p.ej., **people say** se dice; **my people** los míos; mi familia; mis allegados; *ssg* (*pl:* **peoples**) pueblo, nación, raza; *va* poblar
**pep** [pɛp] *s* (slang) brío, ánimo, vigor; **to be full of pep** (slang) estar muy jaque; (*pret & pp:* **pepped;** *ger:* **pepping**) *va* (slang) animar; **to pep up** (slang) animar, dar vigor a
**peplum** ['pɛpləm] *s* (*pl:* **-lums** o **-la** [lə]) (hist.) peplo; faldillas
**pepo** ['pipo] *s* (bot.) pepónide
**pepper** ['pɛpər] *s* (bot.) pimentero (*Piper nigrum*); (bot.) pimiento (*Capsicum*); pimienta (*condimento*); pimentero (*vasija*); *va* sazonar con pimienta; acribillar; salpicar; motear
**pepper-and-salt** ['pɛpərənd'sɔlt] *adj* mezclado de negro y blanco
**pepperbox** ['pɛpər,bɑks] *s* pimentero
**peppercorn** ['pɛpər,kɔrn] *s* grano de pimienta; chuchería, bagatela
**pepper cress** *s* (bot.) mastuerzo
**peppergrass** ['pɛpər,græs] o ['pɛpər,grɑs] *s* (bot.) mastuerzo; (bot.) sabelección, lepidio
**peppermint** ['pɛpərmɪnt] *s* (bot.) menta piperita; esencia de menta; pastilla de menta
**peppermint drop** *s* pastilla de menta
**pepper pot** *s* sopa de callos, carne y legumbres condimentada con pimientos, ají, etc.
**pepper tree** *s* (bot.) turbinto, pimentero falso
**peppery** ['pɛpərɪ] *adj* que tiene mucha o demasiada pimienta; picante, mordaz; enojado, de malas pulgas
**peppy** ['pɛpɪ] *adj* (*comp:* **-pier;** *super:* **-piest**) (slang) brioso, animoso, vigoroso
**pepsin** ['pɛpsɪn] *s* (biochem.) pepsina
**pep talk** *s* (slang) palabras para alentar y confortar
**peptic** ['pɛptɪk] *adj* péptico; *s* substancia péptica
**peptic ulcer** *s* (path.) úlcera péptica
**peptide** ['pɛptaɪd] o ['pɛptɪd] *s* (biochem.) péptido
**peptize** ['pɛptaɪz] *va* (chem.) peptizar
**peptone** ['pɛpton] *s* (biochem.) peptona
**per** [pʌr] *prep* por; **as per** según
**peradventure** [,pʌrəd'vɛntʃər] *s* duda, incertidumbre; **beyond peradventure** sin posibilidad de duda
**perambulate** [pər'æmbjəlet] *va* recorrer andando; recorrer para inspeccionar; *vn* pasearse
**perambulation** [pər,æmbjə'leʃən] *s* visita de inspección; paseo
**perambulator** [pər'æmbjə,letər] *s* paseante; cochecillo de niño
**per annum** [pər 'ænəm] por año, al año
**perborate** [pər'boret] *s* (chem.) perborato
**percale** [pər'kel] o [pər'kæl] *s* percal
**percaline** [,pʌrkə'lin] *s* percalina
**per capita** [pər 'kæpɪtə] por cabeza, por persona
**perceive** [pər'siv] *va* percibir
**per cent** o **percent** [pər'sɛnt] por ciento
**percentage** [pər'sɛntɪdʒ] *s* porcentaje; (slang) provecho, ventaja
**percentile** [pər'sɛntɪl] *s* percentil
**per centum** [pər 'sɛntəm] var. de **per cent**
**percept** ['pʌrsɛpt] *s* percepción (*efecto de percibir; objeto percibido*)
**perceptibility** [pər,sɛptɪ'bɪlɪtɪ] *s* perceptibilidad
**perceptible** [pər'sɛptɪbəl] *adj* perceptible
**perceptibly** [pər'sɛptɪblɪ] *adv* perceptiblemente
**perception** [pər'sɛpʃən] *s* percepción; comprensión, penetración
**perceptive** [pər'sɛptɪv] *adj* perceptivo (*que tiene virtud de percibir*)
**perceptual** [pər'sɛptʃʊəl] *adj* perceptivo (*perteneciente a la percepción*)
**Perceval** ['pʌrsɪvəl] *s* var. de **Percival**
**perch** [pʌrtʃ] *s* percha, varilla, rama (*en la que posa un ave*); pescante (*del cochero*); sitio o posición elevada; medida de longitud que equivale a 5,18 metros; medida de área que equivale a 23,3 metros cuadrados; (ichth.) perca; *va* colocar o situar en un sitio algo elevado; *vn* posar (*un ave*); sentarse en un sitio algo elevado, encaramarse
**perchance** [pər'tʃæns] o [pər'tʃɑns] *adv* (archaic & poet.) quizá, por ventura
**Percheron** ['pʌrtʃərɑn] o ['pʌrʃərɑn] *adj & s* percherón
**perchlorate** [pər'kloret] *s* (chem.) perclorato
**perchloric** [pər'klorɪk] *adj* perclórico
**perchloric acid** *s* (chem.) ácido perclórico
**perchloride** [pər'kloraɪd] o [pər'klorɪd] o **perchlorid** [pər'klorɪd] *s* (chem.) percloruro
**percipient** [pər'sɪpɪənt] *adj & s* perceptor
**Percival** o **Percivale** ['pʌrsɪvəl] *s* Perceval
**percolate** ['pʌrkəlet] *va* infiltrarse por entre los poros de; *vn* infiltrarse
**percolation** [,pʌrkə'leʃən] *s* infiltración
**percolator** ['pʌrkə,letər] *s* colador; cafetera filtradora
**percuss** [pər'kʌs] *va* percutir
**percussion** [pər'kʌʃən] *s* percusión; (med.) percusión
**percussion cap** *s* cápsula fulminante
**percussion hammer** *s* martillo neumático; (med.) martillo percusor
**percussion instrument** *s* (mus.) instrumento de percusión
**percussion lock** *s* llave de percusión
**percussor** [pər'kʌsər] *s* (med.) percusor
**Percy** ['pʌrsɪ] *s* nombre abreviado de **Percival**
**per diem** [pər 'daɪəm] (Lat.) por día; *s* cantidad que se da cada día
**perdition** [pər'dɪʃən] *s* perdición; infierno
**peregrinate** ['pɛrɪgrɪnet] *va* recorrer; *vn* peregrinar
**peregrination** [,pɛrɪgrɪ'neʃən] *s* peregrinación
**peregrine** o **peregrin** ['pɛrɪgrɪn] *adj* extranjero; *s* (orn.) halcón peregrino
**peregrine falcon** *s* (orn.) halcón peregrino
**peremptory** [pə'rɛmptərɪ] o ['pɛrəmp,torɪ] *adj* perentorio; autoritario, imperioso
**perennial** [pə'rɛnɪəl] *adj* perenne; (bot.) perenne, vivaz; *s* (bot.) planta vivaz
**perennially** [pə'rɛnɪəlɪ] *adv* perennemente
**perf.** abr. de **perfect** y **perforated**
**perfect** ['pʌrfɪkt] *adj* perfecto; (gram.) perfecto; *s* (gram.) perfecto; (gram.) pretérito perfecto; [pər'fɛkt] o ['pʌrfɪkt] *va* perfeccionar
**perfect cadence** *s* (mus.) cadencia perfecta
**perfectibility** [pər,fɛktɪ'bɪlɪtɪ] *s* perfectibilidad
**perfectible** [pər'fɛktɪbəl] *adj* perfectible
**perfection** [pər'fɛkʃən] *s* perfección; **to perfection** a la perfección
**perfectionist** [pər'fɛkʃənɪst] *s* perfeccionista
**perfective** [pər'fɛktɪv] *adj* perfectivo
**perfectly** ['pʌrfɪktlɪ] *adv* perfectamente
**perfecto** [pər'fɛkto] *s* (*pl:* **-tos**) cigarro puro afilado en los dos extremos
**perfect participle** *s* (gram.) participio pasivo o de pretérito
**perfect rhyme** *s* (pros.) rima perfecta
**perfervid** [pər'fʌrvɪd] *adj* fervidísimo
**perfidious** [pər'fɪdɪəs] *adj* pérfido
**perfidy** ['pʌrfɪdɪ] *s* (*pl:* **-dies**) perfidia

**perfoliate** [pər'folɪɪt] o [pər'folɪet] *adj* (bot.) perfoliado
**perforate** ['pʌrfəret] *adj* perforado; *va* perforar
**perforated** ['pʌrfə,retɪd] *adj* (philately) dentado
**perforation** [,pʌrfə'reʃən] *s* perforación; trepado (*línea de puntos taladrados, p.ej., en los sellos de correo*)
**perforator** ['pʌrfə,retər] *s* perforador; perforadora; (telg.) perforador
**perforce** [pər'fors] *adv* por fuerza, necesariamente
**perform** [pər'fɔrm] *va* ejecutar; (theat.) representar; *vn* ejecutar; funcionar (*p.ej., una maquina*)
**performance** [pər'fɔrməns] *s* actuación, ejecución; interpretación, presentación, representación; funcionamiento; (theat.) función; (sport) performance
**performer** [pər'fɔrmər] *s* ejecutante; actor, representante; acróbata
**perfume** ['pʌrfjum] o [pər'fjum] *s* perfume; [pər'fjum] *va* perfumar
**perfumer** [pər'fjumər] *s* perfumero o perfumista
**perfumery** [pər'fjumərɪ] *s* (*pl:* **-ies**) perfumería; perfume, perfumes
**perfunctory** [pər'fʌŋktərɪ] *adj* hecho sin cuidado, hecho a la ligera, perfunctorio; indiferente, negligente
**Pergamum** ['pʌrgəməm] *s* Pérgamo
**pergola** ['pʌrgələ] *s* pérgola
**perhaps** [pər'hæps] *adv* acaso, tal vez, quizá
**peri** ['pɪrɪ] *s* (*pl:* **-ris**) (myth.) peri
**perianth** ['pɛrɪænθ] *s* (bot.) periantio
**pericardiac** [,pɛrɪ'kardɪæk] o **pericardial** [,pɛrɪ'kardɪəl] *adj* pericardíaco
**pericarditis** [,pɛrɪkar'daɪtɪs] *s* (path.) pericarditis
**pericardium** [,pɛrɪ'kardɪəm] *s* (*pl:* **-a** [ə]) (anat.) pericardio
**pericarp** ['pɛrɪkarp] *s* (bot.) pericarpio
**Pericles** ['pɛrɪkliz] *s* Pericles
**pericranium** [,pɛrɪ'krenɪəm] *s* (*pl:* **-a** [ə]) (anat.) pericráneo; (hum.) cabeza
**peridot** ['pɛrɪdat] *s* (mineral.) peridoto
**perigee** ['pɛrɪdʒi] *s* (astr.) perigeo
**perigyny** [pə'rɪdʒɪnɪ] *s* (bot.) periginia
**perihelion** [,pɛrɪ'hilɪən] *s* (*pl:* **-a** [ə]) (astr.) perihelio
**peril** ['pɛrəl] *s* peligro; (*pret & pp:* **-iled** o **-illed;** *ger:* **-iling** o **-illing**) *va* poner en peligro
**perilous** ['pɛrɪləs] *adj* peligroso
**perimeter** [pə'rɪmɪtər] *s* perímetro
**perimysium** [,pɛrɪ'mɪʒɪəm] o [,pɛrɪ'mɪzɪəm] *s* (anat.) perimisio
**perineal** [,pɛrɪ'niəl] *adj* perineal
**perineum** [,pɛrɪ'niəm] *s* (*pl:* **-a** [ə]) (anat.) perineo
**perineurium** [,pɛrɪ'njʊrɪəm] o [,pɛrɪ'nʊrɪəm] *s* (*pl:* **-a** [ə]) (anat.) perineurio
**period** ['pɪrɪəd] *s* período; (gram.) punto; (sport) división (*de ciertos juegos*); hora (*de clase*)
**period costume** *s* traje de época
**period furniture** *s* muebles de estilo
**periodic** [,pɪrɪ'adɪk] *adj* periódico; (lit.) oratorio; [,pʌraɪ'adɪk] *adj* (chem.) peryódico
**periodical** [,pɪrɪ'adɪkəl] *adj* periódico; *s* periódico, revista periódica, publicación periódica
**periodically** [,pɪrɪ'adɪkəlɪ] *adv* periódicamente; de vez en cuando
**periodic fraction** *s* (math.) fracción periódica
**periodicity** [,pɪrɪə'dɪsɪtɪ] *s* (*pl:* **-ties**) periodicidad
**periodic law** *s* (chem.) ley periódica
**periodic motion** *s* (phys.) movimiento periódico
**periodic system** *s* (chem.) sistema periódico
**periodic table** *s* (chem.) tabla periódica, cuadro del sistema periódico
**periodide** [pər'aɪədaɪd] o [pər'aɪədɪd] *s* (chem.) peryoduro
**periodontal** [,pɛrɪə'dantəl] *adj* periodontal
**perioeci** [,pɛrɪ'isaɪ] *spl* periecos
**perioecic** [,pɛrɪ'isɪk] *adj* perieco
**periosteum** [,pɛrɪ'astɪəm] *s* (*pl:* **-a** [ə]) (anat.) periostio
**periostitis** [,pɛrɪas'taɪtɪs] *s* (path.) periostitis
**peripatetic** [,pɛrɪpə'tɛtɪk] *adj & s* paseante; (*cap.*) *adj & s* peripatético
**peripheral** [pə'rɪfərəl] *adj* periférico
**periphery** [pə'rɪfərɪ] *s* (*pl:* **-ies**) periferia
**periphrase** ['pɛrɪfrez] *s* perífrasi; *va* expresar con perífrasis; *vn* perifrasear
**periphrasis** [pə'rɪfrəsɪs] *s* (*pl:* **-ses** [siz]) perífrasi o perífrasis
**periphrastic** [,pɛrɪ'fræstɪk] *adj* perifrástico
**peripteral** [pə'rɪptərəl] *adj* (arch.) períptero
**periscian** [pɪ'rɪʃɪən] o [pɪ'rɪsɪən] *adj* periscio
**periscii** [pɪ'rɪʃɪaɪ] o [pɪ'rɪsɪaɪ] *spl* periscios
**periscope** ['pɛrɪskop] *s* periscopio
**periscopic** [,pɛrɪ'skapɪk] *adj* periscópico
**perish** ['pɛrɪʃ] *vn* perecer; averiarse (*echarse a perder*); **perish the thought!** ¡no lo permita Dios!
**perishable** ['pɛrɪʃəbəl] *adj* perecedero; averiable, deleznable; **perishables** *spl* artículos perecederos
**perishable goods** *spl* artículos perecederos
**perissodactyl** o **perissodactyle** [pɪ,rɪsə'dæktɪl] *adj & s* (zool.) perisodáctilo
**peristalsis** [,pɛrɪ'stælsɪs] *s* (*pl:* **-ses** [siz]) (physiol.) peristalsis o peristaltismo
**peristaltic** [,pɛrɪ'stæltɪk] *adj* peristáltico
**peristome** ['pɛrɪstom] *s* (bot.) perístoma
**peristyle** ['pɛrɪstaɪl] *s* (arch.) peristilo
**peritoneal** [,pɛrɪtə'niəl] *adj* peritoneal
**peritoneum** o **peritonaeum** [,pɛrɪtə'niəm] *s* *s* (*pl:* **-a** [ə]) (anat.) peritoneo
**peritonitis** [,pɛrɪtə'naɪtɪs] *s* (path.) peritonitis
**periwig** ['pɛrɪwɪg] *s* perico (*pelo postizo*)
**periwinkle** ['pɛrɪ,wɪŋkəl] *s* (bot.) pervinca; (zool.) litorina, bígaro
**perjure** ['pʌrdʒər] *va* hacer (*a una persona*) quebrantar el juramento; **to perjure oneself** perjurarse
**perjured** ['pʌrdʒərd] *adj* perjuro
**perjurer** ['pʌrdʒərər] *s* perjuro
**perjury** ['pʌrdʒərɪ] *s* (*pl:* **-ries**) perjurio
**perk** [pʌrk] *va* alzar (*la cabeza*); aguzar (*las orejas*); **to perk out** o **up** engalanar; *vn* pavonearse; engalanarse; **to perk up** reanimarse, sentirse mejor
**perky** ['pʌrkɪ] *adj* (*comp:* **-ier;** *super:* **-iest**) airoso, gallardo
**perlite** ['pʌrlaɪt] *s* (metal. & petrog.) perlita
**permafrost** ['pʌrmə,frɔst] o ['pʌrmə,frast] *s* suelo helado de modo permanente, en las regiones polares
**permalloy** [,pʌrm'ælɔɪ] *s* (trademark) permaleación, permaloy
**permanence** ['pʌrmənəns] *s* permanencia
**permanency** ['pʌrmənənsɪ] *s* (*pl:* **-cies**) permanencia; persona, cosa o posición permanentes
**permanent** ['pʌrmənənt] *adj* permanente; *s* (coll.) permanente, ondulación permanente
**Permanent Court of Arbitration** *s* Tribunal Permanente de Arbitraje
**Permanent Court of International Justice** *s* Tribunal Permanente de Justicia Internacional
**permanent magnetism** *s* (phys.) magnetismo permanente
**permanent tenure** *s* inamovilidad
**permanent wave** *s* ondulación permanente
**permanent way** *s* (rail.) material fijo
**permanganate** [pər'mæŋgənet] *s* (chem.) permanganato
**permanganic** [,pʌrmæŋ'gænɪk] *adj* permangánico
**permanganic acid** *s* (chem.) ácido permangánico
**permeability** [,pʌrmɪə'bɪlɪtɪ] *s* permeabilidad
**permeable** ['pʌrmɪəbəl] *adj* permeable
**permeance** ['pʌrmɪəns] *s* (elec.) permeancia
**permeate** ['pʌrmɪet] *va & vn* penetrar
**permeation** [,pʌrmɪ'eʃən] *s* penetración (*al través de los poros*)
**Permian** ['pʌrmɪən] *adj & s* (geol.) pérmico
**permissible** [pər'mɪsɪbəl] *adj* permisible
**permission** [pər'mɪʃən] *s* permisión, permiso
**permissive** [pər'mɪsɪv] *adj* permisivo; permisible
**permit** ['pʌrmɪt] *s* permiso; (com.) cédula de

aduana; [pər'mɪt] (*pret & pp:* **-mitted;** *ger:* **-mitting**) *va* permitir; **to permit to** + *inf* permitir + *inf,* permitir que + *subj*
**permutable** [pər'mjutəbəl] *adj* permutable
**permutation** [,pʌrmjə'teʃən] *s* permutación; (math.) permutación
**permute** [pər'mjut] *va* permutar
**pernicious** [pər'nɪʃəs] *adj* pernicioso
**pernicious anemia** *s* (path.) anemia perniciosa
**pernickety** [pər'nɪkɪtɪ] *adj* (coll.) descontentadizo, quisquilloso
**perorate** ['pɛrəret] *vn* perorar
**peroration** [,pɛrə'reʃən] *s* peroración
**peroxide** [pər'ɑksaɪd] o **peroxid** [pər'ɑksɪd] *s* (chem.) peróxido; (chem.) peróxido de hidrógeno
**peroxide blonde** *s* (slang) rubia oxigenada
**peroxyacid** [pər,ɑksɪ'æsɪd] *s* (chem.) peroxiácido
**perpend** ['pʌrpənd] *s* (mas.) perpiaño; (pər'pɛnd] *va & vn* (archaic) considerar, reflexionar
**perpendicular** [,pʌrpən'dɪkjələr] *adj & s* perpendicular
**perpendicularity** [,pʌrpən,dɪkjə'lærɪtɪ] *s* perpendicularidad
**perpetrate** ['pʌrpɪtret] *va* perpetrar
**perpetration** [,pʌrpɪ'treʃən] *s* perpetración
**perpetrator** ['pʌrpɪ,tretər] *s* perpetrador
**perpetual** [pər'pɛtʃuəl] *adj* perpetuo
**perpetually** [pər'pɛtʃuəlɪ] *adv* perpetuamente
**perpetual motion** *s* movimiento continuo o movimiento perpetuo
**perpetuate** [pər'pɛtʃuet] *va* perpetuar
**perpetuation** [pər,pɛtʃu'eʃən] *s* perpetuación
**perpetuity** [,pʌrpɪ'tjuɪtɪ] o [,pʌrpɪ'tuɪtɪ] *s* (*pl:* **-ties**) perpetuidad; **in perpetuity** perpetuamente, para siempre
**Perpignan** [pɛrpi'njɑ̃] *s* Perpiñán
**perplex** [pɛr'plɛks] *va* dejar perplejo; embrollar, enredar
**perplexed** [pər'plɛkst] *adj* perplejo
**perplexity** [pər'plɛksɪtɪ] *s* (*pl:* **-ties**) perplejidad; problema
**perquisite** ['pʌrkwɪzɪt] *s* obvención, adehala
**per se** [pər 'si] por sí mismo, en sí mismo, esencialmente
**persecute** ['pʌrsɪkjut] *va* perseguir
**persecution** [,pʌrsɪ'kjuʃən] *s* persecución; *adj* persecutorio
**persecutor** ['pʌrsɪ,kjutər] *s* perseguidor
**Perseid** ['pʌrsɪɪd] *s* (astr.) Perseida
**Persephone** [pər'sɛfənɪ] *s* (myth.) Perséfone
**Perseus** ['pʌrsjus] o ['pʌrsɪəs] *s* (myth. & astr.) Perseo
**perseverance** [,pʌrsɪ'vɪrəns] *s* perseverancia
**persevere** [,pʌrsɪ'vɪr] *vn* perseverar; **to persevere in** + *ger* perseverar en + *inf*
**persevering** [,pʌrsɪ'vɪrɪŋ] *adj* perseverante
**Persian** ['pʌrʒən] o ['pʌrʃən] *adj & s* persa
**Persian Gulf** *s* golfo Pérsico
**Persian lamb** *s* oveja caracul; caracul (*piel*)
**persicary** ['pʌrsɪ,kɛrɪ] *s* (*pl:* **-ies**) (bot.) persicaria, duraznillo
**persiflage** ['pʌrsɪflɑʒ] *s* burla fina, parloteo festivo
**persimmon** [pər'sɪmən] *s* (bot.) placaminero; (bot.) caqui
**persist** [pər'sɪst] o [pər'zɪst] *vn* persistir; **to persist in** + *ger* persistir en + *inf*
**persistence** [pər'sɪstəns] o [pər'zɪstəns] o **persistency** [pər'sɪstənsɪ] o [pər'zɪstənsɪ] *s* persistencia; porfía; pertinacia (*p.ej., de una enfermedad*)
**persistent** [pər'sɪstənt] o [pər'zɪstənt] *adj* persistente; porfiado; pertinaz (*enfermedad*)
**person** ['pʌrsən] *s* persona; (gram. & theol.) persona; **clean about one's person** cuidadoso en su aseo personal; **in the person of** en la persona de; **no person** nadie
**personable** ['pʌrsənəbəl] *adj* bien parecido, presentable
**personage** ['pʌrsənɪdʒ] *s* personaje; persona; (theat.) personaje
**persona grata** [pər'sonə 'gretə] *s* (*pl:* **personae gratae** [pər'soni 'greti]) persona grata
**personal** ['pʌrsənəl] *adj* personal; de uso personal; mueble, mobiliario (*dícese, p.ej., de los bienes*); **to become personal** personalizarse, pasar a hacer alusiones de carácter personal; **to make a personal appearance** aparecer en persona; *s* nota de sociedad; remitido (*en un periódico*)
**personal a** *s* la preposición **a** con el complemento directo de persona
**personal effects** *spl* bienes de uso personal
**personal equation** *s* ecuación personal
**personal estate** *s* bienes muebles
**personality** [,pʌrsə'nælɪtɪ] *s* (*pl:* **-ties**) personalidad
**personality cult** *s* culto a la personalidad
**personalization** [,pʌrsənəlɪ'zeʃən] *s* personalización
**personalize** ['pʌrsənəlaɪz] *va* personalizar
**personally** ['pʌrsənəlɪ] *adv* personalmente; en particular; como cosa personal
**personal pronoun** *s* pronombre personal
**personal property** *s* bienes muebles
**personalty** ['pʌrsənəltɪ] *s* (*pl:* **-ties**) bienes muebles
**personate** ['pʌrsənɪt] o ['pʌrsənet] *adj* (bot.) personada (*corola*); ['pʌrsənet] *va* fingir ser, hacerse pasar por; representar, hacer el papel de; *vn* hacer un papel
**personation** [,pʌrsə'neʃən] *s* personificación; representación (*de un papel*); usurpación del nombre de otra persona
**personification** [pər,sɑnɪfɪ'keʃən] *s* personificación
**personify** [pər'sɑnɪfaɪ] (*pret & pp:* **-fied**) *va* personificar
**personnel** [,pʌrsə'nɛl] *s* personal
**perspective** [pər'spɛktɪv] *adj* perspectivo; *s* perspectiva
**perspicacious** [,pʌrspɪ'keʃəs] *adj* perspicaz
**perspicacity** [,pʌrspɪ'kæsɪtɪ] *s* perspicacia; (archaic) perspicacia (*agudeza de la vista*)
**perspicuity** [,pʌrspɪ'kjuɪtɪ] *s* perspicuidad
**perspicuous** [pər'spɪkjuəs] *adj* perspicuo
**perspiration** [,pʌrspɪ'reʃən] *s* transpiración
**perspire** [pər'spaɪr] *va & vn* transpirar, sudar
**persuade** [pər'swed] *va* persuadir; **to persuade to** + *inf* persuadir a + *inf,* persuadir a que + *subj*
**persuasible** [pər'swesɪbəl] *adj* fácil de convencer
**persuasion** [pər'sweʒən] *s* persuasión; persuasiva; secta, creencia religiosa; creencia fuerte; (hum.) clase, especie
**persuasive** [pər'swesɪv] *adj* persuasivo
**pert** [pʌrt] *adj* atrevido, descarado; (coll.) animado, vivo
**pertain** [pər'ten] *vn* pertenecer; **pertaining to** perteneciente a
**pertinacious** [,pʌrtɪ'neʃəs] *adj* pertinaz
**pertinacity** [,pərtɪ'næsɪtɪ] *s* pertinacia
**pertinence** ['pʌrtɪnəns] o **pertinency** ['pʌrtɪnənsɪ] *s* pertinencia
**pertinent** ['pʌrtɪnənt] *adj* pertinente
**perturb** [pər'tʌrb] *va* perturbar
**perturbation** [,pʌrtər'beʃən] *s* perturbación
**Peru** [pə'ru] *s* el Perú
**Perugia** [pɛ'rudʒɑ] *s* Perusa
**peruke** [pə'ruk] *s* peluquín
**perusal** [pə'ruzəl] *s* lectura, lectura cuidadosa
**peruse** [pə'ruz] *va* leer, leer con atención
**Peruvian** [pə'ruvɪən] *adj & s* peruano
**Peruvian bark** *s* (pharm.) quina, cascarilla
**pervade** [pər'ved] *va* penetrar, esparcirse por, extenderse por
**pervasion** [pər'veʒən] *s* penetración, esparcimiento
**pervasive** [pər'vesɪv] *adj* penetrante
**perverse** [pər'vʌrs] *adj* perverso; avieso, díscolo; contumaz; (psychopath.) pervertido
**perverseness** [pər'vʌrsnɪs] *s* perversidad
**perversion** [pər'vʌrʒən] o [pər'vʌrʃən] *s* perversión; (psychopath.) perversión
**perversity** [pər'vʌrsɪtɪ] *s* (*pl:* **-ties**) perversidad; indocilidad; contumacia
**pervert** ['pʌrvərt] *s* renegado, apóstata; (psychopath.) pervertido; [pər'vʌrt] *va* pervertir; emplear mal (*los talentos que uno tiene*)
**pervious** ['pʌrvɪəs] *adj* permeable; fácil de convencer
**pesky** ['pɛskɪ] *adj* (*comp:* **-kier;** *super:* **-kiest**) (coll.) molesto, cargante
**pessary** ['pɛsərɪ] *s* (*pl:* **-ries**) (med.) pesario
**pessimism** ['pɛsɪmɪzəm] *s* pesimismo
**pessimist** ['pɛsɪmɪst] *s* pesimista
**pessimistic** [,pɛsɪ'mɪstɪk] *adj* pesimista

**pessimistically** [ˌpɛsɪˈmɪstɪkəlɪ] *adv* con pesimismo
**pest** [pɛst] *s* peste; insecto nocivo; (fig.) plaga (*infortunio, contratiempo, etc.*); (fig.) machaca (*persona fastidiosa*)
**Pestalozzian** [ˌpɛstəˈlɑtsɪən] *adj* (educ.) pestalociano
**pester** [ˈpɛstər] *va* molestar, importunar
**pesthouse** [ˈpɛstˌhaʊs] *s* lazareto, hospital de contagiosos
**pestiferous** [pɛsˈtɪfərəs] *adj* pestífero; (coll.) engorroso, molesto
**pestilence** [ˈpɛstɪləns] *s* pestilencia
**pestilent** [ˈpɛstɪlənt] *adj* mortífero; pestilente; engorroso, molesto
**pestilential** [ˌpɛstɪˈlɛnʃəl] *adj* pestilencial; pestilencioso
**pestle** [ˈpɛsəl] o [ˈpɛstəl] *s* mano de almirez o mortero; *va* majar
**pet** [pɛt] *s* animal mimado, animal casero; niño mimado; favorito; fanfurriña, enojo pasajero; *adj* mimado; domesticado; favorito; (*pret & pp:* **petted;** *ger:* **petting**) *va* acariciar, mimar; *vn* (slang) besuquearse
**petal** [ˈpɛtəl] *s* (bot.) pétalo
**petaled** o **petalled** [ˈpɛtəld] *adj* que tiene pétalos
**petard** [pɪˈtɑrd] *s* petardo
**petcock** [ˈpɛtˌkɑk] *s* llave de desagüe, llave de purga
**Pete** [pit] *s* Perico
**Peter** [ˈpitər] *s* Pedro; **to rob Peter to pay Paul** desnudar a un santo para vestir a otro; (*l.c.*) *vn* (coll.) agotarse; **to peter out** (coll.) agotarse, acabarse
**Peter Pan** *s* (lit.) el niño que no quiso crecer, héroe de la famosa comedia infantil de James Barrie
**Peter's pence** *spl* los diezmos de San Pedro
**Peter the Great** *s* Pedro el Grande
**Peter the Hermit** *s* Pedro el Ermitaño
**petiolate** [ˈpɛtɪolet] *adj* peciolado
**petiole** [ˈpɛtɪol] *s* (bot. & zool.) pecíolo
**petit** [ˈpɛtɪ] *adj* (law) menor
**petite** [pəˈtit] *adj* pequeña, chiquita
**petition** [pɪˈtɪʃən] *s* petición; instancia, memorial, solicitud; *va* suplicar; dirigir una instancia o memorial a, solicitar
**petitionary** [pɪˈtɪʃəˌnɛrɪ] *adj* petitorio
**petitio principii** [pɪˈtɪʃɪo prɪnˈsɪpɪaɪ] *s* (log.) petición de principio
**petit jury** *s* (law) jurado de juicio
**pet name** *s* nombre de cariño, sobrenombre familiar
**Petrarch** [ˈpitrɑrk] *s* Petrarca
**Petrarchism** [ˈpitrɑrkɪzəm] *s* petrarquismo
**petrel** [ˈpɛtrəl] *s* (orn.) petrel
**Petri dish** [ˈpetri] *s* caja o disco de Petri
**petrifaction** [ˌpɛtrɪˈfækʃən] o **petrification** [ˌpɛtrɪfɪˈkeʃən] *s* petrificación
**Petrified Forest** *s* Bosque Petrificado
**petrify** [ˈpɛtrɪfaɪ] (*pret & pp:* **-fied**) *va* petrificar; *vn* petrificarse
**petrochemical** [ˌpɛtrəˈkɛmɪkəl] *adj* petroquímico; *s* producto petroquímico
**Petrograd** [ˈpɛtrogræd] *s* Petrogrado
**petrography** [pɪˈtrɑgrəfɪ] *s* petrografía
**petrol** [ˈpɛtrəl] *s* (Brit.) gasolina; (*pret & pp:* **-rolled;** *ger:* **-rolling**) *va* (Brit.) limpiar con gasolina
**petrolatum** [ˌpɛtroˈletəm] *s* (pharm.) petrolato
**petroleum** [pɪˈtrolɪəm] *s* petróleo
**petroleum jelly** *s* petrolato, parafina blanda
**petroliferous** [ˌpɛtrəˈlɪfərəs] *adj* petrolífero
**petrology** [pɪˈtrɑlədʒɪ] *s* petrología
**petronel** [ˈpɛtrənəl] *s* pistola de caballería
**petrous** [ˈpɛtrəs] *adj* petroso; (anat.) petroso
**pet shop** *s* pajarería (*tienda donde se venden pajaros y otros animales domésticos*)
**petticoat** [ˈpɛtɪkot] *s* enaguas; (slang) falda (*mujer, muchacha, moza*); *adj* (slang) de mujer, de mujeres
**pettifogger** [ˈpɛtɪˌfɑgər] *s* picapleitos, trapacista
**pettifoggery** [ˈpɛtɪˌfɑgərɪ] *s* (*pl:* **-ies**) trapacería
**pettifogging** [ˈpɛtɪˌfɑgɪŋ] *adj* trapacero; *s* trapacería
**pettish** [ˈpɛtɪʃ] *adj* malhumorado, enojadizo
**petty** [ˈpɛtɪ] *adj* (*comp:* **-tier;** *super:* **-tiest**) insignificante, menor, pequeño; mezquino; intolerante
**petty cash** *s* caja de menores, efectivo para gastos menores
**petty jury** *s* var. de **petit jury**
**petty larceny** *s* (law) ratería, hurto
**petty officer** *s* (nav.) suboficial
**petty treason** *s* traición menor
**petulance** [ˈpɛtjələns] o **petulancy** [ˈpɛtjələnsɪ] *s* mal humor
**petulant** [ˈpɛtjələnt] *adj* malhumorado, enojadizo
**petunia** [pɪˈtjunɪə] o [pɪˈtunɪə] *s* (bot.) petunia
**pew** [pju] *s* banco de iglesia; *interj* ¡ fo!
**pewee** [ˈpiwi] *s* (orn.) aguador
**pewit** [ˈpiwɪt] *s* (orn.) gaviota de cabeza negra; (orn.) ave fría
**pewter** [ˈpjutər] *s* peltre; vajilla de peltre; *adj* de peltre
**pewterer** [ˈpjutərər] *s* peltrero
**pf.** abr. de **pfennig** y **preferred**
**Pfc.** abr. de **private first class**
**pfd.** abr. de **preferred**
**pfg.** abr. de **pfennig**
**Pg.** abr. de **Portugal** y **Portuguese**
**Phaedra** [ˈfidrə] *s* (myth.) Fedra
**Phaethon** [ˈfeɪθɑn] *s* (myth.) Faetón
**phaeton** o **phaëton** [ˈfeɪtən] *s* faetón
**phagocyte** [ˈfægəsaɪt] *s* (physiol.) fagocito
**phagocytosis** [ˌfægəsaɪˈtosɪs] *s* fagocitosis
**phalangeal** [fəˈlændʒɪəl] *adj* falangiano
**phalanger** [fəˈlændʒər] *s* (zool.) falangero
**phalangette** [ˌfælənˈdʒɛt] *s* (anat.) falangeta
**phalanstery** [ˈfælənˌstɛrɪ] *s* (*pl:* **-ies**) falansterio
**phalanx** [ˈfelæŋks] o [ˈfælæŋks] *s* (*pl:* **phalanxes** o **phalanges** [feˈlændʒiz]) falange; (anat. & zool.) falange
**phalarope** [ˈfælərop] *s* (orn.) falárope
**phallic** [ˈfælɪk] *adj* fálico
**phallicism** [ˈfælɪsɪzəm] o **phallism** [ˈfælɪzəm] *s* falismo
**phallin** [ˈfælɪn] *s* (biochem.) falina
**phallus** [ˈfæləs] *s* (*pl:* **-li** [laɪ]) falo
**phanerogam** [ˈfænərəˌgæm] *s* (bot.) fanerógama
**phanerogamous** [ˌfænəˈrɑgəməs] *adj* (bot.) fanerógamo
**phantasm** [ˈfæntæzəm] *s* fantasma
**phantasmagoria** [fænˌtæzməˈgorɪə] *s* fantasmagoría
**phantasmagorial** [fænˌtæzməˈgorɪəl] o **phantasmagoric** [fænˌtæzməˈgɔrɪk] o [fænˌtæzməˈgɑrɪk] *adj* fantasmagórico
**phantasmal** [fænˈtæzməl] *adj* fantasmal
**phantasy** [ˈfæntəsɪ] o [ˈfæntəzɪ] *s* (*pl:* **-sies**) var. de **fantasy**
**phantom** [ˈfæntəm] *s* fantasma; *adj* fantasmal
**phantom circuit** *s* (elec.) circuito fantasma
**Pharaoh** [ˈfɛro] o [ˈfɛreo] *s* Faraón
**Pharaonic** [ˌfɛreˈɑnɪk] *adj* faraónico
**pharisaic** [ˌfærɪˈseɪk] *adj* farisaico; (*cap.*) *adj* farisaico
**pharisaical** [ˌfærɪˈseɪkəl] *adj* farisaico
**pharisaism** [ˈfærɪseɪzəm] *s* farisaísmo; (*cap.*) *s* farisaísmo
**pharisee** [ˈfærɪsi] *s* fariseo; (*cap.*) *s* fariseo
**phariseeism** [ˈfærɪsiɪzəm] *s* var. de **pharisaism**
**pharmaceutic** [ˌfɑrməˈsutɪk] o [ˌfɑrməˈsjutɪk] *adj* farmacéutico; **pharmaceutics** *ssg* farmacéutica, farmacia
**pharmaceutical** [ˌfɑrməˈsutɪkəl] o [ˌfɑrməˈsjutɪkəl] *adj* farmacéutico
**pharmacist** [ˈfɑrməsɪst] *s* farmacéutico
**pharmacognosy** [ˌfɑrməˈkɑgnəsɪ] *s* farmacognosia
**pharmacologist** [ˌfɑrməˈkɑlədʒɪst] *s* farmacólogo
**pharmacology** [ˌfɑrməˈkɑlədʒɪ] *s* farmacología
**pharmacopoeia** [ˌfɑrməkoˈpiə] *s* farmacopea
**pharmacy** [ˈfɑrməsɪ] *s* (*pl:* **-cies**) farmacia
**pharyngeal** [fəˈrɪndʒɪəl] o [ˌfærɪnˈdʒiəl] *adj* faríngeo
**pharyngitis** [ˌfærɪnˈdʒaɪtɪs] *s* (path.) faringitis
**pharyngoscope** [fəˈrɪŋgəskop] *s* faringoscopio

**pharyngoscopy** [ˌfærɪŋˈgɑskəpɪ] *s* faringoscopia
**pharynx** [ˈfærɪŋks] *s* (*pl:* **pharynxes** o **pharynges** [fəˈrɪndʒiz]) (anat.) faringe
**phase** [fez] *s* fase; (astr., biol., elec. & phys.) fase; **in phase** (elec.) en fase; **out of phase** (elec.) fuera de fase; *va* (elec.) poner en fase; (coll.) inquietar, molestar
**phase lag** *s* (elec.) retraso de fase, corrimiento de fase
**phase modulation** *s* (rad.) modulación de fase
**phaseolin** [fəˈsiəlɪn] *s* (biochem.) faseolina
**phase rule** *s* (physical chem.) ley de las fases
**phase shift** *s* (elec.) decalaje
**phase splitter** *s* (elec.) divisor de fase
**Ph.B.** abr. de **Bachelor of Philosophy**
**Ph.D.** abr. de **Doctor of Philosophy**
**pheasant** [ˈfɛzənt] *s* (orn.) faisán
**phelloderm** [ˈfɛlədʌrm] *s* (bot.) felodermo
**phellogen** [ˈfɛlədʒən] *s* (bot.) felógeno
**phenacetin** [fɪˈnæsɪtɪn] *s* (pharm.) fenacetina
**phenakistoscope** [ˌfɛnəˈkɪstəskop] *s* fenaquistiscopio
**Phenicia** [fɪˈnɪʃə] *s* var. de **Phoenicia**
**phenix** [ˈfinɪks] *s* var. de **phoenix**
**phenobarbital** [ˌfinoˈbɑrbɪtæl] o [ˌfinoˈbɑrbɪtəl] *s* (pharm.) fenobarbital
**phenocryst** [ˈfinəkrɪst] o [ˈfɛnəkrɪst] *s* (geol.) fenocristal
**phenol** [ˈfinol] o [ˈfinɑl] *s* (chem.) fenol
**phenology** [fɪˈnɑlədʒɪ] *s* fenología
**phenolphthalein** [ˌfinɑlˈθælin] *s* (chem.) fenolftaleína
**phenomenal** [fɪˈnɑmɪnəl] *adj* fenomenal; (fig.) fenomenal
**phenomenalism** [fɪˈnɑmənəlɪzəm] *s* (philos.) fenomenalismo
**phenomenally** [fɪˈnɑmɪnəlɪ] *adv* fenomenalmente
**phenomenology** [fɪˌnɑməˈnɑlədʒɪ] *s* (philos.) fenomenología
**phenomenon** [fɪˈnɑmɪnɑn] *s* (*pl:* **-na** [nə]) fenómeno; (philos.) fenómeno
**phenothiazine** [ˌfinəˈθaɪəzin] *s* (chem.) fenotiacina
**phenotype** [ˈfinətaɪp] *s* (biol.) fenotipo
**phenyl** [ˈfɛnɪl] o [ˈfinɪl] *s* (chem.) fenilo
**phenylene** [ˈfɛnɪlin] o [ˈfinɪlin] *s* (chem.) fenileno
**phew** [fju] *interj* ¡puf!; ¡anda!; ¡zape!
**phial** [ˈfaɪəl] *s* frasco, frasco pequeño
**Phidian** [ˈfɪdɪən] *adj* de Fidias
**Phidias** [ˈfɪdɪəs] *s* Fidias
**Phil.** abr. de **Philip, Philippians** y **Philippine**
**Phila.** abr. de **Philadelphia**
**Philadelphia** [ˌfɪləˈdɛlfɪə] *s* Filadelfia
**Philadelphian** [ˌfɪləˈdɛlfɪən] *adj & s* filadelfiano
**philander** [fɪˈlændər] *s* galanteador, tenorio; (zool.) filandro; *vn* galantear
**philanderer** [fɪˈlændərər] *s* galanteador, tenorio
**philanthropic** [ˌfɪlənˈθrɑpɪk] o **philanthropical** [ˌfɪlənˈθrɑpɪkəl] *adj* filantrópico
**philanthropist** [fɪˈlænθrəpɪst] *s* filántropo
**philanthropy** [fɪˈlænθrəpɪ] *s* filantropía
**philatelic** [ˌfɪləˈtɛlɪk] *adj* filatélico
**philatelist** [fɪˈlætəlɪst] *s* filatelista
**philately** [fɪˈlætəlɪ] *s* filatelia
**Philemon** [fɪˈlimən] *s* (myth.) Filemón; (Bib.) Epístola de San Pablo a Filemón
**philharmonic** [ˌfɪlhɑrˈmɑnɪk] *adj* filarmónico; *s* filarmónico; sociedad filarmónica
**philhellene** [fɪlˈhɛlin] *adj & s* filheleno
**Philip** [ˈfɪlɪp] *s* Felipe; Filipo (*p.ej., de Macedonia*)
**Philippi** [fɪˈlɪpaɪ] *s* Filipos
**Philippian** [fɪˈlɪpɪən] *adj & s* filipense; **Philippians** *spl* (Bib.) Epístola de San Pablo a los Filipenses
**philippic** [fɪˈlɪpɪk] *s* filípica; (*cap.*) *s* (hist.) Filípica (*de Demóstenes; de Cicerón*)
**Philippine** [ˈfɪlɪpin] *adj* filipino; **Philippines** *spl* Filipinas (*islas*)
**Philippine Islands** *spl* Islas Filipinas
**Philistine** [fɪˈlɪstin], [ˈfɪlɪstin] o [ˈfɪlɪstaɪn] *adj & s* (Bib. & fig.) filisteo
**Philistinism** [fɪˈlɪstɪnɪzəm] o [ˈfɪlɪstɪnɪzəm] *s* filisteísmo
**Phillips screw** [ˈfɪlɪps] *s* tornillo patente Phillips
**philologian** [ˌfɪləˈlodʒɪən] *s* filólogo
**philological** [ˌfɪləˈlɑdʒɪkəl] *adj* filológico
**philologist** [fɪˈlɑlədʒɪst] *s* filólogo
**philology** [fɪˈlɑlədʒɪ] *s* filología
**philomel** o **Philomel** [ˈfɪləmɛl] *s* (poet.) filomela o filomena (*ruiseñor*)
**Philomela** [ˌfɪləˈmilə] *s* (myth.) Filomela; (*l.c.*) *s* (poet.) filomela o filomena (*ruiseñor*)
**philopena** [ˌfɪləˈpinə] *s* juego de prendas que se inicia compartiendo una nuez; la nuez; la prenda
**philosopher** [fɪˈlɑsəfər] *s* filósofo
**philosopher's stone** *s* piedra filosofal
**philosophic** [ˌfɪləˈsɑfɪk] o **philosophical** [ˌfɪləˈsɑfɪkəl] *adj* filosófico
**philosophize** [fɪˈlɑsəfaɪz] *vn* filosofar
**philosophy** [fɪˈlɑsəfɪ] *s* (*pl:* **-phies**) filosofía
**philter** o **philtre** [ˈfɪltər] *s* filtro (*bebida mágica*); *va* hechizar con filtro
**phimosis** [faɪˈmosɪs] *s* (path.) fimosis
**Phineas** [ˈfɪnɪəs] *s* Fineas
**phlebitis** [flɪˈbaɪtɪs] *s* (path.) flebitis
**phlebosclerosis** [ˌflɛbosklɪˈrosɪs] *s* (path.) flebosclerosis
**phlebotomist** [flɪˈbɑtəmɪst] *s* flebotomiano
**phlebotomy** [flɪˈbɑtəmɪ] *s* flebotomía
**phlegm** [flɛm] *s* (physiol. & fig.) flema
**phlegmatic** [flɛgˈmætɪk] o **phlegmatical** [flɛgˈmætɪkəl] *adj* flemático
**phlegmon** [ˈflɛgmɑn] *s* (path.) flemón
**phlegmonous** [ˈflɛgmənəs] *adj* flemonoso
**phlegmy** [ˈflɛmɪ] *adj* flemoso
**phloem** o **phloëm** [ˈfloɛm] *s* (bot.) floema
**phlogistic** [floˈdʒɪstɪk] *adj* (path. & old chem.) flogístico
**phlogiston** [floˈdʒɪstɑn] *s* (old chem.) flogisto
**phlogopite** [ˈflɑgəpaɪt] *s* (mineral.) flogopita
**phlorizin** [ˈflɑrɪzɪn] o [fləˈraɪzɪn] *s* (chem.) floricina
**phlox** [flɑks] *s* (bot.) cambrina, simpática, flox
**phlyctena** [flɪkˈtinə] *s* (*pl:* **-nae** [ni]) (path.) flictena
**phobia** [ˈfobɪə] *s* fobia
**Phocian** [ˈfoʃən] *adj & s* focense
**Phocis** [ˈfosɪs] *s* la Fócida
**phoebe** [ˈfibɪ] *s* (orn.) aguador; (*cap.*) *s* (myth.) Febe; (poet.) Febe (*la luna*)
**Phoebus** [ˈfibəs] *s* (myth.) Febo; (poet.) Febo (*el sol*)
**Phoenicia** [fɪˈnɪʃə] *s* Fenicia
**Phoenician** [fɪˈnɪʃən] *adj & s* fenicio
**phoenix** [ˈfinɪks] *s* (myth. & fig.) fénix
**phone** [fon] *s* (coll.) teléfono; (phonet.) fon; **to come** o **to go to the phone** acudir al teléfono, ponerse al aparato; *va & vn* (coll.) telefonear
**phone call** *s* llamada telefónica
**phoneme** [ˈfonim] *s* (phonet.) fonema
**phonemic** [foˈnimɪk] *adj* fonémico; **phonemics** *ssg* fonémica
**phonet.** abr. de **phonetics**
**phonetic** [foˈnɛtɪk] *adj* fonético; **phonetics** *ssg* fonética
**phonetically** [foˈnɛtɪkəlɪ] *adv* fonéticamente
**phonetician** [ˌfonɪˈtɪʃən] *s* fonetista
**phoney** [ˈfonɪ] *adj* (*comp:* **-nier;** *super:* **-niest**) var. de **phony;** *s* var. de **phony**
**phonic** [ˈfonɪk] *adj* fónico; **phonics** *ssg* fónica; *spl* sistema fónico, basado en la ortografía ordinaria, que se emplea para enseñar a pronunciar y a leer a los niños
**phonogram** [ˈfonəgræm] *s* fonograma
**phonograph** [ˈfonəgræf] o [ˈfonəgrɑf] *s* fonógrafo; *adj* fonográfico
**phonographic** [ˌfonəˈgræfɪk] *adj* fonográfico
**phonographically** [ˌfonəˈgræfɪkəlɪ] *adv* fonográficamente
**phonograph record** *s* disco de fonógrafo
**phonography** [foˈnɑgrəfɪ] *s* fonografía
**phonolite** [ˈfonəlaɪt] *s* (mineral.) fonolita
**phonologic** [ˌfonəˈlɑdʒɪk] o **phonological** [ˌfonəˈlɑdʒɪkəl] *adj* fonológico
**phonologist** [foˈnɑlədʒɪst] *s* fonólogo
**phonology** [foˈnɑlədʒɪ] *s* fonología
**phonoscope** [ˈfonəskop] *s* fonoscopio
**phony** [ˈfonɪ] *adj* (*comp:* **-nier;** *super:* **-niest**) (slang) falso, contrahecho; *s* (*pl:* **-nies**) (slang) farsa; (slang) farsante

**phosgene** ['fasdʒin] *s* (chem.) fosgeno
**phosphate** ['fasfet] *s* (chem. & agr.) fosfato
**phosphatic** [fas'fætɪk] *adj* fosfático
**phosphatize** ['fasfətaɪz] *va* fosfatar
**phosphaturia** [,fasfə'tjʊrɪə] o [,fasfə'tʊrɪə] *s* (path.) fosfaturia
**phosphene** ['fasfin] *s* (physiol.) fosfeno
**phosphide** ['fasfaɪd] o ['fasfɪd] *s* (chem.) fosfuro
**phosphine** ['fasfin] o ['fasfɪn] *s* (chem.) fosfina
**phosphite** ['fasfaɪt] *s* (chem.) fosfito
**phosphonium** [fas'fonɪəm] *s* (chem.) fosfonio
**Phosphor** ['fasfər] *s* (poet.) Fósforo (*estrella matutina*)
**phosphorate** ['fasfəret] *va* fosforar
**phosphor bronze** *s* (trademark) bronce fosforoso
**phosphoresce** [,fasfə'rɛs] *vn* fosforecer
**phosphorescence** [,fasfə'rɛsəns] *s* fosforescencia
**phosphorescent** [,fasfə'rɛsənt] *adj* fosforescente
**phosphoric** [fas'farɪk] o [fas'fɔrɪk] *adj* (chem.) fosfórico
**phosphoric acid** *s* (chem.) ácido fosfórico
**phosphorite** ['fasfəraɪt] *s* (mineral.) fosforita
**phosphoroscope** [fas'farəskop] o [fas'fɔrəskop] *s* fosforoscopio
**phosphorous** ['fasfərəs] o [fas'forəs] *adj* (chem.) fosforoso
**phosphorous acid** *s* (chem.) ácido fosforoso
**phosphorus** ['fasfərəs] *s* (*pl:* **-ri** [raɪ]) (chem.) fósforo; (*cap.*) *s* (poet.) Fósforo (*estrella matutina*)
**phosphureted** o **phosphuretted** ['fasfjə,rɛtɪd] *adj* (chem.) fosfurado
**phot** [fat] o [fot] *s* (phys.) fotio
**photic** ['fotɪk] *adj* fótico
**photo** ['foto] *s* (*pl:* **-tos**) (coll.) foto; *va* (coll.) fotografiar
**photoactinic** [,fotoæk'tɪnɪk] *adj* fotoactínico
**photocell** ['foto,sɛl] *s* (elec.) fotocelda o fotocélula
**photochemical** [,foto'kɛmɪkəl] *adj* fotoquímico
**photochemistry** [,foto'kɛmɪstrɪ] *s* fotoquímica
**photochrome** ['fotokrom] *s* fotocromo
**photochromy** ['foto,kromɪ] *s* fotocromía
**photoconductivity** [,foto,kandʌk'tɪvɪtɪ] *s* (elec.) fotoconductividad
**photocopy** ['foto,kapɪ] *s* (*pl:* **-ies**) fotocopia
**photodisintegration** [,fotodɪs,ɪntɪ'greʃən] *s* (phys.) fotodesintegración
**photodynamic** [,fotodaɪ'næmɪk] o [,fotodɪ'næmɪk] *adj* fotodinámico; **photodynamics** *ssg* fotodinámica
**photoelectric** [,foto·ɪ'lɛktrɪk] *adj* fotoeléctrico
**photoelectric cell** *s* célula fotoeléctrica
**photoelectron** [,foto·ɪ'lɛktran] *s* (physical chem.) fotoelectrón
**photoengrave** [,fotoɛn'grev] *va* fotograbar
**photoengraver** [,fotoɛn'grevər] *s* fotograbador
**photoengraving** [,fotoɛn'grevɪŋ] *s* fotograbado
**photo finish** *s* (sport) llegada de caballos o corredores a la meta con tan poca diferencia que hay que determinar al vencedor mediante el fotofija
**photofinishing** [,foto'fɪnɪʃɪŋ] *s* (phot.) revelado e impresión
**photoflash lamp** ['fotə,flæʃ] *s* (phot.) relámpago fotogénico eléctrico
**photogen** ['fotodʒɛn] *s* (chem.) fotógeno
**photogene** ['fotodʒin] *s* fotógeno (*impresión visual que dura después que la imagen propia ha cesado de ser visible*); (chem.) fotógeno
**photogenic** [,foto'dʒɛnɪk] *adj* (biol. & phot.) fotogénico
**photogrammetric** [,fotogrə'mɛtrɪk] o **photogrammetrical** [,fotogrə'mɛtrɪkəl] *adj* fotogramétrico
**photogrammetry** [,foto'græmɪtrɪ] *s* fotogrametría
**photograph** ['fotəgræf] o ['fotəgraf] *s* fotografía (*imagen, retrato*); *va & vn* fotografiar; **to photograph well** ser fotogénico
**photographer** [fə'tagrəfər] *s* fotógrafo
**photographic** [,fotə'græfɪk] *adj* fotográfico
**photographically** [,fotə'græfɪkəlɪ] *adv* fotográficamente
**photography** [fə'tagrəfɪ] *s* fotografía (*arte*)
**photogravure** [,fotogrə'vjʊr] o [,foto'grevjər] *s* huecograbado
**photojournalism** [,foto'dʒʌrnəlɪzəm] *s* fotoperiodismo
**photokinesis** [,fotokɪ'nisɪs] *s* (physiol.) fotocinesis
**photokinetic** [,fotokɪ'nɛtɪk] *adj* fotocinético
**photolithograph** [,foto'lɪθəgræf] o [,foto'lɪθəgraf] *s* fotolitografía; *va* fotolitografiar
**photolithography** [,fotolɪ'θagrəfɪ] *s* fotolitografía
**photolysis** [fo'talɪsɪs] *s* fotólisis
**photomechanical** [,fotomɪ'kænɪkəl] *adj* fotomecánico
**photometer** [fo'tamɪtər] *s* fotómetro
**photometry** [fo'tamɪtrɪ] *s* fotometría
**photomicrography** [,fotomaɪ'kragrəfɪ] *s* fotomicrografía
**photomontage** [,fotoman'taʒ] *s* fotomontaje
**photon** ['fotan] *s* (phys.) fotón
**photo-offset** [,foto'ɔf,sɛt] o [,foto'af,sɛt] *s* foto-offset
**photophobia** [,foto'fobɪə] *s* (path.) fotofobia
**photoplay** ['foto,ple] *s* fotodrama, drama cinematográfico
**photoprint** ['foto,prɪnt] *s* fotocalco
**photoprocess** ['foto,prasɛs] o ['foto,prosɛs] *s* procedimiento fotomecánico
**photoreconnaissance** [,fotorɪ'kanɪsəns] *s* fotorreconocimiento
**photorelief** [,fotorɪ'lif] *s* fotografía en relieve, fotorrelieve
**photosensitive** [,foto'sɛnsɪtɪv] *adj* fotosensitivo
**photospectroscope** [,foto'spɛktrəskop] *s* fotospectroscopio
**photosphere** ['foto,sfɪr] *s* (astr.) fotosfera
**photostat** ['fotostæt] *s* (trademark) fotóstato; *va & vn* fotostatar
**photostatic** [,foto'stætɪk] *adj* fotostático
**photosynthesis** [,foto'sɪnθɪsɪs] *s* (bot. & chem.) fotosíntesis
**phototaxis** [,foto'tæksɪs] *s* (biol.) fototactismo o fototaxis
**phototelegraph** [,foto'tɛlɪgræf] o [,foto'tɛlɪgraf] *s* fototelégrafo; *va & vn* fototelegrafiar
**phototelegraphy** [,fototɪ'lɛgrəfɪ] *s* fototelegrafía
**phototherapeutics** [,foto,θɛrə'pjutɪks] o **phototherapy** [,foto'θɛrəpɪ] *s* fototerapia
**phototropism** [fo'tatrəpɪzəm] *s* (biol.) fototropismo
**phototube** ['fotətjub] o ['fotətub] *s* (elec.) fototubo
**phototype** ['fototaɪp] *s* fototipo
**phototypography** [,fototaɪ'pagrəfɪ] *s* fototipografía
**phototypy** ['foto,taɪpɪ] o [fo'tatəpɪ] *s* fototipia
**photovoltaic** [,fotoval'teɪk] *adj* fotovoltaico
**photozincography** [,fotozɪŋ'kagrəfɪ] *s* fotocincografía
**phrase** [frez] *s* frase; (mus.) frase musical; *va* frasear; (mus.) frasear
**phraseology** [,frezɪ'alədʒɪ] *s* (*pl:* **-gies**) fraseología
**phrasing** ['frezɪŋ] *s* fraseo; (mus.) fraseo
**phratry** ['fretrɪ] *s* (*pl:* **-tries**) fratría
**phreatic** [frɪ'ætɪk] *adj* freático
**phrenetic** [frɪ'nɛtɪk] *adj* frenético
**phrenetically** [frɪ'nɛtɪkəlɪ] *adv* frenéticamente
**phrenic** ['frɛnɪk] *adj* frénico; (anat.) frénico
**phrenitis** [frɪ'naɪtɪs] *s* (path.) frenitis
**phrenological** [,frɛnə'ladʒɪkəl] *adj* frenológico
**phrenologist** [frɪ'nalədʒɪst] *s* frenólogo
**phrenology** [frɪ'nalədʒɪ] *s* frenología
**phrenopathy** [frɪ'napəθɪ] *s* (path.) frenopatía
**phrensy** ['frɛnzɪ] *s* (*pl:* **-sies**) var. de **frenzy**
**Phrygia** ['frɪdʒɪə] *s* Frigia
**Phrygian** ['frɪdʒɪən] *adj & s* frigio
**PHS.** abr. de **Public Health Service**
**phthalein** ['θælin], ['θælɪɪn], ['fθælin] o ['fθælɪɪn] *s* (chem.) ftaleína

**phthalic** ['θælɪk] o ['fθælɪk] *adj* (chem.) ftálico
**phthalin** ['θælɪn] o ['fθælɪn] *s* (chem.) ftalina
**phthiocol** ['θaɪəkol] o [θaɪəkəl] *s* (biochem.) ftiocol
**phthisic** ['tɪzɪk] *s* (path.) tisis
**phthisical** ['tɪzɪkəl] *adj* tísico
**phthisis** ['θaɪsɪs] *s* (path.) tisis
**phycology** [faɪ'kɑlədʒɪ] *s* ficología
**phylactery** [fɪ'læktərɪ] *s* (*pl:* **-ies**) filacteria; (f.a.) filacteria
**Phyllis** ['fɪlɪs] *s* Filis
**phyllite** ['fɪlaɪt] *s* (mineral.) filita
**phyllium** ['fɪlɪəm] *s* (ent.) filio
**phyllode** ['fɪlod] *s* (bot.) filodio
**phyllomania** [,fɪlo'menɪə] *s* (bot.) filomanía
**phyllophagous** [fɪ'lɑfəgəs] *adj* filófago
**phyllopod** ['fɪləpɑd] *adj* & *s* (zool.) filópodo
**phyllotaxis** [,fɪlə'tæksɪs] *s* (bot.) filotaxia
**phylloxera** [,fɪlɑk'sɪrə] o [fɪ'lɑksərə] *s* (*pl:* **-rae** [ri]) (ent.) filoxera
**phylogenesis** [,faɪlo'dʒɛnɪsɪs] *s* (biol.) filogénesis
**phylogenetic** [,faɪlodʒɪ'nɛtɪk] o **phylogenic** [,faɪlo'dʒɛnɪk] *adj* filogénico
**phylogeny** [faɪ'lɑdʒɪnɪ] *s* (*pl:* **-nies**) (biol.) filogenia
**phylum** ['faɪləm] *s* (*pl:* **-la** [lə]) (biol.) filo o fílum
**phys.** abr. de **physical, physician, physics, physiological** y **physiology**
**physic** ['fɪzɪk] *s* medicamento; purgante; **physics** *ssg* física; (*pret* & *pp:* **-icked;** *ger:* **-icking**) *va* purgar; medicinar; curar
**physical** ['fɪzɪkəl] *adj* físico
**physical chemistry** *s* química física
**physical culture** *s* cultura física
**physical education** *s* educación física
**physical fitness** *s* buena salud
**physical geography** *s* geografía física
**physically** ['fɪzɪkəlɪ] *adv* físicamente
**physical science** *s* ciencia física
**physical therapy** *s* terapia física
**physician** [fɪ'zɪʃən] *s* médico
**physicist** ['fɪzɪsɪst] *s* físico
**physic nut** *s* (bot.) piñón, piñón de Indias
**physicochemical** [,fɪzɪko'kɛmɪkəl] *adj* físicoquímico
**physicochemist** [,fɪzɪko'kɛmɪst] *s* físicoquímico
**physicochemistry** [,fɪzɪko'kɛmɪstrɪ] *s* físicoquímica
**physiocracy** [,fɪzɪ'ɑkrəsɪ] *s* fisiocracia
**physiocrat** ['fɪzɪəkræt] *s* fisiócrata
**physiocratic** [,fɪzɪə'krætɪk] *adj* fisiócrata; fisiocrático
**physiognomic** [,fɪzɪɑg'nɑmɪk] o [,fɪzɪə'nɑmɪk] o **physiognomical** [,fɪzɪɑg'nɑmɪkəl] o [,fɪzɪə'nɑmɪkəl] *adj* fisonómico
**physiognomist** [,fɪzɪ'ɑgnəmɪst] o [,fɪzɪ'ɑnəmɪst] *s* fisonomista
**physiognomy** [,fɪzɪ'ɑgnəmɪ] o [,fɪzɪ'ɑnəmɪ] *s* fisionomía
**physiographer** [,fɪzɪ'ɑgrəfər] *s* fisiógrafo
**physiographic** [,fɪzɪə'græfɪk] *adj* fisiográfico
**physiography** [,fɪzɪ'ɑgrəfɪ] *s* fisiografía
**physiological** [,fɪzɪə'lɑdʒɪkəl] *adj* fisiológico
**physiological chemistry** *s* química fisiológica
**physiologically** [,fɪzɪə'lɑdʒɪkəlɪ] *adv* fisiológicamente
**physiologist** [,fɪzɪ'ɑlədʒɪst] *s* fisiólogo
**physiology** [,fɪzɪ'ɑlədʒɪ] *s* fisiología
**physiotherapy** [,fɪzɪo'θɛrəpɪ] *s* fisioterapia
**physique** [fɪ'zik] *s* físico (*exterior, talle, constitución de una persona*)
**physostigmine** [,faɪso'stɪgmin] o [,faɪso'stɪgmɪn] *s* (chem.) fisostigmina
**phytin** ['faɪtɪn] *s* (chem.) fitina
**phytogeography** [,faɪtodʒɪ'ɑgrəfɪ] *s* fitogeografía
**phytographer** [faɪ'tɑgrəfər] *s* fitógrafo
**phytographic** [,faɪtə'græfɪk] o **phytographical** [,faɪtə'græfɪkəl] *adj* fitográfico
**phytography** [faɪ'tɑgrəfɪ] *s* fitografía
**phytolaccaceous** [,faɪtolə'keʃəs] *adj* (bot.) fitolacáceo
**phytology** [faɪ'tɑlədʒɪ] *s* fitología
**phytopathology** [,faɪtopə'θɑlədʒɪ] *s* (bot. & med.) fitopatología
**phytophagous** [faɪ'tɑfəgəs] *adj* (zool.) fitófago
**phytoplankton** [,faɪto'plæŋktən] *s* (biol.) fitoplancton
**phytotomy** [faɪ'tɑtəmɪ] *s* fitotomía
**P.I.** abr. de **Philippine Islands**
**pi** [paɪ] *s* (print.) pastel; (math.) pi; mezcolanza; (*pret* & *pp:* **pied;** *ger:* **piing**) *va* (print.) empastelar
**pia mater** ['paɪə'metər] *s* (anat.) piamáter
**pian** [pɪ'æn] o [pjɑn] *s* (path.) pian
**pianist** [pɪ'ænɪst] o ['piənɪst] *s* pianista
**piano** [pɪ'æno] *s* (*pl:* **-os**) piano; *adj* pianístico; [pɪ'ɑno] *adj* (mus.) suave; *adv* (mus.) suavemente
**pianoforte** [pɪ,æno'fɔrtɪ] o [pɪ'ænofort] *s* (mus.) pianoforte
**pianola** [,piə'nolə] *s* (trademark) pianola, autopiano; *adj* (slang) fácil, fácil de ejecutar
**piano stool** *s* taburete de piano
**piano tuner** *s* afinador de pianos
**piano wire** *s* cuerda de piano
**piaster** o **piastre** [pɪ'æstər] *s* piastra
**piazza** [pɪ'æzə] *s* plaza; (arch.) pórtico, galería
**pibroch** ['pibrɑk] *s* (Scotch) música marcial o fúnebre que se toca con la gaita
**pica** ['paɪkə] *s* (print.) cícero; (path. & vet.) pica
**Picard** ['pɪkərd] *adj* & *s* picardo
**Picardy** ['pɪkərdɪ] *s* la Picardía
**picarel** [,pɪkə'rɛl] *s* (ichth.) mena
**picaresque** [,pɪkə'rɛsk] *adj* picaresco
**picaroon** [,pɪkə'run] *s* pícaro; pirata; buque de piratas; *vn* piratear
**picayune** [,pɪkə'jun] *adj* de poca monta, mezquino; *s* medio real; persona insignificante; bagatela, friolera
**piccadilly** [,pɪkə'dɪlɪ] *s* (*pl:* **-lies**) cuello de pajarita, foque (*cuello almidonado*)
**piccalilli** ['pɪkə,lɪlɪ] *s* legumbres en escabeche
**piccolo** ['pɪkəlo] *s* (mus.) (*pl:* **-los**) flautín
**piccoloist** ['pɪkəlo·ɪst] *s* flautín (*músico*)
**piceous** ['pɪsɪəs] o ['paɪsɪəs] *adj* píceo; inflamable
**pick** [pɪk] *s* pico; punzón; cosecha, recolección; (mus.) plectro; flor (*lo más excelente*) ‖ *va* escoger; recoger (*p.ej., flores*); recolectar (*p.ej., algodón*); picar; cavar con un pico; romper (*el hielo*) con un punzón; picotear; escarbarse, mondarse, limpiarse (*los dientes*); descañonar, desplumar (*un ave*); rascarse (*una cicatriz, una pequeña herida, un grano*); roer (*un hueso*); mondar (*las frutas*); falsear, forzar (*una cerradura*); armar (*una pendencia*); (mus.) herir (*las cuerdas de un instrumento*); puntear (*p.ej., la guitarra*); buscar (*defectos*); separar las fibras de (*p.ej., la estopa*); **to pick off** ir matando con tiros sucesivos; **to pick one's way (through)** andar con mucho tiento (por entre); **to pick out** entresacar; ver (*una cosa que no se destaca de otras*); descifrar; **to pick pockets** hurtar de los bolsillos; **to pick someone to pieces** (coll.) no dejarle a uno un hueso sano; **to pick up** recoger; recobrar (*ánimo, velocidad*); hallar o conseguir por casualidad; aprender con la práctica; aprender de oídas; invitar a subir a un coche; entablar conversación con (*sin presentación previa*); captar (*una señal de radio*) ‖ *vn* picar; comer sin gana, comer melindrosamente; escoger esmeradamente; ratear; **to pick at** tirar de; comer sin gana, comer melindrosamente; (coll.) tomarla con, criticar, regañar; **to pick on** escoger, elegir; (coll.) criticar, regañar; (coll.) molestar, hostilizar; **to pick over** (coll.) ir revolviendo y examinando; preparar para el uso; **to pick up** (coll.) ir mejor, sentirse mejor, restablecerse; recobrar velocidad
**pickaback** ['pɪkə,bæk] *adv* a cuestas, en hombros
**pickaninny** ['pɪkə,nɪnɪ] *s* (*pl:* **-nies**) (offensive) negrito, niño negro; niñito
**pickax** o **pickaxe** ['pɪk,æks] *s* piqueta, zapapico
**picker** ['pɪkər] *s* recogedor; escardador; escogedor; (mach.) palanca de tiro; (mach.) sacalanzadera
**pickerel** ['pɪkərəl] *s* (ichth.) sollo norteamericano (*Esox niger y Esox vermiculatus*)

**pickerelweed** [ˈpɪkərəlˌwid] *s* (bot.) flor de la laguna

**picket** [ˈpɪkɪt] *s* piquete (*estaca clavada en la tierra*); (mil.) piquete; piquete de huelguistas; *va* cercar con piquetes o estacas; atar (*un animal*) a una estaca; estacionar piquetes de huelguistas cerca de, poner un cordón de piquetes a; *vn* servir de piquete de huelguistas

**picket fence** *s* cerca de estacas

**picket line** *s* línea de vigilantes huelguistas

**pickings** [ˈpɪkɪŋz] *spl* lo recogido; lo robado, lo pillado; residuos

**pickle** [ˈpɪkəl] *s* encurtido; escabeche, salmuera; (metal.) baño químico para limpiar metales; (coll.) apuro, aprieto; **to get into a pickle** (coll.) meterse en un berenjenal; *va* encurtir; escabechar; (metal.) limpiar con baño químico

**picklock** [ˈpɪkˌlɑk] *s* ganzúa (*garfio; ladrón*)

**pick-me-up** [ˈpɪkmiˌʌp] *s* (coll.) tentempié; (coll.) trago fortificante

**pickpocket** [ˈpɪkˌpɑkɪt] *s* carterista, ratero

**pickup** [ˈpɪkˌʌp] *s* recolección; recobro (*de un motor*); aceleración (*de un automóvil*); (slang) mejora; (coll.) persona conocida por casualidad y sin presentación; (elec.) pick-up, fonocaptor

**pickup truck** *s* camioneta de reparto

**picky** [ˈpɪkɪ] *adj* melindroso en el comer

**picnic** [ˈpɪknɪk] *s* jira, partida de campo, comida campestre; (slang) rato agradable, cosa fácil; (*pret & pp:* **-nicked; *ger:* -nicking**) *vn* hacer una comida campestre, merendar en el campo

**picnicker** [ˈpɪknɪkər] *s* merendante en el campo, excursionista

**picot** [ˈpiko] *s* piquillo, puntilla; (*pret & pp:* **-coted** [kod]; *ger:* **-coting** [ko·ɪŋ] *va* adornar o guarnecer con piquillos

**picrate** [ˈpɪkret] *s* (chem.) picrato

**picric** [ˈpɪkrɪk] *adj* pícrico

**picric acid** *s* (chem.) ácido pícrico

**Pict** [pɪkt] *s* picto

**Pictish** [ˈpɪktɪʃ] *adj* picto

**pictograph** [ˈpɪktəgræf] o [ˈpɪktəgrɑf] *s* pictografía

**pictographic** [ˌpɪktəˈgræfɪk] *adj* pictográfico

**pictorial** [pɪkˈtorɪəl] *adj* pictórico; gráfico; ilustrado; *s* revista ilustrada

**pictorially** [pɪkˈtorɪəlɪ] *adv* pictóricamente; con ilustraciones

**picture** [ˈpɪktʃər] *s* cuadro, pintura; imagen; retrato; ilustración; fotografía; lámina, grabado; película; (fig.) retrato, cuadro; estado general (*de un enfermo*); cuadro completo, visión de conjunto; **picture of despair** cuadro de desolación; **picture of health** salud personificada; *va* dibujar; pintar; describir; representarse; **to picture to oneself** representarse

**picture book** *s* libro con láminas

**picture frame** *s* marco

**picture gallery** *s* galería de pinturas

**picture hat** *s* pamela

**picture house** *s* cine, teatro cine

**picture page** *s* noticiario gráfico (*de un periódico*)

**picture palace** *s* (Brit.) cine, teatro cine

**picture post card** *s* tarjeta postal ilustrada, tarjeta postal con vistas fotográficas

**picture puzzle** *s* var. de **jigsaw puzzle**

**picture show** *s* exhibición de pinturas; cine

**picture signal** *s* (telv.) videoseñal

**picturesque** [ˌpɪktʃəˈrɛsk] *adj* pintoresco

**picturesqueness** [ˌpɪktʃəˈrɛsknɪs] *s* carácter pintoresco

**picture tube** *s* (telv.) tubo de imagen, tubo de televisión

**picture writing** *s* pictografía

**piddle** [ˈpɪdəl] *vn* emplearse en bagatelas; (coll.) orinar

**piddling** [ˈpɪdlɪŋ] *adj* de poca monta, insignificante

**piddock** [ˈpɪdək] *s* (zool.) julán

**pidgin English** [ˈpɪdʒɪn] *s* lengua franca usada en China entre los extranjeros y los indígenas

**pie** [paɪ] *s* pastel; (orn.) picaza, urraca; (print.) pastel; mezcolanza; (*pret & pp:* **pied; *ger:* pieing**) *va* (print.) empastelar

**pie à la mode** [mod] *s* pastel servido con helado encima

**piebald** [ˈpaɪˌbɔld] *adj & s* picazo (*caballo*)

**piece** [pis] *s* pedazo (*fragmento; casco, p.ej., de botella rota; retazo, p.ej., de tela*); pieza (*de una máquina o artefacto; obra dramática; composición suelta de música; cañón; figura que sirve para jugar a las damas, el ajedrez, etc.; moneda*); lote, parcela (*de terreno*); (dial.) rato; (dial.) corta distancia; **a piece of advice** un consejo; **a piece of baggage** un bulto; **a piece of folly** una tontería; **a piece of furniture** un mueble; **a piece of money** una moneda; **a piece of work** un trabajo; **of a piece with** de la misma clase que, lo mismo que; de acuerdo con; **to break to pieces** despedazar, hacer pedazos; despedazarse; **to cut to pieces** desmenuzar; destrozar (*p.ej., un ejército*); **to fall to pieces** desbaratarse, caer en ruina; **to fly to pieces** romperse en mil pedazos; **to give one a piece of one's mind** decirle a uno cuántas son cinco, decirle a uno su parecer con toda franqueza; **to go to pieces** desvencijarse; darse a la desesperación; ir al desastre (*p.ej., un negocio*); sufrir un ataque de nervios; perder por completo la salud; **to pick someone to pieces** (coll.) no dejarle a uno un hueso sano; **to speak one's piece** (coll.) decir su parecer; hablar con franqueza; **to take to pieces** desarmar; refutar punto por punto; *va* juntar las piezas de; formar juntando piezas; remendar; **to piece out** completar a pedacitos; *vn* (coll.) comer a deshora

**pièce de résistance** [ˌpjɛs də rezisˈtɑ̃s] *s* plato principal; lo principal, lo más importante

**piecemeal** [ˈpisˌmil] *adj* hecho a bocaditos; fragmentario; *adv* a bocaditos; en pedazos; a remiendos

**piece of eight** *s* doblón de a ocho (*antigua moneda de oro española*)

**piece wage** *s* remuneración por rendimiento

**piecework** [ˈpisˌwʌrk] *s* destajo, trabajo a destajo

**pieceworker** [ˈpisˌwʌrkər] *s* destajero

**pie crust** *s* pasta de pastel

**pied** [paɪd] *adj* abigarrado; de o con traje abigarrado; pintado, manchado (*pájaro*); pío, remendado (*animal*)

**Piedmont** [ˈpidmɑnt] *s* el Piamonte; llanura del sureste de los EE.UU.

**Piedmontese** [ˌpidmɑnˈtiz] *adj* piamontés; *s* (*pl:* **-tese**) piamontés

**pier** [pɪr] *s* muelle; estribo, sostén (*de puente*); pila, pilastre (*de varias obras de ingeniería*); rompeolas; (arch.) entrepaño (*espacio de pared entre dos huecos*)

**pierce** [pɪrs] *va* agujerear, horadar, taladrar; atravesar, traspasar; picar, pinchar, punzar; (fig.) traspasar (*de dolor*); *vn* penetrar, entrar a la fuerza

**piercing** [ˈpɪrsɪŋ] *adj* penetrante, agudo, desgarrador

**pier glass** *s* espejo de cuerpo entero

**Pierian** [paɪˈɪrɪən] *adj* pierio

**Pierian spring** *s* fuente pieria

**pier table** *s* consola

**pietism** [ˈpaɪətɪzəm] *s* piedad, devoción; mojigatería; (*cap.*) *s* pietismo

**pietist** [ˈpaɪətɪst] *s* beato; (*cap.*) *s* pietista

**pietistic** [ˌpaɪəˈtɪstɪk] *adj* beato

**piety** [ˈpaɪətɪ] *s* (*pl:* **-ties**) piedad, devoción

**piezoelectric** [paɪˌizo·ɪˈlɛktrɪk] *adj* piezoeléctrico

**piezoelectricity** [paɪˌizo·ɪˌlɛkˈtrɪsɪtɪ] *s* piezoelectricidad

**piezometer** [ˌpaɪɪˈzɑmɪtər] *s* piezómetro

**piffle** [ˈpɪfəl] *s* (coll.) disparates, música celestial

**pig** [pɪg] *s* (zool.) cerdo; puerco, cochino (*cerdo domesticado*); lechón; carne de puerco; (metal.) lingote; (coll.) marrano (*hombre sucio e indecente*); **to buy a pig in a poke** cerrar un trato a ciegas

**pigeon** [ˈpɪdʒən] *s* (orn.) paloma; (slang) bobalicón

**pigeon breast** *s* (path.) pecho de pichón

**pigeon hawk** *s* (orn.) halcón palumbario

**pigeonhole** [ˈpɪdʒənˌhol] *s* hornilla, casilla de paloma; casilla; *va* encasillar; clasificar y retener en la memoria; dar carpetazo a

**pigeon house** *s* palomar
**pigeon-toed** ['pɪdʒən,tod] *adj* con los pies torcidos hacia dentro
**pigeonwing** ['pɪdʒən,wɪŋ] *s* figura de danza en forma de ala de paloma; figura que hacen los patinadores en forma de ala de paloma
**piggery** ['pɪgərɪ] *s* (*pl:* **-ies**) pocilga
**piggish** ['pɪgɪʃ] *adj* cochino; glotón, voraz
**piggy** ['pɪgɪ] *s* (*pl:* **-gies**) lechón, lechoncillo; *adj* glotón
**piggyback** ['pɪgɪ,bæk] *adv* a cuestas, en hombros
**piggybacking** ['pɪgɪ,bækɪŋ] *s* transporte de semi-remolques cargados, en vagones de plataforma
**pig-headed** ['pɪg,hɛdɪd] *adj* terco, cabezudo
**pig iron** *s* arrabio, hierro colado en barras
**piglet** ['pɪglɪt] o **pigling** ['pɪglɪŋ] *s* lechón, lechoncillo
**pigment** ['pɪgmənt] *s* pigmento; *va* pigmentar; *vn* pigmentarse
**pigmentary** ['pɪgmən,tɛrɪ] *adj* pigmentario
**pigmentation** [,pɪgmən'teʃən] *s* (biol.) pigmentación
**pigmy** ['pɪgmɪ] *adj* var. de **pygmy;** *s* (*pl:* **-mies**) var. de **pygmy**
**pignut** ['pɪg,nʌt] *s* (bot.) pacanero; pacana (*fruto*)
**pigpen** ['pɪg,pɛn] *s* pocilga; (fig.) corral de vacas (*paraje sucio o destartalado*)
**pigskin** ['pɪg,skɪn] *s* piel de cerdo, pellejo de cerdo; (coll.) silla de montar; (coll.) balón (*con que se juega al fútbol*)
**pigsty** ['pɪg,staɪ] *s* (*pl:* **-sties**) pocilga
**pigtail** ['pɪg,tel] *s* coleta, trenza; andullo (*de tabaco*)
**pigweed** ['pɪg,wid] *s* (bot.) cenizo, quelite; (bot.) quenopodio; (bot.) mercolina; (bot.) amaranto
**pika** ['paɪkə] *s* (zool.) ochotona
**pike** [paɪk] *s* pica; punta (*p.ej., de flecha*); escarpia; carretera; peaje; camino de barrera; (ichth.) lucio; *va* herir o matar con la pica; *vn* (coll.) irse, salir corriendo; **to pike along** (coll.) seguir su camino
**pikeman** ['paɪkmən] *s* (*pl:* **-men**) piquero
**piker** ['paɪkər] *s* (slang) cicatero; (slang) persona de poco fuste; (slang) cobarde
**Pike's Peak** *s* el pico de Pike (*en las Montañas Rocosas*)
**pikestaff** ['paɪk,stæf] o ['paɪk,stɑf] *s* (*pl:* **-staves** [,stevz]) asta de pica; báculo herrado
**pilaf** o **pilaff** [pɪ'lɑf] *s* pilav (*manjar oriental*)
**pilaster** [pɪ'læstər] *s* (arch.) pilastra
**Pilate** ['paɪlət] *s* Pilatos
**pilau** o **pilaw** [pɪ'lɔ] *s* var. de **pilaf**
**pilchard** ['pɪltʃərd] *s* (ichth.) sardina
**pile** [paɪl] *s* pila, montón; mole; conjunto apretado (*p.ej., de edificios*); pilote; lanilla, pelusa; lana; pira; (coll.) caudal, fortuna; (coll.) montón (*número considerable*); (elec., her. & phys.) pila; **piles** *mpl* (path.) almorranas; **to make a pile** (coll.) hacerse su agosto, enriquecerse; *va* apilar; **to pile on** echar encima; **to pile one thing on another** superponer una cosa a otra; **to pile up** apilar, amontonar; **to pile with** cubrir con, cargar de; *vn* apilarse; **to pile in** o **into** entrar atropelladamente en; entrar todos en (*un recinto pequeño*); subir todos a (*p.ej., un automóvil*); **to pile up** apilarse; acumularse
**piled** [paɪld] *adj* de mucho pelillo, de mucha lanilla
**pile driver** *s* martinete
**pile dwelling** *s* vivienda lacustre sostenida por pilares
**pilewort** ['paɪl,wʌrt] *s* (bot.) celidonia menor
**pilfer** ['pɪlfər] *va & vn* ratear
**pilgrim** ['pɪlgrɪm] *s* peregrino, romero
**pilgrimage** ['pɪlgrɪmɪdʒ] *s* peregrinación, romería
**piling** ['paɪlɪŋ] *s* pilotaje (*conjunto de pilotes*)
**pill** [pɪl] *s* píldora; (slang) pelota; (slang) chinche, posma (*persona molesta*); mal trago, sinsabor; **to gild the pill** dorar la píldora
**pillage** ['pɪlɪdʒ] *s* pillaje; *va & vn* pillar
**pillar** ['pɪlər] *s* pilar; (fig.) pilar (*persona*); **from pillar to post** de Herodes a Pilatos; *va* proveer de pilares, sostener con pilares
**pillared** ['pɪlərd] *adj* con pilares; de forma columnar
**Pillars of Hercules** *spl* columnas de Hércules
**pillbox** ['pɪl,bɑks] *s* caja para píldoras; (mil.) fortín armado de ametralladoras
**pillory** ['pɪlərɪ] *s* (*pl:* **-ries**) picota; (*pret & pp:* **-ried**) *va* empicotar; poner a la vergüenza, poner en ridículo
**pillow** ['pɪlo] *s* almohada; cojín; mundillo; (mach.) cojinete; (naut.) almohada (*de las jarcias*); (naut.) tragante, descanso (*del bauprés*); *va* poner sobre una almohada; soportar, servir de almohada a
**pillow block** *s* (mach.) chumacera
**pillowcase** ['pɪlo,kes] *s* almohada, funda de almohada
**pillow lace** *s* encaje de bolillos
**pillow sham** *s* paño bordado (*para cubrir almohadas*)
**pillowslip** ['pɪlo,slɪp] *s* var. de **pillowcase**
**pillowy** ['pɪləwɪ] *adj* blando, suave
**pilocarpine** [,paɪlo'kɑrpin] o [,paɪlo'kɑrpɪn] *s* (chem.) pilocarpina
**pilose** ['paɪlos] *adj* piloso
**pilosity** [paɪ'lɑsɪtɪ] *s* pilosidad
**pilot** ['paɪlət] *s* piloto; práctico (*de puerto*); (rail.) trompa, delantera; mechero encendedor (*de una cocina de gas*); *va* pilotar; conducir (*servir de guía a*)
**pilotage** ['paɪlətɪdʒ] *s* (naut. & aer.) pilotaje
**pilot balloon** *s* globo piloto
**pilot biscuit** o **bread** *s* (naut.) galleta
**pilot chute** *s* paracaídas piloto
**pilot engine** *s* (rail.) máquina piloto
**pilot fish** *s* (ichth.) piloto
**pilot house** *s* (naut.) timonera
**pilot light** *s* lámpara testigo, lámpara de comprobación, lámpara piloto; mechero encendedor (*de una cocina de gas*)
**pilot plant** *s* instalación piloto
**Piltdown man** ['pɪlt,daun] *s* (anthrop.) hombre de Piltdown
**pimento** [pɪ'mɛnto] *s* (*pl:* **-tos**) (bot.) pimienta; pimienta inglesa (*fruto seco y molido*); pimiento dulce
**pimiento** [pɪ'mjɛnto] *s* (*pl:* **-tos**) pimiento dulce
**pimola** [pɪ'molə] *s* aceituna rellena con un taco de pimiento dulce
**pimp** [pɪmp] *s & vn* var. de **pander**
**pimpernel** ['pɪmpərnɛl] *s* (bot.) murajes
**pimple** ['pɪmpəl] *s* grano (*en la piel*)
**pimpled** ['pɪmpəld] *adj* var. de **pimply**
**pimply** ['pɪmplɪ] *adj* (*comp:* **-plier;** *super:* **-pliest**) granujoso
**pin** [pɪn] *s* alfiler; prendedero; clavija; ficha o clavillo (*para sujetar las hojas de las tijeras*); bolo (*del juego de bolos*); asta (*de la bandera que marca cada agujero en el juego de golf*); botón (*de manubrio*); (mach.) gorrón; (naut.) cabilla; (coll.) pierna; **to be on pins and needles** estar en espinas; (*pret & pp:* **pinned;** *ger:* **pinning**) *va* asegurar o prender con un alfiler o con alfileres; clavar, fijar, sujetar; coger y sujetar; **to pin down** sujetar con alfileres; obligar (*a una persona*) a que diga la verdad; **to pin one's faith on** tener puesta su esperanza en; **to pin something on someone** (coll.) acusarle o culparle a uno de una cosa; **to pin up** recoger y apuntar con alfileres, arremangar; fijar en la pared con alfileres
**pinacoid** ['pɪnəkɔɪd] *s* (cryst.) pinacoide
**pinafore** ['pɪnə,for] *s* delantal de niña
**pinaster** [paɪ'næstər] o [pɪ'næstər] *s* (bot.) pinastro, pino rodeno
**pinball** ['pɪn,bɔl] *s* billar romano, bagatela
**pincase** ['pɪn,kes] *s* alfiletero, cañutero
**pince-nez** ['pæns,ne] *s* lentes de nariz, lentes de pinzas
**pincer movement** *s* (mil.) movimiento de pinzas
**pincers** ['pɪnsərz] *ssg* o *spl* pinzas (*instrumento; órgano prensil del cangrejo, etc.*); (mil.) movimiento de pinzas
**pinch** [pɪntʃ] *s* pellizco; apretón; polvo, p.ej., **pinch of snuff** polvo de rapé; aprieto, apuro; tormento (*p.ej., del hambre*); (slang) arresto; (slang) hurto, robo; **in a pinch** en un aprieto; en caso necesario; *va* pellizcar; cogerse

(*los dedos*) en una puerta; apretar, p.ej., **this shoe pinches me** este zapato me aprieta; atenacear; restringir; contraer (*el frío la cara de uno*); adelgazar (*el dolor, el hambre a una persona*); limitar los gastos de; (slang) arrestar, prender; (slang) hurtar, robar; *vn* apretar; economizar, privarse de lo necesario
**pinchbeck** ['pɪntʃ,bɛk] *s* similor; falsificación; *adj* de similor; falsificado
**pinchers** ['pɪntʃərz] *ssg* o *spl* var. de **pincers**
**pinch-hit** ['pɪntʃ,hɪt] (*pret & pp:* **-hit;** *ger:* **-hitting**) *vn* (baseball) batear de emergente; (fig.) substituir a otro en un apuro
**pinch hitter** *s* (baseball) bateador emergente
**pincushion** ['pɪn,kuʃən] *s* acerico
**Pindar** ['pɪndər] *s* Píndaro
**Pindaric** [pɪn'dærɪk] *adj* pindárico
**pindling** ['pɪndlɪŋ] *adj* (coll.) enteco, enfermizo
**Pindus** ['pɪndəs] *s* Pindo
**pine** [paɪn] *s* (bot.) pino; *vn* languidecer; **to pine for** penar por
**pineal** ['pɪnɪəl] *adj* pineal
**pineal body** o **gland** *s* (anat.) glándula pineal
**pineapple** ['paɪn,æpəl] *s* (bot.) ananás, piña (*planta y fruto*)
**pine cone** *s* piña
**pine marten** *s* (zool.) marta
**pine needle** *s* pinocha; **pine needles** *spl* alhumajo
**pinery** ['paɪnərɪ] *s* (*pl:* **-ies**) pinar; piñal
**pine tar** *s* alquitrán de madera
**piney** ['paɪnɪ] *adj* var. de **piny**
**pinfeather** ['pɪn,fɛðər] *s* cañón (*pluma del ave no desarrollada*)
**pinfold** ['pɪn,fold] *s* corral de concejo; *va* encerrar en corral de concejo
**ping** [pɪŋ] *s* silbido de bala; *vn* silbar como una bala
**ping-pong** ['pɪŋ,pɑŋ] *s* (trademark) ping-pong, tenis de mesa, tenis de salón
**pinguin** ['pɪŋgwɪn] *s* (bot.) piña de ratón, piñuela, maya
**pinhead** ['pɪn,hɛd] *s* cabecilla de alfiler; cosa muy pequeña o insignificante; (slang) bobalicón
**pinhole** ['pɪn,hol] *s* agujero que hace un alfiler; agujero para espiga o clavija
**pinion** ['pɪnjən] *s* (mach. & orn.) piñón; (orn.) ala; (orn.) remera; *va* cortar las alas a (*un ave*); maniatar
**pinion gear** *s* (aut.) piñón diferencial
**pink** [pɪŋk] *adj* rosado, sonrosado; *s* color de rosa; estado perfecto; comunistoide; (bot.) clavel, clavellina; *va* herir levemente con daga, espada, etc.; adornar; (sew.) ondear, ojetear, picar
**pinkeye** ['pɪŋk,aɪ] *s* (path.) conjuntivitis catarral aguda
**pinking shears** ['pɪŋkɪŋ] *spl* tijeras picafestones
**pinkish** ['pɪŋkɪʃ] *adj* rosado claro, que tira a rosado
**pin money** *s* alfileres, dinero para alfileres
**pinna** ['pɪnə] *s* (*pl:* **-nae** [ni] o **-nas**) (orn.) pluma; (orn.) ala; (zool.) aleta (*de pez o foca*); (anat.) pabellón del oído; (bot.) folíolo
**pinnace** ['pɪnɪs] *s* (naut.) pinaza; (naut.) bote
**pinnacle** ['pɪnəkəl] *s* pináculo, cumbre; (arch.) pináculo; (fig.) pináculo, cumbre
**pinnate** ['pɪnet] *adj* (bot.) pinado
**pinnatifid** [pɪ'nætɪfɪd] *adj* (bot.) pinatífido
**pinniped** ['pɪnɪpɛd] *adj & s* (zool.) pinnípedo
**pin oak** *s* (bot.) roble de los pantanos
**Pinocchio** [pɪ'nɔkɪo] *s* Pinocho
**pinochle** o **pinocle** ['pi,nʌkəl] *s* pinocle (*juego de naipes*)
**piñon** ['pɪnjən] o ['pinjon] *s* (bot.) pino piñón; piñón (*fruto*)
**pinpoint** ['pɪn,pɔɪnt] *s* punta de alfiler; *adj* exacto, preciso; *va & vn* apuntar con precisión
**pinpoint bombing** *s* (aer.) bombardeo de precisión
**pinprick** ['pɪn,prɪk] *s* alfilerazo
**pint** [paɪnt] *s* pinta (*medida*)
**pintail** ['pɪn,tel] *s* (orn.) pato cuellilargo; (orn.) ganga
**pin-tailed sand grouse** ['pɪn,teld] *s* (orn.) ganga
**pintle** ['pɪntəl] *s* gorrón; perno de un gozne; (naut.) pinzote, macho de timón
**pinto** ['pɪnto] *adj* pintado; *s* (*pl:* **-tos**) caballo pintado; pinto (*frijol*)
**pint pot** *s* olla con capacidad de pinta
**pint-size** ['paɪnt,saɪz] o **pint-sized** ['paɪnt,saɪzd] *adj* diminuto
**pinup girl** ['pɪn,ʌp] *s* fotografía o dibujo artístico de una muchacha linda; muchacha modelo para tal fotografía
**pinwheel** ['pɪn,hwil] *s* rueda de fuego, rueda giratoria (*de fuegos artificiales*); molino de viento, rehilandera (*juguete de niño*)
**pinworm** ['pɪn,wʌrm] *s* (zool.) lombriz de los niños
**piny** ['paɪnɪ] *adj* (*comp:* **-ier;** *super:* **-iest**) pinoso
**pioneer** [,paɪə'nɪr] *s* pionero (*explorador, colonizador; primer promotor*); (mil.) zapador; *va* preparar el camino a; iniciar, promover; abrir o explorar (*el camino*); *vn* abrir nuevos caminos, explorar
**pious** ['paɪəs] *adj* pío, piadoso; mojigato
**pip** [pɪp] *s* pepita (*simiente*); (vet.) pepita; punto (*en un naipe, dado, etc.*); (coll.) enfermedad pasajera; (*pret & pp:* **pipped;** *ger:* **pipping**) *va* romper (*el cascarón el polluelo*); *vn* piar, pipiar
**pipe** [paɪp] *s* caño, conducto, tubo; cañería; pipa (*para fumar tabaco*); fumarada (*tabaco que cabe en la pipa*); (mus.) caramillo, zampoña, pipa, flauta de Pan; (mus.) cañón (*de órgano*); silbo, nota aflautada, voz atiplada; pipa, tonel; (naut.) pito o silbato del contramaestre; **pipes** *spl* (mus.) gaita; *va* conducir por medio de tubos o cañerías; proveer de tuberías o cañerías; instalar tubos o cañerías en; decir o pronunciar con voz atiplada; cantar con voz atiplada; llamar con silbatos; (sew.) adornar con cordoncillos; *vn* tocar el caramillo; hablar o cantar con voz atiplada; tocar su pito (*el contramaestre*); **to pipe down** (slang) callarse; **to pipe up** comenzar a tocar; (slang) comenzar a hablar
**pipe bender** *s* curvatubos
**pipe clamp** *s* sujetatubos
**pipe clay** *s* albero, tierra de pipa
**pipe-clay** ['paɪp,kle] *va* blanquear o limpiar con albero
**pipe cleaner** *s* desobturador de pipa, limpiapipas
**pipe cutter** *s* cortatubos (*herramienta*)
**pipe dream** *s* (coll.) idea o esperanza imposibles, castillo en el aire
**pipe fitter** *s* cañero, montador de tuberías
**pipe fitting** *s* instalación de tuberías; **pipe fittings** *spl* accesorios para tubería, accesorios de cañería
**pipeful** ['paɪpful] *s* fumarada (*tabaco que cabe en la pipa*)
**pipe hanger** *s* portacaño
**pipe line** *s* cañería, tubería; oleoducto; fuente de informes confidenciales
**pipe-line** ['paɪp,laɪn] *va* conducir por medio de un oleoducto; proveer de un oleoducto
**pipe of peace** *s* pipa de paz
**pipe organ** *s* (mus.) órgano
**piper** ['paɪpər] *s* flautista; gaitero; **to pay the piper** pagar los vidrios rotos
**piperaceous** [,pɪpə'reʃəs] *adj* (bot.) piperáceo
**piperine** ['pɪpərin] o ['pɪpərɪn] *s* (chem.) piperina
**pipestem** ['paɪp,stɛm] *s* boquilla de pipa de fumar
**pipe thread** *s* rosca de tubería
**pipe tobacco** *s* tabaco de pipa
**pipette** [paɪ'pɛt] o [pɪ'pɛt] *s* pipeta
**pipe wrench** *s* llave para tubos, llave de caño
**piping** ['paɪpɪŋ] *s* cañería, tubería; canalización; materia para la fabricación de tubos; notas de flauta; música de gaita; notas aflautadas; silbido, sonido agudo; (sew.) cordoncillo; figuras hechas con azúcar en un bollo; *adj* aflautado, agudo
**piping hot** *adj* muy caliente, hirviendo; **to be piping hot** estar que quema
**pipit** ['pɪpɪt] *s* (orn.) bisbita
**pipkin** ['pɪpkɪn] *s* ollita
**pippin** ['pɪpɪn] *s* camuesa (*manzana*); (slang) real moza

**pipsissewa** [pɪp'sɪsɪwə] *s* (bot.) quimafila
**pipy** ['paɪpɪ] *adj* (*comp:* **-ier;** *super:* **-iest**) tubular; agudo, chillón
**piquancy** ['pikənsɪ] *s* picante
**piquant** ['pikənt] *adj* picante
**pique** [pik] *s* pique, resentimiento; **in a pique** resentido; *va* picar, enojar, provocar; despertar, excitar; **to be piqued at** tener un pique con; **to pique oneself on** o **upon** enorgullecerse de
**piqué** [pɪ'ke] *s* piqué (*tela*)
**piquet** [pɪ'kɛt] *s* séptimo, juego de los ciento
**piracy** ['paɪrəsɪ] *s* (*pl:* **-cies**) piratería; publicación fraudulenta
**Piraeus** [paɪ'riəs] *s* el Pireo
**piragua** [pɪ'rɑgwə] o [pɪ'rægwə] *s* var. de **pirogue**
**pirate** ['paɪrɪt] *s* pirata; *va* robar, pillar; publicar fraudulentamente; *vn* piratear
**piratical** [paɪ'rætɪkəl] *adj* pirático
**pirogue** [pɪ'rog] *s* piragua
**pirouette** [,pɪru'ɛt] *s* pirueta; *vn* piruetear
**piscatorial** [,pɪskə'torɪəl] o **piscatory** ['pɪskə,torɪ] *adj* piscatorio
**Pisces** ['pɪsiz] *spl* (astr.) Piscis
**piscina** [pɪ'saɪnə] o [pɪ'sinə] *s* (*pl:* **-nae** [ni]) (eccl.) piscina
**piscivorous** [pɪ'sɪvərəs] *adj* piscívoro
**pish** [pɪʃ] *interj* ¡bah!; *vn* refunfuñar
**pisiform** ['paɪsɪfɔrm] *adj* pisiforme; (anat.) pisiforme
**Pisistratus** [paɪ'sɪstrətəs] *s* Pisístrato
**pismire** ['pɪs,maɪr] *s* (ent.) hormiga
**pistachio** [pɪs'tɑʃɪo] o [pɪs'tæʃɪo] *s* (*pl:* **-os**) (bot.) alfóncigo (*árbol y fruto*); (bot.) pistachero (*árbol*); pistacho (*almendra*); sabor a pistacho; color de pistacho
**pistil** ['pɪstɪl] *s* (bot.) pistilo
**pistillate** ['pɪstɪlet] *adj* (bot.) pistilado
**pistol** ['pɪstəl] *s* pistola (*arma de fuego*)
**pistole** [pɪs'tol] *s* pistola (*moneda*)
**piston** ['pɪstən] *s* (mach.) émbolo, pistón; (mus.) pistón
**piston assembly** *s* conjunto del émbolo
**piston displacement** *s* cilindrada
**piston pin** *s* eje o pasador de émbolo
**piston pump** *s* bomba de émbolo
**piston ring** *s* anillo de émbolo, aro de émbolo
**piston rod** *s* vástago de émbolo
**piston stroke** *s* carrera del émbolo
**piston valve** *s* válvula de émbolo
**pit** [pɪt] *s* hoyo; cárcava, hoya; cacaraña, hoyuelo (*en la piel*); trampa; hueso (*de ciertas frutas*); cancha, reñidero (*para peleas de gallos, etc.*); boca (*del estómago*); fosa común (*de muchos cadáveres*); pozo (*de tirador*); (aut.) fosa; (com.) bolsa (*dedicada a un solo producto*); abismo, infierno; (min.) pozo; (Brit.) foso, parte posterior del patio; (Brit.) mosqueteros (*personas que veían la comedia de pie desde la parte posterior del patio*); (fig.) escollo (*peligro latente*); (*pret & pp:* **pitted;** *ger:* **pitting**) *va* marcar con hoyos; dejar hoyoso (*el rostro*); poner en un hoyo; deshuesar (*p.ej., una ciruela*); **to pit one person against another** oponer una persona a otra
**pitapat** ['pɪtə,pæt] *s* latido rápido; sonido de un trotecito ligero; *adv* con latido rápido; con un trotecito ligero
**pitch** [pɪtʃ] *s* pez *f* (*substancia negra y pegajosa*); echada, lanzamiento; cosa lanzada; pelota lanzada; cabezada (*de un barco*); pendiente (*de un tejado*); elevación (*de un arco de puente*); declive, grado de inclinación; paso (*de hélice, tornillo, etc.*); distancia (*p.ej., entre remaches*); (elec.) paso (*p.ej., de un arrollamiento*); (mus.) tono, altura; (fig.) grado, extremo; *va* echar, lanzar; elevar (*el heno*) con la horquilla, lanzar (*el heno*) al camión; armar o plantar (*una tienda de campaña*); embrear; cantear (*una piedra*); (mus.) graduar el tono de; *vn* caerse, caer de cabeza; fijarse, instalarse; bajar en declive, inclinarse; (naut.) cabecear; **to pitch about** agitarse, sacudirse; **to pitch in** (coll.) poner manos a la obra; (coll.) comenzar a comer; **to pitch into** (coll.) arremeter contra, desatarse contra; (coll.) regañar, reprender; **to pitch on** o **upon** escoger, elegir
**pitch accent** *s* acento de altura
**pitchblende** ['pɪtʃ,blɛnd] *s* (mineral.) pechblenda
**pitch-dark** ['pɪtʃ'dɑrk] *adj* negro u obscuro como la pez
**pitched battle** *s* batalla campal
**pitcher** ['pɪtʃər] *s* jarra; (baseball) lanzador
**pitcherful** ['pɪtʃərfʊl] *s* jarra (*lo que cabe en esta vasija*)
**pitcher plant** *s* (bot.) planta cazadora de insectos (*Sarracenia y Darlingtonia*)
**pitchfork** ['pɪtʃ,fɔrk] *s* (agr.) horca, horquilla; **to rain pitchforks** (coll.) caer o llover chuzos, llover a cántaros; *va* amontonar o elevar (*heno*) con la horquilla
**pitchman** ['pɪtʃmən] *s* (*pl:* **-men**) (slang) buhonero (*con un puesto en las ferias y verbenas*)
**pitch pine** *s* (bot.) pino tea
**pitch pipe** *s* (mus.) diapasón
**pitchstone** ['pɪtʃ,ston] *s* vidrio volcánico
**pitchy** ['pɪtʃɪ] *adj* (*comp:* **-ier;** *super:* **-iest**) peceño
**piteous** ['pɪtɪəs] *adj* lastimero, lastimoso
**pitfall** ['pɪt,fɔl] *s* (hunt.) trampa, callejo; (fig.) escollo
**pith** [pɪθ] *s* (bot.) médula; (fig.) fuerza, vigor; (fig.) médula
**pit head** *s* (min.) boca de pozo
**pithecanthropus** [,pɪθɪkæn'θropəs] *s* (*pl:* **-pi** [paɪ]) (anthrop.) pitecántropo
**pithy** ['pɪθɪ] *adj* (*comp:* **-ier;** *super:* **-iest**) medular; meduloso; enérgico, expresivo, vivo
**pitiable** ['pɪtɪəbəl] *adj* enternecedor, lamentable; despreciable
**pitiably** ['pɪtɪəblɪ] *adv* lamentablemente; de modo despreciable
**pitiful** ['pɪtɪfʊl] lastimero, lastimoso; compasivo; despreciable
**pitiless** ['pɪtɪlɪs] *adj* desapiadado, empedernido, incompasivo
**pitometer** [pɪ'tɑmɪtər] *s* (hyd.) pitómetro
**pitpit** ['pɪt,pɪt] *s* (orn.) pitpit, azucarero
**pittance** ['pɪtəns] *s* jornal miserable; recursos insuficientes; ración de hambre
**pitter** ['pɪtər] *s* deshuesadora
**pitter-patter** ['pɪtər,pætər] *s* chapaleteo (*de la lluvia*); golpeteo suave o ligero; *adv* con chapaleteo; con golpeteo suave o ligero
**Pittsburgh** ['pɪtsbʌrg] *s* Pitsburgo
**pituitary** [pɪ'tjuɪ,tɛrɪ] o [pɪ'tuɪ,tɛrɪ] *adj* pituitario
**pituitary body** *s* (anat.) cuerpo pituitario
**pituitary gland** *s* (anat.) glándula pituitaria
**pituitary membrane** *s* (anat.) membrana pituitaria
**pituitous** [pɪ'tjuɪtəs] o [pɪ'tuɪtəs] *adj* pituitoso
**pity** ['pɪtɪ] *s* (*pl:* **-ies**) piedad, compasión, lástima; **for pity's sake!** ¡por piedad!, ¡por Dios!; **it is a pity (that)** es lástima (que); **to have** o **to take pity on** tener piedad de, apiadarse de, compadecer; **what a pity!** ¡qué lástima!; (*pret & pp:* **-ied**) *va* apiadarse de, compadecer
**pityriasis** [,pɪtɪ'raɪəsɪs] *s* (path.) pitiríasis
**Pius** ['paɪəs] *s* Pío
**pivot** ['pɪvət] *s* pivote, gorrón, eje de rotación; (fig.) eje, punto fundamental; *va* montar sobre un pivote; colocar por medio de un pivote; proveer de pivote; *vn* pivotar; **to pivot on** girar sobre; depender de
**pivotal** ['pɪvətəl] *adj* céntrico; fundamental
**pixilated** ['pɪksɪ,letɪd] *adj* chiflado; (slang) borracho
**pixy** o **pixie** ['pɪksɪ] *s* (*pl:* **-ies**) duende, hada
**pizzle** ['pɪzəl] *s* vergajo
**pk.** abr. de **park, peak** y **peck**
**pkg.** abr. de **package**
**pl.** abr. de **place** y **plural**
**placable** ['plekəbəl] o ['plækəbəl] *adj* placable
**placard** ['plækɑrd] *s* cartel; [plə'kɑrd] o ['plækɑrd] *va* llenar de carteles; fijar carteles en; fijar (*un anuncio*) en sitio público; publicar por medio de carteles
**placate** ['pleket] *va* aplacar
**place** [ples] *s* sitio, lugar; puesto; local (*de un establecimiento*); distrito; parte; (arith.) lugar; (arith.) decimal; calle o plaza de poca extensión; **in place** en su sitio; a propósito, oportuno; **in the first place** en primer lugar; **in the next place** luego, después; **in no place**

en ninguna parte; **in place of** en lugar de, en vez de; **out of place** fuera de su lugar; impropio, inconveniente, fuera de propósito; **to give place** ceder, hacer lugar; **to hold one's place** no cejar, no perder terreno; **to know one's place** quedarse en su lugar, mirarse a sí, ser respetuoso; **to look for a place to live** buscar piso; **to take place** tener lugar; *va* poner, colocar; acordarse bien de; dar colocación o empleo a; (com.) prestar a interés; *vn* (sport) colocarse (*un caballo en las carreras*)

**placebo** [plə'sibo] *s* (*pl:* **-bos** o **-boes**) (eccl. & med.) placebo

**place card** *s* tarjeta (*que indica la colocación de uno en la mesa*)

**place in the sun** *s* la igualdad, su porción de los bienes de este mundo, su porción de gloria

**place kick** *s* (football) puntapié que se da a la pelota después de colocarla en tierra

**place-kick** ['ples,kɪk] *vn* (football) patear la pelota después de colocarla en tierra

**placement** ['plesmənt] *s* colocación; (football) colocación de la pelota en tierra para patearla

**placement test** *s* (educ.) examen selectivo

**place name** *s* nombre de lugar, topónimo

**placenta** [plə'sɛntə] *s* (*pl:* **-tae** [ti] o **-tas**) (anat., bot. & zool.) placenta

**placental** [plə'sɛntəl] *adj* placentario; *s* (zool.) placentario

**place of business** *s* establecimiento, local de negocios

**place of refuge** *s* asilo, refugio

**place of worship** *s* templo, edificio de culto

**placer** ['plæsər] *s* (min.) placer; (min.) lavadero de oro

**placer mining** *s* minería de lavado

**placid** ['plæsɪd] *adj* plácido

**placidity** [plə'sɪdɪtɪ] *s* placidez

**placket** ['plækɪt] *s* abertura en la parte superior de la falda o las enaguas; bolsillo (de falda)

**plagiarism** ['pledʒɪərɪzəm] o ['pledʒərɪzəm] *s* plagio

**plagiarist** ['pledʒɪərɪst] o ['pledʒərɪst] *s* plagiario

**plagiarize** ['pledʒɪəraɪz] o ['pledʒəraɪz] *va* plagiar

**plagioclase** ['pledʒɪə,kles] *s* (mineral.) plagioclasa

**plagiostome** ['pledʒɪə,stom] *adj* & *s* (ichth.) plagiostomo

**plagiotropic** [,pledʒɪə'trɑpɪk] *adj* (bot.) plagiotropo

**plagiotropism** [,pledʒɪ'ɑtrəpɪzəm] *s* (bot.) plagiotropismo

**plague** [pleg] *s* plaga; peste; *va* plagar, apestar, infestar; atormentar, molestar

**plaguey** o **plaguy** ['plegɪ] *adj* (coll.) enfadoso, molesto

**plaice** [ples] *s* (ichth.) platija

**plaid** [plæd] *s* tartán (*tela*); cuadros a la escocesa; plaid (*manta*); *adj* listado a la escocesa

**plaided** ['plædɪd] *adj* listado a la escocesa; con manta de tartán

**plain** [plen] *adj* llano; feo, sin atractivo; ordinario; solo, natural, puro; sencillo; **in plain English** sin rodeos; **in plain sight** o **view** en plena vista; *s* llano, llanura; *vn* (archaic & dial.) quejarse

**plain chant** *s* canto llano

**plain clothes** *spl* traje de calle, traje de paisano

**plain-clothes man** ['plen'kloz] o ['plen'kloðz] *s* agente de policía que no lleva uniforme, agente de policía que lleva traje de calle

**plain dealing** *s* trato sincero, buena fe

**plain knitting** *s* punto de media

**plainness** ['plennɪs] *s* llaneza; fealdad

**plain omelet** *s* tortilla a la francesa

**plain sailing** *s* navegación libre y serena; acción desembarazada

**plainsman** ['plenzmən] *s* (*pl:* **-men**) llanero

**plain song** *s* canto llano

**plain speaking** *s* franqueza

**plain-spoken** ['plen'spokən] *adj* franco, sincero, brusco, directo

**plaint** [plent] *s* quejido, lamento; (law) querella; (archaic & dial.) plañido

**plaintiff** ['plentɪf] *s* (law) demandante

**plaintive** ['plentɪv] *adj* quejumbroso, lastimero

**plait** [plæt] o [plet] *s* trenza; *va* trenzar; [plæt] o [plit] *s* pliegue; *va* plegar

**plan** [plæn] *s* plan (*intento, proyecto*); plan, plano (*representación gráfica*); **to change one's plans** cambiar de proyecto; (*pret* & *pp:* **planned;** *ger:* **planning**) *va* planear, planificar; **to plan to** + *inf* proponerse + *inf; vn* hacer proyectos

**planchette** [plæn'ʃɛt] *s* tabla de escritura espiritista

**plane** [plen] *adj* plano; *s* plano; (aer.) plano o ala; aeroplano, avión; (carp.) cepillo; garlopa (*cepillo grande*); (bot.) plátano de oriente; (bot.) plátano de occidente; (fig.) nivel (*grado de elevación moral, etc.*); *va* acepillar, cepillar; **to plane down** reducir con el cepillo el espesor de; **to plane off** o **away** quitar con el cepillo; *vn* viajar en aeroplano; (aer.) planear; (naut.) elevarse (*el barco*) al ser impulsado por el motor

**plane cell** *s* (aer.) célula (*de avión*)

**plane geometry** *s* geometría plana

**plane of incidence** *s* (opt.) plano de incidencia

**planer** ['plenər] *s* acepillador; acepilladora (*máquina*); (print.) tamborilete

**planer tree** *s* (bot.) planera

**plane sickness** *s* (aer.) mareo del aire, mal de vuelo

**planet** ['plænɪt] *s* (astr. & astrol.) planeta

**plane table** *s* (surv.) plancheta

**planetarium** [,plænɪ'tɛrɪəm] *s* (*pl:* **-a** [ə]) planetario

**planetary** ['plænɪ,tɛrɪ] *adj* planetario; errante, inconstante; mundano, terrestre; (mach.) planetario

**planetesimal** [,plænɪ'tɛsɪməl] *adj* & *s* planetesimal

**planetoid** ['plænɪtɔɪd] *s* (astr.) planetoide

**plane tree** *s* (bot.) plátano de oriente; (bot.) plátano de occidente

**plane trigonometry** *s* trigonometría plana

**planimeter** [plə'nɪmɪtər] *s* planímetro

**planimetric** [,plænɪ'mɛtrɪk] o **planimetrical** [,plænɪ'mɛtrɪkəl] *adj* planimétrico

**planimetry** [plə'nɪmɪtrɪ] *s* planimetría

**planing mill** *s* taller de cepillado; cepilladora

**planish** ['plænɪʃ] *va* aplanar

**planisphere** ['plænɪsfɪr] *s* planisferio

**plank** [plæŋk] *s* tabla gruesa, tablón; artículo de un programa político; **to walk the plank** lanzarse al mar (*pena de muerte que imponían los piratas a sus víctimas*); *va* entablar, entarimar; asar a la brasa en una tabla; **to plank down** (coll.) colocar firmemente; (coll.) arrojar con alguna violencia (*sobre una mesa, un mostrador, etc.*); **to plank out** (coll.) pagar o desembolsar sin vacilación

**planking** ['plæŋkɪŋ] *s* entablación; tablaje; maderamen de cubierta, tablazón de buque

**plank-sheer** ['plæŋk,ʃɪr] *s* (naut.) regala

**plankton** ['plæŋktən] *s* (biol.) plankton o plancton

**planned economy** *s* economía dirigida o planificada

**planned parenthood** *s* natalidad dirigida, procreación planeada

**planner** ['plænər] *s* proyectista

**plano-concave** [,pleno'kɑnkev] *adj* planocóncavo

**plano-convex** [,pleno'kɑnvɛks] *adj* planoconvexo

**plant** [plænt] o [plɑnt] *s* (bot.) planta; fábrica, taller; grupo motor (*de un automóvil*); plantel (*establecimiento de educación*); (slang) proyecto para engañar; *va* plantar; sembrar (*semillas*); inculcar (*doctrinas*); (slang) plantar (*golpes*); (slang) ocultar (*géneros robados*)

**plantaginaceous** [,plæntədʒɪ'neʃəs] *adj* (bot.) plantagináceo

**plantain** ['plæntɪn] *s* (bot.) plátano (*Musa paradisiaca y fruto*); (bot.) llantén (*Plantago major*)

**plantation** [plæn'teʃən] *s* plantío; plantación

**planter** ['plæntər] o ['plɑntər] *s* plantador; plantadora (*máquina*)

**plantigrade** ['plæntɪgred] *adj* & *s* (zool.) plantígrado

**plantlet** ['plæntlɪt] o ['plɑntlɪt] *s* plantilla, planta rudimentaria

**plant louse** *s* (ent.) pulgón

**plant pathology** *s* patología vegetal

**plant physiology** *s* fisiología vegetal

**plaque** [plæk] *s* placa

**plaquette** [plæ'kɛt] *s* (anat.) plaqueta

**plash** [plæʃ] *s* salpicadura; chapoteo; mancha; charco; *va* salpicar; chapotear; manchar; entretejer (*ramas*); hacer o podar (*un seto vivo*) entretejiendo ramas; *vn* chapotear, caer con ruido

**plashy** ['plæʃɪ] *adj* (*comp:* **-ier;** *super:* **-iest**) cenagoso, pantanoso; salpicado, manchado

**plasm** ['plæzəm] *s* var. de **plasma**

**plasma** ['plæzmə] *s* (anat., phys. & physiol.) plasma *m;* (biol.) protoplasma; (mineral.) plasma *f;* suero (*de la leche*)

**plasmatic** [plæz'mætɪk] o **plasmic** ['plæzmɪk] *adj* plasmático

**plasmochin** ['plæzməkɪn] *s* (pharm.) plasmoquina

**plasmodium** [plæz'modɪəm] *s* (*pl:* **-a** [ə]) (biol.) plasmodio

**plasmolysis** [plæz'mɑlɪsɪs] *s* (physiol.) plasmólisis

**plasmoquine** ['plæzməkwaɪn] *s* var. de **plasmochin**

**plasmosome** ['plæzməsom] *s* (biol.) plasmosoma

**plaster** ['plæstər] o ['plɑstər] *s* yeso; argamasa; enlucido (*capa de yeso*); (pharm.) emplasto; *va* enyesar; argamasar; enlucir; emplastar; embadurnar, untar; pegar (*anuncios, carteles*); **to plaster down** pegar (*p.ej., el pelo al cráneo*)

**plasterboard** ['plæstər,bord] o ['plɑstər,bord] *s* cartón de yeso y fieltro

**plaster cast** *s* (surg.) vendaje enyesado

**plasterer** ['plæstərər] o ['plɑstərər] *s* yesero, enlucidor, revocador

**plastering** ['plæstərɪŋ] o ['plɑstərɪŋ] *s* enlucimiento; enlucido, enyesado

**plastering trowel** *s* llana de enlucir

**plaster of Paris** *s* yeso de París

**plastic** ['plæstɪk] *adj* plástico; *s* plástico (*cuerpo*); plástica (*arte de plasmar*)

**plastic bomb** *s* bomba de plástico

**plasticine** ['plæstɪsin] *s* (trademark) arcilla de modelar, plastilina

**plasticity** [plæs'tɪsɪtɪ] *s* plasticidad

**plasticize** ['plæstɪsaɪz] *va* plastificar; *vn* plastificarse

**plastic surgery** *s* cirugía plástica

**plastic wood** *s* (trademark) madera plástica

**plastron** ['plæstrən] *s* pechera; (arm. & zool.) peto; (fencing) plastrón

**plat** [plæt] *s* plan, plano o mapa; parcela, solar; trenza; (*pret & pp:* **platted;** *ger:* **platting**) *va* trazar el plano o mapa de, trasladar al papel; trenzar

**platan** ['plætən] *s* var. de **plane tree**

**platanaceous** [,plætə'neʃəs] *adj* (bot.) platanáceo

**plate** [plet] *s* plato; vajilla de oro, vajilla de plata; cubierto; placa, chapa (*de metal, cristal, etc.*); escudete; lámina; clisé; dentadura postiza, base de la dentadura postiza; pecho delgado (*carne de vaca*); (arch.) viga horizontal; (baseball) puesto meta, puesto del batter; (anat., elec., phot., rad. & zool.) placa; (mach.) plato; *va* chapear; blindar; platear, dorar, niquelar (*por la galvanoplastia*); (print.) clisar

**plateau** [plæ'to] *s* meseta

**plate circuit** *s* (rad.) circuito de placa

**plate current** *s* (rad.) corriente de placa

**plateful** ['pletfʊl] *s* plato (*lo que contiene un plato*)

**plate glass** *s* vidrio o cristal cilindrado

**plateholder** ['plet,holdər] *s* (phot.) almacén de placas, portaplacas, chasis

**platen** ['plætən] *s* platina, rodillo

**plater** ['pletər] *s* (sport) caballo que no gana carreras

**plateresque** [,plætə'rɛsk] *adj* (arch.) plateresco

**platform** ['plæt,fɔrm] *s* plataforma; andén; cargadero; tribuna (*de orador*); (geog.) plataforma; (fig.) plataforma (*programa político*)

**platform car** *s* (rail.) plataforma

**platform carriage** *s* carro fuerte

**Platine** ['plætaɪn] *adj* rioplatense

**plating** ['pletɪŋ] *s* galvanoplastia; capa metálica; blindaje

**platiniridium** [,plætɪnɪ'rɪdɪəm] *s* platiniridio

**platinocyanide** [,plætɪno'saɪənaɪd] o [,plætɪno'saɪənɪd] *s* (chem.) platinocianuro

**platinoid** ['plætɪnɔɪd] *s* platinoide

**platinotype** ['plætɪnə,taɪp] *s* (phot.) platinotipia

**platinum** ['plætɪnəm] *s* (chem.) platino

**platinum black** *s* negro de platino

**platinum blonde** *s* rubia platino

**platitude** ['plætɪtjud] o ['plætɪtud] *s* perogrullada, trivialidad; falta de gracia

**platitudinous** [,plætɪ'tjudɪnəs] o [,plætɪ'tudɪnəs] *adj* trivial, falto de gracia

**Plato** ['pleto] *s* Platón

**Platonic** [plə'tɑnɪk] *adj* platónico

**Platonic love** *s* amor platónico

**Platonism** ['pletənɪzəm] *s* platonismo

**Platonist** ['pletənɪst] *s* platonista

**platoon** [plə'tun] *s* (mil.) pelotón; grupo (*de personas*)

**platter** ['plætər] *s* fuente, platón; (slang) disco de fonógrafo

**platyhelminth** [,plætɪ'hɛlmɪnθ] *s* (zool.) platelminto

**platypus** ['plætɪpəs] *s* (*pl:* **-puses** o **-pi** [paɪ]) (zool.) ornitorrinco

**platyrrhine** ['plætɪraɪn] o ['plætɪrɪn] *adj & s* (zool.) platirrino

**plaudit** ['plɔdɪt] *s* aplauso

**plausibility** [,plɔzɪ'bɪlɪtɪ] *s* especiosidad; (coll.) credibilidad

**plausible** ['plɔzɪbəl] *adj* especioso, aparente; bien hablado; (coll.) creíble

**Plautine** ['plɔtaɪn] o ['plɔtɪn] *adj* plautino

**Plautus** ['plɔtəs] *s* Plauto

**play** [ple] *s* juego; jugada (*lance de juego*); pieza, obra dramática; juego (*de aguas, de colores, de luces, etc.*); (mach.) juego; **at play** jugando; **to be full of play** ser retozón, ser travieso; **to come into play** entrar en juego; **to give full play to** dar rienda suelta a ‖ *va* jugar (*p.ej., un naipe, una partida de juego*); jugar a (*p.ej., los naipes*); jugar con (*un contrario*); dar (*un chasco*); hacer (*una mala jugada*); dirigir (*agua, una manguera*); hacer o desempeñar (*un papel*); hacer o desempeñar el papel de; representar (*una obra dramática, un film*); dar representaciones en (*una ciudad*); apostar por (*un caballo*); darse al juego en (*las carreras de caballo*); dejar que se canse (*un pez que ha picado en el anzuelo*); gastar (*una broma*); (mus.) tocar (*un instrumento, una pieza, un disco de fonógrafo*); **to be played out** estar agotado; estar estropeado por el uso, estar inservible; **to play back** retocar (*un disco de fonógrafo*); **to play someone false** engañarle a uno; **to play up** ensalzar, dar bombo a ‖ *vn* jugar; representar, desempeñar un papel; correr (*una fuente*); rielar (*la luz en la superficie del agua*); vagar (*p.ej., una sonrisa por los labios*); hacerse el (o la), p.ej., **to play sick** hacerse el enfermo; **to play on** continuar jugando; continuar tocando; aprovecharse de, valerse de; agitar (*emociones*) por provecho propio; (mus.) tocar (*un instrumento*); **to play out** cansarse, rendirse; agotarse; acabarse; **to play safe** tomar sus precauciones; **to play up to** hacer la rueda a, halagar servilmente

**playable** ['pleəbəl] *adj* servible; (theat.) representable

**play-act** ['ple,ækt] *vn* (coll.) actuar, hacer un papel; (coll.) hacer la comedia

**playback** ['ple,bæk] *s* (elec.) lectura (*de una grabación fonográfica acabada de registrar*); (elec.) aparato de lectura

**playback head** *s* cabeza de lectura (*del magnetófono*)

**playbill** ['ple,bɪl] *s* cartel; programa (*de una pieza dramática*)

**playboy** ['ple,bɔɪ] *s* (slang) amante de los placeres, niño bonito

**player** ['pleər] *s* jugador; actor; ejecutante; autopiano

**player piano** *m* autopiano

**playfellow** ['ple,fɛlo] *s* compañero de juego

**playful** ['plefəl] *adj* juguetón; dicho en broma

**playfulness** ['plefəlnɪs] *s* travesura, retozo; jovialidad
**playgoer** ['ple,goər] *s* aficionado al teatro, persona que frecuenta el teatro
**playground** ['ple,graʊnd] *s* patio de recreo, campo de juego
**playhouse** ['ple,haʊs] *s* casita de juguete para niños, casita de muñecas; teatro
**playing card** *s* naipe
**playing field** *s* campo de deportes, terreno de juego
**playlet** ['plelɪt] *s* (theat.) juguete cómico, paso de comedia
**playmate** ['ple,met] *s* compañero de juego
**play-off** ['ple,ɔf] o ['ple,ɑf] *s* (sport) partido de desempate
**play on words** *s* juego de palabras, retruécano
**play pen** *s* parque, corralito plegable (*para bebés*)
**playroom** ['ple,rum] o ['ple,rʊm] *s* cuarto de juegos
**plaything** ['ple,θɪŋ] *s* juguete; (fig.) juguete
**playtime** ['ple,taɪm] *s* hora de recreo, hora de juego
**playwright** ['ple,raɪt] *s* autor dramático, dramaturgo
**plaza** ['plɑzə] o ['plæzə] *s* plaza
**plea** [pli] *s* ruego, súplica; disculpa, excusa; (law) contestación a la demanda
**pleach** [plitʃ] *va* entretejer (*p.ej., ramas de árboles*)
**plead** [plid] (*pret & pp:* **pleaded** o **pled**) *va* alegar; (law) defender (*una causa*); *vn* suplicar; argumentar; abogar; (law) abogar; **to plead against** abogar contra; **to plead for** abogar por; **to plead guilty** (law) confesarse culpable; **to plead not guilty** (law) negar la acusación, declararse inocente; **to plead with** suplicar; **to plead with someone for something** rogarle a uno que conceda algo
**pleader** ['plidər] *s* suplicante; (law) abogado
**pleadings** ['plidɪŋz] *spl* (law) alegatos
**pleasance** ['plɛzəns] *s* parque, jardín de recreo; (archaic) placer
**pleasant** ['plɛzənt] *adj* agradable; simpático
**pleasantness** ['plɛzəntnɪs] *s* agradabilidad
**pleasantry** ['plɛzəntrɪ] *s* (*pl:* **-ries**) chanza, chiste, dicho gracioso
**please** [pliz] *va & vn* gustar; **as you please** como Vd. quiera; **if you please** si quiere, si me hace el favor; **to be pleased to** + *inf* alegrarse de + *inf*, complacerse en + *inf;* **to be pleased with** estar satisfecho de o con; **to be pleased with oneself** estar satisfecho de sí mismo; **to do as one pleases** hacer su voluntad; **to please oneself** darse gusto, no hacer más que lo que se le antoja; **please God** si Dios lo quiere; **please** + *inf* tenga Vd. la bondad de + *inf*, hágame Vd. el favor de + *inf*, sírvase + *inf*
**pleasing** ['plizɪŋ] *adj* agradable, grato
**pleasurable** ['plɛʒərəbəl] *adj* agradable
**pleasure** ['plɛʒər] *s* placer, goce, deleite, gusto; **what is your pleasure?** ¿en qué puedo servirle?, ¿qué es lo que Vd. desea?; **with pleasure** con mucho gusto
**pleasure boat** *s* bote de recreo
**pleasure car** *s* (aut.) coche de paseo, coche de deporte
**pleasure seeker** *s* persona que anda tras los placeres, amigo de los placeres
**pleasure trip** *s* viaje de recreo, viaje de placer
**pleat** [plit] *s* pliegue, plisado; *va* plegar, plisar
**pleating** ['plitɪŋ] *s* plisado
**plebe** [plib] *s* (mil.) cadete de primer año (*en la Academia Militar de los EE.UU.*); (nav.) guardia marina de primer año (*en la Academia Naval de los EE.UU.*)
**plebeian** [plɪ'biən] *adj & s* plebeyo
**plebeianism** [plɪ'biənɪzəm] *s* plebeísmo
**plebiscite** ['plɛbɪsaɪt] o ['plɛbɪsɪt] *s* plebiscito
**plebs** [plɛbz] *s* (*pl:* **plebes** ['plibiz]) plebe; (hist.) plebe
**plectognath** ['plɛktɑgnæθ] *adj & s* (zool.) plectognato
**plectrum** ['plɛktrəm] *s* (*pl:* **-trums** o **-tra** [trə]) (mus.) plectro
**pled** [plɛd] *pret & pp de* **plead**
**pledge** [plɛdʒ] *s* promesa; voto (*promesa que se hace a Dios*); prenda; brindis; **as a pledge of** en prenda de; **to take the pledge** comprometerse a no catar bebidas alcohólicas; *va* prometer; empeñar; dar (*la palabra*); brindar por; **to pledge to secrecy** exigir promesa de secreto o silencio a
**pledgee** [plɛdʒ'i] *s* depositario
**Pleiad** ['pliæd] o ['plaɪæd] *s* (*pl:* **Pleiades** ['pliədiz] o ['plaɪədiz]) Pléyade; **Pleiades** *spl* (myth. & astr.) Pléyades
**Pleiocene** ['plaɪəsin] *adj & s* var. de **Pliocene**
**Pleistocene** ['plaɪstəsin] *adj & s* (geol.) pleistoceno
**plenary** ['plinərɪ] o ['plɛnərɪ] *adj* plenario
**plenary indulgence** *s* (eccl.) indulgencia plenaria
**plenary session** *s* sesión plenaria
**plenipotentiary** [,plɛnɪpə'tɛnʃɪ,ɛrɪ] o [,plɛnɪpə'tɛnʃərɪ] *adj* plenipotenciario; *s* (*pl:* **-ies**) plenipotenciario
**plenitude** ['plɛnɪtjud] o ['plɛnɪtud] *s* plenitud
**plenteous** ['plɛntɪəs] o **plentiful** ['plɛntɪfəl] *adj* abundante, copioso
**plenty** ['plɛntɪ] *s* copia, abundancia; cantidad suficiente; *adj* suficiente; *adv* (coll.) completamente, muy
**plenum** ['plinəm] *s* (*pl:* **-nums** o **-na** [nə]) pleno
**plenum chamber** *s* cámara de pleno
**pleochroism** [plɪ'ɑkro·ɪzəm] *s* (cryst.) pleocroísmo
**pleonasm** ['pliənæzəm] *s* pleonasmo; palabra o frase superfluas
**pleonastic** [,pliə'næstɪk] *adj* pleonástico
**plesiosaur** ['plisɪə,sɔr] *s* (pal.) plesiosauro
**plethora** ['plɛθərə] *s* plétora; (path.) plétora
**plethoric** [plɛ'θɑrɪk], [plɛ'θɔrɪk] o ['plɛθərɪk] *adj* pletórico; (fig.) ampuloso, hinchado
**plethysmograph** [plɪ'θɪzmogræf] o [plɪ'θɪzmogrɑf] *s* (physiol.) pletismógrafo
**pleura** ['plʊrə] *s* (*pl:* **-rae** [ri]) (anat. & zool.) pleura
**pleural** ['plʊrəl] *adj* pleural
**pleurisy** ['plʊrɪsɪ] *s* (path.) pleuresía
**pleuritic** [plʊ'rɪtɪk] *adj* pleurítico
**pleuritis** [plʊ'raɪtɪs] *s* (path.) pleuritis
**pleurodont** ['plʊrədɑnt] *adj* (zool.) pleurodonto
**pleuronectid** [,plʊrə'nɛktɪd] *adj & s* (ichth.) pleuronecto
**pleuropneumonia** [,plʊronju'monɪə] o [,plʊronu'monɪə] *s* (path.) pleuroneumonía
**plexiglass** ['plɛksɪ,glæs] o ['plɛksɪ,glɑs] *s* (trademark) plexiglás
**plexus** ['plɛksəs] *s* (*pl:* **-uses** o **-us**) (anat. & zool.) plexo
**pliability** [,plaɪə'bɪlɪtɪ] *s* flexibilidad, docilidad
**pliable** ['plaɪəbəl] *adj* flexible, plegable, dócil
**pliancy** ['plaɪənsɪ] *s* flexibilidad, docilidad
**pliant** ['plaɪənt] *adj* flexible; manejable, sumiso
**plicate** ['plaɪket] *adj* plegado (*en forma de abanico*)
**pliers** ['plaɪərz] *ssg* o *spl* alicates, pinzas
**plight** [plaɪt] *s* estado, situación; apuro, aprieto; promesa, compromiso solemne; *va* empeñar o dar (*su palabra*); prometer en matrimonio; **to plight one's troth** prometer fidelidad; dar palabra de casamiento, contraer esponsales
**Plimsoll line** o **mark** ['plɪmsɑl] o ['plɪmsəl] *s* (naut.) marca Plimsoll (*línea de carga máxima*)
**plinth** [plɪnθ] *s* (arch.) plinto
**Pliny** ['plɪnɪ] *s* Plinio
**Pliny the Elder** *s* Plinio el Antiguo
**Pliny the Younger** *s* Plinio el Joven
**Pliocene** ['plaɪəsin] *adj & s* (geol.) pliocénico
**plod** [plɑd] (*pret & pp:* **plodded;** *ger:* **plodding**) *va* recorrer (*un camino*) pausada y pesadamente; *vn* caminar pausada y pesadamente; trabajar laboriosamente; **to plod away at** dedicarse laboriosamente a, ocuparse laboriosamente en
**plodder** ['plɑdər] *s* persona que camina pausada y pesadamente; persona que trabaja con más aplicación que talento; estudiante más aplicado que brillante
**plop** [plɑp] *s* paf (*ruido de la caída de un objeto plano que cae sin violencia al agua*); *adv* dejando oír un paf; (*pret & pp:* **plopped;** *ger:*

**plopping**) *va* arrojar dejando oír un paf; **to plop down** arrojar sobre el mostrador; *vn* dejar oír un paf; caer dejando oír un paf
**plot** [plɑt] *s* complot, conspiración; argumento, trama (*de una novela, etc.*); parcela, solar; plano, mapa; cuadro de flores; cuadro de hortalizas; (*pret & pp:* **plotted;** *ger:* **plotting**) *va* fraguar, tramar, urdir, maquinar; dividir en parcelas o solares; trazar el plano de; trazar, tirar (*líneas*); *vn* conspirar
**Plotinus** [plo'taɪnəs] *s* Plotino
**plotter** ['plɑtər] *s* conjurado, conspirador; maquinador
**plough** [plaʊ] *s, va & vn* var. de **plow**
**plover** ['plʌvər] o ['plovər] *s* (orn.) chorlito
**plow** [plaʊ] *s* arado; quitanieve, barredora de nieve; *va* arar; surcar; quitar o barrer (*la nieve*); **to plow back** reinvertir (*ganancias*); **to plow under** cubrir arando; **to plow up** arrancar con un arado; romper (*p.ej., un pavimento*) como con un arado; *vn* arar; avanzar como un arado
**plowboy** ['plaʊ,bɔɪ] *s* yuguero; gañancico
**plowland** ['plaʊ,lænd] *s* tierra labrantía; tierra labrada
**plowman** ['plaʊmən] *s* (*pl:* **-men**) arador, labrador, yuguero; gañán
**plowshare** ['plaʊ,ʃɛr] *s* reja de arado
**plowshare bone** *s* (anat.) vómer
**plowstaff** ['plaʊ,stæf] o ['plaʊ,stɑf] *s* abéstola, aguijada
**plowtail** ['plaʊ,tel] *s* esteva o estevas
**ploy** [plɔɪ] *s* maniobra, manejo, artimaña; *vn* (mil.) pasar del orden abierto al compacto
**pluck** [plʌk] *s* ánimo, coraje, valor; asadura; tirón; *va* arrancar, coger; herir, puntear (*las cuerdas de un instrumento con los dedos*); desplumar (*un ave*); (coll.) dar calabazas a (*en un examen*); (slang) estafar, robar; *vn* tirar, dar un tirón; **to pluck up** recobrar ánimo, envalentonarse
**plucky** ['plʌkɪ] *adj* (*comp:* **-ier;** *super:* **-iest**) animoso, valiente
**plug** [plʌg] *s* taco, tarugo; boca de agua; tableta de tabaco; (slang) chistera; (elec.) tapón fusible; (elec.) clavija, toma, ficha; (aut.) bujía; (coll.) rocín, penco; (slang) elogio incidental; (*pret & pp:* **plugged;** *ger:* **plugging**) *va* atarugar; (slang) pegar; (slang) taladrar con una bala; calar (*un melón*); **to plug in** (elec.) enchufar; *vn* (coll.) trabajar con ahinco; **to plug along** (coll.) trabajar con ahinco
**plug fuse** *s* (elec.) tapón fusible
**plugger** ['plʌgər] *s* (coll.) trabajador diligente, estudiante diligente; (dent.) orificador
**plug hat** *s* (slang) chistera, sombrero de copa alta
**plug-in** ['plʌg,ɪn] *adj* enchufable
**plug tobacco** *s* tabaco torcido
**plug-ugly** ['plʌg,ʌglɪ] *s* (*pl:* **-lies**) (slang) bullanguero, matón
**plum** [plʌm] *s* (bot.) ciruelo; ciruela (*fruto*); pasa (*en un bollo, etc.*); confite; la cosa mejor; turrón, pingüe destino; *adj* morado
**plumage** ['plumɪdʒ] *s* plumaje
**plumb** [plʌm] *s* plomada; **in plumb** a plomo; **out of plumb** fuera de plomo; *adj* vertical; (coll.) completo; *adv* a plomo, verticalmente; (coll.) completamente; (coll.) directamente; *va* aplomar; sondear
**plumbaginaceous** [plʌm,bædʒɪ'neʃəs] *adj* (bot.) plumbagináceo
**plumbago** [plʌm'bego] *s* plombagina
**plumb bob** *s* plomada, perpendículo
**plumber** ['plʌmər] *s* cañero, instalador de cañería, plomero
**plumbery** ['plʌmərɪ] *s* (*pl:* **-ies**) plomería
**plumbic** ['plʌmbɪk] *adj* plúmbeo; (chem.) plúmbico
**plumbing** ['plʌmɪŋ] *s* plomería; instalación sanitaria; conjunto de cañerías; sondeo
**plumbing fixtures** *spl* artefactos o efectos sanitarios
**plumb line** *s* cuerda de plomada
**plum cake** *s* pastel aderezado con pasas de Corinto y ron
**plume** [plum] *s* pluma (*de ave*); penacho; *va* emplumar; componerse (*las plumas*); **to plume oneself on** enorgullecerse de
**plume grass** *s* (bot.) carricera, vulpino
**plumelet** ['plumlɪt] *s* plumilla
**plummet** ['plʌmɪt] *s* plomada; *vn* caer a plomo, precipitarse
**plumose** ['plumos] *adj* plumoso
**plump** [plʌmp] *s* (coll.) caída pesada; (coll.) ruido sordo; *adj* rechoncho, regordete; brusco, directo, franco; *adv* de golpe, de sopetón; francamente, sin rodeos; *va* engordar; hinchar; *vn* engordar; hincharse; caer a plomo, desplomarse, dejarse caer pesadamente
**plum pudding** *s* pudín inglés con pasas de Corinto, piel de limón, huevos, ron, etc.
**plum tree** *s* (bot.) ciruelo
**plumule** ['plumjul] *s* (bot.) plúmula; (orn.) plumón
**plumy** ['plumɪ] *adj* plumoso; empenachado
**plunder** ['plʌndər] *s* pillaje, saqueo; botín; *va* pillar, saquear
**plunge** [plʌndʒ] *s* zambullida; caída a plomo; tumbo, sacudida violenta; salto; corcovo (*de un animal encorvando el lomo*); baño en agua fría; piscina natatoria; cabeceo (*de un buque*); *va* zambullir; sumergir; hundir (*p.ej., un puñal*); *vn* zambullirse; sumergirse; abismarse, hundirse (*p.ej., en la tristeza*); caer a plomo; dar un tumbo, empezar a dar tumbos; arrojarse, precipitarse; corcovear (*un animal encorvando el lomo*); cabecear (*un buque*); (slang) entregarse al juego, entregarse a las especulaciones
**plunger** ['plʌndʒər] *s* zambullidor; (mach.) émbolo buzo; obús (*de una válvula de neumático*); persona impetuosa; (slang) jugador o especulador desenfrenado
**plunk** [plʌŋk] *s* (coll.) golpe seco; (coll.) ruido seco; *adv* (coll.) con un golpe seco; (coll.) con un ruido de golpe seco; *va* puntear (*p.ej., la guitarra*); (coll.) arrojar, empujar o dejar caer pesadamente; **to plunk down** (coll.) arrojar pesadamente; *vn* sonar o caer con un ruido de golpe seco
**pluperfect** ['plu,pʌrfɪkt] o [,plu'pʌrfɪkt] *adj & s* (gram.) pluscuamperfecto
**plupf.** abr. de **pluperfect**
**plur.** abr. de **plural**
**plural** ['plʊrəl] *adj & s* (gram.) plural
**plurality** [plʊ'rælɪtɪ] *s* (*pl:* **-ties**) pluralidad
**pluralize** ['plʊrəlaɪz] *va* pluralizar
**plurally** ['plʊrəlɪ] *adv* en el plural
**plus** [plʌs] *s* más (*signo*); añadidura; *adj* más; y pico; **to be plus** (coll.) tener además, tener por añadidura; *prep* más
**plus fours** *spl* pantalones holgados de media pierna
**plush** [plʌʃ] *s* felpa; *adj* afelpado; (slang) lujoso, suntuoso
**plushy** ['plʌʃɪ] *adj* (*comp:* **-ier;** *super:* **-iest**) felpudo
**plus sign** *s* signo más
**Plutarch** ['plutɑrk] *s* Plutarco
**Pluto** ['pluto] *s* (myth. & astr.) Plutón
**plutocracy** [plu'tɑkrəsɪ] *s* (*pl:* **-cies**) plutocracia
**plutocrat** ['plutəkræt] *s* plutócrata
**plutocratic** [,plutə'krætɪk] *adj* plutocrático
**Plutonian** [plu'tonɪən] *adj* plutoniano
**plutonic** [plu'tɑnɪk] *adj* (geol.) plutónico; (*cap.*) *adj* (myth. & geol.) plutónico
**plutonium** [plu'tonɪəm] *s* (chem.) plutonio
**Plutus** ['plutəs] *s* (myth.) Pluto
**pluvial** ['pluvɪəl] *adj* pluvial
**pluviometer** [,pluvɪ'ɑmɪtər] *s* pluviómetro
**pluvious** ['pluvɪəs] *adj* pluvioso
**ply** [plaɪ] *s* (*pl:* **plies**) capa o doblez (*de una tela, manguera, etc.*); cordón (*de un cable*); (*pret & pp:* **plied**) *va* manejar (*la aguja, un instrumento, etc.*); ejercer (*un oficio*); batir (*el agua con los remos*); no dejar descansar, no dar descanso a; trabajar con ahinco en; acosar, importunar; navegar por (*un río*); *vn* estar en movimiento incesante, funcionar constantemente; avanzar, moverse; (naut.) barloventear; **to ply between** hacer el servicio entre
**plywood** ['plaɪ,wʊd] *s* chapeado, madera contrachapada, madera laminada
**p.m.** abr. de **post meridiem** (Lat.) **after noon** y **post mortem**
**P.M.** abr. de **post meridiem** (Lat.) **after noon, Postmaster** y **Provost Marshal**

**pneumatic** [nju'mætɪk] o [nu'mætɪk] *adj* neumático; **pneumatics** *ssg* neumática
**pneumatically** [nju'mætɪkəlɪ] o [nu'mætɪkəlɪ] *adv* neumáticamente
**pneumatic drill** *s* perforadora de aire comprimido
**pneumococcus** [ˌnjumə'kɑkəs] o [ˌnumə'kɑkəs] *s* (*pl:* **-cocci** ['kɑksaɪ]) (bact.) neumococo
**pneumonia** [nju'monɪə] o [nu'monɪə] *s* (path.) pulmonía o neumonía; **an attack of pneumonia** o **a case of pneumonia** una pulmonía; **to get pneumonia** coger una pulmonía
**pneumonic** [nju'mɑnɪk] o [nu'mɑnɪk] *adj* neumónico
**pneumothorax** [ˌnjumo'θoræks] o [ˌnumo'θoræks] *s* (path. & med.) neumotórax
**P.O.** abr. de **post office**
**poach** [potʃ] *va* coger en vedado; (cook.) escalfar (*huevos*); *vn* cazar o pescar en vedado
**poached egg** *s* huevo escalfado
**poacher** ['potʃər] *s* cazador furtivo, pescador furtivo
**pock** [pɑk] *s* hoyuelo (*en la piel*)
**pocket** ['pɑkɪt] *s* bolsillo, faltriquera; cavidad; talega (*saco de lienzo basto*); tronera (*de la mesa de billar*); (aer.) bolsa de aire, vacío; (mil.) bolsón; (min.) depósito de pepitas de oro, cueva mineralizada; **in pocket** con ganancia; **out of pocket** perdidoso; **to pick pockets** hurtar de los bolsillos; *va* embolsar; tragarse (*injurias*); disimular (*emociones*); apropiarse (*ganancias sin tener derecho a ellas*)
**pocket battleship** *s* acorazado de bolsillo
**pocket billiards** *ssg* trucos (*juego*)
**pocketbook** ['pɑkɪtˌbʊk] *s* portamonedas, cartera; bolsa (*de mujer*)
**pocketful** ['pɑkɪtfʊl] *s* bolsillo, lo que cabe en el bolsillo
**pocket handkerchief** *s* pañuelo de bolsillo o de mano
**pocketknife** ['pɑkɪtˌnaɪf] *s* (*pl:* **-knives** [ˌnaɪvz]) navaja, cortaplumas
**pocket money** *s* alfileres, dinero de bolsillo
**pocket veto** *s* (U.S.A.) veto indirecto o implícito (*que consiste en no firmar el Presidente una ley dentro del plazo legal*)
**pockmark** ['pɑkˌmɑrk] *s* var. de **pock**
**pock-marked** ['pɑkˌmɑrkt] *adj* apedreado, picado de viruelas, varioloso, picoso
**pod** [pɑd] *s* (bot.) vaina; (*pret & pp:* **podded;** *ger:* **podding**) *vn* (bot.) criar vainas; llenarse, henchirse
**podgy** ['pɑdʒɪ] *adj* (*comp:* **-ier;** *super:* **-iest**) gordinflón, rechoncho
**podiatrist** [po'daɪətrɪst] *s* podíatra
**podiatry** [po'daɪətrɪ] *s* podiatría
**podium** ['podɪəm] *s* (*pl:* **-a** [ə]) (arch.) podio; (anat. & zool.) pie; (bot.) pecíolo; estrado (*de director de orquesta*)
**podophyllin** [ˌpɑdə'fɪlɪn] *s* (pharm.) podofilino
**podophyllotoxin** [ˌpɑdəˌfɪlə'tɑksɪn] *s* (chem.) podofilotoxina
**podophyllum** [ˌpɑdə'fɪləm] *s* podofilo
**poem** ['po·ɪm] *s* poema; (fig.) poesía (*cosa muy hermosa*)
**poesy** ['po·ɪsɪ] o ['po·ɪzɪ] *s* (*pl:* **-sies**) (archaic) poesía; (obs.) poema
**poet** ['po·ɪt] *s* poeta
**poetaster** ['po·ɪtˌæstər] *s* poetastro
**poetess** ['po·ɪtɪs] *s* poetisa
**poetic** [po'ɛtɪk] *adj* poético; **poetics** *ssg* poética
**poetical** [po'ɛtɪkəl] *adj* poético
**poetic justice** *s* justicia ideal
**poetic license** *s* licencia poética
**poetic vein** *s* numen poético
**poetize** ['po·ɪtaɪz] *va & vn* poetizar
**poet laureate** *s* (*pl:* **poets laureate**) poeta laureado
**poetry** ['po·ɪtrɪ] *s* poesía
**pogrom** ['pogrɑm] *s* pogrom, levantamiento contra los judíos
**poignancy** ['pɔɪnənsɪ] o ['pɔɪnjənsɪ] *s* picante; viveza, intensidad
**poignant** ['pɔɪnənt] o ['pɔɪnjənt] *adj* picante; vivo, intenso
**poikilothermal** [ˌpɔɪkɪlo'θʌrməl] *adj* (zool.) poiquilotermo
**poilu** ['pwɑlu] *s* soldado francés
**poinsettia** [pɔɪn'sɛtɪə] *s* (bot.) flor de la Pascua, pastora
**point** [pɔɪnt] *s* punta (*de espada, lápiz, tierra*); punto; pico (*de la pluma de escribir*); puntilla (*de la plumafuente*); gracia (*del chiste*); rasgo, peculiaridad; propósito; tanto o punto (*unidad de cuenta en los juegos*); (coll.) indirecta, insinuación; (elec.) punta; (print. & math.) punto; (naut.) cuarta (*de la rosa náutica*); (hunt.) punta (*del perro de caza*); (Brit.) aguja (*riel*); **at the point of** a punto de; **at the point of death** a punto de morir, en artículo de muerte; **beside the point** fuera de propósito; **from the point of view of** bajo el punto de vista de; **in point** a propósito; **in point of** por lo que toca a; **in point of fact** en realidad; **just the point** lo que importa; **to a certain point** hasta cierto punto; **to be beside the point** no venir al caso; **to be on the point of** estar a punto de; **to carry one's point** salirse con la suya; **to come** o **to get to the point** venir al caso o al grano, llegar al punto fundamental; **to get the point** caer en la cuenta; **to make a point of** hacer hincapié de; **to make a point of** + *ger* insistir en + *inf*, no dejar de + *inf*, esmerarse en + *inf*; **to speak to the point** hablar al caso; **to strain** o **stretch a point** exceder el límite; excederse haciendo concesiones, hacer una excepción; **to the point** a propósito; **up to a certain point** hasta cierto punto ‖ *va* aguzar, sacar punta a; apuntar (*p.ej. un arma de fuego*); señalar, señalar con el dedo; puntuar; rejuntar, resanar (*una pared*); reforzar; puntar (*las letras hebreas y árabes*); (hunt.) parar (*la caza*); **to point one's finger at** señalar con el dedo; **to point a gun at** apuntar con el fusil; **to point off** indicar con un punto o con puntos; **to point out** señalar, indicar, hacer notar; **to point up** poner de realce o de relieve, destacar ‖ *vn* apuntar; apostemarse; pararse (*el perro de muestra*); **to point at** apuntar; apuntar o señalar con el dedo; **to point to** señalar; indicar, pronosticar
**point-blank** ['pɔɪntˌblæŋk] *adj & adv* a quema ropa; **to ask a question point-blank** hacer una pregunta a quema ropa
**pointed** ['pɔɪntɪd] *adj* puntiagudo; picante; directo, acentuado
**pointedly** ['pɔɪntɪdlɪ] *adv* directamente, enfáticamente; a propósito
**pointer** ['pɔɪntər] *s* indicador; puntero; manecilla del reloj; perro de muestra; fiel (*de la balanza*); (coll.) indicación, dirección
**point lace** *s* encaje de punto, puntas
**pointless** ['pɔɪntlɪs] *adj* sin punta; sin sentido, insubstancial; sin tantos
**point of honor** *s* punto de honor, pundonor
**point of order** *s* cuestión de procedimiento
**point of view** *s* punto de vista
**poise** [pɔɪz] *s* equilibrio, aplomo, serenidad, balance; *va* equilibrar; sopesar; considerar; *vn* equilibrarse; estar suspendido; cernerse
**poison** ['pɔɪzən] *s* veneno, ponzoña; (fig.) ponzoña; *adj* venenoso, ponzoñoso; *va* envenenar
**poisoner** ['pɔɪzənər] *s* envenenador
**poison gas** *s* (mil.) gas tóxico, gas de guerra
**poison hemlock** *s* (bot.) cicuta, cicuta mayor
**poisoning** ['pɔɪzənɪŋ] *s* envenenamiento
**poison ivy** *s* (bot.) hiedra venenosa, chechén, tosiguero
**poison oak** *s* (bot.) hiedra venenosa, chechén; (bot.) zumaque venenoso
**poisonous** ['pɔɪzənəs] *adj* venenoso
**poison-pen letter** ['pɔɪzənˌpɛn] *s* paulina (*carta ofensiva anónima*)
**poison sumac** *s* (bot.) zumaque venenoso
**poke** [pok] *s* empuje, empujón; codazo; hurgonazo; tardón; papalina de ala abovedada; (bot.) hierba carmín, grana encarnada; *va* empujar; hacer (*un agujero*) a empujones; abrirse (*paso*) a empujones, abrirse (*paso*) a fuerza de codazos; atizar, hurgar; introducir, meter; **to poke fun at** burlarse de; **to poke one's nose into** entremeterse en; **to poke someone in the ribs** darle a uno un codazo en las costillas; *vn* fisgar, husmear; andar perezosamente; **to poke along** andar perezosamente; **to poke**

**around** fisgar, husmear; andar buscando algo; **to poke into** hurgar en
**pokeberry** ['pok,bɛrɪ] *s* (*pl:* **-ries**) (bot.) hierba carmín, grana encarnada (*planta y baya*)
**poke bonnet** *s* papalina de ala abovedada
**poker** ['pokər] *s* hurgón; tardón; póker o pócar (*juego de naipes*)
**poker face** *s* (coll.) cara de jugador de póker (*cara impasible*); **to keep a poker face** (coll.) disfrazar la expresión del rostro
**pokeweed** ['pok,wid] *s* (bot.) hierba carmín, grana encarnada
**poky** o **pokey** ['pokɪ] *adj* (*comp:* **-ier;** *super:* **-iest**) roncero, lerdo, perezoso, tardo; insignificante; desaliñado
**polacre** [po'lɑkər] *s* (naut.) polacra
**Poland** ['polənd] *s* Polonia
**polar** ['polər] *adj* polar
**polar bear** *s* (zool.) oso blanco
**polar cap** *s* casquete polar (*del planeta Marte*)
**polarimeter** [,polə'rɪmɪtər] *s* polarímetro
**Polaris** [po'lɛrɪs] *s* (astr.) la estrella polar, la polar norte
**polariscope** [po'lærɪskop] *s* polariscopio
**polarity** [po'lærɪtɪ] *s* polaridad
**polarization** [,polərɪ'zeʃən] *s* polarización
**polarize** ['poləraɪz] *va* polarizar
**polarizer** ['polə,raɪzər] *s* (opt.) polarizador
**polaroid** ['polərɔɪd] *s* (trademark) polaroide
**polaroid lenses** *spl* lentes polarizantes
**pole** [pol] *s* pértiga; poste, piquete, jalón; asta (*de bandera*); botador (*para mover los barcos*); (astr., geog., biol., elec. & math.) polo; medida lineal equivalente a 5,03 metros; medida de superficie equivalente a 25,2 metros cuadrados; (*cap.*) *s* polaco; (*l.c.*) *va* finear, impeler (*una embarcación*) con botador; *vn* silgar, singar
**poleax** o **poleaxe** ['pol,æks] *s* hachuela de mano; jifero
**polecat** ['pol,kæt] *s* (zool.) turón, veso (*Putorius putorius*); (zool.) mofeta (*Mephitis*); (zool.) vormela (*Putorius sarmaticus*)
**pole gap** *s* (phys.) entrehierro, entrehierro polar (*del ciclotrón*)
**polemic** [po'lɛmɪk] *adj* polémico; *s* polémica (*controversia*); polemista; **polemics** *ssg* polémica (*arte*)
**polemical** [po'lɛmɪkəl] *adj* polémico
**polemist** ['pɑlɪmɪst] *s* polemista
**polemoniaceous** [,pɑlɪ,monɪ'eʃəs] *adj* (bot.) polemoniáceo
**polenta** [po'lɛntə] *s* polenta
**pole piece** *s* parhilera; (elec.) pieza polar
**pole pitch** *s* (elec.) paso polar, distancia interpolar
**polestar** ['pol,stɑr] *s* (astr.) estrella polar; (fig.) norte (*guía*); (fig.) miradero (*centro de interés*)
**pole vault** *s* (sports) salto con garrocha, salto con pértiga
**police** [pə'lis] *s* policía; (mil.) limpieza; *va* poner o mantener servicio de policía en; (mil.) limpiar
**police action** *s* (int. law) acción de policía
**police car** *s* coche de policía
**police court** *s* tribunal de policía
**police dog** *s* perro policía
**police force** *s* cuerpo de policía, servicio de policía
**police headquarters** *s* jefatura de policía
**policeman** [pə'lismən] *s* (*pl:* **-men**) policía, agente o guardia de policía, guardia urbano
**police record** *s* ficha
**police state** *s* estado-policía, estado policial
**police station** *s* oficina de policía, prefectura
**policewoman** [pə'lis,wumən] *s* (*pl:* **-women**) mujer policía
**policy** ['pɑlɪsɪ] *s* (*pl:* **-cies**) política; (ins.) póliza; (U.S.A.) lotería
**policyholder** ['pɑlɪsɪ,holdər] *s* asegurado, tenedor de una póliza
**policy of encirclement** *s* política de cerco, política de acorralamiento
**policy racket** *s* var. de **numbers game**
**polio** ['polɪo] *s* (coll.) polio (*poliomielitis*)
**poliomyelitis** [,polɪo,maɪə'laɪtɪs] *s* (path.) poliomielitis
**Polish** ['polɪʃ] *adj* polaco; *spl* polacos; *ssg* polaco (*idioma*); (*l.c.*) ['pɑlɪʃ] *s* pulimento (*acción o efecto; ingrediente*); cera de lustrar; bola, betún, crema; elegancia, pulidez; cultura, urbanidad; *va* pulir; embolar, dar bola, betún o brillo a (*los zapatos*); (fig.) pulir; **to polish off** (coll.) terminar de prisa, acabar con, sin más ni más; (slang) engullir; **to polish up** mejorar, perfeccionar; *vn* pulirse
**Polish Corridor** ['polɪʃ] *s* Corredor Polaco
**polished** ['pɑlɪʃt] *adj* pulido, terso, brillante; cortés, distinguido, urbano
**polisher** ['pɑlɪʃər] *s* pulidor; pulidora (*máquina*)
**polishing wax** *s* cera de lustrar
**polishing wheel** *s* rueda de bruñir, muela pulidora
**Politburo** [pɑ'lɪt,bjurɑ] *s* Politburó
**polite** [pə'laɪt] *s* cortés; culto
**politeness** [pə'laɪtnɪs] *s* cortesía; cultura
**Politian** [po'lɪʃən] *s* Policiano
**politic** ['pɑlɪtɪk] *adj* prudente, sagaz; astuto, ladino; político; **politics** *ssg* o *spl* política
**political** [pə'lɪtɪkəl] *adj* político
**political economy** *s* economía política
**political science** *s* ciencia política
**politician** [,pɑlɪ'tɪʃən] *s* político; politiquero (*político de propósitos ruines*)
**polity** ['pɑlɪtɪ] *s* (*pl:* **-ties**) gobierno; estado
**polka** ['polkə] *s* (mus.) polca; *vn* polcar
**polka dot** ['pokə] *s* punto (*en un diseño de puntos*); diseño de puntos
**poll** [pol] *s* encuesta; votación; nómina, lista electoral; cabeza; **polls** *spl* colegio electoral, urnas electorales; **to go to the polls** ir a las urnas, acudir a los comicios; **to take a poll** hacer una encuesta; *va* dar (*un voto*); recibir (*votos*); encuestar (*la opinión pública*); recibir en la urna los votos de; podar, desmochar (*un árbol*); descornar; trasquilar; *vn* votar
**pollack** ['pɑlək] *s* (ichth.) gado (*de los géneros Pollachius y Theragra*)
**pollard** ['pɑlərd] *s* árbol desmochado; res descornada; *va* acotar, desmochar (*un árbol*); descornar
**pollen** ['pɑlən] *s* (bot.) polen
**pollinate** ['pɑlɪnet] *va* polinizar
**pollination** [,pɑlɪ'neʃən] *s* polinización
**polling booth** *s* cabina o caseta de votar
**polling place** *s* urnas electorales, lugar donde se vota
**pollinic** [pə'lɪnɪk] o **pollinical** [pə'lɪnɪkəl] *adj* polínico
**polliniferous** [,pɑlɪ'nɪfərəs] *adj* polinífero
**pollinium** [pə'lɪnɪəm] *s* (*pl:* **-a** [ə]) (bot.) polinio
**pollinosis** [,pɑlɪ'nosɪs] *s* (path.) polinosis
**polliwog** ['pɑlɪwɑg] *s* (zool.) renacuajo; (slang) persona que atraviesa el ecuador en un barco por primera vez
**pollock** ['pɑlək] *s* var. de **pollack**
**poll tax** *s* capitación
**pollute** [pə'lut] *va* contaminar, ensuciar, corromper
**pollution** [pə'luʃən] *s* contaminación, corrupción; (path.) polución
**Pollux** ['pɑləks] *s* (myth. & astr.) Pólux
**Polly** ['pɑlɪ] *s* Mariquita
**pollywog** ['pɑlɪwɑg] *s* var. de **polliwog**
**polo** ['polo] *s* (sport) polo
**polonaise** [,pɑlə'nez] o [,polə'nez] *s* polonesa (*prenda de vestir*); (mus.) polonesa
**polonium** [pə'lonɪəm] *s* (chem.) polonio
**polo player** *s* polista, jugador de polo
**polo shirt** *s* pulóver con cuello abotonado
**poltergeist** ['poltər,gaɪst] *s* espíritu que golpea y mueve mesas y otros objetos para indicar su presencia
**poltroon** [pɑl'trun] *s* cobarde
**poltroonery** [pɑl'trunərɪ] *s* cobardía
**poly** ['polɪ] *s* (*pl:* **-lies**) (bot.) polio
**polyandrous** [,pɑlɪ'ændrəs] *adj* poliándrico; (bot.) poliandro
**polyandry** ['pɑlɪ,ændrɪ] *s* poliandria; (bot.) poliandria
**polyanthus** [,pɑlɪ'ænθəs] *s* (bot.) hierba de San Pablo mayor; (bot.) narciso de manojo
**polyarchy** ['pɑlɪ,ɑrkɪ] *s* poliarquía
**polybasic** [,pɑlɪ'besɪk] *adj* (chem.) polibásico
**polybasite** [,pɑlɪ'besaɪt] o [pə'lɪbəsaɪt] *s* (mineral.) polibasita
**polycarpic** [,pɑlɪ'kɑrpɪk] o **polycarpous** [,pɑlɪ'kɑrpəs] *adj* (bot.) policárpico

**polychromatic** [ˌpɑlɪkroˈmætɪk] *adj* policromo
**polychrome** [ˈpɑlɪkrom] *adj* policromo; *s* combinación de varios colores; obra policroma; *va* policromar
**polychromy** [ˈpɑlɪˌkromɪ] *s* policromía
**polyclinic** [ˌpɑlɪˈklɪnɪk] *s* policlínica
**Polydorus** [ˌpɑlɪˈdorəs] *s* (myth.) Polidoro
**polyethylene** [ˌpɑlɪˈɛθɪlin] (chem) polietileno
**polygamist** [pəˈlɪgəmɪst] *s* polígamo
**polygamous** [pəˈlɪgəməs] *adj* polígamo
**polygamy** [pəˈlɪgəmɪ] *s* poligamia
**polygenism** [pəˈlɪdʒɪnɪzəm] *s* poligenismo
**polyglot** [ˈpɑlɪglɑt] *adj & s* poligloto; *s* libro poligloto; Biblia poliglota
**polygon** [ˈpɑlɪgɑn] *s* (geom.) polígono
**polygonal** [pəˈlɪgənəl] *adj* poligonal
**polygraph** [ˈpɑlɪgræf] o [ˈpɑlɪgrɑf] *s* polígrafo (*autor; aparato multicopista*); (med.) polígrafo
**polygraphy** [pəˈlɪgrəfɪ] *s* poligrafía
**polyhedral** [ˌpɑlɪˈhidrəl] *adj* poliédrico
**polyhedron** [ˌpɑlɪˈhidrən] *s* (*pl:* **-drons** o **-dra** [drə]) (geom.) poliedro
**Polyhymnia** [ˌpɑlɪˈhɪmnɪə] *s* (myth.) Polimnia
**polymer** [ˈpɑlɪmər] *s* (chem.) polímero
**polymeric** [ˌpɑlɪˈmɛrɪk] *adj* polímero
**polymerism** [ˈpɑlɪmərɪzəm] o [pəˈlɪmərɪzəm] *s* polimeria
**polymerization** [ˌpɑlɪmərɪˈzeʃən] o [pəˌlɪmərɪˈzeʃən] *s* polimerización
**polymerize** [ˈpɑlɪməraɪz] o [pəˈlɪməraɪz] *va* polimerizar; *vn* polimerizarse
**polymorphic** [ˌpɑlɪˈmɔrfɪk] *adj* var. de **polymorphous**
**polymorphism** [ˌpɑlɪˈmɔrfɪzəm] *s* polimorfismo
**polymorphous** [ˌpɑlɪˈmɔrfəs] *adj* polimorfo
**Polynesia** [ˌpɑlɪˈniʃə] o [ˌpɑlɪˈniʒə] *s* la Polinesia
**Polynesian** [ˌpɑlɪˈniʃən] o [ˌpɑlɪˈniʒən] *adj & s* polinesio
**polyneuritis** [ˌpɑlɪnjʊˈraɪtɪs] o [ˌpɑlɪnʊˈraɪtɪs] *s* (path.) polineuritis
**polynomial** [ˌpɑlɪˈnomɪəl] *adj* polinómico; *s* (alg.) polinomio
**polynuclear** [ˌpɑlɪˈnjuklɪər] o [ˌpɑlɪˈnuklɪər] *adj* polinuclear
**polyp** [ˈpɑlɪp] *s* (zool. & path.) pólipo
**polypary** [ˈpɑlɪˌpɛrɪ] *s* (*pl:* **-ies**) (zool.) polipero
**polypetalous** [ˌpɑlɪˈpɛtələs] *adj* (bot.) polipétalo
**polyphagia** [ˌpɑlɪˈfedʒɪə] *s* (path.) polifagía
**polyphase** [ˈpɑlɪfez] *adj* (elec.) polifásico
**Polyphemus** [ˌpɑlɪˈfiməs] *s* (myth.) Polifemo
**polyphone** [ˈpɑlɪfon] *s* (phonet.) letra polífona, símbolo polífono
**polyphonic** [ˌpɑlɪˈfɑnɪk] *adj* polifónico
**polyphony** [pəˈlɪfənɪ] *s* (mus. & phonet.) polifonía
**polyphyletic** [ˌpɑlɪfaɪˈlɛtɪk] *adj* polifilético
**polypody** [ˈpɑlɪˌpodɪ] *s* (*pl:* **-dies**) (bot.) polipodio
**polypus** [ˈpɑlɪpəs] *s* (*pl:* **-pi** [paɪ]) (path.) pólipo
**polysemous** [ˌpɑlɪˈsiməs] *adj* polisémico o polisemo
**polysemy** [ˈpɑlɪˌsimɪ] *s* polisemia
**polystyle** [ˈpɑlɪstaɪl] *adj & s* (arch.) polistilo
**polystylous** [ˌpɑlɪˈstaɪləs] *adj* (bot.) polistilo
**polystyrene** [ˌpɑlɪˈstaɪrin] o [ˌpɑlɪˈstɪrin] *s* (chem.) polistireno
**polysyllabic** [ˌpɑlɪsɪˈlæbɪk] *adj* polisílabo, polisilábico
**polysyllable** [ˈpɑlɪˌsɪləbəl] *s* polisílabo
**polysyndeton** [ˌpɑlɪˈsɪndətən] *s* (rhet.) polisíndeton
**polysynthetic** [ˌpɑlɪsɪnˈθɛtɪk] *adj* polisintético
**polytechnic** [ˌpɑlɪˈtɛknɪk] *adj* politécnico; *s* escuela politécnica
**polytheism** [ˈpɑlɪθiɪzəm] *s* politeísmo
**polytheist** [ˈpɑlɪθiɪst] *s* politeísta
**polytheistic** [ˌpɑlɪθiˈɪstɪk] *adj* politeísta
**polytonal** [ˌpɑlɪˈtonəl] *adj* politonal
**polytonality** [ˌpɑlɪtoˈnælɪtɪ] *s* (mus.) politonalidad
**polyuria** [ˌpɑlɪˈjʊrɪə] *s* (path.) poliuria
**polyvalence** [ˌpɑlɪˈveləns] o [pəˈlɪvələns] *s* (bact. & chem.) polivalencia
**polyvalent** [ˌpɑlɪˈvelənt] o [pəˈlɪvələnt] *adj* (bact. & chem.) polivalente
**pomace** [ˈpʌmɪs] *s* bagazo de manzanas; bagazo
**pomaceous** [poˈmeʃəs] *adj* (bot.) pomáceo
**pomade** [pəˈmed] o [pəˈmɑd] *s* pomada
**pomander** [poˈmændər] o [ˈpomændər] *s* poma, bola aromática
**pomatum** [poˈmetəm] o [poˈmɑtəm] *s* var. de **pomade**
**pome** [pom] *s* (bot.) pomo
**pomegranate** [ˈpɑmˌgrænɪt], [pɑmˈgrænɪt] o [ˈpʌmˌgrænɪt] *s* (bot.) granado; granada (*fruto*)
**pomelo** [ˈpɑməlo] *s* (*pl:* **-los**) (bot.) pomelo
**Pomeranian** [ˌpɑməˈrenɪən] *adj* pomeranio o pomerano; *s* pomeranio o pomerano; perro pomerano
**pomfret** [ˈpɑmfrɪt] *s* (ichth.) castañola
**pommel** [ˈpʌməl] o [ˈpɑməl] *s* pomo (*de la guarnición de la espada*); perilla (*del arzón*); (*pret & pp:* **-meled** o **-melled;** *ger:* **-meling** o **-melling**) *va* apuñear, aporrear
**pomology** [poˈmɑlədʒɪ] *s* pomología
**pomp** [pɑmp] *s* pompa
**pompadour** [ˈpɑmpədor] o [ˈpɑmpədʊr] *s* copete
**pompano** [ˈpɑmpəno] *s* (*pl:* **-nos**) (ichth.) pampanito
**Pompeian** [pɑmˈpeən] *adj & s* pompeyano
**Pompeii** [pɑmˈpe] o [pɑmˈpe·i] *s* Pompeya
**Pompey** [ˈpɑmpɪ] *s* Pompeyo
**pompon** [ˈpɑmpɑn] *s* pompón
**pomposity** [pɑmˈpɑsɪtɪ] *s* (*pl:* **-ties**) pomposidad
**pompous** [ˈpɑmpəs] *adj* pomposo
**poncho** [ˈpɑntʃo] *s* (*pl:* **-chos**) capote de monte, poncho
**pond** [pɑnd] *s* estanque, charco; vivero; (hum.) charco (*mar, océano*)
**ponder** [ˈpɑndər] *va* ponderar, considerar con particular cuidado; *vn* meditar, pensar con cuidado; **to ponder on** u **over** ponderar, considerar con particular cuidado
**ponderable** [ˈpɑndərəbəl] *adj* ponderable; (fig.) ponderable
**ponderosity** [ˌpɑndəˈrɑsɪtɪ] *s* ponderosidad; pesadez
**ponderous** [ˈpɑndərəs] *adj* ponderoso; pesado
**pond lily** *s* (bot.) ninfea, nenúfar
**pondweed** [ˈpɑndˌwid] *s* (bot.) acaxaxán, zacatillo
**pone** [pon] *s* pan de maíz
**pongee** [pɑnˈdʒi] *s* tela suave de seda
**poniard** [ˈpɑnjərd] *s* puñal; *va* apuñalar
**pontederiaceous** [ˌpɑntɪˌdɪrɪˈeʃəs] *adj* (bot.) pontederiáceo
**Pontic** [ˈpɑntɪk] *adj* póntico
**pontifex** [ˈpɑntɪfɛks] *s* (*pl:* **pontifices** [pɑnˈtɪfɪsiz]) (hist. & eccl.) pontífice
**pontiff** [ˈpɑntɪf] *s* (hist. & eccl.) pontífice; sumo sacerdote; Sumo Pontífice
**pontifical** [pɑnˈtɪfɪkəl] *adj* pontifical, pontificio; *s* pontifical (*libro litúrgico*); **pontificals** *spl* pontificales
**pontificate** [pɑnˈtɪfɪkɪt] o [pɑnˈtɪfɪket] *s* pontificado; [pɑnˈtɪfɪket] *vn* pontificar; hablar con ampulosidad
**pontil** [ˈpɑntɪl] *s* var. de **punty**
**Pontine Marshes** [ˈpɑntɪn] o [ˈpɑntaɪn] *spl* Pantanos Pontinos
**Pontius** [ˈpɑnʃəs] o [ˈpɑntɪəs] *s* Poncio
**pontlevis** [pɑntˈlɛvɪs] *s* puente levadizo
**pontonier** [ˌpɑntəˈnɪr] *s* (mil.) pontonero
**pontoon** [pɑnˈtun] *s* pontón; flotador (*de hidroavión*)
**pontoon bridge** *s* puente de barcas, puente de pontones
**Pontus** [ˈpɑntəs] *s* (myth.) Ponto; **the Pontus** el Ponto (*país*)
**Pontus Euxinus** [jukˈsaɪnəs] *s* Ponto Euxino (*antiguo nombre del mar Negro*)
**pony** [ˈponɪ] *s* (*pl:* **-nies**) jaca, caballito; (coll.) traducción usada ilícitamente en las lecciones o exámenes; pequeño vaso (*para licor alcohólico*); (*pret & pp:* **-nied**) *va & vn* (coll.) traducir con clave o ayuda; (slang) pagar; **to pony up** (slang) pagar

**pony engine** *s* pequeña locomotora de maniobras
**pony express** *s* sistema de correo utilizando hombres a caballo
**pooch** [putʃ] *s* (coll.) perro
**poodle** ['pudəl] *s* perro de lanas
**pooh** [pu] *interj* ¡bah!, ¡qué va!
**pooh-pooh** [,pu'pu] *va* negar importancia a; *vn* mofar; *interj* ¡bah!, ¡qué va!
**pooh-pooh theory** *s* (philol.) teoría de las expresiones afectivas
**pool** [pul] *s* cuerpo de agua estancado; charco (*en el pavimento*); piscina; hoya (*en un río*); trucos (*juego*); polla o puesta (*en ciertos juegos*); mancomunidad, combinación de intereses con un propósito común; caudales unidos para un fin; *va* mancomunar
**poolroom** ['pul,rum] o ['pul,rʊm] *s* sala de trucos; sala de apuestas
**pool table** *s* mesa de trucos
**poop** [pup] *s* (naut.) popa; (naut.) toldilla (*cubierta*); *va* (naut.) embarcar (*agua*) por la popa
**poop deck** *s* (naut.) toldilla
**poop royal** *s* (naut.) chopeta
**poor** [pʊr] *adj* pobre; malo; **the poor** los pobres; **poor as a church mouse** más pobre que las ratas o una rata; **poor in spirit** pobre de espíritu
**poor box** *s* caja de limosnas, cepillo
**poor farm** *s* granja o finca sostenida por la caridad pública donde se recluye a los menesterosos
**poorhouse** ['pʊr,haʊs] *s* asilo de pobres, casa de caridad
**poor law** *s* ley acerca de los menesterosos
**poorly** ['pʊrlɪ] *adj* (coll.) malo, enfermo; *adv* pobremente; mal
**poor rate** *s* diezmos pagados para el socorro de los menesterosos
**Poor Richard** *s* el buenhombre Ricardo (*seudónimo de Benjamín Franklin*)
**poor-spirited** ['pʊr'spɪrɪtɪd] *adj* cobarde, pusilánime
**poor thing** *s* pobrecito o pobrecita
**poor white** *s* pobre de la raza blanca (*en el sur de los EE.UU.*)
**pop.** abr. de **popular** y **population**
**pop** [pɑp] *s* estallido, taponazo; bebida gaseosa; *interj* ¡paf!; (*pret & pp:* **popped**; *ger:* **popping**) *va* disparar; hacer estallar; hacer (*una pregunta*); **to pop the question** (coll.) hacer una declaración de amor; *vn* estallar (*como un cohete*); reventarse; suceder de repente; **to pop at** tirar a; **to pop in and out** entrar y salir súbita e inesperadamente; **to pop up** aparecer súbita o inesperadamente
**pop concert** *s* concierto popular
**popcorn** ['pɑp,kɔrn] *s* rosetas, palomitas
**pope** o **Pope** [pop] s papa
**popedom** ['popdəm] *s* papado
**Pope Joan** *s* Juana la papisa, la papisa Juana
**popery** ['popərɪ] *s* (scornful) papismo
**popess** ['popɪs] *s* papisa
**popeyed** ['pɑp,aɪd] *adj* de ojos saltones
**popgun** ['pɑp,gʌn] *s* tirabala, taco
**popinjay** ['pɑpɪndʒe] *s* pisaverde, galancete; (orn.) pito real
**popish** ['popɪʃ] *adj* (scornful) papista, católico
**poplar** ['pɑplər] *s* (bot.) álamo
**poplin** ['pɑplɪn] *s* popelina
**popliteal** [pɑp'lɪtɪəl] *adj* (anat.) poplíteo
**popover** ['pɑp,ovər] *s* panecillo hueco de masa muy fina
**popper** ['pɑpər] *s* persona o cosa que produce un estallido; canasto de alambre o cacerola de metal donde se tuesta el maíz
**poppet** ['pɑpɪt] *s* (mach.) válvula de disco con movimiento vertical
**poppy** ['pɑpɪ] *s* (*pl:* **-pies**) (bot.) amapola, ababa
**poppycock** ['pɑpɪ,kɑk] *s* (coll.) necedad, tontería; *interj* ¡necedades!, ¡tonterías!
**popsicle** ['pɑpsɪkəl] *s* polo (*pequeño sorbete en el extremo de un palito*)
**populace** ['pɑpjəlɪs] *s* populacho
**popular** ['pɑpjələr] *adj* popular
**popular etymology** *s* etimología popular
**popularity** [,pɑpjə'lærɪtɪ] *s* popularidad
**popularization** [,pɑpjələrɪ'zeʃən] *s* popularización, vulgarización
**popularize** ['pɑpjələraɪz] *va* popularizar, vulgarizar
**popularly** ['pɑpjələrlɪ] *adv* popularmente
**populate** ['pɑpjəlet] *va* poblar
**population** [,pɑpjə'leʃən] *s* población
**Populism** ['pɑpjəlɪzəm] *s* populismo
**Populist** ['pɑpjəlɪst] *s* populista
**populous** ['pɑpjələs] *adj* populoso
**populousness** ['pɑpjələsnɪs] *s* (lo) populoso
**porbeagle** ['pɔr,bigəl] *s* (ichth.) tiburón (*Lamna nasus*)
**porcelain** ['pɔrsəlɪn] o ['pɔrslɪn] *s* porcelana
**porcelain crab** *s* (zool.) liebre de mar o liebre marina
**porch** [portʃ] *s* porche, pórtico, cobertizo
**porcine** ['pɔrsaɪn] o ['pɔrsɪn] *adj* porcino
**porcupine** ['pɔrkjəpaɪn] *s* (zool.) puerco espín
**pore** [por] *s* poro; *vn* mirar con mirada intensa y sostenida; **to pore over** meditar (*un asunto*) cuidadosamente; estudiar larga y detenidamente
**porgy** ['pɔrgɪ] *s* (*pl:* **-gies**) (ichth.) pagro
**poricidal** [,porɪ'saɪdəl] *adj* (bot.) poricida
**pork** [pork] *s* carne de cerdo, carne de puerco; (slang) dinero del estado usado para conferir favores políticos
**pork barrel** *s* (slang) política que sigue un diputado para conseguir beneficios para la región que representa, asegurándose así los votos; fondos votados por los diputados para el cumplimiento de esta política
**pork chop** *s* chuleta de puerco
**porker** ['porkər] *s* cerdo, cerdo cebado
**porky** ['porkɪ] *adj* porcuno; gordo
**pornographer** [pɔr'nɑgrəfər] *s* pornógrafo
**pornographic** [,pɔrnə'græfɪk] *adj* pornográfico
**pornography** [pɔr'nɑgrəfɪ] *s* pornografía
**porosity** [po'rɑsɪtɪ] *s* porosidad
**porous** ['porəs] *adj* poroso
**porous plaster** *s* parche poroso
**porphyritic** [,pɔrfɪ'rɪtɪk] *adj* porfídico
**porphyry** ['pɔrfɪrɪ] *s* (*pl:* **-ries**) pórfido
**porpoise** ['pɔrpəs] *s* (zool.) marsopa, puerco de mar
**porraceous** [pə'reʃəs] *adj* porráceo
**porridge** ['pɑrɪdʒ] o ['pɔrɪdʒ] *s* gachas
**porringer** ['pɑrɪndʒər] o ['pɔrɪndʒər] *s* escudilla
**port** [port] *s* puerto; (naut.) portilla; (nav.) tronera; (naut.) babor; (mach.) lumbrera; porte; oporto, vino de Oporto; **to put into port** entrar a puerto; *adj* portuario; *vn* (naut.) virar hacia el lado de babor
**portable** ['portəbəl] *adj* portátil
**portable typewriter** *s* máquina de escribir portátil
**portage** ['portɪdʒ] *s* porteo (*acción de llevar por tierra y a cuestas barcos, provisiones, etc., de una corriente de agua a otra*); porte; *va* portear
**portal** ['portəl] *s* portada; boca o portal (*de túnel*)
**portal vein** *s* (anat.) vena porta
**Port Arthur** *s* Puerto Arturo
**Port-au-Prince** [,porto'prɪns] *s* Puerto Príncipe
**port authority** *s* autoridad portuaria, autoridad del puerto
**portcullis** [port'kʌlɪs] *s* (fort.) rastrillo
**Porte** [port] *s* Puerta (*Turquía*)
**porte-cochere** o **porte-cochère** ['portko'ʃɛr] *s* puerta cochera
**porte-monnaie** [,portmə'ne] o ['port,mʌnɪ] *s* portamonedas
**portend** [por'tɛnd] *va* presagiar, anunciar de antemano
**portent** ['portɛnt] *s* presagio, augurio
**portentous** [por'tɛntəs] *adj* amenazante, ominoso; portentoso, extraordinario
**porter** ['portər] *s* mozo de servicio (*en trenes y hoteles*); portero, conserje; pórter (*cerveza de color obscuro y sabor amargo*)
**porterage** ['portərɪdʒ] *s* oficio o trabajo de mozo de servicio; portería; porte (*lo que se paga por el transporte*)

**porterhouse** ['portər,haus] o **porterhouse steak** *s* biftec de filete
**porter's lodge** *s* portería, conserjería
**portfolio** [port'folɪo] *s* (*pl:* **-os**) cartera (*estuche para papeles; empleo de ministro; valores comerciales*)
**porthole** ['port,hol] *s* (naut.) porta, portilla; (nav.) tronera
**Portia** ['porʃɪə] o ['porʃə] *s* Porcia
**portico** ['portɪko] *s* (*pl:* **-coes** o **-cos**) pórtico
**portiere** o **portière** [por'tjɛr] *s* antepuerta, portier
**portion** ['porʃən] *s* porción; dote; *va* dividir, repartir; dotar
**Portland cement** ['portlənd] *s* cemento pórtland
**portly** ['portlɪ] *adj* (*comp:* **-lier;** *super:* **-liest**) corpulento; grave, majestuoso
**portmanteau** [port'mænto] *s* (*pl:* **-teaus** o **-teaux** [toz]) portamanteo
**portmanteau word** *s* palabra de enchufamiento
**port of call** *s* (naut.) escala
**Port of Spain** *s* Puerto de España (*en la isla de la Trinidad*)
**Porto Rican** ['porto 'rikən] *adj* & *s* var. de **Puerto Rican**
**Porto Rico** ['porto 'riko] *s* var. de **Puerto Rico**
**portrait** ['portret] o ['portrɪt] *s* retrato
**portraitist** ['portretɪst] *s* retratista
**portrait painter** *s* pintor retratista
**portraiture** ['portrɪtʃər] *s* acción de retratar; retrato
**portray** [por'tre] *va* retratar; (fig.) retratar
**portrayal** [por'treəl] *s* representación gráfica; descripción acertada, retrato
**portress** ['portrɪs] *s* portera
**Portugal** ['portʃəgəl] *s* Portugal
**Portuguese** ['portʃəgiz] *adj* portugués; *s* (*pl:* **-guese**) portugués
**Portuguese East Africa** *s* el África Oriental Portuguesa
**Portuguese Guinea** *s* la Guinea Portuguesa
**Portuguese India** *s* la India Portuguesa
**Portuguese West Africa** *s* el África Occidental Portuguesa
**portulaca** [,portʃə'lækə] *s* (bot.) verdolaga
**port wine** *s* vino de Oporto
**pose** [poz] *s* pose (*postura del cuerpo; afectación*); *va* colocar en cierta postura; formular, hacer, proponer, plantear (*una pregunta, cuestión, etc.*); confundir; *vn* posar (*para retratarse; como modelo*); fachendear; **to pose as** dárselas de, hacerse pasar por
**Poseidon** [po'saɪdən] *s* (myth.) Poseidón
**poser** ['pozər] *s* presuntuoso; problema de difícil comprensión
**poseur** [po'zʌr] *s* poseur (*persona afectada, persona que emplea afectación con el propósito de causar sensación*)
**posh** [pɑʃ] *adj* (slang) elegante, gracioso; (slang) lujoso, suntuoso
**posit** ['pɑzɪt] *va* colocar, disponer; (philos.) aceptar como hecho, proponer como principio
**position** [pə'zɪʃən] *s* posición; empleo, puesto; opinión; **to be in a position to** + *inf* estar en condiciones de + *inf*
**positive** ['pɑzɪtɪv] *adj* positivo; *s* (math.) término positivo; (elec.) electricidad positiva, borne positivo; (gram.) positivo; (phot.) positiva o positivo
**positivism** ['pɑzɪtɪvɪzəm] *s* positivismo
**positivist** ['pɑzɪtɪvɪst] *s* positivista
**positivistic** [,pɑzɪtɪ'vɪstɪk] *adj* positivista
**positron** ['pɑzɪtrɑn] *s* (phys.) positrón
**posology** [pə'sɑlədʒɪ] *s* (med.) posología
**posse** ['pɑsɪ] *s* grupo de hombres llamados a las armas por el jefe local para ayudarle a ejercer su autoridad
**possess** [pə'zɛs] *va* poseer
**possession** [pə'zɛʃən] *s* posesión
**possessive** [pə'zɛsɪv] *adj* posesivo; deseoso de poseer; (gram.) posesivo; *s* (gram.) posesivo
**possessor** [pə'zɛsər] *s* poseedor, posesor
**possessory** [pə'zɛsərɪ] *adj* posesorio
**posset** ['pɑsɪt] *s* bebida caliente hecha con leche, licor y especias
**possibility** [,pɑsɪ'bɪlɪtɪ] *s* (*pl:* **-ties**) posibilidad; persona o cosa posibles
**possible** ['pɑsɪbəl] *adj* posible
**possibly** ['pɑsɪblɪ] *adv* posiblemente; tal vez
**possum** ['pɑsəm] *s* (zool.) zarigüeya; **to act** o **play possum** (coll.) fingir estar dormido, hacer la mortecina, hacer o hacerse el muerto
**post** [post] *s* poste; puesto; cargo, destino; correo; casa de postas; cartero; casa de correos; buzón; (mil.) apostadero, puesto militar; (mil.) campamento, guarnición; *adv* por la posta, a toda prisa; *va* fijar (*carteles*); poner en lista; echar al correo; apostar, situar; enterar, tener al corriente; nombrar (*a una persona*) para desempeñar un cargo determinado; (com.) pasar (*un asiento*) del libro diario al libro mayor; **post no bills** se prohíbe fijar carteles; *vn* correr la posta; viajar en posta
**postage** ['postɪdʒ] *s* porte, franqueo
**postage stamp** *s* sello de correo; estampilla, timbre (Am.)
**postal** ['postəl] *adj* postal; *s* postal (*tarjeta*)
**postal car** *s* (rail.) coche de correos
**postal card** *s* tarjeta postal
**postal permit** *s* franqueo concertado
**postal savings bank** *s* caja postal de ahorros
**postboy** ['post,bɔɪ] *s* cartero; postillón
**postbox** ['post,bɑks] *s* buzón
**post card** *s* tarjeta postal
**post chaise** *s* silla de posta
**postdate** ['post,det] *s* posfecha; [,post'det] *va* posfechar; seguir, acontecer después de
**postdiluvian** [,postdɪ'luvɪən] *adj* postdiluviano
**posted** ['postɪd] *adj* con postes o pilares; (coll.) enterado, al corriente
**poster** ['postər] *s* cartel, cartelón, letrero; fijador de carteles; caballo de posta
**poste restante** [,post rɛs'tɑnt] *s* (Fr.) lista de correos
**posterior** [pɑs'tɪrɪər] *adj* posterior; *s* nalgas
**posteriority** [pɑs,tɪrɪ'ɔrɪtɪ] o [pɑs,tɪrɪ'ɑrɪtɪ] *s* posterioridad
**posterity** [pɑs'tɛrɪtɪ] *s* posteridad
**postern** ['postərn] *s* portillo, postigo; (fort.) poterna
**Post Exchange** *s* (U.S.A.) cantina y tienda de variedades para los militares en los campamentos
**postfix** ['postfɪks] *s* (gram.) posfijo
**postgraduate** [post'grædʒuɪt] *adj* & *s* postgraduado
**posthaste** ['post'hest] *adv* por la posta, a toda prisa
**posthole** ['post,hol] *s* agujero de poste
**posthole digger** *s* barrena para practicar hoyos en la colocación de postes, cavador de agujeros de poste
**post horse** *s* caballo de posta
**posthouse** ['post,haus] *s* posta, casa de postas
**posthumous** ['pɑstʃuməs] *adj* póstumo
**posthumously** ['pɑstʃuməslɪ] *adv* póstumamente
**posthypnotic** [,posthɪp'nɑtɪk] *adj* posthipnótico
**postiche** [pɔs'tiʃ] *adj* postizo
**postilion** o **postillion** [pos'tɪljən] o [pɑs'tɪljən] *s* postillón
**postimpressionism** [,postɪm'prɛʃənɪzəm] *s* postimpresionismo
**postimpressionist** [,postɪm'prɛʃənɪst] *s* postimpresionista
**postliminy** [post'lɪmɪnɪ] *s* (law) postliminio
**postlude** ['postlud] *s* (mus.) postludio
**postman** ['postmən] *s* (*pl:* **-men**) cartero
**postmark** ['post,mɑrk] *s* matasellos, timbre de correos (*que marca la fecha, hora y lugar de salida o recibo del correo*); *va* matasellar, timbrar (*el correo*)
**postmaster** ['post,mæstər] o ['post,mɑstər] *s* administrador de correos
**postmaster general** *s* (*pl:* **postmasters general**) director general de correos
**postmastership** ['post,mæstərʃɪp] o ['post,mɑstərʃɪp] *s* administración de correos
**postmeridian** [,postmə'rɪdɪən] *adj* postmeridiano
**post meridiem** [,post mə'rɪdɪəm] (Lat.) por la tarde
**postmistress** ['post,mɪstrɪs] *s* administradora de correos
**post-mortem** [,post'mɔrtəm] *adj* posterior a la muerte; *s* autopsia, examen de un cadáver

**postnatal** [post'netəl] *adj* postnatal
**post-obit** [ˌpost'obɪt] o [ˌpost'ɑbɪt] *adj* válido después de la muerte de una persona
**post office** *s* casa de correos
**post-office box** ['postˌɑfɪs] *s* apartado de correos, casilla postal
**post-office branch** *s* estafeta, sucursal de correos
**post-office savings bank** *s* var. de **postal savings bank**
**postoperative** [post'ɑpəˌretɪv] o [post'ɑpərətɪv] *adj* postoperatorio
**postorbital** [post'ɔrbɪtəl] *adj* postorbital
**postpaid** ['postˌped] *adj* con porte pagado, franco de porte
**postpalatal** [post'pælətəl] *adj & s* (phonet.) postpalatal
**postpone** [post'pon] *va* aplazar
**postponement** [post'ponmənt] *s* aplazamiento
**postprandial** [post'prændɪəl] *adj* postprandial
**postprandial speech** *s* discurso de sobremesa
**postrider** ['postˌraɪdər] *s* corredor de posta
**post road** *s* camino de postas; ruta por donde pasa el correo
**postscript** ['postskrɪpt] *s* posdata (*a una carta*); suplemento a un escrito
**posttonic** [post'tɑnɪk] *adj* (phonet.) postónico
**postulant** ['pɑstʃələnt] *s* (rel.) postulante, postulanta
**postulate** ['pɑstʃəlɪt] *s* postulado; ['pɑstʃəlet] *va* postular, pedir, solicitar; (eccl.) postular; admitir sin pruebas
**postulation** [ˌpɑstʃə'leʃən] *s* postulación, petición; (eccl.) postulación; admisión sin pruebas
**postulator** ['pɑstʃəˌletər] *s* (eccl.) postulador
**posture** ['pɑstʃər] *s* postura; *va* poner en una postura o en posturas; *vn* adoptar una postura
**posturer** ['pɑstʃərər] *s* poseur; contorsionista
**postwar** ['postˌwɔr] *adj* de la postguerra
**posy** ['pozɪ] *s* (*pl:* **-sies**) flor; ramillete de flores; verso grabado en una sortija
**pot** [pɑt] *s* pote, tiesto; caldera, olla, puchero (*de cocina*); puesta (*en el juego*); bebida alcohólica; (found.) crisol de horno; (coll.) cantidad considerable de dinero; vaso de noche, orinal; **to go to pot** (coll.) fracasar, tronarse, arruinarse; **to keep the pot boiling** (coll.) ganar el pan de cada día; (coll.) mantener las cosas en marcha; (*pret & pp:* **potted;** *ger:* **potting**) *va* plantar en tiestos o macetas; cocer y conservar en olla; conservar en botes o marmitas; disparar contra; (coll.) ganar, apoderarse de; *vn* disparar; beber cerveza, empinar el codo
**potable** ['potəbəl] *adj* potable; *s* cosa que puede beberse
**potash** ['pɑtˌæʃ] *s* (chem.) potasa
**potassic** [pə'tæsɪk] *adj* potásico
**potassium** [pə'tæsɪəm] *s* (chem.) potasio
**potassium bromide** *s* (chem.) bromuro de potasio
**potassium carbonate** *s* (chem.) carbonato de potasio
**potassium chlorate** *s* (chem.) clorato de potasio
**potassium cyanide** *s* (chem.) cianuro de potasio
**potassium hydroxide** *s* (chem.) hidróxido de potasio
**potassium nitrate** *s* (chem.) nitrato de potasio
**potassium permanganate** *s* (chem.) permanganato de potasio
**potation** [po'teʃən] *s* potación
**potato** [pə'teto] *s* (*pl:* **-toes**) (bot.) patata (*planta y tubérculo*); papa (Am.); (bot.) batata (*Ipomoea batatas*); (coll.) nulidad, persona o cosa insignificante
**potato beetle** o **bug** *s* (ent.) chinche de la patata, chaquetudo, escarabajo patatero
**potato blight** *s* plaga de la patata
**potato chip** *s* rebanada de patata frita
**potato omelet** *s* tortilla a la española
**potbellied** ['pɑtˌbelɪd] *adj* barrigón, panzudo
**potbelly** ['pɑtˌbelɪ] *s* (*pl:* **-lies**) barriga, panza; persona panzuda
**potboiler** ['pɑtˌbɔɪlər] *s* obra artística o literaria hecha con el solo propósito de ganar dinero
**potboy** ['pɑtˌbɔɪ] *s* mozo de servicio de una fonda o taberna; lavaplatos
**pot cheese** *s* requesón
**pot companion** *s* compañero de taberna
**potency** ['potənsɪ] *s* (*pl:* **-cies**) potencia
**potent** ['potənt] *adj* potente
**potentate** ['potəntet] *s* potentado
**potent cross** *s* (her.) cruz potenzada
**potential** [pə'tenʃəl] *adj* potencial; (gram.) potencial; *s* potencial; (elec., gram., math. & phys.) potencial
**potential energy** *s* (phys.) energía potencial
**potential function** *s* (math.) función potencial
**potentiality** [pəˌtenʃɪ'ælɪtɪ] *s* (*pl:* **-ties**) potencialidad
**potentially** [pə'tenʃəlɪ] *adv* potencialmente
**potential mood** *s* (gram.) modo potencial
**potentilla** [ˌpotən'tɪlə] *s* (bot.) potentila
**potentiometer** [pəˌtenʃɪ'ɑmɪtər] *s* (elec.) potenciómetro
**pothanger** ['pɑtˌhæŋər] *s* llares
**pother** ['pɑðər] *s* agitación, confusión, barahunda; nube de polvo o humo asfixiante; *va* agitar, confundir, molestar; *vn* agitarse, confundirse, molestarse
**potherb** ['pɑtˌʌrb] o ['pɑtˌhʌrb] *s* hortaliza, verdura; hierba que se emplea para sazonar
**potholder** ['pɑtˌholdər] *s* portaollas
**pothole** ['pɑtˌhol] *s* bache, hoyo redondo (*en el camino*); (geol.) marmita de gigante
**pothook** ['pɑtˌhuk] *s* garabato (*gancho; letra mal hecha*)
**pothouse** ['pɑtˌhaus] *s* cervecería, taberna
**pothunter** ['pɑtˌhʌntər] *s* persona que caza para obtener alimento sin preocuparse por las reglas de la caza; persona que toma parte en concursos, contiendas y torneos con el solo propósito de ganar premios
**potion** ['poʃən] *s* poción
**pot lead** [led] *s* grafito
**potlid** ['pɑtˌlɪd] *s* cobertera, tapadera
**potluck** ['pɑtˌlʌk] *s* comida sin preparación ni cumplidos, lo que haya de comer; **to take potluck** hacer penitencia
**potpie** ['pɑtˌpaɪ] *s* pastelón de carne; estofado con bollos de harina
**potpourri** [popu'ri] o [pɑt'purɪ] *s* mezcolanza aromática de pétalos secos y especias; (mus.) popurrí
**pot roast** *s* asado hecho en marmita
**potsherd** ['pɑtˌʃʌrd] *s* tiesto, casco (*pedazo roto*)
**pot shot** *s* tiro a corta distancia; tiro en contra de las reglas del juego limpio
**pottage** ['pɑtɪdʒ] *s* potaje
**potted** ['pɑtɪd] *adj* cocido y conservado en botes u ollas; de maceta, p.ej., **potted plants** plantas de maceta; (slang) borracho
**potter** ['pɑtər] *s* alfarero; *vn* ocuparse en fruslerías
**potter's clay** *s* arcilla figulina, barro de alfarería
**potter's field** *s* cementerio de los pobres, hoyanca
**potter's wheel** *s* rueda o torno de alfarero
**pottery** ['pɑtərɪ] *s* (*pl:* **-ies**) alfarería; cacharros (de alfarería)
**pottle** ['pɑtəl] *s* azumbre (*medida*); licor alcohólico; (Brit.) cesto para frutas
**pot-valiant** ['pɑtˌvæljənt] *adj* valiente por el licor que le anima
**pouch** [pautʃ] *s* bolsa, saquillo; bolsa (*del canguro*); valija; petaca; cartuchera; *va* embolsar; formar una bolsa en; fruncir; *vn* formar una bolsa; hacer pucheros; deglutir, saciarse
**poulard** [pu'lɑrd] *s* polla capona que se ceba para comerla
**poulterer** ['poltərər] *s* pollero
**poultice** ['poltɪs] *s* cataplasma; *va* poner una cataplasma a
**poultry** ['poltrɪ] *s* aves de corral
**poultry dealer** *s* recovero
**pounce** [pauns] *s* grasilla, arenilla (*para secar escritos*); carbón molido que se usa para traspasar dibujos picados a otra tela o papel; golpe súbito, zarpada; zarpa de ave de rapiña; *va* alisar, preparar o rociar (*una superficie*) con

grasilla o arenilla; estarcir con arenilla; *vn* entrar súbita e inesperadamente; **to pounce at, on** o **upon** saltar sobre, precipitarse sobre

**pounce bag** *s* cisquero

**pounce box** *s* cajita de polvos de arenilla

**pouncet box** ['paʊnsɪt] *s* cajita agujereada para perfumes

**pound** [paʊnd] *s* libra (*peso*); golpazo, martilleo; corral de concejo (*para encerrar animales descarriados*); *va* golpear, golpetear, martillar; machacar, moler; encerrar en el corral de concejo; bombardear incesantemente; (fig.) desempedrar (*pasear mucho por*); *vn* golpear, golpetear

**poundage** ['paʊndɪdʒ] *s* impuesto, comisión, etc. exigida por cada libra esterlina o cada libra de peso

**poundal** ['paʊndəl] *s* (phys.) poundal

**poundcake** ['paʊnd,kek] *s* pastel en que entra una libra de cada ingrediente; ponqué

**pounder** ['paʊndər] *s* martillador; machaca; persona o cosa que pesa determinado número de libras o que está relacionada con determinado número de libras, p.ej., **a ten-pounder** un cañón de a diez; **a five-pounder** un pescado de cinco libras

**pound-foolish** ['paʊnd'fulɪʃ] *adj* incapaz de guardar o manejar grandes sumas de dinero

**poundkeeper** ['paʊnd,kipər] *s* guardián de corral de concejo

**pound net** *s* red de pesca, nasa de pescar

**pound sterling** *s* libra esterlina

**pour** [por] *s* lluvia torrencial; *va* vaciar, verter, derramar; hacer fluir; hacer salir profusamente; **to pour out** verter (*p.ej., agua*); *vn* fluir rápidamente; llover a torrentes; **to pour into** entrar a montones en; **to pour out** salir a chorros; salir a montones; **to pour out of** inclinar para vaciar, verter (*un recipiente*); salir a montones de (*p.ej., el teatro*)

**pourboire** [pur'bwɑr] *s* propina

**pourparler** [pur'pɑrlɪ] *s* coloquio, conferencia

**pout** [paʊt] *s* mala cara, mal gesto, puchero; (ichth.) gado; (ichth.) zoarce; *vn* poner mala cara, hacer gesto de enojo y desagrado, hacer pucheros

**pouter** ['paʊtər] *s* persona que hace pucheros, persona que pone cara de enfado; (orn.) paloma buchona

**poverty** ['pɑvərtɪ] *s* pobreza

**poverty-stricken** ['pɑvərtɪ,strɪkən] *adj* extremadamente pobre

**POW** abr. de **prisoner of war**

**powder** ['paʊdər] *s* polvo; polvos (*de tocador*); pólvora (*mezcla explosiva*); *va* pulverizar; empolvar, polvorear; *vn* hacerse polvo; empolvarse

**powder blue** *s* azul pálido

**powdered milk** *s* leche en polvo

**powdered sugar** *s* azúcar en polvo

**powder flask** *s* polvorín

**powder horn** *s* chifle

**powder magazine** *s* (naut.) santabárbara

**powder maker** *s* polvorista

**powder monkey** *s* mozo que antiguamente iba en los barcos de guerra para ocuparse de transportar la pólvora a los cañones

**powder puff** *s* borla para empolvarse

**powder room** *s* cuarto tocador, cuarto de aseo

**powdery** ['paʊdərɪ] *adj* polvoriento, polvoroso; empolvado; deleznable, quebradizo

**power** ['paʊər] *s* poder, poderío, potencia; (math., mech., opt. & phys.) potencia; (fig.) energía; **Powers** *spl* potestades (*sexta orden de los ángeles*); **in power** en el poder; **the Great Powers** las grandes potencias; **the powers that be** las autoridades, los que mandan; **to the best of one's power** cuanto esté en el poder de uno; *va* accionar, impulsar

**power amplifier** *s* (rad.) amplificador de poder o de potencia

**power behind the throne** *s* poder oculto

**powerboat** ['paʊər,bot] *s* autobote, bote automóvil, gasolinera

**power brake** *s* (aut.) servofreno

**power company** *s* empresa de fuerza motriz

**power cord** *s* (elec.) cordón de alimentación

**power dive** (aer.) picado con motor

**power drill** *s* taladradora de fuerza

**power factor** *s* (elec.) factor de potencia

**powerful** ['paʊərfəl] *adj* poderoso

**powerhouse** ['paʊər,haʊs] *s* (elec.) estación generadora, central eléctrica; (slang) manantial de fuerza, persona llena de energía, fuerza arrolladora

**powerless** ['paʊərlɪs] *adj* impotente

**power line** *s* (elec.) línea de fuerza; (elec.) sector de distribución (*en las ciudades*)

**power mower** *s* motosegadora

**power of attorney** *s* (law) poder

**power of the keys** *s* (eccl.) llaves de la iglesia

**power pack** *s* (rad.) fuente surtidora, fuente de alimentación, fuente de poder

**power plant** *s* (elec.) estación generadora, central eléctrica; (aut.) grupo motor; (aer.) grupo motopropulsor

**power play** *s* maniobra ofensiva concentrada

**power politics** *ssg* o *spl* política de poder

**power reactor** *s* (phys.) reactor generador de energía

**power saw** *s* motosierra

**power shovel** *s* excavadora

**power station** *s* (elec.) estación generadora, central eléctrica

**power steering** *s* (aut.) servodirección

**power stroke** *s* carrera motriz

**power supply** *s* (rad.) suministro de potencia

**power tool** *s* herramienta motriz

**power transformer** *s* (elec.) transformador de fuerza

**power transmission** *s* (elec.) transmisión de energía

**power tube** *s* (rad.) válvula de fuerza o de poder

**powwow** ['paʊ,waʊ] *s* ceremonia de los indios norteamericanos que consiste en bailes y fiestas para ahuyentar las enfermedades y tener éxito en las empresas; conferencia acerca de o con los indios norteamericanos; conferencia; curandero indio; santiguadera; *vn* conferenciar

**pox** [pɑks] *s* enfermedad que afecta la piel creando una erupción de pústulas; sífilis

**pozzolana** [,pɑtsə'lɑnɑ] o **pozzuolana** [,pɑtswə'lɑnɑ] *s* (geol.) puzolana

**pp.** abr. de **pages, past participle** y **pianissimo**

**p.p.** abr. de **parcel post, past participle** y **postpaid**

**ppr.** o **p.pr.** abr. de **present participle**

**pr.** abr. de **pair, present** y **price**

**P.R.** abr. de **Puerto Rico**

**practicability** [,præktɪkə'bɪlɪtɪ] *s* factibilidad

**practicable** ['præktɪkəbəl] *adj* practicable

**practical** ['præktɪkəl] *adj* práctico

**practicality** [,præktɪ'kælɪtɪ] *s* (*pl:* **-ties**) espíritu práctico; cosa práctica

**practical joke** *s* burla de consecuencias

**practically** ['præktɪkəlɪ] *adv* prácticamente; casi, poco más o menos

**practical nurse** *s* enfermera práctica (*que ejerce la profesión sin haber terminado el curso oficial*)

**practice** ['præktɪs] *s* práctica; ensayo; ejercicio (*p.ej., de la medicina*); **in practice** en la práctica; **to make a practice of** + *inf* acostumbrar + *inf; va* practicar; ejercitar (*p.ej., caridad*); ejercer (*una profesión*); hacer ejercicios en, estudiar (*p.ej., el piano*); tener por costumbre; **to practice** + *ger* ensayarse a + *inf;* **to practice what one preaches** predicar con el ejemplo; *vn* ejercitarse; ejercer; practicar la medicina; ensayarse; entrenarse; conducirse; **to practice as** ejercer de (*p.ej., abogado*)

**practiced** ['præktɪst] *adj* práctico

**practician** [præk'tɪʃən] *s* practicón

**practise** ['præktɪs] *s, va & vn* var. de **practice**

**practitioner** [præk'tɪʃənər] *s* profesional; práctico (*médico*)

**praedial** ['pridɪəl] *adj* predial

**praefect** ['prifɛkt] *s* var. de **prefect**

**praefloration** [,priflo'reʃən] *s* (bot.) prefloración

**praefoliation** [,prifolɪ'eʃən] *s* (bot.) prefoliación

**praenomen** [pri'nomɛn] *s* (*pl:* **-nomina** ['nɑmɪnə]) prenombre

**praetor** ['pritər] o ['pritɔr] *s* pretor

**praetorian** [pri'torɪən] *adj & s* pretoriano

**pragmatic** [præg'mætɪk] o **pragmatical** [præg'mætɪkəl] *adj* pragmático; dogmático, engreído; oficioso, entremetido; activo, ocupado; práctico

**pragmatic sanction** *s* sanción pragmática o pragmática sanción

**pragmatism** ['prægmətɪzəm] *s* (philos.) pragmatismo; dogmatismo; oficiosidad; positivismo

**pragmatist** ['prægmətɪst] *adj & s* (philos.) pragmatista

**Prague** [prɑg] o [preg] *s* Praga

**prairie** ['prɛrɪ] *s* llanura, pampa, pradera

**prairie chicken** *s* (orn.) gallina de las praderas

**prairie dog** *s* (zool.) ardilla ladradora, perro de las praderas

**prairie schooner** *s* carromato de cuatro ruedas y toldo, que se usaba para viajar en el oeste de los EE.UU. antes del ferrocarril transcontinental

**prairie wolf** *s* (zool.) coyote

**praise** [prez] *s* alabanza, elogio; elogios; **to heap praises on** amontonar alabanzas sobre; **to sing the praise** o **the praises of** alabar o elogiar con efusión y entusiasmo; *va* alabar, elogiar; **to praise to the skies** poner sobre las estrellas, poner por las nubes

**praiseworthy** ['prez,wʌrðɪ] *adj* laudable, elogiable

**Prakrit** ['prɑkrɪt] *s* prácrito

**praline** ['prɑlin] *s* almendra garapiñada, almendra confitada, pacana garapiñada

**pram** [præm] *s* (coll.) cochecillo de niño

**prance** [præns] o [prɑns] *s* cabriola; trenzado; *vn* cabriolar; trenzar; pavonearse al caminar

**prancer** ['prænsər] o ['prɑnsər] *s* caballo trenzador

**prandial** ['prændɪəl] *adj* prandial

**prank** [præŋk] *s* travesura, picardía; broma; *va* adornar con exceso; *vn* adornarse con exceso, sobrecargarse en el vestir

**prankish** ['præŋkɪʃ] *adj* travieso, pícaro

**prankster** ['præŋkstər] *s* (coll.) bromista

**prase** [prez] *s* (mineral.) prasio

**praseodymium** [,prezɪo'dɪmɪəm] *s* (chem.) praseodimio

**prate** [pret] *s* charla, parloteo; *vn* charlar, parlotear

**prater** ['pretər] *s* charlatán

**pratique** [præ'tik] *s* (naut.) libre plática

**prattle** ['prætəl] *s* charla, parloteo; charla necia y sin sentido (*imitando a los niños en la pronunciación*); *vn* charlar, parlotear; hablar como los niños

**prattler** ['prætlər] *s* charlatán, parlanchín

**prawn** [prɔn] *s* (zool.) camarón (*Palaemon*); (zool.) langostín (*Peneus*); (zool.) gamba, quisquilla (*Pandalus*)

**Praxiteles** [præks'ɪtəliz] *s* Praxiteles

**pray** [pre] *va* implorar, rogar, suplicar; rezar (*una oración*); *vn* orar, rezar; **to pray for** orar por; **pray** + *inf* sírvase + *inf*, p.ej., **pray tell me** sírvase decirme

**prayer** [prɛr] *s* oración, rezo; ruego, súplica; oficio (*rezo diario*); **to say one's prayers** decir sus oraciones; ['preər] *s* rezador

**prayer book** [prɛr] *s* devocionario, oracional

**prayerful** ['prɛrfəl] *adj* rezador, devoto

**prayerless** ['prɛrlɪs] *adj* sin rezo; que no reza

**prayer meeting** [prɛr] *s* reunión para orar y alabar a Dios

**prayer rug** [prɛr] *s* alfombra de rezo

**praying mantis** *s* (ent.) mantis religiosa, predicador, rezadora

**preach** [pritʃ] *va* predicar; aconsejar (*p.ej., la paciencia*); *vn* predicar

**preacher** ['pritʃər] *s* predicador; pastor espiritual; sermoneador

**preachify** ['pritʃɪfaɪ] (*pret & pp:* **-fied**) *vn* predicar o sermonear molestamente

**preaching** ['pritʃɪŋ] *s* predicación; sermón, sermoneo

**preachment** ['pritʃmənt] *s* prédica, sermón, arenga

**preachy** ['pritʃɪ] *adj* (*comp:* **-ier;** *super:* **-iest**) (coll.) inclinado a predicar, moralizador

**preadamic** [,priə'dæmɪk] *adj* preadamítico

**preadamite** [pri'ædəmaɪt] *s* preadamita

**preadaptation** [,priædæp'teʃən] *s* (biol.) preadaptación

**preamble** ['pri,æmbəl] *s* preámbulo

**preamplifier** [pri'æmplɪ,faɪər] *s* (rad.) preamplificador

**prearrange** [,priə'rendʒ] *va* arreglar de antemano

**prearrangement** [,priə'rendʒmənt] *s* arreglo previo

**prebend** ['prɛbənd] *s* prebenda; prebendado

**prebendary** ['prɛbən,dɛrɪ] *s* (*pl:* **-ies**) prebendado

**Pre-Cambrian** [,pri'kæmbrɪən] *adj & s* (geol.) precámbrico

**precarious** [prɪ'kɛrɪəs] *adj* precario

**precariousness** [prɪ'kɛrɪəsnɪs] *s* precariedad

**precaution** [prɪ'kɔʃən] *s* precaución

**precautionary** [prɪ'kɔʃən,ɛrɪ] *adj* precaucionado, precavido

**precautious** [prɪ'kɔʃəs] *adj* precavido

**precede** [pri'sid] *va & vn* preceder

**precedence** [pri'sidəns] o ['prɛsɪdəns] *s* precedencia

**precedency** [pri'sidənsɪ] o ['prɛsɪdənsɪ] *s* (*pl:* **-cies**) var. de **precedence**

**precedent** [pri'sidənt] o ['prɛsɪdənt] *adj* precedente; ['prɛsɪdənt] *s* precedente

**preceding** [pri'sidɪŋ] *adj* precedente

**precentor** [prɪ'sɛntər] *s* chantre

**precept** ['prisɛpt] *s* precepto

**preceptive** [prɪ'sɛptɪv] *adj* preceptivo

**preceptor** [prɪ'sɛptər] *s* preceptor

**preceptorial** [,prisɛp'torɪəl] *adj* preceptoral

**preceptress** [prɪ'sɛptrɪs] *s* preceptora

**precession** [pri'sɛʃən] *s* precedencia; (mech.) precesión

**precessional** [pri'sɛʃənəl] *adj* de la precesión de los equinoccios, causado por la precesión de los equinoccios

**precession of the equinoxes** *s* (astr.) precesión de los equinoccios

**precinct** ['prisɪŋkt] *s* barriada, recinto; distrito electoral

**preciosity** [,prɛʃɪ'ɑsɪtɪ] *s* (*pl:* **-ties**) (lit.) preciosismo

**precious** ['prɛʃəs] *adj* precioso; caro, amado; (coll.) considerable; *adv* (coll.) muy, p.ej., **precious little** muy poco

**preciously** ['prɛʃəslɪ] *adv* preciosamente; extremadamente; con mucho cuidado

**precious stone** *s* piedra preciosa

**precipice** ['prɛsɪpɪs] *s* precipicio

**precipitance** [prɪ'sɪpɪtəns] o **precipitancy** [prɪ'sɪpɪtənsɪ] *s* precipitación

**precipitant** [prɪ'sɪpɪtənt] *adj* precipitado; *s* (chem.) precipitante

**precipitate** [prɪ'sɪpɪtɪt] o [prɪ'sɪpɪtet] *adj* precipitado; *s* (chem.) precipitado; [prɪ'sɪpɪtet] *va* precipitar; (chem.) precipitar; *vn* precipitarse; (chem.) precipitarse

**precipitation** [prɪ,sɪpɪ'teʃən] *s* precipitación; (chem., meteor. & fig.) precipitación

**precipitin** [prɪ'sɪpɪtɪn] *s* (immun.) precipitina

**precipitous** [prɪ'sɪpɪtəs] *adj* empinado, escarpado; precipitoso, precipitado

**precipitron** [prɪ'sɪpɪtrɑn] *s* (trademark) precipitrón

**precise** [prɪ'saɪs] *adj* preciso; escrupuloso, meticuloso

**precision** [prɪ'sɪʒən] *s* precisión

**precision bombing** *s* (aer.) bombardeo de precisión

**precision instrument** *s* instrumento de precisión, aparato de precisión

**preclude** [prɪ'klud] *va* excluir, imposibilitar

**preclusion** [prɪ'kluʒən] *s* exclusión, evitación

**precocious** [prɪ'koʃəs] *adj* precoz

**precocity** [prɪ'kɑsɪtɪ] *s* precocidad

**precognition** [,prikɑg'nɪʃən] *s* precognición

**pre-Columbian** [,prikə'lʌmbɪən] *adj* precolombino

**preconceive** [,prikən'siv] *va* preconcebir

**preconception** [,prikən'sɛpʃən] *s* preconcepción

**preconcert** [,prikən'sʌrt] *va* concertar de antemano

**precontract** [pri'kɑntrækt] *s* contrato previo; [,prikən'trækt] o [pri'kɑntrækt] *va & vn* contratar de antemano

**precool** [pri'kul] *va* preenfriar

**precordial** [pri'kɔrdʒəl] o [pri'kɔrdjəl] *adj* (anat.) precordial

**precursor** [pri'kʌrsər] *s* precursor
**precursory** [pri'kʌrsərɪ] *adj* precursor
**pred.** abr. de **predicate**
**predacious** [prɪ'deʃəs] o **predatory** ['prɛdə,torɪ] *adj* rapaz; predador, predator, depredador
**predeceased** [,pridɪ'sist] *adj* predifunto, premuerto
**predecessor** ['prɛdɪ,sɛsər] o [,prɛdɪ'sɛsər] *s* predecesor
**predestinarian** [pri,dɛstɪ'nɛrɪən] *adj & s* predestinaciano, predestinador
**predestinate** [pri'dɛstɪnɪt] *s* (theol.) predestinado; [pri'dɛstɪnet] *va* predestinar
**predestination** [pri,dɛstɪ'neʃən] *s* predestinación; (theol.) predestinación
**predestine** [pri'dɛstɪn] *va* predestinar
**predeterminate** [,pridɪ'tʌrmɪnɪt] *adj* predeterminado
**predetermination** [,pridɪ,tʌrmɪ'neʃən] *s* predeterminación
**predetermine** [,pridɪ'tʌrmɪn] *va* predeterminar
**predial** ['pridɪəl] *adj* predial
**predicable** ['prɛdɪkəbəl] *adj* predicable; *s* (log.) predicable
**predicament** [prɪ'dɪkəmənt] *s* trance apurado, situación difícil; (log.) predicamento
**predicant** ['prɛdɪkənt] *adj & s* predicante
**predicate** ['prɛdɪkɪt] *s* predicado; ['prɛdɪket] *va & vn* predicar
**predication** [,prɛdɪ'keʃən] *s* aserción, afirmación
**predicative** ['prɛdɪ,ketɪv] *adj* predicativo
**predict** [prɪ'dɪkt] *va* predecir
**predictable** [prɪ'dɪktəbəl] *adj* pronosticable
**prediction** [prɪ'dɪkʃən] *s* predicción
**predictive** [prɪ'dɪktɪv] *adj* profético
**predictor** [prɪ'dɪktər] *s* predictor; (aer.) predictor
**predigest** [,pridɪ'dʒɛst] o [,pridaɪ'dʒɛst] *va* predigerir
**predigestion** [,pridɪ'dʒɛstʃən] o [,pridaɪ'dʒɛstʃən] *s* predigestión
**predilection** [,pridɪ'lɛkʃən] o [,prɛdɪ'lɛkʃən] *s* predilección
**predispose** [,pridɪs'poz] *va* predisponer
**predisposition** [,pridɪspə'zɪʃən] *s* predisposición
**predominance** [prɪ'dɑmɪnəns] *s* predominancia
**predominant** [prɪ'dɑmɪnənt] *adj* predominante
**predominate** [prɪ'dɑmɪnet] *va & vn* predominar
**predomination** [prɪ,dɑmɪ'neʃən] *s* predominación
**preëlection** [,priɪ'lɛkʃən] *s* preelección; *adj* preelectoral
**preëminence** [pri'ɛmɪnəns] *s* preeminencia
**preëminent** [pri'ɛmɪnənt] *adj* preeminente
**preëminently** [pri'ɛmɪnəntlɪ] *adv* preeminentemente
**preëmpt** [pri'ɛmpt] *va* asegurarse de (*una cosa*) antes que nadie; apropiarse (*terreno*) con el derecho de comprarlo antes que nadie
**preëmption** [pri'ɛmpʃən] *s* preempción
**preëmptor** [pri'ɛmptər] o [pri'ɛmptɔr] *s* comprador por derecho de prioridad
**preen** [prin] *va* arreglarse (*las plumas*) con el pico; **to preen oneself** atildarse, componerse, vestirse cuidadosamente
**preëngage** [,priɛn'gedʒ] *va* contratar o comprometer de antemano
**preëstablish** [,priɛs'tæblɪʃ] *va* establecer de antemano
**preëxist** [,priɛg'zɪst] *vn* preexistir
**preëxistence** [,priɛg'zɪstəns] *s* preexistencia
**preëxistent** [,priɛg'zɪstənt] *adj* preexistente
**pref.** abr. de **preface, preferred** y **prefix**
**prefabricate** [pri'fæbrɪket] *va* prefabricar
**preface** ['prɛfɪs] *s* prefacio; *va* introducir, empezar; decir a modo de introducción; prologar
**prefatorial** [,prɛfə'torɪəl] o **prefatory** ['prɛfə,torɪ] *adj* introductor, preliminar; como prefacio
**prefect** ['prifɛkt] *s* prefecto
**prefecture** ['prifɛktʃər] *s* prefectura
**prefer** [prɪ'fʌr] (*pret & pp:* **-ferred;** *ger:* **-ferring**) *va* preferir; presentar; promover; **to prefer to** + *inf* preferir + *inf*
**preferable** ['prɛfərəbəl] *adj* preferible
**preferably** ['prɛfərəblɪ] *adv* preferiblemente
**preference** ['prɛfərəns] *s* preferencia
**preferential** [,prɛfə'rɛnʃəl] *adj* preferente
**preferential tariff** *s* aranceles preferenciales
**preferential voting** *s* votación en la cual el elector indica un segundo candidato en caso de que el de su primera elección sea derrotado
**preferment** [prɪ'fʌrmənt] *s* preferencia; ascenso, promoción; dignidad
**preferred stock** *s* (com.) acción preferente, acciones preferentes
**prefiguration** [,prifɪgjə'reʃən] *s* prefiguración
**prefigure** [pri'fɪgjər] *va* prefigurar; representarse de antemano
**prefix** ['prifɪks] *s* (gram.) prefijo; [pri'fɪks] *va* prefijar; (gram.) prefijar
**preformation** [,prifɔr'meʃən] *s* preformación
**pregnable** ['prɛgnəbəl] *adj* expugnable
**pregnancy** ['prɛgnənsɪ] *s* (*pl:* **-cies**) preñez, embarazo
**pregnant** ['prɛgnənt] *adj* preñado; fértil; (fig.) preñado
**preheat** [pri'hit] *va* precalentar, calentar previamente
**prehensile** [prɪ'hɛnsɪl] *adj* prensil
**prehension** [prɪ'hɛnʃən] *s* prensión
**prehistoric** [,prihɪs'tɑrɪk] o [,prihɪs'tɔrɪk] o **prehistorical** [,prihɪs'tɑrɪkəl] o [,prihɪs'tɔrɪkəl] *adj* prehistórico
**prehistorically** [,prihɪs'tɑrɪkəlɪ] o [,prihɪs'tɔrɪkəlɪ] *adv* prehistóricamente
**prehistory** [pri'hɪstərɪ] *s* prehistoria
**preignition** [,priɪg'nɪʃən] *s* preignición
**prejudge** [pri'dʒʌdʒ] *va* prejuzgar
**prejudgment** o **prejudgement** [pri'dʒʌdʒmənt] *s* prejuicio
**prejudice** ['prɛdʒədɪs] *s* prejuicio, preocupación; perjuicio (*daño*); **to the prejudice of** con perjuicio de; **without prejudice** (law) sin detrimento de sus propios derechos; *va* predisponer, prevenir; perjudicar (*dañar*)
**prejudicial** [,prɛdʒə'dɪʃəl] *adj* perjudicial
**prejudicially** [,prɛdʒə'dɪʃəlɪ] *adv* perjudicialmente
**prelacy** ['prɛləsɪ] *s* (*pl:* **-cies**) prelacía
**prelate** ['prɛlɪt] *s* prelado
**prelature** ['prɛlətʃər] *s* prelatura
**pre-Lenten** [pri'lɛntən] *adj* carnavalesco
**prelim.** abr. de **preliminary**
**preliminary** [prɪ'lɪmɪ,nɛrɪ] *adj* preliminar; *s* (*pl:* **-ies**) preliminar
**prelude** ['prɛljud], ['prilud] o ['priljud] *s* preludio; (mus.) preludio; *va* preludiar; *vn* preludiar; (mus.) preludiar
**premarital** [pri'mærɪtəl] *adj* premarital
**premature** [,primə'tjʊr] o [,primə'tʊr] *adj* prematuro
**prematurely** [,primə'tjʊrlɪ] o [,primə'tʊrlɪ] *adv* prematuramente
**premedical** [pri'mɛdɪkəl] *adj* premédico
**premeditate** [pri'mɛdɪtet] *va* premeditar
**premeditated** [pri'mɛdɪ,tetɪd] *adj* premeditado
**premeditation** [,primɛdɪ'teʃən] *s* premeditación
**premier** ['primɪər] o ['prɛmjər] *adj* primero; principal, superior; [prɪ'mɪr] o ['primɪər] *s* primer ministro, jefe del estado, presidente del consejo
**première** [prə'mjɛr] o [prɪ'mɪr] *s* estreno; actriz principal
**premiership** [prɪ'mɪrʃɪp] o ['primɪər,ʃɪp] *s* jefatura del estado, presidencia del consejo
**premise** ['prɛmɪs] *s* (law & log.) premisa; **premises** *spl* predio, local; **major premise** (log.) premisa mayor; **minor premise** (log.) premisa menor; *va* sentar o establecer como premisa; *vn* establecer una premisa
**premium** ['primɪəm] *s* premio; (ins.) prima; **at a premium** a premio; en gran demanda, muy solicitado
**premolar** [pri'molər] *adj & s* (anat.) premolar
**premonish** [prɪ'mɑnɪʃ] *va* advertir, prevenir
**premonition** [,primə'nɪʃən] *s* advertencia; presentimiento
**premonitory** [prɪ'mɑnɪ,torɪ] *adj* premonitorio

**Premonstratensian** [prɪˌmɑnstrəˈtɛnʃən] *adj & s* (eccl.) premonstratense
**prenatal** [priˈnetəl] *adj* prenatal
**preoccupancy** [priˈɑkjəpənsɪ] *s* (*pl:* **-cies**) preocupación
**preoccupation** [priˌɑkjəˈpeʃən] *s* preocupación
**preoccupied** [priˈɑkjəpaɪd] *adj* preocupado
**preoccupy** [priˈɑkjəpaɪ] (*pret & pp:* **-pied**) *va* preocupar
**preordain** [ˌpriɔrˈden] *va* preordinar
**preordination** [ˌpriɔrdɪˈneʃən] *s* preordinación
**prep.** abr. de **preparatory** y **preposition**
**prepaid** [priˈped] *adj* pagado por adelantado; con porte pagado; *pret & pp de* **prepay**
**prepalatal** [priˈpælətəl] *adj & s* (phonet.) prepalatal
**preparation** [ˌprɛpəˈreʃən] *s* preparación
**preparative** [prɪˈpærətɪv] *adj & s* preparativo
**preparatory** [prɪˈpærəˌtorɪ] *adj* preparatorio
**preparatory school** *s* escuela preparatoria
**prepare** [prɪˈpɛr] *va* preparar, prevenir; *vn* prepararse, prevenirse; **to prepare against** prevenirse a o contra; **to prepare to** + *inf* prepararse a o para + *inf*
**preparedness** [prɪˈpɛrɪdnɪs] o [prɪˈpɛrdnɪs] *s* preparación; preparación militar, armamentismo
**prepay** [prɪˈpe] (*pret & pp:* **-paid**) pagar por adelantado
**prepayment** [prɪˈpemənt] *s* pago adelantado
**prepense** [prɪˈpɛns] *adj* premeditado; **with malice prepense** (law) con malicia y premeditación
**preponderance** [prɪˈpɑndərəns] *s* preponderancia
**preponderant** [prɪˈpɑndərənt] *adj* preponderante
**preponderate** [prɪˈpɑndəret] *vn* preponderar
**preposition** [ˌprɛpəˈzɪʃən] *s* preposición
**prepositional** [ˌprɛpəˈzɪʃənəl] *adj* preposicional
**prepositionally** [ˌprɛpəˈzɪʃənəlɪ] *adv* de manera preposicional, como preposición
**prepositive** [priˈpɑzɪtɪv] *adj* prepositivo; *s* (gram.) partícula prepositiva
**prepossess** [ˌpripəˈzɛs] *va* preocupar, predisponer favorablemente
**prepossessing** [ˌpripəˈzɛsɪŋ] *adj* agradable, simpático
**prepossession** [ˌpripəˈzɛʃən] *s* preocupación, predisposición favorable
**preposterous** [prɪˈpɑstərəs] *adj* absurdo, ridículo
**preposterously** [prɪˈpɑstərəslɪ] *adv* absurdamente, ridículamente
**prepotency** [priˈpotənsɪ] *s* (*pl:* **-cies**) prepotencia
**prepotent** [priˈpotənt] *adj* prepotente
**prep school** [prɛp] *s* (slang) escuela preparatoria
**prepuce** [ˈpripjus] *s* (anat.) prepucio
**Pre-Raphaelite** [ˌpriˈræfɪəlaɪt] [ˌpriˈrefɪəlaɪt] *adj & s* prerrafaelista
**Pre-Raphaelitism** [ˌpriˈræfɪəˌlaɪtɪzəm] o [ˌpriˈrefɪəˌlaɪtɪzəm] *s* prerrafaelismo
**prerecorded** [ˌpririˈkɔrdɪd] *adj* (rad. & telv.) grabado anteriormente, grabado de antemano
**prerequisite** [priˈrɛkwɪzɪt] *adj* necesario de antemano; *s* requisito previo, requisito prescrito de antemano
**prerogative** [prɪˈrɑgətɪv] *adj* privilegiado; *s* prerrogativa
**preromanticism** [ˌpriroˈmæntɪsɪzəm] *s* prerromanticismo
**pres.** abr. de **present**
**Pres.** abr. de **Presbyterian** y **President**
**presage** [ˈprɛsɪdʒ] *s* presagio; [prɪˈsedʒ] *va* presagiar
**presbyope** [ˈprɛzbɪop] o [ˈprɛsbɪop] *s* presbiope
**presbyopia** [ˌprɛzbɪˈopɪə] o [ˌprɛsbɪˈopɪə] *s* (path.) presbiopía
**presbyopic** [ˌprɛzbɪˈɑpɪk] o [ˌprɛsbɪˈɑpɪk] *adj* presbiope
**presbyte** [ˈprɛzbaɪt] o [ˈprɛsbaɪt] *s* présbita
**presbyter** [ˈprɛzbɪtər] o [ˈprɛsbɪtər] *s* presbítero
**Presbyterian** [ˌprɛzbɪˈtɪrɪən] o [ˌprɛsbɪˈtɪrɪən] *adj & s* presbiteriano
**Presbyterianism** [ˌprɛzbɪˈtɪrɪənɪzəm] o [ˌprɛsbɪˈtɪrɪənɪzəm] *s* presbiterianismo
**presbytery** [ˈprɛzbɪˌtɛrɪ] o [ˈprɛsbɪˌtɛrɪ] *s* (*pl:* **-ies**) presbiterio
**presbytia** [prɛzˈbɪtɪə] o [prɛsˈbɪtɪə] *s* (path.) presbicia
**presbytic** [prɛzˈbɪtɪk] o [prɛsˈbɪtɪk] *adj* présbita
**preschool** [ˈpriˌskul] *adj* preescolar
**prescience** [ˈpriʃɪəns] o [ˈprɛʃɪəns] *s* presciencia
**prescient** [ˈpriʃɪənt] o [ˈprɛʃɪənt] *adj* presciente
**prescribe** [prɪˈskraɪb] *va & vn* prescribir; (pharm.) recetar
**prescript** [prɪˈskrɪpt] o [ˈpriskrɪpt] *adj* prescrito; [ˈpriskrɪpt] *s* regla, precepto
**prescriptible** [prɪˈskrɪptɪbəl] *adj* prescriptible
**prescription** [prɪˈskrɪpʃən] *s* prescripción; (law & med.) prescripción; (pharm.) receta
**prescriptive** [prɪˈskrɪptɪv] *adj* directivo; sancionado por la costumbre; adquirido o establecido por prescripción
**preselector** [ˌprisɪˈlɛktər] *s* (telp.) preselector
**presence** [ˈprɛzəns] *s* presencia; **in the presence of** en presencia de; **saving your presence** con excusas por haber dicho (o hecho) esto en su presencia
**presence chamber** *s* salón de recepciones, salón donde recibe un soberano u otra persona de alto rango
**presence of mind** *s* presencia de ánimo
**present** [ˈprɛzənt] *adj* presente (*que está aquí*); presente, actual; *s* presente, regalo; (gram.) presente; **at present** al presente, actualmente; **by these presents** por las presentes, por las escrituras presentes; **for the present** por lo presente; [prɪˈzɛnt] *va* presentar; **to present arms** (mil.) presentar armas; **to present oneself** presentarse; **to present with** obsequiar con
**presentable** [prɪˈzɛntəbəl] *adj* presentable; bien apersonado
**presentation** [ˌprɛzənˈteʃən] o [ˌprizənˈteʃən] *s* presentación; **on presentation** (com.) a presentación
**presentation copy** *s* ejemplar de cortesía con dedicatoria del autor
**present-day** [ˈprɛzəntˌde] *adj* de hoy en día
**presentiment** [prɪˈzɛntɪmənt] *s* presentimiento
**presently** [ˈprɛzəntlɪ] *adv* luego, dentro de poco
**presentment** [prɪˈzɛntmənt] *s* presentación; retrato; representación teatral; (law) acusación por el gran jurado
**present participle** *s* (gram.) participio activo o de presente
**present perfect** *s* (gram.) pretérito perfecto
**preservation** [ˌprɛzərˈveʃən] *s* conservación; preservación
**preservative** [prɪˈzʌrvətɪv] *adj & s* preservativo
**preserve** [prɪˈzʌrv] *s* conserva, confitura, compota; vedado; *va* conservar; preservar, proteger; *vn* hacer conservas
**preserved fruit** *s* dulce de almíbar
**preserve jar** *s* bote de conservas
**preserver** [prɪˈzʌrvər] *s* preservador
**preside** [prɪˈzaɪd] *vn* presidir; **to preside over** presidir
**presidency** [ˈprɛzɪdənsɪ] *s* (*pl:* **-cies**) presidencia
**president** [ˈprɛzɪdənt] *s* presidente; rector (*de una universidad*)
**president-elect** [ˈprɛzɪdəntɪˈlɛkt] *s* presidente electo
**presidential** [ˌprɛzɪˈdɛnʃəl] *adj* presidencial
**presidium** [prɪˈsɪdɪəm] *s* presidio
**press** [prɛs] *s* apretón, empujón, presión; prisa, urgencia; apiñamiento, muchedumbre; prensa (*máquina para prensar, comprimir o imprimir; conjunto de periódicos o periodistas*); imprenta (*acción o arte de imprimir*); pliegue (*de una prenda planchada*); armario; **in press** en prensa; **to have a good** (o **bad**) **press** tener buena (o mala) prensa; **to go to**

**press** entrar en prensa; *va* apretar; prensar; planchar (*la ropa*); apresurar; abrumar, acosar, instar; insistir en; abrazar; imprimir (*discos de fonógrafo*); **to press into service** poner a trabajar; **to press one's point** insistir en su punto de vista; *vn* pesar, ejercer presión; urgir; apiñarse; apresurarse; **to press forward** avanzar, adelantarse; **to press through the crowd** abrirse paso por entre la multitud
**press agent** *s* agente de publicidad
**pressboard** ['prɛs,bord] *s* cartón prensado
**press box** *s* tribuna de la prensa
**press conference** *s* entrevista de prensa, conferencia de prensa
**press gang** *s* (mil.) levadores; (nav.) ronda de matrícula
**pressing** ['prɛsɪŋ] *adj* apremiante, urgente; *s* planchado (*de la ropa*)
**pressing boards** *spl* (b.b.) tablillas de encuadernar
**pressman** ['prɛsmən] *s* (*pl:* **-men**) prensador; (print.) prensista
**pressmark** ['prɛs,mɑrk] *s* marca de biblioteca; *va* poner marca de biblioteca en
**press proof** *s* (print.) prueba de impresión
**press release** *s* comunicado de prensa
**pressroom** ['prɛs,rum] o ['prɛs,rum] *s* salón de prensas, taller de imprenta
**pressure** ['prɛʃər] *s* presión; opresión; urgencia; tensión de nervios; (elec.) tensión, fuerza electromotriz; **to exert pressure on** ejercer presión sobre
**pressure cooker** *s* cocina de presión, olla a o de presión
**pressure gage** o **pressure gauge** *s* manómetro, indicador de presión
**pressure group** *s* minoría que ejerce influencia en los cuerpos legislativos
**pressure suit** *s* traje a presión
**pressure tunnel** *s* (aer.) túnel a presión
**pressurize** ['prɛʃəraɪz] *va* (aer.) sobrecargar, sobrecomprimir, presurizar
**presswork** ['prɛs,wʌrk] *s* impresión, tirada; trabajo de impresor; chapas de madera encoladas y prensadas
**prester** ['prɛstər] *s* (obs.) sacerdote
**Prester John** *s* el Preste Juan
**prestidigitation** [,prɛstɪ,dɪdʒɪ'teʃən] *s* prestidigitación
**prestidigitator** [,prɛstɪ'dɪdʒɪ,tetər] *s* prestidigitador
**prestige** [prɛs'tiʒ] o ['prɛstɪdʒ] *s* prestigio
**presumable** [prɪ'zuməbəl] o [prɪ'zjuməbəl] *adj* presumible
**presumably** [prɪ'zuməblɪ] o [prɪ'zjuməblɪ] *adv* probablemente, verosímilmente
**presume** [prɪ'zum] o [prɪ'zjum] *va* presumir; suponer, dar por sentado; **to presume to** + *inf* tomar la libertad de + *inf; vn* suponer; **to presume on** o **upon** abusar de
**presumedly** [prɪ'zumɪdlɪ] o [prɪ'zjumɪdlɪ] *adv* supuestamente
**presumption** [prɪ'zʌmpʃən] *s* presunción; pretensión; (law) presunción
**presumptive** [prɪ'zʌmptɪv] *adj* presuntivo; presunto (*supuesto*)
**presumptively** [prɪ'zʌmptɪvlɪ] *adv* presuntivamente
**presumptuous** [prɪ'zʌmptʃʊəs] *adj* confianzudo, desenvuelto
**presuppose** [,prisə'poz] *va* presuponer
**presupposition** [,prisʌpə'zɪʃən] *s* presuposición
**pret.** abr. de **preterit**
**pretence** [prɪ'tɛns] o ['pritɛns] *s* var. de **pretense**
**pretend** [prɪ'tɛnd] *va* aparentar, fingir (*alegría, dolor, etc.*); **to pretend to** + *inf* fingir + *inf*, aparentar que + *ind;* **to pretend to be** fingirse, p.ej., **to pretend to be a friend** fingirse amigo; *vn* fingir; **to pretend to** pretender (*p.ej., el trono*)
**pretended** [prɪ'tɛndɪd] *adj* pretendido
**pretender** [prɪ'tɛndər] *s* pretendiente
**pretense** [prɪ'tɛns] o ['pritɛns] *s* pretensión; fingimiento; presunción; **under false pretenses** con falsas apariencias, con apariencias fingidas; **under pretense of** so pretexto de
**pretension** [prɪ'tɛnʃən] *s* pretensión
**pretentious** [prɪ'tɛnʃəs] *adj* pretencioso, aparatoso; ambicioso, vasto
**preterit** o **preterite** ['prɛtərɪt] *adj & s* (gram.) pretérito
**preterition** [,prɛtə'rɪʃən] *s* preterición; (law & rhet.) preterición
**pretermission** [,pritər'mɪʃən] *s* pretermisión
**pretermit** [,pritər'mɪt] (*pret & pp:* **-mitted;** *ger:* **-mitting**) *va* pretermitir
**preternatural** [,pritər'nætʃərəl] *adj* preternatural
**pretext** ['pritɛkst] *s* pretexto; *va* pretextar
**pretonic** [pri'tɑnɪk] *adj* (gram.) pretónico
**pretor** ['pritər] o ['pritɔr] *s* var. de **praetor**
**pretorian** [pri'torɪən] *adj & s* var. de **praetorian**
**prettify** ['prɪtɪfaɪ] (*pret & pp:* **-fied**) *va* embellecer
**pretty** ['prɪtɪ] *adj* (*comp:* **-tier;** *super:* **-tiest**) bonito, lindo; bello; (scornful) bueno, grande; (coll.) bueno, bastante, considerable; *adv* algo, bastante; **sitting pretty** (slang) en buena posición; (slang) acomodado; *s* (*pl:* **-ties**) persona linda, cosa linda
**pretty penny** *s* (coll.) dineral, ojo de la cara
**pretzel** ['prɛtsəl] *s* galleta tostada hecha en forma de rosquilla y polvoreada con sal
**prevail** [prɪ'vel] *vn* prevalecer; **to be prevailed on** o **upon to** + *inf* dejarse persuadir a + *inf;* **to prevail against** u **over** prevalecer sobre, triunfar de; **to prevail on, upon** o **with** persuadir
**prevailing** [prɪ'velɪŋ] *adj* prevaleciente, reinante, imperante; común, corriente
**prevalence** ['prɛvələns] *s* frecuencia, uso corriente, boga, costumbre
**prevalent** ['prɛvələnt] *adj* común, corriente, en boga
**prevaricate** [prɪ'værɪket] *vn* mentir, usar de lenguaje ambiguo para engañar; (law) prevaricar
**prevarication** [prɪ,værɪ'keʃən] *s* mentira, lenguaje ambiguo; (law) prevaricación
**prevaricator** [prɪ'værɪ,ketər] *s* mentiroso; (law) prevaricador
**prevent** [prɪ'vɛnt] *va* impedir, estorbar; **to prevent from** + *ger* impedir + *inf* o impedir que + *subj; vn* obstar
**preventable** [prɪ'vɛntəbəl] *adj* evitable
**preventative** [prɪ'vɛntətɪv] *adj & s* var. de **preventive**
**preventer** [prɪ'vɛntər] *s* (naut.) contraamura
**preventible** [prɪ'vɛntɪbəl] *adj* var. de **preventable**
**prevention** [prɪ'vɛnʃən] *s* prevención; estorbo, obstáculo
**preventive** [prɪ'vɛntɪv] *adj* impeditivo, preventivo; profiláctico, preservativo; *s* preservativo
**preventive medicine** *s* medicina profiláctica, medicina preventiva
**preview** ['pri,vju] *s* vista anticipada, inspección previa; (mov.) avance; (mov.) preestreno; [pri'vju] o ['pri,vju] *va* ver de antemano, inspeccionar de antemano
**previous** ['priviəs] *adj* previo, anterior; *adv* previamente; **previous to** antes de
**previously** ['priviəslɪ] *adv* previamente, anteriormente
**previous question** *s* petición que se hace en una asamblea legislativa para saber si se ha de hacer una votación para dar término al debate
**prevision** [pri'vɪʒən] *s* previsión
**previsional** [pri'vɪʒənəl] *adj* previsor
**prewar** ['pri,wɔr] *adj* prebélico, de antes de la guerra, de preguerra
**prey** [pre] *s* presa; víctima; **to be prey to** ser presa de; *vn* cazar; **to prey on** o **upon** apresar y devorar; pillar, robar; tener preocupado, tener en zozobra, agobiar
**Priam** ['praɪəm] *s* (myth.) Príamo
**priapism** ['praɪəpɪzəm] *s* (path.) priapismo
**Priapus** [praɪ'epəs] *s* (myth.) Príapo
**price** [praɪs] *s* precio; **at any price** a toda costa; de cualquier manera; **beyond** o **without price** tan valioso que no puede comprarse; **to set a price on someone's head** poner a precio la cabeza de uno; *va* apreciar, esti-

mar, fijar el precio de, poner precio a; averiguar el precio de
**price ceiling** *s* precio tope
**price control** *s* control de precios, intervención de los precios
**price cutting** *s* reducción de precios (*a un nivel inferior a la tarifa establecida*)
**price fixing** *s* fijación de precios, tarificación; acuerdo secreto para la fijación de precios
**price freezing** *s* congelación de precios
**priceless** ['praɪslɪs] *adj* inapreciable, sin precio; (coll.) divertido, absurdo; **to be priceless** no tener precio
**price list** *s* lista de precios
**price mark** *s* marbete o etiqueta (*que expresa el precio de un artículo*)
**price stabilization** *s* estabilización de precios
**price war** *s* guerra de precios
**prick** [prɪk] *s* espiche (*arma o instrumento puntiagudo*); púa (*punta aguda*); agujerillo (*hecho con una punta aguda*); pinchazo, punzada (*herida; dolor*); aguijón; **to kick against the pricks** tener rebeldía que sólo es motivo de sufrimiento, cocear contra el aguijón; *va* pinchar; marcar con agujerillos; punzar (*herir*); dar una punzada a; clavar o enclavar (*a las caballerías*); **to prick up** aguzar (*p.ej., las orejas*); *vn* causar una punzada; sentir una punzada; sentir comezón; erguirse; picarse (*el vino*)
**pricket** ['prɪkɪt] *s* candelero que termina en punta aguda donde se clava la bujía; gamo de un año de edad
**prickle** ['prɪkəl] *s* espina, pincho, púa; pinchazo, punzada; *va* causar una punzada a; *vn* sentir una punzada
**prickly** ['prɪklɪ] *adj* (*comp:* **-lier;** *super:* **-liest**) espinoso, puado, lleno de púas; agudo, punzante
**prickly heat** *s* (path.) salpullido causado por exceso de calor
**prickly pear** *s* (bot.) chumbera, higuera chumba, higuera de tuna; higo chumbo, higo de tuna (*fruto*)
**prickly poppy** *s* (bot.) adormidera espinosa
**pride** [praɪd] *s* orgullo; arrogancia, altivez; *va* enorgullecer; **to pride oneself on** o **upon** enorgullecerse de; **to pride oneself on** + *ger* enorgullecerse de + *inf*
**prideful** ['praɪdfəl] *adj* orgulloso
**Pride's Purge** *s* (hist.) la purificación de Pride
**prie-dieu** [pri'djœ] *s* reclinatorio
**prier** ['praɪər] *s* hurón (*persona que todo lo averigua*)
**priest** [prist] *s* sacerdote
**priestcraft** ['prist,kræft] o ['prist,krɑft] *s* trapisondas eclesiásticas
**priestess** ['pristɪs] *s* sacerdotisa
**priesthood** ['pristhʊd] *s* sacerdocio; clero
**priestly** ['pristlɪ] *adj* (*comp:* **-lier;** *super:* **-liest**) sacerdotal
**priest-ridden** ['prist,rɪdən] *adj* abarrotado de curas
**prig** [prɪg] *s* pedante, presuntuoso, mojigato
**priggery** ['prɪgərɪ] *s* (*pl:* **-ies**) pedantería, presuntuosidad, mojigatería
**priggish** ['prɪgɪʃ] *adj* pedante, presuntuoso, mojigato
**prim** [prɪm] *adj* (*comp:* **primmer;** *super:* **primmest**) estirado, relamido
**primacy** ['praɪməsɪ] *s* (*pl:* **-cies**) primacía
**prima donna** ['primə 'dɑnə] *s* (*pl:* **prima donnas**) (mus.) prima donna (*la cantante principal en una ópera*)
**prima-facie** ['praɪmə'feʃɪi] *adj* (law) suficiente para justificar la presunción del hecho
**primage** ['praɪmɪdʒ] *s* (naut.) capa, quintalada
**primal** ['praɪməl] *adj* primitivo; básico, principal
**primarily** ['praɪmɛrɪlɪ] o ['praɪmərɪlɪ] *adv* primariamente (*en primer lugar; principalmente*)
**primary** ['praɪmɛrɪ] o ['praɪmərɪ] *adj* primario; *s* (*pl:* **-ries**) (lo) principal; color primario; elección preliminar para nombrar candidatos para las elecciones generales; reunión de electores para nombrar candidatos para las elecciones generales; (orn.) pluma primaria; (elec.) primario (*arrollamiento*)
**primary accent** *s* (phonet.) acento primario
**primary cell** *s* (elec.) elemento primario
**primary coil** *s* (elec.) carrete primario
**primary colors** *spl* colores primarios
**primary education** *s* enseñanza primaria
**primary election** *s* elección preliminar para nombrar candidatos para las elecciones generales
**primary feather** *s* (orn.) pluma primaria
**primary planet** *s* (astr.) planeta primario
**primary point** *s* (com.) lugar de distribución del grano
**primary school** *s* escuela de primera enseñanza
**primary union** *s* (surg.) unión de primera intención
**primate** ['praɪmet] *s* (eccl.) primado; (zool.) primate
**primateship** ['praɪmetʃɪp] *s* primacía
**primatial** [praɪ'meʃəl] *adj* primacial
**prime** [praɪm] *adj* primero, principal; básico; primo (*excelente, de primera calidad*); (arith.) primo; (print.) marcado con virgulilla; *s* flor, juventud, primavera; alba, aurora; (la) flor y nata; (arith.) número primo; (eccl.) prima; (phys.) minuto (*de un grado*); (print.) virgulilla; **prime of life** edad viril, flor de edad; *va* preparar, instruir, informar de antemano; cebar (*un arma de fuego, una bomba, un carburador*); poner la primera capa o la primera mano a; poner virgulilla a; **to be primed for an examination** (coll.) ir bien empollado
**prime meridian** *s* primer meridiano
**prime minister** *s* primer ministro
**prime mover** *s* fuente de fuerza; máquina motriz; palanca (*de una empresa*); (philos.) primer motor
**prime number** *s* (arith.) número primo
**primer** ['praɪmər] *s* persona que ceba un arma; persona que cubre con una primera mano de pintura; cápsula detonante, cebador; ['prɪmər] *s* cartilla
**primeval** [praɪ'mivəl] *adj* prístino
**prime vertical** *s* (astr.) primer vertical
**priming** ['praɪmɪŋ] *s* preparación; cebo; (mas. & paint.) primera capa
**primipara** [praɪ'mɪpərə] *s* (*pl:* **-rae** [ri]) (obstet.) primípara
**primitive** ['prɪmɪtɪv] *adj* primitivo; *s* (f.a.) primitivo
**primogenitor** [,praɪmo'dʒɛnɪtər] *s* progenitor
**primogeniture** [,praɪmo'dʒɛnɪtʃər] *s* primogenitura
**primordial** [praɪ'mɔrdɪəl] *adj* primordial
**primp** [prɪmp] *va* acicalar, engalanar; *vn* acicalarse, engalanarse
**primrose** ['prɪm,roz] *s* (bot.) primavera; (bot.) primavera de la China; (bot.) hierba del asno; color amarillo claro; *adj* de color amarillo claro; alegre, florido
**primrose path** *s* sendero alfombrado de flores, sendero fácil y agradable; vida dada a los placeres de los sentidos
**primula** ['prɪmjʊlə] *s* (bot.) primavera
**primulaceous** [,prɪmjə'leʃəs] *adj* (bot.) primuláceo
**prin.** abr. de **principal**
**prince** [prɪns] *s* príncipe; **to live like a prince** portarse como un príncipe
**Prince Albert** *s* gabán largo y cruzado
**prince consort** *s* príncipe consorte
**princedom** ['prɪnsdəm] *s* principado
**Prince Edward Island** *s* la Isla del príncipe Eduardo
**princeling** ['prɪnslɪŋ] *s* principito
**princely** ['prɪnslɪ] *adj* (*comp:* **-lier;** *super:* **-liest**) principesco
**Prince of Darkness** *s* príncipe de las tinieblas (*demonio*)
**Prince of Peace** *s* (Bib.) príncipe de paz (*Jesucristo*)
**prince of the blood** *s* príncipe de la sangre
**Prince of the Church** *s* príncipe de la Iglesia (*cardenal*)
**Prince of Wales** *s* príncipe de Gales
**prince royal** *s* hijo mayor de un soberano
**princess** ['prɪnsɪs] *s* princesa
**princesse dress** [prɪn'sɛs] o ['prɪnsɪs] *s* princesa
**princess royal** *s* hija mayor de un soberano
**principal** ['prɪnsɪpəl] *adj* principal; *s* principal, jefe; director (*de una escuela*); (com. &

law) principal; criminal; (arch.) jamba de fuerza
**principal clause** *s* (gram.) proposición dominante
**principality** [ˌprɪnsɪˈpælɪtɪ] *s* (*pl:* **-ties**) principado; **principalities** *spl* (rel.) principados
**principally** [ˈprɪnsɪpəlɪ] *adv* por lo general; principalmente
**principal parts** *spl* (gram.) partes principales
**principalship** [ˈprɪnsɪpəlˌʃɪp] *s* dirección; dirección de una escuela
**principate** [ˈprɪnsɪpet] *s* supremacía; principado
**principle** [ˈprɪnsɪpəl] *s* principio; (chem.) principio; **in principle** en principio; **on principle** por principio
**principled** [ˈprɪnsɪpəld] *adj* escrupuloso, de principios
**prink** [prɪŋk] *va & vn* var. de **primp**
**print** [prɪnt] *s* tipo, letra de molde; estampa; grabado, lámina; estampado (*tejido*); diseño (*estampado*); impresión; tirada, edición; (phot.) impresión; **in print** en letra de molde; impreso, publicado; **out of print** agotado; *va* imprimir; estampar; hacer imprimir; publicar; escribir en letra de molde, escribir en caracteres de imprenta; (phot.) tirar, imprimir; (fig.) imprimir o grabar (*en la memoria*); *vn* imprimir; ser impresor
**printable** [ˈprɪntəbəl] *adj* imprimible
**printed circuit** *s* (elec.) circuito impreso
**printed matter** *s* impresos
**printer** [ˈprɪntər] *s* impresor
**printer's devil** *s* aprendiz de imprenta
**printer's ink** *s* tinta de imprenta
**printer's mark** *s* (print.) pie de imprenta
**printing** [ˈprɪntɪŋ] *s* impresión; caracteres impresos; tirada, edición; letras de mano imitación de las impresas; (phot.) tiraje
**printing frame** *s* (phot.) marco de imprimir, prensa
**printing press** *s* prensa de imprenta
**print shop** *s* imprenta; estampería
**prior** [ˈpraɪər] *adj* anterior; *adv* anteriormente; **prior to** antes de; *s* prior
**priorate** [ˈpraɪərɪt] o [ˈpraɪəret] *s* priorato
**prioress** [ˈpraɪərɪs] *s* priora
**priority** [praɪˈɑrɪtɪ] o [praɪˈɔrɪtɪ] *s* (*pl:* **-ties**) prioridad
**priory** [ˈpraɪərɪ] *s* (*pl:* **-ries**) priorato
**prise** [praɪz] *va* levantar o mover por fuerza
**prism** [ˈprɪzəm] *s* (geom., opt. & cryst.) prisma
**prismatic** [prɪzˈmætɪk] *adj* prismático
**prismatic colors** *spl* colores prismáticos
**prism binocular** *s* anteojo prismático
**prison** [ˈprɪzən] *s* cárcel, prisión; *va* encarcelar
**prison camp** *s* campamento para prisioneros, campo de prisioneros
**prisoner** [ˈprɪzənər] o [ˈprɪznər] *s* preso; (mil.) prisionero; **to take prisoner** coger preso a; (mil.) hacer prisionero
**prisoner of war** *s* prisionero de guerra
**prisoner's base** *s* rescate (*juego de muchachos*)
**prison reform** *s* reforma penitenciaria
**prison van** *s* coche celular
**prissy** [ˈprɪsɪ] *adj* (*comp:* **-sier;** *super:* **-siest**) (coll.) remilgado, melindroso, estirado
**pristine** [ˈprɪstin] o [ˈprɪstaɪn] *adj* prístino
**prithee** [ˈprɪðɪ] *interj* (archaic) ¡te ruego!
**privacy** [ˈpraɪvəsɪ] *s* (*pl:* **-cies**) aislamiento, retiro; secreto, reserva; **to have no privacy** no poder estar a solas, no poder retirarse de la vista del público
**private** [ˈpraɪvɪt] *adj* particular; privado, íntimo; confidencial, secreto; retirado; *s* soldado raso; **privates** *spl* partes pudendas; **in private** privadamente; en secreto
**private enterprise** *s* empresa privada (*dirección y control de la industria por personas privadas*)
**privateer** [ˌpraɪvəˈtɪr] *s* (naut.) corsario (*embarcación; marino*); *vn* (naut.) corsear
**privateering** [ˌpraɪvəˈtɪrɪŋ] *adj* (naut.) corsario; *s* (naut.) corso
**privateersman** [ˌpraɪvəˈtɪrzmən] *s* (*pl:* **-men**) (naut.) corsario
**private first class** *s* soldado de primera, aspirante a cabo
**private hospital** *s* clínica, casa de salud
**private individual** *s* particular
**private life** *s* vida privada
**private line** *s* línea (telefónica) particular
**privately** [ˈpraɪvɪtlɪ] *adv* privadamente; secretamente
**private property** *s* propiedad privada, bienes particulares
**private sale** *s* venta directa (*sin licitación y sin corredor*)
**private view** *s* (f.a.) día de inauguración
**privation** [praɪˈveʃən] *s* privación
**privative** [ˈprɪvətɪv] *adj* privativo; (gram.) privativo; *s* (gram.) prefijo privativo, sufijo privativo
**privet** [ˈprɪvɪt] *s* (bot.) aligustre, ligustro; *adj* ligustrino
**privilege** [ˈprɪvɪlɪdʒ] *s* privilegio; *va* privilegiar
**privily** [ˈprɪvɪlɪ] *adv* privadamente, secretamente
**privy** [ˈprɪvɪ] *s* (*pl:* **-ies**) privada, letrina; *adj* privado; **privy to** enterado secretamente de
**privy council** *s* consejo privado
**privy seal** *s* (Brit.) sello pequeño
**prize** [praɪz] *s* premio; presa; botín; **to take the prize** llevarse el premio; (fig.) llevarse la mapa; *adj* premiado; digno de premio; dado como premio; *va* apreciar, estimar; tasar; levantar o mover por fuerza
**prize court** *s* tribunal de presas marítimas
**prize crew** *s* (naut.) tripulación encargada de llevar a puerto la nave apresada
**prize fight** *s* partido de boxeo profesional
**prize fighter** *s* boxeador profesional
**prize fighting** *s* boxeo profesional
**prizeman** [ˈpraɪzmən] *s* (*pl:* **-men**) laureado, premiado
**prize money** *s* premio en metálico; (box.) bolsa; (naut.) parte de presa
**prize ring** *s* cuadrilátero de boxeo
**prize winner** *s* ganador del premio
**pro** [pro] *prep* en pro de; *s* (*pl:* **pros**) razón en favor; voto afirmativo; (coll.) deportista profesional; **the pros and the cons** el pro y el contra
**proa** [ˈproə] *s* prao (*embarcación malaya*)
**pro-Ally** [ˌproəˈlaɪ] o [ˌproˈælaɪ] *adj & s* aliadófilo
**probabilism** [ˈprɑbəbɪlɪzəm] *s* (philos.) probabilismo
**probability** [ˌprɑbəˈbɪlɪtɪ] *s* (*pl:* **-ties**) probabilidad; acontecimiento probable; (meteor.) tiempo probable; **in all probability** según toda probabilidad
**probable** [ˈprɑbəbəl] *adj* probable
**probably** [ˈprɑbəblɪ] *adv* probablemente
**probang** [ˈprobæŋ] *s* (surg.) sonda esofágica
**probate** [ˈprobet] *adj* (law) testamentario; *s* (law) prueba legal de la autenticidad de un testamento; (law) copia auténtica de un testamento; *va* (law) probar por proceso legal la autenticidad de (*un testamento*)
**probate court** *s* (law) tribunal encargado de probar la autenticidad de testamentos
**probation** [proˈbeʃən] *s* probación; libertad vigilada; **to put on probation** dar el azul a
**probational** [proˈbeʃənəl] o **probationary** [proˈbeʃəˌnerɪ] *adj* probatorio; de libertad vigilada; tutelar
**probationer** [proˈbeʃənər] *s* persona que está a prueba; liberto, delincuente puesto bajo vigilancia
**probationership** [proˈbeʃənərˌʃɪp] *s* período de prueba, condición del que está a prueba
**probation officer** *s* (law) agente de vigilancia (*de los delincuentes juveniles*)
**probative** [ˈprobətɪv] o [ˈprɑbətɪv] *adj* probatorio
**probe** [prob] *s* sonda; encuesta, indagación; (surg.) sonda; *va* indagar; (surg.) sondar, tentar
**probity** [ˈprobɪtɪ] o [ˈprɑbɪtɪ] *s* probidad
**problem** [ˈprɑbləm] *s* problema
**problematic** [ˌprɑbləˈmætɪk] o **problematical** [ˌprɑbləˈmætɪkəl] *adj* problemático
**problematically** [ˌprɑbləˈmætɪkəlɪ] *adv* problemáticamente
**proboscidian** [ˌprobəˈsɪdɪən] *adj & s* (zool.) proboscidio

**proboscis** [pro'basɪs] *s* (*pl:* **-boscises** o **-boscides** ['basɪdiz]) *s* (zool. & ent.) probóscide; (hum.) trompa (*nariz del hombre*)
**proboscis monkey** *s* (zool.) nasica
**procedure** [pro'sidʒər] *s* procedimiento
**proceed** [pro'sid] *vn* proceder; **to proceed against** proceder contra; **to proceed from** proceder de; **to proceed to** + *inf* proceder a + *inf;* **to proceed to blows** ir a las manos; **proceeds** ['prosidz] *spl* producto, ganancia
**proceeding** [pro'sidɪŋ] *s* procedimiento; **proceedings** *spl* actas; (law) procedimiento
**process** ['prasɛs] o ['prosɛs] *s* procedimiento; proceso (*transcurso del tiempo*); (anat. & biol.) proceso; (law) comparendo; **in process** haciéndose; **in the process of time** andando el tiempo, con el tiempo; *adj* de elaboración; fotomecánico; *va* preparar o tratar mediante un procedimiento especial; (law) procesar
**procession** [pro'sɛʃən] *s* procesión
**processional** [pro'sɛʃənəl] *adj* procesional; *s* procesional, libro procesional
**proclaim** [pro'klem] *va* proclamar
**proclamation** [,praklə'meʃən] *s* proclamación
**proclitic** [pro'klɪtɪk] *adj & s* (gram.) proclítico
**proclivity** [pro'klɪvɪtɪ] *s* (*pl:* **-ties**) inclinación, propensión
**Procne** ['praknɪ] *s* (myth.) Procne o Progne
**procommunist** [pro'kamjənɪst] *adj & s* filocomunista
**proconsul** [pro'kansəl] *s* procónsul
**proconsular** [pro'kansələr] o [pro'kansjələr] *adj* proconsular
**proconsulate** [pro'kansəlɪt] o [pro'kansjəlɪt] o **proconsulship** [pro'kansəlʃɪp] *s* proconsulado
**procrastinate** [pro'kræstɪnet] *va* procrastinar, diferir de un día para otro; *vn* tardar, ser moroso, no decidirse
**procrastination** [pro,kræstɪ'neʃən] *s* tardanza; falta de decisión
**procrastinator** [pro'kræstɪ,netər] *s* tardador; persona que no se decide pronto
**procreate** ['prokrɪet] *va* procrear
**procreation** [,prokrɪ'eʃən] *s* procreación
**procreative** ['prokrɪ,etɪv] *adj* procreador, procreante
**procreator** ['prokrɪ,etər] *s* procreador
**Procrustean** [pro'krʌstɪən] *adj* de Procusto
**Procrustes** [pro'krʌstiz] *s* (myth.) Procustes o Procusto
**proctology** [prak'talədʒɪ] *s* proctología
**proctor** ['praktər] *s* (educ.) censor; (law) procurador
**proctorial** [prak'torɪəl] *adj* del guardián de la disciplina
**proctorship** ['praktərʃɪp] *s* (educ.) cargo u oficio del censor; (law) procuración
**proctoscope** ['praktəskop] *s* proctoscopio
**procumbent** [pro'kʌmbənt] *adj* boca abajo; (bot.) procumbente
**procurable** [pro'kjurəbəl] *adj* asequible
**procurator** ['prakjə,retər] *s* procurador
**procure** [pro'kjur] *va* conseguir, obtener; causar, ocasionar; solicitar y obtener (*mujeres*) para casas de prostitución; *vn* alcahuetear
**procurement** [pro'kjurmənt] *s* consecución, obtención
**procurer** [pro'kjurər] *s* alcahuete
**procuress** [pro'kjurɪs] *s* alcahueta
**Procyon** ['prosɪan] *s* (astr.) Proción
**prod** [prad] *s* empuje; aguijada, pincho; (*pret & pp:* **prodded;** *ger:* **prodding**) *va* aguijar, pinchar; (fig.) aguijar, pinchar
**prodigal** ['pradɪgəl] *adj* pródigo; *s* pródigo; (law) pródigo
**prodigality** [,pradɪ'gælɪtɪ] *s* (*pl:* **-ties**) prodigalidad
**prodigal son** *s* hijo pródigo
**prodigious** [pro'dɪdʒəs] *adj* prodigioso, maravilloso; enorme, inmenso
**prodigy** ['pradɪʒɪ] *s* (*pl:* **-gies**) prodigio
**prodromal** ['pradrəməl] *adj* prodrómico
**prodrome** ['prodrom] *s* (path.) pródromo
**produce** ['prodjus] o ['produs] *s* producción, producto; productos agrícolas; [pro'djus] o [pro'dus] *va* producir; presentar (*p.ej., un drama*) al público; (geom.) prolongar (*p.ej., una línea*)
**producer** [pro'djusər] o [pro'dusər] *s* productor; gasógeno; (theat.) realizador
**producer gas** *s* gas pobre
**producers' goods** *spl* bienes de producción
**product** ['pradəkt] *s* producto; (chem. & math.) producto
**production** [pro'dʌkʃən] *s* producción
**productive** [pro'dʌktɪv] *adj* productivo
**productivity** [,prodʌk'tɪvɪtɪ] *s* productividad
**proem** ['proɛm] *s* proemio
**proemial** [pro'imɪəl] *adj* proemial
**Prof.** abr. de **Professor**
**profanation** [,prafə'neʃən] *s* profanación
**profanatory** [pro'fænə,torɪ] *adj* profanador
**profane** [pro'fen] *adj* profano; injurioso (*lenguaje*); *s* profano; *va* profanar
**profanity** [pro'fænɪtɪ] *s* (*pl:* **-ties**) profanidad; blasfemia
**profess** [pro'fɛs] *va & vn* profesar
**professed** [pro'fɛst] *adj* alegado, declarado, imputado; (rel.) profeso; *s* (rel.) profeso
**professedly** [pro'fɛsɪdlɪ] *adv* declaradamente; concedidamente; supuestamente
**profession** [pro'fɛʃən] *s* profesión
**professional** [pro'fɛʃənəl] *adj & s* profesional
**professionalism** [pro'fɛʃənəlɪzəm] *s* profesionalismo
**professionalize** [pro'fɛʃənəlaɪz] *va* hacer profesional; *vn* hacerse profesional
**professorate** [pro'fɛsərɪt] *s* profesorado
**professor** [pro'fɛsər] *s* catedrático, profesor; (coll.) profesor, maestro
**professorial** [,profɛ'sorɪəl] o [,prafɪ'sorɪəl] *adj* profesoral
**professorship** [pro'fɛsərʃɪp] *s* profesorado
**proffer** ['prafər] *s* oferta, propuesta; *va* ofrecer, proponer
**proficiency** [pro'fɪʃənsɪ] *s* (*pl:* **-cies**) pericia, destreza, habilidad
**proficient** [pro'fɪʃənt] *adj* perito, diestro, hábil; *s* perito
**profile** ['profaɪl] *s* perfil; contorno; bosquejo biográfico conciso y vivo; *va* perfilar
**profit** ['prafɪt] *s* provecho, beneficio, utilidad, ganancia; **at a profit** con ganancia; *va* servir, ser de utilidad a; *vn* sacar provecho, ganar; adelantar, mejorar; **to profit by** aprovechar, sacar provecho de
**profitable** ['prafɪtəbəl] *adj* provechoso
**profitably** ['prafɪtəblɪ] *adv* provechosamente
**profit and loss** *s* (com.) ganancias y pérdidas
**profiteer** [,prafɪ'tɪr] *s* logrero, usurero, explotador; *vn* logrear, explotar, usurear
**profit sharing** *s* participación en los beneficios, división de los beneficios entre dueño y empleados
**profit squeeze** *s* (coll.) var. de **cost-price squeeze**
**profligacy** ['praflɪgəsɪ] *s* libertinaje; prodigalidad
**profligate** ['praflɪgɪt] *adj & s* libertino; pródigo
**pro forma** [pro 'fɔrmə] *adv* (Lat.) por mera forma; *adj* (com.) simulado
**pro forma invoice** *s* factura simulada
**profound** [pro'faund] *adj* profundo
**profundity** [pro'fʌndɪtɪ] *s* (*pl:* **-ties**) profundidad
**profuse** [pro'fjus] *adj* profuso; pródigo
**profusion** [pro'fjuʒən] *s* profusión
**progenitor** [pro'dʒɛnɪtər] *s* progenitor
**progeniture** [pro'dʒɛnɪtʃər] *s* engendramiento; prole
**progeny** ['pradʒɪnɪ] *s* (*pl:* **-nies**) prole
**pro-German** [,pro'dʒʌrmən] *adj* pro-alemán; *s* (*pl:* **-mans**) pro-alemán
**progesterone** [pro'dʒɛstəron] *s* (biochem.) progesterona
**proglottid** [pro'glatɪd] *s* (zool.) proglotis
**prognathism** ['pragnəθɪzəm] o [prag'neθɪzəm] *s* prognatismo
**prognathous** ['pragnəθəs] o [prag'neθəs] *adj* prognato
**prognosis** [prag'nosɪs] *s* (*pl:* **-ses** [siz]) pronóstico (*especialmente de una enfermedad*)
**prognostic** [prag'nastɪk] *adj* pronosticador; *s* pronóstico
**prognosticate** [prag'nastɪket] *va* pronosticar
**prognostication** [prag,nastɪ'keʃən] *s* pronosticación

**prognosticator** [prɑg'nɑstɪ,ketər] *s* pronosticador
**program** o **programme** ['progræm] *s* programa; *adj* de programa; programático; (*pret & pp:* **-gramed** o **-grammed;** *ger:* **-graming** o **-gramming**) *va* programar
**programing** o **programming** ['progræmɪŋ] *s* programación
**program music** *s* música de programa
**progress** ['prɑgrɛs] o ['progrɛs] *s* progreso; progresos (*de una enfermedad, de un alumno, etc.*); **to make progress** hacer progresos; [pro'grɛs] *vn* progresar
**progression** [pro'grɛʃən] *s* progresión; (math.) progresión
**progressive** [pro'grɛsɪv] *adj* progresivo; (gram.) durativo; (pol.) progresista; *s* (pol.) progresista
**prohibit** [pro'hɪbɪt] *va* prohibir
**prohibition** [,pro·ɪ'bɪʃən] *s* prohibición
**prohibitionist** [,pro·ɪ'bɪʃənɪst] *adj & s* prohibicionista
**prohibitive** [pro'hɪbɪtɪv] *adj* prohibitivo
**prohibitory** [pro'hɪbɪ,torɪ] *adj* prohibitorio
**project** ['prɑdʒɛkt] *s* proyecto; [pro'dʒɛkt] *va* proyectar (*una bala; un film; un plan; una sombra*); hacer resaltar o sobresalir; (geom.) proyectar; *vn* resaltar, sobresalir
**project administrator** *s* proyectista
**projectile** [pro'dʒɛktɪl] *adj* arrojadizo; arrojador; *s* proyectil
**projection** [pro'dʒɛkʃən] *s* proyección; saliente, resalte
**projection machine** *s* (mov.) proyector
**projective** [pro'dʒɛktɪv] *adj* proyectivo
**projective geometry** *s* geometría proyectiva
**projector** [pro'dʒɛktər] *s* proyector (*aparato*); proyectista (*persona*)
**prolan** ['prolæn] *s* (biochem.) prolán
**prolapse** [pro'læps] o **prolapsus** [pro'læpsəs] *s* (path.) prolapso
**prolate** ['prolet] *adj* (geom.) alargado en la dirección del diámetro polar
**prolegomenon** [,prolɪ'gɑmɪnɑn] *s* (*pl:* **-na** [nə]) prolegómeno
**prolepsis** [pro'lɛpsɪs] *s* (*pl:* **-ses** [siz]) (rhet.) prolepsis
**proletarian** [,prolɪ'tɛrɪən] *adj & s* proletario
**proletarianize** [,prolɪ'tɛrɪənaɪz] *va* proletarizar
**proletariat** [,prolɪ'tɛrɪət] *s* proletariado
**proliferate** [pro'lɪfəret] *va* (biol.) multiplicar (*células, tejidos, etc.*); *vn* (biol.) proliferar (*células, tejidos, etc.*); proliferar
**proliferation** [pro,lɪfə'reʃən] *s* proliferación
**proliferous** [pro'lɪfərəs] *adj* (bot.) prolífero
**prolific** [pro'lɪfɪk] *adj* prolífico
**prolificacy** [pro'lɪfɪkəsɪ] *s* prolificación
**prolifically** [pro'lɪfɪkəlɪ] *adv* prolíficamente
**proline** ['prolin] o ['prolɪn] *s* (biochem.) prolina
**prolix** ['prolɪks] o [pro'lɪks] *adj* difuso, verboso
**prolixity** [pro'lɪksɪtɪ] *s* difusión, verbosidad
**prolocutor** [pro'lɑkjətər] *s* portavoz; presidente (*de una asamblea*)
**prologue** o **prolog** ['prolɔg] o ['prolɑg] *s* prólogo
**prologuize** ['prolɔgaɪz] o ['prolɑgaɪz] *vn* prologar
**prolong** [pro'lɔŋ] o [pro'lɑŋ] *va* prolongar
**prolongation** [,prolɔŋ'geʃən] o [,prolɑŋ'geʃən] *s* prolongación
**prolonge** [pro'lɑndʒ] *s* (arti.) prolonga
**prom** [prɑm] *s* (U.S.A.) baile de gala bajo los auspicios de los alumnos de una clase colegial o universitaria
**promenade** [,prɑmɪ'ned] o [,prɑmɪ'nɑd] *s* paseo; baile de gala; *vn* pasear o pasearse
**promenade concert** *s* concierto durante el cual la gente pasea o baila
**promenade deck** *s* (naut.) cubierta de paseo
**Promethean** [pro'miθɪən] *adj* de Prometeo
**Prometheus** [pro'miθus] o [pro'miθɪəs] *s* (myth.) Prometeo
**promethium** [pro'miθɪəm] *s* (chem.) prometio
**prominence** ['prɑmɪnəns] *s* prominencia; eminencia
**prominent** ['prɑmɪnənt] *adj* prominente; eminente
**prominently** ['prɑmɪnəntlɪ] *adv* prominentemente; eminentemente
**promiscuity** [,prɑmɪs'kjuɪtɪ] o [,promɪs'kjuɪtɪ] *s* promiscuidad
**promiscuous** [pro'mɪskjuəs] *adj* promiscuo
**promiscuous intercourse** *s* promiscuidad
**promise** ['prɑmɪs] *s* promesa; (fig.) promesa (*señal que hace esperar un bien*); **to give promise** prometer; *va & vn* prometer; **to promise to** + *inf* prometer + *inf*
**Promised Land** *s* (Bib.) Tierra de promisión; (*l.c.*) *s* (fig.) tierra de promisión
**promising** ['prɑmɪsɪŋ] *adj* prometedor, prometiente
**promissory** ['prɑmɪ,sorɪ] *s* promisorio
**promissory note** *s* pagaré
**promontory** ['prɑmən,torɪ] *s* (*pl:* **-ries**) promontorio; (anat.) promontorio
**promote** [prə'mot] *va* promover; fomentar
**promoter** [prə'motər] *s* promotor; fomentador
**promotion** [prə'moʃən] *s* promoción; fomento
**prompt** [prɑmpt] *adj* pronto, puntual; listo, dispuesto; *va* incitar, mover; inspirar, sugerir; soplar; (theat.) apuntar; **to prompt someone to** + *inf* mover a alguien a + *inf*
**promptbook** ['prɑmpt,bʊk] *s* (theat.) apunte
**prompter** ['prɑmptər] *s* (theat.) apuntador
**prompter's box** *s* (theat.) concha
**promptitude** ['prɑmptɪtjud] o ['prɑmptɪtud] *s* prontitud, puntualidad
**promptly** ['prɑmptlɪ] *adv* pronto, puntualmente
**promptness** ['prɑmptnɪs] *s* prontitud, puntualidad
**promulgate** [pro'mʌlget] o ['prɑməlget] *va* promulgar
**promulgation** [,promʌl'geʃən] o [,prɑməl'geʃən] *s* promulgación
**promulgator** [pro'mʌlgetər] o ['prɑməl,getər] *s* promulgador
**pron.** abr. de **pronoun** y **pronunciation**
**pronation** [pro'neʃən] *s* (physiol.) pronación
**pronator** [pro'netər] *s* (anat.) pronador
**prone** [pron] *adj* postrado boca abajo; extendido sobre el suelo; dispuesto, propenso
**proneness** ['pronnɪs] *s* postración; disposición, propensión
**pronephros** [pro'nɛfrɑs] *s* (embryol.) pronefros
**prong** [prɔŋ] o [prɑŋ] *s* punta (*de tenedor, horquilla, etc.*); *va* hincar con punta, traspasar
**prongbuck** ['prɔŋ,bʌk] o ['prɑŋ,bʌk] *s* (zool.) berrendo; (zool.) gacela del sur de África (*Antidorcas marsupialis*)
**pronged** [prɔŋd] o [prɑŋd] *adj* provisto de puntas o dientes
**pronghorn** ['prɔŋ,hɔrn] o ['prɑŋ,hɔrn] *s* (zool.) berrendo
**pronominal** [pro'nɑmɪnəl] *adj* pronominal
**pronominally** [pro'nɑmɪnəlɪ] *adv* pronominalmente
**pronoun** ['pronaʊn] *s* pronombre
**pronounce** [prə'naʊns] *va* pronunciar
**pronounceable** [prə'naʊnsəbəl] *adj* pronunciable
**pronounced** [prə'naʊnst] *adj* marcado, definido, decidido
**pronouncement** [prə'naʊnsmənt] *s* declaración, manifiesto; decisión, opinión
**pronouncing** [prə'naʊnsɪŋ] *adj* pronunciador, de pronunciación
**pronto** ['prɑnto] *adv* (coll.) pronto, en seguida
**pronunciamento** [prə,nʌnsɪə'mɛnto] *s* (*pl:* **-tos**) proclama, manifiesto
**pronunciation** [prə,nʌnsɪ'eʃən] o [prə,nʌnʃɪ'eʃən] *s* pronunciación
**proof** [pruf] *s* prueba; graduación normal de las bebidas alcohólicas; (law, math., phot. & print.) prueba; **to be proof against** ser o estar a prueba de; **to put to the proof** poner a prueba; *adj* de prueba; a prueba de; de graduación normal (*dícese de las bebidas alcohólicas*)
**proof plane** *s* (phys.) plano de prueba
**proofread** ['pruf,rid] (*pret & pp:* **-read** [,rɛd]) *va* (print.) corregir (*pruebas*), corregir prueba de
**proofreader** ['pruf,ridər] *s* (print.) corrector de pruebas

**proofreading** ['pruf,ridɪŋ] *s* (print.) corrección de pruebas
**proof sheet** *s* (print.) pliego de prueba
**proof spirit** *s* licor de prueba
**prop** [prɑp] *s* apoyo, sostén, puntal; riostra; rodrigón (*para sostener una planta*); (min.) entibo; **props** *spl* (theat.) accesorios; (*pret & pp:* **propped;** *ger:* **propping**) *va* apoyar, sostener, apuntalar; poner un rodrigón a; (min.) entibar
**propaganda** [,prɑpə'gændə] *s* propaganda; *adj* propagandístico
**propagandism** [,prɑpə'gændɪzəm] *s* propagandismo
**propagandist** [,prɑpə'gændɪst] *adj & s* propagandista
**propagate** ['prɑpəget] *va* propagar; *vn* propagarse
**propagation** [,prɑpə'geʃən] *s* propagación
**propagative** ['prɑpə,getɪv] *adj* propagativo
**propagator** ['prɑpə,getər] *s* propagador
**propane** ['propen] *s* (chem.) propano
**proparoxytone** [,propær'ɑksɪton] *adj & s* (phonet.) proparoxítono
**propel** [pro'pɛl] (*pret & pp:* **-pelled;** *ger:* **-pelling**) *va* propulsar, impeler hacia adelante
**propellant** [pro'pɛlənt] *s* propulsante
**propellent** [pro'pɛlənt] *adj & s* propulsor
**propeller** [pro'pɛlər] *s* propulsor
**propensity** [pro'pɛnsɪtɪ] *s* (*pl:* **-ties**) propensión
**proper** ['prɑpər] *adj* propio, conveniente; decente, decoroso; exacto, justo; propio, p.ej., **China proper** China propia; (coll.) excelente
**proper fraction** *s* (math.) fracción propia
**properly** ['prɑpərlɪ] *adv* propiamente, convenientemente; decentemente, decorosamente; exactamente; **properly speaking** hablando en términos precisos
**proper noun** *s* (gram.) nombre propio
**propertied** ['prɑpərtɪd] *adj* propietario; adinerado
**property** ['prɑpərtɪ] *s* (*pl:* **-ties**) propiedad; **properties** *spl* (theat.) accesorios
**property line** *s* línea de edificación
**property man** *s* (theat.) encargado de los accesorios
**property owner** *s* propietario de bienes raíces
**prophecy** ['prɑfɪsɪ] *s* (*pl:* **-cies**) profecía
**prophesy** ['prɑfəsaɪ] (*pret & pp:* **-sied**) *va & vn* profetizar
**prophet** ['prɑfɪt] *s* profeta; **the Prophet** el Profeta (*Mahoma*); **the Prophets** (Bib.) las Profecías
**prophetess** ['prɑfɪtɪs] *s* profetisa
**prophetic** [pro'fɛtɪk] *adj* profético
**prophetically** [pro'fɛtɪkəlɪ] *adv* proféticamente
**prophylactic** [,profɪ'læktɪk] o [,prɑfɪ'læktɪk] *adj & s* profiláctico
**prophylaxis** [,profɪ'læksɪs] o [,prɑfɪ'læksɪs] *s* profilaxis
**propinquity** [pro'pɪŋkwɪtɪ] *s* propincuidad
**propitiate** [pro'pɪʃɪet] *va* propiciar
**propitiation** [pro,pɪʃɪ'eʃən] *s* propiciación
**propitiatory** [pro'pɪʃɪə,torɪ] *adj* propiciatorio
**propitious** [pro'pɪʃəs] *adj* propicio
**propolis** ['prɑpəlɪs] *s* propóleos, aleda, cera aleda
**proponent** [pro'ponənt] *s* proponedor; defensor, patrocinador
**proportion** [prə'porʃən] *s* proporción; (math.) proporción; **proportions** *spl* proporciones (*tamaño; dimensiones*); **in proportion as** a medida que; **in proportion to** a medida de; **out of proportion** desproporcionado; *va* proporcionar
**proportionable** [prə'porʃənəbəl] *adj* proporcionable
**proportional** [prə'porʃənəl] *adj* proporcional; *s* (math.) número o cantidad proporcional
**proportionality** [prə,porʃə'nælɪtɪ] *s* proporcionalidad
**proportionally** [prə'porʃənəlɪ] *adv* proporcionalmente
**proportional representation** *s* (pol.) representación proporcional
**proportionate** [prə'porʃənɪt] *adj* proporcionado
**proportionately** [prə'porʃənɪtlɪ] *adv* proporcionadamente
**proportioned** [prə'porʃənd] *adj* proporcionado
**proportionment** [prə'porʃənmənt] *s* (el) proporcionar
**proposal** [prə'pozəl] *s* propuesta; oferta de matrimonio
**propose** [prə'poz] *va* proponer; *vn* proponer; proponer matrimonio; **to propose to** pedir la mano a; **to propose to** + *inf* proponer o proponerse + *inf*
**proposition** [,prɑpə'zɪʃən] *s* proposición; (coll.) empresa; (coll.) asunto, cosa, problema; (coll.) sujeto, tipo
**propound** [prə'paʊnd] *va* proponer (*una adivinanza, problema, teoría, etc.*)
**proprietary** [prə'praɪə,tɛrɪ] *adj* propietario; patentado (*aplícase a las medicinas de patente*); *s* (*pl:* **-ies**) propietario; grupo de propietarios; posesión
**proprietor** [prə'praɪətər] *s* propietario
**proprietorship** [prə'praɪətər,ʃɪp] *s* propiedad, posesión
**proprietress** [prə'praɪətrɪs] *s* propietaria
**propriety** [prə'praɪətɪ] *s* (*pl:* **-ties**) corrección, conducta decorosa; conveniencia; **proprieties** *spl* cánones sociales, convenciones
**propulsion** [pro'pʌlʃən] *s* propulsión
**propulsive** [pro'pʌlsɪv] *adj* propulsor
**propyl** ['propɪl] *s* (chem.) propilo
**pro rata** [pro 'retə] *adv* a prorrateo, a prorrata
**prorate** ['pro,ret] *s* prorrata; [pro'ret] o ['pro,ret] *va* prorratear
**prorogation** [,proro'geʃən] *s* prorrogación
**prorogue** [pro'rog] *va* prorrogar
**prosaic** [pro'zeɪk] *adj* prosaico; (fig.) prosaico
**prosaically** [pro'zeɪkəlɪ] *adv* prosaicamente
**proscenium** [pro'sinɪəm] *s* proscenio
**proscribe** [pro'skraɪb] *va* proscribir
**proscription** [pro'skrɪpʃən] *s* proscripción
**proscriptive** [pro'skrɪptɪv] *adj* proscriptor
**prose** [proz] *s* prosa; *adj* prosaico, prosístico
**prosector** [pro'sɛktər] *s* prosector
**prosecute** ['prɑsɪkjut] *va* (law) procesar; desempeñar (*un cargo*); llevar a cabo
**prosecution** [,prɑsɪ'kjuʃən] *s* (law) procesamiento; (law) parte actora, parte acusadora; prosecución
**prosecutor** ['prɑsɪ,kjutər] *s* (law) fiscal; (law) acusador, demandante
**proselyte** ['prɑsəlaɪt] *s* prosélito; *va* convertir de una creencia u opinión a otra; *vn* ganar prosélitos
**proselytism** ['prɑsəlaɪtɪzəm] o ['prɑsəlɪtɪzəm] *s* proselitismo
**proselytize** ['prɑsəlaɪtaɪz] o ['prɑsəlɪtaɪz] *va* convertir de una creencia u opinión a otra; *vn* ganar prosélitos
**prosenchyma** [prɑs'ɛŋkɪmə] *s* (bot.) prosénquima
**prose poem** *s* poema en prosa
**Proserpina** [pro'sʌrpɪnə] o **Proserpine** [pro'sʌrpɪni] o ['prɑsərpaɪn] *s* (myth.) Proserpina
**prose writer** *s* prosista
**prosimian** [pro'sɪmɪən] *adj & s* (zool.) prosimiano
**prosit** ['prosɪt] o ['prozɪt] *interj* (Lat.) ¡salud!
**proslavery** [pro'slevərɪ] *adj* esclavista
**prosodist** ['prɑsədɪst] *s* persona diestra en el arte métrica
**prosody** ['prɑsədɪ] *s* métrica
**prosopopoeia** [pro,sopə'piə] *s* (rhet.) prosopopeya
**prospect** ['prɑspɛkt] *s* perspectiva, vista; expectativa, esperanza; probabilidad de éxito; cliente o comprador probable; **in prospect** anticipado, esperado; *va* prospectar (*un terreno*); *vn* prospectar; **to prospect for** buscar (*p.ej., oro, petróleo*)
**prospective** [prə'spɛktɪv] *adj* anticipado, esperado, probable
**prospector** ['prɑspɛktər] *s* prospector (*explorador de minas, petróleo*); gambusino (Am.)
**prospectus** [prə'spɛktəs] *s* prospecto
**prosper** ['prɑspər] *va & vn* prosperar
**prosperity** [prɑs'pɛrɪtɪ] *s* (*pl:* **-ties**) prosperidad

**prosperous** ['prɑspərəs] *adj* próspero; prosperado (*rico*)
**prostate** ['prɑstet] *s* (anat.) próstata; *adj* prostático
**prostatectomy** [,prɑstə'tɛktəmɪ] *s* (surg.) prostatectomía
**prostate gland** *s* (anat.) glándula prostática
**prosthesis** ['prɑsθɪsɪs] *s* (gram.) prótesis o próstesis; (surg.) prótesis
**prosthetic** [prɑs'θɛtɪk] *adj* (gram.) protético o prostético; (surg.) protético
**prostitute** ['prɑstɪtjut] o ['prɑstɪtut] *s* prostituta; persona que prostituye su talento y habilidad por dinero; *va* prostituir
**prostitution** [,prɑstɪ'tjuʃən] o [,prɑstɪ'tuʃən] *s* prostitución
**prostrate** ['prɑstret] *adj* postrado; postrado boca abajo, postrado en el suelo; *va* postrar; **to prostrate oneself** postrarse
**prostration** [prɑs'treʃən] *s* postración
**prostyle** ['prostaɪl] *s* (arch.) próstilo
**prosy** ['prozɪ] *adj* (*comp:* **-ier**; *super:* **-iest**) prosaico
**Prot.** abr. de **Protestant**
**protactinium** [,protæk'tɪnɪəm] *s* (chem.) var. de **protoactinium**
**protagonist** [pro'tægənɪst] *s* protagonista
**Protagoras** [pro'tægərəs] *s* Protágoras
**protasis** ['prɑtəsɪs] *s* (gram.) prótasis
**protean** ['protɪən] o [pro'tiən] *adj* proteico (*que cambia de formas o de ideas*); (*cap.*) *adj* (myth.) proteico
**protect** [prə'tɛkt] *va* proteger
**protection** [prə'tɛkʃən] *s* protección; pasaporte, salvoconducto
**protectionism** [prə'tɛkʃənɪzəm] *s* proteccionismo
**protectionist** [prə'tɛkʃənɪst] *adj* & *s* proteccionista
**protective** [prə'tɛktɪv] *adj* protector
**protective coloration** *s* (biol.) homocromía, mimetismo
**protective custody** *s* custodia preventiva
**protective tariff** *s* protección aduanera, tarifa proteccionista
**protector** [prə'tɛktər] *s* protector; (sport) coraza
**protectorate** [prə'tɛktərɪt] *s* protectorado
**protectory** [prə'tɛktərɪ] *s* (*pl:* **-ries**) asilo (*para la protección de menores*)
**protectress** [prə'tɛktrɪs] *s* protectora o protectriz
**protégé** ['protəʒe] *s* ahijado, protegido
**protégée** ['protəʒe] *s* ahijada, protegida
**proteid** ['protiɪd] *s* (biochem.) proteido; *adj* (biochem.) proteico
**protein** ['protiɪn] o ['protin] *s* (biochem.) proteína
**pro tem.** abr. de **pro tempore**
**pro tempore** [pro'tɛmpərɪ] *adv* (Lat.) interinamente
**pro-tempore** [pro'tɛmpərɪ] *adj* interino
**Proterozoic** [,prɑtəro'zo·ɪk] *adj* & *s* (geol.) proterozoico
**protest** ['protɛst] *s* protesta; (com.) protesto; (law) protesta; **under protest** de mala gana, haciendo objeciones; [pro'tɛst] *va* protestar, declarar enérgicamente; protestar de, contra o por (*mostrar disconformidad con*); (com.) prostestar; *vn* protestar
**protestant** ['prɑtɪstənt] o [pro'tɛstənt] *adj* & *s* protestante; (*cap.*) ['prɑtɪstənt] *adj* & *s* protestante
**Protestantism** ['prɑtɪstəntɪzəm] *s* protestantismo
**protestation** [,prɑtɛs'teʃən] *s* protestación
**Proteus** ['protjus] o ['protɪəs] *s* (myth. & fig.) Proteo
**prothallium** [pro'θælɪəm] *s* (*pl:* **-a** [ə]) (bot.) protalo
**prothesis** ['prɑθɪsɪs] *s* (gram.) prótesis o próstesis; (surg.) prótesis
**prothetic** [pro'θɛtɪk] *adj* (gram.) protético o prostético; (surg.) protético
**prothonotary** [pro'θɑnə,tɛrɪ] o [,proθə'notərɪ] *s* (*pl:* **-ies**) escribano principal (*de un tribunal*); (eccl.) protonotario
**prothorax** [pro'θoræks] *s* (*pl:* **-raxes** o **-races** [rəsiz]) (ent.) protórax

**protium** ['protɪəm] o ['proʃɪəm] *s* (chem.) procio
**protoactinium** [,protoæk'tɪnɪəm] *s* (chem.) protoactinio
**protocol** ['protəkɑl] *s* protocolo; *va* protocolar
**protogine** ['protədʒɪn] o ['protədʒin] *s* (geol.) protógina
**protomartyr** [,proto'mɑrtər] *s* protomártir
**proton** ['protɑn] *s* (phys. & chem.) protón
**protonema** [,protə'nimə] *s* (*pl:* **-mata** [mətə]) (bot.) protonema
**protoplasm** ['protəplæzəm] *s* (biol.) protoplasma
**protoplasmic** [,protə'plæzmɪk] *adj* protoplásmico
**prototype** ['protətaɪp] *s* prototipo
**protozoan** [,protə'zoən] *adj* & *s* (zool.) protozoario o protozoo
**protozoölogy** [,protəzo'ɑlədʒɪ] *s* protozoología
**protozoön** [,protə'zoɑn] *s* (*pl:* **-a** [ə]) (zool.) protozoo
**protract** [pro'trækt] *va* prolongar; (surv.) dibujar con la escala y el transportador
**protractile** [pro'træktɪl] *adj* protráctil
**protraction** [pro'trækʃən] *s* prolongación; (surv.) dibujo hecho con la escala y el transportador
**protractor** [pro'træktər] *s* prolongador; (surv.) transportador
**protrude** [pro'trud] *va* empujar hacia afuera, sacar fuera; *vn* resaltar, sobresalir
**protrusion** [pro'truʒən] *s* avanzamiento hacia afuera; saliente, resalte
**protrusive** [pro'trusɪv] *adj* saliente, protuberante
**protuberance** [pro'tjubərəns] o [pro'tubərəns] *s* protuberancia
**protuberant** [pro'tjubərənt] o [pro'tubərənt] *adj* protuberante
**proud** [praʊd] *adj* orgulloso; soberbio
**proud flesh** *s* (path.) carnosidad, bezo
**prov.** abr. de **provincialism**
**Prov.** abr. de **Provence, Provençal, Proverbs, Province** y **Provost**
**provable** ['pruvəbəl] *adj* comprobable, demostrable
**prove** [pruv] (*pret:* **proved**; *pp:* **proved** o **proven**) *va* probar; *vn* resultar; **to prove to be** venir a ser; resultar, salir
**Provençal** [,provən'sɑl] *adj* & *s* provenzal
**Provence** [pro'vɑns] *s* la Provenza
**provender** ['prɑvəndər] *s* forraje; (coll.) comida
**prover** ['pruvər] *s* probador, ensayador
**proverb** ['prɑvərb] *s* proverbio; ejemplo típico, ejemplo notorio; **Proverbs** *spl* (Bib.) Proverbios, Libro de los Proverbios
**proverbial** [pro'vʌrbɪəl] *adj* proverbial
**proverbially** [pro'vʌrbɪəlɪ] *adv* proverbialmente
**provide** [prə'vaɪd] *va* proporcionar; suministrar; *vn* precaverse; prepararse; disponer, estipular; **to provide against** precaverse contra o de; **to provide for** proveer a; asegurarse (*el porvenir*); proveer lo necesario para (*p.ej., la educación de un hijo*)
**provided** [prə'vaɪdɪd] *conj* a condición (de) que, con tal (de) que
**providence** ['prɑvɪdəns] *s* providencia; (*cap.*) *s* Providencia
**provident** ['prɑvɪdənt] *adj* providente
**providential** [,prɑvɪ'dɛnʃəl] *adj* providencial
**provider** [prə'vaɪdər] *s* proveedor
**providing** [prə'vaɪdɪŋ] *conj* var. de **provided**
**province** ['prɑvɪns] *s* provincia; competencia
**provincial** [prə'vɪnʃəl] *adj* provincial (*perteneciente a la provincia*); provinciano (*campesino; perteneciente a una provincia en contraposición a la capital*); intolerante; *s* provinciano; (eccl.) provincial
**provincialism** [prə'vɪnʃəlɪzəm] *s* provincialismo; intolerancia
**provinciality** [prə,vɪnʃɪ'ælɪtɪ] *s* (*pl:* **-ties**) provincialismo; provincianismo
**proving ground** *s* campo de ensayos
**provision** [prə'vɪʒən] *s* provisión; condición, estipulación; **provisions** *spl* provisiones; **to make provision for** providenciar; asegurar el porvenir de (*p.ej., la familia de uno*); ase-

gurarse (*el porvenir*); proveer lo necesario para (*p. ej., la educación de un hijo*); *va* aprovisionar
**provisional** [prəˈvɪʒənəl] *adj* provisional
**provisionally** [prəˈvɪʒənəlɪ] *adv* provisionalmente
**proviso** [prəˈvaɪzo] *s* (*pl:* **-sos** o **-soes**) condición, estipulación, salvedad
**provisory** [prəˈvaɪzərɪ] *adj* condicional, provisorio
**provitamin** [proˈvaɪtəmɪn] *s* (biochem.) provitamina
**provocation** [ˌpravəˈkeʃən] *s* provocación
**provocative** [prəˈvakətɪv] *adj* provocativo; *s* provocación
**provoke** [prəˈvok] *va* provocar; **to provoke to** + *inf* provocar a + *inf*
**provoking** [prəˈvokɪŋ] *adj* provocador (*irritante*)
**provost** [ˈpravəst] *s* preboste; (eccl.) prepósito; (educ.) preboste (*jefe educacional en algunas universidades norteamericanas*)
**provost marshal** [ˈprovo] *s* (mil.) capitán preboste; (nav.) oficial de vigilancia
**provostship** [ˈpravəstʃɪp] *s* prebostazgo; (eccl.) prepositura
**prow** [praʊ] *s* (naut.) proa
**prowess** [ˈpraʊɪs] *s* proeza; destreza
**prowl** [praʊl] *s* ronda en busca de presa o pillaje, vagabundeo; *vn* rondar en busca de presa o pillaje, cazar al acecho, vagabundear, rodar
**prowler** [ˈpraʊlər] *s* rondador; ladrón
**proximal** [ˈpraksɪməl] *adj* (anat.) proximal
**proximate** [ˈpraksɪmɪt] *adj* próximo
**proximately** [ˈpraksɪmɪtlɪ] *adv* próximamente
**proximity** [prakˈsɪmɪtɪ] *s* proximidad
**proximity fuse** *s* espoleta de proximidad por radio
**proximo** [ˈpraksɪmo] *adv* del o en el mes que viene
**proxy** [ˈpraksɪ] *s* (*pl:* **-ies**) poder; apoderado, poderhabiente; **by proxy** por poderes
**prude** [prud] *s* mojigato, gazmoño
**prudence** [ˈprudəns] *s* prudencia
**prudent** [ˈprudənt] *adj* prudente
**prudential** [pruˈdenʃəl] *adj* prudencial
**prudery** [ˈprudərɪ] *s* (*pl:* **-ies**) mojigatería, gazmoñería
**prudish** [ˈprudɪʃ] *adj* mojigato, gazmoño
**prune** [prun] *s* ciruela pasa; *va* escamondar, podar; (fig.) escamondar
**pruning hook** o **knife** *s* podadera
**prurience** [ˈprʊrɪəns] o **pruriency** [ˈprʊrɪənsɪ] *s* lascivia
**prurient** [ˈprʊrɪənt] *adj* lascivo; anheloso
**pruriginous** [prʊˈrɪdʒɪnəs] *adj* pruriginoso
**prurigo** [prʊˈraɪgo] *s* (path.) prurigo
**pruritus** [prʊˈraɪtəs] *s* (path.) prurito
**Prussia** [ˈprʌʃə] *s* Prusia
**Prussian** [ˈprʌʃən] *adj* & *s* prusiano
**Prussian blue** *s* azul de Prusia
**Prussianism** [ˈprʌʃənɪzəm] *s* prusianismo
**prussiate** [ˈprʌʃɪet] o [ˈprʌsɪet] *s* (chem.) prusiato
**prussic** [ˈprʌsɪk] *adj* prúsico
**prussic acid** *s* (chem.) ácido prúsico
**pry** [praɪ] *s* (*pl:* **pries**) palanca, alzaprima; persona entremetida; (*pret & pp:* **pried**) *va* alzaprimar; conseguir con gran dificultad; **to pry open** forzar (*p.ej., una tapa*) con la alzaprima o palanca; **to pry out of** arrancar (*p.ej., un secreto*) a (*una persona*); *vn* entremeterse; **to pry into** meterse en, entremeterse en
**pryer** [ˈpraɪər] *s* var. de **prier**
**prying** [ˈpraɪɪŋ] *adj* curioso, entremetido
**prythee** [ˈprɪðɪ] *interj* (archaic) ¡ te ruego!
**Ps.** abr. de **Psalm** o **Psalms**
**P.S.** abr. de **postscript** y **Privy Seal**
**psalm** [sam] *s* salmo; **the Psalms** (Bib.) los Salmos
**psalmbook** [ˈsamˌbʊk] *s* libro de Salmos versificados
**psalmist** [ˈsamɪst] *s* salmista; **the Psalmist** el Salmista
**psalmody** [ˈsamədɪ] o [ˈsalmədɪ] *s* (*pl:* **-dies**) salmodia; salmos
**Psalter** [ˈsɔltər] *s* Salterio
**psaltery** [ˈsɔltərɪ] *s* (*pl:* **-ies**) (mus.) salterio
**pseudo** [ˈsudo] o [ˈsjudo] *adj* supuesto, falso, fingido
**pseudohermaphroditism** [ˌsudohʌrˈmæfrədaɪtɪzəm] o [ˌsjudohʌrˈmæfrədaɪtɪzəm] *s* seudohermafroditismo
**pseudomorphism** [ˌsudəˈmɔrfɪzəm] o [ˌsjudəˈmɔrfɪzəm] *s* (mineral.) seudomorfismo
**pseudonym** [ˈsudənɪm] o [ˈsjudənɪm] *s* seudónimo
**pseudonymous** [suˈdanɪməs] o [sjuˈdanɪməs] *adj* seudónimo
**pseudopod** [ˈsudəpad] o [ˈsjudəpad] *s* (zool.) seudópodo
**pseudopodium** [ˌsudəˈpodɪəm] o [ˌsjudəˈpodɪəm] *s* (*pl:* **-a** [ə]) var. de **pseudopod**
**pshaw** [ʃɔ] *interj* ¡ pche!
**psilosis** [saɪˈlosɪs] *s* (path.) psilosis (*caída del pelo; esprue*)
**psittacism** [ˈsɪtəsɪzəm] *s* psitacismo
**psittacosis** [ˌsɪtəˈkosɪs] *s* (path.) psitacosis
**psoas** [ˈsoəs] *s* (anat.) psoas
**psoriasis** [soˈraɪəsɪs] *s* (path.) soríasis
**P.S.T.** abr. de **Pacific Standard Time**
**pst** [pst] *interj* ¡ chis, chis!, ¡ ce!
**psych.** abr. de **psychology** y **psychological**
**psychasthenia** [ˌsaɪkæsˈθinɪə] *s* (path.) psicastenia
**psyche** [ˈsaɪkɪ] *s* psiquis (*alma, inteligencia*); (*cap.*) *s* (myth.) Psiquis
**psychiatric** [ˌsaɪkɪˈætrɪk] *adj* psiquiátrico
**psychiatrist** [saɪˈkaɪətrɪst] *s* psiquíatra
**psychiatry** [saɪˈkaɪətrɪ] *s* psiquiatría
**psychic** [ˈsaɪkɪk] *adj* psíquico; mediúmnico; *s* médium
**psychical** [ˈsaɪkɪkəl] *adj* var. de **psychic**
**psychoanalysis** [ˌsaɪkoəˈnælɪsɪs] *s* psicoanálisis
**psychoanalyst** [ˌsaɪkoˈænəlɪst] *s* psicoanalista
**psychoanalytic** [ˌsaɪkoˌænəˈlɪtɪk] o **psychoanalytical** [ˌsaɪkoˌænəˈlɪtɪkəl] *adj* psicoanalítico
**psychoanalytically** [ˌsaɪkoˌænəˈlɪtɪkəlɪ] *adv* psicoanalíticamente
**psychoanalyze** [ˌsaɪkoˈænəlaɪz] *va* psicoanalizar
**psychodynamic** [ˌsaɪkodaɪˈnæmɪk] *adj* psicodinámico; **psychodynamics** *ssg* psicodinámica
**psychognosis** [saɪˈkagnəsɪs] *s* psicognostia
**psychologic** [ˌsaɪkəˈladʒɪk] o **psychological** [ˌsaɪkəˈladʒɪkəl] *adj* psicológico
**psychologically** [ˌsaɪkəˈladʒɪkəlɪ] *adv* psicológicamente
**psychological moment** *s* momento psicológico
**psychological warfare** *s* guerra psicológica
**psychologist** [saɪˈkalədʒɪst] *s* psicólogo
**psychology** [saɪˈkalədʒɪ] *s* psicología
**psychometric** [ˌsaɪkoˈmetrɪk] *adj* psicométrico; **psychometrics** *ssg* psicometría
**psychometry** [saɪˈkamɪtrɪ] *s* psicometría
**psychoneurosis** [ˌsaɪkonjʊˈrosɪs] o [ˌsaɪkonʊˈrosɪs] *s* (*pl:* **-ses** [siz]) (path.) psiconeurosis
**psychopath** [ˈsaɪkopæθ] *s* psicópata
**psychopathic** [ˌsaɪkoˈpæθɪk] *adj* psicopático
**psychopathology** [ˌsaɪkopəˈθalədʒɪ] *s* psicopatología
**psychopathy** [saɪˈkapəθɪ] *s* psicopatía
**psychophysics** [ˌsaɪkoˈfɪzɪks] *ssg* psicofísica
**psychosis** [saɪˈkosɪs] *s* (*pl:* **-ses** [siz]) (path.) psicosis; (psychol.) estado mental
**psychosomatic** [ˌsaɪkosoˈmætɪk] *adj* psicosomático
**psychotherapy** [ˌsaɪkoˈθerəpɪ] *s* psicoterapia
**psychrometer** [saɪˈkramɪtər] *s* psicrómetro
**pt.** abr. de **part, pint** o **pints** y **point**
**ptarmigan** [ˈtarmɪgən] *s* (orn.) perdiz blanca
**pteridophyte** [ˈterɪdoˌfaɪt] *s* (bot.) pteridófita o teridófita
**pterodactyl** [ˌteroˈdæktɪl] *s* (pal.) pterodáctilo
**Ptolemaic** [ˌtalɪˈmeɪk] *adj* ptolemaico; *s* partidario de Tolomeo
**Ptolemaic system** *s* (astr.) sistema de Tolomeo
**Ptolemy** [ˈtalɪmɪ] *s* Tolomeo
**ptomaine** o **ptomain** [ˈtomen] *s* (biochem.) ptomaína o tomaína
**ptomaine poisoning** *s* envenenamiento ptomaínico
**pts.** abr. de **parts, pints** y **points**

**ptyalin** [ˈtaɪəlɪn] *s* (path.) ptialina
**ptyalism** [ˈtaɪəlɪzəm] *s* (path.) ptialismo
**pub** [pʌb] *s* (Brit. slang) taberna
**puberty** [ˈpjubərtɪ] *s* pubertad
**pubes** [ˈpjubiz] *s* (anat.) pubis (*parte inferior del vientre; vello que la cubre*); *pl de* **pubis**
**pubescence** [pjuˈbɛsəns] *s* pubescencia
**pubescent** [pjuˈbɛsənt] *adj* pubescente
**pubic** [ˈpjubɪk] *adj* púbico
**pubis** [ˈpjubɪs] *s* (*pl:* **-bes** [biz]) (anat.) pubis (*parte del hueso coxal*)
**public** [ˈpʌblɪk] *adj* público; *s* público; **in public** en público
**public-address system** [ˈpʌblɪkəˈdrɛs] *s* sistema amplificador de discursos públicos
**publican** [ˈpʌblɪkən] *s* (hist.) publicano; (Brit.) tabernero
**publication** [ˌpʌblɪˈkeʃən] *s* publicación
**public charge** *s* carga pública
**public conveyance** *s* vehículo de servicio público, vehículo de transporte urbano
**public debt** *s* deuda pública
**public enemy** *s* enemigo público
**public health** *s* higiene pública
**public house** *s* posada, hotel; (Brit.) taberna
**publicist** [ˈpʌblɪsɪst] *s* publicista
**publicity** [pʌbˈlɪsɪtɪ] *s* publicidad; *adj* publicitario
**publicize** [ˈpʌblɪsaɪz] *va* publicar
**public library** *s* biblioteca municipal
**publicly** [ˈpʌblɪklɪ] *adv* públicamente
**public official** *s* funcionario público
**public opinion** *s* opinión pública
**public relations** *spl* relaciones públicas
**public school** *s* (U.S.A.) escuela pública; (Brit.) internado privado con dote
**public servant** *s* funcionario público
**public speaking** *s* elocución, oratoria
**public spirit** *s* celo patriótico del buen ciudadano
**public-spirited** [ˈpʌblɪkˈspɪrɪtɪd] *adj* cívico, patriótico
**public square** *s* plaza; plaza de armas (Am.)
**public thoroughfare** *s* vía pública
**public toilet** *s* quiosco de necesidad
**public utility** *s* empresa de servicio público; **public utilities** *spl* acciones emitidas por empresas de servicio público
**public works** *spl* obras públicas
**publish** [ˈpʌblɪʃ] *va* publicar; (eccl.) publicar
**publisher** [ˈpʌblɪʃər] *s* editor
**publishing house** *s* casa editorial
**puccoon** [pəˈkun] *s* (bot.) litospermo; (bot.) sanguinaria del Canadá
**puce** [pjus] *adj* de color castaño rojizo; *s* color castaño rojizo
**puck** [pʌk] *s* duende malicioso; (sport) disco de caucho
**pucker** [ˈpʌkər] *s* pliegue mal hecho; frunce; *va* plegar mal; fruncir; *vn* plegarse mal
**puckish** [ˈpʌkɪʃ] *adj* travieso, juguetón
**pudding** [ˈpʊdɪŋ] *s* pudín; chorizo
**pudding stone** *s* (geol.) pudinga
**puddle** [ˈpʌdəl] *s* aguazal, charco; mezcla de arcilla húmeda y arena en una pasta; *va* mojar, enlodar, enfangar; hacer una pasta de (*arcilla húmeda y arena*); tapar u obstruir con una mezcla de arcilla húmeda y arena; (found.) pudelar
**puddler** [ˈpʌdlər] *s* (found.) pudelador
**puddling** [ˈpʌdlɪŋ] *s* (found.) pudelación; arcilla pastosa
**puddling furnace** *s* horno de pudelar
**puddly** [ˈpʌdlɪ] *adj* encharcado
**pudency** [ˈpjudənsɪ] *s* pudicicia
**pudgy** [ˈpʌdʒɪ] *adj* (*comp:* **-ier;** *super:* **-iest**) gordinflón, rechoncho
**pueblo** [ˈpwɛblo] *s* (*pl:* **-los**) (U.S.A.) pueblo indio
**puerile** [ˈpjuərɪl] *adj* pueril
**puerility** [ˌpjuəˈrɪlɪtɪ] *s* (*pl:* **-ties**) puerilidad
**puerperal** [pjuˈʌrpərəl] *adj* puerperal
**puerperal fever** *s* (path.) fiebre puerperal
**puerperium** [ˌpjuərˈpɪrɪəm] *s* (obstet.) puerperio
**Puerto Rican** [ˈpwɛrto ˈrikən] *adj & s* puertorriqueño
**Puerto Rico** [ˈpwɛrto ˈriko] *s* Puerto Rico
**puff** [pʌf] *s* resoplido, soplo vivo; bocanada (*de humo*); bullón (*de vestido*); borla de polvos; pastelillo de crema o jalea; masa redonda y suave; alabanza exagerada; ráfaga, ventolera; *va* soplar; hinchar; alabar exageradamente; *vn* soplar; resollar; echar bocanadas (*p.ej., una chimenea*); hincharse; enorgullecerse exageradamente
**puff adder** *s* (zool.) víbora puff
**puffball** [ˈpʌfˌbɔl] *s* (bot.) bejín, cuesco de lobo
**puffer** [ˈpʌfər] *s* soplador; (ichth.) pez globo; (ichth.) diodón; (ichth.) tamboril
**puffin** [ˈpʌfɪn] *s* (orn.) frailecillo (*Fratercula arctica*)
**puffing adder** *s* (zool.) heterodón
**puff paste** *s* pasta de harina muy fina que se usa para hacer pasteles y tortas, hojaldre
**puff sleeve** *s* manga de bullón
**puffy** [ˈpʌfɪ] *adj* (*comp:* **-ier;** *super:* **-iest**) hinchado; que viene en bocanadas; corto de resuello; (fig.) hinchado, engreído; (fig.) campanudo
**pug** [pʌg] *s* doguino, perro carlín
**pugilism** [ˈpjudʒɪlɪzəm] *s* pugilismo o pugilato
**pugilist** [ˈpjudʒɪlɪst] *s* púgil o pugilista
**pugilistic** [ˌpjudʒɪˈlɪstɪk] *adj* de pugilato, pugilístico
**pugnacious** [pʌgˈneʃəs] *adj* pugnaz, belicoso
**pugnacity** [pʌgˈnæsɪtɪ] *s* pugnacidad, belicosidad
**pug nose** *s* nariz roma y levantada
**pug-nosed** [ˈpʌgˌnozd] *adj* braco
**puissance** [ˈpjuɪsəns], [pjuˈɪsəns] o [ˈpwɪsəns] *s* fuerza grande, pujanza
**puissant** [ˈpjuɪsənt], [pjuˈɪsənt] o [ˈpwɪsənt] *adj* fuerte, pujante
**puke** [pjuk] *s* (slang) vómito; *va & vn* (slang) vomitar
**pulchritude** [ˈpʌlkrɪtjud] o [ˈpʌlkrɪtud] *s* belleza, hermosura
**pule** [pjul] *vn* gemir, quejarse, llorar con voz débil (*como hacen los niños*)
**pull** [pʊl] *s* tirón, estirón; chupada (*p.ej., a un cigarro*); tirador (*de una puerta*); cuerda (*con que se tira de una cosa*); esfuerzo penoso o prolongado; (slang) enchufe, buenas aldabas; (fig.) tirón (*atracción*) ‖ *va* tirar de; arrancar, coger; rasgar; estirar, dislocar, torcer (*p.ej., un ligamento*); chupar; beber; reservar (*p.ej., las fuerzas*); (print.) sacar (*una impresión o prueba*); (slang) llevar a cabo; (slang) arrestar; **to pull apart** separar por tracción; romper en dos; **to pull down** demoler, derribar; bajar (*p.ej., la cortinilla*); abatir, degradar, humillar; **to pull in** cobrar (*una cuerda o soga*); **to pull off** (slang) llevar a cabo; **to pull oneself together** componerse, recobrar la calma; **to pull out** arrancar, sacar; **to pull through** sacar de un aprieto, sacar de una enfermedad; **to pull up** arrancar, desarraigar; detener, parar ‖ *vn* moverse despacio, moverse con esfuerzo; remar; **to pull apart** romperse por tracción; **to pull at** tirar de (*p.ej., su corbata*); chupar (*p.ej., un cigarro*); **to pull for** (slang) apoyar, ayudar; **to pull for oneself** tirar por su lado; **to pull in** detenerse; llegar (*un tren*) a la estación; **to pull on** tirar de; **to pull out** partir; partir (*un tren*) de la estación; **to pull through** salir a flote; recobrar la salud; **to pull up** moverse hacia adelante; detenerse, pararse; arrimarse (*p.ej., un auto a la acera*); **pull** tirad (*indicación en una puerta*)
**pull chain** *s* (elec.) cadenilla de tiro, tirador
**pull cord** *s* (elec.) tirador
**pulldevil** [ˈpʊlˌdɛvəl] *s* potera
**puller** [ˈpʊlər] *s* tirador, extractor, arrancador; (slang) atracción
**pullet** [ˈpʊlɪt] *s* polla (*gallina joven*)
**pulley** [ˈpʊlɪ] *s* polea; sistema de poleas; polea de transmisión
**Pullman car** [ˈpʊlmən] *s* coche Pullman
**pull-over** [ˈpʊlˌovər] *s* pulóver (*chaleco de punto de media que se pone comenzando por la cabeza*)
**pull socket** *s* (elec.) portalámparas de cadena
**pullulate** [ˈpʌljəlet] *vn* pulular
**pulmonary** [ˈpʌlməˌnɛrɪ] *adj* pulmonar
**pulmonate** [ˈpʌlmənet] o [ˈpʌlmənɪt] *adj* pulmonado
**pulmotor** [ˈpʌlˌmotər] o [ˈpʊlˌmotər] *s* pulmotor
**pulp** [pʌlp] *s* pulpa; pasta (*para hacer papel*);

(anat.) bulbo (*de diente*); *va* hacer pulpa (*una cosa*)
**pulpit** ['pulpɪt] *s* púlpito; (fig.) púlpito
**pulpit glasses** *spl* anteojos de predicador
**pulpwood** ['pʌlp,wud] *s* madera de pulpa; madera hecha pulpa para hacer papel
**pulpy** ['pʌlpɪ] *adj* (*comp:* **-ier;** *super:* **-iest**) pulposo
**pulque** ['pulkɪ] *s* pulque
**pulsate** ['pʌlset] *vn* pulsar; vibrar
**pulsatile** ['pʌlsətɪl] *adj* pulsátil
**pulsation** [pʌl'seʃən] *s* pulsación; (phys. & physiol.) pulsación
**pulsative** ['pʌlsətɪv] *adj* pulsativo
**pulse** [pʌls] *s* pulso; legumbres (*garbanzos, habas, lentejas*); **to feel** o **take the pulse of** tomar el pulso a; *vn* pulsar
**pulsimeter** [pʌl'sɪmɪtər] *s* pulsímetro
**pulsometer** [pʌl'sɑmɪtər] *s* pulsómetro; pulsímetro
**pulverizable** ['pʌlvə,raɪzəbəl] *adj* pulverizable
**pulverization** [,pʌlvərɪ'zeʃən] *s* pulverización
**pulverize** ['pʌlvəraɪz] *va* pulverizar; *vn* pulverizarse
**puma** ['pjumə] *s* (zool.) puma
**pumice** ['pʌmɪs] *s* piedra pómez; *va* apomazar
**pumice stone** *s* piedra pómez
**pummel** ['pʌməl] (*pret & pp:* **-meled** o **-melled;** *ger:* **-meling** o **-melling**) *va* apuñear, aporrear
**pump** [pʌmp] *s* bomba; servilla, zapatilla; *va* elevar (*agua*) por medio de una bomba; sacar (*agua*) por medio de una bomba; llenar de aire por medio de una bomba; mover de arriba para abajo (*como el guimbalete de una bomba*); sonsacar; tirar de la lengua a; **to pump up** hinchar, inflar (*el neumático*); *vn* trabajar elevando agua por medio de una bomba; moverse de arriba para abajo
**pump box** *s* cuerpo de bomba; émbolo de bomba
**pump dale** *s* (naut.) dala, adala
**pumper** ['pʌmpər] *s* bombero; ganzúa, sonsacador
**pumpernickel** ['pʌmpər,nɪkəl] *s* pan de centeno entero
**pump handle** *s* guimbalete
**pump house** *s* casa de bombas
**pumping station** *s* estación de bombas, estación elevadora
**pumpkin** ['pʌmpkɪn] o ['pʌŋkɪn] *s* (bot.) calabaza común; (coll.) cachazudo; **some pumpkins** (coll.) persona de muchas campanillas
**pump piston** *s* émbolo de bomba
**pump-priming** ['pʌmp,praɪmɪŋ] *s* (econ.) inyección económica (*por parte del gobierno*)
**pun** [pʌn] *s* retruécano, equívoco, juego de palabras; (*pret & pp:* **punned;** *ger:* **punning**) *vn* jugar del vocablo, decir equívocos
**punch** [pʌntʃ] *s* puñetazo; punzón; sacabocado; perforación; ponche (*bebida*); (coll.) empuje, fuerza, vigor; **to pull one's punches** (box.) moderar los puñetazos; (slang) moderar el ataque; (*cap.*) *s* Polichinela; **pleased as Punch** muy satisfecho; (*l.c.*) *va* pegar con los puños; punzonar; picar, taladrar, perforar (*p.ej., un billete*)
**Punch-and-Judy show** ['pʌntʃənd'dʒudɪ] *s* función de títeres en la cual Polichinela se pelea con su mujer
**punch bowl** *s* ponchera
**punch card** *s* tarjeta perforada
**punch-drunk** ['pʌntʃ,drʌnk] *adj* atontado (*p.ej,. por una tunda de golpes*); completamente aturdido
**punched card** [pʌntʃt] *s* var. de **punch card**
**punched tape** *s* cinta perforada
**puncheon** ['pʌntʃən] *s* pipa, tonel; punzón; pie derecho; pedazo de un tronco dividido por la mitad y con la superficie pulida rudamente
**punchinello** [,pʌntʃɪ'nɛlo] *s* (*pl:* **-los** o **-loes**) polichinela, pulchinela
**punching bag** *s* (sport) boxibalón
**punch line** *s* broche de oro, colofón del artículo (*frase que sintetiza el escrito*)
**punch press** *s* (mach.) prensa punzonadora
**punctilio** [pʌŋk'tɪlɪo] *s* (*pl:* **-os**) puntillo, pundonor
**punctilious** [pʌŋk'tɪlɪəs] *adj* puntilloso, pundonoroso
**punctual** ['pʌŋktʃuəl] *adj* puntual
**punctuality** [,pʌŋktʃu'ælɪtɪ] *s* puntualidad
**punctually** ['pʌŋktʃuəlɪ] *adv* puntualmente
**punctuate** ['pʌŋktʃuet] *va* puntuar; acentuar, destacar; interrumpir; *vn* puntuar
**punctuation** [,pʌŋktʃu'eʃən] *s* puntuación
**punctuation mark** *s* signo de puntuación
**puncture** ['pʌŋktʃər] *s* puntura; (aut.) pinchazo, picadura, perforación; (surg.) punción; **to have a puncture** tener un neumático pinchado; *va* pinchar, picar, perforar; (surg.) puncionar; *vn* ser pinchado
**puncture-proof** ['pʌŋktʃər,pruf] *adj* (aut.) imperforable, a prueba de pinchazos
**pundit** ['pʌndɪt] *s* erudito, sabio
**pungency** ['pʌndʒənsɪ] *s* picante; estímulo, vivacidad
**pungent** ['pʌndʒənt] *adj* picante; estimulante, vivaz
**Punic** ['pjunɪk] *adj* púnico; (fig.) púnico
**Punic Wars** *spl* guerras púnicas
**punish** ['pʌnɪʃ] *va* castigar; (coll.) maltratar
**punishable** ['pʌnɪʃəbəl] *adj* castigable, punible
**punishment** ['pʌnɪʃmənt] *s* castigo; (coll.) maltrato
**punitive** ['pjunɪtɪv] o **punitory** ['pjunɪ,torɪ] *adj* punitivo
**Punjab** [pʌn'dʒɑb] o ['pʌndʒɑb] *s* Penyab
**punk** [pʌŋk] *s* yesca, pebete; hupe; (slang) pillo, gamberro; *adj* (slang) malo, de mala calidad
**punster** ['pʌnstər] *s* vocablista, equivoquista
**punt** [pʌnt] *s* batea, pontón (*barco chato*); (football) puntapié dado al balón en el aire; *va* impeler (*un barco*) con un botador; (football) dar un puntapié a (*el balón*) antes que llegue al suelo; *vn* pasear o pescar en una batea; jugar por dinero; apostar contra el banquero
**punter** ['pʌntər] *s* hombre que impele un barco con el botador; (football) jugador que da un puntapié al balón en el aire; jugador que apuesta contra el banquero
**punty** ['pʌntɪ] *s* (*pl:* **-ties**) puntel
**puny** ['pjunɪ] *adj* (*comp:* **-nier;** *super:* **-niest**) encanijado, débil; insignificante, mezquino
**pup** [pʌp] *s* var. de **puppy**
**pupa** ['pjupə] *s* (*pl:* **-pae** [pi]) (ent.) pupa, ninfa
**pupal** ['pjupəl] *adj* (ent.) pupal
**puparium** [pju'perɪəm] *s* (ent.) pupario
**pupil** ['pjupəl] *s* alumno; (anat.) pupila
**pupillary** ['pjupɪ,lerɪ] *adj* pupilar (*perteneciente al pupilo o huérfano*); (anat.) pupilar
**Pupin system** [pju'pin] *s* (elec.) pupinización
**puppet** ['pʌpɪt] *s* títere; muñeca pequeña; (fig.) maniquí; (mach.) muñeca
**puppeteer** [,pʌpɪ'tɪr] *s* titiritero
**puppet government** *s* gobierno títere, gobierno de monigotes
**puppet regime** *s* régimen títere
**puppet show** *s* función de títeres
**puppy** ['pʌpɪ] *s* (*pl:* **-pies**) cachorro; pisaverde
**puppyish** ['pʌpɪɪʃ] *adj* de cachorro; fatuo
**puppy love** *s* (coll.) primeros amores
**pup tent** *s* (mil.) tienda de abrigo
**pur** [pʌr] *s* ronroneo; (*pret & pp:* **purred;** *ger:* **purring**) *va* decir murmurando; *vn* ronronear (*el gato; el avión*)
**purblind** ['pʌr,blaɪnd] *adj* cegato; miope, falto de comprensión
**purchasable** ['pʌrtʃəsəbəl] *adj* comprable; sobornable
**purchase** ['pʌrtʃəs] *s* compra; agarre firme; **you have no purchase** Vd. no tiene donde agarrarse; *va* comprar
**purchaser** ['pʌrtʃəsər] *s* comprador
**purchasing power** *s* poder adquisitivo, poder de adquisición (*del dinero*)
**pure** [pjur] *adj* puro
**pure-blooded** ['pjur,blʌdɪd] *adj* castizo, de sangre pura
**purée** [pju're] o ['pjure] *s* puré
**pure line** *s* (biol.) linaje puro
**pureness** ['pjurnɪs] *s* pureza
**purfle** ['pʌrfəl] *s* orla; *va* orlar
**purgation** [pʌr'geʃən] *s* purgación

**purgative** [ˈpʌrgətɪv] *adj* purgativo o purgante; *s* purgante
**purgatorial** [ˌpʌrgəˈtorɪəl] *adj* purgatorio
**purgatory** [ˈpʌrgəˌtorɪ] *s* (*pl:* **-ries**) (theol. & fig.) purgatorio
**purge** [pʌrdʒ] *s* purgación; purgante; *va* purgar; *vn* purgarse
**purification** [ˌpjurɪfɪˈkeʃən] *s* purificación
**purify** [ˈpjurɪfaɪ] (*pret & pp:* **-fied**) *va* purificar; *vn* purificarse
**Purim** [ˈpjurɪm] o [ˈpurɪm] *s* (rel.) Purim
**purine** [ˈpjurin] o [ˈpjurɪn] *s* (chem.) purina
**purism** [ˈpjurɪzəm] *s* casticismo, purismo
**purist** [ˈpjurɪst] *adj* purista; *s* casticista, purista
**puristic** [pjuˈrɪstɪk] *adj* purista
**puritan** [ˈpjurɪtən] *adj & s* puritano; (*cap.*) *adj & s* puritano
**puritanic** [ˌpjurɪˈtænɪk] o **puritanical** [ˌpjurɪˈtænɪkəl] *adj* puritano
**Puritanism** [ˈpjurɪtənɪzəm] *s* puritanismo
**purity** [ˈpjurɪtɪ] *s* pureza
**purl** [pʌrl] *s* flujo y murmullo; inversión de la puntada al tejer; guarnición rizada de tela, encaje o cinta; *va* tejer invirtiendo la puntada; bordar u orlar con guarnición rizada; *vn* fluir murmurando
**purlieu** [ˈpʌrlu] *s* terreno contiguo a un bosque; territorio lindante; jurisdicción; guarida, nidal; **purlieus** *spl* alrededores, inmediaciones
**purlin** o **purline** [ˈpʌrlɪn] *s* (carp.) correa
**purloin** [pərˈlɔɪn] *va & vn* robar, hurtar
**purple** [ˈpʌrpəl] *s* púrpura; *adj* purpúreo; *va* purpurar; *vn* purpurear
**purple loosestrife** *s* (bot.) salicaria
**purple martin** *s* (orn.) golondrina purpúrea
**purplish** [ˈpʌrplɪʃ] *adj* algo purpúreo
**purport** [ˈpʌrport] *s* significado, idea principal; [pərˈport] o [ˈpʌrport] *va* significar, querer decir; **to purport to** + *inf* pretender + *inf*
**purpose** [ˈpʌrpəs] *s* intención, propósito; fin, objeto; **for the purpose** al efecto; **for what purpose?** ¿con qué fin?; **on purpose** adrede, de propósito; **to good purpose** con buenos resultados; **to little purpose** con pocos resultados; **to no purpose** sin resultado; **to serve one's purpose** servir para el caso; *va* proponer, proyectar; proponerse
**purposeful** [ˈpʌrpəsfəl] *adj* porfiador; intencional; que obra con propósito
**purposeless** [ˈpʌrpəslɪs] *adj* sin propósito, sin fin determinado
**purposely** [ˈpʌrpəslɪ] *adv* adrede, de propósito
**purposive** [ˈpʌrpəsɪv] *adj* intencional; funcional; que obra con propósito
**purr** [pʌr] *s, va & vn* var. de **pur**
**purse** [pʌrs] *s* bolsa; colecta (*recaudación con fin caritativo*); *va* fruncir (*p.ej., los labios*)
**purse crab** *s* (zool.) cobo
**purse-proud** [ˈpʌrsˌpraud] *adj* envanecido por tener mucho dinero, orgulloso por ser rico
**purser** [ˈpʌrsər] *s* (naut.) contador de navío, comisario de a bordo
**purse strings** *spl* cordones de la bolsa
**purslane** [ˈpʌrslen] o [ˈpʌrslɪn] *s* (bot.) verdolaga
**pursuance** [pərˈsuəns] o [pərˈsjuəns] *s* prosecución
**pursuant** [pərˈsuənt] o [pərˈsjuənt] *adj* consiguiente; *adv* conforme; **pursuant to** conforme a, de acuerdo con
**pursue** [pərˈsu] o [pərˈsju] *va* perseguir; proseguir; seguir (*una carrera*)
**pursuit** [pərˈsut] o [pərˈsjut] *s* persecución; prosecución; busca o búsqueda (*p.ej., de la felicidad*); empleo, ocupación, oficio
**pursuit plane** *s* (aer.) caza, avión de caza
**pursuivant** [ˈpʌrswɪvənt] *s* persevante; acompañante, secuaz
**pursy** [ˈpʌrsɪ] *adj* (*comp:* **-sier**; *super:* **-siest**) obeso; asmático; flojo, holgado; fruncido, plegado
**purulence** [ˈpjurələns] o [ˈpjurjələns] o **purulency** [ˈpjurələnsɪ] o [ˈpjurjələnsɪ] purulencia
**purulent** [ˈpjurələnt] o [ˈpjurjələnt] *adj* purulento
**purvey** [pərˈve] *va* abastecer, proveer, suministrar
**purveyance** [pərˈveəns] *s* abastecimiento, proveimiento, suministro
**purveyor** [pərˈveər] *s* abastecedor, proveedor
**purview** [ˈpʌrvju] *s* alcance
**pus** [pʌs] *s* pus
**push** [puʃ] *s* empuje, empujón; (fig.) empuje (*fuerza, vigor*); *va* empujar; extender (*p.ej., conquistas*); **to push around** (coll.) tratar a empujones; **to push aside** hacer a un lado; **to push away** empujar, rechazar; apartar con la mano; **to push back** echar atrás; **to push through** forzar (*p.ej., una resolución*); *vn* empujar, moverse o apresurarse dando empujones; **to push ahead** adelantarse dando empujones; avanzar; **to push off** irse, salir; comenzar; apartarse de la orilla dando empujones; **to push on** avanzar, seguir adelante; **push** empujad (*indicación en una puerta*)
**pushball** [ˈpuʃˌbɔl] *s* (sport) juego en que se emplea una pelota pesada y de grandes dimensiones que se empuja con cualquier parte del cuerpo excepto las manos
**push button** *s* pulsador, botón de llamada, botón interruptor
**push-button control** [ˈpuʃˌbʌtən] *s* mando por botón
**push-button starter** *s* (aut.) botón de arranque
**push-button tuning** *s* (rad.) sintonización de botón
**push-button war** *s* guerra por botón
**pushcart** [ˈpuʃˌkart] *s* carretilla de mano
**push drill** *s* taladro de empuje
**pusher** [ˈpuʃər] *s* empujador; (coll.) persona emprendedora; (aer.) avión que lleva el motor propulsor en la parte de atrás
**pusher engine** *s* (rail.) locomotora de empuje
**pushing** [ˈpuʃɪŋ] *adj* emprendedor; entremetido, agresivo
**push-over** [ˈpuʃˌovər] *s* (slang) cosa muy fácil de hacer; (slang) persona muy fácil de dominar
**pushpin** [ˈpuʃˌpɪn] *s* crucillo (*juego de los alfileres*); chinche (*clavito*)
**push-pull** [ˈpuʃˈpul] *adj* (rad.) simétrico, de contrafase, de empuja-tira, de tira y empuje
**push-pull amplification** *s* (rad.) amplificación en disposición simétrica, contrafase
**pusillanimity** [ˌpjusɪləˈnɪmɪtɪ] *s* pusilanimidad
**pusillanimous** [ˌpjusɪˈlænɪməs] *adj* pusilánime
**puss** [pus] *s* gato; liebrecilla; chica, muchacha; (slang) cara, boca
**Puss in Boots** *s* El gato con botas
**pussy** [ˈpusɪ] *s* (*pl:* **-ies**) michito, gatito (*pequeño gato*); (bot.) amento
**pussyfoot** [ˈpusɪˌfut] *s* (*pl:* **-foots**) (slang) persona que anda a paso de gato, persona de evasivas; *vn* (slang) moverse a paso de gato, andar con cautela, no declararse
**pussy willow** *s* (bot.) sauce norteamericano de amentos muy sedosos (*Salix discolor*)
**pustular** [ˈpʌstʃələr] *adj* pustuloso
**pustulation** [ˌpʌstʃəˈleʃən] *s* pustulación
**pustule** [ˈpʌstʃul] *s* (bot. & path.) pústula
**put** [put] *s* echada; (com.) privilegio u opción de venta dentro de un plazo determinado por un precio estipulado ‖ (*pret & pp:* **put**; *ger:* **putting**) *va* poner, colocar; exponer, expresar; proponer para ser discutido; hacer (*una pregunta*); estimar, valuar; poner en ejercicio; imponer (*impuestos, multas*); arrojar, echar, lanzar; **to put across** llevar a cabo; hacer aceptar; **to put aside** poner aparte; rechazar; ahorrar (*dinero*); **to put away** guardar (*p.ej., en un cajón*); ahorrar (*dinero*); **to put by** ahorrar (*dinero*); **to put down** anotar, apuntar; sofocar (*una insurrección*); rebajar (*los precios*); **to put forth** echar, producir; extender; dar a luz; ejercer, emplear; proponer; **to put in** introducir en; interponer (*palabras*); pasar (*el tiempo*); **to put off** posponer, dejar para más tarde; deshacerse de; hacer guardar; **to put on** ponerse (*la ropa*); calzarse (*las botas*); poner en escena; llevar (*p.ej., un drama a la pantalla*); accionar (*p.ej., un freno*); fingir; atribuir; cargar (*impuestos*); **to put oneself out** incomodarse, molestarse; desvivirse, afanarse; **to put out** poner en la

calle; extender (*la mano*); sacar (*p.ej., un ojo*); apagar (*un fuego, la luz*); dar a luz, publicar; plantar; decepcionar, frustrar; (sport) sacar fuera de la partida; **to put over** (slang) llevar a cabo; **to put through** llevar a cabo; **to put to it** forzar a seguir un camino difícil, causar dificultad a; **to put up** mostrar, ofrecer; construir, edificar; poner a un lado; poner en el sitio acostumbrado; abrir (*un paraguas*); conservar (*fruta, legumbres, etc.*); hospedar; (coll.) incitar; (slang) proyectar con malicia; **put it here!** (coll.) ¡dame esa mano! ‖ *vn* dirigirse; **to put about** (naut.) cambiar de rumbo; **to put in** (naut.) entrar a puerto; **to put on** fingir; **to put up** parar, hospedarse; **to put up with** aguantar, tolerar

**putamen** [pju'temɪn] *s* (*pl:* **-tamina** ['tæmɪnə]) (bot.) putamen (*cuesco, huesco, núcleo*)

**putative** ['pjutətɪv] *adj* reputado, supuesto; putativo

**putative marriage** *s* (canon law) matrimonio putativo

**putlog** ['pʌt,lɔg] o ['pʌt,lɑg] *s* (carp.) almojaya

**putlog hole** *s* mechinal

**put-out** ['pʊt,aut] *adj* contrariado, enojado, ofendido

**putrefaction** [,pjutrɪ'fækʃən] *s* putrefacción

**putrefactive** [,pjutrɪ'fæktɪv] *adj* putrefactivo

**putrefy** ['pjutrɪfaɪ] (*pret & pp:* **-fied**) *va* pudrir; *vn* pudrirse

**putrescence** [pju'trɛsəns] *s* pudrición, putrefacción

**putrescent** [pju'trɛsənt] *adj* putrescente

**putrescible** [pju'trɛsɪbəl] *adj* putrescible

**putrescine** [pju'trɛsin] o [pju'trɛsɪn] *s* (biochem.) putrescina

**putrid** ['pjutrɪd] *adj* pútrido; corrompido, perverso

**putridity** [pju'trɪdɪtɪ] *s* putridez; podredumbre

**Putsch** [pʊtʃ] *s* intentona de sublevación; insurrección, sublevación

**putt** [pʌt] *s* (golf) golpe que hace meterse la pelota en el agujero o cerca de él; *va* (golf) golpear (*la pelota*) con cuidado para que corra a meterse en el agujero o cerca de él

**puttee** [pə'ti] o ['pʌtɪ] *s* polaina (*de cuero o paño*)

**putter** ['pʌtər] *vn* trabajar sin orden ni sistema; **to putter around** ocuparse en fruslerías, temporizar

**putting green** *s* (golf) campo de juego nivelado que circunda cada agujero

**putty** ['pʌtɪ] *s* (*pl:* **-ties**) masilla; (*pret & pp:* **-tied**) *va* enmasillar

**putty knife** *s* cuchillo de enmasillar, cuchillo de vidriero, espátula

**putty powder** *s* polvos de estaño, cenizas de estaño

**put-up** ['pʊt,ʌp] *adj* (coll.) proyectado y preparado de antemano, premeditado con malicia

**puzzle** ['pʌzəl] *s* enigma; acertijo, rompecabezas; *va* confundir, poner perplejo; **to puzzle out** descifrar, desenredar; *vn* estar confundido, estar perplejo; **to puzzle over** tratar de resolver, tratar de descifrar

**puzzlement** ['pʌzəlmənt] *s* confusión, perplejidad

**puzzler** ['pʌzlər] *s* quisicosa (*objeto de pregunta muy dudosa*)

**puzzling** ['pʌzlɪŋ] *adj* enigmático

**Pvt.** abr. de **Private**

**PW** abr. de **prisoner of war**

**pwt.** abr. de **pennyweight**

**PX** ['pi'ɛks] *s* var. de **Post Exchange**

**pyaemia** [paɪ'imɪə] *s* (path.) pioemia

**pycnostyle** ['pɪknostaɪl] *s* (arch.) picnóstilo

**pyemia** [paɪ'imɪə] *s* var. de **pyaemia**

**Pygmalion** [pɪg'melɪən] *s* (myth.) Pigmalión

**pygmy** ['pɪgmɪ] *adj* pigmeo; *s* (*pl:* **-mies**) pigmeo

**pyjamas** [pɪ'dʒɑməz] o [pɪ'dʒæməz] *spl* var. de **pajamas**

**pylon** ['paɪlɑn] *s* pilón

**pyloric** [paɪ'lɑrɪk] o [paɪ'lɔrɪk] *adj* pilórico

**pylorus** [paɪ'lorəs] *s* (*pl:* **-ri** [raɪ]) (anat.) píloro

**pyogenic** [,paɪə'dʒɛnɪk] *adj* piogénico

**pyorrhea** o **pyorrhoea** [,paɪə'riə] *s* (path.) piorrea

**pyramid** ['pɪrəmɪd] *s* pirámide; **the Pyramids** las Pirámides; *va* dar forma de pirámide a; aumentar (*su dinero*) comprando o vendiendo al crédito y empleando las ganancias para comprar o vender más; *vn* tener forma de pirámide

**pyramidal** [pɪ'ræmɪdəl] *adj* piramidal

**Pyramus** ['pɪrəməs] *s* (myth.) Píramo

**pyran** ['paɪræn] o [paɪ'ræn] *s* (chem.) pirano

**pyre** [paɪr] *s* pira

**Pyrenean** [,pɪrɪ'niən] *adj* pirenaico

**Pyrenees** ['pɪrɪniz] *spl* Pirineos

**pyretic** [paɪ'rɛtɪk] *adj* pirético

**pyretology** [,paɪrɪ'tɑlədʒɪ] *s* piretología

**pyrex** ['paɪrɛks] *s* (trademark) cristal que resiste el calor del horno

**pyrexia** [paɪ'rɛksɪə] *s* (path.) pirexia

**pyribenzamine** [,pɪrɪ'bɛnzəmin] o [,pɪrɪ'bɛnzəmɪn] *s* (pharm.) piribenzamina

**pyridine** ['pɪrɪdin] o ['pɪrɪdɪn] *s* (chem.) piridina

**pyriform** ['pɪrɪfɔrm] *adj* piriforme

**pyrites** [paɪ'raɪtiz], [pɪ'raɪtiz] o ['paɪraɪts] *s* (mineral.) pirita

**pyrogallic** [,paɪro'gælɪk] *adj* pirogálico

**pyrogallol** [,paɪro'gælol] o [,paɪro'gælɑl] *s* (chem.) pirogalol

**pyrography** [paɪ'rɑgrəfɪ] *s* pirograbado

**pyrolusite** [,paɪrə'lusaɪt] o [paɪ'rɑljəsaɪt] *s* (mineral.) pirolusita

**pyromancy** ['paɪro,mænsɪ] *s* piromancía

**pyromania** [,paɪro'menɪə] *s* piromanía

**pyrometer** [paɪ'rɑmɪtər] *s* (phys.) pirómetro

**pyrophorus** [paɪ'rɑfərəs] *s* (*pl:* **-ri** [raɪ]) (chem.) piróforo

**pyroscope** ['paɪrəskop] *s* (phys.) piroscopio

**pyrosis** [paɪ'rosɪs] *s* (path.) pirosis

**pyrosphere** ['paɪrosfɪr] *s* pirosfera

**pyrotechnic** [,paɪro'tɛknɪk] *adj* pirotécnico; **pyrotechnics** *spl* pirotecnia

**pyrotechnical** [,paɪro'tɛknɪkəl] *adj* pirotécnico

**pyrotechnist** [,paɪro'tɛknɪst] *s* pirotécnico

**pyroxene** ['paɪrɑksin] *s* (mineral.) piroxena

**pyroxylin** o **pyroxyline** [paɪ'rɑksɪlɪn] *s* piroxilina

**Pyrrha** ['pɪrə] *s* (myth.) Pirra

**pyrrhic** ['pɪrɪk] *adj* pírrico; (*cap.*) *adj* pírrico

**Pyrrhic victory** *s* triunfo pírrico, victoria pírrica

**Pyrrhonism** ['pɪrənɪzəm] *s* pirronismo

**Pyrrhus** ['pɪrəs] *s* Pirro

**pyrrole** [pɪ'rol] o ['pɪrol] *s* (chem.) pirrol

**Pythagoras** [pɪ'θægərəs] *s* Pitágoras

**Pythagorean** [pɪ,θægə'riən] *adj & s* pitagórico

**Pythian** ['pɪθɪən] *adj* pitio

**Pythian games** *spl* juegos pitios

**Pythias** ['pɪθɪəs] *s* (myth.) Pitias

**python** ['paɪθɑn] o ['paɪθən] *s* (zool.) pitón; (*cap.*) *s* (myth.) Pitón

**pythoness** ['paɪθənɪs] *s* pitonisa

**pyuria** [paɪ'jurɪə] *s* (path.) piuria

**pyx** [pɪks] *s* (eccl.) píxide, copón; (Brit.) caja que se guarda en la casa de moneda para conservar especímenes para probarlos en peso y pureza

**pyxidium** [pɪks'ɪdɪəm] *s* (*pl:* **-a** [ə]) (bot.) pixidio

# Q

**Q, q** [kju] *s* (*pl:* **Q's, q's** [kjuz]) décimaséptima letra del alfabeto inglés

**Q.** abr. de **quarto, queen, question** y **quire**

**Q.E.D.** abr. de **quod erat demonstrandum** (Lat.) **which was to be proved**

**Q.M.** abr. de **quartermaster**

**Q.M.G.** abr. de **Quartermaster General**

**qr.** abr. de **quarter** y **quire**

**qt.** abr. de **quantity** y **quart** o **quarts**

**qts.** abr. de **quarts**

**qu.** abr. de **quart, quarter, quarterly, queen, query** y **question**

**quack** [kwæk] *s* graznido del pato; charlatán; medicastro, curandero; ignorante que se las echa de tener conocimientos en una materia; *adj* falso; *vn* parpar (*el pato*)

**quackery** ['kwækərɪ] *s* (*pl:* **-ies**) charlatanismo

**quacksalver** ['kwæk,sælvər] *s* medicastro, curandero

**quad** [kwɑd] *s* (print.) cuadratín; (coll.) plaza cuadrangular, patio cuadrangular (*en las universidades*)

**quadragenarian** [,kwɑdrədʒɪ'nɛrɪən] *adj & s* cuadragenario

**Quadragesima** [,kwɑdrə'dʒɛsɪmə] *s* (eccl.) cuadragésima

**Quadragesimal** [,kwɑdrə'dʒɛsɪməl] *adj* cuadragesimal

**quadrangle** ['kwɑd,ræŋgəl] *s* cuadrángulo; plaza cuadrangular, patio cuadrangular

**quadrangular** [kwɑd'ræŋgjələr] *adj* cuadrangular

**quadrant** ['kwɑdrənt] *s* (astr. & geom.) cuadrante

**quadrat** ['kwɑdræt] *s* (print.) cuadratín

**quadrate** ['kwɑdret] o ['kwɑdrɪt] *adj & s* cuadrado; ['kwɑdret] *va* cuadrar; *vn* cuadrar (*conformarse*)

**quadratic** [kwɑ'drætɪk] *adj* (alg.) de segundo grado, cuadrático; **quadratics** *spl* ramo del álgebra que trata de las ecuaciones de segundo grado

**quadratic equation** *s* (alg.) ecuación de segundo grado, ecuación cuadrática

**quadrature** ['kwɑdrətʃər] *s* (astr., elec. & math.) cuadratura

**quadrature of the circle** *s* (math.) cuadratura del círculo

**quadrennial** [kwɑd'rɛnɪəl] *adj & s* cuadrienal

**quadrennially** [kwɑd'rɛnɪəlɪ] *adv* cada cuatro años

**quadriceps** ['kwɑdrɪsɛps] *s* (anat.) cuadríceps

**quadriga** [kwɑd'raɪgə] *s* (*pl:* **-gae** [dʒi]) (hist.) cuadriga

**quadrilateral** [,kwɑdrɪ'lætərəl] *adj & s* cuadrilátero

**quadrille** [kwə'drɪl] *adj* cuadriculado; *s* cuadrícula; cuadrilla (*baile*); (taur.) cuadrilla; *va* cuadricular; *vn* bailar una cuadrilla; cuadrillar (Am.)

**quadrille ruling** *s* cuadrícula

**quadrillion** [kwɑd'rɪljən] *s* (Brit.) cuatrillón

**quadrinomial** [,kwɑdrɪ'nomɪəl] *s* (alg.) cuadrinomio

**quadripartite** [,kwɑdrɪ'pɑrtaɪt] *adj* cuadripartido, cuatripartito

**quadrivium** [kwɑd'rɪvɪəm] *s* cuadrivio (*en la edad media, las cuatro artes matemáticas*)

**quadroon** [kwɑd'run] *s* cuarterón

**quadrumanous** [kwɑd'rumənəs] *adj* (zool.) cuadrúmano

**quadruped** ['kwɑdrupɛd] *adj & s* cuadrúpedo

**quadrupedal** [kwɑd'rupədəl] *adj* cuadrupedal

**quadruple** ['kwɑdrupəl] o [kwɑd'rupəl] *adj & s* cuádruple; *adv* cuatro veces; cuatro veces mayor; *va* cuadruplicar; *vn* cuadruplicarse

**quadruplet** ['kwɑdruplɛt] o [kwɑd'ruplɛt] *s* grupo de cuatro; cuatrillizo (*cada uno de los cuatro hijos de un mismo parto*)

**quadruplicate** [kwɑd'ruplɪkɪt] o [kwɑd'ruplɪket] *adj* cuadruplicado; [kwɑd'ruplɪket] *va* cuadruplicar

**quadruplication** [kwɑd,ruplɪ'keʃən] *s* cuadruplicación

**quaestor** ['kwɛstər] o ['kwistər] *s* cuestor

**quaestorship** ['kwɛstərʃɪp] o ['kwistərʃɪp] *s* cuestura

**quaff** [kwɑf] o [kwæf] *s* trago grande; *va & vn* beber en gran cantidad

**quagga** ['kwægə] *s* (zool.) cuaga

**quaggy** ['kwægɪ] *adj* (*comp:* **-gier;** *super:* **-giest**) pantanoso; blando como lodo

**quagmire** ['kwæg,maɪr] o ['kwɑg,maɪr] *s* cenagal; (coll.) cenagal (*negocio de difícil salida*)

**quahog** ['kwɔhɑg] o [kwə'hɑg] *s* (zool.) almeja redonda (*Venus mercenaria*)

**quail** [kwel] *s* (orn.) codorniz; *vn* acobardarse, cejar por temor

**quaint** [kwent] *adj* curioso, raro; afectado, rebuscado; fantástico, singular

**quake** [kwek] *s* temblor, terremoto; *vn* temblar

**Quaker** ['kwekər] *adj & s* cuáquero

**Quakeress** ['kwekərɪs] *s* cuáquera

**Quakerish** ['kwekərɪʃ] *adj* parecido a los cuáqueros; de cuáquero

**Quakerism** ['kwekərɪzəm] *s* cuaquerismo

**quaker-lady** ['kwekər,ledɪ] *s* (*pl:* **-dies**) (bot.) houstonia cerúlea

**Quaker meeting** *s* reunión de cuáqueros; (coll.) reunión en que hay poca conversación

**quaking bog** *s* tremadal

**quaking grass** *s* (bot.) tembladera, zarcillitos

**qualifiable** ['kwɑlɪ,faɪəbəl] *adj* calificable

**qualification** [,kwɑlɪfɪ'keʃən] *s* calificación; capacidad, idoneidad; requisito

**qualified** ['kwɑlɪfaɪd] *adj* calificado

**qualifier** ['kwɑlɪ,faɪər] *s* calificador; (gram.) calificativo

**qualify** ['kwɑlɪfaɪ] (*pret & pp:* **-fied**) *va* calificar; capacitar, habilitar; *vn* capacitarse, habilitarse

**qualitative** ['kwɑlɪ,tetɪv] *adj* cualitativo

**qualitative analysis** *s* (chem.) análisis cualitativo

**quality** ['kwɑlɪtɪ] *s* (*pl:* **-ties**) calidad; cualidad (*característica de una persona o cosa*); (dial.) gente de categoría; (phonet.) timbre; **in quality of** en calidad de; *adj* (coll.) de calidad, p.ej., **quality goods** mercancías de calidad

**qualm** [kwɑm] *s* escrúpulo de conciencia; duda, inquietud; basca (*malestar de estómago*)

**qualmish** ['kwɑmɪʃ] *adj* escrupuloso; bascoso

**quandary** ['kwɑndərɪ] *s* (*pl:* **-ries**) incertidumbre, perplejidad

**quantify** ['kwɑntɪfaɪ] (*pret & pp:* **-fied**) *va* cuantificar

**quantimeter** [kwɑn'tɪmɪtər] *s* cuantímetro

**quantitative** ['kwɑntɪ,tetɪv] *adj* cuantitativo

**quantitative analysis** *s* (chem.) análisis cuantitativo

**quantity** ['kwɑntɪtɪ] *s* (*pl:* **-ties**) cantidad

**quantum** ['kwɑntəm] *s* (*pl:* **-ta** [tə]) (phys.) quántum o cuanto; *adj* (phys.) cuántico

**quantum mechanics** *ssg* (phys.) mecánica cuántica

**quantum theory** *s* (phys.) teoría de los cuanta, teoría cuántica

**quarantine** ['kwɑrəntin] o ['kwɔrəntin] *s* cuarentena; estación de cuarentena; *va* poner en cuarentena

**quarrel** ['kwɑrəl] o ['kwɔrəl] *s* disputa, riña, pelea; cuadrillo (*saeta de cuatro aristas*); pequeño vidrio (*de vidriera*); cincel de albañil; **to have no quarrel with** no estar en desacuerdo con; **to pick a quarrel with** tomarse con; (*pret & pp:* **-reled** o **-relled;** *ger:* **-reling** o **-relling**) *vn* disputar, reñir, pelear

**quarrelsome** ['kwarəlsəm] o ['kwɔrəlsəm] *adj* pendenciero

**quarrier** ['kwarɪər] o ['kwɔrɪər] *s* cantero, picapedrero

**quarry** ['kwarɪ] o ['kwɔrɪ] *s* (*pl:* **-ries**) cantera, pedrera; caza, presa; rombo (*de vidrio, loza, teja, etc.*); (*pret & pp:* **-ried**) *va* sacar (*piedras*) de una cantera; sacar como de una cantera

**quart** [kwɔrt] *s* cuarto de galón

**quartan** ['kwɔrtən] *s* (path.) cuartana; *adj* cuartanal

**quarter** ['kwɔrtər] *adj* cuarto; *s* cuarto; trimestre; moneda de 25 centavos; pierna y partes adyacentes; calcañar; (astr.) cuarto de luna; (mil.) cuartel (*buen trato a los vencidos*); (naut.) cuadra; región, lugar; fuente, origen; **quarters** *spl* morada, vivienda; local; (aer.) compartimiento (*de tripulación*); (mil.) cuarteles; **at close quarters** pegados, muy cerca; **from all quarters** de todas partes; **to give no quarter to** no dar cuartel a; **to take up quarters at** alojarse en; (mil.) acuartelarse en; *va* cuartear; descuartizar; alojar, hospedar; (her. & mil.) acuartelar; *vn* alojarse, hospedarse; (mil.) acuartelarse

**quarterback** ['kwɔrtər,bæk] *s* (football) uno de cuatro jugadores que juegan detrás de la línea

**quarter day** *s* (Brit.) día en que empieza un trimestre; (Brit.) día en que se paga un trimestre

**quarterdeck** ['kwɔrtər,dɛk] *s* (naut.) alcázar

**quartered** ['kwɔrtərd] *adj* dividido en cuartos; aserrado en cuartos (*para mostrar la veta*); alojado, hospedado; (mil.) acuartelado; (her.) cuartelado

**quartered oak** *s* roble aserrado en cuartos

**quarter-hour** ['kwɔrtər'aʊr] *s* cuarto de hora; **on the quarter-hour** al cuarto en punto, cada cuarto de hora

**quartering** ['kwɔrtərɪŋ] *s* división en cuartos; acuartelamiento; (her.) acuartelamiento; (her.) cuartel

**quarterly** ['kwɔrtərlɪ] *adj* trimestral; *adv* trimestralmente; (her.) en cruz; *s* (*pl:* **-lies**) publicación o revista trimestral

**quartermaster** ['kwɔrtər,mæstər] o ['kwɔrtər,mastər] *s* (mil.) comisario; (nav.) cabo de brigadas

**quartermaster corps** *s* (mil.) cuerpo de administración militar, intendencia

**quartern** ['kwɔrtərn] *s* cuarterón (*cuarta parte*)

**quarter note** *s* (mus.) negra, semínima

**quarter round** *s* cuarto bocel

**quartersaw** ['kwɔrtər,sɔ] (*pret:* **-sawed;** *pp:* **-sawed** o **-sawn**) *va* aserrar (*un tronco*) longitudinalmente en cruz y luego en tablas

**quarter section** *s* terreno, por lo general, cuadrado, que tiene 160 acres

**quarter sessions** *spl* tribunal que se reúne trimestralmente

**quarterstaff** ['kwɔrtər,stæf] o ['kwɔrtər,staf] *s* (*pl:* **-staves** [,stevz]) pica (*lanza larga*)

**quartet** o **quartette** [kwɔr'tɛt] (mus.) cuarteto; cuarteto (*grupo de cuatro*)

**quarto** ['kwɔrto] *adj* en cuarto; *s* (*pl:* **-tos**) libro en cuarto

**quartz** [kwɔrts] *s* (mineral.) cuarzo; (min.) quijo (*mineral de oro o plata*)

**quartz glass** *s* vidrio de cuarzo

**quartziferous** [kwɔrt'sɪfərəs] *adj* cuarcífero

**quartzite** ['kwɔrtsaɪt] *s* (mineral.) cuarcita

**quartz lamp** *s* lámpara de cuarzo

**quartzose** ['kwɔrtsos] o **quartzous** ['kwɔrtsəs] *adj* cuarzoso

**quartz plate** *s* (elec.) placa de cuarzo

**quartz sand** *s* arena cuarzosa

**quash** [kwaʃ] *va* sofocar, reprimir; anular, invalidar

**quasi** ['kwesaɪ] o ['kwasɪ] *adv* cuasi

**quasi contract** *s* (law) cuasicontrato

**Quasimodo** [,kwæsɪ'modo] *s* (eccl.) cuasimodo, domingo de cuasimodo

**quassia** ['kwaʃə] *s* (bot. & pharm.) cuasia

**quaternary** [kwa'tʌrnərɪ] *adj* cuaternario; (chem.) cuaternario; *s* (*pl:* **-ries**) cuaternario; (*cap.*) *adj & s* (geol.) cuaternario

**quatrain** ['kwatren] *s* cuarteto (*verso*)

**quatrefoil** ['kætər,fɔɪl] o ['kætrə,fɔɪl] *s* (bot.) hoja cuadrifoliada, flor cuadrifoliada; (arch.) cuadrifolio

**quaver** ['kwevər] *s* temblor, estremecimiento, vibración; (mus.) trémolo, trino; (mus.) corchea; *vn* temblar, estremecerse, vibrar; (mus.) trinar

**quavery** ['kwevərɪ] *adj* tembloroso, trémulo, vibrante

**quay** [ki] *s* muelle, desembarcadero

**Que.** abr. de **Quebec**

**quean** [kwin] *s* prostituta; moza o mujer atrevida y descocada; (Scotch) moza, muchacha

**queasy** ['kwizɪ] *adj* (*comp:* **-sier;** *super:* **-siest**) bascoso; nauseabundo; fastidioso, delicado; remilgado

**queen** [kwin] *s* reina; dama o reina (*en el ajedrez*); dama (*naipe que corresponde al caballo*); abeja reina, abeja maestra; (fig.) reina; *vn* ser reina; conducirse como reina

**Queen Anne** *s* Ana Estuardo

**Queen Anne's lace** *s* (bot.) dauco, zanahoria silvestre

**queen bee** *s* abeja maestra, abeja reina; (slang) marimandona, la que lleva la voz cantante

**queen cell** *s* maestril, realera

**queen consort** *s* esposa del rey

**queendom** ['kwindəm] *s* dominio de la reina; dignidad de reina

**queen dowager** *s* reina viuda

**queenhood** ['kwinhʊd] *s* dignidad de reina

**queenly** ['kwinlɪ] *adj* (*comp:* **-lier;** *super:* **-liest**) de reina, propio de una reina; como reina; como de reina

**queen mother** *s* reina madre

**Queen of Sheba** *s* reina de Sabá

**queen olive** *s* aceituna de la reina, aceituna gordal

**queen post** *s* péndola

**queen regent** *s* reina regente (*durante la ausencia del rey*); reina reinante

**queen regnant** *s* reina reinante

**queen's English** *s* inglés castizo

**queen's ware** *s* loza inglesa de color de crema

**queer** [kwɪr] *adj* curioso, raro; estrambótico, estrafalario; indispuesto, aturdido; (coll.) sospechoso, misterioso; (slang) falso; **queer in the head** (coll.) chiflado; *va* (slang) echar a perder; (slang) comprometer

**queer fish** *s* estrafalario

**quell** [kwɛl] *va* sofocar, reprimir; mitigar (*una pena o dolor*)

**quench** [kwɛntʃ] *va* apagar; templar (*el acero*)

**quenched gap** *s* (elec.) entrehierro de chispa amortiguada

**quenching bath** *s* (metal.) baño para templar

**quenchless** ['kwɛntʃlɪs] *adj* inextinguible

**quercine** ['kwʌrsɪn] o ['kwʌrsaɪn] *adj* (bot.) cuercíneo o quercíneo

**quercitrin** ['kwʌrsɪtrɪn] *s* (chem.) quercitrina

**quercitron** ['kwʌrsɪtrən] *s* (bot.) cuercitrón o quercitrón (*árbol, corteza y colorante*)

**quern** [kwʌrn] *s* molinillo de mano

**querulous** ['kwɛrələs] o ['kwɛrjələs] *adj* querelloso, quejoso; cojijoso

**query** ['kwɪrɪ] *s* (*pl:* **-ries**) pregunta; signo de interrogación; duda, incertidumbre; (*pret & pp:* **-ried**) *va* preguntar, interrogar; marcar con signo de interrogación; dudar, expresar duda acerca de; *vn* hacer preguntas; expresar duda

**ques.** abr. de **question**

**quest** [kwɛst] *s* búsqueda; demanda (*p.ej., del Santo Grial*); **in quest of** en busca de; *va & vn* buscar

**question** ['kwɛstʃən] *s* pregunta; cuestión (*objeto de discusión*); proposición; **beside the question** que no viene al caso; **beyond question** fuera de duda; **in question** en cuestión; **out of the question** imposible, indiscutible, impensable; **to ask a question** hacer una pregunta; **to be a question of** tratarse de, ser cuestión de; **to call in question** (law) emplazar; (law) recusar; poner en duda; poner en tela de juicio; **without question** sin

duda; *va* interrogar; preguntar; cuestionar, poner en tela de juicio; *vn* interrogar, hacer preguntas
**questionable** [ˈkwɛstʃənəbəl] *adj* cuestionable
**question mark** *s* (gram.) interrogación, signo de interrogación, punto interrogante
**questionnaire** [ˌkwɛstʃənˈɛr] *s* cuestionario
**quetzal** [kɛtˈsɑl] *s* (orn.) quezal
**queue** [kju] *s* coleta; cola (*hilera de personas*); *vn* hacer cola
**quibble** [ˈkwɪbəl] *s* sutileza, subterfugio; *vn* sutilizar, emplear subterfugios
**quibbler** [ˈkwɪblər] *s* sutilizador
**quick** [kwɪk] *adj* rápido, veloz; ágil, vivo; despierto, listo, penetrante; súbito; fácil de convertir en efectivo; **quick on the draw** u **on the trigger** agudo, listo, vivo, impetuoso; *adv* aprisa, pronto; rápidamente, velozmente; *s* carne viva; (lo) más hondo del ser, (lo) más profundo del alma; **the quick** los vivos; **the quick and the dead** los vivos y los muertos; **to cut** o **to sting to the quick** herir en lo vivo, tocar en la herida
**quick-acting** [ˈkwɪkˈæktɪŋ] *adj* de acción rápida
**quick assets** *spl* (com.) disponibilidades, activo disponible
**quick-break switch** [ˈkwɪkˌbrek] *s* (elec.) interruptor de ruptura brusca
**quick-burning** [ˈkwɪkˈbʌrnɪŋ] *adj* de quema rápida
**quick-change artist** [ˈkwɪkˌtʃendʒ) *s* (theat.) transformista
**quick-change gear** *s* (mach.) engranaje de cambio rápido
**quicken** [ˈkwɪkən] *va* acelerar, avivar; aguzar, animar; *vn* acelerarse, avivarse; aguzarse, animarse
**quick-freeze** [ˈkwɪkˈfriz] (*pret:* **-froze;** *pp:* **-frozen**) *va* congelar rápidamente
**quick grass** *s* (bot.) grama del norte
**quicklime** [ˈkwɪkˌlaɪm] *s* cal viva
**quick lunch** *s* servicio rápido, servicio de la barra
**quickly** [ˈkwɪklɪ] *adv* aprisa, pronto; rápidamente, velozmente
**quickness** [ˈkwɪknɪs] *s* rapidez, velocidad; agilidad, viveza; penetración, sagacidad
**quick return** *s* (mach.) retroceso rápido
**quicksand** [ˈkwɪkˌsænd] *s* arena movediza
**quickset** [ˈkwɪkˌsɛt] *s* arbusto vivo; seto vivo; *adj* hecho de arbustos vivos
**quick-setting** [ˈkwɪkˈsɛtɪŋ] *adj* de fraguado rápido
**quicksilver** [ˈkwɪkˌsɪlvər] *s* azogue; *va* azogar
**quickstep** [ˈkwɪkˌstɛp] *s* pasacalle; marcha escrita en compás acelerado; paso acelerado
**quick-tempered** [ˈkwɪkˈtɛmpərd] *adj* vivo de genio, irascible
**quick time** *s* (mil.) paso redoblado, paso forzado
**quick trick** *s* (cards) baza rápida
**quick-witted** [ˈkwɪkˈwɪtɪd] *adj* despierto, listo, perspicaz
**quid** [kwɪd] *s* mascada de tabaco; (*pl:* **quid**) (Brit. slang) libra esterlina
**quiddity** [ˈkwɪdɪtɪ] *s* (*pl:* **-ties**) esencia, quid; quisquilla, sutileza
**quidnunc** [ˈkwɪdˌnʌŋk] *s* correveidile, curioso
**quiescence** [kwaɪˈɛsəns] *s* quietud, reposo; (gram.) quiescencia
**quiescent** [kwaɪˈɛsənt] *adj* quieto, reposado; (gram.) quiescente
**quiet** [ˈkwaɪət] *adj* quieto; silencioso, callado; (com.) encalmado (*mercado*); **to keep quiet** estarse callado; *adv* quietamente; calladamente; *s* quietud; silencio; **on the quiet** a las calladas, de callada; *va* aquietar; *vn* aquietarse
**quietism** [ˈkwaɪətɪzəm] *s* quietismo
**quietist** [ˈkwaɪətɪst] *adj & s* quietista
**quietness** [ˈkwaɪətnɪs] *s* quietud; silencio
**quietude** [ˈkwaɪətjud] o [ˈkwaɪətud] *s* quietud
**quietus** [kwaɪˈitəs] *s* golpe decisivo; muerte
**quill** [kwɪl] *s* pluma de ave; cañón de pluma; púa (*del erizo, puerco espín, etc.*)
**quill driver** *s* (scornful) cagatintas
**quillwort** [ˈkwɪlˌwʌrt] *s* (bot.) isoete; (bot.) eupatorio purpúreo
**quilt** [kwɪlt] *s* edredón; *va* acolchar
**quilting** [ˈkwɪltɪŋ] *s* trabajo de acolchado; género acolchado; material para edredones
**quilting bee** *s* grupo de damas reunidas para hacer edredones
**quince** [kwɪns] *s* (bot.) membrillo (*árbol y fruto*)
**quincunx** [ˈkwɪnkʌŋks] *s* (hort.) quincunce; **in a quincunx** o **in quincunxes** a o al tresbolillo
**quinin** [ˈkwɪnɪn] o **quinine** [ˈkwaɪnaɪn] o [kwɪˈnin] *s* (chem.) quinina
**quinoline** [ˈkwɪnəlin] *s* (chem.) quinoleína o quinolina
**quinquagenarian** [ˌkwɪnkwədʒɪˈnɛrɪən] *adj & s* quincuagenario
**Quinquagesima** [ˌkwɪnkwəˈdʒɛsɪmə] *s* (eccl.) quincuagésima
**quinquennial** [kwɪnˈkwɛnɪəl] *adj* quinquenal
**quinquennium** [kwɪnˈkwɛnɪəm] *s* (*pl:* **-a** [ə]) quinquenio
**quinquereme** [ˈkwɪnkwɪrim] *s* quinquerreme
**quinsy** [ˈkwɪnzɪ] *s* (path.) esquinencia, cinanquia
**quint** [kwɪnt] *s* (coll.) quintillizo
**quintal** [ˈkwɪntəl] *s* quintal
**quinte** [kæ̃t] *s* (fencing) quinta
**quintessence** [kwɪnˈtɛsəns] *s* quintaesencia
**quintessential** [ˌkwɪntɛˈsɛnʃəl] *adj* quintaesenciado
**quintet** o **quintette** [kwɪnˈtɛt] *s* (mus.) quinteto; quinteto (*grupo de cinco*)
**quintile** [ˈkwɪntɪl] o [ˈkwɪntaɪl] *s* quintilo
**Quintilian** [kwɪnˈtɪljən] *s* Quintiliano
**quintillion** [kwɪnˈtɪljən] *s* (U.S.A.) trillón; (Brit.) quintillón
**quintuple** [ˈkwɪntjupəl], [ˈkwɪntupəl], [kwɪnˈtjupəl] o [kwɪnˈtupəl] *adj & s* quíntuplo; *adv* cinco veces; cinco veces mayor; *va* quintuplicar; *vn* quintuplicarse
**quintuplet** [ˈkwɪntjuplɛt], [ˈkwɪntuplɛt], [kwɪnˈtjuplɛt] o [kwɪnˈtuplɛt] *s* grupo de cinco; quintillizo
**quintuplication** [kwɪnˌtjuplɪˈkeʃən] o [kwɪnˌtuplɪˈkeʃən] *s* quintuplicación
**quip** [kwɪp] *s* agudeza, ocurrencia; pulla, chufleta; sutileza, subterfugio; (*pret & pp:* **quipped;** *ger:* **quipping**) *va* decir en son de burla; *vn* burlarse, echar pullas
**quipster** [ˈkwɪpstər] *s* chistoso, pullista
**quire** [kwaɪr] *s* mano de papel; (b.b.) alzado
**Quirinal** [ˈkwɪrɪnəl] *adj* quirinal; *s* Quirinal
**quirk** [kwʌrk] *s* rareza (*acción caprichosa*); agudeza, ocurrencia; sutileza, subterfugio; vuelta repentina; rasgo (*en la escritura*)
**quirt** [kwʌrt] *s* látigo con mango corto y correa de cuero crudo retorcido
**quisling** [ˈkwɪzlɪŋ] *s* quisling (*traidor a la patria*)
**quit** [kwɪt] *adj* libre, descargado, sin obligaciones; **quits** *adj* en paz, corrientes (*por medio del pago o venganza*); **to be quits** estar desquitados; **to cry quits** pedir treguas; (*pret & pp:* **quit** o **quitted;** *ger:* **quitting**) *va* dejar; pagar (*una deuda*); **to quit** + *ger* dejar de + *inf; vn* irse, marcharse; parar; (coll.) dejar de trabajar
**quitch** [kwɪtʃ] o **quitch grass** *s* (bot.) grama del norte
**quitclaim** [ˈkwɪtˌklem] *s* (law) renuncia; *va* (law) renunciar (*p.ej., una herencia*)
**quite** [kwaɪt] *adv* absolutamente, enteramente; verdaderamente; (coll.) bastante, muy
**quitrent** [ˈkwɪtˌrɛnt] *s* (feud.) censo que se pagaba en dinero en vez de trabajo
**quittance** [ˈkwɪtəns] *s* quitanza; pago, retorno
**quitter** [ˈkwɪtər] *s* remolón, persona que deja fácilmente lo empezado, persona que se da fácilmente por vencida; desertor (*de una causa*)
**quiver** [ˈkwɪvər] *s* temblor, estremecimiento; aljaba, carcaj; *vn* temblar, estremecerse
**quiverleaf** [ˈkwɪvərˌlif] *s* (bot.) alamillo
**qui vive** [kiˈviv] (Fr.) ¿quién vive?; **to be on the qui vive** estar alerta
**Quixote** [ˈkwɪksət] *s* (fig.) quijote (*hombre quijotesco*)
**quixotic** [kwɪksˈɑtɪk] *adj* quijotesco
**quixotically** [kwɪksˈɑtɪkəlɪ] *adv* quijotescamente

**quixotism** ['kwɪksətɪzəm] *s* quijotismo; quijotada (*acto*)
**quixotry** ['kwɪksətrɪ] *s* quijotería
**quiz** [kwɪz] *s* (*pl:* **quizzes**) examen escrito u oral; broma pesada; bromista; (*pret & pp:* **quizzed;** *ger:* **quizzing**) *va* examinar; interrogar; burlarse de; mirar con aire burlón
**quiz game** *s* torneo de preguntas y respuestas
**quiz master** *s* (rad. & telv.) animador de un programa de preguntas y respuestas
**quiz program** *s* (rad. & telv.) programa de preguntas y respuestas, torneo radiofónico
**quiz section** *s* (educ.) clase dedicada a preguntas y respuestas, grupo de práctica
**quizzical** ['kwɪzɪkəl] *adj* curioso, raro; cómico; burlón, gracioso
**quizzing glass** *s* monóculo con mango
**quodlibet** ['kwadlɪbɛt] *s* cuodlibeto; (mus.) fantasía, miscelánea
**quodlibetic** [ˌkwadlɪ'bɛtɪk] o **quodlibetical** [ˌkwadlɪ'bɛtɪkəl] *adj* cuodlibético
**quoin** [kɔɪn] o [kwɔɪn] *s* esquina; piedra angular; cuña; (print.) cuña; *va* (print.) acuñar
**quoin post** *s* poste de quicio, poste de esclusa
**quoit** [kwɔɪt] o [kɔɪt] *s* herrón, tejo; **quoits** *ssg* hito (*juego de tejos*)
**quondam** ['kwandæm] *adj* antiguo, de otro tiempo
**Quonset hut** ['kwansɪt] *s* cobertizo de metal semicilíndrico
**quorum** ['kworəm] *s* quórum
**quot.** abr. de **quotation**
**quota** ['kwotə] *s* cuota
**quotable** ['kwotəbəl] *adj* citable
**quota system** *s* sistema de cuotas
**quotation** [kwo'teʃən] *s* cita (*de un texto*); (com.) cotización
**quotation marks** *spl* comillas
**quote** [kwot] *s* (coll.) cita; (coll.) cotización; **quotes** *spl* (coll.) comillas; **close quote** fin de la cita; *va & vn* citar; cotizar; **quote** cito
**quoteworthy** ['kwotˌwʌrðɪ] *adj* digno de citarse
**quoth** [kwoθ] *1ª y 3ª personas del sg del pret* (archaic) dije, dijo
**quotha** ['kwoθə] *interj* (archaic) ¡no digas!, ¡vaya!
**quotidian** [kwo'tɪdɪən] *adj* cotidiano; *s* fiebre cotidiana
**quotient** ['kwoʃənt] *s* (math.) cociente
**quo warranto** [kwo wa'rænto] *s* (law) notificación legal por la cual se pregunta a una persona con qué derecho tiene ciertos privilegios y franquicias; (law) proceso legal emprendido contra tal persona
**q.v.** abr. de **quod vide** (Lat.) **which see**
**qy.** abr. de **query**

# R

**R, r** [ɑr] *s* (*pl:* **R's, r's** [ɑrz]) décimoctava letra del alfabeto inglés; **the three R's (reading, 'riting, and 'rithmetic)** lectura, escritura y aritmética
**r.** abr. de **railroad, railway, road, rod, ruble** y **rupee**
**R.** abr. de **railroad, railway, Regina** (Lat.) **Queen, Republican, response, Rex** (Lat.) **King, River** y **Royal**
**R.A.** abr. de **Rear Admiral, Royal Academy** y **Royal Artillery**
**rabbet** ['ræbɪt] *s* (carp.) barbilla, rebajo, muesca; (carp.) embarbillado; *va* (carp.) embarbillar, rebajar; (carp.) cortar una muesca en
**rabbi** ['ræbaɪ] *s* (*pl:* **-bis** o **-bies**) rabino
**rabbinic** [rə'bɪnɪk] o **rabbinical** [rə'bɪnɪkəl] *adj* rabínico; **Rabbinic** *s* lengua rabínica
**rabbinism** ['ræbɪnɪzəm] *s* rabinismo
**rabbinist** ['ræbɪnɪst] *s* rabinista
**rabbit** ['ræbɪt] *s* (zool.) conejo
**rabble** ['ræbəl] *s* canalla, chusma; multitud turbulenta; (found.) hurgón
**rabble rouser** *s* populachero, alborotapueblos
**rabble-rousing** ['ræbəl,raʊzɪŋ] *adj* populachero
**Rabelaisian** [,ræbə'lezɪən] *adj & s* rabelesiano
**rabic** ['ræbɪk] *adj* (med. & vet.) rábico
**rabid** ['ræbɪd] *adj* rabioso
**rabies** ['rebiz] o ['rebɪiz] *s* (path.) rabia
**raccoon** [ræ'kun] *s* (zool.) mapache, oso lavador; piel de mapache
**race** [res] *s* raza; buena casta, buen abolengo; carrera; sabor o gusto particular (*del vino*); certamen (*que sugiere una carrera*); movimiento progresivo; corriente de agua fuerte y veloz; caz (*para tomar y conducir el agua*); **to run a race** correr una carrera; *va* competir con, en una carrera; hacer correr de prisa; acelerar (*un motor*) al máximo, hacer funcionar (*un motor*) a velocidad excesiva; **I'll race you to the corner** a ver quién llega primero a la esquina; *vn* correr de prisa; correr en una carrera; competir en una carrera; embalarse (*un motor*); (naut.) regatear
**race course** *s* pista de carreras; autódromo
**race hatred** *s* odio de razas
**race horse** *s* caballo de carreras
**raceme** [ræ'sim] *s* (bot.) racimo
**racemose** ['ræsɪmos] *adj* (bot.) racimoso
**racer** ['resər] *s* corredor; caballo de carreras; auto de carrera
**race riot** *s* disturbio racista, motín entre gentes de razas distintas
**race suicide** *s* suicidio de la raza
**race track** *s* carrera, pista de carreras, hipódromo
**race wire service** *s* servicio telegráfico y telefónico de noticias turfistas
**Rachel** ['retʃəl] *s* Raquel
**rachialgia** [,rekɪ'ældʒɪə] *s* (path.) raquialgia
**rachidian** [rə'kɪdɪən] *adj* raquídeo
**rachis** ['rekɪs] *s* (*pl:* **rachises** o **rachides** ['rækɪdiz] o ['rekɪdiz]) (anat. & bot.) raquis; cañón de pluma
**rachitic** [rə'kɪtɪk] *adj* raquítico
**rachitis** [rə'kaɪtɪs] *s* (path.) raquitis
**rachitome** ['rekɪtom] *s* (surg.) raquítomo
**rachitomy** [rə'kɪtəmɪ] *s* (surg.) raquitomía
**racial** ['reʃəl] *adj* racial
**racing car** *s* (aut.) coche de carreras
**racing form** *s* programa de las carreras de caballos
**racism** ['resɪzəm] *s* racismo
**racist** ['resɪst] *adj & s* racista
**rack** [ræk] *s* estante; percha (*en que se cuelga la ropa*); red de equipaje (*en los trenes*); pesebre; astillero; armero; rambla (*para estirar los paños*); paso fino (*del caballo*); nube pasajera que el viento arrastra en girones; recorrido de una tempestad; destrucción, ruina; dolor, tormento; caballete (*en que se daba tormento*); vestigio; (mach.) cremallera; **on the rack** en gran dolor, en gran sufrimiento; **to go to rack and ruin** caer en un estado de ruina total; **rack and pinion** cremallera y piñón; *va* estirar, forzar; atormentar; torturar en el caballete; despedazar; agobiar, oprimir; **to rack off** trasegar (*el vino*); **to rack one's brains** calentarse la cabeza, devanarse los sesos; *vn* caminar (*el caballo*) a paso fino
**rack-and-pinion jack** ['rækənd'pɪnjən] *s* gato de cremallera
**racket** ['rækɪt] *s* (sport) raqueta; raqueta (*para andar por la nieve*); alboroto, baraúnda; esfuerzo, pena, trabajo; (slang) trapisonda, trapacería; **rackets** *ssg* juego parecido al tenis que se juega en una cancha rodeada de paredes altas; **to raise a racket** armar un alboroto
**racketeer** [,rækɪ'tɪr] *s* trapisondista, trapacista; *vn* trapacear
**rack rail** *s* carril de cremallera
**rack railway** *s* ferrocarril de cremallera
**raconteur** [,rækɑn'tʌr] *s* cuentista
**racoon** [ræ'kun] *s* var. de **raccoon**
**racquet** ['rækɪt] *s* (sport) raqueta; raqueta (*para andar por la nieve*); **racquets** *ssg* var. de **rackets**
**racy** ['resɪ] *adj* (*comp:* **-ier;** *super:* **-iest**) espiritoso, vivo de genio; chispeante; que tiene aroma, fragancia, sabor especial; picante (*algo libre*)
**rad.** abr. de **radical**
**radar** ['redɑr] *s* (elec.) radar
**radar-controlled** ['redɑrkən'trold] *adj* mandado por radar
**radarscope** ['redɑrskop] *s* radarscopio o radaroscopio
**radar screen** *s* antena de radar
**raddle** ['rædəl] *s* almagre; *va* pintar o marcar con almagre; pintar (*el rostro*); entrelazar
**radial** ['redɪəl] *adj* radial
**radial engine** *s* motor radial
**radial-flow turbine** ['redɪəl,flo] *s* turbina radial
**radian** ['redɪən] *s* (math.) radián
**radiance** ['redɪəns] o **radiancy** ['redɪənsɪ] *s* brillo, resplandor; (phys.) radiación
**radiant** ['redɪənt] *adj* radiante, resplandeciente; (phys.) radiante; (fig.) radiante (*alegre, sonriente*); *s* (astr.) radiante
**radiant energy** *s* (phys.) energía radiante
**radiant-panel heat** ['redɪənt,pænəl] *s* calefacción a panel radiante
**radiate** ['redɪet] *adj* radiado; (bot. & zool.) radiado; *s* (zool.) radiado; *va* radiar; difundir (*p.ej., felicidad*); *vn* radiar, irradiar; extenderse de un punto central
**radiation** [,redɪ'eʃən] *s* radiación
**radiation sickness** *s* (path.) enfermedad de radiación, mal de rayos
**radiator** ['redɪ,etər] *s* radiador
**radiator cap** *s* (aut.) tapón de radiador
**radical** ['rædɪkəl] *adj* radical; (bot., chem., math., philol. & pol.) radical; *s* raíz, principio fundamental; (chem., math., philol. & pol.) radical
**radical-changing verb** ['rædɪkəl'tʃendʒɪŋ] *s* (gram.) verbo que cambia la vocal de la raíz
**radicalism** ['rædɪkəlɪzəm] *s* radicalismo
**radical sign** *s* (math.) signo de radicación
**radicle** ['rædɪkəl] *s* (bot.) radícula
**radio** ['redɪo] *s* (*pl:* **-os**) radio (*emisión; aparato*); (coll.) radiograma; **on the radio** en la radio; *adj* de radio; *va* radiar, radiodifundir

**radioactive** [ˌredɪoˈæktɪv] *adj* radiactivo
**radioactive carbon** *s* (phys.) radiocarbono
**radioactivity** [ˌredɪoækˈtɪvɪtɪ] *s* radiactividad
**radio amateur** *s* radioaficionado
**radio announcer** *s* locutor de la radio
**radioastronomy** [ˌredɪoəˈstrɑnəmɪ] *s* radioastronomía
**radio beacon** *s* radiofaro
**radio beam** *s* haz del radiofaro
**radiobiology** [ˌredɪobaɪˈɑlədʒɪ] *s* radiobiología
**radiobroadcasting** [ˌredɪoˈbrɔdˌkæstɪŋ] o [ˌredɪoˈbrɔdˌkɑstɪŋ] *s* radiodifusión
**radiobroadcasting station** *s* radiodifusora, radioemisora
**radiochemistry** [ˌredɪoˈkɛmɪstrɪ] *s* radioquímica
**radio commentator** *s* comentarista de la radio
**radio compass** *s* radiobrújula
**radioelement** [ˌredɪoˈɛlɪmənt] *s* (chem.) radioelemento
**Radio Free Europe** *s* Radio Europa Libre
**radio frequency** *s* (rad.) radiofrecuencia
**radio-frequency** [ˌredɪoˈfrikwənsɪ] *adj* (rad.) de radiofrecuencia
**radiogoniometer** [ˌredɪoˌgonɪˈɑmɪtər] *s* radiogoniómetro
**radiogoniometry** [ˌredɪoˌgonɪˈɑmɪtrɪ] *s* radiogoniometría
**radiogram** [ˈredɪoˌgræm] *s* radiograma
**radiograph** [ˈredɪoˌgræf] o [ˈredɪoˌgrɑf] *s* radiografía; *va* radiografiar
**radiographic** [ˌredɪoˈgræfɪk] *adj* radiográfico
**radiography** [ˌredɪˈɑgrəfɪ] *s* radiografía
**radioisotope** [ˌredɪoˈaɪsotop] *s* radioisótopo
**radiolarian** [ˌredɪoˈlɛrɪən] *s* (zool.) radiolario
**radio listener** *s* radioyente, radioescucha
**radiolocation** [ˌredɪoloˈkeʃən] *s* radiolocalización
**radiologist** [ˌredɪˈɑlədʒɪst] *s* radiólogo
**radiology** [ˌredɪˈɑlədʒɪ] *s* radiología
**radiometer** [ˌredɪˈɑmɪtər] *s* radiómetro
**radiometry** [ˌredɪˈɑmɪtrɪ] *s* radiometría
**radio network** *s* red de emisoras, red radioemisora, cadena de radiodifusoras
**radio newscaster** *s* cronista de radio
**radiopaque** [ˌredɪoˈpek] *adj* radiopaco
**radiophone** [ˈredɪoˌfon] *s* (phys.) radiófono; (rad.) radioteléfono
**radiophonic** [ˌredɪoˈfɑnɪk] *adj* radiofónico
**radiophonograph** [ˌredɪoˈfonəgræf] o [ˌredɪoˈfonəgrɑf] *s* radiofonógrafo, radiogramófono
**radiophony** [ˌredɪˈɑfənɪ] *s* (phys. & rad.) radiofonía
**radiophoto** [ˌredɪoˈfoto] *s* (*pl:* **-tos**) radiofoto; *adj* de radiofoto
**radio receiver** *s* radiorreceptor, radiorreceptora
**radio repairs** *spl* radiorreparaciones
**radioscopy** [ˌredɪˈɑskəpɪ] *s* radioscopia
**radiosensitive** [ˌredɪoˈsɛnsɪtɪv] *adj* radiosensitivo
**radio set** *s* aparato de radio; radiorreceptor
**radiosonde** [ˈredɪoˌsɑnd] *s* (meteor.) radiosonda
**radio spectrum** *s* (phys.) espectro de radio, espectro electromagnético
**radio station** *s* radioestación, estación emisora
**radiotelegraph** [ˌredɪoˈtɛlɪgræf] o [ˌredɪoˈtɛlɪgrɑf] *s* radiotelégrafo; *va* radiotelegrafiar
**radiotelegraphy** [ˌredɪotɪˈlɛgrəfɪ] *s* radiotelegrafía
**radiotelephone** [ˌredɪoˈtɛlɪfon] *s* radioteléfono; *va* radiotelefonear
**radiotelephony** [ˌredɪotɪˈlɛfənɪ] *s* radiotelefonía
**radio telescope** *s* radiotelescopio
**radiotherapy** [ˌredɪoˈθɛrəpɪ] *s* radioterapia
**radiothermy** [ˈredɪoˌθʌrmɪ] *s* radiotermia
**radiothorium** [ˌredɪoˈθorɪəm] *s* (chem.) radiotorio
**radio transmitter** *s* radiotransmisor
**radiotron** [ˈredɪətrɑn] *s* (trademark) radiotrón
**radio tube** *s* lámpara termoiónica, tubo radiógeno, tubo de radio
**radio wave** *s* onda de radio, radioonda
**radish** [ˈrædɪʃ] *s* (bot.) rábano
**radium** [ˈredɪəm] *s* (chem.) radio
**radius** [ˈredɪəs] *s* (*pl:* **-i** [aɪ] o **-uses**) (anat. & geom.) radio; radio (*p.ej., de acción*); **within a radius of** en . . . a la redonda, p.ej., **within a radius of five kilometers** en cinco kilómetros a la redonda
**radix** [ˈredɪks] *s* (*pl:* **radices** [ˈrædɪsiz] o [ˈredɪsiz] o **radixes**) (bot. & gram.) raíz; (math.) base (*para un sistema de números*)
**radome** [ˈredom] *s* (electron.) cúpula protectora de la antena
**radon** [ˈredɑn] *s* (chem.) radón
**radula** [ˈrædʒʊlə] *s* (*pl:* **-lae** [li]) (zool.) rádula
**R.A.F.** abr. de **Royal Air Force**
**raffia** [ˈræfɪə] *s* (bot.) rafia (*palmera y fibra*)
**raffle** [ˈræfəl] *s* rifa; *va & vn* rifar
**raft** [ræft] o [rɑft] *s* balsa, armadía; (coll.) gran número; *va* convertir en balsa; transportar en balsa; pasar en balsa
**rafter** [ˈræftər] o [ˈrɑftər] *s* par (*de un cuchillo de armadura*); cabrio, contrapar
**rag** [ræg] *s* trapo; (slang) fisga (*burla*); **rags** *spl* trapos (*prendas de vestir*); andrajos, harapos; **to be in rags** estar en andrajos; **to chew the rag** (slang) dar la lengua; (*pret & pp:* **ragged**; *ger:* **ragging**) *va* (slang) regañar; (slang) hacer fisga a
**ragamuffin** [ˈrægəˌmʌfɪn] *s* pelagatos; golfo, chiquillo haraposo
**rag baby** o **rag doll** *s* muñeca de trapo
**rage** [redʒ] *s* rabia; ardor, entusiasmo; violencia; boga, moda; **to be all the rage** estar en boga, estar de moda, hacer furor; **to fly into a rage** montar en cólera, montar en furor; *vn* arrebatarse; entusiasmarse
**ragged** [ˈrægɪd] *adj* andrajoso, harapiento, haraposo; áspero, desigual, raspado; cortado en dientes
**raglan** [ˈræglən] *s* raglán
**ragman** [ˈrægˌmæn] *s* (*pl:* **-men**) andrajero, trapero
**ragout** [ræˈgu] *s* (cook.) guisado
**ragpicker** [ˈrægˌpɪkər] *s* andrajero, trapero
**ragtag** [ˈrægˌtæg] *s* chusma, populacho; **ragtag and bobtail** canalla, gentuza
**ragtime** [ˈrægˌtaɪm] *s* (coll.) ritmo musical con acentos irregulares; (coll.) música popular de acentos irregulares
**ragweed** [ˈrægˌwid] *s* (bot.) ambrosía
**ragwort** [ˈrægˌwʌrt] *s* (bot.) hierba de Santiago
**rah** [rɑ] *interj* ¡ viva!, ¡ hurra!
**raid** [red] *s* ataque inesperado; invasión, incursión; *va* atacar inesperadamente; invadir; capturar (*p.ej., la policía un garito*)
**raider** [ˈredər] *s* invasor; buque corsario
**rail** [rel] *s* carril, riel; barandilla; guardalado (*p.ej., de un puente*); apoyo para los pies (*en un bar*); listón de madera; (naut.) obra muerta; (orn.) rascón, ralo acuático; bance (*para cerrar un portillo*); (carp.) peinazo (*p.ej., de una puerta*); **rails** *spl* títulos o valores de ferrocarril; **by rail** por ferrocarril; **off the rails** descarrilado; *adj* ferroviario; *va* poner barandilla a; **to rail off** cercar con barandilla; *vn* quejarse amargamente; **to rail at** injuriar, ultrajar
**rail car** *s* automotriz
**rail center** *s* centro ferroviario
**rail chair** *s* (rail.) cojinete
**rail fence** *s* cerca hecha de palos horizontales
**railhead** [ˈrelˌhɛd] *s* término de vía de un ferrocarril en construcción; cabeza de carril; (mil.) estación ferroviaria de víveres y municiones
**railing** [ˈrelɪŋ] *s* barandilla, pasamano
**raillery** [ˈrelərɪ] o [ˈrælərɪ] *s* (*pl:* **-ies**) burla, chanza, zumba
**railroad** [ˈrelˌrod] *s* ferrocarril; *adj* ferroviario; *va* enviar por ferrocarril; llevar o transportar por ferrocarril; (coll.) llevar a cabo con demasiada precipitación; (slang) encarcelar falsamente; *vn* trabajar en el ferrocarril, ser ferrocarrilero
**railroad car** *s* coche o vagón ferroviario
**railroad crossing** *s* paso a nivel
**railroader** [ˈrelˌrodər] *s* ferrocarrilero, ferroviario
**railroading** [ˈrelˌrodɪŋ] *s* construcción y manejo de ferrocarriles; trabajo en el ferrocarril; (coll.) ejecución demasiado apresurada
**railway** [ˈrelˌwe] *s* ferrocarril; *adj* ferroviario
**raiment** [ˈremənt] *s* prendas de vestir
**rain** [ren] *s* lluvia; (fig.) lluvia; **the rains** la época de las lluvias; *va* llover (*enviar como llu-*

*via*); *vn* llover; **it is raining** llueve; **to rain on** llover sobre; **rain or shine** llueva o no, con buen o mal tiempo
**rainbow** ['ren,bo] *s* arco iris; *adj* irisado
**rainbow trout** *s* (ichth.) trucha arco iris
**rain check** *s* billete que se devuelve a los espectadores de un espectáculo al aire libre en caso de lluvia
**rain cloud** *s* nube de lluvia
**raincoat** ['ren,kot] *s* impermeable, chubasquero
**raindrop** ['ren,drɑp] *s* gota de lluvia
**rainfall** ['ren,fɔl] *s* lluvia repentina; precipitación acuosa
**rain gage** o **gauge** *s* pluviómetro
**rainproof** ['ren,pruf] *adj* impermeable, a prueba de lluvia
**rainstorm** ['ren,stɔrm] *s* tempestad de lluvia
**rain water** *s* agua lluvia, agua llovediza
**rainy** ['renɪ] *adj* (*comp:* **-ier;** *super:* **-iest**) lluvioso
**rainy day** *s* día lluvioso; tiempo futuro de posible necesidad; **to save up for a rainy day** ahorrar dinero para asegurarse el porvenir
**rainy season** *s* estación de las lluvias
**raise** [rez] *s* aumento; alza, subida; *va* levantar; criar (*a niños, animales*); cultivar (*plantas*); reunir (*dinero*); suscitar (*una duda*); resucitar (*a los muertos*); avistar, columbrar; dejarse (*barba, bigote*); poner (*una objeción*); plantear (*una pregunta*); aumentar; aumentar fraudulentamente el valor de (*un cheque*); levantar (*tropas; un sitio*); (math.) elevar (*a potencias*)
**raised** [rezd] *adj* saliente, en relieve, de realce
**raiser** ['rezər] *s* criador (*p.ej., de ganado*); cultivador (*p.ej., de legumbres*)
**raisin** ['rezən] *s* pasa (*uva seca*)
**raison d'être** ['rezɔn 'dɛtrə] *s* razón de ser
**rajah** o **raja** ['rɑdʒə] *s* rajá
**rake** [rek] *s* rastro, rastrillo; rastrilladora (*rastro montado sobre dos ruedas*); raqueta (*de la mesa de juego*); calavera, libertino; desviación de la vertical; *va* rastrillar; escudriñar; atizar, avivar; barrer (*p.ej., una línea de soldados con una ametralladora*); **to rake together** acumular (*p.ej., dinero*); *vn* rastrear
**rake-off** ['rek,ɔf] o ['rek,ɑf] *s* (slang) dinero u otra cosa obtenida ilícitamente
**rakish** ['rekɪʃ] *adj* airoso, gallardo; listo, vivo; libertino
**râle** [rɑl] *s* estertor
**rally** ['rælɪ] *s* (*pl:* **-lies**) reunión popular, reunión política; recuperación, recobro; (tennis) acción de pegar la pelota de un lado para otro repetidas veces; (*pret & pp:* **-lied**) *va* reunir; reanimar; recobrar (*la fuerza, la salud, el ánimo*); ridiculizar, embromar; *vn* reunirse; reunirse y rehacerse; recobrarse (*p.ej., los precios en la Bolsa*); recobrar la fuerza, la salud, el ánimo; **to rally to the side of** acudir a, ir en socorro de
**Ralph** [rælf] *s* Rodolfo
**ram** [ræm] *s* (zool.) carnero; pisón; (naut.) espolón; (naut.) buque con espolón; émbolo de percusión (*de una bomba*); ariete hidráulico; (*cap.*) *s* (astr.) Aries; (*l.c.*) (*pret & pp:* **rammed;** *ger:* **ramming**) *va* dar contra, pegar contra, chocar en (*p.ej., un camión*); atestar, rellenar; apisonar; (naut.) atacar con espolón; *vn* chocar; **to ram into** chocar en
**Ramadan** [,ræmə'dɑn] *s* el Ramadán
**ramble** ['ræmbəl] *s* paseo; *vn* pasear; divagar (*andar a la ventura; hablar apartándose del asunto*); serpentear (*p.ej., un río*); extenderse serpenteando (*como hacen las enredaderas*)
**rambler** ['ræmblər] *s* paseador, vagabundo; divagador; (bot.) rosal de enredadera
**rambling** ['ræmblɪŋ] *adj* divagador; encantado (*dícese de una casa grande*); *s* divagación
**rambunctious** [ræm'bʌŋkʃəs] *adj* (slang) revoltoso, inmanejable; (slang) alborotado, turbulento
**ramekin** o **ramequin** ['ræmɪkɪn] *s* quesadilla; pequeña cazuela para quesadillas
**Rameses** ['ræmɪsiz] *s* Ramsés
**ramie** ['ræmɪ] *s* (bot.) ramio; ramina (*fibra*)
**ramification** [,ræmɪfɪ'keʃən] *s* ramificación
**ramify** ['ræmɪfaɪ] (*pret & pp:* **-fied**) *va* ramificar; *vn* ramificarse
**ram-jet engine** ['ræm,dʒɛt] *s* (aer.) motor autorreactor, estatorreactor, pulsorreactor
**rammer** ['ræmər] *s* pisón; baqueta de fusil
**rammish** ['ræmɪʃ] *adj* carneruno; maloliente; libidinoso
**ramose** ['remos] o [rə'mos] *adj* ramoso
**ramous** ['reməs] *adj* ramoso; ramiforme
**ramp** [ræmp] *s* rampa; *vn* moverse con violencia; saltar o precipitarse con furia; pararse en las patas traseras con la mano abierta y las garras tendidas
**rampage** ['ræmpedʒ] *s* alboroto; **to go on a rampage** alborotar, comportarse como un loco; [ræm'pedʒ] o ['ræmpedʒ] *vn* alborotar, comportarse como un loco
**rampancy** ['ræmpənsɪ] *s* exuberancia, extravagancia; violencia, desenfreno
**rampant** ['ræmpənt] *adj* exuberante, extravagante; violento, desenfrenado; (her.) rampante
**rampant arch** *s* (arch.) arco por tranquil, arco en rampa
**rampart** ['ræmpɑrt] *s* (fort.) terraplén; muralla; defensa, amparo
**rampion** ['ræmpɪən] *s* (bot.) rapónchigo
**ramrod** ['ræm,rɑd] *s* baqueta, atacador
**ramshackle** ['ræm,ʃækəl] *adj* desvencijado, destartalado
**ran** [ræn] *pret de* **run**
**ranch** [ræntʃ] *s* hacienda, granja; hacendados; *vn* trabajar en una hacienda; dirigir una hacienda
**rancher** ['ræntʃər] *s* hacendado
**ranchman** ['ræntʃmən] *s* (*pl:* **-men**) hacendado
**rancid** ['rænsɪd] *adj* rancio
**rancidity** [ræn'sɪdɪtɪ] *s* rancidez, ranciedad
**rancor** ['ræŋkər] *s* rencor
**rancorous** ['ræŋkərəs] *adj* rencoroso
**Randolph** ['rændɑlf] *s* Randolfo
**random** ['rændəm] *adj* casual, fortuito, sin proyectar; **at random** al azar, a la ventura
**ranee** ['rɑnɪ] *s* raní
**rang** [ræŋ] *pret de* **ring**
**range** [rendʒ] *s* escala (*p.ej., de velocidades, precios*); fila, hilera, ringlera; alcance; divagación; línea de tiro; campo de tiro; terreno de pasto; cordillera; línea de dirección; campo de actividad; autonomía (*p.ej., de un buque o avión*); cocina económica, hornillo; extensión (*de la voz*); serie o gama (*de colores*); clase, orden; **at close range** a quema ropa; **within range** a tiro; **within range of** al alcance de; *va* alinear; recorrer (*un terreno, el bosque*); ir a lo largo de (*la costa*); arreglar, ordenar; *vn* variar, fluctuar (*entre ciertos límites*); extenderse; divagar, errar; ponerse en fila; **to range over** recorrer
**range finder** *s* telémetro
**range pole** *s* (surv.) jalón
**ranger** ['rendʒər] *s* guardamayor de bosque; recorredor; perro ventor
**Rangoon** [ræŋ'gun] *s* Rangún
**rangy** ['rendʒɪ] *adj* (*comp:* **-ier;** *super:* **-iest**) ágil; de patas largas y fino de ancas; ancho, espacioso
**rani** ['rɑnɪ] *s* (*pl:* **-nis**) raní
**rank** [ræŋk] *s* fila; (mil.) grado, empleo; categoría, rango; condición, posición; distinción; **the ranks** los soldados de fila; el pueblo, la gente común; **to break ranks** (mil.) romper filas; **to close ranks** estrechar las distancias; (mil.) cerrar las filas; **to reduce to the ranks** degradar; **to rise from the ranks** llegar a oficial (*de soldado raso*); *adj* lozano, exuberante; denso, espeso; grosero; maloliente; excesivo, extremado; incorregible, rematado; indecente, vulgar; *va* alinear; ordenar; tener posición o grado más alto que; *vn* tener (cierta) posición o grado; ocupar el último grado; **to rank high** ocupar alta posición; ser tenido en alta estima; sobresalir; **to rank low** ocupar baja posición; **to rank with** estar al nivel de; tener el mismo grado que
**rank and file** *spl* soldados de fila; pueblo, gente común
**rankle** ['ræŋkəl] *va* enconar, agriar; *vn* enconarse
**ransack** ['rænsæk] *va* registrar, escudriñar; robar, saquear
**ransom** ['rænsəm] *s* rescate; *va* rescatar; redimir (*del pecado*)

**rant** [rænt] *s* lenguaje alborotado y retumbante; *vn* despotricar, delirar, hablar a gritos
**ranula** [ˈrænjələ] *s* (path. & vet.) ránula
**ranunculaceous** [rəˌnʌŋkjəˈleʃəs] *adj* (bot.) ranunculáceo
**ranunculus** [rəˈnʌŋkjələs] *s* (*pl:* **-luses** o **-li** [laɪ]) (bot.) ranúnculo
**rap** [ræp] *s* golpe corto y seco; taque (*ruido de golpe con que se llama a una puerta*); (slang) crítica mordaz; (coll.) bledo; **I don't care a rap** (coll.) no se me da un bledo de ello; **to take the rap** (slang) pagar la multa, sufrir las consecuencias; (*pret & pp:* **rapped;** *ger:* **rapping**) *va* golpear con golpe corto y seco; decir vivamente; (slang) criticar mordazmente; *vn* golpear con golpe corto y seco; **to rap at the door** tocar a la puerta
**rapacious** [rəˈpeʃəs] *adj* rapaz
**rapaciousness** [rəˈpeʃəsnɪs] *s* rapacidad
**rapacity** [rəˈpæsɪtɪ] *s* rapacidad
**rape** [rep] *s* rapto; estupro, violación; (bot.) naba; *va* raptar; estuprar, violar
**rape oil** *s* aceite de colza
**rapeseed** [ˈrepˌsid] *s* semillas de colza
**Raphael** [ˈræfɪəl] o [ˈrefɪəl] *s* Rafael
**Raphaelesque** [ˌræfɪəˈlɛsk] *adj* rafaelesco
**raphania** [rəˈfenɪə] *s* (path.) rafania
**raphe** [ˈrefi] *s* (*pl:* **-phae** [fi]) (anat. & bot.) rafe
**rapid** [ˈræpɪd] *adj* rápido; **rapids** *spl* rápidos (*de un río*)
**rapid-fire** [ˈræpɪdˈfaɪr] *adj* de tiro rápido; hecho vivamente
**rapidity** [rəˈpɪdɪtɪ] *s* rapidez
**rapid transit** *s* transporte rápido de viajeros
**rapier** [ˈrepɪər] *s* estoque, espadín
**rapine** [ˈræpɪn] *s* rapiña
**rapping** [ˈræpɪŋ] *s* (el) golpear (*de los espíritus*)
**rapport** [ræˈport] o [rɑˈpɔr] *s* relación, conformidad; **en rapport** de acuerdo
**rapprochement** [rɑprɔʃˈmɑ̃] *s* acercamiento, aproximación
**rapscallion** [ræpˈskæljən] *s* canalla, golfo, pícaro
**rapt** [ræpt] *adj* arrebatado, extático, transportado; absorto
**Raptores** [ræpˈtoriz] *spl* (zool.) rapaces
**raptorial** [ræpˈtorɪəl] *adj* predador; propio para asir y retener la presa; rapaz
**rapture** [ˈræptʃər] *s* rapto, éxtasis
**rapturous** [ˈræptʃərəs] *adj* extático
**rare** [rɛr] *adj* raro; poco usado (*dícese de una palabra o locución*); (cook.) poco asado
**rare bird** *s* mirlo blanco, rara avis
**rarebit** [ˈrɛrbɪt] o [ˈræbɪt] *s* var. de **Welsh rabbit**
**rare earth** *s* (chem.) tierra rara
**raree show** [ˈrɛri] *s* mundonuevo; espectáculo
**rarefaction** [ˌrɛrɪˈfækʃən] *s* rarefacción
**rarefy** [ˈrɛrɪfaɪ] (*pret & pp:* **-fied**) *va* enrarecer, rarefacer; *vn* enrarecerse, rarefacerse
**rare gas** *s* (chem.) gas raro
**rarely** [ˈrɛrlɪ] *adv* raramente, rara vez; excelentemente; extremadamente
**rareness** [ˈrɛrnɪs] *s* rareza
**rarity** [ˈrɛrɪtɪ] *s* (*pl:* **-ties**) rareza; (phys.) raridad
**rascal** [ˈræskəl] *s* bellaco, bribón, pícaro
**rascality** [ræsˈkælɪtɪ] *s* (*pl:* **-ties**) bellaquería, bribonada, picardía
**rascally** [ˈræskəlɪ] *adj* bellaco, bribón, pícaro
**rase** [rez] *va* var. de **raze**
**rash** [ræʃ] *adj* temerario; *s* brote (*erupción cutánea*)
**rasher** [ˈræʃər] *s* torrezno (*lonja de tocino*)
**rashness** [ˈræʃnɪs] *s* temeridad
**rasp** [ræsp] o [rɑsp] *s* escofina; sonido de escofina, ronquido; *va* escofinar; irritar, molestar; decir con voz ronca; *vn* hacer sonido áspero
**raspberry** [ˈræzˌbɛrɪ] o [ˈrɑzˌbɛrɪ] *s* (*pl:* **-ries**) (bot.) frambueso, sangüeso; frambuesa, sangüesa (*fruto*)
**raspberry bush** *s* (bot.) frambueso, sangüeso
**rat** [ræt] *s* (zool.) rata; (coll.) postizo; (slang) canalla; (slang) desertor; (slang) esquirol; (slang) soplón; **to smell a rat** olerse una trama, sospechar una intriga; (*pret & pp:* **ratted;** *ger:* **ratting**) *vn* cazar ratas; (slang) portarse como un canalla; (slang) soplar, delatar
**ratable** [ˈretəbəl] *adj* tasable, valuable; (Brit.) sujeto a impuestos o contribuciones
**ratan** [ræˈtæn] *s* var. de **rattan**
**rat-a-tat** [ˌrætəˈtæt] *interj* ¡ta, ta!, ¡tras, tras!
**ratcatcher** [ˈrætˌkætʃər] *s* cazarratas (*persona y animal*)
**ratch** [rætʃ] o **ratchet** [ˈrætʃɪt] *s* (mach.) rueda de trinquete, barra de trinquete; (mach.) trinquete (*garfio*); (mach.) mecanismo de trinquete
**ratchet brace** *s* berbiquí de trinquete
**ratchet drill** *s* taladro de trinquete
**ratchet jack** *s* cric de cremallera
**ratchet screwdriver** *s* destornillador de trinquete
**ratchet wheel** *s* rueda de trinquete
**ratchet wrench** *s* llave de trinquete
**rate** [ret] *s* razón (*cantidad medida por otra cosa tomada como unidad*); tipo (*p.ej., de interés*); velocidad; tarifa; clase, calidad; manera, modo; (Brit.) impuesto local; **at any rate** de todos modos; **at the rate of** a razón de; **at that rate** de ese modo, en ese caso; **at the same rate** al mismo ritmo; *va* valuar; estimar, juzgar; clasificar; regañar; *vn* ser considerado, ser tenido; estar clasificado; regañar
**rateable** [ˈretəbəl] *adj* var. de **ratable**
**ratel** [ˈretəl] o [ˈrɑtəl] *s* (zool.) ratel
**rate of climb** *s* (aer.) velocidad ascensional
**rate of exchange** *s* tipo de cambio
**ratepayer** [ˈretˌpeər] *s* (Brit.) contribuyente
**rather** [ˈræðər] o [ˈrɑðər] *adv* algo, un poco; bastante; antes, más bien; mejor dicho; por el contrario; muy, mucho; **had rather** preferiría; **would have rather** hubiera preferido; **rather than** antes que, más bien que; *interj* ¡ya lo creo!
**rathskeller** [ˈrɑtsˌkɛlər] *s* taberna o restaurante de sótano
**ratification** [ˌrætɪfɪˈkeʃən] *s* ratificación
**ratify** [ˈrætɪfaɪ] (*pret & pp:* **-fied**) *va* ratificar
**ratiné** [ˌrætɪˈne] *s* ratina (*tela*)
**rating** [ˈretɪŋ] *s* grado, clase, rango; justiprecio; clasificación; (Brit.) marinero
**ratio** [ˈreʃo] o [ˈreʃɪo] *s* (*pl:* **-tios**) (math.) razón; (math.) cociente
**ratiocinate** [ˌræʃɪˈɑsɪnet] *vn* raciocinar
**ratiocination** [ˌræʃɪˌɑsɪˈneʃən] *s* raciocinación
**ration** [ˈreʃən] o [ˈræʃən] *s* ración; (mil.) ración; *va* racionar; (mil.) racionar
**rational** [ˈræʃənəl] *adj* racional; (math.) racional; *s* (eccl.) racional
**rationale** [ˌræʃənˈɑlɪ] *s* razón fundamental; exposición razonada
**rationalism** [ˈræʃənəlɪzəm] *s* racionalismo
**rationalist** [ˈræʃənəlɪst] *s* racionalista
**rationalistic** [ˌræʃənəˈlɪstɪk] *adj* racionalista
**rationality** [ˌræʃəˈnælɪtɪ] *s* (*pl:* **-ties**) racionalidad; ademán o uso razonables
**rationalization** [ˌræʃənəlɪˈzeʃən] *s* acción de hacer racional; busca de excusas; (com. & math.) racionalización
**rationalize** [ˈræʃənəlaɪz] *va* hacer racional; cohonestar; (math.) racionalizar; *vn* buscar excusas
**ration book** *s* cartilla de racionamiento
**rationing** [ˈreʃənɪŋ] o [ˈræʃənɪŋ] *s* racionamiento
**Ratisbon** [ˈrætɪsbɑn] *s* Ratisbona
**ratite** [ˈrætaɪt] *adj* (orn.) corredor; *s* (orn.) corredora
**ratline** o **ratlin** [ˈrætlɪn] *s* (naut.) flechaste
**ratoon** [ræˈtun] *s* (agr.) retoño; (agr.) soca (*retoño de la caña de azúcar*)
**ratsbane** [ˈrætsˌben] *s* veneno para matar las ratas; trióxido de arsénico
**rattail file** [ˈrætˌtel] *s* lima de cola de rata
**rattan** [ræˈtæn] *s* (bot.) rota, roten; caña de la rota; roten (*bastón*)
**ratter** [ˈrætər] *s* cazador de ratas
**rattle** [ˈrætəl] *s* carraca, matraca; sonajero (*de niño*); matraqueo; traqueteo (*de una cosa que se transporta*); baraúnda; estertor (*del que agoniza*); anillos o discos de la punta de la cola de la serpiente de cascabel; *va* traquetear; atortolar, confundir; **to rattle off** decir rápida-

mente; *vn* traquetear; moverse o funcionar con traqueteo; hablar rápida y tontamente
**rattlebrain** [ˈrætəlˌbren] *s* cascabel, casquivano
**rattlepate** [ˈrætəlˌpet] *s* casquivano, charlador necio
**rattler** [ˈrætlər] *s* (zool.) serpiente de cascabel; (coll.) tren de carga rápido
**rattlesnake** [ˈrætəlˌsnek] *s* (zool.) serpiente de cascabel
**rattletrap** [ˈrætəlˌtræp] *s* trasto viejo; coche destartalado; (slang) tarabilla, parlanchín; (slang) boca; **rattletraps** *spl* chucerías, fruslerías
**rattling** [ˈrætlɪŋ] *adj* que traquetea, ruidoso; vivo, alegre; (coll.) enorme, extraordinario; *adv* (coll.) muy, sumamente
**rattly** [ˈrætlɪ] *adj* ruidoso, que traquetea
**rattrap** [ˈrætˌtræp] *s* ratonera (*para cazar ratas*); trance apurado, atolladero
**ratty** [ˈrætɪ] *adj* (*comp:* **-tier;** *super:* **-tiest**) de ratas, como ratas; lleno de ratas; (slang) vil, ruin
**raucous** [ˈrɔkəs] *adj* ronco
**rauwolfia** [rɔˈwʊlfɪə] *s* (bot.) rauwulfia; (pharm.) rauwulfina
**ravage** [ˈrævɪdʒ] *s* estrago, destrucción, ruina; *va* estragar, destruir, arruinar
**rave** [rev] *vn* desvariar, delirar, disparatar; bramar, enfurecerse; **to rave about** hacerse lenguas de, deshacerse en elogios de
**ravehook** [ˈrevˌhʊk] *s* (naut.) descalcador
**ravel** [ˈrævəl] *s* hilacha sin destorcer; (*pret & pp:* **-eled** o **-elled;** *ger:* **-eling** o **-elling**) *va* deshilar, destorcer; desenredar; enredar, confundir; *vn* deshilarse, destorcerse; desenredarse; enredarse
**ravelin** [ˈrævlɪn] *s* (fort.) revellín
**raveling** o **ravelling** [ˈrævəlɪŋ] *s* hilacha
**raven** [ˈrevən] *s* (orn.) cuervo; (*cap.*) *s* (astr.) Cuervo; (*l.c.*) *adj* negro y lustroso (*como el plumaje del cuervo*)
**ravening** [ˈrævənɪŋ] *adj* voraz
**ravenous** [ˈrævənəs] *adj* voraz, hambriento, famélico; rapaz
**ravin** [ˈrævɪn] *s* var. de **rapine**
**ravine** [rəˈvin] *s* hondonada, cañón
**raving** [ˈrevɪŋ] *s* desvarío, delirio; *adj* desvariado, delirante; (coll.) extraordinario
**ravioli** [ˌrɑvɪˈolɪ] o [ˌrævɪˈolɪ] *spl* (cook.) rabioles
**ravish** [ˈrævɪʃ] *va* encantar, entusiasmar; raptar; violar (*a una mujer*)
**ravishing** [ˈrævɪʃɪŋ] *adj* encantador, pasmoso
**ravishment** [ˈrævɪʃmənt] *s* encanto, transporte; rapto; violación (*de una mujer*)
**raw** [rɔ] *adj* crudo; principiante, inexperto; ulceroso, en carne viva; crudo (*día, tiempo*); (slang) injusto, severo; *s* carne viva; llaga, úlcera
**raw-boned** [ˈrɔˌbond] *adj* descarnado, demacrado
**raw cotton** *s* algodón en rama
**raw deal** *s* (slang) mala pasada; **to give someone a raw deal** (slang) jugarle a uno una mala pasada
**rawhide** [ˈrɔˌhaɪd] *s* cuero en verde; látigo hecho de cuero en verde; *va* azotar con látigo de cuero en verde
**raw material** *s* primera materia, materia prima
**raw silk** *s* seda en rama
**raw sugar** *s* azúcar amarillo, azúcar sin refinar
**raw umber** *s* tierra de sombra cruda
**ray** [re] *s* rayo (*de luz*); raya (*línea fina*); (bot.) bráctea; (zool.) radio; (ichth.) raya; (fig.) vislumbre; *va* radiar; tratar con rayos; *vn* irradiar; extenderse de un punto central
**Raymond** [ˈremənd] *s* Ramón, Raimundo
**rayon** [ˈreɑn] *s* rayón
**raze** [rez] *va* arrasar, asolar
**razor** [ˈrezər] *s* navaja de afeitar
**razorback** [ˈrezərˌbæk] *s* (zool.) puerco cimarrón; (zool.) rorcual; sierra, cordillera
**razor blade** *s* hoja u hojita de afeitar
**razor clam** *s* (zool.) mango de cuchillo, muergo
**razor strop** *s* asentador, suavizador
**razz** [ræz] *s* (slang) irrisión; *va* (slang) mofarse de
**razzia** [ˈræzɪə] *s* razzia
**R.C.** abr. de **Red Cross, Reserve Corps** y **Roman Catholic**
**r-colored vowel** [ˈɑrˌkʌlərd] *s* (phonet.) vocal de colorido de r
**rd.** abr. de **road** y **rod** o **rods**
**R.D.** abr. de **Rural Delivery**
**reach** [ritʃ] *s* alcance; estirón; extensión; extensión de un canal entre dos compuertas; extensión de un río entre dos recodos; (naut.) bordada; **beyond reach (of)** u **out of reach (of)** fuera del alcance (de); **within reach** al alcance de la mano; a tiro; **within reach of** al alcance de; *va* alcanzar; estirar; alargar, extender; pasar o entregar con la mano; ponerse en contacto con; llegar a; influenciar; cumplir (*cierto número de años*); *vn* alcanzar; alargar o extender la mano o el brazo; extenderse; (naut.) navegar de bolina; **to reach after** o **for** esforzarse por coger; echar mano a; **to reach into** meter la mano en; penetrar en
**reachable** [ˈritʃəbəl] *adj* alcanzadizo
**react** [rɪˈækt] *vn* reaccionar
**re-act** [riˈækt] *va* volver a representar (*una escena, un drama*)
**reactance** [rɪˈæktəns] *s* (elec.) reactancia
**reaction** [rɪˈækʃən] *s* reacción
**reactionary** [rɪˈækʃənˌɛrɪ] *adj* reaccionario; *s* (*pl:* **-ies**) reaccionario
**reaction turbine** *s* turbina de reacción
**reactive** [rɪˈæktɪv] *adj* reactivo
**reactor** [rɪˈæktər] *s* (elec. & phys.) reactor
**read** [rid] (*pret & pp:* **read** [rɛd]) *va* leer; recitar (*poesía*); rezar; interpretar (*atribuir cierto fin a*); estudiar (*derecho*); leer en, adivinar (*el pensamiento ajeno*); **to read out of** despedir de (*p.ej., un partido político*); **to read over** recorrer, repasar (*un escrito*); *vn* leer; rezar, p.ej., **this page reads thus** esta página reza así; leerse, p.ej., **this book reads easily** este libro se lee con facilidad; **to read about** leer sobre; **to read between the lines** leer entre líneas; **to read of** leer acerca de; aprender o saber leyendo; **to read on** seguir leyendo; **to read up on** informarse por la lectura acerca de; [rɛd] *adj* leído (*enterado mediante la lectura*)
**readable** [ˈridəbəl] *adj* leíble, legible; ameno, interesante (*libro*)
**readapt** [ˌriəˈdæpt] *va* readaptar
**readdress** [ˌriəˈdrɛs] *va* volver a dirigir (*una carta*); poner nueva dirección a (*una carta*)
**reader** [ˈridər] *s* lector; libro de lectura
**readily** [ˈrɛdɪlɪ] *adv* pronto; fácilmente, sin esfuerzo; de buena gana
**readiness** [ˈrɛdɪnɪs] *s* preparación; disposición; propensión; agilidad, destreza; disponibilidad; vivacidad (*de ingenio*)
**reading** [ˈridɪŋ] *adj* lector; de lectura, **para** leer; *s* lectura; recitación, declamación; lectura o lección (*interpretación de un pasaje*)
**reading book** *s* libro de lectura
**reading desk** *s* atril
**reading glass** *s* lente para leer, vidrio de aumento; **reading glasses** *spl* anteojos para la lectura
**reading lamp** *s* lámpara de sobremesa
**reading material** *s* material de lectura
**reading room** *s* gabinete de lectura; sala de lectura
**readjustment** [ˌriəˈdʒʌstmənt] *s* reajuste, reacomodo
**readmit** [ˌriədˈmɪt] (*pret & pp:* **-mitted;** *ger:* **-mitting**) *va* readmitir
**ready** [ˈrɛdɪ] *adj* (*comp:* **-ier;** *super:* **-iest**) listo, preparado, pronto; dispuesto; propenso; ágil, diestro; disponible; vivo; **to make ready** preparar; prepararse; (*pret & pp:* **-ied**) *va* preparar; *vn* prepararse
**ready cash** *s* dinero a la mano, fondos disponibles, dinero contante y sonante
**ready-made** [ˈrɛdɪˌmed] *adj* hecho, confeccionado, p.ej., **a ready-made suit** un traje hecho
**ready-made clothes** *spl* ropa hecha
**ready-made clothier** *s* ropero, confeccionista
**ready-made clothing** *s* ropa hecha
**ready-mixed paint** [ˈrɛdɪˌmɪkst] *s* pintura preparada o hecha
**ready money** *s* dinero contante

**reaffirm** [ˌriəˈfʌrm] *va* reafirmar
**reaffirmation** [ˌriæfərˈmeʃən] *s* reafirmación
**reagent** [rɪˈedʒənt] *s* (chem.) reactivo
**real** [ˈriəl] *adj* real; auténtico; inmueble
**real estate** *s* bienes raíces
**real-estate** [ˈriəlɪˌstet] *adj* inmobiliario
**real-estate broker** *s* corredor de bienes raíces
**realgar** [rɪˈælgər] *s* (mineral.) rejalgar
**real image** *s* (phys.) imagen real
**realism** [ˈriəlɪzəm] *s* realismo
**realist** [ˈriəlɪst] *s* realista
**realistic** [ˌriəˈlɪstɪk] *adj* realista
**realistically** [ˌriəˈlɪstɪkəlɪ] *adv* de manera realista
**reality** [rɪˈælɪtɪ] *s* (*pl:* **-ties**) realidad; **in reality** en realidad
**realization** [ˌriəlɪˈzeʃən] *s* comprensión; realización; adquisición (*de dinero*)
**realize** [ˈriəlaɪz] *va* darse cuenta de, hacerse cargo de; realizar; hacer aparecer real; adquirir (*ganancias*); reportar (*ganancias*); *vn* realizar (*vender bienes rápidamente*)
**really** [ˈriəlɪ] *adv* realmente
**realm** [rɛlm] *s* reino
**realtor** [ˈriəltɔr] o [ˈriəltər] *s* corredor de bienes raíces
**realty** [ˈriəltɪ] *s* bienes raíces, bienes inmuebles
**real wages** *spl* salario real
**ream** [rim] *s* resma; **reams** *spl* (coll.) montones; *va* escariar
**reamer** [ˈrimər] *s* escariador; exprimidor (*para extraer el jugo de las frutas*)
**reanimate** [riˈænɪmet] *va* reanimar; *vn* reanimarse
**reap** [rip] *va* segar; cosechar; *vn* cosechar
**reaper** [ˈripər] *s* segador; segadora, máquina segadora
**reaping machine** *s* máquina segadora
**reappear** [ˌriəˈpɪr] *vn* reaparecer
**reappearance** [ˌriəˈpɪrəns] *s* reaparición
**reappoint** [ˌriəˈpɔɪnt] *va* volver a nombrar
**reappointment** [ˌriəˈpɔɪntmənt] *s* nuevo nombramiento
**reapportion** [ˌriəˈporʃən] *s* volver a prorratear
**reapportionment** [ˌriəˈporʃənmənt] *s* nuevo prorrateo
**rear** [rɪr] *adj* posterior, trasero; de atrás; de retaguardia; *s* parte posterior, parte de atrás; espalda; fondo (*de una sala*); cola (*de una fila, de un automóvil*); retaguardia; (slang) culo, trasero; **at** o **in the rear of** detrás de; al fondo de; *va* alzar, levantar; edificar, erigir; criar, educar; *vn* encabritarse, suspenderse (*un caballo*)
**rear admiral** *s* contraalmirante
**rear axle** *s* eje trasero
**rear-axle housing** [ˈrɪrˈæksəl] *s* (aut.) caja de puente trasero
**rear-end** [ˈrɪrˌɛnd] *adj* de cola, p.ej., **rear-end collision** colisión de cola
**rear guard** *s* retaguardia
**rearm** [riˈɑrm] *va* rearmar; *vn* rearmarse
**rearmament** [riˈɑrməmənt] *s* rearme
**rearmost** [ˈrɪrmost] *adj* último de atrás, último de todos
**rearrange** [ˌriəˈrendʒ] *va* volver a arreglar o disponer; (mus.) volver a adaptar
**rearrangement** [ˌriəˈrendʒmənt] *s* nuevo arreglo, nueva disposición; (mus.) nueva adaptación
**rear-view mirror** [ˈrɪrˈvju] *s* (aut.) retrovisor, espejo de retrovisión
**rearward** [ˈrɪrwərd] *adj* postrero, último; *adv* hacia atrás
**rear wheel** *s* (aut.) rueda trasera
**rear window** *s* (aut.) luneta, luneta posterior
**reason** [ˈrizən] *s* razón; **by reason of** a causa de, en virtud de; **in all reason** con razón; **in reason** dentro de lo razonable; **out of reason** fuera de razón; **to bring to reason** meter en razón; **to listen to reason** meterse en razón; **to stand to reason** ser razonable; *va & vn* razonar
**reasonable** [ˈrizənəbəl] *adj* razonable
**reasonably** [ˈrizənəblɪ] *adv* razonablemente
**reasoner** [ˈrizənər] *s* razonador
**reasoning** [ˈrizənɪŋ] *adj* razonador; *s* razonamiento
**reason of state** *s* razón de estado
**reassemble** [ˌriəˈsɛmbəl] *va* volver a reunir; (mach.) volver a armar o montar; *vn* volver a reunirse
**reassess** [ˌriəˈsɛs] *va* volver a amillarar; volver a apreciar, volver a estimar
**reassessment** [ˌriəˈsɛsmənt] *s* nuevo amillaramiento; nueva apreciación, nueva estimación
**reassume** [ˌriəˈsum] o [ˌriəˈsjum] *va* reasumir
**reassumption** [ˌriəˈsʌmpʃən] *s* reasunción
**reassurance** [ˌriəˈʃurəns] *s* afirmación reiterada, certeza restablecida; nueva confianza
**reassure** [ˌriəˈʃur] *va* volver a asegurar; tranquilizar
**reassuring** [ˌriəˈʃurɪŋ] *adj* tranquilizador
**reattach** [ˌriəˈtætʃ] *va* reatar
**reawaken** [ˌriəˈwekən] *va* volver a despertar; *vn* volver a despertarse
**rebaptize** [ˌribæpˈtaɪz] *va* rebautizar
**rebate** [ˈribet] o [rɪˈbet] *s* rebaja; *va* rebajar
**rebec** o **rebeck** [ˈribɛk] *s* (mus.) rabel
**Rebecca** [rɪˈbɛkə] *s* Rebeca
**rebel** [ˈrɛbəl] *adj & s* rebelde; [rɪˈbɛl] (*pret & pp:* **-belled;** *ger:* **-belling**) *vn* rebelarse
**rebellion** [rɪˈbɛljən] *s* rebelión
**rebellious** [rɪˈbɛljəs] *adj* rebelde
**rebind** [ˈriˌbaɪnd] *s* libro reencuadernado; [riˈbaɪnd] (*pret & pp:* **-bound**) *va* reatar; (sew.) ribetear; (b.b.) reencuadernar
**rebinding** [riˈbaɪndɪŋ] *s* (b.b.) reencuadernación
**rebirth** [ˈriˌbʌrθ] o [riˈbʌrθ] *s* renacimiento
**rebore** [riˈbor] *va* rectificar, retaladrar (*un cilindro*)
**reborn** [riˈbɔrn] *adj* renacido
**rebound** [ˈriˌbaund] o [rɪˈbaund] *s* rebote, repercusión; [rɪˈbaund] *vn* rebotar, repercutir; [riˈbaund] *adj* reatado; reencuadernado; *pret & pp de* **rebind**
**rebroadcast** [riˈbrɔdkæst] o [riˈbrɔdkɑst] *s* retransmisión; (*pret & pp:* **-cast** o **-casted**) *va* retransmitir
**rebuff** [rɪˈbʌf] *s* rechazo, desaire; *va* rechazar, desairar
**rebuild** [riˈbɪld] (*pret & pp:* **-built**) *va* reconstruir, reedificar
**rebuke** [rɪˈbjuk] *s* reprensión; *va* reprender
**rebus** [ˈribəs] *s* jeroglífico; (her.) armas parlantes
**rebush** [riˈbuʃ] *va* rellenar (*los cojinetes*) con metal blanco
**rebut** [rɪˈbʌt] (*pret & pp:* **-butted;** *ger:* **-butting**) *va* rebatir, refutar (*un argumento*)
**rebuttal** [rɪˈbʌtəl] *s* rebatimiento, refutación
**rebutter** [rɪˈbʌtər] *s* (law) dúplica, contrarréplica
**rec.** abr. de **receipt, recipe, record** y **recorder**
**recalcitrance** [rɪˈkælsɪtrəns] o **recalcitrancy** [rɪˈkælsɪtrənsɪ] *s* obstinación, terquedad
**recalcitrant** [rɪˈkælsɪtrənt] *adj* recalcitrante
**recalescence** [ˌrikəˈlɛsəns] *s* (metal.) recalescencia
**recall** [rɪˈkɔl] o [ˈrikɔl] *s* aviso, llamada (*para hacer volver*); recordación; revocación, anulación; retirada (*de un diplomático*); deposición de un funcionario público por votación popular; [rɪˈkɔl] *va* hacer volver, mandar volver; recordar; revocar, anular; retirar (*a un diplomático*); deponer
**recant** [rɪˈkænt] *va* retractar; *vn* retractarse
**recantation** [ˌrikænˈteʃən] *s* retractación, recantación
**recap** [ˈriˌkæp] o [riˈkæp] (*pret & pp:* **-capped;** *ger:* **-capping**) *va* recauchutar (*un neumático*)
**recapitalization** [riˌkæpɪtəlɪˈzeʃən] *s* recapitalización
**recapitalize** [riˈkæpɪtəlaɪz] *va* recapitalizar
**recapitulate** [ˌrikəˈpɪtʃəlet] *va & vn* recapitular
**recapitulation** [ˌrikəˌpɪtʃəˈleʃən] *s* recapitulación
**recapture** [riˈkæptʃər] *s* recobro; recordación; represa (*de una embarcación de los enemigos*); *va* recobrar; recordar (*a la memoria*); represar (*una embarcación*)
**recast** [ˈriˌkæst] o [ˈriˌkɑst] *s* refundición; reconstrucción (*p.ej., de una frase*); [riˈkæst] o

[ri'kast] (*pret & pp:* **-cast**) *va* refundir; reconstruir (*p.ej., una frase*)
**recd.** o **rec'd.** abr. de **received**
**recede** [rɪ'sid] *vn* retroceder; deprimirse; retirarse
**receipt** [rɪ'sit] *s* recepción; recibo; recibí; receta, fórmula; **receipts** *spl* entradas, ingresos; **on receipt of** al recibo de; **to acknowledge receipt of** acusar recibo de; **to be in receipt of a letter** obrar una carta en mi (nuestro) poder, p.ej., **I am in receipt of your letter** obra en mi poder su carta; **receipt in full** finiquito; *va* poner el recibí a (*una cuenta*)
**receivable** [rɪ'sivəbəl] *adj* recibidero; por cobrar, p.ej., **bills receivable** cuentas por cobrar
**receive** [rɪ'siv] *va* recibir; receptar (*cosas que son materia de delito*); **received payment** recibí; *vn* recibir; comulgar; (rad.) recibir; (sport) ser restador
**receiver** [rɪ'sivər] *s* receptor; recipiente; (telg., telp. & rad.) receptor; (telp.) receptor telefónico, auricular; (rad.) estación receptora; auricular de casco, receptor de cabeza; (phys.) recipiente (*de la máquina neumática*); receptador (*de cosas que son materia de delito*); (law) síndico (*en un concurso de acreedores o en una quiebra*); (law) receptor (*que hace cobranzas*); (sport) restador
**receivership** [rɪ'sivərʃɪp] *s* (law) sindicatura; (law) receptoría
**receiving set** *s* (telg., telp. & rad.) receptor, aparato receptor
**receiving teller** *s* recibidor (*de un banco*)
**recency** ['risənsɪ] *s* novedad, (lo) reciente
**recension** [rɪ'sɛnʃən] *s* recensión
**recent** ['risənt] *adj* reciente; **the recent past** el pasado próximo; (*cap.*) *adj* (geol.) holoceno, diluvial
**recently** ['risəntlɪ] *adv* recientemente; recién, p.ej., **recently arrived** recién llegado
**receptacle** [rɪ'sɛptəkəl] *s* receptáculo; recipiente (*vasija*); (bot.) receptáculo; (elec.) receptáculo, caja de contacto
**receptacle plate** *s* (elec.) escudete de receptáculo
**receptacle plug** *s* (elec.) clavija o ficha de receptáculo
**reception** [rɪ'sɛpʃən] *s* recepción
**reception center** *s* (mil.) centro de recepción
**reception hall** *s* sala de recepción, sala de recibo
**receptionist** [rɪ'sɛpʃənɪst] *s* (coll.) persona encargada de recibir visitantes a la entrada de una oficina, consultorio, etc.
**receptive** [rɪ'sɛptɪv] *adj* receptivo
**receptivity** [,risɛp'tɪvɪtɪ] *s* receptividad
**receptor** [rɪ'sɛptər] *s* receptador (*p.ej., de delincuentes*); (physiol.) receptor
**recess** [rɪ'sɛs] o ['risɛs] *s* intermisión, tregua; descanso; recreo, hora de recreo; hueco, nicho; depresión; retiro, escondrijo; [rɪ'sɛs] *va* ahuecar; empotrar; deprimir; hacer un nicho en; apartar, retirar; *vn* (coll.) tomar una recreación; (coll.) prorrogarse, suspenderse
**recess hour** *s* hora de recreo
**recession** [rɪ'sɛʃən] *s* retroceso; retirada; baja; depresión (*p.ej., de una pared*); contracción económica; procesión que vuelve a la sacristía; [ri'sɛʃən] *s* restitución; cesión de bienes a un propietario anterior
**recessional** [rɪ'sɛʃənəl] *s* himno que se canta al retirarse el sacerdote y el coro a la sacristía; *adj* cantado o tocado al retirarse el sacerdote y el coro a la sacristía; (geol.) de retroceso
**recessive** [rɪ'sɛsɪv] *adj* regresivo; (biol.) recesivo
**recessive character** *s* (biol.) carácter recesivo
**recharge** [ri'tʃardʒ] *s* (elec.) recarga; carga de recambio (*p.ej., de extintor*); *va* recargar; (elec.) recargar
**recheck** [ri'tʃɛk] *s* nueva comprobación o verificación; *va* volver a comprobar o verificar
**recherché** [rəʃɛr'ʃe] o [rə'ʃɛrʃe] *adj* muy buscado, solicitado; esmerado, exquisito; alambicado, rebuscado
**recidivism** [rɪ'sɪdɪvɪzəm] *s* recidivismo
**recidivist** [rɪ'sɪdɪvɪst] *s* recidivista
**recipe** ['rɛsɪpɪ] *s* fórmula, receta, receta de cocina
**recipient** [rɪ'sɪpɪənt] *adj & s* recibidor; recipiente
**reciprocal** [rɪ'sɪprəkəl] *adj* recíproco; (gram.) recíproco; *s* cosa recíproca; (math.) recíproca
**reciprocally** [rɪ'sɪprəkəlɪ] *adv* recíprocamente
**reciprocate** [rɪ'sɪprəket] *va* intercambiar, trocar; corresponder a (*p.ej., la amistad de una persona*); reciprocar, hacer corresponder; (mach.) dar movimiento alternativo o de vaivén a; *vn* alternar; reciprocarse, corresponder; (mach.) tener movimiento alternativo o de vaivén
**reciprocating** [rɪ'sɪprə,ketɪŋ] *adj* alternativo, de vaivén; de movimiento alternativo
**reciprocating engine** *s* máquina de movimiento alternativo
**reciprocation** [rɪ,sɪprə'keʃən] *s* intercambio; reciprocación, correspondencia; alternación
**reciprocity** [,rɛsɪ'prasɪtɪ] *s* reciprocidad; (com.) reciprocidad (*entre dos naciones*)
**recital** [rɪ'saɪtəl] *s* narración; (mus.) recital
**recitation** [,rɛsɪ'teʃən] *s* recitación; narración
**recitative** ['rɛsɪ,tetɪv] o [rɪ'saɪtətɪv] *adj* recitativo; [,rɛsɪtə'tiv] *adj* (mus.) recitativo; *s* (mus.) recitado
**recite** [rɪ'saɪt] *va* recitar; narrar
**reck** [rɛk] *va* preocuparse por; *vn* preocuparse; (archaic) importar
**reckless** ['rɛklɪs] *adj* atolondrado, inconsiderado, temerario
**recklessness** ['rɛklɪsnɪs] *s* atolondramiento, inconsideración, temeridad
**reckon** ['rɛkən] *va* calcular; considerar, estimar; (coll.) calcular (*pensar, conjeturar*); *vn* calcular; **to reckon on** contar con; **to reckon with** tener en cuenta, tomar en serio
**reckoning** ['rɛkənɪŋ] *s* cálculo, cómputo; cuenta; arreglo o ajuste de cuentas; (naut.) estima; **to be out of one's reckoning** estar lejos de la cuenta, engañarse en el cálculo
**reclaim** [ri'klem] *va* reclamar (*lo que pertenece a uno*); [rɪ'klem] *va* hacer utilizable; hacer labrantío (*un terreno*); ganar (*terreno*) a la mar; recuperar (*materiales usados*); conducir o guiar (*a los que hacen mala vida*); (law) reclamar; *vn* reclamar (*protestar*)
**reclamation** [,rɛklə'meʃən] *s* utilización (*de materiales usados*); recuperación; reclamación (*protesta*); (law) reclamación
**recline** [rɪ'klaɪn] *va* reclinar; *vn* reclinarse
**reclining** [rɪ'klaɪnɪŋ] *adj* reclinable
**reclothe** [ri'kloð] *va* volver a vestir
**recluse** [rɪ'klus] *adj* solitario; [rɪ'klus] o ['rɛklus] *s* solitario, ermitaño
**reclusion** [rɪ'kluʒən] *s* reclusión, encierro
**recognition** [,rɛkəg'nɪʃən] *s* reconocimiento; (dipl.) reconocimiento
**recognizable** ['rɛkəg,naɪzəbəl] *adj* reconocible
**recognizance** [rɪ'kagnɪzəns] o [rɪ'kanɪzəns] *s* (law) obligación (*escritura en que uno se obliga a cumplir un acto determinado*); (law) suma que uno tiene que perder por incumplimiento de una obligación
**recognize** ['rɛkəgnaɪz] *va* reconocer
**recoil** [rɪ'kɔɪl] *s* reculada; reculada, culatazo (*de un arma de fuego*); *vn* recular, apartarse; recular (*un arma de fuego*); reaccionar
**recollect** [,rɛkə'lɛkt] *va & vn* recordar
**re-collect** [,rikə'lɛkt] *va* recoger, reunir; recobrar; **to re-collect oneself** componerse, recobrar la calma; *vn* reunirse, volver a juntarse
**recollection** [,rɛkə'lɛkʃən] *s* recordación; recolección, recogimiento
**recommence** [,rikə'mɛns] *va* recomenzar
**recommend** [,rɛkə'mɛnd] *va* recomendar
**recommendation** [,rɛkəmɛn'deʃən] *s* recomendación
**recommendatory** [,rɛkə'mɛndə,torɪ] *adj* recomendatorio
**recommender** [,rɛkə'mɛndər] *s* recomendante
**recommit** [,rikə'mɪt] (*pret & pp:* **-mitted;** *ger:* **-mitting**) *va* volver a confiar, volver a entregar; volver a cometer; volver a someter; volver a comprometer; volver a internar
**recommitment** [,rikə'mɪtmənt] o **recommittal** [,rikə'mɪtəl] *s* nueva comisión; nueva internación; nuevo compromiso

**recompense** ['rɛkəmpɛns] *s* recompensa; *va* recompensar
**recompose** [,rikəm'poz] *va* recomponer
**recomposition** [,rikɑmpə'zɪʃən] *s* recomposición
**reconcilable** ['rɛkən,saɪləbəl] *adj* reconciliable
**reconcile** ['rɛkənsaɪl] *va* reconciliar; (eccl.) reconciliar; **to become reconciled** reconciliarse (*dos o más personas*); **to reconcile oneself** resignarse, someterse
**reconcilement** ['rɛkən,saɪlmənt] o **reconciliation** [,rɛkən,sɪlɪ'eʃən] *s* reconciliación
**reconciliatory** [,rɛkən'sɪlɪə,torɪ] *adj* reconciliador
**recondite** ['rɛkəndaɪt] o [rɪ'kɑndaɪt] *adj* recóndito
**recondition** [,rikən'dɪʃən] *va* reacondicionar
**reconnaissance** [rɪ'kɑnɪsəns] *s* (mil.) reconocimiento
**reconnoiter** o **reconnoitre** [,rɛkə'nɔɪtər] o [,rikə'nɔɪtər] *va & vn* (mil.) reconocer
**reconquer** [ri'kɑŋkər] *va* reconquistar
**reconquest** [ri'kɑŋkwɛst] *s* reconquista; *va* reconquistar
**reconsider** [,rikən'sɪdər] *va* reconsiderar
**reconsideration** [,rikən,sɪdə'reʃən] *s* reconsideración
**reconstituent** [,rikən'stɪtjuənt] *adj & s* reconstituyente
**reconstitute** [ri'kɑnstɪtjut] o [ri'kɑnstɪtut] *va* reconstituir
**reconstitution** [ri,kɑnstɪ'tjuʃən] o [ri,kɑnstɪ'tuʃən] *s* reconstitución
**reconstruct** [,rikən'strʌkt] *va* reconstruir
**reconstruction** [,rikən'strʌkʃən] *s* reconstrucción
**reconstructive** [,rikən'strʌktɪv] *adj* reconstructor; reconstructivo
**reconvene** [,rikən'vin] *va* convocar de nuevo; *vn* convenir de nuevo, volver a juntarse o reunirse
**reconvention** [,rikən'vɛnʃən] *s* (law) reconvención
**reconversion** [,rikən'vʌrʒən] o [,rikən'vʌrʃən] *s* reconversión
**reconvert** [,rikən'vʌrt] *va* reconvertir
**reconveyance** [,rikən'veəns] *s* devolución; escritura de traspaso al poseedor anterior
**record** ['rɛkərd] *s* registro; anotación; ficha, historia personal; protocolo (*de un notario*); disco (fonográfico); cilindro (fonográfico); (educ.) expediente académico; (sport) record, plusmarca; **records** *spl* anales, memorias; archivo; **off the record** confidencialmente; **on record** registrado; **to break a record** batir un record; superar precedentes; **to make a record** establecer un record; grabar un disco; *adj* máximo; notable, sin precedentes; [rɪ'kɔrd] *va* registrar; asentar; inscribir; protocolar; grabar (*un disco fonográfico*); grabar en disco fonográfico
**record breaker** *s* (sport) plusmarquista
**record changer** *s* cambiadiscos, tocadiscos automático
**recorder** [rɪ'kɔrdər] *s* registrador; contador, indicador; grabador, grabadora o registrador (*de fonógrafo*); juez recopilador
**recorder of deeds** *s* registrador de la propiedad
**recordership** [rɪ'kɔrdərʃɪp] *s* cargo u oficio de registrador
**record holder** *s* (sport) recordman
**recording** [rɪ'kɔrdɪŋ] *adj* registrador; magnetofónico (*alambre o cinta*); *s* registro; grabación o grabado (*de discos fonográficos*)
**recording head** *s* cabeza de registro o cabeza grabadora
**recording secretary** *s* secretario escribiente, secretario de actas
**recording tape** *s* cinta magnetofónica
**record library** *s* discoteca
**record player** *s* tocadiscos
**re-count** ['rikaʊnt] o [ri'kaʊnt] *s* recuento; [ri'kaʊnt] *va* recontar
**recount** [rɪ'kaʊnt] *va* recontar, referir
**recoup** [rɪ'kup] *va* recobrar; resarcir; **to recoup oneself** recobrarse; *vn* recobrarse
**recourse** [rɪ'kors] o ['rikors] *s* recurso; paño de lágrimas; **to have recourse to** recurrir a
**recover** [rɪ'kʌvər] *va* recobrar; recuperar; libertar, rescatar; (law) reivindicar; **to recover oneself** contenerse; recobrar el equilibrio; *vn* recobrarse; recobrarse de la enfermedad, recobrar la salud; (law) ganar un pleito
**re-cover** [ri'kʌvər] *va* recubrir
**recovery** [rɪ'kʌvərɪ] *s* (*pl:* **-ies**) recobro; recuperación; (law) reivindicación; **past recovery** sin remedio
**recreancy** ['rɛkrɪənsɪ] *s* pusilanimidad; deslealtad, traición
**recreant** ['rɛkrɪənt] *adj & s* cobarde; traidor
**recreate** ['rɛkrɪet] *va* recrear (*divertir*); *vn* recrearse
**re-create** [,rikri'et] *va* recrear (*crear o producir de nuevo*)
**recreation** [,rɛkrɪ'eʃən] *s* recreación, recreo
**recreational** [,rɛkrɪ'eʃənəl] *adj* de recreación
**recreation hall** *s* salón de recreo
**recreative** ['rɛkrɪ,etɪv] *adj* recreativo
**recrement** ['rɛkrɪmənt] *s* (physiol.) recremento
**recriminate** [rɪ'krɪmɪnet] *va* recriminar (*una acusación*); recriminar contra (*un acusador*); *vn* recriminar
**recrimination** [rɪ,krɪmɪ'neʃən] *s* recriminación
**recriminative** [rɪ'krɪmɪ,netɪv] o **recriminatory** [rɪ'krɪmɪnə,torɪ] *adj* recriminatorio
**recross** [ri'krɔs] o [ri'krɑs] *va* recruzar; *vn* recruzarse
**recrudescence** [,rikru'dɛsəns] *s* recrudescencia
**recrudescent** [,rikru'dɛsənt] *adj* recrudescente
**recruit** [rɪ'krut] *s* recluta; *va* reclutar; reforzar con reclutas, proveer de reclutas; aumentar o mantener el número de; restablecer, rehacer; abastecer; *vn* alistar reclutas; ganar reclutas; restablecerse, rehacerse, reponerse
**recruitment** [rɪ'krutmənt] *s* reclutamiento
**rect.** abr. de **receipt, rector** y **rectory**
**rectal** ['rɛktəl] *adj* rectal
**rectangle** ['rɛktæŋgəl] *s* (geom.) rectángulo
**rectangular** [rɛk'tæŋgjələr] *adj* rectangular
**rectification** [,rɛktɪfɪ'keʃən] *s* rectificación
**rectifier** ['rɛktɪ,faɪər] *s* rectificador; (chem. & elec.) rectificador
**rectify** ['rɛktɪfaɪ] (*pret & pp:* **-fied**) rectificar; (chem. & elec.) rectificar
**rectilinear** [,rɛktɪ'lɪnɪər] *adj* rectilíneo
**rectinerved** ['rɛktɪ,nʌrvd] *adj* (bot.) rectinervio
**rectitude** ['rɛktɪtjud] o ['rɛktɪtud] *s* rectitud, probidad, corrección
**recto** ['rɛkto] *s* (*pl:* **-tos**) (print.) recto
**rectocele** ['rɛktəsil] *s* (path.) rectocele
**rector** ['rɛktər] *s* rector
**rectorate** ['rɛktərɪt] *s* rectorado
**rectory** ['rɛktərɪ] *s* (*pl:* **-ries**) casa del rector; (Brit.) rectoría
**rectrix** ['rɛktrɪks] *s* (*pl:* **rectrices** [rɛk'traɪsiz]) (orn.) rectriz
**rectum** ['rɛktəm] *s* (*pl:* **-ta** [tə]) (anat.) recto
**rectus** ['rɛktəs] *s* (*pl:* **-ti** [taɪ]) (anat.) recto (*músculo*)
**recumbency** [rɪ'kʌmbənsɪ] *s* reclinación
**recumbent** [rɪ'kʌmbənt] *adj* reclinado
**recuperate** [rɪ'kjupəret] *va* recuperar; restablecer, reponer; *vn* recuperarse, recobrarse
**recuperation** [rɪ,kjupə'reʃən] *s* recuperación; restablecimiento
**recuperative** [rɪ'kjupə,retɪv] *adj* recuperativo
**recuperator** [rɪ'kjupə,retər] *s* (mach.) recuperador
**recur** [rɪ'kʌr] (*pret & pp:* **-curred;** *ger:* **-curring**) *vn* volver a ocurrir, repetirse; volver (*a un asunto*); volver a presentarse (*a la memoria*)
**recurrence** [rɪ'kʌrəns] *s* repetición
**recurrent** [rɪ'kʌrənt] *adj* repetido; periódico; (anat., math. & path.) recurrente
**recurve** [rɪ'kʌrv] *va* recorvar; *vn* recorvarse
**recusancy** ['rɛkjuzənsɪ] o [rɪ'kjuzənsɪ] *s* recusación; (hist.) falta de sumisión a la Iglesia anglicana por parte de un católico
**recusant** ['rɛkjuzənt] o [rɪ'kjuzənt] *adj & s* recusante; (hist.) no conformista (*con el anglicanismo*)
**recuse** [rɪ'kjuz] *va* (law) recusar
**red** [rɛd] *adj* (*comp:* **redder;** *super:* **reddest**)

rojo; ruboroso; enrojecido, inflamado; tinto (*vino*); *s* rojo, color rojo; **in the red** (coll.) endeudado; **to see red** (coll.) enfurecerse, echar chispas; (*cap.*) *adj & s* rojo (*comunista*)
**redact** [rɪˈdækt] *va* redactar
**redaction** [rɪˈdækʃən] *s* redacción
**redan** [rɪˈdæn] *s* (fort.) rediente
**red ant** *s* (ent.) hormiga roja (*Formica rufa*)
**redbait** [ˈrɛdˌbet] *va* motejar (*a uno*) de rojo o comunista
**redbird** [ˈrɛdˌbʌrd] *s* (orn.) cardenal; (orn.) piranga
**red-blooded** [ˈrɛdˌblʌdɪd] *adj* fuerte, valiente, vigoroso
**red brass** *s* latón rojo
**redbreast** [ˈrɛdˌbrɛst] *s* (orn.) petirrojo
**redbud** [ˈrɛdˌbʌd] *s* (bot.) árbol del amor
**redcap** [ˈrɛdˌkæp] *s* (Brit.) policía militar; (U.S.A.) mozo de estación (*que suele llevar gorra roja*); (orn.) jilguero
**red cedar** *s* (bot.) cedro rojo, cedro de Virginia
**red cell** *s* (physiol.) hematíe, glóbulo rojo
**red cent** *s* (coll.) centavo; **to be not worth a red cent** (coll.) no valer un pito
**red clover** *s* (bot.) trébol rojo
**redcoat** [ˈrɛdˌkot] *s* soldado inglés
**red corpuscle** *s* (physiol.) glóbulo rojo
**red cross** *s* cruz roja; (*caps.*) *s* Cruz Roja
**redd** [rɛd] (*pret & pp:* **redd** o **redded**) *va* (coll. & dial.) asear, poner en orden
**red deer** *s* (zool.) ciervo común; ciervo de Virginia (*cuando ostenta su pelaje rojizo de verano*)
**redden** [ˈrɛdən] *va* enrojecer; *vn* enrojecerse
**reddish** [ˈrɛdɪʃ] *adj* rojizo
**red dogwood** *s* (bot.) sanguiñuelo, sanapudio blanco, cornejo hembra
**redeem** [rɪˈdim] *va* redimir; cumplir (*una promesa*); compensar
**redeemable** [rɪˈdiməbəl] *adj* redimible
**redeemer** [rɪˈdimər] *s* redentor; (*cap.*) *s* Redentor
**redemption** [rɪˈdɛmpʃən] *s* redención
**redemptive** [rɪˈdɛmptɪv] o **redemptory** [rɪˈdɛmptərɪ] *adj* redentor
**redevelop** [ˌridɪˈvɛləp] *va* desarrollar de nuevo; (phot.) volver a revelar; *vn* desarrollarse de nuevo
**redevelopment** [ˌridɪˈvɛləpmənt] *s* nuevo desarrollo
**red-eyed** [ˈrɛdˌaɪd] *adj* con los ojos inyectados
**red fire** *s* fuego rojo (*compuesto de estroncio*)
**red flag** *s* bandera roja; provocación
**red fox** *s* (zool.) zorra roja; zorro rojo (*piel*)
**red-haired** [ˈrɛdˌhɛrd] *adj* pelirrojo
**red-handed** [ˈrɛdˈhændɪd] *adj* con las manos ensangrentadas; en flagrante
**red hat** *s* capelo (*sombrero rojo de los cardenales; dignidad de cardenal*)
**redhead** [ˈrɛdˌhɛd] *s* pelirrojo; (orn.) pato de cabeza colorada (*Nyroca americana*)
**redheaded** [ˈrɛdˌhɛdɪd] *adj* pelirrojo; de cabeza roja; colérico
**red heat** *s* calor rojo; **to a red heat** al rojo
**red herring** *s* arenque seco y ahumado; (fig.) artificio para distraer la atención del asunto de que se trata
**red-hot** [ˈrɛdˈhɑt] *adj* calentado al rojo, candente; ardiente, entusiasta; nuevo, fresco
**redingote** [ˈrɛdɪŋgot] *s* redingote
**redintegrate** [rɛdˈɪntɪgret] *va* reintegrar; *vn* reintegrarse
**redintegration** [rɛdˌɪntɪˈgreʃən] *s* reintegración
**redirect** [ˌridɪˈrɛkt] o [ˌridaɪˈrɛkt] *adj* (law) del segundo interrogatorio de un testigo por su abogado después de las repreguntas; *va* volver a dirigir
**rediscount** [riˈdɪskaʊnt] *s* redescuento; *va* redescontar
**rediscount rate** *s* tipo de redescuento
**rediscover** [ˌridɪsˈkʌvər] *va* redescubrir
**rediscovery** [ˌridɪsˈkʌvərɪ] *s* (*pl:* **-ies**) redescubrimiento
**redistribute** [ˌridɪsˈtrɪbjut] *va* redistribuir
**redistribution** [ˌridɪstrɪˈbjuʃən] *s* redistribución
**redistrict** [riˈdɪstrɪkt] *va* volver a dividir en distritos
**red lead** [lɛd] *s* rojo de plomo
**red-letter** [ˈrɛdˌlɛtər] *adj* marcado con letra roja; (fig.) feliz, memorable
**red light** *s* luz roja; (fig.) señal amonestadora
**red-light district** [ˈrɛdˈlaɪt] *s* barrio de los lupanares
**red man** *s* piel roja (*indio norteamericano*)
**red mullet** *s* (ichth.) salmonete
**redness** [ˈrɛdnɪs] *s* rojez; inflamación
**redo** [ˈriˈdu] *s* repetición; refundición; reforma; (*pret:* **-did;** *pp:* **-done**) *va* repetir, rehacer; refundir; reformar
**red oak** *s* (bot.) roble rojo
**red ocher** *s* (mineral.) ocre rojo, almagre
**redolence** [ˈrɛdələns] *s* fragancia, perfume
**redolent** [ˈrɛdələnt] *adj* fragante, perfumado; **redolent of** que huele a (*que despide un fuerte olor de; que hace pensar en*)
**redouble** [riˈdʌbəl] *va* redoblar; (bridge) decir recontra a; *vn* redoblarse; (bridge) decir recontra; volver atrás
**redoubt** [rɪˈdaʊt] *s* (fort.) reducto
**redoubtable** [rɪˈdaʊtəbəl] *adj* formidable, temible
**redound** [rɪˈdaʊnd] *vn* redundar; **to redound to** redundar en
**redowa** [ˈrɛdəwə] o [ˈrɛdəvə] *s* redova
**red pepper** *s* pimentón
**red periwinkle** *s* (bot.) dominica, flor de príncipe
**redpoll** [ˈrɛdˌpol] *s* (orn.) pajarel, pardillo
**redraft** [ˈriˌdræft] o [ˈriˌdrɑft] *s* nuevo dibujo, diseño o plan; nuevo borrador, nueva copia; (com.) resaca; [riˈdræft] o [riˈdrɑft] *va* volver a dibujar; hacer un nuevo borrador de; volver a trazar
**redress** [rɪˈdrɛs] o [ˈridrɛs] *s* reparación, resarcimiento; corrección, enmienda; alivio, remedio; equilibrio; [rɪˈdrɛs] *va* reparar, resarcir; corregir, enmendar; aliviar, remediar; equilibrar (*una balanza*)
**Red Ridinghood** [ˈraɪdɪŋˌhʊd] *s* Caperucita Roja
**red sandalwood** *s* (bot.) sándalo rojo
**Red Sea** *s* mar Rojo
**red shift** *s* (phys.) desviación hacia el rojo del espectro
**redskin** [ˈrɛdˌskɪn] *s* piel roja (*indio norteamericano*)
**red snapper** *s* (ichth.) huachinango
**red squirrel** *s* (zool.) ardilla roja de Norteamérica
**redstart** [ˈrɛdˌstɑrt] *s* (orn.) colirrojo (*Phoenicurus phoenicurus*); (orn.) candelita
**red tape** *s* balduque; (fig.) formalismo, expedienteo, papeleo
**redtop** [ˈrɛdˌtɑp] *s* (bot.) agróstide
**reduce** [rɪˈdjus] o [rɪˈdus] *va* reducir; (chem., math., surg. & phot.) reducir; (mil.) degradar; *vn* reducirse; reducir peso
**reducer** [rɪˈdjusər] o [rɪˈdusər] *s* reductor; (chem. & phot.) reductor; (mach.) reducción (*para unir dos tubos o árboles de calibres diferentes*)
**reducible** [rɪˈdjusɪbəl] o [rɪˈdusɪbəl] *adj* reducible
**reducing agent** *s* (chem.) agente reductor
**reducing exercises** *spl* ejercicios físicos para adelgazar o para reducir peso
**reducing flame** *s* (chem.) llama reductora
**reductase** [rɪˈdʌktes] o [rɪˈdʌktez] *s* (biochem.) reductasa
**reductio ad absurdum** [rɪˈdʌkʃɪo æd æbˈsʌrdəm] *s* reducción al absurdo
**reduction** [rɪˈdʌkʃən] *s* reducción
**redundance** [rɪˈdʌndəns] *s* var. de **redundancy**
**redundancy** [rɪˈdʌndənsɪ] *s* (*pl:* **-cies**) redundancia
**redundant** [rɪˈdʌndənt] *adj* redundante
**reduplicate** [rɪˈdjuplɪket] o [rɪˈduplɪket] *adj* reduplicado; (bot.) reduplicado; *va* reduplicar
**reduplication** [rɪˌdjuplɪˈkeʃən] o [rɪˌduplɪˈkeʃən] *s* reduplicación; (gram.) reduplicación
**red valerian** *s* (bot.) milamores
**red wine** *s* vino tinto
**redwing** [ˈrɛdˌwɪŋ] *s* (orn.) tordo alirrojo; (orn.) arrocero (*Agelaius phoeniceus*)
**red-winged blackbird** [ˈrɛdˌwɪŋd] *s* (orn.) arrocero

**redwood** ['rɛd,wud] *s* (bot.) secoya; madera de secoya
**reëcho** [ri'ɛko] *s* (*pl:* **-oes**) eco repetido; *va* repetir el eco de; repetir como eco; *vn* responder el eco; resonar
**reed** [rid] *s* (bot.) carrizo (*Phragmites communis*); (bot.) caña (*Arundo donax*); caña; flecha o saeta de caña; (mus.) instrumento de lengüeta; peine (*de los telares*); *adj* (mus.) de lengüeta
**reedbird** ['rid,bʌrd] *s* (orn.) chambergo
**reed instrument** *s* (mus.) instrumento de lengüeta
**reëdit** [ri'ɛdɪt] *va* refundir
**reed mace** *s* (bot.) espadaña
**reed organ** *s* (mus.) órgano de lengüetas
**reed pipe** *s* (mus.) tubo de lengüeta
**reëducate** [ri'ɛdʒəket] o [ri'ɛdʒuket] *va* reeducar
**reëducation** [,riɛdʒə'keʃən] o [,riɛdʒu'keʃən] *s* reeducación
**reedy** ['ridɪ] *adj* (*comp:* **-ier;** *super:* **-iest**) lleno de cañas; hecho de caña o cañas; agudo, de tono delgado y agudo
**reef** [rif] *s* arrecife, escollo; (min.) veta, filón; (naut.) parte de la vela que se puede aferrar con rizos; **to let out the reef** (naut.) largar rizos; **to take in the reef** (naut.) tomar rizos; *va* arrizar; **to reef one's sails** (fig.) aflojar en un empeño
**reef band** *s* (naut.) faja de rizos
**reefer** ['rifər] *s* (naut.) el que arriza las velas; chaquetón; (slang) pitillo de mariguana
**reef knot** *s* (naut.) nudo llano, nudo de rizos
**reef point** *s* (naut.) rizo
**reek** [rik] *s* vaho; *va* ahumar; despedir; oler a; *vn* vahear, humear; estar bañado en sudor; estar mojado con sangre; **to reek of** o **with** oler a
**reel** [ril] *s* carrete; tambor; carretel; devanadera; rollo; broca; baile escocés o virginiano muy vivo; película o cinta (*de cine*); tambaleo; **off the reel** (coll.) fácil y prestamente; *va* aspar (*en carretel*); tirar de (*un pez*) haciendo girar el carretel; devanar, enrollar; hacer tambalear; **to reel off** decir o narrar fácil y prestamente; *vn* tambalear, dar vueltas; cejar (*andar hacia atrás, p.ej., el enemigo*)
**reëlect** [,riɪ'lɛkt] *va* reelegir
**reëlection** [,riɪ'lɛkʃən] *s* reelección
**reëligible** [ri'ɛlɪdʒɪbəl] *adj* reelegible
**reëmbark** [,riɛm'bark] *va* reembarcar; *vn* reembarcar o reembarcarse
**reënact** [,riɛn'ækt] *va* volver a decretar; volver a promulgar; volver a desempeñar el papel de; reproducir, volver a representar; *vn* volver a actuar, volver a desempeñar un papel
**reënactment** [,riɛn'æktmənt] *s* ley o estatuto nuevo; nueva promulgación; nueva representación
**reënforce** [,riɛn'fors] *va* var. de **reinforce**
**reënforcement** [,riɛn'forsmənt] *s* var. de **reinforcement**
**reënlist** [,riɛn'lɪst] *va* reenganchar; *vn* reengancharse
**reënlistment** [,riɛn'lɪstmənt] *s* reenganche
**reënter** [ri'ɛntər] *va* reentrar en; volver a asentar; volver a matricular; volver a matricularse en; *vn* reentrar, reingresar; volver a matricularse
**reëntering** [ri'ɛntərɪŋ] *adj* (math. & mil.) entrante
**reëntry** [ri'ɛntrɪ] *s* (*pl:* **-tries**) reingreso, nueva entrada; vuelta a la atmósfera terrestre
**reëntry permit** *s* permiso de regreso
**reëstablish** [,riɛs'tæblɪʃ] *va* restablecer
**reëstablishment** [,riɛs'tæblɪʃmənt] *s* restablecimiento
**reeve** [riv] (*pret & pp:* **rove** o **reeved**) *va* (naut.) pasar en un ojal, jareta, etc.; (naut.) asegurar (*p.ej., un cabo*); (naut.) asegurar con cabo; *vn* (naut.) laborear
**reëxamination** [,riɛg,zæmɪ'neʃən] *s* reexaminación
**reëxamine** [,riɛg'zæmɪn] *va* reexaminar
**reëxport** [ri'ɛksport] *s* reexportación; [,riɛks'port] o [ri'ɛksport] *va* reexportar
**ref.** abr. de **referee, reference, referred, reformation, reformed** y **reformer**
**refection** [rɪ'fɛkʃən] *s* refacción o refección (*alimento*)
**refectory** [rɪ'fɛktərɪ] *s* (*pl:* **-ries**) refectorio
**refer** [rɪ'fʌr] (*pret & pp:* **-ferred;** *ger:* **-ferring**) *va* referir; *vn* referirse
**referee** [,rɛfə'ri] *s* (sport) árbitro; (law) juez árbitro; *va & vn* arbitrar
**reference** ['rɛfərəns] *s* referencia; persona a quien se puede acudir para referencias; **in** o **with reference to** en cuanto a, respecto de; **to make reference to** hacer alusión a
**reference frame** *s* var. de **frame of reference**
**reference library** *s* biblioteca de consulta
**reference mark** *s* (print.) llamada
**reference work** *s* obra de consulta
**referendum** [,rɛfə'rɛndəm] *s* (*pl:* **-da** [də]) referéndum
**refill** ['rifɪl] *s* relleno; [ri'fɪl] *va* rellenar
**refillable** [ri'fɪləbəl] *adj* rellenable
**refine** [rɪ'faɪn] *va* refinar; *vn* refinarse; sutilizar; **to refine on** o **upon** mejorar; aventajar, superar
**refined** [rɪ'faɪnd] *adj* refinado; fino, cortés, sutil; esmerado, exacto
**refinement** [rɪ'faɪnmənt] *s* refinamiento (*acción de refinar; buen gusto; perfeccionamiento*); sutileza
**refiner** [rɪ'faɪnər] *s* refinador
**refinery** [rɪ'faɪnərɪ] *s* (*pl:* **-ies**) refinería
**refit** [ri'fɪt] (*pret & pp:* **-fitted;** *ger:* **-fitting**) *va* componer, reparar, restaurar
**reflect** [rɪ'flɛkt] *va* reflejar; echar, traer consigo; *vn* reflejar o reflexionar; **to reflect on** o **upon** reflexionar en o sobre; tachar, notar
**reflecting telescope** *s* telescopio de espejo
**reflection** [rɪ'flɛkʃən] *s* reflexión; reflejo (*imagen*); tacha, reproche; (physiol.) reflejo
**reflective** [rɪ'flɛktɪv] *adj* reflexivo; (fig.) reflexivo
**reflector** [rɪ'flɛktər] *s* reflector
**reflex** ['riflɛks] *adj & s* reflejo; (physiol.) reflejo; [rɪ'flɛks] *va* replegar
**reflexible** [rɪ'flɛksɪbəl] *adj* reflexible
**reflexive** [rɪ'flɛksɪv] *adj & s* (gram.) reflexivo (*pronombre o verbo*)
**refloat** [ri'flot] *va* poner a flote nuevamente; *vn* flotar nuevamente
**refluent** ['rɛfluənt] *adj* refluente
**reflux** ['riflʌks] *s* reflujo
**reforest** [ri'fɑrɪst] o [ri'fɔrɪst] *va* volver a repoblar (*un monte*)
**reforestation** [,rifɑrɪs'teʃən] o [,rifɔrɪs'teʃən] *s* reforestación, nueva repoblación (*de un monte*)
**reform** [rɪ'fɔrm] *s* reforma; *va* reformar; *vn* reformarse
**re-form** [ri'fɔrm] *va* reformar; *vn* reformarse
**reformation** [,rɛfər'meʃən] *s* reformación; (*cap.*) *s* (hist.) Reforma
**reformative** [rɪ'fɔrmətɪv] *adj* reformativo
**reformatory** [rɪ'fɔrmə,torɪ] *adj* reformatorio; *s* (*pl:* **-ries**) reformatorio
**reformed** [rɪ'fɔrmd] *adj* reformado: (*cap.*) *adj & s* reformado
**reformer** [rɪ'fɔrmər] *s* reformador
**reformist** [rɪ'fɔrmɪst] *adj & s* reformista
**reform school** *s* casa de correción, reformatorio
**refract** [rɪ'frækt] *va* refractar; determinar la condición refractiva de (*un ojo*); determinar el poder refractor de (*un lente*)
**refraction** [rɪ'frækʃən] *s* (phys. & opt.) refracción; determinación de la condición refractiva del ojo
**refractive** [rɪ'fræktɪv] *adj* refractivo
**refractive index** *s* (opt.) índice de refracción
**refractometer** [,rifræk'tɑmɪtər] *s* refractómetro
**refractor** [rɪ'fræktər] *s* (opt.) refractor
**refractory** [rɪ'fræktərɪ] *adj* refractario
**refrain** [rɪ'fren] *s* estribillo; *vn* abstenerse, refrenarse; **to refrain from** abstenerse de
**refrangibility** [rɪ,frændʒɪ'bɪlɪtɪ] *s* refrangibilidad
**refrangible** [rɪ'frændʒɪbəl] *adj* refrangible
**refresh** [rɪ'frɛʃ] *va* refrescar; **to refresh the memory** refrescar la memoria; *vn* refrescarse
**refresher course** [rɪ'frɛʃər] *s* curso de repaso

**refreshing** [rɪ'frɛʃɪŋ] *adj* refrescante; alentador, confortante
**refreshment** [rɪ'frɛʃmənt] *s* refrescadura (*acción*); refresco (*alimento o bebida*)
**refrigerant** [rɪ'frɪdʒərənt] *adj* & *s* refrigerante
**refrigerate** [rɪ'frɪdʒəret] *va* refrigerar
**refrigeration** [rɪ,frɪdʒə'reʃən] *s* refrigeración
**refrigeration coil** *s* serpentín de refrigeración
**refrigerator** [rɪ'frɪdʒə,retər] *s* refrigerador, heladera, nevera
**refrigerator car** *s* (rail.) carro o vagón frigorífico
**refringency** [rɪ'frɪndʒənsɪ] *s* refringencia
**refringent** [rɪ'frɪndʒənt] *adj* refringente
**refuel** [ri'fjuəl] *va* reaprovisionar de combustible; *vn* reaprovisionarse de combustible
**refuge** ['rɛfjudʒ] *s* refugio; expediente, subterfugio; **to take refuge** refugiarse
**refugee** [,rɛfju'dʒi] *s* refugiado
**refulgence** [rɪ'fʌldʒəns] *s* refulgencia
**refulgent** [rɪ'fʌldʒənt] *adj* refulgente
**refund** ['rifʌnd] *s* reembolso; [rɪ'fʌnd] *va* reembolsar; [ri'fʌnd] *va* consolidar
**refurbish** [ri'fʌrbɪʃ] *va* restaurar, retocar, repulir
**refurnish** [ri'fʌrnɪʃ] *va* amueblar de nuevo
**refusal** [rɪ'fjuzəl] *s* denegación, negativa; opción exclusiva
**refuse** ['rɛfjus] *s* basura, desecho; hez, zupia; [rɪ'fjuz] *va* rehusar; rechazar, no querer aceptar; **to refuse to** + *inf* negarse a + *inf*, rehusar + *inf*
**refutation** [,rɛfjʊ'teʃən] *s* refutación
**refute** [rɪ'fjut] *va* refutar
**reg.** abr. de **register, registered, registrar, registry, regular** y **regularly**
**regain** [rɪ'gen] *va* recobrar, recuperar; volver a alcanzar
**regal** ['rigəl] *adj* regio
**regale** [rɪ'gel] *va* regalar; **to regale oneself** regalarse
**regalement** [rɪ'gelmənt] *s* regalamiento
**regalia** [rɪ'geliə] *s* cigarro de regalía; *spl* regalías (*derechos o privilegios pertenecientes al rey*); insignias reales; insignias o distintivos (*de una asociación, orden, etc.*); galas, trajes de lujo
**regalism** ['rigəlɪzəm] *s* regalismo
**regalist** ['rigəlɪst] *s* regalista
**regality** [rɪ'gælɪtɪ] *s* (*pl:* **-ties**) realeza; soberanía; reino
**regard** [rɪ'gɑrd] *s* mirada; consideración; respeto; respecto, relación; **regards** *spl* recuerdos; **in** o **with regard to** en cuanto a, respecto a o de; **without regard to** sin considerar, sin hacer caso de; **without any regard for** sin miramientos por; *va* mirar; considerar; tocar a, referirse a; **as regards** en cuanto a; *vn* mirar
**regardful** [rɪ'gɑrdfəl] *adj* atento; mirado, respetuoso
**regarding** [rɪ'gɑrdɪŋ] *prep* tocante a, respecto a o de
**regardless** [rɪ'gɑrdlɪs] *adj* desatento, descuidado, indiferente; *adv* (coll.) pese a quien pese, cueste lo que cueste; **regardless of** sin hacer caso de; a pesar de
**regatta** [rɪ'gætə] *s* regata
**regency** ['ridʒənsɪ] *s* (*pl:* **-cies**) regencia
**regeneracy** [rɪ'dʒɛnərəsɪ] *s* regeneración
**regenerate** [rɪ'dʒɛnərɪt] *adj* regenerado; [rɪ'dʒɛnəret] *va* regenerar; *vn* regenerarse
**regeneration** [rɪ,dʒɛnə'reʃən] *s* regeneración
**regenerative** [rɪ'dʒɛnə,retɪv] *adj* regenerativo
**regenerative braking** *s* (elec.) frenaje de regeneración
**regenerative furnace** *s* horno de regeneración
**regenerator** [rɪ'dʒɛnə,retər] *s* regenerador; (mach.) regenerador
**regent** ['ridʒənt] *adj* regente; *s* regente; miembro de una junta directiva
**regentship** ['ridʒəntʃɪp] *s* regencia
**regicidal** [,rɛdʒɪ'saɪdəl] *adj* regicida
**regicide** ['rɛdʒɪsaɪd] *s* regicidio (*acción*); regicida (*persona*)
**regild** [ri'gɪld] *va* volver a dorar
**regime** o **régime** [re'ʒim] o **regimen** ['rɛdʒɪmɛn] *s* régimen
**regiment** ['rɛdʒɪmənt] *s* (mil.) regimiento; ['rɛdʒɪmɛnt] *va* regimentar
**regimental** [,rɛdʒɪ'mɛntəl] *adj* regimental; **regimentals** *spl* uniforme militar
**regimentation** [,rɛdʒɪmɛn'teʃən] *s* regimentación
**Reginald** ['rɛdʒɪnəld] *s* Reginaldo
**region** ['ridʒən] *s* región
**regional** ['ridʒənəl] *adj* regional
**regionalism** ['ridʒənəlɪzəm] *s* regionalismo
**regionalist** ['ridʒənəlɪst] *adj* & *s* regionalista
**register** ['rɛdʒɪstər] *s* registro; registrador (*aparato*); registro parroquial; reja regulable de calefacción; índice, tabla de materias; (mus.) extensión (*de la voz, de un instrumento*); (naut.) matrícula; (print.) registro; *va* registrar; manifestar, dar a conocer; certificar; (print.) registrar; *vn* registrarse; inscribirse
**registered letter** *s* carta certificada
**registered nurse** *s* (U.S.A.) enfermera titulada
**registrable** ['rɛdʒɪstrəbəl] *adj* registrable
**registrar** ['rɛdʒɪstrɑr] o [,rɛdʒɪ'strɑr] *s* registrador, archivero
**registration** [,rɛdʒɪ'streʃən] *s* registro, inscripción; matrícula
**registration fee** *s* derechos de matrícula
**registry** ['rɛdʒɪstrɪ] *s* (*pl:* **-tries**) registro
**regnant** ['rɛgnənt] *adj* reinante
**regress** ['rigrɛs] *s* retroceso; (astr.) retrogradación; (eccl.) regreso; [rɪ'grɛs] *vn* retroceder; (astr.) retrogradar
**regression** [rɪ'grɛʃən] *s* regresión
**regressive** [rɪ'grɛsɪv] *adj* regresivo
**regret** [rɪ'grɛt] *s* pesar, sentimiento; pesadumbre, remordimiento; **regrets** *spl* excusas (*que se envían para rehusar una invitación*); (*pret* & *pp:* **-gretted;** *ger:* **-gretting**) *va* sentir, lamentar; lamentar la pérdida de; arrepentirse de; **to regret to** + *inf* sentir + *inf*
**regretful** [rɪ'grɛtfəl] *adj* pesaroso; deplorable
**regrettable** [rɪ'grɛtəbəl] *adj* lamentable
**regrettably** [rɪ'grɛtəblɪ] *adv* lamentablemente
**regroup** [ri'grup] *va* reagrupar; *vn* reagruparse
**Regt.** abr. de **regent** y **regiment**
**regular** ['rɛgjələr] *adj* regular; (bot., eccl., geom., gram. & mil.) regular; (coll.) cabal, completo, verdadero; *s* obrero permanente; parroquiano regular; (eccl. & mil.) regular; **regulars** *spl* (mil.) tropas regulares
**regularity** [,rɛgjə'lærɪtɪ] *s* regularidad
**regularization** [,rɛgjələrɪ'zeʃən] *s* regularización
**regularize** ['rɛgjələraɪz] *va* regularizar
**regulate** ['rɛgjəlet] *va* regular; graduar (*p.ej., un grifo*)
**regulation** [,rɛgjə'leʃən] *s* regulación; regla, ordenanza; *adj* regular; de regla, de ordenanza
**regulative** ['rɛgjə,letɪv] *adj* regulativo
**regulator** ['rɛgjə,letər] *s* regulador; (mach. & elec.) regulador
**regulatory** ['rɛgjələ,torɪ] *adj* regulador
**regulus** ['rɛgjələs] *s* (*pl:* **-luses** o **-li** [laɪ]) régulo; (chem. & metal.) régulo; (*cap.*) *s* (astr.) Régulo
**regurgitate** [ri'gʌrdʒɪtet] *va* volver a arrojar (*un líquido*); vomitar sin esfuerzo; *vn* regurgitar
**regurgitation** [ri,gʌrdʒɪ'teʃən] *s* regurgitación
**rehabilitate** [,rihə'bɪlɪtet] *va* rehabilitar
**rehabilitation** [,rihə,bɪlɪ'teʃən] *s* rehabilitación
**rehandle** [ri'hændəl] *va* manejar de nuevo
**rehash** ['rihæʃ] *s* rehacimiento; repetición (*p.ej., de viejos argumentos*); refundición, refrito (*especialmente de una obra dramática*); [ri'hæʃ] *va* rehacer; repetir una y otra vez
**rehearsal** [rɪ'hʌrsəl] *s* ensayo; repetición detallada
**rehearse** [rɪ'hʌrs] *va* ensayar; repetir detalladamente; *vn* ensayarse; **to rehearse** + *ger* ensayarse a + *inf*
**reheat** [ri'hit] *va* recalentar
**reign** [ren] *s* reino; reinado; dominio, imperio; **in the reign of** durante el reinado de; *vn* reinar
**reignite** [,riɪg'naɪt] *va* reencender; *vn* reencenderse
**Reign of Terror** *s* (hist.) Terror

**reimburse** [ˌriɪmˈbʌrs] *va* reembolsar
**reimbursement** [ˌriɪmˈbʌrsmənt] *s* reembolso
**reimport** [riˈɪmport] *s* reimportación; [ˌriɪmˈport] o [riˈɪmport] *va* reimportar
**reimportation** [ˌriɪmporˈteʃən] *s* reimportación
**reimpression** [ˌriɪmˈprɛʃən] *s* reimpresión
**rein** [ren] *s* rienda; **to draw rein** tener las riendas; detener el paso, parar; **to give rein to** aflojar las riendas a; **to give free rein to** dar rienda suelta a; **to take the reins** tomar las riendas; **with free rein** a rienda suelta; *va* dirigir por medio de riendas; contener, gobernar, refrenar; *vn* obedecer a las riendas; detener el paso
**reincarnate** [ˌriɪnˈkɑrnet] *va* reencarnar
**reincarnation** [ˌriɪnkɑrˈneʃən] *s* reencarnación
**reindeer** [ˈrenˌdɪr] *s* (zool.) reno
**reinfect** [ˌriɪnˈfɛkt] *va* reinfectar
**reinfection** [ˌriɪnˈfɛkʃən] *s* reinfección
**reinflate** [ˌriɪnˈflet] *va* reinflar
**reinforce** [ˌriɪnˈfors] *va* reforzar
**reinforced concrete** *s* cemento armado, hormigón armado
**reinforcement** [ˌriɪnˈforsmənt] *s* refuerzo; **reinforcements** *spl* (mil.) refuerzos
**reinoculate** [ˌriɪnˈɑkjəlet] *va* reinocular; *vn* reinocularse
**reinoculation** [ˌriɪnˌɑkjəˈleʃən] *s* reinoculación
**reinstall** [ˌriɪnˈstɔl] *va* reinstalar
**reinstate** [ˌriɪnˈstet] *va* reinstalar; renovar
**reinstatement** [ˌriɪnˈstetmənt] *s* reinstalación; renovación
**reinsurance** [ˌriɪnˈʃurəns] *s* reaseguro
**reinsure** [ˌriɪnˈʃur] *va* reasegurar
**reinvest** [ˌriɪnˈvɛst] *va* reinvertir
**reinvestment** [ˌriɪnˈvɛstmənt] *s* reinversión
**reiterate** [riˈɪtəret] *va* reiterar
**reiteration** [riˌɪtəˈreʃən] *s* reiteración
**reiterative** [riˈɪtəˌretɪv] *adj* reiterativo
**reject** [rɪˈdʒɛkt] *va* rechazar; arrojar (*vomitar*)
**rejection** [rɪˈdʒɛkʃən] *s* rechazamiento; vómito; **rejections** *spl* excremento
**rejoice** [rɪˈdʒɔɪs] *va* regocijar; *vn* regocijarse
**rejoicing** [rɪˈdʒɔɪsɪŋ] *s* regocijo
**rejoin** [riˈdʒɔɪn] *va* volver a juntar o unir; volver a juntarse con, volver a la compañía de; [rɪˈdʒɔɪn] *va* contestar; *vn* contestar; (law) duplicar
**rejoinder** [rɪˈdʒɔɪndər] *s* contestación; (law) contrarréplica
**rejuvenate** [rɪˈdʒuvɪnet] *va* rejuvenecer; *vn* rejuvenecerse
**rejuvenation** [rɪˌdʒuvɪˈneʃən] *s* rejuvenecimiento
**rekindle** [riˈkɪndəl] *va* reencender; *vn* reencenderse
**rel.** abr. de **relating, relative, relatively, religion** y **religious**
**relaid** [riˈled] *pret & pp de* **relay**
**relapse** [rɪˈlæps] *s* recaída; *vn* recaer
**relate** [rɪˈlet] *va* relacionar; contar, relatar; *vn* relacionarse
**related** [rɪˈletɪd] *adj* relacionado
**relation** [rɪˈleʃən] *s* relación; narración, relato; pariente; parentesco; **relations** *spl* cópula; **in relation to** o **with relation to** respecto de
**relational** [rɪˈleʃənəl] *adj* que expresa relación; de parentesco
**relationship** [rɪˈleʃənʃɪp] *s* relación; parentesco
**relative** [ˈrɛlətɪv] *adj* relativo; (gram.) relativo; *s* deudo, pariente; (gram.) relativo
**relative clause** *s* (gram.) oración de relativo
**relative humidity** *s* (meteor.) humedad relativa
**relatively** [ˈrɛlətɪvlɪ] *adv* relativamente
**relativism** [ˈrɛlətɪvɪzəm] *s* relativismo
**relativity** [ˌrɛləˈtɪvɪtɪ] *s* relatividad; (phys.) relatividad
**relator** [rɪˈletər] *s* relator
**relax** [rɪˈlæks] *va* relajar; esparcir, desahogar; *vn* relajar (*aflojarse; hacerse menos severo*); esparcirse, desahogarse, despreocuparse
**relaxation** [ˌrilækˈseʃən] *s* relajación; esparcimiento, desahogo, despreocupación
**relaxation of tension** *s* disminución de la tirantez internacional
**relaxative** [rɪˈlæksətɪv] *adj & s* relajante
**relaxedly** [rɪˈlæksɪdlɪ] *adv* relajadamente; desahogadamente
**relaxing** [rɪˈlæksɪŋ] *adj* despreocupante
**relay** [ˈrile] o [rɪˈle] *s* relevo, remuda; parada, posta (*de caballos*); (mil. & sport) relevo; (sport) carrera de relevos o de equipos; (elec.) relai o relais; (*pret & pp:* **-layed**) *va* transmitir relevándose; enviar por la posta; transmitir con un relais; retransmitir (*una emisión*); reexpedir (*un radiotelegrama*); [riˈle] (*pret & pp:* **-laid**) *va* volver a colocar
**relay race** *s* (sport) carrera de relevos o de equipos
**release** [rɪˈlis] *s* liberación; excarcelación; alivio; finiquito; desprendimiento; (mach.) escape, disparador; (law) cesión; (law) acta o escritura de cesión; permiso de publicación, venta, etc.; obra o pieza lista para la publicación, venta, etc.; (aer.) lanzamiento; *va* soltar; aliviar; relevar; (law) ceder; permitir la publicación, venta, etc. de; (aut.) soltar (*el embrague, el freno*); (aer.) lanzar (*una bomba*)
**re-lease** [riˈlis] *va* arrendar de nuevo
**relegate** [ˈrɛlɪget] *va* relegar
**relegation** [ˌrɛlɪˈgeʃən] *s* relegación
**relent** [rɪˈlɛnt] *vn* ablandarse, aplacarse
**relentless** [rɪˈlɛntlɪs] *adj* implacable
**relevance** [ˈrɛlɪvəns] o **relevancy** [ˈrɛlɪvənsɪ] *s* pertinencia
**relevant** [ˈrɛlɪvənt] *adj* pertinente
**reliability** [rɪˌlaɪəˈbɪlɪtɪ] *s* confiabilidad
**reliable** [rɪˈlaɪəbəl] *adj* confiable, fidedigno
**reliable sources** *spl* fuentes fidedignas
**reliably** [rɪˈlaɪəblɪ] *adv* de un modo confiable
**reliance** [rɪˈlaɪəns] *s* confianza
**reliant** [rɪˈlaɪənt] *adj* confiado
**relic** [ˈrɛlɪk] *s* reliquia
**relict** [rɪˈlɪkt] *adj* (biol.) relicto; [ˈrɛlɪkt] *s* (biol.) reliquia, forma relicta; viuda; **relicts** *spl* restos mortales
**relief** [rɪˈlif] *s* relevación; alivio; caridad; relieve (*labor que resalta sobre un plano*); (fort.) relieve; (mil.) relevo; **in relief** en relieve; **on relief** viviendo de socorro, recibiendo manutención gratuita
**relief map** *s* mapa en relieve
**relieve** [rɪˈliv] *va* relevar; aliviar; auxiliar (*a los necesitados*); (mil.) relevar
**relievo** [rɪˈlivo] *s* (*pl:* **-vos**) relieve
**relight** [riˈlaɪt] *va* reencender
**religion** [rɪˈlɪdʒən] *s* religión
**religiosity** [rɪˌlɪdʒɪˈɑsɪtɪ] *s* religiosidad; beatería
**religious** [rɪˈlɪdʒəs] *adj* religioso; *s* religioso; *spl* religiosos
**reline** [riˈlaɪn] *va* reforrar, revestir; (aut.) reforrar (*los frenos*)
**relinquish** [rɪˈlɪŋkwɪʃ] *va* abandonar, dejar, renunciar
**relinquishment** [rɪˈlɪŋkwɪʃmənt] *s* abandono, dejación, renuncia
**reliquary** [ˈrɛlɪˌkwɛrɪ] *s* (*pl:* **-ies**) relicario
**relique** [ˈrɛlɪk] o [rɛˈlik] *s* var. de **relic**
**relish** [ˈrɛlɪʃ] *s* buen sabor, gusto; condimento, sazón; dejo, gustillo, saborcillo; entremés; *va* saborear; gustar de; comer o beber con placer; *vn* saber bien; agradar, gustar
**relive** [riˈlɪv] *va* volver a llevar (*tal o cual vida*); repasar en la memoria (*un tiempo pasado*); *vn* renacer, volver a la vida
**reload** [riˈlod] *va* recargar, volver a cargar
**reluctance** [rɪˈlʌktəns] *s* renuencia, aversión; (elec.) reluctancia; **with reluctance** de mala gana
**reluctancy** [rɪˈlʌktənsɪ] *s* renuencia, aversión
**reluctant** [rɪˈlʌktənt] *adj* renuente, maldispuesto
**reluctivity** [ˌrɛləkˈtɪvɪtɪ] *s* (elec.) reluctividad
**relume** [riˈlum] *va* reencender
**rely** [rɪˈlaɪ] (*pret & pp:* **-lied**) *vn* depender, confiar; **to rely on** depender de, confiar en
**remade** [riˈmed] *pret & pp de* **remake**
**remain** [rɪˈmen] *vn* permanecer, quedarse; restar; continuar; **to remain to be** + *pp* quedar por + *inf*, p.ej., **more than half of the railroad remains to be built** aún queda más de la mitad del ferrocarril por construir;

**remains** *spl* desechos, residuos, restos; restos mortales; obra póstuma
**remainder** [rɪˈmendər] *s* resto, restante, residuo; (math.) resta, resto o residuo; libro casi invendible; *va* saldar (*libros que ya no se venden*)
**remake** [riˈmek] (*pret & pp:* **-made**) *va* rehacer
**remand** [rɪˈmænd] o [rɪˈmɑnd] *va* reencarcelamiento; persona reencarcelada; *va* reencarcelar
**remanent magnetism** [ˈrɛmənənt] *s* (phys.) magnetismo remanente
**remark** [rɪˈmɑrk] *s* observación, nota; *va & vn* observar, notar; **to remark on** o **upon** aludir a, comentar
**remarkable** [rɪˈmɑrkəbəl] *adj* notable, extraordinario
**remarkably** [rɪˈmɑrkəblɪ] *adv* notablemente, extraordinariamente
**remarriage** [riˈmærɪdʒ] *s* segundas (o terceras, etc.) nupcias
**remarry** [riˈmærɪ] (*pret & pp:* **-ried**) *vn* volver a casarse
**remediable** [rɪˈmidɪəbəl] *adj* remediable
**remediably** [rɪˈmidɪəblɪ] *adv* remediablemente
**remedial** [rɪˈmidɪəl] *adj* remediador
**remediless** [ˈrɛmɪdɪlɪs] *adj* irremediable, sin remedio
**remedy** [ˈrɛmɪdɪ] *s* (*pl:* **-dies**) remedio; (*pret & pp:* **-died**) *va* remediar
**remember** [rɪˈmɛmbər] *va* acordarse de, recordar; **to remember to** + *inf* acordarse de + *inf*, recordar + *inf*, p.ej., **he remembered to do it** se acordó de hacerlo, recordó hacerlo; **to remember** + *ger* acordarse de + *perf inf*, recordar + *perf inf*, p.ej., **he remembered doing it** se acordaba de haberlo hecho, recordaba haberlo hecho; **remember me to your brother** recuerdos a su hermano, déle Vd. a su hermano recuerdos o memorias de mi parte; *vn* acordarse, recordar; **if I remember correctly** si mal no me acuerdo, si mal no recuerdo
**remembrance** [rɪˈmɛmbrəns] *s* recuerdo; **remembrances** *spl* recuerdos, saludos
**remembrancer** [rɪˈmɛmbrənsər] *s* recordatorio, recordativo
**remiges** [ˈrɛmɪdʒiz] *spl* (orn.) rémiges, remeras
**remind** [rɪˈmaɪnd] *va* recordar; **to remind someone of something** recordar algo a alguien; **to remind to** + *inf* recordar que + *subj*, p.ej., **remind him to write** recuérdele Vd. que escriba
**reminder** [rɪˈmaɪndər] *s* recordatorio, recordativo
**Remington gun** [ˈrɛmɪŋtən] *s* rémington
**reminisce** [ˌrɛmɪˈnɪs] *vn* contar sus recuerdos, entregarse a los recuerdos
**reminiscence** [ˌrɛmɪˈnɪsəns] *s* reminiscencia; (philos.) reminiscencia
**reminiscent** [ˌrɛmɪˈnɪsənt] *adj* recordativo; evocador
**remiss** [rɪˈmɪs] *adj* descuidado, negligente
**remissible** [rɪˈmɪsɪbəl] *adj* remisible
**remission** [rɪˈmɪʃən] *s* remisión
**remission of sins** *s* remisión de los pecados
**remissness** [rɪˈmɪsnɪs] *s* descuido, negligencia
**remit** [rɪˈmɪt] (*pret & pp:* **-mitted;** *ger:* **-mitting**) *va* remitir; devolver, restituir; reencarcelar; *vn* remitir dinero; remitir o remitirse
**remittal** [rɪˈmɪtəl] *s* remisión
**remittance** [rɪˈmɪtəns] *s* remesa
**remittent** [rɪˈmɪtənt] *adj* remitente
**remnant** [ˈrɛmnənt] *adj* remanente; *s* remanente, resto; retal, retazo; saldo (*resto de mercancías*)
**remodel** [riˈmɑdəl] (*pret & pp:* **-eled** o **-elled;** *ger:* **-eling** o **-elling**) *va* modelar de nuevo; rehacer, reconstruir; convertir, transformar
**remonetize** [riˈmɑnɪtaɪz] o [riˈmʌnɪtaɪz] *va* volver a monetizar
**remonstrance** [rɪˈmɑnstrəns] *s* protesta, reconvención
**remonstrant** [rɪˈmɑnstrənt] *adj & s* protestante
**remonstrate** [rɪˈmɑnstret] *vn* protestar; **to remonstrate with** reconvenir
**remonstration** [ˌrimɑnˈstreʃən] o [ˌrɛmɑnˈstreʃən] *s* protesta, reconvención
**remonstrative** [rɪˈmɑnstrətɪv] *adj* protestante
**remonstrator** [rɪˈmɑnstretər] *s* protestante
**remora** [ˈrɛmərə] *s* (ichth.) rémora
**remorse** [rɪˈmɔrs] *s* remordimiento
**remote** [rɪˈmot] *adj* remoto
**remote control** *s* comando a distancia, telecontrol, control remoto
**remotely** [rɪˈmotlɪ] *adv* remotamente
**remount** [riˈmaʊnt] *s* caballo de remonta; remonta (*conjunto de caballos*); *va* volver a subir (*p.ej., una escalera*); (mil.) remontar; *vn* volver a subir
**removal** [rɪˈmuvəl] *s* sacamiento; remoción; mudanza, traslado; eliminación; deposición (*de un empleo*)
**remove** [rɪˈmuv] *s* grado, paso, escalón; mudanza; *va* remover; quitar de en medio, apartar matando; *vn* removerse
**removed** [rɪˈmuvd] *adj* distante, apartado; **first cousin once removed** hijo de primo carnal
**remunerate** [rɪˈmjunəret] *va* remunerar
**remuneration** [rɪˌmjunəˈreʃən] *s* remuneración
**remunerative** [rɪˈmjunəˌretɪv] *adj* remunerativo
**Remus** [ˈriməs] *s* (myth.) Remo
**renaissance** [ˌrɛnəˈsɑns] o [rɪˈnesəns] *s* renacimiento; (*cap.*) *s* Renacimiento
**renal** [ˈrinəl] *adj* renal
**rename** [riˈnem] *va* volver a nombrar, dar nuevo nombre a
**Renard** [ˈrɛnərd] *s* var. de **Reynard**
**renascence** [rɪˈnæsəns] *s* renacimiento; (*cap.*) *s* Renacimiento
**renascent** [rɪˈnæsənt] *adj* renaciente
**rencounter** [rɛnˈkaʊntər] *s* altercado, refriega; encuentro fortuito
**rend** [rɛnd] (*pret & pp:* **rent**) *va* desgarrar; hender, rajar; arrancar; estremecer (*un ruido el aire*)
**render** [ˈrɛndər] *va* rendir (*gracias, obsequios, homenaje*); prestar, suministrar (*p.ej., ayuda*); pagar (*p.ej., un tributo*); desempeñar (*un papel*); traducir (*p.ej., sentimientos*); verter (*de un idioma a otro*); derretir (*cera, manteca, etc.*); extraer o clarificar derritiendo; extraer la grasa o el sebo a; dar la primera capa de enlucido a; volver, poner; hacer (*p.ej., justicia*); (mus.) ejecutar
**rendezvous** [ˈrɑndəvu] *s* (*pl;* **-vous** [vuz]) cita; encuentro, reunión (*en el espacio*); (*pret & pp:* **-voused** [vud]; *ger:* **-vousing** [vuɪŋ]) *va* reunir a una cita; *vn* reunirse a una cita
**rendition** [rɛnˈdɪʃən] *s* rendición; traducción; (mus.) ejecución
**renegade** [ˈrɛnɪged] *adj & s* renegado; traidor; desertor
**renege** [rɪˈnɪg] *s* renuncio; *va* renunciar; *vn* renunciar; (coll.) volverse atrás, no cumplir su promesa
**renegotiation** [ˌrinɪˌgoʃɪˈeʃən] *s* renegociación
**renew** [rɪˈnju] o [rɪˈnu] *va* renovar; *vn* renovarse; obtener o conceder una renovación o extensión de contrato, cuenta, etc.
**renewable** [rɪˈnjuəbəl] o [rɪˈnuəbəl] *adj* renovable
**renewal** [rɪˈnjuəl] o [rɪˈnuəl] *s* renovación
**renewedly** [rɪˈnjuɪdlɪ] o [rɪˈnuɪdlɪ] *adv* de nuevo, otra vez
**reniform** [ˈrɛnɪfɔrm] o [ˈrinɪfɔrm] *adj* reniforme
**rennet** [ˈrɛnɪt] *s* cuajo
**rennet bag** *s* (zool.) cuajar
**rennin** [ˈrɛnɪn] *s* (biochem.) quimosina
**renomination** [riˌnɑmɪˈneʃən] *s* nueva nominación, nuevo nombramiento
**renounce** [rɪˈnaʊns] *va* renunciar (*p.ej., una herencia, un ofrecimiento, un derecho*); renunciar a (*un proyecto*); desconocer; *vn* renunciar
**renouncement** [rɪˈnaʊnsmənt] *s* renunciación; desconocimiento
**renovate** [ˈrɛnovet] *va* renovar; reformar (*p.ej., una tienda, una casa*)
**renovation** [ˌrɛnoˈveʃən] *s* renovación; reforma
**renovator** [ˈrɛnoˌvetər] *s* renovador

**renown** [rɪˈnaʊn] *s* renombre
**renowned** [rɪˈnaʊnd] *adj* renombrado
**rent** [rɛnt] *s* alquiler, arriendo; renta de la tierra; desgarro, rasgón; cisma, desavenencia; **for rent** se alquila; *adj* desgarrado, rasgado; andrajoso, haraposo; *va* alquilar, arrendar; *vn* alquilarse, arrendarse; *pret & pp de* **rend**
**rentable** [ˈrɛntəbəl] *adj* arrendable
**rental** [ˈrɛntəl] *s* alquiler, arriendo
**rent control** *s* control de alquileres
**renter** [ˈrɛntər] *s* inquilino, arrendatario
**rent roll** *s* lista de rentas
**renumber** [riˈnʌmbər] *va* volver a numerar, corregir la numeración de
**renunciation** [rɪˌnʌnsɪˈeʃən] o [rɪˌnʌnʃɪˈeʃən] *s* renunciación, renunciamiento; desconocimiento
**reopen** [riˈopən] *va* reabrir; *vn* reabrirse
**reopening** [riˈopənɪŋ] *s* reapertura
**reorganization** [ˌriɔrgənɪˈzeʃən] *s* reorganización
**reorganize** [riˈɔrgənaɪz] *va* reorganizar; *vn* reorganizarse
**reorient** [riˈorɪɛnt] *va* reorientar
**rep.** abr. de **report, reported, reporter, representative** y **republic**
**Rep.** abr. de **Republic** y **Republican**
**rep** [rɛp] *s* reps (*tela*); (slang) reputación
**repack** [riˈpæk] *va* reempacar; (mach.) reempaquetar
**repaid** [rɪˈped] *pret & pp de* **repay**
**repaint** [riˈpent] *s* repinte; *va & vn* repintar
**repair** [rɪˈpɛr] *s* reparación; remonta (*de las botas*); **in repair** en buen estado; **in bad repair** en mal estado; **in good repair** en buen estado; *va* reparar; remontar (*botas*); *vn* dirigirse; volver
**repairable** [rɪˈpɛrəbəl] *adj* var. de **reparable**
**repairman** [rɪˈpɛrˌmæn] o [rɪˈpɛrmən] *s* (*pl:* **-men**) reparador, mecánico
**repair service** *s* servicio de reparaciones
**repair shop** *s* taller de reparaciones
**repaper** [riˈpepər] *va* empapelar de nuevo
**reparable** [ˈrɛpərəbəl] *adj* reparable
**reparation** [ˌrɛpəˈreʃən] *s* reparación
**reparative** [rɪˈpærətɪv] *adj* reparativo
**repartee** [ˌrɛpɑrˈti] *s* respuesta viva y bien sentada; agudeza y gracia en responder
**repartition** [ˌripɑrˈtɪʃən] o [ˌripərˈtɪʃən] *s* reparto; *va* repartir
**repass** [riˈpæs] o [riˈpɑs] *va* repasar; hacer repasar; volver a aprobar (*un proyecto de ley*); *vn* repasar
**repast** [rɪˈpæst] o [rɪˈpɑst] *s* comida, comilona
**repatriate** [riˈpetrɪet] *s* repatriado; *va* repatriar
**repatriation** [riˌpetrɪˈeʃən] *s* repatriación
**repave** [riˈpev] *va* repavimentar
**repay** [rɪˈpe] (*pret & pp:* **-paid**) *va* reembolsar; resarcir; compensar
**repayable** [rɪˈpeəbəl] *adj* reembolsable; resarcible; compensable
**repayment** [rɪˈpemənt] *s* reembolso; resarcimiento; compensación
**repeal** [rɪˈpil] *s* abrogación, revocación; *va* abrogar, revocar
**repeat** [rɪˈpit] *s* repetición; (mus.) repetición; *va* repetir; **to repeat oneself** repetirse; *vn* repetir; (path.) repetir; (U.S.A.) volver a votar en la misma elección (*ilegalmente*)
**repeatedly** [rɪˈpitɪdlɪ] *adv* repetidamente
**repeater** [rɪˈpitər] *s* repetidor; rifle de repetición; reloj de repetición; (U.S.A.) persona que vota más de una vez en una elección; (telp.) repetidor
**repeating decimal** *s* (math.) fracción decimal periódica
**repeating rifle** *s* rifle de repetición
**repeating watch** *s* reloj de repetición
**repel** [rɪˈpɛl] (*pret & pp:* **-pelled;** *ger:* **-pelling**) *va* rechazar; repugnar
**repellent** [rɪˈpɛlənt] *adj* repulsivo; (med.) repercusivo; *s* tela impermeable; (med.) repercusivo
**repent** [rɪˈpɛnt] *va* arrepentirse de; *vn* arrepentirse; **to repent having** + *pp* arrepentirse de haber + *pp*
**repentance** [rɪˈpɛntəns] *s* arrepentimiento
**repentant** [rɪˈpɛntənt] *adj* arrepentido; de arrepentimiento
**repeople** [riˈpipəl] *va* repoblar
**repercussion** [ˌripərˈkʌʃən] *s* repercusión
**repertoire** [ˈrɛpərtwɑr] *s* repertorio
**repertory** [ˈrɛpərˌtorɪ] *s* (*pl:* **-ries**) repertorio
**repertory theater** *s* teatro de repertorio
**repetend** [ˈrɛpɪtɛnd] o [ˌrɛpɪˈtɛnd] *s* (math.) período
**repetition** [ˌrɛpɪˈtɪʃən] *s* repetición
**repetitious** [ˌrɛpɪˈtɪʃəs] *adj* repetidor
**repetitive** [rɪˈpɛtɪtɪv] *adj* reiterativo
**rephrase** [riˈfrez] *va* volver a expresar o formular; expresar o formular de modo diferente
**repine** [rɪˈpaɪn] *vn* apurarse, afligirse, quejarse
**replace** [rɪˈples] *va* reponer; reemplazar
**replaceable** [rɪˈplesəbəl] *adj* reemplazable
**replacement** [rɪˈplesmənt] *s* reposición; reemplazo; repuesto; pieza de repuesto; (mil.) soldado reemplazante
**replacement center** *s* (mil.) centro de substitución
**replant** [riˈplænt] o [riˈplɑnt] *va* replantar; resembrar
**replenish** [rɪˈplɛnɪʃ] *va* llenar, henchir; rellenar, rehenchir; reaprovisionar; colmar de inspiración
**replenishment** [rɪˈplɛnɪʃmənt] *s* henchimiento; relleno; reaprovisionamiento
**replete** [rɪˈplit] *adj* repleto
**repletion** [rɪˈpliʃən] *s* repleción
**replevin** [rɪˈplɛvɪn] *s* (law) reivindicación; (law) auto de desembargo; *va* (law) reivindicar
**replevy** [rɪˈplɛvɪ] (*pret & pp:* **-ied**) *va* (law) reivindicar
**replica** [ˈrɛplɪkə] *s* (f.a.) réplica; (mus.) repetición; segunda edición (*persona o cosa muy semejante a otra*)
**reply** [rɪˈplaɪ] *s* (*pl:* **-plies**) contestación, respuesta; (*pret & pp:* **-plied**) *va* contestar, responder; *vn* contestar, responder; (law) replicar
**reply coupon** *s* cupón-respuesta
**report** [rɪˈport] *s* relato; informe; denuncia; detonación, tiro; rumor; reputación; *va* relatar; informar acerca de, redactar un informe acerca de; denunciar; **to report out** devolver o presentar (*p.ej., un proyecto de ley*) con dictamen o informes; *vn* hacer un relato; redactar un informe; ser repórter; presentarse; **to report on** notificar
**reportable** [rɪˈportəbəl] *adj* digno de ser relatado
**report card** *s* certificado escolar
**reportedly** [rɪˈportɪdlɪ] *adv* según se informa
**reporter** [rɪˈportər] *s* relator; repórter o reportero (*de un periódico*)
**reporting** [rɪˈpɔrtɪŋ] *s* reportaje
**reportorial** [ˌrɛpərˈtorɪəl] *adj* reporteril
**repose** [rɪˈpoz] *s* descanso; *va* descansar; poner (*confianza*); *vn* descansar
**reposeful** [rɪˈpozfəl] *adj* reposado
**repository** [rɪˈpɑzɪˌtorɪ] *s* (*pl:* **-ries**) almacén, depósito, repositorio; depositario (*persona*); mina o almacén (*de información*); filón
**repossess** [ˌripəˈzɛs] *va* recobrar; **to repossess of** o **in** restaurar en la posesión de
**repossession** [ˌripəˈzɛʃən] *s* recobro
**repoussé** [rəpuˈse] *adj & s* repujado
**repp** [rɛp] *s* reps (*tela*)
**reprehend** [ˌrɛprɪˈhɛnd] *va* reprender
**reprehensible** [ˌrɛprɪˈhɛnsɪbəl] *adj* reprensible
**reprehension** [ˌrɛprɪˈhɛnʃən] *s* reprensión
**represent** [ˌrɛprɪˈzɛnt] *va* representar
**re-present** [ˌriprɪˈzɛnt] *va* volver a presentar
**representation** [ˌrɛprɪzɛnˈteʃən] *s* representación
**representative** [ˌrɛprɪˈzɛntətɪv] *adj* representativo; *s* representante
**repress** [rɪˈprɛs] *va* reprimir
**repressible** [rɪˈprɛsɪbəl] *adj* reprimible
**repression** [rɪˈprɛʃən] *s* represión; (psychoanal.) represión
**repressive** [rɪˈprɛsɪv] *adj* represivo
**reprieve** [rɪˈpriv] *s* suspensión temporal de un castigo, suspensión temporal de la pena de

muerte; respiro, alivio temporal; *va* suspender temporalmente el castigo de, suspender temporalmente la pena de muerte de; aliviar temporalmente
**reprimand** ['rɛprɪmænd] o ['rɛprɪmɑnd] *s* reprimenda; *va* reconvenir, reprender
**reprint** ['ri,prɪnt] *s* reimpresión; tirada aparte; [ri'prɪnt] *va* reimprimir
**reprisal** [rɪ'praɪzəl] *s* represalia o represalias; **to make reprisals** tomar represalias
**reproach** [rɪ'protʃ] *s* reproche; oprobio; *va* reprochar; oprobiar; **to reproach someone for something** reprochar algo a alguien
**reproachable** [rɪ'protʃəbəl] *adj* reprochable
**reproachful** [rɪ'protʃfəl] *adj* reprochador, reprensor
**reproachless** [rɪ'protʃlɪs] *adj* irreprochable
**reprobate** ['rɛprobet] *adj & s* malvado; (theol.) réprobo; *va* reprobar
**reprobation** [,rɛpro'beʃən] *s* reprobación
**reproduce** [,riprə'djus] o [,riprə'dus] *va* reproducir; *vn* reproducirse
**reproducer** [,riprə'djusər] o [,riprə'dusər] *s* reproductor; (mach. & elec.) reproductor
**reproducible** [,riprə'djusɪbəl] o [,riprə'dusɪbəl] *adj* reproductible
**reproduction** [,riprə'dʌkʃən] *s* reproducción
**reproductive** [,riprə'dʌktɪv] *adj* reproductor
**reproof** [rɪ'pruf] *s* reprobación
**reprovable** [rɪ'pruvəbəl] *adj* reprobable
**reproval** [rɪ'pruvəl] *s* reprobación
**reprove** [rɪ'pruv] *va* reprobar
**reptile** ['rɛptɪl] *adj & s* (zool. & fig.) reptil
**reptilian** [rɛp'tɪlɪən] *adj* (zool. & fig.) reptil; *s* (zool.) reptil
**Repub.** abr. de **Republic** y **Republican**
**republic** [rɪ'pʌblɪk] *s* república; **The Republic** la República de Platón
**republican** [rɪ'pʌblɪkən] *adj & s* republicano
**republicanism** [rɪ'pʌblɪkənɪzəm] *s* republicanismo
**republication** [,ripʌblɪ'keʃən] *s* nueva publicación
**republic of letters** *s* república de las letras o república literaria
**republish** [ri'pʌblɪʃ] *va* volver a publicar
**repudiate** [rɪ'pjudɪet] *va* repudiar; no reconocer (*p.ej., una deuda*)
**repudiation** [rɪ,pjudɪ'eʃən] *s* repudiación; desconocimiento (*p.ej., de una deuda*)
**repugnance** [rɪ'pʌgnəns] o **repugnancy** [rɪ'pʌgnənsɪ] *s* repugnancia
**repugnant** [rɪ'pʌgnənt] *adj* repugnante
**repulse** [rɪ'pʌls] *s* repulsión, rechazo; *va* repeler, rechazar
**repulsion** [rɪ'pʌlʃən] *s* repulsión; (phys.) repulsión; (fig.) repulsión (*antipatía*)
**repulsive** [rɪ'pʌlsɪv] *adj* (phys. & fig.) repulsivo; feúcho
**repurchase** [ri'pʌrtʃəs] *s* recompra; *va* recomprar
**reputable** ['rɛpjətəbəl] *adj* bien reputado, de buena reputación; castizo (*vocablo*)
**reputation** [,rɛpjə'teʃən] *s* reputación; buena reputación
**repute** [rɪ'pjut] *s* reputación; buena reputación; **by repute** según la opinión común; *va* reputar
**reputed** [rɪ'pjutɪd] *adj* supuesto; **highly reputed** bien reputado
**reputedly** [rɪ'pjutɪdlɪ] *adv* según la opinión común
**request** [rɪ'kwɛst] *s* petición, solicitud; **at the request of** a petición de; **by request** a petición; **on** o **upon request** a pedido, a solicitud; *va* pedir; **to request something from someone** pedir algo a alguien; **to request someone to do something** pedir a alguien que haga algo
**requiem** o **Requiem** ['rikwɪɛm] o ['rɛkwɪɛm] *s* réquiem (*misa y música*)
**requiem mass** *s* misa de réquiem
**requiescat** [,rɛkwɪ'ɛskæt] *s* oración o voto por un difunto
**require** [rɪ'kwaɪr] *va* requerir, exigir
**requirement** [rɪ'kwaɪrmənt] *s* requisito; necesidad
**requisite** ['rɛkwɪzɪt] *adj & s* requisito
**requisition** [,rɛkwɪ'zɪʃən] *s* demanda, exacción; demanda de extradición; (mil.) requisición; *va* demandar, exigir; (mil.) requisar
**requital** [rɪ'kwaɪtəl] *s* compensación, retorno
**requite** [rɪ'kwaɪt] *va* corresponder a (*los beneficios, el amor, etc.*); corresponder con (*el bienhechor*); **to requite a person for his efforts** compensar a una persona sus esfuerzos
**reran** [ri'ræn] *pret de* **rerun**
**reread** [ri'rid] (*pret & pp:* **-read** ['rɛd]) *va* releer
**rerebrace** ['rɪr,bres] *s* (arm.) brafonera
**reredos** ['rɪrdɑs] *s* (eccl.) retablo
**reroute** [ri'rut] o [ri'raʊt] *va* reencaminar
**rerun** ['ri,rʌn] *s* nueva exhibición de una película; (telv.) programa grabado repetido; [ri'rʌn] (*pret:* **-ran;** *pp;* **-run;** *ger:* **-running**) *va* volver a exhibir (*una película*)
**resale** ['ri,sel] o [ri'sel] *s* reventa
**rescind** [rɪ'sɪnd] *va* rescindir
**rescission** [rɪ'sɪʒən] *s* rescisión
**rescript** ['riskrɪpt] *s* rescripto; refundición
**rescue** ['rɛskju] *s* salvación; liberación; rescate; liberación violenta de un preso; recuperación ilegal de una cosa retenida por la autoridad; **to go to the rescue of** acudir al socorro de; *va* salvar, librar; libertar; rescatar; libertar violenta e ilegalmente; recobrar violenta e ilegalmente
**rescue party** *s* pelotón de salvamento
**rescuer** ['rɛskjʊər] *s* salvador
**reseal** [ri'sil] *va* resellar
**research** [rɪ'sʌrtʃ] o ['risʌrtʃ] *s* investigación; *vn* investigar
**researcher** [rɪ'sʌrtʃər] o ['risʌrtʃər] *s* investigador
**research professor** *s* profesor o catedrático investigador
**reseat** [ri'sit] *va* volver a sentar; poner un asiento o fondo nuevo a (*una silla*)
**resect** [rɪ'sɛkt] *va* (surg.) resecar
**resection** [rɪ'sɛkʃən] *s* resección
**resedaceous** [,rɛsɪ'deʃəs] *adj* (bot.) resedáceo
**resell** [ri'sɛl] (*pret & pp:* **-sold**) *va* revender
**reseller** [ri'sɛlər] *s* revendedor
**resemblance** [rɪ'zɛmbləns] *s* parecido, semejanza
**resemble** [rɪ'zɛmbəl] *va* asemejarse a, parecerse a
**resent** [rɪ'zɛnt] *va* resentirse de o por
**resentful** [rɪ'zɛntfəl] *adj* resentido
**resentment** [rɪ'zɛntmənt] *s* resentimiento
**reserpine** ['rɛsərpɪn], ['rɛsərpin], [rə'sʌrpɪn] o [rə'sʌrpin] *s* (pharm.) reserpina
**reservation** [,rɛzər'veʃən] *s* reservación; reserva; **without reservation** sin reserva
**reserve** [rɪ'zʌrv] *adj* (mil.) reservista; *s* reserva; (com. & mil.) reserva; *va* reservar
**reserve bank** *s* (U.S.A.) banco de reserva
**reserved** [rí'zʌrvd] *adj* reservado
**reservedly** [rɪ'zʌrvɪdlɪ] *adv* reservadamente
**reserve officer** *s* (mil.) oficial de complemento, oficial de reserva
**reservist** [rɪ'zʌrvɪst] *s* (mil.) reservista
**reservoir** ['rɛzərvwɑr] *s* depósito, reservorio; embalse, pantano; (fig.) mina; (fig.) fondo (*p.ej., de sabiduría*)
**reset** ['ri,sɛt] *s* nuevo engaste, nueva montadura; reducción (*de un hueso dislocado*); (print.) recomposición; [ri'sɛt] (*pret & pp:* **-set;** *ger:* **-setting**) *va* volver a engastar o a montar; volver a encajar (*un hueso dislocado*); (print.) recomponer (*un texto*); (print.) volver a disponer (*los tipos*)
**resettle** [ri'sɛtəl] *va* volver a arreglar; volver a determinar; volver a colonizar; llegar a un nuevo acuerdo sobre; *vn* volver a arreglarse; volver a determinarse; restablecerse; hacer nuevo asiento (*un edificio*); llegar a un nuevo acuerdo
**resettlement** [ri'sɛtəlmənt] *s* nuevo arreglo; nueva determinación; nueva colonización; restablecimiento; nuevo acuerdo
**reshape** [ri'ʃep] *va* reformar
**reship** [ri'ʃɪp] (*pret & pp:* **-shipped;** *ger:* **-shipping**) *va* reembarcar; reenviar, reexpedir; *vn* reembarcarse
**reshipment** [ri'ʃɪpmənt] *s* reembarco (*de personas*); reembarque (*de mercancías*); reenvío, reexpedición

**reshuffle** [ri'ʃʌfəl] *s* nueva barajadura; recomposición; *va* volver a barajar; mezclar y revolver otra vez
**reside** [rɪ'zaɪd] *vn* residir
**residence** ['rɛsɪdəns] *s* residencia; (educ.); residencia
**residency** ['rɛzɪdənsɪ] *s* (*pl:* **-cies**) residencia
**resident** ['rɛzɪdənt] *adj* residente; (orn.) no migratorio; *s* residente; médico interno, médico residente
**residential** [,rɛzɪ'dɛnʃəl] *adj* residencial
**residual** [rɪ'zɪdʒuəl] *adj* residual
**residual magnetism** *s* var. de **remanent magnetism**
**residuary** [rɪ'zɪdʒu,ɛrɪ] *adj* residual
**residue** ['rɛzɪdju] o ['rɛzɪdu] *s* resto, residuo
**residuum** [rɪ'zɪdʒuəm] *s* (*pl:* **-a** [ə]) residuo
**resign** [rɪ'zaɪn] *va* dimitir, resignar, renunciar; **to resign command to another person** resignar el mando en otra persona; **to resign oneself** resignarse; **to resign oneself to** + *inf* resignarse a + *inf; vn* dimitir; separarse (*p.ej., de un club*); resignarse
**resignation** [,rɛzɪg'neʃən] *s* dimisión, renuncia; resignación
**resigned** [rɪ'zaɪnd] *adj* resignado
**resignedly** [rɪ'zaɪnɪdlɪ] *adv* resignadamente
**resilience** [rɪ'zɪlɪəns] o **resiliency** [rɪ'zɪlɪənsɪ] *s* elasticidad; alegría, viveza; (mech.) resiliencia
**resilient** [rɪ'zɪlɪənt] *adj* elástico; alegre, vivo
**resin** ['rɛzɪn] *s* resina; *va* tratar con resina, aplicar una capa de resina a
**resinate** ['rɛzɪnet] *s* (chem.) resinato
**resinoid** ['rɛzɪnɔɪd] *adj* resinoide, resinoideo; *s* resinoide; gomorresina
**resinous** ['rɛzɪnəs] *adj* resinoso
**resist** [rɪ'zɪst] *va* resistir (*la tentación*); resistir a (*la violencia; la risa*); **to resist** + *ger* resistir a + *inf; vn* resistirse
**resistance** [rɪ'zɪstəns] *s* resistencia; (elec.) resistencia; **to offer resistance** oponer resistencia
**resistance box** *s* (elec.) caja de resistencias
**resistance coil** *s* (elec.) bobina o carrete de resistencia
**resistance movement** *s* movimiento de resistencia
**resistant** [rɪ'zɪstənt] *adj* resistente
**resistibility** [rɪ,zɪstɪ'bɪlɪtɪ] *s* resistibilidad
**resistible** [rɪ'zɪstɪbəl] *adj* resistible
**resistive** [rɪ'zɪstɪv] *adj* resistivo
**resistivity** [,rizɪs'tɪvɪtɪ] *s* resistencia; (elec.) resistividad
**resistless** [rɪ'zɪstlɪs] *adj* irresistible
**resistor** [rɪ'zɪstər] *s* (elec.) resistor
**resnatron** ['rɛznətrɑn] *s* (elec.) resnatrón
**resold** [ri'sold] *pret & pp de* **resell**
**resole** [ri'sol] *va* sobresolar (*un zapato*)
**resoluble** ['rɛzəlubəl] *adj* resoluble
**resolute** ['rɛzəlut] *adj* resuelto
**resolution** [,rɛzə'luʃən] *s* resolución; **good resolutions** buenos propósitos
**resolvable** [rɪ'zɑlvəbəl] *adj* resoluble
**resolve** [rɪ'zɔlv] *s* resolución; *va* resolver; *vn* resolverse; **to resolve on** o **upon** resolverse por; **to resolve to** + *inf* resolverse a + *inf*
**resolved** [rɪ'zɔlvd] *adj* resuelto
**resonance** ['rɛzənəns] *s* resonancia
**resonant** ['rɛzənənt] *adj* resonante
**resonate** ['rɛzənet] *vn* resonar
**resonator** ['rɛzə,netər] *s* resonador
**resorb** [ri'sɔrb] *va* resorber
**resorcin** [rɛ'zɔrsɪn] o **resorcinol** [rɛ'zɔrsɪnɑl] *s* (chem.) resorcina
**resorption** [rɪ'sɔrpʃən] *s* resorción
**resort** [rɪ'zɔrt] *s* concurrencia; recreo; lugar muy frecuentado; estación (*p.ej., de verano*); recurso; **as a last resort** como último recurso; **to have resort to** recurrir a; *vn* concurrir; recurrir; **to resort to** recurrir a
**resound** [rɪ'zaund] *va* hacer resonar; cantar, celebrar; *vn* resonar
**resource** [rɪ'sors] o ['risors] *s* recurso
**resourceful** [rɪ'sorsfəl] *adj* despejado, ingenioso, listo
**respect** [rɪ'spɛkt] *s* respeto (*veneración*); respecto (*relación, concepto*); **respects** *spl* recuerdos, saludos; **in that respect** bajo ese respecto; **in respect of** respecto a o de; **in respect that** puesto que, ya que; **to pay one's respects to** ofrecer sus respetos a; **with respect to** respecto a o de; *va* respetar (*venerar*); respectar (*tocar*)
**respectability** [rɪ,spɛktə'bɪlɪtɪ] *s* respetabilidad
**respectable** [rɪ'spɛktəbəl] *adj* respetable; **at a respectable distance** a respetable distancia
**respectful** [rɪ'spɛktfəl] *adj* respetuoso
**respectfully** [rɪ'spɛktfəlɪ] *adv* respetuosamente; **respectfully yours** de Vd. atento y seguro servidor
**respecting** [rɪ'spɛktɪŋ] *prep* con respecto a, respecto de
**respective** [rɪ'spɛktɪv] *adj* respectivo
**respectively** [rɪ'spɛktɪvlɪ] *adv* respectivamente
**respell** [ri'spɛl] (*pret & pp:* **-spelled** o **-spelt**) *va* volver a deletrear; transcribir (*en letras de otro alfabeto*)
**respiration** [,rɛspɪ'reʃən] *s* respiración
**respirator** ['rɛspɪ,retər] *s* respirador; máscara respiratoria
**respiratory** [rɪ'spaɪrə,torɪ] o ['rɛspɪrə,torɪ] *adj* respiratorio
**respire** [rɪ'spaɪr] *va & vn* respirar
**respite** ['rɛspɪt] *s* respiro; suspensión (*especialmente de la pena de muerte*); **without respite** sin respirar; *va* dar treguas a; aplazar, diferir; dar suspensión a
**resplendence** [rɪ'splɛndəns] o **resplendency** [rɪ'splɛndənsɪ] *s* resplandor
**resplendent** [rɪ'splɛndənt] *adj* resplandeciente
**respond** [rɪ'spɑnd] *vn* responder
**respondent** [rɪ'spɑndənt] *adj* respondedor; *s* respondedor; (law) demandado (*especialmente en pleito de divorcio*)
**response** [rɪ'spɑns] *s* respuesta; (eccl.) respuesta que da la congregación a las palabras del oficiante; (eccl.) responsorio; (rad.) respuesta
**responsibility** [rɪ,spɑnsɪ'bɪlɪtɪ] *s* (*pl:* **-ties**) responsabilidad
**responsible** [rɪ'spɑnsɪbəl] *adj* responsable; de confianza, p.ej., **a responsible position** un puesto de confianza; **responsible for** responsable de
**responsive** [rɪ'spɑnsɪv] *adj* responsivo; sensible
**responsory** [rɪ'spɑnsərɪ] *s* (*pl:* **-ries**) (eccl.) responsorio
**rest** [rɛst] *s* descanso; reposo (*falta de movimiento*); descansadero; paz (*de los muertos*); (mach.) luneta; (mus.) pausa; resto (*lo que queda*); (billiards & pool) diablo; **at rest** en reposo (*sin movimiento*); tranquilo; dormido; en paz (*muerto*); **the rest** lo demás, lo restante; los demás; **to come to rest** venir a parar; **to lay to rest** enterrar; **without rest** sin descanso; *va* descansar; parar; poner (*p.ej., confianza*); (law) terminar la presentación de pruebas en (*un pleito*); *vn* descansar; residir, estar, hallarse; (law) terminar la presentación de pruebas; **to rest assured** estar seguro, tener la seguridad; **to rest from** descansar de (*p.ej., fatigas*); **to rest on** descansar en o sobre, estribar en
**restate** [ri'stet] *va* volver a declarar; volver a exponer; volver a formular; volver a plantear (*p.ej., un problema*)
**restatement** [ri'stetmənt] *s* nueva declaración; nueva exposición
**restaurant** ['rɛstərənt] o ['rɛstərɑnt] *s* restaurante
**restaurateur** [,rɛstərɑ'tʌr] *s* dueño de un restaurante, fondista
**rest cure** *s* cura de reposo
**restful** ['rɛstfəl] *adj* descansado, reposado, tranquilo
**restharrow** ['rɛst,hæro] *s* (bot.) detienebuey
**resting place** *s* lugar de descanso; última morada; descansadero (*de escalera*)
**restitution** [,rɛstɪ'tjuʃən] o [,rɛstɪ'tuʃən] *s* restitución
**restive** ['rɛstɪv] *adj* intranquilo; rebelón
**restless** ['rɛstlɪs] *adj* intranquilo; insomne
**restlessness** ['rɛstlɪsnɪs] *s* intranquilidad; insomnio

**restock** [ri'stɑk] *va* reaprovisionar; repoblar (*p.ej., un acuario*)
**restoration** [,rɛstə'reʃən] *s* restauración
**restorative** [rɪ'storətɪv] *adj & s* restaurativo
**restore** [rɪ'stor] *va* restaurar; devolver
**restorer** [rɪ'storər] *s* restaurador
**restrain** [rɪ'stren] *va* refrenar; aprisionar, encerrar
**restrainedly** [rɪ'strenɪdlɪ] o [rɪ'strendlɪ] *adv* comedidamente
**restraint** [rɪ'strent] *s* restricción; freno; comedimiento
**restraint of trade** *s* limitación de la libre competencia
**restrict** [rɪ'strɪkt] *va* restringir
**restriction** [rɪ'strɪkʃən] *s* restricción
**restrictive** [rɪ'strɪktɪv] *adj* restrictivo; (gram.) restrictivo
**restring** [ri'strɪŋ] (*pret & pp:* **-strung**) *va* volver a enhebrar o ensartar; volver a atar con cuerdas; volver a proveer de cuerdas; volver a tender (*un alambre*); volver a encordar (*un violín, una raqueta*)
**restringent** [rɪ'strɪndʒənt] *adj & s* restringente
**rest room** *s* sala de descanso; excusado, retrete; (theat.) saloncillo
**restrung** [ri'strʌŋ] *pret & pp de* **restring**
**result** [rɪ'zʌlt] *s* resultado; **as a result of** de resultas de; *vn* resultar; **to result from** resultar de; **to result in** dar por resultado, parar en
**resultant** [rɪ'zʌltənt] *adj* resultante; *s* resultado; (mech.) resultante
**resume** [rɪ'zum] o [rɪ'zjum] *va* reasumir; reanudar (*el viaje, el vuelo, etc.*); volver a tomar (*asiento*); *vn* continuar; recomenzar; recomenzar a hablar
**résumé** [,rɛzʊ'me] o [,rɛzjʊ'me] *s* resumen
**resumption** [rɪ'zʌmpʃən] *s* reasunción; renovación; continuación
**resurface** [ri'sʌrfɪs] *va* volver a allanar o alisar; dar nueva superficie a; *vn* volver a emerger (*un submarino*)
**resurge** [rɪ'sʌrdʒ] *vn* resurgir
**resurgence** [rɪ'sʌrdʒəns] *s* resurgimiento
**resurrect** [,rɛzə'rɛkt] *va & vn* resucitar
**resurrection** [,rɛzə'rɛkʃən] *s* resurrección; (*cap.*) *s* (theol.) Resurrección
**resuscitate** [rɪ'sʌsɪtet] *va & vn* resucitar
**resuscitation** [rɪ,sʌsɪ'teʃən] *s* resucitación
**resuscitative** [rɪ'sʌsɪ,tetɪv] *adj* resucitador
**ret** [rɛt] (*pret & pp:* **retted**; *ger:* **retting**) *va* enriar
**retable** [rɪ'tebəl] *s* (eccl.) retablo
**retail** ['ritel] *s* venta al por menor; **at retail** al por menor; *adj* al por menor, p.ej., **retail price** precio al por menor; **retail trade** comercio al por menor; *va* detallar, vender al por menor; repetir (*p.ej., calumnias*); *vn* vender al por menor; venderse al por menor
**retailer** ['ritelər] *s* revendedor, detallista, comerciante al por menor
**retain** [rɪ'ten] *va* retener; contratar (*a un abogado*) pagándole honorarios anticipados
**retainer** [rɪ'tenər] *s* criado, dependiente; adherente, partidario; (law) ajuste con un abogado; cantidad que se da a un abogado en virtud de ajuste; (law) retención
**retaining wall** *s* muro de retención
**retake** ['ri,tek] *s* nueva toma (*p.ej., de vistas cinematográficas*); [ri'tek] (*pret:* **-took**; *pp:* **-taken**) *va* volver a tomar
**retaliate** [rɪ'tælɪet] *vn* vengarse, desquitarse; **to retaliate on** o **upon** desquitarse con, represaliar
**retaliation** [rɪ,tælɪ'eʃən] *s* venganza, desquite, represalia
**retaliative** [rɪ'tælɪ,etɪv] o **retaliatory** [rɪ'tælɪə,torɪ] *adj* vengador; vengativo
**retard** [rɪ'tɑrd] *s* retardo; *va* retardar; atrasar o retrasar (*un reloj*); *vn* retardarse; atrasarse o retrasarse (*un reloj*)
**retardation** [,ritɑr'deʃən] *s* retardación
**retarded** [rɪ'tɑrdɪd] *adj* atrasado; **mentally retarded** mentalmente atrasado
**retaught** [ri'tɔt] *pret & pp de* **reteach**
**retch** [rɛtʃ] *va* vomitar; *vn* arquear, esforzarse por vomitar
**retching** ['rɛtʃɪŋ] *s* esfuerzo de vómito
**ret'd.** abr. de **returned**
**reteach** [ri'titʃ] (*pret & pp:* **-taught**) *va* volver a enseñar
**retell** [ri'tɛl] (*pret & pp:* **-told**) *va* volver a decir; recontar (*volver a relatar; volver a sumar o adicionar*); dar nueva versión de
**retention** [rɪ'tɛnʃən] *s* retención
**retentive** [rɪ'tɛntɪv] *adj* retentivo
**retentivity** [,ritɛn'tɪvɪtɪ] *s* retención; (phys.) retentividad
**retiarius** [,riʃɪ'ɛrɪəs] *s* (*pl:* **-i** [aɪ]) (hist.) reciario
**reticence** ['rɛtɪsəns] *s* reserva (*inclinación a guardar silencio*); (rhet.) reticencia
**reticent** ['rɛtɪsənt] *adj* reservado (*inclinado a guardar silencio*)
**reticle** ['rɛtɪkəl] *s* (opt.) retículo
**reticular** [rɪ'tɪkjələr] *adj* reticular
**reticulate** [rɪ'tɪkjəlet] o [rɪ'tɪkjəlɪt] *adj* reticulado; [rɪ'tɪkjəlet] *va* disponer en forma de red; marcar con líneas que forman red; *vn* formar red, tener figura de red
**reticulation** [rɪ,tɪkjə'leʃən] *s* reticulación; malla (*del tejido de la red*)
**reticule** ['rɛtɪkjul] *s* retícula (*bolsillito de mano*); (opt.) retícula; (*cap.*) *s* (astr.) Retícula
**reticulum** [rɪ'tɪkjələm] *s* (*pl:* **-la** [lə]) retículo; (anat. & bot.) retículo; (zool.) redecilla, retículo
**retina** ['rɛtɪnə] *s* (anat.) retina
**retinal** ['rɛtɪnəl] *adj* retiniano
**retinitis** [,rɛtɪ'naɪtɪs] *s* (path.) retinitis
**retinue** ['rɛtɪnju] *s* comitiva, séquito
**retire** [rɪ'taɪr] *va* retirar; jubilar (*a un empleado*); (baseball) retirar (*a un batter o equipo*); *vn* retirarse; jubilarse; recogerse (*retirarse a dormir*); (mil.) retirarse
**retired** [rɪ'taɪrd] *adj* retirado; jubilado
**retirement** [rɪ'taɪrmənt] *s* retiro; jubilación (*de un empleado*); (mil.) retirada (*retroceso en buen orden*)
**retirement annuity** *s* jubilación, pensión de retiro
**retiring** [rɪ'taɪrɪŋ] *adj* reservado; retraído, tímido; dimitente
**retold** [ri'told] *pret & pp de* **retell**
**retook** [ri'tʊk] *pret de* **retake**
**retool** [ri'tul] *vn* instalar nuevas máquinas-herramientas
**retorsion** [rɪ'tɔrʃən] *s* retorsión; (law) retorsión
**retort** [rɪ'tɔrt] *s* réplica, respuesta pronta y aguda; (chem.) retorta; *va* rebatir, redargüir (*un argumento*); devolver (*un insulto u ofensa*); *vn* replicar
**retort stand** *s* portarretorta
**retouch** [ri'tʌtʃ] *va* retocar; (phot.) retocar
**retrace** [rɪ'tres] *va* repasar; volver a seguir las huellas de; **to retrace one's steps** volver sobre sus pasos
**re-trace** [ri'tres] *va* volver a trazar
**retract** [rɪ'trækt] *va* retraer; retractar o retractarse de (*lo que se ha dicho*); *vn* retraerse; retractarse
**retractable** [rɪ'træktəbəl] *adj* retractable; (aer.) replegable, retráctil
**retractation** [,ritræk'teʃən] *s* retractación
**retractile** [rɪ'træktɪl] *adj* retráctil
**retraction** [rɪ'trækʃən] *s* retracción; retractación (*de lo que se ha dicho*)
**retractive** [rɪ'træktɪv] *adj* retractor
**retractor** [rɪ'træktər] *s* (surg.) retractor; (anat.) músculo retractor
**retranslate** [,ritræns'let] o [ri'trænslet] *va* retraducir
**retread** ['ri,trɛd] *s* neumático recauchutado; neumático ranurado; [ri'trɛd] (*pret & pp:* **-treaded**) *va* recauchutar (*un neumático*); volver a ranurar (*un neumático*); (*pret:* **-trod**; *pp:* **-trod** o **-trodden**) *va* desandar; *vn* volverse atrás
**retreat** [rɪ'trit] *s* retiro; retraimiento (*habitación retirada*); refugio; manicomio; casa para alcohólicos; (eccl.) retiro; (mil.) retirada, retreta; (mil.) retreta (*toque*); **in full retreat** en plena retirada; **to beat a retreat** retraerse, retirarse; (mil.) batirse o marchar en retirada, emprender la retirada; *vn* retraerse, retirarse; deprimirse; (aer.) inclinarse hacia atrás

**retrench** [rɪ'trɛntʃ] *va* cercenar; (mil.) atrincherar; *vn* recogerse (*moderarse en los gastos*)
**retrenchment** [rɪ'trɛntʃmənt] *s* cercenadura; (mil.) atrincheramiento
**retrial** [ri'traɪəl] *s* reensayo; (law) revista; nuevo proceso
**retribution** [,rɛtrɪ'bjuʃən] *s* justo castigo; (theol.) juicio final
**retributive** [rɪ'trɪbjətɪv] o **retributory** [rɪ'trɪbjə,torɪ] *adj* castigador; justiciero
**retrieval** [rɪ'trivəl] *s* recobro; reparación; (hunt.) cobra
**retrieve** [rɪ'triv] *va* cobrar; reparar (*p.ej., un daño*); desquitarse de (*una pérdida, una derrota*); (hunt.) cobrar, portar; *vn* (hunt.) cobrar, portar
**retriever** [rɪ'trivər] *s* perro cobrador, perro traedor
**retroactive** [,rɛtro'æktɪv] *adj* retroactivo
**retroactivity** [,rɛtroæk'tɪvɪtɪ] *s* retroactividad
**retrocede** [,rɛtro'sid] *va* hacer retrocesión de; *vn* retroceder
**retrocession** [,rɛtro'sɛʃən] *s* retrocesión
**retrochoir** ['rɛtro,kwaɪr] *s* (arch.) trascoro
**retrod** [ri'trɑd] *pret & pp de* **retread**
**retrodden** [ri'trɑdən] *pp de* **retread**
**retrofiring** [,rɛtro'faɪrɪŋ] *s* retrodisparo
**retroflex** ['rɛtroflɛks] *adj* desviado hacia atrás
**retroflexion** [,rɛtro'flɛkʃən] *s* retroflexión; (path.) retroflexión
**retrogradation** [,rɛtrogrə'deʃən] *s* retrogradación; (astr.) retrogradación
**retrograde** ['rɛtrogred] *adj* retrógrado; *vn* retroceder, volver atrás; decaer, degenerar; (astr.) retrogradar
**retrogress** ['rɛtrogrɛs] *vn* retroceder; empeorar
**retrogression** [,rɛtro'grɛʃən] *s* retrogresión; empeoramiento
**retrogressive** [,rɛtro'grɛsɪv] *adj* regresivo, retrógrado
**retrorocket** [,rɛtro'rɑkɪt] *s* retrocohete
**retrospect** ['rɛtrospɛkt] *s* retrospección; consideración de lo pasado; **in retrospect** retrospectivamente; *va* recorrer en la memoria
**retrospection** [,rɛtro'spɛkʃən] *s* retrospección; consideración de lo pasado
**retrospective** [,rɛtro'spɛktɪv] *adj* retrospectivo; retroactivo
**retroussé** [,rɛtru'se] o [rə'truse] *adj* arremangado
**retroversion** [,rɛtro'vʌrʃən] *s* (path.) retroversión
**retry** [ri'traɪ] (*pret & pp:* **-tried**) *va* reensayar; rever (*un caso legal*); (law) procesar de nuevo (*a una persona*)
**retting** ['rɛtɪŋ] *s* enriamiento
**return** [rɪ'tʌrn] *s* vuelta; devolución; recompensa; respuesta; informe, noticia; ganancia, provecho; rédito; resultado (*de las elecciones*); reportaje (*de las elecciones*); declaración (*de impuestos*); **in return** en cambio; en recompensa; en resarcimiento; **many happy returns of the day** feliz cumpleaños, que cumpla muchos más; *adj* repetido; de vuelta; **by return mail** a vuelta de correo; *va* volver, devolver; rendir; dar en cambio; corresponder a (*un favor*); dar (*un fallo, una respuesta, las gracias*); anunciar oficialmente; elegir (*a cuerpo legislativo*); restar (*la pelota*); devolver (*un naipe del palo que acaba de jugar el compañero*); **to return to** + *inf* volver a, regresar a + *inf; vn* volver; responder
**returnable** [rɪ'tʌrnəbəl] *adj* restituíble; (law) devolutivo
**return address** *s* dirección del remitente
**return game** *s* (sport) desquite, juego de desquite
**return ticket** *s* billete de vuelta; billete de ida y vuelta
**return trip** *s* viaje de vuelta
**retuse** [rɪ'tjus] o [rɪ'tus] *adj* (bot.) retuso
**Reuben** ['rubɪn] *s* (Bib.) Rubén
**reunification** [ri,junɪfɪ'keʃən] *s* reunificación
**reunify** [ri'junɪfaɪ] (*pret & pp:* **-fied**) *va* reunificar
**reunion** [ri'junjən] *s* reunión; (*cap.*) *s* la Isla de la Reunión
**reunite** [,rijʊ'naɪt] *va* reunir; *vn* reunirse

**rev.** abr. de **revenue, reverse, review, revised, revision** y **revolution**
**Rev.** abr. de **Revelation** y **Reverend**
**rev** [rɛv] *s* (coll.) revolución; (*pret & pp:* **revved;** *ger:* **revving**) *va* (coll.) cambiar la velocidad de; **to rev up** (coll.) acelerar; *vn* (coll.) acelerarse
**revaccinate** [ri'væksɪnet] *va* revacunar
**revaccination** [,rivæksɪ'neʃən] *s* revacunación
**revaluation** [,rivælju'eʃən] *s* nueva valoración; (econ.) revaloración
**revalue** [ri'vælju] *va* revalorizar
**revamp** [ri'væmp] *va* renovar, componer, remendar
**revanchist** [rɪ'vɑntʃɪst] *adj & s* revanchista
**reveal** [rɪ'vil] *va* revelar
**revealed religion** *s* (theol.) religión revelada
**revealment** [rɪ'vilmənt] *s* revelamiento
**reveille** ['rɛvəlɪ] *s* (mil.) diana, toque de diana
**revel** ['rɛvəl] *s* jarana, regocijo tumultuoso; (*pret & pp:* **-eled** o **-elled;** *ger:* **-eling** o **-elling**) *vn* jaranear; deleitarse; **to revel in** deleitarse en
**revelation** [,rɛvə'leʃən] *s* revelación; (*cap.*) *s* (Bib.) libro de la Revelación
**reveler** o **reveller** ['rɛvələr] *s* jaranero
**revelry** ['rɛvəlrɪ] *s* (*pl:* **-ries**) jarana, diversión tumultuosa
**revenant** ['rɛvənənt] *s* persona que vuelve; espectro, aparecido
**revenge** [rɪ'vɛndʒ] *s* venganza; *va* vengar; **to be revenged** o **to revenge oneself** vengarse; *vn* vengarse
**revengeful** [rɪ'vɛndʒfəl] *adj* vengativo
**revenue** ['rɛvənju] o ['rɛvənu] *s* renta, rédito; rentas públicas
**revenue cutter** *s* (naut.) escampavía
**revenue officer** *s* agente fiscal
**revenue stamp** *s* sello fiscal
**reverberant** [rɪ'vʌrbərənt] *adj* reverberante
**reverberate** [rɪ'vʌrbəret] *va* reflejar; *vn* reverberar
**reverberation** [rɪ,vʌrbə'reʃən] *s* reverberación
**reverberatory** [rɪ'vʌrbərə,torɪ] *adj* reverberatorio
**reverberatory furnace** *s* horno de reverbero
**revere** [rɪ'vɪr] *va* reverenciar, venerar
**reverence** ['rɛvərəns] *s* reverencia; (*cap.*) *s* Reverencia (*título*); (*l.c.*) *va* reverenciar
**reverend** ['rɛvərənd] *adj* reverendo; *s* (coll.) clérigo, eclesiástico, pastor
**reverent** ['rɛvərənt] *adj* reverente
**reverential** [,rɛvə'rɛnʃəl] *adj* reverencial
**reverie** ['rɛvərɪ] *s* ensueño, ensueños
**revers** [rə'vɪr] o [rə'vɛr] *s* (*pl:* **revers** [rə'vɪrz] o [rə'vɛrz]) (sew.) solapa
**reversal** [rɪ'vʌrsəl] *s* inversión; cambio (*p.ej., de opinión*); (law) revocación
**reverse** [rɪ'vʌrs] *adj* invertido; contrario; de marcha atrás; *s* revés; contrario; contramarcha, marcha atrás, mecanismo de marcha atrás; (fig.) revés, contratiempo; **in reverse** en marcha atrás; **quite the reverse** todo lo contrario; **to put a car in reverse** invertir la marcha de un coche; *va* invertir; dar vuelta a; poner en marcha atrás; dar contravapor a (*una máquina de vapor*); (law) revocar; **to reverse oneself** cambiar de opinión, contradecirse; **to reverse the charges** (telp.) cobrar al número llamado; (telg.) cobrar al destinatario; *vn* invertirse; cambiarse al sentido opuesto (*en los bailes*)
**reverse gear** *s* (aut.) (engranaje de) marcha atrás
**reversely** [rɪ'vʌrslɪ] *adv* al revés
**reverse pedal** *s* pedal de marcha atrás
**reverser** [rɪ'vʌrsər] *s* (elec.) inversor
**reverse turn** *s* (aer.) cambio de dirección hacia atrás
**reversibility** [rɪ,vʌrsɪ'bɪlɪtɪ] *s* reversibilidad
**reversible** [rɪ'vʌrsɪbəl] *adj* reversible
**reversible lock** *s* cerradura que cierra por ambos lados
**reversible reaction** *s* (chem.) reacción reversible
**reversion** [rɪ'vʌrʒən] o [rɪ'vʌrʃən] *s* reversión; (biol. & law) reversión; (law) futura
**reversional** [rɪ'vʌrʒənəl] o [rɪ'vʌrʃənəl] o **re-**

**versionary** [rɪˈvʌrʒəˌnɛrɪ] o [rɪˈvʌrʃəˌnɛrɪ] *adj* de reversión, de la reversión
**revert** [rɪˈvʌrt] *vn* revertir, recudir; (biol.) saltar atrás; (law) revertir
**revery** [ˈrɛvərɪ] *s* (*pl:* **-ies**) var. de **reverie**
**revet** [rɪˈvɛt] (*pret & pp:* **-vetted;** *ger:* **-vetting**) *va* revestir (*un muro, un terraplén, etc.*)
**revetment** [rɪˈvɛtmənt] *s* revestimiento
**revictual** [riˈvɪtəl] (*pret & pp:* **-ualed** o **-ualled;** *ger:* **-ualing** o **-ualling**) *va* reavituallar; *vn* reavituallarse
**review** [rɪˈvju] *s* revista (*reexaminación; reconocimiento; publicación periódica*); reseña, revista (*de un libro*); repaso (*de una lección*); (mil.) revista, reseña; (theat.) revista; *va* rever, revisar; reseñar (*un libro*); repasar (*una lección*); (mil.) revistar
**reviewer** [rɪˈvjuər] *s* revisor; revistero, crítico
**revile** [rɪˈvaɪl] *va* ultrajar, vilipendiar
**revilement** [rɪˈvaɪlmənt] *s* ultraje, vilipendio
**revise** [rɪˈvaɪz] *s* revisión; refundición; (print.) segunda prueba; *va* rever, revisar; refundir (*un libro*); enmendar
**Revised Version** *s* versión enmendada de la Biblia (*de 1881 y 1885*)
**revision** [rɪˈvɪʒən] *s* revisión; refundición (*de un libro*); enmienda
**revisionism** [rɪˈvɪʒənɪzəm] *s* revisionismo
**revisionist** [rɪˈvɪʒənɪst] *adj & s* revisionista
**revisory** [rɪˈvaɪzərɪ] *adj* revisor
**revitalize** [rɪˈvaɪtəlaɪz] *va* revitalizar
**revival** [rɪˈvaɪvəl] *s* resucitación; reanimación; restablecimiento; renacimiento; despertamiento religioso; servicios especiales destinados a despertar el interés por la religión; (theat.) reestreno, reposición
**revivalist** [rɪˈvaɪvəlɪst] *s* predicador que dirige servicios especiales para despertar el sentimiento religioso
**Revival of Learning** *s* Renacimiento literario, Renacimiento humanista
**revive** [rɪˈvaɪv] *va* revivir; (theat.) reestrenar; *vn* revivir; volver en sí, recordar
**revivification** [rɪˌvɪvɪfɪˈkeʃən] *s* revivificación
**revivify** [rɪˈvɪvɪfaɪ] (*pret & pp:* **-fied**) *va* revivificar
**revocable** [ˈrɛvəkəbəl] *adj* revocable
**revocation** [ˌrɛvəˈkeʃən] *s* revocación
**revocatory** [ˈrɛvəkəˌtorɪ] *adj* revocatorio
**revoke** [rɪˈvok] *s* renuncio (*en algunos juegos de naipes*); *va* revocar; *vn* renunciar
**revolt** [rɪˈvolt] *s* rebelión; *va* dar o causar asco a; repugnar, indignar; *vn* rebelarse; sentir asco
**revolting** [rɪˈvoltɪŋ] *adj* asqueroso, repugnante; abominable, odioso; rebelde, insurrecto
**revolution** [ˌrɛvəˈluʃən] *s* revolución
**revolutionary** [ˌrɛvəˈluʃənˌɛrɪ] *adj* revolucionario; *s* (*pl:* **-ies**) revolucionario
**Revolutionary War** *s* (U.S.A.) guerra de la Independencia
**revolutionist** [ˌrɛvəˈluʃənɪst] *s* revolucionario
**revolutionize** [ˌrɛvəˈluʃənaɪz] *va* revolucionar
**revolve** [rɪˈvɑlv] *va* hacer girar; revolver (*en la mente*); *vn* girar; (astr.) revolverse (*un astro en su órbita*)
**revolver** [rɪˈvɑlvər] *s* revólver
**revolving** [rɪˈvɑlvɪŋ] *adj* giratorio; rotativo
**revolving bookcase** *s* giratoria
**revolving door** *s* puerta giratoria
**revolving fund** *s* fondo rotativo
**revue** [rɪˈvju] *s* (theat.) revista
**revulsion** [rɪˈvʌlʃən] *s* cambio repentino, reacción fuerte (*sobre todo en los sentimientos o las ideas*); (med.) revulsión
**revulsive** [rɪˈvʌlsɪv] *adj & s* revulsivo
**Rev. Ver.** abr. de **Revised Version**
**reward** [rɪˈwərd] *s* premio, recompensa; hallazgo, p.ej., **five dollars reward** cinco dólares de hallazgo; *va* premiar, recompensar, gratificar
**rewarding** [rɪˈwərdɪŋ] *adj* provechoso, útil, valioso
**rewind** [riˈwaɪnd] (*pret & pp:* **-wound**) *va* rebobinar, redevanar
**rewire** [riˈwaɪr] *va* reatar con alambre; cambiar el alambre a; reinstalar alambre conductor en; telegrafiar de nuevo; *vn* telegrafiar de nuevo
**reword** [riˈwʌrd] *va* volver a formular; formular en otras palabras; repetir
**rewrite** [ˈriˌraɪt] *s* (U.S.A.) artículo preparado para la publicación; [riˈraɪt] (*pret* **-wrote;** *pp:* **-written**) *va* escribir de nuevo; refundir (*un escrito*); (U.S.A.) preparar (*un escrito o relato de otra persona*) para la publicación
**Reynard** [ˈrɛnərd] o [ˈrenɑrd] *s* maese Renarte
**R.F.** o **r.f.** abr. de **radio frequency**
**R.F.D.** abr. de **Rural Free Delivery**
**R.H.** abr. de **Royal Highlanders** y **Royal Highness**
**Rhadamanthus** [ˌrædəˈmænθəs] *s* (myth.) Radamanto
**Rhaetia** [ˈriʃɪə] *s* la Recia
**Rhaetian** [ˈriʃən] *adj & s* rético
**Rhaetian Alps** *spl* Alpes réticos
**Rhaeto-Romanic** [ˌritoroˈmænɪk] *adj & s* retorromano
**rhamnaceous** [ræmˈneʃəs] *adj* (bot.) ramnáceo
**rhapsodic** [ræpˈsɑdɪk] o **rhapsodical** [ræpˈsɑdɪkəl] *adj* rapsódico; extático, locamente entusiasmado
**rhapsodist** [ˈræpsədɪst] *s* (hist.) rapsoda; (lit.) rapsodista; persona que se expresa con extravagante entusiasmo
**rhapsodize** [ˈræpsədaɪz] *va* recitar con extravagante entusiasmo; *vn* expresarse con extravagante entusiasmo
**rhapsody** [ˈræpsədɪ] *s* (*pl:* **-dies**) (mus. & lit.) rapsodia; expresión o escritura caracterizadas por extravagante entusiasmo
**rhatany** [ˈrætənɪ] *s* (*pl:* **-nies**) (bot.) ratania (*planta y raíz*)
**rhea** [ˈriə] *s* (orn.) ñandú o avestruz de la pampa; (*cap.*) *s* (myth.) Rea
**Rheingold** [ˈraɪnˌgold] *s* (myth.) el oro del Rin
**Rhenish** [ˈrɛnɪʃ] *adj* renano; *s* vino del Rin
**rhenium** [ˈrinɪəm] *s* (chem.) renio
**rheometer** [riˈɑmɪtər] *s* reómetro
**rheophore** [ˈriofor] *s* (elec.) reóforo
**rheostat** [ˈriostæt] *s* (elec.) reóstato
**rhesus** [ˈrisəs] *s* (zool.) macaco de la India
**rhetor** [ˈritər] o [ˈritɔr] *s* rétor; orador
**rhetoric** [ˈrɛtərɪk] *s* retórica
**rhetorical** [rɪˈtɑrɪkəl] o [rɪˈtɔrɪkəl] *adj* retórico
**rhetorically** [rɪˈtɑrɪkəlɪ] o [rɪˈtɔrɪkəlɪ] *adv* retóricamente
**rhetorical question** *s* comunicación
**rhetorician** [ˌrɛtəˈrɪʃən] *s* retórico
**rheum** [rum] *s* (path.) reuma, corrimiento; (path.) catarro; (poet.) lágrimas
**rheumatic** [ruˈmætɪk] *adj & s* reumático; **rheumatics** *spl* (dial.) reumatismo
**rheumatic fever** *s* (path.) fiebre reumática
**rheumatism** [ˈrumətɪzəm] *s* (path.) reumatismo
**rheumatoid** [ˈrumətɔɪd] *adj* reumatoideo
**rheumatoid arthritis** *s* (path.) artritis reumatoidea
**rheumy** [ˈrumɪ] *adj* catarroso; húmedo y frío
**Rh factor** *s* (biochem.) factor Rh
**rhinal** [ˈraɪnəl] *adj* rinal
**Rhine** [raɪn] *s* Rin
**Rhinegold** [ˈraɪnˌgold] *s* var. de **Rheingold**
**Rhineland** [ˈraɪnˌlænd] *s* Renania
**rhinencephalon** [ˌraɪnɛnˈsɛfəlɑn] *s* (*pl:* **-la** [lə]) (anat.) rinencéfalo
**Rhine Province** *s* Provincia del Rin
**rhinestone** [ˈraɪnˌston] *s* diamante de imitación hecho de vidrio
**Rhine wine** *s* vino del Rin
**rhinitis** [raɪˈnaɪtɪs] *s* (path.) rinitis
**rhino** [ˈraɪno] *s* (*pl:* **-nos**) (coll.) rinoceronte; (Brit.) dinero
**rhinoceros** [raɪˈnɑsərəs] *s* (zool.) rinoceronte
**rhinoceros hornbill** *s* (orn.) cálao rinoceronte
**rhinoplasty** [ˈraɪnoˌplæstɪ] *s* (surg.) rinoplastia
**rhinoscope** [ˈraɪnəskop] *s* rinoscopio
**rhinoscopy** [raɪˈnɑskəpɪ] *s* rinoscopia
**rhizoid** [ˈraɪzɔɪd] *adj* rizoide; *s* (bot.) rizoide
**rhizome** [ˈraɪzom] *s* (bot.) rizoma
**rhizophagous** [raɪˈzɑfəgəs] *adj* (zool.) rizófago

**rhizophoraceous** [ˌraɪzəfəˈreʃəs] *adj* (bot.) rizoforáceo
**rhizopod** [ˈraɪzopɑd] *s* (zool.) rizópodo
**rhizotomy** [raɪˈzɑtəmɪ] *s* (*pl:* **-mies**) (surg.) rizotomía
**Rhodes** [rodz] *s* Rodas
**Rhodesia** [roˈdiʒə] *s* la Rodesia
**Rhodian** [ˈrodɪən] *adj & s* rodio o rodano
**rhodium** [ˈrodɪəm] *s* (chem.) rodio
**rhododendron** [ˌrodəˈdɛndrən] *s* (bot.) rododendro
**rhodophyceous** [ˌrodəˈfaɪʃəs] *adj* (bot.) rodofíceo
**rhodopsin** [roˈdɑpsɪn] *s* (physiol.) rodopsina
**rhodora** [roˈdorə] *s* (bot.) rodora
**rhomb** [rɑm] o [rɑmb] *s* (geom.) rombo
**rhombencephalon** [ˌrɑmbɛnˈsɛfəlɑn] *s* (anat.) rombencéfalo
**rhombic** [ˈrɑmbɪk] *adj* (geom.) rombal; (cryst.) rómbico
**rhombohedron** [ˌrɑmbəˈhidrən] *s* (*pl:* **-dra** [drə]) (geom.) romboedro
**rhomboid** [ˈrɑmbɔɪd] *adj* romboidal; *s* (geom.) romboide
**rhomboidal** [rɑmˈbɔɪdəl] *adj* romboidal
**rhombus** [ˈrɑmbəs] *s* (*pl:* **-buses** o **-bi** [baɪ]) (geom.) rombo
**rhonchus** [ˈrɑŋkəs] *s* (*pl:* **-chi** [kaɪ]) estertor
**Rhone** o **Rhône** [ron] *s* Ródano; *adj* rodánico
**rhopalic** [roˈpælɪk] *adj* (pros.) ropálico
**rhotacism** [ˈrotəsɪzəm] *s* (philol.) rotacismo
**rhubarb** [ˈrubɑrb] *s* (bot. & pharm.) ruipóntico (*Rheum rhaponticum*); (bot. & pharm.) ruibarbo (*Rheum palmatum y Rheum officinale*); (cook.) ruipóntico; (slang) disputa, pendencia
**rhumb** [rʌm] o [rʌmb] *s* (naut.) rumbo de la aguja, cuarta (*de la rosa náutica*)
**rhumb line** *s* (naut.) loxodromia
**rhyme** [raɪm] *s* rima; **without rhyme or reason** sin ton ni son; *va & vn* rimar
**rhymer** [ˈraɪmər] *s* rimador
**rhymester** [ˈraɪmstər] *s* rimador (*poeta de mediano valor*)
**rhynchocephalian** [ˌrɪŋkosɪˈfelɪən] *adj & s* rincocéfalo
**rhyolite** [ˈraɪolaɪt] *s* (mineral.) riolita
**rhythm** [ˈrɪðəm] *s* ritmo
**rhythmic** [ˈrɪðmɪk] *adj* rítmico; **rhythmics** *ssg* rítmica
**rhythmical** [ˈrɪðmɪkəl] *adj* rítmico
**rhyton** [ˈraɪtɑn] *s* (*pl:* **-ta** [tə]) (archeol.) ritón
**R.I.** abr. de **Royal Institute** y **Rhode Island**
**rialto** [rɪˈælto] (*pl:* **-tos**) mercado; (*cap.*) *s* puente del Rialto (*de Venecia*); centro teatral de Nueva York
**rib** [rɪb] *s* costilla; (anat., bot. & naut.) costilla; varilla (*del abanico, paraguas, etc.*); cuerda (*de neumático*); (sew.) canilla, vivo; (zool.) nervio (*del ala de los insectos*); (fig.) costilla (*mujer propia*); (*pret & pp:* **ribbed;** *ger:* **ribbing**) *va* proveer de costillas; (sew.) hacer vivos en; (slang) tomar el pelo a
**ribald** [ˈrɪbəld] *adj* grosero y obsceno (*especialmente en el lenguaje*); *s* persona grosera y obscena
**ribaldry** [ˈrɪbəldrɪ] *s* lenguaje grosero y obsceno
**riband** o **ribband** [ˈrɪbənd] *s* (archaic) var. de **ribbon**
**ribbed** [rɪbd] *adj* acostillado; acanalado, rayado; nervudo
**ribbing** [ˈrɪbɪŋ] *s* costillaje; varillaje; nervadura
**ribbon** [ˈrɪbən] *s* cinta; *va* encintar; *vn* extenderse como cinta, serpentear
**ribboned** [ˈrɪbənd] *adj* encintado
**riboflavin** [ˌraɪboˈflevɪn] *s* (biochem.) riboflavina
**ribwort** [ˈrɪbˌwʌrt] *s* (bot.) lancéola
**rice** [raɪs] *s* (bot.) arroz (*planta y fruto*); *va* pasar por una hilera
**ricebird** [ˈraɪsˌbʌrd] *s* (orn.) chambergo; (orn.) pájaro conirrostro de Malasia (*Munia oryzivora*)
**rice field** *s* arrozal
**rice paper** *s* papel de paja de arroz
**rice powder** *s* polvos de arroz
**rice pudding** *s* arroz con leche
**ricer** [ˈraɪsər] *s* hilera
**rich** [rɪtʃ] *adj* rico; vivo (*color*); sonoro (*dícese de la voz*); azucarado o condimentado; generoso (*vino*); (coll.) divertido, entretenido; (coll.) ridículo; **the rich** los ricos; **to strike it rich** descubrir un buen filón, tener un golpe de fortuna; **riches** *spl* riqueza
**Richard** [ˈrɪtʃərd] *s* Ricardo
**Richard Coeur de Lion** [ˈkʌr də ˈliən] *s* Ricardo, Corazón de León
**richly** [ˈrɪtʃlɪ] *adv* ricamente; abundantemente, completamente
**richness** [ˈrɪtʃnɪs] *s* riqueza; viveza (*de color*); sonoridad (*de la voz*); crasitud, suculencia
**rick** [rɪk] *s* montón de paja, heno, grano, etc. al raso y frecuentemente bardado; *va* hacer montones de (*paja, heno, grano, etc.*)
**rickets** [ˈrɪkɪts] *s* (path.) raquitis
**rickettsia** [rɪˈkɛtsɪə] *s* (*pl:* **-ae** [i]) (bact.) rickettsia
**rickety** [ˈrɪkɪtɪ] *adj* (path.) raquítico; tambaleante, vacilante; destartalado, desvencijado
**ricksha** [ˈrɪkʃɔ] o [ˈrɪkʃɑ] o **rickshaw** [ˈrɪkʃɔ] *s* rikscha (*pequeño carruaje chino y japonés de dos ruedas y tirado por uno o más hombres*)
**ricochet** [ˌrɪkəˈʃe] o [ˌrɪkəˈʃɛt] *s* rebote; (*pret & pp:* **-cheted** [ˈʃed] o **-chetted** [ˈʃɛtɪd]; *ger:* **-cheting** [ˈʃeɪŋ] o **-chetting** [ˈʃɛtɪŋ]) *vn* rebotar
**ricochet fire** *s* (gun.) fuego de rebote
**rid** [rɪd] (*pret & pp:* **rid** o **ridded;** *ger:* **ridding**) *va* desembarazar, librar; **to be rid of** estar libre de; **to get rid of** desembarazarse de, deshacerse de; matar; **to rid oneself of** desembarazarse de, deshacerse de
**riddance** [ˈrɪdəns] *s* supresión, libramiento; **good riddance!** ¡adiós, gracias! (*¡de buena me he librado!*)
**ridden** [ˈrɪdən] *pp de* **ride**
**riddle** [ˈrɪdəl] *s* acertijo, adivinanza; enigma (*persona o cosa difíciles de comprender*); garbillo, criba gruesa; *va* adivinar; solucionar; garbillar, cribar; acribillar; **to riddle with bullets** acribillar a balazos; **to riddle with questions** acribillar a preguntas; *vn* hablar enigmáticamente
**ride** [raɪd] *s* paseo; **to thumb a ride** pedir ser llevado en automóvil indicando la dirección con el pulgar ‖ (*pret:* **rode;** *pp:* **ridden**) *va* montar (*un caballo, una bicicleta, los hombros de una persona, etc.*); recorrer a caballo; flotar sobre (*las olas*); hender o surcar (*las olas*); correr a caballo en (*una carrera*); luchar felizmente contra; cabalgar (*cubrir el caballo u otro animal a su hembra*); dominar, tiranizar; (coll.) llevar, transportar; (coll.) llevar a horcajadas; (coll.) burlarse de; (coll.) molestar criticando o poniendo en ridículo; **to ride down** revolcar, atropellar; rendir, vencer; alcanzar (*a una persona*) andando a caballo; **to ride out** luchar felizmente con (*una tempestad*); aguantar o soportar con buen éxito (*una desgracia*) ‖ *vn* montar; pasear en coche o carruaje; montar en bicicleta; flotar (*en la superficie del agua o en el aire*); marchar, funcionar; rodar (*alrededor del eje*); **to let ride** (slang) dejar correr; **to ride in** entrar a caballo; entrar en coche; **to ride out** salir a caballo; salir en coche; **to take riding** llevar de paseo
**rider** [ˈraɪdər] *s* caballero, jinete; pasajero; (law) aditamento a un documento; (law) cláusula añadida a un proyecto de ley; (naut.) sobreplán
**ridge** [rɪdʒ] *s* espinazo; caballete (*del tejado; de tierra entre dos surcos*); cordoncillo (*de un tejido*); cordillera; arista, intersección (*de dos planos*); *va* formar caballetes, cordoncillos, etc. en; cubrir o marcar con caballetes, cordoncillos, etc.; *vn* estar marcado con caballetes, cordoncillos, etc.
**ridgeband** [ˈrɪdʒˌbænd] *s* sufra
**ridgepole** [ˈrɪdʒˌpol] *s* parhilera
**ridge purlin** *s* (carp.) correa de cumbrera
**ridgy** [ˈrɪdʒɪ] *adj* (*comp:* **-ier;** *super:* **-iest**) acanalado, alomado, rugoso; cerril
**ridicule** [ˈrɪdɪkjul] *s* irrisión; **to expose to ridicule** poner en ridículo; *va* ridiculizar
**ridiculous** [rɪˈdɪkjələs] *adj* ridículo
**riding academy** *s* escuela de equitación

**riding boot** *s* bota de montar
**riding breeches** *spl* pantalones de equitación
**riding crop** *s* látigo de montar
**riding habit** *s* traje de montar
**riding master** *s* maestro de equitación
**riding saddle** *s* silla de montar
**riding whip** *s* fusta
**Rif** [rɪf], **Er** [ɛr] El Rif
**rife** [raɪf] *adj* frecuente, común, corriente, general; abundante, lleno; **rife with** abundante en, lleno de
**Riff** [rɪf] *s* rifeño
**Riffian** ['rɪfɪən] *adj & s* rifeño
**riffle** ['rɪfəl] *s* recial; rizo (*de agua*); *va* peinar (*la baraja*)
**riffraff** ['rɪf,ræf] *s* bahorrina; *adj* ruin, vil; de ningún valor
**rifle** ['raɪfəl] *s* rifle, fusil; *va* rayar (*un rifle*); hurtar, robar; escudriñar y robar; desnudar, despojar
**rifleman** ['raɪfəlmən] *s* (*pl:* **-men**) tirador armado de rifle; riflero (*soldado*)
**rifle pit** *s* pozo para rifleros
**rifle range** *s* tiro de rifle
**rifling** ['raɪflɪŋ] *s* rayado (*de un rifle*)
**rift** [rɪft] *s* raja, abertura; desavenencia, desacuerdo; *va* rajar; *vn* rajarse
**rifty** ['rɪftɪ] *adj* rajado
**rig** [rɪg] *s* (naut.) aparejo; equipaje; aparejos; (coll.) traje, traje extraño y poco conveniente; carruaje con caballo o caballos; mala partida, mala jugada; timo, robo, engaño; (*pret & pp:* **rigged;** *ger:* **rigging**) *va* (naut.) aparejar, enjarciar; equipar; (coll.) vestir, vestir de una manera extraña y poco conveniente; aprestar, disponer; improvisar; arreglar o manejar de una manera artificiosa o fraudulenta
**rigadoon** [,rɪgə'dun] *s* rigodón (*danza y música*)
**rigger** ['rɪgər] *s* (naut.) aparejador; (aer.) montador
**rigging** ['rɪgɪŋ] *s* (naut.) aparejo; avíos, equipo, todo género de instrumentos
**right** [raɪt] *adj* derecho; verdadero; conveniente; favorable; sano, normal; bien, p.ej., **his work is right** su trabajo está bien; que se busca, p.ej., **this is the right house** ésta es la casa que se busca; que se necesita, p.ej., **this is the right train** éste es el tren que se necesita; que debe, p.ej., **he is going the right way** sigue el camino que debe; (pol.) de derecha; correcto; señalado; correspondiente; (geom.) rectángulo; **to be right** tener razón; **to be all right** estar bien; estar bien de salud; **right or wrong** con razón o sin ella, bueno o malo, a tuertas o a derechas ‖ *adv* derechamente; directamente; correctamente; exactamente; convenientemente; favorablemente; en orden, en buen estado; a la derecha, hacia la derecha; completamente; (coll.) muy; (archaic) muy, p.ej., **right honorable** muy honorable; mismo, p.ej., **right here** aquí mismo; **right now** ahora mismo; **right in Spain** en España mismo; **right from Seville** desde Sevilla mismo; **all right** muy bien; **right afterwards** acto seguido; **right along** sin cesar, sin interrupción; **right away** en seguida; **right off** en seguida ‖ *interj* ¡bien!, ¡bueno!; **right about!** (mil.) ¡derecha! ‖ *s* derecho (*justicia, razón*); derecha (*mano derecha*); (box.) derechazo; (com.) derecho de subscribirse a la compra de acciones o bonos; (com.) certificado que da derecho a comprar acciones o bonos; (pol.) derecha; **by right** o **by rights** según derecho; **on the right** a la derecha; **to be in the right** tener razón; **to have the right to** tener derecho a; **to the right** a la derecha; **to rights** (coll.) en orden ‖ *va* enderezar; corregir, rectificar; hacer justicia a; deshacer (*un entuerto*); (naut.) adrizar ‖ *vn* enderezarse; (naut.) adrizarse
**rightabout-face** ['raɪtə,baut'fes] *s* media vuelta a la derecha; *vn* dar media vuelta a la derecha
**right-and-left** ['raɪtənd'lɛft] *adj* derecho e izquierdo; *adv* a diestra y siniestra; a diestro y siniestro (*sin tino, sin orden*)
**right angle** *s* ángulo recto
**right-angled** ['raɪt'æŋgəld] *adj* rectangular
**right ascension** *s* (astr.) ascensión recta
**righteous** ['raɪtʃəs] *adj* recto, justo; virtuoso
**righteousness** ['raɪtʃəsnɪs] *s* rectitud, justicia; virtud
**right field** *s* (baseball) jardín derecho
**rightful** ['raɪtfəl] *adj* justo; legítimo
**rightfully** ['raɪtfəlɪ] *adv* justamente; legítimamente; a justo título
**right-hand** ['raɪt,hænd] *adj* derecho; de, con o para la mano derecha; de movimiento, funcionamiento, etc. hacia la derecha
**right-hand drive** *s* (aut.) conducción a derecha
**right-handed** ['raɪt'hændɪd] *adj* que usa la mano derecha; con o para la mano derecha; para los que usan la mano derecha; de movimiento hacia la derecha
**right-hand man** *s* mano derecha, brazo derecho
**rightism** ['raɪtɪzəm] *s* derechismo
**rightist** ['raɪtɪst] *adj & s* derechista
**right jab** *s* (box.) inverso de derecha
**rightly** ['raɪtlɪ] *adv* derechamente; correctamente; con razón; convenientemente; **rightly or wrongly** con razón o sin ella; **rightly so** a justo título
**right mind** *s* entero juicio
**right-minded** ['raɪt'maɪndɪd] *adj* honrado, recto
**rightness** ['raɪtnɪs] *s* derechura
**righto** ['raɪto] *interj* (coll.) ¡muy bien!, ¡con mucho gusto!
**right of assembly** *s* derecho de reunión
**right of asylum** *s* derecho de asilo
**right of search** o **right of visit** *s* (int. law) derecho de visita
**right of way** *s* derecho de tránsito o de paso; (law) servidumbre de paso; (rail.) servidumbre de vía
**right shoulder arms** *interj* (mil.) ¡arma al hombro!
**rights of man** *spl* derechos del hombre
**right to work** *s* libertad de trabajo
**right triangle** *s* (geom.) triángulo rectángulo
**right wing** *s* ala derecha (*de un ejército*); (pol.) derecha
**right-wing** ['raɪt,wɪŋ] *adj* derechista
**right-winger** ['raɪt,wɪŋər] *s* (coll.) derechista
**rigid** ['rɪdʒɪd] *adj* rígido
**rigidity** [rɪ'dʒɪdɪtɪ] *s* rigidez
**rigmarole** ['rɪgmərol] *s* galimatías
**rigor** ['rɪgər] *s* rigor; (path. & physiol.) rigor
**rigorism** ['rɪgərɪzəm] *s* rigorismo
**rigorist** ['rɪgərɪst] *s* rigorista
**rigor mortis** ['raɪgɔr 'mɔrtɪs] o ['rɪgər 'mɔrtɪs] *s* rigor de la muerte, rigidez cadavérica
**rigorous** ['rɪgərəs] *adj* riguroso
**rile** [raɪl] *va* (coll.) exasperar, irritar con exceso
**rill** [rɪl] *s* arroyuelo o riachuelo; *vn* correr (*el agua*) en un arroyuelo o riachuelo
**rim** [rɪm] *s* canto, borde; llanta (*de la rueda*); (aut.) aro (*de neumático*); (*pret & pp:* **rimmed;** *ger:* **rimming**) *va* proveer de un canto o borde; correr alrededor del canto de; cercar, rodear
**rime** [raɪm] *s* rima; escarcha; **without rime or reason** sin ton ni son; *va* rimar; cubrir con escarcha; *vn* rimar
**rimer** ['raɪmər] *s* var. de **rhymer**
**rimester** ['raɪmstər] *s* var. de **rhymester**
**rim lock** *s* cerradura guarnecida al revés
**rimy** ['raɪmɪ] *adj* (*comp:* **-ier;** *super:* **-iest**) escarchado
**rind** [raɪnd] *s* corteza; *va* descortezar
**rinderpest** ['rɪndər,pɛst] *s* (vet.) fiebre biliosa hematúrica, ictericia hematúrica
**ring** [rɪŋ] *s* anillo; sortija; círculo; corona (*de un vaso, copa, etc.*); reborde (*de una moneda*); círculo de goma (*para tarros de frutas*); anilla (*que se emplea en la gimnasia*); argolla (*que se pone en la nariz a un animal*); arena (*para carreras, juegos deportivos, etc.*); circo (*para ejercicios ecuestres o acrobáticos*); (taur.) redondel; cuadrilátero o ruedo (*para el boxeo*); boxeo, pugilato; corro (*de gente*); cuadrilla (*grupo de personas*); pandilla (*grupo de personas con un fin censurable o ilícito*); ojera (*bajo el párpado inferior*); (naut.) arganeo (*de la caña del ancla*); (chem.) núcleo; campanada (*toque de campana; sonido de reloj*); campanilleo; tañido; tintineo (*de choque de*

*copas, de campanilla, timbre, etc.*); llamada (*aviso acústico*); (fig.) tono (*carácter, espíritu*); **the rings of Saturn** (astr.) los anillos de Saturno; **to be in the ring (for)** ser candidato (a); **to run rings around** dar cien vueltas a, vencer completamente ‖ *adj* anular ‖ (*pret & pp:* **ringed**) *va* cercar, rodear; anillar; quitar a (*un árbol*) una tira circular de corteza; (sport); meter el herrón o la herradura en (*el clavo*); (sport) meter (*el herrón o la herradura*) en el clavo ‖ *vn* anillarse; formar círculo o corro ‖ (*pret:* **rang** o **rung**; *pp:* **rung**) *va* sonar; tañer, repicar; tocar; llamar o convocar repicando o tocando campanas; llamar al timbre; anunciar o celebrar con repique de campanas; entonar (*las alabanzas de una persona*); dar (*las horas la campana del reloj*); llamar por teléfono; **to ring in** (coll.) introducir con maña o fraudulentamente; **to ring up** llamar por teléfono; marcar (*una compra*) con el timbre ‖ *vn* sonar (*una campana, un timbre, el teléfono*); campanear; campanillear; repicar; tintinear (*el choque de copas, una campanilla*); llamar; resonar, retumbar; ser celebrado, tener fama; zumbar (*los oídos*); (fig.) sonar (*tener cierta apariencia*); **to ring for** llamar, llamar al timbre; **to ring off** terminar una llamada por teléfono; **to ring up** llamar por teléfono

**ring-around-a-rosy** [ˈrɪŋəˌraʊndəˈrozɪ] *s* corro, juego del corro

**ringbolt** [ˈrɪŋˌbolt] *s* perno con anillo, cáncamo de argolla

**ringdove** [ˈrɪŋˌdʌv] *s* (orn.) paloma torcaz; (orn.) tórtola (*Streptopelia risoria*)

**ringed** [rɪŋd] *adj* anillado; que lleva anillo; que lleva anillo de matrimonio; casado

**ringer** [ˈrɪŋər] *s* campanero; dispositivo de llamada; impulsador de campanilla de teléfono; herrón o herradura metida en el clavo; (slang) jugador que toma parte en una competencia atlética representándose falsamente; (slang) segunda edición (*persona o cosa que se parece mucho a otra*)

**ring finger** *s* dedo anular, dedo médico

**ring formation** *s* (chem.) ciclización

**ringing** [ˈrɪŋɪŋ] *s* anillamiento; campaneo; repique; tintineo; retintín o silbido (*de oídos*); *adj* resonante, retumbante

**ringleader** [ˈrɪŋˌlidər] *s* cabecilla

**ringlet** [ˈrɪŋlɪt] *s* anillejo; rizo

**ringleted** [ˈrɪŋlɪtɪd] *adj* rizado

**ringmaster** [ˈrɪŋˌmæstər] o [ˈrɪŋˌmɑstər] *s* hombre encargado de los ejercicios ecuestres y acrobáticos de un circo

**Ring of the Nibelung** *s* Anillo del Nibelungo

**ring shake** *s* acebolladura

**ringside** [ˈrɪŋˌsaɪd] *s* lugar junto al cuadrilátero de boxeo; lugar desde el cual se puede ver de cerca

**ringworm** [ˈrɪŋˌwʌrm] *s* (path.) tiña

**rink** [rɪŋk] *s* patinadero

**rinse** [rɪns] *s* enjuague, aclaración; *va* enjuagar, aclarar

**riot** [ˈraɪət] *s* alboroto, desorden, tumulto; regocijos ruidosos, orgía; exhibición brillante (*de colores*); **to read the riot act** mandar que cese la agitación; reprender vehementemente, protestar vehementemente; **to run riot** desenfrenarse; crecer lozanamente (*las plantas*)

**rioter** [ˈraɪətər] *s* alborotador; jaranero, libertino

**riotous** [ˈraɪətəs] *adj* alborotado, desenfrenado, bullicioso; desenfrenado, libertino

**riot squad** *s* pelotón de asalto, escuadra de choque

**R.I.P.** abr. de **Requiescat** (o **Requiescant**) **in pace** (Lat.) **May he** o **she** (o **they**) **rest in peace**

**rip** [rɪp] *s* rasgón; (sew.) descosido; corriente rápida hecha por la marea; agua que se ha puesto revuelta por la confluencia de corrientes o mareas; (coll.) holgazán; (coll.) jamelgo; (*pret & pp:* **ripped**; *ger:* **ripping**) *va* rasgar, desgarrar; (sew.) descoser; (carp.) aserrar (*la madera*) al hilo; **to rip off** quitar rasgando; arrebatar, quitar violentamente; **to rip open** abrir desgarrando; abrir violentamente; **to rip out** arrancar o sacar desgarrando; arrancar o sacar violentamente; (coll.) decir con violencia; **to rip up** rasgar, desgarrar; desarraigar con violencia; *vn* rasgarse, desgarrarse; (coll.) adelantar o moverse de prisa o con violencia; **to rip out with** (coll.) decir con violencia

**riparian** [rɪˈpɛrɪən] o [raɪˈpɛrɪən] *adj & s* ribereño

**rip cord** *s* (aer.) cabo de desgarre; (aer.) cuerda de apertura

**ripe** [raɪp] *adj* maduro; rosado, colorado; hecho, acabado; dispuesto, preparado, pronto; madurado (*divieso, tumor*); negro (*dícese de una aceituna*)

**ripen** [ˈraɪpən] *va & vn* madurar

**ripeness** [ˈraɪpnɪs] *s* madurez

**riposte** [rɪˈpost] *s* (fencing) estocada que se da después de parar; (fig.) respuesta pronta y aguda; *vn* (fencing) reparar y dar la estocada a un mismo tiempo; (fig.) responder con viveza

**rip panel** *s* (aer.) faja de desgarre

**ripper** [ˈrɪpər] *s* rasgador; descosedor

**ripping** [ˈrɪpɪŋ] *s* rasgadura, desgarro; *adj* (slang) espléndido, excelente, magnífico

**ripple** [ˈrɪpəl] *s* rizo, temblor, ondulación; murmullo; *va* rizar; *vn* rizarse; correr con rizos u olas pequeñas; murmurar

**ripplet** [ˈrɪplɪt] *s* rizo pequeño (*de agua*)

**ripply** [ˈrɪplɪ] *adj* rizado; murmullante

**riprap** [ˈrɪpˌræp] *s* ripio; muro hecho con ripio; (*pret & pp:* **-rapped**; *ger:* **-rapping**) *va* reforzar con ripio; construir con ripio

**rip-roaring** [ˈrɪpˈrorɪŋ] *adj* (slang) alborozado, bullicioso

**ripsaw** [ˈrɪpˌsɔ] *s* sierra de hilar o hender; *va* aserrar al hilo

**rise** [raɪz] *s* subida (*p.ej., de la temperatura, de precios, de un pez a la superficie del agua para coger cebo; cuesta ascendiente*); elevación (*p.ej., del terreno, de la voz*); salida (*de un astro*); ascenso (*en un empleo*); altura (*de peldaño*); montea (*de arco*); nacimiento (*de un manantial*); crecida; (mach.) levantamiento (*de una válvula*); (slang) réplica mordaz; **to get a rise out of** (slang) sacar una réplica mordaz a; **to give rise to** dar origen a; (*pret:* **rose**; *pp:* **risen**) *vn* levantarse; subir; salir (*un astro*); asomar (*p.ej., un peligro*); brotar (*un manantial, una planta*); resucitar; ganar (*en la estimación de uno*); **to rise above** alzarse por encima de; mostrarse superior a; **to rise early** madrugar; **to rise to** ser capaz de, sentirse con fuerzas para

**risen** [ˈrɪzən] *pp de* **rise**

**riser** [ˈraɪzər] *s* contrahuella, contraescalón (*frente del peldaño*); **early riser** madrugador; **late riser** dormilón

**risibility** [ˌrɪzɪˈbɪlɪtɪ] *s* (*pl:* **-ties**) risibilidad; **risibilities** *spl* ganas de reírse, reideras

**risible** [ˈrɪzɪbəl] *adj* risible; **risibles** *spl* reideras

**rising** [ˈraɪzɪŋ] *adj* ascendiente; naciente; creciente; saliente (*Sol*); venidero; (phonet.) creciente (*diptongo*)

**risk** [rɪsk] *s* riesgo; **at the risk of** + *ger* a riesgo de + *inf;* **to run** o **take a risk** correr riesgo; **to run** o **take the risk of** + *ger* correr riesgo de + *inf;* *va* arriesgar; arriesgarse en (*una empresa dudosa*); **to risk** + *ger* arriesgarse a + *inf*

**risky** [ˈrɪskɪ] *adj* (*comp:* **-ier**; *super:* **-iest**) arriesgado; escabroso

**risqué** [rɪsˈke] *adj* escabroso

**rissole** [ˈrɪsol] o [riˈsɔl] *s* (cook.) risol (*torta tostada hecha de carne picada o pescado, huevos, migas de pan y otros ingredientes*)

**rite** [raɪt] *s* rito

**ritornel** o **ritornelle** [ˌrɪtərˈnɛl] *s* (mus.) retornelo

**ritual** [ˈrɪtʃʊəl] *adj & s* ritual

**ritualism** [ˈrɪtʃʊəlɪzəm] *s* ritualismo

**ritualist** [ˈrɪtʃʊəlɪst] *adj & s* ritualista

**ritualistic** [ˌrɪtʃʊəlˈɪstɪk] *adj* ritualista

**ritually** [ˈrɪtʃʊəlɪ] *adv* según el ritual

**ritual murder** *s* asesinato ritual

**riv.** abr. de **river**

**rival** [ˈraɪvəl] *adj & s* rival; (*pret & pp:* **-valed** o **-valled**; *ger:* **-valing** o **-valling**) *va* rivalizar con

**rivalry** [ˈraɪvəlrɪ] *s* (*pl:* **-ries**) rivalidad

**rivalship** ['raɪvəlʃɪp] *s* rivalidad
**rive** [raɪv] (*pret:* **rived;** *pp:* **rived** o **riven**) *va* rajar; *vn* rajarse
**riven** ['rɪvən] *adj* rajado; *pp de* **rive**
**river** ['rɪvər] *s* río; (fig.) río (*p.ej., de sangre*); **down the river** río abajo; **up the river** río arriba; *adj* fluvial
**river basin** *s* cuenca de río
**river bed** *s* cauce
**river front** *s* orilla del río
**river-god** ['rɪvər,gad] *s* dios del río
**riverhead** ['rɪvər,hɛd] *s* nacimiento de un río
**river horse** *s* (zool.) caballo marino (*hipopótamo*)
**riverside** ['rɪvər,saɪd] *s* ribera; *adj* ribereño
**rivet** ['rɪvɪt] *s* roblón, remache; *va* remachar; clavar (*p.ej., los ojos en una persona*)
**riveter** ['rɪvɪtər] *s* remachador; remachadora (*máquina*)
**rivulet** ['rɪvjəlɪt] *s* riachuelo
**rm.** abr. de **ream** y **room**
**rms.** abr. de **reams** y **rooms**
**R.N.** abr. de **registered nurse** y **Royal Navy**
**roach** [rotʃ] *s* (ent.) cucaracha; (ichth.) leucisco
**road** [rod] *s* camino; (naut.) rada; **in the road** estorbando el paso; incomodando; **to be on the road** viajar de lugar en lugar (*en el ejercicio de un empleo*); **to get out of the road** quitarse de en medio; **to take to the road** (archaic) hacerse salteador de caminos
**road agent** *s* (U.S.A.) salteador de caminos
**roadbed** ['rod,bɛd] *s* firme; (rail.) infraestructura; (rail.) capa de balastro
**roadblock** ['rod,blak] *s* (mil.) barricada; (fig.) obstáculo
**roadhouse** ['rod,haus] *s* posada en el camino, venta
**road laborer** *s* peón caminero
**road map** *s* mapa itinerario
**road metal** *s* grava, piedra triturada para caminos
**road roller** *s* cilindro de caminos, apisonador
**road runner** *s* (orn.) correcamino
**road scraper** *s* traílla
**road service** *s* (aut.) auxilio en carretera
**roadside** ['rod,saɪd] *s* borde del camino, borde de la carretera
**roadside inn** *s* posada en el camino, venta
**road sign** *s* señal de carretera, poste indicador
**roadstead** ['rod,stɛd] *s* (naut.) rada
**roadster** ['rodstər] *s* caminante; caballo de campo; (aut.) roadster, coche de caja abierta y de dos plazas
**roadway** ['rod,we] *s* camino, vía
**roam** [rom] *s* vagabundeo; *va* vagar por, recorrer a la ventura; *vn* vagar, andar errante
**roan** [ron] *adj* roano; *s* color roano; caballo roano
**roar** [ror] *s* rugido, bramido; *va* decir a gritos; **to roar oneself hoarse** ponerse ronco gritando; *vn* rugir, bramar; reírse a carcajadas
**roast** [rost] *s* asado; carne para asar; variedad de café tostado; (coll.) fiesta en que se comen manjares asados directamente al o en el fuego; (coll.) burla o censura severa, despellejadura; *adj* asado; tostado (*café*); *va* asar; tostar (*café*); (coll.) burlarse de, mofarse de, despellejar; *vn* asarse; tostarse (*café*)
**roast beef** *s* rosbif
**roaster** ['rostər] *s* asador; tostador; pollo o lechón propio para asar
**roast of beef** *s* carne de vaca asada o para asar
**rob** [rab] (*pret & pp:* **robbed;** *ger:* **robbing**) *va* robar; **to rob someone of something** o **to rob something from someone** robarle algo a alguien; **to rob Peter to pay Paul** desnudar a un santo para vestir a otro; *vn* robar; (*cap.*) *s* nombre abreviado de **Robert**
**robber** ['rabər] *s* robador, ladrón
**robbery** ['rabərɪ] *s* (*pl:* **-ies**) robo
**robe** [rob] *s* manto; abrigo; toga, túnica (*del letrado, juez, etc.*); traje talar (*del sacerdote*); manta (*de coche*); traje, vestido (*de mujer*); *va* vestir; *vn* vestirse
**Robert** ['rabərt] *s* Roberto
**robin** ['rabɪn] *s* (orn.) petirrojo; (orn.) primavera (*Turdus migratorius*)
**robin's-egg blue** ['rabɪnz,ɛg] *s* color azul verdoso
**robot** ['robat] o ['rabət] *s* robot; (fig.) robot (*persona*)
**robot bomb** *s* (mil.) bomba volante, bomba cohete
**robust** [ro'bʌst] *adj* robusto; arduo, vigoroso; grosero
**robustious** [ro'bʌstʃəs] *adj* (archaic & hum.) robusto; (archaic & hum.) alborotado, ruidoso, grosero
**roc** [rak] *s* (myth.) roc o rocho (*ave*)
**rocambole** ['rakəmbol] *s* (bot.) rocambola
**Rochelle salt** [ro'ʃɛl] *s* (pharm.) sal de la Rochela
**rochet** ['ratʃɪt] *s* (eccl.) roquete
**rock** [rak] *s* roca; escollo (*a flor de agua*); (coll.) piedra (*que se tira*); (slang) diamante, piedra preciosa; (orn.) paloma zorita; (ichth.) pez anadromo (*Roccus saxatilis*); mecedura; (*cap.*) *s* Peñón (*de Gibraltar*); **on the rocks** (coll.) arruinado, quebrado, en pobreza extrema; (coll.) con sólo trocitos de hielo, sobre hielo (*dícese de ciertas bebidas alcohólicas*); *adj* de roca, formado de rocas; entre las rocas; *va* mecer; acunar; arrullar; calmar, sosegar; sacudir; **to rock the boat** mover el barco de un modo temerario; (fig.) perturbar la armonía; **to rock to sleep** arrullar, adormecer meciendo; *vn* mecerse; sacudirse
**rock bottom** *s* el fondo, lo más profundo
**rock-bottom** ['rak,batəm] *adj* (el) mínimo, (el) más bajo
**rock-bound** ['rak,baund] *adj* rodeado de rocas; inaccesible
**rock candy** *s* azúcar cande, azúcar candi
**rock crystal** *s* cristal de roca
**rock dove** *s* (orn.) paloma zorita
**rocker** ['rakər] *s* mecedora (*silla*); arco (*de mecedora o cuna*); (mach.) eje de balancín; (mach.) balancín
**rocker arm** *s* (mach.) balancín
**rockershaft** ['rakər,ʃæft] o ['rakər,ʃaft] *s* (mach.) eje de balancín
**rocket** ['rakɪt] *s* cohete; (bot.) roqueta, ruca; (bot.) juliana, violeta; *vn* subir como un cohete, lucirse y desaparecer; alcanzar gran altura rápida y súbitamente
**rocket bomb** *s* bomba cohete
**rocketeer** [,rakɪ'tɪr] *s* cohetero
**rocket gun** *s* (mil.) cañón cohete
**rocket larkspur** *s* (bot.) espuela de caballero
**rocket launcher** *s* (mil.) lanzacohetes
**rocket motor** *s* motor cohete
**rocket plane** *s* (aer.) avión cohete
**rocket-powered** ['rakɪt,pauərd] *adj* propulsado por cohetes
**rocket propulsion** *s* propulsión a cohete
**rocketry** ['rakɪtrɪ] *s* cohetería
**rocket salad** *s* (bot.) roqueta, ruca
**rocket ship** *s* aeronave cohete
**rock garden** *s* jardín entre rocas
**Rockies** ['rakɪz] *spl* Montañas Rocosas o Roqueñas
**rocking chair** *s* mecedora, sillón de hamaca
**rocking horse** *s* caballo mecedor
**rock of ages** *s* Cristo; la fe de Cristo
**Rock of Gibraltar** *s* peñón de Gibraltar
**rock ptarmigan** *s* (orn.) perdiz blanca
**rock-ribbed** ['rak,rɪbd] *adj* que tiene costillas de roca; fuerte, inflexible
**rockrose** ['rak,roz] *s* (bot.) estepa
**rock salt** *s* sal de compás, sal gema
**rockshaft** ['rak,ʃæft] o ['rak,ʃaft] *s* (mach.) eje de balancines; (min.) pozo de relleno
**rockweed** ['rak,wid] *s* (bot.) fuco
**rock wool** *s* lana mineral
**rocky** ['rakɪ] *adj* (*comp:* **-ier;** *super:* **-iest**) roqueño; despiadado, inflexible; (slang) que bambolea; (slang) débil, poco firme
**Rocky Mountains** *spl* Montañas Rocosas o Roqueñas
**Rocky Mountain spotted fever** *s* (path.) fiebre purpúrea de las Montañas Rocosas
**rococo** [ro'koko] o ['rokəko] *adj & s* (f.a.) rococó
**rod** [rad] *s* vara; varilla; barra; vara buscadora; vara de medir; caña de pescar; medida inglesa de longitud que equivale a cinco yardas y media; (anat.) bastoncillo (*de la retina*); (bact.)

bastoncito; (mach.) vástago; (surv.) jalón; vara alta (*autoridad*); opresión, tiranía; (Bib.) linaje, raza, vástago; (slang) revólver, pistola; **to spare the rod** excusar la vara (*no castigar a un niño*)
**rode** [rod] *pret de* **ride**
**rodent** [ˈrodənt] *adj & s* (zool.) roedor
**rodeo** [roˈdeo] o [ˈrodɪo] *s* (*pl:* **-os**) rodeo (*recogida de los ganados; espectáculo de los vaqueros norteamericanos*)
**Roderick** [ˈrɑdərɪk] *s* Rodrigo
**rodman** [ˈrɑdmən] *s* (*pl:* **-men**) (surv.) portamira
**rodomontade** [ˌrɑdəmɑnˈted] o [ˌrɑdəmɑnˈtɑd] *s* rodomontada, fanfarronada; *adj* fanfarrón; *vn* fanfarronear
**roe** [ro] *s* (zool.) corzo; hueva (*masa de huevecillos de ciertos peces*)
**roebuck** [ˈroˌbʌk] o **roe deer** *s* (zool.) corzo
**roentgenogram** [ˈrɛntgənəˌgræm] *s* roentgenograma
**roentgenologist** [ˌrɛntgəˈnɑlədʒɪst] *s* roentgenólogo
**roentgenology** [ˌrɛntgəˈnɑlədʒɪ] *s* roentgenología
**roentgenotherapy** [ˌrɛntgənoˈθɛrəpɪ] *s* roentgenoterapia
**Roentgen rays** [ˈrɛntgən] *spl* (phys.) rayos Roentgen
**rogation** [roˈgeʃən] *s* (hist.) rogación; (eccl.) rogativa; **rogations** *spl* (eccl.) rogativas (*especialmente las que caen en los tres días antes de la Ascensión*)
**rogatory** [ˈrogəˌtorɪ] *adj* rogatorio
**Roger** [ˈrɑdʒər] *s* Rogelio
**rogue** [rog] *s* bribón, pícaro; elefante u otro animal bravo que vive separado del rebaño
**roguery** [ˈrogərɪ] *s* (*pl:* **-ies**) bribonería, picardía; travesura, diablura
**rogues' gallery** *s* colección de retratos de malhechores para uso de la policía
**roguish** [ˈrogɪʃ] *adj* bribón, pícaro; travieso, retozón
**roil** [rɔɪl] *va* enturbiar; irritar, vejar
**roily** [ˈrɔɪlɪ] *adj* enturbiado; irritado, vejado
**roister** [ˈrɔɪstər] *vn* jaranear; fanfarronear
**roisterer** [ˈrɔɪstərər] *s* jaranero; fanfarrón
**roisterous** [ˈrɔɪstərəs] *adj* jaranero; fanfarrón
**Roland** [ˈrolənd] *s* Rolando, Roldán
**rôle** o **role** [rol] *s* papel; **to play a rôle** desempeñar un papel
**roll** [rol] *s* rollo; rodillo; rodadura; echada (*de los dados*); panecillo; ondulación; bamboleo; balance (*del barco*); redoble (*del tambor*); retumbo (*p.ej., del trueno*); rol, lista; (slang) fajo (*de papel moneda*); **to call the roll** pasar lista; **to strike off the rolls** excluir de la lista de miembros ‖ *va* arrollar; envolver; hacer rodar; empujar sobre rodillos; empujar hacia adelante; rodillar; cilindrar; laminar; entintar con rodillo; liar (*un cigarrillo*); mover (*p.ej., el cuerpo*) de un lado a otro; mover o menear (*los ojos*) de uno a otro lado, mover (*los ojos*) hacia arriba, poner (*los ojos*) en blanco; tocar redobles con (*el tambor*); hacer resonar; vibrar (*la voz*); pronunciar (*la r*) vibrando la lengua; meditar cuidadosamente, pesar detenidamente; **to roll one's own** hacérselos o liárselos (*liarse sus propios cigarrillos*); (slang) arreglárselas bien solo; **to roll the bones** (slang) echar o tirar los dados, jugar a los dados; **to roll the eye over** echar una mirada a; **to roll the eyes** poner los ojos en blanco; **to roll up** arrollar; arremangar (*p.ej., las mangas*); amontonar (*p.ej., fortuna*) ‖ *vn* rodar; bambolear o bambolearse; balancear o balancearse (*un barco*); ondear; girar; moverse (*los ojos*) de uno a otro lado, moverse (*los ojos*) hacia arriba; retumbar (*el trueno*); redoblar (*un tambor*); **to roll in** entrar rodando; entrar bamboleándose; avanzar ondeando (*el agua*); (coll.) arroparse en la cama; (coll.) nadar en (*p.ej., dinero*); **to roll out** salir bamboleándose; (slang) levantarse desarropándose; **to roll up** arrollar; llegar en vehículo; amontonarse (*p.ej., dinero*)
**roll call** *s* lista, (el) pasar lista
**rolled oats** *spl* copos de avena
**roller** [ˈrolər] *s* rodillo; tambor; ruedecilla (*de un mueble*); rueda (*de patines*); venda (*para cubrir una herida*); ola larga y creciente; (orn.) pichón volteador; (orn.) canario de canto sostenido
**roller bearing** *s* cojinete de rodillos
**roller blind** *s* cortina de resorte
**roller coaster** *s* montaña rusa
**roller mill** *s* molino de cilindros, trituradora de cilindros
**roller skate** *s* patín de ruedas
**roller-skate** [ˈrolərˌsket] *vn* patinar con patines de ruedas
**roller towel** *s* toalla sin fin, toalla continua
**roll film** *s* (phot.) película en carretes
**rollick** [ˈrɑlɪk] *vn* jugetear, retozar, divertirse de manera turbulenta
**rollicking** [ˈrɑlɪkɪŋ] o **rollicksome** [ˈrɑlɪksəm] *adj* juguetón, retozón, alegre, turbulento
**rolling** [ˈrolɪŋ] *adj* rodante; rodadero; girante; retumbante; undulante u ondulado; doblegado, plegado; *s* rodadura; bamboleo; balanceo; retumbo; undulación; redoble (*del tambor*)
**rolling barrage** *s* (mil.) cortina de fuego rodante
**rolling kitchen** *s* (mil.) cocina rodante
**rolling mill** *s* laminadero, taller de laminación; laminador, tren de laminadores
**rolling pin** *s* hataca, rodillo, rodillo de pastelero
**rolling stock** *s* (rail.) material móvil, material rodante
**rolling stone** *s* (fig.) piedra movediza
**roll sulfur** *s* azufre cañón, azufre en canuto
**roll-top desk** [ˈrolˌtɑp] *s* escritorio norteamericano
**roly-poly** [ˈrolɪˈpolɪ] *adj* regordete, rechoncho; *s* (*pl:* **-lies**) persona regordeta; pudín en forma de rollo, cocido, horneado o sometido a la acción del vapor
**Rom.** abr. de **Roman, Romance** y **Romans** (Bib.)
**rom** o **Rom** [rʌm] *s* rom, hombre o muchacho gitano
**Romaean** [roˈmiən] *adj* romeo (*griego bizantino*)
**Romaic** [roˈmeɪk] *adj & s* romaico
**romaine** [roˈmen] *s* lechuga romana
**Roman** [ˈromən] *adj & s* romano; **Romans** *spl* (Bib.) Epístola a los romanos; (*l.c.*) *adj* (print.) redondo; *s* (print.) letra redonda
**Roman candle** *s* vela romana
**Roman Catholic** *adj & s* católico romano
**Roman Catholicism** *s* catolicismo romano
**Romance** [roˈmæns] o [ˈromæns] *adj* romance o románico (*neolatino*); (*l.c.*) *s* romance (*libro o novela de caballerías*); cuento de aventuras; cuento de amor, cuento de enamorados; (lo) pintoresco (*p.ej., de la historia*); interés en las aventuras, el amor o lo pintoresco; intriga amorosa; ficción, invención; (mus.) romanza; [roˈmæns] *vn* contar o escribir romances, contar o escribir cuentos de aventuras o de amor; pensar o hablar de un modo romántico o fantástico; exagerar; mentir
**romance of chivalry** *s* libro de caballerías
**romancer** [roˈmænsər] *s* romancero; visionario; embustero
**Roman Curia** *s* Curia romana
**Roman Empire** *s* Imperio romano
**Romanesque** [ˌromənˈɛsk] *adj & s* (arch.) románico
**Romanic** [roˈmænɪk] *adj* románico (*neolatino*)
**Romanism** [ˈromənɪzəm] *s* romanismo; (offensive) romanismo (*la religión católica*)
**Romanist** [ˈromənɪst] *s* romanista; (offensive) romanista (*persona que profesa la religión católica*)
**Romanization** [ˌromənɪˈzeʃən] *s* romanización; conversión al catolicismo
**Romanize** [ˈromənaɪz] *va* romanizar; convertir al catolicismo; *vn* romanizarse; convertirse al catolicismo
**Roman law** *s* derecho romano
**Roman nose** *s* nariz aguileña
**Roman numeral** *s* número romano
**Roman rite** *s* rito romano
**Romansh** [roˈmænʃ] o [roˈmɑnʃ] *s* romanche o rumanche
**romantic** [roˈmæntɪk] *adj* romántico; encantado (*sitio*); *s* romántico
**romantically** [roˈmæntɪkəlɪ] *adv* románticamente

**romanticism** [roˈmæntɪsɪzəm] *s* romanticismo
**romanticist** [roˈmæntɪsɪst] *s* romántico
**romanticize** [roˈmæntɪsaɪz] *va* hacer romántico; *vn* ser romántico, hablar o escribir de un modo romántico
**Romantic Movement** *s* Romanticismo
**Romany** [ˈrɑmənɪ] *adj* romany; *s* (*pl:* **-nies**) romany
**Rom. Cath.** abr. de **Roman Catholic**
**Rome** [rom] *s* Roma
**Rome-Berlin axis** [ˈrombʌrˈlɪn] *s* eje Roma-Berlín
**romp** [rɑmp] *s* trisca, retozo; saltabardales; *vn* triscar, corretear
**rompers** [ˈrɑmpərz] *spl* traje holgado de juego para niños
**Romulus** [ˈrɑmjələs] *s* (myth.) Rómulo
**rondeau** [ˈrɑndo] o [rɑnˈdo] *s* rondó o rondeau
**rondel** [ˈrɑndəl] *s* rondel
**rondo** [ˈrɑndo] o [rɑnˈdo] *s* (*pl:* **-dos**) (mus.) rondó
**rood** [rud] *s* crucifijo; cruz en que murió Cristo
**rood screen** *s* (arch.) jube
**roof** [ruf] o [rʊf] *s* tejado (*cubierta de un edificio*); techo (*de paja, bálago, etc.*); azotea (*cubierta llana de un edificio*); imperial (*de un coche*); paladar (*de la boca*); techo interior, cielo raso; cubierta; bóveda (*del cielo*); (fig.) techo (*domicilio, morada*); **to raise the roof** (slang) poner el grito en el cielo; *va* techar
**roofer** [ˈrufər] o [ˈrʊfər] *s* constructor de techos o tejados, techador
**roof garden** *s* pérgola; azotea de baile y diversión
**roofing** [ˈrufɪŋ] o [ˈrʊfɪŋ] *s* material para techos
**roofless** [ˈruflɪs] o [ˈrʊflɪs] *adj* sin techo; mostrenco
**rooftree** [ˈruf,tri] o [ˈrʊf,tri] *s* cumbrera o parhilera; tejado; (fig.) techo (*domicilio*)
**rook** [rʊk] *s* (orn.) chova, grajo, cuervo merendero; embustero; torre, roque (*en el ajedrez*); *va & vn* trampear
**rookery** [ˈrʊkərɪ] *s* (*pl:* **-ies**) bosque grajero; criadero de focas, grullas, aves marinas, etc.; casa o habitación baja y escuálida; vecindario bajo y escuálido
**rookie** [ˈrʊkɪ] *s* (slang) bisoño, novato
**room** [rum] o [rʊm] *s* aposento, cuarto, habitación, pieza; espacio, sitio, lugar; ocasión; **to make room** abrir paso, hacer lugar, despejar la vía; **there is no room for doubt** no cabe duda; **there is no more room** no cabe(n) más; *vn* alojarse, hospedarse
**room and board** *s* pensión completa
**roomer** [ˈrumər] o [ˈrʊmər] *s* inquilino
**roomful** [ˈrumfʊl] o [ˈrʊmfʊl] *s* cuarto lleno; gente en un cuarto, cosas en un cuarto
**rooming house** *s* casa donde se alquilan cuartos
**roommate** [ˈrum,met] o [ˈrʊm,met] *s* compañero de cuarto
**room service** *s* servicio de los cuartos, servicio de restaurante en las habitaciones de un hotel
**roomy** [ˈrumɪ] o [ˈrʊmɪ] *adj* (*comp:* **-ier;** *super:* **-iest**) amplio, espacioso, holgado
**roorback** [ˈrʊrbæk] *s* (U.S.A.) libelo contra un candidato, que se circula por su efecto político
**roost** [rust] *s* percha de gallinero; gallinero; lugar de descanso; **to rule the roost** mandar, tener el mando y el palo (*especialmente en la casa de uno*); *vn* descansar (*las aves*) en la percha; estar alojado; pasar la noche
**rooster** [ˈrustər] *s* gallo
**roosterfish** [ˈrustər,fɪʃ] *s* (ichth.) papagayo
**root** [rut] o [rʊt] *s* raíz; (bot., gram. & math.) raíz; (anat.) raigón (*del diente*); (mus.) base, nota fundamental; **to get to the root of** profundizar; **to take root** echar raíces; *va* plantar firmemente; hocicar u hozar; desarraigar; **to root out** o **up** desarraigar; *vn* arraigar; hocicar u hozar; **to root about** andar buscando; **to root for** (slang) aplaudir o gritar ruidosamente por el éxito de
**rootage** [ˈrutɪdʒ] o [ˈrʊtɪdʒ] *s* arraigo
**root and branch** *adv* por completo
**root beer** *s* bebida no alcohólica hecha de extractos de varias raíces
**root canal** *s* (anat. & dent.) conducto radicular
**rooter** [ˈrutər] o [ˈrʊtər] *s* hozador (*animal*); (slang) hincha (*entusiasta que aplaude o grita ruidosamente por el éxito de un jugador, equipo, etc.*)
**root hair** *s* (bot.) pelos absorbentes
**rootlet** [ˈrutlɪt] o [ˈrʊtlɪt] *s* raicilla
**rootstock** [ˈrut,stɑk] o [ˈrʊt,stɑk] *s* (bot.) rizoma
**rooty** [ˈrutɪ] o [ˈrʊtɪ] *adj* (*comp:* **-ier;** *super:* **-iest**) lleno de raíces; radicoso
**rope** [rop] *s* cuerda; dogal (*para ahorcar a un reo*); lazo (*para coger animales*); muerte en la horca; masa fibrosa y viscosa; **to be at the end of one's rope** estar sin recursos, andar o estar en las últimas; no saber qué hacer; **to give a person rope** (coll.) dar libertad de acción a una persona, dejar que una persona actúe u obre libremente; **to jump** o **to skip rope** saltar a la comba; **to know the ropes** conocer la jarcia o las cuerdas de un buque; (slang) saber cuántas son cinco, saber todas las tretas; *va* atar o amarrar con una cuerda; cercar con cuerdas, rodear con soga; **to rope in** (slang) embaucar o engañar con arte y maña; **to rope off** cercar con cuerdas, rodear con soga; *vn* hacer madeja (*un licor*)
**ropedancer** [ˈrop,dænsər] o [ˈrop,dɑnsər] *s* bailarín de cuerda
**rope ladder** *s* escala de cuerda
**rope railway** *s* alambrecarril
**ropewalk** [ˈrop,wɔk] *s* cordelería
**ropewalker** [ˈrop,wɔkər] *s* volatinero; bailarín de cuerda
**ropeway** [ˈrop,we] *s* cablecarril, teleférico
**ropy** [ˈropɪ] *adj* (*comp:* **-ier;** *super:* **-iest**) correoso, fibroso, viscoso; de cuerda, como una cuerda
**Roquefort** [ˈrokfərt] *s* queso de Roquefort
**roquet** [roˈke] (*pret & pp:* **-queted** [ˈked]; *ger:* **-queting** [ˈkeɪŋ]) *va & vn* (croquet) enrocar
**roquette** [roˈkɛt] *s* (bot.) roqueta
**rorqual** [ˈrɔrkwəl] *s* (zool.) rorcual
**rosaceous** [roˈzeʃəs] *adj* rosáceo; (bot.) rosáceo
**Rosalie** [ˈrɑzəlɪ] o [ˈrozəlɪ] *s* Rosalía
**Rosalind** [ˈrɑzəlɪnd] o [ˈrɑzəlaɪnd] *s* Rosalinda
**rosary** [ˈrozərɪ] *s* (*pl:* **-ries**) rosario; macizo de rosales; jardín de rosales
**rose** [roz] *s* rosa (*flor*); (bot.) rosal (*planta*); rosa (*color; lazo de cintas; piedra preciosa; perfume*); roseta (*de una regadera*); mujer muy hermosa; (arch.) rosa o rosetón; **under the rose** secretamente; *adj* rosado, de color de rosa; *va* hacer rosado; *pret de* **rise**
**rose acacia** *s* (bot.) acacia rosa
**roseate** [ˈrozɪet] o [ˈrozɪɪt] *adj* róseo, rosado; alegre, jovial, vivo
**rosebay** [ˈroz,be] *s* (bot.) adelfa, baladre, rododafne; (bot.) rododendro
**rose beetle** *s* (ent.) macrodáctilo; (ent.) cetoína dorada
**rosebud** [ˈroz,bʌd] *s* pimpollo, capullo de rosa
**rose bug** *s* (ent.) macrodáctilo
**rosebush** [ˈroz,bʊʃ] *s* (bot.) rosal
**rose chafer** *s* (ent.) cetoína dorada
**rose-colored** [ˈroz,kʌlərd] *adj* róseo, rosado; alegre, jovial, vivo; **to see everything in rose-colored spectacles** verlo todo de color de rosa
**rose diamond** *s* diamante rosa
**rose geranium** *s* (bot.) geranio de rosa
**rose hip** *s* (bot.) cinarrodón, eterio
**rose leaf** *s* pétalo de rosa
**roselle** [roˈzɛl] o **rosella** [roˈzɛlə] *s* (bot.) agrio, jamaica, viña
**rose mallow** *s* (bot.) malva rósea; (bot.) amor al uso, flor de la vida
**rosemary** [ˈroz,mɛrɪ] *s* (*pl:* **-ies**) (bot.) romero
**rose of China** *s* (bot.) rosa de China, tulipán (*Hibiscus rosa-sinensis*)
**rose of Jericho** *s* (bot.) rosa de Jericó
**rose of Sharon** [ˈʃɛrən] *s* (bot.) rosa de Siria; (bot.) hipericón; (Bib.) flor del campo
**roseola** [roˈziələ] *s* (path.) roséola; (path.) rubéola
**Rosetta stone** [roˈzɛtə] *s* piedra de Roseta

**rosette** [ro'zɛt] *s* rosa (*lazo de cintas*); (arch.) rosetón; (metal.) roseta
**rose water** *s* agua de rosas
**rose window** *s* (arch.) rosetón
**rosewood** ['roz,wʊd] *s* palo de rosa; (bot.) palisandro; (bot.) leño de Botany
**Rosicrucian** [,rozɪ'kruʃən] *adj & s* rosicruciano o rosacruz
**rosily** ['rozɪlɪ] *adv* con color de rosa; alegremente
**rosin** ['rɑzɪn] *s* colofonia, brea seca; resina; *va* frotar con colofonia
**Rosinante** [,rɑzɪ'næntɪ] *s* rocinante (*rocín matalón*)
**rosolio** [rɔ'zɔljɔ] *s* rosoli
**roster** ['rɑstər] *s* catálogo, lista, registro; horario escolar, horas de clase; (mil.) lista o reglamento que indica los deberes de los oficiales
**rostral** ['rɑstrəl] *adj* rostral
**rostral column** *s* columna rostral
**rostrate** ['rɑstret] *adj* rostrado
**rostrum** ['rɑstrəm] *s* (*pl:* **-trums** o **-tra** [trə]) *s* tribuna; (anat., naut. & zool.) rostro
**rosy** ['rozɪ] *adj* (*comp:* **-ier;** *super:* **-iest**) rosado; sonrosado; alegre
**rot** [rɑt] *s* podredumbre; (bot.) úlcera; (vet.) comalía, morriña; (slang) tontería; (*pret & pp:* **rotted;** *ger:* **rotting**) *va* pudrir; enriar; *vn* pudrirse
**Rotarian** [ro'tɛrɪən] *adj & s* rotario
**rotary** ['rotərɪ] *adj* rotatorio, rotativo
**rotary press** *s* (print.) rotativa, prensa rotativa
**rotate** ['rotet] o [ro'tet] *va* hacer girar; alternar; *vn* girar, rodar; alternar
**rotation** [ro'teʃən] *s* rotación; **in rotation** por turno
**rotational** [ro'teʃənəl] *adj* rotatorio
**rotation of crops** *s* rotación de cosechas o de cultivos
**rotator** ['rotetər] o [ro'tetər] *s* (*pl:* **rotators**) persona o cosa que da vueltas; (*pl:* **rotatores** [,rotə'toriz]) (anat.) rotador
**rotatory** ['rotə,torɪ] *adj* rotatorio
**rote** [rot] *s* rutina, repetición maquinal; **by rote** de memoria; maquinalmente
**rotgut** ['rɑt,gʌt] *s* (slang) matarratas
**rotifer** ['rotɪfər] *s* (zool.) rotífero
**rotiferous** [ro'tɪfərəs] *adj* rotífero
**rotogravure** [,rotəgrə'vjʊr] o [,rotə'grevjʊr] *s* rotograbado
**rotor** ['rotər] *s* (mach. & elec.) rotor
**rotor ship** *s* (naut.) buque a rotores
**rotten** ['rɑtən] *adj* podrido; fétido; viciado (*aire*); poco firme, en mal estado; despreciable; corrompido, no honrado; (slang) vil, ruin
**rotten borough** *s* (Brit.) pueblo antes de 1832 que, a pesar de sus pocos votantes, tuvo el derecho de representación en el Parlamento
**rottenness** ['rɑtənnɪs] *s* podredumbre; fetidez
**rottenstone** ['rɑtən,ston] *s* (mineral.) trípol; *va* tripolizar
**rotter** ['rɑtər] *s* (slang) sinvergüenza
**rotular** ['rɑtʃələr] *adj* rotular
**rotulian** [ro'tjulɪən] *adj* rotuliano
**rotund** [ro'tʌnd] *adj* redondo de cuerpo; rotundo (*lenguaje*)
**rotunda** [ro'tʌndə] *s* rotonda o rotunda
**rotundity** [ro'tʌndɪtɪ] *s* (*pl:* **-ties**) redondez de cuerpo; rotundidad; cosa redonda
**rouble** ['rubəl] *s* var. de **ruble**
**roué** [ru'e] *s* libertino
**Rouen** [ru'ɑn] *s* Ruán
**rouge** [ruʒ] *s* arrebol, alconcilla, colorete; colcótar, rojo de pulir; *va* arrebolar, pintar; *vn* arrebolarse, pintarse
**rough** [rʌf] *adj* áspero; borrascoso, tempestuoso; agitado (*mar*); peludo, velludo; chapucero, tosco; aproximativo; alborotado, turbulento; brutal; bruto; (phonet.) aspirado; *s* brutal, matón; terreno áspero, maleza; cosa áspera o tosca; **in the rough** en bruto (*sin pulimento*); *va* poner áspero; tratar ásperamente; bosquejar o trazar rudamente; labrar toscamente; **to rough it** vivir sin comodidades, hacer vida campestre; *vn* ponerse áspero
**roughage** ['rʌfɪdʒ] *s* material áspero o grosero; alimento o forraje poco digeribles
**rough-and-ready** ['rʌfənd'rɛdɪ] *adj* tosco pero eficaz; desenvuelto; vigoroso pero poco fino
**rough-and-tumble** ['rʌfənd'tʌmbəl] *adj* desordenado, violento; *s* lucha o pelea desordenada y violenta
**roughcast** ['rʌf,kæst] o ['rʌf,kɑst] *s* modelo tosco; mezcla gruesa, mortero grueso; (*pret & pp:* **-cast**) *va* bosquejar; dar a (*la pared*) una capa de mezcla gruesa
**rough copy** *s* borrador
**rough diamond** *s* diamante en bruto; (fig.) diamante en bruto
**rough draft** *s* bosquejo; borrador
**rough-dry** [,rʌf'draɪ] *adj* seco y sin planchar; (*pret & pp:* **-dried**) *va* secar (*ropa*) sin planchar
**roughen** ['rʌfən] *va* poner áspero o tosco; *vn* ponerse áspero o tosco
**rough-hew** [,rʌf'hju] (*pret:* **-hewed;** *pp:* **-hewed** o **-hewn**) *va* desbastar; modelar toscamente
**roughhouse** ['rʌf,haʊs] *s* (slang) trapatiesta, conducta bulliciosa; *va* (slang) molestar o perturbar por conducta bulliciosa; *vn* (slang) conducirse de un modo bullicioso; **to start roughhousing** armar una trapatiesta
**roughing-in** ['rʌfɪŋ'ɪn] *s* capa de mezcla gruesa; instalación de tubos, conductos, cajas de salida, etc. (*dentro de los pisos y paredes*)
**roughish** ['rʌfɪʃ] *adj* algo áspero
**roughly** ['rʌflɪ] *adv* ásperamente; toscamente; aproximadamente; turbulentamente; brutalmente
**roughneck** ['rʌf,nɛk] *s* (slang) canalla
**roughness** ['rʌfnɪs] *s* aspereza, tosquedad; rigor (*del tiempo*); agitación (*del mar*); chapucería; brutalidad
**roughrider** ['rʌf,raɪdər] *s* domador de caballos; hombre acostumbrado a montar caballos indómitos; soldado irregular a caballo; **Roughriders** *spl* regimiento de caballería voluntario norteamericano, organizado por Teodoro Roosevelt, que tomó parte en la guerra entre España y los Estados Unidos
**roughshod** ['rʌf,ʃɑd] *adj* herrado con ramplones (*que impiden resbalar*); **to ride** o **run roughshod over** traer a redopelo, tratar sin miramiento
**rough sketch** *s* bosquejo; borrador
**roulade** [ru'lɑd] *s* (mus.) trino; rebanada de carne arrollada, con relleno de carne picada
**roulette** [ru'lɛt] *s* ruleta (*juego; ruedecilla con puntas*)
**Roumania** [ru'menɪə] *s* var. de **Rumania**
**Roumanian** [ru'menɪən] *adj & s* var. de **Rumanian**
**round** [raʊnd] *adj* redondo; rechoncho; rotundo (*categórico; sonoro*); franco; fuerte, vigoroso; (phonet.) redondeado ‖ *adv* redondamente; alrededor; acá y allá; de boca en boca, de una persona a otra; de un lado para otro; por todas partes; **round about** en contorno ‖ *prep* alrededor de, en torno de; por todos lados de; a la vuelta de (*p.ej., la esquina*); cerca de, cosa de, como; acá y allá en; a todas las partes de; **to come** o **to get round** sobrepujar en astucia a; engatusar ‖ *s* redondo (*cosa redonda o circular*); camino, circuito, ruta; recorrido (*de un policía*); jira (*viaje circular*); redondez; revolución; serie, rutina; ronda (*de cigarros o bebidas*); salva (*de muchas armas de fuego a un tiempo; de aplausos*); disparo o tiro (*de un arma de fuego*); cartucho con bala; corro, círculo (*de personas*); rodaja de carne de vaca; (box.) asalto o suerte; canción corta cantada por varias voces, que empiezan a intervalos sucesivos; danza en que los bailadores se mueven en círculo; **rounds** *spl* recorrido (*de un policía*); **to go the round** ir de boca en boca; ir de mano en mano ‖ *va* redondear; doblar (*una esquina, un promontorio*); cercar, circundar, rodear; (phonet.) redondear; **to round in** (naut.) halar; **to round off** u **out** redondear; acabar, completar, perfeccionar; **to round up** juntar, recoger ‖ *vn* redondearse; girar; **to round off** u **out** redondearse; **to round to** (naut.) orzar
**roundabout** ['raʊndə,baʊt] *adj* indirecto, ambagioso; *s* modo indirecto, curso indirecto; chaqueta; tío vivo
**round dance** *s* baile que ejecutan las parejas con movimiento circular
**roundel** ['raʊndəl] *s* figura redonda; (arch.) nicho, panel o ventana circular; rondel; rondó

**roundelay** ['raʊndəle] *s* melodía que se canta en rueda; baile en círculo
**rounder** ['raʊndər] *s* (coll.) pródigo, malgastador; (coll.) criminal habitual, borrachín habitual, catavinos
**roundheaded** ['raʊnd'hɛdɪd] *adj* de cabeza redondeada; de cabeza de hongo (*dícese de un tornillo*)
**roundhouse** ['raʊnd,haʊs] *s* (rail.) cocherón, casa de máquinas, depósito de locomotoras; (naut.) chupeta, toldilla
**rounding** ['raʊndɪŋ] *s* redondeamiento; (phonet.) redondeamiento
**roundish** ['raʊndɪʃ] *adj* redondete
**roundly** ['raʊndlɪ] *adv* redondamente
**roundness** ['raʊndnɪs] *s* redondez
**round number** *s* número redondo
**round robin** *s* petición firmada en rueda o con las firmas en rueda; competencia atlética en la cual varios equipos o jugadores compiten en una serie de partidos, cada equipo o jugador compitiendo con cada uno de los demás
**round-shouldered** ['raʊnd'ʃoldərd] *adj* cargado de espaldas
**roundsman** ['raʊndzmən] *s* (*pl:* **-men**) rondador de policía
**round steak** *s* tajada de carne de vaca
**Round Table** *s* (myth.) Mesa Redonda (*en que tenían asiento el rey Artús y sus caballeros*); (myth.) Tabla Redonda (*caballeros del rey Artús*)
**round-table discussion** ['raʊnd,tebəl] *s* discusión de mesa redonda
**round tower** *s* torre redonda aislada con remate cónico
**round trip** *s* viaje de ida y vuelta, viaje redondo
**round-trip ticket** ['raʊnd'trɪp] *s* billete de ida y vuelta
**roundup** ['raʊnd,ʌp] *s* rodeo (*del ganado mayor*); redada (*de criminales*); reunión (*p.ej., de viejos amigos*)
**roundworm** ['raʊnd,wʌrm] *s* (zool.) ascáride
**roup** [rup] *s* ronquera; catarro de las aves domésticas
**rouse** [raʊz] *va* despertar; excitar, provocar; levantar (*la caza*); *vn* despertarse, despabilarse, animarse
**rouser** ['raʊzər] *s* despertador; excitador; (coll.) cosa extraordinaria, fenómeno
**rousing** ['raʊzɪŋ] *adj* conmovedor; activo, animado, vigoroso; (coll.) extraordinario
**Roussillon, the** [ro'sɪljən] o [rusi'jõ] el Rosellón
**rout** [raʊt] *s* derrota; derrota completa, fuga desordenada; comitiva, séquito; canalla, gentuza; alboroto, tumulto; *va* derrotar; derrotar completamente, poner en fuga desordenada; arrancar hozando; arrojar, echar o hacer salir con violencia; *vn* hozar
**route** [rut] o [raʊt] *s* ruta; itinerario; *va* encaminar
**routine** [ru'tin] *adj* rutinario; *s* rutina
**routinist** [ru'tinɪst] *s* rutinero
**rove** [rov] *s* madeja de algodón, lana o seda tirada; arandela de remache; *va* torcer (*el hilo*) antes de encanillarlo; *vn* andar errante, errar, vagar; *pret & pp de* **reeve**
**rover** ['rovər] *s* vagabundo; pirata; buque de piratas; (croquet) corsario (*jugador*); (croquet) corsaria (*bola*)
**row** [ro] *s* fila, hilera; crujía (*de casas*); remadura; paseo en bote de remos; **in a row** seguidos, p.ej., **five hours in a row** cinco horas seguidas; [raʊ] *s* (coll.) camorra, pendencia, riña; (coll.) alboroto, bullicio; **to raise a row** (coll.) armar camorra; [ro] *va* conducir o transportar en un bote de remos; mover o impeler remando; manejar (*el remo*); competir con (*una persona*) en una regata a remo; competir en (*una regata a remo*); *vn* remar; **to row hard** hacer fuerza de remos; [raʊ] *va* (coll.) regañar, reñir; *vn* (coll.) armar camorra, pelearse
**rowan** ['roən] o ['raʊən] *s* (bot.) serbal de los cazadores
**rowboat** ['ro,bot] *s* bote, bote de remos
**rowdy** ['raʊdɪ] *adj* (*comp:* **-dier;** *super:* **-diest**) gamberro; *s* (*pl:* **-dies**) gamberro
**rowdyish** ['raʊdɪɪʃ] *adj* gamberro
**rowdyism** ['raʊdɪɪzəm] *s* gamberrismo
**rowel** ['raʊəl] *s* rodaja (*de espuela*); (vet.) sedal; (*pret & pp:* **-eled** o **-elled;** *ger:* **-eling** o **-elling**) *va* espolear con la rodaja; (vet.) poner sedal a
**rower** ['roər] *s* remero
**row house** [ro] *s* casa de una fila de casas seguidas
**rowing** ['ro·ɪŋ] *s* (sport) remo
**rowlock** ['rolɑk] o ['rʌlək] *s* (naut.) escalamera, chumacera; (mas.) sardinel
**royal** ['rɔɪəl] *adj* real; *s* tamaño de papel, de 19 por 24 pulgadas para escribir y de 20 por 25 para imprenta; (naut.) sobrejuanete
**Royal Air Force College** *s* (Brit.) Academia General del Aire
**royal fern** *s* (bot.) helecho real
**royal flush** *s* flux real
**royalism** ['rɔɪəlɪzəm] *s* realismo
**royalist** ['rɔɪəlɪst] *s* realista
**royalistic** [,rɔɪə'lɪstɪk] *adj* realista
**Royal Military College** *s* (Brit.) Academia General Militar
**Royal Naval College** *s* (Brit.) Escuela Naval Militar
**royal palm** *s* (bot.) palma real, palmiche
**royalty** ['rɔɪəltɪ] *s* (*pl:* **-ties**) realeza; personaje real, personajes reales; derechos (*pagados a un autor o inventor*)
**r.p.m.** abr. de **revolutions per minute**
**R.R.** abr. de **railroad** y **Right Reverend**
**R.S.F.S.R.** abr. de **Russian Socialist Federated Soviet Republic**
**R.S.V.P.** abr. de **répondez s'il vous plaît** (Fr.) **please answer** sírvase enviar respuesta
**Rt. Hon.** abr. de **Right Honorable**
**Rt. Rev.** abr. de **Right Reverend**
**rub** [rʌb] *s* roce, frotación; rozadura (*de la piel*); sarcasmo; obstáculo, estorbo; busilis; desigualdad (*de la superficie*); **there's the rub** ahí está el busilis; (*pret & pp:* **rubbed;** *ger:* **rubbing**) *va* restregar, frotar; pasar la mano sobre la superficie de; limpiar, fregar o pulir frotando o rascando; irritar frotando; **to rub away** quitar frotando; **to rub down** amasar; almohazar (*un caballo*); **to rub elbows with** rozarse mucho con; **to rub it in** (slang) reiterar demasiado una cosa desagradable; **to rub in** hacer penetrar por los poros frotando; **to rub off** quitar o limpiar frotando; **to rub out** borrar; (slang) asesinar; **to rub the right way** apaciguar, sosegar; **to rub the wrong way** contrariar, irritar; *vn* restregar, frotar; restregarse, frotarse; **to rub along, on** o **through** ir viviendo con apuros o con trabajo; **to rub off** quitarse o limpiarse frotando; borrarse
**rub-a-dub** ['rʌbə,dʌb] *s* rataplán, tantarantán
**rubber** ['rʌbər] *s* caucho, goma; goma de borrar; chanclo, zapato de goma; jugada final que decide un empate; (bridge) robre; *adj* de caucho, de goma; *vn* (slang) estirar el cuello o volver la cabeza para ver, mirar estirando el cuello o volviendo la cabeza
**rubber band** *s* liga de goma
**rubber cement** *s* cemento de goma
**rubber-covered** ['rʌbər,kʌvərd] *adj* cauchotado
**rubber dam** *s* (dent.) dique de caucho o goma
**rubber heel** *s* tacón de goma
**rubber hose** *s* manguera de goma
**rubberize** ['rʌbəraɪz] *va* engomar, cauchotar
**rubberneck** ['rʌbər,nɛk] *s* (slang) turista que trata de verlo todo; *vn* (slang) estirar el cuello o volver la cabeza para ver, mirar estirando el cuello o volviendo la cabeza
**rubberoid** ['rʌbərɔɪd] *s* ruberoide
**rubber plant** *s* (bot.) árbol del caucho (*planta que produce caucho; planta de adorno*)
**rubber plantation** *s* cauchal
**rubber stamp** *s* sello de goma, cajetín; estampilla (*de la firma de una persona*); (coll.) persona que aprueba sin reflexionar
**rubber-stamp** [,rʌbər'stæmp] *va* estampar con un sello de goma; estampillar (*con la firma de una persona*); (coll.) aprobar sin reflexionar
**rubbery** ['rʌbərɪ] *adj* elástico (*como el caucho*)
**rubbing alcohol** *s* alcohol para fricciones

**rubbish** [ˈrʌbɪʃ] *s* basura, desecho, desperdicios; disparate, necedad, tontería
**rubble** [ˈrʌbəl] *s* ripio; mampostería; desecho; disparate; *va* ripiar
**rubblework** [ˈrʌbəlˌwʌrk] *s* mampostería
**rubdown** [ˈrʌbˌdaʊn] *s* amasamiento o masaje
**rube** [rub] *s* (slang) campesino, rústico, aldeano
**rubefacient** [ˌrubɪˈfeʃənt] *adj* & *s* (med.) rubefaciente
**rubefaction** [ˌrubɪˈfækʃən] *s* rubefacción
**rubescent** [ruˈbɛsənt] *adj* rubescente
**rubiaceous** [ˌrubɪˈeʃəs] *adj* (bot.) rubiáceo
**rubican** [ˈrubɪkən] *adj* rubicán
**rubicel** [ˈrubɪsɛl] *s* (mineral.) rubicela
**Rubicon** [ˈrubɪkɑn] *s* Rubicón; **to cross the Rubicon** pasar el Rubicón
**rubicund** [ˈrubɪkʌnd] *adj* rubicundo
**rubicundity** [ˌrubɪˈkʌndɪtɪ] *s* rubicundez
**rubidium** [ruˈbɪdɪəm] *s* (chem.) rubidio
**ruble** [ˈrubəl] *s* rublo
**rubric** [ˈrubrɪk] *s* rúbrica
**rubrical** [ˈrubrɪkəl] *adj* escrito o impreso de color rojo; marcado con encarnado; de rúbrica
**rubricate** [ˈrubrɪket] *va* rubrificar, poner de color rojo; proveer de rúbricas; dirigir con rúbricas
**rubrician** [ruˈbrɪʃən] *s* rubriquista
**ruby** [ˈrubɪ] *s* (*pl:* **-bies**) rubí; (horol.) rubí; *adj* de color de rubí
**ruby silver** *s* (mineral.) plata roja
**ruby spinel** *s* (mineral.) rubí espinela
**ruche** [ruʃ] *s* (sew.) lechuga de encaje o de malla
**ruching** [ˈruʃɪŋ] *s* (sew.) guarnición que consiste en lechugas de encaje o malla
**ruck** [rʌk] *s* vulgo; arruga; *va* arrugar; *vn* arrugarse
**rucksack** [ˈrʌkˌsæk] o [ˈrʊkˌsæk] *s* barjuleta, mochila
**ruckus** [ˈrʌkəs] o **ruction** [ˈrʌkʃən] *s* (coll.) alboroto, bullicio, tumulto
**rudder** [ˈrʌdər] *s* timón, gobernalle; veleta (*de molino de viento*)
**ruddle** [ˈrʌdəl] *s* almagre; *va* marcar con almagre
**ruddy** [ˈrʌdɪ] *adj* (*comp:* **-dier;** *super:* **-diest**) rubicundo, coloradote
**ruddy turnstone** *s* (orn.) playero turco
**rude** [rud] *adj* rudo; inculto, salvaje
**rudeness** [ˈrudnɪs] *s* rudeza; incultura
**rudiment** [ˈrudɪmənt] *s* rudimento
**rudimental** [ˌrudɪˈmɛntəl] *adj* rudimental
**rudimentary** [ˌrudɪˈmɛntərɪ] *adj* rudimentario
**Rudolph** [ˈrudɑlf] *s* Rodolfo
**rue** [ru] *s* (bot.) ruda; *va* sentir o lamentar; *vn* arrepentirse
**rueful** [ˈrufəl] *adj* lamentable
**ruff** [rʌf] *s* (sew.) lechuguilla; (cards) fallada; collar (*de plumas o de pelo de distinto color alrededor del cuello*); arrebato de cólera; (ichth.) acerina; (orn.) combatiente; *va* (cards) fallar
**ruffed grouse** [rʌft] *s* (orn.) bonasa americana (*Bonasa umbellus*)
**ruffian** [ˈrʌfɪən] *adj* grosero y brutal; *s* hombre grosero y brutal
**ruffianism** [ˈrʌfɪənɪzəm] *s* conducta grosera y brutal, brutalidad
**ruffianly** [ˈrʌfɪənlɪ] *adj* grosero y brutal
**ruffle** [ˈrʌfəl] *s* arruga; (sew.) volante; enojo, molestia; confusión, desorden; redoble (*del tambor*); *va* arrugar; (sew.) fruncir un volante en; (sew.) adornar o guarnecer con volante; erizar (*las plumas*); agitar, descomponer; enojar, molestar; confundir; barajar (*los naipes*); redoblar (*el tambor*); *vn* arrugarse; enojarse, molestarse
**rufous** [ˈrufəs] *adj* rufo, rojizo, rojizo parduzco
**rug** [rʌg] *s* alfombra; alfombrilla; manta (*de coche, de viaje, etc.*)
**Rugby** [ˈrʌgbɪ] *s* (sport) rugby (*clase de fútbol*)
**rugged** [ˈrʌgɪd] *adj* áspero, rugoso; fuerte, recio, vigoroso; rudo, tempestuoso
**rugosity** [ruˈgɑsɪtɪ] *s* rugosidad
**Ruhmkorff coil** [ˈrumkɔrf] *s* (phys.) carrete de Ruhmkorff, carrete de inducción
**Ruhr** [rʊr] *s* Ruhr; región del Ruhr
**ruin** [ˈruɪn] *s* ruina; *va* arruinar; *vn* arruinarse
**ruination** [ˌruɪˈneʃən] *s* arruinamiento
**ruinous** [ˈruɪnəs] *adj* ruinoso
**rule** [rul] *s* regla; código; autoridad, mando, poder; regla de imprenta; (law) fallo o decisión (*de un tribunal*); **as a rule** por regla general; **to be the rule** ser de regla; **to make it a rule to** + *inf* hacerse una regla de + *inf; va* gobernar, mandar, regir; dirigir, guiar; contener, moderar, reprimir; reglar (*marcar con rayas o líneas*); (law) decidir según leyes o reglas; **to rule out** excluir, rechazar, no admitir; *vn* gobernar, mandar, regir; prevalecer, estar en boga; **to rule over** gobernar, mandar, regir
**rule of law** *s* régimen de justicia
**rule of three** *s* (math.) regla de oro, regla de proporción, regla de tres
**rule of thumb** o **rule o' thumb** *s* regla empírica; método empírico
**ruler** [ˈrulər] *s* gobernante; regla (*para trazar líneas*)
**ruling** [ˈrulɪŋ] *adj* gobernante, dirigente, imperante; *s* fallo o decisión de un tribunal o juez; rayado (*de papel*)
**ruling pen** *s* tiralíneas
**rum** [rʌm] *s* ron, aguardiente de caña; (U.S.A.) aguardiente (*cualquier licor alcohólico*); *adj* (slang) extraño, singular
**Rumania** [ruˈmenɪə] *s* Rumania
**Rumanian** [ruˈmenɪən] *adj* & *s* rumano
**rumba** [ˈrʌmbə] *s* rumba (*baile y música*)
**rumble** [ˈrʌmbəl] *s* retumbo; rugido (*de las tripas*); compartimiento posterior (*de un vehículo*); asiento situado detrás de un carruaje (*para los criados*); (aut.) asiento trasero descubierto; (slang) riña entre pandillas; *va* expresar o pronunciar con un sonido sordo y prolongado; *vn* retumbar; avanzar o moverse retumbando
**rumble seat** *s* (aut.) asiento trasero descubierto
**rumen** [ˈrumɛn] *s* (*pl:* **-mina** [mɪnə]) (zool.) rumen; bolo alimenticio
**ruminant** [ˈrumɪnənt] *adj* (zool. & fig.) rumiante; *s* (zool.) rumiante
**ruminate** [ˈrumɪnet] *va* & *vn* rumiar; (fig.) rumiar
**rumination** [ˌrumɪˈneʃən] *s* rumia, rumiación
**ruminative** [ˈrumɪˌnetɪv] *adj* rumiante, rumión
**rummage** [ˈrʌmɪdʒ] *s* búsqueda desordenada; *va* buscar revolviéndolo todo; descubrir, sacar a luz; *vn* buscar revolviéndolo todo; alborotar
**rummage sale** *s* venta de prendas usadas (*con el fin de recoger fondos para obras caritativas*)
**rummy** [ˈrʌmɪ] *adj* (*comp:* **-mier;** *super:* **-miest**) (slang) extraño, raro, singular; *s* rummy (*juego de naipes*); (slang) borracho
**rumor** [ˈrumər] *s* rumor; *va* rumorear; **it is rumored that** se rumorea que
**rumormongering** [ˈrumərˌmʌŋgərɪŋ] *s* (el) propalar rumores
**rump** [rʌmp] *s* anca, nalga; rabadilla u obispillo (*de ave*); (cook.) cuarto trasero (*p.ej., de vaca*); resto, residuo
**rumple** [ˈrʌmpəl] *s* arruga; *va* arrugar, ajar, chafar; *vn* arrugarse
**rumpot** [ˈrʌmpɑt] *s* (slang) cuba, pellejo, odre (*borracho*)
**rumpus** [ˈrʌmpəs] *s* (coll.) batahola, la de San Quintín; (coll.) alboroto, tumulto; **to raise a rumpus** (coll.) armar la de San Quintín
**rumrunner** [ˈrʌmˌrʌnər] *s* importador contrabandista de licores alcohólicos
**run** [rʌn] *s* carrera; curso; corrida; adelantamiento, progreso; clase, género, tipo; libertad de ir y venir a voluntad; carrera (*en las medias*); curso (*de un líquido*); arroyo; migración (*de peces*); terreno de pasto; tubo, caño; descarga de mercancías de contrabando; asedio (*de un banco por los depositantes*); serie (*de representaciones teatrales; de repetidos éxitos*); (baseball & mus.) carrera; (naut.) racel; **a run for one's money** competencia fuerte; satisfacción por sus esfuerzos; **day's run** (naut.) singladura; **in the long run** a la larga; **on the run** a escape, apresurándose; en fuga desordenada; **the common run of people** el común de las gentes; **the general run of** la generalidad de; **to be on the run** darse a la fuga; ceder; volverse atrás; **to have a long run** (theat.) permanecer en cartel du-

rante mucho tiempo; **to have** o **to get the run of** hallar el secreto de, hallar el modo de hacer; tener libertad de ir y venir por ‖ (*pret:* **ran;** *pp:* **run;** *ger:* **running**) *va* correr; dirigir o manejar; trazar o tirar (*una línea*); hacer entrar; introducir o pasar (*mercancías de contrabando*); introducir por fuerza; derretir o fundir (*un metal*); exhibir (*un cine*); proyectar (*una película cinematográfica*); hacer (*mandados*); tener como candidato; gobernar (*un país, una ciudad*); burlar o violar (*un bloqueo*); tener (*calentura*); **to run down** cazar y matar, cazar y destruir; derribar; atropellar (*p.ej., a un peatón*); (coll.) denigrar, desacreditar, desprestigiar; **to run in** (print.) insertar, poner de seguido, sin párrafo; (slang) meter en la cárcel; **to run off** tocar (*una pieza de música*); tirar, imprimir; **to run through** traspasar (*p.ej., con una espada*); **to run up** (coll.) aumentar (*p.ej., gastos*) ‖ *vn* correr; rodar (*sobre ruedas*); apresurarse, darse prisa; trepar (*la vid*); ir y venir, hacer viajes (*un vapor*); supurar (*una llaga*); colar (*un líquido*); correrse (*un color o tinte*); continuar, seguir; ocurrir, suceder; presentar su candidatura; andar, marchar, funcionar; rezar (*decirse un escrito*); desenfrenarse; derretirse o fundirse; migrar (*los peces*); deshilarse (*las medias*); estar en fuerza; **to run about** correr de lugar en lugar; **to run across** dar con, tropezar con; **to run after** seguir, rondar; anhelar por; **to run against** chocar, topar; oponerse a (*otro aspirante a un cargo político*); **to run along** correr; correr a lo largo de; **to run around with** asociarse con; tener amores con; **to run away** correr, huir; desbocarse (*un caballo*); **to run away with** arrebatar; fugarse con; ganar (*p.ej., un campeonato*) fácilmente; **to run back** correr hacia atrás; remontarse; **to run behind** correr detrás; atrasarse; **to run down** escurrir, gotear (*un líquido*); dejar de funcionar; descargarse (*un acumulador*); soltarse (*un muelle*); distenderse (*el muelle del reloj*); acabarse la cuerda, p.ej., **the watch ran down** se acabó la cuerda; agotarse; deteriorarse; **to run dry** secarse (*p.ej., un pozo*); funcionar en seco (*p.ej., engranajes*); **to run empty** marchar desalquilado (*p.ej., un autobús*); **to run flat** (aut.) rodar desinflado, marchar con un neumático deshinchado; **to run for** presentar su candidatura a; **to run for it** correr para librarse; **to run in** entrar al pasar; **to run in the blood** estar en la sangre; **to run in the family** venir de familia; **to run into** dar con, tropezar con; chocar con, topar con; **to run off the road** desviarse de la carretera; **to run off the track** descarrilar (*un tren*); **to run on** continuar; **to run out** salir; expirar, terminar; acabarse; agotarse; **to run out of** no tener más, acabársele a uno, p.ej., **I have run out of money** se me ha acabado el dinero; **to run out on** (coll.) dejar colgado; **to run over** atropellar (*p.ej., a un peatón*); recorrer; registrar a la ligera; pasar por encima; leer rápidamente; rebosar (*un líquido*); **to run through** disipar rápidamente (*una fortuna*); estar difundido en; registrar a la ligera; **to run up and down** correr de una parte a otra; subir y bajar corriendo; **to run with** abundar en; estar empapado de

**runabout** [ˈrʌnəˌbaut] *s* coche pequeño de dos asientos; carruaje pequeño; autobote pequeño; callejero

**runagate** [ˈrʌnəget] *s* (archaic) fugitivo; (archaic) vagabundo

**runaround** [ˈrʌnəˌraund] *s* desviación, vía de paso; (path.) panadizo; (print.) líneas acortadas para intercalar una ilustración; (slang) trato evasivo; **to give the runaround** (slang) tratar evasivamente

**runaway** [ˈrʌnəˌwe] *s* fugitivo; caballo desbocado; fuga o huída; (sport) partida ganada fácilmente; *adj* fugitivo; desbocado (*caballo*); (sport) ganado fácilmente

**runaway marriage** *s* casamiento que sigue a una fuga

**runcinate** [ˈrʌnsɪnet] o [ˈrʌnsɪnɪt] *adj* (bot.) runcinado

**rundle** [ˈrʌndəl] *s* escalón; rueda

**rundown** [ˈrʌnˌdaun] *s* informe detallado

**run-down** [ˈrʌnˈdaun] *adj* desmantelado; inculto; desmedrado, desmirriado; distendido (*muelle de un reloj*); descargado (*acumulador*)

**rune** [run] *s* runa (*carácter*); escrito rúnico; poema escandinavo escrito en runas; misterio, magia

**rung** [rʌŋ] *s* escalón; travesaño de silla; radio o rayo (*de rueda*); *pret & pp de* **ring**

**runic** [ˈrunɪk] *adj* rúnico o runo

**run-in** [ˈrʌnˌɪn] *s* (print.) palabra o palabras insertadas en un párrafo; (slang) encuentro, riña

**runlet** [ˈrʌnlɪt] o **runnel** [ˈrʌnəl] *s* arroyuelo

**runner** [ˈrʌnər] *s* corredor; caballo de carreras; mensajero; maquinista, operador; cuchilla (*de un patín*); patín (*de un trineo*); agente, factor; pasacaminos (*alfombra larga y angosta*); tapete, camino (*de mesa*); pasador (*de contrabando*); carrera (*en las medias*); (bot.) brote rastrero

**runner-up** [ˈrʌnərˈʌp] *s* (*pl:* **runners-up**) (sport) subcampeón, jugador o equipo clasificado después del campeón

**running** [ˈrʌnɪŋ] *adj* corriente; corredor (*caballo*); corredizo (*lazo*); trepador; continuo; repetido continuamente; cursivo (*dícese de la escritura*); supurante; seguido, p.ej., **four times running** cuatro veces seguidas; en marcha; (sport) lanzado (*dícese de la salida de una carrera*); *s* carrera, corrida; administración, dirección; marcha, funcionamiento; flujo; **to be in the running** tener esperanzas o posibilidades de ganar; **to be out of the running** no tener esperanzas ni posibilidades de ganar

**running board** *s* (aut.) estribo

**running expenses** *spl* gastos corrientes

**running gear** *s* rodamientos

**running head** *s* var. de **running title**

**running knot** *s* lazo corredizo

**running mate** *s* caballo establecedor del paso (*en una carrera de caballos*); (U.S.A.) compañero de candidatura, candidato a la vicepresidencia (*respecto del candidato a la presidencia*); (coll.) compañero

**running start** *s* (sport) salida lanzada

**running title** *s* titulillo (*título de página*)

**running water** *s* agua viva; agua corriente

**runny** [ˈrʌnɪ] coladizo; supurante (*llaga*)

**run-off** [ˈrʌnˌɔf] o [ˈrʌnˌɑf] *s* agua de desagüe; (sport) carrera decisiva o final

**run-of-mine coal** [ˈrʌnəvˈmaɪn] *s* carbón tal como sale de la mina

**runproof** [ˈrʌnˌpruf] *adj* indesmallable

**runt** [rʌnt] *s* enano, hombrecillo; redrojo; animal achaparrado

**runty** [ˈrʌntɪ] *adj* enano; achaparrado

**runway** [ˈrʌnˌwe] *s* cauce (*de un arroyo*); vía; senda trillada; (aer.) pista de aterrizaje

**rupee** [ruˈpi] *s* rupia

**Rupert** [ˈrupərt] *s* Ruperto

**rupestrian** [ruˈpɛstrɪən] *adj* rupestre

**rupia** [ˈrupɪə] *s* (path.) rupia

**rupture** [ˈrʌptʃər] *s* ruptura, rompimiento; (path.) quebradura; (fig.) ruptura (*cesación de relaciones*); *va* romper; causar una hernia en; *vn* romperse; padecer hernia

**rural** [ˈrurəl] *adj* rural

**rural free delivery** *s* distribución gratuita del correo en el campo

**ruralist** [ˈrurəlɪst] *s* rurícola

**ruralize** [ˈrurəlaɪz] *va* hacer rural; *vn* hacerse rural; rusticar

**Rus.** abr. de **Russia** y **Russian**

**ruse** [ruz] *s* astucia

**rush** [rʌʃ] *s* acometida, ataque; precipitación, prisa grande; demanda extraordinaria; agolpamiento de gente; friolera, bagatela; (bot.) junco (*planta y tallo*); (U.S.A.) lucha entre dos grupos de estudiantes; **with a rush** de repente; *adj* urgente; juncoso; *va* acometer o atacar con violencia o prisa; empujar con violencia o prisa; despachar con prontitud; (slang) cortejar insistentemente (*a una muchacha*); (slang) solicitar insistentemente a (*los estudiantes de primer año*) para que se inscriban en una sociedad estudiantil; **to rush through** ejecutar de prisa; *vn* lanzarse, precipitarse; venir de prisa, ir de prisa; actuar con prontitud; **to rush about** dar vueltas de un lado para otro; **to rush forward** lanzarse, precipitarse; **to rush in** entrar precipitadamente; **to rush out** salir precipitadamente; **to rush through** lanzarse a través de, lanzarse por entre

**rush-bottomed chair** [ˈrʌʃˈbɑtəmd] *s* silla de junco

**rush hour** *s* hora de tránsito intenso, hora de aglomeración

**rushlight** [ˈrʌʃˌlaɪt] *s* vela con pábilo de junco

**rushlike** [ˈrʌʃˌlaɪk] *adj* juncoso

**rush order** *s* pedido urgente

**rushy** [ˈrʌʃɪ] *adj* (*comp:* **-ier**; *super:* **-iest**) juncoso; juncino

**rusk** [rʌsk] *s* galleta dulce; pedazo de pan tostado en el horno

**Russ** [rʌs] *adj* ruso; *s* (*pl:* **Russ**) ruso

**russet** [ˈrʌsɪt] *adj* canelo; *s* color de canela; paño burdo canelo; variedad de manzana de color de canela

**Russia** [ˈrʌʃə] *s* Rusia; (*l.c.*) *s* piel de Rusia

**Russia leather** *s* piel de Rusia

**Russian** [ˈrʌʃən] *adj* & *s* ruso

**Russian Church** *s* Iglesia rusa

**Russianization** [ˌrʌʃənɪˈzeʃən] *s* rusificación

**Russianize** [ˈrʌʃənaɪz] *va* rusificar

**Russian olive** *s* (bot.) cinamomo

**Russian Revolution** *s* Revolución rusa

**Russian Socialist Federated Soviet Republic** *s* República Federativa Socialista Soviética Rusa

**Russian thistle** *s* (bot.) barrilla pestífera

**Russian Turkestan** *s* el Turquestán Ruso

**Russian turnip** *s* (bot.) col de Laponia

**Russian wolfhound** *s* galgo ruso

**Russo-Japanese** [ˌrʌsoˌdʒæpəˈniz] *adj* rusojaponés

**Russophile** [ˈrʌsofaɪl] *adj* & *s* rusófilo

**Russophobe** [ˈrʌsofob] *adj* & *s* rusófobo

**Russophobia** [ˌrʌsoˈfobɪə] *s* rusofobia

**rust** [rʌst] *s* orín, moho, herrumbre; (bot.) roña, roya; inacción, ociosidad; influencia dañosa; color rojizo o anaranjado; *adj* rojizo, anaranjado; *va* aherrumbrar; hacer entrar la roya en (*una planta*); *vn* aherrumbrarse; tener la roya (*una planta*); deteriorarse por falta de uso

**rustic** [ˈrʌstɪk] *adj* rústico; sencillo, sin artificio; *s* rústico

**rustically** [ˈrʌstɪkəlɪ] *adv* rústicamente

**rusticate** [ˈrʌstɪket] *va* enviar al campo, desterrar al campo; (Brit.) suspender temporalmente (*a un alumno de la universidad*); *vn* rusticar

**rustication** [ˌrʌstɪˈkeʃən] *s* destierro al campo; rusticación; (Brit.) suspensión temporal de la universidad

**rusticity** [rʌsˈtɪsɪtɪ] *s* rusticidad; vida campestre

**rustle** [ˈrʌsəl] *s* susurro, crujido; *va* hacer susurrar, hacer crujir; hurtar (*ganado*); *vn* susurrar, crujir; (slang) proceder con energía, trabajar con ahinco

**rustler** [ˈrʌslər] *s* (slang) buscavidas; (coll.) ladrón de ganado, cuatrero

**rustless** [ˈrʌstlɪs] *adj* sin herrumbre, inoxidable; a prueba de herrumbre

**rustproof** [ˈrʌstˌpruf] *adj* a prueba de herrumbre

**rustre** [ˈrʌstər] *s* (her.) rustro

**rusty** [ˈrʌstɪ] *adj* (*comp:* **-ier**; *super:* **-iest**) oxidado, mohoso, herrumbroso; rojizo; raído, usado; (bot.) herrumbroso; **to be rusty** estar oxidado, desusado, empolvado, p.ej., **my French is rusty** mi francés está oxidado, mi francés se ha oxidado; estar remoto (*estar uno casi olvidado de una cosa que aprendió*)

**rut** [rʌt] *s* rodada, bache; hábito arraigado, rutina; celo; brama (*época de celo*); **in rut** en celo; (*pret* & *pp:* **rutted**; *ger:* **rutting**) *va* hacer rodadas en, surcar; *vn* estar en celo

**rutabaga** [ˌrutəˈbegə] *s* (bot.) rutabaga

**rutaceous** [ruˈteʃəs] *adj* (bot.) rutáceo

**Ruth** [ruθ] *s* Rut

**Ruthenia** [ruˈθinɪə] *s* Rutenia

**Ruthenian** [ruˈθinɪən] *adj* & *s* ruteno

**ruthenium** [ruˈθinɪəm] *s* (chem.) rutenio

**ruthless** [ˈruθlɪs] *adj* despiadado, cruel

**rutile** [ˈrutil] o [ˈrutaɪl] *s* (mineral.) rutilo

**rutin** [ˈrutɪn] *s* (chem.) rutina

**rutty** [ˈrʌtɪ] *adj* (*comp:* **-tier**; *super:* **-tiest**) lleno de rodadas, surcado

**R.V.** abr. de **Revised Version**

**Ry.** abr. de **railway**

**rye** [raɪ] *s* (bot.) centeno; whisky de centeno

**rye grass** *s* (bot.) ballico perenne; (bot.) cizaña vivaz

**rye whiskey** *s* whisky de centeno

# S

**S, s** [ɛs] *s* (*pl:* **S's, s's** [ˈɛsɪz]) décimonona letra del alfabeto inglés
**s.** abr. de **second, shilling, shillings, singular** y **south**
**S.** abr. de **Saint, Saturday, September, South** y **southern**
**S** abr. de **South**
**-'s** desinencia del posesivo singular, p.ej., **the girl's book** el libro de la muchacha; contracción de **is,** p.ej., **he's here** él está aquí; de **has,** p.ej., **she's gone** ella ha ido; de **us** en **let's,** p.ej., **let's go** vámonos
**-s'** desinencia del posesivo plural, p.ej., **a girls' school** una escuela de muchachas
**S.A.** abr. de **Salvation Army, South Africa, South America** y **South Australia**
**Saar** [sɑr] *s* Sarre (*río*); Sarre o territorio del Sarre
**Saar Basin** *s* territorio del Sarre
**Saarland** [ˈsɑrlænd] *s* Sarre o territorio del Sarre
**Saarlander** [ˈsɑrlændər] *s* sarrés
**sabadilla** [ˌsæbəˈdɪlə] *s* (bot.) cebadilla (*planta y semillas*)
**Sabaean** [səˈbiən] *adj & s* sabeo
**Sabaeanism** [səˈbiənɪzəm] *s* sabeísmo
**Sabbatarian** [ˌsæbəˈtɛrɪən] *adj* sabatario; dominical; *s* sabatario (*persona que guarda la fiesta del sábado*); partidario de guardar santamente el domingo
**Sabbatarianism** [ˌsæbəˈtɛrɪənɪzəm] *s* sabatismo; observancia estricta del descanso dominical
**Sabbath** [ˈsæbəθ] *s* sábado (*de los judíos*); dominica (*de los cristianos*); **to keep the Sabbath** guardar el domingo, observar el descanso dominical; *adj* sabático; dominical
**sabbatic** [səˈbætɪk] o **sabbatical** [səˈbætɪkəl] *adj* sabático; dominical; de descanso
**sabbatical year** *s* (Jewish hist.) año sabático; (U.S.A.) año de licencia (*concedido a un profesor universitario*)
**sabella** [səˈbɛlə] *s* (zool.) sabela
**saber** [ˈsebər] *s* sable; *va* golpear con sable, herir a sablazos, matar a sablazos
**saber-toothed tiger** [ˈsebərˌtuθt] *s* (pal.) maquerodo
**Sabine** [ˈsebaɪn] *adj & s* sabino
**sable** [ˈsebəl] *s* (zool.) marta cebellina; marta cebellina (*piel*); (her.) sable; **sables** *spl* vestidos de luto; *adj* negro
**sabot** [ˈsæbo] o [sɑˈbo] *s* zueco
**sabotage** [ˈsæbətɑʒ] *s* sabotaje; *va & vn* sabotear
**saboteur** [ˌsæbəˈtʌr] *s* saboteador
**sabre** [ˈsebər] *s & va* var. de **saber**
**sabulous** [ˈsæbjələs] *adj* sabuloso
**saburra** [səˈbʌrə] *s* saburra
**saburral** [səˈbʌrəl] *adj* saburral
**sac** [sæk] *s* (anat., bot. & zool.) saco
**saccharification** [səˌkærɪfɪˈkeʃən] *s* sacarificación
**saccharify** [səˈkærɪfaɪ] (*pret & pp:* **-fied**) *va* sacarificar
**saccharimeter** [ˌsækəˈrɪmɪtər] *s* sacarímetro
**saccharimetry** [ˌsækəˈrɪmɪtrɪ] *s* sacarimetría
**saccharin** [ˈsækərɪn] *s* (chem.) sacarina
**saccharine** [ˈsækərɪn] o [ˈsækəraɪn] *adj* sacarino; (fig.) azucarado; *s* (chem.) sacarina
**saccharoid** [ˈsækərɔɪd] *adj* sacaroideo
**saccharose** [ˈsækəros] *s* (chem.) sacarosa
**saccule** [ˈsækjul] *s* (anat.) sáculo
**sacerdotal** [ˌsæsərˈdotəl] *adj* sacerdotal
**sacerdotalism** [ˌsæsərˈdotəlɪzəm] *s* sistema sacerdotal; clericalismo
**sachem** [ˈsetʃəm] *s* cacique
**sachet** [ˈsæʃe] o [sæˈʃe] *s* saquito de perfumes; polvo oloroso
**sack** [sæk] *s* saco; americana, saco; vino blanco generoso; (mil.) saco, saqueo; (slang) despedida (*de un empleado*); **to hold the sack** (coll.) quedarse con la carga en las costillas; *va* ensacar; saquear; (slang) despedir (*a un empleado*)
**sackbut** [ˈsækˌbʌt] *s* sacabuche (*instrumento o músico*)
**sackcloth** [ˈsækˌklɔθ] o [ˈsækˌklɑθ] *s* harpillera; cilicio (*usado para la penitencia*); **in sackcloth and ashes** en hábito de penitencia; en señal de arrepentimiento o humildad
**sack coat** *s* saco, americana
**sacker** [ˈsækər] *s* ensacador; saqueador
**sackful** [ˈsækfʊl] *s* saco
**sacking** [ˈsækɪŋ] *s* tela de saco, harpillera
**sacque** [sæk] *s* saco (*prenda de vestir holgada*); bata (*vestido holgado de mujer*)
**sacral** [ˈsekrəl] *adj* (anat.) sacro
**sacrament** [ˈsækrəmənt] *s* sacramento; sacramento del altar (*eucaristía*); juramento solemne
**sacramental** [ˌsækrəˈmɛntəl] *adj & s* sacramental
**Sacramentarian** [ˌsækrəmɛnˈtɛrɪən] *adj & s* sacramentario
**sacred** [ˈsekrɪd] *adj* sagrado
**Sacred College** *s* (eccl.) colegio de cardenales
**sacred cow** *s* vaca sagrada (*persona o cosa inmunes a la crítica*)
**sacred ear** o **sacred earflower** [ˈɪrˌflaʊər] *s* flor de la oreja
**sacred music** *s* música sagrada o sacra
**sacrifice** [ˈsækrɪfaɪs] *s* sacrificio; **at a sacrifice** con pérdida; *va* sacrificar; malvender; *vn* sacrificar; sacrificarse
**Sacrifice of the Mass** *s* sacrificio de la misa, sacrificio del altar
**sacrificial** [ˌsækrɪˈfɪʃəl] *adj* sacrificador, sacrificatorio; de sacrificio
**sacrificially** [ˌsækrɪˈfɪʃəlɪ] *adv* por sacrificio
**sacrilege** [ˈsækrɪlɪdʒ] *s* sacrilegio
**sacrilegious** [ˌsækrɪˈlɪdʒəs] o [ˌsækrɪˈlidʒəs] *adj* sacrílego
**sacristan** [ˈsækrɪstən] *s* sacristán
**sacristy** [ˈsækrɪstɪ] *s* (*pl:* **-ties**) sacristía
**sacroiliac** [ˌsekroˈɪlɪæk] *adj* (anat.) sacroilíaco
**sacroiliac joint** *s* (anat.) sínfisis sacroilíaca
**sacrosanct** [ˈsækrosæŋkt] *adj* sacrosanto
**sacrosanctity** [ˌsækroˈsæŋktɪtɪ] *s* (lo) sacrosanto
**sacrum** [ˈsekrəm] *s* (*pl:* **-cra** [krə]) (anat.) sacro
**sad** [sæd] *adj* (*comp:* **sadder;** *super:* **saddest**) triste; (slang) malo; (dial.) pesado (*al paladar*)
**sadden** [ˈsædən] *va* entristecer; *vn* entristecerse
**saddle** [ˈsædəl] *s* silla de montar; sillín (*de bicicleta*); cincha (*del arnés*); cuarto trasero (*de una res*); paso, puerto (*entre dos montañas*); **in the saddle** en el poder; listo; *va* ensillar; **to saddle on** o **upon** cargar en; **to saddle with** gravar con, echar a cuestas a
**saddleback** [ˈsædəlˌbæk] *s* ensillada (*collado*)
**saddle-backed** [ˈsædəlˌbækt] *adj* ensillado
**saddlebags** [ˈsædəlˌbægz] *spl* alforjas, bizazas
**saddle blanket** *s* sudadero
**saddlebow** [ˈsædəlˌbo] *s* arzón delantero, fuste delantero
**saddlecloth** [ˈsædəlˌklɔθ] o [ˈsædəlˌklɑθ] *s* sudadero
**saddle horse** *s* caballo de silla
**saddler** [ˈsædlər] *s* sillero, talabartero
**saddlery** [ˈsædlərɪ] *s* (*pl:* **-ies**) talabartería; guarniciones de caballería

**saddle strap** *s* ación
**saddle tree** [ˈsædəl,tri] *s* arzón, fuste
**Sadducee** [ˈsædʒəsi] o [ˈsædjʊsi] *s* saduceo
**Sadduceeism** [ˈsædʒəsiɪzəm] o [ˈsædjʊsiɪzəm] *s* saduceísmo
**sadiron** [ˈsæd,aɪərn] *s* plancha pesada
**sadism** [ˈsædɪzəm] o [ˈsedɪzəm] *s* sadismo
**sadist** [ˈsædɪst] o [ˈsedɪst] *s* sádico
**sadistic** [sæˈdɪstɪk] o [seˈdɪstɪk] *adj* sádico
**sadness** [ˈsædnɪs] *s* tristeza
**sad sack** *s* (slang) soldado raso, manso y torpe; (slang) persona inadaptada y ridícula
**safari** [səˈfɑrɪ] *s* (*pl:* **-ris**) safari
**safe** [sef] *s* caja fuerte, caja de caudales; caja; alacena, despensa; *adj* seguro, ileso, salvo; cierto, digno de confianza; innocuo; intacto; sin peligro, a salvo; hecho cuidadosamente; **safe and sound** sano y salvo; **safe from** a salvo de
**safeblower** [ˈsef,bloər] *s* ladrón dinamitero de cajas fuertes
**safebreaker** [ˈsef,brekər] *s* ladrón que abre cajas fuertes por la fuerza
**safe-conduct** [ˈsefˈkɑndʌkt] *s* salvoconducto
**safe-deposit box** [ˈsefdɪˈpɑzɪt] *s* caja de seguridad
**safeguard** [ˈsef,gɑrd] *s* salvaguardia, medida de seguridad; *va* salvaguardar
**safekeeping** [ˈsef,kipɪŋ] *s* custodia, protección
**safely** [ˈseflɪ] *adv* seguramente; a salvo, felizmente
**safety** [ˈseftɪ] *s* (*pl:* **-ties**) seguridad; confianza; innocuidad; salud pública; **to parachute to safety** salvarse en paracaídas; **to reach safety** ponerse a salvo, llegar a lugar seguro; *adj* de seguridad
**safety belt** *s* cinturón de seguridad (*de reparadores de líneas telegráficas*); (aer. & aut.) correa de seguridad; (naut.) cinturón salvavidas
**safety bolt** *s* cerrojo de seguridad
**safety curtain** *s* (theat.) telón de seguridad, telón contra incendios
**safety film** *s* (phot.) película de seguridad
**safety fuse** *s* espoleta de seguridad; (elec.) fusible de seguridad
**safety glass** *s* vidrio de seguridad
**safety island** *s* isla de seguridad, burladero
**safety lamp** *s* lámpara de seguridad
**safety mask** *s* máscara de seguridad
**safety match** *s* fósforo de seguridad
**safety nut** *s* tuerca de seguridad
**safety pin** *s* imperdible, alfiler de seguridad
**safety rail** *s* guardarriel
**safety razor** *s* máquina de afeitar, maquinilla de seguridad
**safety stop** *s* mecanismo de detención automático
**safety valve** *s* válvula de seguridad
**safety zone** *s* zona de seguridad, burladero
**safflower** [ˈsæ,flaʊər] *s* (bot.) alazor; flores de alazor
**saffron** [ˈsæfrən] *s* (bot.) azafrán; azafrán (*estigma y color*); *adj* azafranado; *va* azafranar (*teñir; poner azafrán en*)
**saffroned** [ˈsæfrənd] *adj* azafranado
**sag** [sæg] *s* combadura, comba; flecha (*p.ej., de un cable*); baja (*p.ej., de los precios*); (*pret & pp:* **sagged;** *ger:* **sagging**) *vn* combarse; ceder, doblegarse, aflojar; bajar (*los precios*)
**saga** [ˈsɑgə] *s* saga
**sagacious** [səˈgeʃəs] *adj* sagaz
**sagacity** [səˈgæsɪtɪ] *s* (*pl:* **-ties**) sagacidad
**sagamore** [ˈsægəmor] *s* cacique
**sagapenum** [,sægəˈpinəm] *s* sagapeno
**sagathy** [ˈsægəθɪ] *s* sagatí
**sage** [sedʒ] *adj* sabio, grave, solemne, cuerdo; *s* sabio; (bot.) salvia; (bot.) artemisa
**sagebrush** [ˈsedʒ,brʌʃ] *s* (bot.) artemisa
**sagittal** [ˈsædʒɪtəl] *adj* sagital; (anat. & zool.) sagital
**Sagittarius** [,sædʒɪˈtɛrɪəs] *s* (astr.) Sagitario
**sagittate** [ˈsædʒɪtet] *adj* (bot.) sagitado
**sago** [ˈsego] *s* (*pl:* **-gos**) sagú (*fécula*); (bot.) sagú
**sago palm** *s* (bot.) sagú
**saguaro** [səˈgwɑro] *s* (*pl:* **-ros**) (bot.) saguaro
**Sahara** [səˈhɛrə] o [səˈhɑrə] *s* Sahara; *adj* sahárico
**Sahara Desert** *s* Desierto de Sahara
**Sahib** [ˈsɑ·ɪb] *s* Sahib (*señor, amo—tratamiento que dan los habitantes de la India a los europeos*)
**said** [sɛd] *pret & pp de* **say**
**sail** [sel] *s* vela; barco de vela; brazo (*del molino de viento*); paseo en barco de vela, viaje en barco de vela; **in sail** en barco de vela; **to make sail** alzar velas; **to set sail** hacerse a la vela; empezar un viaje en una embarcación; **to take in sail** apocar las velas; (fig.) recoger velas; **under full sail** a vela llena; **under sail** con las velas alzadas; *va* gobernar (*un barco de vela*); navegar (*un mar, río, etc.*); *vn* navegar, navegar a la vela; salir, salir del puerto, salir de viaje; deslizarse, flotar, volar; **to sail along** volar, ir muy de prisa; **to sail along the coast** costear; **to sail back** tomar puerto; **to sail into** (slang) atacar, azotar; (slang) regañar, reñir
**sailboat** [ˈsel,bot] *s* buque de vela, barco de vela, velero
**sailcloth** [ˈsel,klɔθ] o [ˈsel,klɑθ] *s* (naut.) lona, paño
**sailer** [ˈselər] *s* velero; **good sailer** barco marinero
**sailfish** [ˈsel,fɪʃ] *s* (ichth.) aguja de mar, pez vela
**sailing** [ˈselɪŋ] *s* navegación; paseo en barco de vela; salida (*de un buque*)
**sailing orders** *spl* últimas instrucciones (*dadas al capitán de un buque*)
**sailing vessel** *s* buque velero
**sail loft** *s* velería
**sailmaker** [ˈsel,mekər] *s* velero
**sail needle** *s* aguja capotera
**sailor** [ˈselər] *s* marinero, marino; canotié; (nav.) marino (*que no tiene categoría de oficial*); *adj* marinero, marinesco
**sailor-fashion** [ˈselər,fæʃən] *adv* a la marinera
**sailoring** [ˈselərɪŋ] *s* marinería
**sailorly** [ˈselərlɪ] *adj* marinesco
**sailplane** [ˈsel,plen] *s* (aer.) velero
**sainfoin** [ˈsenfɔɪn] o [ˈsænfɔɪn] *s* (bot.) pipirigallo, esparceta
**saint** [sent] *s & adj* santo; *va* (eccl.) canonizar; **Saint** se abrevia **St.** en la toponimia, y tales palabras se encuentran alfabetizadas bajo **St.**
**Saint Agnes's Eve** *s* vigilia del día de Santa Inés (*20 de enero*)
**Saint Andrew's cross** *s* cruz de San Andrés
**Saint-Andrew's-cross** [sentˈændruzˈkrɔs] o [sentˈændruzˈkrɑs] *s* (bot.) arrayanilla
**Saint Anthony's fire** *s* (path.) fuego de San Antón, fuego de San Marcial
**Saint Bernard** [bərˈnɑrd] *s* perro de San Bernardo
**sainted** [ˈsentɪd] *adj* santo; bendito, canonizado
**sainthood** [ˈsenthʊd] *s* santidad
**Saint James the Greater** *s* Santiago el Mayor
**Saint James the Less** *s* Santiago el Menor
**saintliness** [ˈsentlɪnɪs] *s* santidad
**saintly** [ˈsentlɪ] *adj* santo
**Saint Patrick's Day** *s* día de San Patricio (*17 de marzo*)
**saintship** [ˈsentʃɪp] *s* santidad
**Saint-Simonian** [,sentsaɪˈmonɪən] *adj & s* sansimoniano
**Saint-Simonianism** [,sentsaɪˈmonɪənɪzəm] *s* sansimonismo
**Saint-Simonist** [sentˈsaɪmənɪst] *s* sansimoniano
**Saint Swithin's Day** [ˈswɪðɪnz] *s* día de San Swithin (*que corresponde al día de San Regalado por la tradición que sostiene que si llueve este día, lo hace 40 días seguidos*)
**Saint Valentine's Day** *s* día de San Valentín (*14 de febrero, día en que en los países del norte se ofrecen felicitaciones y regalos los amantes en señal de cariño y amor*)
**Saint Vitus's dance** [ˈvaɪtəsɪz] *s* (path.) baile de San Vito
**sake** [sek] *s* motivo; respeto, bien, amor; **for his sake** por su bien; **for the sake of** por, por motivo de, por amor a; **for your own sake** por su propio bien
**saker** [ˈsekər] *s* (orn. & arti.) sacre

**salaam** [sə'lɑm] *s* zalema; *va* saludar con zalema, hacer zalema a
**salability** [,selə'bɪlɪtɪ] *s* facilidad de venta, salida
**salable** ['seləbəl] *adj* venable, vendible
**salacious** [sə'leʃəs] *adj* salaz
**salacity** [sə'læsɪtɪ] *s* salacidad
**salad** ['sæləd] *s* ensalada; hortaliza, verdura
**salad bowl** *s* ensaladera
**salad days** *spl* ingenuidad juvenil
**salad dressing** *s* aderezo, aliño
**Saladin** ['sælədɪn] *s* Saladino
**salad oil** *s* aceite de comer
**salamander** ['sælə,mændər] *s* salamandra (*estufa*); (zool. & myth.) salamandra; (zool.) tuza; (fig.) pirófago
**Salamis** ['sæləmɪs] *s* Salamina
**sal ammoniac** [sæl] *s* sal amoníaca, sal amoníaco
**salaried** ['sælərɪd] *adj* a sueldo; retribuído (*empleo*)
**salary** ['sælərɪ] *s* (*pl:* **-ries**) sueldo
**salary scale** *s* escala de sueldos
**salary worker** *s* persona que trabaja a sueldo
**sale** [sel] *s* venta; almoneda, subasta; demanda, mercado; **for sale, on sale** de venta, en venta; se vende(n)
**saleable** ['seləbəl] *adj* var. de **salable**
**salep** ['sælɛp] *s* salep
**saleratus** [,sælə'retəs] *s* bicarbonato de sosa, bicarbonato de potasa, salerato
**salesclerk** ['selz,klʌrk] *s* vendedor, dependiente de tienda
**sales commission** *s* comisión de ventas
**salesgirl** ['selz,gʌrl] *s* vendedora, dependienta de tienda
**Salesian** [sə'liʃən] *adj & s* salesiano (*de las órdenes fundadas por Dom Bosco*); salesa (*de la orden de la Visitación de Nuestra Señora*)
**saleslady** ['selz,ledɪ] *s* (*pl:* **-dies**) (coll.) vendedora
**salesman** ['selzmən] *s* (*pl:* **-men**) vendedor, dependiente de tienda
**sales manager** *s* gerente de ventas
**salesmanship** ['selzmənʃɪp] *s* venta, ocupación de vendedor; arte de vender
**salespeople** ['selz,pipəl] *spl* vendedores
**salesperson** ['selz,pʌrsən] *s* vendedor
**salesroom** ['selz,rum] o ['selz,rʊm] *s* salón de ventas; salón de exhibición
**sales talk** *s* argumento para inducir a comprar
**sales tax** *s* impuesto sobre ventas
**saleswoman** ['selz,wʊmən] *s* (*pl:* **-women**) vendedora, dependienta de tienda
**Salian** ['selɪən] *adj & s* salio
**Salic** ['sælɪk] o ['selɪk] *adj* sálico
**salicaceous** [,sælɪ'keʃəs] *adj* (bot.) salicáceo
**salicin** ['sælɪsɪn] *s* (chem.) salicina
**Salic law** *s* ley sálica
**salicylate** ['sælɪ,sɪlet] o [sə'lɪsɪlet] *s* (chem.) salicilato
**salicylic** [,sælɪ'sɪlɪk] *adj* (chem.) salicílico
**salicylic acid** *s* (chem.) ácido salicílico
**salience** ['selɪəns] o **saliency** ['selɪənsɪ] *s* énfasis; saliente (*parte que sobresale*)
**salient** ['selɪənt] *adj* saliente; sobresaliente; (her.) empinado
**saliferous** [sə'lɪfərəs] *adj* salífero
**salifiable** [,sælɪ'faɪəbəl] *adj* (chem.) salificable
**salification** [,sælɪfɪ'keʃən] *s* (chem.) salificación
**salify** ['sælɪfaɪ] (*pret & pp:* **-fied**) *va* (chem.) salificar
**saline** ['selaɪn] *adj* salino; *s* saladar; substancia salina
**salinity** [sə'lɪnɪtɪ] *s* salinidad
**saliva** [sə'laɪvə] *s* saliva
**salivary** ['sælɪ,vɛrɪ] *adj* salival
**salivary gland** *s* (anat.) glándula salival
**salivate** ['sælɪvet] *va* hacer salivar; *vn* salivar
**salivation** [,sælɪ'veʃən] *s* salivación
**salivous** [sə'laɪvəs] *adj* salivoso
**sallet** ['sælɪt] *s* (arm.) celada
**sallow** ['sælo] *adj* cetrino; *s* (bot.) sauce cabruno; *va* poner cetrino
**sallowish** ['sælo·ɪʃ] *adj* algo cetrino
**Sallust** ['sæləst] *s* Salustio
**sally** ['sælɪ] *s* (*pl:* **-lies**) paseo, viaje; ímpetu, arranque; salida, ocurrencia, humorada; (arch.) saledizo, vuelo; (mil.) salida; (*pret & pp:* **-lied**) *vn* salir, hacer una salida; ir de paseo, ir de viaje; **to sally forth** avanzar, avanzar con denuedo; (*cap.*) *s* Sara
**salmagundi** [,sælmə'gʌndɪ] *s* salpicón; mescolanza, olla podrida
**salmi** ['sælmɪ] *s* guisado de caza asado, salmorejo
**salmon** ['sæmən] *s* salmón (*color*); (ichth.) salmón; (ichth.) salmón de California (*Oncorhynchus tschawytscha*); *adj* salmonado (*de color parecido al de la carne del salmón*)
**salmon pink** *s* salmón, rojo amarillento
**salmon trout** *s* (ichth.) trucha salmonada
**salol** ['sælol] o ['sælɑl] *s* (trademark) salol
**Salome** [sə'lomɪ] *s* (Bib.) Salomé
**salon** [sæ'lɑn] *s* salón
**saloon** [sə'lun] *s* cantina, taberna; salón (*p.ej., de un buque*)
**saloon deck** *s* (naut.) cubierta de salón
**saloonkeeper** [sə'lun,kipər] *s* tabernero
**salpa** ['sælpə] *s* (zool.) salpa
**salsify** ['sælsɪfɪ] *s* (bot.) salsifí
**salt** [sɔlt] *s* sal; purgante de sal; salero; (coll.) marinero; **salts** *spl* sales medicinales; **to not be worth one's salt** no valer uno el pan que come; *adj* salado; *va* salar; marinar (*el pescado*); salgar (*el ganado*); (min.) poner mineral en (*una mina*) para hacer creer que es productiva; (fig.) avivar, aguzar; **to salt away o down** conservar con sal; (slang) ahorrar, guardar para uso futuro
**saltant** ['sæltənt] o ['sɔltənt] *adj* saltante; (her.) empinado
**salt cedar** *s* (bot.) taray
**saltcellar** ['sɔlt,sɛlər] *s* salero
**salted peanuts** *spl* saladillos
**salter** ['sɔltər] *s* salador (*de carne o pescado*); salinero (*persona que prepara o vende la sal*)
**salt-free diet** ['sɔlt'fri] *s* régimen desclorurado
**salthouse** ['sɔlt,haʊs] *s* salero, salín
**saltier** ['sæltɪr] *s* (her.) sotuer
**saltine** [sɔl'tin] *s* galletita salada
**salting** ['sɔltɪŋ] *s* saladura, salazón
**saltish** ['sɔltɪʃ] *adj* salobre, sabroso
**salt lick** *s* salero, lamedero
**salt mackerel** *s* caballa marinada
**salt marsh** *s* saladar, salina
**salt of sorrel** *s* sal de acederas
**salt of the earth, the** lo mejor del mundo, de lo mejor del mundo; (Bib.) la sal de la tierra
**saltpeter** o **saltpetre** [,sɔlt'pitər] *s* nitro o salitre (*nitrato potásico*); nitro de Chile (*nitrato sódico*)
**saltpetrous** [,sɔlt'pitrəs] *adj* salitrado, salitral, salitroso
**salt pit** *s* hoyo salobre, saladar
**salt rheum** *s* (coll.) eczema
**salt shaker** *s* salero
**salt water** *s* agua salada
**salt-water** ['sɔlt,wɔtər] o ['sɔlt,wɑtər] *adj* de agua salada; marino
**saltworks** ['sɔlt,wʌrks] *ssg* o *spl* salina
**saltwort** ['sɔlt,wʌrt] *s* (bot.) barrilla
**salty** ['sɔltɪ] *adj* (*comp:* **-ier;** *super:* **-iest**) salado; (fig.) salado, saleroso
**salubrious** [sə'lubrɪəs] *adj* salubre
**salubrity** [sə'lubrɪtɪ] *s* salubridad
**salutary** ['sæljə,tɛrɪ] o ['sælju,tɛrɪ] *adj* saludable
**salutation** [,sæljə'teʃən] o [,sælju'teʃən] *s* saludo, salutación
**salutatorian** [sə,lutə'torɪən] *s* (U.S.A.) graduando que pronuncia el discurso de salutación (*en las ceremonias de graduación*)
**salutatory** [sə'lutə,torɪ] *s* (*pl:* **-ries**) (U.S.A.) discurso de salutación; *adj* (U.S.A.) de salutación
**salute** [sə'lut] *s* saludo; (mil.) saludo; *va* saludar; (mil.) saludar; alcanzar, llegar a
**Salv.** abr. de **Salvador**
**Salvador** ['sælvədɔr] *s* var. de **El Salvador**
**Salvadoran** [,sælvə'dorən] o **Salvadorian** [,sælvə'dorɪən] *adj & s* salvadoreño
**salvage** ['sælvɪdʒ] *s* salvamento; *va* salvar; recobrar
**salvarsan** ['sælvərsæn] *s* (trademark) salvarsán
**salvation** [sæl'veʃən] *s* salvación
**Salvation Army** *s* ejército de Salvación

**Salvationist** [sæl'veʃənɪst] *s* salutista
**salve** [sæv] o [sɑv] *s* ungüento; (fig.) ungüento, alivio; *va* curar con ungüento; preservar, proteger; aliviar; salvar (*buque, carga, etc.*)
**salver** ['sælvər] *s* bandeja
**salvia** ['sælvɪə] *s* (bot.) salvia
**salvo** ['sælvo] *s* (*pl:* **-vos** o **-voes**) salva
**sal volatile** [ˌsælvə'lætɪlɪ] *s* sal volátil
**S.Am.** abr. de **South America** y **South American**
**Sam** [sæm] *s* nombre abreviado de **Samuel**
**samara** ['sæmərə] o [sə'mɛrə] *s* (bot.) sámara
**Samaritan** [sə'mærɪtən] *adj & s* samaritano
**samarium** [sə'mɛrɪəm] *s* (chem.) samario
**sambuke** ['sæmbjuk] *s* (mus.) sambuca
**same** [sem] *adj & pron indef* mismo; **all the same** a pesar de todo; **it is all the same to me** lo mismo me da; **just the same** lo mismo, sin embargo; **much the same** casi lo mismo; **same . . . as** mismo . . . que
**sameness** ['semnɪs] *s* igualdad, indentidad; monotonía
**Samian** ['semɪən] *adj & s* samio
**samisen** ['sæmɪsɛn] *s* (mus.) samisén
**samite** ['sæmaɪt] o ['semaɪt] *s* jamete
**samlet** ['sæmlɪt] *s* (ichth.) salmoncillo, esguín
**Samoan** [sə'moən] *adj & s* samoano
**Samos** ['semɑs] *s* Samos
**Samothrace** ['sæmoθres] *s* Samotracia
**Samothracian** [ˌsæmo'θreʃən] *adj & s* samotracio
**samovar** ['sæməvɑr] o [ˌsæmə'vɑr] *s* samovar
**samp** [sæmp] *s* maíz molido grueso
**sampan** ['sæmpæn] *s* sampán
**samphire** ['sæmfaɪr] *s* (bot.) empetro, hinojo marino
**sample** ['sæmpəl] *s* muestra; *va* catar, probar
**sample copy** *s* ejemplar muestra
**sampler** ['sæmplər] *s* catador, probador; dechado, marcador (*pedazo de tela con diferentes estilos de labor*)
**sampling** ['sæmplɪŋ] *s* catadura, probadura; (statistics) muestreo
**Samson** ['sæmsən] *s* (Bib. & fig.) Sansón
**Samuel** ['sæmjuəl] *s* Samuel
**samurai** ['sæmuraɪ] *s* samurai
**sanative** ['sænətɪv] *adj* sanativo
**sanatorium** [ˌsænə'torɪəm] *s* (*pl:* **-ums** o **-a** [ə]) sanatorio
**sanatory** ['sænəˌtorɪ] *adj* sanativo
**sanbenito** [ˌsænbə'nito] *s* sambenito
**sanctification** [ˌsæŋktɪfɪ'keʃən] *s* santificación
**sanctify** ['sæŋktɪfaɪ] (*pret & pp:* **-fied**) *va* santificar
**sanctimonious** [ˌsæŋktɪ'monɪəs] *adj* santurrón
**sanctimony** ['sæŋktɪˌmonɪ] *s* santurronería
**sanction** ['sæŋkʃən] *s* sanción; *va* sancionar (*aprobar; confirmar*)
**sanctity** ['sæŋktɪtɪ] *s* (*pl:* **-ties**) santidad
**sanctuary** ['sæŋktʃuˌɛrɪ] *s* (*pl:* **-ies**) santuario; sanctasanctórum; asilo, refugio; **to take sanctuary** acogerse a sagrado
**sanctum** ['sæŋktəm] *s* lugar sagrado; asilo, refugio
**sanctum sanctorum** [sæŋk'torəm] *s* sanctasanctórum; asilo, lugar retirado
**Sanctus** ['sæŋktəs] *s* (eccl. & mus.) Sanctus
**Sanctus bell** *s* (eccl.) campanilla con la que toca a Sanctus el acólito
**sand** [sænd] *s* arena; (slang) valentía, resolución; dinero; **sands** *spl* arenal; (fig.) momentos de la vida; *va* enarenar; polvorear con arena; lijar con papel de lija
**sandal** ['sændəl] *s* sandalia; abarca (*sandalia rústica*); alpargata (*de cáñamo o de esparto*); cacle, guarache, huarache (Am.); zapatilla; chanclo bajito de goma ligera; tira o correa para asegurar la zapatilla; cendal; (bot.) sándalo
**sandaled** o **sandalled** ['sændəld] *adj* calzado con sandalias; abarcado
**sandalwood** ['sændəlˌwud] *s* (bot.) sándalo; *adj* sandalino
**sandarac** ['sændəræk] *s* sandáraca (*resina; rejalgar*); (bot.) tuya articulada
**sandbag** ['sændˌbæg] *s* saco de arena; (fort.) saco terrero; (*pret & pp:* **-bagged**; *ger:* **-bagging**) *va* obstruir con sacos de arena; atacar o golpear con sacos de arena
**sandbank** ['sændˌbæŋk] *s* banco de arena
**sand bar** *s* barra de arena
**sandblast** ['sændˌblæst] o ['sændˌblɑst] *s* soplador de arena; chorro de arena; *va* limpiar con o por medio de chorro de arena, moler por chorro de arena
**sandbox** ['sændˌbɑks] *s* caja para arena; salvadera; (rail.) arenero
**sandbox tree** *s* (bot.) jabillo, árbol del diablo
**sand dollar** *s* (zool.) equinaracnio
**sand dome** *s* (rail.) cúpula de arena
**sand dune** *s* duna, médano
**sander** ['sændər] *s* arenadora (*p.ej., de locomotora*); soplador de arena; lijador; lijadora (*máquina*)
**sanderling** ['sændərlɪŋ] *s* (orn.) chorlito
**sand flea** *s* (ent.) nigua
**sand fly** *s* (ent.) jijene
**sandglass** ['sændˌglæs] o ['sændˌglɑs] *s* reloj de arena
**sand hill** *s* colina de arena, médano
**sandhog** ['sændˌhɑg] o ['sændˌhɔg] *s* obrero que cava arena; obrero que trabaja en cámaras de sumersión
**sand hopper** *s* (zool.) pulga de mar
**sanding block** *s* taco de alisar
**sand launce** [læns] o [lɑns] *s* (ichth.) cebo de fango
**sand lot** *s* (U.S.A.) campo o terreno en una ciudad o cerca de ella que se usa para el béisbol y otros deportes
**sandman** ['sændˌmæn] *s* genio de la fábula que da sueño a los niños
**San Domingo** [sændo'mɪŋgo] *s* var. de **Santo Domingo**
**sandpaper** ['sændˌpepər] *s* papel de lija; *va* lijar
**sandpaper tree** *s* (bot.) vacabuey
**sandpiper** ['sændˌpaɪpər] *s* (orn.) caballero de vientre blanco, lavandera (*Tringoides hypoleucus*)
**sand pit** *s* hoyo de arena; mina de arena
**sand shoe** *s* (Brit.) playera (*calzado*)
**sandstone** ['sændˌston] *s* (mineral.) arenisca, piedra arenisca
**sandstorm** ['sændˌstɔrm] *s* tempestad de arena
**sand viper** *s* (zool.) heterodón; (zool.) víbora cornuda
**sand wasp** *s* (ent.) amófilo
**sandwich** ['sændwɪtʃ] *s* emparedado; *va* intercalar
**Sandwich Islands** *spl* islas Sandwich
**sandwich man** *s* anunciador ambulante que lleva dos cartelones colgados uno por delante y otro por detrás
**sandwort** ['sændˌwʌrt] *s* (bot.) arenaria
**sandy** ['sændɪ] *adj* (*comp:* **-ier**; *super:* **-iest**) arenoso, arenisco; rufo (*pelo*); inconstante, cambiante, movible
**sane** [sen] *adj* cuerdo, sensato; sano (*p.ej., principio*)
**sang** [sæŋ] *pret de* **sing**
**sangaree** [ˌsæŋgə'ri] *s* sangría
**sang-froid** [sɑ̃'frwɑ] *s* sangre fría
**sangsue** ['sæŋsju] *s* sanguijuela
**sanguinary** ['sæŋgwɪnˌɛrɪ] *adj* sanguinario; sangriento
**sanguine** ['sæŋgwɪn] *adj* confiado, esperanzado, optimista; coloradote; sanguinario; *s* sanguina (*lápiz rojo; dibujo hecho con lápiz rojo*)
**sanguineous** [sæŋ'gwɪnɪəs] *adj* sanguíneo; confiado, optimista
**Sanhedrim** ['sænhɪdrɪm] o **Sanhedrin** ['sænhɪdrɪn] *s* sanedrín
**sanicle** ['sænɪkəl] *s* (bot.) sanícula
**sanidine** ['sænɪdɪn] o ['sænɪdin] *s* (mineral.) sanidina
**sanies** ['senɪiz] *s* (path.) sanie o sanies
**sanious** ['senɪəs] *adj* (path.) sanioso
**sanitarian** [ˌsænɪ'tɛrɪən] *adj* sanitario; *s* perito de sanidad
**sanitarium** [ˌsænɪ'tɛrɪəm] *s* (*pl:* **-ums** o **-a** [ə]) sanatorio
**sanitary** ['sænɪˌtɛrɪ] *adj* sanitario
**sanitary cordon** *s* cordón sanitario
**sanitary corps** *s* cuerpo de sanidad
**sanitary napkin** *s* compresa higiénica, paño higiénico

**sanitation** [ˌsænɪˈteʃən] *s* sanidad (*métodos sanitarios*); saneamiento (*acción de dar condiciones de salubridad a un terreno, edificio, etc.*)
**sanity** [ˈsænɪtɪ] *s* cordura, sensatez
**San Jose scale** [ˈsæn hoˌze] *s* (ent.) cochinilla de San José
**San Juan Hill** [sæn ˈhwɑn] *s* la loma de San Juan
**sank** [sæŋk] *pret de* **sink**
**San Salvador** [sæn ˈsælvədɔr] *s* San Salvador (*isla de las Bahamas; capital de la républica de El Salvador*)
**Sanscrit** [ˈsænskrɪt] *adj & s* sánscrito
**sansevieria** [ˌsænsɪvɪˈɪrɪə] *s* (bot.) sanseviera
**Sanskrit** [ˈsænskrɪt] *adj & s* sánscrito
**Sanskritist** [ˈsænskrɪtɪst] *s* sanscritista
**Santa Claus** [ˈsæntəklɔz] o [ˈsæntɪklɔz] *s* San Nicolás, el Papá Noel (*que en los países del norte ocupa el lugar de los Reyes Magos*)
**santalaceous** [ˌsæntəˈleʃəs] *adj* (bot.) santaláceo
**Santo Domingo** [ˈsæntodoˈmɪŋgo] *s* Santo Domingo (*antiguo nombre de la República Dominicana; nombre de su capital*)
**santonica** [sænˈtɑnɪkə] *s* (bot.) santónico; (pharm.) semencontra
**santonin** [ˈsæntənɪn] *s* (pharm.) santonina
**Saône** [son] *s* Saona
**sap** [sæp] *s* savia (*de las plantas*); (bot.) sámago; (fort.) zapa; (slang) necio, tonto; (fig.) savia; (*pret & pp:* **sapped;** *ger:* **sapping**) *va* zapar, socavar; atacar por medio de una zapa; agotar, consumir, desgastar; *vn* hacer trabajos de zapa, cavar una zapa
**sap green** *s* verdevejiga
**saphead** [ˈsæpˌhɛd] *s* (coll.) cabeza de chorlito
**saphenous** [səˈfinəs] *adj* (anat.) safeno
**sapid** [ˈsæpɪd] *adj* sápido; interesante, sabroso
**sapidity** [səˈpɪdɪtɪ] *s* sapidez; interés, sabor
**sapience** [ˈsepɪəns] o **sapiency** [ˈsepɪənsɪ] *s* sapiencia
**sapient** [ˈsepɪənt] *adj* sapiente
**sapindaceous** [ˌsæpɪnˈdeʃəs] *adj* (bot.) sapindáceo
**sapless** [ˈsæplɪs] *adj* seco, sin savia; débil, falto de vigor
**sapling** [ˈsæplɪŋ] *s* árbol muy joven; jovenzuelo, mozuelo
**sapodilla** [ˌsæpəˈdɪlə] *s* (bot.) zapote (*árbol y fruto*)
**saponaceous** [ˌsæpəˈneʃəs] *adj* saponáceo
**saponifiable** [səˈpɑnɪˌfaɪəbəl] *adj* saponificable
**saponification** [səˌpɑnɪfɪˈkeʃən] *s* saponificación
**saponify** [səˈpɑnɪfaɪ] (*pret & pp:* **-fied**) *va* saponificar; *vn* saponificarse
**saponin** [ˈsæpənɪn] *s* (chem.) saponina
**saponite** [ˈsæpənaɪt] *s* (mineral.) saponita
**sapor** [ˈsepər] o [ˈsepɔr] *s* sabor
**saporific** [ˌsæpəˈrɪfɪk] *adj* saporífero
**sapotaceous** [ˌsæpəˈteʃəs] *adj* (bot.) sapotáceo
**sapper** [ˈsæpər] *s* (mil.) zapador
**Sapphic** [ˈsæfɪk] *adj & s* sáfico
**Sapphira** [səˈfaɪrə] *s* (Bib.) Safira
**sapphire** [ˈsæfaɪr] *s* zafiro; *adj* zafirino
**Sappho** [ˈsæfo] *s* Safo
**sappy** [ˈsæpɪ] *adj* (*comp:* **-pier;** *super:* **-piest**) jugoso, lleno de savia; fuerte, enérgico; (slang) necio, tonto, estúpido; (slang) sensiblero
**saprophagous** [səˈprɑfəgəs] *adj* (zool.) saprófago
**saprophyte** [ˈsæprofaɪt] *s* (biol.) saprófito
**saprophytic** [ˌsæproˈfɪtɪk] *adj* (bot.) saprófito
**sapsucker** [ˈsæpˌsʌkər] *s* (orn.) pequeño picamaderos norteamericano
**sapwood** [ˈsæpˌwʊd] *s* sámago, alborno, madera alburente
**saraband** [ˈsærəbænd] *s* (mus.) zarabanda
**Saracen** [ˈsærəsən] *adj & s* sarraceno
**Saracenic** [ˌsærəˈsɛnɪk] o **Saracenical** [ˌsærəˈsɛnɪkəl] *adj* sarracénico
**Saragossa** [ˌsærəˈgɑsə] *s* Zaragoza
**Sarah** [ˈsɛrə] *s* Sara
**Saratoga trunk** [ˌsærəˈtogə] *s* baúl mundo
**sarcasm** [ˈsɑrkæzəm] *s* sarcasmo
**sarcastic** [sɑrˈkæstɪk] *adj* sarcástico
**sarcastically** [sɑrˈkæstɪkəlɪ] *adv* sarcásticamente
**sarcenet** [ˈsɑrsnɛt] *s* tafetán de Florencia
**sarcina** [ˈsɑrsɪnə] *s* (*pl:* **-nae** [ni]) (bact.) sarcina
**sarcocarp** [ˈsɑrkokɑrp] *s* (bot.) sarcocarpio
**sarcocele** [ˈsɑrkosil] *s* (path.) sarcocele
**sarcocolla** [ˌsɑrkoˈkɑlə] *s* sarcocola (*goma*)
**sarcolemma** [ˌsɑrkoˈlɛmə] *s* (anat.) sarcolema
**sarcology** [sɑrˈkɑlədʒɪ] *s* sarcología
**sarcoma** [sɑrˈkomə] *s* (path.) sarcoma
**sarcophagus** [sɑrˈkɑfəgəs] *s* (*pl:* **-gi** [dʒaɪ] o **-guses**) sarcófago
**sard** [sɑrd] *s* sardio
**Sardanapalian** [ˌsɑrdənəˈpelɪən] *adj* sardanapalesco
**Sardanapalus** [ˌsɑrdənəˈpeləs] *s* Sardanápalo
**sardine** [sɑrˈdin] *s* (ichth.) sardina; sardio (*piedra, joya*); **packed like sardines** como sardinas en banasta o en lata
**Sardinia** [sɑrˈdɪnɪə] *s* Cerdeña
**Sardinian** [sɑrˈdɪnɪən] *adj & s* sardo
**sardius** [ˈsɑrdɪəs] *s* sardio
**sardonic** [sɑrˈdɑnɪk] *adj* burlón, sarcástico
**sardonically** [sɑrˈdɑnɪkəlɪ] *adv* sarcásticamente
**sardonyx** [ˈsɑrdənɪks] *s* (mineral.) sardónice
**sargasso** [sɑrˈgæso] *s* (bot.) sargazo
**Sargasso Sea** *s* mar de Sargazos
**sargo** [ˈsɑrgo] *s* (*pl:* **-gos**) (ichth.) sargo
**sark** [sɑrk] *s* (Scotch) camisa
**sarsaparilla** [ˌsɑrsəpəˈrɪlə] *s* (bot.) zarzaparrilla (*arbusto, extracto y bebida*)
**sarsenet** [ˈsɑrsnɛt] *s* var. de **sarcenet**
**sartorial** [sɑrˈtorɪəl] *adj* de sastre, de sastrería; (anat.) sartorio
**sash** [sæʃ] *s* (sew.) banda, echarpe, faja; fajín (*insignia*); (carp.) marco de ventana; *va* proveer de marcos
**sash bar** *s* (arch.) parteluz
**sash chain** *s* cadena para contrapesos de ventana, cadena para hojas de ventana
**sash cord** *s* cuerda para contrapesos de ventana
**sash lift** *s* manija para ventana de guillotina, levantaventana
**sash plane** *s* cepillo rebajador
**sash tool** *s* brocha para pintar marcos de ventana
**sash weight** *s* contrapeso de ventana
**sash window** *s* ventana de guillotina
**sassafras** [ˈsæsəfræs] *s* (bot.) sasafrás (*árbol y corteza de las raíces*)
**Sat.** abr. de **Saturday**
**sat** [sæt] *pret & pp de* **sit**
**Satan** [ˈsetən] *s* Satán o Satanás
**satanic** o **Satanic** [seˈtænɪk] *adj* satánico
**satanically** [seˈtænɪkəlɪ] *adv* satánicamente
**satchel** [ˈsætʃəl] *s* maletín; cartapacio (*de los muchachos de escuela*)
**sate** [set] *va* saciar, hartar, hastiar
**sateen** [sæˈtin] *s* satén
**sateless** [ˈsetlɪs] *adj* insaciable
**satellite** [ˈsætəlaɪt] *s* (astr. & fig.) satélite; *adj* satélite, satelitario
**satellite country** *s* país satélite
**satellite pinion** *s* (mach.) satélite
**satiable** [ˈseʃɪəbəl] o [ˈseʃəbəl] *adj* saciable
**satiate** [ˈseʃɪɪt] o [ˈseʃɪet] *adj* ahito, harto; [ˈseʃɪet] *va* saciar
**satiation** [ˌseʃɪˈeʃən] *s* saciedad
**satiety** [səˈtaɪətɪ] *s* saciedad
**satin** [ˈsætən] *s* raso; *adj* satinado; *va* satinar (*p.ej., el papel*)
**satinet** o **satinette** [ˌsætɪˈnɛt] *s* rasete
**satinwood** [ˈsætənˌwʊd] *s* madera satinada de las Indias; doradillo, satín
**satiny** [ˈsætənɪ] *adj* arrasado, satinado
**satire** [ˈsætaɪr] *s* sátira
**satiric** [səˈtɪrɪk] o **satirical** [səˈtɪrɪkəl] *adj* satírico
**satirist** [ˈsætɪrɪst] *s* satírico
**satirize** [ˈsætɪraɪz] *va & vn* satirizar
**satisfaction** [ˌsætɪsˈfækʃən] *s* satisfacción; **to the satisfaction of** a satisfacción de
**satisfactory** [ˌsætɪsˈfæktərɪ] *adj* satisfactorio
**satisfy** [ˈsætɪsfaɪ] (*pret & pp:* **-fied**) *va & vn* satisfacer
**satrap** [ˈsetræp] o [ˈsætræp] *s* sátrapa
**satrapy** [ˈsetrəpɪ] o [ˈsætrəpɪ] *s* (*pl:* **-ies**) satrapía
**saturable** [ˈsætʃərəbəl] *adj* saturable
**saturate** [ˈsætʃəret] *va* saturar

**saturation** [ˌsætʃəˈreʃən] *s* saturación
**saturation bombing** *s* (aer.) bombardeo de saturación
**saturation current** *s* (phys.) corriente de saturación
**saturation point** *s* punto de saturación
**saturator** [ˈsætʃəˌretər] *s* saturador
**Saturday** [ˈsætərdɪ] o [ˈsætərde] *s* sábado; *adj* sabatino
**Saturn** [ˈsætərn] *s* (myth. & astr.) Saturno
**saturnalia** [ˌsætərˈnelɪə] *ssg* o *spl* saturnal (*orgía desenfrenada*); (*cap.*) *ssg* saturnales (*fiestas en honor de Saturno*)
**saturnalian** [ˌsætərˈnelɪən] *adj* desenfrenado; (*cap.*) *adj* saturnal
**Saturnian** [səˈtʌrnɪən] *adj* saturniano (*perteneciente a Saturno; perteneciente a una forma poética en uso entre los romanos*); feliz, dichoso
**saturnine** [ˈsætərnaɪn] *adj* saturnino
**saturnism** [ˈsætərnɪzəm] *s* (path.) saturnismo
**satyr** [ˈsætər] o [ˈsetər] *s* (myth.) sátiro; sátiro (*hombre lascivo*)
**sauce** [sɔs] *s* salsa; crema (*p.ej., de chocolate*); compota; jugo (*de caramelo*); gracia, viveza; (coll.) insolencia; (coll.) lenguaje descomedido; *va* condimentar, sazonar; (coll.) ser insolente con, desvergonzarse con
**saucebox** [ˈsɔsˌbɑks] *s* (coll.) insolente, descarado
**saucepan** [ˈsɔsˌpæn] *s* cacerola
**saucer** [ˈsɔsər] *s* platillo
**saucer-eyed** [ˈsɔsərˌaɪd] *adj* de ojos de platillo
**saucisson** [ˌsosiˈsõ] *s* (fort. & mil.) salchicha, salchichón
**saucy** [ˈsɔsɪ] *adj* (*comp:* **-cier;** *super:* **-ciest**) insolente, descarado; gracioso, vivo
**Saudi Arabia** [sɑˈudɪ əˈrebɪə] *s* la Arabia Saudita
**sauerkraut** [ˈsaʊrˌkraʊt] *s* chucruta
**Saul** [sɔl] *s* (Bib.) Saúl; (Bib.) Saulo (*nombre de San Pablo antes de su conversión*)
**saunter** [ˈsɔntər] *s* paseo; paso tranquilo y alegre; *vn* pasearse; pasearse con paso tranquilo y alegre
**saurian** [ˈsɔrɪən] *adj & s* (zool.) saurio
**sausage** [ˈsɔsɪdʒ] *s* salchicha
**sauté** [soˈte] *adj* (cook.) salteado; *va* (cook.) saltear
**savage** [ˈsævɪdʒ] *adj & s* salvaje
**savageness** [ˈsævɪdʒnɪs] *s* salvajismo
**savagery** [ˈsævɪdʒrɪ] *s* (*pl:* **-ries**) salvajería, salvajismo
**savanna** o **savannah** [səˈvænə] *s* sabana
**savant** [ˈsævənt] *s* sabio, erudito
**save** [sev] *prep* (lit.) salvo, excepto; *conj* (lit.) a no ser que; *va* salvar (*p.ej., una vida, un alma, un edificio del incendio*); ahorrar (*dinero*); guardar, conservar; amparar, proteger; **God save the Queen!** ¡Dios guarde a la Reina!; **to save face** salvar las apariencias; **to save oneself the trouble** ahorrarse la molestia; **to save one's eyes** cuidarse la vista; *vn* economizar
**save-all** [ˈsevˌɔl] *s* adminículo; alcancía; pantalones de trabajo; delantal de niño
**saveloy** [ˈsævəlɔɪ] *s* salchicha seca y bien sazonada
**savin** o **savine** [ˈsævɪn] *s* (bot. & pharm.) sabina
**saving** [ˈsevɪŋ] *adj* ahorrativo, económico; calificativo; *prep* salvo, excepto; con el debido respeto a; **saving your presence** con excusas por mi conducta en su presencia; **savings** *spl* ahorros, economías
**saving clause** *s* (law) cláusula que contiene una salvedad
**saving grace** *s* mérito especial
**savings account** *s* cuenta de ahorros
**savings and loan association** *s* sociedad de ahorros y préstamos
**savings bank** *s* banco de ahorros, caja de ahorros
**savior** [ˈsevjər] *s* salvador
**Saviour** [ˈsevjər] *s* Salvador
**savoir-faire** [sævwɑrˈfɛr] *s* maña, habilidad, destreza
**savoir-vivre** [sævwɑrˈvivrə] *s* mundo, trato de gentes
**savor** [ˈsevər] *s* sabor; *va* saborear; *vn* heder; oler; **to savor of** oler a, saber a
**savory** [ˈsevərɪ] *adj* (*comp:* **-ier;** *super:* **-iest**) sabroso; salado, picante; fragante; *s* (*pl:* **-ies**) (bot.) ajedrea de jardín; (bot.) tomillo real; (Brit.) digestivo
**savour** [ˈsevər] *s, va & vn* (Brit.) var. de **savor**
**savoy** [səˈvɔɪ] *s* col de Saboya; (*cap.*) *s* la Saboya
**Savoyard** [səˈvɔɪərd] *adj* saboyano; *s* saboyano; partidario de las operetas de Gilbert y Sullivan
**savvy** [ˈsævɪ] *s* (slang) comprensión; (*pret & pp:* **-vied**) *va & vn* (slang) comprender
**saw** [sɔ] *s* sierra; refrán, dicho, proverbio; (*pret:* **sawed;** *pp:* **sawed** o **sawn**) *va* aserrar, serrar; *vn* serrar; serrarse; moverse de atrás para delante como una sierra; *pret de* **see**
**sawbuck** [ˈsɔˌbʌk] *s* cabrilla, borrico, burro
**sawdust** [ˈsɔˌdʌst] *s* aserrín, serrín
**sawfish** [ˈsɔˌfɪʃ] *s* (ichth.) sierra, pez sierra
**sawfly** [ˈsɔˌflaɪ] *s* (*pl:* **-flies**) (ent.) mosca de sierra
**sawhorse** [ˈsɔˌhɔrs] *s* cabrilla, borrico, burro
**sawings** [ˈsɔ·ɪŋz] *spl* aserraduras
**sawmill** [ˈsɔˌmɪl] *s* aserradero, serrería
**sawn** [sɔn] *pp de* **saw**
**saw set** *s* triscador
**sawyer** [ˈsɔjər] *s* aserrador
**Saxe-Coburg-Gotha** [ˈsæksˈkobʌrgˈgoθə] *s* Sajonia-Coburgo-Gotha
**saxhorn** [ˈsæksˌhɔrn] *s* (mus.) bombardón
**saxifragaceous** [ˌsæksɪfrəˈgeʃəs] *adj* (bot.) saxifragáceo
**saxifrage** [ˈsæksɪfrɪdʒ] *s* (bot.) saxífraga
**Saxon** [ˈsæksən] *adj & s* sajón
**Saxony** [ˈsæksənɪ] *s* Sajonia
**saxophone** [ˈsæksəfon] *s* (mus.) saxofón
**saxophonist** [ˈsæksəˌfonɪst] *s* saxofonista
**saxtuba** [ˈsæksˌtjubə] o [ˈsæksˌtubə] *s* (mus.) bombardón
**say** [se] *s* decir; **to have one's say** decir su parecer; (*pret & pp:* **said**) *va* decir; **I should say so!** ¡ya lo creo!; **it is said** se dice; **no sooner said than done** dicho y hecho; **that is to say** es decir, esto es; **to go without saying** caerse de su peso; **to say nothing of** eso sin tomar en cuenta; **to say over again** repetir, volver a decir; **to say the least** por lo menos; **to say to oneself** decir para sí; **say when** (coll.) Vd. dirá
**saying** [ˈseɪŋ] *s* refrán, proverbio; **as the saying goes** como dice el refrán
**says** [sɛz] *tercera persona del sg del pres de ind de* **say**
**say-so** [ˈseˌso] *s* (coll.) voz no confirmada, rumor sin fundamento; (coll.) decir, autoridad
**sb.** abr. de **substantive**
**S.B.** abr. de **Scientiarum Baccalaureus** (Lat.) **Bachelor of Science**
**'sblood** [zblʌd] *interj* (archaic) ¡sangre de Cristo!
**sc.** abr. de **scene, science, scruple** y **scilicet** (Lat.) **to wit, namely**
**S.C.** abr. de **Sanitary Corps, Signal Corps, South Carolina, Staff Corps** y **Supreme Court**
**scab** [skæb] *s* costra, postilla; (vet.) roña; (bot.) escabro; esquirol (*obrero que substituye a un huelguista*); (slang) golfo, bribón; (*pret & pp:* **scabbed;** *ger:* **scabbing**) *vn* formar costra; trabajar como esquirol
**scabbard** [ˈskæbərd] *s* vaina, funda
**scabble** [ˈskæbəl] *va* desbastar
**scabby** [ˈskæbɪ] *adj* (*comp:* **-bier;** *super:* **-biest**) costroso, postilloso, tiñoso, roñoso; (coll.) vil, ruin
**scabies** [ˈskebɪiz] o [ˈskebiz] *s* (path.) sarna, escabiosis
**scabiosa** [ˌskebɪˈosə] *s* var. de **scabious**
**scabious** [ˈskebɪəs] *adj* escabioso; *s* (bot.) escabiosa; (bot.) viuda de jardín, escabiosa de Indias (*Scabiosa atropurpurea*)
**scabrous** [ˈskebrəs] *adj* escabroso
**scads** [skædz] *spl* (slang) montones
**scaffold** [ˈskæfəld] *s* andamio; cadalso (*para dar pena de muerte a un criminal*); *va* proveer de andamio; proveer de cadalso; sostener por medio de un andamio

**scaffolding** [ˈskæfəldɪŋ] *s* andamiada o andamiaje
**scalawag** [ˈskæləwæg] *s* (coll.) tuno, bribón, golfo
**scald** [skɔld] *s* escaldadura; *va* escaldar
**scale** [skel] *s* escama; (bot.) escama; balanza; platillo de balanza; escala (*p.ej., de un mapa*); (mus.) escala; (ent.) cóccido; **scales** *spl* balanza; **Scales** *spl* (astr.) Balanza; **on a scale of** en escala de (*p.ej., 1 por 100*); **on a large scale** en grande escala; **on a small scale** en pequeña escala; **to tip the scales** inclinar la balanza; **to turn the scales** decidir, determinar; **to scale** según escala; *va* escamar; descortezar, descostrar; cubrir con escamas; pesar; escalar, subir, trepar; medir con escala; graduar; reducir de acuerdo con una escala; tirar (*una piedra*) de manera que corte la superficie del agua; *vn* descamarse; descortezarse, descostrarse; cubrirse de escamas; formarse escamas, formarse incrustaciones; subir, trepar
**scale fern** *s* (bot.) doradilla
**scale insect** *s* (ent.) cóccido
**scale model** *s* maqueta o modelo a escala
**scalene** [skeˈlin] o [ˈskelin] *adj* (geom. & anat.) escaleno
**scalenohedron** [ske,linoˈhidrən] *s* (cryst.) escalenoedro
**scalenus** [skeˈlinəs] *s* (anat.) escaleno, músculo escaleno
**scaling** [ˈskelɪŋ] *s* escamadura (*acción de quitar las escamas*); escalamiento (*acción de entrar por medio de escalas; medición por escala*)
**scaling ladder** *s* escala de sitio
**scallion** [ˈskæljən] *s* chalote, escalluna; (bot.) puerro; (bot.) cebolleta
**scallop** [ˈskɑləp] o [ˈskæləp] *s* (zool.) concha de peregrino; concha de peregrino, pechina, venera (*que llevaban los peregrinos*); concha (*en que se sirve el pescado*); (sew.) festón; *va* hornear a la crema y con pan rallado; cocer (*p.ej., ostras*) en su concha; festonear
**scalloping** [ˈskɑləpɪŋ] o [ˈskæləpɪŋ] *s* festón bordado, borde adornado con festones
**scallop shell** *s* concha de peregrino, pechina, venera
**scalp** [skælp] *s* cuero cabelludo; (fig.) trofeo; *va* escalpar; comprar y revender (*p.ej., billetes de teatro*)
**scalpel** [ˈskælpəl] *s* (surg.) escalpelo
**scalper** [ˈskælpər] *s* revendedor de billetes de teatro
**scaly** [ˈskelɪ] *adj* (*comp:* **-ier;** *super:* **-iest**) escamoso; (coll.) vil, ruin, mezquino
**scammony** [ˈskæmənɪ] *s* (bot. & pharm.) escamonea
**scamp** [skæmp] *s* golfo, bribón; *va* hacer descuidada y chapuceramente
**scamper** [ˈskæmpər] *s* huída precipitada, carrera rápida; *vn* escaparse precipitadamente, correr rápidamente; **to scamper away** escaparse precipitadamente, correr rápidamente
**scampish** [ˈskæmpɪʃ] *adj* bribón
**scan** [skæn] (*pret & pp:* **scanned;** *ger:* **scanning**) *va* escudriñar; escandir (*versos*); (telv.) explorar; (coll.) dar un vistazo a
**Scand.** abr. de **Scandinavia** y **Scandinavian**
**scandal** [ˈskændəl] *s* escándalo; campanada (*suceso ruidoso*)
**scandalize** [ˈskændəlaɪz] *va* escandalizar
**scandalmonger** [ˈskændəl,mʌŋgər] *s* maldiciente, murmurador
**scandalous** [ˈskændələs] *adj* escandaloso; maldiciente, murmurador
**Scandinavia** [,skændɪˈnevɪə] *s* Escandinavia
**Scandinavian** [,skændɪˈnevɪən] *adj & s* escandinavo
**scandium** [ˈskændɪəm] *s* (chem.) escandio
**scanning disk** *s* (telv.) disco explorador
**scansion** [ˈskænʃən] *s* escansión
**scant** [skænt] *adj* escaso, limitado, insuficiente; mero, solo, apenas suficiente; escaso, p.ej., **a scant half-hour** media hora escasa; **scant of** escaso de; *va* reducir, limitar, escatimar
**scantling** [ˈskæntlɪŋ] *s* (carp.) cuartón; cuartones
**scanty** [ˈskæntɪ] *adj* (*comp:* **-ier;** *super:* **-iest**) escaso, limitado, insuficiente, poco suficiente; ligero (*dícese de la ropa*)

**scape** [skep] *s* (arch., bot. & zool.) escapo
**'scape** o **scape** [skep] *s, va & vn* (archaic) var. de **escape**
**scapegoat** [ˈskep,got] *s* (Bib.) cabrón-emisario; cabeza de turco, víctima propiciatoria, víctima inocente
**scapegrace** [ˈskep,gres] *s* pícaro, truhán, bribón
**scaphoid** [ˈskæfɔɪd] *s* (anat.) escafoides
**scapula** [ˈskæpjələ] *s* (*pl:* **-lae** [li] o **-las**) (anat.) escápula, omóplato
**scapular** [ˈskæpjələr] *adj* escapular; *s* escapulario; pluma escapular; (surg.) vendaje para el omóplato
**scar** [skɑr] *s* cicatriz, señal; paraje rocoso, escollo; (fig.) cicatriz; (*pret & pp:* **scarred;** *ger:* **scarring**) *va* señalar; *vn* cicatrizarse
**scarab** [ˈskærəb] *s* (ent. & f.a.) escarabajo
**scarabaeus** [,skærəˈbiəs] *s* (*pl:* **-i** [aɪ]) var. de **scarab**
**scaramouch** [ˈskærə,mautʃ] o [ˈskærə,muʃ] *s* fanfarrón; truhán, bribón
**scarce** [skɛrs] *adj* escaso, raro; **to make oneself scarce** (coll.) no dejarse ver, hacerse el perdidizo
**scarcely** [ˈskɛrslɪ] *adv* apenas; probablemente no; ciertamente no; **scarcely ever** raramente
**scarcity** [ˈskɛrsɪtɪ] *s* (*pl:* **-ties**) escasez, carestía, rareza
**scare** [skɛr] *s* susto, alarma; *va* asustar, espantar; **to scare away** espantar, ahuyentar; **to scare up** (coll.) juntar, recoger (*dinero*); **scared stiff** muerto de miedo
**scarecrow** [ˈskɛr,kro] *s* espantajo (*figura; persona; cosa que infunde temor*); espantapájaros (*figura*)
**scarf** [skɑrf] *s* (*pl:* **scarfs** o **scarves**) bufanda, chal; pañuelo para el cuello; chalina (*corbata de caídas largas*); tapete (*adorno o protección de los muebles*); *s* (*pl:* **scarfs**) (carp.) ensambladura francesa; *va* unir con ensambladura francesa
**scarfpin** [ˈskɑrf,pɪn] *s* alfiler de corbata
**scarfskin** [ˈskɑrf,skɪn] *s* epidermis
**scarification** [,skærɪfɪˈkeʃən] *s* (agr. & surg.) escarificación
**scarificator** [ˈskærɪfɪ,ketər] *s* (surg.) escarificador
**scarifier** [ˈskærɪ,faɪər] *s* (agr. & surg.) escarificador
**scarify** [ˈskærɪfaɪ] (*pret & pp:* **-fied**) *va* (agr. & surg.) escarificar; criticar severamente
**scarious** [ˈskɛrɪəs] *adj* (bot.) escarioso
**scarlatina** [,skɑrləˈtinə] *s* (path.) escarlatina; (path.) escarlatina de forma benigna
**scarlet** [ˈskɑrlɪt] *adj* escarlata; *s* escarlata (*color y tela*)
**scarlet fever** *s* (path.) escarlata
**scarlet lychnis** *s* (bot.) cruz de Malta
**scarlet oak** *s* (bot.) coscoja, roble escarlata
**scarlet runner** *s* (bot.) judía de España, judía escarlata
**scarlet tanager** *s* (orn.) piranga
**scarp** [skɑrp] *s* escarpa, declive; (fort.) escarpa; *va* escarpar; *vn* hacer escarpa, tener escarpa
**scary** [ˈskɛrɪ] *adj* (*comp:* **-ier;** *super:* **-iest**) (coll.) asustadizo; (coll.) espantoso
**scat** [skæt] *interj* ¡zape!
**scathe** [skeð] *va* (archaic & dial.) hacer daño a; abrasar; criticar acerbamente
**scatheless** [ˈskeðlɪs] *adj* sano y salvo, ileso
**scathing** [ˈskeðɪŋ] *adj* acerbo, duro
**scatological** [,skætəˈlɑdʒɪkəl] *adj* escatológico
**scatology** [skəˈtɑlədʒɪ] *s* escatología
**scatter** [ˈskætər] *s* esparcimiento, dispersión; *va* esparcir, dispersar
**scatterbrain** [ˈskætər,bren] *s* (coll.) cabeza de chorlito
**scatterbrained** [ˈskætər,brend] *adj* (coll.) alegre de cascos, casquivano
**scattered** [ˈskætərd] *adj* esparcido; irregular, intermitente; despeinado; divagador
**scattering** [ˈskætərɪŋ] *s* esparcimiento, dispersión; pequeño número, pequeña cantidad
**scaup** [skɔp] o **scaup duck** *s* (orn.) coquinero
**scaur** [skɔr] *s* paraje rocoso; roca a flor del agua
**scavenge** [ˈskævɪndʒ] *va* limpiar, barrer

**scavenger** ['skævɪndʒər] *s* basurero; animal que se alimenta de carroña; *vn* recoger la basura
**scenario** [sɪ'nɛrɪo] o [sɪ'nɑrɪo] *s* (*pl:* **-os**) (mov. & theat.) guión
**scenarist** [sɪ'nɛrɪst] o [sɪ'nɑrɪst] *s* (mov.) guionista
**scene** [sin] *s* escena (*en literatura, arte, teatro y cine*); vista, paisaje; arrebato, escándalo, demostración de pasión; **behind the scenes** (theat. & fig.) entre bastidores; **to make a scene** dar un espectáculo, causar escándalo
**scenery** ['sinərɪ] *s* (*pl:* **-ies**) paisaje; (theat.) decoraciones
**scene shifter** *s* tramoyista
**scenic** ['sinɪk] o ['sɛnɪk] *adj* escénico (*perteneciente a la escena*); pintoresco; gráfico
**scenographer** [si'nɑgrəfər] *s* escenógrafo
**scenography** [si'nɑgrəfɪ] *s* escenografía
**scent** [sɛnt] *s* olor; perfume; olfato; rastro, pista; *va* oler; perfumar; rastrear; sospechar
**scentless** ['sɛntlɪs] *adj* inodoro; sin olfato
**scepter** ['sɛptər] *s* cetro; *va* proveer de cetro
**sceptered** ['sɛptərd] *adj* que lleva cetro; regio, imperial
**sceptic** ['skɛptɪk] *adj & s* escéptico
**sceptical** ['skɛptɪkəl] *adj* escéptico
**scepticism** ['skɛptɪsɪzəm] *s* escepticismo
**sceptre** ['sɛptər] *s & va* var. de **scepter**
**Schaffhausen** [,ʃɑf'haʊzən] *s* Escafusa
**schappe** ['ʃɑpə] *s* sedalina
**schedule** ['skɛdʒʊl] *s* lista, cuadro, catálogo; plan, programa; horario (*p.ej., de los trenes*); *va* catalogar; proyectar; fijar la hora de, fijar el tiempo de
**Scheherazade** [ʃə,hɛrə'zɑdə] *s* Scherezada
**Scheldt** [skɛlt] *s* Escalda (*río*)
**schema** ['skimə] *s* (*pl:* **-mata** [mətə]) esquema; (philos.) esquema
**schematic** [ski'mætɪk] *adj* esquemático
**scheme** [skim] *s* esquema; plan, proyecto, designio; ardid, treta; *va & vn* proyectar, tramar
**schemer** ['skimər] *s* proyectista; intrigante
**scheming** ['skimɪŋ] *adj* astuto, mañoso, intrigante
**Schick test** [ʃɪk] *s* (med.) prueba de Schick
**schilling** ['ʃɪlɪŋ] *s* chelín austríaco
**schism** ['sɪzəm] *s* cisma; facción cismática, secta cismática
**schismatic** [sɪz'mætɪk] *adj & s* cismático
**schismatical** [sɪz'mætɪkəl] *adj* cismático
**schist** [ʃɪst] *s* (geol.) esquisto
**schistose** ['ʃɪstos] o **schistous** ['ʃɪstəs] *adj* esquistoso
**schizocarp** ['skɪzokɑrp] *s* (bot.) esquizocarpio
**schizomycete** [,skɪzomaɪ'sit] *s* (bot.) esquizomiceto
**schizophrenia** [,skɪzo'frinɪə] *s* (path.) esquizofrenia
**schizophrenic** [,skɪzo'frɛnɪk] *adj & s* esquizofrénico
**schmaltz** [ʃmɑlts] *s* (slang) sensiblería
**schnapps** o **schnaps** [ʃnɑps] *s* ginebra de Holanda; aguardiente
**schnorkel** o **schnorkle** ['ʃnɔrkəl] *s* var. de **snorkel**
**scholar** ['skɑlər] *s* escolar (*estudiante*); sabio, erudito; becario (*estudiante que disfruta una beca*)
**scholarly** ['skɑlərlɪ] *adj* erudito; *adv* eruditamente
**scholarship** ['skɑlərʃɪp] *s* erudición; beca (*plaza gratuita en una escuela o universidad*)
**scholastic** [skə'læstɪk] *adj & s* escolástico
**scholastically** [skə'læstɪkəlɪ] *adv* escolásticamente
**scholasticism** [skə'læstɪsɪzəm] *s* escolasticismo; (philos.) escolasticismo
**scholiast** ['skolɪæst] *s* escoliador o escoliasta
**scholiastic** [,skolɪ'æstɪk] *adj* de los escoliastas
**scholium** ['skolɪəm] *s* (*pl:* **-a** [ə]) escolio
**school** [skul] *s* escuela; facultad (*de la universidad*); banco o cardume (*de peces*); **in school** en la escuela; *adj* de escuela, para escuela, escolar; *va* enseñar, instruir, adiestrar, disciplinar; *vn* nadar (*los peces*) en bancos
**school age** *s* edad escolar
**school board** *s* junta de instrucción pública
**schoolbook** ['skul,bʊk] *s* libro escolar
**schoolboy** ['skul,bɔɪ] *s* alumno de escuela
**school day** *s* día lectivo
**schoolfellow** ['skul,fɛlo] *s* condiscípulo, compañero de escuela
**schoolgirl** ['skul,gʌrl] *s* alumna de escuela
**schoolhouse** ['skul,haʊs] *s* escuela (*edificio*)
**schooling** ['skulɪŋ] *s* instrucción, enseñanza; experiencia; coste de la instrucción escolar
**schoolman** ['skulmən] *s* (*pl:* **-men**) maestro; (philos.) escolástico
**schoolmarm** ['skul,mɑrm] *s* (coll.) maestra de escuela
**schoolmaster** ['skul,mæstər] o ['skul,mɑstər] *s* maestro de escuela
**schoolmate** ['skul,met] *s* condiscípulo, compañero de escuela
**schoolmistress** ['skul,mɪstrɪs] *s* maestra de escuela
**school of thought** *s* escuela (*doctrina, sistema*); (coll.) punto de vista, modo de ver
**schoolroom** ['skul,rum] o ['skul,rʊm] *s* aula, sala de clase
**school ship** *s* buque escuela
**schoolteacher** ['skul,titʃər] *s* maestro de escuela
**schoolyard** ['skul,jɑrd] *s* patio de recreo de la escuela
**school year** *s* año escolar, año lectivo
**school zone** *s* zona escolar
**schooner** ['skunər] *s* (naut.) goleta; (U.S.A.) carromato de cuatro ruedas y con toldo; (coll.) vaso grande de cerveza
**schooner-rigged** ['skunər,rɪgd] *adj* (naut.) de velas cangrejas
**schottische** ['ʃɑtɪʃ] *s* chotis (*baile y música*)
**schwa** [ʃwɑ] *s* (phonet.) e relajada
**sci.** abr. de **science** y **scientific**
**sciatic** [saɪ'ætɪk] *adj* ciático
**sciatica** [saɪ'ætɪkə] *s* (path.) ciática
**sciatic nerve** *s* (anat.) nervio ciático
**science** ['saɪəns] *s* ciencia; (*cap.*) *s* ciencia cristiana
**science fiction** *s* novela científica, novela de divulgación científica
**scientific** [,saɪən'tɪfɪk] *adj* científico
**scientifically** [,saɪən'tɪfɪkəlɪ] *adv* científicamente
**scientific management** *s* gestión científica, organización científica del trabajo
**scientism** ['saɪəntɪzəm] *s* cientismo
**scientist** ['saɪəntɪst] *s* científico, hombre de ciencia, sabio; (*cap.*) *s* adepto de la ciencia cristiana
**scil.** abr. de **scilicet** (Lat.) **to wit, namely**
**scimitar** o **scimiter** ['sɪmɪtər] *s* cimitarra
**scintilla** [sɪn'tɪlə] *s* centella, chispa; partícula, vestigio
**scintillate** ['sɪntɪlet] *vn* centellear, chispear
**scintillation** [,sɪntɪ'leʃən] *s* centelleo
**scintillation counter** *s* (phys.) centellador, contador de centelleo
**sciolism** ['saɪəlɪzəm] *s* erudición superficial, pseudoerudición
**sciolist** ['saɪəlɪst] *s* erudito superficial, pseudoerudito
**scion** ['saɪən] *s* (hort. & fig.) vástago
**Scipio** ['sɪpɪo] *s* Escipión
**scirrhous** ['skɪrəs] o ['sɪrəs] *adj* escirroso
**scirrhus** ['skɪrəs] o ['sɪrəs] *s* (*pl:* **-rhi** [raɪ] o **-rhuses**) (path.) escirro
**scission** ['sɪʒən] o ['sɪʃən] *s* escisión
**scissor** ['sɪzər] *va* cortar con tijeras; **scissors** *ssg* o *spl* tijeras
**scissors-grinder** ['sɪzərz'graɪndər] *s* afilador de tijeras; (orn.) chotacabras
**scissors kick** *s* (swimming) golpe de tijera
**sclerenchyma** [sklɪ'rɛŋkɪmə] *s* (bot.) esclerénquima
**scleroderma** [,sklɪro'dʌrmə] *s* (path.) esclerodermia
**scleroma** [sklɪ'romə] *s* (*pl:* **-mata** [mətə]) (path.) escleroma
**sclerometer** [sklɪ'rɑmɪtər] *s* esclerómetro
**sclerosis** [sklɪ'rosɪs] *s* (*pl:* **-ses** [siz]) (path. & bot.) esclerosis
**sclerotic** [sklɪ'rɑtɪk] *adj* (anat.) esclerótico; (path.) escleroso; *s* (anat.) esclerótica
**sclerotitis** [,sklɪro'taɪtɪs] *s* (path.) esclerotitis
**sclerotium** [sklɪ'roʃɪəm] *s* (*pl:* **-a** [ə]) (bot.) esclerocio

**sclerotomy** [sklɪˈrɑtəmɪ] *s* (*pl:* **-mies**) (surg.) esclerotomía
**sclerous** [ˈsklɪrəs] *adj* escleroso
**scoff** [skɔf] o [skɑf] *s* mofa, burla; *vn* mofarse, burlarse; **to scoff at** mofarse de, burlarse de
**scoffer** [ˈskɔfər] o [ˈskɑfər] *s* mofador, burlador
**scoffingly** [ˈskɔfɪŋlɪ] o [ˈskɑfɪŋlɪ] *adv* con mofa y escarnio
**scold** [skold] *s* regañón, regañona; *va & vn* regañar
**scolex** [ˈskolɛks] *s* (*pl:* **scoleces** [skoˈlisiz]) (zool.) escólex
**scoliosis** [ˌskolɪˈosɪs] o [ˌskɑlɪˈosɪs] *s* (path.) escoliosis
**scollop** [ˈskɑləp] *s & va* var. de **scallop**
**scolopendra** [ˌskɑloˈpɛndrə] *s* (zool.) escolopendra
**sconce** [skɑns] *s* defensa, cobertizo; baluarte, fortín; (coll.) cabeza; (coll.) agudeza, inteligencia; candelabro de pared, candelero de pared; *va* defender, cubrir; fortificar con baluarte
**scone** [skon] o [skɑn] *s* bizcocho chato cocido en una plancha metálica
**scoop** [skup] *s* cuchara (*de excavadora; cualquier instrumento en forma de cuchara*); paleta (*utensilio de cocina*); achicador (*para extraer el agua*); cucharada, palada, paletada (*porción recogida de una vez*); hueco (*lugar ahuecado con la cuchara, etc.*); (coll.) buena ganancia; (slang) primera publicación de una noticia; *va* sacar con pala, paleta o cuchara; achicar (*agua*); ahuecar; **to scoop out** ahuecar, vaciar
**scoopful** [ˈskupfʊl] *s* cucharada, palada, paletada
**scoop net** *s* esparavel, manga
**scoot** [skut] *s* (coll.) carrera precipitada; *vn* (coll.) correr precipitadamente
**scooter** [ˈskutər] *s* monopatín o patinete (*plancha montada sobre ruedas*); motoneta; lancha rápida; velero que se desliza rápidamente por el hielo o el agua; (orn.) negreta; *vn* correr en monopatín o patinete; deslizar
**scope** [skop] *s* alcance, extensión; oportunidad; indicador visual
**scopolamine** [skoˈpɑləmin] o [ˌskopoˈlæmɪn] *s* (chem.) escopolamina
**scops owl** [skɑps] *s* (orn.) buharro, corneja
**scorbutic** [skɔrˈbjutɪk] *adj & s* escorbútico
**scorbutus** [skɔrˈbjutəs] *s* (path.) escorbuto
**scorch** [skɔrtʃ] *s* chamusco (*quemadura leve*); *va* chamuscar; abrasar (*secar, marchitar*); criticar acerbamente; *vn* chamuscarse; abrasarse; (coll.) correr muy rápidamente
**scorched-earth policy** [ˈskɔrtʃtˈʌrθ] *s* (mil.) política de tierra abrasada
**scorcher** [ˈskɔrtʃər] *s* (coll.) día de mucho calor; (coll.) reproche acerbo; (coll.) jinete o biciclista que va a toda velocidad
**scorching** [ˈskɔrtʃɪŋ] *adj* abrasador; acerbo, duro, mordaz
**score** [skor] *s* cuenta, tantos (*en un juego*); nota (*en un examen*); muesca, entalladura; línea, raya; (mus.) partitura; veintena; **on that score** a ese respecto; **on the score of** a título de, con motivo de; **to keep score** tantear, apuntar los tantos; **to pay off a score** o **to settle a score** desquitarse de un agravio; *va* anotar (*los tantos*); ganar, tantear (*tantos*); señalar, rayar; (mus.) instrumentar; criticar severamente, regañar acerbamente; **to score a cylinder** (aut.) rayar un cilindro; **to score a point** ganar un punto; *vn* ganar tantos; marcar los tantos; hacer rayas, hacer señales
**score board** *s* pizarrón anotador, cuadro indicador, marcador
**score card** *s* anotador
**score keeper** *s* tanteador
**scoria** [ˈskorɪə] *s* (*pl:* **-ae** [i]) escoria; (petrog.) escoria
**scoriaceous** [ˌskorɪˈeʃəs] *adj* escoriáceo
**scorify** [ˈskorɪfaɪ] (*pret & pp:* **-fied**) *va* escorificar
**scorn** [skɔrn] *s* desprecio, desdén; **to cast scorn upon** denigrar; *va & vn* despreciar, desdeñar; **to scorn to** + *inf* no dignarse + *inf*
**scornful** [ˈskɔrnfəl] *adj* desdeñoso
**scorpene** [ˈskɔrpin] *s* (ichth.) escorpina, raño
**Scorpio** [ˈskɔrpɪo] *s* (astr.) Escorpión
**scorpion** [ˈskɔrpɪən] *s* (ent.) alacrán, escorpión; escorpión (*azote; ballesta de los antiguos*)
**scorpion grass** *s* (bot.) alacranera
**Scot.** abr. de **Scotch, Scotland** y **Scottish**
**scot** [skɑt] *s* escote; (*cap.*) *s* escocés
**scotch** [skɑtʃ] *s* corte, incisión; marca, señal; calce, cuña; obstáculo, impedimento; (*cap.*) *adj* escocés; *s* escocés (*dialecto; whisky*); *spl* escoceses; (*l.c.*) *va* cortar; marcar; herir ligeramente; calzar; detener, frustrar; engalgar (*una rueda*)
**Scotch-Irish** [ˈskɑtʃˈaɪrɪʃ] *adj* de descendencia irlandesa y escocesa
**Scotchman** [ˈskɑtʃmən] *s* (*pl:* **-men**) escocés
**Scotch pine** *s* (bot.) pino albar
**Scotch tape** *s* (trademark) cinta adhesiva transparente
**Scotch terrier** *s* perro escocés
**Scotch thistle** *s* (bot.) acantio, cardo borriqueño, toba
**Scotch whiskey** *s* whisky escocés
**scoter** [ˈskotər] *s* (orn.) negreta, pato negro
**scot-free** [ˈskɑtˈfri] *adj* impune
**scotia** [ˈskoʃɪə] o [ˈskoʃə] *s* (arch.) escocia, nacela; (*cap.*) [ˈskoʃə] *s* (poet.) Escocia
**Scotism** [ˈskotɪzəm] *s* escotismo
**Scotland** [ˈskɑtlənd] *s* Escocia
**Scotland Yard** *s* cuerpo de detectives de Londres
**Scots** [skɑts] *adj* escocés; *ssg* escocés (*dialecto*); *spl* escoceses
**Scotsman** [ˈskɑtsmən] *s* (*pl:* **-men**) escocés
**Scotticism** [ˈskɑtɪsɪzəm] *s* acento del habla escocesa
**Scottish** [ˈskɑtɪʃ] *adj* escocés; *ssg* escocés (*dialecto*); *spl* escoceses
**scoundrel** [ˈskaʊndrəl] *s* pícaro, bribón
**scoundrelly** [ˈskaʊndrəlɪ] *adj* pícaro, bribón
**scour** [skaʊr] *s* fregado, estregamiento; *va* fregar, estregar (*frotar con fuerza para limpiar*); escurar (*el paño*); purgar; limpiar con un chorro de agua; formar (*un cauce el agua corriente*); recorrer rápidamente, explorar detenidamente; batir (*el monte*)
**scourge** [skʌrdʒ] *s* azote, flagelo; *va* azotar; flagelar
**Scourge of God, the** el azote de Dios (*Atila*)
**scouring** [ˈskaʊrɪŋ] *s* fregadura; **scourings** *spl* residuo de la fregadura; pulpa inservible que se saca al grano; (fig.) escoria, canalla
**scout** [skaʊt] *s* (mil.) escucha, explorador; niño explorador, niña exploradora; exploración, reconocimiento; (slang) tipo, individuo, sujeto; *va* explorar, reconocer (*un territorio*); observar (*al enemigo*); negarse a creer, burlarse de; *vn* explorar, reconocer; **to scout at** mofarse de; **to scout for** (coll.) buscar
**scouting** [ˈskaʊtɪŋ] *s* exploración, reconocimiento; actividades de los niños exploradores
**scoutmaster** [ˈskaʊtˌmæstər] o [ˈskaʊtˌmɑstər] *s* jefe de tropa de niños exploradores
**scow** [skaʊ] *s* (U.S.A.) lanchón de carga
**scowl** [skaʊl] *s* ceño, semblante ceñudo; *vn* mirar con ceño, poner mal gesto
**scrabble** [ˈskræbəl] *s* pataleo; garrapatos (*mala escritura*); *va* arañar; garrapatear (*escribir mal*); *vn* patalear; garrapatear
**scrag** [skræg] *s* persona delgada y pellejuda, animal delgado y pellejudo; (slang) pescuezo; (*pret & pp:* **scragged;** *ger:* **scragging**) *va* (slang) ahorcar, torcer el pescuezo a
**scraggly** [ˈskræglɪ] *adj* (*comp:* **-glier;** *super:* **-gliest**) áspero, dentado, harapiento, desgreñado
**scraggy** [ˈskrægɪ] *adj* (*comp:* **-gier;** *super:* **-giest**) áspero, nudoso; flaco, delgado, huesoso
**scram** [skræm] (*pret & pp:* **scrammed;** *ger:* **scramming**) *vn* (slang) largarse, salir de naja
**scramble** [ˈskræmbəl] *s* lucha, contienda; arrebatiña; trepa; *va* arrebatar; recoger de prisa, recoger con confusión; revolver; hacer un revoltillo de (*huevos*); trepar; (rad.) invertir o cambiar de otra manera el espectro de frecuencias de (*una señal*) de modo que no pueda ser recobrada sino por el aparato receptor que tenga la clave electrónica; *vn* luchar; trepar
**scrambled eggs** *spl* revoltillo, huevos revueltos

**scrannel** ['skrænəl] *adj* delgado, descarnado; chillón, rechinante

**scrap** [skræp] *s* pedazo, fragmento, migaja; desecho, metal viejo, chatarra; (slang) riña, contienda, camorra; **scraps** *spl* sobras (*de la mesa*); ripios, desperdicios; parte seca de la grasa animal, chicharrón; *adj* desechado, viejo; (*pret & pp:* **scrapped;** *ger:* **scrapping**) *va* desechar, descartar, echar a la basura; despedazar; reducir a hierro viejo; *vn* (slang) reñir, pelear

**scrapbook** ['skræp,bʊk] *s* álbum de recortes, libro de recuerdos

**scrape** [skrep] *s* raspadura; raspazo (*lugar que se ha raspado*); aprieto, enredo; reverencia hecha con un pie echado hacia atrás; *va* raspar; arañar (*recoger con mucho afán*); **to scrape acquaintance** trabar amistad; **to scrape together, to scrape up** arañar; *vn* raspar; rascar (*tocar un instrumento de cuerda y arco haciendo un sonido de raspadura*); hacer una reverencia echando el pie hacia atrás; arreglárselas, desenvolverse en un aprieto; amontonar dinero poco a poco; **to scrape along** ir tirando; **to scrape through** aprobar justo

**scraper** ['skrepər] *s* raedera, raspador; arañador (*de dinero; del violín*); rascatripas (*del violín*); desuellacaras (*barbero malo*); limpiabarros, estregadera (*para estregar los pies*)

**scrap heap** *s* montón de cachivaches, montón de desechos

**scrap iron** *s* hierro de desecho, desecho de hierro, chatarra

**scrapple** ['skræpəl] *s* pasta (frita) de harina de maíz con pedazos de carne de puerco

**scrappy** ['skræpɪ] *adj* (*comp:* **-pier;** *super:* **-piest**) fragmentario, inconexo, misceláneo; (slang) peleador

**scratch** [skrætʃ] *s* arañazo, rasguño; (coll.) garrapato; (sport) línea de partida; prueba de valor; (billiards) bambarria, chiripa; **to be up to scratch** estar en buena condición; **to start from scratch** empezar sin nada, empezar sin ventaja, empezar desde el principio; *va* arañar, rasguñar; (coll.) garrapatear; borrar, raspar (*lo escrito*); (sport) borrar (*un corredor o caballo*); **to scratch out** borrar; sacar (*ojos*) con las uñas; *vn* arañar, rasguñar; (coll.) garrapatear; raspear (*una pluma al escribir*); juntar dinero con gran dificultad

**scratch hit** *s* (baseball) golpe por casualidad o por chamba

**scratch pad** *s* cuadernillo de apuntes

**scratch test** *s* medida de dureza al rayado; (med.) reacción de la escarificación

**scratchy** ['skrætʃɪ] *adj* (*comp:* **-ier;** *super:* **-iest**) arañador, raspador; áspero, irregular

**scrawl** [skrɔl] *s* garrapatos; *va & vn* garrapatear

**scrawny** ['skrɔnɪ] *adj* (*comp:* **-nier;** *super:* **-niest**) descarnado, huesudo

**screak** [skrik] *s* chirrido, rechinamiento; *vn* chirriar, rechinar

**scream** [skrim] *s* chillido, alarido, grito; (slang) persona o cosa muy divertidas; *va* vociferar; *vn* chillar, gritar; reírse a gritos

**screamer** ['skrimər] *s* chillón, gritón; (slang) persona sobresaliente, cosa sobresaliente; (slang) persona muy divertida, escrito muy divertido; (orn.) anhima, palamedea; (orn.) chajá (*Chauna chavaria*)

**screaming** ['skrimɪŋ] *s* chillido, alarido, grito; *adj* chillón, gritón; llamativo; cómico, chistoso, divertidísimo; (slang) excelente

**screech** [skritʃ] *s* chillido; *vn* chillar

**screech owl** *s* (orn.) corneja, buharro; (orn.) lechuza, lechuza norteamericana; profeta del mal

**screechy** ['skritʃɪ] *adj* (*comp:* **-ier;** *super:* **-iest**) chillón

**screed** [skrid] *s* tirada; diatriba; (mas.) maestra

**screen** [skrin] *s* mampara, biombo; pantalla (*delante de la chimenea*); alambrera (*para evitar que las moscas se introduzcan en las habitaciones*); tamiz (*para pasar arena, carbón, etc.*); retícula, trama (*para obtener fotograbados*); (mov., phys. & telv.) pantalla; (fig.) pantalla (*cine, arte del cine*); **to put on the screen** llevar a la pantalla, llevar al celuloide; *va* defender, proteger; cubrir, ocultar; cinematografiar; rodar, proyectar (*una película*); adaptar para el cine; tamizar (*p.ej., arena*); dividir, separar

**screen grid** *s* (rad.) rejilla blindada

**screen-grid tube** ['skrin'grɪd] *s* (rad.) válvula de rejilla blindada, válvula de rejilla-pantalla

**screenings** ['skrinɪŋz] *spl* residuos de criba, desperdicios de criba

**screen play** ['skrin,ple] *s* cinedrama

**screw** [skru] *s* tornillo; rosca (*filete; vuelta espiral*); tuerca (*pieza taladrada en que se encaja el tornillo*); hélice (*de un vapor*); tacaño; **to have a screw loose** (slang) faltarle a uno un tornillo, tener flojos los tornillos; **to put the screws on** apretar los tornillos a; *va* atornillar; enroscar (*torcer en forma de tornillo*); obligar; obtener por fuerza; **to screw from** u **out of** sonsacar; **to screw up** torcer (*el rostro*); **to screw up courage** animarse, cobrar ánimo; *vn* atornillarse; enroscarse

**screwball** ['skru,bɔl] *adj & s* (slang) extravagante, excéntrico, estrafalario

**screw bolt** *s* perno roscado

**screw conveyor** *s* transportador de tornillo sin fin

**screwdriver** ['skru,draɪvər] *s* destornillador

**screw eye** *s* armella

**screwhead** ['skru,hɛd] *s* cabeza de tornillo

**screw jack** *s* gato de tornillo

**screw key** *s* desvolvedor

**screw propeller** *s* hélice

**screw tap** *s* macho de terraja

**screw thread** *s* filete de tornillo

**scribal error** ['skraɪbəl] *s* error de escribiente

**scribble** ['skrɪbəl] *s* garrapatos; *va & vn* garrapatear

**scribbler** ['skrɪblər] *s* garrapateador; mal escritor, autorzuelo despreciable

**scribe** [skraɪb] *s* escriba (*intérprete de la ley entre los judíos*); amanuense; escribiente; autor, escritor; *va* arañar, rayar; trazar con punzón

**scriber** ['skraɪbər] *s* punzón de trazar

**scrim** [skrɪm] *s* tejido de algodón o lino ligero y basto

**scrimmage** ['skrɪmɪdʒ] *s* lucha, pelea; (football) jugada en que, los equipos estando juntos, se lanza la pelota hacia atrás

**scrimp** [skrɪmp] *va* escatimar; **to scrimp someone for food** escatimar a uno la comida; *vn* escatimar

**scrimpy** ['skrɪmpɪ] *adj* (*comp:* **-ier;** *super:* **-iest**) escaso, escatimoso

**scrip** [skrɪp] *s* cédula, documento; vale, abonaré

**script** [skrɪpt] *s* escritura, letra cursiva; (print.) plumilla inglesa; manuscrito; texto, palabras (*de un drama, cine, etc.*); (rad. & telv.) guión; (law) escritura

**scriptorium** [skrɪp'torɪəm] *s* (*pl:* **-ums** o **-a** [ə]) escritorio

**scriptural** o **Scriptural** ['skrɪptʃərəl] *adj* bíblico

**scripturally** ['skrɪptʃərəlɪ] *adv* conforme a la Biblia

**scripture** ['skrɪptʃər] *s* escrito sagrado; (*cap.*) *s* Escritura; **Scriptures** *spl* Escrituras; **Holy Scriptures** Sagradas Escrituras

**scriptwriter** ['skrɪpt,raɪtər] *s* guionista

**scrivener** ['skrɪvnər] *s* (archaic) escribano; (archaic) escribiente

**scrod** [skrɑd] *s* (ichth.) cría del abadejo común

**scrofula** ['skrɑfjələ] *s* (path.) escrófula

**scrofulous** ['skrɑfjələs] *adj* escrofuloso

**scroll** [skrol] *s* rollo de papel, rollo de pergamino; (arch.) voluta

**scroll saw** *s* sierra de calar, sierra para contornear

**scrollwork** ['skrol,wʌrk] *s* dibujo de volutas, adornos de voluta, obra con volutas

**scrotal** ['skrotəl] *adj* escrotal

**scrotum** ['skrotəm] *s* (*pl:* **-ta** [tə] o **-tums**) (anat.) escroto

**scrub** [skrʌb] *s* monte bajo; persona de poca altura; (sport) jugador no oficial, no adiestrado; fregado; *adj* achaparrado; (sport) no ofi-

cial, no adiestrado; (*pret & pp:* **scrubbed;** *ger:* **scrubbing**) *va* fregar, restregar
**scrubbing brush** *s* cepillo de fregar, estregadera
**scrubby** ['skrʌbɪ] *adj* (*comp:* **-bier;** *super:* **-biest**) achaparrado, bajo, pequeño; vil, miserable, despreciable; erizado, mal afeitado
**scrub oak** *s* (bot.) chaparro
**scrub woman** *s* fregona
**scruff** [skrʌf] *s* nuca; piel que cubre la nuca; capa, superficie; espuma, escoria
**scrumptious** ['skrʌmpʃəs] *adj* (slang) elegante, magnífico
**scrunch** [skrʌntʃ] *s* (coll.) crujido; *va & vn* (coll.) ronzar
**scruple** ['skrupəl] *s* escrúpulo; (pharm.) escrúpulo; cantidad ínfima; *va* tener escrúpulos acerca de; *vn* escrupulizar
**scrupulosity** [,skrupjə'lɑsɪtɪ] *s* (*pl:* **-ties**) escrupulosidad
**scrupulous** ['skrupjələs] *adj* escrupuloso
**scrutinize** ['skrutɪnaɪz] *va* escrutar, escudriñar
**scrutiny** ['skrutɪnɪ] *s* (*pl:* **-nies**) escrutinio, escudriñamiento
**scud** [skʌd] *s* carrera rápida; salpicaduras de agua que lleva el viento; nube correo; (*pret & pp:* **scudded;** *ger:* **scudding**) *vn* correr rápidamente, deslizarse precipitadamente
**scuff** [skʌf] *s* rascadura; desgaste; *va* rascar; desgastar; arrastrar (*los pies*); *vn* rascarse; desgastarse; arrastrar los pies
**scuffle** ['skʌfəl] *s* sarracina, lucha; *vn* luchar, forcejear; arrastrar los pies
**scull** [skʌl] *s* espadilla; remo; bote; *va* impulsar con espadilla; *vn* cinglar, remar con espadilla
**sculler** ['skʌlər] *s* bote de espadilla; remero de bote
**scullery** ['skʌlərɪ] *s* (*pl:* **-ies**) espetera, sollastría; trascocina
**scullery maid** *s* fregona
**scullion** ['skʌljən] *s* (archaic) sollastre (*mozo de cocina; pícaro*)
**sculpin** ['skʌlpɪn] *s* (ichth.) coto; individuo despreciable
**sculptor** ['skʌlptər] *s* escultor
**sculptress** ['skʌlptrɪs] *s* escultora
**sculptural** ['skʌlptʃərəl] *adj* escultural
**sculpture** ['skʌlptʃər] *s* escultura; *va & vn* esculpir
**sculptured** ['skʌlptʃərd] *adj* esculpido, ornado de esculturas
**sculpturesque** [,skʌlptʃə'rɛsk] *adj* escultural
**scum** [skʌm] *s* espuma, nata; (fig.) escoria, canalla, gente baja; (*pret & pp:* **scummed;** *ger:* **scumming**) *va & vn* espumar
**scummy** ['skʌmɪ] *adj* (*comp:* **-mier;** *super:* **-miest**) espumoso; vil, ruin
**scup** [skʌp] *s* (ichth.) pagro
**scupper** ['skʌpər] *s* imbornal; (naut.) imbornal o embornal
**scuppernong** ['skʌpərnɑŋ] *s* moscatel norteamericano
**scurf** [skʌrf] *s* caspa; costra
**scurfy** ['skʌrfɪ] *adj* (*comp:* **-ier;** *super:* **-iest**) casposo; costroso
**scurrility** [skə'rɪlɪtɪ] *s* (*pl:* **-ties**) procacidad, insolencia, grosería
**scurrilous** ['skʌrɪləs] *adj* procaz, insolente, grosero, chocarrero
**scurry** ['skʌrɪ] *s* fuga, carrera precipitada; ventolera, remolino; ráfaga, nevisca; (*pret & pp:* **-ried**) *va* poner en fuga, hacer correr; *vn* echar a correr, escabullirse; **to scurry around** menearse; **to scurry off** escabullirse; **to scurry through** pasar precipitadamente por; hacer de prisa, leer de prisa, terminar rápidamente
**scurvy** ['skʌrvɪ] *s* (path.) escorbuto; *adj* (*comp:* **-vier;** *super:* **-viest**) vil, ruin, despreciable
**scurvy grass** *s* (bot.) coclearia, hierba de las cucharas
**scut** [skʌt] *s* rabito
**Scutari** ['skutɑrɪ] *s* Escútari
**scutate** ['skjutet] *adj* escutiforme
**scutch** [skʌtʃ] *s* agramadera; agramaduras; martillo cortador de ladrillos; *va* agramar
**scutcheon** ['skʌtʃən] *s* var. de **escutcheon**
**scutch grass** *s* (bot.) grama; (bot.) grama del norte
**scute** [skjut] *s* (zool.) escudo
**scutellate** ['skjutəlet] o [skju'tɛlet] *adj* (bot., zool. & orn.) escutelado
**scutellum** [skju'tɛləm] *s* (*pl:* **-la** [lə]) (bot. & zool.) escutelo
**scutiform** ['skjutɪfɔrm] *adj* escutiforme
**scuttle** ['skʌtəl] *s* cubo, balde; escotillón; (naut.) escotilla; abertura, agujero; fuga, paso acelerado; *va* (naut.) barrenar, dar barreno a; (naut.) agujerear la cubierta de; *vn* echar a correr, correr con precipitación
**scuttlebutt** ['skʌtəl,bʌt] *s* (naut.) pipa o tonel de agua de beber; (naut.) fuente de beber; (slang) runrún, chismes
**scutum** ['skjutəm] *s* (*pl:* **-ta** [tə]) (zool.) escudo
**scybalum** ['sɪbələm] *s* (*pl:* **-la** [lə]) (path.) esquíbala
**Scylla** ['sɪlə] *s* (geog. & myth.) Escila; **to be between Scylla and Charybdis** estar entre Escila y Caribdis
**scythe** [saɪð] *s* guadaña, dalla; *va* guadañar
**Scythia** ['sɪθɪə] *s* la Escitia
**Scythian** ['sɪθɪən] *adj* escita, escítico; *s* escita
**S. Dak.** abr. de **South Dakota**
**'sdeath** [zdɛθ] *interj* (archaic) ¡vive Dios!
**S.E.** o **SE** abr. de **southeast**
**sea** [si] *s* mar; fig.) mar (*p.ej., de lágrimas*); **at sea** en el mar; perplejo, confuso; **beyond the sea** allende el mar; **by the sea** a la orilla del mar; **by sea** por mar; **in the open sea** en pleno mar; **to follow the sea** ser marinero; **to go to sea** hacerse marinero; emprender un viaje por mar; **to put to sea** hacerse a la mar
**sea anemone** *s* (zool.) anemone de mar
**sea bass** [bæs] *s* (ichth.) serrano, perca de mar
**sea bird** *s* ave marina, ave de mar
**seaboard** ['si,bord] *s* costa del mar, litoral; playa; *adj* costanero, costero
**sea-born** ['si,bɔrn] *adj* nacido en el mar, nacido del mar, que sale del mar
**sea-borne** ['si,born] *adj* transportado por mar
**sea bread** *s* galleta, bizcocho (*de marinero*)
**sea bream** *s* (ichth.) besugo
**sea breeze** *s* brisa de mar
**sea calf** *s* (zool.) becerro marino
**sea coal** *s* (archaic) carbón de piedra
**seacoast** ['si,kost] *s* litoral, costa marítima
**sea cow** *s* (zool.) manatí; (zool.) ternera marina (*morsa*)
**sea cucumber** *s* (zool.) cohombro de mar
**sea daffodil** *s* (bot.) nardo marítimo, amormío
**sea dog** *s* (zool.) foca; (zool.) perro de mar; marinero viejo, lobo de mar
**sea eagle** *s* (orn.) águila marina; (orn.) quebrantahuesos
**sea elephant** *s* (zool.) foca de trompa, elefante marino
**seafarer** ['si,fɛrər] *s* marinero; navegante
**seafaring** ['si,fɛrɪŋ] *adj* marinero; navegante; *s* marinería; navegación
**sea foam** *s* espuma de mar
**seafood** ['si,fud] *s* pescado de mar, mariscos
**seafowl** ['si,faʊl] *s* ave de mar
**seagirt** ['si,gʌrt] *adj* cercado por el mar
**seagoing** ['si,go·ɪŋ] *adj* de alta mar, de la navegación marítima
**sea goose** *s* (orn.) barnacla
**sea grape** *s* (bot.) cocobolo, uvero
**sea green** *s* verdemar
**sea gull** *s* (orn.) gaviota
**sea hare** *s* (zool.) liebre de mar o liebre marina
**sea hedgehog** *s* (zool.) apancora
**sea hog** *s* (zool.) puerco de mar
**sea horse** *s* (ichth.) caballito de mar; (ichth. & zool.) caballo marino; (her.) monstruo mitad caballo y mitad pez
**sea kale** *s* (bot.) col marina
**sea king** *s* rey del mar (*pirata noruego de la Edad Media*)
**seal** [sil] *s* sello; (zool.) foca; (zool.) león marino; **to set one's seal to** poner el sello a; aprobar; **seals** *spl* sellos (*símbolo de la autoridad*); *va* sellar; cerrar herméticamente; decidir irrevocablemente; lacrar; **to seal in** cerrar herméticamente; *vn* cazar focas
**sea lavender** *s* (bot.) acelga silvestre, limonio
**sealed-in** ['sild,ɪn] *adj* hermético
**sea legs** *spl* pie marino
**sealer** ['silər] *s* sellador; cierre hermético; ca-

zador de focas; embarcación en que se cazan focas
**sealery** ['silərɪ] *s* (*pl:* **-ies**) caza de focas; lugar donde se cazan focas
**sea level** *s* nivel del mar
**sea lily** *s* (zool.) lirio de mar (*crinoideo*)
**sealing wax** *s* lacre; **to seal with sealing wax** lacrar
**sea lion** *s* (zool.) león marino
**seal ring** *s* sortija con sello, anillo sigilar
**sealskin** ['sil,skɪn] *s* piel de foca
**seam** [sim] *s* costura; metido (*tela sobrante en las costuras de una prenda de ropa*); costurón (*cicatriz o línea semejante en la piel*); arruga (*pliegue en la piel*); grieta, juntura; (min.) filón, veta; *va* coser; señalar con cicatrices; arrugar; *vn* agrietarse
**seaman** ['simən] *s* (*pl:* **-men**) marinero; (nav.) marino (*que no tiene categoría de oficial*)
**seamanlike** ['simən,laɪk] o **seamanly** ['simənlɪ] *adj* de buen marinero
**seamanship** ['simənʃɪp] *s* náutica, marinería
**seamark** ['si,mɑrk] *s* línea de límite de la marea; (naut.) marca de reconocimiento
**sea mew** *s* (orn.) gaviota
**sea mile** *s* milla náutica
**seamless** ['simlɪs] *adj* inconsútil, sin costura
**sea monster** *s* monstruo marino
**seamstress** ['simstrɪs] *s* costurera; modistilla
**seamy** ['simɪ] *adj* (*comp:* **-ier;** *super:* **-iest**) con costuras; basto; ruin, miserable
**séance** ['seɑns] *s* sesión, reunión; sesión de espiritistas
**Sea of Galilee** *s* mar de Galilea
**Sea of Japan** *s* mar del Japón
**Sea of Marmara** o **Marmora** ['mɑrmərə] *s* mar de Mármara
**Sea of Tiberias** [taɪ'bɪrɪəs] *s* lago de Tiberíades
**sea otter** *s* (zool.) lataz
**sea pink** *s* (bot.) césped de Olimpo, estátice
**seaplane** ['si,plen] *s* hidroplano
**seaport** ['si,port] *s* puerto, puerto de mar
**sea power** *s* potencia naval
**sea purse** *s* cáscara córnea del huevo de la raya
**sear** [sɪr] *s* chamusco, socarra; gacheta (*de un arma de fuego*); *adj* seco, marchito; raído, gastado; *va* chamuscar, socarrar; cauterizar; endurecer; *vn* chamuscarse, socarrarse; endurecerse; marchitarse
**search** [sʌrtʃ] *s* busca, búsqueda; pesquisa, indagación; **in search of** en busca de; *va* buscar; explorar, averiguar; registrar; **to search out** buscar; examinar; descubrir buscando; *vn* buscar; **to search after** buscar; explorar, averiguar; preguntar por; **to search for** buscar; **to search into** indagar, investigar
**searching** ['sʌrtʃɪŋ] *adj* escrutador; agudo, penetrante, minucioso
**searching party** *s* grupo de personas que se envían en busca de alguien
**searchlight** ['sʌrtʃ,laɪt] *s* reflector, proyector; luz de un proyector
**search warrant** *s* (law) orden de allanamiento, auto de registro domiciliario
**sea robber** *s* pirata, corsario
**sea robin** *s* (ichth.) rubio volador
**sea room** *s* espacio para maniobrar sin peligro
**sea rover** *s* pirata, corsario
**sea salt** *s* sal marina
**seascape** ['siskep] *s* vista del mar; (paint.) marina
**seascapist** ['si,skepɪst] *s* marinista
**sea serpent** *s* monstruo marino; (zool.) hidrófido
**sea shell** *s* concha marina, caracol marino
**seashore** ['si,ʃor] *s* ribera del mar, playa
**seasick** ['si,sɪk] *adj* mareado
**seasickness** ['si,sɪknɪs] *s* mareo
**seaside** ['si,saɪd] *s* ribera del mar, orilla del mar, playa; *adj* costanero; de playa, de mar
**sea snake** *s* (zool.) hidrófido
**season** ['sizən] *s* estación (*una de las cuatro partes del año*); temporada (*espacio de tiempo formando un conjunto; tiempo en que un lugar está más frecuentado*); sazón (*tiempo oportuno; tiempo de madurez*); **for a season** durante una temporada; **in good season** con tiempo; **in season** a su tiempo; en sazón; con tiempo; **in season and out of season** en tiempo y a destiempo; **out of season** fuera de sazón; a destiempo; **to dress according to the season** vestir con la estación; *va* sazonar; curar (*la madera*); acostumbrar; moderar, templar; *vn* sazonarse; curarse (*p.ej., la madera*); acostumbrarse
**seasonable** ['sizənəbəl] *adj* oportuno, tempestivo, conveniente
**seasonal** ['sizənəl] *adj* estacional
**seasoning** ['sizənɪŋ] *s* aliño, aderezo, condimento; sal, chiste; cura (*de la madera*)
**season ticket** *s* billete de abono
**sea squirt** *s* (zool.) ascidia
**seat** [sit] *s* asiento; fondillos (*de los calzones o pantalones*); morada, residencia; sitio, lugar, paraje; sede (*p.ej., del gobierno*); escaño (*en las Cortes*); teatro, (*p.ej., de una guerra*); centro (*p.ej., de la erudición*); batalla (*de la silla de montar*); **to take a seat** tomar asiento; *va* sentar; tener asientos para, tener cabida para; poner asiento a (*una silla*); ajustar (*una válvula*) en su asiento; echar fondillos a (*pantalones*); arraigar, fijar, establecer, afianzar; **to seat oneself** sentarse; **to be seated** estar sentado; sentarse; estar situado
**seat belt** *s* cinturón de asiento
**seat cover** *s* funda de asiento
**seating capacity** *s* aforo, cabida, número de asientos
**Seato** ['sito] *s* la O.T.A.S.E. (*la Organización del Tratado del Sudeste Asiático*)
**sea trout** *s* (ichth.) trucha marina, trucha de mar
**sea urchin** *s* (zool.) erizo de mar
**sea wall** *s* dique marítimo
**seaward** ['siwərd] *s* dirección hacia el mar; *adj* dirigido hacia el mar; *adv* hacia el mar
**seawards** ['siwərdz] *adv* hacia el mar
**seaway** ['si,we] *s* ruta marítima; mar ancha, alta mar; mar gruesa, mar alborotada; avance de una embarcación por mar; vía de agua interior para buques de alta mar
**seaweed** ['si,wid] *s* plantas marinas; algas; (bot.) alga marina
**sea wind** *s* viento que sopla del mar
**seaworthy** ['si,wʌrðɪ] *adj* marinero, en condiciones de navegar
**sebaceous** [sɪ'beʃəs] *adj* sebáceo
**sebaceous gland** *s* (anat.) glándula sebácea
**Sebastian** [sɪ'bæstʃən] *s* Sebastián
**sebesten** [sɪ'bɛstən] *s* (bot.) sebestén (*árbol y fruto*)
**sec.** abr. de **secant, second, secondary, secretary, section** y **sector**
**SEC** abr. de **Securities and Exchange Commission**
**secant** ['sikənt] *adj* & *s* (geom. & trig.) secante
**secede** [sɪ'sid] *vn* separarse, retirarse
**secession** [sɪ'sɛʃən] *s* secesión
**secessionism** [sɪ'sɛʃənɪzəm] *s* secesionismo
**secessionist** [sɪ'sɛʃənɪst] *adj* & *s* secesionista
**seckel** ['sɛkəl] *s* pera pequeña de color rojizo
**seclude** [sɪ'klud] *va* recluir
**secluded** [sɪ'kludɪd] *adj* recluso; solitario, retirado
**seclusion** [sɪ'kluʒən] *s* reclusión, soledad
**seclusive** [sɪ'klusɪv] *adj* solitario; exclusivo
**second** ['sɛkənd] *adj* segundo; **to be second to none** ser sin segundo, no ir en zaga a nada, no ir en zaga a nadie; **to play second fiddle** desempeñar un papel secundario; *s* segundo; artículo de segunda calidad; padrino (*p.ej., en un certamen, desafío*); segundante (*en el boxeo*); (mus.) segunda; (aut.) segunda (velocidad); dos (*en las fechas*); *adv* en segundo lugar; *va* secundar; apoyar (*una moción en junta deliberante*)
**Second Advent** *s* segundo advenimiento, segunda venida (*de Jesucristo*)
**secondary** ['sɛkən,dɛrɪ] *adj* secundario; *s* (*pl:* **-ies**) (elec.) secundario
**secondary accent** *s* (phonet.) acento secundario
**secondary cell** *s* (elec.) elemento secundario
**secondary coil** *s* (elec.) carrete secundario
**secondary feather** *s* (orn.) pluma secundaria
**secondary school** *s* escuela de segunda enseñanza

**second base** *s* (baseball) segunda base *f* (*puesto*); (baseball) segunda base *m* (*jugador*)
**second baseman** *s* (baseball) segunda base *m* (*jugador*)
**second best** *s* (el) mejor después del primero
**second childhood** *s* segunda niñez
**second-class** ['sɛkənd,klæs] o ['sɛkənd,klɑs] *adj* de segunda clase; de clase inferior
**second-class matter** *s* correspondencia de segunda clase
**seconder** ['sɛkəndər] *s* persona que apoya una moción
**second hand** *s* segundero (*de reloj*)
**second-hand** ['sɛkənd,hænd] *adj* de segunda mano, de ocasión
**second-hand bookshop** *s* librería de viejo
**second-hand dealer** *s* prendero
**second-hand shop** *s* prendería
**second lieutenant** *s* (mil.) alférez, subteniente
**second nature** *s* segunda naturaleza
**second person** *s* (gram.) segunda persona
**second-rate** ['sɛkənd,ret] *adj* de segundo orden; de calidad inferior, de menor cuantía
**second-run wine** ['sɛkənd,rʌn] *s* vino de segunda
**second sight** *s* doble vista, segunda vista
**seconds pendulum** *s* péndulo de segundos
**second violin** *s* segundo violín
**second wind** [wɪnd] *s* nuevo aliento
**secrecy** ['sikrəsɪ] *s* (*pl:* **-cies**) secreto; **in secrecy** en secreto
**secret** ['sikrɪt] *adj* secreto; *s* secreto; (eccl.) secreta (*oración*); **in secret** en secreto
**secret agent** *s* agente secreto, agente de la policía secreta
**secretarial** [,sɛkrɪ'tɛrɪəl] *adj* de secretario, para secretarios
**secretariat** o **secretariate** [,sɛkrɪ'tɛrɪɪt] *s* secretaría
**secretary** ['sɛkrɪ,tɛrɪ] *s* (*pl:* **-ies**) secretario; secreter, escritorio
**secretary bird** *s* (orn.) secretario, serpentario
**Secretary of State** *s* (U.S.A.) ministro de Asuntos Exteriores
**secretaryship** ['sɛkrɪ,tɛrɪʃɪp] *s* secretaría
**secret ballot** *s* voto secreto
**secrete** [sɪ'krit] *va* esconder, encubrir; (physiol.) secretar
**secretin** [sɪ'kritɪn] *s* (biochem.) secretina
**secretion** [sɪ'kriʃən] *s* (physiol.) secreción
**secretive** [sɪ'kritɪv] *adj* callado, reservado; (physiol.) secretorio
**secretory** [sɪ'kritərɪ] *adj* (physiol.) secretorio; *s* órgano secretorio, glándula secretoria
**secret service** *s* servicio secreto; servicio de espionaje
**secret society** *s* sociedad secreta
**secs.** abr. de **seconds** y **sections**
**sect.** abr. de **section**
**sect** [sɛkt] *s* secta
**sectarian** [sɛk'tɛrɪən] *adj* & *s* sectario
**sectarianism** [sɛk'tɛrɪənɪzəm] *s* sectarismo
**sectary** ['sɛktərɪ] *adj* sectario; *s* (*pl:* **-ries**) sectario
**sectile** ['sɛktɪl] *adj* sectil
**section** ['sɛkʃən] *s* sección; (arch., geom. & mil.) sección; región (*de un país*); barrio (*de una ciudad*); (rail.) distrito, tramo; *va* seccionar
**sectional** ['sɛkʃənəl] *adj* seccional; regional, local
**sectionalism** ['sɛkʃənəlɪzəm] *s* regionalismo
**sectionalize** ['sɛkʃənəlaɪz] *va* dividir en secciones; (U.S.A.) dividir según los intereses locales
**sectionally** ['sɛkʃənəlɪ] *adv* en secciones, por secciones; en una región
**section foreman** *s* (rail.) capataz de tramo
**section gang** *s* (rail.) cuadrilla de tramo
**section hand** *s* (rail.) peón ferrocarrilero
**sector** ['sɛktər] *s* sector; (geom., math. & mil.) sector
**secular** ['sɛkjələr] *adj* secular; *s* seglar
**secularism** ['sɛkjələrɪzəm] *s* secularismo
**secularist** ['sɛkjələrɪst] *s* secularista
**secularity** [,sɛkjə'lærɪtɪ] *s* secularidad
**secularization** [,sɛkjələrɪ'zeʃən] *s* secularización
**secularize** ['sɛkjələraɪz] *va* secularizar
**secure** [sɪ'kjʊr] *adj* seguro; *va* asegurar; obtener, conseguir; *vn* asegurarse
**security** [sɪ'kjʊrɪtɪ] *s* (*pl:* **-ties**) seguridad; segurador (*persona*); **securities** *spl* valores, obligaciones, títulos
**Security Council** *s* Consejo de Seguridad
**security risk** *s* riesgo a la seguridad nacional (*persona*)
**secy.** o **sec'y.** abr. de **secretary**
**sedan** [sɪ'dæn] *s* silla de manos; (aut.) sedán
**sedan chair** *s* silla de manos
**sedate** [sɪ'det] *adj* sentado, sosegado, tranquilo
**sedation** [sɪ'deʃən] *s* (med.) sedación
**sedative** ['sɛdətɪv] *adj* & *s* (med.) sedativo
**sedentary** ['sɛdən,tɛrɪ] *adj* sedentario
**sedge** [sɛdʒ] *s* (bot.) juncia
**sedged** [sɛdʒd] *adj* júnceo; hecho de juncias
**sedge warbler** *s* (orn.) saltamimbres
**sedgy** ['sɛdʒɪ] *adj* júnceo; abundante en juncias
**sediment** ['sɛdɪmənt] *s* sedimento; *va* sedimentar; *vn* sedimentarse
**sedimental** [,sɛdɪ'mɛntəl] *adj* sedimentario
**sedimentary** [,sɛdɪ'mɛntərɪ] *adj* sedimentario; (geol.) sedimentario
**sedimentation** [,sɛdɪmɛn'teʃən] *s* sedimentación
**sedimentation test** *s* (physiol.) velocidad de sedimentación globular
**sedition** [sɪ'dɪʃən] *s* sedición
**seditionary** [sɪ'dɪʃə,nɛrɪ] *adj* & *s* sedicioso
**seditious** [sɪ'dɪʃəs] *adj* sedicioso
**seduce** [sɪ'djus] o [sɪ'dus] *va* seducir
**seducement** [sɪ'djusmənt] o [sɪ'dusmənt] *s* seducción
**seducer** [sɪ'djusər] o [sɪ'dusər] *s* seductor
**seducible** [sɪ'djusɪbəl] o [sɪ'dusɪbəl] *adj* seducible
**seduction** [sɪ'dʌkʃən] *s* seducción
**seductive** [sɪ'dʌktɪv] *adj* seductivo
**sedulity** [sɪ'djulɪtɪ] o [sɪ'dulɪtɪ] *s* diligencia, cuidado
**sedulous** ['sɛdjələs] *adj* diligente, cuidadoso
**sedum** ['sidəm] *s* (bot.) hierba callera (*Sedum telephium*); (bot.) uva de gato (*Sedum acre*)
**see** [si] *s* (eccl.) sede; (*pret:* **saw;** *pp:* **seen**) *va* ver; recibir; acompañar (*a casa, a la puerta, etc.*); (poker) aceptar (*una apuesta*) apostando una cantidad igual; (poker) aceptar la apuesta de (*un jugador*) apostando una cantidad igual; **to see** + *inf* ver + *inf*, p.ej., **I saw the train go by** ví pasar el tren; **to see** + *pp* ver + *inf*, p.ej.,**I saw the criminal hanged** ví ahorcar al criminal; **to see off** ir a despedir (*a una persona*); **to see out** llevar a cabo; (coll.) aventajar, beber más que; **to see through** llevar a cabo; ayudar en un trance difícil; *vn* ver; **let's see** a ver, veamos; **to see about** + *ger* ver de + *inf;* **to see after** cuidar, cuidar de; buscar; **to see into** conocer el juego de; **to see that** atender a que, ver que; **to see through** conocer el juego de; **to see to** atender a; tener cuidado de; **to see to it that** atender a que, ver que; **see here!** ¡mire Vd.!
**seed** [sid] *s* simiente; **to go to seed** dar semilla; dar en grana; echarse a perder; *adj* seminal; *va* sembrar; despepitar (*quitar las semillas de*); *vn* sembrar; dejar caer semillas
**seedcake** ['sid,kek] *s* torta de semillas aromáticas
**seed capsule** *s* (bot.) pericarpio
**seedcase** ['sid,kes] *s* (bot.) pericarpio
**seed coat** *s* (bot.) tegumento seminal, cubierta de la semilla
**seed corn** *s* maíz para sembrar
**seeder** ['sidər] *s* sembrador; sembradora (*máquina*); máquina de despepitar
**seeding** ['sidɪŋ] *s* siembra, sementera; caída de semilla
**seed-lac** ['sid,læk] *s* laca en grano
**seed leaf** *s* (bot.) cotiledón
**seedling** ['sidlɪŋ] *s* planta de semilla; árbol de pie; arbolito que no pasa de tres pies de alto
**seed oysters** *spl* ostras muy jóvenes
**seed pearl** *s* perlita, aljófar
**seed plant** *s* planta de semilla
**seedsman** ['sidzmən] *s* (*pl:* **-men**) sembrador; vendedor de semillas
**seedtime** ['sid,taɪm] *s* siembra
**seed vessel** *s* (bot.) pericarpio

**seedy** ['sidɪ] *adj* (*comp:* **-ier;** *super:* **-iest**) lleno de granos; (coll.) raído, andrajoso
**seeing** ['siɪŋ] *adj* vidente; *s* vista, visión; (el) ver; *conj* visto que
**Seeing Eye dog** *s* perro-lazarillo
**seek** [sik] (*pret & pp:* **sought**) *va* buscar; recorrer buscando; procurar; dirigirse a; **to seek a person's life** tratar de matar a una persona; *vn* buscar; **to seek after** tratar de obtener; solicitar; **to seek to** + *inf* esforzarse por + *inf*
**seem** [sim] *vn* parecer; **I still seem to hear the music** todavía me parece oír la música
**seeming** ['simɪŋ] *adj* aparente; *s* apariencia
**seemingly** ['simɪŋlɪ] *adv* aparentemente, al parecer
**seemly** ['simlɪ] *adj* (*comp:* **-lier;** *super:* **-liest**) decente, decoroso, correcto; bien parecido; *adv* decentemente, decorosamente, correctamente
**seen** [sin] *pp de* **see**
**seep** [sip] *vn* percolarse, rezumarse, escurrirse, filtrar
**seepage** ['sipɪdʒ] *s* percolación, filtración
**seer** [sɪr] *s* vidente, profeta
**seeress** ['sɪrɪs] *s* vidente, profetisa
**seersucker** ['sɪr,sʌkər] *s* sirsaca
**seesaw** ['si,sɔ] *s* balancín, columpio de tabla; vaivén (*movimiento*); *adj* de balancín; *vn* columpiarse (*en el balancín*); alternar; vacilar
**seethe** [sið] *va* empapar, embeber; (pharm.) elijar; *vn* hervir; (fig.) hervir
**segment** ['sɛgmənt] *s* segmento; *va* dividir en segmentos
**segmental** [sɛg'mɛntəl] *adj* segmental; (arch. & zool.) segmental
**segmental arch** *s* (arch.) arco escarzano
**segmentally** [sɛg'mɛntəlɪ] *adv* en segmentos
**segmentary** ['sɛgmən,tɛrɪ] *adj* segmentario
**segmentation** [,sɛgmən'teʃən] *s* segmentación
**sego** ['sigo] *s* (*pl:* **-gos**) (bot.) ayatito
**sego lily** *s* (bot.) ayatito
**segregate** ['sɛgrɪget] o ['sɛgrɪgɪt] *adj* segregado; ['sɛgrɪget] *va* segregar
**segregation** [,sɛgrɪ'geʃən] *s* segregación
**segregationist** [,sɛgrɪ'geʃənɪst] *s* segregacionista
**segregative** ['sɛgrɪ,getɪv] *adj* segregativo
**Seidlitz powder** ['sɛdlɪts] *s* polvos de Seidlitz
**seigneur** [sin'jʌr] *s* señor (*feudal*)
**seignior** ['sinjər] *s* señor
**seigniorage** ['sinjərɪdʒ] *s* señoreaje
**seigniory** ['sinjərɪ] *s* (*pl:* **-ies**) señorío (*en la época feudal*)
**seignorial** [sin'jorɪəl] o [sin'jɔrɪəl] señoril
**Seine** [sen] *s* Sena; (*l.c.*) *s* red barredera; *va & vn* pescar con red barredera
**seism** ['saɪzəm] *s* sismo o seísmo
**seismic** ['saɪzmɪk] *adj* sísmico
**seismogram** ['saɪzməgræm] *s* sismograma
**seismograph** ['saɪzməgræf] o ['saɪzməgrɑf] *s* sismógrafo
**seismographic** [,saɪzmə'græfɪk] o **seismographical** [,saɪzmə'græfɪkəl] *adj* sismográfico
**seismography** [saɪz'mɑgrəfɪ] *s* sismografía
**seismologic** [,saɪzmə'lɑdʒɪk] o **seismological** [,saɪzmə'lɑdʒɪkəl] *adj* sismológico
**seismologist** [saɪz'mɑlədʒɪst] *s* sismologista
**seismology** [saɪz'mɑlədʒɪ] *s* sismología
**seismometer** [saɪz'mɑmɪtər] *s* sismómetro
**seize** [siz] *va* asir, agarrar, coger; comprender; embargar, secuestrar; aprovecharse de (*una oportunidad*); apoderarse de; atar, prender, sujetar; *vn* agarrar, coger; **to seize on** o **upon** asir de repente, coger de repente; apoderarse de
**seizin** ['sizən] *s* (law) posesión, toma de posesión
**seizing** ['sizɪŋ] *s* agarro, captura; atadura, ligadura, aferramiento; cuerda
**seizure** ['siʒər] *s* asimiento, prendimiento, prisión; captura, presa, toma; embargo, secuestro; ataque (*de una enfermedad*)
**selachian** [sɪ'lekɪən] *adj & s* (ichth.) selacio
**seldom** ['sɛldəm] *adv* raramente, rara vez
**select** [sɪ'lɛkt] *adj* selecto, escogido; *va* seleccionar
**selectee** [sɪ,lɛk'ti] *s* (mil.) quinto
**selection** [sɪ'lɛkʃən] *s* selección; trozo escogido; (com.) surtido
**selective** [sɪ'lɛktɪv] *adj* selectivo; (rad.) selectivo
**selective service** *s* servicio militar obligatorio
**selectivity** [sɪ,lɛk'tɪvɪtɪ] *s* (rad.) selectividad
**selectman** [sɪ'lɛktmən] *s* (*pl:* **-men**) concejal, miembro del ayuntamiento, miembro del concejo municipal
**selector** [sɪ'lɛktər] *s* escogedor; (telp.) selector (*órgano del teléfono automático*)
**Selene** [sɛ'lini] *s* (myth.) Selene
**selenide** ['sɛlɪnaɪd] o ['sɛlɪnɪd] *s* (chem.) seleniuro
**selenite** ['sɛlɪnaɪt] o [sɛ'linaɪt] *s* (mineral.) selenita
**selenium** [sɛ'linɪəm] *s* (chem.) selenio
**selenium cell** *s* (elec.) célula de selenio
**selenium rectifier** *s* (elec.) rectificador de selenio
**selenographer** [,sɛlɪ'nɑgrəfər] o **selenographist** [,sɛlɪ'nɑgrəfɪst] *s* selenógrafo
**selenography** [,sɛlɪ'nɑgrəfɪ] *s* selenografía
**self** [sɛlf] *adj* mismo; *pron* sí mismo; *s* (*pl:* **selves**) uno mismo; **all by one's self** sin ayuda de nadie; **one's other self** su otro yo; **the self** el yo, el propio yo
**self-abasement** [,sɛlfə'besmənt] *s* rebajamiento de sí mismo
**self-abhorrence** [,sɛlfæb'hɑrəns] o [,sɛlfæb'hɔrəns] *s* aborrecimiento de sí mismo
**self-abnegation** [,sɛlf,æbnɪ'geʃən] *s* abnegación
**self-absorption** [,sɛlfæb'sɔrpʃən] o [,sɛlfæb'zɔrpʃən] *s* ensimismamiento
**self-abuse** [,sɛlfə'bjus] *s* abuso de sí mismo; masturbación
**self-acting** [,sɛlf'æktɪŋ] *adj* automático
**self-addressed** [,sɛlfə'drɛst] *adj* dirigido a sí mismo
**self-analysis** [,sɛlfə'nælɪsɪs] *s* autoanálisis
**self-appointed** [,sɛlfə'pɔɪntɪd] *adj* designado por sí mismo
**self-assertion** [,sɛlfə'sʌrʃən] *s* agresividad
**self-assertive** [,sɛlfə'sʌrtɪv] *adj* agresivo
**self-assurance** [,sɛlfə'ʃurəns] *s* confianza en sí mismo
**self-assured** [,sɛlfə'ʃurd] *adj* seguro de sí
**self-centered** o **self-centred** [,sɛlf'sɛntərd] *adj* egocéntrico, concentrado en sí mismo
**self-cleaning** [,sɛlf'klinɪŋ] *adj* autolimpiador
**self-colored** [,sɛlf'kʌlərd] *adj* de color uniforme; de color natural
**self-command** [,sɛlfkə'mænd] o [,sɛlfkə'mɑnd] *s* dominio sobre sí mismo
**self-communion** [,sɛlfkə'mjunjən] *s* comunión consigo mismo
**self-complacence** [,sɛlfkəm'plesəns] o **self-complacency** [,sɛlfkəm'plesənsɪ] *s* complacencia en sí mismo
**self-conceit** [,sɛlfkən'sit] *s* presunción, arrogancia, vanagloria
**self-confidence** [,sɛlf'kɑnfɪdəns] *s* confianza en sí mismo
**self-conscious** [,sɛlf'kɑnʃəs] *adj* consciente de sí, cohibido, apocado, tímido
**self-consciousness** [,sɛlf'kɑnʃəsnɪs] *s* conciencia de sí, apocamiento, timidez; autoconciencia
**self-consequence** [,sɛlf'kɑnsɪkwɛns] *s* conciencia de su propia importancia
**self-consistent** [,sɛlfkən'sɪstənt] *adj* consecuente
**self-contained** [,sɛlfkən'tend] *adj* callado, reservado, silencioso; dueño de sí mismo; independiente, autónomo, completo en sí mismo
**self-contradiction** ['sɛlf,kɑntrə'dɪkʃən] *s* proposición que envuelve contradicción
**self-control** [,sɛlfkən'trol] *s* dominio de sí mismo, señorío de sí mismo
**self-controlled** [,sɛlfkən'trold] *adj* dueño de sí mismo; automático
**self-cooling** [,sɛlf'kulɪŋ] *adj* enfriado automáticamente; *s* autoenfriamiento
**self-criticism** [,sɛlf'krɪtɪsɪzəm] *s* autocrítica
**self-deception** [,sɛlfdɪ'sɛpʃən] *s* autoengaño
**self-defeating** [,sɛlfdɪ'fitɪŋ] *adj* contraproducente
**self-defense** [,sɛlfdɪ'fɛns] *s* autodefensa; **in self-defense** en defensa propia
**self-denial** [,sɛlfdɪ'naɪəl] *s* abnegación

**self-destruction** [ˌsɛlfdɪsˈtrʌkʃən] *s* autodestrucción
**self-determination** [ˈsɛlfdɪˌtʌrmɪˈneʃən] *s* (pol.) autodeterminación o autodeterminismo
**self-devotion** [ˌsɛlfdɪˈvoʃən] *s* sacrificio de sí mismo
**self-discipline** [ˌsɛlfˈdɪsɪplɪn] *s* autodisciplina, disciplina de sí mismo
**self-educated** [ˌsəlfˈɛdjəˌketɪd] *adj* autodidacto
**self-effacement** [ˌsɛlfɪˈfesmənt] *s* modestia, recogimiento
**self-employed** [ˌsɛlfɛmˈplɔɪd] *adj* que trabaja por su propia cuenta
**self-esteem** [ˌsɛlfɛsˈtim] *s* amor propio, respeto de sí mismo
**self-evident** [ˌsɛlfˈɛvɪdənt] *adj* patente, manifiesto, evidente por sí mismo
**self-examination** [ˈsɛlfɛgˌzæmɪˈneʃən] *s* autocrítica
**self-existent** [ˌsɛlfɛgˈzɪstənt] *adj* existente por sí mismo
**self-explanatory** [ˌsɛlfɛksˈplænəˌtorɪ] *adj* que se explica por sí mismo
**self-expression** [ˌsɛlfɛksˈprɛʃən] *s* expresión de la personalidad propia
**self-filling** [ˌsɛlfˈfɪlɪŋ] *adj* que se llena automáticamente
**self-governing** [ˌsɛlfˈgʌvərnɪŋ] *adj* autónomo
**self-government** [ˌsɛlfˈgʌvərnmənt] *s* autogobierno, autonomía; dominio sobre sí mismo
**selfheal** [ˈsɛlfˌhil] *s* (bot.) sanícula; (bot.) hierba de las heridas
**self-help** [ˌsɛlfˈhɛlp] *s* ayuda de sí mismo, ayuda propia
**selfhood** [ˈsɛlfhʊd] *s* individualidad; personalidad; egoísmo
**self-ignition** [ˌsɛlfɪgˈnɪʃən] *s* encendido automático; autoencendido
**self-importance** [ˌsɛlfɪmˈpɔrtəns] *s* altivez, arrogancia, imperio
**self-important** [ˌsɛlfɪmˈpɔrtənt] *adj* altivo, arrogante, imperioso
**self-imposed** [ˌsɛlfɪmˈpozd] *adj* que uno se impone a sí mismo
**self-improvement** [ˌsɛlfɪmˈpruvmənt] *s* perfeccionamiento de sí mismo
**self-inductance** [ˌsɛlfɪnˈdʌktəns] *s* (elec.) autoinductancia
**self-induction** [ˌsɛlfɪnˈdʌkʃən] *s* (elec.) autoinducción
**self-induction coil** *s* (elec.) self
**self-indulgence** [ˌsɛlfɪnˈdʌldʒəns] *s* desenfreno, falta de sobriedad, intemperancia
**self-inflicted** [ˌsɛlfɪnˈflɪktɪd] *adj* que uno se ha infligido a sí mismo
**self-instruction** [ˌsɛlfɪnˈstrʌkʃən] *s* autoenseñanza
**self-interest** [ˌsɛlfˈɪntərɛst] o [ˌsɛlfˈɪntrɪst] *s* interés personal, egoísmo
**selfish** [ˈsɛlfɪʃ] *adj* egoísta
**selfishness** [ˈsɛlfɪʃnɪs] *s* egoísmo
**self-knowledge** [ˌsɛlfˈnɑlɪdʒ] *s* conocimiento de sí mismo
**selfless** [ˈsɛlflɪs] *adj* generoso, desinteresado
**self-liquidating** [ˌsɛlfˈlɪkwɪˌdetɪŋ] *adj* que se liquida por sí mismo, autoamortizable
**self-loading** [ˌsɛlfˈlodɪŋ] *adj* autocargador
**self-locking** [ˌsɛlfˈlɑkɪŋ] *adj* autocerrador
**self-love** [ˌsɛlfˈlʌv] *s* amor propio, egoísmo
**self-made man** [ˈsɛlfˌmed] *s* hijo de sus propias obras, hombre que ha logrado éxito por sus propios esfuerzos
**self-moving** [ˌsɛlfˈmuvɪŋ] *adj* automotor
**self-opinionated** [ˌsɛlfəˈpɪnjəˌnetɪd] *adj* orgulloso, vanidoso; porfiado en su parecer
**self-pity** [ˌsɛlfˈpɪtɪ] *s* compasión de sí mismo
**self-pollinate** [ˌsɛlfˈpɑlɪnet] *va* (bot.) autopolinizar
**self-pollination** [ˈsɛlfˌpɑlɪˈneʃən] *s* (bot.) autopolinización
**self-pollution** [ˌsɛlfpəˈluʃən] *s* polución voluntaria
**self-portrait** [ˌsɛlfˈportret] *s* autorretrato
**self-possessed** [ˌsɛlfpəˈzɛst] *adj* sereno, dueño de sí mismo
**self-possession** [ˌsɛlfpəˈzɛʃən] *s* serenidad, dominio sobre sí mismo, tranquilidad del ánimo
**self-preservation** [ˈsɛlfˌprɛzərˈveʃən] *s* propia conservación
**self-propagating** [ˌsɛlfˈprɑpəˌgetɪŋ] *adj* autopropagado
**self-propelled** [ˌsɛlfproˈpɛld] *adj* autopropulsado, de propulsión automática
**self-propelling** [ˌsɛlfproˈpɛlɪŋ] *adj* autopropulsor
**self-propulsion** [ˌsɛlfproˈpʌlʃən] *s* autopropulsión
**self-protection** [ˌsɛlfprəˈtɛkʃən] *s* autoprotección
**self-recording** [ˌsɛlfrɪˈkɔrdɪŋ] *adj* autorregistrador
**self-regulating** [ˌsɛlfˈrɛgjəˌletɪŋ] *adj* autorregulador
**self-reliance** [ˌsɛlfrɪˈlaɪəns] *s* confianza en sí mismo
**self-reliant** [ˌsɛlfrɪˈlaɪənt] *adj* confiado en sí mismo
**self-reproach** [ˌsɛlfrɪˈprotʃ] *s* culpa que uno se echa a sí mismo
**self-respect** [ˌsɛlfrɪˈspɛkt] *s* decoro, dignidad, respeto de sí mismo
**self-respecting** [ˌsɛlfrɪˈspɛktɪŋ] *adj* decoroso, lleno de dignidad
**self-restraint** [ˌsɛlfrɪˈstrent] *s* dominio sobre sí mismo
**self-righteous** [ˌsɛlfˈraɪtʃəs] *adj* santurrón
**self-sacrifice** [ˌsɛlfˈsækrɪfaɪs] *s* sacrificio de sí mismo
**selfsame** [ˈsɛlfˌsem] *adj* mismísimo
**self-satisfaction** [ˈsɛlfˌsætɪsˈfækʃən] *s* satisfacción de sí mismo
**self-satisfied** [ˌsɛlfˈsætɪsfaɪd] *adj* satisfecho de sí
**self-sealing** [ˌsɛlfˈsilɪŋ] *adj* autotaponador
**self-seeker** [ˌsɛlfˈsikər] *s* egoísta
**self-seeking** [ˌsɛlfˈsikɪŋ] *adj* egoísta; *s* egoísmo
**self-service** [ˈsɛlfˈsʌrvɪs] *s* autoservicio; *adj* de autoservicio
**self-starter** [ˌsɛlfˈstɑrtər] *s* (aut.) arrancador automático, arranque automático
**self-starting** [ˌsɛlfˈstɑrtɪŋ] *adj* de arranque automático
**self-styled** [ˌsɛlfˈstaɪld] *adj* llamado por sí mismo
**self-sufficiency** [ˌsɛlfsəˈfɪʃənsɪ] *s* confianza desmedida en sí mismo; autosuficiencia
**self-sufficient** [ˌsɛlfsəˈfɪʃənt] *adj* excesivamente confiado en sí mismo; autosuficiente
**self-support** [ˌsɛlfsəˈport] *s* mantenimiento económico propio
**self-sustaining** [ˌsɛlfsəsˈtenɪŋ] *adj* que se gana la vida; autosostenido, automantenido
**self-tapping screw** [ˌsɛlfˈtæpɪŋ] *s* tornillo que labra la rosca por sí mismo
**self-taught** [ˌsɛlfˈtɔt] *adj* autodidacto
**self-will** [ˌsɛlfˈwɪl] *s* voluntariedad
**self-willed** [ˌsɛlfˈwɪld] *adj* obstinado, terco
**self-winding clock** [ˌsɛlfˈwaɪndɪŋ] *s* reloj de cuerda automática, reloj de autocuerda
**sell** [sɛl] *s* (slang) estafa, engaño; *va* vender; (slang) hacer aceptar (*p.ej., una idea, un sistema*); **to sell out** realizar, saldar; (slang) vender, traicionar; **to sell someone on something** (slang) hacer aceptar una cosa a una persona, convencer a una persona del valor de una cosa; *vn* venderse, estar de venta; ser aceptado; **to sell for** correr a o por, venderse en (*tantos dólares*); **to sell off** bajar (*el mercado de valores*); **to sell out** venderlo todo, realizar
**seller** [ˈsɛlər] *s* vendedor
**seller's market** *s* mercado del vendedor
**selling race** *s* carrera a reclamar, carrera de ventas
**sellout** [ˈsɛlˌaut] *s* (slang) saldo, realización; (slang) traición; (slang) función de teatro para la que están vendidos todos los asientos
**seltzer** [ˈsɛltsər] *s* agua de seltz
**selvage** o **selvedge** [ˈsɛlvɪdʒ] *s* orillo, vendo, borde; (min.) salbanda
**Sem.** abr. de **Seminary** y **Semitic**
**semantic** [sɪˈmæntɪk] *adj* semántico; **semantics** *ssg* semántica
**semanticist** [sɪˈmæntɪsɪst] *s* semantista
**semaphore** [ˈsɛməfor] *s* semáforo; *va & vn* comunicar por medio de un semáforo
**semaphoric** [ˌsɛməˈfɑrɪk] o **semaphorical** [ˌsɛməˈfɑrɪkəl] *adj* semafórico

**semasiological** [sɪˌmesɪə'lɑdʒɪkəl] *adj* semasiológico
**semasiology** [sɪˌmesɪ'ɑlədʒɪ] *s* semasiología
**semblance** ['sɛmbləns] *s* simulacro, apariencia, imagen
**semeiology** [ˌsimaɪ'ɑlədʒɪ] *s* semiología
**semeiotic** [ˌsimaɪ'ɑtɪk] o **semeiotical** [ˌsimaɪ'ɑtɪkəl] *adj* semiótico; **semeiotics** *ssg* semiótica
**Semele** ['sɛməli] *s* (myth.) Semele
**semen** ['simɛn] (bot. & physiol.) semen
**semester** [sɪ'mɛstər] *s* semestre; *adj* semestral
**semester hour** *s* (educ.) hora semestral
**semiannual** [ˌsɛmɪ'ænjuəl] *adj* semianual
**semiarid** [ˌsɛmɪ'ærɪd] *adj* semiárido
**semiautomatic** [ˌsɛmɪˌɔtə'mætɪk] *adj* semiautomático
**semibreve** ['sɛmɪˌbriv] *s* (mus.) semibreve
**semicadence** [ˌsɛmɪ'kedəns] *s* (mus.) semicadencia
**semicentennial** [ˌsɛmɪsɛn'tɛnɪəl] *adj & s* cincuentenario
**semicircle** ['sɛmɪˌsʌrkəl] *s* semicírculo
**semicircular** [ˌsɛmɪ'sʌrkjələr] *adj* semicircular
**semicircular arch** *s* (arch.) arco de medio punto
**semicircular canal** *s* (anat.) canal semicircular
**semicivilized** [ˌsɛmɪ'sɪvɪlaɪzd] *adj* semicivilizado
**semicoke** ['sɛmɪ'kok] *s* semicoque
**semicolon** ['sɛmɪˌkolən] *s* (gram.) punto y coma
**semiconductor** [ˌsɛmɪkən'dʌktər] *s* (elec.) semiconductor
**semiconscious** [ˌsɛmɪ'kɑnʃəs] *adj* semiconsciente
**semiconsonant** [ˌsɛmɪ'kɑnsənənt] *s* semiconsonante
**semiconsonantal** [ˌsɛmɪˌkɑnsə'næntəl] *adj* semiconsonante
**semicylindrical** [ˌsɛmɪsɪ'lɪndrɪkəl] *adj* semicilíndrico
**semidaily** [ˌsɛmɪ'delɪ] *adv* dos veces al día
**semideponent** [ˌsɛmɪdɪ'ponənt] *adj* (gram.) semideponente
**semidetached** [ˌsɛmɪdɪ'tætʃt] *adj* semiseparado
**semideveloped** [ˌsɛmɪdɪ'vɛləpt] *adj* desarrollado incompletamente, a medio desarrollar
**semidiameter** [ˌsɛmɪdaɪ'æmɪtər] *s* (astr. & geom.) semidiámetro
**semi-Diesel engine** [ˌsɛmɪ'dizəl] *s* semidiesel
**semidivine** [ˌsɛmɪdɪ'vaɪn] *adj* semidivino
**semielliptical** [ˌsɛmɪ·ɪ'lɪptɪkəl] *adj* semielíptico
**semifinal** [ˌsɛmɪ'faɪnəl] *adj & s* (sport) semifinal
**semifluid** [ˌsɛmɪ'fluɪd] *adj* semiflúido
**semilearned** [ˌsɛmɪ'lʌrnɪd] *adj* (philol.) semiculto
**semiliquid** [ˌsɛmɪ'lɪkwɪd] *adj & s* semilíquido
**semilunar** [ˌsɛmɪ'lunər] *adj* semilunar
**semimonthly** [ˌsɛmɪ'mʌnθlɪ] *adj* quincenal; *adv* quincenalmente; *s* (*pl:* **-lies**) periódico quincenal, revista quincenal
**seminal** ['sɛmɪnəl] *adj* seminal; (fig.) primigenio, primordial
**seminar** ['sɛmɪnɑr] o [ˌsɛmɪ'nɑr] *s* seminario
**seminarist** ['sɛmɪˌnɛrɪst] *s* seminarista
**seminary** ['sɛmɪˌnɛrɪ] *s* (*pl:* **-ies**) seminario
**semination** [ˌsɛmɪ'neʃən] *s* sembradura; propagación, diseminación
**seminiferous** [ˌsɛmɪ'nɪfərəs] *adj* seminífero
**Seminole** ['sɛmɪnol] *adj & s* semínola
**semiofficial** [ˌsɛmɪə'fɪʃəl] *adj* semioficial
**semiology** [ˌsimaɪ'ɑlədʒɪ] *s* var. de **semeiology**
**semiotic** [ˌsimaɪ'ɑtɪk] *adj* var. de **semeiotic**
**semipedal** [sɪ'mɪpɪdəl] o [ˌsɛmɪ'pidəl] *adj* semipedal
**Semi-Pelagian** [ˌsɛmɪpɪ'ledʒɪən] *adj & s* semipelagiano
**Semi-Pelagianism** [ˌsɛmɪpɪ'ledʒɪənɪzəm] *s* semipelagianismo
**semipermeable** [ˌsɛmɪ'pʌrmɪəbəl] *adj* semipermeable
**semipopular** [ˌsɛmɪ'pɑpjələr] *adj* semipopular
**semiprecious** [ˌsɛmɪ'prɛʃəs] *adj* semiprecioso, fino
**semiquaver** ['sɛmɪˌkwevər] *s* (mus.) semicorchea
**Semiramis** [sə'mɪrəmɪs] *s* Semíramis
**semirigid** [ˌsɛmɪ'rɪdʒɪd] *adj* (aer.) semirrígido
**semiskilled** [ˌsɛmɪ'skɪld] *adj* medio mecánico
**semisolid** [ˌsɛmɪ'sɑlɪd] *adj & s* semisólido
**Semite** ['sɛmaɪt] o ['simaɪt] *s* semita
**Semitic** [sɪ'mɪtɪk] *adj* semítico; *s* semita (*individuo*); lengua semítica; semítico (*grupo de lenguas*)
**Semitism** ['sɛmɪtɪzəm] o ['simɪtɪzəm] *s* semitismo
**Semitist** ['sɛmɪtɪst] o ['simɪtɪst] *s* semitista
**semitone** ['sɛmɪˌton] *s* (mus.) semitono
**semitrailer** ['sɛmɪˌtrelər] *s* semi-remolque
**semitropical** [ˌsɛmɪ'trɑpɪkəl] *adj* semitropical
**semivocalic** [ˌsɛmɪvo'kælɪk] *adj* semivocal
**semivowel** ['sɛmɪˌvauəl] *s* semivocal
**semiweekly** [ˌsɛmɪ'wiklɪ] *adj* bisemanal; *adv* bisemanalmente; *s* (*pl:* **-lies**) periódico bisemanal, revista bisemanal
**semiyearly** [ˌsɛmɪ'jɪrlɪ] *adj* semestral; *adv* semestralmente
**semolina** [ˌsɛmə'linə] *s* sémola
**sempiternal** [ˌsɛmpɪ'tʌrnəl] *adj* sempiterno
**sempstress** ['sɛmpstrɪs] *s* var. de **seamstress**
**Sen.** o **sen.** abr. de **Senate, Senator** y **Senior**
**senate** ['sɛnɪt] *s* senado
**senator** ['sɛnətər] *s* senador
**senatorial** [ˌsɛnə'torɪəl] *adj* senatorial
**senatorship** ['sɛnətərʃɪp] *s* senaduría
**senatus consultum** [sɪ'netəskən'sʌltəm] *s* (*pl:* **senatus consulta**) senadoconsulto
**send** [sɛnd] (*pret & pp:* **sent**) *va* enviar, mandar; remitir, expedir; lanzar (*una bola, flecha, etc.*); poner (*un telegrama*); **to send away** despedir; despachar; **to send back** reenviar, devolver; **to send down** enviar abajo; mandar bajar; **to send packing** despedir con cajas destempladas; **to send up** enviar arriba; mandar subir; (coll.) enviar a la cárcel; **to send word** mandar recado; **to send to** + *inf* enviar a + *inf; vn* (rad.) transmitir; **to send for** enviar por, enviar a buscar
**sendal** ['sɛndəl] *s* cendal
**sender** ['sɛndər] *s* remitente; (telg.) transmisor
**sending** ['sɛndɪŋ] *s* remisión; (telg.) transmisión
**sending key** *s* (telg.) manipulador
**send-off** ['sɛndˌɔf] o ['sɛndˌɑf] *s* (coll.) empujón; (coll.) despedida afectuosa
**Senegal** [ˌsɛnɪ'gɔl] *s* el Senegal
**Senegalese** [ˌsɛnɪgɔ'liz] *adj* senegalés; *s* (*pl:* **-ese**) senegalés
**senescence** [sɪ'nɛsəns] *s* senescencia
**senescent** [sɪ'nɛsənt] *adj* senescente
**seneschal** ['sɛnɪʃəl] *s* senescal
**senile** ['sinaɪl] o ['sinɪl] *adj* senil
**senility** [sɪ'nɪlɪtɪ] *s* senilidad
**senior** ['sinjər] *adj* mayor, de mayor edad; viejo; del último año; padre, p.ej., **John Jones, Senior,** Juan Jones, padre; *s* mayor; socio más antiguo; alumno del último año
**seniority** [sin'jɑrɪtɪ] o [sin'jɔrɪtɪ] *s* antigüedad, ancianidad; prioridad, precedencia
**senna** ['sɛnə] *s* (bot. & pharm.) sen
**Sennacherib** [sə'nækərɪb] *s* Senaquerib
**sennight** ['sɛnaɪt] *s* (archaic) semana
**sennit** ['sɛnɪt] *s* (naut.) cajeta
**sensation** [sɛn'seʃən] *s* sensación; **to cause a sensation** hacer sensación
**sensational** [sɛn'seʃənəl] *adj* sensacional
**sensationalism** [sɛn'seʃənəlɪzəm] *s* sensacionalismo; (philos.) sensacionalismo, sensacionismo, sensualismo
**sensationalist** [sɛn'seʃənəlɪst] *s* persona que causa sensación; (philos.) sensacionalista, sensacionista
**sense** [sɛns] *s* sentido; opinión; (geom. & mech.) sentido; **in a sense** en cierto sentido; **to be out of one's senses** haber perdido el juicio; **to come to one's senses** volver en sí; recobrar el sentido común; **to make sense** tener sentido, ser razonable; **to make sense out of** comprender, explicarse; *va* intuir, sentir, sospechar; (coll.) comprender
**senseless** ['sɛnslɪs] *adj* falto de sentido, sin

sentido; desmayado, inconsciente; insensato, necio
**sense of guilt** *s* cargo de conciencia
**sense of humor** *s* sentido del humor
**sense organ** *s* órgano sensorio
**sensibility** [ˌsɛnsɪˈbɪlɪtɪ] *s* (*pl:* **-ties**) sensibilidad; susceptibilidad; **sensibilities** *spl* sentimientos delicados
**sensible** [ˈsɛnsɪbəl] *adj* sensato, cuerdo; sensible
**sensitive** [ˈsɛnsɪtɪv] *adj* sensible; susceptible; sensitivo, sensorio; (phot. & rad.) sensible; (phot.) sensibilizado
**sensitiveness** [ˈsɛnsɪtɪvnɪs] *s* sensibilidad; susceptibilidad; (phot. & rad.) sensibilidad
**sensitive plant** *s* (bot.) sensitiva, mimosa vergonzosa
**sensitivity** [ˌsɛnsɪˈtɪvɪtɪ] *s* (*pl:* **-ties**) sensibilidad; susceptibilidad; (phot. & rad.) sensibilidad
**sensitization** [ˌsɛnsɪtɪˈzeʃən] *s* sensibilización
**sensitize** [ˈsɛnsɪtaɪz] *va* sensibilizar; (phot.) sensibilizar
**sensorial** [sɛnˈsorɪəl] *adj* sensorio
**sensorium** [sɛnˈsorɪəm] *s* (*pl:* **-ums** o **-a** [ə]) sensorio
**sensory** [ˈsɛnsərɪ] *adj* sensorio
**sensual** [ˈsɛnʃʊəl] *adj* sensual
**sensualism** [ˈsɛnʃʊəlɪzəm] *s* sensualismo; (philos.) sensualismo
**sensualist** [ˈsɛnʃʊəlɪst] *adj & s* sensualista; (philos.) sensualista
**sensuality** [ˌsɛnʃʊˈælɪtɪ] *s* (*pl:* **-ties**) sensualidad
**sensualize** [ˈsɛnʃʊəlaɪz] *va* hacer sensual; *vn* volverse sensual
**sensually** [ˈsɛnʃʊəlɪ] *adv* sensualmente
**sensuous** [ˈsɛnʃʊəs] *adj* sensual; voluptuoso
**sent** [sɛnt] *pret & pp de* **send**
**sentence** [ˈsɛntəns] *s* frase, oración; sentencia; (law) sentencia; *va* sentenciar, condenar
**sentential** [sɛnˈtɛnʃəl] *adj* (gram.) oracional
**sententious** [sɛnˈtɛnʃəs] *adj* sentencioso
**sentience** [ˈsɛnʃəns] *s* sensibilidad
**sentient** [ˈsɛnʃənt] *adj* sensitivo, sensible; *s* ser sensitivo; conciencia
**sentiment** [ˈsɛntɪmənt] *s* sentimiento
**sentimental** [ˌsɛntɪˈmɛntəl] *adj* sentimental
**sentimentalism** [ˌsɛntɪˈmɛntəlɪzəm] *s* sentimentalismo
**sentimentalist** [ˌsɛntɪˈmɛntəlɪst] *s* sentimentalista
**sentimentality** [ˌsɛntɪmɛnˈtælɪtɪ] *s* (*pl:* **-ties**) sentimentalismo
**sentimentalize** [ˌsɛntɪˈmɛntəlaɪz] *va* hacer sentimental; tratar sentimentalmente; *vn* obrar sentimentalmente, afectar sentimiento
**sentinel** [ˈsɛntɪnəl] *s* centinela; **to stand sentinel** estar de centinela, hacer centinela
**sentry** [ˈsɛntrɪ] *s* (*pl:* **-tries**) centinela
**sentry box** *s* garita de centinela
**Seoul** [seˈul] o [sol] *s* Seúl
**sepal** [ˈsipəl] o [ˈsɛpəl] *s* (bot.) sépalo
**separable** [ˈsɛpərəbəl] *adj* separable
**separably** [ˈsɛpərəblɪ] *adv* separablemente
**separate** [ˈsɛpərɪt] *adj* separado; suelto; [ˈsɛpəret] *va* separar; *vn* separarse
**separately** [ˈsɛpərɪtlɪ] *adv* separadamente
**separation** [ˌsɛpəˈreʃən] *s* separación
**separatism** [ˈsɛpərɪtɪzəm] *s* separatismo
**separatist** [ˈsɛpərɪtɪst] *adj & s* separatista
**separative** [ˈsɛpəˌretɪv] *adj* separativo
**separator** [ˈsɛpəˌretər] *s* separador (*persona; máquina*); (elec.) separador (*de las placas de un acumulador*)
**Sephardic** [sɪˈfɑrdɪk] *adj* sefardí o sefardita
**Sephardim** [sɪˈfɑrdɪm] *spl* sefardíes
**sepia** [ˈsipɪə] *s* sepia (*pez, tinta, pigmento, color, estampado*); *adj* sepia, a la sepia
**sepia paper** *s* (phot.) papel sepia
**sepoy** [ˈsipɔɪ] *s* cipayo
**seps** [sɛps] *s* (zool.) eslizón, sepedón
**sepsis** [ˈsɛpsɪs] *s* (path.) sepsis
**Sept.** abr. de **September**
**septal** [ˈsɛptəl] *adj* septal
**September** [sɛpˈtɛmbər] *s* septiembre
**septenary** [ˈsɛptɪˌnɛrɪ] *adj* septenario; *s* (*pl:* **-ies**) septena; septenio
**septennial** [sɛpˈtɛnɪəl] *adj* que dura siete años; que ocurre una vez en siete años
**septentrional** [sɛpˈtɛntrɪənəl] *adj* septentrional
**septet** o **septette** [sɛpˈtɛt] *s* septena; (mus.) septeto
**septfoil** [ˈsɛptˌfɔɪl] *s* (bot.) sieteenrama
**septic** [ˈsɛptɪk] *adj* séptico
**septicemia** o **septicaemia** [ˌsɛptɪˈsimɪə] *s* (path.) septicemia
**septicidal** [ˌsɛptɪˈsaɪdəl] *adj* (bot.) septicida
**septic tank** *s* fosa séptica, pozo séptico
**septifragal** [sɛpˈtɪfrəgəl] *adj* (bot.) septífrago
**septillion** [sɛpˈtɪljən] *s* (U.S.A.) cuatrillón; (Brit.) septillón
**septimole** [ˈsɛptɪmol] *s* (mus.) septillo
**septuagenarian** [ˌsɛptʃʊədʒɪˈnɛrɪən] *adj & s* septuagenario
**septuagenary** [ˌsɛptʃʊˈædʒɪˌnɛrɪ] *adj* septuagenario; *s* (*pl:* **-ies**) septuagenario
**Septuagesima** [ˌsɛptʃʊəˈdʒɛsɪmə] o **Septuagesima Sunday** *s* (eccl.) septuagésima
**Septuagint** [ˈsɛptuədʒɪnt] o [ˈsɛptʃʊədʒɪnt] *s* (Bib.) versión de los Setenta
**septum** [ˈsɛptəm] *s* (*pl:* **-ta** [tə]) (anat.) septo
**septuple** [ˈsɛptʊpəl], [ˈsɛptjʊpəl], [sɛpˈtupəl] o [sɛpˈtjupəl] *adj & s* séptuplo; *va* septuplicar
**septuplication** [sɛpˌtuplɪˈkeʃən] o [sɛpˌtjuplɪˈkeʃən] *s* septuplicación
**sepulcher** [ˈsɛpəlkər] *s* sepulcro; (arch.) sepulcro; *va* sepultar en sepulcro
**sepulchral** [sɪˈpʌlkrəl] *adj* sepulcral; (fig.) sepulcral
**sepulture** [ˈsɛpəltʃər] *s* sepultura (*acción y lugar*); *va* sepultar
**seq.** abr. de **sequentia** (Lat.) **the following**
**sequel** [ˈsikwəl] *s* resultado, secuela; continuación; capítulo final (*de un cuento*)
**sequela** [sɪˈkwilə] *s* (*pl:* **-lae** [li]) secuaz, secuaces; secuela; (med.) secuela
**sequence** [ˈsikwəns] *s* sucesión, orden de sucesión; resultado, consecuencia; secansa, runfla, escalera (*en los naipes*); (eccl., mov. & mus.) secuencia
**sequent** [ˈsikwənt] *adj* subsiguiente; consecutivo; consiguiente; *s* resultado, consecuencia
**sequential** [sɪˈkwenʃəl] *adj* consecutivo; consiguiente
**sequester** [sɪˈkwɛstər] *va* apartar, alejar, segregar; (law) secuestrar
**sequestration** [ˌsikwɛsˈtreʃən] *s* apartamiento; retiro, reclusión; (law) secuestro
**sequestrum** [sɪˈkwɛstrəm] *s* (*pl:* **-tra** [trə]) (med.) secuestro
**sequin** [ˈsikwɪn] *s* lentejuela; cequí (*moneda*)
**sequoia** [sɪˈkwɔɪə] *s* (bot.) secoya
**seraglio** [sɛˈræljo] *s* (*pl:* **-ios**) serrallo
**serape** [sɛˈrɑpe] *s* sarape
**seraph** [ˈsɛrəf] *s* (*pl:* **-aphs** o **-aphim** [əfɪm]) (Bib. & theol.) serafín
**seraphic** [sɪˈræfɪk] *adj* seráfico
**seraphim** [ˈsɛrəfɪm] *pl de* **seraph**
**Serb** [sʌrb] *adj & s* servio
**Serbia** [ˈsʌrbɪə] *s* Servia
**Serbian** [ˈsʌrbɪən] *adj & s* var. de **Serb**
**Serbo-Croatian** [ˌsʌrbokroˈeʃən] *adj & s* servocroata
**sere** [sɪr] *adj* seco, marchito; gastado
**serenade** [ˌsɛrəˈned] *s* serenata; *va* dar serenata a; *vn* dar serenatas
**serendipity** [ˌsɛrənˈdɪpɪtɪ] *s* don de acertar sin buscar
**serene** [sɪˈrin] *adj* sereno
**serenity** [sɪˈrɛnɪtɪ] *s* (*pl:* **-ties**) serenidad; (*cap.*) *s* Serenidad (*título*)
**serf** [sʌrf] *s* siervo de la gleba
**serfdom** [ˈsʌrfdəm] *s* servidumbre de la gleba
**serge** [sʌrdʒ] *s* sarga
**sergeancy** [ˈsɑrdʒənsɪ] *s* (*pl:* **-cies**) sargentía
**sergeant** [ˈsɑrdʒənt] *s* (mil.) sargento; alguacil
**sergeant-at-arms** [ˈsɑrdʒəntətˈɑrmz] *s* (*pl:* **sergeants-at-arms**) oficial de orden
**sergeant major** *s* (*pl:* **sergeant majors**) (mil.) sargento auxiliar del ayudante, suboficial
**sergt.** abr. de **sergeant**
**serial** [ˈsɪrɪəl] *adj* serial; publicado por entregas; (rad.) seriado; *s* cuento por entregas, novela por entregas; (rad.) serial, drama en episodios
**serially** [ˈsɪrɪəlɪ] *adv* en serie, por series; por entregas

**serial number** *s* número de serie
**seriate** ['sɪrɪet] *adj* serial
**seriatim** [,sɪrɪ'etɪm] o [,sɛrɪ'etɪm] *adv* en serie
**sericulture** ['sɛrɪ,kʌltʃər] *s* sericicultura, sericultura
**sericulturist** [,sɛrɪ'kʌltʃərɪst] *s* sericicultor, sericultor
**series** ['sɪrɪz] *s* serie; *adj* (elec.) en serie
**series-wound** ['sɪrɪz,waʊnd] *adj* (elec.) arrollado en serie
**serif** ['sɛrɪf] *s* (print.) trazo fino de adorno (*de una letra*)
**serin** ['sɛrɪn] *s* (orn.) verdecillo
**seriocomic** [,sɪrɪo'kɑmɪk] *adj* jocoserio
**serious** ['sɪrɪəs] *adj* serio
**seriously** ['sɪrɪəslɪ] *adv* seriamente
**seriousness** ['sɪrɪəsnɪs] *s* seriedad
**serjeant** ['sɑrdʒənt] *s* var. de **sergeant**
**sermon** ['sʌrmən] *s* sermón; (fig.) sermón
**sermonize** ['sʌrmənaɪz] *va & vn* sermonear
**sermonizing** ['sʌrmə,naɪzɪŋ] *adj* sermoneador; *s* sermoneo
**Sermon on the Mount** *s* (Bib.) sermón de la Montaña
**serology** [sɪ'rɑlədʒɪ] *s* serología
**seroon** [sə'run] *s* churla
**serosity** [sɪ'rɑsɪtɪ] *s* (med. & physiol.) serosidad
**serotinous** [sɪ'rɑtɪnəs] *adj* (bot.) serondo o serótino
**serous** ['sɪrəs] *adj* seroso
**serous membrane** *s* (anat.) membrana serosa
**serpent** ['sʌrpənt] *s* serpiente; buscapiés, carretilla (*cohete*); (mus.) serpentón (*instrumento de viento*); (fig.) serpiente (*persona traidora; el demonio*); (*cap.*) *s* (astr.) Serpiente
**Serpent Bearer** *s* (astr.) Serpentario
**serpentine** ['sʌrpəntin] *s* (mineral.) serpentina; ['sʌrpəntin] o ['sʌrpəntaɪn] *adj* serpentino; *vn* serpentear
**serpiginous** [sər'pɪdʒɪnəs] *adj* serpiginoso
**serpigo** [sər'paɪgo] *s* (path.) serpigo
**serrate** ['sɛret] o **serrated** ['sɛretɪd] *adj* serrado
**serration** [sɛ'reʃən] *s* endentadura
**serratus** [sɛ'retəs] *s* (anat.) serrato
**serried** ['sɛrɪd] *adj* apretado
**serrulate** ['sɛrjəlet] *adj* dentelado
**serum** ['sɪrəm] *s* (*pl:* **-rums** o **-ra** [rə]) (biol. & med.) suero; suero de la leche
**serum therapy** *s* seroterapia
**serval** ['sʌrvəl] *s* (zool.) serval
**servant** ['sʌrvənt] *s* criado, servidor, sirviente
**servant girl** *s* muchacha de servir
**servant problem** *s* crisis del servicio doméstico
**serve** [sʌrv] *s* (tennis) servicio, saque; *va* servir; abastecer, proporcionar; maniobrar (*un cañón*); cubrir (*a la hembra*); cumplir (*una condena*); (law) entregar (*una citación*); (naut.) aforrar (*un cable*); (tennis) servir; **to serve right** merecerlo bien, p.ej., **it serves me right** bien me lo merezco; *vn* servir; (tennis & mil.) servir; **to serve as** servir de
**server** ['sʌrvər] *s* criado, servidor; mozo de comedor, mozo de café; (tennis) sacador, servidor; (eccl.) acólito; bandeja
**Servia** ['sʌrvɪə] *s* var. de **Serbia**
**Servian** ['sʌrvɪən] *adj & s* var. de **Serbian**
**service** ['sʌrvɪs] *s* servicio; (naut.) forro de cable; (law) entrega; **at your service** para servir a Vd.; **in service** funcionando; **out of service** descompuesto; **the service** el ejército; la marina; la aviación; **the services** las fuerzas armadas; **to be of service (to)** servir; *va* instalar; mantener, reparar
**serviceability** [,sʌrvɪsə'bɪlɪtɪ] *s* utilidad; estabilidad; complacencia
**serviceable** ['sʌrvɪsəbəl] *adj* servible, útil; duradero; servicial, complaciente
**serviceberry** ['sʌrvɪs,bɛrɪ] *s* (*pl:* **-ries**) (bot.) guillomo (*arbusto y fruto*); (bot.) serbal (*árbol*); serba (*fruto*)
**service ceiling** *s* (aer.) techo de servicio
**service dress** *s* (mil. & nav.) uniforme diario
**service entrance** *s* entrada para el servicio
**service line** (tennis) línea de saque o servicio; (tennis) línea de fondo
**serviceman** ['sʌrvɪs,mæn] *s* (*pl:* **-men**) empleado de servicio, reparador, mecánico; (mil.) militar
**service record** *s* hoja de servicios
**service station** *s* estación de servicio, taller de reparaciones, gasolinera
**service stripe** *s* galón de servicio
**service tree** *s* (bot.) acafresna, serbal
**serviette** [,sʌrvɪ'ɛt] *s* servilleta
**servile** ['sʌrvɪl] *adj* servil
**servility** [sər'vɪlɪtɪ] *s* (*pl:* **-ties**) servilismo
**serving** ['sʌrvɪŋ] *s* porción (*de un alimento*)
**serving mallet** *s* (naut.) maceta de aforrar
**serving table** *s* pequeño aparador, mesa para el servicio de los manjares
**servitor** ['sʌrvɪtər] *s* servidor; secuaz, partidario
**servitude** ['sʌrvɪtjud] o ['sʌrvɪtud] *s* servidumbre; trabajos forzados; (law) servidumbre
**servo brake** ['sʌrvo] *s* servofreno
**servo control** *s* (aer.) servocontrol
**servomechanism** [,sʌrvo'mɛkənɪzəm] *s* servomecanismo
**servomotor** [,sʌrvo'motər] *s* (mach.) servomotor
**sesame** ['sɛsəmɪ] *s* (bot.) sésamo, ajonjolí; sésamo (*palabra mágica*); **open sesame** sésamo ábrete
**sesamoid** ['sɛsəmɔɪd] o **sesamoidal** [,sɛsə'mɔɪdəl] *adj* sesamoideo
**sesquialtera** [,sɛskwɪ'æltərə] *s* (mus.) sesquiáltera (*intervalo; juego de órgano*)
**sesquialteral** [,sɛskwɪ'æltərəl] *adj* sesquiáltero
**sesquicentennial** [,sɛskwɪsɛn'tɛnɪəl] *adj & s* sesquicentenario
**sesquipedalian** [,sɛskwɪpɪ'delɪən] *adj* sesquipedal (*de pie y medio de largo; excesivamente largo*); que emplea palabras sesquipedales; *s* palabra sesquipedal
**sessile** ['sɛsɪl] *adj* (bot.) sésil, sentado
**session** ['sɛʃən] *s* sesión; período escolar; **to be in session** sesionar
**sessional** ['sɛʃənəl] *adj* de una sesión; de cada sesión
**sestet** [sɛs'tɛt] *s* (mus.) sexteto; dos tercetos (*de un soneto*)
**set** [sɛt] *s* juego (*de libros, sillas, etc.*); tren (*p.ej., de engranajes*); aderezo (*p.ej., de diamantes*); pareja (*p.ej., de caballos*); partida (*de tenis*); servicio (*de mesa*); equipo; grupo, clase; batería (*de utensilios de cocina*); (mov.) plató; (rad., telg. & telp.) aparato; (theat.) decoración; colocación, disposición; porte, postura; caída, ajuste (*de una prenda de vestir*); dirección, tendencia; vuelta; muestra (*del perro en acecho de la caza*); planta de transplantar; pie de árbol; triscamiento de los dientes (*de una sierra*); endurecimiento (*de la cola*); fraguado (*del cemento o yeso*); **set of artificial teeth** caja de dientes postizos, dentadura artificial; **set of dishes** servicio de mesa, vajilla; **set of teeth** dentadura ‖ *adj* resuelto, determinado; inflexible, obstinado; fijo, firme, sólido; meditado, estudiado; **set price** precio fijo; ‖ (*pret & pp:* **set;** *ger:* **setting**) *va* poner; asentar, colocar; establecer, instalar; arreglar, preparar; adornar; apostar; poner (*un reloj*) en hora; reenvidar (*en el juego de bridge*); poner, meter, pegar (*fuego*); fijar, determinar (*el precio*); expresar, escribir; poner a empollar (*una gallina*); montar, engastar (*una piedra preciosa*); cuajar (*un líquido*); encasar (*un hueso dislocado*); disponer (*los tipos*); triscar, trabar (*los dientes de la sierra*); armar, colocar (*una trampa*); fijar (*el peinado*); poner (*la mesa*); **to be set** perder (*en el juego de bridge*); **to set afire** poner fuego a, pegar fuego a; **to set an example** dar ejemplo; **to set apart** o **aside** reservar, poner a un lado; **to set back** parar, detener; poner obstáculos a; hacer retroceder; atrasar o retrasar (*p.ej., un reloj*); **to set down** deponer, depositar; poner por escrito; atribuir; **to set forth** exponer, dar a conocer; **to set off** hacer estallar, hacer saltar; poner de relieve; **to set on** azuzar; **to set one's jaws** apretar las quijadas; **to set one's heart on** tener la esperanza puesta en; **to set one's teeth** apretar los dientes; **to set out** sacar y disponer; **to set right** enmendar, corregir; **to set sail** hacerse a la vela; **to set someone against** poner a una persona mal con; **to set store by** dar mucha importancia a; **to set to music** poner música a; **to set**

**up** levantar, construir; armar, montar; comenzar, emprender; ensalzar; regocijar; (print.) componer; **to set up shop** poner tienda; **to set up the drinks** (coll.) convidar a beber ‖ *vn* ponerse (*dícese del Sol, la Luna, etc.*); cuajarse (*un líquido*); endurecerse (*la cola*); fraguar (*el cemento, el yeso*); empollar (*una gallina*); estar de muestra (*un perro de caza*); caer, sentar (*una prenda de vestir*); tender; **to set about** + *ger* ponerse a + *inf;* **to set forth** ponerse en camino; **to set in** aparecer, comenzar, declararse; fluir (*la marea*); **to set off** salir, partir; **to set out** ponerse en camino; emprender un negocio; **to set out for** salir para, partir para; **to set out to** + *inf* ponerse a + *inf;* **to set to work** poner manos a la obra; **to set upon** atacar, acometer

**setaceous** [sɪˈteʃəs] *adj* cerdoso; setáceo

**setback** [ˈsɛt,bæk] *s* revés, contrariedad; (arch.) retraqueo

**set-in** [ˈsɛt,ɪn] *adj* empotrado

**setoff** [ˈsɛt,ɔf] o [ˈsɛt,ɑf] *s* salida, partida; adorno; compensación

**setscrew** [ˈsɛt,skru] *s* tornillo de presión

**settee** [sɛˈti] *s* canapé, sofá; banco (*con respaldo y brazos*)

**settee bed** *s* canapé cama, sofá cama

**setter** [ˈsɛtər] *s* (print.) compositor, cajista; sétter (*perro de muestra*)

**setting** [ˈsɛtɪŋ] *s* armadura, marco; engaste, montadura; fraguado (*del cemento*); puesta, ocaso (*p.ej., del Sol*); (theat.) puesta en escena, decoración; (theat.) escena

**setting-up exercises** [ˈsɛtɪŋˈʌp] *spl* ejercicios sin aparatos, gimnasia sueca

**settle** [ˈsɛtəl] *s* banco largo; *va* asentar, colocar; asegurar, fijar; acabar; componer, conciliar; templar, moderar, calmar; determinar, decidir; hacer compacto; solidificar; hacer depositar; matar (*el polvo*); dar una profesión a; casar; poblar, colonizar; ajustar, arreglar (*cuentas*); **to settle on** o **upon** dar en dote, dar en propiedad; *vn* asentarse (*un líquido, un edificio*); arraigar, establecerse; componerse; templarse, moderarse, calmarse; hacerse compacto; solidificarse; **to settle down** irse lentamente a fondo (*un buque*); aflojar el paso; formalizarse; **to settle down to work** ponerse seriamente a trabajar; **to settle on** fijar, señalar (*p.ej., una fecha*); escoger

**settlement** [ˈsɛtəlmənt] *s* establecimiento; composición; determinación, decisión; colonización; colonia; caserío, poblado; pago, arreglo, ajuste (*de cuentas*); casa de beneficencia; (law) asignación, traspaso (*de bienes*)

**settlement house** *s* casa de beneficencia

**settlement worker** *s* persona que se consagra al servicio de una casa de beneficiencia

**settler** [ˈsɛtlər] *s* fundador; colono, poblador; (coll.) fin, golpe de gracia

**settling** [ˈsɛtlɪŋ] *s* asiento, sentamiento; colonización; **settlings** *spl* heces, zurrapas

**set-to** [ˈsɛt,tu] *s* (*pl:* **-tos**) (coll.) lucha, combate, disputa

**setup** [ˈsɛt,ʌp] *s* porte, postura; disposición (*p.ej., de las partes de una máquina*); (coll.) organización; (slang) invitación a beber, bebida

**setwall** [ˈsɛtwɔl] *s* (bot.) valeriana

**seven** [ˈsɛvən] *adj* siete; *s* siete; **seven o'clock** las siete

**seven deadly sins** *spl* siete pecados capitales

**sevenfold** [ˈsɛvən,fold] *adj & s* séptuplo; *adv* siete veces

**Seven Hills** *spl* siete colinas (*de Roma*)

**seven hundred** *adj & s* setecientos

**seven seas** *spl* todos los mares del mundo

**seventeen** [ˈsɛvənˈtin] *adj & s* diecisiete o diez y siete

**seventeenth** [ˈsɛvənˈtinθ] *adj* décimoséptimo; diecisieteavo; *s* décimoséptimo; diecisieteavo; diecisiete (*en las fechas*)

**seventeen-year locust** [ˈsɛvən,tin,jɪr] *s* (ent.) cigarra norteamericana cuya larva vive hasta diecisiete años (*Cicada septendecim*)

**seventh** [ˈsɛvənθ] *adj* séptimo; *s* séptimo; siete (*en las fechas*); (mus.) séptima

**seventh day** *s* sábado, el séptimo día de la semana

**seventh-day** [ˈsɛvənθ,de] *adj* sabatino

**Seventh-Day Adventist** *s* adventista del séptimo día

**seventh heaven** *s* séptimo cielo; (coll.) séptimo cielo (*felicidad suprema*); **to be in seventh heaven** (coll.) estar en sus glorias

**seventieth** [ˈsɛvəntɪɪθ] *adj & s* septuagésimo; setentavo

**seventy** [ˈsɛvəntɪ] *adj* setenta; *s* (*pl:* **-ties**) setenta

**Seven Wonders of the World** *spl* siete maravillas del mundo

**Seven Years' War** *s* guerra de los Siete Años

**sever** [ˈsɛvər] *va* separar, desunir; romper (*relaciones*); *vn* separarse, desunirse

**several** [ˈsɛvərəl] *adj* varios, diversos; distintos, respectivos; *spl* varios; algunos

**severally** [ˈsɛvərəlɪ] *adv* separadamente; respectivamente

**severalty** [ˈsɛvərəltɪ] *s* (*pl:* **-ties**) singularidad; (law) posesión privativa

**severance** [ˈsɛvərəns] *s* separación; ruptura (*p.ej., de las relaciones diplomáticas*)

**severance pay** *s* indemnización por despido

**severe** [sɪˈvɪr] *adj* severo; riguroso (*tiempo*); violento, recio

**severity** [sɪˈvɛrɪtɪ] *s* (*pl:* **-ties**) severidad; rigor; violencia

**Severn** [ˈsɛvərn] *s* Severna

**Seville** [səˈvɪl] o [ˈsɛvɪl] *s* Sevilla

**Sevillian** [səˈvɪljən] *adj & s* sevillano

**sew** [so] (*pret:* **sewed;** *pp:* **sewed** o **sewn**) *va & vn* coser

**sewage** [ˈsuɪdʒ] o [ˈsjuɪdʒ] *s* aguas de albañal, aguas fecales

**sewage disposal** *s* depuración de aguas fecales

**sewer** [ˈsuər] o [ˈsjuər] *s* albañal, cloaca, alcantarilla; mayordomo de comedor, jefe de los mozos; *va* alcantarillar; [ˈsoər] *s* persona que cose, costurera, sastre, etc.; (ent.) arrolladora, torcedora

**sewerage** [ˈsuərɪdʒ] o [ˈsjuərɪdʒ] *s* desagüe; alcantarillado (*sistema*); aguas de albañal

**sewer gas** [ˈsuər] o [ˈsjuər] *s* gas cloacal

**sewing** [ˈso·ɪŋ] *s* costura; *adj* de coser, para coser

**sewing basket** *s* cesta de costura, canastilla de la costura

**sewing bee** *s* reunión para hacer costura

**sewing circle** *s* círculo de costura

**sewing machine** *s* máquina de coser

**sewing press** *s* (b.b.) telar

**sewn** [son] *pp de* **sew**

**sex** [sɛks] *s* sexo; **the fair sex** o **the gentle sex** el bello sexo; **the sterner sex** o **the stronger sex** el sexo feo o el sexo fuerte; **the weaker sex** el sexo débil; *adj* sexual

**sexagenarian** [,sɛksədʒɪˈnɛrɪən] *adj & s* sexagenario

**sexagenary** [sɛksˈædʒɪ,nɛrɪ] *adj* sexagenario; *s* (*pl:* **-ies**) sexagenario

**Sexagesima** [,sɛksəˈdʒɛsɪmə] o **Sexagesima Sunday** *s* (eccl.) sexagésima

**sexagesimal** [,sɛksəˈdʒɛsɪməl] *adj* sexagesimal

**sexangle** [ˈsɛks,æŋgəl] *s* (geom.) sexángulo

**sex appeal** *s* atracción sexual; atracción o encanto femenino

**sex chromosome** *s* (biol.) cromosoma sexual

**sexennial** [sɛksˈɛnɪəl] *adj* sexenal

**sex hygiene** *s* higiene sexual

**sex-linkage** [ˈsɛks,lɪŋkɪdʒ] *s* (biol.) herencia ligada al sexo

**sex-linked** [ˈsɛks,lɪŋkt] *adj* (biol.) ligado al sexo

**sexologist** [sɛksˈɑlədʒɪst] *s* sexólogo

**sexology** [sɛksˈɑlədʒɪ] *s* sexología

**sext** [sɛkst] *s* (eccl.) sexta

**sextain** [ˈsɛksten] *s* sextilla

**sextan** [ˈsɛkstən] *adj* sextano; *s* (path.) fiebre sextana

**sextant** [ˈsɛkstənt] *s* (math.) sexta parte del círculo; sextante (*instrumento*); (*cap.*) *s* (astr.) Sextante

**sextet** o **sextette** [sɛksˈtɛt] *s* grupo de seis; (mus.) sexteto

**sextile** [ˈsɛkstɪl] *adj* (astrol.) sextil

**sextillion** [sɛksˈtɪljən] *s* (Brit.) sextillón

**sexton** [ˈsɛkstən] *s* sacristán

**sextuple** [ˈsɛkstupəl], [ˈsɛkstjupəl], [sɛks-

'tupəl] o [sɛks'tjupəl] *adj & s* séxtuplo; *va* sextuplicar; *vn* sextuplicarse
**sextuplet** ['sɛkstuplɛt], ['sɛkstjuplɛt], [sɛks'tuplɛt] o [sɛks'tjuplɛt] *s* grupo de seis; uno de seis nacidos a un tiempo; (mus.) seisillo
**sextuplication** [sɛks,tuplɪ'keʃən] o [sɛks,tjuplɪ'keʃən] *s* sextuplicación
**sexual** ['sɛkʃuəl] *adj* sexual
**sexual intercourse** *s* comercio sexual
**sexuality** [,sɛkʃu'ælɪtɪ] *s* sexualidad
**sexy** ['sɛksɪ] *adj* (*comp:* **-ier;** *super:* **-iest**) (slang) sicalíptico
**sfumato** [sfu'mato] *adj* (paint.) esfumado
**s.g.** abr. de **specific gravity**
**sgraffito** [zgraf'fito] *s* (f.a.) esgrafiado
**Sgt.** abr. de **Sergeant**
**shabby** ['ʃæbɪ] *adj* (*comp:* **-bier;** *super:* **-biest**) raído, usado, gastado; andrajoso, desaseado; vil, ruin
**shabby-genteel** ['ʃæbɪdʒen'til] *adj* pobre pero de aspecto digno
**shack** [ʃæk] *s* choza, casucha
**shackle** ['ʃækəl] *s* grillete, grillo; maniota (*con que se ata un animal*); (fig.) traba, impedimento; **shackles** *spl* grillos, cadenas, esposas; *va* poner grilletes a, poner esposas a; encadenar; (fig.) trabar, poner obstáculos a
**shackle bolt** *s* perno de horquilla, bulón de grillete
**shad** [ʃæd] *s* (ichth.) sábalo
**shadberry** ['ʃæd,bɛrɪ] *s* (*pl:* **-ries**) (bot.) cornillo, cornijuelo, guillomo; (bot.) níspero del Canadá (*arbusto y fruto*)
**shadblossom** ['ʃæd,blɑsəm] *s* flor de níspero del Canadá
**shadbush** ['ʃæd,buʃ] *s* (bot.) cornillo, cornijuelo, guillomo; (bot.) níspero del Canadá
**shaddock** ['ʃædək] *s* (bot.) pamplemusa (*árbol y fruto*)
**shade** [ʃed] *s* sombra; pantalla (*de lámpara*); cortina, visillo, estor (*de una ventana*); cortina de resorte; matiz (*diferencia muy pequeña*); **in the shade** o **into the shade** a la sombra; (fig.) en condición inferior; **the shades** las tinieblas; las sombras (*de los muertos*); *va* sombrear; obscurecer; rebajar ligeramente (*el precio*); (f.a.) sombrear; *vn* cambiar poco a poco
**shadeless** ['ʃedlɪs] *adj* privado de sombra
**shade tree** *s* árbol de sombra
**shad fly** *s* (ent.) cachipolla
**shading** ['ʃedɪŋ] *s* sombreo; sombreado; matiz; ligera rebaja (*en los precios*)
**shadow** ['ʃædo] *s* sombra; (fig.) sombra (*vestigio; espectro; amparo, protección; parte obscura; persona que sigue a otra por todas partes*); aspecto triste; **in the shadow of** dentro de la sombra de; muy cerca de; **the shadows** las tinieblas; *va* sombrear; representar o indicar vagamente; simbolizar; acechar, espiar, seguir (*a una persona*) como su propia sombra; (f.a.) sombrear, matizar; entristecer; **to shadow forth** representar vagamente, representar de un modo profético
**shadowboxing** ['ʃædo,bɑksɪŋ] *s* (sport) boxeo con un adversario imaginario
**shadowgraph** ['ʃædo,græf] o ['ʃædo,grɑf] *s* radiografía; sombras chinescas
**shadowless** ['ʃædolɪs] *adj* sin sombra
**shadow play** *s* (theat.) sombras chinescas
**shadowy** ['ʃædo·ɪ] o ['ʃædəwɪ] *adj* sombroso; vago, ligero, indefinido; imaginario, quimérico; simbólico
**shady** ['ʃedɪ] *adj* (*comp:* **-ier;** *super:* **-iest**) sombrío, umbroso; (coll.) sospechoso; (coll.) deshonroso, de mala fama; (coll.) verde (*cuento*); **on the shady side of** más allá de (*cierta edad*); **to keep shady** (slang) no dejarse ver
**shaft** [ʃæft] o [ʃɑft] *s* dardo, flecha, saeta; astil (*de flecha; de pluma*); mango (*p.ej., de martillo*); rayo (*de luz*); vara alcándara, limonera, fuste (*de un coche o carro*); pozo (*de mina; de ascensor*); caña, fuste (*de columna*); asta (*de una bandera*); (mach.) árbol, eje; (bot.) tallo, vástago; (bot.) pezón, pedúnculo; (fig.) dardo (*para ridiculizar a una persona*)
**shaft furnace** *s* horno de cuba
**shag** [ʃæg] *s* pelo áspero y lanudo; lana áspera; felpa; tripe (*tejido*); picadura de tabaco muy ordinario
**shagbark** ['ʃæg,bɑrk] *s* (bot.) nuez dura
**shaggy** ['ʃægɪ] *adj* (*comp:* **-gier;** *super:* **-giest**) peludo, velludo, hirsuto; lanudo; afelpado; áspero
**shagreen** [ʃə'grin] *s* chagrín; lija, zapa; *adj* achagrinado
**shah** [ʃɑ] *s* chah
**shake** [ʃek] *s* sacudida, sacudimiento; (coll.) temblor, terremoto; (coll.) apretón de manos; (slang) instante, momento; grieta, hendedura; (mus.) trino; (coll.) batido (*de leche*); **no great shakes** (coll.) poco extraordinario, poco importante; (*pret:* **shook;** *pp:* **shaken**) *va* sacudir; arrojar con una sacudida; agitar; volver (*la cabeza*) de un lado a otro (*en señal de negación*); hacer temblar; estrechar, apretar (*la mano a uno*); hacer ondear; perturbar, inquietar; (slang) zafarse de; **to shake down** bajar sacudiendo; hacer depositar; poner en condiciones de funcionar; (slang) sacar dinero a; **to shake off** sacudir; arrojar con una sacudida; dar esquinazo a, zafarse de; **to shake up** agitar, sacudir con violencia; cambiar bruscamente, trastornar; reorganizar; *vn* sacudirse, agitarse; ondear, bambolearse; temblar; (mus.) trinar; (fig.) agitarse, perturbarse, inquietarse; **to shake with cold** tiritar de frío; **shake!** (coll.) ¡vengan esos cinco!, ¡estrechémoslas!, ¡choque Vd. esos cinco!
**shakedown** ['ʃek,daun] *s* cama improvisada; prueba, ensayo; (slang) concusión, exacción de dinero por compulsión
**shakedown cruise** *s* (nav.) crucero de ensayo (*para comprobar la nave o aclimatar al personal*)
**shaken** ['ʃekən] *pp de* **shake**
**shaker** ['ʃekər] *s* sacudidor; agitador (*aparato*); espolvoreador (*utensilio*)
**Shakespearian** o **Shakesperian** [ʃek'spɪrɪən] *adj & s* shakespeariano o shakespiriano
**shake-up** ['ʃek,ʌp] *s* profunda conmoción; cambio de personal, reorganización completa
**shako** ['ʃæko] o ['ʃeko] *s* (*pl:* **-os**) chacó
**Shaksperian** [ʃek'spɪrɪən] *adj & s* var. de **Shakespearian**
**shaky** ['ʃekɪ] *adj* (*comp:* **-ier;** *super:* **-iest**) trémulo, vacilante; débil; falto de crédito, indigno de confianza
**shale** [ʃel]] *s* pizarra
**shale oil** *s* aceite de pizarra bituminosa, aceite esquistoso
**shall** [ʃæl] (*cond:* **should**) *v aux* se emplea para formar (1) el futuro de ind, p.ej., **I shall arrive** llegaré; (2) el futuro perfecto de ind, p.ej., **I shall have arrived** habré llegado; y (3) el modo potencial, p.ej., **what shall he do?** ¿qué ha de hacer?, ¿qué debe hacer?
**shalloon** [ʃæ'lun] *s* chalón
**shallop** ['ʃæləp] *s* chalupa
**shallot** [ʃə'lɑt] *s* (bot.) chalote
**shallow** ['ʃælo] *adj* bajo, poco profundo; (fig.) superficial, frívolo; *s* bajo, bajío; *va* hacer menos profundo; *vn* hacerse menos profundo
**shaly** ['ʃelɪ] *adj* pizarreño
**sham** [ʃæm] *s* fingimiento, pretexto, engaño, falsificación; farsante; cubierta de adorno; *adj* fingido, falso; postizo; (*pret & pp:* **shammed;** *ger:* **shamming**) *va & vn* fingir
**shaman** ['ʃɑmən] o ['ʃæmən] *s* chamán; hechicero
**sham battle** *s* simulacro de combate
**shamble** ['ʃæmbəl] *s* bamboleo; **shambles** *spl* o *ssg* matadero, degolladero; matanza, carnicería, lugar de gran matanza; **to leave a shambles** dejar (*un sitio*) arruinado, en desorden; *vn* andar bamboleándose
**shame** [ʃem] *s* vergüenza; deshonra; **for shame!** ¡qué vergüenza! **to be a shame** ser una mala vergüenza; **to bring shame upon** deshonrar; **to put to shame** avergonzar; superar, aventajar; **what a shame!** ¡qué lástima!; **shame on you!** ¡qué vergüenza!, ¡eso está feo para Vd.!; *va* avergonzar; deshonrar
**shamefaced** ['ʃem,fest] *adj* vergonzoso; tímido
**shameful** ['ʃemfəl] *adj* vergonzoso
**shameless** ['ʃemlɪs] *adj* desvergonzado, descarado

**shammer** [ˈʃæmər] *s* fingidor, impostor
**shammy** [ˈʃæmɪ] *s* (*pl:* **-mies**) gamuza (*animal y piel*)
**shampoo** [ʃæmˈpu] *s* champú, lavado de la cabeza; *va* lavar (*la cabeza*); lavar la cabeza a
**shamrock** [ˈʃæmrɑk] *s* (bot.) trébol irlandés; (bot.) trébol blanco; (bot.) acedera menor (*Oxalis acetosella*); (bot.) lupulina (*Medicago lupulina*)
**shanghai** [ˈʃæŋhaɪ] o [ʃæŋˈhaɪ] (*pret & pp:* **-haied;** *ger:* **-haiing**) *va* embarcar emborrachando, embarcar narcotizando; llevarse con violencia, llevarse con engaño
**Shangrila** [ˈʃæŋgrɪˈlɑ] *s* Jauja (*país maravilloso*)
**shank** [ʃæŋk] *s* caña o cañilla de la pierna; pierna (*de un animal*); zanca (*de un ave*); astil, caña, fuste; mango, vástago; caña (*del ancla*); enfranque (*de la suela del zapato*); (print.) árbol; remate, extremidad; **to go** o **to ride on shank's mare** caminar en coche de San Francisco
**shan't** [ʃænt] o [ʃɑnt] contracción de **shall not**
**shantung** [ʃænˈtʌŋ] *s* shantung
**shanty** [ˈʃæntɪ] *s* (*pl:* **-ties**) cabaña pobre o ruda, chabola, choza; (naut.) saloma
**shape** [ʃep] *s* forma; (iron mfg.) perfil; **in bad shape** (coll.) arruinado, descompuesto; (coll.) muy malo, muy enfermo; **out of shape** deformado; descompuesto, desarreglado; **to lick into shape** (coll.) preparar (*una cosa*) para que pueda hacer su servicio; **to put into shape** ordenar, poner en orden; **to take shape** tomar forma; *va* formar; definir, determinar; dirigir; idear, dibujar; *vn* formarse; **to shape up** formarse; desarrollarse bien
**shapeless** [ˈʃeplɪs] *adj* informe
**shapely** [ˈʃeplɪ] *adj* (*comp:* **-lier;** *super:* **-liest**) bien formado, bien hecho, esbelto
**shard** [ʃɑrd] *s* fragmento, tiesto, casco; élitro (*de los coleópteros*)
**share** [ʃɛr] *s* parte, porción; reja (*del arado*); (com.) acción; **on shares** participando en los riesgos y la ganancia; **to go shares** participar; *va* repartir; tener parte en, usar juntos de, poseer en común; *vn* participar, tener parte
**sharecropper** [ˈʃɛrˌkrɑpər] *s* aparcero, mediero
**shareholder** [ˈʃɛrˌholdər] *s* (com.) accionista
**shark** [ʃɑrk] *s* (ichth.) tiburón; estafador, gato; (slang) experto, perito
**sharkskin** [ˈʃɑrkˌskɪn] *s* lija, zapa; tejido de algodón o rayón (*para trajes*)
**sharp** [ʃɑrp] *adj* agudo, afilado; anguloso; fuerte, pronunciado (*dícese de una curva o pendiente*); nítido (*dícese de una fotografía*); rápido, veloz (*dícese del paso de una persona*); fogoso, violento; fuerte, vehemente; atento, despierto; picante, mordaz; penetrante; vivo, listo; fino (*oído*); (phonet.) sordo; (mus.) sostenido; (slang) elegante; **sharp features** facciones bien marcadas; **sharp taste** sabor acre; **sharp temper** genio áspero; **sharp tuning** (rad.) sintonía afilada; **sharp turn** vuelta repentina; *adv* agudamente; en punto, p.ej., **at three o'clock sharp** a las tres en punto; *s* (mus.) sostenido; estafador; (coll.) experto, perito; **sharps** *spl* parte del trigo a la que hay que dar la segunda molienda
**sharpen** [ˈʃɑrpən] *va* aguzar, afilar, sacar punta a; *vn* afilarse
**sharpener** [ˈʃɑrpənər] *s* aguzador, afilador; máquina de afilar
**sharper** [ˈʃɑrpər] *s* fullero, caballero de industria
**sharpie** [ˈʃɑrpɪ] *s* embarcación de fondo plano con una o dos velas triangulares
**sharpness** [ˈʃɑrpnɪs] *s* agudeza; angulosidad; nitidez; rapidez, velocidad; fuerza, violencia
**sharp-nosed** [ˈʃɑrpˌnozd] *adj* de nariz puntiaguda; de finísimo olfato
**sharp-set** [ˈʃɑrpˌsɛt] *adj* famélico, hambriento; ávido, ansioso; de borde afilado
**sharpshooter** [ˈʃɑrpˌʃutər] *s* tirador certero; (mil.) tirador distinguido
**sharp-sighted** [ˈʃɑrpˌsaɪtɪd] *adj* de vista penetrante; listo, perspicaz
**sharp-witted** [ˈʃɑrpˌwɪtɪd] *adj* penetrante, perspicaz
**shatter** [ˈʃætər] *va* romper, hacer astillas, hacer pedazos, romper de un golpe; destruir, destrozar; quebrantar (*la salud*); agitar, perturbar; *vn* romperse, hacerse pedazos; **shatters** *spl* fragmentos, pedazos
**shatterproof** [ˈʃætərˈpruf] *adj* inastillable
**shattery** [ˈʃætərɪ] *adj* saltadizo
**shave** [ʃev] *s* afeitado; raedura; rascador; rebanada delgada; **to have a close shave** (coll.) escapar en una tabla; (*pret:* **shaved;** *pp:* **shaved** o **shaven**) *va* afeitar (*la cara*); raer, raspar; rebanar (*en porciones muy delgadas*); rozar (*raer la superficie de; pasar tocando la superficie de; cortar muy justo*); (carp.) cepillar, alisar, rascar; (taur.) afeitar (*las astas del toro*); *vn* afeitarse; estafar, ser duro en un negocio
**shaveling** [ˈʃevlɪŋ] *s* jovenzuelo; (scornful) fraile, monje
**shaven** [ˈʃevən] *pp de* **shave**
**shaver** [ˈʃevər] *s* barbero; máquina de afeitar; alisador, rascador; (coll.) muchachito
**Shavian** [ˈʃevɪən] *adj & s* shaviano
**shaving** [ˈʃevɪŋ] *s* afeitado; viruta (*de madera, metal, etc.*)
**shaving brush** *s* brocha de afeitar, escobilla de afeitar o de barba
**shaving cream** *s* crema de afeitar
**shaving foam** *s* espuma de afeitar
**shaving soap** *s* jabón de afeitar, jabón para la barba
**shawl** [ʃɔl] *s* chal, mantón
**shawm** [ʃɔm] *s* (mus.) caramillo
**shay** [ʃe] *s* (coll.) silla volante (*coche ligero*)
**she** [ʃi] *pron pers* (*pl:* **they**) ella; *s* (*pl:* **shes**) hembra
**sheaf** [ʃif] *s* (*pl:* **sheaves**) gavilla; *va* agavillar
**shear** [ʃɪr] *s* esquileo, trasquila; lana que se ha esquilado; hoja de la tijera; **shears** *spl* tijeras grandes; cizallas (*para cortar metales*); grúa de tijera; (*pret:* **sheared;** *pp:* **sheared** o **shorn**) *va* esquilar, trasquilar (*las ovejas*); cortar con tijeras, cizallar, cortar con cizallas; quitar cortando, cortar muy cerca; romper o cortar por fuerza del cizallamiento
**shearwater** [ˈʃɪrˌwɔtər] o [ˈʃɪrˌwɑtər] *s* (orn.) pufino, fardela del Atlántico; (orn.) pico tijera, meauca (*Rhynchops*)
**sheatfish** [ˈʃitˌfɪʃ] *s* (ichth.) siluro
**sheath** [ʃiθ] *s* (*pl:* **sheaths** [ʃiðz]) vaina; envoltura, cubierta, estuche; (bot.) vaina
**sheathe** [ʃið] *va* envainar; enfundar; embonar (*el casco de un buque*)
**sheathing** [ˈʃiðɪŋ] *s* forro, revestimiento; enfundadura; entablado, entarimado; (naut.) embono
**sheathing board** *s* cartón de yeso
**sheathing nail** *s* clavo de entablar
**sheath knife** *s* cuchillo encerrado en una vaina
**sheave** [ʃiv] *s* roldana; *va* agavillar
**Sheba** [ˈʃibə] *s* Sabá; **Queen of Sheba** reina de Sabá
**shebang** [ʃəˈbæŋ] *s* (slang) equipo, apresto; **the whole shebang** (coll.) la totalidad, el todo
**she'd** [ʃid] contracción de **she had** y de **she would**
**shed** [ʃɛd] *s* cobertizo; vertiente (*de agua*); (*pret & pp:* **shed;** *ger:* **shedding**) *va* verter, derramar; largar, desprenderse de; dar, echar, esparcir (*luz*); mudar (*la pluma, el pellejo, etc.*); *vn* pelechar (*los animales*)
**shedder** [ˈʃɛdər] *s* derramador; cangrejo o langosta que comienza a mudar el caparazón; cangrejo que acaba de mudar el caparazón
**shedding** [ˈʃɛdɪŋ] *s* vertimiento, derramamiento; desprendimiento; esparcimiento (*de luz*); muda (*p.ej., de plumas*)
**sheen** [ʃin] *s* lustre, brillo, resplandor; prensado (*lustre de los tejidos prensados*)
**sheeny** [ˈʃinɪ] *adj* lustroso, brillante
**sheep** [ʃip] *s* (*pl:* **sheep**) carnero; oveja (*hembra*); badana (*piel*); tonto, simplón, papanatas; **to make sheep's eyes** mirar con ojos de carnero degollado; *adj* ovejero
**sheep botfly** *s* (ent.) estro o moscardón de carnero

**sheepcote** [ˈʃip,kot] o [ˈʃip,kɑt] *s* aprisco, redil, ovil
**sheep dog** *s* perro de pastor, perro ovejero
**sheepfold** [ˈʃip,fold] *s* aprisco, redil, ovil
**sheephook** [ˈʃip,hʊk] *s* cayada, cayado
**sheepish** [ˈʃipɪʃ] *adj* avergonzado, corrido; tonto, tímido, pulsilánime
**sheepman** [ˈʃip,mæn] *s* (*pl:* **-men**) dueño y criador de ganado lanar; pastor
**sheep range** *s* pasto de ovejas
**sheepshead** [ˈʃips,hɛd] *s* cabeza de oveja; papanatas, simplón; (ichth.) sargo, salema
**sheepshearer** [ˈʃip,ʃɪrər] *s* esquilador (*persona*); esquiladora (*máquina*)
**sheepskin** [ˈʃip,skɪn] *s* zalea (*cuero que conserva la lana*); badana (*piel curtida*); (coll.) diploma
**sheep sorrel** *s* (bot.) acederilla
**sheep tick** *s* (ent.) mosca del carnero
**sheepwalk** [ˈʃip,wɔk] *s* pasto de ovejas, dehesa de ovejas
**sheer** [ʃɪr] *s* (naut.) desviación (*de un buque de su rumbo*); (naut.) arrufadura (*curvatura*); *adj* fino, delgado, ligero; puro, sin mezcla; cabal, completo; casi transparente; escarpado; *adv* cabalmente, completamente; de un golpe, directamente; en cuesta; *va* desviar; *vn* desviarse
**sheet** [ʃit] *s* sábana (*para la cama*); hoja (*de papel, metal, etc.*); hoja impresa; diario, periódico; extensión (de agua); (naut.) escota; (poet.) vela (*de navío*); **to be** o **to have a sheet in the wind** (slang) estar entre dos velas, estar chispado, estar borrachuelo; **sheet of paper** papel; **sheets** *spl* espacio a proa o a popa de bote abierto; *va* ensabanar; proveer de sábana; *vn* extenderse en hojas
**sheet anchor** *s* (naut.) ancla de la esperanza; (fig.) áncora de salvación
**sheeting** [ˈʃitɪŋ] *s* lencería para sábanas; encofrado (*revestimiento de planchas*); cobertura de placas, laminado
**sheet iron** *s* palastro, hierro laminado
**sheet lightning** *s* fucilazo, relámpago difuso
**sheet metal** *s* metal laminado, metal en láminas
**sheet music** *s* música en hojas sueltas
**Sheffield plate** [ˈʃɛfild] *s* plateado de Sheffield
**sheik** o **sheikh** [ʃik] *s* jeque; (slang) galanteador irresistible, sultán
**sheikdom** [ˈʃikdəm] *s* principado (de jeque)
**shekel** [ˈʃɛkəl] *s* siclo; **shekels** *spl* (slang) dinero
**sheldrake** [ˈʃɛl,drek] *s* (orn.) tadorna; (orn.) pato canelo; (orn.) pato sierra
**shelf** [ʃɛlf] *s* (*pl:* **shelves**) estante, anaquel, entrepaño; bajío, banco de arena; roca subyacente; **on the shelf** arrinconado, desechado, olvidado; en prenda
**shelflist** [ˈʃɛlf,lɪst] *s* catálogo topográfico (*de una biblioteca*)
**shelf warmer** *s* artículo de venta morosa, artículo invendible
**she'll** [ʃil] contracción de **she shall** y de **she will**
**shell** [ʃɛl] *s* cáscara (*de huevo, nuez, etc.*); concha, caparazón (*p.ej., de crustáceo*); vaina (*de legumbre*); cubierta, corteza; armazón, esqueleto; bomba, proyectil; cápsula (*para cartuchos*); cuerpo (*p.ej., de caldera*); (sport) piragua, yola; **to come out of one's shell** salir del carapacho o de la concha; **to retire into one's shell** meterse en su carapacho o en su concha; *va* descascarar; desvainar; desgranar (*p.ej., guisantes*); cañonear, bombardear; **to shell out** (coll.) entregar (*dinero*); *vn* desencascararse; desconcharse; **to shell out** (coll.) entregar el dinero, pagar
**shellac** [ʃəˈlæk] o [ˈʃɛlæk] *s* laca, goma laca; (*pret & pp:* **-lacked**; *ger:* **-lacking**) *va* barnizar con goma laca
**shellacking** [ʃəˈlækɪŋ] *s* (slang) paliza, zurra; (slang) derrota
**shellback** [ˈʃɛl,bæk] *s* (slang) lobo de mar; (slang) persona que ha atravesado el ecuador en un barco
**shellbark** [ˈʃɛl,bɑrk] *s* (bot.) nuez dura
**sheller** [ˈʃɛlər] *s* descascarador; desgranador; descascaradora (*máquina*)
**shellfire** [ˈʃɛl,faɪr] *s* cañoneo, fuego de bomba
**shellfish** [ˈʃɛl,fɪʃ] *s* marisco, mariscos
**shellfishery** [ˈʃɛl,fɪʃərɪ] *s* (*pl:* **-ies**) marisqueo
**shell hole** *s* (mil.) embudo
**shellproof** [ˈʃɛl,pruf] *adj* a prueba de bomba
**shell shock** *s* conmoción psiconeurótica del soldado, neurosis de guerra
**shelly** [ˈʃɛlɪ] *adj* (*comp:* **-ier**; *super:* **-iest**) conchado, conchudo
**shelter** [ˈʃɛltər] *s* abrigo, amparo, refugio, resguardo, asilo; **to take shelter** abrigarse, refugiarse; *va* abrigar, amparar, proteger, guarecer; *vn* abrigarse, refugiarse, guarecerse
**shelter tent** *s* (mil.) tienda de abrigo
**shelve** [ʃɛlv] *va* poner sobre un estante o anaquel; proveer de estantes o anaqueles; arrinconar, desechar, dejar a un lado; diferir indefinidamente; *vn* estar en declive
**shelving** [ˈʃɛlvɪŋ] *s* anaquelería, estantería; material para anaqueles o estantes
**Shemite** [ˈʃɛmaɪt] *s* var. de **semite**
**shenanigans** [ʃɪˈnænɪgənz] *spl* (coll.) artificios, embustes
**sheol** [ˈʃiol] *s* (coll.) infierno, báratro
**shepherd** [ˈʃɛpərd] *s* pastor; (fig.) pastor; *va* pastorear (*a las ovejas o los fieles*)
**shepherd dog** *s* perro de pastor, perro ovejero
**shepherd god** *s* dios de los pastores (*el dios Pan*)
**shepherdess** [ˈʃɛpərdɪs] *s* pastora
**Shepherd kings** *spl* reyes pastores
**shepherd's pipe** *s* zampoña
**shepherd's-purse** [ˈʃɛpərdz,pʌrs] *s* (bot.) bolsa de pastor, zurrón de pastor, pan y quesillo
**sherbet** [ˈʃʌrbət] *s* sorbete
**sherd** [ʃʌrd] *s* var. de **shard**
**shereef** o **sherif** [ʃɛˈrif] *s* jerife
**sheriff** [ˈʃɛrɪf] *s* oficial de justicia inglés o norteamericano
**sherifian** [ʃɛˈrifɪən] *adj* jerifiano
**sherry** [ˈʃɛrɪ] *s* (*pl:* **-ries**) jerez, vino de Jerez
**sherry cobbler** *s* bebida compuesta de agua y vino de Jerez con azúcar, limón, naranja y pedacitos de hielo (*sírvese con pajas*)
**sherry reception** *s* vino (*reunión donde se ofrece vino de Jerez*)
**she's** [ʃiz] contracción de **she is** y de **she has**
**shew** [ʃo] *s, va & vn* var. de **show**
**shewbread** [ˈʃo,brɛd] *s* (Bib.) panes de la proposición
**shibboleth** [ˈʃɪbəlɛθ] *s* lema, santo y seña; habla, jerga; rasgo distintivo
**shield** [ʃild] *s* escudo; (bot., zool., her. & fig.) escudo; (elec.) blindaje; sobaquera (*con que se resguarda del sudor la parte del vestido correspondiente al sobaco*); *va* amparar, defender, escudar; (elec.) blindar
**shield-bearer** [ˈʃild,bɛrər] *s* escudero
**shift** [ʃɪft] *s* cambio; tanda (*grupo de obreros*); turno (*orden del trabajo*); maña, subterfugio, fraude; **to make shift** ayudarse, ingeniarse, componérselas; ingeniarse a duras penas; hacer lo posible; *va* cambiar; deshacerse de; **to shift gears** cambiar de marcha; **to shift the blame** echar la culpa a otro; **to shift the blame on** echar la culpa a; *vn* cambiar, cambiar de puesto; mañear, tergiversar; ayudarse, ingeniarse; **to shift for oneself** ayudarse, ingeniarse
**shifting engine** *s* (rail.) locomotora de maniobras
**shift key** *s* tecla de cambio, tecla de mayúsculas, palanca de mayúsculas
**shiftless** [ˈʃɪftlɪs] *adj* inútil, galbanoso
**shifty** [ˈʃɪftɪ] *adj* (*comp:* **-ier**; *super:* **-iest**) ingenioso; tramoyista; huyente (*vistazo*)
**shill** [ʃɪl] *s* (slang) cómplice de un fullero
**shillalah** o **shillelagh** [ʃɪˈlelə] o [ʃɪˈlelɪ] *s* palo, cachiporra
**shilling** [ˈʃɪlɪŋ] *s* chelín
**shilly-shally** [ˈʃɪlɪ,ʃælɪ] *adj* irresoluto; *adv* irresolutamente; (*pret & pp:* **-lied**) *vn* estar irresoluto, no saber qué hacer
**shily** [ˈʃaɪlɪ] *adv* tímidamente
**shim** [ʃɪm] *s* cuña, calza; (*pret & pp:* **shimmed**; *ger:* **shimming**) *va* acuñar, calzar
**shimmer** [ˈʃɪmər] *s* luz trémula, débil resplandor; *vn* rielar
**shimmery** [ˈʃɪmərɪ] *adj* trémulo, resplandeciente

**shimmy** [ˈʃɪmɪ] *s* (*pl:* **-mies**) shimmy (*baile*); (coll.) camisa de mujer; vibración excesiva; (aut.) abaniqueo (*de las ruedas delanteras*); (*pret & pp:* **-mied**) *vn* bailar el shimmy; vibrar; (aut.) bambolear
**shin** [ʃɪn] *s* (anat.) espinilla; (*pret & pp:* **shinned;** *ger:* **shinning**) *va & vn* trepar; **to shin up** trepar
**shinbone** [ˈʃɪn,bon] *s* (anat.) tibia, espinilla
**shindig** [ˈʃɪndɪg] *s* (slang) juerga, fiesta ruidosa
**shindy** [ˈʃɪndɪ] *s* (*pl:* **-dies**) (slang) alboroto, zacapela; (slang) juerga, fiesta ruidosa
**shine** [ʃaɪn] *s* luz, brillo; lustre, bruñido; buen tiempo; (coll.) lustre (*que se da al calzado*); (slang) simpatía; (slang) alboroto; (slang) travesura; **to take a shine to** (slang) tomar simpatía por; (*pret & pp:* **shined**) *va* (coll.) embetunar, embolar, limpiar (*el calzado*); bruñir, pulir; dar lustre a, poner lustroso; (*pret & pp:* **shone**) *va* hacer brillar, abrillantar; *vn* lucir, brillar, resplandecer; hacer sol, hacer buen tiempo; (fig.) brillar, lucir (*distinguirse, sobresalir*); **to shine up to** (slang) tratar de conquistar la amistad de
**shiner** [ˈʃaɪnər] *s* cosa que brilla; limpiabotas; (ichth.) pececillo plateado; (slang) ojo; (slang) ojo morado; (slang) guinea o soberano (*monedas inglesas*)
**shingle** [ˈʃɪŋgəl] *s* ripia (*usada como una teja para cubrir el tejado de las casas*); tejamaní (Am.); pelo a la garçonne; (coll.) letrero de oficina; guijo, guijarro, cascajo; guijarral (*playa u otro terreno*); **to hang out one's shingle** (coll.) abrir una oficina; (coll.) abrir un consultorio médico; **shingles** *spl* (path.) zona; *va* cubrir con ripias; cortar (*el pelo*) a la garçonne; cinglar (*el hierro*); *vn* ripiar
**shingly** [ˈʃɪŋglɪ] *adj* guijarroso, cascajoso
**shin guard** *s* (sport) espinillera
**shining** [ˈʃaɪnɪŋ] *adj* brillante, luciente; (fig.) brillante, distinguido
**shinny** [ˈʃɪnɪ] *s* (*pl:* **-nies**) cachava (*juego y palo*); (*pret & pp:* **-nied**) *vn* (coll.) trepar valiéndose de las espinillas
**Shinto** [ˈʃɪnto] *s* sintoísmo; sintoísta; *adj* sintoísta
**Shintoism** [ˈʃɪnto·ɪzəm] *s* sintoísmo
**Shintoist** [ˈʃɪnto·ɪst] *adj & s* sintoísta
**shiny** [ˈʃaɪnɪ] *adj* (*comp:* **-ier;** *super:* **-iest**) brillante, lustroso; glaseado (*p.ej., papel*); brilloso (*que brilla por el mucho uso*)
**-ship** *suffix s* -ato, p.ej., **deanship** decanato; **generalship** generalato; -ción p.ej., **horsemanship** equitación; **scholarship** erudición; -ía, p.ej., **chancellorship** cancillería; **lordship** señoría; **secretaryship** secretaría
**ship** [ʃɪp] *s* nave, buque, barco, navío; nave aérea, aeronave; tripulación; (*pret & pp:* **shipped;** *ger:* **shipping**) *va* embarcar; enviar, remitir; armar (*p.ej., los remos*); **to ship water** embarcar agua; *vn* embarcarse (*ir a bordo de un buque; aceptar un empleo a bordo de un buque*); **to ship on** tripular (*ir de tripulación en*)
**ship biscuit** *s* galleta, pan de marinero
**shipboard** [ˈʃɪp,bord] *s* bordo; **on shipboard** a bordo
**ship bread** *s* var. de **ship biscuit**
**shipbuilder** [ˈʃɪp,bɪldər] *s* arquitecto naval, ingeniero naval; constructor de buques
**shipbuilding** [ˈʃɪp,bɪldɪŋ] *s* arquitectura naval; construcción de buques; *adj* armador
**ship canal** *s* canal de navegación
**ship carpenter** *s* carpintero de ribera
**ship chandler** *s* abastecedor de buques
**shipload** [ˈʃɪp,lod] *s* cargamento completo de un buque
**shipman** [ˈʃɪpmən] *s* (*pl:* **-men**) capitán de buque, patrón
**shipmaster** [ˈʃɪp,mæstər] o [ˈʃɪp,mɑstər] *s* capitán de buque, patrón
**shipmate** [ˈʃɪp,met] *s* camarada de a bordo
**shipment** [ˈʃɪpmənt] *s* embarque (*por agua*); envío, remesa
**ship money** *s* (Brit.) impuesto de guerra para la construcción de buques
**ship of the desert** *s* nave del desierto (*camello*)
**ship of the line** *s* navío de línea, navío de alto bordo
**ship of war** *s* navío de guerra
**shipowner** [ˈʃɪp,onər] *s* naviero, armador
**shipper** [ˈʃɪpər] *s* embarcador (*en una embarcación*); expedidor, remitente
**shipping** [ˈʃɪpɪŋ] *s* embarque; envío, remesa; navegación; marina, flota
**shipping clerk** *s* dependiente encargado de envíos y transportes de mercancías
**shipping memo** *s* nota de remisión
**shipping room** *s* local de donde se hacen envíos
**shipplane** [ˈʃɪp,plen] *s* avión de cubierta
**ship-rigged** [ˈʃɪp,rɪgd] *adj* (naut.) aparejado con velas cuadradas y tres mástiles
**shipshape** [ˈʃɪp,ʃep] *adj & adv* en buen orden
**ship's husband** *s* director de una empresa naviera; encargado de un buque en el puerto
**shipside** [ˈʃɪp,saɪd] *adj & adv* al costado del buque; *s* zona de embarque y desembarque; muelle
**ship's papers** *spl* documentación del buque
**ship's time** *s* hora local del buque
**shipworm** [ˈʃɪp,wʌrm] *s* (zool.) broma, tiñuela
**shipwreck** [ˈʃɪp,rɛk] *s* naufragio; barco náufrago; (fig.) naufragio; *va* hacer naufragar; *vn* naufragar; (fig.) naufragar
**shipwright** [ˈʃɪp,raɪt] *s* carpintero de ribera, carpintero de navío
**shipyard** [ˈʃɪp,jɑrd] *s* astillero
**shire** [ʃaɪr] *s* (Brit.) condado
**shirk** [ʃʌrk] *s* persona que evita trabajar; *va* evitar (*el trabajo*); faltar a (*un deber*); *vn* evitar trabajar; faltar a sus obligaciones, escurrir el hombro
**shirr** [ʃʌr] *s* (sew.) frunce; *va* (sew.) fruncir; cocer (*huevos*) en un plato chato con crema o pan rallado
**shirred egg** *s* huevo al plato
**shirring** [ˈʃʌrɪŋ] *s* (sew.) frunce
**shirt** [ʃʌrt] *s* camisa; camiseta (*ropa interior*); **to keep one's shirt on** (slang) quedarse sereno, no perder la paciencia; **to lose one's shirt** (slang) perder hasta la camisa
**shirtband** [ˈʃɪrt,bænd] *s* cuello de camisa, tira del cuello de la camisa de hombre
**shirt front** *s* pechera de camisa
**shirting** [ˈʃʌrtɪŋ] *s* tela para camisas de hombre
**shirt sleeve** *s* manga de camisa; **in shirt sleeves** en camisa, en mangas de camisa
**shirt-sleeve** [ˈʃʌrt,sliv] *adj* (coll.) sencillo, directo
**shirttail** [ˈʃʌrt,tel] *s* pañal, faldón
**shirtwaist** [ˈʃʌrt,west] *s* blusa (*de mujer*)
**shivaree** [,ʃɪvəˈri] *s* cantaleta, cencerrada
**shiver** [ˈʃɪvər] *s* tiritón, estremecimiento, temblor; *va* estrellar, hacer astillas; *vn* tiritar, estremecerse; estrellarse, hacerse pedazos
**shivery** [ˈʃɪvərɪ] *adj* estremecido, trémulo; estremecedor; frío; friolento (*sensible al frío*); quebradizo, saltadizo
**shoal** [ʃol] *s* bajo, bajío, banco de arena; muchedumbre, gran cantidad; *adj* bajo, poco profundo; *vn* disminuir en profundidad; reunirse en gran número
**shoaly** [ˈʃolɪ] *adj* bajo, poco profundo, vadoso
**shoat** [ʃot] *s* cochinillo, gorrino
**shock** [ʃɑk] *s* choque (*encuentro violento y repentino*); temblor de tierra; (elec.) sacudida; (med. & fig.) choque; (path.) choque (*depresión profunda*); sobresalto (*conmoción nerviosa o mental repentina*); (coll.) parálisis; (agr.) tresnal, hacina; greña (*de pelo*); *va* chocar; sobresaltar (*asustar, alterar profundamente*); dar una sacudida eléctrica a; chocar, escandalizar (*causar extrañeza, enfado, etc.*); (agr.) hacinar; *vn* chocar
**shock absorber** *s* amortiguador
**shock-headed** [ˈʃɑk,hɛdɪd] *adj* greñudo
**shocking** [ˈʃɑkɪŋ] *adj* chocante, escandalizador
**shockproof** [ˈʃɑk,pruf] *adj* a prueba de sacudidas
**shock therapy** o **treatment** *s* shockterapia, convulsoterapia
**shock troops** *spl* (mil.) tropas de asalto
**shock wave** *s* (aer.) onda de choque
**shod** [ʃɑd] *pret & pp de* **shoe**
**shoddy** [ˈʃɑdɪ] *s* lana mecánica sin fieltrar; caedura de lana; paño burdo de lana; imitación, ostentación vulgar; *adj* (*comp:* **-dier;** *super:*

**-diest**) hecho de lana desechada; falso, de imitación
**shoe** [ʃu] *s* bota, botina (*calzado que sube más arriba del tobillo*); zapato (*calzado que no pasa del tobillo*); cubierta (*de un neumático*); zapata (*de un freno; del carruaje eléctrico para sacar la corriente del tercer carril*); regatón (*remate de metal*); **in the shoes of** en el pellejo de; **to die with one's shoes on** morir al pie del cañón; **to put on one's shoes** calzarse; **where the shoe pinches** donde está el busilis; (*pret & pp:* **shod**) *va* calzar; herrar (*un caballo*); poner regatón a; *vn* calzarse
**shoebill** [ˈʃuˌbɪl] *s* (orn.) picozapato
**shoeblack** [ˈʃuˌblæk] *s* limpiabotas
**shoe blacking** *s* betún, bola
**shoehorn** [ˈʃuˌhɔrn] *s* calzador
**shoelace** [ˈʃuˌles] *s* cordón de zapato, lazo de zapato
**shoe leather** *s* cuero para zapatos; correjel
**shoemaker** [ˈʃuˌmekər] *s* zapatero; zapatero remendón
**shoemaking** [ˈʃuˌmekɪŋ] *s* zapatería
**shoe mender** *s* zapatero remendón
**shoe polish** *s* betún, bola
**shoeshine** [ˈʃuˌʃaɪn] *s* brillo, lustre; limpiabotas
**shoe store** *s* zapatería
**shoestring** [ˈʃuˌstrɪŋ] *s* agujeta, cordón de zapato, lazo de zapato; pequeña cantidad de dinero; **on a shoestring** con muy poco dinero
**shoe tree** *s* horma
**shogun** [ˈʃogun] *s* shogún
**shogunate** [ˈʃogunet] *s* shogunado
**shone** [ʃon] o [ʃɑn] *pret & pp de* **shine**
**shoo** [ʃu] *interj* ¡ox! (*para espantar las aves de corral*); *va & vn* oxear
**shook** [ʃʊk] *pret de* **shake**
**shoot** [ʃut] *s* renuevo, retoño, pimpollo, vástago; conducto inclinado; tolva (*para agua, granos, carbón, etc.*); tiro; tiro al blanco, certamen de tiradores; lanzamiento (*de un cohete al espacio*) ‖ (*pret & pp:* **shot**) *va* tirar, disparar (*un arma*); herir o matar con arma de fuego, herir o matar con arma arrojadiza; fusilar (*ejecutar con descarga de fusilería*); fotografiar; rodar, filmar; echar (*los dados*); descargar, verter, vaciar de golpe; medir la altura de (*p.ej., el Sol*); **to shoot craps** jugar a los dados; **to shoot down** derribar (*un avión*); **to shoot the rapids** bajar por los rápidos, salvar los rápidos; **to shoot to death** matar a tiros; **to shoot trouble** buscar desperfectos, localizar averías; **to shoot up** (slang) destrozar echando balas a diestra y siniestra ‖ *vn* tirar; nacer, brotar, germinar; lanzarse, precipitarse, moverse rápidamente; punzar (*dícese de un dolor, una llaga, etc.*); **to shoot at** tirar a; (coll.) hacer tiro a (*desear, ambicionar*); **to shoot up** nacer, brotar; moverse rápidamente hacia arriba
**shooter** [ˈʃutər] *s* tirador; (coll.) arma de fuego, revólver
**shooting** [ˈʃutɪŋ] *s* tiro; caza con escopeta; fusilería; cañoneo; rodaje (*de un cine o film*)
**shooting box** *s* (Brit.) pabellón de caza
**shooting gallery** *s* galería de tiro al blanco, galería de tirar al blanco
**shooting match** *s* certamen de tiro al blanco; (slang) totalidad, conjunto, todo
**shooting pain** *s* punzada
**shooting season** *s* tiempo de caza
**shooting star** *s* estrella fugaz, estrella filante; (bot.) sarapico
**shooting war** *s* guerra verdadera
**shop** [ʃɑp] *s* tienda; taller (*oficina de trabajo manual*); **to set up shop** abrir tienda; emprender un negocio; **to shut up shop** cerrar, alzar o levantar tienda; desistir de una empresa; **to talk shop** hablar de su oficio, hablar del propio trabajo (*fuera de tiempo*); (*pret & pp:* **shopped**; *ger:* **shopping**) *vn* ir de compras, ir de tiendas; **to go shopping** ir de compras, ir de tiendas; **to send shopping** mandar a la compra; **to shop around** ir de tienda en tienda buscando gangas
**shopgirl** [ˈʃɑpˌgʌrl] *s* muchacha de tienda, dependienta
**shopkeeper** [ˈʃɑpˌkipər] *s* tendero
**shoplifter** [ˈʃɑpˌlɪftər] *s* ratero de tiendas, mechera
**shoplifting** [ˈʃɑpˌlɪftɪŋ] *s* ratería en las tiendas (*por parte de personas que se fingen parroquianos*)
**shopman** [ˈʃɑpmən] *s* (*pl:* **-men**) tendero; vendedor, mancebo de tienda
**shopper** [ˈʃɑpər] *s* comprador
**shopping center** *s* agrupación de tiendas, con parque para automóviles
**shopping district** *s* barrio comercial
**shopwalker** [ˈʃɑpˌwɔkər] *s* (Brit.) vigilante de almacén
**shopwindow** [ˈʃɑpˌwɪndo] *s* escaparate; vidriera (Am.)
**shopwork** [ˈʃɑpˌwʌrk] *s* trabajo de taller
**shopworn** [ˈʃɑpˌworn] *adj* desgastado con el trajín de la tienda
**shore** [ʃor] *s* orilla, ribera; costa, playa; (min.) entibo, ademe; (naut.) escora; **in shore** muy cerca de la tierra; **off shore** a lo largo de la costa; **on shore** en tierra; **shores** *spl* (poet.) clima, región; *va* apuntalar; (min.) entibar; (naut.) escorar
**shore dinner** *s* comida de mariscos
**shore leave** *s* (naut.) permiso para ir a tierra
**shoreless** [ˈʃorlɪs] *adj* sin costa; ilimitado
**shore line** *s* línea de la playa; línea de barcos costeros
**shore patrol** *s* (naut.) patrulla en tierra
**shoreward** [ˈʃorwərd] *adj & adv* hacia la playa
**shoring** [ˈʃorɪŋ] *s* apuntalamiento; puntales
**shorn** [ʃorn] *adj* esquilado; mocho, pelado; **shorn of** privado de, despojado de; *pp de* **shear**
**short** [ʃɔrt] *adj* corto (*en espacio, tiempo y cantidad*); breve (*en tiempo*); bajo (*de cuerpo*); poco (*tiempo*); (fig.) corto, sucinto, lacónico; brusco, seco; friable, quebradizo; (com.) que vende sin posesión; (phonet.) breve; **for short** para abreviar, para ser más breve; **in a short time** en breve, dentro de poco; **in short** en fin; **in short order** prontamente; **on short notice** con poco tiempo de aviso; **to be short of** estar escaso de; no responder a; estar lejos de; **short of breath** corto de resuello ‖ *adv* brevemente; sucintamente, lacónicamente; bruscamente; corto; (com.) sin posesión; **to cut short** interrumpir bruscamente; acabar bruscamente; **to fall short** ser insuficiente; **to fall short of** no alcanzar, no llegar a; **to run short** ser insuficiente; **to run short of** acabársele a uno, p.ej., **I am running short of gasoline** se me acaba la gasolina; **to sell short** (com.) vender al descubierto; **to stop short** parar de repente ‖ *s* (mov.) cortometraje, cinta de corto metraje; (com.) persona que vende al descubierto; (com.) venta al descubierto; (com.) valores vendidos al descubierto; (elec.) cortocircuito; **shorts** *spl* calzones cortos; calzoncillos; mezcla de salvado y harina basta ‖ *va* (elec.) poner en cortocircuito ‖ *vn* (elec.) ponerse en cortocircuito
**shortage** [ˈʃɔrtɪdʒ] *s* déficit; escasez, carestía, falta
**shortbread** [ˈʃɔrtˌbrɛd] *s* torta dulce y friable hecha con manteca
**shortcake** [ˈʃɔrtˌkek] *s* torta de frutas
**short-change** [ˌʃɔrtˈtʃendʒ] *va* (coll.) no devolver la vuelta debida a; (coll.) estafar, engañar
**short circuit** *s* (elec.) cortocircuito
**short-circuit** [ˌʃɔrtˈsʌrkɪt] *va* (elec.) cortocircuitar; *vn* (elec.) cortocircuitarse
**shortcoming** [ˈʃɔrtˌkʌmɪŋ] *s* defecto, desperfecto
**short-commons** [ˈʃɔrtˈkɑmənz] *spl* ración escasa, comida insuficiente
**short cut** *s* atajo; (fig.) atajo
**shorten** [ˈʃɔrtən] *va* acortar; hacer más friable con grasa; *vn* acortarse
**shortening** [ˈʃɔrtənɪŋ] o [ˈʃɔrtnɪŋ] *s* acortamiento; grasa para hacer la pastelería más friable
**shorthand** [ˈʃɔrtˌhænd] *s* taquigrafía; **to take shorthand** escribir al dictado; *adj* taquigráfico
**short-handed** [ˈʃɔrtˈhændɪd] *adj* escaso de mano de obra, escaso de ayudantes
**shorthand-typist** [ˈʃɔrtˌhændˈtaɪpɪst] *s* taquimecanógrafo, taquimeca
**shorthorn** [ˈʃɔrtˌhɔrn] *s* ganado vacuno de cuernos cortos

**shortish** [ˈʃɔrtɪʃ] *adj* algo corto, algo pequeño
**short-legged** [ˈʃɔrt,lɛgɪd] o [ˈʃɔrt,lɛgd] *adj* de piernas cortas
**short-lived** [ˈʃɔrtˈlaɪvd] o [ˈʃɔrtˈlɪvd] *adj* de breve vida, de breve duración
**shortly** [ˈʃɔrtlɪ] *adv* luego, en breve; en pocas palabras; descortésmente; **shortly after** poco tiempo después; **shortly after** + *ger* a poco de + *inf*
**short money** *s* (com.) dinero prestado a corto plazo
**shortness** [ˈʃɔrtnɪs] *s* cortedad, brevedad; escasez, insuficiencia; friabilidad
**short-range** [ˈʃɔrt,rendʒ] *adj* de poco alcance
**short sale** *s* (com.) venta al descubierto, venta a plazo
**short shrift** *s* tiempo muy breve para confesarse; breve tregua; **to make short shrift of** despachar de prisa, enviar noramala
**short-sighted** [ˈʃɔrtˈsaɪtɪd] *adj* miope, corto de vista; falto de perspicacia, falto de previsión
**shortstop** [ˈʃɔrt,stɑp] *s* (baseball) medio (*jugador que está entre la segunda y tercera bases*); guardabosque, torpedero (Am.)
**short story** *s* cuento
**short suit** *s* (cards) fallo
**short-tempered** [ˈʃɔrtˈtɛmpərd] *adj* de mal genio
**short-term** [ˈʃɔrt,tʌrm] *adj* (com.) a corto plazo
**short ton** *s* tonelada corta o menor (*2000 libras o 907,2 kilogramos*)
**short-waisted** [ˈʃɔrtˈwestɪd] *adj* corto de talle
**short wave** *s* (rad.) onda corta
**short-wave** [ˈʃɔrt,wev] *adj* (rad.) de onda corta
**short-winded** [ˈʃɔrtˈwɪndɪd] *adj* corto de resuello
**short-witted** [ˈʃɔrtˈwɪtɪd] *adj* corto de alcances
**shot** [ʃɑt] *s* tiro, disparo; balazo (*golpe de bala y herida*); alcance (*distancia*); golpe, tirada, jugada (*en ciertos juegos*); lanzamiento (*de un cohete al espacio*); (min.) barreno; (phot.) instantánea, fotografía; escote (*parte que hay que pagar*); tentativa, conjetura; (sport) pesa (*bola de metal muy pesada*); (slang) dosis, jeringazo, trago; (fig.) tiro (*tirador; indirecta desfavorable contra una persona*); perdigones (*granos de plomo*); munición; **like a shot** como una bala; **long shot** esfuerzo por hacer algo muy difícil; **not by a long shot** ni con mucho, ni por pienso; **to be a good shot** ser un buen tiro, tener buena puntería; **to put the shot** (sport) tirar la pesa; **to start like a shot** salir disparado; **to take a shot at** disparar un tiro a; hacer una tentativa de; **within pistol shot** a tiro de pistola; *adj* tornasolado; **shot through with** cargado de; (*pret & pp:* **shotted;** *ger:* **shotting**) *va* cargar con perdigones, cargar con munición; tornasolar (*un tejido*); *pret & pp de* **shoot**
**shote** [ʃot] s var. de **shoat**
**shotgun** [ˈʃɑt,gʌn] *s* escopeta
**shot-put** [ˈʃɑt,pʊt] *s* (sport) tiro de la pesa
**should** [ʃʊd] *v aux* se emplea para formar (1) el condicional presente, p.ej., **if I should wait for him, I should miss the train** si yo le esperase, perdería el tren; (2) el condicional pasado, p.ej., **if I had waited for him, I should have missed the train** si yo le hubiese esperado, habría perdido el tren; y (3) el modo potencial, p.ej., **he should go at once** debiera salir en seguida; **he should have gone at once** debiera haber salido en seguida
**shoulder** [ˈʃoldər] *s* hombro; brazuelo (*de res muerta*); (print.) hombro; saliente (*de un bastión; de un camino*); hombrera (*de una prenda de vestir*); **across the shoulder** en bandolera; **on the shoulders of** a hombros de; **straight from the shoulder** con toda franqueza; **to have broad shoulders** tener buenas espaldas; **to put one's shoulders to the wheel** arrimar el hombro; **to square one's shoulders** enderezar los hombros, cuadrarse; **to turn a cold shoulder to** volver las espaldas a, negarse al trato de; **shoulder to shoulder** hombro a hombro; *va* llevar a hombros, cargar sobre los hombros, echar sobre las espaldas; cargar con (*el fusil*); tomar sobre sí, hacerse responsable de; aceptar con resignación; empujar con los hombros para abrirse paso; **shoulder arms** (mil.) armas al hombro
**shoulder blade** *s* (anat.) escápula, omóplato
**shoulder knot** *s* dragona
**shoulder padding** *s* hombrera
**shoulder strap** *s* (mil.) charretera; presilla (*p.ej., de ropa interior*)
**shouldn't** [ˈʃʊdənt] contracción de **should not**
**shout** [ʃaʊt] *s* voz, grito; alboroto, gritería; *va* vocear, gritar; **to shout down** hacer sentar a gritos, hacer callar haciendo mucho alboroto; *vn* dar voces, gritar; alborotar
**shove** [ʃʌv] *s* empujón; *va* empujar; *vn* dar empujones, avanzar a empujones; **to shove off** alejarse de la costa; (slang) salir, ponerse en marcha
**shovel** [ˈʃʌvəl] *s* pala; palada (*cantidad que se recoge en una pala de una vez*); sombrero de teja; (*pret & pp:* **-eled** o **-elled;** *ger:* **-eling** o **-elling**) *va* traspalar; construir con pala; espalar (*p.ej., la nieve*); abrir con pala; limpiar con pala; echar en grandes cantidades; *vn* trabajar con pala
**shovelboard** [ˈʃʌvəl,bord] *s* var. de **shuffleboard**
**shoveler** o **shoveller** [ˈʃʌvələr] *s* paleador; (orn.) espátula; (orn.) pato cuchareta, ánade cucharetero (*Spatula clypeata*)
**shovelful** [ˈʃʌvəlfʊl] *s* palada
**shovel hat** *s* sombrero de teja
**show** [ʃo] *s* exhibición, exposición, muestra; espectáculo; (coll.) función (*en el teatro*); sesión (*cada representación de un drama o película*); ostentación; falsa apariencia; prueba, demostración; indicación, signo, señal; apariencia, exterior; alarde (*p.ej., de confianza*); (coll.) ocasión, oportunidad; (slang) equipo, apresto; (coll.) tercer puesto en una carrera; espectáculo ridículo; hazmerreír; **to be the whole show** (coll.) ser el todo; **to make a show of** hacer gala de; **to steal the show from** robar la obra a (*otro actor*) ‖ (*pret:* **showed;** *pp:* **shown** o **showed**) *va* mostrar, enseñar; probar, demostrar; marcar (*p.ej., la hora*); acompañar (*p.ej., a la puerta*); **to show off** hacer alarde de; **to show up** hacer subir; (coll.) desenmascarar ‖ *vn* mostrarse, aparecer, asomar; salir (*p.ej., la combinación*); (coll.) llegar en tercer puesto en una carrera; (theat.) actuar; (theat.) representarse; **to show off** alardear, fachendear; **to show up** destacarse; (coll.) presentarse, dejarse ver
**show bill** *s* cartel
**show biz** [bɪz] *s* (slang) var. de **show business**
**showboat** [ˈʃo,bot] *s* barco teatro, buque teatro
**showbread** [ˈʃo,brɛd] *s* var. de **shewbread**
**show business** *s* comercio de los espectáculos; ocupación de actor, empresario, etc.
**showcase** [ˈʃo,kes] *s* vitrina, vitrina de exposición
**showdown** [ˈʃo,daʊn] *s* cartas boca arriba; (coll.) revelación forzosa, arreglo terminante
**shower** [ˈʃaʊər] *s* ducha; aguacero, chaparrón; reunión o fiesta para obsequiar con regalos a una novia próxima a casarse; (fig.) rociada (*p.ej., de balas*); *va* regar; **to shower with favors** colmar de favores; *vn* llover
**shower bath** *s* ducha, baño de ducha
**showery** [ˈʃaʊərɪ] *adj* chubascoso, lluvioso
**show girl** *s* (theat.) corista
**showiness** [ˈʃo·ɪnɪs] *s* vistosidad, aparatosidad; cursería
**showing** [ˈʃo·ɪŋ] *s* demostración; exhibición
**showman** [ˈʃomən] *s* (*pl:* **-men**) director de espectáculos, empresario de teatro, empresario de circo
**showmanship** [ˈʃomənʃɪp] *s* habilidad para presentar espectáculos; teatralidad
**show-off** [ˈʃo,ɔf] o [ˈʃo,ɑf] *s* ostentación; (coll.) pinturero, persona muy ostentosa
**show of hands** *s* votación por manos levantadas
**show of strength** *s* demostración de fuerza, despliegue de poder

**showpiece** ['ʃo,pis] *s* objeto expuesto a la vista; objeto de arte sobresaliente
**show place** *s* sitio o edificio que se exhibe al público por su belleza o lujo
**showroom** ['ʃo,rum] o ['ʃo,rʊm] *s* sala de muestras, sala de exhibición
**show window** *s* escaparate de tienda; vidriera (Am.)
**showy** ['ʃo·ɪ] *adj* (*comp:* **-ier;** *super:* **-iest**) vistoso, ostentoso, aparatoso; cursi
**shrank** [ʃræŋk] *pret de* **shrink**
**shrapnel** ['ʃræpnəl] *s* granada de metralla; metralla
**shred** [ʃrɛd] *s* triza, jirón, tira; pizca, fragmento; **to be in shreds** estar hecho trizas, estar raído, estar andrajoso; **to tear to shreds** hacer trizas; (*pret & pp:* **shredded** o **shred;** *ger:* **shredding**) *va* hacer trizas, hacer tiras, desmenuzar; deshilar (*carne*)
**shrew** [ʃru] *s* arpía, mujer regañona, fierecilla; (zool.) musaraña
**shrewd** [ʃrud] *adj* astuto; vivo, listo, despierto
**shrewdness** ['ʃrudnɪs] *s* astucia; viveza
**shrewish** ['ʃruɪʃ] *adj* regañona, de mal genio
**shrewmouse** ['ʃru,maʊs] *s* (*pl:* **-mice** [,maɪs]) (zool.) musaraña
**shriek** [ʃrik] *s* chillido, grito agudo; risotada chillona; *vn* chillar
**shrievalty** ['ʃrivəltɪ] *s* (*pl:* **-ties**) cargo y jurisdicción de sheriff
**shrift** [ʃrɪft] *s* confesión
**shrike** [ʃraɪk] *s* (orn.) alcaudón, verdugo
**shrill** [ʃrɪl] *adj* chillón, agudo y penetrante; *s* chillido; *vn* chillar
**shrilly** ['ʃrɪllɪ] *adv* de manera chillona, con un ruido agudo y penetrante
**shrimp** [ʃrɪmp] *s* (zool.) camarón; (zool.) crustáceo del género *Crangon;* (fig.) renacuajo (*hombrecillo; persona muy pequeña*)
**shrimpfish** ['ʃrɪmp,fɪʃ] *s* (ichth.) centrisco, chocha de mar
**shrine** [ʃraɪn] *s* relicario; sepulcro de santo; santuario; lugar sagrado (*por ciertos recuerdos, por su historia, etc.*); *va* guardar en un relicario
**shrink** [ʃrɪŋk] *s* contracción, encogimiento; (*pret:* **shrank** o **shrunk;** *pp:* **shrunk** o **shrunken**) *va* contraer, encoger; **to shrink on** montar en caliente, zunchar en caliente; *vn* contraerse, encogerse; moverse hacia atrás; rehuirse, acobardarse, retirarse
**shrinkable** ['ʃrɪŋkəbəl] *adj* contráctil, que se puede contraer o encoger
**shrinkage** ['ʃrɪŋkɪdʒ] *s* contracción, encogimiento; disminución, reducción; merma, pérdida
**shrive** [ʃraɪv] (*pret:* **shrove** o **shrived;** *pp:* **shriven** o **shrived**) *va* imponer la penitencia a, dar la absolución a; confesar; oír en confesión; **to shrive oneself** confesarse y hacer penitencia; *vn* confesarse; oír al penitente
**shrivel** ['ʃrɪvəl] (*pret & pp:* **-eled** o **-elled;** *ger:* **-eling** o **-elling**) *va* arrugar, marchitar, fruncir; *vn* arrugarse, marchitarse, fruncirse; **to shrivel up** avellanarse; consumirse
**shriven** ['ʃrɪvən] *pp de* **shrive**
**shroud** [ʃraʊd] *s* mortaja, sudario; cubierta, velo; cuerda de suspensión (*del paracaídas*); (naut.) obenque; *va* amortajar; cubrir, velar
**shroud line** *s* cuerda de suspensión (*del paracaídas*)
**shrove** [ʃrov] *pret de* **shrive**
**Shrove Monday** *s* lunes de carnaval
**Shrove Sunday** *s* domingo de carnaval
**Shrovetide** ['ʃrov,taɪd] *s* carnestolendas
**Shrove Tuesday** *s* martes de carnaval
**shrub** [ʃrʌb] *s* (bot.) arbusto; ponche (*bebida*)
**shrubbery** ['ʃrʌbərɪ] *s* (*pl:* **-ies**) arbustos; plantío de arbustos
**shrubby** ['ʃrʌbɪ] *adj* (*comp:* **-bier;** *super:* **-biest**) arbustivo
**shrug** [ʃrʌg] *s* encogimiento de hombros; (*pret & pp:* **shrugged;** *ger:* **shrugging**) *va* contraer; **to shrug one's shoulders** encogerse de hombros; *vn* encogerse de hombros
**shrunk** [ʃrʌŋk] *pret & pp de* **shrink**
**shrunken** ['ʃrʌŋkən] *adj* mermado, encogido, arrugado, seco; *pp de* **shrink**
**sh-sh** [ʃʃ] *interj* ¡chitón!
**shuck** [ʃʌk] *s* cáscara, vaina, hollejo; *va* descascarar, descortezar; quitar la concha a (*una ostra*)
**shudder** ['ʃʌdər] *s* estremecimiento; *vn* estremecerse
**shuffle** ['ʃʌfəl] *s* arrastramiento de pies; barajadura (*de naipes*); turno de barajar; movimiento rápido de un lado a otro; evasiva, mala jugada; recomposición; *va* mezclar, mezclar desordenadamente, revolver; arrastrar (*los pies*); barajar (*naipes*); **to shuffle off** deshacerse de; *vn* caminar arrastrando los pies; bailar arrastrando los pies; moverse rápidamente de un lado a otro; barajar; esquivarse por medio de jugarretas; **to shuffle along** ir arrastrando los pies; ir tirando; **to shuffle off** irse arrastrando los pies
**shuffleboard** ['ʃʌfəl,bord] *s* juego de tejo; mesa de tejo
**shun** [ʃʌn] (*pret & pp:* **shunned;** *ger:* **shunning**) *va* esquivar, evitar, apartarse de
**shunt** [ʃʌnt] *s* desviación; (elec.) derivación; (rail.) aguja, cambio de vía; *va* desviar; apartar, deshacerse de; (rail.) desviar; (elec.) poner en derivación
**shunt-wound** ['ʃʌnt,waʊnd] *adj* (elec.) arrollado en derivación
**shut** [ʃʌt] *adj* cerrado; (phonet.) cerrado; (*pret & pp:* **shut;** *ger:* **shutting**) *va* cerrar, tapar; **to shut down** cerrar (*p.ej., una fábrica*); **to shut in** encerrar; **to shut off** cortar (*electricidad, gas, agua*); **to shut out** impedir la entrada de, cerrar la puerta a; (sport) no permitir a (*el equipo enemigo*) ganar tantos; **to shut up** cerrar bien, tapar; acorralar, aprisionar; (coll.) hacer callar; **to shut up shop** cerrar, alzar o levantar tienda; desistir de una empresa; *vn* cerrarse; **to shut down** parar; **to shut down on** o **upon** (coll.) reprimir, suprimir; **to shut up** (coll.) callarse la boca
**shut-down** ['ʃʌt,daʊn] *s* cierre, cesación de trabajo
**shut-in** ['ʃʌt,ɪn] *adj* recluso; (psychopath.) aislado; *s* recluso, valetudinario que vive encerrado en su casa o el hospital
**shut-out** ['ʃʌt,aʊt] *s* cierre para impedir la entrada; (sport) triunfo en que el contrario no gana un solo tanto
**shutter** ['ʃʌtər] *s* cerrador; persiana, celosía; contraventana (*para el exterior de las vidrieras*); cierre metálico (*de escaparate*); (phot.) obturador
**shuttle** ['ʃʌtəl] *s* lanzadera; *vn* ir y venir acompasadamente; hacer viajes cortos de ida y vuelta
**shuttlecock** ['ʃʌtəl,kɑk] *s* volante
**shuttle service** *s* servicio de ida y vuelta entre dos estaciones cercanas
**shuttle train** *s* tren que hace viajes cortos de ida y vuelta
**shy** [ʃaɪ] *adj* (*comp:* **shyer** *o* **shier;** *super:* **shyest** o **shiest**) tímido, recatado, arisco; asustadizo; cauteloso, prudente; escaso, pobre; (slang) adeudado; **to be shy a dollar** (slang) faltarle a uno un dólar; **to be shy on** (slang) estar escaso de; **to fight shy of** evitar, tratar de evitar; *s* (*pl:* **shies**) echada; respingo; (*pret & pp:* **shied**) *va* arrojar, lanzar; *vn* esquivarse, hacerse a un lado; respingar, espantarse; **to shy at** retroceder ante, respingar al ver, espantarse con; **to shy away** alejarse asustado
**shyly** ['ʃaɪlɪ] *adv* tímidamente
**shyness** ['ʃaɪnɪs] *s* timidez, recato; miedo; cautela, prudencia, reserva
**shyster** ['ʃaɪstər] *s* (coll.) abogado trampista
**S.I.** abr. de **Staten Island**
**si** [si] *s* (mus.) si
**Siam** [saɪ'æm] o ['saɪæm] *s* Siam
**Siamese** [,saɪə'miz] *adj* siamés; *s* (*pl:* **-mese**) siamés
**Siamese twins** *spl* hermanos siameses
**sib** [sɪb] *adj* emparentado; *s* parentela; pariente; hermano, hermana
**Siberia** [saɪ'bɪrɪə] *s* Siberia
**Siberian** [saɪ'bɪrɪən] *adj & s* siberiano
**Siberian sable** *s* (zool.) marta cebellina
**sibilance** ['sɪbɪləns] o **sibilancy** ['sɪbɪlənsɪ] *s* calidad sibilante

**sibilant** ['sɪbɪlənt] *adj* sibilante; *s* sonido sibilante; letra sibilante
**sibilate** ['sɪbɪlet] *vn* silbar
**sibling** ['sɪblɪŋ] *s* hermano, hermana
**sibyl** ['sɪbɪl] *s* sibila
**sibylline** ['sɪbɪlaɪn] o ['sɪbɪlɪn] *adj* sibilino; (fig.) sibilino
**Sibylline Books** *spl* Libros sibilinos
**sic** [sɪk] *va* (*pret & pp:* **sicked;** *ger:* **sicking**) atacar; azuzar, abijar (*a un perro*)
**Sicanian** [sɪ'kenɪən] *adj* sicano
**siccative** ['sɪkətɪv] *adj & s* secante
**Sicilian** [sɪ'sɪljən] *adj & s* siciliano
**Sicilian Vespers** *spl* (hist.) Vísperas sicilianas
**Sicily** ['sɪsɪlɪ] *s* Sicilia
**sick** [sɪk] *adj* enfermo; nauseado; pálido, demacrado; cansado, agotado; **the sick** los enfermos; **to be sick of** estar cansado de, estar harto de; **to be sick at one's stomach** tener náuseas; **to take sick** caer enfermo; **sick and tired of** (coll.) harto y cansado de; **sick at heart** afligido de corazón, angustiado; *va* var. de **sic**
**sick bay** *s* (naut.) enfermería
**sickbed** ['sɪk,bɛd] *s* lecho de enfermo
**sick call** *s* visita del médico o clérigo a un enfermo; (mil.) toque de visita médica
**sicken** ['sɪkən] *va & vn* enfermar
**sickening** ['sɪkənɪŋ] *adj* nauseabundo; achacoso; repelente
**sick headache** *s* (path.) jaqueca con náuseas
**sickish** ['sɪkɪʃ] *adj* enfermucho; nauseabundo
**sickle** ['sɪkəl] *s* hoz
**sick leave** *s* licencia por enfermo
**sickly** ['sɪklɪ] *adj* (*comp:* **-lier;** *super:* **-liest**) enfermizo; pálido, demacrado; apestado
**Sick Man of Europe, the** el enfermo de Europa (*Turquía*)
**sickness** ['sɪknɪs] *s* enfermedad; náusea
**sick nurse** *s* enfermera
**sickroom** ['sɪk,rum] o ['sɪk,rʊm] *s* cuarto del enfermo
**side** [saɪd] *s* lado; cara (*de un sólido; de un disco de fonógrafo*); falda (*de una colina*); orilla, margen; facción, partido; campo (*en algún desafío*); bando (*en el bridge*); (geom.) lado; (naut.) costado; **by the side of** al lado de; **on all sides** por todos lados, por todas partes; **on the side** (slang) por añadidura; **the other side of the picture** el revés de la medalla; **to split one's sides** desternillarse de risa; **to take sides** tomar partido; **to take sides with** tomar el partido de, ponerse al lado de; **side by side** juntos, lado a lado; *adj* lateral; de lado; indirecto, oblicuo; secundario; suplementario; *va* echar a un lado; poner costados a; *vn* tomar partido; **to side with** declararse por
**side arms** *spl* armas de cinto
**sidebands** ['saɪd,bændz] *spl* (rad.) bandas laterales
**sideboard** ['saɪd,bord] *s* aparador; adral, tablar (*de un carro*)
**sideburns** ['saɪd,bʌrnz] *spl* patillas
**sidecar** ['saɪd,kɑr] *s* cochecito lateral de una motocicleta
**side chain** *s* (chem.) cadena lateral
**side dish** *s* plato de entrada
**side door** *s* puerta lateral; puerta excusada o falsa
**side effect** *s* (med.) efecto secundario perjudicial de ciertos medicamentos
**side face** *s* perfil
**side glance** *s* mirada de soslayo, mirada de través
**side issue** *s* cuestión secundaria
**side-kick** ['saɪd,kɪk] *s* (slang) a látere
**side light** *s* luz lateral; detalle incidental, información incidente
**side line** *s* línea lateral; negocio accesorio, actividad suplementaria; (tennis) línea de lado; **side lines** *spl* (sport) sitio fuera de las líneas; **on the side lines** sin participar, sin tomar parte
**sidelock** ['saɪd,lɑk] *s* tufo
**sidelong** ['saɪd,lɔŋ] o ['saɪd,lɑŋ] *adj* lateral; *adv* lateralmente
**side meat** *s* tocino, tocino salado
**sidenote** ['saɪd,not] *s* (print.) ladillo
**sidepiece** ['saɪd,pis] *s* pieza lateral, parte lateral
**sidereal** [saɪ'dɪrɪəl] *adj* sidéreo
**siderite** ['sɪdəraɪt] *s* (mineral.) siderosa, siderita
**siderosis** [,sɪdə'rosɪs] *s* (path.) siderosis
**siderurgical** [,sɪdər'ʌrdʒɪkəl] *adj* siderúrgico
**siderurgy** ['sɪdər,ʌrdʒɪ] *s* siderurgia
**sidesaddle** ['saɪd,sædəl] *s* sillón, silla de mujer; *adv* a asentadillas, a mujeriegas
**side show** *s* feria, espectáculo de atracciones, espectáculo del circo; asunto de importancia secundaria
**sideslip** ['saɪd,slɪp] *s* resbalamiento lateral (*de un neumático*); deslizamiento lateral (*de un avión*); (*pret & pp:* **-slipped;** *ger:* **-slipping**) *vn* resbalar hacia un lado; deslizar hacia un lado
**sidesplitting** ['saɪd,splɪtɪŋ] *adj* desternillante
**side step** *s* paso hacia un lado; escalón para subir a un carruaje, embarcación, etc.; (box.) esquivada lateral
**side-step** ['saɪd,stɛp] (*pret & pp:* **-stepped;** *ger:* **-stepping**) *va* evitar, evadir, esquivar; *vn* dar un paso hacia un lado, hacerse a un lado, esquivarse; retirarse
**sideswipe** ['saɪd,swaɪp] *s* (coll.) rozadura, tocamiento oblicuo; *va* (coll.) rozar, tocar oblicuamente
**sidetrack** ['saɪd,træk] *s* (rail.) vía muerta, desviadero, apartadero; *va* desviar (*un tren*); echar a un lado, hacer desviar
**side view** *s* vista de perfil, vista de lado
**sidewalk** ['saɪd,wɔk] *s* acera; banqueta, vereda (Am.)
**sidewalk café** *s* terraza (*café en la acera*)
**sidewall** ['saɪd,wɔl] *s* (aut.) flanco (*de un neumático*)
**sideward** ['saɪdwərd] *adj* oblicuo, sesgado; *adv* de lado, hacia un lado
**sidewards** ['saɪdwərdz] *adv* de lado, hacia un lado
**sideway** ['saɪd,we] *s* vereda; callejuela; acera; *adj* oblicuo, sesgado; *adv* de lado, oblicuamente; al través; hacia un lado
**sideways** ['saɪd,wez] *adj* oblicuo, sesgado; *adv* de lado, oblicuamente; al través; hacia un lado
**side-wheel** ['saɪd,hwil] *adj* de ruedas laterales (*dícese de un barco de vapor*)
**side-wheeler** ['saɪd,hwilər] *s* (coll.) vapor de ruedas laterales
**side whiskers** *spl* patillas
**sidewinder** ['saɪd,waɪndər] *s* (zool.) cerasta, víbora cornuda; (slang) puñetazo fuerte dado de lado; (mil.) proyectil antiaéreo de propulsante sólido (*aire-aire*)
**sidewise** ['saɪd,waɪz] *adj* oblicuo, sesgado; *adv* de lado, oblicuamente, sesgadamente; al través; hacia un lado
**siding** ['saɪdɪŋ] *s* (rail.) vía muerta, desviadero, apartadero; entablado de los costados
**sidle** ['saɪdəl] *vn* ir de lado, moverse de lado y furtivamente; **to sidle up** acercarse de lado para no ser visto
**Sidonian** [saɪ'donɪən] *adj & s* sidonio
**siege** [sidʒ] *s* sitio, cerco; (coll.) paso interminable; **to lay siege to** (mil.) poner sitio o cerco a; (fig.) asediar (*p.ej., al corazón de una mujer*); **to raise the siege** (mil.) alzar el cerco, levantar el sitio
**siege artillery** *s* artillería de sitio
**Siege Perilous** *s* Silla peligrosa (*en la mesa redonda del rey Artús*)
**Siegfried** ['sigfrid] *s* Sigfrido
**Sienese** [,siə'niz] *adj* sienés; *s* (*pl:* **-ese**) sienés
**sienna** [sɪ'ɛnə] *s* siena, tierra de siena
**sierra** [sɪ'ɛrə] *s* sierra (*cadena de montes y peñascos cortados*); (ichth.) pintada, sierra
**siesta** [sɪ'ɛstə] *s* siesta; *vn* sestear
**Sieva bean** ['sivə] *s* (bot.) frijol iztagapa; chilipuca (*semilla*)
**sieve** [sɪv] *s* cedazo, tamiz; persona que no sabe guardar secretos; *va* cerner, tamizar
**sieve cell** *s* (bot.) célula cribosa
**sieve disk** o **plate** *s* (bot.) placa acribillada
**sieve tissue** *s* (bot.) tejido criboso
**sieve tube** o **vessel** *s* (bot.) tubo criboso
**sift** [sɪft] *va* cerner, cribar; escudriñar, examinar; *vn* servirse de un cedazo; caer de un cedazo, caer como de un cedazo

**sifter** ['sɪftər] *s* cribador; cedazo, criba, tamiz
**sigh** [saɪ] *s* suspiro; **to breathe a sigh of relief** respirar, cobrar aliento; *va* decir con suspiros; lamentar; *vn* suspirar; **to sigh for** suspirar por
**sight** [saɪt] *s* vista, visión; cosa digna de verse; (coll.) espantajo; (coll.) horror, atrocidad; mira (*de arma de fuego, telescopio, etc.*); opinión, juicio; (coll.) gran cantidad, montón; (com.) vista, p.ej., **thirty days sight** treinta días vista; **at first sight** al primer contacto; **at sight** a primera vista; a libro abierto (*dícese de una traducción*); (com.) a la vista; **in sight** visible; **in sight of** a la vista de; **on sight** a primera vista; **out of sight** fuera del alcance de la vista; por las nubes (*dícese de los precios*); **out of sight of** sin ver; sin ser visto por; **to catch sight of** avistar, alcanzar a ver; **to come into sight** aparecer; asomar; **to heave in sight** (naut.) aparecer en el horizonte; **to keep out of sight** no dejar ver; no dejarse ver; **to know by sight** conocer de vista; **to lose sight of** perder de vista; **to not be able to stand the sight of** no poder ver ni en pintura; **to see the sights** visitar los puntos de interés; **sight unseen** sin haberlo visto; *va* avistar, alcanzar con la vista; descubrir con un instrumento óptico, localizar con la vista por medio de un instrumento; *vn* apuntar con una mira; dirigir una visual
**sight draft** *s* (com.) giro a la vista, letra a la vista
**sightless** ['saɪtlɪs] *adj* ciego; invisible
**sightly** ['saɪtlɪ] *adj* (*comp:* **-lier;** *super:* **-liest**) vistoso, hermoso
**sight-read** ['saɪt,rid] (*pret & pp:* **-read** [,rɛd]) *va* leer a libro abierto; (mus.) ejecutar a la primera lectura; *vn* leer a libro abierto; (mus.) repentizar
**sight reader** *s* lector a libro abierto; (mus.) repentista
**sight reading** *s* lectura a libro abierto (*de un idioma extranjero*); (mus.) ejecución a la primera lectura
**sightseeing** ['saɪt,siɪŋ] *s* excursionismo, turismo, visita de puntos de interés; **to go sightseeing** ir a ver los puntos de interés
**sightseeing bus** *s* autocar, ómnibus de excursión
**sightseer** ['saɪt,siər] *s* excursionista, turista
**sigma** ['sɪgmə] *s* sigma
**sigmoid** ['sɪgmɔɪd] *adj* sigmoideo
**sign** [saɪn] *s* signo (*p.ej., de la lluvia*); (astr., math., med., mus. & print.) signo; señal, marca, huella, vestigio; letrero, muestra; **to show signs of** dar muestras de, tener trazas de; **sign of the cross** señal de la cruz; *va* firmar; contratar, hacer firmar; ceder, traspasar mediante escritura; **to sign away** u **over** firmar el traspaso de, firmar la cesión de; **to sign up** ajustar (*para un trabajo o servicio*); *vn* firmar; **to sign off** (rad.) terminar la transmisión; **to sign up** (coll.) firmar el contrato
**signal** ['sɪgnəl] *s* señal; (rad.) señal; *adj* señalado, notable; (*pret & pp:* **-naled** o **-nalled;** *ger:* **-naling** o **-nalling**) *va* señalar, hacer saber por medio de señales; *vn* hacer señales
**signal code** *s* código de señales
**signal corps** *s* (mil.) cuerpo de señales
**signal flag** *s* bandera de señales
**signalize** ['sɪgnəlaɪz] *va* distinguir, singularizar
**signally** ['sɪgnəlɪ] *adv* señaladamente, notablemente
**signalman** ['sɪgnəl,mæn] *s* (*pl:* **-men**) hombre de señal, señalero; (rail.) guardavía, (rail.) semaforista
**signal strength** *s* (rad.) fuerza de señal
**signal tower** *s* torre de señales
**signatory** ['sɪgnə,torɪ] *adj* signatario, firmante; *s* (*pl:* **-ries**) signatario, firmante
**signature** ['sɪgnətʃər] *s* firma; (print.) signatura; (print.) pliego con signatura; **over one's signature** bajo su firma
**signboard** ['saɪn,bord] *s* letrero, cartelón, muestra; (fig.) muestra
**signer** ['saɪnər] *s* firmante, signatario
**signet** ['sɪgnɪt] *s* sello; signáculo
**signet ring** *s* sortija de sello, anillo sigilar
**significance** [sɪg'nɪfɪkəns] *s* significación
**significant** [sɪg'nɪfɪkənt] *adj* significativo
**signification** [,sɪgnɪfɪ'keʃən] *s* significación
**significative** [sɪg'nɪfɪ,ketɪv] *adj* significativo
**signify** ['sɪgnɪfaɪ] (*pret & pp:* **-fied**) *va & vn* significar
**sign language** *s* lenguaje de los signos, dactilología
**sign manual** *s* firma rubricada, firma de propio puño; sello de individualidad
**signory** ['sinjərɪ] *s* (*pl:* **-ries**) señorío (*mando; dominio feudal*); señoría (*gobierno de ciertas ciudades italianas medievales; república italiana medieval*)
**sign painter** *s* pintor de muestras
**signpost** ['saɪn,post] *s* hito, poste de guía
**Sikh** [sik] *s* sij
**silage** ['saɪlɪdʒ] *s* ensilaje
**silence** ['saɪləns] *s* silencio; **in silence** en silencio; *interj* ¡silencio!; *va* acallar, silenciar, imponer silencio a; (mil.) apagar el fuego de; (mil.) apagar (*el fuego del enemigo*)
**silencer** ['saɪlənsər] *s* silenciero (*persona*); silenciador (*aparato para armas de fuego, motores de explosión, etc.*)
**silent** ['saɪlənt] *adj* silencioso; (phonet.) mudo
**silent movie** *s* (coll.) cine mudo
**silent partner** *s* (com.) socio comanditario
**Silenus** [saɪ'linəs] *s* (myth.) Sileno
**Silesian** [sɪ'liʃən] o [saɪ'liʃən] *adj & s* silesiano o silesio
**silex** ['saɪlɛks] *s* (mineral.) sílex; (chem.) sílice
**silhouette** [,sɪlu'ɛt] *s* silueta; **in silhouette** en silueta; *va* siluetar
**silica** ['sɪlɪkə] *s* (chem.) sílice
**silicate** ['sɪlɪket] o ['sɪlɪkɪt] *s* (chem.) silicato
**siliceous** [sɪ'lɪʃəs] *adj* silíceo
**silicic** [sɪ'lɪsɪk] *adj* (chem.) silícico
**silicide** ['sɪlɪsaɪd] o ['sɪlɪsɪd] *s* (chem.) siliciuro
**silicious** [sɪ'lɪʃəs] *adj* var. de **siliceous**
**silicle** ['sɪlɪkəl] *s* (bot.) silícula
**silicon** ['sɪlɪkən] *s* (chem.) silicio
**silicone** ['sɪlɪkon] *s* (chem.) silicón
**silicosis** [,sɪlɪ'kosɪs] *s* (path.) silicosis
**silique** [sɪ'lik] o ['sɪlɪk] *s* (bot.) silicua
**siliquose** ['sɪlɪkwos] o **siliquous** ['sɪlɪkwəs] *adj* (bot.) silicuoso
**silk** [sɪlk] *s* seda; **to hit the silk** (slang) lanzarse en paracaídas; *adj* sedeño
**silkaline** [,sɪlkə'lin] *s* sedalina
**silk-cotton tree** ['sɪlk'kɑtən] *s* (bot.) capoquero
**silken** ['sɪlkən] *adj* sedeño; asedado; vestido de seda
**silk hat** *s* sombrero de copa
**silk-stocking** ['sɪlk,stɑkɪŋ] *adj* aristocrático; *s* aristócrata
**silkworm** ['sɪlk,wʌrm] *s* gusano de seda
**silky** ['sɪlkɪ] *adj* (*comp:* **-ier;** *super:* **-iest**) sedoso
**sill** [sɪl] *s* travesaño, solera; umbral (*de puerta*); antepecho (*de ventana*)
**sillabub** ['sɪləbʌb] *s* postre hecho de nata, huevos, vino y azúcar
**silliness** ['sɪlɪnɪs] *s* necedad, tontería
**silly** ['sɪlɪ] *adj* (*comp:* **-lier;** *super:* **-liest**) necio, tonto; (coll.) patidifuso
**silo** ['saɪlo] *s* (*pl:* **-los**) (agr.) silo; *va* (agr.) asilar
**Siloam** [sɪ'loəm] o [saɪ'loəm] *s* (Bib.) Siloé
**silt** [sɪlt] *s* cieno, sedimento; *va* obstruir con cieno, obstruir con sedimentos; *vn* obstruirse con cieno, obstruirse con sedimentos
**silty** ['sɪltɪ] *adj* (*comp:* **-ier;** *super:* **-iest**) cenagoso, sedimentoso
**Silurian** [sɪ'lurɪən] *adj & s* (geol.) siluriano o silúrico
**silva** ['sɪlvə] *s* árboles de un país; tratado sobre los árboles de un país
**silvan** ['sɪlvən] *adj* var. de **sylvan;** (*cap.*) *s* Silvano
**silver** ['sɪlvər] *s* (chem.) plata; plata (*moneda o monedas*); plateado (*color*); *adj* plateado; de plata; argentino (*dícese de la voz*); elocuente; *va* platear; azogar (*un espejo*); *vn* platearse
**silver age** *s* (myth.) edad de plata, siglo de plata

**silver fir** *s* (bot.) abeto blanco, abeto de hojas de tejo o abeto plateado
**silverfish** ['sɪlvər,fɪʃ] *s* (ent.) pez de plata; (ichth.) pez de colores
**silver foil** *s* hoja de plata
**silver fox** *s* (zool.) zorro plateado
**silver gilt** *s* plata dorada
**silver leaf** *s* hoja de plata
**silver lining** *s* aspecto agradable de una condición desgraciada o triste
**silver-mounted** ['sɪlvər,maʊntɪd] *adj* montado en plata; adornado de plata
**silver nitrate** *s* (chem.) nitrato de plata
**silver pheasant** *s* (orn.) faisán plateado
**silver plate** *s* plateado; plato de plata; vajilla de plata
**silver-plated** ['sɪlvər'pletɪd] *adj* argentado, plateado
**silver plating** *s* plateado, plateadura
**silver screen** *s* pantalla plateada; (fig.) pantalla (*el cine*)
**silversmith** ['sɪlvər,smɪθ] *s* platero, orfebre
**silver-tongue** ['sɪlvər,tʌŋ] *s* (coll.) pico de oro
**silver-tongued** ['sɪlvər'tʌŋd] *adj* elocuente, con el pico de oro
**silverware** ['sɪlvər,wɛr] *s* plata, vajilla de plata
**silver wedding** *s* bodas de plata
**silvery** ['sɪlvərɪ] *adj* argénteo, argentino
**Silvester** [sɪl'vɛstər] *s* Silvestre
**Simeon** ['sɪmɪən] *s* Simeón
**simian** ['sɪmɪən] *adj* símico; *s* (zool.) simio
**similar** ['sɪmɪlər] *adj* similar, semejante
**similarity** [,sɪmɪ'lærɪtɪ] *s* (*pl:* **-ties**) semejanza
**simile** ['sɪmɪlɪ] *s* (rhet.) símil
**similitude** [sɪ'mɪlɪtjud] o [sɪ'mɪlɪtud] *s* similitud; símil, comparación; imagen, copia
**similor** ['sɪmɪlər] *s* similor
**simitar** ['sɪmɪtər] *s* var. de **scimitar**
**simmer** ['sɪmər] *va* cocer a fuego lento; *vn* cocer a fuego lento; (fig.) estar a punto de estallar; **to simmer down** (coll.) reducirse lentamente; (coll.) tranquilizarse lentamente
**simoleon** [sɪ'molɪən] *s* (slang) dólar
**Simon** ['saɪmən] *s* Simón
**simoniacal** [,saɪmə'naɪəkəl] *adj* simoníaco
**Simoniz** ['saɪmənaɪz] *s* (trademark) simonización; *va* simonizar
**simon-pure** ['saɪmən'pjʊr] *adj* auténtico, puro, genuino, verdadero
**simony** ['sɪmənɪ] o ['saɪmənɪ] *s* simonía
**simoom** [sɪ'mum] o **simoon** [sɪ'mun] *s* simún
**simp** [sɪmp] *s* (slang) bobo, mentecato
**simper** ['sɪmpər] *s* sonrisa boba; *va* decir con sonrisa boba, decir con bobería; *vn* sonreír bobamente
**simple** ['sɪmpəl] *adj* simple; *s* simple (*bobo, mentecato; persona mansa e incauta; planta medicinal*); cosa o idea simples; persona de humilde alcurnia; (eccl.) fiesta simple; (pharm.) simple
**simple engine** *s* máquina de simple expansión
**simple equation** *s* (alg.) ecuación de primer grado
**simple fraction** *s* (math.) fracción incompleja
**simple-hearted** ['sɪmpəl'hɑrtɪd] *adj* inocente, ingenuo
**simple interest** *s* interés simple
**simple machine** *s* mecanismo elemental
**simple-minded** ['sɪmpəl'maɪndɪd] *adj* estúpido, ignorante; candoroso; idiota, imbécil
**simpleness** ['sɪmpəlnɪs] *s* simplicidad
**simple sentence** *s* (gram.) oración simple
**simple substance** *s* (chem.) cuerpo simple (*elemento*)
**simpleton** ['sɪmpəltən] *s* bobo, mentecato
**simplicity** [sɪm'plɪsɪtɪ] *s* (*pl:* **-ties**) simplicidad; simpleza (*bobería, necedad*)
**simplification** [,sɪmplɪfɪ'keʃən] *s* simplificación
**simplify** ['sɪmplɪfaɪ] (*pret & pp:* **-fied**) *va* simplificar
**Simplon tunnel** ['sɪmplɑn] *s* túnel del Simplón
**simply** ['sɪmplɪ] *adv* simplemente, sencillamente; solamente
**simulacrum** [,sɪmjə'lekrəm] *s* (*pl:* **-cra** [krə] o **-crums**) simulacro
**simulate** ['sɪmjəlɪt] o ['sɪmjəlet] *adj* simulado; ['sɪmjəlet] *va* simular
**simulation** [,sɪmjə'leʃən] *s* simulación
**simulative** ['sɪmjə,letɪv] *adj* simulador
**simultaneity** [,saɪməltə'niɪtɪ] o [,sɪməltə'niɪtɪ] *s* simultaneidad
**simultaneous** [,saɪməl'tenɪəs] o [,sɪməl'tenɪəs] *adj* simultáneo
**simultaneous equation** *s* (alg.) ecuación simultánea
**simultaneously** [,saɪməl'tenɪəslɪ] o [,sɪməl'tenɪəslɪ] *adv* simultáneamente
**sin** [sɪn] *s* pecado; (*pret & pp:* **sinned;** *ger:* **sinning**) *vn* pecar
**Sinai** ['saɪnaɪ] o ['saɪnɪaɪ] *s* el Sinaí (*península*); **Mount Sinai** el monte Sinaí
**sinapism** ['sɪnəpɪzəm] *s* sinapismo
**since** [sɪns] *adv* desde entonces, después; **long since** hace mucho tiempo; *prep* desde; después de; **since when?** ¿desde cuándo?; *conj* desde que; después (de) que; ya que, puesto que
**sincere** [sɪn'sɪr] *adj* sincero
**sincerity** [sɪn'sɛrɪtɪ] *s* (*pl:* **-ties**) sinceridad
**sine** [saɪn] *s* (trig.) seno
**sinecure** ['saɪnɪkjʊr] o ['sɪnɪkjʊr] *s* sinecura
**sinecurist** ['saɪnɪ,kjʊrɪst] o ['sɪnɪ,kjʊrɪst] *s* sinecurista
**sine curve** *s* (math.) curva senoidal
**sine die** ['saɪnɪ'daɪi] (Lat.) hasta nueva orden, indefinidamente
**sine qua non** ['saɪnɪkwe'nɑn] *s* (Lat.) condición sin la cual no se hará una cosa, condición indispensable
**sinew** ['sɪnju] *s* tendón; (fig.) fibra, nervio, vigor; (fig.) fuente de energía y vigor
**sine wave** *s* (phys.) onda senoidal
**sinewy** ['sɪnjəwɪ] *adj* nervoso, nervudo; fuerte, vigoroso
**sinful** ['sɪnfəl] *adj* pecador; pecaminoso (*dícese del acto, la intención, etc.*)
**sing.** abr. de **singular**
**sing** [sɪŋ] *s* silbido, zumbido (*p.ej., de un proyectil*); canto; cantata; (*pret:* **sang** o **sung;** *pp:* **sung**) *va* cantar; **to sing to sleep** arrullar, adormecer cantando; *vn* cantar; chillar (*p.ej., los oídos*)
**Singapore** ['sɪŋgəpor], ['sɪŋəpor] o [,sɪŋgə'por] *s* Singapur
**singe** [sɪndʒ] *s* chamusquina, socarra; (*ger:* **singeing**) *va* chamuscar, socarrar; quemar ligeramente, quemar las puntas de; sollamar (*un ave*); perjudicar, dañar
**singer** ['sɪŋər] *s* cantante; vocalista (*p.ej., en un café cantante*); pájaro cantor
**Singhalese** [,sɪŋgə'liz] *adj* cingalés; *s* (*pl:* **-lese**) cingalés
**singing** ['sɪŋɪŋ] *s* canto; chillido (*en los oídos*)
**singing school** *s* escuela de canto
**single** ['sɪŋgəl] *adj* uno; único, solo; simple; particular; individual (*p.ej., cuarto en un hotel*); suelto (*ejemplar*); soltero; de soltero; sincero, honrado; (bot.) sencillo; (naut.) single; *s* simple, individuo; (baseball) sencillo; **singles** *spl* (tennis) juego de simples o individuales; *va* escoger, elegir; singularizar; **to single out** separar, entresacar; singularizar, señalar con especialidad; *vn* andar (*un caballo*) a paso fino; (baseball) pasar a primera base
**single-acting** ['sɪŋgəl'æktɪŋ] *adj* (mach.) de simple efecto
**single bed** *s* cama camera
**single blessedness** *s* estado de soltero o soltera
**single-breasted** ['sɪŋgəl'brɛstɪd] *adj* sin cruzar, de una hilera de botones, de un solo pecho
**single-cut file** ['sɪŋgəl,kʌt] *s* lima de picadura sencilla
**single entry** *s* (com.) partida simple
**single-eyed** ['sɪŋgəl,aɪd] *adj* tuerto; clarividente; justo, honrado
**single file** *s* fila india; **in single file** uno tras otro, de uno en uno, de reata
**single-foot** ['sɪŋgəl,fʊt] *s* paso fino (*de un caballo*); *vn* caminar (*un caballo*) a paso fino
**single-handed** ['sɪŋgəl'hændɪd] *adj* de una mano; para una persona; sin ayuda
**single-hearted** ['sɪŋgəl'hɑrtɪd] *adj* sincero, sin doblez; con un solo propósito
**single life** *s* vida de soltero
**single line** *s* (aut.) paso único

**single-minded** ['sɪŋgəl'maɪndɪd] *adj* con un solo propósito; ingenuo, sincero
**singleness** ['sɪŋgəlnɪs] *s* unidad; sencillez, llaneza; sinceridad, honradez; soltería
**single-phase** ['sɪŋgəl'fez] *adj* (elec.) monofásico
**single-pole switch** ['sɪŋgəl'pol] *s* (elec.) interruptor unipolar
**single room** *s* habitación individual, cuarto para una persona
**single-seater** ['sɪŋgəl'sitər] *s* (aer.) monoplaza, avión de una plaza
**single-space** ['sɪŋgəl'spes] *adj* a un solo espacio, escrito a un solo espacio
**single-stage** ['sɪŋgəl'stedʒ] *adj* de etapa única
**singlestick** ['sɪŋgəl,stɪk] *s* (fencing) bastón; esgrima del bastón; *vn* esgrimir el bastón
**singlet** ['sɪŋglɪt] *s* camiseta
**single tax** *s* impuesto único
**single-throw switch** ['sɪŋgəl'θro] *s* (elec.) interruptor de una caída
**singleton** ['sɪŋgəltən] *s* (bridge) única carta de un palo
**single-track** ['sɪŋgəl,træk] *adj* de vía única, de vía sencilla; (coll.) de cortos alcances, de intereses limitados
**singletree** ['sɪŋgəl,tri] *s* balancín
**singsong** ['sɪŋ,sɔŋ] o ['sɪŋ,sɑŋ] *s* salmodia, sonsonete, acento cantante; *adj* monótono; *va & vn* salmodiar
**singular** ['sɪŋgjələr] *adj* singular; (gram.) singular; *s* (gram.) singular
**singularity** [,sɪŋgjə'lærɪtɪ] *s* (*pl:* **-ties**) singularidad
**Sinhalese** [,sɪnhə'liz] *adj & s* var. de **Singhalese**
**Sinic** ['sɪnɪk] *adj* sínico
**sinister** ['sɪnɪstər] *adj* siniestro (*que está a la mano izquierda; malintencionado; funesto*); (her.) siniestro
**sinistral** ['sɪnɪstrəl] *adj* siniestro
**sinistrorse** ['sɪnɪstrɔrs] *adj* (bot.) sinistrorso
**sink** [sɪŋk] *s* fregadero (*de la cocina*); sumidero, desaguadero; área pantanosa; lugar de vicio y mal vivir; (*pret:* **sank** o **sunk**; *pp:* **sunk**) *va* hundir, sumergir; echar a pique; abrir, cavar (*un pozo*); hincar (*p.ej., los dientes*); enterrar (*un poste*); bajar (*la voz; el precio*); calar (*un cajón hidráulico*); invertir (*mucho dinero*); invertir (*mucho dinero*) perdiéndolo todo; ocultar, suprimir; *vn* hundirse; irse a pique; sumirse (*el agua en la tierra*); sentarse (*p.ej., un edificio*); hundirse (*p.ej., el Sol en el horizonte*); dejarse caer (*en una silla*); descender, desaparecer; menguar, disminuir; decaer (*un enfermo; una llama*)
**sinkable** ['sɪŋkəbəl] *adj* hundible, sumergible
**sinker** ['sɪŋkər] *s* plomo (*de las redes de pesca*)
**sinkhole** ['sɪŋk,hol] *s* agujero de desagüe; hoyo de aguas sucias; lugar de vicio y mal vivir
**sinking fund** *s* fondo de amortización
**sinless** ['sɪnlɪs] *adj* impecable, inmaculado, exento de pecado
**sinner** ['sɪnər] *s* pecador
**Sino-American** [,saɪnoə'mɛrɪkən] o [,sɪnoə'mɛrɪkən] *adj* chinoamericano
**Sino-Japanese** [,saɪno,dʒæpə'niz] o [,sɪno,dʒæpə'niz] *adj* sinojaponés
**Sinological** [,saɪnə'lɑdʒɪkəl] o [,sɪnə'lɑdʒɪkəl] *adj* sinológico
**Sinologist** [saɪ'nɑlədʒɪst] o [sɪ'nɑlədʒɪst] *s* sinólogo
**Sinology** [saɪ'nɑlədʒɪ] o [sɪ'nɑlədʒɪ] *s* sinología
**sinuate** ['sɪnjʊet] *adj* sinuoso; (bot.) festoneado
**sinuosity** [,sɪnjʊ'ɑsɪtɪ] *s* (*pl:* **-ties**) sinuosidad
**sinuous** ['sɪnjʊəs] *adj* sinuoso
**sinus** ['saɪnəs] *s* (anat., bot., zool. & path.) seno
**sinusitis** [,saɪnə'saɪtɪs] *s* (path.) sinusitis
**sinusoid** ['saɪnəsɔɪd] *s* (math.) sinusoide
**sinusoidal** [,saɪnə'sɔɪdəl] *adj* sinusoidal
**Sion** ['saɪən] *s* var. de **Zion**
**sip** [sɪp] *s* sorbo, trago; (*pret & pp:* **sipped**; *ger:* **sipping**) *va & vn* sorber, beber a tragos
**siphon** ['saɪfən] *s* sifón; *va* sacar con sifón, trasegar con sifón; pasar a través de un sifón
**siphon bottle** *s* sifón
**siphonogam** ['saɪfənəgæm] *s* (bot.) sifonógama
**siphonogamic** [,saɪfənə'gæmɪk] *adj* (bot.) sifonógamo
**sir** [sʌr] *s* señor; (*cap.*) *s* sir (*tratamiento honorífico en Inglaterra*)
**sire** [saɪr] *s* padre, semental; caballo padre; sire (*tratamiento dado primero a los señores y luego sólo al rey*); (poet.) padre, antecesor; (obs.) señor; *va* engendrar
**siren** ['saɪrən] *s* (aut., phys., myth. & fig.) sirena
**sirenian** [saɪ'rinɪən] *adj & s* (zool.) sirenio
**Sirian** ['sɪrɪən] *adj* (astr.) siríaco
**Sirius** ['sɪrɪəs] *s* (astr.) Sirio
**sirloin** ['sʌrlɔɪn] *s* solomillo
**sirocco** [sɪ'rɑko] *s* (*pl:* **-cos**) siroco
**sirrah** ['sɪrə] *s* (archaic) señoritingo
**sirup** ['sɪrəp] o ['sʌrəp] *s* var. de **syrup**
**sirupy** ['sɪrəpɪ] o ['sʌrəpɪ] *adj* var. de **syrupy**
**sis** [sɪs] *s* (coll.) hermanita
**sisal** ['saɪsəl] o ['sɪsəl] *s* (bot.) sisal, henequén; cáñamo sisal
**sisal hemp** *s* cáñamo sisal
**sissify** ['sɪsɪfaɪ] (*pret & pp:* **-fied**) *va* (coll.) afeminar
**sissy** ['sɪsɪ] *s* (*pl:* **-sies**) (coll.) hermanita, pequeñita; (coll.) afeminado, maricón, santito
**sister** ['sɪstər] *s* hermana; *adj* hermano, p.ej., **sister language** lengua hermana; gemelo, p.ej., **sister ship** buque gemelo
**sisterhood** ['sɪstərhud] *s* hermandad, cofradía de mujeres
**sister-in-law** ['sɪstərɪn,lɔ] *s* (*pl:* **sisters-in-law**) cuñada, hermana política; concuñada
**sisterly** ['sɪstərlɪ] *adj* como hermana, como hermanas
**Sister of Charity** o **Sister of Mercy** *s* hermana de la caridad
**Sistine** ['sɪstin] o ['sɪstɪn] *adj* sixtino
**Sistine Chapel** *s* Capilla sixtina
**sistrum** ['sɪstrəm] *s* (*pl:* **-trums** o **-tra** [trə]) (mus.) sistro
**Sisyphus** ['sɪsɪfəs] *s* (myth.) Sísifo
**sit** [sɪt] *va* (*pret & pp:* **sat**; *ger:* **sitting**) sentar; montar (*un caballo*); empollar (*huevos*); **to sit out** aguantar hasta el fin; permanecer sentado durante; permanecer más tarde que (*otra persona*); *vn* estar sentado; sentarse; posarse (*el ave sobre una rama*); echarse (*un ave sobre los huevos*); reunirse, celebrar junta; descansar; sentar (*bien o mal un vestido*); **to sit down** sentarse; **to sit in** tomar parte en; **to sit on** o **upon** tomar asiento en (*p.ej., una junta*); tomar parte en; (slang) hacer callar, poner en su lugar; (slang) desairar; **to sit still** estarse quieto; **to sit tight** (coll.) mantenerse firme en su puesto; (coll.) callarse, ocultarse; **to sit up** permanecer sentado; incorporarse (*el que estaba echado*); velar, quedarse en vela; **to sit up and take notice** (coll.) despabilarse
**sit-down strike** ['sɪt,daʊn] *s* huelga de sentados, huelga de brazos caídos
**site** [saɪt] *s* sitio, paraje, lugar, local
**sit-in** ['sɪt,ɪn] *s* huelga de brazos caídos; ocupación de asientos en un local sólo para blancos en protesta contra la discriminación racial
**sitology** [saɪ'tɑlədʒɪ] *s* sitología
**sitter** ['sɪtər] *s* persona sentada, pasajero sentado; modelo de pintor o fotógrafo; ave clueca, gallina clueca
**sitting** ['sɪtɪŋ] *adj* sentado; *s* sentada; estadía (*p.ej., ante un pintor*); **at one sitting** de una sentada
**sitting duck** *s* pato sentado en el agua (*fácil de matar a tiro de escopeta*); (coll.) blanco de fácil alcance
**sitting room** *s* sala, sala de estar
**situate** ['sɪtʃʊet] *va* situar
**situation** [,sɪtʃʊ'eʃən] o [,sɪtʃə'weʃən] *s* situación; puesto, colocación
**situs** ['saɪtəs] *s* sitio, situación
**sitz bath** [sɪts] *s* baño de asiento
**six** [sɪks] *adj* seis; *s* seis; **at sixes and sevens** en confusión; en desacuerdo; **six o'clock** las seis
**sixfold** ['sɪks,fold] *adj & s* séxtuplo; *adv* seis veces
**six hundred** *adj & s* seiscientos

**sixpence** ['sɪkspəns] *s* seis peniques
**sixpenny** ['sɪks,pɛnɪ] o ['sɪkspənɪ] *adj* de seis peniques; mezquino, insignificante; de dos pulgadas
**sixshooter** ['sɪks,ʃutər] *s* revólver de seis tiros
**sixteen** ['sɪks'tin] *adj & s* dieciséis o diez y seis
**sixteenth** ['sɪks'tinθ] *adj* décimosexto; dieciseisavo; *s* décimosexto; dieciseisavo; dieciséis (*en las fechas*)
**sixteenth note** *s* (mus.) semicorchea
**sixth** [sɪksθ] *adj* sexto; *s* sexto; seis (*en las fechas*); (mus.) sexta
**sixthly** ['sɪksθlɪ] *adv* en sexto lugar
**sixth sense** *s* sexto sentido
**sixtieth** ['sɪkstɪɪθ] *adj & s* sexagésimo; sesentavo
**Sixtus** ['sɪkstəs] *s* Sixto (*nombre de varios papas*)
**sixty** ['sɪkstɪ] *adj* sesenta; *s* (*pl:* **-ties**) sesenta
**sixty-four dollar question** ['sɪkstɪ'for] *s* (la) pregunta principal y más difícil (*de un programa de radio o televisión*)
**sixty-fourth note** ['sɪkstɪ'forθ] *s* (mus.) semifusa
**sizable** ['saɪzəbəl] *adj* considerable, bastante grande
**size** [saɪz] *s* tamaño; dimensiones; talla (*de una persona, un vestido*); extensión; diámetro (*de un tubo, alambre, etc.*); apresto (*para empapelar, pintar, etc.*); sisa, cola de retazo (*de los doradores*); (coll.) verdadera situación o condición; **of a size** del mismo tamaño; *va* clasificar según el tamaño; medir el tamaño de; aprestar (*para empapelar*); sisar, encolar; **to size up** enfocar (*un problema*); medir con la vista (*a una persona*)
**sizeable** ['saɪzəbəl] *adj* var. de **sizable**
**size stick** *s* cartabón, marco (*para medir la longitud del pie*)
**sizing** ['saɪzɪŋ] *s* apresto (*para empapelar, pintar, etc.*); sisa, cola de retazo
**sizy** ['saɪzɪ] *adj* glutinoso, pegajoso, viscoso
**sizz** [sɪz] *s* silbido, siseo; *vn* silbar, sisear
**sizzle** ['sɪzəl] *s* siseo (*de la manteca al freírse*); *vn* sisear
**S.J.** abr. de **Society of Jesus**
**S.J.D.** abr. de **Scientiae Juridicae Doctor** (Lat.) **Doctor of Juridical Science**
**skald** [skɔld] o [skɑld] *s* escaldo (*bardo de la Escandinavia antigua*)
**skate** [sket] *s* patín; (ichth.) raya; (slang) adefesio, tipo; (slang) caballejo, rocín; *vn* patinar; **to skate on thin ice** buscar el peligro; usar de argumentos infundados; **to skate over** mencionar muy por encima, pasar por alto
**skatemobile** ['sketmo,bil] *s* patinete montado sobre patines
**skater** ['sketər] *s* patinador
**skating** ['sketɪŋ] *s* patinaje
**skating rink** *s* patinadero, pista de patinar
**skedaddle** [skɪ'dædəl] *vn* (coll.) huir precipitadamente
**skee** [ski] *s & vn* var. de **ski**
**skein** [sken] madeja; enredo, maraña; bandada de aves silvestres
**skeletal** ['skɛlɪtəl] *adj* esquelético
**skeleton** ['skɛlɪtən] *s* esqueleto; (fig.) esqueleto (*sujeto muy flaco; bosquejo*); *adj* esquelético; reducido
**skeletonize** ['skɛlɪtənaɪz] *va* reducir a un esqueleto; preparar el esqueleto de; bosquejar; reducir
**skeleton key** *s* llave maestra
**skeptic** ['skɛptɪk] *adj & s* escéptico
**skeptical** ['skɛptɪkəl] *adj* escéptico
**skepticism** ['skɛptɪsɪzəm] *s* escepticismo
**sketch** [skɛtʃ] *s* boceto, croquis, dibujo; bosquejo, esbozo, esquicio; drama corto, pieza corta; *va* hacer el bosquejo de, dibujar; bosquejar, esbozar, esquiciar
**sketchbook** ['skɛtʃ,buk] *s* libro de bocetos; libro de bosquejos
**sketchy** ['skɛtʃɪ] *adj* (*comp:* **-ier;** *super:* **-iest**) bosquejado; incompleto, fragmentario; galopeado
**skew** [skju] *s* esviaje, curso oblicuo, posición oblicua, desviación de la línea recta; *adj* oblicuo, sesgado; *va* sesgar; falsear, tergiversar; *vn* torcerse, ponerse al sesgo
**skewback** ['skju,bæk] *s* (arch.) salmer
**skewer** ['skjuər] *s* (cook.) broqueta; *va* espetar; sujetar por medio de broquetas; traspasar con aguja o estaquilla
**ski** [ski] o [ʃi] *s* (*pl:* **skis** o **ski**) esquí; *vn* esquiar
**skid** [skɪd] *s* resbalón, deslizamiento (*de un coche*); patinaje, patinazo (*de una rueda*); calzo; galga (*palo que sirve de freno*); (naut.) varadera; (aer.) esquí, patín; **to be on the skids** (slang) ir decayendo; ir fatalmente hacia un desastre; (*pret & pp:* **skidded;** *ger:* **skidding**) *va* calzar; *vn* resbalar, deslizarse (*un coche*); patinar (*una rueda*)
**skid chain** *s* cadena para impedir el patinaje
**skiddy** ['skɪdɪ] *adj* (coll.) resbaladizo; (coll.) resbalador
**skid road** *s* camino de arrastre; camino con trozas transversales
**skid row** [ro] *s* barrio de mala vida
**skier** ['skiər] o ['ʃiər] *s* esquiador
**skiff** [skɪf] *s* esquife
**skiing** ['skiɪŋ] o ['ʃiɪŋ] *s* esquiismo
**skijoring** [ski'dʒorɪŋ] *s* esquí remolcado
**ski jump** *s* salto de esquí; cancha de esquiar; trampolín
**skill** [skɪl] *s* pericia, destreza, habilidad
**skilled** [skɪld] *adj* experto, práctico, hábil, diestro; de experto
**skillet** ['skɪlɪt] *s* sartén; cacerola de mango largo
**skillful** o **skilful** ['skɪlfəl] *adj* experto, hábil, diestro, primoroso; de experto, de perito
**skim** [skɪm] *s* nata, escoria; (*pret & pp:* **skimmed;** *ger:* **skimming**) *va* desnatar, escoriar, espumar; rasar, rozar; tocar ligeramente, examinar ligeramente; *vn* deslizar; rozar; **to skim over** pasar rasando, pasar a la ligera; examinar ligeramente
**ski mask** *s* pasamontaña
**skimmer** ['skɪmər] *s* espumador; espumadera (*paleta cóncava*); canotié; (orn.) rayador, picotijera
**skim milk** *s* leche desnatada
**skim-milk** ['skɪm'mɪlk] *adj* débil, flojo, de inferior calidad
**skimp** [skɪmp] *s* escatimar, escasear; chapucear; *vn* economizar, apretarse; chapucear
**skimpy** ['skɪmpɪ] *adj* (*comp:* **-ier;** *super:* **-iest**) escaso; tacaño, mezquino
**skin** [skɪn] *s* piel; pellejo (*receptáculo para líquidos*); forro de acero (*de una nave*); (coll.) pillo, tramposo; (coll.) tacaño, avaro; **in** o **with a whole skin** ileso, sano y salvo; **to be nothing but skin and bones** estar hecho una oblea, estar en los huesos; **to get soaked to the skin** calarse hasta los huesos; **to save one's skin** salvar el pellejo; (*pret & pp:* **skinned;** *ger:* **skinning**) *va* pelar, desollar; escoriarse (*el codo*); (coll.) timar; cubrir de piel; **to skin alive** (coll.) desollar vivo (*hacer pagar más de lo justo*); torturar, martirizar; regañar severamente; vencer completamente; *vn* perder la piel; cubrirse de piel, cubrirse de pellejo; cicatrizarse; (slang) escabullirse
**skin-deep** ['skɪn'dip] *adj* superficial; *adv* superficialmente
**skin diver** *s* submarinista
**skin diving** *s* submarinismo
**skin effect** *s* (elec.) efecto pelicular
**skinflint** ['skɪn,flɪnt] *s* avaro, escasero
**skinful** ['skɪnful] *s* contenido de un pellejo; (coll.) hartazgo, panzada; (coll.) hartazgo de bebida
**skin game** *s* (slang) fullería
**skin grafting** *s* (surg.) injerto cutáneo
**skink** [skɪŋk] *s* (zool.) escinco
**skinner** ['skɪnər] *s* desollador; peletero
**skinny** ['skɪnɪ] *adj* (*comp:* **-nier;** *super:* **-niest**) flaco, magro, seco, enjuto; pellejudo
**skin-tight** ['skɪn'taɪt] *adj* ajustado al cuerpo
**skip** [skɪp] *s* salto; (*pret & pp:* **skipped;** *ger:* **skipping**) *va* saltar; *vn* saltar; saltar espacios (*la máquina de escribir*); irse precipitadamente; moverse saltando; (coll.) escabullirse
**skip bombing** *s* (aer.) bombardeo de rebote
**skip distance** *s* (rad.) distancia de la zona intermedia de mala recepción o silencio

**skipjack** ['skɪp,dʒæk] *s* (ichth.) pez saltador; (ent.) cucuyo
**ski pole** *s* bastón de esquiar
**skipper** ['skɪpər] *s* saltador; jefe, caudillo; patrón (*de barco*); gusano del queso; (ent.) hesperia; *va* patronear (*un barco*)
**skipping rope** *s* comba, saltador
**skip-stop** ['skɪp,stɑp] *adj* (*tren*) que salta ciertas estaciones, (*ascensor*) que salta ciertos pisos
**skirmish** ['skʌrmɪʃ] *s* escaramuza; *vn* escaramuzar
**skirmisher** ['skʌrmɪʃər] *s* escaramuzador
**skirmish line** *s* (mil.) línea de escaramuza
**skirret** ['skɪrɪt] *s* (bot.) escaravia
**skirt** [skʌrt] *s* falda; borde, orilla; oreja de cuero (*de la silla de montar*); (slang) falda (*mujer*); *va* proveer de falda; proveer de borde u orilla; bordear, seguir el borde o la orilla de; mantenerse fuera del alcance de, moverse a lo largo de; *vn* moverse al borde, estar al margen
**skirting** ['skʌrtɪŋ] *s* material para faldas
**ski stick** *s* var. de **ski pole**
**skit** [skɪt] *s* boceto satírico, boceto burlesco, paso cómico, pasillo
**skitter** ['skɪtər] *va* hacer saltar (*el anzuelo*) ligeramente sobre la superficie del agua; *vn* saltar ligeramente, deslizarse saltando
**skittish** ['skɪtɪʃ] *adj* caprichoso; asustadizo; tímido
**skittles** ['skɪtəlz] *s* juego de bolos
**skive** [skaɪv] *s* disco para pulir diamantes; *va* pulir (*diamantes*); raspar (*cueros*); cortar (*cueros*) en capas finas
**Skr.** abr. de **Sanskrit**
**skua** ['skjuə] *s* (orn.) estercorario
**skulduggery** [skʌl'dʌgərɪ] *s* (coll.) trampa, embuste
**skulk** [skʌlk] *s* remolón; *vn* remolonear; moverse en la sombra, acechar sin ser visto
**skull** [skʌl] *s* cráneo, calavera; cabeza; cerebro
**skull and crossbones** *spl* calavera y dos huesos cruzados, calavera con dos tibias cruzadas (*insignia en la bandera de los piratas y ahora señal del veneno y peligro de muerte*)
**skullcap** ['skʌl,kæp] *s* casquete; (anat.) sincipucio, coronilla
**skunk** [skʌŋk] *s* (zool.) mofeta; (zool.) zorrillo, mapurite (Am.); (coll.) canalla (*persona*)
**skunk cabbage** *s* (bot.) simplocarpo
**sky** [skaɪ] *s* (*pl:* **skies**) cielo; (paint.) cielo; **out of a clear sky** de buenas a primeras, inesperadamente; **to praise to the skies** poner por las nubes, poner en el cielo
**sky blue** *s* azul celeste
**sky-blue** ['skaɪ'blu] *adj* celeste
**sky diving** *s* (sport) paracaidismo
**skyey** ['skaɪɪ] *adj* celeste, etéreo
**sky-high** ['skaɪ'haɪ] *adj & adv* tan alto como el cielo; por las nubes
**skylark** ['skaɪ,lɑrk] *s* (orn.) alondra; *vn* jaranear, juguetear, triscar
**skylight** ['skaɪ,laɪt] *s* tragaluz
**skyline** ['skaɪ,laɪn] *s* línea del horizonte, línea de los edificios contra el cielo
**sky pilot** *s* (slang) clérigo, capellán
**skyrocket** ['skaɪ,rɑkɪt] *s* cohete; *vn* subir como un cohete, lucirse y desaparecer; alcanzar gran altura rápida y súbitamente; elevarse súbitamente (*los precios*)
**skysail** ['skaɪsəl] o ['skaɪ,sel] *s* (naut.) periquito, sosobre
**skyscraper** ['skaɪ,skrepər] *s* rascacielos
**skyward** ['skaɪwərd] *adj* que se dirige hacia el cielo; *adv* hacia el cielo
**skywards** ['skaɪwərdz] *adv* hacia el cielo
**skywriting** ['skaɪ,raɪtɪŋ] *s* escritura aérea
**slab** [slæb] *s* losa; tabla, tablón, plancha; tajada gruesa (*p.ej., de carne*); costero (*tabla inmediata a la corteza*)
**slabber** ['slæbər] *s, va & vn* var. de **slobber**
**slack** [slæk] *adj* flojo; tardo, lento, perezoso; negligente, descuidado; inactivo; *s* flojedad; estado flojo; inactividad; estación muerta, temporada inactiva; cisco (*polvo de carbón*); aguas represadas; **slacks** *spl* pantalones flojos o sueltos; *va* aflojar; apagar (*la cal*); *vn* atrasarse; descuidarse; **to slack off** aflojar; **to slack up** aflojar el paso
**slacken** ['slæken] *va* aflojar; atrasar; disminuir; descuidar; apagar (*la cal*); *vn* aflojarse; atrasarse; aflojar, dejarse ir
**slacker** ['slækər] *s* haragán, perezoso; (mil.) prófugo
**slackness** ['slæknɪs] *s* flojedad; negligencia; inactividad
**slack rope** *s* cuerda floja
**slack water** *s* (naut.) repunte de la marea; aguas semiestancadas
**slag** [slæg] *s* escoria; (*pret & pp:* **slagged;** *ger:* **slagging**) *va* convertir en escoria; *vn* formarse escoria; hacerse escoria
**slaggy** ['slægɪ] *adj* escoriáceo
**slain** [slen] *pp de* **slay**
**slake** [slek] *va* aplacar, calmar; apagar (*la cal*); *vn* aflojar, dejarse ir; apagarse (*la cal*)
**slalom** ['slɑlom] *s* eslalom
**slam** [slæm] *s* golpe; portazo; (coll.) crítica acerba; (bridge) bola, slam; (*pret & pp:* **slammed;** *ger:* **slamming**) *va* cerrar de golpe; mover, golpear o empujar estrepitosamente; (coll.) criticar acerbamente; *vn* cerrarse de golpe
**slam-bang** ['slæm'bæŋ] *adv* (coll.) de golpe y porrazo
**slander** ['slændər] *s* calumnia, difamación; *va* calumniar, difamar
**slanderer** ['slændərər] *s* calumniador, difamador
**slanderous** ['slændərəs] *adj* calumnioso, difamatorio
**slang** [slæŋ] *s* vulgarismo; jerga (*lenguaje especial de un grupo*)
**slangy** ['slæŋɪ] *adj* (*comp:* **-ier;** *super:* **-iest**) que emplea vulgarismos; lleno de vulgarismos
**slant** [slænt] *s* inclinación; parecer, punto de vista; *va* inclinar, sesgar; tergiversar, deformar (*p.ej., una noticia*); *vn* inclinarse, sesgarse
**slantways** ['slænt,wez] *adv* inclinadamente, sesgadamente
**slantwise** ['slænt,waɪz] *adj* inclinado, sesgado; *adv* inclinadamente, sesgadamente
**slap** [slæp] *s* palmada, manazo; bofetada (*golpe en la cara*); regaño, recriminación; insulto, desaire; (coll.) prueba, ensayo; *adv* directamente; súbitamente; (*pret & pp:* **slapped;** *ger:* **slapping**) *va* dar una palmada a, dar un manazo a; dar una bofetada a; poner con fuerza y ruidosamente
**slapdash** ['slæp,dæʃ] *s* trabajo descuidado, chapucería; *adj* descuidado, chapucero; *adv* con descuido, apresuradamente
**slap in the back** *s* espaldarazo
**slapjack** ['slæp,dʒæk] *s* torta frita en la sartén
**slapstick** ['slæp,stɪk] *s* paleta de payaso o cómico; comedia de golpe y porrazo, comedia de payasadas; *adj* de golpe y porrazo, de payasadas
**slash** [slæʃ] *s* tajo, tajada; cuchillada; azote; claro en un bosque; montón de hojas y ramas secas; (sew.) cuchillada; *va* acuchillar; dar un tajo a; hacer fuerte rebaja de (*precios, sueldos, etc.*); azotar; criticar acerbamente; cortar extensamente; acuchillar (*una prenda de vestir*)
**slat** [slæt] *s* hoja, lámina, tablilla
**slate** [slet] *s* pizarra; negro azulado, color de pizarra; candidatura, lista de candidatos; **to have a clean slate** tener las manos limpias; **to wipe the slate clean** empezar de nuevo; *adj* negro azulado, color pizarra; *va* empizarrar, cubrir de pizarra; poner en la lista de candidatos
**slate pencil** *s* pizarrín
**slater** ['sletər] *s* pizarrero; (zool.) cochinilla de humedad, cochinilla de tierra
**slate roof** *s* empizarrado
**slattern** ['slætərn] *s* mujer desaliñada
**slatternly** ['slætərnlɪ] *adj* desaliñado
**slaty** ['sletɪ] *adj* (*comp:* **-ier;** *super:* **-iest**) pizarreño
**slaughter** ['slɔtər] *s* matanza, carnicería; *va* matar; carnear (Am.)
**slaughter house** *s* matadero
**slaughter of the innocents** *s* degollación de los inocentes
**slaughterous** ['slɔtərəs] *adj* mortífero, destructivo
**Slav** [slɑv] o [slæv] *adj & s* eslavo
**slave** [slev] *s & adj* esclavo; *vn* trabajar como esclavo
**Slave Coast** *s* Costa de los Esclavos

**slave driver** *s* negrero; (fig.) negrero, persona despótica que agobia de trabajo a otra
**slaveholder** ['slev,holdər] *s* dueño de esclavos
**slaveholding** ['slev,holdɪŋ] *adj* que posee esclavos; *s* posesión de esclavos
**slave labor** *s* trabajo de esclavos; trabajadores forzados
**slaver** ['slevər] *s* negrero; barco negrero; ['slævər] *s* baba; *va* babosear; *vn* babear
**slavery** ['slevərɪ] *s* esclavitud
**slave trade** *s* trata de esclavos, tráfico de esclavos
**slavey** ['slevɪ] *s* (coll.) criada, fregona
**Slavic** ['slɑvɪk] o ['slævɪk] *adj* eslavo; *s* eslavo (*idioma*)
**slavish** ['slevɪʃ] *adj* servil; esclavizado
**Slavonia** [slə'vonɪə] *s* Eslavonia
**Slavonian** [slə'vonɪən] *adj* & *s* eslavonio; eslavo
**Slavonic** [slə'vɑnɪk] *adj* eslavo; eslavonio; *s* eslavo
**slaw** [slɔ] *s* ensalada de col cortada muy fina
**slay** [sle] (*pret:* **slew**; *pp:* **slain**) *va* matar
**slayer** ['sleər] *s* matador, asesino
**sleave** [sliv] *s* hilacha; *va* deshilachar
**sleazy** ['slizɪ] o ['slezɪ] *adj* (*comp:* **-zier**; *super:* **-ziest**) débil, ligero, tenue
**sled** [slɛd] *s* luge, trineo; (*pret & pp:* **sledded**; *ger:* **sledding**) *va* llevar en trineo; *vn* ir en trineo
**sledding** ['slɛdɪŋ] *s* transportación en trineo, uso del trineo; **hard sledding** camino dificultoso, circunstancias poco favorables; **smooth sledding** circunstancias favorables
**sledge** [slɛdʒ] *s* acotillo; trineo; *va* transportar en trineo; *vn* ir o pasear en trineo
**sledge hammer** *s* acotillo; cosa fuerte y aplastante
**sledge-hammer** ['slɛdʒ,hæmər] *adj* fuerte y aplastante; *va* & *vn* golpear con fuerza con acotillo o como si fuera con acotillo
**sleek** [slik] *adj* liso y brillante, alisado y suave; mañoso, zalamero; *va* alisar y pulir; suavizar
**sleep** [slip] *s* sueño; **to be overcome with sleep** caerse de sueño; **to go to sleep** dormirse; dormirse o morirse (*entorpecerse un miembro*); **to put to sleep** adormecer, dormir; matar por anestesia (*p.ej., a un perro enfermo*); **to read someone to sleep** adormecerle a uno leyendo; **to talk to sleep** adormecer hablando; (*pret & pp:* **slept**) *va* pasar durmiendo; **to sleep away** pasar durmiendo; **to sleep off** dormir (*p.ej., una borrachera*); *vn* dormir; **to sleep over** trasnochar, dormir sobre
**sleeper** ['slipər] *s* durmiente (*persona; traviesa de la vía férrea*); coche-cama, coche-dormitorio
**sleeper seat** *s* (aer. & rail.) butacama
**sleepiness** ['slipɪnɪs] *s* somnolencia
**sleeping** ['slipɪŋ] *adj* durmiente; de dormir, para dormir
**sleeping bag** *s* saco para dormir (*a la intemperie*)
**Sleeping Beauty** *s* la Bella durmiente del bosque
**sleeping car** *s* coche-cama, coche-dormitorio, vagón cama
**sleeping partner** *s* (com.) socio comanditario
**sleeping pill** *s* píldora para dormir
**sleeping powder** *s* polvos calmantes, polvos para dormir
**sleeping sickness** *s* (path.) enfermedad del sueño
**sleepless** ['sliplɪs] *adj* insomne, desvelado; despierto, vivo; sin dormir; pasado en vela
**sleeplessness** ['sliplɪsnɪs] *s* insomnio, desvelo
**sleepwalker** ['slip,wɔkər] *s* sonámbulo
**sleepwalking** ['slip,wɔkɪŋ] *s* sonambulismo; *adj* sonámbulo
**sleepy** ['slipɪ] *adj* (*comp:* **-ier**; *super:* **-iest**) soñoliento; **to be sleepy** tener sueño
**sleepyhead** ['slipɪ,hɛd] *s* dormilón
**sleet** [slit] *s* cellisca, nevisca; *vn* cellisquear, neviscar
**sleety** ['slitɪ] *adj* (*comp:* **-ier**; *super:* **-iest**) de cellisca; lleno de cellisca, cubierto de cellisca
**sleeve** [sliv] *s* manga; (mach.) manguito; **to laugh in** o **up one's sleeve** reírse interiormente, reírse para sí; **up one's sleeve** en reserva
**sleeveless** ['slivlɪs] *adj* sin mangas
**sleigh** [sle] *s* trineo; *va* transportar en trineo; *vn* pasearse en trineo
**sleigh bell** *s* cascabel
**sleighing** ['sleɪŋ] *s* paseo en trineo; estado de las carreteras que permite ir en trineo sobre ellas
**sleigh ride** *s* paseo en trineo
**sleight** [slaɪt] *s* destreza, pericia, habilidad; ardid, artificio
**sleight of hand** *s* juego de manos, prestidigitación
**slender** ['slɛndər] *adj* delgado, flaco; escaso, insuficiente
**slept** [slɛpt] *pret & pp de* **sleep**
**sleuth** [sluθ] *s* sabueso (*perro y detective*); *vn* andar espiando, andar acechando, seguir un rastro o una huella
**sleuthhound** ['sluθ,haʊnd] *s* sabueso; (coll.) sabueso (*detective*)
**slew** [slu] *s* ciénaga; vuelta rápida; (coll.) montón, gran cantidad; *va* volver, torcer; *vn* volverse, torcerse; *pret de* **slay**
**slice** [slaɪs] *s* rebanada, tajada; gajo (*p.ej., de naranja*); trozo, pedazo; (cook.) estrelladera, pala; *va* rebanar, tajar; cortar; dividir
**slice bar** *s* limpiaparrilla
**sliced peaches** *spl* melocotones en tajadas
**slicer** ['slaɪsər] *s* rebanador (*persona o máquina*)
**slicing machine** *s* rebanador o rebanadora
**slick** [slɪk] *s* lugar aceitoso y lustroso (*en el agua*); *adj* liso y brillante; aceitoso y lustroso; meloso, suave, pulido; (coll.) astuto, mañoso; *adv* directamente; (coll.) astutamente, con maña; *va* alisar, pulir
**slickenside** ['slɪkən,saɪd] *s* (geol.) espejo de falla, superficie de deslizamiento
**slicker** ['slɪkər] *s* impermeable; (coll.) embaucador, galafate
**slid** [slɪd] *pret & pp de* **slide**
**slidden** ['slɪdən] *pp de* **slide**
**slide** [slaɪd] *s* resbalón; resbaladero; derrumbamiento; derrumbamiento de tierra; alud; portaobjeto, plaquilla de vidrio (*para microscopio*); desliz (*superficie lisa*); diapositiva, transparencia; cursor, reglilla (*de regla de cálculo*); (mus.) tubo en forma de U; (mus.) grupeto (*de notas*); (mus.) trasporte; (mach.) cursor; *adj* de cursor; (*pret & pp:* **slid**; *pp:* **slid** o **slidden**) *va* deslizar, hacer resbalar; *vn* deslizar, resbalar; **to let slide** dejar pasar, no hacer caso de, no ocuparse de; **to slide over** pasar ligeramente, recorrer superficialmente
**slide caliper** *s* pie de rey
**slide fastener** *s* cierre cremallera
**slide rule** *s* nonio, regla de cálculo
**slide valve** *s* (mach.) corredera, distribuidor, válvula corrediza
**sliding** ['slaɪdɪŋ] *s* deslizamiento; *adj* corredizo; móvil, graduado
**sliding contact** *s* (elec.) cursor
**sliding door** *s* puerta de corredera
**sliding scale** *s* (econ.) escala móvil (*p.ej., de salarios*); regla de cálculo
**slight** [slaɪt] *s* descuido, desatención; desaire, menosprecio; *adj* delgado; sutil, delicado; leve, ligero; pequeño, insignificante; escaso; *va* descuidar, desatender; desairar, menospreciar
**slily** ['slaɪlɪ] *adv* var. de **slyly**
**slim** [slɪm] *adj* (*comp:* **slimmer**; *super:* **slimmest**) delgado; leve, débil, pequeño
**slime** [slaɪm] *s* légamo; baba (*de las culebras, los peces, etc.*); porquería
**slimmish** ['slɪmɪʃ] *adj* algo delgado
**slimy** ['slaɪmɪ] *adj* (*comp:* **-ier**; *super:* **-iest**) legamoso, pecinoso; baboso, viscoso; puerco, sucio
**sling** [slɪŋ] *s* honda (*para tirar piedras*); cabestrillo (*para sostener el brazo lastimado*); hondazo, tirada de honda, golpe dado con una honda; (naut.) braga; (naut.) eslinga; **slings** *spl* grátil (*parte central de la verga*); (*pret & pp:* **slung**) *va* lanzar con una honda; lanzar, tirar; poner en cabestrillo; colgar flojamente; (naut.) embragar; (naut.) eslingar
**slinger** ['slɪŋər] *s* hondero; lanzador, pedrero; cargador que emplea eslinga

**slingshot** ['slɪŋ,ʃɑt] *s* honda, tirador
**slink** [slɪŋk] (*pret & pp:* **slunk**) *vn* andar furtivamente; **to slink away** escurrirse, escabullirse
**slip** [slɪp] *s* resbalón, desliz; falta, error, desliz; lapso; embarcadero; grada (*plano inclinado, donde se construyen los barcos*); funda (*de muebles, de almohada*); papeleta, pedazo de papel; sarmiento (*para transplantar*); combinación (*prenda de vestir*); huída, evasión; traílla (*de perro*); (min. & geol.) dislocación; persona joven y menuda de cuerpo; **to give the slip to** escaparse de, burlar la vigilancia de ‖ (*pret & pp:* **slipped; ***ger:* **slipping**) *va* deslizar; dejar escapar; pasar por alto; soltar (*un perro*); poner rápidamente; quitar rápidamente; dislocarse (*un hueso*); decir inadvertidamente; eludir, evadir; **to slip off** (coll.) quitarse de prisa; **to slip on** (coll.) ponerse de prisa; **to slip one over on** (coll.) jugar una mala pasada a; **to slip one's mind** olvidársele a uno ‖ *vn* escurrirse; borrarse de la memoria; deslizarse; tropezar; errar, equivocarse; (coll.) declinar, deteriorarse; **to let slip** dejar pasar; decir inadvertidamente; **to slip away** escurrirse, escabullirse; **to slip by** pasar inadvertido; pasar rápidamente (*p.ej., el tiempo*); **to slip out of one's hands** escurrirse de entre las manos; **to slip through** colarse; **to slip through one's fingers** írsele a uno de entre las manos; **to slip up** (coll.) equivocarse, errar
**slipcase** ['slɪp,kes] *s* estuche (*para guardar libros*)
**slip cover** *s* funda
**slip knot** *s* nudo corredizo
**slip of the pen** *s* error de pluma
**slip of the tongue** *s* error de lengua
**slip-on** ['slɪp,ɑn] *s* prenda de vestir que se pone por la cabeza; prenda de vestir de quitaipón
**slipper** ['slɪpər] *s* zapatilla, babucha
**slippered** ['slɪpərd] *adj* calzado con zapatillas
**slippering** ['slɪpərɪŋ] *s* pantuflazo
**slippery** ['slɪpərɪ] *adj* deslizadizo, resbaladizo; astuto, zorro; **to be as slippery as an eel** escurrirse como una anguila
**slippery elm** (bot.) olmo norteamericano (*Ulmus fulva*); corteza de *Ulmus fulva* empleada como demulcente
**slipshod** ['slɪp,ʃɑd] *adj* en chancletas; desaseado, desaliñado; arrastrando los pies
**slipslop** ['slɪp,slɑp] *s* (coll.) aguachirle
**slip stream** *s* (aer.) viento de la hélice
**slip-up** ['slɪp,ʌp] *s* (coll.) error, equivocación
**slit** [slɪt] *s* raja, hendedura; cortada, incisión; (*pret & pp:* **slit; ***ger:* **slitting**) *va* rajar, hender; cortar
**slit-eyed** ['slɪt,aɪd] *adj* de ojos almendrados
**slither** ['slɪðər] *s* desliz súbito e irregular; *vn* rodar, deslizarse, culebrear
**slit skirt** *s* falda hendida, falda de tubo (*con abertura*)
**sliver** ['slɪvər] *s* raja (*de madera*); fibra de algodón o lana en hebras; *va* cortar en rajas; separar en hebras
**slob** [slɑb] *s* (slang) sujeto desaseado, sujeto desmañado
**slobber** ['slɑbər] *s* baba; sensiblería; *va* babosear; *vn* babear; hablar con sensiblería
**slobbery** ['slɑbərɪ] *adj* baboso; húmedo
**sloe** [slo] *s* (bot.) endrino (*arbusto*); endrina (*fruto*)
**sloe-colored** ['slo,kʌlərd] *adj* endrino
**sloe-eyed** ['slo,aɪd] *adj* de ojos endrinos
**sloe gin** *s* ginebra de endrinas
**slog** [slɑg] *s* golpetazo; (*pret & pp:* **slogged; ***ger:* **slogging**) *va* golpear; *vn* (coll.) afanarse, trabajar con ahinco
**slogan** ['slogən] *s* lema, mote; grito de combate, grito de guerra
**sloop** [slup] *s* (naut.) balandra
**slop** [slɑp] *s* mojadura, líquido derramado en el suelo; zupia, gacha; **slops** *spl* agua sucia; ropa barata y mal hecha; pantalones holgados; (naut.) pacotilla; (*pret & pp:* **slopped; ***ger:* **slopping**) *va* derramar, salpicar, ensuciar, enlodar; *vn* derramarse; chapotear (*con los pies*); **to slop over** derramarse; (slang) hacer demostraciones excesivas de entusiasmo
**slope** [slop] *s* cuesta, pendiente; declive (*grado de inclinación*); vertiente (*de un continente*); *va* inclinar; cortar al sesgo; *vn* inclinarse; desviarse
**sloppy** ['slɑpɪ] *adj* (*comp:* **-pier; ***super:* **-piest**) mojado y sucio; desgalichado (*p.ej., en el vestir*); chapucero (*en el trabajo*)
**slopshop** ['slɑp,ʃɑp] *s* bazar de ropa barata, tienda de pacotilla
**slosh** [slɑʃ] *s* fango; nieve sucia; (coll.) aguachirle; *vn* chapotear; vagabundear
**slot** [slɑt] *s* ranura (*en que se introduce una moneda*); pista; (*pret & pp:* **slotted; ***ger:* **slotting**) *va* hacer una ranura en; seguir la pista de
**sloth** [sloθ] o [slɔθ] *s* pereza; (zool.) perezoso
**sloth bear** *s* (zool.) oso bezudo
**slothful** ['sloθfəl] o ['slɔθfəl] *adj* perezoso
**slot machine** *s* tragamonedas, tragaperras, distribuidor automático, máquina sacaperras
**slot meter** *s* limitador de corriente, contador automático
**slotting machine** *s* ranuradora
**slouch** [slaʊtʃ] *s* postura relajada, postura floja; persona desaseada y torpe de movimientos; **to walk with a slouch** andar con los hombros caídos y la cabeza inclinada; *va* agachar, doblar hacia abajo; *vn* agacharse, encorvarse; andar caído de hombros; **to slouch in a chair** repantigarse
**slouch hat** *s* sombrero gacho
**slouch pocket** *s* bolsillo inclinado
**slouchy** ['slaʊtʃɪ] *adj* (*comp:* **-ier; ***super:* **-iest**) relajado, flojo; desaseado; inclinado, encorvado
**slough** [slaʊ] *s* cenagal, fangal; estado de abandono moral; [slu] *s* ciénaga; ensenada de río; (U.S.A.) charca; [slʌf] *s* camisa, piel que muda la serpiente; (path.) escara; *va* mudar, echar de sí; *vn* caerse, desprenderse
**slough of despond** [slaʊ] *s* abatimiento profundo
**sloughy** ['slaʊɪ] *adj* (*comp:* **-ier; ***super:* **-iest**) cenagoso, fangoso; ['slʌfɪ] *adj* de escara
**Slovak** ['slovæk] o [slo'væk] *adj & s* eslovaco
**Slovakia** [slo'vɑkɪə] o [slo'vækɪə] *s* Eslovaquia
**Slovakian** [slo'vɑkɪən] o [slo'vækɪən] *adj & s* var. de **Slovak**
**sloven** ['slʌvən] *s* persona desaseada; *adj* desaseado, abandonado
**Slovene** [slo'vin] o ['slovin] *adj & s* esloveno
**Slovenia** [slo'vinɪə] *s* Eslovenia
**Slovenian** [slo'vinɪən] *adj & s* var. de **Slovene**
**slovenly** ['slʌvənlɪ] *adj* (*comp:* **-lier; ***super:* **-liest**) desaseado, desaliñado, abandonado; *adv* desaliñadamente
**slow** [slo] *adj* lento; atrasado (*dícese del reloj*); tardío; lerdo, tardo, torpe (*para comprender*); aburrido; *adv* lentamente, despacio; *va* retardar; atrasar (*p.ej., un reloj*); *vn* retardarse, ir más despacio; atrasarse (*p.ej., un reloj*)
**slowdown** ['slo,daʊn] *s* huelga de brazos caídos (*actitud de los obreros cuando trabajan a ritmo lento*)
**slow-drying** ['slo'draɪɪŋ] *adj* de secado lento
**slow match** *s* mecha tardía
**slow-motion** ['slo,moʃən] *adj* a cámara lenta, al ralentí
**slow-moving** ['slo'muvɪŋ] *adj* tardo, lento, de marcha lenta; (com.) de venta morosa, de morosa salida
**slowness** ['slonɪs] *s* lentitud; torpeza
**slow-witted** ['slo'wɪtɪd] *adj* lerdo, tardo, torpe
**slowworm** ['slo,wʌrm] *s* (zool.) lución
**sludge** [slʌdʒ] *s* lodo, cieno, fango; sedimento fangoso; pedazos de hielo flotantes
**slue** [slu] *s* ciénaga; ensenada de río; vuelta rápida; *va* volver, torcer; *vn* volverse, torcerse
**slug** [slʌg] *s* (coll.) porrazo, puñetazo; (coll.) trago (*de aguardiente*); (gun.) posta; ficha; lingote, pedazo de metal; (print.) lingote; (print.) línea de linotipia; (zool.) babosa; (*pret & pp:* **slugged; ***ger:* **slugging**) *va* aporrear, apuñear
**slugabed** ['slʌgə,bɛd] *s* aficionado a quedarse en la cama
**sluggard** ['slʌgərd] *adj & s* haragán, perezoso, pachón

**sluggish** ['slʌgɪʃ] *adj* inactivo, tardo, indolente; haragán, perezoso, pachorrudo
**sluggishness** ['slʌgɪʃnɪs] *s* inactividad, indolencia, pereza, pachorra
**sluice** [slus] *s* presa; compuerta; muralla, dique; canal; *va* dar paso a, abriendo la compuerta; limpiar, dejando entrar el agua; (min.) lavar (*el oro*); lanzar (*maderos*) por un canal o corriente de agua; *vn* salir el agua a borbotones
**sluice gate** *s* compuerta de presa
**slum** [slʌm] *s* barrio bajo; **the slums** los barrios bajos, los barrios de indigentes; (*pret & pp:* **slummed;** *ger:* **slumming**) *vn* visitar los barrios bajos
**slumber** ['slʌmbər] *s* sueño, sueño ligero, sueño tranquilo; inactividad; *va* pasar (*el tiempo*) durmiendo; *vn* dormir; dormitar; permanecer inactivo
**slumberous** ['slʌmbərəs] o **slumbrous** ['slʌmbrəs] *adj* soñoliento; tranquilo, calmo; inactivo
**slum clearance** *s* eliminación de los barrios bajos
**slummer** ['slʌmər] *s* visitante de los barrios bajos; habitante de los barrios bajos
**slumming** ['slʌmɪŋ] *s* visita a los barrios bajos
**slump** [slʌmp] *s* hundimiento, desplome; fracaso; (com.) baja repentina (*de precios, valores, etc.*); *vn* hundirse, desplomarse; fracasar; bajar repentinamente (*los precios, valores, etc.*)
**slung** [slʌŋ] *pret & pp de* **sling**
**slung shot** *s* rompecabezas (*arma ofensiva*)
**slunk** [slʌŋk] *pret & pp de* **slink**
**slur** [slʌr] *s* farfulla, pronunciación indistinta; borrón, mancha (*en la reputación*); reparo crítico, observación crítica; (mus.) ligado; (*pret & pp:* **slurred;** *ger:* **slurring**) *va* pasar por encima, suprimir, ocultar, pasar ligeramente; pronunciar indistintamente, comerse (*sonidos, sílabas*); farfullar, decir precipitadamente; (mus.) ligar; (mus.) marcar con un ligado; manchar la reputación de, insultar, despreciar, menospreciar
**slush** [slʌʃ] *s* fango muy blando; agua nieve fangosa, nieve a medio derretir; grasa; sentimentalismo tonto
**slush fund** *s* (slang) fondos que se usan para el soborno, especialmente en el comercio de la influencia política
**slushy** ['slʌʃɪ] *adj* (*comp:* **-ier** *super:* **-iest**) fangoso; lleno de nieve a medio derretir; sentimental
**slut** [slʌt] *s* perra; mala mujer, prostituta; mujer sucia
**sluttish** ['slʌtɪʃ] *adj* desaliñado, sucio; malo, inmoral
**sly** [slaɪ] *adj* (*comp:* **slyer** o **slier;** *super:* **slyest** o **sliest**) secreto, furtivo; astuto, socarrón; travieso; **on the sly** a hurtadillas, a escondidas
**slyly** ['slaɪlɪ] *adv* secretamente, furtivamente; astutamente
**smack** [smæk] *s* dejo, gustillo, saborcillo; pizca, pequeña cantidad; manotada, palmada; golpe; chasquido (*de látigo*); beso sonado; (naut.) queche; *adv* violentamente; directamente; *va* dar una manotada a; golpear; hacer chasquidos con (*p.ej., un látigo*); besar sonoramente; **to smack one's lips** chuparse los labios; *vn* **to smack of** saber a, oler a; (fig.) oler a
**smacking** ['smækɪŋ] *adj* vivo, fuerte
**small** [smɔl] *adj* pequeño, chico; bajo; pobre, obscuro, humilde; insignificante; (print.) minúsculo; **to come out on the small end** salir perdiendo, llevarse lo peor; *adv* en miniatura; en pedazos menudos; en tono bajo y suave; tímidamente; **to feel small** sentirse pequeño o insignificante; **to sing small** ponerse modesto y humilde; *s* parte más estrecha (*p.ej., de la espalda*)
**smallage** ['smɔlɪdʒ] *s* apio silvestre
**small arms** *spl* armas ligeras
**small beer** *s* cerveza floja; bagatela; persona de poca monta
**small boy** *s* chico, chico travieso
**small capital** *s* versalilla o versalita
**small change** *s* suelto, dinero menudo
**small circle** *s* (astr. & geom.) círculo menor
**small clothes** *spl* calzones
**small fry** *s* gente menuda, chiquillos; gentecilla de poco más o menos
**small hours** *spl* primeras horas de la mañana
**small intestine** *s* (anat.) intestino delgado
**smallish** ['smɔlɪʃ] *adj* algo pequeño, pequeñito
**small letter** *s* letra minúscula
**small-minded** ['smɔl'maɪndɪd] *adj* tacaño, mezquino; malo, bajo, ruin; intolerante, poco liberal (*en las ideas*)
**smallness** ['smɔlnɪs] *s* pequeñez; (fig.) pequeñez
**small of the back** *s* parte más estrecha de la espalda
**small potatoes** *ssg* persona o cosa insignificante; *spl* personas o cosas insignificantes
**smallpox** ['smɔl,pɑks] *s* (path.) viruela
**small print** *s* tipo menudo, cuerpo pequeño
**small talk** *s* charladuría, charlas frívolas, palique
**small-time** ['smɔl'taɪm] *adj* (slang) insignificante, de poca monta
**small-town** ['smɔl'taʊn] *adj* lugareño, apegado a cosas lugareñas
**smalt** [smɔlt] *s* esmalte (*pigmento y color*)
**smaltite** ['smɔltaɪt] *s* (mineral.) esmaltina
**smart** [smɑrt] *adj* listo, vivo, inteligente; agudo, penetrante, punzante; aseado; majo, elegante; astuto, ladino; fatuo, presuntuoso, sabihondo; (coll.) grande, considerable; *s* escozor; dolor vivo; *va* escocer en (*p.ej., la lengua*); *vn* escocer; sufrir, padecer; sentir irritación en el ánimo
**smart aleck** *s* (coll.) fatuo, presuntuoso, sabihondo
**smarten** ['smɑrtən] *va* abrillantar, hermosear; avivar, animar; *vn* avivarse, animarse
**smartness** ['smɑrtnɪs] *s* vivacidad, inteligencia, agudeza; astucia; elegancia, buen tono; fatuidad, presunción
**smart set** *s* gente chic, gente de buen tono
**smartweed** ['smɑrt,wid] *s* (bot.) pimienta de agua
**smash** [smæʃ] *s* rotura violenta, ruido de una rotura violenta; fracaso, ruina; quiebra, bancarrota; (coll.) choque o tope violento; (coll.) golpe violento; **to go to smash** hacerse pedazos; arruinarse; *va* romper con fuerza; hacer pedazos; arruinar, destrozar; aplastar; (tenis) volear (*la pelota*) con un golpe rápido y fuerte; *vn* romperse con fuerza; hacerse pedazos; arruinarse, destrozarse; aplastarse; **to smash into** topar con, chocar con
**smash hit** *s* (coll.) éxito rotundo
**smash-up** ['smæʃ,ʌp] *s* colisión violenta; ruina, desastre; quiebra, bancarrota
**smatter** ['smætər] o **smattering** ['smætərɪŋ] *s* barniz, tintura, migaja (*noción superficial de algo*)
**smear** [smɪr) *s* embarradura; (bact.) frotis; (fig.) mancha, desdoro; *va* embarrar, untar, manchar; (fig.) manchar, desdorar; *vn* embarrarse, untarse, mancharse
**smear campaign** *s* campaña de calumnias
**smearcase** ['smɪr,kes] *s* naterón, názula, requesón
**smear word** *s* palabra muy insultante, palabra desprestigiadora
**smeary** ['smɪrɪ] *adj* (*comp:* **-ier;** *super:* **-iest**) manchado, graso, grasiento
**smectic** ['smɛktɪk] *adj* esmético
**smell** [smɛl] *s* olor (*bueno o malo*); olfato (*sentido*); perfume, fragancia; hedor; traza, vestigio, señal; (*pret & pp:* **smelled** o **smelt**) *va* oler; olfatear, cazar olfateando; (fig.) olfatear, husmear; **to smell up** (coll.) dar mal olor a; *vn* oler; heder, oler mal; **to smell of** oler a
**smeller** ['smɛlər] *s* oledor; (coll.) nariz
**smelling bottle** *s* redomilla para sales aromáticas
**smelling salts** *spl* sales aromáticas
**smelly** ['smɛlɪ] *adj* (*comp:* **-ier;** *super:* **-iest**) hediondo
**smelt** [smɛlt] *s* (ichth.) esperinque, eperlano; *va & vn* (found.) fundir (*minerales*); *pret & pp de* **smell**
**smelter** ['smɛltər] *s* fundidor; fundición (*fábrica*)

**smelting furnace** *s* horno de fundición
**smilax** ['smaɪlæks] *s* (bot.) zarzaparrilla; (bot.) mirsífilo
**smile** [smaɪl] *s* sonrisa; *va* expresar con una sonrisa; tener (*una sonrisa*); *vn* sonreír o sonreírse
**smiling** ['smaɪlɪŋ] *adj* risueño; (fig.) risueño
**smilingly** ['smaɪlɪŋlɪ] *adv* con cara risueña, con una sonrisa, sonriendo
**smirch** [smʌrtʃ] *s* tiznón; (fig.) deshonra; *va* tiznar; (fig.) tiznar
**smirk** [smʌrk] *s* sonrisa fatua y afectada; *vn* sonreír fatua y afectadamente
**smit** [smɪt] *pp de* **smite**
**smite** [smaɪt] (*pret:* **smote;** *pp:* **smitten** o **smit**) *va* golpear o herir súbitamente y con fuerza; caer con fuerza sobre; apenar, afligir; castigar
**smith** [smɪθ] *s* forjador, herrero
**smithereens** [,smɪðə'rinz] *spl* (coll.) añicos; **to tear to smithereens** (coll.) hacer añicos
**smithy** ['smɪθɪ] *s* (*pl:* **-ies**) herrería
**smitten** ['smɪtən] *adj* herido, afligido; impresionado; muy enamorado; *pp de* **smite**
**smock** [smɑk] *s* bata (*ropa talar para el trabajo de clínica, laboratorio, taller, etc.*); (archaic) camisa de mujer; *va* adornar con frunces que forman dibujo
**smock frock** *s* blusa de obrero
**smocking** ['smɑkɪŋ] *s* adorno de frunces que forman un dibujo
**smog** [smɑg] *s* (coll.) mezcla de humo y niebla
**smoke** [smok] *s* humo; tabaco; **to go up in smoke** irse todo en humo; **to have a smoke** echar un cigarro o cigarrillo; *va* ahumar; cecinar; fumar (*p.ej., cigarros*); pasar (*el tiempo*) fumando; **to smoke out** ahuyentar con humo; dar humazo a; descubrir; *vn* humear; fumar; hacer humo (*una chimenea dentro de la habitación*)
**smokebox** ['smok,bɑks] *s* caja de humos
**smoked glasses** *spl* gafas ahumadas
**smokehouse** ['smok,haʊs] *s* ahumadero
**smokeless** ['smoklɪs] *adj* sin humo
**smokeless powder** *s* pólvora sin humo
**smoker** ['smokər] *s* fumador; fumadero (*local*); (rail.) coche fumador, vagón de fumar; reunión o recepción de fumadores
**smoke rings** *spl* anillos de humo; **to blow smoke rings** sacar humo formando anillos
**smoke screen** *s* cortina de humo, niebla artificial
**smokestack** ['smok,stæk] *s* chimenea
**smoke tree** *s* (bot.) fustete
**smoking** ['smokɪŋ] *adj* fumante; *s* (el) fumar; **no smoking** prohibido fumar, se prohíbe fumar
**smoking car** *s* (rail.) coche fumador, vagón de fumar
**smoking jacket** *s* batín
**smoking room** *s* fumadero, saloncito para fumadores
**smoky** ['smokɪ] *adj* (*comp:* **-ier;** *super:* **-iest**) humeante; humoso, ahumado
**smolder** ['smolder] *s* fuego lento, sin llama y con mucho humo; *vn* arder en rescoldo (*arder sin llama y con mucho humo*); (fig.) estar latente, existir sin manifestarse al exterior, expresar una ira latente; (fig.) resquemarse (*resentirse sin manifestarlo*)
**smolt** [smolt] *s* (ichth.) cría del salmón que baja al mar
**smooth** [smuð] *adj* liso, terso, suave; plano, llano; igual, parejo; afable, blando, meloso; melifluo y sagaz; flúido y fácil (*dícese del estilo*); (phonet.) suave; **smooth as butter** como manteca; *adv* lisamente, suavemente; llanamente; afablemente, blandamente; *va* alisar, suavizar, allanar; facilitar; **to smooth away** quitar (*p.ej., obstáculos*) suavemente; **to smooth down** ablandar, calmar; **to smooth over** atenuar, limar
**smoothbore** ['smuð,bor] *adj* de ánima lisa; *s* arma de ánima lisa
**smooth-faced** ['smuð,fest] *adj* barbilampiño; bien afeitado; liso; de aspecto y palabras agradables
**smooth hound** *s* (ichth.) musola, cazón
**smoothie** ['smuðɪ] *s* var. de **smoothy**
**smoothness** ['smuðnɪs] *s* lisura, tersura; suavidad, blandura; llanura
**smooth-spoken** ['smuð,spokən] *adj* meloso, lisonjero
**smooth-tongued** ['smuð,tʌŋd] *adj* suave y blando en sus palabras; adulador, lisonjero
**smoothy** ['smuðɪ] *s* (*pl:* **-ies**) (coll.) galante (*hombre obsequioso con las damas*); (coll.) elegante, hombre distinguido; (coll.) adulador, lisonjero
**smote** [smot] *pret de* **smite**
**smother** ['smʌðər] *s* humareda, polvareda, nube; sofocación; *va* sofocar, ahogar; (cook.) ahogar, estofar; suprimir, ocultar; contener, reprimir; *vn* sofocarse; estar latente
**smothery** ['smʌðərɪ] *adj* sofocante; polvoroso, humoso
**smoulder** ['smoldər] *s & vn* var. de **smolder**
**smudge** [smʌdʒ] *s* fumigación, humareda; tiznón, mancha hecha con tizne; *va* tiznar, manchar con tizne; ahumar, fumigar (*p.ej., una huerta*)
**smudge pot** *s* vasija nebulizadora (*para proteger las tierras de cultivo contra las heladas*)
**smudgy** ['smʌdʒɪ] *adj* (*comp:* **-ier;** *super:* **-iest**) tiznado
**smug** [smʌg] *adj* (*comp:* **smugger;** *super:* **smuggest**) presumido, relamido; farisaico, pagado de sí mismo; compuesto, pulcro
**smuggle** ['smʌgəl] *va* meter de contrabando; **to smuggle in** meter o pasar de contrabando; **to smuggle out** sacar de contrabando; *vn* contrabandear
**smuggler** ['smʌglər] *s* contrabandista; barco contrabandista
**smuggling** ['smʌglɪŋ] *s* contrabando
**smut** [smʌt] *s* tizne, tiznón; suciedad; sitio sucio; obscenidad, indecencia, dicho obsceno o indecente; (agr.) carbón, tizón, tizoncillo; (*pret & pp:* **smutted;** *ger:* **smutting**) *va* tiznar; (agr.) atizonar; *vn* tiznarse; (agr.) atizonarse
**smutch** [smʌtʃ] *s* mancha, tiznón; *va* manchar, tiznar
**smutty** ['smʌtɪ] *adj* (*comp:* **-tier;** *super:* **-tiest**) tiznado, manchado; verde, obsceno, indecente; (agr.) atizonado
**Smyrna** ['smʌrnə] *s* Esmirna
**snack** [snæk] *s* bocadillo, tentempié; parte, porción
**snack bar** *s* bar o puesto público (*donde no se sirven comidas formales sino bocadillos, dulces, helados, refrescos, etc.*); cantina (*en las estaciones*)
**snaffle** ['snæfəl] *s* bridón del bocado; *va* contener por medio del bridón del bocado
**snafu** [snæ'fu] o ['snæfu] *adj* (slang) caótico; *s* (slang) caos, confusión, desorden; *va* (slang) confundir, enmarañar
**snag** [snæg] *s* tocón; raigón (*de un diente*); tropiezo, obstáculo; **to strike** o **hit a snag** tropezar con un obstáculo; (*pret & pp:* **snagged;** *ger:* **snagging**) *va* arrancar (*troncos*) del fondo del río; encontrar (*un tronco sumergido*); impedir, obstruir, enredar
**snaggletooth** ['snægəl,tuθ] *s* (*pl:* **-teeth**) sobrediente
**snaggle-toothed** ['snægəl,tuθt] *adj* que tiene sobredientes, que tiene dientes rotos o sobresalientes
**snaggy** ['snægɪ] *adj* (*comp:* **-gier;** *super:* **-giest**) nudoso; lleno de troncos, lleno de tocones; sobresaliente; rugoso, desigual
**snail** [snel] *s* (zool.) caracol; (zool.) babosa; (fig.) posma
**snailflower** ['snel,flaʊər] *s* (bot.) caracol real
**snail-paced** ['snel,pest] *adj* lento como una tortuga, lento como un caracol
**snail's pace** *s* paso de tortuga, paso de caracol; **at a snail's pace** a paso de tortuga, a paso de caracol
**snake** [snek] *s* culebra, serpiente; buscapiés, carretilla (*cohete*); (fig.) serpiente (*persona*); *va* arrastrar tirando de; (coll.) sacudir; *vn* culebrear, serpentear; (coll.) sacudirse, moverse a tirones
**snakebird** ['snek,bʌrd] *s* (orn.) anhinga
**snake charmer** *s* encantador de serpientes
**snake in the grass** *s* peligro insospechado, peligro desconocido; amigo pérfido, amigo desleal
**snakeroot** ['snek,rut] o ['snek,rʊt] *s* (bot.)

serpentaria de Virginia; (bot.) polígala de Virginia

**snakeskin** ['snek,skɪn] *s* piel de serpiente

**snakeweed** ['snek,wid] *s* (bot.) bistorta; (bot.) serpentaria de Virginia

**snaky** ['snekɪ] *adj* (*comp:* **-ier;** *super:* **-iest**) serpentino, tortuoso; lleno de serpientes; astuto y traidor

**snap** [snæp] *s* estallido, chasquido; castañetazo (*de los dedos*); mordedura, mordisco; discurso corto y mordaz; movimiento rápido; corto período (*p.ej., de frío agudo*); broche de presión; galletita; disparo rápido sin apuntar; instantánea; ganga, cosa fácil; **not a snap** nada, de ninguna manera ‖ *adj* rápido, hecho de repente ‖ (*pret & pp:* **snapped;** *ger:* **snapping**) *va* asir, cerrar, etc. de golpe; fotografiar instantáneamente; tomar (*una instantánea*); castañetear (*los dedos*); chasquear (*p.ej., el látigo*); **to snap one's fingers at** tratar con desprecio, burlarse de; **to snap up** asir, agarrar; aceptar con avidez, comprar con avidez; cortar la palabra a ‖ *vn* estallar, chasquear; saltar; exclamar; moverse rápidamente; chispear (*los ojos*); (fig.) estallar (*de fatiga*); **to snap at** querer morder; asir (*una oportunidad*); **to snap back at** tirar una mordida a; dar una respuesta grosera a; **to snap off** soltarse; **to snap out of it** (slang) cambiarse repentinamente; **to snap shut** cerrarse de golpe

**snapdragon** ['snæp,drægən] *s* (bot.) dragón, boca de dragón; (bot.) linaria, pajarita

**snap fastener** *s* corchete de presión

**snap hook** *s* mosquetón

**snap judgment** *s* decisión atolondrada

**snap-on** ['snæp,ɑn] *s* (aut.) abrazadera

**snapper** ['snæpər] *s* mordedor; (zool.) chiquiguao, chopontil (*tortuga*); (ichth.) cubera, pargo criollo, pargo colorado

**snapping beetle** *s* (ent.) elatérido (*p.ej., cucuyo, atóo, cardióforo, campilo, corimbites*)

**snapping turtle** *s* (zool.) chiquiguao, chopontil

**snappish** ['snæpɪʃ] *adj* propenso a morder; arisco, mordaz; respondón; irritable

**snappy** ['snæpɪ] *adj* (*comp:* **-pier;** *super:* **-piest**) crepitante; mordaz; (coll.) elegante, garboso; (coll.) fuerte, enérgico; acre y picante (*p.ej., queso*)

**snapshot** ['snæp,ʃɑt] *s* instantánea; disparo rápido sin apuntar; (*pret & pp:* **-shotted;** *ger:* **-shotting**) *va* tomar una instantánea de

**snap switch** *s* (elec.) interruptor de resorte

**snare** [snɛr] *s* lazo, trampa; bordón, tirante, timbre (*de un tambor*); *va* tender lazos a, coger con trampa; (fig.) hacer caer en el lazo

**snare drum** *s* caja clara, tambor con tirantes de cuerda

**snarl** [snɑrl] *s* gruñido; regaño; maraña; greña, pelo enmarañado; *va* decir con un gruñido; enmarañar, enredar; *vn* gruñir; regañar; enmarañarse, enredarse

**snarly** ['snɑrlɪ] *adj* (*comp:* **-ier;** *super:* **-iest**) gruñón; regañón; enredoso, enredado

**snatch** [snætʃ] *s* arrebatamiento; trocito, pedacito; ratito; **by snatches** a ratos; *va & vn* arrebatar; **to snatch at** tratar de asir o agarrar; **to snatch from** arrebatar a

**snatch block** *s* (naut.) pasteca

**snatchy** ['snætʃɪ] *adj* irregular, intermitente

**snath** [snæθ] o **snathe** [sneð] *s* mango de guadaña

**sneak** [snik] *s* entrada furtiva; sujeto solapado; *adj* furtivo; *va* mover a hurtadillas; robar; **to sneak in** introducir a hurtadillas; **to sneak out** llevarse (*algo*) a hurtadillas; *vn* andar furtivamente, moverse a hurtadillas; **to sneak in** entrarse a hurtadillas; **to sneak out** salirse a hurtadillas; **to sneak out of** evitar disimuladamente

**sneaker** ['snikər] *s* sujeto ruin y solapado; (coll.) zapato ligero de lona con suela de goma

**sneaking** ['snikɪŋ] *adj* husmeador; solapado; vil, bajo, ruin; oculto, secreto

**sneak thief** *s* ratero, descuidero

**sneaky** ['snikɪ] *adj* (*comp:* **-ier;** *super:* **-iest**) husmeador; solapado, socarrón; vil, despreciable

**sneer** [snɪr] *s* expresión de burla y desprecio; *va* decir o expresar con burla y desprecio; *vn* hablar con desprecio, hacer un gesto de desprecio, echar una mirada de desprecio; **to sneer at** mofarse de

**sneering** ['snɪrɪŋ] *adj* burlador y despreciativo

**sneeze** [sniz] *s* estornudo; *vn* estornudar; **to sneeze at** (coll.) despreciar, menospreciar, burlarse de

**snell** [snɛl] *s* hilo con que se ata el anzuelo al sedal

**snick** [snɪk] *s* tijeretada; golpe seco; ruido rápido y agudo; pelota golpeada; *va* tijeretear; golpear con fuerza; hacer que (*una cosa*) produzca un ruido como de golpe seco; *vn* producir un ruido como de golpe seco

**snicker** ['snɪkər] *s* risita medio contenida, risa tonta; *vn* reírse tontamente

**snide** [snaɪd] *adj* (slang) socarrón y malicioso

**sniff** [snɪf] *s* husmeo, venteo; sorbo por las narices; *va* husmear, ventear; sorber por las narices; (fig.) husmear, averiguar; sospechar; *vn* ventear; **to sniff at** husmear; menospreciar

**sniffle** ['snɪfəl] *s* resuello fuerte y repetido; **the sniffles** ataque de resoplidos; *vn* resollar fuerte y repetidamente

**sniffy** ['snɪfɪ] *adj* (*comp:* **-ier;** *super:* **-iest**) (coll.) estirado, desdeñoso

**snifter** ['snɪftər] *s* copa para aguardiente; (slang) trago de licor

**snigger** ['snɪgər] *s & vn* var. de **snicker**

**snip** [snɪp] *s* tijeretada; recorte, retazo; pedacito; (coll.) persona pequeña o insignificante; (coll.) sastre; **snips** *spl* tijeras para cortar el metal; (*pret & pp:* **snipped;** *ger:* **snipping**) *va* tijeretear; **to snip off** recortar, cortar de un tijeretazo

**snipe** [snaɪp] *s* (orn.) agachadiza, becacín; *vn* paquear, tirar desde un apostadero, tirar desde un escondite; **to snipe at** paquear, tirar desde un apostadero contra

**snipe eel** *s* (ichth.) anguila agachadiza

**sniper** ['snaɪpər] *s* paco, tirador escondido, tirador emboscado

**sniping** ['snaɪpɪŋ] *s* paqueo

**snippet** ['snɪpɪt] *s* recorte; (coll.) persona pequeña o insignificante

**snippy** ['snɪpɪ] *adj* (*comp:* **-pier;** *super:* **-iest**) compuesto de recortes; (coll.) arrogante, desdeñoso; (coll.) brusco, acre

**snitch** [snɪtʃ] *va & vn* (slang) soplar, ratear, escamotear

**snivel** ['snɪvəl] *s* gimoteo, lloriqueo; moqueo; moquita; (*pret & pp:* **-eled** o **-elled;** *ger:* **-eling** o **-elling**) *vn* gimotear, lloriquear; moquear

**snob** [snɑb] *s* esnob (*persona con pretensiones sociales*)

**snobbery** ['snɑbərɪ] *s* (*pl:* **-ies**) esnobismo

**snobbish** ['snɑbɪʃ] *adj* esnob

**snobbishness** ['snɑbɪʃnɪs] *s* esnobismo

**snood** [snud] *s* cintillo (*alrededor de la cabeza*); red llevada sobre la cabeza; *va* atar (*el cabello*) con un cintillo; recoger (*el cabello*) con una red

**snooded** ['snudɪd] *adj* atado con un cintillo; recogido con una red

**snook** [snuk] *s* (ichth.) róbalo

**snoop** [snup] *s* (coll.) curioso, buscavidas; *vn* (coll.) curiosear, ventear

**snooper** ['snupər] *s* (coll.) curioso, buscavidas

**snoopy** ['snupɪ] *adj* (coll.) curioso, entremetido, furtivo

**snoot** [snut] *s* (slang) cara, narices

**snooty** ['snutɪ] *adj* (*comp:* **-ier;** *super:* **-iest**) (slang) esnob

**snooze** [snuz] *s* (coll.) siestecita, sueñecito; *vn* (coll.) dormitar, echar una siestecita

**snore** [snor] *s* ronquido; *va* pasar roncando; *vn* roncar

**snorkel** ['snɔrkəl] *s* tubo snorkel o respiradero (*de submarino*)

**snort** [snɔrt] *s* bufido; *va* decir o expresar con un bufido; *vn* bufar

**snot** [snɑt] *s* (slang) mocarro

**snotty** ['snɑtɪ] *adj* (coll.) mocoso; (coll.) sucio, asqueroso; (slang) fachedón, engreído, huraño

**snout** [snaʊt] *s* hocico; morro (*cosa parecida a un hocico de animal*); (coll.) hocico (*de una persona*)

**snout beetle** *s* (ent.) rincóforo

**snouted** ['snaʊtɪd] *adj* hocicudo

**snow** [sno] *s* nieve; nevada; (telv.) nieve (*aspecto moteado*); (poet.) nieve (*blancura*); (slang) nieve (*cocaína, heroína*); *va* cubrir u obstruir con nieve; dejar caer como nieve; **to snow in** encerrar mediante la nieve; **to snow under** cubrir u obstruir con nieve; (coll.) derrotar completamente (*a un candidato*); *vn* nevar
**snowball** ['sno,bɔl] *s* bola de nieve; (bot.) bola de nieve; *va* lanzar bolas de nieve a; *vn* aumentar rápidamente (*como una bola de nieve que rueda*)
**snowbank** ['sno,bæŋk] *s* banco de nieve
**snowbell** ['sno,bɛl] *s* (bot.) estoraque norteamericano
**snowberry** ['sno,bɛrɪ] *s* (*pl:* **-ries**) (bot.) bolitas de nieve; (bot.) aceitillo, oreja de ratón, sueldaconsuelda
**snowbird** ['sno,bʌrd] *s* (orn.) pinzón de las nieves; (orn.) junquito; (orn.) echalumbre
**snow-blind** ['snow,blaɪnd] *adj* deslumbrado o cegado por los reflejos de la nieve
**snow blindness** *s* deslumbramiento debido a la nieve
**snow-bound** ['sno,baʊnd] *adj* detenido o aprisionado por la nieve
**snow bunting** *s* (orn.) pinzón de las nieves
**snow-capped** ['sno,kæpt] *adj* coronado de nieve
**snow-clad** ['sno,klæd] *adj* cubierto de nieve
**snowdrift** ['sno,drɪft] *s* ventisquero; nieve movida por el viento
**snowdrop** ['sno,drɑp] *s* (bot.) campanilla de invierno
**snowfall** ['sno,fɔl] *s* nevada
**snow fence** *s* valla paranieves
**snowflake** ['sno,flek] *s* ampo, copo de nieve; (orn.) pinzón de las nieves; (bot.) campanilla
**snow flurry** *s* nevisca
**snow ice** *s* hielo producido por la congelación del agua nieve
**snowiness** ['sno·ɪnɪs] *s* blancura de nieve
**snow line** o **limit** *s* límite de las nieves perpetuas
**snow man** *s* figura de nieve
**snowplow** ['sno,plaʊ] *s* quitanieve, barredora de nieve, expulsanieves
**snowshed** ['sno,ʃɛd] *s* guardanieve
**snowshoe** ['sno,ʃu] *s* raqueta de nieve; *vn* andar sobre la nieve llevando raquetas
**snowslide** ['sno,slaɪd] *s* alud; caída de un alud
**snowstorm** ['sno,stɔrm] *s* nevasca, fuerte nevada
**Snow White** *s* Blanca Nieves
**snow-white** ['sno,hwaɪt] *adj* blanco como la nieve
**snowy** ['sno·ɪ] *adj* (*comp:* **-ier;** *super:* **-iest**) nevoso
**snowy owl** *s* (orn.) lechuza blanca
**snub** [snʌb] *s* desaire; parada brusca; (*pret & pp:* **snubbed;** *ger:* **snubbing**) *va* desairar; parar bruscamente
**snubber** ['snʌbər] *s* persona arrogante; tambor de frenaje; (aut.) amortiguador
**snubby** ['snʌbɪ] *adj* (*comp:* **-bier;** *super:* **-biest**) respingón
**snub-nosed** ['snʌb,nozd] *adj* nacho, de nariz respingona
**snuff** [snʌf] *s* tabaco rapé, tabaco en polvo; costra, moco (*de la mecha de una vela*); **up to snuff** (slang) difícil de engañar; (slang) en buena condición; *va* husmear, olfatear; aspirar, sorber por la nariz; despabilar (*una candela*); **to snuff out** apagar, extinguir
**snuffbox** ['snʌf,bɑks] *s* tabaquera
**snuffer** ['snʌfər] *s* despabilador; **snuffers** *spl* despabiladeras, despabilador, apagavelas
**snuffle** ['snʌfəl] *s* gangueo; **the snuffles** ataque de gangueo; *vn* ganguear; husmear, ventear
**snuffy** ['snʌfɪ] *adj* (*comp:* **-ier;** *super:* **-iest**) tabacoso; desagradable, descortés
**snug** [snʌg] *adj* (*comp:* **snugger;** *super:* **snuggest**) cómodo, abrigado; apañado, ajustado; bien aparejado (*dícese de una embarcación*); muy ceñido (*dícese de una prenda de vestir*); escondido; acomodado; **snug as a bug in a rug** como un pez en el agua; *adv* cómodamente; ajustadamente; a escondidas; bastante pero sin holgura; (*pret & pp:* **snugged;** *ger:* **snugging**) *va* acomodar; apañar, ajustar; aparejar; esconder; hacer suficiente pero no abundante
**snuggery** ['snʌgərɪ] *s* (*pl:* **-ies**) casa cómoda y bien arreglada; sitio cómodo y bien arreglado; posición cómoda y a propósito
**snuggle** ['snʌgəl] *va* apretar, arrimar; *vn* apretarse, arrimarse; dormir bien abrigado; **to snuggle up to** arrimarse a
**snugness** ['snʌgnɪs] *s* comodidad, bienestar, holgura
**So.** abr. de **south**
**so** [so] *s* (mus.) sol; *adv* así; tan + *adj* o *adv;* por tanto, por consiguiente; también; **and so** así pues; también, lo mismo; **and so on** y así sucesivamente; **or so** más o menos; **to think so** creer que sí; **so as to** + *inf* para + *inf;* **so far** hasta aquí; hasta ahora; **so long** (coll.) hasta la vista; **so many** tantos; **so much** tanto; **so so** tal cual; así así; **so that** de modo que, de suerte que, así que; para que; con tal de que; **so to speak** por decirlo así; *conj* así que; *interj* ¡bien!; ¿verdad?
**soak** [sok] *s* mojada, empapamiento; (coll.) potista, borrachín; *va* empapar, remojar; absorber, embeber; (slang) aporrear, castigar severamente; (slang) hacer pagar un precio o precios exorbitantes; **to soak up** absorber, embeber; (fig.) entender; **soaked to the skin** calado hasta los huesos; *vn* empaparse, remojarse; calarse; (coll.) beber mucho, emborracharse; **to soak into** penetrar, filtrarse en
**soakage** ['sokɪdʒ] *s* remojo; líquido rezumado
**so-and-so** ['soənd,so] *s* (*pl:* **-sos**) fulano, fulano de tal; tal; tal cosa; *adj* bien arreglado
**soap** [sop] *s* jabón; *va* jabonar
**soapberry** ['sop,bɛrɪ] *s* (*pl:* **-ries**) (bot.) jaboncillo
**soapbox** ['sop,bɑks] *s* caja de jabón; caja vacía empleada como tribuna en la calle; *vn* hablar en la calle desde una tribuna improvisada
**soapbox orator** *s* orador de plazuela
**soapbox oratory** *s* oratoria de barricada
**soap bubble** *s* burbuja de jabón, pompa de jabón
**soap dish** *s* jabonera
**soap flakes** *spl* copos de jabón
**soapmaker** ['sop,mekər] *s* jabonero
**soap opera** *s* (coll.) drama radiofónico transmitido en una serie de programas de temas doméstico-sentimentales, serial lacrimógeno
**soap powder** *s* jabón en polvo, polvo de jabón
**soapstone** ['sop,ston] *s* (mineral.) esteatita; jabón de sastre
**soapsuds** ['sop,sʌdz] *spl* jabonaduras
**soapwort** ['sop,wʌrt] *s* (bot.) jabonera, saponaria
**soapy** ['sopɪ] *adj* (*comp:* **-ier;** *super:* **-iest**) jabonoso
**soar** [sor] *vn* encumbrarse, subir muy alto, volar a gran altura; aspirar, pretender; (aer.) planear
**sob** [sɑb] *s* sollozo; suspiro (*p.ej., del viento*); *adj* (slang) sentimental; (*pret & pp:* **sobbed;** *ger:* **sobbing**) *va* decir o expresar sollozando; **to sob oneself to sleep** adormecerse sollozando; *vn* sollozar; suspirar (*el viento*)
**sober** ['sobər] *adj* sobrio, moderado; no embriagado; grave, serio; cuerdo, sensato; sereno, tranquilo; apagado (*color*); *va* poner sobrio; desemborrachar; **to sober down** calmar, sosegar; **to sober up** desemborrachar; *vn* volverse sobrio; **to sober down** calmarse, sosegarse; **to sober up** desemborracharse
**sober-minded** ['sobər'maɪndɪd] *adj* cuerdo, sensato, de mente serena, dueño de sí
**soberness** ['sobərnɪs] *s* sobriedad; seriedad; cordura; serenidad
**sobriety** [so'braɪətɪ] *s* (*pl:* **-ties**) sobriedad, moderación; gravedad, seriedad; cordura, sensatez; serenidad
**sobriquet** ['sobrɪke] *s* apodo
**sob sister** *s* (slang) periodista llorona
**sob story** *s* (slang) historia de lagrimitas
**soc.** o **Soc.** abr. de **society**
**socage** o **soccage** ['sɑkɪdʒ] *s* (feud.) ocupación de una tierra por prestación de trabajo pero sin servicio militar
**so-called** ['so,kɔld] *adj* llamado, así llamado; supuesto
**soccer** ['sɑkər] *s* (sport) fútbol asociación

**soccer pool** *s* quiniela (*apuesta mutua de fútbol*)
**sociability** [ˌsoʃəˈbɪlɪtɪ] *s* (*pl:* **-ties**) sociabilidad
**sociable** [ˈsoʃəbəl] *adj* sociable; *s* tertulia; sociable (*coche*)
**social** [ˈsoʃəl] *adj* social; sociable; socialista; de la buena sociedad; *s* reunión social
**social climber** *s* ambicioso de figurar
**social evil** *s* prostitución
**social hygiene** *s* higiene social
**socialism** [ˈsoʃəlɪzəm] *s* socialismo
**socialist** [ˈsoʃəlɪst] *adj & s* socialista
**socialistic** [ˌsoʃəˈlɪstɪk] *adj* socialista
**socialistically** [ˌsoʃəˈlɪstɪkəlɪ] *adv* según el socialismo
**socialite** [ˈsoʃəlaɪt] *s* (coll.) personaje de la buena sociedad
**sociality** [ˌsoʃɪˈælɪtɪ] *s* (*pl:* **-ties**) sociabilidad (*calidad de sociable; índole sociable; tendencia del hombre a la vida social*)
**socialization** [ˌsoʃəlɪˈzeʃən] *s* socialización
**socialize** [ˈsoʃəlaɪz] *va* socializar
**socialized medicine** *s* medicina social
**social register** *s* guía social, registro de la buena sociedad
**social science** *s* ciencia social
**social security** *s* seguro social, retiro obrero, previsión social
**social service** *s* servicio social
**social work** *s* auxilio social
**social worker** *s* persona que se consagra al auxilio social
**society** [səˈsaɪətɪ] *s* (*pl:* **-ties**) sociedad; compañía (*trato*); buena sociedad, mundo elegante; **to be in society** hallarse en sociedad
**society editor** *s* cronista de la vida social
**Society Islands** *spl* islas de la Sociedad
**Society of Jesus** *s* Compañía de Jesús
**sociological** [ˌsosɪəˈlɑdʒɪkəl] o [ˌsoʃɪəˈlɑdʒɪkəl] *adj* sociológico
**sociologically** [ˌsosɪəˈlɑdʒɪkəlɪ] o [ˌsoʃɪəˈlɑdʒɪkəlɪ] *adv* según la sociología
**sociologist** [ˌsosɪˈɑlədʒɪst] o [ˌsoʃɪˈɑlədʒɪst] *s* sociólogo
**sociology** [ˌsosɪˈɑlədʒɪ] o [ˌsoʃɪˈɑlədʒɪ] *s* sociología
**sock** [sɑk] *s* calcetín; zueco (*zapato ligero; comedia*); (slang) golpe fuerte; *adv* (slang) derecho, bien; *va* (slang) pegar, golpear con fuerza
**socket** [ˈsɑkɪt] *s* cuenca (*de los ojos*); alvéolo (*de un diente*); cañón (*de un candelero*); cubo (*de un candelero; de una llave de caja*); (elec.) portalámparas; (rad.) portaválvula, zócalo
**socket wrench** *s* llave de cubo, llave de caja
**socle** [ˈsɑkəl] o [ˈsokəl] *s* (arch.) zócalo
**Socrates** [ˈsɑkrətiz] *s* Sócrates
**Socratic** [soˈkrætɪk] *adj* socrático
**sod** [sɑd] *s* césped; terrón de césped; **under the sod** bajo la tierra; (*pret & pp:* **sodded**; *ger:* **sodding**) *va* cubrir de césped, encespedar
**soda** [ˈsodə] *s* (chem.) sosa, soda; soda (*bebida refrescante*)
**soda ash** *s* cenizas de sosa
**soda cracker** *s* galletita un poco salada, muy friable y sin azúcar ni grasa
**soda fountain** *s* fuente de sodas (*aparato o mostrador con grifos para servir gaseosas y sodas*)
**soda jerk** *s* (slang) mozo que sirve en la fuente de sodas
**soda lime** *s* cal sodada
**sodality** [soˈdælɪtɪ] *s* (*pl:* **-ties**) amistad íntima; hermandad; cofradía
**soda water** *s* agua gaseosa
**sodden** [ˈsɑdən] *adj* empapado, saturado; lerdo, estúpido
**sodium** [ˈsodɪəm] *s* (chem.) sodio; *adj* sódico o de sodio, p.ej., **sodium chloride** cloruro sódico o cloruro de sodio
**sodium bicarbonate** *s* (chem.) bicarbonato sódico
**sodium carbonate** *s* (chem.) carbonato sódico
**sodium cyanide** *s* (chem.) cianuro sódico
**sodium hydrosulfite** *s* (chem.) hidrosulfito sódico (*agente reductor*)
**sodium hydroxide** *s* (chem.) hidróxido de sodio
**sodium hyposulfite** *s* (chem.) hiposulfito de sodio ($S_2O_4Na_2$); (chem. & phot.) hiposulfito de sodio ($S_2O_3Na_2$)
**sodium nitrate** *s* (chem.) nitrato sódico
**Sodom** [ˈsɑdəm] *s* (Bib.) Sodoma
**Sodomite** [ˈsɑdəmaɪt] *s* sodomita; (*l.c.*) *s* sodomita
**sodomy** [ˈsɑdəmɪ] *s* sodomía
**soever** [soˈɛvər] *adv* de cualquier modo; de cualquier clase; en cualquier caso
**sofa** [ˈsofə] *s* sofá
**soffit** [ˈsɑfɪt] *s* (arch.) sofito
**Sofia** [soˈfiə] *s* Sofía (*ciudad*)
**soft** [sɔft] o [sɑft] *adj* blando, muelle; delicado; suave; flojo; flexible (*dícese, p.ej., de un sombrero*); dulce (*metal*); tierno (*dícese de la soldadura*); torpe, estúpido; (phonet.) sonoro; (phonet.) sibilante; (phys.) blando (*rayo; tubo al vacío*); (coll.) fácil; (coll.) fácil de tratar; *adv* blandamente; delicadamente; suavemente; flojamente; *interj* ¡quedo!, ¡sin ruido!, ¡poco a poco!
**softball** [ˈsɔftˌbɔl] o [ˈsɑftˌbɔl] béisbol que se juega con pelota blanda; pelota blanda
**soft-boiled egg** [ˈsɔftˈbɔɪld] o [ˈsɑftˈbɔɪld] *s* huevo pasado por agua
**soft coal** *s* hulla grasa
**soft collar** *s* cuello blando
**soft drink** *s* bebida no alcohólica, refresco
**soften** [ˈsɔfən] o [ˈsɑfən] *va* ablandar; afeminar; **to soften up** ablandar (*por medio del bombardeo*); *vn* ablandarse; afeminarse
**softening of the brain** *s* (path.) reblandecimiento cerebral
**soft-hearted** [ˈsɔftˈhɑrtɪd] o [ˈsɑftˈhɑrtɪd] *adj* de buen corazón
**softish** [ˈsɔftɪʃ] o [ˈsɑftɪʃ] *adj* blandujo
**softness** [ˈsɔftnɪs] o [ˈsɑftnɪs] *s* blandura; suavidad; dulzura; flojedad; debilidad (*de carácter*); (coll.) facilidad
**soft palate** *s* (anat.) paladar blando, velo del paladar
**soft pedal** *s* (mus.) pedal suave, pedal celeste
**soft-pedal** [ˌsɔftˈpɛdəl] o [ˌsɑftˈpɛdəl] *va* (mus.) disminuir la intensidad de, por medio del pedal suave; (slang) moderar; *vn* (mus.) disminuir la intensidad por medio del pedal suave; (slang) moderar
**soft sell** *s* (coll.) método mañoso e indirecto de anunciar o vender mercancías
**soft-shelled crab** [ˈsɔftˌʃɛld] o [ˈsɑftˌʃɛld] *s* cangrejo después de la muda
**soft-shelled turtle** *s* (zool.) triónix espinífero
**soft soap** *s* jabón blando o graso; (coll.) lisonja, adulación
**soft-soap** [ˌsɔftˈsop] o [ˌsɑftˈsop] *va* (coll.) enjabonar, dar jabón a
**soft-spoken** [ˈsɔftˈspokən] o [ˈsɑftˈspokən] *adj* de voz suave; dicho con voz suave
**soft spot** *s* (coll.) afición, simpatía; (coll.) sentimentalismo; (coll.) flaqueza
**soft steel** *s* acero dulce o suave
**soft water** *s* agua blanda, agua suave, agua delgada
**softwood** [ˈsɔftˌwʊd] o [ˈsɑftˌwʊd] *s* árbol conífero; madera de árbol conífero; madera blanda
**softy** [ˈsɔftɪ] o [ˈsɑftɪ] *s* (*pl:* **-ies**) (coll.) mollejón; (coll.) inocentón
**soggy** [ˈsɑgɪ] *adj* (*comp:* **-gier**; *super:* **-giest**) empapado, remojado
**soil** [sɔɪl] *s* suelo, tierra; país, región; mancha; (fig.) mancha, deshonra; *va* manchar, ensuciar; (fig.) manchar, deshonrar; viciar, corromper; *vn* mancharse, ensuciarse; (fig.) mancharse, deshonrarse
**soilage** [ˈsɔɪlɪdʒ] *s* ensuciamiento; (agr.) pasto verde para el ganado
**soil conservation** *s* conservación de suelos
**soil pipe** *s* tubo de desagüe sanitario, cañería de arcilla vitrificada
**soiree** o **soirée** [swɑˈre] *s* sarao, verbena, velada
**sojourn** [ˈsodʒʌrn] *s* estancia, permanencia; [ˈsodʒʌrn] o [soˈdʒʌrn] *vn* estarse, residir por una temporada
**sol.** abr. de **soluble** y **solution**
**Sol.** abr. de **Solomon** y **Solicitor**
**sol** [sɑl] o [sol] *s* (chem. & mus.) sol; (*cap.*) [sɑl] *s* el Sol; (myth.) Sol

**solace** [ˈsɑlɪs] *s* solaz, consuelo; *va* solazar, consolar
**solan** [ˈsolən] *s* (orn.) alcatraz, planga
**solanaceous** [ˌsɑləˈneʃəs] *adj* (bot.) solanáceo
**solanine** [ˈsɑlənin] o [ˈsolənin] *s* (chem.) solanina
**solar** [ˈsolər] *adj* solar
**solarium** [soˈlɛrɪəm] *s* (*pl:* **-a** [ə]) solana
**solar plexus** [ˈplɛksəs] *s* (anat.) plexo solar
**solar protuberances** *spl* (astr.) protuberancias solares
**solar system** *s* sistema solar
**solar year** *s* año solar
**sold** [sold] *pret & pp de* **sell**
**solder** [ˈsɑdər] *s* soldadura; *va* soldar
**soldering** [ˈsɑdərɪŋ] *s* soldadura
**soldering iron** *s* soldador, estañador, cautín
**soldering paste** *s* pasta para soldar
**soldier** [ˈsoldʒər] *s* soldado (*militar sin graduación*); militar (*el que forma parte del ejército*); *vn* militar, servir como soldado; holgazanear; fingirse enfermo
**soldierly** [ˈsoldʒərlɪ] *adj* soldadesco, militar
**soldier of fortune** *s* aventurero militar
**soldiery** [ˈsoldʒərɪ] *s* (*pl:* **-ies**) soldadesca
**sold on** *adj* (slang) convencido del valor o el mérito de
**sold out** *adj* agotado; **the theater is sold out** todas las localidades están vendidas; **we are sold out of those neckties** se nos han agotado esas corbatas
**sole** [sol] *s* planta (*del pie*); suela (*del calzado*); palma (*del casco del caballo*); base, fondo; (ichth.) lenguado; (ichth.) sol, suela, lenguita (*Symphurus plagiusa*); *adj* solo, único; exclusivo; *va* solar
**solecism** [ˈsɑlɪsɪzəm] *s* solecismo; desacierto, patochada
**sole leather** *s* cuero de suela, solería
**solely** [ˈsollɪ] *adv* solamente, únicamente
**solemn** [ˈsɑləm] *adj* solemne
**solemnity** [səˈlɛmnɪtɪ] *s* (*pl:* **-ties**) solemnidad
**solemnization** [ˌsɑləmnɪˈzeʃən] *s* solemnización
**solemnize** [ˈsɑləmnaɪz] *va* solemnizar
**solenoid** [ˈsolɪnɔɪd] *s* (elec.) solenoide
**soleus** [ˈsolɪəs] *s* (anat.) sóleo
**sol-fa** [ˌsolˈfɑ] *s* (mus.) solfa; *va & vn* solfear
**sol-faist** [ˌsolˈfɑ·ɪst] *s* (mus.) solfista
**solfeggio** [sɑlˈfɛdʒo] *s* (*pl:* **-gios**) (mus.) solfeo
**solicit** [səˈlɪsɪt] *va* solicitar; intentar seducir, intentar corromper; *vn* hacer una solicitud, hacer una petición
**solicitation** [səˌlɪsɪˈteʃən] *s* solicitación; incitación, tentación, seducción; tentativa de corrupción
**solicitor** [səˈlɪsɪtər] *s* solicitador; (law) procurador
**solicitor general** *s* (*pl:* **solicitors general**) (U.S.A.) subsecretario de justicia; (U.S.A.) procurador general del Estado; (Brit.) subfiscal de la corona
**solicitous** [səˈlɪsɪtəs] *adj* solícito, ansioso
**solicitude** [səˈlɪsɪtjud] o [səˈlɪsɪtud] *s* solicitud, ansiedad
**solid** [ˈsɑlɪd] *adj* sólido; denso; todo; unánime; impreso sin interlíneas; escrito en una sola palabra; (fig.) sólido, macizo (*p.ej., argumento*); **a solid hour** una hora entera; *s* sólido
**solidarity** [ˌsɑlɪˈdærɪtɪ] *s* (*pl:* **-ties**) solidaridad
**solid geometry** *s* geometría del espacio
**solidification** [səˌlɪdɪfɪˈkeʃən] *s* solidificación
**solidify** [səˈlɪdɪfaɪ] (*pret & pp:* **-fied**) *va* solidificar; *vn* solidificarse
**solidity** [səˈlɪdɪtɪ] *s* (*pl:* **-ties**) solidez
**Solid South** *s* (U.S.A.) conjunto de los estados del Sur (*considerado como unidad política por su apoyo al partido Democrático*)
**solid state** *s* (phys.) estado sólido
**solid-state physics** [ˈsɑlɪdˈstet] *ssg* física del estado sólido
**solid tire** *s* (aut.) macizo
**soliloquize** [səˈlɪləkwaɪz] *vn* soliloquiar
**soliloquy** [səˈlɪləkwɪ] *s* (*pl:* **-quies**) soliloquio
**solipsism** [ˈsɑlɪpsɪzəm] *s* (philos.) solipsismo
**solitaire** [ˈsɑlɪtɛr] *s* solitario (*juego y diamante*); sortija solitario
**solitary** [ˈsɑlɪˌtɛrɪ] *adj* solitario; *s* (*pl:* **-ies**) solitario
**solitary confinement** *s* celda de castigo, aislamiento penal, incomunicación
**solitary sandpiper** *s* (orn.) chorlito de manchas aceneladas
**solleret** [ˈsɑlərɛt] o [ˌsɑləˈrɛt] *s* escarpadura (*de las armaduras antiguas*)
**solmization** [ˌsɑlmɪˈzeʃən] *s* (mus.) solfa
**solo** [ˈsolo] *s* (*pl:* **-los**) (mus.) solo; *adj* (mus.) solista; a solas, hecho a solas
**soloist** [ˈsolo·ɪst] *s* solista
**Solomon** [ˈsɑləmən] *s* Salomón; (fig.) Salomón
**Solomonic** [ˌsɑləˈmɑnɪk] *adj* salomónico
**Solomon Islands** *spl* islas Salomón
**Solomon's seal** *s* sello de Salomón
**Solomon's-seal** [ˈsɑləmənzˌsil] *s* (bot.) sello de Salomón
**Solon** [ˈsolɑn] *s* Solón; (fig.) Solón
**solstice** [ˈsɑlstɪs] *s* (astr.) solsticio
**solstitial** [sɑlˈstɪʃəl] *adj* solsticial
**solubility** [ˌsɑljəˈbɪlɪtɪ] *s* solubilidad
**soluble** [ˈsɑljəbəl] *adj* soluble
**solute** [ˈsɑljut] o [ˈsolut] *s* (chem.) soluto
**solution** [səˈluʃən] *s* solución
**solution of continuity** *s* solución de continuidad
**solvable** [ˈsɑlvəbəl] *adj* soluble
**solve** [sɑlv] *va* resolver, solucionar; adivinar (*un enigma*)
**solvency** [ˈsɑlvənsɪ] *s* (*pl:* **-cies**) solvencia
**solvent** [ˈsɑlvənt] *adj* solvente; (chem.) solvente; *s* (chem.) solvente
**Solyman** [ˈsɑlɪmən] *s* Solimán
**soma** [ˈsomə] *s* (*pl:* **-mata** [mətə]) (biol.) soma
**Somali** [soˈmɑlɪ] *s* (*pl:* **-li** o **-lis**) somalí
**Somaliland** [soˈmɑlɪˌlænd] *s* la Somalía
**somatic** [soˈmætɪk] *adj* somático
**somatology** [ˌsoməˈtɑlədʒɪ] *s* somatología
**somber** o **sombre** [ˈsɑmbər] *adj* sombrío
**sombrero** [sɑmˈbrɛro] *s* (*pl:* **-ros**) sombrero jarano
**some** [sʌm] *adj indef* algún; un poco de; unos; (coll.) grande, bueno, famoso, p.ej., **some crackpot** famoso tarambana; *pron indef pl* algunos; *adv* (coll.) algo; (coll.) muy, mucho
**somebody** [ˈsʌmˌbɑdɪ] *pron indef* alguien; **somebody else** algún otro, otra persona; *s* (*pl:* **-ies**) personaje
**someday** [ˈsʌmde] *adv* algún día
**somehow** [ˈsʌmhaʊ] *adv* de algún modo, de alguna manera; **somehow or other** de un modo u otro
**someone** [ˈsʌmwʌn] *pron indef* alguien; **someone else** algún otro, otra persona
**somersault** [ˈsʌmərˌsɔlt] o **somerset** [ˈsʌmərˌsɛt] *s* salto mortal; **to turn a somersault** dar un salto mortal; *vn* dar un salto mortal, dar saltos mortales
**something** [ˈsʌmθɪŋ] *s* alguna cosa, algo; cosa de importancia, cosa de suposición; **something else** otra cosa; *adv* algo, un poco
**sometime** [ˈsʌmtaɪm] *adj* antiguo, de otro tiempo; *adv* alguna vez, en algún tiempo; antiguamente, en otro tiempo
**sometimes** [ˈsʌmtaɪmz] *adv* a veces, a las veces, algunas veces
**someway** [ˈsʌmwe] *adv* de algún modo
**somewhat** [ˈsʌmhwɑt] *adv* algo, un poco; *s* alguna cosa, algo, un poco
**somewhere** [ˈsʌmhwɛr] *adv* en alguna parte, a alguna parte; en algún tiempo; **somewhere else** en otra parte, a otra parte
**somewhile** [ˈsʌmhwaɪl] *adv* a veces; alguna vez; antiguamente, en otro tiempo
**somewhither** [ˈsʌmhwɪðər] *adv* hacia alguna parte
**somnambulism** [sɑmˈnæmbjəlɪzəm] *s* sonambulismo
**somnambulist** [sɑmˈnæmbjəlɪst] *s* sonámbulo
**somnambulistic** [sɑmˌnæmbjəˈlɪstɪk] *adj* sonámbulo
**somniferous** [sɑmˈnɪfərəs] *adj* somnífero; soñoliento
**somnolence** [ˈsɑmnələns] *s* somnolencia o soñolencia
**somnolent** [ˈsɑmnələnt] *adj* soñoliento
**Somnus** [ˈsɑmnəs] *s* (myth.) el Sueño
**son** [sʌn] *s* hijo; **the Son** el Hijo (*Jesucristo*)
**sonance** [ˈsonəns] *s* sonoridad

**sonant** ['sonənt] *adj* sonante; (phonet.) sonoro; *s* (phonet.) sonora
**sonar** ['sonɑr] *s* sonar
**sonata** [sə'nɑtə] *s* (mus.) sonata
**sonatina** [ˌsɑnə'tinə] *s* (mus.) sonatina
**song** [sɔŋ] o [sɑŋ] *s* canción, canto; bagatela; **for a song** muy barato; **to sing the same old song** volver a la misma canción
**songbird** ['sɔŋˌbʌrd] o ['sɑŋˌbʌrd] *s* ave canora; (fig.) cantora, cantatriz
**songless** ['sɔŋlɪs] o ['sɑŋlɪs] *adj* sin canto
**Song of Solomon** *s* (Bib.) Cantares de Salomón
**Song of Songs** *s* (Bib.) Cantar de los Cantares
**songster** ['sɔŋstər] o ['sɑŋstər] *s* cantor, cantante; cancionista; ave canora
**songstress** ['sɔŋstrɪs] o ['sɑŋstrɪs] *s* cantora, cantatriz; cancionista; poetisa; ave canora
**song thrush** *s* (orn.) malvís, tordo alirrojo
**sonic** ['sɑnɪk] *adj* sónico
**sonic barrier** *s* barrera del sonido, barrera sónica
**sonic boom** *s* estallido que da un avión al atravesar la barrera sónica
**sonic depth finder** *s* sonda acústica
**soniferous** [so'nɪfərəs] *adj* sonoro, sonante
**son-in-law** ['sʌnɪnˌlɔ] *s* (*pl:* **sons-in-law**) yerno
**sonnet** ['sɑnɪt] *s* soneto
**sonneteer** [ˌsɑnɪ'tɪr] *s* sonetista; poetastro; *vn* sonetear, sonetizar
**sonny** ['sʌnɪ] *s* (*pl:* **-nies**) hijito
**Son of God** *s* Hijo de Dios (*Jesucristo*)
**Son of Man** *s* Hijo del Hombre (*Jesucristo*)
**sonometer** [so'nɑmɪtər] *s* sonómetro
**sonorant** [so'norənt] *s* (phonet.) sonante
**sonority** [sə'nɑrɪtɪ] o [sə'nɔrɪtɪ] *s* (*pl:* **-ties**) sonoridad
**sonorous** [sə'norəs] *adj* sonoro, resonante
**soon** [sun] *adv* pronto, en breve; temprano; de buena gana; **soon after** poco después, poco después de; **as soon as** así que, luego que, tan pronto como; **as soon as possible** cuanto antes, lo más pronto posible; **had sooner** preferiría; **how soon?** ¿cuándo?; **sooner or later** tarde o temprano
**soot** [sʊt] o [sut] *s* hollín; *va* manchar o cubrir de hollín, ensuciar con hollín
**soothe** [suð] *va* calmar, sosegar, aliviar
**soothsayer** ['suθˌseər] *s* adivino
**soothsaying** ['suθˌseɪŋ] *s* adivinación, adivinanza
**sooty** ['sʊtɪ] o ['sutɪ] *adj* (*comp:* **-ier;** *super:* **-iest**) holliniento
**sop** [sɑp] *s* sopa (*pan u otra cosa empapada en un líquido*); regalo (*para acallar, apaciguar o sobornar*); persona muy mojada, cosa muy mojada; (*pret & pp:* **sopped;** *ger:* **sopping**) *va* empapar, ensopar; **to sop up** absorber
**Sophia** [so'faɪə] o ['sofɪə] *s* Sofía (*nombre de mujer*)
**sophism** ['sɑfɪzəm] *s* sofisma
**sophist** ['sɑfɪst] *s* sofista; sabio, filósofo
**sophistic** [sə'fɪstɪk] o **sophistical** [sə'fɪstɪkəl] *adj* sofista; sofístico
**sophisticate** [sə'fɪstɪket] *s* mundano, hombre mundano; *va* hacer mundano; envolver en sofisterías; engañar; *vn* valerse de sofismas
**sophisticated** [sə'fɪstɪˌketɪd] *adj* mundano, falto de simplicidad; engañoso, fraudulento
**sophistication** [səˌfɪstɪ'keʃən] *s* mundanería, falta de simplicidad; sofistería
**sophistry** ['sɑfɪstrɪ] *s* sofistería
**Sophoclean** [ˌsɑfə'kliən] *adj* sofocleo
**Sophocles** ['sɑfəkliz] *s* Sófocles
**sophomore** ['sɑfəmor] *s* estudiante de segundo año
**sophomoric** [ˌsɑfə'mɑrɪk] o [ˌsɑfə'mɔrɪk] *adj* de los estudiantes de segundo año; engreído e ignorante
**soporiferous** [ˌsopə'rɪfərəs] o [ˌsɑpə'rɪfərəs] *adj* soporífero
**soporific** [ˌsopə'rɪfɪk] o [ˌsɑpə'rɪfɪk] *adj* soporífero, soporífico; soporoso; *s* soporífero
**sopping** ['sɑpɪŋ] *adj* empapado; **sopping wet** hecho una sopa
**soppy** ['sɑpɪ] *adj* (*comp:* **-pier;** *super:* **-piest**) empapado; lluvioso
**soprano** [sə'præno] o [sə'prɑno] *s* (*pl:* **-os**) soprano; *adj* de soprano, para soprano
**sorb** [sɔrb] *s* (bot.) serbal; serba (*fruto*)
**Sorbonne** [sɔr'bɑn] *s* Sorbona
**sorcerer** ['sɔrsərər] *s* hechicero, brujo
**sorceress** ['sɔrsərɪs] *s* hechicera, bruja
**sorcery** ['sɔrsərɪ] *s* (*pl:* **-ies**) hechicería, brujería, sortilegio
**sordid** ['sɔrdɪd] *adj* sórdido
**sore** [sor] *s* llaga, úlcera; pena, dolor, disgusto, aflicción; **to open an old sore** renovar la herida; *adj* enrojecido, inflamado; dolorido; susceptible, irritable; (coll.) sentido, picado, resentido; penoso; fuerte, vehemente; **to be sore at** (coll.) estar enojado con
**sore ears** *spl* mal o dolor de oídos
**sore eyes** *spl* dolor de ojos
**sorehead** ['sorˌhɛd] *s* (coll.) persona resentida
**sorely** ['sorlɪ] *adv* penosamente; con urgencia
**soreness** ['sornɪs] *s* dolor, inflamación; amargura de una pena
**sore throat** *s* mal o dolor de garganta
**sorghum** ['sɔrgəm] *s* (bot.) alcandía, sorgo, zahína
**sorority** [sə'rɑrɪtɪ] o [sə'rɔrɪtɪ] *s* (*pl:* **-ties**) hermandad (*de mujeres; de estudiantas*)
**sorosis** [sə'rosɪs] *s* (bot.) sorosis
**sorrel** ['sɑrəl] o ['sɔrəl] *adj* alazán; *s* (bot.) acedera; alazán (*color y caballo de este color*)
**sorrow** ['sɑro] o ['sɔro] *s* dolor, pesar, pena; arrepentimiento; *vn* dolerse, apenarse, sentir pena; arrepentirse; **to sorrow for** añorar
**sorrowful** ['sɑrofəl] o ['sɔrofəl] *adj* doloroso, pesaroso, afligido, penoso
**sorry** ['sɑrɪ] o ['sɔrɪ] *adj* (*comp:* **-rier;** *super:* **-riest**) pesaroso, afligido, apenado; arrepentido; malo, pésimo; despreciable, ridículo; **to be** o **feel sorry** sentir; arrepentirse; **to be** o **feel sorry for** compadecer; **to be sorry to** + *inf* sentir + *inf*
**sort** [sɔrt] *s* clase, especie; tipo; modo, manera; (print.) tipo; **a sort of** uno a modo de; **of sorts** de varias clases; de poco valor, de mala muerte; **out of sorts** de mal humor; indispuesto; incómodo; **sort of** (coll.) algo, en cierta medida; *va* clasificar, separar; escoger; entresacar; *vn* asociarse; concordar, estar de acuerdo
**sortie** ['sɔrtɪ] *s* (mil.) salida, surtida
**sorus** ['sorəs] *s* (*pl:* **-ri** [[raɪ]) (bot.) soro
**S O S** ['ɛsˌo'ɛs] *s* (rad.) S O S (*señal de peligro*); (coll.) llamada de auxilio
**so-so** ['soˌso] *adj* mediano, regular, talcualillo; *adv* así así, tal cual
**sot** [sɑt] *s* borracho
**soteriology** [səˌtɪrɪ'ɑlədʒɪ] *s* (theol.) soteriología
**sottish** ['sɑtɪʃ] *adj* embrutecido por la mucha bebida, hecho una uva
**sotto voce** ['sɑto 'votʃe] a sovoz, en voz baja
**soubrette** [su'brɛt] *s* (theat.) camarera o confidenta de comedia; (theat.) doncella coqueta
**soubriquet** ['subrɪke] *s* var. de **sobriquet**
**Soudan** [su'dæn] *s* var. de **Sudan**
**soufflé** [su'fle] o ['sufle] *s* flan, soufflé
**sough** [sʌf] o [saʊ] *s* susurro, suspiro, murmullo; *vn* susurrar, suspirar, murmullar
**sought** [sɔt] *pret & pp de* **seek**
**soul** [sol] *s* alma; **upon my soul!** ¡por vida mía!
**soulful** ['solfəl] *adj* conmovedor, sentimental
**soulless** ['sollɪs] *adj* desalmado
**sound** [saʊnd] *s* sonido; ruido; tañido (*de las campanas*); (surg.) sonda, tienta; (geog.) estrecho, brazo de mar; vejiga natatoria (*de los peces*); **within sound of** al alcance de; *adj* sano; profundo (*dícese, p.ej., del sueño*); sólido, firme; puro; perfecto; solvente; sonoro; **sound of mind** en su juicio cabal; *adv* profundamente; *va* sonar; tocar (*p.ej., campanas*); tantear, sondear; auscultar (*p.ej., los pulmones*); entonar (*p.ej., alabanzas*); (surg.) sondar, tentar; **to sound the call to arms** tocar llamada; *vn* sonar, resonar; sondar; sumergirse (*una ballena*); parecer; **to sound like** sonar como (*p.ej., un trueno*)
**sound barrier** *s* (aer.) barrera del sonido
**soundboard** ['saʊndˌbord] *s* secreto, caja de resonancia (*de un instrumento musical*); tornavoz (*para dirigir el sonido hacia el público*); (fig.) caja de resonancia

**sound effects** *spl* (mov. & rad.) efectos sonoros
**sounder** ['saʊndər] *s* sonador; sondeador; (telg.) resonador
**sound film** *s* film sonoro, película sonora
**sounding** ['saʊndɪŋ] *adj* sonante, resonante; *s* sondeo; **soundings** *spl* sondas
**sounding balloon** *s* globo sonda
**sounding board** *s* var. de **soundboard**
**sounding line** *s* (naut.) sondaleza
**soundless** ['saʊndlɪs] *adj* silencioso; insondable
**soundly** ['saʊndlɪ] *adv* sanamente; profundamente; a fondo; sólidamente; violentamente
**soundproof** ['saʊnd'pruf] *adj* antisonoro; *va* insonorizar
**soundproofing** ['saʊnd'prufɪŋ] *s* aislación de sonido
**sound track** *s* (mov.) huella de sonido, banda sonora, pista sonora
**sound wave** *s* (phys.) onda sonora
**soup** [sup] *s* sopa; **in the soup** (slang) en apuros, en aprietos
**soup dish** *s* plato sopero
**soup kitchen** *s* comedor de beneficencia, dispensario de alimentos (*para los pobres*); (mil.) cocina de campaña
**soup ladle** *s* cucharón
**soup spoon** *s* cuchara de sopa
**soup tureen** *s* sopera
**soupy** ['supɪ] *adj* (*comp:* **-ier;** *super:* **-iest**) parecido a la sopa; brumoso
**sour** [saʊr] *adj* agrio; (fig.) agrio, acre, desapacible; *va* agriar; *vn* agriarse; malearse (*la tierra*)
**source** [sors] *s* fuente
**source book** *s* texto original; colección de textos originales
**source material** *s* fuentes originales
**sour cherry** *s* (bot.) guindo (*árbol*); guinda (*fruto*)
**sourdough** ['saʊr,do] *s* (coll.) explorador en el Canadá y Alaska
**sour grapes** *spl* agraz; (fig.) las uvas verdes (*de la fábula "La zorra y las uvas" de Esopo, es decir, algo que se finge despreciar porque no se puede conseguir*); **sour grapes!** ¡están verdes las uvas!
**sour gum** *s* (bot.) tupelo
**sourish** ['saʊrɪʃ] *adj* agrete
**sourness** ['saʊrnɪs] *s* agrura
**sourpuss** ['saʊr,pʊs] *s* (slang) cascarrabias, vinagre (*persona*)
**souse** [saʊs] *s* zambullida, chapuz; salmuera; adobo; escabeche; cabeza, patas y orejas de cerdo en escabeche; (slang) borrachín; *va* zambullir, chapuzar; adobar; escabechar; verter; **to get soused** (slang) emborracharse; *vn* zambullirse; (slang) embriagarse habitualmente
**soutache** ['sutæʃ] o [su'tæʃ] *s* trencilla
**soutane** [su'tɑn] *s* sotana
**south** [saʊθ] *s* sur, mediodía; *adj* meridional, del sur; *adv* al sur
**South Africa** *s* Sudáfrica; la Unión Sudafricana
**South African** *adj & s* sudafricano
**South America** *s* Sudamérica, la América del Sur
**South American** *adj & s* sudamericano
**South Australia** *s* la Australia Meridional
**South Carolina** [,kærə'laɪnə] *s* la Carolina del Sur
**South China Sea** *s* mar de la China Meridional
**South Dakota** [də'kotə] *s* el Dakota del Sur
**southeast** [,saʊθ'ist] *adj* sudeste, sudestal; *s* sudeste; *adv* al sudeste, hacia el sudeste
**Southeast Asia** *s* el Asia sudoriental, el Sudeste Asiático, el Sudeste de Asia
**southeaster** [,saʊθ'istər] *s* sudeste (*viento*); sudestada (*viento fuerte*)
**southeasterly** [,saʊθ'istərlɪ] *adj* sudestal; *adv* hacia el sudeste; desde el sudeste
**southeastern** [,saʊθ'istərn] *adj* sudeste, suroriental
**southeastward** [,saʊθ'istwərd] *adj* que va hacia el sudeste; *s* sudeste; *adv* hacia el sudeste
**southeastwardly** [,saʊθ'istwərdlɪ] *adj* que va hacia el sudeste; *adv* hacia el sudeste
**southeastwards** [,saʊθ'istwərdz] *adv* hacia el sudeste
**souther** ['saʊðər] *s* sur (*viento*)
**southerly** ['sʌðərlɪ] *adj* meridional; que viene desde el sur; que va hacia el sur; *adv* desde el sur; hacia el sur
**southern** ['sʌðərn] *adj* meridional
**Southern Cross** *s* (astr.) Cruz del Sur
**southerner** ['sʌðərnər] *s* meridional, habitante del sur
**Southern Hemisphere** *s* hemisferio austral
**southernmost** ['sʌðərnmost] *adj* (el) más meridional
**southernwood** ['sʌðərn,wʊd] *s* (bot.) abrótano
**southing** ['saʊðɪŋ] *s* movimiento hacia el sur; diferencia de latitud sur
**South Island** *s* la Isla del Sur (*Nueva Zelanda*)
**South Korea** *s* la Corea del Sur
**South Korean** *adj & s* surcoreano
**southland** ['saʊθlənd] o ['saʊθ,lænd] *s* región meridional
**southlander** ['saʊθləndər] o ['saʊθ,lændər] *s* meridional
**South Magnetic Pole** *s* polo sur magnético
**southpaw** ['saʊθ,pɔ] *adj & s* (sport & slang) zurdo
**South Pole** *s* polo sur
**southron** ['sʌðrən] *adj & s* meridional
**South Sea Islander** *s* oceánico
**South Sea Islands** *spl* la Oceanía
**South Seas** *spl* Grande Océano (*el Pacífico Sur*); mares del sur (*al sur del ecuador*)
**south-southeast** ['saʊθ,saʊθ'ist] *s* sudsudeste
**south-southwest** ['saʊθ,saʊθ'wɛst] *s* sudsudoeste
**southward** ['saʊθwərd] *adj* que va hacia el sur; *s* sur; *adv* hacia el sur
**southwardly** ['saʊθwərdlɪ] *adj* que va hacia el sur; *adv* hacia el sur
**southwards** ['saʊθwərdz] *adv* hacia el sur
**southwest** [,saʊθ'wɛst] *adj & s* sudoeste; *adv* al sudoeste, hacia el sudoeste
**Southwest Africa** *s* el África del Sudoeste
**southwester** [,saʊθ'wɛstər] *s* sudoeste (*viento*); sudoestada (*viento fuerte*); sueste (*sombrero impermeable*)
**southwesterly** [,saʊθ'wɛstərlɪ] *adj* sudoeste; *adv* hacia el sudoeste; desde el sudoeste
**southwestern** [,saʊθ'wɛstərn] *adj* sudoeste
**southwestward** [,saʊθ'wɛstwərd] *adj* que va hacia el sudoeste; *s* sudoeste; *adv* hacia el sudoeste
**southwestwardly** [,saʊθ'wɛstwərdlɪ] *adj* que va hacia el sudoeste; *adv* hacia el sudoeste
**southwestwards** [,saʊθ'wɛstwərdz] *adv* hacia el sudoeste
**south wind** *s* austro, noto
**souvenir** [,suvə'nɪr] o ['suvənɪr] *s* recuerdo, memoria
**souvenir sheet** *s* (philately) hoja-bloque
**sou'wester** [,saʊ'wɛstər] *s* var. de **southwester**
**sovereign** ['sɑvrɪn] o ['sʌvrɪn] *adj* soberano; *s* soberano (*rey; moneda*); soberana (*reina*)
**sovereignly** ['sɑvrɪnlɪ] o ['sʌvrɪnlɪ] *adv* soberanamente; eficazmente
**sovereignty** ['sɑvrɪntɪ] o ['sʌvrɪntɪ] *s* (*pl:* **-ties**) soberanía
**soviet** ['sovɪɛt] *s* soviet; *adj* soviético
**sovietism** ['sovɪɛtɪzəm] *s* sovietismo
**sovietization** [,sovɪ,ɛtɪ'zeʃən] *s* sovietizacíon
**sovietize** ['sovɪɛtaɪz] *va* sovietizar
**Soviet Russia** *s* la Rusia Soviética
**Soviet Union** *s* Unión Soviética
**sow** [saʊ] *s* puerca; (found.) galápago (*lingote*); (found.) fosa, reguera; [so] (*pret:* **sowed;** *pp:* **sown** o **sowed**) *va* sembrar; **to sow with mines** plagar de minas; *vn* sembrar
**sowbread** ['saʊ,brɛd] *s* (bot.) pamporcino
**sow bug** [saʊ] *s* (zool.) cochinilla de humedad
**sower** ['soər] *s* sembrador
**sown** [son] *pp de* **sow**
**sow thistle** [saʊ] *s* (bot.) cerraja
**soy** [sɔɪ] *s* (bot.) soja; semilla de soja; (cook.) salsa de soja
**soybean** ['sɔɪ,bin] *s* (bot.) soja; semilla de soja
**sp.** abr. de **special, species, specific, specimen** y **spelling**
**Sp.** abr. de **Spain, Spaniard** y **Spanish**
**spa** [spɑ] *s* caldas, manantial de agua mineral; balneario

**space** [spes] *s* espacio; (mus. & print.) espacio; **in the space of** por espacio de (*p.ej., un año*); *adj* espacial; de espacios; *va* espaciar; (print.) espaciar; (print.) regletear

**space age** *s* era del espacio

**space bar** o **space key** *s* tecla de espacios, llave espacial, espaciador

**space charge** *s* (elec.) carga de espacio, carga interespacial

**spacecraft** [ˈspesˌkræft] o [ˈspesˌkrɑft] *s* var. de **spaceship**

**space exploration** *s* exploración del espacio

**space flight** *s* vuelo espacial

**space helmet** *s* casco espacial, escafandra espacial

**space-lattice** [ˈspesˌlætɪs] *s* (physical chem.) estructura del cristal (*ordenamiento de los átomos de un cristal mediante la aplicación de los rayos X*)

**spaceless** [ˈspeslɪs] *adj* infinito; que no ocupa espacio

**spaceman** [ˈspesˌmæn] *s* (*pl:* **-men**) navegador del espacio; visitante a la Tierra del espacio exterior

**space mark** *s* (print.) signo para indicar el espaciado

**space medicine** *s* medicina del espacio

**space probe** *s* sondaje del espacio

**spacer** [ˈspesər] *s* (print.) espaciador; (telg.) separador

**space race** *s* carrera espacial

**space science** *s* ciencia del espacio

**spaceship** [ˈspesˌʃɪp] *s* nave del espacio, nave espacial, astronave

**space suit** *s* traje espacial

**space-time continuum** [ˈspesˌtaɪm] *s* (phys.) continuo espacio tiempo, continuo espaciotemporal

**space travel** *s* viajes por el espacio, astronavegación

**space vehicle** *s* vehículo espacial

**spacing** [ˈspesɪŋ] *s* espaciamiento

**spacious** [ˈspeʃəs] *adj* espacioso

**spade** [sped] *s* laya; (mil.) zapa; pique (*naipe que corresponde a la espada*); **spades** *spl* piques (*palo que corresponde al de espadas*); **to call a spade a spade** llamar al pan pan y al vino vino; *va* layar; *vn* layar; (mil.) zapar

**spadework** [ˈspedˌwʌrk] *s* trabajo hecho con la laya; (fig.) trabajo preliminar y fundamental

**spadix** [ˈspedɪks] *s* (*pl:* **spadixes** o **spadices** [speˈdaɪsiz]) (bot.) espádice

**spaghetti** [spəˈgɛtɪ] *s* macarrones delgados; (elec.) tubería aisladora

**spahi** o **spahee** [ˈspɑhi] *s* espahí

**Spain** [spen] *s* España

**spake** [spek] (archaic) *pret de* **speak**

**spall** [spɔl] *s* lasca, astilla de piedra; *va* romper (*piedras*) con la almádena

**span** [spæn] *s* palmo, llave de la mano; extensión completa; (arch.) ojo; pareja (*de caballos*); (aer.) envergadura; (*pret & pp:* **spanned**; *ger:* **spanning**) *va* medir a palmos; atravesar, extenderse sobre, abrazar

**spandrel** [ˈspændrəl] *s* (arch.) enjuta, embecadura

**spangle** [ˈspæŋgəl] *s* lentejuela; *va* estrellar; adornar con lentejuelas; *vn* brillar, resplandecer

**Spaniard** [ˈspænjərd] *s* español o española

**spaniel** [ˈspænjəl] *s* perro de aguas; persona rastrera que sirve de instrumento a otra

**Spanish** [ˈspænɪʃ] *adj* español; *spl* españoles; *ssg* español (*idioma*)

**Spanish American** *adj & s* hispanoamericano (*de la América española*)

**Spanish-American** [ˈspænɪʃəˈmɛrɪkən] *adj* hispanoamericano (*perteneciente a España y América o España y los Estados Unidos*)

**Spanish-American War** *s* guerra hispanoamericana

**Spanish Armada** *s* Armada Invencible

**Spanish bayonet** *s* (bot.) bayoneta

**Spanish broom** *s* (bot.) retama de China, retama de olor, gayomba

**Spanish dagger** *s* (bot.) bayoneta

**Spanish fir** *s* (bot.) pinsapo

**Spanish fly** *s* (ent.) abadejo, mosca de España, cantárida

**Spanish Guinea** *s* la Guinea Española

**Spanish Inquisition** *s* Inquisición de España

**Spanish mackerel** *s* (ichth.) caballa con manchas parduscas por los lados (*Scomberomorus maculatus*)

**Spanish Main** *s* Costa Firme, Tierra Firme; mar Caribe

**Spanish-Moroccan** [ˈspænɪʃməˈrɑkən] *adj* hispanomarroquí

**Spanish Morocco** *s* el Marruecos Español

**Spanish moss** *s* (bot.) barba española

**Spanish n** *s* la letra eñe

**Spanish omelet** *s* tortilla de tomate

**Spanish onion** *s* cebolla grande de sabor dulce

**Spanish oyster plant** *s* (bot.) cardillo, tagarnina

**Spanish paprika** *s* (bot.) asnaucho

**Spanish plum** *s* (bot.) jocotal (*árbol*); jocote (*fruto*)

**Spanish-speaking** [ˈspænɪʃˈspikɪŋ] *adj* hispanohablante, de habla española

**spank** [spæŋk] *s* azote, manotada; *va* azotar, manotear; *vn* correr rápidamente, galopar

**spanker** [ˈspæŋkər] *s* (coll.) cosa muy grande, hermosa o extraordinaria; (coll.) caballo muy veloz; (naut.) cangreja de popa

**spanker boom** *s* (naut.) verga de popa

**spanker gaff** *s* (naut.) cangrejo, pico de cangrejo

**spanking** [ˈspæŋkɪŋ] *s* azote, manotada; *adj* rápido, veloz; fuerte; (coll.) muy grande, muy hermoso, extraordinario

**spanless** [ˈspænlɪs] *adj* que no se puede medir, atravesar o abrazar

**spanner** [ˈspænər] *s* llave de tuercas, llave de manguera

**spar** [spɑr] *s* (naut.) mástil, verga, palo; (aer.) viga mayor; (mineral.) espato; boxeo; combate de gallos a espolonazos; riña, pelea; (*pret & pp:* **sparred**; *ger:* **sparring**) *va* proveer de mástiles, vergas o palos; *vn* reñir, pelear; boxear; luchar a espolonazos (*los gallos*)

**spar deck** *s* (naut.) cubierta de guindaste

**spare** [spɛr] *adj* sobrante, de repuesto; libre, disponible; flaco, enjuto, delgado; escaso; sobrio, frugal; *va* pasar sin, pasarse sin; perdonar; exonerar; salvar, guardar; ahorrar; **to have . . . to spare** tener de sobra, p.ej., **they have money to spare** tienen dinero de sobra; **to have no time to spare** no tener tiempo que perder; **to spare oneself** ahorrarse esfuerzo; *vn* economizar; ser clemente

**spare bed** *s* cama de sobra

**spare hours** *spl* horas de recreo, horas de ocio

**spare money** *s* dinero de reserva

**spare parts** *spl* piezas de recambio o de repuesto

**sparerib** [ˈspɛrˌrɪb] *s* costilla de cerdo con poca carne

**spare room** *s* cuarto del huésped, habitación del forastero

**spare time** *s* tiempo desocupado

**spare tire** *s* neumático de repuesto, goma de recambio

**spare wheel** *s* rueda de recambio

**sparing** [ˈspɛrɪŋ] *adj* económico; escaso

**spark** [spɑrk] *s* chispa; (coll.) galán, cortejador; (coll.) petimetre; (fig.) centellita (*p.ej., de verdad*); *va* (coll.) galantear, cortejar (*a una mujer*); *vn* chispear; (coll.) ser galante

**spark arrester** *s* parachispas; (elec.) parachispas; (rail.) chispero

**spark coil** *s* bobina de chispas, bobina de encendido

**sparker** [ˈspɑrker] *s* artificio chispero; bujía, encendedor; (elec.) apagachispas, parachispas; (slang) galán, enamorado

**spark gap** *s* (elec.) entrehierro (*del carrete de inducción*); (elec.) espacio de chispa (*de la bujía de encendido*)

**sparkish** [ˈspɑrkɪʃ] *adj* galante, elegante

**sparkle** [ˈspɑrkəl] *s* chispita, destello; viveza, alegría; chispa (*diamante muy pequeño*); *va* hacer chispear; *vn* chispear; ser vivaz, ser alegre; espumar, ser efervescente, ser espumoso

**spark lead** [lid] *s* (mach.) avance del encendido

**sparkler** [ˈspɑrklər] *s* piedra preciosa muy brillante, diamante; fuegos artificiales que echan chispitas; ojo muy brillante

**sparklet** [ˈspɑrklɪt] *s* chispa, centella; (trademark) cápsula metálica, llena de ácido carbó-

nico líquido y con la cual se pueden fabricar bebidas gaseosas en la mesa
**sparkling** ['spɑrklɪŋ] *adj* chispeante, centelleante; espumante, espumoso (*vino*); **gaseoso** (*agua*)
**spark plug** *s* bujía
**sparrow** ['spæro] *s* (orn.) gorrión, pardal
**sparrow hawk** *s* (orn.) gavilán, cernícalo
**sparse** [spɑrs] *adj* esparcido, disperso; escaso, poco abundante; ralo (*dícese del pelo*)
**sparsity** ['spɑrsɪtɪ] *s* dispersión; escasez; raleza
**Sparta** ['spɑrtə] *s* Esparta
**Spartacus** ['spɑrtəkəs] *s* Espártaco
**Spartan** ['spɑrtən] *adj & s* espartano; (fig.) espartano
**Spartanism** ['spɑrtənɪzəm] *s* severidad de espartano
**spasm** ['spæzəm] *s* (path.) espasmo; ataque súbito y violento, esfuerzo súbito y de breve duración
**spasmodic** [spæz'mɑdɪk] *adj* espasmódico; irregular, intermitente
**spasmodically** [spæz'mɑdɪkəlɪ] *adv* espasmódicamente; irregularmente, intermitentemente
**spastic** ['spæstɪk] *adj* espástico
**spasticity** [spæs'tɪsɪtɪ] *s* (path.) espasticidad
**spat** [spæt] *s* manotada, bofetada; palmadita; riña, disputa; botín, polaina corta; ostra joven; masa de ostras jóvenes; (*pret & pp:* **spatted;** *ger:* **spatting**) *va* dar una manotada a; golpear ligeramente; *vn* reñir, disputar; desovar (*las ostras*); *pret & pp de* **spit**
**spate** [spet] *s* (Brit.) avenida (*de agua*); (Brit.) chaparrón; gran cantidad; torrente de palabras; emoción intensa
**spathe** [speð] *s* (bot.) espata
**spathic** ['spæθɪk] *adj* (mineral.) espático
**spatial** ['speʃəl] *adj* espacial
**spatter** ['spætər] *s* salpicadura; *va* salpicar; (fig.) manchar; *vn* chorrear; chapotear
**spatterdash** ['spætər,dæʃ] *s* polaina larga
**spatterdock** ['spætər,dɑk] *s* (bot.) nenúfar amarillo
**spatula** ['spætʃələ] *s* espátula; (cook. & paint.) espátula
**spatulamancy** ['spætʃələ,mænsɪ] *s* espatulomancía
**spatulate** ['spætʃəlet] *adj* espatulado
**spavin** ['spævɪn] *s* (vet.) esparaván
**spavined** ['spævɪnd] *adj* que tiene esparaván
**spawn** [spɔn] *s* (ichth.) freza; pececillos; producto, resultado; prole; germen, fuente; (bot.) micelio; *va* engendrar, producir; *vn* frezar (*los peces*); producir en abundancia
**spawning** ['spɔnɪŋ] *s* freza, desove
**spawning time** *s* freza, desove
**spay** [spe] *va* sacar los ovarios a (*un animal*)
**spaying** ['speɪŋ] *s* castración femenina
**S.P.C.A.** abr. de **Society for the Prevention of Cruelty to Animals**
**speak** [spik] (*pret:* **spoke;** *pp:* **spoken**) *va* hablar (*un idioma*); decir (*la verdad*); *vn* hablar; **so to speak** por decirlo así; **to know to speak to** conocer de pocas palabras; **to not speak to** negar o quitar el habla a, no hablar con (*por haber reñido*); **to speak for** hablar por, hablar en favor de; pedir, solicitar; representar; **to speak out** elevar la voz, osar hablar, hablar alto; **to speak well for** demostrar el mérito de; **to speak well of** hablar bien de; **speaking!** ¡al habla! (*contestación telefónica*)
**speakeasy** ['spik,izɪ] *s* (*pl:* **-ies**) (slang) taberna clandestina
**speaker** ['spikər] *s* hablante; orador; presidente (*p.ej., de una asamblea legislativa*); (rad.) altavoz
**Speaker of the House** *s* (U.S.A.) presidente de la Cámara de Representantes
**speakership** ['spikərʃɪp] *s* presidencia de una asamblea legislativa
**speaking** ['spikɪŋ] *s* habla; elocuencia; *adj* hablante; viviente; **to be on speaking terms** hablarse
**speaking tube** *s* tubo acústico
**spear** [spɪr] *s* lanza; arpón (*para pescar*); hoja (*de hierba*); *va* alancear, herir con lanza; *vn* brotar
**spearhead** ['spɪr,hɛd] *s* punta de lanza; (fig.) punta de lanza
**spearman** ['spɪrmən] *s* (*pl:* **-men**) lancero
**spearmint** ['spɪr,mɪnt] *s* (bot.) menta verde, menta romana
**spec.** abr. de **special**
**special** ['spɛʃəl] *adj* especial; *s* tren especial
**special delivery** *s* correspondencia urgente, correo urgente, entrega inmediata
**special-delivery** ['spɛʃəldɪ'lɪvərɪ] *adj* urgente, de urgencia
**specialism** ['spɛʃəlɪzəm] *s* especialización
**specialist** ['spɛʃəlɪst] *adj & s* especialista
**speciality** [,spɛʃɪ'ælɪtɪ] *s* (*pl:* **-ties**) especialidad
**specialization** [,spɛʃəlɪ'zeʃən] *s* especialización
**specialize** ['spɛʃəlaɪz] *va* especializar; especificar; *vn* especializar o especializarse
**specially** ['spɛʃəlɪ] *adv* especialmente
**special pleading** *s* (law) alegación parcial
**specialty** ['spɛʃəltɪ] *s* (*pl:* **-ties**) especialidad
**specie** ['spiʃɪ] *s* efectivo, numerario, metálico
**species** ['spiʃɪz] *s* (*pl:* **-cies**) especie; (eccl.) especies sacramentales; **the species** la especie humana
**specif.** abr. de **specifically**
**specific** [spɪ'sɪfɪk] *adj & s* específico
**specifically** [spɪ'sɪfɪkəlɪ] *adv* específicamente; especificadamente
**specification** [,spɛsɪfɪ'keʃən] *s* especificación; presupuesto o plan detallado (*de un edificio*)
**specificative** [spɪ'sɪfɪ,ketɪv] *adj* especificativo
**specific gravity** *s* (phys.) peso específico
**specific heat** *s* calor específico
**specify** ['spɛsɪfaɪ] (*pret & pp:* **-fied**) *va* especificar; designar en el presupuesto
**specimen** ['spɛsɪmən] *s* espécimen; (coll.) tipo (*persona estrafalaria*)
**speciosity** [,spiʃɪ'ɑsɪtɪ] *s* (*pl:* **-ties**) especiosidad
**specious** ['spiʃəs] *adj* especioso (*engañoso*)
**speck** [spɛk] *s* manchita; partícula, pizca; *va* manchar, salpicar de manchas
**speckle** ['spɛkəl] *s* mota, punto; *va* motear, puntear
**specs** [spɛks] *spl* (coll.) anteojos, gafas
**spectacle** ['spɛktəkəl] *s* espectáculo; **spectacles** *spl* anteojos, gafas
**spectacle case** *s* funda de gafas
**spectacled** ['spɛktəkəld] *adj* que lleva anteojos o gafas
**spectacular** [spɛk'tækjələr] *adj* espectacular, aparatoso, ostentoso
**spectator** ['spɛktetər] o [spɛk'tetər] *s* espectador
**specter** ['spɛktər] *s* espectro
**spectral** ['spɛktrəl] *adj* espectral; (phys.) espectral
**spectrograph** ['spɛktrəgræf] o ['spɛktrəgrɑf] *s* espectrógrafo
**spectroscope** ['spɛktrəskop] *s* espectroscopio
**spectroscopic** [,spɛktrə'skɑpɪk] *adj* espectroscópico
**spectroscopy** [spɛk'trɑskəpɪ] *s* espectroscopia
**spectrum** ['spɛktrəm] *s* (*pl:* **-tra** [trə] o **-trums**) (phys.) espectro
**spectrum analysis** *s* análisis espectral
**specular** ['spɛkjələr] *adj* especular
**specular iron** *s* (mineral.) hierro especular
**speculate** ['spɛkjəlet] *vn* especular; (com.) especular
**speculation** [,spɛkjə'leʃən] *s* especulación; (com.) especulación
**speculative** ['spɛkjə,letɪv] *adj* especulativo; arriesgado, aventurado
**speculator** ['spɛkjə,letər] *s* especulador
**speculum** ['spɛkjələm] *s* (*pl:* **-la** [lə] o **-lums**) *s* espejo; (med. & surg.) espéculo
**sped** [spɛd] *pret & pp de* **speed**
**speech** [spitʃ] *s* habla (*facultad de hablar; manera de hablar; idioma, lenguaje; arenga, discurso*); conferencia; parlamento (*de un actor*)
**speech clinic** *s* clínica de la palabra, clínica para la corrección de defectos del habla
**speech correction** *s* rehabilitación del habla, corrección de defectos del habla
**speechify** ['spitʃɪfaɪ] (*pret & pp:* **-fied**) *vn* (hum. & scornful) arengar, perorar
**speechless** ['spitʃlɪs] *adj* sin habla; mudo, silencioso; estupefacto

**speed** [spid] *s* velocidad; velocidad máxima; (aut.) marcha, velocidad (*de los engranajes*); **at full speed** a toda velocidad; **to make speed** marchar a gran velocidad; (*pret & pp:* **sped**) *va* apresurar, dar prisa a; despedir, despachar; ayudar, favorecer; *vn* apresurarse, darse prisa; adelantar, progresar; ir con exceso de velocidad, exceder la velocidad permitida
**speedboat** ['spid,bot] *s* lancha de gran velocidad, lancha de carreras
**speeder** ['spidər] *s* persona o cosa que anda a gran velocidad; automovilista que excede la velocidad permitida
**speeding** ['spidɪŋ] *s* exceso de velocidad
**speed king** *s* (aut.) as del volante
**speed limit** *s* velocidad permitida, velocidad máxima
**speedometer** [spi'dɑmɪtər] *s* velocímetro; (aut.) taquímetro y cuentakilómetros unidos
**speed record** *s* marca de velocidad
**speed-up** ['spid,ʌp] *s* aumento de producción; (coll.) aceleración; (aut.) acelerada (*del motor*)
**speedway** ['spid,we] *s* vía de tráfico rápido; carretera para carreras
**speedwell** ['spidwɛl] *s* (bot.) verónica
**speedy** ['spidɪ] *adj* (*comp:* **-ier;** *super:* **-iest**) veloz, rápido; pronto, vivo
**speleologist** [,spilɪ'ɑlədʒɪst] *s* espeleólogo
**speleology** [,spilɪ'ɑlədʒɪ] *s* espeleología
**spell** [spɛl] *s* encanto, hechizo; turno, tanda, revezo; rato, poco tiempo; temporada (*p.ej., de buen tiempo*); **by spells** a ratos; **to cast a spell on** encantar, hechizar; **under a spell** bajo el poder de un encanto; (*pret & pp:* **spelled** o **spelt**) *va* deletrear; descifrar; indicar, significar; **to spell it out to someone** (coll.) decírselo a uno deletreando; **to spell out** (coll.) explicar detalladamente; *vn* deletrear; (*pret & pp:* **spelled**) *va* relevar, revezar, reemplazar
**spellbind** ['spɛl,baɪnd] (*pret & pp:* **-bound**) *va* fascinar (*especialmente con su oratoria*)
**spellbinder** ['spɛl,baɪndər] *s* (coll.) orador fascinante, orador persuasivo
**spellbinding** ['spɛl,baɪndɪŋ] *adj* fascinante, persuasivo
**spellbound** ['spɛl,baʊnd] *pret & pp de* **spellbind**
**speller** ['spɛlər] *s* deletreador (*persona*); abecedario, silabario; cartilla de deletrear
**spelling** ['spɛlɪŋ] *s* deletreo; ortografía; grafía
**spelling bee** *s* concurso o certamen de ortografía
**spelt** [spɛlt] *s* (bot.) espelta; *pret & pp de* **spell**
**spelter** ['spɛltər] *s* peltre
**spelunker** [spɪ'lʌŋkər] *s* aficionado a la espeleología, espeleólogo de afición
**spencer** ['spɛnsər] *s* chaqueta corta de punto
**spend** [spɛnd] (*pret & pp:* **spent**) *va* gastar; pasar (*una hora, un día, etc.*); **to spend a mast** (naut.) perder un palo; *vn* gastar dinero; consumirse
**spender** ['spɛndər] *s* gastador
**spending money** *s* dinero para gastos menudos
**spendthrift** ['spɛnd,θrɪft] *s & adj* gastador, derrochador, pródigo
**Spenserian** [spɛn'sɪrɪən] *adj* spenseriano
**spent** [spɛnt] *adj* gastado; pasado; consumido, agotado; *pret & pp de* **spend**
**sperm** [spʌrm] *s* esperma; espermatozoo; (zool.) cachalote; esperma de ballena
**spermaceti** [,spʌrmə'sɛtɪ] o [,spʌrmə'sitɪ] *s* espermaceti
**spermatic** [spər'mætɪk] *adj* espermático
**spermatic cord** *s* (anat.) cordón espermático
**spermatophyte** ['spʌrmətə,faɪt] *s* (bot.) espermatofita
**spermatorrhea** [,spʌrmətə'riə] (path.) espermatorrea
**spermatozoön** [,spʌrmətə'zoɑn] *s* (*pl:* **-zoa** ['zoə]) (zool.) espermatozoo
**spermogonium** [,spʌrmə'gonɪəm] *s* (*pl:* **-a** [ə]) (bot.) espermogonio
**sperm oil** *s* aceite de esperma
**sperm whale** *s* (zool.) cachalote
**spew** [spju] *va & vn* vomitar
**sp. gr.** abr. de **specific gravity**
**sphacelate** ['sfæsəlet] *vn* (path.) esfacelarse
**sphacelus** ['sfæsələs] *s* (path.) esfacelo
**sphagnum** ['sfægnəm] *s* (*pl:* **-na** [nə]) (bot.) esfágnea
**sphene** [sfin] *s* (mineral.) esfena o esfeno
**sphenoid** ['sfinɔɪd] *s* (anat.) esfenoides
**sphenoidal** [sfɪ'nɔɪdəl] *adj* esfenoidal
**sphere** [sfɪr] *s* (geom.) esfera; (astr.) astro; (astr.) esfera celeste; (fig.) esfera (*ambiente, círculo*); (poet.) esfera (*cielo*)
**sphere of influence** *s* (dipl.) esfera de influencia
**spherical** ['sfɛrɪkəl] *adj* esférico
**spherical trigonometry** *s* trigonometría esférica
**spherical vault** *s* (arch.) bóveda de casquete esférico
**sphericity** [sfɪ'rɪsɪtɪ] *s* (*pl:* **-ties**) esfericidad
**spheroid** ['sfɪrɔɪd] *s* (geom.) esferoide
**spheroidal** [sfɪ'rɔɪdəl] *adj* esferoidal
**spherometer** [sfɪ'rɑmɪtər] *s* (phys.) esferómetro
**spherule** ['sfɛrul] *s* esférula
**sphincter** ['sfɪŋktər] *s* (anat.) esfínter
**sphinx** [sfɪŋks] *s* (*pl:* **sphinxes** o **sphinges** ['sfɪndʒiz]) esfinge; (fig.) esfinge (*personaje impenetrable*)
**sphragistic** [sfrə'dʒɪstɪk] *adj* esfragístico; **sphragistics** *ssg* esfragística
**sphygmograph** ['sfɪgməgræf] o ['sfɪgməgrɑf] *s* (physiol.) esfigmógrafo
**spica** ['spaɪkə] *s* (*pl:* **-cae** [si]) (archeol. & surg.) espiga; (*cap.*) *s* (astr.) espiga de la Virgen
**spicate** ['spaɪket] *adj* (bot.) espigado
**spice** [spaɪs] *s* especia; sainete, picante; aroma, fragancia; punta, pequeña cantidad; (fig.) sainete; *va* especiar; dar gusto o picante a
**spiceberry** ['spaɪs,bɛrɪ] *s* (*pl:* **-ries**) (bot.) gaulteria o té del Canadá
**spice box** *s* especiero
**spicebush** ['spaɪs,bʊʃ] *s* (bot.) benjoin
**Spice Islands** *spl* islas de las Especias
**spicery** ['spaɪsərɪ] *s* (*pl:* **-ies**) especiería (*conjunto de especias*); aroma, picante
**spiciform** ['spaɪsɪfɔrm] *adj* (bot.) espiciforme
**spiciness** ['spaɪsɪnɪs] *s* picante, aroma; (fig.) picante; (fig.) sicalipsis
**spick-and-span** ['spɪkənd'spæn] *adj* flamante; bien arreglado; impecablemente limpio
**spicular** ['spɪkjələr] o **spiculate** ['spɪkjəlet] *adj* espicular
**spicule** ['spɪkjul] *s* aguja (*p.ej., de hielo*); (anat., bot. & zool.) espícula
**spicy** ['spaɪsɪ] *adj* (*comp:* **-ier;** *super:* **-iest**) especiado; aromático, picante; (fig.) sabroso, picante; (fig.) sicalíptico
**spider** ['spaɪdər] *s* (ent. & mach.) araña; trébedes (*cazo con pies*); sartén de mango largo
**spider crab** *s* (zool.) araña de mar
**spider lines** *spl* retículo
**spider monkey** *s* (zool.) mono araña
**spider web** *s* tela de araña, telaraña
**spiderwort** ['spaɪdər,wʌrt] *s* (bot.) pasajera
**spidery** ['spaɪdərɪ] *adj* de araña; lleno de arañas; semejante a una telaraña; largo y delgado
**spiel** [spil] *s* (slang) arenga, discurso; *vn* (slang) arengar, hacer un discurso
**spiffy** ['spɪfɪ] *adj* (*comp:* **-ier;** *super:* **-iest**) (slang) guapo, elegante
**spigot** ['spɪgət] *s* grifo; espiche (*taco para tapar un agujero*)
**spike** [spaɪk] *s* perno (*clavo muy largo*); alcayata, escarpia; espigón (*cosa puntiaguda*); (bot.) espiga; *va* empernar; sujetar con alcayatas o escarpias; herir con un clavo; clavar (*un cañón*); acabar, poner fin a; inutilizar
**spikelet** ['spaɪklɪt] *s* (bot.) espiguita o espiguilla
**spikenard** ['spaɪknərd] o ['spaɪknɑrd] *s* (bot.) espicanardo; (bot.) aralia; nardo (*de los antiguos*)
**spiky** ['spaɪkɪ] *adj* espigado; erizado, puntiagudo
**spile** [spaɪl] *s* pilote; espiche; caño para sacar el azúcar del arce azucarero; *va* proveer de pilote; proveer de espiche; poner espiche a; afirmar con pilotes; cerrar con tarugo
**spilikin** ['spɪlɪkɪn] *s* pajita o astilla (*que se usan en ciertos juegos*); **spilikins** *spl* juego de pajitas
**spill** [spɪl] *s* derramamiento; líquido derramado; (coll.) vuelco, caída; astilla; alegrador (*tira de papel para encender*); (*pret & pp:* **spilled** o **spilt**) *va* derramar, verter; esparcir; (coll.)

volcar, hacer caer; (naut.) hacer relingar, quitarle el viento a (*una vela*); **to spill the beans** (slang) revelar el secreto; *vn* derramarse, verterse
**spillikin** ['spɪlɪkɪn] *s* var. de **spilikin**
**spillway** ['spɪl,we] *s* derramadero, vertedero, canal de desagüe
**spilt** [spɪlt] *pret & pp de* **spill**
**spin** [spɪn] *s* vuelta, giro muy rápido; (coll.) paseo en coche, bicicleta, etc.; (phys.) giro electrónico; (aer.) barrena; **to go into a spin** (aer.) entrar en barrena; (*pret & pp:* **spun;** *ger:* **spinning**) *va* hacer dar vueltas, hacer girar; hilar (*lino, el capullo, etc.*); bailar (*un trompo*); **to spin out** alargar, extender, prolongar; **to spin yarns** contar cuentos increíbles; *vn* dar vueltas, girar; hilar; bailar (*dícese del trompo*); (coll.) correr rápidamente; (aer.) entrar en barrena
**spinach** ['spɪnɪtʃ] o ['spɪnɪdʒ] *s* (bot.) espinaca; espinacas (*hojas que se comen*)
**spinal** ['spaɪnəl] *adj* espinal
**spinal anesthesia** *s* (med.) anestesia espinal
**spinal column** *s* (anat.) espina dorsal, columna vertebral
**spinal cord** *s* (anat.) médula espinal
**spindle** ['spɪndəl] *s* huso; eje; (carp.) mazorca (*de un balustre*); *vn* crecer muy alto y delgado
**spindle-legged** ['spɪndəl,lɛgɪd] o ['spɪndəl,lɛgd] *adj* zanquilargo, zanquivano
**spindlelegs** ['spɪndəl,lɛgz] *spl* piernas largas y delgadas; *ssg* (coll.) zanquivano
**spindle-shanked** ['spɪndəl,ʃæŋkt] *adj* var. de **spindle-legged**
**spindleshanks** ['spɪndəl,ʃæŋks] *spl & ssg* var. de **spindlelegs**
**spindle tree** *s* (bot.) bonetero
**spindling** ['spɪndlɪŋ] *adj* largo y delgado; flaco y demasiado alto
**spindly** ['spɪndlɪ] *adj* (*comp:* **-dlier;** *super:* **-dliest**) largo y delgado; flaco y demasiado alto
**spindrift** ['spɪn,drɪft] *s* (naut.) rocío (*de las olas*)
**spine** [spaɪn] *s* espina, púa; cordoncillo; loma, cerro; (anat., bot. & zool.) espina; (anat.) espina, espinazo; (b.b.) lomo; (fig.) valor, ánimo
**spined** [spaɪnd] *adj* espinoso
**spinel** [spɪ'nɛl] o ['spɪnəl] *s* (mineral.) espinela
**spineless** ['spaɪnlɪs] *adj* sin espinas; sin espinazo; sin firmeza de carácter
**spinet** ['spɪnɪt] *s* (mus.) espineta
**spinnaker** ['spɪnəkər] *s* (naut.) spinnaker (*vela grande triangular de un yate, opuesta a la vela mayor*)
**spinnaker boom** *s* (naut.) botalón del spinnaker
**spinner** ['spɪnər] *s* hilador, hilandero; máquina de hilar
**spinneret** ['spɪnərɛt] *s* (zool.) hilera
**spinney** ['spɪnɪ] *s* (Brit.) bosquete (*para cazar*)
**spinning** ['spɪnɪŋ] *s* hila (*acción*); hilandería (*arte*); *adj* hilador
**spinning frame** *s* hilandería
**spinning jenny** *s* máquina de hilar de múltiples husos
**spinning machine** *s* máquina hiladora, máquina de hilar
**spinning wheel** *s* torno de hilar
**spin-off** ['spɪn,ɑf] o ['spɪn,ɔf] *s* (com.) traspaso de ciertas actividades de una compañía a otra compañía nueva e independiente, recibiendo los accionistas originales acciones de la nueva compañía libres de impuestos
**spinose** ['spaɪnos] *adj* espinoso
**spinous** ['spaɪnəs] *adj* espinoso; espíneo
**Spinozism** [spɪ'nozɪzəm] *s* espinosismo
**Spinozist** [spɪ'nozɪst] *s* espinosista
**spinster** ['spɪnstər] *s* solterona, doncellueca; hilandera
**spinsterhood** ['spɪnstərhud] *s* soltería de mujer
**spintight** ['spɪn,taɪt] *s* (trademark) aprietatuercas
**spinule** ['spaɪnjul] o ['spɪnjul] *s* espínula
**spiny** ['spaɪnɪ] *adj* (*comp:* **-ier;** *super:* **-iest**) espinoso; puntiagudo; (fig.) espinoso (*enmarañado, difícil*)
**spiny lobster** *s* (zool.) langosta
**spiraea** [spaɪ'riə] *s* (bot.) espirea
**spiracle** ['spaɪrəkəl] o ['spɪrəkəl] *s* (zool.) espiráculo
**spiral** ['spaɪrəl] *adj & s* espiral; (*pret & pp:* **-raled** o **-ralled;** *ger:* **-raling** o **-ralling**) *va* mover formando espiras; torcer en espiral; *vn* moverse formando espiras; dar vueltas como una espiral; (aer.) volar en espiral
**spiral nebula** *s* (astr.) nebulosa espiral
**spiral staircase** *s* escalera de caracol, escalera espiral
**spirant** ['spaɪrənt] *adj & s* (phonet.) espirante
**spire** [spaɪr] *s* (arch.) aguja, chapitel; peñasco, cúspide, cima; espira; espiral; (geom. & zool.) espira; tallo (*de hierba*); *vn* crecer hacia arriba en forma espiral; rematar en punta; germinar
**spirea** [spaɪ'riə] *s* var. de **spiraea**
**spirillum** [spaɪ'rɪləm] *s* (*pl:* **-la** [lə]) (bact.) espirilo
**spirit** ['spɪrɪt] *s* espíritu; humor, temple; personaje; licor; **spirits** *spl* humor, genio; espíritu, brío, vivacidad; espíritu (*solución alcohólica*); licor; **out of spirits** triste, abatido, desalentado; **the Spirit** Dios; el Espíritu Santo; **to break the spirit of** desalentar; reprimir, sujetar; **to keep up one's spirits** no desalentarse, no desanimarse; *va* alentar, animar; **to spirit away** llevarse misteriosamente
**spirited** ['spɪrɪtɪd] *adj* espiritoso, fogoso
**spiritism** ['spɪrɪtɪzəm] *s* espiritismo
**spirit lamp** *s* lámpara de alcohol
**spiritless** ['spɪrɪtlɪs] *adj* apocado, tímido, sin ánimo
**spirit level** *s* nivel de burbuja, nivel de aire
**spiritual** ['spɪrɪtʃuəl] *adj* espiritual; *s* espiritual (*tonada religiosa de los negros*)
**spiritual director** *s* director espiritual
**spiritualism** ['spɪrɪtʃuəlɪzəm] *s* espiritismo; espiritualismo (*contrario de materialismo*)
**spiritualist** ['spɪrɪtʃuəlɪst] *s* espiritista; espiritualista
**spiritualistic** [,spɪrɪtʃuə'lɪstɪk] *adj* espiritista; espiritualista
**spiritualistic séance** *s* sesión de espiritistas
**spirituality** [,spɪrɪtʃu'ælɪtɪ] *s* (*pl:* **-ties**) espiritualidad
**spiritualization** [,spɪrɪtʃuəlɪ'zeʃən] *s* espiritualización
**spiritualize** ['spɪrɪtʃuəlaɪz] *va* espiritualizar
**spirituel** [,spɪrɪtʃu'ɛl] *adj* ingenioso, agudo, gracioso; etéreo, espiritual
**spirituelle** [,spɪrɪtʃu'ɛl] *adj fem de* **spirituel**
**spirituous** ['spɪrɪtʃuəs] *adj* espiritoso o espirituoso
**spirituous liquors** *spl* licores espirituosos
**spirochete** ['spaɪrokit] *s* (bact.) espiroqueta
**spirogyra** [,spaɪro'dʒaɪrə] *s* (bot.) espirogira
**spirometer** [spaɪ'rɑmɪtər] *s* espirómetro
**spirt** [spʌrt] *s, va & vn* var. de **spurt**
**spiry** ['spaɪrɪ] *adj* espiral, acaracolado; afilado, puntiagudo; con muchos chapiteles
**spit** [spɪt] *s* saliva, esputo; espuma (*de un insecto*); llovizna; nevisca; asador, espetón; punta o lengua de tierra; **the spit of** o **the spit and image of** la segunda edición de, el retrato de; (*pret & pp:* **spat** o **spit;** *ger:* **spitting**) *va* escupir; **to spit forth** escupir (*p.ej., metralla*); *vn* escupir; lloviznar; neviscar; fufar (*el gato*); (*pret & pp:* **spitted;** *ger:* **spitting**) *va* espetar
**spitball** ['spɪt,bɔl] *s* pelotilla de papel mascado; (baseball) curva conseguida mojando la pelota con saliva
**spitchcock** ['spɪtʃ,kɑk] *s* anguila tajada y asada o frita; *va* tajar y asar o freír; maltratar
**spit curl** *s* (coll.) caracol (*rizo aplastado sobre la sien*)
**spite** [spaɪt] *s* despecho, rencor, inquina, mala voluntad; molestia, fastidio; **in spite of** a pesar de, a despecho de; **out of spite** por despecho; *va* despechar, picar, molestar
**spiteful** ['spaɪtfəl] *adj* despechado, rencoroso
**spitfire** ['spɪt,faɪr] *s* fierabrás; mujer de mal genio; artificio que echa chispas y fuego
**spittle** ['spɪtəl] *s* saliva, esputo
**spittoon** [spɪ'tun] *s* escupidera
**spitz** [spɪts] *s* perro de Pomerania, perro lulú
**spiv** [spɪv] *s* (Brit. coll.) estraperlista muy guapo, galafate, gorrón, parásito

**splanchnic** ['splæŋknɪk] *adj* espláenico
**splash** [splæʃ] *s* salpicadura, rociada; chapoteo; mancha; **to make a splash** (coll.) hacer impresión, llamar la atención; *va* salpicar; chapotear; manchar; *vn* chapotear, caer con ruido; salpicar; moverse o caer golpeando el agua
**splashboard** ['splæʃ,bord] *s* alero, guardafango (*de un carruaje*)
**splasher** ['splæʃər] *s* salpicador; salpicadero
**splash lubrication** *s* lubricación al chapoteo o al barboteo
**splashy** ['splæʃɪ] *adj* (*comp:* **-ier;** *super:* **-iest**) fangoso, lodoso; (coll.) llamativo
**splat** [splæt] *s* pieza central y vertical del respaldo de una silla
**splatter** ['splætər] *s, va & vn* var. de **spatter**
**splay** [sple] *s* bisel, chaflán; alféizar; extensión, expansión; *adj* ancho, extendido, desplegado; torpe, sin gracia; *va* biselar, achaflanar; extender; *vn* extenderse, extenderse sin gracia
**splayed arch** *s* (arch.) arco abocinado
**splayfoot** ['sple,fut] *s* (*pl:* **-feet**) pie aplastado y torcido; (path.) pie contrahecho, pie zambo
**splay-footed** ['sple,futɪd] *adj* que tiene los pies aplastados y torcidos; torpe, sin gracia
**spleen** [splin] *s* (anat.) baso; mal humor; (archaic) esplín (*tristeza profunda*); **to vent one's spleen** descargar la bilis
**spleenish** ['splinɪʃ] *adj* bilioso, malhumorado, irritable
**spleenwort** ['splin,wʌrt] *s* (bot.) asplenio
**splendent** ['splɛndənt] *adj* esplendente
**splendid** ['splɛndɪd] *adj* espléndido
**splendiferous** [splɛn'dɪfərəs] *adj* (coll.) espléndido, magnífico
**splendor** ['splɛndər] *s* esplendor
**splenectomy** [splɪ'nɛktəmɪ] *s* (*pl:* **-mies**) (surg.) esplenectomía
**splenetic** [splɪ'nɛtɪk] *adj* esplénico; (fig.) bilioso, malhumorado, irritable
**splenetically** [splɪ'nɛtɪkəlɪ] *adv* rencorosamente, de mal humor
**splenic** ['splɛnɪk] o ['splinɪk] *adj* esplénico
**splenitis** [splɪ'naɪtɪs] *s* (path.) esplinitis
**splice** [splaɪs] *s* empalme, junta; *va* empalmar, juntar; (slang) casar
**spline** [splaɪn] *s* tira flexible, tira flexible para dibujar curvas; ranura para una cuña; cuña; *va* ranurar; proveer de cuña
**splint** [splɪnt] *s* astilla, tablilla; launa (*de las armaduras antiguas*); (surg.) cabestrillo, tablilla; (vet.) sobrehueso (*tumor y hueso*); **in a splint** (surg.) entablillado; *va* (surg.) entablillar
**splint bone** *s* (vet.) sobrehueso; (anat.) peroné
**splinter** ['splɪntər] *s* astilla; esquirla (*de piedra, cristal; de hueso*); *va* astillar; *vn* astillarse, hacerse astillas
**splinter group** *s* grupo disidente
**splintery** ['splɪntərɪ] *adj* astilloso
**split** [splɪt] *s* fractura, división; (slang) porción; (coll.) media botella; dulce de fruta fresca, helado, jarabe y nueces; caída acrobática con las piernas en línea recta; *adj* hendido, partido; dividido; (*pret & pp:* **split;** *ger:* **splitting**) *va* partir, dividir; **to split one's sides with laughter** desternillarse de risa; *vn* partirse, dividirse a lo largo; **to split away (from)** separarse (de); **my head is splitting** me duele terriblemente la cabeza; **to split up** (coll.) separarse, desavenirse (*dos o más personas*); **to split with** (coll.) desavenirse con, romper con
**split fee** *s* dicotomía (*entre médicos*)
**split infinitive** *s* (gram.) infinitivo partido (*infinitivo inglés en el que se interponen una o más palabras entre la preposición* **to** *y el verbo*)
**split-level house** ['splɪt'lɛvəl] *s* casa con pisos contiguos construidos en niveles distintos
**split peas** *spl* guisantes majados
**split personality** *s* personalidad desdoblada
**split phase** *s* (elec.) fase partida
**split second** *s* fracción de segundo
**splitter** ['splɪtər] *s* partidor, hendedor, divisor; persona quisquillosa
**splitter wheel** *s* disco abridor (*para facilitar el paso de la sierra*)
**split ticket** *s* (pol.) candidatura dividida, voto dividido (*entre candidatos de dos o más partidos*)
**splitting** ['splɪtɪŋ] *s* hendimiento, fractura, división; escisión (*del átomo*); *adj* partidor; fuerte, violento; enloquecedor (*dolor de cabeza*)
**split-up** ['splɪt,ʌp] *s* (com.) división de las acciones de una empresa en nuevas acciones de menor valor; (coll.) desunión, desavenencia
**splotch** [splɑtʃ] *s* borrón, mancha grande; *va* manchar, salpicar
**splotchy** ['splɑtʃɪ] *adj* (*comp:* **-ier;** *super:* **-iest**) lleno de borrones o manchas
**splurge** [splʌrdʒ] *s* (coll.) fachenda, ostentación; *vn* (coll.) fachendear, hacer ostentación
**splutter** ['splʌtər] *s* chisporroteo; farfulla (*manera de hablar*); *va* farfullar; *vn* chisporrotear; farfullar
**spodumene** ['spɑdʒumin] *s* (mineral.) espodumeno
**spoil** [spɔɪl] *s* despojo, botín, presa; **spoils** *spl* robo, botín, presa; empleos repartidos entre los vencedores; (*pret & pp:* **spoiled** o **spoilt**) *va* echar a perder, estropear, deteriorar; mimar; amargar (*una tertulia, una velada*); **to spoil of** despojar de; *vn* echarse a perder, estropearse; **to spoil for, to be spoiling for** (coll.) ansiar, anhelar
**spoiled** [spɔɪld] *adj* consentido (*dícese de un niño*)
**spoiler** ['spɔɪlər] *s* corruptor; consentidor; despojador
**spoilsman** ['spɔɪlzmən] *s* (*pl:* **-men**) individuo del partido vencedor que toma un empleo público como recompensa
**spoils system** *s* sistema de acaparamiento de los cargos públicos por el partido victorioso en las elecciones
**spoilt** [spɔɪlt] *pret & pp de* **spoil**
**spoke** [spok] *s* radio o rayo (*de rueda*); freno; escalón (*de escalera*); **to put a spoke in one's wheel** ponerle trabas a uno; *pret de* **speak**
**spoken** ['spokən] *pp de* **speak**
**spokeshave** ['spok,ʃev] *s* rebajador de radios (*de ruedas*)
**spokesman** ['spoksmən] *s* (*pl:* **-men**) vocero, portavoz
**spokesmanship** ['spoksmənʃɪp] *s* vocería
**spokewise** ['spok,waɪz] *adv* como un radio de rueda, como radios de rueda
**spoliation** [,spolɪ'eʃən] *s* expoliación, despojo
**spondaic** [spɑn'deɪk] espondaico
**spondee** ['spɑndi] *s* espondeo
**spondulics** [spɑn'dulɪks] *ssg* (slang) cuartos, plata
**spondyl** o **spondyle** ['spɑndɪl] *s* (anat.) espóndil o espóndilo
**spondylitis** [,spɑndɪ'laɪtɪs] *s* (path.) espondilitis
**sponge** [spʌndʒ] *s* esponja; (fig.) esponja (*gorrón, parásito*); **to throw up** (o **in**) o **to toss up** (o **in**) **the sponge** (coll.) tirar la esponja (*darse por vencido*); *va* limpiar con esponja; borrar; absorber; *vn* recoger o pescar esponjas; ser absorbente; **to sponge on** (coll.) vivir a costa de (*otra persona*)
**sponge cake** *s* bizcocho muy ligero, pastaflora
**sponger** ['spʌndʒər] *s* persona que limpia con esponja; máquina para humedecer las telas antes de plancharlas; embarcación que va a la pesca de esponjas; (fig.) esponja (*gorrón, parásito*)
**sponge rubber** *s* caucho esponjoso
**spongin** ['spʌndʒɪn] *s* (biochem.) espongina
**spongy** ['spʌndʒɪ] *adj* (*comp:* **-gier;** *super:* **-giest**) esponjoso
**sponson** ['spɑnsən] *s* barbeta lateral de un buque de guerra; plataforma triangular detrás o delante de la rueda de paletas de un barco de vapor; cámara de aire (*en la borda de una canoa*); flotador (*de un hidroavión*)
**sponsor** ['spɑnsər] *s* patrocinador; padrino, madrina; (rad. & telv.) patrocinador; **to stand sponsor for** apadrinar; *va* patrocinar; apadrinar; (rad. & telv.) patrocinar
**sponsorial** [spɑn'sorɪəl] *adj* patrocinador
**sponsorship** ['spɑnsərʃɪp] *s* patrocinio; padrinazgo; (rad. & telv.) patrocinio

**spontaneity** [ˌspɑntəˈniɪtɪ] *s* (pl: **-ties**) espontaneidad
**spontaneous** [spɑnˈtenɪəs] *adj* espontáneo; (bot. & biol.) espontáneo
**spontaneous combustion** *s* combustión espontánea, inflamación espontánea
**spontaneous generation** *s* (biol.) generación espontánea
**spontoon** [spɑnˈtun] *s* espontón
**spoof** [spuf] *s* (slang) engaño; (slang) broma; *va* (slang) engañar; *vn* (slang) bromear
**spook** [spuk] *s* (coll.) aparecido, espectro
**spooky** [ˈspukɪ] *adj* (*comp:* **-ier;** *super:* **-iest**) (coll.) semejante a un fantasma; (coll.) visitado por fantasmas; (coll.) horripilante
**spool** [spul] *s* carrete; canilla (*de una máquina de tejer*); *va* devanar; encanillar
**spoon** [spun] *s* cuchara; **born with a silver spoon in one's mouth** nacido de pie; *va* cucharear; dar forma de cuchara a; *vn* (slang) besuquearse (*los enamorados*)
**spoonbill** [ˈspunˌbɪl] *s* (orn.) espátula; (orn.) cucharón, ajaja; (ichth.) pez hoja
**spoondrift** [ˈspunˌdrɪft] *s* var. de **spindrift**
**spoonerism** [ˈspunərɪzəm] *s* contrepetterie o contrepèterie (*lapsus linguae en forma de metátesis entre vocablos, que produce un resultado absurdo*)
**spoonful** [ˈspunfʊl] *s* cucharada
**spoon hook** *s* anzuelo de cuchara
**spoony** [ˈspunɪ] *adj* (*comp:* **-ier;** *super:* **-iest**) (coll.) sobón; *s* (*pl:* **-ies**) (coll.) sobón, galán meloso
**spoor** [spʊr] *s* pista de un animal salvaje; *va* seguir la pista de
**sporadic** [spəˈrædɪk] o **sporadical** [spəˈrædɪkəl] *adj* esporádico
**sporangium** [spoˈrændʒɪəm] *s* (*pl:* **-a** [ə]) (bot.) esporangio
**spore** [spor] *s* (biol.) espora
**sporidium** [spoˈrɪdɪəm] *s* (*pl:* **-a** [ə]) (bot.) esporidio
**sporocarp** [ˈsporəkɑrp] *s* (bot.) esporocarpo
**sporophyll** o **sporophyl** [ˈsporəfɪl] *s* (bot.) esporofila
**sporophyte** [ˈsporəfaɪt] *s* (bot.) esporofito
**sporozoan** [ˌsporəˈzoən] *adj & s* (zool.) esporozoo
**sporran** [ˈspɑrən] o [ˈspɔrən] *s* escarcela de los montañeses de Escocia
**sport** [sport] *s* deporte; deportista; juguete (*persona o cosa dominada por algún poder*); hazmerreír; (coll.) jugador, tahur; (coll.) buen perdedor (*en el juego*); (coll.) buen compañero, tipo; (coll.) majo, guapo; (biol.) mutación; **to make sport of** reírse de, burlarse de; *adj* deportivo; *va* (coll.) lucir (*p.ej., un traje nuevo*); *vn* divertirse; estar de burla; juguetear
**sport clothes** *spl* var. de **sportswear**
**sport coat** *s* americana sport
**sport fan** *s* (slang) aficionado al deporte
**sportful** [ˈsportfəl] *adj* juguetón
**sporting** [ˈsportɪŋ] *adj* deportista; deportivo; honrado, leal; temerario; arriesgado
**sporting chance** *s* (coll.) riesgo de buen perdedor
**sporting goods** *spl* artículos de deporte
**sporting house** *s* (coll.) casa de juego; (coll.) casa de rameras
**sportive** [ˈsportɪv] *adj* juguetón; alegre, festivo
**sports** *adj* deportivo
**sports car** *s* coche deportivo
**sportscaster** [ˈsportsˌkæstər] o [ˈsportsˌkɑstər] *s* (rad. & telv.) locutor deportivo
**sport shirt** *s* camisa sport
**sportsman** [ˈsportsmən] *s* (*pl:* **-men**) deportista; persona muy honrada; persona temeraria
**sportsmanlike** [ˈsportsmənˌlaɪk] *adj* de deportista; leal y honrado
**sportsmanship** [ˈsportsmənʃɪp] *s* pericia en los deportes; lealtad y honradez; nobleza, magnanimidad, grandeza
**sports news** *s* noticiario deportivo
**sportswear** [ˈsportsˌwɛr] *s* trajes de sport, trajes deportivos
**sportswoman** [ˈsportsˌwʊmən] *s* (*pl:* **-women**) deportista *f*
**sports writer** *s* cronista deportivo
**sporty** [ˈsportɪ] *adj* (*comp:* **-ier;** *super:* **-iest**) (coll.) alegre, brillante; (coll.) disipado, libertino; (coll.) magnánimo; (coll.) elegante, guapo
**sporulation** [ˌspɑrjəˈleʃən] o [ˌspɔrjəˈleʃən] *s* (biol.) esporulación
**sporule** [ˈspɑrjul] o [ˈspɔrjul] *s* (bot.) espórula
**spot** [spɑt] *s* mancha; sitio, lugar; (coll.) poquito; **in spots** aquí y allí; en algunos respectos; **on the spot** sobre el terreno, allí mismo; al punto; (slang) en dificultad; (slang) destinado a ser matado; **to hit the spot** (coll.) tener razón; (coll.) dar satisfacción; **to put on the spot** poner en un aprieto; *adj* disponible; contante; (*pret & pp:* **spotted;** *ger:* **spotting**) *va* manchar; esparcir, diseminar; (coll.) descubrir, encontrar, reconocer; *vn* mancharse, tener manchas
**spot cash** *s* dinero contante
**spotless** [ˈspɑtlɪs] *adj* inmaculado, sin manchas
**spotlight** [ˈspɑtˌlaɪt] *s* proyector orientable; (aut.) faro piloto, faro giratorio; luz concentrada; atención del público
**spot remover** [rɪˈmuvər] *s* quitamanchas (*persona y substancia*)
**spotted** [ˈspɑtɪd] *adj* manchado; moteado
**spotted fever** *s* (path.) tifus exantemático; (path.) fiebre purpúrea de las Montañas Rocosas
**spotted hyena** *s* (zool.) hiena manchada
**spotted sandpiper** *s* (orn.) chorlo manchado, chorlito playero manchado
**spotter** [ˈspɑtər] *s* vigilante secreto; atalayador, observador; situador
**spotty** [ˈspɑtɪ] *adj* (*comp:* **-tier;** *super:* **-tiest**) manchado; irregular
**spot-weld** [ˈspɑtˌwɛld] *va* soldar por puntos
**spot welding** *s* soldadura por puntos
**spousal** [ˈspaʊzəl] *adj* nupcial; *s* nupcias; **spousals** *spl* nupcias
**spouse** [spaʊz] o [spaʊs] *s* cónyuge, consorte
**spout** [spaʊt] *s* canalón (*para el agua del tejado*); pico (*de cafetera, jarra, etc.*); chorro; **up the spout** (slang) en prenda; (slang) acabado, arruinado; *va* echar en chorro; declamar; *vn* chorrear; declamar; soplar (*echar agua la ballena*)
**sprain** [spren] *s* torcedura, esguince; *va* torcer, torcerse (*p.ej., una cuerda, un tendón*)
**sprang** [spræŋ] *pret de* **spring**
**sprat** [spræt] *s* (ichth.) pequeño arenque (*Clupea sprattus*)
**sprawl** [sprɔl] *s* postura floja; *vn* arrellanarse
**spray** [spre] *s* rociada; espuma (*del mar*); rociador, pulverizador; ramita; *va & vn* rociar
**sprayer** [ˈspreər] *s* rociador, pulverizador, vaporizador
**spray gun** *s* pistola pulverizadora
**spray nozzle** *s* espumadera, lanza regadera
**spread** [sprɛd] *s* extensión; amplitud, anchura; intervalo; diferencia; difusión; colcha, sobrecama, cubrecama; mantel, tapete; (coll.) festín, banquete; envergadura (*de las alas de las aves*); (aer.) envergadura; (*pret & pp:* **spread**) *va* extender; difundir, propagar; untar, dar una capa a; esparcir, desparramar; escalonar; abrir, separar; poner (*la mesa*); **to spread oneself** (coll.) echar el resto; (coll.) tratar de impresionar, tratar de ganarse la buena voluntad; (coll.) lucirse, fachendear, jactarse; *vn* extenderse; difundirse, propagarse; desparramarse; abrirse, separarse
**spread eagle** *s* figura de águila con las alas abiertas (*emblema de los EE.UU.*); bocón, fanfarrón; fanfarronería, chovinismo
**spread-eagle** [ˈsprɛdˌigəl] *adj* con las alas abiertas (*como un águila*); (coll.) fanfarrón; (coll.) patriotero; *va* (naut.) atar con brazos y piernas extendidas (*para flagelar*)
**spread-eagleism** [ˈsprɛdˌigəlɪzəm] *s* (coll.) patriotería
**spreader** [ˈsprɛdər] *s* esparcidor; divulgador; distribuidora de abono
**spree** [spri] *s* juerga, parranda; borrachera; **to go on a spree** ir de juerga; coger una borrachera
**sprig** [sprɪg] *s* ramita; (scornful) jovenzuelo
**sprightly** [ˈspraɪtlɪ] *adj* (*comp:* **-lier;** *super:* **-liest**) vivo, alegre, animado

**spring** [sprɪŋ] *s* primavera (*estación del año*); muelle, resorte (*pieza elástica de metal*); ballesta (*muelle de coche*); fuente, manantial; surtidor (*de petróleo*); salto, brinco; abertura, grieta; tensión, tirantez; (arch.) arranque ‖ *adj* de muelle, de resorte; primaveral; de fuente, de manantial ‖ (*pret:* **sprang** o **sprung**; *pp:* **sprung**) *va* soltar (*un muelle o resorte*); torcer, combar, encorvar; hacer saltar (*una trampa, una mina*); **to spring something on someone** embocarle o soltarle a uno una cosa (*p.ej., una mala noticia*) ‖ *vn* saltar, brincar; moverse rápidamente o de golpe; saltar de golpe a un lado o atrás; brotar, nacer, proceder; torcerse, combarse, encorvarse; **to spring at** abalanzarse sobre; **to spring back** saltar hacia atrás; **to spring to one's feet** levantarse de un salto; **to spring forth** precipitarse; brotar; **to spring forward** arrojarse; **to spring up** levantarse de un salto; brotar, nacer; presentarse a la vista

**springal** [ˈsprɪŋəl] o **springald** [ˈsprɪŋəld] *s* joven, muchacho

**spring beauty** *s* (bot.) claytonia

**springboard** [ˈsprɪŋˌbord] *s* trampolín; (fig.) trampolín

**springbok** [ˈsprɪŋˌbɑk] *s* (zool.) gacela del sur de África (*Antidorcas marsupialis*)

**spring bolt** *s* pestillo de golpe

**spring chicken** *s* polluelo; (coll.) pollita, p.ej., **she's no longer a spring chicken** ya no es una pollita

**springe** [sprɪndʒ] *s* lazo, trampa; *va* coger con un lazo o trampa

**springer** [ˈsprɪŋər] *s* saltador; perro ojeador; (arch.) imposta; (zool.) gacela del sur de África

**spring fever** *s* (hum.) ataque primaveral, galbana

**springhalt** [ˈsprɪŋˌhɔlt] *s* (vet.) cojera de caballo

**spring hook** *s* mosquetón

**springhouse** [ˈsprɪŋˌhaʊs] *s* enfriadero sobre un manantial

**springlet** [ˈsprɪŋlɪt] *s* fuentezuela

**spring lock** *s* cerradura de golpe o de muelle

**spring mattress** *s* colchón de muelles, somier

**springtail** [ˈsprɪŋˌtel] *s* (ent.) tisanuro

**springtide** [ˈsprɪŋˌtaɪd] *s* primavera

**spring tide** *s* (naut.) aguas vivas; corriente o torrente muy impetuoso

**springtime** [ˈsprɪŋˌtaɪm] *s* primavera

**spring water** *s* agua manantial, agua de manantial

**spring wheat** *s* trigo de primavera

**springy** [ˈsprɪŋɪ] *adj* (*comp:* **-ier**; *super:* **-iest**) elástico; lleno de manantiales

**sprinkle** [ˈsprɪŋkəl] *s* rociada; llovizna; poquito, pizca; *va* rociar, regar; salpicar, sembrar; espolvorear (*p.ej., azúcar*); *vn* rociar; lloviznar, gotear (*llover a gotas espaciadas*)

**sprinkler** [ˈsprɪŋklər] *s* rociadera o regadera

**sprinkler system** *s* instalación de rociadura automática (*para la extinción de incendios*)

**sprinkling** [ˈsprɪŋklɪŋ] *s* rociada, rociadura; pequeña cantidad

**sprinkling can** *s* regadera

**sprint** [sprɪnt] *s* (sport) embalaje, carrera corta de velocidad; *vn* (sport) embalarse, lanzarse, correr a toda velocidad sobre un recorrido muy corto

**sprinter** [ˈsprɪntər] *s* (sport) corredor de velocidad a pequeñas distancias

**sprit** [sprɪt] *s* (naut.) botavara, verga de abanico

**sprite** [spraɪt] *s* duende, trasgo

**spritsail** [ˈsprɪtsəl] o [ˈsprɪtˌsel] *s* (naut.) cebadera

**sprocket** [ˈsprɑkɪt] *s* diente de rueda de cadena; rueda de cadena

**sprocket wheel** *s* rueda de cadena

**sprout** [spraʊt] *s* (bot.) retoño, renuevo, brote; **sprouts** *spl* (bot.) bretones; *va* hacer brotar o germinar; (coll.) quitar los brotes o botones a; *vn* brotar o germinar, echar renuevos; crecer rápidamente

**spruce** [sprus] *s* (bot.) abeto del Norte, abeto falso, abeto rojo, pícea; *adj* garboso, apuesto, elegante; *va* ataviar, componer; *vn* ataviarse, componerse; **to spruce up** emperifollarse

**sprue** [spru] *s* (path.) esprue, psilosis; (found.) bebedero

**sprung** [sprʌŋ] *pret & pp de* **spring**

**spry** [spraɪ] *adj* (*comp:* **spryer** o **sprier**; *super:* **spryest** o **spriest**) activo, vivo, listo, ágil

**spt.** abr. de **seaport**

**spud** [spʌd] *s* (agr.) escarda; escoplo (*para quitar la corteza a los árboles*); (coll.) patata

**spue** [spju] *va & vn* var. de **spew**

**spume** [spjum] *s* espuma; *vn* espumar

**spumy** [ˈspjumɪ] *adj* (*comp:* **-ier**; *super:* **-iest**) espumoso, espumajoso

**spun** [spʌn] *pret & pp de* **spin**

**spun glass** *s* vidrio hilado, cristal hilado

**spunk** [spʌŋk] *s* (coll.) corazón, coraje, valor, ánimo; yesca; *vn* encenderse; **to spunk up** (coll.) dar prueba de valor

**spunky** [ˈspʌŋkɪ] *adj* (*comp:* **-ier**; *super:* **-iest**) (coll.) vivo, valiente, animado; (coll.) enfadadizo

**spun silk** *s* seda cardada e hilada

**spun yarn** *s* (naut.) meollar

**spur** [spʌr] *s* espuela; gusanillo (*rosca puntiaguda en que terminan las barrenas*); espolón (*del gallo; de una montaña; de un buque de guerra*); (carp.) espolón; (rail.) ramal corto; (fig.) espuela (*estímulo*); **on the spur of the moment** impulsivamente, sin la reflexión debida; **to win one's spurs** distinguirse; cobrar buena fama sin ayuda ajena; (*pret & pp:* **spurred**; *ger:* **spurring**) *va* espolear; proveer de espuelas; **to spur on** (fig.) espolear; *vn* cabalgar muy aprisa; apretar el paso

**spurgall** [ˈspʌrˌgɔl] *s* espoleadura

**spurge** [spʌrdʒ] *s* (bot.) euforbio

**spur gear** *s* (mach.) rueda dentada recta; engranaje de ruedas dentadas rectas

**spurge flax** *s* (bot.) torvisco

**spurge laurel** *s* (bot.) lauréola

**spurious** [ˈspjʊrɪəs] *adj* espurio

**spurn** [spʌrn] *s* desdén, menosprecio; coz; *va* desdeñar, menospreciar; rechazar a puntapiés; *vn* cocear

**spurred** [spʌrd] *adj* con espuelas; con espolones

**spurry** [ˈspʌrɪ] *s* (bot.) esparcilla

**spur stone** *s* guardacantón

**spurt** [spʌrt] *s* chorro repentino; arranque; esfuerzo extraordinario y breve; *va* hacer salir a borbotones, hacer salir en chorro; *vn* salir a borbotones, salir en chorro; hacer un esfuerzo extraordinario y breve

**spur track** (rail.) ramal corto

**spur wheel** *s* (mach.) engranaje de ruedas dentadas rectas

**sputnik** [ˈspʊtnɪk] o [ˈspʌtnɪk] *s* sputnik (*satélite artificial ruso*)

**sputter** [ˈspʌtər] *s* farfulla (*manera de hablar*); ruido del que farfulla; palabras pronunciadas atropelladamente; chisporroteo; *va* farfullar; escupir farfullando; *vn* farfullar; chisporrotear

**sputum** [ˈspjutəm] *s* (*pl:* **-ta** [tə]) esputo

**spy** [spaɪ] *s* (*pl:* **spies**) espía; (*pret & pp:* **spied**) *va* espiar; columbrar, divisar; *vn* espiar; **to spy on** espiar

**spyglass** [ˈspaɪˌglæs] o [ˈspaɪˌglɑs] *s* catalejo

**sq.** abr. de **square**

**squab** [skwɑb] *s* (orn.) pichón, pichoncillo; (orn.) pollo, pollito; sofá, canapé; cojín; *adj* acabado de nacer (*dícese de las aves*); regordete, rechoncho

**squabble** [ˈskwɑbəl] *s* riña, reyerta; *vn* reñir, disputar

**squabby** [ˈskwɑbɪ] *adj* regordete, rechoncho

**squad** [skwɑd] *s* escuadra; (mil.) escuadra

**squadron** [ˈskwɑdrən] *s* (nav.) escuadra; (aer.) escuadrilla; (mil.) escuadrón (*de caballería*)

**squalid** [ˈskwɑlɪd] *adj* escuálido

**squall** [skwɔl] *s* grupada; chubasco; ráfaga de viento; (coll.) riña; (coll.) chubasco (*adversidad*); chillido; *vn* chillar

**squally** [ˈskwɔlɪ] *adj* (*comp:* **-ier**; *super:* **-iest**) chubascoso; ventoso; (coll.) amenazador

**squalor** [ˈskwɑlər] *s* escualor, escualidez

**squama** [ˈskwemə] *s* (*pl:* **-mae** [mi]) (anat. & biol.) escama

**squamate** [ˈskwemet] *adj* escamoso

**squamose** ['skwemos] o **squamous** ['skweməs] *adj* escamoso
**squander** ['skwɑndər] *va* malgastar, despilfarrar
**square** [skwɛr] *s* (geom. & math.) cuadrado; (carp.) escuadra; (mil.) cuadro; manzana (*de casas*); plaza; casilla o escaque (*del tablero de ajedrez o damas*); **to be on the square** (coll.) obrar en buena fe ‖ *adj* cuadrado, p.ej., **eight square inches** ocho pulgadas cuadradas; en cuadro, de lado, p.ej., **eight inches square** ocho pulgadas en cuadro u ocho pulgadas de lado; rectangular; en ángulo recto; justo, recto, equitativo; saldado; leal, honrado; claro y directo; sólido, fuerte; (coll.) abundante, completo; **to get square with** (coll.) hacérselas pagar a ‖ *adv* en cuadro; en forma de rectángulo; en ángulo recto; lealmente, honradamente ‖ *va* cuadrar; (math.) cuadrar; (carp.) escuadrar; dividir en cuadros; ajustar, nivelar, conformar; (slang) cohechar, sobornar; **to square oneself** compensar un dicho o hecho; pagar con las misma moneda ‖ *vn* cuadrarse, ajustarse, conformarse; (coll.) saldar cuentas; **to square away** (naut.) bracear en cuadro; **to square off** (coll.) colocarse en posición de defensa
**square dance** *s* danza de figuras
**square deal** *s* (coll.) trato equitativo, juego limpio
**square-faced** ['skwɛr,fest] *adj* de cara cuadrada
**square-headed** ['skwɛr'hɛdɪd] *adj* de cabeza cuadrada; de cabeza de diamante (*tuerca*)
**square knot** *s* nudo llano, nudo derecho
**square meal** *s* (coll.) comida abundante
**square measure** *s* medida cuadrada o de superficie
**square piano** *s* piano cuadrado
**square-rigger** ['skwɛr,rɪgər] *s* (naut.) buque de cruz
**square root** *s* (math.) raíz cuadrada
**square sail** *s* (naut.) vela de cruz
**square shooter** *s* (coll.) persona leal y honrada
**square-toed** ['skwɛr,tod] *adj* con los dedos de los pies gruesos y cortos; de ideas anticuadas
**squarish** ['skwɛrɪʃ] *adj* casi cuadrado
**squash** [skwɑʃ] *s* (bot.) calabaza (*planta y fruto*); aplastamiento, despachurramiento; *va* aplastar, despachurrar, apabullar; apiñar, apretar; poner fin a, por la fuerza; confutar (*un argumento*); acallar con un argumento, respuesta, etc.; *vn* aplastarse; apiñarse, apretarse
**squashy** ['skwɑʃɪ] *adj* (*comp:* **-ier;** *super:* **-iest**) aplastado; mojado y blando, lodoso; fácil de aplastar
**squat** [skwɑt] *s* posición del que está en cuclillas; *adj* en cuclillas; rechoncho; (*pret & pp:* **squatted** o **squat;** *ger:* **squatting**) *va* hacer acuclillarse; *vn* acuclillarse, agacharse, acurrucarse; sentarse en el suelo, estar sentado en el suelo; establecerse en terreno ajeno sin derecho; establecerse en un terreno público para crear un derecho
**squatter** [skwɑtər] *s* advenedizo, intruso, colono usurpador; colono que se establece en un terreno público para crear un derecho
**squatty** ['skwɑtɪ] *adj* (*comp:* **-tier;** *super:* **-tiest**) rechoncho, regordete
**squaw** [skwɔ] *s* india norteamericana; mujer, esposa, muchacha
**squawk** [skwɔk] *s* graznido; (slang) queja en voz chillona; *va* (slang) decir en voz chillona; *vn* graznar; (slang) quejarse en voz chillona
**squaw man** *s* blanco casado con india
**squeak** [skwik] *s* chillido; chirrido; **narrow squeak** (coll.) escapada en una tabla; *va* decir con un chillido; hacer chirriar; *vn* dar chillidos; chirriar
**squeaky** ['skwikɪ] *adj* (*comp:* **-ier;** *super:* **-iest**) chillón; chirriador, chirriante
**squeal** [skwil] *s* alarido, chillido; *va* proferir con un alarido o chillido; *vn* dar un alarido o chillido; (slang) soplar, delatar; **to squeal on** (slang) soplar, delatar (*a una persona*)
**squealer** ['skwilər] *s* chillador; (slang) soplón
**squealing** ['skwilɪŋ] *s* (rad.) aullido
**squeamish** ['skwimɪʃ] *adj* delicado, escrupuloso, remilgado; excesivamente modesto
**squeegee** ['skwidʒi] *s* alisador o enjugador de goma (*para secar superficies mojadas*); (*pret & pp:* **-geed;** *ger:* **-geeing**) *va* secar con alisador o enjugador de goma
**squeeze** [skwiz] *s* estrujón, apretón, abrazo fuerte; apiñamiento; impresión; (coll.) forzosa (*presión de hacer algo*); **to put the squeeze on someone** (coll.) poner a uno las peras a cuatro o a ocho, meter en prensa a uno, hacer a uno la forzosa; *va* estrujar, apretar; exprimir; agobiar, oprimir, estrujar; **to squeeze in** meter a estrujones; *vn* tupirse; **to squeeze through** abrirse paso a estrujones por entre, pasar apretadamente a través de
**squeezer** ['skwizər] *s* exprimidera
**squelch** [skwɛltʃ] *s* (coll.) tapaboca; *va* apabullar, despachurrar; *vn* chapotear, andar chapoteando
**squib** [skwɪb] *s* buscapiés, carretilla; cohete que falla con un sonido crepitante; pasquín, escrito satírico; (*pret & pp:* **squibbed;** *ger:* **squibbing**) *va* arrojar; salpicar; pasquinar; *vn* soltar carretillas; estallar; divulgar pasquinadas
**squid** [skwɪd] *s* (zool.) calamar; (zool.) flecha de mar, calamar volante
**squid-jigger** ['skwɪd,dʒɪgər] *s* guadañeta
**squill** [skwɪl] *s* (bot.) escila, esquila, cebolla albarrana; (zool.) esquila
**squint** [skwɪnt] *s* mirada bizca; mirada de soslayo, mirada furtiva; bizquera, estrabismo; propensión, tendencia; *adj* bizco, bisojo; de soslayo, de mal ojo; *va* hacer torcer la vista a; achicar (*los ojos*); *vn* bizquear; torcer la vista; tener los ojos medio cerrados; andar o correr oblicuamente; tener una tendencia indirecta; mirar de mal ojo
**squint-eyed** ['skwɪnt,aɪd] *adj* bizco, bisojo; malévolo, sospechoso
**squire** [skwaɪr] *s* (feud.) escudero; (Brit.) terrateniente de antigua heredad; (U.S.A.) juez de paz, juez local; asistente, sirviente; acompañante (*de una señora*); *va* asistir o servir como escudero; acompañar (*a una señora*); *vn* ser escudero; ser acompañante
**squireen** [skwaɪ'rin] *s* terrateniente de poca monta
**squirm** [skwʌrm] *s* retorcimiento; *vn* retorcerse; **to squirm out of** escaparse de (*p.ej., un aprieto*) haciendo muchas fuerzas
**squirmy** ['skwɪrmɪ] *adj* (*comp:* **-ier;** *super:* **-iest**) retorcido, retorciéndose
**squirrel** ['skwʌrəl] *s* (zool.) ardilla; petigrís (*piel*)
**squirrel-cage motor** ['skwʌrəl,kedʒ] *s* (elec.) motor de jaula de ardilla
**squirt** [skwʌrt] *s* chorro, chisguete; jeringazo; (coll.) mono, presuntuoso; *va* arrojar a chorros; *vn* salir a chorros
**squirting cucumber** *s* (bot.) cohombrillo amargo, pepinillo del diablo
**Sr.** abr. de **senior** y de **Sir**
**S.R.O.** abr. de **standing room only**
**S.S.** abr. de **Secretary of State, Straits Settlements, steamship** y **Sunday school**
**St.** abr. de **Saint, Strait** y **Street**
**stab** [stæb] *s* puñalada; (coll.) tentativa; **stab in the back** puñalada (de traidor) por la espalda; **to make a stab at** (slang) esforzarse por hacer; (*pret & pp:* **stabbed;** *ger:* **stabbing**) *va* apuñalar; traspasar; **to stab to death** escabechar; *vn* apuñalar, dar de puñaladas
**Stabat Mater** ['stɑbɑt 'mɑtər] o ['stebæt 'metər] *s* (eccl. & mus.) stábat máter
**stability** [stə'bɪlɪtɪ] *s* (*pl:* **-ties**) estabilidad
**stabilization** [,stebɪlɪ'zeʃən] o [,stæbɪlɪ'zeʃən] *s* estabilización
**stabilize** ['stebɪlaɪz] o ['stæbɪlaɪz] *va* estabilizar
**stabilizer** ['stebɪ,laɪzər] o ['stæbɪ,laɪzər] *s* estabilizador (*persona o aparato*)
**stable** ['stebəl] *adj* estable; *s* establo, cuadra, caballeriza; caballos de carrera de un particular; *va* poner o guardar en un establo, cuadra o caballeriza; *vn* estar colocado en un establo, cuadra o caballeriza
**stable boy** ['stebəl,bɔɪ] *s* mozo de caballerías, mozo de cuadra

**stable fly** *s* (ent.) mosca picadora de los establos
**stableman** ['stebəl,mæn] *s* (*pl:* **-men**) establero
**stably** ['steblɪ] *adv* establemente
**staccato** [stə'kɑto] *s* (*pl:* **-tos**) (mus.) staccato
**stack** [stæk] *s* niara, hacina, rimero; pila, montón; (mil.) pabellón de fusiles; estantería, depósito (*de libros en una biblioteca*); cañón de chimenea; cuba (*del alto horno*); (coll.) montón, gran número; *va* amontonar, apilar; hacinar; florear (*el naipe*); **to have the cards stacked against one** estar en una situación desventajosa
**staddle** ['stædəl] *s* resalvo
**stadholder** ['stæd,holdər] *s* estatúder
**stadholderate** ['stæd,holdəret] **stadholdership** ['stæd,holdərʃɪp] *s* estatuderato
**stadia** ['stedɪə] *s* (surv.) estadia
**stadia hairs** *spl* (surv.) hilos taquimétricos
**stadia rod** *s* (surv.) mira taquimétrica
**stadium** ['stedɪəm] *s* (*pl:* **-ums** o **-a** [ə]) estadio
**stadtholder** ['stæt,holdər] *s* var. de **stadholder**
**staff** [stæf] o [stɑf] *s* (*pl:* **staves** [stevz] o **staffs**) bastón; apoyo, sostén; (mus.) pentágrama; *s* (*pl:* **staffs**) personal; (mil.) estado mayor; *va* proveer de personal, nombrar personal para
**staff officer** *s* (mil.) oficial de estado mayor
**staff tree** *s* (bot.) celastro
**stag** [stæg] *s* (zool.) ciervo; varón; varón solo (*no acompañado de mujeres*); *adj* exclusivo para hombres
**stag beetle** *s* (ent.) ciervo volante
**stage** [stedʒ] *s* escena; estrado; andamio, tablado; cadalso; teatro (*de cualquier suceso*); etapa, jornada, posta; descansadero, parada; fase, estadio; diligencia (*coche*); portaobjeto (*del microscopio*); (rad.) etapa, escalón; **by easy stages** a pequeñas etapas; lentamente; **on the stage** sobre la escena, en el teatro; **to go on the stage** hacerse actor; *va* poner en escena, representar; preparar, organizar; *vn* ser apropiado al teatro; viajar en diligencia
**stagecoach** ['stedʒ,kotʃ] *s* diligencia
**stagecraft** ['stedʒ,kræft] o ['stedʒ,krɑft] *s* arte teatral
**stage door** *s* (theat.) entrada de los artistas
**stage effect** *s* efecto escénico
**stage fright** *s* miedo al público, trac
**stagehand** ['stedʒ,hænd] *s* tramoyista, metemuertos, metesillas
**stage manager** *s* (theat.) director de escena
**stager** ['stedʒər] *s* hombre experimentado; (coll.) caballo de diligencia
**stage setting** *s* (theat.) arreglo de escena; (theat.) aparato escénico
**stage-struck** ['stedʒ,strʌk] *adj* loco por el teatro
**stage whisper** *s* susurro en voz alta
**stagger** ['stægər] *s* vacilación, tambaleo; (aer.) decalaje; **staggers** *ssg* (vet.) modorra, vértigo; *va* hacer vacilar, hacer tambalear; hacer titubear; sorprender; asustar; escalonar (*las horas de trabajo*); *vn* vacilar, tambalear, hacer eses al andar; titubear; sorprenderse; asustarse; conmoverse mucho
**staggering** ['stægərɪŋ] *adj* tambaleante; derribador; sorprendente; espantoso
**staghound** ['stæg,haʊnd] *s* sabueso
**staging** ['stedʒɪŋ] *s* andamiada; (theat.) representación; viajes en diligencia
**staging area** *s* (mil.) zona de embarco
**stagnancy** ['stægnənsɪ] *s* estancación o estancamiento
**stagnant** ['stægnənt] *adj* estancado, estadizo; (fig.) estancado, inactivo, paralizado
**stagnate** ['stægnet] *va* estancar; *vn* estancarse
**stagnation** [stæg'neʃən] *s* estancación o estancamiento; (fig.) estancamiento
**stag party** *s* tertulia de hombres solos
**stagy** ['stedʒɪ] *adj* (*comp:* **-ier**; *super:* **-iest**) teatral
**staid** [sted] *adj* grave, serio, formal
**stain** [sten] *s* mancha; tinte, tintura; materia colorante; *va* manchar; teñir; colorar; *vn* mancharse; hacer manchas
**stained glass** *s* vidrio de color
**stained-glass window** ['stend,glæs] o ['stend,glɑs] *s* vidriera de colores, vitral (en color)
**stainless** ['stenlɪs] *adj* inoxidable, inmanchable; inmaculado
**stainless steel** *s* acero inoxidable
**stair** [stɛr] *s* escalón (*peldaño de escalera*); escalera; **stairs** *spl* escalera; **below stairs** abajo, al o en el piso bajo; en la cocina, en las viviendas de escalera abajo
**staircase** ['stɛr,kes] *s* escalera, caja de la escalera
**stairway** ['stɛr,we] *s* escalera
**stair well** *s* hueco de escalera
**stake** [stek] *s* estaca; telero (*de un carro*); puesta, posta; rodrigón (*para sostener plantas*); bigorneta; premio del vencedor; **at stake** en juego; en gran peligro; **to die at the stake** morir en la hoguera; **to have much at stake** irle a uno mucho en una cosa; **to pull up stakes** (coll.) irse; (coll.) mudar de casa; *va* estacar; atar a una estaca; rodrigar (*plantas*); apostar; arriesgar, aventurar; **to stake all** jugarse el todo por el todo; **to stake off** o **to stake out** estacar, señalar con estacas
**stakeholder** ['stek,holdər] *s* el que guarda las apuestas y paga al que gana
**stake truck** *s* camión de plataforma con teleros
**Stakhanovism** [stə'xɑnəvɪzəm] *s* stajanovismo
**Stakhanovite** [stə'xɑnəvaɪt] *adj & s* stajanovista
**stalactite** [stə'læktaɪt] o ['stæləktaɪt] *s* estalactita
**stalagmite** [stə'lægmaɪt] o ['stæləgmaɪt] *s* estalagmita
**stale** [stel] *adj* añejo, rancio, viejo; anticuado; viciado (*aire*); mohoso (*chiste*); *va* añejar, enranciar; *vn* añejarse, enranciarse
**stalemate** ['stel,met] *s* mate ahogado (*en el ajedrez*); estancación; **to reach a stalemate** llegar a un punto muerto; *va* dar mate ahogado a; estancar, paralizar
**Stalingrad** ['stɑlɪn,grɑd] *s* Stalingrado
**Stalinism** ['stɑlɪnɪzəm] *s* stalinismo
**Stalinist** ['stɑlɪnɪst] *adj & s* stalinista
**stalk** [stɔk] *s* (bot.) tallo; (bot., anat. & zool.) pedúnculo; (el) cazar al acecho; paso majestuoso; (obs.) paso furtivo; *va* cazar al acecho; acechar, espiar; *vn* cazar al acecho; andar con paso majestuoso; andar con paso altivo; (obs.) andar con paso furtivo; **to stalk out** salir con paso airado
**stalking-horse** ['stɔkɪŋ,hɔrs] *s* caballo o figura que representa un caballo que usan los cazadores al acecho para esconderse; (pol.) candidato que sirve para encubrir la candidatura de otra persona; disfraz, pretexto, máscara
**stall** [stɔl] *s* establo, pesebre; puesto (*para la venta*); caseta (*de una feria*); (Brit.) butaca; (slang) pretexto; *va* encerrar en un establo; estancar, poner trabas a; parar (*un motor*); **to stall off** (coll.) eludir, evitar; *vn* estar o vivir en un establo; atascarse, atollarse; pararse (*un motor*); (slang) eludir para engañar o demorar; **to stall for time** (slang) tardar para ganar tiempo
**stall-fed** ['stɔl,fed] *adj* cebado o engordado en un establo
**stallion** ['stæljən] *s* caballo padre, caballo semental
**stalwart** ['stɔlwərt] *s* persona fornida; partidario leal; *adj* fornido, forzudo; valiente; leal, constante
**Stambul** o **Stamboul** [stɑm'bul] *s* Estambul
**stamen** ['stemən] *s* (bot.) estambre
**stamina** ['stæmɪnə] *s* fuerza, nervio, vigor, resistencia
**staminate** ['stæmɪnet] *adj* (bot.) estaminado (*que sólo tiene estambres*); (bot.) estaminífero
**staminode** ['stæmɪnod] *s* var. de **staminodium**
**staminodium** [,stæmɪ'nodɪəm] *s* (*pl:* **-dia** [dɪə]) (bot.) estaminodio o estaminodo
**stammer** ['stæmər] *s* balbuceo, tartamudeo; *va* balbucear (*p.ej., excusas*); *vn* balbucear o balbucir; tartamudear
**stamp** [stæmp] *s* sello; estampilla (*sello con letrero para estampar*); marca, impresión, rastro; pisón; cuño, troquel (*para estampar las monedas, etc.*); tipo, clase, calaña; *va* hollar, pisotear; imprimir, estampar; sellar; troquelar; pa-

tear; indicar, señalar; poner el sello a; bocartear (*el mineral*); **to stamp out** apagar pateando; extinguir con la fuerza; suprimir; *vn* patalear

**Stamp Act** *s* (hist.) ley del Timbre

**stampede** [stæm'pid] *s* estampida; movimiento precipitado y unánime; *va* hacer huir en desorden; provocar a pánico, provocar a obrar impulsivamente; *vn* huir en desorden; obrar por común impulso

**stamping grounds** *spl* (slang) guarida (*sitio frecuentado por una persona*)

**stamp mill** *s* (min.) bocarte

**stamp pad** *s* tampón

**stamp-vending machine** ['stæmp,vɛndɪŋ] *s* máquina expendedora de sellos

**stance** [stæns] *s* (sport) postura, planta

**stanch** [stɑntʃ] *adj* firme, fuerte; leal, constante; estanco; *va* estancar; restañar (*la sangre de una herida*); *vn* apagarse; restañarse

**stanchion** ['stænʃən] *s* puntal, montante, pie derecho; cornadiza (*en las vaquerías*); *va* proveer de puntales, montantes o pies derechos; sujetar a puntales

**stand** [stænd] *s* parada; estancia (*entre dos etapas*); postura, posición; resistencia; tribuna, estrado; sostén, soporte, pie, pedestal; puesto, quiosco ‖ (*pret & pp:* **stood**) *va* poner derecho, colocar verticalmente; tolerar, soportar, resistir; (coll.) aguantar (*a una persona*); (coll.) sufragar (*un gasto*); **to stand off** tener a raya; **to stand on end** poner de punta; **to stand one's ground** mantenerse firme, mantenerse en su puesto ‖ *vn* estar, estar situado; estar parado; estacionarse; estar de pie, estar derecho; ponerse de pie, levantarse; resultar; navegar; mostrar la caza (*un perro*); persistir; mantenerse; quedarse; surgir, nacer; pararse; **to stand aloof** mantenerse apartado; **to stand apart** o **aside** apartarse, mantenerse apartado; **to stand back of** colocarse detrás de; garantizar, respaldar; **to stand by** mantenerse a corta distancia; estar alerta; (rad. & telv.) esperar la continuación de un programa interrumpido; apoyar, defender; **to stand for** significar, representar; apoyar, defender; apadrinar; mantener (*p.ej., una opinión*); presentarse como candidato de; (coll.) tolerar; navegar hacia; **to stand forth** destacarse; **to stand in** (coll.) tener buenas aldabas, estar en buenas relaciones; **to stand in for** substituir (*a una persona*); **to stand in line** hacer cola; **to stand in the way** cerrar el paso; estorbar; **to stand off** apartarse, quedar a distancia; **to stand on** depender de, basarse en; pedir con insistencia; **to stand on end** ponerse de punta; erizarse, encresparse (*el pelo*); **to stand out** sobresalir; resaltar, destacarse; no ceder; **to stand to reason** ser lógico, ser razonable; **to stand up** ponerse de pie, levantarse; durar, conservarse; **to stand up for** apoyar, defender; **to stand up to** hacer resueltamente frente a

**standard** ['stændərd] *s* patrón; norma, regla establecida; bandera, estandarte; emblema, símbolo; (bot.) árbol o arbusto de tronco o tallo alto y derecho; *adj* normal; corriente, regular; legal; clásico

**standardbearer** ['stændərd,bɛrər] *s* abanderado o portaestandarte; jefe (*de un movimiento*); (orn.) chotacabras africano

**standard broadcasting** *s* difusión normal

**standard candle** *s* (phys.) bujía normal o patrón

**standard gauge** *s* (rail.) vía normal

**standard gold** *s* oro de ley

**standardization** [,stændərdɪ'zeʃən] *s* normalización, estandardización

**standardize** ['stændərdaɪz] *va* normalizar, estandardizar

**standard keyboard** *s* teclado universal (*de la máquina de escribir*)

**standard meter** *s* metro patrón

**standard of living** *s* nivel de vida

**standard time** *s* hora legal

**stand-by** ['stænd,baɪ] *s* (*pl:* **-bys**) adherente fiel, recurso seguro, paño de lágrimas

**standee** [stæn'di] *s* (coll.) espectador que asiste de pie

**stand-in** ['stænd,ɪn] *s* (mov.) doble; (coll.) buenas aldabas

**standing** ['stændɪŋ] *s* posición, condición; reputación; duración; parada; **in good standing** en posición acreditada; **of long standing** de mucho tiempo, de antigua fecha; **of standing** de prestigio; *adj* derecho, en pie; de pie; permanente, estable, fijo; parado, inmóvil; encharcado, estancado; vigente

**standing army** *s* ejército permanente

**standing committee** *s* comisión permanente

**standing rigging** *s* (naut.) jarcia de firme, jarcia muerta

**standing room** *s* sitio para estar de pie

**stand-off** ['stænd,ɔf] o ['stænd,ɑf] *s* reserva, aislamiento; empate; *adj* retraído, reservado, indiferente

**stand-offish** [,stænd'ɔfɪʃ] o [,stænd'ɑfɪʃ] *adj* retraído, reservado, indiferente, huraño

**standpat** ['stænd,pæt] *adj & s* (coll.) conservador

**standpatter** ['stænd,pætər] *s* (coll.) conservador

**standpipe** ['stænd,paɪp] *s* columna de alimentación, columna de alimentación de agua

**standpoint** ['stænd,pɔɪnt] *s* punto de vista

**standstill** ['stænd,stɪl] *s* parada, detención, alto; descanso, inactividad; **to come to a standstill** cesar, pararse

**stand-up** ['stænd,ʌp] *adj* derecho; estando de pie, p.ej., **a stand-up meal** una comida de pie

**stanhope** ['stænhop] o ['stænəp] *s* cabriolé ligero

**stank** [stæŋk] *pret de* **stink**

**stannate** ['stænet] *s* (chem.) estannato

**stannic** ['stænɪk] *adj* (chem.) estánnico

**stannous** ['stænəs] *adj* (chem.) estannoso

**stanza** ['stænzə] *s* estancia, estrofa

**stapedius** [stə'pidɪəs] *s* (anat.) estapedio

**stapes** ['stepiz] *s* (anat.) estribo

**staphylococcus** [,stæfɪlə'kɑkəs] *s* (*pl:* **-cocci** ['kɑksaɪ]) (bact.) estafilococo

**staphyloma** [,stæfɪ'lomə] *s* (*pl:* **-mata** [mətə]) (path.) estafiloma

**staple** ['stepəl] *s* grapa (*para clavar; para sujetar papeles*); artículo o producto principal; materia prima; fibra textil; *adj* primero, principal; corriente, reconocido, establecido; *va* sujetar con grapas; clasificar (*hebras textiles*) según su longitud

**stapler** ['steplər] *s* surtidor de lanas; engrapador, cose-papeles

**star** [stɑr] *s* astro (*cuerpo celeste*); estrella (*cualquier astro, a excepción del Sol y la Luna; figura con que se representa una estrella; cosa que tiene esta figura*); estrellón (*fuego artificial*); (mov. & theat.) estrella (*mujer u hombre*); (elec.) estrella; (print.) estrella o asterisco; (fig.) estrella o astro (*persona que sobresale*); (fig.) as (*p.ej., de fútbol*); (fig.) estrella (*hado, destino; pelos blancos en la frente del caballo*); **to see stars** (coll.) ver las estrellas; **to thank one's lucky stars** estar agradecido por su buena suerte; *adj* estelar; principal; sobresaliente; (*pret & pp:* **starred;** *ger:* **starring**) *va* estrellar, adornar o señalar con estrellas; marcar con asterisco; presentar como estrella (*a un actor o una actriz*); *vn* ser la estrella; ser el astro; lucirse; sobresalir

**star apple** *s* (bot.) caimito (*árbol y fruto*)

**starboard** ['stɑrbərd] o ['stɑrbord] *s* (naut.) estribor; *adj* de estribor; *adv* a estribor; *va & vn* volver a estribor

**star boarder** *s* huésped principal o predilecto (*en una casa de huéspedes*)

**starch** [stɑrtʃ] *s* almidón, fécula; entono, arrogancia; (slang) fuerza, vigor; *va* almidonar

**Star Chamber** *s* (Brit. hist.) cámara estrellada; tribunal secreto y arbitrario

**starchy** ['stɑrtʃɪ] *adj* (*comp:* **-ier;** *super:* **-iest**) feculento, feculoso; almidonado; (fig.) tieso, entonado

**star connection** *s* (elec.) conexión en estrella

**stardom** ['stɑrdəm] *s* (theat.) estrellato (*categoría o condición de estrella*); actores eminentes

**star drill** *s* barrena de filo en cruz, taladro estrella

**star dust** *s* nebulosas; partículas de meteoritos; (coll.) encanto
**stare** [stɛr] *s* mirada fija; *va* mirar fijamente, mirar de hito en hito, clavar la vista en; **to stare down** o **to stare out of countenance** desconcertar mirando fijamente, avergonzar con la mirada; **to stare one in the face** darle a uno en la cara, estar a la vista, saltar a la vista; deber acontecer; *vn* mirar fijamente, fijar estrechamente la mirada
**starfish** ['stɑr,fɪʃ] *s* (zool.) estrella de mar
**star gauge** *s* (gun.) calibrador de ánima
**stargaze** ['stɑr,gez] *vn* mirar las estrellas; ser distraído, soñar despierto
**stargazer** ['stɑr,gezər] *s* el que mira las estrellas; astrólogo; astrónomo; (ichth.) uranóscopo
**stargazing** ['stɑr,gezɪŋ] *s* observación de las estrellas; abstracción, ensimismamiento
**staring** ['stɛrɪŋ] *adj* mirando fijamente; llamativo, vistoso
**stark** [stɑrk] *adj* completo, cabal, puro; tieso, rígido; duro, severo; *adv* completamente, enteramente; rígidamente, severamente
**stark-naked** ['stɑrk'nekɪd] *adj* en pelota, en cueros
**starless** ['stɑrlɪs] *adj* sin estrellas
**starlet** ['stɑrlɪt] *s* estrellita
**starlight** ['stɑr,laɪt] *s* luz de las estrellas; *adj* estrellado
**starlike** ['stɑr,laɪk] *adj* estrellado; brillante como una estrella
**starling** ['stɑrlɪŋ] *s* (orn.) estornino; (orn.) trupial
**starlit** ['stɑr,lɪt] *adj* iluminado por las estrellas
**Star of Bethlehem** *s* estrella de Belén
**star-of-Bethlehem** ['stɑrəv'bɛθlɪəm] *s* (bot.) leche de gallina, estrella de Belén
**star-of-night** ['stɑrəv'naɪt] *s* (bot.) copey
**star polygon** *s* (geom.) estrella poligonal
**starred** [stɑrd] *adj* estrellado; (theat.) presentado como estrella; afortunado
**starry** ['stɑrɪ] *adj* (*comp:* **-rier;** *super:* **-riest**) estrellado; brillante, rutilante
**starry-eyed** ['stɑrɪ,aɪd] *adj* soñador, quimérico
**Stars and Bars** *spl* (hist.) bandera de la Confederación de los estados del Sur de Norteamérica
**Stars and Stripes** *spl* estrellas y listas, barras y estrellas, franjas y estrellas (*bandera de los EE.UU.*)
**star sapphire** *s* zafiro asteriado, zafiro de ojo de gato
**star shell** *s* (mil.) bomba luminosa
**star shower** *s* lluvia de estrellas
**star-spangled** ['stɑr,spæŋgəld] *adj* estrellado
**Star-Spangled Banner** *s* bandera estrellada (*bandera de los EE.UU.*)
**start** [stɑrt] *s* principio, comienzo; salida, partida; lugar de partida; ventaja (*en una carrera*); sobresalto; respingo (*de un caballo*); arranque (*de un coche, tren, etc.*); (sport) salida; **to give a start** sobresaltar; **to give a start to** poner en marcha; hacer que empiece a funcionar; ayudar (*a un joven*) a establecerse en los negocios; **to make a fresh start** volver a empezar; *va* principiar, empezar; poner en marcha, hacer andar; hacer arrancar; dar la señal de partida a; entablar (*una conversación*); levantar (*la caza*); *vn* principiar, empezar; sobresaltar; nacer, provenir; aflojarse; ponerse en marcha; arrancar; **starting with** a partir de; **to start after** salir en busca de; **to start in, out** o **up** principiar, empezar; ponerse en marcha; **to start to** + *inf* principiar a + *inf*, empezar a + *inf;* ponerse a + *inf;* echarse a (*reír, llorar, correr*)
**starter** ['stɑrtər] *s* iniciador; primero (*de una serie*); (aut.) arranque, motor de arranque; (elec.) encebador, encendedor (*de tubos fluorescentes*); (sport) stárter, juez de salida
**star thistle** *s* (bot.) cardo estrellado, calcitrapa
**starting** ['stɑrtɪŋ] *s* puesta en marcha
**starting crank** *s* manivela de arranque
**starting motor** *s* motor de arranque
**starting point** *s* punto de partida
**starting post** *s* (sport) poste o línea de partida
**startle** ['stɑrtəl] *s* susto; *va* asustar, sorprender, sobrecoger; *vn* asustarse, sorprenderse, sobrecogerse
**startling** ['stɑrtlɪŋ] *adj* alarmante, asombroso, sorprendente
**starvation** [stɑr'veʃən] *s* hambre, inanición
**starvation diet** *s* régimen de hambre
**starvation wages** *spl* salario de hambre
**starve** [stɑrv] *va* hambrear; hacer morir de hambre; obligar mediante el hambre; **to starve out** hacer rendirse por hambre; *vn* hambrear; morir de hambre; (coll.) tener hambre; **to starve for** sufrir por la falta de
**starveling** ['stɑrvlɪŋ] *adj & s* hambrón
**starving** ['stɑrvɪŋ] *adj* hambriento, famélico
**stash** [stæʃ] *va* ocultar, guardar en lugar seguro
**stat.** abr. de **statuary, statute** y **statue**
**statable** ['stetəbəl] *adj* enunciable, formulable
**state** [stet] *s* estado; fausto, pompa, ceremonia; **to lie in state** estar expuesto en capilla ardiente, estar de cuerpo presente (*el cadáver de un muerto*); **to live in state** gastar mucho lujo; **to ride in state** pasear en carruaje de lujo; *adj* de estado, del estado; estatal (*del Estado*); público; de gala, de lujo; *va* declarar, afirmar; exponer, manifestar; formular; plantear (*p.ej., un problema*)
**statecraft** ['stet,kræft] o ['stet,krɑft] *s* política, arte de gobernar
**stated** ['stetɪd] *adj* fijo, establecido; dicho
**statehood** ['stethʊd] *s* estatidad
**Statehouse** o **statehouse** ['stet,haʊs] *s* (U.S.A.) edificio del Estado (*en que tiene reuniones la legislatura de uno de los estados de los EE.UU.*)
**stateless** ['stetlɪs] *adj* apátrida
**stateliness** ['stetlɪnɪs] *s* majestuosidad
**stately** ['stetlɪ] *adj* (*comp:* **-lier;** *super:* **-liest**) imponente, majestuoso
**statement** ['stetmənt] *s* declaración; exposición, informe, relación; (com.) estado de cuentas
**state of mind** *s* estado de ánimo
**state of siege** *s* estado de sitio
**State rights** *spl* var. de **States' rights**
**stateroom** ['stet,rum] o ['stet,rʊm] *s* (naut.) camarote; (rail.) compartimiento particular
**state room** *s* sala para las ceremonias
**state secret** *s* secreto de estado
**state's evidence** *s* (law) testimonio aducido por el procurador del Estado en un juicio criminal; testimonio de un cómplice o de cómplices; **to turn state's evidence** (law) atestar en un juicio en contra de un cómplice o de cómplices, convertirse en testigo del estado
**States-General** ['stets'dʒɛnərəl] *s* (hist.) estados generales (*de Francia*); parlamento de los Países Bajos
**stateside** ['stet,saɪd] *adj* (coll.) estadounidense; *adv* (coll.) a o en los Estados Unidos; a o en la parte continental de los Estados Unidos
**statesman** ['stetsmən] *s* (*pl:* **-men**) estadista, hombre de estado
**statesmanlike** ['stetsmən,laɪk] *adj* de estadista, propio de estadista
**statesmanly** ['stetsmənlɪ] *adj* de estadista, digno de un estadista
**statesmanship** ['stetsmənʃɪp] *s* habilidad de estadista
**state socialism** *s* socialismo del estado
**States' rights** *spl* (U.S.A.) derechos de los Estados
**state-wide** ['stet,waɪd] *adj* por todo el estado, de todo el estado
**static** ['stætɪk] *adj* estático; (rad.) atmosférico; *s* (rad.) parásitos atmosféricos; **statics** *ssg* (mech.) estática
**static electricity** *s* electricidad estática
**static machine** *s* (elec.) máquina electrostática
**station** ['steʃən] *s* estación; condición, situación; (astr. & eccl.) estación; *va* estacionar, apostar, colocar
**station agent** *s* (rail.) jefe de estación
**stationary** ['steʃən,ɛrɪ] *adj* estacionario
**station break** *s* (rad.) descanso, intermedio
**stationer** ['steʃənər] *s* papelero; (archaic) estacionario (*librero*)
**stationery** ['steʃən,ɛrɪ] *s* efectos de escritorio
**stationery store** *s* papelería
**station house** *s* paradero; estación de ferrocarril; cuartelillo de policía

**station identification** *s* (rad. & telv.) indicativo de la emisora
**stationmaster** [ˈsteʃən,mæstər] o [ˈsteʃən,mɑstər] *s* (rail.) jefe de estación
**stations of the cross** *spl* (eccl.) estaciones, estaciones de la cruz
**station wagon** *s* rubia, coche rural
**statism** [ˈstetɪzəm] *s* estatismo
**statist** [ˈstetɪst] *adj* estatista; *s* estatista; estadístico
**statistic** [stəˈtɪstɪk] *adj* estadístico; **statistics** *ssg* estadística (*ciencia*); *spl* estadística o estadísticas
**statistical** [stəˈtɪstɪkəl] *adj* estadístico
**statistician** [,stætɪsˈtɪʃən] *s* estadístico
**statocyst** [ˈstætəsɪst] *s* (zool.) estatocisto
**statolith** [ˈstætəlɪθ] *s* (zool.) estatolito
**stator** [ˈstetər] *s* (mach. & elec.) estator
**statoscope** [ˈstætəskop] *s* (phys.) estatoscopio o estatóscopo
**statuary** [ˈstætʃu,ɛrɪ] *adj* estatuario; *s* (*pl:* **-ies**) estatuario (*persona*); estatuaria (*arte*); estatuas
**statue** [ˈstætʃu] *s* estatua; *va* estatuar
**Statue of Liberty** *s* estatua de la Libertad
**statuesque** [,stætʃuˈɛsk] *adj* escultural
**statuette** [,stætʃuˈɛt] *s* figurilla, estatuita
**stature** [ˈstætʃər] *s* estatura, talla; habilidad, carácter
**status** [ˈstetəs] *s* estado, condición; situación social, profesional o legal; categoría (*distinción, elevada condición*)
**status quo** [kwo] *s* statu quo (*la situación presente; la situación de antes*)
**status seeker** *s* persona que trata de adquirir categoría
**status seeking** *s* esfuerzo por adquirir categoría
**status symbol** *s* símbolo de categoría social
**statute** [ˈstætʃut] *s* estatuto, ley
**statute mile** *s* milla ordinaria (*5280 pies*)
**statute of limitations** *s* (law) ley de la prescripción
**statutory** [ˈstætʃu,torɪ] *adj* estatutario, legal
**St. Augustine** [sent ˈɔgəstin] *s* San Agustín (*ciudad de la Florida*)
**staunch** [stɔntʃ] o [stɑntʃ] *adj, va & vn* var. de **stanch**
**staurolite** [ˈstɔrəlaɪt] *s* (mineral.) estaurolita
**stave** [stev] *s* duela (*de barril*); palo, bastón; peldaño (*de escala*); estrofa; (mus.) pentagrama; (*pret & pp:* **staved** o **stove**) *va* romper, destrozar; desfondar; romper las duelas a; proveer de duelas; **to stave off** impedir, evitar, diferir; *vn* romperse, destrozarse, desfondarse
**staves** [stevz] *pl de* **staff** y de **stave**
**stavesacre** [ˈstevzekər] *s* (bot.) estafisagria, albarraz
**stay** [ste] *s* morada, permanencia, estancia; parada, detención, suspensión; (law) dilación, prórroga; paciencia, resistencia; (naut.) estay; varilla o ballena (*de corsé*); apoyo, sostén; **stays** *spl* corsé; **in stays** (naut.) en la virada; *va* asentar, fijar, fundar; apoyar, sostener; soportar, tolerar; aplazar, detener; esperar; poner freno a; *vn* quedar, quedarse, permanecer; hospedarse; habitar; parar, pararse, detenerse; esperar; resistir; (naut.) virar o cambiar de rumbo o bordada; **to stay away** quedarse apartado, quedarse fuera; **to stay in** quedarse en casa; **to stay out** quedarse fuera; **to stay up** velar, no acostarse
**stay-at-home** [ˈsteət,hom] *adj & s* hogareño; acaserado (Am.)
**staying power** *s* resistencia, fortaleza, aguante
**staysail** [ˈstesəl] o [ˈste,sel] *s* (naut.) vela de estay
**St. Croix** [sent ˈkrɔɪ] *s* Santa Cruz (*isla*)
**S.T.D.** abr. de **Sacrae Theologiae Doctor** (Lat.) **Doctor of Sacred Theology**
**stead** [stɛd] *s* lugar; **in his stead** en su lugar, en lugar de él; **to stand in good stead** ser ventajoso, ser de provecho, ayudar, servir
**steadfast** [ˈstɛdfæst] o [ˈstɛdfɑst] *adj* resuelto; constante; fijo
**steadfastness** [ˈstɛdfæstnɪs] o [ˈstɛdfɑstnɪs] *s* resolución; constancia; fijeza
**steadiness** [ˈstɛdɪnɪs] *s* constancia, fijeza, seguridad; uniformidad; resolución; seriedad
**steady** [ˈstɛdɪ] *adj* (*comp:* **-ier;** *super:* **-iest**) constante, fijo, firme, seguro; regular, uniforme; resuelto; asentado, serio; (com.) en calma (*dícese de la Bolsa*); (naut.) estable, en calma; (*pret & pp:* **-ied**) *va* estabilizar, reforzar; calmar (*los nervios*); *vn* estabilizarse; calmarse
**steady state** *s* (phys.) régimen permanente
**steak** [stek] *s* lonja o tajada (*de carne o pescado*); biftec
**steal** [stil] *s* (coll.) robo, hurto; (*pret:* **stole;** *pp:* **stolen**) *va* robar, hurtar; atraer, cautivar; *vn* robar, hurtar; **to steal away** escabullirse; **to steal into** meterse a hurtadillas en; **to steal out of** salirse a escondidas de; **to steal upon** aproximarse sin ruido a
**stealth** [stɛlθ] *s* cautela, recato; **by stealth** a hurtadillas, a escondidas
**stealthy** [ˈstɛlθɪ] *adj* (*comp:* **-ier;** *super:* **-iest**) astuto, taimado; secreto, furtivo, clandestino
**steam** [stim] *s* vapor, vapor de agua; vaho; (coll.) potencia, energía; **to blow off steam** dejar escapar vapor; (coll.) desfogarse, desahogarse, soltar la lengua; **to get up steam** dar presión; **to let off steam** descargar vapor; (fig.) desahogarse; **under steam** bajo presión; *adj* de vapor; *va* cocer al vapor; dar un baño de vapor a, saturar de vapor; empañar (*p.ej., las ventanas*); **to get steamed up** empañarse (*p.ej., un vidrio, un cristal*); (coll.) excitarse, animarse; (slang) emborracharse; *vn* emitir vapor, echar vapor; evaporarse; marchar o funcionar a vapor; **to steam ahead** avanzar, adelantar por medio de vapor; (fig.) hacer grandes progresos; **to steam away** salir (*la locomotora, el buque de vapor*)
**steamboat** [ˈstim,bot] *s* vapor, buque de vapor
**steam boiler** *s* caldera de vapor
**steam box** o **chest** *s* caja o cámara de vapor
**steam dome** *s* (rail.) cúpula de toma de vapor
**steam engine** *s* máquina de vapor
**steamer** [ˈstimər] *s* vapor, buque de vapor; automóvil de vapor
**steamer rug** *s* manta de viaje
**steamer trunk** *s* baúl de camarote
**steam fitter** *s* tubero, cañero, montador de calderas de vapor
**steam heat** *s* calefacción por vapor
**steaming** [ˈstimɪŋ] *adj* vaporoso; humeante; *adv* **steaming hot** intensamente caliente
**steam organ** *s* (mus.) órgano de vapor
**steam power plant** *s* estación termoeléctrica, central térmica
**steam roller** *s* apisonadora (*movida a vapor*); (coll.) fuerza arrolladora
**steam-roller** [ˈstim,rolər] *adj* (coll.) arrollador; *va* allanar y afirmar (*la carretera*) con apisonadora; (coll.) aplastar con fuerza arrolladora
**steamship** [ˈstim,ʃɪp] *s* vapor, buque de vapor
**steam shovel** *s* pala mecánica de vapor, máquina excavadora de vapor
**steam table** *s* plancha caliente
**steamtight** [ˈstim,taɪt] *adj* a prueba de vapor
**steam turbine** *s* turbina de vapor
**steamy** [ˈstimɪ] *adj* (*comp:* **-ier;** *super:* **-iest**) vaporoso; humeante; empañado; (coll.) muy excitado
**steapsin** [stɪˈæpsɪn] *s* (biochem.) esteapsina
**stearate** [ˈstiəret] *s* (chem.) estearato
**stearic** [stɪˈærɪk] o [ˈstɪrɪk] *adj* (chem.) esteárico
**stearic acid** *s* (chem.) ácido esteárico
**stearin** [ˈstiərɪn] o [ˈstɪrɪn] *s* (chem.) estearina
**stearoptene** [,stiəˈrɑptin] *s* (chem.) estearopteno
**steatite** [ˈstiətaɪt] *s* (mineral.) esteatita
**steatitic** [,stiəˈtɪtɪk] *adj* (mineral.) esteatitoso
**steatopygia** [,stiətoˈpaɪdʒɪə] o [,stiətoˈpɪdʒɪə] *s* (anthrop.) esteatopigia
**stedfast** [ˈstɛdfæst] o [ˈstɛdfɑst] *adj* var. de **steadfast**
**steed** [stid] *s* caballo; corcel; caballo de combate; caballo de carrera
**steel** [stil] *s* acero; ballena de acero; eslabón (*hierro acerado para sacar fuego de un pedernal; cilindro de acero para afilar cuchillas*); (fig.) acero (*fuerza; valor*); *adj* acerado; (fig.) frío, duro; *va* acerar; (fig.) acerar; **to steel oneself** (fig.) acerarse, acorazarse

**steel blue** *s* azul acerado
**steel mill** *s* acería, fábrica de acero
**steel wool** *s* virutillas de acero, estopa de acero
**steelwork** [ˈstil,wʌrk] *s* artículos, partes, instrumentos de acero; montaje de acero; **steelworks** *ssg* o *spl* fábrica de acero
**steelworker** [ˈstil,wʌrkər] *s* herrero de obra; obrero en una fábrica de acero
**steely** [ˈstilɪ] *adj* (*comp:* **-ier;** *super:* **-iest**) acerado; (fig.) fuerte, inflexible, duro
**steelyard** [ˈstiljɑrd] o [ˈstiljərd] *s* romana
**steenbok** [ˈstin,bɑk] o [ˈsten,bɑk] *s* (zool.) antílope africano
**steep** [stip] *adj* escarpado, empinado; (coll.) alto, excesivo (*precio*); *s* cuesta empinada; empapamiento, remojo; (found.) brasca; *va* empapar, remojar, poner en infusión; **steeped in** absorbido en; lleno de; *vn* (coll.) empaparse, estar en infusión
**steeple** [ˈstipəl] *s* aguja, campanario (*de iglesia*)
**steeplebush** [ˈstipəl,bʊʃ] *s* (bot.) espirea norteamericana (*Spiraea tomentosa*)
**steeplechase** [ˈstipəl,tʃes] *s* carrera del campanario, carrera (de caballos) de obstáculos
**steeplejack** [ˈstipəl,dʒæk] *s* (coll.) reparador de altas chimeneas, torres, etc.
**steer** [stɪr] *s* buey (*de cualquier edad*); novillo; *va* guiar, conducir, gobernar; *vn* gobernar, p.ej., **this boat does not steer well** este buque no gobierna bien; conducirse; **to steer clear of** (coll.) evitar, eludir
**steerage** [ˈstɪrɪdʒ] *s* dirección; (naut.) proa, entrepuente
**steerage passenger** *s* (naut.) pasajero de proa
**steerageway** [ˈstɪrɪdʒ,we] *s* (naut.) empuje del buque necesario para gobernar
**steering column** *s* (aut.) columna de dirección
**steering committee** *s* comisión de iniciativas
**steering gear** *s* mecanismo de dirección
**steering knuckle** *s* (aut.) charnela de dirección, muñón de dirección
**steering wheel** *s* (naut.) rueda del timón; (aut.) volante o volante de dirección
**steersman** [ˈstɪrzmən] *s* (*pl:* **-men**) piloto, timonero; conductor (*de automóvil*)
**steeve** [stiv] *s* (naut.) lanzamiento
**stegomyia** [,stɛgəˈmaɪə] *s* (ent.) estegomía
**stegosaurus** [,stɛgəˈsɔrəs] *s* (*pl:* **-ri** [raɪ]) (pal.) estegosauro
**stein** [staɪn] *s* pichel para cerveza
**steinbok** [ˈstaɪn,bɑk] *s* (zool.) antílope africano; (zool.) íbice
**stele** [ˈstilɪ] *s* (*pl:* **-lae** [li] o **-les**) (arch. & bot.) estela
**stellar** [ˈstɛlər] *adj* estelar, estelario
**stellate** [ˈstɛlet] *adj* estrellado
**St. Elmo's fire** o **St. Elmo's light** [ˈɛlmoz] *s* fuego de Santelmo
**stem** [stɛm] *s* (bot.) tallo, vástago; (bot.) pedúnculo; pie (*de una copa*); cañón (*de una pipa; de una pluma*); (mach.) varilla, vástago; fuste (*de una columna*); tija o espiga (*de una llave*); botón (*de un reloj de bolsillo*); (naut.) roda, tajamar; (gram.) tema; **from stem to stern** de proa a popa; (*pret & pp:* **stemmed;** *ger:* **stemming**) *va* desgranar, despalillar; estancar, represar; detener, refrenar; hacer frente a; embestir con la proa; **to stem the tide** rendir la marea; **to stem the torrent** detener el torrente; *vn* provenir, nacer; **to stem from** provenir de, originarse en, traer su origen de
**stemless** [ˈstɛmlɪs] *adj* sin vástago; (bot.) sin tallo, sin pedúnculo; que no se puede desgranar
**stemma** [ˈstɛmə] *s* (*pl:* **-mas** o **-mata** [mətə]) (zool.) estema (*ojo simple de los insectos*)
**stemmed** [stɛmd] *adj* (bot.) con tallo, con pedúnculo; desgranado
**stemmer** [ˈstɛmər] *s* máquina de despalillar
**stemple** [ˈstɛmpəl] *s* (min.) estemple
**stemson** [ˈstɛmsən] *s* (naut.) contrabranque, contrarroda
**stem-winder** [ˈstɛm,waɪndər] *s* (coll.) remontuar
**stem-winding** [ˈstɛm,waɪndɪŋ] *adj* de remontuar
**stench** [stɛntʃ] *s* hedor, hediondez
**stencil** [ˈstɛnsəl] *s* patrón picado; estarcido (*dibujo*); (*pret & pp:* **-ciled** o **-cilled;** *ger:* **-ciling** o **-cilling**) *va* estarcir
**stenocardia** [,stɛnəˈkɑrdɪə] *s* (path.) estenocardia
**stenograph** [ˈstɛnəgræf] o [ˈstɛnəgrɑf] *s* escritura taquigráfica; máquina para taquigrafiar; *va & vn* estenografiar, taquigrafiar
**stenographer** [stəˈnɑgrəfər] *s* estenógrafo
**stenographic** [,stɛnəˈgræfɪk] *adj* estenográfico
**stenographically** [,stɛnəˈgræfɪkəlɪ] *adv* estenográficamente
**stenography** [stəˈnɑgrəfɪ] *s* estenografía
**stenosis** [stɪˈnosɪs] *s* (path.) estenosis
**stenotype** [ˈstɛnətaɪp] *s* (trademark) máquina estenotipiadora o de estenotipiar; estenotipia (*letra o grupo de letras*)
**stenotypy** [ˈstɛnə,taɪpɪ] *s* estenotipia
**Stentor** [ˈstɛntər] *s* (myth.) Estentor; (*l.c.*) *s* persona con voz estentórea
**stentorian** [stɛnˈtorɪən] *adj* estentóreo
**step** [stɛp] *s* paso; escalón, grada, peldaño; grado; medida, gestión; (mus.) intervalo; (naut.) carlinga; estribo (*de un coche*); **steps** *spl* escalera de mano; **in step** llevando el paso; de acuerdo; (elec.) en fase; **out of step** no llevando el paso; en desacuerdo; **to break step** romper paso; **to take steps** dar pasos; tomar medidas, gestionar; **to watch one's step** mirarse en ello, ser prudente, proceder con cautela, andarse con tiento; **step by step** paso a paso ‖ (*pret & pp:* **stepped;** *ger:* **stepping**) *va* escalonar, colocar de trecho en trecho; plantar (*el pie*); **to step down** reducir, disminuir; **to step off** medir a pasos; **to step up** elevar, aumentar ‖ *vn* dar un paso, dar pasos; andar, caminar, ir; (coll.) andar de prisa; **to step aside** hacerse a un lado; retirarse; **to step back** dar un paso atrás; volver hacia atrás, retroceder; **to step down** bajar; dimitir; **to step in** entrar; (coll.) visitar al pasar; tomar parte (en); **to step lively** darse prisa; **to step on** pisar; **to step on it** (coll.) acelerar la marcha, darse prisa; (coll.) pisar fuertemente el acelerador, apretar el acelerador a fondo; **to step on the starter** pisar el arranque; **to step out** salir; bajar (*de un coche*); apretar el paso; entregarse al lujo, los placeres o los vicios; andar de parranda; **to step up** subir; avanzar
**stepbrother** [ˈstɛp,brʌðər] *s* medio hermano, hermanastro
**stepchild** [ˈstɛp,tʃaɪld] *s* (*pl:* **-children**) hijastro, alnado
**stepdaughter** [ˈstɛp,dɔtər] *s* hijastra
**step-down transformer** [ˈstɛp,daʊn] *s* (elec.) transformador reductor
**stepfather** [ˈstɛp,fɑðər] *s* padrastro
**stephanite** [ˈstɛfənaɪt] *s* (mineral.) estefanita, plata agria
**Stephen** [ˈstivən] *s* Esteban
**step-in** [ˈstɛp,ɪn] *adj* que se pone comenzando por los pies (*dícese de ciertas prendas de vestir*); **step-ins** *spl* bragas (*pantalones de mujer*)
**stepladder** [ˈstɛp,lædər] *s* escala, escalera doble, escalera de tijera
**stepmother** [ˈstɛp,mʌðər] *s* madrastra; (dial.) padrastro (*de las uñas*)
**stepparent** [ˈstɛp,pɛrənt] *s* padrastro o madrastra
**steppe** [stɛp] *s* estepa
**stepping stone** *s* estriberón, pasadera; escalón (*para la realización de un deseo*); escabel (*para medrar*)
**stepsister** [ˈstɛp,sɪstər] *s* media hermana, hermanastra
**stepson** [ˈstɛp,sʌn] *s* hijastro
**step terrace** *s* parata
**step-up transformer** [ˈstɛp,ʌp] *s* (elec.) transformador elevador
**stercoraceous** [,stʌrkəˈreʃəs] *adj* estercóreo
**sterculiaceous** [stʌr,kjulɪˈeʃəs] *adj* (bot.) esterculiáceo
**stere** [stɪr] *s* estéreo
**stereo** [ˈstɛrɪo] o [ˈstɪrɪo] *adj* (coll.) estereofónico; (coll.) estereoscópico; *s* (*pl:* **-os**) (coll.) música estereofónica, disco estereofónico, radiodifusión estereofónica; (coll.) fotografía estereoscópica
**stereobate** [ˈstɛrɪəbet] *s* (arch.) estereóbato

**stereo camera** *s* verascopio, cámara estereoscópica
**stereochemical** [ˌsterɪo'kemɪkəl] *s* estereoquímico
**stereochemistry** [ˌsterɪo'kemɪstrɪ] *s* estereoquímica
**stereochromy** ['sterɪəˌkromɪ] *s* estereocromía
**stereogram** ['sterɪəˌgræm] *s* estereograma
**stereographic** [ˌsterɪə'græfɪk] o **stereographical** [ˌsterɪə'græfɪkəl] *adj* estereográfico
**stereography** [ˌsterɪ'ɑgrəfɪ] *s* estereografía
**stereoisomerism** [ˌsterɪoaɪ'sɑmərɪzəm] *s* (chem.) estereoisomería
**stereometry** [ˌsterɪ'ɑmɪtrɪ] *s* estereometría
**stereophonic** [ˌsterɪə'fɑnɪk] *adj* estereofónico
**stereophony** [ˌsterɪ'ɑfənɪ] *s* estereofonía
**stereophotography** [ˌsterɪəfə'tɑgrəfɪ] *s* estereofotografía
**stereopsis** [ˌsterɪ'ɑpsɪs] *s* esteriopsis
**stereopticon** [ˌsterɪ'ɑptɪkən] *s* estereóptico
**stereoscope** ['sterɪəˌskop] *s* estereoscopio
**stereoscopic** [ˌsterɪə'skɑpɪk] *adj* estereoscópico
**stereoscopically** [ˌsterɪə'skɑpɪkəlɪ] *adv* estereoscópicamente
**stereoscopy** [ˌsterɪ'ɑskəpɪ] *s* estereoscopia
**stereotomy** [ˌsterɪ'ɑtəmɪ] *s* estereotomía
**stereotropism** [ˌsterɪ'ɑtrəpɪzəm] *s* (biol.) estereotropismo
**stereotype** ['sterɪəˌtaɪp] *s* estereotipo; estereotipia; *va* estereotipar; (fig.) estereotipar
**stereotyped** ['sterɪəˌtaɪpt] *adj* estereotipado; (fig.) estereotipado (*fijo e invariable; gastado, trillado*)
**stereotypy** ['sterɪəˌtaɪpɪ] *s* estereotipia
**stereo viewer** *s* verascopio (*estereoscopio para diapositivas*)
**stereovision** ['sterɪoˌvɪʒən] o ['stɪrɪoˌvɪʒən] *s* estereovisión
**sterile** ['sterɪl] *adj* estéril
**sterility** [stə'rɪlɪtɪ] *s* (*pl:* **-ties**) esterilidad
**sterilization** [ˌsterɪlɪ'zeʃən] *s* esterilización
**sterilize** ['sterɪlaɪz] *va* esterilizar
**sterilizer** ['sterɪˌlaɪzər] *s* esterilizador (*persona y aparato*)
**sterling** ['stʌrlɪŋ] *s* libras esterlinas; plata de ley; vajilla de plata; *adj* fino, de ley; verdadero, genuino, puro, excelente
**sterling area** o **bloc** *s* área de la libra esterlina
**sterling silver** *s* plata de ley
**stern** [stʌrn] *s* (naut.) popa; *adj* severo, austero; firme, decidido
**sternal** ['stʌrnəl] *adj* (anat.) esternal
**stern chase** *s* (naut.) caza en que una nave persigue a otra marchando en la estela de ésta
**stern chaser** *s* (naut.) guardatimón
**stern fast** *s* (naut.) codera
**stern gallery** *s* (naut.) galería de popa
**sternmost** ['stʌrnmost] *adj* (naut.) popel
**sternpost** ['stʌrnˌpost] *s* (naut.) codaste
**stern sheets** *spl* (naut.) cámara a popa
**sternum** ['stʌrnəm] *s* (*pl:* **-na** [nə] o **-nums**) (anat.) esternón
**sternutative** [stər'njutətɪv] o [stər'nutətɪv] *adj* estornutativo o estornutatorio
**sternward** ['stʌrnwərd] o **sternwards** ['stʌrnwərdz] *adv* (naut.) a popa, hacia la popa
**sternway** ['stʌrnˌwe] *s* (naut.) cía
**stern-wheeler** ['stʌrnˌhwilər] *s* bote de rueda de paletas a popa
**stertor** ['stʌrtər] *s* estertor
**stertorous** ['stʌrtərəs] *adj* estertoroso
**stet** [stet] *s* (print.) indicación de no suprimir lo ya cancelado; (*pret & pp:* **stetted;** *ger:* **stetting**) *va* (print.) marcar para que no se suprima
**stethoscope** ['steθəskop] *s* (med.) estetoscopio
**stethoscopic** [ˌsteθə'skɑpɪk] *adj* estetoscópico
**stethoscopy** [ste'θɑskəpɪ] *s* (med.) estetoscopia
**stevedore** ['stivədor] *s* (naut.) estibador
**stew** [stju] o [stu] *s* guisado, estofado; **to be in a stew** (coll.) estar apurado; *va* guisar, estofar; *vn* abrasarse; (coll.) estar apurado, estar preocupado; **to stew in one's own juice** cocer en su propia salsa, freír en su aceite
**steward** ['stjuərd] o ['stuərd] *s* administrador; mayordomo, senescal; despensero; camarero (*de buque o avión*)
**stewardess** ['stjuərdɪs] o ['stuərdɪs] *s* mayordoma; camarera (*de buque o avión*); azafata, aeromoza (*de avión*)
**stewardship** ['stjuərdʃɪp] o ['stuərdʃɪp] *s* administración; mayordomía
**stewed fruit** *s* compota de frutas
**stewed tomatoes** *spl* puré de tomates
**stewpan** ['stjuˌpæn] o ['stuˌpæn] *s* cazuela, cacerola
**St. George's Channel** *s* el canal de San Jorge
**St. Gotthard** [sent 'gɑtərd] *s* San Gotardo (*montaña, cuello y túnel*)
**St. Helena** [sent he'linə] *s* Santa Elena (*isla y colonia inglesas en el Atlántico Meridional*)
**sthenic** ['sθenɪk] *adj* (med.) esténico
**stibine** ['stɪbin] o ['stɪbɪn] *s* (chem.) estibina
**stibium** ['stɪbɪəm] *s* (chem.) estibio
**stibonium** [stɪ'bonɪəm] *s* (chem.) estibonio
**stick** [stɪk] *s* palillo, palito; vara, bastón; barra (*de dinamita*); (aer.) mango de escoba, palanca de mando; (naut.) mástil, verga; (coll.) bodoque; (coll.) dosis de licor muy fuerte que se añade a una bebida; (print.) componedor; (print.) texto contenido en el componedor; puñalada, estocada; parada, demora; pegadura; **sticks** *spl* (coll.) monte, afueras del poblado ‖ (*pret & pp:* **sticked**) *va* proveer de palo, sostener con un palo; (print.) componer, colocar (*letras*) en el componedor ‖ (*pret & pp:* **stuck**) *va* picar, punzar; apuñalar; clavar, hincar; poner, meter; parar, detener; pegar; (coll.) confundir, aturrullar; **to stick out** asomar (*la cabeza*); sacar (*la lengua*); **to stick up** (slang) atracar, asaltar (*para robar*); **to stick one's hands up** alzar las manos (*en señal de sumisión*) ‖ *vn* estar prendido, estar hincado; pegarse; agarrarse (*la pintura*); encastillarse (*p.ej., una ventana*); asomarse; resaltar, sobresalir; continuar, persistir; permanecer; atascarse; quedarse parado; dudar, vacilar; **to stick around** (slang) quedarse, demorarse; **to stick at** persistir en; sentir escrúpulo por; **to stick at it** persistir; **to stick out** salir (*p.ej., el pañuelo del bolsillo*); sobresalir, proyectarse; velar (*un escollo, peñasco, etc.*); resultar evidente; (coll.) perseverar hasta el fin; **to stick to** aferrarse a, con o en (*p.ej., una opinión*); **to stick together** (coll.) quedarse unidos, no abandonarse; **to stick to one's guns** mantenerse firme, no cejar; **to stick up** destacarse; estar de punta (*el pelo*); **to stick up for** (coll.) defender
**sticker** ['stɪkər] *s* etiqueta engomada, marbete engomado; punta, espina; fijador; persona perseverante; (coll.) misterio, problema arduo
**sticking plaster** *s* esparadrapo
**stick-in-the-mud** ['stɪkɪnðəˌmʌd] *adj & s* perezoso, tardón; conservador, chapado a la antigua
**stick-lac** ['stɪkˌlæk] *s* laca en palo o en rama
**stickle** ['stɪkəl] *vn* porfiar o disputar por menudencias, sentir escrúpulos por menudencias
**stickleback** ['stɪkəlˌbæk] *s* (ichth.) espinoso
**stickler** ['stɪklər] *s* rigorista; problema arduo
**stickpin** ['stɪkˌpɪn] *s* alfiler de corbata
**sticktight** ['stɪkˌtaɪt] *s* (bot.) bidente
**stick-up** ['stɪkˌʌp] *s* (slang) atraco, asalto
**sticky** ['stɪkɪ] *adj* (*comp:* **-ier;** *super:* **-iest**) pegajoso; (coll.) bochornoso; (coll.) húmedo, mojado; (coll.) azucarado, sentimental; (coll.) difícil
**stiff** [stɪf] *adj* tieso; anquilosado (*músculo*); entorpecido, entumecido; arduo, difícil; (coll.) excesivo (*precio*); (fig.) tieso, ceremonioso, severo; *s* (slang) cadáver; (slang) persona tiesa y afectada
**stiff collar** *s* cuello almidonado
**stiffen** ['stɪfən] *va* atiesar; endurecer; espesar; (elec.) aumentar la inductancia de; *vn* atiesarse; endurecerse; espesarse; arrecirse (*de frío*); (fig.) obstinarse
**stiffening** ['stɪfənɪŋ] *s* atiesamiento; atiesador (*lo que pone tieso*)
**stiff-jointed** ['stɪfˌdʒɔɪntɪd] *adj* de junturas rígidas
**stiff neck** *s* tortícolis (*dolor*); obstinación; persona obstinada
**stiff-necked** ['stɪfˌnekt] *adj* terco, obstinado

**stiffness** [ˈstɪfnɪs] *s* tiesura; (fig.) tiesura
**stiff shirt** *s* camisola
**stifle** [ˈstaɪfəl] *s* (vet.) babilla; *va* ahogar, sofocar; apagar, suprimir; *vn* ahogarse, sofocarse
**stifle joint** *s* (vet.) babilla
**stifling** [ˈstaɪflɪŋ] *adj* ahogado, sofocante, bochornoso
**stigma** [ˈstɪgmə] *s* (*pl:* **-mas** o **-mata** [mətə]) (bot., hist., path., zool. & fig.) estigma; **stigmata** *spl* estigmas (*señales de las llagas de Jesucristo*)
**stigmatic** [stɪgˈmætɪk] *adj* estigmático; manchado; deforme; (opt.) anastigmático; *s* (eccl.) estigmático (*persona que presenta los estigmas de Jesucristo*)
**stigmatism** [ˈstɪgmətɪzəm] *s* (opt. & path.) estigmatismo
**stigmatization** [ˌstɪgmətɪˈzeʃən] *s* estigmatización
**stigmatize** [ˈstɪgmətaɪz] *va* estigmatizar
**St.-Ignatius's-bean** [sentɪgˈneʃəsɪzˈbin] *s* haba de San Ignacio
**stile** [staɪl] *s* escalera para atravesar una empalizada, tapia, etc.; torniquete; (arch.) montante
**stiletto** [stɪˈlɛto] *s* (*pl:* **-tos**) estilete, puñal
**still** [stɪl] *adj* inmóvil; quieto, tranquilo; callado, silencioso; bajo, suave; no espumoso; **to hold still** estarse quieto o callado; *adv* tranquilamente; silenciosamente; todavía, aún; *conj* sin embargo, con todo; *s* alambique, destiladera; destilería; vista fija, fotografía de lo inmóvil; (poet.) silencio; *va* acallar, hacer callar; amortiguar; calmar; *vn* callar; calmarse
**stillbirth** [ˈstɪlˌbʌrθ] *s* parto muerto
**stillborn** [ˈstɪlˌbɔrn] *adj* nacido muerto
**still hunt** *s* caza al acecho; empeño secreto o escondido; indagación clandestina; (pol.) solicitación clandestina de votos
**still-hunt** [ˈstɪlˌhʌnt] *va & vn* cazar al acecho, sin perros
**still life** *s* (*pl:* **still lifes** o **still lives**) (paint.) bodegón, naturaleza muerta
**still-life** [ˈstɪlˌlaɪf] *adj* de naturaleza muerta
**stillness** [ˈstɪlnɪs] *s* inmovilidad; tranquilidad, silencio
**Stillson wrench** [ˈstɪlsən] *s* llave Stillson, llave para tubos
**stilly** [ˈstɪlɪ] *adj* (*comp:* **-ier**; *super:* **-iest**) (poet.) quieto, silencioso, calmo; [ˈstɪllɪ] *adv* quietamente, silenciosamente
**stilt** [stɪlt] *s* zanco; pilote (*en el agua*); (orn.) cigoñuela
**stilted** [ˈstɪltɪd] *adj* elevado; tieso, hinchado, pomposo
**stilted arch** *s* (arch.) arco peraltado
**Stilton cheese** [ˈstɪltən] *s* queso Stilton
**stilt sandpiper** *s* (orn.) chorlito palmeado de pico largo
**stimulant** [ˈstɪmjələnt] *adj & s* estimulante
**stimulate** [ˈstɪmjəlet] *va & vn* estimular; **to stimulate to** + *inf* estimular a + *inf*, estimular a que + *subj*
**stimulation** [ˌstɪmjəˈleʃən] *s* estímulo, excitación
**stimulative** [ˈstɪmjəˌletɪv] *adj* estimulador; *s* estímulo
**stimulus** [ˈstɪmjələs] *s* (*pl:* **-li** [laɪ]) estímulo
**sting** [stɪŋ] *s* picadura; picazón (*dolor*); estímulo; (bot. & zool.) aguijón; (*pret & pp:* **stung**) *va* picar, pinchar, punzar; aguijonear, espolear; **to sting to the quick** herir en lo vivo; *vn* picar
**stingaree** [ˈstɪŋəri] *s* (ichth.) pastinaca
**stingbull** [ˈstɪŋˌbul] *s* (ichth.) pez víbora, araña
**stinger** [ˈstɪŋər] *s* aguijón, púa (*de un animal o planta*); (coll.) dicho mordaz
**stinginess** [ˈstɪndʒɪnɪs] *s* ahorratividad, tacañería, mezquindad; escasez
**sting ray** *s* (ichth.) pastinaca
**stingy** [ˈstɪndʒɪ] *adj* (*comp:* **-gier**; *super:* **-giest**) avariento, mezquino, tacaño; escaso, poco; [ˈstɪŋɪ] *adj* (*comp:* **-ier**; *super:* **-iest**) picante, punzante; aguijonado
**stink** [stɪŋk] *s* hedor, mal olor; **to raise a stink** (slang) armar una trapisonda; (*pret:* **stank** o **stunk**; *pp:* **stunk**) *va* dar mal olor a, hacer oler mal; **to stink out** ahuyentar con humo o vapores hediondos; *vn* heder, oler muy mal; (fig.) tener muy mala reputación; **to stink in one's nostrils** repugnar muchísmo; **to stink of** (slang) poseer (*p.ej., dinero*) en un grado que da asco
**stink bomb** *s* bomba fétida
**stinkbug** [ˈstɪŋkˌbʌg] *s* (ent.) chinche de jardín
**stinker** [ˈstɪŋkər] *s* pebete (*cosa hedionda*); persona hedionda; (orn.) petrel gigante; (slang) sinvergüenza, canalla
**stinking camomile** *s* (bot.) manzanilla fétida o hedionda
**stinking iris** *s* (bot.) lirio hediondo, íride
**stint** [stɪnt] *s* límite, restricción; ahorro; tarea, faena; *va* limitar, restringir; *vn* ser económico, ahorrar con mezquindad
**stipe** [staɪp] *s* (bot. & zool.) estipe
**stipel** [ˈstaɪpəl] *s* (bot.) estipulilla
**stipend** [ˈstaɪpɛnd] *s* estipendio; *va* estipendiar
**stipendiary** [staɪˈpɛndɪˌɛrɪ] *adj* estipendiario; *s* (*pl:* **-ies**) estipendiario
**stipple** [ˈstɪpəl] *s* graneo, punteado; *va & vn* granear, puntear
**stippling** [ˈstɪplɪŋ] *s* graneo, punteado
**stipular** [ˈstɪpjələr] *adj* (bot.) estipular
**stipulate** [ˈstɪpjəlet] *adj* (bot.) estipulado; *va* estipular
**stipulation** [ˌstɪpjəˈleʃən] *s* estipulación
**stipule** [ˈstɪpjul] *s* (bot.) estípula
**stir** [stʌr] *s* agitación, movimiento, meneo; alboroto, tumulto; empuje, hurgonada; **to create a stir** hacer o meter ruido; (*pret & pp:* **stirred**; *ger:* **stirring**) *va* mover, agitar; revolver; excitar, emocionar, conmover; atizar o avivar (*el fuego*); remover (*un líquido*); **to stir up** revolver; despertar; excitar, conmover; fomentar, suscitar (*discordias, rebeliones, etc.*); *vn* moverse, bullirse, agitarse; tener lugar; (coll.) estar levantado
**stirps** [stʌrps] *s* (*pl:* **stirpes** [ˈstʌrpiz]) estirpe; progenitor
**stirring** [ˈstʌrɪŋ] *adj* activo, despierto; conmovedor, emocionante
**stirrup** [ˈstʌrəp] o [ˈstɪrəp] *s* estribo
**stirrup bone** *s* (anat.) estribo
**stirrup cup** *s* trago de partida, copa de despedida
**stirrup pump** *s* (Brit.) bomba de mano
**stirrup strap** *s* ación
**stitch** [stɪtʃ] *s* punto, puntada; pedazo de tela; (coll.) pizca, poquito; punzada, dolor punzante; **to be in stitches** (coll.) desternillarse de risa; *va* coser, bastear, hilvanar, unir, puntear, dar puntadas en; *vn* coser, bordar
**stithy** [ˈstɪðɪ] o [ˈstɪθɪ] *s* (*pl:* **-ies**) yunque; herrería
**St. John Lateran** *s* San Juan de Letrán (*iglesia*)
**St.-John's-wort** [sentˈdʒɑnzˌwʌrt] *s* (bot.) hierba de San Juan
**St. Lawrence** [sent ˈlɔrəns] o [sent ˈlɑrəns] *s* San Lorenzo (*río*)
**stoat** [stot] *s* (zool.) armiño de verano; (zool.) comadreja
**stock** [stɑk] *s* surtido, existencias; capital comercial; acciones, valores; caldo (*de carne*); ganado; tronco (*p.ej., de árbol*); cepo (*del yunque*); cepa (*de tronco de árbol*); palo, madero; leño; mango, manija; culata, caja (*de fusil*); (naut.) cepo (*del ancla*); materias primas; alzacuello; familia, estirpe; (bot.) patrón (*en que se injerta una rama*); (bot.) injerto; (bot.) alhelí; (mach.) terraja; (theat.) programa, repertorio; (fig.) tronco (*persona torpe*); **stocks** *spl* cepo, corma (*castigo*); (naut.) astillero, grada de construcción; potro (*para sujetar los caballos para herrarlos*); **in stock** en existencia, en almacén; **on the stocks** en preparación; (naut.) en vía de construcción; **out of stock** agotado; **to take stock** hacerse el inventario; **to take stock in** (coll.) interesarse en, sentir interés por; dar importancia a; (coll.) confiar en; (com.) comprar acciones de ‖ *adj* común, regular; consagrado; banal, vulgar; (theat.) de repertorio; bursátil; ganadero, del ganado ‖ *va* surtir, abastecer; tener en existencias, tener existencias de; encepar; acumular, acopiar; sembrar hierba en; poblar (*un estanque, una colmena, etc.*)

**stockade** [stɑ'ked] *s* estacada, empalizada, palanquera; *va* empalizar
**stockbreeder** ['stɑk,bridər] *s* criador de ganado
**stockbroker** ['stɑk,brokər] *s* bolsista, corredor de bolsa, agente de bolsa, agente de cambio
**stockbrokerage** ['stɑk,brokərɪdʒ] o **stockbroking** ['stɑk,brokɪŋ] *s* correduría de bolsa
**stock car** *s* (rail.) vagón para el ganado; (aut.) coche de serie
**stock company** *s* (com.) sociedad anónima; (theat.) teatro de repertorio
**stock dividend** *s* dividendo en acciones
**stock dove** *s* (orn.) paloma brava o silvestre
**stock exchange** *s* bolsa
**stock farm** *s* hacienda de ganado
**stockfish** ['stɑk,fɪʃ] *s* pescado aplastado y secado al aire sin salar
**stockholder** ['stɑk,holdər] *s* accionista, tenedor de acciones
**stockholder of record** *s* accionista que como tal figura en el libro-registro de la compañía
**Stockholm** ['stɑkhom] *s* Estocolmo
**stockinet** [,stɑkɪ'nɛt] *s* elástica, tela de punto
**stocking** ['stɑkɪŋ] *s* media; **in one's stocking feet** con medias pero sin zapatos
**stock in trade** *s* artículos que se venden en una tienda; existencias de un comercio; útiles, herramienta; recursos
**stockjobber** ['stɑk,dʒɑbər] *s* corredor de bolsa; agente de corredores de bolsa
**stockman** ['stɑk,mæn] *s* (*pl:* **-men**) ganadero; almacenero, almacenista
**stock market** *s* bolsa, mercado de valores; **to play the stock market** jugar en bolsa, jugar a la bolsa
**stockpile** ['stɑk,paɪl] *s* reserva de materias primas; acopio de materiales estratégicos; *va* acumular, reunir (*materias primas*); hacer acopio de (*materiales estratégicos*); *vn* acumular, reunir materias primas; hacer acopio de materiales estratégicos
**stockpiling** ['stɑk,paɪlɪŋ] *s* almacenaje de reservas; acumulación de materiales estratégicos
**stock raising** *s* ganadería
**stockroom** ['stɑk,rum] o ['stɑk,rʊm] *s* almacén; sala de exposición para los viajantes en los hoteles
**stock split** *s* (com.) división de las acciones de una empresa en nuevas acciones de menor valor
**stock-still** ['stɑk'stɪl] *adj* completamente inmóvil
**stocktaking** ['stɑk,tekɪŋ] *s* (el) inventariar
**stocky** ['stɑkɪ] *adj* (*comp:* **-ier;** *super:* **-iest**) bajo, grueso y fornido
**stockyard** ['stɑk,jɑrd] *s* corral de concentración de ganado
**stodgy** ['stɑdʒɪ] *adj* (*comp:* **-ier;** *super:* **-iest**) pesado, indigesto, aburrido; repleto, muy lleno, rollizo
**stogie** o **stogy** ['stogɪ] *s* (*pl:* **-gies**) cigarro barato, largo y delgado
**stoic** ['sto·ɪk] *adj & s* estoico; (*cap.*) *adj & s* estoico
**stoical** ['sto·ɪkəl] *adj* estoico
**stoicheiology** [,stɔɪkɪ'ɑlədʒɪ] *s* var. de **stoichiology**
**stoicheiometry** [,stɔɪkɪ'ɑmɪtrɪ] *s* var. de **stoichiometry**
**stoichiology** [,stɔɪkɪ'ɑlədʒɪ] *s* estequiología
**stoichiometry** [,stɔɪkɪ'ɑmɪtrɪ] *s* estequiometría
**stoicism** ['sto·ɪsɪzəm] *s* estoicismo; (*cap.*) *s* estoicismo
**stoke** [stok] *va* atizar, avivar (*el fuego*); cebar, alimentar (*un horno*); *vn* atizar el fuego; cebar el horno; (fig.) comer
**stokehold** ['stok,hold] *s* (naut.) cuarto de calderas; (naut.) boca del horno
**stokehole** ['stok,hol] *s* boca del horno; plataforma del fogonero
**stoker** ['stokər] *s* fogonero; alimentador de hogar (*aparato*)
**stole** [stol] *s* estola; *pret de* **steal**
**stolen** ['stolən] *pp de* **steal**
**stolen base** *s* (baseball) base robada
**stolid** ['stɑlɪd] *adj* impasible, insensible
**stolidity** [stə'lɪdɪtɪ] *s* (*pl:* **-ties**) impasibilidad, insensibilidad
**stolon** ['stolɑn] *s* (bot. & zool.) estolón
**stoma** ['stomə] *s* (*pl:* **stomata** ['stomətə] o ['stɑmətə]) (anat., bot. & zool.) estoma
**stomach** ['stʌmək] *s* (anat.) estómago; barriga, vientre; apetito; deseo, inclinación; **to turn the stomach** revolver el estómago, dar asco; *va* tragar (*recibir en el estómago; aguantar, tolerar*)
**stomacher** ['stʌməkər] *s* peto
**stomachic** [sto'mækɪk] *adj* estomacal; *s* (med.) estomacal
**stomach pump** *s* bomba estomacal
**stomate** ['stomet] *adj* provisto de estoma o estomas; *s* (bot.) estoma
**stomatic** [sto'mætɪk] *adj* estomático (*perteneciente a la boca*)
**stomatitis** [,stomə'taɪtɪs] *s* (path.) estomatitis
**stomatology** [,stomə'tɑlədʒɪ] *s* estomatología
**stomatoplasty** ['stomətə,plæstɪ] *s* estomatoplastia
**stone** [ston] *s* piedra; hueso (*de la fruta*); (path.) piedra o cálculo; (path.) mal de piedra; (Brit.) 14 libras (*peso*); **to cast the first stone** lanzar la primera piedra; **to leave no stone unturned** no dejar piedra por mover; *va* revestir de piedra; lapidar, apedrear; deshuesar
**Stone Age** *s* (archeol.) edad de piedra
**stone-blind** ['ston'blaɪnd] *adj* completamente ciego
**stone-broke** ['ston'brok] *adj* (slang) arrancado, sin blanca
**stone bruise** *s* contusión producida por una piedra bajo la planta del pie; (aut.) rotura superficial (*de un neumático*) producida por una piedra
**stonechat** ['ston,tʃæt] *s* (orn.) culiblanco
**stonecrop** ['ston,krɑp] *s* (bot.) pan de cuco
**stone crusher** *s* quebradora de roca, trituradora
**stone curlew** *s* (orn.) alcaraván
**stonecutter** ['ston,kʌtər] *s* cantero, picapedrero; máquina de labrar piedras
**stone-deaf** ['ston'dɛf] *adj* sordo como una tapia
**stone fruit** *s* (bot.) drupa, fruta de hueso
**stone marten** *s* (zool.) garduña
**stonemason** ['ston,mesən] *s* albañil; cantero
**stone pine** *s* (bot.) pino piñonero (*Pinus pinea*); (bot.) pino cembro
**stone's throw** *s* tiro de piedra; **within a stone's throw** a tiro de piedra
**stoneware** ['ston,wɛr] *s* gres
**stonework** ['ston,wʌrk] *s* cantería, obra de sillería
**stoneworker** ['ston,wʌrkər] *s* cantero, picapedrero
**stoneyard** ['ston,jɑrd] *s* cantería
**stony** ['stonɪ] *adj* (*comp:* **-ier;** *super:* **-iest**) pedregoso; pétreo; empedernido, duro
**stony-hearted** ['stonɪ,hɑrtɪd] *adj* de corazón empedernido
**stood** [stʊd] *pret & pp de* **stand**
**stooge** [studʒ] *s* (slang) preguntador apostado en el auditorio para hacer preguntas preparadas de antemano a un comediante que las contesta de manera divertida para el público; (slang) paniaguado, hombre de paja
**stool** [stul] *s* escabel, banquillo; planta madre; grupo de vástagos; añagaza, señuelo; cimillo (*palo a que se ata el señuelo*); inodoro, sillico, retrete; cámara, evacuación de vientre; solera o repisa de ventana; *vn* brotar, echar tallos; obrar, hacer del cuerpo, exonerar el vientre
**stool pigeon** *s* cimbel (*ave*); soplón, espía
**stoop** [stup] *s* inclinación, encorvada; dignación; descenso rápido; escalinata de entrada; *va* inclinar, bajar; *vn* doblarse, inclinarse, encorvarse; andar encorvado; humillarse, rebajarse; bajar rápidamente sobre la presa; **to stoop to** + *inf* rebajarse a + *inf*
**stoop-shouldered** ['stup'ʃoldərd] *adj* cargado de espaldas
**stop** [stɑp] *s* parada, alto, pausa; estada, estancia; detención; fin, cesación, suspensión; cerradura, tapadura; obstáculo, impedimento; freno; tope, retén, paleta, fiador; (mus.) llave, traste (*de guitarra*); (mus.) registro (*de órgano*); (gram.) punto; (phonet.) oclusión; (phonet.) consonante oclusiva; punto (*en los tele-*

*gramas*); **to put a stop to** poner fin a ‖ (*pret & pp:* **stopped;** *ger:* **stopping**) *va* parar, detener; acabar, terminar; estorbar, obstruir; interceptar, interrumpir, suspender; cerrar, tapar; rechazar (*un golpe*); retener (*un sueldo o parte de él*); (sport) poner fuera de combate; **to stop up** tapar, obstruir, cegar ‖ *vn* parar, pararse, detenerse; quedarse, permanecer; hospedarse, alojarse; acabarse, terminarse; **to stop** + *ger* cesar de, dejar de + *inf;* **to stop at** pararse en, hospedarse en; **to stop at nothing** no pararse en escrúpulos; **to stop off** quedarse un poco; **to stop over** quedarse un poco; detenerse durante un viaje; **to stop short** pararse de sopetón, detenerse de golpe; **to stop to** + *inf* detenerse a + *inf*

**stopcock** [ˈstapˌkak] *s* llave de cierre, llave de paso

**stope** [stop] *s* (min.) grada, obra en escalones; *va & vn* (min.) excavar en escalones

**stopgap** [ˈstapˌgæp] *s* tapadero; substituto provisional; *adj* provisional

**stop light** *s* luz de parada, luz de paro

**stop-loss order** [ˈstapˌlɔs] o [ˈstapˌlas] *s* orden a un corredor de Bolsa para que compre o venda al ser alcanzada determinada cotización

**stopover** [ˈstapˌovər] *s* (rail.) parada intermedia, billete de parada intermedia

**stoppage** [ˈstapɪdʒ] *s* parada, detención; cesación; interrupción, interceptación; suspensión; obstrucción; obstáculo; resistencia; retención (*de un sueldo o parte de él*); embargo por el vendedor de mercancías en tránsito; (path.) obstrucción

**stop payment** *s* orden a un banco de detener el pago de un cheque

**stopper** [ˈstapər] *s* tapón; tapador; taco, tarugo; (naut.) boza; *va* entaponar

**stopple** [ˈstapəl] *s* tapón; *va* entaponar

**stop sign** o **stop signal** *s* señal de alto, señal de parada

**stop watch** *s* reloj de segundos muertos, cronómetro

**storage** [ˈstorɪdʒ] *s* almacenaje, depósito; (aut.) pupilaje

**storage battery** *s* (elec.) acumulador

**storage space** *s* espacio de almacenaje

**storax** [ˈstoræks] *s* (bot.) estoraque (*árbol y bálsamo*)

**store** [stor] *s* tienda; almacén; provisión, repuesto; **I know what is in store for you** sé lo que le espera a Vd.; **to have in store** tener guardado, tener reservado; **to set store by** dar mucha importancia a, confiarse en; *va* abastecer; tener guardado, tener en reserva, almacenar; **to store away** acumular

**storehouse** [ˈstorˌhaʊs] *s* almacén, depósito; (fig.) mina (*p.ej., de sabiduría*)

**storekeeper** [ˈstorˌkipər] *s* guardaalmacén; tendero; (naut.) pañolero

**storeroom** [ˈstorˌrum] o [ˈstorˌrʊm] *s* cuarto de almacenar; (naut.) despensa, pañol de víveres

**storey** [ˈstorɪ] *s* piso

**storied** [ˈstorɪd] *adj* celebrado en la historia; (f.a.) historiado (*cuadro, dibujo, etc.*); de (*tantos*) pisos, p.ej., **two-storied house** casa de dos pisos

**storiette** [ˌstorɪˈɛt] *s* cuentecillo

**stork** [stɔrk] *s* (orn.) cigüeña; **to have a visit from the stork** (fig.) recibir a la cigüeña

**stork's-bill** [ˈstɔrkzˌbɪl] *s* (bot.) geranio; (bot.) pico de cigüeña

**storm** [stɔrm] *s* tormenta, tempestad, borrasca; huracán, vendaval; (mil.) asalto; (naut.) borrasca; (fig.) tempestad, agitación, tumulto; **to take by storm** tomar por asalto; *va* asaltar; *vn* tempestear, haber tormenta, haber tempestad; (fig.) tempestear (*rabiar, impacientarse*); (fig.) precipitarse

**storm cellar** *s* sótano que sirve de asilo durante las tempestades

**storm center** *s* centro de la tempestad, zona de presión mínima; (fig.) centro de la agitación

**storm cloud** *s* nubarrón

**storm door** *s* contrapuerta, guardapuerta, cancel

**storm hood** *s* pasamontaña

**storm troops** *spl* tropas de asalto

**storm window** *s* sobrevidriera

**stormy** [ˈstɔrmɪ] *adj* (*comp:* **-ier;** *super:* **-iest**) borrascoso, tempestuoso; (fig.) borrascoso, turbulento, violento

**stormy petrel** *s* (orn.) petrel de la tempestad; (fig.) persona pendenciera, persona que anuncia el mal

**story** [ˈstorɪ] *s* (*pl:* **-ries**) historia, historieta, cuento, anécdota; trama, enredo, argumento; (coll.) mentira, embuste; piso, alto; (*pret & pp:* **-ried**) *va* historiar

**storyteller** [ˈstorɪˌtɛlər] *s* narrador; (coll.) mentiroso, embustero

**storytelling** [ˈstorɪˌtɛlɪŋ] *s* narración de cuentos; (coll.) mentira, impostura, embustes

**stoup** [stup] *s* copa, frasco; (eccl.) pila de agua bendita

**stout** [staʊt] *adj* corpulento, gordo, robusto, fornido; animoso, valiente; leal; terco, obstinado; *s* cerveza obscura fuerte

**stout-hearted** [ˈstaʊtˌhartɪd] *adj* valiente, intrépido

**stoutness** [ˈstaʊtnɪs] *s* corpulencia, gordura, robustez; ánimo, valor; obstinación

**stove** [stov] *s* estufa (*para calentar*); hornillo, cocina de gas, cocina eléctrica; invernáculo, estufa; horno cerámico; cuarto de secar; *pret & pp de* **stave**

**stovepipe** [ˈstovˌpaɪp] *s* tubo de estufa, tubo de hornillo; (coll.) chistera, chimenea (*sombrero*)

**stow** [sto] *va* meter, guardar, esconder; (naut.) estibar, arrumar; (slang) acabar con; *vn* (naut.) estar arrumado; **to stow away** esconderse en un barco o avión, embarcarse clandestinamente

**stowage** [ˈsto·ɪdʒ] *s* (naut.) estiba, arrumaje; (naut.) bodega

**stowaway** [ˈstoəˌwe] *s* polizón, pasajero clandestino, llovido

**St. Peter's** *s* San Pedro de Roma (*basílica*)

**St. Petersburg** [sent ˈpitərzbʌrg] *s* San Petersburgo

**str.** abr. de **strait** y **steamer**

**strabismal** [strəˈbɪzməl] o **strabismic** [strəˈbɪzmɪk] *adj* estrábico

**strabismus** [strəˈbɪzməs] *s* (path.) estrabismo

**Strabo** [ˈstrebo] *s* Estrabón

**strabotomy** [strəˈbatəmɪ] *s* (*pl:* **-mies**) (surg.) estrabotomía

**straddle** [ˈstrædəl] *s* separación de las piernas, esparrancamiento; *va* montar a horcajadas; (coll.) favorecer a ambos lados en (*un pleito, controversia, etc.*); *vn* ponerse a horcajadas; esparrancarse; (coll.) favorecer a ambos lados

**Stradivarius** [ˌstrædɪˈvɛrɪəs] *s* Estradivario; estradivario (*violín*)

**strafe** [straf] o [stref] *s* (slang) bombardeo violento; *va* (slang) bombardear violentamente

**straggle** [ˈstrægəl] *vn* vagar, errar; extraviarse, andar perdido; separarse; estar esparcido

**straggler** [ˈstræglər] *s* extraviado; rezagado; rama extendida; objeto aislado

**straggly** [ˈstræglɪ] *adj* dispersado por todas partes, desordenado

**straight** [stret] *adj* derecho; recto; erguido; lacio (*cabello*); seguido, continuo; sincero, honrado; exacto, correcto; decidido, intransigente; solo (*p.ej., whisky*); en orden; **to set a person straight** mostrar el camino a una persona; mostrar a una persona el modo de proceder; dar consejo a una persona; *adv* derecho, derechamente; sin interrupción; sinceramente, con franqueza; exactamente; en seguida; **to go straight** (coll.) enmendarse; **to talk straight from the shoulder** hablar con toda franqueza; **straight ahead** todo derecho, todo seguido; *s* rectitud; recta (*de un camino*); (poker) escalera

**straight angle** *s* ángulo derecho

**straight-arm** [ˈstretˌarm] *va* (football) rechazar (*al adversario*) tendiendo los brazos

**straight away** *adv* luego, en seguida

**straightaway** [ˈstretəˌwe] *s* derechera, parte recta de un camino; (rail.) recta; *adj* derecho, directo, en línea recta

**straightedge** [ˈstretˌɛdʒ] *s* regla de borde recto

**straighten** [ˈstretən] *va* enderezar; arreglar, poner en orden; *vn* enderezarse; **to straighten up** enderezarse

**straight face** *s* cara seria
**straightforward** [ˌstretˈfɔrwərd] *adj* franco, sincero; honrado; derecho, recto, en línea recta; *adv* en derechura
**straightforwards** [ˌstretˈfɔrwərdz] *adv* en derechura
**straight grain** *s* veta recta, fibra derecha
**straight-grained** [ˈstretˌgrend] *adj* veteado en línea recta
**straight line** *s* recta, línea recta
**straight man** *s* (coll.) actor cuyas preguntas, hechas con cara seria, ponen de relieve los chistes de un actor cómico
**straight off** *adv* luego, en seguida
**straight-out** [ˈstretˌaʊt] *adv* (coll.) cabal, completo, entero
**straight ticket** *s* (pol.) candidatura completa
**straightway** [ˈstretˌwe] *adv* luego, inmediatamente
**strain** [stren] *s* tensión, tirantez; esfuerzo muy grande; agotamiento, fatiga excesiva; torcedura (*de un músculo*); (mach.) deformación; aire, melodía; cepa (*de una familia o linaje*); raza, linaje, rasgo racial; vena, genio; traza, huella, rastro; clase (*de plantas o animales*); *va* estirar, tender con fuerza, poner tirante, hacer fuerza a; torcer o torcerse (*p.ej., la muñeca*); forzar (*los nervios, la vista, etc.*); apretar, exprimir; deformar; colar, tamizar; *vn* esforzarse, hacer un esfuerzo excesivo; deformarse; colarse, tamizarse; filtrarse; exprimirse (*un jugo*); poner dificultades, resistirse; **to strain at** hacer grandes esfuerzos por
**strained** [strend] *adj* forzado (*dícese, p.ej., de una risa*); tirante (*dícese de las relaciones de amistad*)
**strainer** [ˈstrenər] *s* colador
**strait** [stret] *s* (geog.) estrecho; **straits** *spl* (geog.) estrecho; aprieto, apuro; **to be in dire straits** estar en el mayor apuro, hallarse en gran estrechez
**straiten** [ˈstretən] *va* estrechar, contraer, rodear; apremiar, embarazar; **in straitened circumstances** estrecho de medios
**strait jacket** *s* camisa de fuerza
**strait-laced** [ˈstretˌlest] *adj* gazmoño, estrecho de conciencia
**Strait of Dover** *s* Paso de Calais
**Strait of Gibraltar** *s* estrecho de Gibraltar
**Strait of Magellan** *s* estrecho de Magallanes
**Straits Settlements** *spl* Establecimientos de los Estrechos (*Malaca*)
**strake** [strek] *s* (naut.) traca
**stramonium** [strəˈmonɪəm] *s* (bot.) estramonio; (pharm.) daturina
**strand** [strænd] *s* playa, ribera; hebra, filamento; torón, ramal (*de cuerda, cable, etc.*); hilo (*de perlas*); pelo; (poet.) tierra lejana; *va* deshebrar, deshilar; trenzar, retorcer (*cuerda, cable, etc.*); zurcir (*una media o calceta*); dejar perdido o desamparado; (naut.) varar; *vn* andar perdido o desamparado; (naut.) varar, encallar
**stranded** [ˈstrændɪd] *adj* encallado (*buque*); desprovisto, desamparado; en cordones, trenzado, retorcido (*dícese de la cuerda, cable o alambre*)
**strange** [strendʒ] *adj* extraño; esquivo, retraído; nuevo, desconocido; novel, no acostumbrado
**strangeness** [ˈstrendʒnɪs] *s* extrañeza, rareza; esquivez; novedad; maravilla
**stranger** [ˈstrendʒər] *s* forastero; visitador; intruso; desconocido; principiante; **to be no stranger to** no ser ignorante de, no desconocer
**strangle** [ˈstræŋgəl] *va* estrangular; reprimir, suprimir; *vn* estrangularse
**strangle hold** *s* (sport) collar de fuerza; (fig.) aprieto, opresión, dominio completo
**strangulate** [ˈstræŋgjəlet] *va* (path. & surg.) estrangular
**strangulated hernia** *s* (path.) hernia estrangulada
**strangulation** [ˌstræŋgjəˈleʃən] *s* estrangulación; (path. & surg.) estrangulación
**strangullion** [strænˈgʌljən] *s* (vet.) estrangol
**strangury** [ˈstræŋgjərɪ] *s* (path.) estangurria o estranguria
**S trap** *s* sifón en S
**strap** [stræp] *s* correa (*de cuero*); banda, tira (*de tela, metal, etc.*); trabilla (*debajo del zapato*); asentador (*para afilar las navajas*); (*pret & pp:* **strapped;** *ger:* **strapping**) *va* atar o liar con correa, banda o tira; azotar con una correa; fajar, vendar; asentar (*una navaja*)
**straphanger** [ˈstræpˌhæŋər] *s* (coll.) pasajero colgado (*pasajero agarrado a las anillas de soporte*)
**strap iron** *s* fleje, flejes
**strapped** [stræpt] *adj* (slang) alcanzado
**strapper** [ˈstræpər] *s* atador; mozo de cuadra; asentador; (coll.) persona alta y fuerte; (slang) mentira enorme
**strapping** [ˈstræpɪŋ] *adj* (coll.) alto y fuerte; (coll.) enorme, grandísimo
**Strasbourg** o **Strassburg** [ˈstræsbʌrg] *s* Estrasburgo
**stratagem** [ˈstrætədʒəm] *s* estratagema
**strategic** [strəˈtidʒɪk] *adj* estratégico; **strategics** *ssg* estrategia
**strategical** [strəˈtidʒɪkəl] *adj* estratégico
**strategist** [ˈstrætɪdʒɪst] *s* estratega
**strategy** [ˈstrætɪdʒɪ] *s* (*pl:* **-gies**) estrategia
**stratification** [ˌstrætɪfɪˈkeʃən] *s* estratificación
**stratify** [ˈstrætɪfaɪ] (*pret & pp:* **-fied**) *va* estratificar; *vn* estratificarse
**stratigraphic** [ˌstrætɪˈgræfɪk] o **stratigraphical** [ˌstrætɪˈgræfɪkəl] *adj* estratigráfico
**stratigraphy** [strəˈtɪgrəfɪ] *s* estratigrafía
**stratocruiser** [ˈstrætoˌkruzər] *s* transaéreo estratosférico
**strato-cumulus** [ˌstretoˈkjumjələs] *s* (*pl:* **-li** [laɪ]) (meteor.) estratocúmulo
**stratoliner** [ˈstrætoˌlaɪnər] *s* transaéreo estratosférico
**stratosphere** [ˈstrætəsfɪr] o [ˈstretəsfɪr] *s* estratosfera
**stratospheric** [ˌstrætəsˈfɛrɪk] o [ˌstretəsˈfɛrɪk] *adj* estratosférico
**stratovision** [ˈstrætəˌvɪʒən] *s* estratovisión
**stratum** [ˈstretəm] o [ˈstrætəm] *s* (*pl:* **-ta** [tə] o **-tums**) (anat. & geol.) estrato; clase, categoría (*de la sociedad*)
**stratus** [ˈstretəs] *s* (*pl:* **-ti** [taɪ]) (meteor.) estrato
**straw** [strɔ] *s* paja; pajita (*para beber*); chispazo (*indicación*); **I don't care a straw** no se me da un bledo; **to be the last straw** ser el colmo; **to catch at a straw** obrar con desesperación; *adj* pajizo; baladí, de poca importancia; falso, ficticio
**straw ballot** *s* var. de **straw vote**
**strawberry** [ˈstrɔˌbɛrɪ] *s* (*pl:* **-ries**) (bot.) fresa (*planta y fruto*)
**strawberry patch** *s* fresal
**strawberry shortcake** *s* torta de fresa, ponqué de fresa
**strawberry tomato** *s* (bot.) tomate de invierno
**strawberry tree** *s* (bot.) madroño; (bot.) bonetero
**strawboard** [ˈstrɔˌbord] *s* cartón de paja
**straw hat** *s* sombrero de paja; canotié (*el de copa plana y baja*)
**straw man** *s* figura de paja; testaferro; testigo falso; persona de poca monta
**straw vote** *s* voto informativo
**strawy** [ˈstrɔ·ɪ] *adj* (*comp:* **-ier;** *super:* **-iest**) pajizo; baladí
**stray** [stre] *adj* perdido, extraviado; disperso, aislado, suelto; (elec.) parásito; *s* vagabundo; animal perdido o extraviado; **strays** *spl* (rad.) ruidos parásitos; *vn* perderse, extraviarse
**streak** [strik] *s* raya, lista; vena, veta; traza, rasgo; rayo (*de luz*); (coll.) tiempo muy breve; racha (*de fortuna*); **like a streak** (coll.) como un rayo; *va* rayar, listar; abigarrar; *vn* rayarse; (coll.) andar o pasar como un rayo
**streaky** [ˈstrikɪ] *adj* (*comp:* **-ier;** *super:* **-iest**) rayado, listado, veteado; abigarrado; desigual, irregular
**stream** [strim] *s* corriente; río, arroyo; flujo, chorro; torrente (*de personas*); desfile (*de autos*); **against the stream** contra la corriente; *va* arrojar, derramar; hacer ondear; (min.) lavar con un chorro de agua; *vn* correr, manar (*un líquido*); chorrear; ondear, flotar; correr rápidamente; **to stream out** salir a torrentes
**streamer** [ˈstrimər] *s* flámula; cinta ondeante; rayo de luz, faja de luz; cola o cabellera de co-

meta; extensión de la corona solar (*durante los eclipses de Sol*); título que ocupa todo el ancho del periódico
**streamlet** ['strimlɪt] *s* arroyuelo; hilo de agua
**streamline** ['strim,laɪn] *s* línea aerodinámica; *adj* aerodinámico; *va* aerodinamizar, hacer aerodinámico
**streamlined** ['strim,laɪnd] *adj* aerodinámico, perfilado
**streamliner** ['strim,laɪnər] *s* tren aerodinámico de lujo
**street** [strit] *s* calle; *adj* callejero
**street Arab** *s* pillete de calle
**streetcar** ['strit,kɑr] *s* tranvía
**street cleaner** *s* basurero; barredera (*aparato*)
**street cleaning** *s* limpieza de calles, servicio de riego
**street clothes** *spl* traje de calle
**street floor** *s* piso bajo
**street lamp** *s* farol (de la calle)
**street lighting** *s* alumbrado público
**street railway** *s* tranvía, ferrocarril urbano
**street sprinkler** *s* carricuba, carro de riego, regadera
**street sweeper** *s* barredera, raspadora
**streetwalker** ['strit,wɔkər] *s* cantonera, carrerista, prostituta de calle
**strength** [strɛŋθ] *s* fuerza; intensidad; (mil.) número (*de soldados o fuerzas militares*); (com.) tendencia a la subida; **by main strength** con todas sus fuerzas; **on the strength of** fundándose en; confiando en
**strengthen** ['strɛŋθən] *va* fortificar, reforzar, fortalecer; confirmar, corroborar; *vn* fortificarse, reforzarse, fortalecerse
**strenuous** ['strɛnjuəs] *adj* estrenuo, vigoroso; arduo, difícil, activo
**streptococcic** [,strɛptə'kɑksɪk] *adj* estreptocócico
**streptococcus** [,strɛptə'kɑkəs] *s* (*pl:* **-cocci** ['kɑksaɪ]) (bact.) estreptococo
**streptomycin** [,strɛpto'maɪsɪn] *s* (pharm.) estreptomicina
**streptotrichin** [strɛp'tɑtrɪkɪn] *s* (pharm.) estreptotricina
**stress** [strɛs] *s* tensión, fuerza, esfuerzo; compulsión; importancia; acento; (mech.) tensión (*resistencia molecular a fuerzas exteriores*); **to lay stress on** o **upon** hacer hincapié en; *va* someter a esfuerzo, ejercer coerción sobre; hacer hincapié en; acentuar
**stress accent** *s* acento prosódico
**stretch** [strɛtʃ] *s* estiramiento, estirón; trecho (*distancia de lugar o tiempo*); tramo (*de carretera*); tensión, extensión; esfuerzo (*de la imaginación*); (slang) condena (*extensión de la pena*); **at a stretch** de un tirón, p.ej., **three hours at a stretch** tres horas de un tirón; *va* estirar; alargar, extender; tender; forzar, violentar; (fig.) estirar (*el dinero*); **to stretch a point** hacer una concesión; **to stretch oneself** desperezarse; *vn* estirarse; alargarse, extenderse; tenderse; desperezarse; **to stretch out** echarse
**stretcher** ['strɛtʃər] *s* ensanchador (*para los guantes*); camilla (*para los heridos y enfermos*); (mas.) soga; (mach.) tensor, estirador; (paint.) bastidor
**stretcher-bearer** ['strɛtʃər,bɛrər] *s* camillero
**stretchy** ['strɛtʃɪ] *adj* (coll.) estirable, extensible; (coll.) propenso a desperezarse
**strew** [stru] (*pret:* **strewed**; *pp:* **strewed** o **strewn**) *va* esparcir, derramar; sembrar, salpicar; polvorear
**strewn** [strun] *pp de* **strew**
**stria** ['straɪə] *s* (*pl:* **-ae** [i]) estría; (arch. & med.) estría
**striated** ['straɪetɪd] *adj* estriado
**striation** [straɪ'eʃən] *s* estriación
**stricken** ['strɪkən] *adj* herido; afligido; inhabilitado; rasado (*con el rasero*); **stricken in age** o **in years** debilitado por los años; *pp de* **strike**
**strickle** ['strɪkəl] *s* rasero; escantillón; *va* rasar
**strict** [strɪkt] *adj* estricto, riguroso
**strictness** ['strɪktnɪs] *s* rigor, severidad, exactitud
**stricture** ['strɪktʃər] *s* crítica severa, censura; (path.) estrictura, estenosis
**stridden** ['strɪdən] *pp de* **stride**
**stride** [straɪd] *s* zancada, trancada, tranco; **to hit one's stride** alcanzar la actividad o velocidad acostumbrada; **to make great** o **rapid strides** avanzar a grandes pasos; **to take in one's stride** hacer sin esfuerzo, hacer con mucha desenvoltura; (*pret:* **strode**; *pp:* **stridden**) *va* pasar a zancadas, cruzar de un tranco; montar a horcajadas; *vn* dar zancadas, andar a trancos, caminar a paso largo
**stridence** ['straɪdəns] o **stridency** ['straɪdənsɪ] *s* estridencia, estridor
**strident** ['straɪdənt] *adj* estridente
**stridor** ['straɪdər] *s* (path.) estridor
**stridulant** ['strɪdʒələnt] *adj* estriduloso
**stridulate** ['strɪdʒəlet] *vn* estridular
**stridulation** [,strɪdʒə'leʃən] *s* estridulación; (zool.) estridulación
**stridulous** ['strɪdʒələs] *adj* estriduloso; (path.) estriduloso
**strife** [straɪf] *s* contienda, refriega; rivalidad, emulación
**strike** [straɪk] *s* golpe; huelga; (min.) descubrimiento repentino; golpe de fortuna; hembra (*de una cerradura*); rasero; (baseball) golpe (*pelota que pasa sobre el puesto meta y entre el hombro y la rodilla del batter*); acto de tragar el anzuelo; (bowling) pleno; **to go on strike** ir a la huelga, ponerse en huelga ‖ (*pret:* **struck**; *pp:* **struck** *o* **stricken**) *va* golpear; pulsar (*una tecla*); herir, percutir; topar, dar con; acuñar (*monedas*); echar (*raíces*); frotar, rayar o encender (*un fósforo*); (min.) descubrir repentinamente; cerrar (*un trato*), hacer (*un pacto*); (naut.) arriar (*las velas*); rasar, nivelar; coger con el anzuelo; arponear; dar (*la hora*); afligir, herir; impresionar; tomar o asumir (*una postura*); quitar de un golpe; borrar, cancelar; **to strike a snag** encontrar un obstáculo; **to strike camp** batir tiendas; **to strike for a loan** dar un sablazo a; **to strike it rich** descubrir un buen filón, tener un golpe de fortuna; **to strike off** quitar de golpe; borrar; deducir; impresionar; (print.) tirar; **to strike one's attention** atraer la atención; **to strike one's fancy** antojársele a uno; **to strike out** borrar, tachar, cancelar; (baseball) hacer golpear mal la pelota tres veces; **to strike up** trabar (*conversación, amistad*); entablar (*una conversación*); empezar a cantar, empezar a tocar; **to strike with terror** sobrecoger de terror ‖ *vn* dar, sonar (*una campana, un reloj*); encenderse (*un fósforo*); declararse o estar en huelga; agarrarse, fijarse; echar raíces; tragar o coger el anzuelo; (mil.) dar el asalto; **to strike at** tratar de golpear; acometer; **to strike out** ponerse en marcha, echar camino adelante; (baseball) golpear mal la pelota tres veces
**strikebreaker** ['straɪk,brekər] *s* rompehuelgas, esquirol
**striker** ['straɪkər] *s* golpeador; huelguista; (mach.) percutor
**striking** ['straɪkɪŋ] *adj* percutor; impresionante, llamativo, sorprendente; en huelga
**striking mechanism** *s* sonería (*del reloj*)
**striking power** *s* potencia de choque, poder ofensivo
**striking range** *s* alcance agresivo
**string** [strɪŋ] *s* cuerdecilla; hilo o hebra fuerte; sarta (*de perlas; de mentiras*); hebra (*de habichuelas*); (arch.) limón; (mus.) cuerda; lazo; (coll.) condición (*de una concesión*); **strings** *spl* (mus.) instrumentos de cuerda; **on a string** en su poder; **to have two strings to one's bow** tener dos cuerdas en su arco; **to pull strings** ejercer su influencia secretamente; utilizar apoyos secretos; (*pret & pp:* **strung**) *va* enhebrar, ensartar; atar con cuerdas; proveer de cuerdas; colgar de una cuerda; tender (*un cable, un alambre*); encordar (*un violín, una raqueta*); templar (*un violín*); desfibrar, quitar las fibras a; extender, colocar en fila; (slang) hacer fisga a; **to string along** (slang) traer al retortero; **to string up** (coll.) ahorcar
**string bean** *s* (bot.) habichuela, judía; habichuela verde, judía verde
**stringcourse** ['strɪŋ,kors] *s* (arch.) cordón

**stringed instrument** *s* (mus.) instrumento de cuerda
**stringency** ['strɪndʒənsɪ] *s* (*pl:* **-cies**) rigor, severidad; fuerza de persuasión; (com.) tirantez
**stringent** ['strɪndʒənt] *adj* riguroso, severo, estricto; convincente; (com.) tirante
**stringer** ['strɪŋər] *s* encordador; ensartador; (carp.) riostra; (rail.) durmiente longitudinal
**stringhalt** ['strɪŋ,hɔlt] *s* (vet.) ancado
**stringhalted** ['strɪŋ,hɔltɪd] *adj* (vet.) ancado
**string orchestra** *s* orquesta de cuerdas
**stringpiece** ['strɪŋ,pis] *s* riostra
**string quartet** *s* (mus.) cuarteto de cuerdas
**string tie** *s* corbatín angosto
**stringy** ['strɪŋɪ] *adj* (*comp:* **-ier;** *super:* **-iest**) fibroso, filamentoso; correoso, duro; viscoso
**strip** [strɪp] *s* tira; lámina (*de metal*); faja (*de tierra*); (*pret & pp:* **stripped;** *ger:* **stripping**) *va* desnudar; despojar, desmantelar, robar; desforrar; deshacer (*la cama*); estropear (*el engranaje, un tornillo*); ordeñar hasta agotar; desvenar (*tabaco*); descortezar; **to strip of** despojar de; **to strip down** desguarnecer; *vn* desnudarse; despojarse; descortezarse
**stripe** [straɪp] *s* raya, lista, banda; gaya; cinta, franja; (mil. & nav.) galón; tipo, índole; latigazo; *va* rayar, listar; gayar
**striped** [straɪpt] o ['straɪpɪd] *adj* rayado, a rayas
**striped hyena** *s* (zool.) hiena rayada
**striped mullet** *s* (ichth.) mújol
**stripling** ['strɪplɪŋ] *s* rapagón, mozuelo
**strip mining** *s* mineraje a tajo abierto
**stripped-down** ['strɪpt,daun] *adj* desguarnecido
**stripteaser** ['strɪp'tizər] *s* desnudista *f*
**strive** [straɪv] (*pret:* **strove;** *pp:* **striven**) *vn* esforzarse; hacer lo posible; luchar; **to strive to** + *inf* esforzarse por + *inf*
**striven** ['strɪvən] *pp de* **strive**
**strobile** ['strɑbɪl] *s* (bot. & zool.) estróbilo
**stroboscope** ['strɑbəskop] *s* estroboscopio
**strode** [strod] *pret de* **stride**
**stroke** [strok] *s* golpe; campanada (*de un reloj o campana*); plumada; pincelada; brochada; brazada (*en la natación*); jugada; caricia (*hecha con la mano*); raya; raquetazo; (mach.) embolada, carrera; palada, remada; primer remero; ataque de parálisis, apoplejía; buen éxito inesperado; golpe (*de fortuna*); rasgo (*de ingenio*); **at one stroke** de un golpe, de una sola vez; **at the stroke of** al dar las (*p.ej., tres*); **to keep stroke** remar al compás (*dos o más bogadores*); **to not do a stroke of work** no dar golpe, no levantar paja del suelo; **with one fell stroke** de un plumazo; **stroke of fortune** golpe de fortuna; **stroke of wit** chiste, agudeza; *va* frotar suavemente, acariciar con la mano; rayar
**stroke oar** *s* primer remero, bogavante
**stroll** [strol] *s* paseo; **to take a stroll** dar un paseo; *va* pasearse por; **to stroll the streets** callejear; *vn* pasear, pasearse; vagar, errar, callejear
**stroller** ['strolər] *s* paseante; vagabundo; cómico ambulante; andaderas, cochecito para niños
**stroma** ['stromə] *s* (*pl:* **-mata** [mətə]) (anat., biol. & bot.) estroma
**Stromboli** ['strɔmbəli] *s* Estrómboli
**strong** [strɔŋ] o [strɑŋ] *adj* (*comp:* **stronger** ['strɔŋgər] o ['strɑŋgər]; *super:* **strongest** ['strɔŋgɪst] o ['strɑŋgɪst]) fuerte, resistente; intenso; firme (*mercado*); violento; enérgico; marcado; celoso, acérrimo; picante; rancio; (gram.) fuerte (*vocal; verbo*); ascendiendo a, p.ej., **a thousand strong** ascendiendo a mil; *adv* fuertemente, vigorosamente
**strong-arm** ['strɔŋ,ɑrm] o ['strɑŋ,ɑrm] *adj* (coll.) violento; *va* (coll.) usar violencia contra
**strongbox** ['strɔŋ,bɑks] o ['strɑŋ,bɑks] *s* cofre fuerte, caja de caudales
**strong breeze** *s* (naut.) viento fresco
**strong drink** *s* bebida alcohólica, bebida fuerte
**strong gale** *s* (naut.) viento muy duro
**stronghold** ['strɔŋ,hold] o ['strɑŋ,hold] *s* fuerte, fortaleza; plaza fuerte
**strong man** *s* hércules; (coll.) promotor, alma (*el que da aliento y fuerza a una cosa*)
**strongman** ['strɔŋ,mæn] o ['strɑŋ,mæn] *s* (*pl:* **-men**) hombre fuerte (*dictador*)
**strong-minded** ['strɔŋ'maɪndɪd] o ['strɑŋ'maɪndɪd] *adj* de inteligencia vigorosa; independiente; hombruna (*dícese de una mujer*)
**strontia** ['strɑnʃɪə] *s* (chem.) estronciana
**strontianite** ['strɑnʃɪənaɪt] *s* (mineral.) estroncianita
**strontium** ['strɑnʃɪəm] *s* (chem.) estroncio
**strop** [strɑp] *s* suavizador; (*pret & pp:* **stropped;** *ger:* **stropping**) *va* suavizar (*una navaja*)
**strophe** ['strofɪ] *s* estrofa
**strophic** ['strɑfɪk] o ['strofɪk] *adj* estrófico
**strove** [strov] *pret de* **strive**
**struck** [strʌk] *pret & pp de* **strike**
**structural** ['strʌktʃərəl] *adj* estructural
**structure** ['strʌktʃər] *s* estructura; construcción
**struggle** ['strʌgəl] *s* lucha; esfuerzo, forcejeo; *vn* luchar; esforzarse, forcejear; **to struggle to** + *inf* luchar por + *inf*
**struggle for existence** *s* lucha por la vida o por la existencia
**strum** [strʌm] *s* cencerreo; (*pret & pp:* **strummed;** *ger:* **strumming**) *va* arañar (*un instrumento músico*) sin arte; *vn* cencerrear
**struma** ['strumə] *s* (*pl:* **-mae** [mi]) *s* (path.) estruma (*escrófula; bocio*); (bot.) apófisis
**strumous** ['struməs] *adj* estrumoso
**strumpet** ['strʌmpɪt] *s* ramera, prostituta
**strung** [strʌŋ] *pret & pp de* **string**
**strut** [strʌt] *s* (carp.) tornapunta, riostra, jabalcón; contoneo, pavoneo; (*pret & pp:* **strutted;** *ger:* **strutting**) *vn* contonearse, pavonearse
**strychnin** ['strɪknɪn] o **strychnine** ['strɪknɪn], ['strɪknaɪn] o ['strɪknin] *s* (chem.) estricnina
**St. Sophia** [sent so'faɪə] *s* Santa Sofía (*mezquita*)
**St. Thomas** [sent 'tɑməs] *s* Santo Tomás (*isla*)
**Stuart, Mary** ['stjuərt] o ['stuərt] María Estuardo
**stub** [stʌb] *s* trozo, fragmento; colilla (*de cigarro*); zoquete (*de madera no labrada*); tocón (*de un árbol cortado*); cepa (*de árbol*); pluma de escribir corta y de punta gruesa; talón (*de un cheque*); *adj* embotado; (*pret & pp:* **stubbed;** *ger:* **stubbing**) *va* rozar, limpiar, arrancar los tocones de; desarraigar; aplastar; **to stub off** embotar; **to stub one's toe** dar un tropezón
**stub axle** *s* (aut.) mangueta
**stubble** ['stʌbəl] *s* (agr.) rastrojo; *va* (agr.) rastrojar
**stubbly** ['stʌblɪ] *adj* lleno de rastrojo; cerdoso, hirsuto
**stubborn** ['stʌbərn] *adj* terco, testarudo, obstinado; porfiado, cabezón; intratable
**stubbornness** ['stʌbərnnɪs] *s* terquedad, testarudez, obstinación; porfía
**stubby** ['stʌbɪ] *adj* (*comp:* **-bier;** *super:* **-biest**) cachigordete; corto, grueso y cerdoso; lleno de troncos, lleno de tocones
**stub nail** *s* clavo de herrar viejo
**stub-pointed** ['stʌb,pɔɪntɪd] *adj* mocho
**stucco** ['stʌko] *s* (*pl:* **-coes** o **-cos**) estuco; *va* estucar
**stuccowork** ['stʌko,wʌrk] *s* estuco, obra de estuco
**stuck** [stʌk] *pret & pp de* **stick**
**stuck-up** ['stʌk,ʌp] *adj* (coll.) tieso, estirado, espetado, orgulloso
**stud** [stʌd] *s* tachón; botón de camisa; montante, pie derecho, poste de tabique; refuerzo de eslabón; perno prisionero, espárrago; clavo de adorno; yeguada (*rebaño; establecimiento*); caballeriza; caballada; caballo padre; **at stud** destinado a padrear; *adj* semental; (*pret & pp:* **studded;** *ger:* **studding**) *va* tachonar
**stud bolt** *s* perno prisionero, espárrago
**studbook** ['stʌd,bʊk] *s* registro genealógico de caballos, libro de oro de los caballos de pura sangre
**studding** ['stʌdɪŋ] *s* montantes de tabique; madera para construir montantes
**studdingsail** ['stʌdɪŋsəl] o ['stʌdɪŋ,sel] *s* (naut.) ala

**student** ['stjudənt] o ['studənt] *s* estudiante; investigador
**student body** *s* estudiantado
**student lamp** *s* quinqué
**stud farm** *s* acaballadero
**studhorse** ['stʌd,hɔrs] *s* caballo padre, caballo semental
**studied** ['stʌdɪd] *adj* estudiado (*afectado*); premeditado, hecho adrede
**studio** ['stjudɪo] o ['studɪo] *s* (*pl:* **-os**) taller, estudio; (mov. & rad.) estudio
**studious** ['stjudɪəs] o ['studɪəs] *adj* estudioso; asiduo, solícito
**study** ['stʌdɪ] *s* (*pl:* **-ies**) estudio; meditación profunda; solicitud; **to be in a brown study** estar absorto en la meditación; (*pret & pp:* **-ied**) *va* estudiar; *vn* estudiar; **to study to** + *inf* esforzarse por + *inf*
**study hall** *s* sala de estudio o de lectura
**stuff** [stʌf] *s* materia, material; tela, género, paño; cosa o cosas; efectos, muebles, baratijas, bagatelas; medicina; fruslerías; índole, carácter; *va* rellenar, atestar, colmar; atascar, tapar, cerrar; embutir; atracar (*de comida*); (cook.) rellenar; meter sin orden, llenar sin orden; disecar (*un animal muerto para conservar su apariencia*); *vn* atracarse, hartarse
**stuffed olives** *spl* aceitunas rellenas
**stuffed shirt** *s* (slang) tragavirotes
**stuffing** ['stʌfɪŋ] *s* relleno
**stuffing box** *s* caja de estopas, prensaestopas
**stuffing nut** *s* (mach.) tuerca del prensaestopas
**stuffy** ['stʌfɪ] *adj* (*comp:* **-ier;** *super:* **-iest**) sofocante, mal ventilado; aburrido, sin interés; cerrado, tapado; (coll.) etiquetero, relamido; (coll.) picajoso
**Stuka** ['stukə] o ['ʃtukə] *s* stuka (*avión alemán de combate en picado*)
**stultification** [,stʌltɪfɪ'keʃən] *s* posición ridícula, apariencia estulta; descrédito
**stultify** ['stʌltɪfaɪ] (*pret & pp:* **-fied**) *va* poner en ridículo, hacer parecer ridículo; quitar importancia a; **to stultify oneself** ponerse en ridículo
**stumble** ['stʌmbəl] *s* tropiezo, tropezón, traspié; desatino, desliz; *va* hacer tropezar, hacer dar un traspié; confundir; extraviar; *vn* tropezar, dar un traspié; errar; moverse a tropezones, hablar a tropezones; **to stumble on** o **upon** tropezar con
**stumbling block** *s* tropezadero, escollo
**stumbly** ['stʌmblɪ] *adj* tropezoso
**stump** [stʌmp] *s* cepa (*tronco próximo a las raíces*); tocón (*tronco que queda de un árbol*); muñón (*p.ej., de brazo cortado*); raigón (*de muela*); colilla (*de cigarro*); fragmento, resto; rabo (*de una cola*); paso pesado; (coll.) desafío, reto; (slang) pierna; (f.a.) esfumino; tribuna pública; **up a stump** perplejo, en un apuro; *va* arrancar los tocones de; cortar, amputar; (coll.) confundir, dejar confuso, dejar sin habla; (coll.) desafiar; recorrer pronunciando discursos políticos; (f.a.) esfumar; *vn* cojear, renquear; pronunciar discursos políticos
**stump puller** *s* destroncadora
**stump speaker** *s* orador callejero
**stump speech** *s* arenga electoral
**stumpy** ['stʌmpɪ] *adj* (*comp:* **-ier;** *super:* **-iest**) lleno de tocones; cachigordete, achaparrado
**stun** [stʌn] (*pret & pp:* **stunned:** *ger:* **stunning**) *va* aturdir, atolondrar, dejar pasmado
**stung** [stʌŋ] *pret & pp de* **sting**
**stunk** [stʌŋk] *pret & pp de* **stink**
**stunner** ['stʌnər] *s* golpe que aturde; (coll.) cosa pasmosa, persona maravillosa
**stunning** ['stʌnɪŋ] *adj* aturdidor; (coll.) brutal (*pasmoso, estupendo, pistonudo, elegante, hermoso, lujoso*)
**stunsail** ['stʌnsəl] *s* var. de **studdingsail**
**stunt** [stʌnt] *s* atrofia, falta de crecimiento o desarrollo; engendro (*animal, planta u otra cosa*); (coll.) suerte acrobática, maniobra sensacional; (coll.) faena, hazaña, proeza, recurso (*para lograr un fin*); (coll.) anuncio de reclamo; (aer.) vuelo acrobático; *va* atrofiar, impedir el crecimiento o desarrollo de; (coll.) hacer suertes con; *vn* (coll.) hacer suertes acrobáticas, hacer maniobras sensacionales; (aer.) lucirse haciendo maniobras acrobáticas
**stunt man** *s* (mov.) doble que hace suertes peligrosas
**stupe** [stjup] o [stup] *s* (med.) fomento, compresa pequeña
**stupefacient** [,stjupɪ'feʃənt] o [,stupɪ'feʃənt] *adj & s* estupefaciente
**stupefaction** [,stjupɪ'fækʃən] o [,stupɪ'fækʃən] *s* estupefacción
**stupefy** ['stjupɪfaɪ] o ['stupɪfaɪ] (*pret & pp:* **-fied**) *va* dejar estupefacto, pasmar; causar estupor a
**stupendous** [stju'pɛndəs] o [stu'pɛndəs] *adj* estupendo; enorme
**stupid** ['stjupɪd] o ['stupɪd] *adj & s* estúpido
**stupidity** [stju'pɪdɪtɪ] o [stu'pɪdɪtɪ] *s* (*pl:* **-ties**) estupidez
**stupor** ['stjupər] o ['stupər] *s* estupor
**sturdiness** ['stʌrdɪnɪs] *s* fuerza, robustez; firmeza, tenacidad
**sturdy** ['stʌrdɪ] *adj* (*comp:* **-dier;** *super:* **-diest**) fuerte, robusto, fornido; firme, tenaz
**sturgeon** ['stʌrdʒən] *s* (ichth.) esturión
**stutter** ['stʌtər] *s* tartamudeo; *va* decir tartamudeando; *vn* tartamudear
**St. Vincent** [sent 'vɪnsənt] *s* San Vicente (*isla*)
**sty** [staɪ] *s* (*pl:* **sties**) pocilga, zahurda; (path.) orzuelo
**Stygian** ['stɪdʒɪən] *adj* estigio, estigioso
**style** [staɪl] *s* estilo; moda; elegancia; título, epíteto; (bot. & print.) estilo; modelo, p.ej., **latest style** último modelo; **in style** de moda; **in the style of** al estilo de; **to live in great style** vivir en gran lujo; *va* adaptar a la moda, cortar a la moda; nombrar, intitular
**stylebook** ['staɪl,bʊk] *s* (print.) libro de ejemplos de impresión y modelos de ortografía, etc.
**stylet** ['staɪlɪt] *s* estilete; (surg.) estilete
**stylish** ['staɪlɪʃ] *adj* de moda, elegante
**stylist** ['staɪlɪst] *s* estilista
**stylistic** [staɪ'lɪstɪk] *adj* estilístico; **stylistics** *ssg* estilística
**stylite** ['staɪlaɪt] *s* estilita
**stylize** ['staɪlaɪz] *va* estilizar
**stylograph** ['staɪləgræf] o ['staɪləgrɑf] *s* estilógrafo
**stylographic** [,staɪlə'græfɪk] *adj* estilográfico
**styloid** ['staɪlɔɪd] *adj* (anat.) estiloides
**stylus** ['staɪləs] *s* estilo; aguja (*de fonógrafo*)
**stymie** ['staɪmɪ] *s* (golf) condición en que una pelota se encuentra entre la del adversario y el agujero; (*pret & pp:* **-mied;** *ger:* **-mieing**) *va* (golf) estorbar con una pelota entre la del adversario y el agujero; (fig.) frustrar
**stymy** ['staɪmɪ] *s* (*pl:* **-mies**) var. de **stymie;** (*pret & pp:* **-mied**) *va* var. de **stymie**
**styptic** ['stɪptɪk] *adj & s* estíptico
**styptic pencil** *s* lápiz estíptico
**styracaceous** [,staɪrə'keʃəs] *adj* (bot.) estiracáceo
**styrene** ['staɪrin] o ['stɪrin] *s* (chem.) estireno
**Styria** ['stɪrɪə] *s* Estiria
**Styx** [stɪks] *s* (myth.) Estigia
**suasion** ['sweʒən] *s* persuasión
**suasive** ['swesɪv] *adj* suasorio, persuasor
**suave** [swɑv] o [swev] *adj* suave; afable, fino, zalamero, pulido
**suavity** ['swævɪtɪ] o ['swɑvɪtɪ] *s* (*pl:* **-ties**) suavidad; afabilidad, finura
**sub.** abr. de **subscription, substitute** y **suburban**
**sub** [sʌb] *s & adj* (coll.) substituto; (coll.) submarino; (coll.) subordinado; (coll.) subalterno; (*pret & pp:* **subbed;** *ger:* **subbing**) *va* (coll.) atacar o hundir con submarino; *vn* (coll.) ser substituto; **to sub for** (coll.) hacer las veces de
**subacetate** [sʌb'æsɪtet] *s* (chem.) subacetato
**subacid** [sʌb'æsɪd] *adj* (chem.) subácido
**subagent** [sʌb'edʒənt] *s* subagente
**subaltern** [səb'ɔltərn] o ['sʌbəltərn] *adj & s* subalterno
**subantarctic** [,sʌbænt'ɑrktɪk] *adj* subantártico
**subaquatic** [,sʌbə'kwætɪk] o [,sʌbə'kwɑtɪk] *adj* subacuático
**subaqueous** [sʌb'ekwɪəs] o [sʌb'ækwɪəs] *adj* subácueo
**subarctic** [sʌb'ɑrktɪk] *adj* subártico
**subarid** [sʌb'ærɪd] *adj* medianamente árido
**subatom** [sʌb'ætəm] *s* (chem. & phys.) subátomo
**subatomic** [,sʌbə'tɑmɪk] *adj* subatómico

**subcellar** ['sʌb,sɛlər] *s* sótano inferior
**subchaser** ['sʌb,tʃesər] *s* cazasubmarinos
**subclass** ['sʌb,klæs] o ['sʌb,klɑs] *s* (biol.) subclase
**subclavian** [sʌb'kleviən] *adj* (anat.) subclavio
**subcommittee** ['sʌbkə,mɪtɪ] *s* subcomisión
**subconscious** [sʌb'kɑnʃəs] *adj* subconsciente; *s* subconsciencia
**subconsciousness** [sʌb'kɑnʃəsnɪs] *s* subconsciencia
**subcontinent** [sʌb'kɑntɪnənt] *s* subcontinente
**subcontract** [sʌb'kɑntrækt] *s* subcontrato; [sʌb'kɑntrækt] o [,sʌbkən'trækt] *va & vn* subcontratar
**subcontractor** [sʌb'kɑntræktər] o [,sʌbkən'træktər] *s* subcontratista
**subcostal** [sʌb'kɑstəl] *adj* (anat. & zool.) subcostal
**subcritical** [sʌb'krɪtɪkəl] *adj* subcrítico
**subcutaneous** [,sʌbkju'tenɪəs] *adj* subcutáneo
**subdeacon** [sʌb'dikən] *s* subdiácono
**subdeaconry** [sʌb'dikənrɪ] *s* subdiaconato
**subdean** ['sʌb,din] *s* subdecano
**subdeb** [sʌb'dɛb] *s* (coll.) tobillera, chica muy joven, ya casi en edad de ponerse de largo
**subdelirium** [,sʌbdɪ'lɪrɪəm] *s* (path.) subdelirio
**subdivide** [,sʌbdɪ'vaɪd] o ['sʌbdɪ,vaɪd] *va* subdividir; *vn* subdividirse
**subdivision** [,sʌbdɪ'vɪʒən] o ['sʌbdɪ,vɪʒən] *s* subdivisión
**subdominant** [sʌb'dɑmɪnənt] *s* (mus.) subdominante
**subdouble** [sʌb'dʌbəl] *adj* (math.) subduplo
**subdue** [səb'dju] o [səb'du] *va* subyugar, sojuzgar; dominar, sujetar; amansar, suavizar; mejorar (*tierras*)
**subereous** [su'bɪrɪəs] o [sju'bɪrɪəs] *adj* suberoso
**suberin** ['subərɪn] o ['sjubərɪn] *s* (biochem.) suberina
**subfamily** [sʌb'fæmɪlɪ] o ['sʌb,fæmɪlɪ] *s* (*pl:* **-lies**) (biol.) subfamilia
**subgenus** [sʌb'dʒinəs] o ['sʌb,dʒinəs] *s* (*pl:* **-genera** ['dʒɛnərə] o **-genuses**) (biol.) subgénero
**subgroup** ['sʌb,grup] *s* subgrupo
**subhead** ['sʌb,hɛd] *s* subtítulo; subdirector
**subheading** ['sʌb,hɛdɪŋ] *s* subtítulo
**subhuman** [sʌb'hjumən] *adj* inferior a lo humano; casi humano
**subindex** [sʌb'ɪndɛks] *s* (*pl:* **-dices** [dɪsiz]) subíndice
**subj.** abr. de **subject, subjective** y **subjunctive**
**subjacent** [sʌb'dʒesənt] *adj* subyacente
**subject** ['sʌbdʒɪkt] *s* asunto, materia; objeto (*de un experimento*); (mus.) tema; súbdito (*persona sujeta a la autoridad de un superior*); (gram., med., philos., psychol. & log.) sujeto; *adj* súbdito; sujeto; [səb'dʒɛkt] *va* sujetar, someter
**subject index** *s* índice de materias
**subjection** [səb'dʒɛkʃən] *s* sujeción
**subjective** [səb'dʒɛktɪv] *adj* subjetivo
**subjectivism** [səb'dʒɛktɪvɪzəm] *s* (philos.) subjetivismo
**subjectivity** [,sʌbdʒɛk'tɪvɪtɪ] *s* subjetividad
**subject matter** *s* asunto, materia, objeto
**subject pronoun** *s* pronombre sujeto
**subjoin** [səb'dʒɔɪn] *va* añadir, adjuntar
**subjugate** ['sʌbdʒəget] *va* subyugar
**subjugation** [,sʌbdʒə'geʃən] *s* subyugación
**subjugator** ['sʌbdʒə,getər] *s* subyugador
**subjunctive** [səb'dʒʌŋktɪv] *adj & s* (gram.) subjuntivo
**subkingdom** [sʌb'kɪŋdəm] o ['sʌb,kɪŋdəm] *s* (biol.) subreino
**sublease** ['sʌb,lis] *s* subarriendo; [,sʌb'lis] o ['sʌb,lis] *va & vn* subarrendar
**sublet** [sʌb'lɛt] o ['sʌb,lɛt] (*pret & pp:* **-let;** *ger:* **-letting**) *va & vn* subarrendar, realquilar
**sublieutenant** [,sʌblu'tɛnənt] *s* subteniente
**sublimate** ['sʌblɪmet] *adj* sublimado; *s* (chem.) sublimado; *va* sublimar
**sublimation** [,sʌblɪ'meʃən] *s* sublimación
**sublime** [sə'blaɪm] *adj* sublime; **the sublime** lo sublime; *va* sublimar
**Sublime Porte** [port] *s* Sublime Puerta (*Turquía*)
**subliminal** [sʌb'lɪmɪnəl] o [sʌb'laɪmɪnəl] *adj & s* (psychol.) subliminar
**sublimity** [səb'lɪmɪtɪ] *s* (*pl:* **-ties**) sublimidad
**sublingual** [sʌb'lɪŋgwəl] *adj* (anat.) sublingual
**sublunar** [sʌb'lunər] o **sublunary** ['sʌblu,nɛrɪ] o [sʌb'lunərɪ] *adj* sublunar
**submachine gun** [,sʌbmə'ʃin] *s* subfusil ametrallador
**submarginal** [sʌb'mɑrdʒɪnəl] *adj* submarginal; improductivo
**submarine** ['sʌbmə,rin] *adj & s* submarino; *va* (coll.) atacar o hundir con un submarino
**submaxilla** [,sʌbmæks'ɪlə] *s* (*pl:* **-lae** [li]) (anat. & zool.) mandíbula submaxilar
**submaxillary** [sʌb'mæksɪ,lɛrɪ] *adj* submaxilar; *s* (*pl:* **-ies**) mandíbula submaxilar; glándula submaxilar
**submaxillary gland** *s* (anat.) glándula submaxilar
**submerge** [səb'mʌrdʒ] *va* sumergir; *vn* sumergirse
**submergence** [səb'mʌrdʒəns] *s* sumersión
**submerse** [səb'mʌrs] *va & vn* var. de **submerge**
**submersible** [səb'mʌrsɪbəl] *adj* sumergible, hundible; *s* sumergible (*buque*)
**submersion** [səb'mʌrʒən] o [səb'mʌrʃən] *s* sumersión
**submicroscopic** [,sʌbmaɪkrə'skɑpɪk] *adj* submicroscópico
**submission** [səb'mɪʃən] *s* sumisión
**submissive** [səb'mɪsɪv] *adj* sumiso
**submit** [səb'mɪt] (*pret & pp:* **-mitted;** *ger:* **-mitting**) *va* someter (*razones, reflexiones, etc.; un negocio*); proponer, permitirse decir; *vn* someterse
**submultiple** [sʌb'mʌltɪpəl] *adj & s* (math.) submúltiplo
**subnormal** [sʌb'nɔrməl] *adj* subnormal; *s* (geom.) subnormal
**suborbital** [sʌb'ɔrbɪtəl] *adj* suborbital
**suborder** ['sʌb,ɔrdər] o [sʌb'ɔrdər] *s* suborden
**subordinate** [səb'ɔrdɪnɪt] *adj* subordinado; (gram.) subordinado (*aplícase a la oración*); (gram.) subordinante (*aplícase a la conjunción*); [səb'ɔrdɪnet] *va* subordinar
**subordinating conjunction** *s* (gram.) conjunción subordinante
**subordination** [səb,ɔrdɪ'neʃən] *s* subordinación
**suborn** [sə'bɔrn] *va* sobornar
**subornation** [,sʌbɔr'neʃən] *s* soborno
**subornation of perjury** *s* (law) soborno de testigo
**subplot** ['sʌb,plɑt] *s* trama secundaria
**subpoena** o **subpena** [sʌb'pinə] o [sə'pinə] *s* (law) comparendo; *va* (law) mandar comparecer
**sub rosa** [sʌb 'rozə] *adv* en secreto, en confianza
**subsatellite** [sʌb'sætəlaɪt] *s* subsatélite
**subscapular** [sʌb'skæpjələr] *adj* (anat.) subscapular
**subscribe** [səb'skraɪb] *va* subscribir; *vn* subscribir; subscribirse, abonarse; **to subscribe for** o **to** subscribir (*un número de acciones u obligaciones*); subscribirse a, abonarse a (*una publicación periódica*); **to subscribe to** subscribir (*una opinión o dictamen*)
**subscriber** [səb'skraɪbər] *s* subscriptor; abonado
**subscription** [səb'skrɪpʃən] *s* subscripción; firma; abono (*p.ej., a una revista*)
**subsection** ['sʌb,sɛkʃən] o [sʌb'sɛkʃən] *s* subdivisión
**subsequence** ['sʌbsɪkwəns] *s* subsecuencia, posterioridad; acontecimiento subsiguiente
**subsequent** ['sʌbsɪkwənt] *adj* subsecuente o subsiguiente, posterior
**subserve** [səb'sʌrv] *va* adelantar, ayudar
**subservience** [səb'sʌrvɪəns] o **subserviency** [səb'sʌrvɪənsɪ] *s* servilismo; subordinación; utilidad
**subservient** [səb'sʌrvɪənt] *adj* servil; subordinado; útil
**subside** [səb'saɪd] *vn* apaciguarse, calmarse; cesar, acabarse; bajar (*el nivel de un líquido*); hundirse, irse al fondo; (coll.) caer
**subsidence** [səb'saɪdəns] o ['sʌbsɪdəns] *s* apaciguamiento, calma; cesación; bajada; hundimiento, sumersión
**subsidiary** [səb'sɪdɪ,ɛrɪ] *adj* subsidiario, auxi-

liar; afiliado; *s* (*pl:* **-ies**) suplemento; (com.) filial
**subsidiary company** *s* (com.) filial
**subsidize** [ˈsʌbsɪdaɪz] *va* subsidiar, subvencionar; comprar la ayuda de; sobornar
**subsidy** [ˈsʌbsɪdɪ] *s* (*pl:* **-dies**) subsidio, subvención
**subsist** [səbˈsɪst] *va* alimentar, mantener; *vn* subsistir
**subsistence** [səbˈsɪstəns] *s* subsistencia; (philos.) subsistencia
**subsistent** [səbˈsɪstənt] *adj* subsistente
**subsoil** [ˈsʌbˌsɔɪl] *s* subsuelo
**subsonic** [sʌbˈsɑnɪk] *adj* subsónico
**subspecies** [ˈsʌbˌspiʃɪz] o [sʌbˈspiʃɪz] *s* (*pl:* **-cies**) (biol.) subespecie
**subst.** abr. de **substantive** y **substitute**
**substance** [ˈsʌbstəns] *s* substancia; **in substance** en substancia
**substandard** [sʌbˈstændərd] o [ˈsʌbˌstændərd] *adj* inferior al nivel normal, inferior a la norma
**substantial** [səbˈstænʃəl] *adj* substancial; substancioso; fuerte, sólido; rico, acomodado; **to be in substantial agreement** estar de acuerdo en substancia
**substantiality** [səbˌstænʃɪˈælɪtɪ] *s* (*pl:* **-ties**) substancialidad; fuerza, solidez; opulencia, riqueza
**substantiate** [səbˈstænʃɪet] *va* verificar, comprobar, establecer; dar cuerpo a
**substantiation** [səbˌstænʃɪˈeʃən] *s* verificación, comprobación; incorporación
**substantival** [ˌsʌbstænˈtaɪvəl] *adj* (gram.) substantivo
**substantive** [ˈsʌbstəntɪv] *adj* substantivo; (gram.) substantivo; *s* (gram.) substantivo
**substantivize** [ˈsʌbstəntɪvaɪz] *va* (gram.) substantivar
**substation** [ˈsʌbˌsteʃən] *s* dependencia; (elec.) subcentral, subestación
**substitute** [ˈsʌbstɪtjut] o [ˈsʌbstɪtut] *adj* substitutivo, sucedáneo; *s* substituto (*persona*); substitutivo, sucedáneo; (mil.) reemplazo (*hombre que sirve en lugar de otro*); **beware of substitutes** desconfíe de substitutivos; *va* poner (*a una persona o cosa*) en lugar de otra, p.ej., **we substituted margarine for butter** pusimos (o usamos) margarina en lugar de mantequilla; *vn* actuar de substituto; **to substitute for** substituir (*a una persona o cosa*), p.ej., **John substituted for Peter** Juan substituyó a Pedro
**substitution** [ˌsʌbstɪˈtjuʃən] o [ˌsʌbstɪˈtuʃən] *s* empleo o uso de una persona o cosa en lugar de otra; (alg., chem. & law) substitución; (coll.) imitación fraudulenta
**substitutional** [ˌsʌbstɪˈtjuʃənəl] o [ˌsʌbstɪˈtuʃənəl] *adj* substituidor, sucedáneo
**substitutive** [ˈsʌbstɪˌtjutɪv] o [ˈsʌbstɪˌtutɪv] *adj* substitutivo
**substrate** [ˈsʌbstret] *s* substrato; (biochem.) substrato
**substratum** [sʌbˈstretəm] o [sʌbˈstrætəm] *s* (*pl:* **-ta** [tə] o **-tums**) substrato
**substructure** [ˈsʌbˌstrʌktʃər] o [sʌbˈstrʌktʃər] *s* subestructura
**subsume** [səbˈsum] o [səbˈsjum] *va* subsumir
**subsumption** [səbˈsʌmpʃən] *s* subsumpción
**subtenancy** [sʌbˈtɛnənsɪ] *s* (*pl:* **-cies**) subarriendo
**subtenant** [sʌbˈtɛnənt] *s* subarrendatario
**subtend** [səbˈtɛnd] *va* (geom. & bot.) subtender
**subterfuge** [ˈsʌbtərfjudʒ] *s* subterfugio, escapatoria
**subterranean** [ˌsʌbtəˈrenɪən] *adj* subterráneo; *s* subterráneo (*lugar o espacio*); habitante subterráneo
**subterraneous** [ˌsʌbtəˈrenɪəs] *adj* subterráneo
**subtile** [ˈsʌtəl] o [ˈsʌbtɪl] *adj* sutil; astuto
**subtility** [sʌbˈtɪlɪtɪ] o **subtilty** [ˈsʌtəltɪ] o [ˈsʌbtɪltɪ] *s* (*pl:* **-ties**) sutileza o sutilidad
**subtitle** [ˈsʌbˌtaɪtəl] *s* subtítulo; *va* subtitular
**subtle** [ˈsʌtəl] *adj* sutil; astuto; insidioso
**subtlety** [ˈsʌtəltɪ] *s* (*pl:* **-ties**) sutileza o sutilidad; astucia; distinción sutil
**subtly** [ˈsʌtlɪ] *adv* sutilmente; astutamente; insidiosamente
**subtract** [səbˈtrækt] *va & vn* substraer o sustraer
**subtraction** [səbˈtrækʃən] *s* substracción o sustracción
**subtrahend** [ˈsʌbtrəhɛnd] *s* (math.) substraendo
**subtreasury** [ˈsʌbˌtrɛʒərɪ] o [sʌbˈtrɛʒərɪ] *s* (*pl:* **-ies**) subtesorería
**subtropical** [sʌbˈtrɑpɪkəl] *adj* subtropical
**subtropics** [ˈsʌbˌtrɑpɪks] o [sʌbˈtrɑpɪks] *spl* subtrópicos
**suburb** [ˈsʌbʌrb] *s* suburbio, arrabal; **the suburbs** las afueras, los alrededores, los barrios externos
**suburban** [səˈbʌrbən] *adj & s* suburbano
**suburbanite** [səˈbʌrbənaɪt] *s* suburbano
**subvention** [sʌbˈvɛnʃən] *s* subvención
**subversion** [sʌbˈvʌrʒən] o [sʌbˈvʌrʃən] *s* subversión
**subversive** [sʌbˈvʌrsɪv] *adj* subversivo; *s* subversor
**subvert** [sʌbˈvʌrt] *va* subvertir
**subway** [ˈsʌbˌwe] *s* galería subterránea; paso subterráneo; ferrocarril subterráneo, metro
**succeed** [səkˈsid] *va* suceder (*a una persona o cosa*), p.ej., **autumn succeeds summer** el otoño sucede al verano; *vn* tener buen éxito, salir bien; **to succeed in** tener éxito en, salir bien en; **to succeed in** + *ger* conseguir o lograr + *inf;* **to succeed to** suceder a (*p.ej., la corona*)
**succeeding** [səkˈsidɪŋ] *adj* subsiguiente; sucesor
**success** [səkˈsɛs] *s* buen éxito; éxito, resultado; persona o cosa que tiene buen éxito; **to make a success of** tener éxito en
**successful** [səkˈsɛsfəl] *adj* próspero, feliz; logrado; acertado; **to be successful** tener buen éxito
**succession** [səkˈsɛʃən] *s* sucesión; **in succession** uno tras otro, seguidos
**successive** [səkˈsɛsɪv] *adj* sucesivo
**successor** [səkˈsɛsər] *s* sucesor
**succinct** [səkˈsɪŋkt] *adj* sucinto
**succinic** [səkˈsɪnɪk] *adj* succínico
**succor** [ˈsʌkər] *s* socorro; *va* socorrer
**succory** [ˈsʌkərɪ] *s* var. de **chicory**
**succotash** [ˈsʌkətæʃ] *s* guiso de maíz tierno y habas
**succubus** [ˈsʌkjəbəs] *s* (*pl:* **-bi** [baɪ] o **-buses**) súcubo, demonio súcubo
**succulence** [ˈsʌkjələns] *s* suculencia
**succulency** [ˈsʌkjələnsɪ] *s* (*pl:* **-cies**) var. de **succulence**
**succulent** [ˈsʌkjələnt] *adj* suculento
**succumb** [səˈkʌm] *vn* sucumbir
**succuss** [səˈkʌs] *va* sacudir; (med.) sacudir (*a un paciente para descubrir la presencia de un líquido*)
**succussation** [ˌsʌkəˈseʃən] o **succussion** [səˈkʌʃən] *s* sucusión
**such** [sʌtʃ] *adj indef & pron indef* tal, semejante; **as such** como tal; **one such** un tal; **such a** tal, semejante; **such a** + *adj* un tan + *adj;* **such and such** tal o cual; **such as** quienes, los que
**suchlike** [ˈsʌtʃˌlaɪk] *adj indef* tal, semejante; *pron indef* tales personas, tales cosas
**suck** [sʌk] *s* chupada; mamada; *va & vn* chupar; aspirar (*el aire*); mamar
**sucker** [ˈsʌkər] *s* chupador; mamón, mamantón; (bot.) serpollo, pimpollo; (bot.) mamón, chupón; (ichth.) catostomo; (mach.) chupón (*émbolo*); (mach.) válvula de bomba; (mach.) caño de bomba; (zool.) ventosa; (coll.) primo, bobo; *va* (bot.) cortar los chupones de; *vn* (bot.) echar chupones
**suckle** [ˈsʌkəl] *va* lactar; criar, educar; *vn* lactar
**suckling** [ˈsʌklɪŋ] *adj & s* mamón, mamantón
**sucrose** [ˈsukros] o [ˈsjukros] *s* (chem.) sacarosa
**suction** [ˈsʌkʃən] *s* succión; *adj* aspirante
**suction cup** *s* copa de succión
**suction pump** *s* bomba aspirante
**suctorial** [sʌkˈtorɪəl] *adj* suctorio
**Sudan** [suˈdæn] *s* Sudán
**Sudanese** [ˌsudəˈniz] *adj* sudanés; *s* (*pl:* **-nese**) sudanés
**Sudan grass** (bot.) hierba del Sudán, sorgo del Sudán
**sudatorium** [ˌsudəˈtorɪəm] o [ˌsjudəˈtorɪəm] *s* (*pl:* **-a** [ə]) sudadero; (hist.) sudatorio

**sudatory** ['sudə,torɪ] o ['sjudə,torɪ] *adj* sudatorio
**sudden** ['sʌdən] *adj* súbito, repentino; **all of a sudden** de repente
**suddenness** ['sʌdənnɪs] *s* rapidez, precipitación, brusquedad
**Sudeten** [su'detən] *spl* sudetas o sudetes (*naturales*); montes Sudetes
**Sudetenland** [su'detən,lænd] *s* región de los Sudetes
**sudoriferous** [,sudə'rɪfərəs] o [,sjudə'rɪfərəs] *adj* sudorífero
**sudorific** [,sudə'rɪfɪk] o [,sjudə'rɪfɪk] *adj & s* sudorífico
**sudoriparous** [,sudə'rɪpərəs] o [,sjudə'rɪpərəs] *adj* (anat.) sudoríparo
**suds** [sʌdz] *spl* jabonaduras; (slang) espuma, cerveza
**sudsy** ['sʌdzɪ] *adj* espumoso, jabonoso
**sue** [su] o [sju] *va* demandar; pedir; (law) procesar; **to sue out** (law) rogar y obtener; *vn* (law) poner pleito, entablar juicio; **to sue for damages** demandar por daños y perjuicios; **to sue for peace** pedir la paz
**suede** [swed] *s* suecia, gamuza, ante
**suet** ['suɪt] o ['sjuɪt] *s* sebo
**Suetonius** [swɪ'tonɪəs] *s* Suetonio
**suety** ['suɪtɪ] o ['sjuɪtɪ] *adj* seboso; sebáceo
**Suevian** ['swivɪən] *adj & s* suevo
**Suez Canal** [su'ɛz] o ['suɛz] *s* canal de Suez
**suffer** ['sʌfər] *va* sufrir, padecer; *vn* sufrir, padecer; **to suffer from** padecer de, adolecer de; (fig.) adolecer de
**sufferable** ['sʌfərəbəl] *adj* sufrible
**sufferance** ['sʌfərəns] *s* sufrimiento, tolerancia; paciencia; **on sufferance** por tolerancia
**sufferer** ['sʌfərər] *s* sufridor; doliente; víctima
**suffering** ['sʌfərɪŋ] *s* sufrimiento, dolencia; *adj* doliente
**suffice** [sə'faɪs] *va* satisfacer; ser suficiente a o para; *vn* bastar, ser suficiente
**sufficiency** [sə'fɪʃənsɪ] *s* (*pl:* **-cies**) suficiencia
**sufficient** [sə'fɪʃənt] *adj* suficiente
**suffix** ['sʌfɪks] *s* (gram.) sufijo; [sə'fɪks] *va* añadir como sufijo
**suffocate** ['sʌfəket] *va* sofocar; *vn* sofocarse
**suffocation** [,sʌfə'keʃən] *s* sofocación
**suffocative** ['sʌfə,ketɪv] *adj* sofocante
**suffragan** ['sʌfrəgən] *adj* sufragáneo; *s* obispo sufragáneo
**suffragan bishop** *s* obispo sufragáneo
**suffrage** ['sʌfrɪdʒ] *s* sufragio; aprobación, voto favorable; (eccl.) sufragio
**suffragette** [,sʌfrə'dʒɛt] *s* (coll.) sufragista (*mujer*)
**suffragist** ['sʌfrədʒɪst] *s* sufragista
**suffuse** [sə'fjuz] *va* difundir, bañar, llenar
**suffusion** [sə'fjuʒən] *s* difusión, baño; (path.) sufusión
**Sufi** ['sufɪ] *s* (*pl:* **-fis** [fɪz]) sufí
**Sufism** ['sufɪzəm] *s* sufismo
**sugar** ['ʃʊgər] *s* azúcar; *adj* azucarero; *va* azucarar; (fig.) azucarar; *vn* formar azúcar; **to sugar off** hacer el azúcar de arce; (slang) salirse a hurtadillas
**sugar beet** *s* (bot.) remolacha azucarera
**sugar bowl** *s* azucarero
**sugarbush** ['ʃʊgər,bʊʃ] *s* bosquecillo de arces del azúcar
**sugar cane** *s* (bot.) caña de azúcar
**sugar-coat** ['ʃʊgər,kot] *va* azucarar; endulzar, dorar (*lo desagradable*)
**sugar-coating** ['ʃʊgər,kotɪŋ] *s* capa de azúcar, garapiña; dorado (*de lo desagradable*)
**sugar daddy** *s* (slang) viejo verde que prodiga regalos a las chicas
**sugar loaf** *s* pan de azúcar (*cono de azúcar; sombrero; colina*)
**sugar-loaf** ['ʃʊgər,lof] *adj* de forma de pan de azúcar, cónico
**sugar maple** *s* (bot.) arce del azúcar
**sugar mill** *s* ingenio de azúcar
**sugar of lead** [lɛd] *s* (chem.) azúcar de plomo
**sugar of milk** *s* azúcar de leche
**sugarplum** ['ʃʊgər,plʌm] *s* confite, dulce
**sugar tongs** *spl* tenacillas (*para coger terrones de azúcar*)
**sugary** ['ʃʊgərɪ] *adj* azucarado
**suggest** [səg'dʒɛst] *va* sugerir; sugestionar (*por hipnosis*); **to suggest** + *ger* sugerir + *inf*
**suggestible** [səg'dʒɛstɪbəl] *adj* sugerible (*cosa*); sugestionable (*persona*)
**suggestion** [səg'dʒɛstʃən] *s* sugerencia; (psychol.) sugestión; sombra, traza ligera
**suggestive** [səg'dʒɛstɪv] *adj* sugestivo; sicalíptico, sugestivo de lo indecente
**suicidal** [,suɪ'saɪdəl] o [,sjuɪ'saɪdəl] *adj* suicida
**suicide** ['suɪsaɪd] o ['sjuɪsaɪd] *s* suicidio (*acción*); suicida (*persona*); **to commit suicide** suicidarse
**suint** ['suɪnt] o [swɪnt] *s* suarda (*grasa de la lana*)
**suit** [sut] o [sjut] *s* juego (*de cosas relacionadas entre sí*); traje, terno; traje sastre (*de mujer*); súplica, petición; cortejo, galanteo; palo (*de la baraja*); (law) pleito, proceso; **to follow suit** servir del palo; seguir el ejemplo de otro, seguir la corriente; **suit of armor** armadura completa; *va* adaptar, ajustar, acomodar; adaptarse a; proveer de traje o trajes; sentar, ir o venir bien a; favorecer; satisfacer; **to suit oneself** hacer (*uno*) lo que guste; *vn* convenir, ser a propósito
**suitability** [,sutə'bɪlɪtɪ] o [,sjutə'bɪlɪtɪ] *s* conveniencia, adaptabilidad
**suitable** ['sutəbəl] o ['sjutəbəl] *adj* conveniente, apropiado, satisfactorio, adecuado
**suitably** ['sutəblɪ] o ['sjutəblɪ] *adv* convenientemente, apropiadamente, a propósito
**suitcase** ['sut,kes] o ['sjut,kes] *s* maleta, valija
**suite** [swit] *s* séquito, comitiva; juego (*de cosas relacionadas entre sí*); serie; crujía (*de piezas*); habitación salón (*en un hotel*); (mus.) suite
**suiting** ['sutɪŋ] o ['sjutɪŋ] *s* tela para trajes, corte de traje
**suit of clothes** *s* traje completo (*de hombre*)
**suitor** ['sutər] o ['sjutər] *s* suplicante; galán, cortejador, enamorado; (law) demandante, parte actora
**sulcus** ['sʌlkəs] *s* (*pl:* **-ci** [saɪ]) surco; (anat.) cisura
**Suleiman** [,sule'mɑn] *s* var. de **Solyman**
**sulfadiazine** [,sʌlfə'daɪəzin] o [,sʌlfə'daɪəzɪn] *s* (pharm.) sulfadiacina
**sulfa drugs** ['sʌlfə] *spl* (pharm.) medicamentos sulfas
**sulfanilamide** [,sʌlfə'nɪləmaɪd] o [,sʌlfə'nɪləmɪd] *s* (pharm.) sulfanilamida
**sulfapyridine** [,sʌlfə'pɪrɪdin] o [,sʌlfə'pɪrɪdɪn] *s* (pharm.) sulfapiridina
**sulfarsphenamine** [,sʌlfɑrsfɛnə'min] o [,sʌlfɑrsfə'næmɪn] *s* (pharm.) sulfarsfenamina
**sulfas** ['sʌlfəz] *spl* (pharm.) sulfas
**sulfate** ['sʌlfet] *s* (chem.) sulfato; *va* sulfatar; (elec.) sulfatar
**sulfathiazole** [,sʌlfə'θaɪəzol] *s* (pharm.) sulfatiazol
**sulfation** [sʌl'feʃən] *s* sulfatación; (elec.) sulfatación
**sulfhydric acid** [sʌlf'haɪdrɪk] *s* (chem.) ácido sulfhídrico
**sulfid** ['sʌlfɪd] o **sulfide** ['sʌlfaɪd] o ['sʌlfɪd] *s* (chem.) sulfuro
**sulfite** ['sʌlfaɪt] *s* (chem.) sulfito
**sulfonal** ['sʌlfənæl] o [,sʌlfə'næl] *s* (pharm.) sulfonal
**sulfonamide** [sʌl'fɑnəmaɪd] o [sʌl'fɑnəmɪd] *s* (chem.) sulfonamida
**sulfur** ['sʌlfər] *s* (chem.) azufre; véase **sulphur**
**sulfurate** ['sʌlfjəret] o ['sʌlfəret] *va* sulfurar (*combinar con el azufre*); azufrar (*echar azufre sobre; sahumar con azufre*)
**sulfuration** [,sʌlfjə'reʃən] o [,sʌlfə'reʃən] *s* sulfuración; azuframiento
**sulfur dioxide** *s* (chem.) dióxido de azufre
**sulfuret** ['sʌlfjərɪt] *s* (chem.) sulfuro; ['sʌlfjərɛt] (*pret & pp:* **-reted** o **-retted**; *ger:* **-reting** o **-retting**) *va* azufrar; sulfurar
**sulfuric** [sʌl'fjurɪk] *adj* sulfúrico, sulfúreo; (chem.) sulfúrico
**sulfuric acid** *s* (chem.) ácido sulfúrico
**sulfur mine** *s* azufrera
**sulfurous** ['sʌlfərəs] *adj* sulfuroso, sulfúreo; ['sʌlfərəs] o [sʌl'fjʊrəs] *adj* (chem.) sulfuroso
**sulfurous acid** *s* (chem.) ácido sulfuroso

**sulk** [sʌlk] *s* enfurruñamiento, murria; *vn* enfurruñarse
**sulky** [ˈsʌlkɪ] *adj* (*comp:* **-ier;** *super:* **-iest**) enfurruñado, murrio, resentido; *s* (*pl:* **-ies**) coche de dos ruedas y un solo asiento
**Sulla** [ˈsʌlə] *s* Sila (*general romano*)
**sulla clover** [ˈsʌlə] o [ˈsulə] *s* (bot.) zulla
**sullen** [ˈsʌlən] *adj* hosco, malhumorado, taciturno, resentido, triste
**sullenness** [ˈsʌlənnɪs] *s* hosquedad, mal humor, resentimiento, tristeza
**sully** [ˈsʌlɪ] *s* (*pl:* **-lies**) mancha, tacha; (*pret & pp:* **-lied**) *va* manchar, empañar
**sulphadiazine** [ˌsʌlfəˈdaɪəzin] o [ˌsʌlfəˈdaɪəzɪn] *s* var. de **sulfadiazine**
**sulpha drugs** [ˈsʌlfə] *spl* var. de **sulfa drugs**
**sulphanilamide** [ˌsʌlfəˈnɪləmaɪd] o [ˌsʌlfəˈnɪləmɪd] *s* var. de **sulfanilamide**
**sulphapyridine** [ˌsʌlfəˈpɪrɪdin] o [ˌsʌlfəˈpɪrɪdɪn] *s* var. de **sulfapyridine**
**sulphas** [ˈsʌlfəz] *spl* var. de **sulfas**
**sulphate** [ˈsʌlfet] *s & va* var. de **sulfate**
**sulphathiazole** [ˌsʌlfəˈθaɪəzol] *s* var. de **sulfathiazole**
**sulphid** [ˈsʌlfɪd] o **sulphide** [ˈsʌlfaɪd] o [ˈsʌlfɪd] *s* var. de **sulfid** o **sulfide**
**sulphite** [ˈsʌlfaɪt] *s* var. de **sulfite**
**sulphur** [ˈsʌlfər] *s* (chem.) azufre; color de azufre; *adj* azufrado; *va* azufrar
**sulphurate** [ˈsʌlfjəret] o [ˈsʌlfəret] *va* var. de **sulfurate**
**sulphureous** [sʌlˈfjurɪəs] *adj* sulfúreo
**sulphuret** [ˈsʌlfjərɪt] *s* var. de **sulfuret;** [ˈsʌlfjərɛt] (*pret & pp:* **-reted** o **-retted;** *ger:* **-reting** o **-retting**) *va* var. de **sulfuret**
**sulphuric** [sʌlˈfjurɪk] *adj* var. de **sulfuric**
**sulphurize** [ˈsʌlfjəraɪz] *va* azufrar
**sulphurous** [ˈsʌlfərəs] *adj* sulfuroso, sulfúreo; infernal; ardiente, abrasador; [ˈsʌlfərəs] o [sʌlˈfjurəs] *adj* (chem.) sulfuroso
**sulphury** [ˈsʌlfərɪ] o [ˈsʌlfrɪ] *adj* sulfúreo, azufroso
**sulphydric acid** [sʌlˈfaɪdrɪk] *s* (chem.) ácido sulfhídrico
**sultan** [ˈsʌltən] *s* sultán
**sultana** [sʌlˈtænə] o [sʌlˈtɑnə] *s* sultana; (orn.) calamón; uva sultanina; pasa sultanina
**sultanate** [ˈsʌltənet] *s* sultanato
**sultaness** [ˈsʌltənɪs] o [sʌlˈtɑnɪs] *s* sultana
**sultanic** [sʌlˈtænɪk] *adj* sultánico
**sultry** [ˈsʌltrɪ] *adj* (*comp:* **-trier;** *super:* **-triest**) bochornoso
**Sulu** [ˈsulu] *s* joloano
**Suluan** [suˈluən] *adj & s* joloano
**Sulu Archipelago** *s* archipiélago de Sulú o Joló
**sum** [sʌm] *s* suma; (coll.) problema de aritmética; (*pret & pp:* **summed;** *ger:* **summing**) *va* sumar; **to sum up** sumar, resumir, compendiar; *vn* sumar; **to sum to** ascender a
**sumac** o **sumach** [ˈʃumæk] o [ˈsumæk] *s* (bot.) zumaque; hojas de zumaque secas
**Sumatran** [suˈmɑtrən] *adj & s* sumatrino
**Sumerian** [suˈmɪrɪən] o [sjuˈmɪrɪən] *adj & s* sumerio
**summarization** [ˌsʌmərɪˈzeʃən] *s* resumen, recapitulación
**summarize** [ˈsʌməraɪz] *va* resumir, recapitular
**summary** [ˈsʌmərɪ] *adj* sumario; *s* (*pl:* **-ries**) sumario, resumen
**summation** [sʌmˈeʃən] *s* adición; recapitulación; suma, total
**summer** [ˈsʌmər] *s* verano, estío; viga maestra; sotabanco (*piedra*); dintel; abril (*es decir, año*), p.ej., **to have seen fifteen summers** tener quince abriles; *adj* veraniego, estival; *va* preservar o mantener durante el verano; *vn* veranear
**summer camp** *s* campamento de veraneo
**summer colony** *s* colonia veraniega
**summerhouse** [ˈsʌmərˌhaus] *s* cenador, glorieta
**summer house** *s* casa para veranear, casa de verano
**summering** [ˈsʌmərɪŋ] *adj* veraneante; *s* veraneo
**summer resort** *s* lugar de veraneo, estación de verano
**summersault** [ˈsʌmərˌsɔlt] *s & vn* var. de **somersault**
**summer sausage** *s* salchicha cruda seca, salchicha cruda ahumada
**summer savory** *s* (bot.) ajedrea de jardín
**summer school** *s* escuela de verano
**summer solstice** *s* (astr.) solsticio de verano
**summer squash** *s* calabaza (*variedad de Cucurbita Pepo que se come en el verano*)
**summertime** [ˈsʌmərˌtaɪm] *s* verano, estío
**summer wheat** *s* trigo de primavera
**summery** [ˈsʌmərɪ] *adj* veraniego, estival
**summing up** *s* recapitulación, resumen
**summit** [ˈsʌmɪt] *s* cima, cumbre; sumidad
**summit conference** *s* conferencia en la cumbre
**summitry** [ˈsʌmɪtrɪ] *s* reuniones en la cumbre, esfuerzo por resolver los problemas internacionales mediante conferencias en la cumbre
**summon** [ˈsʌmən] *va* llamar, convocar; (law) emplazar, citar; evocar
**summoner** [ˈsʌmənər] *s* (law) emplazador; (law) ujier
**summons** [ˈsʌmənz] *s* (*pl:* **-monses**) orden, señal; (law) emplazamiento, citación; *va* (coll.) emplazar, citar
**sump** [sʌmp] *s* sumidero; (mach.) colector de aceite
**sumpter** [ˈsʌmptər] *s* acémila
**sumptuary** [ˈsʌmptʃuˌɛrɪ] *adj* suntuario
**sumptuary laws** *spl* leyes suntuarias
**sumptuous** [ˈsʌmptʃuəs] *adj* suntuoso
**Sun.** abr. de **Sunday**
**sun** [sʌn] *s* sol; año solar; **from sun to sun** de sol a sol; **to have a place in the sun** ocupar su puesto en el mundo; **under the sun** debajo del sol, en este mundo; (*pret & pp:* **sunned;** *ger:* **sunning**) *va* asolear; *vn* asolearse
**sun bath** *s* baño de sol
**sunbeam** *s* [ˈsʌnˌbim] *s* rayo de sol
**sunbird** [ˈsʌnˌbʌrd] *s* (orn.) suimanga; (orn.) pájaro sol, tigana (*Eurypyga helias*)
**sun bittern** *s* (orn.) tigana, pájaro sol
**sunbonnet** [ˈsʌnˌbɑnɪt] *s* papalina
**sunburn** [ˈsʌnˌbʌrn] *s* quemadura de sol, solanera; (*pret & pp:* **-burned** o **-burnt**) *va* quemar al sol, tostar al sol; *vn* quemarse al sol, tostarse al sol
**sunburnt** [ˈsʌnˌbʌrnt] *adj* requemado, bronceado
**sunburst** [ˈsʌnˌbʌrst] *s* resplandor repentino del sol en medio de las nubes; broche en forma de sol
**sundae** [ˈsʌndɪ] *s* helado con frutas, jarabes o nueces
**Sunda Islands** [ˈsʌndə] *spl* islas de la Sonda
**sun dance** *s* danza del sol
**Sunda Strait** [ˈsʌndə] *s* estrecho de la Sonda
**Sunday** [ˈsʌndɪ] *s* domingo; *adj* dominical; dominguero (*que se usa en domingo*)
**Sunday best** *s* (coll.) trapos de cristianar, ropa dominguera
**Sunday law** *s* ley del descanso dominical
**Sunday's child** *s* niño nacido de pies, niño mimado de la fortuna
**Sunday school** *s* escuela dominical, doctrina dominical
**sunder** [ˈsʌndər] *s* separación; **in sunder** en dos, en partes; *va* separar; romper; *vn* separarse; romperse
**sundew** [ˈsʌnˌdju] o [ˈsʌnˌdu] *s* (bot.) rocío de sol, rosolí, drosera
**sundial** [ˈsʌnˌdaɪəl] *s* reloj de sol, cuadrante solar
**sundog** [ˈsʌnˌdɔg] o [ˈsʌnˌdɑg] *s* parhelio; arco iris incompleto
**sundown** [ˈsʌnˌdaun] *s* puesta del sol
**sun-dried** [ˈsʌnˌdraɪd] *adj* secado al sol
**sundries** [ˈsʌndrɪz] *spl* artículos diversos
**sundry** [ˈsʌndrɪ] *adj* varios, diversos
**sunfast** [ˈsʌnˌfæst] o [ˈsʌnˌfɑst] *adj* inalterable al sol
**sunfish** [ˈsʌnˌfɪʃ] *s* (ichth.) luna, pez luna; (ichth.) pomotio
**sunflower** [ˈsʌnˌflauər] *s* (bot.) girasol
**sung** [sʌŋ] *pret & pp de* **sing**
**sunglasses** [ˈsʌnˌglæsɪz] o [ˈsʌnˌglɑsɪz] *spl* gafas para sol, gafas de sol
**sunglow** [ˈsʌnˌglo] *s* arrebol
**sun god** *s* dios del sol, divinidad solar
**sunk** [sʌŋk] *pret & pp de* **sink**

**sunken** [ˈsʌŋkən] *adj* hundido, sumido
**sun lamp** *s* (med.) lámpara de rayos ultravioletas, lámpara de cuarzo
**sunless** [ˈsʌnlɪs] *adj* nublado, sin sol
**sunlight** [ˈsʌn,laɪt] *s* luz del sol
**sunlit** [ˈsʌn,lɪt] *adj* iluminado por el sol
**sunn** [sʌn] *s* var. de **sunn hemp**
**Sunna** o **Sunnah** [ˈsʊnə] *s* zuna
**sunn hemp** *s* (bot.) cáñamo de Bengala
**sunny** [ˈsʌnɪ] *adj* (*comp:* **-nier**; *super:* **-niest**) de sol; asoleado, bañado de sol; brillante, resplandeciente; alegre, risueño; **to be sunny** hacer sol
**sunny side** *s* sol, lado del sol; (fig.) lado bueno, lado favorable
**sun parlor** *s* solana, mirador
**sun porch** *s* solana
**sunproof** [ˈsʌn,pruf] *adj* a prueba de sol
**sunrise** [ˈsʌn,raɪz] *s* salida del sol, orto del sol
**sunroom** [ˈsʌn,rum] o [ˈsʌn,rʊm] *s* solana
**sunset** [ˈsʌn,sɛt] *s* puesta del sol, ocaso del sol
**sunshade** [ˈsʌn,ʃed] *s* quitasol, sombrilla; toldo, marquesina; visera contra el sol
**sunshine** [ˈsʌn,ʃaɪn] *s* día, claridad del sol; alegría, contento; **in the sunshine** al sol
**sunshine roof** *s* (aut.) techo corredizo
**sunshiny** [ˈsʌn,ʃaɪnɪ] *adj* (*comp:* **-ier**; *super:* **-iest**) lleno de sol; brillante, resplandeciente; alegre, risueño
**sunspot** [ˈsʌn,spɑt] *s* mancha solar, mácula solar
**sun spurge** *s* (bot.) lechetrezna
**sunstroke** [ˈsʌn,strok] *s* (path.) insolación
**sun-up** [ˈsʌn,ʌp] *s* salida o nacimiento del sol
**sunward** [ˈsʌnwərd] *adj* que va hacia el sol; *adv* hacia el sol
**sunwards** [ˈsʌnwərdz] *adv* hacia el sol
**sunwise** [ˈsʌn,waɪz] *adj & adv* con el sol (*en su aparente movimiento diurno*)
**sup.** abr. de **superior, superlative, supine** y **supplement**
**sup** [sʌp] *s* sorbo; (*pret & pp:* **supped**; *ger:* **supping**) *va* sorber; dar de cenar a; *vn* cenar
**super** [ˈsupər] o [ˈsjupər] *s* (coll.) figurante, comparsa; (coll.) superintendente; *adj* (coll.) súper, archi (*excelente, muy bueno*)
**superable** [ˈsupərəbəl] o [ˈsjupərəbəl] *adj* superable
**superabound** [,supərəˈbaund] o [,sjupərəˈbaund] *vn* sobreabundar o superabundar
**superabundance** [,supərəˈbʌndəns] o [,sjupərəˈbʌndəns] *s* sobreabundancia o superabundancia
**superabundant** [,supərəˈbʌndənt] o [,sjupərəˈbʌndənt] *adj* sobreabundante o superabundante
**superadd** [,supərˈæd] o [,sjupərˈæd] *va* sobreañadir
**superannuate** [,supərˈænjuet] o [,sjupərˈænjuet] *va* inhabilitar; jubilar (*por motivo de ancianidad o enfermedad*); *vn* inhabilitarse; jubilarse
**superannuated** [,supərˈænjʊ,etɪd] o [,sjupərˈænjʊ,etɪd] *adj* inhabilitado; jubilado; añejo, anticuado, fuera de moda
**superannuation** [,supər,ænjʊˈeʃən] o [,sjupər,ænjʊˈeʃən] *s* inhabilitación; jubilación
**superb** [sʊˈpʌrb] o [sjʊˈpʌrb] *adj* soberbio, estupendo, magnífico
**superbomb** [ˈsupər,bɑm] o [ˈsjupər,bɑm] *s* superbomba
**supercargo** [ˈsupər,kɑrgo] o [ˈsjupər,kɑrgo] *s* (*pl:* **-goes** o **-gos**) (naut.) sobrecargo
**supercharge** [,supərˈtʃɑrdʒ] o [,sjupərˈtʃɑrdʒ] *va* sobrealimentar
**supercharger** [ˈsupər,tʃɑrdʒər] o [ˈsjupər,tʃɑrdʒər] *s* (mach.) compresor de sobrealimentación, superalimentador
**superciliary** [,supərˈsɪlɪ,ɛrɪ] o [,sjupərˈsɪlɪ,ɛrɪ] *adj* (anat.) superciliar
**supercilious** [,supərˈsɪlɪəs] o [,sjupərˈsɪlɪəs] *adj* arrogante, altanero, desdeñoso
**supercolumniation** *s* [,supərkə,lʌmnɪˈeʃən] o [,sjupərkə,lʌmnɪˈeʃən] *s* (arch.) superposición de columnas
**superconductivity** [,supər,kɑndʌkˈtɪvɪtɪ] o [,sjupər,kɑndʌkˈtɪvɪtɪ] *s* superconductividad
**superconductor** [,supərkənˈdʌktər] o [,sjupərkənˈdʌktər] *s* (elec.) superconductor
**superdominant** [,supərˈdɑmɪnənt] o [,sjupərˈdɑmɪnənt] *s* (mus.) superdominante
**superego** [,supərˈigo], [,supərˈɛgo], [,sjupərˈigo] o [,sjupərˈɛgo] *s* (psychoanal.) super-yo
**superelevation** [,supər,ɛlɪˈveʃən] o [,sjupər,ɛlɪˈveʃən] *s* (rail.) peralte
**supereminent** [,supərˈɛmɪnənt] o [,sjupərˈɛmɪnənt] *adj* supereminente
**supererogation** [,supər,ɛroˈgeʃən] o [,sjupər,ɛroˈgeʃən] *s* supererogación
**supererogatory** [,supərɪˈrɑgə,torɪ] o [,sjupərɪˈrɑgə,torɪ] *adj* supererogatorio
**superfetation** [,supərfɪˈteʃən] o [,sjupərfɪˈteʃən] *s* superfetación
**superficial** [,supərˈfɪʃəl] o [,sjupərˈfɪʃəl] *adj* superficial
**superficiality** [,supər,fɪʃɪˈælɪtɪ] o [,sjupər,fɪʃɪˈælɪtɪ] *s* (*pl:* **-ties**) superficialidad
**superficiary** [,supərˈfɪʃɪ,ɛrɪ] o [,sjupərˈfɪʃɪ,ɛrɪ] *adj* (law) superficiaro
**superficies** [,supərˈfɪʃɪiz] o [,sjupərˈfɪʃɪiz] *s* (*pl:* **-cies**) superficie
**superfine** [ˈsupər,faɪn] o [ˈsjupər,faɪn] *adj* superfino
**superfluity** [,supərˈfluɪtɪ] o [,sjupərˈfluɪtɪ] *s* (*pl:* **-ties**) superfluidad
**superfluous** [sʊˈpʌrfluəs] o [sjʊˈpʌrfluəs] *adj* superfluo
**superfort** [ˈsupər,fɔrt] o [ˈsjupər,fɔrt] o **superfortress** [ˈsupər,fɔrtrɪs] o [ˈsjupər,fɔrtrɪs] *s* (aer.) superfortaleza
**superheat** [,supərˈhit] o [,sjupərˈhit] *va* recalentar, sobrecalentar
**superheater** [,supərˈhitər] o [,sjupərˈhitər] *s* recalentador de vapor
**superheterodyne** [,supərˈhɛtərədaɪn] o [,sjupərˈhɛtərədaɪn] *adj & s* (rad.) superheterodino
**superhighway** [,supərˈhaɪ,we] o [,sjupərˈhaɪ,we] *s* supercarretera
**superhuman** [,supərˈhjumən] o [,sjupərˈhjumən] *adj* sobrehumano
**superhumeral** [,supərˈhjumərəl] o [,sjupərˈhjumərəl] *s* (eccl.) superhumeral
**superimpose** [,supərɪmˈpoz] o [,sjupərɪmˈpoz] *va* sobreponer
**superincumbent** [,supərɪnˈkʌmbənt] o [,sjupərɪnˈkʌmbənt] *adj* superyacente
**superinduce** [,supərɪnˈdjus] o [,sjupərɪnˈdjus] *va* sobreañadir
**superinduction** [,supərɪnˈdʌkʃən] o [,sjupərɪnˈdʌkʃən] *s* sobreañadidura
**superintend** [,supərɪnˈtɛnd] o [,sjupərɪnˈtɛnd] *va* superentender
**superintendence** [,supərɪnˈtɛndəns] o [,sjupərɪnˈtɛndəns] *s* superintendencia
**superintendency** [,supərɪnˈtɛndənsɪ] o [,sjupərɪnˈtɛndənsɪ] *s* (*pl:* **-cies**) var. de **superintendence**
**superintendent** [,supərɪnˈtɛndənt] o [,sjupərɪnˈtɛndənt] *s* superintendente
**superior** [səˈpɪrɪər] o [sʊˈpɪrɪər] *adj* superior; sereno, indiferente; arrogante; *s* superior; superiora
**superioress** [səˈpɪrɪərɪs] o [sʊˈpɪrɪərɪs] *s* superiora
**superiority** [sə,pɪrɪˈɑrɪtɪ] o [sʊ,pɪrɪˈɑrɪtɪ] *s* superioridad; serenidad, indiferencia; arrogancia
**superl.** abr. de **superlative**
**superlative** [səˈpʌrlətɪv] o [sʊˈpʌrlətɪv] *adj* superlativo; (gram.) superlativo; *s* (gram.) superlativo; **to talk in superlatives** exagerar
**superman** [ˈsupər,mæn] o [ˈsjupər,mæn] *s* (*pl:* **-men**) sobrehombre, superhombre
**supermarket** [ˈsupər,mɑrkɪt] o [ˈsjupər,mɑrkɪt] *s* supermercado
**supermundane** [,supərˈmʌnden] o [,sjupərˈmʌnden] *adj* sobremundano o supramundano
**supernal** [sʊˈpʌrnəl] o [sjʊˈpʌrnəl] *adj* superno, excelso, celestial
**supernatant** [,supərˈnetənt] o [,sjupərˈnetənt] *adj* sobrenadante
**supernatural** [,supərˈnætʃərəl] o [,sjupərˈnætʃərəl] *adj* sobrenatural
**supernaturalism** [,supərˈnætʃərəlɪzəm] o [,sjupərˈnætʃərəlɪzəm] *s* sobrenaturalismo
**supernumerary** [,supərˈnumə,rɛrɪ] o [,sjupərˈnjumə,rɛrɪ] *adj* supernumerario; *s* (*pl:* **-ies**) supernumerario; (theat.) figurante, comparsa

**superorganic** [ˌsupərɔrˈgænɪk] o [ˌsjupərɔrˈgænɪk] *adj* sobreorgánico
**superphosphate** [ˌsupərˈfɑsfet] o [ˌsjupərˈfɑsfet] *s* (chem. & agr.) superfosfato
**superpose** [ˌsupərˈpoz] o [ˌsjupərˈpoz] *va* sobreponer, superponer
**superposition** [ˌsupərpəˈzɪʃən] o [ˌsjupərpəˈzɪʃən] *s* superposición; (geom.) superposición
**superpower** [ˈsupərˌpaʊər] o [ˈsjupərˌpaʊər] *s* (dipl. & elec.) superpotencia
**superproduction** [ˌsupərprəˈdʌkʃən] o [ˌsjupərprəˈdʌkʃən] *s* superproducción
**superregeneration** [ˌsupərrɪˌdʒɛnəˈreʃən] o [ˌsjupərrɪˌdʒɛnəˈreʃən] *s* (rad.) superreacción, superregeneración
**superregenerative** [ˌsupərrɪˈdʒɛnəˌretɪv] o [ˌsjupərrɪˈdʒɛnəˌretɪv] *adj* (rad.) superregenerativo
**supersaturate** [ˌsupərˈsætʃəret] o [ˌsjupərˈsætʃəret] *va* sobresaturar
**supersaturation** [ˌsupərˌsætʃəˈreʃən] o [ˌsjupərˌsætʃəˈreʃən] *s* (chem.) sobresaturación
**superscribe** [ˌsupərˈskraɪb] o [ˌsjupərˈskraɪb] *va* sobrescribir
**superscript** [ˈsupərskrɪpt] o [ˈsjupərskrɪpt] *adj* sobrescrito; *s* (math.) índice sobrescrito
**superscription** [ˌsupərˈskrɪpʃən] o [ˌsjupərˈskrɪpʃən] *s* sobrescrito; (pharm.) superscripción
**supersede** [ˌsupərˈsid] o [ˌsjupərˈsid] *va* reemplazar, substituir; desalojar; (law) sobreseer
**supersensible** [ˌsupərˈsɛnsɪbəl] o [ˌsjupərˈsɛnsɪbəl] *adj* suprasensible
**supersensitive** [ˌsupərˈsɛnsɪtɪv] o [ˌsjupərˈsɛnsɪtɪv] *adj* supersensible
**supersonic** [ˌsupərˈsɑnɪk] o [ˌsjupərˈsɑnɪk] *adj* supersónico; **supersonics** *ssg* supersónica
**superspy** [ˈsupərˌspaɪ] o [ˈsjupərˌspaɪ] *s* (*pl:* **-spies**) superespía
**superstate** [ˈsupərˌstet] o [ˈsjupərˌstet] *s* superestado
**superstition** [ˌsupərˈstɪʃən] o [ˌsjupərˈstɪʃən] *s* superstición
**superstitious** [ˌsupərˈstɪʃəs] o [ˌsjupərˈstɪʃəs] *adj* supersticioso
**superstructure** [ˈsupərˌstrʌktʃər] o [ˈsjupərˌstrʌktʃər] *s* superstructura o superestructura
**supertax** [ˈsupərˌtæks] o [ˈsjupərˌtæks] *s* sobretasa, impuesto adicional
**supervene** [ˌsupərˈvin] o [ˌsjupərˈvin] *vn* sobrevenir
**supervention** [ˌsupərˈvɛnʃən] o [ˌsjupərˈvɛnʃən] *s* sobrevenida o superveniencia
**supervise** [ˈsupərvaɪz] o [ˈsjupərvaɪz] *va* superentender, supervisar
**supervision** [ˌsupərˈvɪʒən] o [ˌsjupərˈvɪʒən] *s* superintendencia, supervisión
**supervisor** [ˈsupərˌvaɪzər] o [ˈsjupərˌvaɪzər] *s* superintendente, supervisor
**supervisory** [ˌsupərˈvaɪzərɪ] o [ˌsjupərˈvaɪzərɪ] *adj* vigilante, supervisor, de superintendente
**supervoltage** [ˌsupərˈvoltɪdʒ] o [ˌsjupərˈvoltɪdʒ] *s* (phys.) supervoltaje
**supination** [ˌsupɪˈneʃən] o [ˌsjupɪˈneʃən] *s* supinación; (anat. & physiol.) supinación
**supinator** [ˌsupɪˈnetər] o [ˌsjupɪˈnetər] *s* (anat.) supinador
**supine** [suˈpaɪn] o [sjuˈpaɪn] *adj* supino; [ˈsupaɪn] o [ˈsjupaɪn] *s* (gram.) supino
**supp.** abr. de **supplement**
**supper** [ˈsʌpər] *s* cena; **to eat supper** tomar la cena, cenar
**suppl.** abr. de **supplement**
**supplant** [səˈplænt] *va* reemplazar, substituir; suplantar (*con malas artes*)
**supple** [ˈsʌpəl] *adj* flexible; dócil, servil; *va* hacer flexible; hacer dócil o servil; *vn* volverse flexible; volverse dócil o servil
**supplement** [ˈsʌplɪmənt] *s* suplemento (*lo que se añade para completar; parte que se añade a un diccionario, periódico u otro escrito*); (trig.) suplemento; [ˈsʌplɪmɛnt] *va* suplir, completar
**supplemental** [ˌsʌplɪˈmɛntəl] *adj* suplemental
**supplementary** [ˌsʌplɪˈmɛntərɪ] *adj* suplementario; (geom.) suplementario
**suppliance** [ˈsʌplɪəns] *s* súplica, suplicación
**suppliant** [ˈsʌplɪənt] o **supplicant** [ˈsʌplɪkənt] *adj & s* suplicante
**supplicate** [ˈsʌplɪket] *va & vn* suplicar
**supplication** [ˌsʌplɪˈkeʃən] *s* súplica, suplicación
**supplicator** [ˈsʌplɪˌketər] *s* suplicante
**supplicatory** [ˈsʌplɪkəˌtorɪ] *adj* suplicatorio
**supply** [səˈplaɪ] *s* (*pl:* **-plies**) suministro, provisión, aprovisionamiento; surtido, repuesto; suplente, substituto; oferta, existencia; **supplies** *spl* pertrechos; provisiones, víveres; artículos, efectos, materiales; **to be in short supply** escasear, ir a menos; (*pret & pp:* **-plied**) *va* abastecer, suministrar, proveer, aprovisionar; reemplazar; [ˈsʌplɪ] *adv* flexiblemente; dócilmente
**supply and demand** [səˈplaɪ] *spl* oferta y demanda
**support** [səˈport] *s* apoyo, soporte, sostén; sustento; *va* apoyar, soportar, sostener; sustentar; aguantar; (theat.) hacer el papel de; (theat.) acompañar (*a un actor principal*)
**supportable** [səˈportəbəl] *adj* soportable
**supporter** [səˈportər] *s* defensor, mantenedor, partidario; apoyo, soporte, sostén; tirante (*para medias*); suspensorio (*para sostener el escroto*); faja medical; (her.) tenante (*del escudo*)
**suppose** [səˈpoz] *va* suponer; creer; **to be supposed to** + *inf* deber + *inf*, p.ej., **he is supposed to arrive by three o'clock** debe llegar para las tres; **to be supposed to be** tener fama de (ser); **suppose we take a walk?** ¿qué será si damos un paseo?; **to suppose so** suponer que sí
**supposed** [səˈpozd] *adj* supuesto
**supposedly** [səˈpozɪdlɪ] *adv* según lo que se supone
**supposition** [ˌsʌpəˈzɪʃən] *s* suposición, creencia, opinión
**suppositional** [ˌsʌpəˈzɪʃənəl] *adj* supositivo, hipotético
**supposititious** [səˌpɑzɪˈtɪʃəs] *adj* supositicio (*fingido*); supositivo
**suppository** [səˈpɑzɪˌtorɪ] *s* (*pl:* **-ries**) supositorio
**suppress** [səˈprɛs] *va* suprimir
**suppresser** [səˈprɛsər] *s* var. de **suppressor**
**suppressible** [səˈprɛsɪbəl] *adj* suprimible
**suppression** [səˈprɛʃən] *s* supresión
**suppressive** [səˈprɛsɪv] *adj* supresivo
**suppressor** [səˈprɛsər] *s* supresor; eliminador (*de ruidos, de parásitos atmosféricos, etc.*)
**suppurate** [ˈsʌpjəret] *vn* supurar
**suppuration** [ˌsʌpjəˈreʃən] *s* supuración
**suppurative** [ˈsʌpjəˌretɪv] *adj* supurativo; supurante; *s* supurativo
**supranational** [ˌsuprəˈnæʃənəl] o [ˌsjuprəˈnæʃənəl] *adj* supranacional
**supraorbital** [ˌsuprəˈɔrbɪtəl] o [ˌsjuprəˈɔrbɪtəl] *adj* (anat.) supraorbital
**suprarenal** [ˌsuprəˈrinəl] o [ˌsjuprəˈrinəl] *adj* (anat.) suprarrenal; *s* (anat.) glándula suprarrenal
**supraspinous** [ˌsuprəˈspaɪnəs] o [ˌsjuprəˈspaɪnəs] *adj* supraspinoso
**supraspinous fossa** *s* (anat.) supraspina
**supremacy** [səˈprɛməsɪ], [sʊˈprɛməsɪ] o [sjʊˈprɛməsɪ] *s* supremacía
**supreme** [səˈprim], [sʊˈprim] o [sjʊˈprim] *adj* supremo; **supreme moment** momento supremo, hora suprema (*muerte*); **supreme sacrifice** sacrificio supremo
**Supreme Being** *s* Ser Supremo
**Supreme Court** *s* Tribunal Supremo; Corte Suprema (Am.)
**supt.** o **Supt.** abr. de **superintendent**
**surah** [ˈsurə] *s* surá (*tejido*)
**sural** [ˈsjʊrəl] *adj* (anat.) sural
**surcease** [sʌrˈsis] *s* (archaic) cesación
**surcharge** [ˈsʌrˌtʃɑrdʒ] *s* sobrecarga; (philately) sobrecarga; [ˌsʌrˈtʃɑrdʒ] o [ˈsʌrˌtʃɑrdʒ] *va* sobrecargar; (philately) sobrecargar
**surcingle** [ˈsʌrˌsɪŋgəl] *s* sobrecincha
**surcoat** [ˈsʌrˌkot] *s* gabán, sobretodo; sobrevesta (*sobre la armadura*)
**surd** [sʌrd] *adj* (math. & phonet.) sordo; *s* (math.) número sordo; (phonet.) sonido sordo, consonante sorda
**sure** [ʃur] *adj* seguro; **for sure** seguramente,

sin duda; **to be sure** seguramente, sin duda; **to be sure to** + *inf* no dejar de + *inf;* **to make sure** asegurar; asegurarse, cerciorarse; *adv* (coll.) seguramente; **sure enough** efectivamente
**sure-fire** [ˈʃʊr‚faɪr] *adj* (slang) seguro, de éxito seguro
**sure-footed** [ˈʃʊrˈfʊtɪd] *adj* de pie firme
**sure thing** *s* (slang) sacabocados; *adv* (slang) seguramente; *interj* (slang) ¡claro!, ¡seguro!
**surety** [ˈʃʊrtɪ] o [ˈʃʊrɪtɪ] *s* (*pl:* **-ties**) seguridad, fiador
**suretyship** [ˈʃʊrtɪʃɪp] o [ˈʃʊrɪtɪʃɪp] *s* seguridad, fianza
**surf** [sʌrf] *s* cachones, olas que rompen en la playa
**surface** [ˈsʌrfɪs] *s* superficie; *adj* superficial; *va* alisar, allanar; recubrir; cepillar (*madera*); emplastecer (*para pintar*); *vn* emerger (*un submarino*)
**surface mail** *s* correo por vía ordinaria
**surface tension** *s* (phys.) tensión superficial
**surfbird** [ˈsʌrf‚bʌrd] *s* (orn.) afriza, chorlo de las playas
**surfboard** [ˈsʌrf‚bord] *s* (sport) patín de mar
**surfboat** [ˈsʌrf‚bot] *s* (naut.) bote que puede resistir a las marejadas fuertes
**surf duck** *s* (orn.) negreta
**surfeit** [ˈsʌrfɪt] *s* exceso; hastío, hartura; empacho, indigestión; *va* atracar, hastiar, hartar; encebadar (*las bestias*); *vn* atracarse, hartarse; encebadarse
**surf-riding** [ˈsʌrf‚raɪdɪŋ] *s* (sport) patinaje sobre las olas
**surfy** [ˈsʌrfɪ] *adj* agitado, espumoso, undoso
**surge** [sʌrdʒ] *s* oleada; (elec.) sobretensión; *va* hacer undular; (naut.) aflojar, lascar, soltar poco a poco; *vn* agitarse, undular
**surgeon** [ˈsʌrdʒən] *s* cirujano
**surgeonfish** [ˈsʌrdʒən‚fɪʃ] *s* (ichth.) cirujano
**Surgeon General** *s* (*pl:* **Surgeons General**) médico mayor, jefe de la sanidad militar o naval
**surgery** [ˈsʌrdʒərɪ] *s* (*pl:* **-ies**) cirugía; gabinete de cirujano, sala de operaciones
**surgical** [ˈsʌrdʒɪkəl] *adj* quirúrgico
**surgy** [ˈsʌrdʒɪ] *adj* (*comp:* **-ier;** *super:* **-iest**) agitado, onduloso
**surly** [ˈsʌrlɪ] *adj* (*comp:* **-lier;** *super:* **-liest**) áspero, rudo, hosco, insolente
**surmise** [sʌrˈmaɪz] o [ˈsʌrmaɪz] *s* conjetura, suposición; [sʌrˈmaɪz] *va & vn* conjeturar, suponer
**surmount** [sərˈmaʊnt] *va* levantarse sobre; coronar; aventajar, sobrepujar; superar
**surmullet** [sərˈmʌlɪt] *s* (ichth.) mullo, salmonete
**surname** [ˈsʌr‚nem] *s* apellido; sobrenombre (*nombre que se añade al apellido*); *va* apellidar; sobrenombrar, dar un sobrenombre a
**surpass** [sərˈpæs] o [sərˈpɑs] *va* sobrepasar, aventajar
**surpassing** [sərˈpæsɪŋ] o [sərˈpɑsɪŋ] *adj* sobresaliente, extraordinario, incomparable
**surplice** [ˈsʌrplɪs] *s* (eccl.) sobrepelliz
**surpliced** [ˈsʌrplɪst] *adj* con sobrepelliz
**surplus** [ˈsʌrplʌs] *s* exceso, demasía, sobrante; (com.) superávit; *adj* sobrante, de sobra, excedente
**surplusage** [ˈsʌrplʌsɪdʒ] *s* exceso, demasía, sobrante; superfluidades (*palabras*)
**surplus property** *s* excedentes
**surprisal** [sərˈpraɪzəl] *s* sorpresa
**surprise** [sərˈpraɪz] *s* sorpresa; **to take by surprise** coger o tomar por sorpresa; *adj* inesperado, improviso; *va* sorprender; **to be surprised at** estar sorprendido de
**surprise attack** *s* ataque por sorpresa
**surprise package** *s* sorpresa
**surprise party** *s* reunión improvisada para felicitar a alguien
**surprising** [sərˈpraɪzɪŋ] *adj* sorprendente, sorpresivo
**surrealism** [səˈriəlɪzəm] *s* surrealismo
**surrealist** [səˈriəlɪst] *adj & s* surrealista
**surrealistic** [sə‚riəlˈɪstɪk] *adj* surrealista
**surrender** [səˈrɛndər] *s* rendición, entrega; dejación, abandono; sumisión; *va* rendir, entregar; dejar, abandonar; *vn* rendirse, entregarse
**surrender value** *s* (ins.) valor de rescate
**surreptitious** [‚sʌrɛpˈtɪʃəs] *adj* subrepticio
**surrey** [ˈsʌrɪ] *s* birlocho
**surrogate** [ˈsʌrəget] *s* substituto; (eccl.) vicario; (law) juez de testamentarías
**surround** [səˈraʊnd] *va* cercar, rodear, circundar; (mil.) sitiar
**surrounding** [səˈraʊndɪŋ] *adj* circundante, circunvecino; **surroundings** *spl* alrededores, contornos; ambiente, medio
**surtax** [ˈsʌrtæks] *s* impuesto adicional sobre rentas que pasan de cierta cantidad
**surveillance** [sərˈveləns] o [sərˈveljəns] *s* vigilancia
**survey** [ˈsʌrve] *s* examen, reconocimiento, inspección, estudio; medición, agrimensura, plano; levantamiento de planos; encuesta (*p.ej., de opinión*); bosquejo (*p.ej., de literatura*); [sʌrˈve] o [ˈsʌrve] *va* examinar, reconocer, inspeccionar, estudiar; medir; levantar el plano de; *vn* levantar el plano
**surveying** [sʌrˈveɪŋ] *s* agrimensura, planimetría
**surveyor** [sʌrˈveər] *s* examinador, inspector; sobrestante, vigilante; agrimensor, topógrafo; vista, inspector de aduanas
**surveyorship** [sʌrˈveərʃɪp] *s* agrimensura, empleo de agrimensor
**surveyor's measure** *s* sistema de medidas usado por los agrimensores (*la unidad es la cadena de 66 pies de largo, hecha de eslabones de 7,92 pulgadas de largo*)
**survival** [sərˈvaɪvəl] *s* supervivencia
**survival of the fittest** *s* (biol.) supervivencia de los más aptos
**survive** [sərˈvaɪv] *va* sobrevivir a (*otra persona, un desastre*); *vn* sobrevivir
**surviving** [sərˈvaɪvɪŋ] *adj* sobreviviente
**survivor** [sərˈvaɪvər] *s* sobreviviente
**Susan** [ˈsjuzən] o [ˈsuzən] *s* Susana
**susceptibility** [sə‚sɛptɪˈbɪlɪtɪ] *s* (*pl:* **-ties**) susceptibilidad; impresionabilidad; (elec.) susceptibilidad
**susceptible** [səˈsɛptɪbəl] *adj* susceptible; enamoradizo
**suspect** [ˈsʌspɛkt] o [səsˈpɛkt] *s* sospechoso; *adj* sospechado; [səsˈpɛkt] *va & vn* sospechar
**suspend** [səsˈpɛnd] *va* suspender; **to suspend payment** suspender pagos; *vn* dejar de obrar, dejar de funcionar; suspender pagos
**suspenders** [səsˈpɛndərz] *spl* tirantes (*de pantalón*)
**suspense** [səsˈpɛns] *s* suspensión; duda, incertidumbre; ansiedad; indecisión, irresolución; **in suspense** en suspenso (*pendiente de alguna resolución*); en la incertidumbre
**suspension** [səsˈpɛnʃən] *s* suspensión; (rhet.) suspensión
**suspension bridge** *s* puente colgante, puente de suspensión
**suspension of arms** *s* suspensión de armas
**suspension points** *spl* puntos suspensivos
**suspensive** [səsˈpɛnsɪv] *adj* suspensivo; indeciso, irresoluto
**suspensory** [səsˈpɛnsərɪ] *adj* suspensorio; *s* (*pl:* **-ries**) suspensorio
**suspicion** [səsˈpɪʃən] *s* sospecha, suspicacia; sombra, traza ligera; **above suspicion** superior a la sospecha, por encima de toda sospecha; **on suspicion** por ser sospechado; **under suspicion** sospechado
**suspicious** [səsˈpɪʃəs] *adj* sospechoso
**suspiration** [‚sʌspɪˈreʃən] *s* suspiro; respiración muy larga
**suspire** [səsˈpaɪr] *va* expresar con un suspiro; *vn* (poet.) suspirar, respirar con fuerza
**sustain** [səsˈten] *va* sostener, sustentar; apoyar, defender; confirmar, probar; sufrir (*p.ej., un daño, una pérdida*)
**sustaining program** *s* (rad. & telv.) programa sin patrocinador
**sustenance** [ˈsʌstɪnəns] *s* sustento, alimentos, subsistencia; sostenimiento
**sutler** [ˈsʌtlər] *s* vivandero
**suture** [ˈsutʃər] o [ˈsjutʃər] *s* costura; (anat., bot., surg. & zool.) sutura; *va* unir mediante sutura
**suzerain** [ˈsuzəren] o [ˈsjuzəren] *adj* soberano, supremo; *s* (feud.) suzerano; (dipl.) estado que ejerce la soberanía sobre otro
**suzerainty** [ˈsuzərentɪ] o [ˈsjuzərentɪ] *s*

(feud.) suzeranía; (dipl.) soberanía de un estado sobre otro
**svelte** [svɛlt] *adj* sutil, flexible, delgado, esbelto
**s.w., S.W.** o **SW** abr. de **southwest**
**swab** [swɑb] *s* escobón, estropajo, aljofifa, esponja; (surg.) algodón, esponja, tapón de algodón; (naut.) lampazo; (gun.) escobillón; (slang) patán; (*pret & pp:* **swabbed;** *ger:* **swabbing**) *va* limpiar, fregar; (surg.) limpiar con algodón; (naut.) lampacear
**swabber** [ˈswɑbər] *s* escobón; (surg.) algodón, esponja, tapón de algodón; (naut.) lampazo; (naut.) lampacero
**Swabia** [ˈswebɪə] *s* Suabia
**Swabian** [ˈswebɪən] *adj & s* suabo
**swaddle** [ˈswɑdəl] *s* faja, pañal; *va* fajar, envolver, empañar
**swaddling clothes** *spl* envoltura, pañales, mantillas
**swag** [swæg] *s* (slang) robo, hurto, botín; (f.a.) guirnalda
**swage** [swedʒ] *s* estampa, tas; *va* estampar, forjar en estampa, formar en el yunque
**swagger** [ˈswægər] *s* fanfarronada; contoneo, paso jactancioso; *adj* (coll.) muy elegante; *va* intimidar; decir fanfarroneando; *vn* fanfarronear; contonearse
**swagger stick** *s* bastón ligero de paseo
**swain** [swen] *s* zagal; (slang) amante, enamorado
**swale** [swel] *s* pantano, prado
**swallow** [ˈswɑlo] *s* trago, deglución; tragadero; (orn.) golondrina; *va* tragar, deglutir; (fig.) tragar o tragarse (*cosas inverosímiles; cosas repulsivas o vejatorias*); (fig.) suprimir, retractar, desdecir; engullir (*paparruchas*); *vn* tragar, deglutir
**swallow-tail** [ˈswɑloˌtel] *s* frac; (carp.) cola de milano
**swallow-tailed coat** [ˈswɑloˌteld] *s* frac
**swallowwort** [ˈswɑloˌwʌrt] *s* (bot.) golondrinera, celidonia
**swam** [swæm] *pret de* **swim**
**swamp** [swɑmp] *s* pantano, marisma; *va* sumergir, encharcar, inundar; abrumar (*p.ej., de trabajo*); *vn* sumergirse, hundirse
**swampland** [ˈswɑmpˌlænd] *s* pantanal
**swamp oak** *s* (bot.) roble blanco de California (*Quercus lobata*); (bot.) casuarina; (bot.) roble de los pantanos (*Quercus palustris*); (bot.) viminaria
**swampy** [ˈswɑmpɪ] *adj* (*comp:* **-ier;** *super:* **-iest**) pantanoso
**swan** [swɑn] *s* (orn.) cisne; (fig.) cisne (*poeta*); (*cap.*) *s* (astr.) Cisne
**swan dive** *s* salto de ángel
**swank** [swæŋk] *s* (coll.) jactancia, ostentación, elegancia vistosa; *adj* (slang) vistoso, ostentoso, elegante; *vn* (coll.) fanfarronear, pavonearse
**swan knight** *s* (myth.) caballero del cisne
**swanky** [ˈswæŋkɪ] *adj* (*comp:* **-ier;** *super:* **-iest**) (slang) brioso, vistoso, ostentoso, elegante
**swan mussel** *s* (zool.) almeja de los estanques
**swanneck** [ˈswɑnˌnɛk] *s* cuello de cisne
**swan's-down** [ˈswɑnzˌdaʊn] *s* plumón de cisne; moletón, paño de vicuña
**swanskin** [ˈswɑnˌskɪn] *s* piel de cisne; moletón, lanilla
**swan song** *s* canto del cisne
**swap** [swɑp] *s* (coll.) trueque, cambalache; (*pret & pp:* **swapped;** *ger:* **swapping**) *va & vn* (coll.) trocar, cambalachear
**sward** [swɔrd] *s* césped
**swarm** [swɔrm] *s* enjambre; (fig.) enjambre; *va* enjambrar; trepar; *vn* enjambrar; trepar; volar o moverse en enjambres; hormiguear (*una multitud de gente o animales*)
**swarming** [ˈswɔrmɪŋ] *adj* hormigueante; *s* enjambrazón (*de abejas*)
**swart** [swɔrt] *adj* var. de **swarthy**
**swarthy** [ˈswɔrðɪ] o [ˈswɔrθɪ] *adj* (*comp:* **-ier;** *super:* **-iest**) moreno, atezado, carinegro
**swash** [swɑʃ] *s* chorretada, golpe de agua; ruido del agua movida; canalizo; *va* salpicar; *vn* chapotear; hacer ruido (*el agua*); baladronear, hacer ruido
**swashbuckler** [ˈswɑʃˌbʌklər] *s* espadachín, valentón, matón, matasiete
**swashbuckling** [ˈswɑʃˌbʌklɪŋ] *adj* fanfarrón, jactancioso; *s* fanfarronada, jactancia
**swash plate** *s* (mach.) placa oscilante
**swastika** [ˈswɑstɪkə] o [ˈswæstɪkə] *s* svástica
**swat** [swɑt] *s* (coll.) golpe violento; (*pret & pp:* **swatted;** *ger:* **swatting**) *va* (coll.) golpear con fuerza; (coll.) aporrear, aplastar (*una mosca*)
**swatch** [swɑtʃ] *s* muestra de tela, cuero, etc.; muestrario
**swath** [swɔθ] o [swɑθ] *s* guadañada; ringlera de hierba o mies acabada de segar; faja, tira; **to cut a swath** hacer gran papel
**swathe** [sweð] *s* envoltura; vendaje; guadañada; ringlera de hierba o mies acabada de segar; *va* envolver, fajar; atar, liar; vendar
**sway** [swe] *s* sacudimiento, oscilación, vaivén; inclinación, ladeo; imperio, mando, dominio; **to hold sway** tener dominio; **to hold sway over** dominar; *va* sacudir, hacer oscilar; conmover; disuadir; dominar, gobernar; *vn* inclinarse, ladearse; desviarse; oscilar; tambalear, flaquear
**swayback** [ˈsweˌbæk] *s* corcova con prominencia anterior; *adj* deslomado, derrengado
**sway-backed** [ˈsweˌbækt] *adj* deslomado, derrengado
**swear** [swɛr] (*pret:* **swore;** *pp:* **sworn**) *va* jurar; juramentar; prestar (*juramento*); **to swear in** tomar juramento a, hacer prestar juramento; **to swear off** jurar renunciar a; **to swear out** obtener mediante juramento; *vn* jurar; **to swear at** decir juramentos a, maldecir; **to swear by** jurar por; poner toda su confianza en; **to swear to** prestar juramento a; declarar bajo juramento; **to swear to** + *inf* jurar + *inf*, p.ej., **he swore to tell the truth** juró decir la verdad
**sweat** [swɛt] *s* sudor; (coll.) sudor, trasudor; (*pret & pp:* **sweat** o **sweated**) *va* sudar (*agua por los poros; la ropa*); hacer sudar; (slang) hacer sudar (*es decir, hacer dar a disgusto*); (slang) someter a un interrogatorio brutal para arrancar informes o una confesión; (metal.) fundir, soldar, calentar hasta la fusión; **to sweat it out** (slang) aguantarlo hasta el fin; *vn* sudar; (coll.) sudar (*trabajar con fatiga*)
**sweatband** [ˈswɛtˌbænd] *s* badana del forro del sombrero, tafilete
**sweater** [ˈswɛtər] *s* sudante (*persona*); suéter
**sweat gland** *s* (anat.) glándula sudorípara
**sweatily** [ˈswɛtɪlɪ] *adv* con sudor
**sweat shirt** s (sport) pulóver de mangas largas
**sweatshop** [ˈswɛtˌʃɑp] *s* taller donde hacen sudar al obrero todo lo que puede rendir por un salario de miseria
**sweaty** [ˈswɛtɪ] *adj* (*comp:* **-ier;** *super:* **-iest**) sudoriento, sudoroso; (fig.) penoso, laborioso
**Swed.** abr. de **Sweden** y **Swedish**
**Swede** [swid] *s* sueco
**Sweden** [ˈswidən] *s* Suecia
**Swedish** [ˈswidɪʃ] *adj* sueco; *spl* suecos; *ssg* sueco (*idioma*)
**Swedish clover** *s* (*bot.*) trébol sueco
**Swedish turnip** *s* (bot.) nabo de Suecia
**sweep** [swip] *s* barrido; soplo (*del viento*); extensión; alcance; barrendero; deshollinador; remo largo y pesado; cigoñal (*de pozo*); (sport) carrera que decide las apuestas; (*pret & pp:* **swept**) *va* barrer; arrastrar, arrebatar; tocar, rozar; recorrer con la mirada, los dedos, etc.; *vn* barrer; pasar o moverse rápidamente; pasar arrasando; extenderse; precipitarse; andar con paso majestuoso
**sweepback** [ˈswipˌbæk] *s* (aer.) flecha
**sweeper** [ˈswipər] *s* barrendero (*persona*); barredera (*máquina para barrer las calles*); barredera de alfombra; (nav.) dragaminas
**sweep generator** *s* (telv.) generador de barrido
**sweeping** [ˈswipɪŋ] *adj* arrebatador; comprensivo, extenso, vasto; *s* barredura; **sweepings** *spl* barreduras
**sweep second hand** *s* segundero central
**sweepstake** [ˈswipˌstek] *s* ganancia por una persona de todas las apuestas; **sweepstakes** *ssg & spl* lotería en la cual una persona gana todas las apuestas; carrera que decide todas las apuestas; premio en las carreras de caballos
**sweet** [swit] *s* persona querida; dulzura; **sweets**

*spl* dulces, golosinas; *adj* dulce; oloroso; fresco; bueno, fértil; querido; lindo; amable; **to be sweet on** (coll.) estar enamorado de; *adv* dulcemente; **to smell sweet** tener buen olor
**sweet alyssum** *s* (bot.) alhelicillo
**sweet basil** *s* (bot.) albahaca
**sweet bay** *s* (bot.) laurel; (bot.) magnolia
**sweetbread** ['swit,brɛd] *s* lechecillas, mollejas
**sweetbriar** o **sweetbrier** ['swit,braɪər] *s* (bot.) eglantina (*Rosa eglanteria*)
**sweet cicely** *s* (bot.) perifollo oloroso
**sweet cider** *s* sidra dulce
**sweet clover** *s* (bot.) trébol oloroso
**sweet corn** *s* maíz tierno, maíz de grano dulce
**sweeten** ['switən] *va* endulzar, azucarar; suavizar; purificar; *vn* endulzarse, azucararse; suavizarse
**sweetening** ['switənɪŋ] *s* dulcificación; (cook.) dulcificante
**sweet fern** *s* (bot.) polipodio común; (bot.) perifollo oloroso
**sweet flag** *s* (bot.) ácoro, iris amarillo
**sweet gale** *s* (bot.) mirto de Brabante
**sweet gum** *s* (bot.) ocozol
**sweetheart** ['swit,hɑrt] *s* enamorado o enamorada; querida, amiga querida; galán, cortejo
**sweetie** ['switɪ] *s* (coll.) var. de **sweetheart**
**sweeting** ['switɪŋ] *s* camuesa (*manzana*)
**sweetish** ['switɪʃ] *adj* algo dulce
**sweet marjoram** *s* (bot.) mejorana
**sweetmeats** ['swit,mits] *spl* confitura, confites, dulces
**sweetness** ['switnɪs] *s* dulzura; suavidad
**sweet oil** *s* aceite de oliva
**sweet pea** *s* (bot.) guisante de olor
**sweet pepper** *s* (bot.) pimiento dulce
**sweet pepper bush** *s* (bot.) cletra
**sweet potato** *s* batata, camote; (coll.) ocarina
**sweet scabious** *s* (bot.) escabiosa de Indias
**sweet-scented** ['swit,sɛntɪd] *adj* oloroso, perfumado
**sweet sixteen** *s* los dieciséis abriles
**sweetsop** ['swit,sɑp] *s* (bot.) chirimoyo del Senegal; chirimoya del Senegal (*fruto*)
**sweet spirit of niter** *s* (pharm.) espíritu de nitro dulce
**sweet-tempered** ['swit'tɛmpərd] *adj* complaciente, de carácter dulce
**sweet tooth** *s* gusto por los dulces
**sweet-toothed** ['swit,tuθt] *adj* goloso
**sweet william** o **sweet William** *s* (bot.) clavel de ramillete, clavel de San Isidro, minutisa
**swell** [swɛl] *s* hinchazón; entumecimiento; oleada, marejada; oleaje; mar tendida, mar de fondo o de leva; ondulación del terreno; (mus.) reguladores; (mus.) pedal de expresión (*del órgano*); (coll.) persona muy elegante; *adj* (coll.) muy elegante; (slang) de órdago, magnífico, excelente; (*pret:* **swelled;** *pp:* **swelled** o **swollen**) *va* hinchar, inflar (*con aire*); abultar, aumentar, acrecentar; elevar, levantar; (mus.) aumentar gradualmente la fuerza de; (fig.) hinchar, engreír; *vn* hincharse; inflarse; abultarse, aumentar, crecer; elevarse, levantarse; (mus.) aumentar gradualmente en fuerza; (fig.) hincharse, engreírse; embravecerse (*el mar*)
**swelled head** *s* entono, soberbia; **to have a swelled head** estar muy pagado de sí mismo
**swelling** ['swɛlɪŋ] *s* hinchazón; bulto, chichón, protuberancia
**swelter** ['swɛltər] *s* calor abrumador; sudor abundante; *va* abrumar, sofocar; sudar, hacer sudar; *vn* abrumarse, sofocarse de calor; chorrear de sudor
**swept** [swɛpt] *pret & pp de* **sweep**
**sweptback wing** ['swɛpt,bæk] *s* var. de **backswept wing**
**swerve** [swʌrv] *s* desvío brusco; *va* desviar; *vn* desviarse, torcer, cambiar repentinamente de dirección
**swift** [swɪft] *adj* veloz, rápido; pronto, presto; repentino; vivo, activo; *adv* velozmente, rápidamente; *s* (orn.) vencejo (*Apus apus*); (orn.) salangana (*Collocalia esculenta*)
**swift-footed** ['swɪft'futɪd] *adj* ligero, veloz, de paso rápido
**swiftly** ['swɪftlɪ] *adv* velozmente, rápidamente; pronto
**swiftness** ['swɪftnɪs] *s* velocidad, rapidez; prontitud
**swig** [swɪg] *s* (coll.) tragantada; (*pret & pp:* **swigged;** *ger:* **swigging**) *va & vn* (coll.) beber a grandes tragos
**swill** [swɪl] *s* bazofia; basura, inmundicia; tragantada; *va* lavar, inundar de agua; beber a grandes tragos; llenar; emborrachar; *vn* chapotear, salpicar; beber a grandes tragos; emborracharse
**swim** [swɪm] *s* natación; nadada (Am.); distancia recorrida nadando; vahido, desmayo; (ichth.) vejiga natatoria, nadadera de pez; **the swim** (coll.) la corriente (*p.ej., de los negocios*); (*pret:* **swam;** *pp:* **swum;** *ger:* **swimming**) *va* pasar a nado; hacer nadar o flotar; *vn* nadar; deslizarse, escurrirse; padecer vahidos; dar vueltas (*la cabeza*); **to go swimming** ir a nadar, ir a bañarse; **to swim across** atravesar a nado
**swimmer** ['swɪmər] *s* nadador
**swimmeret** ['swɪmərɛt] *s* (zool.) pleópodo
**swimming** ['swɪmɪŋ] *s* natación; vahido, vértigo; *adj* nadante; lleno de lágrimas
**swimmingly** ['swɪmɪŋlɪ] *adv* lisamente, sin tropiezo, sin dificultad
**swimming pool** *s* piscina, piscina natatoria
**swimming suit** *s* traje de baño, traje de natación
**swimwear** ['swɪm,wɛr] *s* ropa de natación, trajes de natación
**swindle** ['swɪndəl] *s* estafa, timo; *va & vn* estafar, timar
**swindler** ['swɪndlər] *s* estafador, timador
**swine** [swaɪn] *s* cerdo, puerco; (fig.) puerco, cochino; *spl* ganado de cerda
**swineherd** ['swaɪn,hʌrd] *s* porquero, porquerizo
**swing** [swɪŋ] *s* oscilación, balance, vaivén; columpio; hamaca; anchura, libertad de acción; alcance; turno, período; jira; fuerza, ímpetu; vuelta; (boxing) golpe lateral, golpe de lado; (mus. & poet.) ritmo constantemente repetido; **in full swing** en plena marcha, en pleno vigor; (*pret & pp:* **swung**) *va* blandir (*p.ej., un arma*); menear (*los brazos*); hacer oscilar, hacer dar vueltas a; colgar (*una cosa*) para que oscile; columpiar; manejar con éxito; *vn* oscilar; balancearse, bambolear; columpiarse; estar colgado; dar una vuelta; **to swing open** abrirse de pronto (*una puerta*)
**swing drawbridge** *s* puente giratorio
**swingeing** ['swɪndʒɪŋ] *adj* (coll.) muy grande, extraordinario
**swinging boom** *s* (naut.) tangón
**swinging door** *s* batiente oscilante
**swingle** ['swɪŋgəl] *s* espadilla; *va* espadillar
**swingletree** ['swɪŋgəl,tri] *s* var. de **singletree**
**swing music** *s* música de baile de ritmo repetido y con improvisaciones
**swing shift** *s* (coll.) turno desde las quince hasta medianoche
**swinish** ['swaɪnɪʃ] *adj* porcuno; (fig.) puerco, cochino
**swipe** [swaɪp] *s* (coll.) golpe fuerte; *va* (coll.) dar un golpe fuerte a; (slang) hurtar, robar
**swirl** [swʌrl] *s* remolino, torbellino; vuelta, movimiento giratorio; *va* hacer girar; *vn* remolinar, arremolinarse; girar
**swish** [swɪʃ] *s* silbido, zumbido; chasquido (*p. ej., de látigo*); crujido (*de un vestido*); *va* chasquear (*p.ej., el látigo*); *vn* moverse produciendo un silbido o zumbido; chasquear; crujir (*un vestido*)
**Swiss** [swɪs] *adj & ssg* suizo; *spl* suizos
**Swiss chard** *s* (bot.) acelga
**Swiss cheese** *s* queso suizo, Gruyère
**Swiss Guards** *spl* guardia suiza
**Swiss mountain pine** *s* (bot.) pino negro
**Swiss pine** *s* (bot.) pino cembro
**switch** [swɪtʃ] *s* varilla, bastoncillo, latiguillo; golpe, latigazo; coletazo; cabellera, trenza o moño postizo, añadido (*de mujer*); (elec.) llave; (elec.) interruptor; (elec.) conmutador; (rail.) agujas; desviación, conmutación, cambio; *va* azotar, fustigar; (elec.) conmutar; (rail.) desviar; **to switch off** (elec.) cortar, desconectar; **to switch on** (elec.) cerrar (*el*

*circuito*); poner, encender (*la luz, la radio, etc.*); *vn* cambiarse, moverse; desviarse
**switchback** ['swɪtʃ,bæk] *s* (rail.) pendiente de vaivén; deslizador circular, montaña rusa
**switchboard** ['swɪtʃ,bord] *s* (elec. & telp.) cuadro de distribución
**switching engine** *s* (rail.) locomotora de maniobras
**switchman** ['swɪtʃmən] *s* (*pl:* **-men**) (rail.) guardagujas, agujetero
**switch plate** *s* (elec.) placa de interruptor, placa de llave
**switch tender** *s* (rail.) guardagujas, agujetero
**switch tower** *s* (rail.) garita o torre de control
**switchyard** ['swɪtʃ,jɑrd] *s* (rail.) patio de maniobras
**Switzerland** ['swɪtsərlənd] *s* Suiza
**swivel** ['swɪvəl] *s* eslabón giratorio; torniquete (*de silla giratoria*); enganche giratorio; (gun.) colisa; (*pret & pp:* **-eled** o **-elled; *ger:* -eling** o **-elling**) *va* hacer girar sobre un eje; enganchar con un eslabón giratorio; *vn* girar sobre un eje
**swivel chair** *s* silla giratoria
**swivel gun** *s* colisa
**swob** [swɑb] *s* var. de **swab;** (*pret & pp:* **swobbed;** *ger:* **swobbing**) *va* var. de **swab**
**swollen** ['swolən] *adj* hinchado; crecido; **swollen with pride** hinchado de orgullo; *pp de* **swell**
**swoon** [swun] *s* desmayo, deliquio; *vn* desmayarse, desvanecerse
**swoop** [swup] *s* arremetida, descenso súbito; *va* arrebatar, coger al vuelo; *vn* bajar rápidamente, precipitarse; abatirse (*el ave de rapiña*)
**swop** [swɑp] *s* var. de **swap;** (*pret & pp:* **swopped;** *ger:* **swopping**) *va & vn* var. de **swap**
**sword** [sord] *s* espada; **at swords' points** enemistados a sangre y fuego; **the sword** el poder de la espada; **to cross swords** luchar, reñir; **to draw the sword** tirar de la espada, desnudar la espada; **to measure swords** medir las espadas; **to put to the sword** pasar al filo de la espada; **to sheathe the sword** envainar la espada
**sword-and-cloak** ['sordənd'klok] *adj* de capa y espada
**sword arm** *s* brazo derecho
**sword bayonet** *s* bayoneta espada, sable-bayoneta
**sword bean** *s* (bot.) caraota grande (*Canavalia gladiata*)
**swordbearer** ['sord,bɛrər] *s* paje que llevaba la espada al caballero
**sword belt** *s* cinturón
**sword cane** *s* bastón de estoque
**sword dance** *s* danza de espadas
**sword fern** *s* (bot.) cola de quetzal
**swordfish** ['sord,fɪʃ] *s* (ichth.) pez espada
**sword handler** *s* (taur.) mozo de estoques
**sword knot** *s* borla de espada
**sword lily** *s* (bot.) estoque
**swordman** ['sordmən] *s* (*pl:* **-men**) var. de **swordsman**
**Sword of Damocles** *s* espada de Dámocles
**swordplay** ['sord,ple] *s* esgrima; danza de espadas
**sword rattling** *s* fanfarronería
**sword side** *s* lado del padre, varones de la familia
**swordsman** ['sordzmən] *s* (*pl:* **-men**) espada; esgrimidor
**swordsmanship** ['sordzmənʃɪp] *s* esgrima, habilidad en el manejo de la espada
**sword swallower** ['swɑloər] *s* tragasable
**sword thrust** *s* estocada, golpe de espada
**swore** [swor] *pret de* **swear**
**sworn** [sworn] *pp de* **swear**
**sworn enemy** *s* enemigo jurado
**swum** [swʌm] *pp de* **swim**
**swung** [swʌŋ] *pret & pp de* **swing**
**Sybarite** ['sɪbəraɪt] *adj & s* sibarita
**Sybaritic** [,sɪbə'rɪtɪk] *adj* sibarítico
**sybaritism** ['sɪbəraɪtɪzəm] *s* sibaritismo
**sycamore** ['sɪkəmor] *s* (bot.) sicómoro; (bot.) plátano; (bot.) falso plátano, arce blanco
**sycamore fig** *s* (bot.) sicómoro
**sycamore maple** *s* (bot.) falso plátano, arce blanco
**sycon** ['saɪkɑn] *s* (zool.) sicón
**syconium** [saɪ'konɪəm] *s* (bot.) sicono
**sycophancy** ['sɪkəfənsɪ] *s* adulación, servilismo; parasitismo
**sycophant** ['sɪkəfənt] *s* adulador; parásito; (hist.) sicofanta (*denunciador; impostor*)
**sycophantic** [[,sɪkə'fæntɪk] *adj* adulatorio; parasítico
**sycosis** [saɪ'kosɪs] *s* (path.) sicosis (*afección de la piel*)
**syenite** ['saɪənaɪt] *s* (mineral.) sienita
**syll.** abr. de **syllable** y **syllabus**
**syllabary** ['sɪlə,bɛrɪ] *s* (*pl:* **-ies**) silabario
**syllabic** [sɪ'læbɪk] *adj* silábico
**syllabicate** [sɪ'læbɪket] *va* silabear
**syllabication** [sɪ,læbɪ'keʃən] o **syllabification** [sɪ,læbɪfɪ'keʃən] *s* silabeo
**syllabify** [sɪ'læbɪfaɪ] (*pret & pp:* **-fied**) *va* silabear
**syllabize** ['sɪləbaɪz] *va* var. de **syllabify**
**syllable** ['sɪləbəl] *s* sílaba; *va* silabear
**syllabub** ['sɪləbʌb] *s* var. de **sillabub**
**syllabus** ['sɪləbəs] *s* (*pl:* **-buses** *o* **-bi** [baɪ]) sílabo
**syllepsis** [sɪ'lɛpsɪs] *s* (*pl:* **-ses** [siz]) (rhet.) silepsis
**syllogism** ['sɪlədʒɪzəm] *s* silogismo
**syllogistic** [,sɪlə'dʒɪstɪk] *adj* silogístico
**syllogize** ['sɪlədʒaɪz] *va* deducir mediante silogismos; *vn* silogizar
**sylph** [sɪlf] *s* (myth.) silfo, sílfide; (fig.) sílfide
**sylva** ['sɪlvə] *s* var. de **silva**
**sylvan** ['sɪlvən] *adj* selvoso, selvático
**sylvanite** ['sɪlvənaɪt] *s* (mineral.) silvanita
**Sylvia** ['sɪlvɪə] *s* Silvia
**sylviculture** [,sɪlvɪ'kʌltʃər] *s* silvicultura
**sylvite** ['sɪlvaɪt] *s* (mineral.) silvina
**Sylvanus** [sɪl'venəs] *s* Silvano
**sym.** abr. de **symbol, symmetrical, symphony** y **symptom**
**symbiont** ['sɪmbaɪɑnt] o ['sɪmbɪɑnt] *s* (biol.) simbión o simbiota
**symbiosis** [,sɪmbaɪ'osɪs] o [,sɪmbɪ'osɪs] *s* (biol.) simbiosis
**symbiotic** [,sɪmbaɪ'ɑtɪk] o [,sɪmbɪ'ɑtɪk] *adj* (biol.) simbiótico
**symbol** ['sɪmbəl] *s* símbolo; *va* simbolizar
**symbolic** [sɪm'bɑlɪk] o **symbolical** [sɪm'bɑlɪkəl] *adj* simbólico
**symbolism** ['sɪmbəlɪzəm] *s* simbolismo
**symbolist** ['sɪmbəlɪst] *s* simbolista
**symbolistic** [,sɪmbəl'ɪstɪk] *adj* simbolístico
**symbolization** [,sɪmbəlɪ'zeʃən] *s* simbolización
**symbolize** ['sɪmbəlaɪz] *va* simbolizar
**symmetric** [sɪ'mɛtrɪk] o **symmetrical** [sɪ'mɛtrɪkəl] *adj* simétrico
**symmetrically** [sɪ'mɛtrɪkəlɪ] *adv* simétricamente
**symmetrize** ['sɪmɪtraɪz] *va* simetrizar
**symmetry** ['sɪmɪtrɪ] *s* (*pl:* **-tries**) simetría
**sympathectomy** [,sɪmpə'θɛktəmɪ] *s* (surg.) simpaticectomía
**sympathetic** [,sɪmpə'θɛtɪk] *adj* simpático (*p.ej., sentimiento*); compasivo; (anat., mus., phys. & physiol.) simpático; **sympathetic to** o **toward** favorablemente dispuesto a o hacia
**sympathetically** [,sɪmpə'θɛtɪkəlɪ] *adv* simpáticamente; compasivamente
**sympathetic ink** *s* tinta simpática
**sympathetic nervous system** *s* (anat. & physiol.) gran simpático, sistema nervioso simpático, sistema del gran simpático
**sympathetic strike** *s* huelga para ayuda a otros huelguistas
**sympathize** ['sɪmpəθaɪz] *vn* simpatizar, compadecerse; **to sympathize with** compadecer, compadecerse de; comprender
**sympathizer** ['sɪmpə,θaɪzər] *s* simpatizador; partidario
**sympathy** ['sɪmpəθɪ] *s* (*pl:* **-thies**) simpatía; compasión, conmiseración; **to be in sympathy with** estar de acuerdo con, ser partidario de; **to extend one's sympathies to** dar el pésame a
**sympetalous** [sɪm'pɛtələs] *adj* (bot.) simpétalo
**symphonic** [sɪm'fɑnɪk] *adj* sinfónico
**symphonic poem** *s* (mus.) poema sinfónico

**symphonious** [sɪm'fonɪəs] *adj* armonioso
**symphonist** ['sɪmfənɪst] *s* sinfonista
**symphony** ['sɪmfənɪ] *s* (*pl:* **-nies**) sinfonía
**symphony orchestra** *s* orquesta sinfónica o gran orquesta
**symphysis** ['sɪmfɪsɪs] *s* (*pl:* **-ses** [siz]) (anat. & zool.) sínfisis
**sympodium** [sɪm'podɪəm] *s* (*pl:* **-a** [ə]) (bot.) simpodio
**symposium** [sɪm'pozɪəm] *s* (*pl:* **-a** [ə]) coloquio; colección de artículos sobre un mismo tema; (hist.) simposio
**symptom** ['sɪmptəm] *s* (med. & fig.) síntoma
**symptomatic** [,sɪmptə'mætɪk] *adj* sintomático
**symptomatology** [,sɪmptəmə'tɑlədʒɪ] *s* sintomatología
**syn.** abr. de **synonym** y **synonymous**
**synaeresis** [sɪ'nɛrɪsɪs] *s* sinéresis
**synaesthesia** [,sɪnɛs'θiʒə] o [,sɪnɛs'θiʒɪə] *s* var. de **synesthesia**
**synagogue** ['sɪnəgɑg] *s* sinagoga
**synalepha** o **synaloepha** [,sɪnə'lifə] *s* sinalefa
**synapse** [sɪ'næps] *s* (physiol.) sinapsis
**synapsis** [sɪ'næpsɪs] *s* (*pl:* **-ses** [siz]) (biol. & physiol.) sinapsis
**synarthrosis** [,sɪnɑr'θrosɪs] *s* (anat.) sinartrosis
**sync** [sɪŋk] *s* (coll.) sincronización (*en la cinematografía y la telecomunicación*); (*pret & pp:* **synced** [sɪŋkt]; *ger:* **syncing** ['sɪŋkɪŋ]) *va & vn* (coll.) sincronizar
**syncarp** ['sɪnkɑrp] *s* (bot.) sincarpo
**syncarpous** [sɪn'kɑrpəs] *adj* (bot.) sincárpeo
**synchromesh** ['sɪŋkro,mɛʃ] *s* (aut.) engranaje sincronizado; (aut.) cambio de velocidades sincronizado
**synchronal** ['sɪŋkrənəl] *adj* var. de **synchronous**
**synchronic** [sɪn'krɑnɪk] *adj* sincrónico
**synchronism** ['sɪŋkrənɪzəm] *s* sincronismo; cuadro sincrónico
**synchronization** [,sɪŋkrənɪ'zeʃən] *s* sincronización
**synchronize** ['sɪŋkrənaɪz] *va & vn* sincronizar
**synchronizer** ['sɪŋkrə,naɪzər] *s* sincronizador
**synchronoscope** [sɪn'krɑnəskop] *s* (elec.) sincronoscopio
**synchronous** ['sɪŋkrənəs] *adj* síncrono; (elec.) síncrono
**synchronous converter** *s* (elec.) convertidor sincrónico
**synchronous motor** *s* (elec.) motor sincrónico
**synchronous speed** *s* (elec.) velocidad de sincronismo
**synchrony** ['sɪŋkrənɪ] o ['sɪnkrənɪ] *s* sincronía
**synchrotron** ['sɪŋkrətrɑn] *s* (phys.) sincrotrón
**synchro unit** ['sɪŋkro] *s* (elec.) motor sincronizador
**synclastic** [sɪn'klæstɪk] *adj* (math.) sinclástico
**synclinal** [sɪn'klaɪnəl] o ['sɪŋklɪnəl] *adj* sinclinal; (geol.) sinclinal
**syncline** ['sɪŋklaɪn] *s* (geol.) sinclinal
**syncopal** ['sɪŋkəpəl] *adj* sincopal
**syncopate** ['sɪŋkəpet] *va* (mus. & phonet.) sincopar
**syncopated** ['sɪŋkə,petɪd] *adj* sincopado
**syncopation** [,sɪŋkə'peʃən] *s* (mus. & phonet.) síncopa
**syncope** ['sɪŋkəpɪ] *s* (mus. & phonet.) síncopa; (path. & phonet.) síncope
**syncretic** [sɪn'krɛtɪk] *adj* sincrético
**syncretism** ['sɪŋkrətɪzəm] *s* sincretismo
**syncrisis** ['sɪŋkrɪsɪs] *s* (rhet.) sincrisis
**syndactyl** o **syndactyle** [sɪn'dæktɪl] *adj & s* sindáctilo
**syndesmosis** [,sɪndɛs'mosɪs] *s* (*pl:* **-ses** [siz]) (anat.) sindesmosis
**syndic** ['sɪndɪk] *s* síndico
**syndical** ['sɪndɪkəl] *adj* sindical
**syndicalism** ['sɪndɪkəlɪzəm] *s* sindicalismo
**syndicalist** ['sɪndɪkəlɪst] *adj & s* sindicalista
**syndicate** ['sɪndɪkɪt] o ['sɪndɪket] *s* sindicato; ['sɪndɪket] *va* sindicar; dirigir mediante un sindicato; publicar mediante un sindicato; *vn* sindicarse
**syndication** [,sɪndɪ'keʃən] *s* sindicación
**syndrome** ['sɪndrəmi] o ['sɪndrom] *s* (path.) síndrome
**synecdoche** [sɪ'nɛkdəkɪ] (rhet.) sinécdoque
**syneresis** [sɪ'nɛrɪsɪs] *s* var. de **synaeresis**
**synergy** ['sɪnərdʒɪ] *s* sinergia
**synesthesia** [,sɪnɛs'θiʒə] o [,sɪnɛs'θiʒɪə] *s* (physiol. & psychol.) sinestesia
**syngamy** ['sɪŋgəmɪ] *s* (biol.) singamia
**syngenesious** [,sɪndʒɪ'niʃəs] *adj* (bot.) singenésico
**syngenesis** [sɪn'dʒɛnɪsɪs] *s* (biol.) singénesis
**synizesis** [,sɪnɪ'zisɪs] *s* (gram., biol. & path.) sinizesis
**synod** ['sɪnəd] *s* sínodo; (astr. & astrol.) sínodo
**synodal** ['sɪnədəl] *adj* sinodal
**synodic** [sɪ'nɑdɪk] o **synodical** [sɪ'nɑdɪkəl] *adj* sinódico; (astr.) sinódico
**synonym** ['sɪnənɪm] *s* sinónimo
**synonymity** [,sɪnə'nɪmɪtɪ] *s* sinonimia
**synonymous** [sɪ'nɑnɪməs] *adj* sinónimo
**synonymy** [sɪ'nɑnɪmɪ] *s* (*pl:* **-mies**) sinonimia; (rhet.) sinonimia
**synop.** abr. de **synopsis**
**synopsis** [sɪ'nɑpsɪs] *s* (*pl:* **-ses** [siz]) sinopsis
**synoptic** [sɪ'nɑptɪk] o **synoptical** [sɪ'nɑptɪkəl] *adj* sinóptico
**synorchism** [sɪ'nɔrkɪzəm] *s* (path.) sinorquismo
**synovia** [sɪ'novɪə] *s* (anat.) sinovia
**synovial** [sɪ'novɪəl] *adj* sinovial
**synovitis** [,sɪnə'vaɪtɪs] *s* (path.) sinovitis
**syntactic** [sɪn'tæktɪk] o **syntactical** [sɪn'tæktɪkəl] *adj* sintáctico
**syntax** ['sɪntæks] *s* sintaxis
**synthesis** ['sɪnθɪsɪs] *s* (*pl:* **-ses** [siz]) síntesis
**synthesize** ['sɪnθɪsaɪz] *va* sintetizar
**synthetic** [sɪn'θɛtɪk] o **synthetical** [sɪn'θɛtɪkəl] *adj* sintético
**synthetically** [sɪn'θɛtɪkəlɪ] *adv* sintéticamente
**synthetic rubber** *s* caucho sintético
**syntonic** [sɪn'tɑnɪk] o **syntonical** [sɪn'tɑnɪkəl] *adj* (elec.) sintónico
**syntonin** ['sɪntənɪn] *s* (biochem.) sintonina
**syntony** ['sɪntənɪ] *s* (elec.) sintonía
**syphilide** ['sɪfɪlɪd] *s* (path.) sifílide
**syphilis** ['sɪfɪlɪs] *s* (path.) sífilis
**syphilitic** [,sɪfɪ'lɪtɪk] *adj & s* sifilítico
**syphilologist** [,sɪfɪ'lɑlədʒɪst] *s* sifilólogo
**syphilology** [,sɪfɪ'lɑlədʒɪ] *s* sifilología
**syphilosis** [,sɪfɪ'losɪs] *s* (path.) sifilosis
**syphon** ['saɪfən] *s & va* var. de **siphon**
**syr.** abr. de **syrup**
**Syracusan** [,sɪrə'kjuzən] *adj & s* siracusano
**Syracuse** ['sɪrəkjus] *s* Siracusa
**Syria** ['sɪrɪə] *s* Siria
**Syriac** ['sɪrɪæk] *adj & s* siríaco (*dialecto*)
**Syrian** ['sɪrɪən] *adj & s* sirio
**syringa** [sɪ'rɪŋgə] *s* (bot.) jeringuilla, celinda
**syringe** ['sɪrɪndʒ] o [sɪ'rɪndʒ] *s* jeringa; (med.) jeringa, jeringuilla; (med.) jeringa, mangueta (*para echar ayudas*); *va* jeringar
**syringin** [sɪ'rɪndʒɪn] *s* (chem.) siringina
**syringomyelia** [sɪ,rɪŋgomaɪ'ilɪə] *s* (path.) siringomielia
**syringotomy** [,sɪrɪŋ'gɑtəmɪ] *s* (surg.) siringotomía
**syrinx** ['sɪrɪŋks] *s* (*pl:* **syringes** [sɪ'rɪndʒiz] o **syrinxes**) (anat.) trompa de Eustaquio; siringa (*zampoña, flauta de Pan*); siringe (*órgano cantor de los pájaros*)
**syrt** [sʌrt] *s* sirte
**syrtis** ['sʌrtɪs] *s* (*pl:* **-tes** [tiz]) sirte
**syrup** ['sɪrəp] o ['sʌrəp] *s* almíbar; jarabe (*almíbar con zumos refrescantes o medicinales*)
**syrupy** ['sɪrəpɪ] o ['sʌrəpɪ] *adj* almibarado; espeso como jarabe
**syssarcosis** [,sɪsɑr'kosɪs] *s* (anat.) sisarcosis
**Syst.** abr. de **system**
**systaltic** [sɪs'tæltɪk] *adj* sistáltico
**system** ['sɪstəm] *s* sistema
**systematic** [,sɪstə'mætɪk] *adj* sistemático; **systematics** *ssg* sistemática
**systematical** [,sɪstə'mætɪkəl] *adj* var. de **systematic**
**systematically** [,sɪstə'mætɪkəlɪ] *adv* sistemáticamente

**systematization** [ˌsɪstəmətɪˈzeʃən] *s* sistematización
**systematize** [ˈsɪstəmətaɪz] *va* sistematizar
**systematology** [ˌsɪstəməˈtɑlədʒɪ] *s* sistematología
**systemic** [sɪsˈtɛmɪk] *adj* (anat. & physiol.) sistemático
**systemize** [ˈsɪstəmaɪz] *va* var. de **systematize**
**systole** [ˈsɪstəlɪ] *s* (gram., biol. & physiol.) sístole
**systolic** [sɪsˈtɑlɪk] *adj* sistólico
**systyle** [ˈsɪstaɪl] *s* (arch.) sístilo
**syzygy** [ˈsɪzɪdʒɪ] *s* (*pl:* **-gies**) (astr.) sicigia

# T

**T, t** [ti] *s* (*pl:* **T's, t's** [tiz]) vigésima letra del alfabeto inglés
**t.** abr. de **teaspoon, temperature, tempore, tenor, tense, territory, time, ton** o **tons, town** y **transitive**
**T.** abr. de **Territory, Testament** y **Tuesday**
**tab** [tæb] *s* apéndice; marbete; lengüeta; (coll.) cuenta; (aer.) aleta compensadora; **to keep tab on** (coll.) verificar, tener a la vista; **to pick up the tab** (coll.) pagar la cuenta
**tabard** ['tæbərd] *s* tabardo
**tabasco** [tə'bæsko] *s* (trademark) tabasco
**tabby** ['tæbɪ] *adj* atigrado; *s* (*pl:* **-bies**) gato atigrado; gata; solterona; chismosa maldiciente; tabí, tafetán
**tabernacle** ['tæbər,nækəl] *s* tabernáculo; templo, santuario; (*cap.*) *s* (Bib.) Tabernáculo
**table** ['tebəl] *s* mesa; tabla (*lista, cuadro o catálogo, etc.*); (arch.) tablero; (anat.) tabla; **on the table** sobre la mesa del presidente; **to clear the table** alzar o levantar la mesa; **to help at table** servir en la mesa; **to set the table** poner la mesa; **to turn the tables** volver las tornas; **under the table** completamente emborrachado; **tables of the law** (Bib.) tablas de la ley; *va* poner sobre la mesa; poner índice a; disponer en una tabla; dar carpetazo a, aplazar la discusión de
**tableau** ['tæblo] *s* (*pl:* **-leaus** o **-leaux** [loz]) cuadro vivo; espectáculo
**tablecloth** ['tebəl,klɔθ] o ['tebəl,klɑθ] *s* mantel; tela para manteles
**table cover** *s* carpeta, cubierta de mesa, sobremesa, tapete
**table d'hôte** ['tɑbəl'dot] *s* mesa redonda; comida a precio fijo
**table lamp** *s* lámpara de mesa
**tableland** ['tebəl,lænd] *s* meseta; planicie
**table linen** *s* mantelería
**table manners** *spl* modales que uno tiene en la mesa
**table of contents** *s* índice de materias, tabla de materias
**table oil** *s* aceite de comer
**table rapping** *s* (el) golpear (*de los espíritus*)
**tables of the law** *spl* (Bib.) tablas de la ley
**tablespoon** ['tebəl,spun] *s* cuchara de sopa, cuchara grande
**tablespoonful** ['tebəl,spunfʊl] *s* cucharada de sopa, cucharada grande
**tablet** ['tæblɪt] *s* tableta, comprimido, pastilla; lápida, placa; taco o bloc de papel
**table talk** *s* conversación de sobremesa
**table tennis** *s* tenis de mesa, tenis de salón
**table tilting, tipping** o **turning** *s* movimientos de las mesas (*atribuídos a los espíritus*)
**table top** *s* tablero
**tableware** ['tebəl,wɛr] *s* servicio, artículos para la mesa
**tabloid** ['tæblɔɪd] *adj* condensado, conciso, breve; *s* diario ilustrado de noticias condensadas y sensacionales; (pharm.) tableta, pastilla
**taboo** [tə'bu] *s* tabú; *adj* prohibido; *va* prohibir
**tabor** ['tebər] *s* tamboril
**taboret** o **tabouret** ['tæbəret] *s* taburete (*asiento*); bastidor de bordar; (mus.) tamborilete
**tabu** [tə'bu] *s, adj & va* var. de **taboo**
**tabular** ['tæbjələr] *adj* tabular
**tabulate** ['tæbjəlet] *va* tabular, poner en forma de tabla
**tabulation** [,tæbjə'leʃən] *s* tabulación
**tabulator** ['tæbjə,letər] *s* tabulador
**tabulator key** *s* tecla tabulatoria, tecla del tabulador
**tacamahac** ['tækəmə,hæk] *s* (bot.) tacamaca (*árbol y resina*)
**tachistoscope** [tə'kɪstəskop] *s* taquistoscopio
**tachometer** [tə'kɑmɪtər] *s* tacómetro
**tachycardia** [,tækɪ'kɑrdɪə] *s* (path.) taquicardia
**tachygraph** ['tækɪgræf] o ['tækɪgrɑf] *s* taquigrafía; taquígrafo
**tachygrapher** [tæ'kɪgrəfər] *s* taquígrafo
**tachygraphic** [,tækɪ'græfɪk] o **tachygraphical** [,tækɪ'græfɪkəl] *adj* taquigráfico
**tachygraphy** [tæ'kɪgrəfɪ] *s* taquigrafía
**tachylyte** ['tækɪlaɪt] *s* (mineral.) taquilita
**tachymeter** [tæ'kɪmɪtər] *s* taquímetro; (surv.) taquímetro
**tachymetric** [,tækɪ'metrɪk] *adj* taquimétrico
**tachymetry** [tæ'kɪmɪtrɪ] *s* taquimetría
**tachysterol** [tə'kɪstərol] *s* (biochem.) taquisterol
**tacit** ['tæsɪt] *adj* tácito
**tacitly** ['tæsɪtlɪ] *adv* tácitamente
**taciturn** ['tæsɪtərn] *adj* taciturno
**taciturnity** [,tæsɪ'tʌrnɪtɪ] *s* taciturnidad
**Tacitus** ['tæsɪtəs] *s* Tácito
**tack** [tæk] *s* tachuela, puntilla; (sew.) hilván; (naut.) bordada, virada; (naut.) amura; cambio de dirección; política, línea de conducta; alimento; *va* clavar con tachuelas; (sew.) coser, hilvanar; unir, añadir; *vn* (naut.) virar, cambiar de bordada; cambiar de política, cambiar de línea de conducta
**tackle** ['tækəl] *s* aparejo, avíos, enseres; polea, poleame; (football) atajo y agarrada; (football) atajador; *va* asir, agarrar; atacar, embestir; abordar (*un problema*); (football) atajar
**tacky** ['tækɪ] *adj* (*comp:* **-ier;** *super:* **-iest**) pegajoso; (coll.) mal vestido, desaseado, descuidado
**tact** [tækt] *s* tacto, discreción
**tactful** ['tæktfəl] *adj* discreto, político
**tactical** ['tæktɪkəl] *adj* táctico
**tactically** ['tæktɪkəlɪ] *adv* tácticamente
**tactician** [tæk'tɪʃən] *s* táctico
**tactics** ['tæktɪks] *spl* táctica; *ssg* (mil.) táctica
**tactile** ['tæktɪl] o ['tæktaɪl] *adj* táctil; tangible, palpable
**tactility** [tæk'tɪlɪtɪ] *s* tactilidad; tangibilidad
**tactless** ['tæktlɪs] *adj* indiscreto
**tactual** ['tæktʃʊəl] *adj* tactivo, táctil
**tactually** ['tæktʃʊəlɪ] *adv* mediante el tacto; respecto al tacto
**tadpole** ['tæd,pol] *s* (zool.) renacuajo
**ta'en** [ten] (poet.) var. de **taken**
**taenia** ['tinɪə] *s* (*pl:* **-ae** [i]) (anat., arch. & zool.) tenia
**taeniacide** ['tinɪə,saɪd] *s* (med.) tenicida
**taeniafuge** ['tinɪə,fjudʒ] *adj & s* (med.) tenífugo
**taeniasis** [ti'naɪəsɪs] *s* (path.) teniasis
**taffeta** ['tæfɪtə] *s* tafetán; *adj* de tafetán; muy delicado; florido (*estilo*)
**taffrail** ['tæfrel] *s* (naut.) coronamiento; (naut.) pasamano de la borda a popa
**taffy** ['tæfɪ] *s* melcocha, arropía; (coll.) lisonja
**tag** [tæg] *s* marbete, etiqueta; cola, rabito, pingajo; copo, mechón; vedija; herrete; sentencia o cita que se añade a una composición literaria; (theat.) palabra o frase de efecto contenida en un discurso; **to play tag** jugar al tócame tú; (*pret & pp:* **tagged;** *ger:* **tagging**) *va* pegar un marbete a; marcar con marbete o etiqueta; proveer de etiqueta o etiquetas; (coll.) perseguir, seguir los pasos de; añadir para producir efecto; alcanzar, tocar (*como en un juego de niños*); *vn* (coll.) seguir de cerca; **to tag after** (coll.) seguir de cerca
**Tagalog** [tɑ'gɑlɑg] *s* tagalo
**tag day** *s* (U.S.A.) día de cartelas (*día en que se solicitan en las calles contribuciones para obras de caridad, poniendo una cartela o flor en el ojal del contribuyente*)

**tag end** *s* cabo flojo; retal, retazo
**tagrag** [ˈtæg,ræg] *s* canalla; harapo, andrajo
**Tagus** [ˈtegəs] *s* Tajo
**Tahitian** [tɑˈhitɪən] *adj & s* taitiano
**tail** [tel] *s* cola; (fig.) cola (*de un cometa, una chaqueta*); trenza (*de pelo*); **tails** *spl* (coll.) cruz (*de una moneda*); (coll.) frac; **to turn tail** volver la espalda, mostrar los talones; **with his tail between his legs** con el rabo entre las piernas; **tails, you lose** cruz y pierde Vd.; *adj* de cola; *va* proveer de cola; seguir como una cola; añadir; atar, juntar; *vn* formar cola; llegar al fin; disminuir poco a poco; **to tail after** seguir de cerca, pisar los talones a
**tail assembly** *s* (aer.) empenaje, planos de cola
**tailboard** [ˈtel,bord] *s* tabla en la parte posterior de un carro, camión, etc., que se puede bajar o quitar para cargar o descargar
**tail end** *s* cola, parte de atrás; conclusión; **at the tail end** al final
**tail fin** *s* (aer.) plano de deriva
**tail gunner** *s* (aer.) artillero de cola
**tailing** [ˈtelɪŋ] *s* (mas.) entrega, tizón; **tailings** *spl* desechos, restos; (min.) colas
**tail lamp** o **tail light** *s* farol de cola, farol trasero
**tailor** [ˈtelər] *s* sastre; *va* entallar (*un traje*); proveer de trajes o vestidos; *vn* ser sastre
**tailorbird** [ˈtelər,bʌrd] *s* (orn.) sutora, pájaro sastre
**tailoring** [ˈtelərɪŋ] *s* sastrería, costura
**tailor-made** [ˈtelər,med] *adj* hecho por sastre, hecho con corte de sastre
**tailpiece** [ˈtel,pis] *s* apéndice, cabo; (arch.) viga que entra en una pared sostenida por un sillar o tizón; (mus.) cordal (*de un instrumento de cuerda*); (print.) florón, marmosete
**tail plane** *s* (aer.) plano de cola
**tailrace** [ˈtel,res] *s* cauce de salida, caz de descarga; (min.) canal que arrastra el agua con el material de desecho
**tail skid** *s* (aer.) patín de cola
**tail spin** *s* (aer.) barrena picada
**tailstock** [ˈtel,stɑk] *s* (mach.) contrapunta
**tail wind** *s* (aer.) viento de cola, viento trasero; (naut.) viento en popa
**tain** [ten] *s* hoja de estaño
**taint** [tent] *s* mancha; corrupción, infección; *va* manchar; corromper, viciar; *vn* mancharse; corromperse, viciarse
**take** [tek] *s* toma; presa, redada; (mov.) toma; (slang) entradas, ingresos ‖ (*pret:* **took**; *pp:* **taken**) *va* tomar; quedarse con; coger; llevarse; llevar; aceptar; arrebatar, quitar; comer (*una pieza, en el juego de ajedrez y en el de damas*); cobrar, percibir; ganar; aguantar, tolerar; deducir, substraer; soportar; cautivar, deleitar; tener, sentir; saltar por encima de; dar (*un salto, un paso, un paseo*); hacer (*un viaje; ejercicio*); seguir (*un consejo; una asignatura*); sacar (*fotografías*); necesitar; usar, calzar (*cierto tamaño de zapatos*); estudiar (*p.ej., historia, francés, matemáticas*); echar (*una siesta*); tomar (*un tren, tranvía, etc.*); sufrir (*un examen*); **to take amiss** llevar a mal, tomar en mala parte; **to take apart** descomponer, desarmar, desmontar; **to take away** llevarse; quitar; **to take back** recibir devuelto; devolver; retractar, desdecirse de; **to take down** bajar; descolgar; poner por escrito; tomar nota de; desmontar; tragar; (coll.) quitar los humos a, humillar; **to take for** considerar, suponer, tomar por, p.ej., **I took you for someone else** le tomé a Vd. por otra persona; **to take from** quitar a; restar de; **to take in** acoger, admitir; recibir (*en su casa, en la sociedad, etc.*); abarcar; comprender; ganar (*dinero*); visitar (*los puntos de interés*); cazar (*captarse la voluntad de, con halagos y engaños*); meter (*p.ej., las costuras de una prenda de vestir*); **to take it out on** (coll.) desquitarse a costa de, desahogarse riñendo (*a una persona*); **to take it that** suponer que; **to take it upon oneself to** + *inf* encargarse de + *inf;* **to take off** quitarse (*p.ej., el sombrero*); descontar; (coll.) imitar, parodiar; **to take on** tomar, contratar; empezar; cargar con, tomar sobre sí; desafiar; **to take out** sacar; pasear (*a un niño, un caballo*); llevar fuera, poner fuera; omitir; obtener; quitar; extraer, separar; (bridge) sacar (*al compañero*); escoltar (*a una muchacha*); (coll.) tener amores con (*una muchacha*); para la calle, p.ej., **give me a sandwich to take out** me da un sandwich para la calle; **to take over** tomar posesión de; tomar la dirección de; **to take seriously** tomar en serio; **to take up** subir; apretar, atiesar; levantar; coger, prender; recoger; absorber; amortiguar; rebajar, disminuir; emprender, comenzar; tomar, estudiar; ocupar, llenar (*un espacio*); tomar posesión de; pagar; consultar (*un asunto*); **to take upon oneself** tomar sobre sí, encargarse de ‖ *vn* arraigar, prender; cuajar; tomar posesión; actuar, obrar; salir, resultar; tomar (*por la derecha, por la izquierda*); adherirse; pegar; darse, dedicarse; (coll.) tener éxito; **to take after** parecerse a, ser semejante a; seguir el ejemplo de; **to take off** levantarse; salir; (aer.) despegar; **to take on** (coll.) excitarse, quejarse; **to take to** aficionarse a, tomar cariño a; dedicarse a; dirigirse a; **to take to** + *ger* ponerse a + *inf;* **to take up with** (coll.) relacionarse con, estrechar amistad con; (coll.) vivir con; **to take well** (coll.) sacar buen retrato
**take-down** [ˈtek,daʊn] *adj* desmontable; *s* desmontaje; mecanismo de desmontar; rifle desmontable; (coll.) humillación
**take-home pay** [ˈtekˈhom] *s* salario menos impuestos, etc.
**taken** [ˈtekən] *pp de* **take**
**take-in** [ˈtek,ɪn] *s* (coll.) abuso, engaño
**take-off** [ˈtek,ɑf] *s* salto; raya de donde se salta; (coll.) imitación burlesca, parodia; (mach.) toma de fuerza; (aer.) despegue
**take-out** [ˈtek,aʊt] *s* (bridge) sacada
**take-out bid** *s* (bridge) declaración de sacada
**take-over** [ˈtek,ovər] *s* toma
**take-up** [ˈtek,ʌp] *s* apretadura; apretador; atesador (*p.ej., de correa*); tensor; canal de llamas ascendente; (sew.) frunce
**taking** [ˈtekɪŋ] *adj* atractivo, encantador; (coll.) contagioso; *s* toma; toma de posesión; **takings** *spl* ingresos
**talbot** [ˈtɔlbət] *s* perro de San Huberto
**talc** [tælk] *s* (mineral.) talco; (*pret & pp:* **talcked** o **talced** [tælkt]; *ger:* **talcking** o **talcing** [ˈtælkɪŋ]) *va* tratar con talco, aplicar talco a
**talcose** [ˈtælkos] o [tælˈkos] o **talcous** [ˈtælkəs] *adj* talcoso
**talcum** [ˈtælkəm] *s* (mineral.) talco; talco en polvo
**talcum powder** *s* talco en polvo; polvos de talco, polvos blancos faciales
**tale** [tel] *s* cuento (*relato; enredo; mentira*); cuenta; **to tell tales** contar cuentos
**talebearer** [ˈtel,bɛrər] *s* cuentista, chismoso
**talebearing** [ˈtel,bɛrɪŋ] *adj* cuentista, chismoso; *s* chismería
**talent** [ˈtælənt] *s* talento; gente de talento
**talented** [ˈtæləntɪd] *adj* talentoso
**talent scout** *s* buscador de nuevas figuras (*para la televisión, el cine, etc.*)
**talesman** [ˈtelizmən] o [ˈtelzmən] *s* (*pl:* **-men**) (law) jurado suplente
**taleteller** [ˈtel,tɛlər] *s* var. de **talebearer**
**talion** [ˈtælɪən] *s* talión
**talipot** [ˈtælɪpɑt] *s* (bot.) palmera de sombrilla
**talisman** [ˈtælɪsmən] o [ˈtælɪzmən] *s* (*pl:* **-mans**) talismán
**talismanic** [,tælɪsˈmænɪk] o [,tælɪzˈmænɪk] *adj* talismánico
**talk** [tɔk] *s* charla, plática (*conversación; conferencia, discurso*); fábula, comidilla (*p.ej., de la ciudad*); **to cause talk** dar que hablar; *va* hablar (*cierto idioma; disparates*); hablar de; convencer hablando; **to be talked out** (coll.) haber hablado hasta no poder más; **to talk down** tapar la boca a, hacer callar hablando más o en voz más alta; **to talk into** + *ger* persuadir a + *inf;* **to talk out of** conseguir hablando a; **to talk out of** + *ger* disuadir de + *inf;* **to talk over** convencer o persuadir discutiendo; **to talk up** ensalzar; *vn* hablar; parlar (*p.ej., el loro*); **to talk back** replicar, responder con malos modales; **to talk on** discutir (*un asunto*); hablar sin parar; continuar hablando; **to talk over** discutir; **to talk to**

(coll.) reprender; **to talk up** elevar la voz, osar hablar, hablar alto
**talkative** [ˈtɔkətɪv] *adj* hablador, locuaz
**talked-about** [ˈtɔktəˌbaʊt] *adj* sonado
**talker** [ˈtɔkər] *s* hablador; orador; parlón, charlatán
**talkie** [ˈtɔkɪ] *s* (coll.) cine hablado, cine parlante
**talking doll** *s* muñeca parlante
**talking film** *s* (mov.) película hablada
**talking machine** *s* máquina parlante
**talking picture** *s* cine hablado, cine parlante
**talking point** *s* (slang) argumento (*para inducir a comprar*)
**talking-to** [ˈtɔkɪŋˌtu] *s* (*pl:* **-tos**) (coll.) reprensión, rapapolvo
**tall** [tɔl] *adj* alto; (coll.) exagerado, extraordinario
**tallish** [ˈtɔlɪʃ] *adj* un poco alto
**tallith** [ˈtælɪθ] *s* taled
**tallow** [ˈtælo] *s* sebo; *va* ensebar
**tallowy** [ˈtælo·ɪ] o [ˈtæləwɪ] *adj* seboso
**tally** [ˈtælɪ] *s* (*pl:* **-lies**) tara o tarja (*palo partido en dos donde se marca con muescas las ventas*); muesca en una tarja; cuenta; unidad (*en un cómputo hecho por grupos*); etiqueta, rótulo; contraparte; duplicado; (*pret & pp:* **-lied**) *va* marcar, notar; tarjar; echar la cuenta de; ajustar, acomodar; *vn* echar una cuenta; concordar, corresponder, conformarse
**tallyho** [ˈtælɪˌho] *s* (*pl:* **-hos**) coche de cuatro caballos; grito de cazador de zorras; [ˌtælɪˈho] *interj* grito del cazador
**tally sheet** *s* hoja en que se anota una cuenta, especialmente en una elección
**Talmudic** [tælˈmʌdɪk] *adj* talmúdico
**Talmudist** [ˈtælmədɪst] *s* talmudista
**talon** [ˈtælən] *s* garra; (arch.) talón (*moldura*); **talons** *spl* dedos o manos rapaces
**talus** [ˈteləs] *s* (*pl:* **-li** [laɪ]) (anat.) astrágalo; (*pl:* **-luses**) *s* talud; (geol.) talud detrítico
**tam** [tæm] *s* boina escocesa
**tamale** [təˈmɑlɪ] *s* tamal (*manjar mejicano*)
**tamarack** [ˈtæməræk] *s* (bot.) alerce americano (*Larix laricina*)
**tamaricaceous** [ˌtæmərɪˈkeʃəs] *adj* (bot.) tamaricáceo
**tamarin** [ˈtæmərɪn] *s* (zool.) saguino
**tamarind** [ˈtæmərɪnd] *s* (bot.) tamarindo (*árbol y fruto*)
**tamarisk** [ˈtæmərɪsk] *s* (bot.) tamariz o tamarisco
**tambo** [ˈtæmbo] *s* (theat.) var. de **end man;** [ˈtɑmbo] *s* tambo (Am.)
**tambour** [ˈtæmbʊr] *s* tambor; (sew.) tambor (*para hacer bordados*); *va & vn* bordar a tambor
**tambourine** [ˌtæmbəˈrin] *s* (mus.) pandereta; (orn.) tamboreta
**tame** [tem] *adj* amansado, domesticado; dócil, sumiso; aburrido, insípido; *va* amansar, domesticar; someter, avasallar; suavizar
**tameless** [ˈtemlɪs] *adj* indomable; indómito
**Tamerlane** [ˈtæmərlen] *s* Tamerlán
**Tamil** [ˈtæməl] *adj & s* tamul
**tammy** [ˈtæmɪ] *s* (*pl:* **-mies**) estameña
**tam-o'-shanter** [ˈtæməˈʃæntər] *s* boina escocesa
**tamp** [tæmp] *va* atacar (*un barreno*); apisonar
**tamper** [ˈtæmpər] *s* apisonador (*persona*); pisón; *vn* entremeterse; **to tamper with** manosear, tocar ajando; tratar de forzar (*una cerradura*); falsificar (*un documento*); corromper
**tampion** [ˈtæmpɪən] *s* (arm.) tapabocas; (mus.) tapón de cañón de órgano
**tampon** [ˈtæmpɑn] *s* (surg.) tapón; *va* (surg.) taponar
**tamponage** [ˈtæmpənɪdʒ] o **tamponment** [ˈtæmpənmənt] *s* (surg.) taponamiento
**tan** o **tan.** abr. de **tangent**
**tan** [tæn] *adj* requemado, tostado; de color; de color de canela; marrón; *s* casca (*corteza que se usa para curtir*); tanino; (*pret & pp:* **tanned;** *ger:* **tanning**) *va* curtir, adobar, zurrar; quemar, tostar; (coll.) zurrar, dar una paliza a
**tanager** [ˈtænədʒər] *s* (orn.) tángara
**tanbark** [ˈtænˌbɑrk] *s* casca
**tandem** [ˈtændəm] *s* tándem; *adj & adv* en tándem
**tang** [tæŋ] *s* sabor u olor fuerte y picante; dejo, gustillo; espiga o cola (*de un formón, lima, etc.*); tañido (*sonido vibrante*); *va* hacer retiñir; *vn* retiñir
**tangency** [ˈtændʒənsɪ] *s* tangencia
**tangent** [ˈtændʒənt] *adj* tangente; (geom.) tangente; *s* (geom., trig. & mus.) tangente; **to fly off** o **go off at a tangent** cambiar de repente, tomar súbitamente nuevo rumbo
**tangential** [tænˈdʒenʃəl] *adj* tangencial; divergente; apenas contiguo
**Tangerine** [ˌtændʒəˈrin] *adj & s* tangerino; (*l.c.*) *s* mandarina (*fruto*)
**tangibility** [ˌtændʒɪˈbɪlɪtɪ] *s* tangibilidad
**tangible** [ˈtændʒɪbəl] *adj* tangible; **tangibles** *spl* bienes materiales
**tangibly** [ˈtændʒɪblɪ] *adv* tangiblemente
**Tangier** [tænˈdʒɪr] *s* Tánger
**tangle** [ˈtæŋgəl] *s* enredo, maraña, lío; *va* enredar, enmarañar; *vn* enredarse, enmarañarse
**tangly** [ˈtæŋglɪ] *adj* enredado, enmarañado
**tango** [ˈtæŋgo] *s* (*pl:* **-gos**) tango (*baile y música*); *vn* bailar el tango
**tangram** [ˈtæŋgrəm] *s* jugete chino que consiste en un cuadrado dividido en siete piezas de forma variada, tales que con ellas dispuestas de varias maneras se puedan formar diversas figuras
**tangy** [ˈtæŋɪ] *adj* fuerte y picante
**tank** [tæŋk] *s* tanque; cisterna; (aut.) depósito; (mil.) tanque, carro de combate; (rail.) ténder; (slang) barriga; (slang) bodega (*hombre que bebe mucho*); *va* almacenar o poner en tanques; *vn* **to tank up** (slang) emborracharse
**tankage** [ˈtæŋkɪdʒ] *s* cabida de un tanque; depósito en tanques; precio del depósito en tanques; (agr.) residuos animales que se emplean como abono o alimento para los animales
**tankard** [ˈtæŋkərd] *s* jarro grande con asa y tapa
**tank car** *s* (rail.) carro cuba, vagón cisterna, vagón tanque
**tank engine** *s* (rail.) locomotora-ténder
**tanker** [ˈtæŋkər] *s* (naut.) barco tanque, buque cisterna; (aer.) avión nodriza
**tanker plane** *s* (aer.) aeroplano-nodriza, avión-nodriza
**tank farming** *s* quimicultura, cultivo hidropónico
**tank locomotive** *s* (rail.) locomotora-ténder
**tank truck** *s* camión cisterna, camión tanque
**tannate** [ˈtænet] *s* (chem.) tanato
**tanner** [ˈtænər] *s* noquero, curtidor
**tannery** [ˈtænərɪ] *s* (*pl:* **-ies**) tenería, curtiduría
**tannic** [ˈtænɪk] *adj* (chem.) tánico
**tannic acid** *s* (chem.) ácido tánico
**tannin** [ˈtænɪn] *s* (chem.) tanino
**tanning** [ˈtænɪŋ] *s* curtido, curtimiento; quemadura o tostadura (*del cutis por el sol*); (coll.) zurra, paliza
**tansy** [ˈtænzɪ] *s* (*pl:* **-sies**) (bot.) tanaceto, hierba lombriguera
**tantalate** [ˈtæntəlet] *s* (chem.) tantalato
**tantalic** [tænˈtælɪk] *adj* (chem.) tantálico
**tantalic acid** *s* (chem.) ácido tantálico
**tantalite** [ˈtæntəlaɪt] *s* (mineral.) tantalita
**tantalization** [ˌtæntəlɪˈzeʃən] *s* exasperación, tentación sin satisfacción posible
**tantalize** [ˈtæntəlaɪz] *va* exasperar, atormentar mostrando lo que no se puede conseguir
**tantalum** [ˈtæntələm] *s* (chem.) tántalo o tantalio
**tantalus** [ˈtæntələs] *s* frasquera; (*cap.*) *s* (myth.) Tántalo
**tantamount** [ˈtæntəˌmaʊnt] *adj* equivalente
**tantara** [tænˈtærə] o [ˈtæntərə] *s* toque de trompeta, cuerno de caza, etc.
**tantivy** [tænˈtɪvɪ] *adj* rápido, veloz; *adv* a galope tendido; *interj* (hunt.) ¡a galope!; *s* (*pl:* **-ies**) galopada
**tantrum** [ˈtæntrəm] *s* berrinche, rabieta
**Taoism** [ˈtaʊɪzəm] *s* taoísmo
**Taoist** [ˈtaʊɪst] *adj & s* taoísta
**tap** [tæp] *s* golpecito, palmadita; canilla, espita; grifo; remiendo del tacón (*de un calzado*); calidad o clase (*de vino*); (elec.) toma; (mach.) macho de terraja; (coll.) taberna, mostrador de taberna; **taps** *spl* silencio (*toque que manda que cada cual se acueste*); **on tap** sacado del

barril, servido al grifo; listo, a mano; (*pret & pp:* **tapped; ***ger:* **tapping**) *va* dar golpecitos o palmaditas a o en; poner la espita a; sacar o tomar (*quitando la espita*); sangrar (*un árbol*); (surg.) sajar; remontar, remendar el tacón de; unir, hacer comunicar; (elec.) hacer una derivación en; intervenir (*un teléfono*); (mach.) aterrajar; *vn* dar golpecitos, golpear ligeramente

**tap dance** *s* zapateo, zapateado

**tap-dance** [ˈtæp,dæns] o [ˈtæp,dɑns] *vn* zapatear

**tape** [tep] *s* cinta; (sport) cinta tendida para marcar el final de una carrera; *va* proveer de cinta o cintas; medir con cinta; (coll.) grabar en cinta magnetofónica

**tapeline** [ˈtep,laɪn] *s* cinta de medir

**tape measure** *s* cinta de medir, cinta métrica

**taper** [ˈtepər] *s* cerilla, velita larga y delgada; ahusamiento; *adj* ahusado; *va* ahusar; *vn* ahusarse; ir disminuyendo

**tape recorder** *s* grabador o grabadora de cinta, magnetófono

**tape recording** *s* grabación sobre cinta

**tapestry** [ˈtæpɪstrɪ] *s* (*pl:* **-tries**) tapiz; (*pret & pp:* **-tried**) *va* entapizar, tapizar

**tapeworm** [ˈtep,wʌrm] *s* solitaria, lombriz solitaria

**tapioca** [,tæpɪˈokə] *s* tapioca

**tapir** [ˈtepər] *s* (zool.) tapir, danta

**tapis** [ˈtæpɪ] o [ˈtæpɪs] *s* (obs.) tapiz; **on** o **upon the tapis** sobre el tapete

**tapper** [ˈtæpər] *s* macito (*de un timbre, descohesor, etc.*); (telg.) manipulador; instrumento de aterrajar

**tappet** [ˈtæpɪt] *s* (mach.) botador; (aut.) alzaválvulas, taqué

**tappet rod** *s* varilla levantaválvula, varilla empujadora

**taproom** [ˈtæp,rum] o [ˈtæp,rʊm] *s* bodegón, taberna

**taproot** [ˈtæp,rut] o [ˈtæp,rʊt] *s* (bot.) raíz central o maestra

**tapster** [ˈtæpstər] *s* mozo de taberna

**tap water** *s* agua corriente, agua de grifo

**tap wrench** *s* volvedor de machos

**tar** [tɑr] *s* alquitrán; (coll.) marinero; *adj* alquitranado; (*pret & pp:* **tarred;** *ger:* **tarring**) *va* alquitranar; **to tar and feather** embrear y emplumar, untar de brea y cubrir de plumas (*por castigo*)

**tarantella** [,tærənˈtɛlə] *s* tarantela (*baile y música*)

**tarantula** [təˈræntʃələ] *s* (zool.) tarántula

**tarboosh** [tɑrˈbuʃ] *s* fez (*gorro turco rojo*)

**tardigrade** [ˈtɑrdɪgred] *adj* (zool.) tardígrado

**tardily** [ˈtɑrdɪlɪ] *adv* tardiamente

**tardiness** [ˈtɑrdɪnɪs] *s* tardanza

**tardy** [ˈtɑrdɪ] *adj* (*comp:* **-dier;** *super:* **-diest**) tardío

**tare** [tɛr] *s* tara (*rebaja en el peso*); (bot.) arveja o veza; (Bib.) cizaña; *va* tarar

**tarente** [təˈrɛnte] *s* (zool.) estelión

**targe** [tɑrdʒ] *s* (archaic) tarja (*escudo*)

**target** [ˈtɑrgɪt] *s* blanco; (rail.) placa de señal; (phys.) blanco (*foco de emisión*); (surv.) corredera; (fig.) blanco (*de la burla*), objeto (*de risa, críticas, etc.*); (obs.) tarja, rodela

**target area** *s* zona a batir

**target practice** *s* tiro al blanco

**tariff** [ˈtærɪf] *s* tarifa; arancel; *adj* arancelario

**tarlatan** [ˈtɑrlətən] *s* tarlatana

**tarmac** [ˈtɑrmæk] *s* (trademark) tarmac; (aer.) tarmac (*frente a un hangar*)

**tarn** [tɑrn] *s* lago pequeño de montaña

**tarnish** [ˈtɑrnɪʃ] *s* deslustre; *va* deslustrar; *vn* deslustrarse

**taro** [ˈtɑro] *s* (*pl:* **-ros**) (bot.) taro, colocasia

**tar paper** *s* papel alquitranado, cartón alquitranado o embreado

**tarpaulin** [tɑrˈpɔlɪn] *s* alquitranado; encerado; abrigo o sombrero impermeables hechos de encerado

**Tarpeia** [tɑrˈpiə] *s* Tarpeya

**Tarpeian** [tɑrˈpiən] *adj* tarpeyo

**Tarpeian Rock** *s* roca Tarpeya

**tarpon** [ˈtɑrpɑn] *s* (ichth.) tarpón

**Tarquin** [ˈtɑrkwɪn] *s* Tarquino

**tarragon** [ˈtærəgɑn] *s* (bot.) dragoncillo, estragón

**tarry** [ˈtɑrɪ] *adj* alquitranado, embreado; [ˈtærɪ] (*pret & pp:* **-ried**) *va* (archaic) esperar; *vn* detenerse, pararse, quedarse; esperar; tardar

**tarry-fingered** [ˈtɑrɪˈfɪŋgərd] *adj* largo de uñas

**tarsal** [ˈtɑrsəl] *adj* tarsiano; *s* (anat. & zool.) tarso

**tarsier** [ˈtɑrsɪər] *s* (zool.) mago

**tarsus** [ˈtɑrsəs) *s* (*pl:* **-si** [saɪ]) (anat. & zool.) tarso; (*cap.*) *s* Tarso

**tart** [tɑrt] *adj* acre, agrio; (fig.) áspero, mordaz; *s* tarta

**tartan** [ˈtɑrtən] *s* tartán; dibujo escocés; (naut.) tartana; *adj* de tartán; hecho de tartán

**tartar** [ˈtɑrtər] *s* (chem.) tártaro; tártaro o sarro (*de los dientes*); mujer regañona; **to catch a tartar** meterse con uno muy fuerte; (*cap.*) *adj & s* tártaro

**Tartarean** [tɑrˈtɛrɪən] *adj* tartáreo

**tartar emetic** *s* (chem.) tártaro emético

**tartare sauce** [ˈtɑrtər] *s* salsa tártara

**tartaric** [tɑrˈtærɪk] o [tɑrˈtɑrɪk] *adj* tártrico

**tartaric acid** *s* (chem.) ácido tártrico

**tartarize** [ˈtɑrtəraɪz] *va* tartarizar

**Tartarus** [ˈtɑrtərəs] *s* (myth.) Tártaro (*infierno*)

**Tartary** [ˈtɑrtərɪ] *s* Tartaria

**tartlet** [ˈtɑrtlɪt] *s* tarta o pastel pequeño

**tartrate** [ˈtɑrtret] *s* (chem.) tartrato

**task** [tæsk] o [tɑsk] *s* tarea; **to bring** o **take to task** llamar a capítulo; *va* atarear; abrumar, exigir demasiado de; acusar, tachar

**task force** *s* (mil. & nav.) agrupación de fuerzas para una misión especial

**taskmaster** [ˈtæsk,mæstər] o [ˈtɑsk,mɑstər] *s* persona que señala las tareas, amo, superintendente; ordenancista

**Tasmanian** [tæzˈmenɪən] *adj & s* tasmanio

**Tasmanian wolf** *s* (zool.) lobo marsupial

**tassel** [ˈtæsəl] *s* borla; (bot.) penacho (*inflorescencia macho, especialmente del maíz*); (*pret & pp:* **-seled** o **-selled;** *ger:* **-seling** o **-selling**) *va* adornar con borlas; hacer borlas de; *vn* echar penachos (*el maíz*)

**tassel hyacinth** *s* (bot.) jacinto de penacho

**taste** [test] *s* gusto, sabor; sorbo, trago; muestra, ejemplar; gusto, buen gusto; **in bad taste** de mal gusto; **in good taste** de buen gusto; **to acquire a taste for** tomar gusto a; **to have a taste for** tener gusto a; **to taste** a gusto, a sabor; **to the king's** o **queen's taste** perfectamente; *va* gustar; probar; *vn* saber; **to taste like** u **of** saber a

**taste bud** *s* (anat.) papila del gusto

**tasteful** [ˈtestfəl] *adj* de buen gusto, elegante

**tasteless** [ˈtestlɪs] *adj* desabrido, insípido; de mal gusto

**taster** [ˈtestər] *s* catador, probador; catavino (*taza*)

**tasty** [ˈtestɪ] *adj* (*comp:* **-ier;** *super:* **-iest**) (coll.) sabroso; (coll.) de buen gusto

**tat** [tæt] (*pret & pp:* **tatted;** *ger:* **tatting**) *vn* (sew.) hacer frivolité

**Tatar** [ˈtɑtər] *adj & s* tártaro, tátaro

**tatouay** [ˈtætue] o [,tɑtuˈaɪ] *s* (zool.) tatú

**tatter** [ˈtætər] *s* andrajo, harapo, guiñapo; *va* hacer andrajos

**tatterdemalion** [,tætərdɪˈmeljən] o [,tætərdɪˈmæljən] *s* zaparrastroso, guiñapo

**tattered** [ˈtætərd] *adj* andrajoso, haraposo

**tatting** [ˈtætɪŋ] *s* (sew.) frivolité

**tattle** [ˈtætəl] *s* charla; chismografía; *va* descubrir (*secretos*) charlando; *vn* charlar; chismear

**tattler** [ˈtætlər] *s* charlador; chismoso; (orn.) sarapico

**tattletale** [ˈtætəl,tel] *s* cuentista, chismoso; *adj* revelador

**tattoo** [tæˈtu] *s* tatuaje; (mil.) retreta, toque de retreta; retreta (*fiesta nocturna en la cual las tropas recorren las calles*); *va* tatuar o tatuarse (*p.ej., el brazo o algo en el brazo*)

**taught** [tɔt] *pret & pp de* **teach**

**taunt** [tɔnt] o [tɑnt] *s* dicterio; mofa, pulla; *va* reprochar o provocar con insultos; **to taunt a person into doing something** conseguir con insultos que una persona haga algo

**taupe** [top] *adj & s* gris obscuro amarillento

**taurine** ['tɔraɪn] o ['tɔrɪn] *adj* taurino; *s* (chem.) taurina
**Taurus** ['tɔrəs] *s* (astr. & geog.) Tauro
**taut** [tɔt] *adj* tieso, tirante; aseado, bien arreglado
**tautog** [tɔ'tɑg] *s* (ichth.) tautoga
**tautological** [,tɔtə'lɑdʒɪkəl] *adj* tautológico
**tautology** [tɔ'tɑlədʒɪ] *s* tautología
**tautomer** ['tɔtəmər] *s* (chem.) tautómero
**tautomerism** [tɔ'tɑmərɪzəm] *s* (chem.) tautomería
**tavern** ['tævərn] *s* taberna; mesón, posada
**taw** [tɔ] *s* bolita de mármol; juego de las bolitas de mármol; línea desde donde se tiran las bolitas de mármol
**tawdry** ['tɔdrɪ] *adj* cursi, charro, vistoso
**tawny** ['tɔnɪ] *adj* (*comp:* **-nier;** *super:* **-niest**) leonado
**tawny owl** *s* (orn.) cárabo
**tax** [tæks] *s* impuesto, contribución; esfuerzo; *va* poner impuestos a (*una persona*); poner impuestos sobre (*la propiedad*); abrumar, someter a esfuerzo excesivo; agotar (*la paciencia de uno*); censurar, reprender; (law) tasar (*las costas*); (coll.) cobrar
**taxable** ['tæksəbəl] *adj* imponible; sujeto a impuesto
**taxation** [tæk'seʃən] *s* impuestos, contribuciones; imposición de contribuciones; (law) tasación de costas
**tax collector** *s* recaudador de impuestos
**tax cut** *s* reducción de impuestos
**tax evader** *s* burlador de impuestos
**tax-exempt** ['tæksɪg,zɛmpt] *adj* exento de impuesto
**tax-free** ['tæks,fri] *adj* libre de impuesto
**taxi** ['tæksɪ] *s* (*pl:* **-is**) taxi; (*pret & pp:* **-ied;** *ger:* **-iing** o **-ying**) *va* (aer.) carretear; *vn* ir en taxi; (aer.) carretear, correr por tierra, taxear
**taxicab** ['tæksɪ,kæb] *s* taxi
**taxi dancer** *s* taxi (*muchacha empleada para bailar con los clientes en salas de baile y cabarets*)
**taxidermal** [,tæksɪ'dʌrməl] *adj* taxidérmico
**taxidermist** ['tæksɪ,dʌrmɪst] *s* taxidermista
**taxidermy** ['tæksɪ,dʌrmɪ] *s* taxidermia
**taxi driver** *s* taxista, conductor de taxi
**taxilight** ['tæksɪ,laɪt] *s* (aer.) luz de rodaje
**taximeter** ['tæksɪ,mitər] *s* taxímetro
**taxiplane** ['tæksɪ,plen] *s* (aer.) avioneta de alquiler
**taxis** ['tæksɪs] *s* (biol.) tactismo, taxia o taxis; (surg.) taxis
**taxi service** *s* servicio de taxis; (aer.) servicio regular de aviones de alquiler
**taxi stand** *s* parada de taxis
**taxiway** ['tæksɪ,we] *s* (aer.) pista de rodaje
**taxonomic** [,tæksə'nɑmɪk] *adj* taxonómico
**taxonomist** [tæks'ɑnəmɪst] *s* taxonomista
**taxonomy** [tæks'ɑnəmɪ] *s* taxonomía
**taxpayer** ['tæks,peər] *s* contribuyente
**tax rate** *s* tipo (*porcentaje*) de impuesto, tipo impositivo
**t.b.** abr. de **tuberculosis**
**tbs.** o **tbsp.** abr. de **tablespoon** o **tablespoons**
**tea** [ti] *s* (bot.) té; té (*hoja seca; bebida; reunión por la tarde*); tisana (*bebida medicinal*); caldo de carne
**tea bag** *s* muñeca
**tea ball** *s* huevo del té, bolita (perforada) para té; bolsita de té
**teaboard** ['ti,bord] *s* bandeja para servir el té
**tea caddy** *s* bote para té
**teacart** ['ti,kɑrt] *s* mesita de té con ruedas
**teach** [titʃ] (*pret & pp:* **taught**) *va* enseñar; dar (*una lección*); (coll.) dar una lección a (*una persona para que comprenda la falta que ha cometido*); **to teach how to** + *inf* o **to teach to** + *inf* enseñar a + *inf;* **to teach someone something** enseñar algo a alguien; *vn* enseñar
**teachability** [,titʃə'bɪlɪtɪ] *s* docilidad
**teachable** ['titʃəbəl] *adj* dócil, educable, enseñable
**teacher** ['titʃər] *s* maestro, instructor; (fig.) maestra (*p.ej., la desgracia*)
**teacher's pet** *s* alumno mimado
**teaching** ['titʃɪŋ] *adj* docente; *s* enseñanza; doctrina
**teaching staff** *s* personal docente
**tea cozy** *s* cubretetera
**teacup** ['ti,kʌp] *s* taza de té, taza para té
**teacupful** ['tɪkʌpfʊl] *s* taza de té
**tea dance** *s* té bailable
**teahouse** ['ti,haʊs] *s* salón de té, sitio donde se vende y sirve té y refrescos
**teak** [tik] *s* (bot.) teca (*árbol y madera*)
**teakettle** ['ti,kɛtəl] *s* tetera
**teakwood** ['tik,wʊd] *s* teca (*madera*)
**teal** [til] *s* (orn.) pato chiquito; (orn.) cerceta, trullo
**tea leaf** *s* hoja de té
**team** [tim] *s* atelaje, tiro, tronco; yunta (*de bueyes*); (sport) equipo; *va* enyugar, uncir, enganchar juntos; acarrear, transportar o conducir con un tronco; *vn* conducir un tronco; ser tronquista; **to team up** asociarse, unirse; formar un equipo
**teammate** ['tim,met] *s* compañero de equipo, equipier
**teamster** ['timstər] *s* tronquista; carretero; camionista
**teamwork** ['tim,wʌrk] *s* solidaridad, cooperación; espíritu de equipo
**tea party** *s* reunión para tomar el té
**teapot** ['ti,pɑt] *s* tetera
**tear** [tɪr] *s* lágrima; **in tears** en llanto; **to burst into tears** romper a llorar; **to fill with tears** arrasarse (*los ojos*) de o en lágrimás; **to hold back one's tears** beberse las lágrimas; **to laugh away one's tears** convertir las lágrimas en risas; **to move to tears** mover a lágrimas ‖ [tɛr] *s* rasgón, desgarro; raja, hendedura; precipitación, prisa; (slang) borrachera ‖ [tɛr] (*pret:* **tore;** *pp:* **torn**) *va* rasgar, desgarrar; rajar; lacerar; herir; arrancar; acongojar, afligir; mesarse (*los cabellos*); **to tear apart** romper en dos; **to tear down** derribar (*un edificio*); desarmar (*una máquina*); **to tear oneself away** (coll.) irse o separarse de mala gana; **to tear open** abrir rasgando; **to tear out** arrancar; **to tear up** romper (*un papel*) ‖ *vn* rasgarse, desgarrarse; lacerarse; correr, precipitarse; **to tear along** correr a toda velocidad
**tear bomb** [tɪr] *s* bomba lacrimógena
**teardrop** ['tɪr,drɑp] *s* lágrima
**tearful** ['tɪrfəl] *adj* lacrimoso
**tear gas** [tɪr] *s* gas lacrimógeno
**tear-jerker** ['tɪr,dʒʌrkər] *s* (slang) drama o cine que arranca lágrimas
**tear-off** ['tɛr,ɔf] o ['tɛr,ɑf] *adj* exfoliador
**tearoom** ['ti,rum] o ['ti,rʊm] *s* salón de té
**tear sheet** [tɛr] *s* hoja del anunciante
**teary** ['tɪrɪ] *adj* lloroso
**tease** [tiz] *s* embromador; broma continua; *va* embromar, fastidiar, azuzar; cardar (*el paño*)
**teasel** ['tizəl] *s* (bot.) cardencha; (bot.) cardo de cardadores; carda (*cabeza del tallo de la cardencha; instrumento para cardar*); (*pret & pp:* **-seled** o **-selled;** *ger:* **-seling** o **-selling**) *va* cardar, rebotar (*el paño*)
**teaser** ['tizər] *s* embromador; broma continua; (coll.) rompecabezas, problema difícil
**tea set** *s* servicio para té
**teaspoon** ['ti,spun] *s* cucharilla o cucharita
**teaspoonful** ['tispunfʊl] *s* cucharada pequeña o de café, cucharadita
**teat** [tit] *s* teta; pezón (*extremidad de la teta*)
**tea time** *s* hora de té
**tea wagon** *s* var. de **teacart**
**teazel** ['tizəl] *s* var. de **teasel;** (*pret & pp:* **-zeled** o **-zelled;** *ger:* **-zeling** o **-zelling**) *va* var. de **teasel**
**tech.** abr. de **technical** y **technology**
**technetium** [tɛk'niʃɪəm] *s* (chem.) tecnetio
**technic** ['tɛknɪk] *adj* técnico; *s* técnica (*ciencia de un arte; habilidad*); término técnico; **technics** *ssg* técnica (*ciencia de un arte*); *spl* técnica (*habilidad*)
**technical** ['tɛknɪkəl] *adj* técnico
**technicality** [,tɛknɪ'kælɪtɪ] *s* (*pl:* **-ties**) tecnicismo (*término técnico*); tecnicidad (*carácter técnico*); cosa técnica, procedimiento técnico
**technically** ['tɛknɪkəlɪ] *adv* técnicamente
**technician** [tɛk'nɪʃən] *s* técnico
**technicolor** ['tɛknɪ,kʌlər] *s* (trademark) tecnicolor

**technique** [tɛk'nik] *s* técnica (*método; habilidad*)
**technocracy** [tɛk'nɑkrəsɪ] *s* tecnocracia
**technocrat** ['tɛknəkræt] *s* tecnócrata
**technocratic** [,tɛknə'krætɪk] *adj* tecnocrático
**technologic** [,tɛknə'lɑdʒɪk] o **technological** [,tɛknə'lɑdʒɪkəl] *adj* tecnológico
**technologist** [tɛk'nɑlədʒɪst] *s* tecnólogo
**technology** [tɛk'nɑlədʒɪ] *s* tecnología
**techy** ['tɛtʃɪ] *adj* (*comp:* **-ier;** *super:* **-iest**) (coll.) cosquilloso, picajón
**tectonic** [tɛk'tɑnɪk] *adj* tectónico; **tectonics** *ssg* tectónica
**ted** [tɛd] (*pret & pp:* **tedded;** *ger:* **tedding**) *va* henear; esparcir; disipar
**tedder** ['tɛdər] *s* heneador (*persona o aparato*)
**Teddy** ['tɛdɪ] *s* nombre abreviado de **Theodore**
**Teddy bear** *s* oso de juguete, oso de trapo
**Te Deum** [ti'diəm] *s* tedeum
**tedious** ['tidɪəs] o ['tidʒəs] *adj* tedioso
**tedium** ['tidɪəm] *s* tedio
**tee** [ti] *s* (sport) hito (*p.ej., en el juego de tejos*); (golf) tee (*punto de saque*); te (*empalme para tubos en forma de T*); *va* (golf) colocar (*la pelota*) en el tee; **to tee off** (golf) golpear (*la pelota*) desde el tee
**teem** [tim] *vn* hormiguear, abundar; llover a cántaros; **to teem with** abundar en, hervir de
**teeming** ['timɪŋ] *adj* hormigueante; torrencial (*lluvia*)
**teen age** [tin] *s* edad de 13 a 19 años
**teen-ager** ['tin,edʒər] *s* joven de 13 a 19 años de edad
**teens** [tinz] *spl* números ingleses que terminan en **-teen** (de 13 a 19); edad de 13 a 19 años; **to be in one's teens** tener de 13 a 19 años
**teeny** ['tinɪ] *adj* (*comp:* **-nier;** *super:* **-niest**) (coll.) diminuto, menudo, pequeñito
**teepee** ['tipi] *s* var. de **tepee**
**teeter** ['titər] *s* vaivén, balanceo; columpio; *vn* balancear, oscilar; estar temblando
**teeth** [tiθ] *pl de* **tooth**
**teethe** [tið] *vn* endentecer
**teething** ['tiðɪŋ] *s* dentición
**teething ring** *s* chupador
**teetotal** [ti'totəl] *adj* teetotalista; (coll.) absoluto, completo
**teetotaler** o **teetotaller** [ti'totələr] *s* teetotalista
**teetotalism** [ti'totəlɪzəm] *s* teetotalismo (*templanza que excluye por completo las bebidas alcohólicas*)
**teetotum** [ti'totəm] *s* perinola
**tegmen** ['tɛgmɛn] *s* (*pl:* **-mina** [mɪnə]) (bot. & zool.) tegmen
**tegula** ['tɛgjələ] *s* (*pl:* **-lae** [li]) (zool.) tégula
**tegular** ['tɛgjələr] *adj* tegular
**tegument** ['tɛgjəmənt] *s* (anat., bot. & zool.) tegumento
**tegumentary** [,tɛgjə'mɛntərɪ] *adj* tegumentario
**te-hee** [ti'hi] *s* risita entre dientes; *vn* reírse entre dientes; *interj* ¡ ji, ji!
**tektite** ['tɛktaɪt] *s* (geol.) tectita
**tel.** abr. de **telegram, telegraph** y **telephone**
**telamon** ['tɛləmɑn] *s* (*pl:* **telamones** [,tɛlə'moniz]) (arch.) telamón
**telangiectasis** [tɛl,ændʒɪ'ɛktəsɪs] *s* (*pl:* **-ses** [siz]) (path.) telangiectasia
**telautograph** [tɛl'ɔtəgræf] o [tɛl'ɔtəgrɑf] *s* telautógrafo
**telecamera** [,tɛlɪ'kæmərə] *s* cámara televisora
**telecast** ['tɛlɪ,kæst] o ['tɛlɪ,kɑst] *s* teledifusión; (*pret & pp:* **-cast** o **-casted**) *va & vn* teledifundir
**telecommunication** [,tɛlɪkə,mjunɪ'keʃən] *s* telecomunicación
**teledu** ['tɛlɪdu] *s* (zool.) tejón teledu
**telega** [tɛ'lɛgə] *s* telega
**telegony** [tɪ'lɛgənɪ] *s* (biol.) telegonía
**telegram** ['tɛlɪgræm] *s* telegrama
**telegraph** ['tɛlɪgræf] o ['tɛlɪgrɑf] *s* telégrafo; *va & vn* telegrafiar
**telegraph code** *s* código telegráfico
**telegrapher** [tɪ'lɛgrəfər] *s* telegrafista
**telegrapher's cramp** *s* calambre de los telegrafistas
**telegraphic** [,tɛlɪ'græfɪk] *adj* telegráfico
**telegraphically** [,tɛlɪ'græfɪkəlɪ] *adv* telegráficamente
**telegraph pole** *s* poste telegráfico
**telegraphy** [tɪ'lɛgrəfɪ] *s* telegrafía
**telekinesis** [,tɛlɪkɪ'nisɪs] *s* telequinesia
**telelectric** [,tɛlɪ'lɛktrɪk] *adj* teleléctrico
**Telemachus** [tɪ'lɛməkəs] *s* (myth.) Telémaco
**telemechanic** [,tɛlɪmɪ'kænɪk] *adj* telemecánico; **telemechanics** *ssg* telemecánica
**telemeter** [tɪ'lɛmɪtər] *s* telémetro; *va & vn* telemetrar
**telemetric** [,tɛlɪ'mɛtrɪk] *adj* telemétrico
**telemetry** [tɪ'lɛmɪtrɪ] *s* telemetría
**telencephalon** [,tɛlɛn'sɛfəlɑn] *s* (anat.) telencéfalo
**teleological** [,tɛlɪə'lɑdʒɪkəl] o [,tilɪə'lɑdʒɪkəl] *adj* teleológico
**teleology** [,tɛlɪ'ɑlədʒɪ] o [,tilɪ'ɑlədʒɪ] *s* teleología
**teleost** ['tɛlɪɑst] o ['tilɪɑst] *adj & s* (ichth.) teleósteo
**telepathic** [,tɛlɪ'pæθɪk] *adj* telepático
**telepathically** [,tɛlɪ'pæθɪkəlɪ] *adv* telepáticamente
**telepathist** [tɪ'lɛpəθɪst] *s* telepatista
**telepathy** [tɪ'lɛpəθɪ] *s* telepatía
**telephone** ['tɛlɪfon] *s* teléfono; *va & vn* telefonear
**telephone book** *s* libro de teléfonos
**telephone booth** *s* locutorio, cabina telefónica
**telephone call** *s* llamada telefónica
**telephone directory** *s* anuario telefónico, guía telefónica
**telephone exchange** *s* estación telefónica, central de teléfonos
**telephone girl** *s* señorita telefonista
**telephone message** *s* telefonema, despacho telefónico
**telephone number** *s* número de teléfono
**telephone operator** *s* telefonista
**telephone receiver** *s* receptor telefónico
**telephone switchboard** *s* cuadro de control telefónico
**telephone table** *s* mesita portateléfono
**telephonic** [,tɛlɪ'fɑnɪk] *adj* telefónico
**telephony** [tɪ'lɛfənɪ] *s* telefonía
**telephote** ['tɛlɪfot] *s* (elec.) telefoto *m*
**telephoto** [,tɛlɪ'foto] *adj* telefotográfico; *s* telefoto *f* (*imagen*); telefotógrafo (*aparato*); lente telefotográfico
**telephotograph** [,tɛlɪ'fotəgræf] o [,tɛlɪ'fotəgrɑf] *s* telefotografía; *va & vn* telefotografiar
**telephotographic** [,tɛlɪ,fotə'græfɪk] *adj* telefotográfico
**telephotography** [,tɛlɪfə'tɑgrəfɪ] *s* telefotografía
**telephoto lens** *s* lente telefotográfico, teleobjetivo
**teleprinter** ['tɛlɪ,prɪntər] *s* teleimpresor
**teleprompter** ['tɛlɪ,prɑmptər] *s* (trademark) apuntador automático (*para ayudar a un actor u orador*)
**teleran** ['tɛlɪræn] *s* (elec.) telerán
**telescope** ['tɛlɪskop] *s* telescopio; catalejo (*anteojo de larga vista*); *va* telescopar; acortar; *vn* telescoparse
**telescope word** *s* var. de **portmanteau word**
**telescopic** [,tɛlɪ'skɑpɪk] *adj* telescópico
**telescopically** [,tɛlɪ'skɑpɪkəlɪ] *adv* telescópicamente
**Telescopium** [,tɛlɪ'skopɪəm] *s* (astr.) Telescopio
**telescopy** [tɪ'lɛskəpɪ] *s* arte de hacer o manejar el telescopio
**telestereoscope** [,tɛlɪ'stɛrɪə,skop] *s* telestereoscopio
**telesthesia** [,tɛlɪs'θiʒə] o [,tɛlɪs'θiʒɪə] *s* telestesia
**telethermometer** [,tɛlɪθər'mɑmɪtər] *s* teletermómetro
**teletype** ['tɛlɪtaɪp] *s* (trademark) teletipo; *va* transmitir por teletipo
**teletyper** ['tɛlɪ,taɪpər] *s* teletipista
**teletypewriter** [,tɛlɪ'taɪp,raɪtər] *s* teletipia
**teleview** ['tɛlɪ,vju] *va & vn* ver por televisión
**televiewer** ['tɛlɪ,vjuər] *s* televidente, telespectador
**televise** ['tɛlɪvaɪz] *va* televisar
**television** ['tɛlɪ,vɪʒən] *s* televisión
**television camera** *s* cámara televisora

**television screen** *s* pantalla televisora
**television set** *s* televisor, telerreceptor
**telfordize** ['tɛlfərdaɪz] *va* recubrir con pavimento télford
**telford pavement** *s* pavimento télford (*superficie compuesta de una mezcla de piedras grandes y pequeñas y una capa dura de grava*)
**tell** [tɛl] (*pret & pp:* **told**) *va* decir; contar (*narrar; computar*); determinar; conocer, distinguir; **to tell someone off** (coll.) decirle a uno cuántas son cinco; **to tell someone to** + *inf* decirle a uno que + *subj; vn* hablar; surtir efecto; **to tell on** dejarse ver en (*p.ej., la salud de uno*); (coll.) denunciar, contar chismes de
**tellable** ['tɛləbəl] *adj* decible
**teller** ['tɛlər] *s* narrador, relator; cajero (*de un banco*); escrutador (*de votos*)
**telling** ['tɛlɪŋ] *adj* eficaz; *s* narración; **there is no telling** no es posible decir
**telltale** ['tɛl,tel] *s* soplón, chismoso; indicio, señal; reloj registrador; (naut.) axiómetro; *adj* revelador; indicador
**tellurate** ['tɛljəret] *s* (chem.) telurato
**telluric** [tɛ'lurɪk] *adj* telúrico; (chem.) telúrico
**telluride** ['tɛljəraɪd] o ['tɛljərɪd] *s* (chem.) telururo
**tellurite** ['tɛljəraɪt] *s* (chem.) telurito; (mineral.) telurita
**tellurium** [tɛ'lurɪəm] *s* (chem.) telurio
**tellurous** ['tɛljərəs] *adj* (chem.) teluroso
**telly** ['tɛlɪ] *s* (*pl:* **-lies**) (Brit.) televisión
**telolecithal** [,tɛlə'lɛsɪθəl] *adj* (embryol.) telolecito
**telophase** ['tɛləfez] *s* (biol.) telofase
**telpher** ['tɛlfər] *adj & s* teleférico; *va* teleferar
**telpherage** ['tɛlfərɪdʒ] *s* teleferaje
**temblor** [tɛm'blor] *s* temblor de tierra
**temerarious** [,tɛmə'rɛrɪəs] *adj* temerario
**temerity** [tɪ'mɛrɪtɪ] *s* temeridad
**temper** ['tɛmpər] *s* temple (*natural, genio; dureza del acero*); mal genio, cólera; punto (*de una mezcla*); **to fly into a temper** montar en cólera; **to keep one's temper** dominar su mal genio; **to lose one's temper** perder la paciencia, encolerizarse; *va* templar; (mus.) templar; *vn* templarse
**tempera** ['tɛmpərə] *s* (paint.) temple (*procedimiento*)
**temperament** ['tɛmpərəmənt] *s* temperamento (*naturaleza particular de un individuo*); disposición, genialidad; (mus.) temperamento
**temperamental** [,tɛmpərə'mɛntəl] *adj* temperamental; original, genial
**temperance** ['tɛmpərəns] *s* templanza; *adj* de templanza, p.ej., **temperance society** sociedad de templanza
**temperate** ['tɛmpərɪt] *adj* templado (*en comer y beber; en clima*)
**temperately** ['tɛmpərɪtlɪ] *adv* templadamente
**temperate zone** *s* zona templada
**temperature** ['tɛmpərətʃər] *s* temperatura; (path.) temperatura (*fiebre*)
**tempered** ['tɛmpərd] *adj* templado; (mus.) templado
**tempest** ['tɛmpɪst] *s* tempestad; *va* agitar violentamente
**tempest in a teapot** *s* más el ruido que las nueces
**tempestuous** [tɛm'pɛstʃuəs] *adj* tempestuoso; (fig.) tempestuoso
**Templar** ['tɛmplər] *s* Templario, caballero del Temple; (U.S.A.) caballero templario
**template** ['tɛmplɪt] *s* var. de **templet**
**temple** ['tɛmpəl] *s* templo; templén (*de un telar*); gafa (*enganche con que se afianzan los anteojos en las sienes*); (anat.) sien
**templet** ['tɛmplɪt] *s* plantilla; (constr.) solera; (naut.) gálibo
**tempo** ['tɛmpo] *s* (*pl:* **-pos** o **-pi** [pi]) (mus.) tiempo; (fig.) ritmo (*p.ej., de la vida*)
**temporal** ['tɛmpərəl] *adj* temporal; (anat. & gram.) temporal
**temporal bone** *s* (anat.) hueso temporal
**temporality** [,tɛmpə'rælɪtɪ] *s* (*pl:* **-ties**) temporalidad; cosa temporal; **temporalities** *spl* (eccl.) temporalidades
**temporally** ['tɛmpərəlɪ] *adv* temporalmente (*en el orden de lo temporal o terreno*)
**temporarily** ['tɛmpə,rɛrɪlɪ] *adv* temporalmente (*por algún tiempo*)
**temporary** ['tɛmpə,rɛrɪ] *adj* temporal, temporáneo, temporario
**temporization** [,tɛmpərɪ'zeʃən] *s* contemporización
**temporize** ['tɛmpəraɪz] *vn* contemporizar, temporizar
**tempt** [tɛmpt] *va* tentar; **to tempt a person into a house** tentar a una persona a que entre en una casa; **to tempt someone to** + *inf* tentar a uno a + *inf*, tentar a uno a que + *subj*
**temptation** [tɛmp'teʃən] *s* tentación
**tempter** ['tɛmptər] *s* tentador; **the Tempter** el tentador (*el diablo*)
**tempting** ['tɛmptɪŋ] *adj* tentador
**temptress** ['tɛmptrɪs] *s* tentadora
**ten** [tɛn] *adj* diez; *s* diez; **ten o'clock** las diez; **the tens** las decenas (*los números 10, 20, 30, etc.*)
**tenability** [,tɛnə'bɪlɪtɪ] o [,tinə'bɪlɪtɪ] *s* defendibilidad
**tenable** ['tɛnəbəl] o ['tinəbəl] *adj* defendible
**tenace** ['tɛnes] *s* (bridge) tenaza (*reina y as o rey y sota*)
**tenacious** [tɪ'neʃəs] *adj* tenaz
**tenacity** [tɪ'næsɪtɪ] *s* tenacidad; (phys.) tenacidad
**tenaculum** [tɪ'nækjələm] *s* (*pl:* **-la** [lə]) (surg.) tenáculo
**tenaille** [tɛ'nel] *s* (fort.) tenaza
**tenancy** ['tɛnənsɪ] *s* (*pl:* **-cies**) tenencia; propiedad arrendada
**tenant** ['tɛnənt] *s* arrendatario, inquilino; morador, residente; *va* arrendar, alquilar
**tenant farmer** *s* colono
**tenantry** ['tɛnəntrɪ] *s* (*pl:* **-ries**) arrendatarios, inquilinos; tenencia; propiedad arrendada
**tench** [tɛntʃ] *s* (ichth.) tenca
**Ten Commandments** *spl* (Bib.) diez mandamientos
**tend** [tɛnd] *va* cuidar, vigilar; servir; *vn* tender; dirigirse; **to tend to** atender a (*p.ej., los negocios*); **to tend to** + *inf* tender a + *inf*
**tendance** ['tɛndəns] *s* atención, cuidado
**tendency** ['tɛndənsɪ] *s* (*pl:* **-cies**) tendencia
**tendentious** [tɛn'dɛnʃəs] *adj* tendencioso
**tender** ['tɛndər] *s* oferta; (naut.) alijador, falúa; (naut.) nodriza; (rail.) ténder; *adj* tierno; dolorido; *va* ofrecer; tender
**tenderfoot** ['tɛndər,fut] *s* (*pl:* **-foots** o **-feet**) *s* recién llegado (*en condiciones de vida muy ásperas*); principiante, novato
**tender-hearted** ['tɛndər'hɑrtɪd] *adj* compasivo, tierno de corazón
**tenderloin** ['tɛndər,lɔɪn] *s* filete (*de carne de vaca o cerdo*); (*cap.*) *s* barrio de mala vida (*en las grandes ciudades*)
**tenderness** ['tɛndərnɪs] *s* ternura, terneza; sensibilidad
**tendinous** ['tɛndɪnəs] *adj* tendinoso
**tendon** ['tɛndən] *s* (anat.) tendón
**tendril** ['tɛndrɪl] *s* (bot.) zarcillo, tijereta; rizo (*de pelo*)
**Tenebrae** ['tɛnɪbri] *spl* (eccl.) tinieblas
**tenebrous** ['tɛnɪbrəs] *adj* tenebroso
**tenement** ['tɛnɪmənt] *s* habitación, vivienda; aposento; casa de vecindad
**tenement house** *s* casa de vecindad
**tenesmus** [tə'nɛzməs] o [tə'nɛsməs] *s* (path.) tenesmo, pujo
**tenet** ['tɛnɪt] o ['tinɪt] *s* credo, dogma, principio
**tenfold** ['tɛn,fold] *adj & s* décuplo; *adv* diez veces
**Tenn.** abr. de **Tennessee**
**tennis** ['tɛnɪs] *s* (sport) tenis; *adj* tenístico
**tennis ball** *s* pelota de tenis
**tennis court** *s* (sport) campo de tenis, cancha de tenis
**tennis player** *s* tenista
**tenon** ['tɛnən] *s* (carp.) espiga, almilla; *va* (carp.) espigar, despatillar, desquijerar; (carp.) ensamblar con espiga
**tenor** ['tɛnər] *s* tenor, carácter, curso, tendencia; (mus.) tenor (*persona; voz; instrumento*); *adj* (mus.) de tenor, para el tenor
**tenotomy** [tɪ'nɑtəmɪ] *s* (*pl:* **-mies**) (surg.) tenotomía

**tenpenny** [ˈtɛn,pɛnɪ] o [ˈtɛnpənɪ] *adj* de diez peniques, que vale diez peniques
**tenpenny nail** *s* clavo de tres pulgadas
**tenpins** [ˈtɛn,pɪnz] *ssg* juego de bolos en que se juega con diez bolos de madera dispuestos en triángulo; *spl* los diez bolos
**tense** [tɛns] *adj* tenso, tieso; tenso (*dícese de una persona o de una situación dramática*); tirante (*dícese de las relaciones de amistad próximas a romperse*); *s* (gram.) tiempo; *va* estirar
**tenseness** [ˈtɛnsnɪs] *s* tensión, tirantez
**tensible** [ˈtɛnsɪbəl] *adj* tensible
**tensile** [ˈtɛnsɪl] o [ˈtɛnsaɪl] *adj* tensor; de tensión; dúctil, flexible
**tensile strength** *s* (phys.) resistencia a la tensión
**tension** [ˈtɛnʃən] *s* tensión; (mech.) tracción; esfuerzo mental, ansia, congoja; tirantez (*de amistad, de relaciones diplomáticas próximas a romperse*); tensor, regulador de la tensión (*dispositivo*)
**tensional** [ˈtɛnʃənəl] *adj* de tensión
**tensity** [ˈtɛnsɪtɪ] *s* tensión
**tenson** [ˈtɛnsən] *s* (lit.) tensón o tensión
**tensor** [ˈtɛnsər] o [ˈtɛnsɔr] *s* (anat.) tensor
**ten-strike** [ˈtɛn,straɪk] *s* (sport) golpe con que se derriban todos los bolos (*en el juego de diez bolos*); (coll.) golpe o jugada muy difícil y de mucho éxito
**tent** [tɛnt] *s* tienda, tienda de campaña; (surg.) lechino, tapón; *va* acampar bajo tiendas; (surg.) tener abierto con tapón; *vn* acampar bajo una tienda
**tentacle** [ˈtɛntəkəl] *s* (bot. & zool.) tentáculo
**tentacular** [tɛnˈtækjələr] *adj* tentacular
**tentative** [ˈtɛntətɪv] *adj* tentativo
**tent caterpillar** *s* (ent.) falsa lagarta
**tenter** [ˈtɛntər] *s* tendedor, bastidor; escarpia o alcayata (*de tendedor*); *va* enramblar; *vn* enramblarse
**tenterhook** [ˈtɛntər,hʊk] *s* escarpia o alcayata (*de tendedor*); **on tenterhooks** en ascuas, ansioso
**tenth** [tɛnθ] *adj* décimo; *s* décimo; diez (*en las fechas*); (mus.) décima
**tenuity** [tɛˈnjuɪtɪ] *s* tenuidad; raridad (*p.ej., del aire*)
**tenuous** [ˈtɛnjuəs] *adj* tenue; raro (*poco denso*)
**tenure** [ˈtɛnjər] *s* tenencia; ejercicio (*de un cargo*); inamovilidad (*de un cargo*)
**tepee** [ˈtipi] *s* tipi (*tienda de los indios norteamericanos*)
**tepid** [ˈtɛpɪd] *adj* tibio; (fig.) tibio
**tepidity** [tɪˈpɪdɪtɪ] *s* tibieza; (fig.) tibieza
**ter.** abr. de **territory**
**teratological** [,tɛrətəˈlɑdʒɪkəl] *adj* teratológico
**teratology** [,tɛrəˈtɑlədʒɪ] *s* teratología
**terbium** [ˈtʌrbɪəm] *s* (chem.) terbio
**tercel** [ˈtʌrsəl] *s* (orn.) halcón macho, terzuelo
**tercentenary** [tʌrˈsɛntə,nɛrɪ] *adj* de trescientos años; *s* (*pl:* **-ies**) tricentenario
**tercet** [ˈtʌrsɪt] *s* terceto; (mus.) tresillo
**terebinth** [ˈtɛrɪbɪnθ] *s* (bot.) terebinto, albotín
**teredo** [tɛˈrido] *s* (*pl:* **-dos**) (zool.) teredo
**Terence** [ˈtɛrəns] *s* Terencio
**tergiversate** [ˈtʌrdʒɪvər,set] *vn* tergiversar
**tergiversation** [,tʌrdʒɪvərˈseʃən] *s* tergiversación
**tergiversator** [ˈtʌrdʒɪvər,setər] *s* tergiversador
**term** [tʌrm] *s* término; condena, período (*de prisión*); semestre, período escolar; período o mandato (*p.ej., del presidente de los EE.UU.*); (arch., log. & math.) término; **terms** *spl* términos (*expresiones, palabras; relaciones mutuas*); condiciones; **to be on good terms with** estar en buenos términos con; **to bring to terms** imponer condiciones a; someter, vencer; **to come to terms** ponerse de acuerdo; someterse; *va* llamar, nombrar
**termagancy** [ˈtʌrməgənsɪ] *s* mal genio (*de mujer*)
**termagant** [ˈtʌrməgənt] *adj* regañona, de mal genio; *s* mujer regañona, mujer de mal genio
**terminability** [,tʌrmɪnəˈbɪlɪtɪ] *s* terminabilidad
**terminable** [ˈtʌrmɪnəbəl] *adj* terminable
**terminal** [ˈtʌrmɪnəl] *adj* terminal; *s* término, fin; (elec.) terminal; (rail.) estación de cabeza, estación de fin de línea
**terminally** [ˈtʌrmɪnəlɪ] *adv* al final, finalmente
**terminate** [ˈtʌrmɪnet] *va & vn* terminar
**termination** [,tʌrmɪˈneʃən] *s* terminación; (gram.) terminación, desinencia
**terminative** [ˈtʌrmɪ,netɪv] *adj* terminativo
**terminological** [,tʌrmɪnəˈlɑdʒɪkəl] *adj* terminológico
**terminology** [,tʌrmɪˈnɑlədʒɪ] *s* (*pl:* **-gies**) terminología
**term insurance** *s* seguro a plazo fijo
**terminus** [ˈtʌrmɪnəs] *s* (*pl:* **-ni** [naɪ] o **-nuses**) término; (rail.) estación de cabeza, estación extrema; (*cap.*) *s* (myth.) Término
**termite** [ˈtʌrmaɪt] *s* (ent.& fig.) termita
**term of service** *s* período de servicio
**tern** [tʌrn] *s* (orn.) gaviotín (*Sterna hirundo*); (orn.) golondrina de mar (*Hydrochelidon*)
**ternary** [ˈtʌrnərɪ] *adj* ternario
**ternate** [ˈtʌrnet] *adj* ternario; (bot.) ternado
**terpene** [ˈtʌrpin] *s* (chem.) terpeno
**terpineol** [tərˈpɪnɪol] o [tərˈpɪnɪɑl] *s* (chem.) terpineol
**Terpsichore** [tərpˈsɪkərɪ] *s* (myth.) Terpsícore
**terpsichorean** [,tʌrpsɪkəˈriən] *adj* de Terpsícore
**terr.** abr. de **terrace** y **territory**
**terrace** [ˈtɛrəs] *s* terraplén; terraza; azotea, terrado; hilera de casas dispuestas a lo largo de una serie de gradas o terraplenes; *va* terraplenar
**terra cotta** [ˈtɛrə ˈkɑtə] *s* terracota; color rojo oscuro
**terra firma** [ˈtɛrə ˈfʌrmə] *s* tierra firme; **on terra firma** sobre suelo firme
**terrain** [tɛˈren] o [ˈtɛren] *s* terreno; (geol.) terreno
**terra incognita** [ˈtɛrə ɪnˈkɑgnɪtə] *s* tierra desconocida
**terra japonica** [ˈtɛrə dʒəˈpɑnɪkə] *s* (pharm.) tierra japónica
**terramycin** [,tɛrəˈmaɪsɪn] *s* (pharm.) terramicina
**terrane** [tɛˈren] o [ˈtɛren] *s* (geol.) terreno
**terrapin** [ˈtɛrəpɪn] *s* (zool.) terrapene
**terraqueous** [tɛrˈekwɪəs] *adj* terráqueo
**terrazzo** [tɛˈrɑtso] *s* piso veneciano
**terreplein** [ˈtɛr,plen] *s* (fort.) terraplén
**terrestrial** [təˈrɛstrɪəl] *adj* terrestre
**terrestrial globe** *s* globo terráqueo o terrestre (*la Tierra; mapa de la Tierra en forma de bola*)
**terrestrial magnetism** *s* magnetismo terrestre
**terret** [ˈtɛrɪt] *s* anillo de collera, portarriendas
**terrible** [ˈtɛrɪbəl] *adj* terrible; (coll.) muy malo, muy desagradable
**terribly** [ˈtɛrɪblɪ] *adv* terriblemente; (coll.) muy, excesivamente
**terrier** [ˈtɛrɪər] *s* terrier
**terrific** [təˈrɪfɪk] *adj* terrífico; (coll.) brutal (*extraordinariamente grande, intenso, lujoso, hermoso, excelente, etc.*)
**terrifically** [təˈrɪfɪkəlɪ] *adv* terriblemente; (coll.) enormemente, extraordinariamente
**terrify** [ˈtɛrɪfaɪ] (*pret & pp:* **-fied**) *va* aterrorizar
**territorial** [,tɛrɪˈtorɪəl] *adj* territorial; (*cap.*) *s* (Brit.) soldado territorial
**territoriality** [,tɛrɪ,torɪˈælɪtɪ] *s* territorialidad
**territorially** [,tɛrɪˈtorɪəlɪ] *adv* territorialmente
**territory** [ˈtɛrɪ,torɪ] *s* (*pl:* **-ries**) territorio
**terror** [ˈtɛrər] *s* terror
**terrorism** [ˈtɛrərɪzəm] *s* terrorismo
**terrorist** [ˈtɛrərɪst] *adj & s* terrorista
**terroristic** [,tɛrəˈrɪstɪk] *adj* de terrorismo, de terrorista
**terrorization** [,tɛrərɪˈzeʃən] *s* terror, terrorismo
**terrorize** [ˈtɛrəraɪz] *va* aterrorizar
**terror-stricken** [ˈtɛrər,strɪkən] *adj* aterrorizado
**terry cloth** [ˈtɛrɪ] *s* albornoz
**terse** [tʌrs] *adj* breve, sucinto, vivo
**tertian** [ˈtʌrʃən] *adj* terciano; *s* (path.) terciana

**tertiary** [ˈtʌrʃɪˌɛrɪ] o [ˈtʌrʃərɪ] *adj* terciario; (*cap.*) *adj* (geol.) terciario; *s* (*pl:* **-ies**) (geol.) terciario
**Tertullian** [tərˈtʌlɪən] *s* Tertuliano
**terza rima** [ˈtɛrtsɑ ˈrimɑ] *s* (pros.) tercia rima
**tessellate** [ˈtɛsəlet] *adj* teselado; *va* formar con teselas
**tessera** [ˈtɛsərə] *s* (*pl:* **-ae** [i]) tesela; (hist.) tésera
**Test.** abr. de **Testament**
**test** [tɛst] *s* prueba, ensayo; examen; (educ. & psychol.) test; (zool.) testa; *va* probar, poner a prueba; examinar
**testa** [ˈtɛstə] *s* (*pl:* **-tae** [ti]) (bot. & zool.) testa
**testacean** [tɛsˈteʃən] *adj* & *s* (zool.) testáceo
**testacy** [ˈtɛstəsɪ] *s* estado de testado
**testament** [ˈtɛstəmənt] *s* testamento; (*cap.*) *s* Testamento
**testamentary** [ˌtɛstəˈmɛntərɪ] *adj* testamentario
**testate** [ˈtɛstet] *adj* testado
**testator** [tɛsˈtetər] o [ˈtɛstetər] *s* testador
**testatrix** [tɛsˈtetrɪks] *s* (*pl:* **-trices** [trɪsiz]) testadora
**test ban** *s* proscripción de las pruebas nucleares
**tester** [ˈtɛstər] *s* probador, ensayador; baldaquín, dosel
**test flight** *s* (aer.) vuelo de ensayo o de prueba
**testicle** [ˈtɛstɪkəl] *s* (anat.) testículo
**testicular** [tɛsˈtɪkjələr] *adj* testicular
**testify** [ˈtɛstɪfaɪ] (*pret & pp:* **-fied**) *va & vn* testificar
**testimonial** [ˌtɛstɪˈmonɪəl] *adj* de recomendación; de homenaje; *s* recomendación, certificado; homenaje
**testimony** [ˈtɛstɪˌmonɪ] *s* (*pl:* **-nies**) testimonio; (Bib.) testimonio; **testimonies** *spl* Sagradas Escrituras; **in testimony whereof** en testimonio de lo cual
**testing bench** *s* banco de pruebas
**testing grounds** *spl* campo de prueba
**testis** [ˈtɛstɪs] *s* (*pl:* **-tes** [tiz]) (anat.) teste
**test of strength** *s* prueba de fuerza
**testosterone** [tɛsˈtɑstəron] *s* (biochem.) testosterona
**test pilot** *s* (aer.) piloto de pruebas
**test tube** *s* probeta, tubo de ensayo
**testudinal** [tɛsˈtjudɪnəl] o [tɛsˈtudɪnəl] *adj* (zool.) testudinal
**testudinous** [tɛsˈtjudɪnəs] o [tɛsˈtudɪnəs] *adj* testudíneo
**testudo** [tɛsˈtjudo] o [tɛsˈtudo] *s* (*pl:* **-dines** [dɪniz]) (hist.) testudo
**testy** [ˈtɛstɪ] *adj* (*comp:* **-tier**; *super:* **-tiest**) enojadizo, picajoso, quisquilloso
**tetanic** [tɪˈtænɪk] *adj* tetánico
**tetanize** [ˈtɛtənaɪz] *va* tetanizar
**tetanus** [ˈtɛtənəs] *s* (path.) tétanos
**tetany** [ˈtɛtənɪ] *s* (path.) tetania
**tetartohedral** [tɪˌtɑrtoˈhidrəl] *adj* (cryst.) tetartoédrico
**tetartohedron** [tɪˌtɑrtoˈhidrən] *s* (cryst.) tetartoedro
**tetchy** [ˈtɛtʃɪ] *adj* (*comp:* **-ier**; *super:* **-iest**) pelilloso, enojadizo
**tête-à-tête** [ˈtetəˈtet] *s* conversación a solas entre dos; confidente (*mueble*); *adj* de persona a persona; *adv* a solas, cara a cara
**tête-bêche** [tɛtˈbɛʃ] *adj* (philately) capiculado
**tether** [ˈtɛðər] *s* traba, atadura; **at the end of one's tether** al límite de las posibilidades o paciencia de uno; *va* apersogar
**tetrachlorid** [ˌtɛtrəˈklorɪd] o **tetrachloride** [ˌtɛtrəˈkloraɪd] o [ˌtɛtrəˈklorɪd] *s* (chem.) tetracloruro
**tetrachord** [ˈtɛtrəkɔrd] *s* (mus.) tetracordio
**tetrachordal** [ˌtɛtrəˈkɔrdəl] *adj* (mus.) tetracordal
**tetracycline** [ˌtɛtrəˈsaɪklɪn] *s* (pharm.) tetraciclina
**tetradymite** [tɛˈtrædɪmaɪt] *s* (mineral.) tetradimita
**tetraethyl lead** [ˌtɛtrəˈɛθɪl lɛd] *s* (chem.) tetraetilo de plomo
**tetragon** [ˈtɛtrəgɑn] *s* (geom.) tetrágono
**tetragonal** [tɛˈtrægənəl] *adj* tetragonal
**tetrahedral** [ˌtɛtrəˈhidrəl] *adj* tetraédrico
**tetrahedron** [ˌtɛtrəˈhidrən] *s* (*pl:* **-drons** o **-dra** [drə]) (geom.) tetraedro
**tetralogy** [tɛˈtræləd͡ʒɪ] *s* (*pl:* **-gies**) (theat.) tetralogía
**tetrameter** [tɛˈtræmɪtər] *adj* & *s* tetrámetro
**tetrapetalous** [ˌtɛtrəˈpɛtələs] *adj* (bot.) tetrapétalo
**tetrarch** [ˈtɛtrɑrk] *s* tetrarca
**tetrarchy** [ˈtɛtrɑrkɪ] *s* (*pl:* **-chies**) tetrarquía
**tetrasyllabic** [ˌtɛtrəsɪˈlæbɪk] *adj* tetrasílabo o tetrasilábico
**tetrasyllable** [ˌtɛtrəˈsɪləbəl] *s* tetrasílabo
**tetravalent** [ˌtɛtrəˈvelənt] o [tɛˈtrævələnt] *adj* (chem.) tetravalente
**tetrode** [ˈtɛtrod] *s* (elec.) tetrodo
**tetroxide** [tɛˈtrɑksaɪd] o [tɛˈtrɑksɪd] *s* (chem.) tetróxido
**tetryl** [ˈtɛtrɪl] *s* tetrilo
**tetter** [ˈtɛtər] *s* (path.) empeine, herpes, culebrilla
**Teucer** [ˈtjusər] o [ˈtusər] *s* (myth.) Teucro
**Teucrian** [ˈtjukrɪən] o [ˈtukrɪən] *adj* & *s* teucro
**Teuton** [ˈtjutən] o [ˈtutən] *adj* & *s* teutón
**Teutonic** [tjuˈtɑnɪk] o [tuˈtɑnɪk] *adj* teutónico; *s* teutónico (*idioma*)
**Tex.** abr. de **Texas**
**Texan** [ˈtɛksən] *adj* & *s* tejano
**Texas** [ˈtɛksəs] *s* Tejas
**Texas fever** *s* (vet.) fiebre de Tejas
**text** [tɛkst] *s* texto; lema, tema
**textbook** [ˈtɛkstˌbʊk] *s* libro de texto
**textile** [ˈtɛkstɪl] o [ˈtɛkstaɪl] *adj* textil; *s* textil (*materia que puede tejerse*); tejido
**textual** [ˈtɛkstʃuəl] *adj* textual
**textual criticism** *s* crítica textual
**textualist** [ˈtɛkstʃuəlɪst] *s* textualista
**textually** [ˈtɛkstʃuəlɪ] *adv* textualmente
**textural** [ˈtɛkstʃərəl] *adj* textural
**textura** [ˈtɛkstʃər] *s* textura; (fig.) textura (*estructura*)
**Th.** abr. de **Thomas** y **Thursday**
**T.H.** abr. de **Territory of Hawaii**
**Thaddeus** [ˈθædɪəs] *s* Tadeo
**Thai** [ˈtɑ·i] o [taɪ] *adj* & *s* tailandés
**Thailand** [ˈtaɪlənd] *s* Tailandia
**thalamic** [θəˈlæmɪk] *adj* talámico
**thalamus** [ˈθæləməs] *s* (*pl:* **-mi** [maɪ]) (anat.) tálamo
**thalassic** [θəˈlæsɪk] *adj* talásico
**Thales** [ˈθeliz] *s* Tales
**Thalia** [θəˈlaɪə] *s* (myth.) Talía
**thallium** [ˈθælɪəm] *s* (chem.) talio
**thallophyte** [ˈθæləfaɪt] *s* (bot.) talófita
**thallophytic** [ˌθæləˈfɪtɪk] *adj* talofítico
**thallus** [ˈθæləs] *s* (*pl:* **-li** [laɪ] o **-luses**) (bot.) talo
**thalweg** [ˈtɑlˌvex] *s* vaguada
**Thames** [tɛmz] *s* Támesis
**than** [ðæn] *conj* que, p.ej., **he is richer than I** es más rico que yo; **than** + *numeral* de + *numeral*, p.ej., **more than twenty** más de veinte; **than** + *verb* de lo que + *verb*, p.ej., **he writes better than he speaks** escribe mejor de lo que habla; **than** + *verb with direct object understood* del (de la, de los, de las) que, p.ej., **they sent us more coffee than we ordered** nos enviaron más café del que pedimos; *prep* **than which** o **than whom** comparado con el cual
**thane** [θen] *s* (Brit. hist.) caballero, gentilhombre; (Scottish hist.) barón, señor
**thank** [θæŋk] *s* (archaic) gracia; **thanks** *spl* gracias; agradecimiento, gratitud; **thanks to** gracias a (*merced a, por intervención de*); **thanks** *interj* ¡gracias!; *va* agradecer, dar las gracias a; **to have oneself to thank** tener la culpa, ser responsable; **to thank someone for something** agradecerle a uno una cosa; **to thank someone to** + *inf* agradecerle a uno (que) + *subj*, p.ej., **we will thank you to fill out the enclosed card** le agradeceremos llene la adjunta tarjeta
**thankful** [ˈθæŋkfəl] *adj* agradecido
**thankfully** [ˈθæŋkfəlɪ] *adv* con agradecimiento
**thankfulness** [ˈθæŋkfəlnɪs] *s* agradecimiento, gratitud
**thankless** [ˈθæŋklɪs] *adj* ingrato (*desagradecido; que no corresponde al trabajo que cuesta*)
**thanksgiving** [θæŋksˈgɪvɪŋ] *s* acción de gracias; (*cap.*) *s* (U.S.A.) día de acción de gracias

**Thanksgiving Day** *s* (U.S.A.) día de acción de gracias, día de gracias
**that** [ðæt] *adj dem* (*pl:* **those**) ese; aquel; *pron dem* (*pl:* **those**) ése; aquél; eso; aquello; **at that** (coll.) sin más; (coll.) considerándolo todo; **in that** porque; **upon that** sobre eso; luego; **that's that** (coll.) así es; *pron rel* que, quien, el cual, el que; en que, cuando; *adv* tan; **that far** tan lejos; hasta allí; **that much** tanto; *conj* que; para que; **so that** de modo que; para que
**thatch** [θætʃ] *s* paja, barda, bálago; techo de paja o bálago; (coll.) pelo (*de la cabeza*); *va* cubrir de paja, bardar, poner un techo de paja a
**thatched roof** *s* techo de paja o bálago
**thaumaturge** [ˈθɔmətʌrdʒ] *s* taumaturgo
**thaumaturgic** [ˌθɔməˈtʌrdʒɪk] o **thaumaturgical** [ˌθɔməˈtʌrdʒɪkəl] *adj* taumatúrgico
**thaumaturgy** [ˈθɔməˌtʌrdʒɪ] *s* taumaturgia
**thaw** [θɔ] *s* deshielo, derretimiento; (fig.) ablandamiento, enternecimiento; *va* deshelar, derretir; *vn* deshelarse, derretirse; (fig.) ablandarse, enternecerse
**the** [ðə], [ðɪ] o [ði] *art def* el; el más a propósito; [ðə] o [ðɪ] *adv* cuanto, p.ej., **the more the merrier** cuanto más mejor; **the more . . . the more** cuanto más . . . tanto más
**theaceous** [θiˈeʃəs] *adj* (bot.) teáceo
**theanthropism** [θiˈænθrəpɪzəm] *s* teantropía
**theater** [ˈθiətər] *s* teatro; (fig.) teatro (*p.ej., de una guerra*)
**theater-in-the-round** [ˈθiətərɪnðəˈraʊnd] *s* teatro circular
**theater of war** *s* (mil.) teatro de la guerra
**theatre** [ˈθiətər] *s* var. de **theater**
**theatric** [θɪˈætrɪk] *adj* teatral
**theatrical** [θɪˈætrɪkəl] *adj* teatral; **theatricals** *spl* funciones teatrales; asuntos teatrales; modales artificiales o exagerados
**theatricalism** [θɪˈætrɪkəlɪzəm] *s* teoría y método dramático; calidad teatral, estilo teatral
**theatricality** [θɪˌætrɪˈkælɪtɪ] *s* teatralidad
**thebaine** [ˈθibəin], [θɪˈbein] o [θɪˈbeɪn] *s* (chem.) tebaína
**Theban** [ˈθibən] *adj & s* tebano o tebeo
**Thebes** [θibz] *s* Tebas (*de Egipto; de Grecia*)
**theca** [ˈθikə] *s* (*pl:* **-cae** [si]) (anat. & bot.) teca
**thé dansant** [tedɑ̃ˈsɑ̃] *s* (*pl:* **thés dansants** [tedɑ̃ˈsɑ̃]) té baile, té bailable
**thee** [ði] *pron pers* (archaic, poet. & Bib.) te; ti; (en el lenguaje familiar entre los cuáqueros) tú; **with thee** contigo
**theelin** [θilɪn] *s* (biochem.) teelina
**theft** [θɛft] *s* hurto, robo
**thegn** [θen] *s* var. de **thane**
**thein** [ˈθiɪn] o **theine** [ˈθiin] o [ˈθiɪn] *s* (chem.) teína
**their** [ðɛr] *adj poss* su; el (o su) . . . de ellos
**theirs** [ðɛrz] *pron poss* el suyo, el de ellos
**theism** [ˈθiɪzəm] *s* teísmo
**theist** [ˈθiɪst] *s* teísta
**theistic** [θiˈɪstɪk] *adj* teísta
**them** [ðɛm] *pron pers* los; ellos; **to them** les; a ellos
**thematic** [θiˈmætɪk] *adj* temático
**theme** [θim] *s* tema; (mus.) tema
**theme song** *s* (mus.) tema central; (rad.) sintonía
**Themistocles** [θɪˈmɪstəkliz] *s* Temístocles
**themselves** [ðɛmˈsɛlvz] *pron pers* ellos mismos; se; sí, sí mismos; **with themselves** consigo
**then** [ðɛn] *s* aquel tiempo; *adj* de entonces; *adv* entonces (*en aquel tiempo*); después, luego, en seguida; además, también; **but then** pero al mismo tiempo, pero por otro lado; **by then** para entonces; **from then on** desde entonces, de allí en adelante; **then and there** ahí mismo, al momento
**thenar** [ˈθinɑr] *adj & s* (anat.) tenar
**thence** [ðɛns] *adv* desde allí; desde entonces; por eso, por esa razón
**thenceforth** [ˌðɛnsˈforθ] o **thenceforward** [ˌðɛnsˈfɔrwərd] *adv* de allí en adelante; desde entonces
**theobromine** [ˌθiəˈbromin] o [ˌθiəˈbromɪn] *s* (chem.) teobromina
**theocracy** [θiˈɑkrəsɪ] *s* (*pl:* **-cies**) teocracia
**theocrat** [ˈθiəkræt] *s* teócrata
**theocratic** [ˌθiəˈkrætɪk] *adj* teocrático
**Theocritus** [θiˈɑkrɪtəs] *s* Teócrito
**theodicy** [θiˈɑdɪsɪ] *s* (*pl:* **-cies**) teodicea
**theodolite** [θiˈɑdəlaɪt] *s* teodolito
**Theodore** [ˈθiədor] *s* Teodoro
**Theodoric** [θiˈɑdərɪk] *s* Teodorico
**Theodosius** [ˌθiəˈdoʃɪəs] *s* Teodosio
**theogonic** [ˌθiəˈgɑnɪk] *adj* teogónico
**theogony** [θiˈɑgənɪ] *s* (*pl:* **-nies**) teogonía
**theologian** [ˌθiəˈlodʒɪən] *s* teólogo
**theological** [ˌθiəˈlɑdʒɪkəl] *adj* teológico
**theologically** [ˌθiəˈlɑdʒɪkəlɪ] *adv* teológicamente
**theologize** [θiˈɑlədʒaɪz] *va* hacer teológico; discurrir teológicamente sobre; *vn* teologizar
**theologue** [ˈθiəlɔg] o [ˈθiəlɑg] *s* (coll.) teólogo (*estudiante*)
**theology** [θiˈɑlədʒɪ] *s* (*pl:* **-gies**) teología
**Theophilus** [θiˈɑfɪləs] *s* Teófilo
**Theophrastus** [ˌθiəˈfræstəs] *s* Teofrasto
**theorem** [ˈθiərəm] *s* teorema
**theoretic** [ˌθiəˈrɛtɪk] o **theoretical** [ˌθiəˈrɛtɪkəl] *adj* teórico
**theoretically** [ˌθiəˈrɛtɪkəlɪ] *adv* teóricamente
**theoretician** [ˌθiərəˈtɪʃən] *s* teórico
**theorist** [ˈθiərɪst] *s* teorizante; teórico
**theorize** [ˈθiəraɪz] *vn* teorizar
**theory** [ˈθiərɪ] *s* (*pl:* **-ries**) teoría
**theory of knowledge** *s* (philos.) teoría del conocimiento
**theosophic** [ˌθiəˈsɑfɪk] o **theosophical** [ˌθiəˈsɑfɪkəl] *adj* teosófico
**theosophist** [θiˈɑsəfɪst] *s* teósofo
**theosophy** [θiˈɑsəfɪ] *s* teosofía
**therapeutic** [ˌθɛrəˈpjutɪk] *adj* terapéutico; **therapeutics** *ssg* terapéutica
**therapeutical** [ˌθɛrəˈpjutɪkəl] *adj* terapéutico
**therapeutically** [ˌθɛrəˈpjutɪkəlɪ] *adv* terapéuticamente
**therapeutist** [ˌθɛrəˈpjutɪst] *s* terapeuta
**therapist** [ˈθɛrəpɪst] *s* terapeuta
**therapy** [ˈθɛrəpɪ] *s* (*pl:* **-pies**) terapia
**there** [ðɛr] *adv* ahí, allí, allá; **all there** (coll.) despierto, vigilante, vivo; **to not be all there** (coll.) no estar en sus cabales; **there is** o **there are** hay; aquí tiene Vd.; usado enfáticamente con un verbo, se omite en la traducción al español, p.ej., **there appeared a man dressed in black** apareció un hombre vestido de negro; *interj* ¡ eso es!, ¡ mira!, ¡ vaya!
**thereabout** [ˈðɛrəˌbaʊt] o **thereabouts** [ˈðɛrəˌbaʊts] *adv* por ahí, por allí; cerca, aproximadamente
**thereafter** [ðɛrˈæftər] o [ðɛrˈɑftər] *adv* después de eso, de allí en adelante; conforme, en conformidad
**thereat** [ðɛrˈæt] *adv* entonces, en eso; en aquel lugar; por eso, por esa razón
**thereby** [ðɛrˈbaɪ] o [ˈðɛrbaɪ] *adv* con eso; así, de tal modo; cerca de ahí, por allí cerca
**therefor** [ðɛrˈfɔr] *adv* para esto, para eso
**therefore** [ˈðɛrfor] *adv* por lo tanto, por consiguiente
**therefrom** [ðɛrˈfrɑm] o [ðɛrˈfrʌm] *adv* de eso, de ahí, de allí
**therein** [ðɛrˈɪn] *adv* en esto, en eso; en ese respecto
**thereinto** [ðɛrˈɪntu] o [ˌðɛrɪnˈtu] *adv* dentro de esto, dentro de eso
**thereof** [ðɛrˈɑv] *adv* de esto, de eso
**thereon** [ðɛrˈɑn] o [ðɛrˈɔn] *adv* en eso, sobre eso, encima de eso; en seguida
**there's** [ðɛrz] contracción de **there is** y **there has**
**Theresa** [təˈrisə] o [təˈrɛsə] *s* Teresa
**thereto** [ðɛrˈtu] *adv* a eso; además, además de eso
**theretofore** [ˌðɛrtuˈfor] *adv* antes de eso, hasta entonces
**thereunder** [ðɛrˈʌndər] *adv* bajo eso, debajo de eso; debajo, por debajo
**thereupon** [ˌðɛrəˈpɑn] o [ˌðɛrəˈpɔn] *adv* sobre eso, encima de eso; por eso, por consiguiente; al momento, en seguida
**therewith** [ðɛrˈwɪð] o [ðɛrˈwɪθ] *adv* con esto, con eso; luego, en seguida
**therewithal** [ˌðɛrwɪðˈɔl] *adv* con esto, con eso; a más, además
**therianthropic** [ˌθɪrɪænˈθrɑpɪk] *adj* teriantrópico

**theriomorphic** [ˌθɪrɪəˈmɔrfɪk] o **theriomorphous** [ˌθɪrɪəˈmɔrfəs] *adj* teriomórfico
**therm** [θʌrm] *s* (phys.) termia o termio
**thermae** [ˈθʌrmi] *spl* termas
**thermal** [ˈθʌrməl] *adj* termal
**thermal barrier** *s* barrera térmica
**thermalize** [ˈθʌrməlaɪz] o **thermatize** [ˈθʌrmətaɪz] *va* (phys.) termatizar
**thermesthesia** [ˌθʌrmɪsˈθiʒə] o [ˌθʌrmɪsˈθiʒɪə] *s* (physiol.) termoestesia
**thermic** [ˈθʌrmɪk] *adj* térmico
**thermion** [ˈθʌrmˌaɪən] o [ˈθʌrmɪən] *s* (phys.) termión
**thermionic** [ˌθʌrmaɪˈɑnɪk] o [ˌθʌrmɪˈɑnɪk] *adj* termiónico; **thermionics** *ssg* termiónica
**thermistor** [θərˈmɪstər] *s* (elec.) termistor
**thermit** [ˈθʌrmɪt] o **thermite** [ˈθʌrmaɪt] *s* (trademark) termita
**thermobarograph** [ˌθʌrmoˈbærəgræf] o [ˌθʌrmoˈbærəgrɑf] *s* termobarógrafo
**thermobarometer** [ˌθʌrmobəˈrɑmɪtər] *s* termobarómetro
**thermocautery** [ˌθʌrmoˈkɔtərɪ] *s* termocauterio
**thermochemical** [ˌθʌrmoˈkɛmɪkəl] *adj* termoquímico
**thermochemistry** [ˌθʌrmoˈkɛmɪstrɪ] *s* termoquímica
**thermocouple** [ˈθʌrmoˌkʌpəl] *s* (elec.) termopar, par térmico
**thermodynamic** [ˌθʌrmodaɪˈnæmɪk] o [ˌθʌrmodɪˈnæmɪk] *adj* termodinámico; **thermodynamics** *ssg* termodinámica
**thermoelectric** [ˌθʌrmo·ɪˈlɛktrɪk] o **thermoelectrical** [ˌθʌrmo·ɪˈlɛktrɪkəl] *adj* termoeléctrico
**thermoelectric couple** *s* (elec.) par termoeléctrico
**thermoelectricity** [ˌθʌrmo·ɪˌlɛkˈtrɪsɪtɪ] *s* termoelectricidad
**thermoelectromotive** [ˌθʌrmo·ɪˌlɛktroˈmotɪv] *adj* termoelectromotor
**thermoelement** [ˌθʌrmoˈɛlɪmənt] *s* (elec.) termoelemento
**thermofission** [ˌθʌrmoˈfɪʃən] *s* (phys.) termofisión
**thermofusion** [ˌθʌrmoˈfjuʒən] *s* (phys.) termofusión
**thermogenesis** [ˌθʌrmoˈdʒɛnɪsɪs] *s* (physiol.) termogénesis
**thermogenetic** [ˌθʌrmodʒɪˈnɛtɪk] *adj* termógeno
**thermograph** [ˈθʌrməgræf] o [ˈθʌrməgrɑf] *s* termógrafo
**thermolabile** [ˌθʌrmoˈlebɪl] *adj* (biochem.) termolábil
**thermology** [θərˈmɑlədʒɪ] *s* termología
**thermolysis** [θərˈmɑlɪsɪs] *s* (chem. & physiol.) termólisis
**thermometer** [θərˈmɑmɪtər] *s* termómetro
**thermometric** [ˌθʌrmoˈmɛtrɪk] *adj* termométrico
**thermometry** [θərˈmɑmɪtrɪ] *s* termometría
**thermomotive** [ˌθʌrmoˈmotɪv] *adj* termomotor
**thermonuclear** [ˌθʌrmoˈnjuklɪər] o [ˌθʌrmoˈnuklɪər] *adj* termonuclear
**thermopile** [ˈθʌrməpaɪl] *s* (phys.) termopila
**thermoplastic** [ˌθʌrməˈplæstɪk] *adj* termoplástico
**Thermopylae** [θərˈmɑpɪli] *s* las Termópilas
**thermos bottle** [ˈθʌrməs] *s* termos, botella termos
**thermoscope** [ˈθʌrməskop] *s* termoscopio
**thermosiphon** [ˌθʌrmoˈsaɪfən] *s* termosifón
**thermostat** [ˈθʌrməstæt] *s* termóstato
**thermostatic** [ˌθʌrməˈstætɪk] *adj* termostático
**thermostatically** [ˌθʌrməˈstætɪkəlɪ] *adv* mediante un termóstato
**thermotropism** [θərˈmɑtrəpɪzəm] *s* (biol.) termotropismo
**Thersites** [θərˈsaɪtiz] *s* (myth.) Tersites
**thesaurus** [θɪˈsɔrəs] *s* (*pl:* **-ri** [raɪ]) tesoro; tesauro o tesoro (*catálogo, diccionario, etc.*)
**these** [ðiz] *pl de* **this**
**Theseus** [ˈθisus] o [ˈθisɪəs] *s* (myth.) Teseo
**thesis** [ˈθisɪs] *s* (*pl:* **-ses** [siz]) tesis; (mus.) tesis
**thesis play** *s* pieza de tesis
**Thespian** [ˈθɛspɪən] *adj* de Tespis; dramático, trágico; *s* actor dramático o trágico
**Thespis** [ˈθɛspɪs] *s* Tespis
**Thess.** abr. de **Thessalonians**
**Thessalian** [θɛˈselɪən] *adj & s* tesaliano
**Thessalonian** [ˌθɛsəˈlonɪən] *adj & s* tesalonicense; **Thessalonians** *spl* (Bib.) Epístola a los Tesalonicenses (*cada una de dos*)
**Thessalonica** [ˌθɛsəloˈnaɪkə] o [ˌθɛsəˈlɑnɪkə] *s* (hist.) Tesalónica
**Thessaly** [ˈθɛsəlɪ] *s* la Tesalia
**Thetis** [ˈθitɪs] *s* (myth.) Tetis
**theurgic** [θiˈʌrdʒɪk] o **theurgical** [θiˈʌrdʒɪkəl] *adj* teúrgico
**theurgist** [ˈθiʌrdʒɪst] *s* teurgo
**theurgy** [ˈθiʌrdʒɪ] *s* (*pl:* **-gies**) teurgia
**thews** [θuz] o [θjuz] *spl* músculos; fuerza muscular
**they** [ðe] *pron pers* ellos
**they'd** [ðed] contracción de **they had** y **they would**
**they'll** [ðel] contracción de **they will** y **they shall**
**they're** [ðɛr] contracción de **they are**
**they've** [ðev] contracción de **they have**
**thiamine** [ˈθaɪəmin] o [ˈθaɪəmɪn] *s* (biochem.) tiamina
**thiazole** [ˈθaɪəzol] *s* (chem.) tiazol
**Thibetan** [tɪˈbɛtən] *adj & s* var. de **Tibetan**
**thick** [θɪk] *adj* espeso, grueso, denso; de espesor, p.ej., **three inches thick** de tres pulgadas de espesor; abundante; cubierto, lleno; brumoso, nebuloso; torpe, estúpido; basto, burdo, grosero; (coll.) íntimo; (coll.) insoportable, insolente; **to be thick with** (coll.) tener mucha intimidad con; *adv* espesamente, densamente; abundantemente; **to lay it on thick** (coll.) exagerar en los reproches o las alabanzas; **to talk thick** tener la lengua gorda; *s* espesor, grueso; **the thick of** lo más denso de (*p.ej., la multitud*); lo más reñido de (*p.ej., el combate*); **through thick and thin** a toda prueba, por las buenas y las malas
**thicken** [ˈθɪkən] *va* espesar; *vn* espesarse; complicarse (*el enredo*)
**thickener** [ˈθɪkənər] *s* espesador
**thickening** [ˈθɪkənɪŋ] *adj* espesativo; *s* espesamiento; espesante, espesador
**thicket** [ˈθɪkɪt] *s* espesura, soto, matorral
**thickhead** [ˈθɪkˌhɛd] *s* (coll.) cabeza dura (*persona*)
**thick-headed** [ˈθɪkˈhɛdɪd] *adj* (coll.) torpe, estúpido
**thick-knee** [ˈθɪkˌni] *s* (orn.) alcaraván
**thickly** [ˈθɪklɪ] *adv* espesamente, densamente; abundantemente; repetidamente; muy, sumamente
**thickness** [ˈθɪknɪs] *s* espesura (*calidad*); espesor (*dimensión; densidad de un flúido*); lo más denso; lo más reñido; capa, estrato
**thick-set** [ˈθɪkˌsɛt] *adj* denso, muy poblado; grueso, rechoncho; *s* espesura, soto, matorral; seto espeso
**thick-skinned** [ˈθɪkˈskɪnd] *adj* de pellejo espeso; duro, insensible
**thick-witted** [ˈθɪkˈwɪtɪd] *adj* torpe, estúpido, imbécil
**thief** [θif] *s* (*pl:* **thieves**) ladrón
**thieve** [θiv] *vn* hurtar, robar
**thievery** [ˈθivərɪ] *s* (*pl:* **-ies**) hurto, robo, latrocinio
**thieves' Latin** *s* caló o jerga de los ladrones
**thievish** [ˈθivɪʃ] *adj* engatado, ratero, rapaz
**thigh** [θaɪ] *s* (anat.) muslo
**thighbone** [ˈθaɪˌbon] *s* (anat.) fémur
**thigmotaxis** [ˌθɪgməˈtæksɪs] *s* (biol.) tigmotaxia
**thigmotropism** [θɪgˈmɑtrəpɪzəm] *s* (biol.) tigmotropismo
**thill** [θɪl] *s* limonera o lanza
**thimble** [ˈθɪmbəl] *s* dedal; (mach.) manguito; (naut.) guardacabo
**thimbleberry** [ˈθɪmbəlˌbɛrɪ] *s* (*pl:* **-ries**) (bot.) frambueso norteamericano (*Rubus occidentalis, R. parviflorus y R. argutus*); frambuesa (*fruto*)
**thimbleful** [ˈθɪmbəlfʊl] *s* dedal (*cantidad que cabe en un dedal*)
**thimblerig** [ˈθɪmbəlˌrɪg] *s* fullería hecha jugando con tres tacitas y un guisante; (*pret &*

*pp:* **-rigged;** *ger:* **-rigging**) *va & vn* engañar con la fullería de tres tacitas y un guisante; engañar
**thin** [θɪn] *adj* (*comp:* **thinner;** *super:* **thinnest**) delgado, tenue, flaco; fino (*paño, papel, suela de zapato, etc.*); ralo (*pelo*); aguado (*caldo*); transparente; claro, ligero, escaso; *adv* delgadamente; ligeramente; poco; (*pret & pp:* **thinned;** *ger:* **thinning**) *va* adelgazar, enflaquecer; enrarecer; aclarar; aguar; desleír (*los colores*); *vn* adelgazarse; enflaquecerse; enrarecerse
**thine** [ðaɪn] *adj poss* (archaic & poet.) tu; *pron poss* (archaic & poet.) tuyo; el tuyo
**thing** [θɪŋ] *s* cosa; **of all things!** ¡qué sorpresa!; **the thing** lo que está de moda; lo debido, lo importante; **to be the real thing** estar muy de veras; **to know a thing or two** (coll.) saber cuántas son cinco; (coll.) tener experiencia; **to make a good thing of** (coll.) sacar provecho de; **to not know the first thing about** no saber nada de; **to see things** ver visiones, padecer alucinaciones; **to tell someone a thing or two** (coll.) decirle a uno dos gracias
**thing-in-itself** [ˌθɪŋɪnɪtˈsɛlf] *s* (philos.) cosa en sí
**thingumbob** [ˈθɪŋəmbɑb] *s* (coll.) cosa, negocillo (*cosa cuyo nombre se ha olvidado o no se quiere pronunciar*)
**think** [θɪŋk] (*pret & pp:* **thought**) *va* pensar; acordarse de; **to think it over** pensarlo; **to think nothing of** tener en poco; creer fácil; no dar importancia a; **to think of** pensar de (*tener cierta opinión de*); **to think out** imaginar, idear, descubrir, resolver; **to think up** imaginar; inventar (*p.ej., una excusa*); *vn* pensar; **to think aloud** pensar en alta voz, expresar lo que uno piensa; **to think ill of** tener mala opinión de; **to think not** creer que no; **to think of** pensar en (*tener el pensamiento concentrado en*); pensar (*un número, un naipe, etc.*); **to think out loud** pensar en alta voz, expresar lo que uno piensa; **to think over** pensar detenidamente; **to think so** creer que sí; **to think twice** pensar dos veces; **to think well of** tener buena opinión de; **you think so!** (iron.) ¡que te crees tú eso!
**thinkable** [ˈθɪŋkəbəl] *adj* pensable, concebible
**thinker** [ˈθɪŋkər] *s* pensador
**thinking** [ˈθɪŋkɪŋ] *adj* pensante; pensador (*meditabundo*); *s* pensamiento; parecer
**thinner** [ˈθɪnər] *s* diluente
**thinnish** [ˈθɪnɪʃ] *adj* flacucho; algo ralo
**thin-skinned** [ˈθɪnˈskɪnd] *adj* de pellejo delgado; sensible, susceptible
**thiocyanate** [ˌθaɪoˈsaɪənet] *s* (chem.) tiocianato
**thiocyanic** [ˌθaɪosaɪˈænɪk] *adj* tiociánico
**thiocyanic acid** *s* (chem.) ácido tiociánico
**thionic** [θaɪˈɑnɪk] *adj* tiónico
**thionic acid** *s* (chem.) ácido tiónico
**thiophene** [ˈθaɪəfin] *s* (chem.) tiofeno
**thiosinamine** [ˌθaɪəsɪˈnæmɪn] *s* (chem.) tiosinamina
**thiosulfate** [ˌθaɪoˈsʌlfet] *s* (chem.) tiosulfato
**thiosulfuric** [ˌθaɪosʌlˈfjʊrɪk] *adj* tiosulfúrico
**thiosulfuric acid** *s* (chem.) ácido tiosulfúrico
**thiourea** [ˌθaɪojʊˈriə] o [ˌθaɪoˈjʊrɪə] *s* (chem.) tiourea
**third** [θʌrd] *adj* tercero; *s* tercero; tercio (*una de tres partes iguales*); tres (*en las fechas*); (mus.) tercera; (aut.) tercera (velocidad)
**third base** *s* (baseball) tercera base *f* (*puesto*); (baseball) tercera base *m* (*jugador*)
**third baseman** *s* (baseball) tercera base *m* (*jugador*)
**third-class** [ˈθʌrdˌklæs] o [ˈθʌrdˌklɑs] *adj* de tercera clase
**third degree** *s* (coll.) interrogatorio de un preso, hecho de una manera brutal, interrogatorio bajo tortura
**thirdly** [ˈθʌrdlɪ] *adv* en tercer lugar
**third person** *s* (gram.) tercera persona
**third rail** *s* (rail.) tercer carril
**third-rate** [ˈθʌrdˌret] *adj* de tercer orden; de mala calidad, de última clase
**thirst** [θʌrst] *s* sed; (fig.) sed; *vn* tener sed; **to thirst for** tener sed de; (fig.) tener sed de
**thirsty** [ˈθʌrstɪ] *adj* (*comp:* **-ier;** *super:* **-iest**) sediento; **to be thirsty** tener sed; **to be thirsty for** tener sed de
**thirteen** [ˈθʌrˈtin] *adj & s* trece
**thirteenth** [ˈθʌrˈtinθ] *adj* décimotercero o décimotercio; trezavo; *s* decimotercero o décimotercio; trezavo; trece (*en las fechas*)
**thirtieth** [ˈθʌrtɪɪθ] *adj* trigésimo; treintavo; *s* trigésimo; treintavo; treinta (*en las fechas*)
**thirty** [ˈθʌrtɪ] *adj* treinta; *s* (*pl:* **-ties**) treinta; **thirty all** (tennis) treinta iguales
**thirty-second note** [ˈθʌrtɪˈsɛkənd] *s* (mus.) fusa
**thirty-twomo** [ˌθʌrtɪˈtuˌmo] *adj* en treintaidosavo; *s* libro en treintaidosavo
**Thirty Years' War** *s* guerra de los Treinta Años
**this** [ðɪs] *adj dem* (*pl:* **these**) este; *pron dem* (*pl:* **these**) éste; esto; *adv* tan
**Thisbe** [ˈθɪzbɪ] *s* (myth.) Tisbe
**thistle** [ˈθɪsəl] *s* (bot.) cardo
**thistledown** [ˈθɪsəlˌdaʊn] *s* borrilla de cardo
**thistly** [ˈθɪslɪ] *adj* lleno de cardos; espinoso
**thither** [ˈθɪðər] o [ˈðɪðər] *adj* más lejano, al otro lado; *adv* allá, hacia allá, para allá
**thitherward** [ˈθɪðərwərd] o [ˈðɪðərwərd] *adv* allá, hacia allá, para allá
**tho** o **tho'** [ðo] *adv & conj* var. de **though**
**thole** [θol] o **tholepin** [ˈθolˌpɪn] *s* (naut.) escálamo o tolete
**Thomas** [ˈtɑməs] *s* Tomás
**Thomism** [ˈtomɪzəm] o [ˈθomɪzəm] *s* tomismo
**Thomist** [ˈtomɪst] o [ˈθomɪst] *adj & s* tomista
**thong** [θɔŋ] o [θɑŋ] *s* correa, tira de cuero
**thoracic** [θoˈræsɪk] *adj* torácico
**thoracic duct** *s* (anat.) conducto torácico
**thorax** [ˈθoræks] *s* (*pl:* **-raxes** o **-races** [rəsiz]) (anat. & zool.) tórax
**thoric** [ˈθɑrɪk] o [ˈθorɪk] *adj* (chem.) tórico
**thorite** [ˈθoraɪt] *s* (mineral.) torita
**thorium** [ˈθorɪəm] *s* (chem.) torio
**thorn** [θɔrn] *s* espina; (bot.) espino u oxcicanto; (bot.) endrino; (fig.) espina (*ansia, tormento*); **thorn in the flesh** o **side** espina en el dedo, motivo de continuo enojo
**thorn apple** *s* (bot.) manzana espinosa, higuera loca
**thornback** [ˈθɔrnˌbæk] *s* (ichth.) raya espinosa; (zool.) centolla
**thorny** [ˈθɔrnɪ] *adj* (*comp:* **-ier;** *super:* **-iest**) espinoso; (fig.) espinoso
**thoro** [ˈθʌro] *adj* var. de **thorough**
**thoron** [ˈθorɑn] *s* (chem.) torón
**thorough** [ˈθʌro] *adj* cabal, completo; cuidadoso, concienzudo
**thoroughbred** [ˈθʌroˌbrɛd] *adj* de pura raza o sangre; bien nacido, bien educado; *s* pura sangre *m*; persona bien nacida, persona bien educada
**thoroughfare** [ˈθʌroˌfɛr] *s* carretera, vía pública; tránsito, pasaje; **no thoroughfare** se prohibe el paso
**thoroughgoing** [ˈθʌroˌgo·ɪŋ] *adj* cabal, completo, esmerado, perfecto
**thoroughly** [ˈθʌrolɪ] *adv* a fondo
**thoroughness** [ˈθʌronɪs] *s* entereza, perfección, minuciosidad
**thoroughwort** [ˈθʌroˌwʌrt] *s* (bot.) eupatorio
**thorp** [θɔrp] *s* (archaic) aldea
**those** [ðoz] *pl de* **that**
**thou** [ðaʊ] *pron pers* (archaic, poet. & Bib.) tú; *va & vn* (archaic) tutear
**though** [ðo] *adv* sin embargo; *conj* aun cuando, aunque, bien que, si bien; **as though** como si
**thought** [θɔt] *s* pensamiento; consideración; (coll.) pizca, muy poco; *pret & pp de* **think**
**thought control** *s* control del pensamiento
**thoughtful** [ˈθɔtfəl] *adj* pensativo; atento, considerado
**thoughtfulness** [ˈθɔtfəlnɪs] *s* atención, consideración, solicitud
**thoughtless** [ˈθɔtlɪs] *adj* irreflexivo; descuidado; inconsiderado
**thought transference** *s* transmisión del pensamiento
**thousand** [ˈθaʊzənd] *adj & s* mil; **a thousand** u **one thousand** mil
**Thousand and One Nights, The** las Mil y una noches
**thousandfold** [ˈθaʊzəndˌfold] *adj* multiplicado por mil; *adv* mil veces más

**Thousand Islands, the** las Mil Islas
**thousandth** [ˈθaʊzəndθ] *adj & s* milésimo
**Thrace** [θres] *s* la Tracia
**Thracian** [ˈθreʃən] *adj & s* traciano o tracio
**thrall** [θrɔl] *s* esclavo; esclavitud, servidumbre
**thralldom** o **thraldom** [ˈθrɔldəm] *s* esclavitud, servidumbre
**thrash** [θræʃ] *va* (agr.) trillar; azotar, zurrar; **to thrash out** decidir después de una discusión cabal; **to thrash over** discutir repetidas veces; *vn* (agr.) trillar; dar vueltas, sacudirse, menearse
**thrasher** [ˈθræʃər] *s* (agr.) trillador; (agr.) trilladora mecánica; (orn.) cuicacoche; (ichth.) raposa de mar, zorra de mar
**thread** [θrɛd] *s* hilo; (mach.) filete o rosca; (zool.) hilo (*de la araña*); (fig.) hilo (*de un discurso, de la vida, etc.*); **to hang by a thread** estar colgado de un hilo; **to lose the thread of** perder el hilo de; *va* enhebrar; ensartar (*p.ej., cuentas*); (mach.) aterrajar, filetear; **to thread one's way through** serpentear por, abrirse camino por; *vn* (cook.) formar filamentos; serpentear, abrirse camino
**threadbare** [ˈθrɛd,bɛr] *adj* raído; andrajoso; gastado, viejo
**threadworm** [ˈθrɛd,wʌrm] *s* (zool.) lombriz de los niños (*Oxyuris vermicularis*); (zool.) filaria
**thready** [ˈθrɛdɪ] *adj* filiforme; fibroso, correoso, viscoso; débil, tenue (*voz*); (med.) débil (*pulso*)
**threat** [θrɛt] *s* amenaza
**threaten** [ˈθrɛtən] *va & vn* amenazar; **to threaten to** + *inf* amenazar + *inf* o amenazar con + *inf*
**threatening** [ˈθrɛtənɪŋ] *adj* amenazador, amenazante
**three** [θri] *adj* tres; *s* tres; **three o'clock** las tres
**three-banded armadillo** [ˈθri,bændɪd] *s* (zool.) armadillo de tres fajas, apar
**three-color process** [ˈθri,kʌlər] *s* tricromía, procedimiento tricromo
**three-cornered** [ˈθriˈkɔrnərd] *adj* triangular; ternario; tricornio, de tres picos (*sombrero*)
**three-D** [ˈθriˈdi] *adj* (coll.) tridimensional; *s* (coll.) película cinematográfica tridimensional, cinestéreo, estereocinema
**three-decker** [ˈθriˈdɛkər] *s* (naut.) navío de tres puentes; cosa que tiene tres capas, partes, pisos, etc.; (coll.) novela de tres tomos, novela muy larga
**three-dimensional** [ˈθridɪˈmɛnʃənəl] *adj* tridimensional
**three-element vacuum tube** [ˈθri,ɛlɪmənt] *s* (rad.) tubo al vacío de tres electrodos
**threefold** [ˈθri,fold] *adj & s* triple; *adv* tres veces más
**three-four time** [ˈθriˈfor] *s* (mus.) compás de tres por cuatro
**three hundred** *adj & s* trescientos
**three-mile limit** [ˈθri,maɪl] *s* (int. law) límite de tres millas
**threepence** [ˈθrɛpəns] o [ˈθrɪpəns] *s* suma de tres peniques; moneda de tres peniques
**threepenny** [ˈθrɛpənɪ], [ˈθrɪpənɪ] o [ˈθri,pɛnɪ] *adj* de tres peniques; barato, vil, ruin
**three-phase** [ˈθri,fez] *adj* (elec.) trifásico
**three-ply** [ˈθri,plaɪ] *adj* de tres capas
**three-point landing** [ˈθri,pɔɪnt] *s* (aer.) aterrizaje sobre tres puntos
**three R's** [ɑrz] *spl* lectura, escritura y aritmética
**threescore** [ˈθriˈskor] *adj* tres veintenas de, sesenta
**threesome** [ˈθrisəm] *s* grupo de tres personas; grupo de tres jugadores; juego de tres jugadores
**three-square file** [ˈθriˈskwɛr] *s* lima triangular
**three-way cock** [ˈθri,we] *s* grifo de tres vías
**three-way switch** *s* (elec.) conmutador de tres terminales
**three-wire** [ˈθri,waɪr] *adj* (elec.) trifilar
**Three Wise Men** *spl* Reyes Magos
**threnody** [ˈθrɛnədɪ] *s* (*pl:* **-dies**) treno (*canto fúnebre*)
**threonine** [ˈθriənin] o [ˈθriənɪn] *s* (biochem.) treonina
**thresh** [θrɛʃ] *va* (agr.) trillar; **to thresh out** decidir después de una discusión cabal; **to thresh over** discutir repetidas veces; *vn* (agr.) trillar; dar vueltas, sacudirse, menearse
**thresher** [ˈθrɛʃər] *s* (agr.) trillador; (agr.) trilladora; (ichth.) raposa de mar, zorra de mar
**thresher shark** *s* (ichth.) raposa de mar, zorra de mar
**threshing floor** *s* era
**threshing machine** *s* máquina trilladora
**threshold** [ˈθrɛʃold] *s* umbral; (psychol. & fig.) umbral, limen; **to be on the threshold of** estar en los umbrales de; **to cross the threshold** atravesar los umbrales
**threw** [θru] *pret de* **throw**
**thrice** [θraɪs] *adv* tres veces; muy, sumamente, repetidamente
**thrift** [θrɪft] *s* economía, parquedad; (bot.) estática, césped de Olimpo
**thriftiness** [ˈθrɪftɪnɪs] *s* economía, parquedad
**thriftless** [ˈθrɪftlɪs] *adj* manirroto, malgastador
**thrifty** [ˈθrɪftɪ] *adj* (*comp:* **-ier;** *super:* **-iest**) económico, parco; floreciente, próspero
**thrill** [θrɪl] *s* emoción viva; *va* emocionar, conmover; *vn* emocionarse, conmoverse
**thriller** [ˈθrɪlər] *s* persona o cosa emocionante; cuento o pieza de teatro espeluznante
**thrilling** [ˈθrɪlɪŋ] *adj* emocionante; espeluznante
**thrippence** [ˈθrɪpəns] *s* var. de **threepence**
**thrips** [θrɪps] *s* (ent.) tripso
**thrive** [θraɪv] (*pret:* **throve** o **thrived;** *pp:* **thriven** o **thrived**) *vn* medrar, prosperar
**thriven** [ˈθrɪvən] *pp de* **thrive**
**thro'** o **thro** [θru] *adj, adv & prep* var. de **through**
**throat** [θrot] *s* garganta; (bot.) garganta; (arch.) goterón; (fig.) garganta (*de un río, una vasija, etc.*); **to clear one's throat** aclarar la voz; **to cut one's throat** degollarle a uno; desacreditarle a uno; degollarse; desacreditarse; **to jump down one's throat** enfadarse violentamente contra una persona; **to stick in one's throat** clavársele a uno en la garganta (*p.ej., una espina*); ser difícil de decir
**throatband** [ˈθrot,bænd] *s* ahogadero
**throated** [ˈθrotɪd] *adj* que tiene garganta; que tiene cierta garganta, p.ej., **white-throated** de garganta blanca
**throatful** [ˈθrotfʊl] *s* gargantada (*trago*)
**throatlatch** [ˈθrot,lætʃ] *s* var. de **throatband**
**throatwort** [ˈθrot,wʌrt] *s* (bot.) hermosilla
**throaty** [ˈθrotɪ] *adj* (*comp:* **-ier;** *super:* **-iest**) gutural, ronco
**throb** [θrɑb] *s* latido, palpitación, pulsación; (*pret & pp:* **throbbed;** *ger:* **throbbing**) *vn* latir, palpitar, pulsar
**throbbing** [ˈθrɑbɪŋ] *adj* palpitante
**throe** [θro] *s* dolor, congoja; **throes** *spl* angustia, agonía; esfuerzo penoso
**thrombin** [ˈθrɑmbɪn] *s* (biochem.) trombina
**thrombocyte** [ˈθrɑmbosaɪt] *s* (physiol.) trombocito
**thrombosis** [θrɑmˈbosɪs] *s* (path.) trombosis
**thrombus** [ˈθrɑmbəs] *s* (*pl:* **-bi** [baɪ]) (path.) trombo
**throne** [θron] *s* trono; **thrones** *spl* (eccl.) tronos; *va* entronizar
**throne room** *s* salón del trono
**throng** [θrɔŋ] o [θrɑŋ] *s* gentío, tropel, muchedumbre; *va* apretar, atestar; *vn* agolparse, apiñarse
**throstle** [ˈθrɑsəl] *s* (orn.) malvís, tordo alirrojo; (mach.) telar continuo
**throttle** [ˈθrɑtəl] *s* garganta, gaznate; (mach.) válvula de estrangulación, válvula reguladora; regulador (*de locomotora*); acelerador (*de automóvil*); *va* ahogar, sofocar; impedir, suprimir; (mach.) estrangular; (mach.) regular; **to throttle down** reducir la velocidad de
**through** [θru] *adj* de paso; directo, sin paradas, con pocas paradas; acabado, terminado; **to be through with** haber acabado con; no querer ocuparse más de; *adv* a través, de un lado a otro, de parte a parte; desde el principio hasta el fin; completamente; **through and through** de punta a cabo; de todo en todo, hasta los tuétanos; *prep* por, a través de; me-

diante, por medio de; a causa de; por entre; durante todo; todo lo largo de
**throughout** [θru'aʊt] *adv* en todas partes; por todas partes; en todo, en todos respectos; desde el principio hasta el fin; *prep* en todo; durante todo; a lo largo de
**throughway** ['θru,we] *s* carretera troncal, carretera de acceso limitado
**throve** [θrov] *pret de* **thrive**
**throw** [θro] *s* echada, tirada, lance; riesgo, ventura; capita, bufanda, chal; cobertor o colcha ligera ‖ (*pret:* **threw;** *pp:* **thrown**) *va* arrojar, echar, lanzar; disparar; lanzar (*p.ej., la jabalina*); dirigir, lanzar (*p.ej., una mirada*); tirar (*los dados*); derribar; desarzonar; proyectar (*una sombra*); dar a luz, parir; dar forma a (*las vasijas de barro*); perder con premeditación (*un juego, una carrera*); torcer (*hilo*); tender (*un puente*); **to throw away** tirar; malgastar; perder, no aprovechar; **to throw back** rechazar; **to throw down** echar por tierra, derribar; **to throw in** añadir, dar de más; **to throw off** desechar, deshacerse de; (coll.) producir (*p.ej., poesías*) con desenvoltura; **to throw on** echarse (*una prenda de vestir*); **to throw oneself at** asediar (*p.ej., una mujer a un hombre*); **to throw out** botar, arrojar, desechar; echar a la calle; **to throw over** abandonar, dejar; **to throw up** abandonar, dejar; renunciar; levantar rápidamente; echar en cara; (coll.) vomitar ‖ *vn* arrojar, echar, lanzar; **to throw back** parecerse a un antepasado, retroceder a un tipo anterior; **to throw up** vomitar
**throwback** ['θro,bæk] *s* salto atrás, retroceso; (biol.) reversión; (mov.) escena retrospectiva
**thrower** ['θroər] *s* tirador, lanzador; torcedor de seda
**thrown** [θron] *pp de* **throw**
**thru** [θru] *adj, adv & prep* var. de **through**
**thrum** [θrʌm] *s* rasgueo; hilo basto, hilo destorcido; **thrums** *spl* cadillos; (*pret & pp:* **thrummed;** *ger:* **thrumming**) *va* rasguear sin arte (*un instrumento de cuerda*); golpear ociosamente; repetir de modo monótono; *vn* zangarrear; teclear
**thrush** [θrʌʃ] *s* (orn.) tordo; (orn.) arandillo, malvís; (path.) ubrera; (vet.) higo
**thrust** [θrʌst] *s* empuje; acometida; cuchillada, estocada, puñalada; (phys.) empuje; (*pret & pp:* **thrust**) *va* empujar; acometer; atravesar, traspasar; clavar, hincar; imponer (*una tarea a una persona*); *vn* dar un empujón; abrirse paso por fuerza
**thrust fault** *s* (geol.) falla acostada
**Thucydides** [θu'sɪdɪdiz] o [θju'sɪdɪdiz] *s* Tucídides
**thud** [θʌd] *s* baque, ruido sordo; (*pret & pp:* **thudded;** *ger:* **thudding**) *va & vn* golpear con ruido sordo
**thug** [θʌg] *s* malhechor, ladrón, asesino
**thuja** ['θudʒə] *s* (bot.) tuya
**Thule** ['θulɪ] o ['θjulɪ] *s* Tule
**thulium** ['θulɪəm] o ['θjulɪəm] *s* (chem.) tulio
**thumb** [θʌm] *s* pulgar, dedo gordo; **all thumbs** (coll.) desmañado, chapucero, torpe; **to twiddle one's thumbs** menear ociosamente los pulgares; no hacer nada, estar ocioso; **under the thumb of** bajo la férula de, bajo el zapato de; **thumbs down** con el pulgar vuelto hacia abajo (*en señal de desaprobación*); **thumbs up** con el pulgar vuelto hacia arriba (*en señal de aprobación*); *va* manosear sin cuidado; ensuciar con los dedos; **to thumb a ride** pedir ser llevado en automóvil indicando la dirección con el pulgar; **to thumb one's nose at** (coll.) señalar (*a una persona*) poniendo el pulgar sobre la nariz en son de burla; (coll.) tratar con sumo desprecio; *vn* zangarrear; **to thumb through** hojear (*un libro*) con el pulgar
**thumb index** *s* índice recortado, índice en el corte
**thumbnail** ['θʌm,nel] *s* uña del pulgar; cosa muy pequeña o breve; *adj* muy pequeño, muy pequeño pero completo, en miniatura
**thumb notch** *s* uñero
**thumb nut** *s* tuerca de orejetas; tuerca moleteada
**thumbprint** ['θʌm,prɪnt] *s* impresión del pulgar; *va* marcar con impresión del pulgar
**thumbscrew** ['θʌm,skru] *s* tornillo de mariposa, tornillo de orejas; empulgueras (*instrumento para dar tormento*)
**thumbstall** ['θʌm,stɔl] *s* funda para el pulgar
**thumbtack** ['θʌm,tæk] *s* chinche, chincheta
**thump** [θʌmp] *s* golpazo, porrazo, trastazo; *va* dar un golpe pesado a; golpear, aporrear; *vn* dar un porrazo; caer con golpe pesado; andar con pasos pesados; latir (*el corazón*) con golpes pesados
**thumping** ['θʌmpɪŋ] *adj* (coll.) pesado, enorme
**thunder** ['θʌndər] *s* trueno; estruendo (*p.ej., de aplausos*); amenaza, denunciación; **to steal one's thunder** robar la idea o el método de uno; *va* fulminar (*censuras, amenazas, etc.*); arrojar o lanzar con estruendo; expresar con estruendo; *vn* tronar; **it is thundering** truena; **to thunder along** pasar con estruendo; **to thunder at** tronar contra
**thunder and lightning** *s* rayos y truenos
**thunderbolt** ['θʌndər,bolt] *s* rayo; (fig.) rayo
**thunderclap** ['θʌndər,klæp] *s* tronido
**thundercloud** ['θʌndər,klaʊd] *s* nube cargada de electricidad
**thunderer** ['θʌndərər] *s* tronador; **the Thunderer** Júpiter tonante o tronante
**thunderhead** ['θʌndər,hɛd] *s* cúmulo (*que se resuelve en lluvia con truenos*)
**thundering** ['θʌndərɪŋ] *adj* tronador; tronitoso, estrepitoso; (coll.) enorme, extraordinario
**thunderous** ['θʌndərəs] *adj* tronante, tronitoso
**thundershower** ['θʌndər,ʃaʊər] *s* chubasco con truenos
**thundersquall** ['θʌndər,skwɔl] *s* ráfaga o racha de viento, acompañada de lluvia y truenos
**thunderstorm** ['θʌndər,stɔrm] *s* tronada, tempestad de truenos
**thunderstruck** ['θʌndər,strʌk] *adj* atónito, estupefacto, pasmado
**Thur.** abr. de **Thursday**
**thurible** ['θʊrɪbəl] o ['θjʊrɪbəl] *s* (eccl.) turíbulo
**thurifer** ['θʊrɪfər] o ['θjʊrɪfər] *s* (eccl.) turiferario
**thurify** ['θʊrɪfaɪ] o ['θjʊrɪfaɪ] (*pret & pp:* **-fied**) *va & vn* turificar
**Thuringia** [θʊ'rɪndʒɪə] o [θjʊ'rɪndʒɪə] *s* Turingia
**Thuringian** [θʊ'rɪndʒɪən] o [θjʊ'rɪndʒɪən] *adj & s* turingiano
**Thursday** ['θʌrzdɪ] *s* jueves
**thus** [ðʌs] *adv* así; **thus far** hasta aquí, hasta ahora
**thwack** [θwæk] *s* golpe, porrazo; sequete; *va* golpear, pegar; dar un golpe seco a
**thwart** [θwɔrt] *s* riostra (*de una canoa*); bancada, banco de remeros; *adj* transversal, oblicuo; *adv* de través; *va* desbaratar, impedir, frustrar
**thy** [ðaɪ] *adj poss* (archaic & poet.) tu
**thylacine** ['θaɪləsaɪn] o ['θaɪləsɪn] *s* (zool.) lobo marsupial
**thyme** [taɪm] *s* (bot.) tomillo
**thymelaeaceous** [,θɪmɪlɪ'eʃəs] *adj* (bot.) timeleáceo
**thymic** ['taɪmɪk] *adj* tímico (*perteneciente al tomillo*); ['θaɪmɪk] *adj* tímico (*perteneciente al timo*)
**thymol** ['θaɪmɑl] *s* (chem.) timol
**thymus** ['θaɪməs] *s* (anat.) timo; *adj* tímico
**thymus gland** *s* (anat.) timo
**thyroid** ['θaɪrɔɪd] *adj* tiroides; *s* (anat.) tiroides (*glándula, cartílago*); (pharm.) tiroidina
**thyroidectomy** [,θaɪrɔɪ'dɛktəmɪ] *s* (*pl:* **-mies**) (surg.) tiroidectomía
**thyroid extract** *s* (pharm.) tiroidina
**thyroid gland** *s* (anat.) glándula tiroides
**thyroxin** [θaɪ'rɑksɪn] o **thyroxine** [θaɪ'rɑksin] *s* (biochem.) tiroxina
**thyrse** [θʌrs] *s* (bot.) tirso
**thyrsus** ['θʌrsəs] *s* (*pl:* **-si** [saɪ]) (bot. & myth.) tirso
**thyself** [ðaɪ'sɛlf] *pron* (archaic & poet.) tú mismo; ti mismo; te, ti
**tiara** [taɪ'ɛrə] o [tɪ'ɑrə] *s* tiara; diadema (*adorno femenino de cabeza*)
**Tiber** ['taɪbər] *s* Tíber
**Tiberius** [taɪ'bɪrɪəs] *s* Tiberio
**Tibet** [tɪ'bɛt] o ['tɪbɛt] *s* el Tibet
**Tibetan** [tɪ'bɛtən] *adj & s* tibetano

**tibia** [ˈtɪbɪə] *s* (*pl:* **-ae** [i] o **-as**) (anat. & mus.) tibia
**tibial** [ˈtɪbɪəl] *adj* tibial
**tic** [tɪk] *s* (path.) tic
**tic douloureux** [ˌduluˈru] *s* (path.) tic doloroso de la cara
**tick** [tɪk] *s* tictac; contramarca, contraseña; (coll.) instante, momento; cutí, terliz; funda (*de almohada o colchón*); (coll.) crédito; (ent.) garrapata, mosca borriquera, pito; **on tick** (coll.) al fiado; *va* marcar, notar o contar con un tictac como el del reloj; marcar, poner una contraseña a; *vn* hacer tictac; latir (*el corazón*)
**ticker** [ˈtɪkər] *s* teleimpresor; (slang) reloj; (slang) corazón
**ticker tape** *s* cinta de teleimpresor
**ticket** [ˈtɪkɪt] *s* billete; localidad, entrada; papeleta de empeño; talón; marbete; (coll.) aviso de multa (*por estacionar un auto indebidamente*); (U.S.A.) candidatura; **that's the ticket** (coll.) eso es, eso es lo que se necesita; *va* poner marbete a
**ticket agent** *s* taquillero
**ticket collector** *s* revisor
**ticket office** *s* taquilla, despacho de billetes
**ticket of leave** *s* (Brit.) libertad bajo palabra
**ticket-of-leave man** [ˈtɪkɪtəvˈliv] *s* (Brit.) penado libre bajo palabra
**ticket scalper** *s* revendedor de billetes
**ticket window** *s* ventanilla, taquilla
**tick fever** *s* (path.) fiebre de garrapatas; (vet.) fiebre de Tejas
**ticking** [ˈtɪkɪŋ] *s* cutí, terliz
**tickle** [ˈtɪkəl] *s* cosquillas; cosquilleo; *va* cosquillear; gustar, divertir; *vn* cosquillear; tener o sentir cosquillas
**tickler** [ˈtɪklər] *s* persona que cosquillea; libro borrador o de apuntes; (coll.) problema difícil
**tickler coil** *s* (rad.) bobina de regeneración
**ticklish** [ˈtɪklɪʃ] *adj* cosquilloso; picajoso, quisquilloso, cosquilloso; difícil, delicado; inseguro, inestable
**tick-tack-toe** [ˌtɪktækˈto] *s* juego, parecido al tres en raya, en el cual dos jugadores ponen su señal alternativamente en uno de nueve espacios de una figura de líneas cruzadas, cada jugador intentando llenar primero tres espacios seguidos
**tick-tock** [ˈtɪkˌtɑk] *s* tictac (*del reloj*)
**tidal** [ˈtaɪdəl] *adj* de marea
**tidal wave** *s* ola de marea; (fig.) ola (*p.ej., de indignación popular*)
**tidbit** [ˈtɪdˌbɪt] *s* buen bocado, bocado rico, bocadito
**tiddledywinks** [ˈtɪdəldɪˌwɪŋks] o **tiddlywinks** [ˈtɪdlɪˌwɪŋks] *s* juego de la pulga, juego que consiste en hacer saltar un disco en una taza
**tide** [taɪd] *s* (naut.) marea; temporada; corriente; **to go with the tide** seguir la corriente; **to turn the tide** hacer cambiar las cosas; cambiar el curso (*p.ej., de la batalla*); **the tide turned** dió vuelta la tortilla; *va* llevar, hacer flotar; **to tide over** ayudar un poco; superar (*una dificultad*); *vn* levantarse (*la superficie de las aguas del mar*); navegar o flotar con la marea
**tide-driven power plant** [ˈtaɪdˌdrɪvən] *s* usina mareamotriz
**tide gate** *s* compuerta de marea
**tideland** [ˈtaɪdˌlænd] *s* terreno inundado por la marea, estero
**tide power** *s* hulla azul
**tidewater** [ˈtaɪdˌwɔtər] o [ˈtaɪdˌwɑtər] *s* agua de marea; orilla del mar; *adj* costanero
**tideway** [ˈtaɪdˌwe] *s* canal de marea; corriente de marea
**tidings** [ˈtaɪdɪŋz] *spl* noticias, informes
**tidy** [ˈtaɪdɪ] *s* (*pl:* **-dies**) pañito bordado, cubierta de respaldar; *adj* (*comp:* **-dier**; *super:* **-diest**) aseado, limpio, pulcro, ordenado; (*pret & pp:* **-died**) *va* asear, limpiar, arreglar, poner en orden; *vn* asearse; poner las cosas en orden
**tie** [taɪ] *s* atadura; lazo, nudo; corbata; empate (*en elecciones, juegos, etc.*); tirante, estay; (mus.) ligado; (rail.) traviesa; (fig.) lazo, vínculo; **ties** *spl* zapatos bajos de lazos; **to tie a tie** hacer una corbata; (*pret & pp:* **tied**; *ger:* **tying**) *va* atar, liar; enlazar; hacer (*la corbata*); confinar, limitar; empatar (*p.ej., una elección*); empatársela a (*una persona*); (mus.) ligar; **to be tied up** estar ocupado; **to tie down** confinar, limitar; **to tie up** atar; envolver; obstruir (*el tráfico*); (com.) embargar; *vn* atar; empatar o empatarse
**tieback** [ˈtaɪˌbæk] *s* alzapaño (*tira de tela o cordonería*)
**tie bar** *s* barra tirante, varilla de tensión; (rail.) barra separadora (*de las dos agujas de cambio*)
**tie beam** *s* tirante, viga tensora
**tiepin** [ˈtaɪˌpɪn] *s* alfiler de corbata
**tier** [ˈtaɪər] *s* atador; (dial.) delantal de niña atado con cintas; [tɪr] *s* fila, ringlera; tonga; (theat.) fila de palcos; *va* formar en filas o tongas
**tierce** [tɪrs] *s* tercerola (*barril*); tercera o tercia (*tres cartas del mismo palo*); (eccl.) tercia; (mus.) tercera; posición de mano en tercera (*en la esgrima*)
**tie rod** *s* barra tirante, varilla de tensión; (aut.) biela, barra de acoplamiento de dirección
**tie-up** [ˈtaɪˌʌp] *s* enlace, unión; parada o paralización (*causada por una huelga u otros motivos*); bloqueo, embotellamiento (*del tráfico*)
**tiff** [tɪf] *s* riña ligera, quimera; pique, resentimiento; *vn* reñir; picarse, irritarse
**tiffin** [ˈtɪfɪn] *s* (Brit.) almuerzo; *va* (Brit.) dar de almorzar a; *vn* (Brit.) almorzar
**tiger** [ˈtaɪgər] *s* tigre; (fig.) tigre (*persona muy cruel*)
**tiger beetle** *s* (ent.) cicindela
**tiger cat** *s* (zool.) gato montés, ocelote, serval; gato doméstico atigrado
**tiger-eye** [ˈtaɪgərˌaɪ] *s* ojo de gato (*piedra*)
**tigerflower** [ˈtaɪgərˌflaʊər] *s* (bot.) flor de un día, flor de la maravilla
**tigerish** [ˈtaɪgərɪʃ] *adj* atigrado, tigrino, feroz
**tiger lily** *s* (bot.) azucena atigrada
**tiger moth** *s* (ent.) artia
**tiger's-eye** [ˈtaɪgərzˌaɪ] *s* var. de **tiger-eye**
**tiger shark** *s* (ichth.) pez zorro; (ichth.) alecrín
**tight** [taɪt] *adj* apretado, estrecho; tieso, tirante; bien cerrado, hermético; estanco; ajustado, ceñido; compacto, denso; fijo, firme, sólido; complicado, difícil; duro, severo; (com.) escaso, difícil de obtener; (paint.) mal manejado; (sport) casi igual; (coll.) agarrado, tacaño; (slang) borracho; (dial.) aseado, pulido; *adv* firmemente; **to hold tight** mantener fijo; agarrarse bien; **to sit tight** (coll.) estarse quieto; (coll.) tener la misma postura; **tights** *spl* traje de malla (*p.ej., de los acróbatas*)
**tighten** [ˈtaɪtən] *va* apretar; atiesar, estirar; *vn* apretarse; atiesarse, estirarse
**tight-fisted** [ˈtaɪtˈfɪstɪd] *adj* agarrado, tacaño
**tight-fitting** [ˈtaɪtˈfɪtɪŋ] *adj* ceñido, muy ajustado
**tight-lipped** [ˈtaɪtˈlɪpt] *adj* que tiene los labios apretados; callado, silencioso, hermético
**tightrope** [ˈtaɪtˌrop] *s* cuerda tirante; *vn* andar en la cuerda tirante
**tight squeeze** *s* (coll.) brete, aprieto
**tightwad** [ˈtaɪtˌwɑd] *s* (slang) cicatero
**tigress** [ˈtaɪgrɪs] *s* tigresa
**tigrish** [ˈtaɪgrɪʃ] *adj* var. de **tigerish**
**tike** [taɪk] *s* var. de **tyke**
**til** [tɪl] o [til] *s* (bot.) ajonjolí; (bot.) til (*de las Canarias*); [til] *s* (phonet.) tilde
**tilbury** [ˈtɪlbərɪ] *s* (*pl:* **-ries**) tílburi
**tile** [taɪl] *s* azulejo; baldosa (*para solar*); teja (*para cubrir por fuera los techos*); tubo de barro cocido, canal de barro cocido; (coll.) chistera, sombrero de copa; *va* azulejar; embaldosar; tejar
**tilefish** [ˈtaɪlˌfɪʃ] *s* (ichth.) lofolátilo
**tile kiln** *s* tejar, tejería
**tiler** [ˈtaɪlər] *s* azulejero; tejero
**tile roof** *s* tejado (de tejas)
**tiliaceous** [ˌtɪlɪˈeʃəs] *adj* (bot.) tiliáceo
**tiling** [ˈtaɪlɪŋ] *s* azulejos; baldosas; tejas; azulejería; embaldosado
**till** [tɪl] *s* cajón o gaveta del dinero; *prep* hasta; *conj* hasta que; *va* labrar, cultivar
**tillable** [ˈtɪləbəl] *adj* labrantío
**tillage** [ˈtɪlɪdʒ] *s* cultivo, labranza; agricultura; tierra labrada; cosecha

**tiller** ['tɪlər] *s* agricultor, labrador; palanca, mango; (naut.) barra o caña del timón; (hort.) sierpe
**tilt** [tɪlt] *s* inclinación; declive; tienda, entalamadura; justa, torneo; martinete de báscula; lanzada; **at tilt** en posición inclinada; dando una lanzada; **full tilt** a toda velocidad; *va* inclinar, volcar; asestar (*una lanza*); acometer; forjar o martillar con martinete; entoldar; *vn* inclinarse; justar, tornear; luchar; **to tilt at** luchar con, arremeter contra; protestar contra
**tilth** [tɪlθ] *s* cultivo, labranza; tierra labrada; capa cultivable (*de un terreno*)
**tilt hammer** *s* martinete de báscula
**tiltyard** ['tɪlt,jɑrd] *s* palestra, lugar de una justa o torneo
**Tim.** abr. de **Timothy**
**timbal** ['tɪmbəl] *s* (mus.) timbal; membrana del aparato estridulante (*de los cicádidos*)
**timbale** ['tɪmbəl] *s* (cook.) timbal
**timber** ['tɪmbər] *s* madera de construcción; maderaje; viga, madero; bosque, árboles de monte; (naut.) cuaderna; *va* enmaderar
**timber hitch** *s* (naut.) vuelta de braza
**timberland** ['tɪmbər,lænd] *s* tierras maderables
**timber line** *s* altura o límite de la vegetación, límite del bosque maderable
**timber wolf** *s* (zool.) lobo norteamericano (*Canis lupus lycaon*)
**timbre** ['tɪmbər] o ['tæmbər] *s* (her., phonet. & phys.) timbre
**timbrel** ['tɪmbrəl] *s* (mus.) adufe, pandereta
**time** [taɪm] *s* tiempo; hora, p.ej., **time to go to bed** hora de acostarse; vez, p.ej., **that was the last time I saw him** ésa era la última vez que le ví; rato, p.ej., **he had a nice time** pasó un buen rato; plazo; horas de trabajo; sueldo; tiempo de parir, término del embarazo; hora, última hora; (phot.) tiempo de exposición; **against time** esforzándose por acabar antes de cierto tiempo; **at no time** ninguna vez; **at the same time** a un tiempo; a la vez; todavía, sin embargo; **at the time of** en tiempo de; **at the wrong time** fuera de tiempo; **at times** a tiempos, a veces; **behind time** atrasado; **behind the times** anticuado, fuera de moda; **between times** en los intervalos; **for some time (past)** de algún tiempo a esta parte; **for the time being** por el momento, por ahora; **from time to time** de tiempo en tiempo; **in due time** a su tiempo, en su día; **in good time** en tiempo; pronto; **in no time** en muy poco tiempo, en un abrir y cerrar de ojos; **in time** con tiempo; (mus.) a compás; **in time to** + *inf* a tiempo para + *inf;* **on time** a la hora (debida); con puntualidad; a plazo; **to bide one's time** esperar la hora propicia, tomarse tiempo; **to do time** (coll.) cumplir una condena; **to have a good time** darse buen tiempo, divertirse; **to have no time for** no poder tolerar; **to keep time** contar el tiempo; andar bien (*un reloj*); (mus.) llevar el compás; **to kill time** matar el tiempo; **to know how to tell time** saber o conocer el reloj; **to lose time** atrasarse (*el reloj*); **to make time** ganar tiempo, avanzar con rapidez; **to mark time** hacer tiempo; trabajar en vano; (mil.) marcar el paso; **to pass the time away** matar el tiempo; **to pass the time of day** saludarse (*dos personas*); **to pass the time of day with** saludar, dar los buenos días a; **to take one's time** no darse prisa, ir despacio; **to tell the time** decir la hora, p.ej., **tell me the time** dígame la hora; **to tell time** decir la hora (*p.ej., el reloj de sol*); **to waste time** gastar o perder el tiempo; **what time is it?** ¿qué hora es?; **within a short time** al poco tiempo; **time after time** o **time and again** repetidas veces; **times** (math.) por (*multiplicado por*); *adj* de tiempo, del tiempo; a plazo; *va* calcular el tiempo de; medir el tiempo de; hacer a tiempo oportuno; regular; hacer a compás; (mach.) graduar la distribución de; (sport) cronometrar
**time bomb** *s* bomba-reloj, bomba a reloj
**timecard** ['taɪm,kɑrd] *s* hoja de presencia, tarjeta registradora (*de la hora de llegada y salida*); horario
**time clock** *s* reloj registrador
**time-consuming** ['taɪmkən,sumɪŋ] o ['taɪmkən,sjumɪŋ] *adj* que toma mucho tiempo
**time-delay relay** ['taɪmdɪ'le] *s* (elec.) relai de retardo
**time draft** *s* (com.) letra de cambio a plazo, orden de pago a plazo
**time exposure** *s* (phot.) pose
**time fuse** *s* espoleta de tiempos
**time-honored** ['taɪm,ɑnərd] *adj* consagrado, tradicional
**time immemorial** *s* tiempo inmemorable; (law) tiempo inmemorial
**timekeeper** ['taɪm,kipər] *s* listero, apuntador, alistador de tiempo; reloj, cronómetro; (mus.) marcador de tiempo; (sport) cronometrador, juez de tiempo
**timeless** ['taɪmlɪs] *adj* eterno, infinito; sin fecha, sin limitación de tiempo; intemporal
**timely** ['taɪmlɪ] *adj* (*comp:* **-lier;** *super:* **-liest**) oportuno
**time off** *s* permiso, asueto
**time out** *s* (coll.) descanso, intermisión
**time out of mind** *s* tiempo inmemorable
**timepiece** ['taɪm,pis] *s* reloj, cronómetro
**timer** ['taɪmər] *s* contador de tiempo; (mach.) distribuidor del encendido
**timesaver** ['taɪm,sevər] *s* economizador de tiempo
**timeserver** ['taɪm,sʌrvər] *s* contemporizador
**timeserving** ['taɪm,sʌrvɪŋ] *adj* contemporizador; *s* contemporización
**time signal** *s* señal horaria
**time signature** *s* (mus.) signatura
**time switch** *s* (elec.) interruptor de reloj, interruptor horario
**timetable** ['taɪm,tebəl] *s* guía, horario, itinerario
**timework** ['taɪm,wʌrk] *s* trabajo a jornal
**timeworn** ['taɪm,worn] *adj* traqueado, gastado por el tiempo
**time zone** *s* huso horario
**timid** ['tɪmɪd] *adj* tímido
**timidity** [tɪ'mɪdɪtɪ] *s* timidez
**timing** ['taɪmɪŋ] *s* medida del tiempo; regulación del tiempo; puesta a punto; selección del momento oportuno (*para producir un efecto deseado*); (aut.) regulación del encendido; (aut.) regulación de la distribución; (mus.) regulación del compás (*ritmo*); (sport) cronometraje; (theat.) sincronización; (theat.) velocidad de la acción
**timing gears** *spl* (mach.) distribución, engranaje de distribución, mando de las válvulas
**timocracy** [taɪ'mɑkrəsɪ] *s* (*pl:* **-cies**) timocracia
**timocratic** [,taɪmə'krætɪk] o **timocratical** [,taɪmə'krætɪkəl] *adj* timocrático
**timorous** ['tɪmərəs] *adj* temeroso, tímido
**timothy** ['tɪməθɪ] *s* (bot.) fleo; (*cap.*) Timoteo; (Bib.) Epístola de San Pablo a Timoteo (*cada una de dos*)
**timpano** ['tɪmpəno] *s* (*pl:* **-ni** [ni]) (mus.) atabal, tímpano
**tin** [tɪn] *s* (chem.) estaño; hojalata, hoja de lata; lata (*envase*); *adj* de estaño; de hojalata; pobre, inferior; (*pret & pp:* **tinned;** *ger:* **tinning**) *va* estañar; recubrir de estaño; (Brit.) enlatar, conservar en latas
**tinamou** ['tɪnəmu] *s* (orn.) tinamú
**tincal** ['tɪŋkɑl] o ['tɪŋkɔl] *s* tincal
**tin can** *s* lata, envase de hojalata
**tinctorial** [tɪŋk'torɪəl] *adj* tintóreo
**tincture** ['tɪŋktʃər] *s* (pharm.) tintura; (her.) esmalte; (fig.) tintura (*noticia superficial*); *va* tinturar; (fig.) tinturar
**tin cup** *s* taza de hojalata
**tinder** ['tɪndər] *s* yesca; mecha
**tinderbox** ['tɪndər,bɑks] *s* lumbres, yescas, yesquero; (fig.) persona muy excitable
**tine** [taɪn] *s* púa (*p.ej., de tenedor*)
**tinea** ['tɪnɪə] *s* (path.) tiña
**tin foil** *s* hojuela de estaño, papel de estaño
**ting** [tɪŋ] *s* tintín; *va* hacer tintinear; *vn* tintinear
**ting-a-ling** ['tɪŋə,lɪŋ] *s* tilín
**tinge** [tɪndʒ] *s* matiz, tinte; dejo, gustillo; (*ger:* **tingeing** o **tinging**) *va* matizar, teñir; dar gusto o sabor a
**tingle** ['tɪŋgəl] *s* comezón, hormigueo; *va* pro-

ducir comezón u hormigueo a; *vn* sentir comezón u hormigueo; zumbar (*los oídos*); estremecerse (*p.ej., de entusiasmo*)
**tin hat** *s* (coll.) yelmo de acero, casco de acero
**tinker** ['tɪŋkər] *s* calderero remendón; chapucero, chafallón; chapuz, chafallo; *va* remendar chapuceramente; chafallar; *vn* ocuparse vanamente; **to tinker at** o **with** ocuparse vanamente con o en
**tinker's damn** o **dam** *s* (slang) cosa de ningún valor; **to not be worth a tinker's damn** (slang) no valer un pito; **to not care a tinker's damn** (slang) no importarle a uno un pito
**tinkle** ['tɪŋkəl] *s* retintín; *va* hacer retiñir; marcar con un retintín; *vn* retiñir
**tinman** ['tɪnmən] *s* (*pl:* **-men**) var. de **tinsmith**
**tinner** ['tɪnər] *s* minero de estaño; estañero; hojalatero; (Brit.) envasador de latas
**tinnitus** [tɪ'naɪtəs] *s* (path.) zumbido de oídos
**tinny** ['tɪnɪ] *adj* (*comp:* **-nier;** *super:* **-niest**) de estaño; que tintina como los objetos de estaño o de hojalata; que sabe a estaño; débil, endeble
**tin-pan alley** ['tɪn,pæn] *s* barrio, especialmente en la ciudad de Nueva York, donde se publica la mayor parte de la música popular; conjunto de compositores de música popular
**tin plate** *s* hojalata
**tin-plate** ['tɪn,plet] *va* estañar
**tin roof** *s* tejado de hojalata
**tinsel** ['tɪnsəl] *s* oropel; (fig.) oropel; lentejuelas o tiritas de hoja de estaño (*que se usan como ornamento, p.ej., para el árbol de Navidad*); lama, restaño, brocadillo; *adj* de oropel; (*pret & pp:* **-seled** o **-selled;** *ger:* **-seling** o **-selling**) *va* oropelar
**tinsmith** ['tɪn,smɪθ] *s* estañero; hojalatero
**tin soldier** *s* soldadito de plomo (*juguete*)
**tint** [tɪnt] *s* tinte, matiz; media tinta; *va* teñir, matizar, colorar ligeramente
**tintinnabulation** [,tɪntɪ,næbjə'leʃən] *s* campanilleo
**tintype** ['tɪn,taɪp] *s* (phot.) ferrotipo
**tinware** ['tɪn,wɛr] *s* objetos de hojalata
**tin wedding** *s* décimo aniversario (*del matrimonio*)
**tinwork** ['tɪn,wʌrk] *s* estañadura; hojalatería
**tiny** ['taɪnɪ] *adj* (*comp:* **-nier;** *super:* **-niest**) diminuto, menudo, pequeñito
**tip** [tɪp] *s* extremo, extremidad; herrete, casquillo; punta (*p.ej., de la lengua*); puntera (*del zapato*); embocadura (*de cigarrillo*); inclinación, ladeo; palmadita, golpecito; propina (*gratificación*); soplo (*informe dado en secreto*); (*pret & pp:* **tipped;** *ger:* **tipping**) *va* herretear, poner herrete o casquillo a; inclinar, ladear; golpear ligeramente; volcar; dar propina a; informar por debajo de cuerda; tocar (*el sombrero*) con los dedos; quitarse (*el sombrero en señal de cortesía*); **to tip in** (print.) encañonar (*un pliego*); **to tip off** (coll.) informar por debajo de cuerda; (coll.) advertir; **to tip over** volcar; *vn* dar una propina o propinas; inclinarse, ladearse; **to tip over** volcarse
**tipcart** ['tɪp,kɑrt] *s* volquete
**tip-in** ['tɪp,ɪn] *s* (print.) pliego encañonado
**tip-off** ['tɪp,ɔf] o ['tɪp,ɑf] *s* (coll.) informe dado por debajo de cuerda; (coll.) advertencia
**tipped** [tɪpt] *adj* aboquillado (*cigarrillo*); herreteado
**tippet** ['tɪpɪt] *s* palatina; esclavina
**tipping** ['tɪpɪŋ] *s* costumbre de dar propinas
**tipple** ['tɪpəl] *s* bebida alcohólica; volcadero; *va* beber a menudo y en poca cantidad; *vn* beborrotear
**tippler** ['tɪplər] *s* bebedor
**tipstaff** ['tɪp,stæf] o ['tɪp,stɑf] *s* vara de justicia; ministril, alguacil de vara
**tipster** ['tɪpstər] *s* (coll.) individuo que vende informes secretos, especialmente a los jugadores
**tipsy** ['tɪpsɪ] *adj* (*comp:* **-sier;** *super:* **-siest**) vacilante; achispado
**tipsy cake** *s* bizcocho borracho
**tiptoe** ['tɪp,to] *s* punta del pie; puntas de los pies; **on tiptoe** de puntillas; alerta, sobre aviso; furtivamente; (*pret & pp:* **-toed;** *ger:* **-toeing**) *vn* andar de puntillas
**tiptop** ['tɪp,tɑp] *s* cumbre, cima; *adj* al punto más alto; (coll.) superior, excelente
**tirade** ['taɪred] o [tɪ'red] *s* diatriba, invectiva
**tire** [taɪr] *s* neumático, llanta de goma; llanta o calce (*cerco metálico de las ruedas*); *va* cansar; aburrir, fastidiar; poner llantas o neumáticos a; *vn* cansarse; aburrirse, fastidiarse
**tire chain** *s* cadena de llanta, cadena antirresbaladiza
**tired** [taɪrd] *adj* cansado, rendido
**tire gauge** *s* indicador de presión de neumáticos, medidor para neumáticos
**tire iron** *s* (aut.) desmontable
**tireless** ['taɪrlɪs] *adj* incansable, infatigable
**tire pressure** *s* presión de inflado
**tire pump** *s* bomba para inflar neumáticos
**tire rack** *s* (aut.) portaneumático
**tiresome** ['taɪrsəm] *adj* cansado, aburrido, pesado
**tire spreader** *s* ensanchador de neumáticos
**Tirol, the** [tɪ'rol] o ['tɪrɑl] var. de **the Tyrol**
**'tis** [tɪz] contracción de **it is**
**tissue** ['tɪʃʊ] *s* tejido fino, gasa, tisú; (biol.) tejido; papel de seda; (fig.) tejido (*p.ej., de mentiras*)
**tissue culture** *s* (bact.) cultivo de tejidos
**tissue paper** *s* papel de seda
**tit** [tɪt] *s* teta; pezón (*extremidad de la teta*); (orn.) paro, herrerillo; **tit for tat** pata es la traviesa, guájete por guájete, ojo por ojo
**titan** ['taɪtən] *s* titán; (*cap.*) *s* (myth.) Titán; *adj* titánico
**titanate** ['taɪtənet] *s* (chem.) titanato
**titan crane** *s* (mach.) titán
**Titania** [tɪ'tenɪə] *s* Titania
**titanic** [taɪ'tænɪk] *adj* titánico; (chem.) titánico; (*cap.*) *adj* (myth.) titánico
**titanite** ['taɪtənaɪt] *s* (mineral.) titanita
**titanium** [taɪ'tenɪəm] o [tɪ'tenɪəm] *s* (chem.) titanio o titano
**titbit** ['tɪt,bɪt] *s* var. de **tidbit**
**titer** ['taɪtər] *s* (chem., immun. & physiol.) título
**tithable** ['taɪðəbəl] *adj* diezmable
**tithe** ['taɪð] *s* décimo (*décima parte*); diezmo (*impuesto pagado a la iglesia*); impuesto muy pequeño; pizca; *va* diezmar
**tither** ['taɪðər] *s* diezmero
**tithing** ['taɪðɪŋ] *s* diezmo; recaudación o pago del diezmo; (Brit.) pequeña división administrativa, formada por diez familias de vecinos
**Tithonus** [tɪ'θonəs] *s* (myth.) Titono
**Titian** ['tɪʃən] *s* El Ticiano; *adj* castaño rojizo, rubio rojizo
**titillate** ['tɪtɪlet] *va* titilar (*cosquillear*)
**titillation** [,tɪtɪ'leʃən] *s* titilación
**titivate** ['tɪtɪvet] *va* (coll.) ataviar, vestir con mucha elegancia; *vn* (coll.) ataviarse, vestirse con mucha elegancia
**titlark** ['tɪt,lɑrk] *s* (orn.) bisbita
**title** ['taɪtəl] *s* título; (sport) campeonato; *va* titular, intitular
**titled** ['taɪtəld] *adj* titulado
**title deed** *s* (law) título de propiedad
**titleholder** ['taɪtəl,holdər] *s* titulado; (sport) campeón
**title page** *s* portada, frontispicio
**title rôle** *s* (theat.) papel principal (*el que corresponde al título de la obra*)
**titmouse** ['tɪt,maʊs] *s* (*pl:* **-mice**) (orn.) paro; (orn.) paro carbonero, herrerillo
**Titoism** ['tito·ɪzəm] *s* titoísmo
**Titoist** ['tito·ɪst] *adj & s* titoísta
**titrate** ['taɪtret] o ['tɪtret] *va & vn* (chem.) titrar o titular
**titration** [taɪ'treʃən] o [tɪ'treʃən] *s* (chem.) titración o titulación
**titter** ['tɪtər] *s* risita ahogada o disimulada; *vn* reír a medias, reír con disimulo
**tittivate** ['tɪtɪvet] *va & vn* (coll.) var. de **titivate**
**tittle** ['tɪtəl] *s* ápice (*pequeño signo; parte mínima*)
**tittle-tattle** ['tɪtəl,tætəl] *s* charla, chismes; *vn* charlar, chismear
**titular** ['tɪtʃələr] *adj* titular; nominal (*que sólo tiene el nombre de un cargo sin poder real*)
**Titus** ['taɪtəs] *s* Tito; (Bib.) Epístola de San Pablo a Tito
**tmesis** ['tmisɪs] *s* (rhet.) tmesis
**tn.** abr. de **ton**

**TNT** o **T.N.T.** abr. de **trinitrotoluene**
**to** [tu], [tʊ] o [tə] *adv* hacia adelante; **to and fro** alternativamente; yendo y viniendo; **to come to** volver en sí; *prep* a, p.ej., **he is going to Buenos Aires** va a Buenos Aires; **they gave something to the beggar** dieron algo al pobre; **we are learning to dance** aprendemos a bailar; para, p.ej., **he is reading to himself** lee para sí; por, p.ej., **work to do** trabajo por hacer; hasta, p.ej., **to a certain extent** hasta cierto punto; en, p.ej., **from door to door** de puerta en puerta; con, p.ej., **kind to her** amable con ella; según, p.ej., **to my way of thinking** según mi modo de pensar; menos, p.ej., **five minutes to ten** las diez menos cinco
**toad** [tod] *s* (zool.) sapo; (zool.) rana
**toadeater** [ˈtod,itər] *s* adulador servil
**toadfish** [ˈtod,fɪʃ] *s* (ichth.) sapo
**toadflax** [ˈtod,flæks] *s* (bot.) linaria
**toadstone** [ˈtod,ston] *s* estelión, estelón
**toadstool** [ˈtod,stul] *s* (bot.) agárico, seta; seta venenosa
**toady** [ˈtodɪ] *s* (*pl:* **-ies**) adulador servil; (*pret & pp:* **-ied**) *va & vn* adular servilmente
**toadyism** [ˈtodɪɪzəm] *s* adulación servil
**to-and-fro** [ˈtuəndˈfro] *adj* alternativo, de vaivén
**toast** [tost] *s* tostadas; brindis; **a piece of toast** una tostada; *va* tostar; brindar a o por; *vn* tostarse; brindar
**toaster** [ˈtostər] *s* tostador; brindador
**toastmaster** [ˈtost,mæstər] o [ˈtost,mɑstər] *s* brindador; el que presenta a los oradores en un banquete
**Tob.** abr. de **Tobit**
**tobacco** [təˈbæko] *s* (*pl:* **-cos**) (bot.) tabaco; tabaco (*hojas secas*)
**tobacco dove** *s* (orn.) paloma tojosa
**tobaccoism** [təˈbæko·ɪzəm] *s* (path.) tabaquismo
**tobacco mosaic** *s* (plant path.) mosaico del tabaco
**tobacconist** [təˈbækənɪst] *s* tabaquero, estanquero
**tobacco pipe** *s* pipa para fumar
**tobacco pouch** *s* petaca
**tobacco worm** *s* (zool.) larva de la esfinge
**Tobias** [toˈbaɪəs] *s* Tobías
**Tobit** [ˈtobɪt] *s* Tobías; (Bib.) Libro de Tobías
**toboggan** [təˈbɑgən] *s* tobogán; *vn* deslizarse en tobogán; (com.) caer, precipitarse, disminuir en valor súbitamente
**toboggan slide** *s* pista para tobogán
**Toby** [ˈtobɪ] *s* (*pl:* **-bies**) vaso o pichel con asa, en forma de un hombre que lleva un gabán y un sombrero de tres picos; (slang) cigarro largo, delgado y barato
**toccata** [təˈkɑtə] *s* (mus.) tocata
**tocologist** [toˈkɑlədʒɪst] *s* tocólogo
**tocology** [toˈkɑlədʒɪ] *s* tocología
**tocopherol** [toˈkɑfərol] o [toˈkɑfərɑl] *s* (biochem.) tocoferol
**tocsin** [ˈtɑksɪn] *s* campana de alarma; campanada de alarma
**today** o **to-day** [tʊˈde] *adv & s* hoy
**toddle** [ˈtɑdəl] *s* tambaleo, pasillos inciertos; *vn* tambalear, andar con pasillos inciertos; hacer pinitos; andar, caminar; bailar; (slang) dar un paseo
**toddler** [ˈtɑdlər] *s* persona que anda con pasillos inciertos; niño que hace pinitos
**toddy** [ˈtɑdɪ] *s* (*pl:* **-dies**) ponche; vino de palmera
**to-do** [tʊˈdu] *s* (coll.) confusión, alboroto, alharaca
**toe** [to] *s* dedo del pie; punta del pie; puntera (*remiendo a la media; refuerzo de cuero del zapato*); lumbre (*de la herradura*); pesuño (*de los animales de pata hendida*); **on one's toes** alerta; **to tread on the toes of** estorbar, ofender; (*pret & pp:* **toed**; *ger:* **toeing**) *va* tocar o alcanzar con la punta del pie; echar punteras a; (carp.) clavar oblicuamente; (carp.) clavar con clavos hincados oblicuamente; **to toe the line** o **the mark** ponerse a la raya; obrar como se debe; *vn* golpear con las puntas de los pies; **to toe in** andar con las puntas de los pies hacia adentro; (aut.) convergir (*las ruedas*)
**toe dancer** *s* bailarina clásica
**toenail** [ˈto,nel] *s* uña del dedo del pie; (carp.) clavo oblicuo; *va* (carp.) clavar oblicuamente
**toffee** o **toffy** [ˈtɔfɪ] o [ˈtɑfɪ] *s* melcocha, arropía
**tog** [tɑg] *s* (coll.) prenda de vestir; **togs** *spl* (coll.) ropa, vestidos; (*pret & pp:* **togged**; *ger:* **togging**) *va* (coll.) vestir, engalanar, acicalar
**toga** [ˈtogə] *s* (hist.) toga
**together** [tʊˈgɛðər] *adv* juntos; juntamente; en común; a un tiempo, al mismo tiempo; sin interrupción; de acuerdo; **to get together** acopiar; reunir; reunirse; ponerse de acuerdo; **to go together** ir juntos; ser novios; armonizar entre sí; **together with** junto con
**toggery** [ˈtɑgərɪ] *s* (coll.) ropa, vestidos
**toggle** [ˈtɑgəl] *s* cazonete de aparejo; fiador atravesado; palanca acodillada; *va* asegurar con cazonete; proveer de cazonete
**toggle bolt** *s* tornillo de fiador
**toggle chain** *s* cadena de ajuste, cadena con fiador y anillo
**toggle joint** *s* junta de codillo
**toggle plate** *s* placa de articulación
**toggle press** *s* prensa de palanca acodillada
**toggle switch** *s* (elec.) interruptor a palanca, interruptor de rótula
**toil** [tɔɪl] *s* afán, fatiga; faena, obra laboriosa; **toils** *spl* red, lazo; *vn* afanarse, fatigarse; moverse con fatiga
**toiler** [ˈtɔɪlər] *s* trabajador
**toilet** [ˈtɔɪlɪt] *s* tocador (*mesa con espejo*); utensilio de tocador, juego de tocador; tocado, atavío; traje; retrete, inodoro, excusado; (surg.) limpiadura de una herida; **to make one's toilet** asearse, acicalarse
**toilet articles** *spl* artículos de tocador
**toilet bowl** *s* cubeta del inodoro
**toilet paper** *s* papel higiénico
**toilet powder** *s* polvos de tocador
**toiletry** [ˈtɔɪlɪtrɪ] *s* (*pl:* **-ries**) artículos de tocador
**toilet service** *s* juego de tocador
**toilet soap** *s* jabón de olor, jabón de tocador
**toilet tank** *s* tanque o depósito del inodoro
**toilette** [tɔɪˈlɛt] o [twɑˈlɛt] *s* atavío; traje, vestido (*de mujer*)
**toilet water** *s* agua de tocador
**toilsome** [ˈtɔɪlsəm] *s* fatigoso, laborioso, penoso
**toilworn** [ˈtɔɪl,worn] *adj* rendido por la fatiga
**token** [ˈtokən] *s* señal, símbolo; prenda, recuerdo; prueba, muestra; tanto, ficha o medalla (*usada como moneda*); **by the same token** por el mismo motivo; además; **in token of** en señal de
**token payment** *s* pago nominal
**told** [told] *pret & pp de* **tell**; **all told** todo incluído, en junto
**Toledan** [təˈlidən] *adj & s* toledano
**Toledo** [təˈlido] *s* (*pl:* **-dos**) arma toledana, hoja toledana
**tolerable** [ˈtɑlərəbəl] *adj* tolerable; mediano, regular
**tolerably** [ˈtɑlərəblɪ] *adv* tolerablemente; medianamente
**tolerance** [ˈtɑlərəns] *s* tolerancia; (mach. & med.) tolerancia; tolerancia, permiso (*en el monedaje*)
**tolerant** [ˈtɑlərənt] *adj* tolerante
**tolerate** [ˈtɑləret] *va* tolerar
**toleration** [,tɑləˈreʃən] *s* tolerancia, tolerantismo
**tolerationism** [,tɑləˈreʃənɪzəm] *s* tolerantismo
**toll** [tol] *s* doble (*de las campanas*); peaje, portazgo; pontazgo; maquila (*de molinero*); (telp.) tarifa; impuesto, derecho; derechos de paso (*por un canal*); baja, mortalidad (*número de víctimas*); *va* cobrar o pagar como peaje; imponer peaje a; tocar a muerto (*una campana*); tocar a muerto para; llamar con toque de difuntos; *vn* doblar
**toll bar** *s* barrera de peaje
**toll bridge** *s* puente de peaje
**toll call** *s* (telp.) llamada a larga distancia
**tollgate** [ˈtol,get] *s* barrera de peaje
**tollkeeper** [ˈtol,kipər] *s* peajero, portazguero
**Toltec** [ˈtɑltɛk] *adj & s* tolteca
**tolu** [toˈlu] *s* (pharm.) bálsamo de Tolú
**toluene** [ˈtɑljuin] *s* (chem.) tolueno
**toluic** [təˈluɪk] o [ˈtɑljuɪk] *adj* (chem.) toluico

**toluidine** [tə'luidin] o [tə'luɪdɪn] *s* (chem.) toluidina
**toluol** ['taljuɑl] *s* (chem.) toluol
**tolyl** ['talɪl] *s* (chem.) tolilo
**tom** o **Tom** [tam] *s* macho del gato, del pavo y de algún otro animal; (*cap.*) *s* nombre abreviado de **Thomas**
**tomahawk** ['taməhɔk] *s* tomahawk; **to bury the tomahawk** envainar la espada, hacer la paz; *va* herir o matar con tomahawk
**tomato** [tə'meto] o [tə'mato] *s* (*pl:* **-toes**) (bot.) tomatera o tomate (*planta*); tomate (*fruto*); *adj* tomatero
**tomato tree** *s* (bot.) árbol del tomate
**tomb** [tum] *s* tumba, sepulcro; (fig.) muerte; *va* sepultar
**tombac** ['tambæk] *s* tombac
**tomboy** ['tam,bɔɪ] *s* moza retozona, muchacha traviesa
**tombstone** ['tum,ston] *s* piedra o lápida sepulcral
**tomcat** ['tam,kæt] *s* gato (*macho*)
**tomcod** ['tam,kad] *s* (ichth.) microgado, pez escarchada
**Tom, Dick, and Harry** *s* fulano, zutano y mengano
**tome** [tom] *s* tomo; libro grueso
**tomentose** [tə'mɛntos] o ['tomɛntos] *adj* tomentoso
**tomentum** [tə'mɛntəm] *s* (*pl:* **-ta** [tə]) (bot.) tomento
**tomfool** [,tam'ful] *s* necio, payaso
**tomfoolery** [,tam'fuləri] *s* (*pl:* **-ies**) necedad, payasada
**tommy** o **Tommy** ['tamɪ] *s* (*pl:* **-mies**) soldado raso inglés
**Tommy gun** *s* (slang) pistola ametralladora (*de la marca Thompson*)
**tommyrot** ['tamɪ,rat] *s* (slang) mentecatería, música celestial
**tomorrow** o **to-morrow** [tu'maro] o [tu'mɔro] *adv & s* mañana; **the day after tomorrow** pasado mañana
**Tom Thumb** *s* Pulgarcito (*enano de los cuentos de hadas*)
**tomtit** ['tam,tɪt] *s* (orn.) herrerillo, trepatroncos; (orn.) coletero, rey de zarza
**tom-tom** ['tam,tam] *s* tantán
**ton** [tʌn] *s* tonelada; (naut.) tonelada; **tons** *spl* (coll.) montones
**tonal** ['tonəl] *adj* tonal
**tonality** [to'nælɪtɪ] *s* (*pl:* **-ties**) (mus. & f.a.) tonalidad
**tone** [ton] *s* tono; (f.a., mus., phonet. & physiol.) tono; **to change one's tone** mudar de tono; **to lower one's tone** bajar el tono; *va* entonar (*el cuerpo*); (mus. & paint.) entonar; (phot.) entonar, virar; **to tone down** suavizar el tono de; **to tone up** elevar el tono de; *vn* armonizar; **to tone down** moderarse; **to tone in with** armonizar con; **to tone up** reforzarse
**tone arm** *s* brazo sonoro, brazo para fonógrafo
**tone color** *s* (mus.) timbre
**tone control** *s* (rad.) regulación del tono
**tone-deaf** ['ton,dɛf] *adj* duro de oído
**tone deafness** *s* sordera musical
**tone poem** *s* (mus.) poema sinfónico
**tong** [tɔŋ] o [taŋ] *s* asociación secreta china; **tongs** *spl* tenazas; tenazas de rizar; tenacillas (*p.ej., para azúcar*); *va* asir, sujetar o arrancar con tenazas; *vn* emplear tenazas, trabajar con tenazas
**Tongking** ['taŋ'kɪŋ] *s* var. de **Tonkin**
**tongue** [tʌŋ] *s* (anat.) lengua; vara o lanza (*de carro*); tarabilla (*de la hebilla de la correa*); lengüeta de balanza; (carp. & mus.) lengüeta; (fig.) lengua (*idioma; badajo de campana; lengua de un animal usada como alimento*); (fig.) lengua (*de tierra, de fuego, de zapato*); **to give tongue** (hunt.) comenzar a ladrar; **to hold one's tongue** morderse la lengua; **to stick one's tongue out at** sacar la lengua a; *va* lamer; (carp.) sacar lengüeta a (*una tabla*); (carp.) ensamblar a lengüeta y ranura; (mus.) producir (*tonos*) con la lengua; *vn* extenderse (*p.ej., una lengua de tierra*); echar llamas; (mus.) producir tonos con la lengua
**tongue and groove** *s* (carp.) lengüeta y ranura
**tongue-and-groove joint** ['tʌŋənd'gruv] *s* (carp.) ensambladura de lengüeta y ranura
**tongue depressor** *s* (med.) depresor de la lengua
**tonguefish** ['tʌŋ,fɪʃ] *s* (ichth.) lengüita
**tongue-lashing** ['tʌŋ,læʃɪŋ] *s* (coll.) latigazo (*reprensión áspera*)
**tongue-tied** ['tʌŋ,taɪd] *adj* mudo, con la lengua atada; que tiene impedimento al hablar
**tongue twister** *s* trabalenguas
**tonic** ['tanɪk] *adj* tónico; *s* (med.) tónico; (mus. & phonet.) tónica
**tonic accent** *s* acento tónico
**tonicity** [to'nɪsɪtɪ] *s* tonicidad
**tonight** o **to-night** [tu'naɪt] *adv & s* esta noche
**tonite** ['tonaɪt] *s* tonita
**tonka bean** ['taŋkə] *s* (bot.) sarapia; haba tonca (*semilla de la sarapia*)
**Tonkin** ['tan'kɪn] *s* el Tonquín
**tonnage** ['tʌnɪdʒ] *s* tonelaje
**tonneau** [tʌ'no] *s* (*pl:* **-neaus** o **-neaux** ['noz]) (aut.) compartimiento posterior
**tonometer** [to'namɪtər] *s* tonómetro
**tonsil** ['tansəl] *s* (anat.) tonsila, amígdala
**tonsillar** ['tansɪlər] *adj* tonsilar
**tonsillectomy** [,tansɪ'lɛktəmɪ] *s* (*pl:* **-mies**) (surg.) tonsilectomía, amigdalotomía
**tonsillitis** [,tansɪ'laɪtɪs] *s* (path.) tonsilitis, amigdalitis
**tonsorial** [tan'sorɪəl] *adj* barberil
**tonsure** ['tanʃər] *s* (eccl.) tonsura; *va* (eccl.) tonsurar
**tontine** ['tantin] o [tan'tin] *s* tontina; *adj* de tontina
**tony** ['tonɪ] *adj* (*comp:* **-ier**; *super:* **-iest**) (slang) aristocrático, elegante; (*cap.*) *s* Antoñito
**too** [tu] *adv* también; demasiado; **it is too bad** es lástima; **only too** muy; **too bad!** ¡qué lástima!; **too many** demasiados; **too much** demasiado
**took** [tʊk] *pret de* **take**
**tool** [tul] *s* herramienta; (fig.) instrumento; *adj* herramental; *va* trabajar con herramienta; adornar con una herramienta; (b.b.) filetear; *vn* instalar máquinas-herramientas
**tool bag** *s* bolsa de herramientas
**toolbox** ['tul,baks] *s* caja de herramientas
**tool cabinet** *s* armario para herramientas
**tool chest** *s* caja de herramientas
**toolholder** ['tul,holdər] *s* portaherramientas
**tooling** ['tulɪŋ] *s* trabajo hecho con herramienta; (b.b.) fileteado
**tool kit** *s* juego de herramientas
**toolmaker** ['tul,mekər] *s* tallador de herramientas, herrero de herramientas
**toolmaking** ['tul,mekɪŋ] *s* talladura de herramientas
**tool steel** *s* acero de herramientas
**toot** [tut] *s* sonido breve (*de la bocina, el pito, etc.*); *va* sonar; *vn* sonar la bocina, tocar el cuerno, pitar
**tooth** [tuθ] *s* (*pl:* **teeth**) (anat.) diente; diente (*de sierra, rastrillo, peine, etc.*); **armed to the teeth** armado hasta los dientes; **by the skin of one's teeth** por poco, por milagro; **in the teeth of** en la cara de; a despecho de; **to cast in one's teeth** darle o echarle en cara a uno; **to cut teeth** endentecer; **to fight tooth and nail** luchar a brazo partido, luchar encarnizadamente; **to set one's teeth** apretar los dientes (*preparar a resistir*); **to show one's teeth** enseñar o mostrar los dientes; **to throw in one's teeth** darle o echarle en cara a uno; *va* dentar (*formar dientes en*); *vn* endentar
**toothache** ['tuθ,ek] *s* dolor de muelas
**toothbrush** ['tuθ,brʌʃ] *s* cepillo para los dientes
**toothed** [tuθt] o [tuðd] *adj* dentado; dentellado
**tooth edge** *s* dentera
**toothing** ['tuθɪŋ] *s* (mas.) adaraja
**toothing plane** *s* (carp.) cepillo dentado
**toothless** ['tuθlɪs] *adj* desdentado, desmolado
**tooth mark** *s* dentellada
**tooth paste** *s* pasta dentífrica
**toothpick** ['tuθ,pɪk] *s* palillo, mondadientes
**tooth powder** *s* polvo dentífrico
**toothsome** ['tuθsəm] *adj* gustoso, sabroso

**toothwort** ['tuθ,wʌrt] *s* (bot.) madrona, hierba de la madre, dentaria
**toothy** ['tuθɪ] *adj* (*comp:* **-ier;** *super:* **-iest**) que tiene dientes grandes, que muestra sus dientes; hambriento, voraz; (coll.) gustoso, sabroso
**top** [tɑp] *s* ápice (*extremo superior*); cabeza; cima (*de una montaña, un árbol; tallo de ciertas verduras*); cumbre (*de montaña; punto culminante*); copa (*de un árbol*); fuelle (*de un carruaje*); parche (*de un tambor*); tapa (*de un cilindro, un barril, una caja*); remate (*de un tejado*); principio (*de una página*); cabecera (*de un río*); coronilla (*de la cabeza*); coronamiento (*de un muro*); tablero (*de una mesa*); copete (*de una bota; adorno en la parte superior de un mueble*); cabeza, jefe; colmo (*último grado*); tope (*máximo*); camiseta (*del traje de baño*); peón, peonza, trompo (*juguete*); mapa (*lo que sobresale en algo*); galopo (*usado para formar maromas*); (aut.) capota; (naut.) cofa; (dial.) copete, moño; **at the top of** a la cabeza de (*p.ej., la clase*); **at the top of one's voice** a voz en grito; **from top to bottom** de arriba abajo; de alto a bajo; completamente; **from top to toe** de pies a cabeza; **on top** con el mayor éxito, victorioso; **on top of** encima de, en lo alto de; **on top of the world** en el tejado del mundo (*en el polo norte*); (coll.) en el colmo de la riqueza, la felicidad, etc.; **over the top** (mil.) al ataque, saliendo de las trincheras; **the tops** (slang) la flor de la canela; **to sleep like a top** dormir como un leño; *adj* cimero; máximo; último (*piso*); (él) más alto; tope (*precio*); alto; superior; superficial (*que está en la superficie*); (*pret & pp:* **topped;** *ger:* **topping**) *va* coronar, rematar; llegar a la cima de; cubrir; aventajar, superar; descopar (*p.ej., un árbol*); **to top off** rematar, terminar; (naut.) embicar (*una verga*); *vn* predominar, ser excelente; encumbrarse
**topaz** ['topæz] *s* topacio
**top billing** *s* (theat.) cabecera de cartel
**top boot** *s* bota de campaña; bota con vueltas
**topcoat** ['tɑp,kot] *s* abrigo, sobretodo; abrigo de entretiempo
**top-drawer** ['tɑp,drɔr] *adj* (coll.) de las altas clases, de primer rango
**top-dress** ['tɑp,drɛs] *va* recebar; (agr.) estercolar la superficie de
**top-dressing** ['tɑp,drɛsɪŋ] *s* recebo; (agr.) estercoladura aplicada a la superficie
**tope** [top] *va & vn* beber con exceso
**toper** ['topər] *s* borrachín
**topflight** ['tɑp,flaɪt] *adj* sobresaliente, destacado, más eminente
**topgallant** [tə'gælənt] *s* (naut.) juanete; *adj* (naut.) de juanete; [,tɑp'gælənt] *s* ápice, cumbre; cosa sobresaliente; *adj* sobresaliente
**topgallant mast** [tə'gælənt] *s* (naut.) mastelerillo
**topgallant sail** [tə'gælənt] *s* (naut.) juanete
**top hat** *s* chistera, sombrero de copa
**top-heavy** ['tɑp,hɛvɪ] *adj* demasiado pesado por arriba, más pesado arriba que abajo; (com.) que tiene capitalización inflada; (naut.) alteroso
**tophus** ['tofəs] *s* (*pl:* **-phi** [faɪ]) (path.) tofo
**topiary** ['topɪ,ɛrɪ] *adj* topiario; *s* (*pl:* **-ies**) topiaria
**topic** ['tɑpɪk] *s* asunto, tema, materia, tópico
**topical** ['tɑpɪkəl] *adj* corriente; del asunto; (med.) tópico
**topknot** ['tɑp,nɑt] *s* moño (*de pelo, de cintas; de plumas de algunas aves*)
**toplofty** ['tɑp,lɔftɪ] o ['tɑp,lɑftɪ] *adj* (coll.) copetudo, vanidoso
**topman** ['tɑpmən] *s* (*pl:* **-men**) (naut.) gaviero
**topmast** ['tɑpməst], ['tɑp,mæst] o ['tɑp,mɑst] *s* (naut.) mastelero
**topmost** ['tɑpmost] *adj* (el) más alto
**top notch** *s* (coll.) colmo, disloque
**top-notch** ['tɑp'nɑtʃ] *adj* superior, sobresaliente, de primera clase
**top-notcher** ['tɑp'nɑtʃər] *s* (coll.) persona sobresaliente, cosa sobresaliente
**top of the morning** *s* primeras horas de la mañana; (Irish) buenos días
**topographer** [tə'pɑgrəfər] *s* topógrafo
**topographic** [,tɑpə'græfɪk] o **topographical** [,tɑpə'græfɪkəl] *adj* topográfico
**topographically** [,tɑpə'græfɪkəlɪ] *adv* topográficamente
**topography** [tə'pɑgrəfɪ] *s* (*pl:* **-phies**) topografía
**topology** [tə'pɑlədʒɪ] *s* (anat. & math.) topología
**toponym** ['tɑpənɪm] *s* topónimo
**toponymic** [,tɑpə'nɪmɪk] *adj* toponímico; **toponymics** *ssg* toponimia
**toponymy** [tə'pɑnɪmɪ] *s* (*pl:* **-mies**) toponimia; (anat.) toponimia
**topper** ['tɑpər] *s* (coll.) persona o cosa de primera clase; (coll.) chistera, sombrero de copa
**topping** ['tɑpɪŋ] *adj* sobresaliente; (coll.) sobresaliente, de primera clase; *s* copete, moño; **toppings** *spl* desmocho (*p.ej., de los árboles*)
**topping lift** *s* (naut.) perigallo
**topple** ['tɑpəl] *va* derribar, volcar; *vn* derribarse, volcarse; caerse, venirse abajo
**topsail** ['tɑpsəl] o ['tɑp,sel] *s* (naut.) gavia
**top-secret** ['tɑp'sikrɪt] *adj* extremadamente secreto
**top sergeant** *s* (coll.) primer sargento
**topsides** ['tɑp,saɪdz] *spl* (naut.) borda (*parte superior del costado*)
**topsoil** ['tɑp,sɔɪl] *s* capa superficial del suelo
**topsy-turvy** ['tɑpsɪ'tʌrvɪ] *adj* desbarajustado, desordenado; *adv* en cuadro, patas arriba; *s* desbarajuste, desorden
**top-timber** ['tɑp,tɪmbər] *s* (naut.) barraganete
**toque** [tok] *s* toca
**torah** ['torə] *s* tora (*de los judíos*); **the Torah** la Tora
**torch** [tɔrtʃ] *s* antorcha; antorcha a soplete, lámpara de soldar; lámpara de bolsillo; **to carry a** o **the torch for** (slang) amar (*a una persona*) desesperadamente
**torchbearer** ['tɔrtʃ,bɛrər] *s* portahachón, hachero; (fig.) adicto, partidario, defensor
**torchlight** ['tɔrtʃ,laɪt] *s* luz de antorcha
**torchlight procession** *s* desfile de portahachones
**torch singer** *s* cantante de canciones de amor no correspondido
**torch song** *s* canción lenta y melancólica de amor no correspondido
**torchwood** ['tɔrtʃ,wud] *s* (bot.) amírida, ñámbar
**tore** [tor] *pret de* **tear**
**toreador** ['tɔrɪədɔr] *s* toreador
**toric** ['tɑrɪk] *adj* tórico
**toric lens** *s* lente tórica
**torment** ['tɔrmɛnt] *s* tormento; [tɔr'mɛnt] *va* atormentar
**tormenter** o **tormentor** [tɔr'mɛntər] *s* atormentador
**torn** [torn] *pp de* **tear**
**tornado** [tɔr'nedo] *s* (*pl:* **-does** o **-dos**) (meteor.) tornado, tromba terrestre; (fig.) explosión violenta
**toroid** ['torɔɪd] *s* (geom.) toroide
**torpedo** [tɔr'pido] *s* (*pl:* **-does**) (nav., ichth. & rail.) torpedo; *va* (nav. & fig.) torpedear
**torpedo boat** *s* (nav.) torpedero, lancha torpedera
**torpedo-boat destroyer** [tɔr'pido,bot] *s* (nav.) cazatorpedero, contratorpedero
**torpedoist** [tɔr'pido·ɪst] *s* torpedista
**torpedo tube** *s* (nav.) tubo lanzatorpedos
**torpid** ['tɔrpɪd] *adj* torpe; entorpecido; aletargado; indiferente, insensible
**torpidity** [tɔr'pɪdɪtɪ] o **torpor** ['tɔrpər] *s* torpeza; entorpecimiento; letargo; indiferencia, insensibilidad
**torque** [tɔrk] *s* (mech.) esfuerzo de rotación, par motor; torques (*collar*)
**torque arm** *s* (aut.) brazo de par
**torque converter** *s* (aut.) convertidor de par
**torrefaction** [,tɑrɪ'fækʃən] o [,tɔrɪ'fækʃən] *s* torrefacción
**torrefy** ['tɑrɪfaɪ] o ['tɔrɪfaɪ] (*pret & pp:* **-fied**) *va* abrasar, asar, tostar
**torrent** ['tɑrənt] o ['tɔrənt] *s* torrente (*corriente de aguas impetuosas*); chaparrón violento; (fig.) torrente
**torrential** [tɑ'rɛnʃəl] o [tɔ'rɛnʃəl] *adj* torrencial
**torrid** ['tɑrɪd] o ['tɔrɪd] *adj* tórrido

**torridity** [tɑ'rɪdɪtɪ] o [tə'rɪdɪtɪ] *s* extremo calor
**torrid zone** *s* zona tórrida
**torsion** ['tɔrʃən] *s* torsión; (mech.) torsión
**torsional** ['tɔrʃənəl] *adj* torsional
**torsion balance** *s* (phys.) balanza de torsión
**torsion pendulum** *s* péndulo de torsión
**torso** ['tɔrso] *s* (*pl:* **-sos**) torso; (f.a.) torso
**tort** [tɔrt] *s* (law) agravio indemnizable en juicio civil (*excepto infracción de contrato*)
**torticollis** [,tɔrtɪ'kɑlɪs] *s* (path.) tortícolis
**tortoise** ['tɔrtəs] *s* (zool.) tortuga, tortuga de tierra
**tortoise beetle** *s* (ent.) cásida
**tortoise shell** *s* carey, concha
**tortoise-shell** ['tɔrtəs,ʃɛl] *adj* de carey, de concha; abigarrado como el carey o la concha
**tortuosity** [,tɔrtʃʊ'ɑsɪtɪ] *s* (*pl:* **-ties**) tortuosidad
**tortuous** ['tɔrtʃʊəs] *adj* tortuoso; (fig.) tortuoso (*solapado*); (fig.) torcido (*que no obra con rectitud*)
**torture** ['tɔrtʃər] *s* tortura; *va* torturar; torcer, forzar, violentar
**torturous** ['tɔrtʃərəs] *adj* torturador
**torulus** ['tɑrʊləs] *s* (*pl:* **-li** [laɪ]) (ent.) tórulo
**torus** ['torəs] *s* (*pl:* **-ri** [raɪ]) (arch.) torés; (anat., bot. & math.) toro
**tory** ['torɪ] *s* (*pl:* **-ries**) conservador; (*cap.*) *s* tory
**Toryism** ['torɪɪzəm] *s* torismo
**tosh** [tɑʃ] *s* (slang) música celestial
**toss** [tɔs] o [tɑs] *s* echada; alcance de una echada; agitación, meneo; *va* echar (*de una parte a otra*); arrojar ligeramente; arrojar de un tirón; lanzar al aire; agitar, menear; mantear; levantar airosamente (*la cabeza*); echar a cara o cruz; lanzar (*p.ej., un comentario*); **to toss aside** echar a un lado; **to toss off** hacer muy rápidamente; tragar de un golpe; *vn* agitarse, menearse; jugar a cara y cruz; **to toss and turn** revolverse, dar vueltas (*en la cama*)
**toss-up** ['tɔs,ʌp] o ['tɑs,ʌp] *s* cara y cruz; (coll.) probabilidad igual
**tot** [tɑt] *s* párvulo; trago; total; (coll.) adición; (*pret & pp:* **totted;** *ger:* **totting**) *va & vn* (coll.) sumar
**total** ['totəl] *adj & s* total; (*pret & pp:* **-taled** o **-talled;** *ger:* **-taling** o **-talling**) *va* sumar; ascender a; formar un total de
**total abstinence** *s* abstinencia de bebidas alcohólicas
**total eclipse** *s* (astr.) eclipse total
**totalitarian** [to,tælɪ'tɛrɪən] *adj & s* totalitario
**totalitarianism** [to,tælɪ'tɛrɪənɪzəm] *s* totalitarismo
**totality** [to'tælɪtɪ] *s* (*pl:* **-ties**) totalidad
**totalization** [,totəlɪ'zeʃən] *s* totalización
**totalize** ['totəlaɪz] *va* totalizar
**totalizer** ['totə,laɪzər] *s* totalizador
**totally** ['totəlɪ] *adv* totalmente
**total war** *s* guerra total
**tote** [tot] *va* (coll.) cargar, llevar, acarrear
**totem** ['totəm] *s* tótem
**totemic** [to'tɛmɪk] *adj* totémico
**totemism** ['totəmɪzəm] *s* totemismo
**totem pole** *s* pilar totémico
**tother** ['tʌðər] (dial.) contracción de **the other**
**totipalmate** [,totɪ'pælmɪt] o [,totɪ'pælmet] *adj* (zool.) totipalmo
**totter** ['tɑtər] *s* tambaleo; *vn* tambalearse; amenazar ruina, estar para desplomarse
**tottery** ['tɑtərɪ] *adj* tambaleante, vacilante; ruinoso
**toucan** [tʊ'kɑn] o ['tukən] *s* (orn.) tucán
**touch** [tʌtʃ] *s* toque; tacto, tiento; pulsación (*del pianista o dactilógrafo*); tacto (*del piano, el pianista, la máquina de escribir, el dactilógrafo*); pizca, poquito; ramo (*de una enfermedad*); (paint.) toque; **by touch** al tacto; **out of touch with** no al corriente de; sin relaciones con; **to get in touch with** ponerse en comunicación o contacto con; **to keep in touch with** mantenerse en comunicación o contacto con; **to lose one's touch** perder el tiento; *va* tocar; conmover, enternecer; igualar, compararse con; tocar (*con la piedra de toque*); (slang) pedir prestado a; (slang) robar; **to not touch** no catar (*p.ej., vino*); **to touch off** descargar; provocar; representar con la mayor precisión; acabar; **to touch up** retocar; estimular; *vn* tocar; **to touch at** tocar en (*un puerto*); **to touch down** (aer.) aterrizar; **to touch on** o **upon** tocar
**touch-and-go** ['tʌtʃənd'go] *adj* difícil, arriesgado; hecho de prisa, incompleto
**touchback** ['tʌtʃ,bæk] *s* (football) acción de tocar el suelo con el balón detrás de su propia meta
**touchdown** ['tʌtʃ,daʊn] *s* (football) jugada que consiste en tocar el suelo con el balón detrás de la meta del adversario; tantos ganados con tal jugada
**touched** [tʌtʃt] *adj* tocado (*echado a perder; medio loco*); **touched in the head** (coll.) tocado de la cabeza
**touchhole** ['tʌtʃ,hol] *s* fogón, oído del cañón
**touching** ['tʌtʃɪŋ] *adj* conmovedor, enternecedor; *prep* tocante a, en lo que toca a
**touch-me-not** ['tʌtʃmi,nɑt] *s* (bot.) hierba de Santa Catalina; (bot.) cohombrillo amargo; persona altanera y esquiva
**touchstone** ['tʌtʃ,ston] *s* (mineral. & fig.) piedra de toque
**touch typewriting** *s* escritura al tacto, mecanografía al tacto
**touchwood** ['tʌtʃ,wʊd] *s* yesca
**touchy** ['tʌtʃɪ] *adj* (*comp:* **-ier;** *super:* **-iest**) quisquilloso, enojadizo
**tough** [tʌf] *adj* correoso, estropajoso; tenaz; difícil; malvado; alborotador, pendenciero; malo (*dícese de la suerte*); *s* alborotador, pendenciero, bribón
**toughen** ['tʌfən] *va* hacer correoso, endurecer; hacer tenaz; dificultar; *vn* ponerse correoso, endurecerse; hacerse tenaz; hacerse difícil
**toughness** ['tʌfnɪs] *s* correosidad; tenacidad; dificultad; maldad
**Toulon** [tu'lɑn] *s* Tolón
**Toulouse** [tu'luz] *s* Tolosa
**toupee** [tu'pe] o [tu'pi] *s* tupé
**tour** [tʊr] *s* jira, paseo, vuelta; viaje largo; **on tour** de viaje; **the grand tour** un viaje por los países principales de Europa; **to make a tour** hacer un viaje; **to make a tour of** recorrer; *va* viajar por, recorrer; *vn* viajar por distracción o diversión
**Touraine** [tʊ'ren] *s* la Turena
**tour de force** [tʊrdə'fɔrs] *s* juego de destreza
**touring** ['tʊrɪŋ] *s* turismo; *adj* turístico
**touring car** *s* turismo, coche de turismo
**tourist** ['tʊrɪst] *adj* turístico; *s* turista
**tourist camp** *s* campamento de turismo
**tourist class** *s* (aer. & naut.) clase turista
**tourmalin** ['tʊrməlɪn] o **tourmaline** ['tʊrməlɪn] o ['tʊrməlin] *s* (mineral.) turmalina
**tournament** ['tʊrnəmənt] o ['tʌrnəmənt] *s* torneo; (sport) torneo
**tourney** ['tʊrnɪ] o ['tʌrnɪ] *s* torneo, justa; *vn* tornear, justar
**tourniquet** ['tʊrnɪket] o ['tʌrnɪke] *s* (surg.) torniquete
**Tours** [tʊr] *s* Turs
**tousle** ['taʊzəl] *s* enredo de cabello, maraña; *va* enmarañar, despeinar
**tout** [taʊt] *s* (coll.) solicitante; (coll.) espía de las carreras de caballos (*especialmente el que busca y vende informes confidenciales*); *va* (coll.) solicitar; (coll.) importunar, molestar; (coll.) buscar, husmear o dar (*informes confidenciales sobre carreras de caballos*); (coll.) decir mil bienes de; *vn* (coll.) solicitar clientes, destinos, etc.; (coll.) espiar y obtener informes confidenciales sobre carreras de caballos
**tow** [to] *s* remolque (*acción; vehículo remolcado; cabo o sirga*); estopa; **to take a tow** hacerse remolcar, ir remolcado; **to take in tow** dar remolque a, llevar o tomar a remolque; *adj* de estopa; *va* remolcar
**towage** ['to·ɪdʒ] *s* remolque; derechos de remolque
**toward** [tord] o [tə'wɔrd] o **towards** [tordz] o [tə'wɔrdz] *prep* hacia; cerca de; tocante a; para con
**towboat** ['to,bot] *s* remolcador
**towel** ['taʊəl] *s* toalla; (*pret & pp:* **-eled** o **-elled;** *ger:* **-eling** o **-elling**) *va* secar con toalla

**toweling** o **towelling** ['tauəlıŋ] *s* género o tela para toallas
**towel rack** *s* toallero
**tower** ['tauər] *s* torre; *vn* encumbrarse
**tower clock** *s* reloj de torre
**towering** ['tauərıŋ] *adj* elevado, muy alto; sobresaliente; muy grande; muy violento
**Tower of Babel** *s* torre de Babel
**towery** ['tauərı] *adj* torreado; muy alto
**towhead** ['to,hɛd] *s* persona de pelo rubio muy pálido
**towheaded** ['to,hɛdıd] *adj* de pelo rubio muy pálido
**towhee** ['tauhi] o ['tohi] *s* (orn.) tarenga, luis, totochil
**towing service** *s* (aut.) servicio de grúa, servicio de remolque
**towline** ['to,laın] *s* cable de remolque; (naut.) sirga; (naut.) estacha (*atada al arpón ballenero*)
**town** [taun] *s* población, pueblo; **in town** a la ciudad, en la ciudad; al centro de la ciudad, en el centro de la ciudad; **to go to town** (slang) tener gran éxito; **to paint the town red** (slang) correrla, ir de parranda
**town clerk** *s* escribano municipal
**town council** *s* concejo municipal
**town crier** *s* pregonero público, voceador
**town hall** *s* casa de ayuntamiento
**town house** *s* casa de ciudad, casa en la ciudad
**townhouse** ['taun,haus] *s* (Brit.) casa de ayuntamiento
**town meeting** *s* reunión de los habitantes de una población; reunión de los electores de una ciudad (*en la Nueva Inglaterra*)
**townsfolk** ['taunz,fok] *spl* vecinos del pueblo
**township** ['taunʃıp] *s* municipio, sexmo, término municipal; subdivisión de un partido; terreno de seis millas en cuadro
**townsman** ['taunzmən] *s* (*pl:* **-men**) ciudadano, vecino; conciudadano, paisano
**townspeople** ['taunz,pipəl] *spl* vecinos del pueblo
**town talk** *s* comidilla o hablillas del pueblo
**towpath** ['to,pæθ] o ['to,pɑθ] *s* camino de sirga
**tow plane** *s* (aer.) avión de remolque
**towrope** ['to,rop] *s* cable de remolque
**tow target** *s* (aer.) blanco remolcado
**tow truck** *s* camión-grúa, grúa-remolque
**toxaemia** [tɑks'imıə] *s* var. de **toxemia**
**toxalbumin** [,tɑksæl'bjumın] *s* (biochem.) toxialbúmina
**toxemia** [tɑks'imıə] *s* (path.) toxemia
**toxemic** [tɑks'imık] *adj* toxémico
**toxic** ['tɑksık] *adj & s* tóxico
**toxicity** [tɑks'ısıtı] *s* (*pl:* **-ties**) toxicidad
**toxicogenic** [,tɑksıkə'dʒɛnık] *adj* toxicogénico o toxicógeno
**toxicological** [,tɑksıkə'lɑdʒıkəl] *adj* toxicológico
**toxicologist** [,tɑksı'kɑlədʒıst] *s* toxicólogo
**toxicology** [,tɑksı'kɑlədʒı] *s* toxicología
**toxicosis** [,tɑksı'kosıs] *s* (*pl:* **-ses** [siz]) (path.) toxicosis
**toxin** ['tɑksın] *s* (bact.) toxina
**toxiphobia** [,tɑksı'fobıə] *s* (psychopath.) toxofobia
**toy** [tɔı] *s* juguete; bagatela; dije, bujería; *adj* de jugar; de adorno; muy pequeño; miniatura (*perro*); *vn* jugar; divertirse; **to toy with** jugar con (*una persona; los sentimientos de una persona*); acariciar (*una idea*); comer melindrosamente (*p.ej., el desayuno*)
**toy bank** *s* alcancía, hucha
**toy dog** *s* perrillo, perro miniatura
**toyon** ['tojən] *s* (bot.) tollón
**toyshop** ['tɔı,ʃɑp] *s* juguetería
**toy soldier** *s* soldadito de plomo, soldado de juguete
**toy train** *s* tren de juguete
**tp.** abr. de **township**
**tr.** abr. de **transitive, transpose** y **treasurer**
**trabecula** [trə'bɛkjələ] *s* (*pl:* **-lae** [li]) (anat. & bot.) trabécula
**trace** [tres] *s* huella, rastro; indicio, señal; trazo (*delineación*); calco (*obtenido por contacto del original*); tirante (*de los arreos de una caballería*); pizca; (geom.) traza; **to kick over the traces** rebelarse; **without leaving a trace** sin dejar rastro; *va* rastrear; trazar (*p.ej., una curva; los rasgos de una persona o cosa*); calcar; localizar; recorrer (*p.ej., un circuito eléctrico en falla*); averiguar el paradero de; remontar al origen de
**traceable** ['tresəbəl] *adj* trazable
**tracer** ['tresər] *s* trazador; calcador; encargado de buscar los objetos extraviados; cédula de investigación (*para encontrar los objetos extraviados*); (chem. & phys.) trazador; *adj* (chem. & phys.) trazador
**tracer bullet** *s* bala trazante o trazadora
**tracer element** *s* (phys.) radioelemento trazador
**tracery** ['tresərı] *s* (*pl:* **-ies**) (arch.) tracería
**trachea** ['trekıə] o [trə'kiə] *s* (*pl:* **-ae** [i]) (anat., bot. & zool.) tráquea
**tracheal** ['trekıəl] o [trə'kiəl] *adj* traqueal
**tracheid** ['trekııd] *s* (bot.) traqueida
**tracheitis** [,trekı'aıtıs] *s* (path.) traqueítis
**tracheotomy** [,trekı'ɑtəmı] *s* (*pl:* **-mies**) (surg.) traqueotomía
**trachoma** [trə'komə] *s* (path.) tracoma
**trachomatous** [trə'kɑmətəs] o [trə'komətəs] *adj* tracomatoso
**trachyte** ['trekaıt] o ['trækaıt] *s* (geol.) traquita
**tracing** ['tresıŋ] *s* trazo; calco; *adj* de trazar; de calcar
**tracing paper** *s* papel de calcar
**track** [træk]] *s* huella (*que deja el pie; vestigio*); rodada, carril (*que dejan las ruedas al pasar*); estela (*que deja un barco*); vía (*del ferrocarril, los tranvías*); camino, senda; trayectoria (*p.ej., de un avión, un huracán*); llanta de oruga (*de un tractor*); sucesión (*de ideas, acontecimientos, etc.*); derrota (*rumbo que sigue un barco*); (sport) carreras y saltos; (sport) pista (*por donde corren los caballos*); (fig.) camino (*método, procedimiento*); **in one's tracks** allí mismo; **off the track** desviado; descarrilado; **on the right track** en el buen camino; **on the track** en el rastro; **to get off the track** descarrilar; (fig.) descarrilar, salirse del asunto; **to jump the track** descarrilar, salirse fuera del carril; **to keep track of** no olvidar; no perder la cuenta de; no perder de vista; **to lose track of** olvidar; perder de vista; **to make tracks** correr, irse muy de prisa; *va* rastrear, seguir la huella o la pista de; atravesar; manchar pisando, dejar pisadas en; llevar (*p.ej., barro*) con los pies; **to track down** averiguar el origen de; atrapar, seguir y capturar
**trackage** ['trækıdʒ] *s* (rail.) sistema de vías; (rail.) derecho para uso de vía; remolque
**trackhound** ['træk,haund] *s* perro rastrero
**tracking** ['trækıŋ] *adj* rastreador; *s* rastreo (*p.ej., de un satélite*)
**tracking antenna** *s* antena de rastreo
**tracking station** *s* estación de rastreo
**trackless** ['træklıs] *adj* sin rastro; sin caminos, sin tránsito; sin carriles
**trackless trolley** *s* filobús, trolebús
**track meet** *s* (sport) concurso de carreras y saltos
**track tank** *s* (rail.) atarjea de alimentación
**trackwalker** ['træk,wɔkər] *s* (rail.) guardavía, recorredor de vía
**tract** [trækt] *s* espacio (*de terreno, de tiempo*); folleto (*especialmente el de propaganda religiosa o política*); (anat.) sistema (*de órganos*)
**tractability** [,træktə'bılıtı] *s* docilidad
**tractable** ['træktəbəl] *adj* tratable; maleable, dúctil
**tractile** ['træktıl] o ['træktaıl] *adj* dúctil
**traction** ['trækʃən] *s* tracción; adherencia (*de las ruedas*); (physiol.) contracción
**traction company** *s* empresa de tranvías
**traction engine** *s* máquina de tracción
**traction wheel** *s* rueda de tracción
**tractive** ['træktıv] *adj* tractivo, de tracción
**tractor** ['træktər] *s* tractor; (aer.) hélice de tracción; (aer.) avión de tracción
**tractor-trailer** ['træktər'trelər] *s* tractocamión, semi-remolque
**trade** [tred] *s* comercio; contratación, trato, negocio; trueque, canje; oficio; parroquia, clientela; trata (*p.ej., de mujeres*); **the trades** los vientos alisios; *va* trocar, cambiar; **to trade**

in dar como parte del pago; **to trade off** deshacerse de, trocando; *vn* comerciar; comprar; **to trade in** comerciar en; **to trade on** aprovecharse de, explotar
**trade binding** *s* (b.b.) encuadernación mecánica
**trade-in** ['tred,ɪn] *s* cosa dada como pago o pago parcial en la compra de otra; trueque
**trademark** ['tred,mɑrk] *s* marca de fábrica, marca registrada, marca privativa
**trade name** *s* nombre de fábrica; razón social
**trader** ['tredər] *s* comerciante, traficante; negociador; trocador; (naut.) buque mercante
**trade school** *s* escuela de artes y oficios
**tradesman** ['tredzmən] *s* (*pl:* **-men**) tendero; comerciante; (Brit.) artesano
**tradespeople** ['tredz,pipəl] *s* tenderos; comerciantes; (Brit.) gente del oficio
**trades union** o **trade union** *s* sindicato, gremio de obreros
**trade unionism** *s* sindicalismo
**trade unionist** *s* sindicalista
**trade winds** *spl* vientos alisios
**trading account** *s* cuenta de compraventa
**trading post** *s* factoría
**trading stamp** *s* sello de premio, sello de descuento (*que se da al comprador como aliciente*)
**tradition** [trə'dɪʃən] *s* tradición
**traditional** [trə'dɪʃənəl] *adj* tradicional
**traditionalism** [trə'dɪʃənəlɪzəm] *s* tradicionalismo
**traditionally** [trə'dɪʃənəlɪ] *adv* tradicionalmente
**traditionary** [trə'dɪʃən,ɛrɪ] *adj* var. de **traditional**
**traduce** [trə'djus] o [trə'dus] *va* calumniar
**traducer** [trə'djusər] o [trə'dusər] *s* calumniador
**traducianism** [trə'djuʃənɪzəm] o [trə'duʃənɪzəm] *s* (theol.) traducianismo
**traffic** ['træfɪk] *s* tráfico (*comercio; tránsito, circulación de personas y vehículos*); trata (*p.ej., de mujeres*); (*pret & pp:* **-ficked;** *ger:* **-ficking**) *vn* traficar
**traffic circle** *s* glorieta de tráfico, círculo de tráfico
**traffic control** *s* regulación de tráfico
**traffic court** *s* juzgado de tráfico
**traffic jam** *s* bloqueo, embotellamiento, tapón de tráfico
**trafficker** ['træfɪkər] *s* traficante
**traffic light** *s* luz de tráfico, semáforo
**traffic manager** *s* (com.) jefe de expediciones; (rail.) jefe de tráfico
**traffic sign** o **signal** *s* señal de tráfico, señal urbana
**traffic ticket** *s* aviso de multa (*por estacionar un auto indebidamente*)
**tragacanth** ['trægəkænθ] *s* (bot.) tragacanto (*árbol y goma*)
**tragedian** [trə'dʒidɪən] *s* trágico (*autor; actor*)
**tragedienne** o **tragédienne** [trə,dʒidɪ'ɛn] *s* trágica (*actriz*)
**tragedy** ['trædʒɪdɪ] *s* (*pl:* **-dies**) tragedia
**tragic** ['trædʒɪk] o **tragical** ['trædʒɪkəl] *adj* trágico
**tragically** ['trædʒɪkəlɪ] *adv* trágicamente
**tragicomedy** [,trædʒɪ'kɑmədɪ] *s* (*pl:* **-dies**) tragicomedia
**tragicomic** [,trædʒɪ'kɑmɪk] o **tragicomical** [,trædʒɪ'kɑmɪkəl] *adj* tragicómico
**tragus** ['tregəs] *s* (*pl:* **-gi** [dʒaɪ]) (anat.) trago
**trail** [trel] *s* huella, pista, rastro; sendero, vereda (*p.ej., que cruza un yermo*); estela (*de humo, de polvo, de un cometa, cohete, etc.*); cola (*de vestido*); (arti.) gualdera; *va* arrastrar (*llevar por el suelo*); rastrear, seguir la pista de; cazar siguiendo la pista; andar detrás de; pisar (*la hierba*) hasta formar una senda; llevar (*p.ej., barro*) con los pies; (mil.) bajar (*el arma*); *vn* arrastrar (*moverse como las serpientes; colgar, p.ej., un vestido, hasta tocar en el suelo*); rezagarse, ir rezagado; arrastrarse, trepar (*una planta*); **to trail off** desaparecer poco a poco, desvanecerse (*p.ej., el humo*)
**trail blazer** *s* explorador, iniciador, pionero
**trailer** ['trelər] *s* persona o animal que sigue la pista; remolque vivienda, vivienda remolque, autocasa, coche-habitación, casa en ruedas, casa rodante (*que se acopla a un auto*); acoplado, remolque, carretón de remolque; camión acoplado; tranvía acoplado; (bot.) planta rastrera; (mov.) anuncio de próximas atracciones
**trailer camp** *s* campamento para coches-habitaciones
**trailer court** *s* parque de remolques viviendas
**trailing arbutus** *s* (bot.) epigea rastrera
**trailing edge** *s* (aer.) borde de salida
**trail rope** *s* arrastradera (*de globo aerostático*); (mil.) prolonga
**trail spade** *s* (arti.) espolón
**train** [tren] *s* tren (*serie, p.ej., de ondas*); cola (*de un vestido*); hilo (*del pensamiento*); reguero de pólvora; (rail.) tren; *va* adiestrar; apuntar (*un arma*); guiar (*las plantas*); (sport) entrenar; *vn* adiestrarse; (sport) entrenarse
**trainband** ['tren,bænd] *s* (Brit. hist.) banda armada
**trained dog** *s* perro maestro
**trained nurse** *s* enfermera graduada
**trainee** [tre'ni] *s* persona que se entrena; (mil.) recluta
**trainer** ['trenər] *s* amaestrador; (sport) entrenador; (aer.) avión de entrenamiento
**training** ['trenɪŋ] *s* instrucción, preparación; adiestramiento; (sport) entrenamiento
**training camp** *s* (mil.) campamento de instrucción militar, campo de entrenamiento
**training school** *s* escuela práctica; reformatorio
**training ship** *s* (nav.) buque escuela
**trainload** ['tren,lod] *s* carga de un tren completo
**trainman** ['trenmən] *s* (*pl:* **-men**) (rail.) ferroviario; (rail.) guardafrenos
**train oil** *s* aceite de ballena u otro pescado
**train wrecker** *s* descarrilador de trenes
**trait** [tret] *s* rasgo, característica; golpe, toque
**traitor** ['tretər] *s* traidor
**traitorous** ['tretərəs] *adj* traidor, traicionero
**traitress** ['tretrɪs] *s* traidora
**Trajan** ['tredʒən] *s* Trajano
**trajectory** [trə'dʒɛktərɪ] *s* (*pl:* **-ries**) trayectoria
**tram** [træm] *s* trama (*seda para tramar*); (Brit.) tranvía; (min.) vagoneta; (mach.) calibre de alineación
**tramcar** ['træm,kɑr] *s* (Brit.) tranvía
**trammel** ['træməl] *s* impedimento, obstáculo; traba, manea, maniota; red (*para cazar o pescar*); trasmallo; garabato de chimenea; (*pret & pp:* **-meled** o **-melled;** *ger:* **-meling** o **-melling**) *va* impedir, estorbar; trabar, poner trabas a
**trammel net** *s* trasmallo
**tramontane** [trə'mɑnten] o ['træmənten] *adj* tramontano
**tramp** [træmp] *s* vagabundo; marcha pesada, paso pesado; pataleo; paseo largo; vapor volandero; *va* pisar con fuerza; recorrer a pie; *vn* patullar; andar o viajar a pie; vagar; vagabundear
**trample** ['træmpəl] *s* pisoteo; *va* pisotear; *vn* patullar; **to trample on** o **upon** pisotear, hollar
**trampoline** ['træmpəlɪn] *s* trampolín de acróbata o gimnasta
**tramp steamer** *s* vapor volandero, buque trampa
**tramway** ['træm,we] *s* vía aérea, funicular aéreo; (Brit.) tranvía
**trance** [træns] o [trɑns] *s* rapto, arrobamiento; trance, estado hipnótico; ensimismamiento; *va* encantar, enajenar
**tranquil** ['træŋkwɪl] *adj* tranquilo
**tranquilize** ['træŋkwɪlaɪz] *va* tranquilizar; *vn* tranquilizar; tranquilizarse
**tranquilizer** ['træŋkwɪ,laɪzər] *s* (med.) tranquilizador
**tranquillity** o **tranquility** [træŋ'kwɪlɪtɪ] *s* tranquilidad
**trans.** abr. de **transactions, transitive** y **transportation**
**transact** [træn'zækt] o [træns'ækt] *va* tramitar, llevar a cabo
**transaction** [træn'zækʃən] o [træns'ækʃən] *s* tramitación; transacción; **transactions** *spl* actas (*de una sociedad erudita*)
**transactor** [træn'zæktər] o [træns'æktər] *s* tramitador

**transalpine** [træns'ælpɪn] o [træns'ælpaɪn] *adj* transalpino
**trans-Andean** [ˌtrænsæn'diən] o [træns'ændɪən] *adj* transandino
**transatlantic** [ˌtrænsət'læntɪk] *adj & s* transatlántico
**Transcaucasia** [ˌtrænskɔ'keʒə] o [ˌtrænskɔ'keʃə] *s* la Transcaucasia
**transceiver** [træn'sivər] *s* (rad.) transceptor
**transcend** [træn'sɛnd] *va* exceder, sobrepujar, superar; *vn* sobresalir
**transcendence** [træn'sɛndəns] *s* excelencia, superioridad; (philos.) trascendencia
**transcendent** [træn'sɛndənt] *adj* excelente, superior; (philos. & theol.) trascendente
**transcendental** [ˌtrænsɛn'dɛntəl] *adj* sobresaliente; sobrenatural, metafísico; idealista, espiritual; obscuro, incomprensible, vago; (philos. & math.) trascendental
**transcendentalism** [ˌtrænsɛn'dɛntəlɪzəm] *s* (philos.) transcendentalismo
**transcendentalist** [ˌtrænsɛn'dɛntəlɪst] *s* transcendentalista
**transcontinental** [ˌtrænskɑntɪ'nɛntəl] *adj* transcontinental
**transcribe** [træn'skraɪb] *va* transcribir; (mus. & rad.) transcribir
**transcript** ['trænskrɪpt] *s* trasunto, traslado; (educ.) certificado de estudios, copia del expediente académico, hoja de estudios
**transcription** [træn'skrɪpʃən] *s* transcripción; (mus. & rad.) transcripción
**transducer** [træns'djusər] o [træns'dusər] *s* (phys.) transductor
**transect** [træn'sɛkt] *va* cruzar de un lado a otro, dividir cruzando
**transept** ['trænsɛpt] *s* (arch.) crucero, transepto; (arch.) brazo del crucero
**transfer** ['trænsfər] *s* traslado; transbordo; (rail.) vía de transferencia, estación de transferencia; contraseña o billete de transferencia; transporte, reporte (*de litografía*); (law) transferencia; [træns'fʌr] o ['trænsfər] (*pret & pp:* **-ferred**; *ger:* **-ferring**) *va* trasladar, transferir; transbordar; transportar, reportar (*una prueba litográfica a la piedra*); (law) transferir; *vn* cambiar de tren, tranvía, etc.
**transferable** [træns'fʌrəbəl] o ['trænsfərəbəl] *adj* transferible
**transfer agent** *s* (com.) agente de transferencias
**transference** [træns'fʌrəns] o ['trænsfərəns] *s* transferencia
**transferor** [træns'fʌrər] *s* (law) transferidor
**transferrer** [træns'fʌrər] *s* transferidor
**transfer table** *s* (rail.) carro transbordador
**transfiguration** [trænsˌfɪgjə'reʃən] *s* transfiguración; (*cap.*) *s* (Bib. & eccl.) Transfiguración
**transfigure** [træns'fɪgjər] *va* transfigurar
**transfix** [træns'fɪks] *va* traspasar, espetar; dejar atónito o confuso (*por maravilla, dolor, etc.*)
**transfixion** [træns'fɪkʃən] *s* transfixión; (surg.) transfixión
**transform** [træns'fɔrm] *va* transformar; (elec., math. & phys.) transformar; *vn* transformarse
**transformation** [ˌtrænsfər'meʃən] *s* transformación (*acción o efecto de transformar; peluca*)
**transformative** [træns'fɔrmətɪv] *adj* transformativo
**transformer** [træns'fɔrmər] *s* transformador; (elec.) transformador
**transformism** [træns'fɔrmɪzəm] *s* (biol.) transformismo
**transformist** [træns'fɔrmɪst] *adj & s* transformista
**transfuse** [træns'fjuz] *va* transfundir; (med.) hacer una transfusión de (*p.ej., sangre*); (med.) hacer una transfusión a (*una persona*)
**transfuser** [træns'fjuzər] *s* transfusor
**transfusion** [træns'fjuʒən] *s* transfusión; (med.) transfusión de sangre
**transfusionist** [træns'fjuʒənɪst] *s* (med.) transfusionista
**transgress** [træns'grɛs] *va* violar, quebrantar, traspasar; exceder, traspasar (*p.ej., los límites de la prudencia*); *vn* cometer transgresión; prevaricar, pecar
**transgression** [træns'grɛʃən] *s* transgresión; prevaricación, pecado
**transgressor** [træns'grɛsər] *s* transgresor; prevaricador, pecador
**tranship** [træn'ʃɪp] (*pret & pp:* **-shipped**; *ger:* **-shipping**) *va* var. de **transship**
**transhipment** [træn'ʃɪpmənt] *s* var. de **transshipment**
**transiency** ['trænʃənsɪ] *s* transitoriedad
**transient** ['trænʃənt] *adj* pasajero, transitorio; transeúnte; de tránsito; *s* transeúnte; (elec.) corriente momentánea
**transistor** [træn'sɪstər] *s* (elec.) transistor
**transistorize** [træn'sɪstəraɪz] *va* transistorizar
**transit** ['trænsɪt] o ['trænzɪt] *s* tránsito; (astr. & surv.) tránsito; **in transit** de o en tránsito; *va* atravesar; (surv.) invertir; *vn* transitar
**transition** [træn'zɪʃən] *s* transición
**transitional** [træn'zɪʃənəl] *adj* transitivo, de transición
**transitive** ['trænsɪtɪv] *adj* transitivo; (gram.) transitivo; *s* (gram.) verbo transitivo
**transitory** ['trænsɪˌtorɪ] *adj* transitorio
**transit visa** *s* visado de tránsito
**Trans-Jordan** [træns'dʒɔrdən] o **Transjordania** [ˌtrænsdʒɔr'denɪə] *s* la Transjordania
**translatable** [træns'letəbəl] *adj* traducible
**translate** [træns'let] o ['trænslet] *va* traducir (*de una lengua a otra*); trasladar (*de un lugar a otro*); (mech. & telg.) trasladar; (fig.) enajenar, extasiar; *vn* traducir; traducirse
**translation** [træns'leʃən] *s* traducción; (mech. & telg.) traslación
**translator** [træns'letər] o ['trænsletər] *s* traductor; (telg. & telp.) traslator
**transliterate** [træns'lɪtəret] *va* transcribir (*letras, palabras, etc.*)
**transliteration** [trænsˌlɪtə'reʃən] *s* transcripción
**translucence** [træns'lusəns] o **translucency** [træns'lusənsɪ] *s* translucidez
**translucent** [træns'lusənt] *adj* translúcido
**transmarine** [ˌtrænsmə'rin] *adj* transmarino
**transmigrate** [træns'maɪgret] o ['trænsmɪgret] *vn* transmigrar
**transmigration** [ˌtrænsmaɪ'greʃən] o [ˌtrænsmɪ'greʃən] *s* transmigración
**transmissibility** [trænsˌmɪsɪ'bɪlɪtɪ] *s* transmisibilidad
**transmissible** [træns'mɪsɪbəl] *adj* transmisible
**transmission** [træns'mɪʃən] *s* transmisión; (aut.) cambio de marchas o cambio de velocidades
**transmission gear** *s* (aut.) engranaje de transmisión
**transmission-gear box** [træns'mɪʃənˌgɪr] *s* (aut.) caja de cambio de marchas, caja de velocidades
**transmit** [træns'mɪt] (*pret & pp:* **-mitted**; *ger:* **-mitting**) *va & vn* transmitir
**transmittal** [træns'mɪtəl] *s* transmisión
**transmitter** [træns'mɪtər] *s* transmisor; (rad., telg. & telp.) transmisor
**transmitting set** *s* (rad.) aparato transmisor
**transmitting station** *s* (rad.) estación transmisora
**transmogrify** [træns'mɑgrɪfaɪ] (*pret & pp:* **-fied**) *va* (hum.) transformar como por encanto, modificar como por encanto, modificar con una rapidez sorprendente
**transmutable** [træns'mjutəbəl] *adj* transmutable
**transmutation** [ˌtrænsmju'teʃən] *s* transmutación; (alchem. & chem.) transmutación; (biol.) transformismo
**transmute** [træns'mjut] *va* transmutar; *vn* transmutar; transmutarse
**transoceanic** [ˌtrænsoʃɪ'ænɪk] *adj* transoceánico
**transom** ['trænsəm] *s* (carp.) travesaño; montante (*hueco cuadrilongo sobre una puerta*); (naut.) yugo de popa
**transonic** [træn'sɑnɪk] *adj* transónico
**transpacific** [ˌtrænspə'sɪfɪk] *adj* transpacífico
**transpadane** ['trænspəˌden] o [træns'peden] *adj* transpadano
**transparence** [træns'pɛrəns] *s* transparencia

**transparency** [træns'pɛrənsɪ] *s* (*pl:* **-cies**) transparencia; transparente (*figura en un papel translúcido*)
**transparent** [træns'pɛrənt]] *adj* transparente; (fig.) transparente
**transpiration** [,trænspɪ'reʃən] *s* transpiración; (bot. & physiol.) transpiración
**transpire** [træns'paɪr] *va* transpirar; *vn* transpirar; (fig.) transpirar (*dejarse conocer una cosa secreta*); (coll.) acontecer, tener lugar
**transplant** ['trænsplænt] o ['trænsplɑnt] *s* trasplante; [træns'plænt] o [træns'plɑnt] *va* trasplantar; (surg.) trasplantar; *vn* trasplantarse
**transplantable** [træns'plæntəbəl] o [træns'plɑntəbəl] *adj* trasplantable
**transplantation** [,trænsplæn'teʃən] *s* trasplante, trasplantación
**transplanter** [træns'plæntər] o [træns'plɑntər] *s* trasplantador (*persona o instrumento*)
**transpolar** [træns'polər] *adj* traspolar
**transport** ['trænsport] *s* transporte; (aer., naut. & fig.) transporte; deportado, desterrado; [træns'port] *va* transportar; deportar, desterrar; (fig.) transportar
**transportable** [træns'portəbəl] *adj* transportable; pasible o digno de deportación o destierro
**transportation** [,trænspor'teʃən] *s* transporte; deportación, destierro; (U.S.A.) pasaje, billete (*de viaje*); (U.S.A.) coste del transporte, precio de viaje
**transport worker** *s* transportista
**transposal** [træns'pozəl] *s* transposición
**transpose** [træns'poz] *va* transponer; (alg.) transponer; (mus.) transportar
**transposition** [,trænspə'zɪʃən] *s* transposición; (mus.) transposición
**trans-Pyrenean** [,trænspɪrɪ'niən] *adj* transpirenaico
**transship** [træns'ʃɪp] (*pret & pp:* **-shipped; ger: -shipping**) *va* transbordar
**transshipment** [træns'ʃɪpmənt] *s* transbordo
**trans-Siberian** [,trænssaɪ'bɪrɪən] *adj* transiberiano
**transubstantial** [,trænsəb'stænʃəl] *adj* transubstancial
**transubstantiate** [,trænsəb'stænʃɪet] *va* transubstanciar; *vn* transubstanciarse
**transubstantiation** [,trænsəb,stænʃɪ'eʃən] *s* transubstanciación
**transuranic** [,trænsjʊ'rænɪk] *adj* (chem.) transuránico
**transurethral** [,trænsjʊ'riθrəl] *adj* transuretral
**transversal** [træns'vʌrsəl] *adj* transversal; *s* (geom.) línea transversal
**transverse** [træns'vʌrs] o ['trænsvərs] *adj* transverso; *s* transverso; (geom.) eje transverso
**transvestite** [træns'vɛstaɪt] *adj & s* transvestido
**transvestitism** [træns'vɛstɪtɪzəm] *s* transvestismo o transvestitismo
**Transylvania** [,trænsɪl'venɪə] *s* la Transilvania
**Transylvanian** [,trænsɪl'venɪən] *adj & s* transilvano
**trap** [træp] *s* trampa; bombillo, sifón (*tubo doblemente acodado*); coche ligero de dos ruedas; (sport) lanzaplatos, lanzadiscos (*para disparar pichones de barro*); (geol.) trap; (slang) boca; **traps** *spl* (mus.) instrumentos de percusión; (coll.) equipaje, efectos personales; **to fall into the trap** caer en el lazo o la trampa; **to spring a trap** hacer saltar una trampa; (*pret & pp:* **trapped;** *ger:* **trapping**) *va* entrampar; atrapar (*a un ladrón*); proveer o tapar con bombillo; adornar, enjaezar; *vn* entrampar
**trap door** *s* escotillón, trampa; (theat.) escotillón, pescante
**trapeze** [trə'piz] *s* (sport) trapecio; (geom.) trapezoide
**trapeze performer** *s* trapecista
**trapezial** [trə'pizɪəl] *adj* trapecial; (geom.) trapezoidal
**trapezium** [trə'pizɪəm] *s* (*pl:* **-ums** o **-a** [ə]) (anat.) trapecio; (geom.) trapezoide
**trapezius** [trə'pizɪəs] *s* (anat.) trapecio
**trapezohedron** [,træpɪzo'hidrən] *s* (cryst.) trapezoedro
**trapezoid** ['træpɪzɔɪd] *s* (anat.) trapezoide; (geom.) trapecio
**trapezoidal** [,træpɪ'zɔɪdəl] *adj* (geom.) trapecial
**trapper** ['træpər] *s* cazador de alforja, trampero
**trappings** ['træpɪŋz] *spl* jaeces (*de los caballos*); adornos, atavíos
**Trappist** ['træpɪst] *adj & s* trapense
**trapshooter** ['træp,ʃutər] *s* tirador al vuelo
**trapshooting** ['træp,ʃutɪŋ] *s* tiro al vuelo, tiro de pichón
**trash** [træʃ] *s* broza (*despojo de las plantas*); basura, desecho; cachivaches; disparates; gentuza
**trash can** *s* basurero (*recipiente*)
**trash collection** *s* recogida de basuras
**trashy** ['træʃɪ] *adj* (*comp:* **-ier;** *super:* **-iest**) baladí, fútil; vil, despreciable
**Trasteverine** [trɑs'tevərɪn] *adj & s* transtiberino
**trauma** ['trɔmə] *s* (*pl:* **-mata** [mətə] o **-mas**) (path. & psychopath.) trauma
**traumatic** [trɔ'mætɪk] *adj* traumático
**traumaticine** [trɔ'mætɪsin] o [trɔ'mætɪsɪn] *s* (pharm.) traumaticina
**traumatism** ['trɔmətɪzəm] *s* (path.) traumatismo
**travail** ['trævel] o ['trævəl] *s* afán, labor, pena; dolores de parto; *vn* afanarse; estar de parto
**travel** ['trævəl] *s* viaje; circulación, tráfico; (mach.) recorrido; (*pret & pp:* **-eled** o **-elled;** *ger:* **-eling** o **-elling**) *va* hacer viajar; viajar por; recorrer; *vn* viajar; andar, correr
**travel agency** *s* agencia de viajes
**travel bureau** *s* oficina de turismo
**traveled** o **travelled** ['trævəld] *adj* que ha viajado mucho; muy recorrido por los viajeros
**traveler** o **traveller** ['trævələr] *s* viajero; (com.) viajante
**traveler's check** *s* cheque de viajeros
**traveler's-joy** ['trævələrz'dʒɔɪ] *s* (bot.) hierba de pordioseros
**traveler's tree** *s* (bot.) árbol del viajero, ravenala
**traveling** o **travelling** ['trævəlɪŋ] *adj* viajante; de viaje, para viajar
**traveling crane** *s* grúa corredera o corrediza, grúa de puente
**traveling expenses** *spl* gastos de viaje
**traveling fellowship** *s* bolsa de viaje, beca de viaje
**traveling salesman** *s* viajante, agente viajero
**travelog** o **travelogue** ['trævəlɔg] o ['trævəlɑg] *s* conferencia sobre viajes
**traverse** ['trævərs] o [trə'vʌrs] *s* paso, pasaje; travesía (*distancia*); travesío (*lugar*); (arch.) través; (arch.) galería que cruza una iglesia; (carp.) travesaño; (fort.) traversa, través; camino oblicuo o en zigzag; (naut.) ruta oblicua, bordada oblicua; (geom.) línea transversal; (surv.) línea quebrada; (law) objeción legal; obstáculo, oposición; través, revés (*desgracia*); *adj* travieso, transversal; *adv* de través, transversalmente; *va* atravesar, cruzar; pasar por, recorrer; hacer dar vueltas o rodar; estorbar, impedir; (arti.) mover o volver lateralmente; (fig.) escudriñar, examinar con cuidado; (law) negar, oponerse a; *vn* atravesarse; hacer vaivén; rodar, girar
**traverse circle** *s* (arti.) círculo recorrido por la cureña al girar
**traverse drill** *s* taladro de ajuste lateral, taladro ranurador
**traverser** [trə'vʌrsər] *s* (rail.) carro transbordador
**traverse table** *s* (surv.) cuadro de latitudes y desviaciones; (rail.) carro transbordador
**travertin** ['trævərtɪn] o **travertine** ['trævərtɪn] o ['trævərtin] *s* (mineral.) travertino
**travesty** ['trævɪstɪ] *s* (*pl:* **-ties**) parodia; (*pret & pp:* **-tied**) *va* parodiar
**trawl** [trɔl] *s* red barredera, jábega; palangre sostenido por boyas; *va & vn* pescar a la rastra; pescar con palangre
**trawler** ['trɔlər] *s* jabeguero; barco para la pesca a la rastra; palangrero (*persona y barco*)

**trawling** [ˈtrɔlɪŋ] *s* pesca a la rastra
**trawl line** *s* espinal
**tray** [tre] *s* bandeja; batea (*p.ej., de baúl*); (chem. & phot.) cubeta
**tray cloth** *s* cubrebandeja
**treacherous** [ˈtrɛtʃərəs] *adj* traicionero, traidor; incierto, poco seguro
**treachery** [ˈtrɛtʃərɪ] *s* (*pl:* **-ies**) traición
**treacle** [ˈtrikəl] *s* (Brit.) melaza
**tread** [trɛd] *s* pisada; huella, peldaño, grada (*de escalera*); barrote o escalón (*de escala*); suela (*del zapato, del estribo*); horquilla (*de los zancos*); galladura, prendedura (*en la yema del huevo*); (aut.) huella, rodamiento, banda de rodamiento; (aut.) distancia transversal entre las ruedas; (rail.) cara de las ruedas; (rail.) superficie de rodadura; (rail.) entrevía; (*pret:* **trod;** *pp:* **trodden** o **trod**) *va* pisar; pisotear; trillar; apoyar el pie en (*p.ej., un pedal*); abrumar, agobiar, oprimir; seguir (*p.ej., el paso de una persona*); *vn* andar, caminar; poner el pie; **to tread on** pisar; seguir de cerca
**treadle** [ˈtrɛdəl] *s* pedal; *va* hacer funcionar con pedal; *vn* pedalear
**treadmill** [ˈtrɛd,mɪl] *s* rueda de andar; (fig.) noria (*cosa en que, sin adelantar nada, se anda como dando vueltas*)
**treas.** abr. de **treasurer** y **treasury**
**treason** [ˈtrizən] *s* traición
**treasonable** [ˈtrizənəbəl] o **treasonous** [ˈtrizənəs] *adj* traicionero, traidor
**treasure** [ˈtrɛʒər] *s* tesoro; (fig.) tesoro (*persona o cosa de mucho precio*); *va* atesorar; apreciar mucho, considerar o guardar como un tesoro
**treasure house** *s* tesoro (*lugar de riquezas*)
**treasurer** [ˈtrɛʒərər] *s* tesorero
**treasurership** [ˈtrɛʒərər,ʃɪp] *s* tesorería
**treasure-trove** [ˈtrɛʒərˈtrov] *s* tesoro hallado
**treasury** [ˈtrɛʒərɪ] *s* (*pl:* **-ies**) tesorería; tesoro; (fig.) tesoro (*enciclopedia; persona que sabe mucho*); (*cap.*) *s* (Brit.) ministerio de Hacienda
**Treasury Department** *s* (U.S.A.) ministerio de Hacienda
**treasury note** *s* (U.S.A.) bono del ministerio de hacienda
**treat** [trit] *s* convite; regalo; convidada (*invitación a beber*); *va* tratar; regalar; convidar; curar (*un enfermo*); **to treat as** tratar (*a una persona*) de (*p.ej., amigo*); tomar (*una cosa*) de (*p.ej., broma*); *vn* tratar; regalar; convidar; **to treat of** tratar de
**treatise** [ˈtritɪs] *s* tratado (*escrito, libro*)
**treatment** [ˈtritmənt] *s* tratamiento
**treaty** [ˈtritɪ] *s* (*pl:* **-ties**) tratado (*pacto*)
**Trebizond** [ˈtrɛbɪzɑnd] *s* Trebisonda
**treble** [ˈtrɛbəl] *adj* triple; sobreagudo; (mus.) atiplado; (mus.) de tiple; *s* (mus.) tiple; *va* triplicar; *vn* triplicarse
**treble clef** *s* (mus.) clave de sol
**trebly** [ˈtrɛblɪ] *adv* tres veces, triplicadamente
**tree** [tri] *s* árbol; (archaic) horca (*para ahorcar a los condenados*); (archaic) cruz (*en que murió Jesucristo*); **to bark up the wrong tree** ir descaminado, quejarse sin razón; **up a tree** (coll.) arrinconado, en un aprieto, entre la espada y la pared; *va* proveer de puntal u otro apoyo de madera; ahuyentar por un árbol; estirar sobre la horma (*de zapatero*); (coll.) poner en aprieto; *vn* ramificarse; huir por un árbol
**tree-dozer** [ˈtri,dozər] *s* tumbadora
**tree fern** *s* (bot.) helecho arbóreo
**tree frog** *s* (zool.) rana arbórea; (zool.) rubeta, rana de San Antonio
**tree heath** *s* (bot.) brezo albarino, blanco o castellano
**treeless** [ˈtrilɪs] *adj* sin árboles
**treenail** [ˈtri,nel] o [ˈtrɛnəl] *s* clavija, taruguillo de madera
**tree of heaven** *s* (bot.) árbol del cielo, barniz del Japón
**tree of knowledge of good and evil** *s* árbol de la ciencia del bien y del mal
**tree of life** *s* (Bib. & bot.) árbol de la vida
**tree surgeon** *s* cirujano de los árboles
**tree surgery** *s* cirugía de los árboles
**tree toad** *s* (zool.) rubeta, rana de San Antonio
**treetop** [ˈtri,tɑp] *s* copa, cima de árbol
**tréflé cross** [,treˈfle] *s* (her.) cruz trebolada
**trefoil** [ˈtrifɔɪl] *s* (bot. & arch.) trébol
**trefoil arch** *s* (arch.) arco trebolado
**trek** [trɛk] *s* jornada; migración; (*pret & pp:* **trekked;** *ger:* **trekking**) *vn* viajar; emigrar; viajar en carromato
**trellis** [ˈtrɛlɪs] *s* enrejado, espaldera; *va* proveer de enrejado o espaldera; entrelazar, entretejer; fijar sobre una espaldera
**trelliswork** [ˈtrɛlɪs,wʌrk] *s* enrejado, espaldera
**trematode** [ˈtrɛmətod] o [ˈtrimətod] *s* (zool.) tremátodo
**tremble** [ˈtrɛmbəl] *s* temblor; estremecimiento; *vn* temblar; tiritar; estremecerse
**trembler** [ˈtrɛmblər] *s* temblador; (rel.) temblador (*cuáquero*); (elec.) temblador
**trembly** [ˈtrɛmblɪ] *adj* tembloroso, trémulo
**tremendous** [trɪˈmɛndəs] *adj* tremendo; (coll.) tremendo (*muy grande*)
**tremolite** [ˈtrɛməlaɪt] *s* (mineral.) tremolita
**tremolo** [ˈtrɛməlo] *s* (*pl:* **-los**) (mus.) trémolo
**tremor** [ˈtrɛmər] o [ˈtrimər] *s* temblor; conmoción, estremecimiento; (path.) temblor
**tremulous** [ˈtrɛmjələs] *adj* trémulo; tímido, temeroso
**trenail** [ˈtri,nel] o [ˈtrɛnəl] *s* var. de **treenail**
**trench** [trɛntʃ] *s* foso, zanja; acequia, cauce; (mil.) trinchera; *va* hacer fosos o zanjas en; atrincherar; hacer trincheras en; *vn* abrirse camino (*p.ej., un torrente*); hacer trincheras; invadir; **to trench on** o **upon** lindar con, tocar; invadir, pasar los límites de
**trenchancy** [ˈtrɛntʃənsɪ] *s* agudeza; mordacidad; energía
**trenchant** [ˈtrɛntʃənt] *adj* agudo; incisivo, mordaz, punzante; enérgico; bien definido, bien delineado
**trench coat** *s* trinchera
**trencher** [ˈtrɛntʃər] *s* (hist.) tajadero, plato trinchero
**trencherman** [ˈtrɛntʃərmən] *s* (*pl:* **-men**) comilón; gorrón, parásito, pegote; **to be a good trencherman** tener buen diente
**trench fever** *s* (path.) fiebre de las trincheras
**trench foot** *s* (path.) pie de trinchera, micetoma del pie
**trench gun** o **mortar** *s* (arti.) mortero de trinchera
**trench mouth** *s* (path.) estomatitis ulcerosa epidémica
**trench warfare** *s* guerra de trincheras
**trend** [trɛnd] *s* dirección, curso, tendencia; *vn* dirigirse, tender
**Trent** [trɛnt] *s* Trento
**trepan** [trɪˈpæn] *s* (min. & surg.) trépano; (*pret & pp:* **-panned;** *ger:* **-panning**) *va* (mach. & surg.) trepanar
**trepanation** [,trɛpəˈneʃən] *s* trepanación
**trepang** [trɪˈpæŋ] *s* (zool.) holoturia; holoturias desecadas
**trephine** [trɪˈfaɪn] o [trɪˈfin] *s* (surg.) trefina; *va* (surg.) trefinar
**trepidation** [,trɛpɪˈdeʃən] *s* miedo, terror; trepidación (*vibración*); (path.) trepidación (*clonus del pie*)
**trespass** [ˈtrɛspəs] *s* entrada sin derecho; infracción, violación; pecado, culpa; *vn* entrar sin derecho; abusar; pecar; **no trespassing** prohibida la entrada, prohibido el paso; **to trespass against** pecar contra; **to trespass on** entrar o meterse sin derecho en; infringir, violar; abusar de (*p.ej., la paciencia de uno*)
**trespasser** [ˈtrɛspəsər] *s* intruso; infractor, violador; pecador
**tress** [trɛs] *s* trenza; bucle, rizo
**trestle** [ˈtrɛsəl] *s* caballete; puente o viaducto de caballetes
**trestle bridge** *s* puente de caballetes
**trestletree** [ˈtrɛsəl,tri] *s* (naut.) bao de los palos
**trestlework** [ˈtrɛsəl,wʌrk] *s* construcción, estructura u obra de caballetes; castillejo (*andamio*)
**Treves** [trivz] *s* Tréveris
**trey** [tre] *s* tres (*naipe, dado o ficha de dominó con tres señales*)
**triad** [ˈtraɪæd] *s* tríada; (mus.) acorde de tres sonidos
**triadelphous** [,traɪəˈdɛlfəs] *adj* (bot.) triadelfo

**trial** [ˈtraɪəl] *s* ensayo, prueba, experimento; aflicción, desgracia, mortificación; (law) juicio, proceso, vista de una causa; **on trial** a prueba, puesto a prueba; (law) en juicio; **to bring to trial, to put on trial** (law) encausar, poner en tela de juicio; **to stand trial** (law) ser procesado; *adj* de ensayo, de prueba
**trial and error** *s* tanteo, método de tanteos
**trial balance** *s* (com.) balance de prueba, cotejo del déficit y superávit en una cuenta
**trial balloon** *s* globo sonda; (fig.) globo sonda (*anuncio hecho para probar la opinión pública*); **to send up a trial balloon** (fig.) lanzar un globo sonda
**trial by jury** *s* (law) juicio por jurado
**trial jury** *s* (law) jurado procesal
**trial order** *s* (com.) pedido de ensayo
**trial run** *s* marcha de ensayo
**triandrous** [traɪˈændrəs] *adj* (bot.) triandro
**triangle** [ˈtraɪˌæŋgəl] *s* (geom., mus. & fig.) triángulo; escuadra (*del delineante*); (*cap.*) *s* (astr.) Triángulo
**triangular** [traɪˈæŋgjələr] *adj* triangular
**triangulate** [traɪˈæŋgjəlet] *adj* triangulado; *va* triangular
**triangulation** [traɪˌæŋgjəˈleʃən] *s* triangulación
**Triassic** [traɪˈæsɪk] *adj* & *s* (geol.) triásico
**triatomic** [ˌtraɪəˈtɑmɪk] *adj* (chem.) triatómico
**triaxial** [traɪˈæksɪəl] *adj* triaxial
**tribade** [ˈtrɪbəd] *s* tríbada
**tribadism** [ˈtrɪbədɪzəm] *s* tribadismo
**tribal** [ˈtraɪbəl] *adj* tribal
**tribally** [ˈtraɪbəlɪ] *adv* según la tribu; en tribus
**tribasic** [traɪˈbesɪk] *adj* (chem.) tribásico
**tribe** [traɪb] *s* tribu
**tribesman** [ˈtraɪbzmən] *s* (*pl:* **-men**) miembro de una tribu
**tribrach** [ˈtraɪbræk] o [ˈtrɪbræk] *s* (pros.) tribraquio
**tribulation** [ˌtrɪbjəˈleʃən] *s* tribulación
**tribunal** [trɪˈbjunəl] o [traɪˈbjunəl] *s* tribunal; (fig.) tribunal (*de la opinión pública, de la conciencia, etc.*)
**tribunate** [ˈtrɪbjənɪt] o [ˈtrɪbjənet] *s* tribunado
**tribune** [ˈtrɪbjun] *s* tribuna (*plataforma elevada desde donde hablan los oradores*); (arch.) tribuna; (hist.) tribuno; tribuno (*demagogo*)
**tribuneship** [ˈtrɪbjunʃɪp] *s* tribunado
**tributary** [ˈtrɪbjəˌterɪ] *adj* tributario; *s* (*pl:* **-ies**) tributario
**tribute** [ˈtrɪbjut] *s* tributo
**trice** [traɪs] *s* tris (*momento, instante*); **in a trice** en un periquete, en dos trancos; *va* (naut.) izar, izar y liar
**tricentennial** [ˌtraɪsenˈtenɪəl] *adj* de trescientos años; *s* tricentenario
**triceps** [ˈtraɪseps] *s* (anat.) tríceps
**trichiasis** [trɪˈkaɪəsɪs] *s* (path.) triquíasis
**trichina** [trɪˈkaɪnə] *s* (*pl:* **-nae** [ni]) (zool.) triquina
**trichinosis** [ˌtrɪkɪˈnosɪs] *s* (path.) triquinosis
**trichinous** [ˈtrɪkɪnəs] *adj* triquinoso
**trichite** [ˈtrɪkaɪt] *s* (petrog.) triquita
**trichloride** [traɪˈkloraɪd] o [traɪˈklorɪd] *s* (chem.) tricloruro
**trichology** [trɪˈkɑlədʒɪ] *s* tricología
**trichotomic** [ˌtrɪkəˈtɑmɪk] *adj* tricotómico
**trichotomous** [traɪˈkɑtəməs] *adj* tricótomo
**trichotomy** [traɪˈkɑtəmɪ] *s* tricotomía
**trichroic** [traɪˈkro·ɪk] *adj* tricroico
**trichromatic** [ˌtraɪkroˈmætɪk] *adj* tricromático
**trichromatism** [traɪˈkromətɪzəm] *s* tricromatismo
**tricipital** [traɪˈsɪpɪtəl] *adj* tríceps, tricípite
**trick** [trɪk] *s* maña (*habilidad; jugada, embuste; hábito; vicio*); suerte, truco; ilusión; burla, chasco; arte, artificio; travesura; turno, tanda; baza (*número de naipes recogidos por el que gana*); (dial.) chiquito o chiquita; **to be up to one's old tricks** hacer de las suyas; **to do** o **to turn the trick** resolver el problema, dar en el clavo; **to play a dirty trick on** hacer una mala jugada a, hacer un flaco servicio a; *adj* ingenioso; pulcro, acicalado; acrobático; *va* trampear; burlar, engañar; ataviar, vestir; vestir de una manera extraña; **to trick into** + *ger* lograr con engaños que (*una persona*) + *subj;* **to trick out** ataviar, vestir; vestir de una manera extraña; *vn* trampear; mañear; hacer suertes; travesear
**trickery** [ˈtrɪkərɪ] *s* (*pl:* **-ies**) trampería, malas mañas
**trickle** [ˈtrɪkəl] *s* hilo, chorro delgado, goteo; *va* verter gota a gota; *vn* escurrir, gotear; entrar, salir, pasar gradual e irregularmente
**trickster** [ˈtrɪkstər] *s* tramposo, embustero
**tricksy** [ˈtrɪksɪ] *adj* tramposo; engañoso, ilusorio; juguetón, retozón, travieso; garboso, apuesto, elegante
**tricktrack** [ˈtrɪkˌtræk] *s* chaquete
**tricky** [ˈtrɪkɪ] *adj* (*comp:* **-ier;** *super:* **-iest**) tramposo, engañoso; difícil, intrincado; delicado, p.ej., **a tricky situation** una situación delicada; vicioso (*animal*)
**triclinic** [traɪˈklɪnɪk] *adj* (cryst.) triclínico
**triclinium** [traɪˈklɪnɪəm] *s* (*pl:* **-a** [ə]) (hist.) triclinio
**tricolor** [ˈtraɪˌkʌlər] *adj* tricolor; *s* bandera tricolor
**tricolor tube** *s* (telv.) tubo tricolor
**tricorn** [ˈtraɪkɔrn] *adj* & *s* tricornio
**tricot** [ˈtriko] *s* tricot, tejido de punto
**tricotine** [ˌtrɪkəˈtin] *s* tela asargada de lana
**trictrac** [ˈtrɪkˌtræk] *s* var. de **tricktrack**
**tricuspid** [traɪˈkʌspɪd] *adj* tricúspide; (anat.) tricúspide; *s* (anat.) muela tricúspide
**tricuspid valve** *s* (anat.) válvula tricúspide
**tricycle** [ˈtraɪsɪkəl] *s* triciclo
**trident** [ˈtraɪdənt] *adj* tridente; *s* tridente; (hist. & myth.) tridente
**tridentate** [traɪˈdentet] *adj* tridente
**tridimensional** [ˌtraɪdɪˈmenʃənəl] *adj* tridimensional
**tried** [traɪd] *adj* probado, fiel, seguro
**triennial** [traɪˈenɪəl] *adj* trienal; *s* trienio; tercer aniversario
**triennially** [traɪˈenɪəlɪ] *adv* trienalmente
**triennium** [traɪˈenɪəm] *s* (*pl:* **-ums** o **-a** [ə]) trienio
**trifacial** [traɪˈfeʃəl] *adj* trifacial
**trifid** [ˈtraɪfɪd] *adj* trífido
**trifle** [ˈtraɪfəl] *s* bagatela, friolera, nadería, fruslería; baratija, pizca; dulce de bizcocho borracho, crema, conserva de fruta y nata batida; *va* malgastar; **to trifle away** malgastar; *vn* retozar, travesear; chancear, hablar sin seriedad; **to trifle with** manosear; jugar con, burlarse de
**trifler** [ˈtraɪflər] *s* persona frívola; chancero, burlón
**trifling** [ˈtraɪflɪŋ] *adj* frívolo, fútil, ligero; insignificante, sin importancia
**trifocal** [traɪˈfokəl] *adj* trifocal; *s* lente trifocal; **trifocals** *spl* anteojos trifocales
**trifoliate** [traɪˈfolɪɪt] o [traɪˈfolɪet] *adj* (bot.) trifoliado
**trifoliolate** [traɪˈfolɪəlet] *adj* (bot.) trifoliolado
**trifolium** [traɪˈfolɪəm] *s* (bot.) trifolio
**triforium** [traɪˈforɪəm] *s* (*pl:* **-a** [ə]) (arch.) triforio
**triform** [ˈtraɪˌfɔrm] *adj* triforme
**trifurcate** [traɪˈfʌrkɪt] o [traɪˈfʌrket] *adj* trifurcado; [traɪˈfʌrket] *va* trifurcar; *vn* trifurcarse
**trifurcation** [ˌtraɪfərˈkeʃən] *s* trifurcación
**trig.** abr. de **trigonometric** y **trigonometry**
**trig** [trɪg] *adj* acicalado, elegante; estirado, relamido; firme, fuerte, sano; *s* calzo; (*pret & pp:* **trigged;** *ger:* **trigging**) *va* acicalar; calzar (*una rueda*)
**trigeminal** [traɪˈdʒemɪnəl] *adj* trigémino
**trigeminal nerve** *s* (anat.) trigémino
**trigeminous** [traɪˈdʒemɪnəs] *adj* trigémino
**trigger** [ˈtrɪgər] *s* disparador, gatillo (*de pistola, etc.*); (mach.) disparador
**triggerfish** [ˈtrɪgərˌfɪʃ] *s* (ichth.) pez ballesta
**trigger-happy** [ˈtrɪgərˌhæpɪ] *adj* de gatillo alegre, demasiado propenso a tirar; pendenciero
**trigger mechanism** *s* mecanismo de disparo, mecanismo gatillo
**triglyph** [ˈtraɪglɪf] *s* (arch.) tríglifo
**trigon** [ˈtraɪgɑn] *s* (astrol. & geom.) trígono; (mus.) trigón
**trigonal** [ˈtrɪgənəl] *adj* trigonal; (cryst.) trigonal
**trigonometer** [ˌtrɪgəˈnɑmɪtər] *s* trigonómetra

**trigonometric** [ˌtrɪgənə'mɛtrɪk] o **trigonometrical** [ˌtrɪgənə'mɛtrɪkəl] *adj* trigonométrico
**trigonometrically** [ˌtrɪgənə'mɛtrɪkəlɪ] *adv* trigonométricamente
**trigonometry** [ˌtrɪgə'nɑmɪtrɪ] *s* trigonometría
**trigraph** ['traɪgræf] o ['traɪgrɑf] *s* grupo de tres letras que representa un solo sonido
**trihedral** [traɪ'hidrəl] *adj* triedro
**trihedron** [traɪ'hidrən] *s* (*pl:* **-drons** o **-dra** [drə]) (geom.) triedro
**trilateral** [traɪ'lætərəl] *adj* trilátero
**trilingual** [traɪ'lɪŋgwəl] *adj* trilingüe
**triliteral** [traɪ'lɪtərəl] *adj* trilítero
**trilithon** ['trɪlɪθɑn] *s* (archeol.) trilito
**trill** [trɪl] *s* gorjeo; trino, trinado; (phonet.) vibración; (phonet.) consonante vibrante; *va* decir o cantar gorjeando; (phonet.) pronunciar con vibración; *vn* gorjear; trinar; gotear
**trillion** ['trɪljən] *s* (U.S.A.) billón (*un millón de millones*); (Brit.) trillón (*un millón de billones*)
**trillium** ['trɪlɪəm] *s* (bot.) trilio
**trilobate** [traɪ'lobet] *adj* trilobado
**trilobite** ['traɪləbaɪt] *s* (pal.) trilobites
**trilocular** [traɪ'lɑkjələr] *adj* trilocular
**trilogy** ['trɪlədʒɪ] *s* trilogía
**trim** [trɪm] *s* estado, condición; buen estado, buena condición; adorno, atavío; traje, vestido, equipo; aseo, compostura; (naut.) asiento, disposición marinera (*de un buque*); (naut.) orientación; (constr.) chambrana (*adorno alrededor de las puertas y ventanas*); **out of trim** en mal estado; (naut.) mal estivado; *adj* (*comp:* **trimmer;** *super:* **trimmest**) acicalado, compuesto, bonito, elegante; (*pret & pp:* **trimmed;** *ger:* **trimming**) *va* ajustar, adaptar; arreglar, componer, pulir; adornar, decorar; enguirnaldar (*el árbol de Navidad*); recortar (*para dar forma a*); despabilar (*una lámpara o vela*); cambiar, mudar; (agr.) podar, mondar; (carp.) acepillar, alisar, desbastar; (naut.) balancear, equilibrar; (naut.) orientar (*las velas*); (naut.) disponer para la navegación; (coll.) derrotar, vencer; (coll.) regañar, reprender; *vn* nadar entre dos aguas, balancearse entre dos opiniones; (naut.) orientarse (*un buque*)
**trimerous** ['trɪmərəs] *adj* trímero
**trimester** [traɪ'mɛstər] *s* trimestre
**trimestral** [traɪ'mɛstrəl] o **trimestrial** [traɪ'mɛstrɪəl] *adj* trimestral
**trimeter** ['trɪmɪtər] *adj & s* trímetro
**trimmer** ['trɪmər] *s* guarnecedor; contemporizador; máquina de recortar; (carp.) cabio; (rad.) condensador de ajuste, condensador compensador
**trimming** ['trɪmɪŋ] *s* guarnición, adorno; orla, franja, ribete; desbastadura; (coll.) paliza, zurra; (coll.) reprensión; (coll.) derrota; **trimmings** *spl* accesorios, arrequives; recortes
**trimonthly** [traɪ'mʌnθlɪ] *adj* trimestral
**trinal** ['traɪnəl] *adj* trino
**trine** [traɪn] *adj* trino; (astrol.) trino; (*cap.*) *s* (theol.) Trinidad
**Trinitarian** [ˌtrɪnɪ'tɛrɪən] *adj & s* creyente en la Trinidad; (eccl.) trinitario; (*l.c.*) *adj* ternario
**trinitrocresol** [traɪˌnaɪtro'krisol] o [traɪˌnaɪtro'krisɑl] *s* (chem.) trinitrocresol
**trinitrotoluene** [traɪˌnaɪtro'tɑljuin] *s* (chem.) trinitrotolueno
**trinitrotoluol** [traɪˌnaɪtro'tɑljuol] o [traɪˌnaɪtro'tɑljuɑl] *s* (chem.) trinitrotoluol
**trinity** ['trɪnɪtɪ] *s* (*pl:* **-ties**) trinca; (*cap.*) *s* (theol.) Trinidad
**Trinity Sunday** *s* domingo de la santísima Trinidad
**trinket** ['trɪŋkɪt] *s* dije, chuchería; baratija, bujería
**trinomial** [traɪ'nomɪəl] *adj* (alg., bot. & zool.) de tres términos; *s* (alg.) trinomio; (bot. & zool.) nombre de tres términos
**trio** ['trio] *s* (*pl:* **-os**) trío; (mus.) trío
**triode** ['traɪod] *s* (electron.) triodo
**triolet** ['traɪolɛt] o ['triolɛt] *s* composición poética de ocho versos con dos rimas
**trioxide** [traɪ'ɔksaɪd] o [traɪ'ɔksɪd] *s* (chem.) trióxido
**trip** [trɪp] *s* viaje; excursión, recorrido; tropiezo; desliz; traspié, zancadilla; paso o movimiento ágil, rápido y ligero; (mach.) trinquete, escape, disparo; (*pret & pp:* **tripped;** *ger:* **tripping**) *va* trompicar, echar la zancadilla a; detener, estorbar, estorbar el paso a; inclinar, volcar; ejecutar con agilidad (*p.ej., un baile*); coger en falta; coger en una mentira; (mach.) disparar, soltar; (naut.) levar (*el ancla*); **to trip the light fantastic** bailar con agilidad; *vn* ir aprisa, ir con paso rápido y ligero; brincar, saltar, correr; tropezar; viajar; **to trip over** tropezar en
**triparted** [traɪ'pɑrtɪd] *adj* tripartido
**tripartite** [traɪ'pɑrtaɪt] *adj* tripartito
**tripartition** [ˌtraɪpɑr'tɪʃən] *s* tripartición
**tripe** [traɪp] *s* callos, mondongo, ventrón; (slang) barbaridad, disparate, música celestial
**tripetalous** [traɪ'pɛtələs] *adj* (bot.) tripétalo
**triphammer** ['trɪpˌhæmər] *s* martillo de caída, martillo pilón
**triphenylmethane** [traɪˌfɛnɪl'mɛθen] o [traɪˌfinɪl'mɛθen] *s* (chem.) trifenilmetano
**triphthong** ['trɪfθɔŋ] o ['trɪfθɑŋ] *s* triptongo
**tripinnate** [traɪ'pɪnet] *adj* (bot.) tripinado
**triplane** ['traɪˌplen] *s* (aer.) triplano
**triple** ['trɪpəl] *adj* triple; *s* triple; (baseball) golpe con que el bateador gana la tercera base; *va* triplicar; *vn* triplicarse; (baseball) hacer (*el bateador*) un golpe tal que gane la tercera base
**Triple Alliance** *s* Triple Alianza o (la) Tríplice
**triple crown** *s* tiara del papa
**triple-nerved** ['trɪpəl'nʌrvd] *adj* (bot.) trinervado
**triple play** *s* (baseball) jugada que pone fuera de juego a tres jugadores
**triplet** ['trɪplɪt] *s* trillizo (*cada uno de tres hermanos nacidos de un mismo parto*); terceto (*combinación de tres versos*); (mus.) terceto, tresillo
**triple time** *s* (mus.) compás ternario
**triplex** ['trɪplɛks] o ['traɪplɛks] *adj* triple; *s* cosa triple; (mus.) compás ternario
**triplicate** ['trɪplɪkɪt] *adj* triplicado; *s* triplicado; **in triplicate** por triplicado; ['trɪplɪket] *va* triplicar
**triplication** [ˌtrɪplɪ'keʃən] *s* triplicación
**triplicity** [trɪ'plɪsɪtɪ] *s* triplicidad
**triply** ['trɪplɪ] *adv* tres veces
**tripod** ['traɪpɑd] *s* (hist.) trípode; trípode (*para instrumentos geodésicos, fotográficos, etc.*)
**tripoli** ['trɪpəlɪ] *s* (mineral.) trípol
**Tripolitan** [trɪ'pɑlɪtən] *adj & s* tripolino o tripolitano
**tripper** ['trɪpər] *s* corredor; andarín; saltarín; persona que trompica; (mach.) disparador
**tripping** ['trɪpɪŋ] *adj* ágil, rápido, ligero; (mach.) disparador
**triptych** ['trɪptɪk] *s* tríptico
**trireme** ['traɪrim] *s* (hist.) trirreme
**trisect** [traɪ'sɛkt] *va* trisecar
**trisection** [traɪ'sɛkʃən] *s* trisección
**trismus** ['trɪzməs] o ['trɪsməs] *s* (path.) trismo
**trispermous** [traɪ'spʌrməs] *adj* (bot.) trispermo
**Tristan** ['trɪstən] o **Tristram** ['trɪstrəm] *s* (myth.) Tristán
**trisulcate** [traɪ'sʌlket] o [traɪ'sʌlkɪt] *adj* trisulco
**trisulfide** [traɪ'sʌlfaɪd] o [traɪ'sʌlfɪd] *s* (chem.) trisulfuro
**trisyllabic** [ˌtrɪsɪ'læbɪk] o [ˌtraɪsɪ'læbɪk] *adj* trisílabo
**trisyllable** [trɪ'sɪləbəl] o [traɪ'sɪləbəl] *s* trisílabo
**trite** [traɪt] *adj* gastado, trillado, trivial
**tritium** ['trɪtɪəm] o ['trɪʃɪəm] *s* (chem.) tritio
**triton** ['traɪtən] *s* (zool.) tritón; (*cap.*) *s* (myth.) Tritón
**tritone** ['traɪˌton] *s* (mus.) tritono
**triturate** ['trɪtʃəret] *s* cosa triturada; *va* triturar
**trituration** [ˌtrɪtʃə'reʃən] *s* trituración
**triumph** ['traɪəmf] *s* triunfo; **in triumph** en triunfo; *vn* triunfar; **to triumph over** triunfar de

**triumphal** [traɪ'ʌmfəl] *adj* triunfal

**triumphal arch** *s* arco triunfal

**triumphant** [traɪ'ʌmfənt] *adj* triunfante

**triumvir** [traɪ'ʌmvər] *s* triunviro

**triumviral** [traɪ'ʌmvərəl] *adj* triunviral

**triumvirate** [traɪ'ʌmvərɪt] *s* triunvirato

**triune** ['traɪjun] *adj* trino y uno (*que es tres y uno al mismo tiempo*); *s* tríada; (*cap.*) *s* (theol.) Trinidad

**triunity** [traɪ'junɪtɪ] *s* condición o estado de trino y uno

**trivalence** [traɪ'veləns] o ['trɪvələns] o **trivalency** [traɪ'velənsɪ] o ['trɪvələnsɪ] *s* (chem.) trivalencia

**trivalent** [traɪ'velənt] o ['trɪvələnt] *adj* (chem.) trivalente

**trivalve** ['traɪ,vælv] *adj* trivalvo

**trivet** ['trɪvɪt] *s* trébedes; platillo con tres pies

**trivia** ['trɪvɪə] *spl* bagatelas, trivialidades

**trivial** ['trɪvɪəl] *adj* trivial, insignificante

**triviality** [,trɪvɪ'ælɪtɪ] *s* (*pl:* **-ties**) trivialidad

**trivium** ['trɪvɪəm] *s* trivio (*en la edad media, las tres primeras artes liberales*)

**triweekly** [traɪ'wiklɪ] *adj* trisemanal (*que se repite tres veces por semana o cada tres semanas*); *adv* trisemanalmente; *s* (*pl:* **-lies**) periódico o revista trisemanal

**trocar** ['trokar] *s* (surg.) trocar

**trochaic** [tro'keɪk] *adj & s* trocaico

**trochanter** [tro'kæntər] *s* (anat., ent. & zool.) trocánter

**troche** ['trokɪ] *s* (pharm.) trocisco

**trochee** ['troki] *s* troqueo

**trochilus** ['trakɪləs] *s* (*pl:* **-li** [laɪ]) troquilo

**trochlea** ['traklɪə] *s* (*pl:* **-ae** [i]) (anat.) tróclea

**trochlear** ['traklɪər] *adj* (anat.) troclear; (bot.) troclearío

**trochoid** ['trokɔɪd] *adj* trocoideo; *s* (geom.) trocoide

**trod** [trad] *pret & pp de* **tread**

**trodden** ['tradən] *pp de* **tread**

**troglodyte** ['tragləda ɪt] *s* troglodita; mono antropomorfo; (fig.) troglodita (*hombre bárbaro y cruel*); (fig.) ermitaño, solitario

**troglodytic** [,traglə'dɪtɪk] o **troglodytical** [,traglə'dɪtɪkəl] *adj* troglodítico

**troika** ['trɔɪkə] *s* troica

**Troilus** ['tro·ɪləs] o ['trɔɪləs] *s* (myth.) Troilo

**Trojan** ['trodʒən] *adj* troyano; *s* troyano; **to work like a Trojan** trabajar con gran ánimo y esfuerzo

**Trojan horse** *s* caballo de Troya

**Trojan War** *s* (myth.) guerra de Troya

**troll** [trol] *s* rodadura; cantar que se entona en partes sucesivas; repetición, rutina; carrete (*de la caña de pescar*); cebo (*para la pesca*); gnomo, enano, gigante; *va* cantar con voz abultada; cantar en sucesión; pescar a la cacea; pescar a la cacea en (*p.ej., un lago*); atraer, seducir; *vn* cantar o tocar alegremente; pescar a la cacea; hablar rápidamente

**trolley** ['tralɪ] *s* corredera elevada; (elec.) polea o arco de trole; (elec.) tranvía; volquete; (Brit.) carretilla; **off one's trolley** (slang) destornillado, chiflado

**trolley bus** *s* trolebús, ómnibus-tranvía

**trolley car** *s* coche o carruaje de tranvía

**trolley line** *s* línea de tranvías, red de tranvías

**trolley pole** *s* trole

**trolley wire** *s* cable conductor (*del tranvía eléctrico*)

**trolling** ['trolɪŋ] *s* cacea, pesca a la cacea

**trollop** ['traləp] *s* cochina (*mujer sucia y desaliñada*); mujer de mala vida

**trombone** ['trambon] o [tram'bon] *s* trombón (*instrumento y el que lo toca*)

**trombonist** ['trambonɪst] o [tram'bonɪst] *s* trombón (*músico*)

**trommel** ['traməl] *s* (metal.) trómel

**trompe** [tramp] *s* (found.) trompa

**troop** [trup] *s* tropa; compañía (*de actores*); tropa de 32 niños exploradores; (mil.) escuadrón (*de caballería*); **troops** *spl* (mil.) tropas; *va* reunir en tropa; *vn* agruparse, juntarse; marcharse, marcharse en tropel; marchar en orden militar

**troop carrier** *s* (aer.) avión de transporte de tropas

**trooper** ['trupər] *s* soldado de caballería; corcel de guerra; (mil.) transporte (*buque*); agente de policía montado; **to swear like a trooper** jurar como un carretero

**troopship** ['trup,ʃɪp] *s* (mil.) transporte

**troostite** ['trustaɪt] *s* (metal.) troostita

**tropaeolin** [tro'piəlɪn] *s* (chem.) tropeolina

**tropaeolum** [tro'piələm] *s* (*pl:* **-lums** o **-la** [lə]) (bot.) tropeolea

**trope** [trop] *s* (mus. & rhet.) tropo

**tropeine** ['tropɪin] o ['tropɪɪn] *s* (chem.) tropeína

**trophic** ['trafɪk] *adj* (physiol.) trófico

**trophied** ['trofɪd] *adj* adornado, cargado o cubierto de trofeos

**trophoplasm** ['trafəplæzəm] *s* (biol.) trofoplasma

**trophy** ['trofɪ] *s* (*pl:* **-phies**) trofeo; recuerdo

**tropic** ['trapɪk] *adj* tropical; *s* (astr. & geog.) trópico; **tropics** o **Tropics** *spl* zona tropical

**tropical** ['trapɪkəl] *adj* tropical; (rhet.) trópico

**tropical year** *s* (astr.) año trópico

**tropic bird** *s* (orn.) rabijunco, contramaestre

**tropic of Cancer** *s* trópico de Cáncer

**tropic of Capricorn** *s* trópico de Capricornio

**tropine** ['tropin] o ['tropɪn] *s* (chem.) tropina

**tropism** ['tropɪzəm] *s* (biol.) tropismo

**tropistic** [tro'pɪstɪk] *adj* del tropismo

**tropologic** [,trapə'ladʒɪk] o **tropological** [,trapə'ladʒɪkəl] *adj* tropológico

**tropology** [tro'palədʒɪ] *s* (*pl:* **-gies**) tropología

**troposphere** ['trapəsfɪr] *s* (meteor.) troposfera o tropoesfera

**trot** [trat] *s* trote; paso o movimiento vivo o apresurado; niñito; (slang) traducción interlineal que usan los estudiantes para ahorrarse trabajo; (*pret & pp:* **trotted**; *ger:* **trotting**) *va* hacer trotar; pasar al trote por encima de; **to trot out** (slang) sacar para mostrar o enseñar; *vn* trotar

**troth** [trɔθ] o [troθ] *s* fe; verdad; esponsales; **in troth** en verdad; **to plight one's troth** prometer fidelidad; dar palabra de casamiento, contraer esponsales

**trotline** ['trat,laɪn] *s* palangre

**Trotskyism** ['tratskɪɪzəm] *s* trotskismo

**Trotskyite** ['tratskɪaɪt] *adj & s* trotskista

**trotter** ['tratər] *s* trotón; pie de cerdo o carnero (*usado como alimento*)

**troubadour** ['trubədor] o ['trubədur] *s* trovador; *adj* trovadoresco

**trouble** ['trʌbəl] *s* apuro, dificultad; confusión, estorbo, embarazo; conflicto; inquietud, preocupación; pena, molestia, aflicción; avería, falla, pana (*de índole mecánica*); mal, enfermedad; **that's the trouble** ahí está el busilis, ahí está el tope; **the trouble is that . . .** lo malo es que . . .; **to be in trouble** estar en un aprieto o apuro; **to be looking for trouble** buscar tres (o cinco) pies al gato, buscar camorra; **to get into trouble** enredarse, meterse en líos; **to go to the trouble to** + *inf* darse la molestia de + *inf;* **to put oneself to the trouble to** + *inf* o **to take the trouble to** + *inf* tomarse la molestia de + *inf;* **to shoot trouble** localizar averías; **not to be worth the trouble** no valer la pena; **what's the trouble?** ¿qué sucede?, ¿qué hay?; *va* apurar; confundir, estorbar, embarazar; disturbar; inquietar, preocupar; apenar, afligir; molestar, incomodar; dar que hacer a; **may I trouble you?** ¿me hace Vd. el favor?; **to be troubled with** padecer de; **to trouble oneself** molestarse; *vn* apurarse; inquietarse, preocuparse; molestarse, darse molestia, incomodarse; **to trouble to** + *inf* molestarse en + *inf*

**trouble-free** ['trʌbəl,fri] *adj* libre de disturbios; exento de averías

**trouble lamp** *s* lámpara de socorro, lámpara de inspección

**troublemaker** ['trʌbəl,mekər] *s* perturbador, camorrista

**trouble shooting** *s* investigación de fallas o panas, localización de averías, comprobación de averías

**troublesome** ['trʌbəlsəm] *adj* molesto, pesado, gravoso, dificultoso; impertinente; perturbador; camorrista

**troublous** ['trʌbləs] *adj* agitado, inquieto; molesto
**trough** [trɔf] o [trɑf] *s* artesa (*p.ej., para amasar pan*); pesebre; abrevadero, camellón; canal (*curso de agua excavado artificialmente; conducto de las aguas del tejado*); abismo (*de una onda*); seno (*entre dos ondas*); (meteor.) mínimo de presión; (coll.) borrachín
**trounce** [traʊns] *va* zurrar; castigar; (coll.) vencer decisivamente
**troupe** [trup] *s* compañía de actores o de circo
**trouper** ['trupər] *s* miembro de una compañía teatral; viejo actor
**troupial** ['trupɪəl] *s* (orn.) trupial
**trousers** ['traʊzərz] *spl* pantalones; **to wear the trousers** calzarse o ponerse los calzones o los pantalones (*dícese de la mujer que supedita al marido*)
**trousseau** [tru'so] ['truso] *s* (*pl:* **-seaux** ['soz] o [soz] o **-seaus**) ajuar, equipo de novia, canastilla, joyas
**trout** [traʊt] *s* (ichth.) trucha
**trout fishing** *s* pesca de la trucha
**trout stream** *s* arroyo en que abunda la trucha
**trouvère** [tru'vɛr] *s* trovero
**trow** [tro] o [traʊ] *va & vn* (archaic) creer, pensar; (archaic) esperar
**trowel** ['traʊəl] *s* paleta, llana, trulla, desplantador
**Troy** [trɔɪ] *s* Troya
**troy weight** *s* peso troy (*cuya unidad es la libra de doce onzas, que equivale a 373,24 gramos*)
**truancy** ['truənsɪ] *s* (*pl:* **-cies**) ausencia de la clase sin permiso; haraganería
**truant** ['truənt] *adj* haragán; *s* haragán; novillero (*muchacho que no asiste a la clase*); **to play truant** hacer novillos
**truant officer** *s* vigilante escolar
**truce** [trus] *s* tregua
**truck** [trʌk] *s* carro; vagoneta; camión, camioneta; autocamión; carretilla (*carro pequeño de mano*); ruedecilla; remate de asta o mástil; cambio, permuta, trueque; efectos para vender o trocar, baratijas, zupias, hojarasca; pago del salario en especie; (rail.) bogie, carretón (*de locomotora, coche, etc.*); (Brit.) furgón de plataforma; (U.S.A.) hortalizas para el mercado; (coll.) desechos, desperdicios; (coll.) negocio, relaciones; *va* acarrear, transportar en carro, vagoneta, camión, etc.; cambiar, permutar, trocar; traficar en; *vn* conducir un carro, vagoneta, camión, etc.; ser carretero, conductor de camión, etc.
**truckage** ['trʌkɪdʒ] *s* acarreo; camionaje
**truck driver** *s* camionista, conductor de camión
**trucker** ['trʌkər] *s* carretero; camionista, conductor de camión; verdulero
**truck garden** *s* huerto de hortalizas (*para el mercado*)
**truckle** ['trʌkəl] *s* ruedecilla; carriola; *va* mover sobre ruedecillas; *vn* rodar sobre ruedecillas; someterse servilmente
**truckle bed** *s* carriola
**truckload** ['trʌk,lod] *s* carga de un carro; carga de un camión
**truckman** ['trʌkmən] *s* (*pl:* **-men**) carretero; conductor de camión; baratador
**truculence** ['trʌkjələns] o ['trukjələns] o **truculency** ['trʌkjələnsɪ] o ['trukjələnsɪ] *s* truculencia
**truculent** ['trʌkjələnt] o ['trukjələnt] *adj* truculento
**trudge** [trʌdʒ] *s* marcha, paseo; marcha penosa; *va* recorrer con pena y trabajo; *vn* caminar, ir a pie; marchar con pena y trabajo; **to trudge along** marchar con pena y trabajo
**trudgen stroke** ['trʌdʒən] *s* brazada a la marinera
**true** [tru] *adj* (*comp:* **truer** ['truər]; *super:* **truest** ['truɪst]) verdadero; exacto; constante, uniforme; fiel, leal; alineado; a plomo, a nivel; **to come true** hacerse realidad; **to run true to form** obrar como era de esperarse; **true to life** conforme con la realidad; *adv* verdaderamente; exactamente; propiamente, naturalmente; *s* ajuste, posición debida o correcta; **in true** alineado; **out of true** desalineado; **the true** lo verdadero; *va* alinear, rectificar; **to true up** alinear, rectificar
**true bill** *s* (law) acto acusatorio formulado por el gran jurado como base del procesamiento de un acusado, por haberse encontrado indicios suficientes de culpabilidad
**true-blue** ['tru'blu] *adj* fiel, leal, constante
**true copy** *s* copia fiel
**true course** *s* (naut.) rumbo verdadero
**true-hearted** ['tru,hɑrtɪd] *adj* fiel, leal, sincero
**truelove** ['tru,lʌv] *s* fiel amante; enamorado o enamorada; (bot.) hierba de París
**truelove knot** o **true-lover's knot** ['tru'lʌvərz] *s* lazo de amor
**true ribs** *spl* (anat.) costillas verdaderas
**true time** *s* (astr.) tiempo (solar) verdadero
**truffle** ['trʌfəl] o ['trufəl] *s* (bot.) trufa
**truism** ['truɪzəm] *s* perogrullada, verdad trillada, truísmo
**trull** [trʌl] *s* prostituta, mujer de mala vida
**truly** ['trulɪ] *adv* verdaderamente; efectivamente; fielmente; **truly yours** su seguro servidor, de Vd. atto. y S.S.
**trump** [trʌmp] *s* triunfo (*en los juegos de naipes*); (coll.) persona muy simpática, buen chico, buena chica; (archaic & poet.) trompa, toque de trompa; (Scotch & Irish) trompa gallega; **no trump** sin triunfo; *va* matar con un triunfo; aventajar, sobrepujar; (archaic & poet.) tocar (*la trompa*); (archaic & poet.) anunciar a son de trompa; **to trump up** forjar, inventar (*para engañar*); *vn* triunfar (*jugar del palo de triunfo*); (archaic & poet.) tocar la trompa
**trumpery** ['trʌmpərɪ] *s* (*pl:* **-ies**) hojarasca, oropel, relumbrón; baratija, bujería; necedad, tontería; *adj* de oropel; inútil, sin valor; necio, tonto
**trumpet** ['trʌmpɪt] *s* trompeta; toque de trompeta; trompetilla o trompeta acústica; trompeta o trompetero (*músico*); **to blow one's own trumpet** cantar sus propias alabanzas; *va* anunciar con trompetas, pregonar a son de trompeta; abocinar; *vn* trompetear; barritar (*el elefante*)
**trumpet creeper** *s* (bot.) jazmín trompeta
**trumpeter** ['trʌmpɪtər] *s* trompetero, trompeta; (fig.) pregonero; (orn.) agamí, pájaro trompeta
**trumpet flower** *s* (bot.) jazmín trompeta; (bot.) madreselva; (bot.) trompetilla
**trumpet honeysuckle** *s* (bot.) madreselva
**trumpet vine** *s* var. de **trumpet creeper**
**truncate** ['trʌŋket] *adj* truncado; *va* truncar
**truncation** [trʌŋ'keʃən] *s* truncamiento; (cryst.) truncadura
**truncheon** ['trʌntʃən] *s* cachiporra; bastón de mando; *va* zurrar con cachiporra
**trundle** ['trʌndəl] *s* rodadura; ruedecilla; ruedecilla de mueble; carriola; *va* hacer rodar; *vn* rodar
**trundle bed** *s* carriola
**trunk** [trʌŋk] *s* tronco (*del cuerpo humano o animal, del árbol, de una familia, del ferrocarril, etc.*); baúl; cofre de equipajes, portaequipaje (*del automóvil*); trompa (*del elefante*); vivero; (anat. & arch.) tronco; **trunks** *spl* taparrabo (*usado como traje de baño, etc.*); *adj* troncal; principal
**trunk hose** *spl* trusas
**trunk line** *s* (rail.) línea troncal; (telp.) línea principal
**trunk piston** *s* (mach.) émbolo de tronco
**trunnion** ['trʌnjən] *s* (arti.) muñón
**truss** [trʌs] *s* armadura; braguero (*para contener las hernias*); haz, paquete, lío; (Brit.) 60 libras de heno; (Brit.) 36 libras de paja; (hort.) mazorca, racimo; (naut.) troza; *va* armar; empaquetar, liar; espetar; apretar (*barriles*); (naut.) aferrar (*las velas*); (archaic) apretar (*el vestido*); (archaic) atar (*cordones, cintas, etc.*); (archaic) arreglar o componer (*el cabello*); *vn* (archaic) irse, marcharse
**trust** [trʌst] *s* confianza; esperanza (*persona o cosa en que se confía*); cargo, custodia; depósito; crédito; obligación; (law) fideicomiso; (econ.) trust, cartel; **in trust** en confianza; en depósito; **on trust** a crédito, al fiado; haciendo confianza; *va* confiar; confiar en; vender a crédito a; *vn* confiar; fiar (*vender sin tomar el precio al contado*); **to trust in** fiarse a o de

**trust buster** *s* (slang) fiscal anticartel
**trust company** *s* banco fideicomisario, banco de depósitos
**trustee** [trʌs'ti] *s* administrador, comisario; regente (universitario); fideicomisario; depositario
**trusteeship** [trʌs'tiʃɪp] *s* cargo de administrador, fideicomisario, depositario, etc.; fideicomiso (*de la ONU*)
**trustful** ['trʌstfəl] o **trusting** ['trʌstɪŋ] *adj* confiado
**trustworthiness** ['trʌst,wʌrðɪnɪs] *s* confiabilidad
**trustworthy** ['trʌst,wʌrðɪ] *adj* confiable, fidedigno
**trusty** ['trʌstɪ] *adj* (*comp:* **-ier;** *super:* **-iest**) fiel, honrado, leal, seguro; *s* (*pl:* **-ies**) persona fiel, segura, digna de confianza; (U.S.A.) preso que se ha merecido algunos privilegios
**truth** [truθ] *s* (*pl:* **truths** [truðz] o [truθs]) verdad; **in truth** a la verdad, en verdad
**truthful** ['truθfəl] *adj* verídico, veraz
**truthfulness** ['truθfəlnɪs] *s* veracidad
**try** [traɪ] *s* (*pl:* **tries**) intento, ensayo, prueba; (*pret & pp:* **tried**) *va* intentar, ensayar, probar; comprobar, verificar; exasperar, irritar; cansar, fatigar; forzar (*p.ej., la vista, los nervios*); (law) procesar; (law) ver (*un pleito*); refinar o purificar derritiendo o hirviendo; **to try on** probarse (*una prenda de vestir*); **to try out** someter a prueba; refinar o purificar derritiendo o hirviendo; *vn* ensayar, probar; esforzarse; tratar; **to be trying to** + *inf* querer + *inf, p.ej.,* **it is trying to rain** quiere llover; **to try out** (sport) presentarse como competidor; **to try to** + *inf* tratar de + *inf,* intentar + *inf*
**trying** ['traɪɪŋ] *adj* penoso; molesto, cansado, difícil de soportar
**tryout** ['traɪ,aut] *s* (coll.) experimento, prueba, prueba de competencia
**trypaflavine** [,trɪpə'flevɪn] o [,trɪpə'flevin] *s* (pharm.) tripaflavina
**trypanosome** ['trɪpənəsom] *s* (zool.) tripanosoma
**tryparsamide** [,trɪpɑr'sæmɪd] o [trɪp'ɑrsəmɪd] *s* (trademark) triparsamida
**trypsin** ['trɪpsɪn] *s* (biochem.) tripsina
**tryptic** ['trɪptɪk] *adj* (physiol.) tríptico
**tryptophan** ['trɪptəfæn] o **tryptophane** ['trɪptəfen] *s* (biochem.) triptófano
**trysail** ['traɪsəl] o ['traɪ,sel] *s* (naut.) vela mayor de capa
**try square** *s* escuadra de comprobación
**tryst** [trɪst] o [traɪst] *s* cita; lugar de cita; *va* dar una cita a; *vn* acudir a una cita
**trysting place** *s* lugar de cita
**tsar** [tsɑr] *s* var. de **czar**
**tsarevitch** ['tsɑrɪvɪtʃ] *s* var. de **czarevitch**
**tsarina** [tsɑ'rinə] *s* var. de **czarina**
**tsetse** ['tsɛtsɪ] *s* (ent.) tsetsé
**tsetse fly** *s* (ent.) mosca tsetsé
**tsp.** abr. de **teaspoon**
**T square** *s* te, regla T
**Tu.** abr. de **Tuesday**
**tub** [tʌb] *s* tina, cuba; artesón; (coll.) baño; (coll.) cuba (*persona de mucho vientre*); (coll.) carcamán, trompo (*buque malo y pesado*); (*pret & pp:* **tubbed;** *ger:* **tubbing**) *va* entinar, encubar; bañar en bañera; *vn* bañarse, bañarse en bañera
**tuba** ['tjubə] o ['tubə] *s* (mus.) tuba
**Tubal-cain** ['tjubəl,ken] o ['tubəl,ken] *s* (Bib.) Tubalcaín
**tubbing** ['tʌbɪŋ] *s* baño
**tubby** ['tʌbɪ] *adj* (*comp:* **-bier;** *super:* **-biest**) rechoncho; sordo (*ruido*)
**tube** [tjub] o [tub] *s* tubo; túnel; (coll.) ferrocarril subterráneo; (anat.) tubo, trompa; (elec. & rad.) tubo; cámara (*de un neumático*); *va* entubar; meter en un tubo; proveer de tubos; dar forma de tubo a
**tubeless** ['tjublɪs] o ['tublɪs] *adj* sin tubo; (aut.) sin cámara
**tuber** ['tjubər] o ['tubər] *s* (anat. & bot.) tubérculo
**tubercle** ['tjubərkəl] o ['tubərkəl] *s* (anat., bot., path. & zool.) tubérculo
**tubercle bacillus** *s* (bact.) bacilo de Koch
**tubercular** [tju'bʌrkjələr] o [tu'bʌrkjələr] *adj* tubercular; tuberculoso; *s* tuberculoso (*persona que padece tuberculosis*)
**tubercularization** [tju,bʌrkjələrɪ'zeʃən] o [tu,bʌrkjələrɪ'zeʃən] *s* tuberculización
**tuberculin** [tju'bʌrkjəlɪn] o [tu'bʌrkjəlɪn] *s* (bact.) tuberculina
**tuberculosis** [tju,bʌrkjə'losɪs] o [tu,bʌrkjə'losɪs] *s* (path.) tuberculosis
**tuberculous** [tju'bʌrkjələs] o [tu'bʌrkjələs] *adj* tuberculoso
**tuberose** ['tjub,roz] o ['tub,roz] *s* (bot.) tuberosa
**tuberosity** [,tjubə'rɑsɪtɪ] o [,tubə'rɑsɪtɪ] *s* (*pl:* **-ties**) tuberosidad
**tuberous** ['tjubərəs] o ['tubərəs] *adj* tuberoso
**tube tester** *s* (rad.) probador de válvulas
**tubeworks** ['tjub,wʌrks] o ['tub,wʌrks] *spl* tubería
**tubicolous** [tju'bɪkələs] o [tu'bɪkələs] *adj* (zool.) tubícola
**tubing** ['tjubɪŋ] o ['tubɪŋ] *s* tubería; material para tubos; trozo de tubo
**Tübingen** ['tybɪŋən] *s* Tubinga
**tubular** ['tjubjələr] o ['tubjələr] *adj* tubular
**tubular boiler** *s* caldera tubular
**tubulate** ['tjubjəlet] o ['tubjəlet] *adj* tubular; tubulado
**tubulation** [,tjubjə'leʃən] o [,tubjə'leʃən] *s* tubulación
**tubule** ['tjubjul] o ['tubjul] *s* tubito
**tubulous** ['tjubjələs] o ['tubjələs] *adj* (bot.) tubuloso
**tubulure** ['tjubjələr] o ['tubjələr] *s* (chem.) tubulura
**tuck** [tʌk] *s* pliegue o doblez (horizontal), alforza; (b.b.) cartera; (coll.) energía, vivacidad; (slang) banquete, festín; (slang) dulce, confitura; (slang) ganas de comer; (naut.) arca de popa; *va* echar un pliegue (horizontal) a, alforzar; doblar (*como para encubrir*); arremangar; apretar; arropar; **to tuck away** encubrir, ocultar; (slang) comer o beber vorazmente; **to tuck in** arropar, enmantar; remeter (*p.ej., la ropa de cama*); **to tuck up** arremangar (*un vestido*); guarnecer (*la cama*); *vn* alforzar
**tucker** ['tʌkər] *s* alforzador; alforzador de la máquina de coser; escote, pañoleta; *va* (coll.) agotar, cansar
**Tues.** abr. de **Tuesday**
**Tuesday** ['tjuzdɪ] o ['tuzdɪ] *s* martes
**tufa** ['tjufə] o ['tufə] *s* (geol.) toba (*piedra caliza porosa*)
**tufaceous** [tju'feʃəs] o [tu'feʃəs] *adj* toboso
**tuff** [tʌf] *s* (geol.) toba (*piedra volcánica*)
**tuft** [tʌft] *s* copete (*de plumas, cabellos, etc.*); moño; borla; manojo, racimo, ramillete; grupo de árboles o arbustos; *va* empenachar; poner borlas a; *vn* crecer formando mechones
**tufted** ['tʌftɪd] *adj* copetudo; empenachado
**tufthunter** ['tʌft,hʌntər] *s* ambicioso de figurar, zalamero
**tufting needle** *s* aguja colchonera
**tug** [tʌg] *s* estirón, tirón; esfuerzo; remolcador (*barco*); tirante (*correa*); (*pret & pp:* **tugged;** *ger:* **tugging**) *va* arrastrar, tirar con fuerza de; remolcar (*un barco*); *vn* tirar con fuerza; esforzarse, luchar
**tugboat** ['tʌg,bot] *s* remolcador
**tug of war** *s* (sport) lucha de la cuerda; (fig.) lucha suprema, lucha decisiva
**Tuileries** ['twilərɪz] o [twil'ri] *spl* Tullerías
**tuition** [tju'ɪʃən] o [tu'ɪʃən] *s* enseñanza; precio de la enseñanza, cuota
**tuitional** [tju'ɪʃənəl] o [tu'ɪʃənəl] *adj* de enseñanza; del precio de la enseñanza
**tularemia** [,tulə'rimɪə] *s* (path.) tularemia
**tule** ['tulɛ] *s* (bot.) junco de laguna, tule
**tule goose** *s* (orn.) ánsar, guanana prieta
**tulip** ['tjulɪp] o ['tulɪp] *s* (bot.) tulipán (*planta, raíz bulbosa y flor*)
**tulip tree** *s* (bot.) tulipanero o tulipero
**tulipwood** ['tjulɪp,wud] o ['tulɪp,wud] *s* madera del tulipero; (bot.) palo de rosa (*árbol y madera*)
**tulle** [tul] *s* tul
**Tully** ['tʌlɪ] *s* Tulio
**tumble** ['tʌmbəl] *s* caída; voltereta; confusión,

desorden; **to take a tumble** rodar, caerse; *va* derribar, derrocar, volcar; revolver; arrojar, tirar; ajar, arrugar; desarreglar, trastornar; *vn* caer o caerse; voltear; derribarse, derrocarse, volcarse; brincar, dar saltos, precipitarse; echarse (*en la cama*); (slang) caer, comprender; **to tumble down** desplomarse, hundirse, venir abajo
**tumblebug** ['tʌmbəl,bʌg] *s* (ent.) escarabajo pelotero o bolero
**tumble-down** ['tʌmbəl,daʊn] *adj* destartalado, destrozado, desvencijado
**tumbler** ['tʌmblər] *s* vaso (*para beber*); volteador, volatinero; dominguillo, tentemozo (*juguete*); rodete, fiador (*p.ej., de la cerradura*); seguro de escopeta; (orn.) pichón volteador
**tumbler switch** *s* (elec.) interruptor de volquete
**tumbleweed** ['tʌmbəl,wid] *s* (bot.) planta rodadora
**tumbrel** o **tumbril** ['tʌmbrəl] *s* chirrión; carro de artillería
**tumefaction** [,tjumɪ'fækʃən] o [,tumɪ'fækʃən] *s* tumefacción
**tumefy** ['tjumɪfaɪ] o ['tumɪfaɪ] (*pret & pp:* **-fied**) *va* tumefacer; *vn* tumefacerse
**tumescence** [tju'mɛsəns] o [tu'mɛsəns] *s* tumescencia
**tumescent** [tju'mɛsənt] o [tu'mɛsənt] *adj* tumescente
**tumid** ['tjumɪd] o ['tumɪd] *adj* túmido; (fig.) túmido
**tumor** ['tjumər] o ['tumər] *s* (path.) tumor
**tumorous** ['tjumərəs] o ['tumərəs] *adj* tumoroso
**tumular** ['tjumjələr] o ['tumjələr] *adj* tumulario
**tumult** ['tjumʌlt] o ['tumʌlt] *s* tumulto
**tumultuary** [tju'mʌltʃʊ,ɛrɪ] o [tu'mʌltʃʊ,ɛrɪ] *adj* tumultuario
**tumultuous** [tju'mʌltʃʊəs] o [tu'mʌltʃʊəs] *adj* tumultuoso
**tumulus** ['tjumjələs] o ['tumjələs] *s* (*pl:* **-luses** o **-li** [laɪ]) túmulo
**tun** [tʌn] *s* tonel, barril; tonelada (*medida que equivale a 252 galones*); (*pret & pp:* **tunned;** *ger:* **tunning**) *va* entonelar, embarrilar
**tuna** ['tunə] *s* (ichth.) atún; (bot.) tuna
**tunable** ['tjunəbəl] o ['tunəbəl] *adj* armonioso, melodioso; cantable; afinado, templado; que se puede templar; (rad.) sintonizable
**tuna fishery** *s* atunara, almadraba
**tundra** ['tʌndrə] o ['tundrə] *s* tundra
**tune** [tjun] o [tun] *s* tonada, aire; armonía; tono (*manera de actuar o hablar*); (rad.) sintonía; **in tune** afinado; afinadamente; **out of tune** desafinado; desafinadamente; **to change one's tune** o **to sing a different tune** mudar de tono; **to the tune of** (coll.) por la suma de; *va* acordar, afinar; armonizar; (rad.) sintonizar; **to tune in** (rad.) sintonizar; **to tune out** (rad.) desintonizar; **to tune up** ajustar, poner a punto; poner a tono (*un motor de automóvil*); (mus.) acordar; *vn* armonizar; **to tune up** (coll.) empezar a cantar, llorar, etc.
**tuneable** ['tjunəbəl] o ['tunəbəl] *adj* var. de **tunable**
**tuneful** ['tjunfəl] o ['tunfəl] *adj* armonioso, melodioso
**tuneless** ['tjunlɪs] o ['tunlɪs] *adj* discorde, disonante
**tuner** ['tjunər] o ['tunər] *s* (mus.) afinador (*persona*); (rad.) sintonizador
**tung oil** [tʌŋ] *s* aceite de tung
**tungstate** ['tʌŋstet] *s* (chem.) tungstato
**tungsten** ['tʌŋstən] *s* (chem.) tungsteno
**tungsten steel** *s* acero al tungsteno
**tungstic** ['tʌŋstɪk] *adj* (chem.) túngstico
**tunic** ['tjunɪk] o ['tunɪk] *s* túnica; (anat., bot. & zool.) túnica; (eccl.) tunicela
**tunicate** ['tjunɪket] o ['tunɪket] *adj* tunicado; *s* (zool.) tunicado
**tunicle** ['tjunɪkəl] o ['tunɪkəl] *s* (eccl.) tunicela
**tuning** ['tjunɪŋ] o ['tunɪŋ] *s* afinación; armonización; (rad.) sintonización
**tuning coil** *s* (rad.) bobina sintonizadora, bobina de sintonía
**tuning condenser** *s* (rad.) condensador de sintonía, condensador sintonizador
**tuning dial** *s* (rad.) cuadrante de sintonización
**tuning fork** *s* (mus.) diapasón
**tuning hammer** o **key** *s* (mus.) afinador, martillo, templador
**tuning knob** *s* (rad.) botón de sintonización, perilla sintonizadora
**Tunis** ['tjunɪs] o ['tunɪs] *s* Túnez (*ciudad*)
**Tunisia** [tju'nɪʃɪə] o [tu'nɪʃɪə] *s* Túnez (*país*)
**Tunisian** [tju'nɪʃɪən] o [tu'nɪʃɪən] *adj & s* tunecino
**tunnel** ['tʌnəl] *s* túnel; (min.) galería; (*pret & pp:* **-neled** o **-nelled;** *ger:* **-neling** o **-nelling**) *va* atravesar por túnel; construir un túnel a través de o debajo de; *vn* construir o perforar un túnel
**tunnel disease** *s* (path.) anemia de los túneles; (path.) enfermedad de los cajones de aire comprimido
**tunny** ['tʌnɪ] *s* (*pl:* **-nies**) (ichth.) atún
**tupelo** ['tupɪlo] *s* (*pl:* **-los**) (bot.) tupelo
**tuppence** ['tʌpəns] *s* var. de **twopence**
**tuque** [tjuk] o [tuk] *s* gorra de punto de los canadienses
**Turanian** [tjʊ'renɪən] o [tʊ'renɪən] *adj & s* turanio
**turban** ['tʌrbən] *s* turbante
**turbaned** ['tʌrbənd] *adj* tocado con turbante
**turbid** ['tʌrbɪd] *adj* turbio
**turbidimeter** [,tʌrbɪ'dɪmɪtər] *s* turbidímetro
**turbidimetric** [,tʌrbɪdɪ'mɛtrɪk] *adj* turbidimétrico
**turbidity** [tʌr'bɪdɪtɪ] *s* turbiedad
**turbinate** ['tʌrbɪnet] o ['tʌrbɪnɪt] *adj* turbinado (*que afecta la figura de un cono inverso*); (anat.) turbinado; *s* concha espiral; (anat.) hueso turbinado
**turbine** ['tʌrbɪn] o ['tʌrbaɪn] *s* turbina
**turbine-electric** ['tʌrbɪnɪ'lɛktrɪk] o ['tʌrbaɪnɪ'lɛktrɪk] *adj* turboeléctrico
**turbit** ['tʌrbɪt] *s* (orn.) paloma de corbata
**turboblower** ['tʌrbo,bloər] *s* turbosoplador
**turbocompressor** [,tʌrbokəm'prɛsər] *s* turbocompresor
**turbodynamo** [,tʌrbo'daɪnəmo] *s* (*pl:* **-mos**) turbodínamo
**turbofan** ['tʌrbo,fæn] *s* turboventilador
**turbogenerator** ['tʌrbo'dʒɛnə,retər] *s* turbogenerador
**turbojet** ['tʌrbo,dʒɛt] *s* turborreactor, motor de turborreacción; avión de turborreacción
**turbomotor** ['tʌrbo,motər] *s* turbomotor
**turbo-prop bomber** ['tʌrbo,prɑp] *s* (aer.) bombardero turbohélice
**turbo-propeller engine** [,tʌrbopro'pɛlər] o **turbo-prop engine** ['tʌrbo,prɑp] *s* (aer.) turbohélice, motor de turbohélice
**turbopump** ['tʌrbo,pʌmp] *s* turbobomba
**turbo-ram-jet** [,tʌrbo'ræm'dʒɛt] *s* (aer.) turborreactor a postcombustión
**turbosupercharger** ['tʌrbo'supər,tʃɑrdʒər] o ['tʌrbo'sjupər,tʃɑrdʒər] *s* turbosupercargador
**turbot** ['tʌrbət] *s* (ichth.) rodaballo
**turboventilator** ['tʌrbo'vɛntɪ,letər] *s* turboventilador
**turbulence** ['tʌrbjələns] o **turbulency** ['tʌrbjələnsɪ] *s* turbulencia
**turbulent** ['tʌrbjələnt] *adj* turbulento
**Turco** ['tʌrko] *s* (*pl:* **-cos**) (mil.) turco (*tirador argelino*)
**tureen** [tʊ'rin] o [tjʊ'rin] *s* sopera
**turf** [tʌrf] *s* (*pl:* **turfs** o **turves**) césped (*hierba menuda*); tepe, terrón de tierra (*con césped*); turba; hipódromo; carreras de caballos
**turfman** ['tʌrfmən] *s* (*pl:* **-men**) turfista
**turfy** ['tʌrfɪ] *adj* (*comp:* **-ier;** *super:* **-iest**) encespedado; turboso; turfista
**turgescence** [tʌr'dʒɛsəns] *s* turgescencia
**turgescent** [tʌr'dʒɛsənt] *s* turgescente
**turgid** ['tʌrdʒɪd] *adj* (path. & fig.) turgente
**turgidity** [tʌr'dʒɪdɪtɪ] *s* turgencia
**Turin** ['tjʊrɪn] o ['tʊrɪn] *s* Turín
**turion** ['tjʊrɪɑn] o ['tʊrɪɑn] *s* (bot.) turión
**Turk.** abr. de **Turkey** y **Turkish**
**Turk** [tʌrk] *s* turco; (offensive) persona bárbara y feroz
**Turkestan** [,tʌrkə'stæn] o [,tʌrkə'stɑn] *s* el Turquestán
**turkey** ['tʌrkɪ] *s* (orn.) pavo; (*cap.*) *s* Turquía; **to talk turkey** (coll.) no tener pelos en la lengua
**turkey buzzard** *s* (orn.) aura, gallinazo

**turkey cock** *s* pavo (*macho*); persona vanagloriosa
**turkey gobbler** *s* (coll.) pavo (*macho*)
**turkey hen** *s* pava
**Turkey in Asia** *s* la Turquía de Asia, la Turquía Asiática
**Turkey in Europe** *s* la Turquía de Europa, la Turquía Europea
**turkey oak** *s* (bot.) roble rojo; (bot.) roble ahorquillado; **Turkey oak** *s* (bot.) rebollo (*Quercus cerris*)
**Turkey red** *s* rojo turco; tela de algodón de color rojo turco
**Turkic languages** ['tʌrkɪk] *spl* (philol.) idiomas turcos
**Turkish** ['tʌrkɪʃ] *adj* turco; *s* turco (*idioma*)
**Turkish bath** *s* baño turco
**Turkish Empire** *s* Imperio otomano
**Turkish towel** *s* toalla rusa
**Turkmen Soviet Socialist Republic, the** ['tʌrkmɛn] el Turkmenistán
**Turkoman** ['tʌrkomən] *s* (*pl:* **-mans**) turcomano
**Turkomanic** [,tʌrko'mænɪk] *adj* turcomano
**Turkophile** ['tʌrkofaɪl] *adj & s* turcófilo
**Turkophobe** ['tʌrkofob] *adj & s* turcófobo
**Turk's-cap lily** ['tʌrks,kæp] *s* (bot.) martagón
**Turk's-head** ['tʌrks,hɛd] *s* tortera con tubo central; deshollinador, escobón; (bot.) melón de costa; (naut.) cabeza de turco
**turmeric** ['tʌrmərɪk] *s* (bot.) cúrcuma (*planta y raíz*)
**turmeric paper** *s* (chem.) papel de cúrcuma
**turmoil** ['tʌrmɔɪl] *s* alboroto, disturbio, tumulto
**turn** [tʌrn] *s* vuelta; ocasión, oportunidad; fase; proceder, comportamiento; aspecto, figura, forma; estilo; expresión; vahido, vértigo, desvanecimiento; ensayo, prueba; exigencia; inclinación, propensión; giro (*de la frase*); turno (*alternativa entre dos o más personas*); espira (*de una hélice o una espiral*); (coll.) sacudida, susto; (elec.) espira (*de un rollo de alambre*); (mus.) grupeto; **turns** *spl* (coll.) reglas (*de la mujer*); **at every turn** a cada paso, en todo momento; **at the turn of** a la vuelta de; **bad turn** mala pasada; **by turns** por turnos; **good turn** favor, servicio; **in turn** por turno; **one good turn deserves another** bien con bien se paga; **out of turn** fuera de turno; **to a turn** exactamente; con suma perfección; **to be one's turn** tocarle a uno, p.ej., **it's your turn** le toca a Vd.; **to have a turn for** tener habilidad en, tener inclinación a; **to take a turn** dar una vuelta; cambiar de aspecto; **to take a turn for the better** estar mejorando; **to take a turn for the worse** estar empeorando; **to take turns** turnar, alternar; **to wait one's turn** aguardar turno, esperar vez ‖ *va* volver; dar vuelta a (*p.ej., una llave*); trastornar; torcer (*p.ej., el tobillo*); doblar (*la esquina, la calle*); aplicar, emplear, utilizar; dirigir (*p.ej., los ojos*); agriar; tornear (*labrar al torno*); pasar, sobrepasar; tener (*p.ej., veinte años cumplidos*); (elec.) dar vuelta a (*un interruptor*); **to turn against** predisponer en contra de; **to turn around** volver (*hacer girar*); voltear (*poner al revés*); torcer, dar otro sentido a (*las palabras de una persona*); **to turn aside** desviar; **to turn away** desviar; despachar, despedir; **to turn back** devolver; hacer retroceder; retrasar (*el reloj*); **to turn down** doblar o plegar hacia abajo; invertir; rechazar, rehusar; bajar (*p.ej., el gas*); **to turn in** doblar o plegar hacia adentro; entregar; **to turn into** volver en, p.ej., **he turned the water into wine** volvió el agua en vino; plantar (*a una persona*) en (*p.ej., la calle*); **to turn off** desviar; despedir; hacer, ejecutar; apagar (*la luz, la radio*); cortar (*el agua, gas, etc.*); cerrar (*la llave del agua, gas, etc.; la radio, la televisión*); interrumpir (*la corriente eléctrica*); **to turn on** encender (*la luz*); poner (*la luz, la radio, etc.*); abrir la llave de (*p.ej., el agua, gas*); abrir (*la llave del agua, gas, etc.*); establecer (*la corriente eléctrica*); **to turn out** echar; despedir; sacar hacia afuera; echar al campo (*a los animales*); volver al revés; apagar (*la luz*); hacer, ejecutar, fabricar, producir; **to turn over** entregar; invertir, volcar; doblar, plegar; considerar, revolver; hacer girar (*el motor de un automóvil*); hojear (*un libro*); pasar (*las hojas de un libro*); **to turn to** enderezar (*a una persona*) a o hacia; **to turn up** doblar o plegar hacia arriba; levantar; arremangar; revolver (*la tierra*); volver (*un naipe*); abrir la llave de (*p.ej., el gas*); abrir (*la llave del gas, etc.*); poner más alto o más fuerte (*la radio*) ‖ *vn* volver, p.ej., **the road turns to the right** el camino vuelve hacia la derecha; virar (*un automóvil, un avión, etc.*); girar (*moverse circularmente*); volverse (*inclinar, p.ej., la conversación a determinados asuntos; hacerse, ponerse, resultar; agriarse ciertos licores; mudar de opinión*); doblarse, plegarse; dar vueltas (*la cabeza*); cambiar (*el viento*); **to turn about** dar vuelta, dar una vuelta completa; cambiar de frente; mudar de opinión; voltearse; **to turn against** cobrar aversión a; rebelarse contra; **to turn around** dar vuelta, dar una vuelta completa; **to turn aside** o **away** desviarse; alejarse; **to turn back** volver, regresar; retroceder; **to turn down** doblarse hacia abajo; invertirse; **to turn in** doblarse hacia adentro, replegarse; entrar, dar la vuelta y entrar; recogerse, volver a casa; (coll.) recogerse, acostarse; **to turn into** entrar en; convertirse en; **to turn off** desviarse, cambiar de camino; **to turn on** volverse contra; depender de; versar sobre; ocuparse de; **to turn out** salir a la calle; dejarse ver; acontecer; venir a ser; resultar, salir, p.ej., **he will turn out a good doctor** saldrá un buen médico; (coll.) levantarse (*salir de cama*); **to turn out badly** salir mal; **to turn out right** acabar bien; **to turn out to be** venir a ser; resultar, salir; **to turn out well** salir bien; **to turn over** volcar, derribarse (*un vehículo*); cambiar de posición; **to turn over and over** dar repetidas vueltas; **to turn to** acudir a; recurrir a, dirigirse a; redundar en; convertirse en; **to turn to and fro** volver de un lado a otro; **to turn up** doblarse hacia arriba; levantarse; acontecer; acudir, aparecer, dejarse ver; **to turn upon** volverse contra; depender de; versar sobre; ocuparse en
**turnbuckle** ['tʌrn,bʌkəl] *s* tensor roscado, tornillo tensor; torniquete (*para mantener abiertas las hojas de las ventanas*)
**turncoat** ['tʌrn,kot] *s* tránsfuga, apóstata, renegado
**turndown** ['tʌrn,daʊn] *s* rechazamiento; *adj* doblado hacia abajo, caído (*cuello*)
**turner** ['tʌrnər] *s* volvedor; torneador; tornero (*obrero que labra al torno*); gimnasta, volatinero
**turning** ['tʌrnɪŋ] *adj* giratorio, rotatorio; *s* vuelta; giro, viraje; tornería; invención (*de una frase*); **turnings** *spl* torneaduras; piezas torneadas
**turning point** *s* punto de transición, punto decisivo, punto crucial; (surv.) punto de cambio (*en la nivelación*)
**turnip** ['tʌrnɪp] *s* (bot.) nabo (*planta y raíz*); (bot.) colinabo o rutabaga; (slang) calentador (*reloj de bolsillo*); (slang) tipo, sujeto; (coll.) tonto, necio
**turnkey** ['tʌrn,ki] *s* llavero de una cárcel, carcelero
**turn of life** *s* (physiol.) menopausia
**turn of mind** *s* natural, inclinación, propensión
**turnout** ['tʌrn,aʊt] *s* concurrencia; entrada (*número de personas que asisten a un espectáculo*); apartadero (*para dejar pasar otros automóviles, trenes, etc.*); producción (*cantidad producida*); equipaje; carruaje de lujo; (coll.) huelga; (coll.) huelguista
**turnover** ['tʌrn,ovər] *s* vuelco; cambio de personal; movimiento de mercancías; ciclo de compra y venta; (cook.) pastel con repulgo; *adj* doblado hacia abajo
**turnpike** ['tʌrn,paɪk] *s* carretera de peaje, camino de portazgo, autopista de portazgo; barrera de portazgo
**turn signals** *spl* (aut.) señales de dirección, indicadores de dirección
**turnspit** ['tʌrn,spɪt] *s* persona o perro que da vueltas al asador

**turnstile** ['tʌrn,staɪl] *s* torniquete
**turnstone** ['tʌrn,ston] *s* (orn.) revuelvepiedras
**turntable** 'tʌrn,tebəl] *s* placa giratoria, plataforma giratoria (*de ferrocarril*); placa giratoria, plato giratorio (*de gramófono*)
**turpentine** ['tʌrpəntaɪn] *s* trementina; esencia de trementina
**turpeth** ['tʌrpɪθ] *s* (bot.) turbit; (pharm.) turbino
**turpitude** ['tʌrpɪtjud] o ['tʌrpɪtud] *s* torpeza, infamia, vileza
**turquoise** ['tʌrkɔɪz] o ['tʌrkwɔɪz] *s* (mineral.) turquesa
**turquoise blue** *s* azul turquesa
**turret** ['tʌrɪt] *s* torrecilla; (arch.) torreón; (arti.) torre; (hist.) torre móvil; (nav.) torreta
**turreted** ['tʌrɪtɪd] *adj* torreado; (zool.) turriculado
**turret lathe** *s* torno revolvedor, torno de torrecilla
**turtle** ['tʌrtəl] *s* (zool.) tortuga; **to turn turtle** derribarse patas arriba; volcar (*un coche*); zozobrar (*un buque*)
**turtleback** ['tʌrtəl,bæk] *s* caparazón de tortuga; (naut.) cubierta de caparazón
**turtledove** ['tʌrtəl,dʌv] *s* (orn.) tórtola; (fig.) tórtolo (*persona enamorada*)
**Tuscan** ['tʌskən] *adj & s* toscano
**Tuscany** ['tʌskənɪ] *s* la Toscana
**Tusculum** ['tʌskjələm] *s* Túsculo
**tush** [tʌʃ] *s* colmillo; *interj* ¡ bah!
**tusk** [tʌsk] *s* colmillo (*p.ej., del elefante*); *va* herir con los colmillos; cavar o rasgar con los colmillos
**tusker** ['tʌskər] *s* animal colmilludo
**tussah** ['tʌsə] *s* tusor (*seda*); (ent.) anterea
**tussle** ['tʌsəl] *s* agarrada, riña; *vn* agarrarse, asirse, reñir
**tussock** ['tʌsək] *s* montecillo de hierbas crecientes
**tussock moth** *s* (ent.) lagarta, monja
**tut** [tʌt] *interj* ¡ bah!
**tutelage** ['tjutɪlɪdʒ] o ['tutɪlɪdʒ] *s* tutela; enseñanza, instrucción
**tutelar** ['tjutɪlər] o ['tutɪlər] *adj* tutelar
**tutelary** ['tjutɪ,lɛrɪ] o ['tutɪ,lɛrɪ] *adj* tutelar; *s* (*pl:* **-ies**) divinidad tutelar, santo tutelar, genio tutelar, numen tutelar
**tutor** ['tjutər] o ['tutər] *s* (law) tutor; preceptor; maestro particular; (Brit.) guardián de la disciplina; *va* ser tutor de; enseñar; dar enseñanza particular a; tratar con severidad; *vn* ser tutor; dar lecciones particulares; (coll.) tomar lecciones particulares
**tutorial** [tju'torɪəl] o [tu'torɪəl] *adj* tutelar; preceptoral
**tutorship** ['tjutərʃɪp] o ['tutərʃɪp] *s* tutela; preceptorado
**tutsan** ['tʌtsən] *s* (bot.) todasana, todabuena
**tutti-frutti** ['tutɪ'frutɪ] *s* helado de varias frutas; conserva de varias frutas; *adj* hecho con varias frutas
**tutty** ['tʌtɪ] *s* atutía, tucía
**tuxedo** [tʌk'sido] *s* (*pl:* **-dos**) smoking
**tuyère** [twi'jɛr] o [twɪr] *s* (found.) tobera
**TV** abr. de **television**
**twaddle** ['twɑdəl] *s* charla, habladuría; tonterías, disparates; *va* decir tontamente; *vn* charlar, decir tonterías
**twain** [twen] *adj & s* (archaic & poet.) dos
**twang** [twæŋ] *s* tañido (*de un instrumento músico*); timbre nasal; *va* tocar con un tañido; arrojar con un sonido agudo; decir con timbre nasal; tirar (*una flecha*); *vn* producir un sonido agudo; hablar por la nariz, hablar con voz nasal
**'twas** [twɑz] o [twʌz] contracción de **it was**
**tweak** [twik] *s* pellizco retorcido; *va* pellizcar retorciendo; *vn* dar un pellizco retorcido
**tweed** [twid] *s* mezcla de lana; traje de mezcla de lana; **tweeds** *spl* ropa de mezcla de lana
**tweedledum and tweedledee** [,twidəl'dʌm ənd ,twidəl'di] *spl* dos cosas entre las cuales no hay diferencia; **it's tweedledum and tweedledee** llámele Vd. hache, da lo mismo perro que gato
**tweedy** ['twidɪ] *adj* de mezcla de lana; aficionado a la ropa de mezcla de lana; directo, franco, prosaico
**'tween** [twin] *prep* (poet.) var. de **between**
**tweet** [twit] *s* pío; *vn* piar
**tweeter** ['twitər] *s* (rad.) altavoz para altas audiofrecuencias, altavoz agudos
**tweezers** ['twizərz] *spl* pinzas, tenacillas, bruselas
**twelfth** [twɛlfθ] *adj* duodécimo; dozavo; *s* duodécimo; dozavo; doce (*en las fechas*)
**Twelfth-day** ['twɛlfθ,de] *s* var. de **Twelfth-tide**
**Twelfth-night** ['twɛlfθ,naɪt] *s* día de Reyes, Epifanía; víspera del día de Reyes
**Twelfth-tide** ['twɛlfθ,taɪd] *s* día de Reyes, Epifanía
**twelve** [twɛlv] *adj* doce; *s* doce; **twelve o'clock** las doce; **the Twelve** (Bib.) los doce apóstoles (*de Jesucristo*)
**Twelve Apostles** *spl* (Bib.) doce apóstoles (*de Jesucristo*)
**twelvefold** ['twɛlv,fold] *adj* doce veces mayor o más; de doce partes; *adv* doce veces más
**twelvemo** ['twɛlvmo] *adj* en dozavo; *s* (*pl:* **-mos**) libro en dozavo
**twelvemonth** ['twɛlv,mʌnθ] *s* año (*doce meses*)
**Twelve Tables** *spl* doce tablas (*antigua ley romana*)
**twentieth** ['twɛntɪɪθ] *adj* vigésimo; veintavo; *s* vigésimo; veintavo; veinte (*en las fechas*)
**twenty** ['twɛntɪ] *adj* veinte; *s* (*pl:* **-ties**) veinte
**twentyfold** ['twɛntɪ,fold] *adj* veinte veces mayor o más; de veinte partes; *adv* veinte veces más
**twenty-one** ['twɛntɪ'wʌn] *s* veintiuna (*juego de naipes*)
**'twere** [twʌr] contracción de **it were**
**twice** [twaɪs] *adv* dos veces; **twice as large as** dos veces más grande que
**twice-told** ['twaɪs,told] *adj* dicho dos veces; trillado, sabido
**twiddle** ['twɪdəl] *s* vuelta ligera; *va* menear o revolver ociosamente; *vn* ocuparse de tonterías; girar; temblar
**twig** [twɪg] *s* ramito; varilla de virtudes, **twigs** *spl* leña menuda
**twilight** ['twaɪ,laɪt] *s* crepúsculo; *adj* crepuscular
**twilight sleep** *s* (med.) sueño crepuscular (*narcosis obstétrica parcial*)
**twill** [twɪl] *s* tela cruzada; cruzado (*dibujo de tela*); *va* cruzar (*la tela*)
**'twill** [twɪl] contracción de **it will**
**twin** [twɪn] *adj & s* gemelo; **the Twins** (astr.) los Gemelos; (*pret & pp:* **twinned**; *ger:* **twinning**) *va* parir (*gemelos*); parear; emparejar; *vn* parir gemelos; nacer gemelo; emparejarse
**twin beds** *spl* camas gemelas
**Twin Cities** *spl* ciudades gemelas (*Saint Paul y Minneápolis, EE.UU.*)
**twin-cylinder** ['twɪn'sɪlɪndər] *adj* de dos cilindros, de cilindros gemelos
**twine** [twaɪn] *s* bramante, guita; enroscadura; retorcedura; *va* enroscar; retorcer; *vn* enroscarse; retorcerse
**twinflower** ['twɪn,flaʊər] *s* (bot.) té de Suecia
**twinge** [twɪndʒ] *s* punzada; *va* causar un dolor agudo a; *vn* sentir una punzada
**twin-jet plane** ['twɪn'dʒɛt] *s* (aer.) avión birreactor
**twinkle** ['twɪŋkəl] *s* centelleo; pestañeo; movimiento muy rápido; instante; *va* hacer centellear; abrir y cerrar (*los ojos*) rápidamente; *vn* centellear; pestañear; moverse rápidamente
**twinkling** ['twɪŋklɪŋ] *s* centelleo; pestañeo; movimiento muy rápido; instante; **in the twinkling of an eye** en un abrir y cerrar de ojos
**twin lead** [lid] *s* (telv.) alambre gemelo
**twin-motor** ['twɪn'motər] *adj* (aer.) bimotor
**twin-screw** ['twɪn'skru] *adj* (naut.) de dos hélices, de doble hélice
**twirl** [twʌrl] *s* vuelta, giro; rasgo (*trazado con la pluma*); *va* hacer girar; (baseball) arrojar (*la pelota*); *vn* girar, dar vueltas; hacer piruetas
**twist** [twɪst] *s* torcedura; enroscadura; curva, recodo; giro, vuelta; torzal; rosca (*de pan*); rollo de tabaco; propensión, prejuicio; sesgo (*de la mente*); *va* torcer; retorcer; enroscar;

hacer girar; entrelazar; desviar; (baseball) arrojar (*la pelota*) haciéndola dar vueltas; (fig.) torcer (*dar diverso sentido a*); *vn* torcerse; retorcerse; enroscarse; dar vueltas; entrelazarse; desviarse; serpentear; **to twist and turn** dar vueltas (*en la cama, por no poder dormir*)
**twister** ['twɪstər] *s* torcedor (*persona y aparato*); torcedero (*aparato*); (baseball) pelota arrojada con efecto; (meteor.) tromba, tornado
**twit** [twɪt] *s* reprensión; advertencia recordativa; (*pret & pp:* **twitted;** *ger:* **twitting**) *va* reprender; reprender (*a uno*) recordando algo desagradable o poniéndole en ridículo; **to twit with** reprender (*a uno*) recordando (*p.ej., un error o estupidez*)
**twitch** [twɪtʃ] *s* estirón repentino; crispadura; ligero temblor; acial (*instrumento para oprimir el hocico de las bestias para sujetarlas*); *va* arrancar; mover de un tirón; *vn* crisparse; temblar (*p.ej., los párpados*); dar un tirón
**twitter** ['twɪtər] *s* gorjeo (*de los pájaros*); risita sofocada; excitación, inquietud; *vn* gorjear (*los pájaros*); reír sofocadamente; agitarse, temblar de inquietud
**'twixt** [twɪkst] *prep* (poet. & dial.) var. de **betwixt**
**two** [tu] *adj* dos; *s* dos; **in two** en dos; **to put two and two together** atar cabos, sacar la conclusión evidente; **two o'clock** las dos; **two of a kind** tal para cual
**two-bagger** ['tu,bægər] *s* (baseball) doblete (*golpe con que el bateador gana la segunda base*)
**two-base hit** ['tu,bes] *s* var. de **two-bagger**
**two-by-four** ['tubaɪ,for] *adj* de dos por cuatro (*pulgadas, pies, etc.*); (coll.) pequeño, insignificante; *s* madero de dos por cuatro pulgadas
**two-cycle** ['tu,saɪkəl] *adj* (mach.) de dos tiempos; *s* (mach.) ciclo de dos tiempos
**two-cylinder** ['tu,sɪlɪndər] *adj* (mach.) de dos cilindros, bicilíndrico; **a two-cylinder motor** un dos cilindros
**two-edged** ['tu,ɛdʒd] *adj* de dos filos
**two-faced** ['tu,fest] *adj* de dos caras; (fig.) de dos caras (*doble, falso*)
**two-fisted** ['tu,fɪstɪd] *adj* de dos puños; (coll.) fuerte, vigoroso, valiente
**two-fold** ['tu,fold] *adj* doble; *adv* dos veces
**two-four** ['tu'for] *adj* (mus.) de dos por cuatro
**two-handed** ['tu,hændɪd] *adj* de dos manos; para dos manos; ambidextro
**two hundred** *adj & s* doscientos
**two-part** ['tu,pɑrt] *adj* de dos partes
**two-part time** *s* (mus.) compás a dos tiempos
**twopence** ['tʌpəns] *s* dos peniques; moneda de dos peniques
**two-penny** ['tʌpənɪ] *adj* de dos peniques; despreciable, sin valor
**two-phase** ['tu,fez] *adj* (elec.) bifásico
**two-ply** ['tu,plaɪ] *adj* de dos capas; de dos tramas; de dos hilos o hebras
**twosome** ['tusəm] *s* pareja; pareja de jugadores; juego de dos
**two-step** ['tu,stɛp] *s* paso doble (*baile y música*)
**two-stroke cycle** ['tu,strok] *s* (mach.) ciclo de dos tiempos
**two-time** ['tu,taɪm] *va* (slang) engañar en amor, ser infiel a (*una persona del otro sexo*)
**'twould** [twʊd] contracción de **it would**
**two-way** ['tu,we] *adj* de dos sentidos o direcciones
**two-way radio** *s* equipo emisor y receptor, aparato receptor y transmisor
**two-way switch** *s* (elec.) cada uno de dos conmutadores de tres terminales
**two-way valve** *s* (mach.) válvula de dos pasos
**two-wire** ['tu,waɪr] *adj* (elec.) bifilar
**tycoon** [taɪ'kun] *s* taicún (*señor feudal del Japón*); (coll.) magnate
**tying** ['taɪɪŋ] *ger de* **tie**
**tyke** [taɪk] *s* (coll.) chiquillo, niño travieso; perro, gozque; (archaic & dial.) patán
**tympan** ['tɪmpən] *s* tambor; (arch.) tímpano; (print.) tímpano

**tympanic** [tɪm'pænɪk] *adj* (anat. & med.) timpánico
**tympanic antrum** *s* (anat.) antro timpánico
**tympanic membrane** *s* (anat.) membrana timpánica
**tympanist** ['tɪmpənɪst] *s* atabalero
**tympanites** [,tɪmpə'naɪtiz] *s* (path.) timpanitis (*hinchazón producida por gases*)
**tympanitic** [,tɪmpə'nɪtɪk] *adj* timpanítico
**tympanitis** [,tɪmpə'naɪtɪs] *s* (path.) timpanitis (*inflamación del tímpano del oído*)
**tympanum** ['tɪmpənəm] *s* (*pl:* **-nums** o **-na** [nə]) (arch. & anat.) tímpano
**type** [taɪp] *s* tipo; (print.) tipo; (print.) letra (*conjunto de letras o tipos*); letras impresas, letras escritas a máquina; tipo (*figura de una moneda o medalla*); (physiol.) grupo; *va* escribir a máquina, mecanografiar; imprimir; representar, simbolizar; (med.) determinar el grupo de (*un espécimen de sangre*); *vn* escribir a máquina
**type bar** *s* línea de linotipia; palanca portatipos (*de la máquina de escribir*)
**type face** *s* forma de letra, estilo de letra
**type founder** *s* fundidor de letra
**type founding** *s* fundición de letras de imprenta
**type gauge** *s* tipómetro
**type genus** *s* (biol.) género tipo
**type metal** *s* metal de imprenta
**typescript** ['taɪp,skrɪpt] *s* material escrito a máquina
**typesetter** ['taɪp,sɛtər] *s* (print.) cajista; (print.) máquina de componer
**typesetting** ['taɪp,sɛtɪŋ] *s* (print.) composición; *adj* (print.) para componer tipos
**typewrite** ['taɪp,raɪt] (*pret:* **-wrote;** *pp:* **-written**) *va & vn* escribir a máquina, mecanografiar
**typewriter** ['taɪp,raɪtər] *s* máquina de escribir; mecanógrafo o mecanógrafa, dactilógrafo o dactilógrafa
**typewriter ribbon** *s* cinta para máquinas de escribir
**typewriting** ['taɪp,raɪtɪŋ] *s* mecanografía o dactilografía; trabajo hecho con máquina de escribir
**typewritten** ['taɪp,rɪtən] *adj* escrito a máquina; *pp de* **typewrite**
**typewrote** ['taɪp,rot] *pret de* **typewrite**
**typhoid** ['taɪfɔɪd] *adj* tifoideo; *s* (path.) fiebre tifoidea
**typhoidal** [taɪ'fɔɪdəl] *adj* tifoideo
**typhoid bacillus** *s* (bact.) bacilo tífico
**typhoid fever** (path.) fiebre tifoidea
**typhoon** [taɪ'fun] *s* tifón
**typhous** ['taɪfəs] *adj* tífico
**typhus** ['taɪfəs] *s* (path.) tifus
**typical** ['tɪpɪkəl] *adj* típico
**typically** ['tɪpɪkəlɪ] *adv* típicamente
**typification** [,tɪpɪfɪ'keʃən] *s* simbolización
**typify** ['tɪpɪfaɪ] (*pret & pp:* **-fied**) *va* simbolizar; ser ejemplo o modelo de
**typing** ['taɪpɪŋ] *s* mecanografía o dactilografía; trabajo hecho con máquina de escribir
**typist** ['taɪpɪst] *s* mecanógrafo o mecanógrafa, dactilógrafo o dactilógrafa
**typographer** [taɪ'pɑgrəfər] *s* tipógrafo
**typographic** [,taɪpə'græfɪk] o **typographical** [,taɪpə'græfɪkəl] *adj* tipográfico
**typographical error** *s* error de máquina
**typographically** [,taɪpə'græfɪkəlɪ] *adv* tipográficamente
**typography** [taɪ'pɑgrəfɪ] *s* tipografía
**typolithography** [,taɪpəlɪ'θɑgrəfɪ] *s* tipolitografía
**typometry** [taɪ'pɑmɪtrɪ] *s* (print.) tipometría
**tyrannic** [tɪ'rænɪk] o [taɪ'rænɪk] o **tyrannical** [tɪ'rænɪkəl] o [taɪ'rænɪkəl] *adj* tiránico
**tyrannicidal** [tɪ,rænɪ'saɪdəl] *adj* tiranicida
**tyrannicide** [tɪ'rænɪsaɪd] o [taɪ'rænɪsaɪd] *s* tiranicidio (*acción*); tiranicida (*persona*)
**tyrannize** ['tɪrənaɪz] *va & vn* tiranizar
**tyrannous** ['tɪrənəs] *adj* tirano
**tyranny** ['tɪrənɪ] *s* (*pl:* **-nies**) tiranía
**tyrant** ['taɪrənt] *s* tirano
**Tyre** [taɪr] *s* Tiro
**Tyrian** ['tɪrɪən] *adj & s* tirio
**Tyrian purple** *s* púrpura de Tiro

**tyro** [ˈtaɪro] *s* (*pl:* **-ros**) tirón, novicio
**Tyrol, the** [tɪˈrol] o [ˈtɪrɑl] el Tirol
**Tyrolean** [tɪˈrolɪən] *adj & s* var. de **Tyrolese**
**Tyrolese** [ˌtɪroˈliz] *adj* tirolés; *s* (*pl:* **-lese**) tirolés
**tyrosinase** [ˈtaɪrosɪˌnes] o [ˈtɪrosɪˌnes] *s* (biochem.) tirosinasa
**tyrosine** [ˈtaɪrəsin] o [ˈtɪrəsin] *s* (biochem.) tirosina
**tyrothricin** [ˌtaɪrəˈθraɪsɪn] o [ˌtaɪrəˈθrɪsɪn] *s* (pharm.) tirotricina
**Tyrrhenian** [tɪˈrinɪən] *adj* tirreno
**Tyrrhenian Sea** *s* mar Tirreno
**tzar** [tsɑr] *s* var. de **czar**
**tzarevitch** [ˈtsɑrɪvɪtʃ] *s* var. de **czarevitch**
**tzarina** [tsɑˈrinə] *s* var. de **czarina**
**tzetze** [ˈtsɛtsɪ] *s* var. de **tsetse**
**tzigane** [ˌtsiˈgɑn] *adj & s* gitano (*de Hungría*)

# U

**U, u** [ju] *s* (*pl:* **U's, u's** [juz]) vigésima primera letra del alfabeto inglés

**U.** abr. de **University**

**Ubiquitarian** [ju,bɪkwɪ'tɛrɪən] *adj & s* (eccl.) ubiquitario

**ubiquitous** [ju'bɪkwɪtəs] *adj* ubicuo

**ubiquity** [ju'bɪkwɪtɪ] *s* ubicuidad

**U-boat** ['ju,bot] *s* submarino, submarino alemán

**U bolt** *s* perno en U

**u.c.** abr. de **upper case**

**udder** ['ʌdər] *s* ubre

**udometer** [ju'dɑmɪtər] *s* udómetro

**ugh** [ʊ] o [ʌ] *interj* ¡puf!, ¡buf!

**ugliness** ['ʌglɪnɪs] *s* fealdad; (coll.) malhumor

**ugly** ['ʌglɪ] *adj* (*comp:* **-lier;** *super:* **-liest**) feo; (coll.) malhumorado, pendenciero

**ugly duckling** *s* niño poco prometedor que sale un adulto interesante; **the Ugly Duckling** el Patito Feo

**UHF** abr. de **ultrahigh frequency**

**uhlan** ['ulɑn] o [u'lɑn] *s* (mil.) ulano

**U.K.** abr. de **United Kingdom**

**ukase** [ju'kes] *s* ucase

**Ukraine** ['jukren] o [ju'kren] *s* Ucrania

**Ukrainian** [ju'krenɪən] *adj & s* ucranio

**ulcer** ['ʌlsər] *s* (path.) úlcera; (fig.) llaga

**ulcerate** ['ʌlsəret] *va* ulcerar; *vn* ulcerarse

**ulceration** [,ʌlsə'reʃən] *s* ulceración

**ulcerous** ['ʌlsərəs] *adj* ulceroso

**ulema** [,ulə'mɑ] *s* ulema

**uliginose** [ju'lɪdʒɪnos] o **uliginous** [ju'lɪdʒɪnəs] *adj* uliginoso

**ulitis** [ju'laɪtɪs] *s* (path.) ulitis

**ulluco** [u'juko] *s* (bot.) ulluco (*tubérculo comestible de Sudamérica semejante a la patata*)

**ulmaceous** [ʌl'meʃəs] *adj* (bot.) ulmáceo

**ulna** ['ʌlnə] *s* (*pl:* **-nae** [ni] o **-nas**) (anat.) ulna

**ulnar** ['ʌlnər] *adj* ulnar

**ulster** ['ʌlstər] *s* úlster

**ult.** abr. de **ultimo** (Lat.) **in the past month**

**ulterior** [ʌl'tɪrɪər] *adj* ulterior; escondido, oculto

**ultima** ['ʌltɪmə] *s* (gram.) última sílaba

**ultimate** ['ʌltɪmɪt] *adj* último, final; fundamental, esencial; sumo, extremo

**ultimately** ['ʌltɪmɪtlɪ] *adv* últimamente, por último

**ultima Thule** *s* última Tule

**ultimatum** [,ʌltɪ'metəm] *s* (*pl:* **-tums** o **-ta** [tə]) ultimátum

**ultimo** ['ʌltɪmo] *adv* del mes próximo pasado, en el mes próximo pasado

**ultra** ['ʌltrə] *s* ultraísta, extremista; *adj* extremo, excesivo; *prep* ultra

**ultrahigh frequency** [,ʌltrə'haɪ] *s* (rad.) frecuencia ultraelevada

**ultraliberal** [,ʌltrə'lɪbərəl] *adj & s* ultraliberal

**ultramarine** [,ʌltrəmə'rin] *adj* ultramarino; *s* ultramar, azul de ultramar, azul ultramarino

**ultramarine blue** *s* azul de ultramar, azul ultramarino

**ultramicroscope** [,ʌltrə'maɪkrəskop] *s* ultramicroscopio

**ultramicroscopic** [,ʌltrə,maɪkrə'skɑpɪk] *adj* ultramicroscópico

**ultramicroscopy** [,ʌltrəmaɪ'krɑskəpɪ] o [,ʌltrə'maɪkrə,skopɪ] *s* ultramicroscopia

**ultramodern** [,ʌltrə'mɑdərn] *adj* ultramoderno

**ultramontane** [,ʌltrə'mɑnten] *adj & s* ultramontano

**ultramontanism** [,ʌltrə'mɑntənɪzəm] *s* ultramontanismo

**ultramundane** [,ʌltrə'mʌnden] *adj* ultramundano

**ultraradical** [,ʌltrə'rædɪkəl] *adj* ultrarradical

**ultrarapid** [,ʌltrə'ræpɪd] *adj* ultrarrápido

**ultrared** [,ʌltrə'rɛd] *adj* ultrarrojo

**ultrasonic** [,ʌltrə'sɑnɪk] *adj* ultrasónico; **ultrasonics** *ssg* ultrasónica

**ultratropical** [,ʌltrə'trɑpɪkəl] *adj* ultratropical

**ultraviolet** [,ʌltrə'vaɪəlɪt] *adj* (phys.) ultraviolado o ultravioleta

**ultraviolet rays** *spl* (phys.) rayos ultravioletas

**ultravirus** [,ʌltrə'vaɪrəs] *s* ultravirus

**ultrazodiacal** [,ʌltrəzo'daɪəkəl] *adj* (astr.) ultrazodiacal

**ululant** ['juljələnt] o ['ʌljələnt] *adj* ululante

**ululate** ['juljəlet] o ['ʌljəlet] *vn* ulular

**ululation** [,juljə'leʃən] o [,ʌljə'leʃən] *s* ululación

**Ulysses** [jʊ'lɪsiz] *s* (myth.) Ulises

**umbel** ['ʌmbəl] *s* (bot.) umbela

**umbellar** ['ʌmbələr] o **umbellate** ['ʌmbəlet] *adj* umbelado, umbeliforme

**umbelliferous** [,ʌmbə'lɪfərəs] *adj* umbelífero

**umber** ['ʌmbər] *s* tierra de sombra; *adj* de color ocre obscuro

**umbilical** [ʌm'bɪlɪkəl] *adj* umbilical

**umbilical cord** *s* (anat.) cordón umbilical

**umbilicate** [ʌm'bɪlɪkɪt] *adj* umbilicado

**umbilicus** [ʌm'bɪlɪkəs] o [,ʌmbɪ'laɪkəs] *s* (*pl:* **-ci** [saɪ]) (anat.) ombligo

**umbo** ['ʌmbo] *s* (*pl:* **umbones** [ʌm'boniz] o **umbos**) umbón (*del escudo*); (anat. & zool.) umbo

**umbra** ['ʌmbrə] *s* (*pl:* **-brae** [bri]) sombra; (astr.) región sombra, cono de sombra; (astr.) núcleo (*de las manchas solares*); (ichth.) ombrina, ombrina barbuda

**umbrage** ['ʌmbrɪdʒ] *s* sombra, umbría; resentimiento; **to take umbrage at** resentirse por

**umbrageous** [ʌm'bredʒəs] *adj* umbroso, sombroso; resentido

**umbra tree** *s* (bot.) ombú

**umbrella** [ʌm'brɛlə] *s* paraguas; (zool.) umbrela; (mil.) sombrilla protectora

**umbrella man** *s* paragüero

**umbrella stand** *s* paragüero

**umbrella tree** *s* (bot.) magnolia tripétala

**Umbria** ['ʌmbrɪə] *s* la Umbría

**Umbrian** ['ʌmbrɪən] *adj & s* umbro

**umiak** ['umɪæk] *s* barca de la mujer (*de los esquimales*)

**umlaut** ['ʊmlaʊt] *s* (phonet.) metafonía; diéresis; *va* modificar por metafonía; escribir con diéresis

**umpire** ['ʌmpaɪr] *s* árbitro; (sport) árbitro; *va & vn* arbitrar; (sport) arbitrar

**UMT** abr. de **Universal Military Training**

**un-** *prefix* in-, p.ej., **uncertain** incierto; **unhappy** infeliz; **unheard-of** inaudito; des-, p.ej., **unequal** desigual; **unfortunate** desgraciado; **unbutton** desabotonar; **unhook** desenganchar; anti-, p.ej., **uneconomic** antieconómico; **unscientific** anticientífico; **unsportsmanlike** antideportivo; poco, p.ej., **unintelligent** poco inteligente

**UN** ['ju'ɛn] *s* ONU (*organización de las Naciones Unidas*)

**unabashed** [,ʌnə'bæʃt] *adj* desvergonzado

**unable** [ʌn'ebəl] *adj* incapaz, inhábil; imposibilitado; **to be unable to** + *inf* no poder + *inf;* **to be unable to make up one's mind** no acabar de decidirse

**unabridged** [,ʌnə'brɪdʒd] *adj* no abreviado, íntegro, completo

**unaccented** [ʌn'æksɛntɪd] o [,ʌnæk'sɛntɪd] *adj* inacentuado

**unacceptable** [,ʌnæk'sɛptəbəl] *adj* inaceptable

**unaccompanied** [,ʌnə'kʌmpənɪd] *adj* sin acompañamiento

**unaccountable** [ˌʌnəˈkaʊntəbəl] *adj* inexplicable; irresponsable
**unaccountably** [ˌʌnəˈkaʊntəblɪ] *adv* inexplicablemente; irresponsablemente
**unaccounted-for** [ˌʌnəˈkaʊntɪdˌfɔr] *adj* no explicado; no hallado
**unaccustomed** [ˌʌnəˈkʌstəmd] *adj* no acostumbrado; desacostumbrado
**unadaptability** [ˌʌnəˌdæptəˈbɪlɪtɪ] *s* inadaptabilidad
**unadaptable** [ˌʌnəˈdæptəbəl] *adj* inadaptable
**unadoptable** [ˌʌnəˈdɑptəbəl] *adj* inadoptable
**unadulterated** [ˌʌnəˈdʌltəˌretɪd] *adj* no adulterado, puro
**unadvised** [ˌʌnədˈvaɪzd] *adj* desaconsejado, desatentado
**unadvisedly** [ˌʌnədˈvaɪzɪdlɪ] *adv* inconsideradamente, imprudentemente
**unaffected** [ˌʌnəˈfɛktɪd] *adj* inafectado
**unafraid** [ˌʌnəˈfred] *adj* desaprensivo, sin miedo
**unaligned** [ˌʌnəˈlaɪnd] *adj* no comprometido, no empeñado
**unallowable** [ˌʌnəˈlaʊəbəl] *adj* inadmisible
**unalterability** [ʌnˌɔltərəˈbɪlɪtɪ] *s* inalterabilidad
**unalterable** [ʌnˈɔltərəbəl] *adj* inalterable
**unalterably** [ʌnˈɔltərəblɪ] *adv* inalterablemente
**unaltered** [ʌnˈɔltərd] *adj* inalterado
**unambiguous** [ˌʌnæmˈbɪgjʊəs] *adj* inequívoco
**un-American** [ˌʌnəˈmɛrɪkən] *adj* antiamericano, antinorteamericano
**unanalyzable** [ʌnˈænəˌlaɪzəbəl] *adj* inanalizable
**unanimism** [juˈnænɪmɪzəm] *s* unanimismo
**unanimity** [ˌjunəˈnɪmɪtɪ] *s* unanimidad
**unanimous** [juˈnænɪməs] *adj* unánime
**unanswerable** [ʌnˈænsərəbəl] o [ʌnˈɑnsərəbəl] *adj* incontestable
**unanswered** [ʌnˈænsərd] o [ʌnˈɑnsərd] *adj* por contestar; no correspondido
**unappealable** [ˌʌnəˈpiləbəl] *adj* inapelable
**unappetizing** [ʌnˈæpɪˌtaɪzɪŋ] *adj* poco apetitoso
**unappreciative** [ˌʌnəˈpriʃɪˌetɪv] *adj* ingrato, desagradecido
**unapprehensive** [ʌnˌæprɪˈhɛnsɪv] *adj* desaprensivo
**unapproachable** [ˌʌnəˈprotʃəbəl] *adj* inaccesible, inabordable; sin igual
**unapt** [ʌnˈæpt] *adj* inepto, inhábil; improbable; inadecuado
**unarm** [ʌnˈɑrm] *va* desarmar
**unarmed** [ʌnˈɑrmd] *adj* desarmado, inerme; (biol.) inerme
**unascertainable** [ʌnˌæsərˈtenəbəl] *adj* inaveriguable
**unasked** [ʌnˈæskt] o [ʌnˈɑskt] *adj* no solicitado; sin pedir; no convidado
**unassembled** [ˌʌnəˈsɛmbəld] *adj* desarmado, desmontado
**unassimilable** [ˌʌnəˈsɪmɪləbəl] *adj* inasimilable
**unassuming** [ˌʌnəˈsumɪŋ] o [ˌʌnəˈsjumɪŋ] *adj* modesto, sin pretensiones
**unattached** [ˌʌnəˈtætʃt] *adj* suelto; libre; no prometido; (law) no embargado; (mil. & nav.) de reemplazo
**unattainable** [ˌʌnəˈtenəbəl] *adj* inasequible, inalcanzable
**unattended** [ˌʌnəˈtɛndɪd] *adj* desatendido; inasistido
**unattractive** [ˌʌnəˈtræktɪv] *adj* sin atractivo, desairado
**unauthorized** [ʌnˈɔθəraɪzd] *adj* desautorizado
**unavailable** [ˌʌnəˈveləbəl] *adj* indisponible
**unavailing** [ˌʌnəˈvelɪŋ] *adj* vano, inútil, ineficaz
**unavoidable** [ˌʌnəˈvɔɪdəbəl] *adj* inevitable
**unaware** [ˌʌnəˈwɛr] *adj* inconsciente; **to be unaware of** estar ajeno de; *adv* de improviso; sin saberlo
**unawares** [ˌʌnəˈwɛrz] *adv* de improviso; sin saberlo; **to catch somebody unawares** coger a una persona desprevenida
**unbacked** [ʌnˈbækt] *adj* sin ayuda; sin respaldo; sin domar; sin apuesta
**unbaked** [ʌnˈbekt] *adj* no cocido; no maduro
**unbalance** [ʌnˈbæləns] *s* desequilibrio; *va* desequilibrar; trastornar
**unbalanced** [ʌnˈbælənst] *adj* desequilibrado; (fig.) desequilibrado
**unbandage** [ʌnˈbændɪdʒ] *va* desvendar
**unbar** [ʌnˈbɑr] (*pret & pp:* **-barred;** *ger:* **-barring**) *va* desatrancar
**unbearable** [ʌnˈbɛrəbəl] *adj* inaguantable, intolerable
**unbearably** [ʌnˈbɛrəblɪ] *adv* inaguantablemente, intolerablemente
**unbeatable** [ʌnˈbitəbəl] *adj* imbatible
**unbeaten** [ʌnˈbitən] *adj* no batido; no pisado, no trillado; invicto, insuperado, imbatido
**unbecoming** [ˌʌnbɪˈkʌmɪŋ] *adj* impropio, indecoroso; que sienta mal
**unbeknown** [ˌʌnbɪˈnon] *adj* (coll.) no sabido, no conocido; **unbeknown to me** (coll.) sin saberlo yo
**unbelief** [ˌʌnbɪˈlif] *s* descreimiento
**unbeliever** [ˌʌnbɪˈlivər] *s* descreído
**unbelieving** [ˌʌnbɪˈlivɪŋ] *adj* descreído
**unbelt** [ʌnˈbɛlt] *va* desceñir
**unbend** [ʌnˈbɛnd] (*pret & pp:* **-bent** o **-bended**) *va* enderezar, desencorvar; aflojar, soltar; (naut.) desenvergar; *vn* enderezarse; suavizarse, ponerse afable
**unbending** [ʌnˈbɛndɪŋ] *adj* inflexible, inconquistable, poco afable
**unbent** [ʌnˈbɛnt] *pret & pp de* **unbend**
**unbiased** o **unbiassed** [ʌnˈbaɪəst] *adj* imparcial, despreocupado
**unbidden** [ʌnˈbɪdən] *adj* no convidado; espontáneo
**unbind** [ʌnˈbaɪnd] (*pret & pp:* **-bound**) *va* desatar
**unbleached** [ʌnˈblitʃt] *adj* crudo, sin blanquear
**unblessed** o **unblest** [ʌnˈblɛst] *adj* no bendecido; maldito; desgraciado; malo, infame
**unblushing** [ʌnˈblʌʃɪŋ] *adj* desvergonzado
**unbodied** [ʌnˈbɑdɪd] *adj* incorpóreo
**unbolt** [ʌnˈbolt] *va* desempernar; desatrancar
**unbolted** [ʌnˈboltɪd] *adj* desatrancado; sin cerner
**unbonnet** [ʌnˈbɑnɪt] *va* quitar el bonete o el sombrero a; *vn* descubrirse
**unbonneted** [ʌnˈbɑnɪtɪd] *adj* sin bonete, sin sombrero
**unborn** [ʌnˈbɔrn] *adj* no nacido aún, venidero, futuro
**unbosom** [ʌnˈbʊzəm] *va* confesar; **to unbosom oneself** desahogarse, abrir su pecho; **to unbosom oneself of** desahogarse de; *vn* desahogarse, abrir su pecho
**unbound** [ʌnˈbaʊnd] *adj* desatado, suelto, libre; (b.b.) sin encuadernar; *pret & pp de* **unbind**
**unbounded** [ʌnˈbaʊndɪd] *adj* ilimitado; desenfrenado
**unbowed** [ʌnˈbaʊd] *adj* no inclinado; no domado
**unbraid** [ʌnˈbred] *va* destrenzar, destejer
**unbreakable** [ʌnˈbrekəbəl] *adj* irrompible
**unbred** [ʌnˈbrɛd] *adj* malcriado
**unbridle** [ʌnˈbraɪdəl] *va* desembridar
**unbridled** [ʌnˈbraɪdəld] *adj* desembridado; desenfrenado
**unbroken** [ʌnˈbrokən] *adj* intacto, entero; no interrumpido; no adiestrado, no domado, cerrero
**unbuckle** [ʌnˈbʌkəl] *va* deshebillar; desatar
**unburden** [ʌnˈbʌrdən] *va* descargar; aliviar; **to unburden oneself of** aliviarse de; desahogarse de
**unburied** [ʌnˈbɛrɪd] *adj* insepulto
**unburned** [ʌnˈbʌrnd] o **unburnt** [ʌnˈbʌrnt] *adj* incombusto
**unbusinesslike** [ʌnˈbɪznɪsˌlaɪk] *adj* poco práctico, descuidado
**unbutton** [ʌnˈbʌtən] *va* desabotonar
**uncage** [ʌnˈkedʒ] *va* sacar de la jaula; libertar
**uncalled-for** [ʌnˈkɔldˌfɔr] *adj* no buscado; gratuito, inmerecido; insolente
**uncanceled** [ʌnˈkænsəld] *adj* sin cancelar (*dícese de los sellos de correo*)
**uncanny** [ʌnˈkænɪ] *adj* misterioso, espectral; fantástico
**uncap** [ʌnˈkæp] (*pret & pp:* **-capped;** *ger:* **-capping**) *va* destapar; *vn* descubrirse
**uncared-for** [ʌnˈkɛrdˌfɔr] *adj* abandonado, descuidado, desamparado
**unceasing** [ʌnˈsisɪŋ] *adj* incesante

**unceremonious** [ˌʌnserɪ'monɪəs] *adj* inceremonioso
**uncertain** [ʌn'sʌrtən] *adj* incierto
**uncertainty** [ʌn'sʌrtəntɪ] *s* (*pl:* **-ties**) incertidumbre
**unchain** [ʌn'tʃen] *va* desencadenar
**unchangeable** [ʌn'tʃendʒəbəl] *adj* incambiable
**uncharitable** [ʌn'tʃærɪtəbəl] *adj* poco caritativo, duro
**uncharted** [ʌn'tʃartɪd] *adj* inexplorado
**unchaste** [ʌn'tʃest] *adj* incasto
**unchastity** [ʌn'tʃæstɪtɪ] *s* incontinencia
**unchecked** [ʌn'tʃekt] *adj* no verificado; no refrenado, inestorbado; desenfrenado
**unchristian** [ʌn'krɪstʃən] *adj* no cristiano; anticristiano; impropio, indecoroso
**unchurch** [ʌn'tʃʌrtʃ] *va* expulsar de la iglesia, excomulgar
**uncial** ['ʌnʃɪəl] o ['ʌnʃəl] *adj & s* uncial
**unciform** ['ʌnsɪfɔrm] *adj* unciforme; *s* (anat.) unciforme
**uncinate** ['ʌnsɪnet] *adj* uncinado
**uncircumcised** [ʌn'sʌrkəmsaɪzd] *adj* incircunciso
**uncircumscribed** [ʌn'sʌrkəmskraɪbd] *adj* incircunscripto
**uncivil** [ʌn'sɪvɪl] *adj* incivil
**uncivilized** [ʌn'sɪvɪlaɪzd] *adj* incivilizado, inculto
**unclad** [ʌn'klæd] *adj* no vestido, desnudo
**unclaimed** [ʌn'klemd] *adj* sin reclamar
**unclaimed letter** *s* carta rechazada, carta sobrante
**unclasp** [ʌn'klæsp] o [ʌn'klɑsp] *va* desabrochar; *vn* desabrocharse
**unclassifiable** [ʌn'klæsɪˌfaɪəbəl] *adj* inclasificable
**unclassified** [ʌn'klæsɪfaɪd] *adj* no clasificado; no clasificado como secreto
**uncle** ['ʌŋkəl] *s* tío; (coll.) tío (*hombre entrado en edad*); (slang) prestamista
**unclean** [ʌn'klin] *adj* sucio
**uncleanly** [ʌn'klenlɪ] *adj* (*comp:* **-lier;** *super:* **-liest**) sucio; [ʌn'klinlɪ] *adv* suciamente
**uncleanness** [ʌn'klinnɪs] *s* suciedad
**unclench** [ʌn'klentʃ] *va* desasir, desagarrar, soltar
**Uncle Sam** *s* el tío Sam
**uncloak** [ʌn'klok] *va* desencapotar; *vn* desencapotarse
**unclog** [ʌn'klɑg] (*pret & pp:* **-clogged;** *ger:* **-clogging**) *va* desatrancar, desatancar
**unclose** [ʌn'kloz] *va* desencerrar
**unclothe** [ʌn'kloð] *va* desarropar
**unclouded** [ʌn'klaudɪd] *adj* despejado, sin nubes
**uncoated** [ʌn'kotɪd] *adj* sin capa (*p.ej., de pintura*)
**uncoil** [ʌn'kɔɪl] *va* desarrollar, desenrollar
**uncollectible** [ˌʌnkə'lektɪbəl] *adj* incobrable
**uncombed** [ʌn'komd] *adj* despeinado
**uncomfortable** [ʌn'kʌmfərtəbəl] *adj* incómodo; con malestar
**uncommercial** [ˌʌnkə'mʌrʃəl] *adj* no comercial; no comerciante
**uncommitted** [ˌʌnkə'mɪtɪd] *adj* no cometido; no comprometido, no empeñado
**uncommon** [ʌn'kɑmən] *adj* poco común, raro
**uncommonly** [ʌn'kɑmənlɪ] *adv* raramente; extraordinariamente
**uncommunicative** [ˌʌnkə'mjunɪˌketɪv] *adj* poco comunicativo, inconversable
**uncompromising** [ʌn'kɑmprəˌmaɪzɪŋ] *adj* inflexible, intransigente
**unconcern** [ˌʌnkən'sʌrn] *s* indiferencia, despreocupación
**unconcerned** [ˌʌnkən'sʌrnd] *adj* indiferente, despreocupado
**unconcernedly** [ˌʌnkən'sʌrnɪdlɪ] *adv* indiferentemente, sin preocuparse
**unconditional** [ˌʌnkən'dɪʃənəl] *adj* incondicional
**unconditionally** [ˌʌnkən'dɪʃənəlɪ] *adv* incondicionalmente
**unconditioned** [ˌʌnkən'dɪʃənd] *adj* incondicional; natural, no adquirido
**unconducive** [ˌʌnkən'djusɪv] o [ˌʌnkən'dusɪv] *adj* inconducente
**unconfessed** [ˌʌnkən'fest] *adj* inconfeso
**unconformity** [ˌʌnkən'fɔrmɪtɪ] *s* (*pl:* **-ties**) disconformidad
**uncongealable** [ˌʌnkən'dʒiləbəl] *adj* incongelable
**uncongealed** [ˌʌnkən'dʒild] *adj* incongelado
**uncongenial** [ˌʌnkən'dʒinɪəl] *adj* antipático; incompatible; desagradable
**uncongeniality** [ˌʌnkənˌdʒinɪ'ælɪtɪ] *s* antipatía; incompatibilidad; desagrado
**unconnected** [ˌʌnkə'nektɪd] *adj* inconexo; desconectado
**unconquerable** [ʌn'kɑŋkərəbəl] *adj* inconquistable
**unconquered** [ʌn'kɑŋkərd] *adj* invicto
**unconscionable** [ʌn'kɑnʃənəbəl] *adj* desrazonable, desmedido, excesivo, inmoral
**unconscionably** [ʌn'kɑnʃənəblɪ] *adv* desrazonablemente, desmedidamente, con exceso, inmoralmente
**unconscious** [ʌn'kɑnʃəs] *adj* inconsciente; desmayado; ignorante; no intencional; **the unconscious** lo inconsciente
**unconsciousness** [ʌn'kɑnʃəsnɪs] *s* inconsciencia
**unconstitutional** [ˌʌnkɑnstɪ'tjuʃənəl] o [ˌʌnkɑnstɪ'tuʃənəl] *adj* inconstitucional
**unconstitutionality** [ˌʌnkɑnstɪˌtjuʃən'ælɪtɪ] o [ˌʌnkɑnstɪˌtuʃən'ælɪtɪ] *s* inconstitucionalidad
**uncontaminated** [ˌʌnkən'tæmɪˌnetɪd] *adj* incontaminado
**uncontrollable** [ˌʌnkən'troləbəl] *adj* ingobernable
**uncontrolled** [ˌʌnkən'trold] *adj* incontrolado
**unconventional** [ˌʌnkən'venʃənəl] *adj* informal, despreocupado, original
**unconventionality** [ˌʌnkənˌvenʃən'ælɪtɪ] *s* informalidad, despreocupación, originalidad
**uncooked** [ʌn'kukt] *adj* crudo, sin cocer
**uncork** [ʌn'kɔrk] *va* destapar, descorchar
**uncorrupted** [ˌʌnkə'rʌptɪd] *adj* incorrupto
**uncountable** [ʌn'kauntəbəl] *adj* incontable
**uncounted** [ʌn'kauntɪd] *adj* no contado; innumerable
**uncouple** [ʌn'kʌpəl] *va* desatraillar (*los perros*); desacoplar, desenganchar; desaparejar
**uncourteous** [ʌn'kʌrtɪəs] *adj* descortés
**uncourtly** [ʌn'kortlɪ] *adj* grosero, rústico, inurbano
**uncouth** [ʌn'kuθ] *adj* tosco, rústico; extraño, raro
**uncover** [ʌn'kʌvər] *va* descubrir; *vn* descubrirse (*quitarse el sombrero*)
**uncreated** [ˌʌnkri'etɪd] *adj* increado
**uncrown** [ʌn'kraun] *va* destronar
**uncrowned** [ʌn'kraund] *adj* sin corona
**unction** ['ʌŋkʃən] *s* unción; efusión o entusiasmo poco sinceros, fervor fingido
**unctuous** ['ʌŋktʃuəs] *adj* untuoso; (fig.) zalamero
**uncultivated** [ʌn'kʌltɪˌvetɪd] *adj* inculto (*no cultivado; tosco, rústico*)
**uncultured** [ʌn'kʌltʃərd] *adj* inculto (*tosco, rústico*)
**uncurl** [ʌn'kʌrl] *va* desrizar; *vn* desrizarse
**uncut** [ʌn'kʌt] *adj* sin cortar; sin labrar; intonso (*libro o revista*)
**undamaged** [ʌn'dæmɪdʒd] *adj* indemne, ileso, intacto
**undamped** [ʌn'dæmpt] *adj* no humedecido; no refrenado; (phys.) no amortiguado
**undated** [ʌn'detɪd] *adj* sin fecha; sin acontecimientos notables
**undaunted** [ʌn'dɔntɪd] *adj* impávido, denodado
**undecagon** [ʌn'dekəgɑn] *s* (geom.) undecágono, endecágono
**undeceive** [ˌʌndɪ'siv] *va* desengañar
**undecided** [ˌʌndɪ'saɪdɪd] *adj* indeciso
**undeclinable** [ˌʌndɪ'klaɪnəbəl] *adj* indeclinable; (gram.) indeclinable
**undefeated** [ˌʌndɪ'fitɪd] *adj* invicto
**undefended** [ˌʌndɪ'fendɪd] *adj* indefenso
**undefensible** [ˌʌndɪ'fensɪbəl] *adj* indefendible
**undefiled** [ˌʌndɪ'faɪld] *adj* impoluto, inmaculado
**undefinable** [ˌʌndɪ'faɪnəbəl] *adj* indefinible
**undefined** [ˌʌndɪ'faɪnd] *adj* indefinido
**undelivered** [ˌʌndɪ'lɪvərd] *adj* sin entregar

**undelivered letter** *s* carta rechazada, carta sobrante
**undemonstrable** [ˌʌndɪˈmɑnstrəbəl] o [ʌnˈdɛmənstrəbəl] *adj* indemostrable
**undemonstrative** [ˌʌndɪˈmɑnstrətɪv] *adj* reservado, callado, poco expresivo
**undeniable** [ˌʌndɪˈnaɪəbəl] *adj* innegable, inconcuso; excelentísimo
**undeniably** [ˌʌndɪˈnaɪəblɪ] *adv* innegablemente
**undenominational** [ˌʌndɪˌnɑmɪˈneʃənəl] *adj* no sectario
**undependable** [ˌʌndɪˈpɛndəbəl] *adj* no confiable
**under-** *prefix* sub-, p.ej., **underdeveloped** subdesarrollado; **underlying** subyacente; infra-, p.ej., **underconsumption** infraconsumo; **underworld** inframundo; des-, p.ej., **underfed** desnutrido; menos-, p.ej., **underrate** menospreciar; bajo, p.ej., **underneath** parte baja; inferior, p.ej., **underpass** paso inferior
**under** [ˈʌndər] *adj* inferior; interior (*ropa*); *adv* debajo; más abajo; **to bring under** dominar, someter; **to go under** fracasar; hundirse; **to keep under** oprimir; *prep* bajo; debajo de; inferior a; **under arms** sobre las armas; **under full sail** (naut.) a vela llena; **under lock and key** bajo llave; **under oath** bajo juramento; **under penalty of death** so pena de muerte; **under sail** (naut.) a la vela; **under separate cover** bajo cubierta separada, por separado; **under steam** bajo presión; **under the hand and seal of** firmado y sellado por; **under the necessity of** en la necesidad de; **under one's nose** (coll.) en las barbas de uno; **under way** en camino; principiando
**underage** [ˈʌndərˌedʒ] *adj* menor de edad; no de la edad a propósito
**underbid** [ˌʌndərˈbɪd] (*pret & pp:* **-bid**; *ger:* **-bidding**) *va* ofrecer menos que
**underbodice** [ˈʌndərˌbɑdɪs] *s* cubrecorsé
**underbred** [ˌʌndərˈbrɛd] *adj* de raza impura; vulgar, rudo
**underbrush** [ˈʌndərˌbrʌʃ] *s* maleza
**undercarriage** [ˈʌndərˌkærɪdʒ] *s* carro inferior; (aer.) tren de aterrizaje
**undercharge** [ˈʌndərˌtʃɑrdʒ] *s* cargo insuficiente, precio insuficiente; [ˌʌndərˈtʃɑrdʒ] *va* hacer pagar menos del valor, no cargar bastante en la cuenta a; cargar . . . de menos, p.ej., **you have undercharged me one dollar** me ha cargado Vd. un dólar de menos
**underclassman** [ˌʌndərˈklæsmən] o [ˌʌndərˈklɑsmən] *s* (*pl:* **-men**) alumno universitario de los dos primeros años
**underclothes** [ˈʌndərˌkloz] *spl* o **underclothing** [ˈʌndərˌkloðɪŋ] *s* ropa interior
**undercoat** [ˈʌndərˌkot] *s* chaqueta interior; pelaje corto; capa de fondo, primera mano (*de pintura*)
**underconsumption** [ˈʌndərkənˈsʌmpʃən] *s* infraconsumo
**undercover** [ˌʌndərˈkʌvər] *adj* secreto, confidencial
**undercurrent** [ˈʌndərˌkʌrənt] *s* corriente submarina, corriente subfluvial; (fig.) tendencia oculta, tendencia obscura
**undercut** [ˈʌndərˌkʌt] *adj* socavado; *s* socava, socavación; filete, solomillo; [ˌʌndərˈkʌt] (*pret & pp:* **-cut**; *ger:* **-cutting**) *va* socavar
**underdevelop** [ˌʌndərdɪˈvɛləp] *s* desarrollar incompletamente; (phot.) revelar incompletamente
**underdeveloped countries** [ˌʌndərdɪˈvɛləpt] *spl* países subdesarrollados
**underdevelopment** [ˌʌndərdɪˈvɛləpmənt] *s* desarrollo incompleto; (phot.) revelado incompleto
**underdog** [ˈʌndərˌdɔg] o [ˈʌndərˌdɑg] *s* perro perdedor; perdidoso, víctima; desvalido
**underdone** [ˈʌndərˌdʌn] o [ˌʌndərˈdʌn] *adj* soasado, a medio asar
**underestimate** [ˈʌndərˌɛstɪmɪt] *s* apreciación o estimación demasiado baja; presupuesto demasiado bajo; menosprecio; [ˌʌndərˈɛstɪmet] *va* avaluar o estimar en valor demasiado bajo; subestimar, menospreciar, tener (*a una persona o cosa*) en menos de lo que merece
**underestimated** [ˌʌndərˈɛstɪˌmetɪd] *adj* inestimado
**underexpose** [ˌʌndərɛkˈspoz] *va* (phot.) exponer insuficientemente
**underexposure** [ˌʌndərɛkˈspoʒər] *s* (phot.) subexposición
**underfed** [ˌʌndərˈfɛd] *pret & pp de* **underfeed**
**underfeed** [ˌʌndərˈfid] (*pret & pp:* **-fed**) *va* desnutrir
**underfeeding** [ˌʌndərˈfidɪŋ] *s* desnutrición
**underfoot** [ˌʌndərˈfʊt] *adj* debajo de los pies; en el suelo; (coll.) estorbando
**undergarment** [ˈʌndərˌgɑrmənt] *s* prenda de vestir interior
**undergo** [ˌʌndərˈgo] (*pret:* **-went**; *pp:* **-gone**) *va* experimentar, sufrir, padecer
**undergraduate** [ˌʌndərˈgrædʒʊɪt] *adj* no graduado; *s* alumno no graduado, estudiante del bachillerato
**undergraduate course** *s* asignatura o curso para el bachillerato
**underground** [ˈʌndərˈgraʊnd] *adj* subterráneo; clandestino; *adv* bajo tierra; clandestinamente; [ˈʌndərˌgraʊnd] *s* subterráneo; ferrocarril subterráneo; movimiento clandestino, fuerzas ocultas, resistencia
**underground movement** *s* movimiento oculto
**underground railroad** *s* ferrocarril subterráneo; (fig.) método clandestino de ayudar a los fugitivos
**undergrowth** [ˈʌndərˌgroθ] *s* maleza; pelaje corto
**underhand** [ˈʌndərˌhænd] *adj* taimado, socarrón, clandestino; (sport) hecho con las manos debajo de los hombros; *adv* taimadamente, socarronamente, clandestinamente; (sport) con las manos debajo de los hombros
**underhanded** [ˈʌndərˈhændɪd] *adj* taimado, socarrón, clandestino
**underhung** [ˈʌndərˌhʌŋ] *adj* suspendido; sobresaliente (*dícese de la quijada inferior*); con la quijada inferior sobresaliente
**underlaid** [ˌʌndərˈled] *pret & pp de* **underlay**
**underlain** [ˌʌndərˈlen] *pp de* **underlie**
**underlap** [ˌʌndərˈlæp] (*pret & pp:* **-lapped**; *ger:* **-lapping**) *va* extender por debajo de; *vn* extender por debajo
**underlay** [ˈʌndərˌle] *s* (print.) calzo, realce; [ˌʌndərˈle] (*pret & pp:* **-laid**) *va* (print.) calzar; poner por debajo; levantar, reforzar; *pret de* **underlie**
**underlie** [ˌʌndərˈlaɪ] (*pret:* **-lay**; *pp:* **-lain**; *ger:* **-lying**) *va* estar debajo de, extenderse debajo de; ser la razón fundamental de, ser la base de; sustentar, sostener
**underline** [ˌʌndərˈlaɪn] o [ˈʌndərˌlaɪn] *va* subrayar
**underling** [ˈʌndərlɪŋ] *s* inferior, subordinado; suboficial; paniaguado, secuaz servil
**underlying** [ˈʌndərˌlaɪɪŋ] *adj* subyacente; fundamental
**undermine** [ˌʌndərˈmaɪn] o [ˈʌndərˌmaɪn] *va* socavar, minar; (fig.) socavar, minar (*p.ej., la salud*)
**undermost** [ˈʌndərmost] *adj* (el) más bajo; *adv* a lo más bajo
**underneath** [ˌʌndərˈniθ] *s* parte baja, superficie inferior; *adj* inferior, más bajo; *adv* debajo; *prep* debajo de
**undernourished** [ˌʌndərˈnʌrɪʃt] *adj* desnutrido
**undernourishment** [ˌʌndərˈnʌrɪʃmənt] *s* desnutrición, subalimentación
**underofficer** [ˈʌndərˌɔfɪsər] o [ˈʌndərˌɑfɪsər] *s* subalterno, oficial subalterno; [ˌʌndərˈɔfɪsər] o [ˌʌndərˈɑfɪsər] *va* proveer de un número insuficiente de oficiales
**underpants** [ˈʌndərˌpænts] *spl* (coll.) calzoncillos
**underpass** [ˈʌndərˌpæs] o [ˈʌndərˌpɑs] *s* paso inferior; vía por bajo tierra
**underpay** [ˌʌndərˈpe] *s* pago insuficiente; (*pret & pp:* **-paid**) *va & vn* pagar insuficientemente
**underpin** [ˌʌndərˈpɪn] (*pret & pp:* **-pinned**; *ger:* **-pinning**) *va* apuntalar, socalzar
**underpinning** [ˈʌndərˌpɪnɪŋ] *s* apuntalamiento, socalzado; (coll.) las piernas de uno

**underplot** ['ʌndər,plɑt] *s* trama secundaria
**underprivileged** [,ʌndər'prɪvɪlɪdʒd] *adj* desamparado, desvalido
**underproduction** [,ʌndərprə'dʌkʃən] *s* baja producción
**underrate** [,ʌndər'ret] *va* menospreciar
**underriver** ['ʌndər,rɪvər] *adj* subfluvial
**underscore** ['ʌndər,skor] *s* línea de subrayar; [,ʌndər'skor] o ['ʌndər,skor] *va* subrayar
**undersea** ['ʌndər,si] *adj* submarino; [,ʌndər'si] *adv* bajo la superficie del mar
**underseas** [,ʌndər'siz] *adv* bajo la superficie del mar
**undersecretary** [,ʌndər'sɛkrɪ,tɛrɪ] *s* (*pl:* **-ies**) subsecretario
**undersecretaryship** [,ʌndər'sɛkrɪ,tɛrɪʃɪp] *s* subsecretaría
**undersell** [,ʌndər'sɛl] (*pret & pp:* **-sold**) *va* vender a menor precio que; malbaratar
**underservant** ['ʌndər,sʌrvənt] *s* criado inferior
**undershirt** ['ʌndər,ʃʌrt] *s* camiseta
**undershot** ['ʌndər,ʃɑt] *adj* que tiene saliente la mandíbula inferior; de corriente baja o inferior
**undershot water wheel** *s* rueda (hidráulica) de corriente baja o inferior
**underside** ['ʌndər,saɪd] *s* superficie inferior, superficie de fondo
**undersign** [,ʌndər'saɪn] o ['ʌndər,saɪn] *va* subscribir
**undersigned** ['ʌndər,saɪnd] *adj* infraescrito, abajo firmado
**undersized** ['ʌndər,saɪzd] *adj* de baja dimensión, de dimensión insuficiente, de infratamaño
**underskirt** ['ʌndər,skʌrt] *s* enaguas, refajo
**undersleeve** ['ʌndər,sliv] *s* manga interior
**underslung** ['ʌndər,slʌŋ] *adj* colgante, debajo del eje, debajo de los muelles
**undersold** [,ʌndər'sold] *pret & pp de* **undersell**
**undersong** ['ʌndər,sɔŋ] o ['ʌndər,sɑŋ] *s* canción acompañante; (fig.) sentido subyacente, sentido latente
**understand** [,ʌndər'stænd] (*pret & pp:* **-stood**) *va* comprender, entender; subentender, sobrentender (*una cosa que no está expresa*); (gram.) suplir; **be it understood** entiéndase; **to give to understand** dar a entender; **to understand each other** entenderse; *vn* comprender, entender
**understandable** [,ʌndər'stændəbəl] *adj* comprensible
**understanding** [,ʌndər'stændɪŋ] *adj* entendedor, inteligente; benévolo, tolerante; *s* entendimiento; comprensión; acuerdo; (philos.) entendimiento; **to come to an understanding** entenderse; **to come to an understanding with** llegar a un acuerdo con
**understate** [,ʌndər'stet] *va* exponer de un modo demasiado débil
**understatement** [,ʌndər'stetmənt] *s* exposición demasiado débil
**understood** [,ʌndər'stʊd] *pret & pp de* **understand**
**understudy** ['ʌndər,stʌdɪ] *s* (*pl:* **-ies**) (theat.) sobresaliente; (*pret & pp:* **-ied**) *va* aprender (*un papel*) para poder suplir a otro actor; aprender un papel para poder suplir (*a otro actor*); *vn* aprender un papel para poder suplir a otro actor
**undertake** [,ʌndər'tek] (*pret:* **-took;** *pp:* **-taken**) *va* emprender; comprometerse a; *vn* comprometerse; **to undertake to** + *inf* comprometerse a + *inf*
**undertaker** [,ʌndər'tekər] o ['ʌndər,tekər] *s* empresario; ['ʌndər,tekər] *s* empresario de pompas fúnebres, director de funeraria
**undertaking** [,ʌndər'tekɪŋ] *s* empresa; empeño; garantía; ['ʌndər,tekɪŋ] *s* funeraria, empresa funeraria
**undertone** ['ʌndər,ton] *s* voz baja; matiz suave, color apagado; fondo
**undertook** [,ʌndər'tʊk] *pret de* **undertake**
**undertow** ['ʌndər,to] *s* resaca; contracorriente
**undervaluation** ['ʌndər,væljʊ'eʃən] *s* estimación baja
**undervalue** [,ʌndər'vælju] *va* estimar demasiado bajo
**undervest** ['ʌndər,vɛst] *s* camiseta
**underwaist** ['ʌndər,west] *s* jubón, corpiño
**underwater** ['ʌndər,wɔtər] o ['ʌndər,wɑtər] *adj* subacuático, submarino; inundado; entre aguas
**underwear** ['ʌndər,wɛr] *s* ropa interior
**underweight** ['ʌndər,wet] *s* peso escaso; *adj* de peso escaso
**underwent** [,ʌndər'wɛnt] *pret de* **undergo**
**underwood** ['ʌndər,wʊd] *s* maleza
**underworld** ['ʌndər,wʌrld] *s* mundo terrenal; mundo submarino; antípoda; averno, infierno; gente de mal vivir, mundo del vicio, bajos fondos sociales, inframundo
**underwrite** [,ʌndər'raɪt] o ['ʌndər,raɪt] (*pret:* **-wrote;** *pp:* **-written**) *va* subscribir; asegurar
**underwriter** ['ʌndər,raɪtər] *s* subscritor; asegurador; compañía aseguradora
**underwritten** [,ʌndər'rɪtən] o ['ʌndər,rɪtən] *pp de* **underwrite**
**underwrote** [,ʌndər'rot] o ['ʌndər,rot] *pret de* **underwrite**
**undescribable** [,ʌndɪ'skraɪbəbəl] *adj* indescriptible
**undeserved** [,ʌndɪ'zʌrvd] *adj* inmerecido
**undesirable** [,ʌndɪ'zaɪrəbəl] *adj & s* indeseable
**undetachable** [,ʌndɪ'tætʃəbəl] *adj* inamovible, inseparable
**undeterminable** [,ʌndɪ'tʌrmɪnəbəl] *adj* indeterminable
**undevout** [,ʌndɪ'vaʊt] *adj* indevoto
**undigested** [,ʌndɪ'dʒɛstɪd] *adj* indigesto
**undid** [ʌn'dɪd] *pret de* **undo**
**undine** [ʌn'din] o ['ʌndin] *s* (myth.) ondina
**undiplomatic** [,ʌndɪplə'mætɪk] *adj* poco diplomático
**undiscernible** [,ʌndɪ'zʌrnɪbəl] o [,ʌndɪ'sʌrnɪbəl] *adj* imperceptible, invisible
**undisciplined** [ʌn'dɪsɪplɪnd] *adj* indisciplinado
**undiscriminating** [,ʌndɪs'krɪmɪ,netɪŋ] *adj* sin sentido crítico, incapaz de distinguir bien
**undisguised** [,ʌndɪs'gaɪzd] *adj* sin disfraz; abierto, franco
**undismayed** [,ʌndɪs'med] *adj* impávido, intrépido; no desanimado
**undisputed** [,ʌndɪs'pjutɪd] *adj* incontestable, sin disputa
**undistinguishable** [,ʌndɪ'stɪŋgwɪʃəbəl] *adj* indistinguible
**undistinguished** [,ʌndɪ'stɪŋgwɪʃt] *adj* deslucido; no distinguido
**undistorted** [,ʌndɪs'tɔrtɪd] *adj* sin falsificación; (elec.) sin distorsión
**undistorted output** *s* (elec.) potencia de salida sin distorsión
**undisturbed** [,ʌndɪ'stʌrbd] *adj* sin tocar; imperturbado
**undivided** [,ʌndɪ'vaɪdɪd] *adj* indiviso
**undo** [ʌn'du] (*pret:* **-did;** *pp:* **-done**) *va* deshacer; anular; resolver, explicar
**undoing** [ʌn'duɪŋ] *s* desatadura; anulación; ruina, pérdida, destrucción
**undone** [ʌn'dʌn] *adj* sin hacer, por hacer; **to come undone** desatarse, deshacerse; **to leave nothing undone** no dejar nada por hacer; *pp de* **undo**
**undoubted** [ʌn'daʊtɪd] *adj* indudable
**undoubtedly** [ʌn'daʊtɪdlɪ] *adv* indudablemente
**undramatic** [,ʌndrə'mætɪk] *adj* no dramático, poco dramático
**undraw** [ʌn'drɔ] (*pret:* **-drew;** *pp:* **-drawn**) *va* abrir, tirar hacia fuera
**undress** ['ʌn,drɛs] o [ʌn'drɛs] *s* ropa de casa; (mil.) traje de cuartel; ['ʌn,drɛs] *adj* de trapillo, informal; [ʌn'drɛs] *va* desnudar; desadornar; desvendar (*una herida*); *vn* desnudarse
**undrew** [ʌn'dru] *pret de* **undraw**
**undrinkable** [ʌn'drɪŋkəbəl] *adj* impotable
**undue** [ʌn'dju] o [ʌn'du] *adj* indebido, impropio; excesivo
**undulant** ['ʌndjələnt] *adj* undulante, ondulante
**undulant fever** *s* (path.) fiebre ondulante

**undulate** ['ʌndjəlet] *adj* ondulado; *va* ondular (*el pelo*); hacer ondas en; *vn* ondular, undular
**undulation** [ˌʌndjə'leʃən] *s* ondulación, undulación
**undulatory** ['ʌndjələˌtori] *adj* ondulatorio, undulatorio
**unduly** [ʌn'djulɪ] o [ʌn'dulɪ] *adv* indebidamente, impropiamente; excesivamente
**undying** [ʌn'daɪɪŋ] *adj* imperecedero
**unearned** [ʌn'ʌrnd] *adj* no ganado; inmerecido
**unearned increment** *s* mayor valía
**unearth** [ʌn'ʌrθ] *va* desenterrar; (fig.) descubrir
**unearthly** [ʌn'ʌrθlɪ] *adj* sobrenatural; espectral, fantástico
**uneasy** [ʌn'izɪ] *adj* inquieto; desgarbado; incómodo, no bien
**uneatable** [ʌn'itəbəl] *adj* no comestible, incomible
**uneconomic** [ˌʌnikə'nɑmɪk] o [ˌʌnɛkə'nɑmɪk] o **uneconomical** [ˌʌnikə'nɑmɪkəl] o [ˌʌnɛkə'nɑmɪkəl] *adj* antieconómico
**uneducable** [ʌn'ɛdʒəkəbəl] *adj* ineducable
**uneducated** [ʌn'ɛdʒəˌketɪd] *adj* ineducado
**unemployable** [ˌʌnɛm'plɔɪəbəl] *adj* inutilizable; inútil para el trabajo
**unemployed** [ˌʌnɛm'plɔɪd] *adj* cesante, desocupado; inutilizado; (com.) improductivo; *s* cesante, desocupado
**unemployment** [ˌʌnɛm'plɔɪmənt] *s* cesantía, desocupación, desempleo
**unemployment compensation** *s* subsidios de paro
**unemployment insurance** *s* seguro de desocupación, seguro contra el paro obrero
**unending** [ʌn'ɛndɪŋ] *adj* inacabable, interminable
**unenlightened** [ˌʌnɛn'laɪtənd] *adj* poco instruído, ignorante
**unequal** [ʌn'ikwəl] *adj* desigual; insuficiente; injusto, parcial; **unequal to** insuficiente para; no al nivel de; sin fuerzas para
**unequaled** o **unequalled** [ʌn'ikwəld] *adj* inigualado
**unequally** [ʌn'ikwəlɪ] *adv* desigualmente; injustamente, parcialmente
**unequivocal** [ˌʌnɪ'kwɪvəkəl] *adj* inequívoco
**unequivocally** [ˌʌnɪ'kwɪvəkəlɪ] *adv* inequívocamente
**unerring** [ʌn'ʌrɪŋ] o [ʌn'ɛrɪŋ] *adj* infalible, seguro
**Unesco** [ju'nɛsko] *s* Unesco
**unessential** [ˌʌnɛ'sɛnʃəl] *adj* no esencial
**unestimated** [ʌn'ɛstɪˌmetɪd] *adj* inestimado
**unethical** [ʌn'ɛθɪkəl] *adj* poco ético
**uneven** [ʌn'ivən] *adj* desigual, irregular; (math.) impar
**unevenness** [ʌn'ivənnɪs] *s* desigualdad, irregularidad; (math.) imparidad
**uneventful** [ˌʌnɪ'vɛntfəl] *adj* sin acontecimientos notables, tranquilo
**unexampled** [ˌʌnɛg'zæmpəld] o [ˌʌnɛg'zɑmpəld] *adj* sin ejemplo, sin igual, sin par
**unexceptionable** [ˌʌnɛk'sɛpʃənəbəl] *adj* irreprensible, irrecusable
**unexceptional** [ˌʌnɛk'sɛpʃənəl] *adj* ordinario, usual; sin excepción
**unexchangeable** [ˌʌnɛks'tʃendʒəbəl] *adj* incambiable
**unexhausted** [ˌʌnɛg'zɔstɪd] *adj* inexhausto
**unexpected** [ˌʌnɛk'spɛktɪd] *adj* inesperado
**unexpectedly** [ˌʌnɛk'spɛktɪdlɪ] *adv* inesperadamente
**unexpired** [ˌʌnɛk'spaɪrd] *adj* no expirado
**unexplainable** [ˌʌnɛk'splenəbəl] *adj* inexplicable
**unexplained** [ˌʌnɛk'splend] *adj* inexplicado
**unexploited** [ˌʌnɛk'splɔɪtɪd] *adj* inexplotado
**unexplored** [ˌʌnɛk'splord] *adj* inexplorado
**unexposed** [ˌʌnɛk'spozd] *adj* (phot.) inexpuesto
**unexpurgated** [ʌn'ɛkspərˌgetɪd] *adj* no expurgado, sin expurgar
**unextinguishable** [ˌʌnɛk'stɪŋgwɪʃəbəl] *adj* inapagable, inextinguible
**unextinguished** [ˌʌnɛk'stɪŋgwɪʃt] *adj* inextinto
**unfading** [ʌn'fedɪŋ] *adj* sin descolorar; inmarcesible; (rad.) sin desvanecerse
**unfailing** [ʌn'felɪŋ] *adj* indefectible; inagotable
**unfair** [ʌn'fɛr] *adj* inicuo, injusto; falso, doble, desleal; desfavorable (*viento*); (sport) sucio
**unfaithful** [ʌn'feθfəl] *adj* infiel
**unfaltering** [ʌn'fɔltərɪŋ] *adj* resuelto, firme
**unfamiliar** [ˌʌnfə'mɪljər] *adj* poco familiar; poco conocedor, no familiarizado
**unfamiliarity** [ˌʌnfəˌmɪlɪ'ærɪtɪ] *s* falta de familiaridad; desconocimiento
**unfasten** [ʌn'fæsən] o [ʌn'fɑsən] *va* desatar, desligar, desabrochar, soltar, desatacar
**unfathomable** [ʌn'fæðəməbəl] *adj* insondable
**unfavorable** [ʌn'fevərəbəl] *adj* desfavorable
**unfeasible** [ʌn'fizəbəl] *adj* impracticable
**unfeathered** [ʌn'fɛðərd] *adj* implume
**unfeeling** [ʌn'filɪŋ] *adj* insensible
**unfeigned** [ʌn'fend] *adj* sincero, verdadero
**unfeignedly** [ʌn'fenɪdlɪ] *adv* sinceramente, sin fingimiento
**unfetter** [ʌn'fɛtər] *va* desencadenar
**unfilled** [ʌn'fɪld] *adj* no lleno, vacante; por cumplir, pendiente
**unfindable** [ʌn'faɪndəbəl] *adj* inencontrable
**unfinished** [ʌn'fɪnɪʃt] *adj* sin acabar; mal acabado, imperfecto
**unfit** [ʌn'fɪt] *adj* incapaz, inhábil; impropio; (*pret & pp:* **-fitted;** *ger:* **-fitting**) *va* inhabilitar
**unfitting** [ʌn'fɪtɪŋ] *adj* impropio; indecoroso
**unfix** [ʌn'fɪks] *va* desatar, desprender, soltar
**unflagging** [ʌn'flægɪŋ] *adj* incansable, persistente
**unfledged** [ʌn'flɛdʒd] *adj* implume; inmaturo, inexperimentado
**unflinching** [ʌn'flɪntʃɪŋ] *adj* impávido, resuelto
**unfold** [ʌn'fold] *va* desplegar; *vn* desplegarse
**unfordable** [ʌn'fordəbəl] *adj* invadeable
**unforeseeable** [ˌʌnfor'siəbəl] *adj* imprevisible
**unforeseen** [ˌʌnfor'sin] *adj* imprevisto, inesperado
**unforgettable** [ˌʌnfər'gɛtəbəl] *adj* inolvidable
**unforgivable** [ˌʌnfər'gɪvəbəl] *adj* imperdonable
**unformed** [ʌn'fɔrmd] *adj* informe; crudo; rudimentario
**unfortunate** [ʌn'fɔrtʃənɪt] *adj & s* desgraciado
**unfounded** [ʌn'faʊndɪd] *adj* infundado
**unfrequented** [ˌʌnfrɪ'kwɛntɪd] *adj* poco frecuentado
**unfriended** [ʌn'frɛndɪd] *adj* desamparado, sin amigos
**unfriendly** [ʌn'frɛndlɪ] *adj* inamistoso, poco amistoso; desfavorable
**unfrock** [ʌn'frɑk] *va* expulsar, degradar (*a un sacerdote*)
**unfruitful** [ʌn'frutfəl] *adj* infructuoso
**unfulfilled** [ˌʌnfʊl'fɪld] *adj* incumplido
**unfurl** [ʌn'fʌrl] *va* desenrollar
**unfurnished** [ʌn'fʌrnɪʃt] *adj* desamueblado
**ungainly** [ʌn'genlɪ] *adj* desgarbado, torpe, feo
**ungenerous** [ʌn'dʒɛnərəs] *adj* poco generoso
**ungentlemanly** [ʌn'dʒɛntəlmənlɪ] *adj* poco caballeroso, malcriado, descortés
**ungird** [ʌn'gʌrd] *va* desceñir, descinchar
**unglazed** [ʌn'glezd] *adj* no vidriado; deslustrado; no satinado (*papel*); sin cristales (*ventana*)
**ungodliness** [ʌn'gɑdlɪnɪs] *s* impiedad, irreligión; maldad, perversidad; (coll.) atrocidad
**ungodly** [ʌn'gɑdlɪ] *adj* impío, irreligioso; malvado, perverso; (coll.) atroz
**ungovernable** [ʌn'gʌvərnəbəl] *adj* ingobernable; indisciplinado
**ungraceful** [ʌn'gresfəl] *adj* desgraciado, desgarbado
**ungracious** [ʌn'greʃəs] *adj* descortés; desgraciado, desagradable, sin gracia
**ungrammatical** [ˌʌngrə'mætɪkəl] *adj* ingramatical
**ungrateful** [ʌn'gretfəl] *adj* ingrato, desagradecido
**ungrounded** [ʌn'graʊndɪd] *adj* infundado, inmotivado; poco instruído; (elec.) sin toma a tierra, sin retorno terrestre
**ungrudgingly** [ʌn'grʌdʒɪŋlɪ] *adv* de buena gana, sin quejarse

**ungual** ['ʌŋgwəl] *adj* unguinal, unguiculado
**unguarded** [ʌn'gɑrdɪd] *adj* indefenso; descuidado, imprudente
**unguent** ['ʌŋgwənt] *s* ungüento
**unguiculate** [ʌŋ'gwɪkjəlɪt] *adj* unguiculado
**unguis** ['ʌŋgwɪs] *s* (*pl:* **-gues** [gwiz]) (anat.) unguis
**ungula** ['ʌŋgjələ] *s* (*pl:* **-lae** [li]) uña; (bot.) uña; (zool. & geom.) úngula
**ungular** ['ʌŋgjələr] *adj* ungular
**ungulate** ['ʌŋgjəlet] o ['ʌŋgjəlɪt] *adj & s* (zool.) ungulado
**unhallowed** [ʌn'hælod] *adj* profano; malvado
**unhand** [ʌn'hænd] *va* quitar las manos a; soltar
**unhandsome** [ʌn'hænsəm] *adj* feo, desaliñado; descortés, indecoroso; poco generoso
**unhandy** [ʌn'hændɪ] *adj* desmañado; incómodo
**unhappily** [ʌn'hæpɪlɪ] *adv* infelizmente; desgraciadamente
**unhappiness** [ʌn'hæpɪnɪs] *s* infelicidad; desgracia
**unhappy** [ʌn'hæpɪ] *adj* infeliz; desgraciado
**unharmed** [ʌn'hɑrmd] *adj* incólume, ileso, indemne, sano y salvo
**unharmonious** [,ʌnhɑr'monɪəs] *adj* inarmónico
**unharness** [ʌn'hɑrnɪs] *va* desenjaezar, desguarnecer; desarmar; desenganchar
**unhealthful** [ʌn'hɛlθfəl] *adj* insalubre
**unhealthy** [ʌn'hɛlθɪ] *adj* malsano
**unheard** [ʌn'hʌrd] *adj* no oído; desconocido; sin ser oído
**unheard-of** [ʌn'hʌrd,ɑv] *adj* inaudito, nunca oído, nunca visto
**unheeded** [ʌn'hidɪd] *adj* desatendido
**unheedful** [ʌn'hidfəl] *adj* desatento
**unhesitating** [ʌn'hɛzɪ,tetɪŋ] *adj* resuelto, pronto, listo
**unhinge** [ʌn'hɪndʒ] *va* desgonzar; (fig.) desequilibrar, trastornar
**unhitch** [ʌn'hɪtʃ] *va* desenganchar
**unholy** [ʌn'holɪ] *adj* impío, malo
**unhonored** [ʌn'ɑnərd] *adj* sin honores, despreciado; protestado (*cheque*)
**unhook** [ʌn'hʊk] *va* desabrochar; desenganchar; descolgar; *vn* desabrocharse; desengancharse; descolgarse
**unhoped-for** [ʌn'hopt,fɔr] *adj* inesperado, no esperado
**unhorse** [ʌn'hɔrs] *va* desarzonar, desmontar
**unhurriedly** [ʌn'hʌrɪdlɪ] *adv* sin prisa
**unhurt** [ʌn'hʌrt] *adj* incólume, ileso
**Uniat** ['junɪæt] *adj & s* uniato
**uniaxial** [,junɪ'æksɪəl] *adj* uniáxico
**unicameral** [,junɪ'kæmərəl] *adj* unicameral
**unicellular** [,junɪ'sɛljələr] *adj* unicelular
**unicorn** ['junɪkɔrn] *adj* unicornio; *s* (myth. & Bib.) unicornio
**unification** [,junɪfɪ'keʃən] *s* unificación
**uniflorous** [,junɪ'florəs] *adj* (bot.) unifloro
**unifoliate** [,junɪ'folɪɪt] *adj* (bot.) unifoliado
**uniform** ['junɪfɔrm] *adj & s* uniforme; *va* uniformar
**uniformity** [,junɪ'fɔrmɪtɪ] *s* (*pl:* **-ties**) uniformidad
**unify** ['junɪfaɪ] (*pret & pp:* **-fied**) *va* unificar
**unilateral** [,junɪ'lætərəl] *adj* unilateral
**unimpeachable** [,ʌnɪm'pitʃəbəl] *adj* irrecusable, intachable
**unimportance** [,ʌnɪm'pɔrtəns] *s* poca importancia
**unimportant** [,ʌnɪm'pɔrtənt] *adj* poco importante
**uninflammable** [,ʌnɪn'flæməbəl] *adj* ininflamable
**uninflected** [,ʌnɪn'flɛktɪd] *adj* (gram.) sin inflexiones
**uninhabitable** [,ʌnɪn'hæbɪtəbəl] *adj* inhabitable
**uninhabited** [,ʌnɪn'hæbɪtɪd] *adj* inhabitado
**uninspired** [,ʌnɪn'spaɪrd] *adj* no inspirado, sin inspiración; aburrido, fastidioso
**unintelligent** [,ʌnɪn'tɛlɪdʒənt] *adj* ininteligente
**unintelligible** [,ʌnɪn'tɛlɪdʒɪbəl] *adj* ininteligible
**uninterested** [ʌn'ɪntərəstɪd] o [ʌn'ɪntrɪstɪd] *adj* desinteresado, poco interesado
**uninteresting** [ʌn'ɪntərɛstɪŋ] o [ʌn'ɪntrɪstɪŋ] *adj* poco interesante, falto de interés
**uninterrupted** [,ʌnɪntə'rʌptɪd] *adj* ininterrumpido, no interrumpido
**union** ['junjən] *s* unión; emblema de unión; sindicato, gremio obrero; (mach.) unión; *adj* gremial; (*cap.*) *s* Unión (*EE.UU.*)
**union catalogue** *s* catálogo colectivo (*de varias bibliotecas*)
**unionism** ['junjənɪzəm] *s* gremios obreros, sindicalismo, unionismo; (*cap.*) *s* Unionismo
**unionist** ['junjənɪst] *s* agremiado, sindicalista, unionista; (*cap.*) *s* Unionista
**unionization** [,junjənɪ'zeʃən] *s* agremiación
**unionize** ['junjənaɪz] *va* agremiar; *vn* agremiarse
**Union Jack** *s* pabellón nacional de la Gran Bretaña
**Union of South Africa** *s* Unión Sudafricana
**Union of Soviet Socialist Republics** *s* Unión de Repúblicas Socialistas Soviéticas
**union shop** *s* fábrica de obreros agremiados
**union suit** *s* traje interior de una sola pieza
**uniparous** [jʊ'nɪpərəs] *adj* (zool. & bot.) uníparo
**uniped** ['junɪpɛd] *adj* unípede
**unipersonal** [,junɪ'pʌrsənəl] *adj* unipersonal
**unipolar** [,junɪ'polər] *adj* (elec.) unipolar
**unique** [jʊ'nik] *adj* único (*en su género*)
**uniqueness** [jʊ'niknɪs] *s* unicidad
**unisexual** [,junɪ'sɛkʃʊəl] *adj* unisexual
**unison** ['junɪsən] o ['junɪzən] *s* concordancia, armonía; (mus.) unisonancia; **in unison** al unísono; **in unison with** al unísono de; *adj* (mus.) unísono
**unit** ['junɪt] *s* unidad; (mach. & elec.) grupo; *adj* unitario
**Unitarian** [,junɪ'tɛrɪən] *adj & s* unitario
**Unitarianism** [,junɪ'tɛrɪənɪzəm] *s* unitarismo
**unitary** ['junɪ,tɛrɪ] *adj* unitario
**unitary theory** *s* (chem.) teoría unitaria
**unite** [jʊ'naɪt] *va* unir; reunir, juntar; *vn* reunirse, juntarse
**united** [jʊ'naɪtɪd] *adj* unido
**United Arab Republic** *s* República Árabe Unida
**United Kingdom** *s* Reino Unido
**United Nations** *spl* Naciones Unidas
**United States** *adj* estadounidense; **the United States** *ssg* Estados Unidos *msg* o los Estados Unidos *mpl*
**unitive** ['junɪtɪv] *adj* unitivo
**unity** ['junɪtɪ] *s* (*pl:* **-ties**) unidad
**univ.** abr. de **universal** y **university**
**Univ.** abr. de **Universalist** y **University**
**univalence** [,junɪ'veləns] o [jʊ'nɪvələns] *s* (chem.) univalencia
**univalent** [,junɪ'velənt] o [jʊ'nɪvələnt] *adj* (chem.) univalente
**univalve** ['junɪ,vælv] *adj* (zool.) univalvo
**universal** [,junɪ'vʌrsəl] *adj* universal; *s* (log.) universal; (log.) proposición universal
**Universal Bishop** *s* obispo universal
**universalism** [,junɪ'vʌrsəlɪzəm] *s* universalismo; (*cap.*) *s* universalismo
**universalist** [,junɪ'vʌrsəlɪst] *s* universalista; (*cap.*) *s* universalista
**universality** [,junɪvʌr'sælɪtɪ] *s* (*pl:* **-ties**) universalidad
**universalize** [,junɪ'vʌrsəlaɪz] *va* universalizar
**universal joint** *s* (aut.) articulación universal, junta universal, cardán
**universal language** *s* lengua universal
**universally** [,junɪ'vʌrsəlɪ] *adv* universalmente
**universe** ['junɪvʌrs] *s* universo
**university** [,junɪ'vʌrsɪtɪ] *s* (*pl:* **-ties**) universidad; *adj* universitario
**univocal** [jʊ'nɪvəkəl] *adj* unívoco
**unjoint** [ʌn'dʒɔɪnt] *va* desunir; desencajar, desensamblar
**unjust** [ʌn'dʒʌst] *adj* injusto
**unjustifiable** [ʌn'dʒʌstɪ,faɪəbəl] *adj* injustificable
**unjustified** [ʌn'dʒʌstɪfaɪd] *adj* injustificado
**unkempt** [ʌn'kɛmpt] *adj* despeinado
**unkind** [ʌn'kaɪnd] *adj* poco amable; despiadado, brutal
**unkindness** [ʌn'kaɪndnɪs] *s* falta de amabilidad; tratamiento despiadado, acción brutal

**unknit** [ʌn'nɪt] (*pret & pp:* **-knitted** o **-knit;** *ger:* **-knitting**) *va* destejer; desfruncir
**unknowable** [ʌn'noəbəl] *adj* inconocible, incognoscible; insabible
**unknowingly** [ʌn'no·ɪŋlɪ] *adv* desconocidamente, sin saberlo
**unknown** [ʌn'non] *adj* desconocido, ignoto, incógnito; *s* desconocido; (math.) incógnita
**unknown quantity** *s* (math. & fig.) incógnita
**unknown soldier** *s* soldado desconocido
**unlace** [ʌn'les] *va* desenlazar; desatar (*p.ej., los cordones del zapato*)
**unlade** [ʌn'led] *va* descargar
**unlatch** [ʌn'lætʃ] *va* abrir levantando el picaporte
**unlawful** [ʌn'lɔfəl] *adj* ilegal; ilegítimo
**unlawfully** [ʌn'lɔfəlɪ] *adv* ilegalmente; ilegítimamente
**unlearn** [ʌn'lʌrn] *va* desaprender
**unlearned** [ʌn'lʌrnɪd] *adj* indocto; ignorante; [ʌn'lʌrnd] *adj* innato, no aprendido
**unleash** [ʌn'liʃ] *va* destraillar; soltar
**unleavened** [ʌn'lɛvənd] *adj* ázimo, sin levadura
**unless** [ʌn'lɛs] *prep* excepto; *conj* a menos que, a no ser que
**unlettered** [ʌn'lɛtərd] *adj* indocto, iletrado; analfabeto
**unlike** [ʌn'laɪk] *adj* desemejante; desemejante de; (dial.) improbable; (elec.) de nombres contrarios (*dícese, p.ej., de los polos de un imán*); (elec.) de signo contrario; *prep* a diferencia de
**unlikelihood** [ʌn'laɪklɪhʊd] *s* inverosimilitud, improbabilidad
**unlikely** [ʌn'laɪklɪ] *adj* inverosímil, improbable
**unlikeness** [ʌn'laɪknɪs] *s* disimilitud, desemejanza, diferencia
**unlimber** [ʌn'lɪmbər] *va* quitar el avantrén a (*un cañón*); preparar para la acción; *vn* prepararse para la acción
**unlimited** [ʌn'lɪmɪtɪd] *adj* ilimitado; indefinido
**unlined** [ʌn'laɪnd] *adj* sin forro; sin rayar (*papel*); sin arrugas (*rostro*)
**unliquidated** [ʌn'lɪkwɪ,detɪd] *adj* ilíquido
**unload** [ʌn'lod] *va* descargar (*una carga; un cañón*); exonerar, aliviar; (coll.) deshacerse de (*p.ej., mercancías*); *vn* descargar
**unlock** [ʌn'lɑk] *va* abrir; (print.) desapretar; (fig.) descubrir, revelar; *vn* abrirse
**unlooked-for** [ʌn'lʊkt,fɔr] *adj* inesperado, inopinado
**unloose** [ʌn'lus] *va* desatar, desencadenar, aflojar, soltar; *vn* desatarse, desencadenarse, aflojarse
**unloosen** [ʌn'lusən] *va* desatar, desencadenar, aflojar, soltar
**unlosable** [ʌn'luzəbəl] *adj* inamisible, imperdible
**unloved** [ʌn'lʌvd] *adj* desamado
**unlovely** [ʌn'lʌvlɪ] *adj* desgraciado, desgarbado
**unloving** [ʌn'lʌvɪŋ] *adj* desamorado
**unlucky** [ʌn'lʌkɪ] *adj* de mala suerte; desgraciado, desdichado; aciago, nefasto; **to be unlucky** tener mala suerte
**unmake** [ʌn'mek] (*pret & pp:* **-made**) *va* deshacer; arruinar, destruir
**unman** [ʌn'mæn] (*pret & pp:* **-manned;** *ger:* **-manning**) acobardar, desanimar; afeminar; privar de hombres; (mil.) desguarnecer (*una plaza, un castillo*)
**unmanageable** [ʌn'mænɪdʒəbəl] *adj* inmanejable
**unmanly** [ʌn'mænlɪ] *adj* afeminado, enervado; bajo, cobarde
**unmannerly** [ʌn'mænərlɪ] *adj* descortés, malcriado, mal educado; *adv* descortésmente
**unmarketable** [ʌn'mɑrkɪtəbəl] *adj* incomerciable
**unmarriageable** [ʌn'mærɪdʒəbəl] *adj* incasable
**unmarried** [ʌn'mærɪd] *adj* soltero
**unmask** [ʌn'mæsk] o [ʌn'mɑsk] *va* desenmascarar; *vn* desenmascararse
**unmatchable** [ʌn'mætʃəbəl] *adj* sin igual, incomparable
**unmatched** [ʌn'mætʃt] *adj* incomparable, único; desapareado
**unmeaning** [ʌn'minɪŋ] *adj* falto de significación; vacío, sin expresión, sin sentido
**unmeasurable** [ʌn'mɛʒərəbəl] *adj* inmensurable
**unmeasured** [ʌn'mɛʒərd] *adj* ilimitado; desenfrenado, inmoderado
**unmeet** [ʌn'mit] *adj* impropio, inconveniente
**unmentionable** [ʌn'mɛnʃənəbəl] *adj* que no se puede mencionar; infando; **unmentionables** *spl* cosas que no se deben mencionar; (hum.) prendas íntimas (*calzones, pantalones, etc.*)
**unmerciful** [ʌn'mʌrsɪfəl] *adj* inclemente, despiadado
**unmerited** [ʌn'mɛrɪtɪd] *adj* inmerecido
**unmesh** [ʌn'mɛʃ] *va* desengranar; *vn* desengranarse
**unmindful** [ʌn'maɪndfəl] *adj* desatento, descuidado; **to be unmindful of** no pensar en, olvidar (*p.ej., la hora*)
**unmistakable** [,ʌnmɪs'tekəbəl] *adj* inequívoco
**unmitigated** [ʌn'mɪtɪ,getɪd] *adj* no mitigado, duro; absoluto, redomado
**unmixed** o **unmixt** [ʌn'mɪkst] *adj* puro, sin mezcla
**unmodulated** [ʌn'mɑdjə,letɪd] *adj* sin modular
**unmoor** [ʌn'mʊr] *va* (naut.) desamarrar (*un buque*); (naut.) desaferrar (*las áncoras*)
**unmoral** [ʌn'mɑrəl] o [ʌn'mɔrəl] *adj* amoral
**unmotivated** [ʌn'motɪ,vetɪd] *adj* inmotivado
**unmounted** [ʌn'maʊntɪd] *adj* desmontado
**unmovable** [ʌn'muvəbəl] *adj* inmoble
**unmoved** [ʌn'muvd] *adj* inmoto; impasible, frío; inmoble, constante
**unmuzzle** [ʌn'mʌzəl] *va* desbozalar; (fig.) dejar hablar
**unnatural** [ʌn'nætʃərəl] *adj* innatural, contranatural, desnaturalizado; anormal; afectado
**unnavigable** [ʌn'nævɪgəbəl] *adj* innavegable
**unnecessary** [ʌn'nɛsə,sɛrɪ] *adj* innecesario
**unnegotiable** [,ʌnnɪ'goʃɪəbəl] *adj* innegociable; (coll.) incomerciable, intransitable
**unnerve** [ʌn'nʌrv] *va* acobardar, desconcertar, trastornar
**unnoticeable** [ʌn'notɪsəbəl] *adj* imperceptible
**unnoticed** [ʌn'notɪst] *adj* inadvertido
**unnumbered** [ʌn'nʌmbərd] *adj* innumerable; sin número
**unobliging** [,ʌnə'blaɪdʒɪŋ] *adj* poco amable, poco servicial
**unobservant** [,ʌnəb'zʌrvənt] *adj* inobservante
**unobserved** [,ʌnəb'zʌrvd] *adj* inadvertido
**unobtainable** [,ʌnəb'tenəbəl] *adj* inasequible
**unobtrusive** [,ʌnəb'trusɪv] *adj* discreto, reservado
**unoccasioned** [,ʌnə'keʒənd] *adj* inmotivado
**unoccupied** [ʌn'ɑkjəpaɪd] *adj* vacante, libre; desocupado, ocioso
**unofficial** [,ʌnə'fɪʃəl] *adj* oficioso, extraoficial
**unopened** [ʌn'opənd] *adj* no abierto, sin abrir; no cortado (*libro*)
**unorganized** [ʌn'ɔrgənaɪzd] *adj* inorganizado
**unorthodox** [ʌn'ɔrθədɑks] *adj* inortodoxo
**unpack** [ʌn'pæk] *va* desembalar, desempaquetar; vaciar
**unpaid** [ʌn'ped] *adj* sin pagar, por pagar
**unpalatable** [ʌn'pælətəbəl] *adj* desabrido, ingustable
**unparalleled** [ʌn'pærəlɛld] *adj* sin par, sin igual, incomparable
**unpardonable** [ʌn'pɑrdənəbəl] *adj* imperdonable
**unparliamentary** [,ʌnpɑrlə'mɛntərɪ] *adj* no parlamentario
**unpatriotic** [,ʌnpetrɪ'ɑtɪk] o [,ʌnpætrɪ'ɑtɪk] *adj* poco patriótico, antipatriótico
**unpayable** [ʌn'peəbəl] *adj* impagable
**unpeople** [ʌn'pipəl] *va* despoblar
**unpeopled** [ʌn'pipəld] *adj* despoblado
**unperceived** [,ʌnpər'sivd] *adj* inadvertido
**unperturbable** [,ʌnpər'tʌrbəbəl] *adj* imperturbable
**unperturbed** [,ʌnpər'tʌrbd] *adj* imperturbado
**unpin** [ʌn'pɪn] (*pret & pp:* **-pinned;** *ger:* **-pinning**) *va* desprender; desenclavijar
**unplait** [ʌn'plæt] o [ʌn'plet] *va* destrenzar

**unplayable** [ʌn'pleəbəl] *adj* irrepresentable
**unpleasant** [ʌn'plɛzənt] *adj* antipático, desagradable
**unpleasantness** [ʌn'plɛzəntnɪs] *s* molestia; disgusto, desavenencia
**unplumbed** [ʌn'plʌmd] *adj* no sondado; sin cañerías
**unpolarized** [ʌn'poləraɪzd] *adj* no polarizado
**unpolluted** [,ʌnpə'lutɪd] *adj* impoluto
**unpopular** [ʌn'pɑpjələr] *adj* impopular
**unpopularity** [ʌn,pɑpjə'lærɪtɪ] *s* impopularidad
**unpopulated** [ʌn'pɑpjə,letɪd] *adj* despoblado
**unpractical** [ʌn'præktɪkəl] *adj* impráctico
**unpracticed** o **unpractised** [ʌn'præktɪst] *adj* inexperto; no practicado
**unprecedented** [ʌn'prɛsɪ,dɛntɪd] *adj* inaudito, sin precedente
**unpredictable** [,ʌnprɪ'dɪktəbəl] *adj* imposible de predecir; incierto, inconstante
**unprejudiced** [ʌn'prɛdʒədɪst] *adj* imparcial; no perjudicado
**unpremeditated** [,ʌnprɪ'mɛdɪ,tetɪd] *adj* impremeditado
**unpremeditation** [,ʌnprɪ,mɛdɪ'teʃən] *s* impremeditación
**unprepossessing** [,ʌnprɪpə'zɛsɪŋ] *adj* poco atrayente
**unpresentable** [,ʌnprɪ'zɛntəbəl] *adj* mal apersonado; impresentable
**unpretending** [,ʌnprɪ'tɛndɪŋ] *adj* modesto
**unpretentious** [,ʌnprɪ'tɛnʃəs] *adj* modesto, sencillo; poco ambicioso
**unpreventable** [ʌnprɪ'vɛntəbəl] *adj* inevitable
**unprincipled** [ʌn'prɪnsɪpəld] *adj* malo, sin conciencia
**unprintable** [ʌn'prɪntəbəl] *adj* que no puede imprimirse
**unprinted** [ʌn'prɪntɪd] *adj* sin imprimir
**unproductive** [,ʌnprə'dʌktɪv] *adj* improductivo
**unprofessional** [,ʌnprə'fɛʃənəl] *adj* no profesional
**unprofitable** [ʌn'prɑfɪtəbəl] *adj* inútil, infructuoso
**unpronounceable** [,ʌnprə'naʊnsəbəl] *adj* impronunciable
**unpropitious** [,ʌnprə'pɪʃəs] *adj* impropicio
**unprovoked** [,ʌnprə'vokt] *adj* no provocado, sin provocación
**unpublishable** [ʌn'pʌblɪʃəbəl] *adj* impublicable
**unpublished** [ʌn'pʌblɪʃt] *adj* inédito
**unpunished** [ʌn'pʌnɪʃt] *adj* impune
**unpurchasable** [ʌn'pʌrtʃəsəbəl] *adj* incomprable
**unqualifiable** [ʌn'kwɑlɪ,faɪəbəl] *adj* incalificable
**unqualified** [ʌn'kwɑlɪfaɪd] *adj* inepto, incompetente; absoluto, completo, ilimitado
**unquenchable** [ʌn'kwɛntʃəbəl] *adj* inextinguible; insaciable
**unquestionable** [ʌn'kwɛstʃənəbəl] *adj* incuestionable
**unquestionably** [ʌn'kwɛstʃənəblɪ] *adv* incuestionablemente
**unquestioned** [ʌn'kwɛstʃənd] *adj* no interrogado; no indagado; incontestable
**unquiet** [ʌn'kwaɪət] *adj* agitado; inquieto
**unquote** [ʌn'kwot] *va & vn* dejar de citar; **unquote** fin de la cita
**unravel** [ʌn'rævəl] (*pret & pp:* **-eled** o **-elled;** *ger:* **-eling** o **-elling**) *va* desenredar, desenmarañar; *vn* desenredarse, desenmarañarse
**unreachable** [ʌn'ritʃəbəl] *adj* inalcanzable
**unread** [ʌn'rɛd] *adj* no leído; indocto
**unreadable** [ʌn'ridəbəl] *adj* ilegible
**unready** [ʌn'rɛdɪ] *adj* desprevenido; lento, lerdo
**unreal** [ʌn'riəl] *adj* irreal
**unreality** [,ʌnrɪ'ælɪtɪ] *s* (*pl:* **-ties**) irrealidad
**unrealizable** [ʌn'riə,laɪzəbəl] *adj* irrealizable
**unreasonable** [ʌn'rizənəbəl] *adj* irrazonable, desrazonable
**unreasonably** [ʌn'rizənəblɪ] *adv* irrazonablemente, desrazonablemente
**unreasoning** [ʌn'rizənɪŋ] *adj* irracional
**unrecognizable** [ʌn'rɛkəg,naɪzəbəl] *adj* irreconocible
**unreconcilable** [ʌn'rɛkən,saɪləbəl] *adj* irreconciliable
**unreconciled** [ʌn'rɛkənsaɪld] *adj* irreconciliado
**unreconstructed** [ʌn,rikən'strʌktɪd] *adj* no reconstruído; (coll.) irreconciliado
**unreel** [ʌn'ril] *va* desenrollar; *vn* desenrollarse
**unreeve** [ʌn'riv] *va* (naut.) despasar; *vn* (naut.) despasarse
**unrefined** [,ʌnrɪ'faɪnd] *adj* no refinado, impuro; tosco, grosero, rudo
**unreflecting** [,ʌnrɪ'flɛktɪŋ] *adj* irreflexivo
**unregarded** [,ʌnrɪ'gɑrdɪd] *adj* desatendido
**unregenerate** [,ʌnrɪ'dʒɛnərɪt] *adj* irregenerado; impío, malvado
**unrelenting** [,ʌnrɪ'lɛntɪŋ] *adj* inflexible, implacable, inexorable
**unreliability** [,ʌnrɪ,laɪə'bɪlɪtɪ] *s* falta de confiabilidad, informalidad
**unreliable** [,ʌnrɪ'laɪəbəl] *adj* indigno de confianza, informal
**unreligious** [,ʌnrɪ'lɪdʒəs] *adj* irreligioso
**unremitting** [,ʌnrɪ'mɪtɪŋ] *adj* incesante; infatigable
**unremunerated** [,ʌnrɪ'mjunə,retɪd] *adj* irremunerado
**unrenewable** [,ʌnrɪ'njuəbəl] o [,ʌnrɪ'nuəbəl] *adj* irrenovable; (com.) improrrogable
**unrented** [ʌn'rɛntɪd] *adj* desalquilado
**unrepaired** [,ʌnrɪ'pɛrd] *adj* descompuesto
**unrepentant** [,ʌnrɪ'pɛntənt] *adj* impenitente
**unreplaceable** [,ʌnrɪ'plesəbəl] *adj* irreemplazable
**unrequited love** [,ʌnrɪ'kwaɪtɪd] *s* amor no correspondido
**unreserved** [,ʌnrɪ'zʌrvd] *adj* libre, no reservado; franco, abierto
**unreservedly** [,ʌnrɪ'zʌrvɪdlɪ] *adv* sin reserva; sin restricción
**unresistant** [,ʌnrɪ'zɪstənt] *adj* no resistente
**unresponsive** [,ʌnrɪ'spɑnsɪv] *adj* insensible, desinteresado; desobediente
**unrest** [ʌn'rɛst] *s* intranquilidad, desorden
**unrevoked** [,ʌnrɪ'vokt] *adj* irrevocado
**unrhymed** [ʌn'raɪmd] *adj* no rimado
**unriddle** [ʌn'rɪdəl] *va* descifrar, adivinar, explicar
**unrig** [ʌn'rɪg] (*pret & pp:* **-rigged;** *ger:* **-rigging**) *va* (naut.) desaparejar
**unrighteous** [ʌn'raɪtʃəs] *adj* malo, malvado, vicioso, injusto
**unrighteousness** [ʌn'raɪtʃəsnɪs] *s* maldad, vicio, injusticia
**unrightful** [ʌn'raɪtfəl] *adj* ilegítimo, injusto
**unrimed** [ʌn'raɪmd] *adj* var. de **unrhymed**
**unripe** [ʌn'raɪp] *adj* inmaturo; crudo
**unrivaled** o **unrivalled** [ʌn'raɪvəld] *adj* sin rival, incomparable
**unrobe** [ʌn'rob] *va* desarropar; *vn* desarroparse
**unroll** [ʌn'rol] *va* desenrollar; desplegar; *vn* desenrollarse; desplegarse
**unromantic** [,ʌnro'mæntɪk] *adj* poco romántico
**unroof** [ʌn'ruf] o [ʌn'rʊf] *va* destechar
**unroot** [ʌn'rut] o [ʌn'rʊt] *va* desarraigar; *vn* desarraigarse
**unruffled** [ʌn'rʌfəld] *adj* sin fruncir, sin arrugar; tranquilo, sereno
**unruled** [ʌn'ruld] *adj* no gobernado; no rayado (*papel*)
**unruly** [ʌn'rulɪ] *adj* ingobernable, revoltoso
**unsaddle** [ʌn'sædəl] *va* desensillar (*un caballo*); desarzonar (*a una persona*)
**unsafe** [ʌn'sef] *adj* inseguro
**unsaid** [ʌn'sɛd] *adj* callado, no dicho; *pret & pp de* **unsay**
**unsalable** o **unsaleable** [ʌn'seləbəl] *adj* invendible
**unsanitary** [ʌn'sænɪ,tɛrɪ] *adj* insalubre, antihigiénico
**unsatisfactory** [ʌn,sætɪs'fæktərɪ] *adj* insatisfactorio, poco satisfactorio
**unsatisfied** [ʌn'sætɪsfaɪd] *adj* insatisfecho
**unsavory** [ʌn'sevərɪ] *adj* desabrido; (fig.) infame, deshonroso
**unsay** [ʌn'se] (*pret & pp:* **-said**) *va* desdecirse de
**unscathed** [ʌn'skeðd] *adj* ileso, incólume, sano y salvo

**unscholarly** [ʌn'skɑlərlɪ] *adj* falto de erudición; indigno de un erudito
**unschooled** [ʌn'skuld] *adj* indocto, ignorante
**unscientific** [,ʌnsaɪən'tɪfɪk] *adj* no científico, poco científico, anticientífico
**unscramble** [ʌn'skræmbəl] *va* desenredar, desembrollar
**unscrew** [ʌn'skru] *va* destornillar; *vn* destornillarse
**unscrupulous** [ʌn'skrupjələs] *adj* inescrupuloso, poco escrupuloso
**unseal** [ʌn'sil] *va* desellar; (fig.) abrir
**unsearchable** [ʌn'sʌrtʃəbəl] *adj* inescrutable
**unseasonable** [ʌn'sizənəbəl] *adj* intempestivo
**unseat** [ʌn'sit] *va* quitar del asiento; desarzonar; destituir; echar abajo
**unseaworthy** [ʌn'si,wʌrðɪ] *adj* innavegable
**unseemly** [ʌn'simlɪ] *adj* impropio, indecoroso; *adv* impropiamente, indecorosamente
**unseen** [ʌn'sin] *adj* no visto; invisible
**unselfish** [ʌn'sɛlfɪʃ] *adj* desinteresado, altruísta
**unselfishness** [ʌn'sɛlfɪʃnɪs] *s* desinterés, altruísmo
**unsettle** [ʌn'sɛtəl] *va* desarreglar, descomponer; inquietar, trastornar; *vn* desarreglarse, descomponerse; inquietarse, trastornarse
**unsettled** [ʌn'sɛtəld] *adj* desarreglado, descompuesto; inconstante; indeciso; inhabitado, despoblado; sin residencia fija; (com.) por pagar, no liquidado
**unsex** [ʌn'sɛks] *va* privar de la sexualidad
**unshackle** [ʌn'ʃækəl] *va* desherrar, desencadenar
**unshakable** o **unshakeable** [ʌn'ʃekəbəl] *adj* insacudible; firme; imperturbable
**unshapely** [ʌn'ʃeplɪ] *adj* contrahecho, deforme, desproporcionado
**unshatterable** [ʌn'ʃætərəbəl] *adj* inastillable
**unshaven** [ʌn'ʃevən] *adj* sin afeitar
**unsheathe** [ʌn'ʃið] *va* desenvainar
**unshell** [ʌn'ʃɛl] *va* descascarar
**unship** [ʌn'ʃɪp] (*pret & pp:* **-shipped;** *ger:* **-shipping**) *va* desembarcar; (coll.) deshacerse de; (naut.) desarmar (*un remo*); (naut.) desmontar (*el timón*)
**unshod** [ʌn'ʃɑd] *adj* descalzo; desherrado (*caballo*)
**unshowy** [ʌn'ʃo·ɪ] *adj* deslucido
**unshrinkable** [ʌn'ʃrɪŋkəbəl] *adj* inencogible
**unshroud** [ʌn'ʃraʊd] *va* desamortajar
**unsightly** [ʌn'saɪtlɪ] *adj* feo, repugnante
**unsinkable** [ʌn'sɪŋkəbəl] *adj* insumergible
**unskilled** [ʌn'skɪld] *adj* inexperto; desmañado
**unskilled laborer** *s* peón, bracero, operario no especializado
**unskillful** [ʌn'skɪlfəl] *adj* desmañado
**unsling** [ʌn'slɪŋ] (*pret & pp:* **-slung**) *va* descolgar; quitar del cabestrillo; (naut.) deslingar
**unsnap** [ʌn'snæp] (*pret & pp:* **-snapped;** *ger:* **-snapping**) *va* desabrochar
**unsnarl** [ʌn'snɑrl] *va* desenredar, desenmarañar
**unsociability** [ʌn,soʃə'bɪlɪtɪ] *s* insociabilidad
**unsociable** [ʌn'soʃəbəl] *adj* insociable
**unsold** [ʌn'sold] *adj* invendido
**unsolder** [ʌn'sɑdər] *va* desoldar; (fig.) dividir, separar
**unsolvable** [ʌn'sɑlvəbəl] *adj* insoluble, irresoluble
**unsophisticated** [,ʌnsə'fɪstɪ,ketɪd] *adj* cándido, natural, sencillo
**unsound** [ʌn'saʊnd] *adj* poco firme; falso, erróneo; podrido; ligero (*sueño*)
**unsparing** [ʌn'spɛrɪŋ] *adj* liberal, generoso; cruel, despiadado
**unspeakable** [ʌn'spikəbəl] *adj* indecible; incalificable (*infame, atroz*)
**unsportsmanlike** [ʌn'sportsmən,laɪk] *adj* antideportivo
**unspotted** [ʌn'spɑtɪd] *adj* sin manchas, inmaculado
**unstable** [ʌn'stebəl] *adj* inestable
**unsteady** [ʌn'stɛdɪ] *adj* inseguro, inestable; inconstante, irresoluto; poco juicioso
**unstep** [ʌn'stɛp] (*pret & pp:* **-stepped;** *ger:* **-stepping**) *va* (naut.) desmontar (*p.ej., un mástil*)
**unstinted** [ʌn'stɪntɪd] *adj* ilimitado, liberal
**unstinting** [ʌn'stɪntɪŋ] *adj* porfiado, tenaz; generoso, liberal
**unstitch** [ʌn'stɪtʃ] *va* descoser
**unstop** [ʌn'stɑp] (*pret & pp:* **-stopped;** *ger:* **-stopping**) *va* destaponar (*una botella, las fosas nasales*)
**unstrap** [ʌn'stræp] (*pret & pp:* **-strapped;** *ger:* **-strapping**) *va* aflojar las correas de
**unstressed** [ʌn'strɛst] *adj* sin énfasis; (phonet.) inacentuado
**unstring** [ʌn'strɪŋ] (*pret & pp:* **-strung**) *va* desencordar, desencordelar; desensartar; debilitar, trastornar
**unstrung** [ʌn'strʌŋ] *adj* debilitado, trastornado, nervioso; *pret & pp de* **unstring**
**unstudied** [ʌn'stʌdɪd] *adj* natural, no afectado
**unsubdued** [,ʌnsəb'djud] o [,ʌnsəb'dud] *adj* indomado, insumiso
**unsubmissive** [,ʌnsəb'mɪsɪv] *adj* insumiso
**unsubstantial** [,ʌnsəb'stænʃəl] *adj* insubstancial
**unsuccessful** [,ʌnsək'sɛsfəl] *adj* fracasado, sin éxito, impróspero, desairado
**unsufferable** [ʌn'sʌfərəbəl] *adj* inaguantable
**unsuitability** [,ʌnsutə'bɪlɪtɪ] o [,ʌnsjutə'bɪlɪtɪ] *s* inconveniencia; incompetencia
**unsuitable** [ʌn'sutəbəl] o [ʌn'sjutəbəl] *adj* inconveniente, inadecuado; incompetente
**unsuited** [ʌn'sutɪd] o [ʌn'sjutɪd] *adj* inadecuado; incompetente
**unsullied** [ʌn'sʌlɪd] *adj* inmaculado
**unsung** [ʌn'sʌŋ] *adj* no cantado
**unsure** [ʌn'ʃʊr] *adj* incierto; inseguro
**unsurmised** [,ʌnsər'maɪzd] *adj* no conjeturado
**unsurpassed** [,ʌnsər'pæst] o [,ʌnsər'pɑst] *adj* insuperado, sin par
**unsuspected** [,ʌnsə'spɛktɪd] *adj* insospechado
**unsweetened** [ʌn'switənd] *adj* no endulzado
**unswept** [ʌn'swɛpt] *adj* no barrido
**unswerving** [ʌn'swʌrvɪŋ] *adj* firme, inmutable, resoluto
**unsymmetrical** [,ʌnsɪ'mɛtrɪkəl] *adj* asimétrico, disimétrico
**unsympathetic** [,ʌnsɪmpə'θɛtɪk] *adj* incompasivo, indiferente
**unsystematic** [,ʌnsɪstə'mætɪk] o **unsystematical** [,ʌnsɪstə'mætɪkəl] *adj* sin sistema, no metódico
**untactful** [ʌn'tæktfəl] *adj* sin tacto, indiscreto
**untainted** [ʌn'tentɪd] *adj* incorrupto, sin mancha
**untamable** o **untameable** [ʌn'teməbəl] *adj* indomable
**untamed** [ʌn'temd] *adj* indomado
**untangle** [ʌn'tæŋgəl] *va* desenredar, desenmarañar
**untaught** [ʌn'tɔt] *adj* sin instrucción; natural, espontáneo
**untaxed** [ʌn'tækst] *adj* libre de impuesto
**unteachable** [ʌn'titʃəbəl] *adj* indócil
**untempered** [ʌn'tɛmpərd] *adj* sin templar
**untenable** [ʌn'tɛnəbəl] o [ʌn'tinəbəl] *adj* insostenible
**untenanted** [ʌn'tɛnəntɪd] *adj* sin arrendar, desocupado
**unthankful** [ʌn'θæŋkfəl] *adj* ingrato, desagradecido
**unthatch** [ʌn'θætʃ] *va* desbardar; (fig.) descubrir
**unthinkable** [ʌn'θɪŋkəbəl] *adj* impensable
**unthinking** [ʌn'θɪŋkɪŋ] *adj* irreflexivo; instintivo
**unthoughtful** [ʌn'θɔtfəl] *adj* irreflexivo; inconsiderado; aturdido
**unthought-of** [ʌn'θɔt,ɑv] *adj* no soñado, no imaginado; olvidado
**unthread** [ʌn'θrɛd] *va* desensartar; deshebrar, desenhebrar; desenredar; abrirse camino por
**unthrifty** [ʌn'θrɪftɪ] *adj* gastador, pródigo
**untidy** [ʌn'taɪdɪ] *adj* desaliñado, desaseado
**untie** [ʌn'taɪ] (*pret & pp:* **-tied;** *ger:* **-tying**) *va* desatar; soltar; *vn* desatarse
**until** [ʌn'tɪl] *prep* hasta; *conj* hasta que; **to wait until** + *ind* aguardar a que + *subj,* esperar a que + *subj*
**untillable** [ʌn'tɪləbəl] *adj* incultivable
**untilled** [ʌn'tɪld] *adj* inculto
**untimely** [ʌn'taɪmlɪ] *adj* intempestivo; pre-

maturo; *adv* intempestivamente; prematuramente
**untiring** [ʌnˈtaɪrɪŋ] *adj* incansable, infatigable
**untitled** [ʌnˈtaɪtəld] *adj* sin título
**unto** [ˈʌntu] *prep* (archaic) a; (archaic) hasta
**untold** [ʌnˈtold] *adj* nunca dicho; inenarrable; incalculable
**untouchable** [ʌnˈtʌtʃəbəl] *adj* intangible; *s* intocable (*individuo de una casta inferior en la India*)
**untoward** [ʌnˈtord] *adj* desfavorable; terco, indócil; adverso, contrario, desdichado
**untrained** [ʌnˈtrend] *adj* indócil, indisciplinado; no adiestrado; no entrenado
**untrammeled** o **untrammelled** [ʌnˈtræməld] *adj* libre, sin trabas
**untransferable** [ˌʌntrænsˈfʌrəbəl] *adj* intransferible
**untranslatable** [ˌʌntrænsˈletəbəl] *adj* intraducible
**untranslated** [ˌʌntrænsˈletɪd] *adj* sin traducir
**untraveled** o **untravelled** [ʌnˈtrævəld] *adj* que no ha viajado; aislado, inexplorado
**untried** [ʌnˈtraɪd] *adj* no probado
**untrod** [ʌnˈtrɑd] *adj* no pisado, no trillado
**untrue** [ʌnˈtru] *adj* falso; inexacto; infiel; desalineado; desplomado
**untruss** [ʌnˈtrʌs] *va* desatar, desempaquetar; descargar; desarmar
**untrustworthy** [ʌnˈtrʌstˌwʌrðɪ] *adj* indigno de confianza
**untruth** [ʌnˈtruθ] *s* falsedad, mentira
**untruthful** [ʌnˈtruθfəl] *adj* falso, mentiroso
**untuck** [ʌnˈtʌk] *va* desenfaldar
**untutored** [ʌnˈtjutərd] o [ʌnˈtutərd] *adj* sin instrucción
**untwine** [ʌnˈtwaɪn] *va* desenroscar; desenmarañar; *vn* desenroscarse; desenmarañarse
**untwist** [ʌnˈtwɪst] *va* destorcer; desenmarañar; *vn* destorcerse; desenmarañarse
**unused** [ʌnˈjuzd] *adj* inutilizado, inusitado; deshabituado, no acostumbrado
**unusual** [ʌnˈjuʒuəl] *adj* inusual, extraordinario
**unusually** [ʌnˈjuʒuəlɪ] *adv* extraordinariamente
**unutterable** [ʌnˈʌtərəbəl] *adj* indecible, inexpresable
**unutterably** [ʌnˈʌtərəblɪ] *adv* indeciblemente, inexpresablemente
**unvaccinated** [ʌnˈvæksɪˌnetɪd] *adj* sin vacunar
**unvanquished** [ʌnˈvæŋkwɪʃt] *adj* invicto
**unvarnished** [ʌnˈvɑrnɪʃt] *adj* sin barnizar; (fig.) sencillo, sin adornos
**unveil** [ʌnˈvel] *va* quitar el velo a; descubrir; inaugurar, develar, descubrir (*p.ej., una estatua*); *vn* quitarse el velo; descubrirse, revelarse
**unveiling** [ʌnˈvelɪŋ] *s* inauguración, develación (*de una estatua*)
**unventilated** [ʌnˈventɪˌletɪd] *adj* sin ventilación
**unverified** [ʌnˈverɪfaɪd] *adj* sin verificar, sin comprobar
**unvoice** [ʌnˈvɔɪs] *va* (phonet.) ensordecer, afonizar; *vn* (phonet.) ensordecerse, afonizarse
**unvoiced** [ʌnˈvɔɪst] *adj* no expresado; (phonet.) insonoro, afonizado
**unvoicing** [ʌnˈvɔɪsɪŋ] *s* (phonet.) afonización
**unwanted** [ʌnˈwɑntɪd] *adj* indeseado
**unwarrantable** [ʌnˈwɑrəntəbəl] o [ʌnˈwɔrəntəbəl] *adj* injustificable
**unwarranted** [ʌnˈwɑrəntɪd] o [ʌnˈwɔrəntɪd] *adj* no justificado; desautorizado; no asegurado, sin garantía
**unwary** [ʌnˈwerɪ] *adj* incauto, imprudente
**unwashed** [ʌnˈwɑʃt] o [ʌnˈwɔʃt] *adj* sucio, sin lavar; **the great unwashed** la canalla, el populacho
**unwavering** [ʌnˈwevərɪŋ] *adj* firme, resuelto, determinado
**unweaned** [ʌnˈwind] *adj* sin destetar
**unwearied** [ʌnˈwɪrɪd] *adj* no cansado; incansable
**unweave** [ʌnˈwiv] (*pret:* **-wove;** *pp:* **-woven**) *va* destejer; desenmarañar; *vn* destejerse; desenmarañarse
**unwed** [ʌnˈwed] o **unwedded** [ʌnˈwedɪd] *adj* soltero, no casado
**unwelcome** [ʌnˈwelkəm] *adj* no bienvenido, mal acogido; importuno, molesto
**unwell** [ʌnˈwel] *adj* enfermo, indispuesto; menstruante
**unwept** [ʌnˈwept] *adj* no llorado; no vertido (*dícese de las lágrimas*)
**unwholesome** [ʌnˈholsəm] *adj* insalubre
**unwieldy** [ʌnˈwildɪ] *adj* pesado, abultado, inmanejable
**unwilling** [ʌnˈwɪlɪŋ] *adj* desinclinado, maldispuesto; **willing or unwilling** que quiera o que no quiera
**unwillingness** [ʌnˈwɪlɪŋnɪs] *s* desinclinación, mala gana
**unwillingly** [ʌnˈwɪlɪŋlɪ] *adv* de mala gana
**unwind** [ʌnˈwaɪnd] (*pret & pp:* **-wound**) *va* desenvolver; (fig.) desenvolver (*p.ej., un cuento*); *vn* desenvolverse; distenderse (*el muelle del reloj*)
**unwired** [ʌnˈwaɪrd] *adj* sin alambres
**unwise** [ʌnˈwaɪz] *adj* mal aconsejado, indiscreto; tonto
**unwitnessed** [ʌnˈwɪtnɪst] *adj* sin testigos
**unwitting** [ʌnˈwɪtɪŋ] *adj* inconsciente, inadvertido
**unwittingly** [ʌnˈwɪtɪŋlɪ] *adv* inconscientemente, inadvertidamente
**unwomanly** [ʌnˈwumənlɪ] *adj* indigno de una mujer, poco propio de una mujer
**unwonted** [ʌnˈwʌntɪd] *adj* desacostumbrado; inusitado
**unworkable** [ʌnˈwʌrkəbəl] *adj* impracticable; irresoluble
**unworkmanlike** [ʌnˈwʌrkmənˌlaɪk] *adj* chapucero; *adv* chapuceramente
**unworldly** [ʌnˈwʌrldlɪ] *adj* no terrenal, no mundano, espiritual
**unworthily** [ʌnˈwʌrðɪlɪ] *adv* indignamente
**unworthiness** [ʌnˈwʌrðɪnɪs] *s* indignidad, desmerecimiento
**unworthy** [ʌnˈwʌrðɪ] *adj* indigno, desmerecedor
**unwound** [ʌnˈwaund] *pret & pp de* **unwind**
**unwounded** [ʌnˈwundɪd] *adj* ileso, sin heridas
**unwrap** [ʌnˈræp] (*pret & pp:* **-wrapped;** *ger:* **-wrapping**) *va* desenvolver; desempaquetar, desempapelar; *vn* desempaquetarse
**unwrinkle** [ʌnˈrɪŋkəl] *va* desarrugar; *vn* desarrugarse
**unwritten** [ʌnˈrɪtən] *adj* no escrito; en blanco; tradicional
**unwritten law** *s* ley no escrita; derecho de matar al seductor de la esposa o hija
**unyielding** [ʌnˈjildɪŋ] *adj* terco; inflexible; insumiso
**unyoke** [ʌnˈjok] *va* desuncir; *vn* desuncirse; desunirse
**U.P.** abr. de **United Press**
**up** [ʌp] *adv* arriba, en lo alto, en el aire; hacia arriba; para arriba; al norte; **to be all up with** no haber remedio para; **to be up** estar en lo alto, estar en el aire; estar levantado; vencer (*un plazo*); **to be up in arms** estar sobre las armas; protestar vehementemente; **to be up to a person** tocarle a uno; **to get up** levantarse; **to go up** subir; **to keep up** mantener; mantenerse firme; continuar; **to keep up with** correr parejas con; **up above** allá arriba; **up against it** (slang) en apuros; **up to** hasta; a la altura de; dispuesto para; al corriente de; armando, tramando; **what is up?** ¿qué pasa?; *prep* a lo alto de, en lo alto de; encima de; arriba de, hacia arriba de; sobre; subiendo; aguas arriba de (*cierto río*); **up the river** río arriba; **up the street** calle arriba; **up a tree** (slang) en apuros; *adj* ascendente; alto, elevado; en pie, derecho; de pie, levantado; levantado de la cama; acabado, terminado; cumplido; cercano; versado, al corriente; bajo consideración; **to be up and about** estar levantado (*dícese de uno que ha estado enfermo*); *s* altura; subida; prosperidad; **ups and downs** altibajos, vaivenes, vicisitudes; *va* levantar; (coll.) aumentar; *vn* levantarse; subir; animarse; **to up and** + *inf* (coll.) ponerse de repente a + *inf*
**up-and-coming** [ˈʌpənˈkʌmɪŋ] *adj* (coll.) emprendedor y prometedor
**up-and-doing** [ˈʌpənˈduɪŋ] *adj* (coll.) emprendedor

**up-and-down** [ˈʌpənˈdaʊn] *adj* vertical, perpendicular; (coll.) absoluto, categórico
**up-and-up** [ˈʌpənˈʌp] *s* subida progresiva; **on the up-and-up** (coll.) mejorándose; sin dolo, abiertamente
**upas** [ˈjupəs] *s* (bot.) upas (*árbol y resina*); (fig.) ponzoña
**upborne** [ʌpˈborn] *adj* sostenido; levantado en alto
**upbraid** [ʌpˈbred] *va* reconvenir; **to upbraid for** o **with** reconvenir con, de, por o sobre
**upbraiding** [ʌpˈbredɪŋ] *adj* recriminador; *s* recriminación, reconvención
**upbringing** [ˈʌpˌbrɪŋɪŋ] *s* educación
**upbuild** [ʌpˈbɪld] (*pret & pp:* **-built**) *va* construir, establecer, componer, armar
**upcountry** [ˈʌpˌkʌntrɪ] *s* (coll.) interior (del país); *adj* (coll.) del interior; *adv* en el interior, hacia el interior, tierra adentro
**update** [ʌpˈdet] *va* poner al día
**upend** [ʌpˈɛnd] *va* poner de punta, poner derecho; *vn* ponerse de punta, ponerse derecho
**upgrade** [ˈʌpˌgred] *s* pendiente en subida; **on the upgrade** ascendente; progresivo; *adj* ascendente; *adv* cuesta arriba; [ʌpˈgred] *va* mejorar la calidad de, adelantar a un nivel más alto, substituir un producto superior por (*uno inferior*)
**upgrowth** [ˈʌpˌgroθ] *s* crecimiento
**upheaval** [ʌpˈhivəl] *s* solevantamiento; (geol.) solevantamiento; (fig.) trastorno, cataclismo
**upheave** [ʌpˈhiv] *va* solevantar; *vn* solevantarse
**upheld** [ʌpˈhɛld] *pret & pp de* **uphold**
**uphill** [ˈʌpˌhɪl] *adj* ascendente; difícil, penoso; [ˌʌpˈhɪl] *adv* cuesta arriba
**uphold** [ʌpˈhold] (*pret & pp:* **-held**) *va* levantar en alto; sostener, apoyar; defender
**upholster** [ʌpˈholstər] *va* tapizar
**upholsterer** [ʌpˈholstərər] *s* tapicero
**upholstery** [ʌpˈholstərɪ] *s* (*pl:* **-ies**) tapicería
**upkeep** [ˈʌpˌkip] *s* conservación; gastos de conservación, gastos de entretenimiento
**upland** [ˈʌplənd] o [ˈʌpˌlænd] *s* terreno elevado, tierra alta; *adj* elevado, alto
**upland cotton** *s* algodón de altura, algodón de la Luisiana
**upland plover** *s* (orn.) batitú
**uplift** [ˈʌpˌlɪft] *s* levantamiento, elevación; mejora social; edificación; [ʌpˈlɪft] *va* levantar, elevar; edificar
**upmost** [ˈʌpmost] *adj* var. de **uppermost**
**upon** [əˈpɑn] *prep* en, sobre, encima de; hacia; contra; tras; **upon my honor!** ¡a fe mía!; **upon my word!** ¡por mi palabra!
**upper** [ˈʌpər] *adj* superior, alto; interior; exterior (*dícese de la ropa*); *s* pala (*del calzado*); **on one's uppers** con los zapatos sin suelas; (coll.) andrajoso, pobre
**upper berth** *s* litera alta
**Upper Canada** *s* el Alto Canadá (*hoy la provincia de Ontario*)
**upper case** *s* (print.) letra de caja alta
**upper-case** [ˈʌpərˌkes] *adj* (print.) de caja alta
**upper-class** [ˈʌpərˌklæs] o [ˈʌpərˌklɑs] *adj* de las altas clases, aristocrático; de tercer o cuarto año (*en las escuelas*)
**upper classes** *spl* altas clases
**upperclassman** [ˌʌpərˈklæsmən] o [ˌʌpərˈklɑsmən] *s* (*pl:* **-men**) estudiante de tercer o cuarto año
**upper crust** *s* (coll.) altas clases, alta sociedad
**uppercut** [ˈʌpərˌkʌt] *s* (box.) golpe de abajo arriba; (*pret & pp:* **-cut;** *ger:* **-cutting**) *va & vn* golpear de abajo arriba
**upper hand** *s* dominio, ventaja; **to have the upper hand** tener vara alta
**Upper House** *s* Cámara alta
**upper lip** *s* labio superior
**upper middle class** *s* alta burguesía
**uppermost** [ˈʌpərmost] *adj* (el) más alto, más elevado, supremo, último; predominante, principal; *adv* en lo más alto; en primer lugar
**uppish** [ˈʌpɪʃ] *adj* (coll.) arrogante, copetudo
**upraise** [ʌpˈrez] *va* levantar
**uprear** [ʌpˈrɪr] *va* levantar; *vn* levantarse
**upright** [ˈʌpˌraɪt] *adj* vertical, derecho; (fig.) recto, probo; *adv* verticalmente; *s* montante
**uprightness** [ˈʌpˌraɪtnɪs] *s* verticalidad; (fig.) rectitud, probidad
**upright piano** *s* piano vertical, piano recto
**uprise** [ˈʌpˌraɪz] *s* subida; [ʌpˈraɪz] (*pret:* **-rose;** *pp:* **-risen**) *vn* levantarse; subir; sublevarse
**uprisen** [ʌpˈrɪzən] *pp de* **uprise**
**uprising** [ʌpˈraɪzɪŋ] o [ˈʌpˌraɪzɪŋ] *s* levantamiento, alboroto popular, sublevación; pendiente en subida
**uproar** [ˈʌpˌror] *s* tumulto, alboroto, conmoción; rugido
**uproarious** [ʌpˈrorɪəs] *adj* tumultuoso
**uproot** [ʌpˈrut] o [ʌpˈrʊt] *va* desarraigar, descepar; (fig.) desarraigar
**uprose** [ʌpˈroz] *pret de* **uprise**
**uprouse** [ʌpˈraʊz] *va* despertar, excitar, mover
**upset** [ˈʌpˌsɛt] *s* vuelco; contratiempo, trastorno; enfermedad; disputa; [ʌpˈsɛt] o [ˈʌpˌsɛt] *adj* volcado; trastornado, perturbado; indispuesto; [ʌpˈsɛt] (*pret & pp:* **-set;** *ger:* **-setting**) *va* volcar; trastornar, perturbar; enfermar, indisponer; *vn* volcar
**upset price** *s* precio mínimo fijado en una subasta
**upsetting** [ʌpˈsɛtɪŋ] *adj* inquietante, desconcertante
**upshot** [ˈʌpˌʃɑt] *s* resultado; quid, esencia, toque
**upside** [ˈʌpˌsaɪd] *s* parte superior; **to turn upside down** volcar; trastornar; volcarse; trastornarse; **upside down** al revés, lo de arriba abajo; en confusión, revuelto
**upstage** [ˈʌpˌstedʒ] *adj* situado al fondo de la escena; (coll.) altanero, arrogante; [ˌʌpˈstedʒ] *adv* al fondo de la escena, hacia el fondo de la escena
**upstairs** [ˌʌpˈstɛrz] *adv* arriba; [ˈʌpˌstɛrz] *adj* de arriba; *s* piso de arriba; pisos superiores
**upstanding** [ʌpˈstændɪŋ] *adj* derecho, erguido; (fig.) recto, probo
**upstart** [ˈʌpˌstɑrt] *adj & s* advenedizo; presuntuoso
**upstate** [ˈʌpˌstet] *adj* (U.S.A.) interior, septentrional
**upstream** [ˈʌpˌstrim] *adv* aguas arriba, río arriba, contra la corriente
**upstroke** [ˈʌpˌstrok] *s* plumada ascendente; (mach.) carrera ascendente
**upsurge** [ˈʌpˌsʌrdʒ] *s* subida repentina (*p.ej., de precios*); [ʌpˈsʌrdʒ] *vn* subir repentinamente
**upswing** [ˈʌpˌswɪŋ] *s* movimiento hacia arriba; (fig.) mejora notable; **on the upswing** mejorando notablemente
**uptake** [ˈʌpˌtek] *s* levantamiento, subida; comprensión; canal de llamas ascendente; canal de ventilación; captación (*de un trazador radiactivo*)
**upthrust** [ˈʌpˌθrʌst] *s* solevantamiento; (geol.) solevantamiento
**up-to-date** [ˈʌptʊˌdet] *adj* que va hasta la fecha; moderno, reciente, de última moda, de última hora; al corriente
**up-to-the-minute** [ˈʌptʊðəˈmɪnɪt] *adj* moderno; al corriente
**uptown** [ˈʌpˌtaʊn] *adj* de arriba, de la parte alta de la ciudad; [ˈʌpˈtaʊn] *adv* arriba, hacia la parte alta de la ciudad
**uptrend** [ˈʌpˌtrɛnd] *s* tendencia al alza
**upturn** [ˈʌpˌtʌrn] *s* vuelta hacia arriba; mejora (*en los negocios, precios, etc.*); [ʌpˈtʌrn] *va* volver hacia arriba; *vn* volverse hacia arriba
**upturned** [ʌpˈtʌrnd] *adj* revuelto, invertido; arremangado; respingado
**upward** [ˈʌpwərd] *adj* ascendente; *adv* hacia arriba; **upward of** más de
**upwardly** [ˈʌpwərdlɪ] *adv* hacia arriba
**upwards** [ˈʌpwərdz] *adv* hacia arriba; **upwards of** más de
**Ural** [ˈjʊrəl] *adj* ural; **Urals** *spl* Urales, montes Urales
**Ural-Altaic** [ˈjʊrəlælˈteɪk] *adj & s* uraloaltaico
**Uralian** [jʊˈrelɪən] *adj* urálico
**Ural Mountains** *spl* montes Urales
**Urania** [jʊˈrenɪə] *s* (myth.) Urania
**Uranian** [jʊˈrenɪən] *adj* uranio
**uranic** [jʊˈrænɪk] *adj* (chem.) uránico
**uraninite** [jʊˈrænɪnaɪt] *s* (mineral.) uraninita
**uranite** [ˈjʊrənaɪt] *s* (mineral.) uranita
**uranium** [jʊˈrenɪəm] *s* (chem.) urano o uranio

**uranographer** [ˌjurəˈnɑgrəfər] *s* uranógrafo
**uranography** [ˌjurəˈnɑgrəfɪ] *s* uranografía
**uranometry** [ˌjurəˈnɑmɪtrɪ] *s* uranometría
**uranous** [ˈjurənəs] *adj* (chem.) uranoso
**Uranus** [ˈjurənəs] *s* (astr. & myth.) Urano
**urao** [uˈrɑo] *s* (mineral.) urao
**urate** [ˈjuret] *s* (chem.) urato
**urban** [ˈʌrbən] *adj* urbano (*perteneciente a la ciudad*); (*cap.*) *s* Urbano
**urbane** [ʌrˈben] *adj* urbano (*cortés, fino*)
**urbanistic** [ˌʌrbəˈnɪstɪk] *adj* urbanístico
**urbanite** [ˈʌrbənaɪt] *s* ciudadano
**urbanity** [ʌrˈbænɪtɪ] *s* urbanidad
**urbanization** [ˌʌrbənɪˈzeʃən] *s* urbanización
**urbanize** [ˈʌrbənaɪz] *va* urbanizar
**urban renewal** *s* renovación urbanística
**urceolate** [ˈʌrsɪəlet] *adj* urceolado
**urchin** [ˈʌrtʃɪn] *s* chiquillo, pilluelo, galopín; (ichth.) erizo; (mach.) erizo (*de la carda mecánica*)
**Urdu** [ˈurdu], [urˈdu] o [ʌrˈdu] *s* urdú
**urea** [juˈriə] o [ˈjurɪə] *s* (biochem.) urea
**urease** [ˈjurɪes] o [ˈjurɪez] *s* (biochem.) ureasa
**uremia** [juˈrimɪə] *s* (path.) uremia
**uremic** [juˈrimɪk] *adj* urémico
**ureter** [juˈritər] *s* (anat. & zool.) uréter
**urethra** [juˈriθrə] *s* (*pl:* **-thras** o **-thrae** [θri]) (anat.) uretra
**urethral** [juˈriθrəl] *adj* uretral
**urethritis** [ˌjurɪˈθraɪtɪs] *s* (path.) uretritis
**urethroscope** [juˈriθrəskop] *s* uretroscopio
**urethroscopy** [ˌjurɪˈθrɑskəpɪ] *s* uretroscopia
**urge** [ʌrdʒ] *s* impulso, instinto; *va* impeler, empujar; impulsar, incitar; apremiar, instar; pedir instantemente; **to urge to** + *inf* instar **a** que + *subj*; *vn* apresurarse; apremiar; presentar argumentos o pretensiones
**urgency** [ˈʌrdʒənsɪ] *s* (*pl:* **-cies**) urgencia; instancia, insistencia
**urgent** [ˈʌrdʒənt] *adj* urgente; insistente, apremiante
**Uriah** [juˈraɪə] *s* (Bib.) Urías
**uric** [ˈjurɪk] *adj* úrico
**uric acid** *s* (chem.) ácido úrico
**urinal** [ˈjurɪnəl] *s* orinal (*vaso*); urinal o urinario (*lugar*)
**urinalysis** [ˌjurɪˈnælɪsɪs] *s* (*pl:* **-ses** [siz]) urinálisis
**urinary** [ˈjurɪˌnerɪ] *adj* urinario; *s* (*pl:* **-ies**) urinal (*lugar*)
**urinary calculus** *s* (path.) cálculo urinario
**urinary tract** *s* (anat.) vías urinarias
**urinate** [ˈjurɪnet] *va* orinar (*p.ej., sangre*); *vn* orinar u orinarse
**urination** [ˌjurɪˈneʃən] *s* urinación, micción
**urine** [ˈjurɪn] *s* orina, orines
**urn** [ʌrn] *s* urna; cafetera o tetera con hornillo y grifo; (arch.) jarrón
**urodelan** [ˌjuroˈdilən] *adj* & *s* (zool.) urodelo
**urogenital** [ˌjuroˈdʒenɪtəl] *adj* urogenital
**urolith** [ˈjurolɪθ] *s* (path.) urolito
**urolithiasis** [ˌjurolɪˈθaɪəsɪs] *s* (path.) urolitiasis
**urologic** [ˌjuroˈlɑdʒɪk] o **urological** [ˌjuroˈlɑdʒɪkəl] *adj* urológico
**urologist** [jurˈɑlədʒɪst] *s* urólogo
**urology** [jurˈɑlədʒɪ] *s* urología
**uropygial** [ˌjuroˈpɪdʒɪəl] *adj* uropigal
**uropygium** [ˌjuroˈpɪdʒɪəm] *s* uropigio, rabadilla (*de las aves*)
**uroscopy** [jurˈɑskəpɪ] *s* uroscopia
**urosis** [jurˈosɪs] *s* (path.) urosis
**Ursa Major** [ˈʌrsəˈmedʒər] *s* (astr.) Osa Mayor
**Ursa Minor** [ˈʌrsəˈmaɪnər] *s* (astr.) Osa Menor
**ursine** [ˈʌrsaɪn] o [ˈʌrsɪn] *adj* ursino; velloso
**ursine dasyure** [ˈdæsɪjur] *s* (zool.) diablo de Tasmania
**ursine howler** *s* (zool.) aluato
**Ursula** [ˈʌrsjulə] *s* Úrsula
**Ursuline** [ˈʌrsjulɪn] o [ˈʌrsjulaɪn] *adj* ursulino; *s* ursulina
**urticaceous** [ˌʌrtɪˈkeʃəs] *adj* (bot.) urticáceo
**urticant** [ˈʌrtɪkənt] *adj* urticante
**urticaria** [ˌʌrtɪˈkerɪə] *s* (path.) urticaria
**urtication** [ˌʌrtɪˈkeʃən] *s* (med.) urticación
**Uru.** abr. de **Uruguay**
**Uruguay** [ˈjurəgwe] o [ˈjurəgwaɪ] *s* el Uruguay
**Uruguayan** [ˌjurəˈgweən] o [ˌjurəˈgwaɪən] *adj* & *s* uruguayo
**urus** [ˈjurəs] *s* (zool.) uro
**U.S.** abr. de **United States**
**us** [ʌs] *pron pers* nos; nosotros
**U.S.A.** abr. de **United States of America, United States Army** y **Union of South Africa**
**usability** [ˌjuzəˈbɪlɪtɪ] *s* disponibilidad
**usable** [ˈjuzəbəl] *adj* utilizable, aprovechable, usual
**usage** [ˈjusɪdʒ] o [ˈjuzɪdʒ] *s* uso
**usance** [ˈjuzəns] *s* (econ.) interés o renta (*beneficio sacado del dinero invertido o prestado*); (com.) plazo a que se debe pagar una letra de cambio; **at usance** al usado
**U.S.C.G.** abr. de **United States Coast Guard**
**use** [jus] *s* uso, empleo; **in use** en uso; **out of use** desusado; **to be of no use** no servir para nada; **to have no use for** no necesitar; no servirse de; (coll.) no tener buena opinión de, tener en poco; **to make use of** servirse de; **to put to use** servirse de, poner en uso; [juz] *va* usar, emplear; tratar; agotar, consumir; acostumbrar; **to use language** decir blasfemias; **to use up** agotar, consumir; (coll.) agotar, cansar, rendir; *vn* ir con frecuencia, concurrir con frecuencia; soler, p.ej., **I used to go out for a walk every morning** solía salir de paseo todas las mañanas o salía de paseo todas las mañanas
**useable** [ˈjuzəbəl] *adj* var. de **usable**
**used** [juzd] *adj* usado (*empleado; gastado por el uso; acostumbrado*); **used to** [ˈjustu] acostumbrado a
**used car** *s* coche usado, coche de segunda mano, coche de ocasión
**useful** [ˈjusfəl] *adj* útil
**usefulness** [ˈjusfəlnɪs] *s* utilidad
**useless** [ˈjuslɪs] *adj* inútil, inservible
**uselessness** [ˈjuslɪsnɪs] *s* inutilidad
**user** [ˈjuzər] *s* usuario; (law) usufructuario
**U-shaped** [ˈjuˌʃept] *adj* en forma de U
**usher** [ˈʌʃər] *s* acomodador (*p.ej., en el teatro*); ujier, portero; (Brit.) repetidor; *va* acomodar; anunciar, introducir; **to usher in** anunciar, introducir
**usherette** [ˌʌʃəˈret] *s* acomodadora
**U.S.M.** abr. de **United States Mail** y **United States Marine**
**U.S.M.A.** abr. de **United States Military Academy**
**U.S.M.C.** abr. de **United States Marine Corps**
**U.S.N.** abr. de **United States Navy**
**U.S.N.A.** abr. de **United States Naval Academy**
**U.S.N.G.** abr. de **United States National Guard**
**U.S.S.** abr. de **United States Senate** y **United States Ship, Steamer** o **Steamship**
**U.S.S.R.** o **USSR** abr. de **Union of Soviet Socialist Republics**
**ustulation** [ˌʌstʃəˈleʃən] *s* chamusquina, socarrina; (pharm.) ustulación
**usu.** abr. de **usual** y **usually**
**usual** [ˈjuʒuəl] *adj* usual; **as usual** como de costumbre
**usually** [ˈjuʒuəlɪ] *adv* usualmente
**usucapion** [ˌjuzjuˈkepɪɑn] *s* (law) usucapión
**usucapt** [ˈjuzjukæpt] *va* (law) usucapir
**usufruct** [ˈjuzjufrʌkt] *s* (law) usufructo; *va* usufructuar
**usurer** [ˈjuʒərər] *s* usurero
**usurious** [juˈʒurɪəs] *adj* usurario
**usurp** [juˈzʌrp] *va* usurpar
**usurpation** [ˌjuzʌrˈpeʃən] *s* usurpación
**usurper** [juˈzʌrpər] *s* usurpador
**usury** [ˈjuʒərɪ] *s* (*pl:* **-ries**) usura
**Ut.** abr. de **Utah**
**utensil** [juˈtensəl] *s* utensilio
**uterine** [ˈjutərɪn] o [ˈjutəraɪn] *adj* uterino
**uterus** [ˈjutərəs] *s* (*pl:* **-i** [aɪ]) (anat.) útero
**utilitarian** [ˌjutɪlɪˈterɪən] *adj* utilitario; utilitarista; *s* utilitarista
**utilitarianism** [ˌjutɪlɪˈterɪənɪzəm] *s* utilitarismo
**utility** [juˈtɪlɪtɪ] *s* (*pl:* **-ties**) utilidad; empresa de servicio público; *adj* para uso general

**utility man** *s* factótum, criado para todo; (baseball) suplente; (theat.) racionista
**utilization** [ˌjutɪlɪˈzeʃən] *s* utilización
**utilize** [ˈjutɪlaɪz] *va* utilizar
**utmost** [ˈʌtmost] *adj* sumo, supremo, extremo, último; más grande, mayor posible; más distante, más lejano; *s* más alto grado; **the utmost** lo sumo, lo mayor, lo más; **to do one's utmost** hacer todo lo posible; **to the utmost** a más no poder
**utopia** o **Utopia** [juˈtopɪə] *s* utopia o utopía
**utopian** o **Utopian** [juˈtopɪən] *adj* utópico; utopista; *s* utopista
**utopianism** [juˈtopɪənɪzəm] *s* utopismo
**utricle** [ˈjutrɪkəl] *s* (anat.) utrículo; (bot.) utrícula
**utricular** [juˈtrɪkjələr] *adj* utricular
**utter** [ˈʌtər] *adj* total, completo, absoluto, terminante; *va* proferir, pronunciar, lanzar; expresar, manifestar, dar a conocer; poner en circulación (*p.ej., moneda falsa*)
**utterable** [ˈʌtərəbəl] *adj* decible, articulable, pronunciable
**utterance** [ˈʌtərəns] *s* pronunciación; expresión, manifestación; declaración, palabras
**utterly** [ˈʌtərlɪ] *adv* totalmente, completamente, absolutamente, terminantemente
**uttermost** [ˈʌtərmost] *adj & s* var. de **utmost**
**uvea** [ˈjuvɪə] *s* (anat.) úvea
**uvula** [ˈjuvjələ] *s* (*pl:* **-las** o **-lae** [li]) (anat.) úvula
**uvular** [ˈjuvjələr] *adj* (anat. & phonet.) uvular
**uvulitis** [ˌjuvjəˈlaɪtɪs] *s* (path.) uvulitis
**uxorial** [ʌkˈsoriəl] *adj* uxorio (*perteneciente a la esposa*)
**uxoricide** [ʌkˈsorɪsaɪd] *s* uxoricida (*marido*); uxoricidio (*acción*)
**uxorious** [ʌkˈsorɪəs] *adj* uxorio (*muy amante de su mujer y demasiado complaciente con ella*)
**Uz** [ʌz] *s* (Bib.) tierra de Hus
**Uzbeg** [ˈʌzbɛg] o **Uzbek** [ˈʌzbɛk] *s* uzbeco
**Uzbekistan** [ˌuzbɛkɪˈstɑn] *s* el Uzbekistán

# V

**V, v** [vi] *s* (*pl:* **V's, v's** [viz]) vigésima segunda letra del alfabeto inglés.

**v.** abr. de **verb, verse, versus, vice-, vide** (Lat.) **see, voice, volt, voltage, volume** y **von**

**v** abr. de **volt**

**V.** abr. de **Venerable, Vice, Victoria, Viscount** y **Volunteer**

**Va.** abr. de **Virginia** (*EE.UU.*)

**V.A.** abr. de **Veterans' Administration, Vicar Apostolic** y **Vice-Admiral**

**vacancy** ['vekənsɪ] *s* (*pl:* **-cies**) vacío; vacancia, vacante (*empleo sin proveer*); apartamento o cuarto vacante; desocupación, ociosidad; vacuidad, vaciedad

**vacant** ['vekənt] *adj* vacío; vacante (*empleo, cuarto*); distraído, necio; vago (*dícese, p.ej., de la mirada*)

**vacate** ['veket] *va* dejar vacante, desocupar; anular, revocar; *vn* marcharse

**vacation** [ve'keʃən] *s* vacación; vacaciones; **to be on vacation** estar de vacaciones; **to go away on a vacation** o **to leave for a vacation** marcharse de vacaciones; *vn* tomar vacaciones

**vacationist** [ve'keʃənɪst] *s* vacacionista

**vacations with pay** *spl* vacaciones retribuídas, vacaciones en el trabajo

**vaccinate** ['væksɪnet] *va* vacunar

**vaccination** [,væksɪ'neʃən] *s* vacunación

**vaccine** ['væksin] o ['væksɪn] *s* vacuna

**vaccine therapy** *s* vacunoterapia

**vacillate** ['væsɪlet] *vn* vacilar

**vacillating** ['væsɪ,letɪŋ] *adj* vacilante

**vacillation** [,væsɪ'leʃən] *s* vacilación

**vacuity** [væ'kjuɪtɪ] *s* (*pl:* **-ties**) vacuidad

**vacuo** ['vækjuo]; **in vacuo** en el vacío

**vacuole** ['vækjuol] *s* (biol.) vacuola

**vacuous** ['vækjuəs] *adj* vacío; fatuo, necio

**vacuum** ['vækjuəm] *s* (*pl:* **-ums** o **-a** [ə]) vacío; *va* (coll.) limpiar con el aspirador, aspirar (*el polvo, las migajas*)

**vacuum bottle** *s* botella de vacío

**vacuum brake** *s* freno al vacío, freno de vacío

**vacuum cleaner** *s* aspirador de polvo

**vacuum cup** *s* ventosa

**vacuum filter** *s* filtro al vacío

**vacuum pump** *s* bomba al vacío

**vacuum tank** *s* (aut.) aspirador de gasolina, nodriza

**vacuum tube** *s* (elec.) tubo al vacío, tubo de vacío

**vade mecum** [,vedɪ'mikəm] *s* vademécum

**vagabond** ['vægəbɑnd] *adj & s* vagabundo

**vagabondage** ['vægəbɑndɪdʒ] *s* vagabundaje, vagabundeo

**vagary** [və'gɛrɪ] *s* (*pl:* **-ies**) capricho, extravagancia

**vagina** [və'dʒaɪnə] *s* (bot. & anat.) vagina

**vaginal** ['vædʒɪnəl] o [və'dʒaɪnəl] *adj* vaginal

**vaginate** ['vædʒɪnet] *adj* vaginado

**vaginitis** [,vædʒɪ'naɪtɪs] *s* (path.) vaginitis

**vaginula** [və'dʒɪnjələ] *s* (bot. & zool.) vagínula

**vagitus** [və'dʒaɪtəs] *s* (med.) vagido

**vagrancy** ['vegrənsɪ] *s* (*pl:* **-cies**) vagancia, vagabundaje

**vagrant** ['vegrənt] *adj* vagante, vagabundo; *s* vagabundo

**vague** [veg] *adj* vago

**vagueness** ['vegnɪs] *s* vaguedad

**vagus** ['vegəs] *s* (*pl:* **-gi** [dʒaɪ]) (anat.) vagus

**vain** [ven] *adj* vano; vanidoso; **in vain** en vano

**vainglorious** [,ven'glorɪəs] *adj* vanaglorioso

**vainglory** [,ven'glorɪ] *s* vanagloria

**vainly** ['venlɪ] *adv* vanamente; vanidosamente

**vair** [vɛr] *s* vero (*piel*); (her.) veros

**valance** ['væləns] *s* doselera (*cenefa del dosel*); guardamalleta (*sobre la cortina*)

**vale** [vel] *s* valle

**valediction** [,vælɪ'dɪkʃən] *s* despedida

**valedictorian** [,vælɪdɪk'torɪən] *s* alumno que pronuncia el discurso de despedida

**valedictory** [,vælɪ'dɪktərɪ] *s* (*pl:* **-ries**) discurso de despedida; *adj* de despedida

**valence** ['veləns] *s* (chem.) valencia

**Valenciennes** [,vælənsɪ'ɛnz] *s* encaje de Valenciennes

**valency** ['velənsɪ] *s* (*pl:* **-cies**) var. de **valence**

**valentine** ['væləntaɪn] *s* tarjeta (*afectuosa o jocosa anónima*) del día de San Valentín; amado o amada (*escogida en ese día*); **St. Valentine** San Valentín

**Valentine's Day** *s* día de San Valentín; día de los enamorados, día de los corazones (*14 de febrero*)

**vale of tears** *s* valle de lágrimas

**Vale of Tempe** ['tɛmpɪ] *s* (hist.) valle de Tempe

**valerian** [və'lɪrɪən] *s* (bot. & pharm.) valeriana

**valet** ['vælɪt] o ['væle] *s* paje, sirviente

**valet de chambre** [væ'lɛdə'ʃɑ̃brə] *s* paje de cámara, ayuda de cámara

**valetudinarian** [,vælɪ,tjudɪ'nɛrɪən] o [,vælɪtudɪ'nɛrɪən] *adj & s* valetudinario

**Valhalla** [væl'hælə] *s* (myth.) el Valhala

**valiancy** ['væljənsɪ] *s* (*pl:* **-cies**) valentía (*valor, ánimo; hazaña heroica*)

**valiant** ['væljənt] *adj* valiente

**valid** ['vælɪd] *adj* válido; vigente

**validate** ['vælɪdet] *va* validar

**validation** [,vælɪ'deʃən] *s* validación

**validity** [və'lɪdɪtɪ] *s* (*pl:* **-ties**) validez; vigencia

**valise** [və'lis] *s* maleta; velís (Am.)

**Valkyrie** [væl'kɪrɪ], ['vælkɪrɪ] o [væl'kaɪrɪ] *s* valquiria

**vallation** [væ'leʃən] *s* vallado

**valley** ['vælɪ] *s* valle; (arch.) lima hoya

**valor** ['vælər] *s* valor, coraje, ánimo

**valorization** [,vælərɪ'zeʃən] *s* valorización

**valorize** ['væləraɪz] *va* valorizar

**valorous** ['vælərəs] *adj* valeroso

**valour** ['vælər] *s* (Brit.) var. de **valor**

**valse** [vɑls] *s* var. de **waltz**

**valuable** ['væljuəbəl] o ['væljəbəl] *adj* valioso (*que vale mucho*); valorable, estimable; **valuables** *spl* objetos de valor, joyas, alhajas

**valuation** [,vælju'eʃən] *s* valuación, valoración

**value** ['vælju] *s* valor; (mus.) valor; adquisición, inversión, p.ej., **a wonderful value** una adquisición extraordinaria, una inversión maravillosa; *va* valuar, valorar; estimar, tener en mucho

**valued** ['væljud] *adj* estimado, apreciado; valorado

**valueless** ['væljulɪs] *adj* sin valor

**valuta** [və'lutə] *s* (econ.) valuta

**valvate** ['vælvet] *adj* valvulado; valviforme

**valve** [vælv] *s* (anat., mach. & rad.) válvula; (biol.) valva; (bot.) ventalla (*de la vaina de una legumbre*); (mus.) llave; *va* gobernar por medio de válvulas

**valve box** *s* (mach.) caja de distribución

**valve cap** *s* tapita de válvula (*de neumático*)

**valve chest** *s* var. de **valve box**

**valve gears** *spl* distribución, mecanismo de distribución

**valve-in-head** ['vælvɪn'hɛd] *adj* con válvulas en la culata

**valveless** ['vælvlɪs] *adj* sin válvulas

**valve lifter** *s* levantaválvulas

**valve seat** *s* asiento de válvula

**valve spring** *s* muelle de válvula

**valve stem** *s* vástago de válvula

**valvular** ['vælvjələr] *adj* valvular

**vamoose** [væ'mus] *va* (slang) dejar rápidamente; *vn* (slang) marcharse rápidamente

**vamp** [væmp] *s* empella (*del calzado*); remiendo; (mus.) acompañamiento improvisado; (slang) vampiresa, mujer fatal; *va* poner empella a; remendar; enmendar, componer; (mus.) improvisar (*un acompañamiento*); (slang) coquetear con; **to vamp up** enmendar, componer; urdir para engañar; *vn* (mus.) improvisar; (slang) coquetear
**vampire** ['væmpaɪr] *s* vampiro; (zool.) vampiro; (fig.) vampiro (*concusionario*); mujer coqueta; vampiresa, mujer fatal (*mujer que sacrifica a su capricho a los hombres*)
**van** [væn] *s* carro de carga, camión, camión de mudanzas; (Brit.) furgón de equipajes; (mil.) vanguardia
**vanadium** [və'nedɪəm] *s* (chem.) vanadio
**vanadium steel** *s* acero al vanadio
**Vandal** ['vændəl] *adj* vándalo, vandálico; *s* vándalo; (*l.c.*) *adj* vandálico; *s* vándalo
**vandalism** ['vændəlɪzəm] *s* vandalismo
**Vandyke beard** [væn'daɪk] *s* barba puntiaguda
**Vandyke collar** *s* valona
**vane** [ven] *s* veleta (*para marcar la dirección del viento*); paleta (*de hélice*); barba (*de pluma*); aspa (*de molino*)
**vang** [væŋ] *s* (naut.) osta
**vanguard** ['væn,gɑrd] *s* (mil. & fig.) vanguardia; **in the vanguard** a vanguardia
**vanilla** [və'nɪlə] *s* (bot.) vainilla (*planta, fruto y extracto*)
**vanillin** ['vænɪlɪn] o [və'nɪlɪn] *s* (chem.) vainillina
**vanish** ['vænɪʃ] *vn* desvanecerse, desaparecer
**vanishing cream** *s* crema desvanecedora
**vanishing point** *s* punto de fuga, punto de desaparición; (perspective) punto de la vista
**vanity** ['vænɪtɪ] *s* (*pl:* **-ties**) vanidad; neceser de belleza, estuche de afeites; tocador
**vanity case** *s* neceser de belleza
**vanity dresser** o **table** *s* tocador
**vanquish** ['væŋkwɪʃ] *va* vencer, sujetar, dominar
**vantage** ['væntɪdʒ] o ['vɑntɪdʒ] *s* ventaja, superioridad
**vantage ground** *s* posición ventajosa
**vanward** ['vænwərd] *adj & adv* hacia el frente
**vapid** ['væpɪd] *adj* insípido
**vapidity** [væ'pɪdɪtɪ] *s* insipidez
**vapor** ['vepər] *s* vapor; niebla, bruma; vaho, exhalación; humo, quimera, sueño; *va* vaporizar; *vn* vaporear; jactarse
**vaporable** ['vepərəbəl] *adj* vaporable
**vapor bath** *s* baño de vapor
**vapor heat** *s* calefacción a vapor de muy baja presión
**vaporish** ['vepərɪʃ] *adj* vaporoso; melancólico
**vaporization** [,vepərɪ'zeʃən] *s* vaporización; (med.) vaporización
**vaporize** ['vepəraɪz] *va* vaporizar; *vn* vaporizarse
**vaporizer** ['vepə,raɪzər] *s* vaporizador
**vaporous** ['vepərəs] *adj* vaporoso; fugaz, inútil; vano, quimérico
**vapor trail** *s* (aer.) estela de vapor, rastro de condensación
**vapory** ['vepərɪ] *adj* vaporoso; melancólico, atrabilioso
**var.** abr. de **variant**
**variability** [,verɪə'bɪlɪtɪ] *s* variabilidad
**variable** ['verɪəbəl] *adj* variable; *s* (math.) variable
**variable condenser** *s* (elec.) condensador variable
**variance** ['verɪəns] *s* variación, modificación, diferencia; desavenencia, desacuerdo; **at variance** en desacuerdo
**variant** ['verɪənt] *adj & s* variante
**variation** [,verɪ'eʃən] *s* variación
**varicella** [,værɪ'sɛlə] *s* (path.) varicela
**varicocele** ['værɪkə,sil] *s* (path.) varicocele
**varicolored** ['verɪ,kʌlərd] *adj* abigarrado
**varicose** ['værɪkos] *adj* varicoso
**varicose veins** *spl* (path.) varices
**varicosis** [,værɪ'kosɪs] *s* (path.) varicosis
**varicosity** [,værɪ'kɑsɪtɪ] *s* (*pl:* **-ties**) varicosidad (*estado varicoso; varice*)
**varied** ['verɪd] *adj* variado
**variegate** ['verɪəget] o ['verɪget] *va* jaspear, abigarrar
**variegated** ['verɪə,getɪd] o ['verɪ,getɪd] *adj* jaspeado, abigarrado
**variegation** [,verɪə'geʃən] o [,verɪ'geʃən] *s* jaspeado, abigarramiento
**variety** [və'raɪətɪ] *s* (*pl:* **-ties**) variedad; (theat.) variedades
**variocoupler** [,verɪo'kʌplər] *s* (rad.) varioacoplador
**variola** [və'raɪələ] *s* (path.) viruela
**varioloid** ['verɪələɪd] *s* (path.) varioloide
**variolous** [və'raɪələs] *adj* varioloso
**variometer** [,verɪ'ɑmɪtər] *s* (elec., meteor. & rad.) variómetro
**variorum** [,verɪ'orəm] *adj & s* variórum
**various** ['verɪəs] *adj* vario; *adj pl* varios
**varix** ['verɪks] *s* (*pl:* **varices** ['verɪsiz]) (path.) varice o várice
**varlet** ['vɑrlɪt] *s* (archaic) lacayo, paje; (archaic) truhán, golfo
**varmint** ['vɑrmɪnt] *s* (coll. & dial.) bicho, sabandija; (coll. & dial.) golfo, bribón
**varnish** ['vɑrnɪʃ] *s* barniz; (fig.) capa, máscara, apariencia; *va* barnizar; (fig.) adornar, dar apariencia falsa a, encubrir
**varnishing day** *s* (f.a.) barnizado
**varsity** ['vɑrsɪtɪ] *s* (*pl:* **-ties**) (sport) universidad; (sport) equipo principal (*de la universidad*); *adj* (sport) universitario
**varsovienne** [,vær,so'vjɛn] *s* varsoviana (*baile y música*)
**vary** ['verɪ] (*pret & pp:* **-ied**) *va & vn* variar
**vas** [væs] *s* (*pl:* **vasa** ['vesə]) (anat.) vaso
**vascular** ['væskjələr] *adj* (bot. & zool.) vascular
**vasculous** ['væskjələs] *adj* vasculoso
**vase** [ves] o [vez] *s* florero, jarrón; (arch.) copa, vaso
**vasectomy** [væ'sɛktəmɪ] *s* (*pl:* **-mies**) (surg.) vasectomía
**vaseline** ['væsəlin] *s* (trademark) vaselina
**vasoligation** [,væsolaɪ'geʃən] *s* (surg.) vasoligatura
**vasomotor** [,væso'motər] *adj* (physiol.) vasomotor
**vassal** ['væsəl] *adj & s* vasallo
**vassalage** ['væsəlɪdʒ] *s* vasallaje
**vast** [væst] o [vɑst] *adj* vasto
**vastly** ['væstlɪ] o ['vɑstlɪ] *adv* en sumo grado, sumamente
**vastness** ['væstnɪs] o ['vɑstnɪs] *s* vastedad
**vat** [væt] *s* tina, cuba
**Vatican** ['vætɪkən] *s* Vaticano
**Vatican City** *s* Ciudad del Vaticano, Ciudad Vaticana
**vaticinate** [və'tɪsɪnet] *va* vaticinar
**vaudeville** ['vodvɪl] o ['vɔdɪvɪl] *s* (theat.) variedades, teatro de variedades; (theat.) vaudeville, zarzuela
**vault** [vɔlt] *s* (arch. & anat.) bóveda; bóveda (*cripta*); bodega; cámara acorazada (*de un banco*); sepultura, tumba; bóveda celeste; salto; *va* abovedar; saltar; *vn* saltar
**vaulted** ['vɔltɪd] *adj* abovedado
**vaulting** ['vɔltɪŋ] *s* abovedado; salto
**vaulting horse** *s* potro de madera
**vaunt** [vɔnt] o [vɑnt] *s* jactancia; *va* jactarse de; *vn* jactarse
**vb.** abr. de **verb** y **verbal**
**V.C.** abr. de **Vice-Chancellor** y **Victoria Cross**
**V.D.** abr. de **venereal disease**
**veal** [vil] *s* carne de ternera
**veal chop** *s* chuleta de ternera
**vector** ['vɛktər] *adj* vectorial; *s* (biol. & math.) vector
**Veda** ['vedə] *s* Veda
**Vedaic** [ve'deɪk] *adj & s* védico
**vedette** [vɪ'dɛt] *s* centinela de avanzada; buque escucha
**Vedic** ['vedɪk] *adj & s* var. de **Vedaic**
**Vedism** ['vedɪzəm] *s* vedismo
**veer** [vɪr] *s* virada; *va* virar; soltar (*p.ej., un cabo*); *vn* virar; desviarse
**veery** ['vɪrɪ] *s* (*pl:* **-ies**) (orn.) tordo norteamericano (*Hylocichla fuscescens*)
**Vega** ['vigə] *s* (astr.) Vega
**vegetable** ['vɛdʒɪtəbəl] *adj* vegetal; *s* vegetal (*planta*); hortaliza, legumbre (*planta comestible*)

**vegetable garden** *s* huerto de hortalizas, huerto de legumbres, huerto de verduras
**vegetable horsehair** *s* crin vegetal
**vegetable ivory** *s* marfil vegetal
**vegetable kingdom** *s* reino vegetal
**vegetable marrow** *s* (bot.) calabaza (*variedad de Cucurbita Pepo*); (bot.) aguacate
**vegetable mold** *s* tierra vegetal, mantillo
**vegetable oil** *s* aceite vegetal
**vegetable soup** *s* sopa de hortelano, sopa de legumbres
**vegetal** ['vɛdʒɪtəl] *adj* vegetal
**vegetarian** [,vɛdʒɪ'tɛrɪən] *adj & s* vegetariano
**vegetarianism** [,vɛdʒɪ'tɛrɪənɪzəm] *s* vegetarianismo
**vegetate** ['vɛdʒɪtet] *vn* vegetar; (fig.) vegetar
**vegetation** [,vɛdʒɪ'teʃən] *s* vegetación
**vegetative** ['vɛdʒɪ,tetɪv] *adj* vegetativo
**vehemence** ['viɪməns] *s* vehemencia
**vehement** ['viɪmənt] *adj* vehemente
**vehicle** ['viɪkəl] *s* vehículo
**vehicular** [vɪ'hɪkjələr] *adj* vehicular
**vehicular traffic** *s* circulación rodada
**Veii** ['vijaɪ] *s* Veyos
**veil** [vel] *s* velo; (fig.) velo; **to take the veil** tomar el velo; *va* velar
**veiling** ['velɪŋ] *s* velo; material para velos
**vein** [ven] *s* vena; (fig.) rasgo; *va* jaspear, vetear
**veined** [vend] *adj* venoso, veteado
**veining** ['venɪŋ] *s* jaspeado; disposición a manera de venas
**veinstone** ['ven,ston] *s* (min.) ganga
**velar** ['vilər] *adj & s* (phonet.) velar
**velarization** [,vilərɪ'zeʃən] *s* (phonet.) velarización
**velarize** ['viləraɪz] *va* (phonet.) velarizar
**velatura** [,vɛlə'turə] *s* (paint.) veladura
**vellum** ['vɛləm] *s* vitela; papel avitelado; *adj* de vitela; avitelado
**vellum paper** *s* papel vitela, papel avitelado
**velocipede** [vɪ'lɑsɪpid] *s* velocípedo
**velocity** [vɪ'lɑsɪtɪ] *s* (*pl:* **-ties**) velocidad
**velodrome** ['vilədrom] *s* velódromo
**velum** ['viləm] *s* (*pl:* **-la** [lə]) (biol.) velo; (anat.) velo del paladar
**velure** [və'lur] *s* terciopelado; cepillo de pana; *va* cepillar con cepillo de pana
**velvet** ['vɛlvɪt] *s* terciopelo; vello, piel velluda; (slang) ganancia limpia; *adj* de terciopelo; aterciopelado
**velvet glove** *s* guante de terciopelo; **to handle with velvet gloves** tratar con cortesía superficial que encubre determinación inflexible
**velvet grass** *s* (bot.) heno blanco
**velveteen** [,vɛlvɪ'tin] *s* velludillo
**velvet weaver** *s* terciopelero
**velvety** ['vɛlvɪtɪ] *adj* aterciopelado
**Ven.** abr. de **Venerable** y **Venice**
**venal** ['vinəl] *adj* venal (*que se deja sobornar*)
**venality** [vi'nælɪtɪ] *s* venalidad
**venation** [vi'neʃən] *s* venación (*disposición de las venas*)
**vend** [vend] *va* vender como buhonero; *vn* ser buhonero
**Vendean** [vɛn'diən] *adj & s* vandeano
**vendee** [vɛn'di] *s* comprador
**vender** ['vɛndər] *s* vendedor, buhonero
**vendetta** [vɛn'dɛtə] *s* vendetta, venganza entre una familia y otra
**vending machine** *s* distribuidor automático, tragaperras
**vendor** ['vɛndər] *s* vendedor, buhonero
**vendue** [vɛn'dju] o [vɛn'du] *s* almoneda, venduta
**veneer** [və'nɪr] *s* chapa, enchapado; (fig.) apariencia; *va* enchapar; (fig.) disfrazar
**venerability** [,vɛnərə'bɪlɪtɪ] *s* venerabilidad
**venerable** ['vɛnərəbəl] *adj* venerable
**venerate** ['vɛnəret] *va* venerar
**veneration** [,vɛnə'reʃən] *s* veneración
**venereal** [vɪ'nɪrɪəl] *adj* venéreo
**venereal disease** *s* enfermedad venérea
**venery** ['vɛnərɪ] *s* venus (*acto carnal*); (archaic) venación (*caza*)
**Venetia** [vɪ'niʃɪə] o [vɪ'niʃə] *s* Venecia (*provincia o distrito*)
**Venetian** [vɪ'niʃən] *adj & s* veneciano
**Venetian blind** *s* persiana de tiro, persiana interior americana
**Venezuela** [,vɛnɪ'zwilə] *s* Venezuela
**Venezuelan** [,vɛnɪ'zwilən] *adj & s* venezolano
**Venezuelanism** [,vɛnɪ'zwilənɪzəm] *s* venezolanismo
**vengeance** ['vɛndʒəns] *s* venganza; **with a vengeance** con violencia; con extremo, con creces
**vengeful** ['vɛndʒfəl] *adj* vengativo
**venial** ['vinɪəl] *adj* venial
**veniality** [,vinɪ'ælɪtɪ] *s* (*pl:* **-ties**) venialidad
**venial sin** *s* pecado venial
**Venice** ['vɛnɪs] *s* Venecia (*ciudad*)
**venire** [vɪ'naɪrɪ] *s* (law) auto de convocación del jurado
**venireman** [vɪ'naɪrɪmən] *s* (*pl:* **-men**) (law) persona convocada para jurado
**venison** ['vɛnɪzən] o ['vɛnzən] *s* carne de venado
**venom** ['vɛnəm] *s* veneno
**venomous** ['vɛnəməs] *adj* venenoso
**venous** ['vinəs] *adj* venal, venoso
**vent** [vɛnt] *s* orificio, agujero; ventosa, fogón (*oído del arma de fuego*); venteo; respiradero (*de un barril*); tapón; (found.) bravera; (mus.) orificio, agujero (*de un instrumento músico de viento*); (zool.) ano; abertura (*en una prenda de vestir*); chimenea (*del paracaídas*); **to give vent to** desahogar; *va* proveer de abertura; desahogar, expresar; **to vent one's spleen** descargar la bilis
**ventage** ['vɛntɪdʒ] *s* orificio, agujero
**venthole** ['vɛnt,hol] *s* venteo, respiradero (*en un barril*)
**ventilate** ['vɛntɪlet] *va* ventilar; (fig.) ventilar
**ventilation** [,vɛntɪ'leʃən] *s* ventilación
**ventilator** ['vɛntɪ,letər] *s* ventilador; extractor de aire
**ventral** ['vɛntrəl] *adj* ventral
**ventrally** ['vɛntrəlɪ] *adv* en posición ventral, en dirección ventral
**ventricle** ['vɛntrɪkəl] *s* (anat. & zool.) ventrículo
**ventricular** [vɛn'trɪkjələr] *adj* ventricular
**ventriloquial** [,vɛntrɪ'lokwɪəl] *adj* ventrílocuo
**ventriloquism** [vɛn'trɪləkwɪzəm] *s* ventriloquia
**ventriloquist** [vɛn'trɪləkwɪst] *s* ventrílocuo
**ventriloquy** [vɛn'trɪləkwɪ] *s* var. de **ventriloquism**
**venture** ['vɛntʃər] *s* empresa arriesgada, especulación; **at a venture** a la ventura; *va* aventurar; **to venture a guess** aventurar una suposición; *vn* aventurarse; **to venture on** arriesgarse en; **to venture out** arriesgarse fuera
**venturesome** ['vɛntʃərsəm] *adj* aventurero (*audaz, osado*); aventurado (*azaroso, peligroso*)
**Venturi meter** [vɛn'turɪ] *s* (trademark) venturímetro, medidor Venturi
**Venturi tube** *s* (hyd.) tubo Venturi
**venturous** ['vɛntʃərəs] *adj* aventurero; aventurado, peligroso
**venue** ['vɛnju] *s* (law) jurisdicción en que se ha cometido un crimen; (law) lugar donde se reúne el jurado
**Venus** ['vinəs] *s* (myth. & astr.) Venus; (fig.) Venus (*mujer de gran belleza*)
**Venus's-flytrap** ['vinəsɪz'flaɪ,træp] *s* (bot.) atrapamoscas, dionea
**Venus's-looking-glass** ['vinəsɪz'lukɪŋ,glæs] o ['vinəsɪz'lukɪŋ,glɑs] *s* (bot.) espejo de Venus
**veracious** [vɪ'reʃəs] *adj* veraz
**veracity** [vɪ'ræsɪtɪ] *s* (*pl:* **-ties**) veracidad
**veranda** o **verandah** [və'rændə] *s* terraza, galería
**veratrine** ['vɛrətrin] *s* (chem.) veratrina
**verb** [vʌrb] *s* (gram.) verbo; *adj* verbal
**verbal** ['vʌrbəl] *adj* verbal; (gram.) verbal; *s* (gram.) verbal
**verbalism** ['vʌrbəlɪzəm] *s* expresión verbal; verbalismo (*propensión a dar más importancia a las palabras que a los conceptos*); frase sin sentido o con poco sentido
**verbalize** ['vʌrbəlaɪz] *va* expresar por medio de palabras; (gram.) transformar en verbo; *vn* hablar con verbosidad, expresarse con verbosidad
**verbatim** [vər'betɪm] *adj* textual; *adv* **al pie de la letra, palabra por palabra**
**verbena** [vər'binə] *s* (bot.) verbena

**verbenaceous** [ˌvʌrbɪˈneʃəs] *adj* (bot.) verbenáceo
**verbiage** [ˈvʌrbɪɪdʒ] *s* verbosidad, palabrería
**verbose** [vərˈbos] *adj* verboso
**verbosity** [vərˈbɑsɪtɪ] *s* verbosidad
**verdancy** [ˈvʌrdənsɪ] *s* (*pl:* **-cies**) verdor; inocencia, sencillez
**verdant** [ˈvʌrdənt] *adj* verde; inocente, sencillo
**verdict** [ˈvʌrdɪkt] *s* veredicto
**verdigris** [ˈvʌrdɪgris] *s* cardenillo, verdete
**verdure** [ˈvʌrdʒər] *s* verdor
**verdurous** [ˈvʌrdʒərəs] *adj* verde y fresco, lozano, frondoso
**verge** [vʌrdʒ] *s* borde, margen; confín; báculo, vara; fuste (*de una columna*); **on the verge of** al borde de; **on the verge of** + *ger* a punto de + *inf; vn* acercarse; propender; **to verge on** o **upon** llegar casi hasta, rayar en; **to verge towards** propender a
**verger** [ˈvʌrdʒər] *s* sacristán; macero
**Vergil** [ˈvʌrdʒɪl] *s* var. de **Virgil**
**Vergilian** [vərˈdʒɪlɪən] *adj* var. de **Virgilian**
**veriest** [ˈverɪɪst] *adj* extremo, sumo
**verifiable** [ˈverɪˌfaɪəbəl] *adj* verificable
**verification** [ˌverɪfɪˈkeʃən] *s* verificación
**verify** [ˈverɪfaɪ] (*pret & pp:* **-fied**) *va* verificar, comprobar; (law) afirmar bajo juramento
**verily** [ˈverɪlɪ] *adv* en verdad
**verisimilar** [ˌverɪˈsɪmɪlər] *adj* verisímil
**verisimilitude** [ˌverɪsɪˈmɪlɪtjud] o [ˌverɪsɪˈmɪlɪtud] *s* verisimilitud
**verism** [ˈvɪrɪzəm] *s* verismo
**veritable** [ˈverɪtəbəl] *adj* verdadero
**veritably** [ˈverɪtəblɪ] *adv* verdaderamente
**verity** [ˈverɪtɪ] *s* (*pl:* **-ties**) verdad
**verjuice** [ˈvʌrˌdʒus] *s* agrazada; acrimonia
**verjuiced** [ˈvʌrˌdʒust] *adj* agrio; de agrazada
**vermeil** [ˈvʌrmɪl] *s* plata, bronce o cobre sobredorados; (poet.) bermellón
**vermicelli** [ˌvʌrmɪˈselɪ] *s* fideos
**vermicidal** [ˌvʌrmɪˈsaɪdəl] *adj* vermicida
**vermicide** [ˈvʌrmɪsaɪd] *s* vermicida
**vermicular** [vərˈmɪkjələr] *adj* vermicular
**vermiform** [ˈvʌrmɪfɔrm] *adj* vermiforme
**vermiform appendix** *s* (anat.) apéndice vermiforme
**vermifuge** [ˈvʌrmɪfjudʒ] *adj & s* (med.) vermífugo
**vermilion** [vərˈmɪljən] *s* bermellón; *adj* bermejo
**vermilion flycatcher** *s* (orn.) rubí
**vermin** [ˈvʌrmɪn] *spl* sabandijas (*animales o personas*); *ssg* sabandija (*persona*)
**verminous** [ˈvʌrmɪnəs] *adj* verminoso
**vermis** [ˈvʌrmɪs] *s* (anat.) vermis
**vermouth** [vərˈmuθ] o [ˈvʌrmuθ] *s* vermut
**vernacular** [vərˈnækjələr] *adj* vernáculo; *s* idioma vernáculo; idioma corriente; jerga (*lenguaje especial de un oficio o profesión*)
**vernal** [ˈvʌrnəl] *adj* vernal
**vernal equinox** *s* (astr.) equinoccio vernal o de primavera
**vernal grass** *s* (bot.) grama de olor o de los prados
**vernally** [ˈvʌrnəlɪ] *adv* primaveralmente
**vernation** [vərˈneʃən] *s* (bot.) vernación, prefoliación
**vernier** [ˈvʌrnɪər] o [ˈvʌrnɪr] *s* vernier
**veronal** [ˈverənəl] *s* (trademark) veronal
**Veronese** [ˌveroˈniz] *adj* veronés; *s* (*pl:* **-nese**) veronés; el Veronés (*pintor*)
**veronica** [vəˈrɑnɪkə] *s* (bot.) verónica; lienzo de la Verónica; (taur.) verónica
**Versailles** [verˈsaɪ] o [vərˈselz] *s* Versalles
**versatile** [ˈvʌrsətɪl] *adj* flexible, universal, hábil para muchas cosas; versátil (*inconstante*); (bot. & zool.) versátil
**versatility** [ˌvʌrsəˈtɪlɪtɪ] *s* (*pl:* **-ties**) flexibilidad, universalidad, variedad de habilidades; versatilidad (*inconstancia*)
**verse** [vʌrs] *s* verso; versículo (*en la Biblia*)
**versed** [vʌrst] *adj* versado; **versed in** versado en
**versed sine** *s* (trig.) seno verso
**versemaker** [ˈvʌrsˌmekər] *s* versificador
**versicle** [ˈvʌrsɪkəl] *s* (eccl.) versículo
**versification** [ˌvʌrsɪfɪˈkeʃən] *s* versificación
**versifier** [ˈvʌrsɪˌfaɪər] *s* versificador; poetastro
**versify** [ˈvʌrsɪfaɪ] (*pret & pp:* **-fied**) *va & vn* versificar
**version** [ˈvʌrʒən] o [ˈvʌrʃən] *s* versión; (obstet.) versión
**verso** [ˈvʌrso] *s* (*pl:* **-sos**) dorso, reverso; (print.) verso, vuelto
**verst** [vʌrst] *s* versta (*medida rusa igual a 3500 pies*)
**versus** [ˈvʌrsəs] *prep* contra
**vertebra** [ˈvʌrtɪbrə] *s* (*pl:* **-brae** [bri] o **-bras**) (anat. & zool.) vértebra
**vertebral** [ˈvʌrtɪbrəl] *adj* vertebral
**vertebral column** *s* (anat.) columna vertebral
**vertebrate** [ˈvʌrtɪbret] o [ˈvʌrtɪbrɪt] *adj & s* vertebrado
**vertebrated** [ˈvʌrtɪˌbretɪd] *adj* vertebrado
**vertebration** [ˌvʌrtɪˈbreʃən] *s* vertebración
**vertex** [ˈvʌrteks] *s* (*pl:* **-texes** o **-tices** [tɪsiz]) (math. & anat.) vértice; (astr.) cenit; ápice
**vertical** [ˈvʌrtɪkəl] *adj & s* vertical
**vertical circle** *s* (astr.) vertical
**vertical hold** *s* (telv.) bloqueo vertical
**vertically** [ˈvʌrtɪkəlɪ] *adv* verticalmente
**vertical rudder** *s* (aer.) timón de dirección
**vertical stabilizer** *s* (aer.) plano de dirección
**verticil** [ˈvʌrtɪsɪl] *s* (bot.) verticilo
**verticilate** [vərˈtɪsɪlet] *adj* (bot. & zool.) verticilado
**vertiginous** [vərˈtɪdʒɪnəs] *adj* vertiginoso
**vertigo** [ˈvʌrtɪgo] *s* (*pl:* **-gos** o **-goes**) vértigo; (vet.) modorra, vértigo
**vervain** [ˈvʌrven] *s* (bot.) verbena
**verve** [vʌrv] *s* energía, vigor, ánimo, viveza
**very** [ˈverɪ] *adj* mismo, mismísimo; mero, puro; verdadero; *adv* muy; mucho, p.ej., **to be very hot** tener mucho calor
**very high frequency** *s* (rad. & telv.) frecuencia muy alta
**vesical** [ˈvesɪkəl] *adj* vesical
**vesicant** [ˈvesɪkənt] *adj & s* vesicante
**vesicate** [ˈvesɪket] *va* avejigar; *vn* avejigarse
**vesicle** [ˈvesɪkəl] *s* (anat., bot., path. & zool.) vesícula
**vesicular** [vɪˈsɪkjələr] *adj* vesicular
**vesiculate** [vɪˈsɪkjəlet] *adj* vesiculado
**Vespasian** [vesˈpeʒən] *s* Vespasiano
**vesper** [ˈvespər] *s* tarde, anochecer; oración de la tarde; campana que llama a vísperas; (*cap.*) *s* Véspero; **vespers** o **Vespers** *spl* (eccl.) vísperas; *adj* vespertino
**vesper mouse** *s* (zool.) rata de monte, rata silvestre
**vespertine** [ˈvespərtɪn] o [ˈvespərtaɪn] *adj* vespertino
**vessel** [ˈvesəl] *s* vasija, recipiente; bajel, buque, embarcación; (anat. & bot.) vaso
**vest** [vest] *s* chaleco; chaquetilla (*de mujer*); camiseta; *va* vestir; investir; conceder (*p.ej., poder*); **to vest with** investir de; *vn* vestirse; tener validez
**Vesta** [ˈvestə] *s* (myth.) Vesta
**vestal** [ˈvestəl] *adj* vestal; *s* vestal; virgen; monja
**vestal virgin** *s* vestal
**vested** [ˈvestɪd] *adj* revestido (*dícese, p.ej., de un prelado*); establecido por la ley
**vested interests** *spl* intereses creados
**vestee** [vesˈti] *s* pechera
**vestibular** [vesˈtɪbjələr] *adj* (anat.) vestibular
**vestibule** [ˈvestɪbjul] *s* vestíbulo; zaguán (*de una casa*); (anat.) vestíbulo (*del oído*)
**vestibule car** *s* (rail.) coche de vestíbulo
**vestibule door** *s* contrapuerta, portón
**vestige** [ˈvestɪdʒ] *s* vestigio; (biol.) vestigio
**vestigial** [vesˈtɪdʒɪəl] *adj* vestigial
**vestment** [ˈvestmənt] *s* vestidura
**vest pocket** *s* bolsillo de chaleco
**vest-pocket** [ˈvestˌpɑkɪt] *adj* diminuto, en miniatura
**vestry** [ˈvestrɪ] *s* (*pl:* **-tries**) sacristía; capilla; junta parroquial; reunión de la junta parroquial
**vestryman** [ˈvestrɪmən] *s* (*pl:* **-men**) miembro de la junta parroquial
**vesture** [ˈvestʃər] *s* vestidura; cubierta
**Vesuvian** [vɪˈsuvɪən] o [vɪˈsjuvɪən] *adj* vesubiano
**Vesuvius** [vɪˈsuvɪəs] o [vɪˈsjuvɪəs] *s* el Vesubio
**vet.** abr. de **veteran** y **veterinary**
**vetch** [vetʃ] *s* (bot.) vicia; (bot.) veza, arveja

**veteran** [ˈvɛtərən] *adj* veterano; *s* veterano; (mil.) veterano, ex combatiente
**veterinarian** [ˌvɛtərɪˈnɛrɪən] *s* veterinario
**veterinary** [ˈvɛtərɪˌnɛrɪ] *adj* veterinario; *s* (*pl:* **-ies**) veterinario
**veterinary medicine** *s* medicina veterinaria
**vetiver** [ˈvɛtɪvər] *s* (bot.) vetiver
**veto** [ˈvito] *s* (*pl:* **-toes**) veto; *adj* del veto; *va* vetar
**vex** [vɛks] *va* vejar
**vexation** [vɛksˈeʃən] *s* vejación
**vexatious** [vɛksˈeʃəs] *adj* vejante, vejatorio
**vexedly** [ˈvɛksɪdlɪ] *adv* irritadamente, con molestia
**vexed question** *s* cuestión batallona
**V.F.W.** abr. de **Veterans of Foreign Wars**
**v.g.** abr. de **verbi gratia** (Lat.) **for example**
**VHF** abr. de **very high frequency**
**v.i.** abr. de **intransitive verb**
**V.I.** abr. de **Virgin Islands**
**via** [ˈvaɪə] *prep* vía, p.ej., **via New York** vía Nueva York
**viability** [ˌvaɪəˈbɪlɪtɪ] *s* viabilidad
**viable** [ˈvaɪəbəl] *adj* viable
**viaduct** [ˈvaɪədʌkt] *s* viaducto
**vial** [ˈvaɪəl] *s* frasco pequeño
**viand** [ˈvaɪənd] *s* vianda; **viands** *spl* manjares delicados, platos selectos
**viaticum** [vaɪˈætɪkəm] *s* (*pl:* **-cums** o **-ca** [kə]) viático; (eccl.) viático
**vibrant** [ˈvaɪbrənt] *adj* vibrante; (phonet.) sonoro; (fig.) vibrante (*p.ej., estilo*); *s* (phonet.) sonora
**vibrate** [ˈvaɪbret] *va & vn* vibrar
**vibratile** [ˈvaɪbrətɪl] *adj* vibrátil
**vibration** [vaɪˈbreʃən] *s* vibración
**vibrative** [ˈvaɪbrətɪv] *adj* vibratorio
**vibrator** [ˈvaɪbretər] *s* vibrador
**vibratory** [ˈvaɪbrəˌtorɪ] *adj* vibratorio
**vibrio** [ˈvɪbrɪo] *s* (*pl:* **-os**) (bact.) vibrio
**vibrion** [ˈvɪbrɪɑn] *s* (bact.) vibrión
**viburnum** [vaɪˈbʌrnəm] *s* (bot.) viburno, mundillo
**vicar** [ˈvɪkər] *s* vicario
**vicarage** [ˈvɪkərɪdʒ] *s* vicaría, vicariato; beneficio del vicario
**vicar-general** [ˈvɪkərˈdʒɛnərəl] *s* (*pl:* **vicars-general**) vicario general
**vicarial** [vaɪˈkɛrɪəl] o [vɪˈkɛrɪəl] *adj* vicarial
**vicarious** [vaɪˈkɛrɪəs] o [vɪˈkɛrɪəs] *adj* vicario; sufrido por otro, experimentado por otro; (physiol.) vicario
**vicarship** [ˈvɪkərʃɪp] *s* vicaría, vicariato
**vice** [vaɪs] *s* vicio; (mach.) tornillo (*para sujetar el objeto que se ha de trabajar*)
**vice-admiral** [ˌvaɪsˈædmɪrəl] *s* vicealmirante
**vice-admiralty** [ˌvaɪsˈædmɪrəltɪ] *s* vicealmirantazgo
**vice-chancellor** [ˌvaɪsˈtʃænsələr] o [ˌvaɪsˈtʃɑnsələr] *s* vicecanciller
**vice-Christ** [ˌvaɪsˈkraɪst] *s* vicecristo
**vice-consul** [ˌvaɪsˈkɑnsəl] *s* vicecónsul
**vice-consulate** [ˌvaɪsˈkɑnsəlɪt] *s* viceconsulado
**vice-counsellor** [ˌvaɪsˈkaʊnsələr] *s* viceconsiliario
**vicegerency** [ˌvaɪsˈdʒɪrənsɪ] *s* vicegerencia
**vicegerent** [ˌvaɪsˈdʒɪrənt] *adj & s* vicegerente
**vice-God** [ˌvaɪsˈgɑd] *s* vicediós
**vice-governor** [ˌvaɪsˈgʌvərnər] *s* vicegobernador
**vice-king** [ˌvaɪsˈkɪŋ] *s* virrey
**vicennial** [vaɪˈsɛnɪəl] *adj* vicenal
**Vice Pres.** abr. de **Vice-President**
**vice-presidency** [ˌvaɪsˈprɛzɪdənsɪ] *s* vicepresidencia
**vice-president** [ˌvaɪsˈprɛzɪdənt] *s* vicepresidente
**vice-presidential** [ˌvaɪsprɛzɪˈdɛnʃəl] *adj* vicepresidencial
**vice-queen** [ˌvaɪsˈkwin] *s* virreina
**vice-rector** [ˌvaɪsˈrɛktər] *s* vicerrector
**viceregal** [ˌvaɪsˈrigəl] *adj* virreinal
**viceregent** [ˌvaɪsˈridʒənt] *s* vicerregente
**viceroy** [ˈvaɪsrɔɪ] *s* virrey
**viceroyalty** [ˌvaɪsˈrɔɪəltɪ] *s* virreinato
**vice-secretary** [ˌvaɪsˈsɛkrɪˌtɛrɪ] *s* vicesecretario
**vice-secretaryship** [ˌvaɪsˈsɛkrɪˌtɛrɪʃɪp] *s* vicesecretaría
**vice-treasurer** [ˌvaɪsˈtrɛʒərər] *s* vicetesorero
**vice versa** [ˈvaɪsɪˈvʌrsə] *adv* viceversa
**Vichy water** [ˈvɪʃɪ] *s* agua de Vichy
**vici** [ˈvaɪsaɪ] *s* gamuza
**vicinage** [ˈvɪsɪnɪdʒ] *s* vecindad
**vicinal** [ˈvɪsɪnəl] *adj* vecinal
**vicinity** [vɪˈsɪnɪtɪ] *s* (*pl:* **-ties**) vecindad
**vicious** [ˈvɪʃəs] *adj* vicioso; ruin, arisco (*caballo*); bravo (*perro*)
**vicious circle** *s* círculo vicioso
**vicissitude** [vɪˈsɪsɪtjud] o [vɪˈsɪsɪtud] *s* vicisitud
**victim** [ˈvɪktɪm] *s* víctima
**victimization** [ˌvɪktɪmɪˈzeʃən] *s* inmolación; engaño, estafa
**victimize** [ˈvɪktɪmaɪz] *va* inmolar, hacer víctima; engañar, estafar
**victor** [ˈvɪktər] *s* vencedor
**victoria** [vɪkˈtorɪə] *s* victoria (*coche*); (bot.) victoria
**Victorian** [vɪkˈtorɪən] *adj & s* victoriano
**Victorian age** *s* época victoriana
**victorious** [vɪkˈtorɪəs] *adj* victorioso
**victory** [ˈvɪktərɪ] *s* (*pl:* **-ries**) victoria
**victrola** [vɪkˈtrolə] *s* (trademark) fonógrafo
**victual** [ˈvɪtəl] *s* (dial.) vitualla, alimento; **victuals** *spl* (coll. & dial.) vituallas, alimentos, víveres; (*pret & pp:* **-ualed** o **-ualled**; *ger:* **-ualing** o **-ualling**) *va* avituallar; *vn* avituallarse
**victualer** o **victualler** [ˈvɪtələr] *s* abastecedor; (mil.) comisario; hostelero
**vicuña** [vɪˈkunjə] o [vɪˈkjunə] *s* (zool.) vicuña (*animal, lana y tela*)
**vid.** abr. de **vide** (Lat.) **see**
**videlicet** [vɪˈdɛlɪsɛt] *adv* a saber, es decir
**video** [ˈvɪdɪo] *s* vídeo; *adj* de vídeo
**videocast** [ˈvɪdɪoˌkæst] o [ˈvɪdɪoˌkɑst] *s* teledifusión; (*pret & pp:* **-cast** o **-casted**) *va* teledifundir
**video signal** *s* videoseñal
**video tape** *s* cinta grabada de televisión
**video-tape recording** [ˈvɪdɪoˌtep] *s* videograbación
**video telephony** *s* visiotelefonía
**vidette** [vɪˈdɛt] *s* var. de **vedette**
**vie** [vaɪ] (*pret & pp:* **vied**; *ger:* **vying**) *vn* competir, rivalizar
**Vienna** [vɪˈɛnə] *s* Viena
**Viennese** [ˌviəˈniz] *adj* vienés; *s* (*pl:* **-nese**) vienés
**Viet-Namese** [viˈɛtnɑˈmiz] o [ˈvitnəˈmiz] *adj* vietnamés o vietnamita; *s* (*pl:* **-ese**) vietnamés o vietnamita
**view** [vju] *s* vista; panorama, paisaje; opinión, parecer; inspección; intento, propósito; **in view of** en vista de; **on view** en exhibición; **to be on view** estar expuesto (*p.ej., un cadáver*); **to take a dim view of** mirar escépticamente, no entusiasmarse por; **with a view to** con el propósito de; en cuanto a; **with a view to** + *ger* con vistas a + *inf; va* ver, mirar; contemplar, considerar, pesar; examinar, inspeccionar
**viewer** [ˈvjuər] *s* espectador; inspector; televidente, telespectador; mirador para transparencias, proyector de transparencias
**view finder** *s* (phot.) visor
**viewless** [ˈvjulɪs] *adj* invisible; sin opinión
**viewpoint** [ˈvjuˌpɔɪnt] *s* punto de la vista (*sitio*); punto de vista (*opinión, ademán*)
**vigesimal** [vaɪˈdʒɛsɪməl] *adj* vigésimo; vigesimal
**vigil** [ˈvɪdʒɪl] *s* vigilia; **vigils** *spl* (eccl.) vigilia
**vigilance** [ˈvɪdʒɪləns] *f* vigilancia
**vigilant** [ˈvɪdʒɪlənt] *adj* vigilante
**vigilante** [ˌvɪdʒɪˈlæntɪ] *s* vigilante
**vignette** [vɪnˈjɛt] *s* viñeta
**vigor** [ˈvɪgər] *s* vigor
**vigorous** [ˈvɪgərəs] *adj* vigoroso
**vigour** [ˈvɪgər] *s* (Brit.) var. de **vigor**
**viking** o **Viking** [ˈvaɪkɪŋ] *s* vikingo, pirata escandinavo
**vile** [vaɪl] *adj* vil; repugnante
**vilification** [ˌvɪlɪfɪˈkeʃən] *s* vilipendio, difamación
**vilify** [ˈvɪlɪfaɪ] (*pret & pp:* **-fied**) *va* vilipendiar, difamar
**villa** [ˈvɪlə] *s* villa, quinta
**village** [ˈvɪlɪdʒ] *s* aldea

**villager** ['vɪlɪdʒər] *s* aldeano
**villain** ['vɪlən] *s* malvado; malo, traidor (*de una novela o drama*); (hist.) villano
**villainous** ['vɪlənəs] *adj* malvado, villano
**villainy** ['vɪlənɪ] *s* (*pl:* **-ies**) villanía, maldad
**villanelle** [,vɪlə'nɛl] *s* villanela
**villein** ['vɪlən] *s* (hist.) villano
**villeinage** ['vɪlənɪdʒ] *s* (hist.) villanaje
**villous** ['vɪləs] *adj* velloso
**villus** ['vɪləs] *s* (*pl:* **-li** [laɪ]) (anat., bot. & zool.) vello
**vim** [vɪm] *s* fuerza, vigor, energía
**vinaigrette** [,vɪne'grɛt] *s* vinagrera
**Vincennes** [vɪn'sɛnz] *s* Vincenas
**Vincent** ['vɪnsənt] *s* Vicente
**vincible** ['vɪnsɪbəl] *adj* vencible
**vinculum** ['vɪŋkjələm] *s* (*pl:* **-la** [lə]) vínculo
**vindicate** ['vɪndɪket] *va* vindicar; (law) vindicar, reivindicar
**vindication** [,vɪndɪ'keʃən] *s* vindicación; (law) vindicación, reivindicación
**vindicative** [vɪn'dɪkətɪv] o ['vɪndɪ,ketɪv] *adj* vindicativo
**vindicator** ['vɪndɪ,ketər] *s* vindicador
**vindictive** [vɪn'dɪktɪv] *adj* vindicativo, vengativo
**vine** [vaɪn] *s* (bot.) enredadera; (bot.) vid, parra (*de uvas*)
**vinedresser** ['vaɪn,drɛsər] *s* viñador
**vinegar** ['vɪnɪgər] *s* vinagre
**vinegar eel** *s* (zool.) anguílula del vinagre
**vinegarer** ['vɪnɪgərər] *s* vinagrero
**vinegar fly** *s* (ent.) mosca del vinagre
**vinegarish** ['vɪnɪgərɪʃ] *adj* avinagrado
**vinegary** ['vɪnɪgərɪ] *adj* vinagroso (*gusto o genio*)
**vinegrower** ['vaɪn,groər] *s* vinícola, viñador
**vineyard** ['vɪnjərd] *s* viña, viñedo
**vineyardist** ['vɪnjərdɪst] *s* viñador
**vinic** ['vaɪnɪk] o ['vɪnɪk] *adj* vínico
**vinification** [,vɪnɪfɪ'keʃən] *s* vinificación
**vinous** ['vaɪnəs] *adj* vinoso
**vintage** ['vɪntɪdʒ] *s* vendimia; cosecha de vino; (coll.) categoría, tipo, clase
**vintager** ['vɪntɪdʒər] *s* vendimiador
**vintage wine** *s* vino de buena cosecha
**vintage year** *s* año de buen vino
**vintner** ['vɪntnər] *s* vinatero
**vinyl** ['vaɪnɪl] o ['vɪnɪl] *s* (chem.) vinilo
**vinyl acetate** *s* (chem.) acetato de vinilo
**vinyl alcohol** *s* (chem.) alcohol vinílico
**viol** ['vaɪəl] *s* (mus.) viola; (naut.) virador
**viola** [vaɪ'olə] o [vɪ'olə] *s* (mus.) viola (*instrumento y persona*); ['vaɪolə] o [vaɪ'olə] *s* (bot.) viola
**violable** ['vaɪələbəl] *adj* violable
**violaceous** [,vaɪə'leʃəs] *adj* violáceo
**viola d'amore** [vi'ɔlɑ dɑ'more] *s* (mus.) viola de amor
**violate** ['vaɪəlet] *va* violar
**violation** [,vaɪə'leʃən] *s* violación
**violator** ['vaɪə,letər] *s* violador
**violence** ['vaɪələns] *s* violencia
**violent** ['vaɪələnt] *adj* violento
**violet** ['vaɪəlɪt] *s* (bot.) violeta; violado (*color*); violeta (*color; colorante*); *adj* violado (*color*); violeta (*color y perfume*)
**violet ray** *s* rayo violeta
**violet shift** *s* (phys.) desviación hacia el violado del espectro
**violin** [,vaɪə'lɪn] *s* violín (*instrumento y el que lo toca*)
**violinist** [,vaɪə'lɪnɪst] *s* violinista
**violist** ['vaɪəlɪst] *s* viola (*persona*)
**violle** [vjəl] *s* violle (*unidad fotométrica*)
**violoncellist** [,vaɪələn'tʃɛlɪst] o [,viələn'tʃɛlɪst] *s* violoncelista
**violoncello** [,vaɪələn'tʃɛlo] o [,viələn'tʃɛlo] *s* (*pl:* **-los**) (mus.) violoncelo
**viosterol** [vaɪ'ɑstərɑl] *s* (pharm.) viosterol
**viper** ['vaɪpər] *s* (zool.) víbora; (fig.) víbora
**viperine** ['vaɪpərɪn] o ['vaɪpəraɪn] *adj* vipéreo o viperino
**viperish** ['vaɪpərɪʃ] o **viperous** ['vaɪpərəs] *adj* viperino; (fig.) viperino
**viper's bugloss** *s* (bot.) viborera
**viper's-grass** ['vaɪpərz,græs] o ['vaɪpərz,grɑs] *s* (bot.) escorzonera
**virago** [vɪ'rego] *s* (*pl:* **-goes** o **-gos**) mujer regañona
**viral** ['vaɪrəl] *adj* viral
**virelay** ['vɪrɪle] *s* virolai (*verso*)
**vireo** ['vɪrɪo] *s* (*pl:* **-os**) (orn.) vireo
**virescence** [vaɪ'rɛsəns] *s* (bot.) virescencia
**virescent** [vaɪ'rɛsənt] *adj* virescente
**Virgil** ['vʌrdʒɪl] *s* Virgilio
**Virgilian** [vər'dʒɪlɪən] *adj* virgiliano
**virgin** ['vʌrdʒɪn] *s* virgen; (*cap.*) *s* (astr.) Virgen; **the Virgin** la Santísima Virgen; (*l.c.*) *adj* virgen
**virginal** ['vʌrdʒɪnəl] *adj* virginal; *s* (mus.) virginal, espineta
**virgin birth** *s* (theol.) parto virginal de María; (zool.) reproducción virginal o asexual (*partenogénesis*)
**virgin cork** *s* corcho bornizo, corcho virgen
**Virginia** [vər'dʒɪnjə] *s* Virginia (*uno de los estados de los EE.UU.; nombre de mujer*)
**Virginia creeper** *s* (bot.) guau (*Parthenocissus quinquefolia*)
**Virginian** [vər'dʒɪnjən] *adj* & *s* virginiano
**Virginia snakeroot** *s* (bot.) serpentaria virginiana, viperina de Virginia
**Virginia stock** *s* (bot.) mahonesa
**Virgin Islands** *spl* islas Vírgenes
**virginity** [vər'dʒɪnɪtɪ] *s* virginidad
**virginium** [vər'dʒɪnɪəm] *s* (chem.) virginio
**Virgin Mary** *s* Virgen María
**Virgin Queen, the** la reina virgen (*Isabel I de Inglaterra*)
**virgin's-bower** ['vʌrdʒɪnz'baʊər] *s* (bot.) clemátide
**Virgo** ['vʌrgo] *s* (astr.) Virgo
**viridescence** [,vɪrɪ'dɛsəns] *s* verdor
**viridescent** [,vɪrɪ'dɛsənt] *adj* verdoso
**virile** ['vɪrɪl] *adj* viril
**virile member** *s* (anat.) miembro viril
**virility** [vɪ'rɪlɪtɪ] *s* (*pl:* **-ties**) virilidad
**virole** [vɪ'rol] *s* (her.) virol
**viroled** [vɪ'rold] *adj* (her.) virolado
**virological** [,vaɪrə'lɑdʒɪkəl] *adj* virológico
**virologist** [vaɪ'rɑlədʒɪst] *s* virólogo
**virology** [vaɪ'rɑlədʒɪ] *s* virología
**virtual** ['vʌrtʃʊəl] *adj* virtual
**virtual image** *s* (phys.) imagen virtual
**virtuality** [,vʌrtʃʊ'ælɪtɪ] *s* virtualidad
**virtually** ['vʌrtʃʊəlɪ] *adv* virtualmente
**virtue** ['vʌrtʃʊ] *s* virtud; **by** o **in virtue of** en virtud de
**virtuosity** [,vʌrtʃʊ'ɑsɪtɪ] *s* (*pl:* **-ties**) virtuosismo
**virtuoso** [,vʌrtʃʊ'oso] *s* (*pl:* **-sos** o **-si** [si]) virtuoso
**virtuous** ['vʌrtʃʊəs] *adj* virtuoso
**virulence** ['vɪrʊləns] o ['vɪrjələns] o **virulency** ['vɪrʊlənsɪ] o ['vɪrjələnsɪ] *s* virulencia
**virulent** ['vɪrʊlənt] o ['vɪrjələnt] *adj* virulento
**virus** ['vaɪrəs] *s* virus
**Vis.** o **Visc.** abr. de **Viscount**
**visa** ['vizə] *s* visa; *va* visar
**visage** ['vɪzɪdʒ] *s* semblante; apariencia
**vis-à-vis** [,vizə'vi] *s* persona que está enfrente; coche con dos asientos enfrentados; sillón con dos asientos enfrentados; *adj* enfrentado; *adv* frente a frente; *prep* enfrente de; respecto de
**Visayan** [vɪ'sɑjən] *adj* & *s* bisayo o visayo
**Visayan Islands** *spl* islas Bisayas o Visayas
**viscera** ['vɪsərə] *spl* vísceras
**visceral** ['vɪsərəl] *adj* visceral
**viscid** ['vɪsɪd] *adj* viscoso
**viscose** ['vɪskos] *adj* viscoso; *s* viscosa
**viscosity** [vɪs'kɑsɪtɪ] *s* viscosidad
**viscount** ['vaɪkaʊnt] *s* vizconde
**viscountcy** ['vaɪkaʊntsɪ] *s* (*pl:* **-cies**) vizcondado
**viscountess** ['vaɪkaʊntɪs] *s* vizcondesa
**viscountship** ['vaɪkaʊntʃɪp] *s* vizcongado
**viscounty** ['vaɪkaʊntɪ] *s* (*pl:* **-ties**) var. de **viscountship**
**viscous** ['vɪskəs] *adj* viscoso
**vise** [vaɪs] *s* (mach.) tornillo, torno
**visé** ['vize] o [vi'ze] *s* & *va* var. de **visa**
**Vishnu** ['vɪʃnu] *s* Visnú
**visibility** [,vɪzɪ'bɪlɪtɪ] *s* visibilidad
**visible** ['vɪzɪbəl] *adj* visible
**visibly** ['vɪzɪblɪ] *adv* visiblemente
**Visigoth** ['vɪzɪgɑθ] *s* visigodo
**Visigothic** [,vɪzɪ'gɑθɪk] *adj* visigótico; *s* letra visigótica

**vision** [ˈvɪʒən] *s* visión; *va* ver en una visión, ver como en una visión; *vn* aparecer en una visión
**visionary** [ˈvɪʒən,ɛrɪ] *adj* visionario; *s* (*pl:* **-ies**) visionario
**visit** [ˈvɪzɪt] *s* visita; *va* visitar; mandar (*la peste, un castigo, etc.*); *vn* hacer visitas; visitarse
**visitant** [ˈvɪzɪtənt] *adj & s* visitante
**visitation** [,vɪzɪˈteʃən] *s* visitación; disposición divina, gracia o castigo del cielo; (*cap.*) *s* Visitación
**visiting** [ˈvɪzɪtɪŋ] *adj* visitador; de visita
**visiting card** *s* tarjeta de visita
**visiting fireman** *s* (coll.) personaje recibido con gran agasajo en país ajeno; (slang) forastero que se divierte en una gran ciudad
**visiting hours** *spl* horas de consulta
**visiting nurse** *s* enfermera ambulante
**visiting professor** *s* profesor visitante
**visitor** [ˈvɪzɪtər] *s* visitante; (sport) visitante
**visor** [ˈvaɪzər] o [ˈvɪzər] *s* visera (*del yelmo, de las gorras, del parabrisas del automóvil, etc.*); (fig.) máscara
**vista** [ˈvɪstə] *s* vista, panorama, perspectiva
**Vistula** [ˈvɪstjʊlə] *s* Vístula
**visual** [ˈvɪʒʊəl] *adj* visual; visible
**visual acuity** *s* acuidad
**visualization** [,vɪʒʊəlɪˈzeʃən] *s* representación en la mente, visualización
**visualize** [ˈvɪʒʊəlaɪz] *va* visualizar, representarse en la mente; *vn* representarse en la mente; (med.) hacerse visible
**visual line** *s* visual
**visually** [ˈvɪʒʊəlɪ] *adv* visualmente
**visual purple** *s* (biochem.) púrpura visual
**vitaceous** [vaɪˈteʃəs] *adj* (bot.) vitáceo
**vital** [ˈvaɪtəl] *adj* vital; mortal; **vitals** *spl* vísceras, partes vitales
**vital force** *s* fuerza vital
**vitalism** [ˈvaɪtəlɪzəm] *s* vitalismo
**vitalist** [ˈvaɪtəlɪst] *s* vitalista
**vitalistic** [,vaɪtəˈlɪstɪk] *adj* vitalista
**vitality** [vaɪˈtælɪtɪ] *s* vitalidad
**vitalization** [,vaɪtəlɪˈzeʃən] *s* vitalización
**vitalize** [ˈvaɪtəlaɪz] *va* vitalizar
**vital statistics** *ssg* estadística demográfica; *spl* estadísticas demográficas
**vitamin** o **vitamine** [ˈvaɪtəmɪn] *s* vitamina
**vitamin deficiency** *s* avitaminosis, carencia de vitaminas
**vitaminic** [,vaɪtəˈmɪnɪk] *adj* vitamínico
**vitellin** [vɪˈtɛlɪn] o [vaɪˈtɛlɪn] *s* (biochem.) vitelina
**vitellus** [vɪˈtɛləs] o [vaɪˈtɛləs] *s* vitelo, yema del huevo
**vitiate** [ˈvɪʃɪet] *va* viciar; (law) viciar
**vitiation** [,vɪʃɪˈeʃən] *s* viciación
**viticultural** [,vɪtɪˈkʌltʃərəl] o [,vaɪtɪˈkʌltʃərəl] *adj* vitícola
**viticulture** [ˈvɪtɪ,kʌltʃər] o [ˈvaɪtɪ,kʌltʃər] *s* viticultura
**viticulturist** [,vɪtɪˈkʌltʃərɪst] o [,vaɪtɪˈkʌltʃərɪst] *s* vitícola, viticultor
**vitiligo** [,vɪtɪˈlaɪgo] *s* (path.) vitíligo
**vitreous** [ˈvɪtrɪəs] *adj* vítreo
**vitreous electricity** *s* electricidad vítrea
**vitreous humor** *s* (anat.) humor vítreo
**vitrifaction** [,vɪtrɪˈfækʃən] *s* vitrificación
**vitrifiable** [,vɪtrɪˈfaɪəbəl] *adj* vitrificable
**vitrification** [,vɪtrɪfɪˈkeʃən] *s* var. de **vitrifaction**
**vitrify** [ˈvɪtrɪfaɪ] (*pret & pp:* **-fied**) *va* vitrificar; *vn* vitrificarse
**vitriol** [ˈvɪtrɪəl] *s* (chem.) vitriolo; (fig.) crítica cáustica
**vitriolic** [,vɪtrɪˈɑlɪk] *adj* (chem.) vitriólico; (fig.) cáustico, mordaz
**vitriolize** [ˈvɪtrɪəlaɪz] *va* vitriolizar (*impregnar de vitriolo*); vitriolar (*arrojar vitriolo a*)
**vituperable** [vaɪˈtjupərəbəl] o [vaɪˈtupərəbəl] *adj* vituperable
**vituperate** [vaɪˈtjupəret] o [vaɪˈtupəret] *va* vituperar
**vituperation** [vaɪ,tjupəˈreʃən] o [vaɪ,tupəˈreʃən] *s* vituperación, vituperio
**vituperative** [vaɪˈtjupə,retɪv] o [vaɪˈtupə,retɪv] *adj* vituperioso
**vituperator** [vaɪˈtjupə,retər] o [vaɪˈtupə,retər] *s* vituperador
**viva** [ˈvivɑ] *s* viva; *interj* ¡ viva!
**vivacious** [vɪˈveʃəs] o [vaɪˈveʃəs] *adj* vivo, alegre, vivaracho, vivaz
**vivacity** [vɪˈvæsɪtɪ] o [vaɪˈvæsɪtɪ] *s* (*pl:* **-ties**) viveza, alegría
**vivandière** [vivɑ̃ˈdjɛr] *s* cantinera, vivandera
**vivarium** [vɪˈvɛrɪəm] *s* (*pl:* **-iums** o **-ia** [ɪə]) vivario
**viva voce** [ˈvaɪvəˈvosɪ] *adv* de viva voz
**vive** [viv] *interj* ¡ viva!
**Vivian** [ˈvɪvɪən] *s* Viviana
**vivid** [ˈvɪvɪd] *adj* vivo
**vivification** [,vɪvɪfɪˈkeʃən] *s* vivificación
**vivify** [ˈvɪvɪfaɪ] (*pret & pp:* **-fied**) *va* vivificar
**viviparous** [vaɪˈvɪpərəs] *adj* vivíparo
**vivisect** [ˈvɪvɪsɛkt] o [,vɪvɪˈsɛkt] *va* disecar (*un animal vivo*); *vn* practicar la vivisección
**vivisection** [,vɪvɪˈsɛkʃən] *s* vivisección
**vivisectionist** [,vɪvɪˈsɛkʃənɪst] *s* viviseccionista
**vivisector** [ˈvɪvɪ,sɛktər] o [,vɪvɪˈsɛktər] *s* vivisector
**vivisectorium** [,vɪvɪsɛkˈtorɪəm] *s* vivisectorio
**vixen** [ˈvɪksən] *s* zorra (*hembra*); mujer regañona y colérica
**vixenish** [ˈvɪksənɪʃ] *adj* zorruno; regañona y colérica
**viz.** abr. de **videlicet** (Lat.) **to wit, namely**
**vizard** [ˈvɪzərd] *s* var. de **visor**
**vizier** [vɪˈzɪr] o [ˈvɪzjər] o **vizir** [vɪˈzɪr] *s* visir
**vizor** [ˈvaɪzər] o [ˈvɪzər] *s* var. de **visor**
**vocab.** abr. de **vocabulary**
**vocable** [ˈvokəbəl] *s* vocablo, voz
**vocabulary** [voˈkæbjə,lɛrɪ] *s* (*pl:* **-ies**) vocabulario
**vocabulist** [voˈkæbjəlɪst] *s* vocabulista, lexicógrafo
**vocal** [ˈvokəl] *adj* vocal; vocálico; expresivo
**vocal cords** *spl* (anat.) cuerdas vocales
**vocalic** [voˈkælɪk] *adj* vocálico
**vocalism** [ˈvokəlɪzəm] *s* (phonet.) vocalismo; canto, arte de cantar
**vocalist** [ˈvokəlɪst] *s* cantante, vocalista
**vocalization** [,vokəlɪˈzeʃən] *s* (mus. & phonet.) vocalización
**vocalize** [ˈvokəlaɪz] *va* (phonet.) vocalizar; emitir con la voz; cantar; *vn* (mus.) vocalizar; (phonet.) vocalizarse
**vocally** [ˈvokəlɪ] *adv* vocalmente; expresivamente
**vocal music** *s* música vocal
**vocal organ** *s* (anat.) órgano de la voz
**vocation** [voˈkeʃən] *s* vocación; (theol.) vocación
**vocational** [voˈkeʃənəl] *adj* práctico, vocacional
**vocational guidance** *s* guía vocacional
**vocational school** *s* escuela de artes y oficios
**vocative** [ˈvɑkətɪv] *adj & s* vocativo
**vociferant** [voˈsɪfərənt] *adj & s* vociferante
**vociferate** [voˈsɪfəret] *va & vn* vociferar
**vociferation** [vo,sɪfəˈreʃən] *s* vociferación, vocería
**vociferous** [voˈsɪfərəs] *adj* vociferador, vocinglero
**vodka** [ˈvɑdkə] *s* vodka
**vogue** [vog] *s* boga, moda; **in vogue** en boga, de moda
**voice** [vɔɪs] *s* voz; (gram. & mus.) voz; **in a loud voice** en voz alta; **in a low voice** en voz baja; **in voice** (mus.) en voz; **to raise one's voice** alzar la voz; **with one voice** a una voz; *va* expresar; divulgar; (mus.) regular el tono de (*un órgano*); (mus.) escribir la parte vocal de; (phonet.) sonorizar; *vn* (phonet.) sonorizarse
**voice coil** *s* (rad.) bobina móvil
**voiceless** [ˈvɔɪslɪs] *adj* mudo; (phonet.) mudo (*dícese de las consonantes oclusivas*)
**voicing** [ˈvɔɪsɪŋ] *s* (phonet.) sonorización
**void** [vɔɪd] *adj* vacío; nulo, inválido; vano; **void of** falto de, desprovisto de; *s* vacío, hueco; *va* vaciar; anular; evacuar
**voidable** [ˈvɔɪdəbəl] *adj* evacuable; anulable
**voidance** [ˈvɔɪdəns] *s* vaciamiento, evacuación; (eccl.) vacante
**voile** [vɔɪl] *s* espumilla
**vol.** abr. de **volume**
**volant** [ˈvolənt] *adj* volante; ligero; (her.) volante

**volatile** ['vɑlətɪl] *adj* volátil
**volatile oil** *s* aceite volátil
**volatility** [,vɑlə'tɪlɪtɪ] *s* volatilidad
**volatilization** [,vɑlətɪlɪ'zeʃən] *s* volatilización
**volatilize** ['vɑlətɪlaɪz] *va* volatilizar; *vn* volatilizarse
**volcanic** [vɑl'kænɪk] *adj* volcánico
**volcanic ashes** *spl* (geol.) cenizas volcánicas
**volcanic cone** *s* (geol.) cono volcánico
**volcanic mud** *s* (geol.) lodo volcánico
**volcanic neck** *s* (geol.) cuello volcánico
**volcanic rocks** *spl* (geol.) rocas volcánicas
**volcanism** ['vɑlkənɪzəm] *s* volcanismo
**volcano** [vɑl'keno] *s* (*pl:* **-noes** o **-nos**) volcán; (fig.) volcán; **to be on the edge of a volcano** (fig.) estar sobre un volcán
**volcanology** [,vɑlkən'ɑlədʒɪ] *s* vulcanología
**vole** [vol] *s* (zool.) arvícola, rata de agua, campañol
**volition** [vo'lɪʃən] *s* volición
**volitional** [vo'lɪʃənəl] *adj* volitivo
**volley** ['vɑlɪ] *s* descarga, lluvia (*de piedras, balas, etc.*); (mil.) descarga; (tennis) voleo; *va* (tennis) volear; *vn* lanzar una descarga
**volleyball** ['vɑlɪ,bɔl] *s* volibol
**volplane** ['vɑl,plen] *s* (aer.) planeo, vuelo planeado; *vn* (aer.) planear
**vols.** abr. de **volumes**
**Volscian** ['vɑlʃən] *adj* & *s* volsco
**volt** [volt] *s* (elec.) voltio
**voltage** ['voltɪdʒ] *s* (elec.) voltaje
**voltage amplification** *s* (elec.) amplificación de tensión
**voltage divider** *s* (rad.) divisor de voltaje, partidor de tensión
**voltage drop** *s* (elec.) caída de tensión
**voltage regulator** *s* (elec.) regulador de tensión
**voltage transformer** *s* (elec.) transformador de tensión
**voltaic** [vɑl'teɪk] *adj* voltaico
**voltaic battery** *s* (elec.) pila voltaica
**voltaic cell** *s* (elec.) célula voltaica
**voltaic current** *s* (elec.) corriente voltaica
**voltaic electricity** *s* electricidad voltaica
**voltaic pile** *s* (elec.) pila voltaica
**Voltairian** [vɑl'tɛrɪən] *adj* & *s* volteriano
**Voltairianism** [vɑl'tɛrɪənɪzəm] o **Voltairism** [vɑl'tɛrɪzəm] *s* volterianismo
**voltameter** [vɑl'tæmɪtər] *s* (phys.) voltámetro
**voltammeter** ['volt'æm,mitər] *s* (phys.) voltamperímetro
**volt-ampere** ['volt'æmpɪr] *s* (elec.) voltamperio
**volte-face** [,vɔlt'fɑs] *s* cambio de dirección; cambio de opinión; *vn* cambiar de dirección; cambiar de opinión
**voltmeter** ['volt,mitər] *s* (elec.) voltímetro
**volubility** [,vɑljə'bɪlɪtɪ] *s* facundia; volubilidad
**voluble** ['vɑljəbəl] *adj* facundo; voluble (*que fácilmente se puede mover alrededor*); (bot.) voluble
**volume** ['vɑljəm] *s* volumen (*libro; bulto; masa, p.ej., de agua*); tomo (*cada libro que forma parte de una obra*); volumen sonoro; (geom.) volumen; **to speak volumes** ser de suma significación
**volume control** *s* (rad.) regulación del volumen (sonoro); (rad.) regulador de volumen, control de volumen
**volumeter** [və'lumɪtər] *s* volúmetro
**volumetric** [,vɑljə'mɛtrɪk] *adj* volumétrico
**voluminous** [və'lumɪnəs] *adj* voluminoso
**voluntarily** ['vɑlən,tɛrɪlɪ] *adv* voluntariamente
**voluntarism** ['vɑləntərɪzəm] *s* (philos.) voluntarismo
**voluntary** ['vɑlən,tɛrɪ] *adj* voluntario; *s* (*pl:* **-ies**) acción voluntaria; (mus.) solo de órgano
**voluntary manslaughter** *s* (law) homicidio intencional sin premeditación
**volunteer** [,vɑlən'tɪr] *adj* voluntario; de voluntarios; *va* ofrecer (*sus servicios*); *vn* servir como voluntario; ofrecerse
**voluptuary** [və'lʌptʃu,ɛrɪ] *s* (*pl:* **-ies**) voluptuoso; *adj* voluptuoso
**voluptuous** [və'lʌptʃuəs] *adj* voluptuoso
**voluptuousness** [və'lʌptʃuəsnɪs] *s* voluptuosidad
**volute** [və'lut] *s* (arch.) voluta; (fig.) voluta; (zool.) voluta (*cualquiera de los volútidos*); (zool.) vuelta (*de una concha en espiral*)
**volva** ['vɑlvə] *s* (bot.) volva
**volvulus** ['vɑlvjələs] *s* (path.) vólvulo
**vomer** ['vomər] *s* (anat.) vómer
**vomicine** ['vɑmɪsin] o ['vɑmɪsɪn] *s* (chem.) vomicina
**vomit** ['vɑmɪt] *s* vómito; vomitivo (*emético*); *va* & *vn* vomitar
**vomitive** ['vɑmɪtɪv] *adj* & *s* vomitivo
**vomitory** ['vɑmɪ,torɪ] *adj* vomitorio; *s* (*pl:* **-ries**) (arch.) vomitorio
**vomiturition** [,vɑmɪtʃu'rɪʃən] *s* (path.) vomiturición
**voodoo** ['vudu] *s* vodú; *adj* voduísta
**voodooism** ['vuduɪzəm] *s* voduísmo
**voodooist** ['vuduɪst] *s* voduísta
**voodooistic** [,vudu'ɪstɪk] *adj* voduísta
**voracious** [və'reʃəs] *adj* voraz
**voracity** [və'ræsɪtɪ] *s* voracidad
**vortex** ['vɔrtɛks] *s* (*pl:* **-texes** o **-tices** [tɪsiz]) vórtice
**vorticella** [,vɔrtɪ'sɛlə] *s* (*pl:* **-lae** [li]) (zool.) vorticela
**Vosges** [voʒ] *spl* Vosgos
**votaress** ['votərɪs] *s* partidaria, aficionada; monja, religiosa, mujer ligada por votos solemnes
**votary** ['votərɪ] *s* (*pl:* **-ries**) partidario, aficionado; monje, religioso, persona ligada por votos solemnes
**vote** [vot] *s* voto; *va* votar; **to vote down** derrotar por votación; **to vote in** elegir por votación; *vn* votar
**vote-getter** ['vot,gɛtər] *s* acaparador de votos; consigna que gana votos
**vote of confidence** *s* voto de confianza
**voter** ['votər] *s* votante
**voting machine** *s* máquina de votar, máquina electoral
**voting paper** *s* (Brit.) papeleta de votación
**voting precinct** *s* distrito electoral
**votive** ['votɪv] *adj* votivo
**votive Mass** *s* (eccl.) misa votiva
**votive offering** *s* voto, exvoto
**vouch** [vautʃ] *va* garantizar, atestiguar; *vn* salir fiador; **to vouch for** responder de (*una cosa*); responder por (*una persona*)
**voucher** ['vautʃər] *s* fiador, garante; comprobante (de pago); resguardo (*documento justificativo*)
**vouchsafe** [vautʃ'sef] *va* conceder, otorgar; servirse hacer o dar, dignarse hacer o dar; *vn* dignarse; **to vouchsafe to** + *inf* dignarse + *inf*
**voussoir** [vu'swɑr] *s* (arch.) dovela
**vow** [vau] *s* promesa solemne; voto (*a Dios, un santo, etc.*); *va* prometer solemnemente; votar; jurar; *vn* hacer voto; **to vow to** + *inf* hacer voto de + *inf*
**vowel** ['vauəl] *s* vocal; *adj* vocálico
**vowel harmony** *s* (philol.) armonía vocálica
**vowelize** ['vauəlaɪz] *va* vocalizar; puntar (*un texto hebreo o árabe*)
**vowel point** *s* punto vocálico (*de las lenguas hebrea, árabe, etc.*)
**vowel system** *s* sistema vocálico
**voyage** ['vɔɪɪdʒ] *s* viaje por mar, viaje por aire; *va* atravesar (*p.ej., el mar*); *vn* viajar por mar, viajar por aire
**voyager** ['vɔɪɪdʒər] *s* viajero por mar, viajero por aire
**V.P.** abr. de **Vice-President**
**vs.** abr. de **versus**
**v.s.** abr. de **vide supra** (Lat.) **see above**
**V.S.** abr. de **Veterinary Surgeon**
**V-shaped** ['vi,ʃept] *adj* en forma de V
**v.t.** abr. de **transitive verb**
**Vt.** abr. de **Vermont**
**V-type engine** ['vi,taɪp] *s* (aut.) motor tipo V
**vug** [vʌg] o [vug] *s* (min.) drusa, bolsa
**Vul.** abr. de **Vulgate**
**Vulcan** ['vʌlkən] *s* (myth.) Vulcano
**Vulcanian** [vʌl'kenɪən] *adj* vulcanio; (*l.c.*) *adj* vulcanio
**vulcanism** ['vʌlkənɪzəm] *s* vulcanismo
**vulcanist** ['vʌlkənɪst] *s* vulcanista
**vulcanite** ['vʌlkənaɪt] *s* vulcanita
**vulcanization** [,vʌlkənɪ'zeʃən] *s* vulcanización

**vulcanize** ['vʌlkənaɪz] *va* vulcanizar
**vulcanized rubber** *s* caucho vulcanizado
**vulcanizer** ['vʌlkən,aɪzər] *s* vulcanizador
**vulcanology** [,vʌlkən'ɑlədʒɪ] *s* var. de **volcanology**
**vulg.** abr. de **vulgar** y **vulgarly**
**Vulg.** abr. de **Vulgate**
**vulgar** ['vʌlgər] *adj* grosero; vulgar; *s* vulgo
**vulgar fraction** *s* (math.) fracción común
**vulgarian** [vʌl'gɛrɪən] *s* persona grosera; advenedizo, nuevo rico
**vulgarism** ['vʌlgərɪzəm] *s* grosería; vulgarismo; vulgaridad
**vulgarity** [vʌl'gærɪtɪ] *s* (*pl:* **-ties**) grosería; vulgaridad
**vulgarization** [,vʌlgərɪ'zeʃən] *s* vulgarización
**vulgarize** ['vʌlgəraɪz] *va* vulgarizar
**vulgarizer** ['vʌlgə,raɪzər] *s* vulgarizador
**Vulgar Latin** *s* latín vulgar, latín rústico
**Vulgate** ['vʌlget] *s* Vulgata
**vulnerability** [,vʌlnərə'bɪlɪtɪ] *s* vulnerabilidad
**vulnerable** ['vʌlnərəbəl] *adj* vulnerable
**vulnerary** ['vʌlnə,rɛrɪ] *s* (*pl:* **-ies**) vulnerario; *adj* vulnerario
**vulpine** ['vʌlpaɪn] o ['vʌlpɪn] *adj* vulpino
**vulpinite** ['vʌlpɪnaɪt] *s* (mineral.) vulpinita
**vulture** ['vʌltʃər] *s* (orn.) buitre
**vulturine** ['vʌltʃəraɪn] o ['vʌltʃərɪn] *adj* buitrero
**vulva** ['vʌlvə] *s* (*pl:* **-vae** [vi] o **-vas**) (anat.) vulva
**vulvar** ['vʌlvər] *adj* vulvar
**vulvitis** [vʌl'vaɪtɪs] *s* (path.) vulvitis
**vying** ['vaɪɪŋ] *adj* emulador; *ger de* **vie**
**vyingly** ['vaɪɪŋlɪ] *adv* rivalizando

**W, w** [ˈdʌbəlju] *s* (*pl:* **W's, w's** [ˈdʌbəljuz]) vigésima tercera letra del alfabeto inglés
**w** abr. de **watt**
**w.** abr. de **week, west, wide, width** y **wife**
**W** abr. de **watt** y **west**
**W.** abr. de **Wales, Wednesday, Welsh, west** y **western**
**wabble** [ˈwɑbəl] *s & vn* var. de **wobble**
**wabbly** [ˈwɑblɪ] *adj* var. de **wobbly**
**wacky** [ˈwækɪ] *adj* (*comp:* **-ier;** *super:* **-iest**) (slang) excéntrico, estrafalario
**wad** [wɑd] *s* bolita de algodón; fajo o lío (*de billetes, papeles, etc.*); taco (*que se pone en las escopetas*); (*pret & pp:* **wadded;** *ger:* **wadding**) *va* colocar algodón en; enliar; atapar; acolchonar, rellenar; atacar (*una escopeta*)
**wadding** [ˈwɑdɪŋ] *s* algodón (*bolitas de hebras de algodón*); taco; tapón; guata (*que se usa para acolchar*)
**waddle** [ˈwɑdəl] *s* anadeo; *vn* anadear
**wade** [wed] *s* vadeamiento; *va* vadear (*una corriente de agua*); *vn* caminar por terreno difícil, agua, nieve o barro; chapotear, andar descalzo por el agua; **to wade into** (coll.) meter el hombro a; (coll.) embestir con violencia; **to wade through** ir con dificultad por; leer con dificultad
**wader** [ˈwedər] *s* vadeador; bota alta impermeable; (orn.) zancuda, ave zancuda
**wadi** [ˈwɑdɪ] *s* (*pl:* **-dis**) uadi
**wading bird** *s* (orn.) ave zancuda
**wady** [ˈwɑdɪ] *s* (*pl:* **-dies**) var. de **wadi**
**wafer** [ˈwefər] *s* oblea (*para pegar sobres; píldora*); hostia (*oblea comestible*); (eccl.) hostia
**wafery** [ˈwefərɪ] *adj* delgado, ligero; fino y fácil de partir
**waffle** [ˈwɑfəl] *s* barquillo
**waffle iron** *s* barquillero (*molde*)
**waft** [wæft] o [wɑft] *s* ráfaga de aire, viento, olor, etc.; mecedura, fluctuación; movimiento (*de la mano*); *va* llevar por el aire; llevar a flote; *vn* moverse o flotar de un sitio a otro
**wag** [wæg] *s* meneo; bromista; (*pret & pp:* **wagged;** *ger:* **wagging**) *va* menear (*la cabeza; la cola*); *vn* menearse
**wage** [wedʒ] *s* salario, paga; **wages** *spl* salario, paga; galardón, premio; *va* emprender y continuar, perseguir; hacer (*guerra*), dar (*batalla*)
**wage earner** *s* asalariado
**wager** [ˈwedʒər] *s* apuesta; **to lay a wager** hacer una apuesta; *va & vn* apostar
**wage scale** *s* escala de salarios
**wageworker** [ˈwedʒˌwʌrkər] *s* asalariado
**wageworking** [ˈwedʒˌwʌrkɪŋ] *adj* asalariado
**waggery** [ˈwægərɪ] *s* (*pl:* **-ies**) broma, chanza; jocosidad
**waggish** [ˈwægɪʃ] *adj* bromista; divertido, gracioso
**waggle** [ˈwægəl] *s* meneo rápido; *va* menear rápidamente; *vn* menearse rápidamente
**Wagnerian** [vɑgˈnɪrɪən] *adj & s* vagneriano
**wagon** [ˈwægən] *s* carro, furgón; (Brit.) vagón o coche (*de ferrocarril*); **on the wagon** (slang) sin tomar bebidas alcohólicas; **to hitch one's wagon to a star** poner el tiro muy alto
**wagoner** [ˈwægənər] *s* carretero
**wagonette** [ˌwægəˈnɛt] *s* break, carricoche
**wagonload** [ˈwægənˌlod] *s* carretada
**wagon train** *s* tren de furgones; (mil.) tren de equipajes
**wagtail** [ˈwægˌtel] *s* (orn.) aguanieves, aguzanieves, nevatilla
**wahoo** [ˈwɑhu] o [wɑˈhu] *s* (bot.) evónimo; (bot.) tilio; (bot.) olmo; (ichth.) peto
**waif** [wef] *s* expósito; granuja (*chiquillo vagabundo*); animal extraviado o abandonado; (law) cosa robada y soltada por el ladrón
**wail** [wel] *s* gemido, lamento; *vn* gemir, lamentarse, llorar quejándose de dolor
**Wailing Wall** *s* muro de los lamentos
**wainscot** [ˈwenskət] o [ˈwenskɑt] *s* arrimadillo, friso (*de madera*); (*pret & pp:* **-scoted** o **-scotted;** *ger:* **-scoting** o **-scotting**) *va* poner arrimadillo o friso a (*la parte inferior de una pared*)
**wainscoting** o **wainscotting** [ˈwenskətɪŋ] o [ˈwenskɑtɪŋ] *s* arrimadillo, friso; madera de entablado
**wainwright** [ˈwenˌraɪt] *s* carretero
**waist** [west] *s* cintura, talle (*del cuerpo humano y del vestido*); blusa, corpiño
**waistband** [ˈwestˌbænd] *s* pretina
**waistcloth** [ˈwestˌklɔθ] o [ˈwestˌklɑθ] *s* taparrabo
**waistcoat** [ˈwestˌkot] o [ˈwɛskət] *s* chaleco
**waistline** [ˈwestˌlaɪn] *s* talle
**wait** [wet] *s* espera; **waits** *spl* murga de nochebuena; **to have a good wait** (coll.) esperar sentado; **to lie in wait** estar al acecho; **to lie in wait for** acechar, preparar una emboscada a; *va* esperar, aguardar; (coll.) aplazar, diferir; *vn* esperar, aguardar; **to wait for** esperar, aguardar; **to wait on** servir, despachar (*p.ej., a los parroquianos en una tienda*); visitar, ir a ver; acompañar, velar sobre; presentar respetos a; **to wait until** + *ind* esperar a que + *subj*
**waiter** [ˈwetər] *s* mozo de restaurante, camarero; azafate, bandeja; aguardador
**waiting** [ˈwetɪŋ] *s* espera; servicio; **in waiting** de honor (*dícese del caballero o la dama que sirve a un personaje real*); *adj* que espera; que sirve; de espera
**waiting list** *s* lista de espera
**waiting maid** *s* criada de servicio, doncella
**waiting man** *s* criado de servicio
**waiting room** *s* sala de espera; antesala (*p.ej., de un consultorio médico*)
**waiting woman** *s* criada de servicio, doncella
**waitress** [ˈwetrɪs] *s* moza de restaurante, camarera
**waive** [wev] *va* renunciar a (*p.ej., un derecho*); diferir, dilatar, poner a un lado
**waiver** [ˈwevər] *s* (law) renuncia
**wake** [wek] *s* vigilia; velatorio (*acción de velar a un difunto*); estela (*de un barco u otro objeto en movimiento*); **in the wake of** en la estela de; inmediatamente detrás de; (*pret:* **waked** o **woke;** *pp:* **waked**) *va & vn* despertar; resucitar; velar
**wakeful** [ˈwekfəl] *adj* desvelado
**wakefulness** [ˈwekfəlnɪs] *s* desvelo
**wake knot** *s* (her.) lago de amor
**waken** [ˈwekən] *va & vn* despertar
**wake-robin** [ˈwekˌrɑbɪn] *s* (bot.) arisema; (bot.) aro; (bot.) trilio
**Walachia** [wɑˈlekɪə] *s* Valaquia
**Walachian** [wɑˈlekɪən] *adj & s* valaco
**Waldenses** [wɑlˈdɛnsiz] *spl* valdenses
**Waldensian** [wɑlˈdɛnsɪən] *adj & s* valdense
**waldgrave** [ˈwɔldgrev] *s* valdgrave
**Waldo** [ˈwɔldo] o [ˈwɑldo] *s* Ubaldo
**wale** [wel] *s* verdugón; (naut.) cinta; relieve (*que sobresale del tejido*); *va* levantar verdugones a
**Wales** [welz] *s* Gales, el país de Gales
**walk** [wɔk] *s* caminata (*distancia*); paseo (*acción*); andar, paso (*manera de andar o caminar*); andadura (*de una caballería*); alameda, paseo, vereda; cercado (*para animales*): carrera, condición; oficio, empleo; **at a walk** caminando; **to go for a walk** salir a pasear; **to take a walk** dar un paseo; *va* pasear (*a un niño, un caballo*); caminar (*recorrer caminando*); correr (*un espacio determinado*); ha-

cer andar (*y no correr*); llevar caminando; **to walk off** deshacerse de (*p.ej., un dolor de cabeza*) caminando; *vn* andar, caminar; pasear; ir despacio (*no corriendo*); conducirse, portarse; (baseball) pasar a primera base; **to walk away (from)** alejarse caminando (de); **to walk off with** cargar con, llevarse, robarse; **to walk out** salir repentinamente; declararse en huelga; **to walk out on** (coll.) abandonar, dejar airadamente, salir airadamente de

**walkaway** ['wɔkə,we] *s* (coll.) triunfo fácil

**walker** ['wɔkər] *s* caminante; paseante; peatón; andaderas

**walkie-lookie** ['wɔkɪ'lʊkɪ] *s* cámara televisora portátil

**walkie-talkie** ['wɔkɪ'tɔkɪ] *s* (rad.) transmisor-receptor portátil

**walking beam** *s* (mach.) balancín

**walking delegate** *s* delegado viajante de un gremio obrero

**walking encyclopedia** *s* (coll.) enciclopedia ambulante

**walking papers** *spl* (coll.) despedida (*de un empleo o cargo*)

**walking stick** *s* bastón; (ent.) espectro

**walking typhoid fever** *s* (path.) fiebre tifoidea ambulante o ambulatoria

**walk-on** ['wɔk,ɑn] *s* (theat.) parte de por medio

**walkout** ['wɔk,aʊt] *s* (coll.) huelga

**walkover** ['wɔk,ovər] *s* (coll.) triunfo fácil

**wall** [wɔl] *s* muro; pared (*entre dos habitaciones*); cerca (*muro que rodea, p.ej., un jardín*); muralla (*p.ej., de una fortificación*); pared (*de un tubo, vaso, caldera, etc.*); **to drive to the wall** poner entre la espada y la pared; **to go to the wall** entregarse, rendirse; fracasar; **to push to the wall** poner entre la espada y la pared; *va* emparedar, murar; amurallar; **to wall up** cerrar con muro

**wallaby** ['wɑləbɪ] *s* (*pl:* **-bies**) (zool.) ualabi (*especie de canguro*)

**Wallachia** [wɑ'lekɪə] *s* var. de **Walachia**

**wallaroo** [,wɑlə'ru] *s* (zool.) canguro de talla mayor (*del subgénero Osphranter*)

**wallboard** ['wɔl,bord] *s* cartón de yeso, cartón tabla

**wallet** ['wɑlɪt] *s* cartera de bolsillo; morral (*saco de provisiones*)

**walleye** ['wɔl,aɪ] *s* ojo de color muy pálido; ojo desviado hacia afuera; ojo saltón; estrabismo divergente; pez de ojos saltones

**walleyed** ['wɔl,aɪd] *adj* de ojos incoloros; de ojos desviados hacia afuera; de ojos saltones; de mirada vaga

**walleyed herring** *s* (ichth.) arenque de ojos grandes

**wallflower** ['wɔl,flaʊər] *s* (bot.) alhelí amarillo; (coll.) mujer que se queda sin bailar (*por no haber sido invitada a ello*); **to be a wallflower** (coll.) comer pavo

**wall knot** *s* (naut.) piña

**Walloon** [wɑ'lun] *adj & s* valón

**wallop** ['wɑləp] *s* (coll.) golpazo; (coll.) fuerza; (coll.) tunda, zurra; *va* (coll.) golpear fuertemente; (coll.) tundir, zurrar

**wallow** ['wɑlo] *s* revuelco (*acción*); revolcadero (*sitio*); *vn* revolcarse (*en el lodo; en los vicios*); nadar (*en riquezas*)

**wallpaper** ['wɔl,pepər] *s* papel de empapelar, papel pintado; *va* empapelar

**wall plate** *s* carrera, solera, viga de apoyo

**wall rock** *s* (geol. & min.) roca de respaldo

**wall rocket** *s* (bot.) jaramago

**wall rue** *s* (bot.) ruda de muros

**wallwort** ['wɔl,wʌrt] *s* (bot.) cañarroya

**walnut** ['wɔlnət] *s* (bot.) nogal (*árbol y madera*); nuez (*de nogal*)

**Walpurgis night** [vɑl'pʊrgɪs] *s* noche de Walpurgis

**walpurgite** [wɑl'pʌrdʒaɪt] o [wɑl'pʌrgaɪt] *s* (mineral.) valpurgita

**walrus** ['wɔlrəs] o ['wɑlrəs] *s* (zool.) morsa

**Walter** ['wɔltər] *s* Gualterio

**waltz** [wɔlts] *s* vals; *adj* de vals; *va* hacer valsar; *vn* valsar; girar, dar vueltas

**wambly** ['wɑmlɪ] o ['wæmlɪ] *adj* (dial.) trémulo, vacilante; (dial.) mareado, nauseado

**wampum** ['wɑmpəm] *s* cuentas de concha que usaban los pieles rojas como dinero; (slang) dinero

**wan** [wɑn] *adj* (*comp:* **wanner;** *super:* **wannest**) macilento; plomizo (*cielo*); obscuro, empañado

**wand** [wɑnd] *s* vara; varita de virtudes

**wander** ['wɑndər] *va* (poet.) atravesar o recorrer a la ventura; *vn* errar, vagar; extraviarse, perderse; **to wander about** o **around** errar o vagar de una parte a otra, andar acá y allá

**wanderer** ['wɑndərər] *s* vago, vagamundo; peregrino; prevaricador

**wandering Jew** *s* (bot.) matalí o sangría; (*caps.*) *s* Judío errante

**wanderlust** ['wɑndər,lʌst] *s* pasión de viajar, ansia de vagar

**wane** [wen] *s* mengua, disminución; decadencia, declinación; gema (*de un madero*); menguante (*de la luna*); **in** u **on the wane** menguando; decayendo, declinando; *vn* menguar, disminuir; decaer, declinar

**wangle** ['wæŋgəl] *va* sacudir; (coll.) mamar o mamarse (*p.ej., un buen destino*); (coll.) cazar (*adquirir con maña*); (coll.) adulterar (*p.ej., cuentas*); **to wangle into** + *ger* (coll.) persuadir con artimañas a + *inf; vn* (coll.) barajárselas; **to wangle through** (coll.) sacudirse bien (*salir con maña de un apuro*)

**wanigan** ['wɑnɪgən] *s* (U.S.A.) caja en que los gancheros guardan sus pertrechos; (U.S.A.) vivienda tosca de los gancheros, que flota en una balsa

**wannish** ['wɑnɪʃ] *adj* algo macilento

**want** [wɑnt] o [wɔnt] *s* deseo; necesidad; falta, carencia; **to be in want** estar necesitado; *va* desear; necesitar; carecer de; *vn* faltar; estar necesitado; **to want for** carecer de; necesitar; **to want to** + *inf* desear + *inf*

**want ad** *s* (coll.) anuncio clasificado

**wanting** ['wɑntɪŋ] o ['wɔntɪŋ] *adj* faltante (*que falta*); defectuoso, deficiente; **to be wanting** faltar; *prep* sin, menos, salvo

**wanton** ['wɑntən] *adj* insensible, perverso; caprichoso, irreflexivo; licencioso; lujoso; (poet.) lozano; (poet.) retozón; *s* libertino; *va* malgastar; *vn* retozar, juguetear

**wantonness** ['wɑntənnɪs] *s* insensibilidad, perversidad; capricho, irreflexión; libertinaje; lujo; (poet.) lozanía; (poet.) travesura

**wapiti** ['wɑpɪtɪ] *s* (*pl:* **-tis**) (zool.) uapití

**war** [wɔr] *s* guerra; **to be at war** estar en guerra; **to go to war** declarar la guerra, entrar en guerra; ir a la guerra (*como soldado*); (*pret & pp:* **warred;** *ger:* **warring**) *vn* guerrear; **to war on** guerrear con, hacer la guerra a

**war baby** *s* hijo de soldado, nacido durante una guerra; (coll.) industria o comercio fomentados por la guerra

**War between the States** *s* (U.S.A.) guerra entre Norte y Sur

**warble** ['wɔrbəl] *s* gorjeo, trino; *vn* gorjear, trinar

**warbler** ['wɔrblər] *s* gorjeador; (orn.) curruca; (orn.) candelita (*Setophaga ruticilla*)

**war bond** *s* bono de guerra

**war bride** *s* novia de guerra (*la recién casada con un soldado en tiempo de guerra*); (slang) industria o comercio fomentados por la guerra

**war cloud** *s* amenaza de guerra

**war club** *s* maza usada como arma

**war crime** *s* crimen de guerra

**war criminal** *s* criminal de guerra

**war cry** *s* grito de guerra

**ward** [wɔrd] *s* pupilo, menor o huérfano (*bajo tutela*); tutela, custodia; barrio, distrito (*de una ciudad*); crujía (*de un hospital*); guarda o rodaplancha (*de una llave*); guarda (*de la cerradura*); defensa, posición defensiva; *va* (archaic) guardar, vigilar; **to ward off** parar, detener, desviar

**war dance** *s* danza de guerra, danza guerrera

**warden** ['wɔrdən] *s* guardián; carcelero; alcalde; alcaide (*de una fortaleza*); capillero (*de una iglesia*); director (*de ciertas escuelas*)

**warder** ['wɔrdər] *s* guardián; (Brit.) carcelero

**ward heeler** *s* (coll.) muñidor (*de un cacique político*)

**wardrobe** ['wɔrd,rob] *s* guardarropa (*local; armario*); vestuario; (theat.) guardarropía

**wardrobe trunk** *s* baúl ropero, baúl perchero
**wardroom** ['wɔrd,rum] o ['wɔrd,rʊm] *s* (nav.) cuartel de oficiales; (Brit.) cuarto de guardia
**wardship** ['wɔrdʃɪp] *s* pupilaje, tutela
**ware** [wɛr] *s* loza de barro, artículos de alfarería; **wares** *spl* mercancías, efectos, géneros
**war effort** *s* esfuerzo bélico
**warehouse** ['wɛr,haʊs] *s* almacén; guardamuebles
**warehouseman** ['wɛr,haʊsmən] *s* (*pl:* **-men**) almacenero, guardalmacén; almacenista (*dueño*)
**warfare** ['wɔr,fɛr] *s* guerra
**war game** *s* supuesto táctico; juego de guerra
**war god** *s* dios de la guerra
**war head** *s* cabeza de combate, punta de combate (*de torpedo*)
**war horse** *s* caballo guerrero; (coll.) veterano, persona que ha tomado parte en muchas luchas y batallas
**warily** ['wɛrɪlɪ] *adv* cautelosamente
**wariness** ['wɛrɪnɪs] *s* cautela
**warlike** ['wɔr,laɪk] *adj* guerrero
**war loan** *s* empréstito de guerra
**warlock** ['wɔrlɑk] *s* (archaic) brujo, hechicero; (archaic) adivino, sortílego
**war lord** *s* jefe militar
**warm** [wɔrm) *adj* caliente (*que da calor*); templado (*ni frío ni caliente*); cálido, caluroso (*clima, país*); abrigador (*vestido, traje*); cálido (*color*); desagradable; (coll.) acomodado, bien de fortuna; (coll.) caliente (*cercano a lo que se busca*); (fig.) caluroso; **to be warm** hacer calor (*dícese del tiempo*); tener calor (*p.ej., una persona*); *va* calentar; hacer más amistoso, expresivo, etc.; acalorar; calentar (*una silla*); (coll.) zurrar; **to warm over** recalentar (*comida fría*); **to warm up** recalentar (*comida fría*); hacer más amistoso, expresivo, etc.; acalorar; *vn* calentarse; **to warm up** templar (*el tiempo*); hacerse más amistoso, expresivo, etc.; acalorarse; (sport) hacer ejercicios para entrar en calor
**warm-blooded** ['wɔrm'blʌdɪd] *adj* apasionado, ardiente; (zool.) de sangre caliente
**war memorial** *s* monumento a los caídos
**warm front** *s* (meteor.) frente caliente
**warm-hearted** ['wɔrm'hɑrtɪd] *adj* afectuoso, bondadoso, simpático
**warming pan** *s* mundillo, calentador de cama
**warmish** ['wɔrmɪʃ] *adj* algo caliente; algo caluroso
**warmonger** ['wɔr,mʌŋgər] *s* atizador de la guerra, fomentador de la guerra
**warmth** [wɔrmθ] *s* calor; ardor, entusiasmo; cordialidad, simpatía
**warn** [wɔrn] *va* avisar, advertir; aconsejar; amonestar
**warning** ['wɔrnɪŋ] *s* aviso, advertencia; *adj* amonestador
**War Office** *s* (Brit.) ministerio del Ejército
**War of Independence** *s* guerra de la Independencia
**war of nerves** *s* guerra de nervios
**War of Secession** *s* (U.S.A.) guerra de Secesión
**War of the Roses** *s* guerra de las dos Rosas
**warp** [wɔrp] *s* urdimbre (*de un tejido*); comba, alabeo (*de una tabla*); sesgo (*de la mente*); prejuicio; (naut.) espía; *va* combar, alabear, torcer; desviar; pervertir (*a una persona; el juicio de una persona; un texto*); (naut.) mover (*una embarcación*) con espía; *vn* combarse, alabearse, torcerse; desviarse; (naut.) espiarse
**war paint** *s* pintura que se ponen los pieles rojas para ir a la batalla; (coll.) ademán de amenaza; (coll.) colorete, atavíos, galas, trajes de lujo
**warpath** ['wɔr,pæθ] o ['wɔr,pɑθ] *s* senda que siguen los indios norteamericanos para atacar al enemigo; **to be on the warpath** estar preparado para la guerra; estar buscando pendencia
**warplane** ['wɔr,plen] *s* avión de guerra, avión militar
**warrant** ['wɑrənt] o ['wɔrənt] *s* autorización; decreto, orden; cédula, certificación; citación (*ante un juez*); justificación; garantía, promesa; *va* autorizar; justificar; garantizar, prometer; afirmar, asegurar
**warrantable** ['wɑrəntəbəl] o ['wɔrəntəbəl] *adj* garantizable; justificable
**warrantee** [,wɑrən'ti] o [,wɔrən'ti] *s* persona garantizada o afianzada
**warranter** ['wɑrəntər] o ['wɔrəntər] *s* garante
**warrant officer** *s* (mil.) suboficial de la clase de tropa; (nav.) contramaestre
**warrantor** ['wɑrəntɔr] o ['wɔrəntɔr] *s* (law) garante
**warranty** ['wɑrəntɪ] o ['wɔrəntɪ] *s* (*pl:* **-ties**) autorización; justificación; seguridad; (law) garantía
**warren** ['wɑrən] o ['wɔrən] *s* conejera; vivar (*donde se crían animales pequeños*); vedado; barrio o edificio densamente poblado
**warrior** ['wɑrɪər] o ['wɔrɪər] *s* guerrero
**war risk insurance** *s* seguros contra el riesgo de guerra
**Warsaw** ['wɔrsɔ] *s* Varsovia
**Warsaw Pact** *s* Tratado de Varsovia
**war scare** *s* psicosis de guerra
**warship** ['wɔr,ʃɪp] *s* buque de guerra
**war strength** *s* efectivos de guerra
**wart** [wɔrt] *s* verruga; (bot.) verruga
**wart hog** *s* (zool.) jabalí de verrugas
**wartime** ['wɔr,taɪm] *s* tiempo de guerra
**war-torn** ['wɔr,torn] *adj* devastado por la guerra
**war to the death** *s* guerra a muerte
**warty** ['wɔrtɪ] *adj* (*comp:* **-ier**; *super:* **-iest**) verrugoso
**war whoop** *s* grito de guerra (*especialmente de los pieles rojas*)
**wary** ['wɛrɪ] *adj* (*comp:* **-ier**; *super:* **-iest**) cauteloso (*dícese de una persona o de sus actos o dichos*); **wary of** cauteloso con
**was** [wɑz] o [wʌz] *primera y tercera personas del sg del pret de* **be**
**Wash.** abr. de **Washington**
**wash** [wɑʃ] o [wɔʃ] *s* lavado; jabonado (*ropa blanca que se ha de jabonar o se ha jabonado*); loción; alimento líquido; lavazas, despojos líquidos; batiente del agua; ruido del agua al batir; aluvión (*materia arrastrada y depositada por el agua*); charco, pantano; (aer.) disturbio aerodinámico, estela turbulenta; (paint.) lavado; (min.) grava aurífera; venta ficticia de acciones con el fin de manejar el mercado; *adj* lavable; *va* lavar; bañar, mojar; fregar (*la vajilla*); (mas., min., paint. & fig.) lavar; **to wash away** quitar lavando; derrubiar; llevarse (*el agua o las olas*); **to wash off** quitar lavando; *vn* lavarse; lavar la ropa; ser arrastrado y depositado por el agua; gastarse por la acción del agua: moverse, batir (*el agua*); (coll.) mantenerse firme
**washable** ['wɑʃəbəl] o ['wɔʃəbəl] *adj* lavable
**wash-and-wear** ['wɑʃənd'wɛr] o ['wɔʃənd'wɛr] *adj* de lava y pon
**washbasin** ['wɑʃ,besən] o ['wɔʃ,besən] *s* var. de **washbowl**
**washbasket** ['wɑʃ,bæskɪt] o ['wɔʃ,bæskɪt] *s* cesto de la colada
**washboard** ['wɑʃ,bord] o ['wɔʃ,bord] *s* lavadero, tabla de lavar; rodapié; (naut.) falca
**wash bottle** *s* (chem.) frasco lavador
**washbowl** ['wɑʃ,bol] o ['wɔʃ,bol] *s* jofaina, palangana
**washcloth** ['wɑʃ,klɔθ] o ['wɔʃ,klɔθ] *s* paño para lavarse
**washday** ['wɑʃ,de] o ['wɔʃ,de] *s* día de colada
**washed-out** ['wɑʃt,aʊt] o ['wɔʃt,aʊt] *adj* desteñido, descolorido; (coll.) debilitado, extenuado
**washed-up** ['wɑʃt,ʌp] o ['wɔʃt,ʌp] *adj* (slang) deslomado, derrengado; (slang) fracasado
**washer** ['wɑʃər] o ['wɔʃər] *s* lavador; lavadora o lavadora mecánica; arandela; disco de goma, zapatilla (*de una llave o grifo*); (phot.) lavador
**washerwoman** ['wɑʃər,wʊmən] o ['wɔʃər,wʊmən] *s* (*pl:* **-women**) lavandera
**wash goods** *spl* tejidos lavables, prendas lavables
**washing** ['wɑʃɪŋ] o ['wɔʃɪŋ] *s* lavado (*lavamiento; ropa lavada o por lavar*); (min.) lava;

**washings** *spl* lavadura (*agua sucia; rozadura de un cabo*)
**washing machine** *s* lavadora, lavadora mecánica, máquina de lavar
**washing soda** *s* sosa de lavar (*bicarbonato de sodio que se usa para blanquear la ropa*)
**wash leather** *s* gamuza (*piel*)
**wash line** *s* cordón de tender ropa
**washout** ['wɑʃ,aut] o ['wɔʃ,aut] *s* derrubio; (coll.) desilusión, fracaso
**washrag** ['wɑʃ,ræg] o ['wɔʃ,ræg] *s* paño para lavarse; paño de cocina
**washroom** ['wɑʃ,rum] o ['wɔʃ,rum] *s* gabinete de aseo, lavabo
**wash sale** *s* venta ficticia de acciones con el fin de manejar el mercado
**washstand** ['wɑʃ,stænd] o ['wɔʃ,stænd] *s* lavamanos (*palanganero; lavabo*)
**washtub** ['wɑʃ,tʌb] o ['wɔʃ,tʌb] *s* tina de lavar, cuba de colada; lavadero
**wash water** *s* agua de lavado; lavazas (*agua sucia*)
**washwoman** ['wɑʃ,wumən] o ['wɔʃ,wumən] *s* (*pl:* **-women**) lavandera
**washy** ['wɑʃɪ] o ['wɔʃɪ] *adj* (*comp:* **-ier;** *super:* **-iest**) aguado, diluído, débil; insulso, flojo
**wasn't** ['wɑzənt] o ['wʌzənt] contracción de **was not**
**wasp** [wɑsp] *s* (ent.) avispa
**waspish** ['wɑspɪʃ] *adj* colérico, rencoroso, irascible; como una avispa; ceñido, delgado
**wasp-waisted** ['wɑsp,westɪd] *adj* de talle de avispa
**wassail** ['wɑsəl] o ['wæsəl] *s* juerga de borrachera; cerveza o vino condimentados con especias (*que se toman en una juerga*); *interj* ¡salud!; *va* beber a la salud de; *vn* tomar parte en una juerga de borrachera
**wassailer** ['wɑsələr] o ['wæsələr] *s* juerguista, borrachón; brindador
**wastage** ['westɪdʒ] *s* pérdida, derroche, desgaste
**waste** [west] *s* derroche; pérdida (*p.ej., de tiempo*); decaimiento; basura, despojo, desecho, desperdicio; desgaste; despoblado, yermo; hilacha de algodón; (law) perjuicio causado por descuido del inquilino; **to go to waste** perderse, ser desperdiciado; **to lay waste** asolar, devastar, poner a fuego y sangre; *adj* desechado, inútil, sobrante; arruinado, desolado; yermo; (physiol.) excrementicio; *va* derrochar, malgastar, desperdiciar; desgastar; asolar, devastar; *vn* perderse; consumirse; mermar; **to waste away** decaer, consumirse
**wastebasket** ['west,bæskɪt] o ['west,bɑskɪt] *s* papelera (*cesto para papeles inútiles y desechos*)
**wasteful** ['westfəl] *adj* derrochador, manirroto, pródigo; devastador, ruinoso
**waste paper** *s* papel viejo, papeles usados
**waste pipe** *s* tubo de desagüe
**waste product** *s* producto de desecho; materia excretada
**wastrel** ['westrəl] *s* derrochador, malgastador; pródigo, perdido; cosa defectuosa o inútil, desecho
**watch** [wɑtʃ] *s* vigilancia; velación, vigilia; guardia; vigía; vigilante; reloj (*de bolsillo o de pulsera*); (mil.) centinela; (mil.) vigilia; (naut.) guardia; **to be on the watch for** estar a la mira de; tener cuidado con; **to keep watch** estar de guardia; **to keep watch over** velar (*p.ej., el sueño de una persona*); vigilar por o sobre; *adj* relojero; *va* mirar; velar, vigilar; guardar; tener cuidado con; *vn* mirar; velar (*no dormir*); **to watch for** acechar, esperar; **to watch out** tener cuidado; **to watch out for** estar a la mira de; guardarse de; tener cuidado con; **to watch over** velar (*p.ej., el sueño de una persona*); vigilar o velar por o sobre
**watchcase** ['wɑtʃ,kes] *s* caja de reloj
**watch chain** *s* cadena de reloj
**watch charm** *s* dije
**watchdog** ['wɑtʃ,dɔg] o ['wɑtʃ,dɑg] *s* perro de guarda, perro guardián; (fig.) fiel guardián
**watch fire** *s* hoguera encendida durante la noche (*p.ej., en un campamento*)
**watchful** ['wɑtʃfəl] *adj* desvelado, vigilante
**watchfulness** ['wɑtʃfəlnɪs] *s* desvelo, vigilancia
**watchful waiting** *s* espera vigilante
**watch glass** *s* cristal de reloj; (naut.) ampolleta de media hora
**watchmaker** ['wɑtʃ,mekər] *s* relojero
**watchmaking** ['wɑtʃ,mekɪŋ] *adj* relojero; *s* relojería
**watchman** ['wɑtʃmən] *s* (*pl:* **-men**) velador, vigilante, sereno
**watchman's clock** *s* reloj para vigilantes
**watch meeting** *s* oficio de noche vieja
**watch night** *s* noche vieja; oficio de noche vieja
**watch pocket** *s* relojera
**watch spring** *s* muelle de reloj
**watch strap** *s* pulsera
**watchtower** ['wɑtʃ,tauər] *s* garita, atalaya, vigía
**watchword** ['wɑtʃ,wʌrd] *s* santo y seña, contraseña; lema
**watchwork** ['wɑtʃ,wʌrk] *s* aparato de relojería
**water** ['wɔtər] o ['wɑtər] *s* agua; (com.) acciones emitidas sin el equivalente aumento de capital; **waters** *spl* aguas (*agua fluyente; agua batiente; agua mineral; agua de manantial; alta mar; visos de la seda, de las piedras preciosas*); **above water** (fig.) flotante; **by water** por agua, por barco; **like water** como agua (*pródigamente*); **of the first water** de lo mejor; **to back water** (naut. & fig.) ciar; **to carry water on both shoulders** nadar entre dos aguas, ser pancista; **to fish in troubled waters** pescar en río revuelto, pescar en agua turbia; **to go by water** ir por mar; **to hold water** retener el agua; (coll.) tener base firme, ser bien fundado; **to make water** hacer aguas (*orinar*); (naut.) hacer agua; **to pour** o **throw cold water on** echar un jarro de agua (fría) a, desanimar mostrando indiferencia; **to tread water** mantenerse a flote pataleando en el agua ‖ *adj* acuático; de agua; para agua ‖ *va* regar, rociar; aguar (*p.ej., el vino*); abrevar (*p.ej., el ganado*); proveer de agua; proveer de visos; (com.) emitir (*acciones*) sin el correspondiente aumento de capital ‖ *vn* llenarse de agua; abrevarse (*el ganado*); tomar agua (*p.ej., una locomotora*); llorar (*los ojos*); (naut.) hacer aguada
**water back** *s* caja de agua caliente
**water ballast** *s* (naut. & aer.) lastre de agua
**water bath** *s* baño de agua; baño maría
**water beetle** *s* (ent.) ditisco
**water bird** *s* ave acuática
**water bottle** *s* bolsa o botella para agua; cantimplora; vasija para recoger muestras de agua
**water brain** *s* (vet.) tornada
**waterbuck** ['wɔtər,bʌk] o ['wɑtər,bʌk] *s* (zool.) antílope acuático (*Kobus*)
**water buffalo** *s* (zool.) búfalo común; (zool.) carabao
**water bug** *s* (ent.) chinche de agua; (ent.) cucaracha
**water carrier** *s* aguador; barco para transporte de agua; cañería de agua; depósito de agua; nube de lluvia
**water clock** *s* reloj de agua
**water closet** *s* excusado, retrete, váter
**water color** *s* acuarela; color para acuarela
**water-color** ['wɔtər,kʌlər] o ['wɑtər,kʌlər] *adj* hecho a la acuarela
**water-colorist** ['wɔtər,kʌlərɪst] o ['wɑtər,kʌlərɪst] *s* acuarelista
**water column** *s* indicador de nivel del agua; (rail.) columna de agua
**water-cooling** ['wɔtər,kulɪŋ] o ['wɑtər,kulɪŋ] *s* refrigeración por agua
**watercourse** ['wɔtər,kors] o ['wɑtər,kors] *s* corriente de agua; lecho de corriente
**watercraft** ['wɔtər,kræft] o ['wɑtər,kræft] *s* embarcación, embarcaciones; destreza en la navegación; destreza en la natación o en los deportes acuáticos
**water cress** *s* (bot.) berro (*planta y hojas que se comen en ensalada*)
**water cure** *s* cura de aguas
**water dog** *s* perro de aguas; (coll.) buen nadador

**water dropwort** *s* (bot.) nabo del diablo
**waterfall** ['wɔtər,fɔl] o ['wɑtər,fɔl] *s* caída de agua, cascada
**water fennel** *s* (bot.) hinojo acuático, felandrio, enante
**water flea** *s* (ent.) pulga de agua
**waterfowl** ['wɔtər,faʊl] o ['wɑtər,faʊl] *s* ave acuática, aves acuáticas (*especialmente las palmípedas*)
**water front** *s* terreno ribereño (*especialmente de una ciudad*)
**water gap** *s* garganta u hondonada (*entre montañas por donde corre una corriente*)
**water gas** *s* gas de agua
**water gate** *s* abertura para el agua; compuerta
**water germander** *s* (bot.) escordio, ajote, camedrio acuático
**water glass** *s* vidrio soluble; vaso para beber agua
**water hammer** *s* choque de ariete, choque de agua; (phys.) martillo de agua (*tubo de vidrio*)
**water heater** *s* calentador de agua
**water hemlock** *s* (bot.) cicuta acuática; (bot.) felandrio, nabo del diablo
**water hole** *s* charco
**water horehound** *s* (bot.) marrubio acuático
**water ice** *s* sorbete, helado; hielo solidificado directamente del agua
**wateriness** ['wɔtərɪnɪs] o ['wɑtərɪnɪs] *s* acuosidad
**watering can** *s* regadera
**watering place** *s* aguadero, abrevadero; aguas minerales; baños, balneario
**watering pot** *s* regadera
**watering trough** *s* abrevadero, aguadero; (rail.) atarjea de alimentación
**water jacket** *s* camisa de agua
**water level** *s* nivel de agua; (naut.) línea de agua
**water lily** *s* (bot.) ninfea, nenúfar
**water line** *s* (naut.) línea de flotación, línea de agua; nivel de agua
**water-logged** ['wɔtər,lɔgd] o ['wɑtər,lɔgd] *adj* anegado, inundado; empapado
**water main** *s* cañería maestra
**waterman** ['wɔtərmən] o ['wɑtərmən] *s* (*pl:* **-men**) barquero; remero
**watermark** ['wɔtər,mɑrk] o ['wɑtər,mɑrk] *s* marca de agua, filigrana; marca de nivel de agua; *va* marcar (*papel*) al agua
**watermelon** ['wɔtər,mɛlən] o ['wɑtər,mɛlən] *s* (bot.) sandía (*planta y fruto*)
**water meter** *s* contador de agua
**water mill** *s* molino de agua
**water moccasin** *s* (zool.) mocasín de agua
**water nymph** *s* (myth.) ninfa de las aguas; (bot.) nenúfar
**water of crystallization** *s* (chem.) agua de cristalización
**water ouzel** *s* (orn.) tordo de agua, mirlo de agua
**water parsnip** *s* (bot.) berrera, arsáfraga
**water pipe** *s* cañería de agua
**water plantain** *s* (bot.) alisma
**water polo** *s* (sport) polo de agua, polo acuático
**water power** *s* fuerza de agua, fuerza hidráulica, hulla blanca
**waterproof** ['wɔtər,pruf] o ['wɑtər,pruf] *adj* impermeable; *s* material impermeable; impermeable (*sobretodo*); *va* impermeabilizar
**waterproofing** ['wɔtər,prufɪŋ] o ['wɑtər,prufɪŋ] *s* impermeabilización (*acción*); impermeabilizante (*material*)
**water rat** *s* (zool.) rata de agua, arvícola; (zool.) rata almizclada u ondatra
**water seal** *s* cierre hidráulico
**watershed** ['wɔtər,ʃɛd] o ['wɑtər,ʃɛd] *s* línea divisoria de las aguas; cuenca
**water shrew** *s* (zool.) musaraña de agua (*Neomys fodiens*)
**waterside** ['wɔtər,saɪd] o ['wɑtər,saɪd] *s* orilla, borde del agua
**water ski** *s* esquí acuático
**water skiing** *s* esquí acuático, esquiismo acuático
**water skipper** *s* var. de **water strider**
**water snake** *s* (zool.) culebra de agua
**water-soak** ['wɔtər,sok] o ['wɑtər,sok] *va* empapar de agua
**water spaniel** *s* perro de aguas
**waterspout** ['wɔtər,spaʊt] o ['wɑtər,spaʊt] *s* canalón (*para el agua del tejado*); manguera, boquilla de manguera; tromba marina; turbión, manga de agua
**water sprite** *s* espíritu de las aguas
**water strider** ['straɪdər] *s* (ent.) tejedor, zapatero
**water supply** *s* abastecimiento de agua
**water-supply system** ['wɔtərsə,plaɪ] o ['wɑtərsə,plaɪ] *s* fontanería
**water table** *s* (arch.) retallo de derrame; (eng.) capa freática
**watertight** *adj* ['wɔtər,taɪt] o ['wɑtər,taɪt] *adj* hermético, estanco; (fig.) seguro, que no deja lugar a malas interpretaciones
**watertight compartment** *s* (naut.) compartimiento estanco
**water tower** *s* arca de agua; torre de agua contra incendios
**water-tube boiler** ['wɔtər,tjub] o ['wɑtər,tjub] *s* caldera tubular de agua
**water turkey** *s* (orn.) anhinga
**water vapor** *s* vapor de agua
**water wagon** *s* (mil.) carro de agua; **to be on the water wagon** (slang) haber dejado de tomar bebidas alcohólicas
**water wave** *s* ondulación al agua (*en el peinado*)
**waterway** ['wɔtər,we] o ['wɑtər,we] *s* vía de agua, vía fluvial; canal (*para dejar pasar el agua*); (naut.) trancanil
**water wheel** *s* rueda hidráulica; turbina de agua; rueda de agua (*de la noria*); rueda de paletas (*del buque de ruedas*)
**water wings** *spl* nadaderas
**waterworks** ['wɔtər,wʌrks] o ['wɑtər,wʌrks] *ssg* o *spl* establecimiento para la distribución de las aguas; edificio con máquinas y bombas para la distribución de las aguas
**waterworn** ['wɔtər,worn] o ['wɑtər,worn] *adj* gastado o pulido por la acción del agua
**watery** ['wɔtərɪ] o ['wɑtərɪ] *adj* acuoso; aguado; mojado; lagrimoso, lloroso; evaporado, insípido; débil, pálido; que amenaza lluvia
**watery grave** *s* aguas en que tiene sepultura un cadáver
**Watling Island** ['wɑtlɪŋ] *s* Guanahaní o San Salvador (*isla de las Bahamas*)
**watt** [wɑt] *s* (elec.) vatio
**wattage** ['wɑtɪdʒ] *s* (elec.) vatiaje
**watt-hour** ['wɑt'aʊr] *s* (*pl:* **watt-hours**) (elec.) vatio-hora
**watt-hour meter** *s* (elec.) vatihorímetro
**wattle** ['wɑtəl] *s* zarzo, sebe; barba (*de ave*); barbilla (*de pez*); (bot.) acacia; *adj* construído con zarzo; *va* construir con zarzo; entretejer en forma de zarzo; amarrar con tiras de zarzo
**wattmeter** ['wɑt,mitər] *s* (elec.) vatímetro
**wave** [wev] *s* onda; onda u ondulación (*del cabello*); ola (*de calor o frío*); oleada (*p.ej., de huelgas*); señal hecha con la mano; (phys.) onda; (poet.) aguas, mar; *va* agitar, blandir (*p.ej., la espada*); ondear u ondular (*el cabello*); hacer señales con (*la mano o el pañuelo*); decir (*adiós*) con la mano; **to wave aside** apartar, rechazar; *vn* ondear, ondearse; hacer señales con la mano o el pañuelo
**wave band** *s* (rad.) banda de ondas
**wave front** *s* (phys.) frente de ondas
**wave length** *s* (phys.) longitud de onda
**wavelet** ['wevlɪt] *s* olita
**wave motion** *s* (phys.) ondulación, movimiento ondulatorio
**waver** ['wevər] *s* oscilación, vacilación; *vn* oscilar, vacilar
**wave theory** *s* (phys.) teoría ondulatoria (*de la luz*)
**wave train** *s* (phys.) tren de ondas
**wave trap** *s* (rad.) trampa de ondas
**wavy** ['wevɪ] *adj* (*comp:* **-ier**; *super:* **-iest**) ondeado; ondulado
**wax** [wæks] *s* cera; **to be wax in one's hands** ser como una cera; *va* encerar; cerotear (*el hilo*); *vn* hacerse, ponerse; crecer (*la luna*)
**wax bean** *s* habichuela, frijolillo
**waxen** ['wæksən] *adj* ceroso; plástico
**wax myrtle** *s* (bot.) árbol de la cera (*Myrica cerifera*)

**wax palm** *s* (bot.) palma de cera; (bot.) carnauba, palma negra (*Copernicia cerifera*)
**wax paper** *s* papel parafinado, papel encerado
**wax plant** *s* (bot.) monotropa; (bot.) flor de la cera (*Hoya carnosa*); (bot.) árbol de la cera (*Myrica cerifera*)
**wax privet** *s* (bot.) aligustre del Japón
**wax taper** *s* cerilla
**wax tree** *s* (bot.) trueno (*Ligustrum lucidum*); (bot.) fresno chino; (bot.) árbol de la cera (*Rhus verniciflua; Myrica cerifera*)
**waxwing** [ˈwæksˌwɪŋ] *s* (orn.) ampélido
**waxwork** [ˈwæksˌwʌrk] *s* figura o figuras de cera; **waxworks** *spl* museo de cera
**waxy** [ˈwæksɪ] *adj* (*comp:* **-ier;** *super:* **-iest**) ceroso
**way** [we] *s* vía, camino; pasaje; manera, modo; medio; costumbre, hábito; condición, estado; distancia; dirección, sentido; respecto; voluntad, p.ej., **he always wants his own way** quiere hacer siempre su voluntad; **ways** *spl* maneras, modales; anguilas (*para botar un barco al agua*); **across the way from** enfrente de, frente a; **a good way** un buen trecho; **a great way off** muy lejos; **all the way** por todo el camino; hasta el fin del camino; **all the way down to** o **up to** toda la distancia hasta; **any way** de cualquier modo, de todas maneras; **by the way** de paso; a propósito, dicho sea de paso; **by way of** por la vía de; por vía de, por modo de; a título de; a guisa de; **in a bad way** en mal estado; en malas condiciones; **in a big way** en gran escala; **in a small way** en pequeña escala; **in a way** de cierta manera, hasta cierto punto; **in every way** en todos respectos; **in my own way** a mi modo; **in no way** de ningún modo; **in the way of** en el ramo de, en la línea de; como; **in this way** de este modo; **once in a way** de vez en cuando; **on one's way** camino adelante; **on the way** en el camino; de paso; **on the way to** camino de, rumbo a; **on the way out** en dirección a la salida; saliendo; desapareciendo; **out of the way** hecho, despachado; fuera de lo común; fuera de orden; a un lado; escondido; inconveniente, impropio; **that way** por allí; de ese modo; **this way** por aquí; de este modo; **to be in the way** estorbar, incomodar; **to come one's way** seguir el mismo camino; caerle a uno en suerte, acontecerle a uno; **to feel one's way** tantear el camino; proceder con tiento; **to feel the same way** pasarle a uno lo mismo; ser de la misma opinión; **to find one's way** hallar el camino; **to force one's way** abrirse paso por fuerza; **to get into the way of** contraer la costumbre de; **to get out of the way** quitarse de en medio; quitarse de encima (*p.ej., un trabajo atrasado*); **to give way** ceder, retroceder; romperse (*p.ej., una cuerda*); fracasar; entregarse a las emociones propias; **to give way to** entregarse a (*p.ej., el dolor, el resentimiento*); **to go a long way towards** contribuir mucho a; **to go out of one's way** dar un rodeo; dar un rodeo innecesario; **to go out of one's way (for)** darse molestia (por), molestarse (por); **to go out of one's way to please** desvivirse por complacer; **to go the same way** llevar el mismo camino; **to have a way with** manejar bien, tener poder de persuasión con; **to have one's way** salirse con la suya; **to keep on one's way** seguir su camino; **to keep out of the way** estarse a un lado, no obstruir el paso; **to know one's way around** saber cómo entendérselas; **to lead the way** enseñar el camino, ir o entrar primero; **to lose one's way** perderse, andar perdido; **to make one's way** abrirse paso; avanzar; hacer carrera, acreditarse; **to make way** hacer lugar; ceder el paso; avanzar; **to make way for** dar paso a, hacer lugar para; **to mend one's ways** mejorar de conducta, mudar de vida; **to not know one's way around** estar en ayunas; **to not know which way to turn** no saber dónde meterse, no saber a qué atenerse; **to pave the way** preparar el terreno; **to put out of the way** poner (*una cosa*) donde no estorbe; quitar de en medio (*matar*); **to see one's way to** + *inf* ver el modo de, encontrar la manera de + *inf;* **to take one's way** irse, marcharse; **to wend one's way** seguir camino; **to wind one's way through** serpentear por; **to wing one's way** ir o avanzar volando; **to work one's way** abrirse camino, abrirse paso; **to work one's way through** pagar con su trabajo los gastos de (*p.ej., la universidad*); **under way** en marcha, en camino; pendiente; **which way?** ¿por dónde?
**waybill** [ˈweˌbɪl] *s* hoja de ruta
**way down** *s* bajada
**wayfarer** [ˈweˌfɛrər] *s* caminante
**wayfaring** [ˈweˌfɛrɪŋ] *adj* caminante
**wayfaring tree** *s* (bot.) barbadejo, morrionera
**way in** *s* entrada
**waylaid** [ˌweˈled] *pret & pp de* **waylay**
**waylay** [ˌweˈle] (*pret & pp:* **-laid**) *va* asechar; detener en el camino
**way of life** *s* manera de ser, modo de vivir
**Way of St. James** *s* Camino de Santiago (*Vía láctea*)
**way out** *s* salida
**wayside** [ˈweˌsaɪd] *adj* del borde del camino, junto al camino; *s* borde del camino; **to fall by the wayside** desaparecer; fracasar
**way station** *s* (rail.) estación de paso, estación de tránsito, apeadero
**way train** *s* (rail.) tren ómnibus, tren carreta
**way up** *s* subida, subidero
**wayward** [ˈwewərd] *adj* descarriado; díscolo, voluntarioso; voltario, voluble
**waywardness** [ˈwewərdnɪs] *s* descarrío; voluntariedad; voltariedad
**wayworn** [ˈweˌworn] *adj* cansado de viajar, fatigado del viaje
**w.c.** abr. de **water closet** y **without charge**
**W.C.T.U.** abr. de **Women's Christian Temperance Union**
**we** [wi] *pron pers* nosotros
**weak** [wik] *adj* débil; (gram.) débil (*vocal; verbo*)
**weaken** [ˈwikən] *va* debilitar, enflaquecer; atenuar; *vn* debilitarse, enflaquecer; atenuarse
**weaker sex** *s* sexo débil
**weakfish** [ˈwikˌfɪʃ] *s* (ichth.) pescadilla
**weak-kneed** [ˈwikˌnid] *adj* flojo de rodillas; débil, cobarde
**weakling** [ˈwiklɪŋ] *adj & s* canijo, cobarde
**weakly** [ˈwiklɪ] *adj* (*comp:* **-lier;** *super:* **-liest**) débil, enfermizo, achacoso; *adv* débilmente
**weak-minded** [ˈwikˈmaɪndɪd] *adj* imbécil, mentecato; irresoluto, vacilante
**weakness** [ˈwiknɪs] *s* debilidad; lado débil; gusto, inclinación
**weak side** *s* lado débil
**weal** [wil] *s* verdugón; (archaic) bienestar
**weald** [wild] *s* (poet.) campo abierto
**wealth** [wɛlθ] *s* riqueza; abundancia
**wealthy** [ˈwɛlθɪ] *adj* (*comp:* **-ier;** *super:* **-iest**) rico
**wean** [win] *va* destetar; **to wean away from** apartar gradualmente de
**weanling** [ˈwinlɪŋ] *adj* recién destetado; *s* niño o animal recién destetado
**weapon** [ˈwɛpən] *s* arma
**weaponeer** [ˌwɛpənˈɪr] *s* perito en materia de armas nucleares
**weaponry** [ˈwɛpənrɪ] *s* (*pl:* **-ries**) armamento, sistema de armas
**wear** [wɛr] *s* uso (*de ropa*); ropa; desgaste, deterioro; durabilidad; estilo, moda; **for all kinds of wear** a todo llevar; **for everyday wear** para todo trote ‖ (*pret:* **wore;** *pp:* **worn**) *va* llevar o traer puesto, llevar, usar; calzar (*cierto tamaño de zapato o guante*); exhibir, mostrar; desgastar, deteriorar; agotar, cansar; hacer (*p.ej., un agujero*) por el roce o frotando; **to wear away** consumir, gastar; **to wear down** desgastar frotando; agotar, cansar (*p. ej., la paciencia de uno*); cansar hasta rendir (*a una persona*); **to wear out** consumir, gastar; agotar, cansar (*p.ej., la paciencia de uno*); acabar con; abusar de (*la hospitalidad de uno*) ‖ *vn* desgastarse, deteriorarse; durar; pasar, desaparecer; (naut.) virar; **to wear off** pasar, desaparecer; **to wear out** gastarse, usarse
**wear and tear** [tɛr] *s* desgaste o deterioro causado por el uso
**weariness** [ˈwɪrɪnɪs] *s* cansancio; aburrimiento

**wearing apparel** *s* ropaje, prendas de vestir
**wearisome** [ˈwɪrɪsəm] *adj* aburrido, fastidioso
**weary** [ˈwɪrɪ] *adj* (*comp:* **-rier;** *super:* **-riest**) cansado; aburrido; (*pret & pp:* **-ried**) *va* cansar; aburrir; *vn* cansarse; aburrirse
**weasand** [ˈwizənd] *s* tráquea; garganta
**weasel** [ˈwizəl] *s* (zool.) comadreja
**weaseler** [ˈwizələr] *s* pancista
**weasel words** *spl* palabras ambiguas (*dichas para quedar bien con todos*)
**weather** [ˈwɛðər] *s* tiempo; mal tiempo; **to be bad weather** hacer mal tiempo; **to be good weather** hacer buen tiempo; **to be under the weather** (coll.) estar indispuesto, sentirse mal; (coll.) estar borracho; *adj* meteorológico; atmosférico; (naut.) de barlovento; **to keep one's weather eye open** estar a la mira, espiar el peligro; *va* airear; solear; curar (*madera*) exponiéndola al aire, sol o lluvia; intemperizar; aguantar (*el temporal, la adversidad*); doblar (*un cabo*); dar inclinación a (*tablas, tejas, etc. para hacer caer el agua*); *vn* curtirse a la intemperie, desgastarse por la intemperie; resistir a la intemperie
**weather beam** *s* (naut.) costado de barlovento
**weather-beaten** [ˈwɛðərˌbitən] *adj* curtido por la intemperie
**weatherboard** [ˈwɛðərˌbord] *s* tabla de chilla, tabla solapada; *va* cubrir con tablas de chilla, cubrir con tablas solapadas
**weather-bound** [ˈwɛðərˌbaʊnd] *adj* atrasado o detenido por el mal tiempo
**Weather Bureau** *s* departamento de señales meteorológicas
**weathercock** [ˈwɛðərˌkɑk] *s* veleta; (fig.) veleta (*persona mudable*)
**weathered oak** *s* roble ahumado
**weather gauge** *s* (naut.) barlovento
**weatherglass** [ˈwɛðərˌglæs] o [ˈwɛðərˌglɑs] *s* barómetro, baroscopio u otro instrumento que indica la presión de la atmósfera, y por lo tanto, el estado del tiempo
**weathering** [ˈwɛðərɪŋ] *s* descomposición de la roca por los agentes atmosféricos; (constr.) declive de derrame
**weatherman** [ˈwɛðərˌmæn] *s* (*pl:* **-men**) (coll.) pronosticador del tiempo, meteorologista; (coll.) oficina meteorológica
**weather map** *s* mapa meteorológico
**weatherproof** [ˈwɛðərˌpruf] *adj* a prueba de la intemperie, a prueba del mal tiempo
**weather strip** *s* burlete, cierre hermético
**weather-strip** [ˈwɛðərˌstrɪp] (*pret & pp:* **-stripped;** *ger:* **-stripping**) *va* proveer de burletes
**weather stripping** *s* burlete, cierre hermético; burletes
**weather vane** *s* veleta
**weather-wise** [ˈwɛðərˌwaɪz] *adj* hábil en la pronosticación del tiempo
**weave** [wiv] *s* tejido; (*pret:* **wove** o **weaved;** *pp:* **woven** o **wove**) *va* tejer; (fig.) tejer (*un cuento, una intriga*); **to weave one's way** avanzar virando y cambiando de dirección; **to weave together** entrelazar; combinar; *vn* tejer; zigzaguear
**weaver** [ˈwivər] *s* tejedor; (orn.) tejedor
**weaverbird** [ˈwivərˌbʌrd] *s* (orn.) tejedor
**web** [wɛb] *s* tela, tejido; tela (*p.ej., de araña*); membrana (*entre los dedos de ciertas aves*); barba (*de una pluma*); alma (*de los carriles, etc.*); paletón (*de la llave*); hoja (*de sierra, de espada*); (print.) rollo de papel continuo; (rad. & telv.) red; (fig.) tela, tejido, enredo, maraña
**webbed** [wɛbd] *adj* tejido; palmeado
**webbing** [ˈwɛbɪŋ] *s* tiras de tela (*que sirven para cinchas y para tapizar muebles*); borde tejido que se pone como refuerzo a las alfombras; membrana (*entre los dedos de ciertas aves*)
**webfoot** [ˈwɛbˌfʊt] *s* (*pl:* **-feet**) pie palmeado; palmípedo
**web-footed** [ˈwɛbˌfʊtɪd] *adj* palmípedo, de pie palmeado
**web frame** *s* (naut.) cuaderna
**web press** *s* prensa que imprime en rollo de papel continuo
**web-toed** [ˈwɛbˌtod] *adj* var. de **web-footed**
**Wed.** abr. de **Wednesday**
**we'd** [wid] contracción de **we had, we should** y **we would**
**wed** [wɛd] (*pret:* **wedded;** *pp:* **wedded** o **wed;** *ger:* **wedding**) *va* casar (*unir en matrimonio*); casarse con; *vn* casarse
**wedding** [ˈwɛdɪŋ] *s* bodas, matrimonio; *adj* de boda, nupcial
**wedding cake** *s* torta de boda
**wedding day** *s* día de bodas
**wedding march** *s* (mus.) marcha nupcial
**wedding night** *s* noche de bodas
**wedding ring** *s* anillo de boda
**wedding trip** *s* viaje de novios
**wedge** [wɛdʒ] *s* cuña; (mil.) cúneo; (fig.) cuña; *va* acuñar; apretar con cuña; apretar; encajar; *vn* avanzar con fuerza; estar encajado
**wedlock** [ˈwɛdlɑk] *s* matrimonio
**Wednesday** [ˈwɛnzdɪ] *s* miércoles
**wee** [wi] *adj* diminuto, menudo, pequeñito
**weed** [wid] *s* mala hierba; (coll.) cigarro, tabaco; (archaic) prenda de vestir; **weeds** *spl* ropa de luto; *va* desherbar, escardar; **to weed out** (fig.) escardar; (fig.) arrancar, extirpar
**weeder** [ˈwidər] *s* desherbador, escardador (*persona*); escarda (*azada para escardar*)
**weeding hoe** *s* almocafre, escardillo
**weed killer** *s* matazarzas, matamalezas, herbicida
**weedy** [ˈwidɪ] *adj* (*comp:* **-ier;** *super:* **-iest**) lleno de malas hierbas; débil, flaco; (coll.) torpe, lerdo, desgarbado
**wee folk** *spl* hadas
**week** [wik] *s* semana; **this day week** de hoy en ocho días; **week in, week out** semana tras semana
**weekday** [ˈwikˌde] *s* día laborable, día de la semana que no sea el domingo; *adj* de o en un día laborable
**weekend** [ˈwikˌɛnd] *s* fin de semana; *adj* de o durante el fin de semana; *vn* pasar el fin de semana
**weekly** [ˈwiklɪ] *adj* semanal; *adv* semanalmente; *s* (*pl:* **-lies**) semanario
**ween** [win] *vn* (archaic) creer, imaginar, suponer
**weep** [wip] *s* (coll.) lloro; (orn.) ave fría; (*pret & pp:* **wept**) *va* llorar (*p.ej., la muerte de un amigo*); derramar (*lágrimas*); **to weep away** pasar (*la noche, la vida, etc.*) llorando; *vn* llorar; (plant path.) llorar
**weeper** [ˈwipər] *s* llorón; llorona, plañidera (*mujer alquilada para llorar en los entierros*)
**weep hole** *s* (eng.) cantimplora
**weeping** [ˈwipɪŋ] *adj* llorón, lloroso; (bot.) llorón; *s* lloro
**weeping willow** *s* (bot.) sauce llorón
**weepy** [ˈwipɪ] *adj* (*comp:* **-ier;** *super:* **-iest**) (coll.) lloroso
**weevil** [ˈwivəl] *s* (ent.) gorgojo (*de las familias Curculionidae y Lariidae*)
**weevily** o **weevilly** [ˈwivəlɪ] *adj* gorgojoso
**weft** [wɛft] *s* trama; tejido; humo
**weigh** [we] *va* pesar; agobiar, sobrecargar; (naut.) levantar (*el ancla*); (fig.) pesar; **to weigh down** agravar, hacer doblar bajo un peso; **to weigh one's words** pesar sus palabras; *vn* pesar; (naut.) levantar el ancla; (fig.) pesar (*tener influencia en el ánimo*); **to weigh in** (sport) pesarse (*un jockey*); **to weigh on** ser gravoso a
**weighmaster** [ˈweˌmæstər] o [ˈweˌmɑstər] *s* encargado de la báscula; balanzario (*en las casas de moneda*)
**weight** [wet] *s* peso; pesa (*de la balanza, el reloj, etc.; en la gimnasia*); (fig.) peso (*importancia; carga o gravamen*); **by weight** por peso; **to be worth its weight in gold** valer su peso en oro; **to lose weight** rebajar de peso; **to pull one's weight** hacer su parte; **to put on weight** ponerse gordo; **to throw one's weight around** (coll.) mandar arbitrariamente, hacer valer su poder; *va* cargar, gravar; sobrecargar; ponderar (*estadísticamente*)
**weightless** [ˈwetlɪs] *adj* ingrávido
**weightlessness** [ˈwetlɪsnɪs] ingravidez, gravedad nula
**weighty** [ˈwetɪ] *adj* (*comp:* **-ier;** *super:* **-iest**) pesado; gravoso; importante, influyente
**weir** [wɪr] *s* presa, vertedero; encañizada, pesquera

**weird** [wɪrd] *adj* misterioso, sobrenatural, horripilante; (coll.) extraño, raro
**welch** [wɛltʃ] *va* (slang) dejar de cumplir con; *vn* (slang) dejar de cumplir una apuesta u obligación; **to welch on** (slang) dejar de cumplir con
**welcome** [ˈwɛlkəm] *s* bienvenida, buena acogida; acogida; **to wear out one's welcome** abusar de la hospitalidad de una persona hasta serle molesto; *adj* bienvenido; grato, agradable; **you are welcome** sea Vd. bienvenido; no hay de qué; **you are welcome to it** está a la disposición de Vd., buen provecho le haga; *interj* ¡bienvenido!; *va* dar la bienvenida a; acoger, recibir con amabilidad y gusto
**weld** [wɛld] *s* autógena, soldadura autógena; (bot.) gualda; *va* soldar con autógena; (fig.) unificar, unir; *vn* soldarse; ser soldable
**welder** [ˈwɛldər] *s* soldador (*persona*); soldadora (*máquina*)
**welding** [ˈwɛldɪŋ] *s* autógena, soldadura autógena
**welding torch** *s* soplete soldador, antorcha soldadora
**welfare** [ˈwɛlˌfɛr] *s* bienestar; asistencia (*trabajo de auxilio social*)
**welfare state** *s* estado de beneficencia, estado socializante
**welfare work** *s* asistencia (*trabajo de auxilio social*)
**welkin** [ˈwɛlkɪn] *s* (archaic) bóveda celeste, firmamento
**we'll** [wil] contracción de **we shall** y **we will**
**well** [wɛl] *adj* bien; bien de salud; *adv* (*comp:* **better;** *super:* **best**) bien; muy; muy bien; mucho, p.ej., **he earned well over a hundred dollars** ganó mucho más de cien dólares; pues; pues bien; **as well** también; igualmente; **as well as** además de; así como, tanto como; *interj* ¡vaya!; *s* pozo; fuente, manantial; depósito (*de una pluma fuente*); *va* manar; *vn* manar, salir a borbotones
**well-appointed** [ˈwɛləˈpɔɪntɪd] *adj* bien amueblado, bien equipado
**well-balanced** [ˈwɛlˈbælənst] *adj* bien ajustado; (fig.) bien equilibrado, cuerdo, sensato
**well-behaved** [ˈwɛlbɪˈhevd] *adj* de buena conducta
**well-being** [ˈwɛlˈbiɪŋ] *s* bienestar
**wellborn** [ˈwɛlˈbɔrn] *adj* bien nacido
**well-bred** [ˈwɛlˈbrɛd] *adj* bien criado, cortés
**well-content** [ˈwɛlkənˈtɛnt] *adj* muy contento
**well digger** *s* pocero
**well-disposed** [ˈwɛldɪsˈpozd] *adj* bien dispuesto, bien intencionado
**well-done** [ˈwɛlˈdʌn] *adj* bien hecho; (cook.) bien asado
**well-favored** [ˈwɛlˈfevərd] *adj* bien parecido
**well-featured** [ˈwɛlˈfitʃərd] *adj* bien agestado, de buena cara
**well-fed** [ˈwɛlˈfɛd] *adj* bien comido, regordete
**well-fixed** [ˈwɛlˈfɪkst] *adj* (coll.) acomodado, próspero
**well-found** [ˈwɛlˈfaʊnd] *adj* bien provisto, bien equipado
**well-founded** [ˈwɛlˈfaʊndɪd] *adj* bien fundado
**well-groomed** [ˈwɛlˈgrumd] *adj* acicalado, de mucho aseo
**wellhead** [ˈwɛlˌhɛd] *s* venero, fuente, manantial
**well-heeled** [ˈwɛlˈhild] *adj* (slang) acomodado; **to be well-heeled** (slang) tener bien cubierto el riñón
**well-informed** [ˈwɛlɪnˈfɔrmd] *adj* bien enterado (*de un asunto*); culto
**well-informed sources** *spl* fuentes bien informadas
**well-intentioned** [ˈwɛlɪnˈtɛnʃənd] *adj* bien intencionado
**well-kept** [ˈwɛlˈkɛpt] *adj* bien cuidado, bien atendido
**well-known** [ˈwɛlˈnon] *adj* familiar; bien conocido
**well-mannered** [ˈwɛlˈmænərd] *adj* de buenos modales, cortés, urbano
**well-meaning** [ˈwɛlˈminɪŋ] *adj* bienintencionado
**well-nigh** [ˈwɛlˈnaɪ] *adv* casi
**well-off** [ˈwɛlˈɔf] o [ˈwɛlˈɑf] *adj* en buenas condiciones; acomodado, adinerado
**well-ordered** [ˈwɛlˈɔrdərd] *adj* bien ordenado, bien arreglado
**well-preserved** [ˈwɛlprɪˈzʌrvd] *adj* bien conservado
**well-proportioned** [ˈwɛlprəˈporʃənd] *adj* bien proporcionado
**well-read** [ˈwɛlˈrɛd] *adj* leído, muy leído
**well-shaped** [ˈwɛlˈʃept] *adj* bien formado; perfilado (*dícese de la nariz*)
**well-spent** [ˈwɛlˈspɛnt] *adj* bien empleado
**well-spoken** [ˈwɛlˈspokən] *adj* bienhablado; bien dicho
**wellspring** [ˈwɛlˌsprɪŋ] *s* fuente; fuente inagotable
**well-stocked** [ˈwɛlˈstɑkt] *adj* bien provisto
**well-suited** [ˈwɛlˈsjutɪd] o [ˈwɛlˈsutɪd] *adj* apropiado, conveniente
**well sweep** *s* cigoñal
**well-tempered** [ˈwɛlˈtɛmpərd] *adj* bien templado; (mus.) bien templado
**well-thought-of** [ˈwɛlˈθɔtˌɑv] *adj* bienquisto, bien mirado
**well-thought-out** [ˈwɛlˌθɔtˈaʊt] *adj* bien razonado
**well-timed** [ˈwɛlˈtaɪmd] *adj* oportuno
**well-to-do** [ˈwɛltəˈdu] *adj* acaudalado, acomodado
**well-wisher** [ˈwɛlˈwɪʃər] *s* amigo (*que desea suerte y fortuna a otra persona o empresa*)
**well-worn** [ˈwɛlˈworn] *adj* desgastado por el uso; trillado, vulgar
**Welsh** [wɛlʃ] *adj* galés; *spl* galeses; *ssg* galés (*idioma*); (*l.c.*) *va* (slang) defraudar, dejando de cumplir una apuesta u obligación; *vn* (slang) dejar de cumplir una apuesta u obligación; **to welsh on** (slang) defraudar, dejando de cumplir una apuesta u obligación
**Welshman** [ˈwɛlʃmən] *s* (*pl:* **-men**) galés
**Welsh onion** *s* (bot.) cebolleta, cebollino inglés
**Welsh rabbit** o **rarebit** *s* salsa de queso derretido con cerveza que se come sobre tostadas
**welt** [wɛlt] *s* vira (*del zapato*); ribete; (coll.) verdugón; (coll.) latigazo; *va* poner vira a; poner ribete a; (coll.) dar una paliza a
**welter** [ˈwɛltər] *s* confusión, conmoción; revuelco; *vn* revolcar; estar empapado
**welterweight** [ˈwɛltərˌwet] *s* (box.) peso mediano ligero, peso medio ligero; peso que se le pone a un caballo como ventaja para los otros que corren en la misma carrera
**wen** [wɛn] *s* lobanillo
**wench** [wɛntʃ] *s* muchacha; criada, moza; (archaic) ramera
**wend** [wɛnd] *va* seguir (*su camino*); *vn* seguir su camino; (*cap.*) *s* vendo
**Wendish** [ˈwɛndɪʃ] *adj* vendo; *s* vendo (*idioma*)
**went** [wɛnt] *pret de* **go**
**wept** [wɛpt] *pret & pp de* **weep**
**we're** [wɪr] contracción de **we are**
**were** [wʌr] *segunda persona del sg y primera, segunda y tercera personas del pl del pret de* **be; as it were** como si fuese, por decirlo así
**weren't** [wʌrnt] contracción de **were not**
**werewolf** [ˈwɪrˌwʊlf] o **werwolf** [ˈwʌrˌwʊlf] *s* (*pl:* **-wolves**) hombre convertido en lobo
**Wesleyan** [ˈwɛslɪən] *adj & s* wesleyano
**west** [wɛst] *s* oeste, occidente; *adj* occidental, del oeste; *adv* al oeste
**West Berlin** *s* el Berlín-Oeste
**westerly** [ˈwɛstərlɪ] *adj* occidental; que viene desde el oeste; que va hacia el oeste; *adv* desde el oeste; hacia el oeste; *s* (*pl:* **-lies**) viento del oeste
**western** [ˈwɛstərn] *adj* occidental; *s* cinta cinematográfica o historieta que se desarrolla en el oeste de los EE.UU.
**Western Australia** *s* la Australia Occidental
**Western Church** *s* Iglesia occidental
**Western civilization** *s* la civilización de occidente
**Western Empire** *s* Imperio de Occidente
**westerner** [ˈwɛstərnər] *s* habitante del oeste
**Western Hemisphere** *s* hemisferio occidental
**westernization** [ˌwɛstərnɪˈzeʃən] *s* occidentalización
**westernize** [ˈwɛstərnaɪz] *va* occidentalizar
**westernmost** [ˈwɛstərnmost] *adj* (el) más occidental
**Western Roman Empire** *s* var. de **Western Empire**

**West Germany** *s* la Alemania Occidental
**West Indian** *adj & s* antillano
**West Indies** *spl* Indias Occidentales
**Westminster Abbey** ['wɛst,mɪnstər] *s* la abadía de Wéstminster
**west-northwest** ['wɛst,nɔrθ'wɛst] *s* oesnoroeste, oesnorueste
**Westphalia** [wɛst'felɪə] *s* Vestfalia
**Westphalian** [wɛst'felɪən] *adj & s* vestfaliano
**west-southwest** ['wɛst,sauθ'wɛst] *s* oessudoeste, oessudueste
**West Virginia** *s* la Virginia Occidental, la Virginia del Oeste
**westward** ['wɛstwərd] *adj* que va hacia el oeste; *adv* hacia el oeste; *s* oeste
**westwardly** ['wɛstwərdlɪ] *adj* que va hacia el oeste; *adv* hacia el oeste
**westwards** ['wɛstwərdz] *adv* hacia el oeste
**wet** [wɛt] *adj* (*comp:* **wetter;** *super:* **wettest**) mojado; húmedo; fresco (*dícese de la pintura*); (coll.) antiprohibicionista; *s* líquido; humedad, lluvia; (coll.) antiprohibicionista; (*pret & pp:* **wet** *o* **wetted;** *ger:* **wetting**) *va* mojar; *vn* mojarse
**wetback** ['wɛt,bæk] *s* mojado (*bracero mejicano que ha pasado la frontera ilegalmente*)
**wet battery** *s* (elec.) batería líquida; (elec.) pila líquida
**wet blanket** *s* aguafiestas
**wet cell** *s* (elec.) pila húmeda
**wet goods** *spl* (com.) líquidos envasados; (coll.) licores, bebidas espiritosas
**wether** ['wɛðər] *s* carnero llano, carnero castrado
**wetness** ['wɛtnɪs] *s* humedad
**wet nurse** *s* ama de cría, nodriza
**wet-nurse** ['wɛt,nʌrs] *va* criar (*la nodriza al niño*)
**wet season** *s* estación de las lluvias
**wettish** ['wɛtɪʃ] *adj* algo mojado, húmedo
**wet way** *s* (chem.) vía húmeda
**we've** [wiv] contracción de **we have**
**w.f.** abr. de **wrong font**
**w.g.** abr. de **wire gauge**
**whack** [hwæk] *s* (coll.) golpe ruidoso; (coll.) prueba, tentativa; (coll.) parte; *va* (coll.) golpear ruidosamente
**whacking** ['hwækɪŋ] *adj* (coll.) desmesurado, enorme
**whale** [hwel] *s* (zool.) ballena; **a whale at tennis** (coll.) un as de tenis; **a whale for figures** (coll.) un genio para los números; **a whale of a difference** (coll.) una enorme diferencia; **a whale of a story** (coll.) una historia extraordinaria; **the Whale** (astr.) la Ballena; *va* (coll.) azotar; *vn* pescar ballenas
**whaleback** ['hwel,bæk] *s* (naut.) buque de carga con la cubierta superior redondeada en forma de lomo de ballena
**whaleboat** ['hwel,bot] *s* (naut.) ballenero (*embarcación menor de extremidades agudas*)
**whalebone** ['hwel,bon] *s* ballena (*lámina córnea; tira de tal lámina*)
**whale louse** *s* (zool.) piojo de mar
**whale oil** *s* aceite de ballena
**whaler** ['hwelər] *s* ballenero (*persona y embarcación*)
**whaling** ['hwelɪŋ] *adj* ballenero; *s* pesca de ballenas
**whammy** ['hwæmɪ] *s* (*pl:* **-mies**) (slang) mal de ojo; **to put a** *o* **the whammy on** (slang) hacer mal de ojo a
**whang** [hwæŋ] *s* (coll.) golpe resonante; *va & vn* (coll.) golpear de modo resonante
**wharf** [hwɔrf] *s* (*pl:* **wharves** *o* **wharfs**) muelle
**wharfage** ['hwɔrfɪdʒ] *s* empleo de un muelle; muellaje (*derecho o impuesto*); muelles
**wharfinger** ['hwɔrfɪndʒər] *s* dueño de muelle; encargado de un muelle
**what** [hwɑt] *pron interr* ¿qué?, p.ej., **what do you have in your hand?** ¿qué tiene Vd. en la mano?; ¿cuál?, p.ej., **what is the capital of Japan?** ¿cuál es la capital del Japón?; **what else?** ¿qué más?; *pron rel* lo que; *adj interr* ¿qué . . . ?; *adj rel* el (la, etc.) . . . que; *interj* ¡qué!; **and what not** y qué sé yo que más; **but what** que no, p.ej., **she is not so rich but what she needs help** no es tan rica que no necesite ayuda; **what a . . . !** ¡qué . . . !, p.ej., **what a man!** ¡qué hombre!; ¡qué . . . más o tan . . . !, p.ej, **what a beautiful day!** ¡qué día más hermoso!; **what about . . . ?** ¿qué le parece . . . ?; ¿qué hay en cuanto a . . . ?; **what for?** ¿para qué?, ¿por qué?; **what if?** ¿y si?; ¿qué será si?; **what of it?** ¿eso qué importa?; **what's what** (coll.) lo que hay, cuántas son cinco
**whate'er** [hwɑt'ɛr] *pron & adj* (poet.) var. de **whatever**
**whatever** [hwɑt'ɛvər] *pron* lo que, todo lo que, cualquier cosa que, sea lo que sea que; (coll.) ¿qué?, p.ej., **whatever do you mean?** ¿qué quiere Vd. decir?; *adj* cualquier . . . que
**whatnot** ['hwɑt,nɑt] *s* juguetero (*mueble*)
**what's** [hwɑts] contracción de **what is**
**whatsoe'er** [,hwɑtso'ɛr] *pron & adj* (poet.) var. de **whatsoever**
**whatsoever** [,hwɑtso'ɛvər] *pron & adj* var. de **whatever**
**wheal** [hwil] *s* roncha; *va* levantar roncha en
**wheat** [hwit] *s* (bot.) trigo (*planta y grano*)
**wheatear** ['hwit,ɪr] *s* (orn.) culiblanco
**wheaten** ['hwitən] *adj* triguero; hecho de trigo
**wheat field** *s* trigal
**wheat smut** *s* tizón del trigo
**wheedle** ['hwidəl] *va* engatusar; conseguir por medio de halagos
**wheel** [hwil] *s* rueda; (coll.) bicicleta; **wheels** *spl* maquinaria; **at the wheel** en el volante; (fig.) en el timón; *va* proveer de ruedas; mover por medio de ruedas; pasear (*a un niño en un cochecito*); hacer girar; dar forma por medio de una rueda de alfarero; *vn* girar, rodar; moverse suavemente; moverse por medio de ruedas; (coll.) ir o correr en bicicleta; **to wheel about** (mil.) conversar; **to wheel around** dar una vuelta; girar sobre los talones; cambiar de opinión
**wheelbarrow** ['hwil,bæro] *s* carretilla
**wheel base** *s* (aut.) batalla, distancia entre ejes
**wheel chair** *s* silla de ruedas, sillón de ruedas, cochecillo para inválidos
**wheeler** ['hwilər] *s* girador, rodador; caballo de varas; vapor de ruedas; (coll.) biciclista
**wheel horse** *s* caballo de varas; (fig.) persona que trabaja mucho y con eficiencia
**wheelhouse** ['hwil,haus] *s* (naut.) timonera, caseta del timón
**wheel puller** *s* (aut.) extractor de rueda, sacarruedas
**wheelwright** ['hwil,raɪt] *s* carretero, ruedero, carpintero de carretas
**wheeze** [hwiz] *s* resuello ruidoso; (slang) cuento viejo, chiste viejo; (slang) truco; *va* decir resollando con ruido; *vn* resollar con ruido, gañir
**wheezy** ['hwizɪ] *adj* (*comp:* **-ier;** *super:* **-iest**) que resuella con ruido
**whelk** [hwɛlk] *s* (zool.) buccino; pústula, barro
**whelm** [hwɛlm] *va* sobrepujar, subyugar; sumergir
**whelp** [hwɛlp] *s* cachorro (*de perro, león, oso, etc.*); calavera; diente (*de rueda de cadena*); **whelps** *spl* guardainfante (*del cabrestante*); *va & vn* parir
**when** [hwɛn] *adv* ¿cuándo?, p.ej., **when will he arrive?** ¿cuándo llegará? **I don't know when he will arrive** no sé cuándo llegará; *conj* cuando, p.ej., **I shall be here when he arrives** estaré aquí cuando llegue; en que, p.ej., **there are times when I like to be alone** hay ocasiones en que me gusta estar solo; que, p.ej., **the day when you were born** el dia que tú naciste
**whence** [hwɛns] *adv* ¿de dónde?; por eso, por tanto; de dónde; *conj* de donde
**whencesoever** [,hwɛnsso'ɛvər] *adv* de dondequiera; *conj* de dondequiera que
**whene'er** [hwɛn'ɛr] *conj* (poet.) var. de **whenever**
**whenever** [whɛn'ɛvər] *conj* cuando, cuando quiera que, siempre que
**whensoever** [,hwɛnso'ɛvər] *adv* cuando quiera; *conj* cuando quiera que
**where** [hwɛr] *adv* ¿dónde?, ¿adónde?, ¿en dónde?, p.ej., **where does he live?** ¿dónde vive?; **tell me where he lives** dígame dónde vive; *conj* donde, adonde, en donde, p.ej., **I can't find the house where he lives** no puedo hallar la casa donde vive

**whereabout** ['hwɛrə,baʊt] *adv & s* var. de **whereabouts**
**whereabouts** ['hwɛrə,baʊts] *adv* en qué parte, dónde; *s* paradero
**whereas** [hwɛr'æz] *conj* mientras que; por cuanto, considerando que; *s* considerando
**whereat** [hwɛr'æt] *adv* con lo cual
**whereby** [hwɛr'baɪ] *adv* ¿cómo?; *conj* por donde, por medio del cual
**where'er** [hwɛr'ɛr] *conj* (poet.) dondequiera que
**wherefore** ['hwɛrfor] *adv* ¿por qué?; por eso, por tanto; *conj* por lo cual; *s* motivo, razón
**wherefrom** [hwɛr'frɑm] *adv* de dónde; ¿de dónde?
**wherein** [hwɛr'ɪn] *adv* ¿dónde?, ¿en qué?, ¿cómo?; *conj* donde, en el (la, etc.) que; en que, en lo cual
**whereinto** [hwɛr'ɪntu] o [,hwɛrɪn'tu] *conj* dentro de que, dentro de lo que
**whereof** [hwɛr'ɑv] *adv* ¿de qué?; *conj* de qué; de que
**whereon** [hwɛr'ɑn] *adv* ¿en qué?; *conj* en qué; en que
**wheresoe'er** [,hwɛrso'ɛr] *conj* (poet.) var. de **wheresoever**
**wheresoever** [,hwɛrso'ɛvər] *conj* dondequiera que
**whereto** [hwɛr'tu] *adv* ¿adónde?; ¿por qué?, ¿para qué?; *conj* adonde
**whereunto** [hwɛr'ʌntu] o [,hwɛrʌn'tu] *adv & conj* (archaic) var. de **whereto**
**whereupon** [,hwɛrə'pɑn] *adv* entonces, con lo cual, después de lo cual
**wherever** [hwɛr'ɛvər] *adv* (coll.) ¿dónde?; *conj* dondequiera que
**wherewith** [hwɛr'wɪð] o [hwɛr'wɪθ] *adv* ¿con qué?; *conj* con que, con el cual
**wherewithal** [,hwɛrwɪð'ɔl] *adv* (archaic) ¿con qué?; *conj* (archaic) con que, con el cual; ['hwɛrwɪðɔl] *s* cumquibus, dinero, medios
**wherry** ['hwɛrɪ] *s* (*pl:* **-ries**) esquife; (Brit.) chalana
**whet** [hwɛt] *s* afiladura, aguzadura; aperitivo; (*pret & pp:* **whetted**; *ger:* **whetting**) *va* afilar, aguzar; despertar, estimular; abrir (*el apetito*)
**whether** ['hwɛðər] *pron* (archaic) ¿cuál?; *conj* si, p.ej., **I don't know whether he will come** no sé si vendrá; **whether or no** en todo caso, de todas maneras; **whether or not** si . . . o no, ya sea que . . . o no
**whetstone** ['hwɛt,ston] *s* piedra de afilar
**whew** [hwju] *interj* ¡vaya!; ¡uf!
**whey** [hwe] *s* suero de la leche
**which** [hwɪtʃ] *pron interr* ¿cuál?; *pron rel* que, el (la, etc.) que; *adj interr* ¿qué . . . ?, ¿cuál de los (las) . . . ?; *adj rel* el (la, etc.) . . . que; **which is which** cuál es el uno y cuál el otro
**whichever** [hwɪtʃ'ɛvər] *pron rel* cualquiera; *adj rel* cualquier
**whichsoever** [,hwɪtʃso'ɛvər] *pron & adj rel* var. de **whichever**
**whidah** ['hwɪdə] o **whidah bird** *s* (orn.) viuda; (orn.) viuda de pecho rojo (*Steganura paradisea*)
**whiff** [hwɪf] *s* soplo, ráfaga; soplo fugaz, vaharada; bocanada, fumada; acceso, arranque; pizca, gustillo; descarga de metralla; (coll.) periquete, santiamén; **to get a whiff of** percibir un olor fugaz de; *va* soplar; fumar (*p.ej., una pipa*); fumar echando (*bocanadas de humo*); *vn* soplar; echar bocanadas
**whiffet** ['hwɪfɪt] *s* perrillo; soplillo; (coll.) mequetrefe
**whiffle** ['hwɪfəl] *va* soplar en ráfagas ligeras; *vn* soplar en ráfagas ligeras; cambiar de dirección; cambiar de opinión
**whiffletree** ['hwɪfəl,tri] *s* var. de **whippletree**
**Whig** [hwɪg] *s* whig (*miembro de un partido progresista*)
**Whiggery** ['hwɪgərɪ] *s* principios y prácticas políticas de los whigs
**Whiggish** ['hwɪgɪʃ] *adj* de los whigs, semejante a los whigs
**while** [hwaɪl] *conj* mientras que (*durante el tiempo que; a la vez que*); *s* rato; **a great while** o **a long while** largo rato; **a while ago** hace un rato; **between whiles** de vez en cuando; **the while** entretanto, mientras tanto; *va* pasar; **to while away** engañar o entretener (*el tiempo*); pasar (*p.ej. la mañana*) de un modo entretenido
**whiles** [hwaɪlz] *adv* (archaic & dial.) algunas veces; (archaic & dial.) mientras tanto; *conj* (archaic & dial.) mientras que
**whilom** ['hwaɪləm] *adj* antiguo, de antes; *adv* (archaic) antiguamente, en otro tiempo
**whilst** [hwaɪlst] *conj* mientras que
**whim** [hwɪm] *s* capricho, antojo; (min.) malacate
**whimper** ['hwɪmpər] *s* lloriqueo; *va* decir o expresar lloriqueando; *vn* lloriquear
**whimsey** ['hwɪmzɪ] *s* var. de **whimsy**
**whimsical** ['hwɪmzɪkəl] *adj* caprichoso, fantástico, extravagante
**whimsicality** [,hwɪmzɪ'kælɪtɪ] *s* (*pl:* **-ties**) capricho, fantasía, extravagancia
**whimsy** ['hwɪmzɪ] *s* (*pl:* **-sies**) capricho, antojo; amenidad arcaica, fantasía arcaica, humorismo anticuado
**whin** [hwɪn] *s* (bot.) tojo
**whine** [hwaɪn] *s* gimoteo, quejido lastimoso; *va* decir gimoteando, decir con quejidos lastimosos; *vn* gimotear, dar quejidos lastimosos
**whinny** ['hwɪnɪ] *s* (*pl:* **-nies**) relincho; (*pret & pp:* **-nied**) *vn* relinchar
**whinstone** ['hwɪn,ston] *s* roca basáltica
**whiny** ['hwaɪnɪ] *adj* quejicoso, quejumbroso
**whip** [hwɪp] *s* látigo; azote (*golpe*); batimiento; fusta (*de tronquista*); postre de nata y huevos batidos; mayoral (*pastor a cargo de los perros de caza*); carretero, cochero; miembro de un cuerpo legislativo que dirige y domina a sus copartidarios; cuerda y polea; (*pret & pp:* **whipped** o **whipt**; *ger:* **whipping**) *va* azotar, fustigar; mover, poner o sacar súbita y rápidamente; batir (*nata o huevos*); envolver (*un palo o cuerda*) con hilo o cuerda; pescar con caña en; sobrecoser; (coll.) derrotar, vencer; **to whip up** asir de repente; batir; hacer de prisa; avivar; **to whip out** sacar de repente; *vn* agitarse; arrojarse; moverse rápidamente; echar el anzuelo azotando el agua
**whipcord** ['hwɪp,kɔrd] *s* tralla; género basto y fuerte con costurones diagonales
**whip hand** *s* mano que maneja el látigo; dominio, mando, ventaja
**whiplash** ['hwɪp,læʃ] *s* tralla (*trencilla del extremo del látigo*)
**whiplash injury** *s* (path.) concusión de la espina cervical
**whipped cream** *s* crema o nata batida
**whipper** ['hwɪpər] *s* azotador; batidor
**whipper-snapper** ['hwɪpər,snæpər] *s* arrapiezo, títere, mequetrefe
**whippet** ['hwɪpɪt] *s* perro lebrel
**whipping** ['hwɪpɪŋ] *s* flagelación, paliza; (naut.) filástica, meollar
**whipping boy** *s* cabeza de turco, víctima inocente
**whipping post** *s* poste de flagelación
**whippletree** ['hwɪpəl,tri] *s* volea
**whippoorwill** [,hwɪpər'wɪl] *s* (orn.) chotacabras norteamericano, tapacamino, guabairo
**whipsaw** ['hwɪp,sɔ] *s* sierra cabrilla; *va* serrar con sierra cabrilla; (fig.) vencer sin remedio
**whip snake** *s* (zool.) chirrionera; (zool.) filodríada
**whipstitch** ['hwɪp,stɪtʃ] *s* sobrepuntada; *va* coser con sobrepuntada
**whipstock** ['hwɪp,stɑk] *s* puño del látigo
**whir** [hwʌr] *s* zumbido (*de algo que vuela o gira*); (*pret & pp:* **whirred**; *ger:* **whirring**) *va* hacer volar o girar zumbando; *vn* volver o girar zumbando
**whirl** [hwʌrl] *s* vuelta, giro; remolino, alboroto, ajetreo; vahido, vértigo; *va* hacer girar; llevar muy rápidamente; remolinear; *vn* dar vueltas, girar; remolinear; **my head whirls** siento vahido o vértigo
**whirlibird** ['hwʌrlɪ,bʌrd] *s* (slang) helicóptero
**whirligig** ['hwʌrlɪ,gɪg] *s* (ent.) escribano del agua, girino, tejedera; tiovivo; molinete, rehilandera
**whirlpool** ['hwʌrl,pul] *s* remolino; (fig.) remolino
**whirlwind** ['hwʌrl,wɪnd] *s* torbellino, manga de viento; (fig.) torbellino
**whirr** [hwʌr] *s, va & vn* var. de **whir**
**whish** [hwɪʃ] *s* zumbido suave; *vn* zumbar suavemente; moverse con zumbido suave

**whisk** [hwɪsk] *s* escobilla, cepillo; movimiento rápido; movimiento de la escobilla; batidor metálico; manojo de paja o heno; *va* cepillar; barrer; mover rápidamente; batir (*nata, huevos, etc.*); **to whisk out of sight** escamotear; *vn* moverse rápidamente
**whisk broom** *s* escobilla, cepillo de ropa
**whisker** ['hwɪskər] *s* pelo de la barba; (coll.) bigote o bigotes; **whiskers** *spl* barba o barbas (*pelo en la barba y en los carrillos*); patillas; bigotes (*p.ej., del gato*)
**whiskered** ['hwɪskərd] *adj* barbado; bigotudo
**whiskey** ['hwɪskɪ] *s* whisky; *adj* (coll.) aguardentoso (*dícese de la voz*)
**whisky** ['hwɪskɪ] *s* (*pl:* **-kies**) var. de **whiskey**
**whisper** ['hwɪspər] *s* cuchicheo, susurro; (fig.) susurro (*p.ej., del aura*); *va* decir al oído; decir al oído a; llevar susurrando; *vn* cuchichear, susurrar; (fig.) susurrar (*p.ej., el aura*)
**whispering** ['hwɪspərɪŋ] *s* cuchicheo; *adj* susurrador; susurrón (*que murmura en secreto*)
**whist** [hwɪst] *s* whist (*juego de naipes*); *adj* (archaic) callado; *interj* (archaic) ¡chitón!
**whistle** ['hwɪsəl] *s* silbido, silbo; silbato, pito; **to wet one's whistle** (coll.) remojar la palabra; *va* silbar (*una canción*); enviar, traer, llamar con un silbido; *vn* silbar (*una persona, una bala, el viento, etc.*); **to whistle for** (coll.) tener que arreglárselas sin; **to whistle for a taxi** silbarle a un taxi
**whistler** ['hwɪslər] *s* silbador; (zool.) marmota norteamericana (*Marmota caligata*)
**whistle stop** *s* (rail.) apeadero que el maquinista reconoce con una pitada; pueblecito
**whit** [hwɪt] *s* pizca; **not a whit** ni una pizca; **to not care a whit** no importarle a uno un bledo
**white** [hwaɪt] *adj* blanco (*como la nieve; aplícase también a las uvas, el vino, etc.*); reaccionario, realista; (coll.) honorable, justo; *s* blanco; vestido blanco; clara de huevo; blanco del ojo; reaccionario, realista; **whites** *spl* (path.) pérdidas blancas, flujo blanco; *va* blanquear; *vn* emblanquecerse
**white ant** *s* (ent.) comején, hormiga blanca
**whitebait** ['hwaɪt,bet] *s* arenque de menor tamaño, arenque joven
**whitebeam** ['hwaɪt,bim] *s* (bot.) mojera, mostellar
**whitecap** ['hwaɪt,kæp] *s* cabrilla o paloma
**white cedar** *s* (bot.) cedro blanco de los pantanos; (bot.) tuya
**white clover** *s* (bot.) trébol blanco, trébol rampante
**white coal** *s* hulla blanca
**white-collar** ['hwaɪt,kɑlər] *adj* de oficina; oficinesco (*empleo*)
**white corpuscle** *s* (physiol.) glóbulo blanco
**whited sepulcher** *s* sepulcro blanqueado (*hipócrita*)
**white elephant** *s* (fig.) elefante blanco
**white feather** *s* símbolo de cobardía; **to show the white feather** mostrarse cobarde
**whitefish** ['hwaɪt,fɪʃ] *s* (ichth.) corégono
**white flag** *s* bandera blanca, bandera de paz
**white flax** *s* (bot.) camelina
**white friar** *s* fraile carmelita
**white gold** *s* oro blanco
**white goods** *spl* tejidos de hilo o algodón; ropa blanca; aparatos electrodomésticos
**white goosefoot** *s* (bot.) cenizo
**white-haired** ['hwaɪt,hɛrd] *adj* peliblanco; favorito, predilecto
**white-headed** ['hwaɪt'hɛdɪd] *adj* de cabeza blanca; rubio (*de pelo*); (coll.) favorito
**white-headed eagle** *s* (orn.) águila de cabeza blanca
**white heat** *s* calor blanco; (fig.) fiebre, viva y ardorosa agitación; **to heat to a white heat** calentar al blanco
**white horehound** *s* (bot.) marrubio blanco
**white horse** *s* var. de **whitecap**
**white-hot** ['hwaɪt'hɑt] *adj* calentado al blanco; (fig.) ardoroso, violento, excesivamente entusiasmado
**White House** *s* Casa Blanca
**white lead** [lɛd] *s* albayalde, blanco de plomo
**white lie** *s* mentira inocente, mentira oficiosa
**white-livered** ['hwaɪt'lɪvərd] *adj* macilento; cobarde, pusilánime
**white magic** *s* magia blanca
**white mangrove** *s* (bot.) mangle blanco
**white matter** *s* (anat.) materia blanca
**white meat** *s* pechuga, carne de la pechuga del ave; carne de ternera, carne de cerdo
**whiten** ['hwaɪtən] *va* blanquear, emblanquecer; *vn* blanquear, emblanquecerse; palidecer
**whiteness** ['hwaɪtnɪs] *s* blancura
**white oak** *s* (bot.) roble (*Quercus sessiliflora*); (bot.) roble blanco de América (*Quercus alba*)
**white-of-egg** ['hwaɪtəv'ɛg] *s* clara de huevo, blanco de huevo
**white of the eye** *s* blanco del ojo
**white paper** *s* papel blanco (*informe oficial*)
**white pepper** *s* pimienta blanca
**white pine** *s* (bot.) pino blanco (*Pinus strobus*)
**white plague** *s* peste blanca (*tisis*)
**white poplar** *s* (bot.) álamo blanco
**White Russia** *s* la Rusia Blanca
**White Russian** *s* ruso blanco
**white sauce** *s* salsa blanca
**White Sea** *s* mar Blanco
**white slave** *s* esclavo blanco; mujer vendida en la trata de blancas
**white slavery** *s* trata de blancas
**white-tailed deer** ['hwaɪt,teld] *s* (zool.) ciervo de Virginia
**white-tailed eagle** *s* (orn.) águila marina
**whitethorn** ['hwaɪt,θɔrn] *s* (bot.) espino, oxiacanto
**whitethroat** ['hwaɪt,θrot] *s* (orn.) andahuertas, curruca (*Sylvia*); (orn.) gorrión de Pensilvania (*Zonotrichia albicollis*)
**white-throated sparrow** ['hwaɪt,θrotɪd] *s* (orn.) gorrión de Pensilvania
**white tie** *s* corbatín blanco, traje de etiqueta
**white vitriol** *s* vitriolo blanco
**whitewash** ['hwaɪt,waʃ] o ['hwaɪt,wɔʃ] *s* jalbegue, encalado; encubrimiento de faltas; *va* enjalbegar, encalar, blanquear; encubrir (*faltas*); absolver sin justicia; (coll.) vencer (*a una persona*) sin que haya hecho tantos
**white willow** *s* (bot.) sauce blanco
**white-winged dove** ['hwaɪt'wɪŋd] *s* (orn.) aliblanca, paloma de pitahaya
**whitewood** ['hwaɪt,wʊd] *s* (bot.) liriodendro; (bot.) tilo
**whither** ['hwɪðər] *adv* ¿adónde?; adónde; *conj* adonde
**whithersoever** [,hwɪðərso'ɛvər] *conj* adondequiera que
**whiting** ['hwaɪtɪŋ] *s* blanco de España; (ichth.) merluza; (ichth.) merlango; (ichth.) esciénido
**whitish** ['hwaɪtɪʃ] *adj* blanquecino, blancuzco
**whitlow** ['hwɪtlo] *s* (path.) panadizo
**whitlow grass** *s* (bot.) draba
**whitlowwort** ['hwɪtlo,wʌrt] *s* (bot.) nevadilla
**Whitmonday** ['hwɪt'mʌndɪ] *s* lunes de Pentecostés
**Whitsun** ['hwɪtsən] *adj* de o del domingo de Pentecostés; de o de la semana de Pentecostés
**Whitsunday** ['hwɪt'sʌndɪ] o ['hwɪtsən,de] *s* domingo de Pentecostés
**Whitsuntide** ['hwɪtsən,taɪd] *s* semana de Pentecostés
**whittle** ['hwɪtəl] *s* (archaic) cuchillo; *va* sacar pedazos a (*un trozo de madera*) con un cuchillo o navaja; **to whittle away** o **down** rebajar o reducir poco a poco
**whity** ['hwaɪtɪ] *adj* var. de **whitish**
**whiz** o **whizz** [hwɪz] *s* sonido entre silbido y zumbido; (slang) fenómeno, perito; (*pret & pp:* **whizzed**; *ger:* **whizzing**) *va* mover produciendo un silbido; *vn* silbar; moverse produciendo un silbido, ir zumbando por el aire; **to whiz by** rehilar (*un arma arrojadiza*); pasar como una flecha
**who** [hu] *pron interr* ¿quién?; **who else?** ¿quién más?; *pron rel* que, quien; el que; **who's who** quién es el uno y quién el otro; quiénes son gente de importancia; **Who's Who** ¿Quién es quién? (*libro de biografías*)
**whoa** [hwo] o [wo] *interj* ¡so!
**whodunit** [hu'dʌnɪt] *s* (slang) novela policíaca corta
**whoever** [hu'ɛvər] *pron interr* (coll.) ¿quién?; *pron rel* quienquiera que, cualquiera que; **whoever else** cualquier otro que
**whole** [hol] *adj* entero, todo; único, p.ej., **the**

**whole interest for me was the money I made** el único interés para mí era el dinero que gané; **made out of whole cloth** enteramente falso o imaginario; *s* conjunto, todo, total; **as a whole** en conjunto; **on the whole** en general; por la mayor parte

**whole gale** *s* (naut.) temporal

**wholehearted** ['hol,hɑrtɪd] *adj* francote, cordial

**whole hog; to go the whole hog** (slang) entregarse sin reservas, llegar hasta el último límite, comprometerse a ultranza

**wholeness** ['holnɪs] *s* integridad, totalidad

**whole note** *s* (mus.) semibreve

**whole number** *s* número entero

**whole rest** *s* (mus.) pausa de semibreve

**wholesale** ['hol,sel] *s* venta al por mayor; *adj* al por mayor, mayorista; general; *va* vender al por mayor; *vn* vender al por mayor; venderse al por mayor

**wholesaler** ['hol,selər] *s* comerciante al por mayor, mayorista

**wholesome** ['holsəm] *adj* saludable; fresco, rollizo, lozano

**whole step** o **whole tone** *s* (mus.) tono completo

**whole-wheat** ['hol,hwit] *adj* hecho con harina de trigo entero

**who'll** [hul] contracción de **who shall** y de **who will**

**wholly** ['holɪ] *adv* enteramente, completamente

**whom** [hum] *pron interr* ¿a quién?; *pron rel* que, a quien; al que

**whomsoever** [,humso'ɛvər] *pron rel* a quienquiera que

**whoop** [hup] o [hwup] *s* alarido, chillido; ululato; estertor, ruido jadeante (*peculiar de la tos ferina*); *va* decir a gritos; acosar gritando; **to whoop it up** (slang) armar una gritería, alborotar; *vn* gritar, chillar; ulular; toser con ruido jadeante

**whoopee** ['hwupi] o ['hwʊpi] *interj* (slang) ¡hurra!; *s* (slang) parranda; **to make whoopee** (slang) andar de parranda

**whooping cough** ['hupɪŋ] o ['hʊpɪŋ] *s* (path.) tos ferina, tos convulsiva

**whooping crane** *s* (orn.) toquilcoyote

**whopper** ['hwɑpər] *s* (coll.) enormidad; (coll.) mentirón

**whopping** ['hwɑpɪŋ] *adj* (coll.) enorme, grandísimo

**whore** [hor] *s* puta; *vn* putañear, putear

**whorish** ['horɪʃ] *adj* putesco

**whorl** [hwʌrl] *s* espiral; espiral del caracol; (bot.) verticilo

**whorled** [hwʌrld] *adj* (bot.) verticilado

**whortleberry** ['hwʌrtəl,bɛrɪ] *s* (*pl:* **-ries**) (bot.) arándano, anavia

**who's** [huz] contracción de **who is**

**whose** [huz] *pron interr* ¿de quién?; *pron rel* de quien, cuyo

**whosesoever** [,huzso'ɛvər] *pron rel* de quienquiera que

**whoso** ['huso] *pron rel* (archaic) quienquiera que

**whosoever** [,huso'ɛvər] *pron rel* quienquiera que

**why** [hwaɪ] *adv* ¿por qué?; por qué; por lo que; por el que; **why not?** ¿cómo no?; *s* (*pl:* **whys**) porqué; *interj* ¡toma!; **why, certainly!** ¡desde luego!, ¡por supuesto!; **why, yes!** ¡claro!, ¡pues sí!

**W.I.** abr. de **West Indies** y **West Indian**

**wick** [wɪk] *s* pabilo, mecha

**wicked** ['wɪkɪd] *adj* malo, inicuo; travieso, revoltoso; (coll.) riguroso; (coll.) arisco; (coll.) molesto, desagradable

**wickedness** ['wɪkɪdnɪs] *s* maldad, iniquidad

**wicker** ['wɪkər] *s* mimbre; *adj* mimbroso; de mimbre

**wickerwork** ['wɪkər,wʌrk] *s* artículos de mimbre; cestería

**wicket** ['wɪkɪt] *s* portillo, postigo; ventanilla; (croquet) aro

**wicking** ['wɪkɪŋ] *s* torcida para pabilos y mechas

**wide** [waɪd] *adj* ancho; de ancho, p.ej., **two feet wide** dos pies de ancho; extenso; muy abierto; *adv* de par en par; **wide of** lejos de; **wide of the mark** errado (*tiro*); fuera de propósito; alejado de la verdad; *s* espacio ancho

**wide-angle** ['waɪd,æŋgəl] *adj* (opt.) granangular, de ángulo ancho

**wide-awake** ['waɪdə,wek] *adj* despabilado; (fig.) despabilado, listo, advertido

**wide-eyed** ['waɪd,aɪd] *adj* con los ojos desmesuradamente abiertos

**widely** ['waɪdlɪ] *adv* extensamente; completamente; muy; mucho

**widen** ['waɪdən] *va* ensanchar; *vn* ensancharse

**wide-open** ['waɪd'opən] *adj* de par en par, abierto de par en par; **to be wide-open** tener (*una ciudad*) mano abierta para el juego

**widespread** ['waɪd,sprɛd] *adj* extendido (*dícese de los brazos, alas, etc.*); difundido, dilatado, extenso; corriente

**widgeon** ['wɪdʒən] *s* (orn.) silbón, ánade silbador (*Anas penelope*); (orn.) lavanco (*Anas americana*)

**widow** ['wɪdo] *s* viuda; baceta o fondo (*en los naipes*); *va* dejar viuda

**widow bird** *s* var. de **whidah**

**widower** ['wɪdoər] *s* viudo

**widowhood** ['wɪdohʊd] *s* viudez

**widow's mite** *s* limosna dada gustosamente por una persona pobre

**widow's weeds** *spl* luto de viuda

**width** [wɪdθ] *s* anchura, ancho; extensión

**wield** [wild] *va* esgrimir (*la espada*); ejercer (*autoridad, el poder*)

**wiener** ['winər] *s* embutido de carne de vaca y cerdo

**wienerwurst** ['winər,wʌrst] *s* salchicha de carne de vaca y cerdo

**wife** [waɪf] *s* (*pl:* **wives**) esposa; (archaic) mujer; **to take a wife** tomar mujer; **to take to wife** casarse con

**wifehood** ['waɪfhʊd] *s* estado de mujer casada

**wifely** ['waɪflɪ] *adj* (*comp:* **-lier;** *super:* **-liest**) de esposa, de mujer casada

**wig** [wɪg] *s* peluca; (coll.) peluca (*persona que trae peluca; reprensión severa*)

**wigged** [wɪgd] *adj* de peluca, que trae peluca

**wiggle** ['wɪgəl] *s* meneo rápido; culebreo; *va* menear rápidamente; *vn* menearse rápidamente; culebrear

**wiggler** ['wɪglər] *s* persona que menea; persona o cosa que se menea; larva de mosquito

**wiggly** ['wɪglɪ] *adj* que se menea; ondulante

**wigwag** ['wɪg,wæg] *s* (nav.) comunicación por banderas; (*pret & pp:* **-wagged;** *ger:* **-wagging**) *va* mover de un lado para otro; (nav.) señalar moviendo banderas; *vn* moverse de un lado para otro; (nav.) hacer señales moviendo banderas

**wigwam** ['wɪgwɑm] *s* choza de forma cónica (*de los pieles rojas*)

**wild** [waɪld] *adj* salvaje; feroz, fiero; violento; frenético; descabellado; impetuoso; travieso; perdido (*tiro, bala, etc.*); (naut.) loco (*barco*); (coll.) loco; **wild about** (coll.) loco por; *adv* violentamente; disparatadamente; locamente; **to run wild** vivir desenfrenadamente; crecer salvaje o libre; *s* yermo, desierto, soledad; monte; **wilds** *spl* despoblado, monte

**wild boar** *s* (zool.) jabalí

**wild card** *s* comodín

**wild carrot** *s* (bot.) zanahoria silvestre

**wildcat** ['waɪld,kæt] *s* (zool.) gato montés; (zool.) lince; luchador feroz; empresa arriesgada; locomotora sin tren; pozo de petróleo de exploración; *adj* quimérico; ilícito, ilegal; sin dominio; (*pret & pp:* **-catted;** *ger:* **-catting**) *va & vn* explorar por cuenta propia

**wildcat strike** *s* huelga no sancionada por el sindicato

**wild duck** *s* pato bravío

**wildebeest** ['wɪldə,bist] *s* (zool.) ñu, gnu

**wilder** ['wɪldər] *va* (archaic & poet.) confundir; (archaic & poet.) extraviar; *vn* (archaic & poet.) confundirse; (archaic & poet.) extraviarse

**wilderness** ['wɪldərnɪs] *s* yermo, desierto, soledad; gran cantidad, inmensidad

**wild-eyed** ['waɪld,aɪd] *adj* con los ojos fijos locamente

**wild fig** *s* (bot.) higuera silvestre, cabrahigo; higo silvestre, cabrahigo (*fruto*)

**wildfire** ['waɪld,faɪr] *s* fuego griego; fuego

fatuo; relámpago difuso (*sin trueno*); **to spread like wildfire** ser un reguero de pólvora, correr como pólvora en reguero
**wild flower** *s* flor del campo, flor silvestre
**wild fowl** *spl* aves de caza, ánades
**wild goat** *s* (zool.) cabra montés
**wild goose** *s* ganso bravo
**wild-goose chase** ['waɪld'gus] *s* caza de grillos, búsqueda o empresa hecha sin provecho
**wild hazel** *s* (bot.) nochizo
**wild marjoram** *s* (bot.) orégano
**wildness** ['waɪldnɪs] *s* selvatiquez; ferocidad, fiereza; violencia; travesura; locura, desvarío
**wild oats** *spl* avena loca, ballueca; (fig.) excesos juveniles, mocedad; **to sow one's wild oats** llevar (*los mozos*) una vida de excesos
**wild olive** *s* (bot.) acebuche, olivo silvestre; (bot.) ácana (*Sideroxylon mastichodendron*); acebuchina (*fruto*)
**wild pansy** *s* (bot.) trinitaria
**wild rice** *s* (bot.) arroz de los pieles rojas
**wild sage** *s* (bot.) gallocresta
**wild thyme** *s* (bot.) serpol
**Wild West** *s* oeste de los Estados Unidos durante la época de los pioneros
**wildwood** ['waɪld,wʊd] *s* bosque, floresta
**wile** [waɪl] *s* ardid, engaño; astucia; *va* engatusar; **to wile away** engañar o entretener (*el tiempo*)
**wilful** ['wɪlfəl] *adj* var. de **willful**
**Wilhelmina** [,wɪlhɛl'minə] o [,wɪlə'minə] *s* Guillermina
**will** [wɪl] *s* voluntad; (law) testamento; **at will** a voluntad; **to do the will of** cumplir la voluntad de; **with a will** con mucha voluntad; *va* querer; legar; *vn* querer; (*cond:* **would**) *v aux* se emplea para formar (1) el futuro de ind, p.ej., **he will arrive** llegará; (2) el futuro perfecto de ind, p.ej., **he will have arrived** habrá llegado; (3) el modo potencial, p.ej., **we cannot always do as we will** no siempre podemos hacer lo que queremos; y (4) el pres de ind, indicando costumbre, p.ej., **he will go for days without smoking** pasa días enteros sin fumar
**willet** ['wɪlɪt] *s* (orn.) sinfemia
**willful** ['wɪlfəl] *adj* voluntarioso; voluntario
**willfully** ['wɪlfəlɪ] *adv* voluntariosamente; voluntariamente
**willfulness** ['wɪlfəlnɪs] *s* voluntariedad
**William** ['wɪljəm] *s* Guillermo
**William the Conqueror** *s* Guillermo el Conquistador
**willing** ['wɪlɪŋ] *s* dispuesto; gustoso, pronto
**willingly** ['wɪlɪŋlɪ] *adv* de buena gana, gustosamente
**willingness** ['wɪlɪŋnɪs] *s* buena gana, buena voluntad, complacencia
**will-o'-the-wisp** ['wɪləðə'wɪsp] *s* fuego fatuo; ilusión, quimera
**willow** ['wɪlo] *s* (bot.) sauce
**willow herb** *s* (bot.) camenerio; (bot.) lisimaquia roja; (bot.) adelfilla pelosa
**willowy** ['wɪlo·ɪ] o ['wɪləwɪ] *adj* juncal, mimbreño; lleno de sauces; (fig.) juncal, esbelto, cimbreño
**will power** *s* fuerza de voluntad
**will to power** *s* (philos.) voluntad de poder
**willy-nilly** ['wɪlɪ'nɪlɪ] *adj* indeciso, vacilante; *adv* por malas o por buenas, quieras o no quieras
**wilt** [wɪlt] *va* marchitar; *vn* marchitarse; (fig.) marchitarse, languidecer; (coll.) acobardarse, perder el ánimo
**wily** ['waɪlɪ] *adj* (*comp:* **-ier**; *super:* **-iest**) artero, engañoso, astuto
**wimble** ['wɪmbəl] *s* barrena, taladro
**wimple** ['wɪmpəl] *s* griñón, impla; *va* cubrir con griñón o impla; rizar; (archaic) hacer caer en pliegues; *vn* rizarse (*p.ej., la superficie del agua*); (archaic) caer en pliegues
**win** [wɪn] *s* (coll.) triunfo, éxito; (*pret & pp:* **won**; *ger:* **winning**) *va* ganar; **to win over** conquistar (*ganar la voluntad de*); **to win something from someone** ganar algo a alguien; *vn* ganar, triunfar; **to win out** (coll.) ganar, triunfar; (coll.) tener éxito
**wince** [wɪns] *s* sobresalto; *vn* sobresaltarse (*de miedo, ante un peligro, etc.*)
**winch** [wɪntʃ] *s* torno, maquinilla; manubrio; *va* izar o cobrar con la maquinilla
**wind** [wɪnd] *s* viento (*corriente de aire; olor que deja la caza; ventosidad; vanidad y jactancia*); resuello, respiración; (mus.) instrumento de viento; **against the wind** contra el viento; **before the wind** (naut.) con el viento; **between wind and water** (naut.) cerca de la línea de flotación; (fig.) en sitio peligroso; **down the wind** con el viento; **in the eye** o **the teeth of the wind** (naut.) contra el viento; **into the wind** contra el viento; **off the wind** (naut.) de espalda al viento, con el viento; **on the wind** (naut.) de bolina; **to be in the wind** estar en el aire (*estar pendiente*); **to break wind** ventosear; **to get wind of** husmear, ventear; sospechar, descubrir; **to sail close to the wind** (naut.) ceñir el viento, navegar de bolina; rayar en lo inmoral o lo ilegal; ser formalista; **to take the wind out of one's sails** apagarle a uno los fuegos, dejar a uno súbitamente sin ventaja o sin apoyo ‖ *va* exponer al aire o al viento; husmear, ventear; dejar sin aliento; dejar recobrar el aliento ‖ [waɪnd] *s* vuelta, recodo; torcedura ‖ (*pret & pp:* **wound**) *va* enrollar, envolver; devanar; enroscar; torcer; ovillar (*el hilo*); dar cuerda a (*un reloj*); levantar con el cabrestante; rodear, ceñir (*p.ej., con los brazos*); entrelazar (*los brazos*); **to wind off** desenrollar, desenvolver; **to wind one's way through** serpentear por; **to wind up** enrollar, envolver; (coll.) poner punto final a ‖ *vn* enrollarse, envolverse; serpentear (*un camino*); dar vueltas; enroscarse; torcerse; alabearse, combarse; **to wind up** enrollarse; enroscarse; (baseball) tomar impulso; (coll.) acabar, terminar ‖ [waɪnd] o [wɪnd] (*pret & pp:* **winded** o **wound**) *va* sonar (*un instrumento de viento*)
**windage** ['wɪndɪdʒ] *s* (arti.) fuerza del viento para desviar el curso de un proyectil; (arti.) desvío de un proyectil por efecto del viento; (arti.) viento (*huelgo entre la bala y el ánima del cañón*); (mach.) fricción del aire
**windbag** ['wɪnd,bæg] *s* saco lleno de viento; (coll.) charlatán, palabrero
**wind-blown** ['wɪnd,blon] *adj* llevado por el viento; con el pelo cortado muy corto y peinado hacia la frente
**windbreak** ['wɪnd,brek] *s* guardavientos, abrigo o protección contra el viento
**wind-broken** ['wɪnd,brokən] *adj* (vet.) enfisematoso
**wind cone** *s* (aer.) cono de viento, indicador cónico de la dirección del viento
**winded** ['wɪndɪd] *adj* falto de respiración, sin resuello
**windfall** ['wɪnd,fɔl] *s* fruta caída del árbol (*por efecto del viento*); fortunón, golpe de suerte inesperado, cosa llovida del cielo
**windflower** ['wɪnd,flaʊər] *s* (bot.) anemone
**windgall** ['wɪnd,gɔl] *s* (vet.) aventadura
**windiness** ['wɪndɪnɪs] *s* ventosidad; vaciedad; vanidad, jactancia; verbosidad
**winding** ['waɪndɪŋ] *s* vuelta; torcedura; arrollamiento (*p.ej., de un alambre*); cuerda (*acción de dar cuerda al reloj*); (elec.) bobinado; *adj* sinuoso, tortuoso
**winding machine** *s* bobinadora
**winding sheet** *s* mortaja, sudario; chorro de cera que se ha corrido y endurecido en un lado de la vela o bujía
**winding stairs** *spl* escalera espiral, escalera de caracol
**wind instrument** *s* (mus.) instrumento de viento
**windjammer** ['wɪnd,dʒæmər] *s* (coll.) buque de vela; (coll.) tripulante de buque de vela
**windlass** ['wɪndləs] *s* torno, maquinilla; *va* izar o cobrar con el torno o la maquinilla
**windless** ['wɪndlɪs] *adj* sin viento; sin aliento
**windmill** ['wɪnd,mɪl] *s* molino de viento (*máquina; juguete de papel*); aeromotor, motor de viento; **windmills** *spl* (fig.) molinos de viento (*enemigos imaginarios*); **to tilt at windmills** luchar con los molinos de viento
**window** ['wɪndo] *s* ventana (*abertura en la pared; hoja u hojas de cristales con que se cierra*); ventanilla (*de coche; de los despachos de bille-*

*tes; de un sobre*); escaparate (*en la fachada de una tienda*); transparencia de celofán (*de una cartera*); *va* proveer de ventanas
**window dresser** *s* decorador de vitrinas o escaparates, escaparatista
**window dressing** *s* decoración de vitrinas o escaparates; (fig.) adorno de escaparate
**window envelope** *s* sobre de ventanilla
**window frame** *s* alfajía, marco de ventana
**windowpane** ['wɪndo,pen] *s* cristal, vidrio, hoja de vidrio
**window regulator** *s* (aut.) elevacristales
**window sash** *s* marco de vidriera
**window screen** *s* sobrevidriera; alambrera
**window seat** *s* asiento en la parte interior de un ventanal
**window shade** *s* visillo, transparente
**window-shop** ['wɪndo,ʃɑp] (*pret & pp:* **-shopped;** *ger:* **-shopping**) *vn* curiosear en las tiendas o mirando las vitrinas sin comprar
**window-shopper** ['wɪndo,ʃɑpər] *s* persona que curiosea en las tiendas o mirando las vitrinas sin comprar
**window-shopping** ['wɪndo,ʃɑpɪŋ] *s* curioseo en las tiendas o mirando las vitrinas sin comprar
**window shutter** *s* contraventana
**window sill** *s* repisa de ventana
**window trimmer** *s* decorador de vitrinas
**windpipe** ['wɪnd,paɪp] *s* (anat.) tráquea
**windrow** ['wɪndro] *s* hilera de heno puesto a secar; hilera de gavillas; hilera de hojas secas, hierba, árboles, etc., formada por el viento; *va* colocar o arreglar en hileras para secar
**wind sail** *s* (naut.) manguera
**wind scale** *s* escala de los vientos
**wind shake** *s* venteadura
**windshield** ['wɪnd,ʃild] *s* parabrisas o guardabrisa
**windshield washer** *s* lavaparabrisas, limpiacristales
**windshield wiper** *s* enjugaparabrisas, limpiaparabrisas, limpiavidrio
**wind sock** *s* (aer.) cono de viento
**Windsor tie** ['wɪnzər] *s* corbata ancha de seda atada en lazo
**windstorm** ['wɪnd,stɔrm] *s* ventarrón, viento impetuoso
**wind tunnel** *s* (aer.) túnel aéreo, túnel aerodinámico
**wind-up** ['waɪnd,ʌp] *s* acabóse; conclusión; arreglo; (sport) final de partida; (baseball) movimiento circular del brazo del lanzador antes de lanzar la pelota
**windward** ['wɪndwərd] o ['wɪndərd] *adj* (naut.) de barlovento; *adv* (naut.) a barlovento; *s* (naut.) barlovento; **to turn to windward** (naut.) barloventear
**Windward Islands** ['wɪndwərd] *spl* islas de Barlovento
**Windward Passage** ['wɪndwərd] *s* paso de los Vientos
**windy** ['wɪndɪ] *adj* (*comp:* **-ier;** *super:* **-iest**) ventoso; vacío; palabrero; **it is windy** hace viento
**wine** [waɪn] *s* vino; *va* regalar u obsequiar con vino; *vn* beber vino
**winebibber** ['waɪn,bɪbər] *s* bebedor de vino
**wine cellar** *s* bodega, candiotera
**wine-colored** ['waɪn,kʌlərd] *adj* de color de vino, rojo obscuro
**wine cooler** *s* enfriadera, garapiñera
**wine gallon** *s* galón de 231 pulgadas cúbicas
**wineglass** ['waɪn,glæs] o ['waɪn,glɑs] *s* copa para vino
**winegrower** ['waɪn,groər] *s* vinicultor
**winegrowing** ['waɪn,gro·ɪŋ] *s* vinicultura; *adj* vinicultor
**wine press** *s* lagar; prensa de vino, prensa de lagar
**winery** ['waɪnərɪ] *s* (*pl:* **-ies**) lagar (*edificio*)
**winesap** ['waɪn,sæp] *s* manzana roja invernal
**wineskin** ['waɪn,skɪn] *s* odre
**wine steward** *s* maestro de vinos
**winetaster** ['waɪn,testər] *s* catavinos (*persona*); catavino (*tubo*)
**wing** [wɪŋ] *s* ala; facción, bando; vuelo; (theat.) bastidor, ala; (sport) ala (*jugador que está a un lado*); (hum.) brazo, pata delantera; **to be on the wing** estar volando; estar para irse; estar en pie y activo; **to be under the wing of** estar bajo el ala de; **to take wing** alzar el vuelo, irse volando; *va* dar alas a; herir en el ala o el brazo; volar a través de; acelerar; *vn* volar
**wing case** *s* (ent.) élitro
**wing chair** *s* sillón de orejas
**wing collar** *s* cuello doblado, cuello de pajarita
**wing cover** *s* var. de **wing case**
**winged** [wɪŋd] o ['wɪŋɪd] *adj* alado (*que tiene alas; rápido*); herido en el ala; (coll.) herido en el brazo; (poet.) elevado, sublime
**wing load** *s* (aer.) carga alar
**wing nut** *s* tuerca de aletas
**wing-shaped** ['wɪŋ,ʃept] *adj* alado
**wingspread** ['wɪŋ,sprɛd] *s* envergadura (*de ave o avión*)
**Winifred** ['wɪnɪfrɪd] *s* Genoveva
**wink** [wɪŋk] *s* guiño; parpadeo, pestañeo; parpadeo (*p.ej., de las estrellas*); **to not sleep a wink** no pegar los ojos; **to take forty winks** (coll.) descabezar el sueño; *va* guiñar (*el ojo*); expresar con un guiño; **to wink away** secar (*las lágrimas*) parpadeando; *vn* guiñar; parpadear, pestañear; señalar con un guiño; parpadear (*p.ej., las estrellas*); **to wink at** guiñar el ojo a; fingir no ver
**winker** ['wɪŋkər] *s* guiñador; anteojera (*de caballo*); (coll.) pestaña
**winkle** ['wɪŋkəl] *s* (zool.) litorina; (zool.) bucición
**winner** ['wɪnər] *s* ganador; premiado
**Winnie** ['wɪnɪ] *s* nombre abreviado de **Winifred**
**winning** ['wɪnɪŋ] *adj* ganancioso; triunfante, victorioso; atrayente, simpático, persuasivo; **winnings** *spl* ganancias
**winning number** *s* número premiado
**winning post** *s* (sport) poste de llegada
**winning ways** *spl* modales simpáticos, gracia, atractivo
**winnow** ['wɪno] *va* aventar; entresacar; batir (*las alas*); *vn* aventar; aletear
**winnower** ['wɪnoər] *s* aventador; máquina aventadora
**winsome** ['wɪnsəm] *adj* atrayente, simpático, gracioso
**winter** ['wɪntər] *s* invierno; *adj* invernal; *va* hacer invernar; *vn* invernar
**winter cherry** *s* (bot.) vejiga de perro, alquequenje, vejiguilla
**wintergreen** ['wɪntər,grin] *s* (bot.) pirola; (bot.) gaulteria, té del Canadá; aceite de gaulteria
**winterkill** ['wɪntər,kɪl] *va* matar por exposición a la intemperie durante el invierno; *vn* morir por exposición a la intemperie durante el invierno
**winter rose** *s* (bot.) eléboro negro
**winter savory** *s* (bot.) tomillo real, hisopillo
**Winter's bark** *s* canela de Magallanes, corteza de Winter
**winter solstice** *s* (astr.) solsticio hiemal
**wintertide** ['wɪntər,taɪd] *s* (poet.) invernada
**wintertime** ['wɪntər,taɪm] *s* invernada
**winter wheat** *s* trigo otoñal, trigo de invierno
**wintery** ['wɪntərɪ] *adj* invernal; frío, helado
**wintriness** ['wɪntrɪnɪs] *s* frío de invierno
**wintry** ['wɪntrɪ] *adj* (*comp:* **-trier;** *super:* **-triest**) invernal; frío, helado
**winy** ['waɪnɪ] *adj* vinoso; vinolento
**winze** [wɪnz] *s* (min.) coladero
**wipe** [waɪp] *s* frotadura, limpiadura; *va* frotar para limpiar; enjugar (*p.ej., la cara, el sudor*); soldar frotando la juntura con un pedazo de cuero; **to wipe away** limpiar (*p.ej., las lágrimas*); **to wipe off** quitar frotando; **to wipe on** frotar (*una cosa*) sobre; **to wipe out** (coll.) borrar, cancelar; (coll.) aniquilar, destruir; (coll.) enjugar (*una deuda*)
**wiper** ['waɪpər] *s* limpiador; paño, trapo; (elec.) contacto deslizante; (mach.) leva, álabe
**wire** [waɪr] *s* alambre; telégrafo; telegrama; **hold the wire** (coll.) no descuelgue; **to get under the wire** llegar o terminar con tiempo; **to pull wires** (coll.) tocar o mover resortes (*para lograr un fin*); (coll.) dirigir secretamente a otros; *adj* de alambre, hecho de alambre; *va* proveer de alambres; atar con alambre; atrapar por medio de alambres; alambrar (*ins-*

*talar alambre conductor en*); telegrafiar; *vn* telegrafiar
**wire brush** *s* cepillo de alambre
**wire cutter** *s* cortaalambres (*herramienta*)
**wiredraw** ['waɪr,drɔ] (*pret:* **-drew;** *pp:* **-drawn**) *va* trefilar; estrangular (*el agua o el vapor*); (fig.) prolongar con exceso; (fig.) torcer, falsear
**wiredrawn** ['waɪr,drɔn] *adj* trefilado; tratado con excesiva exactitud y precisión; *pp de* **wiredraw**
**wiredrew** ['waɪr,dru] *pret de* **wiredraw**
**wired wireless** *s* var. de **line radio**
**wire fence** *s* alambrada
**wire gauge** *s* calibre para alambres, calibrador de alambre
**wire gauze** *s* gasa de alambre
**wire-haired** ['waɪr,hɛrd] *adj* de pelo áspero (*perro*)
**wireless** ['waɪrlɪs] *adj* (elec.) inalámbrico, sin hilos; (Brit.) radiofónico; *s* (Brit.) receptor radiofónico; (Brit.) emisión radiofónica, comunicación radiofónica; *va* (Brit.) enviar o transmitir por radiofonía o radiotelegrafía
**wireless telegraphy** *s* telegrafía inalámbrica o sin hilos
**wireless telephony** *s* telefonía inalámbrica o sin hilos
**wire mesh** *s* malla de alambre
**wire nail** *s* alfiler de París, clavo de alambre
**wire netting** *s* tela metálica, red de alambre
**wirephoto** ['waɪr,foto] *s* (*pl:* **-tos**) (trademark) foto telegráfica
**wire puller** *s* (coll.) persona que mueve resortes (*para lograr un fin*)
**wire pulling** *s* (coll.) empleo de resortes (*para lograr un fin*)
**wire recorder** *s* magnetófono, aparato de grabación de alambre, aparato impresor del sonido en alambre, grabadora de alambre
**wire recording** *s* grabación de alambre
**wire screen** *s* tela de alambre
**wire service** *s* servicio telegráfico y telefónico; servicio telegráfico y telefónico de noticias turfistas
**wire solder** *s* alambre de soldadura
**wire tapping** *s* conexión telefónica o telegráfica secreta para interceptar mensajes
**wire wheel** *s* rueda de rayos de alambre
**wirework** ['waɪr,wʌrk] *s* alambrado, tela metálica; **wireworks** *spl* fábrica de objetos de alambre o de tela metálica; trefilería
**wireworker** ['waɪr,wʌrkər] *s* alambrero; trefilero
**wireworm** ['waɪr,wʌrm] *s* (zool.) larva de elatérido
**wiring** ['waɪrɪŋ] *s* (elec.) instalación de alambres eléctricos; (elec.) canalización, alambrado; (surg.) costura con alambre
**wiry** ['waɪrɪ] *adj* (*comp:* **-ier;** *super:* **-iest**) hecho de alambre; como alambre; cimbreante, delgado pero fuerte
**Wis.** o **Wisc.** abr. de **Wisconsin**
**wis** [wɪs] *va* (archaic) saber
**wisdom** ['wɪzdəm] *s* sabiduría, cordura
**Wisdom of Solomon** *s* (Bib.) Sabiduría de Salomón (*libro de la Apócrifa*)
**wisdom tooth** *s* muela del juicio, muela cordal; **to cut one's wisdom teeth** (coll.) salirle a uno las muelas del juicio (*ser prudente y mirado en sus acciones*)
**wise** [waɪz] *adj* sabio; listo; enterado, informado; juicioso, acertado (*p.ej., paso*); **to be wise to** (slang) estar al tanto de; (slang) conocer el juego de; **to get wise** (slang) caer en el chiste; **to put wise (to)** (slang) poner al tanto (de); (slang) poner al tanto del juego (de); *s* modo, manera, guisa; **in any wise** de cualquier modo; **in no wise** de ningún modo; **in this wise** así, en esta forma; *va* **to wise up** (slang) hacer caer en la cuenta; *vn* **to wise up** (slang) caer en la cuenta, caer en el chiste
**wiseacre** ['waɪz,ekər] *s* sabihondo
**wisecrack** ['waɪz,kræk] *s* (slang) cuchufleta, pulla; *vn* (slang) cuchufletear
**wisecracker** ['waɪz,krækər] *s* (slang) cuchufletero, pullista
**wise guy** *s* (slang) sábelotodo
**Wise Men of the East** *s* magos de Oriente

**wish** [wɪʃ] *s* deseo; **to make a wish** pensar en algo que se desea; *va* desear; dar (*p.ej., los buenos días*); **to wish something on someone** (coll.) lograr que una persona acepte una cosa que no desea; *vn* desear; **to wish for** desear, anhelar
**wishbone** ['wɪʃ,bon] *s* espoleta, hueso de la suerte
**wishful** ['wɪʃfəl] *adj* deseoso
**wishful thinking** *s* optimismo a ultranza; **to indulge in wishful thinking** forjarse ilusiones
**wishing well** *s* fuentecilla de los deseos
**wishy-washy** ['wɪʃɪ,wɑʃɪ] o ['wɪʃɪ,wɔʃɪ] *adj* aguado, diluído; débil, flojo, pobre
**wisp** [wɪsp] *s* manojito, puñado; jirón, mechón; rastro, vestigio; bandada; escobilla, cepillo
**wispy** ['wɪspɪ] *adj* (*comp:* **-ier;** *super:* **-iest**) sutil, ligero, delicado
**wist** [wɪst] *pret & pp de* **wit**
**wistaria** [wɪs'tɛrɪə] o **wisteria** [wɪs'tɪrɪə] *s* (bot.) vistaria
**wistful** ['wɪstfəl] *adj* ansioso, tristón, melancólico, pensativo
**wistfulness** ['wɪstfəlnɪs] *s* ansiedad, tristeza, melancolía
**wit** [wɪt] *s* ingenio; juicio, sentido; agudeza; chistoso; **to be at one's wits' end** estar para volverse loco, no saber qué hacer o decir; **to be out of one's wits** estar fuera de sí; **to have** o **to keep one's wits about one** conservar su presencia de ánimo; **to have the wit to** + *inf* tener el tino de + *inf;* **to live by one's wits** campar de golondro, vivir de gorra; **to lose one's wits** perder el juicio; **to use one's wits** valerse de su ingenio; (*primera y tercera personas del sg del pres de ind:* **wot;** *pl del pres de ind:* **wit;** *pret & pp:* **wist;** *ger:* **witting**) *va & vn* (archaic) saber; **to wit** a saber, es decir
**witch** [wɪtʃ] *s* bruja, hechicera; (fig.) hechicera (*mujer de encantos irresistibles*); (fig.) bruja (*mujer vieja y fea*); *adj* brujesco; *va* embrujar, hechizar
**witchcraft** ['wɪtʃ,kræft] o ['wɪtʃ,krɑft] *s* brujería
**witch doctor** *s* médico brujo (*en ciertas tribus africanas*)
**witchery** ['wɪtʃərɪ] *s* (*pl:* **-ies**) brujería; (fig.) hechicería
**witches' Sabbath** *s* aquelarre, junta nocturna de brujas, sábado
**witch hazel** *s* (bot.) hamamelis de Virginia, nogal de la brujería, planta del sortilegio; (bot.) carpe (*Carpinus betulus*); agua o loción de hamamelis, hamamelina
**witch hunt** *s* persecución de supuestos subversores, con fines políticos
**witching** ['wɪtʃɪŋ] *adj* hechicero, mágico, encantador
**witenagemot** ['wɪtənəgə,mot] *s* concejo de los antiguos anglosajones
**with** [wɪð] o [wɪθ] *prep* con; de, p.ej., **covered with snow** cubierto de nieve
**withal** [wɪð'ɔl] *adv* (archaic) además, también; *prep* (archaic) con
**withdraw** [wɪð'drɔ] o [wɪθ'drɔ] (*pret:* **-drew;** *pp:* **-drawn**) *va* retirar; *vn* retirarse; **to withdraw within oneself** recogerse en sí mismo
**withdrawal** [wɪð'drɔəl] o [wɪθ'drɔəl] *s* retiro; retirada
**withdrawn** [wɪð'drɔn] o [wɪθ'drɔn] *pp de* **withdraw**
**withdrew** [wɪð'dru] o [wɪθ'dru] *pret de* **withdraw**
**withe** [wɪθ], [wɪð] o [waɪð] *s* mimbre, junco
**wither** ['wɪðər] *va* marchitar; avergonzar, confundir; *vn* marchitarse; avergonzarse, confundirse; **withers** *spl* cruz (*del cuadrúpedo*)
**withheld** [wɪθ'hɛld] o [wɪð'hɛld] *pret & pp de* **withhold**
**withhold** [wɪθ'hold] o [wɪð'hold] (*pret & pp:* **-held**) *va* negar (*p.ej., un permiso*); suspender (*pago*); detener, retener, contener
**withholding tax** *s* descuento anticipado de los impuestos
**within** [wɪð'ɪn] *adv* dentro; *prep* dentro de; al alcance de; poco menos de; con un margen de,

con una diferencia de . . . más o menos, p.ej., **I can tell you when he will arrive within ten minutes** puedo decirle cuándo llegará con una diferencia de diez minutos más o menos
**without** [wɪ'ðaʊt] *adv* fuera; *prep* fuera de; más allá de; sin; **to do without** pasar sin; **without** + *ger* sin + *inf*, p.ej., **he left without saying good-bye** salió sin despedirse; sin que + *subj*, p.ej., **he came in without my seeing him** entró sin que yo le viese; *conj* (dial.) a menos que + *subj*
**withstand** [wɪθ'stænd] o [wɪð'stænd] (*pret & pp:* **-stood**) *va* aguantar, soportar, resistir
**withstood** [wɪθ'stʊd] o [wɪð'stʊd] *pret & pp de* **withstand**
**withy** ['wɪðɪ] o ['wɪθɪ] *s* (*pl:* **-ies**) mimbre, junco; banda o cabestro hechos de mimbre o junco; *adj* mimbreño
**witless** ['wɪtlɪs] *adj* insensato, estúpido, tonto
**witness** ['wɪtnɪs] *s* testigo (*persona*); testimonio (*evidencia*); **in witness whereof** en fe de lo cual; **to bear witness** dar testimonio; **to call to witness** nombrar testigo, tomar por testigo; *va* atestiguar o testimoniar; firmar como testigo; presenciar; mostrar; *vn* dar testimonio, servir de testigo
**witness stand** *s* puesto o mesa de los testigos
**witticism** ['wɪtɪsɪzəm] *s* agudeza, ocurrencia, dicho agudo
**wittingly** ['wɪtɪŋlɪ] *adv* adrede, a sabiendas
**witty** ['wɪtɪ] *adj* (*comp:* **-tier;** *super:* **-tiest**) agudo, ingenioso; chistoso, ocurrente
**wive** [waɪv] *va* casar, proveer de esposa; casarse con; *vn* casarse
**wivern** ['waɪvərn] *s* (her.) dragón
**wizard** ['wɪzərd] *s* brujo, hechicero, mago; (coll.) as, experto; *adj* mágico
**wizardry** ['wɪzərdrɪ] *s* magia
**wizened** ['wɪzənd] *adj* marchito; acartonado
**wk.** abr. de **week**
**wks.** abr. de **weeks** y **works**
**w.l.** abr. de **wave length**
**w.long.** abr. de **west longitude**
**WNW, W.N.W.** o **w.n.w.** abr. de **west-northwest**
**wo** [wo] *s & interj* var. de **woe**
**woad** [wod] *s* (bot.) glasto, hierba pastel
**wobble** ['wɑbəl] *s* bamboleo, tambaleo; *vn* bambolear, tambalear; bailar (*p.ej., una silla, una baldosa*); vacilar, cambiar, ser inconstante
**wobbly** ['wɑblɪ] *adj* tambaleante, inseguro
**wobegone** ['wobɪ,gɔn] o ['wobɪ,gɑn] *adj* var. de **woebegone**
**woe** [wo] *s* miseria, aflicción, pesar, infortunio; *interj* ¡ay!; **woe is me!** ¡ay de mí!
**woebegone** ['wobɪ,gɔn] o ['wobɪ,gɑn] *adj* cariacontecido, abatido
**woeful** o **woful** ['wofəl] *adj* miserable, triste, abatido; lastimoso
**woke** [wok] *pret de* **wake**
**wold** [wold] *s* rasa ondulada y sin bosques; (bot.) gualda
**wolf** [wʊlf] *s* (*pl:* **wolves**) (zool.) lobo; glotón cruel (*persona*); **to cry wolf** gritar ¡el lobo!, dar falsa alarma; **to keep the wolf from the door** defenderse de la pobreza, guardarse del hambre; *va* comer vorazmente; dar falsa alarma a; *vn* comer vorazmente; vivir como lobo; cazar lobos
**wolf dog** *s* perro lobero; perro de los esquimales; híbrido de perro y lobo
**wolf fish** *s* (ichth.) lobo de mar
**wolfhound** ['wʊlf,haʊnd] *s* galgo lobero
**wolfish** ['wʊlfɪʃ] *adj* lobuno; cruel, rapaz
**wolf pack** *s* grupo submarino a caza de presa
**wolfram** ['wʊlfrəm] *s* (chem.) volframio; (mineral.) volframita
**wolframite** ['wʊlfrəmaɪt] *s* (mineral.) volframita
**wolf's-bane** o **wolfsbane** ['wʊlfs,ben] *s* (bot.) matalobos
**wolverine** o **wolverene** [,wʊlvə'rin] o ['wʊlvərin] *s* (zool.) carcayú, glotón de América; (*cap.*) *s* natural o habitante del estado de Michigan, EE.UU.
**woman** ['wʊmən] *s* (*pl:* **women** ['wɪmɪn]) *s* mujer; criada; *adj* femenino; de mujer
**woman hater** *s* misógino, enemigo de las mujeres
**womanhood** ['wʊmənhʊd] *s* el sexo femenino, la mujer; las mujeres, la feminidad
**womanish** ['wʊmənɪʃ] *adj* mujeril, femenil, afeminado
**womankind** ['wʊmən,kaɪnd] *s* el sexo femenino, la mujer
**womanlike** ['wʊmən,laɪk] *adj* mujeril
**womanly** ['wʊmənlɪ] *adj* (*comp:* **-lier;** *super:* **-liest**) femenil, mujeril; *adv* femenilmente
**woman of the world** *s* mujer mundana
**woman's rights** *spl* derechos de la mujer
**woman suffrage** *s* sufragismo, sufragio femenino
**woman-suffragist** ['wʊmən'sʌfrədʒɪst] *s* sufragista
**womb** [wum] *s* (anat.) útero, matriz; (fig.) entrañas, seno
**wombat** ['wɑmbæt] *s* (zool.) tejón de Australia, fascólomo
**women** ['wɪmɪn] *pl de* **woman**
**womenfolk** ['wɪmɪn,fok] *spl* las mujeres
**won** [wʌn] *pret & pp de* **win**
**wonder** ['wʌndər] *s* maravilla; admiración; **for a wonder** por milagro; **no wonder** no es extraño; **to do wonders with** hacer maravillas con; **to work wonders** hacer milagros; *va* preguntarse, p.ej., **I wonder if it is true** me pregunto ¿será verdad?; *vn* maravillarse, admirarse; **to wonder at** maravillarse con o de, admirarse de
**wonder drugs** *spl* drogas prodigiosas, drogas milagrosas, drogas mágicas
**wonderful** ['wʌndərfəl] *adj* maravilloso
**wonderland** ['wʌndər,lænd] *s* tierra de las maravillas, reino de las hadas
**wonderment** ['wʌndərmənt] *s* asombro, sorpresa, admiración
**wondrous** ['wʌndrəs] *adj* maravilloso; *adv* maravillosamente
**won't** [wont] contracción de **will not**
**wont** [wʌnt] *adj* habituado, acostumbrado; **to be wont to** + *inf* soler + *inf*, acostumbrar + *inf*; *s* hábito, costumbre
**wonted** ['wʌntɪd] *adj* habitual, ordinario, acostumbrado
**woo** [wu] *va* cortejar (*a una mujer*); tratar de conquistar; tratar de persuadir
**wood** [wʊd] *s* madera; leña (*madera cortada para quemar*); objeto de madera; barril o pipa de madera; bosque; (mus.) instrumento de viento de madera; (print.) bloque de madera; **woods** *spl* bosque; (mus.) instrumentos de viento de madera; **out of the woods** libre de incertidumbre, libre de dificultades, libre de compromisos; fuera de peligro; **to take to the woods** andar a monte; *adj* de madera; *va* proveer de madera; obtener madera para
**wood alcohol** *s* alcohol de madera, alcohol metílico
**wood anemone** *s* (bot.) anemona silvestre
**woodbine** ['wʊd,baɪn] *s* (bot.) madreselva; (bot.) guau (*Parthenocissus quinquefolia*)
**wood block** *s* bloque de madera; adoquín de madera; (print.) grabado en madera
**wood borer** *s* (ent.) carcoma
**wood carver** *s* tallista
**wood carving** *s* labrado de madera
**woodchuck** ['wʊd,tʃʌk] *s* (zool.) marmota de América
**woodcock** ['wʊd,kɑk] *s* (orn.) chocha, becada
**woodcraft** ['wʊd,kræft] o ['wʊd,krɑft] *s* conocimiento de la vida del bosque; destreza en trabajos de madera
**woodcut** ['wʊd,kʌt] *s* (print.) grabado en madera
**woodcutter** ['wʊd,kʌtər] *s* leñador
**wood duck** *s* (orn.) juyuyo
**wooded** ['wʊdɪd] *adj* enselvado
**wooden** ['wʊdən] *adj* de madera, hecho de madera; vago (*dícese, p.ej., de la mirada*); torpe, estúpido; sin ánimo, sin color
**wood engraving** *s* (print.) grabado en madera
**wooden-headed** ['wʊdən,hɛdɪd] *adj* (coll.) torpe, estúpido
**wooden horse** *s* caballo de madera (*de que se sirvieron los griegos para invadir a Troya*); potro (*castigo*)
**wooden shoe** *s* zueco
**woodenware** ['wʊdən,wɛr] *s* utensilios de madera

**wood germander** *s* (bot.) camedrio de los bosques
**wood grouse** *s* (orn.) gallo de bosque
**wood ibis** *s* (orn.) bato, tántalo
**woodland** ['wudlənd] *s* bosque, arbolado; *adj* selvático
**woodlander** ['wudləndər] *s* habitante del bosque
**wood lot** *s* terreno de bosque
**wood louse** *s* (zool.) cochinilla de humedad; (ent.) reloj de la muerte
**woodman** ['wudmən] *s* (*pl:* **-men**) habitante del bosque; leñador; (Brit.) guardabosque
**wood note** *s* canto de pájaro silvestre
**wood nymph** *s* (myth.) napea, ninfa de los bosques; (ent.) mariposa (*del género Euthisanotia*); (orn.) colibrí sudamericano (*del género Thalurania*)
**woodpecker** ['wud,pɛkər] *s* (orn.) carpintero, picocarpintero
**wood pigeon** *s* (orn.) paloma torcaz (*Columba palumbus*); (orn.) paloma volcanera (*Columba fasciata*)
**woodpile** ['wud,paɪl] *s* montón de leña
**wood pulp** *s* pulpa de madera
**woodruff** ['wud,rʌf] *s* (bot.) asperilla, hepática estrellada, reina de los bosques
**wood screw** *s* tornillo para madera, tirafondo
**woodshed** ['wud,ʃɛd] *s* leñera
**woodsman** ['wudzmən] *s* (*pl:* **-men**) leñador; hombre acostumbrado a la vida del bosque
**wood sorrel** *s* (bot.) acederilla, acedera menor
**woodsy** ['wudzɪ] *adj* boscoso, selvático
**wood tar** *s* alquitrán vegetal
**wood thrush** *s* (orn.) tordo norteamericano (*Hylocichla mustelina*)
**wood turning** *s* torneo de madera
**wood vinegar** *s* vinagre de madera
**woodwaxen** ['wud,wæksən] *s* (bot.) retama de tintes o de tintoreros
**wood wind** *s* (mus.) instrumento de viento de madera; *spl* (mus.) instrumentos de viento de madera
**wood-wind instrument** ['wud,wɪnd] *s* (mus.) instrumento de viento de madera
**woodwork** ['wud,wʌrk] *s* ebanistería, obra de carpintería; maderaje
**woodworker** ['wud,wʌrkər] *s* ebanista, carpintero
**woodworking** ['wud,wʌrkɪŋ] *s* ebanistería, elaboración de maderas
**woodworm** ['wud,wʌrm] *s* (ent.) carcoma
**woody** ['wudɪ] *adj* (*comp:* **-ier**; *super:* **-iest**) arbolado, enselvado; leñoso
**wooer** ['wuər] *s* pretendiente, galán
**woof** [wuf] *s* trama; género, tejido; [wuf] *s* gruñido; *vn* gruñir (*p.ej., el perro*)
**woofer** ['wufər] *s* (rad.) altavoz para bajas audiofrecuencias, altavoz graves
**wool** [wul] *s* lana; **to pull the wool over one's eyes** (coll.) engañar a uno como un chino, hacerle chino a uno; *adj* de lana, hecho de lana
**woold** [wuld] *va* (naut.) encarcelar
**woolen** ['wulən] *adj* lanero; de lana, hecho de lana; *s* hilo de lana; tejido de lana; **woolens** *spl* géneros de lana, ropa de lana
**woolgathering** ['wul,gæðərɪŋ] *adj* absorto, distraído; *s* absorción, distracción
**woolgrower** ['wul,groər] *s* ganadero de ganado lanar
**woollen** ['wulən] *adj & s* var. de **woolen; woollens** *spl* var. de **woolens**
**woolly** ['wulɪ] *adj* (*comp:* **-lier**; *super:* **-liest**) lanoso, lanudo
**woolman** ['wulmən] *s* (*pl:* **-men**) lanero (*el que trata en lanas*)
**woolpack** ['wul,pæk] *s* fardo para llevar la lana; paquete de lana de 240 libras; cúmulo (*nubes amontonadas*)
**woolsack** ['wul,sæk] *s* saco de lana; (Brit.) cojín en el cual se sienta el Gran Canciller en la Cámara de los Lores; (Brit.) cargo o dignidad de Gran Canciller
**wool stapler** *s* lanero
**wooly** ['wulɪ] *adj* (*comp:* **-ier**; *super:* **-iest**) var. de **woolly**
**woozy** ['wuzɪ] o ['wuzɪ] *adj* (slang) confuso, vaguido; (slang) indispuesto

**Worcestershire sauce** ['wustərʃɪr] *s* salsa inglesa
**word** [wʌrd] *s* palabra; santo y seña, palabra de pase; orden *f*; (*cap.*) *s* (theol.) Verbo o Palabra (*segunda persona de la Santísima Trinidad*); **words** *spl* palabras mayores (*las injuriosas y ofensivas*); letra, palabra (*palabras de una canción*); **by word of mouth** de palabra, verbalmente; **in a word** en una palabra; **in other words** en otros términos; **mark my words!** ¡advierta lo que digo!; **my word!** ¡válgame Dios!; **the Word** la palabra de Dios (*la Escritura*); **to be as good as one's word** cumplir lo prometido; **to bring word** dar noticia; **to have a word with** hablar cuatro palabras con; **to have word from** recibir noticias de; **to have words** tener palabras, tener palabras mayores; **to keep one's word** cumplir su palabra; **to leave word** dejar dicho; **to put in a good word for** decir unas palabras en favor de; **to send word** mandar recado; **to send word that** mandar decir que; **to take a person at his word** tomarle la palabra a una persona; **to take the words out of one's mouth** quitarle a uno las palabras de la boca; **upon my word** palabra de honor; **upon my word!** ¡válgame Dios!; **word for word** palabra por palabra; *va* redactar, formular, expresar en palabras
**wordage** ['wʌrdɪdʒ] *s* palabras; fraseología; palabrería, verbosidad; número de palabras
**word blindness** *s* ceguera verbal, alexia
**wordbook** ['wʌrd,buk] *s* diccionario, vocabulario
**word count** *s* recuento de vocabulario
**word deafness** *s* sordera verbal, sordera psíquica, afasia sensorial
**word element** *s* (gram.) elemento de compuestos
**word formation** *s* (gram.) formación de palabras
**word-for-word** ['wʌrdfər'wʌrd] *adj* literal, ajustado palabra por palabra
**wordiness** ['wʌrdɪnɪs] *s* verbosidad
**wording** ['wʌrdɪŋ] *s* fraseología, manera de expresarse por medio de palabras
**wordless** ['wʌrdlɪs] *adj* falto de palabras; sin expresar
**Word of God** *s* palabra de Dios (*la Escritura*)
**word of honor** *s* palabra de honor
**word order** *s* (gram.) orden *m* de colocación
**word picture** *s* pintura por medio de la palabra
**wordplay** ['wʌrd,ple] *s* juego de palabras
**word salad** *s* esquizofasia (*lenguaje incoherente e incomprensible de la esquizofrenia*)
**word sign** *s* signo (*de la escritura jeroglífica; de la taquigrafía; del sistema Braille*)
**word-slinger** ['wʌrd,slɪŋər] *s* escritorcillo, escritor mercenario
**word square** *s* palabras cruzadas
**wordstock** ['wʌrd,stɑk] s léxico, vocabulario
**wordy** ['wʌrdɪ] *adj* (*comp:* **-ier**; *super:* **-iest**) verboso; verbal
**wore** [wor] *pret de* **wear**
**work** [wʌrk] *s* trabajo; obra (*resultado del trabajo; producción del espíritu; estructura en construcción; fortificación*); (sew.) labor; (phys.) trabajo; **works** *ssg* o *spl* fábrica, usina; *spl* mecanismo; movimiento (*p.ej., de un reloj*); (Bib.) obras; **at work** trabajando; en la oficina, en el taller, en la tienda, etc. (*es decir, no en casa*); **out of work** desempleado, sin trabajo; **to make short work of** concluir con prontitud; deshacerse de, sin rodeos; **to shoot the works** (slang) envidar el resto, jugar el todo por el todo; (slang) comprometerse a ultranza; **to throw out of work** privar de trabajo; quitar el empleo a ‖ *va* hacer trabajar; trabajar, obrar (*p.ej., la madera*); conseguir con esfuerzo; causar, producir; obrar (*p.ej., un milagro*); influir, persuadir; resolver; laborear, explotar (*una mina*); **to work in** meter, hacer entrar; **to work into** intercalar en (*p.ej., un discurso*); **to work it** (coll.) manejar las cosas, darse traza; **to work off** deshacerse de; **to work out** desarrollar, preparar; resolver; determinar (*su destino*); agotar (*una mina*); **to work up** preparar; estimular, excitar ‖ *vn* trabajar; funcionar, marchar; dar resultado;

obrar (*p.ej., un remedio*); **to work against** obrar en contra de; **to work free** o **loose** aflojarse (*con el movimiento o el uso*); **to work on** o **upon** tratar de influir o persuadir; **to work out** resultar; resolverse; (sport) entrenarse

**workable** ['wʌrkəbəl] *adj* practicable; manuable; explotable; laborable

**workaday** ['wʌrkə,de] *adj* de cada día; práctico; ordinario, vulgar, prosaico

**workbag** ['wʌrk,bæg] *s* saco de trabajo

**workbench** ['wʌrk,bentʃ] *s* banco o mesa de trabajo, banco de taller

**workbook** ['wʌrk,bʊk] *s* libro de trabajo; libro de reglas; libro de ejercicios

**workbox** ['wʌrk,bɑks] *s* caja de herramientas; caja de labor

**workday** ['wʌrk,de] *s* día de trabajo, día laborable; jornada (*tiempo de duración del trabajo diario*); *adj* de cada día; práctico; ordinario, vulgar

**worker** ['wʌrkər] *s* trabajador, obrero; (ent.) obrera

**work force** *s* mano de obra, personal obrero

**work horse** *s* caballo de carga; yunque, trabajador esforzado

**workhouse** ['wʌrk,haʊs] *s* taller penitenciario; (Brit.) asilo de pobres donde los recogidos tienen que trabajar en el obrador

**working** ['wʌrkɪŋ] *s* funcionamiento; operación; explotación; **workings** *spl* (min.) labores; *adj* obrero; de trabajo; en funcionamiento

**working agreement** *s* ajuste, arreglo, modo de vivir

**working capital** *s* capital en giro

**working class** *s* clase obrera

**working clothes** *spl* traje de faena

**working day** *s* día de trabajo, día laborable; jornada (*tiempo de duración del trabajo diario*)

**working-day** ['wʌrkɪŋ,de] *adj* de cada día; práctico; ordinario, vulgar

**working drawing** *s* dibujo de trabajo, dibujo de guía

**working face** *s* (min.) fondo de laboreo

**workinggirl** ['wʌrkɪŋ,gʌrl] *s* trabajadora joven: obrera joven

**working hours** *spl* horas laborables, horas de trabajo, horas de jornada

**working hypothesis** *s* hipótesis de guía

**working majority** *s* mayoría suficiente

**workingman** ['wʌrkɪŋ,mæn] *s* (*pl:* **-men**) trabajador; obrero

**working model** *s* modelo de guía

**working order** *s* orden *m* de marcha

**working speed** *s* velocidad de régimen

**working stroke** *s* (mach.) carrera de trabajo

**working voltage** *s* (elec.) voltaje de régimen

**workingwoman** ['wʌrkɪŋ,wʊmən] *s* (*pl:* **-women**) trabajadora; obrera

**workman** ['wʌrkmən] *s* (*pl:* **-men**) trabajador; obrero; artífice

**workmanlike** ['wʌrkmən,laɪk] *adj* esmerado, primoroso, bien ejecutado; *adv* esmeradamente, primorosamente

**workmanship** ['wʌrkmənʃɪp] *s* destreza o habilidad en el trabajo; confección; hechura, obra

**work of art** *s* obra de arte

**workout** ['wʌrk,aʊt] *s* ejercicio; prueba, ensayo

**workpeople** ['wʌrk,pipəl] *spl* obreros

**workroom** ['wʌrk,rum] o ['wʌrk,rʊm] *s* obrador; sala de trabajo; gabinete de trabajo

**workshop** ['wʌrk,ʃɑp] *s* taller; (educ.) taller

**work stoppage** *s* paro

**worktable** ['wʌrk,tebəl] *s* mesa de trabajo; mesa de labor

**workwoman** ['wʌrk,wʊmən] *s* (*pl:* **-women**) trabajadora; obrera

**world** [wʌrld] *s* mundo; **a world of** la mar de; **for all the world** exactamente; **half the world** medio mundo (*mucha gente*); **in the world** en el mundo entero; alguna vez; **not for all the world** por nada del mundo; **since the world began** desde que el mundo es mundo; **the other world** el otro mundo (*la vida futura*); **the world over** por el mundo entero; **to bring into the world** echar al mundo; **to come into the world** venir al mundo; **to see the world** ver mundo; **to think the world of** tener un alto concepto de; **world without end** por los siglos de los siglos; *adj* mundial; mundano

**world affairs** *spl* asuntos internacionales

**World Court** *s* Tribunal Permanente de Justicia Internacional

**world-famous** ['wʌrld'feməs] *adj* mundialmente famoso

**worldling** ['wʌrldlɪŋ] *s* persona mundana

**worldly** ['wʌrldlɪ] *adj* (*comp:* **-lier;** *super:* **-liest**) mundano

**worldly-minded** ['wʌrldlɪ'maɪndɪd] *adj* mundano, apegado a las cosas del mundo

**worldly-wise** ['wʌrldlɪ'waɪz] *adj* que tiene mucho mundo

**world map** *s* mapamundi

**world power** *s* potencia mundial

**World Series** *s* (baseball) Serie Mundial

**world view** *s* concepto del mundo

**World War** *s* Guerra Mundial

**world-weary** ['wʌrld,wɪrɪ] *adj* cansado de la vida

**world-wide** ['wʌrld,waɪd] *adj* mundial, global

**worm** [wʌrm] *s* gusano; serpentín; tornillo sin fin; (fig.) gusano (*persona despreciable*); (fig.) gusano (*de la conciencia*); **worms** *spl* (path.) lombrices; *va* limpiar de lombrices; conseguir o lograr por medio de artimañas; **to worm a secret out of a person** arrancar mañosamente un secreto a una persona; **to worm oneself into** insinuarse en; **to worm one's way through** atravesar serpenteando; *vn* arrastrarse, deslizarse, serpentear como un gusano

**worm-eaten** ['wʌrm,itən] *adj* carcomido; apolillado; desgastado, inservible, viejo

**worm gear** *s* engranaje de tornillo sin fin

**wormhole** ['wʌrm,hol] *s* agujero que deja la carcoma; apolilladura; agujero que hace el gusano

**wormseed** ['wʌrm,sid] *s* (bot.) apasote, pazote

**worm wheel** *s* rueda de tornillo sin fin

**wormwood** ['wʌrm,wʊd] *s* (bot.) ajenjo; (fig.) amargura

**wormy** ['wʌrmɪ] *adj* (*comp:* **-ier;** *super:* **-iest**) gusaniento, gusanoso; carcomido; apolillado; rastrero, servil

**worn** [worn] *adj* gastado, roto, raído; cansado, rendido; *pp de* **wear**

**worn-out** ['worn,aʊt] *adj* muy gastado, inservible; consumido (*por el trabajo, las enfermedades, los vicios, etc.*)

**worriment** ['wʌrɪmənt] *s* (coll.) inquietud, preocupación; (coll.) molestia

**worrisome** ['wʌrɪsəm] *adj* inquietante; inquieto, aprensivo

**worry** ['wʌrɪ] *s* (*pl:* **-ries**) inquietud, preocupación; molestia; (*pret & pp:* **-ried**) *va* inquietar, preocupar; molestar; acosar; morder y sacudir; querer morder; **to be worried** estar inquieto; *vn* inquietarse, preocuparse; **don't worry** pierda Vd. cuidado; **to worry along** arreglárselas de algún modo

**worse** [wʌrs] *adj & adv comp* peor; **worse and worse** de mal en peor, cada vez peor; **worse than ever** peor que nunca; más que nunca; *s* peor

**worsen** ['wʌrsən] *va & vn* empeorar

**worsening** ['wʌrsənɪŋ] *s* empeoramiento

**worship** ['wʌrʃɪp] *s* adoración, culto; **your worship** vuestra merced; (*pret & pp:* **-shiped** o **-shipped;** *ger:* **-shiping** o **-shipping**) *va & vn* adorar, venerar

**worshiper** o **worshipper** ['wʌrʃɪpər] *s* adorador; devoto

**worshipful** ['wʌrʃɪpfəl] *adj* reverenciable; adorador

**worst** [wʌrst] *adj & adv super* peor; *s* (lo) peor; **at worst** a lo más; **if worst comes to worst** si pasa lo peor; **to get the worst of it** llevar la peor parte, salir perdiendo; **to give one the worst of it** darle a uno la peor parte, derrotar a uno; *va* derrotar, vencer

**worsted** ['wʊstɪd] *s* estambre; tela de estambre; *adj* de estambre

**wort** [wʌrt] *s* (bot.) planta, hierba; mosto de cerveza

**worth** [wʌrθ] *s* valor; valía; mérito; **a dollar's worth of** un dólar de; *adj* del valor de; digno de; **to be worth** valer; tener una fortuna de; **to be worth** + *ger* valer la pena de + *inf*, p.ej., **that city is not worth visiting** aquella ciudad no vale la pena de visitarse
**worthiness** [ˈwʌrðɪnɪs] *s* mérito
**worthless** [ˈwʌrθlɪs] *adj* sin valor, inútil, inservible; despreciable, indigno
**worth while** *adj;* **to be worth while** ser de mérito; valer la pena; **to be worth while to** + *inf* valer la pena + *inf*, p.ej., **it isn't worth while to go to the theater this evening** no vale la pena ir al teatro esta noche
**worth-while** [ˈwʌrθˈhwaɪl] *adj* de mérito, digno de atención, p.ej., **a worth-while book** un libro de mérito, un libro digno de atención
**worthy** [ˈwʌrðɪ] *adj* (*comp:* **-thier;** *super:* **-thiest**) digno; benemérito, meritorio; **worthy of** + *ger* digno de + *inf;* **worthy of note** digno de notarse; *s* (*pl:* **-thies**) benemérito, notable; (hum.) personaje
**wot** [wɑt] *primera y tercera personas del sg del pres de ind de* **wit**
**would** [wud] *v aux* se emplea para formar (1) el condicional presente, p.ej., **he said he would come** dijo que vendría; **he would come if he could** vendría si pudiese; (2) el condicional pasado, p.ej., **he would have come if he had been able** habría venido si hubiese podido; (3) el modo potencial, p.ej., **would that I knew it!** ¡ojalá que lo supiese!; (4) el imperf de ind, indicando costumbre, p.ej., **he would go for days without smoking** pasaba días enteros sin fumar
**would-be** [ˈwud,bi] *adj* llamado; supuesto, p.ej., **a would-be pianist** un supuesto pianista; *s* presumido
**wouldn't** [ˈwudənt] contracción de **would not**
**wound** [wund] *s* herida; *va* herir; [waund] *pret & pp de* **wind**
**wounded** [ˈwundɪd] *adj* herido; **the wounded** los heridos
**wove** [wov] *pret & pp de* **weave**
**woven** [ˈwovən] *pp de* **weave**
**wow** [wau] *interj* (coll.) ¡ax!; *s* ululación (*del disco fonográfico*); (slang) cosa muy graciosa; (slang) éxito rotundo; *va* (slang) arrebatar, entusiasmar
**wrack** [ræk] *s* naufragio; destrucción, ruina; (bot.) varec, quelpo, fuco, zostera de mar; algas que arroja el mar a la playa; **to go to wrack and ruin** arruinarse
**wraith** [reθ] *s* aparecido, espectro, fantasma
**wrangle** [ˈræŋgəl] *s* disputa, riña, pelotera; *va* disputar; pasar disputando; lograr disputando; rodear (*el ganado o las caballerías*); *vn* disputar, reñir, pelotear
**wrangler** [ˈræŋglər] *s* disputador, pendenciero; (Brit.) graduado con altos honores en matemáticas; (U.S.A.) ganadero, manadero
**wrap** [ræp] *s* abrigo; (*pret & pp:* **wrapped;** *ger:* **wrapping**) *va* envolver; **to be wrapped up in** estar prendado de, estar entregado a; estar envuelto en; **to wrap up** envolver; arropar; *vn* envolverse; **to wrap up** arroparse
**wrap-around windshield** [ˈræpə,raund] *s* (aut.) parabrisas curvilíneo o panorámico
**wrapper** [ˈræpər] *s* envolvedor; envoltura; bata, peinador; faja (*de periódico o revista*); capa (*de tabaco*)
**wrapping** [ˈræpɪŋ] *s* envoltura; arropamiento
**wrapping paper** *s* papel de envolver o embalar, papel de estraza
**wrasse** [ræs] *s* (ichth.) labro; (ichth.) durdo (*Labrus bergylta*); (ichth.) tordo de mar (*Labrus mixtus*)
**wrath** [ræθ] o [rɑθ] *s* ira, cólera muy grande; venganza
**wrathful** [ˈræθfəl] o [ˈrɑθfəl] *adj* iracundo, colérico, furioso
**wrathy** [ˈræθɪ] o [ˈrɑθɪ] *adj* (*comp:* **-ier;** *super:* **-iest**) var. de **wrathful**
**wreak** [rik] *va* descargar (*la cólera*); infligir (*pena, castigo, venganza*)
**wreath** [riθ] *s* (*pl:* **wreaths** [riðz]) guirnalda; corona de laurel; corona (*funeral*); espiral (*p.ej., de humo*)
**wreathe** [rið] *va* enguirnaldar; tejer (*guirnaldas*); ceñir, envolver; *vn* enroscarse, moverse en anillos, elevarse en espirales (*p.ej., el humo*)
**wreck** [rɛk] *s* destrucción, ruina; naufragio; colisión o descarrilamiento (*p.ej., de un tren*); **to be a wreck** estar hecho un cascajo, estar hecho una ruina; *va* derribar; destruir, arruinar; hacer naufragar (*a un buque o una persona*); descarrilar (*un tren*); arrasar; *vn* arruinarse
**wreckage** [ˈrɛkɪdʒ] *s* destrucción, ruina; naufragio; despojos, restos; escombros (*de un edificio*); (fig.) naufragio (*p.ej., de las esperanzas de uno*)
**wrecker** [ˈrɛkər] *s* demoledor; descarrilador (*de trenes*); (aut.) camión de auxilio; (rail.) carro de auxilio, carro de grúa; (naut.) salvador de buques
**wrecking ball** *s* bola rompedora
**wrecking car** *s* (aut.) camión de auxilio; (rail.) carro de auxilio, carro de grúa
**wrecking crane** *s* grúa destructora; grúa de auxilio o de salvamento
**wren** [rɛn] *s* (orn.) buscareta, coletero, rey de zarza; (orn.) reyezuelo
**wrench** [rɛntʃ] *s* llave; torcedura violenta; dolor, pena, sufrimiento; *va* torcer violentamente; hacer daño a, torciendo; arrebatar torciendo; torcer (*el sentido de una frase*)
**wrest** [rɛst] *s* torsión violenta; llave para afinar pianos, arpas, etc.; *va* torcer violentamente, arrancar violentamente, arrebatar; torcer (*el sentido de una frase*); **to wrest something from someone** arrebatarle a uno una cosa
**wrestle** [ˈrɛsəl] *s* lucha; partido de lucha; *vn* (sport & fig.) luchar
**wrestler** [ˈrɛslər] *s* luchador
**wrestling** [ˈrɛslɪŋ] *s* lucha (*combate cuerpo a cuerpo*)
**wrestling match** *s* partido de lucha
**wrest pin** *s* clavija de piano
**wrest plank** *s* (mus.) clavijero (*del piano*)
**wretch** [rɛtʃ] *s* miserable (*persona desdichada; persona vil y despreciable*)
**wretched** [ˈrɛtʃɪd] *adj* miserable; pésimo, malísimo (*p.ej., trabajo*)
**wretchedness** [ˈrɛtʃɪdnɪs] *s* miseria; bajeza, ruindad, vileza
**wrick** [rɪk] *s* torcedura (*de un músculo o miembro*); *va* torcerse (*un músculo o miembro*)
**wriggle** [ˈrɪgəl] *s* meneo serpentino, culebreo; *va* menear rápidamente; introducir mañosamente; **to wriggle one's way into** colarse en; (fig.) colarse en; *vn* menearse rápidamente; culebrear, moverse serpenteando; **to wriggle away** escaparse culebreando; **to wriggle out of** escabullirse de, escaparse de
**wriggler** [ˈrɪglər] *s* persona que se menea; larva de mosquito
**wriggly** [ˈrɪglɪ] *adj* que se menea; sinuoso, tortuoso
**wright** [raɪt] *s* artífice
**wring** [rɪŋ] *s* torsión; expresión (*p.ej., del zumo*); (*pret & pp:* **wrung**) *va* torcer; retorcer (*las manos*); exprimir (*el zumo, la ropa, etc.*); arrancar (*dinero*); sacar por fuerza (*la verdad*); acongojar, afligir; **to wring out** exprimir (*la ropa*)
**wringer** [ˈrɪŋər] *s* exprimidor o secadora (*de la ropa acabada de lavar*)
**wrinkle** [ˈrɪŋkəl] *s* arruga; (coll.) truco, ardid; *va* arrugar; *vn* arrugarse
**wrinkly** [ˈrɪŋklɪ] *adj* (*comp:* **-klier;** *super:* **-kliest**) arrugado
**wrist** [rɪst] *s* (anat.) muñeca; codillo (*de los cuadrúpedos*)
**wristband** [ˈrɪst,bænd] o [ˈrɪzbənd] *s* puño, bocamanga
**wristlet** [ˈrɪstlɪt] *s* brazalete; muñequera (*en la cual se lleva sujeto un reloj*); manguito para la muñeca
**wrist pin** *s* (mach.) eje o pasador de émbolo
**wrist watch** *s* reloj de pulsera
**writ** [rɪt] *s* escrito; (law) auto, mandato, orden *f* (*de la corte*)
**write** [raɪt] (*pret:* **wrote;** *pp:* **written**) *va* escribir; **to write down** poner por escrito; bajar el precio de; **to write off** cancelar (*una deuda*); **to write out** poner por escrito; escribir sin abreviar; **to write up** describir;

escribir en detalle; escribir una crónica de; poner al día (*un escrito*); subir el precio de; dar bombo a; *vn* escribir; **to write away** dejar correr la pluma, escribir a vuela pluma; **to write back** contestar por carta o por escrito; **to write on** seguir escribiendo; escribir acerca de

**writer** ['raɪtər] *s* escritor

**writer's cramp** *s* calambre de los escribientes

**write-up** ['raɪt,ʌp] *s* (coll.) relato; (coll.) crónica; (coll.) bombo; (coll.) valoración excesiva

**writhe** [raɪð] *vn* contorcerse; retorcerse (*a causa de un dolor*); sufrir angustia

**writing** ['raɪtɪŋ] *s* el escribir; escritura; profesión de escritor; escrito; **at this writing** al escribir ésta; **in one's own writing** de su puño y letra; **to put in writing** poner por escrito; *adj* de escribir

**writing desk** *s* escritorio

**writing materials** *spl* recado de escribir

**writing pad** *s* taco de escribir

**writing paper** *s* papel de escribir, papel de cartas

**writing room** *s* sala de escritura

**writing table** *s* mesa de escribir

**writ of execution** *s* (law) auto de ejecución

**written** ['rɪtən] *pp de* **write**

**written accent** *s* acento ortográfico

**wrong** [rɔŋ] o [rɑŋ] *adj* injusto; malo; equivocado; erróneo; impropio, poco conveniente; no . . . que se busca, p.ej., **this is the wrong house** ésta no es la casa que se busca; no . . . que se necesita, p.ej., **this is the wrong train** éste no es el tren que se necesita; no . . . que debe, p.ej., **he is going the wrong way** no sigue el camino que debe; **in the wrong place** descolocado, mal colocado; **to be wrong** no tener razón; tener la culpa; **to be wrong with** pasar algo a, p.ej., **something is wrong with the telephone** algo le pasa al teléfono; *adv* mal; por error; sin razón; al revés; **to go wrong** salir mal; ir por mal camino; darse a la mala vida; *s* mal, daño, perjuicio; agravio, injusticia; error; **to be in the wrong** no tener razón; tener la culpa; **to do wrong** obrar mal; *va* agraviar, ofender, hacer mal a, ser injusto con

**wrongdoer** ['rɔŋ,duər] o ['rɑŋ,duər] *s* malvado, malhechor

**wrongdoing** ['rɔŋ,duɪŋ] o ['rɑŋ,duɪŋ] *s* maldad, perversidad

**wrongful** ['rɔŋfəl] o ['rɑŋfəl] *adj* injusto, malo; equivocado; ilegal

**wrong-headed** ['rɔŋ,hɛdɪd] o ['rɑŋ,hɛdɪd] *adj* equivocado; terco, obstinado

**wrongly** ['rɔŋlɪ] o ['rɑŋlɪ] *adv* mal; por error; sin razón; al revés

**wrongness** ['rɔŋnɪs] o ['rɑŋnɪs] *s* injusticia; maldad; error; inexactitud

**wrong number** *s* (telp.) número errado, número equivocado

**wrong side** *s* revés, contrahaz; lado contrario (*del camino*); **to get out of bed on the wrong side** levantarse del izquierdo; **wrong side out** al revés

**wrote** [rot] *pret de* **write**

**wroth** [rɔθ] o [rɑθ] *adj* iracundo, colérico, furioso

**wrought** [rɔt] *adj* forjado; labrado; hecho al martillo

**wrought iron** *s* hierro dulce

**wrought-up** ['rɔt'ʌp] *adj* sobreexcitado, muy conmovido

**wrung** [rʌŋ] *pret & pp de* **wring**

**wry** [raɪ] *adj* (*comp:* **wrier;** *super:* **wriest**) torcido; tuerto; desviado, pervertido; terco; equivocado

**wrybill** ['raɪ,bɪl] *s* (orn.) anarrinco

**wry face** *s* mueca, mohín, gesto

**wryneck** ['raɪ,nɛk] *s* (orn.) torcecuello o tuercecuello; (path.) torticolis

**WSW, W.S.W.** o **w.s.w.** abr. de **west-southwest**

**wt.** abr. de **weight**

**wulfenite** ['wʊlfənaɪt] *s* (mineral.) wulfenita

**W.Va.** abr. de **West Virginia**

**Wy.** abr. de **Wyoming**

**wych-elm** ['wɪtʃ'ɛlm] *s* (bot.) olmo escocés

**wych-hazel** ['wɪtʃ'hezəl] *s* var. de **witch hazel**

**Wycliffite** o **Wyclifite** ['wɪklɪfaɪt] *adj & s* viclefita

**wye level** [waɪ] *s* (surv.) nivel de horquetas

**Wyo.** abr. de **Wyoming**

**wyvern** ['waɪvərn] *s* var. de **wivern**

**X, x** [ɛks] *s* (*pl:* **X's, x's** [ˈɛksɪz]) vigésima cuarta letra del alfabeto inglés
**xanthaline** [ˈzænθəlin] *s* (chem.) xantalina
**xanthate** [ˈzænθet] *s* (chem.) xantato
**xanthein** [ˈzænθɪɪn] *s* (chem.) xanteína
**xanthene** [ˈzænθin] *s* (chem.) xanteno
**xanthin** [ˈzænθɪn] *s* (chem.) xantina
**xanthine** [ˈzænθin] o [ˈzænθɪn] *s* (biochem.) xantina
**Xanthippe** [zænˈtɪpɪ] *s* Jantipa o Jantipe; mujer pendenciera
**xanthochroid** [ˈzænθokrɔɪd] *adj & s* (anthrop.) xantocroide
**xanthoderm** [ˈzænθodʌrm] *s* (anthrop.) xantodermo
**xanthogen** [ˈzænθodʒɛn] *s* (chem.) xantógeno
**xanthoma** [zænˈθomə] *s* (*pl:* **-mata** [mətə] o **-mas**) (path.) xantoma
**xanthophyll** [ˈzænθofɪl] *s* (biochem.) xantofila
**xanthopsia** [zænˈθɑpsɪə] *s* (path.) xantopsia
**xanthopsin** [zænˈθɑpsɪn] *s* xantopsina
**xanthosis** [zænˈθosɪs] *s* (path.) xantosis
**xanthous** [ˈzænθəs] *adj* amarillo
**xanthoxylin** [zænˈθɑksɪlɪn] *s* (chem. & pharm.) xantoxilina
**Xavier** [ˈzævɪər] o [ˈzevɪər] *s* Javier
**xebec** [ˈzibɛk] *s* (naut.) jabeque
**xenia** [ˈzinɪə] *s* (bot.) xenia
**xenogenesis** [ˌzɛnəˈdʒɛnɪsɪs] *s* (biol.) xenogénesis
**xenon** [ˈzinɑn] o [ˈzɛnɑn] *s* (chem.) xeno o xenón
**xenophobe** [ˈzɛnofob] *s* xenófobo
**xenophobia** [ˌzɛnoˈfobɪə] *s* xenofobia
**Xenophon** [ˈzɛnəfən] *s* Jenofonte
**xerophthalmia** [ˌzɪrɑfˈθælmɪə] *s* (path.) xeroftalmía
**xerophyte** [ˈzɪrəfaɪt] *s* (bot.) xerófita
**xerophytic** [ˌzɪrəˈfɪtɪk] *adj* (bot.) xerófito
**Xerxes** [ˈzʌrksiz] *s* Jerjes
**xiphisternum** [ˌzɪfɪˈstʌrnəm] *s* (*pl:* **-na** [nə]) (anat.) xifisternón
**xiphoid** [ˈzɪfɔɪd] *adj & s* (anat.) xifoides
**xiphosuran** [ˌzɪfəˈsurən] *s* (zool.) jifosuro
**Xmas** [ˈkrɪsməs] *s* var. de **Christmas**
**X ray** *s* rayo X; radiografía; **X rays** *spl* rayos X
**X-ray** [ˈɛksˌre] *adj* radiográfico; [ˈɛksˈre] *va* radiografiar; tratar por medio de los rayos X
**X-ray photograph** *s* radiografía (*fotografía por los rayos X*)
**xylan** [ˈzaɪlæn] *s* (chem.) xilán
**xylem** [ˈzaɪlɛm] *s* (bot.) xilema
**xylene** [ˈzaɪlin] *s* (chem.) xileno
**xylidine** [ˈzaɪlɪdin] o [ˈzɪlɪdin] *s* (chem.) xilidina
**xylobalsamum** [ˌzaɪloˈbɔlsəməm] o [ˌzaɪloˈbælsəməm] *s* xilobálsamo
**xylograph** [ˈzaɪləgræf] o [ˈzaɪləgrɑf] *s* xilografía (*grabado*)
**xylographer** [zaɪˈlɑgrəfər] *s* xilógrafo
**xylographic** [ˌzaɪləˈgræfɪk] o **xylographical** [ˌzaɪləˈgræfɪkəl] *adj* xilográfico
**xylography** [zaɪˈlɑgrəfɪ] *s* xilografía (*arte*)
**xylol** [ˈzaɪlol] o [ˈzaɪlɑl] *s* (chem.) xilol
**xylophagous** [zaɪˈlɑfəgəs] *adj* xilófago
**xylophone** [ˈzaɪləfon] o [ˈzɪləfon] *s* (mus.) xilófono
**xylose** [ˈzaɪlos] *s* (chem.) xilosa
**xyster** [ˈzɪstər] *s* (surg.) xister

# Y

**Y, y** [waɪ] *s* (*pl:* **Y's, y's** [waɪz]) vigésima quinta letra del alfabeto inglés

**-y** *suffix adj* -ado, p.ej., **wavy** ondulado; -iento, p.ej., **hungry** hambriento; **dusty** polvoriento; -izo, p.ej., **coppery** cobrizo; **strawy** pajizo; -oso, p.ej., **juicy** jugoso; **rocky** rocoso; -udo, p.ej., **fleshy** carnudo; **hairy** peludo; *suffix s* -ia, p.ej., **glory** gloria; **victory** victoria; -ía, p.ej., **geology** geología; **philosophy** filosofía; *suffix dim* -ito, p.ej., **pussy** michito; **Johnny** Juanito

**y.** abr. de **yard** o **yards** y **year**

**yacht** [jɑt] *s* yate; *vn* pasear en yate; tomar parte en regatas en yate

**yacht club** *s* club náutico

**yachting** ['jɑtɪŋ] *adj* aficionado al deporte de los yates; *s* navegación en yate, paseo en yate

**yacht race** *s* regata de yates

**yachtsman** ['jɑtsmən] *s* (*pl:* **-men**) aficionado al deporte de los yates

**yachtsmanship** ['jɑtsmənʃɪp] *s* arte de navegar un yate

**yackety-yack** ['jækɪtɪ'jæk] *s* (slang) charla, palique

**yah** [jɑ] *interj* ¡bah!; ¡puf!

**yahoo** ['jɑhu] o ['jehu] *s* patán

**Yahveh** o **Yahweh** ['jɑwe] *s* (Bib.) Yahvé

**yak** [jæk] *s* (zool.) yac (*bóvido del Tibet*)

**yam** [jæm] *s* (bot.) ñame (*planta y raíz*); batata, camote, boniato

**yank** [jæŋk] *s* (coll.) tirón; (*cap.*) *adj & s* (slang) yanqui; (*l.c.*) *va* (coll.) sacar de un tirón; *vn* (coll.) dar un tirón, dar tirones

**Yankee** ['jæŋkɪ] *adj & s* yanqui

**Yankeedom** ['jæŋkɪdəm] *s* los yanquis; Yanquilandia

**Yankeeism** ['jæŋkɪɪzəm] *s* característica de los yanquis; yanquismo

**yap** [jæp] *s* (slang) ladrido corto; (slang) conversación necia y ruidosa; (*pret & pp:* **yapped;** *ger:* **yapping**) *vn* (slang) ladrar con ladrido corto; (slang) charlar necia y ruidosamente

**yard** [jɑrd] *s* yarda (*medida*); cercado, corral, patio; (naut.) verga; (rail.) patio; **to man the yards** (naut.) disponer la gente sobre las vergas; (naut.) disponerse sobre las vergas; **to square the yards** (naut.) poner las vergas en cruz; *va* acorralar

**yardage** ['jɑrdɪdʒ] *s* yardaje

**yardarm** ['jɑrd,ɑrm] *s* (naut.) penol, singlón

**yardmaster** ['jɑrd,mæstər] o ['jɑrd,mɑstər] *s* (rail.) superintendente del patio

**yardstick** ['jɑrd,stɪk] *s* yarda, vara de medir; (fig.) criterio, norma

**yarn** [jɑrn] *s* hilado, hilaza; (coll.) cuento, burlería; *vn* (coll.) inventar y contar historietas

**yarn tester** *s* cuentahilos

**yarrow** ['jæro] *s* (bot.) milenrama

**yataghan** ['jætəgæn] *s* yatagán

**yaupon** ['jɔpən] *s* (bot.) apalachina

**yaw** [jɔ] *s* (naut.) guiñada; (aer.) desvío; **yaws** *spl* (path.) frambesia; *vn* (naut.) guiñar; (aer.) desviarse; (fig.) desviarse del camino

**yawl** [jɔl] *s* (naut.) queche; (naut.) bote; (dial.) alarido, aullido; *vn* (dial.) dar alaridos, aullar

**yawn** [jɔn] *s* bostezo; abertura; *va* decir bostezando; *vn* bostezar; abrirse desmesuradamente

**yawning** ['jɔnɪŋ] *adj* bostezante; abierto desmesuradamente; *s* bostezos

**yawp** [jɔp] *s* (coll.) alarido; (coll.) plática ruidosa; *vn* (coll.) dar alaridos; (coll.) charlar ruidosamente; (coll.) bostezar ruidosamente

**y-cleped** o **y-clept** [ɪ'klɛpt] *adj* (archaic) llamado, nombrado

**yd.** abr. de **yard** o **yards**

**yds.** abr. de **yards**

**ye** [ji] *pron pers* (archaic) vosotros; [ðɪ] *art def* (archaic) el, la

**yea** [je] *s* sí (*voto afirmativo*); *adv* sí; sin duda; (archaic) además

**yean** [jin] *va & vn* parir (*la cabra, la oveja*)

**yeanling** ['jinlɪŋ] *s* cordero o cabrito mamantón

**year** [jɪr] *s* año; **years** *spl* años (*edad; época de la vida*); muchos años; **of late years** en estos últimos años; **year by year** año por año; **year in, year out** año tras año

**yearbook** ['jɪr,buk] *s* anuario

**yearling** ['jɪrlɪŋ] *adj & s* primal

**yearlong** ['jɪr,lɔŋ] o ['jɪr,lɑŋ] *adj* que dura un año; que dura años

**yearly** ['jɪrlɪ] *adj* anual; *adv* anualmente

**yearn** [jʌrn] *vn* suspirar; **to yearn for** suspirar por, anhelar por; sentir lástima por; **to yearn to** + *inf* anhelar + *inf*

**yearning** ['jʌrnɪŋ] *s* anhelo, deseo vivo

**year of grace** *s* año de gracia

**yeast** [jist] *s* levadura, fermento; espuma, jiste; pastilla de levadura

**yeast cake** *s* pastilla de levadura, levadura comprimida

**yeasty** ['jistɪ] *adj* de la levadura; espumoso; casquivano, frívolo

**yegg** [jɛg] *s* (slang) ladrón; (slang) ladrón de cajas fuertes

**yelk** [jɛlk] *s* var. de **yolk**

**yell** [jɛl] *s* grito, voz; *va* decir a gritos; *vn* gritar, dar voces

**yellow** ['jɛlo] *adj* amarillo; escandaloso, sensacional (*periodismo*); (coll.) blanco (*cobarde, miedoso*); *s* amarillo; yema de huevo; *vn* amarillecer

**yellow-billed cuckoo** ['jɛlo,bɪld] *s* (orn.) cuclillo de las lluvias

**yellowbird** ['jɛlo,bʌrd] *s* (orn.) jilguero de América; (orn.) dominguito; (orn.) oropéndola

**yellow elder** *s* (bot.) tronadora, trompetilla

**yellow fever** *s* (path.) fiebre amarilla

**yellow flag** *s* bandera amarilla; (bot.) lirio amarillo

**yellowhammer** ['jɛlo,hæmər] *s* (orn.) ave tonta; (orn.) picamaderos norteamericano

**yellow goatsbeard** *s* (bot.) salsifí de los prados

**yellowish** ['jɛlo·ɪʃ] *adj* amarillento

**yellow jack** *s* fiebre amarilla; bandera amarilla de cuarentena; (bot.) junquillo; (ichth.) jurel

**yellow jacket** *s* (ent.) avispa; (ent.) avispón

**yellow jasmine** *s* (bot.) jazmín; (bot.) jazmín silvestre (*Gelsemium sempervirens*)

**yellow journalism** *s* periodismo sensacional

**yellowlegs** ['jɛlo,lɛgz] *s* (*pl:* **-legs**) (orn.) sarapico (*Totanus flavipes*)

**yellowness** ['jɛlonɪs] *s* amarillez

**yellow ocher** *s* (mineral.) ocre amarillo

**yellow oxide** *s* óxido amarillo

**yellow peril** *s* peligro amarillo

**yellow pine** *s* (bot.) pino amarillo; (bot.) liriodendro

**yellow poplar** *s* (bot.) liriodendro

**yellow poppy** *s* (bot.) pamplina

**Yellow River** *s* río Amarillo

**yellow sandalwood** *s* (bot.) sándalo

**Yellow Sea** *s* mar Amarillo

**yellow spot** *s* (anat.) mancha amarilla

**yellow streak** *s* vena de cobarde, trazas de cobarde

**yellowthroat** ['jɛlo,θrot] *s* (orn.) pecho amarillo

**yelp** [jɛlp] *s* gañido (*del perro*); *va* decir con gritos; ahuyentar con gritos; *vn* gañir

**yen** [jɛn] *s* (coll.) deseo vivo; (*pret & pp:* **yenned;** *ger:* **yenning**) *vn* (coll.) anhelar

**yeoman** ['jomən] *s* (*pl:* **-men**) (Brit.) labrador acomodado, pequeño terrateniente; (archaic) guardia del rey, sirviente del rey; (naut.) oficinista de a bordo; (naut.) pañolero
**yeomanly** ['jomənlɪ] *adj* honrado, leal; firme, porfiado; *adv* valerosamente
**yeoman of the guard** *s* (Brit.) continuo
**yeomanry** ['jomənrɪ] *s* (Brit.) labradores acomodados, pequeños terratenientes; (archaic) guardias del rey; (naut.) pañoleros; (Brit.) caballería voluntaria
**yeoman's service** *s* buen servicio, ayuda leal
**yes** [jɛs] *adv* sí; además, aun; *s* (*pl:* **yeses**) sí; **to say yes** dar el sí (*convenir en el matrimonio*); (*pret & pp:* **yessed;** *ger:* **yessing**) *va* decir sí a; *vn* decir sí
**yes man** *s* (slang) hombre que asiente siempre y lo acepta todo
**yesterday** ['jɛstərdɪ] o ['jɛstərde] *adv & s* ayer; **the day before yesterday** anteayer
**yestereve** [,jɛstər'iv] o **yesterevening** [,jɛstər'ivnɪŋ] *adv* (archaic & poet.) ayer tarde; *s* (archaic & poet.) la tarde de ayer
**yestermorn** [,jɛstər'mɔrn] *adv* (archaic & poet.) ayer por la mañana; *s* (archaic & poet.) la mañana de ayer
**yesternight** [,jɛstər'naɪt] *adv* (archaic & poet.) anoche; *s* (archaic & poet.) la noche de ayer
**yesteryear** [,jɛstər'jɪr] *adv* (archaic & poet.) antaño; *s* (archaic & poet.) el año pasado
**yestreen** [,jɛs'trin] *adv* (Scottish & poet.) ayer tarde; *s* (Scottish & poet.) la tarde de ayer
**yet** [jɛt] *adv* todavía, aun; **as yet** hasta ahora; **not yet** todavía no; *conj* con todo, sin embargo
**yew** [ju] *s* (bot.) tejo
**Yiddish** ['jɪdɪʃ] *s* yídish
**yield** [jild] *s* producción; rédito; rendimiento; *va* producir; rendir, redituar; *vn* producir; rendir; rendirse, entregarse, someterse; acceder, ceder, consentir
**yielding** ['jildɪŋ] *adj* complaciente, dócil, sumiso; productivo; *s* sumisión, rendimiento
**yipe** [jaɪp] *interj* (coll.) grito de dolor, miedo, sorpresa, etc.
**Y.M.C.A.** abr. de **Young Men's Christian Association**
**Y.M.H.A.** abr. de **Young Men's Hebrew Association**
**yod** [jod] o [jɑd] *s* (philol.) yod
**yodel** ['jodəl] *s* canto que se hace cambiando frecuentemente de la voz natural a la voz de falsete y viceversa; (*pret & pp:* **-deled** o **-delled;** *ger:* **-deling** o **-delling**) *va & vn* cantar cambiando frecuentemente de la voz natural a la voz de falsete y viceversa
**yodle** ['jodəl] *s, va & vn* var. de **yodel**
**yoga** ['jogə] *s* yoga
**yogi** ['jogɪ] *s* yogui
**yogurt** ['jogʊrt] *s* yogurt
**yo-heave-ho** ['jo'hiv'ho] *interj* (naut.) ¡iza!
**yoicks** [jɔɪks] *interj* grito que se emplea para excitar los perros en la caza
**yoke** [jok] *s* yugo; yunta (*de bestias de trabajo*); percha para llevar cargas; hombrillo (*de la camisa*); parte superior de la falda en las caderas; (elec.) culata; (mach.) horquilla; **to throw off the yoke** sacudir el yugo; *va* uncir; acoplar, unir; oprimir, subyugar; *vn* estar unidos
**yoke elm** *s* (bot.) carpe, ojaranzo
**yokefellow** ['jok,fɛlo] *s* compañero de yugo; compañero de trabajo y sufrimiento; cónyuge (*marido o mujer*)
**yokel** ['jokəl] *s* patán
**yokemate** ['jok,met] var. de **yokefellow**
**yolk** [jok] *s* yema de huevo; churre en la lana de oveja
**Yom Kippur** [jɑm 'kɪpər] *s* día de propiciación que celebran los judíos al principio del año hebreo
**yon** [jɑn] o **yond** [jɑnd] *adj & adv* (archaic & dial.) var. de **yonder**
**yonder** ['jɑndər] *adj* aquel; de más allá; *adv* allí a la vista
**yore** [jor] *adv* (obs.) hace mucho tiempo, hace muchos años; *s* (obs.) otro tiempo; **of yore** antiguamente, en otro tiempo, antaño
**Yorkshire pudding** ['jɔrkʃɪr] *s* bizcocho de masa
**you** [ju] *pron pers sg & pl* tú, te; vosotros; usted, ustedes; le, la, les; **with you** contigo; consigo, p.ej., **you took it with you** lo llevó consigo; *pron indef* se, p.ej., **you cannot smoke here** no se puede fumar aquí
**you'd** [jud] contracción de **you had** y **you would**
**you'll** [jul] contracción de **you shall** y **you will**
**young** [jʌŋ] *adj* (*comp:* **younger** ['jʌŋgər]; *super:* **youngest** ['jʌŋgɪst]) joven; menor (de edad); reciente, temprano; tierno; inexperto; **the young** los jóvenes, la gente joven, la juventud; **with young** encinta, preñada; *spl* hijuelos
**younger set** *s* generación nueva, (los) jóvenes
**young hopeful** *s* muchacho que promete
**youngish** ['jʌŋɪʃ] *adj* bastante joven
**youngling** ['jʌŋlɪŋ] *adj & s* jovenzuelo; primal; novato
**Young Men's Christian Association** *s* Asociación de jóvenes cristianos, Asociación cristiana de jóvenes
**young people** *spl* jóvenes, gente joven, juventud
**youngster** ['jʌŋstər] *s* jovencito; niño, chiquito
**younker** ['jʌŋkər] *s* (archaic) niño, chiquito; (obs.) señorito
**your** [jʊr] *adj poss* tu, vuestro, su, el (o su) de Vd. o de Vds.
**yours** [jʊrz] *pron poss* tuyo, vuestro; suyo; de Vd., de Vds.; el tuyo, el vuestro; el suyo; el de Vd., el de Vds.; **of yours** tuyo, vuestro; suyo; de Vd., de Vds., p.ej., **a friend of yours** un amigo suyo, un amigo de Vd.; **yours truly** su seguro servidor, de Vd. atto. y S. S.; (coll.) este cura (*yo*)
**yourself** [jʊr'sɛlf] *pron* (*pl:* **-selves**) tú mismo; usted mismo; sí mismo; se; sí
**youth** [juθ] *s* (*pl:* **youths** [juθs] o [juðz]) juventud; jovenzuelo; *spl* jóvenes, gente joven, juventud
**youthful** ['juθfəl] *adj* juvenil
**you've** [juv] contracción de **you have**
**yowl** [jaʊl] *s* aullido, alarido; *vn* aullar, dar alaridos
**yo-yo** ['jo,jo] *s* (*pl:* **-yos**) diábolo
**yr.** abr. de **year** o **years**
**yrs.** abr. de **years**
**ytterbium** [ɪ'tʌrbɪəm] *s* (chem.) iterbio
**yttrium** ['ɪtrɪəm] *s* (chem.) itrio
**Yucatan** [,jukɑ'tɑn] o [,jukə'tæn] *s* el Yucatán
**yucca** ['jʌkə] *s* (bot.) yuca
**Yugoslav** ['jugo'slɑv] *adj & s* yugoeslavo
**Yugoslavia** ['jugo'slɑvɪə] *s* Yugoeslavia
**Yugoslavic** [,jugo'slɑvɪk] *adj* yugoeslavo
**Yule** [jul] *s* la Navidad; la pascua de Navidad
**Yule log** *s* nochebueno (*leño*)
**Yuletide** ['jul,taɪd] *s* la pascua de Navidad
**Y.W.C.A.** abr. de **Young Women's Christian Association**
**Y.W.H.A.** abr. de **Young Women's Hebrew Association**
**ywis** [ɪ'wɪs] *adv* (archaic) sin duda, ya lo creo

# Z

**Z, z** [zi] *s* (*pl:* **Z's, z's** [ziz]) vigésima sexta letra del alfabeto inglés
**Zaccheus** [zæ'kiəs] *s* (Bib.) Zaqueo
**Zachariah** [,zækə'raɪə] *s* (Bib.) Zacarías
**zaffer** ['zæfər] *s* (mineral.) zafre
**zany** ['zenɪ] *s* (*pl:* **-nies**) tonto, necio; bufón, payaso
**zeal** [zil] *s* celo
**Zealand** ['zilənd] *s* la isla de Seeland (*Dinamarca*)
**zealot** ['zɛlət] *s* fanático
**zealotry** ['zɛlətrɪ] *s* fanatismo
**zealous** ['zɛləs] *adj* celoso (*que tiene gran entusiasmo*)
**zebec** ['zibɛk] *s* var. de **xebec**
**Zebedee** ['zɛbɪdi] *s* (Bib.) Zebedeo
**zebra** ['zibrə] *s* (zool.) cebra
**zebra parakeet** *s* (orn.) periquito de Australia
**zebu** ['zibju] *s* (zool.) cebú
**Zech.** abr. de **Zechariah**
**Zechariah** [,zɛkə'raɪə] *s* (Bib.) Zacarías
**Zedekiah** [,zɛdɪ'kaɪə] *s* (Bib.) Sedecías
**zedoary** ['zɛdo,ɛrɪ] *s* (pharm.) cedoaria
**Zeeland** ['zilənd] *s* la Zelanda o la Zelandia (*Holanda*)
**Zeelander** ['ziləndər] *s* celandés
**zein** ['ziɪn] *s* (biochem.) zeína
**Zeitgeist** ['tsaɪt,gaɪst] *s* espíritu de la época
**zenith** ['zinɪθ] *s* (astr. & fig.) cenit
**Zeno** ['zino] *s* Zenón
**zeolite** ['ziəlaɪt] *s* (mineral.) ceolita
**Zeph.** abr. de **Zephaniah**
**Zephaniah** [,zɛfə'naɪə] *s* (Bib.) Sofonías
**zephyr** ['zɛfər] *s* céfiro (*viento; tela*)
**zeppelin** o **Zeppelin** ['zɛpəlɪn] *s* zepelín
**zero** ['zɪro] *s* (*pl:* **-ros** o **-roes**) cero; *adj* nulo
**zero gravity** *s* gravedad nula
**zero hour** *s* (mil.) hora cero
**zero weather** *s* tiempo de cero grados, tiempo muy frío
**zest** [zɛst] *s* entusiasmo; gusto, sabor; cáscara de limón o naranja; *va* dar gusto o sabor a, sazonar
**zeugma** ['zjugmə] o ['zugmə] *s* (rhet.) zeugma; (rhet.) zeugma en que uno de los elementos de la construcción no es apropiado al sentido del verbo
**Zeus** [zus] o [zjus] *s* (myth.) Zeus
**zigzag** ['zɪg,zæg] *s* zigzag; *adj & adv* en zigzag; (*pret & pp:* **-zagged;** *ger:* **-zagging**) *va* mover en zigzag; *vn* zigzaguear
**zinc** [zɪŋk] *s* (chem.) cinc; (elec.) vara o cilindro de cinc (*de una pila húmeda*); (*pret & pp:* **zinced** [zɪŋkt] o **zincked;** *ger:* **zincing** ['zɪŋkɪŋ] o **zincking**) *va* cubrir con cinc; platear con cinc, cincar
**zinc carbonate** *s* (chem.) carbonato de cinc
**zinc chloride** *s* (chem.) cloruro de cinc
**zinc etching** *s* cincograbado; cincografía
**zincograph** ['zɪŋkəgræf] o ['zɪŋkəgrɑf] *s* cincograbado
**zincography** [zɪŋ'kɑgrəfɪ] *s* cincografía
**zinc ointment** *s* (pharm.) pomada o ungüento de cinc
**zincous** ['zɪŋkəs] *adj* cincoso
**zinc oxide** *s* (chem.) óxido de cinc
**zinc sulfate** *s* (chem.) sulfato de cinc
**zinc sulfide** *s* (chem.) sulfuro de cinc
**zinc white** *s* blanco de cinc
**zingaro** ['tsɪŋgɑro] *s* (*pl:* -ri [ri]) cíngaro
**zingiberaceous** [,zɪndʒɪbə'reʃəs] *adj* (bot.) cingiberáceo
**zinnia** ['zɪnɪə] *s* (bot.) rascamoño
**Zion** ['zaɪən] *s* Sión
**Zionism** ['zaɪənɪzəm] *s* sionismo
**Zionist** ['zaɪənɪst] *adj & s* sionista
**zip** [zɪp] *s* silbido, zumbido; (coll.) energía, vitalidad; (*pret & pp:* **zipped;** *ger:* **zipping**) *va* cerrar con cierre relámpago; *vn* silbar, zumbar; (coll.) actuar con energía, moverse con energía; **to zip by** (coll.) pasar rápidamente
**zipper** ['zɪpər] *s* cierre relámpago, cierre cremallera; (trademark) chanclo con cierre relámpago
**zippy** ['zɪpɪ] *adj* (*comp:* **-pier;** *super:* **-piest**) (coll.) animado, vivo, alegre
**zircon** ['zʌrkɑn] *s* (mineral.) circón
**zirconate** ['zʌrkənet] *s* (chem.) circonato
**zirconia** [zər'konɪə] *s* (chem.) circona
**zirconium** [zər'konɪəm] *s* (chem.) circonio
**zither** ['zɪθər] *s* (mus.) cítara (*instrumento músico con cuerdas tendidas horizontalmente*)
**zithern** ['zɪθərn] o **zittern** ['zɪtərn] *s* (mus.) cítara (*instrumento músico parecido a la guitarra; instrumento músico con cuerdas tendidas horizontalmente*)
**zoanthropy** [zo'ænθrəpɪ] *s* (path.) zoantropía
**zodiac** ['zodɪæk] *s* (astr.) zodíaco
**zodiacal** [zo'daɪəkəl] *adj* zodiacal
**zoetrope** ['zo·itrop] *s* zootropo (*juguete*)
**zona** ['zonə] *s* (*pl:* **-nae** [ni]) zona (*lista; ceñidor*); (path.) zona
**zonal** ['zonəl] *adj* zonal
**zone** [zon] *s* zona; distrito postal; (poet.) zona (*ceñidor*); *va* dividir en zonas; marcar con zonas; ceñir
**zoned** [zond] *adj* zonado (*señalado con listas*); dividido en zonas; que lleva ceñidor
**zone number** *s* número del distrito postal
**zoning** ['zonɪŋ] *s* zonificación
**zonule** ['zonjul] *s* zonula
**zoo** [zu] *s* zoo (*parque zoológico*)
**zoöcecidium** [,zoəsɪ'sɪdɪəm] *s* (*pl:* **-a** [ə]) (zool.) zoocecidia
**zoöchemical** [,zoo'kɛmɪkəl] *adj* zooquímico
**zoöchemistry** [,zoo'kɛmɪstrɪ] *s* zooquímica
**zoögeography** [,zoodʒɪ'ɑgrəfɪ] *s* zoogeografía
**zoögloea** [,zoo'gliə] *s* (bact.) zooglea
**zoögraphy** [zo'ɑgrəfɪ] *s* zoografía
**zoölogical** [,zoə'lɑdʒɪkəl] *adj* zoológico
**zoölogical garden** *s* parque zoológico, jardín zoológico
**zoölogist** [zo'ɑlədʒɪst] *s* zoólogo
**zoölogy** [zo'ɑlədʒɪ] *s* zoología
**zoom** [zum] *s* zumbido; (aer.) empinadura; *va* (aer.) empinar; *vn* zumbar; (aer.) empinarse
**zoömetric** [,zoə'mɛtrɪk] *adj* zoométrico
**zoömetry** [zo'ɑmɪtrɪ] *s* zoometría
**zoömorphism** [,zoə'mɔrfɪzəm] *s* zoomorfismo
**zoönosis** [zo'ɑnəsɪs] *s* (path.) zoonosis
**zoöparasite** [,zoə'pærəsaɪt] *s* (zool.) zooparásito
**zoöpathology** [,zoəpə'θɑlədʒɪ] *s* zoopatología
**zoöpery** [zo'ɑpərɪ] *s* zooperia
**zoöphilia** [,zoə'fɪlɪə] *s* zoofilia
**zoöphilous** [zo'ɑfɪləs] *adj* zoófilo
**zoöphyte** ['zoəfaɪt] *s* (zool.) zoófito
**zoöplankton** [,zoə'plæŋktən] *s* (zool.) zooplancton
**zoöplasty** ['zoə,plæstɪ] *s* (surg.) zooplastia
**zoöpsychology** [,zoəsaɪ'kɑlədʒɪ] *s* zoopsicología
**zoösporangium** [,zoəspə'rændʒɪəm] *s* (*pl:* **-a** [ə]) (bot.) zoosporangio
**zoöspore** ['zoəspor] *s* (bot.) zoospora
**zoötaxy** ['zoə,tæksɪ] *s* zootaxia
**zoötechny** ['zoo,tɛknɪ] *s* zootecnia
**zoötomy** [zo'ɑtəmɪ] *s* zootomía
**zoötoxin** [,zoə'tɑksɪn] *s* zootoxina
**zoot suit** [zut] *s* (slang) traje con saco muy largo y pantalones holgados pero muy estrechos en los tobillos
**Zoroaster** [,zoro'æstər] *s* Zoroastro
**Zoroastrian** [,zoro'æstrɪən] *adj* zoroástrico, zoroastriano; *s* zoroastriano

**Zoroastrianism** [ˌzoroˈæstrɪənɪzəm] *s* zoroastrismo
**zoster** [ˈzɑstər] *s* (path.) zoster, zona
**Zouave** [zuˈɑv] *s* (mil.) zuavo
**zounds** [zaʊndz] *interj* (archaic) ¡voto al diablo!
**zucchetto** [tsukˈkɛto] *s* (*pl:* **-tos**) (eccl.) solideo
**Zulu** [ˈzulu] *adj* zulú; *s* (*pl:* **-lus**) zulú
**Zululand** [ˈzuluˌlænd] *s* Zululandia
**zwieback** [ˈtswiˌbɑk] o [ˈswiˌbɑk] *s* bizcocho retostado
**Zwinglian** [ˈzwɪŋglɪən] o [ˈtsvɪŋlɪən] *adj* & *s* zuingliano
**zygal** [ˈzaɪgəl] *adj* cigal
**zygodactyl** [ˌzaɪgəˈdæktɪl] o [ˌzɪgəˈdæktɪl] *adj* (orn.) zigodáctilo; *s* (orn.) zigodáctila
**zygoma** [zaɪˈgomə] o [zɪˈgomə] *s* (*pl:* **-mata** [mətə]) (anat.) cigoma
**zygomatic** [ˌzaɪgoˈmætɪk] o [ˌzɪgoˈmætɪk] *adj* (anat.) cigomático
**zygomatic arch** *s* (anat.) arco cigomático
**zygomatic bone** *s* (anat.) hueso cigomático
**zygomatic muscle** *s* (anat.) músculo cigomático
**zygomorphic** [ˌzaɪgoˈmɔrfɪk] o [ˌzɪgoˈmɔrfɪk] o **zygomorphous** [ˌzaɪgoˈmɔrfəs] o [ˌzɪgoˈmɔrfəs] *adj* (biol.) zigomorfo
**zygophyllaceous** [ˌzaɪgofɪˈleʃəs] o [ˌzɪgofɪˈleʃəs] *adj* (bot.) cigofiláceo
**zygosis** [zaɪˈgosɪs] o [zɪˈgosɪs] *s* (bot. & zool.) cigosis
**zygospore** [ˈzaɪgəspor] o [ˈzɪgəspor] *s* (bot.) zigospora
**zygote** [ˈzaɪgot] o [ˈzɪgot] *s* (biol.) cigoto
**zygotene** [ˈzaɪgotin] o [ˈzɪgotin] *adj* (biol.) cigoteno
**zymase** [ˈzaɪmes] *s* (biochem.) zimasa
**zyme** [zaɪm] *s* (path.) cimo
**zymogen** [ˈzaɪmodʒən] o **zymogene** [ˈzaɪmodʒin] *s* (biochem.) cimógeno; (biol.) cimógeno, cimo excitador
**zymogenesis** [ˌzaɪmoˈdʒɛnɪsɪs] *s* (biochem.) cimogénesis
**zymogenic** [ˌzaɪmoˈdʒɛnɪk] *adj* cimógeno
**zymogenic organism** *s* (biol.) organismo cimógeno
**zymology** [zaɪˈmɑlədʒɪ] *s* cimología
**zymolysis** [zaɪˈmɑlɪsɪs] *s* (biochem.) cimólisis
**zymometer** [zaɪˈmɑmɪtər] *s* cimómetro
**zymoplastic** [ˌzaɪmoˈplæstɪk] *adj* (biochem.) cimoplástico
**zymoscope** [ˈzaɪmoskop] *s* cimoscopio
**zymosimeter** [ˌzaɪmoˈsɪmɪtər] *s* cimosímetro
**zymosis** [zaɪˈmosɪs] *s* (*pl:* **-ses** [siz]) cimosis
**zymotic** [zaɪˈmɑtɪk] *adj* cimótico
**zymurgy** [ˈzaɪmʌrdʒɪ] *s* cimurgia o cimotecnia
**Zyrian** [ˈzɪrɪən] *s* ziriano (*idioma finoúgrio*)

# LABELS AND ABBREVIATIONS

abr. **abbreviation—abreviatura**
*adj* **adjective—adjetivo**
*adv* **adverb—adverbio**
(aer.) **aeronautics—aeronáutica**
(agr.) **agriculture—agricultura**
(alchem.) **alchemy—alquimia**
(alg.) **algebra—álgebra**
(Am.) **Spanish-American—hispanoamericano**
(anat.) **anatomy—anatomía**
(anthrop.) **anthropology—antropología**
(api.) **apiculture—apicultura**
(Arab.) **Arabic—arábigo**
(arch.) **architecture—arquitectura**
(archeol.) **archeology—arqueología**
(arith.) **arithmetic—aritmética**
(arm.) **armor—armadura**
*art* **article—artículo**
(arti.) **artillery—artillería**
(astr.) **astronomy—astronomía**
(astrol.) **astrology—astrología**
*aug* **augmentative—aumentativo**
(aut.) **automobiles—automóviles**
(bact.) **bacteriology—bacteriología**
(b.b.) **bookbinding—encuadernación**
(Bib.) **Biblical—bíblico**
(bibliog.) **bibliography—bibliografía**
(biochem.) **biochemistry—bioquímica**
(biog.) **biography—biografía**
(biol.) **biology—biología**
(bot.) **botany—botánica**
(box.) **boxing—boxeo**
(Brit.) **British—británico**
(*cap.*) **capital—mayúscula**
(carp.) **carpentry—carpintería**
(cf.) **compare—compárese**
(chem.) **chemistry—química**
(chron.) **chronology—cronología**
(coll.) **colloquial—familiar**
(com.) **commerce—comercio**
*comp* **comparative—comparativo**
*conj* **conjunction—conjunción**
(constr.) **construction—construcción**
(cook.) **cooking—cocina**
(cryst.) **crystallography—cristalografía**
*def* **definite—definido**
*dem* **demonstrative—demostrativo**
(dent.) **dentistry—dentistería**
(dial.) **dialectal—dialectal**
*dim* **diminutive—diminutivo**
(dipl.) **diplomacy—diplomacia**
(eccl.) **ecclesiastical—eclesiástico**
(econ.) **economics—economía**
(educ.) **education—educación**
(elec.) **electricity—electricidad**
(electron.) **electronics—electrónica**
(embryol.) **embryology—embriología**
(eng.) **engineering—ingeniería**
(ent.) **entomology—entomología**
(equit.) **horsemanship—equitación**
*expl* **expletive—partícula expletiva**
*f* **feminine noun—nombre femenino**
(f.a.) **fine arts—bellas artes**
(falc.) **falconry—cetrería**
*fem* **feminine—femenino**
(feud.) **feudalism—feudalismo**
(fig.) **figurative—figurado**
(fort.) **fortification—fortificación**
(found.) **foundry—fundición**
*fpl* **feminine noun plural—nombre femenino plural**
*fsg* **feminine noun singular—nombre femenino singular**
*Fr.* **French—francés**
*fut* **future—futuro**
(geog.) **geography—geografía**
(geol.) **geology—geología**
(geom.) **geometry—geometría**
*ger* **gerund—gerundio**
(gram.) **grammar—gramática**
(gun.) **gunnery—artillería**
(her.) **heraldry—heráldica**
(hist.) **history—historia**
(horol.) **horology—horología**
(hort.) **horticulture—horticultura**
(hum.) **humorous—jocoso**
(hunt.) **hunting—caza**
(hyd.) **hydraulics—hidráulica**
(ichth.) **ichthyology—ictiología**
(illit.) **illiterate—iliterato**
(immun.) **immunology—inmunología**
*imperf* **imperfect—imperfecto**
*impers* **impersonal—impersonal**
*impv* **imperative—imperativo**
*ind* **indicative—indicativo**
*indecl* **indeclinable—indeclinable**
*indef* **indefinite—indefinido**
*inf* **infinitive—infinitivo**
(ins.) **insurance—seguros**
(int. law) **international law—derecho internacional**
*interj* **interjection—interjección**
*interr* **interrogative—interrogativo**
*invar* **invariable—invariable**
(iron.) **ironical—irónico**
(jewel.) **jewelry—joyería**
(journ.) **journalism—periodismo**
(Lat.) **Latin—latín**
(*l.c.*) **lower case—letra de caja baja**